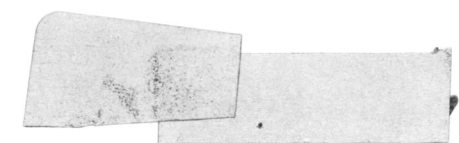
W9-AWG-039

HOLT, RINEHART AND WINSTON SPECIAL EDITION

Merriam-Webster's

MIDDLE SCHOOL
DICTIONARY

A Merriam-Webster®

MERRIAM-WEBSTER INC., *Publishers*
SPRINGFIELD, MASSACHUSETTS, U.S.A.

A GENUINE MERRIAM-WEBSTER

The name *Webster* alone is no guarantee of excellence. It is used by a number of publishers and may serve mainly to mislead an unwary buyer.

Merriam-Webster™ is the name you should look for when you consider the purchase of dictionaries or other fine reference books. It carries the reputation of a company that has been publishing since 1831 and is your assurance of quality and authority.

Library of Congress Cataloging in Publication Data
Main entry under title:

Merriam-Webster's intermediate dictionary.

Previously published as: Webster's Intermediate Dictionary

1. English languages—Dictionaries,   Juvenile. [1. English language—Dictionaries]
I. Merriam-Webster Inc.   II. Title: Intermediate dictionary.
PE1628.5.W387   1994   423—dc20   93-30427
ISBN 0-87779-479-0   CIP

Merriam-Webster's Intermediate Dictionary principal copyright 1986

Printed in the United States of America

ISBN 0-03-096483-0

12   062   01

Contents

Preface

◆

MERRIAM-WEBSTER'S MIDDLE SCHOOL DICTIONARY

is the middle book of a three-dictionary series prepared especially for elementary and secondary students. It is preceded by *Merriam-Webster's Elementary Dictionary* and followed by *Merriam-Webster's High School Dictionary. Merriam-Webster's Middle School Dictionary* is intended for use primarily by students in junior high schools and middle schools. The range of the vocabulary covered is suited to the needs of older students, but definitions have been written in everyday language that young students will find clear.

This dictionary has been edited by the permanent Merriam-Webster staff of trained and experienced lexicographers. They have selected the entries chiefly on the basis of their occurrence in textbooks and other school materials in all subjects. The editors have also had access to the many millions of examples of English words used in context that form the extensive Merriam-Webster citation files and that underlie *Webster's Third New International Dictionary, Merriam-Webster's Collegiate Dictionary,* and other Merriam-Webster® dictionaries. Reliance on this broad base of evidence has helped the editors make sure that the current general vocabulary of English has received its proper share of attention, while still giving the language of special school subjects—traditional ones like mathematics, science, and social studies and newer ones like computers—the full coverage that today's students need.

Merriam-Webster's Middle School Dictionary will give you all the information you would expect to have about how words are spelled, how they are pronounced, and what they mean; moreover, it also has a number of features found in more advanced Merriam-Webster® dictionaries. For example, the fascinating study of where words come from is deepened here: Many formal etymologies in square brackets have been added to the word history paragraphs, which may already be familiar to you. Other paragraphs that follow definitions discuss the small but important differences in meaning that help keep synonyms distinct and make one more appropriate than another in a particular context. One thousand illustrations of animals, plants, vehicles, musical instruments, articles of clothing, and many other kinds of things supplement and enrich the information given in definitions. In addition, special tables answer your questions about such matters as the name of a book of the Bible, the relation of a U.S. measure to its metric equivalent, or the diameter of a planet in our solar system. In the back of your dictionary, you will find separate sections giving you information about common abbreviations; names of figures from history, mythology, and the Bible; names of places; signs and symbols; and a list of commonly misspelled words.

Merriam-Webster's Middle School Dictionary can become a very valuable book to you, helping you with your studies and answering many of your questions about words in the English language. It is not a book to be read once and then set aside; instead, you will want to pick it up again and again. The more you use it, of course, the more useful it will become to you. Using a dictionary well is not always an easy and obvious matter, however. The editors of your dictionary have used a variety of type styles and a number of special words, abbreviations, and symbols to help them pack as much information as they possibly could into a small space for you. These signals are explained fully in the next section, called "Using Your Dictionary." You need to read it carefully and become familiar with what it tells you. Then you will be able to get the most from your dictionary. ◆

Merriam-Webster Inc.

Using Your Dictionary

 DICTIONARY ENTRIES

The entries in the dictionary are all the words printed in **boldface** type. The **main entries** are the entries that are listed in alphabetical order at the extreme left in a column. Most main entries are provided with a pronunciation, a part-of-speech label, and a definition. **Run-on entries** are the entries that can be found at the end of the definition of a main entry. When a run-on entry is a single word, no definition is given. An undefined run-on entry contains a form of the main entry word. If you were unsure about the meaning of the run-on, you would look up the meaning of the suffix and combine it with an appropriate meaning of the main entry word. When a run-on entry consists of a commonly used phrase, a definition is provided.

> ¹**talk** . . . *vb* **1 :** to express in speech (*talk* sense)
>   **2** . . . **3** . . . **4** . . . **5 a** . . . **b** . . . **6 a** . . **b** . . .
>   — **talk·er** *n* — **talk back :** to answer disrespectfully

In the above example, both **talker** and **talk back** are run-on entries. **Variant spellings** and **inflected forms** (such as plurals of nouns and past tenses of verbs), which are discussed later in separate sections, are also given in boldface type and are considered dictionary entries.

Most main entries are single words, but some are not. A main entry can also be a prefix like ¹**a–** on page 1, a suffix like **–ability** on page 2, a combining form like **bio–** on page 72, a combination of words like **abominable snowman** and **about-face** on page 2, a combination of letters like **IOU** on page 400, or a combination of a numeral and a letter like **3-D** on page 794.

 ORDER OF ENTRIES

Throughout the dictionary, main entries are alphabetized by first letter, then second letter, and so on, regardless of any spaces or hyphens that may appear in them. When a main entry contains a numeral, consider the numeral as though it were a spelled-out word, and you will find it at its alphabetical place. For example, **4-H** appears on page 299 between **four-footed** and **four-in-hand.** Likewise, when a word is usually spelled with an abbreviation, such as **St. Bernard,** consider the spelled-out form (in this case **Saint**), and you will find it at its alphabetical place (on page 666 between **Saint Andrew's cross** and **sainted**).

When main entries are spelled exactly alike but have different functions in a sentence (such as noun and verb) or have different origins, they are called **homographs.** Each homograph is indicated by a small raised numeral at the very beginning of the word. For example, on page 6 ¹**account** and ²**account** are entered as separate homographs because they have different functions (the first is a noun, the second is a verb). The entries ¹**calf** and ²**calf** (on page 103) are separate homographs because they have different origins (the first from an Old English word, the second from a Norse word). In general, homographs are listed and numbered in the order in which they came into the language. The word *calf* meaning a young cow came into the language before the word *calf* meaning a part of the leg.

When main entries are spelled alike except that one of them is capitalized, the one not capitalized is listed first. For example, on page 300 **frank** is listed before **Frank.**

When main entries are compounds, such as **standby, stand by, stand-in,** and **stand in,** the solid form is entered first, then the hyphenated form, and then the open form, with a space between its parts. Thus, **standby** comes before **stand by,** and **stand-in** comes before **stand in.**

 GUIDE WORDS

At the top of each page are two large boldface words separated by a dot. These are called **guide words.** They show the alphabetical range of the entries on that page, and you can use them to help you find a word quickly. For example, if you are looking up the word *famine,* look at the guide words as you flip through the pages. Stop when you come to the guide words between which the word *famine*

alphabetically falls. The page having the guide words **fall • famously** (page 272) is the page you want. If you stop at the preceding page (page 271), the guide words **fail • fall** tell you that you are not yet where you want to be. If you stop at the following page (page 273), the guide words **fan • farthest** tell you that you have gone too far.

The guide words are usually the first and last main entries on the page, but there are exceptions. Actually, the guide words are the first and last entries alphabetically on the page, and this includes all the boldface entries, not just the main entries. A guide word is most often a main entry, but it may also be a variant spelling, an inflected form, or a run-on entry.

Look, for example, at the guide words on page 802. The first guide word, **together,** is also the first main entry. But the second guide word is **tonally,** while the last main entry on the page is **tonality. Tonally** is actually a run-on entry at the main entry **tonal,** but it is alphabetically the last entry on the page and so is the proper guide word.

Like main entries, guide words are always in alphabetical order from page to page throughout the book. Once in a while, this system presents a problem where the alphabetically last entry on a page—the one that would normally be chosen as the second guide word—is actually later in alphabetical order than the first guide word on the next page. In such cases, a different second guide word must be chosen, one that does not disturb the alphabetical order of the guide words from page to page.

Look, for example, at pages 556 and 557. Notice that the first guide word on page 557 is the run-on entry **perceiver,** because it is the alphabetically first entry on the page. Now look at the bottom of page 556: You can see that the alphabetically last entry on the page is the inflected form **perceiving,** yet it is not the second guide word. The second guide word is the inflected form **perceived,** which is in alphabetical order with **perceiver** on the next page. If **perceiving** were used as the second guide word, alphabetical order would be broken, so **perceiving** is ignored.

 ## VARIANT SPELLINGS

A number of main entries have a second, and sometimes a third, spelling also shown in boldface. These alternate spellings are called **variants.**

Variants that are separated by the word *or* are equal variants. Either spelling of such variants is equally acceptable with the other in current English. Equal variants are usually listed in alphabetical order, such as **fan·ta·sy** *or* **phan·ta·sy.** However, if one of the equal variants is used slightly more frequently, that one is entered first even though it may not fall alphabetically first, such as **di·a·logue** *or* **di·a·log.**

Variants that are separated by the word *also* are not equal variants, and the one listed before the word *also* is considerably more common than the one that follows the word *also.* Thus, at the entry **glam·or·ous** *also*

glam·our·ous, the first spelling is used more often than the second, but both spellings are considered acceptable.

Occasionally, both *or* and *also* are used to separate a number of variants at a single entry. For example, three variants are shown for the following entry: **bo·gey** *also* **bo·gy** *or* **bo·gie.** This indicates that neither **bogy** nor **bogie** is as commonly used as **bogey,** but all three are considered acceptable.

Some variants are entered separately at their own alphabetical places. These are followed by the italicized words *variant of* and a cross-reference in small capital letters to the more common spelling or form.

> **despatch** *variant of* DISPATCH

> **aeroplane** *chiefly British variant of* AIRPLANE

Variants that are standard in American English are given at the main entry and are entered again at their own alphabetical places only if they fall one column or more away from the main entry. Variants that are restricted in some way (as by being chiefly British or dialect) are found only at their own alphabetical places.

When one variant is more common for a particular meaning than for other meanings, it is given before the definition with an indication of how common it is.

> ¹**disk** *or* **disc** . . . **2** . . . **b** *usually disc* : a phonograph record

> ¹**nick·el** . . . **2 a** *also* **nick·le** : the U.S. five-cent piece made of nickel and copper

If the variant is shown in boldface at the beginning of the entry, as **disc** is, it appears in italic before the definition. If it is not shown at the beginning of the entry, as **nickle** is not, it appears in boldface before the definition.

CENTERED DOTS AND HYPHENATION

In this dictionary, the boldface centered dots in entries indicate the acceptable places to put a hyphen when the word is divided at the end of a line. For example, the dots in the entry **in·ter·con·ti·nen·tal** indicate that the word may be broken at the end of a line as follows:

in-
tercontinental

inter-
continental

intercon-
tinental

interconti-
nental

intercontinen-
tal

It is customary to avoid dividing a word so that a single letter is left at the end of one line or the beginning of the next line. For this reason, this dictionary does not show any division in such words as **eject, away, lily,** and **risky.** Thus, the dots that show end-of-line division do not always separate the syllables of a word. Syllables are shown only in the pronunciation, explained in the next section.

In the case of homographs, the divisions are usually indicated only in the first homograph, but these apply to all the following homographs.

¹par·al·lel . . . *adj* . . .

²parallel *n* . . .

³parallel *vt* . . .

A word in a compound made up of two or more separate words is divided only when no individual entry exists for that word.

Dew·ey decimal system . . . *n* . . .

diabetes mel·li·tus . . . *n* . . .

pri·ma don·na . . . *n* . . .

There are no separate entries for *Dewey, mellitus, prima,* or *donna.*

This dictionary also uses a special double hyphen ⸗ at the end of a line when the word being broken is usually spelled with a hyphen at that point. For example, at the entry **out-of-bounds** on page 533, the word is broken at the end of the second line with a double hyphen so as to show that the word is spelled *out-of-bounds* rather than *outofbounds.*

 PRONUNCIATION

It is often difficult to tell how a word is pronounced from its spelling. For example, in *bat, late, any,* and *above,* the letter *a* stands for a different sound in each word. In addition, many words are pronounced in more than one way, even though they may have only one accepted spelling.

To represent the sounds of spoken English in a written form, a special set of pronunciation symbols is used. Each symbol stands for only one sound, and each sound is represented by only one symbol.

The pronunciation of most entry words is shown immediately following the boldface entry. To make it clear that pronunciation symbols are being used and not regular letters, the symbols are always shown between slant lines \ \.

A complete list of pronunciation symbols used in this dictionary appears on page 14A. For ready reference, a shorter list of symbols is printed at the bottom of the right column on odd-numbered pages throughout the dictionary. Following most of the symbols in the chart are words containing the sound of that symbol. The boldface letters in these words are the letters that have the same sound as the symbol.

For example, following the symbol **j** are the words **j**ob, **g**em, e**dge.** The boldface **j** in **j**ob, the **g** in **g**em, and the

dge in e**dge** are all pronounced \j\.

At the beginning of the list of pronunciation symbols is the symbol **ə,** called a **schwa** \'shwä\. This symbol often represents the sound of an unstressed vowel (as the first and last vowels in *America*), but it may also represent the sound of a stressed vowel (as the first vowel of *brother*).

Hyphens are used in the pronunciation to indicate the syllables of a word.

noisy \'nȯi-zē\ (2 syllables)

no·tice·able \'nōt-ə-sə-bəl\ (4 syllables)

Of course, the syllables of words are not separated when we speak. One sound follows right after another without pause. It is obvious in the example *noticeable* above that the number and position of hyphens are not the same as the number and position of dots in the entry word. Only the hyphens show syllables; the dots mark acceptable places to divide the word at the end of a line.

Some syllables are spoken with greater force or stress than others. In this dictionary the primary (strongest) stress is shown by a high-set vertical mark \'\ placed immediately *before* the stressed syllable. Secondary (slightly weaker) stress is shown by a low-set vertical mark \ˌ\ also placed immediately *before* the stressed syllable. In the word *notify,* for example, the first syllable receives primary stress, and the last syllable receives secondary stress. The middle syllable receives weak stress and is not marked in this dictionary. All of this information is shown in the pronunciation \'nōt-ə-ˌfī\.

Many words have more than one acceptable pronunciation. Variant pronunciations are separated by commas, and sometimes groups of variants are separated by semicolons. When the word *also* separates variant pronunciations, the one following the *also* is not as common as the one preceding it. All the variant pronunciations shown in this dictionary are quite acceptable and are used by educated speakers of English.

When a variant pronunciation is shown, sometimes only part of the pronunciation of the word changes. In such cases, only the part that changes may be shown. To get the full pronunciation, add the part that changes to the part that stays the same.

ec·o·nom·ic \ˌek-ə-'näm-ik, ˌē-kə-\

ei·ther \'ē-t͟hər *also* 'ī-\

ex·pi·ra·to·ry \ik-'spī-rə-ˌtōr-ē, ek-, -tȯr-; 'ēk-sp(ə-)rə-\

If a variant is used mostly in a particular region of the United States or in a part of the English-speaking world outside the United States, that location is identified.

¹sure \'shu̇(ə)r, *especially Southern* 'shō(ə)r\

¹sched·ule \'skej-ü(ə)l, -əl, *Canadian also* 'shej-, *British usually* 'shed-yü(ə)l\

When a pronunciation symbol is enclosed in parentheses, as at **¹sure,** that sound may or may not be pronounced. Thus, **sure** may be pronounced as \'shur\ or \'shu̇ər\ and in the South as \'shōr\ or \'shōər\.

If an incomplete pronunciation is given for an entry word, the missing portion may be found at a preceding entry.

sword \'sō(ə)rd, 'sȯ(ə)rd\

sword·fish \-ˌfish\

Thus, the full pronunciation of *swordfish* is \'sō(ə)rd-ˌfish, 'sȯ(ə)rd-ˌfish\. In the case of homographs, if the pronunciation is the same for each homograph, the pronunciation is given only for the first.

¹**quack** \'kwak\ *n*   ¹**short** \'shȯ(ə)rt\ *adj*

²**quack** *vb*   ²**short** *adv*

Many entries for compounds made up of two or more separate words will also have missing pronunciations. Look at the entries for the separate words to determine their pronunciation. If one of the words has no entry of its own, however, the pronunciation of that word will be shown at the entry for the compound.

monarch butterfly *n* . . .

hog·nose snake \ˌhȯg-ˌnōz-, ˌhäg-\ *n* . . .

Some undefined run-on entries show no pronunciation. In these cases, the pronunciation of the run-on is the pronunciation of the main entry plus the pronunciation of the suffix, which may be found at its own alphabetical place.

bossy \'bȯ-sē\ *adj* . . . — **bos·si·ness** *n*

Thus, the pronunciation of **bossiness** is \'bȯ-sē-nəs\, which is not shown because it is simply \'bȯ-sē\ plus \nəs\.

 THE FUNCTIONS OF WORDS

The several different grammatical functions of words are known as **parts of speech.** This dictionary identifies the function of most entry words with one of the eight traditional part-of-speech labels, abbreviated, italicized, and placed after the boldface entry itself or after the pronunciation, when one is given.

bur·glar . . . *n* (noun)

cease . . . *vb* (verb)

de·li·cious . . . *adj* (adjective)

fair·ly . . . *adv* (adverb)

you . . . *pron* (pronoun)

in·to . . . *prep* (preposition)

or . . . *conj* (conjunction)

ouch . . . *interj* (interjection)

When a noun is always used in the plural, the label *n pl* is used. A noun so labeled always takes a plural verb.

she·nan·i·gans . . . *n pl*

trou·sers . . . *n pl*

Sometimes, an entry word that is spelled as a plural may take either a singular or a plural verb, depending on its use. For example, although the word *acrobatics* is plural in form, it may be singular in such uses as "Acrobatics is a strenuous activity" or plural in "You make these acrobatics look easy." To indicate such uses, the word *acrobatics* is given the label *n sing or pl*.

In addition to the traditional part-of-speech labels, there are a number of other functional labels used in this dictionary.

> **may**   . . . *helping verb*
> **me·thinks**   . . . *impersonal verb*
> **avast**   . . . *imperative verb*
> **an**   . . . *indefinite article*
> **the**   . . . *definite article*
> **Fris·bee**   . . . *trademark*
> **Re·al·tor** . . . *collective mark*
> **—gram**   . . . *n combining form*
> **—ous**   . . . *adj suffix*
> **non—**   . . . *prefix*

 INFLECTED FORMS

Inflected forms include the plural forms of nouns; the past tense, past participle, and present participle forms of verbs; and the comparative and superlative forms of adjectives and adverbs. In most instances, these forms are regular (that is, they are formed by the addition of *-s* or *-es* to nouns, *-ed* and *-ing* to verbs, and *-er* and *-est* to adjectives and adverbs). These regular inflected forms are not shown in this dictionary. Irregular inflected forms, such as those that involve a change in the spelling of the root word or a doubling of a final letter, are shown in boldface.

As with variants of main entries, variants of inflected forms are equal when they are separated by *or*. If they are out of alphabetical order, the one shown first is slightly more common. Variants separated by *also* are not equal, however, and the one shown first is considerably more common than the other. Even so, both variants are acceptable.

An effort is usually made to save space in showing inflected forms by showing only the last part for words of more than two syllables. The form is usually cut back to the point that corresponds to the last end-of-line division indicated in the main entry.

the·o·ry . . . *n, pl* **-ries** . . .

or·ga·nize . . . *vb* **nized; -niz·ing** . . .

Inflected forms whose own alphabetical places are more than one column away from the main entry are given separate entry there with a cross-reference in small capital letters to the main entry.

geese *pl of* GOOSE

brought *past and past participle of* BRING

A. Plurals of Nouns

Nouns that form their plurals simply by the addition of *–s* or *–es* are not shown unless there is a chance that they may be mistaken or misspelled.

mon·key . . . *n, pl* **monkeys** [not *monkies*]

mon·goose . . . *n, pl* **mon·goos·es** [not *mongeese*]

Nouns that form their plurals in any other way than by the addition of *–s* or *–es* to an unchanged base have such plurals shown.

cad·dy . . . *n, pl* **caddies** [*–y* changes to *–i–*]

child . . . *n, pl* **chil·dren** [irregular ending]

knife . . . *n, pl* **knives** [*–f–* changes to *–v–*]

oa·sis . . . *n, pl* **oa·ses** [Greek plural]

se·ta . . . *n, pl* **se·tae** [Latin plural]

ser·aph . . . *n, pl* **ser·a·phim** [Hebrew plural]

deer . . . *n, pl* **deer** [no change at all]

Most compound nouns form their plural by pluralizing the final element. Such plurals are not shown when the final element is a recognizable word entered at its own place (such as *blueberry* and *eyetooth*). Plurals for compounds that pluralize any but the last element are shown.

son-in-law . . . *n, pl* **sons-in-law**

secretary-general . . . *n, pl* **secretaries-general**

Plurals are also given for all entries that have variant plural forms.

in·dex . . . *n, pl* **in·dex·es** *or* **in·di·ces**

mon·si·gnor . . . *n, pl* **monsignors** *or* **mon·si·gno·ri**

ban·jo . . . *n, pl* **banjos** *also* **banjoes**

Irregular plural forms are also entered at their own alphabetical place in this dictionary when they fall more than one column away from the singular entry. You will find **feet,** for example, entered on page 276 because it falls more than a column away from the singular **foot.** However, the irregular plural **oxen** is not shown at its own place because it does not fall more than a column away from **ox.** Irregular plurals that are shown at their own alphabetical place have a cross-reference in small capital letters to the singular form.

lice *pl of* LOUSE

media *pl of* MEDIUM

B. Forms of Verbs

Some inflected forms of a verb are especially important because they are used to form all the verb tenses. These forms are the present tense, past tense, past participle, and present participle. Most verbs in English form the past tense and past participle by the addition of *–ed* to the base form, which is also the present tense form. They form the present participle by the addition of *–ing* to the base form. These verbs are considered to be regular, and their inflected forms are not shown in this dictionary.

Inflected forms are shown if they are created in any other way, even if it is no more than a matter of dropping a final *–e* before the ending is added. Variants of inflected forms are always shown. When the past participle has the same form as the past tense, only one form is shown.

grow . . . *vb* **grew** . . . ; **grown** . . . ; **grow·ing**

¹**fade** . . . *vb* **fad·ed**; **fad·ing**

¹**chop** . . . *vb* **chopped**; **chop·ping**

²**bias** *vb* **bi·ased** *or* **bi·assed**; **bi·as·ing** *or* **bi·as·sing**

²**picnic** *vb* **pic·nicked**; **pic·nick·ing**

¹**fry** . . . **fried**; **fry·ing**

C. Forms of Adjectives and Adverbs

Most adjectives and adverbs form their comparative and superlative forms with the words *more* or *most* or with the addition of *–er* and *–est* to the simple form. These adjectives and adverbs are considered regular, and such forms are not shown in this dictionary. Any other spelling changes (such as changing *–y* to *–i–*, doubling the final consonant, or dropping *–e*) are shown. All variant forms are shown. To save space, superlative forms are often cut back to the ending *–est*.

¹**good** . . . *adj* **bet·ter** . . . ; **best**

¹**red** . . . *adj* **red·der**; **red·dest**

sandy . . . *adj* **sand·i·er**; **–est**

³**fine** *adj* **fin·er**; **fin·est**

¹**ear·ly** . . . *adv* **ear·li·er**; **–est**

²**much** *adv* **more**; **most**

spry . . . *adv* **spri·er** *or* **spry·er** . . . ; **spri·est** *or* **spry·est**

◆ DEFINITIONS

A **definition** is the statement of the meaning of an entry word. In this dictionary each definition is set off by a bold-face colon.

¹**fan** *n* : an enthusiastic follower or admirer

op·ti·mis·tic . . . *adj* : showing optimism : expecting everything to come out all right : HOPEFUL

Often, instead of a statement or in addition to it, one or more cross-references to synonyms are given in small capital letters. A full definition can be found at the entry that is referred to.

law·mak·er . . . *n* : LEGISLATOR

mer·i·to·ri·ous . . . *adj* : deserving reward or honor : PRAISEWORTHY

When an entry word has more than one sense, the appropriate number precedes each sense.

hoax . . . *n* **1** : an act intended to trick or deceive **2** : something false passed off or accepted as genuine

Sometimes, a definition is so closely related to the definition preceding it that, instead of a number, an italic *also* or *esp* (for *especially*) separates the two definitions. The divider *esp* is used to introduce the most common meaning included in the more general definition just before it. The divider *also* is used to introduce a meaning that is closely related to and derived from the preceding meaning.

opus . . . *n* . . . : ¹WORK 7; *esp* : a musical composition or set of compositions

sand·bur . . . *n* : any of a genus of grasses native to warm sandy areas that produce spine-covered seeds; *also* : one of these seeds

A numbered sense can be further divided into subsenses preceded by small boldface letters. Sometimes, an unnumbered sense is divided into lettered subsenses.

erode . . . *vb* . . . **1 a** : to destroy gradually by chemical means : CORRODE **b** : to wear away by or as if by the action of water, wind, or glacial ice **2** : to undergo erosion

²**scope** *n* : any of various instruments for viewing: as **a** : MICROSCOPE **b** : ¹TELESCOPE **c** : OSCILLOSCOPE

In this dictionary, the definitions of senses of a word are listed in historical order, just as homographs are. Listing by historical order means that sense **1** was used in English before sense **2**, sense **2** before sense **3**, and so forth. It does not mean, however, that sense **3** necessarily developed from sense **2**. It may have done so, or sense **2** and sense **3** may have developed independently from sense **1**. Sometimes, you can tell just by the way definitions are worded that one sense developed out of another.

¹**branch** . . . *n* **1** : a natural division of a plant stem (as a bough growing from a trunk or twig from a bough) **2** : something extending from a main line or source ⟨river *branch*⟩ a ⟨railroad *branch*⟩ **3** : a separate or subordinate division or part of a central system ⟨executive *branch* of the government⟩ ⟨a *branch* of a bank⟩

In the above entry, phrases are provided within angle brackets ⟨ ⟩ to illustrate common ways of using the entry word in the indicated sense. These phrases are called **verbal illustrations.**

Sometimes, in addition to or in place of a definition, you will find a cross-reference to a table that lists other similar terms or a cross-reference that sends you to another entry for related information.

Sag·it·tar·i·us . . . *n* . . . **2 a** : the ninth sign of the zodiac — see ZODIAC table

Dan·iel . . . *n* — see BIBLE table

digital computer *n* : a computer that operates with numbers expressed as digits (as in the binary system) — compare ANALOG COMPUTER

 CAPITALIZATION

When an entry word is usually capitalized in ordinary writing, it is entered in this dictionary with a capital letter. Other entries begin with a lowercase letter. A few such entries also have an italic label *often cap*. This label indicates that the word is capitalized about as often as it is lowercased.

Oc·to·ber . . . *n* . . .

ver·dant . . . *adj* . . .

an·gli·cize . . . *vb* . . . *often cap* . . .

Some words have special meanings when capitalized that they do not have when they are written without a capital letter. This dictionary shows the use of the capital with such entries by putting the label *cap* or *often cap* at the appropriate sense.

col·os·se·um . . . *n* **1** *cap* : an outdoor arena built in Rome in the first century A.D. **2** : COLISEUM

Occasionally, some words that are almost always capitalized in their usual meanings have special meanings in which they are not capitalized. In this dictionary the labels *not cap* or *often not cap* are given at the proper sense.

Re·nais·sance . . . *n* **1** : the period of European history between the 14th and 17th centuries marked by a fresh interest in ancient art and literature and by the beginnings of modern science **2** *often not cap* : a movement or period of great activity (as in literature, science, and the arts)

²**Roman** *adj* **1** : of or relating to Rome or the Romans or the empire of which Rome was the original capital **2 a** . . . **b** . . . **3** *not cap* : of or relating to a type style with upright characters (as in "these definitions")

SPECIAL USAGE LABELS AND GUIDE PHRASES

For many entries, italic labels identify the kind of context in which the word or a sense of the word is usually found. Some of the most commonly used labels in this dictionary are

archaic (once standard but now used only in special contexts)

slang (very informal usage not usually found in formal writing)

substandard (not normally used by educated speakers and writers) *nonstandard* (sometimes used by well-educated people but not always considered appropriate for good usage)

British (common only in Great Britain or the British Commonwealth countries)

Scottish (common only in Scotland)

dialect (common only in one or more regions of the United States.)

Regional labels like the last three in the list above are often preceded by the word *chiefly*. This modifier indicates that the word or meaning is most common in the named region but has some use outside it.

The following examples illustrate the use of such special usage labels:

thou . . . *pron, archaic* : the person addressed

lid . . . *n* . . . **3** *slang* : HAT

ain't . . . **2** *substandard* **a** : have not **b** : has not

lay . . . *vb* . . . **4** *nonstandard* : ¹LIE

¹sis·ter . . . *n* . . . **6** *chiefly British* : ¹NURSE 2

auld . . . *adj, chiefly Scottish* : OLD

craw·dad . . . *n, dialect* : CRAYFISH 1

At a few entries, an italicized **guide phrase** may be provided before a definition to identify the reference of a special meaning.

PG . . . *adj, of a motion picture* : . . .

oblique . . . *adj* . . . **2** *of a solid* : . . .

USAGE NOTES

For some entries, a note beginning with a phrase such as "used as," "used in," or "used to" may be added to a definition. This **usage note** is set off by a dash.

le·ga·to . . . *adv or adj* : in a manner that is smooth and connected — used as a direction in music

³slow *vb* : to make or go slow or slower — often used with *down* or *up*

²shear *n* **1 a** : a cutting tool similar or identical to a pair of scissors but typically larger — usually used in pl.

When a word has a special use that cannot easily or clearly be explained in a definition, a usage note may take the place of a definition.

ouch . . . *interj* — used to express sudden pain

²let *vb* . . . **3** . . . **b** — used to introduce a request

SYNONYM PARAGRAPHS

At selected entries, the boldface abbreviation **syn** (for *synonym*) introduces a paragraph of explanation at the end of the definition. This **synonym paragraph** explains and illustrates with examples the relation of words that are similar in meaning to the main entry. Here is the synonym paragraph for *decline*:

¹de·cline . . . *vb* . . . **5** . . .

syn DECLINE, REFUSE, REJECT mean to express unwillingness to go along with a demand or request. DECLINE suggests a polite negative response 〈*decline* an invitation to a party〉 REFUSE suggests a forceful or absolute denial 〈*refused* to see him at all〉 REJECT may suggest an unwillingness even to consider a demand or request 〈*rejected* her plan before she had finished speaking〉

Notice that the words being discussed are listed at the beginning of the paragraph in small capital letters, followed by a statement of the meaning that they have in common. Next, something is said about the special element of meaning each word has that makes it different from the other words in the list. A verbal illustration follows, showing the special meaning of the word in action.

At the main entries for these words (except the first word), you will find a cross-reference to this synonym paragraph. This cross-reference is also introduced by the boldface abbreviation **syn** following the definition.

¹re·fuse . . . *vb* . . . **3** . . . **syn** see DECLINE

¹re·ject . . . *vb* . . . **4** . . . **syn** see DECLINE

ETYMOLOGIES

At many entries, the origin of the entry word is shown by tracing it or its parts back to the earliest known forms and meanings. Such information is called an **etymology.** In this dictionary the etymologies are shown within square brackets [ ] generally just after the definition.

Names of languages in etymologies are given in full rather than abbreviated. No attempt has been made to distinguish the major historical periods of languages other than English. The appearance of the phrase "derived from" before a new language name and form indicates that one or more minor states of development have been omitted for clarity and simplicity. Language forms within etymologies are given in italics, and their meanings are placed inside quotation marks.

li·co·rice . . . *n* . . . [Middle English *licorice* "licorice," from early French *licorice* (same meaning), from Latin *liquiritia* (same meaning), derived from Greek *glykyrrhiza*, literally "sweet root"]

If no language name appears before a form, the language is the last one named. Thus, in the etymology of **abbreviate,** *abbreviare* and *brevis* are Latin words and *ad–* is a Latin prefix.

ab·bre·vi·ate . . . *vb* . . . [Middle English *abbreviaten* "abbreviate," from Latin *abbreviatus* "made short," from *abbreviare* "to shorten," from earlier *ad–* "to" and *brevis* "short" — related to ABRIDGE, BRIEF]

Sometimes, an etymology explains how the word came to be applied to something.

red·let·ter . . . *adj* **:** worth remembering especially in a happy or joyful way a *red-letter* day [from the practice of marking holy days in red letters in church calendars]

When a word comes from the name of a person, the name of a place, or some other proper name, this fact is often given in the etymology.

sax·o·phone . . . *n* [named for Antoine "Adolph" *Sax* 1814–1894 a Belgian maker of musical instruments]

pan·de·mo·ni·um . . . *n* . . . [from *Pandemonium*, name of the place of demons in *Paradise Lost* by John Milton, derived from Greek *pan–* "all, every, completely" and Greek *daimon* "devil, demon"]

Wal·dorf salad . . . *n* . . . [named for the *Waldorf-Astoria Hotel* in New York City]

To some extent, words exist in families, just as people do. Particularly with borrowings into English from Latin and Greek, many words may be derived from a single ancestor. Sometimes, the connection is evident when you see the words together, as in the case of *final, define, finish,* and *infinity.* Sometimes, however, the connection may have been blurred somewhat by changes in spelling and meaning over the centuries, as in the case of *nautical, nausea,* and *noise.* Such connections between words are interesting in themselves, and they can also be helpful to you in learning new words. Your attention is drawn to such connections in etymologies by a note that begins "— related to" and continues with one or more cross-references (in small capital letters) to the related entries. Each of the entries named will have its own etymology and a similar note.

[1]cross . . . *n* . . . [Old English *cros,* probably from an early Norse or an early Irish word derived from Latin *crux* "cross" — related to CRUCIAL, CRUISE, CRUSADE, CRUX, EXCRUCIATING]

cru·cial . . . *adj* . . . [from French *crucial* "having the form of a cross, being or involving a crisis," from Latin *cruc–, crux* "cross, trouble, torture" —related to CROSS, CRUCIFY, CRUX]

cruise . . . *vb* . . . [from Dutch *kruisen* "to cruise, move crosswise," from early Dutch *crūce* "cross," from Latin *crux* "cross" — related to CROSS, CRUCIAL]

[1]cru·sade . . . *n* . . . [derived from early French *croisade* and Spanish *cruzada,* both meaning literally "an expedition of persons marked with or bearing the sign of the cross" and both derived from Latin *cruc–, crux* "cross" — related to CROSS]

crux . . . *n* . . . [from Latin *crux* "cross, torture, trouble" — related to CROSS, CRUCIAL, CRUCIFY]

ex·cru·ci·at·ing . . . *adj* . . . [derived from Latin *excruciatus,* past participle of *excruciare* "to torture," from *ex–* "out of, from" and *cruciare* "to torment, crucify," from *cruc–, crux* "cross" — related to CROSS, CRUCIAL, CRUCIFY]

 ## WORD HISTORIES

Some of the many English words that have interesting histories are provided with a **Word History** paragraph. Such a paragraph follows the definition and is followed by the etymology.

ca·nary . . . *n* . . .
Word History The small bird we call a canary owes its name to big dogs. Early explorers of a group of islands off the northwest coast of Africa reported seeing many large dogs there. Romans reading these reports gave the islands the Latin name *Canariae insulae,* meaning "dog islands," which was borrowed into English as *Canary islands.* The dogs from which the islands got their name were probably not native to the islands but brought there from Africa. Truly native to the islands were small greenish brown birds. Some of these were taken to Europe in the 16th century for pets. Since they came from the Canary islands, they were called *canary birds* in England. The yellow bird kept as a pet today is a descendant of the wild greenish birds of the "dog islands." [from *Canary (islands),* from Spanish *Islas Canarias* "Canary islands," from Latin *Canariae insulae,* literally "dog islands," from *canis* "dog" — related to CANINE]

 ## LISTS OF UNDEFINED WORDS

Lists of words appear without definitions at the following prefix entries in this dictionary:

non–	**re–**
over–	**un–**

The meanings of the listed compounds formed with these prefixes are easily understandable from the meaning of the prefix combined with the meaning of the base word. Compounds that are not easily understandable in this way are entered at their own place with definitions. For example, **nonobjective** is entered and defined at its own place because its meaning is not easily understandable as the sum of the meanings of **non–** and **objective.**

PRONUNCIATION SYMBOLS

ə	(called *schwa* \\'shwä\\) b**a**n**a**n**a**, c**o**llide, **a**but; in stressed syllables as in h**u**mdr**u**m, m**o**ther, ab**u**t	k	used for a rasping sound between \\k\\ and \\h\\, as in German i**ch,** Bu**ch,** one pronunciation of lo**ch, ch**utzpah
ə	used before \\l\\, \\n\\, and \\m\\, as in batt**le,** mitt**en,** and one pronunciation of op**en** \\'ōp-ᵊm\\	l	**l**i**l**y, poo**l,** morta**l**
		m	**m**ur**m**ur
ər	f**ur**ther, m**er**ger	n	**n**i**n**e, cotto**n**
a	**a**x, m**a**p	ŋ	si**ng,** si**ng**er, fi**ng**er, i**nk**
ā	**a**ge, v**a**c**a**tion, d**ay**	ō	l**ow,** b**o**ne, c**oo**perate
ä	f**a**ther, c**o**t, c**a**rt	ȯ	m**o**th, l**a**w, s**o**rt, **a**ll
à	used for a sound between \\a\\ and \\ä\\, as in an eastern New England pronunciation of **au**nt, h**a**lf	ȯi	c**oi**n, destr**oy**
		p	**p**e**pp**er, li**p**
		r	**r**a**r**ity
au̇	**ou**t, n**ow**	s	**s**pice, le**ss**
b	**b**a**b**y, ri**b**	sh	**sh**y, di**sh,** ma**ch**ine, mi**ss**ion, spe**ci**al
ch	**ch**in, ma**tch,** nature \\'nā-chər\\	t	**t**igh**t,** la**tt**er
d	**d**i**d,** la**dd**er	th	**th**in, e**th**er
e	l**e**ss	t͟h	**th**is, ei**th**er
ē	s**ea**w**ee**d, **a**ny, s**e**rial, c**e**r**ea**l	ü	b**oo**t, r**u**le
f	**f**i**f**ty, cu**ff, ph**one	u̇	f**oo**t, p**u**ll
g	**g**ift, pi**g,** bi**gg**er	v	gi**v**e, **v**i**v**id
h	**h**at, a**h**ead	w	**w**e, a**w**ay
i	tr**i**p	y	**y**ou, **y**et
ī	l**i**fe, b**uy,** m**y**	yü	f**ew, u**nion, m**u**le, **you**th
j	**j**ob, **g**em, e**dge**	yu̇	f**u**rious
k	**k**in, **c**oo**k, ch**asm	z	**z**one, rai**s**e
		zh	vi**s**ion, bei**g**e

\\ \\   slant lines used in pairs to mark the beginning and end of a pronunciation: \\'pen\\

ˈ   mark at the beginning of a syllable that has primary (strongest) stress: \\'pen-ə-ˌtrāt\\

ˌ   mark at the beginning of a syllable that has secondary (next-strongest) stress: \\'pen-ə-ˌtrāt\\

-      mark of syllable division in pronunciations [the mark of end-of-line division in boldface entry words is a centered dot · and the position of the two kinds of division often does not agree, as in **build·ing** \\'bil-diŋ\\, **spe·cial** \\'spesh-əl\\, **ca·ter** \\'kāt-ər\\]

( )   parentheses used to indicate that what is between them is present in some utterances but not in others: at **fac·to·ry,** \\'fak-t(ə-)rē\\ = \\'fak-tə-rē, 'fak-trē\\ or \\'fak-trē, 'fak-tə-rē\\

A

¹a \'ā\ *n, often cap* **1** : the first letter of the English alphabet **2** : a musical note referred to by the letter A : the sixth tone of a C-major scale **3** : a grade rating a student's work as superior

²a \ə, (')ā\ *indefinite article* **1** : some one unspecified ⟨a man overboard⟩ ⟨a dozen⟩ **2** : the same : ONE ⟨two of a kind⟩ ⟨birds of a feather⟩ **3** : of whatever kind : ANY ⟨a person who is sick can't work well⟩ **4** : in each : to each : for each ⟨twice a week⟩ — used in all senses before words beginning with a consonant sound; compare AN [Old English *ān* "one"]

¹a- \ə\ *prefix* **1** : on : in : at ⟨abed⟩ **2** : in a specified state or condition ⟨afire⟩ **3** : in (such) a manner ⟨aloud⟩ **4** : in the act or process of ⟨gone a-hunting⟩ [Old English *a-* "on, in, at"]

²a- \(')ā\ *or* **an-** \(')an\ *prefix* : not : without ⟨asexual⟩ — *a-* before consonants and sometimes before *h*, *an-* before vowels and usually before *h* ⟨anhydrate⟩ [derived from Greek *a-, an-* "not"]

aard·vark \'ärd-,värk\ *n* : a large burrowing African mammal that feeds on ants and termites with its long sticky tongue [from obsolete Afrikaans (South African Dutch), literally "earth pig"]

aardvark

ab- *prefix* : from : away : departing from ⟨abnormal⟩ [derived from Latin *ab-* "from, away"]

ab·a·ca \,ab-ə-'kä, 'ab-ə-,kä\ *n* : a fiber that comes from a banana tree native to the Philippines — called also *Manila hemp*

aback \ə-'bak\ *adv* **1** *archaic* : ²BACK 1, BACKWARD **2** : by surprise : UNAWARES ⟨taken *aback* by the turn of events⟩

aba·cus \'ab-ə-kəs, ə-'bak-əs\ *n, pl* **aba·ci** \'ab-ə-sī, -,kē; ə-'bak-,ī\ *or* **aba·cus·es** : an instrument for making calculations by sliding counters along rods or in grooves

¹abaft \ə-'baft\ *adv* : toward the stern : at the stern

²abaft *prep* : to the rear of; *esp* : toward the stern from

ab·a·lo·ne \,ab-ə-'lō-nē\ *n* : a mollusk with a flattened slightly spiral shell that has holes along the edge and is lined with mother-of-pearl

¹aban·don \ə-'ban-dən\ *vb* **1** : to give up completely **2** : to withdraw from often in the face of danger ⟨abandon ship⟩ **3** : to withdraw protection, support, or help from **4** : to give oneself up to an emotion — **aban·don·ment** \-mənt\ *n*

syn ABANDON, DESERT, FORSAKE mean to leave without intending to return. ABANDON suggests that the person or thing left behind is helpless or needs protection ⟨the baby was *abandoned* on the steps of the church⟩ DESERT suggests the breaking of a promise, duty, or relationship ⟨*deserted* the cause when there was trouble⟩ ⟨mining towns that were *deserted* after the gold rush⟩ FORSAKE stresses leaving behind something known or loved well ⟨brave soldiers *forsaking* their families and going off to war⟩

²abandon *n* **1** : a complete yielding to natural impulses **2** : ENTHUSIASM 1, EXUBERANCE

aban·doned \ə-'ban-dənd\ *adj* **1** : that has been deserted : left empty or unused ⟨an *abandoned* house⟩ **2** : completely free from restraint ⟨*abandoned* laughter⟩

abase \ə-'bās\ *vb* **abased; abas·ing** : to lower in rank or position : HUMBLE, DEGRADE — **abase·ment** \-mənt\ *n*

abash \ə-'bash\ *vb* : to destroy the self-control or self-confidence of **syn** see EMBARRASS — **abash·ment** \-mənt\ *n*

abate \ə-'bāt\ *vb* **abat·ed; abat·ing** : to make or become less ⟨the wind *abated*⟩ ⟨the excitement has *abated*⟩ — **abat·er** *n*

abate·ment \ə-'bāt-mənt\ *n* **1** : the act or process of abating : the state of being abated **2** : an amount abated (as from a tax)

ab·at·toir \'ab-ə-,twär\ *n* : SLAUGHTERHOUSE

ab·bess \'ab-əs\ *n* : the head of an abbey for women

ab·bey \'ab-ē\ *n, pl* **abbeys** **1 a** : MONASTERY **b** : CONVENT **2** : a church that once belonged to an abbey ⟨Westminster *Abbey*⟩

ab·bot \'ab-ət\ *n* : the head of an abbey for men

ab·bre·vi·ate \ə-'brē-vē-,āt\ *vb* **-at·ed; -at·ing** : to make briefer : SHORTEN; *esp* : to reduce (as a word) to a shorter form intended to stand for the whole [Middle English *abbreviaten* "abbreviate", from Latin *abbreviatus* "made short", from *abbreviare* "to shorten", from earlier *ad-* "to" and *brevis* "short" — related to ABRIDGE, BRIEF]

ab·bre·vi·a·tion \ə-,brē-vē-'ā-shən\ *n* **1** : the act or result of abbreviating : ABRIDGMENT **2** : a shortened form of a written word or phrase used in place of the whole

Ab·di·as \ab-'dī-əs\ *n* — see BIBLE table

ab·di·cate \'ab-di-,kāt\ *vb* **-cat·ed; -cat·ing** : to give up sovereign power, office, or responsibility formally — **ab·di·ca·tion** \,ab-di-'kā-shən\ *n*

ab·do·men \'ab-də-mən, ab-'dō-mən\ *n* **1 a** : the part of the body between the chest and the hips **b** : the body cavity containing the chief digestive organs — called also *abdominal cavity* **2** : the hind portion of the body behind the thorax in an arthropod — see INSECT illustration — **ab·dom·i·nal** \ab-'däm-ən-ᵊl, -nᵊl\ *adj* — **ab·dom·i·nal·ly** \-ē\ *adv*

ab·duct \ab-'dəkt\ *vb* **1** : to carry (a person) off by force **2** : to draw (a part of the body) away from a middle plane or line that divides the body or a bodily part into right and left halves — **ab·duc·tion** \-'dək-shən\ *n*

ab·duc·tor \ab-'dək-tər\ *n* : one that abducts; *esp* : a muscle that draws a body part (as an arm or finger) away from a plane or a line that divides the body or a hand or foot into right and left halves

abeam \ə-'bēm\ *adv or adj* : at right angles to a ship's keel

abed \ə-'bed\ *adv or adj* : in bed

Ab·er·deen An·gus \,ab-ər-,dē-'naŋ-gəs\ *n* : any of a breed of usually black hornless beef cattle originating in Scotland

Aberdeen Angus

ab·er·rant \ə-'ber-ənt, 'ab-ə-rənt\ *adj* : being different from the usual or natural type

ab·er·ra·tion \,ab-ə-'rā-shən\ *n* **1** : the act of differing especially from a moral standard or normal state **2** : unsoundness or disorder of the mind **3** : a small regularly occurring change of apparent position in heavenly bodies due to the combined effect of the motion of light and the motion of the observer

abet \ə-'bet\ *vb* **abet·ted; abet·ting** : to actively encourage or aid — **abet·ment** \-mənt\ *n* — **abet·tor** *or* **abet·ter** \-'bet-ər\ *n*

abey·ance \ə-'bā-ən(t)s\ *n* : a temporary interruption of activity ⟨plans held in *abeyance*⟩

ab·hor \ab-'hȯ(ə)r, ab-\ *vb* **ab·horred; ab·hor·ring** : to shrink from in disgust **syn** *see* HATE — **ab·hor·rence** \-'hȯr-ən(t)s, -'här-\ *n* — **ab·hor·rer** \-'hȯr-ər\ *n*

ab·hor·rent \ab-'hȯr-ənt, -'här-, ab-\ *adj* : causing or deserving strong dislike — **ab·hor·rent·ly** *adv*

abide \ə-'bīd\ *vb* **abode** \-'bōd\ *or* **abid·ed; abid·ing** **1** *archaic* : to wait for **2** : to bear patiently : TOLERATE **3** : ¹LAST 1, ENDURE ⟨an *abiding* friendship⟩ **4** : DWELL 1, 2 — **abid·ance** \ə-'bīd-ən(t)s\ *n* — **abid·er** *n* — **abide by** : to accept the terms of : be obedient to ⟨*abide by* the rules⟩

abil·i·ty \ə-'bil-ət-ē\ *n, pl* **-ties** **1 a** : the quality or state of being able : power to do something **b** : competence in doing : SKILL **2** : natural or acquired skill
  syn ABILITY, APTITUDE, TALENT mean unusual capacity for doing or achieving something. ABILITY suggests having from birth the power to do a thing especially well ⟨always has had the *ability* to run fast⟩ APTITUDE suggests a quickness to learn and a natural liking usually for a field or activity ⟨people with a natural *aptitude* for computers⟩ TALENT suggests a great ability to create things and one that needs to be developed ⟨you should work on your *talent* for writing short stories⟩

-abil·i·ty *also* **-ibil·i·ty** \ə-'bil-ət-ē\ *n suffix, pl* **-ties** : ability, fitness, or likeliness to act or be acted on in (such) a way ⟨read*ability*⟩ [derived from Latin *-abilitas, -ibilitas* "-ability"]

ab·ject \'ab-ˌjekt\ *adj* : very low in spirit or hope : WRETCHED ⟨*abject* misery⟩ ⟨an *abject* coward⟩ — **ab·ject·ly** \'ab-ˌjek-(t)lē, ab-'jek-\ *adv* — **ab·ject·ness** \-ˌjek(t)-nəs, -'jek(t)-\ *n*

ab·jure \ab-'jů(ə)r\ *vb* **ab·jured; ab·jur·ing** : to renounce solemnly ⟨*abjure* allegiance⟩

ab·late \a-'blāt\ *vb* **ab·lat·ed; ab·lat·ing** : to remove or become removed by cutting, eating or wearing away, evaporating, or vaporizing

ab·la·tion \a-'blā-shən\ *n* : the process of ablating : as **a** : surgical cutting and removal **b** : removal of a part (as the outside of a nose cone) by melting or vaporization

ablaze \ə-'blāz\ *adj* **1** : being on fire **2** : radiant with light or bright color

able \'ā-bəl\ *adj* **abler** \-b(ə-)lər\; **ablest** \-b(ə-)ləst\ **1 a** : having enough power, skill, or resources to do something ⟨*able* to swim⟩ **b** : not prevented ⟨*able* to vote⟩ **2** : SKILLFUL, COMPETENT ⟨an *able* editor⟩ [Middle English *able* "able", from early French *able* (same meaning), from Latin *habilis* "easily managed, skillful", from *habēre* "to have"]

-able *also* **-ible** \ə-bəl\ *adj suffix* **1** : fit for or worthy of being ⟨collect*ible*⟩ **2** : likely to or capable of ⟨break*able*⟩ ⟨perish*able*⟩ **3** : having a certain quality ⟨knowledge*able*⟩ ⟨peace*able*⟩ [derived from Latin *-abilis, -ibilis* "-able"]

able–bod·ied \ˌā-bəl-'bäd-ēd\ *adj* : having a healthy strong body : physically fit

abloom \ə-'blüm\ *adj* : being in bloom

ab·lu·tion \ə-'blü-shən, a-'blü-\ *n* : washing oneself especially as a religious rite

ably \'ā-blē\ *adv* : in an able manner

ABM \ˌā-(ˌ)bē-'em\ *n* : ANTIBALLISTIC MISSILE

ab·ne·gate \'ab-ni-ˌgāt\ *vb* **-gat·ed; -gat·ing** **1** : to give up a right or privilege **2** : to deny to oneself : RENOUNCE — **ab·ne·ga·tion** \ˌab-ni-'gā-shən\ *n*

ab·nor·mal \(')ab-'nȯr-məl\ *adj* : differing from the normal or average; *esp* : noticeably irregular — **ab·nor·mal·ly** \-mə-lē\ *adv*

ab·nor·mal·i·ty \ˌab-nər-'mal-ət-ē, -(ˌ)nȯr-\ *n, pl* **-ties** **1** : the state of being abnormal **2** : something abnormal

¹aboard \ə-'bōrd, -'bȯrd\ *adv* : on, onto, or within a vehicle (as a car, ship, or airplane)

²aboard *prep* : on or into especially for passage ⟨go *aboard* ship⟩

abode \ə-'bōd\ *n* : the place where one stays or lives

abol·ish \ə-'bäl-ish\ *vb* : to do away with completely : put an end to — **abol·ish·able** \-ə-bəl\ *adj* — **abol·ish·er** *n* — **abol·ish·ment** \-mənt\ *n*

ab·o·li·tion \ˌab-ə-'lish-ən\ *n* **1** : the act of abolishing : the state of being abolished **2** : the abolishing of slavery

ab·o·li·tion·ist \ˌab-ə-'lish-(ə-)nəst\ *n* : a person who is in favor of abolishing especially slavery — **ab·o·li·tion·ism** \-'lish-ə-ˌniz-əm\ *n*

A–bomb \'ā-ˌbäm\ *n* : ATOM BOMB

abom·i·na·ble \ə-'bäm-(ə-)nə-bəl\ *adj* **1** : deserving or causing disgust : HATEFUL, DETESTABLE ⟨*abominable* behavior⟩ **2** : quite disagreeable ⟨*abominable* weather⟩ — **abom·i·na·bly** \-blē\ *adv*

abominable snow·man \-'snō-mən, -,man\ *n, often cap A&S* : a creature thought to exist in the Himalayas and held to be a primitive relative of human beings, an ape, or more commonly a bear

abom·i·nate \ə-'bäm-ə-,nāt\ *vb* **-nat·ed; -nat·ing** : HATE, LOATHE — **abom·i·na·tor** \-,nāt-ər\ *n*

abom·i·na·tion \ə-,bäm-ə-'nā-shən\ *n* **1** : something detestable **2** : extreme disgust and hatred : LOATHING

ab·orig·i·nal \ˌab-ə-'rij-nəl, -ən-ᵊl\ *adj* **1** : being the first of its kind in a region : INDIGENOUS **2** : of, relating to, or being aborigines — **ab·orig·i·nal·ly** \-ē\ *adv*

ab·orig·i·ne \ˌab-ə-'rij-ə-(ˌ)nē\ *n* : a member of the original race to live in an area : NATIVE [from Latin *aborigines* "original inhabitants", from *ab origine* "from the beginning", from *origin-, origo* "beginning, source", from *oriri* "to rise" — related to ORIGIN]

abort \ə-'bȯrt\ *vb* **1** : to bring forth premature or stillborn offspring **2** : to become checked in development **3** : to put an end to prematurely ⟨*abort* a project⟩

abor·tion \ə-'bȯr-shən\ *n* **1** : a premature birth occurring before the fetus can survive — compare MISCARRIAGE 3 **2** : failure of a project or action to reach full development; *also* : a result of such failure

abor·tion·ist \ə-'bȯr-sh(ə-)nəst\ *n* : one who produces abortions

abor·tive \ə-'bȯrt-iv\ *adj* **1** : failing to achieve the desired end : UNSUCCESSFUL ⟨an *abortive* attempt to escape⟩ **2** : imperfectly formed or developed : RUDIMENTARY — **abor·tive·ly** *adv* — **abor·tive·ness** *n*

abound \ə-'baůnd\ *vb* **1** : to be present in large numbers or in great quantity **2** : to be filled or abundantly supplied ⟨a stream *abounding* in fish⟩

¹about \ə-'baůt\ *adv* **1** : on all sides : AROUND ⟨wander *about*⟩ ⟨people standing *about*⟩ **2** : reasonably close to : APPROXIMATELY, NEARLY ⟨*about* three years⟩ ⟨*about* ready to go⟩ **3** : in succession : ALTERNATELY ⟨turn *about* is fair play⟩ **4** : in the opposite direction ⟨face *about*⟩

²about *prep* **1** : on every side of : AROUND **2 a** : ²NEAR **b** : on or near the person of ⟨has no knife *about* him⟩ **c** : at the command of ⟨keeps her wits *about* her⟩ **3 a** : in the act or process of doing ⟨do it well while you're *about* it⟩ **b** : on the point of ⟨*about* to join our friends⟩ **4** : having to do with : CONCERNING ⟨tell me *about* it⟩ ⟨a book *about* birds⟩ **5** : over or in different parts of ⟨traveled *about* the country⟩

about–face \ə-'baůt-'fās\ *n* **1** : a reversal of direction **2** : a reversal of attitude or point of view — **about–face** *vb*

¹above \ə-'bəv\ *adj* **1** : in or to a higher place : OVERHEAD **2** : higher on the same or a preceding page **3** : in or to a higher rank or number

²above *prep* **1** : in or to a higher place than : OVER **2** : superior to ⟨a captain is *above* a lieutenant⟩ ⟨*above* criticism⟩ **3** : too proud or honorable to stoop to ⟨*above* such mean tricks⟩ **4** : exceeding in number, quantity, or size : more than ⟨*above* the average⟩

³**above** *adj* : written above

above·board \ə-'bəv-ˌbȯrd, -ˌbȯrd\ *adv or adj* : without concealment or deceit

ab·ra·ca·dab·ra \ˌab-rə-kə-'dab-rə\ *n* **1** : a magical charm or word **2** : unintelligible language : JARGON

abrade \ə-'brād\ *vb* **abrad·ed; abrad·ing** **1** : to rub or wear away especially by friction **2** : to irritate or roughen by rubbing — **abrad·er** *n*

abra·sion \ə-'brā-zhən\ *n* **1** : a rubbing, grinding, or wearing away by friction **2** : a place where the surface has been rubbed or scraped off ⟨an *abrasion* on her knee⟩

¹**abra·sive** \ə-'brā-siv, -ziv\ *adj* : having the effect of abrading — **abra·sive·ly** *adj* — **abra·sive·ness** *n*

²**abrasive** *n* : a substance (as emery) used for abrading, smoothing, or polishing

abreast *adv or adj* **1** : side by side with bodies in line ⟨lined up three *abreast*⟩ **2** : up to a standard or level especially of knowledge ⟨keep *abreast* of the times⟩

abridge \ə-'brij\ *vb* **abridged; abridg·ing** **1** : to make less : DIMINISH ⟨forbidden to *abridge* the rights of citizens⟩ **2** : to shorten in duration or extent **3** : to shorten by omission of words : CONDENSE [Middle English *abregen* "deprive, reduce", from early French *abregier* (same meaning), from Latin *abbreviare* "to shorten" — related to ABBREVIATE] — **abridg·er** *n*

abridg·ment *or* **abridge·ment** \ə-'brij-mənt\ *n* **1 a** : the action of abridging **b** : the state of being abridged **2** : a shortened form of a written work

abroad \ə-'brȯd\ *adv or adj* **1** : over a wide area **2** : away from one's home ⟨doesn't go *abroad* at night⟩ **3** : in or to foreign countries ⟨travel *abroad*⟩ **4** : in wide circulation ⟨rumors were *abroad*⟩

ab·ro·gate \'ab-rə-ˌgāt\ *vb* **-gat·ed; -gat·ing** : to do away with or cancel by authority ⟨*abrogate* a law⟩ — **ab·ro·ga·tion** \ˌab-rə-'gā-shən\ *n*

abrupt \ə-'brəpt\ *adj* **1 a** : SUDDEN 1a ⟨an *abrupt* change in the weather⟩ **b** : rudely brief : CURT ⟨an *abrupt* manner⟩ **2** : ¹STEEP 1 ⟨the high *abrupt* bank of a stream⟩ — **abrupt·ly** \ə-'brəp-(t)lē\ *adv* — **abrupt·ness** \ə-'brəp(t)-nəs\ *n*

> **Word History** If a person is rudely brief in speech or manner or stops you before you finish talking, you could say that that person is abrupt. If a road ends suddenly, you could say that the road comes to an abrupt end. In both of these cases you might think of something that is abrupt as "breaking off". *Abrupt* comes from the Latin word *abruptus*, meaning "broken off, ending suddenly". That word is formed (with the addition of the prefix *ab-*, meaning "from") from the Latin word *rumpere*, meaning "to break". Latin *rumpere* has given us several other English words that carry the idea of breaking: *interrupt, rupture,* and *corrupt*. [from Latin *abruptus* "abrupt", derived from *abrumpere* "to break off", from *ab-* "from" and *rumpere* "to break" — related to CORRUPT, INTERRUPT, RUPTURE]

ab·scess \'ab-ˌses\ *n* : a collection of pus surrounded by inflamed tissue at some point in the body — **ab·scessed** \-ˌsest\ *adj*

ab·scis·sa \ab-'sis-ə\ *n* : the first number of an ordered pair of numbers locating a point in a plane coordinate system that is the distance of the point from the y-axis found by measuring along a line parallel to the x-axis — compare ORDINATE

ab·scis·sion \ab-'sizh-ən\ *n* **1** : the act or process of cutting off **2** : the natural separation of flowers, fruit, or leaves from plants

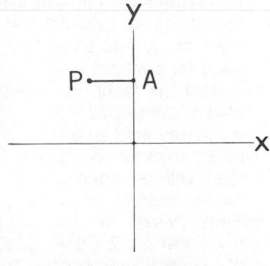

abscissa: *AP* is abscissa of point *P*

ab·scond \ab-'skänd, əb-\ *vb* : to depart secretly and hide oneself — **ab·scond·er** *n*

ab·sence \'ab-sən(t)s\ *n* **1** : the state of being absent **2** : the time that one is absent **3** : ²WANT 1a, LACK ⟨*absence* of detail⟩

¹**ab·sent** \'ab-sənt\ *adj* **1** : not present or attending : MISSING **2** : not existing ⟨enthusiasm was *absent*⟩ **3** : PREOCCUPIED 1, INATTENTIVE — **ab·sent·ly** *adv*

²**ab·sent** \ab-'sent\ *vb* : to keep (oneself) away

ab·sen·tee \ˌab-sən-'tē\ *n* : a person who is absent

ab·sent·mind·ed \ˌab-sənt-'mīn-dəd\ *adj* : lost in thought and unaware of one's surroundings or action — **ab·sent·mind·ed·ly** *adv* — **ab·sent·mind·ed·ness** *n*

ab·so·lute \'ab-sə-ˌlüt, ˌab-sə-'lüt\ *adj* **1 a** : free from imperfection : PERFECT **b** : free or nearly free from mixture : PURE ⟨*absolute* alcohol⟩ **2** : free from restraint or limitation ⟨*absolute* power⟩ ⟨an *absolute* monarch⟩ **3** : having no exceptions : UNQUALIFIED ⟨an *absolute* requirement⟩ ⟨*absolute* freedom⟩ **4** : free from doubt : CERTAIN ⟨*absolute* proof⟩ **5 a** : independent of standards of measurement that reflect individual choice : ACTUAL ⟨*absolute* brightness of a star⟩ ⟨*absolute* motion⟩ **b** : relating to or coming from the basic units of length, mass, and time ⟨*absolute* electric units⟩ **c** : relating to the absolute-temperature scale ⟨10° *absolute*⟩ — **ab·so·lute·ly** \'ab-sə-ˌlē, ˌab-sə-'lüt-\ *adv* — **ab·so·lute·ness** \-ˌlüt-nəs, -'lüt-\ *n*

absolute error *n* : the difference between the true value of a quantity and the value found by experiment

absolute music *n* : music that is free of any associations or ideas (as a plot or narrative) outside the music itself ⟨a fugue is an example of *absolute music*⟩

absolute temperature *n* : temperature measured on a scale that has absolute zero as the zero point

absolute value *n* : the numerical value of a number that for a number which is positive or zero is equal to the number itself and for a negative number is equal to the additive inverse of the number

absolute zero *n* : a hypothetical temperature that has never been reached, represents no heat at all, and is equal to approximately $-273.15°C$ or $-459.67°F$

ab·so·lu·tion \ˌab-sə-'lü-shən\ *n* : the act of absolving; *esp* : a forgiving of sins

ab·solve \əb-'zälv, -'sälv, -'zȯlv, -'sȯlv\ *vb* **ab·solved; ab·solv·ing** : to set free from an obligation or from the consequences of guilt — **ab·solv·er** *n*

ab·sorb \əb-'sȯrb, -'zȯrb\ *vb* **1** : to take in or suck or swallow up ⟨a sponge *absorbs* water⟩ ⟨plant roots *absorb* water⟩ **2** : to hold the interest of : ENGROSS ⟨*absorbed* in thought⟩ **3 a** : to receive without giving back ⟨a sound-*absorbing* surface⟩ **b** : to transform (radiant energy) into a different form usually with a resulting rise in temperature ⟨the earth *absorbs* the sun's rays⟩ — **ab·sorb·abil·i·ty** \əb-ˌsȯr-bə-'bil-ət-ē, -ˌzȯr-\ *n* — **ab·sorb·able** \əb-'sȯr-bə-bəl, -'zȯr-\ *adj* — **ab·sorb·er** *n*

ab·sor·bent \əb-'sȯr-bənt, -'zȯr-\ *adj* : able to absorb ⟨*absorbent* cotton⟩ — **ab·sor·ben·cy** \əb-'sȯr-bən-sē, -'zȯr-\ *n* — **absorbent** *n*

ab·sorp·tion \əb-'sȯrp-shən, -'zȯrp-\ *n* **1** : the process of absorbing or being absorbed: as **a** : the passing of digested food through the wall of the intestines into the blood or lymph **b** : the stopping and taking in especially of radiant energy or sound waves **2** : entire occupation of the mind — **ab·sorp·tive** \-'sȯrp-tiv, -'zȯrp-\ *adj*

ab·stain \əb-'stān\ *vb* : to keep oneself from doing something ⟨*abstain* from voting⟩ — **ab·stain·er** *n*

\ə\	abut	\au̇\	out	\i\	tip	\ȯ\	saw	\u̇\	foot
\ər\	further	\ch\	chin	\ī\	life	\ȯi\	coin	\y\	yet
\a\	mat	\e\	pet	\j\	job	\th\	thin	\yü\	few
\ā\	take	\ē\	easy	\ŋ\	sing	\th\	this	\yu̇\	cure
\ä\	cot, cart	\g\	go	\ō\	bone	\ü\	food	\zh\	vision

ab·ste·mi·ous \ab-'stē-mē-əs\ *adj* : not eating and drinking much — **ab·ste·mi·ous·ly** *adv*

ab·sten·tion \əb-'sten-chən, ab-\ *n* : the act or practice of abstaining; *esp* : a formal refusal to vote ⟨3 ayes, 5 nays, and 2 *abstentions*⟩

ab·sti·nence \'ab-stə-nən(t)s\ *n* : an abstaining especially from drinking alcoholic beverages — **ab·sti·nent** \-nənt\ *adj* — **ab·sti·nent·ly** *adv*

¹**ab·stract** \ab-'strakt, 'ab-,strakt\ *adj* **1** : expressing a quality or idea without reference to an actual person or thing ⟨*honesty* is an *abstract* word⟩ **2** : difficult to understand : HARD ⟨*abstract* problems⟩ **3** : using elements of form (as color, line, or texture) with little or no attempt at creating a realistic picture ⟨*abstract* art⟩ [from Latin *abstractus* "abstract", from earlier *abstrahere* "to draw away", from *abs-, ab-* "from, away" and *trahere* "to draw" — related to ATTRACT, ¹TRACE, ³TRACE] — **ab·stract·ly** \ab-'strak-(t)lē, 'ab-,strak-\ *adv* — **ab·stract·ness** \ab-'strak(t)-nəs, 'ab-,strak(t)-\ *n*

²**ab·stract** \'ab-,strakt\ *n* : a brief statement of the main points or facts : SUMMARY

³**ab·stract** \ab-'strakt, 'ab-,strakt, *in sense 3 usually* 'ab-,strakt\ *vb* **1** : to take out : REMOVE ⟨*abstract* a diamond from a pile of sand⟩ **2** : to consider apart from a particular instance ⟨*abstract* the idea of roundness from a ball⟩ **3** : to make an abstract of : SUMMARIZE **4** : to draw away the attention of — **ab·strac·tor** *or* **ab·stract·er** \-'strak-tər, -,strak-\ *n*

ab·stract·ed \ab-'strak-təd, 'ab-,strak-\ *adj* : PREOCCUPIED 1, ABSENTMINDED — **ab·stract·ed·ly** *adv* — **ab·stract·ed·ness** *n*

ab·strac·tion \ab-'strak-shən\ *n* **1 a** : the act or process of abstracting : the state of being abstracted **b** : an abstract idea or term **2** : an artistic composition or creation having designs that do not represent actual objects — **ab·strac·tive** \-'strak-tiv\ *adj*

ab·struse \əb-'strüs, ab-\ *adj* : hard to understand — **ab·struse·ly** *adv* — **ab·struse·ness** *n*

ab·surd \əb-'sərd, -'zərd\ *adj* : completely unreasonable or untrue : RIDICULOUS — **ab·sur·di·ty** \-'sərd-ət-ē, -'zərd-\ *n* — **ab·surd·ly** *adv* — **ab·surd·ness** *n*

abun·dance \ə-'bən-dən(t)s\ *n* **1** : a large quantity : PLENTY **2** : WEALTH 1

abun·dant \ə-'bən-dənt\ *adj* : existing in or possessing abundance : ABOUNDING **syn** see PLENTIFUL — **abun·dant·ly** *adv*

¹**abuse** \ə-'byüz\ *vb* **abused; abus·ing** **1** : to use wrongly : MISUSE ⟨*abuse* a privilege⟩ **2** : to treat cruelly : MISTREAT ⟨*abuse* a dog⟩ **3** : to attack in words : scold rudely — **abus·er** *n*

²**abuse** \ə-'byüs\ *n* **1** : a corrupt practice or custom ⟨election *abuses*⟩ **2 a** : improper use or treatment : MISUSE ⟨*abuse* of privileges⟩ ⟨drug *abuse*⟩ **b** : physical mistreatment **3** : harsh insulting language

abu·sive \ə-'byü-siv, -ziv\ *adj* : using or characterized by abuse — **abu·sive·ly** *adv* — **abu·sive·ness** *n*

abut \ə-'bət\ *vb* **abut·ted; abut·ting** : to touch along a border or with a part that sticks out — **abut·ter** *n*

abut·ment \ə-'bət-mənt\ *n* **1** : the action or place of abutting **2** : something against which another thing rests its weight or pushes with force ⟨*abutments* that support a bridge⟩

abutment 2

abys·mal \ə-'biz-məl\ *adj* **1** : resembling an abyss ⟨*abysmal* ignorance⟩ **2** : ABYSSAL — **abys·mal·ly** \-mə-lē\ *adv*

abyss \ə-'bis\ *n* : a gulf so deep or a space so great that it cannot be measured

abys·sal \ə-'bis-əl\ *adj* : of or relating to the bottom waters of the ocean depths

ac- — see AD-

aca·cia \ə-'kā-shə\ *n* **1** : GUM ARABIC **2** : any of numerous woody legumes with globe-shaped white or yellow flower clusters and often fernlike leaves

ac·a·dem·ic \,ak-ə-'dem-ik\ *adj* **1** : of or relating to school or college **2** : literary or general rather than technical ⟨took the *academic* course⟩ **3** : having no practical importance : THEORETICAL ⟨an *academic* question⟩ — **ac·a·dem·i·cal·ly** \-'dem-i-k(ə-)lē\ *adv*

acad·e·my \ə-'kad-ə-mē\ *n, pl* **-mies** **1 a** : ¹SCHOOL 1a; *esp* : a private high school **b** : an institution for training in special subjects or skills ⟨military *academy*⟩ **2** : a society of learned persons

Word History Our word *academy* comes from the Greek word *Akadēmeia,* the name of the park or grove outside of ancient Athens where the philosopher Plato taught his students. Just as schools and parks today are often named after famous persons, the Akadēmeia had been named in honor of a Greek hero, Akadēmos. [Greek *Akadēmeia,* the grove outside Athens where Plato had his school]

a cap·pel·la *also* **a ca·pel·la** \,äk-ə-'pel-ə\ *adv or adj* : without accompanying instrumental music ⟨sing *a cappella*⟩ [from Italian *a cappella* "in chapel style"]

ac·cede \ak-'sēd, ik-\ *vb* **ac·ced·ed; ac·ced·ing** **1** : to give consent : AGREE ⟨*accede* to a proposed plan⟩ **2** : to enter upon an office or position ⟨*acceded* to the throne in 1838⟩

ac·ce·le·ran·do \(,)ä-,chel-ə-'rän-dō\ *adv or adj* : gradually faster — used as a direction in music

ac·cel·er·ate \ik-'sel-ə-,rāt, ak-\ *vb* **-at·ed; -at·ing** **1** : to bring about earlier ⟨*accelerated* our departure⟩ **2** : to move or cause to move faster; *also* : to cause to change velocity — **ac·cel·er·a·tive** \-,rāt-iv\ *adj*

ac·cel·er·a·tion \ik-,sel-ə-'rā-shən, ak-\ *n* **1** : the act or process of accelerating : the state of being accelerated **2** : the rate of change of velocity with respect to time; *also* : change in velocity

acceleration of gravity : the acceleration of a freely falling body under the influence of gravity that is expressed as the rate of increase of velocity per unit of time and that amounts to a value of about 9.806 meters per second per second

ac·cel·er·a·tor \ik-'sel-ə-,rāt-ər, ak-\ *n* **1** : one that accelerates **2** : a device (as a pedal) in a motor vehicle used to control the speed of the motor **3** : a device that is used to give high velocities to charged particles (as electrons and protons)

ac·cel·er·om·e·ter \ik-,sel-ə-'räm-ət-ər, ak-\ *n* : an instrument for measuring acceleration or for detecting and measuring vibrations

¹**ac·cent** \'ak-,sent\ *n* **1** : a way of talking shared by a group (as the people of a country) **2** : greater stress or force given to a syllable of a word in speaking ⟨*before* has the *accent* on the last syllable⟩ **3** : a mark (as ' or ,) identifying a syllable that is accented in speaking **4** : greater stress given to a beat in music **5** : something used for contrast

²**ac·cent** \ak-'sent, 'ak-,sent\ *vb* **1** : to make more noticeable : EMPHASIZE **2 a** : to say with an accent : STRESS **b** : to mark with a written or printed accent

accent mark *n* **1** : ¹ACCENT 3 **2** : one of several symbols used to indicate musical stress

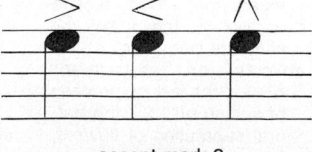
accent mark 2

ac·cen·tu·ate \ik-'sen-chə-ˌwāt, ak-\ vb **-at·ed; -at·ing** : ²ACCENT — **ac·cen·tu·a·tion** \ik-ˌsen-chə-'wā-shən, (ˌ)ak-\ n

ac·cept \ik-'sept, ak-\ vb **1 a** : to receive or take willingly ⟨accept a gift⟩ ⟨accepted her as a member⟩ **b** : to be able or designed to take or hold (something applied or added) ⟨a surface that will not accept ink⟩ ⟨a computer program ready to accept commands⟩ ⟨the body's ability to accept skin grafts⟩ **2 a** : to agree to ⟨accept an offer⟩ **b** : to think of as proper or normal ⟨the idea is widely accepted⟩ [Middle English accepten "receive, accept", from early French accepter (same meaning), derived from Latin accipere "receive", from ac-, ad- "to" and capere "to take" — related to CAPTURE, EXCEPT, RECEIVE] — **ac·cept·er** or **ac·cep·tor** \-'sep-tər\ n

ac·cept·able \ik-'sep-tə-bəl, ak-\ adj **1** : capable or worthy of being accepted : SATISFACTORY ⟨an acceptable excuse⟩ **2** : barely good enough ⟨plays an acceptable game⟩ — **ac·cept·abil·i·ty** \ik-ˌsep-tə-'bil-ət-ē, ak-\ n — **ac·cept·ably** \ik-'sep-tə-blē, ak-\ adv

ac·cep·tance \ik-'sep-tən(t)s, ak-\ n **1** : the act of accepting **2** : the quality or state of being accepted or acceptable

ac·cep·ta·tion \ˌak-ˌsep-'tā-shən\ n : the generally understood meaning of a word or expression

¹ac·cess \'ak-ˌses\ n **1** : permission or power to enter, approach, or make use of ⟨access to secret information⟩ **2** : a way or means of approach ⟨a nation's access to the sea⟩

²access vb : to get at : gain access to

ac·ces·si·ble \ik-'ses-ə-bəl, ak-\ adj **1** : capable of being reached ⟨a resort accessible by train or bus⟩ **2** : capable of being used, seen, or known : OBTAINABLE ⟨accessible information⟩ — **ac·ces·si·bil·i·ty** \ik-ˌses-ə-'bil-ət-ē, ak-\ n — **ac·ces·si·bly** \-blē\ adv

ac·ces·sion \ik-'sesh-ən, ak-\ n **1** : something added : ACQUISITION **2** : increase by something added **3** : the act of agreeing ⟨accession to a proposal⟩ **4** : the act of coming to office or power ⟨the accession of a king⟩

¹ac·ces·so·ry \ik-'ses-(ə-)rē, ak-\ n, pl **-ries** **1** : something (as an object or device) that is not necessary in itself but adds to the beauty, convenience, or effectiveness of something else **2** : a person who aids another in doing wrong or in an attempt to escape justice

²accessory adj : aiding or helping in a secondary way : SUPPLEMENTARY

accessory fruit n : a fruit (as the strawberry, apple, or fig) of which a conspicuous part consists of tissue other than that of the ripened ovary

access time n : the time lag between the time stored information (as in a computer) is requested and the time it is delivered

ac·ci·dent \'ak-səd-ənt, -sə-ˌdent\ n **1 a** : an event occurring by chance or from unknown causes **b** : ¹CHANCE 1 **2** : an unintended and usually sudden and unexpected event resulting in loss of injury ⟨an automobile accident⟩

¹ac·ci·den·tal \ˌak-sə-'dent-ᵊl\ adj **1** : happening unexpectedly or by chance ⟨an accidental discovery of oil⟩ **2** : not happening or done on purpose ⟨an accidental shooting⟩ — **ac·ci·den·tal·ly** \-'dent-lē, -'dent-ᵊl-ē\ adv

²accidental n : a musical note whose pitch is changed (as by a sharp or a flat) from the pitch shown in the key signature

ac·cip·i·ter \ak-'sip-ət-ər\ n : any of various low-flying hawks that have short wings and long legs

¹ac·claim \ə-'klām\ vb **1** : to welcome with applause or great praise ⟨a novel acclaimed by the critics⟩ **2** : to proclaim by or as if by acclamation [from Latin acclamare, literally "to shout at", from ac-, ad- "to, toward" and clamare "to shout" — related to CLAIM, CLAMOR] — **ac·claim·er** n

²acclaim n **1** : the act of acclaiming **2** : APPLAUSE, PRAISE

ac·cla·ma·tion \ˌak-lə-'mā-shən\ n **1** : a loud eager expression of approval, praise, or agreement **2** : an overwhelming positive vote by voice ⟨elected by acclamation⟩

ac·cli·mate \'ak-lə-ˌmāt, ə-'klī-mət, -ˌmāt\ vb **-mat·ed; -mat·ing** : ACCLIMATIZE — **ac·cli·ma·tion** \ˌak-lə-'mā-shən, ˌak-ˌlī-\ n

ac·cli·ma·tize \ə-'klī-mə-ˌtīz\ vb **-tized; -tiz·ing** : to adapt to a new climate or environment — **ac·cli·ma·ti·za·tion** \ə-ˌklī-mət-ə-'zā-shən\ n

ac·co·lade \'ak-ə-ˌlād\ n **1** : a formal salute (as a tap on the shoulder with the blade of a sword) that marks the conferring of knighthood **2** : a mark of recognition of merit : PRAISE

ac·com·mo·date \ə-'käm-ə-ˌdāt\ vb **-dat·ed; -dat·ing** **1** : ADAPT **2** : to bring into agreement ⟨accommodate the differences⟩ **3** : OBLIGE 2b ⟨accommodated me with a ride⟩ **4** : to provide with something desired: as **a** : to provide with lodgings **b** : to make or have room for ⟨the table accommodates 12 comfortably⟩ **5** : to undergo visual accommodation ⟨the lens of the eye accommodates⟩ syn see CONTAIN — **ac·com·mo·da·tive** \-ˌdāt-iv\ adj — **ac·com·mo·da·tive·ness** n

ac·com·mo·dat·ing adj : ready and willing to help : OBLIGING

ac·com·mo·da·tion \ə-ˌkäm-ə-'dā-shən\ n **1 a** : something supplied that is useful and handy **b** pl : lodging and meals or traveling space and related services ⟨overnight accommodations⟩ **2** : the act of accommodating : the state of being accommodated **3** : the automatic adjustment of the eye for seeing at different distances **4** : an adjustment of differences : SETTLEMENT

ac·com·pa·ni·ment \ə-'kəmp-(ə-)nē-mənt\ n **1** : music played along with a solo part to enrich it **2** : an accompanying object, situation, or event

ac·com·pa·nist \ə-'kəmp-(ə-)nəst\ n : a musician who plays an accompaniment

ac·com·pa·ny \ə-'kəmp-(ə-)nē\ vb **-nied; -ny·ing** **1** : to go with or attend as a companion **2** : to perform an accompaniment to or for **3** : to occur at the same time as or along with ⟨a thunderstorm accompanied by high winds⟩ [Middle English accompanien "to accompany", from early French acompaignier (same meaning), from a- "to" and compaing, compain "companion", from Latin companio "companion" — related to COMPANION, COMPANY]

syn ACCOMPANY, ATTEND, ESCORT mean to go along with. ACCOMPANY stresses the closeness of the relationship and stresses that the people are equals ⟨would you like to accompany me to the movies?⟩ ATTEND suggests waiting upon and serving someone of higher rank ⟨assistants and bodyguards attended the President⟩ ESCORT suggests that one is going along as a matter of protection, ceremony, or courtesy ⟨a marching band escorted the heroes⟩

ac·com·plice \ə-'käm-pləs, -'kəm-\ n : one associated with another in wrongdoing

ac·com·plish \ə-'käm-plish, -'kəm-\ vb : to bring to a successful finish : PERFORM — **ac·com·plish·able** \-ə-bəl\ adj

ac·com·plished adj **1** : shown or known to be true ⟨an accomplished fact⟩ **2 a** : skilled or polished through practice or training : EXPERT ⟨an accomplished pianist⟩ **b** : having many accomplishments

ac·com·plish·ment \ə-'käm-plish-mənt, -'kəm-\ n **1** : the act of accomplishing : COMPLETION **2** : something accomplished : ACHIEVEMENT **3** : an ability, social quality, or skill

\ə\ abut	\au̇\ out	\i\ tip	\ȯ\ saw	\u̇\ foot	
\ər\ further	\ch\ chin	\ī\ life	\ȯi\ coin	\y\ yet	
\a\ mat	\e\ pet	\j\ job	\th\ thin	\yü\ few	
\ā\ take	\ē\ easy	\ŋ\ sing	\th\ this	\yu̇\ cure	
\ä\ cot, cart	\g\ go	\ō\ bone	\ü\ food	\zh\ vision	

acquired by training or practice

¹ac·cord \ə-'kȯrd\ *vb* **1** : to grant as suitable or proper ⟨rights not *accorded* to foreigners⟩ **2** : to be in harmony : AGREE

²accord *n* **1 a** : AGREEMENT 1b, HARMONY **b** : an agreement between parties ⟨reach an *accord*⟩ **2** : willingness to act or do something ⟨went of their own *accord*⟩

ac·cor·dance \ə-'kȯrd-ᵊn(t)s\ *n* : AGREEMENT 1b, CONFORMITY ⟨in *accordance* with a rule⟩

ac·cord·ing as *conj* **1** : in accord with the way in which **2** : depending on how or whether

ac·cord·ing·ly \ə-'kȯrd-iŋ-lē\ *adv* **1** : in accordance : CORRESPONDINGLY **2** : CONSEQUENTLY, SO

according to *prep* **1** : in agreement with ⟨did everything *according to* the rules⟩ **2** : as stated by ⟨*according to* the experts⟩ **3** : depending on

¹ac·cor·di·on \ə-'kȯrd-ē-ən\ *n* : a musical instrument that has a keyboard and a bellows and that produces tones when air is forced past metal reeds — **ac·cor·di·on·ist** \-ē-ə-nəst\ *n*

²accordion *adj* : creased to fold like an accordion ⟨*accordion* pleats⟩

accordion

ac·cost \ə-'kȯst, -'käst\ *vb* : to approach and speak first to often in a challenging or aggressive way

¹ac·count \ə-'kaȯnt\ *n* **1** : a record of money paid out and money received **2** : a statement listing purchases and credits : BILL **3 a** : ¹VALUE 3 ⟨a man of little *account*⟩ **b** : ¹REGARD 2a ⟨held in high *account*⟩ **4** : ¹PROFIT 1, ADVANTAGE ⟨labored to no *account*⟩ **5 a** : a statement of reasons, causes, or motives ⟨gave an *account* of her actions⟩ **b** : a statement of facts ⟨*accounts* of the game⟩ **c** : a reason for an action ⟨on that *account* I must refuse⟩ **6** : a sum of money deposited in a bank [Middle English *acount, accompt* "the act or result of counting", from early French *aconte, accompte* (same meaning), from *aconter, accompter* (verb) "to add, count", from *a-* "to" and *conter, compter* "to count", derived from Latin *computare* "to count, compute" — related to COMPUTE, ¹COUNT] **syn** see NARRATIVE — **on account of** : for the sake of : by reason of : BECAUSE OF — **on no account** : in no circumstances

²account *vb* **1** : to think of as ⟨*accounts* herself lucky⟩ **2** : to give an explanation ⟨have to *account* for the money I spent⟩ **3** : to be the cause ⟨illness *accounts* for so many absences⟩

ac·count·able \ə-'kaȯnt-ə-bəl\ *adj* **1** : responsible for giving an account (as of one's acts) ⟨will be held *accountable*⟩ **2** : capable of being accounted for : EXPLAINABLE — **ac·count·abil·i·ty** \-,kaȯnt-ə-'bil-ət-ē\ *n* — **ac·count·ably** \-'kaȯnt-ə-blē\ *adv*

ac·coun·tant \ə-'kaȯnt-ᵊnt\ *n* : a person professionally trained in accounting

ac·count·ing \ə-'kaȯnt-iŋ\ *n* **1** : the skill, system, or practice of recording the amounts of money made and spent by a person or business **2** : the action of giving an account

ac·cou·tre *or* **ac·cou·ter** \ə-'küt-ər\ *vb* **-cou·tred** *or* **-cou·tered; -cou·tring** *or* **-cou·ter·ing** \-'küt-ə-riŋ, -'kü-triŋ\ : to provide with equipment : OUTFIT

ac·cou·tre·ment *or* **ac·cou·ter·ment** \ə-'kü-trə-mənt, -'küt-ər-mənt\ *n* **1** : the act of equipping : the state of being equipped **2** : an accessory item of clothing or equipment — usually used in pl.

ac·cred·it \ə-'kred-ət\ *vb* **1** : to send with credentials and authority to act as representative ⟨*accredit* an ambassador to France⟩ **2** : to certify as in agreement with a standard

⟨an *accredited* school⟩ **3** : ²CREDIT 3 — **ac·cred·i·ta·tion** \ə-,kred-ə-'tā-shən, -'dā-\ *n*

ac·cre·tion \ə-'krē-shən\ *n* **1** : the process of growth or enlargement; *esp* : increase or growth by addition on the outside **2** : a product or result of accretion

ac·crue \ə-'krü\ *vb* **ac·crued; ac·cru·ing** **1** : to come about as a natural growth or addition ⟨benefits *accrue* to society from education⟩ **2** : to accumulate over a period of time ⟨*accrued* interest⟩ — **ac·cru·al** \-'krü-əl\ *n*

ac·cu·mu·late \ə-'kyü-myə-,lāt\ *vb* **-lat·ed; -lat·ing** **1** : to gather or pile up especially little by little : AMASS ⟨*accumulate* a fortune⟩ **2** : to increase in quantity, number, or amount ⟨rubbish *accumulates* quickly⟩

ac·cu·mu·la·tion \ə-,kyü-myə-'lā-shən\ *n* **1** : a collecting together : AMASSING **2** : increase or growth by addition **3** : something accumulated : COLLECTION

ac·cu·mu·la·tor \ə-'kyü-m(y)ə-,lāt-ər\ *n* : one that accumulates; *esp* : a part (as in a computer) where numbers are totaled or stored

ac·cu·ra·cy \'ak-yə-rə-sē\ *n, pl* **-cies** **1** : freedom from error : CORRECTNESS **2** : conformity to a standard : EXACTNESS

ac·cu·rate \'ak-yə-rət\ *adj* **1** : free from mistakes especially as the result of care **2** : agreeing exactly with truth or a standard [from Latin *accuratus* "accurate", derived from *accurare* "to take care of", from *ac-, ad-* "to" and *cura* "care" — related to CURE, CURIOUS; see *Word History* at CURE] **syn** see CORRECT — **ac·cu·rate·ly** \-yə-rət-lē, -yərt-\ *adv* — **ac·cu·rate·ness** \-nəs\ *n*

ac·cursed \ə-'kərst, -'kər-səd\ *or* **ac·curst** \ə-'kərst\ *adj* **1** : being under a curse **2** : DAMNABLE 2, DETESTABLE — **ac·curs·ed·ly** \-'kər-səd-lē\ *adv* — **ac·curs·ed·ness** \-'kər-səd-nəs\ *n*

ac·cu·sa·tion \,ak-yə-'zā-shən, -yü-\ *n* **1** : the act of accusing : the fact of being accused **2** : a charge of wrongdoing

ac·cu·sa·tive \ə-'kyü-zət-iv\ *adj* : of, relating to, or being the grammatical case that marks the direct object of a verb or the object of a preposition — **accusative** *n*

ac·cuse \ə-'kyüz\ *vb* **ac·cused; ac·cus·ing** : to charge with a fault and especially with a crime — **ac·cus·er** *n* — **ac·cus·ing·ly** \-'kyü-ziŋ-lē\ *adv*

ac·cused \ə-'kyüzd\ *n, pl* **accused** : one charged with an offense; *esp* : the defendant in a criminal case

ac·cus·tom \ə-'kəs-təm\ *vb* : to make familiar

ac·cus·tomed \ə-'kəs-təmd\ *adj* **1** : CUSTOMARY ⟨my *accustomed* lunch hour⟩ **2** : familiar with **3** : being in the habit or custom ⟨*accustomed* to making decisions⟩

¹ace \'ās\ *n* **1** : a playing card with one large figure in its center **2** : a very small amount or degree ⟨within an *ace* of winning⟩ **3** : a point scored on a serve (as in tennis) that an opponent fails to touch **4** : a golf hole made in one stroke **5 a** : a combat pilot who has shot down at least five enemy airplanes **b** : a person who is expert at something

²ace *vb* **aced; ac·ing** **1** : to score an ace against ⟨the tennis player *aced* her opponent⟩ **2** : to earn the grade of A on (an examination)

³ace *adj* : of first or high rank or quality

acel·lu·lar \(')ā-'sel-yə-lər\ *adj* : not made up of cells

-a·ceous \'ā-shəs\ *adj suffix* : consisting of ⟨carbon*aceous*⟩ : having the nature or form of ⟨herb*aceous*⟩ [from Latin *-aceus* "consisting of"]

ac·e·tate \'as-ə-,tāt\ *n* **1** : a chemical compound formed by the reaction of acetic acid with another substance **2 a** : a textile fiber made from cellulose and acetate **b** : a fabric or plastic made of this fiber

ace·tic \ə-'sēt-ik\ *adj* : of, relating to, or producing acetic acid or vinegar

acetic acid *n* : a colorless strong-smelling liquid acid that gives the sour taste to vinegar and that is used especially in making chemical compounds (as plastics)

ac·e·tone \'as-ə-,tōn\ *n* : an easily evaporated fragrant flammable liquid compound used chiefly to dissolve or make chemical compounds

ace·tyl·cho·line \ə-,set-ᵊl-'kō-,lēn, -,sēt-; 'as-ə-,tēl-\ *n* : a compound released at autonomic nerve endings that functions in carrying nerve impulses

acet·y·lene \ə-'set-ᵊl-ən, -ᵊl-,ēn\ *n* : a compound of carbon and hydrogen that is a colorless gas used chiefly in welding and soldering and in making chemical compounds

ace·tyl·sal·i·cyl·ic acid \ə-'sēt-ᵊl-,sal-ə-,sil-ik-\ *n* : ASPIRIN 1

¹ache \'āk\ *vb* **ached; ach·ing 1** : to suffer a dull persistent pain **2** : to long earnestly : YEARN

²ache *n* : a dull persistent pain — **achy** \'ā-kē\ *adj*

achene \ə-'kēn\ *n* : a small dry one-seeded fruit (as of the buttercup) that ripens without bursting — **ache·ni·al** \ə-'kē-nē-əl\ *adj*

achieve \ə-'chēv\ *vb* **achieved; achiev·ing 1** : ACCOMPLISH ⟨*achieved* our purpose⟩ **2** : to get by effort ⟨*achieve* greatness⟩ [Middle English *acheven* "achieve", from early French *achever* "to finish", from *a-* "to" and *chief* "end, head", from Latin *caput* "head" — related to CAPITAL, CHIEF] — **achiev·able** \-'chē-və-bəl\ *adj*

achieve·ment \ə-'chēv-mənt\ *n* **1** : the act of achieving **2** : something achieved

Achil·les' heel \ə-,kil-ēz-\ *n* : a special or personal weakness

> **Word History** In Greek legend, Achilles' mother protected him from harm by dipping him in the river Styx. However, she held him by the heel while doing it. As a result this heel did not get wet and thus was not protected. Later, during the Trojan War, Achilles was killed by Paris, a Trojan prince, who shot him in the unprotected heel with an arrow. The term *Achilles' heel* has since come to refer to any weak spot or point. [named for *Achilles,* warrior in Greek legend]

Achilles tendon *n* : the strong tendon joining the muscles in the calf of the leg to the bone of the heel

ach·ro·mat·ic \,ak-rə-'mat-ik\ *adj* **1** : giving an image practically free from colors not in the object ⟨an *achromatic* lens⟩ **2** : being black, gray, or white

¹ac·id \'as-əd\ *adj* **1** : sour, bitter, or stinging to the taste : resembling vinegar in taste **2** : sour in temper : CROSS ⟨*acid* remarks⟩ **3** : of, relating to, or having the characteristics of an acid ⟨*acid* soil⟩ ⟨*acid* indigestion⟩ — **ac·id·ly** *adv* — **ac·id·ness** *n*

²acid *n* **1** : a sour substance **2** : a compound that usually dissolves in water, has a sour taste, reacts with a base to form a salt, and turns litmus paper red **3** : LSD

ac·id–fast \'as-əd-,fast\ *adj* : not easily made to lose color by acids

acid·ic \ə-'sid-ik, a-\ *adj* **1** : acid-forming **2** : ACID

acid·i·fy \ə-'sid-ə-,fī\ *vb* **-fied; -fy·ing 1** : to make or become acid **2** : to change into an acid — **acid·i·fi·ca·tion** \ə-,sid-ə-fə-'kā-shən\ *n*

acid·i·ty \ə-'sid-ət-ē, a-\ *n, pl* **-ties 1** : the quality, state, or degree of being acid **2** : the state of being extremely acid

acid precipitation *n* : precipitation (as rain or snow) with increased acidity that is caused by environmental factors

acid rain *n* : rain with increased acidity that is caused by environmental factors (as atmospheric pollutants)

ac·knowl·edge \ik-'näl-ij, ak-\ *vb* **-edged; -edg·ing 1** : to recognize the rights or authority of **2** : to admit the truth or existence of **3** : to make known that something has been received or noticed ⟨*acknowledge* a letter⟩

> **syn** ACKNOWLEDGE, ADMIT, OWN, CONFESS mean to make public something one would rather keep private. ACKNOWLEDGE suggests revealing something that has been or might be concealed ⟨the company *acknowledged* that it had been polluting the lake⟩ ADMIT stresses a demand to reveal and an unwillingness to do so ⟨why don't

you *admit* that you made a mistake?⟩ OWN suggests acknowledging something of a personal nature ⟨I *own* that I can be rude sometimes⟩ CONFESS suggests an admission of weakness, failure, or guilt ⟨criminals forced to *confess* their crimes⟩

ac·knowl·edged \ik-'näl-ijd, ak-\ *adj* : generally recognized or accepted ⟨the *acknowledged* leader⟩

ac·knowl·edg·ment *also* **ac·knowl·edge·ment** \ik-'näl-ij-mənt, ak-\ *n* **1 a** : the act of acknowledging **b** : an act of acknowledging some deed or achievement **2** : something done or given in return for something received

ac·me \'ak-mē\ *n* : the highest point : PEAK ⟨the *acme* of perfection⟩

ac·ne \'ak-nē\ *n* : a disorder of the skin caused by inflammation of skin glands and hair follicles and marked by pimples especially on the face

ac·o·lyte \'ak-ə-,līt\ *n* : a person who assists a member of the clergy in a service

ac·o·nite \'ak-ə-,nīt\ *n* **1** : any of a genus of poisonous usually blue-flowered or purple-flowered plants related to the buttercups **2** : a drug obtained from the common Old World monkshood

acorn \'ā-,kȯrn, -kərn\ *n* : the nut of the oak tree

acorn squash *n* : an acorn-shaped winter squash with ridges on its dark green outer surface and sweet yellow to orange flesh

acous·tic \ə-'kü-stik\ *or* **acous·ti·cal** \-sti-kəl\ *adj* **1** : of or relating to the sense or organs of hearing, to sound, or to the science of sounds: as **a** : deadening or absorbing sound **b** : operated by or using sound waves **2** : of, relating to, or being a musical instrument whose sound is not electronically modified ⟨*acoustic* guitar⟩ — **acous·ti·cal·ly** \-sti-k(ə-)lē\ *adv*

aconite 1

acous·tics \ə-'kü-stiks\ *n sing or pl* **1** : a science dealing with sound **2** *also* **acous·tic** \-stik\ : the qualities in an enclosed space (as an auditorium) that make it easy or hard for a person in it to hear distinctly

ac·quaint \ə-'kwānt\ *vb* **1** : to cause to know socially ⟨became *acquainted* at school⟩ **2** : to cause to know firsthand : INFORM ⟨*acquaint* her with her duties⟩

ac·quain·tance \ə-'kwānt-ᵊn(t)s\ *n* **1** : knowledge gained by personal experience ⟨had some *acquaintance* with the subject⟩ **2** : a person one knows slightly — **ac·quain·tance·ship** \-,ship\ *n*

ac·qui·esce \,ak-wē-'es\ *vb* **-esced; -esc·ing** : to accept, agree, or give consent by keeping silent or by not raising objections — **ac·qui·es·cence** \-'es-ᵊn(t)s\ *n*

ac·qui·es·cent \,ak-wē-'es-ᵊnt\ *adj* : acquiescing or tending to acquiesce — **ac·qui·es·cent·ly** *adv*

ac·quire \ə-'kwī(ə)r\ *vb* **ac·quired; ac·quir·ing** : to come to have often by one's own efforts : GAIN — **ac·quir·able** \-'kwī-rə-bəl\ *adj*

ac·quired *adj* **1** : gained by or as a result of effort or experience **2** : caused by environmental forces and not passed from parent to offspring in the genes ⟨*acquired* characteristics⟩

acquired immune deficiency syndrome *n* : AIDS

acquired immunity *n* : immunity that is taken on following an attack of disease or caused by injection

\ə\ abut		\au̇\ out	\i\ tip	\ȯ\ saw	\u̇\ foot
\ər\ further		\ch\ chin	\ī\ life	\ȯi\ coin	\y\ yet
\a\ mat		\e\ pet	\j\ job	\th\ thin	\yü\ few
\ā\ take		\ē\ easy	\ŋ\ sing	\th\ this	\yu̇\ cure
\ä\ cot, cart		\g\ go	\ō\ bone	\ü\ food	\zh\ vision

ac·quire·ment \ə-'kwī(ə)r-mənt\ *n* **1** : the act of acquiring **2** : ACCOMPLISHMENT 3

ac·qui·si·tion \,ak-wə-'zish-ən\ *n* **1** : the act of acquiring **2** : something acquired

ac·quis·i·tive \ə-'kwiz-ət-iv\ *adj* : having a strong wish to acquire things : GRASPING — **ac·quis·i·tive·ness** *n*

ac·quit \ə-'kwit\ *vb* **ac·quit·ted; ac·quit·ting** **1** : to declare innocent of a crime or wrongdoing **2** : to conduct (oneself) usually satisfactorily

ac·quit·tal \ə-'kwit-°l\ *n* : the freeing (as by verdict) of a person from the charge of an offense

acre \'ā-kər\ *n* **1** *pl* : property consisting of land : ESTATE **2** : a unit of area equal to 43,560 square feet (about 4047 square meters) — see MEASURE table [Old English *æcer* "field, cultivated land"]

acre·age \'ā-k(ə-)rij\ *n* : area in acres

acre–foot *n* : the volume (as of irrigation water) that would cover one acre to a depth of one foot

ac·rid \'ak-rəd\ *adj* **1** : biting or bitter in taste or odor **2** : bitterly irritating to the feelings ⟨an *acrid* remark⟩ — **ac·rid·ly** *adv* — **ac·rid·ness** *n*

ac·ri·mo·ny \'ak-rə-,mō-nē\ *n, pl* **-nies** : harsh or biting sharpness especially of words, manner, or disposition — **ac·ri·mo·ni·ous** \,ak-rə-'mō-nē-əs\ *adj* — **ac·ri·mo·ni·ous·ly** *adv* — **ac·ri·mo·ni·ous·ness** *n*

ac·ro·bat \'ak-rə-,bat\ *n* : a person (as a circus performer) who is very good at stunts like jumping, balancing, tumbling, and swinging from things — **ac·ro·bat·ic** \,ak-rə-'bat-ik\ *adj*

ac·ro·bat·ics \,ak-rə-'bat-iks\ *n sing or pl* **1** : the art or performance of an acrobat **2** : stunts of or resembling those of an acrobat ⟨airplane *acrobatics*⟩

acro·le·in \ə-'krō-lē-ən\ *n* : a colorless irritating liquid

ac·ro·nym \'ak-rə-,nim\ *n* : a word (as *radar*) formed from the beginning letter or letters of each or most of the parts of a compound term

acrop·o·lis \ə-'kräp-ə-ləs\ *n* : the upper fortified part of an ancient Greek city

acropolis

¹across \ə-'krȯs\ *adv* **1** : from one side to the other ⟨boards sawed directly *across*⟩ **2** : to or on the opposite side ⟨got *across* in a boat⟩ **3** : so as to be understandable or successful ⟨get the message *across*⟩

²across *prep* **1** : to or on the opposite side of ⟨*across* the street⟩ **2** : so as to cross or pass at an angle ⟨lay one stick *across* another⟩

acryl·ic \ə-'kril-ik\ *n* **1** : ACRYLIC FIBER **2** : a paint containing an acrylic resin

acrylic fiber *n* : a quick-drying synthetic fiber used for woven and knitted cloth

acrylic resin *n* : a glassy synthetic organic plastic used for cast and molded parts or as coatings and adhesives

¹act \'akt\ *n* **1** : something that is done ⟨an *act* of kindness⟩ **2** : the doing of something ⟨caught in the *act*⟩ **3 a** : a law made by a governing body ⟨an *act* of Congress⟩ **4 a** : one of the main divisions of a play or opera **b** : one of the parts of a variety show or circus **5** : a display of behavior that is not sincere ⟨just putting on an *act*⟩ [Middle English *act* "act, deed", from Latin *actus* "action of doing" and from Latin *actum* "something done", both from *agere* "to drive, do" — related to AGENT]

²act *vb* **1** : to perform by action especially on the stage **2** : to play the part of ⟨*act* the man of the world⟩ **3 a** : to behave in a manner suitable to ⟨*act* your age⟩ **b** : to conduct oneself ⟨*act* like a fool⟩ **4** : to take action : MOVE ⟨think before you *act*⟩ **5 a** : to perform a function : SERVE

⟨*act* as mayor⟩ **b** : to produce an effect : WORK ⟨wait for a medicine to *act*⟩

ac·tin \'ak-tən\ *n* : a protein of muscle that with myosin is active in muscular contraction

act·ing \'ak-tiŋ\ *adj* : serving temporarily or in place of another ⟨*acting* president⟩

ac·ti·nism \'ak-tə-,niz-əm\ *n* : the property of radiant energy especially in the visible and ultraviolet regions by which chemical changes are produced — **ac·tin·ic** \ak-'tin-ik\ *adj*

ac·tin·i·um \ak-'tin-ē-əm\ *n* : a radioactive metallic element found especially in pitchblende — see ELEMENT table

ac·tion \'ak-shən\ *n* **1** : a legal proceeding in a court by which one demands one's right or the correction of a wrong **2** : the working of one thing on another so as to produce a change ⟨the *action* of acids on metals⟩ **3** : the process or manner of acting or functioning; *also* : such an action expressed by a verb **4 a** : a thing done : DEED **b** *pl* : BEHAVIOR, CONDUCT **5** : combat in war : BATTLE **6** : the plot of a drama or work of fiction

action verb *n* : a verb that expresses action ⟨*lingered* in "they lingered over dinner" and *bring* in "bring me the broom" are *action verbs*⟩ — compare LINKING VERB

ac·ti·vate \'ak-tə-,vāt\ *vb* **-vat·ed; -vat·ing** **1** : to make active **2** : to make (as molecules) more chemically active **3** : to make (a substance) give off radioactive particles, give off light at low temperatures, be easily affected by light, or carry an electric charge under the influence of light or other electromagnetic radiation **4** : to treat (as carbon or alumina) so as to improve the amount of adsorption **5** : to mix (sewage) with air so as to favor the growth of organisms that cause decomposition **6** : to place on active duty ⟨*activate* the reserves⟩ — **ac·ti·va·tion** \,ak-tə-'vā-shən\ *n* — **ac·ti·va·tor** \'ak-tə-,vāt-ər\ *n*

activation energy *n* : the least amount of energy required to change a normal stable molecule into a reactive molecule

ac·tive \'ak-tiv\ *adj* **1** : producing or involving action or movement **2** : representing the subject as performing the action expressed by the verb ⟨*hits* in "she hits the ball" is an *active* verb⟩ **3** : having or requiring quick or energetic movements ⟨an *active* child⟩ ⟨*active* sports⟩ **4 a** : ready for action ⟨takes an *active* interest⟩ **b** : engaged or participating in an action or activity ⟨an *active* member⟩ **c** : erupting or likely to erupt ⟨an *active* volcano⟩ **5** : engaged in or requiring full-time service especially in the armed forces ⟨*active* duty⟩ **6** : marked by present action or use ⟨an *active* account⟩ ⟨a student's *active* vocabulary⟩ **7 a** : capable of acting or reacting **b** : tending to progress or increase ⟨*active* tuberculosis⟩ — **ac·tive·ly** *adv* — **ac·tive·ness** *n*

active immunity *n* : immunity produced by the individual when exposed to an antigen — compare PASSIVE IMMUNITY

active transport *n* : the movement (as across a cell membrane) of substances from regions of lower concentration to regions of higher concentration by the use of metabolic energy

ac·tiv·ist \'ak-ti-vəst\ *n* : a person who believes in forceful action (as a mass demonstration) for political purposes

ac·tiv·i·ty \ak-'tiv-ət-ē\ *n, pl* **-ties** **1** : the quality or state of being active **2** : forceful or energetic action **3** : a natural, normal, or assigned function: as **a** : a process that an organism carries on or participates in by virtue of being alive **b** : a similar process that involves or is capable of involving mental function **4** : an educational exercise designed to teach by firsthand experience **5** : an active force ⟨solar *activity*⟩ **6 a** : something done especially for relaxation or fun **b** : a form of organized recreation

ac·tor \'ak-tər\ *n* : one that acts; *esp* : a person who acts especially in a play or movie or on television

ac·tress \'ak-trəs\ *n* : a woman or girl who acts especially in a play or movie or on television

Acts \'ak(t)s\ *or* **Acts of the Apostles** — see BIBLE table

ac·tu·al \'ak-ch(ə-w)əl, 'ak-sh(ə-w)əl\ *adj* : existing in fact and not merely as a possibility   **syn** see REAL — **ac·tu·al·i·ty** \ˌak-chə-'wal-ət-ē, -shə-\ *n* — **ac·tu·al·ize** \-ˌīz\ *vb*

ac·tu·al·ly \'ak-ch(ə-w)ə-lē, 'ak-sh(ə-w)ə-lē\ *adv* : in fact or in truth : REALLY ⟨she *actually* spoke Spanish⟩ ⟨*actually*, I didn't want to go⟩

ac·tu·ary \'ak-chə-ˌwer-ē, -shə-\ *n, pl* **-ar·ies** : one who calculates insurance premiums and dividends — **ac·tu·ar·i·al** \ˌak-chə-'wer-ē-əl\ *adj*

ac·tu·ate \'ak-chə-ˌwāt, -shə-\ *vb* **-at·ed; -at·ing**   **1** : to put into action ⟨the windmill *actuates* the pump⟩   **2** : to arouse to action ⟨*actuated* by the hope of winning⟩

act up *vb* : to act in an unruly, abnormal, or annoying way

acu·ity \ə-'kyü-ət-ē\ *n* : keenness of perception

acu·men \ə-'kyü-mən, 'ak-yə-mən\ *n* : keenness of mind : SHREWDNESS

acute \ə-'kyüt\ *adj* **acut·er; acut·est**   **1 a** : SEVERE 3, SHARP ⟨*acute* pain⟩   **b** : having a sudden onset and short duration ⟨*acute* disease⟩   **2** : measuring less than a right angle ⟨*acute* angle⟩   **3 a** : marked by keen awareness : SHREWD ⟨an *acute* observation⟩   **b** : having sharp perceptions : OBSERVANT   **4** : [2]SHRILL, HIGH ⟨an *acute* sound⟩   **5** : needing speedy attention : CRITICAL ⟨an *acute* shortage of blood plasma⟩   **syn** see SHARP — **acute·ly** *adv* — **acute·ness** *n*

ad \'ad\ *n* : ADVERTISEMENT 2

ad- *or* **ac-** *or* **ag-** *or* **al-** *or* **ap-** *or* **as-** *or* **at-** *prefix* : to : toward — usually *ac-* before *c, k,* or *q* and *ag-* before *g* and *al-* before *l* and *ap-* before *p* and *as-* before *s* and *at-* before *t* and *ad-* before other sounds but sometimes *ad-* even before one of the listed consonants [derived from Latin *ad-* "to, toward"]

ad·age \'ad-ij\ *n* : an old familiar saying : PROVERB

[1]ada·gio \ə-'däj-ō, -'däj-ē-ˌō, -'däzh-\ *adv or adj* : in an easy graceful manner : SLOWLY — used as a direction in music

[2]adagio *n*   **1** : a musical composition or movement in adagio tempo   **2** : a ballet duet or trio displaying difficult feats of balance, lifting, or spinning

[1]ad·a·mant \'ad-ə-mənt, -ˌmant\ *n*   **1** : an imaginary stone of great hardness   **2** : an unbreakable or extremely hard substance [Middle English *adamant* "an imaginary stone of great hardness, diamond", from early French *adamant* (same meaning), from Latin *adamant-, adamas* "hardest metal, diamond", from Greek *adamant-, adamas* (same meaning) — related to DIAMOND; see *Word History* at DIAMOND]

[2]adamant *adj* : firmly fixed or decided especially against something : UNYIELDING — **ad·a·mant·ly** *adv*

ad·a·man·tine \ˌad-ə-'man-ˌtēn, -ˌtīn\ *adj*   **1** : made of or having the quality of adamant   **2** : [2]ADAMANT

Ad·am's apple \ˌad-əmz-\ *n* : the lump in the front of the neck formed by the largest cartilage of the larynx [derived from a translation of Hebrew *tappûaḥ hā ādhām* "lump on a man" but mistaken for "apple of Adam" because Hebrew *tappûaḥ* means both "lump" and "apple" and *ādhām* means both "man" and "Adam"]

adapt \ə-'dapt\ *vb* : to make or become suitable; *esp* : to change so as to fit a new or specific use or situation ⟨*adapt* to life in a new school⟩ ⟨*adapt* the novel for children⟩ [from French *adapter* and Latin *adaptare*, both meaning "to adapt", from Latin *ad-* "to" and *aptus* "apt, fit" — related to APT] — **adapt·abil·i·ty** \-ˌdap-tə-'bil-ət-ē\ *n* — **adapt·able** \-'dap-tə-bəl\ *adj*

ad·ap·ta·tion \ˌad-ˌap-'tā-shən, -əp-\ *n*   **1 a** : the act or process of adapting   **b** : the state of being adapted   **2** : adjustment to environmental conditions: as   **a** : adjustment of a sense organ to the degree or quality of stimulation   **b** : change in an organism or its parts that fits it better for the conditions of its environment; *also* : a structure resulting from this change   **3** : something that is adapted;

esp : a composition rewritten into a new form — **ad·ap·ta·tion·al** \-shnəl, -shən-ᵊl\ *adj* — **ad·ap·ta·tion·al·ly** \-ē\ *adv*

adapt·ed \ə-'dap-təd\ *adj* : suited by nature or design to a particular use, purpose, or situation

adapt·er *also* **adap·tor** \ə-'dap-tər\ *n*   **1** : someone or something that adapts   **2 a** : a device for connecting two parts (as of different diameters) of a usually larger device   **b** : an attachment for adapting a device for uses not originally intended

add \'ad\ *vb*   **1 a** : to join or unite to a thing so as to increase or improve it ⟨*add* a wing to the house⟩   **b** : to unite or combine in a single whole   **2** : to put or say something more ⟨*add* one cup of sugar⟩ ⟨*add* to her remarks⟩   **3 a** : to perform the mathematical operation of addition   **b** : to combine (as numbers) into a single sum — **add·able** *or* **add·ible** \'ad-ə-bəl\ *adj*

ad·dend \'ad-ˌend\ *n* : a number that is to be added to another

ad·den·dum \ə-'den-dəm\ *n, pl* **-den·da** \-'den-də\ : something added (as to a book)

[1]ad·der \'ad-ər\ *n*   **1** : a poisonous European viper; *also* : any of several related snakes   **2** : any of several harmless North American snakes (as the hognose snakes)

[2]add·er \'ad-ər\ *n* : one that adds

ad·der's–tongue \'ad-ərz-ˌtəŋ\ *n*   **1** : a fern whose fruiting spike resembles a serpent's tongue   **2** : DOGTOOTH VIOLET

[1]ad·dict \ə-'dikt\ *vb*   **1** : to devote or surrender oneself to something habitually ⟨*addicted* to detective stories⟩   **2** : to cause (a person) to make a habit of using a drug ⟨a pusher tries to *addict* others⟩

[1]adder 1

[2]ad·dict \'ad-(ˌ)ikt\ *n* : one who is addicted (as to a drug)

ad·dic·tion \ə-'dik-shən, a-\ *n* : the quality or state of being addicted; *esp* : uncontrollable use of habit-forming drugs

ad·dic·tive \ə-'dik-tiv, a-\ *adj* : causing or characterized by addiction

ad·di·tion \ə-'dish-ən, a-\ *n*   **1** : the result of adding : INCREASE   **2** : the act, process, or operation of adding   **3** : a part added (as to a building) — **in addition** : as something more : BESIDES — **in addition to** : [2]BESIDES

ad·di·tion·al \ə-'dish-nəl, -ən-ᵊl\ *adj* : being an addition : EXTRA — **ad·di·tion·al·ly** \-ē\ *adv*

[1]ad·di·tive \'ad-ət-iv\ *adj* : relating to or produced by addition — **ad·di·tive·ly** *adv*

[2]additive *n* : a substance added to another in small amounts to give or improve desirable qualities or decrease unwanted qualities ⟨a gasoline *additive*⟩ ⟨*additives* which color, flavor, or preserve food⟩

additive identity element *n* : an element (as zero in the set of real numbers) of a mathematical set that leaves every element of the set unchanged when added to it

additive inverse *n* : a number that when added to a given number gives zero ⟨the *additive inverse* of 4 is −4⟩ — compare [2]OPPOSITE 3

ad·dle \'ad-ᵊl\ *vb* **ad·dled; ad·dling** \'ad-liŋ, -ᵊl-iŋ\   **1** : to make or become confused   **2** : to become rotten : SPOIL ⟨*addled* eggs⟩

[1]ad·dress \ə-'dres, a-\ *vb*   **1 a** : to direct the attention of oneself ⟨*addressed* themselves to the problem⟩   **b** : to

\ə\ abut	\aú\ out	\i\ tip	\ó\ saw	\ú\ foot
\ər\ further	\ch\ chin	\ī\ life	\ói\ coin	\y\ yet
\a\ mat	\e\ pet	\j\ job	\th\ thin	\yü\ few
\ā\ take	\ē\ easy	\ŋ\ sing	\t̲h̲\ this	\yú\ cure
\ä\ cot, cart	\g\ go	\ō\ bone	\ü\ food	\zh\ vision

deal with ⟨prepares to *address* the problem⟩ **2 a** : to communicate directly ⟨*address* a petition to the governor⟩ **b** : to deliver a formal speech to ⟨*address* the convention⟩ **3** : to mark directions for delivery on ⟨*address* a letter⟩ **4** : to greet by a prescribed form **5** : to identify (as a peripheral or a piece of information) by an address — **ad·dress·er** *n*

²ad·dress \ə-'dres, 'ad-ˌres\ *n* **1** : manner of speaking : DELIVERY **2** : a rehearsed speech **3 a** : a place where a person or organization can usually be reached **b** : the directions for delivery on mail **4** : a location (as in the memory of a computer) where particular information is stored; *also* : the symbols (as numerals or letters) that identify such a location

ad·dress·able \ə-'dres-ə-bəl\ *adj* : able to be reached through an address ⟨*addressable* registers in a computer⟩

ad·dress·ee \ˌad-ˌres-'ē, ə-ˌdres-'ē\ *n* : one to whom mail is addressed

ad·duce \ə-'d(y)üs\ *vb* **ad·duced; ad·duc·ing** : to offer as example, reason, or proof

ad·duct \ə-'dəkt\ *vb* : to draw (a part of the body) toward or past a middle plane or line that divides the body or a bodily part into right and left halves

ad·duc·tor \ə-'dək-tər\ *n* : a muscle that draws a body part (as an arm or finger) toward or past a plane or a line that divides the body or a hand or foot into right and left halves

add up *vb* **1 a** : to come to a total and especially the expected total **b** : to make sense ⟨her story just doesn't *add up*⟩ **2** : to amount to a lot ⟨just a little each time, but it all *adds up*⟩

ad·e·nine \'ad-ᵊn-ēn\ *n* : one of the bases which make up the genetic code of DNA and RNA — compare CYTOSINE, GUANINE, THYMINE, URACIL

¹ad·e·noid \'ad-ᵊn-ˌoid, 'ad-ˌnoid\ *or* **ad·e·noi·dal** \ˌad-ᵊn-'oid-ᵊl\ *adj* **1** : of, relating to, or resembling glands or the tissue of glands **2** : of or relating to adenoids or adenoid disorder

²adenoid *n* : an abnormally enlarged mass of tissue at the back of the pharynx that usually interferes with breathing — usually used in pl.

aden·o·sine di·phos·phate \ə-'den-ə-ˌsēn-dī-'fäs-ˌfāt\ *n* : ADP

adenosine tri·phos·phate \-trī-'fäs-ˌfāt\ *n* : ATP

¹ad·ept \'ad-ˌept\ *n* : a highly skilled or well-trained individual : EXPERT

²adept \ə-'dept\ *adj* : very good at something **syn** see SKILLFUL — **adept·ly** *adv* — **adept·ness** \-'dep(t)-nəs\ *n*

ad·e·qua·cy \'ad-i-kwə-sē\ *n, pl* **-cies** : the quality or state of being adequate

ad·e·quate \'ad-i-kwət\ *adj* **1** : suitable or enough for a requirement ⟨food and water *adequate* for six people⟩ **2** : good enough ⟨your grades are barely *adequate*⟩ — **ad·e·quate·ly** *adv* — **ad·e·quate·ness** *n*

ad·here \ad-'hi(ə)r, əd-\ *vb* **ad·hered; ad·her·ing** **1** : to stay loyal (as to a cause or promise) **2** : to stick by or as if by gluing, suction, grasping, or melting

ad·her·ence \ad-'hir-ən(t)s, əd-\ *n* **1** : the action or quality of adhering **2** : steady or faithful attachment ⟨*adherence* to the truth⟩

¹ad·her·ent \ad-'hir-ənt, əd-\ *adj* : able or tending to adhere

²adherent *n* : a person who adheres to a leader, belief, or group

ad·he·sion \ad-'hē-zhən, əd-\ *n* **1** : steady or firm attachment; *esp* : a sticking together **2** : abnormal union of tissues following inflammation (as after surgery) **3** : the molecular attraction between surfaces of bodies in contact

¹ad·he·sive \ad-'hē-siv, əd-, -ziv\ *adj* : tending to adhere : prepared for adhering — **ad·he·sive·ness** *n*

²adhesive *n* : an adhesive substance (as glue or cement)

adhesive tape *n* : tape that is coated on one side with an adhesive and is used especially for medical purposes

adi·a·bat·ic \ˌad-ē-ə-'bat-ik, ˌā-, dī-ə-\ *adj* : occurring without loss or gain of heat ⟨*adiabatic* expansion⟩ — **ad·i·a·bat·i·cal·ly** \-'bat-i-k(ə-)lē\ *adv*

adieu \ə-'d(y)ü, a-\ *n, pl* **adieus** *or* **adieux** \-'d(y)üz\ : ²FAREWELL 1 — often used interjectionally [Middle English *adieu* "farewell", from early French *adieu* (same meaning), from *a Dieu*, literally "(I commit you) to God", from Latin *Deus* "God" — related to ADIOS, DEITY]

adi·os \ˌad-ē-'ōs, ˌäd-\ *interj* — used to express farewell [from Spanish *adiós* "farewell", from *a Dios*, literally "(I commit you) to God", from Latin *Deus* "God" — related to ADIEU, DEITY]

ad·i·pose \'ad-ə-ˌpōs\ *adj* : of or relating to animal fat : FATTY — **ad·i·pos·i·ty** \ˌad-ə-'päs-ət-ē\ *n*

ad·ja·cent \ə-'jās-ᵊnt\ *adj* **1** : lying next or near : having a border or point in common ⟨a field *adjacent* to the road⟩ **2** : having a common vertex and side ⟨*adjacent* angles⟩ — **ad·ja·cent·ly** *adv*

ad·jec·tive \'aj-ik-tiv\ *n* : a word that modifies a noun by describing a quality of the thing named, indicating its quantity or extent, or specifying a thing as distinct from something else — **adjective** *adj* — **ad·jec·ti·val** \ˌaj-ik-'tī-vəl\ *adj or n* — **ad·jec·ti·val·ly** \-və-lē\ *adv*

ad·join \ə-'join, a-\ *vb* **1** : to add or attach by joining **2** : to lie next to or in contact with

ad·journ \ə-'jərn\ *vb* : to bring or come to a close for a period of time ⟨Congress *adjourned*⟩ ⟨*adjourn* a meeting⟩ — **ad·journ·ment** \-mənt\ *n*

ad·judge \ə-'jəj\ *vb* **ad·judged; ad·judg·ing** **1** : ADJUDICATE **2** : to consider or say to be : DEEM ⟨they *adjudged* the play a success⟩

ad·ju·di·cate \ə-'jüd-i-ˌkāt\ *vb* **-cat·ed; -cat·ing** : to decide, award, or sentence judicially ⟨*adjudicate* a claim⟩ — **ad·ju·di·ca·tion** \-ˌjüd-i-'kā-shən\ *n*

ad·junct \'aj-ˌəŋ(k)t\ *n* : ¹ACCESSORY 1

ad·jure \ə-'ju(ə)r\ *vb* **ad·jured; ad·jur·ing** : to command solemnly under or as if under oath — **ad·ju·ra·tion** \ˌaj-ə-'rā-shən\ *n*

ad·just \ə-'jəst\ *vb* **1** : to bring to a better state : set right ⟨*adjust* conflicts⟩ ⟨*adjust* the error⟩ **2** : to move the parts of an instrument or a piece of machinery until they fit together in the best working order ⟨*adjust* a watch⟩ ⟨*adjust* the brakes on a car⟩ **3** : to determine the amount of an insurance claim **4** : to adapt oneself to conditions ⟨had trouble *adjusting* to the new job⟩ — **ad·just·able** \-'jəs-tə-bəl\ *adj* — **ad·just·er** *also* **ad·jus·tor** \-'jəs-tər\ *n*

ad·just·ment \ə-'jəs(t)-mənt\ *n* **1** : the act or process of adjusting **2** : a settlement of a claim or debt **3** : the state of being adjusted **4** : a means of adjusting one part (as in a machine) to another ⟨an *adjustment* for focusing a microscope⟩

ad·ju·tant \'aj-ət-ənt\ *n* **1** : an officer (as in the army) who assists the commanding officer in clerical work **2** : ASSISTANT

¹ad–lib \(')ad-'lib\ *vb* **ad–libbed; ad–lib·bing** : to improvise lines, or a speech, or music

²ad–lib *adj* : spoken, composed, or performed without preparation

ad lib *adv* : without restraint or limit

ad li·bi·tum \(')ad-'lib-ət-əm\ *adv* : freely as one wishes — used as a direction in music [modern Latin, "according to one's desire"]

ad·min·is·ter \əd-'min-ə-stər\ *vb* **ad·min·is·tered; ad·min·is·ter·ing** \-st(ə-)riŋ\ **1** : to direct the affairs of : MANAGE ⟨*administer* a government⟩ **2** : SETTLE 5 ⟨*administer* an estate⟩ **3** : to give out as deserved ⟨*administer* justice⟩ **4** : to give formally or ceremonially ⟨*administer* the sacraments⟩ **5** : to give as treatment ⟨*administer* a drug⟩

ad·min·is·tra·tion \əd-ˌmin-ə-'strā-shən, ad-\ *n* **1** : the act or process of administering **2** : performance of executive duties : MANAGEMENT **3** : the work involved in managing public affairs as distinguished from policy-making **4**

a : a group of persons who administer **b** *cap* : the executive branch of a government

ad·min·is·tra·tive \əd-'min-ə-,strāt-iv, -strət-\ *adj* : of or relating to administration ⟨working in an *administrative* position⟩

ad·min·is·tra·tor \əd-'min-ə-,strāt-ər\ *n* : a person who administers

ad·min·is·tra·trix \əd-,min-ə-'strā-triks\ *n, pl* **-is·tra·tri·ces** \-'strā-trə-,sēz\ : a woman who is an administrator

ad·mi·ra·ble \,ad-mə-rə-bəl, -mrə-bəl\ *adj* : deserving to be admired : EXCELLENT — **ad·mi·ra·ble·ness** *n* — **ad·mi·ra·bly** \-blē\ *adv*

ad·mi·ral \'ad-mə-rəl, -mrəl\ *n* **1** : a naval commissioned officer with a rank above that of captain; *esp* : an officer with a rank just above that of vice admiral **2** : any of several brightly colored butterflies

> **Word History** English can trace a number of words back to Arabic. One of the areas in which the Arabs taught Europeans a few things was sailing. It should thus come as no surprise that the English word *admiral,* meaning "a high-ranking naval officer", comes from Arabic. In Arabic, *amīr-al-baḥr* means literally "commander of the sea". (The first part of the compound, *amīr,* was taken into English as *emir,* meaning "a Muslim prince".) When *amīr-al-baḥr* was borrowed by the French, they dropped the last part, *baḥr,* meaning "sea", and thus used *amiral* to mean "naval commander". Probably because an admiral was such an impressive person, the word became associated with Latin *admirari,* meaning "to admire", and thus in English it became *admiral.* [Middle English *admiral* "naval commander", from early French *amiral* and Latin *admirallus* (both, same meaning), from Arabic *amīr-al-baḥr* "commander of the sea"]

ad·mi·ral·ty \'ad-mə-rəl-tē, -mrəl-\ *adj* : of or relating to conduct on the sea : MARITIME ⟨*admiralty* court⟩ ⟨*admiralty* law⟩

Admiralty *n* : a group of officials formerly in charge of the British navy

ad·mi·ra·tion \,ad-mə-'rā-shən\ *n* **1** : an object of admiring regard **2** : a feeling of great and delighted approval

ad·mire \əd-'mī(ə)r\ *vb* **ad·mired; ad·mir·ing** **1** : to look at with admiration ⟨*admire* the scenery⟩ **2** : to have high regard for ⟨*admired* her courage⟩ [from early French *admirer* "to view with wonder", from Latin *admirari* (same meaning), from *ad-* "at" and *mirari* "to wonder" — related to MIRACLE] — **ad·mir·er** \-'mīr-ər\ *n*

ad·mis·si·ble \əd-'mis-ə-bəl\ *adj* : that can be or is worthy to be admitted ⟨*admissible* evidence⟩ — **ad·mis·si·bil·i·ty** \-,mis-ə-'bil-ət-ē\ *n*

ad·mis·sion \əd-'mish-ən, ad-\ *n* **1** : the act of admitting; *esp* : an admitting of something that has not been proved ⟨an *admission* of guilt⟩ **2** : the right or permission to enter ⟨standards of *admission* to a school⟩ **3** : the price of entrance

ad·mit \əd-'mit, ad-\ *vb* **ad·mit·ted; ad·mit·ting** **1 a** : to allow room for : PERMIT ⟨a question that *admits* two answers⟩ **b** : to make known usually with some unwillingness ⟨*admitted* that he really didn't know⟩ ⟨*admit* a mistake⟩ **2** : to allow entry : let in ⟨*admit* a state to the Union⟩ **syn** see ACKNOWLEDGE — **ad·mit·ted·ly** \-'mit-əd-lē\ *adv*

ad·mit·tance \əd-'mit-ən(t)s, ad-\ *n* : permission to enter : ENTRANCE

ad·mix·ture \ad-'miks-chər\ *n* **1 a** : the act of mixing **b** : the fact of being mixed **2 a** : something added by mixing **b** : a product of mixing

ad·mon·ish \ad-'män-ish\ *vb* **1** : to criticize or warn gently but seriously : warn of a fault **2** : to give friendly advice or encouragement to ⟨*admonished* them to keep trying⟩ **syn** see REBUKE — **ad·mon·ish·ment** \-mənt\ *n*

ad·mo·ni·tion \,ad-mə-'nish-ən\ *n* : a gentle or friendly criticism or warning

ad·mon·i·to·ry \ad-'män-ə-,tōr-ē, -,tor-\ *adj* : expressing admonition : WARNING

ado \ə-'dü\ *n* : ¹FUSS 1, TROUBLE ⟨much *ado* about nothing⟩

ado·be \ə-'dō-bē\ *n* **1** : a brick or building material made of a sun-dried mixture of earth and straw **2** : a building made of adobe bricks [Spanish]

ad·o·les·cence \,ad-əl-'es-°n(t)s\ *n* : the state or process of growing up; *also* : the period of life from puberty to maturity [Middle English *adolescence* "adolescence", from early French *adolescence* (same meaning), from Latin *adolescentia* (same meaning), from *adolescere* "to grow up" — related to ADULT] — **ad·o·les·cent** \-°nt\ *adj or n*

adobe 2

adopt \ə-'däpt\ *vb* **1** : to take legally as one's own child ⟨*adopt* an orphan⟩ **2** : to take as one's own ⟨*adopt* a point of view⟩ **3** : to accept formally ⟨the assembly *adopted* a constitution⟩ — **adopt·able** \ə-'däp-tə-bəl\ *adj* — **adopt·er** *n* — **adop·tion** \ə-'däp-shən\ *n*

adop·tive \ə-'däp-tiv\ *adj* : made by or associated with adoption ⟨the *adoptive* parents⟩

ador·able \ə-'dōr-ə-bəl, -'dor-\ *adj* **1** : deserving to be adored **2** : CHARMING, LOVELY ⟨an *adorable* child⟩ — **ador·able·ness** *n* — **ador·ably** \-blē\ *adv*

adore \ə-'dō(ə)r, -'do(ə)r\ *vb* **adored; ador·ing** **1** : ²WORSHIP 1 **2** : to be very fond of [from early French *adorer* "to adore", from Latin *adorare* (same meaning), from *ad-* "to" and *orare* "to speak, pray" — related to ORACLE, ORATION] — **ad·o·ra·tion** \,ad-ə-'rā-shən\ *n* — **ador·er** \ə-'dōr-ər, -'dor-\ *n*

adorn \ə-'dorn\ *vb* : to heighten the appearance of with ornaments

> **syn** ADORN, DECORATE, EMBELLISH, BEAUTIFY mean to improve the appearance by adding something that is not essential. ADORN suggests that the thing added is beautiful in itself ⟨a gold star *adorned* the tree⟩ DECORATE suggests adding color or design to something that is plain or dull ⟨*decorated* her room with posters⟩ EMBELLISH stresses the adding of something not needed ⟨dishes *embellished* with a leaf design⟩ BEAUTIFY stresses the improvement of something plain or ugly ⟨flower boxes *beautify* the street⟩

adorn·ment \ə-'dorn-mənt\ *n* **1** : the action of adorning : the state of being adorned **2** : something that adorns

ADP \,ā-,dē-'pē, ā-'dē-,pē\ *n* : a compound formed in living cells that reacts to form ATP

¹ad·re·nal \ə-'drē-nəl\ *adj* : of, relating to, located near, or derived from the adrenal glands or their secretions

²adrenal *n* : ADRENAL GLAND

adrenal gland *n* : either of a pair of complex endocrine glands that are located near the kidney and produce the hormone epinephrine

adren·a·line \ə-'dren-°l-ən\ *n* : EPINEPHRINE

adrift \ə-'drift\ *adv or adj* **1** : without power or anchor ⟨a ship *adrift* in the storm⟩ **2** : without guidance or purpose ⟨alone and *adrift* in the city⟩

adroit \ə-'dròit\ *adj* : having or showing great skill or cleverness ⟨an *adroit* leader⟩ ⟨*adroit* at handling problems⟩ ⟨the candidate's *adroit* use of television⟩ — **adroit·ly** *adv*

\ə\ abut	\aú\ out	\i\ tip	\ò\ saw	\ú\ foot
\ər\ further	\ch\ chin	\ī\ life	\òi\ coin	\y\ yet
\a\ mat	\e\ pet	\j\ job	\th\ thin	\yü\ few
\ā\ take	\ē\ easy	\ŋ\ sing	\th\ this	\yü\ cure
\ä\ cot, cart	\g\ go	\ō\ bone	\ü\ food	\zh\ vision

— **adroit·ness** n

ad·u·late \'aj-ə-,lāt\ vb **-lat·ed; -lat·ing** : to flatter or admire — **ad·u·la·tion** \,aj-ə-'lā-shən\ n — **ad·u·la·tor** \'aj-ə-,lāt-ər\ n — **ad·u·la·to·ry** \'aj-ə-lə-,tōr-ē, -,tȯr-\ adj

¹**adult** \ə-'dəlt, 'ad-,əlt\ adj **1** : fully developed and mature **2** : of, relating to, or characteristic of adults [from Latin adultus "having grown up", from adolescere "to grow up" — related to ADOLESCENCE] — **adult·hood** \ə-'dəlt-,hu̇d\ n — **adult·ness** \ə-'dəlt-nəs, 'ad-,əlt-\ n

²**adult** n : a fully grown person, animal, or plant — **adult·like** \ə-'dəlt-,līk\ adj

adul·ter·ant \ə-'dəl-tə-rənt\ n : something used to adulterate another thing

adul·ter·ate \ə-'dəl-tə-,rāt\ vb **-at·ed; -at·ing** : to make impure or weaker by adding an unnecessary or lower-grade substance; esp : to prepare for sale by using in whole or in part a substance that reduces value or strength [from Latin adulteratus "to make impure", from ad- "to" and alter "other" — related to ALTER] — **adul·ter·a·tion** \ə-,dəl-tə-'rā-shən\ n — **adul·ter·a·tor** \ə-'dəl-tə-,rāt-ər\ n

adul·tery \ə-'dəl-t(ə-)rē\ n, pl **-ter·ies** : voluntary sexual intercourse between a married person and someone other than his or her spouse — **adul·ter·er** \-tər-ər\ n — **adul·ter·ess** \-t(ə-)rəs\ n — **adul·ter·ous** \-t(ə-)rəs\ adj

¹**ad·vance** \əd-'van(t)s\ vb **ad·vanced; ad·vanc·ing** **1** : to move forward ⟨advance a few yards⟩ **2** : to help the progress of ⟨sacrifices that advance the cause of freedom⟩ **3** : to raise to a higher rank or position : PROMOTE ⟨was advanced from clerk to assistant manager⟩ **4** : to give and expect to be paid back ⟨advance a loan⟩ **5** : SUGGEST 1, PROPOSE ⟨advance a new plan⟩ — **ad·vanc·er** n

²**advance** n **1** : a forward movement **2** : progress in development : IMPROVEMENT ⟨recent advances in medicine⟩ **3** : a rise in price, value, or amount **4** : a first step or approach ⟨an unfriendly look discourages advances⟩ **5 a** : the giving of something (as money) before a return is received ⟨I need an advance on my salary⟩ **b** : the money or goods given — **in advance** : ¹BEFORE, BEFOREHAND ⟨knew of the change two weeks in advance⟩ — **in advance of** : AHEAD OF

³**advance** adj **1** : made, sent, or furnished ahead of time ⟨an advance payment⟩ **2** : going or situated before ⟨an advance guard⟩ ⟨an advance scout⟩

ad·vanced \əd-'van(t)st\ adj **1** : being beyond the elementary or introductory level ⟨advanced mathematics⟩ **2** : being far along in progress or development ⟨an advanced civilization⟩ ⟨advanced paralysis⟩ **3** : having altered from a more primitive ancestral state ⟨advanced insects like the wasps and bees⟩

ad·vance·ment \əd-'van(t)s-mənt\ n **1** : the action of advancing : the state of being advanced **2** : a raising or being raised to a higher rank or position

ad·van·tage \əd-'vant-ij\ n **1** : the fact of being in a better position or condition ⟨gain the advantage⟩ **2** : ¹BENEFIT 1, GAIN **3** : something that helps the one it belongs to ⟨speed is an advantage in sports⟩ — **to advantage** : so as to give a favorable impression

ad·van·ta·geous \,ad-,van-'tā-jəs, -vən-\ adj : giving an advantage : HELPFUL, FAVORABLE — **ad·van·ta·geous·ly** adv — **ad·van·ta·geous·ness** n

ad·vent \'ad-,vent\ n **1** cap : the season beginning four Sundays before Christmas **2** : the first appearance : ARRIVAL ⟨the advent of spring⟩ [Middle English advent "Christmas season", from Latin adventus (same meaning), from earlier adventus "arrival"]

ad·ven·ti·tious \,ad-(,)ven-'tish-əs, -vən-\ adj **1** : coming from an outside source and not an essential part : ACCIDENTAL **2** : appearing out of the usual or normal place ⟨adventitious buds⟩ — **ad·ven·ti·tious·ly** adv — **ad·ven·ti·tious·ness** n

¹**ad·ven·ture** \əd-'ven-chər\ n **1** : an action involving unknown or extraordinary dangers **2** : the encountering of risks ⟨the spirit of adventure⟩ **3** : an unusual or exciting experience ⟨the field trip was an adventure⟩

²**adventure** vb **-ven·tured; -ven·tur·ing** \-'vench-(ə-)riŋ\ **1** : ²RISK 1, VENTURE **2** : to venture upon ⟨explorers adventuring the wilderness⟩

ad·ven·tur·er \əd-'vench-(ə-)rər\ n **1** : a person who looks for adventures **2** : a person who tries to become wealthy or powerful by trickery

ad·ven·ture·some \əd-'ven-chər-səm\ adj : ADVENTUROUS 1

ad·ven·tur·ous \əd-'vench-(ə-)rəs\ adj **1** : ready to take risks or to deal with the new and unknown ⟨adventurous explorers⟩ **2** : having unknown dangers and risks ⟨an adventurous voyage⟩ — **ad·ven·tur·ous·ly** adv — **ad·ven·tur·ous·ness** n

    syn ADVENTUROUS, VENTURESOME, DARING mean exposing oneself to more danger than one has to. ADVENTUROUS suggests a willingness to accept risks but does not rule out showing good sense ⟨adventurous campers backpacking in the mountains⟩ VENTURESOME suggests a lively eagerness for dangerous undertakings ⟨venturesome deep-sea explorers⟩ DARING stresses lack of fear and even boldness in looking for danger ⟨racing-car drivers are often very daring⟩

ad·verb \'ad-,vərb\ n : a word used to modify a verb, an adjective, another adverb, a preposition, a phrase, a clause, or a sentence and often used to show degree, manner, place, or time — **adverb** adj — **ad·ver·bi·al** \ad-'vər-bē-əl\ adj or n — **ad·ver·bi·al·ly** \-bē-ə-lē\ adv

¹**ad·ver·sary** \'ad-və(r)-,ser-ē\ n, pl **-sar·ies** : someone or something that struggles with, opposes, or resists : ENEMY, OPPONENT

²**adversary** adj : involving two persons or two sides who oppose each other ⟨our adversary system of justice⟩

ad·verse \ad-'vərs, 'ad-,vərs\ adj **1** : acting in an opposite direction ⟨adverse winds⟩ **2** : opposed to one's interests ⟨adverse testimony⟩; esp : not friendly or favorable ⟨adverse criticism⟩ ⟨adverse remarks⟩ **3** : causing harm : HARMFUL ⟨adverse effects of a drug⟩ — **ad·verse·ly** adv — **ad·verse·ness** n

ad·ver·si·ty \ad-'vər-sət-ē\ n, pl **-ties** : an instance or condition of serious or continued misfortune

ad·vert \ad-'vərt\ vb : to make a reference : REFER

ad·ver·tise \'ad-vər-,tīz\ vb **-tised; -tis·ing** **1** : to announce publicly especially by a printed notice or a broadcast ⟨advertise a sale⟩ **2** : to call public attention to especially by pointing out desirable qualities so as to create a desire to buy or to do business ⟨advertise a cereal⟩ ⟨advertise a store⟩ **3** : to give a public notice or advertisement ⟨advertise for a lost dog⟩ — **ad·ver·tis·er** n

ad·ver·tise·ment \,ad-vər-'tīz-mənt, əd-'vərt-əz-\ n **1** : the act or process of advertising **2** : a public notice; esp : one published or broadcast

ad·ver·tis·ing \'ad-vər-,tī-ziŋ\ n **1** : the action of calling something to the attention of the public especially by paid announcements **2** : published or broadcast advertisements **3** : the business of preparing advertisements

ad·vice \əd-'vīs\ n : an opinion or suggestion offered about a decision or course of conduct : COUNSEL

ad·vis·able \əd-'vī-zə-bəl\ adj : reasonable or proper under the circumstances : WISE, PRUDENT — **ad·vis·abil·i·ty** \-,vī-zə-'bil-ət-ē\ n — **ad·vis·ably** \-'vī-zə-blē\ adv

ad·vise \əd-'vīz\ vb **ad·vised; ad·vis·ing** **1 a** : to give advice to : COUNSEL ⟨advised them to save their money⟩ **b** : RECOMMEND 3 ⟨advised caution⟩ **2** : INFORM 1 ⟨were advised of bad flying conditions⟩ **3** : to talk over a problem or decision : CONSULT ⟨the woman advised with her parents⟩ — **ad·vis·er** or **ad·vi·sor** \-'vī-zər\ n

ad·vised \əd-'vīzd\ adj : thought about : CONSIDERED ⟨an ill-advised plan⟩ — **ad·vis·ed·ly** \-'vī-zəd-lē\ adv

ad·vise·ment \əd-'vīz-mənt\ n : careful consideration ⟨take

a matter under *advisement*⟩

ad·vi·so·ry \əd-'vīz-(ə-)rē\ *adj* **1** : having the power or right to advise ⟨an *advisory* committee⟩ **2** : giving or containing advice ⟨an *advisory* opinion⟩

ad·vo·ca·cy \'ad-və-kə-sē\ *n* : the act or process of advocating : SUPPORT

¹ad·vo·cate \'ad-və-kət, -,kāt\ *n* **1** : a person who argues for the cause of another especially in a court of law **2 a** : a person who argues for, recommends, or supports a cause or policy ⟨an *advocate* of civil rights⟩ [Middle English *advocat* "one that pleads a case for another (in court)", from early French *advocat* (same meaning), from Latin *advocatus* (same meaning), derived from *advocare* "to call to one's aid, summon", from *ad-* "to, toward, near" and *vocare* "to call" — related to PROVOKE, REVOKE, VOCATION]

²ad·vo·cate \'ad-və-,kāt\ *vb* **-cat·ed; -cat·ing** : to speak in favor of : argue for

adz *or* **adze** \'adz\ *n* : a cutting tool that has a thin arched blade set at right angles to the handle and is used chiefly for shaping wood

ae͏̈·des \ā-'ēd-ēz\ *n, pl* **aëdes** : any of a genus of mosquitoes including carriers of disease (as yellow fever)

ae·gis \'ē-jəs\ *n* **1** : PROTECTION 1a, DEFENSE ⟨under the *aegis* of the law⟩ **2** : PATRONAGE 1, SPONSORSHIP

ae·on \'ē-ən, 'ē-,än\ *n* : a very long period of time : AGE

aer- *or* **aero-** *combining form* **1** : air : atmosphere ⟨*aerate*⟩ ⟨*aerobic*⟩ **2** : gas ⟨*aerosol*⟩ **3** : aviation ⟨*aeronautics*⟩ [derived from Greek *aer-, aero-* "air"]

aer·ate \'a(-ə)r-,āt, 'e(-ə)r-\ *vb* **aer·at·ed; aer·at·ing** **1** : to supply (blood) with oxygen by respiration **2 a** : to supply or fill to the limit (as soil) with air **b** : to expose to air (as for purifying or ventilation) **3** : to combine or fill with gas — **aer·a·tion** \,a(-ə)r-'ā-shən, ,e(-ə)r-\ *n* — **aer·a·tor** \'a(-ə)r-,āt-ər, 'e(-ə)r-\ *n*

¹ae·ri·al \'ar-ē-əl, 'er-\ *adj* **1 a** : of, relating to, or occurring in the air or atmosphere ⟨an *aerial* display on a trapeze⟩ **b** : living or growing in the air rather than on the ground or in water **c** : running on cables or rails that are raised above the ground ⟨an *aerial* railway⟩ **2 a** : of or relating to aircraft ⟨*aerial* navigation⟩ **b** : designed for use in, taken from, or operating from aircraft ⟨*aerial* photograph⟩ — **aer·i·al·ly** \-ē-ə-lē\ *adv*

²aerial *n* **1** : ANTENNA 2 **2** : FORWARD PASS

aerial root *n* : a root (as for clinging to a wall) that does not enter the soil

aer·ie \'a(ə)r-ē, 'e(ə)r-, 'i(ə)r-\ *n* **1** : the nest of a bird on a cliff or a mountaintop **2** : a dwelling on a height [derived from Latin *area* "open ground, feeding place for animals" — related to AREA]

aerial root

aer·o·bat·ics \,ar-ə-'bat-iks, ,er-\ *n sing or pl* : spectacular flying feats and maneuvers — **aer·o·bat·ic** \-ik\ *adj*

aer·o·bic \,a(-ə)r-'ō-bik, ,e(-ə)r-\ *adj* **1** : living, active, or occurring only in the presence of oxygen **2** : of, relating to, or caused by aerobic organisms (as bacteria) — **aer·o·bi·cal·ly** \-bi-k(ə-)lē\ *adv*

aer·o·bics \,a(-ə)r-'ō-biks, ,e(-ə)r-\ *n sing or pl* : a system of exercises intended to develop the body's ability to take in and use oxygen

aero·drome \'ar-ə-,drōm, 'er-\ *n, British* : AIRPORT, AIRFIELD

aero·dy·nam·ics \,ar-ō-dī-'nam-iks, ,er-\ *n* : a science that deals with the motion of fluids (as air) that are gases and with the forces acting on bodies exposed to them — **aero·dy·nam·ic** \-ik\ *adj*

aer·om·e·ter \,a(-ə)r-'äm-ət-ər, ,e(-ə)r-\ *n* : an instrument for finding out the weight or the mass per volume of air or other gases

aero·naut \'ar-ə-,nȯt, 'er-, -,nät\ *n* : a person who operates or travels in a dirigible or balloon

aeronautical engineering *n* : engineering that deals with aeronautics and flight control — **aeronautical engineer** *n*

aero·nau·tics \,ar-ə-'nȯt-iks, ,er-\ *n* **1** : a science dealing with the operation of aircraft **2** : the art or science of flight — **aero·nau·ti·cal** \-'nȯt-i-kəl\ *adj*

aero·plane \'ar-ə-,plān, 'er-\ *chiefly British variant of* AIRPLANE

aero·sol \'ar-ə-,sȯl, 'er-, -,säl\ *n* : a mixture of fine solid or liquid particles and gas ⟨smoke, fog, and mist are *aerosols*⟩

¹aero·space \'ar-ō-,spās, 'er-\ *n* **1** : the earth's atmosphere and the space beyond **2** : a science dealing with aerospace

²aerospace *adj* : of or relating to aerospace, to the vehicles used in aerospace or their manufacture, or to travel in aerospace ⟨*aerospace* medicine⟩

aes·thet·ic *or* **es·thet·ic** \es-'thet-ik, is-\ *adj* : of or relating to beauty or what is beautiful — **aes·thet·i·cal·ly** \-i-k(ə-)lē\ *adv*

aes·thet·ics *also* **es·thet·ics** \es-'thet-iks, is-\ *n* : a branch of philosophy that studies and explains the principles and forms of beauty especially in art and literature

aes·ti·vate, aes·ti·va·tion *variant of* ESTIVATE, ESTIVATION

¹afar \ə-'fär\ *adv* : from, to, or at a great distance

²afar *n* : a great distance ⟨a voice from *afar*⟩

af·fa·ble \'af-ə-bəl\ *adj* : being at ease and pleasant especially in conversation ⟨an *affable* host⟩ **syn** see GRACIOUS — **af·fa·bil·i·ty** \,af-ə-'bil-ət-ē\ *n* — **af·fa·bly** \'af-ə-blē\ *adv*

af·fair \ə-'fa(ə)r, -'fe(ə)r\ *n* **1 a** *pl* : commercial, professional, public, or personal business ⟨government *affairs*⟩ ⟨must arrange my *affairs* before I can leave⟩ **b** : ²CONCERN 1, MATTER ⟨not your *affair* at all⟩ **2 a** : EVENT 1b, ACTIVITY ⟨a social *affair*⟩ **b** : PRODUCT 2, THING ⟨a flimsy *affair* of ropes bridging the river⟩ **3** : a brief romantic relationship

¹af·fect \ə-'fekt, a-\ *vb* **1** : to show a liking for : FANCY ⟨*affect* flashy clothes⟩ **2** : FEIGN 1, PRETEND ⟨*affect* indifference⟩

²affect *vb* : to produce an effect upon: as **a** : to produce a significant and usually harmful influence upon or change in ⟨paralysis *affected* his limbs⟩ **b** : to act upon (as a person or a person's feelings) so as to cause a response ⟨the criticism *affected* her deeply⟩

af·fec·ta·tion \,af-,ek-'tā-shən\ *n* : an unnatural form of behavior intended to impress others ⟨the accent was an *affectation*⟩

af·fect·ed \ə-'fek-təd, a-\ *adj* : not natural or genuine — **af·fect·ed·ly** *adv* — **af·fect·ed·ness** *n*

af·fect·ing \ə-'fek-tiŋ, a-\ *adj* : causing a feeling of pity, sympathy, or sorrow — **af·fect·ing·ly** \-tiŋ-lē\ *adv*

¹af·fec·tion \ə-'fek-shən\ *n* : a quality or feeling of liking and caring for another

²affection *n* : DISEASE, DISORDER ⟨an *affection* of the brain⟩

af·fec·tion·ate \ə-'fek-sh(ə-)nət\ *adj* : feeling or showing a great liking for a person or thing : LOVING — **af·fec·tion-**

adz

\ə\ abut	\au̇\ out	\i\ tip	\ȯ\ saw	\u̇\ foot
\ər\ further	\ch\ chin	\ī\ life	\ȯi\ coin	\y\ yet
\a\ mat	\e\ pet	\j\ job	\th\ thin	\yu̇\ few
\ā\ take	\ē\ easy	\ŋ\ sing	\th\ this	\yu̇\ cure
\ä\ cot, cart	\g\ go	\ō\ bone	\ü\ food	\zh\ vision

ate·ly *adv*

af·fer·ent \'af-ə-rənt, 'af-,er-ənt\ *adj* : bearing or conducting inward; *esp* : conveying impulses toward a nerve center — **af·fer·ent·ly** *adv*

af·fi·ance \ə-'fī-ən(t)s\ *vb* **-anced; -anc·ing** : to promise in marriage

af·fi·da·vit \,af-ə-'dā-vət\ *n* : a sworn statement in writing

¹**af·fil·i·ate** \ə-'fil-ē-,āt\ *vb* **-at·ed; -at·ing** : to connect closely often as a member, branch, or associate — **af·fil·i·a·tion** \-,fil-ē-'ā-shən\ *n*

²**af·fil·i·ate** \ə-'fil-ē-ət\ *n* : an affiliated person or organization

af·fin·i·ty \ə-'fin-ət-ē\ *n, pl* **-ties** **1** : relationship by marriage **2 a** : a feeling of closeness or sympathy because of shared interests **b** : ATTRACTION; *esp* : an attractive force between substances or particles that causes them to enter into and remain in chemical combination

af·firm \ə-'fərm\ *vb* : to state positively or with confidence **syn** see ASSERT — **af·fir·ma·tion** \,af-ər-'mā-shən\ *n*

¹**af·fir·ma·tive** \ə-'fər-mət-iv\ *adj* **1** : declaring that the fact is so ⟨gave an *affirmative* answer⟩ **2** : being positive or helpful ⟨take an *affirmative* approach⟩ — **af·fir·ma·tive·ly** *adv*

²**affirmative** *n* **1** : an expression (as the word *yes*) of agreement **2** : the affirmative side in a debate or vote

affirmative action *n* : an active effort to improve the educational and employment opportunities of members of minority groups and women

¹**af·fix** \ə-'fiks, a-\ *vb* **1** : to attach physically : FASTEN ⟨*affix* a stamp to a letter⟩ **2** : to attach in any way : ADD ⟨*affix* a signature to a document⟩

²**af·fix** \'af-,iks\ *n* : a letter or a group of letters attached to the beginning or end of a word that serves to produce a derivative word or an inflectional form

af·flict \ə-'flikt\ *vb* : to cause suffering or unhappiness to

af·flic·tion \ə-'flik-shən\ *n* **1** : the state of being afflicted : SORROW, SUFFERING **2** : something that causes pain or unhappiness

af·flu·ence \'af-,lü-ən(t)s *also* a-'flü-, ə-'flü-\ *n* : the state of having much wealth or property

af·flu·ent \'af-,lü-ənt *also* a-'flü-, ə-'flü-\ *adj* : having plenty of money and the things money can buy [Middle English *affluent* "abundant", from early French *affluent* (same meaning), derived from Latin *ad-* "to" and *fluere* "to flow" — related to FLUID] — **af·flu·ent·ly** *adv*

af·ford \ə-'förd, -'förd\ *vb* **1** : to be able to do or to bear without serious harm ⟨you can't *afford* to waste your strength⟩ **2** : to be able to pay for ⟨unable to *afford* a new car⟩ **3** : to supply one with : PROVIDE, FURNISH ⟨tennis *affords* good exercise⟩

af·fray \ə-'frā\ *n* : a noisy quarrel or fight

af·fright \ə-'frīt\ *vb* : FRIGHTEN 1, ALARM

¹**af·front** \ə-'frənt\ *vb* : to insult openly : OFFEND

²**affront** *n* : a deliberately offensive act or utterance : INSULT

Af·ghan \'af-,gan\ *n* **1** : a person born or living in Afghanistan **2** *not cap* : a blanket or shawl made of knitted or crocheted colored wool — **Afghan** *adj*

Afghan hound *n* : a tall swift hunting dog native to the Near East with a coat of long silky hair and a long silky bunch of hair on the head

afi·cio·na·do \ə-,fish-(ē-)ə-'näd-ō, -,fis-ē-\ *n, pl* **-dos** : a person who really likes and appreciates something ⟨an *aficionado* of Mexican food⟩ ⟨science fiction *aficionados*⟩ [Spanish, derived from Latin *affectio* "affection"]

Afghan hound

afield \ə-'fēld\ *adv* **1** : to, in, or on the field **2** : away from home **3** : out of a regular, planned, or proper course : ASTRAY

afire \ə-'fī(ə)r\ *adj or adv* : being on fire

aflame \ə-'flām\ *adj or adv* : AFIRE

afloat \ə-'flōt\ *adj or adv* **1 a** : carried on or as if on the water **b** : being at sea **2** : circulating about : RUMORED ⟨there was a story *afloat*⟩ **3** : being flooded : AWASH ⟨the decks were *afloat*⟩

aflut·ter \ə-'flət-ər\ *adj* **1** : flapping quickly **2** : nervously excited

afoot \ə-'fut\ *adv or adj* **1** : on foot ⟨travels *afoot*⟩ **2** : in the process of development : UNDER WAY ⟨a plan was *afoot* to seize power⟩

afore \ə-'fō(ə)r, -'fó(ə)r\ *adv or conj or prep, chiefly dialect* : BEFORE

afore·men·tioned \-,men-chənd\ *adj* : mentioned before

afore·said \-,sed\ *adj* : said or named before

afore·thought \-,thöt\ *adj* : thought of or planned beforehand : PREMEDITATED ⟨with malice *aforethought*⟩

afoul of \ə-'faú-ləv\ *prep* **1** : in or into collision or entanglement with ⟨one ship ran *afoul of* the other⟩ **2** : in or into conflict with ⟨they fell *afoul of* the law⟩

afraid \ə-'frād, *Southern also* -'fre(ə)d\ *adj* **1** : filled with fear or dread ⟨*afraid* of snakes⟩ **2** : filled with concern or regret ⟨*afraid* she might be late⟩ **3** : UNWILLING, RELUCTANT ⟨not *afraid* to work hard⟩ [Middle English *affraied* "filled with fear", derived from *affraien* "to frighten", from early French *affreer* "to frighten" — related to ¹FRAY]

afresh \ə-'fresh\ *adv* : from a new start : AGAIN

Af·ri·can \'af-ri-kən\ *n* **1** : a person born or living in Africa **2** : a person of African ancestry — **African** *adj*

African elephant *n* : the tall large-eared elephant of tropical Africa

African sleeping sickness *n* : SLEEPING SICKNESS 1

African violet *n* : a tropical African plant widely grown as a houseplant for its velvety fleshy leaves and showy purple, pink, or white flowers

Af·ri·kaans \,af-ri-'kän(t)s, -'känz\ *n* : a language developed from 17th century Dutch and used in the Republic of South Africa

Af·ri·ka·ner \,af-ri-'kän-ər\ *n* : a person born in South Africa whose ancestors were Dutch settlers there

¹**Af·ro** \'af-rō\ *adj* : of or relating to African or Afro-American fashion or culture ⟨an *Afro* wig⟩

²**Afro** *n* : an Afro haircut

Af·ro–Amer·i·can \,af-rō-ə-'mer-ə-kən\ *adj* : of or relating to Americans having African and especially black ancestors — **Afro–American** *n*

aft \'aft\ *adv* : near, toward, or in the stern of a ship or the tail of an aircraft

Afro

¹**af·ter** \'af-tər\ *adv* : following in time or place : AFTERWARD, BEHIND [Old English *æfter* "behind, later"]

²**after** *prep* **1 a** : behind in time or place ⟨following *after* us⟩ ⟨*after* dinner⟩ **b** : below in rank or order ⟨the highest mountain *after* Mount Everest⟩ **2** : for the reason of catching, seizing, or getting ⟨ran *after* the ball⟩ ⟨go *after* gold⟩ **3** : with the name of or a name derived from that of ⟨named *after* his father⟩ **b** : in imitation of ⟨patterned *after* a Gothic cathedral⟩

³**after** *conj* : later than the time when

⁴**after** *adj* **1** : later in time ⟨in *after* years⟩ **2** : located aft

after all *adv* : in spite of what was indicated or expected ⟨decided to go *after all*⟩ ⟨it rained *after all*⟩

af·ter·birth \'af-tər-,bərth\ *n* : the placenta and membranes of the fetus that are expelled after childbirth

af·ter·burn·er \-,bər-nər\ *n* : a burner attached to the tail pipe of a turbojet engine for forcing fuel into the hot exhaust gases and burning it to provide extra forward push

af·ter·deck \-,dek\ *n* : the rear half of the deck of a ship

af·ter·ef·fect \-ə-,fekt\ *n* : an effect that arises after the first or immediate effect has decreased or disappeared ⟨a medicine with no noticeable *aftereffects*⟩

af·ter·glow \-,glō\ *n* : a glow remaining (as in the sky after sunsets) where a light has disappeared

af·ter·im·age \-,im-ij\ *n* : a usually visual sensation continuing after the stimulus causing it has ended

af·ter·life \-,līf\ *n* **1** : an existence after death **2** : a later period in one's life

af·ter·math \'af-tər-,math\ *n* **1** : ²RESULT 1, CONSEQUENCE ⟨felt tired as an *aftermath* of the race⟩ **2** : the period immediately following a usually destructive event ⟨the *aftermath* of war⟩

> **Word History** The second part of *aftermath* comes from the Old English word *mæth,* meaning "the result of a mowing or harvesting", that is, a crop. This word was derived from the Old English verb *māwan,* which survives today as our modern English *mow.* During a good growing season in England, a second and sometimes a third crop of hay could be grown after the first mowing. When this crop was cut, it was the aftermath. Since the 17th century, the meaning of *aftermath* has broadened to include all kinds of results, not just those of a second mowing. [Old English *mæth* "mowing", from *māwan* "to mow"]

af·ter·noon \,af-tər-'nün\ *n* : the part of day between noon and sunset — **afternoon** *adj*

af·ter–shave \'af-tər-,shāv\ *n* : a lotion for use on the face after shaving

af·ter·taste \-,tāst\ *n* : a sensation (as of flavor) continuing after the stimulus causing it has ended

af·ter·thought \-,thȯt\ *n* : a later thought about something one has done or said

af·ter·ward \'af-tə(r)-wərd\ *or* **af·ter·wards** \-wərdz\ *adv* : at a later time

ag- — see AD-

again \ə-'gen, -'gin, -'gān\ *adv* **1** : in return ⟨bring us word *again*⟩ **2** : another time : ANEW ⟨come see us *again*⟩ **3** : in addition ⟨half as much *again*⟩ **4** : on the other hand ⟨I may, and *again* I may not⟩ **5** : MOREOVER, FURTHER ⟨*again,* there is another matter to consider⟩ [Old English *ongēan* "opposite, back"]

against \ə-'gen(t)st, -'gin(t)st, -'gān(t)st\ *prep* **1** : ⁴OPPOSITE ⟨over *against* the park⟩ **2 a** : opposed to ⟨campaign *against* disease⟩ **b** : as a protection from ⟨a shield *against* aggression⟩ **3** : in preparation for ⟨storing food *against* the winter⟩ **4** : in or into contact with ⟨ran *against* a tree⟩ ⟨leaning *against* the wall⟩ **5** : in a direction opposite to ⟨*against* the wind⟩ **6** : before the background of ⟨green trees *against* the blue sky⟩

agape \ə-'gāp *also* ə-'gap\ *adj* : having the mouth open in wonder or surprise ⟨the crowd stood *agape* at the speaker⟩

agar \'äg-ər\ *or* **agar–agar** \'äg-ə-'räg-ər\ *n* **1** : a jellylike substance obtained from a red alga and used especially in culture media or to give firmness to foods **2** : a culture medium containing agar

ag·ate \'ag-ət\ *n* **1** : a smooth-looking quartz having its colors arranged in stripes or forms that look like clouds or moss **2** : a playing marble of agate or glass

aga·ve \ə-'gäv-ē\ *n* : any of a genus of plants (as the century plant) related to the amaryllis that have spiny-edged leaves and flowers in tall branched clusters and include some cultivated for fiber or for ornament

¹age \'āj\ *n* **1 a** : the time from birth to a specified date ⟨a child six years of *age*⟩ **b** : the time of life when a person attains some right or capacity ⟨the voting *age* is 18⟩; *esp* : MAJORITY 1 ⟨come of *age*⟩ **c** : normal lifetime **d** : the later part of life ⟨youth and *age*⟩ **2** : a period of time as-

sociated with a particular person or thing ⟨machine *age*⟩ ⟨*Age* of Discovery⟩ **3** : a long period of time ⟨did it *ages* ago⟩ **syn** see PERIOD

²age *vb* **aged; ag·ing** *or* **age·ing** **1** : to become or cause to become old or old in appearance ⟨his troubles *aged* him⟩ **2** : to become or cause to become mellow or mature : RIPEN

-age \ij\ *n suffix* **1** : total amount : collection ⟨mile*age*⟩ **2 a** : action : process ⟨cover*age*⟩ **b** : result of ⟨break*age*⟩ **c** : rate of ⟨dos*age*⟩ **3** : house or place of ⟨orphan*age*⟩ **4** : state : status ⟨bond*age*⟩ **5** : fee : charge ⟨post*age*⟩ [Middle English *-age* "collection", from early French *-age* (same meaning), from Latin *-aticum* "collection"]

agave

aged *adj* **1** \'ā-jəd\ : very old ⟨an *aged* oak⟩ **2** \'ājd\ : having reached a specified age ⟨a child *aged* ten⟩ — **ag·ed·ness** \'ā-jəd-nəs\ *n*

age·ism \'ā-(,)jiz-əm\ *n* : prejudice or discrimination against people of a particular age and especially against the elderly — **age·ist** \-jist\ *adj*

age·less \'āj-ləs\ *adj* **1** : not growing old or showing the effects of age **2** : ETERNAL 1, TIMELESS ⟨an *ageless* story⟩ — **age·less·ly** *adv*

agen·cy \'ā-jən-sē\ *n, pl* **-cies** **1** : a person or thing through which power is used or something is achieved : MEANS **2** : the office or function of an agent **3** : an establishment doing business for another ⟨an insurance *agency*⟩ **4** : a part of a government that manages projects in a certain area ⟨a health *agency*⟩

agen·da \ə-'jen-də\ *n* : a list of items of business to be considered (as at a meeting)

agent \'ā-jənt\ *n* **1 a** : something that produces an effect ⟨a cleansing *agent*⟩ **b** : a chemically, physically, or biologically active substance **2** : a person who acts or does business for another ⟨government *agents*⟩ ⟨a real estate *agent*⟩ [Middle English *agent* "one that produces an effect", derived from Latin *agere* "to drive, act, do" — related to ACT, AGILE]

Age of Fishes : the Devonian period

Age of Mammals : the Cenozoic era

Age of Reptiles : MESOZOIC

age–old \'a-'jōld\ *adj* : having existed for ages : ANCIENT ⟨an *age-old* story⟩

ag·er·a·tum \,aj-ə-'rāt-əm\ *n* : any of a large genus of tropical American herbs related to the daisies and often cultivated for their small showy heads of blue or white flowers

Ag·ge·us \a-'gē-əs\ *n* — see BIBLE table

¹ag·glom·er·ate \ə-'gläm-ə-,rāt\ *vb* **-at·ed; -at·ing** : to gather into a ball, mass, or cluster

²ag·glom·er·ate \ə-'gläm-ə-rət\ *n* **1** : a jumbled mass or collection **2** : a rock composed of volcanic pieces of various sizes

ag·glom·er·a·tion \ə-,gläm-ə-'rā-shən\ *n* **1** : the action or process of collecting in a mass **2** : a heap or cluster of dissimilar elements — **ag·glom·er·a·tive** \ə-'gläm-ə-,rāt-iv\ *adj*

ag·glu·ti·nate \ə-'glüt-ᵊn-āt\ *vb* **-nat·ed; -nat·ing** **1** : to cause to stick : FASTEN **2** : to cause to clump or experience agglutination **3** : to unite into a group or gather into a mass

ag·glu·ti·na·tion \ə-,glüt-ᵊn-'ā-shən\ *n* **1** : the action or

\ə\ abut	\au̇\ out	\i\ tip	\ȯ\ saw	\u̇\ foot
\ər\ further	\ch\ chin	\ī\ life	\ȯi\ coin	\y\ yet
\a\ mat	\e\ pet	\j\ job	\th\ thin	\yü\ few
\ā\ take	\ē\ easy	\ŋ\ sing	\th\ this	\yu̇\ cure
\ä\ cot, cart	\g\ go	\ō\ bone	\ü\ food	\zh\ vision

process of agglutinating   **2** : a mass or group formed by the union of separate elements   **3** : a reaction in which particles (as red blood cells or bacteria) suspended in a liquid collect into clumps usually as a response to a specific antibody — **ag·glu·ti·na·tive** \-'glüt-°n-,āt-iv, -ət-\ adj

ag·glu·ti·nin \ə-'glüt-°n-ən\ n : an antibody causing agglutination

ag·glu·ti·no·gen \ə-'glüt-°n-ə-jən\ n : an antigen whose presence results in the formation of an agglutinin

ag·gran·dize \ə-'gran-,dīz also 'ag-rən-\ vb **-dized; -diz·ing** : to make great or greater (as in power, wealth, or reputation) — **ag·gran·dize·ment** \ə-'gran-dəz-mənt, -,dīz- also ,ag-rən-'dīz-mənt\ n — **ag·gran·diz·er** n

ag·gra·vate \'ag-rə-,vāt\ vb **-vat·ed; -vat·ing**   **1** : to make more serious or severe (aggravate an injury)   **2** : to make angry by bothering again and again [from Latin aggravare "to make heavier", from ad- "to" and gravare "to burden", from gravis "heavy" — related to ³GRAVE, GRAVITY, GRIEVE]

ag·gra·va·tion \,ag-rə-'vā-shən\ n   **1** : the act or result of aggravating   **2** : something that aggravates

¹**ag·gre·gate** \'ag-ri-gət\ adj   **1** : formed by the collection together of units or particles into one mass or sum   **2** : clustered in a dense mass or head (an aggregate flower) [Middle English aggregat "made up of a collection", derived from Latin aggregare "to add to", from ag-, ad- "to, toward" and gregare "gather into a flock or herd", from greg-, grex "flock, herd" — related to CONGREGATE, SEGREGATE]

²**ag·gre·gate** \'ag-ri-,gāt\ vb **-gat·ed; -gat·ing**   **1** : to collect or gather into a mass or whole   **2** : to amount to as a whole

³**ag·gre·gate** \'ag-ri-gət\ n   **1** : a collection or sum of units or parts   **2** : a clustered mass of individual soil particles considered the basic structural unit of soil

aggregate fruit n : a compound fruit (as a raspberry) made up of the several separate ripened ovaries of a single flower

ag·gre·ga·tion \,ag-ri-'gā-shən\ n   **1** : the collecting of units or parts into a mass or whole   **2** : a group, body, or mass composed of many distinct parts

ag·gres·sion \ə-'gresh-ən\ n   **1** : an attack made without reasonable cause   **2** : the practice of making attacks   **3** : hostile or destructive behavior or outlook [derived from Latin aggredi "to attack", from ad- "to" and gradi "to attack, approach, step"]

ag·gres·sive \ə-'gres-iv\ adj   **1 a** : showing readiness to attack (an aggressive dog)   **b** : practicing aggression (an aggressive nation)   **2** : being forceful in getting things done (an aggressive sales campaign) — **ag·gres·sive·ly** adv — **ag·gres·sive·ness** n

ag·gres·sor \ə-'gres-ər\ n : a person or country that attacks without reasonable cause

ag·grieved \ə-'grēvd\ adj   **1** : troubled or distressed in spirit   **2** : having a cause for complaint; esp : suffering from injury or loss

aghast \ə-'gast\ adj : struck with terror, amazement, or horror

ag·ile \'aj-əl, -,īl\ adj   **1** : able to move quickly and easily : NIMBLE (an agile gymnast)   **2** : mentally quick (an agile thinker) [from early French agile "agile", derived from Latin agere "to drive, act, do" — related to ACT, AGENT] — **ag·ile·ly** \-ə(l)-lē, -,ī(l)-lē\ adv — **agil·i·ty** \ə-'jil-ət-ē\ n

aging present participle of AGE

ag·i·tate \'aj-ə-,tāt\ vb **-tat·ed; -tat·ing**   **1** : to move with an irregular, rapid, or violent action (water agitated by wind)   **2** : to stir up : EXCITE, DISTURB (agitated by bad news)   **3** : to try to stir up public feeling (agitate for equal rights) — **ag·i·tat·ed·ly** \-,tāt-əd-lē\ adv — **ag·i·ta·tion** \,aj-ə-'tā-shən\ n

ag·i·ta·tor \'aj-ə-,tāt-ər\ n   **1** : a person who stirs up public

feeling   **2** : a device for stirring or shaking

agleam \ə-'glēm\ adj : BRIGHT 1, SHINING

aglit·ter \ə-'glit-ər\ adj : reflecting light by glittering

aglow \ə-'glō\ adj : radiant with warmth or excitement

ag·nos·tic \ag-'näs-tik, əg-\ n : a person who believes that whether God exists is not known and probably cannot be known [from Greek agnōstos "unknown", from a- "not" and gnōstos "known"] — **agnostic** adj — **ag·nos·ti·cism** \-'näs-tə-,siz-əm\ n

ago \ə-'gō\ adj or adv : earlier than the present time (many years ago)

agog \ə-'gäg\ adj : full of interest or excitement

ag·o·nize \'ag-ə-,nīz\ vb **-nized; -niz·ing** : to suffer or cause to suffer extreme pain or anguish of body or mind — **ag·o·niz·ing·ly** \-,nī-ziŋ-lē\ adv

ag·o·ny \'ag-ə-nē\ n, pl **-nies**   **1** : intense pain of mind or body   **2** : a strong sudden display of emotion : OUTBURST (an agony of delight)

> **Word History** In ancient Greece a public gathering for a festival was called agōn. Since the Greeks placed a high value on sports and athletic competition, there were almost always athletic events at these gatherings. The struggle to win the prize in such contests came to be called agōnia. This term came also to be used for any difficult physical struggle and then for the pain that went with it, physical or mental. Our English word agony, meaning "intense pain of mind or body", thus comes from a word that originally meant a happy celebration. [Middle English agonie "agony", from Latin agonia (same meaning), from Greek agōnia "struggle", from agōn "gathering, contest for a prize"]

ag·o·ra \'ag-ə-rə\ n, pl **agoras** \-rəz\ or **ag·o·rae** \-,rē, -,rī\ : the marketplace or gathering place in an ancient Greek city

agou·ti \ə-'güt-ē\ n   **1** : a tropical American rodent about the size of a rabbit   **2** : a gray-streaked color of fur resulting from the barring of each hair in several alternate dark and light bands

agouti 1

agrar·i·an \ə-'grer-ē-ən, -'grar-\ adj   **1** : of or relating to fields or lands or their ownership (agrarian reforms)   **2** : of, relating to, or concerned with farmers or farming interests (an agrarian political party)   **3** : AGRICULTURAL 2 (an agrarian country)

agree \ə-'grē\ vb **agreed; agree·ing**   **1** : to give one's approval : CONSENT (agree to a plan)   **2** : ADMIT 1b, CONCEDE (all agreed they had been wrong)   **3** : to be alike : CORRESPOND   **4** : to get along well   **5** : to come to an understanding (agree on a price)   **6** : to be fitting, pleasing, or healthful : SUIT (the climate agrees with you)   **7** : to be alike or correspond grammatically in gender, number, case, or person (a verb should agree with its subject) [Middle English agreen "admit, accept", from early French agreer (same meaning), from a- "to, toward" and gre "will, pleasure", derived from Latin gratus "pleasing, thankful, agreeable" — related to GRACE]

agree·able \ə-'grē-ə-bəl\ adj   **1** : pleasing to the mind or senses : PLEASANT (an agreeable taste)   **2** : ready or willing to agree (I'm agreeable to the idea)   **3** : being in harmony : CONSONANT — **agree·able·ness** n — **agree·ably** \-blē\ adv

agreed \ə-'grēd\ adj : settled by agreement

agree·ment \ə-'grē-mənt\ n   **1 a** : the act of agreeing   **b** : harmony of opinion, action, or character : CONCORD   **2 a** : an arrangement or understanding (as a contract or treaty) about action to be taken   **b** : a written record of such an agreement   **3** : the fact of agreeing grammatically

syn AGREEMENT, CONTRACT, BARGAIN mean an arrangement between persons on a matter of common interest. AGREEMENT suggests a shared understanding that is arrived at after some discussion ⟨an *agreement* to work as a team⟩ CONTRACT suggests a formal often written agreement ⟨a *contract* with a recording studio⟩ BARGAIN applies to a firm agreement especially about purchase and sale ⟨we made a *bargain* to sell the land⟩

ag·ri·cul·tur·al \ˌag-ri-ˈkəlch-(ə-)rəl\ *adj* **1** : of, relating to, or used in agriculture ⟨*agricultural* machinery⟩ **2** : engaged in or concerned with agriculture ⟨an *agricultural* society⟩ — **ag·ri·cul·tur·al·ly** \-ē\ *adv*

ag·ri·cul·ture \ˈag-ri-ˌkəl-chər\ *n* : the science or occupation of cultivating the soil, producing crops, and raising livestock : FARMING — **ag·ri·cul·tur·ist** \ˌag-ri-ˈkəlch-(ə-)rəst\ *or* **ag·ri·cul·tur·al·ist** \-(ə-)rə-ləst\ *n*

agron·o·my \ə-ˈgrän-ə-mē\ *n* : a branch of agriculture that deals with the raising of crops and the care of the soil — **agron·o·mist** \-məst\ *n*

aground \ə-ˈgraúnd\ *adv or adj* : on or onto the shore or the bottom of a body of water ⟨the ship ran *aground*⟩

ague \ˈā-gyü\ *n* **1** : a fever (as malaria) marked by outbreaks of chills, fever, and sweating that recur at regular intervals **2** : a fit of shivering : CHILL

ah \ˈä\ *interj* — used to express delight, relief, regret, or scorn

aha \ä-ˈhä\ *interj* — used to express surprise, triumph, or scorn

ahead \ə-ˈhed\ *adv or adj* **1** : in or toward the front ⟨the road *ahead*⟩ ⟨go *ahead*⟩ **2** : in, into, or for the future ⟨think *ahead*⟩ **3** : in or toward a better position ⟨came out $20 *ahead* on the deal⟩ **4** : at or to an earlier time ⟨set the clock *ahead*⟩ ⟨make payments *ahead*⟩

ahead of *prep* : in or at a place or time before ⟨got *ahead of* me⟩ ⟨we're *ahead of* schedule⟩

A–ho·ri·zon \ˈā-hə-ˌrī-zən\ *n* : the outer dark-colored soil with a light texture consisting usually of soil rich in organic debris in various stages of disintegration

ahoy \ə-ˈhói\ *interj* — used in calling out to a passing ship or boat

¹aid \ˈād\ *vb* : to provide with what is useful or necessary : HELP, ASSIST — **aid·er** *n*

²aid *n* **1 a** : the act of helping **b** : help given **2** : ASSISTANT **3** : someone or something that is of help or assistance

aide \ˈād\ *n* : a person who acts as an assistant

aide–de–camp \ˌād-di-ˈkamp, -ˈkän\ *n, pl* **aides–de–camp** \ˌād(z)-di-\ : an aide to a high military or naval officer

AIDS \ˈādz\ *n* : a serious disease of the human immune system marked by destruction of a large proportion of the helper T cells in the body due to infection by a virus commonly transmitted especially in blood and semen.

ail \ˈāl\ *vb* **1** : to be the matter with : TROUBLE ⟨what *ails* you?⟩ **2** : to have something the matter; *esp* : to suffer ill health ⟨has been *ailing* for years⟩

ai·lan·thus \ā-ˈlan(t)-thəs\ *n* : a quick-growing Asian tree with fernlike leaves and ill-scented greenish flowers

ai·le·ron \ˈā-lə-ˌrän\ *n* : a movable part (as a flap) of an airplane wing or a movable body apart from the wing for giving a rolling motion and as a result providing control sideways

ail·ment \ˈāl-mənt\ *n* : a bodily disorder : SICKNESS

¹aim \ˈām\ *vb* **1** : to point a weapon **2** : ASPIRE, INTEND ⟨*aims* to please⟩ **3** : to direct to or toward an object or goal ⟨*aim* a camera⟩

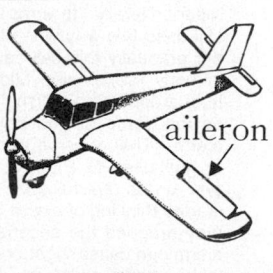

aileron

²aim *n* **1** : the directing of a weapon or a missile at a mark **2** : GOAL 2, PURPOSE

aim·less \ˈām-ləs\ *adj* : lacking a goal or purpose ⟨*aimless* wandering⟩ — **aim·less·ly** *adv* — **aim·less·ness** *n*

ain't \(ˈ)ānt\ **1 a** : are not **b** : is not **c** : am not — used by many educated speakers and writers in certain phrases (as "ain't I" or "and that ain't hay") and to catch attention but more common in less educated speech **2** *substandard* **a** : have not **b** : has not

¹air \ˈa(ə)r, ˈe(ə)r\ *n* **1 a** : the invisible mixture of odorless tasteless gases (as nitrogen and oxygen) that surrounds the earth **b** : a light breeze **2** : COMPRESSED AIR ⟨put *air* in a soft bicycle tire⟩ **3 a** : AIRCRAFT ⟨travel by *air*⟩ ⟨*air* attack⟩ **b** : AVIATION ⟨*air* safety⟩ **4 a** : the substance through which radio waves travel **b** : a radio or television broadcast ⟨went on the *air*⟩ **5 a** : outward appearance : apparent nature ⟨an *air* of mystery⟩ **b** *pl* : an artificial way of acting ⟨put on *airs*⟩ **6** : ¹TUNE 1, MELODY

²air *vb* **1** : to place in the air for cooling, freshening, or cleaning ⟨*air* blankets⟩ **2** : to make known in public ⟨*air* one's complaints⟩

air bag *n* : an automobile safety device consisting of a bag designed to inflate automatically in front of a rider in case of a collision.

air base *n* : a base of operations for military aircraft

air bladder *n* **1** : a cavity in a fish containing gases (as oxygen and nitrogen) and serving in respiration or the regulation of its ability to float **2** : a cavity found in various algae that contains gases and serves to keep the plant afloat

air·borne \ˈa(ə)r-ˌbôrn, -ˌbôrn, ˈe(ə)r-\ *adj* : supported or transported by air ⟨*airborne* troops⟩

air brake *n* **1** : a brake operated by a piston driven by compressed air **2** : a surface that may be quickly positioned into the air for lowering the speed of an airplane

air·brush \ˈa(ə)r-ˌbrəsh, ˈe(ə)r-\ *n* : a device that uses compressed air to apply a liquid (as paint or a protective coating) as a fine spray — **airbrush** *vb*

air–con·di·tion \ˌa(ə)r-kən-ˈdish-ən, ˌe(ə)r-\ *vb* : to equip with a device for cleaning air and controlling its humidity and temperature — **air con·di·tion·er** \-ˈdish-(ə-)nər\ *n* — **air–conditioning** \-ˈdish-(ə-)niŋ\ *n*

air–cool \ˈa(ə)r-ˌkül, ˈe(ə)r-\ *vb* : to cool (as an internal-combustion engine) by air

air·craft \ˈa(ə)r-ˌkraft, ˈe(ə)r-\ *n, pl* **aircraft** : a machine (as an airplane, glider, or helicopter) that can travel through the air and that is supported either by its own buoyancy or by the action of the air against its surfaces

aircraft carrier *n* : a warship with a deck from which airplanes can take off and on which they can land

air–cushion vehicle *n* : HOVERCRAFT

air·drome \ˈa(ə)r-ˌdröm, ˈe(ə)r-\ *n* : AIRPORT

air·drop \-ˌdräp\ *n* : delivery of cargo or people by parachute from an airplane — **air–drop** \-ˌdräp\ *vb*

Aire·dale \ˈa(ə)r-ˌdāl, ˈe(ə)r-\ *n* : any of a breed of large terriers with a black and tan coat

air·field \ˈa(ə)r-ˌfēld, ˈe(ə)r-\ *n* **1** : the landing field of an airport **2** : AIRPORT

air·flow \-ˌflō\ *n* : a flow of air; *esp* : the motion of

Airedale

\ə\ abut	\aú\ out	\i\ tip	\ó\ saw	\ú\ foot
\ər\ further	\ch\ chin	\ī\ life	\ói\ coin	\y\ yet
\a\ mat	\e\ pet	\j\ job	\th\ thin	\yü\ few
\ā\ take	\ē\ easy	\ŋ\ sing	\th\ this	\yú\ cure
\ä\ cot, cart	\g\ go	\ō\ bone	\ü\ food	\zh\ vision

air (as around parts of an airplane in flight) compared to the surface of a body surrounded by the air

air·foil \-,fóil\ *n* : an airplane surface (as a wing or rudder) designed to produce reaction from the air through which it moves

air force *n* : the military organization of a nation for air warfare

air·frame \'a(ə)r-,frām, 'e(ə)r-\ *n* : the structure of an aircraft, rocket vehicle, or missile without the engine and related parts

air gun *n* **1** : a gun that fires with a compressed gas (as air or carbon dioxide) **2** : any of various hand tools that work by compressed air; *esp* : AIRBRUSH

air hammer *n* : JACKHAMMER

air lane *n* : a route followed by airplanes

air letter *n* **1** : an airmail letter **2** : a sheet of airmail writing paper that can be folded and sealed with the message inside and the address outside

air·lift \'a(ə)r-,lift, 'e(ə)r-\ *n* : a system of transporting cargo or passengers by aircraft to or from an area otherwise impossible to reach — **airlift** *vb*

air·line \-,līn\ *n* : a system of transportation by airplanes including its routes, equipment, and workers

air·lin·er \-,lī-nər\ *n* : a large passenger airplane operated by an airline

air lock *n* : an air space with two airtight doors that permits movement between two spaces with different pressures or different temperatures

air·mail \'a(ə)r-'māl, 'e(ə)r-, -,māl\ *n* **1** : the system of transporting mail by aircraft **2** : mail transported by air — **airmail** *vb*

air·man \-mən\ *n* **1 a** : an enlisted person in the air force **b** : an enlisted person in the air force with a rank below that of sergeant; *esp* : one with the rank just below that of airman first class **2** : ¹PILOT 3, AVIATOR

airman basic *n* : an enlisted person of the lowest rank in the air force

airman first class *n* : an enlisted person in the air force with a rank just below that of sergeant

air mass *n* : a body of air extending hundreds or thousands of miles sideways and sometimes as high as the stratosphere and having nearly the same conditions of temperature and humidity at any single level

air·plane \'a(ə)r-,plān, 'e(ə)r-\ *n* : a fixed-wing aircraft heavier than air that is driven by a propeller or by a forceful stream of gases backward and is supported by the reaction of the air against its wings

air plant *n* **1** : EPIPHYTE **2** : BRYOPHYLLUM

air pocket *n* : a condition of the atmosphere that causes an airplane to drop suddenly

air·port \'a(ə)r-,pōrt, 'e(ə)r-, -,pòrt\ *n* : an area of land or water where airplanes may land to take on and let off passengers or cargo and that usually has equipment for the shelter, supply, and repair of planes

air pressure *n* : the pressure resulting from the weight of the atmosphere

air pump *n* : a pump for removing air from a closed space or for compressing air or forcing it through other equipment

air raid *n* : an attack by airplanes (as bombers) on a surface target

air sac *n* **1** : one of the air-filled spaces connected with the lungs of a bird **2** : one of the thin-walled microscopic pouches in which gases are exchanged in the lungs

air·ship \'a(ə)r-,ship, 'e(ə)r-\ *n* : a lighter-than-air aircraft with its own power and steering

air·sick \-,sik\ *adj* : sick to one's stomach while riding in an airplane because of its motion — **air·sick·ness** *n*

air·speed \-,spēd\ *n* : the speed of an airplane according to measurements of the surrounding air rather than of the ground below

air·strip \-,strip\ *n* : a runway without normal air base or airport equipment

air·tight \-'tīt\ *adj* **1** : so tightly sealed that no air can get in or out ⟨an *airtight* container⟩ **2** : leaving no opening for attack ⟨an *airtight* argument⟩

air·wave \-,wāv\ *n* : ¹AIR 4a — usually used in pl.

air·way \-,wā\ *n* **1** : a passage for a current of air **2** : a regular route for aircraft; *esp* : one equipped with aids for guiding aircraft **3** : AIRLINE

air·wor·thy \-,wər-_thē_\ *adj* : fit or safe for operation in the air — **air·wor·thi·ness** *n*

airy \'a(ə)r-ē, 'e(ə)r-\ *adj* **air·i·er; -est** **1 a** : of or relating to air : ATMOSPHERIC **b** : high in the air : LOFTY ⟨*airy* perches⟩ **c** : performed in air ⟨*airy* leaps⟩ **2** : lacking a sound or solid basis ⟨*airy* romance⟩ **3** : resembling air in lightness : DELICATE, ETHEREAL **4** : open to the air : BREEZY ⟨an *airy* room⟩ — **air·i·ly** \'ar-ə-lē, 'er-\ *adv* — **air·i·ness** \'ar-ē-nəs, 'er-\ *n*

aisle \'ī(ə)l\ *n* : a passage between sections of seats (as in a church or theater)

ajar \ə-'jär\ *adv or adj* : slightly open ⟨left the door *ajar*⟩

akim·bo \ə-'kim-bō\ *adj or adv* **1** : having the hand on the hip and the elbow turned outward **2** : set in a bent position ⟨legs *akimbo*⟩ [Middle English *in kenebowe* "akimbo"]

akin \ə-'kin\ *adj* **1** : related by blood **2** : essentially similar or related

Ak·ka·di·an \ə-'kād-ē-ən\ *n* **1** : an ancient Semitic language of Mesopotamia used from about the 28th to the 1st century B.C. **2** : a member of a Semitic people living in Mesopotamia before 2000 B.C. — **Akkadian** *adj*

al- — see AD-

¹-al \əl, °l\ *adj suffix* : of, relating to, or characterized by ⟨direction*al*⟩ ⟨fiction*al*⟩ [Middle English *-al* "relating to", from early French *-al* (same meaning), from Latin *-alis* "relating to"]

²-al *n suffix* : action : process ⟨rehears*al*⟩ [Middle English *-aille* "action, process", from early French *-aille* (same meaning), derived from Latin *-alis* "relating to"]

al·a·bas·ter \'al-ə-,bas-tər\ *n* **1** : a smooth usually white and nearly transparent gypsum used for carving (as vases) **2** : a hard calcite that is nearly transparent and sometimes has stripes

à la carte \,al-ə-'kärt, ,äl-\ *adv or adj* : with a separate price for each item on the menu [from French *à la carte*, literally "by the bill of fare"]

alac·ri·ty \ə-'lak-rət-ē\ *n* : a cheerful readiness to do something ⟨accepted with *alacrity*⟩ — **alac·ri·tous** \-rət-əs\ *adj*

à la mode \,al-ə-'mōd, ,äl-\ *adj* **1** : STYLISH, FASHIONABLE **2** : topped with ice cream ⟨pie *à la mode*⟩ [from French *à la mode*, literally "according to the fashion"]

al·a·nine \'al-ə-,nēn\ *n* : an amino acid formed especially from proteins

¹alarm \ə-'lärm\ *n* **1** : a warning of danger **2** : a device that warns or signals (as by a bell, buzzer or whistle) ⟨sound the *alarm*⟩ ⟨set the *alarm* for six o'clock⟩ **3** : the fear caused by a sudden sense of danger **syn** see FEAR

Word History Today we usually think of an alarm as a loud noise that awakens us or warns us of fire or some other danger. Its first use, however, was as a call to arms to soldiers in Italy. The Italian phrase *all'arme!* means literally "to arms" or "to your weapons". It was still used this way when borrowed into other languages, but gradually this call came to be shortened to *alarme* in early French and Middle English. The final *-e* was later dropped in English. The word also came to be used as the name for the cry, as for example to "give the alarm". Then it came to be used for any warning. A bell or gun used to sound a warning was called an *alarm bell* or an *alarm gun*. It wasn't long before people started thinking of *alarm* as the signal device itself. Then they dropped the second part of the phrase. Since an alarm can cause fright or worry, such feelings also came to be known as *alarm*. By the 17th century, the word was used as a verb, meaning "to warn of danger" and then "to frighten". [Middle English *alarme* "a call to arms", from early French *alarme* (same meaning), derived from early Italian *all'arme,* literally "to arms", from *all'* "to the" and *arme* "weapon", from Latin *arma* "weapon" — related to ³ARM]

²**alarm** *vb*   **1** : to warn of danger   **2** : to cause to feel a sense of danger : FRIGHTEN — **alarm·ing·ly** \ə-'lär-miŋ-lē\ *adv*

alarm clock *n* : a clock that can be set to sound an alarm at any desired time

alarm·ist \ə-'lär-məst\ *n* : a person who alarms others especially needlessly — **alarm·ism** \-,miz-əm\ *n*

alas \ə-'las\ *interj* — used to express unhappiness, pity, or concern

Alas·kan malamute \ə-,las-kən-\ *n* : any of a breed of strong heavy-coated working dogs developed in Alaska for pulling sleds

Alas·ka time \ə-'las-kə-\ *n* : the time of the ninth time zone west of Greenwich that includes most of Alaska

alb \'alb\ *n* : a full-length white linen vestment worn by priests at the Eucharist

al·ba·core \'al-bə-,kō(ə)r, -,kȯ(ə)r\ *n, pl* **-core** *or* **-cores** : a large tuna with long pectoral fins and white flesh used especially for canning

Al·ba·nian \al-'bā-nē-ən, -nyən\ *n*   **1** : a person born or living in Albania   **2** : the Indo-European language of the Albanian people — **Albanian** *adj*

al·ba·tross \'al-bə-,trȯs, -, träs\ *n, pl* **-tross** *or* **-tross·es** : any of various large web-footed seabirds that are related to the petrels and include the largest birds of the sea

al·be·it \ȯl-'bē-ət, al-\ *conj* : even though : ALTHOUGH

al·bi·no \al-'bī-nō\ *n, pl* **-nos** : an organism deficient in coloring matter; *esp* : a human being or lower animal that has an inherited lack of pigment and usually a milky skin, white or colorless hair, and eyes with pink or blue iris and deep red pupil — **al·bi·nism** \'al-bə-,niz-əm, al-'bī-\ *n* — **albino** *adj*

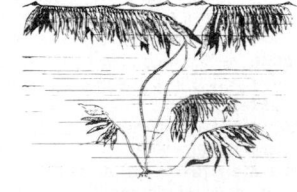
albatross

al·bite \'al-,bīt\ *n* : a usually white feldspar containing sodium

al·bum \'al-bəm\ *n*   **1 a** : a book with blank pages in which to put a collection (as of autographs, stamps, or photographs)   **b** : a container for a phonograph record   **c** : one or more phonograph records or tape recordings carrying a major work or a group of selections   **2** : a collection usually in book form of literary selections, musical compositions, or pictures

al·bu·men \al-'byü-mən\ *n*   **1** : the white of an egg   **2** : ALBUMIN

al·bu·min \al-'byü-mən\ *n* : any of numerous proteins that dissolve in water and are found especially in blood, the whites of eggs, and various animal and plant tissues

al·bu·mi·nous \al-'byü-mə-nəs\ *adj* : relating to, containing, or having the properties of albumen or albumin

al·che·my \'al-kə-mē\ *n* : a medieval chemical science with the goals of changing less valuable metals into gold, discovering a single cure for all diseases, and discovering how to live forever [Middle English *alkamie, alquemie,* from early French *alquemie* or Latin *alchymia* (both same meaning), from Arabic *al-kīmiyā'* (same meaning), from *al* "the" and *kīmiyā'* "alchemy", from Greek *chēmeia* "alchemy" — related to CHEMO-, CHEMISTRY]

al·co·hol \'al-kə-,hȯl\ *n*   **1 a** : a colorless flammable easily evaporated liquid that is used to dissolve things and that is the substance in fermented and distilled liquors (as beer,

wine, whiskey) that can make one drunk — called also *ethanol, ethyl alcohol, grain alcohol*   **b** : any of various carbon compounds that are similar to ethyl alcohol in having at least one hydroxyl group   **2** : drink (as beer, wine, or whiskey) containing alcohol

¹**al·co·hol·ic** \,al-kə-'hȯl-ik, -'häl-\ *adj*   **1** : of, relating to, or containing alcohol   **2** : affected with alcoholism — **al·co·hol·i·cal·ly** \-i-k(ə-)lē\ *adv*

²**alcoholic** *n* : one affected with alcoholism

al·co·hol·ism \'al-kə-,hȯ-,liz-əm\ *n* : continued, uncontrolled, and greater than normal use of alcoholic drinks; *also* : an abnormal bodily state associated with such use

al·cove \'al-,kōv\ *n*   **1** : a small section of a room set back from the rest of it   **2** : an arched opening (as in a wall) : NICHE

Al·deb·a·ran \al-'deb-ə-rən\ *n* : a very bright red star in Taurus

al·der \'ȯl-dər\ *n* : any of a genus of toothed-leaved trees or shrubs related to the birches

al·der·man \'ȯl-dər-mən\ *n* : a member of a legislative body in a U.S. city — **al·der·man·ic** \,ȯl-dər-'man-ik\ *adj*

al·drin \'ȯl-drən, al-\ *n* : a long-acting insecticide that is related to naphthalene but has added chlorine atoms

ale \'ā(ə)l\ *n* : an alcoholic drink made from malt and flavored with hops that is usually more bitter than beer

alee \ə-'lē\ *adv or adj* : on or toward the lee

¹**alert** \ə-'lərt\ *adj*   **1 a** : being watchful and ready to meet danger   **b** : quick to understand and act   **2** : ACTIVE 3, BRISK   **syn** see INTELLIGENT — **alert·ly** *adv* — **alert·ness** *n*

²**alert** *n*   **1** : a signal of danger   **2** : the period during which an alert is in effect — **on the alert** : on the lookout especially for danger or opportunity

³**alert** *vb* : to call to a state of readiness : WARN

A level *n* : the later of two British examinations in a secondary school subject

ale·wife \'ā(ə)l-,wīf\ *n* : a food fish that is related to the herrings and is very common along the Atlantic coast of the U.S.

al·fal·fa \al-'fal-fə\ *n* : a deep-rooted European plant of the legume family with purple flowers and leaves like clover that is widely grown for hay and forage

al·ga \'al-gə\ *n, pl* **al·gae** \'al-(,)jē\ : any plant (as a seaweed) of a group that forms the lowest division of the plant kingdom and includes forms mostly growing in water, lacking a system of vessels for carrying fluids, and often having chlorophyll masked by brown or red coloring matter — **al·gal** \'al-gəl\ *adj*

alga

al·ge·bra \'al-jə-brə\ *n* : a branch of mathematics that explores the relationships between numbers and the operations used to work with them and that uses letters or other symbols to represent them — **al·ge·bra·ic** \,al-jə-'brā-ik\ *adj* — **al·ge·bra·i·cal·ly** \-'brā-ə-k(ə-)lē\ *adv*

al·gin \'al-jən\ *n* : a substance obtained from marine brown algae that is used especially in food and paints to give thickness or firmness or to make a stable liquid mixture in which drops of one liquid are scattered evenly throughout the other

\ə\ **abut**	\au̇\ **out**	\i\ **tip**	\ȯ\ **saw**	\u̇\ **foot**
\ər\ **further**	\ch\ **chin**	\ī\ **life**	\ȯi\ **coin**	\y\ **yet**
\a\ **mat**	\e\ **pet**	\j\ **job**	\th\ **thin**	\yü\ **few**
\ā\ **take**	\ē\ **easy**	\ŋ\ **sing**	\th\ **this**	\yu̇\ **cure**
\ä\ **cot, cart**	\g\ **go**	\ō\ **bone**	\ü\ **food**	\zh\ **vision**

AL·GOL *or* **Al·gol** \'al-,gäl, -,gȯl\ *n* : an algebraic computer programming language stressing algorithms that is used especially in mathematics and science and related fields [from *algo*rithm and *l*anguage]

Al·gon·qui·an \al-'gän-kwē-ən, -'gäŋ-\ *n* **1** : a stock of Indian languages spoken from Labrador to the Carolinas and westward to the Great Plains **2** : a member of any of the American Indian peoples speaking Algonquian languages

al·go·rithm \'al-gə-,rith-əm\ *n* : a step-by-step method often with repeated series of steps for solving a problem (as finding the greatest common divisor) or accomplishing a goal

¹alias \'ā-lē-əs, 'āl-yəs\ *adv* : otherwise called : otherwise known as ⟨John Doe *alias* Richard Roe⟩

²alias *n* : an assumed or additional name

¹al·i·bi \'al-ə-,bī\ *n, pl* **-bis** \-,bīz\ **1** : the plea made by a person accused of a crime of having been at another place when the crime occurred **2** : a believable excuse [from Latin *alibi* "elsewhere"]

²alibi *vb* **-bied; -bi·ing** **1** : to make an excuse for **2** : to offer an excuse ⟨tried to *alibi* for showing up late⟩

¹alien \'ā-lē-ən, 'āl-yən\ *adj* **1** : relating or belonging to another country : FOREIGN ⟨*alien* residents⟩ **2** : wholly different in nature or character ⟨opinions *alien* to his outlook⟩

²alien *n* **1** : a resident who was born elsewhere and is not a citizen of the country in which he or she now lives **2** : a being that comes from or lives in another world

alien·ate \'ā-lē-ə-,nāt, 'āl-yə-,nāt\ *vb* **-at·ed; -at·ing** **1** : to transfer (as a title, property, or right) to another **2** : to cause (one who used to be friendly or loyal) to become unfriendly or disloyal — **alien·ation** \,ā-lē-ə-'nā-shən, ,āl-yə-'nā-\ *n*

¹alight \ə-'līt\ *vb* **alight·ed** \-'līt-əd\ *also* **alit** \ə-'lit\; **alight·ing** **1** : to get down : DISMOUNT **2** : to descend from the air and settle : LAND ⟨the bird *alighted* on a twig⟩

²alight *adj* : full of light : lighted up ⟨the sky was *alight* with stars⟩

align *also* **aline** \ə-'līn\ *vb* **1** : to bring into or be in line or alignment **2** : to cause to be for or against something (as a belief or political party) — **align·er** *n*

align·ment *also* **aline·ment** \ə-'līn-mənt\ *n* **1 a** : the act of aligning : the state of being aligned **b** : the proper adjustment of parts in relation to each other **2** : an arrangement of groups or forces ⟨a new political *alignment*⟩

¹alike \ə-'līk\ *adj* : SIMILAR 1 — **alike·ness** *n*

²alike *adv* : in the same manner, form, or degree ⟨we think *alike*⟩

al·i·ment \'al-ə-mənt\ *n* : FOOD 1, NUTRIMENT; *also* : SUSTENANCE 1a

al·i·men·ta·ry \,al-ə-'ment-ə-rē, -'men-trē\ *adj* : of or relating to nourishment or nutrition [from Latin *alimentarius* "relating to or involving the nourishing process", derived from *alere* "to nourish" — related to ALUMNUS, ALMA MATER]

alimentary canal *n* : a long tube made up of the esophagus, stomach, small intestine, and large intestine into which food is taken and digested and from which wastes are passed out

al·i·mo·ny \'al-ə-,mō-nē\ *n* : money paid to one spouse by the other for support during or after divorce or separation

A–line \'ā-,līn\ *adj* : having a flared bottom and a close-fitting top ⟨an *A-line* skirt⟩

alive \ə-'līv\ *adj* **1** : having life : not dead **2** : still in existence, force, or operation : ACTIVE ⟨kept hope *alive*⟩ **3** : extremely aware or conscious : SENSITIVE ⟨*alive* to the beauty of life⟩ **4** : marked by much life or activity ⟨blossoms *alive* with bees⟩ — **alive·ness** *n*

aliz·a·rin \ə-'liz-ə-rən\ *n* : a compound of orange or red crystals that is used as a red dye and in making red pigments

al·ka·li \'al-kə-,lī\ *n, pl* **-lies** *or* **-lis** **1** : a substance (as a hydroxide) that has a bitter taste and neutralizes acids **2** : ALKALI METAL **3** : a salt or mixture of salts easily dissolved in water and present in some soils of very dry regions [Middle English *alkali* "alkali", from Latin *alkali* (same meaning), from Arabic *al-qili* "ashes of a particular plant"]

alkali metal *n* : any of the metals in the group that consists of lithium, sodium, potassium, rubidium, cesium, and francium

al·ka·line \'al-kə-lən, -,līn\ *adj* : of, relating to, or having the characteristics of an alkali : BASIC — **al·ka·lin·i·ty** \,al-kə-'lin-ət-ē\ *n*

alkaline earth *n* **1** : an oxide of any of several strongly basic metals consisting of calcium, strontium, and barium and sometimes magnesium, radium, or beryllium **2** : ALKALINE-EARTH METAL

alkaline–earth metal *n* : any of the metals whose oxides are the alkaline earths

al·kane \'al-,kān\ *n* : any of a series of compounds of carbon and hydrogen atoms in which each carbon atom is attached to four other atoms

al·kyd \'al-kəd\ *n* : any of numerous synthetic resins used especially for protective coatings (as paint)

¹all \'ȯl\ *adj* **1 a** : the whole of ⟨sat up *all* night⟩ **b** : as much as possible ⟨in *all* seriousness⟩ **2** : every one of ⟨*all* students can go⟩ **3** : any whatever ⟨beyond *all* doubt⟩

²all *adv* **1** : WHOLLY, ALTOGETHER ⟨sat *all* alone⟩ ⟨*all* across the country⟩ **2** : so much ⟨*all* the better for it⟩ **3** : for each side : APIECE ⟨the score is two *all*⟩

³all *pron* **1** : the whole number, quantity, or amount ⟨*all* that I have⟩ ⟨*all* of us⟩ **2** : EVERYBODY, EVERYTHING ⟨known to *all*⟩ ⟨sacrificed *all* for love⟩

Al·lah \'al-ə, 'äl-ə, 'äl-,ä, ä-'lä\ *n* : the Supreme Being of Islam [Arabic]

all–Amer·i·can \,ȯ-lə-'mer-ə-kən\ *adj* **1** : representing or typical of the U.S. or its ideals ⟨an *all-American* boy⟩ **2** : selected as the best in the U.S. ⟨the *all-American* football team⟩ — **all–American** *n*

al·lar·gan·do \,äl-,är-'gän-dō\ *adv or adj* : gradually slower with crescendo — used as a direction in music

all–around \,ȯ-lə-'raùnd\ *or* **all–round** *adj* **1** : good in many fields ⟨an *all-around* athlete⟩ **2** : having general usefulness

al·lay \a-'lā, ə-\ *vb* **-layed; -lay·ing** **1** : to make less severe : RELIEVE ⟨*allay* pain⟩ **2** : to make quiet : CALM ⟨*allay* fears⟩

al·le·ga·tion \,al-i-'gā-shən\ *n* **1** : the act of alleging **2** : something alleged; *esp* : a statement not supported by proof or evidence ⟨*allegations* of criminal involvement⟩

al·lege \ə-'lej\ *vb* **al·leged; al·leg·ing** **1** : to state as a fact but without proof ⟨*allege* a person's guilt⟩ **2** : to offer as a reason or excuse ⟨*allege* illness to avoid work⟩ — **al·leg·ed·ly** \-'lej-əd-lē\ *adv*

al·le·giance \ə-'lē-jən(t)s\ *n* **1** : loyalty and obedience owed to one's country or government **2** : devotion or loyalty to a person, group, or cause

al·le·go·ry \'al-ə-,gōr-ē, -,gȯr-\ *n, pl* **-ries** : a story in which the characters and events are symbols that stand for truths about human life — **al·le·gor·i·cal** \,al-ə-'gȯr-i-kəl, -'gär-\ *adj* — **al·le·gor·i·cal·ly** \-i-k(ə-)lē\ *adv*

al·le·gret·to \,al-ə-'gret-ō, ,äl-\ *adv or adj* : faster than andante but not so fast as allegro — used as a direction in music

¹al·le·gro \ə-'leg-rō, -'lā-grō\ *adv or adj* : in a brisk lively manner — used as a direction in music

²allegro *n, pl* **-gros** : a piece or movement in allegro tempo

al·lele \ə-'lē(ə)l\ *n* **1** : either of a pair of characters inherited alternatively **2** : one of several forms of a gene that occur at one locus and determine alternate forms of one or more genetic traits — **al·le·lic** \-'lē-lik, -'lel-ik\ *adj*

al·le·lu·ia \,al-ə-'lü-yə\ *interj* : ¹HALLELUJAH

al·ler·gen \'al-ər-jən\ *n* : a substance that causes allergy

— **al·ler·gen·ic** \,al-ər-'jen-ik\ adj

al·ler·gic \ə-'lər-jik\ adj **1** : of, relating to, or causing allergy ⟨an allergic reaction⟩ **2** : having a dislike for something ⟨allergic to hard work⟩

al·ler·gist \'al-ər-jəst\ n : a specialist in allergy

al·ler·gy \'al-ər-jē\ n, pl **-gies 1 a** : altered bodily reactivity (as to antigens) **b** : exaggerated or abnormal reaction (as by sneezing, itching, or rashes) to substances, situations, or physical states that are harmless to most people **2** : a feeling of dislike

al·le·vi·ate \ə-'lē-vē-,āt\ vb **-at·ed; -at·ing** : to make easier to put up with : RELIEVE — **al·le·vi·a·tion** \ə-,lē-vē-'ā-shən\ n

al·ley \'al-ē\ n, pl **alleys 1** : a garden or park walk bordered by trees or bushes **2** : a narrow wooden floor on which balls are rolled in bowling; also : a room or building housing a number of such alleys **3** : a narrow street or passageway between buildings

al·ley·way \'al-ē-,wā\ n : ALLEY 3

All Fools' Day n : APRIL FOOLS' DAY

all fours n pl : all four legs of a four-legged animal or the two legs and two arms of a person ⟨got down on all fours⟩

All·hal·lows \ȯl-'hal-ōz, -əz\ n : ALL SAINTS' DAY

al·li·ance \ə-'lī-ən(t)s\ n **1** : the state of being allied **2 a** : a union between persons, families, or parties **b** : a union between nations for assistance and protection **3** : a treaty of alliance

al·lied \ə-'līd, 'al-,īd\ adj **1** : being related or connected in some way ⟨chemistry and allied subjects⟩ **2 a** : joined in alliance ⟨allied nations⟩ **b** cap : of or relating to the nations united against Germany and its allies in World War I or World War II

allies pl of ALLY

al·li·ga·tor \'al-ə-,gāt-ər\ n **1** : either of two large short-legged reptiles resembling crocodiles but having a shorter and broader snout **2** : leather made from alligator's hide [from Spanish el lagarto "the lizard"]

alligator 1

alligator clip n : a clip that has jaws something like an alligator's and is used to make temporary electrical connections

alligator gar n : a large freshwater gar of the central U.S. that grows to a length of 2 meters and weighs as much as 68 kilograms

alligator pear n : AVOCADO

all–im·por·tant \,ȯ-lim-'pȯrt-°nt, -ənt\ adj : of very great importance

al·lit·er·a·tion \ə-,lit-ə-'rā-shən\ n : the repetition of a sound at the beginning of two or more neighboring words (as in wild and woolly or a babbling brook) — **al·lit·er·a·tive** \ə-'lit-ə-,rāt-iv, -rət-\ adj — **al·lit·er·a·tive·ly** adv

al·lo·cate \'al-ə-,kāt\ vb **-cat·ed; -cat·ing 1** : to divide and distribute for a special reason or to particular persons or things ⟨allocate funds among charities⟩ **2** : to set apart for a particular purpose ⟨allocate materials for a project⟩ — **al·lo·ca·tion** \,al-ə-'kā-shən\ n

al·lot \ə-'lät\ vb **al·lot·ted; al·lot·ting** : to assign as a share or portion

al·lot·ment \ə-'lät-mənt\ n **1** : the act of allotting **2** : something allotted

al·lot·ro·py \ə-'lä-trə-pē\ n : the existence of a substance and especially a chemical element in two or more different forms ⟨diamond and graphite show the allotropy of carbon⟩ — **al·lo·trope** \'al-ə-,trōp\ n — **al·lo·trop·ic** \,al-ə-'träp-ik\ adj

all–out \'ȯ-'laut\ adj : made with maximum effort : EXTREME

⟨an all-out attempt to finish on time⟩

all out adv : with maximum effort ⟨went all out to win⟩

all·over \'ȯ-,lō-vər\ adj : covering the whole surface of something ⟨a sweater with an allover pattern⟩

all over adv : EVERYWHERE

al·low \ə-'lau\ vb **1 a** : to assign as a share or suitable amount (as of time or money) **b** : to take into consideration as a deduction or an addition ⟨allow a gallon for leakage⟩ **2** : ADMIT 1b, CONCEDE ⟨allowed that the situation was serious⟩ **3** : ¹PERMIT ⟨gaps allow passage⟩ ⟨will not allow smoking⟩ **4** : to give thought to present conditions and to what will probably happen later ⟨allow for growth⟩ — **al·low·able** \-ə-bəl\ adj

al·low·ance \ə-'lau-ən(t)s\ n **1 a** : a share or portion given out **b** : a sum given ⟨gets a weekly allowance⟩ ⟨an allowance for expenses⟩ **c** : a reduction from a stated price ⟨a trade-in allowance on a car⟩ **2** : an allowed difference between parts that fit together in a machine **3** : the act of allowing : PERMISSION **4** : an allowing for things that may partly excuse an offense or mistake or for things that may happen ⟨make allowance for age⟩ ⟨make allowance for differences of opinion⟩

¹al·loy \'al-,ȯi, ə-'lȯi\ n : a substance consisting of two or more metals or of a metal and a nonmetal united usually by being melted together

²al·loy \ə-'lȯi, 'al-,ȯi\ vb **1** : to reduce the purity of by mixing with a less valuable metal **2** : to mix so as to form an alloy **3** : to lower or damage by mixing with something else

all–pow·er·ful \'ȯl-'pau(-ə)r-fəl\ adj : having complete power

all–pur·pose \-'pər-pəs\ adj : suitable for many uses ⟨an all-purpose tool⟩

¹all right adv **1** : reasonably well ⟨does all right in school⟩ **2** : very well : YES ⟨all right, I'll come⟩ **3** : beyond doubt : CERTAINLY ⟨that's the one all right⟩

²all right adj **1** : SATISFACTORY, CORRECT **2** : ¹SAFE 1, WELL

all–round \'ȯl-'raund\ variant of ALL-AROUND

All Saints' Day n : November 1 observed as a church festival in honor of the Christian saints

All Souls' Day n : November 2 observed in some Christian churches as a day of prayer for the dead

all·spice \'ȯl-,spīs\ n **1** : the berry of a West Indian tree related to the myrtle **2** : a spice made from allspice berries

all–star \,ȯl-,stär\ adj : made up chiefly or entirely of stars ⟨an all-star team⟩ — **all–star** \'ȯl-,stär\ n

al·lude \ə-'lüd\ vb **al·lud·ed; al·lud·ing** : to speak of or hint at without mentioning directly

¹al·lure \ə-'lü(ə)r\ vb **al·lured; al·lur·ing** : to try to attract or influence by offering what seems to be a benefit or pleasure — **al·lure·ment** \-mənt\ n

²allure n : power of attraction : CHARM

al·lu·sion \ə-'lü-zhən\ n : a reference made to something that is not directly mentioned ⟨the book contains many allusions to earlier books⟩ — **al·lu·sive** \-'lü-siv, -ziv\ adj — **al·lu·sive·ly** adv — **al·lu·sive·ness** n

al·lu·vi·al \ə-'lü-vē-əl\ adj : relating to, composed of, or found in alluvium

al·lu·vi·um \ə-'lü-vē-əm\ n, pl **-vi·ums** or **-via** \-vē-ə\ : soil material (as clay, silt, sand, or gravel) deposited by running water

¹al·ly \ə-'lī, 'al-,ī\ vb **al·lied; al·ly·ing** : to form a connection between : UNITE; esp : to join in an alliance [Middle English allien "unite", from early French alier (same meaning), derived from Latin *al-, ad-* "to" and *ligare* "to bind" — related to LIGAMENT]

²al·ly \'al-,ī, ə-'lī\ *n, pl* **al·lies**   **1** : a plant or animal linked to another by genetic or evolutionary relationship ⟨ferns and their *allies*⟩   **2 a** : one associated or united with another for some common purpose   **b** *pl, cap* : the Allied nations in World War I or World War II

-al·ly \(ə-)lē\ *adv suffix* : ²-LY [from ¹-*al* + -*ly*]

al·ma ma·ter \,al-mə-'mät-ər\ *n* : a school, college, or university that one has attended [Latin, literally "fostering mother", from *almus* "nourishing" (from *alire* "to nourish") and *mater* "mother" — related to ALIMENTARY, MATERNAL]

al·ma·nac \'ól-mə-,nak, 'al-\ *n* : a book containing a calendar of days, weeks, and months and usually facts about the rising and setting of the sun and moon, changes in the tides, and information of general interest

al·man·dine \'al-mən-,dēn, -,dīn\ *n* : ALMANDITE

al·man·dite \'al-mən-,dīt\ *n* : a deep red garnet containing iron and aluminum

al·mighty \ól-'mīt-ē\ *adj, often cap* : having unlimited power ⟨*Almighty* God⟩

Almighty *n* : GOD 1— used with *the*

al·mond \'äm-ənd, 'am-; 'äl-mənd, 'al-\ *n* : a small tree having flowers like those of a peach tree; *also* : the edible kernel of its fruit used as a nut

al·mo·ner \'al-mə-nər, 'äm-ə-\ *n* : a person who gives out alms

al·most \'ól-,mōst, ól-'mōst\ *adv* : only a little less than : NEARLY ⟨we're *almost* finished⟩

alms \'ämz, 'älmz\ *n, pl* **alms** : something and especially money given to help the poor : CHARITY — **alms·giv·er** \-,giv-ər\ *n* — **alms·giv·ing** \-,giv-iŋ\ *n*

alms·house \-,haus\ *n* : POORHOUSE

al·ni·co \'al-ni-,kō\ *n* : a powerful permanent-magnet alloy containing iron, nickel, aluminum, and one or more of the elements cobalt, copper, and titanium

al·oe \'al-ō\ *n* : any of a large genus of chiefly southern African plants related to lilies and having spikes of often showy flowers; *also* : the dried bitter juice of the leaves of an aloe used as a strong laxative and tonic — usually used in pl.

aloft \ə-'lóft\ *adv or adj*   **1** : in the air; *esp* : in flight   **2** : at, on, or to the higher rigging of a sailing ship

alo·ha \ə-'lō-ə, -,hä; ä-'lō-,hä\ *interj* — used to express greeting or farewell [from Hawaiian *aloha* "love"]

¹alone \ə-'lōn\ *adj*   **1** : separated from others ⟨*alone* in her room⟩   **2** : not including anyone or anything else ⟨money *alone* is not enough⟩

aloe

²alone *adv*   **1** : SOLELY 1 ⟨the proof rests on that statement *alone*⟩   **2** : without company, aid, or support ⟨did it *alone*⟩

¹along \ə-'lóŋ\ *prep*   **1** : on or near in a lengthwise direction : parallel with the length of ⟨walk *along* the beach⟩ ⟨lined up *along* the wall⟩   **2** : at a point on ⟨stopped *along* the way⟩

²along *adv*   **1** : ¹ONWARD, FORWARD ⟨move *along*⟩   **2** : as a companion or associate ⟨brought my best friend *along*⟩   **3** : throughout the time ⟨knew the truth all *along*⟩   **4** : in addition : ALSO ⟨the bill came *along* with the package⟩   **5** : at or on hand ⟨had a camera *along*⟩

along·shore \-,shō(ə)r, -,shó(ə)r\ *adv or adj* : along the shore or coast

¹along·side \-,sīd\ *adv* : along or close at the side : in parallel position

²alongside *prep* : side by side with; *esp* : parallel to ⟨boats *alongside* the dock⟩

¹aloof \ə-'lüf\ *adv* : at a distance : out of involvement

²aloof *adj* : removed or distant in interest or feeling : RESERVED — **aloof·ly** *adv* — **aloof·ness** *n*

aloud \ə-'laud\ *adv* : so as to be clearly heard ⟨read *aloud*⟩

alp \'alp\ *n* : a high rugged mountain

al·paca \al-'pak-ə\ *n*   **1** : a mammal with fine long woolly hair domesticated in Peru and related to the llama   **2** : wool of the alpaca or a cloth made of it; *also* : a rayon or cotton imitation of this cloth [Spanish]

al·pha \'al-fə\ *n*   **1** : the first letter of the Greek alphabet — A or α   **2** : something that is first : BEGINNING

al·pha·bet \'al-fə-,bet, -bət\ *n*   **1** : the letters of a language arranged in their usual order

alpaca 1

2 : a system of signs or signals that serve as equivalents for letters [Middle English *alphabete* "alphabet", derived from Greek *alphabētos* "alphabet", from *alpha* "first letter" (in Greek) and *bēta* "second letter" (in Greek)]

al·pha·bet·i·cal \,al-fə-'bet-i-kəl\ *or* **al·pha·bet·ic** \-'bet-ik\ *adj* : arranged in the order of the letters of the alphabet — **al·pha·bet·i·cal·ly** \-i-k(ə-)lē\ *adv*

al·pha·bet·ize \'al-fə-bə-,tīz\ *vb* **-ized; -iz·ing** : to arrange in alphabetical order — **al·pha·bet·iza·tion** \,al-fə-,bet-ə-'zā-shən\ *n*

alpha particle *n* : a positively charged particle that is identical with the nucleus of a helium atom, consists of 2 protons and 2 neutrons, and is thrown at high speed from a radioactive atomic nucleus

alpha ray *n*   **1** : an alpha particle moving at high speed   **2** : a stream of alpha particles — called also *alpha radiation*

al·pine \'al-,pīn\ *adj, often cap*   **1** : of, relating to, or resembling mountains and especially the Alps   **2** : of, relating to, or growing on upland slopes above the highest elevation where trees grow

al·ready \ól-'red-ē, 'ól-,red-ē\ *adv* : before a certain time : by the time ⟨I had *already* left when you called⟩

al·right \ól-'rīt, 'ól-,rīt\ *adv or adj* : ALL RIGHT

Al·sa·tian \al-'sā-shən\ *n* : GERMAN SHEPHERD

al·sike clover \,al-,sak-, -,sīk-\ *n* : a European perennial clover widely grown as food for browsing or grazing animals

al·so \'ól-sō\ *adv*   **1** : LIKEWISE 1   **2** : in addition : TOO

al·so–ran \-,ran\ *n*   **1** : a horse or dog that does not finish in the first three places in a race   **2** : a contestant that does not win

al·tar \'ól-tər\ *n*   **1** : a raised place on which sacrifices are offered   **2** : a platform or table used as a center of worship

al·ter \'ól-tər\ *vb*   **1** : to change partly but usually not completely ⟨*alter* a dress⟩   **2** : CASTRATE, SPAY [Middle English *alteren* "to make different", from early French *alterer* (same meaning), derived from Latin *alter* "other (of two)" — related to ADULTERATE] — **al·ter·able** \'ól-t(ə-)rə-bəl\ *adj*

al·ter·ation \,ól-tə-'rā-shən\ *n*   **1 a** : the act or process of altering   **b** : the state of being altered   **2** : the result of altering : MODIFICATION

al·ter·ca·tion \,ól-tər-'kā-shən\ *n* : a noisy or angry dispute

¹al·ter·nate \'ól-tər-,nāt *also* 'al-\ *vb* **-nat·ed; -nat·ing**   **1** : to do, occur, or act by turns   **2** : to cause to alternate

²al·ter·nate \'ól-tər-nət *also* 'al-\ *adj*   **1** : occurring or following by turns ⟨*alternate* sunshine and rain⟩   **2 a** : occurring first on one side and then on the other at different levels along an axis ⟨*alternate* leaves on a plant stem⟩   **b** : arranged one above, beside, or next to another ⟨*alternate* layers of meat and cheese⟩   **3** : every other : every second ⟨works on *alternate* days⟩   **4** : being one of the things between which a choice is to be made ⟨we took an *alternate* route⟩ — **al·ter·nate·ly** *adv*

³**alternate** *n* : a person named to take the place of another when necessary

alternate angle *n* **1** : one of a pair of angles on opposite sides of a line intersecting two other lines and between the two intersected lines — called also *alternate interior angle* **2** : one of a pair of angles on opposite sides of a line intersecting two other lines and outside the two intersected lines — called also *alternate exterior angle*

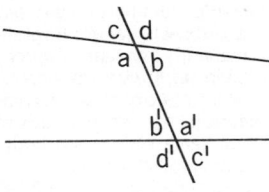

alternate angle 1 and 2: alternate interior angles *a, a', b, b'*; alternate exterior angles *c, c', d, d'*

alternating current *n* : an electric current that reverses its direction at regular intervals — abbr. *AC*

al·ter·na·tion \ˌȯl-tər-'nā-shən *also* ˌal-\ *n* **1** : the act or process of alternating **2** : alternate position or occurrence : SUCCESSION **3** : regular reversal in direction of flow ⟨an *alternation* of an electric current⟩

alternation of generations : the alternate occurrence of two or more forms and especially of a sexual and an asexual generation in the life cycle of a plant or animal

¹**al·ter·na·tive** \ȯl-'tər-nət-iv *also* al-\ *adj* **1** : offering or expressing a choice ⟨*alternative* plans⟩ **2** : being one of the things between which a choice is to be made : ALTERNATE ⟨an *alternative* route⟩ — **al·ter·na·tive·ly** *adv* — **al·ter·na·tive·ness** *n*

²**alternative** *n* **1** : a chance to choose between two or more things only one of which may be chosen ⟨the *alternative* of going by bus or car⟩ **2** : one of the things between which a choice is to be made

al·ter·na·tor \'ȯl-tər-ˌnāt-ər *also* 'al-\ *n* : an electric generator for producing alternating current

alt·horn \'alt-ˌhȯ(ə)rn\ *n* : an alto horn often used in bands in place of the French horn

al·though *also* **al·tho** \ȯl-'thō\ *conj* : in spite of the fact that : THOUGH

al·tim·e·ter \al-'tim-ət-ər, 'al-tə-ˌmēt-ər\ *n* : an instrument for measuring altitude; *esp* : a barometer that registers changes in atmospheric pressure accompanying changes in altitude

al·ti·tude \'al-tə-ˌt(y)üd\ *n* **1 a** : the angular height of a celestial object above the horizon **b** : the vertical distance of an object above a given level (as sea level) **c** : the perpendicular distance in a geometric figure from the point opposite to and farthest from the base to the base, from the vertex of an angle to the side opposite, or from the base to a parallel side or face **2** : an elevated region — usually used in pl. **syn** see HEIGHT

al·to \'al-tō\ *n, pl* **altos 1 a** : CONTRALTO **b** : the second highest of the four voice parts of a mixed chorus — compare ²BASS 1a, ²SOPRANO 1, TENOR 2a **2** : the second highest member of a family of musical instruments; *esp* : ALTHORN

al·to·cu·mu·lus \ˌal-tō-'kyü-myə-ləs\ *n* : a fleecy cloud formation consisting of large whitish globular cloudlets with shaded portions

al·to·geth·er \ˌȯl-tə-'geth-ər\ *adv* **1** : WHOLLY, THOROUGHLY **2** : on the whole

al·to·stra·tus \ˌal-tō-'strāt-əs, -'strat-\ *n* : a cloud formation similar to cirrostratus but darker and at a lower level

al·tru·ism \'al-trü-ˌiz-əm\ *n* : unselfish interest in the welfare of others — **al·tru·ist** \-trü-əst\ *n* — **al·tru·is·tic** \ˌal-trü-'is-tik\ *adj* — **al·tru·is·ti·cal·ly** \-'is-ti-k(ə-)lē\ *adv*

al·um \'al-əm\ *n* **1** : either of two colorless compounds containing aluminum that are used in medicine (as to check local sweating or to stop bleeding) **2** : ALUMINUM SULFATE

alu·mi·na \ə-'lü-mə-nə\ *n* : the oxide of aluminum that occurs in nature as corundum and in bauxite and is used as a source of aluminum, as an abrasive, and as an absorbent

alu·min·i·um \ˌal-yə-'min-ē-əm\ *n, chiefly British* : ALUMINUM

alu·mi·nize \ə-'lü-mə-ˌnīz\ *vb* **-nized; -niz·ing** : to treat or coat with aluminum

alu·mi·num \ə-'lü-mə-nəm\ *n* : a silver-white malleable light element that conducts electricity and heat well, is highly resistant to oxidation, and is the most abundant metal in the earth's crust — see ELEMENT table

aluminum oxide *n* : ALUMINA

aluminum sulfate *n* : a white salt made from bauxite and used in making paper, purifying water, and tanning

alum·na \ə-'ləm-nə\ *n, pl* **-nae** \-(ˌ)nē\ : a girl or woman who has attended or graduated from a particular school, college, or university

alum·nus \ə-'ləm-nəs\ *n, pl* **-ni** \-ˌnī\ : one who has attended or has graduated from a particular school, college, or university [Latin, literally "foster son", from *alere* "to nourish" — related to ALIMENTARY, ALMA MATER]

al·ve·o·lar \al-'vē-ə-lər\ *adj* : of, relating to, resembling, or having alveoli

al·ve·o·lus \al-'vē-ə-ləs\ *n, pl* **-li** \-ˌlī, -ˌ(ˌ)lē\ : a small cavity or pit; *esp* : an air cell of the lungs

al·ways \'ȯl-wēz, -wəz, -ˌwāz\ *adv* **1** : at all times : INVARIABLY ⟨*always* ready for a party⟩ **2** : throughout all time : FOREVER, PERPETUALLY ⟨I'll remember you *always*⟩

Alz·hei·mer's disease \'älts-ˌhī-mərz, 'alts-\ *n* : a disease of the central nervous system characterized by the wasting away of brain tissue with gradual loss of memory and mental abilities — called also *Alzheimer's*

am *present 1st sing of* BE

AM \'ā-ˌem\ *n* : a system of broadcasting using amplitude modulation; *also* : a receiver of radio waves broadcast by such a system — **AM** *adj*

amain \ə-'mān\ *adv* **1** : with all one's might **2 a** : at full speed **b** : in great haste

amal·gam \ə-'mal-gəm\ *n* **1** : an alloy of mercury with some other metal or metals that is used esp. for tooth filling **2** : a combination or mixture of different elements ⟨an *amalgam* of fact and fiction⟩

amal·gam·ate \ə-'mal-gə-ˌmāt\ *vb* **-at·ed; -at·ing 1** : to unite in an amalgam **2** : to combine into a single body : MERGE

amal·gam·ation \ə-ˌmal-gə-'mā-shən\ *n* **1 a** : the act or process of amalgamating ⟨made by the *amalgamation* of mercury with silver⟩ **b** : the state of being amalgamated **2** : a combination of different elements into a single body

am·a·ni·ta \ˌam-ə-'nīt-ə, -'nēt-\ *n* : any of various mostly poisonous fungi with white spores and a globe-shaped swelling about the base of the stem

aman·u·en·sis \ə-ˌman-yə-'wen(t)-səs\ *n, pl* **-u·en·ses** \-'wen(t)-ˌsēz\ : a person employed to write from dictation or to copy manuscript : SECRETARY

am·a·ranth \'am-ə-ˌran(t)th\ *n* : any of a large genus of coarse herbs having leaves arranged singly along the stem and small flowers and are sometimes cultivated for color

am·a·ryl·lis \ˌam-ə-'ril-əs\ *n* : any of various plants of a group related to the lilies; *esp* : any of several African herbs having bulbs and grown for their clusters of large

\ə\ abut	\au̇\ out	\i\ tip	\ȯ\ saw	\u̇\ foot
\ər\ further	\ch\ chin	\ī\ life	\ȯi\ coin	\y\ yet
\a\ mat	\e\ pet	\j\ job	\th\ thin	\yü\ few
\ā\ take	\ē\ easy	\ŋ\ sing	\th\ this	\yu̇\ cure
\ä\ cot, cart	\g\ go	\ō\ bone	\ü\ food	\zh\ vision

showy flowers

amass \ə-'mas\ *vb* : to collect into a mass : ACCUMULATE — **amass·er** *n*

am·a·teur \'am-ə-,tər, -ət-ər, -ə-,t(y)ù(ə)r, -ə-chù(ə)r, -ə-chər\ *n* 1 : a person who takes part in an activity (as a study or sport) for pleasure and not for pay 2 : a person who engages in something without experience or skill ⟨mistakes made only by an *amateur*⟩ [from French *amateur* "one who admires or is devoted to something", derived from Latin *amare* "to love" — related to AMOROUS] — **ama·teur** *adj* — **am·a·teur·ish** \,am-ə-'tər-ish, -'t(y)ù(ə)r-ish\ *adj* — **am·a·teur·ish·ly** *adv* — **am·a·teur·ish·ness** *n*

amaryllis

am·a·to·ry \'am-ə-,tōr-ē, -,tòr-\ *adj* : of, relating to, or expressing sexual love

amaze \ə-'māz\ *vb* **amazed; amaz·ing** : to surprise or astonish greatly : fill with wonder — **amaz·ing·ly** *adv*

amaze·ment \ə-'māz-mənt\ *n* : great surprise or astonishment

am·a·zon \'am-ə-,zän, -ə-zən\ *n* 1 *cap* : a member of a race of female warriors of ancient Greek mythology 2 : a tall strong woman

Am·a·zo·nian \,am-ə-'zō-nē-ən, -'zō-nyən\ *adj* 1 : of or resembling an Amazon 2 : of or relating to the Amazon river or its valley

am·bas·sa·dor \am-'bas-əd-ər, əm-, -'bas-ə-dò(ə)r\ *n* 1 : a person sent as the chief representative of his or her own government in another country 2 : an official representative or messenger — **am·bas·sa·do·ri·al** \(,)am-,bas-ə-'dōr-ē-əl, -,dòr-, əm-\ *adj* — **am·bas·sa·dor·ship** \am-'bas-əd-ər-,ship, əm-\ *n*

am·ber \'am-bər\ *n* 1 : a hard yellowish partly transparent resin from trees long dead that can be highly polished and is used for ornamental objects (as beads) 2 : a dark orange yellow — **amber** *adj*

am·ber·gris \'am-bər-,gris, -,grēs\ *n* : a waxy substance from the sperm whale that is used to make perfumes

am·bi·dex·trous \,am-bi-'dek-strəs\ *adj* : using both hands with equal ease — **am·bi·dex·trous·ly** *adv*

am·bi·ent \'am-bē-ənt\ *adj* : surrounding on all sides

am·bi·gu·ity \,am-bə-'gyü-ət-ē\ *n, pl* **-ities** 1 : the fact or state of being ambiguous 2 : something ambiguous

am·big·u·ous \am-'big-yə-wəs\ *adj* : able to be understood in more than one way [from Latin *ambiguus* "ambiguous", from *ambigere* "to wander around", from *ambi* "around, both", and *agere* "to drive, do" — related to ACT, AGENT] — **am·big·u·ous·ly** *adv* — **am·big·u·ous·ness** *n*

am·bi·tion \am-'bish-ən\ *n* 1 **a** : an eager desire for social standing, fame, or power **b** : desire to achieve a particular goal : ASPIRATION 2 : the particular goal of ambition

Word History When candidates for public office in ancient Rome wanted to be elected, they had to do just what modern candidates must do. They had to spend most of their time going around the city urging the citizens to vote for them. The Latin word for this effort was *ambitio*, which came from *ambire*, a verb meaning "to go around". Since this "ambition" was caused by a desire for honor or power, the word eventually came to mean "the desire for honor or power". This word came into French and English as *ambition* in the late Middle Ages. Later its meaning broadened to include "an admirable desire for advancement or improvement" and still later "the object of this desire". [Middle English *ambi-*

tion "desire for power", from early French *ambition* (same meaning), derived from Latin *ambire* "to go around", from *ambi-* "around" and *ire* "to go"]

am·bi·tious \am-'bish-əs\ *adj* 1 : stirred by or possessing ambition ⟨*ambitious* to be captain of the team⟩ 2 : showing ambition ⟨an *ambitious* plan⟩ — **am·bi·tious·ly** *adv*

¹am·ble \'am-bəl\ *vb* **am·bled; am·bling** \-b(ə-)liŋ\ : to go at an amble [Middle English *amblen* "to walk in a leisurely manner", from early French *ambler* (same meaning), from Latin *ambulare* "to walk" — related to AMBULANCE; see *Word History* at AMBULANCE] — **am·bler** \-b(ə-)lər\ *n*

²amble *n* 1 : an easy gait of a horse in which the legs on the same side of the body move together 2 : a gentle easy way of walking

am·bro·sia \am-'brō-zh(ē-)ə\ *n* 1 : the food of the Greek and Roman gods 2 : something extremely pleasing to taste or smell 3 : a dessert made of oranges and shredded coconut — **am·bro·sial** \-zh(ē-)əl\ *adj*

am·bu·lance \'am-byə-lən(t)s\ *n* : a vehicle that is equipped for transporting the injured or the sick

Word History When the term *ambulance* first came into use, it did not refer to a vehicle. To meet the urgent needs of the wounded during war, the French about 200 years ago set up temporary movable hospitals close to the battlefields. They called such a hospital *hôpital ambulant*, meaning literally "walking hospital". The French adjective *ambulant* can be traced back to the Latin verb *ambulare*, meaning "to walk". In time the French dropped the word *hôpital* from the phrase and changed the adjective to the noun *ambulance*. This word was also later applied to the wagon used for transporting the wounded to the field hospital. Before long, the word *ambulance* came to be used for civilian temporary hospitals set up during emergencies and also for the vehicles used to take the sick and injured to the hospital. English borrowed the word from the French to refer to such vehicles. [from French *ambulance* "field hospital", from *(hôpital) ambulant*, literally "traveling hospital", derived from Latin *ambulare* "to walk" — related to AMBLE]

am·bu·la·to·ry \'am-byə-lə-,tōr-ē, -,tòr-\ *adj* 1 : of or relating to walking 2 : able to walk about ⟨*ambulatory* patients in a hospital⟩

am·bus·cade \'am-bə-,skād, ,am-bə-'skād\ *n* : ²AMBUSH — **ambuscade** *vb* — **am·bus·cad·er** *n*

¹am·bush \'am-,bùsh\ *vb* : to attack from an ambush

²ambush *n* : a trap in which hidden persons wait to attack by surprise

ame·ba, ame·bic, ame·boid *variant of* AMOEBA, AMOEBIC, AMOEBOID

am·e·bi·a·sis \,am-i-'bī-ə-səs\ *n, pl* **-bi·a·ses** \-'bī-ə-,sēz\ : infection with or disease caused by amoebas

amebic dysentery *n* : severe amebiasis affecting the intestines of human beings and marked by dysentery, pain in the bowels, and injury to the intestinal wall

ame·lio·rate \ə-'mēl-yə-,rāt\ *vb* **-rat·ed; -rat·ing** : to make or grow better or more tolerable — **ame·lio·ra·tion** \-,mēl-yə-'rā-shən, -,mē-lē-ə-\ *n* — **ame·lio·ra·tive** \-'mēl-yə-,rāt-iv, -'mē-lē-ə-\ *adj*

amen \(')ā-'men, (')ā-; 'ā- *when sung*\ *interj* — used to express agreement or approval

ame·na·ble \ə-'mē-nə-bəl, -'men-ə-\ *adj* : readily giving in or agreeing ⟨*amenable* to our wishes⟩ — **ame·na·bil·i·ty** \ə-,mē-nə-'bil-ət-ē, -,men-ə-\ *n* — **ame·na·bly** \ə-'mē-nə-blē, -'men-ə-\ *adv*

amend \ə-'mend\ *vb* 1 : to change for the better : IMPROVE 2 : to change the wording or meaning of : ALTER ⟨*amend* a legislative bill⟩ **syn** *see* CORRECT — **amend·able** \-'men-də-bəl\ — **amend·er** *n*

amend·ment \ə-'men(d)-mənt\ *n* 1 : the act or process of amending especially for the better 2 : a change in wording or meaning especially in a law, bill, or motion

amends \ə-'men(d)z\ *n sing or pl* : something done or

given by a person to make up for a loss or injury he or she has caused 〈make *amends*〉

ame·ni·ty \ə-'men-ət-ē, -'mē-nət-\ *n, pl* **-ties** **1** : the quality of being pleasant or agreeable **2** : something (as good manners or household appliances) that makes life easier or more pleasant — usually used in pl.

ament \'am-ənt, 'ā-mənt\ *n* : a flower cluster in which flowers all of one sex and without petals grow in close circular rows on a slender stalk (as in the alder, willow, birch, and poplar) : CATKIN

ament

¹Amer·i·can \ə-'mer-ə-kən\ *n* **1** : a person born or living in North America or South America; *esp* : a citizen of the U.S. **2** : the English language used in the U.S.

²American *adj* **1** : of or relating to North or South America or their residents 〈*American* coastline〉 **2** : of or relating to the U.S. or its citizens

American chameleon *n* : a long-tailed lizard of the southeastern U.S. that can change its color

American elm *n* : a large ornamental tree common in the eastern U.S.

American Indian *n* : a member of any of the native peoples of the western hemisphere except usually the Eskimos; *esp* : an American Indian of North America and especially the U.S.

Amer·i·can·ism \ə-'mer-ə-kə-,niz-əm\ *n* **1** : a word or meaning of a word that is common only in American English **2** : loyalty to the traditions, interests, or standards of the U.S. **3** : a custom or attitude common only to Americans

Amer·i·can·ize \ə-'mer-ə-kə-,nīz\ *vb* **-ized; -iz·ing** : to make or become American (as in customs, habits, dress, or speech) — **Amer·i·can·iza·tion** \ə-,mer-ə-kə-nə-'zā-shən\ *n*

American Sign Language *n* : a sign language for the deaf

American Spanish *n* : any of the varieties of Spanish used in North, Central, and South America and in the West Indies

American Standard Version *n* : an American revision of the Authorized Version of the Bible published in 1901 — called also *American Revised Version*

am·er·i·ci·um \,am-ə-'ris-ē-əm, -'rish-\ *n* : a radioactive metallic element produced by bombardment of plutonium with high-energy helium nuclei — see ELEMENT table

Am·er·in·di·an \,am-ə-'rin-dē-ən\ *n* : AMERICAN INDIAN — **Amerindian** *adj*

am·e·thyst \'am-ə-thəst, -(,)thist\ *n* **1** : a clear purple or bluish violet variety of crystallized quartz used as a gem **2** : a medium purple

   Word History Gems were once believed to have magical qualities. An amethyst, for example, was supposed to have the power to prevent or cure drunkenness in its wearer. For this reason the Greeks gave it the name *amethystos*, which comes from the prefix *a-*, meaning "not", and *methyein* "to be drunk". [Middle English *amatiste* "amethyst", from early French *amatiste* and Latin *amethystus* (both with the same meaning), from Greek *amethystos*, literally "remedy against drunkenness", from *a-* "not" and *methyein* "to be drunk", from *methy* "wine"]

ami·a·ble \'ā-mē-ə-bəl\ *adj* : generally agreeable : having a friendly and pleasant manner — **ami·a·bil·i·ty** \,ā-mē-ə-'bil-ət-ē\ *n* — **ami·a·ble·ness** \'ā-mē-ə-bəl-nəs\ *n* — **ami·a·bly** \-blē\ *adv*

am·i·ca·ble \'am-i-kə-bəl\ *adj* : showing kindness or good-

will : PEACEABLE — **am·i·ca·bil·i·ty** \,am-i-kə-'bil-ət-ē\ *n* — **am·i·ca·bly** \'am-i-kə-blē\ *adv*

amicable number *n* : either of a pair of numbers (as 220 and 284) each of which is equal to the sum of all the exact divisors of the other

am·ice \'am-əs\ *n* : a white linen cloth worn around the neck and shoulders under other vestments by a priest at Mass

amid \ə-'mid\ *or* **amidst** \-'midst\ *prep* : in or into the middle of

amid·ships \ə-'mid-,ships\ *adv* : in or near the middle of a ship

amine \ə-'mēn, 'am-,ēn\ *n* : any of various carbon compounds derived from ammonia

ami·no acid \ə-'mē-nō-\ *n* : any of numerous organic acids that include some which are the building blocks of proteins and are made by living cells from simpler compounds or are obtained in the diet

Amish \'äm-ish, 'am-, 'ām-\ *adj* : of or relating to the Mennonites who settled in America — **Amish** *n*

¹amiss \ə-'mis\ *adv* : in the wrong way 〈now, don't take this remark *amiss*〉

²amiss *adj* : ²WRONG 2, 5, FAULTY, IMPROPER 〈something is *amiss* here〉

am·i·ty \'am-ət-ē\ *n, pl* **-ties** : FRIENDSHIP; *esp* : friendly relations between nations

am·me·ter \'am-,ēt-ər\ *n* : an instrument for measuring electric current in amperes

am·mo·nia \ə-'mō-nyə\ *n* **1** : a colorless gas that is a compound of nitrogen and hydrogen, has a sharp smell and taste, is easily dissolved in water, can easily be made a liquid by cold and pressure, is used to make ice, fertilizers, and explosives, and is the chief nitrogen-containing waste product of many organisms that live in water **2** : a solution of ammonia in water [from Latin *sal ammoniacus* "ammonium chloride", literally "salt of Ammon", named for the Egyptian god Ammon near whose temple the salt was produced] — **am·mo·ni·a·cal** \,am-ə-'nī-ə-kəl\ *adj*

am·mo·nite \'am-ə-,nīt\ *n* : any of numerous flat spiral fossil shells of mollusks similar to the nautilus that are especially abundant in the Mesozoic period of geological history — **am·mo·nit·ic** \,am-ə-'nit-ik\ *adj*

am·mo·ni·um \ə-'mō-nē-əm\ *n* : an ion that comes from the combination of ammonia with a hydrogen ion

ammonium chloride *n* : a white crystalline volatile salt used in dry cells and to cause the discharge of mucus from the respiratory tract

ammonium cy·a·nate \-'sī-ə-,nāt\ *n* : a white salt that changes into urea on standing or on heating in a solution with water

ammonium hydroxide *n* : a compound that is formed when ammonia dissolves in water and that exists only in solution

ammonium nitrate *n* : a colorless crystalline salt used in explosives and fertilizers

ammonium sulfate *n* : a colorless crystalline salt used chiefly as a fertilizer

am·mu·ni·tion \,am-yə-'nish-ən\ *n* **1 a** : objects (as bullets) fired from guns **b** : explosive objects (as bombs) used in war **2** : material that may be used in attacking or defending a position

am·ne·sia \am-'nē-zhə\ *n* : severe loss of memory — **am·ne·si·ac** \-z(h)ē-,ak\ *adj or n*

am·nes·ty \'am-nə-stē\ *n, pl* **-ties** : the granting of pardon (as by a government) to a large number of persons

am·nio·cen·te·sis \,am-nē-ō-(,)sen-'tē-səs\ *n, pl* **-te·ses** \-'tē-,sēz\ : the operation of inserting a hollow needle

\ə\ abut	\au̇\ out	\i\ tip	\ȯ\ saw	\u̇\ foot
\ər\ further	\ch\ chin	\ī\ life	\ȯi\ coin	\y\ yet
\a\ mat	\e\ pet	\j\ job	\th\ thin	\yü\ few
\ā\ take	\ē\ easy	\ŋ\ sing	\th\ this	\yu̇\ cure
\ä\ cot, cart	\g\ go	\ō\ bone	\ü\ food	\zh\ vision

through the wall of the abdomen and into the uterus of a pregnant female especially to withdraw a sample of the fluid surrounding the fetus that is used to find out its sex and especially to check for abnormal cells, chromosomes, and chemicals which may predict a birth defect

amoe·ba \ə-'mē-bə\ *n, pl* **-bas** *or* **-bae** \-(,)bē\ : any of a large genus of proto- zoans that have no per- manent cell organs or structures, that change shape to form temporary lobes for moving and tak- ing in food, and that are widespread in fresh and salt water and in moist soils — **amoe·bic** \-bik\ *adj*

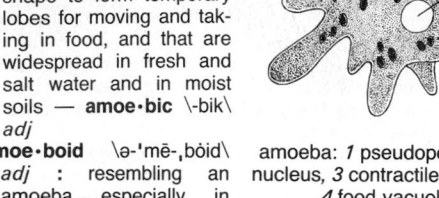

amoeba: *1* pseudopodium, *2* nucleus, *3* contractile vacuole, *4* food vacuole

amoe·boid \ə-'mē-,bóid\ *adj* : resembling an amoeba especially in moving or changing shape by means of the flow of protoplasm

amok \ə-'mək, -'mäk\ *or* **amuck** \ə-'mək\ *adv* : in a vio- lently excited state ⟨run *amok*⟩

among \ə-'məŋ\ *also* **amongst** \-'məŋ(k)st\ *prep* **1** : in or through the midst of ⟨*among* the crowd⟩ **2** : in company with ⟨you're *among* friends⟩ **3** : through all or most of ⟨discontent *among* the poor⟩ **4** : in the class of ⟨*among* my good qualities is modesty⟩ **5** : in shares to each of ⟨divided *among* the heirs⟩

amon·til·la·do \ə-,män-tə-'läd-(,)ō\ *n, pl* **-dos** : a medium dry sherry

am·o·rous \'am-(ə-)rəs\ *adj* **1** : tending to love : easily falling in love ⟨an *amorous* nature⟩ **2** : of, relating to, or caused by love ⟨an *amorous* glance⟩ [Middle English *am- orous* "moved by love", from early French *amorous* (same meaning), derived from Latin *amare* "to love" — related to AMATEUR] — **am·o·rous·ly** *adv* — **am·o- rous·ness** *n*

amor·phous \ə-'mòr-fəs\ *adj* : having no fixed form — **amor·phous·ly** *adv* — **amor·phous·ness** *n*

Amos \'ā-məs\ *n* — see BIBLE table

¹amount \ə-'maunt\ *vb* **1** : to add up ⟨the bill *amounted* to ten dollars⟩ **2** : to be the same in meaning or effect ⟨acts that *amount* to treason⟩

²amount *n* : the total number or quantity : AGGREGATE ⟨the *amount* to be paid⟩ **2** : a given or particular quantity or number ⟨add the same *amount* to both columns⟩

amour \ə-'mù(ə)r, ä-, a-\ *n* : a love affair; *esp* : a secret love affair

am·per·age \'am-p(ə-)rij, -,pi(ə)r-ij\ *n* : the rate of flow of a current of electricity expressed in amperes

am·pere \'am-,pi(ə)r\ *n* : a unit for measuring the rate of flow of an electric current

am·per·sand \'am-pər-,sand\ *n* : a character & standing for the word *and* [from older *and per se and*, spoken form of the phrase *& per se and*, which followed *Z* in early lists of letters of the alphabet and meant "(the character) & by itself (stands for) *and*"]

am·phet·amine \am-'fet-ə-,mēn, -mən\ *n* : a compound or one made from it used especially to increase the activity of the central nervous system and formerly to relieve a stuffy nose

am·phib·ia \am-'fib-ē-ə\ *n pl* : AMPHIBIANS

am·phib·i·an \am-'fib-ē-ən\ *n* **1** : any organism that is able to live both on land and in water; *esp* : any of a class of cold-blooded animals (as frogs and newts) with back- bones that in many respects are between fishes and rep- tiles **2** : an airplane designed to take off from and land on either land or water — **amphibian** *adj*

am·phib·i·ous \am-'fib-ē-əs\ *adj* **1** : able to live both on land and in water ⟨*amphibious* plants⟩ **2 a** : designed for use on both land and water ⟨*amphibious* vehicles⟩ **b** : carried out by land, sea, and air forces acting together ⟨an *amphibious* assault⟩ [from Greek *amphibios* "living a double life", from *amphi-* "around, on both sides" and *bios* "mode of life"] — **am·phib·i·ous·ly** *adv* — **am- phib·i·ous·ness** *n*

am·phi·bole \'am(p)-fə-,bōl\ *n* : any of a group of rock- forming minerals of similar crystal structure that contain calcium, magnesium, iron, aluminum, and sodium or a combination of them with silicon and oxygen

am·phi·ox·us \,am(p)-fē-'äk-səs\ *n, pl* **-oxi** \-'äk-,sī\ *or* **-ox·us·es** : LANCELET

am·phi·pod \'am(p)-fi-,päd\ *n* : any of a large group of crustaceans including the sand fleas and related forms — **amphipod** *adj*

am·phi·the·a·ter \'am(p)-fə-,thē-ət-ər\ *n* **1** : a building with seats rising in curved rows around an open space on which games and plays take place **2** : something (as a piece of level ground surrounded by hills) that resembles an amphitheater

am·pho·ra \'am(p)-fə-rə\ *n, pl* **-pho·rae** \-fə-,rē, -,rī\ *or* **-pho·ras** \-rəz\ : an ancient Greek or Roman jar with two handles

am·ple \'am-pəl\ *adj* **am·pler** \-p(ə-)lər\; **am·plest** \-p(ə-)ləst\ **1** : generous in size, scope, or capacity : CO- PIOUS **2** : enough to satisfy a need **syn** see PLENTIFUL — **am·ple·ness** *n* — **am·ply** \-plē\ *adv*

am·pli·fi·ca·tion \,am-plə-fə-'kā-shən\ *n* : an act, exam- ple, or product of amplifying

am·pli·fi·er \'am-plə-,fī(-ə)r\ *n* : one that amplifies; *esp* : a device usually using electron tubes or transistors to obtain an increase of voltage, current, or power

am·pli·fy \'am-plə-,fī\ *vb* **-fied; -fy·ing** **1** : ENLARGE 2; *esp* : to add details or illustrations to ⟨*amplify* a statement⟩ **2** : to increase (voltage, current, or power) in magnitude or strength

am·pli·tude \'am-plə-,t(y)üd\ *n* **1** : the quality or state of being ample : FULLNESS **2** : EXTENT 1, RANGE **3 a** : the extent of a back-and-forth movement (as of a pendulum) measured from the midpoint to an extreme **b** : one half of the up-and-down extent of the vibration of a wave (as of alternating current)

amplitude modulation *n* **1** : changes in the amplitude of a radio carrier wave according to the strength of the signal **2** : a broadcasting system using amplitude modulation

am·pu·tate \'am-pyə-,tāt\ *vb* **-tat·ed; -tat·ing** : to cut off; *esp* : to cut off an arm or leg from the body — **am·pu·ta- tion** \,am-pyə-'tā-shən\ *n*

am·pu·tee \,am-pyə-'tē\ *n* : one that has had an arm or leg amputated

amuck *variant of* AMOK

am·u·let \'am-yə-lət\ *n* : a small object worn as a charm against evil

amuse \ə-'myüz\ *vb* **amused; amus·ing** **1** : to occupy with something pleasant ⟨*amuse* a child with a toy⟩ **2** : to please the sense of humor of ⟨the story *amused* everyone⟩ — **amus·ed·ly** \-'myü-zəd-lē\ *adv* — **amus·ing·ly** \-'myü-ziŋ-lē\ *adv*

syn AMUSE, DIVERT, ENTERTAIN mean to pass or cause to pass the time pleasantly. AMUSE suggests that one's at- tention is lightly held ⟨*amused* herself by playing soli- taire⟩ DIVERT suggests turning the attention from worry or routine to something funny ⟨the patients found the play *diverting*⟩ ENTERTAIN suggests amusing with spe- cially prepared activity or performance ⟨put on a show to *entertain* the troops⟩

amuse·ment \ə-'myüz-mənt\ *n* **1** : something that amuses **2** : the condition of being amused

amusement park *n* : a park with many rides (as a roller coaster or merry-go-round) and games for entertainment

am·yl acetate \'am-əl-\ *n* : BANANA OIL

am·y·lase \'am-ə-,lās, -,lāz\ *n* : an enzyme that speeds up the digestion of starch or glycogen — called also *diastase*

an \ən, (')an\ *indefinite article* : ²A — used before words beginning with a vowel sound ⟨*an* oak⟩ ⟨*an* hour⟩

an- — see ²A-

¹**-an** *or* **-ian** *also* **-ean** *n suffix* **1** : one that belongs to ⟨American⟩ ⟨Boston*ian*⟩ **2** : one skilled in or specializing in ⟨magic*ian*⟩ [derived from Latin *-anus, -ianus* (adjective and noun suffixes)]

²**-an** *or* **-ian** *also* **-ean** *adj suffix* **1** : of or belonging to ⟨American⟩ **2** : characteristic of : resembling ⟨Hercul*ean*⟩

ana- *or* **an-** *prefix* : up : upward ⟨*ana*bolism⟩ [derived from Greek *an* "up, back"]

anab·o·lism \ə-'nab-ə-,liz-əm\ *n* : the part of metabolism concerned with the building up of the substance of plants and animals — **an·a·bol·ic** \,an-ə-'bäl-ik\ *adj*

anach·ro·nism \ə-'nak-rə-,niz-əm\ *n* **1** : the placing of persons, events, objects, or customs in times to which they do not belong **2** : a person or a thing out of place in time and especially the present time [probably from Greek *anachronismos* "anachronism", derived from earlier *anachronizein* "to be late", from *ana-* "up" and *chronizein* "to spend time, linger", from *chronos* "time" — related to CHRONIC, CHRONICLE, SYNCHRONOUS] — **anach·ro·nis·tic** \ə-,nak-rə-'nis-tik\ *adj* — **anach·ro·nis·ti·cal·ly** \-ti-k(ə-)lē\ *adv*

an·a·con·da \,an-ə-'kän-də\ *n* : a large South American snake that crushes its prey in its coils; *also* : any large snake that crushes its prey like an anaconda

anaconda

anaemia, anaemic *variant of* ANEMIA, ANEMIC

an·aer·o·bic \,an-ə-'rō-bik; ,an-,a-(ə-)'rō-, -,e-(ə-)'rō-\ *adj* : living, active, or occurring in the absence of free oxygen — **an·aer·obe** \'an-ə-,rōb; (')an-'a(-ə)r-,ōb, -'e(-ə)r-\ *n* — **an·aer·o·bi·cal·ly** \,an-ə-'rō-bi-k(ə-)lē; ,an-,a-(ə-)'rō-, -,e-(ə-)'rō-\ *adv*

anaesthesia, anaesthetic *variant of* ANESTHESIA, ANESTHETIC

ana·gram \'an-ə-,gram\ *n* : a word or phrase made out of another by changing the order of the letters ⟨"rebate" is an *anagram* of "beater"⟩

anal \'ān-°l\ *adj* : of, relating to, or situated near the anus — **anal·ly** \-°l-ē\ *adv*

anal fin *n* : a single fin located on the lower back part of the body of a fish behind the excretory opening

an·al·ge·sia \,an-°l-'jē-zhə, -z(h)ē-ə\ *n* : loss of the ability to feel pain while awake — **an·al·ge·sic** \-'jē-zik, -sik\ *adj or n*

an·a·log \'an-°l-,òg, -,äg\ *adj* : of or relating to an analog computer

analog computer *n* : a computer that works with numbers represented by directly measurable quantities (as voltages or resistances) — compare DIGITAL COMPUTER

anal·o·gous \ə-'nal-ə-gəs\ *adj* **1** : showing analogy : SIMILAR **2** : related by analogy — **anal·o·gous·ly** *adv* — **anal·o·gous·ness** *n*

an·a·logue *or* **an·a·log** \'an-°l-,òg, -,äg\ *n* **1** : something that is analogous to something else **2** : an organ similar in function to an organ of another animal or plant but different in structure and origin

anal·o·gy \ə-'nal-ə-jē\ *n, pl* **-gies** **1** : resemblance in some details between things otherwise unlike : SIMILARITY **2** : similarity in function between bodily parts of different structure and origin — **an·a·log·i·cal** \,an-°l-'äj-i-kəl\ *adj*

— an·a·log·i·cal·ly \-k(ə-)lē\ *adv*

anal·y·sis \ə-'nal-ə-səs\ *n, pl* **-y·ses** \-ə-,sēz\ **1 a** : an examination of a whole to discover its elements and their relations **b** : a statement of such an analysis **2** : an explanation of the nature and meaning of something ⟨*analysis* of the news⟩ **3** : the identification or separation of the parts of a substance **4** : PSYCHOANALYSIS

an·a·lyst \'an-°l-əst\ *n* **1** : a person who analyzes or who is skilled in analysis ⟨news *analyst*⟩ **2** : PSYCHOANALYST

an·a·lyt·ic \,an-ə-'lit-ik\ *or* **an·a·lyt·i·cal** \-i-kəl\ *adj* **1 a** : of or relating to analysis **b** : separating something into its parts or elements **2** : skilled in or using analysis — **an·a·lyt·i·cal·ly** \-i-k(ə-)lē\ *adv*

analytical balance *n* : a very precise balance used to weigh very tiny amounts of substances

an·a·lyze \'an-°l-,īz\ *vb* **-lyzed; -lyz·ing** : to study or find out the nature and relationship of the parts of by analysis — **an·a·lyz·able** \-,ī-zə-bəl\ *adj*

an·a·pest \'an-ə-,pest\ *n* : a metrical foot consisting of two unaccented syllables followed by one accented syllable (as in *the accused*) — **an·a·pes·tic** \,an-ə-'pes-tik\ *adj*

ana·phase \'an-ə-,fāz\ *n* : a stage of mitosis or meiosis in which the chromosomes move from the center toward the opposite ends of a dividing cell

an·ar·chic \a-'när-kik, ə-\ *adj* : of or relating to anarchy — **an·ar·chi·cal·ly** \-ki-k(ə-)lē\ *adv*

an·ar·chism \'an-ər-,kiz-əm, -,är-\ *n* : a political theory that government is not necessary

an·ar·chist \'an-ər-kəst, -,är-\ *n* : a person who believes in anarchism or anarchy or practices anarchy — **anarchist** *or* **an·ar·chis·tic** \,an-ər-'kis-tik, -,(,)är-\ *adj*

an·ar·chy \'an-ər-kē, -,är-\ *n* **1** : the condition of a country where there is no government **2** : a state of lawlessness, confusion, or disorder

anas·to·mose \ə-'nas-tə-,mōz, -,mōs\ *vb* **-mosed; -mos·ing** : to connect or communicate by anastomosis

anas·to·mo·sis \ə-,nas-tə-'mō-səs\ *n, pl* **-mo·ses** \-'mō-,sēz\ : the union of parts or branches (as of streams or blood vessels) so as to communicate with each other; *also* : NETWORK 2, MESH

anath·e·ma \ə-'nath-ə-mə\ *n* **1 a** : a curse declared by church authority and accompanied by excommunication **b** : ¹CURSE 1 **2** : a person or thing that is cursed or strongly disliked

anat·o·mize \ə-'nat-ə-,mīz\ *vb* **-mized; -miz·ing** : to cut up carefully so as to show or to examine the structure and use of the parts

anat·o·my \ə-'nat-ə-mē\ *n, pl* **-mies** **1** : a branch of knowledge that deals with the structure of organisms; *also* : a book on bodily structure **2** : structural makeup especially of an organism or any of its parts — **an·a·tom·ic** \,an-ə-'täm-ik\ *or* **an·a·tom·i·cal** \-'täm-i-kəl\ *adj* — **an·a·tom·i·cal·ly** \-i-k(ə-)lē\ *adv* — **anat·o·mist** \ə-'nat-ə-məst\ *n*

-ance \ən(t)s, °n(t)s\ *n suffix* **1** : action or process ⟨avoid*ance*⟩ ⟨perform*ance*⟩ **2** : quality or state : instance of a quality or state ⟨protuber*ance*⟩ **3** : amount or degree ⟨conduct*ance*⟩ [derived from Latin *-antia* "-ancy"]

an·ces·tor \'an-,ses-tər\ *n* **1** : one from whom an individual, group, or species is descended **2** : something from which something else has developed : FORERUNNER [Middle English *ancestre* "ancestor", from early French *ancestre* (same meaning), from Latin *antecessor* "one that goes before", derived from earlier *antecedere* "to go before", from *ante-* "before" and *cedere* "to go, yield" — related to CONCEDE, PREDECESSOR]

\ə\ abut	\au̇\ out	\i\ tip	\ȯ\ saw	\u̇\ foot
\ər\ further	\ch\ chin	\ī\ life	\ȯi\ coin	\y\ yet
\a\ mat	\e\ pet	\j\ job	\th\ thin	\yü\ few
\ā\ take	\ē\ easy	\ŋ\ sing	\th̲\ this	\yu̇\ cure
\ä\ cot, cart	\g\ go	\ō\ bone	\ü\ food	\zh\ vision

an·ces·tral \an-'ses-trəl\ adj : of, relating to, or developed from an ancestor ⟨ancestral home⟩ — **an·ces·tral·ly** \-trə-lē\ adv

an·ces·try \'an-,ses-trē\ n 1 : line of descent 2 : one's ancestors

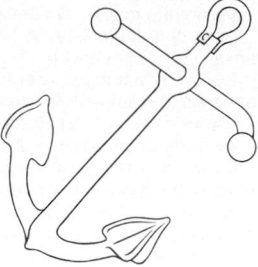

anchor 1

¹**an·chor** \'aŋ-kər\ n 1 : a device usually of metal that is attached to a boat or ship by a cable and that when thrown overboard digs into the earth and holds the boat or ship in place 2 : something that serves to hold an object firmly or that gives a feeling of stability ⟨the anchor of a bridge⟩ 3 : ANCHOR-PERSON

²**anchor** vb **an·chored; an·chor·ing** \-k(ə-)riŋ\ 1 : to hold in place by means of an anchor ⟨anchor a ship⟩ 2 : to fasten by a firm foundation ⟨anchor the cables of a bridge⟩ 3 : to drop anchor : become anchored ⟨the boat anchored in the harbor⟩

an·chor·age \'aŋ-k(ə-)rij\ n 1 : a place where boats may be anchored 2 : a firm hold to resist a strong pull 3 : a means of security

an·cho·rite \'aŋ-kə-,rīt\ n : HERMIT 1

an·chor·man \'aŋ-kər-,man\ n 1 : one who competes or is placed last 2 : an anchorperson who is a man

an·chor·per·son \-,pər-sⁿn\ n : a broadcaster who reads the news and introduces the reports of other broadcasters

an·chor·wom·an \-,wùm-ən\ n 1 : a woman who competes or is placed last 2 : an anchorperson who is a woman

an·cho·vy \'an-,chō-vē, an-'chō-vē\ n, pl **-vies** or **-vy** : any of numerous small fishes resembling herrings; esp : a common Mediterranean fish used especially for sauces and relishes

¹**an·cient** \'ān-shənt, -chənt; 'āŋ(k)-shənt\ adj 1 : having existed for many years ⟨ancient customs⟩ 2 : of or relating to a period of time long past 3 a : AGED, VENERABLE b : OLD-FASHIONED 1, ANTIQUE syn see OLD — **an·cient·ness** n

²**ancient** n 1 : an aged person 2 pl : the civilized peoples of ancient times and especially of Greece and Rome

an·cient·ly \'ān-shənt-lē, -chənt-; 'āŋ(k)-shənt-lē\ adv : in ancient times

-an·cy \ən-sē, ⁿn-sē\ n suffix, pl **-ancies** : quality or state ⟨vacancy⟩ [derived from Latin -antia "quality or state"]

and \ən(d), (')an(d)\ conj 1 : added to ⟨2 and 2 make 4⟩ 2 : AS WELL AS, ALSO — used to join words or word groups ⟨ice cream and cake⟩ ⟨strong and healthy⟩ ⟨swerved and avoided an accident⟩

¹**an·dan·te** \än-'dän-,tā, an-'dant-ē\ adv or adj : slow but not too slow — used as a direction in music

²**andante** n : a musical piece or movement in andante tempo

an·des·ite \'an-di-zīt\ n : a usually dark grayish rock of feldspar that is formed from lava — **an·des·it·ic** \,an-di-'zit-ik\ adj

and·iron \'an-,dī(-ə)rn\ n : one of a pair of metal supports for firewood in a fireplace

an·dra·dite \an-'drād-,īt, 'an-drə-,dīt\ n : a garnet ranging from yellow and green to brown and black and containing calcium and iron

An·drom·e·da \an-'dräm-əd-ə\ n : a northern group of stars in a straight line south of Cassiopeia between Pegasus and Perseus [from Greek Andromedē, a mythological princess]

-ane \,ān\ n suffix : a carbon compound in which each carbon atom is attached to four atoms [altered form of -ene]

an·ec·dote \'an-ik-,dōt\ n : a brief story about something interesting or funny in a person's life — **an·ec·dot·al** \,an-ik-'dōt-ⁿl\ adj — **an·ec·dot·al·ly** \-ⁿl-ē\ adv

ane·mia or **anae·mia** \ə-'nē-mē-ə\ n : a condition in which the blood has less than the normal amount of red blood cells, hemoglobin, or total volume and which is usually marked by pale skin, shortness of breath, and uneven heart action — **ane·mic** \-mik\ adj

an·e·mom·e·ter \,an-ə-'mäm-ət-ər\ n : an instrument for measuring the force or speed of the wind

anem·o·ne \ə-'nem-ə-nē\ n 1 : any of a large genus of herbs related to the buttercups that have showy flowers without petals but with conspicuous often colored sepals 2 : SEA ANEMONE

an·er·oid \'an-ə-,ròid\ adj : containing no liquid or put into motion without the use of liquid

aneroid barometer n : an instrument in which atmospheric pressure bends a metallic surface which in turn moves a pointer

an·es·the·sia or **an·aes·the·sia** \,an-əs-'thē-zhə\ n : loss of bodily sensation with or without loss of consciousness

¹**an·es·thet·ic** or **an·aes·thet·ic** \,an-əs-'thet-ik\ adj : of, relating to, or capable of producing anesthesia — **an·es·thet·i·cal·ly** \-'thet-i-k(ə)lē\ adv

²**anesthetic** or **anaesthetic** n : a substance that produces anesthesia in part or all of the body

anes·the·tist \ə-'nes-thət-əst\ n : one who gives anesthetics to patients

anes·the·tize \ə-'nes-thə-,tīz\ vb **-tized; -tiz·ing** : to make insensible to pain especially by the use of an anesthetic

anew \ə-'n(y)ü\ adv 1 : over again : AFRESH ⟨begin anew⟩ 2 : in a new or different form

an·gel \'ān-jəl\ n 1 : a spiritual being serving God especially as a messenger or as a guardian of human beings 2 : MESSENGER, HARBINGER ⟨angel of death⟩ 3 : a person as pure, lovely, or good as an angel [Middle English angel "spiritual being", from Old English engel and early French angele (both, same meaning), derived from Greek angelos, literally "messenger"] — **an·gel·ic** \an-'jel-ik\ or **an·gel·i·cal** \-i-kəl\ adj — **an·gel·i·cal·ly** \-i-k(ə-)lē\ adv

an·gel·fish \'ān-jəl-,fish\ n 1 : any of several bright-colored bony fishes that are very thin from side to side and live in warm seas 2 : a black and silver South American fish popular in aquariums — called also scalare

angel food cake n : a usually white sponge cake made of flour, sugar, and whites of eggs

¹**an·ger** \'aŋ-gər\ n : a strong feeling of displeasure and usually of opposition toward someone or something

syn ANGER, RAGE, FURY, WRATH mean an intense emotional state caused by displeasure. ANGER is a broad term that applies to various levels of emotion that may or may not be shown ⟨kept her anger inside herself⟩ RAGE suggests loss of self-control from great anger ⟨screaming with rage⟩ FURY suggests destructive rage that comes close to madness ⟨in their fury they smashed all the dishes⟩ WRATH suggests a desire to gain revenge or to punish ⟨in his wrath the king ordered the rebels executed⟩

²**anger** vb **an·gered; an·ger·ing** \-g(ə-)riŋ\ : to make angry

an·gi·na \an-'jī-nə, 'an-jə-nə\ n : a disorder marked by sudden bursts of intense pain; esp : ANGINA PECTORIS — **an·gi·nal** \an-'jīn-ⁿl, 'an-jən-\ adj

angina pec·to·ris \-'pek-t(ə-)rəs\ n : a heart disorder in which the heart muscle receives too little oxygen and which is marked by brief attacks of intense chest pain that occur again and again

an·gio·sperm \'an-jē-ə-,spərm\ n : any of a class of vascular plants with the seeds in a closed ovary : FLOWERING PLANT — **an·gio·sper·mous** \,an-jē-ə-'spər-məs\ adj

¹**an·gle** \'aŋ-gəl\ n 1 : the figure formed by two lines extending from the same point 2 : a measure of the amount of turning that would be required to bring one line of an angle over to meet the other at all points 3 : a sharp

projecting corner   **4** : POINT OF VIEW, ASPECT ⟨consider a problem from a new *angle*⟩   **5** : a sharply curving course or direction [Middle English *angle* "corner", from early French *angle* (same meaning), from Latin *angulus* "angle"] — **an·gled** \-gəld\ *adj*

²**angle** *vb* **an·gled; an·gling** \-g(ə-)liŋ\   **1** : to turn, move, or direct at an angle   **2** : to present (as a news story) from a particular point of view : SLANT

³**angle** *vb* **an·gled; an·gling** \-g(ə-)liŋ\   **1** : to fish with hook and line   **2** : to try to get what one wants in a sly way [derived from Old English *angel* "fishhook", from *anga* "hook"]

angle bracket *n* : BRACKET 3b

angle of incidence : the angle that a ray meeting a surface makes with a perpendicular to the surface at the point of contact

angle of reflection : the angle between a reflected ray and the perpendicular to a reflecting surface drawn at the point of contact

angle of repose : the angle of maximum slope at which a heap of any loose solid material (as earth) will stand without sliding

an·gler \'aŋ-glər\ *n*   **1** : a person who fishes with hook and line especially for pleasure   **2** : a bottom-dwelling marine fish that has a large flat head with parts that stick out and lure other fish within reach of its broad mouth

An·gles \'aŋ-gəlz\ *n pl* : a Germanic people conquering England with the Saxons and Jutes in the 5th century A.D. and joining with them to form the Anglo-Saxon people [from Latin *Angli* "the Angles"; of Germanic origin]

an·gle·worm \'aŋ-gəl-,wərm\ *n* : EARTHWORM

An·gli·can \'aŋ-gli-kən\ *adj* : of or relating to the established Church of England — **Anglican** *n* — **An·gli·can·ism** \-kə-,niz-əm\ *n*

an·gli·cize \'aŋ-glə-sīz\ *vb* **-cized; -ciz·ing** *often cap* : to make English (as in habits, speech, or outlook)

an·gling \'aŋ-gliŋ\ *n* : fishing with hook and line for pleasure

An·glo *combining form*   **1** \'aŋ-,glō, -glə\ : English ⟨*Anglo*-Norman⟩   **2** \-,glō\ : English and ⟨*Anglo*-Japanese⟩ [derived from Latin *Angli* "the Angles"]

An·glo–Amer·i·can \,aŋ-glō-ə-'mer-ə-kən\ *n*   **1** : a person living in the U.S. who was born in or whose ancestors were born in England   **2** : a North American whose native language is English and whose culture is basically English — **Anglo–American** *adj*

An·glo–Sax·on \,aŋ-glō-'sak-sən\ *n*   **1** : a member of the Germanic people who conquered England in the 5th century A.D.   **2** : a person whose ancestors were English   **3** : OLD ENGLISH — **Anglo–Saxon** *adj*

an·go·ra \aŋ-'gōr-ə, an-, -'gor-\ *n*   **1** : yarn or cloth made from the hair of the Angora goat or the Angora rabbit   **2** : ANGORA CAT

Angora cat *n* : a long-haired domestic cat [from *Angora* (former spelling of Ankara, Turkey)]

Angora goat *n* : any of a breed or variety of the domestic goat raised for its long silky hair which is used to make true mohair fabrics

Angora rabbit *n* : a usually white rabbit raised for its long fine soft hair

an·gry \'aŋ-grē\ *adj* **an·gri·er; -est**   **1 a** : feeling or showing anger   **b** : threatening as if in anger   **2** : painfully inflamed ⟨an *angry* rash⟩ — **an·gri·ly** \-grə-lē\ *adv* — **an·gri·ness** \-grē-nəs\ *n*

ang·strom \'aŋ-strəm\ *n* : a unit of length used especially of wavelengths (as of light) and equal to one ten-billionth

Angora goat

of a meter — abbr. Å

an·guish \'aŋ-gwish\ *n* : extreme pain or distress of body or mind — **an·guished** \-gwisht\ *adj*

an·gu·lar \'aŋ-gyə-lər\ *adj*   **1** : having one or more angles : sharp-cornered : POINTED ⟨an *angular* mountain peak⟩   **2** : measured by an angle ⟨*angular* distance⟩   **3** : being lean and bony ⟨an *angular* face⟩ — **an·gu·lar·i·ty** \,aŋ-gyə-'lar-ət-ē\ *n* — **an·gu·lar·ly** \'aŋ-gyə-lər-lē\ *adv*

An·gus \'aŋ-gəs\ *n* : ABERDEEN ANGUS

an·hy·dride \(')an-'hī-,drīd\ *n* : a compound that comes from another (as an acid) by removal of water

an·hy·drite \(')an-'hī-,drīt\ *n* : a mineral consisting of calcium sulfate free from water

an·hy·drous \(')an-'hī-drəs\ *adj* : free from water

an·i·line \'an-ᵊl-ən\ *n* : an oily poisonous liquid that is used in making dyes

¹**an·i·mal** \'an-ə-məl\ *n*   **1** : any of a kingdom of living beings typically differing from plants in capacity for active movement, in rapid response to stimulation, and in lack of cellulose cell walls   **2 a** : one of the lower animals as distinguished from human beings   **b** : MAMMAL

> **Word History** Latin *anima* means "breath" or "soul", and *animalis,* the adjective that comes from it, means "having breath or soul". An animal such as a cat or dog can be seen to breathe. Plants breathe too, by taking in certain gases from the atmosphere and releasing others. However, this process cannot be observed by the naked eye. So the noun *animal,* which comes from *animalis,* was borrowed from Latin for that group of living beings that breathe visibly. [from Latin *animal* "living being that can move", derived from *animalis* "animate", from *anima* "soul, breath" — related to ANIMATE; see *Word History* at ANIMATE]

²**animal** *adj*   **1** : of, relating to, or derived from animals   **2** : of or relating to the body rather than the mind

an·i·mal·cule \,an-ə-'mal-kyül\ *n* : a very small animal that is invisible or nearly invisible to the naked eye — **an·i·mal·cu·lar** \-'mal-kyə-lər\ *adj*

animal heat *n* : heat produced in the body of a living animal by its chemical and physical activity

animal husbandry *n* : a branch of agriculture concerned with raising domestic animals

animal kingdom *n* : the one of the three or sometimes four basic groups of natural objects that includes all living and extinct animals — compare MINERAL KINGDOM, PLANT KINGDOM, PROTIST

¹**an·i·mate** \'an-ə-mət\ *adj*   **1** : having life : ALIVE   **2** : ANIMATED 1, LIVELY — **an·i·mate·ly** *adv* — **an·i·mate·ness** *n*

> **Word History** The same Latin word *anima* meaning "breath, soul" that gave us *animal* has given us other words. The English adjective *animate* meaning "alive" comes from the Latin verb *animare* meaning "to give life to", which in turn came from *anima.* A characteristic of animals is their ability to move about. When a cartoon is drawn and filmed in such a way that lifelike movement is produced, we say it is *animated.* An *animated* film seems to have a life of its own. [Middle English *animate* "alive", from Latin *animatus* (same meaning), derived from *anima* "soul, breath" — related to ANIMAL; see *Word History* at ANIMAL]

²**an·i·mate** \'an-ə-,māt\ *vb* **-mat·ed; -mat·ing**   **1** : to give life to : make alive   **2** : to give spirit and vigor to : ENLIVEN   **3** : to make as an animated cartoon

an·i·mat·ed \'an-ə-,māt-əd\ *adj*   **1** : full of life and energy : LIVELY   **2** : appearing to be alive or moving   **syn** see

\ə\ abut		\au̇\ **out**	\i\ **tip**	\ȯ\ **saw**	\u̇\ **foot**
\ər\ **further**		\ch\ **chin**	\ī\ **life**	\ȯi\ **coin**	\y\ **yet**
\a\ **mat**		\e\ **pet**	\j\ **job**	\th\ **thin**	\yü\ **few**
\ā\ **take**		\ē\ **easy**	\ŋ\ **sing**	\th\ **this**	\yu̇\ **cure**
\ä\ **cot, cart**		\g\ **go**	\ō\ **bone**	\ü\ **food**	\zh\ **vision**

LIVELY — **an·i·mat·ed·ly** adv

animated cartoon n : a movie made from a series of drawings that give the appearance of motion by small changes in each drawing

an·i·ma·tion \,an-ə-'mā-shən\ n **1** : the state of being animate or animated **2 a** : a film made by photographing a series of positions of objects (as puppets) **b** : ANIMATED CARTOON **3** : the making of animations

an·i·mos·i·ty \,an-ə-'mäs-ət-ē\ n, pl **-ties** : a feeling of dislike or hatred

an·ion \'an-,ī-ən\ n : a negatively charged ion

an·ise \'an-əs\ n : an herb that is related to the carrot and produces seeds with an aroma; also : ANISEED

ani·seed \'an-ə(s)-,sēd\ n : the seed of anise often used as a flavoring

an·iso·trop·ic \,an-,ī-sə-'träp-ik\ adj : having properties that change in measurement with change in direction about a point ⟨an anisotropic crystal⟩

an·kle \'aŋ-kəl\ n : the joint between the foot and the leg; also : the region of this joint

an·kle·bone \-'bōn, -,bōn\ n : the bone that in human beings bears the weight of the body and with the tibia and fibula forms the ankle joint

an·klet \'aŋ-klət\ n **1** : something (as an ornament) worn around the ankle **2** : a short sock reaching slightly above the ankle

an·ky·lo·saur \'aŋ-kə-lō-,sòr\ n : any of several plant-eating dinosaurs having a thickset body with bony plates covering the back

an·nal·ist \'an-ᵊl-əst\ n : a writer of annals : HISTORIAN — **an·nal·is·tic** \,an-ᵊl-'is-tik\ adj

an·nals \'an-ᵊlz\ n pl **1** : a record of events arranged in yearly order **2** : historical records

an·nat·to \ə-'nät-ō\ n, pl **-tos** : a yellowish red substance used for dyeing that is made from the pulp around the seeds of a tropical tree

an·neal \ə-'nē(ə)l\ vb : to heat and then cool so as to toughen and make less brittle

an·ne·lid \'an-ᵊl-əd, 'an-ə-lid\ n : any of a phylum of long animals without backbones that have segments and a body cavity and include the earthworms, leeches, and related forms — **annelid** adj

¹an·nex \ə-'neks, 'an-,eks\ vb **1** : to attach as an addition : APPEND **2** : to add (a territory) to one's own territory to form a larger country ⟨the United States annexed Texas in 1845⟩ — **an·nex·a·tion** \,an-,ek-'sā-shən\ n — **an·nex·a·tion·ist** \-sh(ə-)nəst\ n

²an·nex \'an-,eks, 'an-iks\ n : something annexed; esp : an added part of a building

an·ni·hi·late \ə-'nī-ə-,lāt\ vb **-lat·ed; -lat·ing** : to destroy completely — **an·ni·hi·la·tion** \ə-,nī-ə-'lā-shən\ n — **an·ni·hi·la·tor** \ə-'nī-ə-,lāt-ər\ n

an·ni·ver·sa·ry \,an-ə-'vərs-(ə-)rē\ n, pl **-ries** **1** : the annual return of the date of a special event **2** : the celebration of an anniversary [Middle English anniversarie "anniversary", from Latin anniversaria (same meaning), literally "the year has turned", from annus "year" and versus "turned", from vertere "to turn" — related to CONVERSE, UNIVERSE, VERSATILE]

an·no Do·mi·ni \,an-ō-'däm-ə-nē, -'dō-mə-, -,nī\ adv, often cap A — used to indicate that a time division falls within the period dating from the birth of Chirst [Latin, literally "in the year of the Lord"]

an·no·tate \'an-ə-,tāt\ vb **-tat·ed; -tat·ing** : to make or add explanatory notes — **an·no·ta·tor** \-,tāt-ər\ n

an·no·ta·tion \,an-ə-'tā-shən\ n **1** : the act of annotating **2** : a note added as a comment or explanation

an·nounce \ə-'naún(t)s\ vb **an·nounced; an·nounc·ing** **1** : to make known publicly : PROCLAIM **2** : to give notice of the coming, arrival, or presence of ⟨announce dinner⟩

an·nounce·ment \ə-'naún(t)s-mənt\ n **1** : the act of announcing **2** : a public notice announcing something

an·nounc·er \ə-'naún(t)-sər\ n : a person who introduces television or radio programs, makes announcements, and gives the news and station identification

an·noy \ə-'nòi\ vb : to disturb or irritate especially by repeated disagreeable acts : VEX — **an·noy·er** n

an·noy·ance \ə-'nòi-ən(t)s\ n **1 a** : the act of annoying **b** : the feeling of being annoyed **2** : a source of annoyance : NUISANCE

an·noy·ing \ə-'nòi-iŋ\ adj : causing annoyance ⟨an annoying habit⟩ — **an·noy·ing·ly** adv

¹an·nu·al \'an-y(ə-w)əl\ adj **1** : covering the period of a year ⟨annual rainfall⟩ **2** : occurring or performed once a year : YEARLY ⟨an annual meeting⟩ **3** : completing the life cycle in one growing season [Middle English annual "for a year", from early French annuel and Latin annualis (both, same meaning), derived from Latin annus "year"] — **an·nu·al·ly** \-ē\ adv

²annual n **1** : a publication appearing yearly **2** : an annual plant

annual ring n : the layer of wood produced by a single year's growth of a woody plant — called also tree ring

an·nu·ity \ə-'n(y)ü-ət-ē\ n, pl **-ities** **1** : a sum of money paid at regular intervals **2** : an insurance contract providing for the payment of an annuity

an·nul \ə-'nəl\ vb **an·nulled; an·nul·ling** **1** : to make ineffective : NEUTRALIZE, CANCEL ⟨annul the drug's effect⟩ **2** : to bring to an end legally ⟨annul a marriage⟩ — **an·nul·ment** \ə-'nəl-mənt\ n

an·nu·lar \'an-yə-lər\ adj : of, relating to, or forming a ring

annular eclipse n : an eclipse in which a thin outer ring of the sun's disk is not covered by the moon's dark disk that appears smaller

An·nun·ci·a·tion \ə-,nən(t)-sē-'ā-shən\ n : the announcement to the Virgin Mary that she was to be the mother of the Messiah; also : March 25 observed as a church festival in honor of the Annunciation

an·ode \'an-,ōd\ n **1** : the positive electrode of an electrolytic cell to which the negative ions are attracted — compare CATHODE **2** : the negative terminal of a battery that is delivering electric current **3** : the electron-collecting electrode of an electron tube — **an·od·ic** \a-'näd-ik\ adj

an·od·ize \'an-ə-,dīz\ vb **-ized; -iz·ing** : to cause (a metal) to undergo electrolytic action as the anode of a cell in order to coat with a protective or decorative film

anoint \ə-'nòint\ vb **1** : to rub over with oil or an oily substance **2** : to put oil on as part of a religious ceremony — **anoint·er** n — **anoint·ment** \-mənt\ n

anom·a·lous \ə-'näm-ə-ləs\ adj : not following a general rule or method — **anom·a·lous·ly** adv — **anom·a·lous·ness** n

anom·a·ly \ə-'näm-ə-lē\ n, pl **-lies** **1** : an act or instance of not following the general rule or method **2** : something anomalous

anon \ə-'nän\ adv : SOON 1; also : at a later time

an·o·nym·i·ty \,an-ə-'nim-ət-ē\ n, pl **-ties** : the quality or state of being anonymous

anon·y·mous \ə-'nän-ə-məs\ adj **1** : not named or identified ⟨the donor wishes to remain anonymous⟩ **2** : made or done by someone unknown ⟨anonymous gifts⟩ ⟨an anonymous phone call⟩ [from Latin anonymus "anonymous", from Greek anonymos (same meaning), from an-, a- "not, without" and onyma, onoma "name" — related to SYNONYMOUS] — **anon·y·mous·ly** adv — **anon·y·mous·ness** n

anoph·e·les \ə-'näf-ə-,lēz\ n : any of a genus of mosquitoes that includes all mosquitoes which transmit malaria to human beings — **anoph·e·line** \-,līn\ adj or n

an·orex·ia \,an-ə-'rek-sē-ə\ n : ANOREXIA NERVOSA

anorexia ner·vo·sa \-(,)nər-'vō-sə, -zə\ n : a serious eating disorder especially of young women in their teens in which an abnormal fear of weight gain leads to faulty eating habits and extreme weight loss

an·orex·ic \ˌan-ə-'rek-sik\ *adj* : affected with anorexia nervosa

an·or·thite \ə-'nȯr-ˌthīt\ *n* : a white, grayish, or reddish calcium-containing feldspar

¹**an·oth·er** \ə-'nəth-ər\ *adj* **1** : some other ⟨at *another* time⟩ ⟨choose *another* book⟩ **2** : one more in addition ⟨have *another* piece of toast⟩

²**another** *pron* **1** : one more of the same kind ⟨I've had one piece, but I think I'll have *another*⟩ **2** : one that is different : someone or something else ⟨living in *another's* house⟩ ⟨wanting new songs is one thing, but writing them is *another*⟩ **3** : one of a group that is not specified ⟨at one time or *another*⟩

an·ox·ia \a-'näk-sē-ə\ *n* : a condition in which too little oxygen (as at high altitudes) reaches the tissues

¹**an·swer** \'an(t)-sər\ *n* **1 a** : something spoken or written in reply especially to a question   **b** : a solution of a problem   **2** : something said or done in response

²**answer** *vb* **an·swered; an·swer·ing** \'an(t)s-(ə-)riŋ\ **1** : to speak or write in reply   **2** : to take responsibility for something ⟨*answered* for the children's safety⟩   **3** : CONFORM 2, CORRESPOND ⟨*answered* to the description⟩   **4** : to be what is needed for : SERVE ⟨*answer* the purpose⟩   **5** : to find a solution for — **an·swer·er** \'an(t)-sər-ər\ *n*

an·swer·able \'an(t)s-(ə-)rə-bəl\ *adj* **1** : getting the credit or blame for one's acts or decisions : RESPONSIBLE   **2** : capable of being answered or proved wrong

ant \'ant\ *n* : any of a family of small insects that are related to the bees and wasps and live in colonies in which different types of individuals perform special duties

ant- — see ANTI-

¹**-ant** \ənt, °nt\ *n suffix* **1** : one that performs a specified action ⟨cool*ant*⟩ ⟨deodor*ant*⟩   **2** : thing that is acted upon in a specified manner ⟨inhal*ant*⟩ [derived from Latin *-ant* (verb or adjective suffix)]

²**-ant** *adj suffix* **1** : performing a specified action or being in a specified condition ⟨propell*ant*⟩   **2** : causing a specified action or process

ant·ac·id \(')ant-'as-əd\ *adj* : tending to prevent or neutralize acidity ⟨*antacid* tablets⟩ — **antacid** *n*

an·tag·o·nism \an-'tag-ə-ˌniz-əm\ *n* : a state of being opposed to something or unfriendly toward someone

an·tag·o·nist \an-'tag-ə-nəst\ *n* : one that opposes another

an·tag·o·nis·tic \(ˌ)an-ˌtag-ə-'nis-tik\ *adj* : showing antagonism — **an·tag·o·nis·ti·cal·ly** \-ti-k(ə-)lē\ *adv*

an·tag·o·nize \an-'tag-ə-ˌnīz\ *vb* **-nized; -niz·ing** : to stir up dislike or anger in

ant·arc·tic \(')ant-'ärk-tik, -'ärt-ik\ *adj, often cap* : of or relating to the South Pole or to the region near it

antarctic circle *n, often cap A&C* : the parallel of latitude that is approximately 66½ degrees south of the equator

ant bear *n* : a large South American anteater with shaggy gray fur, a black band across the breast, and a white shoulder stripe

ant cow *n* : an aphid which secretes a sugary substance used by ants

ant bear

ante- *prefix* **1** : prior : earlier ⟨*ante*date⟩   **2** : in front of ⟨*ante*room⟩ [derived from Latin *ante* "before, in front"]

ant·eat·er \ 'ant-ˌēt-ər\ *n* : any of several mammals (as an echidna or aardvark) that feed on ants

an·te·bel·lum \ˌant-i-'bel-əm\ *adj* : existing before a war; *esp* : existing before the Civil War

¹**an·te·ced·ent** \ˌant-ə-'sēd-ənt\ *n* **1** : a noun, pronoun, phrase, or clause referred to by a pronoun ⟨in "the house that we live in", "house" is the *antecedent* of "that"⟩   **2** : an event or cause coming before something   **3** *pl* : one's ancestors or parents

²**antecedent** *adj* : coming earlier in time or order — **an·te·ced·ent·ly** *adv*

an·te·cham·ber \'ant-i-ˌchām-bər\ *n* : ANTEROOM

an·te·date \'ant-i-ˌdāt\ *vb* **1** : to date with a date earlier than that of actual writing ⟨*antedate* a check⟩   **2** : to come before in time ⟨automobiles *antedate* airplanes⟩

an·te·di·lu·vi·an \ˌant-i-də-'lü-vē-ən, -dī-\ *adj* **1** : of or relating to the period before the Flood described in the Bible   **2** : very old or old-fashioned — **antediluvian** *n*

an·te·lope \'ant-°l-ˌōp\ *n, pl* **-lope** *or* **-lopes** **1** : any of various Old World cud-chewing mammals that are related to the goats and oxen but differ from the true oxen especially by a more graceful build and horns directed upward and backward   **2** : PRONGHORN

an·te me·ri·di·em \ˌant-i-mə-'rid-ē-əm, -ē-ˌem\ *adj* : being before noon — abbr. **a.m.** [Latin]

an·ten·na \an-'ten-ə\ *n, pl* **-ten·nae** \-'ten-(ˌ)ē\ *or* **-tennas** **1** *pl usually* antennae : any of one or two pairs of long slender organs of sensation on the head of an arthropod (as an insect or a crab) that are made up of segments   **2** *pl usually* antennas : a device (as a rod or wire) for sending or receiving radio waves

an·ten·nule \an-'ten-(ˌ)yü(ə)l\ *n* : a small antenna (as of a crayfish)

an·te·ri·or \an-'tir-ē-ər\ *adj* **1** : placed or being before or toward the front   **2** : coming before in time — **an·te·ri·or·ly** *adv*

an·te·room \'ant-i-ˌrüm, -ˌru̇m\ *n* : a room used as an entrance to another

an·them \'an(t)-thəm\ *n* **1** : a sacred composition with words usually from the Scriptures   **2** : a song of praise or gladness

an·ther \'an(t)-thər\ *n* : the part of a flower that produces and contains pollen and is usually borne on a stalk

ant·hill \'ant-ˌhil\ *n* : a mound made by ants in digging their nest

an·tho·cy·a·nin \ˌan(t)-thə-'sī-ə-nən\ *n* : any of various soluble pigments producing blue to red coloring in flowers and plants

an·thol·o·gy \an-'thäl-ə-jē\ *n, pl* **-gies** : a collection of literary pieces — **an·thol·o·gist** \-jəst\ *n*

an·thra·cite \'an(t)-thrə-ˌsīt\ *n* : a hard glossy coal that burns without much smoke or flame

an·thrax \'an-ˌthraks\ *n* : an infectious and usually fatal disease of warm-blooded animals (as cattle and sheep) caused by a bacterium; *also* : a bacterium causing anthrax

¹**an·thro·poid** \'an(t)-thrə-ˌpȯid\ *adj* **1** : resembling a human being   **2** : resembling an ape

²**anthropoid** *n* : any of several large tailless apes (as a gorilla or chimpanzee)

an·thro·pol·o·gy \ˌan(t)-thrə-'päl-ə-jē\ *n* : the science of human beings and especially of their physical characteristics, their origin and the distribution of races, their environment and social relations, and their culture — **an·thro·po·log·i·cal** \-pə-'läj-i-kəl\ *adj* — **an·thro·pol·o·gist** \-'päl-ə-jəst\ *n*

anti- \ˌant-i, ˌant-ē, ˌan-, ˌtī\ *or* **ant-** *or* **anth-** *prefix* **1** : opposite in kind, position, or action ⟨*anti*histamine⟩   **2** : opposed to ⟨*anti*social⟩   **3** : working against ⟨*anti*bacterial⟩ ⟨*anti*pollution⟩ [derived from Greek *anti-* "against"]

an·ti·air·craft \ˌant-ē-'a(ə)r-ˌkraft, -'e(ə)r-\ *adj* : designed or used for defense against aircraft ⟨an *antiaircraft* gun⟩

an·ti·bac·te·ri·al \ˌant-ē-ˌbak-'tir-ē-əl, ˌan-, ˌtī-ˌbak-\ *adj* : directed or effective against bacteria

an·ti·bal·lis·tic missile \ˌant-i-bə-ˌlis-tik-, ˌan-ˌtī-\ *n* : a

\ə\ abut	\au̇\ out	\i\ tip	\ȯ\ saw	\u̇\ foot
\ər\ further	\ch\ chin	\ī\ life	\ȯi\ coin	\y\ yet
\a\ mat	\e\ pet	\j\ job	\th\ thin	\yü\ few
\ā\ take	\ē\ easy	\ŋ\ sing	\t̲h̲\ this	\yu̇\ cure
\ä\ cot, cart	\g\ go	\ō\ bone	\ü\ food	\zh\ vision

missile for stopping and destroying ballistic missiles

an·ti·bi·ot·ic \,ant-i-bī-'ät-ik, ,an-,tī-, ,ant-i-bē-\ *n* : a substance produced by an organism (as a fungus or bacterium) that in dilute solution inhibits or kills a harmful microscopic plant or animal and especially one that causes disease — **antibiotic** *adj*

an·ti·body \'ant-i-,bäd-ē\ *n* : a substance produced by the body that combines with an antigen and counteracts its effects or those of the microscopic plant or animal on which the antigen occurs

¹an·tic \'ant-ik\ *n* : a wildly playful or funny act or action

²antic *adj* : wildly playful : FROLICSOME

an·tic·i·pate \an-'tis-ə-,pāt\ *vb* **-pat·ed; -pat·ing** **1** : to foresee and deal with or provide for beforehand ⟨*anticipated* their objections⟩ ⟨*anticipated* my every need⟩ **2** : to expect especially with pleasure ⟨*anticipate* the pleasure of your visit next week⟩ [from Latin *anticipatus* "having dealt with ahead of time", from *anticipare* "anticipate", literally "to take before", from *anti-*, altered form of *ante-* "before" and *-cipare*, derived from *capere* "to take" — related to ACCEPT, CAPTURE] — **an·tic·i·pa·tor** \-,pāt-ər\ *n*

an·tic·i·pa·tion \(,)an-,tis-ə-'pā-shən\ *n* **1** : an earlier action that takes into account and deals with or prevents a later action **2** : pleasurable expectation **3** : the act of providing for an expected event or state — **an·tic·i·pa·to·ry** \an-'tis-ə-pə-,tōr-ē, -,tȯr-\ *adj*

an·ti·cli·max \,ant-i-'klī-,maks\ *n* **1** : a shift in writing or speaking from an important idea to an unimportant or silly one **2** : an event at the end of a series that is strikingly less important than what has preceded it — **an·ti·cli·mac·tic** \-klī-'mak-tik, -klə-\ *adj*

an·ti·cline \'ant-i-,klīn\ *n* : an arch of rock arranged in layers that bend downward in opposite directions from the top — compare SYNCLINE

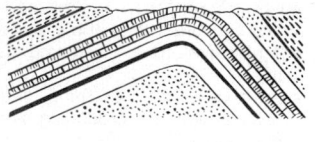

anticline

an·ti·cy·clone \,ant-i-'sī-,klōn\ *n* : a system of winds that rotates about a center of high atmospheric pressure clockwise in the northern hemisphere, that usually advances at 32 to 45 kilometers per hour, and that usually has a diameter of 2500 to 4000 kilometers — **an·ti·cy·clon·ic** \-sī-'klän-ik\ *adj*

an·ti·dote \'ant-i-,dōt\ *n* : a remedy to counteract the effects of poison — **an·ti·dot·al** \,ant-i-'dōt-°l\ *adj* — **an·ti·dot·al·ly** \-°l-ē\ *adv*

an·ti–fed·er·al·ist \,ant-i-'fed-(ə-)re-ləst\ *n, often cap A&F* : a member of the group that opposed the adoption of the U.S. Constitution

an·ti·freeze \'ant-i-,frēz\ *n* : a substance added to a liquid (as the water in an automobile radiator) to prevent freezing

an·ti·gen \'ant-i-jən, -,jen\ *n* : a chemical substance (as a protein) that causes the body to form antibodies against it when it is introduced into the body either alone or as part of a microscopic plant or animal — **an·ti·gen·ic** \,ant-i-'jen-ik\ *adj*

an·ti·his·ta·mine \,ant-i-'his-tə-,mēn, -mən, ,an-,tī-\ *n* : any of various drugs used for treating allergic reactions and cold symptoms

an·ti·knock \,ant-i-'näk, ,an-,tī-\ *n* : a substance that is used as the fuel or as something to be added to the fuel of an internal-combustion engine to help prevent knocking

an·ti·lock \'an-,tī-,läk, 'an-ti-\ *adj* : being a braking system for a motor vehicle designed to keep the wheels from locking and skidding

an·ti·mag·net·ic \,ant-i-mag-'net-ik, ,an-,tī-\ *adj* : having a balance unit made of alloys that will not remain magnetized ⟨an *antimagnetic* watch⟩

an·ti·ma·lar·i·al \,ant-i-mə-'ler-ē-əl, ,an-,tī-\ *adj* : serving to prevent, check, or cure malaria — **antimalarial** *n*

an·ti·mat·ter \'ant-i-,mat-ər\ *n* : matter whose parts match parts of ordinary matter except in having some opposite properties (as a positive instead of a negative charge)

an·ti·mo·ny \'ant-ə-,mō-nē\ *n* : a metallic silvery white brittle element made of crystals that is used especially in alloys and medicine — see ELEMENT table

an·ti·neu·tron \,ant-i-'n(y)ü-,trän, ,an-,tī-\ *n* : the uncharged part of antimatter that is related to the neutron

an·ti·ox·i·dant \,ant-ē-'äk-səd-ənt, ,an-,tī-\ *n* : a substance that opposes oxidation or prevents or makes difficult reactions made easier by oxygen

an·ti·par·ti·cle \'ant-i-,pärt-i-kəl, 'an-,tī-\ *n* : an elementary particle identical to another elementary particle in mass but opposite to it in electric or magnetic properties

an·tip·a·thy \an-'tip-ə-thē\ *n, pl* **-thies** **1** : a strong dislike **2** : a person or thing that arouses strong dislike — **an·ti·pa·thet·ic** \,ant-i-pə-'thet-ik\ *adj*

an·ti·per·spi·rant \,ant-i-'pər-sp(ə-)rənt, ,an-,tī-\ *n* : a preparation used to stop or reduce perspiration

an·ti·pode \'ant-ə-,pōd\ *n, pl* **an·tip·o·des** \an-'tip-ə-,dēz\ **1** : the parts of the earth opposite each other at a distance of the earth's diameter — usually used in pl. **2** : the exact opposite — **an·tip·o·dal** \an-'tip-əd-°l\ *adj* — **an·tip·o·de·an** \(,)an-tip-ə-'dē-ən\ *adj*

an·ti·pol·lu·tion \,ant-i-pə-'lü-shən, ,an-,tī-\ *adj* : designed to stop or reduce pollution ⟨an *antipollution* device on a car⟩

an·ti·pro·ton \,ant-i-'prō-,tän, ,an-,tī-\ *n* : the part of antimatter related to the proton

¹an·ti·quar·i·an \,ant-ə-'kwer-ē-ən\ *n* : ANTIQUARY

²antiquarian *adj* : of or relating to antiquaries or antiquities

an·ti·quary \'ant-ə-,kwer-ē\ *n, pl* **-quar·ies** : a person who collects or studies antiquities

an·ti·quate \'ant-ə-,kwāt\ *vb* **-quat·ed; -quat·ing** : to make old or obsolete

¹an·tique \an-'tēk\ *adj* **1** : belonging to antiquity **2** : belonging to earlier periods ⟨*antique* furniture⟩ **3** : belonging to or resembling a former style or fashion ⟨silver of an *antique* design⟩ **syn** see OLD

²antique *n* : an object of an earlier period; *esp* : a work of art, piece of furniture, or decorative object made at an earlier period

an·tiq·ui·ty \an-'tik-wət-ē\ *n, pl* **-ties** **1** : ancient times; *esp* : those before the Middle Ages **2** : very great age **3** *pl* : objects or monuments from ancient times

an·ti·sep·tic \,ant-ə-'sep-tik\ *adj* **1** : killing or making harmless germs that cause disease or decay **2** : relating to or characterized by the use of antiseptic substances — **antiseptic** *n* — **an·ti·sep·ti·cal·ly** \-ti-k(ə-)lē\ *adv*

an·ti·se·rum \'ant-i-,sir-əm, 'an-,tī-\ *n* : a serum containing antibodies

an·ti·so·cial \,ant-i-'sō-shəl, ,an-,tī-\ *adj* **1** : being against or bad for society **2** : UNFRIENDLY 1

an·ti·stat·ic \,ant-i-'stat-ik, ,an-,tī-\ *adj* : reducing, removing, or preventing the collection of static electricity

an·ti·tank \,ant-i-'taŋk\ *adj* : designed to destroy or stop tanks

an·tith·e·sis \an-'tith-ə-səs\ *n, pl* **-tith·e·ses** \-'tith-ə-,sēz\ : the exact opposite : CONTRARY — **an·ti·thet·i·cal** \,ant-ə-'thet-i-kəl\ *adj*

an·ti·tox·in \,ant-i-'täk-sən\ *n* : any of various specific antibodies that are formed in response to a foreign and usually poisonous substance introduced into the body and that can often be produced in lower animals for use in treating human diseases by injection — **an·ti·tox·ic** \-sik\ *adj*

an·ti·ven·in \,ant-i-'ven-ən, ,an-,tī-\ *n* : a serum containing an antitoxin to a poison of an animal (as a snake)

ant·ler \'ant-lər\ *n* : the solid often branched horn of a deer or one of its close relatives that is cast off and grown anew each year; *also* : a branch of such horn — **ant·lered**

\-lərd\ *adj*

ant lion *n* : a four-winged insect that when a larva digs a cone-shaped pit in which it lies in wait to catch insects (as ants) on which it feeds

ant·onym \'ant-ə-ˌnim\ *n* : a word of opposite meaning ⟨"hot" and "cold" are *antonyms*⟩ — **an·ton·y·mous** \an-'tän-ə-məs\ *adj*

anus \'ā-nəs\ *n* : the lower or posterior opening of the alimentary canal

an·vil \'an-vəl\ *n* **1** : a heavy iron block on which metal is shaped (as by hammering) **2** : the middle bone of the chain of three small bones in the ear of a mammal — called also *incus*

anx·i·ety \aŋ-'zī-ət-ē\ *n, pl* **-eties** **1** : fear or nervousness about what might happen **2** : fearful concern or interest

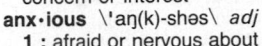

anvil 1

anx·ious \'aŋ(k)-shəs\ *adj* **1** : afraid or nervous about what may happen : WORRIED ⟨*anxious* about their son's health⟩ **2** : desiring earnestly ⟨*anxious* to make good⟩ **syn** see EAGER — **anx·ious·ly** *adv* — **anx·ious·ness** *n*

¹any \'en-ē\ *adj* **1** : one taken at random ⟨*any* person you meet⟩ **2** : EVERY 1 ⟨*any* child knows that⟩ **3** : of whatever number or amount ⟨haven't *any* money⟩ ⟨are there *any* nails left⟩

²any *pron* **1** : any individuals ⟨are *any* of you ready⟩ **2** : any amount ⟨there isn't *any* left⟩

³any *adv* : to the least amount or degree ⟨can't get it *any* clearer⟩ ⟨was never *any* good⟩

any·body \'en-ē-ˌbäd-ē, -bəd-ē\ *pron* : ANYONE

any·how \'en-ē-ˌhaú\ *adv* **1** : in any way, manner, or order **2** : without regard to or in spite of other considerations

any·more \ˌen-ē-'mō(ə)r, -'mò(ə)r\ *adv* : at the present time : NOWADAYS ⟨never see them *anymore*⟩

any·one \'en-ē-(ˌ)wən\ *pron* : any person at all

any·place \'en-ē-ˌplās\ *adv* : ANYWHERE

any·thing \'en-ē-ˌthiŋ\ *pron* : a thing of any kind

any·way \'en-ē-ˌwā\ *adv* : ANYHOW

any·where \'en-ē-ˌ(h)we(ə)r, -ˌ(h)wa(ə)r\ *adv* : in, at, or to any place

any·wise \'en-ē-ˌwīz\ *adv* : in any way whatever

A1 \'ā-'wən\ *adj* : of the very best kind

aor·ta \ā-'òrt-ə\ *n, pl* **aortas** *or* **aor·tae** \-'òrt-ē\ : the main artery that carries blood from the heart to branch arteries by which it is carried throughout the body — **aor·tic** \-'òrt-ik\ *adj*

aortic arch *n* : one of the paired branches of the aorta in fish and the embryos of higher animals with backbones that are reduced in the adult of amphibians and reptiles to a single pair and in the adult of birds and mammals to a single arch

aou·dad \'aú-ˌdad, 'ä-ú-\ *n* : a wild sheep of North Africa

¹ap- — see AD-

²ap- — see APO-

apace \ə-'pās\ *adv* : at a quick pace : FAST

Apache \ə-'pach-ē\ *n* : a member of an American Indian people of the American Southwest

¹apart \ə-'pärt\ *adv* **1** : away from each other ⟨towns five miles *apart*⟩

aoudad

2 : as a separate unit : SEPARATELY ⟨considered *apart* from other points⟩ **3** : into parts : to pieces ⟨took the clock *apart*⟩ **4** : one from another ⟨can't tell the twins *apart*⟩

²apart *adj* : separate from others ⟨in a place *apart*⟩ — **apart·ness** *n*

apart·heid \ə-'pär-ˌtāt, -ˌtīt\ *n* : a policy of racial segregation practiced in the Republic of South Africa

apart·ment \ə-'pärt-mənt\ *n* **1** : a room or set of rooms used as a dwelling **2** : APARTMENT HOUSE

apartment house *n* : a building containing several individual apartments

ap·a·thet·ic \ˌap-ə-'thet-ik\ *adj* : having or showing little or no feeling or interest — **ap·a·thet·i·cal·ly** \-'thet-i-k(ə-)lē\ *adv*

ap·a·thy \'ap-ə-thē\ *n* : lack of feeling or of interest

ap·a·tite \'ap-ə-ˌtīt\ *n* : any of a group of variously colored minerals that are phosphates of calcium and that are used as a source of phosphorus and its compounds

apato·sau·rus \ə-ˌpat-ə-'sòr-əs\ *n* : BRONTOSAURUS

¹ape \'āp\ *n* **1 a** : MONKEY 1; *esp* : one of the larger tailless or short-tailed forms **b** : any of a family of large primates (as the chimpanzee or gorilla) **2** : ³MIMIC 1

²ape *vb* **aped; ap·ing** : to copy closely or blindly **syn** see IMITATE — **ap·er** *n*

ape–man \'āp-ˌman, -ˌman\ *n* : a primate (as a pithecanthropine) between human beings and the higher apes in character

ap·er·ture \'ap-ə(r)-ˌchú(ə)r, -chər\ *n* : an opening or open space : HOLE

apex \'ā-ˌpeks\ *n, pl* **apex·es** *or* **api·ces** \'ā-pə-ˌsēz, 'ap-ə-\ **1** : the uppermost point : TOP ⟨*apex* of a mountain⟩ **2** : ³TIP 1 ⟨*apex* of the tongue⟩ **3** : the highest point ⟨at the *apex* of her career⟩

aph·elion \a-'fēl-yən\ *n, pl* **aph·elia** \-yə\ : the point in the orbit of a heavenly body (as a planet) that is farthest from the sun

aphid \'ā-fəd *also* 'af-əd\ *n* : any of numerous small slow-moving insects that suck the juices of plants

aphis \'ā-fəs, 'af-əs\ *n, pl* **aphi·des** \'ā-fə-ˌdēz, 'af-ə-\ : APHID

aphis lion *n* : any of several insect larvae (as a lacewing or ladybug larva) that feed on aphids

aph·o·rism \'af-ə-ˌriz-əm\ *n* : a short statement of a general truth or idea — **aph·o·rist** \-rəst\ *n* — **aph·o·ris·tic** \ˌaf-ə-'ris-tik\ *adj* — **aph·o·ris·ti·cal·ly** \-ti-k(ə-)lē\ *adv*

api·ary \'ā-pē-ˌer-ē\ *n, pl* **-ar·ies** : a place where bees are kept; *esp* : a collection of beehives — **api·a·rist** \'ā-pē-ə-rəst\ *n*

apiece \ə-'pēs\ *adv* : for each one

ap·ish \'ā-pish\ *adj* : imitating closely or blindly — **ap·ish·ly** *adv* — **ap·ish·ness** *n*

APL \ˌā-(ˌ)pē-'el\ *n* : an algebraic computer programming language designed especially for use in mathematics [*a* *p*rogramming *l*anguage]

aplomb \ə-'pläm, -'pləm\ *n* : complete freedom from nervousness or uncertainty

apo- *or* **ap-** *prefix* : away from : off ⟨*aphelion*⟩ [derived from Greek *apo* "away, off"]

Apoc·a·lypse \ə-'päk-ə-ˌlips\ *n* — see BIBLE table

Apoc·ry·pha \ə-'päk-rə-fə\ *n sing or pl* — see BIBLE table

apo·gee \'ap-ə-(ˌ)jē\ *n* : the point farthest from the center of a heavenly body (as the earth or the moon) reached by an object (as a satellite) orbiting it — compare PERIGEE

apol·o·get·ic \ə-ˌpäl-ə-'jet-ik\ *adj* **1** : offered by way of apology ⟨an *apologetic* smile⟩ **2** : sorry for having done something wrong ⟨they were *apologetic* about the mis-

\ə\ abut	\aú\ out	\i\ tip	\ò\ saw	\ú\ foot
\ər\ further	\ch\ chin	\ī\ life	\òi\ coin	\y\ yet
\a\ mat	\e\ pet	\j\ job	\th\ thin	\yü\ few
\ā\ take	\ē\ easy	\ŋ\ sing	\th\ this	\yú\ cure
\ä\ cot, cart	\g\ go	\ō\ bone	\ü\ food	\zh\ vision

take) — **apol·o·get·i·cal·ly** \-'jet-i-k(ə-)lē\ *adv*

apol·o·gist \ə-'päl-ə-jəst\ *n* : one who speaks or writes in defense of a faith, cause, or institution

apol·o·gize \ə-'päl-ə-,jīz\ *vb* **-gized; -giz·ing** : to make an apology — **apol·o·giz·er** *n*

apol·o·gy \ə-'päl-ə-jē\ *n, pl* **-gies** **1** : an expression of regret (as for a mistake or a discourtesy) **2** : a poor substitute

ap·o·plec·tic \,ap-ə-'plek-tik\ *adj* **1** : of, relating to, or caused by stroke ⟨*apoplectic* symptoms⟩ **2** : affected with or inclined to stroke ⟨*apoplectic* patients⟩ **3** : seeming likely to cause stroke ⟨an *apoplectic* rage⟩; *also* : very excited or angry

ap·o·plexy \'ap-ə-,plek-sē\ *n, pl* **-plex·ies** : [2]STROKE 5

apos·ta·sy \ə-'päs-tə-sē\ *n, pl* **-sies** : a giving up of a religious faith or a previous loyalty

apos·tate \ə-'päs-,tāt, -tət\ *n* : one who commits apostasy — **apostate** *adj*

apos·tle \ə-'päs-əl\ *n* **1 a** : one of a group made up of Christ's twelve original disciples and Paul   **b** : the first Christian missionary to a region **2** : the person who first puts forward an important belief or starts a great reform [Middle English *apostle* "teacher sent out by Christ", from Old English *apostol* and early French *apostle* (both, same meaning), derived from Greek *apostolos* "one sent on a mission"] — **apos·tle·ship** \-,ship\ *n*

ap·os·tol·ic \,ap-ə-'stäl-ik\ *adj* **1** : of or relating to an apostle or the apostles **2** : PAPAL

[1]apos·tro·phe \ə-'päs-trə-(,)fē\ *n* : the addressing of an absent person as if present or of an object or abstract idea as if capable of understanding (as in an "O grave, where is thy victory?")

[2]apostrophe *n* : a mark ' used to show that letters or figures are missing (as in *can't* for *cannot* or *'76* for *1776*) or to show the possessive case (as in *James's*) or the plural of letters or figures (as in "cross your *t's*")

apoth·e·car·ies' measure \ə-'päth-ə-,ker-ēz-\ *n* : a measure of capacity used chiefly by pharmacists

apothecaries' weight *n* : a system of weights used chiefly by pharmacists — see MEASURE table

apoth·e·cary \ə-'päth-ə-,ker-ē\ *n, pl* **-car·ies** : DRUGGIST

ap·pall \ə-'pól\ *vb* : to overcome or shock with horror

ap·pall·ing \ə-'pól-iŋ\ *adj* : inspiring horror or dismay : SHOCKING — **ap·pall·ing·ly** *adv*

Ap·pa·loo·sa \,ap-ə-'lü-sə\ *n* : any of a breed of saddle horses developed in northwestern North America that have small dark spots or blotches on a white coat

ap·pa·nage \'ap-ə-nij\ *n* **1** : a grant (as of land) made by a ruler to a member of the royal family **2** : a customary right or privilege

Appaloosa

ap·pa·ra·tus \,ap-ə-'rat-əs, -'rāt-\ *n, pl* **-tus·es** or **-tus** **1** : the equipment or material for a particular use or job ⟨gymnasium *apparatus*⟩ ⟨laboratory *apparatus*⟩ **2** : a complicated instrument or device

[1]ap·par·el \ə-'par-əl\ *vb* **-eled** or **-elled; -el·ing** or **-el·ling** : [1]DRESS 2a

[2]apparel *n* : things that are worn : CLOTHING

ap·par·ent \ə-'par-ənt, -'per-\ *adj* **1** : open to view : VISIBLE **2** : clear to the understanding : EVIDENT ⟨*apparent* that the road was little used⟩ **3** : appearing to be true or real ⟨the *apparent* meaning of the speech⟩

ap·par·ent·ly \ə-'par-ənt-lē, -'per-\ *adv* : it seems apparent : EVIDENTLY ⟨the window had *apparently* been forced open⟩ ⟨*apparently*, we're supposed to wait here⟩

ap·pa·ri·tion \,ap-ə-'rish-ən\ *n* **1** : an unusual or unexpected sight **2** : GHOST

[1]ap·peal \ə-'pē(ə)l\ *n* **1** : a legal proceeding by which a case is brought to a higher court for review **2** : an asking for something badly needed or wanted : PLEA **3** : the power to cause enjoyment : ATTRACTION

[2]appeal *vb* **1** : to make a legal appeal **2** : to call upon another for a decision ⟨*appealed* to the umpire⟩ **3** : to ask for something badly needed or wanted **4** : to be pleasing or attractive

ap·pear \ə-'pi(ə)r\ *vb* **1** : to come into sight : become plain : SHOW ⟨stars *appeared* in the sky⟩ **2** : to present oneself formally (as to answer a charge) ⟨*appear* in court⟩ **3** : SEEM 1, LOOK ⟨things are not always as they *appear*⟩ ⟨*appears* to be tired⟩ **4** : to come before the public ⟨*appears* on television⟩

ap·pear·ance \ə-'pir-ən(t)s\ *n* **1** : the act, process, or an instance of appearing **2** : the way someone or something looks ⟨the room has a cool *appearance*⟩ ⟨gave every *appearance* of being healthy⟩ ⟨keep up *appearances*⟩ **3** : something that appears

ap·pease \ə-'pēz\ *vb* **ap·peased; ap·peas·ing** **1** : to make calm or quiet **2** : to give in to even when it is wrong to do so   **syn** see PACIFY [Middle English *appesen* "to appease", from early French *apaisier* (same meaning), from *a-* "to" and *pais* "peace", from Latin *pac-*, *pax* "peace" — related to PACIFY, PEACE] — **ap·pease·ment** \-mənt\ *n* — **ap·peas·er** *n*

ap·pel·lant \ə-'pel-ənt\ *n* : one that appeals; *esp* : one that appeals a judicial decision

ap·pel·late \ə-'pel-ət\ *adj* : having the power to review the decisions of a lower court ⟨an *appellate* court⟩

ap·pel·la·tion \,ap-ə-'lā-shən\ *n* : an identifying or descriptive name or title

ap·pend \ə-'pend\ *vb* : to add as something extra ⟨*append* a postscript to a letter⟩

ap·pend·age \ə-'pen-dij\ *n* **1** : something attached to a larger or more important thing **2** : a projecting part of the body (as an antenna) especially when paired with one on each side

ap·pen·dec·to·my \,ap-ən-'dek-tə-mē, ,ap-,en-\ *n, pl* **-mies** : surgical removal of the human appendix

ap·pen·di·ci·tis \ə-,pen-də-'sīt-əs\ *n* : inflammation of the appendix

ap·pen·dix \ə-'pen-diks\ *n, pl* **-dix·es** or **-di·ces** \-də-,sēz\ **1** : additional material attached at the end of a piece of writing **2** : a bodily process or outgrowth; *esp* : a small tube that is closed at one end and projects from the pouch marking the beginning of the large intestine in the lower right side of the abdomen

appendix 2

ap·per·tain \,ap-ər-'tān\ *vb* : PERTAIN 1

ap·pe·tite \'ap-ə-,tīt\ *n* **1** : a natural desire especially for food **2** : [2]TASTE 4 ⟨an *appetite* for adventure⟩

ap·pe·tiz·er \'ap-ə-,tī-zər\ *n* : a food or drink usually served before a meal to make one hungrier

ap·pe·tiz·ing \'ap-ə-,tī-ziŋ\ *adj* : appealing to the appetite — **ap·pe·tiz·ing·ly** *adv*

ap·plaud \ə-'plód\ *vb* **1** : PRAISE 1, APPROVE ⟨*applaud* their efforts⟩ **2** : to show approval especially by clapping the hands [from early French *applaudir* "to applaud", from Latin *applaudere* (same meaning), from *ap-*, *ad-* "to, toward", and *plaudere* "to clap" — related to EXPLODE, PLAUDIT, PLAUSIBLE; see *Word History* at EXPLODE, PLAUSIBLE] — **ap·plaud·able** \-ə-bəl\ *adj* — **ap·plaud·er** *n*

ap·plause \ə-ˈplȯz\ *n* : approval shown especially by clapping the hands

ap·ple \ˈap-əl\ *n* : a rounded fruit with a red, yellow, or green skin, firm white flesh and a seedy core; *also* : the tree of the rose family that bears this fruit

ap·ple–pie \ˌap-əl-ˈpī\ *adj* : just right : PERFECT ⟨in *apple- pie* order⟩

ap·ple·sauce \-ˌsȯs\ *n* : a sauce made of sweetened stewed apples

ap·pli·ance \ə-ˈplī-ən(t)s\ *n* **1** : a piece of equipment for making a tool or machine suitable for a special purpose : ATTACHMENT **2** : a device designed for a particular use ⟨a fire-fighting *appliance*⟩ ⟨an *appliance* serving as an artificial arm⟩ **3** : a piece of household or office equipment that runs on gas or electricity

ap·pli·ca·ble \ˈap-li-kə-bəl *also* ə-ˈplik-ə-\ *adj* : capable of being put to use or put into practice : APPROPRIATE — **ap·pli·ca·bil·i·ty** \ˌap-li-kə-ˈbil-ət-ē *also* ə-ˌplik-ə-\ *n*

ap·pli·cant \ˈap-li-kənt\ *n* : one who applies for something ⟨an *applicant* for work⟩

ap·pli·ca·tion \ˌap-lə-ˈkā-shən\ *n* **1 a** : an act of applying ⟨*application* of paint to a house⟩ **b** : an act of putting to use ⟨*application* of a new method⟩ **c** : the use to which something is put ⟨new *applications* for the computer⟩ ⟨an *application* program is meant to solve a particular problem⟩ **2** : ability to fix one's attention on a task **3 a** : a request made personally or in writing ⟨an *application* for a job⟩ **b** : an application form **4** : something put or spread on a surface ⟨hot *applications* on a sprained ankle⟩ **5** : ability to be put to practical use

ap·pli·ca·tor \ˈap-lə-ˌkāt-ər\ *n* : a device for applying a substance (as medicine or polish)

ap·plied \ə-ˈplīd\ *adj* : put to use in practice or action; *esp* : applying general principles to solve problems that have clear limits ⟨*applied* sciences⟩

¹ap·pli·qué \ˌap-lə-ˈkā\ *n* : a cutout decoration fastened to a larger piece of material

²appliqué *vb* **-quéd; -qué·ing** : to apply an appliqué to a larger surface

ap·ply \ə-ˈplī\ *vb* **ap·plied; ap·ply·ing** **1 a** : to put to use ⟨*apply* knowledge⟩ **b** : to lay or spread on ⟨*apply* a coat of paint⟩ **c** : to place in contact ⟨*apply* heat⟩ **d** : to put into operation or effect ⟨*apply* a law⟩ **2** : to give one's full attention ⟨*applied* myself to the work⟩ **3** : to have relation or a connection ⟨this law *applies* to everyone⟩ **4** : to make an application : make a request ⟨*apply* for a job⟩ — **ap·pli·er** \-ˈplī-(-ə)r\ *n*

ap·point \ə-ˈpȯint\ *vb* **1** : to decide on usually from a position of authority ⟨the teacher *appointed* a time for our meeting⟩ **2** : to choose for some job or offices ⟨I was *appointed* to wash the dishes⟩ ⟨the school board *appointed* three new teachers⟩ ⟨the president *appoints* a cabinet⟩

ap·point·ed *adj* : provided with furnishings and equipment ⟨a well-*appointed* house⟩

ap·poin·tee \ə-ˌpȯin-ˈtē, ˌa-ˌpȯin-\ *n* : a person appointed to a position or an office

ap·point·ive \ə-ˈpȯint-iv\ *adj* : of, relating to, or filled by appointment ⟨an *appointive* office⟩

ap·point·ment \ə-ˈpȯint-mənt\ *n* **1** : the act or an instance of appointing ⟨holds office by *appointment*⟩ **2** : a position or office to which a person is named ⟨holds an *appointment* from the president⟩ **3** : an agreement to meet at a fixed time ⟨an *appointment* with the dentist⟩ **4** : FURNISHINGS — usually used in pl.

ap·por·tion \ə-ˈpōr-shən, -ˈpȯr-\ *vb* **-tioned; -tion·ing** \-sh(ə-)niŋ\ : to divide and distribute in proportion — **ap·por·tion·ment** \-shən-mənt\ *n*

ap·po·site \ˈap-ə-zət\ *adj* : highly appropriate : PERTINENT, APT

ap·po·si·tion \ˌap-ə-ˈzish-ən\ *n* : a grammatical construction in which a noun or noun equivalent is followed by another that explains it ⟨in "my friend the doctor", the word "doctor" is in *apposition* with "friend"⟩

¹ap·pos·i·tive \ə-ˈpäz-ət-iv, a-\ *adj* : of, relating to, or standing in apposition — **ap·pos·i·tive·ly** *adv*

²appositive *n* : the second of a pair of nouns or noun equivalents in apposition

ap·prais·al \ə-ˈprā-zəl\ *n* : an act or instance of appraising

ap·praise \ə-ˈprāz\ *vb* **ap·praised; ap·prais·ing** **1** : to set a value on **2** : to judge how good someone or something is — **ap·praise·ment** \-mənt\ *n* — **ap·prais·er** *n*

ap·pre·cia·ble \ə-ˈprē-shə-bəl, ə-ˈprish(-ē)-ə-bəl\ *adj* : large enough to be noticed or measured — **ap·pre·cia·bly** \-blē\ *adv*

ap·pre·ci·ate \ə-ˈprē-shē-ˌāt, ə-ˈprish-ē-ˌāt\ *vb* **-at·ed; -at·ing** **1** : to see the worth, quality, or significance of ⟨*appreciate* the difference between right and wrong⟩ **2** : to admire highly ⟨thinks no one *appreciates* her paintings⟩ **3** : to be fully aware of ⟨must experience it to *appreciate* it⟩ **4** : to be grateful for ⟨we *appreciate* your help⟩ **5** : to increase in number or value [from Latin *appretiatus* "having put a value on," derived from *ap-*, *ad-* "to" and *pretium* "price" — related to PRICE] — **ap·pre·ci·a·tion** \ə-ˌprē-shē-ˈā-shən, -ˌprish-ē-\ *n* — **ap·pre·cia·tive** \ə-ˈprē-shət-iv, -ˌprish-ət-\ *adj* — **ap·pre·cia·tive·ly** *adv* — **ap·pre·cia·tive·ness** *n*

ap·pre·hend \ˌap-ri-ˈhend\ *vb* **1** : ¹ARREST 2 ⟨*apprehend* a burglar⟩ **2** : to look forward to with fear and uncertainty **3** : UNDERSTAND 1a

ap·pre·hen·sion \ˌap-ri-ˈhen-chən\ *n* **1** : ²ARREST 2 **2** : an understanding of something **3** : fear of or uncertainty about what may be coming

ap·pre·hen·sive \ˌap-ri-ˈhen(t)-siv\ *adj* : fearful of what may be coming — **ap·pre·hen·sive·ly** *adv* — **ap·pre·hen·sive·ness** *n*

¹ap·pren·tice \ə-ˈprent-əs\ *n* : a person who is learning a trade or art by experience under a skilled worker

²apprentice *vb* **-ticed; -tic·ing** : to set at work as an apprentice

ap·pren·tice·ship \ə-ˈprent-əs-ˌship\ *n* **1** : service as an apprentice **2** : the period during which a person serves as an apprentice

ap·prise \ə-ˈprīz\ *vb* **ap·prised; ap·pris·ing** : to give notice to : INFORM

¹ap·proach \ə-ˈprōch\ *vb* **1** : to come near or nearer **2** : to begin to deal with ⟨*approach* a problem⟩

²approach *n* **1** : an act or instance of approaching **2** : a beginning step **3** : way of dealing with something ⟨try a new *approach*⟩ **4** : a way (as a path or road) to get to some place

ap·proach·able \ə-ˈprō-chə-bəl\ *adj* : easy to meet or deal with — **ap·proach·abil·i·ty** \-ˌprō-chə-ˈbil-ət-ē\ *n*

ap·pro·ba·tion \ˌap-rə-ˈbā-shən\ *n* : APPROVAL

¹ap·pro·pri·ate \ə-ˈprō-prē-ˌāt\ *vb* **-at·ed; -at·ing** **1** : to take for one's own often without right **2** : to set apart for a particular purpose or use ⟨*appropriate* funds for research⟩

²ap·pro·pri·ate \ə-ˈprō-prē-ət\ *adj* : especially suitable or fitting **syn** see FIT — **ap·pro·pri·ate·ly** *adv* — **ap·pro·pri·ate·ness** *n*

ap·pro·pri·a·tion \ə-ˌprō-prē-ˈā-shən\ *n* **1** : an act or instance of appropriating **2** : a sum of money appropriated for a specific use

ap·prov·al \ə-ˈprü-vəl\ *n* : an act or instance of approving — **on approval** : for a customer to buy or send back ⟨stamps sent *on approval*⟩

ap·prove \ə-ˈprüv\ *vb* **ap·proved; ap·prov·ing** **1** : to think well of **2** : to accept as satisfactory — **ap-**

\ə\ abut	\au̇\ out	\i\ tip	\ȯ\ saw	\u̇\ foot
\ər\ further	\ch\ chin	\ī\ life	\ȯi\ coin	\y\ yet
\a\ mat	\e\ pet	\j\ job	\th\ thin	\yü\ few
\ā\ take	\ē\ easy	\ŋ\ sing	\th\ this	\yu̇\ cure
\ä\ cot, cart	\g\ go	\ō\ bone	\ü\ food	\zh\ vision

prov·ing·ly \-'prü-viŋ-lē\ *adv*

¹ap·prox·i·mate \ə-'präk-sə-mət\ *adj* : nearly correct or exact ⟨the *approximate* cost⟩ ⟨*approximate* rhyme⟩ — **ap·prox·i·mate·ly** *adv*

²ap·prox·i·mate \ə-'präk-sə-,māt\ *vb* **-mat·ed; -mat·ing** **1** : to bring near or close **2** : to come near : APPROACH

ap·prox·i·ma·tion \ə-,präk-sə-'mā-shən\ *n* **1** : a coming near or close (as in value) **2** : something approximate; *esp* : an estimate or figure that is almost exact

apri·cot \'ap-rə-,kät, 'ā-prə-\ *n* : an oval orange-colored fruit resembling the related peach and plum in flavor; *also* : a tree that bears apricots

April \'ā-prəl\ *n* : the 4th month of the year

> **Word History** The English word *April* comes from the Latin *Aprilis,* the name given to the month by the ancient Romans. No one knows for certain why the Romans named it as they did. One possibility is that *Aprilis* may be related to the Latin verb *aperire* meaning "to open". April is the month when the buds of leaves and flowers begin to open. Another theory is that the name may have been formed originally from the name of the Greek goddess Aphrodite. [Middle English *April* "April", from early French *avrill* and Latin *Aprilis* (both meaning "April")]

April fool *n* : one who is tricked on April Fools' Day

April Fools' Day *n* : April 1 on which many people like to play practical jokes

apron \'ā-prən, -pərn\ *n* **1** : a garment worn on the front of the body to keep the clothing from getting dirty **2** : something that suggests or resembles an apron in shape, position, or use: as **a** : the part of the stage in front of the curtain **b** : the

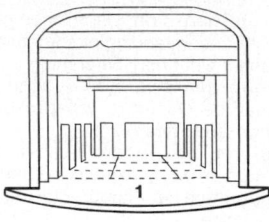

1 apron 2a

paved part of an airport next to the terminal area or hangars [from Middle English *napron* "protective garment" (*a napron* was mistaken for *an apron*), derived from early French *nape* "cloth", from Latin *mappa* "napkin" — related to MAP, NAPKIN]

¹ap·ro·pos \,ap-rə-'pō, 'ap-rə-,pō\ *adv* : at the right time

²apropos *adj* : being to the point : PERTINENT

apropos of *prep* : CONCERNING

apse \'aps\ *n* : a part of a building (as a church) that sticks out from one end of the building, is usually semicircular, has an arched roof, and is often richly decorated especially in Gothic churches

apt \'apt\ *adj* **1** : just right; *esp* : being to the point : RELEVANT ⟨an *apt* remark⟩ **2** : having a tendency : INCLINED, LIKELY ⟨*apt* to become angry⟩ **3** : quick to learn ⟨*apt* in arithmetic⟩ [Middle English *apt* "suitable", from Latin *aptus* "apt, fit" — related to ADAPT] **syn** see QUICK — **apt·ly** *adv* — **apt·ness** \'ap(t)-nəs\ *n*

ap·ti·tude \'ap-tə-,t(y)üd\ *n* **1** : ability to learn : APTNESS **2** : a natural ability ⟨an *aptitude* for mathematics⟩ **syn** see ABILITY

aqua \'ak-wə, 'äk-\ *n* : a light greenish blue

aqua·cade \'ak-wə-,kād, 'äk-\ *n* : a water spectacle that consists usually of exhibitions of swimming and diving accompanied by music

aqua·cul·ture \'ak-wə-,kəl-,chər, 'äk-\ *n* : the cultivation of the natural produce of water (as fish or shellfish) — **aqua·cul·tur·ist** \-'kəlch-(ə-)rəst\ *n*

aqua·ma·rine \,ak-wə-mə-'rēn, ,äk-\ *n* **1** : a transparent beryl that is blue, blue-green, or green **2** : a pale blue to light greenish blue

aqua·naut \'ak-wə-,nòt, 'äk-\ *n* : a person who lives for a long while in an underwater shelter used as a base for research

aqua·plane \'ak-wə-,plān, 'äk-\ *n* : a board towed behind a motorboat and ridden by a person standing on it — **aqua·plane** *vb* — **aqua·plan·er** *n*

aqua re·gia \,ak-wə-'rē-j(ē-)ə, ,äk-\ *n* : a mixture of nitric and hydrochloric acids that dissolves gold or platinum

aquar·ist \ə-'kwar-əst, -'kwer-\ *n* : one who keeps an aquarium

aquar·i·um \ə-'kwar-ē-əm, -'kwer-\ *n, pl* **-i·ums** *or* **-ia** \-ē-ə\ : a container (as a glass tank) or an artificial pond in which living water animals or plants are kept; *also* : an establishment where such collections are kept and shown

Aquar·i·us \ə-'kwar-ē-əs, -'kwer-\ *n* **1** : a group of stars between Capricorn and Pisces usually pictured as a man pouring water **2 a** : the 11th sign of the zodiac — see ZODIAC table **b** : a person whose sign of the zodiac is Aquarius

¹aquat·ic \ə-'kwät-ik, -'kwat-\ *adj* **1** : growing or living in or often found in water ⟨*aquatic* animals⟩ **2** : performed in or on water

²aquatic *n* : an aquatic animal or plant

aq·ue·duct \'ak-wə-,dəkt\ *n* **1** : an artificial channel for water; *esp* : one for carrying a large quantity of flowing water **2** : a structure that carries the water of a canal across a river or hollow [from Latin *aquaeductus* "aqueduct", from *aquae,* form of *aqua* "water", and *ductus* "act of conducting or leading" — related to DUCT]

aque·ous \'ā-kwē-əs, 'ak-wē-\ *adj* **1 a** : of, relating to, or resembling water **b** : made from, by, or with water ⟨an *aqueous* solution⟩ **2** : of or relating to the aqueous humor

aqueous humor *n* : a clear fluid between the lens and the cornea of the eye

aqui·fer \'ak-wə-fər, 'äk-\ *n* : a water-bearing layer of rock, sand, or gravel capable of absorbing water — **aquif·er·ous** \a-'kwif-ə-rəs, ä-\ *adj*

aq·ui·line \'ak-wə-,līn, -lən\ *adj* **1** : of or resembling an eagle **2** : curving like an eagle's beak ⟨an *aquiline* nose⟩ — **aq·ui·lin·i·ty** \,ak-wə-'lin-ət-ē\ *n*

-ar \ər *also* ,är\ *adj suffix* : of or relating to ⟨molecul*ar*⟩ : being ⟨spectacul*ar*⟩ : resembling ⟨oracul*ar*⟩ [derived from Latin *-aris* (adjective suffix)]

Ar·ab \'ar-əb\ *n* **1 a** : a member of the Semitic people of the Arabian peninsula **b** : a member of an Arabic-speaking people **2** : ARABIAN HORSE — **Arab** *adj*

ar·a·besque \,ar-ə-'besk\ *n* : an ornament or style of decoration that uses outlines of flowers, leaves, branches, or fruit and sometimes animal and human figures to produce a pattern of lines that cross over one another — **arabesque** *adj*

Ara·bi·an \ə-'rā-bē-ən\ *adj* : of, relating to, or characteristic of Arabia or its people — **Arabian** *n*

Arabian camel *n* : DROMEDARY

Arabian horse *n* : a horse of a breed originally used in Arabia and nearby areas and noted for its graceful build, intelligence, and spirit

¹Ar·a·bic \'ar-ə-bik\ *adj* **1** : ARABIAN, ARAB **2** : expressed in or making use of Arabic numerals

Arabian horse

²Arabic *n* : a Semitic language that is the chief language of Arabia, Jordan, Lebanon, Syria, Iraq, Egypt, and parts of northern Africa

Arabic numeral *n* : any of the number symbols 1, 2, 3, 4, 5, 6, 7, 8, 9, and 0

ar·a·ble \'ar-ə-bəl\ *adj* : fit for or cultivated by plowing : suitable for producing crops

arach·nid \ə-'rak-nəd, -,nid\ *n* : any of a class of arthropods including the spiders, scorpions, mites, and ticks and having a segmented body divided into two regions of which the front part bears four pairs of legs but no antennae — **arachnid** *adj*

ara·go·nite \ə-'rag-ə-ˌnīt, 'ar-ə-gə-\ *n* : a mineral that is chemically the same as calcite but heavier per unit volume and with different crystalline form

Ar·a·mae·an \ˌar-ə-'mē-ən\ *n* **1** : a member of a Semitic people of the 2d millennium B.C. in Syria and northern Mesopotamia **2** : ARAMAIC — **Aramaean** *adj*

Ar·a·ma·ic \ˌar-ə-'mā-ik\ *n* : a Semitic language of the Aramaeans

ar·a·mid \'ar-ə-məd, -ˌmid\ *n* : any of a group of light but very strong heat-resistant synthetic materials used especially in woven fabrics and plastics

Arap·a·ho *or* **Arap·a·hoe** \ə-'rap-ə-ˌhō\ *n* : a member of an American Indian people of the plains region extending from Saskatchewan and Manitoba to New Mexico and Texas

Ar·a·wak \'ar-ə-ˌwäk\ *n, pl* **-wak** *or* **-waks** : a member of an Indian people chiefly of Guyana

ar·bi·ter \'är-bət-ər\ *n* **1** : ARBITRATOR **2** : a person having the power to decide what is right or proper ⟨an *arbiter* of taste⟩

ar·bi·trary \'är-bə-ˌtrer-ē\ *adj* **1** : coming from or given to free exercise of the will without thought of fairness or right ⟨an *arbitrary* decision⟩ ⟨an *arbitrary* ruler⟩ **2** : seeming to have been chosen by chance ⟨punctuation marks are *arbitrary* symbols⟩ — **ar·bi·trari·ly** \ˌär-bə-'trer-ə-lē\ *adv* — **ar·bi·trari·ness** \'är-bə-ˌtrer-ē-nəs\ *n*

ar·bi·trate \'är-bə-ˌtrāt\ *vb* **-trat·ed; -trat·ing** **1** : to settle a disagreement after hearing the arguments of both sides ⟨*arbitrate* between management and labor⟩ **2** : to refer a dispute to others for settlement : submit to arbitration

ar·bi·tra·tion \ˌär-bə-'trā-shən\ *n* : the act of arbitrating; *esp* : the settling of a dispute in which both sides present their arguments to a third person or group for settlement

ar·bi·tra·tor \'är-bə-ˌtrāt-ər\ *n* : a person chosen to settle differences in a disagreement

ar·bor \'är-bər\ *n* : a shelter of vines or branches or a structure of crossed wood or metal strips covered with climbing shrubs or vines

Arbor Day *n* : a day usually in April or May set aside as a day to plant trees

ar·bo·re·al \är-'bōr-ē-əl, -'bòr-\ *adj* **1** : of, relating to, or resembling a tree **2** : living in or often found in trees

ar·bo·re·tum \ˌär-bə-'rēt-əm\ *n, pl* **-retums** *or* **-re·ta** \-'rēt-ə\ : a place where trees and plants are grown for scientific and educational purposes

ar·bor·ist \'är-bə-rəst\ *n* : a specialist in the care of trees

ar·bor·vi·tae \ˌär-bər-'vīt-ē\ *n* : any of various evergreen trees with closely overlapping scalelike leaves that are often grown for ornament and hedges [modern Latin *arbor vitae*, literally "tree of life"]

ar·bu·tus \är-'byüt-əs\ *n* : TRAILING ARBUTUS

¹arc \'ärk\ *n* **1** : something curved **2** : a glowing flow of electricity across a gap in a circuit or between electrodes **3** : a continuous portion of a curved line (as part of the circumference of a circle)

²arc *vb* **1** : to form an electric arc **2** : to follow an arc-shaped course

ar·cade \är-'kād\ *n* **1** : a row of arches with the columns that support them **2** : an arched or covered passageway (as between shops) **3** : a place with many games to be played by putting coins in them

¹arch \'ärch\ *n* **1** : a usually curved part of a structure that is over an opening and serves as a support **2** : something resembling an arch in form or function; *esp* : either of two portions of the bony structure of the foot that give it flexibility **3** : ARCHWAY [Middle English *arche* "arch", from early French *arche* (same meaning), derived from Latin *arcus* "bow (weapon)"]

²arch *vb* **1** : to cover or provide with an arch **2** : to form into an arch **3** : to take an arch-shaped path

³arch \'ärch\ *adj* **1** : PRINCIPAL, CHIEF ⟨an *arch*-villain⟩ **2** : being clever and mischievous ⟨an *arch* look⟩ [from *arch*-(prefix)] — **arch·ly** *adv* — **arch·ness** *n*

arch- *prefix* : chief : principal ⟨*arch*enemy⟩ [derived from Greek *archein* "to begin, rule"]

ar·chae·ol·o·gy *or* **ar·che·ol·o·gy** \ˌär-kē-'äl-ə-jē\ *n* : the science that deals with past human life as shown by fossil relics and the monuments and tools left by ancient peoples — **ar·chae·o·log·i·cal** \-kē-ə-'läj-i-kəl\ *adj* — **ar·chae·ol·o·gist** \-kē-'äl-ə-jəst\ *n*

ar·chae·op·ter·yx \ˌär-kē-'äp-tə-riks\ *n* : a primitive bird of the Jurassic period of geological history in Europe having characteristics of a reptile

ar·cha·ic \är-'kā-ik\ *adj* : of, relating to, characteristic of, or surviving from an earlier time; *esp* : no longer in general use ⟨the *archaic* words *methinks* and *saith*⟩ **syn** see OLD

ar·cha·ism \'är-kē-ˌiz-əm, -kā-\ *n* **1** : the use of archaic words **2** : an archaic word or expression

arch·an·gel \'ärk-ˌān-jəl\ *n* : an angel of high rank — **arch·an·gel·ic** \ˌärk-ˌan-'jel-ik\ *adj*

arch·bish·op \(')ärch-'bish-əp\ *n* : the bishop of highest rank in a group of dioceses

arch·bish·op·ric \(')ärch-'bish-ə-(ˌ)prik\ *n* : the office or area of authority of an archbishop

arch·dea·con \(')ärch-'dē-kən\ *n* : a church official who assists a bishop

arch·di·o·cese \(')ärch-'dī-ə-səs, -ˌsēz, -ˌsēs\ *n* : the diocese of an archbishop

Ar·che·an *or* **Ar·chae·an** \är-'kē-ən\ *adj* : of, relating to, or being the earliest eon of geological history or the corresponding system of rocks — see GEOLOGIC TIME table — **Archean** *n*

arch·en·e·my \(')ärch-'en-ə-mē\ *n* : a principal enemy

Ar·cheo·zo·ic \ˌär-kē-ə-'zō-ik\ *adj* : ARCHEAN — **Archeozoic** *n*

ar·cher \'är-chər\ *n* : a person who shoots with a bow and arrow

ar·chery \'ärch-(ə-)rē\ *n* : the art, practice, or skill of shooting with bow and arrow

ar·che·type \'är-ki-ˌtīp\ *n* : the original pattern or model from which something is copied — **ar·che·typ·al** \ˌär-ki-'tī-pəl\ *adj*

ar·chi·epis·co·pal \ˌär-kē-ə-'pis-kə-pəl\ *adj* : of or relating to an archbishop

Ar·chi·me·des principle \ˌär-kə-'mēd-ēz-\ *n* : a law of fluid mechanics: a body in a fluid is lifted up with a force equal to the weight of the fluid whose place was taken by the body

ar·chi·pel·a·go \ˌär-kə-'pel-ə-ˌgō, ˌär-chə-\ *n, pl* **-goes** *or* **-gos** : a wide stretch of water with many scattered islands; *also* : a group of islands

ar·chi·tect \'är-kə-ˌtekt\ *n* : a person who designs buildings and advises in their construction

ar·chi·tec·ture \'är-kə-ˌtek-chər\ *n* **1** : the art or science of designing and building structures and especially ones that can be lived in **2** : architectural product or work **3** : a method or style of building — **ar·chi·tec·tur·al** \ˌär-kə-'tek-chə-rəl, -'tek-shrəl\ *adj* — **ar·chi·tec·tur·al·ly** \-ē\ *adv*

ar·chi·trave \'är-kə-ˌtrāv\ *n* : the line of stones resting right on the capital of the column in an ancient Greek or Roman building

ar·chive \'är-ˌkīv\ *n* : a place in which public records or historical documents are preserved; *also* : the material

\ə\ abut		\aú\ **out**	\i\ tip	\ò\ **saw**	\ú\ **foot**
\ər\ **further**		\ch\ **chin**	\ī\ life	\òi\ **coin**	\y\ **yet**
\a\ mat		\e\ **pet**	\j\ **job**	\th\ **thin**	\yü\ **few**
\ā\ take		\ē\ **easy**	\ŋ\ **sing**	\th\ **this**	\yü\ **cure**
\ä\ cot, cart		\g\ **go**	\ō\ **bone**	\ü\ **food**	\zh\ **vision**

preserved — usually used in pl.

ar·chi·vist \'är-kə-vəst, -ˌkī-\ *n* : a person in charge of archives

arch·way \'ärch-ˌwä\ *n* : a passage under an arch; *also* : an arch over a passage

-ar·chy \ˌär-kē, *in some words also* ər-kē\ *n combining form, pl* **-archies** : rule : government [derived from Greek *archein* "to rule"]

arc lamp *n* : a lamp that produces light when an electric current passes between two hot electrodes surrounded by gas — called also *arc light*

¹**arc·tic** \'ärk-tik, 'ärt-ik\ *adj* **1** *often cap* : of or relating to the north pole or the region around it **2** : very cold : FRIGID [Middle English *artik* "arctic", derived from Greek *arktikos* "arctic", from *Arktos* "the Bear", name of the most easily recognizable constellation near the north pole of the sky]

²**arc·tic** \'ärt-ik, 'ärk-tik\ *n* : a rubber overshoe : GALOSH

arctic circle *n, often cap A&C* : the parallel of latitude that is approximately 66½ degrees north of the equator

arctic fox *n* : a small fox of arctic regions having a valuable fur that is blue-gray or brownish in summer and white in winter

arctic hare *n* : a large hare of arctic America that is almost completely white in winter

arctic fox

arctic tern *n* : a tern breeding in arctic regions of both the Old and New World and migrating to South America and Africa

Arc·tu·rus \ärk-'t(y)ùr-əs\ *n* : a very large bright star in Boötes that does not appear to move

ar·dent \'ärd-ᵊnt\ *adj* : showing or having warmth of feeling : PASSIONATE — **ar·dent·ly** *adv*

ar·dor \'ärd-ər\ *n* **1** : a warmth of feeling **2** : great eagerness : ZEAL

ar·du·ous \'ärj-(ə-)wəs\ *adj* : extremely difficult : LABORIOUS ⟨an *arduous* climb⟩ — **ar·du·ous·ly** *adv* — **ar·du·ous·ness** *n*

¹**are** *present 2d sing or present pl of* BE [Old English *earun* "are"]

²**are** \'a(ə)r, 'e(ə)r, 'är\ *n* — see METRIC SYSTEM table [from French *are* (unit of measure), from Latin *area* "open ground, area"]

ar·ea \'ar-ē-ə, 'er-\ *n* **1** : a usually level piece of ground **2** : the amount of surface within a closed figure; *esp* : the number of unit squares equal in measure to the included surface ⟨a circle with *area* of 500 square meters⟩ **3** : REGION 2a ⟨a farming *area*⟩ **4** : a field of activity or study **5** : a part of the brain having a particular function (as vision or hearing) [from Latin "open ground" — related to AERIE]

area code *n* : a three-digit number that represents each telephone service area in a country (as the U.S. or Canada)

area·way \'ar-ē-ə-ˌwä, 'er-\ *n* : a sunken space providing entrance to and air and light for a basement

are·na \ə-'rē-nə\ *n* **1** : an enclosed area used for public entertainment **2** : a building containing an arena **3** : a field of activity ⟨the political *arena*⟩

aren't \(')ärnt, 'är-ənt\ : are not

are·o·la \ə-'rē-ə-lə\ *n, pl* **-lae** \-ˌlē\ *or* **-las** : a colored ring (as about the nipple) — **are·o·lar** \-lər\ *adj*

ar·gent \'är-jənt\ *adj* : resembling silver : SILVERY, WHITE

ar·gen·tite \'är-jən-ˌtīt\ *n* : a dark gray mineral with a metallic luster that is a sulfide of silver and an ore of silver

ar·gil·la·ceous \ˌär-jə-'lā-shəs\ *adj* : of, relating to, or containing clay or the minerals of clay

ar·gi·nine \'är-jə-ˌnēn\ *n* : an amino acid that is found in various proteins

Ar·give \'är-ˌjīv, -ˌgīv\ *adj* : of or relating to the Greeks or Greece and especially to the city of Argos — **Argive** *n*

ar·gon \'är-ˌgän\ *n* : a colorless odorless element that is a gas found in the air and in volcanic gases and used especially in electric bulbs — see ELEMENT table

ar·go·naut \'är-gə-ˌnót, -ˌnät\ *n* **1** *cap* : one of a band of heroes sailing with Jason in search of the Golden Fleece **2** : PAPER NAUTILUS

ar·go·sy \'är-gə-sē\ *n, pl* **-sies** : a large merchant ship

ar·got \'är-gət, -ˌgō\ *n* : a more or less private vocabulary used by a particular class or group

ar·gue \'är-gyü\ *vb* **ar·gued; ar·gu·ing** **1** : to give reasons for or against ⟨*argue* in favor of lowering taxes⟩ **2** : to talk about some matter usually with different points of view ⟨*argue* about politics⟩ **3** : to persuade by giving reasons ⟨tried to *argue* their parents into getting a new car⟩ **syn** see DISCUSS — **ar·gu·er** *n*

ar·gu·ment \'är-gyə-mənt\ *n* **1 a** : a reason for or against something **b** : a discussion in which arguments are presented : DEBATE **2** : an angry disagreement : QUARREL

ar·gu·men·ta·tive \ˌär-gyə-'ment-ət-iv\ *adj* : marked by or given to argument : QUARRELSOME — **ar·gu·men·ta·tive·ly** *adv*

aria \'är-ē-ə\ *n* : a song in an opera sung by a single voice

ar·id \'ar-əd\ *adj* : very dry; *esp* : not having enough rainfall to support agriculture — **arid·i·ty** \ə-'rid-ət-ē, a-\ *n*

Ar·i·es \'er-(ē-)ˌēz, 'ar-\ *n* **1** : a group of stars between Pisces and Taurus usually pictured as a ram **2 a** : the first sign of the zodiac — see ZODIAC table **b** : a person whose sign of the zodiac is Aries

aright \ə-'rīt\ *adv* : so as to be correct : RIGHTLY ⟨If I remember *aright*⟩

arise \ə-'rīz\ *vb* **arose** \-'rōz\; **aris·en** \-'riz-ən\; **aris·ing** \-'rī-ziŋ\ **1** : to get up from sleep or after lying down ⟨*arising* at dawn⟩ **2 a** : to begin at a source ⟨arteries that *arise* from the aorta⟩ **b** : to come into being or to attention ⟨a question *arose*⟩ **3** : to move upward ⟨mist *arose* from the valley⟩

ar·is·toc·ra·cy \ˌar-ə-'stäk-rə-sē\ *n, pl* **-cies** **1** : a government run by a small class of people **2 a** : an upper class that is usually based on birth and is richer and more powerful than the rest of society **b** : persons thought to be better than the rest of the community

aris·to·crat \ə-'ris-tə-ˌkrat, a-; 'ar-ə-stə-\ *n* **1** : a member of an aristocracy **2** : a person who has habits and ideas like those of the aristocracy — **aris·to·crat·ic** \ə-ˌris-tə-'krat-ik, a-ˌris-tə-, ˌar-ə-stə-\ *adj* — **aris·to·crat·i·cal·ly** \-i-k(ə-)lē\ *adv*

arith·me·tic \ə-'rith-mə-ˌtik\ *n* **1** : a branch of mathematics that deals with real numbers and their addition, subtraction, multiplication, and division **2** : an act or method of computing — **ar·ith·met·ic** \ˌar-ith-'met-ik\ *or* **ar·ith·met·i·cal** \-'met-i-kəl\ *adj* — **ar·ith·met·i·cal·ly** \-i-k(ə-)lē\ *adv* — **arith·me·ti·cian** \ə-ˌrith-mə-'tish-ən\ *n*

arithmetic mean \ˌar-ith-ˌmet-ik-\ *n* : a value that is computed by dividing the sum of a set of terms by the number of terms ⟨the *arithmetic mean* of 6, 4, and 5 is 5⟩

ark \'ärk\ *n* **1** : the ship in which Noah and his family were saved from the Flood **2 a** : a sacred chest in which the ancient Hebrews kept the two tablets of the Law **b** : a place in a synagogue for the scrolls of the Torah

¹**arm** \'ärm\ *n* **1 a** : a human upper limb; *esp* : the part between the shoulder and wrist **b** : a corresponding limb of a lower animal with a backbone **2** : something resembling an arm in shape or position ⟨an *arm* of the sea⟩ ⟨the *arm* of a chair⟩ **3** : ¹POWER 1a ⟨the long *arm* of the law⟩ **4** : SLEEVE 1 [Old English *earm* "arm"] — **armed** \'ärmd\ *adj* — **arm·less** \'ärm-ləs\ *adj* — **arm·like** \-ˌlīk\ *adj*

²**arm** *vb* **1** : to provide with weapons ⟨*arm* a regiment⟩ **2** : to provide with a means of defense ⟨*arm* oneself with facts⟩ **3** : to get ready for action or operation ⟨*arm* a bomb⟩

³arm *n* **1 a :** WEAPON; *esp* : FIREARM **b :** a combat branch of an army **c :** a branch of the military forces **2** *pl* : the designs on a shield or flag of a family or a government **3 a** *pl* : actual fighting : WARFARE **b** *pl* : military service [Middle English *armes* "weapons", from early French *armes* (same meaning), from Latin *arma* "weapons" — related to ALARM; see *Word History* at ALARM]

ar·ma·da \är-'mäd-ə, -'mād-\ *n* **1 :** a large fleet of warships **2 :** a large force or group of usually moving things ⟨an *armada* of fishing boats⟩ [from Spanish *armada* "fleet", derived from Latin *arma* "weapons"]

ar·ma·dil·lo \,är-mə-'dil-ō\ *n, pl* **-los :** any of several small burrowing mammals of warm parts of the Americas whose head and body are protected by hard bony armor

armadillo

ar·ma·ment \'är-mə-mənt\ *n* **1 :** the military strength and equipment of a nation **2 :** a supply of war materials **3 :** the process of preparing for war

ar·ma·ture \'är-mə-chər, -,chù(ə)r\ *n* **1 :** a covering or structure (as the spines of a cactus) used for protection or defense **2 :** the part of an electric generator that consists of coils of wire around an iron core and that induces an electric current when it is rotated in a magnetic field **3 :** the part of an electric motor that consists of coils of wire around an iron core and that is caused to rotate in a magnetic field when an electric current is passed through the coils **4 :** the movable part of an electromagnetic device (as a loudspeaker)

arm·chair \'ärm-,che(ə)r, -,cha(ə)r; 'ärm-'che(ə)r, -'cha(ə)r\ *n* **:** a chair with supports for a person's arms

armed forces *n pl* **:** the military, naval, and air forces of a nation

Ar·me·nian \är-'mē-nē-ən, -nyən\ *n* **1 :** a person born or living in Armenia **2 :** the Indo-European language of the Armenians — **Armenian** *adj*

arm·ful \'ärm-,fùl\ *n, pl* **arm·fuls** \-,fùlz\ *or* **arms·ful** \'ärmz-,fùl\ **:** as much as a person's arm can hold ⟨an *armful* of books⟩

arm·hole \'ärm-,hōl\ *n* **:** an opening for the arm in a garment

ar·mi·stice \'är-mə-stəs\ *n* **:** a pause in fighting brought about by agreement between the two sides

Armistice Day *n* **:** VETERANS DAY

arm·let \'ärm-lət\ *n* **:** a band (as of cloth or metal) worn around the upper arm

ar·mor \'är-mər\ *n* **1 :** a covering (as of metal) to protect the body in battle **2 :** a protective covering (as the steel sides of a battleship or the covering of an animal or plant) **3 :** armored forces and vehicles (as tanks)

ar·mored \'är-mərd\ *adj* **1 :** protected by armor ⟨an *armored* car⟩ ⟨*armored* reptiles⟩ **2 :** supplied with armored equipment ⟨an *armored* force⟩

ar·mor·er \'är-mər-ər\ *n* **1 :** one that makes armor or arms **2 :** a person who repairs, puts together, and tests firearms

ar·mo·ri·al \är-'mōr-ē-əl, -'mòr-\ *adj* **:** of, relating to, or carrying designs on a shield or flag of a family or a government

armor 1

ar·mo·ry \'ärm-(ə-)rē\ *n, pl* **ar·mor·ies** **1 :** a supply of arms **2 :** a place where arms are kept and where soldiers are often trained **3 :** a place where arms are made

arm·pit \'ärm-,pit\ *n* **:** the hollow beneath the junction of the arm and shoulder

ar·my \'är-mē\ *n, pl* **ar·mies** **1 a :** a large body of men and women organized for land warfare **b** *often cap* **:** the complete military organization of a nation for land warfare **2 :** a great number of persons or things **3 :** a body of persons organized to advance an idea [Middle English *armee* "army", from early French *armee* (same meaning), derived from Latin *arma* "weapons"]

ar·my·worm \-,wərm\ *n* **:** any of numerous moths that in the larval stage travel in large numbers from field to field destroying crops (as grass or grain)

ar·ni·ca \'är-ni-kə\ *n* **1 :** dried flower heads of a mountain herb related to the daisies and used especially in solution as a liniment **2 :** a solution prepared from arnica that is used as medicine

aro·ma \ə-'rō-mə\ *n* **:** a noticeable and pleasant smell ⟨the *aroma* of coffee⟩

ar·o·mat·ic \,ar-ə-'mat-ik\ *adj* **:** of, relating to, or having aroma — **aromatic** *n*

arose *past of* ARISE

¹around \ə-'raùnd\ *adv* **1 :** in circumference ⟨a tree five feet *around*⟩ **2 :** in or along a curving path **3 :** on all sides ⟨papers lying *around*⟩ **4 :** NEARBY ⟨stay *around* a while⟩ **5 :** here and there in various places ⟨travel *around*⟩ **6 :** to each in turn ⟨pass the fruit *around*⟩ **7 :** from beginning to end ⟨mild the year *around*⟩ **8 :** in or to an opposite direction or position ⟨turn *around*⟩ **9 :** in the neighborhood of : APPROXIMATELY ⟨a price of *around* $20⟩

²around *prep* **1 a :** on all sides of ⟨fields *around* the village⟩ **b :** so as to encircle or enclose ⟨people seated *around* the table⟩ **c :** on or to another side of ⟨voyage *around* Cape Horn⟩ **d :** near to ⟨lives *around* Chicago⟩ **2 :** here and there in or throughout ⟨travel *around* the country⟩

arouse \ə-'raùz\ *vb* **aroused; arous·ing** **1 :** to awaken from sleep **2 :** to rouse to action : EXCITE

ar·peg·gio \är-'pej-ō, -'pej-ē-,ō\ *n, pl* **-gios** **1 :** the playing of the tones of a chord in succession and not at the same time **2 :** a chord played in arpeggio

arquebus *variant of* HARQUEBUS

ar·raign \ə-'rān\ *vb* **:** to call before a court to answer to a charge — **ar·raign·ment** \-mənt\ *n*

ar·range \ə-'rānj\ *vb* **ar·ranged; ar·rang·ing** **1 :** to put in order; *esp* : to put in a particular order ⟨*arrange* books on shelves⟩ **2 :** to make plans for ⟨*arrange* a program⟩ **3 :** to come to an agreement about : SETTLE ⟨*arrange* a time for the meeting⟩ **4 :** to make a musical arrangement of — **ar·rang·er** *n*

ar·range·ment \ə-'rānj-mənt\ *n* **1 :** a putting in order : the order in which things are put ⟨the *arrangement* of furniture in a room⟩ **2 :** preparation or planning done in advance ⟨make *arrangements* for a trip⟩ **3 :** something made by arranging ⟨a flower *arrangement*⟩ **4 :** a changing of a piece of music to suit voices or instruments other than those for which it was first written

ar·rant \'ar-ənt\ *adj* **:** OUT-AND-OUT ⟨an *arrant* knave⟩ — **ar·rant·ly** *adv*

¹ar·ray \ə-'rā\ *vb* **1 :** to set in order : DRAW UP ⟨soldiers *arrayed* for review⟩ **2 :** to dress especially in fine clothing : ADORN — **ar·ray·er** *n*

²array *n* **1 :** regular order or arrangement; *also* : persons (as troops) in array **2 :** rich or beautiful clothing **3 :** an

\ə\ abut	\aù\ out	\i\ tip	\ò\ saw	\ù\ foot
\ər\ further	\ch\ chin	\ī\ life	\òi\ coin	\y\ yet
\a\ mat	\e\ pet	\j\ job	\th\ thin	\yü\ few
\ā\ take	\ē\ easy	\ŋ\ sing	\th\ this	\yù\ cure
\ä\ cot, cart	\g\ go	\ō\ bone	\ü\ food	\zh\ vision

impressive group   **4** : a group of mathematical elements (as numbers or letters) arranged in rows and columns

ar·rears \ə-'ri(ə)rz\ *n pl*   **1** : the state of being behind in the paying of debts ⟨two months in *arrears*⟩   **2** : unpaid and overdue debts

¹ar·rest \ə-'rest\ *vb*   **1** : to stop the progress or movement of : CHECK ⟨*arrest* a disease⟩   **2** : to take or keep in one's control by authority of law ⟨*arrest* someone on suspicion of robbery⟩   **3** : to attract and hold the attention of ⟨colors that *arrest* the eye⟩

²arrest *n*   **1 a** : the act of stopping : CHECK   **b** : the state of being stopped   **2** : the act of taking or holding in one's control by authority of law

ar·rest·ing \ə-'res-tiŋ\ *adj* : catching the attention ⟨an *arresting* painting⟩

ar·riv·al \ə-'rī-vəl\ *n*   **1** : the act of arriving ⟨await the *arrival* of guests⟩   **2** : a person or thing that has arrived ⟨late *arrivals* at a concert⟩

ar·rive \ə-'rīv\ *vb* **ar·rived; ar·riv·ing**   **1** : to reach the place one started out for ⟨*arrive* home at six o'clock⟩   **2** : to gain a goal or object ⟨*arrive* at a decision⟩   **3** : COME   **4** ⟨the time *arrived* to begin⟩   **4** : to be successful

ar·ro·gance \'ar-ə-gən(t)s\ *n* : a sense of one's own importance that shows itself in a proud and insulting way

ar·ro·gant \'ar-ə-gənt\ *adj*   **1** : overly proud of oneself or one's own opinions   **2** : marked by arrogance ⟨*arrogant* remarks⟩ — **ar·ro·gant·ly** *adv*

ar·ro·gate \'ar-ə-ˌgāt\ *vb* **-gat·ed; -gat·ing**   **1** : to take or claim for one's own without right   **2** : to attribute to another especially without good reason — **ar·ro·ga·tion** \ˌar-ə-'gā-shən\ *n*

ar·row \'ar-ō\ *n*   **1** : a weapon that is made to be shot from a bow and is usually a stick with a point at one end and feathers at the other   **2** : a mark (as on a map) to show direction

ar·row·head \-ˌhed\ *n*   **1** : the wedge-shaped striking end of an arrow   **2** : something (as a mark) resembling an arrowhead

ar·row·root \-ˌrüt, -ˌru̇t\ *n*   **1** : any of several tropical American plants with starchy roots   **2** : an edible starch from arrowroot

arrow worm *n* : any of a small phylum of transparent marine worms

ar·royo \ə-'rȯi-ə, -'rȯi-(ˌ)ō\ *n, pl* **-royos**   **1** : a waterway (as a creek) in a dry region   **2** : an often dry gully or channel

ar·se·nal \'ärs-nəl, -ᵊn-əl\ *n*   **1** : a place for the manufacture or storage of arms   **2** : a collection of weapons

ar·se·nic \'ärs-nik, -ᵊn-ik\ *n*   **1** : a solid poisonous element that is commonly metallic steel-gray and brittle — see ELEMENT table   **2** : a white or transparent extremely poisonous oxide of arsenic used in making glass and insecticides

ar·se·no·py·rite \ˌärs-ᵊn-ō-'pī-ˌrīt\ *n* : a hard bluish or grayish white mineral consisting of iron, arsenic, and sulfur

ar·sine \är-'sēn, 'är-ˌsēn\ *n* : a colorless flammable extremely poisonous gas with an odor like garlic

ar·son \'är-sᵊn\ *n* : the illegal burning of a building or other property — **ar·son·ist** \-əst\ *n*

¹art \(')ärt, ərt\ *archaic present 2d sing of* BE [Old English *eart* "art"]

²art \'ärt\ *n*   **1** : skill that comes through experience or study ⟨the *art* of making friends⟩   **2** : a branch of learning; *esp* : one of the liberal arts — usually used in pl. ⟨a degree in *arts*⟩   **3** : an occupation that requires knowledge or skill ⟨cooking is an *art*⟩   **4** : the use of skill and creativity especially in the making of things that are beautiful to look at, listen to, or read   **5** : the works (as pictures, poems, or songs) produced by artists [Middle English *art* "art, skill", from early French *art* (same meaning), from Latin *art-, ars* "skill"]

ar·te·ri·al \är-'tir-ē-əl\ *adj*   **1 a** : of or relating to an artery   **b** : being the bright red oxygen-rich blood present in most arteries   **2** : of, relating to, or being routes for through traffic ⟨*arterial* highways⟩ — **ar·te·ri·al·ly** \-ē-ə-lē\ *adv*

ar·te·ri·ole \är-'tir-ē-ˌōl\ *n* : a very small artery connecting a larger artery to capillaries — **ar·te·ri·o·lar** \är-ˌtir-ē-'ō-ˌlär, -lər\ *adj*

ar·te·rio·scle·ro·sis \är-ˌtir-ē-ō-sklə-'rō-səs\ *n* : a disease characterized by abnormal thickening and hardening of the walls of the arteries — **ar·te·rio·scle·rot·ic** \-'rät-ik\ *adj or n*

ar·tery \'ärt-ə-rē\ *n, pl* **-ter·ies**   **1** : one of the tube-shaped branching muscular-walled and elastic-walled vessels that carry blood from the heart to all parts of the body   **2** : a channel (as a river or highway) of transportation or communication; *esp* : the main channel in a branching system

ar·te·sian well \är-ˌtē-zhən-\ *n*   **1** : a bored well from which water flows up like a fountain   **2** : a deep-bored well

art·ful \'ärt-fəl\ *adj*   **1** : done with or showing art or skill   **2** : clever at taking advantage — **art·ful·ly** \-fə-lē\ *adv* — **art·ful·ness** *n*

ar·thri·tis \är-'thrīt-əs\ *n* : inflammation of the joints — **ar·thrit·ic** \-'thrit-ik\ *adj or n*

ar·thro·pod \'är-thrə-ˌpäd\ *n* : any of a phylum of animals without backbones (as insects, arachnids, and crustaceans) having a segmented body, jointed limbs, and a shell of chitin that is shed periodically — **arthropod** *adj*

ar·ti·choke \'ärt-ə-ˌchōk\ *n* : a tall plant of the aster family with a flower head cooked and eaten as a vegetable

ar·ti·cle \'ärt-i-kəl\ *n*   **1** : a separate part of a document dealing with a single subject ⟨the third *article* of the U.S. Constitution⟩   **2** : a piece of writing other than fiction or poetry that forms an independent part of a publication (as a magazine)   **3** : a word (as *a, an,* or *the*) used with a noun to limit it or make it clearer   **4** : a member of a class of things ⟨*articles* of clothing⟩

ar·tic·u·lar \är-'tik-yə-lər\ *adj* : of or relating to a joint

¹ar·tic·u·late \är-'tik-yə-lət\ *adj*   **1 a** : clearly understandable   **b** : able to express oneself clearly and well   **2** : consisting of segments united by joints : JOINTED ⟨*articulate* animals⟩ — **ar·tic·u·late·ly** *adv* — **ar·tic·u·late·ness** *n*

²ar·tic·u·late \är-'tik-yə-ˌlāt\ *vb* **-lat·ed; -lat·ing**   **1 a** : to speak in clear syllables or words   **b** : to express clearly   **2** : to unite or become united or connected by or as if by a joint — **ar·tic·u·la·tor** \-ˌlāt-ər\ *n*

ar·tic·u·la·tion \(ˌ)är-ˌtik-yə-'lā-shən\ *n*   **1** : the making of articulate sounds (as in pronunciation)   **2** : a joint between rigid parts of an animal; *esp* : one between bones or cartilages

ar·ti·fact \'ärt-i-ˌfakt\ *n* : a usually simple object (as a tool or ornament) showing human work and representing a culture or a stage in the development of a culture

ar·ti·fice \'ärt-ə-fəs\ *n*   **1 a** : a clever device : TRICK   **b** : false or dishonest behavior ⟨social *artifice*⟩   **2** : clever skill ⟨a vase made with much *artifice*⟩

ar·ti·fi·cer \är-'tif-ə-sər, 'ärt-ə-fə-sər\ *n* : a skilled or artistic worker

ar·ti·fi·cial \ˌärt-ə-'fish-əl\ *adj*   **1** : made, produced, or performed by human beings often following a natural model or process ⟨*artificial* flowers⟩ ⟨*artificial* pollination⟩   **2** : not genuine or sincere : FORCED ⟨an *artificial* smile⟩ [Middle English *artificial* "made or done by humans rather than occurring in nature", from early French *artificial* (same meaning) or Latin *artificialis* "according to the rules of art", from Latin *artificium* "the making of something by art or skill", derived from *arti-* (from *art-, ars* "skill") and *facere* "to make, do" — related to FASHION, MANUFACTURE, PERFECT] — **ar·ti·fi·ci·al·i·ty** \ˌärt-ə-ˌfish-ē-'al-ət-ē\ *n* — **ar·ti·fi·cial·ly** \ˌärt-ə-'fish-(ə-)lē\ *adv*

artificial heart *n* : a device designed to maintain the flow of blood to the tissues of the body especially during a surgical operation on the heart

artificial intelligence *n* : the power of a machine to imitate intelligent human behavior

artificial respiration *n* : the rhythmic forcing of air into and out of the lungs of a person whose breathing has stopped

artificial selection *n* : the process of modifying organisms (as domestic plants and animals) by selective breeding controlled by human beings

ar·til·lery \är-'til-(ə-)rē\ *n, pl* **-ler·ies 1** : large firearms (as cannon or rockets) : ORDNANCE **2** : a branch of an army armed with artillery — **ar·til·lery·man** \-mən\ *n*

ar·ti·san \'ärt-ə-zən, -sən\ *n* : a skilled worker; *esp* : one (as a carpenter) whose occupation requires skill with the hands

art·ist \'ärt-əst\ *n* **1** : a person skilled in one of the arts (as painting, sculpture, music, or writing) **2** : a person showing unusual ability in an occupation requiring skill

ar·tis·tic \är-'tis-tik\ *adj* **1** : relating to or characteristic of art or artists **2** : showing skill and imagination — **ar·tis·ti·cal·ly** \-'tis-ti-k(ə-)lē\ *adv*

art·ist·ry \'ärt-ə-strē\ *n* **1** : artistic quality of effect or workmanship ⟨the *artistry* of her novel⟩ **2** : artistic ability

art·less \'ärt-ləs\ *adj* **1** : lacking art, knowledge, or skill : UNCULTURED **2 a** : made without skill : RUDE **b** : being simple and sincere : NATURAL ⟨*artless* grace⟩ **3** : not trying to deceive others — **art·less·ly** *adv* — **art·less·ness** *n*

ar·um \'ar-əm, 'er-\ *n* : any of a family of plants (as the jack-in-the-pulpit or the skunk cabbage) having heart-shaped or sword-shaped leaves and flowers in a fleshy spike enclosed in a leafy covering

arum

¹-ary *usually* ˌer-ē *after an unstressed syllable*, ə-rē *or* rē *after a stressed syllable*\ *n suffix, pl* **-aries** : thing or person belonging to or connected with ⟨bound*ary*⟩ [derived from Latin *-arius*, *-aria*, *-arium* (noun suffix), from *-arius* (adjective suffix)]

²-ary *adj suffix* : of, relating to, or connected with ⟨legend*ary*⟩ [derived from Latin *-arius* (adjective suffix)]

Ary·an \'ar-ē-ən, 'er-, 'är-yən\ *n* **1** : a member of the Indo-European-speaking people first living in Iran and later entering India and conquering the people living there **2 a** : a member of the people speaking the language from which the Indo-European languages are derived **b** : a member of any of the peoples speaking an Indo-European language — **Aryan** *adj*

¹as \əz, (ˌ)az\ *adv* **1** : to the same degree or amount ⟨*as* cold as ice⟩ ⟨a number twice *as* large⟩ **2** : for example ⟨various trees, *as* oak or pine⟩

²as *conj* **1** : in or to the same degree that ⟨mad *as* a hornet⟩ **2** : in the way or manner that ⟨do *as* I say⟩ **3** : at the same time that ⟨WHILE, WHEN⟩ ⟨sang *as* they marched along⟩ **4** : ²THOUGH ⟨improbable *as* it seems, it's true⟩ **5** : BECAUSE, SINCE ⟨stayed home, *as* I had no car⟩ **6** : that the result is ⟨so clearly guilty *as* to leave no doubt⟩— **as is** : in the present condition without any changes ⟨bought the clock at an auction *as is*⟩

³as *pron* **1** : ¹THAT, WHO, WHICH — used after *same* or *such* ⟨had the same name *as* my cousin⟩ **2** : a fact that ⟨they are smart, *as* you know⟩ ⟨*as* I said before, it's time to go⟩

⁴as *prep* **1** : ⁴LIKE **2** ⟨came dressed *as* a clown⟩ **2** : in the position or role of ⟨working *as* an editor⟩

as- — see AD-

asa·fet·i·da *or* **asa·foe·ti·da** \ˌas-ə-'fit-əd-ē, -'fet-əd-ə\ *n* : a hard gum that has an unpleasant smell and taste, comes from several oriental plants related to the carrot, and was once thought to prevent disease

as·bes·tos \as-'bes-təs, az-\ *n* : a grayish mineral that easily separates into long flexible fibers, that is used to make materials that are fireproof, do not conduct electricity, and are chemically resistant, and that can cause serious lung disease if inhaled as a dust

as·cend \ə-'send\ *vb* : to go up : CLIMB, RISE ⟨*ascend* a hill⟩ ⟨smoke *ascends*⟩ — **as·cend·able** *or* **as·cend·ible** \-'sen-də-bəl\ *adj*

as·cen·dan·cy \ə-'sen-dən-sē\ *or* **as·cen·dance** \-dən(t)s\ *n* : controlling influence

¹as·cen·dant \ə-'sen-dənt\ *n* : a state or position of commanding power

²ascendant *adj* **1** : moving up : RISING **2 a** : in a superior position **b** : inclined to control

as·cen·sion \ə-'sen-chən\ *n* : the act or process of ascending

Ascension Day *n* : the Thursday 40 days after Easter observed by Christians in honor of Christ's ascension into heaven after the Resurrection

as·cent \ə-'sent, a-\ *n* **1** : the act of rising or climbing up **2** : an upward slope

as·cer·tain \ˌas-ər-'tān\ *vb* : to learn with certainty : FIND OUT — **as·cer·tain·able** \-'tā-nə-bəl\ *adj* — **as·cer·tain·ment** \-'tān-mənt\ *n*

as·cet·ic \ə-'set-ik, a-\ *adj* **1** : following a practice of not giving in to one's desires especially as a means of religious discipline ⟨an *ascetic* way of life⟩ **2** : harshly simple : AUSTERE ⟨*ascetic* surroundings⟩ — **ascetic** *n* — **as·cet·i·cism** \ə-'set-ə-ˌsiz-əm\ *n*

ASCII \'as-(ˌ)kē\ *n* : a computer code for expressing numerals, letters of the alphabet, and other symbols [*A*merican *S*tandard *C*ode for *I*nformation *I*nterchange]

as·co·my·cete \ˌas-kō-'mī-ˌsēt, -mī-'sēt\ *n* : any of a class of higher fungi (as yeasts and molds) that have the hyphae divided by partitions and the spores produced in sacs — called also *sac fungus*

ascor·bic acid \ə-ˌskȯr-bik-\ *n* : VITAMIN C

as·cot \'as-kət, -ˌkät\ *n* : a broad neck scarf that is looped under the chin

as·cribe \ə-'skrīb\ *vb* **as·cribed; as·crib·ing** : to think of as coming from a specified cause, source, or author — **as·crib·able** \-'skrī-bə-bəl\ *adj*

as·crip·tion \ə-'skrip-shən\ *n* : the act of ascribing : ATTRIBUTION

-ase \ˌās, ˌāz\ *n suffix* : enzyme ⟨malt*ase*⟩ [French *-ase* (suffix), from the enzyme diast*ase*]

asep·sis \(')ā-'sep-səs, ə-\ *n* : the condition of being aseptic; *also* : the methods of making or keeping aseptic

asep·tic \(')ā-'sep-tik, ə-\ *adj* : preventing infection; *also* : free or freed from disease-causing germs — **asep·ti·cal·ly** \-ti-k(ə-)lē\ *adv*

asex·u·al \(')ā-'seksh-(ə-)wəl, -'sek-shəl\ *adj* **1** : lacking sex ⟨*asexual* organisms⟩ **2** : occurring or formed without the production and union of two kinds of germ cells ⟨*asexual* reproduction⟩ ⟨*asexual* spores⟩ — **asex·u·al·ly** \-ē\ *adv*

as for *prep* : CONCERNING ⟨*as for* me⟩

As·gard \'as-ˌgärd, 'az-\ *n* : the home of the Norse gods

¹ash \'ash\ *n* **1** : any of a genus of trees related to the olive and having bark with grooves and ridges and winged seeds **2** : the tough elastic wood of an ash [Old English *æsc* "ash tree"]

²ash *n* **1 a** : the solid that remains after material is thoroughly burned or is oxidized by chemical means **b** : fine particles of mineral matter from a volcanic vent **2** *pl* : the remains of something destroyed : RUINS **3** *pl* : the remains of the dead human body especially after cremation [Old English *asce* "the remains of something burned"]

\ə\ abut		\au̇\ **out**	\i\ **tip**	\ȯ\ **saw**	\u̇\ **foot**
\ər\ **further**	\ch\ **chin**		\ī\ **life**	\ȯi\ **coin**	\y\ **yet**
\a\ **mat**	\e\ **pet**		\j\ **job**	\th\ **thin**	\yü\ **few**
\ā\ **take**	\ē\ **easy**		\ŋ\ **sing**	\th\ **this**	\yu̇\ **cure**
\ä\ **cot, cart**	\g\ **go**		\ō\ **bone**	\ü\ **food**	\zh\ **vision**

ashamed \ə-'shāmd\ *adj* **1** : feeling shame, guilt, or disgrace ⟨*ashamed* of my behavior⟩ **2** : kept from doing something by a sense of shame ⟨*ashamed* to beg⟩ — **asham·ed·ly** \-'shā-məd-lē\ *adv*

Ashan·ti \ə-'shant-ē, -'shänt-\ *n, pl* **Ashanti** *or* **Ashantis** : a member of a people of southern Ghana

ash·en \'ash-ən\ *adj* **1** : of the color of ashes **2** : deadly pale

ashore \ə-'shō(ə)r, -'shö(ə)r\ *adv or adj* : on or to the shore

ash·tray \'ash-,trā\ *n* : a container for tobacco ashes and for cigar and cigarette butts

Ash Wednesday *n* : the first day of Lent

ashy \'ash-ē\ *adj* **ash·i·er; -est** **1** : of, relating to, or resembling ashes **2** : ASHEN 2

Asian \'ā-zhən, 'ā-shən\ *adj* : of, relating to, or characteristic of Asia or its people — **Asian** *n*

Asi·at·ic \,ā-zhē-'at-ik, -zē-\ *adj* : ASIAN — sometimes taken to be offensive — **Asiatic** *n*

¹aside \ə-'sīd\ *adv* **1** : to or toward the side ⟨stepped *aside*⟩ **2** : out of the way especially for future use : AWAY ⟨put money *aside* for school⟩ **3** : away from one's thought or consideration ⟨all kidding *aside*⟩

²aside *n* : words meant not to be heard by someone; *esp* : an actor's words supposedly not heard by others on the stage

aside from *prep* : with the exception of : EXCEPT FOR ⟨*aside from* a few pieces of bread, the food is gone⟩

as if *conj* **1** : the way it would be if ⟨it was *as if* we had never left⟩ **2** : the way one would do if ⟨they acted *as if* they'd never heard of us⟩ **3** : ³THAT 1a ⟨it seemed *as if* the day would never end⟩

as·i·nine \'as-ᵊn-,īn\ *adj* : marked by inexcusable failure to use one's intelligence or sound judgment ⟨an *asinine* excuse⟩ — **as·i·nine·ly** *adv* — **as·i·nin·i·ty** \,as-ᵊn-'in-ət-ē\ *n*

ask \'ask, 'åsk\ *vb* **1** : to seek information : INQUIRE ⟨*asked* about our trip to California⟩ **2 a** : to make a request ⟨*ask* for help⟩ **b** : to make a request to ⟨*ask* your teacher to help you⟩ **3** : to set as a price : DEMAND ⟨*ask* $20 for the bicycle⟩ **4** : ¹INVITE 2a ⟨we are *asking* a few friends to a party⟩ **5** : to behave as if looking ⟨*asking* for trouble⟩ — **ask·er** *n*

askance \ə-'skan(t)s\ *adv* **1** : with a side glance **2** : with distrust or disapproval

askew \ə-'skyü\ *adv or adj* : AWRY 1

aslant \ə-'slant\ *adv or adj* : in a slanting direction

¹asleep \ə-'slēp\ *adj* **1** : being in a state of sleep **2** : lacking sensation : NUMB ⟨my foot was *asleep*⟩

²asleep *adv* : into a state of sleep

as of *prep* : ¹ON 3, AT ⟨we begin work *as of* Tuesday⟩ ⟨*as of* the moment, things are fine⟩

asp \'asp\ *n* : a small poisonous snake of Egypt

as·par·a·gus \ə-'spar-ə-gəs\ *n* : a tall branching long-lived herb related to the lily and widely grown for its thick edible young shoots

as·par·tic acid \ə-,spärt-ik-\ *n* : an amino acid found especially in plants

as·pect \'as-,pekt\ *n* **1** : a position facing a certain direction : EXPOSURE **2** : a certain way in which something appears or may be regarded ⟨studied every *aspect* of the question⟩ **3** : the appearance of an individual : LOOK

aspect ratio *n* : a comparison of one dimension (as width) to another (as height)

as·pen \'as-pən\ *n* : any of several poplars with leaves that flutter in the lightest breeze

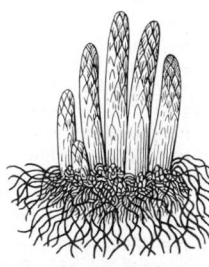

asparagus

as·per·i·ty \a-'sper-ət-ē, ə-'sper-\ *n, pl* **-ties** **1** : something making for hardship : RIGOR, SEVERITY **2** : harshness of temper, manner, or tone

as·perse \ə-'spərs, a-\ *vb* **as·persed; as·pers·ing** : to attack with evil reports or false charges : SLANDER

as·per·sion \ə-'spər-zhən\ *n* : an evil report or false charge ⟨cast *aspersions* on a person⟩

¹as·phalt \'as-,fölt\ *n* **1** : a brown to black substance that is found in natural beds or obtained as something left in petroleum or coal-tar refining and that consists chiefly of compounds of carbon and hydrogen **2** : any of various compositions of asphalt having different uses (as for pavement or for waterproof cement or paint) — **as·phal·tic** \as-'föl-tik\ *adj*

²asphalt *vb* : to cover with asphalt

as·pho·del \'as-fə-,del\ *n* : any of several herbs related to the lilies and bearing white or yellow flowers in long upright spikes

as·phyx·ia \as-'fik-sē-ə\ *n* : a lack of oxygen or excess of carbon dioxide in the body usually caused by interruption of breathing and resulting in unconsciousness

as·phyx·i·ate \as-'fik-sē-,āt\ *vb* **-at·ed; -at·ing** : to cause asphyxia in; *also* : to kill or make unconsious by interference with the normal oxygen intake — **as·phyx·i·a·tion** \(,)as-,fik-sē-'ā-shən\ *n*

as·pic \'as-pik\ *n* : a jelly of fish or meat stock used especially to make a mold of meat, fish, or vegetables

as·pi·dis·tra \,as-pə-'dis-trə\ *n* : an Asian plant related to the lilies, having large leaves at the base of the stem, and often grown as a houseplant

as·pi·rant \'as-p(ə-)rənt, ə-'spī-rənt\ *n* : a person who aspires

¹as·pi·rate \'as-pə-,rāt\ *vb* **-rat·ed; -rat·ing** **1** : to pronounce with an initial *h*-sound **2** : to draw or remove by suction

²as·pi·rate \'as-p(ə-)rət\ *n* : the sound \h\ or a letter or symbol representing it

as·pi·ra·tion \,as-pə-'rā-shən\ *n* **1** : pronunciation with or as an aspirate **2** : a drawing of something in, out, up, or through by suction **3 a** : a strong desire to achieve something high or great **b** : an object of such desire

as·pi·ra·tor \'as-pə-,rāt-ər\ *n* : an apparatus for producing suction or moving or collecting materials by suction

as·pire \ə-'spī(ə)r\ *vb* **as·pired; as·pir·ing** : to work to get something high or great — **as·pir·er** *n*

as·pi·rin \'as-p(ə-)rən\ *n* **1** : a white drug used as a remedy for pain and fever **2** : a tablet of aspirin

ass \'as\ *n* **1** : any of several mammals resembling but smaller than the related horses and having a shorter mane, shorter hair on the tail, and longer ears; *esp* : DONKEY **2** : a stupid or stubborn person

as·sail \ə-'sā(ə)l\ *vb* : to attack violently with blows or words — **as·sail·able** \-'sā-lə-bəl\ *adj* — **as·sail·ant** \-'sā-lənt\ *n*

as·sas·sin \ə-'sas-ən\ *n* : a person who kills another person; *esp* : one who murders a politically important person either for pay or from loyalty to a cause

> **Word History** During the time of the Crusades the members of a secret Muslim group thought it was their religious duty to murder their enemies. Before they killed, members of this group took the drug hashish. The killers thus were known as *hashshāshīn*, an Arabic word meaning "people who smoke or chew hashish". The word was brought back to Europe by the Crusaders and passed into Latin and from there into other European languages. In time the English word *assassin* came to mean any murderer, although it is most often applied to one who murders an important person for money or political reasons. [from Latin *assassinus* "a Muslim murderer", from Arabic *hashshāshīn*, plural of *hashshāsh* "one who smokes or chews hashish"]

as·sas·si·nate \ə-'sas-ᵊn-,āt\ *vb* **-nat·ed; -nat·ing** : to murder a usually important person by a surprise or secret attack   **syn** see KILL — **as·sas·si·na·tion** \ə-,sas-ᵊn-'ā-shən\ *n*

as·sault \ə-'sòlt\ *n*   **1** : a violent or sudden attack   **2** : an unlawful attempt or threat to do harm to another [Middle English *assaut* "assault", from early French *assaut* (same meaning), derived from Latin *assilire, adsilire* "to leap upon", from *as-, ad-* "to, toward" and *salire* "to leap, spring" — related to INSULT, RESILIENT] — **assault** *vb*

¹as·say \'as-,ā, a-'sā\ *n* : examination (as of an ore, metal, or drug) for the purpose of determining the presence, absence, or amount of one or more substances

²as·say \a-'sā, 'as-,ā\ *vb*   **1** : ¹TRY 4, ATTEMPT   **2** : to analyze (as an ore) for one or more valuable substances — **as·say·er** *n*

as·sem·blage \ə-'sem-blij, *for 3 also* ,as-,äm-'bläzh\ *n*   **1** : a collection or gathering of persons or things   **2** : the act of assembling   **3** : an artistic composition made by putting together scraps or junk

as·sem·ble \ə-'sem-bəl\ *vb* **-bled; -bling** \-b(ə-)liŋ\   **1** : to collect into one place or group ⟨*assembled* the crew⟩   **2** : to fit together the parts of ⟨*assemble* a toy⟩   **3** : to meet together ⟨the right to *assemble* peacefully⟩ [Middle English *assemblen* "to bring together, assemble", from early French *assembler* (same meaning), derived from Latin *ad-* "to" and *simul* "together" — related to ENSEMBLE, SIMULTANEOUS]   **syn** see GATHER

as·sem·bler \ə-'sem-b(ə-)lər\ *n*   **1** : one that assembles   **2** : a computer program that turns assembly language into machine language

as·sem·bly \ə-'sem-blē\ *n, pl* **-blies**   **1** : a body of persons gathered together (as to make laws or for discussion, worship, or entertainment)   **2** *often cap* : a governing body; *esp* : the lower house of a legislature   **3** : the act of gathering together or state of being assembled   **4** : a signal for troops to assemble   **5** : a collection of parts that go to make up a complete machine, structure, or unit of a machine   **6** : the translation of assembly language to machine language by an assembler

assembly language *n* : a code for programming a computer that is a close approximation of machine language but is more easily understood by humans

assembly line *n* : an arrangement of machines, equipment, and workers in which work passes from operation to operation in direct line until the product is assembled

as·sem·bly·man \ə-'sem-blē-mən\ *n* : a member of a legislative assembly

as·sem·bly·wom·an \-,wùm-ən\ *n* : a woman who is a member of a legislative assembly

as·sent \ə-'sent, a-\ *vb* : to give one's approval : agree to something — **assent** *n*

as·sert \ə-'sərt, a-\ *vb*   **1** : to state clearly and strongly   **2** : to make others aware of ⟨*assert* your rights⟩

  syn ASSERT, DECLARE, AFFIRM, AVOW mean to state positively usually in the face of denial or objection. ASSERT suggests declaring with confidence often without need for proof or evidence ⟨I *assert* that our team can win the game⟩ DECLARE stresses an open or public statement ⟨*declared* that he would run for the senate⟩ AFFIRM suggests a firm belief based on evidence, experience, or faith ⟨*affirmed* that there is good in everyone⟩ AVOW suggests an open and forceful statement that declares responsibility ⟨the newspaper *avowed* responsibility for its mistake⟩

  —assert oneself : to act or speak up so others are aware of one's interests and opinions

as·ser·tion \ə-'sər-shən, a-\ *n* : the act of asserting; *also* : something asserted : DECLARATION

as·ser·tive \ə-'sərt-iv, a-\ *adj* : having a bold or confident manner — **as·ser·tive·ly** *adv* — **as·ser·tive·ness** *n*

as·sess \ə-'ses, a-\ *vb*   **1** : to set the rate or amount of ⟨the jury *assessed* damages of $5000⟩   **2** : to set a value

on (as property) for tax purposes ⟨a house *assessed* at $63,000⟩   **3** : to put a tax or charge on ⟨the city *assessed* all car owners five dollars⟩   **4** : to find out or decide the importance, size, or value of — **as·sess·able** \-'ses-ə-bəl\ *adj*

as·sess·ment \ə-'ses-mənt, a-\ *n*   **1** : the act of assessing   **2** : the amount or value assessed

as·ses·sor \ə-'ses-ər\ *n* : an official who assesses property for taxes

as·set \'as-,et\ *n*   **1** *pl* : all the property of a person, corporation, or estate that may be used in payment of debts   **2** : a quality or thing that can be used to advantage

as·sid·u·ous \ə-'sij-(ə-)wəs\ *adj* : constantly attentive : DILIGENT — **as·si·du·ity** \,as-ə-'d(y)ü-ət-ē\ *n* — **as·sid·u·ous·ly** *adv* — **as·sid·u·ous·ness** *n*

as·sign \ə-'sīn\ *vb*   **1** : to give (as a title or right) to someone legally   **2** : to pick for a specific use or job ⟨*assign* new campers to work in the kitchen⟩   **3** : to give out as a portion, share, or responsibility ⟨parts in the play were *assigned* to each person⟩ ⟨*assign* homework⟩   **4** : to give a certain quality, role, or importance to ⟨events *assigned* to certain periods of history⟩ ⟨*assign* number values to different letters⟩ — **as·sign·able** \ə-'sī-nə-bəl\ *adj* — **as·sign·er** \ə-'sī-nər\ *or* **as·sign·or** \ə-'sī-nər; ,as-ə-'nò(ə)r, ,as-,ī-, ə-,sī-\ *n* — **as·sign·ment** \ə-'sīn-mənt\ *n*

as·sign·ee \,as-ə-'nē, ,as-,ī-, ə-,sī-\ *n* : a person to whom something is assigned

as·sim·i·late \ə-'sim-ə-,lāt\ *vb* **-lat·ed; -lat·ing** : to take something in and make it part of the thing it has joined

as·sim·i·la·tion \ə-,sim-ə-'lā-shən\ *n* : the act or process of assimilating; *esp* : the bodily process of changing nutrients (as digested food) into protoplasm

¹as·sist \ə-'sist\ *vb* : to give support or aid : HELP

²assist *n*   **1** : an act of assisting   **2** : the action of a player who by passing a ball or puck makes it possible for a teammate to make a putout or score a goal

as·sis·tance \ə-'sis-tən(t)s\ *n* : the act of assisting; *also* : the help given

as·sis·tant \ə-'sis-tənt\ *n* : a person who assists another : HELPER — **assistant** *adj*

as·size \ə-'sīz\ *n* : a session of an English court formerly held by judges traveling on circuit — usually used in pl.

¹as·so·ci·ate \ə-'sō-shē-,āt, -sē-,āt\ *vb* **-at·ed; -at·ing**   **1** : to join or come together as partners, friends, or companions   **2** : to connect in thought ⟨*associate* soldiers with war⟩   **3** : to combine or join with other parts : UNITE [Middle English *associat* "connected, related", derived from Latin *associare* "to write", from *ad-* "to" and *sociare* "to join", from *socius* "companion" — related to SOCIABLE]

²as·so·ci·ate \ə-'sō-shē-ət, -sē-ət, -shət, -shē-,āt, -sē-,āt\ *n*   **1** : a fellow worker : COLLEAGUE   **2** : ¹COMPANION 1, FRIEND   **3** *often cap* : a degree given especially by a junior college ⟨*associate* in arts⟩ — **associate** *adj*

as·so·ci·a·tion \ə-,sō-sē-'ā-shən, -,sō-shē-\ *n*   **1** : the act of associating : the state of being associated   **2** : an organization of persons having a common interest ⟨an athletic *association*⟩   **3** : a feeling, memory, or thought connected with a person, place, or thing ⟨pleasant *associations* with the beach⟩   **4** : the formation of loosely bound groups of ions or molecules

association area *n* : an area of the brain that links and coordinates other areas of the brain

association neuron *n* : INTERNUNCIAL NEURON

as·so·cia·tive \ə-'sō-shē-,āt-iv, -sē-, -shət-iv\ *adj*   **1** : of or relating to association   **2** : of, having, or being the property of producing the same result no matter which pair of

\ə\ abut	\aù\ out	\i\ tip	\ò\ saw	\ù\ foot
\ər\ further	\ch\ chin	\ī\ life	\òi\ coin	\y\ yet
\a\ mat	\e\ pet	\j\ job	\th\ thin	\yü\ few
\ā\ take	\ē\ easy	\ŋ\ sing	\th\ this	\yù\ cure
\ä\ cot, cart	\g\ go	\ō\ bone	\ü\ food	\zh\ vision

elements next to each other in a mathematical expression are used to perform a given operation first if the elements in the expression are listed in a fixed order ⟨addition of the real numbers is *associative* because $(a + b) + c = a + (b + c)$ if *a*, *b*, and *c* are any real numbers⟩ — **as·so·cia·tive·ly** *adv* — **as·so·cia·tiv·i·ty** \ə-ˌsō-shē-ə-'tiv-ət-ē, -ˌsō-sē-, -ˌsō-shə-'tiv-\ *n*

as·so·nance \'as-ə-nən(t)s\ *n* : the repetition of vowel sounds but not consonants in words (as "red hen") for poetic effect — **as·so·nant** \-nənt\ *adj*

as soon as *conj* : immediately at or just after the time that ⟨left *as soon as* the meeting was over⟩

as·sort \ə-'so(ə)rt\ *vb* : to sort into groups

as·sort·ed \ə-'sort-əd\ *adj* **1** : consisting of various kinds ⟨*assorted* cheeses⟩ **2** : matching or fitting together ⟨an ill-*assorted* pair⟩

as·sort·ment \ə-'so(ə)rt-mənt\ *n* **1 a** : arrangement in classes **b** : the quality or state of being made up of various kinds **2** : a collection of different things

as·suage \ə-'swāj\ *vb* **as·suaged; as·suag·ing** **1** : to lessen or make easier to bear; SOOTHE, EASE **2** : SATISFY 2b, QUENCH — **as·suage·ment** \-mənt\ *n*

as·sume \ə-'süm\ *vb* **as·sumed; as·sum·ing** **1** : to take on as a job or responsibility ⟨*assume* control⟩ ⟨*assumed* the presidency⟩ **2** : to take on as a special quality ⟨it *assumes* greater importance now⟩ **3** : to pretend to have or be : PUT ON ⟨immediately *assumed* a look of innocence⟩ **4** : to take for granted : SUPPOSE ⟨I *assumed* he knew⟩

as·sump·tion \ə-'səm(p)-shən\ *n* **1** *cap* : August 15 observed as a church festival to mark the taking up of the Virgin Mary into heaven **2 a** : the act of assuming **b** : the belief that something is true **3** : a fact or statement taken for granted

as·sur·ance \ə-'shür-ən(t)s\ *n* **1** : the act of assuring **2** : the state of being sure or certain **3** *chiefly British* : IN-SURANCE 2 **4** : SELF-CONFIDENCE

as·sure \ə-'shü(ə)r\ *vb* **as·sured; as·sur·ing** **1** : to provide a guarantee of ⟨*assure* security⟩ **2** : to give words of comfort or confidence to : REASSURE ⟨tried to *assure* the worried children⟩ **3** : to cause to be sure or certain ⟨*assure* himself that the door was locked⟩ **4** : to inform positively ⟨can *assure* you of her dependability⟩

as·sured \ə-'shü(ə)rd\ *adj* **1** : made sure or certain **2** : very confident — **as·sur·ed·ly** \-'shür-əd-lē\ *adv* — **as·sur·ed·ness** \-əd-nəs\ *n*

as·ta·tine \'as-tə-ˌtēn\ *n* : a radioactive element discovered by bombarding bismuth with helium nuclei — see ELEMENT table

as·ter \'as-tər\ *n* : any of various mostly fall-blooming leafy-stemmed herbs of the daisy family usually with showy white, pink, purple, or yellow flower heads

as·ter·isk \'as-tə-ˌrisk\ *n* : a symbol * used especially to refer a reader to a note [Middle English *asterichos, asteriscus* "asterisk", derived from Greek *asteriskos*, literally "little star", from *aster-, astēr* "star"]

astern \ə-'stərn\ *adv* **1** : in, at, or toward the stern **2** : in a reverse direction : BACKWARD ⟨full speed *astern*⟩

as·ter·oid \'as-tə-ˌroid\ *n* : one of thousands of small planets between Mars and Jupiter with diameters from a fraction of a kilometer to nearly 800 kilometers

asteroid belt *n* : the region of interplanetary space between the orbits of Mars and Jupiter in which most asteroids are found

asth·ma \'az-mə\ *n* : a condition that is marked by difficulty in breathing with wheezing, a feeling of tightness in the chest, and coughing — **asth·mat·ic** \az-'mat-ik\ *adj or n* — **asth·mat·i·cal·ly** \-'mat-i-k(ə-)lē\ *adv*

as though *conj* : AS IF

astig·ma·tism \ə-'stig-mə-ˌtiz-əm\ *n* : a defect of an optical system (as of the eye) that prevents light from focusing accurately and results in a blurred image or unclear vision — **as·tig·mat·ic** \ˌas-tig-'mat-ik\ *adj*

astir \ə-'stər\ *adj* **1** : being in a state of activity : STIRRING **2** : being out of bed : UP

as to *prep* **1** : with respect to : ABOUT ⟨confused *as to* what happened⟩ **2** : ACCORDING TO 1 ⟨graded *as to* size⟩

as·ton·ish \ə-'stän-ish\ *vb* : to strike with sudden wonder or surprise — **as·ton·ish·ing·ly** \-iŋ-lē\ *adv* — **as·ton·ish·ment** \-mənt\ *n*

as·tound \ə-'staùnd\ *vb* : to fill with puzzled wonder

astrad·dle \ə-'strad-ᵊl\ *adv or prep* : ASTRIDE

as·tra·khan \'as-trə-kən, -ˌkan\ *n, often cap* **1** : sheepskin of the karakul lamb **2** : a cloth made to look like karakul sheepskin

as·tral \'as-trəl\ *adj* : of or relating to the stars

astray \ə-'strā\ *adv or adj* **1** : off the right path or route **2** : in or into error

¹astride \ə-'strīd\ *adv* : with one leg on each side

²astride *prep* : with one leg on each side of ⟨*astride* a horse⟩

as·trin·gen·cy \ə-'strin-jən-sē\ *n* : the quality or state of being astringent

¹as·trin·gent \ə-'strin-jənt\ *adj* : able or tending to shrink body tissues ⟨*astringent* lotions⟩ — **as·trin·gent·ly** *adv*

²astringent *n* : an astringent substance

astro- *combining form* : star : heavens : outer space : astronomical ⟨*astrophysics*⟩ [Middle English *astro-* "star", from early French *astro-* (same meaning), derived from Greek *astēr, astron* "star"]

as·tro·labe \'as-trə-ˌlāb\ *n* : an instrument for observing the positions of heavenly bodies that was used before the sextant was invented

astrolabe

as·trol·o·gy \ə-'sträl-ə-jē\ *n* : the study of the supposed influences of the stars on human affairs by their positions in relation to each other — **as·trol·o·ger** \-jər\ *n* — **as·tro·log·i·cal** \ˌas-trə-'läj-i-kəl\ *adj*

as·tro·naut \'as-trə-ˌnòt, -ˌnät\ *n* : a traveler in a spacecraft [from *astro-* "star, heavens" (derived from Greek *astron* "star") and *-naut* (derived from Greek *nautēs* "sailor", from *naus* "ship") — related to NAUSEA, NAUTICAL; see *Word History* at NAUSEA] — **as·tro·nau·tic** \ˌas-trə-'nòt-ik\ *or* **as·tro·nau·ti·cal** \-i-kəl, -nät-\ *adj*

as·tro·nau·tics \ˌas-trə-'nòt-iks, -nät-\ *n* **1** : the science of the construction and operation of spacecraft **2** : navigation in space

as·tro·nom·i·cal \ˌas-trə-'näm-i-kəl\ *also* **as·tro·nom·ic** \-'näm-ik\ *adj* **1** : of or relating to astronomy **2** : extremely or unbelievably large ⟨the cost was *astronomical*⟩ — **as·tro·nom·i·cal·ly** \-'näm-i-k(ə-)lē\ *adv*

astronomical unit *n* : a unit of length used in astronomy equal to the average distance of the earth from the sun or about 93 million miles (150 million kilometers)

as·tron·o·my \ə-'strän-ə-mē\ *n, pl* **-mies** : the science of the heavenly bodies and of their sizes, motions, and composition — **as·tron·o·mer** \-mər\ *n*

as·tro·phys·ics \ˌas-trə-'fiz-iks\ *n* : a branch of astronomy dealing with the physical and chemical measurements of the heavenly bodies — **as·tro·phys·i·cal** \-'fiz-i-kəl\ *adj* — **as·tro·phys·i·cist** \-'fiz-ə-səst\ *n*

as·tute \ə-'st(y)üt, a-\ *adj* **1** : having understanding and the skill to make good choices or decisions : WISE, SHREWD ⟨an *astute* investor⟩ **2** : done or performed in a clever manner — **as·tute·ly** *adv* — **as·tute·ness** *n*

asun·der \ə-'sən-dər\ *adv or adj* **1** : into parts ⟨torn *asunder*⟩ **2** : far apart

¹as well as *conj* : and in addition ⟨catch fish for food *as well as* for sport⟩ ⟨a fabric that is lightweight *as well as* strong⟩

[2]**as well as** *prep* : in addition to : BESIDES ⟨is a real scholar *as well as* being a poet⟩

as yet *adv* : up to the present time : YET

asy·lum \ə-'sī-ləm\ *n* **1** : a place of safety : SHELTER **2** : protection given especially to political refugees **3** : an institution for the care of those unable to care for themselves and especially for the insane

asym·met·ri·cal \ˌā-sə-'me-tri-kəl\ *or* **asym·met·ric** \-trik\ *adj* : not symmetrical — **asym·met·ri·cal·ly** \-tri-k(ə-)lē\ *adv* — **asym·me·try** \(')ā-'sim-ə-trē\ *n*

at \ət, (')at\ *prep* — used to indicate (1) location in space or time ⟨staying *at* a hotel⟩ ⟨be here *at* six⟩ ⟨sick *at* heart⟩, (2) a goal ⟨aim *at* the target⟩ ⟨laugh *at* him⟩, (3) a condition ⟨*at* work⟩ ⟨*at* liberty⟩ ⟨*at* rest⟩, (4) how or why ⟨sold *at* auction⟩ ⟨angry *at* his answer⟩, or (5) rate, degree, or position in a scale or series ⟨the temperature *at* 90⟩ ⟨retire *at* 65⟩

at- — see AD-

at all \ət-'ȯl, ə-'tȯl, at-'ȯl\ *adv* : in any way : under any circumstances ⟨will go anywhere *at all*⟩ ⟨doesn't mind *at all*⟩ ⟨not *at all* likely⟩

at·a·vis·tic \ˌat-ə-'vis-tik\ *adj* : coming from or associated with one's most primitive ancestors ⟨*atavistic* behavior⟩

atax·ia \ə-'tak-sē-ə, (')ā-\ *n* : inability to coordinate voluntary muscular movements — **atax·ic** \-sik\ *adj*

ate *past of* EAT

[1]**-ate** \ət, ˌāt\ *n suffix* : office : function : rank : group of persons holding a specified office or rank [derived from Latin *-atus* (noun suffix)]

[2]**-ate** *adj suffix* **1** : acted on (in a specified way) : brought into or being in a (specified) state ⟨temper*ate*⟩ **2** : marked by having ⟨chord*ate*⟩ [derived from Latin *-atus* (adjective suffix)]

[3]**-ate** \ˌāt\ *vb suffix* **1** : cause to be modified or affected by ⟨hydrogen*ate*⟩ **2** : cause to become ⟨activ*ate*⟩ **3** : furnish with ⟨aer*ate*⟩ [derived from Latin *-atus* (verb suffix)]

a tem·po \ä-'tem-pō\ *adv or adj* : in time — used as a direction in music to return to the original speed

athe·ism \'ā-thē-ˌiz-əm\ *n* : the belief that there is no God — **athe·ist** \-thē-əst\ *n* — **athe·is·tic** \ˌā-thē-'is-tik\ *adj*

ath·ero·scle·ro·sis \ˌath-ə-rō-sklə-'rō-səs\ *n* : hardening and thickening of the walls of arteries due to deposit of fatty substances in the inner layer

athirst \ə-'thərst\ *adj* : EAGER ⟨*athirst* for knowledge⟩

ath·lete \'ath-ˌlēt\ *n* : a person who is trained in or good at games and exercises that require physical skill, endurance, and strength

athlete's foot *n* : ringworm of the feet

ath·let·ic \ath-'let-ik\ *adj* **1** : of, relating to, or characteristic of athletes or athletics **2** : VIGOROUS 1, ACTIVE **3** : STRONG 1, MUSCULAR — **ath·let·i·cal·ly** \-'let-i-k(ə)lē\ *adv*

ath·let·ics \ath-'let-iks\ *n sing or pl* : games, sports, and exercises requiring strength and skill

athletic supporter *n* : an elastic pouch to support the male genitals worn especially while playing sports

[1]**athwart** \ə-'thwȯ(ə)rt, *nautical often* -thȯ(ə)rt\ *prep* **1** : [2]ACROSS 1 **2** : in opposition to

[2]**athwart** *adv* : [1]ACROSS 1

-a·tion \'ā-shən\ *n suffix* **1** : action or process ⟨flirt*ation*⟩ **2** : something connected with an action or process ⟨discoloration⟩ [derived from Latin *-ation-, -atio* (noun suffix)]

-a·tive \ˌāt-iv, ət-iv\ *adj suffix* **1** : of, relating to, or connected with ⟨authorit*ative*⟩ **2** : tending to ⟨talk*ative*⟩ [derived from Latin *-ativus* (adjective suffix)]

At·lan·tic salmon \ət-'lant-ik-, at-\ *n* : SALMON 1a

Atlantic time *n* : the time of the fourth time zone west of Greenwich that includes the Canadian Maritime Provinces, Puerto Rico, and the Virgin Islands

at·las \'at-ləs\ *n* : a book of maps

> **Word History** Atlas was one of the giants of Greek mythology who ruled the world in an early age. Their rule was overthrown after a mighty battle with other gods.

After his defeat, the story goes, Atlas was forced to hold up the sky on his shoulders. In the 16th century the Flemish mapmaker Gerardus Mercator published a collection of maps. On the title page he showed a picture of Atlas supporting his burden. Mercator gave the book the title *Atlas*. Later collections of maps included similar pictures of Atlas, and such books came to be called *atlases*. [named for Atlas, a giant in Greek mythology]

at·mo·sphere \'at-mə-ˌsfi(ə)r\ *n* **1 a** : the whole mass of air surrounding the earth **b** : a mass of gases surrounding a heavenly body (as a planet) **2** : the air in a particular place ⟨the stuffy *atmosphere* of this room⟩ **3 a** : a surrounding influence or set of conditions ⟨the home *atmosphere*⟩ **b** : the main mood or feeling in a creative work **4** : a unit of pressure equal to the pressure of the air at sea level or about 10 newtons per square centimeter (about 14.7 pounds per square inch) [derived from Greek *atmos* "vapor" and Latin *sphaera* "sphere"]

at·mo·spher·ic \ˌat-mə-'sfi(ə)r-ik, -'sfer-\ *adj* : of or relating to the atmosphere ⟨*atmospheric* pressure⟩ — **at·mo·spher·i·cal·ly** \-i-k(ə-)lē\ *adv*

atoll \'a-ˌtȯl, -ˌtäl, -ˌtōl, 'ā-\ *n* : a coral island consisting of a coral reef surrounding a lagoon

atoll

at·om \'at-əm\ *n* **1** : a tiny particle : BIT **2** : the smallest particle of an element that has the properties of the element and can exist either alone or in combination **3** : the atom considered as a source of vast potential energy [Middle English *atom* "particle", from Latin *atomus* (same meaning), derived from Greek *atomos* "unable to be divided", from *a-* "not" and *temnein* "to cut"]

atom bomb *n* **1** : a bomb whose violent explosive power is due to the sudden release of atomic energy in a very rapid chain reaction of the splitting of nuclei of a heavy chemical element (as plutonium or uranium) by neutrons — called also *atomic bomb, fission bomb* **2** : HYDROGEN BOMB — **atom–bomb** *vb*

atom·ic \ə-'täm-ik\ *adj* **1** : of, relating to, or concerned with atoms, atomic energy, or atom bombs **2** : extremely small **3** : found in the state of separate atoms ⟨*atomic* hydrogen⟩

atomic age *n* : the period of history characterized by the use of atomic energy

atomic clock *n* : an extremely exact clock that depends for its operation on the natural vibrations of atoms or molecules (as of cesium)

atomic energy *n* : energy that can be set free by changes in the nucleus of an atom (as by fission of a heavy nucleus or fusion of light nuclei into heavier ones with accompanying loss of mass)

atomic mass *n* : the mass of any kind of atom usually expressed in atomic mass units

atomic mass unit *n* : a unit of mass for expressing masses of atoms, molecules, or nuclear particles that is equal to $\frac{1}{12}$ of the atomic mass of the most abundant kind of carbon

atomic number *n* : a number that is characteristic of a chemical element and represents the number of protons in the nucleus

atomic reactor *n* : REACTOR 2

\ə\ **abut**	\au̇\ **out**	\i\ **tip**	\ȯ\ **saw**	\u̇\ **foot**
\ər\ **further**	\ch\ **chin**	\ī\ **life**	\ȯi\ **coin**	\y\ **yet**
\a\ **mat**	\e\ **pet**	\j\ **job**	\th\ **thin**	\yü\ **few**
\ā\ **take**	\ē\ **easy**	\ŋ\ **sing**	\th\ **this**	\yu̇\ **cure**
\ä\ **cot, cart**	\g\ **go**	\ō\ **bone**	\ü\ **food**	\zh\ **vision**

atomic theory n **1** : a theory of the nature of matter: all material substances consist of very tiny particles or atoms of not really many kinds and all the atoms of the same kind are uniform in size, weight, and other properties **2** : any of several theories of the structure of the atom; esp : one saying that the atom consists essentially of a small positively charged heavy nucleus in relation to a large arrangement of electrons that surround the nucleus

atomic weight n : the average atomic mass of an element compared to $1/12$ the mass of the most abundant kind of carbon

at·om·ize \'at-ə-ˌmīz\ vb **-ized; -iz·ing** : to reduce to very tiny particles or to a fine spray

at·om·iz·er \'at-ə-ˌmī-zər\ n : a device for giving a very fine spray of a liquid (as a perfume)

atom smasher n : ACCELERATOR 3

aton·al \(')ā-'tōn-əl, (')a-\ adj : being music written without traditional organization based on a tonic — **ato·nal·i·ty** \ˌā-tō-'nal-ət-ē\ n — **aton·al·ly** \(')ā-'tōn-ə-lē, (')a-\ adv

atone \ə-'tōn\ vb **atoned; aton·ing** : to do something to make up for a wrong that has been done

atone·ment \ə-'tōn-mənt\ n **1** : the return to a state of love and harmony between God and human beings through the death of Jesus Christ **2** : something that makes up for an offense or injury

atop \ə-'täp\ prep : on top of

ATP \ˌā-ˌtē-'pē, ā-'tē-ˌpē\ n : a compound that occurs widely in living tissue and serves as a major source of energy

atri·um \'ā-trē-əm\ n, pl **atria** \-trē-ə\ also **atri·ums** : a chamber of the heart that receives blood from the veins that in lung-breathing vertebrates (as frogs and human beings) is one of two chambers of which the right receives blood full of carbon dioxide from the body and the left receives oxygen-rich blood from the lungs but in gill-breathing vertebrates (as fishes) is only a single chamber

atro·cious \ə-'trō-shəs\ adj **1** : savagely wicked, brutal, or cruel **2** : very bad (atrocious weather) — **atro·cious·ly** adv — **atro·cious·ness** n

atroc·i·ty \ə-'träs-ət-ē\ n, pl **-ties** **1** : the quality or state of being atrocious **2** : something that is atrocious

¹at·ro·phy \'a-trə-fē\ n, pl **-phies** : decrease in size or wasting away of a body part or tissue

²atrophy vb **-phied; -phy·ing** : to undergo atrophy

at·ro·pine \'a-trə-ˌpēn\ n : a poisonous white compound from belladonna and related plants used especially to relieve spasms and to dilate the pupil of the eye

at·tach \ə-'tach\ vb **1** : to take money or property by legal authority especially to gain or force payment of a debt (attach a person's salary) **2** : to fasten or join one thing to another : TIE (attach a light to a bicycle) **3** : to tie or bind by feelings of affection (the children were attached to their dog) **4** : to assign by authority : APPOINT (attach an officer to a headquarters) **5** : to think of as belonging to something : ATTRIBUTE (attach no importance to a remark) — **at·tach·able** \-ə-bəl\ adj

at·ta·ché \ˌat-ə-'shā, ˌa-ˌta-, ə-ˌta-\ n : a technical expert on a diplomatic staff (military attaché)

at·ta·ché case \ə-ˌta-'shā-, ˌat-ə-; ə-'tash-(ˌ)ā-\ n : a small suitcase especially for carrying papers and documents

at·tach·ment \ə-'tach-mənt\ n **1** : a seizure by legal process **2** : strong affection : FONDNESS **3** : a device with a special use that is attached to a machine or tool (attachments for a vacuum cleaner) **4** : the connection by which one thing is attached to another **5** : the process of physically attaching

¹at·tack \ə-'tak\ vb **1** : to take strong action against (the dog attacked a skunk) **2** : to use unfriendly or bitter words against **3** : to begin to cause something harmful or destructive to happen to (attacked by fever) **4** : to start work on (attack a problem) — **at·tack·er** n

²attack n **1** : the act or action of attacking : ASSAULT **2** : a

beginning of work on something (as a problem or project) **3** : a spell of sickness; esp : one of a disease that is long-lasting or that tends to occur over and over again

at·tain \ə-'tān\ vb **1** : ACCOMPLISH, ACHIEVE **2** : ²GAIN 1a, OBTAIN **3** : to arrive at : REACH (attain the top of the mountain) — often used with to — **at·tain·abil·i·ty** \ə-ˌtā-nə-'bil-ət-ē\ n — **at·tain·able** \-'tā-nə-bəl\ adj

at·tain·der \ə-'tān-dər\ n : the taking away of a person's civil rights when that person has been declared an outlaw or sentenced to death

at·tain·ment \ə-'tān-mənt\ n **1** : the act of attaining : the state of being attained **2** : something attained : ACCOMPLISHMENT

at·tar \'at-ər, 'a-ˌtär\ n : a fragrant oil that comes from a plant (as the rose) and is used in perfumes or flavorings; also : something (as a perfume) made to give off a sweet or pleasant odor

¹at·tempt \ə-'tem(p)t\ vb **1** : to try to do or perform (attempt an escape) **2** : to make an effort : TRY (attempt to solve the problem)

²attempt n **1** : the act or an instance of attempting; esp : an unsuccessful effort **2** : ²ATTACK 1 (an attempt on the president's life)

at·tend \ə-'tend\ vb **1 a** : to pay attention to (attend my words) (attend to what I say) **b** : to give one's attention (attend to business) **2 a** : to go with especially as a companion or servant **b** : to care for (attend the sick) **3** : to be present with (a cold attended by fever) **4** : to go to or be present at especially to take part in (attend a party) (attend a meeting) (attend school) **5** : to take charge : SEE (I'll attend to that) **syn** see ACCOMPANY

at·ten·dance \ə-'ten-dən(t)s\ n **1** : the act of attending **2 a** : the number of persons attending **b** : a record of how frequently a person attends (perfect attendance)

¹at·ten·dant \ə-'ten-dənt\ adj : accompanying or following as a result

²attendant n **1** : one who goes with or serves another (a bride and her attendants) **2** : an employee who waits on customers (gas station attendant)

at·ten·tion \ə-'ten-chən\ n **1** : the act or power of fixing one's mind upon something : careful listening or watching (pay attention) **2 a** : a state of being aware : AWARENESS, NOTICE (attract attention) **b** : consideration with the idea of taking action (a problem that needs prompt attention) **3** : an act of kindness, care, or courtesy **4** : a military posture with the body stiff and straight, heels together, and arms at the sides

at·ten·tive \ə-'tent-iv\ adj **1** : paying attention **2** : thoughtful for the welfare or comfort of others : COURTEOUS — **at·ten·tive·ly** adv — **at·ten·tive·ness** n

at·ten·u·ate \ə-'ten-yə-ˌwāt\ vb **-at·ed; -at·ing** **1** : to make thin or slender **2** : to make less in amount, force, or value : WEAKEN **3** : to become thin, fine, or less — **at·ten·u·a·tion** \ə-ˌten-yə-'wā-shən\ n

at·test \ə-'test\ vb : to give proof of : testify to (the result attests the truth of that statement) (I can attest to your innocence) — **at·tes·ta·tion** \ˌa-ˌtes-'tā-shən\ n — **at·test·er** \ə-'tes-tər\ n

at·tic \'at-ik\ n : a room or a space just below the roof of a building

> **Word History** In ancient Greece the region around Athens was known as Attica, and many of the buildings in Attica had a special feature of a second wall that extended above the top of the main wall or row of columns supporting the roof. When builders in Europe later copied this feature of Attica's buildings, their buildings were said to be in the style of Attica, or the Attic style. Eventually, the word attic came to be used as a noun to refer to this upper wall and later to a room behind the wall under the roof. Today we refer to any room just underneath the roof as the attic, even when the building is not in the style of those in ancient Attica. [from French at-

tique "attic", from *attique* (an adjective) "of Attica", from Latin *Atticus* "of Attica"]

At·tic \'at-ik\ *adj* : of or relating to Athens

¹at·tire \ə-'tī(ə)r\ *vb* **at·tired; at·tir·ing** : to put clothes and especially special or fine clothes on

²attire *n* : CLOTHING 1; *esp* : fine clothes

at·ti·tude \'at-ə-,t(y)üd\ *n* **1** : a position of the body or a figure **2** : a particular feeling or way of thinking about something **3** : the position of something in relation to something else

at·tor·ney \ə-'tər-nē\ *n*, *pl* **-neys** : a person who acts as agent for another in dealing with business or legal matters

attorney general *n*, *pl* **attorneys general** *or* **attorney generals** : the chief law officer of a nation or state who represents the government in legal matters

at·tract \ə-'trakt\ *vb* **1** : to pull to or toward oneself or itself ⟨a magnet *attracts* iron⟩ **2** : to draw by appealing to interest or feeling ⟨*attract* attention⟩ [Middle English *attracten* "attract, cause to adhere", derived from Latin *attrahere,* literally "to draw near", from *at-, ad-* "to, toward" and *trahere* "to draw" — related to ABSTRACT, ¹TRACE, ³TRACE]

at·trac·tion \ə-'trak-shən\ *n* **1** : the act, process, or power of attracting **2** : something that attracts or pleases **3** : a force acting between particles of matter, tending to draw them together, and resisting their separation

at·trac·tive \ə-'trak-tiv\ *adj* : having the power or quality of attracting — **at·trac·tive·ly** *adv* — **at·trac·tive·ness** *n*

¹at·tri·bute \'a-trə-,byüt\ *n* **1** : a quality belonging to a particular person or thing **2** : a word that indicates a quality; *esp* : ADJECTIVE

²at·trib·ute \ə-'trib-yət, -,yüt\ *vb* **-ut·ed; -ut·ing** **1** : to explain as the cause of ⟨*attribute* our success to hard work⟩ **2** : to think of as likely to be a quality of a person or thing ⟨*attribute* stubbornness to mules⟩ — **at·trib·ut·able** \-yət-ə-bəl\ *adj* — **at·trib·ut·er** *n* — **at·tri·bu·tion** \,a-trə-'byü-shən\ *n*

at·trib·u·tive \ə-'trib-yət-iv\ *adj* : joined directly to a modified noun without a verb ⟨"red" in "red hair" is an *attributive* adjective⟩ — compare PREDICATE

at·tri·tion \ə-'trish-ən, a-\ *n* **1** : the act of wearing down by or as if by friction **2** : a reduction in numbers usually as a result of resignation, retirement, or death

at·tune \ə-'t(y)ün\ *vb* : to bring into harmony : TUNE — **at·tune·ment** \-mənt\ *n*

atyp·i·cal \(')ā-'tip-i-kəl\ *adj* : not typical — **atyp·i·cal·ly** \-i-k(ə-)lē\ *adv*

au·burn \'ò-bərn\ *adj* : of a reddish brown color ⟨*auburn* hair⟩

¹auc·tion \'òk-shən\ *n* : a public sale at which things are sold to those who offer to pay the most [from Latin *auction-, auctio,* literally "increase", derived from *augēre* "to increase" — related to AUGMENT]

²auction *vb* **auc·tioned; auc·tion·ing** \-sh(ə-)niŋ\ : to sell at auction

auc·tion·eer \,òk-shə-'ni(ə)r\ *n* : a person in charge of an auction — **auctioneer** *vb*

au·da·cious \ò-'dā-shəs\ *adj* **1** : very bold and daring : FEARLESS **2** : showing a lack of proper respect — **au·da·cious·ly** *adv* — **au·da·cious·ness** *n*

au·dac·i·ty \ò-'das-ət-ē\ *n*, *pl* **-ties** : the quality or fact of being audacious

au·di·ble \'òd-ə-bəl\ *adj* : heard or capable of being heard ⟨the sound was barely *audible*⟩ — **au·di·bil·i·ty** \,òd-ə-'bil-ət-ē\ *n* — **au·di·bly** \'òd-ə-blē\ *adv*

au·di·ence \'òd-ē-ən(t)s\ *n* **1** : a group that listens or watches (as at a play or concert) **2** : an interview with a person of high rank **3** : those of the general public who give attention to something said, done, or written ⟨books with an *audience* of millions⟩

¹au·dio \'òd-ē-,ō\ *adj* **1** : of or relating to electrical or other frequencies occurring in the range of sound waves that can be heard **2 a** : of or relating to sound or its reproduction and especially accurate reproduction ⟨bought new *audio* equipment⟩ **b** : relating to or used in sending or receiving sound — compare ²VIDEO 1

²audio *n* **1** : the sending, receiving, or reproducing of sound **2** : the part of television or motion-picture equipment that deals with sound

audio- *combining form* **1** : hearing ⟨*audio*meter⟩ **2** : sound ⟨*audio*phile⟩ **3** : auditory and ⟨*audio*visual⟩ [derived from Latin *audire* "to hear"]

au·dio–lin·gual \,òd-ē-ō-'liŋ-g(yə-)wəl\ *adj* : involving the use of listening and speaking drills in language learning

au·di·ol·o·gist \,òd-ē-'äl-ə-jəst\ *n* : a person who specializes in audiology

au·di·ol·o·gy \,òd-ē-'äl-ə-jē\ *n* : a branch of science concerned with hearing and especially with the treatment of individuals having trouble with their hearing

au·di·om·e·ter \,òd-ē-'äm-ət-ər\ *n* : an instrument used to measure the keenness of hearing — **au·dio·met·ric** \,òd-ē-ō-'me-trik\ *adj* — **au·di·om·e·try** \,òd-ē-'äm-ə-trē\ *n*

au·dio·phile \'òd-ē-ō-,fīl\ *n* : a person who is enthusiastic about hi-fi

au·dio·vi·su·al \,òd-ē-ō-'vizh(-ə)-wəl, -'vizh-əl\ *adj* : of, relating to, or using both sound and sight ⟨*audiovisual* teaching aids⟩

¹au·dit \'òd-ət\ *n* **1** : a thorough check of accounts especially of a business **2** : a careful check or review ⟨an energy *audit* of our house⟩

²audit *vb* : to make an audit of

¹au·di·tion \ò-'dish-ən\ *n* **1** : the power or sense of hearing **2** : a short performance to test the talents of a musician, singer, dancer, or actor

²audition *vb* **-di·tioned; -di·tion·ing** \-'dish-(ə-)niŋ\ : to test or try out in an audition

au·di·tor \'òd-ət-ər\ *n* **1** : a person who listens to or hears something or someone; *esp* : a member of an audience **2** : a person who audits accounts

au·di·to·ri·um \,òd-ə-'tōr-ē-əm, -'tòr-\ *n* **1** : the part of a public building where an audience sits **2** : a room, hall, or building used for public gatherings

au·di·to·ry \'òd-ə-,tōr-ē, -,tòr-\ *adj* : of or relating to hearing or to the sense or organs of hearing

auditory canal *n* : the passage leading from the external-ear opening to the eardrum

auditory nerve *n* : a nerve connecting the inner ear with the brain and carrying impulses concerned with hearing and balance

au·ger \'ò-gər\ *n* : any of various tools made like a spiral or screw and used for boring holes or moving loose material

　　Word History The tool called an *auger* has nothing to do with people's navels, but the words *auger* and *navel* are related. This tool was first used to bore a hole for the axle in the nave or hub of a wheel. Such a nave was called *nafu* in Old English. *Nafu* was closely related to the word *nafela,* which has become our word *navel.* In Old English *auger* was spelled *nafogār,* which was made up of *nafu* and *gār,* meaning "spear". *Nafogār* was in time spelled *navegār* and then *nauger.* Since *a nauger* sounds just like *an auger,* many people began to write *an auger.* That is how our modern spelling of the word was born. [Middle English *auger* "auger", an altered form of *nauger,* from Old English *nafogār* "tool for boring holes in the hub of a wheel"]

¹aught \'òt, 'ät\ *pron* : ³ALL 1 ⟨go, for *aught* I care⟩ [Old English *āwiht* "anything", from *ā* "ever, always" and *wiht* "creature, thing"]

\ə\ abut	\aú\ out	\i\ tip	\ò\ saw	\ú\ foot
\ər\ **further**	\ch\ **chin**	\ī\ life	\òi\ **coin**	\y\ **yet**
\a\ mat	\e\ pet	\j\ job	\th\ thin	\yü\ few
\ā\ take	\ē\ **easy**	\ŋ\ sing	\th\ **this**	\yú\ cure
\ä\ cot, cart	\g\ **go**	\ō\ bone	\ü\ food	\zh\ vision

²**aught** n : ¹ZERO 1 [from *naught* "zero", from mistaking *a naught* for *an aught*]

au·gite \'ȯ-,jīt\ n : a black to dark green variety of pyroxene

aug·ment \ȯg-'ment\ vb 1 : to increase especially in size, amount, or degree 2 : to add to : SUPPLEMENT [Middle English *augmenten* "to increase", from early French *augmenter* (same meaning), derived from Latin *augēre* "to increase" — related to AUCTION] — **aug·ment·able** \-ə-bəl\ adj — **aug·men·ta·tion** \,ȯg-mən-'tā-shən, -,men-\ n

au gratin \ō-'grat-ᵉn, ȯ-, -'grät-\ adj : covered with bread crumbs or grated cheese and browned

¹**au·gur** \'ȯ-gər\ n : a person (as in ancient Rome) who foretells the future by omens

²**augur** vb 1 : to predict from signs or omens 2 : to give promise of ⟨this *augurs* well for the future⟩

au·gu·ry \'ȯ-gyə-rē, -gə-\ n, pl **-ries** 1 : predicting the future especially from omens 2 : a sign of the future : OMEN

au·gust \ȯ-'gəst\ adj : being grand and noble : MAJESTIC — **au·gust·ly** adv — **au·gust·ness** n

Au·gust \'ȯ-gəst\ n : the 8th month of the year

Word History The first calendar used by the ancient Romans began the year with March. The month that we now call August was then the sixth month of the year and was known by the name *Sextilis*, a Latin word meaning "sixth." When the emperor Augustus Caesar was in power, however, he wished to have a month named after himself. The Roman senate satisfied him by changing *Sextilis* to *Augustus*. The English word *August* comes from the Latin *Augustus*. [Old English *August* "the eighth month", from Latin *Augustus* "August", from *Augustus (Caesar)*]

auk \'ȯk\ n : any of several stout black-and-white short-necked diving seabirds that breed in colder parts of the northern hemisphere

auld \'ȯl(d), 'äl(d)\ adj, *chiefly Scottish* : OLD

auld lang syne \,ōl-,(d)aŋ-'zīn, ,ȯl-,(d)laŋ-, ,ȯl-\ n : the good old times [from Scottish, literally "old long ago"]

aunt \'ant, 'ȧnt\ n 1 : the sister of one's father or mother 2 : the wife of one's uncle

au·ra \'ȯr-ə\ n : a special quality or impression associated with something ⟨an *aura* of holiness⟩

au·ral \'ȯr-əl\ adj : of or relating to the ear or sense of hearing — **au·ral·ly** \-ə-lē\ adv

au·re·ole \'ȯr-ē-,ōl\ or **au·re·o·la** \ȯ-'rē-ə-lə\ n 1 : a radiant light around the head or body in a picture of a sacred person 2 : a bright area surrounding a bright light (as of the sun's disk) when seen through thin cloud or mist

Au·reo·my·cin \,ȯr-ē-ō-'mīs-ᵉn\ *trademark* — used for an antibiotic

au re·voir \,ōr-əv-'wär, ,ȯr-\ n : GOOD-BYE [French, literally "till seeing again"]

au·ri·cle \'ȯr-i-kəl\ n 1 : PINNA 2 2 : an atrium of the heart

au·ric·u·lar \ȯ-'rik-yə-lər\ adj 1 : of or relating to the ear or the sense of hearing 2 : told privately ⟨*auricular* confession⟩ 3 : learned or recognized through the sense of hearing 4 : of or relating to an auricle

Au·ri·ga \ȯ-'rī-gə\ n : a group of stars between Perseus and Gemini

au·rochs \'au̇(ə)r-,äks, 'ȯ(ə)r-\ n : an extinct large-horned wild ox of Europe that is thought to be a wild ancestor of domestic cattle

au·ro·ra \ə-'rōr-ə, ȯ-'rȯr-, -'rȯr-\ n, pl **-ras** or **-rae** 1 : ²DAWN 1 2 : AURORA BOREALIS 3 : AURORA AUSTRALIS

— **au·ro·ral** \-əl\ adj

aurora aus·tra·lis \-ȯ-'strā-ləs, -ä-'strā-\ n : a display of light that is the same as the aurora borealis but occurs in the southern hemisphere — called also *southern lights*

aurora bo·re·al·is \-,bōr-ē-'al-əs, -,bȯr-\ n : broad bands of light that have a magnetic and electrical source and that appear in the sky at night especially in the arctic region — called also *northern lights*

aus·pice \'ȯ-spəs\ n, pl **aus·pic·es** \-spə-səz, -,sēz\ 1 : predicting the future especially according to the flight of birds 2 : OMEN; *esp* : a favorable sign 3 pl : support and guidance of a sponsor ⟨a concert given under the *auspices* of the school⟩ [from Latin *auspicium* "auspice", derived from *avis* "bird" and *specere* "to look at" — related to AVIARY, EXPECT, SPECTACLE]

aus·pi·cious \ȯ-'spish-əs\ adj 1 : promising success : FAVORABLE ⟨an *auspicious* beginning⟩ 2 : SUCCESSFUL 1, PROSPEROUS ⟨has been an *auspicious* year⟩ — **aus·pi·cious·ly** adv — **aus·pi·cious·ness** n

Word History In ancient Rome the flight of birds was thought to be a sign from the gods. If a bird swooped down or soared up, it might mean good or bad luck for a person. But only special people were thought to be able to read these signs. Such a person was called in Latin an *auspex*, meaning literally "bird observer". The word was formed from Latin *avis*, meaning "bird" and the Latin verb *specere*, meaning "to see". The art of predicting the future in this way came to be called *auspicium*. A reading of bird actions was taken each time a person or the state was about to take an important step, such as marriage, a new business, or war. The word was taken into English by borrowing the Latin stem *auspici-* of *auspicium* and adding the adjective suffix *-ous*. Although *auspicium* could mean either good news or bad news, when *auspicious* came to be used in English, it was always used of something favorable. [from Latin *auspicium* "reading the future from the flight of birds" and English *-ous* (adjective suffix)]

aus·tere \ȯ-'sti(ə)r\ adj 1 : stern and unfriendly in appearance and manner 2 : living a harsh life with few pleasures : ASCETIC 3 : SIMPLE 4a, UNADORNED — **aus·tere·ly** adv

aus·ter·i·ty \ȯ-'ster-ət-ē\ n, pl **-ties** 1 : the quality or state of being austere 2 : an austere act, manner, or attitude 3 : a way of living with few or no luxuries

Aus·tra·lian \ȯ-'strāl-yən, ä-\ adj : of, relating to, or characteristic of Australia or its people — **Aus·tralian** n

Aus·tra·loid \'ȯs-trə-,lȯid, 'äs-\ adj : of or relating to an ethnic group including the Australian aborigines and related peoples — **Australoid** n

aus·tra·lo·pith·e·cine \ȯ-,strā-lō-'pith-ə-,sīn, ä-,strā-; ,ȯs-trə-, ,äs-trə-\ adj : of or relating to a group of extinct southern African apes having teeth somewhat like those of human beings but having a smaller brain — **australopithecine** n

aut- or **auto-** *combining form* : self : same one ⟨autobiography⟩ [derived from Greek *aut-* "self", from *autos* "self, same"]

au·then·tic \ə-'thent-ik, ȯ-\ adj 1 : being really what it seems to be : GENUINE ⟨*authentic* examples of Hopi jewelry⟩ 2 : made to be or look just like an original ⟨*authentic* colonial costumes⟩ ⟨*authentic* French-style mustard⟩ — **au·then·ti·cal·ly** \-'thent-i-k(ə-)lē\ adv — **au·then·tic·i·ty** \,ȯ-,then-'tis-ət-ē, -thən-\ n

au·then·ti·cate \ə-'thent-i-,kāt, ȯ-\ vb **-cat·ed; -cat·ing** : to prove or serve to prove that something is authentic — **au·then·ti·ca·tion** \-,thent-i-'kā-shən\ n

au·thor \'ȯ-thər\ n 1 : a person who creates a written work : WRITER 2 : one that starts or creates ⟨*author* of a plan for education⟩ — **author** vb

au·thor·i·tar·i·an \ȯ-,thär-ə-'ter-ē-ən, ə-, -,thȯr-\ adj 1 : expecting strict obedience to one's authority ⟨had *authoritarian* parents⟩ 2 : based on the principle that the lead-

auk

ers and not the people have the final authority ⟨an *authoritarian* state⟩ — **authoritarian** *n* — **au·thor·i·tar·i·an·ism** \-ē-ə-,niz-əm\ *n*

au·thor·i·ta·tive \ə-'thär-ə-,tāt-iv, ȯ-, -'thȯr-\ *adj* : having or coming from authority — **au·thor·i·ta·tive·ly** *adv* — **au·thor·i·ta·tive·ness** *n*

au·thor·i·ty \ə-'thär-ət-ē, ȯ-, -'thȯr-\ *n, pl* **-ties** **1 a** : a fact or statement that is used to support a position or decision **b** : a person looked to as an expert **2** : the right to give commands : the power to influence the behavior of others **3** : persons having powers of government ⟨local *authorities*⟩ **4** : the quality of being convincing

au·tho·rize \'ȯ-thə-,rīz\ *vb* **-rized; -riz·ing** **1** : to give authority to **2** : to give legal or official approval to — **au·tho·ri·za·tion** \,ȯ-th(ə-)rə-'zā-shən\ *n* — **au·tho·riz·er** \'ȯ-thə-,rī-zər\ *n*

Authorized Version *n* : a revision of the English Bible made under James I, published in 1611, and widely used by Protestants — see BIBLE table

au·thor·ship \'ȯ-thər-,ship\ *n* **1** : writing as an occupation **2** : the origin especially of a written work ⟨a novel of unknown *authorship*⟩

au·to \'ȯt-ō, 'ät-\ *n* : AUTOMOBILE

auto- — see AUT-

au·to·bi·og·ra·phy \,ȯt-ə-bī-'äg-rə-fē, -bē-\ *n* : a biography written by the person it is about — **au·to·bi·og·ra·pher** \-rə-fər\ *n* — **au·to·bi·o·graph·i·cal** \-,bī-ə-'graf-i-kəl\ *also* **au·to·bio·graph·ic** \-'graf-ik\ *adj* — **au·to·bio·graph·i·cal·ly** \-i-k(ə-)lē\ *adv*

au·to·clave \'ȯt-ō-,klāv\ *n* : a device (as for sterilizing) that uses steam under pressure

au·toc·ra·cy \ȯ-'täk-rə-sē\ *n, pl* **-cies** : government in which one person has unlimited power

au·to·crat \'ȯt-ə-,krat\ *n* : a person who rules with unlimited authority

au·to·crat·ic \,ȯt-ə-'krat-ik\ *adj* : of, relating to, or resembling autocracy or an autocrat — **au·to·crat·i·cal·ly** \-'krat-i-k(ə-)lē\ *adv*

¹au·to·graph \'ȯt-ə-,graf\ *n* : a person's signature written by hand

²autograph *vb* : to write one's signature in or on

au·to·mate \'ȯt-ə-,māt\ *vb* **-mat·ed; -mat·ing** **1** : to operate by automation **2** : to convert to mainly automatic operation

¹au·to·mat·ic \,ȯt-ə-'mat-ik\ *adj* **1 a** : largely or wholly involuntary; *esp* : REFLEX **2** **b** : acting or done without conscious thought or intention ⟨an *automatic* reply⟩ ⟨an *automatic* smile⟩ **2 a** : having devices or mechanisms (as timers) that permit operation without help from a person ⟨*automatic* washer⟩ **b** : making use of the firing process or gas pressure to operate the loading mechanism ⟨an *automatic* rifle⟩ — **au·to·mat·i·cal·ly** \-'mat-i-k(ə-)lē\ *adv*

²automatic *n* : an automatic machine or device; *esp* : an automatic firearm

au·to·ma·tion \,ȯt-ə-'mā-shən\ *n* **1** : the method of making a device, a process, or a system operate by itself **2** : automatic operation of a device, process, or system by mechanical or electronic devices that replace human operators

au·tom·a·tize \ȯ-'täm-ə-,tīz\ *vb* **-tized; -tiz·ing** : to make automatic — **au·tom·a·ti·za·tion** \ȯ-,täm-ət-ə-'zā-shən\ *n*

au·tom·a·ton \ȯ-'täm-ət-ən, -'täm-ə-,tän\ *n, pl* **-atons** *or* **-a·ta** \-ət-ə\ : a machine that can move by itself; *esp* : ROBOT 1a

¹au·to·mo·bile \'ȯt-ə-mō-,bēl, ,ȯt-ə-mō-'bē(ə)l, ,ȯt-ə-'mō-,bēl\ *adj* : of or relating to automobiles

²automobile *n* : a usually four-wheeled vehicle with its own power system (as an internal-combustion engine) designed for passenger transportation on streets and roadways — **automobile** *vb* — **au·to·mo·bil·ist** \-mō-'bē-ləst\ *n*

au·to·mo·tive \,ȯt-ə-'mōt-iv\ *adj* **1** : SELF-PROPELLED **2** : of, relating to, or concerned with automobiles, trucks, or buses

au·to·nom·ic \,ȯt-ə-'näm-ik\ *adj* : of, relating to, controlled by, or being part of the autonomic nervous system

autonomic nervous system *n* : the part of the vertebrate nervous system that controls actions that are mostly automatic (as breathing and heart rate), that sends nerves primarily to smooth and cardiac muscle and to the glands, and that helps to maintain the stability of the environment inside the body through the action of its two parts composed of the sympathetic and parasympathetic nervous systems which often send separate sets of nerve fibers to the same organ with opposite effects on its function

au·ton·o·mous \ȯ-'tän-ə-məs\ *adj* **1** : having autonomy : SELF-GOVERNING **2** : existing independent of anything else — **au·ton·o·mous·ly** *adv*

au·ton·o·my \ȯ-'tän-ə-mē\ *n, pl* **-mies** : the power or right of self-government

au·top·sy \'ȯ-,täp-sē, 'ȯt-əp-\ *n, pl* **-sies** : POSTMORTEM EXAMINATION [from Greek *autopsia* "the act of seeing with one's own eyes", from *aut-* "self" and *opsis* "sight", from *opsesthai* "to be going to see" — related to OPTIC] — **autopsy** *vb*

au·to·ra·dio·graph \,ȯt-ō-'rād-ē-ə-,graf\ *n* : an image made on a photographic film or plate by the radiation from a radioactive substance in a nearby object

au·tumn \'ȯt-əm\ *n* **1** : the season between summer and winter including in the northern hemisphere usually the months of September, October, and November — called also *fall* **2** : a time of full maturity and the beginning of decline — **au·tum·nal** \ȯ-'təm-nəl\ *adj*

¹aux·il·ia·ry \ȯg-'zil-yə-rē, -'zil-(ə-)rē\ *adj* : available to provide something extra or additional when needed ⟨a sailboat with an *auxiliary* engine⟩ ⟨*auxiliary* police⟩

²auxiliary *n, pl* **-ries** : an auxiliary person, group, or device

auxiliary verb *n* : HELPING VERB

aux·in \'ȯk-sən\ *n* : a plant hormone that causes the shoot to grow in length and plays a role in water metabolism of plants

¹avail \ə-'vā(ə)l\ *vb* : to be of use or help

²avail *n* : help toward reaching a goal : USE ⟨effort was of little *avail*⟩

avail·able \ə-'vā-lə-bəl\ *adj* **1** : USABLE; *esp* : present in a form that a plant or animal can use ⟨a food that contains *available* iron⟩ **2** : easy or possible to get, get to, or use ⟨kept emergency supplies *available*⟩ ⟨called every *available* hardware store⟩ — **avail·abil·i·ty** \ə-,vā-lə-'bil-ət-ē\ *n, pl* **-ties** — **avail·able·ness** *n* — **avail·ably** \ə-'vā-lə-blē\ *adv*

av·a·lanche \'av-ə-,lanch\ **1** : a large mass of snow and ice or of earth and rock sliding down a mountainside or over a cliff **2** : a sudden overwhelming rush ⟨an *avalanche* of words⟩

av·a·rice \'av-(ə-)rəs\ *n* : strong desire for riches

av·a·ri·cious \,av-ə-'rish-əs\ *adj* : driven by avarice : greedy for riches — **av·a·ri·cious·ly** *adv* — **av·a·ri·cious·ness** *n*

avast \ə-'vast\ *imperative verb* — a command to stop or cease used by sailors

avaunt \ə-'vȯnt, -'vänt\ *adv, archaic* : AWAY 2

avenge \ə-'venj\ *vb* **avenged; aveng·ing** : to take vengeance for (an action) or on behalf of (a person) — **aveng·er** *n*

av·e·nue \'av-ə-,n(y)ü\ *n* **1** : a way or route to a place or goal : PATH **2** : a usually wide street

\ə\ abut	\au̇\ out	\i\ tip	\ȯ\ saw	\u̇\ foot
\ər\ further	\ch\ chin	\ī\ life	\ȯi\ coin	\y\ yet
\a\ mat	\e\ pet	\j\ job	\th\ thin	\yü\ few
\ā\ take	\ē\ easy	\ŋ\ sing	\th\ this	\yu̇\ cure
\ä\ cot, cart	\g\ go	\ō\ bone	\ü\ food	\zh\ vision

aver \ə-'vər\ vb **averred; aver·ring** : to declare positively : ASSERT

¹av·er·age \'av-(ə-)rij\ n **1** : ARITHMETIC MEAN **2** : something typical of a group, class, or series **3** : a ratio of successful tries to total tries ⟨batting *average*⟩

²average adj **1** : equaling or close to an arithmetic mean **2** : being ordinary or usual ⟨the *average* person⟩ ⟨an *average* day⟩ — **av·er·age·ly** adv — **av·er·age·ness** n

³average vb **-aged; -ag·ing 1** : to amount to usually **2** : to do or get usually ⟨*averaged* 40 miles a day⟩ **3** : to find the average of ⟨*average* the grades⟩

averse \ə-'vərs\ adj : having an active and strong dislike ⟨*averse* to exercise⟩ — **averse·ly** adv — **adverse·ness** n

aver·sion \ə-'vər-zhən\ n **1** : a strong dislike **2** : something strongly disliked

avert \ə-'vərt\ vb **1** : to turn away ⟨*avert* one's eyes⟩ **2** : to keep from happening ⟨*averted* an accident⟩

avi·an \'ā-vē-ən\ adj : of, relating to, or derived from birds

avi·ary \'ā-vē-,er-ē\ n, pl **-ar·ies** : a place (as a large cage or a building) where many live birds are kept usually for exhibition [from Latin *aviarium* "place to keep birds", from *avis* "bird"]

avi·a·tion \,ā-vē-'ā-shən, ,av-ē-\ n : the operation of aircraft (as airplanes or helicopters) that are heavier than air

avi·a·tor \'ā-vē-,āt-ər, 'av-ē-\ n : ¹PILOT 3

av·id \'av-əd\ adj **1** : having so much desire for something as to be greedy **2** : very eager : ENTHUSIASTIC ⟨an *avid* football fan⟩ — **avid·ity** \ə-'vid-ət-ē, a-\ n — **av·id·ly** \'av-əd-lē\ adv

av·o·ca·do \,av-ə-'käd-ō, ,äv-\ n, pl **-dos** : the usually green pear-shaped edible fruit of a tropical American tree that has a rich oily flesh; *also* : the tree that bears this fruit

av·o·ca·tion \,av-ə-'kā-shən\ n : an activity one engages in regularly for enjoyment rather than as a job : HOBBY — **av·o·ca·tion·al** \-shnəl, -shən-ᵊl\

av·o·cet \'av-ə-,set\ n : any of several rather large long-legged shorebirds with webbed feet and slender upward-curving bill

avocet

avoid \ə-'void\ vb **1** : to keep away from ⟨*avoid* accidents⟩ **2** : to keep from doing or being ⟨*avoid* getting too tired⟩ — **avoid·able** \-ə-bəl\ adj — **avoid·ably** \-blē\ adv

avoid·ance \ə-'void-ᵊn(t)s\ n : the act or an instance of avoiding something

av·oir·du·pois \,av-ərd-ə-'poiz, 'av-ərd-ə-,poiz\ n **1** : AVOIRDUPOIS WEIGHT **2** : the fact or quality of being heavy : WEIGHT [Middle English *avoir de pois* "goods sold by weight", from early French, literally "goods of weight"]

avoirdupois weight n : the series of units of weight based on the pound of 16 ounces and the ounce of 16 drams — see MEASURE table

avouch \ə-'vaùch\ vb **1** : to declare positively as a fact : AFFIRM **2** : to give a guarantee of : vouch for — **avouch·ment** \-mənt\ n

avow \ə-'vaù\ vb : to declare or acknowledge openly and frankly **syn** see ASSERT

avow·al \ə-'vaù(-ə)l\ n : an open declaration or admission

avowed \ə-'vaùd\ adj : openly declared or admitted — **avowed·ly** \ə-'vaù-əd-lē\ adv

await \ə-'wāt\ vb **1** : to wait for : EXPECT ⟨*await* a train⟩ **2** : to be ready or waiting for ⟨a reward *awaits* you⟩

¹awake \ə-'wāk\ vb **awoke** \-'wōk\ *also* **awaked** \-'wākt\; **awaked** *or* **awo·ken** \-'wō-kən\ *also* **awoke; awak·ing 1** : to arouse from sleep : wake up **2** : to become aware of something ⟨*awoke* to their danger⟩ **3** : to make or become active : STIR

²awake adj **1** : aroused from sleep **2** : ¹ALERT 1a

awak·en \ə-'wā-kən\ vb **awak·ened; awak·en·ing** \-'wāk-(ə-)niŋ\ : ¹AWAKE — **awak·en·er** \-(ə-)nər\ n

¹award \ə-'wo(ə)rd\ vb **1** : to give by court decision (as after a lawsuit) ⟨*award* damages⟩ **2** : to give or grant as a reward ⟨*award* a prize to the best speaker⟩

²award n : something (as a prize) that is awarded

aware \ə-'wa(ə)r, -'we(ə)r\ adj : having or showing understanding or knowledge : CONSCIOUS — **aware·ness** n

awash \ə-'wosh, -'wäsh\ adv or adj **1** : washed by waves or tide **2** : floating about **3** : flooded or covered with water

¹away \ə-'wā\ adv **1** : on the way ⟨get *away* early⟩ **2** : from this or that place ⟨go *away*⟩ **3** : in or to another place or direction ⟨turn *away*⟩ **4** : to an end : out of existence ⟨echoes dying *away*⟩ **5** : from one's possession ⟨gave *away* a fortune⟩ **6** : without stopping or slowing down ⟨talk *away*⟩ **7** : at or to a great distance in space or time : FAR ⟨*away* back in 1910⟩

²away adj **1** : absent from a place : GONE ⟨be *away* from home⟩ **2** : distant in space or time ⟨a lake not far *away*⟩ ⟨the season is two months *away*⟩

¹awe \'o\ n : a feeling of mixed fear, respect, and wonder

²awe vb **awed; aw·ing** : to fill with awe

awe·some \'o-səm\ adj **1** : showing awe **2** : causing a feeling of awe — **awe·some·ly** adv — **awe·some·ness** n

awe·struck \'o-,strək\ adj : filled with awe

¹aw·ful \'o-fəl\ adj **1** : AWESOME 2 **2** : extremely disagreeable or unpleasant **3** : very great ⟨took an *awful* chance⟩ — **aw·ful·ness** n

²awful adv : ²VERY 1 ⟨*awful* tired⟩

aw·ful·ly \usually 'o-fə-lē in sense 1, 'o-flē in sense 2\ adv **1** : in a disagreeable or unpleasant manner **2** : ²VERY 1 ⟨*awfully* nice of you⟩

awhile \ə-'hwī(ə)l, ə-'wī(ə)l\ adv : for a while : for a short time ⟨sit and rest *awhile*⟩

awhirl \ə-'hwərl, ə-wərl\ adv or adj : in a whirl

awk·ward \'o-kwərd\ adj **1** : lacking skill and flexibility (as in the use of the hands) **2** : not graceful : CLUMSY **3** : causing embarrassment ⟨an *awkward* situation⟩ **4** : difficult to use or handle ⟨an *awkward* tool⟩ — **awk·ward·ly** adv — **awk·ward·ness** n

awl \'ol\ n : a pointed tool for marking surfaces or for making small holes (as in leather or wood)

aw·ning \'on-iŋ, 'än-\ n : a cover (as of canvas) that shades or shelters like a roof

awoke past and past participle of AWAKE

awoken past participle of AWAKE

AWOL \'ā-,wol, ,ā-,dəb-əl-yù-,ō-'el\ n : a person who is absent without permission [*absent without leave*] — **AWOL** adv or adj

awl

awry \ə-'rī\ adv or adj **1** : turned or twisted to one side **2** : out of the right course : WRONG ⟨their plans went *awry*⟩

ax *or* **axe** \'aks\ n : a cutting tool that consists of a heavy edged head attached to a handle and that is used for chopping and splitting wood

ax·i·al \'ak-sē-əl\ adj **1** : of, relating to, or having the characteristics of an axis **2** : situated around, in the direction of, on, or along an axis ⟨*axial* flowers⟩ — **ax·i·al·ly** \-sē-ə-lē\ adv

ax·i·om \'ak-sē-əm\ n : a rule or principle widely accepted as obviously true and not needing to be proved

ax·i·om·at·ic \,ak-sē-ə-'mat-ik\ adj **1** : of or relating to an axiom   **2** : resembling an axiom — **ax·i·om·at·i·cal·ly** \-'mat-i-k(ə-)lē\ *adv*

ax·is \'ak-səs\ *n, pl* **ax·es** \'ak-,sēz\   **1 a** : a straight line about which a body or a geometric figure rotates or may be supposed to rotate   **b** : a straight line with respect to which a body or figure is symmetrical — called also *axis of symmetry*   **c** : one of the reference lines of a coordinate system   **2** : a bodily structure around which parts are arranged in a symmetrical way; *esp* : the main stem of a plant from which leaves and branches arise

ax·le \'ak-səl\ *n* : a pin, pole, or bar on or with which a wheel revolves

ax·o·lotl \'ak-sə-,lät-əl\ *n* : any of several salamanders of mountain lakes of Mexico and the western U.S. that ordinarily live and breed while keeping the larval form

ax·on \'ak-,sän\ *also* **ax·one** \-,sōn\ *n* : a usually long and single nerve-cell process that usually carries impulses away from the cell body — compare DENDRITE 2 — **ax·o·nal** \'ak-sən-ᵊl; ak-'sän-, -'sōn-\ *adj*

¹aye *also* **ay** \'ā\ *adv* : FOREVER 1, ALWAYS [Middle English *aye* "always"; of Norse origin]

²aye *also* **ay** \'ī\ *adv* : ¹YES 1 [perhaps from Middle English *ye* "yes, yea"]

³aye *also* **ay** \'ī\ *n, pl* **ayes** : a vote yes or a person who votes yes

aye–aye \'ī-,ī\ *n* : a nocturnal lemur of Madagascar

Ayr·shire \'a(ə)r-,shi(ə)r, 'e(ə)r-, -shər\ *n* : any of a breed of hardy dairy cattle originated in Ayr that vary in color from white to red or brown

Ayrshire

aza·lea \ə-'zāl-yə\ *n* : any of numerous rhododendrons that have funnel-shaped flowers, usually shed their leaves in the fall, and include many grown as ornamental plants

az·i·muth \'az-(ə-)məth\ *n* : horizontal direction of an object from a fixed point expressed as an angle

azo \'az-ō\ *adj* : relating to or containing two nitrogen atoms united to each other and at both ends to carbon ⟨an *azo* dye⟩

AZT \,ā-(,)zē-'tē\ *n* : a drug used to treat AIDS

Az·tec \'az-,tek\ *n* : a member of an American Indian people that founded the Mexican empire conquered by Cortes in 1519

azure \'azh-ər\ *n* : the blue color of the clear sky

azur·ite \'azh-ə-,rīt\ *n* : a blue mineral that is a carbonate of copper and an ore of copper

B

b \'bē\ *n, often cap*   **1** : the second letter of the English alphabet   **2** : a musical note referred to by the letter B : the seventh tone of a C-major scale   **3** : a grade rating a student's work as good

baa \'ba, 'bä\ *n* : the bleat of a sheep — **baa** *vb*

bab·bitt metal \'bab-ət-\ *n* : an alloy used for lining bearings; *esp* : one containing tin, copper, and antimony

¹bab·ble \'bab-əl\ *vb* **bab·bled; bab·bling** \'bab-(ə-)liŋ\   **1 a** : to make meaningless sounds   **b** : to talk foolishly or too much   **2** : to make the sound of a brook — **bab·bler** \'bab-(ə-)lər\ *n*

²babble *n*   **1** : talk that is not clear   **2** : the sound of a brook

babe \'bāb\ *n* : ¹BABY 1a ⟨a *babe* in arms⟩

ba·bel \'bā-bəl, 'bab-əl\ *n, often cap*   **1** : a confusion of sounds or voices   **2** : a scene of noise or confusion [from the Tower of *Babel* in Genesis 11:4–9, the building of which was interrupted by a confusion of languages]

ba·boon \ba-'bün\ *n* : any of several large African and Asian apes having doglike muzzles and usually short tails

ba·bush·ka \bə-'büsh-kə, -'bush-\ *n* : a kerchief usually folded into a triangle and worn on the head [from Russian *babushka*, "grandmother"; probably so called from the frequent wearing of such kerchiefs by elderly Russian peasant women]

baboon

¹ba·by \'bā-bē\ *n, pl* **ba·bies**   **1 a** : a very young child; *esp* : INFANT   **b** : the youngest of a group   **2** : a childish person — **ba·by·hood** \-bē-,hud\ *n* — **ba·by·ish** \-ish\ *adj*

²baby *adj*   **1** : being or relating to a baby ⟨a *baby* deer⟩ ⟨my *baby* sister⟩ ⟨*baby* clothes⟩   **2** : much smaller than usual ⟨a *baby* grand piano⟩ ⟨*baby* carrots⟩ ⟨a *baby* spaceship⟩

³baby *vb* **ba·bied; ba·by·ing**   **1** : to treat as a baby : PET   **2** : to operate or treat with care ⟨*babied* the car⟩

baby boom *n* : a marked rise in a birthrate (as in the United States after World War II) — **baby boom·er** \'bü-mər\ *n*

baby's breath *n* : a tall branching herb related to the carnation and having clusters of small fragrant white or pink flowers

ba·by–sit \'bā-bē-,sit\ *vb* **-sat** \-,sat\; **-sit·ting** : to care for children usually while the parents are away for a short time — **ba·by–sit·ter** *n*

baby talk *n*   **1** : the speech used by very young children learning to talk   **2** : speech like baby talk sometimes used by adults to speak to very young children

baby tooth *n* : MILK TOOTH

bach·e·lor \'bach-(ə-)lər\ *n*   **1** : a person who has received the lowest degree given by a college, university, or professional school ⟨*bachelor* of arts⟩   **2 a** : an unmarried man   **b** : an unmated male animal — **bach·e·lor·hood** \-,hud\ *n*

bachelor's button *n* : a European plant related to the daisies and often grown for its showy blue, pink, or white flower heads — called also *cornflower*

ba·cil·lus \bə-'sil-əs\ *n, pl* **-cil·li** \-'sil-,ī *also* -'sil-ē\ : any of numerous straight rod-shaped bacteria that require oxygen for growth; *also* : a disease-producing bacterium

¹back \'bak\ *n*   **1 a** : the rear part of the human body especially from the neck to the end of the spine   **b** : the corresponding part of a four-footed or lower animal   **2** : the part of something that is opposite or away from the front part   **3** : something at or on the back for support ⟨*back* of a chair⟩   **4 a** : a position in some games (as football or soccer) behind the front line of players   **b** : a player in this position — **backed** \'bakt\ *adj* — **back·less** \'bak-

\ə\ abut		\au̇\ out	\i\ tip	\ȯ\ saw	\u̇\ foot
\ər\ further		\ch\ chin	\ī\ life	\ȯi\ coin	\y\ yet
\a\ mat		\e\ pet	\j\ job	\th\ thin	\yü\ few
\ā\ take		\ē\ easy	\ŋ\ sing	\th\ this	\yu̇\ cure
\ä\ cot, cart		\g\ go	\ō\ bone	\ü\ food	\zh\ vision

ləs\ *adj*

²back *adv* **1 a** : to, toward, or at the rear   **b** : in or into the past : AGO   **c** : in or into a reclining position   **d** : under control : in check ⟨held *back*⟩   **2** : to, toward, or in a place from which a person or thing came   **3** : in return or reply ⟨write *back*⟩ ⟨talk *back*⟩ — **back and forth** : backward and forward : from one place to another

³back *adj* **1 a** : being at or in the back ⟨*back* door⟩   **b** : distant from a central or main area ⟨*back* roads⟩   **2** : not yet paid : OVERDUE ⟨*back* rent⟩   **3** : no longer current ⟨*back* issues of a magazine⟩

⁴back *vb* **1** : to give aid or support to   **2** : to move or cause to move back or backward   **3** : to shift in a counterclockwise direction ⟨the wind *backed* around⟩   **4** : to provide with a back — **back·er** *n*

back·ache \'bak-ˌāk\ *n* : pain in the back; *esp* : dull continuous pain in the lower back

back·bit·ing \'bak-ˌbīt-iŋ\ *n* : mean talk about someone who is not present

back·board \'bak-ˌbōrd, -ˌbord\ *n* : a board placed at the back or serving as a back; *esp* : a rounded or rectangular board behind the basket on a basketball court

back·bone \-'bōn, -ˌbōn\ *n* **1** : the skeleton of the trunk and tail of a vertebrate that consists of a jointed series of vertebrae enclosing and protecting the spinal cord — called also *spinal column*   **2** : the foundation or sturdiest part of something   **3** : firmness of character — **back·boned** \-'bōnd, -ˌbōnd\ *adj*

back down *vb* : to retreat from a stand one has taken or from a challenge one has accepted

back·drop \'bak-ˌdräp\ *n* **1** : a painted cloth hung across the rear of a stage   **2** : BACKGROUND 1, 3a

back·field \-ˌfēld\ *n* : the football players who line up behind the line of scrimmage

¹back·fire \-ˌfī(ə)r\ *n* **1** : a fire that is set to check the spread of a forest fire or a grass fire by burning off a strip of land ahead of it   **2** : a loud noise caused by the improperly timed explosion of fuel in the cylinder of an internal-combustion engine

²backfire *vb* **1** : to make a backfire   **2** : to have a result opposite to what was planned

back·gam·mon \'bak-ˌgam-ən, ˌbak-'gam-\ *n* : a board game for two played with dice in which the object is to be the first to move all one's pieces around and off the board

back·ground \'bak-ˌgraùnd\ *n* **1** : the scenery or ground that is behind a main figure or object (as in a painting)   **2** : a position that attracts little attention ⟨always tries to keep in the *background*⟩   **3 a** : the setting within which something takes place   **b** : the events leading up to a situation   **c** : information needed to understand a problem or situation   **d** : the total of a person's experience, knowledge, and education   **4 a** : a somewhat steady level of radiation in the natural environment (as from cosmic rays or radio activity)   **b** : undesired sound that is heard in a system (as in radio or a tape recording) that produces sound from other sources

background music *n* : music played to go along with and add to the story or mood of a program (as a movie or radio or television show)

¹back·hand \-ˌhand\ *n* **1 a** : a stroke (as in tennis) made with the back of the hand turned in the direction of movement   **b** : a catch made with the arm across the body and the palm turned away from the body   **2** : handwriting in which the letters slant to the left

backhand 1a

²backhand *adj* : using or made with a backhand

³backhand *vb* : to do, hit, or catch with a backhand

⁴backhand *or* **back·hand·ed** \'bak-ˌhan-dəd\ *adv* : with a backhand

back·hand·ed \'bak-'han-dəd\ *adj* **1** : ²BACKHAND   **2** : not sincere ⟨a *backhanded* compliment⟩

back·hoe \-ˌhō\ *n* : a large powerful machine that digs into the earth with a metal scoop drawn down toward the machine

back·ing \'bak-iŋ\ *n* **1** : something forming a back   **2 a** : ²SUPPORT, AID   **b** : ENDORSEMENT 3, APPROVAL

back·lash \'bak-ˌlash\ *n* : a reaction against some political or social development

back·log \-ˌlòg, -ˌläg\ *n* **1** : a large log at the back of a fire in a fireplace   **2** : an accumulation of tasks that have not been finished

back of *prep* : ²BEHIND 1

back off *vb* : BACK DOWN

¹back·pack \'bak-ˌpak\ *n* : a camping pack carried on the back

²backpack *vb* : to hike with a backpack — **back·pack·er** *n*

back·rest \'bak-ˌrest\ *n* : a rest for the back

back·side \'bak-'sīd\ *n* : BUTTOCK 2

backpack

back·slide \'bak-ˌslīd\ *vb* **-slid** \-ˌslid\; **-slid** *or* **-slid·den** \-ˌslid-ᵊn\; **-slid·ing** \-ˌslīd-iŋ\ : to go back to a less religious or less moral condition — **back·slid·er** \-ˌslīd-ər\ *n*

back·spin \-ˌspin\ *n* : a backward spinning motion of a ball

back·stage \'bak-'stāj\ *adv or adj* : in or to an area behind the stage of a theater

back·stop \'bak-ˌstäp\ *n* **1** : a screen or fence to keep a ball from leaving the field of play   **2** : a baseball catcher

back·stretch \-ˌstrech, -'strech\ *n* : the side of a racetrack that is opposite the part between the last turn and the finish line

back·stroke \-ˌstrōk\ *n* : a swimming stroke made by a swimmer who lies in the water facing upward

back swimmer *n* : any of a family of bugs that live in the water and swim on their backs

back talk *n* : a rude or quarrelsome reply

back·track \'bak-ˌtrak\ *vb* **1** : to go back over a course or path   **2** : to reverse a position or stand

back·up \'bak-ˌəp\ *n* : a person or thing ready to take the place of another in an emergency — **backup** *adj*

¹back·ward \'bak-wərd\ *or* **back·wards** \-wərdz\ *adv* **1** : toward the back ⟨look *backward*⟩   **2** : with the back first ⟨ride *backward*⟩   **3** : opposite to the usual way : in reverse ⟨count *backward*⟩   **4** : toward a worse state

²backward *adj* **1 a** : directed or turned toward the back ⟨a *backward* glance⟩   **b** : done backward   **2** : ¹SHY 1, BASHFUL   **3** : slow in learning or development — **back·ward·ly** *adv* — **back·ward·ness** *n*

back·wash \'bak-ˌwòsh, -ˌwäsh\ *n* : backward movement (as of water or air) produced by a propelling force (as the motion of oars)

back·wa·ter \'bak-ˌwòt-ər, -ˌwät-\ *n* **1** : water held or turned back from its course   **2** : a backward place or condition

back·woods \'bak-'wùdz, -ˌwùdz\ *n pl* **1** : wooded or partly cleared areas far from cities   **2** : a place that is slow to adopt the ways of the city

back·yard \-'yärd\ *n* **1** : an area in back of a house   **2** : an area in which one feels at home or in which one has a special interest

ba·con \'bā-kən\ *n* : salted and smoked meat from the sides and the back of a pig

bacteria *pl of* BACTERIUM

bac·te·ri·ol·o·gist \(,)bak-,tir-ē-'äl-ə-jəst\ *n* : a person who specializes in bacteriology

bac·te·ri·ol·o·gy \(,)bak-,tir-ē-'äl-ə-jē\ *n* **1** : a science that deals with bacteria and their relations to medicine, industry, and agriculture **2** : bacterial life, facts, and events of scientific interest — **bac·te·ri·o·log·ic** \-ē-ə-'läj-ik\ *or* **bac·te·ri·o·log·i·cal** \-'läj-i-kəl\ *adj*

bac·te·rio·phage \bak-'tir-ē-ə-,fāj, -,fäzh\ *n* : any of various viruses that specifically attack bacteria — called also *phage*

bac·te·ri·um \bak-'tir-ē-əm\ *n, pl* **-ria** \-ē-ə\ : any of a class of microscopic plants that live in soil, water, organic matter, or the bodies of plants and animals and are important because of their chemical effects and as a cause of disease — **bac·te·ri·al** \-ē-əl\ *adj*

Bac·tri·an camel \,bak-trē-ən-\ *n* : CAMEL b

¹bad \'bad\ *adj* **worse** \'wərs\; **worst** \'wərst\ **1 a** : below standard : POOR **b** : not favorable ⟨a *bad* impression⟩ **c** : ROTTEN 1 ⟨*bad* meat⟩ **2** : not good or right : morally evil or wrong ⟨a *bad* person⟩ ⟨*bad* behavior⟩ **3** : not enough ⟨*bad* lighting⟩ **4** : DISAGREEABLE 1, UNPLEASANT ⟨*bad* news⟩ **5 a** : HARMFUL ⟨*bad* for the health⟩ **b** : SEVERE 3 ⟨a *bad* cold⟩ **6** : INCORRECT, FAULTY ⟨*bad* spelling⟩ **7** : ¹ILL 2c, SICK ⟨feel *bad*⟩ **8** : SORROWFUL 1, SORRY ⟨don't feel *bad* about losing⟩ — **bad·ness** *n*

²bad *n* **1** : a bad thing or part ⟨take the *bad* with the good⟩ **2** : a bad or unhappy state ⟨go to the *bad*⟩

³bad *adv* : BADLY

bade *past of* BID

badge \'baj\ *n* : a mark or sign worn to show that a person belongs to a certain group, class, or rank

¹bad·ger \'baj-ər\ *n* : any of several sturdy burrowing mammals widely distributed in the northern hemisphere; *also* : the pelt or fur of a badger

²badger *vb* **bad·gered; bad·ger·ing** \'baj-(ə-)riŋ\ : to annoy again and again

badger

bad·land \'bad-,land\ *n* : a region where natural forces have worn away the soft rocks into sharp and complicated shapes and where plant life is scarce

bad·ly \'bad-lē\ *adv* **worse** \'wərs\; **worst** \'wərst\ **1** : in a bad manner ⟨played *badly*⟩ **2** : very much ⟨wanted the jeans *badly*⟩

bad·min·ton \'bad-,mint-ᵊn\ *n* : a game in which a shuttlecock is hit back and forth over a net by players using light rackets

bad–mouth \-,maúth, -'maúth\ *vb* : to say bad things about

¹baf·fle \'baf-əl\ *vb* **baf·fled; baf·fling** \'baf-(ə-)liŋ\ **1** : to defeat or check by confusing : PERPLEX **2 a** : to check or break the force or flow of by or as if by a baffle **b** : to prevent (sound waves) from affecting one another (as by a baffle) **syn** *see* FRUSTRATE — **baf·fle·ment** \-əl-mənt\ *n* — **baf·fler** \-(ə)lər\ *n*

²baffle *n* : a device (as a wall or screen) to turn aside, check, or regulate flow (as of a fluid, light, or sound)

¹bag \'bag\ *n* **1 a** : a container made of flexible material (as paper or plastic) **b** : ¹PURSE 1, HANDBAG **c** : SUITCASE **2 a** : a pouched or hanging bodily part or organ (as an udder) **b** : a puffed-out sag or bulge in cloth **c** : a square white stuffed canvas container that marks a base in baseball **3** : the amount contained in a bag **4** : a quantity of game taken or permitted to be taken — **in the bag** : ¹SURE 4, CERTAIN

²bag *vb* **bagged; bag·ging** **1** : to swell out ⟨pants *bag* at the knees⟩ **2** : to put into a bag ⟨*bagging* groceries⟩ **3** : to kill or capture in hunting ⟨the hunter *bagged* a deer⟩

ba·gel \'bā-gəl\ *n* : a hard doughnut-shaped roll

bag·gage \'bag-ij\ *n* : the traveling bags and personal belongings of a traveler : LUGGAGE

bag·gy \'bag-ē\ *adj* **bag·gi·er; -est** : loose, puffed out, or hanging like a bag ⟨*baggy* pants⟩ — **bag·gi·ly** \'bag-ə-lē\ *adv* — **bag·gi·ness** \'bag-ē-nəs\ *n*

bag of waters : the double-walled fluid-filled pouch resembling a bag that encloses and protects the fetus in the womb and that breaks releasing its fluid during the birth process

bag·pipe \'bag-,pīp\ *n* : a musical instrument played especially in Scotland that consists of a bag for air, a mouth tube for blowing up the air bag, and pipes which give a sound when air passes through them — often used in pl. — **bag·pip·er** \-,pī-pər\ *n*

ba·guette \ba-'get\ *n* : a gem (as a diamond) cut in a long narrow rectangle

bag·worm \'bag-,wərm\ *n* : a moth that as a larva lives in a silk case covered with plant debris and is destructive to the leaves of plants

bagpipe

¹bail \'bā(ə)l\ *n* **1** : a promise or a deposit of money needed to free a prisoner until his or her trial **2** : a person who provides bail [Middle English *bail* "custody, bail", derived from early French *baillier* "to have charge, deliver", derived from Latin *bajulare* "to carry a load", from *bajulus* "load carrier"]

²bail *vb* : to get the release of (a prisoner) by giving bail

³bail *n* : a container used to remove water from a boat [Middle English *baille* "bucket, bail", from early French *baille* "bucket", from Latin *bajula* "water container", derived from *bajulus* "load carrier"]

⁴bail *vb* : to remove (water) from a boat by dipping and throwing over the side — usually used with *out*

⁵bail *n* **1** : a semicircular support **2** : the handle of a kettle or pail [Middle English *beil, baile* "half hoop, bail"; probably of Scandinavian origin]

bai·liff \'bā-ləf\ *n* **1** : any of various officials; *esp* : a minor officer of some U.S. courts usually serving as a messenger or doorkeeper **2** *chiefly British* : one who manages an estate or farm

bail out *vb* **1** : to help from a difficult situation **2** : to jump out of an airplane with a parachute

bairn \'ba(ə)rn, 'be(ə)rn\ *n, chiefly Scottish* : CHILD 1, 2a

¹bait \'bāt\ *vb* **1** : to torment by repeated attacks **2** : to torment (an animal) with dogs **3** : to put bait on or in ⟨*bait* a hook⟩ [Middle English *baiten* "to tease, torment", from an early Norse word originally meaning "to cause to bite"] — **bait·er** *n*

²bait *n* **1** : something used to attract animals to a hook or into a trap **2** : a poisonous material put in food to kill pests **3** : LURE 1, TEMPTATION [Middle English *bait* "a lure", from two early Norse words, one meaning "pasture" and the other meaning "food"]

baize \'bāz\ *n* : a fabric made to resemble felt

¹bake \'bāk\ *vb* **baked; bak·ing** **1** : to cook or become cooked by dry heat especially in an oven **2** : to dry or harden by heat ⟨*bake* bricks⟩ — **bak·er** *n*

²bake *n* **1** : the act or process of baking **2** : a social gath-

\ə\ abut		\aú\ **out**		\i\ tip		\ò\ **saw**		\ú\ **foot**
\ər\ **further**		\ch\ **chin**		\ī\ life		\ói\ **coin**		\y\ **yet**
\a\ **mat**		\e\ **pet**		\j\ **job**		\th\ **thin**		\yü\ **few**
\ā\ **take**		\ē\ **easy**		\ŋ\ **sing**		\th\ **this**		\yù\ **cure**
\ä\ **cot, cart**		\g\ **go**		\ō\ **bone**		\ü\ **food**		\zh\ **vision**

ering at which a baked food is served; *esp* : CLAMBAKE **3**
: baked food ⟨a *bake* sale⟩

bakers' dozen *n* : THIRTEEN

bakers' yeast *n* : a yeast used or suitable for use in making
dough rise

bak·ery \'bā-k(ə-)rē\ *n, pl* **-er·ies** : a place where bread,
cakes, and pastry are made or sold

bake·shop \'bāk-,shäp\ *n* : BAKERY

baking powder *n* : a powder that consists of a carbonate,
an acid, and a starch and that makes the dough rise in
baking cakes and biscuits

baking soda *n* : SODIUM BICARBONATE

¹bal·ance \'bal-ən(t)s\
n **1** : an instrument
used for measuring
mass or weight **2**
: a counterbalancing
weight, force, or influ-
ence **3** : a vibrating
wheel operating with
a hairspring to regu-
late the mechanical
motions of a time-
piece **4** : a condition

balance 1

in which opposing forces are equal to each other **5**
: equality between the totals of the two sides of an account
6 : an orderly and artistic arrangement of elements that is
pleasing : HARMONY **7 a** : something left over : REMAIN-
DER **b** : the amount by which one side of an account is
greater than the other ⟨a *balance* of $10 on the credit side⟩
8 : mental and emotional steadiness **9** : the maintenance
(as in a natural habitat) of a population in about the same
condition and numbers

²balance *vb* **bal·anced; bal·anc·ing** **1** : to figure out the
difference between the debits and credits of an account **2
a** : to make two parts exactly equal ⟨*balance* equations⟩
b : to complete (a chemical equation) so that the same
number of atoms and electric charges of each kind appears on each side **3 a** : ²COUNTERBALANCE, OFFSET **b**
: to equal or make equal in weight, number, or proportion
4 : to weigh against one another : COMPARE **5** : to bring
or come to a state or position of balance — **bal·anc·er** *n*

balance beam *n* : a narrow wooden beam supported in a
horizontal position above the floor and used for balancing
feats in gymnastics

balance of nature : the fine state of balance in a natural
ecosystem due to the effects of the living and nonliving
parts of the environment on each other ⟨species of plants
or animals sometimes die out when human beings upset
the *balance of nature*⟩

balance wheel *n* : a wheel that adjusts the motion of a
mechanism (as a timepiece or a sewing machine)

bal·co·ny \'bal-kə-nē\ *n, pl* **-nies** **1** : a platform enclosed
by a low wall or railing and built out from the side of a
building **2** : a platform inside a building extending out
over part of the main floor (as of a theater)

¹bald \'bȯld\ *adj* **1** : lacking a natural or usual covering (as
of hair) **2** : ²PLAIN 1, UNADORNED ⟨the *bald* facts⟩ — **bald-
ly** *adv* — **bald·ness**
\'bȯl(d)-nəs\ *n*

²bald *vb* : to become bald
⟨his head is *balding*⟩

bald cypress *n* : either of
two large swamp trees re-
lated to the pine and found
in the southern U.S.

bald eagle *n* : a North
American eagle which is
mostly dark when young
but has white head and
neck feathers when ma-
ture

bald eagle

bal·dric \'bȯl-drik\ *n* : a belt worn over one shoulder to provide a device from which to hang a sword or bugle at the
opposite hip

¹bale \'bā(ə)l\ *n* : a large bundle of goods tightly tied for
storing or shipping ⟨a *bale* of cotton⟩

²bale *vb* **baled; bal·ing** : to make up into a bale — **bal·er**
n

ba·leen \bə-'lēn, 'bā-,lēn\ *n* : WHALEBONE

baleen whale *n* : WHALEBONE WHALE

bale·ful \'bāl-fəl\ *adj* **1** : deadly or harmful in influence **2**
: threatening harm or evil — **bale·ful·ly** \-fə-lē\ *adv* —
bale·ful·ness *n*

¹balk \'bȯk\ *n* **1** : something that prevents movement or
action **2** : an illegal motion of a baseball pitcher while in
position to pitch with a runner on base

²balk *vb* **1** : to check or stop by or as if by something in
the way : BLOCK **2** : to stop and refuse to go ⟨horse
balked⟩ **3** : to make a balk in baseball — **balk·er** *n*

balky \'bȯ-kē\ *adj* **balk·i·er; -est** : likely to balk

¹ball \'bȯl\ *n* **1 a** : something round or roundish ⟨a *ball* of
twine⟩ **b** : a usually round object used in a game or sport
c : a usually round shot for a firearm **d** : the rounded
bulge at the base of the thumb or big toe **2** : a game or
sport (as baseball) played with a ball **3** : a pitched baseball that fails to pass through the strike zone and is not
struck at by the batter [Middle English *bal* "ball"; of Norse
origin]

²ball *vb* : to make or come together into a ball

³ball *n* : a large formal party for dancing [from French *bal* "a
dance", derived from Latin *ballare* "to dance" — related to
BALLET]

bal·lad \'bal-əd\ *n* **1** : a simple song **2** : a poem that tells
a story of adventure, of romance, or of a hero, that is suitable for singing, and that usually has stanzas of four lines
with a rhyme on the second and fourth lines **3** : a usually
slow or sentimental popular song

ball–and–socket joint *n* : a joint (as in the hip) in which a
rounded part moves within a socket so as to allow movements in many directions

bal·last \'bal-əst\ *n* **1** : heavy material used to make a
ship steady or to control the rising of a balloon **2** : gravel
or broken stone laid in a foundation for a railroad or used
in making concrete — **ballast** *vb*

ball bearing *n* **1** : a bearing in which the revolving part
turns on steel balls that roll easily in a groove **2** : one of
the balls in a ball bearing

ball·car·ri·er \'bȯl-,kar-ē-ər\ *n* : the football player carrying
the ball in an offensive play

bal·le·ri·na \,bal-ə-'rē-nə\ *n* : a female ballet dancer

bal·let \'bal-ā, ba-'lā\ *n* **1** : a stage dance that tells a story
in movement and pantomime **2** : a group that performs
ballets [from French *ballet* "ballet", derived from Italian
ballare "to dance", from Latin *ballare* "to dance" — related to ³BALL]

bal·lis·tic \bə-'lis-tik\ *adj* : of or relating to ballistics

ballistic missile *n* : a missile that moves under its own
power, is guided as it rises in a steeply curving path, and
falls freely on the way back to earth

bal·lis·tics \bə-'lis-tiks\ *n sing or pl* **1** : the science that
deals with the motion of objects (as bullets or rockets) that
are thrown or driven forward **2** : the flight characteristics
of an object (as a bullet or rocket) that is thrown or driven
forward

¹bal·loon \bə-'lün\ *n* **1** : a bag of tough light material filled
with heated gas or a gas lighter than air so as to rise and
float in the atmosphere **2** : a toy consisting of an inflat-
able rubber bag **3** : an outline containing words spoken
or thought by a character (as in a cartoon)

²balloon *vb* **1** : to go up or travel in a balloon **2** : to swell
or puff out **3** : to increase rapidly

¹bal·lot \'bal-ət\ *n* **1** : a small ball used in secret voting or
a sheet of paper used to cast a vote **2 a** : the action or

system of voting **b** : the right to vote **3** : the number of votes cast

> **Word History** When juries voted in ancient Athens, each juror dropped a colored ball into a cup. A white ball meant "not guilty", and a black ball meant "guilty". In modern times, a black ball cast by a member of a social club can mean that a new candidate is rejected. From this practice comes the word *blackball,* meaning "to exclude from membership". When voting was done by the people of Venice during the Renaissance, secrecy was assured by the use of little colored or marked balls. The Italian for "little ball" is *ballotta,* from *balla,* meaning "ball", and the suffix *-otta,* "little". Now any kind of secret voting, by ball, piece of paper, or voting machine, is called a *ballot.* So is the right to vote itself. [from Italian *ballotta* "little ball (used in voting)", from *balla* "ball"]

²ballot *vb* : to vote or decide by ballot

ball·park \'bòl-,pärk\ *n* : a park in which ball games are played

ball·point \-,pòint\ *n* : a pen whose writing point is a small metal ball that inks itself from an inner supply

ball·room \'bòl-,rüm, -,rùm\ *n* : a large room for dances

bal·ly·hoo \'bal-ē-,hü\ *n* : extravagant statements and claims made for publicity — **ballyhoo** *vb*

balm \'bäm, 'bälm\ *n* **1** : a balsamic resin; *esp* : one from small tropical evergreen trees **2** : a fragrant healing or soothing preparation (as an ointment) **3** : something that comforts or refreshes

balm of Gil·e·ad \-'gil-ē-əd\ **1 a** : a small African and Asian tree with fragrant evergreen leaves **b** : a product from balm of Gilead consisting of its oil and resin **2** : either of two poplars often grown in cultivation

balmy \'bäm-ē, 'bäl-mē\ *adj* **balm·i·er; -est 1** : gently soothing **2** : FOOLISH, INSANE — **balm·i·ly** \'bäm-ə-lē, 'bäl-mə-\ *adv* — **balm·i·ness** \'bäm-ē-nəs, 'bäl-mē-\ *n*

bal·sa \'bòl-sə\ *n* **1** : ¹RAFT; *esp* : one made of two cylinders of metal or wood joined by a frame **2** : a tropical American tree with extremely light strong wood used especially for floats; *also* : its wood

bal·sam \'bòl-səm\ *n* **1 a** : a fragrant and usually oily substance that slowly flows from various plants **b** : a preparation containing or smelling like balsam **2 a** : a balsam-yielding tree (as balsam fir) **b** : IMPATIENS; *esp* : one grown as an ornamental **3** : BALM 2 — **bal·sam·ic** \bòl-'sam-ik\ *adj*

balsam fir *n* : an American evergreen tree related to the pines and widely used for pulpwood and as a Christmas tree

balsam poplar *n* : a North American poplar that is often cultivated as a shade tree and has buds thickly coated with a resin

Bal·tic \'bòl-tik\ *adj* **1** : of or relating to the Baltic sea or to the states of Lithuania, Latvia, and Estonia **2** : of or relating to a branch of the Indo-European languages containing Latvian, Lithuanian, and Old Prussian

Bal·ti·more oriole \,bòl-tə-,mō(ə)r-, -,mó(ə)r-, -mər-\ *n* : a common American oriole which builds a finely woven hanging nest of grass and fiber and the male of which is black, white, and brilliant orange

bal·us·ter \'bal-ə-stər\ *n* : a short post that supports a rail (as of a staircase)

bal·us·trade \'bal-ə-,strād\ *n* : a row of balusters topped by a rail; *also* : a low wall or barrier

bam·boo \bam-'bü\ *n, pl* **bam·boos** : any of various chiefly

bamboo

tropical tall woody grasses including some with strong hollow stems used for building, furniture, or utensils — **bamboo** *adj*

¹ban \'ban\ *vb* **banned; ban·ning** : to forbid especially by law or social pressure

²ban *n* **1** : ¹CURSE 1 **2** : an official order forbidding something

ba·nal \bə-'nal, bā-, -'näl; bā-'näl; 'bān-ᵊl\ *adj* : not original, fresh, or exciting : STALE, COMMONPLACE — **ba·nal·i·ty** \bə-'nal-ət-ē *also* bā- *or* ba-\ *n* — **ba·nal·ly** \bə-'nal-lē, ba-, -'näl-; bā-'näl-; 'bān-ᵊl-(l)ē\ *adv*

ba·nana \bə-'nan-ə\ *n* : a treelike tropical plant with large leaves and flower clusters that develop into a bunch of finger-shaped fruit which are yellow or red when ripe; *also* : its fruit

banana oil *n* : a colorless liquid acetate that has a fruity odor and is used to dissolve things and to make artificial fruit scents

ba·nan·as \bə-'nan-əz\ *adj* : CRAZY 1 ⟨you're driving me *bananas*⟩

banana split *n* : ice cream served on a banana split in half lengthwise and usually covered with syrups, fruits, nuts, and whipped cream

¹band \'band\ *n* **1** : something that binds, ties, or goes around while allowing some motion **2** : a strip that can be told (as by color, texture, or composition) from nearby matter ⟨a *band* of nerve fibers⟩ **3** : a range of wavelengths, frequencies, or energies between two specified limits **4** : a strip of grooves on a phonograph record containing recorded sound [partly from a word of Norse origin meaning "something that binds" and partly from early French *bande* "stripe"; of Germanic origin] — **band·ed** \'ban-dəd\ *adj*

²band *vb* **1** : to put a band on **2** : to tie up with a band **3** : to join in a group ⟨*banded* together for protection⟩

³band *n* **1** : a group of persons, animals, or things **2** : a group of musicians playing together [from early French *bande* "troop", derived from an earlier word of Germanic origin]

¹ban·dage \'ban-dij\ *n* : a strip of fabric used especially to dress and bind up wounds

²bandage *vb* **ban·daged; ban·dag·ing** : to bind, dress, or cover with a bandage

Band–Aid \'ban-'dād\ *trademark* — used for a small adhesive strip with a gauze pad for covering minor wounds

ban·dan·na *or* **ban·dana** \ban-'dan-ə\ *n* : a large handkerchief usually with a colorful design printed on it

band·box \'ban(d)-,bäks\ *n* : a usually round box of paperboard or thin wood often used for storing a hat

ban·di·coot \'ban-di-,küt\ *n* : any of various small insect-eating and plant-eating marsupial mammals especially of Australia

ban·dit \'ban-dət\ *n, pl* **bandits** *also* **ban·dit·ti** \ban-'dit-ē\ : a person who lives by stealing often as a member of a band : ROBBER, OUTLAW [from Italian *bandito,* literally "one who is under a ban"] — **ban·dit·ry** \'ban-də-trē\ *n*

band·mas·ter \'ban(d)-,mas-tər\ *n* : a conductor of a musical band

ban·do·lier *or* **ban·do·leer**

bandolier

\ə\ **abut**		\au̇\ **out**	\i\ **tip**	\ȯ\ **saw**	\u̇\ **foot**
\ər\ **further**		\ch\ **chin**	\ī\ **life**	\ȯi\ **coin**	\y\ **yet**
\a\ **mat**		\e\ **pet**	\j\ **job**	\th\ **thin**	\yü\ **few**
\ā\ **take**		\ē\ **easy**	\ŋ\ **sing**	\th\ **this**	\yu̇\ **cure**
\ä\ **cot, cart**		\g\ **go**	\ō\ **bone**	\ü\ **food**	\zh\ **vision**

\,ban-də-'li(ə)r\ *n* : a belt worn over the shoulder and across the body along the length of which items (as cartridges) may be carried in loops or pouches

band saw *n* : a saw in the form of a continuous steel band running over pulleys

band·stand \'ban(d)-,stand\ *n* : an outdoor platform used for band concerts

band·wag·on \'ban-,dwag-ən\ *n* **1** : a wagon carrying musicians in a parade **2** : a popular movement or activity that attracts growing support

¹**ban·dy** \'ban-dē\ *vb* **ban·died; ban·dy·ing** **1** : to exchange (words) in argument **2** : to discuss or mention in gossip or small talk ⟨several names were *bandied* about⟩

²**bandy** *adj* : curved especially outward ⟨*bandy* legs⟩

ban·dy–legged \,ban-dē-'leg(-ə)d\ *adj* : having bandy legs

bane \'bān\ *n* **1** : ¹POISON 1 **2** : a source of harm, ruin, or unhappiness

bane·ful \'bān-fəl\ *adj* : causing destruction or serious harm — **bane·ful·ly** \-fə-lē\ *adv*

¹**bang** \'ban\ *vb* : to beat, strike, or shut with a loud noise [probably of Scandinavian origin]

²**bang** *n* **1** : a violent blow **2** : a sudden loud noise **3 a** : a quick burst of energy ⟨start off with a *bang*⟩ **b** : a feeling of being thrilled or pleased ⟨you'll get a *bang* out of this⟩

³**bang** *n* : hair cut short across the forehead — usually used in pl. [probably derived from earlier *bangtail* "a short tail (on a horse)"]

⁴**bang** *vb* : to cut (front hair) short and squarely across

ban·gle \'ban-gəl\ *n* **1** : a stiff bracelet or anklet **2** : a small ornament hanging from a bracelet or necklace

bang–up \'ban-,əp\ *adj* : FIRST-RATE, EXCELLENT ⟨had a *bang-up* time⟩ ⟨a *bang-up* job⟩

ban·ish \'ban-ish\ *vb* **1** : to force to leave a country **2** : to drive away ⟨*banish* fears⟩ — **ban·ish·ment** \-mənt\ *n*

ban·is·ter \'ban-ə-stər\ *n* **1** : one of the slender posts used to support the handrail of a staircase **2** : a handrail with its supporting posts **3** : the handrail of a staircase

ban·jo \'ban-jō\ *n, pl* **ban·jos** *also* **banjoes** : a musical instrument with a round body like a drum, a long fretted neck, and four or five strings

banjo

¹**bank** \'bank\ *n* **1** : a mound, pile, or ridge of earth **2** : a piled-up mass of cloud or fog **3** : a rise in the sea bottom **4** : the rising ground at the edge of a lake, river, or sea **5** : a steep slope (as of a hill) **6** : the inward tilt of a surface along a curve or of a vehicle (as an airplane) when taking a curve [Middle English *bank* "piled up mass"; probably of Scandinavian origin]

²**bank** *vb* **1** : to raise a bank around **2** : to cover (as a fire) with fresh fuel to reduce the speed of burning **3** : to build with the foundation of a road or railroad sloping upward from the inside edge ⟨*bank* a curve⟩ **4** : to heap or pile in a bank **5** : to rise in or form a bank **6** : to tilt an airplane sideways when turning

³**bank** *n* **1** : a place of business that lends, exchanges, takes care of, or issues money **2** : a small closed container in which money may be saved **3** : a storage place (as for a reserve supply) ⟨a blood *bank*⟩ ⟨a computer's memory *bank*⟩ [Middle English *bank* "table or counter of a money changer", from early French *banque* (same meaning) or early Italian *banca*, literally "bench"; of Germanic origin]

⁴**bank** *vb* **1** : to have an account in a bank **2** : to deposit in a bank ⟨*banks* $10 every week⟩ — **bank on** : to depend on ⟨we're *banking on* fair weather for the trip⟩

⁵**bank** *n* : a group or series of objects arranged close together in a row ⟨a *bank* of seats⟩ [Middle English *bank* "bench for rowers", from early French *banc* "bench"; of Germanic origin]

bank·book \'bank-,bůk\ *n* : the depositor's book in which a bank enters deposits and withdrawals

bank·card \-,kärd\ *n* : a credit card issued by a bank

bank·er \'ban-kər\ *n* : a person who is engaged in the business of a bank

bank·ing \'ban-kin\ *n* : the business of a bank or banker

bank note *n* : a note issued by a bank that must be paid without interest to anyone presenting it at any time and that may be used as money

bank·roll \'bank-,rōl\ *n* : supply of money : FUNDS

¹**bank·rupt** \'ban-(,)krəpt\ *n* : an individual or group who becomes bankrupt; *esp* : one whose property by court order is turned over to be managed for the benefit of the creditors

²**bankrupt** *vb* : to make bankrupt

³**bankrupt** *adj* : unable to pay one's debts

bank·rupt·cy \'ban-(,)krəp-(t)sē\ *n, pl* **-cies** : the condition of being bankrupt

¹**ban·ner** \'ban-ər\ *n* **1** : ²FLAG 1 **2** : a strip of cloth with a design, picture, or writing on it

²**banner** *adj* : unusually good : OUTSTANDING ⟨a *banner* year for apples⟩

banns \'banz\ *n pl* : public announcement especially in church of a proposed marriage

¹**ban·quet** \'ban-kwət, 'ban- *also* -,kwet\ *n* : a formal dinner for many people often in honor of someone

²**banquet** *vb* : to treat or be treated with a banquet : FEAST — **ban·quet·er** *n*

ban·shee \'ban-(,)shē, ban-'shē\ *n* : a female spirit in Gaelic folklore whose wailing warns that a death will occur soon [from Scottish Gaelic (the ancient language of Scotland) *bean-sīth*, literally "woman of the fairyland"]

ban·tam \'bant-əm\ *n* : any of numerous small domestic fowls that are often miniatures of members of the standard breeds — **bantam** *adj*

ban·tam·weight \-,wāt\ *n* : a boxer in a weight division having the approximate range of 51 to 54 kilograms

¹**ban·ter** \'bant-ər\ *vb* : to speak in a friendly but teasing or witty way — **ban·ter·er** \-ər-ər\ *n* — **ban·ter·ing·ly** \'bant-ə-rin-lē\ *adv*

²**banter** *n* : good-natured teasing or joking

Ban·tu \'ban-(,)tü, 'bän-\ *n, pl* **Bantu** *or* **Bantus** **1 a** : a family of Negroid peoples who occupy equatorial and southern Africa **b** : a member of any of these peoples **2** : a group of African languages spoken in equatorial and southern Africa

ban·yan \'ban-yən\ *n* : a large East Indian tree from whose branches roots grow downward into the ground and form new supporting trunks

banyan

bap·tism \'bap-,tiz-əm\ *n* **1** : the act or ceremony of baptizing **2** : an act or experience that baptizes ⟨a soldier's *baptism* of fire⟩ — **bap·tis·mal** \bap-'tiz-məl\ *adj* — **bap·tis·mal·ly** \-mə-lē\ *adv*

Bap·tist \'bap-təst\ *adj* : of or relating to any of several Protestant denominations practicing baptism by immersion — **Baptist** *n*

bap·tize \bap-'tīz, 'bap-,tīz\ *vb* **bap·tized; bap·tiz·ing** **1** : to dip in water or sprinkle water on as a part of the ceremony of receiving into the Christian church **2 a** : to make pure in spirit (as by a painful experience) **b**

: ¹INITIATE 3   **3** : to give a name to as in the ceremony of baptism : CHRISTEN — **bap·tiz·er** *n*

¹**bar** \'bär\ *n*   **1 a** : a straight piece (as of metal or wood) that is longer than it is wide   **b** : a usually rectangular piece or block of material ⟨a *bar* of soap⟩   **2** : something that hinders or blocks : OBSTACLE   **3** : a bank (as of sand) partly or entirely under water along a shore or in a river   **4 a** : the railing in a courtroom around the place where the business of the court is carried on   **b** : a court of law   **c** : the profession of law   **5** : ³STRIPE 1   **6 a** : a counter on which liquor or food is served   **b** : BARROOM   **7 a** : a vertical line across the musical staff before the beginning of a measure   **b** : ¹MEASURE 4c [Middle English *barre* "bar", from early French *barre* (same meaning)]

²**bar** *vb* **barred; bar·ring**   **1** : to fasten with a bar ⟨*bar* the door⟩   **2** : to mark with bars : STRIPE ⟨gray feathers *barred* with brown⟩   **3** : to block off : CLOSE ⟨*bar* the road with a chain⟩   **4 a** : to keep out : EXCLUDE ⟨*bar* reporters from a meeting⟩   **b** : PREVENT 1, FORBID ⟨the judge *barred* them from talking to reporters⟩

³**bar** *prep* : with the exception of ⟨*bar* none⟩

⁴**bar** *n* : a unit of pressure [from German *bar* "unit of pressure", from Greek *baros* "weight, pressure"]

barb \'bärb\ *n*   **1** : a sharp point that sticks out and backward (as from the point of an arrow or fishhook)   **2** : an often witty remark intended to hurt one's feelings [Middle English *barbe* "barb, beard", from early French *barbe* (same meaning), from Latin *barba* "beard" — related to BARBER]

bar·bar·i·an \bär-'ber-ē-ən, bär-'bar-\ *n* : an uncivilized person

bar·bar·ic \bär-'bar-ik\ *adj*   **1** : of, relating to, or characteristic of barbarians   **2** : CRUEL 2, SAVAGE

bar·ba·rism \'bär-bə-ˌriz-əm\ *n* : the state, ideas, or behavior of a barbarian

bar·bar·i·ty \bär-'bar-ət-ē\ *n, pl* **-ties**   **1** : BARBARISM   **2 a** : CRUELTY 1   **b** : a cruel act

bar·ba·rous \'bär-b(ə-)rəs\ *adj*   **1** : UNCIVILIZED 1   **2** : CRUEL 2, SAVAGE — **bar·ba·rous·ly** *adv* — **bar·ba·rous·ness** *n*

¹**bar·be·cue** \'bär-bi-ˌkyü\ *n*   **1** : a large animal (as a hog or steer) roasted or broiled over an open fire   **2** : an outdoor social gathering at which barbecued food is eaten [from American Spanish *barbacoa* "a portable grill"; of Caribbean Indian origin]

²**barbecue** *vb* **-cued; -cu·ing**   **1** : to cook over or before an open source of heat (as hot coals)   **2** : to cook in a highly seasoned sauce

barbed wire \'bä(r)b-'(d)wī(ə)r\ *n* : wire (as for a fence) with sharp points spaced evenly along it

bar·bel \'bär-bəl\ *n* : a slender process on the lip of some fishes (as a catfish) that is used for feeling

bar·bell \'bär-ˌbel\ *n* : a bar with adjustable weighted disks attached to each end that is used for exercise and in weight lifting

bar·ber \'bär-bər\ *n* : a person whose business is cutting and dressing hair and shaving beards [Middle English *barber* "barber", from early French *barbeor* (same meaning), derived from Latin *barba* "beard" — related to BARB] — **barber** *vb*

bar·ber·ry \'bär-ˌber-ē\ *n* : any of a genus of spiny yellow-flowered shrubs often grown for hedges or ornament

bar·ber·shop \'bär-bər-ˌshäp\ *n* : a barber's place of business

bar·bit·u·rate \bär-'bich-ə-rət, -ˌrāt, ˌbär-bə-'t(y)ùr-ət, -'t(y)ù(ə)r-ˌāt\ *n* : any of various compounds related to barbituric acid and used especially to calm or to produce sleep

bar·bi·tu·ric acid \ˌbär-bə-ˌt(y)ùr-ik-\ *n* : an organic acid used in making plastics and drugs

barb·wire \(')bä(r)b-'wī(ə)r\ *n* : BARBED WIRE

bar·ca·role *or* **bar·ca·rolle** \'bär-kə-ˌrōl\ *n*   **1** : a Venetian gondoliers' song   **2** : a piece of music imitating a barcarole

bar chart *n* : BAR GRAPH

bar code *n* : a code made up of a group of printed and variously spaced bars and sometimes numerals that is designed to be scanned and read into computer memory as identification of the object it labels

bard \'bärd\ *n*   **1** : a person in ancient societies skilled at composing and singing or reciting verses about heroes and their deeds   **2** : POET — **bard·ic** \'bärd-ik\ *adj*

¹**bare** \'ba(ə)r, 'be(ə)r\ *adj* **bar·er; bar·est**   **1** : lacking a covering : NAKED ⟨bare of leaves⟩   **2** : open to view ⟨the scandal was laid *bare*⟩   **3** : ¹EMPTY 1 ⟨the cupboard was *bare*⟩   **4 a** : just enough with nothing to spare ⟨a *bare* majority⟩ ⟨the *bare* necessities of life⟩   **b** : not decorated or added to : PLAIN ⟨the *bare* facts⟩ ⟨a *bare* outline of the story⟩ — **bare·ly** *adv* — **bare·ness** *n*

²**bare** *vb* **bared; bar·ing** : to make or lay bare : UNCOVER, REVEAL

bare·back \'ba(ə)r-ˌbak, 'be(ə)r-\ *or* **bare·backed** \-'bakt\ *adv or adj* : on the bare back of a horse : without a saddle ⟨rode *bareback*⟩ ⟨the art of *bareback* riding⟩

bare·faced \-'fāst\ *adj* : not pretending to be anything else : not appearing to be something different ⟨a *bare-faced* lie⟩ ⟨a *bare-faced* liar⟩

bare·foot \-ˌfùt\ *or* **bare·foot·ed** \-'fùt-əd\ *adv or adj* : with the feet bare : without shoes

bare·hand·ed \-'han-dəd\ *adv or adj*   **1** : with the hands bare : without gloves or mittens   **2** : without tools or weapons

bare·head·ed \-'hed-əd\ *adv or adj* : with the head bare : without a hat

¹**bar·gain** \'bär-gən\ *n*   **1** : an agreement between parties settling what each is to give or receive in a business deal   **2** : something bought or offered for sale at a desirable price   **syn** see AGREEMENT

²**bargain** *vb* : to talk over the terms of a purchase or agreement — **bar·gain·er** *n* — **bargain for** : EXPECT 2 ⟨more trouble than we *bargained for*⟩

¹**barge** \'bärj\ *n* : a broad flat-bottomed boat that is usually towed and used chiefly to transport goods in harbors and on rivers and canals

²**barge** *vb* **barged; barg·ing**   **1** : to carry by barge   **2** : to move or push oneself clumsily or rudely ⟨*barged* right in⟩

bar graph *n* : a graphic means of comparing numbers by rectangles whose lengths are proportional to the numbers they represent — called also *bar chart*

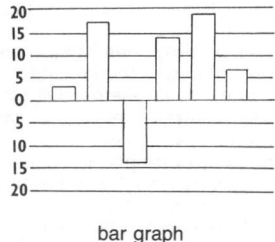

bar graph

bar·ite *or* **bar·yte** \'ba(ə)r-ˌīt, 'be(ə)r-\ *or* **ba·ry·tes** \bə-'rīt-ēz\ *n* : a white, yellow, or colorless mineral consisting of barium sulfate and occurring in crystals or as a mass

bar·i·tone \'bar-ə-ˌtōn\ *n*   **1 a** : a male singing voice between bass and tenor   **b** : a singer having such a voice   **2** : a horn with a range between that of the trumpet and the tuba

bar·i·um \'bar-ē-əm, 'ber-\ *n* : a silver-white poisonous metallic element that occurs only in combination — see ELEMENT table

barium sulfate *n* : a colorless crystalline insoluble sulfate of barium used especially in taking X-ray photographs of the

\ə\ **abut**		\aù\ **out**	\i\ **tip**	\ò\ **saw**	\ù\ **foot**
\ər\ **further**		\ch\ **chin**	\ī\ **life**	\òi\ **coin**	\y\ **yet**
\a\ **mat**		\e\ **pet**	\j\ **job**	\th\ **thin**	\yü\ **few**
\ā\ **take**		\ē\ **easy**	\ŋ\ **sing**	\th\ **this**	\yù\ **cure**
\ä\ **cot, cart**		\g\ **go**	\ō\ **bone**	\ü\ **food**	\zh\ **vision**

digestive tract

¹bark \'bärk\ *vb* **1** : to make the short loud cry of a dog or a similar noise **2** : to shout or speak sharply ⟨*bark* out an order⟩ [Old English *beorcan* "to bark"]

²bark *n* : the sound made by a barking dog

³bark *n* : the tough mostly corky covering of a woody root or stem [Middle English *bark* "tree covering"; of Norse origin]

⁴bark *vb* **1** : to strip the bark from **2** : to rub or scrape the skin of ⟨*barked* her knee⟩

⁵bark *n* **1** : a small sailing ship **2** : a three-masted ship with the first two masts square-rigged and the last fore-and-aft rigged [Middle English *bark* "a small ship", from early French *barque* (same meaning)]

bark beetle *n* : any of a group of beetles that bore under bark of trees both as larvae and adults

bark·er \'bär-kər\ *n* : a person who stands at the entrance to a show and tries to attract customers by loud fast talk

bar·ley \'bär-lē\ *n* : a cereal grass with flowers in dense spikes; *also* : its seed used especially in malt beverages and as food or feed for livestock

bar·ley·corn \-ˌkò(ə)rn\ *n* **1** : a grain of barley **2** : an old unit of length equal to the average length of a grain of barley : a third of an inch (about 8 millimeters)

bar·low \'bär-ˌlō\ *n* : a sturdy inexpensive jackknife [named for Russell *Barlow*, English knife maker]

bar mitz·vah \bär-'mits-və\, *often cap B&M* **1** : a Jewish boy who on his 13th birthday reaches the age of religious duty and responsibility **2** : the ceremony recognizing a boy as a bar mitzvah [from Hebrew *bar miswāh,* literally "son of the (divine) law"]

barn \'bärn\ *n* : a building used chiefly for storing grain and hay and for housing farm animals or farm equipment

bar·na·cle \'bär-ni-kəl\ *n* : any of numerous small saltwater shellfish that are crustaceans, are free-swimming as larvae, and as adults fasten themselves to rocks, wharves, and the bottoms of ships — **bar·na·cled** \-kəld\ *adj*

barn owl *n* : a widely distributed owl with brown, gray, and white feathers that is found near buildings and preys especially on rodents

barn·storm \'bärn-ˌstòrm\ *vb* : to travel through the country making brief stops to entertain (as with shows or flying stunts) or to campaign for political office — **barn·storm·er** *n*

barn swallow *n* : a common swallow that usually nests in barns

barn·yard \'bärn-ˌyärd\ *n* : a usually fenced area around a barn

baro·graph \'bar-ə-ˌgraf\ *n* : a recording barometer

ba·rom·e·ter \bə-'räm-ət-ər\ *n* : an instrument that measures the pressure of the atmosphere to determine probable weather changes — **baro·met·ric** \ˌbar-ə-'me-trik\ *adj*

barometric pressure *n* : the pressure of the atmosphere usually expressed as the height of a column of mercury

bar·on \'bar-ən\ *n* **1** : a member of the lowest rank of the British nobility **2** : a person of great power or influence ⟨a cattle *baron*⟩

bar·on·ess \'bar-ə-nəs\ *n* **1** : the wife or widow of a baron **2** : a woman holding the rank of baron

bar·on·et \'bar-ə-nət *also* ˌbar-ə-'net\ *n* : a man holding a rank of honor below a baron but above a knight

ba·ro·ni·al \bə-'rō-nē-əl\ *adj* : of, relating to, or suitable for a baron ⟨*baronial* splendor⟩

ba·roque \bə-'rōk, ba-, -'räk\ *adj* : of or relating to a style of art and music common in the 17th century that is marked especially by the use of much fancy decoration — **baroque** *n*

bar·racks \'bar-əks, -iks\ *n sing or pl* : a building or group of buildings in which soldiers live

bar·ra·cu·da \ˌbar-ə-'küd-ə\ *n, pl* **-da** *or* **-das** : any of several large fierce marine fishes of warm seas that have strong jaws and sharp teeth and that include some used

for food

bar·rage \bə-'räzh, -'räj\ *n* **1** : a barrier formed by continuous artillery or machine-gun fire directed upon a narrow strip of ground **2** : a rapid or furiously active flow (as of speech or writing)

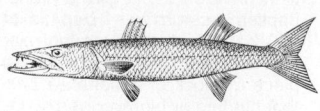
barracuda

barred \'bärd\ *adj* : having alternate bands of different color

¹bar·rel \'bar-əl\ *n* **1** : a round bulging container that is longer than it is wide and has flat ends **2 a** : the amount held by a barrel **b** : a great quantity **3** : a part shaped like a cylinder or tube ⟨gun *barrel*⟩ ⟨the *barrel* of a carburetor⟩ — **bar·reled** \-əld\ *adj*

²barrel *vb* **-reled** *or* **-relled; -rel·ing** *or* **-rel·ling** : to travel at a high speed ⟨*barreling* down the highway⟩

barrel cactus *n* : any of a genus of nearly globe-shaped cacti with many ridges on the outside that are found in Mexico and in nearby parts of the U.S.

barrel organ *n* : a musical instrument having a series of pegs arranged around a revolving cylinder so that they open valves to admit air from a bellows to a set of pipes

¹bar·ren \'bar-ən\ *adj* **1 a** : incapable of producing offspring — used especially of females **b** : usually failing to fruit **2 a** : producing inferior or only a small amount of vegetation ⟨*barren* soils⟩ **b** : not productive of results or gain ⟨a *barren* scheme⟩ — **bar·ren·ly** *adv* — **bar·ren·ness** \-ən-nəs\ *n*

²barren *n* : a tract of barren land

bar·rette \bä-'ret, bə-\ *n* : a clip or bar for holding a girl's or woman's hair in place

¹bar·ri·cade \'bar-ə-ˌkād, ˌbar-ə-'kād\ *vb* **-cad·ed; -cad·ing** : to block off with a barricade

²barricade *n* : a barrier usually made in a hurry for protection against attack or for blocking the way

bar·ri·er \'bar-ē-ər\ *n* **1** : something (as a fence, railing, or natural obstacle) that blocks the way **2** : something not material that keeps apart or makes progress difficult ⟨language *barriers*⟩

barrier reef *n* : a coral reef roughly parallel to a shore and separated from it by a lagoon

bar·ring \'bär-iŋ\ *prep* **1** : with the exception of ⟨*barring* none⟩ **2** : apart from the possibility of ⟨will be there on time, *barring* accidents⟩

bar·rio \'bär-ē-ˌō, 'bar-\ *n* : a neighborhood where most of the people speak Spanish [Spanish]

bar·room \'bär-ˌrüm, -ˌrùm\ *n* : a place of business for the sale of alcoholic drinks

¹bar·row \'bar-ō\ *n* : a large burial mound of earth or stones [Old English *beorg* "mound"]

²barrow *n* **1** : a structure that has handles and sometimes a wheel and is used for carrying things **2** : a cart with a shallow box body, two wheels, and shafts for pushing it : PUSHCART [Old English *bearwe* "barrow"]

bar·tend·er \'bär-ˌten-dər\ *n* : a person who serves alcoholic drinks at a bar

¹bar·ter \'bärt-ər\ *vb* : to trade one thing for another without the use of money — **bar·ter·er** \'bärt-ər-ər\ *n*

²barter *n* : the exchange of goods without the use of money

Ba·ruch \bə-'rük, 'bär-ˌük\ *n* — see BIBLE table

baryte *or* **barytes** *variant of* BARITE

bas·al \'bā-səl, -zəl\ *adj* : relating to, located at, or forming a base — **bas·al·ly** \-sə-lē, -zə-lē\ *adv*

basal metabolic rate *n* : the rate at which heat is given off by an organism at complete rest

basal metabolism *n* : the body's metabolism in a fasting and resting state in which just enough energy is being used for cell activity, respiration, and circulation to maintain life

ba·salt \bə-'sólt, 'bā-ˌsólt\ *n* : a dark gray to black usually fine-grained igneous rock — **ba·sal·tic** \bə-'sól-tik\ *adj*

¹base \'bās\ *n, pl* **bas·es** \'bā-səz\　**1 a** : a thing or part on which something rests : BOTTOM, FOUNDATION ⟨the *base* of a lamp⟩　**b** : a part of a plant or animal organ by which it is attached to a more central structure ⟨leaf *base*⟩　**c** : one of the lines or plane surfaces of a geometric figure from which an altitude is or can be constructed ⟨*bases* of a trapezoid⟩; *esp* : one on which the figure stands ⟨*base* of a triangle⟩　**2** : a main ingredient ⟨paint having a water *base*⟩　**3** : a fundamental part : BASIS　**4 a** : the place from which a start is made　**b** : a line in a survey that is used to calculate numbers　**c** : a place where a military force keeps its supplies or from which it starts its operations ⟨naval *base*⟩ ⟨air *base*⟩　**d** : the number with reference to which a system of numbers is constructed; *esp* : the number of units in a given digit's place of a number system that is required to give one in the next higher place ⟨the decimal system uses a *base* of 10⟩　**e** : ¹ROOT 5　**5 a** : the starting place or goal in various games　**b** : any of the four stations a runner in baseball must touch in order to score　**6** : any of various compounds that react with an acid to form a salt, have a bitter taste, and turn red litmus paper blue　**7** : a number that is multiplied by a rate or of which a percentage or fraction is calculated ⟨to find the interest on $90 at 10% multiply the *base* 90 by .10⟩

²base *vb* **based; bas·ing**　**1** : to make, form, or serve as a base for　**2** : to use as a base or basis for : ESTABLISH

³base *adj*　**1 a** : being of low value and having less desirable properties when compared with something else ⟨a *base* metal such as iron⟩　**b** : containing more than the usual amount of base metals　**2** : not honorable or moral : MEAN ⟨*base* conduct⟩ — **base·ly** *adv* — **base·ness** *n*

base·ball \'bās-,bȯl\ *n* : a game played with a bat and ball by two teams of nine players each on a field with four bases that mark the course a runner must take to score; *also* : the ball used in this game

base·board \-,bōrd, -,bȯrd\ *n* : a board placed at or forming the base of something; *esp* : a molding covering the crack between a wall and floor

base·born \-'bȯrn\ *adj*　**1** : born into a poor family : LOWLY　**2** : of illegitimate birth : BASTARD

based *adj* : having a base or having as a base

base exchange *n* : a store at a naval or air force base that sells to military personnel and authorized civilians

base hit *n* : a hit in baseball that allows the batter to reach base safely with no error made and no base runner forced out

base·less \'bās-ləs\ *adj* : having no basis or reason

base·line \'bās-,līn\ *n*　**1** : a line used as a base　**2 a** : either of two straight lines leading from home plate to first base and third base on a baseball field　**b** : BASE PATH

base·ment \'bās-mənt\ *n* : the part of a building that is entirely or partly below ground level

ba·sen·ji \bə-'sen-jē, -'zen-\ *n* : a small curly-tailed hunting dog native to Africa that does not bark

base on balls : an advance to first base given to a baseball batter who takes four pitches that are balls

base path *n* : the area between the bases of a baseball field used by a base runner

base runner *n* : a baseball player of the team at bat who is on base or is trying to reach a base

basenji

bash \'bash\ *vb*　**1** : to strike violently : BEAT　**2** : to smash by a blow　**3** : ¹CRASH 1a

bash·ful \'bash-fəl\ *adj* : awkward or afraid around other people　**syn** see SHY — **bash·ful·ly** \-fə-lē\ *adv* — **bash·ful·ness** *n*

¹ba·sic \'bā-sik, -zik\ *adj*　**1** : of, relating to, or forming the base or basis : FUNDAMENTAL ⟨*basic* research⟩　**2** : of, relating to, containing, or having the character of a chemical base — **ba·si·cal·ly** \-si-k(ə-)lē, -zi-\ *adv*

²basic *n* : something basic : FUNDAMENTAL

BA·SIC \'bā-sik, -zik\ *n* : a simplified language for programming and interacting with a computer [*B*eginners *A*ll-purpose *S*ymbolic *I*nstruction *C*ode]

ba·sic·i·ty \bā-'sis-ət-ē\ *n, pl* **-ties** : the quality, state, or extent of being a base

basic training *n* : the first few weeks of training for a military recruit

bas·il \'baz-əl, 'bāz-, 'bas-, 'bās-\ *n* : either of two mints with fragrant leaves used in cooking

ba·sin \'bās-ᵊn\ *n*　**1 a** : a wide shallow usually round bowl for holding liquids　**b** : the amount that a basin holds　**2** : a hollow area or enclosure containing water; *esp* : a partly enclosed water area for anchoring ships　**3 a** : the land drained by a river and its branches　**b** : a large or small hollow area in the surface of the land or in the ocean floor　**c** : a great hollow area in the surface of the lithosphere filled by an ocean　**4** : a broad area of the earth beneath which layers of sedimentary rock dip usually from the sides toward the center

ba·sis \'bā-səs\ *n, pl* **ba·ses** \'bā-,sēz\ : something on which some other thing is based or established

bask \'bask\ *vb* : to lie or relax in a pleasant warmth or atmosphere ⟨*bask* in the sun⟩

bas·ket \'bas-kət\ *n*　**1 a** : a container made by weaving together materials (as reeds, straw, or strips of wood)　**b** : the contents of a basket　**2** : something that resembles a basket　**3 a** : a net open at the bottom and hung from a metal ring that is the goal in basketball　**b** : a score made in basketball by tossing the ball through the basket — **bas·ket·like** \-,līk\ *adj*

bas·ket·ball \-,bȯl\ *n* : a court game in which each of two teams tries to toss an inflated ball through a raised goal; *also* : the ball used in this game

bas·ket·ry \'bas-kə-trē\ *n*　**1** : the art or craft of making objects (as baskets) by weaving or braiding long slender pieces　**2** : objects produced by basketry

basking shark *n*　**1** : a large shark that grows to a length of 12 meters, feeds on plankton, and has a large liver that produces much oil　**2** : WHALE SHARK

bas mitz·vah \bä-'smits-və\ *n, often cap B&M*　**1** : a Jewish girl who at about 13 years of age takes on religious responsibilities　**2** : the ceremony recognizing a girl as a bas mitzvah [from Hebrew *bath miṣwāh*, literally "daughter of the (divine) law"]

bas–re·lief \,bä-ri-'lēf, 'bä-ri-,lēf\ *n* : a sculpture in which the design is raised very slightly from the background

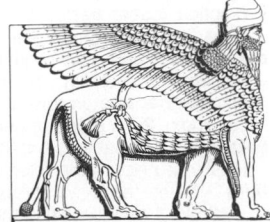
bas-relief

¹bass \'bas\ *n, pl* **bass** *or* **bass·es**　**1** : any of several spiny-finned freshwater sport and food fishes of eastern North America　**2** : any of several saltwater fishes resembling the perch [Old English *bærs* "bass"]

²bass \'bās\ *n*　**1 a** : the lowest musical part in harmony for four parts — compare ALTO 1b, ²SOPRANO 1, TENOR 2a　**b** : the lower half of a

\ə\ abut	\au̇\ out	\i\ tip	\ȯ\ saw	\u̇\ foot
\ər\ further	\ch\ chin	\ī\ life	\ȯi\ coin	\y\ yet
\a\ mat	\e\ pet	\j\ job	\th\ thin	\yü\ few
\ā\ take	\ē\ easy	\ŋ\ sing	\th\ this	\yu̇\ cure
\ä\ cot, cart	\g\ go	\ō\ bone	\ü\ food	\zh\ vision

musical tone range — compare TREBLE **2 a** : the lowest male singing voice or a person who has this voice **b** : a person or instrument performing the bass part [Middle English *bas* (adjective) "being or having a low solemn tone"] — **bass** *adj*

bass clef *n* **1** : a clef that places the F below middle C on the fourth line of the staff **2** : BASS STAFF

bass drum *n* : a large drum that has two heads and that produces a booming sound

bas·set \'bas-ət\ *n* : any of an old French breed of short-legged slow-moving hunting dogs with very long ears and crooked front legs

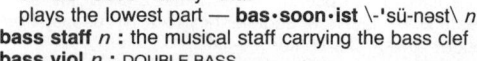

bass horn *n* : TUBA

bas·si·net \,bas-ə-'net\ *n* : an infant's bed often with a hood over one end

bas·soon \bə-'sün, ba-\ *n* : the woodwind instrument of the oboe family that plays the lowest part — **bas·soon·ist** \-'sü-nəst\ *n*

basset

bass staff *n* : the musical staff carrying the bass clef

bass viol *n* : DOUBLE BASS

bass·wood \'bas-,wud\ *n* **1** : LINDEN **2** : TULIP TREE

bast \'bast\ *n* : a strong woody fiber obtained chiefly from the phloem of plants and used especially in fabrics and ropes or cords

bas·tard \'bas-tərd\ *n* : an illegitimate child — **bastard** *adj*

¹baste \'bāst\ *vb* **bast·ed; bast·ing** : to sew with long loose stitches so as to hold the work temporarily in place — **bast·er** *n*

²baste *vb* **bast·ed; bast·ing** : to moisten with liquid (as melted fat or juices) while roasting — **bast·er** *n*

Bas·tille Day \ba-'stē(ə)l-\ *n* : July 14 observed in France as a national holiday in memory of the capture of the Parisian prison the Bastille by revolutionary forces in 1789

bas·tion \'bas-chən\ *n* : some place or something that gives protection against attack ⟨a *bastion* of democracy⟩

¹bat \'bat\ *n* **1** : a stout solid stick : CLUB **2** : a sharp blow **3** : a usually wooden implement used for hitting the ball in various games (as baseball) **4** : a turn at batting [Old English *batt* "club"; probably of Celtic origin]

²bat *vb* **bat·ted; bat·ting** **1** : to strike or hit with or as if with a bat **2** : to take one's turn at bat in baseball **3** : to have a batting average of ⟨is *batting* .300⟩

³bat *n* : any of an order of night-flying mammals with the forelimbs modified to form wings [from Middle English *bakke* "flying bat"; probably of Scandinavian origin]

⁴bat *vb* **bat·ted; bat·ting** : to wink especially in surprise or emotion ⟨never *batted* an eye⟩ [probably an altered form of earlier *bate* "to beat the wings in an impatient manner"]

batch \'bach\ *n* **1 a** : a quantity used or made at one time ⟨a *batch* of cookies⟩ **b** : a group of jobs to be run on a computer at one time with the same program ⟨*batch* processing⟩ **2** : a group of persons or things : LOT

bate \'bāt\ *vb* **bat·ed; bat·ing** : to reduce the force or intensity of : RESTRAIN ⟨listen with *bated* breath⟩

bath \'bath, 'bȧth\ *n, pl* **baths** \'bathz, 'baths, 'bȧthz, 'bȧths\ **1** : a washing of the body **2 a** : water for bathing **b** : a liquid in which objects are placed so that it can act upon them **3 a** : BATHROOM **b** : a building containing rooms for bathing

bathe \'bāth\ *vb* **bathed; bath·ing** **1** : to take a bath **2** : to go swimming **3** : to give a bath to ⟨*bathe* the baby⟩ **4** : to apply a liquid to ⟨*bathe* the eyes⟩ **5** : to cover with or as if with a liquid ⟨a scene *bathed* in moonlight⟩ — **bath·er** \'bā-thər\ *n*

bath·house \'bath-,haus, 'bȧth-\ *n* **1** : BATH 3b **2** : a building containing dressing rooms for swimmers

bathing suit *n* : SWIMSUIT

batho·lith \'bath-ə-,lith\ *n* : a great mass of igneous rock that forced its way into or between other rocks and that stopped in its rise quite a distance below the surface

bath·robe \'bath-,rōb, 'bȧth-\ *n* : a loose robe worn before or after bathing or as a dressing gown

bath·room \-,rüm, -,rum\ *n* **1** : a room containing a bathtub or shower and usually a washbowl and toilet **2** : LAVATORY 2

bath·tub \-,təb\ *n* : a tub in which to take a bath

bathy·scaphe \'bath-i-,skaf, -,skȧf\ *n* : a ship that can be guided underwater for deep-sea exploration and has a round watertight cabin attached to its underside

bathy·sphere \'bath-i-,sfi(ə)r\ *n* : a strongly built steel ball in which a person can dive to great depth for deep-sea observation

bathy·ther·mo·graph \,bath-i-'thər-mə-,graf\ *n* : an instrument that records water temperature in relation to its depth

ba·tik \bə-'tēk, 'bat-ik\ *n* **1** : an Indonesian method of hand-printing textiles by coating with wax the parts not to be dyed **2** : a design or fabric printed by batik

ba·tiste \bə-'tēst, ba-\ *n* : a fine soft sheer fabric of plain weave

ba·ton \bə-'tän, ba-\ *n* **1** : a staff borne as a symbol of office **2** : a stick with which a leader directs a band or orchestra **3** : a hollow rod passed from one member of a relay team to another **4** : a staff with a ball at one or both ends carried by a drum major or baton twirler

bat·tal·ion \bə-'tal-yən\ *n* **1** : a large body of troops : ARMY **2** : a military unit composed of two or more smaller units (as companies or batteries) **3** : a large body of persons organized to act together

¹bat·ten \'bat-ᵊn\ *n* **1** : a thin narrow strip of lumber used especially to seal or strengthen a joint **2** : a strip, bar, or support like or used like a batten

²batten *vb* **bat·tened; bat·ten·ing** \'bat-niŋ, -ᵊn-iŋ\ : to get ready especially for stormy weather by or as if by fastening everything down — usually used with *down*

¹bat·ter \'bat-ər\ *vb* **1** : to beat with repeated violent blows ⟨*batter* down the door⟩ **2** : to wear down or injure by hard use ⟨wore a *battered* old hat⟩ [Middle English *bateren* "to beat"]

²batter *n* : a thin mixture chiefly of flour and liquid beaten together ⟨cake *batter*⟩ [Middle English *bater* "thin mixture", probably derived from *batteren* "to beat"]

³batter *n* : one that bats; *esp* : the baseball player at bat [*bat* and *-er* (noun suffix)]

battering ram *n* **1** : an ancient military machine consisting of a large iron-tipped wooden beam used to beat down walls **2** : a heavy metal bar with handles used (as by fire fighters) to batter down doors and walls

bat·tery \'bat-ə-rē, 'ba-trē\ *n, pl* **-ter·ies** **1 a** : the act of beating **b** : the unlawful beating or use of force upon a person **2**

battering ram 1

: two or more big military guns that are controlled as a unit **3** : an electric cell or connected electric cells for providing electric current ⟨a flashlight *battery*⟩ **4** : a number of similar articles, items, or devices arranged, connected, or used together ⟨a *battery* of tests⟩ **5** : the pitcher and catcher of a baseball team

battery jar *n* : a glass container with straight sides used especially in biology and chemistry laboratories

bat·ting \'bat-iŋ\ *n* : layers or sheets of cotton or wool or of synthetic material used mostly for stuffing quilts or packaging goods

batting average *n* : the average of a baseball batter found by dividing the number of official times at bat into the number of base hits

¹bat·tle \'bat-ᵊl\ *n* **1** : a fight between armies, warships, or airplanes **2** : a fight between two persons ⟨trial by *battle*⟩ **3** : a long or hard struggle or contest ⟨a *battle* of wits⟩

²battle *vb* **bat·tled; bat·tling** \'bat-liŋ, -ᵊl-iŋ\ **1** : to engage in battle **2** : CONTEND 2, STRUGGLE ⟨*battle* for a cause⟩ **3** : to fight against ⟨*battling* a forest fire⟩

bat·tle–ax *or* **bat·tle–axe** \'bat-ᵊl-,aks\ *n* : an ax with a broad blade formerly used as a weapon

bat·tle·field \-,fēld\ *n* : a place where a battle is fought or was once fought

bat·tle·ground \-,graůnd\ *n* : BATTLEFIELD

bat·tle·ment \'bat-ᵊl-mənt\ *n* : a low wall (as at the top of a castle or a tower) with open spaces to shoot through

bat·tle·ship \'bat-ᵊl-,ship\ *n* : a large warship with heavy armor and large guns

bat·ty \'bat-ē\ *adj* **bat·ti·er; -est** : mentally unstable : CRAZY

bau·ble \'bȯ-bəl, 'bäb-əl\ *n* : an object of little value

baud \'bȯd, 'bōd\ *n* : a unit of speed (as one bit per second) at which data is sent in communications

baux·ite \'bȯk-,sīt, 'bäk-\ *n* : a clayey substance that is the principal ore of aluminum

bawdy \'bȯd-ē\ *adj* **bawd·i·er; -est** : morally objectionable : OBSCENE — **bawd·i·ly** \'bȯd-ᵊl-ē\ *adv* — **bawd·i·ness** \'bȯd-ē-nəs\ *n*

¹bawl \'bȯl\ *vb* **1** : to shout or cry out loudly : YELL **2** : to weep noisily — **bawl·er** *n*

²bawl *n* : a loud cry

bawl out *vb* : to scold severely

¹bay \'bā\ *adj* : of the color bay [Middle English *bay* "reddish brown", from early French *bai* (same meaning), from Latin *badius* "reddish brown"]

²bay *n* **1** : a horse with a bay-colored body and black mane, tail, and lower legs **2** : a reddish brown

³bay *n* **1 a** : LAUREL 1 **b** : any of several shrubs or trees resembling the laurel **2** : a laurel wreath given as a prize [Middle English *bay* "berry", from early French *baie* (same meaning), from Latin *baca* "berry"]

⁴bay *n* **1** : a section or compartment of a building or vehicle **2** : BAY WINDOW [Middle English *bay* "main part of a building", from early French *baee* "opening", derived from earlier *baer* "to gape, yawn"]

⁵bay *vb* : to bark with long deep tones [Middle English *baien, abaien* "to bay", from early French *abaiier* (same meaning), originally a word to imitate the sound]

⁶bay *n* **1** : the position of an animal or person forced to face pursuers when it is impossible to escape ⟨brought to *bay*⟩ **2** : the position of pursuers who are held off ⟨kept the hounds at *bay*⟩ **3** : the baying of a dog : a deep bark

⁷bay *n* : an inlet of a body of water (as the sea) that is usually smaller than a gulf [Middle English *baye* "inlet", from early French *baie* "berry" — related to ³BAY]

bay·ber·ry \'bā-,ber-ē\ *n* **1** : a West Indian tree that is related to the myrtles **2 a** : any of several wax myrtles; *esp* : a hardy shrub especially of coastal eastern North America that produces clusters of small berries covered with grayish white wax **b** : the fruit of a bayberry

¹bay·o·net \'bā-ə-nət, -,net, ,bā-ə-'net\ *n* : a weapon like a dagger made to fit on the muzzle end of a rifle

²bayonet *vb* **-net·ed** *also* **-net·ted; -net·ing** *also* **-net·ting** : to stab with a bayonet

bay·ou \'bī-ō, 'bī-ü\ *n* : a marshy or slowly flowing body of water (as a stream or inlet)

bay rum *n* : a fragrant liquid used as a cologne or after-shave lotion

bay window *n* : a window or set of windows that sticks out from the wall of a building

ba·zaar \bə-'zär\ *n* **1** : an oriental marketplace containing rows of small shops **2** : a place where many kinds of goods are sold **3** : a fair for the sale of articles especially to raise money for charity

ba·zoo·ka \bə-'zü-kə\ *n* : a light portable shoulder weapon that consists of an open tube and shoots an explosive rocket able to pierce the armor of tanks [from *bazooka*, name of a homemade musical instrument consisting of pipes and a funnel]

BB \'bē-,bē\ *n* : a small round piece of shot

BCD \,bē-,sē-'dē\ *n* : a computer code for expressing symbols (as numerals and letters of the alphabet) [*b*inary *c*oded *d*ecimal]

B cell \'bē-,sel\ *n* : any of the lymphocytes that are concerned mainly with the formation of antibodies and that do not undergo a stage of development in the thymus

B complex *n* : VITAMIN B COMPLEX

be \(')bē\ *vb, past 1st & 3d sing* **was** \(')wəz, 'wäz\; *2d sing* **were** \(')wər\; *pl* **were;** *past subjunctive* **were;** *past participle* **been** \(')bin, *chiefly British* (')bēn\; *present participle* **be·ing** \'bē-iŋ\; *present 1st sing* **am** \əm, (')am\; *2d sing* **are** \ər, (')är\; *3d sing* **is** \(')iz, əz\; *pl* **are;** *present subjunctive* **be 1 a** : to have the same meaning as : serve as a sign for ⟨January *is* the first month⟩ ⟨let *x* *be* 10⟩ **b** : to have identity with ⟨the first person I met *was* my brother⟩ ⟨she *is* my mother⟩ **c** : to have the quality or character of ⟨the leaves *are* green⟩ **d** : to belong to the class of ⟨the fish *is* a trout⟩ ⟨apes *are* mammals⟩ **2 a** : EXIST 1, LIVE ⟨I think, therefore I *am*⟩ ⟨there *was* an old woman who lived in a shoe⟩ **b** : to occupy a place, situation, or position ⟨the book *is* on the table⟩ ⟨I *was* sick⟩ **c** : to take place : OCCUR ⟨the concert *was* last night⟩ **3** — used with the past participle of transitive verbs to form the passive auxiliary ⟨the money *was* found⟩ ⟨the house is *being* built⟩ **4** — used with the present participle to express continuous action ⟨they *are* studying⟩ ⟨I have *been* sleeping⟩ **5** — used with the infinitive with *to* to express the future or something one must do ⟨she *was* to become famous⟩ ⟨I *am* to go today⟩

be- *prefix* **1** : on : around : over ⟨*be*smear⟩ **2** : provide with or cover with : dress up with ⟨*be*jewel⟩ ⟨*be*whiskered⟩ **3** : about : to : upon ⟨*be*moan⟩ **4** : make : cause to be ⟨*be*little⟩ ⟨*be*friend⟩ [Old English *be-, bi-* "on, over"]

¹beach \'bēch\ *n* : a sandy or gravelly part of the shore of an ocean or lake

²beach *vb* : to run or drive ashore ⟨*beach* a boat⟩

beach buggy *n* : DUNE BUGGY

beach·comb·er \'bēch-,kō-mər\ *n* **1** : a drifter or loafer especially on a south Pacific island **2** : a person who searches along a beach to find lost or discarded articles to sell

beach flea *n* : any of numerous small leaping crustaceans common on sea beaches

beach grass *n* : any of several tough grasses with strong roots that grow on exposed sandy shores; *esp* : one planted to bind the soil on dunes or sandy slopes

beach·head \'bēch-,hed\ *n* : an area on an enemy shore held by an advance force of an invading army to protect the later landing of troops or supplies

beach plum *n* : a shrubby plum with showy white flowers that grows along the Atlantic coast of the northern U.S. and Canada; *also* : its dark purple fruit often used in preserves

bea·con \'bē-kən\ *n* **1** : a signal fire commonly on a hill, tower, or pole **2 a** : a guiding or warning signal (as a lighthouse) **b** : a radio station sending out signals to guide airplanes **3** : something that inspires ⟨a *beacon* light of hope⟩

¹bead \'bēd\ *n* **1** : a small piece of solid material with a

\ə\ abut	\aů\ out	\i\ tip	\ȯ\ saw	\ů\ foot	
\ər\ **further**	\ch\ chin	\ī\ life	\ȯi\ coin	\y\ yet	
\a\ mat	\e\ pet	\j\ job	\th\ thin	\yü\ few	
\ā\ take	\ē\ **easy**	\ŋ\ sing	\th\ **this**	\yů\ cure	
\ä\ cot, cart	\g\ go	\ō\ bone	\ü\ food	\zh\ vision	

hole by which it can be strung on a thread   **2** : a small round mass ⟨*beads* of perspiration⟩   **3** : a small knob on a gun used in taking aim   **4** : a rim or molding (as on a board or tire) that sticks out

Word History The beads you might wear around your neck once represented prayers. The Middle English word *bede* at first meant "a prayer". People then, as now, often kept track of the number and order of a series of prayers with the help of a string of little balls. Because each of these balls stands for a prayer, the word *bede* came to be used for the balls themselves. Today this same word, now spelled *bead,* is used to refer to any small piece of material with a hole in it for threading on a string or wire. It has also been used to refer to any small, round object such as a drop of sweat. [Middle English *bede* "prayer, rosary bead", from Old English *bed* "prayer"]

²bead *vb*   **1** : to cover with beads   **2** : to string together like beads   **3** : to form into a bead

bead·ing \'bēd-iŋ\ *n* : BEADWORK

bead·work \'bēd-,wərk\ *n* : ornamental work made of beads

beady \'bēd-ē\ *adj* **bead·i·er; -est** : resembling beads; *esp* : small, round, and shiny ⟨*beady* eyes⟩

bea·gle \'bē-gəl\ *n* : a small hound with short legs and a smooth coat

beak \'bēk\ *n*   **1 a** : the bill of a bird; *esp* : the bill of a bird of prey adapted for striking and tearing   **b** : any of various rigid mouth structures (as of a turtle or octopus) that stick out; *also* : the long sucking mouth of some insects   **2** : a part shaped like a beak — **beaked** \'bēkt\ *adj*

beagle

bea·ker \'bē-kər\ *n* : a deep cup or glass with a wide mouth and usually a lip for pouring

¹beam \'bēm\ *n*   **1** : a long heavy piece of timber or metal used especially as a main horizontal support of a building or ship   **2** : the bar of a balance from which scales hang   **3** : the width of a ship at its widest part   **4 a** : a ray of light   **b** : a collection of nearly parallel rays (as X rays) or a stream of particles (as electrons)   **5** : a constant radio signal sent out to guide pilots along a course

²beam *vb*   **1** : to send out in beams or as a beam   **2** : to send out beams of light : SHINE   **3** : to smile with joy

bean \'bēn\ *n*   **1 a** : BROAD BEAN   **b** : the seed or pod of various erect or climbing plants related to the pea   **c** : a plant bearing beans   **2** : a seed or fruit like a bean ⟨coffee *beans*⟩

bean·bag \'bēn-,bag\ *n*   **1 a** : a cloth bag filled with dried beans   **b** : a bag filled with pellets that is used as a chair   **2** : a game played with beanbags

bean curd *n* : a food like soft cheese made from soybeans

¹bear \'ba(ə)r, 'be(ə)r\ *n, pl* **bear** *or* **bears**   **1** : any of a family of large heavy mammals that have long shaggy hair and small tails, walk on the soles of their feet, and feed largely on fruit and insects as well as on flesh   **2** : a grumpy or glum person   **3** : a person who sells stocks or bonds in the expectation that the price will go down [Old English *bera* "a bear"] — **bear·ish** \'ba(ə)r-ish, 'be(ə)r-\ *adj*

²bear *vb* **bore** \'bō(ə)r, 'bö(ə)r\; **borne** \'bō(ə)rn, 'bö(ə)rn\ *also* **born** \'bö(ə)rn\; **bear·ing**   **1 a** : to move while holding up and supporting : CARRY ⟨*bear* a burden⟩ ⟨arrived *bearing* gifts⟩   **b** : to hold in the mind ⟨*bear* a grudge⟩   **c** : BEHAVE 1 ⟨*bore* himself like a gentleman⟩   **d** : to give as testimony ⟨*bear* false witness⟩   **e** : to have a feature or

characteristic ⟨*bears* marks of suffering⟩ ⟨*bore* a resemblance to her aunt⟩   **2 a** : to give birth to ⟨*bear* children⟩ ⟨the baby was *born* last week⟩   **b** : to bring forth : PRODUCE ⟨*bear* fruit⟩   **3 a** : to hold up : SUPPORT   **b** : to put up with : STAND ⟨I can't *bear* the suspense⟩   **c** : ASSUME 1 ⟨*bore* the costs⟩ ⟨*bear* the blame⟩   **4** : to push down on : PRESS ⟨*bears* down on her pencil⟩   **5** : to move or lie in an indicated direction ⟨*bear* right at the fork in the road⟩   **6 a** : to have a relation to the matter at hand ⟨facts *bearing* on the question⟩   **b** : to exercise force or influence ⟨bring pressure to *bear*⟩ [Old English *beran* "to carry, support"] — **bear arms**   **1** : to own and carry firearms   **2** : to serve as a soldier

bear·able \'bar-ə-bəl, 'ber-\ *adj* : possible to bear

bear·ber·ry \'ba(ə)r-,ber-ē, 'be(ə)r-\ *n* : a trailing evergreen plant with glossy red berries that is related to the heath

¹beard \'bi(ə)rd\ *n*   **1** : the hair that grows on a man's face   **2** : a hairy or bristly growth or bunch (as on the chin of a goat) — **beard·ed** \-əd\ *adj* — **beard·less** \-ləs\ *adj*

²beard *vb* : to face or challenge boldly ⟨*beard* the lion in his den⟩

bear down *vb* : to use all of one's strength and concentration ⟨the pitcher *bore down* and struck out the last batter⟩

bear·er \'bar-ər, 'ber-\ *n*   **1** : someone or something that bears, supports, or carries   **2** : a person holding a check or order for payment

bear hug *n* : a rough tight hug

bear·ing \'ba(ə)r-iŋ, 'be(ə)r-\ *n*   **1** : the manner in which one carries or conducts oneself   **2** : a machine part in which another turns or slides   **3 a** : the position or direction of one point with respect to another or to the compass   **b** : a calculating of position ⟨take a *bearing*⟩   **c** *pl* : understanding of one's location or situation ⟨lost their *bearings*⟩   **4** : CONNECTION 2 ⟨personal feelings had no *bearing* on our decision⟩

bear out *vb* : CONFIRM 4 ⟨the facts *bore out* her story⟩

bear·skin \'ba(ə)r-,skin, 'be(ə)r-\ *n* : an article made of the skin of a bear

bear up *vb* : to have the strength or courage ⟨*bear up* under the strain⟩

beast \'bēst\ *n*   **1 a** : ¹ANIMAL 1; *esp* : a lower mammal as distinguished from human beings and from lower animals both with and without backbones   **b** : a farm animal especially when kept for work ⟨oxen and horses used as *beasts* of burden⟩   **2** : a mean or brutal person

¹beast·ly \'bēst-lē\ *adj* **beast·li·er; -est**   **1** : of, relating to, or resembling a beast : BESTIAL   **2** : DISAGREEABLE 1, UNPLEASANT ⟨*beastly* weather⟩ — **beast·li·ness** *n*

²beastly *adv* : ²VERY 1 ⟨a *beastly* cold day⟩

¹beat \'bēt\ *vb* **beat; beat·en** \'bēt-ᵊn\ *or* **beat; beat·ing**   **1 a** : to hit again and again ⟨*beat* a drum⟩ ⟨rain *beating* on the roof⟩ — often used with *up* ⟨two bullies *beat* him up⟩   **b** : to flap against ⟨wings *beating* the air⟩   **c** : to mix by stirring : WHIP ⟨*beat* two eggs⟩   **2 a** : to drive or force by blows ⟨*beat* off the intruder⟩   **b** : to make by walking or riding over ⟨*beat* a path⟩   **c** : to shape by blows ⟨*beat* gold into thin strips⟩   **3** : to cause to strike or flap repeatedly ⟨birds *beating* their wings⟩   **4 a** : to win against : DEFEAT   **b** : ¹BAFFLE 1 ⟨it *beats* me where they are⟩   **c** : SURPASS 1 ⟨it *beats* murder as a cause of death⟩ ⟨can you *beat* that?⟩   **5 a** : to act ahead of ⟨*beat* me to the punch⟩   **b** : to arrive before ⟨*beat* us home⟩   **6** : to measure or mark off by strokes ⟨*beat* time to the music⟩   **7** : to glare or strike harshly ⟨the sun *beat* down⟩   **8** : PULSATE, THROB ⟨the heart *beating*⟩ — **beat·er** *n* — **beat about the bush** *or* **beat around the bush** : to fail to get to the point — **beat a retreat** : to leave in haste — **beat it** : to hurry away : SCRAM

²beat *n*   **1 a** : a stroke or blow especially in a series   **b** : PULSATION   **c** : a sound produced by or as if by beating ⟨the *beat* of waves against the rock⟩   **2 a** : a rhythmic stress in poetry or music   **b** : the tempo given to a musical performer   **c** : RHYTHM 2b ⟨likes music with a Latin *beat*⟩   **3** : a place or area regularly visited in the course of work or duty ⟨a police officer's *beat*⟩ ⟨a reporter's *beat*⟩

³beat *adj*   **1** : being tired out   **2** : having lost one's morale

beat·en \'bēt-ᵊn\ *adj* : worn smooth by passing feet ⟨the *beaten* path⟩

be·atif·ic \‚bē-ə-'tif-ik\ *adj* : having a blissful appearance ⟨a *beatific* smile⟩

be·at·i·fy \bē-'at-ə-‚fī\ *vb* **-fied; -fy·ing** : to declare to have reached the blessedness of heaven — **be·at·i·fi·ca·tion** \bē-‚at-ə-fə-'kā-shən\ *n*

be·at·i·tude \bē-'at-ə-‚t(y)üd\ *n* : any of the declarations made in the Sermon on the Mount (Matthew 5:3–12) beginning "Blessed are" [derived from Latin *beatus* "happy"]

beat–up \'bēt-‚əp, -'əp\ *adj* : worn or damaged by use or neglect ⟨a *beat-up* old car⟩

beau \'bō\ *n, pl* **beaux** \'bōz\ *or* **beaus** \'bōz\ : BOYFRIEND 2 [from French *beau* "boyfriend", from *beau* (adjective) "fine, beautiful", derived from Latin *bellus* "pretty" — related to BEAUTY, BELLE]

Beau·fort scale \‚bō-fərt\ *n* : a scale in which the force of the wind is indicated by numbers from 0 to 12

beau ide·al \‚bō-ī-'dē(-ə)l\ *n, pl* **beau ideals** : a perfect model ⟨the *beau ideal* of a basketball player⟩

beau·te·ous \'byüt-ē-əs\ *adj* : BEAUTIFUL 1 — **beau·te·ous·ly** *adv* — **beau·te·ous·ness** *n*

beau·ti·cian \byü-'tish-ən\ *n* : COSMETOLOGIST

beau·ti·ful \'byüt-i-fəl\ *adj*   **1** : having the qualities of beauty   **2** : very good : EXCELLENT — **beau·ti·ful·ly** \-f(ə-)lē\ *adv* — **beau·ti·ful·ness** \-fəl-nəs\ *n*

   syn BEAUTIFUL, PRETTY, LOVELY, HANDSOME mean giving pleasure to the mind or senses. BEAUTIFUL applies to things that give the greatest pleasure and stir the emotions ⟨*beautiful* mountain scenery⟩ PRETTY applies to things that give immediate but often shallow pleasure especially to the senses ⟨a *pretty* dress⟩ LOVELY applies to things that excite the emotions by being very graceful, delicate, or exquisite ⟨a *lovely* melody⟩ HANDSOME applies to things that please the mind because of their good proportions or elegance ⟨the gardens of the mansion are quite *handsome*⟩

beau·ti·fy \'byüt-ə-‚fī\ *vb* **-fied; -fy·ing** : to make beautiful or more beautiful   **syn** see ADORN — **beau·ti·fi·ca·tion** \‚byüt-ə-fə-'kā-shən\ *n*

beau·ty \'byüt-ē\ *n, pl* **beauties**   **1** : the qualities of a person or a thing that give pleasure to the senses   **2** : a lovely person or thing; *esp* : a lovely woman   **3** : an outstanding example ⟨a *beauty* of a black eye⟩ [Middle English *beaute* "beauty", derived from early French *bel* "beautiful", from Latin *bellus* "pretty" — related to BEAU, BELLE]

beauty shop *n* : a place of business for the care of customers' hair, skin, and nails — called also *beauty parlor*

¹bea·ver \'bē-vər\ *n, pl* **beaver** *or* **beavers**   **1** : a large fur-bearing mammal that is related to the rats and mice, has webbed hind feet and a broad flat tail, and builds dams and underwater houses of mud and branches   **2** : the fur of a beaver

¹beaver 1

²beaver *n* : a piece of armor protecting the lower part of the face

be·calm \bi-'käm, -'kälm\ *vb* : to bring to a stop by lack of wind ⟨a ship *becalmed*⟩

be·cause \bi-'kòz, -(')kəz\ *conj* : for the reason that

because of *prep* : by reason of

beck \'bek\ *n* : a beckoning gesture — **at one's beck and**

call : ready to obey any command

beck·on \'bek-ən\ *vb* **beck·oned; beck·on·ing** \'bek-(ə-)niŋ\   **1** : to call or signal to a person usually by a wave or nod ⟨they *beckoned* us to come over⟩   **2** : to appear inviting ⟨new adventures were *beckoning*⟩

be·cloud \bi-'klaůd\ *vb* : to hide as if with a cloud

be·come \bi-'kəm\ *vb* **-came** \-'kām\; **-come; -com·ing**   **1** : to come or grow to be ⟨a tadpole *becomes* a frog⟩ ⟨the days *become* shorter as summer ends⟩   **2** : to look well on : SUIT ⟨her suit *becomes* her⟩ — **become of** : to happen to ⟨whatever *became of* our old friend⟩

be·com·ing \bi-'kəm-iŋ\ *adj* : SUITABLE 2; *also* : looking good on a person ⟨a *becoming* hairstyle⟩ — **be·com·ing·ly** \-iŋ-lē\ *adv*

¹bed \'bed\ *n*   **1 a** : a piece of furniture on which to lie or sleep   **b** : a place or time for sleeping   **2 a** : a plot of ground prepared for plants   **b** : the bottom of a body of water ⟨the *bed* of a river⟩   **3** : a supporting surface or structure   **4** : ¹LAYER 2 ⟨a *bed* of sandstone⟩

²bed *vb* **bed·ded; bed·ding**   **1** : to put or go to bed ⟨*bed* down for the night⟩   **2** : to fix in or on a foundation ⟨an argument *bedded* on good sense⟩   **3** : to plant or arrange in beds

bed–and–breakfast *n* : a place for tourists to stay that offers lodging and breakfast

be·daub \bi-'dòb, -'däb\ *vb* : to smear or soil with something thick, dirty, or sticky

be·daz·zle \bi-'daz-əl\ *vb* : DAZZLE 1 — **be·daz·zle·ment** \-mənt\ *n*

bed·bug \'bed-‚bəg\ *n* : a wingless bloodsucking bug sometimes infesting houses and especially beds

bed·cham·ber \-‚'chäm-bər\ *n* : BEDROOM

bed·clothes \-‚klō(th)z\ *n pl* : coverings (as sheets and blankets) for a bed

bed·ding \'bed-iŋ\ *n*   **1** : BEDCLOTHES   **2** : material for a bed

be·deck \bi-'dek\ *vb* : to dress up with showy things ⟨*bedecked* in furs and jewels⟩

be·dev·il \bi-'dev-əl\ *vb* : to trouble or annoy again and again : PESTER, HARASS ⟨*bedeviled* by problems⟩ — **be·dev·il·ment** \-mənt\ *n*

be·dew \bi-'d(y)ü\ *vb* : to wet with or as if with dew

bed·fast \'bed-‚fast\ *adj* : BEDRIDDEN

bed·fel·low \'bed-‚fel-ō\ *n* : one who shares a bed with another

be·dight \bi-'dīt\ *adj, archaic* : being dressed or decorated

be·dim \bi-'dim\ *vb*   **1** : to make less bright : DIM   **2** : to make indistinct or obscure

be·di·zen \bi-'dīz-ᵊn, -'diz-ᵊn\ *vb* : to dress or decorate especially with showy finery

bed·lam \'bed-ləm\ *n* : a place or scene of uproar and confusion

   Word History Around 1402 the home of a religious community in London was turned into a hospital for the insane. This new hospital kept the name of the community and was known as the Hospital of Saint Mary of Bethlehem. People soon shortened this name to Bethlehem. In Middle English, though, the town of Bethlehem in Palestine was called *Bedlem* or *Bethlem*, so this was the spelling used for the hospital's name. In time the name *Bedlem* or *Bedlam* came to refer to any home for the insane. Today we use *bedlam* for any scene of noise and confusion like that found in the early hospitals for the insane. [from Middle English *Bedlem* "Bethlehem"]

Bed·ling·ton terrier \‚bed-liŋ-tən-\ *n* : a swift lightly built

\ə\ abut	\aů\ out	\i\ tip	\ò\ saw	\ů\ foot
\ər\ further	\ch\ chin	\ī\ life	\òi\ coin	\y\ yet
\a\ mat	\e\ pet	\j\ job	\th\ thin	\yü\ few
\ā\ take	\ē\ easy	\ŋ\ sing	\th\ this	\yů\ cure
\ä\ cot, cart	\g\ go	\ō\ bone	\ü\ food	\zh\ vision

terrier with a narrow head and arched back

bed·ou·in \'bed(-ə)-wən\ *n, pl* **-in** *or* **-ins** *often cap* : a nomadic Arab of the Arabian, Syrian, or north African deserts

Bedlington terrier

bed·pan \'bed-,pan\ *n* : a shallow pan for use as a toilet by a person forced to stay in bed

be·drag·gled \bi-'drag-əld\ *adj* : limp, soggy, or dirty from or as if from rain or mud

bed·rid·den \'bed-,rid-ᵊn\ *adj* : forced to stay in bed by illness or weakness

bed·rock \'bed-'räk, -,räk\ *n* **1** : the solid rock lying under surface materials (as soil) that are not in layers **2** : a solid foundation

bed·roll \'bed-,rōl\ *n* : bedding rolled up for carrying

bed·room \-,rüm, -,rùm\ *n* : a room used for sleeping

bed·sheet \-,shēt\ *n* : ¹SHEET 1

bed·side \-,sīd\ *n* : the place beside a bed especially of a sick or dying person

bed·sore \-,sō(ə)r, -,sò(ə)r\ *n* : a sore caused by constant pressure against a bed (as in an extended illness)

bed·spread \-,spred\ *n* : a decorative cover for a bed

bed·stead \-,sted\ *n* : the framework of a bed

bed·straw \-,strò\ *n* : an herb that is related to madder and has angled stems, leaves arranged in pairs with each opposite the other on the stem or in a circle around the stem, and small flowers

bed·time \'bed-,tīm\ *n* : time to go to bed

¹bee \'bē\ *n* : a social colonial 4-winged insect often kept in hives for the honey that it produces; *also* : any of numerous related insects that differ from the wasps especially in the heavier hairier body and in having sucking as well as chewing mouthparts [Old English *bēo* "bee"]

²bee *n* : a gathering of people for a specific purpose ⟨quilting *bee*⟩ [perhaps from a dialect word *been* "help given by neighbors", derived from Old English *bēn* "prayer"]

bee·bread \'bē-,bred\ *n* : a bitter yellowish brown pollen mixture stored in honeycomb cells and used with honey by bees as food

beech \'bēch\ *n, pl* **beech·es** *or* **beech** : any of a genus of hardwood trees with smooth gray bark and small edible nuts; *also* : its wood — **beech·en** \'bē-chən\ *adj*

¹beef \'bēf\ *n, pl* **beeves** \'bēvz\ *or* **beefs** \'bēfs\ **1** : the flesh of a steer, cow, or bull **2** : a steer, cow, or bull especially when fattened for food **3** *pl* **beefs** : COMPLAINT 1 — **beef·like** \-,līk\ *adj*

²beef *vb* **1** : to add weight, strength, or power to — usually used with *up* **2** : COMPLAIN 1

beef cattle *n pl* : cattle developed primarily for effective production of meat

beef·steak \'bēf-,stāk\ *n* : a slice of beef suitable for broiling or frying

beefy \'bē-fē\ *adj* **beef·i·er; -est** : heavily and powerfully built

¹bee·hive \'bē-,hīv\ *n* **1** : a hive for bees **2** : ¹HIVE 2 ⟨a *beehive* of activity⟩

²beehive *adj* : resembling a dome-shaped beehive

bee·keep·er \'bē-,kē-pər\ *n* : a person who raises bees — **bee·keep·ing** *n*

bee·line \'bē-,līn\ *n* : a straight direct course

been *past participle of* BE

beep \'bēp\ *n* : a sound that signals or warns — **beep** *vb*

beep·er \'bē-pər\ *n* : a small electronic device used to summon the person carrying it that beeps when it receives a special radio signal

beer \'bi(ə)r\ *n* **1** : an alcoholic drink made from malt and flavored with hops **2** : a nonalcoholic drink made from

roots or other parts of plants ⟨birch *beer*⟩

bees·wax \'bēz-,waks\ *n* : ¹WAX 1

beet \'bēt\ *n* : a garden plant with thick long-stalked edible leaves and a swollen root used as a vegetable, as a source of sugar, or as food for livestock; *also* : this root

¹bee·tle \'bēt-ᵊl\ *n* **1** : any of an order of insects having four wings of which the first pair are stiff cases that fold over and protect the second pair when at rest **2** : any of various insects (as a cockroach) resembling a beetle [Old English *bitula* "beetle", from *bītan* "to bite" — related to BITE]

²beetle *adj* : sticking out and hanging over ⟨*beetle* brows⟩ [Middle English *bitel-browed* "having overhanging brows", probably from *bitel*, *betylle* "beetle", from Old English *bitula* "beetle"]

³beetle *vb* **bee·tled; bee·tling** \'bēt-(ə-)liŋ\ : to stick out or hang over ⟨*beetling* cliffs⟩

be·fall \bi-'fól\ *vb* **-fell** \-'fel\; **-fall·en** \-'fó-lən\; **-fall·ing** **1** : to take place : HAPPEN **2** : to happen to

be·fit \bi-'fit\ *vb* **be·fit·ted; be·fit·ting** : to be suitable to or proper for ⟨clothes *befitting* the occasion⟩

be·fog \bi-'fóg, -'fäg\ *vb* **1** : to make foggy : OBSCURE **2** : CONFUSE 2

¹be·fore \bi-'fō(ə)r, -'fó(ə)r\ *adv* **1** : in advance : AHEAD ⟨go on *before*⟩ **2** : at an earlier time ⟨was here *before*⟩

²before *prep* **1 a** : in front of ⟨stood *before* a mirror⟩ **b** : in the presence of ⟨spoke *before* the legislature⟩ **2** : under the consideration of ⟨the case *before* the court⟩ **3** : earlier than ⟨got there *before* me⟩ ⟨come *before* six⟩

³before *conj* **1** : earlier than the time when ⟨think *before* you speak⟩ **2** : more willingly than ⟨I'd starve *before* I'd steal⟩

be·fore·hand \-,hand\ *adv* : ahead of time : in advance

be·foul \bi-'faù(ə)l\ *vb* : to make dirty : SOIL

be·friend \bi-'frend\ *vb* : to act as a friend to

be·fud·dle \bi-'fəd-ᵊl\ *vb* **-fud·dled; -fud·dling** \-'fəd-liŋ, -ᵊl-iŋ\ **1** : to dull the senses of with or as if with too much drink : STUPEFY **2** : CONFUSE 1a, PERPLEX — **be·fud·dle·ment** \-mənt\ *n*

beg \'beg\ *vb* **begged; beg·ging** **1** : to ask for money, food, or help as charity ⟨*beg* in the streets⟩ **2** : to ask earnestly or politely ⟨*beg* a favor⟩ ⟨*beg* pardon⟩

be·get \bi-'get\ *vb* **-got** \-'gät\ *also* **-gat** \-'gat\; **-got·ten** \-'gät-ᵊn\ *or* **-got; -get·ting** **1** : to become the father of **2** : ²CAUSE — **be·get·ter** *n*

¹beg·gar \'beg-ər\ *n* **1** : a person who lives by begging **2** : a very poor person : PAUPER

²beggar *vb* **beg·gared; beg·gar·ing** \'beg-(ə-)riŋ\ **1** : to reduce to beggary **2** : to go beyond the ability of ⟨the costumes almost *beggar* description⟩

beg·gar·ly \'beg-ər-lē\ *adj* : MEASLY — **beg·gar·li·ness** *n*

beg·gar–ticks \'beg-ər-,tiks\ *also* **beg·gar's–ticks** \-ərz-\ *n sing or pl* : BUR MARIGOLD; *also* : its prickly fruits

beg·gary \'beg-(ə)rē\ *n* : extreme poverty

be·gin \bi-'gin\ *vb* **be·gan** \-'gan\; **be·gun** \-'gən\; **be·gin·ning** **1** : to do or be the first part of an action or course : START ⟨*begin* your homework⟩ ⟨it *began* to rain⟩ **2** : to come or bring into existence : ORIGINATE ⟨the war *began* in 1939⟩ **3** : to do or succeed in the least degree ⟨does not *begin* to fill our needs⟩

be·gin·ner \bi-'gin-ər\ *n* : a person who is beginning something or doing something for the first time : an inexperienced person

be·gin·ning \bi-'gin-iŋ\ *n* **1** : the point at which something begins ⟨the *beginning* of the year⟩ **2** : the first part ⟨go back to the *beginning* of the song⟩ **3** : an early stage or period ⟨the *beginnings* of American history⟩

be·gone \bi-'gòn *also* -'gän\ *vb* : to go away — used especially in the imperative mood

be·go·nia \bi-'gō-nyə\ *n* : any of a large genus of tropical herbs often grown for their shining leaves and bright waxy flowers

be·grime \bi-'grīm\ *vb* **be·grimed; be·grim·ing** : to make dirty with grime

be·grudge \bi-'grəj\ *vb* : to give or do reluctantly ⟨*begrudge* a person a favor⟩ — **be·grudg·ing·ly** \-'grəj-iŋ-lē\ *adv*

be·guile \bi-'gī(ə)l\ *vb* **be·guiled; be·guil·ing** **1** : to deceive by cunning means ⟨was *beguiled* into thinking everything was all right⟩ **2** : to draw notice or interest by charm ⟨a *beguiling* manner⟩ ⟨it is the scenery that *beguiles* the tourists⟩ **3** : to cause time to pass pleasantly ⟨*beguile* the time by telling stories⟩ — **be·guile·ment** \-'gī(ə)l-mənt\ *n* — **be·guil·er** \-'gī-lər\ *n*

be·half \bi-'haf, -'háf\ *n* : useful aid : SUPPORT ⟨spoke in my *behalf*⟩ — **in behalf of** *or* **on behalf of** **1** : in the interest of ⟨spoke *in behalf of* the other candidate⟩ **2** : as a representative of ⟨accepted *on behalf of* the whole class⟩

be·have \bi-'hāv\ *vb* **be·haved; be·hav·ing** **1** : to conduct oneself ⟨*behaved* badly at the meeting⟩ **2** : to conduct oneself properly ⟨if you don't *behave* you'll be punished⟩ ⟨I know how to *behave* myself⟩ **3** : to act, function, or react in a particular way ⟨how metals *behave* under heat and pressure⟩

be·hav·ior \bi-'hā-vyər\ *n* **1** : the way in which one conducts oneself **2** : the way in which something (as a machine) behaves **3** : anything that a living being does that involves action and response to stimulation — **be·hav·ior·al** \-'hā-vyə-rəl\ *adj*

be·head \bi-'hed\ *vb* : to cut off the head of

be·he·moth \bi-'hē-məth, 'bē-ə-,məth, -, -,mäth, -,mòth\ *n* **1** *often cap* : an animal described in the Bible that is probably the hippopotamus **2** : something of monstrous size or power

be·hest \bi-'hest\ *n* : ²ORDER 5b, COMMAND ⟨built monuments at their ruler's *behest*⟩

¹be·hind \bi-'hīnd\ *adv or adj* **1 a** : in a place or time that is being or has been departed from ⟨stay *behind*⟩ ⟨left years of poverty *behind*⟩ **b** : at, to, or toward the back ⟨look *behind*⟩ ⟨fall *behind*⟩ **2 a** : not up to the general level ⟨*behind* in school⟩ **b** : not keeping up to a schedule ⟨*behind* in the car payments⟩

²behind *prep* **1** : at, to, or toward the back of ⟨look *behind* you⟩ ⟨a garden *behind* the house⟩ **2** : not up to the level of ⟨sales are *behind* those of last year⟩ ⟨*behind* the rest of the class⟩ **3 a** : in the background of ⟨the reasons *behind* our success⟩ **b** : in support of ⟨we're *behind* you all the way⟩

be·hind·hand \bi-'hīnd-,hand\ *adv or adj* : not keeping up : BEHIND ⟨*behindhand* with the rent⟩

be·hold \bi-'hōld\ *vb* **-held** \-,held\; **-hold·ing** : to look upon : SEE — **be·hold·er** *n*

be·hold·en \bi-'hōl-dən\ *adj* : being indebted for a favor or gift

be·hoof \bi-'hüf\ *n* : ¹ADVANTAGE 1, BENEFIT ⟨acted only for his own *behoof*⟩

be·hoove \bi-'hüv\ *or* **be·hove** \-'hōv\ *vb* **be·hooved** *or* **be·hoved; be·hoov·ing** *or* **be·hov·ing** : to be necessary, fitting, or proper for ⟨such behavior ill *behooves* you⟩ ⟨it *behooves* a good citizen to obey the law⟩

beige \'bāzh\ *n* : a light grayish yellowish brown — **beige** *adj*

be·ing \'bē-iŋ\ *n* **1** : the state of having life or existence **2** : one that exists in fact or thought **3** : a living thing; *esp* : PERSON 1

be·la·bor \bi-'lā-bər\ *vb* **1** : to keep working on to excess ⟨I don't want to *belabor* the point⟩ **2** : ASSAIL, ATTACK

be·lat·ed \bi-'lāt-əd\ *adj* : delayed beyond the usual time — **be·lat·ed·ly** *adv* — **be·lat·ed·ness** *n*

be·lay \bi-'lā\ *vb* **1** : to make (as a rope) fast by turns around a cleat or pin **2** : CEASE, STOP

¹belch \'belch\ *vb* **1** : to force out gas from the stomach through the mouth **2** : to throw out or be thrown out violently ⟨smoke *belching* from the chimney⟩

²belch *n* : a belching of gas

bel·dam *or* **bel·dame** \'bel-dəm\ *n* : an old woman; *esp* : one who is ugly or evil-looking

be·lea·guer \bi-'lē-gər\ *vb* **-guered; -guer·ing** \-g(ə-)riŋ\ **1** : BESIEGE 1 **2** : to subject to troublesome forces : HARASS

bel·fry \'bel-frē\ *n, pl* **belfries** : a tower or a room in a tower for a bell or set of bells

> **Word History** Centuries ago the structure that gives us our word for a bell tower had no bells at all. It was a movable tower used in wartime to protect soldiers attacking a fortress or walled city. The word for this tower was *berfrei* in early French. Middle English borrowed the word and meaning, spelling it *berfrey*. Later *berfrey* was used for the tower that sheltered a guard and then for any tower from which a warning or alarm might be given. The custom of putting bells in these towers made people think *berfrey* should be spelled *bellfrey* or *belfrey*, and in the end this idea changed the spelling and meaning of the word. In Modern English *belfry* means a bell tower or the bell room at the top of a tower usually attached to a church. The word has lost all of its connection with war. [Middle English *belfrey, berfrey* "bell tower, war tower", from early French *berfrei* "war tower", derived from Latin *berfredus* (same meaning); of Greek origin]

Bel·gian \'bel-jən\ *n* **1** : a person born or living in Belgium **2** : any of a Belgian breed of heavy usually roan or chestnut draft horses — **Belgian** *adj*

Belgian hare *n* : any of a breed of slender dark-red domestic rabbits

Belgian sheepdog *n* : any of a breed of active black dogs developed in Belgium for herding sheep

Belgian 2

be·lie \bi-'lī\ *vb* **-lied; -ly·ing** **1** : to give a false idea of ⟨her lively movements *belied* her age⟩ **2** : to show to be false ⟨their actions *belie* their claim to be innocent⟩ — **be·li·er** *n*

be·lief \bə-'lēf\ *n* **1** : a feeling sure that someone or something exists or is true or trustworthy ⟨a *belief* in Santa Claus⟩ ⟨a *belief* in democracy⟩ **2** : religious faith : CREED **3** : something that one thinks is true ⟨political *beliefs*⟩

syn BELIEF, CREDENCE, FAITH mean an accepting of something or someone as true or reliable without asking for proof. BELIEF may suggest going along without careful thought ⟨the widespread *belief* in flying saucers⟩ CREDENCE suggests ready acceptance of rumors, reports, or opinions as a basis for belief ⟨during the panic people gave *credence* to wild stories⟩ FAITH suggests full trust and confidence in the source ⟨the members of the team had great *faith* in their coach's strategy⟩ **syn** see in addition OPINION

be·lieve \bə-'lēv\ *vb* **be·lieved; be·liev·ing** **1** : to have a firm religious faith **2** : to have faith or confidence in the existence or worth of ⟨*believe* in ghosts⟩ ⟨*believe* in regular exercise⟩ **3** : to accept as true ⟨*believe* the reports⟩ **4** : to accept the word or evidence of ⟨they *believed* us⟩ ⟨I could hardly *believe* my ears⟩ **5** : to hold as an opinion : THINK ⟨*believe* it will rain⟩ — **be·liev·able** \-'lē-və-bəl\

\ə\ abut		\aủ\ out	\i\ tip	\ò\ saw	\ủ\ foot
\ər\ further		\ch\ chin	\ī\ life	\òi\ coin	\y\ yet
\a\ mat		\e\ pet	\j\ job	\th\ thin	\yü\ few
\ā\ take		\ē\ easy	\ŋ\ sing	\<u>th</u>\ this	\yủ\ cure
\ä\ cot, cart		\g\ go	\ō\ bone	\ü\ food	\zh\ vision

adj — **be·liev·ably** \-blē\ *adv* — **be·liev·er** *n*

be·like \bi-ˈlīk\ *adv, archaic* : most likely

be·lit·tle \bi-ˈlit-ᵊl\ *vb* **-lit·tled; -lit·tling** \-ˈlit-ᵊl-iŋ, -ˈlit-liŋ\ : to make (a person or a thing) seem little or unimportant ⟨*belittle* the success of a rival⟩ — **be·lit·tle·ment** \-ᵊl-mənt\ *n* — **be·lit·tler** \-ˈlit-ᵊl-ər, -ˈlit-lər\ *n*

¹bell \ˈbel\ *n* **1** : a hollow usually cup-shaped metallic device that makes a ringing sound when struck **2** : the stroke or sound of a bell that tells the hour **3** : a half hour period of a watch on shipboard indicated by the strokes of a bell **4** : something (as a flower or the mouth of a trumpet) shaped like a bell

SHIP'S BELLS

NUMBER OF BELLS	HOUR (A.M. OR P.M.)		
1	12:30	4:30	8:30
2	1:00	5:00	9:00
3	1:30	5:30	9:30
4	2:00	6:00	10:00
5	2:30	6:30	10:30
6	3:00	7:00	11:00
7	3:30	7:30	11:30
8	4:00	8:00	12:00

²bell *vb* **1** : to provide with a bell ⟨*bell* a cat⟩ **2** : to take the form of a bell : FLARE

bel·la·don·na \,bel-ə-ˈdän-ə\ *n* **1** : a European poisonous herb that is related to the nightshade and has reddish bell-shaped flowers, shining black berries, and a root and leaves that are a source of atropine — called also *deadly nightshade* **2** : a drug or extract from the belladonna [from Italian *bella donna,* literally "beautiful lady"; so called because the extract was formerly used in cosmetics]

bell–bot·toms \ˈbel-ˌbät-əmz\ *n pl* : pants with legs that widen out at the bottom — **bell–bottom** *or* **bell–bottomed** \-əmd\ *adj*

bell–boy \ˈbel-ˌbói\ *n* : BELLHOP

bell captain *n* : a person in charge of hotel bellhops

belle \ˈbel\ *n* : a popular attractive girl or woman [French *belle* "a beautiful girl", from *belle* (adjective), feminine form of *beau* "beautiful", from Latin *bellus* "pretty" — related to BEAU, BEAUTY]

bell·flow·er \ˈbel-ˌflaù(-ə)r\ *n* : CAMPANULA

bell·hop \-ˌhäp\ *n* : a hotel or club employee who takes guests to rooms, carries luggage, and runs errands

bel·li·cose \ˈbel-ə-ˌkōs\ *adj* : likely to quarrel or fight — **bel·li·cos·i·ty** \,bel-ə-ˈkäs-ət-ē\ *n*

bel·lig·er·ence \bə-ˈlij-(ə-)rən(t)s\ *n* : a belligerent attitude or disposition

bel·lig·er·en·cy \bə-ˈlij-(ə-)rən-sē\ *n* **1** : the state of being at war **2** : BELLIGERENCE

bel·lig·er·ent \bə-ˈlij-(ə-)rənt\ *adj* **1** : waging war ⟨*belligerent* nations⟩ **2** : eager to or showing eagerness to fight ⟨*belligerent* remarks⟩ — **belligerent** *n* — **bel·lig·er·ent·ly** *adv*

> **syn** BELLIGERENT, PUGNACIOUS, QUARRELSOME, CONTENTIOUS mean having an aggressive or fighting attitude. BELLIGERENT suggests either being actually at war ⟨the *belligerent* nations refused to have peace talks⟩ or having angry aggressive feelings ⟨the new girl at school is *belligerent* and is not making many friends⟩ PUGNACIOUS suggests a nature that takes pleasure in conflict ⟨a *pugnacious* fellow always getting into fights⟩ QUARRELSOME stresses a bad-tempered readiness to fight for no good reason ⟨our neighbors are *quarrelsome*⟩ CONTENTIOUS suggests an odd and annoying fondness for arguing ⟨stayed away from *contentious* people⟩

bell jar *n* : a bell-shaped usually glass container, designed to cover objects, hold gases, or keep a vacuum

bel·low \ˈbel-ō\ *vb* : to make a deep loud roar like that of a bull — **bellow** *n*

bel·lows \ˈbel-ōz, -əz\ *n sing or pl* **1** : a device that produces a strong current of air when it is spread apart and then pressed together **2** : a part of some cameras that is pleated and can expand

bell·pull \ˈbel-ˌpùl\ *n* : a cord or wire or a handle or knob attached to it that one pulls to ring a bell

bells \ˈbelz\ *n pl* : BELL-BOTTOMS

bell·weth·er \ˈbel-ˈweth-ər, -ˌweth-\ *n* : someone or something that leads the way or points out a trend ⟨a *bellwether* of fashion⟩ ⟨a county that is a *bellwether* in national elections⟩ [from earlier *bellwether* "leading sheep (or *wether*) of a flock", from the fact that this sheep wore a bell which told the shepherd where the flock was]

¹bel·ly \ˈbel-ē\ *n, pl* **bellies** **1 a** : ABDOMEN 1 **b** : the undersurface of an animal's body; *also* : hide from this part **c** : ¹STOMACH 1a **2** : an internal cavity : INTERIOR **3** : a curved or rounded surface or object ⟨the *belly* of an airplane⟩

²belly *vb* **bel·lied; bel·ly·ing** : to swell or bulge out

¹bel·ly·ache \ˈbel-ē-ˌāk\ *n* : pain in the abdomen and especially in the bowels : COLIC

²bellyache *vb* : to complain in a whining or irritable way

belly button *n* : NAVEL

belly flop *n* : a dive (as into the water) in which the front of the body lands flat — **belly flop** *vb*

bel·ly–land \ˈbel-ē-ˌland\ *vb* : to land an airplane without use of landing gear — **belly landing** *n*

be·long \bi-ˈlóŋ\ *vb* **1** : to be in a proper place ⟨this book *belongs* on the top shelf⟩ **2 a** : to be the property of a person or group of persons ⟨the watch *belongs* to me⟩ **b** : to be a member ⟨*belongs* to our club⟩ **3** : to be a part of : be connected with : go with ⟨the parts *belonging* to the clock⟩ **4** : to be classified ⟨whales *belong* among the mammals⟩

be·long·ings \bi-ˈlóŋ-iŋz\ *n pl* : the things that belong to a person : POSSESSIONS

be·loved \bi-ˈləv(-ə)d\ *adj* : dearly loved — **be·loved** *n*

¹be·low \bi-ˈlō\ *adv* **1** : in or to a lower place **2** : on a lower floor or deck

²below *prep* : lower than ⟨the diver descends *below* 25 meters⟩ ⟨*below* average⟩ ⟨selling *below* cost⟩

¹belt \ˈbelt\ *n* **1** : a strip of flexible material (as leather) worn around a person's body for holding in or supporting clothing or weapons or for ornament **2** : something resembling a belt : BAND, CIRCLE ⟨a *belt* of trees⟩ **3** : a flexible continuous band running around wheels or pulleys and used for moving or carrying something ⟨a fan *belt* on a car⟩ **4** : a region suited to or producing something or having some special feature ⟨the corn *belt*⟩ ⟨a storm *belt*⟩ — **belt·ed** \ˈbel-təd\ *adj* — **below the belt** : in an unfair way — **under one's belt** : as part of one's experience

²belt *vb* **1** : to put a belt on or around **2** : to hit hard ⟨*belt* a home run⟩ **3** : to mark with a band **4** : to sing in a forceful way ⟨*belt* out a song⟩

³belt *n* : a jarring blow

belt·ing \ˈbel-tiŋ\ *n* : material for making belts

belt–tight·en·ing \ˈbelt-ˌtīt-niŋ, -ᵊn-iŋ\ *n* : a reduction in spending

be·lu·ga \bə-ˈlü-gə\ *n* : a mammal that is related to the dolphins and becomes about 3 meters long and white when adult — called also *beluga whale* [from earlier *beluga* "a white sturgeon", derived from Russian *belyĭ* "white"]

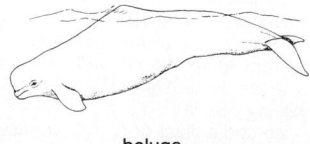

beluga

be·moan \bi-ˈmōn\ *vb* : to express grief over

be·muse \bi-'myüz\ *vb* : CONFUSE 1a

¹bench \'bench\ *n*　**1 a** : a long seat for two or more persons　**b** : a seat where the members of a team wait for a chance to play　**2 a** : the seat where a judge sits in a court of law　**b** : the position or rank of a judge　**c** : a person or persons engaged in judging　**3 a** : a long table for holding tools and work　**b** : SHELF 2

²bench *vb*　**1** : to furnish with benches　**2** : to seat on a bench　**3** : to remove from or keep out of a game

bench mark *n*　**1** : a mark on a permanent object indicating elevation and serving as a reference in geological surveys　**2** *usually* **bench·mark** : something (as a test) that can be used as a standard to check other things (as computer programs) against

bench·warm·er \'bench-,wȯr-mər\ *n* : a reserve player on a sports team

¹bend \'bend\ *vb* **bent** \'bent\; **bend·ing**　**1** : to pull tight ⟨*bend* a bow⟩　**2** : to curve or cause a change of shape ⟨*bend* a wire into a circle⟩　**3** : to turn in a certain direction ⟨*bent* their steps toward town⟩　**4** : to apply or apply oneself closely ⟨*bent* all her strength to force open the door⟩　**5** : to curve out of line ⟨the road *bends* to the left⟩　**6** : to curve downward : STOOP ⟨*bend* over and pick it up⟩

²bend *n*　**1** : the act or process of bending : the state of being bent　**2** : something (as a curved part of a stream) that is bent　**3** *pl* : a severe disorder marked by pain (as in joints), by difficulty in breathing, and often by collapsing and caused by release of gas bubbles in the tissues upon too rapid decrease in air pressure after a stay in a compressed atmosphere — called also *caisson disease*

¹be·neath \bi-'nēth\ *adv* : in or to a lower position : BELOW

²beneath *prep*　**1** : lower than : BELOW　**2** : not worthy of ⟨work *beneath* your dignity⟩

bene·dic·tion \,ben-ə-'dik-shən\ *n*　**1** : an expression of good wishes　**2** : the short blessing at the end of a religious service [Middle English *benediccioun* "an expression of blessing or good wishes", from Latin *benediction-, benedictio* (same meaning), from *benedictus*, past participle of *benedicere* "to bless", from earlier *bene dicere* "to praise, speak well", from *bene* "well" and *dicere* "to say" — related to DICTATE]

Ben·e·dict's solution \'ben-ə-,dik(t)s-\ *n* : a blue liquid that is used to detect some sugars (as glucose) with which it reacts when warmed to produce a red, yellow, or orange solid that separates from the liquid

bene·fac·tion \'ben-ə-,fak-shən, ,ben-ə-'fak-\ *n*　**1** : the action of benefiting　**2** : a benefit given; *esp* : a donation to charity

bene·fac·tor \'ben-ə-,fak-tər\ *n* : one who helps another especially by giving money

bene·fac·tress \'ben-ə-,fak-trəs\ *n* : a woman who is a benefactor

ben·e·fice \'ben-ə-fəs\ *n* : a post held by a member of the clergy that gives the right to use certain property and to receive income from stated sources

be·nef·i·cence \bə-'nef-ə-sən(t)s\ *n*　**1** : the quality or state of being beneficent　**2** : BENEFACTION

be·nef·i·cent \bə-'nef-ə-sənt\ *adj* : doing or producing good; *esp* : performing acts of kindness or charity — **be·nef·i·cent·ly** *adv*

ben·e·fi·cial \,ben-ə-'fish-əl\ *adj* : producing results that are good for health and happiness — **ben·e·fi·cial·ly** \-'fish-ə-lē\ *adv* — **ben·e·fi·cial·ness** *n*

ben·e·fi·ci·ary \,ben-ə-'fish-ē-,er-ē, -'fish-(ə-)rē\ *n, pl* **-ar·ies** : a person who benefits or is expected to benefit from something ⟨the *beneficiary* of life insurance⟩

¹ben·e·fit \'ben-ə-,fit\ *n*　**1 a** : something that does good to a person or thing ⟨the *benefits* of fresh air and sunshine⟩　**b** : useful aid : HELP ⟨had to perform without the *benefit* of a rehearsal⟩　**2** : money paid at death or when sick, retired, or unemployed (as by an insurance company or public agency)　**3** : an entertainment or social event to raise funds for a person or cause [Middle English *benefet, benefit* "good deed", derived from Latin *bene factum* (same meaning), from *bene factus*, past participle of *bene facere* "to do good", from *bene* "well" (from *bonus* "good") and *facere* "to do, make" — related to BONUS, FASHION]

²benefit *vb* **-fit·ed** \-,fit-əd\ *also* **-fit·ted**; **-fit·ing** *also* **-fit·ting**　**1** : to be useful or profitable to ⟨medicines that *benefit* all⟩　**2** : to receive benefit ⟨I *benefited* from the experience⟩

be·nev·o·lence \bə-'nev(-ə)-lən(t)s\ *n* : KINDNESS, GENEROSITY

be·nev·o·lent \bə-'nev(-ə)-lənt\ *adj* : having a desire to do good : KINDLY, CHARITABLE — **be·nev·o·lent·ly** *adv*

Ben·gali \ben-'gȯ-lē, beŋ-\ *n*　**1** : a person born or living in Bengal　**2** : the language of Bengal — **Bengali** *adj*

be·night·ed \bi-'nīt-əd\ *adj* : IGNORANT 1, 2

be·nign \bi-'nīn\ *adj*　**1** : of a gentle disposition : GRACIOUS　**2** : FAVORABLE ⟨a *benign* climate⟩　**3** : of a mild character; *esp* : not malignant ⟨*benign* tumor⟩ — **be·nig·ni·ty** \-'nig-nət-ē\ *n* — **be·nign·ly** \-'nīn-lē\ *adv*

be·nig·nant \bi-'nig-nənt\ *adj*　**1** : showing kindly feelings or intentions　**2** : BENEFICIAL — **be·nig·nant·ly** *adv*

ben·i·son \'ben-ə-sən, -zən\ *n* : BLESSING 1

¹bent \'bent\ *n* : BENT GRASS [Middle English *bent* "grassy place, bent grass"]

²bent *adj*　**1** : changed by bending : CROOKED ⟨a *bent* pin⟩　**2** : strongly favorable to : quite determined ⟨doctors *bent* on finding a cure⟩ [Middle English *bent* "crooked", from *benden* "to bend"]

³bent *n* : a strong natural liking [derived from *bend* "to turn in a certain direction"]

bent grass *n* : any of a genus of stiff or velvety grasses that are used especially for pastures and lawns

ben·thos \'ben-,thäs\ *n* : the plant and animal life that lives on or in the bottom of a body of water (as an ocean)

ben·ton·ite \'bent-ᵊn-,īt\ *n* : an absorbent clay that is used especially as a filler (as in paper)

be·numb \bi-'nəm\ *vb* : to make numb especially by cold

ben·zene \'ben-,zēn, ben-'zēn\ *n* : a colorless flammable liquid that evaporates easily and is used to make or dissolve other chemicals or as a motor fuel — called also *benzol*

ben·zine \'ben-,zēn, ben-'zēn\ *n* : any of various flammable chemicals from petroleum that evaporate easily and are used especially to dissolve fatty substances or as motor fuels

ben·zo·ic acid \ben-,zō-ik-\ *n* : a white crystalline organic acid that is used especially to increase the life of foods, to make other chemicals, and in medicine

ben·zo·yl peroxide \'ben-zə-,wil-, -,zȯil-\ *n* : a white crystalline flammable compound used in bleaching and in medicine especially in the treatement of acne

be·queath \bi-'kwēth, -'kwēth\ *vb*　**1** : to give property by a will　**2** : HAND DOWN 1 — **be·queath·al** \-əl\ *n*

be·quest \bi-'kwest\ *n*　**1** : the action of bequeathing　**2** : something given or left by a will

be·rate \bi-'rāt\ *vb* : to scold forcefully

Ber·ber \'bər-bər\ *n*　**1** : a member of a people of northwestern Africa　**2** : any of a group of languages spoken in northwestern Africa

¹be·reaved \bi-'rēvd\ *adj* : suffering the death of a loved one ⟨*bereaved* parents⟩

²bereaved *n, pl* **bereaved** : a person who is bereaved

be·reave·ment \bi-'rēv-mənt\ *n* : the state or fact of being bereaved

\ə\ abut		\au̇\ out	\i\ tip	\ȯ\ saw	\u̇\ foot
\ər\ further		\ch\ chin	\ī\ life	\ȯi\ coin	\y\ yet
\a\ mat		\e\ pet	\j\ job	\th\ thin	\yü\ few
\ā\ take		\ē\ easy	\ŋ\ sing	\th\ this	\yu̇\ cure
\ä\ cot, cart		\g\ go	\ō\ bone	\ü\ food	\zh\ vision

be·reft \bi-'reft\ adj 1 : not having something needed, wanted, or expected 2 : ¹BEREAVED

be·ret \bə-'rā\ n : a soft flat wool cap without a visor [from French *béret* "beret", derived from a word in an old language of southeastern France meaning "cap", derived from Latin *birrus* "cloak with a hood", of Celtic origin — related to BIRETTA]

beret

berg \'bərg\ n : ICEBERG

ber·i·beri \ˌber-ē-'ber-ē\ n : a disease marked by weakness, wasting, and damage to nerves and caused by a lack of thiamine in the diet or by an inability to absorb and use it

berke·li·um \'bər-klē-əm\ n : an artificially prepared radioactive chemical element — see ELEMENT table

berm or **berme** \'bərm\ n : a shelf or path at the top or bottom of a slope; also : a mound or wall of earth

Ber·mu·da grass \bər-'myüd-ə-\ n : a trailing grass that is native to Europe and is used for lawns and pasture especially in the southern U.S.

¹ber·ry \'ber-ē\ n, pl **berries** 1 : a small pulpy and usually edible fruit (as a strawberry or raspberry) 2 : a simple fruit (as a currant, grape, tomato, or banana) with the wall of the ripened ovary pulpy 3 : the dry seed of some plants (as coffee) — **ber·ry·like** \-ē-ˌlīk\ adj

²berry vb **ber·ried; ber·ry·ing** 1 : to bear or produce berries 2 : to gather or look for berries ⟨go *berrying*⟩

ber·serk \bə(r)-'sərk, ˌbər-, -'zərk; 'bər-ˌsərk, -zərk\ adj : gone out of control : CRAZY, AMOK — **berserk** adv

Word History Many hundreds of years ago in what is now Scandinavia, certain warriors were known for their wild and savage behavior in battle. These fighters wore animal skins, and the early Norse word for such a person was *berserkr,* meaning literally "bear(skin) shirt". The word was borrowed into English in the early 19th century when many people became interested in Norse history and legend. From *berserker,* with the sense of "a Scandinavian warrior", the word became *berserk,* a general term for a person whose behavior is reckless and wild. [from early Norse *berserkr* "warrior", from *ber-* (derived from the word for "bear") and *serkr* "shirt"]

ber·serk·er \bə(r)-'sərk-ər, ˌbər-, -'zərk-; 'bər-ˌsərk-ər, -ˌzərk-\ n : a Scandinavian warrior of ancient times who fought with great fury in battle and was believed impossible to kill or wound

¹berth \'bərth\ n 1 a : enough room to maneuver a ship b : a safe distance ⟨give it wide *berth*⟩ 2 : a place where a ship lies at anchor or at a wharf 3 : a place to sleep on a ship or train 4 : JOB 3, POSITION

²berth vb : to bring or come into a berth

ber·yl \'ber-əl\ n : a mineral consisting of a silicate of beryllium and aluminum that has great hardness and occurs in green, bluish green, yellow, pink, or white crystals

be·ryl·li·um \bə-'ril-ē-əm\ n : a steel-gray light strong brittle toxic metallic element used chiefly to help harden alloys — see ELEMENT table

be·seech \bi-'sēch\ vb **be·sought** \-'sòt\ or **be·seeched; be·seech·ing** : to ask earnestly for

be·seem \bi-'sēm\ vb, archaic : to be proper for

be·set \bi-'set\ vb **-set; -set·ting** 1 : to trouble with problems 2 : ASSAIL, SET UPON

be·set·ting \bi-'set-iŋ\ adj : constantly present or attacking ⟨a *besetting* danger⟩

be·side \bi-'sīd\ prep 1 a : by the side of ⟨walk *beside* me⟩ b : in comparison with ⟨the kitten looks tiny *beside* that big dog⟩ 2 : ¹BESIDES ⟨was the only one, *beside* me,

who objected⟩ 3 : not relating to ⟨*beside* the point⟩ — **beside oneself** : very upset

¹be·sides \bi-'sīdz\ prep 1 : other than : EXCEPT ⟨no one *besides* me knows about it⟩ 2 : in addition to ⟨*besides* being useful, it looks good⟩

²besides adv : in addition : ALSO ⟨had a big dinner and dessert *besides*⟩

be·siege \bi-'sēj\ vb **be·sieged; be·sieg·ing** 1 : to surround with armed forces for the purpose of capturing 2 : to crowd around — **be·sieg·er** n

be·smear \bi-'smi(ə)r\ vb : ²SMEAR

be·smirch \bi-'smərch\ vb : to make soiled or less pure : SULLY

be·som \'bē-zəm\ n : a broom made of twigs

be·spat·ter \bi-'spat-ər\ vb : ¹SPATTER

be·speak \bi-'spēk\ vb **-spoke** \-'spōk\; **-spo·ken** \-'spō-kən\; **-speak·ing** 1 : to ask or arrange for in advance 2 : to make plain : SHOW ⟨her performance *bespeaks* much practice⟩

be·spec·ta·cled \bi-'spek-ti-kəld\ adj : wearing glasses

Bes·se·mer converter \ˌbes-ə-mər-\ n : the furnace used in the Bessemer process

Bessemer process n : a process of making steel from pig iron by burning out impurities (as carbon) by means of a blast of air forced through the hot liquid metal

¹best \'best\ adj, superlative of GOOD 1 : better than all others ⟨my *best* friend⟩ 2 : good or useful in the highest degree : most excellent ⟨my *best* clothes⟩ ⟨the *best* movie I ever saw⟩ — **best part** : ³MOST ⟨it rained for the *best part* of a week⟩

²best adv, superlative of WELL 1 : in the best way 2 : to the highest degree : MOST ⟨*best* able to do the work⟩

³best n 1 : the best state or part ⟨the *best* is yet to come⟩ 2 : one that is best ⟨even the *best* lose once in a while⟩ 3 : one's greatest effort ⟨do your *best*⟩ 4 : best clothes ⟨put on your Sunday *best*⟩ — **at best** : under the best conditions

⁴best vb : to get the better of

bes·tial \'bes-chəl, 'bēs-\ adj 1 : resembling a beast 2 : having or showing qualities like those of a beast : BRUTAL, INHUMAN — **bes·ti·al·i·ty** \ˌbes-chē-'al-ət-ē, ˌbēs-\ n — **bes·tial·ly** \-chə-lē\ adv

be·stir \bi-'stər\ vb : to stir up : rouse to action

be·stow \bi-'stō\ vb : to present as a gift — **be·stow·al** \-'stō-əl\ n

be·strew \bi-'strü\ vb **-strewed; -strewed** or **-strewn** \-'strün\; **-strew·ing** 1 : STREW 2 2 : to lie scattered over

be·stride \bi-'strīd\ vb **-strode** \-'strōd\; **-strid·den** \-'strid-ən\; **-strid·ing** \-'strīd-iŋ\ : to ride, sit, or stand with one leg on each side of

best–sell·er \'bes(t)-'sel-ər\ n : an article (as a book) whose sales are among the highest of its kind — **best–sell·ing** \-'sel-iŋ\ adj

¹bet \'bet\ n 1 : an agreement requiring the person whose guess about the result of a contest or the outcome of an event proves wrong to give something to a person whose guess proves right 2 : the money or thing risked 3 : a choice made by considering what might happen ⟨our best *bet* is to take the back road⟩

²bet vb **bet** also **bet·ted; bet·ting** 1 : to risk in a bet ⟨I'll *bet* a nickel⟩ 2 : to make a bet with ⟨I *bet* you he won't⟩ 3 : to be certain enough to bet ⟨I *bet* it will rain⟩

be·ta \'bāt-ə\ n : the 2d letter of the Greek alphabet — B or β

be·ta–car·o·tene \-'kar-ə-ˌtēn\ n : a form of carotene found in dark green and dark yellow vegetables and fruits

be·take \bi-'tāk\ vb **-took** \-'tůk\; **-tak·en** \-'tā-kən\; **-tak·ing** : to cause (oneself) to go

beta particle n : an electron or positron that is thrown out from the nucleus of an atom during radioactive decay; also : a high-speed electron or positron

beta ray *n* **1** : BETA PARTICLE **2** : a stream of beta particles

be·ta·tron \'bāt-ə-ˌträn\ *n* : a device that speeds up electrons by the action of a rapidly changing magnetic field

be·tel \'bēt-əl\ *n* : a climbing pepper whose dried leaves are chewed together with betel nut and lime as a stimulant especially by southeastern Asians

Be·tel·geuse \'bēt-əl-ˌjüs, 'bet-, -ˌjüz, -ˌjə(r)z\ *n* : a red giant star in Orion that changes in brightness [from French *Bételgeuse* (same meaning); of Arabic origin]

betel nut *n* : the seed of an Asian palm that is chewed with the leaves of betel

bête noire \ˌbet-nə-'wär, ˌbāt-\ *n, pl* **bêtes noires** \ˌbet-nə-'wär(z), ˌbāt-\ : a person or thing strongly disliked or feared

beth·el \'beth-əl\ *n* : a place of worship especially for sailors [from Hebrew *bēth'ēl* "house of God"]

be·think \bi-'think\ *vb* **-thought** \-'thót\; **-think·ing** **1 a** : REMEMBER 1, RECALL **b** : to cause (oneself) to be reminded **2** : to cause (oneself) to consider

be·tide \bi-'tīd\ *vb* **be·tid·ed; be·tid·ing** : to happen or happen to ⟨woe *betide* you if they ever find out⟩

be·times \bi-'tīmz\ *adv* : in time : EARLY ⟨was up *betimes* this morning⟩

be·to·ken \bi-'tō-kən\ *vb* **be·to·kened; be·to·ken·ing** \-'tōk-(ə-)niŋ\ : to be a sign of : INDICATE

be·tray \bi-'trā\ *vb* **1** : to give over to an enemy by treachery **2** : to be unfaithful to ⟨*betrayed* our trust⟩ **3** : to reveal without meaning to ⟨*betrayed* their ignorance⟩ **4** : to tell in violation of a trust ⟨*betray* a secret⟩ **syn** see REVEAL — **be·tray·al** \-'trā-(ə)l\ *n* — **be·tray·er** \-'trā-ər\ *n*

be·troth \bi-'träth, -'tróth, -'tróth, *or with* th\ *vb* : to promise to marry or give in marriage

be·troth·al \-'tróth-əl, -'tróth-, -'tróth-\ *n* : an engagement to be married

be·trothed \-'trätht, -'trótht, -'tróthd\ *n* : the person to whom one is betrothed

bet·ta \'bet-ə\ *n* : any of a genus of small brilliantly colored long-finned freshwater fishes of southeastern Asia

¹bet·ter \'bet-ər\ *adj, comparative of* ¹GOOD **1** : improved in health **2** : of higher quality — **better part** : more than half ⟨the *better part* of an hour⟩

betta

²better *adv, comparative of* WELL **1** : in a more excellent manner **2 a** : to a higher or greater degree **b** : ²MORE ⟨*better* than an hour's drive to the lake⟩

³better *n* **1 a** : a better thing or state ⟨a change for the *better*⟩ **b** : a superior especially in merit or rank **2** : ADVANTAGE 1 ⟨get the *better* of someone⟩

⁴better *vb* **1** : to make better **2** : to surpass in excellence : EXCEL

bet·ter·ment \'bet-ər-mənt\ *n* : IMPROVEMENT 1

bet·tor *or* **bet·ter** \'bet-ər\ *n* : one that bets

¹be·tween \bi-'twēn\ *prep* **1** : by the common action of ⟨ate six pizzas *between* them⟩ **2** : in the time or space that separates ⟨*between* nine and ten o'clock⟩ ⟨*between* the desk and the wall⟩ **3 a** : from one to the other of ⟨flying *between* Miami and Chicago twice a week⟩ **b** : joining or linking in some relationship ⟨the bond *between* friends⟩ ⟨the difference *between* soccer and football⟩ **4** : in comparison of ⟨there's not much to choose *between* the two coats⟩

²between *adv* : in an intermediate space or interval

be·twixt \bi-'twikst\ *adv or prep* : BETWEEN

¹bev·el \'bev-əl\ *n* **1** : the angle that one surface or line makes with another when they are not at right angles **2**

: the slant of a bevel

²bevel *vb* **bev·eled** *or* **bev·elled; bev·el·ing** *or* **bev·el·ling** \'bev-(ə-)liŋ\ : to cut or shape (as an edge) so as to form a bevel

bev·er·age \'bev-(ə-)rij\ *n* : a liquid for drinking

bevy \'bev-ē\ *n, pl* **bev·ies** : a large group ⟨a *bevy* of girls⟩

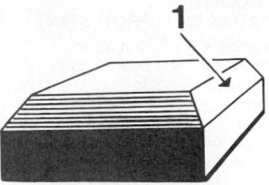

1 bevel 2

be·wail \bi-'wāl\ *vb* : to express great sorrow over ⟨*bewailing* their fate⟩

be·ware \bi-'wa(ə)r, -'we(ə)r\ *vb* **1** : to be on one's guard ⟨*beware* of the dog⟩ **2** : to be suspicious of ⟨*beware* the quick excuse⟩

be·whis·kered \bi-'hwis-kərd, -'wis-\ *adj* : having whiskers

be·wil·der \bi-'wil-dər\ *vb* **-dered; -der·ing** \-d(ə-)riŋ\ : to confuse especially with a great many things to worry about — **be·wil·der·ing·ly** \-d(ə-)riŋ-lē\ *adv* — **be·wil·der·ment** \-dər-mənt\ *n*

be·witch \bi-'wich\ *vb* **1** : to put under a spell **2** : to attract or delight as if by magic — **be·witch·ment** \-mənt\ *n*

be·wray \bi-'rā\ *vb, archaic* : BETRAY, REVEAL

¹be·yond \bē-'änd\ *adv* : on or to the farther side

²beyond *prep* **1** : on or to the farther side of ⟨*beyond* that tree⟩ ⟨*beyond* the sea⟩ **2** : out of the reach or sphere of ⟨*beyond* help⟩ ⟨beautiful *beyond* belief⟩

bi- *prefix* **1** : two ⟨*bi*partisan⟩ **2** : coming or occurring every two ⟨*bi*monthly⟩ **3** : into two parts ⟨*bi*sect⟩ [derived from Latin *bi-* (prefix) "two"]

bi·an·nu·al \(')bī-'an-yə(-wə)l\ *adj* : occurring twice a year — **bi·an·nu·al·ly** \-ē\ *adv*

¹bi·as \'bī-əs\ *n* **1** : a line diagonal to the grain of a fabric **2** : an attitude that always favors one way of feeling or acting over any other : PREJUDICE **3** : a voltage applied to a device (as a transistor control electrode) to establish a reference level for operation

²bias *vb* **bi·ased** *or* **bi·assed; bi·as·ing** *or* **bi·as·sing** : to give a bias to : PREJUDICE

bias tape *n* : a narrow strip of cloth cut on the bias, folded, and used for finishing or decorating clothing

bib \'bib\ *n* **1** : a cloth or plastic shield tied under a child's chin to protect the clothes **2** : the upper part of an apron or of overalls

Bi·ble \'bī-bəl\ *n* **1 a** : a book made up of the writings accepted by Christians as coming from God **b** : a book containing the sacred writings of some other religion **2** *not cap* : a publication widely read and considered very important ⟨the *bible* of show business⟩ [Middle English *Bible* "the Bible", from early French *Bible* (same meaning), from Latin *biblia* (same meaning), from Greek *biblia* (plural) "books", derived from *Byblos*, ancient city in Phoenicia from which the Greeks imported papyrus, an early form of paper]

BOOKS OF THE OLD TESTAMENT

ROMAN CATHOLIC	PROTESTANT	ROMAN CATHOLIC	PROTESTANT
Genesis	Genesis	Wisdom	
Exodus	Exodus	Ecclesiasticus	
Leviticus	Leviticus	Isaias	Isaiah

\ə\ **abut**	\au̇\ **out**	\i\ **tip**	\ȯ\ **saw**	\u̇\ **foot**
\ər\ **further**	\ch\ **chin**	\ī\ **life**	\ȯi\ **coin**	\y\ **yet**
\a\ **mat**	\e\ **pet**	\j\ **job**	\th\ **thin**	\yü\ **few**
\ā\ **take**	\ē\ **easy**	\ŋ\ **sing**	\th\ **this**	\yu̇\ **cure**
\ä\ **cot, cart**	\g\ **go**	\ō\ **bone**	\ü\ **food**	\zh\ **vision**

ROMAN CATHOLIC	PROTESTANT	ROMAN CATHOLIC	PROTESTANT
Numbers	Numbers	Jeremias	Jeremiah
Deuteronomy	Deuteronomy	Lamentations	Lamentations
Josue	Joshua	Baruch	
Judges	Judges	Ezechiel	Ezekiel
Ruth	Ruth	Daniel	Daniel
1 & 2 Kings	1 & 2 Samuel	Osee	Hosea
3 & 4 Kings	1 & 2 Kings	Joel	Joel
1 & 2 Parali-	1 & 2 Chron-	Amos	Amos
pomenon	icles	Abdias	Obadiah
1 Esdras	Ezra	Jonas	Jonah
2 Esdras	Nehemiah	Micheas	Micah
Tobias		Nahum	Nahum
Judith		Habacuc	Habakkuk
Esther	Esther	Sophonias	Zephaniah
Job	Job	Aggeus	Haggai
Psalms	Psalms	Zacharias	Zechariah
Proverbs	Proverbs	Malachias	Malachi
Ecclesiastes	Ecclesiastes	1 & 2 Mach-	
Canticle of	Song of	abees	
Canticles	Solomon		

JEWISH SCRIPTURE

Law	1 & 2 Kings	Nahum	Song of Songs
Genesis	Isaiah	Habakkuk	Ruth
Exodus	Jeremiah	Zephaniah	Lamentations
Leviticus	Ezekiel	Haggai	Ecclesiastes
Numbers	Hosea	Zechariah	Esther
Deuteronomy	Joel	Malachi	Daniel
Prophets	Amos	*Hagiographa*	Ezra
Joshua	Obadiah	Psalms	Nehemiah
Judges	Jonah	Proverbs	1 & 2 Chronicles
1 & 2 Samuel	Micah	Job	

PROTESTANT APOCRYPHA

1 & 2 Esdras	Wisdom of	Baruch	Susanna
Tobit	Solomon	Prayer of Azariah	Bel and the
Judith	Ecclesiasticus	and the Song	Dragon
Additions to	or the Wisdom	of the Three	The Prayer of
Esther	of Jesus Son	Holy Children	Manasses
	of Sirach		1 & 2 Maccabees

BOOKS OF THE NEW TESTAMENT

Matthew	Romans	1 & 2 Thes-	1 & 2 Peter
Mark	1 & 2 Corinthians	salonians	1, 2, 3 John
Luke	Galatians	1 & 2 Timothy	Jude
John	Ephesians	Titus	Revelation (Ro-
Acts of the	Philippians	Philemon	man Catholic:
Apostles	Colossians	Hebrews	Apocalypse)
		James	

bib·li·cal \'bib-li-kəl\ *adj* : relating to, taken from, or found in the Bible

bib·li·og·ra·phy \ˌbib-lē-'äg-rə-fē\ *n, pl* **-phies** : a list of writings about a subject or author or by an author — **bib·lio·graph·ic** \ˌbib-lē-ə-'graf-ik\ *or* **bib·lio·graph·i·cal** \-'graf-i-kəl\ *adj*

bib·u·lous \'bib-yə-ləs\ *adj* **1** : highly absorbent **2** : fond of alcoholic drinks — **bib·u·lous·ly** *adv* — **bib·u·lous·ness** *n*

bi·cam·er·al \(')bī-'kam-(ə-)rəl\ *adj* : consisting of two legislative chambers ⟨a *bicameral* legislature⟩

bi·car·bon·ate \(')bī-'kär-bə-ˌnāt, -nət\ *n* : an acid carbonate

bicarbonate of soda : SODIUM BICARBONATE

bi·cen·te·na·ry \ˌbī-(ˌ)sen-'ten-ə-rē, (')bī-'sent-ᵊn-'er-ē, ˌbī-(ˌ)sen-'tē-nə-rē\ *adj* : BICENTENNIAL — **bicentenary** *n*

bi·cen·ten·ni·al \ˌbī-(ˌ)sen-'ten-ē-əl\ *adj* : relating to a 200th anniversary — **bicentennial** *n*

bi·ceps \'bī-ˌseps\ *n, pl* **biceps** *also* **bicepses** : a muscle having the end at which it begins divided into two parts; *esp* : a large muscle of the front of the upper arm

bick·er \'bik-ər\ *vb* **bick·ered; bick·er·ing** \'bik-(ə-)riŋ\ : to quarrel in an irritating way especially over unimportant things — **bick·er** *n*

bi·col·ored \'bī-ˌkəl-ərd\ *adj* : two-colored — **bicolor** *n*

¹bi·cus·pid \(')bī-'kəs-pəd\ *adj* : having or ending in two points

²bicuspid *n* : ²PREMOLAR

¹bi·cy·cle \'bī-ˌsik-əl,-ˌsīk-\ *n* : a light vehicle with two wheels behind one another, handlebars, a saddle seat, and pedals by which it is made to move

²bicycle *vb* **bi·cy·cled; bi·cy·cling** \-ˌsik-(ə-)liŋ\ : to ride a bicycle — **bi·cy·cler** \-lər\ *n* — **bi·cy·clist** \-ləst\ *n*

¹bid \'bid\ *vb* **bade** \'bad, 'bād\ *or* **bid; bid·den** \'bid-ᵊn\ *or* **bid; bid·ding** **1 a** : ¹ORDER 2a, COMMAND ⟨did as we were *bidden*⟩ **b** : ¹INVITE 2a **2** : to express to ⟨*bade* me farewell⟩ **3** *past and past participle* **bid** : to make an offer for something (as at an auction) ⟨*bid* $10 for a chair⟩ — **bid·der** *n* — **bid fair** : to seem likely

²bid *n* **1** : an offer to pay a certain sum for something or to perform certain work at a stated fee **2** : a turn to bid **3** : INVITATION 2 ⟨received a *bid* to the state tournament⟩ **4 a** : an announcement of what a card player is willing to try for one hand **b** : the amount of such a bid **5** : an attempt to win, achieve, or attract ⟨made a strong *bid* for the job⟩

bid·dy \'bid-ē\ *n, pl* **biddies** : HEN 1; *also* : a young chicken

bide \'bīd\ *vb* **bode** \'bōd\ *or* **bid·ed; bided; bid·ing** : to wait or wait for ⟨*bided* his time before acting⟩

bi·en·ni·al \(')bī-'en-ē-əl\ *adj* **1** : occurring every two years **2** : growing stalks and leaves one year and flowers and fruit the next before dying — **biennial** *n* — **bi·en·ni·al·ly** \-ē-ə-lē\ *adv*

bier \'bi(ə)r\ *n* : a stand on which a coffin is placed

¹bi·fo·cal \(')bī-'fō-kəl\ *adj* : having two focal lengths

²bifocal *n* **1** : a bifocal glass or lens **2** *pl* : eyeglasses with bifocal lenses that correct for near vision and for distant vision

¹big \'big\ *adj* **big·ger; big·gest** **1** : of great force ⟨a *big* storm⟩ **2 a** : large in size, bulk, or extent ⟨a *big* house⟩ ⟨*big* government⟩ ⟨a *big* city⟩ **b** : large in number or amount ⟨a *big* fleet⟩ ⟨*big* money⟩ **3** : of great importance ⟨my *big* chance⟩ ⟨a *big* star in movies⟩ **4** : being older ⟨my *big* sister⟩ — **big·ness** *n* — **big on** : very much in favor of : enthusiastic about ⟨is *big* on stamp collecting⟩

²big *adv* **1** : in a big way ⟨win *big*⟩ **2** : so as to boast ⟨talk *big*⟩

big·a·my \'big-ə-mē\ *n* : the act of marrying one person while still legally married to another [Middle English *bigamie* "bigamy", derived from Latin *bi-* "two" and *gamia* "marriage"] — **big·a·mist** \-məst\ *n* — **big·a·mous** \-məs\ *adj* — **big·a·mous·ly** *adv*

big bang theory *n* : a theory that the universe as it is today is a result of a giant explosion of compacted matter

Big Dipper *n* : DIPPER 3a

big·foot \'big-ˌfût\ *n, often cap* : a large hairy humanlike animal reported to exist in the Pacific Northwest

big game *n* : large animals hunted for sport

big·horn \'big-ˌhorn\ *n, pl* **bighorn** *or* **bighorns** : a usually grayish brown wild sheep of mountainous western North America — called also *Rocky Mountain sheep*

bighorn

bight \'bīt\ *n* **1** : a bend in a coast or the bay it forms **2** : a slack part or loop in a rope

big league *n* : the highest level especially in baseball — **big–league** *adj* — **big leaguer** *n*

big·ot \'big-ət\ *n* : a person who won't listen to anyone whose ideas or beliefs are different from his or her own

big·ot·ed \'big-ət-əd\ *adj* : INTOLERANT 2

big·ot·ry \'big-ə-trē\ *n, pl* **-ries** **1** : the state of mind of a bigot   **2** : bigoted acts or beliefs

big shot *n* : an important person

big toe *n* : the innermost and largest toe of the foot

big top *n*   **1** : the main tent of a circus   **2** : CIRCUS 2

big tree \-,trē\ *n* : a California evergreen tree of the pine family that sometimes exceeds 82 meters (270 feet) in height — called also *giant sequoia, sequoia*

big·wig \'big-,wig\ *n* : BIG SHOT

bike \'bīk\ *n*   **1** : ¹BICYCLE   **2** : MOTORCYCLE — **bike** *vb* — **bik·er** *n*

bi·ki·ni \bə-'kē-nē\ *n* : a scanty two-piece bathing suit for a girl or woman

> **Word History** Why a bathing suit would be named for the site of an atom bomb test in the northern Pacific ocean is hard to see, but that is the case with *bikini*. In July 1946 atom bomb tests were carried out on the small tropical atoll of Bikini in the Marshall islands. In the summer of 1947 the two-piece bathing suit we call a bikini appeared on the beaches of southern France. There is no record of who gave this name to the bathing suit or why. But the bikini fashion became popular, and the word was borrowed from French into English and a number of other languages. [from French *bikini* "two-piece bathing suit", from *Bikini* "atoll in the Marshall islands"]

bi·lat·er·al \(')bī-'lat-ə-rəl, -'la-trəl\ *adj* : having or involving two sides or parties ⟨a *bilateral* treaty⟩ — **bi·lat·er·al·ly** \-ē\ *adv*

bilateral symmetry *n* : plant and animal symmetry in which similar parts are arranged so that one and only one plane can divide the individual into identical or nearly identical halves — compare RADIAL SYMMETRY

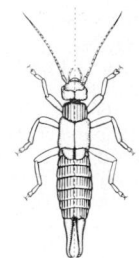

bilateral symmetry

bile \'bī(ə)l\ *n*   **1** : a thick bitter yellow or greenish fluid that is secreted by the liver and aids in the digestion and absorption of fats   **2** : ill humor : ANGER

¹**bilge** \'bilj\ *n*   **1** : the bulging part of a cask or barrel   **2** : the part of a ship's hull between the bottom and the point where the sides begin to rise nearly straight up

²**bilge** *vb* **bilged; bilg·ing**   : to become damaged in the bilge

bilge water *n* : water that collects in a ship's bilge

bil·i·ary \'bil-ē-,er-ē\ *adj* : of, relating to, or conveying bile

bi·lin·gual \(')bī-'liŋ-g(yə-)wəl\ *adj* : of, expressed in, or using two languages ⟨a *bilingual* dictionary⟩ ⟨*bilingual* signs⟩

bil·ious \'bil-yəs\ *adj*   **1 a** : of or relating to bile   **b** : marked by or suffering from a disorder of liver function   **2** : of an irritable disposition : PEEVISH — **bil·ious·ly** *adv* — **bil·ious·ness** *n*

¹**bill** \'bil\ *n*   **1** : the jaws of a bird together with their horny covering   **2** : a mouth structure (as the beak of a turtle) resembling a bird's bill   **3** : the visor of a cap [Old English *bile* "bill (of a bird)"] — **billed** \'bild\ *adj*

²**bill** *vb*   **1** : to touch bills   **2** : to caress affectionately

³**bill** *n*   **1** : a draft of a law presented to a legislature for consideration ⟨introduce a *bill* in Congress⟩   **2** : a record of goods sold, services performed, or work done together with the costs involved ⟨a telephone *bill*⟩   **3** : a sign or poster advertising something   **4** : a piece of paper money ⟨a dollar *bill*⟩ [Middle English *bill* "document", derived from Latin *bulla* "document, seal", from earlier *bulla* "bubble, ornamental knob" — related to ²BOIL, BULLET]

⁴**bill** *vb* : to send a bill to

bill·board \'bil-,bō(ə)rd, -,bȯ(ə)rd\ *n* : a flat surface on which outdoor advertisements are displayed

¹**bil·let** \'bil-ət\ *n*   **1** : an official order that a soldier be put up in a private home   **2** : quarters assigned by or as if by a billet   **3** : JOB 3 [Middle English *bylet* "brief note", from early French *billette*, literally "little document", derived from Latin *bulla* "document"]

²**billet** *vb*   **1** : to assign lodging to : QUARTER   **2** : to have quarters

³**billet** *n*   **1** : a chunky piece of wood (as for firewood)   **2** : a bar of metal; *esp* : one of iron or steel [Middle English *bylet* "chunk of wood", from early French *billete*, literally "little log"; of Celtic origin]

bil·let–doux \,bil-ē-'dü, ,bil-(,)ā-\ *n, pl* **bil·lets–doux** \-'dü(z)\ : a love letter [French, literally "sweet letter"]

bill·fold \'bil-,fōld\ *n* : a folding pocketbook for paper money : WALLET

bil·liards \'bil-yərdz\ *n* : a game played by driving solid balls with a cue into one another or into pockets on a large rectangular table

bil·lion \'bil-yən\ *n*   **1** — see NUMBER table   **2** : a very large number — **billion** *adj* — **bil·lionth** \-yən(t)th\ *adj or n*

bil·lion·aire \,bil-yə-'na(ə)r, -'ne(ə)r; 'bil-yə-,na(ə)r, -,ne(ə)r\ *n* : one who is worth a billion dollars or more

bill of fare : MENU 1

bill of rights *often cap B&R* : a statement of basic rights and privileges guaranteed to a people; *esp* : the first 10 amendments to the U.S. Constitution

¹**bil·low** \'bil-ō\ *n*   **1** : ²WAVE 1; *esp* : a large wave   **2** : a rolling mass like a high wave ⟨*billows* of smoke⟩

²**billow** *vb*   **1** : to rise or roll in waves ⟨the *billowing* ocean⟩   **2** : to bulge or swell out ⟨sails *billowing* in the breeze⟩

bil·lowy \'bil-ə-wē\ *adj* **bil·low·i·er; -est** : full of billows

bil·ly \'bil-ē\ *n, pl* **billies** : a heavy club; *esp* : a police officer's club

billy goat \'bil-ē-\ *n* : a male goat

bi·met·al \'bī-,met-ᵊl\ *adj* : BIMETALLIC

bi·me·tal·lic \,bī-mə-'tal-ik\ *adj* : composed of two different metals — often used of devices having a part in which two metals that expand differently are bonded together

¹**bi·month·ly** \(')bī-'mən(t)th-lē\ *adj*   **1** : occurring every two months   **2** : occurring twice a month : SEMIMONTHLY

²**bimonthly** *adv*   **1** : once every two months   **2** : twice a month

³**bimonthly** *n* : a bimonthly publication

bin \'bin\ *n* : a box, frame, crib, or enclosed place for storage

bi·na·ry \'bī-nə-rē\ *adj*   **1** : compounded or consisting of or marked by two things or parts   **2** : relating to, being, or belonging to a system of numbers having two as its base ⟨*binary* digit⟩   **3** : relating to or being a mathematical operation (as addition) that is used with two elements of a set at a time to produce an element of the set

binary fission *n* : reproduction of a cell by division into two approximately equal parts

binary star *n* : a system of two stars that revolve around each other under the gravitation of both

bin·au·ral \(')bī-'nȯr-əl\ *adj*   **1** : of, relating to, or used with two or both ears ⟨a *binaural* stethoscope⟩   **2** : of, relating to, or making up sound reproduction involving the use of two separated microphones and two channels over which the sound is sent to get a stereophonic effect — **bin·au·ral·ly** \-ə-lē\ *adv*

bind \'bīnd\ *vb* **bound** \'baȯnd\; **bind·ing**   **1 a** : to fasten by tying   **b** : to hold or restrict by force or obligation ⟨*bound* by an oath⟩ ⟨*bound* by friendship⟩   **2** : ²BANDAGE   **3 a** : to stick together   **b** : to form a mass that sticks to-

\ə\ abut		\aȯ\ out	\i\ tip	\ȯ\ saw	\ȯ\ foot
\ər\ further	\ch\ chin	\ī\ life	\ȯi\ coin	\y\ yet
\a\ mat	\e\ pet	\j\ job	\th\ thin	\yü\ few
\ā\ take	\ē\ easy	\ŋ\ sing	\th\ this	\yu̇\ cure
\ä\ cot, cart	\g\ go	\ō\ bone	\ü\ food	\zh\ vision

gether   **c** : to take up and hold (as by chemical forces) : combine with   **4** : to make firm or sure ⟨a deposit *binds* the sale⟩   **5 a** : to finish or decorate with a binding   **b** : to fasten together and enclose in a cover ⟨*bind* a book⟩

bind·er \'bīn-dər\ *n*   **1** : a person who binds books   **2** : a cover for holding together loose sheets of paper   **3** : a machine that cuts grain and ties it in bundles   **4** : something that holds other substances together ⟨use egg as a *binder* in meat loaf⟩ ⟨tar as a *binder* in paving material⟩

bind·ery \'bīn-d(ə-)rē\ *n, pl* **-er·ies** : a place where books are bound

bind·ing \'bīn-diŋ\ *n*   **1** : the cover and fastenings of a book   **2** : a narrow strip of fabric used along the edge of an article of clothing

binding energy *n* : the energy required to break up a molecule, atom, or atomic nucleus completely into the particles that make it up

bind·weed \'bīn-,dwēd\ *n* : any of various twining plants related to the morning glory or to the buckwheat

binge \'binj\ *n* : SPREE

bin·go \'biŋ-,gō\ *n* : a game that is played by covering a numbered space on a card when the number is matched by one chosen at random and that is won by the first player to cover five spaces in a row

bin·na·cle \'bin-i-kəl\ *n* : a box or stand containing a ship's compass and a lamp

¹bin·oc·u·lar \bī-'näk-yə-lər, bə-\ *adj* : of, relating to, using, or adapted to the use of both eyes ⟨*binocular* vision⟩ — **bin·oc·u·lar·ly** *adv*

²bin·oc·u·lar \bə-'näk-yə-lər, bī-\ *n*   **1** : a binocular optical instrument   **2** : a hand-held instrument for seeing at a distance that consists of two telescopes, a focusing device, and usually prisms — usually used in pl. ⟨a pair of *binoculars*⟩

bi·no·mi·al \bī-'nō-mē-əl\ *n*   **1** : a mathematical expression consisting of two terms connected by a plus sign or minus sign   **2** : a biological species name consisting of two terms according to the system of binomial nomenclature — **binomial** *adj* — **bi·no·mi·al·ly** \-mē-ə-lē\ *adv*

binnacle

binomial nomenclature *n* : a system of naming plants and animals in which each species is given a name consisting of two terms of which the first names the genus and the second the species itself

bio- *combining form*   **1** : life ⟨*bio*sphere⟩   **2** : living organisms or tissue ⟨*bio*chemistry⟩ [from Greek *bi-, bio-* "life"]

bio·chem·is·try \,bī-ō-'kem-ə-strē\ *n* : chemistry that deals with the chemical compounds and processes occurring in living things — **bio·chem·i·cal** \-'kem-i-kəl\ *adj* — **bio·chem·i·cal·ly** \-i-k(ə-)lē\ *adv* — **bio·chem·ist** \-'kem-əst\ *n*

bio·de·grad·able \-di-'grād-ə-bəl\ *adj* : capable of being broken down especially into harmless products by the action of living things (as bacteria) ⟨*biodegradable* detergents⟩ — **bio·de·grad·abil·i·ty** \-,grād-ə-'bil-ət-ē\ *n*

bio·di·ver·si·ty \-də-'vər-sət-ē, -dī-\ *n* : biological variety in an environment as indicated by numbers of different species of plants and animals

bi·og·ra·phy \bī-'äg-rə-fē, bē-\ *n, pl* **-phies** : a history of a person's life — **bi·og·ra·pher** \-fər\ *n* — **bio·graph·i·cal** \,bī-ə-'graf-i-kəl\ *adj* — **bio·graph·i·cal·ly** \-i-k(ə-)lē\ *adv*

biological *adj* : of or relating to biology or to life and living beings — **bi·o·log·i·cal·ly** \-'läj-i-k(ə-)lē\ *adv*

biological control *n* : attack upon pests by interference with

their ecology (as by introduction of parasites or diseases)

biological warfare *n* : warfare in which living organisms (as disease germs) are used to harm the enemy or the enemy's livestock and crops

bi·ol·o·gy \bī-'äl-ə-jē\ *n*   **1** : a branch of knowledge that deals with living organisms and life processes   **2 a** : the plant and animal life of a region or environment   **b** : the life processes of an organism or group [from German *biologie* "biology", derived from Greek *bi-, bio-* "life" and *-logia* "study, science"] — **bi·ol·o·gist** \-jəst\ *n*

bi·ome \'bī-,ōm\ *n* : a major type of ecological community ⟨the grassland *biome*⟩

bi·on·ic \bī-'än-ik\ *adj*   **1** : of or relating to bionics   **2** : having the normal biological ability to perform a physical task increased by special devices

bi·on·ics \bī-'än-iks\ *n* : a branch of science concerned with applying facts about the working of biological systems to the solution of engineering problems

bio·phys·ics \,bī-ō-'fiz-iks\ *n* : a branch of science concerned with applying the principles and methods of physics to biological problems — **bio·phys·i·cal** \,bī-ō-'fiz-i-kəl\ *adj* — **bio·phys·i·cist** \-'fiz-ə-səst\ *n*

bi·op·sy \'bī-,äp-sē\ *n, pl* **-sies** : the removal and examination of tissue, cells, or fluids from the living body

bio·sphere \'bī-ə-,sfi(ə)r\ *n* : the part of the world in which life can exist

bio·tech·nol·o·gy \,bī-ō-tek-'näl-ə-jē\ *n* : applied biological science; *esp* : the use of genetic techniques to combine DNA from different sources into one organism in order to produce useful products (as drugs)

bi·ot·ic \bī-'ät-ik\ *adj* : of or relating to life; *esp* : caused by living things

bi·o·tin \'bī-ə-tən\ *n* : a growth vitamin of the vitamin B complex found especially in yeast, liver, and egg yolk

bi·o·tite \'bī-ə-,tīt\ *n* : a generally black or dark green mica containing iron, magnesium, potassium, and aluminum

bi·par·ti·san \(')bī-'pärt-ə-zən, -sən\ *adj* : representing, made up of, or organized by members of two political parties ⟨a *bipartisan* foreign policy⟩

bi·par·tite \(')bī-'pär-,tīt\ *adj*   **1** : being in two parts   **2** : shared by two ⟨*bipartite* treaty⟩

bi·ped \'bī-,ped\ *n* : a two-footed animal — **bi·ped·al** \(')bī-'ped-ᵊl\ *adj*

bi·plane \'bī-,plān\ *n* : an airplane with two sets of wings usually placed one above the other

bi·ra·cial \(')bī-'rā-shəl\ *adj* : of, relating to, or involving people from two races

biplane

¹birch \'bərch\ *n*   **1** : any of a genus of usually short-lived trees or shrubs with typically an outer bark that peels easily in thin layers and leaves that are shed each fall; *also* : its hard pale close-grained wood   **2** : a birch rod or bundle of twigs used as a whip — **birch** *or* **birch·en** \'bər-chən\ *adj*

²birch *vb* : to whip with or as if with a birch

¹bird \'bərd\ *n*   **1** : any of a class of warm-blooded egg-laying vertebrate animals with the body covered with feathers and the forelimbs modified as wings   **2** *slang* : PERSON 1; *esp* : a peculiar person

²bird *vb* : to observe or identify wild birds in their natural environment — **bird·er** *n*

bird·bath \'bərd-,bath, -,båth\ *n* : a basin set up for wild birds to bathe in

bird dog *n* : a dog that has been trained to hunt or bring back game birds

bird·house \'bərd-,haús\ *n* : an artificial nesting place for birds; *also* : AVIARY

bird·like \'bərd-,līk\ *adj* : resembling a bird especially in quickness or voice

bird·man \'bərd-mən *also* -,man\ *n* **1** : one who deals with birds **2** : [1]PILOT 3

bird of paradise : any of numerous brilliantly colored birds of the New Guinea area that often have large graceful tail feathers and are related to the crows

bird of passage : a bird that migrates

bird of prey : a meat-eating bird that feeds partly or completely on the animals it hunts

bird·seed \'bərd-,sēd\ *n* : seeds (as of sunflowers or thistles) used for feeding birds

bird's–eye \'bərd-,zī\ *adj* **1 a** : seen from above as if by a flying bird ⟨*bird's-eye* view⟩ **b** : [1]GENERAL 4, CURSORY ⟨a *bird's-eye* survey of American history⟩ **2** : having spots resembling birds' eyes ⟨*bird's-eye* maple⟩; *also* : made of wood containing such spots

bird's–foot trefoil \,bərdz-,fút-\ *n* : a European plant with claw-shaped pods and yellow flowers that is related to the pea and is widely grown as food for livestock

bird–watch·er \'bərd-,wäch-ər\ *n* : an observer of wild birds

bi·ret·ta \bə-'ret-ə\ *n* : a square cap with three ridges on top worn by Roman Catholic clergymen [from Italian *biretta* "clergyman's cap", derived from a word in an old language of southeastern France meaning "cap", derived from Latin *birrus* "cloak with a hood"; of Celtic origin — related to BERET]

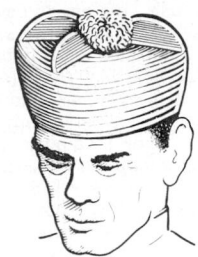

biretta

birth \'bərth\ *n* **1 a** : the coming out of a new individual from the body of its parent **b** : the act or process of bringing forth young from the womb **2** : DESCENT 1, LINEAGE ⟨noble *birth*⟩ **3** : BEGINNING 1, ORIGIN

birth canal *n* : the channel formed by the cervix, vagina, and vulva through which the fetus of a mammal is expelled

birth control *n* : control of the number of births especially by preventing or lessening the occurrence of conception

birth·day \'bərth-,dā\ *n* **1** : the day or anniversary of one's birth **2** : the day or anniversary of a beginning

birth defect *n* : a physical or biochemical defect that is present at birth and is inherited or caused by something that happens or exists in the environment

birth·mark \'bərth-,märk\ *n* : an unusual mark or blemish on the skin at birth — **birthmark** *vb*

birth·place \-,plās\ *n* : place of birth or origin

birth·rate \-,rāt\ *n* : the number of births for every hundred or every thousand persons in a given area or group during a given time

birth·right \-,rīt\ *n* : a right or possession that a person is entitled to by birth

birth·stone \-,stōn\ *n* : a gemstone associated with the month of one's birth

bis·cuit \'bis-kət\ *n, pl* **biscuits** *also* **biscuit 1** : a crisp flat baked product; *esp, British* : CRACKER 2 **2** : a small light bread made with baking powder or baking soda

Word History Long ago it was often a great problem to keep food from spoiling, especially on long journeys. One way to preserve the flat loaves of bread made then was to bake them a second time in order to dry them out. In early French, this bread was known as *pain bescuit* or "bread twice-cooked". Later the term came to be shortened to just *bescuit*. The idea of being "twice-cooked" was lost as the term was used for any crisp, dry, flat bread product or for a type of bread made with baking soda or baking powder instead of yeast. The word was borrowed into Middle English as *bisquite* but later came to be spelled *biscuit* on the model of the French spelling. [Middle English *bisquite* "biscuit", from early French *bescuit* (same meaning), from earlier *pain bescuit* "bread twice-cooked"]

bi·sect \'bī-,sekt, bī-'sekt\ *vb* **1** : to divide into two usually equal parts **2** : [1]INTERSECT 1

bi·sec·tor \'bī-,sek-tər, bī-'sek-tər\ *n* : one that bisects; *esp* : a straight line that bisects an angle or a line segment

bi·sex·u·al \(')bī-'seksh-(ə-)wəl, -'sek-shəl\ *adj* **1** : possessing characters of or having sexual desire for both sexes **2** : of, relating to, or involving two sexes — **bisexual** *n* — **bi·sex·u·al·i·ty** \,bī-,sek-shə-'wal-ət-ē\ *n*

bish·op \'bish-əp\ *n* **1** : a high-ranking member of the clergy usually in charge of a diocese **2** : a chess piece that moves diagonally

Word History The Old English word *bisceop*, from which we get our modern English word *bishop*, comes to us from the Latin word *episcopus*. Like many other Latin words connected with religion and the church, this was borrowed from Greek, the language in which the New Testament was written. The Greek word *episkopos*, meaning literally "overseer", was first used of officials in government and later came to be used for church leaders. In the Bible the word meaning "bishop" and the word meaning "priest" were used for the same thing. It was not until much later that the bishop did indeed become overseer of a large district, or diocese. [Old English *bisceop* "bishop", from Latin *episcopus* (same meaning), from Greek *episkopos*, literally "overseer", from *epi-* "on, over" and *skopos* "watcher, goal, object" — related to EPISCOPAL, HOROSCOPE, SCOPE]

bish·op·ric \'bish-ə-(,)prik\ *n* **1** : DIOCESE **2** : the position of bishop

bis·muth \'biz-məth\ *n* : a heavy brittle grayish white metallic element that is chemically like arsenic and antimony and is used in alloys and drugs — see ELEMENT table

bi·son \'bīs-ᵊn, 'bīz-\ *n, pl* **bison** : any of several large shaggy-maned mammals with a large head, short horns, and a large fleshy hump on the heavy front part of the body; *esp* : BUFFALO b

bisque \'bisk\ *n* : a thick cream soup made with shellfish, meat, or vegetables

bi·sul·fide \(')bī-'səl-,fīd\ *n* : DISULFIDE

[1]bit \'bit\ *n* **1** : the usually metal bar attached to a bridle and put in the mouth of a horse **2** : the biting or cutting edge or part of a tool [Old English *bite* "act of biting"]

[2]bit *n* **1** : a small piece or amount **2** : a short time ⟨rest a *bit*⟩ [earlier *bit* "small piece of food", from Old English *bita* (same meaning)] — **a bit** : [2]SOMEWHAT ⟨was *a bit* tired⟩

[3]bit *n* **1** : a unit of computer information that represents the selection of one of two possible choices (as *yes* or *no*, *on* or *off*) **2** : something (as an electrical pulse, a magnetized spot, or a punched hole) that physically represents a bit [*bi*nary dig*it*]

bitch \'bich\ *n* : a female dog

[1]bite \'bīt\ *vb* **bit** \'bit\; **bit·ten** \'bit-ᵊn\; **bit·ing** \'bīt-iŋ\ **1** : to seize, grip, or cut into with or as if with teeth ⟨*bite* an apple⟩ **2** : to wound, pierce, or sting ⟨*bitten* by a snake⟩ ⟨a mosquito *bit* me⟩ **3** : to cause to smart : STING ⟨pepper *bites* the mouth⟩ **4** : to eat into ⟨acid *biting* into metal⟩ **5** : to take bait ⟨the fish are *biting*⟩ **6** : to respond to something tempting [Old English *bitan* "to bite, grip with the teeth" — related to BEETLE] — **bite the dust** : to fall dead especially in battle

[2]bite *n* **1 a** : a seizing of something by biting **b** : the grip

\ə\ **abut**	\au̇\ **out**	\i\ **tip**	\ȯ\ **saw**	\u̇\ **foot**
\ər\ **further**	\ch\ **chin**	\ī\ **life**	\ȯi\ **coin**	\y\ **yet**
\a\ **mat**	\e\ **pet**	\j\ **job**	\th\ **thin**	\yü\ **few**
\ā\ **take**	\ē\ **easy**	\ŋ\ **sing**	\t̲h̲\ **this**	\yu̇\ **cure**
\ä\ **cot, cart**	\g\ **go**	\ō\ **bone**	\ü\ **food**	\zh\ **vision**

taken in biting   **2 a :** the amount of food taken at a bite   **b :** a small amount of food : SNACK   **3 :** a wound made by biting   **4 :** a sharp penetrating quality or effect ⟨the *bite* of the cold wind on our cheeks⟩

bit·ing \'bīt-iŋ\ *adj* : causing bodily or mental distress : SHARP, CUTTING ⟨*biting* wit⟩

bit·ter \'bit-ər\ *adj*   **1 :** having or being a disagreeable sharp taste that is one of the four basic taste sensations ⟨*bitter* as quinine⟩ — compare ³SALT 1b, ¹SOUR 1, ¹SWEET 1b   **2 :** hard to accept or bear : PAINFUL ⟨*bitter* disappointment⟩   **3 :** sharp and resentful ⟨a *bitter* reply⟩   **4 :** unpleasantly cold ⟨a *bitter* wind⟩ — **bit·ter·ly** *adv* — **bit·ter·ness** *n*

bit·tern \'bit-ərn\ *n* : any of various small or medium-sized herons that are active at night and have a booming cry

¹bit·ter·sweet \'bit-ər-ˌswēt\ *n*   **1 :** a sprawling poisonous weedy nightshade with purple flowers and oval reddish orange berries   **2 :** a North American woody climbing plant with yellow seed-cases that open when ripe to show the scarlet seed covers

²bittersweet *adj* : being both bitter and sweet ⟨a *bittersweet* story⟩

bit·ty \'bit-ē\ *adj* : very small : TINY

bi·tu·mi·nous coal \bə-'t(y)ü-mə-nəs-, bī-\ *n* : a coal that when heated yields considerable matter that escapes as gases — called also *soft coal*

bittern

bi·u·ret reagent \ˌbī-yə-'ret-, 'bī-yə-ˌret-\ *n* : a solution of a base and copper sulfate that is used especially to test for proteins which give a violet color when mixed with it — called also *biuret solution*

¹bi·valve \'bī-ˌvalv\ *adj* : having or being a shell composed of two movable valves ⟨a *bivalve* mollusk⟩

²bivalve *n* : an animal (as a clam) with a bivalve shell

¹biv·ouac \'biv-ˌwak, -ə-ˌwak\ *n* : a temporary camp [French, from a German dialect word *biwake*, literally "on guard"]

²bivouac *vb* **-ouacked; -ouack·ing** : to camp in a bivouac

¹bi·week·ly \(')bī-'wē-klē\ *adj*   **1 :** occurring, done, or produced every two weeks   **2 :** occurring, done, or produced twice a week — **biweekly** *adv*

²biweekly *n* : a biweekly publication

bi·year·ly \(')bī-'yi(ə)r-lē\ *adj*   **1 :** BIENNIAL   **2 :** BIANNUAL

bi·zarre \bə-'zär\ *adj* : strikingly unusual or odd : FANTASTIC — **bi·zarre·ly** *adv* — **bi·zarre·ness** *n*

¹blab \'blab\ *n*   **1 :** TATTLETALE   **2 :** too much talk — **blab·by** \'blab-ē\ *adj*

²blab *vb* **blabbed; blab·bing**   **1 :** to make known by careless talk ⟨*blab* a secret⟩   **2 :** to talk too much : PRATTLE — **blab·ber** *n*

blab·ber·mouth \'blab-ər-ˌmau̇th\ *n* : TATTLETALE

¹black \'blak\ *adj*   **1 a :** of the color black   **b :** very dark   **2 :** having dark skin, hair, and eyes : SWARTHY   **3 :** of or relating to the Negro race ⟨*black* people⟩   **3 a :** ¹EVIL 1, WICKED ⟨a *black* deed⟩   **b :** very sad or gloomy ⟨the outlook was *black*⟩   **c :** SULLEN 1a, HOSTILE — **black·ish** \-ish\ *adj* — **black·ly** *adv* — **black·ness** *n*

²black *n*   **1 :** a black pigment or dye; *esp* : one consisting largely of carbon   **2 :** the characteristic color of soot or coal   **3 :** black clothing ⟨dressed in *black*⟩   **4 :** a black animal (as a horse)   **5 :** a person belonging to a dark-skinned race; *esp* : NEGRO   **6 :** absence of light : DARKNESS ⟨the *black* of night⟩   **7 :** the condition of making a profit ⟨in the *black*⟩

³black *vb* : BLACKEN 1

black·a·moor \'blak-ə-ˌmu̇(ə)r\ *n* : a dark-skinned person;

esp : NEGRO

black–and–blue \ˌblak-ən-'blü\ *adj* : darkly discolored as the result of a bruise

black art *n* : WITCHCRAFT

¹black·ball \'blak-ˌbȯl\ *n*   **1 :** a small black ball used to vote against a person   **2 :** a vote against a person

²blackball *vb* : to vote against; *esp* : to keep (a person) from joining something by voting against

black bass *n* : any of several highly prized freshwater sunfishes native to eastern and central North America

black bear *n* : the usually black-furred bear found in most of the North American forests

black·ber·ry \'blak-ˌber-ē\ *n*   **1** : the usually black or dark purple juicy but seedy edible fruit of various prickly bushes   **2 :** a plant that bears blackberries

black·bird \'blak-ˌbərd\ *n* : any of various birds of which the males are mostly or entirely black: as   **a** : a common and familiar British thrush   **b** : any of several American birds (as a red-winged blackbird) related to the bobolink

black bear

black·board \'blak-ˌbō(ə)rd, -ˌbȯ(ə)rd\ *n* : CHALKBOARD

black·body \'blak-'bäd-ē\ *n* : a body or surface that absorbs all radiant energy falling upon it with no reflection

black book *n* : a book containing a blacklist

black crappie *n* : a silvery black mottled sunfish of the central and eastern U.S. — called also *calico bass*

black death *n* : plague (as bubonic plague) caused by a bacterium and especially in the epidemic form that spread through Asia and Europe in the 14th century; *also* : the 14th century epidemic of plague

black diamond *n* : CARBONADO

black·en \'blak-ən\ *vb* **black·ened; black·en·ing** \'blak-(ə-)niŋ\   **1 :** to make or become dark or black   **2 :** ¹SOIL, DIRTY   **3 :** to hurt the reputation of : DEFAME — **black·en·er** \-(ə-)nər\ *n*

black eye *n* : a dark discoloration of the skin around the eye as the result of a bruise

black–eyed pea \ˌblak-ˌīd-\ *n* : a sprawling herb related to the bean and grown in the southern U.S. especially as food for livestock and for green manure; *also* : its edible seed

black–eyed Su·san \-'süz-ᵊn\ *n* : an American daisy with deep yellow or orange petals and a dark center

black flag *n* : JOLLY ROGER

black·fly \'blak-ˌflī\ *n, pl* **-flies** *or* **-fly** : a two-winged fly that bites and whose larvae live in flowing streams

Black·foot \-ˌfu̇t\ *n, pl* **Black·feet** \-ˌfēt\ *or* **Blackfoot** : a member of a people belonging to an American Indian league of Montana, Alberta, and Saskatchewan

black·guard \'blag-ərd, -ˌärd; 'blak-ˌgärd\ *n* : a rude or dishonest person — **black·guard·ly** \-lē\ *adj or adv*

black·head \'blak-ˌhed\ *n* : a small oily bit of material blocking the outlet of a fat-secreting gland in the skin

black hole *n* : an invisible region believed to exist in space having a very strong gravitational field and thought to be caused by the collapse of a star

black·ing \'blak-iŋ\ *n* : a substance (as a paste or polish) that is applied to an object to make it black

black·jack \'blak-ˌjak\ *n*   **1 :** a small leather-covered club with a flexible handle   **2 :** a common oak of the southern U.S. with black bark

black lead \-'led\ *n* : GRAPHITE

black light *n* : invisible ultraviolet or infrared light

black·list \'blak-ˌlist\ *n* : a list of persons who are disapproved of and are to be punished (as by refusing them jobs) — **blacklist** *vb*

black lung *n* : a disease of the lungs caused by the repeated breathing in of coal dust over a long time — called also *black lung disease*

black magic *n* : WITCHCRAFT

black·mail \'blak-ˌmāl\ *n* **1** : the act of forcing a person to do or pay something especially by a threat to reveal a secret **2** : something (as money) obtained through blackmail — **blackmail** *vb* — **black·mail·er** *n*

> **Word History** The word *blackmail* has no connection at all with the postal system. In the 16th and part of the 17th centuries, the area along the border between England and Scotland was not usually protected by the officials on either side. For this reason it came under the influence of gangs of robbers. The gang leaders demanded payments from the farmers and landholders. These helpless people were told that in return for payment they would not be raided. In Scotland *mail* means "payment, rent, tax", and at that time payment or rent was by custom referred to as "silver" or "white" when paid in coins. Because the robbers usually required payment in cattle or grain rather than money, their payment came to be called "black" mail. [from *black* (the color) and *mail* "rent, payment", from Old English *māl* "agreement"; of Norse origin]

black market *n* **1** : trade that is against government controls (as of prices or rationing) **2** : illegal trade in government property — **black mar·ket·er** \-'mär-kət-ər\ *or* **black mar·ke·teer** \-ˌmär-kə-'ti(ə)r\ *n*

Black Muslim *n* : a member of a black group that follows Islamic religious beliefs and wants a separate black community

black oak *n* : a large timber tree of the central and eastern U.S. with a yellow inner bark used for tanning; *also* : any of several other American oaks

black·out \'blak-ˌaůt\ *n* **1** : a period when lights are kept off to guard against enemy airplane attack in a war **2** : a period when lights are off as a result of an electrical power failure **3** : a temporary dulling or loss of vision or consciousness — **black out** \-'aůt\ *vb*

black pepper *n* : a product that is used to season food and that is made by grinding the fruit of the East Indian pepper with the black husk still on

black plague *n* : BUBONIC PLAGUE

black power *n* : the use of the political and economic power of American blacks especially to achieve racial fairness

black sheep *n* : a person having a bad reputation in a group with a good reputation

black·smith \'blak-ˌsmith\ *n* : a worker who shapes iron (as into horseshoes) by heating it and then hammering it on an iron block — **black·smith·ing** *n*

black·snake \-ˌsnāk\ *n* **1** : any of several snakes largely black or dark in color; *esp* : either of two large harmless snakes of the U.S. **2** : a long braided leather whip

black·thorn \-ˌthȯrn\ *n* **1** : a European spiny plum with hard wood and small white flowers **2** : any of several American hawthorns

black·top \-ˌtäp\ *n* : a bituminous material (as asphalt) used especially for surfacing roads; *also* : a surface paved with blacktop — **blacktop** *vb*

black walnut *n* : a walnut of eastern North America with hard strong heavy dark brown wood and oily edible nuts; *also* : its wood or nut

black widow *n* : a poisonous New World spider the female of which is black with an hourglass-shaped red mark on the underside of the abdomen

blad·der \'blad-ər\ *n* **1** : a pouch in an animal in which a liquid or gas is stored; *esp* : one into which urine passes from the kidneys **2** : something resembling a bladder; *esp* : a bag or container that can be blown up with air — **blad·der·like** \-ˌlīk\ *adj*

blad·der·wort \-ˌwərt, -ˌwȯ(ə)rt\ *n* : any of several slender plants growing in water or on wet shores and having insect-catching bladders on the stem, scalelike leaves, and irregular yellow or purple flowers

blade \'blād\ *n* **1 a** : a leaf of a plant and especially of a grass **b** : the broad flat part of a leaf as distinguished from its stalk **2 a** : the broad flat part of an oar or paddle **b** : an arm of a propeller, electric fan, or steam turbine **3 a** : the cutting part of a tool **b** : SWORD 1 **c** : the runner of an ice skate **4** : a bold lively fellow — **blad·ed** \'blād-əd\ *adj*

¹blame \'blām\ *vb* **blamed; blam·ing** **1** : to find fault with : CENSURE **2 a** : to hold responsible ⟨*blame* them for everything⟩ **b** : to place responsibility for ⟨*blames* it on me⟩ [Middle English *blamen* "to find fault with", from early French *blamer, blasmer* (same meaning), from Latin *blasphemare* "to speak ill of", from Greek *blasphemein* "to blaspheme" — related to BLASPHEME] — **blam·able** \'blā-mə-bəl\ *adj* — **blam·ably** \-blē\ *adv* — **blam·er** *n*

²blame *n* **1** : expression of disapproval ⟨receive both *blame* and praise⟩ **2** : responsibility for something that fails : FAULT ⟨take the *blame* for the defeat⟩

blame·less \'blām-ləs\ *adj* : free from blame or fault — **blame·less·ly** *adv* — **blame·less·ness** *n*

blame·wor·thy \'blām-ˌwər-thē\ *adj* : deserving blame — **blame·wor·thi·ness** *n*

blanch \'blanch\ *vb* **1 a** : to take the color out of : BLEACH **b** : to scald in order to remove the skin from or whiten ⟨*blanch* almonds⟩ **2** : to become white or pale — **blanch·er** *n*

bland \'bland\ *adj* **1** : smooth and soothing in manner : GENTLE ⟨a *bland* smile⟩ **2** : having soft and soothing qualities : not irritating ⟨*bland* diet⟩ — **bland·ly** \'blan(d)lē\ *adv* — **bland·ness** \'blan(d)-nəs\ *n*

blan·dish \'blan-dish\ *vb* : to coax with flattery : CAJOLE — **blan·dish·ment** \-mənt\ *n*

¹blank \'blaŋk\ *adj* **1** : being without writing, printing, or marks ⟨*blank* sheet of paper⟩ **2** : having empty spaces to be filled in ⟨a *blank* form⟩ **3** : having no expression ⟨a *blank* look⟩ **4** : lacking variety, change, or accomplishment : EMPTY ⟨a *blank* day⟩ **5** : ABSOLUTE 3, UNQUALIFIED ⟨*blank* refusal⟩ **6** : not shaped into finished form ⟨a *blank* key⟩ — **blank·ly** *adv* — **blank·ness** *n*

²blank *n* **1 a** : an empty space (as on a paper) or period **b** : a paper with spaces for the entry of information **2** : an empty place ⟨my mind was a *blank*⟩ **3** : a piece of material prepared to be made into something (as a key) **4** : a cartridge loaded with powder but no bullet

³blank *vb* **1** : to keep from scoring **2** : to become confused ⟨*blanked* for a moment⟩

¹blan·ket \'blaŋ-kət\ *n* **1** : a large warm usually oblong covering used for beds **2** : a covering of any kind ⟨a horse *blanket*⟩ ⟨a *blanket* of snow⟩

²blanket *vb* : to cover with or as if with a blanket

³blanket *adj* : covering all instances or members of a group or class ⟨*blanket* approval⟩

blank verse *n* : unrhymed verse; *esp* : unrhymed iambic pentameter verse

¹blare \'bla(ə)r, 'ble(ə)r\ *vb* **blared; blar·ing** **1** : to sound loud and harsh **2** : to sound or say in a harsh noisy manner ⟨loudspeakers *blaring* advertisements⟩

²blare *n* : a loud disagreeable noise ⟨the *blare* of trumpets⟩

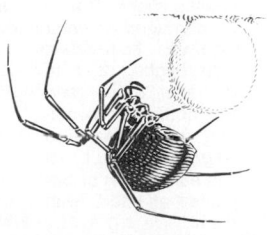

black widow

\ə\ abut	\aů\ out	\i\ tip	\ȯ\ saw	\ů\ foot
\ər\ further	\ch\ chin	\ī\ life	\ȯi\ coin	\y\ yet
\a\ mat	\e\ pet	\j\ job	\th\ thin	\yü\ few
\ā\ take	\ē\ easy	\ŋ\ sing	\th\ this	\yů\ cure
\ä\ cot, cart	\g\ go	\ō\ bone	\ü\ food	\zh\ vision

blar·ney \'blär-nē\ *n* : skillful flattery : BLANDISHMENT [from the *Blarney* stone, a stone in the wall of Blarney Castle, Ireland, said to give skill in flattery to those who kiss it] — **blarney** *vb*

blas·pheme \blas-'fēm, 'blas-,fēm\ *vb* **blas·phemed; blas·phem·ing 1** : to speak of or talk to with disrespect **2** : to speak blasphemy **3** : SWEAR 5 [Middle English *blasfemen* "to blaspheme", from Latin *blasphemare* "to speak ill of, blaspheme", from Greek *blasphēmein* "to blaspheme" — related to BLAME] — **blas·phem·er** *n*

blas·phe·my \'blas-fə-mē\ *n, pl* **-mies** : great disrespect shown to God or to sacred persons or things — **blas·phe·mous** \-məs\ *adj* — **blas·phe·mous·ly** *adv* — **blas·phe·mous·ness** *n*

¹blast \'blast\ *n* **1** : a strong gust of wind **2** : a stream of air or gas forced through an opening **3** : the continuous blowing that ore or metal receives in a blast furnace **4** : the sound made by a wind instrument (as a horn) or by a whistle **5 a** : EXPLOSION 1 **b** : an explosive charge **c** : the sudden air pressure produced in the vicinity of an explosion **6** : a sudden harmful effect from or as if from a hot wind **7** : ¹SPEED 1b, OPERATION ⟨go full *blast*⟩

²blast *vb* **1** : BLARE ⟨music *blasting* from a radio⟩ **2 a** : to use an explosive **b** : SHOOT **3** : to injure or destroy ⟨seedlings *blasted* by the hot dry wind⟩ **4** : to shatter by or as if by an explosive **5** : to attack vigorously ⟨*blasted* by the local press⟩ **6** : to cause to blast off ⟨will *blast* themselves from the moon's surface⟩ — **blast·er** *n*

blast furnace *n* : a furnace in which combustion is forced by a stream of air under pressure; *esp* : one for the reduction of iron ore

blast off \'blas-,tòf\ *vb* : TAKE OFF 5b — used especially of rocket-driven missiles and vehicles — **blast-off** \-,tòf\ *n*

blas·tu·la \'blas-chə-lə\ *n, pl* **-las** \-ləz\ *or* **-lae** \-,lē\ : an early embryo typically having the form of a hollow fluid-filled rounded cavity bounded by a single layer of cells — compare GASTRULA

bla·tant \'blāt-ᵊnt\ *adj* **1** : noisy especially in a rude way **2** : completely obvious especially in a disagreeable way ⟨a *blatant* lie⟩ — **bla·tant·ly** *adv*

¹blaze \'blāz\ *n* **1** : a very strongly burning fire **2** : very bright direct light often accompanied by heat ⟨the *blaze* of TV lights⟩ **3** : a sudden outburst ⟨a *blaze* of flame⟩ ⟨a *blaze* of fury⟩ **4** : a dazzling display ⟨a *blaze* of autumn leaves⟩ [Old English *blæse* "torch"]

²blaze *vb* **blazed; blaz·ing 1 a** : to burn brightly **b** : to flare up : FLAME **2** : to be noticeably brilliant ⟨fields *blazing* with flowers⟩ **3** : to shoot rapidly and repeatedly

³blaze *vb* **blazed; blaz·ing** : to make public : PROCLAIM ⟨*blaze* the news⟩ [Middle English *blasen* "to make public", from early Dutch *blāsen* "to blow"]

⁴blaze *n* **1** : a long white mark running down the face of an animal **2** : a mark made on a tree usually to leave a trail [from German *blas* "a white mark on an animal"]

⁵blaze *vb* **blazed; blaz·ing** : to mark with blazes ⟨*blaze* a trail⟩

blaz·er \'blā-zər\ *n* : a sports jacket in bright stripes or solid color

¹bleach \'blēch\ *vb* **1** : to remove color or stains from **2** : to make whiter or lighter **3** : to grow white : lose color

²bleach *n* **1** : the act or process of bleaching **2** : a chemical used in bleaching

bleach·er \'blē-chər\ *n* : a usually open stand of benches arranged like steps for people to watch from (as at a game) — usually used in pl.

bleak \'blēk\ *adj* **1** : open to wind or weather ⟨a *bleak* coast⟩ **2** : ¹COLD 1, RAW **3** : DREARY, CHEERLESS ⟨the future looks *bleak*⟩ **4** : very plain — **bleak·ly** *adv* — **bleak·ness** *n*

¹blear \'bli(ə)r\ *vb* **1** : to make (the eyes) sore or watery **2** : ²DIM 1, BLUR ⟨*bleared* sight⟩

²blear *adj* : dim with water or tears — **bleary** \'bli(ə)r-ē\ *adj*

bleat \'blēt\ *vb* **1** : to make the sound characteristic of a sheep or goat **2** : to speak in a bleating way — **bleat** *n*

bleed \'blēd\ *vb* **bled** \'bled\; **bleed·ing 1** : to lose or shed blood **2** : to be wounded ⟨*bleed* for one's country⟩ **3** : to feel pain or deep sympathy ⟨my heart *bleeds* for them⟩ **4** : to ooze or flow from a cut surface **5 a** : to draw liquid from ⟨*bleed* a patient⟩ ⟨*bleed* a carburetor⟩ **b** : to run when wetted ⟨dyes that *bleed*⟩ **6** : to get or force money from

bleed·er \'blēd-ər\ *n* : one that bleeds; *esp* : HEMOPHILIAC

bleeding heart *n* **1** : a garden plant related to the poppies and having drooping spikes of deep pink heart-shaped flowers **2** : a person who always shows a great amount of sympathy to victims of misfortune or persecution

blem·ish \'blem-ish\ *n* : a mark that makes something imperfect — **belmish** *vb*

   syn BLEMISH, DEFECT, FLAW mean an imperfection that mars or damages. BLEMISH suggests something that affects only the surface or appearance ⟨peaches with *blemishes* can still be eaten⟩ DEFECT suggests a lack, often hidden, of something that is essential to completeness or perfect functioning ⟨didn't know that the car had major *defects*⟩ FLAW suggests a crack, nick, or break in smoothness or a weak spot ⟨the beam of the roof broke because of a *flaw*⟩

¹blench \'blench\ *vb* : FLINCH

²blench *vb* : to make or grow pale : BLANCH

¹blend \'blend\ *vb* **1** : to mix thoroughly so that the things mixed cannot be recognized **2** : to shade into each other : MERGE **3** : HARMONIZE 2 ⟨furniture that *blends* with the draperies⟩ **syn** see MIX

²blend *n* **1** : a thorough mixture **2** : a product (as coffee) prepared by blending

blend·er \'blen-dər\ *n* : a person or thing that blends; *esp* : an electric appliance with blades for chopping or mixing food

blen·ny \'blen-ē\ *n, pl* **blennies** : any of numerous usually small and relatively long and often scaleless fishes living about rocky seashores

bless \'bles\ *vb* **blessed** \'blest\ *also* **blest** \'blest\; **blessing 1** : to make holy : HALLOW **2** : to make the sign of the cross upon or over **3** : to ask divine care or protection for **4** : to praise or honor as holy **5** : to make successful or happy [Old English *blētsian, blēdsian* "to bless", originally "to sprinkle with blood (of a sacrificial animal)", derived from *blōd* "blood"]

bless·ed \'bles-əd\ *also* **blest** \'blest\ *adj* **1** : HOLY 2 ⟨the *blessed* Trinity⟩ **2** : enjoying happiness — **bless·ed·ly** \'bles-əd-lē\ *adv* — **bless·ed·ness** \'bles-əd-nəs\ *n*

Bless·ed Sacrament \,bles-əd-\ *n* : the objects used in Communion; *esp* : ³HOST

bless·ing \'bles-iŋ\ *n* **1** : the act or words of one that blesses **2** : APPROVAL ⟨gave my *blessing* to the plan⟩ **3** : something that makes one happy or content **4** : grace said at a meal

blew *past of* BLOW

¹blight \'blīt\ *n* **1 a** : a disease of plants resulting in withering and death without rotting **b** : an organism that causes blight **2 a** : something that harms or destroys **b** : a damaged or worsened condition ⟨urban *blight*⟩

²blight *vb* **1** : to affect with blight **2** : to damage or worsen the quality or condition of ⟨slums and *blighted* areas⟩ **3** : to suffer from or become affected with blight

blimp \'blimp\ *n* : a cigar-shaped airship

blimp

filled with gas like a balloon

¹**blind** \'blīnd\ *adj* **1 a :** SIGHTLESS **b :** having less than ¹⁄₁₀ normal vision in the best eye even with the aid of glasses **2 :** lacking in judgment or understanding **3 :** done by using only the instruments within an airplane ⟨a *blind* landing⟩ **4 a :** having only one opening or outlet ⟨a *blind* street⟩ **b :** having no opening ⟨a *blind* wall⟩ — **blind·ly** \'blīn-(d)lē\ *adv* — **blind·ness** \'blīn(d)-nəs\ *n*

²**blind** *vb* **1 :** to make blind **2 :** to make blind for a short time : DAZZLE ⟨*blinded* by the lights⟩ **3 :** to take judgment or understanding away from ⟨*blinded* by love⟩

³**blind** *n* **1 :** a device (as a window shade) to prevent sight or keep out light **2 :** a hiding place for hunters or wildlife observers

⁴**blind** *adv* : without seeing outside of an airplane ⟨fly *blind*⟩

blind·er \'blīn-dər\ *n* : either of two leather flaps on a horse's bridle to keep it from seeing to the side

¹**blind·fold** \'blīn(d)-ˌfōld\ *vb* : to cover the eyes of with or as if with a strip of cloth — **blindfold** *adj*

²**blindfold** *n* : a strip of cloth for covering the eyes

blind·man's buff \ˌblīn(d)-ˌmanz-'bəf\ *n* : a game in which a blindfolded player tries to catch and identify another

blind spot *n* **1 a :** a point in the retina through which the optic nerve enters and which does not respond to light **b :** a part of an area that cannot be seen with available equipment **2 :** an area of weakness (as in judgment) **3 :** a place in which radio signals are not received well at all

¹**blink** \'bliŋk\ *vb* **1 :** to look with half-shut eyes **2 :** to wink quickly ⟨*blink* back tears⟩ **3 :** to shine with a light that goes or seems to go on and off ⟨streetlights *blinking* through rain⟩

²**blink** *n* **1 :** GLIMMER 1a, SPARKLE **2 :** a shutting and opening of the eye — **on the blink** : not working properly ⟨the TV is *on the blink*⟩

blink·er \'bliŋ-kər\ *n* **1 :** one that blinks; *esp* : a blinking light used as a warning or for signaling **2 :** BLINDER

blip \'blip\ *n* : an image on a radar screen

bliss \'blis\ *n* : complete happiness : JOY — **bliss·ful** \-fəl\ *adj* — **bliss·ful·ly** \-fə-lē\ *adv* — **bliss·ful·ness** *n*

¹**blis·ter** \'blis-tər\ *n* **1 :** a raised area of the outer skin containing watery liquid **2 :** a raised spot (as in paint) resembling a blister **3 :** something that causes blistering **4 :** any of various structures (as a gunner's compartment on an airplane) that bulge out — **blis·tery** \-t(ə-)rē\ *adj*

²**blister** *vb* **blis·tered; blis·ter·ing** \-t(ə-)riŋ\ **1 :** to develop a blister : rise in blisters **2 :** to raise a blister on

blister beetle *n* : any of a family of soft-bodied beetles including some whose dried bodies are used in medicine to blister the skin

blister rust *n* : any of several diseases of pines caused by rust fungi and marked by blisters on the outside

blithe \'blīth, 'blīth\ *adj* **1 :** of a happy carefree nature **2 :** HEEDLESS ⟨*blithe* unconcern⟩ — **blithe·ly** *adv*

blithe·some \'blīth-səm, 'blīth-\ *adj* : GAY 1, MERRY — **blith·some·ly** *adv*

blitz \'blits\ *n* **1 a :** an all-out series of air raids **b :** AIR RAID **2 :** a fast thorough campaign ⟨an advertising *blitz* for a new product⟩ — **blitz** *vb*

blitz·krieg \'blits-ˌkrēg\ *n* : a sudden violent enemy attack [German, literally "lightning war"]

bliz·zard \'bliz-ərd\ *n* **1 :** a long heavy snowstorm **2 :** a very strong cold wind filled with fine snow

bloat \'blōt\ *vb* : to swell by filling with or as if with water or air : puff up

blob \'bläb\ *n* : a small lump or drop of something thick (as paste or paint)

bloc \'bläk\ *n* : a combination of persons, groups, or nations united by treaty, agreement, or common interest ⟨the Soviet *bloc*⟩ [French, literally "block"]

¹**block** \'bläk\ *n* **1 a :** a solid piece of material (as stone or wood) usually with one or more flat sides ⟨building *blocks*⟩ **b :** a hollow rectangular piece of material (as of glass or concrete) used for building ⟨cinder *block*⟩ **2 a :** a piece of wood on which condemned persons are beheaded **b :** a mold or support on which something is shaped or displayed **c :** the molded part that contains the cylinders of an internal-combustion engine **3 a :** OBSTACLE **b :** the act of slowing down or stopping an opponent's play in sports **c :** interruption of normal function ⟨a respiratory *block* due to carbon monoxide⟩ **4 :** a wooden or metal case for one or more pulleys **5 :** a number of things forming a group or unit ⟨a *block* of seats⟩ **6 :** a large building divided into separate units ⟨an apartment *block*⟩ **7 a :** a usually rectangular space enclosed by streets **b :** the length of the side of such a block ⟨three *blocks* south⟩ **8 :** a section of railroad track controlled by block signals **9 :** a hand-carved piece of material from which copies are to be printed

²**block** *vb* **1 a :** to stop up or close off : OBSTRUCT **b :** to slow down or stop the progress of; *esp* : to interfere with an opponent (as in football) **c :** to prevent normal functioning of; *esp* : to interrupt the passage of impulses along a nerve **2 :** to mark the main lines of ⟨*block* out a sketch⟩ **3 :** to shape on, with, or as if with a block **4 :** to make (lines of writing or type) even at the left or at both left and right **5 :** to secure, support, or provide with a block — **block·er** *n*

block·ade \blä-'kād\ *n* : the cutting off of an area by means of troops or warships to stop the coming in or going out of people or supplies — **blockade** *vb* — **block·ad·er** *n*

block·age \'bläk-ij\ *n* : an act or instance of blocking : the state of being blocked

block and tackle *n* : an arrangement of pulley blocks and rope or cable for hoisting or hauling

block·bust·er \'bläk-ˌbəs-tər\ *n* : one that is very large, successful, or violent ⟨a *blockbuster* of a movie⟩

block·head \-ˌhed\ *n* : a stupid person

block·house \-ˌhaús\ *n* **1 :** a building of heavy timbers or of concrete built with holes in its sides through which persons inside may fire out at an enemy **2 :** a building used as an observation point for an operation likely to be accompanied by heat, blast, or radiation hazard

blockhouse 1

block letter *n* : a hand-printed usually capital letter; *also* : a printed letter having all lines of equal thickness

block signal *n* : a signal at the entrance of a section of railroad track to regulate trains entering and using it

bloke \'blōk\ *n, chiefly British* : ¹MAN 1a, FELLOW

¹**blond** *or* **blonde** \'bländ\ *adj* **1 :** of a pale yellowish brown color ⟨*blond* hair⟩ **2 :** of a pale white or rosy white color ⟨*blond* skin⟩ **3 :** having blond hair ⟨a *blond* actor⟩ — **blond·ness** \'blän(d)-nəs\ *n*

²**blond** *or* **blonde** *n* **1 :** a blond person **2 :** a light yellowish brown to dark grayish yellow

¹**blood** \'bləd\ *n* **1 a :** the red fluid that circulates in the heart, arteries, capillaries, and veins of a vertebrate animal and that brings nourishment and oxygen to and carries away waste products from all parts of the body **b :** a fluid resembling blood **2 a :** LINEAGE 2, DESCENT; *esp* : royal lineage ⟨a prince of the *blood*⟩ **b :** relationship through a common ancestor : KINSHIP **3 :** ²TEMPER 3d [Old English

\ə\ abut	\aú\ out	\i\ tip	\ó\ saw	\ú\ foot
\ər\ further	\ch\ chin	\ī\ life	\ói\ coin	\y\ yet
\a\ mat	\e\ pet	\j\ job	\th\ thin	\yü\ few
\ā\ take	\ē\ easy	\ŋ\ sing	\th\ this	\yú\ cure
\ä\ cot, cart	\g\ go	\ō\ bone	\ü\ food	\zh\ vision

blōd "blood"]

²blood *vb* : to give experience to ⟨troops already *blooded* in battle⟩ [from an earlier sense, meaning "to smear the face of an inexperienced fox hunter with blood of the fox killed on his first hunt"]

blood bank *n* : a reserve supply of blood or plasma or the place where it is stored

blood cell *n* : a cell normally present in blood

blood count *n* : the counting or estimating of the blood cells in a definite volume of blood; *also* : the number of cells counted or estimated in this way

blood·cur·dling \'bləd-,kərd-liŋ, -ᵊl-iŋ\ *adj* : causing great horror or fear : TERRIFYING ⟨*bloodcurdling* screams⟩

blood·ed \'bləd-əd\ *adj* **1** : entirely or largely purebred ⟨*blooded* horses⟩ **2** : having characteristics (as of body or personality) suggesting (such) blood ⟨warm-*blooded*⟩

blood group *n* : one of the classes into which human beings and some other vertebrates can be separated on the basis of the presence or absence of specific antigens in their blood — called also *blood type* — **blood grouping** *n*

blood·hound \'bləd-,haůnd\ *n* : a large powerful hound with long drooping ears, a wrinkled face, and a very good sense of smell

bloodhound

blood·less \'bləd-ləs\ *adj* **1** : having less blood than normal **2** : done without bloodshed ⟨a *bloodless* revolution⟩ **3** : lacking in spirit or feeling — **blood·less·ly** *adv* — **blood·less·ness** *n*

blood·let·ting \'bləd-,let-iŋ\ *n* : the act or practice of opening a vein for the purpose of drawing blood

blood·line \-,līn\ *n* : a sequence of direct ancestors especially in a pedigree; *also* : FAMILY 1, STRAIN

blood·mo·bile \-mō-,bēl\ *n* : a motor vehicle staffed and equipped for collecting blood from donors

blood plasma *n* : the fluid portion of whole blood

blood platelet *n* : one of the minute disks of the blood of a vertebrate animal that assist in blood clotting

blood poisoning *n* : a diseased condition of the blood caused by poisonous matter or germs in it

blood pressure *n* : pressure of the blood on the walls of blood vessels and especially arteries varying with physical condition and age

blood·root \'bləd-,rüt, -,růt\ *n* : a plant related to the poppies, having a red root and sap, and bearing a single leaf and a white flower in early spring

blood·shed \-,shed\ *n* **1** : the shedding of blood **2** : the taking of life : SLAUGHTER

blood·shot \-,shät\ *adj* : red and inflamed ⟨*bloodshot* eyes⟩

blood·stain \-,stān\ *n* : a discoloration caused by blood — **blood·stained** \-,stānd\ *adj*

blood·stone \-,stōn\ *n* : a green quartz sprinkled with red spots

blood·stream \-,strēm\ *n* : the flowing blood in a living thing with a circulatory system

blood·suck·er \-,sək-ər\ *n* : an animal that sucks blood; *esp* : LEECH 1 — **blood·suck·ing** \-,sək-iŋ\ *adj*

blood sugar *n* : the glucose in the blood; *esp* : the amount or percentage of such sugar normally from 0.08 to 0.11 percent

blood test *n* : a test of the blood; *esp* : a test for syphilis

blood·thirsty \'bləd-,thər-stē\ *adj* : eager to hurt or kill : CRUEL — **blood·thirst·i·ly** \-stə-lē\ *adv* — **blood·thirst·i·ness** \-stē-nəs\ *n*

blood transfusion *n* : the act or operation of transferring blood into a vein or artery of a person or animal

blood type *n* : BLOOD GROUP — **blood–type** *vb*

blood vessel *n* : a vessel in which blood circulates in an animal

bloody \'bləd-ē\ *adj* **blood·i·er; -est** **1 a** : containing, smeared, or stained with blood ⟨a *bloody* handkerchief⟩ **b** : dripping blood ⟨a *bloody* nose⟩ **2** : causing or accompanied by bloodshed ⟨a *bloody* battle⟩ **3** : BLOODTHIRSTY, MURDEROUS ⟨a *bloody* deed⟩ — **blood·i·ly** \'bləd-ᵊl-ē\ *adv* — **blood·i·ness** \'bləd-ē-nəs\ *n* — **bloody** *vb*

¹bloom \'blüm\ *n* **1 a** : ¹FLOWER 1b **b** : flowers or amount of flowers (as of a plant) **c** : the period or state of flowering **2** : a state or time of beauty, freshness, and strength **3 a** : a delicate powdery coating especially on some fruits and leaves **b** : a rosy appearance of the cheeks

²bloom *vb* **1** : to produce flowers : BLOSSOM **2** : to be in a state of youthful beauty or freshness : FLOURISH **3** : to glow with rosy color — **bloom·er** *n*

bloo·mers \'blü-mərz\ *n pl* : full loose pants gathered at the knee and once worn by women for sports; *also* : underpants of similar design worn chiefly by girls [named for Amelia *Bloomer* who introduced the garment]

¹blos·som \'bläs-əm\ *n* **1** : the flower of a seed plant ⟨apple *blossoms*⟩ **2** : the period or state of flowering — **blos·somy** \-ə-mē\ *adj*

²blossom *vb* **1** : ²BLOOM 1 **2** : to grow and do well ⟨a *blossoming* talent⟩

¹blot \'blät\ *n* **1** : ¹SPOT 1, 2a, b, STAIN **2** : ¹DISHONOR 1

²blot *vb* **blot·ted; blot·ting** **1** : ²SPOT 1, STAIN **2** : ²OBSCURE, DIM **3** : ¹DISGRACE **4** : to dry with something absorbent **5** : to become marked with a blot

blotch \'bläch\ *n* **1** : a blemish especially on the skin **2** : a large irregular spot (as of color or ink) — **blotch** *vb* — **blotched** \'blächt\ *adj* — **blotchy** \'bläch-ē\ *adj*

blot out *vb* **1** : to make hard to see or invisible : HIDE **2** : DESTROY 1, KILL

blot·ter \'blät-ər\ *n* **1** : a piece of blotting paper **2** : a book in which entries are made temporarily ⟨a police *blotter*⟩

blotting paper *n* : a soft spongy paper used to absorb wet ink

blouse \'blaůs *also* 'blaůz\ *n* **1** : a loose outer garment like a shirt or smock varying from hip-length to calf-length **2** : a usually loose-fitting garment covering the body from the neck to the waist

¹blow \'blō\ *vb* **blew** \'blü\; **blown** \'blōn\; **blow·ing** **1** : to move or become moved especially rapidly or with power ⟨wind *blowing* from the north⟩ **2** : to send forth a strong stream of air (as from the mouth) ⟨*blow* on one's hands⟩ **3** : to drive or become driven by a stream of air **4** : to make a sound or cause to sound by blowing ⟨*blow* a horn⟩ ⟨*blow* a whistle⟩ **5 a** : to breathe hard or rapidly : PANT **b** *of a whale* : to force moisture-filled air out of the lungs through the blowhole **6 a** : to melt when overloaded ⟨the lights went out when a fuse *blew*⟩ **b** : to cause (a fuse) to blow **7** : to open or break or tear apart by too much pressure ⟨*blew* a gasket⟩ ⟨the tire *blew* out⟩ **8** : to clear by forcing air through ⟨*blew* his nose⟩ **9** : to produce or shape by the action of blown or otherwise forced air ⟨*blow* bubbles⟩ ⟨*blow* glass⟩ **10** : to shatter, burst, or destroy by explosion **11** : to spend recklessly ⟨*blew* all the money in one day⟩ **12** : to lose or miss (an opportunity) by acting in a stupid or clumsy way ⟨*blew* my chance⟩ [Old English *blāwan* "to blow, to move quickly"]

²blow *n* **1** : a blowing of wind especially when strong or violent **2** : a forcing of air from the mouth or nose or through an instrument

³blow *vb* **blew** \'blü\; **blown** \'blōn\; **blow·ing** : ²FLOWER 1, BLOOM [Old English *blōwan* "to bloom"]

⁴blow *n* **1** : a hard hit using a part of the body or an instrument **2** : an unfriendly act : COMBAT ⟨come to *blows*⟩ **3** : a sudden act or effort ⟨solve all our problems with one *blow*⟩ **4** : a sudden disaster ⟨a heavy *blow* to the nation⟩ [Middle English *blaw* "stroke"]

blow–dry \'blō-,drī\ *vb* : to dry and usually style (hair) with a hand-held hair dryer

blow·er \'blō-(ə)r\ *n* **1** : one that blows **2** : a device for producing a stream of air or gas

blow·fish \'blō-,fish\ *n* : any of a family of puffers of which some are poisonous

blow·fly \'blō-,flī\ *n* : any of various two-winged flies (as a bluebottle) that deposit their eggs or maggots on meat or in wounds

blow·gun \-,gən\ *n* : a long narrow tube from which an arrow or dart may be blown

blow·hole \-,hōl\ *n* **1** : a nostril in the top of the head of a whale or related animal **2** : a hole in the ice to which aquatic mammals (as seals) come to breathe

blown \'blōn\ *adj* **1** : being swollen or inflated **2** : FLY-BLOWN **3** : being out of breath

blow·out \'blō-,aút\ *n* **1** : a big festive party **2** : a bursting of a container (as a tire) by pressure of the contents on a weak spot **3** : an eruption of an oil or gas well that is not under control and is the result of too much natural pressure **4** : a valley or hollow blown out by the wind in areas of shifting sand or of light cultivated soil

blow over *vb* : to come to an end without a lasting effect ⟨hoped the problem would *blow over* soon⟩

blow·pipe \'blō-,pīp\ *n* **1** : a small tube for blowing a jet of gas (as air) into a flame so as to increase the heat in a small area **2** : BLOWGUN

blow·torch \-,tòrch\ *n* : a small burner whose flame is made hotter by a blast of air or oxygen

blow·up \'blō-,əp\ *n* **1** : EXPLOSION 1 **2** : an outburst of bad temper **3** : a photographic enlargement

blow up \'blō-'əp\ *vb* **1** : to expand or become expanded to extraordinary size **2** : to fill up or become filled with a gas and especially air ⟨*blow up* a balloon⟩ **3** : to make an enlargement of ⟨*blow up* a photograph⟩ **4 a** : to destroy or become destroyed by explosion **b** : to become violently angry

blowy \'blō-ē\ *adj* **blow·i·er; -est** : WINDY 1

¹**blub·ber** \'bləb-ər\ *n* **1** : the fat of large sea mammals (as whales) **2** : the action of blubbering

²**blubber** *vb* **blub·bered; blub·ber·ing** \-(ə-)riŋ\ **1** : to weep noisily **2** : to talk and weep at the same time

¹**blud·geon** \'bləj-ən\ *n* : a short club with one end thicker and heavier than the other

²**bludgeon** *vb* : to hit very hard : BEAT

¹**blue** \'blü\ *adj* **1** : of the color blue **2** : low in spirits : MELANCHOLY — **blue·ness** *n*

²**blue** *n* **1** : the color of the clear daytime sky or of the colors of light between green and violet **2** : blue clothing or cloth **3 a** : SKY 1 **b** : SEA 1a

³**blue** *vb* **blued; blue·ing** *or* **blu·ing** : to make or turn blue

blue baby *n* : an infant with a bluish tint usually from a defect of the heart

blue·bell \'blü-,bel\ *n* : any of various plants (as a grape hyacinth) with blue bell-shaped flowers; *esp* : HAREBELL

blue·ber·ry \-,ber-ē, -b(ə-)rē\ *n* : the edible blue or blackish small-seeded berry of any of several plants related to the cranberry; *also* : a low or tall shrub producing these berries — compare HUCKLEBERRY 1

blue·bird \-,bərd\ *n* : any of several small North American songbirds related to the robin but more or less blue above

blue·bon·net \'blü-,bän-ət\ *n* : a low-growing lupine of Texas with silky leaves and blue flowers that completes its life cycle in one season

blue·bot·tle \-,bät-ºl\ *n* : any of several blowflies with a shiny blue abdomen or body

blue cheese *n* : strong-flavored cheese streaked with blue mold

blue·fish \'blü-,fish\ *n* : an active saltwater food and sport fish that is related to the pompanos and is bluish above

and silvery below

blue flag *n* : a blue-flowered iris; *esp* : a common wild iris of the eastern U.S.

blue·gill \'blü-,gil\ *n* : a common food and sport sunfish of the eastern and central U.S.

blue·grass \-,gras\ *n* **1** : a valuable pasture and lawn grass with bluish green stems **2** : country music played on a small group of instruments (as banjo, fiddle, and mandolin) with melody or harmony often made up by players during a performance

blue–green alga \,blü-,grēn-\ *n* : any of a class of algae having the chlorophyll masked by bluish green pigments

blue heron *n* : any of several herons with bluish plumage

blueing *or* **bluing** *present participle of* BLUE

blue jay \'blü-,jā\ *n* : any of several largely blue American jays having a small bunch of feathers pointing upward and backward from the top of the head

blue jeans *n pl* : pants or overalls made of blue denim

blue mold *n* : a fungus and especially a penicillium that produces blue or blue-green growths

blue plate \-,plāt\ *n* : a main course (as of meat and vegetable) served as a single menu item

¹**blue·print** \'blü-,print\ *n* **1** : a photographic print made with white lines on a blue background and used especially for copying mechanical drawings, maps, and architects' plans **2** : a detailed plan or program of action

²**blueprint** *vb* : to make a blueprint of or for

blue racer *n* : a blacksnake of a bluish green variety that is found from Ohio to Texas

blue ribbon *n* : a blue ribbon awarded the first-place winner in a competition

blues \'blüz\ *n pl* **1** : low spirits : MELANCHOLY **2** : a song expressing sadness and composed in a style originating among the American blacks

blue shark *n* : a very active shark that is found in the surface waters of warm and temperate seas around the world, may reach a length of 8 meters, and occasionally may attack people

blue·stem \'blü-,stem\ *n* : either of two important grasses of the western U.S. with smooth bluish leaf sheaths that are used to feed livestock

blu·et \'blü-ət\ *n* : a low American herb bearing small bluish flowers usually with one at the end of each slender stem

blue vitriol *n* : a compound of copper sulfate chemically combined with water

blue whale *n* : a whale that may reach a weight of 90 metric tons and a length of 30 meters and is generally considered the largest living animal

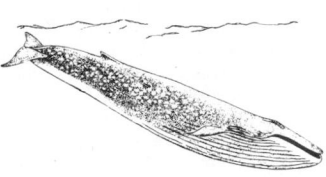

¹**bluff** \'bləf\ *adj* **1** : rising steeply with a broad front ⟨a *bluff* coastline⟩ **2** : frank

blue whale

and outspoken in a good-natured manner [from an obsolete Dutch word *blaf* "flat"] — **bluff·ly** *adv* — **bluff·ness** *n*

syn BLUFF, BLUNT, CURT mean speaking in a frank rough manner. BLUFF usually suggests hearty and good-natured roughness ⟨farmers talking in a *bluff* manner⟩ BLUNT may suggest plain speech that disregards the feelings of others ⟨a *blunt* appraisal of the student's work⟩ CURT usually suggests briefness of speech that is

\ə\ **abut**	\aú\ **out**	\i\ **tip**	\ò\ **saw**	\ú\ **foot**
\ər\ **further**	\ch\ **chin**	\ī\ **life**	\òi\ **coin**	\y\ **yet**
\a\ **mat**	\e\ **pet**	\j\ **job**	\th\ **thin**	\yü\ **few**
\ā\ **take**	\ē\ **easy**	\ŋ\ **sing**	\th\ **this**	\yú\ **cure**
\ä\ **cot, cart**	\g\ **go**	\ō\ **bone**	\ü\ **food**	\zh\ **vision**

upsetting or rude ⟨a *curt* reply to a polite question⟩

²bluff *n* : a high steep bank : CLIFF

³bluff *vb* : to deceive or frighten by pretending to have strength or confidence that one does not really have [probably from Dutch *bluffen* "to boast"] — **bluff·er** *n*

⁴bluff *n* **1 a** : an act or instance of bluffing **b** : the practice of bluffing **2** : one who bluffs

blu·ing *or* **blue·ing** \'blü-iŋ\ *n* : a mixture of blue or violet dyes used in laundering to prevent yellowing of white fabrics

blu·ish \'blü-ish\ *adj* : somewhat blue

¹blun·der \'blən-dər\ *vb* **blun·dered; blun·der·ing** \-d(ə-)riŋ\ **1** : to move unsteadily or blindly **2** : to make a mistake (as through stupidity or carelessness) **3** : to say stupidly or thoughtlessly : BLURT — **blun·der·er** \-dər-ər\ *n*

²blunder *n* : a bad or stupid mistake

blun·der·buss \'blən-dər-,bəs\ *n* : a muzzle-loader with a short barrel and cone-shaped muzzle to make loading easier [derived from an obsolete Dutch word *donderbus*, literally "thundergun"]

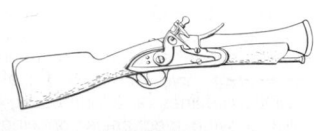

blunderbuss

¹blunt \'blənt\ *adj* **1** : slow or lacking in feeling or understanding **2** : having a thick edge or point **3** : abrupt in speech or manner **syn** see BLUFF — **blunt·ly** *adv* — **blunt·ness** *n*

²blunt *vb* : to make less sharp

¹blur \'blər\ *n* **1** : a smear or stain that dims but does not completely cover **2** : something vague or lacking definite outline — **blur·ry** \-ē\ *adj*

²blur *vb* **blurred; blur·ring** **1** : to make hard to see or read by smearing **2** : to make or become vague or unclear

blurb \'blərb\ *n* : a short description (as in advertising) praising a product highly

blurt \'blərt\ *vb* : to say suddenly and without thinking — usually used with *out* ⟨*blurt* out a secret⟩

¹blush \'bləsh\ *vb* **1** : to become red in the face especially from shame, confusion, or embarrassment **2** : to feel shame or embarrassment **3** : to have a rosy color : BLOOM — **blush·er** *n*

²blush *n* **1** : outward appearance : VIEW ⟨at first *blush*⟩ **2** : a reddening of the face especially from shame, confusion, or embarrassment **3** : a red or rosy tint

¹blus·ter \'bləs-tər\ *vb* **blus·tered; blus·ter·ing** \-t(ə-)riŋ\ **1** : to blow violently and noisily **2** : to talk or act in a noisy boastful way — **blus·ter·er** \-tər-ər\ *n*

²bluster *n* **1** : a violent noise or commotion **2** : loudly boastful or threatening speech — **blus·tery** \-t(ə-)rē\ *adj*

boa \'bō-ə\ *n* **1** : a large snake (as the boa constrictor, anaconda, or python) that crushes its prey **2** : a long fluffy scarf of fur, feathers, or fabric

boa con·stric·tor \-kən-'strik-tər\ *n* : a brown tropical American boa covered with spots and blotches

boar \'bō(ə)r, 'bȯ(ə)r\ *n* **1** : a male pig; *also* : the male of any of several mammals (as a guinea pig or raccoon) **2** : WILD BOAR

¹board \'bō(ə)rd, 'bȯ(ə)rd\ *n* **1** : the side of a ship **2 a** : a long thin flat piece of lumber **b** *pl* : ¹STAGE 2b ⟨trod the *boards* for 40 years⟩ **3 a** : a dining table **b** : daily meals especially when provided for pay ⟨room and *board*⟩ **4** : a group of persons who manage, direct, or investigate ⟨*board* of directors⟩ ⟨*board* of examiners⟩ **5 a** : a flat usually rectangular piece of material designed for a special purpose ⟨cutting *board*⟩ ⟨chess *board*⟩ ⟨diving *board*⟩ **b** : a surface, frame, or device for putting up notices **6** : a sheet of insulating material carrying circuit elements and connectors so that it can be inserted in an electronic de-

vice — **on board** : ABOARD

²board *vb* **1** : to go aboard : get on ⟨*board* a plane⟩ **2** : to cover with boards ⟨*board* up a window⟩ **3** : to provide or be provided with regular meals and often lodging usually for pay

board·er \'bȯrd-ər, 'bȯrd-\ *n* : one who pays for meals and sometimes lodging at another's house

board·ing·house \'bȯrd-iŋ-,haus, 'bȯrd-\ *n* : a house at which persons are boarded

boarding school *n* : a school at which most of the pupils live during the school term

board·walk \'bō(ə)rd-,wȯk, 'bȯ(ə)rd-\ *n* : a walk of planks especially along a beach

¹boast \'bōst\ *n* **1** : the act of boasting **2** : a cause for pride — **boast·ful** \'bōst-fəl\ *adj* — **boast·ful·ly** \-fə-lē\ *adv* — **boast·ful·ness** *n*

²boast *vb* **1** : to praise one's own possessions, qualities, or accomplishments **2** : to have and display proudly — **boast·er** *n*

syn BOAST, BRAG, CROW mean to express pride in oneself or what one has done. BOAST often suggests exaggeration ⟨*boasted* that she was the best runner in the school⟩ but sometimes it applies to claims made with justifiable pride ⟨the town *boasts* one of the best hospitals in the area⟩ BRAG suggests crude praising of oneself ⟨always *bragging* about how much money they had⟩ CROW suggests jubilant and noisy bragging ⟨the team *crowed* over their surprise victory⟩

¹boat \'bōt\ *n* **1** : a small vessel driven by oars or paddles or by sail or power **2** : ¹SHIP 1 **3** : a boat-shaped utensil ⟨gravy *boat*⟩ — **in the same boat** : in the same situation ⟨we're all *in the same boat*⟩

²boat *vb* **1** : to put into or carry in a boat **2** : to travel by boat

boat·er \'bōt-ər\ *n* **1** : a person who travels in a boat **2** : a stiff straw hat

boat·house \'bōt-,haus\ *n* : a shelter for boats

boat·load \-,lōd\ *n* : a boat's full load or an amount equal to such a load ⟨a *boatload* of passengers⟩

boat·man \'bōt-mən\ *n* : a person who manages, works on, or deals in boats

boat·swain *or* **bo·s'n** *or* **bo·sun** \'bō-s°n\ *n* : a sailor in the navy or merchant marine responsible for supervising work related to maintenance of the hull

¹bob \'bäb\ *vb* **bobbed; bob·bing** **1 a** : to move or cause to move up and down in a short quick movement ⟨*bob* the head⟩ ⟨a cork *bobbing* in the water⟩ **b** : to appear suddenly or unexpectedly ⟨may *bob* up anywhere⟩ **2** : to grasp or make a grab with the teeth ⟨*bob* for apples⟩ [Middle English *boben, bobben* "to hit or beat"]

²bob *n* : a short jerky motion ⟨a *bob* of the head⟩

³bob *n* **1** : a woman's or child's short haircut **2** : a weight hanging from a line **3** : ¹FLOAT 2a [from earlier *bob* "a knot or twist of yarn or hair", from Middle English *bobbe* "bunch, cluster"]

⁴bob *vb* **bobbed; bob·bing** **1** : to cut shorter : CROP **2** : to cut (hair) in the style of a bob

bob·ber \'bäb-ər\ *n* : one that bobs; *esp* : ¹FLOAT 2a

bob·bin \'bäb-ən\ *n* : a spool or spindle on which yarn or thread is wound (as in a sewing machine)

bob·ble \'bäb-əl\ *vb* **bob·bled; bob·bling** \'bäb-(ə-)liŋ\ **1** : ¹BOB 1a **2** : to handle in a clumsy or unsure way : FUMBLE — **bobble** *n*

bob·by \'bäb-ē\ *n, pl* **bobbies** *British* : POLICEMAN [named for Sir Robert *(Bobby)* Peel 1788–1850 English politician who first organized the London police force]

bob·by pin \'bäb-ē-\ *n* : a flat metal clip with flexible closed tips for holding the hair in place

bobby socks *or* **bobby sox** *n pl* : girls' thick socks reaching above the ankle

bob·by–sox·er \'bäb-ē-,säk-sər\ *n* : an adolescent girl

bob·cat \'bäb-,kat\ *n* : a common usually rusty-colored

North American lynx

bob·o·link \'bäb-ə-,liŋk\ *n*
: an American songbird
that migrates and has plumage which is streaky
brown above and yellow-
ish brown below except for
the breeding season when
the male is chiefly black
and white

bobcat

bob·sled \'bäb-,sled\ *n* **1**
: a short sled usually used
as one of a joined pair **2** : a racing sled made with two
sets of runners, a hand brake, and often a steering wheel
— **bobsled** *vb* — **bob·sled·der** *n*

bob·tail \-,tāl\ *n* **1** : a short or bobbed tail **2** : a horse,
dog, or cat with a short or bobbed tail — **bobtail** *or* **bob-
tailed** \-,tāld\ *adj*

bob·white \(')bäb-'hwīt, -'wīt\ *n* : any of several American
quails; *esp* : a gray, white, and reddish game bird of the
eastern and central U.S.

¹bode \'bōd\ *vb* **bod·ed; bod·ing** : to indicate (as a future
event) by signs : FORESHADOW

²bode *past of* BIDE

bod·ice \'bäd-əs\ *n* : the upper part of a dress

-bod·ied \'bäd-ēd\ *adj combining form* : having such a
body ⟨long-*bodied*⟩

bodi·less \'bäd-i-ləs, 'bäd-ᵊl-əs\ *adj* : having no body : IN-
CORPOREAL

¹bodi·ly \'bäd-ᵊl-ē\ *adj* : of or relating to the body : PHYSICAL

²bodily *adv* **1** : in the flesh by the body ⟨removed them
bodily⟩ **2** : as a whole : ENTIRELY

bod·kin \'bäd-kən\ *n* **1 a** : DAGGER 1, STILETTO **b** : a
sharp slender instrument for making holes in cloth **2** : a
blunt needle with a large eye for drawing tape or ribbon
through a loop or hem

body \'bäd-ē\ *n, pl* **bod·ies** **1 a** : the physical whole of a
living or dead organism **b** : the trunk or main part of an
organism **c** : a human being : PERSON **2** : the main or
central part ⟨the *body* of a truck⟩ ⟨the *body* of a letter⟩ **3**
: the section of a garment covering the main part of the
body **4** : a mass or portion of matter different from other
masses ⟨a *body* of water⟩ ⟨a *body* of cold air⟩ **5** : a group
of persons or things with a common aim or character ⟨a
body of troops⟩ ⟨a *body* of laws⟩ **6** : richness or fullness
of flavor or texture

body·build·ing \'bäd-ē-,bil-diŋ\ *n* : the developing of the
body through exercise and diet — **body·build·er** \-,bil-
dər\ *n*

body cavity *n* : a cavity within an animal body; *esp* : one
inside the body wall that contains the internal organs (as
the digestive system) and that in mammals is divided by
the diaphragm into a cavity containing the heart, lungs,
and esophagus, and a cavity containing the rest of the
digestive system, the internal parts of the reproductive system, and certain other organs

body·guard \'bäd-ē-,gärd\ *n* : a person or group of persons
whose job is to protect someone

body language *n* : movements (as with the hands) or posture used as a means of expression

body louse *n* : a sucking louse that lives in the clothing and
feeds on the human body

Boer \'bō(ə)r, 'bȯ(ə)r, 'bu̇(ə)r\ *n* : a South African usually of
Dutch descent [Dutch, literally "farmer"]

¹bog \'bäg, 'bȯg\ *n* : wet spongy ground : MARSH — **bog-
gy** \-ē\ *adj*

²bog *vb* **bogged; bog·ging** : to sink or become stuck in or
as if in a bog ⟨get *bogged* down in too much detail⟩

bo·gey *also* **bo·gy** *or* **bo·gie** *n, pl* **bogeys** *also* **bogies** **1**
\'bu̇g-ē, 'bō-gē, 'bü-gē\ : GHOST, PHANTOM **2** \'bō-gē
also 'bu̇g-ē *or* 'bü-gē\ : something one is afraid of especially without reason

bo·gey·man \'bu̇g-ē-,man, 'bō-gē-, 'bü-gē-\ *n* : an imaginary monster used in threatening children

bo·gus \'bō-gəs\ *adj* : not genuine : SPURIOUS, SHAM

Bo·he·mi·an \bō-'hē-mē-ən\ *n* **1 a** : a person born or living in Bohemia **b** : the Czech dialects used in Bohemia
2 *often not cap* **a** : ²VAGABOND, WANDERER **b** : a person
(as an artist or writer) who does not follow ordinary standards of behavior — **bohemian** *adj, often cap* — **bo·he-
mi·an·ism** \-mē-ə-,niz-əm\ *n, often cap*

¹boil \'bȯi(ə)l\ *n* : a painful swollen inflamed area in the skin
resulting from infection — compare CARBUNCLE 2 [an altered form of Middle English *bile* "a boil", from Old English
bȳl (same meaning)]

²boil *vb* **1 a** : to produce bubbles of vapor when heated
⟨the water is *boiling*⟩ **b** : to come or bring to the boiling
point ⟨the coffee *boiled*⟩ **2** : to churn violently as if boiling
⟨*boiling* floodwaters⟩ **3** : to be excited or stirred up ⟨*boil*
with anger⟩ **4** : to go through or cause to go through the
action of a boiling liquid ⟨*boil* eggs⟩ [Middle English *boilen*
"to boil", from early French *boillir*, derived from Latin *bulla*
"a bubble" — related to ³BILL, ²BOWL]

³boil *n* : the act or state of boiling ⟨bring to a *boil*⟩

boil·er \'bȯi-lər\ *n* **1** : a container in which something is
boiled **2** : a strong metal container used in making steam
3 : a tank in which water is heated or hot water is stored

boiling point *n* : the temperature at which a liquid boils

boil over *vb* : to overflow while boiling

bois·ter·ous \'bȯi-st(ə-)rəs\ *adj* **1 a** : noisily rough
: ROWDY ⟨a *boisterous* crowd⟩ **b** : marked by high spirits
⟨*boisterous* laughter⟩ **2** : vigorously active : VIOLENT —
bois·ter·ous·ly *adv* — **bois·ter·ous·ness** *n*

bo·la \'bō-lə\ *or* **bo·las**
\-ləs\ *n, pl* **bo·las** \-ləz\
: a cord with weights at-
tached to the ends for
throwing at and entangling
an animal [American
Spanish *bolas* "bola",
from Spanish *bola* "ball"]

bold \'bōld\ *adj* **1 a** : willing to meet danger or take
risks : DARING **b** : showing daring spirit ⟨a *bold*
plan⟩ **2** : IMPUDENT,
SAUCY **3** : ¹STEEP 1 ⟨*bold*
cliffs⟩ **4** : standing out in
a very noticeable way : CONSPICUOUS ⟨a dress with *bold*
stripes⟩ — **bold·ly** \'bōl-(d)lē\ *adv* — **bold·ness** \'bōl(d)-
nəs\ *n*

bola

bold·face \'bōl(d)-,fās\ *n* **1** : a type having thick dark lines
— compare LIGHTFACE **2** : printing set in boldface

bold–faced \-'fāst\ *adj* **1** : bold in manner or conduct
: IMPUDENT **2** *usually* **bold·faced** : being or set in boldface

bole \'bōl\ *n* : the trunk of a tree

bo·le·ro \bə-'le(ə)r-ō\ *n, pl* **-ros** **1** : a Spanish dance in ¾
time **2** : a loose waist-length jacket open at the front

bo·li·var \bə-'lē-,vär, 'bäl-ə-vər\ *n, pl* **bo·li·vars** *or* **bo·li-
va·res** \,bäl-ə-'vär-,ās, ,bō-li-\ **1** : the basic unit of
money of Venezuela **2** : a silver coin representing one
bolivar [American Spanish *bolívar* "unit of money", named
for Simón *Bolívar*]

boll \'bōl\ *n* : a case or capsule for the seeds of a plant (as
a cotton plant)

boll weevil *n* : a small grayish weevil with a larva that lives
in and feeds on the buds and bolls of the cotton plant

\ə\ **abut**	\au̇\ **out**	\i\ **tip**	\ȯ\ **saw**	\u̇\ **foot**
\ər\ **further**	\ch\ **chin**	\ī\ **life**	\ȯi\ **coin**	\y\ **yet**
\a\ **mat**	\e\ **pet**	\j\ **job**	\th\ **thin**	\yü\ **few**
\ā\ **take**	\ē\ **easy**	\ŋ\ **sing**	\th\ **this**	\yu̇\ **cure**
\ä\ **cot, cart**	\g\ **go**	\ō\ **bone**	\ü\ **food**	\zh\ **vision**

bo·lo \'bō-lō\ *n, pl* **bolos** : a long heavy single-edged knife used in the Philippines

bo·lo·gna \bə-'lō-nē *also* -n(y)ə\ *n* : a large smoked sausage of beef, veal, and pork

Bol·she·vik \'bōl-shə-,vik, 'bȯl-, 'bäl-, -,vēk\ *n, pl* **Bolsheviks** *or* **Bol·she·vi·ki** \,bōl-shə-'vik-ē, ,bȯl-, ,bäl-, -'vē-kē\ **1** : a member of the communist party that seized power in Russia by the Revolution of November 1917 **2** : COMMUNIST 2 — **Bolshevik** *adj*

Bol·she·vism \'bōl-shə-,viz-əm, 'bȯl-, 'bäl-\ *n* : the doctrine or program of the Bolsheviks

¹bol·ster \'bōl-stər\ *n* **1** : a long pillow or cushion **2** : a structural part designed to eliminate friction or provide support

²bolster *vb* **bol·stered; bol·ster·ing** \-st(ə-)riŋ\ : to support with or as if with a bolster; *also* : REINFORCE ⟨came with me to *bolster* my confidence⟩ — **bol·ster·er** \-stər-ər\ *n*

¹bolt \'bōlt\ *n* **1** : a missile (as an arrow) for a crossbow or catapult **2 a** : a lightning stroke : THUNDERBOLT **b** : a sudden surprise ⟨a *bolt* from the blue⟩ **3** : a sliding bar used to fasten a door **4** : the part of a lock worked by a key **5** : a metal pin or rod usually with a head at one end and a screw thread at the other that is used to hold something in place **6** : a roll of cloth or wallpaper **7** : the device that closes the breech of a firearm

²bolt *vb* **1** : to move suddenly or nervously **2** : to move rapidly : DASH ⟨reporters *bolted* for the door⟩ **3** : RUN AWAY 1 ⟨the horse shied and *bolted*⟩ **4** : to break away from or oppose one's political party **5** : to say thoughtlessly : BLURT **6** : to fasten with a bolt **7** : to swallow hastily or without chewing ⟨*bolted* down my dinner and rushed out⟩ — **bolt·er** *n*

³bolt *n* : an act of bolting

¹bomb \'bäm\ *n* **1 a** : an explosive device that has a fuse and is designed to go off under any of various conditions **b** : ATOM BOMB; *also* : nuclear weapons in general — usually used with *the* **2** : a container in which a substance (as an insecticide) is stored under pressure and from which it is released in a fine spray

²bomb *vb* : to attack with bombs

bom·bard \bäm-'bärd *also* bəm-\ *vb* **1** : to attack especially with artillery or bombers **2** : to attack forcefully or continuously (as with questions) **3** : to put under the force of rapidly moving particles (as electrons or alpha rays) — **bom·bard·ment** \-mənt\ *n*

bom·bar·dier \,bäm-bə(r)-'di(ə)r\ *n* : a bomber-crew member who releases the bombs

bombardier beetle *n* : any of numerous beetles that when disturbed discharge an irritating vapor

bom·bast \'bäm-,bast\ *n* : boastful speech or writing — **bom·bas·tic** \bäm-'bas-tik\ *adj* — **bom·bas·ti·cal·ly** \-ti-k(ə-)lē\ *adv*

bomb·er \'bäm-ər\ *n* : one that bombs; *esp* : an airplane designed for dropping bombs

bomb·proof \'bäm-'prüf\ *adj* : safe against the explosive force of bombs

bomb·shell \-,shel\ *n* **1** : ¹BOMB 1a **2** : a great surprise

bo·na fide \'bō-nə-,fīd, 'bä-nə-; ,bō-nə-'fīd-ē, -'fīd-ə\ *adj* **1 a** : made or done in good faith ⟨*bona fide* offer⟩ **b** : acting in good faith ⟨*bona fide* purchaser⟩ **2** : GENUINE 1 ⟨a *bona fide* cowboy⟩ [from Latin *bona fide*, literally "in good faith"; *bona* from *bonus* "good" and *fide* from *fides* "faith" — related to BONUS, FAITH]

bo·nan·za \bə-'nan-zə\ *n* **1** : a rich mass of ore in a mine **2** : something that brings a rich return ⟨a box-office *bonanza*⟩

bon·bon \'bän-,bän\ *n* : a candy with a soft coating (as chocolate) and a creamy center [French, literally "good good", from *bon* "good", from Latin *bonus* "good" — related to BONUS, BOUNTY]

¹bond \'bänd\ *n* **1** : something that binds **2 a** : a material or device for binding **b** : a means by which atoms, ions, or groups of atoms are held together in a molecule or crystal **3** : a uniting or binding force or influence : TIE ⟨the *bonds* of friendship⟩ **4 a** : a pledge to do an act or pay a sum on or before a set date or forfeit a sum if the pledge is not fulfilled **b** : a certificate promising payment of a certain sum on or before a stated day and issued by a government or corporation as an evidence of debt **5** : a binding or connection made by overlapping parts of a structure (as in laying brick)

²bond *vb* **1** : to protect or secure by or operate under a bond **2** : to hold together or make solid by or as if by a bond — **bond·able** \'bän-də-bəl\ *adj* — **bond·er** *n*

bond·age \'bän-dij\ *n* : the state of being a slave or serf

bond·hold·er \'bänd-,hōl-dər\ *n* : one that owns a government or corporation bond

bond·man \'bän(d)-mən\ *n* : ¹SLAVE 1, SERF

¹bonds·man \'bän(d)z-mən\ *n* : BONDMAN

²bondsman *n* : one who gives a bond or bail for another

¹bone \'bōn\ *n* **1 a** : a hard material which is largely calcium phosphate and of which the skeleton of most animals with backbones is formed; *also* : one of the hard pieces in which this material occurs ⟨break a *bone*⟩ **b** : a hard animal substance (as whalebone or ivory) similar to bone **2** : a cause of disagreement — used in the phrases *bone of contention* and *bone to pick* **3** *pl* : something usually or originally made from bone (as dice or clappers) — **bone·less** \-ləs\ *adj* — **bone·like** \-,līk\ *adj*

²bone *vb* **boned; bon·ing** **1** : to remove the bones from ⟨*bone* a fish⟩ **2** : to study hard ⟨*bone* up on math⟩

bone black *n* : the black chiefly carbon matter that is left from bones heated in a closed container and is used especially as a pigment or a material to remove color from other things

bone·meal \'bōn-,mē(ə)l\ *n* : fertilizer or feed made of crushed or ground bone

bon·er \'bō-nər\ *n* : a stupid or ridiculous mistake : BLUNDER

bon·fire \'bän-,fī(ə)r\ *n* : a large outdoor fire

> **Word History** During the Middle Ages in Europe, wars and widespread outbreaks of disease caused the deaths of so many people that it was necessary to burn their corpses in large fires. Such a fire was called a *bonefire* or "fire of bones". Later it became common practice to burn at the stake people who held different religious beliefs. The fires in which these victims died were also *bonefires*. Over the years the word came to be used for outdoor fires lighted for public celebrations. But by this time it was changed to *bonfire*, taking on a less grim spelling and sound. [Middle English *bonefire* "fire of bones"]

bon·go \'bäŋ-gō\ *n, pl* **bongos** *also* **bongoes** : either of a pair of small drums of different sizes fitted together and played with the fingers

bo·ni·to \bə-'nēt-ō, -'nēt-ə\ *n, pl* **-tos** *or* **-to** : any of various medium-sized tunas

bon·net \'bän-ət\ *n* **1** : a child's or woman's hat tied under the chin by ribbons or strings **2** : a soft woolen cap worn in Scotland **3** : the headdress of an American Indian

bon·ny \'bän-ē\ *adj* **bon·ni·er; -est** *chiefly British* : HANDSOME 3, ATTRACTIVE

bon·sai \(')bän-'sī, 'bän-,sī, 'bän-,sī\ *n, pl* **bonsai** : a miniature plant (as a tree) grown in a pot by special methods to restrict its growth; *also* : the art of growing such a plant [Japanese]

bo·nus \'bō-nəs\ *n* : something given to somebody (as a worker) in addition to what is usual or owed [from Latin *bonus* "good" — related to BONA FIDE, BONBON, ²BOON, BOUNTY]

bon voy·age \,bōn-,vwī-'äzh, -,vwä-'yäzh, ,bän-\ *n* : ²FAREWELL 1 — usually used as an interjection [French, literally "good journey"]

bony \'bō-nē\ *adj* **bon·i·er; -est** **1** : of or relating to bone ⟨the *bony* structure of the body⟩ **2** : full of bones **3**

: resembling bone especially in hardness ⟨a *bony* substance⟩   **4** : having large or noticeable bones ⟨a *bony* face⟩   **5** : SKINNY 2, SCRAWNY ⟨*bony* underfed children⟩

bony fish *n* : any of a class that consists of the higher fishes with usually well-developed bony skeletons

¹boo \'bü\ *interj* — used to express contempt or disapproval or to startle or frighten

²boo *n* : a shout of disapproval or contempt — **boo** *vb*

boo·by \'bü-bē\ *n, pl* **boobies**   **1** : a foolish person : DOPE   **2** : any of several gannets of tropical seas

booby trap *n* : a trap for a careless or unsuspecting person; *esp* : a concealed explosive device set to go off when a harmless-looking object is touched — **boo·by·trap** \'bü-bē-,trap\ *vb*

booby 2

¹book \'bük\ *n*   **1** : a set of sheets of paper bound together   **2 a** : a long written work   **b** : a major division of a written work   **3 a** : a volume of business records ⟨the company's *books* show a profit⟩   **b** *pl* : ²RECORD 2b ⟨an outdated law still on the *books*⟩   **4** *cap* : BIBLE 1a   **5** : a pack of items bound together ⟨a *book* of matches⟩ — **in one's book** : in one's own opinion — **one for the book** : an act or event worth noting

Word History Books have not always been made of printed sheets of paper bound between hard covers. Some of the oldest books were written long before paper was known in Europe. Some of these early books were carved in clay or stone, some were written on scrolls made of animal skin, and some were carved on wooden tablets. Wooden tablets were popular in Europe during the Middle Ages, and the wood commonly used was beech. The ancient Germanic word for the beech tree is the same as that for a book. This connection is also found in Old English, where the word *bōc*, which means "book", also means "beech (tree)". [Old English *bōc* "book, beech"; of Germanic origin]

²book *vb*   **1** : ¹RESERVE 3 ⟨*book* a hotel room⟩   **2** : to schedule engagements for ⟨*book* a singer⟩   **3** : to enter charges against in a police register ⟨*book* a suspect⟩

³book *adj*   **1** : gotten from books ⟨*book* learning⟩   **2** : shown by account books ⟨*book* value⟩

book·bind·er \'bük-,bīn-dər\ *n* : BINDER 1

book·bind·ing \-,bīn-diŋ\ *n*   **1** : the binding of a book   **2** : the art or trade of binding books

book·case \'bük-,kās\ *n* : a set of shelves to hold books

book·end \-,end\ *n* : something placed at the end of a row of books to hold them up

book·ish \'bük-ish\ *adj*   **1** : fond of reading   **2** : tending to rely on knowledge from books rather than practical experience   **3** : resembling the language of books : FORMAL — **book·ish·ly** *adv* — **book·ish·ness** *n*

book·keep·er \'bük-,kē-pər\ *n* : a person who keeps accounts for a business — **book·keep·ing** \-,kē-piŋ\ *n*

book·let \'bük-lət\ *n* : a little book; *esp* : PAMPHLET

book louse *n* : any of several minute wingless insects that feed on and injure books

book lung *n* : a specialized breathing organ of spiders and related animals

book·mak·er \'bük-,mā-kər\ *n* : a person who receives and pays off bets

book·mark \-,märk\ *n* : something placed in a book to mark a page

book·mo·bile \'bük-mō-,bēl\ *n* : a truck that serves as a traveling library

book·plate \'bük-,plāt\ *n* : a label pasted inside a book to show who owns it

book·sell·er \-,sel-ər\ *n* : a person who owns or works in a bookstore

book·store \-,stō(ə)r, -,stȯ(ə)r\ *n* : a store that sells mainly books

book·worm \-,wərm\ *n*   **1** : any of various insect larvae that feed on the binding and paste of books   **2** : a person devoted to reading or study

Bool·ean \'bü-lē-ən\ *adj* : of, relating to, or being Boolean algebra

Boolean algebra *n* : any of several logical systems of combining abstract quantities; *esp* : an arithmetic of sets in which the intersection and union of sets are operations [named for George *Boole* 1815–1864 English mathematician]

¹boom \'büm\ *n*   **1** : a long pole used especially to stretch the bottom of a sail   **2 a** : a long beam sticking out from the mast of a derrick to support or guide something that is being lifted   **b** : a long arm used to move a microphone   **3** : a line of connected floating timbers (as across a river) to obstruct passage or catch floating objects [from Dutch *boom* "tree, wooden beam"]

²boom *vb*   **1** : to make a deep hollow rumbling sound   **2 a** : to increase in importance or popularity   **b** : to experience a boom (as in growth) [a word imitating the sound]

³boom *n*   **1** : a booming sound or cry   **2** : a rapid increase in growth or prosperity; *esp* : a rapid widespread expansion of business

boom box *n* : a large portable radio and often tape deck with two attached speakers

¹boo·mer·ang \'bü-mə-,raŋ\ *n* : a curved club that can be thrown so as to return to the thrower [the native word for this club in Australia]

²boomerang *vb* : ²BACKFIRE 2

boom·town \'büm-,taün\ *n* : a town experiencing a sudden growth in business and population

¹boon \'bün\ *n*   **1** : something asked or granted as a favor   **2** : something pleasant or helpful that comes at just the right time : BLESSING [Middle English *boon* "favor", from an early Norse word meaning "a request, plea"]

²boon *adj* : MERRY 1 ⟨a *boon* companion⟩ [Middle English *boon, bon* "favorable", from early French *bon* "good", derived from Latin *bonus* "good" — related to BONUS]

boor \'bü(ə)r\ *n*   **1 a** : PEASANT   **b** : ²RUSTIC   **2** : a crude or impolite person — **boor·ish** \-ish\ *adj* — **boor·ish·ly** *adv* — **boor·ish·ness** *n*

¹boost \'büst\ *vb*   **1** : to push or shove up from below   **2** : to increase in force, power, or amount ⟨*boost* production⟩ ⟨*boost* prices⟩   **3** : ³FURTHER, RAISE ⟨*boost* morale⟩   **4** : to support enthusiastically : PLUG

²boost *n*   **1** : a push upward   **2** : an increase in amount ⟨a *boost* in production⟩   **3** : an act that gives help or encouragement

boost·er \'bü-stər\ *n*   **1** : one that boosts   **2** : an enthusiastic supporter   **3** : an extra dose of an immunizing agent given to maintain or restore the effects of previously established immunity   **4** : a device for strengthening radio or television signals   **5** : the first stage of a multistage rocket providing force for the launching and the first part of the flight

¹boot \'büt\ *n, chiefly dialect* : something given to make a trade equal [Old English *bōt* "remedy"] — **to boot** : ²BESIDES

²boot *n*   **1** : a covering usually of leather or rubber for the foot and part of the leg   **2 a** : ²KICK 1a   **b** : a rude dismissal or discharge — used with *the*   **3** : a new member

\ə\ **abut**	\aü\ **out**	\i\ **tip**	\ȯ\ **saw**	\ü\ **foot**	
\ər\ **further**	\ch\ **chin**	\ī\ **life**	\ȯi\ **coin**	\y\ **yet**	
\a\ **mat**	\e\ **pet**	\j\ **job**	\th\ **thin**	\yü\ **few**	
\ā\ **take**	\ē\ **easy**	\ŋ\ **sing**	\th\ **this**	\yü\ **cure**	
\ä\ **cot, cart**	\g\ **go**	\ō\ **bone**	\ü\ **food**	\zh\ **vision**	

of the Navy or Marine Corps while in boot camp [Middle English *boot* "a covering for the foot"]

³**boot** *vb* **1** : to put boots on **2 a** : ¹KICK 1 **b** : to get rid of or dismiss rudely — often used with *out* ⟨was *booted* out of the office⟩ **3 a** : to load (a program) into a computer from a disk **b** : to start or make ready for use especially by booting a program ⟨*boot* a microcomputer⟩

boot·black \'büt-,blak\ *n* : a person who shines boots and shoes

boot camp *n* : a camp where recently enlisted members of the Navy or Marine Corps receive their basic training

boot·ee *or* **boot·ie** \'büt-ē\ *n* : an infant's knitted or crocheted sock

Bo·ö·tes \bō-'ōt-ēz\ *n* : a northern group of stars including the bright star Arcturus [derived from Greek *Boötes*, literally "plowman"]

booth \'büth\ *n, pl* **booths** \'büthz, 'büths\ **1** : a covered stand for selling or displaying goods (as at a fair or exhibition) or for providing services ⟨information *booth*⟩ **2** : a small enclosure giving privacy for one person ⟨voting *booth*⟩ ⟨telephone *booth*⟩ **3** : a section of a restaurant consisting of a table between two high-backed benches

boot·jack \'büt-,jak\ *n* : a device with a notch used to help pull off one's boots

¹**boot·leg** \-,leg\ *vb* **boot·legged**; **boot·leg·ging** **1** : to make, transport, or sell alcoholic liquor illegally **2 a** : to produce or sell illegally or without permission ⟨*bootlegged* recordings⟩ **b** : SMUGGLE 1 — **boot·leg·ger** *n*

bootjack

²**bootleg** *n* : something bootlegged; *esp* : MOONSHINE 3 — **bootleg** *adj*

boot·less \'büt-ləs\ *adj* : USELESS, UNPROFITABLE

boo·ty \'büt-ē\ *n* **1** : money or goods taken in war or by robbery : SPOILS **2** : a rich gain or prize

booze \'büz\ *n* : alcoholic liquor

¹**bop** \'bäp\ *vb* **bopped; bop·ping** : ¹HIT 1, SOCK

²**bop** *n* : a blow (as from a fist or club) that strikes a person

bo·rate \'bō(ə)r-,āt, 'bȯ(ə)r-\ *n* : a chemical compound formed by the reaction of boric acid with another substance

bo·rax \'bō(ə)r-,aks, 'bȯ(ə)r-\ *n* : a borate of sodium that occurs as a mineral and is used in agricultural chemicals, as a cleansing agent, and as a water softener

¹**bor·der** \'bȯrd-ər\ *n* **1** : an outer part or edge **2** : a boundary especially of a country or state **3** : a narrow bed of plants along the edge of a garden or walk **4** : an ornamental design at the edge of a fabric or rug — **bordered** \-ərd\ *adj*

  syn BORDER, MARGIN, EDGE mean the outermost part of something. BORDER applies to an area on or just within a boundary line ⟨guards were placed along the *border*⟩ MARGIN suggests a border of exact width ⟨do not write in the *margin* of the page⟩ EDGE suggests a sharp line marking a fixed limit ⟨the *edge* of the table⟩

²**border** *vb* **bor·dered; bor·der·ing** \'bȯrd-(ə-)riŋ\ **1** : to put a border on ⟨*border* the garden with flowers⟩ **2** : to be located close to or next to ⟨the U.S. *borders* on Canada⟩ **3** : to come very close to being : VERGE ⟨that remark *borders* on the ridiculous⟩ — **bor·der·er** \-ər-ər\ *n*

bor·der·land \'bȯrd-ər-,land\ *n* **1** : territory at or near a border : FRONTIER **2** : an unclear condition or region separating two clearly different ones ⟨the *borderland* between sleeping and waking⟩

bor·der·line \-,līn\ *adj* : not quite normal or acceptable

¹**bore** \'bō(ə)r, 'bȯ(ə)r\ *vb* **bored; bor·ing** **1** : to make a hole in especially with a drill **2** : to make (as a hole

shaped like a cylinder) by boring or digging away material ⟨*bore* a well⟩ **3** : to move forward steadily especially by overcoming an opposing force ⟨the plane *bored* through the storm⟩ [Old English *borian* "to bore"]

²**bore** *n* **1** : a hole made by or as if by boring **2** : a cavity (as in a gun barrel) shaped like a cylinder **3** : the diameter of a hole or tube; *esp* : the interior diameter of a gun barrel

³**bore** *past of* BEAR

⁴**bore** *n* : a tidal flood with a high abrupt front [probably from Middle English *bore* "wave"; of Norse origin]

⁵**bore** *n* : an uninteresting person or thing [origin unknown]

⁶**bore** *vb* **bored; bor·ing** : to make weary and restless by being dull or monotonous

bore·dom \'bō(ə)rd-əm, 'bȯ(ə)rd-\ *n* : the state of being bored

bor·er \'bōr-ər, 'bȯr-\ *n* **1** : one that bores; *esp* : a tool used for boring **2** : an insect that as a larva or an adult bores in the woody parts of plants

bo·ric acid \,bōr-ik-, ,bȯr-\ *n* : a white boron-containing weak acid that is used as a mild antiseptic

bor·ing \'bō(ə)r-iŋ, 'bȯ(ə)r-\ *adj* : causing boredom : UNINTERESTING, TEDIOUS — **bor·ing·ly** \-iŋ-lē\ *adv*

born \'bȯ(ə)rn\ *adj* **1 a** : brought into life by or as if by birth **b** : ¹NATIVE 2 ⟨American-*born*⟩ **2** : having from birth a certain ability or characteristic ⟨a *born* leader⟩ **3** : meant from or as if from birth ⟨*born* to rule⟩

borne *also* **born** *past participle of* BEAR

born·ite \'bȯ(ə)r-,nīt\ *n* : a brittle metallic-looking mineral consisting of a sulfide of copper and iron and making up a valuable ore of copper

bo·ron \'bō(ə)r-,än, 'bȯ(ə)r-\ *n* : a metalloid element found in nature only in combination (as in borax) — see ELEMENT table

bor·ough \'bər-ō\ *n* **1 a** : a town or urban area in Great Britain that sends one or more members to Parliament **b** : a self-governing urban area in Great Britain **2** : a self-governing town or village in some states **3** : one of the five political divisions of New York City

bor·row \'bär-ō, 'bȯr-\ *vb* **1** : to take or receive something with the promise or intention of returning it **2** : to take for one's own use something begun or thought up by another : ADOPT ⟨*borrow* an idea⟩ **3** : to take 1 from the digit in a given place of a number from which another number is subtracted and add it as 10 to the digit in the next lower place — **bor·row·er** \'bär-ə-wər, 'bȯr-\ *n*

bor·row·ing \'bär-ə-wiŋ, 'bȯr-\ *n* : something borrowed; *esp* : a word or phrase adopted from one language into another

borscht *or* **borsch** \'bȯ(ə)rsh(t)\ *n* : a beet soup that is usually served with sour cream [from Russian *borshch* "beet soup"]

bor·zoi \'bȯr-,zȯi\ *n* : any of a breed of large long-haired dogs developed in Russia especially for hunting wolves [from Russian *borzoĭ* "borzoi dog, swift"]

bos'n *or* **bosun** *variant of* BOATSWAIN

¹**bos·om** \'būz-əm\ *n* **1** : the front of the human chest; *esp* : the female breasts **2** : the chest thought of as the center of secret thoughts and feelings **3** : a close and comforting relationship ⟨in the *bosom* of her family⟩ **4** : the part of a garment covering the breast — **bos·omed** \-əmd\ *adj*

²**bosom** *adj* : ²INTIMATE 3a, CLOSE ⟨*bosom* friends⟩

¹**boss** \'bȯs, 'bäs\ *n* : a raised rounded part often used ornamentally (as on a shield or a ceiling) : STUD [Middle English *boce* "raised rounded part", from early French *boce* (same meaning), probably from Latin]

²**boss** *vb* : to ornament with bosses : EMBOSS

³**boss** \'bȯs\ *n* **1** : the person (as an employer or supervisor) who tells workers what to do **2** : the head of a group; *esp* : a powerful politician who controls all party business [from Dutch *baas* "master"] — **boss** *adj*

⁴**boss** \'bȯs\ *vb* **1** : to be in charge of ⟨*boss* a job⟩ **2** : to

give orders to ⟨don't *boss* me around⟩

⁵**boss** \'bòs\ *adj, slang* : EXCELLENT, FIRST-RATE

bossy \'bò-sē\ *adj* **boss·i·er; -est** : fond of ordering people around : DOMINEERING — **boss·i·ness** *n*

Bos·ton ivy \,bò-stən-\ *n* : a woody Asian vine that is related to the grape, has leaves with three lobes, and often grows over walls

Boston terrier *n* : any of an American breed of small short-haired dogs having erect ears and a broad flat face — called also *Boston bull*

Boston terrier

bot \'bät\ *n* : the larva of a botfly

¹**bo·tan·i·cal** \bə-'tan-i-kəl\ *adj* **1** : of or relating to plants or botany **2** : made or obtained from plants ⟨*botanical* drugs⟩ — **bo·tan·i·cal·ly** \-i-k(ə-)lē\ *adv*

²**botanical** *n* : a vegetable drug especially in the crude state

bot·a·nist \'bät-ᵊn-əst, 'bät-nəst\ *n* : a person who specializes in botany or in a branch of botany

bot·a·ny \'bät-ᵊn-e, 'bät-ne\ *n* **1** : a branch of biology dealing with plant life **2 a** : plant life (as of a given region) **b** : the biology of a plant or plant group

¹**botch** \'bäch\ *vb* : to make or do something in a clumsy or unskillful way : SPOIL, BUNGLE

²**botch** *n* : a botched job : MESS — **botchy** \-ē\ *adj*

bot·fly \'bät-,flī\ *n* : any of various stout two-winged flies whose larvae are parasitic in various mammals

¹**both** \'bōth\ *adj* : the two : the one and the other ⟨*both* feet⟩

²**both** *pron* : the one as well as the other ⟨*both* of us⟩ ⟨we are *both* well⟩

³**both** *conj* — used before two words or phrases connected with *and* to stress that each is included ⟨*both* New York and London⟩

¹**both·er** \'bäth-ər\ *vb* **both·ered; both·er·ing** \-(ə-)riŋ\ **1 a** : to upset often with minor details : ANNOY **b** : to intrude upon : INTERRUPT **2 a** : to cause to be worried or concerned **b** : to become concerned **3** : to take the trouble : make an effort ⟨don't *bother* to knock⟩

²**bother** *n* **1 a** : the state of being bothered **b** : someone or something that bothers in a small way ⟨what a *bother* a cold can be⟩ **2** : COMMOTION 2, FUSS

both·er·some \'bäth-ər-səm\ *adj* : causing bother : TROUBLESOME

¹**bot·tle** \'bät-ᵊl\ *n* **1 a** : a container (as of glass or plastic) with a narrow neck and mouth and usually no handle **b** : a bag made of skin used to hold water or wine **2** : the quantity held by a bottle **3** : NURSING BOTTLE — **bot·tle·ful** \-,fùl\ *n*

²**bottle** *vb* **bot·tled; bot·tling** \'bät-liŋ, -ᵊl-iŋ\ **1** : to put into a bottle **2** : to shut up as if in a bottle : RESTRAIN — **bot·tler** \-lər, -ᵊl-ər\

bottled gas *n* : gas under pressure in portable cylinders

bot·tle–feed \'bät-ᵊl-,fēd\ *vb* **-fed; -feed·ing** : to feed (as an infant) with a nursing bottle

bot·tle·neck \'bät-ᵊl-,nek\ *n* **1** : a narrow passageway **2** : a place, condition, or point where progress is held up ⟨a traffic *bottleneck*⟩

bot·tle–nosed dolphin \,bät-ᵊl-,nōzd-\ *n* : any of various medium-sized stout-bodied whales with teeth and a short conspicuous snout

bot·tle-nose dolphin \,bät-ᵊl-,nōz-\ *n* : BOTTLE-NOSED DOLPHIN

bot·tom \'bät-əm\ *n* **1 a** : the undersurface of something **b** : a supporting surface or part : BASE **c** : BUTTOCK 2, RUMP **2** : the surface on which a body of water lies **3 a**

: the part of a ship's hull lying below the water **b** : ¹BOAT 1, SHIP **4** : the lowest part, place, or point **5** *pl* : the trousers of pajamas **6** : lowland along a river ⟨the Mississippi river *bottoms*⟩ **7** : the most basic or central part : HEART ⟨get to the *bottom* of the problem⟩ — **bot·tomed** \-əmd\ *adj* — **at bottom** : REALLY 1 ⟨no manners, but good-hearted *at bottom*⟩

bottom dollar *n* : one's last dollar ⟨you can bet your *bottom dollar*⟩

bot·tom·land \'bät-əm-,land\ *n* : BOTTOM 6

bot·tom·less \'bät-əm-ləs\ *adj* **1** : having no bottom **2** : very deep ⟨a *bottomless* pit⟩

bot·u·lism \'bäch-ə-,liz-əm\ *n* : poisoning caused by eating food containing a toxin made by a spore-forming bacterium

bou·clé *or* **bou·cle** \bü-'klā\ *n* : an uneven yarn of three fibers one of which forms evenly spaced loops [from French *bouclé* "curly"]

bou·doir \'büd-,wär, 'bùd-\ *n* : a woman's dressing room, bedroom, or private sitting room [from French *boudoir* "lady's dressing room", literally "a place to sulk", from *bouder* "to sulk"]

bough \'baù\ *n* : a branch of a tree; *esp* : a main branch — **boughed** \'baùd\ *adj*

bought *past and past participle of* BUY

bouil·la·baisse \,bü-yə-'bās, 'bü-yə-,bās\ *n* : a spicy stew made from a variety of fish and shellfish

bouil·lon \'bü(l)-,yän, 'bù(l)-; 'bùl-yən\ *n* : a clear seasoned soup made usually from beef [from French *bouillon* "clear soup", derived from early French *bouillir* "to boil", derived from Latin *bulla* "a bubble" — related to ²BOIL]

boul·der \'bōl-dər\ *n* : a large detached and rounded or worn mass of rock

bou·le·vard \'bùl-ə-,värd, 'bül-\ *n* : a wide avenue often having grass strips with trees along its center or sides [from French *boulevard* "walkway lined with trees", derived from early Dutch *bolwerc* "bulwark, rampart"; so called because the earliest boulevards were at sites of abandoned fortifications — related to BULWARK]

¹**bounce** \'baù(n)s\ *vb* **bounced; bounc·ing** **1 a** : to cause to rebound ⟨*bounce* a ball⟩ **b** : to spring back or up after striking a surface **2** : to remove from a place by force **3** : to leap suddenly : BOUND **4** *of a check* : to be returned by a bank as no good (as because of lack of funds)

²**bounce** *n* **1 a** : a sudden leap or bound **b** : a bouncing back : REBOUND **2** : ENTHUSIASM 1, SPIRIT — **bouncy** *adj*

bounc·er \'baù(n)t-sər\ *n* : one that bounces; *esp* : someone employed in a public place to remove troublemakers

bounc·ing \'baù(n)t-siŋ\ *adj* : HEALTHY 1a, LIVELY ⟨a *bouncing* baby⟩ — **bounc·ing·ly** \-siŋ-lē\ *adv*

¹**bound** \'baùnd\ *adj* : going or intending to go ⟨*bound* for home⟩ ⟨college-*bound*⟩ [Middle English *boun* "ready"; of Norse origin]

²**bound** *n* **1** : a boundary line **2** : a point or line beyond which one cannot go : LIMIT ⟨out of *bounds*⟩ **3** : the land within a boundary — usually used in pl. [Middle English *bound* "boundary", from early French *bodne* (same meaning), from Latin *bodina* "boundary"]

³**bound** *vb* **1** : to set limits to : CONFINE **2 a** : to form the boundary of : ENCLOSE **b** : to lie next to **3** : to name the boundaries of

⁴**bound** *past and past participle of* BIND

⁵**bound** *adj* **1** : fastened by or as if by bands : CONFINED ⟨desk-*bound*⟩ **2** : required by law or duty **3** : having a binding ⟨*bound* notebook⟩ **4** : firmly determined ⟨we were *bound* we would succeed⟩ **5** : very likely to do something

\ə\ abut	\aù\ **out**	\i\ tip	\ò\ saw	\ù\ foot	
\ər\ **further**	\ch\ **chin**	\ī\ life	\òi\ coin	\y\ yet	
\a\ mat	\e\ pet	\j\ job	\th\ thin	\yü\ few	
\ā\ take	\ē\ **easy**	\ŋ\ sing	\th\ this	\yù\ cure	
\ä\ cot, cart	\g\ **go**	\ō\ bone	\ü\ food	\zh\ vision	

: CERTAIN, SURE **6** : always found in combination with another word or word part (as *un-* in *unknown* and *-er* in *speaker*) [Middle English *bounden* "fastened, tied", from *binden* "bind"]

⁶bound *n* **1** : a long easy leap **2** : ²BOUNCE 1b, REBOUND [from early French *bond* "a leap", from *bondir* "to leap", probably from Latin]

⁷bound *vb* **1** : to move by leaping **2** : ¹REBOUND 1, BOUNCE

bound·ary \'baún-d(ə-)rē\ *n, pl* **-aries** : something that points out or shows a limit or end : dividing line

bound·en \'baún-dən\ *adj* **1** *archaic* : INDEBTED **2** : required as if by law : NECESSARY ⟨our *bounden* duty⟩

bound·less \'baúnd-ləs\ *adj* : having no boundaries or limits : VAST ⟨the *boundless* sky⟩ — **bound·less·ly** *adv* — **bound·less·ness** *n*

boun·te·ous \'baúnt-ē-əs\ *adj* **1** : giving freely or generously ⟨a *bounteous* host⟩ **2** : given in plenty ⟨*bounteous* gifts⟩ — **boun·te·ous·ly** *adv* — **boun·te·ous·ness** *n*

boun·ti·ful \'baúnt-i-fəl\ *adj* **1** : GENEROUS 1 **2** : PLENTIFUL 2 ⟨a *bountiful* supply⟩ — **boun·ti·ful·ly** \-f(ə-)lē\ *adv* — **boun·ti·ful·ness** \-fəl-nəs\ *n*

boun·ty \'baúnt-ē\ *n, pl* **bounties** **1 a** : GENEROSITY 1 **b** : something given generously **2** : money given as a reward (as for killing a harmful animal or capturing a criminal) [Middle English *bounte* "goodness", from early French *bonté* (same meaning), derived from Latin *bonus* "good" — related to BONUS]

bou·quet \bō-'kā, bü-\ *n* **1** : a bunch of flowers **2** : FRAGRANCE, AROMA

¹bour·geois \'bù(ə)rzh-,wä, bùrzh-'wä\ *adj* **1** : of or relating to townspeople or members of the middle class **2** : marked by a concern for comfort, wealth, and what is respectable

²bourgeois *n, pl* **bour·geois** \-,wä(z), -'wä(z)\ : a person of the middle class of society [from early French *bourgeois* "a resident of a town", from earlier *borjois* (same meaning), from *borc* "town", from Latin *burgus* "fortified place" — related to BURGESS, BURGLAR]

bour·geoi·sie \,bùrzh-,wä-'zē\ *n* : the middle class of society

bourn *or* **bourne** \'bōrn, 'bòrn, 'bù(ə)rn\ *n* **1** *archaic* : BOUNDARY, LIMIT **2** *archaic* : GOAL 2, DESTINATION

bour·rée \bù-'rā\ *n* : a lively 17th century French dance

bout \'baút\ *n* **1** : a spell of activity ⟨nonstop *bout* of reading⟩ **2** : a contest of skill or strength between two people ⟨wrestling *bout*⟩ **3** : ²ATTACK 3 ⟨a *bout* of measles⟩

bou·tique \bü-'tēk\ *n* : a small fashionable store [from French *boutique* "shop"]

bou·ton·niere \,büt-ᵊn-'i(ə)r, ,bü-tən-'ye(ə)r\ *n* : a flower or bouquet worn in a buttonhole

¹bo·vine \'bō-,vīn, -,vēn\ *adj* **1** : of, relating to, or resembling the ox or cow **2** : slow-moving or patient like an ox or cow

²bovine *n* : a bovine animal

¹bow \'baú\ *vb* **1** : to bend the head, body, or knee in greeting, respect, agreement, or obedience **2** : ¹YIELD 5 ⟨*bow* to authority⟩ **3** : ¹BEND 6 ⟨*bowed* with age⟩ **4** : to express by bowing ⟨*bow* one's thanks⟩ [Middle English *bowen* "to bend, yield", from Old English *būgan* "to bend in obedience"]

²bow *n* : a bending of the head or body expressing respect, agreement, obedience, or greeting

³bow \'bō\ *n* **1** : RAINBOW **2** : a weapon used for shooting arrows that is usually made of a strip of wood bent by a cord connecting the two ends **3** : something that is curved like a bow **4** : a wooden rod with horsehairs stretched from end to end used for playing a violin or similar instrument **5** : a knot made with two or more loops ⟨tie the ribbon in a *bow*⟩ [Middle English *bowe* "something curved", from Old English *boga* (same meaning)]

⁴bow \'bō\ *vb* **1** : to bend into a curve **2** : to play a

stringed instrument with a bow

⁵bow \'baú\ *n* : the forward part of a ship [probably from Danish *bov* "shoulder"]

bow·el \'baú(-ə)l\ *n* **1 a** : ²INTESTINE, GUT — usually used in pl. **b** : a division of the intestine **2** *pl* : the interior parts ⟨the *bowels* of the earth⟩ **3** *archaic* : supply of mercy or courage — usually used in pl.

bow·er \'baú(-ə)r\ *n* **1** : a safe and private place for rest **2** : a shelter in a garden made of boughs or vines twisted together — **bow·ery** \-ē\ *adj*

bow·er·bird \'baú(-ə)r-,bərd\ *n* : any of various birds of Australia and nearby islands of which the male builds a chamber or passage arched over with twigs and branches and often ornamented with bright-colored objects especially to attract the female

bowerbird

bow·ie knife \'bü-ē-, 'bō-ē-\ *n* : a large hunting knife with a single-edged blade [named for James *Bowie*]

¹bowl \'bōl\ *n* **1** : a rounded dish generally deeper than a basin and larger than a cup **2** : the contents of a bowl **3** : the bowl-shaped part of something (as a spoon or a tobacco pipe) **4 a** : a rounded valley or geographical region ⟨the dust *bowl*⟩ **b** : a bowl-shaped stadium or theater **5** : BOWL GAME [Old English *bolla* "bowl"] — **bowled** \'bōld\ *adj*

²bowl *n* **1 a** : a ball shaped to roll in a curved path for use in lawn bowling **b** *pl* : LAWN BOWLING **2** : a cast of the ball in bowling or bowls [Middle English *boule* "a weighted ball", from early French *boule* (same meaning), from Latin *bulla* "bubble" — related to ²BOIL]

³bowl *vb* **1** : to roll a ball in bowling or bowls **2** : to move smoothly and rapidly **3 a** : to strike with or as if with a swiftly moving object ⟨almost *bowled* over by the wind⟩ **b** : to overcome with surprise : ASTONISH ⟨the news *bowled* him over⟩

bow·leg·ged \'bō-'leg-(ə)d\ *adj* : having legs that bow outward at or below the knee

¹bowl·er \'bō-lər\ *n* : one that bowls

²bow·ler \'bō-lər\ *n* : DERBY 3

bowl game *n* : a football game played after the regular season between specially invited teams

bow·line \'bō-lən, -,līn\ *n* **1** : a rope used to keep the edge of a sail pulled forward **2** : a knot used for making a loop that will not slip or get stuck

bowl·ing \'bō-liŋ\ *n* **1** : a game played by rolling balls so as to knock down pins set up at the far end of an alley **2** : LAWN BOWLING

bow·man \'bō-mən\ *n* : ARCHER

bow·sprit \'baú-,sprit\ *n* : a large pole for sails sticking out from the bow of a ship

bow·string \'bō-,striŋ\ *n* : the cord connecting the two ends of a bow

bow tie *n* : a short necktie tied in a bow

bow window \'bō-\ *n* : a usually curved window that sticks out from the side of a building

¹box \'bäks\ *n, pl* **box** *or* **box·es** : an evergreen shrub or small tree used especially for hedges [Old English *box* "box (shrub)", from Latin *buxus* (same meaning), from Greek *pyxos* "box tree"]

²box *n* **1 a** : a container usually having four sides, a bottom, and a cover **b** : the amount held by a box ⟨ate a whole *box* of popcorn⟩ **2** : a small compartment for a group of spectators in a theater **3** : the driver's seat on a carriage **4** : a shed that protects **5** : a container (as for a car transmission) that resembles a box **6** : a rectangle which encloses and draws attention to something printed **7** : a space on a baseball diamond where a batter, coach, pitcher, or catcher stands [Old English *box* "container", from Latin *buxis* (same meaning), from Greek *pyxis,* literally "a container made from boxwood"]

³box *vb* : to enclose in or as if in a box

⁴box *n* : a punch or slap especially on the ear [Middle English *box* "a blow or slap on the ear"]

⁵box *vb* **1** : to strike with the hand **2** : to engage in boxing : fight with the fists

box camera *n* : a camera of simple box shape with a simple lens and shutter

box·car \'bäk-,skär\ *n* : a roofed freight car usually with sliding doors in the sides

box elder *n* : a North American maple with compound leaves

¹box·er \'bäk-sər\ *n* : one that engages in the sport of boxing

²boxer *n* : a medium-sized dog of German origin with a smooth coat and a short square face

box·ing \'bäk-siŋ\ *n* : the sport of fighting with the fists

Box·ing Day \'bäk-siŋ-\ *n* : the first weekday after Christmas observed as a legal holiday in parts of the British Commonwealth and celebrated by the giving of Christmas gifts in boxes (as to postmen)

boxing glove *n* : one of a pair of padded leather mittens worn in boxing

box office *n* : an office in a public place (as a theater or stadium) where admission tickets are sold

box score *n* : a printed table giving the score of a game (as baseball), a record of how it was played, and the names and positions of the players

box seat *n* : a seat in a box of a theater or stadium

box stall *n* : a four-sided enclosure within a barn or stable in which an animal can move around freely

box turtle *n* : any of several North American land tortoises able to withdraw completely into the shell and to close it by hinged joints in the lower shell

box·wood \'bäk-,swûd\ *n* : the tough hard wood of the box; *also* : the box tree

box turtle

boy \'bòi\ *n* **1** : a male child from birth to young manhood **2** : SON 1a — **boy·hood** \-,hùd\ *n* — **boy·ish** \-ish\ *adj* — **boy·ish·ly** *adv* — **boy·ish·ness** *n*

¹boy·cott \'bòi-,kät\ *vb* : to join with others in refusing to deal with a person, organization, or country usually to express disapproval or to force acceptance of terms

Word History In 1880 there were many crop failures in Ireland. A famine seemed likely, and the tenants on the farm estates were not able to pay their rents in full. The tenants of one estate asked their estate manager, Charles Boycott, to lower the rents to a level they could pay. He refused and tried to have the tenants removed from the property. As a result, the tenants would not work for Boycott. They went further and forced Boycott's servants to leave him, stopped his mail and food deliveries, and even threatened his life. In short, they made his life wretched without using violence. This treatment of Boycott was reported in the papers, and when other tenants used the same treatment against their estate managers, it was called a "boycott" action. The name was soon being used as a noun and a verb. Now when a boycott is called for, it usually means refusing to do business with someone or to buy a certain product. [named for Charles *Boycott* 1832–1897 estate manager in Ireland]

²boycott *n* : the process or an instance of boycotting

boy·friend \'bòi-,frend\ *n* **1** : a male friend **2** : a regular male companion of a girl or woman

Boy Scout *n* : a member of the Boy Scouts of America

boy·sen·ber·ry \'bòiz-ᵊn-,ber-ē, 'bòis-\ *n* **1** : a very large berry like a blackberry with the flavor of a raspberry that is valued for canning **2** : the trailing hybrid bramble that produces boysenberries

bra \'brä\ *n* : BRASSIERE

¹brace \'brās\ *vb* **braced; brac·ing** **1 a** : to make firm or tight **b** : to get ready : PREPARE ⟨*braced* herself for the test⟩ **2** : to furnish or support with a brace **3** : to give life or energy to : FRESHEN **4** : to place firmly ⟨*bracing* his feet in the stirrups⟩ **5** : to regain one's courage ⟨*brace* up, all is not lost⟩ [Middle English *bracen* "to fasten, bind", from early French *bracier* "to embrace", from *brace* "two arms", derived from Latin *bracchium* "arm" — related to BRACELET, BRASSIERE, EMBRACE; see *Word History* at EMBRACE]

²brace *n, pl* **brac·es** *or* **brace** **1** : two of a kind : PAIR ⟨several *brace* of quail⟩ **2** : something that connects, fastens, or tightens **3** : a tool with a U-shaped bend that is used to turn wood-boring bits **4 a** : something that transfers, resists, or supports weight or pressure; *esp* : a slanted timber used as a support in a structure **b** *pl* : SUSPENDER 2 **c** : a device for supporting a body part (as the shoulders) **d** *pl* : a wire device attached to the teeth to make them straight and pull them into position **5 a** : a mark { or } used to connect words or items or musical staffs that are to be considered together **b** : one of a pair of such marks enclosing words or symbols [Middle English *brace* "pair, clasp", from early French *brace* "two arms", derived from Latin *bracchium* "arm" — related to PRETZEL; see *Word History* at PRETZEL]

brace·let \'brā-slət\ *n* **1** : an ornamental band or chain worn around the wrist **2** : something (as handcuffs) resembling a bracelet [Middle English *bracelet* "band for the arm", from early French *bracelet,* literally "little arm", from *bras* "arm", derived from Latin *bracchium* "arm" — related to BRACE, BRASSIERE]

bra·chio·pod \'brā-kē-ə-,päd\ *n* : any of a phylum of marine animals without backbones that have bivalve shells and a pair of arms bearing tentacles — called also *lampshell* — **brachiopod** *adj*

brack·en \'brak-ən\ *n* : a large coarse branching fern; *also* : a growth of such ferns

¹brack·et \'brak-ət\ *n* **1** : a support for a shelf or other weight usually attached to a wall **2** : a short wall shelf **3 a** : one of a pair of marks [ ] used to enclose words or mathematical symbols to be taken together — called also *square bracket* **b** : one of a pair of marks ⟨ ⟩ used to enclose written or printed matter — called also *angle bracket* **4** : ¹CLASS 3a, GROUP; *esp* : one of a series of groups sorted according to income

²bracket *vb* **1** : to place within or as if within brackets **2** : to put into the same class : ASSOCIATE

bracket fungus *n* : a fungus that forms shelflike fruiting bodies

brack·ish \'brak-ish\ *adj* : somewhat salty

bract \'brakt\ *n* : an often modified leaf associated with a flower or a flower stalk

brad \'brad\ *n* : a slender nail with a small often indented head

brae \'brā\ *n, chiefly Scottish* : a hillside especially along a river

¹brag \'brag\ *n* **1** : a boastful statement **2** : overly proud talk or manner **3** : BRAGGART

²brag *vb* **bragged; brag·ging** : to praise oneself or one's possessions or achievements **syn** see BOAST — **brag·ger**

\ə\ **abut**	\aù\ **out**	\i\ **tip**	\ò\ **saw**	\ù\ **foot**
\ər\ **further**	\ch\ **chin**	\ī\ **life**	\òi\ **coin**	\y\ **yet**
\a\ **mat**	\e\ **pet**	\j\ **job**	\th\ **thin**	\yü\ **few**
\ā\ **take**	\ē\ **easy**	\ŋ\ **sing**	\th\ **this**	\yù\ **cure**
\ä\ **cot, cart**	\g\ **go**	\ō\ **bone**	\ü\ **food**	\zh\ **vision**

\\'brag-ər\\ *n*

brag·ga·do·cio \\,brag-ə-'dō-shē-,ō, -sē-,ō, -shō\\ *n, pl* **-cios** **1** : BRAGGART **2** : loud and empty boasting [from *Braggadochio*, a boasting character in literature]

brag·gart \\'brag-ərt\\ *n* : a person who brags a lot — **brag·gart** *adj*

Brah·man *or* **Brah·min** *n* **1** \\'bräm-ən\\ : a member of the highest priestly class of Hindu society **2** \\'brām-ən, 'bräm-ən, 'bram-ən\\ : any of an Indian breed of humped cattle : ZEBU

¹braid \\'brād\\ *vb* **1** : to form strands into a braid **2** : to ornament especially with ribbon or braid — **braid·er** *n*

²braid *n* : a length of cord, ribbon, or hair formed of three or more strands woven together

braille \\'brā(ə)l\\ *n, often cap* : a system of writing for the blind in which letters are represented by raised dots [named for Louis *Braille* who developed the system]

a	b	c	d	e	f	g	h	i	j
1	2	3	4	5	6	7	8	9	0

k	l	m	n	o	p	q	r	s	t

u	v	x	y	z	w		Capital Sign	Numeral Sign

braille alphabet

¹brain \\'brān\\ *n* **1 a** : the portion of the central nervous system of animals with backbones that is the organ of thought and the central control point for the nervous system, is enclosed within the skull, and is continuous with the spinal cord **b** : a major nervous center in an animal without a backbone **2 a** : INTELLIGENCE 1 — often used in pl. **b** : a very intelligent person — **brainlike** *adj*

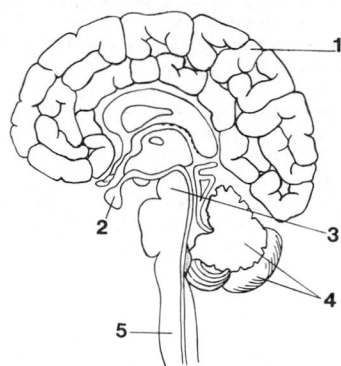

brain 1a: *1* cerebrum, *2* pituitary gland, *3* midbrain, *4* cerebellum, *5* spinal cord

²brain *vb* **1** : to kill by smashing the skull **2** : to hit on the head

brain·case \\'brān-,kās\\ *n* : the cranium enclosing the brain

brain death *n* : the final stopping of activity in the central nervous system as indicated by an electroencephalogram showing no brain waves for a set length of time that is often used as a criterion for human death — **brain–dead** \\'brān-,ded\\ *adj*

brain·less \\'brān-ləs\\ *adj* : UNINTELLIGENT, SILLY — **brain·less·ly** *adv* — **brain·less·ness** *n*

brain stem *n* : the back and lower part of the brain including the midbrain and medulla oblongata

brain·storm \\'brān-,stȯ(ə)rm\\ *n* **1** : a temporary violent attack of mental illness **2** : a sudden inspiration or idea

brain·storm·ing \\-,stȯrm-iŋ\\ *n* : a technique used to solve problems and encourage creativity in which members of a group share their ideas about a subject — **brain·storm** *vb*

brain·teas·er \\-,tē-zər\\ *n* : something demanding mental effort for its solution : PUZZLE

brain·wash \\-,wȯsh, -,wäsh\\ *vb* **1** : to try to change someone's ideas by force ⟨terrorists *brainwashed* the prisoners⟩ **2** : to try to influence someone's habits through sly persuading ⟨advertising that *brainwashes* children⟩

brain wave *n* : rhythmic changes in voltage between parts of the brain

brainy \\'brā-nē\\ *adj* **brain·i·er; -est** : INTELLIGENT 1 — **brain·i·ness** *n*

braise \\'brāz\\ *vb* **braised; brais·ing** : to cook slowly in fat and little moisture in a covered pot

¹brake \\'brāk\\ *n* : a coarse fern often growing several feet high : BRACKEN

²brake *n* : a device for slowing or stopping motion (as of a wheel, vehicle, or engine) especially by friction

³brake *vb* **braked; brak·ing** **1** : to slow or stop by or as if by a brake **2** : to use or operate the brake on a vehicle

⁴brake *n* : rough or marshy overgrown land : THICKET

brake·man \\'brāk-mən\\ *n* : a member of a train crew who inspects the train and assists the conductor

bram·ble \\'bram-bəl\\ *n* : any of a large genus of usually prickly shrubs (as a raspberry or blackberry) that are related to roses — **bram·bly** \\-b(ə-)lē\\ *adj*

bran \\'bran\\ *n* : the broken coat of the seed of a cereal grain left after the grain has been ground and the flour or meal sifted out

¹branch \\'branch\\ *n* **1** : a natural division of a plant stem (as a bough growing from a trunk or twig from a bough) **2** : something extending from a main line or source ⟨river *branch*⟩ ⟨a railroad *branch*⟩ **3** : a separate or subordinate division or part of a central system ⟨executive *branch* of the government⟩ ⟨a *branch* of a bank⟩ — **branched** \\'brancht\\ *adj* — **branch·less** \\'branch-ləs\\ *adj*

²branch *vb* **1** : to send out branches : spread or separate into branches ⟨a great elm *branches* over the yard⟩ **2** : to spring out from a main body or line : DIVERGE ⟨streets *branching* off the highway⟩ **3** : to extend activities ⟨the business is *branching* out all over the state⟩

¹brand \\'brand\\ *n* **1** : a burnt or burning piece of wood **2 a** : a mark made by burning (as on cattle) or by stamping or printing (as on manufactured goods) to show ownership, maker, or quality **b** : TRADEMARK **3 a** : a mark once put on criminals with a hot iron **b** : a mark of disgrace : STIGMA **4 a** : a class of goods identified as the product of a single maker **b** : a particular kind : VARIETY

²brand *vb* **1** : to mark with or as if with a brand **2** : to mark with disapproval : STIGMATIZE

bran·dish \\'bran-dish\\ *vb* : to shake or wave in a threatening or excited manner ⟨*brandish* a stick at a dog⟩

brand–new \\'bran-'n(y)ü\\ *adj* : completely new and unused

bran·dy \\'bran-dē\\ *n, pl* **brandies** : an alcoholic liquor made from wine or fruit juice

brash \\'brash\\ *adj* **1** : RECKLESS, RASH ⟨a *brash* attack⟩ **2** : rudely bold : IMPUDENT ⟨a *brash* youth⟩ — **brash·ly** *adv* — **brash·ness** *n*

brass \\'bras\\ *n* **1** : an alloy containing copper and zinc **2** : the reddish yellow color of brass **3** : the brass instruments of a band or orchestra — often used in pl. **4** : bright metal ornaments, fixtures, or utensils **5** : bold self-assurance : GALL **6** : high-ranking officers especially in the armed forces — **brass** *adj*

brass band *n* : a band made up of brass and percussion instruments

bras·siere \\brə-'zi(ə)r *also* ,bras-ē-'e(ə)r\\ *n* : a woman's close-fitting undergarment having cups for breast support [from obsolete French *brassière* "corset", from early

French *braciere* "arm protector", from *bras* "arm", from Latin *bracchium* (same meaning) — related to BRACE, BRACELET]

brass instrument *n* : any of a group of musical instruments made of curved tubes of brass in various shapes that includes trumpets, trombones, tubas, and French horns — compare PERCUSSION INSTRUMENT, STRINGED INSTRUMENT, WOODWIND 1

brassy \'bras-ē\ *adj* **brass·i·er; -est** **1** : IMPUDENT, SHAMELESS **2** : resembling brass especially in color **3** : resembling the sound of a brass instrument — **brass·i·ly** \'bras-ə-lē\ *adv* — **brass·i·ness** \'bras-ē-nəs\ *n*

brat \'brat\ *n* **1** : CHILD 2a; *esp* : an ill-mannered annoying child — **brat·tish** \'brat-ish\ *adj* — **brat·ty** \'brat-ē\ *adj*

bra·va·do \brə-'väd-ō\ *n, pl* **-does** *or* **-dos** : a display of reckless or pretended bravery

¹brave \'brāv\ *adj* **1** : feeling or displaying no fear : COURAGEOUS **2** : making a fine show : SPLENDID ⟨*brave* banners flying in the wind⟩ — **brave·ly** *adv*

²brave *vb* **braved; brav·ing** : to face or bear with courage ⟨pioneers who *braved* the dangers of the frontier⟩

³brave *n* : a North American Indian warrior

brav·ery \'brāv-(ə-)rē\ *n, pl* **-er·ies** **1 a** : fine clothes **b** : impressive or showy display **2** : the quality or state of being brave : FEARLESSNESS **syn** see COURAGE

¹bra·vo \'bräv-ō\ *n, pl* **bravos** *or* **bravoes** : VILLAIN 2, DESPERADO; *esp* : a hired assassin

²bra·vo \'bräv-ō, brä-'vō\ *n, pl* **bravos** : a shout of approval — often used to applaud a performance

brawl \'brȯl\ *vb* **1** : to quarrel noisily : WRANGLE **2** : to make a loud confused noise — **brawl** *n* — **brawl·er** *n*

brawn \'brȯn\ *n* **1** : full strong muscles **2** : muscular strength **3** *British* : the meat of a boar — **brawn·i·ness** \'brȯ-nē-nəs\ *n* — **brawny** \'brȯ-nē\ *adj*

bray \'brā\ *vb* **1** : to utter the loud harsh cry of a donkey **2** : to produce a sound like the call of a donkey — **bray** *n*

braze \'brāz\ *vb* **brazed; braz·ing** : to join metals with an alloy that melts at a lower temperature than that of the metals joined

¹bra·zen \'brāz-ᵊn\ *adj* **1** : made of brass **2** : sounding harsh and loud like struck brass **3** : not ashamed of or embarrassed by one's bad behavior : IMPUDENT **4** : of the color of polished brass — **bra·zen·ly** *adv* — **bra·zen·ness** \'brāz-ᵊn-(n)əs\ *n*

²brazen *vb* **bra·zened; bra·zen·ing** \'brāz-niŋ, -ᵊn-iŋ\ : to face boldly or defiantly

bra·zier \'brā-zhər\ *n* **1** : a pan for holding burning coals **2** : a utensil on which food is grilled

Bra·zil nut \brə-ˌzil-\ *n* : one of the 3-sided oily edible nuts that occur packed inside the round fruit of a large Brazilian tree

Brazil nut

¹breach \'brēch\ *n* **1** : violation of a law, duty, or tie ⟨a *breach* of trust⟩ **2 a** : a broken or torn condition or area **b** : a gap (as in a wall) made by breaking through **3** : a break in friendly relations

²breach *vb* **1** : to make a breach in **2** : ¹BREAK 2, VIOLATE ⟨*breach* an agreement⟩

¹bread \'bred\ *n* **1** : a baked food made of flour or meal **2** : FOOD 1 **3** *slang* : MONEY 1a

²bread *vb* : to cover food with beaten egg and bread crumbs before cooking ⟨*breaded* pork chop⟩

bread–and–butter \ˌbred-ᵊn-'bət-ər\ *adj* **1 a** : concerned with or being as basic as earning a living ⟨*bread-and-butter* economic issues⟩ **b** : DEPENDABLE ⟨*bread-and-butter* products that always sell⟩ **2** : sent or given as thanks for hospitality ⟨a *bread-and-butter* note⟩

bread·bas·ket \'bred-ˌbas-kət\ *n* **1** : a major cereal-producing region **2** *slang* : ¹STOMACH 1

bread·fruit \-ˌfrüt\ *n* : a round usually seedless fruit that resembles bread in color and texture when baked; *also* : a tall tropical tree that is related to the mulberry and bears this fruit

bread·line \-ˌlīn\ *n* : a line of people waiting to receive free food

bread·stuff \-ˌstəf\ *n* **1** : ¹FLOUR 1, GRAIN **2** : ¹BREAD 1

breadth \'bredth, 'bretth, 'breth\ *n* **1** : distance from side to side : WIDTH **2 a** : something of full width **b** : a wide area **3** : ¹SCOPE 2

bread·win·ner \'bred-ˌwin-ər\ *n* : a person whose wages provide support for his or her family

breadfruit

¹break \'brāk\ *vb* **broke** \'brōk\; **bro·ken** \'brō-kən\; **break·ing** **1a** : to separate into parts suddenly or forcibly ⟨*break* a stick⟩ ⟨glass *breaks* easily⟩ ⟨*break* a bone⟩ **b** : to fracture a bone of ⟨*broke* her arm⟩ **c** : to curl over and fall apart ⟨waves *breaking* against the shore⟩ **2** : to fail to keep : VIOLATE ⟨*broke* the law⟩ ⟨*break* a promise⟩ **3 a** : to force a way ⟨burglars *broke* into the house⟩ ⟨*break* out of jail⟩ **b** : to appear or burst forth suddenly ⟨day was *breaking* in the east⟩ ⟨the storm *broke*⟩ ⟨pandemonium *broke* loose⟩ **c** : to become fair ⟨wait for the weather to *break*⟩ **d** : to run suddenly ⟨*break* for cover⟩ **e** : to penetrate the surface of ⟨fish *breaking* water⟩ **4** : to cut into and turn over the surface of ⟨*break* ground for a new school⟩ **5 a** : to defeat completely : CRUSH ⟨*broke* the revolt⟩ **b** : to lose or cause to lose health, strength, or spirit ⟨*broke* under the strain⟩ ⟨*broken* by grief⟩ ⟨the prisoner *broke* down and confessed⟩ **c** : to lose the ability to function because of damage, wear, or strain ⟨the TV set is *broken*⟩ ⟨my watch *broke*⟩ **6** : to reduce in rank **7 a** : to bring to an end : STOP ⟨*break* a habit⟩ ⟨*broke* silence⟩ **b** : to have or cause an interruption ⟨we'll *break* to let local stations identify themselves⟩ ⟨*broke* in with a comment⟩ **8** : to train an animal ⟨*break* a horse to the saddle⟩ **9** : to make known ⟨*break* the news⟩ **10** : to turn aside or lessen the force of ⟨the bushes *broke* his fall⟩ **11** : to do better than ⟨*broke* the school record⟩ **12** : ²OPEN 1a ⟨*break* an electric circuit⟩ ⟨*broke* the shotgun to load it⟩ **13** : SOLVE ⟨*broke* the code⟩ **14 a** : to curve, drop, or change direction sharply ⟨the pitch *broke* over the plate for a strike⟩ **b** : to change sharply in tone, pitch, or intensity ⟨her voice *broke*⟩ — **break·able** \'brā-kə-bəl\ *adj* — **break camp** : to pack up and leave a camp or campsite — **break even** : to reach a point (as in running a business) where profits match losses — **break into** **1** : to begin suddenly ⟨*broke into* a trot⟩ **2** : to get a start ⟨*break into* show business⟩ — **break the ice** : to make a beginning especially in friendly relations — **break wind** : to expel gas from the intestine

²break *n* **1** : an act, action, or result of breaking **2** : a gap in an electric circuit interrupting the flow of current **3 a** : a short rest from or an interruption of work, duty, or studies **b** : a planned interruption in a radio or television program **c** : a noticeable change (as in a surface, course, movement, or direction) **d** : a sudden run : DASH **4** : a place or situation at which a break occurs : GAP **5** : a stroke of luck ⟨a bad *break*⟩; *esp* : a stroke of good luck ⟨got all the *breaks*⟩

break·age \'brā-kij\ *n* **1 a** : the action of breaking **b** : a quantity broken **2** : an allowance for things broken

break·down \'brāk-,daun\ *n* **1 a** : a failure to function properly **b** : a physical, mental, or nervous collapse **2** : DECOMPOSITION **3** : division into categories : CLASSIFICATION

break down \'brāk-'daun\ *vb* **1** : to stop working properly ⟨the car *broke down* on the highway⟩ **2 a** : to separate (as a chemical compound) into simpler substances : DECOMPOSE **b** : to go through decomposition **3** : to separate or become separated into parts or groups ⟨this report *breaks down* into three sections⟩

break·er \'brā-kər\ *n* **1** : a person or thing that breaks something **2** : a wave breaking into foam against the shore

break·fast \'brek-fəst\ *n* : the first meal of the day — **breakfast** *vb*

break–in \'brā-,kin\ *n* : an act or instance of breaking in

break in \(')brā-'kin\ *vb* **1** : to enter a house or building by force **2 a** : to make used to an activity ⟨*breaking in* a new employee⟩ **b** : to overcome the newness or stiffness of ⟨*breaking in* a new pair of shoes⟩

break·neck \,brāk-,nek\ *adj* : very fast or dangerous ⟨*breakneck* speed⟩

break off *vb* : to stop suddenly

break out *vb* **1** : to develop or erupt suddenly and with force ⟨fire *broke out*⟩ ⟨a riot *broke out*⟩ **2** : to develop a skin rash ⟨*broke out* with the measles⟩

break·through \'brāk-,thrü\ *n* : a sudden advance in knowledge or technique ⟨a *breakthrough* in medical science⟩

break·up \'brā-,kəp\ *n* : an act or an instance of breaking up

break up \(')brā-'kəp\ *vb* **1** : to separate into parts ⟨enzymes help *break up* protein molecules⟩ **2** : to bring or come to an end ⟨the police *broke up* the demonstration⟩ ⟨the party began to *break up*⟩ **3** : to end a romance ⟨they dated for a while but *broke up*⟩ **4** : to go or cause to go into a fit of laughter ⟨that joke always *breaks* me *up*⟩

break·wa·ter \'brāk-,wot-ər, -,wät-\ *n* : an offshore structure (as a wall) to protect a harbor or beach from the force of waves

bream \'brim, 'brēm\ *n, pl* **bream** *or* **breams** : any of various mostly freshwater spiny-finned fishes; *esp* : any of several sunfishes (as a bluegill)

¹breast \'brest\ *n* **1** : either of two milk-producing organs situated on the front of the chest in the human female and some other mammals; *also* : MAMMARY GLAND **2** : the front part of the body between the neck and the abdomen **3** : the center of emotion **4** : something resembling a breast — **breast·ed** \'bres-təd\ *adj*

²breast *vb* : to face or oppose bravely : CONFRONT ⟨*breasted* the waves⟩ ⟨*breast* a storm⟩

breast·bone \'bres(t)-'bōn, -,bōn\ *n* : STERNUM

breast–feed \'brest-,fēd\ *vb* **-fed** \-,fed\; **-feed·ing** : to feed a baby from a mother's breast

breast·plate \'bres(t)-,plāt\ *n* : metal armor for covering the breast

breast·stroke \'bres(t)-,strōk\ *n* : a swimming stroke performed by extending the arms in front of the head while drawing the knees forward and outward and then sweeping the arms back with palms out while kicking backward and outward

breast·work \'brest-,wərk\ *n* : a wall thrown together to serve as a defense in battle

breath \'breth\ *n* **1 a** : air filled with a fragrance or odor **b** : a slight indication : SUGGESTION ⟨a faint *breath* of scandal⟩ **2 a** : the ability to breathe **b** : an act of breathing **c** : BREATHER 2 **3** : a slight breeze **4 a** : air inhaled and exhaled in breathing **b** : something (as moisture on a cold surface) produced by breathing **5** : a spoken sound

— **out of breath** : breathing very rapidly (as from hard exercise)

breathe \'brēth\ *vb* **breathed; breath·ing** **1** : to draw air into and expel it from the lungs **2** : ¹LIVE 1 **3** : to blow softly **4** : to send out by exhaling ⟨*breathe* a sigh of relief⟩ **5** : to bring by or as if by breathing ⟨*breathe* new life into the movement⟩ **6** : to say quietly or softly ⟨don't *breathe* a word to anybody⟩ **7** : to allow to rest after hard work ⟨*breathe* a horse⟩ **8** : to take in in breathing **9** : to allow air or moisture to pass through ⟨a fabric that *breathes*⟩ — **breath·able** \'brē-thə-bəl\ *adj*

breath·er \'brē-thər\ *n* **1** : one that breathes **2** : a pause for rest : BREAK

breath·less \'breth-ləs\ *adj* **1 a** : not breathing **b** : ¹DEAD 1 **2 a** : panting or gasping for breath **b** : BREATHTAKING 1 **3** : difficult to bear because of lack of fresh air or breeze ⟨a hot *breathless* day⟩ **breath·less·ly** *adv* — **breath·less·ness** *n*

breath·tak·ing \'breth-,tā-kiŋ\ *adj* **1** : making one out of breath ⟨*breathtaking* speed⟩ **2** : EXCITING, THRILLING ⟨*breathtaking* beauty⟩ — **breath·tak·ing·ly** \-kiŋ-lē\ *adv*

brec·cia \'brech-(ē-)ə\ *n* : a rock consisting of sharp pieces surrounded by a fine-grained material

breech \'brēch\ *n* **1**
pl \'brich-əz\ *also* 'brē-chəz\ **a** : short trousers fitting snugly at or just below the knee **b** : PANTS 1 **2** : BUTTOCK 2 **3** : the part of a gun at the rear of the barrel

breech 3

breech·cloth \-,klóth\ *n* : LOINCLOTH

breech·clout \'brēch-,klaut\ *n* : LOINCLOTH [from *breech* and *clout* "cloth"]

breech presentation *n* : the appearance of the feet or buttocks of the fetus first at the mouth of the uterus before the rest of the body during the process of birth

¹breed \'brēd\ *vb* **bred** \'bred\; **breed·ing** **1** : to produce or increase (plants or animals) by sexual reproduction ⟨*breed* cattle⟩ **2** : to produce offspring by sexual reproduction **3** : BRING UP 1, TRAIN ⟨born and *bred* in this town⟩ **4** : BRING ABOUT, CAUSE ⟨familiarity *breeds* contempt⟩ **5** : to produce (a fissionable element) by bombarding an element that is not fissionable with neutrons from a radioactive element so that more fissionable material is produced than is used up — **breed·er** *n*

²breed *n* **1** : a kind of plant or animal that is found only under human care and is different from related kinds ⟨a beef *breed* of cattle⟩ **2** : KIND, CLASS

breed·ing *n* **1** : ANCESTRY 1 **2** : training especially in manners **3** : the producing and raising of plants or animals by sexual reproduction

¹breeze \'brēz\ *n* **1** : a gentle wind **2** : something easy to do ⟨it was a *breeze*⟩

²breeze *vb* **breezed; breez·ing** **1** : to move quickly and lightly ⟨look who just *breezed* in⟩ **2** : to proceed easily ⟨*breezed* through the test⟩

breeze·way \'brēz-,wā\ *n* : an open passage connecting two buildings (as a house and garage)

breezy \'brē-zē\ *adj* **breez·i·er; -est** **1** : somewhat windy **2** : lively and somewhat carefree — **breez·i·ly** \-zə-lē\ *adv* — **breez·i·ness** \-zē-nəs\ *n*

brethren *pl of* BROTHER — used chiefly in formal or solemn address

Bret·on \'bret-ən\ *n* : a person born or living in Brittany

breve \'brēv, 'brev\ *n* : a mark ˘ placed over a vowel to show that the vowel is short [from Latin *breve, brevis* "short, brief" — related to BRIEF]

bre·via·ry \'brē-v(y)ə-rē, -vē-,er-ē\ *n, pl* **-ries** : a book containing prayers, hymns, and readings especially for priests for each day of the year

brev·i·ty \'brev-ət-ē\ *n* : the condition of being short or brief

¹brew \'brü\ *vb* **1** : to make (as beer or ale) from water, malt, and hops **2** : to try to bring about : PLOT, PLAN ⟨*brew* mischief⟩ **3** : to prepare (as tea) by soaking in hot water **4** : to start to form ⟨a storm is *brewing*⟩ — **brew·er** \'brü-ər, 'brü(-ə)r\ *n*

²brew *n* : a brewed beverage

brewer's yeast *n* : a yeast used or suitable for use in brewing; *also* : the dried ground-up cells of such a yeast used as a source of the vitamin B complex

brew·ery \'brü-ə-rē, 'brü(-ə)r-ē\ *n, pl* **-er·ies** : a plant where malt liquors are brewed

briar *variant of* BRIER

¹bribe \'brīb\ *n* : something given or promised to a person in order to influence a decision or action dishonestly

²bribe *vb* **bribed; brib·ing** : to influence or try to influence by a bribe — **brib·able** \'brī-bə-bəl\ *adj* — **brib·er** *n*

brib·ery \'brī-b(ə-)rē\ *n, pl* **-er·ies** : the act or practice of bribing

bric–a–brac \'brik-ə-,brak\ *n* : small ornamental articles : KNICKKNACKS

¹brick \'brik\ *n* **1 a** : a building or paving material made from clay molded into blocks and baked **b** : a block made of brick **2** : a block shaped like a brick ⟨a *brick* of ice cream⟩

²brick *vb* : to close, face, or pave with bricks

brick·bat \'brik-,bat\ *n* : a piece of a hard material (as a brick)

brick·lay·er \'brik-,lā-ər, -,le(-ə)r\ *n* : a person who builds with bricks — **brick·lay·ing** \-,lā-iŋ\ *n*

brick·work \'brik-,wərk\ *n* : work made of bricks and mortar

¹brid·al \'brīd-ᵊl\ *n* : WEDDING

²bridal *adj* : of or relating to a bride or a wedding

bride \'brīd\ *n* : a woman just married or about to be married

bride·groom \-,grüm, -,grum\ *n* : a man just married or about to be married

brides·maid \'brīdz-,mād\ *n* : a woman who attends a bride at her wedding

¹bridge \'brij\ *n* **1** : a structure built over something (as a river or a railroad) so people can cross **2** : a platform above and across the deck of a ship for the captain or officer in charge **3 a** : something resembling a bridge ⟨*bridge* of the nose⟩ **b** : music that connects the sections of a song or composition **4** : a curved piece serving to raise the strings of a musical instrument **5** : an artificial replacement for one or more teeth in the mouth that is fastened to the remaining teeth or parts of them permanently or can be removed [Old English *brycg* "bridge"]

²bridge *vb* **bridged; bridg·ing** : to make a bridge over or across ⟨*bridge* a gap⟩ — **bridge·able** \-ə-bəl\ *adj*

³bridge *n* : a card game for four players in two teams [origin unknown]

bridge·head \'brij-,hed\ *n* : a position seized in enemy territory as a place to begin a further advance

¹bri·dle \'brīd-ᵊl\ *n* **1** : a device for controlling a horse made up of a set of straps enclosing the head, a bit, and a pair of reins **2** : something that works or is used like a bridle

²bridle *vb* **bri·dled; bri·dling** \'brīd-liŋ, -ᵊl-iŋ\ **1** : to put a bridle on **2** : to hold back with or as if with a bridle ⟨*bridled* her anger⟩ **3** : to hold the head high and draw in the chin as an expression of resentment ⟨*bridle* at criticism⟩

bridle path *n* : a path for horseback riding

¹brief \'brēf\ *adj* : not very long : SHORT [Middle English *bref, breve* "short, brief", from early French *brief, bref* (same meaning), from Latin *brevis* "short" — related to BREVE] — **brief·ly** *adv* — **brief·ness** *n*

²brief *n* **1** : a brief statement of the case a lawyer will present in court **2** *pl* : short snug underpants [Middle English *bref* "formal letter", from early French *bref* (same meaning), derived from Latin *brevis* "summary", from earlier

brevis (adjective) "short, brief"]

³brief *vb* : to give information or instructions to ⟨*brief* the airplane crew⟩

brief·case \'brēf-,kās\ *n* : a flat case for carrying papers or books

¹bri·er *or* **bri·ar** \'brī(-ə)r\ *n* : a plant (as a blackberry or a wild rose) with a thorny or prickly woody stem [Old English *brēr* "thorny plant"] — **bri·ery** \'brī(-ə)r-ē\ *adj*

²brier *or* **briar** *n* : a heath of southern Europe the root of which is used for making tobacco pipes; *also* : a pipe made of brier [from French *bruyère* "heath", from early French *bruiere* (same meaning), probably derived from Latin *brucus* "heather"]

¹brig \'brig\ *n* : a square-rigged sailing ship with two masts

²brig *n* : a place (as on a ship) for temporary imprisonment of offenders in the U.S. Navy

bri·gade \brig-'ād\ *n* **1** : a body of soldiers consisting of two or more regiments **2** : a group of people organized for acting together ⟨a fire *brigade*⟩

¹brig

brig·a·dier general \,brig-ə-'di(ə)r\ *n* : a military commissioned officer with a rank just below that of major general

brig·and \'brig-ənd\ *n* : BANDIT

brig·an·tine \'brig-ən-,tēn\ *n* : a square-rigged ship with two masts but without a square mainsail

bright \'brīt\ *adj* **1** : giving off or filled with much light **2** : very clear or vivid in color ⟨a *bright* red⟩ **3** : INTELLIGENT 1, CLEVER ⟨a *bright* child⟩ ⟨a *bright* idea⟩ **4** : CHEERFUL 1 ⟨a *bright* smile⟩ **5** : full of promise ⟨a *bright* future⟩ ⟨the prospects for the team are *bright*⟩ — **bright** *adv* — **bright·ly** *adv* — **bright·ness** *n*

syn BRIGHT, SHINING, BRILLIANT, RADIANT mean giving off strong light. BRIGHT applies to a light that is strong when compared to other lights from a similar source ⟨a *bright* star⟩ SHINING suggests steady or constant brightness ⟨the *shining* moon⟩ BRILLIANT suggests the giving off of a striking, strong, or sparkling light ⟨a *brilliant* display of fireworks⟩ RADIANT stresses the giving off or the apparent giving off of rays of light ⟨the sun is a *radiant* body⟩ ⟨*radiant* with joy⟩

bright·en \'brīt-ᵊn\ *vb* **bright·ened; bright·en·ing** \'brīt-niŋ, -ᵊn-iŋ\ : to make or become bright or brighter

bril·liance \'bril-yən(t)s\ *n* : the quality or state of being brilliant

bril·lian·cy \'bril-yən-sē\ *n, pl* **-cies** : BRILLIANCE

¹bril·liant \'bril-yənt\ *adj* **1** : flashing with light : very bright ⟨*brilliant* jewels⟩ **2 a** : very impressive ⟨a *brilliant* career⟩ **b** : very smart or clever ⟨a *brilliant* student⟩ ⟨a *brilliant* idea⟩ — **bril·liant·ly** *adv*

²brilliant *n* : a gem (as a diamond) cut so as to sparkle

¹brim \'brim\ *n* **1** : the edge or rim of something hollow (as a container) ⟨full to the *brim*⟩ **2** : the part of a hat that sticks out around the lower edge — **brim·ful** \-'ful\ *adj* — **brim·less** \-ləs\ *adj* — **brimmed** *adj*

²brim *vb* **brimmed; brim·ming** : to be or become full to overflowing ⟨*brimming* with happiness⟩ ⟨eyes *brimming* with tears⟩ ⟨boats *brimming* with tourists⟩

brim·stone \'brim-,stōn\ *n* : SULFUR

\ə\ abut	\au̇\ **out**	\i\ **tip**	\ȯ\ **saw**	\u̇\ **foot**
\ər\ **further**	\ch\ **chin**	\ī\ **life**	\ȯi\ **coin**	\y\ **yet**
\a\ **mat**	\e\ **pet**	\j\ **job**	\th\ **thin**	\yü\ **few**
\ā\ **take**	\ē\ **easy**	\ŋ\ **sing**	\t̲h̲\ **this**	\yu̇\ **cure**
\ä\ **cot, cart**	\g\ **go**	\ō\ **bone**	\ü\ **food**	\zh\ **vision**

brin·dle \'brin-dᵊl\ *n* : a brindled color or animal

brin·dled \'brin-dᵊld\ *or* **brindle** *adj* : having faint dark streaks or spots on a gray or tawny background

brine \'brīn\ *n* **1** : water containing a great deal of salt **2** : OCEAN 1

brine shrimp *n* : any of a genus of crustaceans found especially in salt lakes

brindle

bring \'brin\ *vb* **brought** \'brȯt\; **bring·ing** \'brin-in\ **1** : to cause to come with oneself by carrying or leading especially to the place from which the action is viewed ⟨*bring* a lunch⟩ ⟨*bring* a friend⟩ **2** : to cause to reach a certain state or take a certain action ⟨*bring* water to a boil⟩ ⟨couldn't *bring* myself to say it⟩ **3** : to cause to arrive or exist ⟨winter will *bring* snow⟩ ⟨*bring* legal action⟩ **4** : to sell for ⟨apples will *bring* a good price⟩ — **bring·er** *n* — **bring forth** : to give birth to : PRODUCE — **bring forward** : to carry (a total) to the next line of an account (as in a checkbook) ⟨what is the balance *brought forward*⟩ — **bring up the rear** : to come last

bring about *vb* : to cause to happen : EFFECT

bring off *vb* : to bring to a successful conclusion ⟨I knew you could *bring* it *off*⟩

bring out *vb* **1** : to show off or develop fully ⟨a difficult task seems to *bring out* your best⟩ **2** : to produce and offer for sale ⟨*bring out* a new book⟩

bring to *vb* : to bring back from unconsciousness : REVIVE

bring up *vb* **1** : to bring to maturity through care and education ⟨*bring up* a child⟩ **2** : to bring to attention : INTRODUCE ⟨I hate to keep *bringing* this *up*⟩

brink \'brink\ *n* **1** : the edge at the top of a steep place **2** : a point of beginning : VERGE ⟨*brink* of war⟩ ⟨on the *brink* of disaster⟩

brink·man·ship \'brink-mən-,ship\ *n* : the practice of pushing a dangerous situation to the limit of safety before stopping

briny \'brī-nē\ *adj* **brin·i·er; -est** : of, relating to, or resembling salt water : SALTY — **brin·i·ness** *n*

bri·quette *or* **bri·quet** \brik-'et\ *n* : a piece made from powdery or ground-up material pressed together and molded ⟨charcoal *briquettes*⟩

brisk \'brisk\ *adj* **1** : very active or alert : LIVELY **2** : very refreshing ⟨*brisk* autumn weather⟩ **3** : ENERGETIC, QUICK ⟨a *brisk* pace⟩ — **brisk·ly** *adv* — **brisk·ness** *n*

bris·ket \'bris-kət\ *n* : the breast or lower chest of a four-footed animal

bris·ling *or* **bris·tling** \'briz-lin, 'bris-\ *n* : a small herring that resembles and is processed like a sardine

¹bris·tle \'bris-əl\ *n* **1** : a short stiff hair **2** : a stiff hair or something like a hair fastened in a brush — **bris·tled** \-əld\ *adj* — **bris·tly** \-(ə-)lē\ *adj*

²bristle *vb* **bris·tled; bris·tling** \-(ə-)lin\ **1** : to rise up and stiffen like bristles ⟨makes your hair *bristle*⟩ ⟨quills *bristling* in all directions⟩ **2** : to show signs of anger ⟨*bristled* at the insult⟩ **3** : to appear as if covered with bristles — **bris·tly** \-(ə-)lē\ *adj*

bris·tle·cone pine \,bris-əl-,kōn-\ *n* : an extremely long-lived pine of the western U.S.

Bri·tan·nia metal \bri-,tan-və-\ *n* : a silver-white alloy

bristlecone pine

that is similar to pewter and consists largely of tin, antimony, and copper

britch·es \'brich-əz\ *n pl* : BREECH 1

¹Brit·ish \'brit-ish\ *n* **1 British** *pl* : the people of Great Britain or their descendants **2** : ²ENGLISH 2

²British *adj* **1** : of or relating to the original people of Britain **2 a** : of or relating to Great Britain or the British **b** : ¹ENGLISH 1

Brit·ish·er \'brit-ish-ər\ *n* : a British person

British thermal unit *n* : the quantity of heat required to raise the temperature of one pound of water one degree Fahrenheit at a specified temperature (as 39°F or 60°F) and equal to about 1055 joules — abbr. *Btu*

Brit·on \'brit-ən\ *n* **1** : a member of one of the peoples living in Britain before the Anglo-Saxon invasions **2** : BRITISHER

Brit·ta·ny spaniel \,brit-ə-nē-\ *n* : any of a French breed of long-legged spaniels

¹brit·tle \'brit-ᵊl\ *adj* **brit·tler** \'brit-lər, -ᵊl-ər\; **brit·tlest** \-ləst, -ᵊl-əst\ : easily broken, cracked, or snapped ⟨*brittle* glass⟩ — **brit·tle·ness** \'brit-ᵊl-nəs\ *n*

Brittany spaniel

²brittle *n* : a hard candy made with nuts and spread in thin sheets ⟨peanut *brittle*⟩

brittle star *n* : any of a group of sea animals similar to the related starfishes but having slender flexible arms

¹broach \'brōch\ *n* : any of various pointed or narrowed tools or parts; *esp* : one used for shaping a hole already bored

²broach *vb* **1** : to make a hole in (as a cask) in order to draw off the contents **2** : to bring up for discussion ⟨*broach* a subject⟩ **3** : to break the surface (as of water) from below

broad \'brȯd\ *adj* **1** : not narrow : WIDE ⟨a *broad* stripe⟩ **2** : extending far and wide : SPACIOUS ⟨*broad* prairies⟩ **3** : ¹FULL 2c ⟨*broad* daylight⟩ **4** : very clear : OBVIOUS ⟨a *broad* hint⟩ **5** : not limited : large in range or amount ⟨a *broad* choice of subjects⟩ ⟨education in its *broadest* sense⟩ **6** : not covering the fine points : GENERAL ⟨*broad* outlines of a problem⟩ **7** : pronounced like the *a* in *father* — **broad·ly** *adv* — **broad·ness** *n*

broad·ax \'brȯd-,aks\ *n* : an ax with a broad blade

broad bean *n* **1** : an Old World upright vetch widely grown for its seeds and as fodder **2** : the large flat edible seed of a broad bean

¹broad·cast \'brȯd-,kast\ *adj* **1** : scattered in all directions **2** : made public by means of radio or television

²broadcast *vb* **broadcast** *also* **broad·cast·ed; broad·cast·ing** **1** : to scatter or sow broadcast **2** : to make widely known **3** : to send out by radio or television — **broad·cast·er** *n*

³broadcast *adv* : so as to spread far and wide

⁴broadcast *n* **1** : the act of sending sound or images by radio or television **2** : a single radio or television program

broad·cloth \'brȯd-,klȯth\ *n* : a fine cloth with a firm smooth surface

broad·en \'brȯd-ᵊn\ *vb* **broad·ened; broad·en·ing** \'brȯd-nin, -ᵊn-in\ : to make or become broad or broader

broad jump *n* : LONG JUMP — **broad jumper** *n*

broad–leaved \'brȯd-'lēvd\ *or* **broad·leaf** \-,lēf\ *also* **broad–leafed** \-'lēft\ *adj* **1** : having broad leaves; *esp* : having leaves that are not needles **2** : composed of broad-leaved plants ⟨*broad-leaved* forests⟩

broad·loom \'brȯd-,lüm\ *adj* : woven on a wide loom especially in a solid color ⟨*broadloom* rug⟩ — **broadloom** *n*

broad–mind·ed \'brȯd-'mīn-dəd\ *adj* : willing to accept opinions, beliefs, or practices that are unusual or different from one's own — **broad–mind·ed·ly** *adv* — **broad–mind·ed·ness** *n*

¹**broad·side** \'bròd-,sīd\ *n* **1** : the part of a ship's side above the waterline **2** : a firing of all of the guns that are on the same side of a ship **3** : a sheet of paper printed usually on one side (as an advertisement) **4** : a strongly worded attack ⟨a *broadside* of criticism⟩

²**broadside** *adv* **1** : with one side forward : SIDEWAYS ⟨turned *broadside*⟩ **2** : from the side ⟨hit the car *broadside*⟩

broad·sword \'bròd-,sō(ə)rd, -,sò(ə)rd\ *n* : sword with a wide blade

Broad·way \'bròd-,wā, -'wā\ *n* : the world of the theater in New York City : the New York stage ⟨a big star on *Broadway*⟩ — **Broadway** *adj*

bro·cade \brō-'kād\ *n* : a cloth with a raised design often in gold or silver thread woven into it – **bro·cad·ed** \-'kād-əd\ *adj*

broc·co·li \'bräk-(ə-)lē\ *n* : an open branching form of cauliflower that bears young flowering shoots used as a vegetable

bro·chure \brō-'shù(ə)r\ *n* : a pamphlet containing advertising or descriptive material

bro·gan \'brō-gən, -,gan; brō-'gan\ *n* : a heavy shoe

¹**brogue** \'brōg\ *n* **1** : BROGAN **2** : a low shoe with decorative holes along the seams and often at the toe [from Irish Gaelic and Scottish Gaelic (ancient languages used before English) *brōg,* derived from an early Norse word meaning "leg covering"]

²**brogue** *n* : a dialect or regional pronunciation; *esp* : an Irish accent [perhaps from Irish Gaelic *barróg* "wrestling hold", probably so called from the idea that unusual pronunciations of words come from a person's not being able to move the tongue freely]

broil \'bròi(ə)l\ *vb* **1** : to cook directly over or under heat **2** : to make or become extremely hot ⟨a *broiling* sun⟩

broil·er \'bròi-lər\ *n* **1** : a rack and pan or an oven equipped with a rack and pan for broiling meat **2** : a young chicken suitable for broiling

¹**broke** *past of* BREAK

²**broke** \'brōk\ *adj* : having no money : PENNILESS

bro·ken \'brō-kən\ *adj* **1** : shattered into pieces ⟨*broken* glass⟩ **2 a** : ¹ROUGH 1a, UNEVEN ⟨*broken* terrain⟩ **b** : having gaps or breaks ⟨a *broken* line⟩ **3** : not kept ⟨a *broken* promise⟩ **4** : subdued completely ⟨a *broken* spirit⟩ **5** : imperfectly spoken ⟨*broken* English⟩ **6** : having one parent missing (as because of divorce) ⟨children from *broken* homes⟩ — **bro·ken·ly** *adv* — **bro·ken·ness** \-kən-(n)əs\ *n*

bro·ken–down \,brō-kən-'daùn\ *adj* : WORN-OUT 1, WEAK

bro·ken·heart·ed \,brō-kən-'härt-əd\ *adj* : overwhelmed by grief

bro·ker \'brō-kər\ *n* : a person who acts as an agent in the purchase and sale of property

bro·ker·age \'brō-k(ə-)rij\ *n* **1** : the business of a broker **2** : the fee or commission charged by a broker

bro·mide \'brō-,mīd\ *n* : any of various compounds of bromine with another element or a chemical group including some used as sedatives

bro·mine \'brō-,mēn\ *n* : a nonmetallic element that is normally found alone as a deep red liquid that has two atoms per molecule, gives off an irritating reddish brown vapor of disagreeable odor, and tends to eat into other matter — see ELEMENT table

brom·thy·mol blue \,brōm-,thī-,mòl-, -,mōl-\ *n* : an acid=base indicator

bronc \'bräŋk\ *n* : BRONCO

bron·chi·al \'bräŋ-kē-əl\ *adj* : of, relating to, or involving the bronchi or their branches

bronchial tube *n* : a primary bronchus or any of its branches

bron·chi·ole \'bräŋ-kē-,ōl\ *n* : a tiny thin-walled branch of a bronchial tube

bron·chi·tis \brän-'kīt-əs, brän-\ *n* : inflammation of the bronchial tubes or a disease marked by this

bron·cho·scope \'bräŋ-kə-,skōp\ *n* : a slender tubelike instrument that may be passed through the trachea into the large bronchi and through which the bronchi can be inspected or worked on

bron·chus \'bräŋ-kəs\ *n, pl* **bron·chi** \'bräŋ-,kī, -,kē\ : either of the main divisions of the trachea each leading to a lung

bron·co *also* **bron·cho** \'bräŋ-kō\ *n, pl* **broncos** *also* **bronchos** **1** : an untamed or partly tamed horse of western North America **2** : MUSTANG 1

bron·to·sau·rus \,bränt-ə-'sòr-əs\ *or* **bron·to·saur** \'bränt-ə-,sò(ə)r\ *n* : any of several very large four=footed and probably plant-eating dinosaurs [derived from Greek *brontē* "thunder" and Greek *sauros* "lizard"]

bronchus: *1* trachea, *2* bronchus

¹**bronze** \'bränz\ *vb* **bronzed; bronz·ing** : to make bronze in color

²**bronze** *n* **1** : an alloy of copper and tin and sometimes other elements (as zinc) **2** : something (as a medal or a statue) made of bronze **3** : a yellowish brown color — **bronzy** \'brän-zē\ *adj*

Bronze Age *n* : a period of human culture marked by the use of bronze (as for weapons and tools) that began between 4000 and 3000 B.C.

brooch \'brōch, 'brüch\ *n* : an ornamental pin or clasp worn on clothing

¹**brood** \'brüd\ *n* : a family of young animals or children; *esp* : the young (as of a bird) hatched or cared for at one time

²**brood** *vb* **1** : to sit on eggs in order to hatch them **2** : to cover young with the wings **3** : to think long and anxiously about something ⟨*brooded* over his mistake⟩ — **brood·ing·ly** \-iŋ-lē\ *adv*

³**brood** *adj* : kept for breeding ⟨*brood* mare⟩ ⟨*brood* flock⟩

brood·er \'brüd-ər\ *n* **1** : a person or animal that broods **2** : a heated structure for raising young poultry

broody \'brüd-ē\ *adj* : being in a condition to brood eggs ⟨a *broody* hen⟩

¹**brook** \'brùk\ *vb* : TOLERATE 1 ⟨*brooks* no interference⟩ [Old English *brūcan* "to use, enjoy"]

²**brook** *n* : a small stream [Old English *brōc* "brook, creek"]

brook·let \'brùk-lət\ *n* : a small brook

brook trout *n* : a common speckled cold-water char of eastern North America

broom \'brüm, 'brùm\ *n* **1** : a plant that is related to the pea and has long slender branches along which grow many drooping yellow flowers **2** : a brush that has a long handle and is used for sweeping

broom·stick \-,stik\ *n* : the handle of a broom

broth \'bròth\ *n, pl* **broths** \'bròths, 'bròthz\ **1** : liquid in which food has been cooked **2** : a fluid culture medium

broth·er \'brəth-ər\ *n, pl* **brothers** *or* **breth·ren** \'breth-(ə-)rən, 'breth-ərn\ **1** : a boy or man related to another person having the same parents **2** : a male relative **3** : a fellow member of a group

broth·er·hood \'brəth-ər-,hùd\ *n* **1** : the state of being brothers or a brother **2** : an association of people for a particular purpose **3** : the persons engaged in the same business or profession

broth·er–in–law \'brəth-(ə)rən-,lȯ, 'brəth-ərn-,lȯ\ *n, pl* **broth·ers–in–law** \'brəth-ər-zən-\ **1** : the brother of one's husband or wife **2** : the husband of one's sister

broth·er·ly \'brəth-ər-lē\ *adj* **1** : of or relating to brothers **2** : ¹KINDLY 2, AFFECTIONATE — **broth·er·li·ness** *n*

brougham \'brü-(ə)m, 'brō-əm\ *n* **1** : a light closed carriage **2** : an automobile having no roof over the driver's seat [named for Henry *Brougham* 1778–1868 Scottish judge who designed the carriage]

brought *past and past participle of* BRING

brow \'braů\ *n* **1 a** : EYEBROW **b** : the ridge on which the eyebrow grows **c** : FOREHEAD **2** : the upper edge of a steep slope

brow·beat \'braů-,bēt\ *vb* **-beat; -beat·en** \-,bēt-ᵊn\; **-beat·ing** : to frighten by a stern manner or threatening speech : BULLY

¹brown \'braůn\ *adj* **1** : of the color brown **2** : of dark or tanned complexion

²brown *n* : a color like that of coffee or chocolate that is a blend of red and yellow darkened by black — **brown·ish** \'braů-nish\ *adj*

³brown *vb* : to make or become brown

brown alga *n* : any of a division of mostly marine algae with the chlorophyll masked by brown coloring matter

¹brown–bag \(')braůn-'bag\ *adj* : carried usually in a brown bag ⟨a *brown-bag* lunch⟩

²brown–bag *vb* **brown–bagged; brown–bag·ging** : to carry a brown-bag lunch ⟨*brown-bagging* it to the game⟩

brown bear *n* : any of several bears that are mostly brown in color, are sometimes lumped together in a single species including the grizzly bear, and at one time inhabited much of North America from Alaska to northern Mexico as well as Europe and Asia

brown coal *n* : LIGNITE

Brown·ian movement \,braů-nē-ən-\ *n* : a random movement of microscopic particles in liquids or gases that results from collisions with molecules of the fluid surrounding the particles — called also *Brownian motion* [named for Robert *Brown* 1773–1858 Scottish scientist]

brown·ie \'braů-nē\ *n* **1** : a good-natured elf believed to perform helpful services at night **2** *cap* : a member of the Girl Scouts of the United States of America from six through eight years of age **3** : a small square or rectangle of rich usually chocolate cake often containing nuts

brown·out \'braů-,naůt\ *n* : a reduction in the use or availability of electric power; *also* : a period of dimmed lighting resulting from such reduction

brown rat *n* : the common rat that is found about human dwellings

brown recluse spider *n* : a spider that has been introduced into the southern U.S., has a dark violin-shaped mark on the front half of its back, and produces a dangerous nerve poison — called also *brown recluse*

brown·stone \'braůn-,stōn\ *n* **1** : a reddish brown sandstone used for building **2** : a dwelling covered with a layer of brownstone

brown sugar *n* : sugar whose crystals are covered by a film of purified dark syrup

brown–tail moth \,braůn-,tāl-\ *n* : a tussock moth whose larvae feed on leaves and are covered with long hairs which are irritating to the skin

brown trout *n* : a speckled European trout widely introduced as a game fish

brow·ridge \'braů-,rij\ *n* : a prominent ridge on the bone above the eye caused by sinuses in the skull

¹browse \'braůz\ *vb* **browsed; brows·ing** **1** : to nibble or feed on leaves and shoots **2** : to read or look over something (as in a book or a store) in a light or careless way — **brows·er** *n*

²browse *n* **1** : tender shoots and leaves used by animals for food **2** : an act or instance of browsing

bru·in \'brü-ən\ *n* : ¹BEAR 1 [from *Bruin*, name of a bear in literature, from early Dutch *bruun* "brown"]

¹bruise \'brüz\ *vb* **bruised; bruis·ing** **1 a** : to cause a bruise on **b** : to become bruised **2** : to crush (as leaves or berries) by pounding **3** : to hurt the feelings of

²bruise *n* **1** : an injury (as from a blow) in which the skin is not broken but is discolored from the breaking of small blood vessels that lie underneath the skin : CONTUSION **2** : an injury to a plant or fruit that resembles a bruise

bruis·er \'brü-zər\ *n* : a big husky person

¹bruit \'brüt\ *n, archaic* : ¹REPORT 1a, RUMOR

²bruit *vb* : to spread by report or rumor

brunch \'brənch\ *n* : a late breakfast, an early lunch, or a combination of the two [*br*eakfast and l*unch*]

bru·net *or* **bru·nette** \brü-'net\ *adj* : having brown or black hair and dark eyes — **brunet** *n*

brunt \'brənt\ *n* : the main force or stress (as of an attack) ⟨the *brunt* of the storm⟩

¹brush \'brəsh\ *n* **1** : BRUSHWOOD 1 **2 a** : short trees or shrubs of poor quality **b** : land covered with brush [Middle English *brusch* "broken or cut twigs or branches", from early French *broce* "small broken branches, brushwood"; possibly of Celtic origin]

²brush *n* **1** : a tool made of bristles set in a back or handle and used for cleaning, smoothing, or painting **2** : a bushy tail (as of a fox or squirrel) **3** : a conductor for an electric current between a moving and a still part of an electric motor or generator **4 a** : an act of brushing **b** : a quick light stroke [Middle English *brusshe* "brush (for sweeping)", derived from early French *broce* "brushwood"] — **brush·like** \-,līk\ *adj*

³brush *vb* **1 a** : to clean, smooth, scrub, or paint with a brush **b** : to apply with or as if with a brush **2 a** : to remove with or as if with a brush ⟨*brush* the lint off your coat⟩ **b** : to pay no attention to : DISMISS ⟨*brush* off criticism⟩ **3** : to pass lightly across : touch gently against in passing ⟨twigs *brushed* my cheek⟩

⁴brush *n* : a brief fight or quarrel [Middle English *brusche* "a rush, collision", from *bruschen* "to rush", from early French *brosser* "to dash through underbrush", from *broce* "brushwood"]

⁵brush *vb* : to move quickly past without stopping or paying attention ⟨*brushed* by the reporters⟩

brush–off \'brəsh-,ȯf\ *n* : a quick dismissal

brush up *vb* : to refresh one's memory, skill, or knowledge ⟨*brush up* your Spanish⟩

brush·wood \'brəsh-,wůd\ *n* **1** : small branches and twigs cut from trees or shrubs **2** : a heavy growth of small trees and bushes

¹brushy \'brəsh-ē\ *adj* **brush·i·er; -est** : SHAGGY

²brushy *adj* **brush·i·er; -est** : covered with or full of brush or brushwood

brusque \'brəsk\ *adj* : so short and frank in manner or speech as to be impolite — **brusque·ly** *adv* — **brusque·ness** *n*

brus·sels sprout \,brəs-əl-\ *n, often cap B* : one of the edible small green heads that grow thickly on the stem of a plant related to the cabbage; *also* : this plant

bru·tal \'brüt-ᵊl\ *adj* : being cruel and inhuman : SAVAGE ⟨a *brutal* attack⟩ — **bru·tal·ly** \-ᵊl-ē\ *adv*

bru·tal·i·ty \brü-'tal-ət-ē\ *n, pl* **-ties** **1** : the quality or state of being brutal **2** : a brutal act or course of action

¹brute \'brüt\ *adj* **1** : of or relating to beasts **2** : typical of beasts : like that of a beast ⟨*brute* force⟩ ⟨*brute* strength⟩

²brute *n* **1** : ¹ANIMAL 2a **2** : a brutal person

brut·ish \'brüt-ish\ *adj* : being unfeeling and stupid — **brut·ish·ness** *n*

bry·o·phyl·lum \,brī-ə-'fil-əm\ *n* : an Old World plant that is often grown for its decorative leaves and forms new plants from its leaves — called also *air plant, life plant*

bry·o·phyte \'brī-ə-,fīt\ *n* : any of a division of nonflowering green plants comprising the mosses and liverworts

¹bub·ble \'bəb-əl\ *vb* **bub·bled; bub·bling** \-(ə-)liŋ\   **1** : to form or produce bubbles   **2** : to flow with a gurgling sound

²bubble *n*   **1** : a tiny round body of air or gas in a liquid ⟨*bubbles* in boiling water⟩   **2** : a thin film of liquid filled with air or gas ⟨soap *bubbles*⟩   **3** : a round body of air inside a solid ⟨a *bubble* in glass⟩   **4** : a tiny movable magnetized element of a thin magnetic material that is shaped like a cylinder and can be used to represent a bit of information (as in a computer)

bubble chamber *n* : a chamber of heated liquid in which the path of a charged particle is made visible by a string of vapor bubbles

bubble gum *n* : a chewing gum that can be blown into large bubbles

bub·bly \'bəb-(ə-)lē\ *adj* **bub·bli·er; -est**   **1** : full of bubbles   **2** : showing lively good spirits

bu·bo \'b(y)ü-bō\ *n, pl* **buboes** : an inflamed swelling of a lymph node especially in the groin — **bu·bon·ic** \b(y)ü-'bän-ik\ *adj*

bubonic plague *n* : a form of plague that is spread especially by rats and marked by chills and fever, weakness, and buboes

buc·ca·neer \,bək-ə-'ni(ə)r\ *n* : ¹PIRATE

> **Word History** In the 17th century French hunters living in the West Indies were known as *boucaniers* because they used the native Indian method of preserving meat by smoking it over a wooden grill. The grill was called a *boucan,* after the Brazilian Indian name for it. Pirates operating in this area used the same method of preserving meat, so they also were called *buccaneers,* the English spelling of the French *boucaniers.* [from French *boucanier* "hunter who smokes meat over a grill"]

¹buck \'bək\ *n, pl* **buck** *or* **bucks**   **1** : a male animal; *esp* : a male deer or antelope   **2 a** : ¹MAN 1a   **b** : DANDY 1   **3** *slang* : DOLLAR 3b

²buck *vb*   **1 a** : to spring into the air with the back arched ⟨a *bucking* horse⟩   **b** : to throw (as a rider) by bucking   **2** : to move or act against the action of ⟨*bucking* a storm⟩ ⟨*buck* a trend⟩   **3** : to move or start jerkily — **buck·er** *n*

³buck *n* : an act or instance of bucking

buck·a·roo \,bək-ə-'rü, 'bək-ə-,rü\ *n, pl* **-roos** : COWBOY [an altered form of Spanish *vaquero* "cowboy" from *vaca* "cow", from Latin *vacca* "cow" — related to VACCINE, VAQUERO; see *Word History* at VACCINE]

buck·board \'bək-,bō(ə)rd, -,bò(ə)rd\ *n* : a four-wheeled vehicle with a floor made of long springy boards

buck·et \'bək-ət\ *n*   **1** : a usually round container for catching, holding, or carrying liquids or solids : PAIL   **2** : an object for collecting, scooping, or carrying something   **3 a** : BUCKETFUL   **b** : a large quantity

buckboard

bucket brigade *n* : a chain of persons acting to put out a fire by passing buckets of water from hand to hand

buck·et·ful \'bək-ət-,fùl\ *n, pl* **buck·et·fuls** \-ət-,fùlz\ *or* **buck·ets·ful** \-əts-,fùl\ : the amount a bucket holds

bucket seat *n* : a low seat for one person used chiefly in automobiles and airplanes

buck·eye \'bək-,ī\ *n* : any of several trees or shrubs of the same genus as the horse chestnut; *also* : the large nutlike seed of a buckeye

¹buck·le \'bək-əl\ *n* : a fastening device which is attached to one end of a belt or strap and through which the other end is passed and held

²buckle *vb* **buck·led; buck·ling** \-(ə-)liŋ\   **1 a** : to fasten with a buckle ⟨*buckle* your seat belt⟩   **b** : to fasten a buckle ⟨*buckle* up for safety⟩   **2** : to apply oneself ⟨*buckle* down to the job⟩   **3** : to give way : BEND, CRUMPLE ⟨the pavement *buckled* in the heat⟩ ⟨knees *buckled*⟩

³buckle *n* : a product of buckling

buck·ler \'bək-lər\ *n* : a small round shield worn on the arm

buck·ram \'bək-rəm\ *n* : a stiff fabric used in garments, hats, and bookbindings

buck·saw \'bək-,sò\ *n* : a saw set in a usually H-shaped frame that is used for sawing wood

buck·shot \-,shät\ *n, pl* **buckshot** *or* **buckshots** : a large shotgun pellet

buck·skin \-,skin\ *n*   **1 a** : the skin of a buck   **b** : a soft flexible leather   **2** *pl* : buckskin breeches   **3** : a horse of a dull yellowish color with black mane and tail

buck·tooth \-'tüth\ *n* : a large front tooth that sticks out — **buck–toothed** \-'tütht\ *adj*

buck·wheat \'bək-,hwēt, -,wēt\ *n* : either of two plants with pinkish or greenish white flowers that are grown for their dark triangular seeds which are used as a cereal grain; *also* : the seeds of a buckwheat

bu·col·ic \byü-'käl-ik\ *adj* : ¹PASTORAL 1a, RURAL

¹bud \'bəd\ *n*   **1** : a small growth at the tip or on the side of a plant stem that later develops into a flower, leaf, or new shoot   **2** : a flower that has not fully opened   **3** : a part that grows out from the body of a plant or animal and develops into a new individual   **4** : a stage in which something is not yet fully developed ⟨trees in *bud*⟩ ⟨a plan still in the *bud*⟩

²bud *vb* **bud·ded; bud·ding**   **1 a** : to set or put forth buds   **b** : to reproduce asexually by forming and developing buds   **2** : to be or develop like a bud (as in freshness and promise of growth) ⟨a *budding* diplomat⟩   **3** : to insert a bud from one plant into an opening cut in the bark of (another plant) in order to grow a desired variety by asexual means

Bud·dhism \'bü-,diz-əm, 'bùd-,iz-\ *n* : a religion of eastern and central Asia growing out of the teaching of Gautama Buddha — **Bud·dhist** \'büd-əst, 'bùd-\ *n or adj* — **Bud·dhis·tic** \bü-'dis-tik, bù-\ *adj*

bud·dy \'bəd-ē\ *n, pl* **buddies** : ¹COMPANION 1, PAL

budge \'bəj\ *vb* **budged; budg·ing**   **1** : to change place or position : MOVE, SHIFT   **2** : GIVE IN, YIELD

bud·ger·i·gar \'bəj-(ə)ri-,gär\ *n* : a small brightly colored Australian parrot often kept as a pet

¹bud·get \'bəj-ət\ *n*   **1** : ²SUPPLY 1a, QUANTITY   **2 a** : a statement of estimated income and expenses   **b** : a plan for using money   **c** : the amount of money available for some purpose [Middle English *bowgette* "small leather pouch", derived from early French *bouge* "leather bag", from Latin *bulga* "leather bag" — related to BULGE] — **bud·get·ary** \'bəj-ə-,ter-ē\ *adj*

²budget *vb*   **1** : to include in a budget ⟨*budget* $50 for entertainment⟩   **2 a** : to provide a budget for ⟨*budget* a trip abroad⟩   **b** : to plan as in a budget ⟨*budget* one's time⟩   **3** : to draw up and operate under a budget ⟨*budget* for a new car⟩

budgerigar

bud scale *n* : one of the leaves resembling scales that form the covering of a plant bud

\ə\ **abut**		\au̇\ **out**	\i\ **tip**	\ȯ\ **saw**	\u̇\ **foot**
\ər\ **further**		\ch\ **chin**	\ī\ **life**	\ȯi\ **coin**	\y\ **yet**
\a\ **mat**		\e\ **pet**	\j\ **job**	\th\ **thin**	\yü\ **few**
\ā\ **take**		\ē\ **easy**	\ŋ\ **sing**	\th\ **this**	\yu̇\ **cure**
\ä\ **cot, cart**		\g\ **go**	\ō\ **bone**	\ü\ **food**	\zh\ **vision**

¹buff \'bəf\ n **1** : an orange yellow **2** : a device (as a stick or wheel) with a soft absorbent surface for applying polishing material **3** : ³FAN, ENTHUSIAST ⟨a tennis *buff*⟩

²buff adj : of the color buff

³buff vb : to polish with or as if with a buff

buf·fa·lo \'bəf-ə-ˌlō\ n, pl **-lo** or **-loes** : any of several wild mammals related to oxen: as **a** : WATER BUFFALO **b** : a large shaggy-maned North American wild bovine mammal with short horns and heavy forequarters with a large muscular hump

buffalo b

Word History The Greeks traveled over much of the ancient world. When in their travels they found unusual animals, they gave them Greek names. The African gazelle they called *boubalos*, deriving part of the name from the Greek word *bous*, meaning "ox". Later the Romans borrowed this Greek word, which they used for "gazelle" and for "wild ox". In Latin they spelled it *bubalus* and later *bufalus*. This Latin word for wild ox later passed into Italian as *bufalo* and into Spanish as *búfalo*. From these languages the English picked it up and gave it the spelling *buffalo*. When English settlers arrived in America, they gave the name *buffalo* to the big, shaggy animal that scientists prefer to call *bison*. [from Italian *bufalo* and Spanish *búfalo*, both meaning "wild ox", from Latin *bubalus, bufalus* "wild ox, African gazelle", from Greek *boubalos* "African gazelle", from *bous* "ox, cow" — related to BUTTER]

buffalo grass n : a low-growing native grass of the American plains and prairies

¹buf·fer \'bəf-ər\ n **1** : a device or material for reducing shock resulting from contact **2** : something that serves as a protective barrier **3** : a substance that in solution can neutralize both acids and bases **4** : a temporary storage unit (as in a computer); esp : one that accepts information at one rate and delivers it at another

²buffer vb **buf·fered; buf·fer·ing** \-(ə-)riŋ\ **1** : to lessen the shock of : CUSHION **2** : to treat (a solution) with a buffer; also : to prepare (aspirin) with an antacid **3** : to collect (as data) in a buffer

³buff·er \'bəf-ər\ n : one that buffs

buffer state n : a small neutral state lying between two larger rival powers

¹buf·fet \'bəf-ət\ n : a blow especially with the hand [Middle English *buffet* "a blow with the hand", derived from early French *buffe* "a blow"]

²buffet vb : to pound repeatedly : BATTER

³buf·fet \(ˌ)bə-'fā, bü-'fā, 'bü-ˌfā\ n **1** : a cabinet or set of shelves for the display of dishes and silver : SIDEBOARD **2** : a meal set out on a buffet or table from which people may serve themselves [French]

buf·foon \(ˌ)bə-'fün\ n : ¹CLOWN 2

buf·foon·ery \(ˌ)bə-'fün-(ə-)rē\ n, pl **-er·ies** : foolish or playful behavior

¹bug \'bəg\ n **1 a** : an insect or other creeping or crawling animal without a backbone ; esp : an insect pest (as a bedbug or head louse) **b** : any of an order of insects with sucking mouthparts and incomplete metamorphosis that includes many destructive plant pests — called also *true bug* **2** : an unexpected mistake or imperfection ⟨a *bug* in a computer program⟩ **3** : a disease-producing germ; also : a disease caused by it **4** : ³FAN, ENTHUSIAST ⟨a camera *bug*⟩ **5** : a concealed listening device

²bug vb **bugged; bug·ging** **1** : ¹BOTHER 1, ANNOY **2** : to place a concealed microphone in

bug·a·boo \'bəg-ə-ˌbü\ n, pl **-boos** **1** : an imaginary object of fear **2** : BUGBEAR 2, BOGEY

bug·bear \'bəg-ˌba(ə)r, -ˌbe(ə)r\ n **1** : an imaginary creature used to frighten children **2** : something one is afraid of

bug–eyed \-ˌīd\ adj : having the eyes bulging (as in astonishment)

¹bug·gy \'bəg-ē\ adj **bug·gi·er; -est** : full of bugs ⟨it's too *buggy* out here — let's go inside⟩

²buggy n, pl **buggies** **1** : a light carriage having a single seat and drawn by one horse **2** : a hand-pushed carriage for a baby

bu·gle \'byü-gəl\ n : a brass musical instrument like the trumpet but without valves — **bugle** vb — **bu·gler** \-glər\ n

bugle

Word History In early English the word *bugle* meant "wild ox". The horns from these animals, called *bugle horns*, were used as signaling devices by soldiers and hunters and also as musical instruments. In time they were called *bugles* as well as *bugle horns*. When horns made of copper or brass began to be used for the same purposes, they were called *bugles* too. [Middle English *bugle* "wild ox", from early French *bugle* (same meaning), from Latin *buculus* "young steer"]

¹build \'bild\ vb **built** \'bilt\; **build·ing** **1** : to make by putting together parts or materials : CONSTRUCT ⟨*build* a house⟩ ⟨*build* a bridge⟩ **2** : to produce or create gradually ⟨*build* a winning team⟩ — often used with *up* ⟨*build* up your strength⟩ **3** : to move or grow toward a peak — often used with *up* ⟨excitement was *building* up⟩

²build n : form or kind of structure : PHYSIQUE

build·er \'bil-dər\ n : one that builds; esp : a person whose business is the construction of buildings

build·ing \'bil-diŋ\ n **1** : a permanent structure built as a dwelling, shelter, or place for human activity or for storage ⟨an office *building*⟩ ⟨an apartment *building*⟩ **2** : the art, work, or business of assembling materials into a structure

building block n : a unit of construction or composition

build·up \'bil-ˌdəp\ n **1** : the act or process of building up **2** : something produced by building up

built–in \'bil-'tin\ adj : forming a permanent part of a structure ⟨*built-in* bookcases⟩

bulb \'bəlb\ n **1 a** : an underground resting stage of a plant consisting of a short stem base bearing one or more buds enclosed in overlapping leaves — compare CORM, TUBER 1 **b** : a fleshy structure (as a tuber or corm) resembling a bulb in appearance or purpose **2** : a rounded object or part shaped more or less like a bulb ⟨a flashlight *bulb*⟩ — **bulb·like** \-ˌlīk\ adj

bulb·ous \'bəl-bəs\ adj **1** : having a bulb : growing from or bearing bulbs **2** : resembling a bulb in being rounded or swollen ⟨a *bulbous* nose⟩

Bul·gar·i·an \ˌbəl-'gar-ē-ən, ˌbùl-, -'ger-\ n **1** : a person born or living in Bulgaria **2** : the Slavic language of the Bulgarians — **Bulgarian** adj

¹bulge \'bəlj\ n : a part that swells or sticks out [from early French *boulge, bouge* "leather bag", from Latin *bulga* "leather bag" — related to BUDGET]

²bulge vb **bulged; bulg·ing** : to swell or curve outward

bul·gur \'bəl-gər, 'bùl-\ n : dried cracked wheat [Turkish]

bu·lim·ia \bü-'lē-mē-ə, byü-\ n : a serious eating disorder mainly of young women that is characterized by compulsive overeating usually followed by intentional vomiting or laxative abuse — **bu·lim·ic** \-'lē-mik\ adj

¹**bulk** \'bəlk\ *n* **1** : greatness of size or mass : VOLUME **2** : a large body or mass **3** : the main or greater part — **in bulk** : not divided into parts or packaged in separate units

²**bulk** *vb* **1** : to cause to swell or bulge **2** : to appear as a consideration

³**bulk** *adj* : being in bulk ⟨*bulk* foods⟩

bulk·head \'bəlk-,hed\ *n* **1** : a wall separating compartments **2** : a structure with a sloping door leading to the cellar stairway of a house

bulky \'bəl-kē\ *adj* **bulk·i·er; -est** **1** : large in size or mass **2** : being large and hard to handle — **bulk·i·ness** *n*

bull \'bul\ *n* **1** : an adult male bovine animal; *also* : an adult male of some other large animals (as an elephant, a moose, or a whale) **2** : a person who buys stocks or bonds in the expectation that the price will go up **3** *slang* : POLICE OFFICER — **bull** *adj* — **bullish** \-ish\ *adj*

¹**bull·dog** \'bul-,dog\ *n* : a stocky short-haired dog with a broad square head and forelegs set widely apart that is of a breed developed in England to fight bulls

²**bulldog** *adj* : resembling or suggestive of a bulldog

³**bulldog** *vb* : to throw a steer by seizing the horns and twisting the neck

bull·doze \'bul-,dōz\ *vb* **bull·dozed; bull·doz·ing** **1** : to move, clear, or level with a bulldozer **2** : to force as if by using a bulldozer

bull·doz·er \'bul-,dō-zər\ *n* : a piece of earth-moving equipment that rides on tracks and has a broad blade for pushing (as in clearing land of trees)

bul·let \'bul-ət\ *n* : a usually cone-shaped lead pellet fixed in the front of a firearms cartridge [from early French *boulette* "small ball" and *boulet* "something thrown or shot", from *boule* "ball", from Latin *bulla* "bubble" — related to BILL] — **bul·let·proof** \,bul-ət-'prüf\ *adj*

bul·le·tin \'bul-ət-ⁿn\ *n* : a brief public notice usually from an informed or official source ⟨news *bulletin*⟩

bulletin board *n* **1** : a board for posting notices (as at a school) **2** : a program on a computer system that allows users to read and write public notices and is accessed usually by modem

bullet train *n* : a very high-speed passenger train

bull·fight \'bul-,fīt\ *n* : a public entertainment in which people excite bulls, display daring in escaping their charges, and finally kill them — **bull·fight·er** *n* — **bull·fight·ing** *n*

bull·frog \-,frog, -,fräg\ *n* : a large heavy frog that makes a booming or bellowing sound

bull·head \-,hed\ *n* : any of various fishes with large heads; *esp* : any of several common freshwater catfishes of the U.S.

bull·head·ed \'bul-'hed-əd\ *adj* : STUBBORN 1 — **bull·head·ed·ness** *n*

bull·horn \'bul-,ho(ə)rn\ *n* : a hand-held combined microphone and loudspeaker

bul·lion \'bul-yən\ *n* : gold or silver especially in bars or blocks

bull·mastiff \'bul-,mas-təf\ *n* : a large powerful dog of a breed developed by crossing bulldogs with mastiffs

bull·ock \'bul-ək\ *n* **1** : a young bull **2** : STEER 1

bull pen *n* **1** : a large cell where prisoners are held until brought into court **2** : a place on a baseball field where relief pitchers warm up

bull's-eye \'bul-,zī\ *n* **1** : a round hard candy **2 a** : the center of a target **b** : a shot that hits the center of a target

bull snake *n* : any of several large harmless North American snakes feeding chiefly on rodents

bull·ter·ri·er \'bul-'ter-ē-ər\ *n* : a short-haired ter-

bullterrier

rier of a breed developed in England by crossing the bulldog with terriers

¹**bul·ly** \'bul-ē\ *n, pl* **bullies** : a person who teases, hurts, or threatens smaller or weaker persons

²**bully** *vb* **bul·lied; bul·ly·ing** : to act like a bully toward

bul·rush \'bul-,rəsh\ *n* : any of several large sedges growing in wet land or water

bul·wark \'bul-(,)wərk, -,wòrk; 'bəl-(,)wərk\ *n* **1** : a solid structure like a wall built for defense **2** : a strong support or protection **3** : the side of a ship above the upper deck — usually used in pl. [Middle English *bulwerke* "bulwark", from early Dutch *bolwerc* (same meaning) — related to BOULEVARD]

¹**bum** \'bəm\ *adj* **1** : INFERIOR 3, WORTHLESS ⟨*bum* advice⟩ **2** : unable to work properly : DISABLED ⟨a *bum* knee⟩

²**bum** *vb* **bummed; bum·ming** **1** : to wander around avoiding work **2** : to obtain by begging ⟨*bum* a ride⟩

³**bum** *n* **1** : a person who avoids work and tries to live off others **2** : ²TRAMP 1, HOBO

bum·ble·bee \'bəm-bəl-,bē\ *n* : any of numerous large hairy social bees

bum·mer \'bəm-ər\ *n* **1** : an unpleasant experience, event, or situation **2** : something that fails : FLOP

¹**bump** \'bəmp\ *vb* **1** : to strike or knock against something with force or violence **2** : to move along unevenly : JOLT — **bump into** : to meet especially by chance

²**bump** *n* **1** : a forceful blow, shock, or jolt **2** : a rounded lump; *esp* : a swelling of tissue (as from a blow or sting)

¹**bum·per** \'bəm-pər\ *adj* : unusually large or fine ⟨a *bumper* crop⟩

²**bump·er** \'bəm-pər\ *n* : a device for absorbing shock or preventing damage (as in collision); *esp* : a usually metal bar at the front or back of a motor vehicle

bumper car *n* : a small electric car made to be driven around in an enclosure and to be bumped into others (as in an amusement park)

bump·kin \'bəm(p)-kən\ *n* : ²RUSTIC, YOKEL

bumpy \'bəm-pē\ *adj* **bump·i·er; -est** : marked by bumps or bumping — **bump·i·ly** \-pə-lē\ *adv* — **bump·i·ness** \-pē-nəs\ *n*

bun \'bən\ *n* **1** : a sweet or plain small bread; *esp* : a round roll **2** : a knot of hair shaped like a bun

¹**bunch** \'bənch\ *n* **1** : a number of things of the same kind growing together ⟨a *bunch* of grapes⟩ **2** : ¹GROUP 1, COLLECTION ⟨a *bunch* of friends⟩ — **bunchy** \'bən-chē\ *adj*

²**bunch** *vb* : to gather in a bunch

bunch·grass \'bənch-,gras\ *n* : any of several grasses chiefly of the western U.S. that grow in bunches

¹**bun·dle** \'bən-dᵊl\ *n* **1** : a number of things fastened or wrapped together : PACKAGE, PARCEL **2 a** : a small band of mostly parallel fibers (as of nerve) **b** : VASCULAR BUNDLE

²**bundle** *vb* **bun·dled; bun·dling** \'bən-(d)liŋ, -dᵊl-iŋ\ **1** : to make into a bundle : WRAP **2** : to hurry off : HUSTLE — **bun·dler** \-dlər, -dᵊl-ər\ *n*

bundle up *vb* : to dress warmly

¹**bung** \'bəŋ\ *n* **1** : the stopper in the bunghole of a barrel **2** : BUNGHOLE

²**bung** *vb* **1** : to plug with or as if with a bung **2** : ¹BATTER 1, BRUISE ⟨got *bunged* up⟩

bun·ga·low \'bəŋ-gə-,lō\ *n* : a house with a single story and a roof with a low slope [from Hindi *baṅglā*, literally "(house) in the style of Bengal"]

bung·hole \'bəŋ-,hōl\ *n* : a hole for filling or emptying a barrel

\ə\ abut	\aú\ out	\i\ tip	\ò\ saw	\ú\ foot
\ər\ further	\ch\ chin	\ī\ life	\òi\ coin	\y\ yet
\a\ mat	\e\ pet	\j\ job	\th\ thin	\yü\ few
\ā\ take	\ē\ easy	\ŋ\ sing	\th\ this	\yu̇\ cure
\ä\ cot, cart	\g\ go	\ō\ bone	\ü\ food	\zh\ vision

bun·gle \'bəŋ-gəl\ *vb* **bun·gled; bun·gling** \-g(ə-)liŋ\ : to act, do, make, or work badly ⟨*bungle* a job⟩ — **bungle** *n* — **bun·gler** \-g(ə-)lər\ *n*

bun·ion \'bən-yən\ *n* : an inflamed swelling on the first joint of the big toe

¹**bunk** \'bəŋk\ *n* **1** : a built-in bed (as on a ship) **2** : a sleeping place [probably a shortened form of *bunker*] — **bunk** *vb*

²**bunk** *n* : NONSENSE 1

Word History The word *bunk* is a shortened form of *bunkum*, which came from the name Buncombe County, North Carolina. Around 1820, the congressman for the district in which this county was located decided to give a very long, boring speech to the Congress. This speech had nothing at all to do with what was under discussion. Still he stubbornly made it, just to please the voters of Buncombe County. The word *buncombe* and its other spelling *bunkum* quickly caught on as a name for empty political nonsense. It didn't take long before its use broadened to include any kind of empty or insincere talk or action. In time it was shortened to the more emphatic *bunk*. [short for *bunkum*, from Buncombe County, North Carolina]

bun·ker \'bəŋ-kər\ *n* **1** : a large bin (as for coal or oil on a ship) **2** : a shelter dug into the ground and made strong against attack **3** : SAND TRAP

bunk·house \'bəŋk-,haůs\ *n* : a simple building providing sleeping quarters

bun·ny \'bən-ē\ *n, pl* **bunnies** : RABBIT

Bun·sen burner \,bən(t)-sən-\ *n* : a gas burner consisting typically of a tube with small holes at the bottom where air enters and mixes with the gas to produce a very hot blue flame [named for Robert *Bunsen* 1811–1899 German chemist]

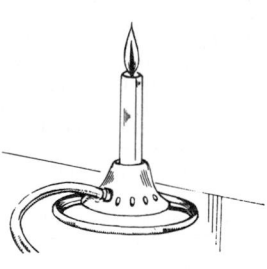
Bunsen burner

bunt \'bənt\ *vb* **1** : to strike or push with the horns or head : BUTT **2** : to push or tap a baseball lightly without swinging the bat — **bunt** *n* — **bunt·er** *n*

¹**bun·ting** \'bənt-iŋ\ *n* : any of various finches that are similar to sparrows in size and habits but have stout bills [Middle English *buntynge* "bunting"]

²**bunting** *n* **1** : a thin cloth used chiefly for making flags and patriotic decorations **2** : flags or decorations made of bunting [possibly derived from a dialect word *bunt* "to sift (meal)"]

¹**buoy** \'bü-ē, 'bói\ *n* **1** : a floating object anchored in a body of water to mark a channel or warn of danger **2** : LIFE BUOY

²**buoy** *vb* **1** : to keep from sinking : keep afloat **2** : to brighten the mood of

buoy·an·cy \'bói-ən-sē, 'bü-yən-\ *n* **1** : the tendency of a body to float or to rise when in a fluid ⟨the *buoyancy* of a cork in water⟩ **2** : the power of a fluid to put an upward force on a body placed in it ⟨the *buoyancy* of seawater⟩

buoy·ant \'bói-ənt, 'bü-yənt\ *adj* **1** : having buoyancy; *esp* : capable of floating **2** : being in a happy mood : CHEERFUL — **buoy·ant·ly** *adv*

bur *variant of* BURR

¹**bur·den** \'bərd-ᵊn\ *n* **1 a** : something carried : LOAD **b** : something taken as a duty or responsibility ⟨tax *burdens*⟩ **2** : something hard to take ⟨a *burden* of sorrow⟩ **3 a** : the carrying of loads ⟨beast of *burden*⟩ **b** : capacity for carrying cargo ⟨a ship of 100 tons *burden*⟩ [Old English *byrthen* "load, burden"] — **burden** *vb*

²**burden** *n* **1** : the refrain or chorus of a song **2** : a main

idea : GIST [an altered form of earlier *bourdon* "a refrain or chorus of a song", from Middle English *bardoun* (same meaning), from early French *bourdon* "bass horn"]

bur·den·some \'bərd-ᵊn-səm\ *adj* : so heavy or hard to take as to be a burden — **bur·den·some·ness** *n*

bur·dock \'bər-,däk\ *n* : any of a genus of coarse herbs that are related to the daisies and have globe-shaped flower heads surrounded by prickly bracts

bu·reau \'byů(ə)r-ō\ *n, pl* **bureaus** *also* **bu·reaux** \-ōz\ **1 a** : a subdivision of a government department ⟨Federal *Bureau* of Investigation⟩ **b** : a business office providing services for the public ⟨travel *bureau*⟩ ⟨credit *bureau*⟩ **2** : a low chest of drawers for use in a bedroom

bu·reau·cra·cy \byů-'räk-rə-sē\ *n, pl* **-cies** **1** : a body of government officials **2** : a system of managing an organization (as a government or business) by strictly following a fixed routine or procedure that often results in delay

bu·reau·crat \'byůr-ə-,krat\ *n* : a member of a bureaucracy — **bu·reau·crat·ic** \,byůr-ə-'krat-ik\ *adj* — **bu·reau·crat·i·cal·ly** \-'krat-i-k(ə-)lē\ *adv*

burg \'bərg\ *n* **1** : a fortress or walled town in the Middle Ages **2** : CITY 1, TOWN

bur·geon \'bər-jən\ *vb* **1 a** : to put forth new growth (as buds) **b** : ²BLOOM 1 **2** : EXPAND 3, FLOURISH

bur·gess \'bər-jəs\ *n* **1** : a citizen of a British borough **2** : a member of the lower house of the legislature of colonial Virginia [Middle English *burgeis* "citizen of a borough", from early French *borjois* "resident of a town", from earlier *borc* "town", from Latin *burgus* "fortified place" — related to BOURGEOIS, BURGLAR]

bur·gher \'bər-gər\ *n* : a person who lives in a borough or a town

bur·glar \'bər-glər\ *n* : a person who commits burglary [from *burgler*, a word meaning "burglar" in the French language used in England during the Middle Ages, from Latin *burglator, burgulator* (same meaning), probably derived from *burgare* "to steal goods by breaking into a building", from *burgus* "fortified place" — related to BOURGEOIS, BURGESS]

bur·glar·ize \'bər-glə-,rīz\ *vb* **-ized; -iz·ing** : to break into and steal from

bur·glary \'bər-glə-rē\ *n, pl* **-glar·ies** : the act of breaking into a building (as a house) especially at night to steal

bur·go·mas·ter \'bər-gə-,mas-tər\ *n* : the mayor of a town in some European countries

buri·al \'ber-ē-əl\ *n* : the act of burying

bur·lap \'bər-,lap\ *n* : a rough fabric made usually from jute or hemp and used mostly for bags and wrappings

¹**bur·lesque** \(,)bər-'lesk\ *n* **1** : a written or dramatic work that makes fun of something by making it appear ridiculous **2** : theatrical entertainment consisting of comic skits and dance — **burlesque** *adj*

²**burlesque** *vb* **bur·lesqued; bur·lesqu·ing** : to mock or make fun of through burlesque

bur·ly \'bər-lē\ *adj* **bur·li·er; -est** : strongly and heavily built — **bur·li·ness** *n*

bur marigold *n* : any of a genus of coarse herbs related to the daisies and having burs that stick to clothing—called also *sticktight*

Bur·mese \,bər-'mēz, -'mēs\ *n, pl* **Burmese** **1** : a person born or living in Burma **2** : the language of the Burmese people — **Burmese** *adj*

¹**burn** \'bərn\ *vb* **burned** \'bərnd, 'bərnt\ *or* **burnt** \'bərnt\; **burn·ing** **1** : to be or set on fire **2 a** : to feel hot or inflamed ⟨the *burning* sand⟩ **b** : to become excited ⟨*burn* with anger⟩ **c** : ¹SCORCH 1 ⟨*burned* the toast⟩ **d** : to appear as if on fire : GLOW ⟨leave a light *burning* in the window⟩ **e** : to destroy by fire ⟨*burn* trash⟩ **f** : to use as fuel ⟨this furnace *burns* gas⟩ ⟨your body *burns* food⟩ **3** : to produce by the action of fire or heat ⟨*burn* a hole in the rug⟩ **4** : to injure or change by or as if by fire or heat ⟨*burn* out a bearing⟩ — **burn·able** \'bər-nə-bəl\ *adj* —

burn·ing·ly \-niŋ-lē\ *adv*

²burn *n* **1** : injury, damage, or effect produced by or as if by burning **2** : the process of burning

burn·er \'bər-nər\ *n* : one that burns; *esp* : the part of a fuel-burning or heat-producing device where a flame or heat is produced

bur·nish \'bər-nish\ *vb* : to make shiny especially by rubbing : POLISH — **bur·nish·er** *n*

bur·noose *or* **bur·nous** \(,)bər-'nüs\ *n* : a hooded cloak worn especially in desert areas (as of northern Africa or eastern Mediterranean countries) [derived from Arabic *burnus* "hooded cloak"]

burn·out \'bər-,naut\ *n* **1** : the ending of operation of a jet or rocket engine as a result of the using up or shutting off of fuel **2** : the point in a flight at which burnout occurs **3** : exhaustion of one's bodily or mental strength

burn out *vb* **1** : to drive out or destroy the property of by fire **2** : to cause to wear out or become exhausted

¹burp \'bərp\ *n* : ²BELCH

²burp *vb* **1** : ¹BELCH 1 **2** : to help a baby expel gas from the stomach especially by patting or rubbing the back

burr \'bər\ *n* **1** *usually* **bur** \'bər\ **a** : a rough or prickly envelope of a fruit **b** : a plant that bears burs **2** : roughness left in cutting or shaping metal **3** *usually* **bur** : a bit used on a dentist's drill **4** : a rough trilled \r\ used by some speakers of English especially in northern England and in Scotland — **burred** \'bərd\ *adj*

bur·ri·to \bə-'rēt-ō\ *n, pl* **-tos** : a flour tortilla rolled or folded around a filling (as of meat, beans, or cheese) and usually baked [American Spanish *burrito* "baked stuffed tortilla", from Spanish *burrito*, literally "little donkey"]

bur·ro \'bər-ō, 'bur-; 'bə-rō\ *n, pl* **burros** : a small donkey often used as a pack animal

¹bur·row \'bər-ō, 'bə-rō\ *n* : a hole in the ground made by an animal (as a rabbit or fox) for shelter or protection

²burrow *vb* **1** : to construct by tunneling **2** : to hide oneself in or as if in a burrow **3** : to move or enter by or as if by digging — **bur·row·er** *n*

bur·sa \'bər-sə\ *n, pl* **bursas** *or* **bur·sae** \-,sē, -,sī\ : a bodily pouch; *esp* : a small fluid-containing pouch between a tendon and a bone

bur·si·tis \(,)bər-'sīt-əs\ *n* : inflammation of a bursa especially of the shoulder or elbow

¹burst \'bərst\ *vb* **burst; burst·ing** **1 a** : to break open or in pieces (as by an explosion from within) ⟨the balloon *burst*⟩ ⟨buds *bursting* open⟩ **b** : to cause to burst **2 a** : to suddenly show one's feelings ⟨*burst* into tears⟩ **b** : to begin to do something suddenly ⟨*burst* into song⟩ **3** : to come or go suddenly ⟨*burst* into the room⟩ **4** : to be filled to the breaking point ⟨just *bursting* with energy⟩

²burst *n* **1** : a sudden release or effort ⟨a *burst* of speed⟩ **2** : a firing of many shots at the same time

bury \'ber-ē\ *vb* **bur·ied; bury·ing** **1** : to place a dead body in the earth, a tomb, or the sea **2** : to place in the ground and cover over for concealment ⟨*buried* treasure⟩ **3** : to cover up : HIDE ⟨*buried* her face in her hands⟩

¹bus \'bəs\ *n, pl* **bus·es** *or* **bus·ses** **1** : a large motor vehicle for carrying passengers **2** : a conductor or group of conductors for collecting electric currents and sending them to outgoing wires

²bus *vb* **bused** *or* **bussed; bus·ing** *or* **bus·sing** : to transport by bus

bus·boy \'bəs-,bȯi\ *n* : a man or boy employed in a restaurant to remove dirty dishes and set tables

bus girl *n* : a woman or girl employed in a restaurant to remove dirty dishes and set tables

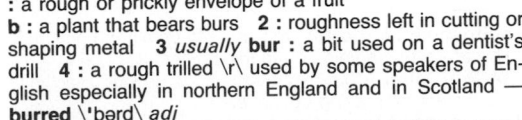

burnoose

bush \'bush\ *n* **1** : SHRUB; *esp* : a low densely branched shrub **2** : a stretch of uncleared or lightly settled country **3** : a bushy tuft or mass

bush baby *n* : any of several small African lemurs

bushed \'busht\ *adj* : ¹WEARY 1, TIRED

bush·el \'bush-əl\ *n* **1** : any of various units of dry capacity — see MEASURE table **2** : a container holding a bushel **3** : a large quantity

bush·ing \'bush-iŋ\ *n* **1** : a usually removable cylindrical lining in an opening of a mechanical part to limit the size of the opening, resist wear (as in a bearing for an axle), or serve as a guide **2** : an electrically insulating lining for a hole to protect a conductor going through the hole

Bush·man \'bush-mən\ *n* : a member of a nomadic hunting people of southern Africa

bush·mas·ter \'bush-,mas-tər\ *n* : a tropical American pit viper that is the largest New World poisonous snake

bush pilot *n* : a pilot who flies a small plane over remote or lightly settled country where commercial airlines don't go

bushy \'bush-ē\ *adj* **bush·i·er; -est** **1** : overgrown with bushes **2** : resembling a bush : being thick and spreading ⟨a *bushy* beard⟩ — **bush·i·ness** *n*

busi·ness \'biz-nəs, -nəz\ *n* **1** : an activity that takes a major part of the time, attention, or effort of a person or group **2 a** : a commercial or industrial activity or organization **b** : the making, buying, and selling of goods and services **3** : something to be dealt with : AFFAIR, MATTER ⟨a strange *business*⟩ **4 a** : personal concern ⟨none of your *business*⟩ **b** : ²RIGHT 2 ⟨you had no *business* saying that⟩

busi·ness·like \'biz-nə-,slīk, -nəz-,līk\ *adj* : having or showing qualities desirable in business

busi·ness·man \'biz-nə-,sman, -nəz-,man\ *n* : a man in business especially as an owner or manager

busi·ness·wom·an \-,swum-ən\ *n* : a woman in business especially as an owner or manager

¹bust \'bəst\ *n* **1** : a piece of sculpture representing the upper part of the human figure including the human head and neck **2** : the upper part of the human body; *esp* : the breasts of a woman [from French *buste* "head and shoulders sculpture", from Italian *busto* (same meaning), from Latin *bustum* "tomb"]

²bust *vb* **bust·ed** *or* **bust; bust·ing** **1** : ¹HIT 1a, PUNCH **2** : to break or smash with force **3** : to ruin or become ruined financially **4** : DEMOTE **5** : to tame an animal ⟨*bust* a bronco⟩ **6** *slang* **a** : ¹ARREST 2 **b** : ²RAID [an altered form of *burst*] — **bust·er** *n*

³bust *n* **1** : ²PUNCH 1 **2** : a complete failure **3** *slang* : a police raid

¹bus·tle \'bəs-əl\ *vb* **bus·tled; bus·tling** \'bəs-(ə-)liŋ\ : to move about busily or noisily

²bustle *n* : noisy or energetic activity

bust·line \'bəst-,līn\ *n* : a line around a woman's body at the bust; *also* : the length of this line

¹busy \'biz-ē\ *adj* **bus·i·er; -est** **1 a** : involved in action : actively at work ⟨too *busy* to eat⟩ **b** : being in use ⟨the

bush baby

line is *busy*⟩ ⟨got a *busy* signal⟩   **2** : full of activity ⟨a *busy* street⟩ — **busi·ly** \'biz-ə-lē\ *adv* — **busy·ness** \'biz-ē-nəs\ *n*

syn BUSY, INDUSTRIOUS, DILIGENT mean seriously involved in doing something. BUSY suggests doing something that requires one's time and attention ⟨*busy* getting the house ready for guests⟩ INDUSTRIOUS suggests working at something steadily or with determination ⟨*industrious* students working on science projects⟩ DILIGENT suggests working toward a particular goal especially over a long period of time ⟨*diligent* scientists accomplished the moon landing⟩

²busy *vb* **bus·ied; busy·ing** : to make or keep busy

busy·body \'biz-ē-,bäd-ē\ *n* : a person who meddles in the affairs of others

¹but \(')bət\ *conj*   **1 a** : except that : UNLESS ⟨it never rains *but* it pours⟩   **b** : ³THAT 1b — used after a negative ⟨there is no doubt *but* he won⟩   **2 a** : while just the opposite ⟨I ski *but* you don't⟩   **b** : yet nevertheless ⟨fell *but* wasn't hurt⟩   **c** : with this exception ⟨no one *but* my sister knows⟩

²but *prep*   **1** : with the exception of ⟨no one there *but* me⟩   **2** : other than ⟨this letter is nothing *but* an insult⟩

³but *adv* : nothing or no more than : ONLY ⟨we have *but* two weeks to get ready⟩

bu·ta·di·ene \,byüt-ə-'dī-,ēn, -,dī-'ēn\ *n* : a flammable gas that is a hydrocarbon used in making synthetic rubbers

bu·tane \'byü-,tān\ *n* : either of two flammable gases that are hydrocarbons obtained usually from petroleum or natural gas and used especially as a fuel

¹butch·er \'bùch-ər\ *n*   **1 a** : one whose business is killing animals for sale as food   **b** : a dealer in meat   **2** : a person who kills in large numbers or in a brutal manner

²butcher *vb* **butch·ered; butch·er·ing** \-(ə-)riŋ\   **1** : to slaughter and prepare for market ⟨*butcher* hogs⟩   **2** : to kill in a barbarous manner : MASSACRE   **3** : to make a mess of : BOTCH

butch·ery \'bùch-(ə-)rē\ *n, pl* **-er·ies** : brutal murder : great slaughter

but·ler \'bət-lər\ *n* : a chief male household servant [Middle English *buteler* "household servant in charge of wines", from early French *bouteillier* "bottle carrier", from *bouteille* "bottle", derived from Latin *buttis* "cask"]

¹butt \'bət\ *vb* : to strike or thrust with the head or horns

²butt *n* : a blow or thrust with the head or horns

³butt *n* : a person who is treated badly or is made fun of ⟨the *butt* of a joke⟩

⁴butt *n*   **1** : BUTTOCK 2   **2** : the thicker or bottom end of something ⟨the *butt* of a rifle⟩   **3** : an unused remainder ⟨a cigarette *butt*⟩

butte \'byüt\ *n* : a hill with steep sides standing in a flat area

¹but·ter \'bət-ər\ *n*   **1** : a solid yellow fatty food made by churning milk or cream   **2** : a substance resembling butter in texture or use ⟨apple *butter*⟩ [Old English *butere* "butter", from Latin *butyrum* (same meaning), from Greek *boutyron,* literally "cow cheese", from *bous* "ox, cow" and *tyros* "cheese" — related to BUFFALO] — **but·tery** \-ə-rē\ *adj*

²butter *vb* : to spread with or as if with butter

but·ter–and–eggs \,bət-ə-rə-'negz, -'nägz\ *n sing or pl* : any of several plants related to the snapdragon and having flowers of two shades of yellow

butter bean *n*   **1** : WAX BEAN   **2** : LIMA BEAN   **3** : a green shell bean especially as opposed to a snap bean

but·ter·cup \'bət-ər-,kəp\ *n* : any of a genus of herbs having cuplike yellow flowers usually with five petals and sepals

but·ter·fat \-,fat\ *n* : the natural fat of milk from which butter is made

but·ter·fin·gered \-,fiŋ-gərd\ *adj* : likely to let things fall or slip through the fingers

but·ter·fish \-,fish\ *n* : any of various fishes with a slippery coating of mucus

but·ter·fly \-,flī\ *n*   **1** : any of numerous slender-bodied day-flying insects with scale-covered often brightly colored wings — compare MOTH, ¹SKIPPER 2   **2** : a swimming stroke performed by moving both arms together in a circular motion while kicking the legs up and down

butterfly fish *n* : any of various fishes having spots or stripes of several colors, broad fins, or both

butterfly weed *n* : a showy orange-flowered milkweed of eastern North America

but·ter·milk \'bət-ər-,milk\ *n*   **1** : the liquid left after the butterfat has been churned from milk or cream   **2** : milk from which all or part of the cream has been removed and which has been soured by adding certain bacteria

but·ter·nut \-,nət\ *n* : the edible oily nut of an American tree related to the walnut; *also* : this tree

but·ter·scotch \-,skäch\ *n* : a candy or dessert topping made from sugar, corn syrup, and water

butt in *vb* : to meddle in someone else's business

but·tock \'bət-ək\ *n*   **1** : the back of the hip which forms one of the fleshy parts on which a person sits   **2** *pl* **a** : the seat of the body   **b** : RUMP 1

¹but·ton \'bət-ⁿn\ *n*   **1 a** : a small knob or disk used for holding parts of a garment together or as an ornament   **b** : a usually round metal or plastic badge   **2** : something (as a small or young mushroom) that resembles a button   **3** : PUSH BUTTON

²button *vb* **but·toned; but·ton·ing** \'bət-niŋ, -ⁿn-iŋ\ : to close or fasten with buttons — **but·ton·er** \-nər, -ⁿn-ər\ *n*

¹but·ton·hole \'bət-ⁿn-,hōl\ *n* : a slit or loop for fastening a button

²buttonhole *vb* **-holed; -hol·ing** : to detain in conversation by or as if by holding on to the clothes of

but·ton·hol·er \'bət-ⁿn-,hō-lər\ *n* : a sewing machine attachment for making buttonholes

but·ton·wood \-,wùd\ *n* : SYCAMORE 2

¹but·tress \'bə-trəs\ *n*   **1** : a structure built against a wall or building to give support and strength   **2** : something that supports, props, or strengthens

²buttress *vb* : to support with or as if with a buttress

bu·tyr·ic acid \byü-,tir-ik-\ *n* : an organic acid with an unpleasant odor found in sweat and spoiling butter

bux·om \'bək-səm\ *adj* : having a healthy plump form — **bux·om·ness** *n*

¹buy \'bī\ *vb* **bought** \'bòt\; **buy·ing** : to get by paying money for : PURCHASE — **buy·er** \'bī(-ə)r\ *n*

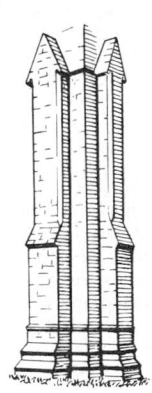

buttress 1

²buy *n* : ¹BARGAIN 2

¹buzz \'bəz\ *vb*   **1** : to make a low continuous humming sound like that of a bee   **2** : to be filled with a low hum or murmur ⟨the room *buzzed* with excitement⟩   **3** : to send for or signal by means of a buzzer   **4** : to fly an airplane low over

²buzz *n*   **1** : a sound of buzzing   **2 a** : a signal given by buzzer   **b** : a telephone call

buz·zard \'bəz-ərd\ *n* : any of various usually large slow-flying birds of prey — compare TURKEY VULTURE

buzz·er \'bəz-ər\ *n* : an electric signaling device that makes a buzzing sound

buzz saw *n* : CIRCULAR SAW

B vitamin *n* : any vitamin of the vitamin B complex

¹by \(')bī, *especially before consonants* bə\ *prep*   **1** : close to : NEAR ⟨*by* the sea⟩   **2 a** : so as to go along or through ⟨*by* a different route⟩   **b** : ²PAST 2 ⟨went right *by* them⟩   **3 a** : AT, DURING ⟨studied *by* night⟩   **b** : not later than ⟨be there *by* 2 p.m.⟩   **4** : through the means or agency of ⟨*by* force⟩   **5** : ACCORDING TO 1 ⟨*by* the rules⟩ ⟨called *by* a different name⟩   **6** : with respect to ⟨a doctor *by* profession⟩   **7** : to or in the amount or length of ⟨win *by* a nose⟩ ⟨sold *by* the pound⟩   **8** : in a series of ⟨walk two *by* two⟩   **9** — used as a function word in multiplication and division and in measurements ⟨divide 6 *by* 2⟩ ⟨a room 15 feet *by* 20 feet⟩   **10** : in the opinion of ⟨it's fine *by* me⟩ — **by oneself** : ²ALONE 2

²**by** \'bī\ *adv*   **1 a** : close at hand : NEAR ⟨lives close *by*⟩   **b** : at or to another's home ⟨stop *by* for a chat⟩   **2** : ⁴PAST ⟨the parade went *by*⟩   **3** : ¹ASIDE 2 ⟨putting some money *by*⟩

³**by** *or* **bye** \'bī\ *n, pl* **byes** \'bīz\ : something incidental — **by the by** : BY THE WAY

by and by \,bī-ən-'bī\ *adv* : before long : SOON

by–and–by \,bī-ən-'bī\ *n* : a future time or occasion

by and large \,bī-ən-'lärj\ *adv* : on the whole : in general

by·gone \'bī-,gȯn *also* -,gän\ *adj* : gone by : PAST — **bygone** *n*

by·law \'bī-,lȯ\ *n* : a rule adopted by an organization for governing its members and regulating its affairs [Middle English *bilawe* "bylaw", probably from an early Norse compound of *bȳr* "town" and *lǫg* "law"]

by·line \'bī-,līn\ *n* : a line at the head of a newspaper or magazine article giving the writer's name

¹**by·pass** \'bī-,pas\ *n* : a passage to one side or around a blocked or very crowded area

²**bypass** *vb* : to make a detour around ⟨*bypass* a city⟩

by·path \'bī-,path, -,pȧth\ *n* : BYWAY

by·place \'bī-,plās\ *n* : a place where few people go

by–prod·uct \'bī-,präd-(,)əkt\ *n* : a product or result produced in addition to the main product or result

by·road \'bī-,rōd\ *n* : BYWAY

by·stand·er \-,stan-dər\ *n* : a person standing near but taking no part in what is happening

by·street \-,strēt\ *n* : a street off a main street

byte \'bīt\ *n* : a group of bits that a computer handles as a unit ⟨an 8-bit *byte*⟩ [possibly an altered form of *bite*]

by the way *adv* : aside or apart from that : INCIDENTALLY ⟨*by the way*, did you hear what happened today⟩

by·way \'bī-,wā\ *n* : a little-traveled side road

by·word \-,wərd\ *n* : PROVERB

¹**Byz·an·tine** \'biz-ən-,tēn, bə-'zan-, 'bīz-ən-; 'biz-ən-,tīn\ *n* : a person born or living in Byzantium or in the Byzantine Empire

²**Byzantine** *adj*   **1** : of, relating to, or typical of Byzantium or the Eastern Roman Empire   **2** : of or relating to a style of architecture developed in the Byzantine Empire especially in the 5th and 6th centuries characterized by a central dome over a square space and by much use of mosaics

C

c \'sē\ *n, often cap*   **1** : the third letter of the English alphabet   **2** : one hundred in Roman numerals   **3** : a musical note referred to by the letter C : the tone on which a C♯ major scale is based   **4** : a grade rating a student's work as fair or mediocre

cab \'kab\ *n*   **1 a** : a light closed carriage (as a hansom)   **b** : a carriage for hire   **2** : TAXICAB   **3 a** : the covered compartment for the engineer and the controls of a locomotive   **b** : a similar compartment on a truck, tractor, or crane [sense 1 from French *cabriolet* "a one-horse carriage", literally "a leap"; sense 2 a shortened form of *taxicab*]

ca·bal \kə-'bal, -'bäl\ *n* : a small group of persons working together secretly (as to take over a government)

ca·bana \kə-'ban-(y)ə\ *n* : a shelter usually with an open side facing the sea or a swimming pool

cab·a·ret \,kab-ə-'rā, 'kab-ə-,rā\ *n* : NIGHTCLUB

cab·bage \'kab-ij\ *n* : a garden plant related to the turnips and mustards that has a round firm head of leaves used as a vegetable

cabbage butterfly *n* : any of several mostly white butterflies whose caterpillars feed on cabbages

cab·bie *or* **cab·by** \'kab-ē\ *n, pl* **cabbies** : CABDRIVER

cab·driv·er \'kab-,drī-vər\ *n* : a driver of a cab

cab·in \'kab-ən\ *n*   **1 a** : a small private room on a ship   **b** : a compartment below deck on a small boat for passengers or crew   **c** : an airplane, airship, or spacecraft compartment for cargo, crew, or passengers   **2** : a small simple dwelling usually having only one story

cabin boy *n* : a boy working as a servant on a ship

cabin cruiser *n* : CRUISER 3

cab·i·net \'kab-(ə-)nət\ *n*   **1 a** : a case or cupboard usually having doors and shelves   **b** : a case for a radio or television   **2** : a group of advisers to the political head of a government ⟨the British *cabinet*⟩ ⟨the president's *cabinet*⟩

cab·i·net·mak·er \-,mā-kər\ *n* : a skilled woodworker who makes fine furniture — **cab·i·net·mak·ing** \-kiŋ\ *n*

cab·i·net·work \-,wərk\ *n* : the finished work made by a cabinetmaker

¹**ca·ble** \'kā-bəl\ *n*   **1** : a very strong thick rope, wire, or chain   **2** : a wire or wire rope by which force is applied to operate a piece of machinery ⟨brake *cable*⟩   **3** : a bundle of electrical wires held together usually around a central core   **4** : CABLEGRAM

²**cable** *vb* **ca·bled; ca·bling** \'kā-b(ə-)liŋ\   **1** : to fasten or provide with a cable   **2** : to telegraph by cable

cable car *n* : a car moved on tracks by an endless cable or along an overhead cable

ca·ble·gram \'kā-bəl-,gram\ *n* : a message sent by a submarine telegraph cable

cable television *n* : a system of television reception in which signals from distant stations are picked up by a main antenna and sent by cable to the sets of paying subscribers — called also *cable TV*

ca·boose \kə-'büs\ *n* : a car usually at the rear of a freight train for the use of the train crew and railroad workers

cab·ri·ole \'kab-rē-,ōl\ *n*   **1** : a ballet leap in which one leg is extended and the other struck quickly against it   **2** : a curved furniture leg ending in an ornamental foot

ca·cao \kə-'kaů, kə-'kā-ō\ *n, pl* **cacaos**   **1** : a South American tree that bears small yellowish flowers followed by fleshy yellow pods containing many seeds   **2** : the dried fatty seeds of the cacao from which cocoa and chocolate are made

¹**cache** \'kash\ *n*   **1** : a place for hiding, storing, or preserv-

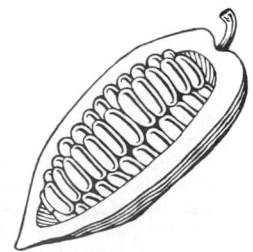

cacao: pod with seeds

ing treasure or supplies   **2** : something hidden or stored in a cache

²**cache** *vb* **cached; cach·ing** : to hide or store in a cache

cack·le \'kak-əl\ *vb* **cack·led; cack·ling** \-(ə-)liŋ\   **1** : to make the sharp broken noise or cry that a hen makes especially after laying an egg   **2** : to laugh or chatter noisily — **cackle** *n* — **cack·ler** \-(ə-)lər\ *n*

ca·coph·o·ny \ka-'käf-ə-nē\ *n, pl* **-nies** : harsh unpleasant sound — **ca·coph·o·nous** \-ə-nəs\ *adj*

cac·tus \'kak-təs\ *n, pl* **cac·ti** \-,tī, -(,)tē\ **cac·tus·es** *or* **cactus** : any of a large family of flowering plants able to live in dry regions and having fleshy stems and branches that bear scales or prickles instead of leaves

cad \'kad\ *n* : a man who does not behave like a gentleman especially toward women [from an earlier dialect word *cad* "an unskilled worker", shortened from Scottish *caddie* (same meaning) — related to CADDIE, CADET; see *Word History* at CADDIE]

ca·dav·er \kə-'dav-ər\ *n* : CORPSE

ca·dav·er·ous \kə-'dav-(ə-)rəs\ *adj* : resembling a corpse: as **a** : ¹PALE 1b, GHASTLY   **b** : ¹THIN 3, HAGGARD — **ca·dav·er·ous·ly** *adv*

cad·die *or* **cad·dy** \'kad-ē\ *n, pl* **caddies** : a person who carries a golfer's clubs — **caddie** *or* **caddy** *vb*

> **Word History** In Scotland in the 18th and 19th centuries, a person who made a living by doing odd jobs was called a *cawdy* or *caddie.* The word *caddie* comes from the French word *cadet,* which was borrowed into English in the 17th century. The chief meaning of *cadet* in both French and English is "a student military officer". The first Scottish caddies formed an organized group, and it may be that the somewhat military structure of the group suggested the name. These caddies looked for odd jobs wherever they could, and after a time the name spread from Scotland into England. Some of the caddies lived near the English universities and took jobs working for students. With scorn the students referred to the lower-class caddies as *cads.* Then they used the term for any person they thought of as having poor manners. That is how we get our modern English word *cad* for "a man who does not behave like a gentleman". Other caddies found jobs carrying clubs for golfers taking up the new game of golf, which began in Scotland. As the popularity of the game grew, so did use of the term *caddie* for one who carries a golfer's clubs. [from Scottish *caddie, cawdy* "one who works at odd jobs", from French *cadet* "one training for military service", derived from Latin *caput* "head" — related to CAD, CADET, CAPTAIN]

cad·dis fly \'kad-əs-\ *n* : any of an order of four-winged insects with a larva which lives in water in a silk case covered with bits of wood or gravel and is often used for fish bait

caddis fly larva

cad·dy \'kad-ē\ *n, pl* **caddies** : a small box or chest; *esp* : one to keep tea in

ca·dence \'kād-ᵊn(t)s\ *n*   **1 a** : rhythmic flow of sounds : the beat of rhythmic motion or activity   **2** : a melodic or rhythmic pattern that serves as the close of a musical phrase or composition — **ca·denced** \-ᵊn(t)st\ *adj*

ca·dent \'kād-ᵊnt\ *adj* : moving in a rhythmic manner

ca·den·za \kə-'den-zə\ *n* : an impressive solo part usually near the close of a musical composition

ca·det \kə-'det\ *n*   **1** : a student military officer   **2** : a student at a military school [from French *cadet* "a younger brother or son, one training for military service", from a dialect word *capdet* "chief, captain", from Latin *capitellum,* literally "little (younger) head or chief", from *caput* "head" — related to CAD, CADDIE, CAPITAL, CAPTAIN, CHIEF;

see *Word History* at CADDIE] — **ca·det·ship** \-,ship\ *n*

Ca·dette scout \kə-'det-\ *n* : a member of the Girl Scouts of the United States of America from 12 through 14 years of age

cad·mi·um \'kad-mē-əm\ *n* : a bluish white metallic element used especially in protective coatings and in storage batteries — see ELEMENT table

cadmium sulfide *n* : a yellow-brown poisonous salt used especially as a pigment in electronic parts, in photoelectric cells, and in medicine

ca·du·ceus \kə-'d(y)ü-sē-əs, -shəs\ *n, pl* **-cei** \-sē-,ī\   **1** : a figure of a staff with two snakes wound around it and two wings at the top   **2** : an emblem bearing a caduceus and symbolizing a physician

caecal, caecum *variant of* CECAL, CECUM

Cae·sar \'sē-zər\ *n* : any of the Roman emperors after Caesar Augustus [from Latin *Caesar* (title of a line of emperors after Caesar Augustus, adopted son of Julius Caesar) — see *Word History* at EMPEROR]

caesarean *variant of* CESAREAN

cae·su·ra \si-'zür-ə, -'zhür-\ *n, pl* **-ras** *or* **-rae** \-'zü(ə)r-(,)ē, -'zhü(ə)r-\ : a break in the flow of sound usually in the middle of a line of verse

ca·fé *also* **ca·fe** \ka-'fā, kə-\ *n*   **1** : a usually small restaurant   **2** : BARROOM   **3** : NIGHTCLUB

caf·e·te·ria \,kaf-ə-'tir-ē-ə\ *n* : a restaurant in which the customers serve themselves or are served at a counter but carry their own food to their tables

caf·feine \ka-'fēn, 'ka-,fēn\ *n* : a bitter stimulating compound found especially in coffee, tea, and kola nuts

caf·tan *or* **kaf·tan** \kaf-'tan, 'kaf-,tan\ *n* : an ankle-length garment with long sleeves that is worn in eastern Mediterranean countries [from Russian *kaftan* "garment"; of Persian origin]

¹**cage** \'kāj\ *n*   **1** : an enclosure that has large openings covered usually with wire net or bars and is used for keeping animals or birds   **2** : an enclosure like a cage in form or purpose

²**cage** *vb* **caged; cag·ing** : to put or keep in or as if in a cage

ca·gey *also* **ca·gy** \'kā-jē\ *adj* **ca·gi·er; -est** : very careful not to be trapped or deceived — **ca·gi·ly** \-jə-lē\ *adv* — **ca·gi·ness** \-jē-nəs\ *n*

cai·man *or* **cay·man** \kā-'man, kī-; 'kā-mən\ *n* : any of several Central and South American reptiles closely related to alligators and crocodiles

ca·ïque \kä-'ēk\ *n*   **1** : a light rowboat used on the Bosporus   **2** : a Greek sailing vessel usually equipped with an engine [from Turkish *kayık* "rowboat"]

cairn \'ka(ə)rn, 'ke(ə)rn\ *n* : a heap of stones piled up as a landmark or as a memorial

cais·son \'kā-,sän, 'kā-sᵊn\ *n*   **1 a** : a chest for ammunition   **b** : a usually two-wheeled vehicle for artillery ammunition   **2** : a watertight chamber used in construction work under water or as a foundation

caisson disease *n* : ²BEND 3

ca·jole \kə-'jōl\ *vb* **ca·joled; ca·jol·ing** : to coax or persuade especially by flattery or false promises : WHEEDLE — **ca·jol·ery** \-'jōl-(ə-)rē\ *n*

¹**Ca·jun** \'kā-jən\ *n* : a Louisianian whose ancestors were French-speaking immigrants from Acadia, Canada [from an altered form of *Acadian*]

²**Cajun** *adj*   **1** : of or relating to the Cajuns   **2** : prepared in a cooking style originating with the Cajuns and marked by the use of hot seasonings (as cayenne pepper)

¹**cake** \'kāk\ *n*   **1** : a small piece of food (as dough or batter, meat, or fish) that is baked or fried   **2** : a baked food made from a sweet batter or dough   **3** : a substance hardened or molded into a solid mass ⟨a *cake* of soap⟩

²**cake** *vb* **caked; cak·ing**   **1** : ENCRUST   **2** : to form or harden into a cake

cal·a·bash \'kal-ə-,bash\ *n* : GOURD 2; *esp* : one whose hard shell is used for a utensil (as a bottle)

cal·a·mine \'kal-ə-,mīn, -mən\ *n* : a mixture of zinc oxide and a small amount of ferric oxide used in lotions, liniments, and ointments

ca·lam·i·tous \kə-'lam-ət-əs\ *adj* : causing or accompanied by calamity — **ca·lam·i·tous·ly** *adv* — **ca·lam·i·tous·ness** *n*

ca·lam·i·ty \kə-'lam-ət-ē\ *n, pl* **-ties** **1** : deep distress or misery **2** : an event that causes great harm

cal·car·e·ous \kal-'kar-ē-əs, -'ker-\ *adj* **1** : resembling calcite or calcium carbonate especially in hardness **2** : consisting of or containing calcium carbonate; *also* : containing calcium

cal·cif·er·ol \kal-'sif-ə-,rȯl, -,rōl\ *n* : a vitamin D that is sometimes added to human and animal diets and is used in medicine to treat various disorders of calcium metabolism

cal·cif·er·ous \kal-'sif-(ə-)rəs\ *adj* : producing or containing calcium carbonate

cal·ci·fy \'kal-sə-,fī\ *vb* **-fied; -fy·ing** : to make or become stony by deposit of calcium salts — **cal·ci·fi·ca·tion** \,kal-sə-fə-'kā-shən\ *n*

cal·cite \'kal-,sīt\ *n* : a mineral substance made up of calcium carbonate and found in numerous forms including limestone, chalk, and marble — **cal·cit·ic** \kal-'sit-ik\ *adj*

cal·ci·um \'kal-sē-əm\ *n* : a silver-white soft metallic element that is found only in combination with other elements (as in limestone) and is one of the necessary elements making up the bodies of most plants and animals — see ELEMENT table [derived from Latin *calc-, calx* "lime", from Greek *chalix* "pebble" — related to CALCULATE, CHALK]

calcium carbonate *n* : a solid substance found in nature as limestone and marble and in plant ashes, bones, and shells and used especially in making lime and portland cement

calcium chloride *n* : a salt that absorbs moisture from the air and is used to dry other substances

calcium hydroxide *n* : a white compound in the form of crystals that is used especially in making mortar and plaster, in softening water, and in bleaching

calcium oxide *n* : an oxide of calcium that is white when pure and makes up the major part of lime

calcium phosphate *n* : any of various phosphates of calcium: as **a** : one used as a fertilizer and in baking powder **b** : a naturally occurring phosphate containing other elements (as fluorine) and occurring as an important part of phosphate-bearing rock, bones, and teeth

calcium sulfate *n* : a white odorless compound of calcium that with water makes up gypsum

cal·cu·late \'kal-kyə-,lāt\ *vb* **-lat·ed; -lat·ing** **1** : to find by performing mathematical operations (as addition, subtraction, multiplication, and division) : COMPUTE **2** : [1]ESTIMATE 1 **3** : to plan by careful thought [from Latin *calculatus* "calculate", derived from *calculus* "pebble (used in counting)", from *calc-, calx* "stone used in gambling, lime", from Greek *chalix* "pebble" — related to CALCIUM, CHALK]

cal·cu·lat·ing \'kal-kyə-,lāt-iŋ\ *adj* **1** : designed to make calculations 〈*calculating* machine〉 **2 a** : tending to plan or study things with much care and caution **b** : SCHEMING — **cal·cu·lat·ing·ly** *adv*

cal·cu·la·tion \,kal-kyə-'lā-shən\ *n* **1 a** : the process or an act of calculating **b** : the result obtained by calculation **2** : care in planning : CAUTION

cal·cu·la·tor \'kal-kyə-,lāt-ər\ *n* **1** : one that calculates **2** : a usually small electronic device for solving mathematical problems

cal·cu·lus \'kal-kyə-ləs\ *n, pl* **-li** \-,lī, -,lē\ *also* **-lus·es** **1** : a mass usually of mineral salts deposited in or around organic material in a hollow organ or bodily duct **2** : a branch of higher mathematics concerned especially with

rates of change and the finding of lengths, areas, and volumes

cal·de·ra \kal-'der-ə, kȯl-, -'dir-\ *n* : a large crater formed by the collapse of a volcanic cone or by an explosion

cal·dron *also* **caul·dron** \'kȯl-drən\ *n* : a large kettle [Middle English *caldron, cauldron* "caldron", from earlier *cauderon* (same meaning), derived from an early French dialect word *caudiere* (same meaning), derived from Latin *caldus* "warm", from *calēre* "to be hot" — related to CALORIE, NONCHALANT]

caldron

[1]cal·en·dar \'kal-ən-dər\ *n* **1 a** : an arrangement of time into days, weeks, months, and years **b** : a chart showing the days, weeks, and months of a year **2 a** : a list of items in proper order **b** : a schedule of coming events [Middle English *calender* "calendar", from early French *calender* and Latin *kalendarium* (both, same meaning), derived from Latin *kalendae* "the first day of the (Roman) month"]

[2]calendar *vb* **-dared; -dar·ing** \-d(ə-)riŋ\ : to enter in a calendar

[1]calf \'kaf, 'kàf\ *n, pl* **calves** \'kavz, 'kàvz\ **1 a** : the young of the domestic cow **b** : the young of various other large animals (as the elephant or whale) **2** *pl* **calfs** : CALFSKIN [Old English *cealf* "young cow"]

[2]calf *n, pl* **calves** : the muscular back part of the leg below the knee [Middle English *calf* "part of the leg"; of Norse origin]

calf·skin \'kaf-,skin, 'kàf-\ *n* : the skin of a calf or leather made from it

cal·i·ber *or* **cal·i·bre** \'kal-ə-bər\ *n* **1** : the diameter of a missile (as a bullet) **2** : the inside diameter of a gun barrel **3** : degree of excellence or importance

cal·i·brate \'kal-ə-,brāt\ *vb* **-brat·ed; -brat·ing** **1** : to measure the caliber of **2 a** : to determine, correct, or put the measuring marks on (as a thermometer tube) **b** : to find out and make corrections for the numerical differences from an accepted or ideal value of — **cal·i·bra·tion** \,kal-ə-'brā-shən\ *n*

cal·i·co \'kal-i-,kō\ *n, pl* **-coes** *or* **-cos** **1** : cotton cloth especially with a colored pattern printed on one side **2** : a blotched or spotted animal (as a piebald horse) [named for *Calicut*, a city in India, where the first calico cloth was made] — **calico** *adj*

calico bass *n* : BLACK CRAPPIE

Cal·i·for·nia condor \,kal-ə-,fȯr-nyə-\ *n* : a very large and rare North American vulture that is related to the condor of South America and is sometimes larger though of lighter build

California poppy *n* : any of a genus of poppies including one widely grown for its pale yellow to red flowers

cal·i·for·ni·um \,kal-ə-'fȯr-nē-əm\ *n* : an artificially prepared radioactive element used as a neutron source in medicine and industry — see ELEMENT table

cal·i·per *or* **cal·li·per** \'kal-ə-pər\

California condor

\ə\ abut	\au̇\ out	\i\ tip	\ȯ\ saw	\u̇\ foot
\ər\ further	\ch\ chin	\ī\ life	\ȯi\ coin	\y\ yet
\a\ mat	\e\ pet	\j\ job	\th\ thin	\yü\ few
\ā\ take	\ē\ easy	\ŋ\ sing	\t͟h\ this	\yu̇\ cure
\ä\ cot, cart	\g\ go	\ō\ bone	\ü\ food	\zh\ vision

n : a measuring instrument with two legs or jaws that can be adjusted to determine thickness, diameter, or distance between surfaces — usually used in pl. ⟨a pair of *calipers*⟩

ca·liph *or* **ca·lif** \'kā-ləf, 'kal-əf\ *n* : an important Muslim political and religious leader — used as a title — **ca·liph·ate** \-,āt, -ət\ *n*

cal·is·then·ics \,kal-əs-'then-iks\ *n sing or pl* **1** : exercises to develop strength and flexibility that are done without special equipment **2** : the art or practice of calisthenics — **cal·is·then·ic** \-ik\ *adj*

Word History People who do regular exercises are often aiming for not just better health and strength but also a fitter and more pleasing look. The benefits that exercise can have for both strength and looks are suggested by the origin of the word *calisthenics*. *Calisthenics* was made by joining the Greek *kalos*, meaning "beautiful", and *sthenos*, meaning "strength". The word was originally used to refer to special exercises done by young women, but it later gained the more general meaning that we now know. [from Greek *kalos* "beautiful" and *sthenos* "strength"]

calk *variant of* CAULK

¹call \'kol\ *vb* **1** : to speak so as to be heard at a distance : SHOUT ⟨*call* for help⟩ **2** : to utter in a loud clear voice ⟨*call* a roll⟩ ⟨*call* out a command⟩ **3** : to announce with authority : PROCLAIM ⟨*call* a halt⟩ **4** : SUMMON 1 ⟨*call* a meeting⟩ **5** : to bring into action or discussion ⟨*call* up reserves⟩ **6 a** : to make a request or demand of or for ⟨*call* for an end to war⟩ ⟨was *called* to testify⟩ **b** : to give temporary control of a computer to a particular set of instructions **7** : to make a telephone call to **8** : to make a brief visit ⟨no salesperson will *call*⟩ **9 a** : to give a name to ⟨*called* the cat "Patches"⟩ **b** : to address by a name ⟨what did you *call* me⟩ **10** : to regard as being of a certain kind ⟨you can *call* them generous⟩ **11** : to estimate as being ⟨*call* it an even dollar⟩ **12 a** : to utter a cry ⟨crows *calling*⟩ **b** : to attract game by imitating its cry **13** : ⁴HALT 2, SUSPEND ⟨*call* a game on account of rain⟩ ⟨*call* time⟩ — **call·er** *n* — **call for** **1** : to stop by (as at one's house) to get ⟨I'll *call for* you later⟩ **2** : ²NEED 2 **3** : ¹ORDER 2a, DIRECT — **call on** *or* **call upon** : to make an appeal to

²call *n* **1** : a loud cry : SHOUT **2 a** : a cry of an animal **b** : an imitation of an animal's cry or a device used to make such an imitation **3 a** : ¹SUMMONS 1, INVITATION **b** : ATTRACTION 1 ⟨the *call* of the wild⟩ **4 a** : ¹DEMAND 1a, CLAIM **b** : ¹REQUEST 1 **5** : a brief visit **6** : the act of calling on the telephone **7** : a ruling made by an official of a sports contest **8** : a temporary transfer of control of computer processing to a particular set of instructions

cal·la lily \'kal-ə-\ *n* : a plant often grown for its large white bract surrounding a fleshy spike of small yellow flowers

call·back \'kol-,bak\ *n* **1** : a return call **2** : a calling back of faulty merchandise (as cars) by a manufacturer for repairs

cal·lig·ra·phy \kə-'lig-rə-fē\ *n* **1 a** : beautiful handwriting **b** : the art of producing such handwriting **2** : PENMANSHIP 2 — **cal·lig·ra·pher** \-rə-fər\ *n*

call·ing \'ko-liŋ\ *n* : OCCUPATION 1, PROFESSION

cal·li·ope \kə-'lī-ə-(,)pē *also* 'kal-ē-,ōp\ *n* : a keyboard musical instrument consisting of a set of whistles sounded usually by steam [named for *Calliope*, one of the nine goddesses in Greek mythology who had control over music and poetry]

call number *n* : a combination of numbers and letters assigned to a library book to indicate its location in the library

call off *vb* **1** : to draw away : DIVERT ⟨*call off* a dog⟩ **2** : CANCEL 2a ⟨*call off* a meeting⟩

cal·los·i·ty \ka-'läs-ət-ē, kə-\ *n, pl* **-ties** : ¹CALLUS 1

cal·lous \'kal-əs\ *adj* **1** : so thickened and usually hardened as to form callus or a callus **2** : feeling no sympathy for others : UNFEELING ⟨a *callous* refusal to help the poor⟩ — **cal·lous·ly** *adv* — **cal·lous·ness** *n*

cal·low \'kal-ō\ *adj* : lacking adult experience : IMMATURE — **cal·low·ness** *n*

call–up \'ko-,ləp\ *n* : an order to report for military service

¹cal·lus \'kal-əs\ *n, pl* **cal·lus·es** **1** : a hard thickened area on skin or bark **2** : a substance that surrounds a break in a bone and is changed into bone in the healing of the break

²callus *vb* : to form callus

¹calm \'käm, 'kälm\ *adj* **1** : marked by calm : STILL **2** : free from excitement or disturbance — **calm·ly** *adv* — **calm·ness** *n*

syn CALM, TRANQUIL, SERENE, PEACEFUL mean quiet and free from disturbance. CALM may suggest that one is free from disturbance even when there is cause for excitement ⟨stayed *calm* during the fire⟩ TRANQUIL suggests a total or lasting state of rest ⟨led a *tranquil* life in a rural area⟩ SERENE suggests a lofty and dignified kind of tranquillity ⟨the queen looks *serene* on her throne⟩ PEACEFUL suggests a quiet state that follows a period of disturbance ⟨after the crisis the country was *peaceful* again⟩

²calm *n* **1 a** : a period or state of freedom from storm, wind, or rough water **b** : complete lack of wind or the presence of wind of no more than one mile per hour **2** : a state of freedom from excitement or disturbance : PEACEFULNESS

³calm *vb* : to make or become calm

cal·o·mel \'kal-ə-məl, -,mel\ *n* : a white tasteless chemical compound of mercury that occurs as a mineral or is made chemically and that is used as a strong laxative, fungicide, and insecticide

ca·lor·ic \kə-'lor-ik, -'lōr-, -'lär-; 'kal-ə-rik\ *adj* **1** : of or relating to heat **2** : of or relating to calories — **ca·lor·i·cal·ly** \-i-k(ə-)lē\ *adv*

cal·o·rie *also* **cal·o·ry** \'kal-(ə-)rē\ *n, pl* **-ries** : a unit of heat: **a** : the heat energy required to raise the temperature of one gram of water one degree Celsius and equal to about 4.19 joules — called also *small calorie* **b** : the amount of energy required to raise the temperature of one kilogram of water one degree Celsius and equal to 1000 small calories — used especially to indicate the value of foods in the production of heat and energy; called also *large calorie, kilocalorie* [from French *calorie* "a unit of heat", from Latin *calor* "heat", from *calēre* "to be hot" — related to CALDRON, NONCHALANT]

cal·o·rif·ic \,kal-ə-'rif-ik\ *adj* : CALORIC

cal·o·rim·e·ter \,kal-ə-'rim-ət-ər\ *n* : a device for measuring quantities of heat given off or taken in

calve \'kav, 'kàv\ *vb* **calved; calv·ing** **1** : to give birth to a calf **2** : to let (as a large piece of a glacier) break off and become separate ⟨icebergs are *calved* in northern seas⟩

calves *pl of* CALF

ca·lyp·so \kə-'lip-sō\ *n, pl* **-sos** : a folk song or style of singing of West Indian origin having a lively rhythm and words which are usually made up by the singer

ca·lyx \'kā-liks *also* 'kal-iks\ *n, pl* **ca·lyx·es** *or* **ca·ly·ces** \'kā-lə-,sēz *also* 'kal-ə-\ : the usually green or leafy outside part of a flower consisting of sepals

cal·zo·ne \kal-'zōn, -'zō-,nē, -'zō-nā; käl-'zòn-ā\ *n, pl* **calzone** *or* **calzones** : a baked or fried turnover of pizza dough with various fillings

cam \'kam\ *n* : a device by which circular motion may be transformed into stop-and-start or back-and-forth motion

ca·ma·ra·de·rie \,käm-(ə-)'räd-ə-rē, kam-(ə-)'rad-\ *n* : good feeling existing between comrades

cam·bi·um \'kam-bē-əm\ *n, pl* **-bi·ums** *or* **-bia** \-bē-ə\ : a thin cell layer between the xylem and phloem of most vascular plants from which new cells (as of wood and bark) develop — **cam·bi·al** \-bē-əl\ *adj*

Cam·bri·an \'kam-brē-ən, 'käm-\ *adj* : of, relating to, or being the earliest period of the Paleozoic era of geological history or the corresponding system of rocks marked by fossils of every major animal type except the vertebrates

— see GEOLOGIC TIME table — **Cambrian** *n*

cam·bric \'kām-brik\ *n* : a fine thin white linen or cotton fabric

came *past of* COME

cam·el \'kam-əl\ *n* : either of two large cud-chewing mammals used for carrying burdens and for riding in desert regions especially of Africa and Asia: **a** : DROMEDARY 2 **b** : a two-humped camel of central Asia — called also *Bactrian camel*

camel: *left* dromedary, *right* Bactrian

camel hair *also* **camel's hair** *n* **1** : the hair of a camel or a substitute for it (as hair from squirrels' tails) **2** : a cloth made of camel hair or of camel hair and wool

ca·mel·lia \kə-'mēl-yə\ *n* : a greenhouse shrub that is related to the tea plant and has glossy evergreen leaves and showy roselike flowers

Ca·mel·o·par·da·lis \kə-,mel-ə-'pärd-ᵊl-əs\ *n* : a northern group of stars between Cassiopeia and Ursa Major

Cam·em·bert \'kam-əm-,be(ə)r\ *n* : a soft cheese with a whitish rind and a yellow inside [named for *Camembert,* a village in France where the cheese was first made]

cam·eo \'kam-ē-,ō\ *n, pl* **-eos** **1** : a carved gem in which the design is higher than its background **2** : a small role (as in a movie) performed by a well-known actor

cam·era \'kam-(ə-)rə\ *n* **1** : a judge's private office ⟨hearings held in *camera*⟩ **2** : a lightproof box fitted with a lens through which the image of an object is recorded on a material sensitive to light **3** : the part of a television sending device in which the image to be televised is changed into electrical signals [from Latin *camera* "room, chamber"; sense 2 from the scientific Latin phrase *camera obscura,* literally "dark chamber" — related to CHAMBER]

camomile *variant of* CHAMOMILE

¹**cam·ou·flage** \'kam-ə-,fläzh, -,fläj\ *n* **1** : the hiding or disguising of something by covering it up or changing the way it looks **2** : the material (as paint or leaves and branches) used for camouflage

²**camouflage** *vb* **-flaged; -flag·ing** : to hide or disguise by camouflage

¹**camp** \'kamp\ *n* **1 a** : a place usually away from cities where tents or buildings are erected for shelter or for living in temporarily **b** : a group of tents, cabins, or huts **c** : a tent or cabin to be lived in temporarily (as during vacation) **d** : a place in the country with tents or cabins for recreation usually during the summer ⟨summer *camp*⟩ ⟨football *camp*⟩ ⟨computer *camp*⟩ **2** : a body of persons in a camp

²**camp** *vb* **1** : to make or occupy a camp **2** : to live in a camp or outdoors especially for recreation — often used with *out*

cam·paign \kam-'pān\ *n* **1** : a series of military operations in a particular area or for a particular purpose as part of a war **2** : a connected series of activities designed to bring about a particular result ⟨an election *campaign*⟩ — **cam-**

paign *vb* — **cam·paign·er** *n*

cam·pa·ni·le \,kam-pə-'nē-lē, ,käm-, -(,)lā, *especially of U.S. structures also* ,kam-pə-'nē(ə)l\ *n* : a bell tower; *esp* : one built separate from another building

cam·pan·u·la \kam-'pan-yə-lə\ *n* : any of a large genus of herbs with bell-shaped flowers including several grown as ornamentals

camp·er \'kam-pər\ *n* **1** : a person who camps **2** : a portable dwelling or a specially equipped vehicle for use during travel and camping

camp·fire \'kamp-,fī(ə)r\ *n* : a fire built outdoors (as at a camp or on a picnic)

Camp Fire Girl *n* : a member of a national organization for girls from 7 to 18

camp·ground \'kamp-,graund\ *n* : the area or place used for a camp or for camping; *esp* : one with facilities for campers

cam·phor \'kam(p)-fər\ *n* : a tough gummy fragrant compound obtained especially from the wood and bark of the camphor tree and used in medicine and as an insect repellent

camphor tree *n* : a large Asian evergreen tree that is related to the laurel and is the source of camphor

camp·o·ree \,kam-pə-'rē\ *n* : a gathering of Boy Scouts or Girl Scouts from a given geographic area

camp·site \'kamp-,sīt\ *n* : a place suitable for or used as the site of a camp; *esp* : one of several in a campground

cam·pus \'kam-pəs\ *n, pl* **cam·pus·es** : the grounds of a college or a school

cam·shaft \'kam-,shaft\ *n* : a shaft to which a cam is fastened or of which a cam forms a part

¹**can** \kən, (')kan\ *helping verb, past* **could** \kəd, (')kud\; *pres sing & pl* **can** **1 a** : know how to ⟨we *can* read⟩ **b** : be able to ⟨I *can* hear you⟩ **c** : be permitted by conscience or feeling ⟨they *can* hardly blame you⟩ **d** : have the power or right to **2** : have permission to : MAY ⟨you *can* go now⟩ [Old English *can* "to know, know how to"]

²**can** \'kan\ *n* **1** : a metal container usually shaped like a cylinder ⟨ash *can*⟩ **2** : the contents of a can ⟨ate the whole *can* of beans⟩ [Old English *canne* "container"]

³**can** \'kan\ *vb* **canned; can·ning** **1** : to prepare for future use by sealing in an airtight can or jar **2** *slang* : to dismiss from a job : FIRE **3** *slang* : to put a stop or end to — **can·ner** *n*

Can·a·da goose \,kan-əd-ə-\ *n* : a common wild goose of North America that is mostly gray and brownish with a black head and neck — called also *Canadian goose*

Canada lynx *n* : LYNX 1

Ca·na·di·an \kə-'nād-ē-ən\ *adj* : of, relating to, or characteristic of Canada or its people — **Canadian** *n*

Canadian bacon *n* : bacon from the loin of a pig that has little fat and is cut into round or oblong slices for cooking

campanile

Canada goose

\ə\ **abut**	\au̇\ **out**	\i\ **tip**	\ȯ\ **saw**	\u̇\ **foot**
\ər\ **further**	\ch\ **chin**	\ī\ **life**	\ȯi\ **coin**	\y\ **yet**
\a\ **mat**	\e\ **pet**	\j\ **job**	\th\ **thin**	\yü\ **few**
\ā\ **take**	\ē\ **easy**	\ŋ\ **sing**	\th\ **this**	\yu̇\ **cure**
\ä\ **cot, cart**	\g\ **go**	\ō\ **bone**	\ü\ **food**	\zh\ **vision**

ca·nal \kə-'nal\ *n* **1** : a tube-shaped bodily passage or channel : DUCT **2** : an artificial waterway for boats or for draining or irrigating land **3** : any of various faint narrow lines on the planet Mars seen through telescopes and formerly thought to be canals built by Martians

ca·nary \kə-'ne(ə)r-ē\ *n, pl* **ca·nar·ies** : a small usually yellow or greenish finch native to the Canary islands that is often kept in a cage

Word History The small bird we call a canary owes its name to big dogs. Early explorers of a group of islands off the northwest coast of Africa reported seeing many large dogs there. Romans reading these reports gave the islands the Latin name *Canariae insulae,* meaning "dog islands", which was borrowed into English as *Canary islands.* The dogs from which the islands got their name were probably not native to the islands but brought there from Africa. Truly native to the islands were small greenish brown birds. Some of these were taken to Europe in the 16th century for pets. Since they came from the Canary islands, they were called *canary birds* in England. The yellow bird kept as a pet today is a descendant of the wild greenish birds of the "dog islands". [from *Canary (islands),* from Spanish *Islas Canarias* "Canary islands", from Latin *Canariae insulae,* literally "dog islands", from *canis* "dog" — related to CANINE]

can·cel \'kan(t)-səl\ *vb* **-celed** *or* **-celled; -cel·ing** *or* **-cel·ling** \-s(ə-)liŋ\ **1** : to cross out or strike out with a line : DELETE **2 a** : to destroy the force or effectiveness of ⟨*cancel* an order⟩ ⟨*cancel* an appointment⟩ **b** : ²OFFSET **3 a** : to divide numerator and denominator by the same number **b** : to remove equivalents on opposite sides of an equation or account **4** : to mark a postage stamp or check so that it cannot be reused — **can·cel·er** *or* **can·cel·ler** \-s(ə-)lər\ *n*

can·cel·la·tion \ˌkan(t)-sə-'lā-shən\ *n* **1** : an act of canceling **2** : a mark made to cancel something

can·cer \'kan(t)-sər\ *n* **1** *cap* : a group of stars between Gemini and Leo usually pictured as a crab **2** *cap* **a** : the fourth sign of the zodiac — see ZODIAC table **b** : a person whose sign of the zodiac is Cancer **3** : a tumor that tends to spread locally and to other parts of the body and often causes death if not treated; *also* : an abnormal state marked by such tumors **4** : a dangerous evil that destroys slowly — **can·cer·ous** \'kan(t)s-(ə-)rəs\ *adj*

Word History The Latin word *cancer,* meaning "crab", was also given as a name to several diseases. One of the diseases was the abnormal, spreading mass of tissue we call a tumor. A possible explanation for this extended use of *cancer* is that the Romans thought some tumors looked like many-legged crabs. A French form of this Latin word was borrowed into English as *canker.* It is now applied to several plant and animal disorders. In the 14th century the Latin word *cancer* in the sense of "tumor" was borrowed directly into English, giving us our modern spelling and sense. [Middle English *Cancer* " 'Crab' star group", from Latin *cancer* "crab, cancer (disease)"; sense 3 directly from Latin *cancer* "crab, cancer" — related to CANKER, CHANCRE]

can·de·la \kan-'dē-lə, -'del-ə\ *n* : a unit of measurement for the intensity of light

can·de·la·bra \ˌkan-də-'läb-rə *also* -'lab-\ : CANDELABRUM

can·de·la·brum \ˌkan-də-'läb-rəm *also* -'lab-\ *n, pl* **-bra** \-rə\ *also* **-brums** : a candlestick that has several branches for holding candles

can·did \'kan-dəd\ *adj* **1** : marked by or showing sincere honesty : FRANK **2** : relating to photography of people acting naturally without being posed ⟨*candid* picture⟩ [from French *candide* "white" and Latin *candidus* "white, bright", from Latin *candēre* "to shine, be bright" — related to CANDIDATE, CANDLE; see *Word History* at CANDIDATE] —

can·did·ly *adv* — **can·did·ness** *n*

can·di·da·cy \'kan-dəd-ə-sē, 'kan-əd-\ *n, pl* **-cies** : the state of being a candidate

can·di·date \'kan-də-ˌdāt, 'kan-ə-, -dət\ *n* : one who runs in an election contest or is proposed for an office or honor

Word History In ancient Rome it was the custom for a person who wanted to be elected to public office to wear a white toga that had been rubbed with chalk to make it bright and spotless. This white toga was a symbol to show that the person did not have any stain on his character or reputation and thus was fit to hold office. The Latin word for "dressed in a bright white toga" was *candidatus.* In time this word came to be used for the person himself, or the candidate. The Latin word *candidatus* came from *candidus,* meaning "bright, shining white". This in turn came from *candēre,* a verb meaning "to shine, be bright". Latin *candēre* has given us two other English words: *candid,* which at first meant "white, free from prejudice" but now usually means "honest, natural", and *candle,* the mass of wax with a wick that is burned to give off a bright light. [from Latin *candidatus* "candidate", from *candidatus* (adjective) "dressed in a white toga", from *candidus* "shining white", from *candēre* "to be bright, shine" — related to CANDID, CANDLE]

can·di·di·a·sis \ˌkan-də-'dī-ə-səs\ *n, pl* **-a·ses** \-ə-ˌsēz\ : infection (as of the sex organs) with a fungus that resembles a yeast

¹can·dle \'kan-dᵊl\ *n* **1** : a mass of tallow or wax containing a wick that is burned to give light **2** : CANDELA [Old English *candel* "candle", from Latin *candela* "candle", from *candēre* "to shine, be bright" — related to CANDID, CANDIDATE; see *Word History* at CANDIDATE]

²candle *vb* **can·dled; can·dling** \'kan-dliŋ, -dᵊl-iŋ\ : to examine an egg by holding it between the eye and a light — **can·dler** \-dlər, -dᵊl-ər\ *n*

can·dle·light \'kan-dᵊl-, ˌ(l)īt\ *n* **1** : the light of a candle **2** : soft artificial light — **can·dle·lit** \-dᵊl-, ˌ(l)it\ *adj*

Can·dle·mas \'kan-dᵊl-məs\ *n* : February 2 observed as a Christian festival in honor of the presentation of Christ in the temple and the purification of the Virgin Mary

can·dle·pow·er \'kan-dᵊl-, paù-(ə)r\ *n* : intensity of light expressed in candelas

can·dle·stick \-, stik\ *n* : a holder with a socket for a candle

can·dor \'kan-dər, -dò(ə)r\ *n* : sincere and honest expression : FRANKNESS

¹can·dy \'kan-dē\ *n, pl* **candies** : a sweet made of sugar often with flavoring and filling

²candy *vb* **can·died; can·dy·ing** : to coat or become coated with sugar; *esp* : to cook (fruit or fruit peel) in sugar syrup

candy strip·er \-, strī-pər\ *n* : a teenage volunteer hospital worker [so called from the fact that the uniform is traditionally striped like some stick candies]

¹cane \'kān\ *n* **1 a** : a jointed plant stem that is usually slender and more or less flexible **b** : any of various tall woody grasses or reeds; *esp* : SUGARCANE **2 a** : WALKING STICK 1 **b** : a rod for flogging **c** : RATTAN 2

²cane *vb* **caned; can·ing** **1** : to beat with a cane **2** : to make with cane ⟨*cane* the seat of a chair⟩

cane·brake \'kān-, brāk\ *n* : a thicket of cane

cane sugar *n* : sugar from sugarcane

¹ca·nine \'kā-, nīn\ *adj* : of or relating to dogs or to the family that includes the dogs, wolves, jackals, and foxes [from Latin *caninus* "having to do with dogs", from *canis* "dog" — related to CANARY, DOG DAYS; see *Word History* at CANARY, DOG DAYS]

²canine *n* **1** : a pointed tooth; *esp* : one located between the outer incisor and the first premolar **2** : ¹DOG 1a, b

can·is·ter *also* **can·nis·ter** \'kan-ə-stər\ *n* : a small box or can for holding a dry product (as coffee, flour, or sugar)

can·ker \'kaŋ-kər\ *n* **1** : an often spreading sore that eats into tissue   **2 a** : an area of dead tissue in a plant   **b** : a plant disease marked by cankers   **3** : any of various animal diseases marked especially by inflammation [Middle English *canker* "spreading sore", from an early French dialect word *cancre* (same meaning), from Latin *cancer* "crab, cancer" — related to CANCER, CHANCRE; see *Word History* at CANCER] — **can·ker·ous** \'kaŋ-k(ə-)rəs\ *adj*

canker sore *n* : a small painful open sore especially of the mouth

can·ker·worm \'kaŋ-kər-,wərm\ *n* : an insect larva (as a looper) that injures plants especially by feeding on buds and leaves

can·na \'kan-ə\ *n* : a tall tropical herb with large leaves and an unbranched stem bearing bright-colored flowers at the end

can·na·bis \'kan-ə-bəs\ *n* : the dried flowering parts of the hemp plant — compare HASHISH, MARIJUANA

canned \'kand\ *adj*   **1** : preserved in a sealed can or jar ⟨*canned* ham⟩   **2 a** : prepared or recorded in advance; *esp* : prepared in one form for ordinary use or wide distribution ⟨*canned* laughter⟩   **b** : lacking originality as if mass-produced ⟨a *canned* speech⟩

can·nery \'kan-(ə-)rē\ *n, pl* **can·ner·ies** : a factory for the canning of food

can·ni·bal \'kan-ə-bəl\ *n* : a human being or an animal that eats its own kind — **cannibal** *adj*

   Word History When Columbus first landed on islands in the sea we now call *Caribbean,* he found native people who spoke different dialects of the same language. These people called themselves *Caniba* or *Carib,* which meant "brave and daring". It is from the form *Carib* that we get our name for the area, the *Caribbean.* The Spanish referred to the people of this area as *Caníbal.* The Spanish explorers believed the *Caníbal* people ate the flesh of other people. By the time the word was borrowed into English as *cannibal,* it had therefore come to mean "a human being that eats the flesh of other human beings". Later the use was broadened to include any "human being or animal that eats its own kind". [from Spanish *caníbal, Caníbal* "cannibal, native people of the Caribbean islands", from *Caniba, Carib,* native words for these people in the Caribbean area]

can·ni·bal·ism \'kan-ə-bə-,liz-əm\ *n*   **1** : the eating of human flesh by a human being   **2** : the eating of the flesh of an animal by another animal of the same kind — **can·ni·bal·is·tic** \,kan-ə-bə-'lis-tik\ *adj*

can·ni·bal·ize \'kan-ə-bə-,līz\ *vb* **-ized; -iz·ing** : to take apart a machine for parts to be used as replacements in other machines

can·non \'kan-ən\ *n, pl* **cannons** *or* **cannon**   **1** : a large heavy gun usually mounted on wheels   **2** : an automatic gun of large caliber on an airplane

can·non·ade \,kan-ə-'nād\ *n* : heavy firing of artillery

can·non·ball \'kan-ən-,bȯl\ *n* : a usually round solid missile for firing from a cannon

can·non·eer \,kan-ə-'ni(ə)r\ *n* : an artillery gunner

can·not \'kan-(,)ät; kə-'nät, ka-'nät\ : can not — **cannot but** : to be unable to do something other than

can·ny \'kan-ē\ *adj* **can·ni·er;   -est** : watchful of one's own interest — **can·ni·ly** \'kan-ᵊl-ē\ *adv* — **can·ni·ness** \'kan-ē-nəs\ *n*

¹ca·noe \kə-'nü\ *n* : a long light narrow boat with sharp ends and curved sides that is usually moved by someone using a paddle

canoe

²canoe *vb* **ca·noed; ca·noe·ing** : to travel or carry in a

canoe — **ca·noe·ist** \-'nü-əst\ *n*

ca·no·la \kə-'nō-lə\ *n*   **1** : a rape plant of an improved variety having seeds that are the source of canola oil   **2** : CANOLA OIL

canola oil *n* : an edible vegetable oil obtained from the seeds of canola that is low in saturated and high in monosaturated fatty acids

¹can·on \'kan-ən\ *n*   **1** : a church law or decree   **2** : an official list (as of the books of the Bible)   **3** : an accepted standard or rule ⟨*canons* of good taste⟩

²canon *n* : a member of the clergy who is on the staff of a cathedral

cañon *variant of* CANYON

ca·non·i·cal \kə-'nän-i-kəl\ *adj*   **1** : relating to or allowed by church law   **2** : accepted as official or genuine — **ca·non·i·cal·ly** \-i-k(ə-)lē\ *adv*

can·on·ize \'kan-ə-,nīz\ *vb* **-ized; -iz·ing**   **1** : to declare to be a saint and worthy of public respect   **2** : to treat something as if it were sacred — **can·on·iza·tion** \,kan-ə-nə-'zā-shən\ *n*

canon law *n* : the body of religious laws that govern a church

Ca·no·pus \kə-'nō-pəs\ *n* : a very bright star not visible north of 37° latitude

¹can·o·py \'kan-ə-pē\ *n, pl* **-pies**   **1 a** : a covering over a bed, throne, or shrine or carried on poles (as over a person of high rank)   **b** : AWNING   **2** : a shade or shelter that hangs over something; *esp* : the uppermost spreading layer of a forest   **3** : the fabric part of a parachute that catches the air

²canopy *vb* **-pied; -py·ing** : to cover with or as if with a canopy

canst \kən(t)st, (')kan(t)st\ *archaic present 2d sing of* CAN

¹cant \'kant\ *n*   **1** : a slanting surface   **2** : ³SLOPE 2, INCLINE [Middle English *cant* "corner", from early Dutch *cant* or early French *cant,* both meaning "edge, corner", from Latin *canthus, cantus* "iron rim on a wheel"; perhaps of Celtic origin]

²cant *vb* : to give a slant to

³cant *n*   **1 a** : ARGOT   **b** : JARGON 2   **2** : insincere speech [probably derived from an early French dialect word *canter* "to tell", from Latin *cantare* "to sing", derived from *canere* "to sing" — related to CANTATA, CHANT, CHANTEY]

can't \'kant, 'kánt, *especially Southern* 'kánt\ : can not

can·ta·loupe *also* **can·te·loupe** \'kant-ᵊl-,ōp\ *n* : a muskmelon with a hard rough skin and reddish orange flesh

can·tan·ker·ous \kan-'taŋ-k(ə-)rəs, kən-\ *adj* : difficult or irritating to deal with — **can·tan·ker·ous·ly** *adv* — **can·tan·ker·ous·ness** *n*

can·ta·ta \kən-'tät-ə\ *n* : a poem, story, or play set to music to be sung by a chorus and soloists [from Italian *cantata* "music for a chorus", from Latin *cantata* (same meaning), derived from *canere* "to sing" — related to CANTOR, CHANT, CHANTEY]

can·teen \kan-'tēn\ *n*   **1** : a store (as in a camp) in which food, drinks, and small supplies are sold   **2** : a place of recreation and entertainment for people in military service   **3** : a small container for carrying liquids (as on a hike)

¹can·ter \'kant-ər\ *n* : a three-beat gait of a horse resembling but smoother and slower than the gallop

²canter *vb* : to go or cause to go at a canter

Can·ter·bury bell \,kant-ə(r)-,ber-ē-\ *n* : a cultivated campanula

can·ti·cle \'kant-i-kəl\ *n* : a song from the Bible used in church services

Canticle of Canticles — see BIBLE table

\ə\ abut	\aú\ out	\i\ tip	\ȯ\ saw	\ú\ foot
\ər\ further	\ch\ chin	\ī\ life	\ȯi\ coin	\y\ yet
\a\ mat	\e\ pet	\j\ job	\th\ thin	\yü\ few
\ā\ take	\ē\ easy	\ŋ\ sing	\t͟h\ this	\yú\ cure
\ä\ cot, cart	\g\ go	\ō\ bone	\ü\ food	\zh\ vision

can·ti·le·ver \'kant-ᵊl-
,ē-vər *also* -ev-ər\ *n*
1 : a beam or support
fastened at only one
end **2** : either of two
beams or structures
that stick out from
piers toward each
other and when
joined form a span in
a bridge

C cantilever 2

can·to \'kan-,tō\ *n, pl*
cantos : a major division of a long poem
can·ton \'kant-ᵊn, 'kan-,tän\ *n* **1** : a division of a country
(as Switzerland) **2** : the top inner quarter of a flag
can·ton·ment \kan-'tōn-mənt, -'tän-\ *n* : a military station
in India
can·tor \'kant-ər\ *n* **1** : a choir leader **2** : a synagogue
official who sings or chants religious music and leads the
congregation in prayer [from Latin *cantor* "singer", derived
from *canere* "to sing" — related to CANTATA, CHANT, CHAN-
TEY]
can·vas \'kan-vəs\ *n* **1 a** : a strong cloth of hemp, flax, or
cotton used for clothing and formerly much used for tents
and sails **b** : a piece of cloth used as a surface for painting; *also* : a painting on such a surface **2** : something
made of canvas
can·vas·back \-,bak\ *n* : a North American wild duck with
a reddish head and grayish back
¹**can·vass** \'kan-vəs\ *vb* : to go through (a district) or go to
(people) to ask for votes, contributions, or orders or to determine public opinion — **can·vass·er** *n*
²**canvass** *n* : an act of convassing
can·yon *or* **ca·ñon** \'kan-yən\ *n* : a deep narrow valley with
steep sides and often with a stream flowing through it
caou·tchouc \kaù-,chùk, -,chük, -,chü\ *n* : ¹RUBBER 2a
¹**cap** \'kap\ *n* **1** : a head covering; *esp* : one that has a
visor and no brim **2** : something that serves as a cover
or protection for something ⟨a bottle *cap*⟩ **3** : a natural
cover or top: as **a** : the umbrella-shaped part that bears
the spores of a mushroom **b** : the top of a bird's head **4**
: a paper or metal container holding a small explosive
charge (as for a toy pistol) [Middle English *cappe* "cap",
from Old English *cæppe* "cap", from Latin *cappa* "head
covering, cloak" — related to ²CAPE, CHAPEL]
²**cap** *vb* **capped; cap·ping 1** : to cover or provide with a
cap **2** : to match with something equal or better
ca·ble \'kā-pə-bəl\ *adj* **1** : having the qualities (as
physical or mental power) to do or accomplish something
⟨you are *capable* of better work⟩ **2** : having qualities or
features permitting ⟨a new train *capable* of very high
speeds⟩ **3** : able to do one's job well : generally efficient
⟨tries to hire *capable* people⟩ — **ca·pa·bil·i·ty** \,kā-pə-
'bil-ət-ē\ *n* — **ca·pa·bly** \'kā-pə-blē\ *adv*
ca·pa·cious \kə-'pā-shəs\ *adj* : able to contain much or
many **syn** *see* SPACIOUS — **ca·pa·cious·ly**
adv — **ca·pa·cious·ness** *n*
ca·pac·i·tor \kə-'pas-ət-ər\ *n* : a device for storing electric
charge — called also *condenser*
ca·pac·i·ty \kə-'pas-ət-ē, -'pas-tē\ *n, pl* **-ties 1** : the ability to hold or contain ⟨the seating *capacity* of a room⟩ **2**
: the largest amount or number that can be contained ⟨a
jug with a *capacity* of four liters⟩ ⟨the auditorium was filled
to *capacity*⟩ **3** : mental or physical ability **4** : ¹POSITION
4a, FUNCTION ⟨in your *capacity* as drama critic⟩
¹**ca·par·i·son** \kə-'par-ə-sən\ *n* **1** : an ornamental covering for a horse **2** : fancy clothing or decoration
²**caparison** *vb* : to dress with or as if with fancy clothes
¹**cape** \'kāp\ *n* : a point of land that extends out into the sea
or a lake [Middle English *cap* "cape, point of land", derived
from an early French dialect word *cap* (same meaning),
from Latin *caput* "head" — related to CAPITAL]

²**cape** *n* : a sleeveless garment worn so as to hang over the
shoulders, arms, and back [probably from Spanish *capa*
"cloak", from Latin *cappa* "head covering, cloak" — related to CAP, CHAPEL, CHAPERON, ¹COPE, ESCAPE]
Cape buffalo \'kāp-\ *n* : a large dangerous and often savage buffalo of grassy and open areas with few trees in
Africa south of the Sahara
Ca·pel·la \kə-'pel-ə\ *n* : a very bright star in Auriga
¹**ca·per** \'kā-pər\ *n* : a pickled flower bud or young berry of
a low prickly shrub of the Mediterranean region that is
used as a relish [from earlier *capers* "caper shrub or
berry" (mistaken for being a plural), from Middle English
caperis (same meaning), from Latin *capperis* "caper
shrub"]
²**caper** *vb* **ca·pered; ca·per·ing** \-p(ə-)riŋ\ : to leap about
in a lively way [probably an altered form of English *capriole* "a playful leap, a leap by a trained horse", from
early French *capriole* or early Italian *capriola* (both, same
meaning), derived from Latin *capreolus* "goat, male deer"]
³**caper** *n* **1** : a gay bounding leap or spring **2** : a playful
or mischievous trick **3** : an illegal or questionable act
cap·il·lar·i·ty \,kap-ə-'lar-ət-ē\ *n* : the action by which the
surface of a liquid where (as in a slender tube) it is in contact with a solid is raised or lowered depending upon how
much the molecules of the liquid are attracted to one another and to those of the solid
¹**cap·il·lary** \'kap-ə-,ler-ē\ *adj* **1** : having a long slender
form and a very small inner diameter ⟨a *capillary* tube⟩ **2**
: of or relating to capillaries or capillarity
²**capillary** *n, pl* **-lar·ies** : a capillary tube; *esp* : any of the
tiny hairlike blood vessels connecting arteries and veins
¹**cap·i·tal** \'kap-ət-ᵊl, 'kap-tᵊl\ *adj* **1 a** : punishable by
death ⟨a *capital* crime⟩ **b** : resulting in death ⟨*capital* pun-
ishment⟩ **2** : belonging to the series A, B, C, etc. rather
than a, b, c, etc. ⟨*capital* letters⟩ **3** : being the location of
a government ⟨the *capital* city⟩ **4** : of or relating to capital
⟨*capital* investment⟩ **5** : EXCELLENT ⟨a *capital* idea⟩ [Mid-
dle English *capital* "relating to or standing at the head of",
from Latin *capitalis* (same meaning); from *caput* "head"
— related to ACHIEVE, CADET, ¹CAPE, CAPRICE, CAPTAIN,
CHIEF; see *Word History* at CAPRICE]
²**capital** *n* **1 a** : accumulated wealth especially as used to
produce more wealth **b** : persons owning or investing
capital **2** : profitable use ⟨make *capital* out of another's
weakness⟩ **3** : a capital letter **4** : a capital city **5** : a
city that is most important for a particular activity or product
⟨the oil *capital* of the country⟩
³**capital** *n* : the top part of an architectural column
cap·i·tal·ism \'kap-ət-ᵊl-,iz-əm, 'kap-tᵊl-\ *n* : an economic
system in which resources and means of production are
privately owned and prices, production, and the distribution
of goods are determined mainly by competition in a free
market — **cap·i·tal·ist** \-əst\ *or* **cap·i·tal·is·tic** \,kap-
ət-ᵊl-'is-tik, ,kap-tᵊl-\ *adj* — **cap·i·tal·is·ti·cal·ly** \-ti-
k(ə-)lē\ *adv*
cap·i·tal·ist \'kap-ət-ᵊl-əst, 'kap-tᵊl-\ *n* **1** : a person who
has capital and especially business capital **2** : a person
who supports capitalism
cap·i·tal·ize \'kap-ət-ᵊl-,īz, 'kap-tᵊl-\ *vb* **-ized; -iz·ing 1**
: to write or print with a beginning capital letter or in capital
letters **2 a** : to supply capital for (as a business or a project) **b** : to use as capital (as in business) **3** : to take an
advantage ⟨*capitalize* on an opponent's mistake⟩ — **cap-
i·tal·iza·tion** \,kap-ət-ᵊl-ə-'zā-shən, ,kap-tᵊl-\ *n*
cap·i·tol \'kap-ət-ᵊl, 'kap-tᵊl\ *n* **1** : the building in which a
state legislature meets **2** *cap* : the building in which the
U.S. Congress meets in Washington, D.C.
ca·pit·u·late \kə-'pich-ə-,lāt\ *vb* **-lat·ed; -lat·ing** : to surrender usually on terms agreed upon in advance — **ca-
pit·u·la·tion** \kə-,pich-ə-'lā-shən\ *n*
ca·po \'kā-pō\ *n, pl* **capos** : a bar that can be fitted on the
fingerboard especially of a guitar to raise the pitch of all

the strings

ca·pon \'kā-ˌpän, -pən\ *n* : a castrated male chicken

ca·price \kə-'prēs\ *n* **1** : a sudden change in feeling, opinion, or action **2** : a disposition to change one's mind suddenly — **ca·pri·cious** \kə-'prish-əs, -'prē-shəs\ *adj* — **ca·pri·cious·ly** *adv* — **ca·pri·cious·ness** *n*

> **Word History** Picture a person shaking in terror and with his or her hair standing on end. To the Italians of long ago such a person looked a bit like a porcupine covered with spines. The Italian word for "a sudden shiver or shudder", *capriccio*, reflects this likeness, for it means literally "head with hair standing on end". The word comes from *capo*, meaning "head" (from Latin *caput* "head") and *riccio*, meaning "porcupine, hedgehog". In time the meaning of *capriccio* changed from "a sudden shiver or shudder" to "a whim or sudden desire to do something". This change in meaning was influenced by the fact that the first part of *capriccio* looks like *capra*, the Italian word for "goat". The goat is an animal known for its sudden actions and frisky behavior. The French borrowed the Italian word *capriccio*, meaning "whim", and spelled it *caprice*. It is from the French that we get our Modern English word *caprice*. [from French *caprice* "a sudden desire or change of mind", from Italian *capriccio* "whim, shudder", literally "head with hair standing on end", from *capo* "head" (from Latin *caput* "head") and *riccio* "porcupine, hedgehog" — related to CAPITAL]

Cap·ri·corn \'kap-ri-ˌkȯ(ə)rn\ *n* **1** : a group of stars between Sagittarius and Aquarius that is usually pictured as a goat **2 a** : the 10th sign of the zodiac — see ZODIAC table **b** : a person whose sign of the zodiac is Capricorn

cap·size \'kap-ˌsīz, kap-'sīz\ *vb* **cap·sized; cap·siz·ing** : to turn over : UPSET ⟨canoes *capsize* easily⟩

cap·stan \'kap-stən, -ˌstan\ *n* : a device that consists of a drum to which a rope is fastened and that is used especially on ships for moving or raising weights

capstan

¹cap·sule \'kap-səl, -(ˌ)sül\ *n* **1** : a surrounding cover of a bodily part ⟨a *capsule* of a joint⟩ **2** : a case bearing spores or seeds **3** : a shell usually of gelatin that is used for packaging something (as a drug); *also* : such a shell together with its contents **4** : an envelope of carbohydrate around a microbe and especially a bacterium **5** : a small compartment with nearly normal atmospheric pressure for a pilot or astronaut; *esp* : SPACECRAFT

²capsule *adj* : very brief ⟨*capsule* movie reviews⟩

¹cap·tain \'kap-tən\ *n* **1 a** : the commanding officer of a military unit **b** : a military commissioned officer with a rank just below that of major **2 a** : the commanding officer of a ship **b** : a naval commissioned officer with a rank just below that of commodore **3** : a fire or police department officer with a rank usually between that of chief and lieutenant **4 a** : the leader of a team or side **b** : a person in charge of several waiters in a restaurant [Middle English *capitane* "military leader", from early French *capitaine* (same meaning), from Latin *capitaneus* "chief", from *caput* "head" — related to CADET, CAPITAL, CHIEF] — **cap·tain·cy** \-sē\ *n*

²captain *vb* : to be captain of

cap·tion \'kap-shən\ *n* **1** : the heading especially of an article or document **2** : the explanation or description accompanying a pictorial illustration (as a cartoon or photograph) **3** : SUBTITLE 2 — **caption** *vb*

cap·tious \'kap-shəs\ *adj* : quick to find fault especially over small things — **cap·tious·ly** *adv* — **cap·tious·ness** *n*

cap·ti·vate \'kap-tə-ˌvāt\ *vb* **-vat·ed; -vat·ing** : to influence or fascinate by some special charm — **cap·ti·va·tion** \ˌkap-tə-'vā-shən\ *n*

¹cap·tive \'kap-tiv\ *adj* **1** : taken and held prisoner especially in war **2** : fastened so as to prevent escape ⟨*captive* balloon⟩ — **cap·tiv·i·ty** \kap-'tiv-ət-ē\ *n*

²captive *n* : one that is captive : PRISONER

cap·tor \'kap-tər, -ˌtȯ(ə)r\ *n* : one that has captured a person or thing

¹cap·ture \'kap-chər, -shər\ *n* **1** : the act of capturing **2** : something or someone captured [from early French *capture* "capture", from Latin *captura* (same meaning), from *captus* "one taken (as a prisoner)", from *capere* "to take" — related to ACCEPT, CATCH, RECEIVE]

²capture *vb* **cap·tured; cap·tur·ing** \'kap-chə-riŋ, 'kap-shriŋ\ **1 a** : to take and hold especially by force ⟨*capture* a city⟩ **b** : to gain or win as if by force ⟨*captured* first prize⟩ **2** : ¹PRESERVE 1 ⟨*captured* her smile on film⟩ **syn** see CATCH

cap·u·chin \'kap-yə-shən, kə-'p(y)ü-\ *n* : a South American monkey with the forehead bare and bordered by a fringe of dark hair

cap·y·bara \ˌkap-i-'bar-ə, -'bär-\ *n* : a tailless South American rodent often exceeding four feet in length that is often found in or near water

capybara

car \'kär\ *n* **1** : a vehicle (as an automobile or part of a passenger train) moving on wheels **2** : the passenger compartment of an elevator **3** : the part of a balloon or an airship that carries the passengers and equipment

ca·rafe \kə-'raf, -'räf\ *n* : a bottle that has a lip and is used to hold water or beverages

car·a·mel \'kär-məl; 'kar-ə-məl, -ˌmel\ *n* **1** : burnt sugar used for coloring and flavoring **2** : a firm chewy candy

car·a·pace \'kar-ə-ˌpās\ *n* : a bony or horny case or shield covering all or part of the back of an animal (as a turtle)

¹carat *variant of* KARAT

²car·at \'kar-ət\ *n* : a unit of weight for precious gems (as diamonds) equal to 200 milligrams

car·a·van \'kar-ə-ˌvan\ *n* **1 a** : a group (as of merchants or pilgrims) traveling together on a long journey through desert or dangerous regions **b** : a group of pack animals or of vehicles traveling together one behind the other **2** : a covered vehicle; *esp* : one equipped as traveling living quarters

car·a·van·sa·ry \ˌkar-ə-'van(t)-sə-rē\ *n, pl* **-ries** **1** : an inn in eastern countries where caravans rest at night **2** : HOTEL, INN

car·a·vel \'kar-ə-ˌvel, -vəl\ *n* : a small 15th and 16th century ship with a broad bow, a high stern, and three or four masts

caravel

\ə\ abut	\au̇\ out	\i\ tip	\ȯ\ saw	\u̇\ foot
\ər\ **further**	\ch\ **chin**	\ī\ **life**	\ȯi\ **coin**	\y\ **yet**
\a\ **mat**	\e\ **pet**	\j\ **job**	\th\ **thin**	\yü\ **few**
\ā\ **take**	\ē\ **easy**	\ŋ\ **sing**	\th\ **this**	\yu̇\ **cure**
\ä\ **cot, cart**	\g\ **go**	\ō\ **bone**	\ü\ **food**	\zh\ **vision**

car·a·way \'kar-ə-,wā\ *n* : a usually white-flowered herb related to the carrot and having fruits used in seasoning and medicine

car·bide \'kär-,bīd\ *n* : a compound of carbon with another element

car·bine \'kär-,bēn, -,bīn\ *n* : a light short-barreled rifle

car·bo·hy·drate \,kär-bō-'hī-,drāt, -drət\ *n* : any of various compounds of carbon, hydrogen, and oxygen (as sugars, starches, or celluloses) most of which are formed by plants and are a major animal food

car·bol·ic acid \kär-,bäl-ik-\ *n* : PHENOL

car·bon \'kär-bən\ *n* **1** : a nonmetallic element found more or less pure in nature (as in diamond and graphite) or as a part of coal and petroleum and of the bodies of living things or obtained artificially — see ELEMENT table **2 a** : a sheet of carbon paper **b** : CARBON COPY 1

car·bo·na·ceous \,kär-bə-'nā-shəs\ *adj* : relating to, containing, or made up of carbon

car·bo·na·do \,kär-bə-'näd-ō, -'näd-\ *n, pl* **-dos** : an impure dark-colored fine-grained mass of diamond particles valuable for great strength and hardness

[1]car·bon·ate \'kär-bə-,nāt\ *n* : a compound formed by the reaction of carbonic acid with another substance

[2]car·bon·ate \'kär-bə-,nāt\ *vb* **-at·ed; -at·ing** **1** : to change into a carbonate **2** : to saturate with carbon dioxide ⟨a *carbonated* beverage⟩ — **car·bon·ation** \,kär-bə-'nā-shən\ *n*

carbon black *n* : any of various black substances consisting of carbon or mostly carbon obtained as soot and used especially as coloring matters

carbon copy *n* **1** : a copy made with carbon paper **2** : [2]DUPLICATE

carbon cycle *n* : the cycle of carbon in living things in which carbon dioxide is used in photosynthesis to form food and growth substances and is later returned to the environment by respiration and decay

carbon dioxide *n* : a heavy colorless gas that does not support burning, dissolves in water to form carbonic acid, is formed especially by the burning and breaking down of organic substances (as in animal respiration), is absorbed from the air by plants in photosynthesis, and has many industrial uses

carbon disulfide *n* : a colorless flammable poisonous liquid used especially to dissolve rubber and as an insecticide — called also *carbon bisulfide*

carbon 14 \-(')fōr(t)-'tēn, -(')fôr-\ *n* : a heavy radioactive form of carbon of mass number 14 used especially in tracer studies and in finding out the age of very old remains (as bones or charcoal) of formerly living materials

car·bon·ic acid \kär-'bän-ik-\ *n* : a weak acid that is formed from water and carbon dioxide, is found only in mixtures with water, and breaks down easily

car·bon·if·er·ous \,kär-bə-'nif-(ə-)rəs\ *adj* **1** : producing or containing carbon or coal **2** *cap* : of, relating to, or being a period of the Paleozoic era of geological history or the corresponding system of rocks that includes coal beds — see GEOLOGIC TIME table — **Carboniferous** *n*

car·bon·ize \'kär-bə-,nīz\ *vb* **-ized; -iz·ing** : to change or become changed into carbon — **car·bon·iza·tion** \,kär-bə-nə-'zā-shən\ *n*

carbon monoxide *n* : a colorless odorless very poisonous gas formed by the incomplete burning of carbon

carbon paper *n* : a thin paper covered with a coloring matter and used for making copies of something written or typed

carbon tet·ra·chlo·ride \-,te-trə-'klō(ə)r-,īd, -'klȯ(ə)r-\ *n* : a colorless nonflammable poisonous liquid used to dissolve things (as grease)

car·bun·cle \'kär-,bəŋ-kəl\ *n* **1** : a rounded and polished garnet **2** : a painful inflammation of the skin and deeper tissues that releases pus from several openings — compare [1]BOIL

car·bu·re·tor \'kär-b(y)ə-,rāt-ər\ *n* : the part of an engine in which liquid fuel (as gasoline) is mixed with air to make it burn easily

car·cass \'kär-kəs\ *n* : a dead body; *esp* : the body of a meat animal prepared for market

car·cin·o·gen \kär-'sin-ə-jən, 'kärs-°n-ə-,jen\ *n* : a substance that causes cancer — **car·ci·no·gen·ic** \,kärs-°n-ō-'jen-ik\ *adj*

car·ci·no·ma \,kärs-°n-'ō-mə\ *n, pl* **-mas** *or* **-ma·ta** \-mət-ə\ : a tumor that consists of epithelial cells and is often fatal if not treated

[1]card \'kärd\ *vb* : to clean and untangle fibers by combing with a card before spinning — **card·er** *n*

[2]card *n* : an instrument for combing fibers (as wool or cotton) [Middle English *carde* "instrument for combing fibers", from early French *carde* (same meaning), derived from Latin *carduus* "thistle"]

[3]card *n* **1** : PLAYING CARD **2** *pl* **a** : a game played with cards **b** : card playing **3** : an amusing person : WAG **4** : a flat stiff usually small and rectangular piece of paper, thin paperboard, or plastic: as **a** : POSTCARD **b** : such a card on which computer information is stored **c** : BANK-CARD **5** : a sports program **6** : a removable circuit board (as in a microcomputer) [Middle English *carde* "playing card", from early French *carte* (same meaning), from early Italian *carta*, literally "leaf of paper", from Latin *charta* "piece of papyrus" — related to CARTON, CARTOON, CHART]

card·board \'kärd-,bō(ə)rd, -,bȯ(ə)rd\ *n* : PAPERBOARD

card catalog *n* : a catalog of library books in which a card for each book is alphabetically filed with its call number usually under the title, author, and subject of the book

car·di·ac \'kärd-ē-,ak\ *adj* : of, relating to, situated near, or acting on the heart

car·di·gan \'kärd-i-gən\ *n* : a usually collarless sweater opening down the front

Car·di·gan Welsh corgi \'kärd-i-gən-\ *n* : a Welsh corgi with rounded ears, a long tail, and forelegs turned slightly outward — called also *Cardigan*

Cardigan Welsh corgi

[1]car·di·nal \'kärd-nəl, -°n-əl\ *n* **1** : a high official of the Roman Catholic Church ranking next below the pope **2** : CARDINAL NUMBER **3** : any of several American finches of which the male is bright red with a black face and a pointed bunch of feathers on its head

Word History Our word *cardinal* can be traced back to the Latin adjective *cardinalis,* which at first meant "of or relating to a hinge". The root of this word is the noun *cardo,* meaning "hinge". Since a hinge is the device on which a door turns, the noun *cardo* also came to be used for "something on which a development turns or depends", or in other words, "something very important". Following this, the adjective took on the meaning "very important, chief, principal". Later the Roman Catholic Church made use of this adjective in referring to principal churches and priests. By the late Middle Ages the word *cardinalis* had come to be used for "a clergyman of the highest rank, next to the pope". When borrowed into English, *cardinalis* became *cardinal.* Then other senses of the word developed. A cardinal's robes are a deep red color, and this color influenced the naming of a type of bird whose color was like that of a cardinal's robes. [Middle English *cardinal* "high church official", from Latin *cardinalis* (same meaning), from *cardinalis* (adjective) "principal, most important, of a hinge", from *cardo* "hinge"]

[2]cardinal *adj* **1** : [2]CHIEF 2, PRIMARY **2** : of or relating to a cardinal number

cardinal flower *n* : a North American plant that belongs to the genus of lobelias and bears brilliant red flowers

car·di·nal·i·ty \ˌkärd-ᵊn-ˈal-ət-ē\ *n, pl* **-ties** : the number of elements in a given mathematical set

cardinal number *n* : a number (as 1, 5, 15) that is used in simple counting and that answers the question "how many?" — see NUMBER table

cardinal point *n* : one of the four principal points of the compass: north, south, east, west

car·di·oid \ˈkärd-ē-ˌȯid\ *n* : a heart-shaped curve traced by a point on the circumference of a circle rolling completely around a circle with the same radius that does not move

car·dio·pul·mo·nary \ˈkärd-ē-ō-ˈpu̇l-mə-ˌner-ē, -ˈpəl-\ *adj* : of or relating to the heart and lungs

cardiopulmonary resuscitation *n* : a procedure used to restore normal breathing when the heart stops beating that includes clearing the air passages to the lungs, applying pressure to the chest to massage the heart, and using drugs

car·dio·vas·cu·lar \ˌkärd-ē-ō-ˈvas-kyə-lər\ *adj* : of, relating to, or involving the heart and blood vessels ⟨*cardiovascular* disease⟩

¹**care** \ˈke(ə)r, ˈka(ə)r\ *n* **1** : a heavy sense of responsibility **2** : serious attention ⟨take *care* in crossing streets⟩ **3** : PROTECTION 1, SUPERVISION ⟨under a doctor's *care*⟩ **4** : an object of one's care

²**care** *vb* **cared; car·ing 1** : to feel interest or concern ⟨we *care* what happens⟩ **2** : to give care ⟨*care* for the sick⟩ **3** : to have a liking or a desire ⟨would you *care* for some pie?⟩ — **car·er** *n*

ca·reen \kə-ˈrēn\ *vb* **1** : to cause a boat to lean or tilt over on one side for cleaning or repairing **2** : to sway from side to side **3** : ²CAREER

¹**ca·reer** \kə-ˈri(ə)r\ *n* **1 a** : ¹COURSE 1, PROGRESS **b** : full speed or activity ⟨in full *career*⟩ **2** : a course of continued progress or activity **3** : a profession followed as a permanent occupation

²**career** *vb* : to go at top speed

care·free \ˈke(ə)r-ˌfrē, ˈka(ə)r-\ *adj* : free from care : LIGHTHEARTED

care·ful \ˈke(ə)r-fəl, ˈka(ə)r-\ *adj* **1** : using care : WATCHFUL ⟨a *careful* driver⟩ **2** : made, done, or said with care ⟨a *careful* examination⟩ — **care·ful·ly** \-f(ə-)lē\ *adv* — **care·ful·ness** \-fəl-nəs\ *n*

  syn CAREFUL, CAUTIOUS, WARY mean taking care to avoid trouble. CAREFUL suggests that one is alert and thus able to prevent mistakes or accidents ⟨be *careful* not to get paint on the rug⟩ CAUTIOUS suggests that one takes special care to avoid problems ahead of time ⟨a *cautious* driver going slowly around the curve⟩ WARY suggests that one is suspicious of danger and sly in avoiding it ⟨be *wary* of strangers⟩

care·less \ˈke(ə)r-ləs, ˈka(ə)r-\ *adj* **1** : CAREFREE **2** : not taking proper care ⟨a *careless* worker⟩ **3** : done, made, or said without proper care ⟨a *careless* mistake⟩ — **care·less·ly** *adv* — **care·less·ness** *n*

ca·ress \kə-ˈres\ *n* **1** : a tender or loving touch or hug **2** : a light stroking, rubbing, or patting — **caress** *vb*

car·et \ˈkar-ət\ *n* : a mark ∧ used to show where something is to be inserted

care·tak·er \ˈke(ə)r-ˌtā-kər, ˈka(ə)r-\ *n* : one that takes care of buildings or land often for an absent owner

care·worn \-ˌwō(ə)rn, -ˌwȯ(ə)rn\ *adj* : showing the effect of grief or worry

car·fare \ˈkär-ˌfa(ə)r, -ˌfe(ə)r\ *n* : the fare charged for carrying a passenger (as on a bus)

car·go \ˈkär-ˌgō\ *n, pl* **cargoes** or **cargos** : the goods transported in a ship, airplane, or vehicle : FREIGHT

Car·ib \ˈkar-əb\ *n* : a member of an Indian people of northern South America and the Lesser Antilles

car·i·bou \ˈkar-ə-ˌbü\ *n, pl* **-bou** or **-bous** : any of several large North American animals of the deer family that are closely related to the reindeer [from Canadian French *caribou* "caribou"; of American Indian origin]

¹**car·i·ca·ture** \ˈkar-i-kə-ˌchu̇(ə)r, -ˌt(y)u̇(ə)r\ *n* **1** : exaggeration of the actions, parts, or features of someone or something usually for comic or satirical effect **2** : something (as a drawing) produced by using caricature **3** : something that seems like a caricature

²**caricature** *vb* **-tured; -tur·ing** : to make or draw a caricature of — **car·i·ca·tur·ist** \-ˌchu̇r-əst, -ˌt(y)u̇r-əst\ *n*

caribou

car·ies \ˈka(ə)r-ēz, ˈke(ə)r-\ *n, pl* **caries** : a progressive destruction of bone or tooth; *esp* : tooth decay

car·il·lon \ˈkar-ə-ˌlän, -lən\ *n* : a set of bells sounded by hammers controlled from a keyboard

car·load \ˈkär-ˈlōd\ *n* : a load that fills a car

car·mine \ˈkär-mən, -ˌmīn\ *n* : a vivid red

car·nage \ˈkär-nij\ *n* : great destruction of life (as in battle) : SLAUGHTER

car·nal \ˈkärn-ᵊl\ *adj* **1** : of or relating to the body **2** : not spiritual : CORPOREAL **3** : SENSUAL 1 — **car·nal·i·ty** \kär-ˈnal-ət-ē\ *n* — **car·nal·ly** \ˈkärn-ᵊl-ē\ *adv*

car·na·tion \kär-ˈnā-shən\ *n* **1** : a moderate red **2** : any of the numerous cultivated herbs of the genus of pinks with reddish, pink, yellow, or white usually double flowers

car·ne·lian \kär-ˈnēl-yən\ *n* : a hard tough reddish quartz used as a gem

car·ni·val \ˈkär-nə-vəl\ *n* **1** : a season or festival of merrymaking before Lent **2** : a noisy merrymaking **3 a** : a traveling group that puts on a variety of amusements **b** : a program of entertainment

car·ni·vore \ˈkär-nə-ˌvō(ə)r, -ˌvȯ(ə)r\ *n* **1** : a flesh-eating animal; *esp* : any of an order of flesh-eating mammals **2** : an insect-eating plant

car·niv·o·rous \kär-ˈniv-(ə-)rəs\ *adj* **1** : feeding on animal tissues **2** : of or relating to the carnivores

car·no·tite \ˈkär-nə-ˌtīt\ *n* : a radioactive mineral from which radium and uranium are obtained

car·ob \ˈkar-əb\ *n* : the sweet pod of a Mediterranean evergreen tree of the legume family that can be prepared to resemble chocolate and is used in various foods

¹**car·ol** \ˈkar-əl\ *n* : a usually religious song of joy

²**carol** *vb* **-oled** or **-olled; -ol·ing** or **-ol·ling 1** : to sing especially in a joyful manner **2** : to sing carols and especially Christmas carols — **car·ol·er** or **car·ol·ler** *n*

¹**car·om** \ˈkar-əm\ *n* : a rebounding especially at an angle

²**carom** *vb* : to strike and rebound at an angle

car·o·tene \ˈkar-ə-ˌtēn\ *n* : any of several orange or red pigments which occur in plants and in the fatty tissues of plant-eating animals and from which vitamin A is formed

ca·rot·id \kə-ˈrät-əd\ *n* : one of the pair of arteries that pass up each side of the neck and supply the head — called also *carotid artery* — **carotid** *adj*

ca·rous·al \kə-ˈrau̇-zəl\ *n* : CAROUSE

ca·rouse \kə-ˈrau̇z\ *n* : a drunken merrymaking — **carouse** *vb* — **ca·rous·er** *n*

car·ou·sel or **car·rou·sel** \ˌkar-ə-ˈsel *also* -ˈzel; ˈkar-ə-ˌsel *also* -ˌzel\ *n* : MERRY-GO-ROUND 1

\ə\ **abut**	\au̇\ **out**	\i\ **tip**	\ȯ\ **saw**	\u̇\ **foot**
\ər\ **further**	\ch\ **chin**	\ī\ **life**	\ȯi\ **coin**	\y\ **yet**
\a\ **mat**	\e\ **pet**	\j\ **job**	\th\ **thin**	\yü\ **few**
\ā\ **take**	\ē\ **easy**	\ŋ\ **sing**	\th\ **this**	\yu̇\ **cure**
\ä\ **cot, cart**	\g\ **go**	\ō\ **bone**	\ü\ **food**	\zh\ **vision**

¹**carp** \'kärp\ vb : to find fault : COMPLAIN — **carp·er** n

²**carp** n, pl **carp** or **carps** : a large variable Old World fresh-water fish noted for its long life and often raised for food; also : any of various related or similar fishes

¹**car·pal** \'kär-pəl\ adj : relating to the wrist or carpus

²**carpal** n : a carpal bone or cartilage

car·pel \'kär-pəl\ n : one of the structures deep inside the flower of a seed plant that together make up the ovary

car·pen·ter \'kär-pən-tər, 'kärp-ᵊm-tər\ n : a worker who builds or repairs wooden structures — **carpenter** vb

carpenter ant n : any of several ants that nest and gnaw passageways in dead or partially decayed wood

car·pen·try \'kär-pən-trē, 'kärp-ᵊm-trē\ n : the work or trade of a carpenter

car·pet \'kär-pət\ n 1 : a heavy fabric used especially as a floor covering 2 : a covering like a carpet — **carpet** vb

¹**car·pet·bag** \-,bag\ n : a traveling bag made of carpeting and very popular in the U.S. in the 19th century

²**carpetbag** adj : of or relating to carpetbaggers

car·pet·bag·ger \'kär-pət-,bag-ər\ n : a Northerner in the South after the Civil War usually seeking private gain under the reconstruction governments

carpet beetle n : a small beetle whose larva damages woolen goods

car·pet·ing \'kär-pət-iŋ\ n : material for carpets; also : CARPET 1 (wall-to-wall carpeting)

car pool n : an arrangement by a group of automobile owners in which each in turn drives his or her own car and carries the others as passengers usually to and from work — **car·pool** \'kär-,pül\ vb — **car·pool·er** n

car·port \'kär-,pō(ə)rt, -,pȯ(ə)rt\ n : an automobile shelter with open sides that is usually attached to the side of a building

car·pus \'kär-pəs\ n, pl **car·pi** \-,pī, -,pē\ : the wrist or its bones

car·ra·geen·an or **car·ra·geen·in** \,kar-ə-'gē-nən\ n : a substance obtained from various red algae (as Irish moss) that is used in foods especially to stabilize and thicken them

car·riage \'kar-ij\ n 1 a : the act of carrying b : manner of holding the body : POSTURE 2 : the cost of carrying 3 : a horse-drawn wheeled vehicle designed for carrying persons 4 : a wheeled support carrying a load (gun carriage) 5 : a movable part of a machine for supporting or carrying some other movable object or part (a typewriter carriage)

car·ri·er \'kar-ē-ər\ n 1 : one that carries (mail carrier) 2 : a person or firm engaged in transporting passengers or goods 3 a : a bearer and transmitter of disease germs; esp : one who carries germs of a disease (as typhoid fever) in his or her system but is immune to the disease b : one who has a gene for a trait or condition (as sickle-cell anemia) that is not expressed in his or her system 4 : an electric wave or alternating current that is used to send signals for radio, television, telephone, and telegraph

car·ri·on \'kar-ē-ən\ n : dead and decaying flesh

car·rot \'kar-ət\ n : the long orange edible root of a common garden plant that is eaten as a vegetable; also : a plant that produces a carrot

¹**car·ry** \'kar-ē\ vb **car·ried; car·ry·ing** 1 : to support and take from one place to another : TRANSPORT (carry a package) 2 : to influence by appeal to the mind or emotions (the speaker carried the audience) 3 : ¹WIN 3b, CAPTURE (carry an election) 4 : to transfer from one place (as a column) to another (carry a number in addition) 5 : to contain and direct the flow of (a pipe carries water) 6 : to wear or have on one's person or within one (carries a camera) (carries a scar) 7 : IMPLY 1, INVOLVE (the crime carries a penalty) 8 : to hold the body or a part of it (carry your head high) 9 : to sing in correct pitch (carry a tune) 10 : to stock for sale (carries three brands of tires) 11 : to keep on a list or record (carrying six drivers

on the payroll) 12 : ¹SUPPORT 4a (pillars carry an arch) 13 a : to succeed in (carry an election) b : to win a majority of votes in (as a state) 14 : to present or publish for the public (a newspaper carries weather reports) (will your local station carry the games) 15 : to reach or travel a distance (a voice that carries well)

²**carry** n, pl **carries** : a quantity that is transferred in addition from one number place to the next one of higher place value

car·ry·all \'kar-ē-,ȯl\ n : a large bag or carrying case

carry away vb : to arouse strong feelings or enthusiasm in

carrying charge n : a charge added to the price of merchandise sold on the installment plan

carry on vb 1 : ²CONDUCT 2, MANAGE (carries on a business) 2 : to behave badly (embarrassed at the way you carried on) 3 : to continue especially in spite of difficulties (still carrying on)

carry out vb : to put into action or effect (carry out a plan)

car·sick \'kär-,sik\ adj : having motion sickness associated with riding in a car — **car sickness** n

¹**cart** \'kärt\ n 1 : a heavy two-wheeled wagon usually pulled by a horse 2 : a light usually two-wheeled vehicle (pony cart)

²**cart** vb : to carry in or as if in a cart — **cart·er** n

car·tel \kär-'tel\ n : a combination of business firms to control world markets and fix prices

car·ti·lage \'kärt-ᵊl-ij, 'kärt-lij\ n 1 : an elastic tissue which composes most of the skeleton of the embryonic and very young vertebrates and much of which is changed to bone later in the life of higher forms but remains throughout life the major part making up the skeleton of primitive forms 2 : a part or structure composed of cartilage

car·ti·lag·i·nous \,kärt-ᵊl-'aj-ə-nəs\ adj : of, relating to, or resembling cartilage

cartilaginous fish n : any of the fishes having the skeleton composed largely of cartilage

car·tog·ra·pher \kär-'täg-rə-fər\ n : a person who makes maps

car·tog·ra·phy \kär-'täg-rə-fē\ n : the making of maps — **car·to·graph·ic** \,kärt-ə-'graf-ik\ adj

car·ton \'kärt-ᵊn\ n : a paperboard box or container [from French carton "cardboard box", from Italian cartone "pasteboard", derived from carta "sheet of paper", from Latin charta "piece of papyrus" — related to ³CARD, CARTOON]

car·toon \kär-'tün\ n 1 : a design, drawing, or painting made as a model for the finished work 2 a : a drawing intended as a humorous comment on public affairs b : COMIC STRIP 3 : ANIMATED CARTOON [from Italian cartone "pasteboard, a sketch of a planned drawing or painting done on heavy paper", derived from carta "sheet of paper", from Latin charta "piece of papyrus" — related to ³CARD, CARTON] — **car·toon·ist** \-'tü-nəst\ n

car·tridge \'kär-trij\ n : a case or container that holds a substance or device which is difficult, troublesome, or awkward to handle and that can be easily changed : as a : a tube containing a complete charge for a firearm b : a holder for photographic film c : a device on a phonograph that changes vibrations of the needle into electrical signals d : a case for holding a magnetic tape or disk e : a case for holding integrated circuits containing a computer program (a video-game cartridge)

cart·wheel \'kärt-,hwēl, -,wēl\ n 1 : a large coin (as a silver dollar) 2 : a sideways handspring with arms and legs extended

carve \'kärv\ vb **carved; carv·ing** 1 : to cut with care or exactness 2 : to cut into pieces or slices 3 : to cut up and serve meat — **carv·er** n

carv·ing \'kär-viŋ\ n 1 : the act or art of a person who carves 2 : a carved object, design, or figure

cary·at·id \,kar-ē-'at-əd\ n, pl **-atids** or **-at·i·des** \-'at-ə-,dēz\ : a sculptured figure of a woman in flowing robes

used as a column in architecture

ca·sa·ba \kə-'säb-ə\ *n* : any of several muskmelons that have a yellow rind and sweet flesh and keep well

¹**cas·cade** \kas-'kād\ *n* : a steep usually small waterfall

²**cascade** *vb* **cas·cad·ed; cas·cad·ing** : to fall in or as if in a cascade

¹**case** \'kās\ *n* **1** : a situation requiring investigation, action, or consideration ⟨a *case* for the police⟩ **2 a** : a form of a noun, pronoun, or adjective showing its grammatical relation to other words ⟨the word "child's" in "a child's shirt" is in the possessive

caryatid

case⟩ **b** : such a relation whether shown by change of form or not ⟨the subject of a verb is in the nominative *case*⟩ **3** : what actually exists or happens : FACT **4** : a question or claim to be settled in a court of law **5** : a convincing argument **6 a** : an instance of disease or injury **b** : ²PATIENT **7** : EXAMPLE 3 ⟨a *case* of injustice⟩ [Middle English *cas* "situation needing action", from early French *cas* (same meaning), from Latin *casus* "a chance", derived from *cadere* "to fall, happen, come by chance"] — **in any case** : no matter what happens ⟨I'll probably go *in any case*⟩ — **in case 1** : IF 1 ⟨*in case* you couldn't figure out the first clue, here's a second⟩ **2** : as a precaution ⟨carry an umbrella just *in case*⟩ **3** : as a precaution against the event that ⟨have extra money *in case* we need it⟩ — **in case of** : in the event of ⟨for use *in case of* fire⟩

²**case** *n* **1 a** : a box or container to hold something **b** : a box with its contents **2** : an outer covering or protective shield **3** : CASING 2 [Middle English *cas* "box, container", from early French *casse* (same meaning), from Latin *capsa* "chest, box", from *capere* "to take, hold" — related to CAPTURE, CASH]

case hard·en \'kās-,härd-ᵊn\ *vb* : to harden (an iron alloy) so that the surface layer is harder than the interior — **case–hard·ened** *adj*

ca·sein \'kā-,sēn, kā-'sēn\ *n* **1** : a phosphorus-containing protein that is separated from milk especially by the action of acid that is used in making paints and adhesives **2** : a phosphorus-containing protein that is produced when milk is made to form curds by rennet, that makes up a major part of cheese, and that is used in making plastics

case knife *n* **1** : SHEATH KNIFE **2** : a table knife

case·ment \'kā-smənt\ *n* **1** : a window frame opening on hinges like a door **2** : a window with a casement

case·work \'kā-,swərk\ *n* : social work involving close contact with the problems and needs of a person or family — **case·work·er** \-,swər-kər\ *n*

¹**cash** \'kash\ *n* **1** : money in the form of coins or bills **2** : money or its equivalent (as a check) paid for goods at the time of purchase or delivery [from early French *casse* or early Italian *cassa*, both meaning "money box", from Latin *capsa* "chest, box" — related to ²CASE]

²**cash** *vb* : to pay or obtain cash for ⟨*cash* a check⟩

ca·shew \'kash-ü, kə-'shü\ *n* : an edible nut that is shaped like a kidney and comes from a tropical American tree that is related

cashew

to the sumacs

¹**cash·ier** \ka-'shi(ə)r\ *n* **1** : an officer of a bank who is responsible for all money received and paid out **2** : an employee of a store or restaurant who receives and records payments made by customers

²**ca·shier** \ka-'shi(ə)r, kə-\ *vb* : to remove from a job; *esp* : to dismiss in disgrace

cashier's check *n* : a check drawn by a bank upon its own funds and signed by its cashier

cash in *vb* **1** : to obtain cash for ⟨*cashed in* her bonds⟩ **2** : to benefit financially ⟨souvenir sellers *cashed in* at the fair⟩ ⟨*cashing in* on their brother's fame⟩

cash·mere *or* **Kash·mir** \'kazh-,mi(ə)r, 'kash-\ *n* **1** : fine wool from the undercoat of cashmere goats **2** : a soft yarn or fabric once made from cashmere wool but now often from sheep's wool

cashmere goat *n* : an Indian goat whose fine soft undercoat forms cashmere wool

cash register *n* : a business machine that usually has a money drawer, records the amount of money received, and exhibits the amount of each sale

cash value *n* : the amount paid to the owner of a life insurance policy if it is cashed in before the person named to receive the benefits is due the full amount

cas·ing \'kā-siŋ\ *n* **1** : something that encloses or surrounds **2** : a frame around a door or window opening

ca·si·no \kə-'sē-nō\ *n, pl* **-nos** : a building or room used for gambling

cask \'kask\ *n* **1** : a barrel-shaped container usually for liquids **2** : the quantity contained in a cask

cas·ket \'kas-kət\ *n* **1** : a small chest or box (as for jewels) **2** : COFFIN

casque \'kask\ *n* : HELMET 1

cas·sa·va \kə-'säv-ə\ *n* : any of several tropical plants with a thick rootstock that yields a nourishing starch; *also* : the rootstock or its starch — compare TAPIOCA

cas·se·role \'kas-ə-,rōl\ *n* **1** : a dish in which food can be baked and served **2** : the food cooked and served in a casserole

cas·sette \kə-'set, ka-\ *n* : a container holding film, photographic plates, or magnetic tape

cas·sia \'kash-ə\ *n* **1** : the coarse bark of any of several cinnamons **2** : any of a genus of herbs, shrubs, and trees of the legume family which grow in warm regions

Cas·si·o·pe·ia \,kas-ē-ə-'pē-(y)ə\ *n* : a northern group of stars between Andromeda and Cepheus

cas·sit·er·ite \kə-'sit-ə-,rīt\ *n* : a brown or black mineral that consists of the dioxide of tin and is the chief source of tin

cas·sock \'kas-ək\ *n* : a close-fitting ankle-length gown worn by clergy (as in the Roman Catholic church)

cas·so·wary \'kas-ə-,wer-ē\ *n, pl* **-war·ies** : any of several tall swift-running birds of New Guinea and Australia that are closely related to the emu

¹**cast** \'kast\ *vb* **cast; cast·ing 1 a** : ¹THROW 1a, TOSS ⟨*cast* a stone⟩ **b** : to throw a fishing line **c** : ¹DIRECT 3, PROJECT ⟨*cast* a glance⟩ ⟨*cast* doubt⟩ **d** : to deposit formally ⟨*cast* a ballot⟩ **e** : to throw off, out, or away ⟨the horse

cassowary

\ə\ **abut**	\aú\ **out**	\i\ **tip**	\ò\ **saw**	\ú\ **foot**
\ər\ **further**	\ch\ **chin**	\ī\ **life**	\òi\ **coin**	\y\ **yet**
\a\ **mat**	\e\ **pet**	\j\ **job**	\th\ **thin**	\yú\ **few**
\ā\ **take**	\ē\ **easy**	\ŋ\ **sing**	\th\ **this**	\yú\ **cure**
\ä\ **cot, cart**	\g\ **go**	\ō\ **bone**	\ü\ **food**	\zh\ **vision**

cast a shoe⟩ ⟨a snake *casts* its skin⟩ **2 a** : COMPUTE **b** : to arrange into parts or into a proper form ⟨*cast* the story in the form of a letter⟩ **3** : to assign parts to actors ⟨*cast* a play⟩ **4** : to shape a substance by pouring it in liquid or very soft form into a mold and letting it harden without pressure ⟨*cast* steel⟩ ⟨*cast* machine parts⟩ — **cast lots** : to draw lots to determine a matter by chance

²cast *n* **1** : an act of casting **2 a** : the form in which a thing is constructed **b** : the characters or the actors in a story or play **3** : the distance to which a thing can be thrown **4 a** : a glance of the eye **b** : APPEARANCE 2, LOOK **5 a** : CASTING 2 **b** : a rigid dressing of plaster of paris for immobilizing a body part **6** : ²FORECAST **7** : a tinge of color : SHADE **8** : one of the characteristics associated with a person or thing ⟨the humorous *cast* of his stories⟩ ⟨her strict *cast* of mind⟩ **9** : something thrown out or off or shed

cast about *vb* : to look around here and there : SEEK

cas·ta·net \,kas-tə-'net\ *n* : a rhythm instrument that consists of two small ivory, wood, or plastic shells fastened together and attached to the thumb and clicked together by the fingers — usually used in pl. [from Spanish *castañeta* "castanet", from *castaña* "chestnut"]

cast around *vb* : CAST ABOUT

cast·away \'kas-tə-,wā\ *adj* **1** : thrown away **2** : cast adrift or ashore — **castaway** *n*

caste \'kast\ *n* **1** : one of the classes into which the Hindu people of India were formerly divided **2 a** : a division of society based upon differences of wealth, rank, or occupation **b** : social rank : PRESTIGE **3** : a specialized form of a social insect that carries out a particular purpose in the colony ⟨the worker *caste* in a colony of honeybees⟩

cas·tel·lat·ed \'kas-tə-,lāt-əd\ *adj* : having battlements like a castle

cast·er \'kas-tər\ *n* **1** : one that casts **2** *or* **cas·tor** \'kas-tər\ : a small container (as for salt) with a top having small holes **3** : a small wheel that turns freely and is used for supporting furniture

cas·ti·gate \'kas-tə-,gāt\ *vb* **-gat·ed; -gat·ing** : to punish, scold, or criticize harshly — **cas·ti·ga·tion** \,kas-tə-'gā-shən\ *n* — **cas·ti·ga·tor** \'kas-tə-,gāt-ər\ *n*

cast·ing \'kas-tin\ *n* **1** : the act of one that casts **2** : something cast in a mold **3** : ²CAST 9

cast iron *n* : a hard brittle alloy of iron, carbon, and silicon shaped by being poured into a mold while melted

cas·tle \'kas-əl\ *n* **1 a** : a large building or group of buildings usually having high walls with towers and a surrounding moat for protection **b** : a large or impressive house **2** : ³ROOK [Middle English *castel* "castle", from early French *castel* (same meaning), derived from Latin *castellum* "castle, fortress" — related to CHÂTEAU]

cast-off \'kas-,tȯf\ *adj* : thrown away or aside ⟨*cast-off* clothes⟩ — **castoff** *n*

Cas·tor \'kas-tər\ *n* : the more northern of the two bright stars in Gemini [from Greek *Kastōr* (name of one of the twin heroes in mythology) — see *Word History* at GEMINI]

cas·tor bean \'kas-tər-\ *n* : the very poisonous seed of the castor-oil plant; *also* : CASTOR-OIL PLANT

castor oil *n* : a pale thick oil obtained from castor beans and used chiefly as a lubricant or a laxative

castor-oil plant *n* : a tropical Old World herb widely grown as an ornamental plant or for its oil-rich seeds

cas·trate \'kas-,trāt\ *vb* **cas·trat·ed; cas·trat·ing** : to remove the sex glands and especially the testes of — **cas·tra·tion** \ka-'strā-shən\ *n*

ca·su·al \'kazh-(ə-)wəl, 'kazh-əl\ *adj* **1** : happening unexpectedly or by chance : not planned or foreseen ⟨a *casual* meeting⟩ **2** : happening without regularity : OCCASIONAL **3 a** : feeling or showing little concern : NONCHALANT **b** : designed for ordinary or informal use ⟨*casual* clothes⟩ — **ca·su·al·ly** \-ē\ *adv* — **ca·su·al·ness** *n*

ca·su·al·ty \'kazh-əl-tē, 'kazh-(ə-)wəl-\ *n, pl* **-ties** **1** : a serious or fatal accident : DISASTER **2 a** : a military person lost (as by death or capture) during warfare **b** : a person or thing injured, lost, or destroyed

cat \'kat\ *n* **1 a** : a small domestic meat-eating mammal kept by people as a pet or for catching rats and mice **b** : an animal (as the lion, tiger, leopard, jaguar, cougar, wildcat, lynx, and cheetah) that belongs to the same family as the domestic cat **2** *slang* : ¹MAN 1a, FELLOW

ca·tab·o·lism \kə-'tab-ə-,liz-əm\ *n* : destructive metabolism that breaks down complex materials within living plants and animals and usually involves the release of energy and formation of waste products — **cat·a·bol·ic** \,kat-ə-'bäl-ik\ *adj*

cat·a·clysm \'kat-ə-,kliz-əm\ *n* **1** : a great flood **2** : a violent and destructive natural event (as an earthquake) **3** : a violent social or political change — **cat·a·clys·mal** \,kat-ə-'kliz-məl\ *or* **cat·a·clys·mic** \-mik\ *adj*

cat·a·comb \'kat-ə-,kōm\ *n* : an underground place of burial — usually used in pl.

cat·a·lep·sy \'kat-ᵊl-,ep-sē\ *n* : a nervous condition in which the muscles become rigid and the body and arms and legs stay in any position in which they are placed

¹cat·a·lep·tic \,kat-ᵊl-'ep-tik\ *adj* : of, having, or being like catalepsy ⟨a *cataleptic* state⟩

²cataleptic *n* : a person who has catalepsy

¹cat·a·log *or* **cat·a·logue** \'kat-ᵊl-,ȯg, -,äg\ *n* **1** : a list of names, titles, or articles arranged according to a system **2** : a book or file containing a catalog

²catalog *or* **catalogue** *vb* **-loged** *or* **-logued; -log·ing** *or* **-logu·ing** **1** : to make a catalog of **2** : to enter in a catalog ⟨*catalog* books⟩ — **cat·a·log·er** *or* **cat·a·logu·er** \-'ȯ-gər, -'ä-gər\ *n*

ca·tal·pa \kə-'tal-pə, -'tȯl-\ *n* : a small tree of America and Asia with broad oval leaves, flowers brightly striped inside and spotted outside, and long narrow pods [derived from an American Indian word meaning literally "head with wings"]

ca·tal·y·sis \kə-'tal-ə-səs\ *n* : the change and especially increase in the rate of a chemical reaction caused by a catalyst

cat·a·lyst \'kat-ᵊl-əst\ *n* : a substance that changes the rate of a chemical reaction but is itself unchanged at the end of the process; *esp* : such a substance that speeds up a reaction or enables it to proceed under milder conditions

cat·a·lyt·ic \,kat-ᵊl-'it-ik\ *adj* : causing, involving, or relating to catalysis ⟨the *catalytic* action of an enzyme⟩

catalytic converter *n* : a device containing a catalyst for changing automobile exhaust into mostly harmless products

cat·a·lyze \'kat-ᵊl-,īz\ *vb* **-lyzed; -lyz·ing** : to bring about or produce by chemical catalysis

cat·a·ma·ran \,kat-ə-mə-'ran, 'kat-ə-mə-,ran\ *n* : a boat with twin hulls

cat·a·mount \'kat-ə-,maunt\ *n* : any of various wild cats: as **a** : COUGAR **b** : LYNX

¹cat·a·pult \'kat-ə-,pəlt, -,pult\ *n* **1** : an ancient military device for hurling missiles **2** : a device for launching an airplane (as from the deck of an aircraft carrier)

²catapult *vb* **1** : to throw or launch by or as if by a catapult **2** : to become catapulted

catapult 1

cat·a·ract \'kat-ə-,rakt\ *n* **1** : a clouding of the lens of the eye or of the transparent cover around it that blocks the passage of light **2 a** : a large waterfall **b** : a sudden rush like a waterfall : FLOOD

ca·tarrh \kə-'tär\ *n* : inflammation of a mucous membrane; *esp* : inflammation of the human nose and air passages that lasts a long time — **ca·tarrh·al** \-'tär-əl\ *adj*

ca·tas·tro·phe \kə-'tas-trə-(,)fē\ *n* **1** : a sudden disaster **2** : complete failure : FIASCO — **cat·a·stroph·ic** \,kat-ə-'sträf-ik\ *adj* — **cat·a·stroph·i·cal·ly** \-i-k(ə-)lē\ *adv*

cat·bird \'kat-,bərd\ *n* : a dark gray American songbird with a black cap and a reddish underside of the base of the tail

cat·boat \-,bōt\ *n* : a sailboat with a single mast set far forward and a single large sail with a long boom

cat·call \-,kól\ *n* : a sound like the cry of a cat or a noise expressing disapproval — **catcall** *vb*

¹catch \'kach, 'kech\ *vb* **caught** \'kót\; **catch·ing** **1 a** : to capture or seize in flight or motion ⟨*catch* butterflies⟩ **b** : ²TRAP 1a **2 a** : to discover unexpectedly ⟨was *caught* in the act⟩ **b** : to stop suddenly ⟨*caught* himself before he gave away the secret⟩ **3** : to take hold of : SNATCH **4 a** : to get entangled ⟨*catch* a sleeve on a nail⟩ **b** : to have the parts connect firmly ⟨this lock will not *catch*⟩ **c** : to attach, join, or fasten tightly **5** : to fall sick with ⟨*catch* a cold⟩ **6** : to take or get for a short time or quickly ⟨*catch* a glimpse of a friend⟩ ⟨*catch* a little sleep⟩ **7 a** : to catch up to ⟨will have to hurry to *catch* the leaders⟩ **b** : to get aboard in time ⟨*catch* the bus⟩ **8** : UNDERSTAND 1a ⟨didn't *catch* what she said⟩ **9** : to play baseball as a catcher [Middle English *cacchen* "to catch", from early French *cachier* "to hunt", probably from Latin *captiare* "to hunt", from earlier *captare* "to chase", derived from *capere* "to take" — related to CAPTURE]

syn CATCH, CAPTURE, TRAP, SNARE mean to come to possess or control by seizing. CATCH suggests the taking of something that is moving, flying, or hiding ⟨*catch* that dog⟩ CAPTURE suggests taking only after overcoming resistance or difficulty ⟨finally *captured* the fort after many days⟩ TRAP and SNARE suggest the use of a device that catches by surprise and then holds the prey ⟨*trapped* bears and other wild animals⟩ ⟨trying to *snare* fish with nets⟩

—**catch fire** **1** : to begin to burn **2** : to become excited or exciting — **catch one's breath** : to pause or rest long enough to regain normal breathing

²catch *n* **1 a** : something caught **b** : the quantity caught at one time ⟨a large *catch* of fish⟩ **2 a** : the act of catching **b** : a pastime in which a ball is thrown and caught **3** : something that checks, fastens, or holds immovable ⟨a *catch* on a door⟩ **4** : one worth catching **5** : a round for three or more voices **6** : a hidden difficulty

catch·all \'kach-,ól, 'kech-\ *n* : something to hold a variety of odds and ends

catch·er \'kach-ər, 'kech-\ *n* : one that catches; *esp* : a baseball player who plays behind home plate

catch·ing *adj* : INFECTIOUS

catch·ment \'kach-mənt, 'kech-\ *n* **1** : the action of catching water **2** : something that catches water

catch on *vb* **1** : to realize something ⟨they had been teasing me, and I never *caught on*⟩ **2** : to become popular ⟨will the new style *catch on*⟩

catchup *variant of* CATSUP

catch up *vb* **1** : to pick up suddenly or quickly ⟨*caught* the mouse *up* by the tail⟩ **2** : to go fast enough to get even with someone ahead ⟨trying to *catch up* with the rest of the class⟩ **3** : to bring oneself up to date ⟨have to *catch up* on my homework⟩ ⟨*catch up* on the news⟩

catchy \'kach-ē, 'kech-ē\ *adj* **catch·i·er; -est** **1** : likely to attract attention **2** : easily remembered ⟨*catchy* music⟩ **3** : TRICKY 2 ⟨a *catchy* question⟩

cat·e·chism \'kat-ə-,kiz-əm\ *n* **1** : a summary of religious doctrine in the form of questions and answers **2** : a set of questions requiring memorized answers put as a test

cat·e·chist \'kat-ə-,kist, -ə-kəst\ *n* : a person who catechizes

cat·e·chize \'kat-ə-,kīz\ *vb* **-chized; -chiz·ing** : to instruct by means of a catechism

cat·e·gor·i·cal \,kat-ə-'gór-i-kəl, -gär-\ *also* **cat·e·gor·ic** \-ik\ *adj* **1** : not restricted or limited in any way : ABSOLUTE ⟨a *categorical* denial⟩ **2** : of, relating to, or being a category — **cat·e·gor·i·cal·ly** \-i-k(ə-)lē\ *adv*

cat·e·go·rize \'kat-i-gə-,rīz\ *vb* **-rized; -riz·ing** : to put into a category : CLASSIFY — **cat·e·go·ri·za·tion** \,kat-i-gə-rə-'zā-shən\ *n*

cat·e·go·ry \'kat-ə-,gōr-ē, -,gór-\ *n, pl* **-ries** **1** : one of the divisions or groupings used in a system of classification ⟨"species" and "genus" are biological *categories*⟩ **2** : ¹CLASS 3a, KIND

ca·ter \'kāt-ər\ *vb* **1** : to provide a supply of food ⟨*cater* for parties⟩ **2** : to supply what is wanted or needed — **ca·ter·er** \-ər-ər\ *n*

cat·er·cor·ner \,kat-ē-'kòr-nər, ,kat-ə-, ,kit-ē-; 'kat-ē-,kòr-nər, 'kat-ə-, 'kit-ē-\ *or* **cat·er–cor·nered** \-nərd\ *or* **cat·ty–cor·ner** *or* **kit·ty–cor·ner** \-nər\ *or* **cat·ty–cor·nered** *or* **kit·ty–cor·nered** \-nərd\ *adv or adj* : in a crosswise position : on a diagonal line

cat·er·pil·lar \'kat-ə(r)-,pil-ər\ *n* : the long wormlike larva of a butterfly or moth; *also* : any of various similar insect larvae (as of a sawfly)

Word History On looking at a fuzzy caterpillar you might see a resemblance to another animal. One kind of caterpillar must have reminded some people of a bear and was at one time called a *bear worm* and later a *woolly bear.* In France long ago, the fuzzy caterpillars probably made some people think of little dogs. The French word for caterpillar is *chenille,* which comes from a Latin word for "little dog". But our word *caterpillar* comes from an early French dialect word, *catepelose,* which is made up of two words meaning "hairy cat". *Pelose,* meaning "hairy", was taken from the Latin *pilus,* "hair". This Latin word is the same root that gives us our modern English word *pile,* meaning "a coat or surface of short furry hairs". Since many caterpillars are covered with such a coat, the name is very fitting. [Middle English *catyrpel* "caterpillar", from an early French dialect word *catepelose* "caterpillar", literally "hairy cat", from *cate* "female cat" and *pelose* "hairy", derived from Latin *pilus* "hair" — related to PILE]

cat·er·waul \'kat-ər-,wól\ *vb* : to make a harsh cry — **caterwaul** *n*

cat·fish \'kat-,fish\ *n* : any of numerous usually stout-bodied large-headed fishes with long thin feelers about the mouth

cat·gut \-,gət\ *n* : a tough cord made from intestines of animals (as sheep) and used for strings of musical instruments and rackets and for sewing in surgery

ca·thar·tic \kə-'thärt-ik\ *n* : a strong laxative — **cathartic** *adj*

ca·the·dral \kə-'thē-drəl\ *n* : the principal church of a district headed by a bishop

cath·ode \'kath-,ōd\ *n* **1** : the negative electrode of an electrolytic cell — compare ANODE 1 **2** : the positive terminal of a battery **3** : the electron-emitting electrode of an electron tube — **ca·thod·ic** \ka-'thäd-ik\ *adj*

cathode ray *n* **1** : one of the high-speed electrons driven in a stream from the heated cathode of a vacuum tube under the force of a strong electric field **2** : a stream of cathode-ray electrons

cathode–ray tube *n* : a vacuum tube in which a beam of electrons is projected upon a fluorescent screen and produces a glowing spot

\ə\ abut	\au̇\ out	\i\ tip	\ȯ\ saw	\u̇\ foot
\ər\ further	\ch\ chin	\ī\ life	\ȯi\ coin	\y\ yet
\a\ mat	\e\ pet	\j\ job	\th\ thin	\yü\ few
\ā\ take	\ē\ easy	\ŋ\ sing	\t̲h̲\ this	\yu̇\ cure
\ä\ cot, cart	\g\ go	\ō\ bone	\ü\ food	\zh\ vision

cath·o·lic \'kath-(ə-)lik\ *adj* **1** : broad in sympathies, tastes, or interests **2** *cap* **a** : of or relating to the Christian church as a whole **b** : ROMAN CATHOLIC — **Ca·thol·i·cism** \kə-'thäl-ə-,siz-əm\ *n*

Catholic *n* **1** : ¹CHRISTIAN 2 **2** : a member of the Roman Catholic church

cat·ion \'kat-,ī-ən\ *n* : the ion in solution during electrolysis that travels to the cathode; *also* : a positively charged ion

cat·kin \'kat-kən\ *n* : a flower cluster (as of the willow or birch) in which the flowers grow in close circular rows along a slender stalk

cat·like \'kat-,līk\ *adj* : resembling a cat especially in being quick and silent

cat·nap \-,nap\ *n* : a short light nap — **catnap** *vb*

cat·nip \-,nip\ *n* : a common strong-scented mint that is especially attractive to cats

cat–o'–nine–tails \,kat-ə-'nīn-,tālz\ *n, pl* **cat–o'–nine–tails** : a whip made of nine knotted cords fastened to a handle

cat's cradle *n* : a game played with a string looped on the fingers so as to resemble a small cradle

cat's–eye \'kats-,ī\ *n* : any of various gems (as chalcedony) with a changeable luster suggestive of reflections from the eye of a cat

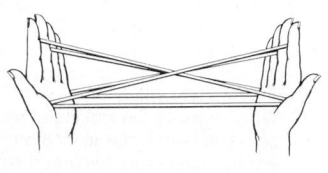
cat's cradle

cat·sup *or* **ketch·up** *or* **catch·up** \'kech-əp, 'kach-; 'kat-səp\ *n* : a thick seasoned sauce usually made of tomatoes

cat·tail \'kat-,tāl\ *n* : a tall marsh plant that bears very tiny flowers and fruit in brown furry spikes at the end of long stalks

cat·tle \'kat-ᵊl\ *n, pl* **cattle** : domestic four-footed animals held as property or raised for use; *esp* : bovine animals (as cows, bulls, or steers) kept on a farm or ranch

cat·tle·man \-mən, -,man\ *n* : a person who raises cattle

cat·ty \'kat-ē\ *adj* **cat·ti·er; -est** **1** : resembling a cat **2** : mean in a sly way ⟨*catty* remarks⟩ — **cat·ti·ly** \'kat-ə-lē\ *adv* — **cat·ti·ness** \'kat-ē-nəs\ *n*

catty–corner *or* **catty–cornered** *variant of* CATERCORNER

cat·walk \'kat-,wòk\ *n* : a narrow walk or way (as along a bridge)

Cau·ca·sian \kò-'kā-zhən, -'kazh-ən\ *adj* **1** : of or relating to the Caucasus or persons living there **2** : of or relating to the white race of humanity — **Caucasian** *n*

cau·cus \'kò-kəs\ *n* : a closed meeting of members of a political party or faction usually to select candidates or decide policy [probably of American Indian origin] — **caucus** *vb*

caught *past and past participle of* CATCH

cauldron *variant of* CALDRON

cau·li·flow·er \'kò-li-,flaù(-ə)r\ *n* : a garden plant closely related to the cabbage and grown for its compact edible head of usually white undeveloped flowers

caulk *or* **calk** \'kòk\ *vb* : to fill up a crack, seam, or joint so as to make it watertight — **caulk·er** *n*

caus·al \'kò-zəl\ *adj* : of, relating to, or being a cause

¹cause \'kòz\ *n* **1** : something or someone that brings about a result or condition **2** : a good or adequate reason ⟨a *cause* for worry⟩ ⟨a *cause* for celebration⟩ **3 a** : a ground of legal action **b** : something supported or deserving support ⟨a worthy *cause*⟩ — **cause·less** \'kòz-ləs\ *adj*
syn CAUSE, REASON, MOTIVE mean something that explains an effect or result. CAUSE applies to any event, circumstance, or condition that brings about or helps bring about a result ⟨slippery roads were the *cause* of many accidents⟩ REASON applies to a traceable or explainable cause of a known effect ⟨too little rain was the *reason* for the poor harvest⟩ MOTIVE applies to actions

explained by a feeling or desire ⟨greater knowledge was her *motive* for studying so hard⟩ ⟨police are trying to find a *motive* for the crime⟩

²cause *vb* **caused; caus·ing** : to be the cause of

cause·way \'kòz-,wā\ *n* : a raised way or road across wet ground or water

¹caus·tic \'kò-stik\ *adj* **1** : capable of eating away by chemical action : CORROSIVE **2** : likely to offend or hurt someone's feelings ⟨a *caustic* remark⟩ — **caus·ti·cal·ly** \-sti-k(ə-)lē\ *adv*

²caustic *n* : a caustic substance (as caustic soda)

caustic potash *n* : POTASSIUM HYDROXIDE

caustic soda *n* : SODIUM HYDROXIDE

cau·ter·ize \'kòt-ə-,rīz\ *vb* **-ized; -iz·ing** : to burn with a hot iron or a chemical substance usually to destroy infected tissue ⟨*cauterize* a wound⟩ — **cau·ter·iza·tion** \,kòt-ə-rə-'zā-shən\ *n*

¹cau·tion \'kò-shən\ *n* **1** : ADMONITION, WARNING **2** : carefulness in regard to danger **3** : someone or something that astonishes or catches one's attention

²caution *vb* **cau·tioned; cau·tion·ing** \'kò-sh(ə-)niŋ\ : to advise caution to : WARN

cau·tion·ary \'kò-shə-,ner-ē\ *adj* : serving as or offering a warning ⟨a *cautionary* tale⟩

cau·tious \'kò-shəs\ *adj* : marked by or given to caution ⟨a *cautious* reply⟩ **syn** see CAREFUL — **cau·tious·ly** *adv* — **cau·tious·ness** *n*

cav·al·cade \,kav-əl-'kād, 'kav-əl-,kād\ *n* **1** : a procession especially of riders or carriages **2** : a dramatic series (as of related events)

¹cav·a·lier \,kav-ə-'li(ə)r\ *n* **1** : a mounted soldier : KNIGHT **2** : a brave and courteous gentleman [from early French *cavalier* "cavalier", from early Italian *cavaliere* (same meaning), derived from Latin *caballarius* "horseman", from earlier *caballus* "horse" — related to CAVALRY, CHIVALRY; see *Word History* at CHIVALRY]

²cavalier *adj* **1** : lighthearted and charming in manner **2** : tending to disregard the rights or feelings of others : ARROGANT, DISDAINFUL — **cav·a·lier·ly** *adv* — **cav·a·lier·ness** *n*

cav·al·ry \'kav-əl-rē\ *n, pl* **-ries** : troops mounted on horseback or moving in motor vehicles or helicopters [from Italian *cavallerie* "cavalry, chivalry", from *cavaliere* "cavalier, knight", derived from Latin *caballarius* "horseman", from earlier *caballus* "horse" — related to CAVALIER, CHIVALRY; see *Word History* at CHIVALRY]

¹cave \'kāv\ *n* : a natural underground chamber or series of chambers open to the surface

²cave *vb* **caved; cav·ing** : to fall or cause to fall in or down : COLLAPSE — usually used with *in*

cave–in \'kā-,vin\ *n* **1** : the action of caving in **2** : a place where earth has caved in

cave·man \'kāv-,man\ *n* : a person living in a cave especially during the Stone Age

cav·ern \'kav-ərn\ *n* : a cave often of large or unknown size

cav·ern·ous \'kav-ər-nəs\ *adj* **1** : having caverns or cavities **2** : resembling a cavern in being large and hollow **3** : composed largely of spaces capable of filling with blood to bring about the enlargement of a body part — compare ERECTILE — **cav·ern·ous·ly** *adv*

cav·i·ar *or* **cav·i·are** \'kav-ē-,är *also* 'käv-\ *n* : the salted eggs of a large fish (as the sturgeon) usually served as an appetizer

cav·il \'kav-əl\ *vb* **-iled** *or* **-illed; -il·ing** *or* **-il·ling** \-(ə-)liŋ\ : to make objections of little worth or importance : QUIBBLE — **cavil** *n* — **cav·il·er** *or* **cav·il·ler** \-(ə-)lər\ *n*

cav·ing \'kā-viŋ\ *n* : the sport of exploring caves : SPELUNKING

cav·i·ta·tion \,kav-ə-'tā-shən\ *n* : the formation of partial vacuums in a liquid by a swiftly moving solid body (as a propeller) or by high-frequency sound waves

cav·i·ty \'kav-ət-ē\ *n, pl* **-ties** **1** : a hollow place; *esp* : an unfilled bodily space ⟨lung *cavity*⟩   **2** : a hole hollowed out in a tooth by decay

ca·vort \kə-'vȯ(ə)rt\ *vb* : to leap or dance about in a lively manner

caw \'kȯ\ *vb* : to utter the harsh call of a crow or a similar cry — **caw** *n*

cay \'kē, 'kā\ *n* : ⁴KEY

cay·enne pepper \,kī-,en-, ,kā-\ *n* : dried ripe hot peppers ground and used to add flavor to food

cayman *variant of* CAIMAN

cay·use \'kī-,(y)üs, kī-'(y)üs\ *n* : a small native horse of the western U.S.

CB \,sē-'bē\ *n* : CITIZENS BAND

C–clamp \'sē-,klamp\ *n* : a clamp shaped like the letter C

cease \'sēs\ *vb* **ceased; ceas·ing** : to come or bring to an end : STOP

cease–fire \'sēs-'fī(ə)r\ *n* : a temporary stopping of warfare

cease·less \'sēs-ləs\ *adj* : ¹CONSTANT 4, CONTINUAL — **cease·less·ly** *adv* — **cease·less·ness** *n*

ce·cro·pia moth \si-,krō-pē-ə-\ *n* : a large red and dark brown or black moth of the eastern U.S. that has a crescent-shaped spot on each wing and a caterpillar which spins a cocoon of coarse silk

cecropia moth

ce·cum *or* **cae·cum** \'sē-kəm\ *n, pl* **ce·ca** *or* **cae·ca** \-kə\ : a cavity open at one end; *esp* : the pouch in which the large intestine begins — **ce·cal** *or* **cae·cal** \-kəl\ *adj*

ce·dar \'sēd-ər\ *n* **1 a** : any of a genus of usually tall trees related to the pines and noted for their fragrant durable wood   **b** : any of numerous cone-bearing trees (as some junipers or arborvitaes) resembling the true cedars especially in having fragrant long-lasting wood   **2** : the wood of a cedar

cedar waxwing *n* : a brown waxwing of North America that has a yellow band on the tip of the tail

cede \'sēd\ *vb* **ced·ed; ced·ing** : to give up especially by treaty ⟨Russia *ceded* Alaska to the U.S. in 1867⟩

ce·dil·la \si-'dil-ə\ *n* : a mark placed under the letter c (as ç) to show that it is to be pronounced like s [from Spanish *cedilla* "mark under a c", originally a name for the obsolete letter ç, from *ceda, zeda* "the letter z", derived from Greek *zēta* "zeta"]

ceil·ing \'sē-liŋ\ *n* **1** : the overhead inside lining of a room   **2** : something that hangs over or is above   **3** : the height above the ground of the base of the lowest layer of clouds when over half of the sky is hidden by clouds   **4** : the greatest height at which an airplane can operate efficiently   **5** : an upper usually prescribed limit ⟨price *ceiling*⟩

cel·an·dine \'sel-ən-,dīn, -,dēn\ *n* **1** : a yellow-flowered herb related to the poppy   **2** : a yellow-flowered European herb of the buttercup family that has been introduced into the U.S. — called also *lesser celandine*

cel·e·brant \'sel-ə-brənt\ *n* : a person who celebrates; *esp* : the priest who is celebrating a mass

cel·e·brate \'sel-ə-,brāt\ *vb* **-brat·ed; -brat·ing** **1** : to perform publicly and according to certain rules ⟨*celebrate* Mass⟩ ⟨*celebrate* a marriage⟩   **2** : to observe in some special way (as by merrymaking or by staying away from work) ⟨*celebrate* a birthday⟩ ⟨*celebrate* Memorial Day⟩   **3** : to praise or make known publicly   **syn** see KEEP — **cel·e·bra·tion** \,sel-ə-'brā-shən\ *n* — **cel·e·bra·tor** \'sel-ə-,brāt-ər\ *n*

cel·e·brat·ed *adj* : widely known and often mentioned   **syn** see FAMOUS

ce·leb·ri·ty \sə-'leb-rət-ē\ *n, pl* **-ties** **1** : the state of being celebrated : FAME   **2** : a celebrated person

ce·ler·i·ty \sə-'ler-ət-ē\ *n, pl* **-ties** : ¹SPEED 1a

cel·ery \'sel-(ə-)rē\ *n, pl* **-er·ies** : a European herb related to the carrot and widely grown for the thick edible stems of its leaves

ce·les·ta \sə-'les-tə\ *n* : a keyboard instrument with hammers that strike steel plates to make ringing sounds

ce·les·tial \sə-'les-chəl\ *adj* **1** : of, relating to, or suggesting heaven ⟨angels are *celestial* beings⟩   **2** : of or relating to the sky ⟨a star is a *celestial* body⟩ — **ce·les·tial·ly** \-chə-lē\ *adv*

celestial equator *n* : the great circle on the celestial sphere midway between the celestial poles

celestial navigation *n* : navigation by observation of the positions of heavenly bodies

celestial pole *n* : one of two points on the celestial sphere around which the daily rotation of the stars appears to take place

celestial sphere *n* : an imaginary sphere of infinite radius against which the celestial bodies appear to be projected

cel·i·ba·cy \'sel-ə-bə-sē\ *n* : the state of not being married; *esp* : the state of one who has taken a vow not to marry

cel·i·bate \'sel-ə-bət\ *n* : one who lives in celibacy — **celibate** *adj*

cell \'sel\ *n* **1** : a very small room (as in a convent or prison) usually for one person   **2** : a small compartment (as in a honeycomb), cavity (as in a plant ovary), or bounded space (as in an insect wing)   **3** : one of the tiny units that are the basic building blocks of living things, that carry on the basic functions of life either alone or in groups, and that include a nucleus and are surrounded by a membrane   **4 a** : a container (as a jar) with electrodes and an electrolyte either for generating electricity by chemical action or for use in electrolysis   **b** : a single unit in a device for changing radiant energy into electrical energy — **celled** \'seld\ *adj*

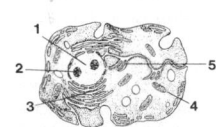
cell 3: *1* nucleus, *2* nucleolus, *3* endoplasmic reticulum, *4* mitochondrion, *5* Golgi apparatus

cel·lar \'sel-ər\ *n* : a room or set of rooms below the surface of the ground : BASEMENT

cell body *n* : the central part of a neuron that includes the nucleus but not the long thin extensions of the cell which carry signals to and from the central part — compare AXON, DENDRITE 2

cell division *n* : a process by which cells increase in number that usually involves division into similar parts of more or less equal size — compare MEIOSIS, MITOSIS

cel·list \'chel-əst\ *n* : a person who plays the cello

cell membrane *n* **1** : a semipermeable outside layer surrounding the protoplasm of a cell   **2** : CELL WALL

cel·lo \'chel-ō\ *n, pl* **cellos** : a large musical instrument of the violin family that plays the bass or tenor part [shortened form of *violoncello*]

cel·lo·phane \'sel-ə-,fān\ *n* : a thin transparent material made from cellulose and used as a wrapping

cell sap *n* : a watery solution of food and wastes that fills the vacuole of most plant cells

cell theory *n* : a general statement in biology that all living things consist of cells each of which has come from a previously existing cell

\ə\ **abut**	\au̇\ **out**	\i\ tip	\ȯ\ saw	\u̇\ foot
\ər\ **further**	\ch\ **chin**	\ī\ life	\ȯi\ coin	\y\ yet
\a\ **mat**	\e\ **pet**	\j\ job	\th\ thin	\yü\ few
\ā\ **take**	\ē\ **easy**	\ŋ\ sing	\th\ this	\yu̇\ cure
\ä\ **cot, cart**	\g\ **go**	\ō\ bone	\ü\ food	\zh\ vision

cel·lu·lar \'sel-yə-lər\ *adj* **1** : of, relating to, or consisting of cells **2** : of, relating to, or being a radiotelephone system in which a geographical area (as a city) is divided into small sections each served by a transmitter of limited range

cel·lu·loid \'sel-(y)ə-,lȯid\ *n* **1** : a tough flammable plastic **2** : a motion-picture film ⟨watch a western on *celluloid*⟩

cel·lu·lose \'sel-yə-,lōs\ *n* : a complex carbohydrate that is the chief part of the cell walls of plants and is commonly obtained as a white stringy substance from vegetable matter (as wood or cotton) which is used in making various products (as rayon and cellophane) — **cel·lu·los·ic** \,sel-yə-'lō-sik\ *adj*

cell wall *n* : the firm nonliving and usually chiefly cellulose wall that encloses and supports most plant cells

Cel·sius \'sel-sē-əs, 'sel-shəs\ *adj* : relating to or having a scale for measuring temperature on which the interval between the triple point and the boiling point of water is divided into 99.99 degrees with 0.01° representing the triple point and 100.00° the boiling point; *also* : CENTIGRADE — abbr. *C*

Celt \'kelt, 'selt\ *also* **Kelt** \'kelt\ *n* : a member of a division of the early Indo-European peoples spread out from the British Isles and Spain to Asia Minor; *also* : a person whose ancestors were Celts

¹Celt·ic \'kel-tik, 'sel-\ *or* **Kelt·ic** \'kel-\ *adj* : of, relating to, or characteristic of the Celts or their languages

²Celtic *or* **Keltic** *n* : a group of languages including Gaelic and Welsh

¹ce·ment \si-'ment\ *n* **1** : a fine powder that is produced from a burned mixture chiefly of clay and limestone and used as an ingredient of mortar and concrete; *also* : CONCRETE **2 a** : a binding element or substance **b** : an adhesive substance **3 a** : CEMENTUM **b** : a material for filling cavities in teeth

²cement *vb* **1** : to unite by or as if by cement **2** : to cover with concrete — **ce·ment·er** *n*

ce·men·tum \si-'ment-əm\ *n* : an outside bony layer that covers the root and neck and sometimes parts of the crown of the teeth of mammals

cem·e·tery \'sem-ə-,ter-ē\ *n, pl* **-ter·ies** : a place where dead people are buried : GRAVEYARD [Middle English *cimitery* "cemetery", from early French *cimitere* (same meaning), from Latin *coemeterium* "cemetery", from Greek *koimētērion* "sleeping chamber, burial place", from *koiman* "to put to sleep"]

Ce·no·zo·ic \,sē-nə-'zō-ik, ,sen-ə-\ *adj* : of, relating to, or being an era of geological history extending from the end that extends to the present time and of the Mesozoic era marked by a rapid evolution of mammals and birds and of flowering plants and especially grasses; *also* : relating to the corresponding system of rocks — see GEOLOGIC TIME table — **Cenozoic** *n*

cen·ser \'sen(t)-sər\ *n* : a container in which incense is burned

¹cen·sor \'sen(t)-sər\ *n* : an official who checks materials (as publications or movies) to take out things thought to be objectionable

²censor *vb* **cen·sored; cen·sor·ing** \'sen(t)s-(ə-)riŋ\ : to examine in order to prevent publication or take out things thought to be objectionable

cen·sor·ship \'sen(t)-sər-,ship\ *n* : the system or practice of censoring

¹cen·sure \'sen-chər\ *n* **1** : the act of blaming or condemning sternly **2** : an official expression of disapproval

²censure *vb* **cen·sured; cen·sur·ing** \'sench-(ə-)riŋ\ **1** : to find fault with **2** : to express formal disapproval of some action of — **cen·sur·able** \'sench-(ə-)rə-bəl\ *adj* — **cen·sur·er** \'sen-chər-ər\ *n*

cen·sus \'sen(t)-səs\ *n* : a counting of the population (as of a country, city, or town) and a gathering of related statistics done by a government every so often

cent \'sent\ *n* **1** : a unit of value equal to ¹⁄₁₀₀ part of a basic unit of money (as in the U.S. and Canada ¹⁄₁₀₀ dollar) **2** : a coin or bill representing one cent [from early French *cent* "hundred", from Latin *centum* "hundred"]

cen·taur \'sen-,tȯ(ə)r\ *n* : a creature in Greek mythology that is half man and half horse

cen·ta·vo \sen-'täv-ō\ *n, pl* **-vos** **1** : a unit of value equal to ¹⁄₁₀₀ part of any of several basic units of money (as the Portuguese escudo or Mexican peso) **2** : a coin representing one centavo

cen·te·nar·i·an \,sent-°n-'er-ē-ən\ *n* : a person 100 years old or older — **centenarian** *adj*

cen·ten·a·ry \sen-'ten-ə-rē, 'sent-°n-,er-ē\ *adj or n* : CENTENNIAL

¹cen·ten·ni·al \sen-'ten-ē-əl\ *n* : a 100th anniversary or its celebration

²centennial *adj* : relating to a period of 100 years — **cen·ten·ni·al·ly** \-ē-ə-lē\ *adv*

¹cen·ter \'sent-ər\ *n* **1** : the point that is an equal distance from all points on the edge of a circle or sphere **2 a** : a place in or around which an activity takes place or from which something begins ⟨a community *center*⟩ **b** : a group of nerve cells that have a common purpose ⟨respiratory *center*⟩ **3** : the middle part (as of a stage) **4** : a player occupying a middle position on a team

²center *vb* **cen·tered; cen·ter·ing** \'sent-ə-riŋ, 'sen-triŋ\ **1** : to place or fix at or around a center or central area **2** : to collect at or around a center

cen·ter·board \'sent-ər-,bō(ə)rd, -,bȯ(ə)rd\ *n* : a keel that can be raised and is used especially in sailboats

center field *n* **1** : the part of the baseball outfield between right field and left field **2** : the position of the player defending center field — **center fielder** *n*

cen·ter·line \,sen-tər-'līn\ *n* : a real or imaginary line that is the same distance from the surface or sides of something (as a machine part or a roadway)

center of gravity : the point at which the entire weight of a body can be thought of as concentrated

center of mass : the point in a body or system of bodies at which the whole mass can be thought of as concentrated

cen·ter·piece \'sent-ər-,pēs\ *n* : a piece put in the center of something and especially a decoration (as flowers) for the center of a table

¹cen·tes·i·mo \chen-'tez-ə-,mō\ *n, pl* **-mi** \-(,)mē\ **1** : a unit of value equal to ¹⁄₁₀₀ lira **2** : a coin representing one centesimo [Italian, literally "hundredth", from Latin *centesimus* "hundredth", from *centum* "hundred"]

²cen·tes·i·mo \sen-'tes-ə-,mō\ *n, pl* **-mos** **1** : a unit of value equal to ¹⁄₁₀₀ part of a Uruguayan peso **2** : a coin representing one centesimo [Spanish *centésimo*, from Latin *centesimus* "hundredth", from *centum* "hundred"]

centi- *combining form* **1** : hundred ⟨*centi*grade⟩ **2** : hundredth part ⟨*centi*meter⟩ — used in terms of the metric system [derived from Latin *centum* "hundred"]

cen·ti·grade \'sent-ə-,grād, 'sänt-\ *adj* : relating to or having a thermometer scale on which the interval between the freezing point and the boiling point of water is divided into 100 degrees with 0° representing the freezing point and 100° the boiling point — abbr. *C;* compare CELSIUS

cen·ti·gram \'sent-ə-,gram, 'sänt-\ *n* — see METRIC SYSTEM table

cen·ti·li·ter \'sent-ə-,lēt-ər, 'sänt-\ *n* — see METRIC SYSTEM table

cen·time \'sän-,tēm, 'sen-\ *n* **1** : a unit of value equal to ¹⁄₁₀₀ franc **2** : a coin representing one centime

cen·ti·me·ter \'sent-ə-,mēt-ər, 'sänt-\ *n* — see METRIC SYSTEM table

centimeter–gram–second *adj* : of, relating to, or being a system of units based upon the centimeter as the unit of length, the gram as the unit of mass, and the second as the unit of time — abbr. *cgs*

cen·ti·mo \'sent-ə-,mō\ *n, pl* **-mos** **1** : a unit of value equal to 1/100 part of a bolivar   **2** : a coin representing one centimo [Spanish *céntimo*]

cen·ti·pede \'sent-ə-,pēd\ *n* : any of a class of long flattened arthropods that have many segments with each segment having one pair of legs except for the first segment which has a pair of poison fangs — compare MILLIPEDE [from Latin *centipeda* "centipede", from *centi-* "hundred" and *-peda,* from *ped-, pes* "foot" — related to PEDESTRIAN]

cen·tral \'sen-trəl\ *adj*   **1** : containing or being a center   **2** : ²CHIEF 2, PRINCIPAL ⟨the *central* figure in a story⟩   **3** : situated at, in, or near the center   **4** : of, relating to, or consisting of the brain and spinal cord; *also* : originating within the central nervous system — **cen·tral·i·ty** \sen-'tral-ət-ē\ *n* — **cen·tral·ly** \'sen-trə-lē\ *adv*

central angle *n* : an angle with its vertex at the center of a circle and with sides that are radii of the circle

cen·tral·ize \'sen-trə-,līz\ *vb* **-ized; -iz·ing** : to bring to a central point or under a single control — **cen·tral·iza·tion** \,sen-trə-lə-'zā-shən\ *n*

central nervous system *n* : the part of the nervous system that in vertebrates consists of the brain and spinal cord

central processing unit *n* : PROCESSOR

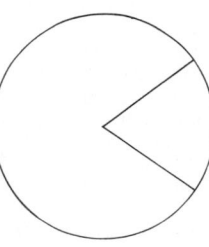
central angle

central tendency *n* : a tendency of statistical data to pile up on or be distributed around some average value

central time *n, often cap C* : the time of the 6th time zone west of Greenwich that includes the central U.S.

cen·tre \'sent-ər\ *chiefly British variant of* CENTER

cen·trif·u·gal \sen-'trif-yə-gəl, -'trif-i-gəl\ *adj*   **1** : proceeding or acting in a direction away from a center or axis   **2** : using or acting by centrifugal force [from scientific Latin *centrifugus* "centrifugal", literally "fleeing from the center", from *centri-* "center" and *-fugus,* from Latin *fugere* "to run away, flee" — related to FUGITIVE, REFUGEE]

centrifugal force *n* : the force that tends to cause a thing or parts of a thing to go outward from a center of rotation

cen·tri·fuge \'sen-trə-,fyüj\ *n* : a machine using centrifugal force for separating substances of different densities, for removing moisture, or for causing gravitational effects

cen·tri·ole \'sen-trē-,ōl\ *n* : one of a pair of minute bodies that are located next to the nucleus of a cell, are important in cell division, and consist of a cylinder-shaped central part surrounded by a circle of nine tiny tubes

cen·trip·e·tal \sen-'trip-ət-ºl\ *adj* : proceeding or acting in a direction toward a center or axis — **cen·trip·e·tal·ly** \-ət-ºl-ē\ *adv*

centripetal force *n* : the force that tends to cause a thing or parts of a thing to go inward toward a center of rotation

cen·tro·mere \'sen-trə-,mi(ə)r\ *n* : the point on a chromosome by which it appears to be attached to the spindle in cell division

cen·tro·some \'sen-trə-,sōm\ *n*   **1** : CENTRIOLE   **2** : the region of a cell that is located next to the nucleus and contains the centrioles

cen·tu·ry \'sench-(ə-)rē\ *n, pl* **-ries**   **1** : a group of 100 things   **2** : a period of 100 years

century plant *n* : a Mexican agave maturing and flowering only once in many years and then dying

ceph·a·lo·pod \'sef-ə-lə-,päd\ *n* : any of a class of mollusks that include the squids, cuttlefishes, and octopuses and have a group of muscular sucker-bearing arms, highly developed eyes, and usually a bag of inky fluid which can be released for defense

ceph·a·lo·tho·rax \,sef-ə-lə-'thō(ə)r-,aks, -'thȯ(ə)r-\ *n* : a combined head and thorax (as of a spider, scorpion, or crustacean)

Ce·phe·id \'sē-fē-əd\ *n* : one of a class of pulsating stars whose changes in brightness are very regular

Ce·pheus \'sē-,fyüs, 'sē-fē-əs\ *n* : a group of stars between Cygnus and the north pole

¹**ce·ram·ic** \sə-'ram-ik\ *adj* : of or relating to the manufacture of a product (as earthenware, porcelain, or brick) made from a nonmetallic mineral by heating at high temperatures

²**ceramic** *n*   **1** *pl* : the art of making ceramic articles   **2** : a product of ceramic manufacture

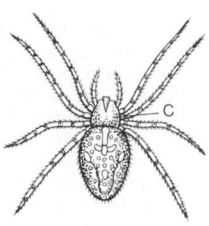
C cephalothorax

cer·cus \'sər-kəs\ *n, pl* **cer·ci** \'sər-,sī\ : a thin manyjointed part of an insect that sticks out from the hind end of its body

¹**ce·re·al** \'sir-ē-əl\ *adj* : relating to grain or to the plants that produce it; *also* : made of grain [derived from Latin *cerealis* "of grain", literally "of Ceres", from *Ceres* (name of Roman goddess of grain)]

²**cereal** *n*   **1** : a plant (as a grass) that produces starchy grain suitable for food; *also* : its grain   **2** : a prepared food of grain

cer·e·bel·lum \,ser-ə-'bel-əm\ *n, pl* **-bellums** *or* **-bel·la** \-'bel-ə\ : a large portion of the back part of the brain that is concerned especially with the action of groups of muscles and with bodily balance

ce·re·bral \sə-'rē-brəl, 'ser-ə-\ *adj*   **1** : of or relating to the brain   **2** : of, relating to, or being the cerebrum   **3** : ¹INTELLECTUAL 1

cerebral hemisphere *n* : either of the two hollow manyridged right or left halves of the cerebrum

cerebral palsy *n* : a disease resulting from damage to the brain usually before or during birth and resulting in imperfect control of muscles, paralysis, and speech disturbances

ce·re·bro·spi·nal fluid \sə-,rē-brō-,spīn-ºl-\ *n* : a fluid that occupies the cavities of the brain and spinal cord and the space between these and the three membranes surrounding them

ce·re·brum \sə-'rē-brəm, 'ser-ə-brəm\ *n, pl* **-brums** *or* **-bra** \-brə\   **1** : ¹BRAIN 1a   **2** : the expanded front or upper part of the brain that consist of the cerebral hemispheres and connecting structures and is reported to be the seat of conscious mental processes

¹**cer·e·mo·ni·al** \,ser-ə-'mō-nē-əl\ *adj* : of, relating to, or forming a ceremony — **cer·e·mo·ni·al·ism** \-nē-ə-,liz-əm\ *n* — **cer·e·mo·ni·al·ist** \-nē-ə-ləst\ *n* — **cer·e·mo·ni·al·ly** \-nē-ə-lē\ *adv* — **cer·e·mo·ni·al·ness** *n*

²**ceremonial** *n* : a ceremonial act, action, or system

cer·e·mo·ni·ous \,ser-ə-'mō-nē-əs\ *adj*   **1** : ¹CEREMONIAL   **2** : careful to observe forms and ceremony : FORMAL — **cer·e·mo·ni·ous·ly** *adv* — **cer·e·mo·ni·ous·ness** *n*

cer·e·mo·ny \'ser-ə-,mō-nē\ *n, pl* **-nies**   **1** : a formal act or series of acts performed in some regular way according to fixed rules ⟨graduation *ceremonies*⟩   **2** : very polite behavior : FORMALITY

ce·ri·um \'sir-ē-əm\ *n* : a metallic element used especially in alloys — see ELEMENT table

cer·met \'sər-,met\ *n* : a strong alloy of a heat-resistant compound (as carbide of titanium) and a metal (as nickel) used especially for turbine blades

\ə\ **abut**	\au̇\ **out**	\i\ **tip**	\ȯ\ **saw**	\u̇\ **foot**
\ər\ **further**	\ch\ **chin**	\ī\ **life**	\ȯi\ **coin**	\y\ **yet**
\a\ **mat**	\e\ **pet**	\j\ **job**	\th\ **thin**	\yü\ **few**
\ā\ **take**	\ē\ **easy**	\ŋ\ **sing**	\th\ **this**	\yu̇\ **cure**
\ä\ **cot, cart**	\g\ **go**	\ō\ **bone**	\ü\ **food**	\zh\ **vision**

¹cer·tain \'sərt-ᵊn\ *adj* **1** : FIXED 1b ⟨receive a *certain* share of the profits⟩ **2** : not to be doubted : known to be true ⟨it is *certain* that diamonds are hard⟩ **3** : known but not named ⟨a *certain* person told me⟩ **4** : RELIABLE, SURE ⟨a *certain* cure⟩ **5 a** : sure to happen : bound to occur : INEVITABLE ⟨defeat was *certain*⟩ **b** : decided in advance by or as if by fate ⟨the plan was *certain* to succeed⟩ **6** : assured in mind or action ⟨feel *certain* they will come⟩

²certain *pron* : certain ones

cer·tain·ly \'sərt-ᵊn-lē\ *adv* **1** : in a manner that is certain : for certain ⟨the earliest voyage of which anything is *certainly* known⟩ **2** : without doubt : SURELY ⟨*certainly* you can do better than that⟩

cer·tain·ty \'sərt-ᵊn-tē\ *n, pl* **-ties 1** : something certain **2** : the quality or state of being or feeling certain

cer·tif·i·cate \(,)sər-'tif-i-kət\ *n* **1** : a document that is proof of some fact; *esp* : one showing that a person has fulfilled the requirements of a school or profession ⟨teaching *certificate*⟩ **2** : a document showing ownership ⟨stock *certificate*⟩ ⟨bond *certificate*⟩

certified milk *n* : milk of high quality produced under the rules and regulations of an authorized medical milk commission

cer·ti·fy \'sərt-ə-,fī\ *vb* **-fied; -fy·ing 1** : to guarantee to be true or valid or as claimed or meeting a standard **2** : ²LICENSE — **cer·ti·fi·able** \-,fī-ə-bəl\ *adj* — **cer·ti·fi·ca·tion** \,sərt-ə-fə-'kā-shən\ *n* — **cer·ti·fi·er** \'sərt-ə-,fī(-ə)r\ *n*

cer·ti·tude \'sərt-ə-,t(y)üd\ *n* : CERTAINTY

ce·ru·le·an \sə-'rü-lē-ən\ *adj* : resembling the blue of the sky

cer·vi·cal \'sər-vi-kəl\ *adj* : of or relating to a neck or cervix

cer·vix \'sər-viks\ *n, pl* **cer·vi·ces** \'sər-və-,sēz\ *or* **cer·vix·es** : the narrow outer end of the uterus that opens into the cavity of the vagina

ce·sar·e·an *or* **cae·sar·e·an** *also* **ce·sar·i·an** \si-'zar-ē-ən, -'zer-\ *n* : CESAREAN SECTION — **cesarean** *or* **caesarean** *also* **cesarian** *adj*

cesarean section *also* **cesarian section** *n* : a surgical operation making an opening in the walls of the abdomen and uterus for delivery of a fetus [from *Cesar,* alternate form of *Caesar,* and *-ean* (adjective suffix); from the belief that Roman Emperor Julius Caesar was born this way]

ce·si·um \'sē-zē-əm\ *n* : a silver-white soft element used especially in photoelectric cells — see ELEMENT table

ces·sa·tion \se-'sā-shən\ *n* : a stopping of action

ces·sion \'sesh-ən\ *n* : a giving over (as of territory or rights) to another

cess·pool \'ses-,pül\ *n* : an underground pit or tank for liquid waste (as household sewage)

ce·ta·cean \si-'tā-shən\ *n* : any of an order of aquatic mammals (as a whale, dolphin, or porpoise) — **cetacean** *adj*

Ce·tus \'sēt-əs\ *n* : a group of stars seen above the equator and south of Pisces and Aries [Latin, literally "whale"]

ce·tyl alcohol \,sēt-ᵊl-\ *n* : a waxy crystalline organic alcohol used especially in cosmetics and detergents

chafe \'chāf\ *vb* **chafed; chaf·ing 1 a** : IRRITATE 1, VEX **b** : to feel irritation : be bothered : FRET **2** : to warm by rubbing **3** : to rub so as to wear away or make sore

cha·fer \'chā-fər\ *n* : any of various large beetles

¹chaff \'chaf\ *n* **1** : the trashy matter (as seed coverings) separated from the seed in threshing grain **2** : something worthless — **chaffy** \-ē\ *adj*

²chaff *n* : light jesting talk : BANTER

³chaff *vb* : to tease good-naturedly

chaf·fer \'chaf-ər\ *vb* **chaf·fered; chaf·fer·ing** \'chaf-(ə-)riŋ\ : to dispute about a price

chaf·ing dish \'chā-fiŋ-\ *n* : a dish for cooking or warming food at the table

¹cha·grin \shə-'grin\ *n* : a feeling of being annoyed by failure or disappointment

²chagrin *vb* **cha·grined** \-'grind\; **cha·grin·ing** \-'grin-iŋ\ : to cause to feel chagrin

¹chain \'chān\ *n* **1 a** : a series of connected links or rings **b** : a measuring instrument of 100 links used in surveying **c** : a unit of length equal to 66 feet **2** : something that restricts or binds : BOND **3 a** : a series of things joined together as if by links ⟨a *chain* of mountains⟩ ⟨a *chain* of events⟩ **b** : a number of atoms united like links in a chain

²chain *vb* : to fasten, bind, or connect with or as if with a chain

chain reaction *n* **1** : a series of events so related to each other that each one sets the next one going **2** : a chemical or nuclear reaction producing energy or products that cause further reactions of the same kind

chain saw *n* : a portable power saw that has teeth linked together to form a continuous chain

chain store *n* : any of a number of stores under the same ownership selling the same lines of goods

chair \'che(ə)r, 'cha(ə)r\ *n* **1** : a seat with legs and a back for use by one person **2 a** : an official seat or a seat of authority or honor **b** : an office or position of authority or honor **c** : an official who conducts a meeting

chair·man \'che(ə)r-mən, 'cha(ə)r-\ *n* : an official who conducts a meeting : CHAIR 2c — **chair·man·ship** \-,ship\ *n*

chair·per·son \-,pər-sən\ *n* : CHAIR 2c

chair·wom·an \-,wùm-ən\ *n* : a woman who conducts a meeting

chaise \'shāz\ *n* : a two-wheeled carriage with a folding top

chaise longue \'shāz-'lóŋ\ *n* : a long chair somewhat like a couch [French, literally "long chair", from *chaise* "chair" and *longue* "long"]

chaise lounge \'shāz-'laùnj, 'chās-\ *n* : CHAISE LONGUE [from *chaise longue;* the spelling *lounge* influenced by the more familiar English word *lounge* "sofa"]

cha·la·za \kə-'lā-zə, -'laz-ə\ *n, pl* **-zae** \-,zē\ *or* **-zas** : either of two twisted bands in the white of a bird's egg that are located at opposite ends of the egg and extend to the yolk

chal·ced·o·ny \kal-'sed-ᵊn-ē, 'chal-sə-,dän-ē\ *n, pl* **-nies** : a nearly transparent quartz commonly pale blue or gray with nearly waxy luster

chal·co·py·rite \,kal-kə-'pī-,rīt\ *n* : a yellow mineral that is a sulfide of copper and iron and an important ore of copper

cha·let \sha-'lā, 'shal-,ā\ *n* **1** : a herdsman's hut in the Alps away from a town or village **2 a** : a Swiss dwelling with a roof that sticks far out past the walls **b** : a cottage built to look like a chalet

chal·ice \'chal-əs\ *n* : GOBLET; *esp* : the cup used in the sacrament of Communion

chalet 2a

¹chalk \'chók\ *n* **1** : a soft white, gray, or buff limestone made up mainly of very small seashells **2** : chalk or material like chalk especially when used in the form of a crayon [Old English *cealc* "chalk", from Latin *calc-, calx* "lime", from Greek *chalix* "pebble" — related to CALCIUM, CALCULATE] — **chalky** \'chó-kē\ *adj*

²chalk *vb* **1** : to rub, mark, write, or draw with chalk **2** : to record or add up with or as if with chalk

chalk·board \'chók-,bō(ə)rd, -,bó(ə)rd\ *n* : a dark smooth surface (as of slate) used for writing or drawing on with chalk

¹chal·lenge \'chal-ənj\ *vb* **chal·lenged; chal·leng·ing 1** : to order to stop and prove identity **2 a** : to object to as bad or incorrect **b** : to demand proof that something is right or legal **3** : to invite or dare to take part in a contest — **chal·leng·er** *n*

²challenge *n* **1** : an objection to something as not being true, genuine, correct, or proper or to a person (as a juror) as not being qualified or approved   **2 :** a sentry's command to halt and prove identity   **3 a :** a demand that someone take part in a duel   **b :** a call or dare for someone to compete in a contest or sport

chal·lis \'shal-ē\ *n, pl* **chal·lises** \'shal-ēz\ **:** a lightweight soft clothing fabric

cha·ly·be·ate \kə-'lē-bē-ət, -'lib-ē-\ *adj* **:** containing salts of iron

¹cham·ber \'chām-bər\ *n* **1 :** a room in a house and especially a bedroom   **2 :** an enclosed space or compartment ⟨the *chamber* of a pistol⟩ ⟨the *chambers* of the heart⟩   **3 a :** a meeting hall of a government body (as an assembly)   **b :** a room where a judge conducts business out of court — usually used in pl.   **4 a :** a group of people organized into a lawmaking body ⟨the lower *chamber* of the legislature⟩   **b :** a board or council of volunteers (as business people) [Middle English *chambre* "chamber", from early French *chambre* (same meaning), from Latin *camera* "room, chamber" — related to CAMERA] — **chambered** \-bərd\ *adj*

²chamber *vb* **cham·bered; cham·ber·ing** \-b(ə-)riṅ\ **:** to place or hold in or as if in a chamber

chambered nautilus *n* **:** NAUTILUS 1

cham·ber·lain \'chām-bər-lən\ *n* **1 :** a chief officer in the household of a ruler or noble   **2 :** TREASURER

cham·ber·maid \'chām-bər-,mād\ *n* **:** a maid who takes care of bedrooms (as in a hotel)

chamber music *n* **:** instrumental music to be performed by a few musicians in a room or small hall

cham·bray \'sham-,brā, -,brē\ *n* **:** a lightweight clothing fabric with colored and white yarns

cha·me·leon \kə-'mēl-yən\ *n* **1 :** a lizard that can vary the color of its skin   **2 :** a person who easily or frequently changes attitude or purpose

    Word History The chameleon of the Old World with its huge, independently movable eyes and a head like a helmet has a fierce look. The Greeks called it *chamaileōn*, combining their words *chamai*, meaning "on the ground, dwarf, lowly" and *leōn* "lion". It may be that the upright ridge of skin behind the head of many of these lizards reminded them of the lion's mane. The Romans borrowed the Greek word for this little creature, and the French later took the Latin word. For a long time after the word was borrowed into Middle English, it was spelled *chamelion*, with the ending like our modern word *lion*. But after a time writers who knew the form of the word in ancient Greek and Latin changed the spelling to *chameleon*, to match the original form. From its basic use as the name of a creature able to change its color with its mood or the temperature, the word came to be used for a person who is changeable, seemingly with the weather. [Middle English *chamelion* "chameleon", from early French *chamelion* (same meaning), from Latin *chamaeleon* (same meaning), from Greek *chamaileōn*, literally "dwarf lion", from *chamai* "on the ground, dwarf, lowly" and *leōn* "lion"]

cham·ois \'sham-ē\ *n, pl* **cham·ois** *also* **cham·oix** \'sham-ē(z)\ **1 :** a small goatlike mountain antelope of Europe and the Caucasus   **2 :** a soft yellowish leather made from the skin of the chamois or from sheepskin

cham·o·mile *or* **cam·o·mile** \'kam-ə-,mīl, -,mēl\ *n* **:** any of a genus of strong-scented herbs related to the daisies with flower heads that contain

chamois 1

a bitter substance used especially in tonics and teas

¹champ \'champ\ *vb* **1 :** to bite and chew noisily ⟨a horse *champing* its bit⟩   **2 :** to show impatience — usually used in the phrase *champing at the bit*

²champ *n* **:** ¹CHAMPION 2, 3

cham·pagne \sham-'pān\ *n* **:** a white sparkling wine

¹cham·pi·on \'cham-pē-ən\ *n* **1 :** a person who fights or speaks for another person or in favor of a cause   **2 :** a person formally acknowledged as better than all others in a sport or in a game of skill   **3 :** the winner of first place in a competition

²champion *vb* **:** to protect or fight for as a champion

cham·pi·on·ship \'cham-pē-ən-,ship\ *n* **1 :** the act of defending as a champion   **2 :** the position or title of champion   **3 :** a contest held to find a champion

¹chance \'chan(t)s\ *n* **1 :** the uncertain course of events   **2 :** OPPORTUNITY 1 ⟨had a *chance* to travel⟩   **3 :** the possibility of loss or injury ⟨took *chances* driving too fast⟩   **4 :** the possibility or probability of something happening ⟨there is a *chance* of rain⟩ ⟨a good *chance* of success⟩   **5 :** a ticket in a raffle

²chance *vb* **chanced; chanc·ing** **1 :** to take place by chance **:** HAPPEN   **2 :** to come unexpectedly — used with *upon* ⟨*chanced* upon a good restaurant⟩   **3 :** ²RISK 2 ⟨*chance* an accident⟩

³chance *adj* **:** happening by chance

chan·cel \'chan(t)-səl\ *n* **:** the part of a church containing the altar and seats for the clergy and choir

chan·cel·lery *or* **chan·cel·lory** \'chan(t)-s(ə-)lə-rē, -səl-rē\ *n, pl* **-ler·ies** *or* **-lor·ies** **1 :** the position or department of a chancellor   **2 :** the building or office where a chancellor works

chan·cel·lor \'chan(t)-s(ə-)lər\ *n* **1 :** a high official of state (as in West Germany)   **2 :** the head of a university

chan·cery \'chan(t)s-(ə-)rē\ *n, pl* **-cer·ies** **:** a record office for public archives

chan·cre \'shaṅ-kər\ *n* **:** a sore at the site of entry of an infectious germ (as one causing syphilis) [from French *chancre* "a sore", from Latin *cancer* "crab, cancer (disease)" — related to CANCER, CANKER]

chan·de·lier \,shan-də-'li(ə)r\ *n* **:** a branched lighting fixture usually hanging from a ceiling

¹change \'chānj\ *vb* **changed; chang·ing** **1 :** to make or become different **:** ALTER   **2 :** to give a different position, course, or direction to   **3 :** to replace with another **:** SWITCH, EXCHANGE ⟨*change* places⟩   **4 :** to give or receive an equal amount of money in usually smaller units of value or in foreign currency ⟨*change* a $10 bill⟩   **5 a :** to put fresh clothes or covering on ⟨*change* a bed⟩   **b :** to put on different clothes — **chang·er** *n* — **change hands :** to pass from one person's possession to another's

²change *n* **1 :** the act, process, or result of changing ⟨a *change* of seasons⟩ ⟨a *change* for the better⟩   **2 :** a fresh set of clothes   **3 a :** money in small units of value received in exchange for an equal amount in larger units   **b :** money returned when a payment is more than the amount due   **c :** money in coins

change·able \'chān-jə-bəl\ *adj* **1 :** likely to change often or suddenly ⟨*changeable* weather⟩   **2 :** appearing different (as in color) from different points of view — **change·abil·i·ty** \,chān-jə-'bil-ət-ē\ *n* — **change·able·ness** \'chān-jə-bəl-nəs\ *n* — **change·ably** \-blē\ *adv*

change·ful \'chānj-fəl\ *adj* **:** CHANGEABLE 1

change·less \'chānj-ləs\ *adj* **:** UNCHANGEABLE, CONSTANT — **change·less·ly** *adv* — **change·less·ness** *n*

change·ling \'chānj-liṅ\ *n* **:** a child of fairies or elves se-

\ə\ abut	\au̇\ out	\i\ tip	\ȯ\ saw	\u̇\ foot
\ər\ further	\ch\ chin	\ī\ life	\ȯi\ coin	\y\ yet
\a\ mat	\e\ pet	\j\ job	\th\ thin	\yü\ few
\ā\ take	\ē\ easy	\ṅ\ sing	\th\ this	\yu̇\ cure
\ä\ cot, cart	\g\ go	\ō\ bone	\ü\ food	\zh\ vision

cretly exchanged in infancy by them for a human child

change of life : MENOPAUSE

change·over \'chān-ˌjō-vər\ *n* : TRANSITION 1

¹**chan·nel** \'chan-ᵊl\ *n* **1** : the bed of a stream **2** : the deeper part of a river, harbor, or strait **3** : a strait or a narrow sea between two close large areas of land ⟨the English *Channel*⟩ **4** : a way of passing something along ⟨the government's complaint had to go through diplomatic *channels*⟩ **5** : a group of frequencies close enough in value for a single radio or television communication **6** : a closed passage through which something flows **7** : a long gutter, groove, or track

²**channel** *vb* **-neled** *or* **-nelled; -nel·ing** *or* **-nel·ling** **1** : to form a channel in **2** : to direct into or through a channel

chan·nel·ize \'chan-ᵊl-ˌīz\ *vb* **-ized; -iz·ing** **1** : ²CHANNEL **2** : to straighten by means of a channel ⟨*channelize* a stream⟩ — **chan·nel·iza·tion** \ˌchan-ᵊl-ə-'zā-shən\ *n*

¹**chant** \'chant\ *vb* **1** : to sing especially in the way a chant is sung **2** : to recite or speak with no change in tone [Middle English *chaunten* "to chant", from early French *chanter* (same meaning), derived from Latin *canere* "to sing" — related to ³CANT, CANTATA, CHANTEY, CHARM]

²**chant** *n* **1** : a melody in which several words or syllables are sung on one tone **2** : something spoken in the style of a chant

chan·tey *or* **chan·ty** \'shant-ē, 'chant-\ *n, pl* **chanteys** *or* **chanties** : a song sung by sailors in rhythm with their work [from French *chanter* "to sing", derived from Latin *canere* "to sing" — related to CANTATA, CHANT, CHARM]

chan·ti·cleer \'chant-ə-ˌkli(ə)r, ˌshant-\ *n* : ¹COCK 1

Cha·nu·kah *variant of* HANUKKAH

cha·os \'kā-ˌäs\ *n* : complete confusion and disorder — **cha·ot·ic** \kā-'ät-ik\ *adj* — **cha·ot·i·cal·ly** \-i-k(ə-)lē\ *adv*

¹**chap** \'chap\ *vb* **chapped; chap·ping** : to open in slits : CRACK ⟨*chapped* lips⟩ [Middle English *chappen* "to chop, crack"]

²**chap** *n* : a crack or a sore roughening of the skin from exposure

³**chap** *n* : ¹FELLOW 4a [shortened form of *chapman* "merchant", from Old English *cēapman* "merchant", from *cēap* "trade" and *man* "man" — related to CHEAP]

chap·ar·ral \ˌshap-ə-'ral, -'rel\ *n* **1** : a thicket of dwarf evergreen oaks; *also* : a dense thicket **2** : an ecological community that is found especially in parts of southern California and is composed of shrubby plants that grow well in dry sunny summers and moist winters

chaparral bird *n* : ROADRUNNER

chaparral cock *n* : ROADRUNNER

chap·el \'chap-əl\ *n* **1** : a building or room or place for prayer or special religious services **2** : a religious service or assembly held in a school or college [Middle English *chapel* "chapel", from early French *chapele* (same meaning), from Latin *cappella* "chapel", literally "little cloak", from earlier *cappa* "cloak, head covering"; so called because a special chapel was built to house a revered cloak of Saint Martin of Tours (a city in France) — related to ²CAPE, CHAPERON]

¹**chap·er·on** *or* **chap·er·one** \'shap-ə-ˌrōn\ *n* : a person who goes with and is responsible for a young woman or a group of young people (as at a dance) [from French *chaperon* "chaperon", literally "hood", derived from early French *chape* "cape", from Latin *cappa* "head covering, cloak" — related to ²CAPE, CHAPEL]

²**chaperon** *or* **chaperone** *vb* **-oned; -on·ing** : to act or go with as a chaperon

chap·lain \'chap-lən\ *n* **1** : a member of the clergy officially attached to a special group (as the army) **2** : a person chosen to conduct religious exercises (as for a club)

chaps \'shaps, 'chaps\ *n pl* : leather leggings worn especially by western ranch workers

chap·ter \'chap-tər\ *n* **1** : a main division of a book or of

a law code **2** : a local branch of an organization

¹**char** \'chär\ *n, pl* **char** *or* **chars** : any of a genus of trouts that have small scales and include the common brook trout

²**char** *vb* **charred; char·ring** **1** : to change or become changed to charcoal or carbon usually by heat : BURN **2** : to burn or become burned partly or slightly : SCORCH

³**char** *n* : a charred substance : CHARCOAL

char·ac·ter \'kar-ik-tər\ *n* **1 a** : a mark or symbol (as a letter or numeral) used in writing or printing **b** : a symbol (as a letter or number) that represents information; *also* : something standing for such a character that may be accepted by a computer **2 a** : a distinguishing feature : CHARACTERISTIC **b** : the group of qualities that make a person, group, or thing different from others **c** : the bodily expression (as eye color or leaf shape) of the action of a gene or group of genes **3** : an odd or peculiar person **4** : a person in a story, novel, or play **5** : REPUTATION 1 **6** : moral excellence and strength — **char·ac·ter·less** \-ləs\ *adj*

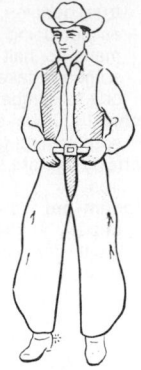

chaps

¹**char·ac·ter·is·tic** \ˌkar-ik-tə-'ris-tik\ *adj* : serving to stress some special quality of an individual or group : TYPICAL — **char·ac·ter·is·ti·cal·ly** \-ti-k(ə-)lē\ *adv*

²**characteristic** *n* : a special quality or appearance that makes an individual or group different from others

syn CHARACTERISTIC, TRAIT, FEATURE mean something that identifies or shows off a person or thing. CHARACTERISTIC suggests a mark or quality that sets an individual or class apart from others of the same kind ⟨poison fangs are a *characteristic* of some snakes⟩ TRAIT applies to an very noticeable often personal characteristic ⟨shyness is a personality *trait*⟩ FEATURE applies to a prominent detail that helps to identify something ⟨her eyes are her most striking *feature*⟩

char·ac·ter·iza·tion \ˌkar-ik-tə-rə-'zā-shən\ *n* **1** : the act of characterizing **2** : the creation of characters (as in a book or play)

char·ac·ter·ize \'kar-ik-tə-ˌrīz\ *vb* **-ized; -iz·ing** **1** : to point out the character of an individual or group : DESCRIBE **2** : to be characteristic of

character sketch *n* : a short written piece describing a character

cha·rade \shə-'rād\ *n* **1** *pl* : a game in which some of the players try to guess a word or phrase from the actions of another player who may not speak **2** : an act that is meaningless or is meant to deceive

char·coal \'chär-ˌkōl\ *n* **1** : a dark or black absorbent carbon made by heating animal or vegetable material in the absence of air **2 a** : a piece or pencil of charcoal used in drawing **b** : a charcoal drawing

chard \'chärd\ *n* : a beet of a variety that does not have a swollen root and forms large leaves and stalks often cooked as a vegetable — called also *Swiss chard*

¹**charge** \'chärj\ *vb* **charged; charg·ing** **1 a** : ²LOAD 1a, FILL **b** : to give an electric charge to **c** : to restore the active materials in a storage battery by the passage of a direct current through in the opposite direction to that of the flowing out of electricity from the battery **2 a** : to give a task, duty, or responsibility to **b** : to give an order by right of authority **3** : to accuse formally ⟨*charged* with speeding⟩ **4** : to rush against : make an assault on **5 a** : to enter as a debt or responsibility on a record ⟨*charged* the purchase to my account⟩ ⟨*charge* books on a library card⟩ **b** : to ask or set as a price ⟨they *charge* too much for everything⟩ ⟨*charged* $100 for repairs⟩ **syn** see COMMAND — **charge·able** \'chär-jə-bəl\ *adj*

²charge *n* **1 a** : the amount (as of ammunition or fuel) needed to load or fill something **b** : ELECTRIC CHARGE **2 a** : a task, duty, or order given to a person : OBLIGATION **b** : the work or duty of managing ⟨has *charge* of the building⟩ **c** : a person or thing given to another person to look after **3** : an instruction, command, or explanation based on authority ⟨a judge's *charge* to the jury⟩ **4 a** : the price demanded especially for a service **b** : an amount listed as a debt on an account **5** : a claim of wrongdoing : ACCUSATION ⟨a *charge* of burglary⟩ **6** : a rush to attack an enemy : ASSAULT **syn** see PRICE — **in charge** : having control of or responsibility for something ⟨*in charge* of the training program⟩

charge account *n* : a customer's account with a creditor (as a store or bank) to which the purchase of goods may be charged

charge card *n* : CREDIT CARD

charged \'chärjd\ *adj* : showing or able to cause strong feelings ⟨an emotionally *charged* book review⟩

¹char·ger \'chär-jər\ *n* : a large flat dish or platter

²charg·er \'chär-jər\ *n* **1** : a cavalry horse **2** : a device for charging storage batteries

char·i·ot \'char-ē-ət\ *n* : a two-wheeled horse-drawn vehicle of ancient times used in battle and also in races and parades

char·i·o·teer \,char-ē-ə-'ti(ə)r\ *n* : a driver of a chariot

cha·ris·ma \kə-'riz-mə\ *n* : a special charm or public appeal

chariot

char·i·ta·ble \'char-ət-ə-bəl\ *adj* **1** : freely giving money or help to poor and needy persons : GENEROUS **2** : given for the needy : of service to the needy ⟨*charitable* funds⟩ ⟨a *charitable* institution⟩ **3** : kindly in judging other people — **char·i·ta·bly** \-blē\ *adv*

char·i·ty \'char-ət-ē\ *n, pl* **-ties** **1** : love for others **2** : kindliness in judging others **3 a** : the giving of aid to the poor and suffering **b** : public aid for the poor **c** : an institution or fund for aiding the needy

char·la·tan \'shär-lə-tən\ *n* : a person who pretends to have knowledge or ability

Word History In the early 16th century people claiming medical skills they did not really have wandered throughout Italy. They sold medicines and treatments of little or no value. Because so many of these fakers seemed to come from a village called Cerreto, the name *cerretano*, meaning literally "inhabitant of Cerreto", became a general name for a medical pretender. Such people always seemed to have a ready line of talk to help them sell their products. Through the influence of the Italian word *ciarlare*, meaning "to chatter", the word *cerretano*, when used to refer to these fakers, came to be spelled *ciarlatano*. It is from this word that we get our English *charlatan*. [from Italian *ciarlatano* "charlatan", an altered form of *cerretano* (same meaning), literally "inhabitant of Cerreto (village in Italy)"]

char·ley horse \'chär-lē-,hòrs\ *n* : pain and stiffness from muscular strain especially in a leg

¹charm \'chärm\ *n* **1** : a word, action, or thing believed to have magic powers **2** : something worn or carried to keep away evil and bring good luck **3** : a small decorative object worn on a chain or bracelet **4** : a quality that attracts and pleases [Middle English *charme* "magic word", from early French *charme* (same meaning), from Latin *carmen* "song", from *canere* "to sing" — related to CHANT, CHANTEY]

²charm *vb* **1** : to affect or influence by or as if by a magic

spell ⟨*charm* a snake⟩ **2** : to protect by or as if by a charm ⟨a *charmed* life⟩ **3 a** : ²DELIGHT 2, FASCINATE **b** : to attract by grace or beauty — **charm·er** *n*

charm·ing \'chärm-iŋ\ *adj* : pleasant and attractive especially in manner

char·nel \'chärn-ᵊl\ *n* : a building or chamber in which dead bodies or bones are deposited — **char·nel** *adj*

¹chart \'chärt\ *n* **1 a** : ¹MAP; *esp* : one showing features (as coasts, shoals, and currents) of importance to sailors **b** : an outline map showing something (as differences in climate or magnetism) according to geography **2** : a sheet giving information in the form of a table or of lists or by means of diagrams or graphs [from early French *charte* "map", from Latin *charta* "piece of papyrus" — related to ³CARD]

²chart *vb* **1** : to make a map or chart of **2** : to lay out a plan for

¹char·ter \'chärt-ər\ *n* **1** : an official document granting, guaranteeing, or showing the limits of the rights and duties of the group to which it is given **2** : a contract by which owners of a ship lease it to others

²charter *vb* **1** : to grant a charter to **2** : to hire (as a ship or a bus) for temporary use — **char·ter·er** \'chärt-ər-ər\ *n*

char·wom·an \'chär-,wùm-ən\ *n* : a woman who does cleaning especially in a large building

chary \'cha(ə)r-ē, 'che(ə)r-\ *adj* **char·i·er; -est** **1** : watchful especially to protect something ⟨*chary* of his reputation⟩ **2** : slow to give, accept, or spend ⟨*chary* of praise⟩ — **char·i·ness** *n*

¹chase \'chās\ *n* **1 a** : the hunting of animals — used with *the* **b** : the act of chasing : PURSUIT ⟨saw the thief and gave *chase*⟩ **2** : something pursued **3** : a scene (as in a movie) where the characters chase one another

²chase *vb* **chased; chas·ing** **1** : to follow in order to capture or overtake ⟨*chase* a thief⟩ ⟨*chase* the bus⟩ **2** : ¹HUNT 1 ⟨*chase* the fox⟩ **3** : to drive away or out ⟨*chase* a dog off the lawn⟩ — **chas·er** *n*

syn CHASE, PURSUE, FOLLOW, TRAIL mean to go after or on the track of someone or something. CHASE suggests going after something that is fleeing or running and trying to catch up with it ⟨*chased* after the runaway cat⟩ PURSUE suggests an extended effort to catch up ⟨the police *pursued* the robbers all over town⟩ FOLLOW may apply to situations in which there is neither speed nor an effort to catch up ⟨a stray dog *followed* me home⟩ TRAIL applies to a following of tracks or other marks rather than the thing itself ⟨*trail* a deer through the snow⟩

³chase *vb* **chased; chas·ing** : to decorate (metal) by indenting with a hammer and tools without cutting edges

chasm \'kaz-əm\ *n* : a deep split or gap in the earth : GORGE

chas·sis \'shas-ē, 'chas-ē\ *n, pl* **chas·sis** \-ēz\ : a supporting frame (as that of the body of an automobile or airplane or the parts of a radio or television receiver)

chaste \'chāst\ *adj* **1 a** : pure in thought and act : MODEST **b** : SPOTLESS **2** : simple or plain in design — **chaste·ly** *adv* — **chaste·ness** \'chās(t)-nəs\ *n*

chas·ten \'chās-ᵊn\ *vb* **chas·tened; chas·ten·ing** \'chās-niŋ, -ᵊn-iŋ\ : to correct by punishment or suffering : DISCIPLINE

chas·tise \(')chas-'tīz\ *vb* **chas·tised; chas·tis·ing** : to punish severely (as by whipping) — **chas·tise·ment** \(')chas-'tīz-mənt *also* 'chas-təz-\ *n* — **chas·tis·er** \(')chas-'tī-zər\ *n*

chas·ti·ty \'chas-tət-ē\ *n* : the quality or state of being chaste

\ə\ abut	\aù\ out	\i\ tip	\ò\ saw	\ù\ foot
\ər\ further	\ch\ chin	\ī\ life	\òi\ coin	\y\ yet
\a\ mat	\e\ pet	\j\ job	\th\ thin	\yü\ few
\ā\ take	\ē\ easy	\ŋ\ sing	\th\ this	\yù\ cure
\ä\ cot, cart	\g\ go	\ō\ bone	\ü\ food	\zh\ vision

cha·su·ble \'chaz-ə-bəl, 'chas-ə-, 'chazh-ə-\ *n* : a sleeveless outer vestment worn by a priest at mass

¹chat \'chat\ *vb* **chat·ted; chat·ting** : to talk in a friendly manner about things that are not serious

²chat *n* **1** : a light friendly conversation **2** : any of several songbirds with a chattering call

châ·teau \sha-'tō\ *n, pl* **châ·teaus** \-'tōz\ *or* **châ·teaux** \-'tō(z)\ : a castle or a large country house especially in France [French, from Latin *castellum* "castle" — related to CASTLE]

chat·tel \'chat-ᵊl\ *n* **1** : a piece of property (as animals, money, or goods) other than real estate **2** : ¹SLAVE 1

chat·ter \'chat-ər\ *vb* **1** : to utter rapid meaningless sounds suggesting speech ⟨squirrels *chattered* angrily⟩ **2** : to talk idly, continually, or rapidly : JABBER **3** : to click again and again without control ⟨teeth *chattering* from the cold⟩ — **chatter** *n* — **chat·ter·er** \'chat-ər-ər\ *n*

chat·ter·box \'chat-ər-ˌbäks\ *n* : a person who talks continually

chat·ty \'chat-ē\ *adj* **chat·ti·er; -est 1** : fond of chatting ⟨a *chatty* neighbor⟩ **2** : having the style of a chat ⟨a *chatty* letter⟩ — **chat·ti·ly** \'chat-ᵊl-ē\ *adv* — **chat·ti·ness** \'chat-ē-nəs\ *n*

¹chauf·feur \'shō-fər, shō-'fər\ *n* : a person hired to drive people around in a car

> **Word History** It seems odd that the word *chauffeur,* meaning "one who drives an automobile for another", should come from the French verb *chauffer,* meaning "to heat". The title comes from the early days of automobiles, when they were still curious, rare, and, to many people, funny. Automobiles were noisy, produced clouds of smoke, and seemed to require a great deal of work to keep them running. To many people they were like the steam engines used to pull trains. *Chauffeur,* the French word for the "stoker", or person who kept the fire going in an engine, was used for anyone driving an automobile. Later the term was used only for a person hired to drive someone else's car. [from French *chauffeur* "driver", literally "stoker", from *chauffer* "to heat"]

²chauffeur *vb* **chauf·feured; chauf·feur·ing** \'shō-f(ə-)riŋ, shō-'fər-iŋ\ : to do the work of a chauffeur : DRIVE

chau·vin·ism \'shō-və-ˌniz-əm\ *n* **1** : exaggerated or unthinking patriotism **2** : an attitude that the members of one's own sex are always better than those of the opposite sex; *also* : behavior that shows such an attitude [from French *chauvinisme* "chauvinism", named for Nicholas Chauvin, a character in a play] — **chau·vin·ist** \-və-nəst\ *n or adj*

cheap \'chēp\ *adj* **1 a** : available at low cost or at less than the true value ⟨potatoes are *cheap* right now⟩ **b** : of low price ⟨always buys the *cheapest* brand⟩ **c** : charging low prices ⟨always wants to go to a *cheap* place⟩ **2** : gained with little effort ⟨a *cheap* victory⟩ **3 a** : of low quality or value ⟨*cheap* material wears out quickly⟩ ⟨a *cheap* joke⟩ **b** : lowered in one's own opinion ⟨feel *cheap*⟩ **c** : STINGY 1 ⟨don't be so *cheap*⟩ [from earlier obsolete *cheap* (noun) "bargain", from Old English *cēap* "trade" — related to ³CHAP] — **cheap** *adv* — **cheap·en** \'chē-pən\ *vb* — **cheap·ly** *adv* — **cheap·ness** *n*

cheap·skate \'chēp-ˌskāt\ *n* : a miserly or stingy person; *esp* : one who tries to avoid paying his or her fair share [*-skate* from earlier *skate* "a person", probably from a dialect word *skite,* meaning "an offensive person"]

¹cheat \'chēt\ *vb* **1** : to deprive of something valuable by dishonest methods ⟨*cheated* them out of their property⟩ **2** : to disappoint in a hope or purpose ⟨the daredevil had *cheated* death again⟩ **3** : to use unfair or dishonest methods to gain an advantage ⟨*cheat* on a test⟩ ⟨*cheat* at cards⟩ — **cheat·er** *n*

²cheat *n* **1** : an act of cheating **2** : a person who cheats

¹check \'chek\ *n* **1** : the exposing of a chess king to attack **2** : a sudden stopping of progress **3** : something that de-lays, stops, or holds back : RESTRAINT ⟨constitutional *checks* and balances⟩ **4** : EXAMINATION 1, INVESTIGATION **5** : a written order telling a bank to pay out money from a person's or company's account to the one named on the order ⟨pay a bill by *check*⟩ ⟨cash a *check*⟩ **6 a** : a ticket or token that shows that the bearer has a claim to something ⟨a baggage *check*⟩ **b** : a slip of paper showing the amount due : BILL ⟨I'll take the *check*⟩ **7 a** : a pattern of squares **b** : a fabric with such a design **8** : a mark √ placed beside an item to show it has been noted [Middle English *chek* "check (in chess), attack" from early French *eschec* (same meaning), from Arabic *shāh* "a check (in chess)", from a Persian word meaning literally "king" — related to CHECKER, CHESS]

²check *vb* **1** : to put a chess king in check **2 a** : to bring to a stop ⟨a product to *check* wetness⟩ **b** : to come to a stop **3** : to hold back : RESTRAIN, CURB ⟨*checked* her temper⟩ **4** : to make sure that something is correct or satisfactory ⟨have a doctor *check* your blood pressure⟩ ⟨*check* it out with your teacher⟩ **5** : to mark with a check ⟨*check* the correct answer⟩ **6** : to mark with a check ⟨a *checked* suit⟩ **7** : to leave or accept for safekeeping or for shipment ⟨*check* baggage⟩ **8** : to be the same on every point : TALLY

check·book \'chek-ˌbùk\ *n* : a book of blank bank checks

¹check·er \'chek-ər\ *n* **1** : a square resembling the markings on a checkerboard **2** : a piece in the game of checkers [Middle English *cheker* "checker (square), board on which chess is played", from early French *eschequier* "board for playing chess", from *eschec* "a check (in chess), attack" — related to CHECK, CHESS]

²checker *vb* **check·ered; check·er·ing** \-(ə-)riŋ\ **1** : to mark with squares of different colors ⟨a *checkered* tablecloth⟩ **2** : to cause to have frequent changes (as of fortune) ⟨a *checkered* career⟩

³checker *n* : one that checks; *esp* : an employee who checks out purchases in a supermarket

check·er·ber·ry \'chek-ə(r)-ˌber-ē\ *n* : WINTERGREEN 1a; *also* : the spicy red fruit of a checkerberry

check·er·board \-ˌbō(ə)rd, -ˌbò(ə)rd\ *n* : a board used in games and marked with 64 squares in two colors

check·ers \'chek-ərz\ *n* : a game played on a checkerboard by two persons each having 12 pieces

check in *vb* : to register at a hotel or motel

checking account *n* : an account in a bank from which the depositor can draw money by writing checks

check·list \'chek-ˌlist\ *n* : a list of items that is easy to refer to

¹check·mate \'chek-ˌmāt\ *vb* **1** : to block completely : THWART **2** : to check a chess opponent's king so that escape is impossible

²checkmate *n* **1 a** : the act of checkmating **b** : the situation of a checkmated king **2** : a complete check

check·out \'chek-ˌaùt\ *n* **1** : the action or an instance of checking out **2** : a counter at which checking out is done

check out \'chek-'aùt\ *vb* **1** : to pay for one's room and leave (as from a hotel) **2** : to satisfy requirements for taking away ⟨*check* a book *out* at the library⟩ **3 a** : to add up the cost of purchases and receive payment for them **b** : to have the cost of purchases added up and pay for them

check·point \'chek-ˌpòint\ *n* : a point at which a check is carried out ⟨vehicles were inspected at different *checkpoints*⟩

check·room \-ˌrüm, -ˌrùm\ *n* : a room at which baggage, parcels, or clothing is checked

check·up \'chek-ˌəp\ *n* : EXAMINATION 1 ⟨a dental *checkup*⟩; *esp* : a general physical examination

ched·dar \'ched-ər\ *n, often cap* : a hard yellow or white cheese of smooth texture [named for *Cheddar,* village in England where the cheese was first made]

cheek \'chēk\ *n* **1** : the fleshy side of the face below the eye and above and to the side of the mouth **2** : disrespectful speech or behavior : NERVE

cheek·bone \'chēk-'bōn, -,bōn\ *n* : the bone or the bony ridge below the eye

cheeky \'chē-kē\ *adj* **cheek·i·er; -est** : showing disrespect : RUDE, IMPUDENT — **cheek·i·ness** *n*

cheep \'chēp\ *vb* : [superscript]1[/superscript]PEEP 1, CHIRP — **cheep** *n*

[superscript]1[/superscript]**cheer** \'chi(ə)r\ *n* **1** : state of mind or heart : SPIRIT ⟨be of good *cheer*⟩ **2** : good spirits ⟨full of *cheer*⟩ **3** : something that gladdens ⟨words of *cheer*⟩ **4** : a shout of praise or encouragement ⟨three *cheers* for our side⟩

[superscript]2[/superscript]**cheer** *vb* **1** : to give hope to or make happier : COMFORT ⟨*cheer* a sick person⟩ **2** : to urge on especially with shouts or cheers ⟨*cheer* the team to victory⟩ **3** : to shout with joy, approval, or enthusiasm ⟨the students *cheered* loudly at the speech⟩ **4** : to grow or be cheerful : REJOICE — usually used with *up* ⟨*cheer* up — things will get better⟩

cheer·ful \'chi(ə)r-fəl\ *adj* **1 a** : full of good spirits ⟨a *cheerful* outlook⟩ **b** : WILLING 3 ⟨*cheerful* obedience⟩ **2** : pleasantly bright ⟨a sunny *cheerful* room⟩ — **cheer·ful·ly** \-f(ə-)lē\ *adv* — **cheer·ful·ness** \-fəl-nəs\ *n*

cheer·lead·er \'chi(ə)r-,lēd-ər\ *n* : a person who leads organized cheering (as at a football or basketball game)

cheer·less \'chi(ə)r-ləs\ *adj* : offering no cheer : GLOOMY — **cheer·less·ly** *adv* — **cheer·less·ness** *n*

cheery \'chi(ə)r-ē\ *adj* **cheer·i·er; -est** : merry and bright in manner or effect : CHEERFUL — **cheer·i·ly** \'chir-ə-lē\ *adv* — **cheer·i·ness** \'chir-ē-nəs\ *n*

cheese \'chēz\ *n* : a food made from milk usually by separating out the curd and molding it

cheese·burg·er \'chēz-,bər-gər\ *n* : a hamburger topped with a slice of cheese

cheese·cake \-,kāk\ *n* : a cake made from cream cheese or cottage cheese, eggs, and sugar

cheese·cloth \-,klȯth\ *n* : a thin loosely woven cotton cloth

cheesy \'chē-zē\ *adj* **chees·i·er; -est** **1** : resembling or suggesting cheese **2** *slang* : CHEAP 3a

chee·tah \'chēt-ə\ *n* : a long-legged spotted African and formerly Asian cat that is the swiftest of all four-footed animals and is often trained to run down game

cheetah

chef \'shef\ *n* **1** : a chief cook **2** : [superscript]1[/superscript]COOK

chef's knife *n* : a large kitchen knife with a triangular blade

che·li·ped \'kē-lə-,ped\ *n* : either of the pair of limbs of a crustacean that bear pincerlike claws

[superscript]1[/superscript]**chem·i·cal** \'kem-i-kəl\ *adj* **1** : of, relating to, used in, or produced by chemistry **2** : acting or operated or produced by chemicals — **chem·i·cal·ly** \-i-k(ə-)lē\ *adv*

[superscript]2[/superscript]**chemical** *n* : a substance (as an element or compound) obtained from a chemical process or used to get a chemical result

chemical engineering *n* : engineering dealing with the use of chemistry in industry — **chemical engineer** *n*

che·mise \shə-'mēz, -'mēs\ *n* **1** : a woman's one-piece undergarment **2** : a loose dress that hangs straight

chem·is·try \'kem-ə-strē\ *n* **1** : a science that deals with the composition, structure, and properties of substances and with the changes that they go through **2** : chemical composition, properties, or processes ⟨the *chemistry* of gasoline⟩ ⟨the *chemistry* of iron⟩ ⟨the *chemistry* of blood⟩ [an altered form of obsolete *chimistry, chymistry* "alchemy", derived from Latin *alchimista* "alchemist", from *alchymia*, from Arabic *al-kīmiyā* (same meaning), from *al* "the" and *kīmiyā'* "alchemy", from Greek *chēmeia* "alchemy" — related to ALCHEMY, CHEMO-] — **chem·ist** \-əst\ *n*

chemo- *combining form* : chemical : chemistry ⟨*chemotaxis*⟩ [scientific Latin, from Greek *chēmeia* "alchemy" — related to ALCHEMY, CHEMISTRY]

che·mo·tax·is \,kē-mō-'tak-səs\ *n* : movement or positioning of cells or organisms in relation to a chemical

che·mo·ther·a·py \,ke-mō-'ther-ə-pē\ *n* : the use of chemical agents in the treatment or control of disease — **che·mo·ther·a·peu·tic** \-,ther-ə-'pyüt-ik\ *adj*

che·mot·ro·pism \kē-'mä-trə-,piz-əm, ke-\ *n* : positioning of cells or organisms in relation to a chemical

che·nille \shə-'nē(ə)l\ *n* : a thick fuzzy fabric

cheque \'chek\ *chiefly British variant of* [superscript]1[/superscript]CHECK 5

cher·ish \'cher-ish\ *vb* **1** : to hold dear : feel or show affection for **2** : to keep with care and affection : NURTURE **3** : to harbor in the mind ⟨*cherish* a hope⟩

Cher·o·kee \'cher-ə-,kē\ *n* : a member of an American Indian people originally from Tennessee and North Carolina

cher·ry \'cher-ē\ *n, pl* **cherries** **1 a** : any of numerous trees and shrubs that are related to the roses and have rather small pale yellow to deep blackish red smooth-skinned fruits **b** : the fruit of a cherry **c** : the wood of a cherry **2** : a medium red [Middle English *chery* "a cherry", from an early French dialect word *cherise* "the cherry" (mistaken as being a plural), derived from Latin *cerasus* "cherry tree"]

chert \'chərt, 'chat\ *n* : a rock resembling flint and consisting mostly of chalcedony that can be separated into fibers and smaller amounts of very fine crystalline quartz and silica that is not crystallized

cher·ub \'cher-əb\ *n* **1** : a painting or drawing of a beautiful child usually with wings **2** : a chubby rosy child — **che·ru·bic** \chə-'rü-bik\ *adj*

Ches·a·peake Bay retriever \,ches-(ə-),pēk-,bā-\ *n* : a large brown wavy-coated bird dog developed in Maryland

Chesh·ire cheese \,chesh-ər-\ *n* : a cheese made in England that is similar to cheddar [named for *Cheshire*, county in England where the cheese was first made]

chess \'ches\ *n* : a game for two players each of whom plays with 16 pieces on a checkerboard [Middle English *ches* "game of chess", from early French *esches* (same meaning), literally "checks", from *eschec* "check" — related to CHECK, CHECKER]

chess·man \'ches-,man, -mən\ *n* : any of the pieces used in chess

chest \'chest\ *n* **1** : a container (as a box or case) for storing, safekeeping, or shipping ⟨tool *chest*⟩ ⟨linen *chest*⟩ **2** : a public fund ⟨community *chest*⟩ **3** : the part of the body enclosed by the ribs and breastbone — **chest·ed** \'ches-təd\ *adj* — **chest·ful** \-,fül\ *n*

ches·ter·field \'ches-tər-,fēld\ *n* **1** : an overcoat with a velvet collar **2** : a sofa with arms [named for a 19th century Earl of *Chesterfield*, English nobleman]

[superscript]1[/superscript]**chest·nut** \'ches-(,)nət\ *n* **1 a** : a sweet edible nut from any of several trees or shrubs related to the beech **b** : a tree or shrub bearing chestnuts; *esp* : an American tree that was formerly common and grew to large size in eastern forests but has been largely wiped out by the chestnut blight and now grows only to the size of a shrub or sapling **c** : the wood of a chestnut tree **2** : HORSE CHESTNUT **3** : a brown or reddish brown horse

[superscript]2[/superscript]**chestnut** *adj* : of a reddish brown color

chestnut blight *n* : a destructive disease of the chestnut of the eastern U.S. marked by infected areas of the bark and cambium and caused by a fungus imported from the Old World

chest of drawers : a piece of furniture containing drawers

\ə\ abut	\au̇\ out	\i\ tip	\ȯ\ saw	\u̇\ foot
\ər\ further	\ch\ chin	\ī\ life	\ȯi\ coin	\y\ yet
\a\ mat	\e\ pet	\j\ job	\th\ thin	\yü\ few
\ā\ take	\ē\ easy	\ŋ\ sing	\th\ this	\yu̇\ cure
\ä\ cot, cart	\g\ go	\ō\ bone	\ü\ food	\zh\ vision

(as for storing clothes)

chev·ron \'shev-rən\ *n* **1** : a figure resembling a V or an upside-down V **2** : a sleeve badge indicating rank (as in the armed forces)

¹chew \'chü\ *vb* : to crush or grind with the teeth — **chew·able** \-ə-bəl\ *adj* — **chew·er** *n* — **chewy** \'chü-ē\ *adj*

²chew *n* **1** : the act of chewing **2** : something for chewing ⟨a *chew* of tobacco⟩

chewing gum *n* : a sweetened and flavored soft material (as of chicle) used for chewing

chew out *vb* : ²REPRIMAND

chew over *vb* : to discuss thoughtfully : think over

Chey·enne \shī-'an, -'en\ *n* : a member of an American Indian people of the western plains of the U.S.

chi \'kī\ *n* : the 22d letter of the Greek alphabet — X or χ

¹chic \'shēk\ *n* : fashionable style

²chic *adj* : STYLISH, SMART ⟨*chic* clothes⟩

chi·ca·nery \shik-'ān-(ə-)rē\ *n, pl* **-ner·ies** : clever trickery

Chi·ca·no \chi-'kän-ō, shi-\ *n* : an American of Mexican ancestry [Mexican Spanish, an altered form of Spanish *mejicano* "Mexican"] — **Chicano** *adj*

chick \'chik\ *n* **1 a** : ¹CHICKEN 1; *esp* : one newly hatched **b** : the young of any bird **2** *slang* : a young woman

chick·a·dee \'chik-ə-(,)dē\ *n* : any of several small American birds with the top of the head black or brown

Chick·a·saw \'chik-ə-,sò\ *n, pl* **-saw** *or* **-saws** : a member of an American Indian people of Mississippi and Alabama

¹chick·en \'chik-ən\ *n* **1** : the common domestic fowl especially when young; *also* : its flesh used as food **2** : any of various birds or their young **3** : COWARD

chickadee

²chicken *adj* : COWARDLY 1

³chicken *vb* **chick·ened; chick·en·ing** \'chik-(ə-)niŋ\ : to lose one's courage — usually used with *out*

chick·en·heart·ed \,chik-ən-'härt-əd\ *adj* : COWARDLY 1, TIMID

chicken pox *n* : a contagious virus disease especially of children marked by low fever and a rash or small watery blisters

chicken wire *n* : a light wire fencing with hexagonal openings

chick–pea \'chik-,pē\ *n* : an Asian herb related to the pea and cultivated for its short pods with one or two edible seeds; *also* : its seed

chick·weed \'chik-,wēd\ *n* : any of several low-growing small-leaved weedy plants related to the pinks

chi·cle \'chik-əl, -lē\ *n* : a gum from the latex of a tropical tree that is used as an important part of chewing gum

chic·o·ry \'chik-(ə-)rē\ *n, pl* **-ries** : a thick-rooted usually blue-flowered European herb related to the daisies and grown for its roots and as a salad plant; *also* : its dried ground roasted root that is sometimes added to coffee

chide \'chīd\ *vb* **chid** \'chid\ *or* **chid·ed** \'chīd-əd\; **chid** *or* **chid·den** \'chid-ᵊn\ *or* **chided; chid·ing** \'chīd-iŋ\ : to express mild disapproval of **syn** see REBUKE

¹chief \'chēf\ *n* : the head of a group : LEADER ⟨an Indian *chief*⟩ ⟨*chief* of police⟩ [Middle English *chief* "top part, head", from early French *chief* "head, chief", from Latin *caput* "head" — related to CAPITAL, CAPTAIN]

²chief *adj* **1** : highest in rank or authority ⟨*chief* executive⟩ **2** : most important : MAIN ⟨your *chief* claim to fame⟩

chief·ly \'chē-flē\ *adv* **1** : above all **2** : for the most part

chief master sergeant *n* : a noncommissioned officer of the highest rank in the air force

chief master sergeant of the air force : a chief master sergeant who advises the senior commanding officer of the air force

chief of state : the head of a country when not the same person as the head of the country's government

chief petty officer *n* : a naval petty officer with a rank just below that of senior chief petty officer

chief·tain \'chēf-tən\ *n* : a chief especially of a band, tribe, or clan — **chief·tain·cy** \-sē\ *n* — **chief·tain·ship** \-,ship\ *n*

chief warrant officer *n* : a military or naval warrant officer of senior rank

¹chif·fon \shif-'än, 'shif-,än\ *n* : a very thin fabric especially of silk

²chiffon *adj* : having a light soft texture ⟨a *chiffon* pie⟩

chif·fo·nier \,shif-ə-'ni(ə)r\ *n* : a high narrow chest of drawers

chig·ger \'chig-ər, 'jig-\ *n* : a six-legged bloodsucking mite larva that causes intense itching

chi·gnon \'shēn-,yän\ *n* : a knot of hair worn at the back of the head

Chi·hua·hua \chə-'wä-(,)wä, shə-, -wə\ *n* : a very small large-eared dog of a breed that originated in Mexico [named for *Chihuahua*, a state in Mexico]

Chihuahua

chil·blain \'chil-,blān\ *n* : redness and swelling sometimes with itching and burning especially of the toes, fingers, nose, and ears caused by being exposed to cold

child \'chīld\ *n, pl* **chil·dren** \'chil-drən, -dərn\ **1** : an unborn or recently born person **2 a** : a young person especially between infancy and youth **b** : a childlike or childish person **3** : a son or daughter of human parents — **child·less** \'chīl(d)-ləs\ *adj* — **with child** : PREGNANT 1

child·bear·ing \'chīl(d)-,bar-iŋ, -,ber-\ *adj* : of or relating to the process of becoming and being pregnant with and giving birth to children ⟨women of *childbearing* age⟩ — **childbearing** *n*

child·birth \'chīl(d)-,bərth\ *n* : the act or process of giving birth to children — called also *parturition*

child·hood \'chīld-,hud\ *n* : the state or time of being a child

child·ish \'chīl-dish\ *adj* **1** : of, resembling, or suitable to a child ⟨*childish* laughter⟩ **2** : showing the less pleasing qualities (as silliness) often thought to be those of children — **child·ish·ly** *adv* — **child·ish·ness** *n*

child·like \'chīl(d)-,līk\ *adj* **1** : of or relating to a child or childhood **2** : showing the more pleasing qualities (as innocence or trustfulness) often thought to be those of children

child·proof \'chīl(d)-,prüf\ *adj* : made to prevent tampering by children ⟨a *childproof* bottle⟩

child's play *n* : something that is very easy to do or is unimportant

chili *or* **chile** *or* **chil·li** \'chil-ē\ *n, pl* **chil·ies** *or* **chil·es** *or* **chil·lies** **1** : HOT PEPPER 1 **2** : CHILI CON CARNE

chili con car·ne \,chil-ē-,kän-'kär-nē, ,chil-ē-kən-\ *n* : a spicy stew made of ground beef, hot peppers or chili powder, and usually beans [from American Spanish *chile con carne*, literally "hot pepper with meat", from *chile* "hot pepper"]

chili dog *n* : a hot dog topped with chili

chili powder *n* : a seasoning made of ground hot peppers and other spices

chili sauce *n* : a spiced tomato sauce usually made with red and green peppers

¹chill \'chil\ *n* **1** : a feeling of cold accompanied by shivering ⟨*chills* and fever⟩ **2** : a moderate but unpleasant amount of cold ⟨there was a *chill* in the air⟩

²chill *adj* **1** : unpleasantly cold : RAW ⟨nights grew *chill*⟩ **2** : not friendly ⟨a *chill* greeting⟩ — **chill·ness** *n*

³chill *vb* **1** : to make or become cold or chilly **2** : to cool without freezing ⟨*chill* the pudding for dessert⟩ **3** : to affect as if with cold ⟨ghost stories that *chill* you in July⟩ **4** : to harden the surface of (as metal) by sudden cooling — **chill·er** — **chill·ing·ly** \-iŋ-lē\ *adv*

chilly \'chil-ē\ *adj* **chill·i·er; -est** : noticeably cold — **chill·i·ness** *n*

¹chime \'chīm\ *n* **1** : a set of bells tuned to play music **2** : the sound of a set of bells — usually used in pl.

²chime *vb* **chimed; chim·ing** **1** : to make the sounds of a chime **2** : to call or indicate by chiming

chime in *vb* : to break into or join in a conversation or discussion

chi·me·ra *or* **chi·mae·ra** \kī-'mir-ə, kə-\ *n* **1** *cap* : a fire-breathing female monster in Greek mythology with a lion's head, a goat's body, and a serpent's tail **2** : something made up by or existing only in the mind — **chi·mer·i·cal** \-'mer-i-kəl, -'mir-\ *adj*

chi·mi·chan·ga \ˌchim-ē-'chäng-gə\ *n* : a tortilla wrapped around a filling (as of meat) and fried in deep fat

chim·ney \'chim-nē\ *n, pl* **chimneys** **1** : a vertical structure extending above the roof of a building for carrying off smoke **2** : a tube usually of glass around a flame (as of a lamp) **3** : something (as a narrow opening in a cliff) resembling a chimney

chimney pot *n* : a pipe usually made of clay placed at the top of a chimney

chimney sweep *n* : a person who cleans soot from chimneys

chimney swift *n* : a small sooty-gray bird with long narrow wings that often attaches its nest to the inside of an unused chimney

chimp \'chimp, 'shimp\ *n* : CHIMPANZEE

chim·pan·zee \ˌchim-ˌpan-'zē, ˌshim-; chim-'pan-zē, shim-\ *n* : an African ape that belongs to the group of higher apes now living that is most closely related to human beings and includes the stronger and larger gorilla

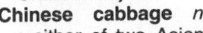

chimpanzee

¹chin \'chin\ *n* : the lower portion of the face lying below the lower lip and including the pointed part of the lower jaw

²chin *vb* **chinned; chin·ning** : to raise oneself with the hands until the chin is level with the support

chi·na \'chī-nə\ *n* **1** : PORCELAIN **2** : dishes of pottery or porcelain for use as tableware

chi·na·ber·ry \'chī-nə-ˌber-ē\ *n* **1** : a soapberry of the southern U.S. and Mexico **2** : a small Asian tree that is related to the mahoganies and has been introduced into the southern U.S.

china clay *n* : KAOLIN

Chi·na·town \'chī-nə-ˌtaun\ *n* : an area of a city where many people of Chinese ancestry live

Chi·na tree \'chī-nə-\ *n* : CHINABERRY 2

chi·na·ware \'chī-nə-ˌwa(ə)r, -ˌwe(ə)r\ *n* : CHINA 2

chinch bug \'chinch-\ *n* : a small black-and-white bug that is very destructive to cereal grasses

chin·chil·la \chin-'chil-ə\ *n* : a South American rodent that is the size of a large squirrel and is widely bred in captivity for its very soft fur of a pearly gray color; *also* : its fur

chine \'chīn\ *n* : BACKBONE 1, SPINE; *also* : a cut of meat or fish including the backbone or part of it and the surrounding flesh

Chi·nese \chī-'nēz, -'nēs\ *n, pl* **Chinese** **1 a** : a person born or living in China **b** : a person of Chinese ancestry **2** : a group of related languages used in China — **Chinese** *adj*

chinchilla

Chinese cabbage *n* : either of two Asian garden plants that are now widely grown in the U.S. and used as green leafy vegetables

Chinese lantern *n* : a collapsible nearly transparent covering for a light

¹chink \'chiŋk\ *n* : a narrow slit or crack

²chink *vb* : to fill the chinks of ⟨log huts *chinked* with mud⟩

³chink *n* : a short sharp sound

⁴chink *vb* : to make or cause to make a short sharp sound

chi·no \'chē-nō, 'shē-\ *n, pl* **chinos** **1** : a usually khaki cotton fabric **2** : an article of clothing made of chino — usually used in pl.

Chi·nook \shə-'nuk, chə-\ *n* : a member of an American Indian people of Oregon

chinook salmon *n* : a large salmon of the northern Pacific ocean that usually has red flesh and is widely sold for food

chintz \'chin(t)s\ *n* : a printed cotton fabric that is usually shiny

¹chip \'chip\ *n* **1** : a small thin flat piece (as of wood, stone, or glass) broken off : FLAKE **2** : a small piece of food ⟨chocolate *chip*⟩: as **a** : a thin crisp piece of food ⟨potato *chip*⟩ **b** : ²FRENCH FRY ⟨fish and *chips*⟩ **3 a** : a counter used in poker **b** *pl* : MONEY 1c ⟨in the *chips*⟩ **4** : a flaw left after a small piece has been broken off ⟨a cup with a *chip* in it⟩ **5** : a very small slice of silicon containing electronic circuits (as for a computer) — **chip off the old block** : a child that resembles his or her parent — **chip on one's shoulder** : an attitude of being eager to fight or quarrel

²chip *vb* **chipped; chip·ping** **1** : to cut or break a chip from something ⟨*chip* a cup⟩ **2** : to break off in small pieces

chip in *vb* : CONTRIBUTE 1

chip·munk \'chip-ˌməŋk\ *n* : any of numerous small striped American animals related to the squirrels

chipped beef \'chip(t)-\ *n* : smoked dried beef sliced thin

chip·per \'chip-ər\ *adj* : being in good health or spirits

Chip·pe·wa \'chip-ə-ˌwȯ, -ˌwä, -ˌwā\ *n* : OJIBWA

chip·ping sparrow \'chip-iŋ-\ *n* : a small eastern North American sparrow whose song is a weak monotonous trill

chi·rop·o·dist \kə-'räp-əd-əst\ *n* : PODIATRIST

chi·rop·o·dy \kə-'räp-əd-ē\ *n* : PODIATRY [from Latin *chir-*, *chiro-* "hand" and Greek *pod-* "foot"; from the fact that this medical practice originally dealt with hands and feet]

chirp \'chərp\ *vb* : to make a short sharp sound like a small bird or cricket — **chirp** *n*

chirr \'chər\ *vb* : to make a vibrating sound like some insects (as a grasshopper or cicada) — **chirr** *n*

chir·rup \'chər-əp, 'chir-\ *vb* : CHIRP — **chirrup** *n*

¹chis·el \'chiz-əl\ *n* : a metal tool with a cutting edge at the end of a blade used to shape or chip away a solid material (as stone, wood, or metal)

²chisel *vb* **-eled** *or* **-elled; -el·ing** *or* **-el·ling** \'chiz-(ə-)liŋ\ **1** : to cut or work with or as if with a chisel **2** : ¹CHEAT 1

\ə\ abut	\au̇\ out	\i\ tip	\ȯ\ saw	\u̇\ foot
\ər\ further	\ch\ chin	\ī\ life	\ȯi\ coin	\y\ yet
\a\ mat	\e\ pet	\j\ job	\th\ thin	\yü\ few
\ā\ take	\ē\ easy	\ŋ\ sing	\th\ this	\yu̇\ cure
\ä\ cot, cart	\g\ go	\ō\ bone	\ü\ food	\zh\ vision

— **chis·el·er** \\'chiz-(ə-)lər\\ *n*

chit·chat \\'chit-,chat\\ *n* : SMALL TALK, GOSSIP

chi·tin \\'kīt-ᵊn\\ *n* : a horny substance that forms part of the hard outer body covering especially of insects and crustaceans — **chi·tin·ous** \\'kīt-ᵊn-əs, 'kīt-nəs\\ *adj*

chi·ton \\'kīt-ᵊn, 'kī-,tän\\ *n* **1** : any of a class of marine mollusks with a shell of calcium-containing plates **2** : a draped garment worn by the ancient Greeks

chit·ter·lings *or* **chit·lins** \\'chit-lənz\\ *n pl* : the intestines of hogs especially prepared as food

chi·val·ric \\shə-'val-rik\\ *adj* : CHIVALROUS 1

chiv·al·rous \\'shiv-əl-rəs\\ *adj* **1** : of or relating to chivalry **2 a** : having or showing honor, generosity, and courtesy **b** : showing special courtesy and regard to women — **chiv·al·rous·ly** *adv* — **chiv·al·rous·ness** *n*

chiv·al·ry \\'shiv-əl-rē\\ *n* **1** : a body of knights **2** : the system, spirit, ways, or customs of knighthood **3** : chivalrous conduct

Word History In the Middle Ages the French referred to a knight as a *chevalier*. This word is derived from the Latin word for "horseman", *caballarius*, which in turn comes from Latin *caballus*, meaning "horse". Knights were supposed to follow a code of conduct which required them to be brave, devoted to duty, and kind to the weak. The French word for these qualities was *chevalerie*. When this noun was borrowed into English, it became *chivalry*. Its adjective forms are *chivalrous* and *chivalric*. The Latin word for "horseman", *caballarius*, has also given us two other common English words. One is *cavalry*, meaning "troops mounted on horseback", and the other is *cavalier*, which as a noun means "mounted knight, gentleman" and as an adjective means "tending to ignore the rights of others". *Cavalier* may be traced back through French and Italian to its Latin source. In English, *cavalier* was used especially to refer to a mounted soldier who was colorful in dress and gallant in manner. During the English Civil War (1641–1649), those who backed the king were called Cavaliers, probably because of their vivid look and stylish manners. Some cavaliers, however, became proud and rude. They showed scorn for the rights and feelings of people of lower social rank. The result was that the adjective *cavalier* came to be used to describe such a scornful person. [Middle English *chivalrie* "group of knights, qualities of knighthood", from early French *chevalerie* (same meaning), from *chevalier* "knight, noble horseman", from Latin *caballarius* "horseman", from earlier *caballus* "horse" — related to CAVALIER, CAVALRY]

chive \\'chīv\\ *n* : an herb related to the onion and used for flavoring

chivy \\'chiv-ē\\ *vb* **chiv·ied; chivy·ing** : to annoy or bother again and again about little things : PESTER

chlor·dane \\'klô(ə)r-,dān\\ *also* **chlor·dan** \\-,dan\\ *n* : an odorless liquid insecticide

chlo·rel·la \\klə-'rel-ə\\ *n* : any of a genus of single-celled green algae; *esp* : one grown as a possible source of food

chlo·ride \\'klō(ə)r-,īd, 'klô(ə)r-\\ *n* : a chemical compound of chlorine with another element, group, or substance

chloride of lime : a white powder used as a bleach, disinfectant, and deodorant

chlo·ri·nate \\'klōr-ə-,nāt, 'klôr-\\ *vb* **-nat·ed; -nat·ing** : to treat or cause to combine with chlorine or a chlorine compound — **chlo·ri·na·tion** \\,klōr-ə-'nā-shən, ,klôr-\\ *n* — **chlo·ri·na·tor** \\'klōr-ə-,nāt-ər, 'klôr-\\ *n*

chiton 2

chlo·rine \\'klō(ə)r-,ēn, 'klô(ə)r-, -ən\\ *n* : a nonmetallic element that is found alone as a heavy greenish yellow irritating gas having two atoms per molecule and a strong odor and that is used especially as a bleach, oxidizing agent, and disinfectant in water purification — see ELEMENT table

chlo·rite \\'klō(ə)r-,īt, 'klô(ə)r-\\ *n* : a usually green mineral associated with and resembling the micas

chlo·ro·flu·o·ro·car·bon \\,klōr-ō-,flú-(ə)r-ō-'kär-bən, ,klôr-\\ *n* : a compound that contains carbon, chlorine, fluorine, and sometimes hydrogen and that is used to help refrigerate things, dissolve other compounds, or make aerosol sprays work and is believed to cause ozone loss in the stratosphere

¹chlo·ro·form \\'klōr-ə-,fôrm, 'klôr-\\ *n* : a colorless heavy poisonous liquid that smells like ether and is used especially to dissolve other compounds or as an anesthetic

²chloroform *vb* : to treat with chloroform especially so as to produce anesthesia or death

chlo·ro·phyll \\'klōr-ə-,fil, 'klôr-, -fəl\\ *n* : the green coloring matter of plants that is found in chloroplasts and is necessary to make plant food from carbon dioxide and water by photosynthesis

chlo·ro·plast \\'klōr-ə-,plast, 'klôr-\\ *n* : a plastid that contains chlorophyll and is the location of photosynthesis and starch formation in a plant cell

¹chock \\'chäk\\ *n* : a wedge or block for steadying or stopping a body (as a barrel), for filling in an unwanted space, or for blocking the movement of a wheel

²chock *vb* : to stop or make steady with or as if with chocks

chock–full \\'chäk-'fúl\\ *or* **chuck–full** \\'chək-'fúl\\ *adj* : full to the limit

choc·o·late \\'chäk-(ə-)lət, 'chók-\\ *n* **1** : a food prepared from ground roasted cacao beans **2** : a beverage of chocolate in water or milk **3** : a candy made or coated with chocolate **4** : a brownish gray — **chocolate** *adj*

Choc·taw \\'chäk-,tò\\ *n* : a member of an American Indian people of Mississippi, Alabama, and Louisiana

¹choice \\'chòis\\ *n* **1** : the act of choosing : SELECTION **2** : the power of choosing : OPTION **3 a** : a person or thing chosen **b** : the best part **4** : a large enough number and variety to choose among

²choice *adj* **1** : very fine ⟨*choice* fruits⟩ **2** : of a grade between prime and good ⟨*choice* meat⟩ — **choice·ly** *adv* — **choice·ness** *n*

choir \\'kwī(-ə)r\\ *n* **1** : an organized group of singers especially in a church **2** : the part of a church where the choir sits

choir·boy \\'kwī(-ə)r-,bòi\\ *n* : a boy member of a church choir

choir·mas·ter \\-,mas-tər\\ *n* : the director of a choir

¹choke \\'chōk\\ *vb* **choked; chok·ing** **1** : to keep from breathing in a normal way by cutting off the supply of air ⟨*choked* by smoke⟩ **2** : to have the windpipe blocked entirely or partly ⟨*choke* on a bone⟩ **3** : to slow or prevent the growth or action of ⟨*choke* back tears⟩ **4** : to block by clogging **5** : to decrease or shut off the air intake of a carburetor to make the fuel mixture richer

²choke *n* **1** : the act or sound of choking **2** : a device for choking a gasoline engine **3** : a portion of a shotgun bore that narrows toward the muzzle; *also* : a device attached to the muzzle that narrows the bore

choke·cher·ry \\'chōk-,cher-ē, -'cher-\\ *n* : any of several American wild cherries with pointed leaves, long clusters of white flowers, and fruit that is nearly black when ripe; *also* : this fruit

chok·er \\'chō-kər\\ *n* **1** : one that chokes **2** : something (as a necklace) that fits closely around the neck

choky \\'chō-kē\\ *adj* **chok·i·er; -est** : tending to cause choking or become choked

chol·era \\'käl-ə-rə\\ *n* : any of several diseases usually marked by severe vomiting and diarrhea

cho·ler·ic \\'käl-ə-rik, kə-'ler-ik\\ *adj* : easily made angry

: hot tempered [from earlier *choler* "yellow bile", from Middle English *coler* (same meaning), from early French *colere* (same meaning), from Latin *cholera* "disease caused by an excess of bile", from Greek *cholē* "bile" — related to MELANCHOLY; see *Word History* at HUMOR]

cho·les·ter·ol \kə-'les-tə-,rōl, -,rol\ *n* : a waxy substance that is present in animal cells and tissues, is important in bodily processes, and may be related to the abnormal thickening and hardening of arteries when too much is present

cho·line \'kō-,lēn\ *n* : a vitamin of the vitamin B complex that is widely distributed in animal and plant products and is necessary for the activities of the liver

chomp \'chämp, 'chȯmp\ *vb* : to chew or bite on something

choose \'chüz\ *vb* **chose** \'chōz\; **cho·sen** \'chōz-ᵊn\; **choos·ing** \'chü-ziŋ\ **1** : to select freely and after consideration ⟨*choose* a leader⟩ **2** : to make a choice : DECIDE ⟨*chose* to go by train⟩ **3** : to see fit ⟨take them if you *choose*⟩ — **choos·er** *n*

choosy *or* **choos·ey** \'chü-zē\ *adj* **choos·i·er; -est** : very careful in choosing : PARTICULAR

¹chop \'chäp\ *vb* **chopped; chop·ping** **1** : to cut by striking especially over and over with something sharp ⟨*chop* down a tree⟩ **2** : to cut into small pieces ⟨*chop* onions⟩ **3** : to strike quickly or again and again [Middle English *chappen* "to cut, crack"]

²chop *n* **1** : a sharp downward blow or stroke (as with an ax) **2** : a small cut of meat often including a part of a rib **3** : a short quick motion (as of a wave)

³chop *vb* **chopped; chop·ping** : to change direction [Middle English *choppe, chappen* "to trade, barter"]

chop·per \'chäp-ər\ *n* **1** : one that chops **2** : HELICOPTER

¹chop·py \'chäp-ē\ *adj* **chop·pi·er; -est** : CHANGEABLE 1, VARIABLE ⟨*choppy* wind⟩

²choppy *adj* **chop·pi·er; -est** **1** : rough with small waves ⟨the lake was *choppy*⟩ **2** : marked by sudden stops and starts : not connected smoothly ⟨short *choppy* sentences⟩ — **chop·pi·ness** *n*

chops \'chäps\ *n pl* : the fleshy covering of the jaws

chop·stick \'chäp-,stik\ *n* : one of a pair of slender sticks used chiefly in oriental countries to lift food to the mouth

chop su·ey \chäp-'sü-ē\ *n* : a dish made chiefly from bean sprouts, bamboo shoots, onions, mushrooms, and meat or fish and served with rice [from Chinese *shap sui*, literally "odds and ends"]

cho·ral \'kōr-əl, 'kȯr-\ *adj* : of, relating to, or sung or recited by a chorus or choir or in chorus — **cho·ral·ly** \-ə-lē\ *adv*

cho·rale \kə-'ral, -'räl\ *n* **1** : a sacred song sung by the choir or congregation or both at a church service : HYMN **2** : ¹CHORUS 1b, CHOIR

¹chord \'kȯrd\ *n* : a group of three or more tones sounded together to form harmony — **chord·al** \-əl\ *adj*

²chord *vb* : to play chords

³chord *n* : a straight line joining two points on a curve

chor·date \'kȯrd-ət, 'kȯr-,dāt\ *n* : any of a major group of animals (as vertebrates and tunicates) having at least at some stage of development a flexible rod of cells forming a support along the back, a central nervous system located in the back, and openings for water to pass over the gills — **chordate** *adj*

³chord: *AC* and *AB*

chord organ *n* : an electronic organ with buttons to play simple chords

chore \'chō(ə)r, 'chȯ(ə)r\ *n* **1** *pl* : the regular light work of a household or farm **2** : an ordinary task **3** : a dull, unpleasant, or difficult task **syn** see TASK

cho·re·og·ra·phy \,kōr-ē-'äg-rə-fē, ,kȯr-\ *n* : the art of arranging dances especially for ballet — **cho·re·og·ra·pher** \-fər\ *n* — **cho·re·o·graph·ic** \-ē-ə-'graf-ik\ *adj*

cho·ri·on \'kōr-ē-,än, 'kȯr-\ *n* : the outer membrane that surrounds the embryo of higher animals with backbones and that in mammals with a placenta contributes to the formation of the placenta

cho·ri·on·ic \,kōr-ē-'än-ik, ,kȯr-\ *adj* **1** : of, relating to, or being part of the chorion ⟨*chorionic* villi⟩ **2** : secreted or produced by chorionic tissue or a related tissue (as in the placenta) ⟨human *chorionic* gonadotropin⟩

cho·ris·ter \'kōr-ə-stər, 'kȯr-, 'kär-\ *n* : a singer in a choir

cho·roid \'kōr-,ȯid, 'kȯr-\ *also* **cho·ri·oid** \-ē-,ȯid\ *adj* : of, relating to, or being the middle layer of the eye of animals with backbones that contains pigment and is located between the sclera and the retina — **choroid** *n*

choroid coat *n* : the choroid layer of the eye

chor·tle \'chȯrt-əl\ *vb* **chor·tled; chor·tling** \'chȯrt-(ə-)liŋ\ : to chuckle especially in satisfaction — **chortle** *n* — **chor·tler** \'chȯrt-lər, -(ə)lər\ *n*

¹cho·rus \'kōr-əs, 'kȯr-\ *n* **1 a** : a group of singers and dancers in Greek drama who take part in or comment on the action **b** : an organized group of singers : CHOIR **c** : a group of dancers and singers (as in a musical comedy) **2 a** : a part of a song or hymn that is repeated every so often : REFRAIN **b** : a song to be sung by a chorus **3** : something uttered by a number of persons or animals all at the same time ⟨a *chorus* of boos⟩ — **in chorus** : in unison

²chorus *vb* : to sing or utter in chorus

chorus girl *n* : a young woman who sings or dances in a chorus (as of a musical)

chose *past of* CHOOSE

chosen *past participle of* CHOOSE

chow \'chaù\ *n* : ¹MEAL 1, FOOD

chow chow \'chaù-,chaù\ *n* : a thick-coated straight-legged muscular dog with a blue-black tongue and a short tail curled close to the back — called also *chow* [from a Chinese dialect word related to *kaú* "dog"]

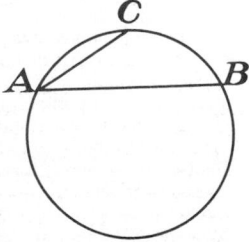
chow chow

chow·der \'chaùd-ər\ *n* : a soup or stew made of seafood or corn with potatoes and onions and milk or tomatoes

chow mein \'chaù-'mān\ *n* : a thick stew of shredded meat, mushrooms, and vegetables served with fried noodles [from Chinese *ch'ao mien*, literally "fried noodles"]

chris·ten \'kris-ᵊn\ *vb* **chris·tened; chris·ten·ing** \'kris-niŋ, -ᵊn-iŋ\ **1** : BAPTIZE 1 **2 a** : to name at baptism ⟨*christened* the baby Robin⟩ **b** : to name or dedicate in a ceremony like that of baptism ⟨*christen* a ship⟩

Chris·ten·dom \'kris-ᵊn-dəm\ *n* **1** : the entire body of Christians **2** : the part of the world where Christianity is most common

¹Chris·tian \'kris-chən, 'krish-\ *n* **1** : a person who believes in Jesus Christ and follows his teachings **2** : a member of a Christian church

²Christian *adj* **1** : of or relating to Jesus Christ or the religion based on his teachings **2** : of or relating to Christians ⟨a *Christian* nation⟩ **3** : being what a Christian should be or do ⟨*Christian* behavior⟩

\ə\ abut	\aù\ out	\i\ tip	\ȯ\ saw	\ù\ foot
\ər\ further	\ch\ chin	\ī\ life	\òi\ coin	\y\ yet
\a\ mat	\e\ pet	\j\ job	\th\ thin	\yü\ few
\ā\ take	\ē\ easy	\ŋ\ sing	\th\ this	\yù\ cure
\ä\ cot, cart	\g\ go	\ō\ bone	\ü\ food	\zh\ vision

Chris·ti·an·i·ty \,kris-chē-'an-ət-ē, ,krish-, -chan-; ,kris-tē-'an-\ *n* **1** : the religion of Christians **2** : Christian belief or practice

Chris·tian·ize \'kris-chə-,nīz, 'krish-\ *vb* **-ized; -iz·ing** : to make Christian — **Chris·tian·i·za·tion** \,kris-chə-nə-'zā-shən, 'krish-\ *n*

christian name *n, often cap C* : the personal name given to a person at birth or christening

Christ·mas \'kris-məs\ *n* **1** : December 25 celebrated in honor of the birth of Christ **2** : CHRISTMASTIME

Christmas cactus *n* : a branching South American cactus with flat stems, short joints, and showy red flowers

Christmas club *n* : a savings account into which deposits are put throughout the year to provide money for Christmas shopping

Christmas fern *n* : a North American evergreen fern often used for winter decorations

Christmas rose *n* : a European herb that is related to the buttercup and produces white or purplish flowers in winter

Christ·mas·tide \'kris-mə-,stīd\ *n* : CHRISTMASTIME

Christ·mas·time \'kris-mə-,stīm\ *n* : the season of Christmas

Christmas tree *n* : a usually evergreen tree decorated at Christmas

¹chro·mat·ic \krō-'mat-ik\ *adj* **1** : of or relating to color; *esp* : being a shade other than black, gray, or white **2** : of or relating to the chromatic scale [from Greek *chrōmatikos* "relating to color", from *chrōma* "color"] — **chro·mat·i·cal·ly** \-i-k(ə-)lē\ *adv*

²chromatic *n* : ²ACCIDENTAL

chromatic aberration *n* : error caused by the differences in refraction of the colored rays into which light can be separated

chromatic scale *n* : a musical scale that has all half steps

chro·ma·tin \'krō-mə-tən\ *n* : a material present in chromosomes that is made up of DNA and protein and stains deeply with certain biological stains

chro·mato·graph \krō-'mat-ə-,graf, krə-\ *n* : an instrument used in chromatography

chro·ma·tog·ra·phy \,krō-mə-'täg-rə-fē\ *n* : separation and detection of chemical compounds as a result of their having traveled at different rates according to their different attractions to matter that carries them (as flowing liquid or gas) and matter that is not moving (as a liquid coating a solid) — **chro·mato·graph·ic** \krō-,mat-ə-'graf-ik, krə-\ *adj*

chrome \'krōm\ *n* **1 a** : CHROMIUM **b** : a chromium pigment **2** : something plated with an alloy of chromium

chro·mite \'krō-,mīt\ *n* : a mineral that consists of an oxide of iron and chromium

chro·mi·um \'krō-mē-əm\ *n* : a blue-white metallic element found in nature only in combination and used especially in alloys and in chrome plating — see ELEMENT table

chro·mo·some \'krō-mə-,sōm, -zōm\ *n* : one of the DNA-containing bodies of a cell nucleus that are usually constant in number in any one kind of plant or animal, and can be seen especially during mitosis and meiosis — **chro·mo·som·al** \,krō-mə-'sō-məl, -'zō-\ *adj*

chromosome number *n* : the number of chromosomes in a cell that is usually constant in the cells making up the body of a particular kind of plant or animal and is usually half as large in sperm cells and egg cells that have gone through meiosis

chro·mo·sphere \'krō-mə-,sfi(ə)r\ *n* : the lower part of the atmosphere of the sun made up chiefly of hydrogen; *also* : a similar part of the atmosphere of any star

chron·ic \'krän-ik\ *adj* **1** : continuing or occurring again and again for a long time ⟨a *chronic* disease⟩ **2** : HABITUAL **2** ⟨a *chronic* complainer⟩ [from `French *chronique* "chronic", from Greek *chronikos* "of time", from *chronos* "time" — related to ANACHRONISM, CHRONICLE, SYNCHRONOUS] — **chron·i·cal·ly** \-i-k(ə-)lē\ *adv*

¹chron·i·cle \'krän-i-kəl\ *n* : an account of events in the order of their happening : HISTORY [Middle English *cronicle* "chronicle", from early French *chronique* (same meaning), derived from Greek *chronikos,* "of time", from *chronos* "time" — related to ANACHRONISM, CHRONIC, SYNCHRONOUS]

²chronicle *vb* **chron·i·cled; chron·i·cling** \-k(ə-)liŋ\ : to record in or as if in a chronicle — **chron·i·cler** \-k(ə-)lər\ *n*

Chron·i·cles \'krän-i-kəlz\ *n* — see BIBLE table

chro·no·graph \'krän-ə-,graf, 'krō-nə-\ *n* : an instrument for measuring and recording stretches of time with exactness —**chro·no·graph·ic** \,krän-ə-'graf-ik, ,krō-nə-\ *adj* — **chro·nog·ra·phy** \krə-'näg-rə-fē\ *n*

chro·no·log·i·cal \,krän-ə-'läj-i-kəl, ,krō-nə-\ *adj* : arranged in or according to the order of time⟨*chronological* order⟩ ⟨a *chronological* table⟩ — **chron·o·log·i·cal·ly** \-i-k(ə-)lē\ *adv*

chro·nol·o·gy \krə-'näl-ə-jē\ *n, pl* **-gies** **1** : the science that deals with measuring time and dating events **2** : a chronological table or list — **chro·nol·o·gist** \-jəst\ *n*

chro·nom·e·ter \krə-'näm-ət-ər\ *n* : an instrument for measuring time; *esp* : one intended to keep time with great exactness — **chro·no·met·ric** \,krän-ə-'me-trik, ,krō-nə-\ *or* **chro·no·met·ri·cal** \-tri-kəl\ *adj*

chro·no·scope \'krän-ə-,skōp, 'krō-nə-\ *n* : an instrument for exact measurement of small stretches of time

chrys·a·lid \'kris-ə-ləd\ *n* : CHRYSALIS

chrys·a·lis \'kris-ə-ləs\ *n, pl* **chrys·al·i·des** \kris-'al-ə-,dēz\ *or* **chrys·a·lis·es** \'kris-ə-lə-səz\ : the pupa of insects (as butterflies) that pass the pupal stage enclosed in a firm case without a cocoon

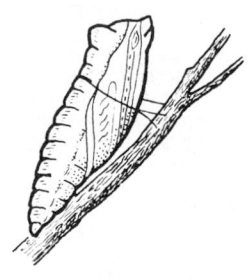

chrysalis

chry·san·the·mum \kris-'an(t)-thə-məm\ *n* **1** : any of a genus of plants that are related to the daisies and include weeds, ornamental plants grown for their brightly colored often double flower heads, and others important as sources of substances used in medicine and as insecticides **2** : a flower head of an ornamental chrysanthemum

chryso·phyte \'kris-ə-,fīt\ *n* : any of a major group of algae (as diatoms) with yellowish green to golden brown pigments

chub·by \'chəb-ē\ *adj* **chub·bi·er; -est** : ⁵PLUMP ⟨a *chubby* baby⟩ — **chub·bi·ness** *n*

¹chuck \'chək\ *vb* **1** : to give a pat or a tap ⟨*chucked* the child under the chin⟩ **2** : TOSS 2 ⟨let's *chuck* the ball around⟩ [origin unknown]

²chuck *n* **1** : a pat or nudge under the chin **2** : an easy throw : TOSS

³chuck *n* **1** : a portion of a side of dressed beef including most of the neck and the parts around the shoulder blade and the first three ribs **2** : a device for holding work or a tool in a machine [English dialect *chuck* "a log or lump", possibly an altered form of *chock*]

chuck–full *variant of* CHOCK-FULL

chuck–hole \'chək-,hōl, 'chəg-\ *n* : POTHOLE

chuck·le \'chək-əl\ *vb* **chuck·led; chuck·ling** \'chək-(ə-)liŋ\ : to laugh in a quiet way — **chuckle** *n*

chuck wagon *n* : a wagon carrying a stove and food for cooking (as on a ranch)

chuck·wal·la \'chək-,wäl-ə\ *n* : a large but harmless lizard of the desert regions of the southwestern U.S.

¹chug \'chəg\ *n* : a dull explosive sound made by or as if by a steam engine pulling a heavy load

²**chug** *vb* **chugged; chug·ging** : to move or go with chugs ⟨a locomotive *chugging* along⟩

¹**chum** \'chəm\ *n* : a close friend : PAL [probably a shortened and altered form of earlier *chamber fellow* "roommate"]

²**chum** *vb* **chummed; chum·ming** : to be chums

chum·my \'chəm-ē\ *adj* **chum·mi·er; -est** : being on close friendly terms — **chum·mi·ly** \'chəm-ə-lē\ *adv* — **chum·mi·ness** \'chəm-ē-nəs\ *n*

chump \'chəmp\ *n* : ¹FOOL 1, DUPE

chunk \'chəŋk\ *n* : a short thick piece or lump

chunky \'chəŋ-kē\ *adj* **chunk·i·er; -est** 1 : STOCKY 2 : full of chunks ⟨*chunky* peanut butter⟩

church \'chərch\ *n* 1 : a building for public worship and especially Christian worship 2 : an organized body of religious believers 3 : public worship — **church·ly** \-lē\ *adj*

church·yard \'chərch-,yärd\ *n* : a yard that belongs to a church and is often used as a burial ground

churl \'chərl\ *n* 1 : a peasant of the Middle Ages 2 : a rude or grumpy person — **churl·ish** \'chər-lish\ *adj* — **churl·ish·ly** *adv* — **churl·ish·ness** *n*

¹**churn** \'chərn\ *n* : a container in which milk or cream is stirred or shaken in making butter

²**churn** *vb* 1 : to stir or shake in a churn (as in making butter) 2 : to stir or shake violently

chute *also* **shute** \'shüt\ *n* 1 : an inclined plane, sloping channel, or passage down or through which things may pass ⟨a coal *chute*⟩ ⟨a mail *chute*⟩ 2 : ¹PARACHUTE 1

chutz·pah \'hut-spə, 'kut-, -(,)spä\ *n* : NERVE 3c [Yiddish; of Hebrew origin]

chyle \'kī(ə)l\ *n* : lymph that is milky from bits of fat and is found especially in the lymphatic vessels surrounding the small intestine and carrying the digested fat to the blood

chyme \'kīm\ *n* : the partly fluid and partly solid mass of incompletely digested food that passes from the stomach into the first part of the small intestine

ci·ca·da \sə-'kād-ə, -'käd-\ *n* : any of a family of stout-bodied insects that are related to the leafhoppers and aphids and have a wide blunt head and large transparent wings

-cide \,sīd\ *n combining form* 1 : killer ⟨pesti*cide*⟩ 2 : killing ⟨geno*cide*⟩ [derived from Latin *-cida* "killer"]

ci·der \'sīd-ər\ *n* : the juice pressed out of fruit (as apples) and used especially as a drink and in the making of vinegar

ci·gar \sig-'är\ *n* : a roll of tobacco leaf for smoking

cig·a·rette \,sig-ə-'ret, 'sig-ə-,ret\ *n* : a small roll of cut tobacco wrapped in paper for smoking [from French *cigarette*, literally "little cigar"]

cil·i·ary \'sil-ē-,er-ē\ *adj* 1 : of or relating to cilia ⟨*ciliary* movement⟩ 2 : of, relating to, or being the muscular body supporting the lens of the eye ⟨the *ciliary* body⟩ ⟨*ciliary* muscles⟩

cil·i·ate \'sil-ē-ət, -,āt\ *n* : any of a group of protozoans that have cilia

cil·i·at·ed \'sil-ē-,āt-əd\ *or* **cil·i·ate** \'sil-ē-ət, -,āt\ *adj* : provided with cilia ⟨a *ciliated* cell⟩

cil·i·um \'sil-ē-əm\ *n, pl* **cil·ia** \-ē-ə\ 1 : EYELASH 2 : one of the tiny hair-like structures of many cells that make lashing movements

¹**cinch** \'sinch\ *n* 1 : a strong girth for a pack or saddle 2 : an easy thing to do 3 : something sure to happen

²**cinch** *vb* 1 : to put a cinch on 2 : to make certain

cin·cho·na \siŋ-'kō-nə, sin-'chō-\ *n* : any of a genus of South American trees and shrubs with bark containing substances (as quinine) that are used in treating malaria

cinc·ture \'siŋ(k)-chər\ *n* : ¹GIRDLE 1, BELT

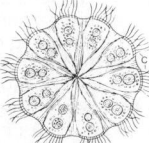

C cilium 2

cin·der \'sin-dər\ *n* 1 : SLAG 2 a : a piece of partly burned coal or wood b : a hot coal without flame 3 : a piece of lava from an erupting volcano — **cin·dery** \-d(ə-)rē\ *adj*

cinder block *n* : a building block made of cement and coal cinders

cin·e·ma \'sin-ə-mə\ *n* 1 a : MOVIE 2a b : a movie theater 2 : MOVIE 3 [derived from French *cinématographe* "motion picture", from Greek *kinēma* "movement" and *graph* "picture", from *kinein* "to move" — related to KINETIC] — **cin·e·mat·ic** \,sin-ə-'mat-ik\ *adj* — **cin·e·mat·i·cal·ly** \-i-k(ə-)lē\ *adv*

cin·e·ma·tog·ra·pher \,sin-ə-mə-'täg-rə-fər\ *n* : a movie photographer

cin·na·bar \'sin-ə-,bär\ *n* : a red mineral that consists of a sulfide of mercury and is the important ore of mercury

cin·na·mon \'sin-ə-mən\ *n* 1 a : a spice consisting of the highly aromatic bark of any of several trees related to the laurel b : a tree that yields cinnamon 2 : a light yellowish brown

cinque·foil \'siŋk-,fòil, 'saŋk-\ *n* : any of a group of plants that have leaves with five lobes and are related to the roses

cion *variant of* SCION

¹**ci·pher** \'sī-fər\ *n* 1 : the symbol 0 denoting the absence of all magnitude or quantity : ZERO — see NUMBER table 2 a : a method of changing a message so as to conceal its meaning b : a message in code [Middle English *cipher* "zero", from early French *cifre* (same meaning), derived from Arabic *ṣifr* "empty"]

²**cipher** *vb* **ci·phered; ci·pher·ing** \-f(ə-)riŋ\ 1 : to use figures in calculating 2 : to change (a message) into cipher

cir·ca \'sər-kə, 'ki(ə)r-,kä\ *prep* : in about ⟨born *circa* 1600⟩

¹**cir·cle** \'sər-kəl\ *n* 1 a : ¹RING 3 b : a closed plane curve every point of which is equally distant from a point within it c : the plane surface bounded by a circle 2 : something in the form of a circle ⟨a traffic *circle*⟩ 3 : ¹CYCLE 2a, ROUND ⟨the wheel had come full *circle*⟩ 4 : a group of people sharing a common interest ⟨our *circle* of friends⟩ [Middle English *cercle* "circle", from early French *cercle* (same meaning), derived from Latin *circus* "circle, ring, arena"]

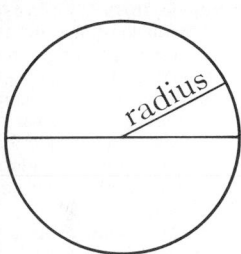

circle 1b

²**circle** *vb* **cir·cled; cir·cling** \-k(ə-)liŋ\ 1 : to enclose in or as if in a circle ⟨*circle* the correct answer⟩ ⟨the trees *circling* our little house⟩ 2 : to move or revolve around ⟨the pilot *circled* the field⟩ ⟨satellites *circling* the earth⟩ 3 : to move in or as if in a circle ⟨the halfback *circled* to the left⟩ — **cir·cler** \-k(ə-)lər\ *n*

circle graph *n* : a circular chart that illustrates size, amount, or frequency by the area of pie-shaped parts of a circle — called also *pie chart*

cir·clet \'sər-klət\ *n* : an ornament in the form of a circle

cir·cuit \'sər-kət\ *n* 1 a : a boundary around an enclosed space b : an enclosed space 2 : a moving or revolving around ⟨the *circuit* of the earth around the sun⟩ 3 : a traveling from place to place in an area (as by a judge) so as to stop in each place at a certain time; *also* : the route so traveled 4 a : ²LEAGUE 2 b : a chain of theaters at which stage shows are shown in turn 5 : the complete

\ə\ abut	\au̇\ out	\i\ tip	\ȯ\ saw	\u̇\ foot
\ər\ further	\ch\ chin	\ī\ life	\ȯi\ coin	\y\ yet
\a\ mat	\e\ pet	\j\ job	\th\ thin	\yü\ few
\ā\ take	\ē\ easy	\ŋ\ sing	\th\ this	\yu̇\ cure
\ä\ cot, cart	\g\ go	\ō\ bone	\ü\ food	\zh\ vision

path of an electric current   **6** : a group of electronic elements : HOOKUP

circuit breaker *n* : a switch that automatically stops the flow of electric current under an abnormal condition

cir·cu·itous \(,)sər-'kyü-ət-əs\ *adj*   **1** : not saying what one means in simple and sincere language   **2** : having a circular or winding course ⟨a *circuitous* route⟩ — **cir·cu·itous·ly** *adv* — **cir·cu·itous·ness** *n*

cir·cuit·ry \'sər-kə-trē\ *n, pl* **-ries** : the plan or the elements of an electric circuit

¹cir·cu·lar \'sər-kyə-lər\ *adj*   **1** : having the form of a circle : ROUND ⟨a *circular* driveway⟩   **2** : passing or going around in a circle ⟨*circular* motion⟩   **3** : CIRCUITOUS 1   **4** : sent around to a number of persons ⟨a *circular* letter⟩ — **cir·cu·lar·i·ty** \,sər-kyə-'lar-ət-ē\ *n* — **cir·cu·lar·ly** \'sər-kyə-lər-lē\ *adv*

²circular *n* : a printed notice or advertisement given or sent to many people

circular cylinder *n* : a cylinder with bases that are circles

circular saw *n* : a power saw with a round cutting blade

cir·cu·late \'sər-kyə-,lāt\ *vb* **-lat·ed; -lat·ing**   **1** : to move or cause to move in a circle or course; *esp* : to follow a course that returns to the starting point ⟨blood *circulates* through the body⟩   **2** : to pass or be passed from person to person or place to place ⟨*circulate* a rumor⟩ ⟨money *circulates*⟩ — **cir·cu·la·tive** \-,lāt-iv\ *adj* — **cir·cu·la·tor** \-,lāt-ər\ *n*

cir·cu·la·tion \,sər-kyə-'lā-shən\ *n*   **1** : orderly movement through a circuit; *esp* : the movement of blood through the vessels of the body caused by the pumping action of the heart   **2 a** : passage from person to person or place to place ⟨coins in *circulation*⟩   **b** : the average number of copies (as of a newspaper) sold over a given period

cir·cu·la·to·ry \'sər-kyə-lə-,tōr-ē, -,tȯr-\ *adj* : of or relating to circulation (as of the blood)

circulatory system *n* : the bodily system of blood, lymph, vessels, and heart concerned with circulation of body fluids

cir·cum·cen·ter \'sər-kəm-,sen-tər\ *n* : the point at which the three perpendicular bisectors of the sides of a triangle intersect and which is the same distance from each of the three vertices of the triangle

cir·cum·cise \'sər-kəm-,sīz\ *vb* **-cised; -cis·ing** : to cut off the foreskin of

cir·cum·ci·sion \,sər-kəm-'sizh-ən, 'sər-kəm-,sizh-\ *n*   **1** : the act of circumcising or being circumcised; *esp* : a Jewish rite performed on male infants as a sign of inclusion in the covenant between God and Abraham   **2** *cap* : January 1 observed as a church festival in honor of the circumcision of Christ

cir·cum·fer·ence \sə(r)-'kəm(p)-fərn(t)s, -f(ə-)rən(t)s\ *n*   **1** : a line that goes around or encloses a circle   **2** : the outer boundary of a figure or area   **3** : the distance around something ⟨the *circumference* of the earth at the equator⟩

cir·cum·flex \'sər-kəm-,fleks\ *n* : a mark ^ over a vowel

cir·cum·lo·cu·tion \,sər-kəm-lō-'kyü-shən\ *n* : the use of many words to express an idea that could be expressed in few — **cir·cum·loc·u·to·ry** \-'läk-yə-,tōr-ē, -,tȯr-\ *adj*

cir·cum·lu·nar \,sər-kəm-'lü-nər\ *adj* : revolving about or surrounding the moon

cir·cum·nav·i·gate \,sər-kəm-'nav-ə-,gāt\ *vb* : to go completely around especially by water ⟨*circumnavigate* the earth⟩ — **cir·cum·nav·i·ga·tion** \-,nav-ə-'gā-shən\ *n*

cir·cum·po·lar \,sər-kəm-'pō-lər\ *adj*   **1** : continually visible above the horizon ⟨a *circumpolar* star⟩   **2** : surrounding or found near a pole of the earth

cir·cum·scribe \'sər-kəm-,skrīb\ *vb* **-scribed; -scrib·ing**   **1** : to hold within narrow limits   **2 a** : to draw a line around   **b** : to put a boundary around [from Latin *circumscribere* "to draw a line around, set limits to", from *circum* "around" and *scribere* "to write, draw" — related to SCRIBE]

cir·cum·spect \'sər-kəm-,spekt\ *adj* : careful to consider everything that might happen — **cir·cum·spec·tion**

\,sər-kəm-'spek-shən\ *n* — **cir·cum·spect·ly** *adv*

cir·cum·stance \'sər-kəm-,stan(t)s\ *n*   **1 a** : a fact or event that must be considered along with another fact or event   **b** : a fact or detail in a chain of events   **2** *pl* : conditions at a certain time or place ⟨impossible under the *circumstances*⟩   **3 a** : the way things happen to be : CHANCE — often used in pl. ⟨a victim of *circumstances*⟩   **b** *pl* : financial condition ⟨in easy *circumstances*⟩

cir·cum·stan·tial \,sər-kəm-'stan-chəl\ *adj*   **1** : consisting of, relating to, or depending on circumstances ⟨*circumstantial* evidence⟩   **2** : containing full details ⟨a *circumstantial* account of what happened⟩ — **cir·cum·stan·tial·ly** \-'stanch-(ə-)lē\ *adv*

cir·cum·vent \,sər-kəm-'vent\ *vb*   **1** : to go around : BYPASS   **2** : to get the better of or avoid the force or effect of by cleverness ⟨*circumvented* the rules⟩ — **cir·cum·ven·tion** \-'ven-chən\ *n*

cir·cus \'sər-kəs\ *n*   **1** : a large arena enclosed by rows of seats (as in ancient Rome)   **2 a** : a show that usually travels from place to place and that has a variety of exhibitions including riding, acrobatic feats, wild animal displays, and performances by jugglers and clowns   **b** : a circus performance   **c** : the performers and equipment of such a circus   **d** : something that suggests a circus [from Latin *circus* "circle, arena"]

ci·ré \sə-'rā\ *n* : a shiny fabric that looks wet [French, literally "waxed"]

cirque \'sərk\ *n* : a deep basin on a mountain that is shaped like half a bowl [French, from Latin *circus* "circle, arena"]

cir·rho·sis \sə-'rō-səs\ *n* : an increase in fiber-containing tissue and hardening especially of the liver

cir·ro·cu·mu·lus \,sir-ō-'kyü-myə-ləs\ *n* : a cloud form of small white rounded masses at a high altitude usually in lines and regular groups

cir·ro·stra·tus \,sir-ō-'strāt-əs, -'strat-\ *n* : a fairly even layer of high stratus darker than cirrus

cir·rus \'sir-əs\ *n, pl* **cir·ri** \'si(ə)r-,ī\ : a thin white cloud usually of tiny ice crystals formed at altitudes of 6,000 to 12,000 meters

cis·lu·nar \(')sis-'lü-nər\ *adj* : lying between the earth and the moon or the moon's orbit

cis·tern \'sis-tərn\ *n* : an artificial reservoir or tank for storing water usually underground

cit·a·del \'sit-əd-ᵊl, -ə-,del\ *n*   **1** : a fortress that sits high above a city   **2** : a strong fortress

ci·ta·tion \sī-'tā-shən\ *n*   **1** : an official order to appear (as before a court)   **2 a** : an act or instance of quoting   **b** : QUOTATION 1   **3** : a formal statement of what a person did to be chosen to receive an award

citadel 1

cite \'sīt\ *vb* **cit·ed; cit·ing**   **1** : to summon to appear before a court   **2** : to quote as an example, authority, or proof   **3** : to refer to especially in praise

cit·i·fy \'sit-i-,fī\ *vb* **-fied; -fy·ing** : to accustom to urban ways : URBANIZE

cit·i·zen \'sit-ə-zən\ *n*   **1** : a person who lives in a city or town   **2 a** : a member of a state   **b** : a person who owes allegiance to a government and is protected by it [Middle English *citizein*, "citizen, resident of a town", derived from early French *citeien* (same meaning), from *cité* "town", derived from Latin *civitas* "state of being a resident of a town, citizenship", from *civis* "citizen" — related to CITY, CIVIL]

cit·i·zen·ry \'sit-ə-zən-rē\ *n, pl* **-ries** : the whole body of citizens

citizens band *n* : a range of radio frequencies set aside for private radio communications

cit·i·zen·ship \'sit-ə-zən-ship\ *n* **1** : possession of the rights and privileges of a citizen **2** : the quality of a person's response to membership in a community

ci·trate \'si-,trāt\ *n* : a salt or ester of citric acid

cit·ric acid \,si-trik-\ *n* : a pleasantly sour-tasting organic acid obtained especially from lemon and lime juices or by the chemical breakdown of sugars and used as a flavoring

cit·ron \'si-trən\ *n* **1 a** : a fruit like the lemon in appearance and structure but larger; *also* : the citrus tree producing this fruit **b** : the preserved rind of the citron used especially in fruitcake **2** : a small watermelon with hard flesh that is used especially in pickles and preserves

cit·ro·nel·la \,si-trə-'nel-ə\ *n* : an oil obtained from a grass of southern Asia and used in perfumes and as an insect repellent

cit·rus \'si-trəs\ *n, pl* **citrus** *or* **cit·rus·es** : any of a genus of often thorny trees and shrubs (as the orange, grapefruit, or lemon) grown in warm regions for their fruits

city \'sit-ē\ *n, pl* **cit·ies** **1** : a place in which people live that is larger or more important than a town **2** : the people of a city [Middle English *citie* "large or small town", from early French *cité* (same meaning), derived from Latin *civitas* "state of being a resident of a town, citizenship", from *civis* "citizen" — related to CITIZEN, CIVIL]

city manager *n* : an official employed by an elected council to direct the administration of a city government

city–state \'sit-ē-'stāt, -,stāt\ *n* : a self-governing state consisting of a city and surrounding territory

civ·et \'siv-ət\ *n* : a thick yellowish strong-smelling substance obtained from the civet cat and used in perfume

civet cat *n* : a long-bodied short-legged African mammal that produces civet

civet cat

civ·ic \'siv-ik\ *adj* : of or relating to a citizen, a city, or citizenship ⟨*civic* pride⟩ — **civ·i·cal·ly** \'siv-i-k(ə-)lē\ *adv*

civ·ics \'siv-iks\ *n* : the study of the rights and duties of citizens

civ·il \'siv-əl\ *adj* **1** : of or relating to citizens ⟨*civil* liberties⟩ **2** : of or relating to the state ⟨*civil* institutions⟩ **3** : of or relating to ordinary or government affairs rather than to those of the military or the church **4** : polite without being friendly ⟨gave a *civil* answer⟩ **5** : relating to court action between individuals having to do with private rights rather than criminal action [Middle English *civil* "relating to a citizen", from early French *civil* (same meaning), from Latin *civilis* "relating to a citizen", from *civis* "citizen" — related to CITIZEN, CITY]

civil defense *n* : protective actions and emergency relief activities carried on by civilians in case of enemy attack or natural disaster

civil engineer *n* : an engineer whose training or occupation is in the designing and construction of public works (as roads or harbors) and of various private works — **civil engineering** *n*

ci·vil·ian \sə-'vil-yən\ *n* : a person not on active duty in a military, police, or fire-fighting force — **civilian** *adj*

ci·vil·i·ty \sə-'vil-ət-ē\ *n, pl* **-ties** **1** : COURTESY 1, POLITENESS **2** : a polite act or expression

civ·i·li·za·tion \,siv-ə-lə-'zā-shən\ *n* **1 a** : an advanced stage (as in art, science, and government) of social development **b** : the way of life of a people ⟨ancient Egyptian *civilization*⟩ **2** : the series of changes involved in becoming civilized **3** : improvement of thought, manners, or taste

civ·i·lize \'siv-ə-,līz\ *vb* **-lized; -liz·ing** : to raise out of a primitive state; *esp* : to bring to an advanced stage (as in art, science, and government) of social development — **civ·i·lized** *adj*

civ·il·ly \'siv-ə(l)-lē\ *adv* : in a civil manner : POLITELY

civil rights *n pl* : the nonpolitical rights of a citizen; *esp* : the rights of personal liberty guaranteed to U.S. citizens by the 13th and 14th amendments to the Constitution and by acts of Congress

civil service *n* : the branch of a government that takes care of the business of running a state but that does not include the lawmaking branch, the military, or the court system

civil war *n* : a war between opposing groups of citizens of the same country or nation

¹clab·ber \'klab-ər\ *n, chiefly dialect* : sour milk that has thickened or curdled

²clabber *vb, chiefly dialect* : CURDLE

clack \'klak\ *vb* : to make or cause to make a clattering or clicking sound — **clack** *n* — **clack·er** *n*

clad \'klad\ *adj* : being covered : wearing clothes

¹claim \'klām\ *vb* **1 a** : to ask for as rightfully belonging to oneself ⟨*claim* an inheritance⟩ **b** : to call for : REQUIRE ⟨business that *claims* attention⟩ **2** : to put an end to life : TAKE ⟨an accident *claimed* his life⟩ **3 a** : to state as a fact : MAINTAIN ⟨*claimed* to have been cheated⟩ **b** : to make a claim ⟨*claimed* to know nothing about it⟩ [Middle English *claimen* "to ask for as a right, claim", from early French *clamer* (same meaning), from Latin *clamare* "to shout" — related to ACCLAIM, CLAMOR] — **claim·able** \'klā-mə-bəl\ — **claim·er** *n*

²claim *n* **1** : a demand for something due or believed to be due ⟨an insurance *claim*⟩ **2 a** : a right or title to something **b** : a statement that may be doubted ⟨a *claim* of authenticity⟩ **3** : something claimed; *esp* : an area of land marked out by a settler or prospector

claim·ant \'klā-mənt\ *n* : a person who claims to have a right to something

clair·voy·ance \kla(ə)r-'vȯi-ən(t)s, kle(ə)r-\ *n* : the power of seeing or knowing about things that are not present to the senses [from French *clairvoyance* "clairvoyance", from *clair* "clear" (from Latin *clarus* "clear") and *voyant* "seeing" (derived from Latin *vidēre* "to see") — related to CLEAR, VISION]

¹clair·voy·ant \kla(ə)r-'vȯi-ənt, kle(ə)r-\ *adj* : of, relating to, or having clairvoyance

²clairvoyant *n* : a person who has clairvoyance

¹clam \'klam\ *n* **1** : any of numerous edible marine mollusks that have two hinged shells and live in sand or mud **2** : a freshwater mussel

²clam *vb* **clammed; clamming** : to dig or gather clams

clam·bake \'klam-,bāk\ *n* : an outdoor party; *esp* : an outing at which food is cooked usually on heated rocks covered by seaweed

clam 1

clam·ber \'klam-bər\ *vb* **clam·bered; clam·ber·ing** \-b(ə-)riŋ\ : to climb awkwardly ⟨*clambered* over the rocks⟩

clam·my \'klam-ē\ *adj* **clam·mi·er; -est** : being damp, soft, sticky, and usually cool — **clam·mi·ness** *n*

\ə\ abut	\au̇\ out	\i\ tip	\ȯ\ saw	\u̇\ foot
\ər\ further	\ch\ chin	\ī\ life	\ȯi\ coin	\y\ yet
\a\ mat	\e\ pet	\j\ job	\th\ thin	\yü\ few
\ā\ take	\ē\ easy	\ŋ\ sing	\th\ this	\yu̇\ cure
\ä\ cot, cart	\g\ go	\ō\ bone	\ü\ food	\zh\ vision

clam·or \\'klam-ər\\ *n* **1 a** : a noisy shouting **b** : a loud continuous noise **2** : strong and active protest or demand [Middle English *clamor* "noisy shouting", from early French *clamour* (same meaning), derived from Latin *clamare* "to shout" — related to ACCLAIM, CLAIM] — **clamor** *vb* — **clam·or·ous** \\-(ə-)rəs\\ *adj* — **clam·or·ous·ly** *adv*

¹clamp \\'klamp\\ *n* : a device that holds or presses parts together firmly

²clamp *vb* : to fasten or tighten with or as if with a clamp

clamp down *vb* : to act in a strict and forceful manner to stop something ⟨police are *clamping down* on drunk driving⟩

clam·shell \\'klam-ˌshel\\ *n* : the shell of a clam

clam up *vb* : to become silent ⟨they *clammed up* when asked for more information⟩

clam worm *n* : any of several large burrowing annelid worms often used as bait

clan \\'klan\\ *n* **1** : a group (as in the Scottish Highlands) made up of households whose heads claim to have a common ancestor **2** : a group of persons united by a common interest

clan·des·tine \\klan-'des-tən\\ *adj* : done in secret ⟨a *clandestine* meeting⟩ — **clan·des·tine·ly** *adv*

¹clang \\'klaŋ\\ *vb* : to make or cause to make a loud ringing sound

²clang *n* : a loud ringing sound like that made by pieces of metal striking together

clan·gor \\'klaŋ-(g)ər\\ *n* : a loud clanging noise — **clan·gor·ous** \\-(g)ə-rəs\\ *adj*

¹clank \\'klaŋk\\ *vb* : to make or move with a clank or series of clanks

²clank *n* : a sharp short ringing sound

clan·nish \\'klan-ish\\ *adj* : tending to associate only with a group of persons like oneself — **clan·nish·ness** *n*

clans·man \\'klanz-mən\\ *n* : a member of a clan

¹clap \\'klap\\ *vb* **clapped; clap·ping** **1** : to strike noisily : BANG ⟨*clap* two boards together⟩ ⟨the door *clapped* shut⟩ **2** : to strike the hands together over and over in applause **3** : to strike with the open hand ⟨*clap* a friend on the shoulder⟩ **4** : to put or set hastily or with force ⟨*clapped* him in jail⟩ ⟨had never *clapped* eyes on me before⟩

²clap *n* **1** : a sound made by or as if by clapping ⟨a *clap* of thunder⟩ **2** : a friendly slap ⟨a *clap* on the shoulder⟩

³clap *n* : GONORRHEA — often used with *the*

clap·board \\'klab-ərd; 'kla(p)-ˌbō(ə)rd, -ˌbȯ(ə)rd\\ *n* : a narrow board thicker at one edge than at the other used to cover the sides of wooden buildings — **clapboard** *vb*

clap·per \\'klap-ər\\ *n* **1** : the tongue of a bell **2** : one that makes a clapping sound

clap·trap \\'klap-ˌtrap\\ *n* : NONSENSE 1

clar·et \\'klar-ət\\ *n* **1** : a dry red table wine **2** : a dark purplish red — **claret** *adj*

clar·i·fy \\'klar-ə-ˌfī\\ *vb* **-fied; -fy·ing** **1** : to make or become pure or clear ⟨*clarify* a liquid⟩ **2** : to make or become easier to understand ⟨*clarify* a statement⟩ — **clar·i·fi·ca·tion** \\ˌklar-ə-fə-'kā-shən\\ *n* — **clar·i·fi·er** \\'klar-ə-ˌfī(-ə)r\\ *n*

clar·i·net \\ˌklar-ə-'net, 'klar-ə-nət\\ *n* : a woodwind musical instrument in the shape of a cylindrical tube having a single-reed mouthpiece — **clar·i·net·ist** *or* **clar·i·net·tist** \\ˌklar-ə-'net-əst\\ *n*

clar·i·on \\'klar-ē-ən\\ *adj* : brilliantly clear ⟨a *clarion* call to action⟩

clar·i·ty \\'klar-ət-ē\\ *n* : the quality or state of being clear ⟨the *clarity*

clarinet

¹clash \\'klash\\ *vb* **1** : to make a clash ⟨*clashing* cymbals⟩ **2 a** : to come into conflict ⟨pickets *clashed* with the police⟩ **b** : to not match well ⟨our ideas *clashed*⟩ ⟨some colors *clash*⟩ — **clash·er** *n*

²clash *n* **1** : a loud sharp sound usually of metal striking metal ⟨the *clash* of swords⟩ **2** : a sharp fight or strong disagreement

¹clasp \\'klasp\\ *n* **1** : a device for holding together objects or parts of something **2** : a holding or embracing with or as if with the hands or arms

²clasp *vb* **1** : to fasten with or as if with a clasp **2** : to enclose and hold with the arms; *esp* : EMBRACE **3** : to seize with or as if with the hand : GRASP — **clasp·er** *n*

¹class \\'klas\\ *n* **1 a** : a group of students meeting regularly to study the same subject **b** : the period during which such a group meets **c** : a course of instruction **d** : a group of students who graduate together ⟨*class* of 1990⟩ **2 a** : a group or rank of society ⟨the working *class*⟩ **b** : high social rank **c** : high quality **3 a** : a group or set alike in some way **b** : a major category in biological classification that is above the order and below the phylum or division **c** : a grouping or standing (as of goods or services) based on quality — **class·less** \\-ləs\\ *adj*

²class *vb* : CLASSIFY

¹clas·sic \\'klas-ik\\ *adj* **1 a** : serving as a standard of excellence **b** : fashionable year after year : TRADITIONAL, ENDURING ⟨a *classic* design⟩ **2** : of or relating to the ancient Greeks or Romans or their culture **3 a** : notable as the best of its kind ⟨a *classic* film⟩ **b** : notable as the most basic of its kind ⟨the *classic* example of a dictator⟩

²classic *n* **1** : a literary work or author of ancient Greece or Rome **2** : a great work of art **3** : something regarded as perfect of its kind **4** : an event that has become a tradition ⟨a football *classic*⟩

clas·si·cal \\'klas-i-kəl\\ *adj* **1** : ¹CLASSIC 1a **2** : of or relating to the classics of literature or art; *esp* : of or relating to the ancient Greek and Roman classics ⟨*classical* studies⟩ **3** : of or relating to serious music in the European tradition **4** : of or relating to tradition : AUTHENTIC **5** : concerned with a general study of the arts and sciences and not specializing in technical studies ⟨a *classical* high school⟩

clas·si·cal·ly \\'klas-i-k(ə-)lē\\ *adv* : in a classic or classical manner

clas·si·cism \\'klas-ə-ˌsiz-əm\\ *n* **1** : the principles or style of the literature, art, or architecture of ancient Greece and Rome **2** : a following of the standards of tradition (as in music or art)

clas·si·fi·ca·tion \\ˌklas-(ə-)fə-'kā-shən\\ *n* **1** : the act or process of classifying **2 a** : systematic arrangement in groups : TAXONOMY **b** : ¹CLASS 3a, CATEGORY — **clas·si·fi·ca·to·ry** \\'klas-(ə-)fə-kə-ˌtōr-ē, -ˌtȯr-\\ *adj*

clas·si·fied \\'klas-ə-ˌfīd\\ *adj* **1** : divided into classes ⟨*classified* ads⟩ **2** : withheld from the knowledge of the general public for reasons of national security ⟨*classified* information⟩

clas·si·fy \\'klas-ə-ˌfī\\ *vb* **-fied; -fy·ing** : to arrange in or assign to classes ⟨*classify* books by subjects⟩ — **clas·si·fi·able** \\-ˌfī-ə-bəl\\ *adj* — **clas·si·fi·er** \\-ˌfī(-ə)r\\ *n*

class·mate \\'klas-ˌmāt\\ *n* : a member of the same class in a school or college

class·room \\-ˌrüm, -ˌrùm\\ *n* : a room in a school or college in which classes meet

¹clat·ter \\'klat-ər\\ *vb* **1** : to make or cause to make a rattling sound **2** : to move with a clatter — **clat·ter·er** \\-ər-ər\\ *n* — **clat·ter·ing·ly** \\'klat-ə-riŋ-lē\\ *adv*

²clatter *n* **1** : a rattling sound (as of hard objects striking together) ⟨the *clatter* of pots and pans⟩ **2** : COMMOTION 2 **3** : noisy chatter — **clat·tery** \\'klat-ə-rē\\ *adj*

clause \\'klȯz\\ *n* **1** : a separate distinct part of an article or document ⟨a *clause* in a will⟩ **2** : a group of words having its own subject and predicate but forming only part of a compound or complex sentence (as "when it rained" or "they went inside" in the sentence "when it rained they went inside")

claus·tro·pho·bia \ˌklȯ-strə-ˈfō-bē-ə\ *n* : abnormal fear of being in closed or narrow spaces — **claus·tro·pho·bic** \-ˈfō-bik\ *adj*

clav·i·chord \ˈklav-ə-ˌkȯ(ə)rd\ *n* : an early keyboard instrument in use before the piano

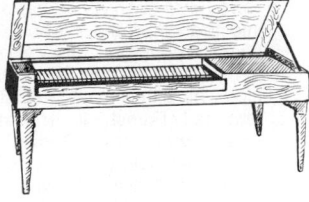
clavichord

clav·i·cle \ˈklav-i-kəl\ *n* : a bone of the shoulder that joins the breastbone and the shoulder blade — called also *collarbone*

¹**claw** \ˈklȯ\ *n* **1 a** : a sharp usually slender and curved nail on the toe of an animal (as a cat or bird) **b** : a sharp curved extension especially if at the end of a limb (as of an insect); *also* : one of the pincerlike organs on some limbs of arthropods (as a lobster or scorpion) **2** : something that resembles a claw in shape or use — **clawed** \ˈklȯd\ *adj* — **claw·like** \ˈklȯ-ˌlīk\ *adj*

²**claw** *vb* : to scratch, seize, or dig with or as if with claws

clay \ˈklā\ *n* **1** : an earthy material that is sticky and easily molded when wet and hard when baked **2** : a plastic substance used like clay for modeling

clay·ey \ˈklā-ē\ *adj* **clay·i·er; -est** : resembling clay or containing much clay (a *clayey* soil)

clay pigeon *n* : a saucer-shaped object made of baked clay and used as a target in trapshooting

¹**clean** \ˈklēn\ *adj* **1** : free from dirt or pollution (*clean* clothes) **2** : free of objectionable behavior or language (led a *clean* life) (a *clean* joke) **3** : being such to the fullest degree : COMPLETE (made a *clean* sweep) **4** : having a simple graceful form : TRIM (a ship with *clean* lines) **5** : ¹SMOOTH 1a (a sharp knife makes a *clean* cut) — **clean·ness** \ˈklēn-nəs\ *n*

²**clean** *adv* **1 a** : so as to clean (a new broom sweeps *clean*) **b** : in a clean manner (fight *clean*) **2** : all the way (tack went *clean* through) (trout leaping *clean* out of the water)

³**clean** *vb* **1** : to make or become clean (*clean* your room) (*cleaned* up for supper) **2** : to take or use up the contents or resources of (tourists *cleaned* out the shops)

clean–cut \ˈklēn-ˈkət\ *adj* : neat and wholesome looking

clean·er \ˈklē-nər\ *n* **1** : one whose work is cleaning **2** : a substance used for cleaning **3** : a device or machine for cleaning

¹**clean·ly** \ˈklēn-lē\ *adv* : in a clean manner

²**clean·ly** \ˈklen-lē\ *adj* **clean·li·er; -est** **1** : careful to keep clean (a *cleanly* animal) **2** : being kept clean by habit (*cleanly* surroundings) — **clean·li·ness** *n*

cleanse \ˈklenz\ *vb* **cleansed; cleans·ing** : to make clean

cleans·er \ˈklen-zər\ *n* : a substance (as a scouring powder or cold cream) used for cleaning

clean·up \ˈklē-ˌnəp\ *n* : an act or instance of cleaning (helped with the *cleanup* after the meal)

¹**clear** \ˈkli(ə)r\ *adj* **1 a** : shining brightly : LUMINOUS (*clear* sunlight) **b** : free from clouds, haze, dust, or mist (a *clear* day) **c** : free from trouble : SERENE (a *clear* gaze) **2 a** : free of blemishes (a *clear* complexion) **b** : easily seen through : TRANSPARENT (*clear* glass) **3** : easily heard, seen, or understood (a *clear* voice) (the meaning was *clear*) **4** : free from doubt : SURE (a *clear* understanding of the issue) **5** : free from guilt : INNOCENT (a *clear* conscience) **6** : free from restriction or entanglement (a *clear* profit) (the coast is *clear*) [Middle English *clere* "clear, bright", from early French *cler* (same meaning), from Latin

clarus "clear, bright" — related to CLAIRVOYANCE, DECLARE] — **clear·ness** *n*

²**clear** *adv* **1** : in a clear manner (shout loud and *clear*) **2** : all the way : COMPLETELY (can see *clear* to the mountains) (the hole goes *clear* through)

³**clear** *vb* **1 a** : to make or become clear (*clear* the water by filtering) (the sky is *clearing*) **b** : to go away : VANISH (clouds *cleared* away after the rain) **2** : to free from blame (*cleared* my name) **3** : to make understandable : EXPLAIN (*cleared* the matter up for me) **4 a** : to free from things blocking (*clear* land for crops) (*clear* a path) **b** : to remove stored or displayed data from (as a computer or calculator) **5** : to give or get approval (*cleared* for secret work) (the proposal *cleared* the committee) **6** : to pay in full : SETTLE (*clear* an account) **7** : to go through customs **8** : ⁴NET (*cleared* a profit) **9** : to get rid of : REMOVE (*clear* the dishes from the table) **10** : to go over or by without touching (*cleared* the fence) — **clear the air** : to remove tension or confusion (*cleared the air* by discussing their differences)

⁴**clear** *n* : a clear space or part — **in the clear** **1** : free of something blocking **2** : free from suspicion or guilt

clear·ance \ˈklir-ən(t)s\ *n* **1 a** : an act or process of clearing **b** : the act of clearing a ship at the customhouse **c** : the papers showing that a ship has cleared **d** : authorization for an airplane to proceed **2** : a sale to clear out stock **3** : the distance by which one object keeps from hitting or touching another or the clear space between them

clear–cut \ˈkli(ə)r-ˈkət\ *adj* : free from doubt or uncertainty : DEFINITE (a *clear-cut* victory)

clear·head·ed \-ˈhed-əd\ *adj* : able to think clearly

clear·ing \ˈkli(ə)r-iŋ\ *n* **1** : the act or process of making or becoming clear **2** : an area of land cleared of wood and brush

clear·ing·house \-ˌhau̇s\ *n* **1** : an institution run by banks for the exchanging of checks and claims **2** : a central agency for collecting and giving out information

clear·ly \ˈkli(ə)r-lē\ *adv* **1** : in a clear manner (was *clearly* visible) **2** : without doubt or question (*clearly* something had to be done)

clear out *vb* **1** : to go or run away often suddenly or secretly (a horse broke loose and *cleared out*) (*cleared out* without paying me back) **2** : to drive out or away usually with force (police *cleared out* the demonstrators)

clear–sight·ed \ˈkli(ə)r-ˈsīt-əd\ *adj* **1** : having good vision **2** : having a clear understanding

cleat \ˈklēt\ *n* **1** : a wooden or metal device around which a rope may be made fast **2** : a strip or projection fastened on or across something to give strength or a place to hold or to prevent slipping (*cleats* on a football shoe)

cleav·age \ˈklē-vij\ *n* **1** : the quality of a crystallized substance or rock of splitting in definite directions **2** : the action of cleaving : the state of being cleaved **3** : the series of mitotic cell divisions of the egg that changes the single cell into a many-celled embryo

¹**cleave** \ˈklēv\ *vb* **cleaved** \ˈklēvd\ *or* **clove** \ˈklōv\; **cleaved; cleav·ing** : to cling to a person or thing closely [Middle English *clevien* "adhere", from Old English *clifian* "adhere"]

²**cleave** *vb* **cleaved** \ˈklēvd\ *also* **cleft** \ˈkleft\ *or* **clove** \ˈklōv\; **cleaved** *also* **cleft** *or* **clo·ven** \ˈklō-vən\; **cleaving** : to split by or as if by a cutting blow (the bow of the ship *cleaving* the water) [Middle English *cleven* "divide", from Old English *clēofan* "divide"]

cleav·er \ˈklē-vər\ *n* : a heavy knife with a wide blade

\ə\ abut	\au̇\ out	\i\ tip	\ȯ\ saw	\u̇\ foot
\ər\ further	\ch\ chin	\ī\ life	\ȯi\ coin	\y\ yet
\a\ mat	\e\ pet	\j\ job	\th\ thin	\yü\ few
\ā\ take	\ē\ easy	\ŋ\ sing	\th\ this	\yu̇\ cure
\ä\ cot, cart	\g\ go	\ō\ bone	\ü\ food	\zh\ vision

clef \'klef\ *n* : a sign placed on the staff in writing music to show what pitch is represented by each line and space

clef

¹cleft \'kleft\ *n* **1** : a space or opening made by splitting : CREVICE **2** : a hollow resembling a cleft

²cleft *adj* : partially split or divided

cleft palate *n* : a split in the roof of the mouth that occurs as a birth defect

clem·a·tis \'klem-ət-əs, kli-'mat-əs\ *n* : a vine or herb related to the buttercups that has leaves with three leaflets and is widely grown for its showy usually white or purple flowers

clem·en·cy \'klem-ən-sē\ *n, pl* **-cies** **1** : disposition to be merciful **2** : an act or instance of mercy **syn** see MERCY

clem·ent \'klem-ənt\ *adj* **1** : inclined to be merciful : LENIENT **2** : not too hot or too cold : MILD ⟨*clement* weather⟩ — **clem·ent·ly** *adv*

clench \'klench\ *vb* **1** : to hold fast : CLUTCH **2** : to set or close tightly ⟨*clench* one's teeth⟩ ⟨*clench* one's fist⟩

clere·sto·ry \'kli(ə)r-ˌstōr-ē, -ˌstȯr-\ *n, pl* **-ries** : an outside wall of a room or building that rises above a roof next to it and contains windows

cler·gy \'klər-jē\ *n, pl* **clergies** : the group of religious officials (as priests, ministers, and rabbis) specially prepared and authorized to conduct religious services

cler·gy·man \'klər-ji-mən\ *n* : a member of the clergy

cler·ic \'kler-ik\ *n* : a member of the clergy

cler·i·cal \'kler-i-kəl\ *adj* **1** : of, relating to, or characteristic of the clergy **2** : of or relating to a clerk or office worker — **cler·i·cal·ly** \-i-k(ə-)lē\ *adv*

clerical collar *n* : a narrow stiffly upright white collar worn by members of the clergy

¹clerk \'klərk\ *n* **1** : a person whose job is to keep records and accounts ⟨town *clerk*⟩ ⟨a stock *clerk*⟩ **2** : a salesperson in a store

²clerk *vb* : to act or work as a clerk

clev·er \'klev-ər\ *adj* **1** : showing skill especially in using one's hands **2** : quick in learning **3** : showing wit or imagination **syn** see INTELLIGENT — **clev·er·ish** \-(ə-)rish\ *adj* — **clev·er·ly** \-ər-lē\ *adv* — **clev·er·ness** \-ər-nəs\ *n*

¹clew \'klü\ *n* **1** : ¹CLUE **2** : a metal loop attached to the lower corner of a sail

²clew *vb* : to haul (a sail) up or down by ropes through the clews

cli·ché \klē-'shā, 'klē-ˌshā, kli-'shā\ *n* : a phrase or expression used so often that it becomes stale; *also* : the idea expressed by it [French, literally "metal printing plate"]

¹click \'klik\ *vb* **1** : to make or cause to make a click **2** : to fit or work together smoothly **3** : SUCCEED 2 ⟨the idea *clicked*⟩

²click *n* : a slight sharp sound

click beetle *n* : any of a family of beetles that are able when turned over to flip into the air by a sudden movement that produces a distinct click

cli·ent \'klī-ənt\ *n* **1** : a person who uses the professional advice or services of another ⟨a lawyer's *clients*⟩ **2** : CUSTOMER 1

cli·en·tele \ˌklī-ən-'tel\ *n* : a group of clients

cliff \'klif\ *n* : a high steep surface of rock, earth, or ice

cli·mac·tic \klī-'mak-tik, klə-\ *adj* : of, relating to, or being a climax

cli·mate \'klī-mət\ *n* **1 a** : a region with specified weather conditions **b** : the average weather conditions of a particular place or region over a period of years **2** : the usual or most widespread mood or conditions ⟨*climate* of fear⟩

— **cli·mat·ic** \klī-'mat-ik, klə-\ *adj*

Word History The ancient Greeks believed that the earth sloped from the equator to the north pole. They thought that this sloping caused the different weather conditions found in different regions of the world. Therefore they called each of the regions a *klima*, which was also the word for "slope" or "inclination". *Klima* was borrowed into Latin as *clima*, and from Latin it was taken into French where it was spelled *climat*. In English it became *climate*, a word which we now use more often to mean the weather conditions themselves than the region where they occur. [Middle English *climat* "climate", from early French *climat* (same meaning), from Latin *climat-, clima* (same meaning), from Greek *klimat-, klima* "slope, latitude, climate", from *klinein* "to lean, recline" — related to CLIMAX, CLINIC]

cli·ma·tol·o·gy \ˌklī-mə-'täl-ə-jē\ *n* : a science that deals with climates — **cli·ma·tol·o·gist** \-jəst\ *n*

¹cli·max \'klī-ˌmaks\ *n* **1 a** : the highest point ⟨the storm had reached its *climax*⟩ **b** : the point of highest dramatic interest or a major turning point in the action (as of a play) **c** : ORGASM **2** : a relatively stable ecological stage or community especially when it is the final one in a series of ecological stages or communities [from Latin *climax* "arrangement of words or phrases in increasing forcefulness", from Greek *klimax* "ladder", from *klinein* "to lean, recline" — related to CLIMATE, CLINIC]

²climax *vb* : to come or bring to a climax

¹climb \'klīm\ *vb* **1 a** : to rise gradually to a higher point ⟨*climb* from poverty to wealth⟩ **b** : to slope upward ⟨the road *climbs* steeply to the summit⟩ **2 a** : to go up or down often with the help of the hands in holding or pulling **b** : to go upward in growing (as by winding around something) ⟨a *climbing* vine⟩ — **climb·able** \'klī-mə-bəl\ *adj* — **climb·er** \-mər\ *n*

²climb *n* **1** : a place where climbing is necessary **2** : the act of climbing

clime \'klīm\ *n* : CLIMATE 1a

¹clinch \'klinch\ *vb* **1 a** : to turn over or flatten the end of something sticking out ⟨*clinch* a nail⟩ **b** : to fasten by clinching **2** : to make final : SETTLE ⟨the evidence *clinched* the case⟩

²clinch *n* **1** : a fastening by means of a clinched nail, rivet, or bolt **2** : the clinched part of a nail, bolt, or rivet

clinch·er \'klin-chər\ *n* : one that clinches; *esp* : a decisive fact or argument

cling \'kliŋ\ *vb* **clung** \'kləŋ\; **cling·ing** \'kliŋ-iŋ\ **1** : to stick to as if glued **2** : to hold or hold on tightly ⟨*clung* desperately to the ladder⟩ **3** : to remain close : be dependent ⟨*clings* to the family⟩

cling peach *n* : a clingstone peach

cling·stone \'kliŋ-ˌstōn\ *n* : a fruit (as a peach) whose flesh sticks strongly to the pit

clin·ic \'klin-ik\ *n* **1** : a medical class in which patients are examined and discussed **2** : a group meeting for teaching a certain skill and working on individual problems ⟨a reading *clinic*⟩ **3** : a place for the treatment of people needing medical help who do not stay overnight [from French *clinique* "medical instruction at a hospital bed", from Greek *klinikē* "medical practice at a sickbed", derived from *klinē* "bed", from *klinein* "to lean, recline" — related to CLIMATE, CLIMAX]

clin·i·cal \'klin-i-kəl\ *adj* **1** : of, relating to, or conducted in or as if in a clinic ⟨*clinical* examination⟩ **2** : involving or based on direct observation of the patient ⟨*clinical* studies⟩ — **clin·i·cal·ly** \-i-k(ə-)lē\ *adv*

clinical thermometer *n* : a thermometer used to measure body temperature that has a narrow place in the tube where the column of liquid separates from the rest as the temperature drops from its highest point and remains in place to keep showing the highest temperature until the thermometer is reset by shaking — called also *fever ther-*

mometer

clink \'kliŋk\ *vb* : to make or cause to make a slight sharp short sound like that of metal being struck ⟨glasses *clinked*⟩ — **clink** *n*

clin·ker \'kliŋ-kər\ *n* : a mass of stony matter that combined during heating (as in a furnace from impurities in the coal) : SLAG

cli·nom·e·ter \klī-'näm-ət-ər\ *n* : an instrument for measuring angles of elevation or slope

¹clip \'klip\ *vb* **clipped; clip·ping** : to fasten with a clip ⟨*clip* the papers together⟩ [Old English *clyppan* "to fasten"]

²clip *n* **1** : a device that grips, clasps, or hooks **2** : a device for loading cartridges into a firearm; *also* : MAGAZINE 4a **3** : a piece of jewelry held by a clip

³clip *vb* **clipped; clip·ping** **1** : to cut or cut off with or as if with shears ⟨*clip* a hedge⟩ ⟨*clip* out a news item⟩ **2** : to cut off or trim the hair or wool of ⟨have the dog *clipped*⟩ [Middle English *clipper* "to cut", of Norse origin]

⁴clip *n* **1** : a two-bladed instrument for cutting especially the nails **2** : an act of clipping **3** : a sharp blow **4** : a rapid pace ⟨move along at a good *clip*⟩

clip·board \'klip-,bō(ə)rd, -,bȯ(ə)rd\ *n* : a small board with a clip at the top for holding papers

clip·per \'klip-ər\ *n* **1** : one that clips **2** *pl* : a device for clipping ⟨hair *clippers*⟩ **3** : a fast sailing ship with usually three tall masts and large square sails

clip·ping \'klip-iŋ\ *n* : something cut out or off ⟨a newspaper *clipping*⟩ ⟨grass *clippings*⟩

clique \'klēk, 'klik\ *n* : a small group of people that keep out outsiders

cli·to·ris \'klit-ə-rəs, kli-'tȯr-əs\ *n, pl* **cli·to·ri·des** \kli-'tȯr-ə-,dēz\ : a small structure in the sex organs of the female mammal that corresponds to the penis in the male — **cli·to·ral** \'klit-ə-rəl\ *adj*

clo·aca \klō-'ā-kə\ *n, pl* **clo·a·cae** \-,kē, -,sē\ : a chamber into which the intestinal, urinary, and reproductive canals empty in birds, reptiles, amphibians, and many fishes; *also* : a chamber like this in an invertebrate animal that serves the same purpose — **clo·acal** \'-ā-kəl\ *adj*

¹cloak \'klōk\ *n* **1** : a long loose outer garment **2** : something that conceals or covers ⟨a *cloak* of secrecy surrounded the talks⟩ [Middle English *cloke* "cloak", from early French *cloque* "cloak, bell"; so named because a cloak resembled a bell in shape — related to CLOCK]

²cloak *vb* : to cover or hide with a cloak

cloak·room \'klō-,krüm, -,krüm\ *n* : a room (as in a school) in which coats and hats may be kept

clob·ber \'kläb-ər\ *vb* **1** : to hit with force **2** : to defeat by a wide margin

¹clock \'kläk\ *n* **1** : a device for measuring or telling the time and especially one not meant to be worn or carried about by a person **2** : a registering device with a dial that is attached to a machine to measure or record what it is doing **3** : a device (as in a computer) that sends out signals at regular spaces of time so that other events can happen in the correct order [Middle English *clok* "clock", from early Dutch *clocke* "bell, clock", from early French *cloque* "bell" or Latin *clocca* "bell"; of Celtic origin — related to CLOAK]

²clock *vb* **1** : to time (as a person or a piece of work) by a timing device **2** : to show (as time or speed) on a recording device

clock arithmetic *n* : MODULAR ARITHMETIC

clock·face \'kläk-,fās\ *n* : the dial face of a clock

clock radio *n* : a clock and radio combined in which the clock can be set to turn on the radio

clock·wise \'kläk-,wīz\ *adv or adj* : in the direction in which the hands of a clock turn

clock·work \'kläk-,wərk\ *n* : machinery (as in a mechanical toy) containing a set of small cogwheels

clod \'kläd\ *n* **1** : a lump or mass especially of earth or clay **2** : a person who is dull or not sensitive — **clod-**

dish \'kläd-ish\ *adj*

clod·hop·per \'kläd-,häp-ər\ *n* **1** : a person who is living or raised in the country **2** : a large heavy shoe

¹clog \'kläg, 'klȯg\ *n* **1** : something that hinders or holds back **2** : a shoe or sandal having a thick usually wooden sole

²clog *vb* **clogged; clog·ging** **1** : to get in the way of **2** : to block passage through **3** : to fill or become filled beyond capacity

clog dance *n* : a dance in which the dancers wear clogs and beat out a rhythm on the floor — **clog dancer** *n* — **clog dancing** *n*

¹clois·ter \'klȯi-stər\ *n* **1 a** : MONASTERY, CONVENT **b** : monastic life **2** : a covered usually arched passage along or around a court

²cloister *vb* **1** : to shut away from the world in or as if in a cloister ⟨leads a *cloistered* life⟩ **2** : to surround with a cloister ⟨*cloistered* gardens⟩

cloister 2

clomp \'klämp, 'klȯmp\ *vb* : ²CLUMP 1

¹clone \'klōn\ *n* **1** : the whole collection of offspring produced asexually from an individual (as a plant increased by grafting) **2** : an individual grown from a single body cell of its parent and having the same genes as its parent — **clon·al** \'klōn-ᵊl\ *adj*

²clone *vb* **cloned; clon·ing** : to make a clone from

clop \'kläp\ *n* : a sound like that of a hoof or wooden shoe against pavement — **clop** *vb*

¹close \'klōz\ *vb* **closed; clos·ing** **1 a** : to move so as to prevent passage through something ⟨*close* the gate⟩ **b** : to block against passage ⟨*close* a street⟩ **2** : to stop the operations of ⟨*close* school⟩ — often used with *down* **3** : to bring or come to an end or conclusion ⟨*close* a deal⟩ ⟨the meeting *closed* with a song⟩ **4** : to bring together the parts or edges of ⟨a *closed* fist⟩ ⟨*close* a switch⟩ **5 a** : to draw near ⟨the second-place runner was *closing* fast⟩ **b** : to engage in a struggle at close quarters ⟨*close* with the enemy⟩

²close \'klōz\ *n* : the point at which something ends

³close \'klōs\ *n* : an enclosed area

⁴close \'klōs\ *adj* **clos·er; clos·est** **1** : having no openings : CLOSED **2 a** : hidden from sight **b** : not open or frank : SECRETIVE **3** : RIGOROUS 1 ⟨keep *close* watch⟩ **4** : hot and stuffy **5** : not generous : STINGY ⟨*close* with money⟩ **6** : having little space between items or units ⟨flying in *close* formation⟩ **7** : fitting tightly or exactly **8** : very short or near the surface ⟨a *close* haircut⟩ **9** : being near in time, space, effect, or degree **10** : having a strong liking each one for the other ⟨a *close* friend⟩ **11** : ACCURATE 2, PRECISE ⟨*close* measurements⟩ ⟨a *close* observer⟩ **12** : decided by a narrow margin ⟨a *close* race⟩ — **close·ly** *adv* — **close·ness** *n*

⁵close \'klōs\ *adv* : in a close position or manner

close call *n* : a narrow escape

closed \'klōzd\ *adj* **1 a** : not open : ENCLOSED **b** : made up entirely of closed tubes or vessels ⟨a *closed* circulatory system⟩ **2** : formed by a line that returns to its starting point ⟨a *closed* curve⟩ **3** : having elements that when subjected to an operation produce only elements of the

\ə\ abut	\au̇\ out	\i\ tip	\ȯ\ saw	\u̇\ foot
\ər\ further	\ch\ chin	\ī\ life	\ȯi\ coin	\y\ yet
\a\ mat	\e\ pet	\j\ job	\th\ thin	\yü\ few
\ā\ take	\ē\ easy	\ŋ\ sing	\th\ this	\yu̇\ cure
\ä\ cot, cart	\g\ go	\ō\ bone	\ü\ food	\zh\ vision

same set ⟨the whole numbers are *closed* under addition⟩ **4** : not admitting or not easily admitting new members ⟨a *closed* meeting⟩ ⟨a *closed* society⟩

closed circuit \'klōz(d)-\ *n* : a television installation in which the signal is sent by wire to a limited number of receivers

close·fist·ed \'klōs-'fis-təd\ *adj* : STINGY 1

close in \(')klō-'zin\ *vb* : to gather in close all around with an oppressing effect ⟨despair *closed in* on her⟩

close–knit \'klō-'snit\ *adj* : bound together by feelings of very close association ⟨a *close-knit* family⟩

close–mouthed \-'maůthd, -'maůtht\ *adj* : not saying very much

¹**clos·et** \'kläz-ət\ *n* **1** : a small private room **2** : a cabinet or small room for china, household utensils, or clothing

²**closet** *vb* **1** : to shut up in or as if in a closet **2** : to take into a private room for an interview

close–up \'klōs-,əp\ *n* : a photograph taken at close range

clos·ing \'klō-zin\ *n* : a concluding part

clo·sure \'klō-zhər\ *n* **1 a** : an act of closing **b** : the condition of being closed **2** : something that closes ⟨a pocket with zipper *closure*⟩ **3** : the property of being closed under a mathematical operation — called also *closure postulate, closure property*

¹**clot** \'klät\ *n* : a mass or lump made by a liquid (as blood) that thickens and sticks together

²**clot** *vb* **clot·ted; clot·ting** : to become or cause to become a clot : form clots

cloth \'klȯth\ *n, pl* **cloths** \'klȯthz, 'klȯths\ **1** : a woven or knitted material (as of cotton or nylon) **2** : a piece of cloth used for a particular purpose ⟨a polishing *cloth*⟩ **3** : TABLECLOTH

clothe \'klōth\ *vb* **clothed** *or* **clad** \'klad\; **cloth·ing** **1 a** : to cover with or as if with clothing : DRESS **b** : to provide with clothes **2** : to express in a certain way

clothes \'klō(th)z\ *n pl* **1** : CLOTHING 1 **2** : BEDCLOTHES

clothes·horse \'klō(th)z-,hȯrs\ *n* : a person who dresses well enough to be noticed

clothes·line \-,līn\ *n* : a line (as of cord) on which clothes may be hung to dry

clothes moth *n* : any of several small moths whose caterpillars eat wool, fur, or feathers

clothes·pin \'klō(th)z-,pin\ *n* : a peg (as of wood) with the lower part slit or a clamp for holding clothes in place on a line

clothes·press \-,pres\ *n* : something (as a tall piece of furniture) in which clothes may be hung

clothes tree *n* : an upright stand with hooks or pegs around the top on which to hang clothes

cloth·ier \'klōth-yər, 'klō-thē-ər\ *n* : a person who makes or sells cloth or clothing

cloth·ing \'klō-thin\ *n* **1** : covering for the human body **2** : something that covers or conceals

¹**cloud** \'klaůd\ *n* **1** : a visible mass of particles of water or ice in the form of fog, mist, or haze usually high in the air **2 a** : a usually visible mass of tiny particles in the air or bits of matter between stars **b** : a group of charged particles (as electrons) **3** : something resembling or thought to be like a cloud ⟨a *cloud* of mosquitoes⟩ ⟨war *clouds* were gathering⟩ — **cloud·less** \-ləs\ *adj*

²**cloud** *vb* **1** : to make or become cloudy **2** : to darken or hide with or as if by a cloud ⟨smog

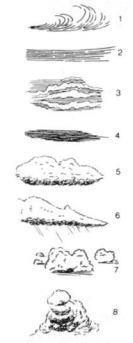

cloud 1: *1* cirrus, *2* cirrostratus, *3* cirrocumulus, *4* altostratus, *5* stratocumulus, *6* nimbostratus, *7* cumulus, *8* cumulonimbus, *9* stratus

clouded our view⟩

cloud·burst \'klaůd-,bərst\ *n* : a sudden heavy rainfall

cloud chamber *n* : a container of air saturated with water vapor whose sudden cooling reveals the path of an ionizing particle (as an electron) by a trail of visible droplets

cloud·let \'klaůd-lət\ *n* : a small cloud

cloudy \'klaůd-ē\ *adj* **cloud·i·er; -est** **1** : darkened by gloom or anxiety **2** : covered over by clouds ⟨a *cloudy* sky⟩ **3** : dimmed or dulled as if by clouds ⟨a *cloudy* mirror⟩ **4** : uneven in color or texture **5** : having visible material in suspension ⟨the water from the faucet was *cloudy*⟩ — **cloud·i·ly** \'klaůd-ᵊl-ē\ *adv* — **cloud·i·ness** \'klaůd-ē-nəs\ *n*

clout \'klaůt\ *n* **1** : a blow especially with the hand or with a baseball bat **2** : ¹INFLUENCE 1 ⟨political *clout*⟩ — **clout** *vb*

¹**clove** \'klōv\ *n* : one of the small bulbs that grows at the base of the scales of a large bulb ⟨a *clove* of garlic⟩ [Old English *clufu* "clove, bulb"]

²**clove** *past of* CLEAVE

³**clove** *n* : the dried flower bud of a tropical tree related to the myrtle that is used as a spice and as the source of an oil used in perfumery and medicine; *also* : this tree [Middle English *clowe* "clove bud", from early French *clou*, shortened form of the phrase *clou de girofle*, literally "nail of clove", from Latin *clavus* "nail"]

clo·ven \'klō-vən\ *past participle of* CLEAVE

cloven foot *n* : a foot (as of a sheep) that has the front part divided into two parts — **clo·ven–foot·ed** \,klō-vən-'fůt-əd\ *adj*

cloven hoof *n* : CLOVEN FOOT — **clo·ven–hoofed** \,klō-vən-'hůft, -'hůft, -'hůvd, -'hůvd\ *adj*

clo·ver \'klō-vər\ *n* : any of a genus of herbs of the legume family that have leaves with three leaflets and flowers in dense heads and that include many plants valuable for forage and as a source of nectar for bees; *also* : any of various related plants

clo·ver·leaf \-,lēf\ *n, pl* **-leafs** \-,lēfs\ *or* **-leaves** \-,lēvz\ : a road plan that resembles a four-leaf clover in shape and is used for passing one highway over another and turning traffic onto connecting roadways which branch only to the right and lead around in a circle to enter the other highway from the right

clover

¹**clown** \'klaůn\ *n* **1** : a rude and often stupid person **2** : a performer (as in a play or circus) who entertains by playing tricks and who usually wears comical clothes and makeup — **clown·ish** \'klaů-nish\ *adj* — **clown·ish·ly** *adv* — **clown·ish·ness** *n*

²**clown** *vb* : to act like a clown

cloy \'klȯi\ *vb* : to supply with too much of something that was originally pleasing — **cloy·ing·ly** \-in-lē\ *adv*

¹**club** \'kləb\ *n* **1 a** : a heavy usually wooden stick used as a weapon **b** : a stick or bat used for hitting a ball in a game ⟨a golf *club*⟩ **2 a** : a black figure resembling a clover leaf used to distinguish a suit of playing cards **b** : a card of the suit bearing clubs **3 a** : a group of people associated because of a common interest **b** : the meeting place of a club

²**club** *vb* **clubbed; club·bing** **1** : to beat or strike with or as if with a club **2** : to unite or combine for a common cause ⟨*club* together to buy a boat⟩

club·foot \'kləb-'fůt\ *n* : a misshapen foot twisted out of position from birth; *also* : this deformed condition — **club-**

foot·ed \-əd\ *adj*

club fungus *n* : any of a large class of fungi that have the hyphae divided by partitions and a special cell for forming spores and that include rusts, smuts, and puffballs

club·house \'kləb-ˌhaus\ *n* **1** : a meeting place (as a house) used by a club for club activities **2** : locker rooms used by an athletic team

club moss *n* : any of an order of low often trailing evergreen plants (as the ground pine) having branching stems covered with small mosslike leaves and reproducing by spores usually borne in club-shaped cones

cluck \'klək\ *n* : the call of a hen especially to her chicks — **cluck** *vb*

¹clue \'klü\ *n* : something that helps a person find something or solve a mystery

²clue *vb* **clued; clu·ing** **1** : to provide with a clue **2** : to give information to ⟨*clue* me in on what happened⟩

¹clump \'kləmp\ *n* **1** : a group of things clustered together ⟨a *clump* of bushes⟩ **2** : a cluster or lump of something **3** : a heavy tramping sound — **clumpy** \'kləm-pē\ *adj*

²clump *vb* **1** : to walk or move clumsily and noisily **2** : to form or cause to form clumps

clum·sy \'kləm-zē\ *adj* **clum·si·er; -est** **1 a** : lacking skill or grace in movement ⟨*clumsy* fingers⟩ **b** : showing social awkwardness or a lack of tact ⟨a *clumsy* attempt at a joke⟩ **2** : awkwardly or poorly made : hard to use ⟨a *clumsy* tool⟩ — **clum·si·ly** \-zə-lē\ *adv* — **clum·si·ness** \-zē-nəs\ *n*

clung *past and past participle of* CLING

¹clus·ter \'kləs-tər\ *n* : a number of similar things growing, collected, or grouped together : BUNCH ⟨a *cluster* of houses⟩ ⟨a flower *cluster*⟩

²cluster *vb* **clus·tered; clus·ter·ing** \-t(ə-)riŋ\ : to grow, collect, or gather in a cluster

¹clutch \'kləch\ *vb* **1** : to grip with or as if with the hand or claws : GRASP **2** : to make a grab ⟨*clutch* at a swinging rope⟩ [Old English *clyccan* "grasp, hold"]

²clutch *n* **1 a** : the claws or a hand in the act of grasping **b** : an often cruel or stern power or control **2** : a device for gripping an object **3 a** : a coupling used to connect and disconnect a driving and a driven part in machinery **b** : a lever or pedal operating a clutch **4** : a tight or critical situation : PINCH

³clutch *adj* : done or doing well in a tight or critical situation ⟨a *clutch* play⟩ ⟨a *clutch* player⟩

⁴clutch *n* : a nest or batch of eggs or a brood of chicks [altered form of dialect word *cletch* "a hatching, brood"]

¹clut·ter \'klət-ər\ *vb* : to fill or cover with a disorderly scattering of things ⟨*clutter* up a room⟩

²clutter *n* : a crowded or confused collection

co- *prefix* **1** : with : together : joint : jointly ⟨*co*exist⟩ ⟨*co*author⟩ **2** : in or to the same degree ⟨*co*extensive⟩ **3** : fellow : partner ⟨*co*worker⟩ [derived from Latin *com-* "with, together"]

¹coach \'kōch\ *n* **1 a** : a large usually closed four-wheeled carriage that has a raised seat in front for the driver and is drawn by horses **b** : a railroad passenger car without berths **c** : ¹BUS 1 **d** : a class of passenger air transportation at a lower fare than first class **2 a** : a private tutor **b** : a person who instructs or trains a performer or team ⟨a football *coach*⟩

²coach *vb* : to act as coach

coach dog *n* : DALMATIAN

coach·man \'kōch-mən\ *n* : a person whose business is driving a coach or carriage

co·ad·ju·tor \ˌkō-ə-'jüt-ər, kō-'aj-ət-ər\ *n* **1** : one who works together with another : ASSISTANT **2** : a bishop assisting a diocesan bishop and often having the right of succession — **coadjutor** *adj*

co·ag·u·late \kō-'ag-yə-ˌlāt\ *vb* **-lat·ed; -lat·ing** : to become or cause to become thickened into a compact mass : CLOT [from Latin *coagulatus*, past participle of *coagulare*

"to curdle", derived from *cogere* "to drive together" — related to ²QUAIL] — **co·ag·u·la·tion** \kō-ˌag-yə-'lā-shən\ *n*

¹coal \'kōl\ *n* **1** : a piece of glowing or charred wood : EMBER **2** : a black or brownish black solid substance that is formed by the partial decay of vegetable matter under the influence of moisture and often increased pressure and temperature within the earth and that is widely used as a fuel

²coal *vb* **1** : to supply with coal **2** : to take in coal

co·alesce \ˌkō-ə-'les\ *vb* **co·alesced; co·alesc·ing** **1** : to grow together ⟨the ends of the broken bones *coalesced*⟩ **2** : to unite into a whole : FUSE **syn** see MIX — **co·ales·cence** \-'les-ᵊn(t)s\ *n*

coal gas *n* : gas from coal; *esp* : gas made from bituminous coal and used for heating and lighting

co·ali·tion \ˌkō-ə-'lish-ən\ *n* : a temporary union of persons, parties, or countries for a common purpose

coal oil *n* **1** : petroleum or a refined oil prepared from it **2** : KEROSENE

coal tar *n* : tar obtained from bituminous coal and used especially in making drugs and dyes

coarse \'kō(ə)rs, 'ko(ə)rs\ *adj* **coars·er; coars·est** **1** : of ordinary or poor quality **2** : made up of large parts or particles ⟨*coarse* sand⟩ **3** : being harsh or rough ⟨*coarse* cloth⟩ **4** : not precise or detailed : roughly approximate **5** : crude in taste, manners, or language — **coarse·ly** *adv* — **coars·en** \'kōrs-ᵊn, 'kórs-\ *vb* — **coarse·ness** *n*

¹coast \'kōst\ *n* **1** : the land near a shore : SEASHORE **2** : a slide down a slope (as on a sled) — **coast·al** \'kōst-ᵊl\ *adj*

²coast *vb* **1** : to sail along the shore of **2 a** : to slide downhill by the force of gravity **b** : to move along (as on a bicycle when not pedaling) without applying power **3** : to proceed easily without special effort

coast·er \'kō-stər\ *n* **1** : one that coasts; *esp* : a ship engaged in coastal trade **2 a** : a round tray usually of silver and sometimes on wheels **b** : a shallow container or a plate or a mat to protect a surface **3** : a small vehicle (as a sled or wagon) for coasting

coast guard *n* **1** : a seagoing force for protecting a coast and lives and property at sea **2** *usually* **coast·guard** *chiefly British* : COASTGUARDSMAN

coast·guards·man \'kōs(t)-ˌgärdz-mən\ *or* **coast·guard·man** \-ˌgärd-mən\ *n* : a member of a coast guard

coast·line \'kōst-ˌlīn\ *n* : the outline or shape of a coast

coast redwood *n* : REDWOOD

coast·wise \'kōst-ˌwīz\ *adv* : by way of or along the coast — **coastwise** *adj*

¹coat \'kōt\ *n* **1** : an outer garment varying in length and style according to fashion and use **2** : the outer covering (as of fur) of an animal **3** : a layer of material covering a surface ⟨a *coat* of paint⟩ — **coat·ed** \-əd\ *adj*

²coat *vb* : to cover with a coat or covering

co·ati \kə-'wät-ē, kwä-'tē\ *n* : a tropical American mammal related to the raccoon but with a longer body and tail and a long flexible snout

coat·ing \'kōt-iŋ\ *n* : ¹COAT 3, COVERING ⟨a *coating* of ice on the pond⟩

coat of arms : the heraldic arms belonging to a person,

coati

family, or group or a representation of these (as on a shield)

coat of mail : a garment of metal scales or rings worn long ago as armor

coat·tail \'kōt-ˌtāl\ *n* : the rear flap of a person's coat — **on one's coattails:** with the help of another person's work, ideas, or political popularity

co·au·thor \(')kō-'ȯ-thər\ *n* : an author who works with another author

coax \'kōks\ *vb* **1** : to influence by gentle urging, special attention, or flattery **2** : to get or win by means of gentle urging or flattery ⟨*coaxed* a raise from the boss⟩

co·ax·i·al cable \kō-ˌak-sē-əl-\ *n* : a cable that consists of a tube of electrically conducting material surrounding a central conductor and is used to send telegraph, telephone, and television signals

cob \'käb\ *n* **1** : a male swan **2** : CORNCOB **3** : a short-legged stocky horse

co·bal·a·min \kō-'bal-ə-mən\ *n* : VITAMIN B$_{12}$

co·balt \'kō-ˌbȯlt\ *n* : a tough shiny silver-white magnetic metallic element that is found with iron and nickel and is used especially in alloys — see ELEMENT table [from German *kobalt* "cobalt", an altered form of *kobold,* literally "goblin"; so called because its appearance in silver ore was thought to have been the work of goblins who left it in place of silver which they stole]

cobalt chloride *n* : a chloride of cobalt; *esp* : one that has two atoms of chlorine per molecule, is blue when dry and deep pink when combined with water, and is used to indicate humidity

cobalt 60 *n* : a heavy radioactive form of cobalt of the mass number 60 made in nuclear reactors and used to produce gamma rays

¹**cob·ble** \'käb-əl\ *vb* **cob·bled; cob·bling** \-(ə-)liŋ\ : to make roughly or hastily — often used with *together* or *up*

²**cobble** *n* : a rounded stone larger than a pebble and smaller than a boulder

cob·bler \'käb-lər\ *n* **1** : a mender or maker of shoes **2** : a deep-dish fruit pie with a thick top crust

cob·ble·stone \'käb-əl-ˌstōn\ *n* : ²COBBLE — **cob·ble·stoned** \-ˌstōnd\ *adj*

CO·BOL *or* **Co·bol** \'kō-ˌbȯl\ *n* : a computer programming language used especially in business [*C*ommon *B*usiness *O*riented *L*anguage]

co·bra \'kō-brə\ *n* : any of several poisonous Asian and African snakes that when excited expand the skin of the neck into a hood; *also* : any of several related African snakes

> **Word History** During the early part of the 16th century, Portuguese traders took control of cities along India's western coast. During this period of contact, the Portuguese became familiar with some of India's animal life. One animal they noticed was a poisonous snake that could expand the skin of its neck to form a hood. The Portuguese called this snake *cobra de capello,* meaning "snake with a hood". The Portuguese name was first borrowed into English in the 17th century. By the 19th century the name had become shortened to *cobra.* [from Portuguese *cobra (de capello)* "snake (with a hood)", from Latin *colubra* "snake"]

cob·web \'käb-ˌweb\ *n* **1** : SPIDERWEB **2** : a single thread spun by a spider or insect larva — **cob·webbed** \-ˌwebd\ *adj* — **cob·web·by** \-ˌweb-ē\ *adj*

co·ca \'kō-kə\ *n* : a South American shrub with leaves resembling tea that are chewed by the natives to give them endurance and are the source of cocaine; *also* : its dried leaves

co·caine \kō-'kān, 'kō-ˌkān\ *n* : a bitter habit-forming drug obtained from coca leaves and used in medicine to deaden pain and illegally to stimulate the central nervous system

coc·cus \'käk-əs\ *n, pl* **coc·ci** \'käk-ˌ(s)ī, 'käk-ˌ(ˌ)(s)ē\ : a bacterium shaped like a sphere — **coc·cal** \'käk-əl\ *adj*

coc·cyx \'käk-siks\ *n, pl* **coc·cy·ges** \'käk-sə-ˌjēz\ *also* **coc·cyx·es** \'käk-sik-səz\ : the bone at the end of the spinal column that is composed of four vertebrae combined into one bone

co·chi·neal \'käch-ə-ˌnēl, 'kō-chə-\ *n* : a red dye consisting of the dried bodies of female cochineal insects used especially as a biological stain

cochineal insect *n* : a small bright red insect that is related to and resembles the mealybug, feeds on cactus, and yields cochineal

co·chlea \'kō-klē-ə, 'käk-lē-\ *n, pl* **co·chle·as** *or* **co·chle·ae** \-klē-ˌē, -lē-ˌē, -ˌī\ : a part of the inner ear of higher vertebrates that is usually coiled like a snail shell and contains the endings of the nerve which carries information about sound to the brain — compare ORGAN OF CORTI — **coch·le·ar** \'kō-klē-ər, 'käk-lē-\ *adj*

¹**cock** \'käk\ *n* **1** : the adult male of a bird and especially the domestic fowl **2** : a device (as a faucet or valve) for controlling the flow of a liquid **3** : the cocked position of the hammer of a firearm ⟨a rifle at half *cock*⟩ [Old English *cocc* "cock, rooster"; probably in imitation of the sound it makes]

²**cock** *vb* **1 a** : to draw back the hammer of (a gun) in readiness for firing ⟨*cock* a pistol⟩ **b** : to set or draw back in readiness for some action ⟨*cock* your arm to throw⟩ **2** : to turn, tip, or tilt upward or to one side

³**cock** *n* : ²TILT 4, SLANT ⟨a *cock* of the head⟩

⁴**cock** *n* : a small pile (as of hay) [Middle English *cok* "small pile"; of Scandinavian origin]

cock·ade \kä-'kād\ *n* : an ornament (as a rosette) worn on the hat as a badge

cock·a·too \'käk-ə-ˌtü\ *n, pl* **-toos** : any of numerous large noisy usually showy chiefly Australasian parrots that have a bunch of feathers on the head

cockatoo

cock·crow \'käk-ˌkrō\ *n* : early morning

cock·er·el \'käk-(ə-)rəl\ *n* : a young male domestic fowl

cock·er spaniel \ˌkäk-ər-\ *n* : any of a breed of small spaniels with long drooping ears and long silky coat

cock·eyed \'käk-'īd\ *adj* **1** : having a squinting eye **2 a** : turned or tilted to one side **b** : slightly crazy : FOOLISH

cock·fight \'käk-ˌfīt\ *n* : a fight between roosters usually fitted with metal spurs

¹**cock·le** \'käk-əl\ *n* : any of several weeds of grain fields [Old English *coccel* "weed"]

²**cockle** *n* **1** : an edible mollusk with a heart-shaped two-valved shell **2** : COCKLESHELL [Middle English *cokille* "cockle, cockleshell", from early French *coquille* "shell", from Latin *conchylia* "shells", derived from Greek *konchylion,* literally "little shell"]

cock·le·bur \'käk-əl-ˌbər, 'kȯk-\ *n* : any of a genus of plants that have prickly fruits and are related to the thistles; *also* : one of its fruits

cock·le·shell \'käk-əl-ˌshel\ *n* **1 a** : a shell or shell valve of a cockle **b** : a shell (as a scallop) that looks like a cockleshell **2** : a light flimsy boat

cock·ney \'käk-nē\ *n, pl* **cockneys** *often cap* **1** : a native of London and especially of the East End of London **2** : the dialect spoken by the cockneys — **cockney** *adj*

cock·pit \'käk-ˌpit\ *n* **1** : an open space in the deck from which a small boat is steered **2** : a space in an airplane or spacecraft for the pilot or pilot and passengers or pilot and crew

cock·roach \-ˌrōch\ *n* : any of an order of swift-running insects that have long antennae and a leathery body wall, are active chiefly at night, and include numerous pests found in houses and ships

cock·sure \'käk-'shù(ə)r\ *adj* **1** : perfectly sure : CERTAIN **2** : COCKY 1

cock·tail \'käk-ˌtāl\ *n* **1** : an iced drink of distilled liquor mixed with flavoring ingredients **2** : an appetizer (as tomato juice) served as a first course at a meal

cocky \'käk-ē\ *adj* **cock·i·er; -est** **1** : being too sure of oneself **2** : being rude usually in a lively and playful way — **cock·i·ly** \'käk-ə-lē\ *adv* — **cock·i·ness** \'käk-ē-nəs\ *n*

co·coa \'kō-kō\ *n* **1** : a cacao tree **2 a** : chocolate ground to a powder after some of its fat has been removed **b** : a beverage made from cocoa powder

cocoa butter *n* : a pale fat obtained from cacao

co·co·nut \'kō-kə-(ˌ)nət\ *n* : the large egg-shaped husk-covered fruit of the coconut palm

coconut oil *n* : a nearly colorless oil or soft white fat that comes from coconuts or copra and is used especially in soaps and foods

coconut palm *n* : a tall tropical palm with finely divided leaves that is probably of American origin

co·coon \kə-'kün\ *n* **1** : an envelope usually of silk which the larva of some insects (as a silk moth or a cecropia moth) forms about itself and in which it passes the pupa stage **2** : a covering suggesting a cocoon

cod \'käd\ *n, pl* **cod** *also* **cods** : a soft-finned fish of the colder parts of the North Atlantic that is a major food fish; *also* : any of several related fishes

co·da \'kōd-ə\ *n* : a closing section in a musical composition [Italian, literally "tail", from Latin *coda, cauda* "tail" — related to COWARD, ³CUE, QUEUE; see *Word History* at COWARD, QUEUE]

coconut palm

cod·dle \'käd-ᵊl\ *vb* **cod·dled; cod·dling** \'käd-liŋ, -ᵊl-iŋ\ **1** : to cook slowly in water below the boiling point ⟨*coddle* eggs⟩ **2** : to treat with extreme care : PAMPER

¹**code** \'kōd\ *n* **1** : a collection of laws arranged in some orderly way ⟨criminal *code*⟩ **2** : a system of principles or rules ⟨moral *code*⟩ **3 a** : a system of signals for communicating **b** : a system of symbols (as letters or numbers) used to represent assigned and often secret meanings **4** : GENETIC CODE

²**code** *vb* **cod·ed; cod·ing** : to put into the form or symbols of a code — **cod·er** *n*

co·deine \'kō-ˌdēn, 'kōd-ē-ən\ *n* : a drug that is obtained from opium, is weaker than morphine, and is used in cough remedies

cod·fish \'käd-ˌfish\ *n* : COD

cod·ger \'käj-ər\ *n* : an odd or cranky fellow

cod·i·fy \'käd-ə-ˌfī, 'kōd-\ *vb* **-fied; -fy·ing** : to arrange (as a collection of laws) in an orderly form — **cod·i·fi·ca·tion** \ˌkäd-ə-fə-'kā-shən, ˌkōd-\ *n*

cod·ling moth \'käd-liŋ-\ *n* : a small stout-bodied moth whose larva lives in fruit and nuts and is a serious pest of numerous orchard-grown crops (as apples, pears, plums, apricots, and walnuts)

cod–liver oil *n* : an oil obtained from the liver of the cod and closely related fishes and used as a source of vitamins A and D

co·ed \'kō-ˌed\ *n* : a student and especially a female student in a coeducational institution

co·ed·u·ca·tion \ˌ(ˌ)kō-ˌej-ə-'kā-shən\ *n* : education of male and female students at the same school or college

— **co·ed·u·ca·tion·al** \-shnəl, -shən-ᵊl\ *adj*

co·ef·fi·cient \ˌkō-ə-'fish-ənt\ *n* **1** : any of the factors of a product considered with respect to one of the factors; *esp* : a constant factor of a term rather than a variable ⟨3 and *k* are *coefficients* of *x* in the term 3*kx*⟩ **2** : a number that serves as a measure of some property (as of a substance or device)

coel·acanth \'sē-lə-ˌkan(t)th\ *n* : a fish or fossil of a family of mostly extinct fishes — **coelacanth** *adj*

coel·en·ter·ate \si-'lent-ə-ˌrāt, -rət\ *n* : any of a phylum of invertebrate animals that include the corals, sea anemones,

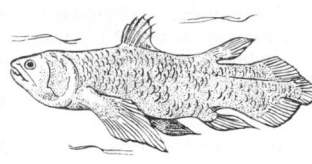

coelacanth

jellyfishes, and hydras and usually have radial body symmetry — **coelenterate** *adj*

co·equal \(ˈ)kō-'ē-kwəl\ *adj* : equal with one another — **co·equal·ly** \-kwə-lē\ *adv*

co·erce \kō-'ərs\ *vb* **co·erced; co·erc·ing** : to cause someone to do something by force or threat — **co·er·cion** \-'ər-zhən, -shən\ *n* — **co·er·cive** \-'ər-siv\ *adj*

co·eval \kō-'ē-vəl\ *adj* : of the same age or duration — **co·eval** *n*

co·ex·ist \ˌkō-ig-'zist\ *vb* **1** : to exist together or at the same time **2** : to live in peace with each other — **co·ex·is·tence** \-'zis-tən(t)s\ *n* — **co·ex·is·tent** \-tənt\ *adj*

co·ex·ten·sive \ˌkō-ik-'sten(t)-siv\ *adj* : having the same length or boundaries in space or time — **co·ex·ten·sive·ly** *adv*

cof·fee \'kò-fē, 'käf-ē\ *n* **1** : a drink made from the roasted and ground seeds of a tropical tree or shrub related to the madder **2** : coffee seeds or a plant producing them [from Italian *caffè* "coffee" and Turkish *kahve* "coffee", both from Arabic *qahwa* "coffee"]

cof·fee·house \'kò-fē-ˌhaus, 'käf-ē-\ *n* : an establishment that sells coffee and usually other refreshments and that commonly serves as an informal club for its regular customers

cof·fee·mak·er \-ˌmā-kər\ *n* : a utensil in which coffee is brewed

cof·fee·pot \-ˌpät\ *n* : a utensil for brewing or serving coffee

coffee table *n* : a low table usually placed in front of a sofa

cof·fer \'kò-fər, 'käf-ər\ *n* **1** : a box used especially to store money and valuables **2** : TREASURY 1, FUNDS — usually used in pl.

cof·fin \'kò-fən\ *n* : a box or case to hold a dead body

cog \'käg\ *n* **1** : a tooth on the rim of a wheel adjusted to fit notches in another wheel or bar and to give or receive motion **2** : a person whose job is of low rank but still important

co·gen·cy \'kō-jən-sē\ *n* : the quality or state of being cogent

co·gent \'kō-jənt\ *adj* **1** : appealing forcibly to the mind : CONVINCING ⟨*cogent* evidence⟩ ⟨a *cogent* argument⟩ **2** : being to the point : PERTINENT ⟨some *cogent* remarks on the situation⟩ — **co·gent·ly** \'kō-jənt-lē\ *adv*

cog·i·tate \'käj-ə-ˌtāt\ *vb* **-tat·ed; -ta·ting** : to think over : PONDER — **cog·i·ta·tion** \ˌkäj-ə-'tā-shən\ *n*

co·gnac \'kōn-ˌyak\ *n* : a French brandy [named for *Cognac*, town in France in and near which it is made]

cog·ni·tion \käg-'nish-ən\ *n* : the act or process of knowing

cog·ni·tive \'käg-nət-iv\ *adj* : of, relating to, or being con-

\ə\ abut	\au̇\ out	\i\ tip	\ò\ saw	\u̇\ foot
\ər\ further	\ch\ chin	\ī\ life	\òi\ coin	\y\ yet
\a\ mat	\e\ pet	\j\ job	\th\ thin	\yü\ few
\ā\ take	\ē\ easy	\ŋ\ sing	\th\ this	\yu̇\ cure
\ä\ cot, cart	\g\ go	\ō\ bone	\ü\ food	\zh\ vision

scious mental activities (as thinking, reasoning, remembering, imagining, learning words, and using language)

cog·ni·zance \'käg-nə-zən(t)s\ *n* **1** : particular knowledge ⟨seemed to have no *cognizance* of the crime⟩ **2** : the act or power of fixing one's mind on something : NOTICE, HEED ⟨take *cognizance* of what is happening⟩ — **cog·ni·zant** \-zənt\ *adj*

cog·no·men \käg-'nō-mən, 'käg-nə-mən\ *n, pl* **-nomens** *or* **-no·mi·na** \-'näm-ə-nə, -'nō-mə-\ **1** : a person's last name : SURNAME **2** : ¹NAME 1; *esp* : ¹NICKNAME

cog·wheel \'käg-,hwēl, -,wēl\ *n* : a wheel with cogs

co·hab·it \kō-'hab-ət\ *vb* : to live together as or as if husband and wife — **co·hab·i·ta·tion** \kō-,hab-ə-'tā-shən\ *n*

co·here \kō-'hi(ə)r\ *vb* **co·hered; co·her·ing** **1 a** : to hold together firmly as parts of the same mass **b** : to consist of parts that cohere **2 a** : to become united in principles, relationships, or interests **b** : to be in agreement between parts — **co·her·ence** \-'hir-ən(t)s, -'her-\ *n* — **co·her·ent** \-ənt\ *adj* — **co·her·ent·ly** *adv*

co·he·sion \kō-'hē-zhən\ *n* **1** : the action or state of sticking together **2** : molecular attraction by which the particles of a body are united throughout the mass — **co·he·sive** \kō-'hē-siv, -ziv\ *adj* — **co·he·sive·ness** *n*

co·hort \'kō-,hȯrt\ *n* **1 a** : one of 10 divisions of an ancient Roman legion **b** : a group of warriors or followers **2** : COMPANION 1, ACCOMPLICE

¹coif \'kȯif, *in sense 2 usually* 'kwäf\ *n* **1** : a close-fitting cap **2** : COIFFURE

²coif \'kȯif, 'kwäf\ *vb* **coiffed** *or* **coifed; coif·fing** *or* **coif·ing** : to cover or dress with a coif

coif·fure \kwä-'fyu̇(ə)r\ *n* : a style or manner of arranging the hair

¹coil \'kȯil\ *vb* **1** : to wind into or lie in loops, rings, or a spiral **2** : to move in a circular, spiral, or winding direction

²coil *n* **1 a** : a series of loops : SPIRAL **b** : a single loop of a coil **2 a** : a number of turns of wire wound around a core (as of iron) to create a magnetic field for an electromagnet or an induction coil **b** : INDUCTION COIL **3** : a series of connected pipes (as in water-heating apparatus) in rows, layers, or windings

¹coin \'kȯin\ *n* **1** : a piece of metal put out by a government authority as money **2** : metal money ⟨three dollars in *coin*⟩

²coin *vb* **1 a** : to make (a coin) especially by stamping : MINT **b** : to convert (metal) into coins **2** : CREATE, INVENT ⟨*coin* a phrase⟩ — **coin·er** *n*

³coin *adj* **1** : of or relating to coins ⟨a *coin* show⟩ **2** : operated by coins ⟨a *coin* laundry⟩

coin·age \'kȯi-nij\ *n* **1** : the act or process of coining **2** : ¹COIN 2 **3** : something (as a word) made up or invented

co·in·cide \,kō-ən-'sīd\ *vb* **-cid·ed; -cid·ing** **1** : to occupy the same place in space or time **2** : to occupy the same positions on a scale **3** : to agree exactly

co·in·ci·dence \kō-'in(t)-səd-ən(t)s\ *n* **1** : the act or condition of coinciding **2 a** : two things that happen at the same time by accident but seem to have some connection **b** : either one of these happenings

co·in·ci·dent \kō-'in(t)-səd-ənt\ *adj* **1** : of similar nature : HARMONIOUS ⟨a theory *coincident* with the facts⟩ **2** : occupying the same space or time ⟨*coincident* events⟩ — **co·in·ci·dent·ly** *adv*

co·in·ci·den·tal \(,)kō-,in(t)-sə-'dent-ᵊl\ *adj* **1** : resulting from a coincidence **2** : occurring or existing at the same time — **co·in·ci·den·tal·ly** \-'dent-lē, -ᵊl-ē\ *adv*

coir \'kȯi(-ə)r\ *n* : a stiff coarse fiber from the outer husk of a coconut

co·i·tus \'kō-ət-əs, kō-'ēt-\ *n* : SEXUAL INTERCOURSE

¹coke \'kōk\ *n* : gray lumps of fuel with pores made by heating soft coal in a closed chamber until some of its gases have passed off

²coke *n* : COCAINE

Coke \'kōk\ *trademark* — used for a cola drink

coke·head \'kōk-,hed\ *n* : a compulsive user of cocaine

col- — see COM-

co·la \'kō-lə\ *n* : a carbonated soft drink usually containing sugar, caffeine, caramel, and a special flavoring

col·an·der \'kəl-ən-dər, 'käl-\ *n* : a utensil with small holes for draining food

col·chi·cine \'käl-chə-,sēn, 'käl-kə-\ *n* : a poisonous substance that is obtained from the corms or seeds of a plant resembling a crocus and that is used on cells to cause changes in chromosome numbers and to produce new varieties of plants

¹cold \'kōld\ *adj* **1** : having a low temperature or one much below normal ⟨a *cold* day⟩ ⟨a *cold* drink⟩ **2** : lacking warmth of feeling : UNFRIENDLY ⟨a *cold* stare⟩ **3** : suffering or uncomfortable from lack of warmth ⟨they feel *cold*⟩ **4 a** : marked by the loss of normal body heat ⟨*cold* hands⟩ **b** : giving the appearance of being dead : UNCONSCIOUS ⟨passed out *cold*⟩ — **cold·ly** *adv* — **cold·ness** \'kōl(d)-nəs\ *n* — **in cold blood** : with planning beforehand : DELIBERATELY

²cold *n* **1 a** : a condition of low temperature **b** : cold weather **2** : bodily sensation produced by loss or lack of heat : CHILL **3** : a bodily disorder popularly associated with chilling; *esp* : COMMON COLD

cold–blood·ed \'kōl(d)-'bləd-əd\ *adj* **1** : lacking or showing a lack of natural human feelings ⟨a *cold-blooded* criminal⟩ **2** : having a body temperature close to that of the environment **3** : sensitive to cold — **cold–blood·ed·ly** *adv*

cold chisel *n* : a strong steel chisel for chipping and cutting cold metal

cold cream *n* : a soothing and cleansing cosmetic

cold cuts *n pl* : sliced cold cooked meats

cold frame *n* : a usually glass-covered frame without artificial heat used to protect plants and seedlings

cold front *n* : an advancing edge of a cold air mass

cold shoulder *n* : treatment that is purposely unfriendly — **cold–shoulder** *vb*

cold frame

cold sore *n* : a group of blisters about or within the mouth caused by a herpesvirus — called also *fever blister*

cold sweat *n* : perspiration and chill occurring together and usually associated with fear, pain, or shock

cold war *n* : a struggle over political differences (as of two nations) carried on by methods short of war and usually without breaking off diplomatic relations

cole \'kōl\ *n* : any of several closely related crop plants (as broccoli, kale, brussels sprouts, and cabbage) of the mustard family

co·le·op·tera \,kō-lē-'äp-tə-rə\ *n pl* : insects that are beetles

cole·slaw \'kōl-,slȯ\ *n* : a salad made of sliced or chopped raw cabbage

co·le·us \'kō-lē-əs\ *n* : any of a large genus of herbs related to the mints and often grown for their leaves of various colors

col·ic \'käl-ik\ *n* : sharp sudden pain in the abdomen — **col·icky** \-i-kē\ *adj*

col·i·se·um \,käl-ə-'sē-əm\ *n* : a large structure (as a stadium) for athletic contests or public entertainment [from the Latin spelling used in the Middle Ages for the *Colosseum*, a great outdoor arena in ancient Rome]

col·lab·o·rate \kə-'lab-ə-,rāt\ *vb* **-rat·ed; -rat·ing** **1** : to work with others (as in writing a book) **2** : to cooperate with an enemy force that has taken over one's country —

col·lab·o·ra·tion \kə-ˌlab-ə-'rā-shən\ n — **col·lab·o·ra·tion·ist** \-sh(ə-)nəst\ n — **col·lab·o·ra·tor** \kə-'lab-ə-ˌrāt-ər\ n

col·lage \kə-'läzh, kò-, kō-\ n : a work of art made by gluing pieces of different materials to a flat surface [from French *collage* "gluing", from *coller* "to glue"]

col·la·gen \'käl-ə-jən\ n : a protein that occurs in the form of fibers, does not dissolve, is found in connective tissue, and forms glue and gelatin on heating for a long time with water

¹**col·lapse** \kə-'laps\ vb **col·lapsed; col·laps·ing** **1** : to fall or shrink together abruptly ⟨a blood vessel that *collapsed*⟩ **2** : to break down completely ⟨the opponent's resistance *collapsed*⟩ **3** : to cave or fall in or give way ⟨the tunnel *collapsed*⟩ **4** : to suddenly lose value or effectiveness ⟨the country's currency *collapsed*⟩ **5** : to break down physically or mentally because of exhaustion or disease **6** : to fold together — **col·laps·ible** \kə-'lap-sə-bəl\ adj

²**collapse** n : the act or an instance of collapsing : BREAKDOWN

¹**col·lar** \'käl-ər\ n **1 a** : a band, strip, or chain worn around the neck or the neckline of a garment **b** : a part of the harness of draft animals fitted over the shoulders **2** : something (as a ring to hold something in place) resembling a collar — **col·lared** \-ərd\ adj — **col·lar·less** \-ər-ləs\ adj

²**collar** vb **1 a** : to seize by the collar **b** : to take possession of : GRAB **2** : to put a collar on

col·lar·bone \'käl-ər-ˌbōn, ˌkäl-ər-'bōn\ n : CLAVICLE

col·lard \'käl-ərd\ n : a kale with smooth leaves that grow at the top of a short thick stalk

¹**col·lat·er·al** \kə-'lat-ə-rəl, -'la-trəl\ adj **1** : associated but of secondary importance **2** : descended from common ancestors but not in the same line ⟨cousins are *collateral* relatives⟩ — **col·lat·er·al·ly** \-ə-rə-lē, -trə-lē\ adv

²**collateral** n : property (as stocks, bonds, or a mortgage) pledged as security for a loan

col·league \'käl-ˌēg\ n : an associate in a profession or office

¹**col·lect** \'käl-ikt also -ˌekt\ n : an opening prayer in the Communion service or the Mass [Middle English *collecte* "prayer", from early French *collecte* (same meaning), from Latin *collecta* "prayer, collect", shortened form of *oratio ad collectam* "prayer upon assembly", derived from earlier *collectus* "was collected", derived from *colligere* "to gather together", from *col-, com-* "together" and *legere* "to gather" — related to LEGEND]

²**col·lect** \kə-'lekt\ vb **1 a** : to bring or come together into one body or place **b** : to gather from a number of sources ⟨*collect* stamps⟩ **2** : to gain or regain control of ⟨*collecting* my thoughts⟩ **3** : to demand and take payment for ⟨*collect* taxes⟩ ⟨*collect* a bill⟩ **4** : to form in a heap or mass : ACCUMULATE ⟨junk *collecting* in the attic⟩ [from Latin *collectus* "was collected", from *colligere* "to gather together", from *col-, com-* "together" and *legere* "to gather" — related to LEGEND] **syn** see GATHER — **col·lect·ible** or **col·lect·able** \kə-'lek-tə-bəl\ adj

³**col·lect** \kə-'lekt\ adv or adj : to be paid for by the receiver ⟨a *collect* phone call⟩ ⟨call *collect*⟩

col·lect·ed \kə-'lek-təd\ adj : being calm and in control of oneself — **col·lect·ed·ly** adv — **col·lect·ed·ness** n

col·lec·tion \kə-'lek-shən\ n **1** : the act or process of collecting **2 a** : something collected; esp : an accumulation of objects gathered for study, comparison, or exhibition **b** : ³SET 7 **3** : a gathering of money ⟨take up a *collection*⟩

¹**col·lec·tive** \kə-'lek-tiv\ adj **1** : having to do with a number of persons or things considered as one group ⟨a *collective* noun⟩ **2** : formed by collecting ⟨the *collective* wisdom of generations⟩ **3** : shared or done by a number of persons as a group ⟨*collective* leadership⟩ ⟨a *collective* effort⟩ — **col·lec·tive·ly** adv

²**collective** n **1** : a collective body : GROUP **2** : a cooperative unit or organization

collective bargaining n : discussion between an employer and union representatives over wages, hours, and working conditions

collective farm n : a farm operated by a group; esp : one under supervision of the government in a communist country

collective mark n : a trademark or a service mark of a group (as a cooperative association)

col·lec·tor \kə-'lek-tər\ n **1** : a person whose job is to collect money due ⟨tax *collector*⟩ ⟨bill *collector*⟩ **2** : one that makes a collection ⟨stamp *collector*⟩ **3** : an object or device that collects ⟨the ornament was just a dust *collector*⟩

col·lege \'käl-ij\ n **1** : a building used for an educational or religious purpose **2 a** : a self-governing body of a university offering living quarters and instruction but not granting degrees ⟨Balliol *College* at Oxford⟩ **b** : a school higher than a high school; esp : an independent institution offering a course of general studies leading to a bachelor's degree **3** : an organized body of persons having common interests or duties ⟨*college* of cardinals⟩

col·le·gian \kə-'lē-jən, -jē-ən\ n : a college student

col·le·giate \kə-'lē-jət, -jē-ət\ adj **1** : of or relating to a college **2** : of, relating to, or characteristic of college students ⟨*collegiate* sports⟩

col·lide \kə-'līd\ vb **col·lid·ed; col·lid·ing** **1** : to come together with solid impact ⟨the football players *collided*⟩ **2** : ¹CLASH 2 a

col·lie \'käl-ē\ n : a large dog of a breed developed in Scotland for herding sheep

collie

col·lier \'käl-yər\ n **1** : a coal miner **2** : a ship for carrying coal

col·liery \'käl-yə-rē\ n, pl **-lier·ies** : a coal mine and the buildings connected with it

col·li·mate \'käl-ə-ˌmāt\ vb **-mat·ed; -mat·ing** : to make (as rays of light) parallel

col·li·sion \kə-'lizh-ən\ n : an act or instance of colliding

col·lo·ca·tion \ˌkäl-ə-'kā-shən\ n : the act or result of placing together

col·loid \'käl-ˌòid\ n : a very finely divided substance which is scattered throughout another substance; also : a mixture consisting of such a substance together with the substance in which it is scattered (as in smoke, gelatin, or marshmallow) — **col·loi·dal** \kä-'lòid-ᵊl, kä-\ adj

col·lo·qui·al \kə-'lō-kwē-əl\ adj **1** : used in or suited to familiar and informal conversation ⟨a *colloquial* word⟩ **2** : using conversational style ⟨a *colloquial* writer⟩ — **col·lo-**

\ə\ **abut**	\au̇\ **out**	\i\ **tip**	\ò\ **saw**	\u̇\ **foot**
\ər\ **further**	\ch\ **chin**	\ī\ **life**	\òi\ **coin**	\y\ **yet**
\a\ **mat**	\e\ **pet**	\j\ **job**	\th\ **thin**	\yü\ **few**
\ā\ **take**	\ē\ **easy**	\ŋ\ **sing**	\th\ **this**	\yu̇\ **cure**
\ä\ **cot, cart**	\g\ **go**	\ō\ **bone**	\ü\ **food**	\zh\ **vision**

qui·al·ly \-kwē-ə-lē\ *adv*

col·lo·qui·al·ism \kə-ˈlō-kwē-ə-ˌliz-əm\ *n* **1** : a colloquial expression **2** : colloquial style

col·lo·quy \ˈkäl-ə-kwē\ *n, pl* **-quies** : CONVERSATION; *esp* : a formal conversation or conference

col·lu·sion \kə-ˈlü-zhən\ *n* : secret agreement or cooperation for an illegal or dishonest purpose — **col·lu·sive** \-ˈlü-siv, -ziv\ *adj*

co·logne \kə-ˈlōn\ *n* : a liquid similar to perfume but not as strongly scented or as long-lasting [named for *Cologne*, city in West Germany where it was first made]

¹co·lon \ˈkō-lən\ *n* : the part of the large intestine between the cecum and the rectum [from Latin *colon* "part of the intestine", from Greek *kolon* (same meaning)] — **co·lon·ic** \kō-ˈlän-ik\ *adj*

²colon *n* : a punctuation mark : used chiefly to direct attention to what follows (as a list, explanation, or quotation) [from earlier *colon* "rhythmic unit in verse", from Latin *colon* "part of a poem", from Greek *kōlon* "limb, part of a poem"]

col·o·nel \ˈkərn-ᵊl\ *n* : a military commissioned officer with a rank just below that of brigadier general [an altered form of earlier *coronel* "colonel", from early French *coronel* (same meaning), from early Italian *colonnello* "colonel, column of soldiers", derived from Latin *columna* "column" — related to COLUMN] — **col·o·nel·cy** \-sē\ *n*

¹co·lo·nial \kə-ˈlō-nē-əl, -nyəl\ *adj* **1** : of, relating to, or characteristic of a colony **2** *often cap* : of or relating to the original 13 colonies forming the United States **3** : possessing, forming, or composed of colonies ⟨a *colonial* nation and its *colonial* empire⟩

²colonial *n* : COLONIST 1

co·lo·nial·ism \kə-ˈlō-nē-ə-ˌliz-əm, -nyə-ˌliz-\ *n* : control by one nation over a dependent area or people; *also* : a policy that favors or is based on such control — **co·lo·nial·ist** \-ləst\ *n or adj*

col·o·nist \ˈkäl-ə-nəst\ *n* **1** : a person who lives in a colony **2** : a person who takes part in founding a colony

col·o·nize \ˈkäl-ə-ˌnīz\ *vb* **-nized; -niz·ing** **1** : to establish a colony in or on ⟨England *colonized* Australia⟩ **2** : to establish in a colony **3** : to settle in a colony — **col·o·ni·za·tion** \ˌkäl-ə-nə-ˈzā-shən\ *n* — **col·o·niz·er** \ˈkäl-ə-ˌnī-zər\ *n*

col·on·nade \ˌkäl-ə-ˈnād\ *n* : an evenly spaced row of columns usually supporting the base of a roof structure — **col·on·nad·ed** \-ˈnād-əd\ *adj*

col·o·ny \ˈkäl-ə-nē\ *n, pl* **-nies** **1 a** : a group of people sent out by a state to a new territory **b** : the territory in which such colonists live **c** : a distant territory belonging to or under the control of a nation **2 a** : a population of plants or animals in a particular place that belong to one species **b** : a mass of microbes usually growing in or on a solid food source (as agar) **3** : a group of people with common qualities or interests located in close association ⟨an artist *colony*⟩

¹col·or \ˈkəl-ər\ *n* **1 a** : a quality of visible things apart from form and from light and shade ⟨the *color* of blood is red⟩ ⟨the green *color* of grass⟩ **b** : the property of objects and light sources that may be described in terms of hue, lightness, and chromatic purity for objects and hue, brightness, and chromatic purity for light sources **c** : a color other than black, white, or gray **2** : an outward and often deceiving appearance ⟨her story has the *color* of truth⟩ **3 a** : COMPLEXION 1; *esp* : a healthy complexion **b** : ²BLUSH 2 **4** : the use or combination of colors ⟨a painter who is a master of *color*⟩ **5** *pl* **a** : an identifying flag, badge, or pennant — usually used in pl. ⟨a ship sailing under Swedish *colors*⟩ **b** : service in the armed forces ⟨a call to the *colors*⟩ **c** : true nature ⟨showed his *colors* during the crisis⟩ **6** : VITALITY 3b, INTEREST ⟨her comments added *color* to the broadcast⟩ **7** : something used to give color : PIGMENT **8** : skin pigmentation other than white that is characteristic

of race

²color *vb* **1 a** : to give color to ⟨the wind *colored* our cheeks⟩ **b** : to change the color of (as by dyeing, staining, or painting) **2** : MISREPRESENT, DISTORT ⟨his story is *colored* by his prejudices⟩ **3** : to take on or change color; *esp* : BLUSH

Col·o·ra·do potato beetle \ˌkäl-ə-ˈrad-ō-, -ˈräd-\ *n* : a black-and-yellow striped beetle that feeds on the leaves of the potato — called also *potato beetle, potato bug*

col·or·ation \ˌkəl-ə-ˈrā-shən\ *n* : use or arrangement of colors or shades : COLORING ⟨study the *coloration* of a flower⟩

col·or–blind \ˈkəl-ər-ˌblīnd\ *adj* : being partly or totally unable to recognize one or more colors — **color blindness** *n*

col·ored \ˈkəl-ərd\ *adj* **1** : having color ⟨*colored* pictures⟩ **2 a** : of a race other than the white; *esp* : of the Negro race **b** : of or relating to colored persons

col·or·fast \ˈkəl-ər-ˌfast\ *adj* : having color that does not fade or run — **col·or·fast·ness** \-ˌfas(t)-nəs\ *n*

color filter *n* : ¹FILTER 3

col·or·ful \ˈkəl-ər-fəl\ *adj* **1** : having noticeable colors **2** : full of variety or interest ⟨a *colorful* personality⟩ — **col·or·ful·ly** \-f(ə-)lē\ *adv* — **col·or·ful·ness** \-fəl-nəs\ *n*

color guard *n* : an honor guard for the colors of an organization

col·or·im·e·ter \ˌkəl-ə-ˈrim-ət-ər\ *n* : a device for determining and specifying colors; *esp* : one used for chemical analysis by comparison of a liquid's color with standard colors

col·or·ing \ˈkəl-(ə-)riŋ\ *n* **1** : the act of applying colors **2** : something that produces color ⟨food *coloring*⟩ **3** : the effect produced by applying or combining colors **4** : COMPLEXION 1, COLORATION **5** : change of appearance (as by adding color)

col·or·less \ˈkəl-ər-ləs\ *adj* **1** : lacking color ⟨a *colorless* liquid⟩ **2** : ¹DULL 8 ⟨*colorless* writing⟩ — **col·or·less·ly** *adv* — **col·or·less·ness** *n*

co·los·sal \kə-ˈläs-əl\ *adj* **1** : of, relating to, or resembling a colossus; *esp* : of very great size **2** : EXTRAORDINARY, EXCEPTIONAL ⟨*colossal* growth⟩ **syn** see MONSTROUS — **co·los·sal·ly** \-ə-lē\ *adv*

col·os·se·um \ˌkäl-ə-ˈsē-əm\ *n* **1** *cap* : an outdoor arena built in Rome in the first century A.D. **2** : COLISEUM [Latin, from *colosseus* "colossal", derived from *colossus* "colossus"]

Co·los·sians \kə-ˈläsh-ənz *also* -ˈläs-ē-ənz, -ˈläsh-ē-ənz\ *n* — see BIBLE table

co·los·sus \kə-ˈläs-əs\ *n, pl* **-los·si** \-ˈläs-ˌī\ *also* **-los·sus·es** **1** : a huge statue **2** : a huge person or thing [from Latin *colossus* "huge statue, colossus"]

co·los·trum \kə-ˈläs-trəm\ *n* : milk secreted for a few days after giving birth and having a high protein and antibody content

col·our \ˈkəl-ər\ *chiefly British variant of* COLOR

colt \ˈkōlt\ *n* **1 a** : ¹FOAL **b** : a young male horse **2** : an inexperienced young person

colt·ish \ˈkōl-tish\ *adj* : FRISKY, PLAYFUL

col·um·bine \ˈkäl-əm-ˌbīn\ *n* : any of a genus of plants that are related to the buttercups and have showy flowers with five petals of which each usually has a long hollow spur

co·lum·bi·um \kə-ˈləm-bē-əm\ *n* : NIOBIUM

Co·lum·bus Day \kə-ˈləm-bəs-\ *n* : the second Monday in October observed as a legal holiday in

columbine

many states of the U.S. in honor of the landing of Columbus in the Bahamas in 1492

col·umn \'käl-əm\ *n* **1 a** : a printed or written vertical arrangement of items ⟨add a *column* of figures⟩ ⟨a mistake in the dollars' *column*⟩ **b** : one of two or more vertical sections of a printed page separated by a rule or blank space **c** : a special regular feature in a newspaper or magazine ⟨a sports *column*⟩ **2** : a supporting pillar; *esp* : one consisting of a usually round shaft, a capital, and a base **3** : something resembling a column in form, position, or function ⟨a *column* of water⟩ **4** : a long row (as of soldiers) [Middle English *columne* "column", from early French *colomne* (same meaning), from Latin *columna* "column" — related to COLONEL] — **col·umned** *adj*

co·lum·nar \kə-'ləm-nər\ *adj* **1** : of, relating to, or being columns **2** : of, relating to, being, or composed of somewhat cylinder-shaped or prism-shaped epithelial cells

col·um·nist \'käl-əm-(n)əst\ *n* : a person who writes a newspaper or magazine column

com- *or* **col-** *or* **con-** *prefix* : with : together : jointly — usually *com-* before *b*, *p*, or *m* ⟨*commingle*⟩, *col-* before *l*, and *con-* before other sounds ⟨*concentrate*⟩ [derived from Latin *com-*, *col-*, *con-* "together, with"]

¹co·ma \'kō-mə\ *n* : a sleeplike state of unconsciousness caused by disease, injury, or poison [scientific Latin, from Greek *kōma* "deep sleep"]

²coma *n, pl* **co·mae** \-,mē, -'mī\ : the head of a comet usually containing a nucleus [from Latin *coma* "hair", from Greek *komē* "hair" — related to COMET]

Co·man·che \kə-'man-chē\ *n, pl* **Comanche** *or* **Comanches** : a member of an American Indian people ranging from Wyoming and Nebraska south into New Mexico and northwestern Texas

Co·man·che·an \kə-'man-chē-ən\ *adj* : of, relating to, or being the period of the Mesozoic era between the Jurassic and the Cretaceous or the system of rocks of that period — **Comanchean** *n*

¹comb \'kōm\ *n* **1 a** : a toothed implement used to smooth and arrange the hair or worn in the hair to hold it in place **b** : a toothed instrument used for separating fibers (as of wool or flax) **2** : a fleshy crest on the head of the domestic fowl and some related birds **3** : ¹HONEYCOMB — **combed** \'kōmd\ *adj*

²comb *vb* **1** : to smooth, arrange, or untangle with a comb ⟨*comb* one's hair⟩ **2** : to go over or through carefully in search of something or someone ⟨we *combed* the beach for shells⟩

¹com·bat \kəm-'bat, 'käm-,bat\ *vb* **-bat·ed** *or* **-bat·ted; -bat·ing** *or* **-bat·ting** **1** : to fight with : BATTLE **2** : to struggle against; *esp* : to strive to reduce or eliminate ⟨*combat* disease⟩

²com·bat \'käm-,bat\ *n* **1** : a fight or contest between individuals or groups **2** : ¹CONFLICT 2 **3** : active fighting in a war : ACTION ⟨soldiers experienced in *combat*⟩

com·bat·ant \kəm-'bat-ᵊnt *also* 'käm-bət-\ *n* : one that is engaged in or ready to engage in combat — **combatant** *adj*

com·bat·ive \kəm-'bat-iv\ *adj* : eager to fight : PUGNACIOUS — **com·bat·ive·ness** *n*

comb·er \'kō-mər\ *n* **1** : one that combs fibers **2** : a long curling wave of the sea

com·bi·na·tion \,käm-bə-'nā-shən\ *n* **1** : a result or product of combining; *esp* : a number of persons or groups joined together to achieve some end **2 a** : a connected series of letters or numbers chosen in setting a lock **b** : any of the possible subsets of a set without regard to the order of their elements **3** : the act or process of combining; *esp* : that of uniting to form a chemical compound

¹com·bine \kəm-'bīn\ *vb* **com·bined; com·bin·ing** **1** : to bring into close relationship : UNIFY **2** : to mix together so that the identity of each part is lost ⟨*combine* the ingredients of a recipe⟩ **3 a** : to become one **b** : to unite to

form a chemical compound **syn** see JOIN — **com·bin·able** \-'bī-nə-bəl\ *adj*

²com·bine \'käm-,bīn\ *n* **1** : a union of persons or groups especially for business or political benefits **2** : a machine that harvests, threshes, and cleans grain while moving over a field

comb·ings \'kō-miŋz\ *n pl* : loose hairs or fibers removed by a comb

combining form \kəm-,bī-niŋ-\ *n* : a linguistic form that occurs only in compounds or derivatives (as *electro-* in *electromagnetic* or *mal-* in *malodorous*)

com·bo \'käm-,bō\ *n, pl* **combos** : a small jazz, dance, or rock band

com·bust \kəm-'bəst\ *vb* : to be or set on fire : BURN

com·bus·ti·ble \kəm-'bəs-tə-bəl\ *adj* **1** : capable of being burned **2** : catching fire or burning easily — **com·bus·ti·bil·i·ty** \-,bəs-tə-'bil-ət-ē\ *n* — **combustible** *n*

com·bus·tion \kəm-'bəs-chən\ *n* **1** : an act or instance of burning **2** : a chemical process in which substances combine with oxygen

com·bus·tor \kəm-'bəs-tər\ *n* : a chamber (as in a jet engine) in which combustion occurs

come \('')kəm\ *vb* **came** \'kām\; **come; com·ing** \'kəm-iŋ\ **1** : to move toward something : APPROACH ⟨*come* here⟩ **2** : to arrive at or enter a scene of action or field of interest ⟨the police *came* to our rescue⟩ **3 a** : to reach the point of being or becoming ⟨the rope *came* untied⟩ **b** : to add up : AMOUNT ⟨the bill *came* to $10⟩ **4** : to take place ⟨the holiday *came* on Thursday⟩ **5** : ORIGINATE 2, ARISE ⟨*comes* from sturdy stock⟩ **6** : to be available ⟨the dress *comes* in three colors⟩ **7** : EXTEND 4, REACH ⟨a coat that *comes* to the knees⟩ **8 a** : to arrive at a place, end, result, or conclusion ⟨*came* to their senses⟩ **b** : HAPPEN 5 ⟨no harm will *come* to you⟩ **9** : to fall within the range or limits of something ⟨*comes* under the terms of the treaty⟩ **10** : to turn out to be : BECOME ⟨her dreams have *come* true⟩ — **com·er** \'kəm-ər\ *n* — **come across** : to meet or find by chance — **come by** : ACQUIRE — **come into one's own** : to reach one's appropriate level of importance, skill, or recognition — **come to be** : to arrive at being : BECOME — **come to pass** : HAPPEN 2 — used with *it* — **come upon** : to meet or find by chance — **come up with** : to produce especially in dealing with a problem or challenge

come about *vb* **1** : to come to pass : HAPPEN **2** : to change direction

come around *vb* : COME ROUND

come·back \'kəm-,bak\ *n* **1** : ²RETORT **2** : a return to a former position or condition (as of health, power, popularity, or prosperity) : RECOVERY

co·me·di·an \kə-'mēd-ē-ən\ *n* **1** : an actor who plays in comedy **2** : a comical individual; *esp* : a humorous professional entertainer

co·me·di·enne \kə-,mēd-ē-'en\ *n* : a female comedian

come·down \'kəm-,daun\ *n* : a falling in status, position, or reputation

come down \(,)kəm-'daun\ *vb* : to fall sick ⟨*came down* with the measles⟩

com·e·dy \'käm-əd-ē\ *n, pl* **-dies** **1** : a light amusing play with a happy ending **2** : a comic literary work **3 a** : an amusing or ridiculous event **b** : humorous entertainment

come·ly \'kəm-lē\ *adj* **come·li·er; -est** : pleasing to the eye : PRETTY, ATTRACTIVE — **come·li·ness** *n*

come out *vb* **1** : to come into public view **2** : to turn out to be ⟨everything *came out* all right⟩

come round *vb* **1** : COME TO 2 : to change direction or opinion

\ə\ abut	\au\ out	\i\ tip	\o\ saw	\u\ foot
\ər\ further	\ch\ chin	\ī\ life	\oi\ coin	\y\ yet
\a\ mat	\e\ pet	\j\ job	\th\ thin	\yü\ few
\ā\ take	\ē\ easy	\ŋ\ sing	\th\ this	\yu\ cure
\ä\ cot, cart	\g\ go	\ō\ bone	\ü\ food	\zh\ vision

com·et \'käm-ət\ *n* : a bright heavenly body that develops a cloudy tail as it moves in an orbit around the sun [Old English *cometa* "comet", from Latin *cometa* (same meaning), from Greek *komētēs*, literally "long-haired", from *komē* "hair" — related to ²COMA]

come to *vb* : to recover consciousness

¹**com·fort** \'kəm(p)-fərt\ *n* **1** : acts or words that comfort **2** : the feeling of the one that is comforted ⟨find *comfort* in a mother's love⟩ **3** : something that makes a person comfortable ⟨the *comforts* of home⟩ — **com·fort·less** \-ləs\ *adj*

²**comfort** *vb* **1** : to give strength and hope to : CHEER **2** : to ease the grief or trouble of : CONSOLE — **com·fort·ing·ly** \'kəm(p)-fər-tiŋ-lē\ *adv*

com·fort·able \'kəm(p)(f)-tə(r)-bəl, 'kəm(p)-fərt-ə-bəl\ *adj* **1** : giving comfort; *esp* : providing physical comfort ⟨a *comfortable* chair⟩ **2** : more than adequate ⟨a *comfortable* income⟩ **3** : enjoying comfort : at ease ⟨are you *comfortable*?⟩ — **com·fort·able·ness** *n* — **com·fort·ably** \-blē\ *adv*

com·fort·er \'kəm(p)-fə(r)t-ər\ *n* **1** : one that gives comfort **2** : a long narrow neck scarf **3** : ¹QUILT

¹**com·ic** \'käm-ik\ *adj* **1** : of or relating to comedy **2** : causing laughter or amusement : FUNNY **3** : of or relating to comic strips

²**comic** *n* **1** : COMEDIAN 2 **2 a** : COMIC STRIP **b** *pl* : the part of a newspaper devoted to comic strips

com·i·cal \'käm-i-kəl\ *adj* : LAUGHABLE, FUNNY — **com·i·cal·ly** \-i-k(ə-)lē\ *adv*

comic book *n* : a magazine made up of a series of comic strips

comic strip *n* : a series of cartoons that tell a story or part of a story

com·ing \'kəm-iŋ\ *adj* **1** : immediately following : NEXT ⟨in the *coming* year⟩ **2** : gaining importance ⟨recognized as a *coming* young star⟩

co·mi·ty \'käm-ət-ē, 'kō-mət-\ *n, pl* **-ties** : courteous behavior : CIVILITY

com·ma \'käm-ə\ *n* : a punctuation mark , used chiefly to show separation of words or word groups within a sentence

comma fault *n* : the error of using a comma between coordinate main clauses not connected by a conjunction

¹**com·mand** \kə-'mand\ *vb* **1 a** : to issue orders by right of authority **b** : to have authority and control over : be commander of ⟨*command* an army⟩ **2** : to have for one's use **3** : to demand or receive as one's due : EXACT ⟨*commands* a high fee⟩ **4** : to look down on especially from a militarily strong position ⟨the hill *commands* the town⟩

syn COMMAND, DIRECT, INSTRUCT, CHARGE mean to issue orders. COMMAND suggests the use of authority and usually some degree of formality ⟨the troops were *commanded* to march forward⟩ DIRECT suggests that obedience is expected and usually applies to definite orders ⟨we were *directed* to write with pencils only⟩ INSTRUCT usually applies to specific methods or points of procedure ⟨the students were *instructed* to complete part one before going on⟩ CHARGE suggests the assigning of a duty or responsibility ⟨the principal is *charged* with keeping the school running smoothly⟩

²**command** *n* **1** : the act of commanding ⟨march on *command*⟩ **2** : an order given ⟨obey a *command*⟩ **3 a** : the ability to control : MASTERY ⟨a good *command* of French⟩ **b** : the authority, right, or power to command **4** : the people, area, or unit under a commander **5** : a position from which military operations are directed

com·man·dant \'käm-ən-,dant, -,dänt\ *n* : an officer in command

com·man·deer \,käm-ən-'di(ə)r\ *vb* : to take possession of by force especially for military purposes

com·mand·er \kə-'man-dər\ *n* **1** : one in official command especially of a military force or base **2** : a naval commis-

sioned officer with a rank just below that of captain — **com·mand·er·ship** \-,ship\ *n*

commander in chief : one who holds the supreme command of an armed force

commanding officer *n* : an officer having charge of a military or naval unit, organization, or base

com·mand·ment \kə-'man(d)-mənt\ *n* : something commanded; *esp* : one of the biblical Ten Commandments

command module *n* : part of a space vehicle designed to carry the crew, the chief communications equipment, and the equipment for return to Earth's atmosphere

com·man·do \kə-'man-dō\ *n, pl* **-dos** *or* **-does** **1** : a military unit trained and organized for surprise raids **2** : a member of a commando

command module separating from service module

com·mem·o·rate \kə-'mem-ə-,rāt\ *vb* **-rat·ed; -rat·ing** **1** : to call to remembrance **2** : to mark by a ceremony **3** : to be a memorial of ⟨a plaque that *commemorates* the battle⟩ **syn** see KEEP — **com·mem·o·ra·tor** \-,rāt-ər\ *n*

com·mem·o·ra·tion \kə-,mem-ə-'rā-shən\ *n* **1** : the act of commemorating **2** : a ceremony that commemorates

com·mem·o·ra·tive \kə-'mem-ə-rət-iv, -,rāt-\ *adj* : intended to commemorate a person, thing, or an event ⟨a *commemorative* postage stamp⟩ — **commemorative** *n*

com·mence \kə-'men(t)s\ *vb* **com·menced; com·menc·ing** : to bring or come into activity, being, or operation : BEGIN, START ⟨*commence* firing⟩ [Middle English *comencen* "to begin", from early French *comencer* (same meaning), probably from a Latin word *cominitiare* "to begin", from *com-* "with, together" and *initiare* "to begin" — related to INITIATE] — **com·menc·er** *n*

com·mence·ment \kə-'men(t)s-mənt\ *n* **1** : an act, instance, or time of commencing **2** : the ceremonies or the day for presenting degrees or diplomas to graduates of a school or college

com·mend \kə-'mend\ *vb* **1** : to give into another's care : ENTRUST **2** : to speak of someone or something with approval : PRAISE ⟨*commended* her for her honesty⟩ — **com·mend·able** \-'men-də-bəl\ *adj* — **com·mend·ably** \-blē\ *adv*

com·men·da·tion \,käm-ən-'dā-shən, -,en-\ *n* **1** : an act of commending **2** : something that commends ⟨was awarded a *commendation* for bravery⟩ — **com·men·da·to·ry** \kə-'men-də-,tōr-ē, -,tòr-\ *adj*

com·men·sal \kə-'men(t)-səl\ *adj* : relating to or living in a state of commensalism

com·men·sal·ism \kə-'men(t)-sə-,liz-əm\ *n* : a relation between two kinds of plants or animals in which one obtains a benefit (as food) from the other without damaging or benefiting it

com·men·su·rate \kə-'men(t)s-(ə-)rət, -'mench-(ə-)rət\ *adj* **1** : equal in measure or extent **2** : PROPORTIONAL 1 ⟨an income *commensurate* with one's needs⟩ — **com·men·su·rate·ly** *adv*

¹**com·ment** \'käm-,ent\ *n* **1** : an expression of opinion or attitude in speech or writing **2** : a remark that explains or criticizes **syn** see REMARK

²**comment** *vb* : to make a comment : REMARK

com·men·tary \'käm-ən-,ter-ē\ *n, pl* **-tar·ies** : a series of comments or notes; *also* : a book made up of such material — often use in pl. ⟨Caesar's *Commentaries* on the Gallic Wars⟩

com·men·ta·tor \'käm-ən-,tāt-ər\ *n* : a person who gives a commentary; *esp* : a person who reports and discusses news on radio or television

com·merce \'käm-(,)ərs\ *n* : buying and selling of goods especially on a large scale and between different places

: TRADE [from early French *commerce* "exchange of ideas or opinions, commerce", from Latin *commercium* (same meaning), from *com-* "with" and *merc-, merx* "merchandise" — related to MARKET, MERCHANT]

¹com·mer·cial \kə-'mər-shəl\ *adj* **1** : of or relating to commerce **2** : designed mainly for profit; *esp* : designed for mass appeal ⟨the *commercial* theater⟩ **3** : paid for by advertisers ⟨*commercial* TV⟩ — **com·mer·cial·ly** \-'mərsh-(ə-)lē\ *adv*

²commercial *n* : an advertisement broadcast on radio or television

commercial bank *n* : a bank that accepts deposits that can be withdrawn without notice and creates credit through loans mainly to businesses

com·mer·cial·ize \kə-'mər-shə-,līz\ *vb* **-ized; -iz·ing** **1** : to manage for the sake of making a profit **2** : to use for profit ⟨*commercialize* Christmas⟩ — **com·mer·cial·iza·tion** \-,mər-shə-lə-'zā-shən\ *n*

com·min·gle \kə-'miŋ-gəl\ *vb* : to mix together : MINGLE

com·mis·er·ate \kə-'miz-ə-,rāt\ *vb* **-at·ed; -at·ing** : to feel or express sorrow or sympathy : SYMPATHIZE — **com·mis·er·a·tion** \-,miz-ə-'rā-shən\ *n*

com·mis·sar \'käm-ə-,sär\ *n* : the head of a government department in the U.S.S.R. before 1946

com·mis·sar·i·at \,käm-ə-'ser-ē-ət\ *n* **1** : a system for supplying an army with food **2** : a government department headed by a commissar

com·mis·sary \'käm-ə-,ser-ē\ *n, pl* **-sar·ies** **1** : a person to whom a duty or office is entrusted by someone of higher rank **2** : a store that provides supplies (as food) especially to members of the military and their families **3** : a lunchroom especially in a motion-picture studio

¹com·mis·sion \kə-'mish-ən\ *n* **1 a** : an order granting the power to perform various acts or duties **b** : a certificate that gives military rank and authority; *also* : the rank and authority so given **2 a** : authority to act as agent for another **b** : a matter entrusted to an agent **3** : a group of persons directed to perform some duty **4** : an act of committing ⟨*commission* of a theft⟩ **5** : a fee paid to an agent or employee for taking care of a piece of business ⟨a 5% sales *commission*⟩ — **in commission** : in use or ready for use ⟨put a ship *in commission*⟩ — **out of commission** **1** : out of service or use **2** : out of working order ⟨the doorbell was *out of commission*⟩

²commission *vb* **-mis·sioned; -mis·sion·ing** \-'mish-(ə-)niŋ\ **1** : to give a commission to **2** : to order to be made ⟨*commissioned* a portrait of himself⟩ **3** : to put (a ship) in commission

com·mis·sion·aire \kə-,mish-ə-'na(ə)r, -'ne(ə)r\ *n, chiefly British* : a uniformed attendant

commissioned officer *n* : a military or naval officer holding by a commission a rank of second lieutenant or ensign or a higher rank

com·mis·sion·er \kə-'mish-(ə-)nər\ *n* **1** : a member of a commission **2** : an official in charge of a government department ⟨Police *Commissioner*⟩

com·mit \kə-'mit\ *vb* **com·mit·ted; com·mit·ting** **1 a** : to make secure or put in safekeeping : ENTRUST ⟨*commit* the poem to memory⟩ **b** : to place in a prison or mental institution **2** : BRING ABOUT, PERFORM ⟨*commit* a crime⟩ **3** : to pledge or assign to some particular course or use ⟨*committed* myself to a meeting on Thursday⟩ — **com·mit·ta·ble** \-'mit-ə-bəl\ *adj*

com·mit·ment \kə-'mit-mənt\ *n* **1** : an act of committing **2 a** : an agreement or pledge to do something in the future **b** : something pledged ⟨financial *commitments*⟩

com·mit·tee \kə-'mit-ē\ *n* : a group of persons appointed or elected to consider or take action on some matter ⟨a legislative *committee*⟩

com·mit·tee·man \-mən, -,man\ *n* : a member of a committee

com·mit·tee·wom·an \-,wum-ən\ *n* : a female member of a committee

com·mode \kə-'mōd\ *n* **1 a** : a low chest of drawers **b** : a movable washstand with a cupboard underneath : TOILET 2b

com·mo·di·ous \kə-'mōd-ē-əs\ *adj* : having a comfortable amount of space **syn** see SPACIOUS — **com·mo·di·ous·ness** *n*

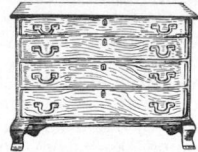

commode 1a

com·mod·i·ty \kə-'mäd-ət-ē\ *n, pl* **-ties** **1** : a product of agriculture or mining **2** : an article that is bought and sold in commerce

com·mo·dore \'käm-ə-,dō(ə)r, -,do(ə)r\ *n* **1** : a naval commissioned officer with a rank just below that of rear admiral **2** : the senior captain of a line of merchant ships

¹com·mon \'käm-ən\ *adj* **1** : relating or belonging to or used by everybody : PUBLIC ⟨the *common* good⟩ **2** : belonging to or shared by two or more individuals or by the members of a group or set ⟨a *common* ancestor⟩ ⟨all points *common* to two intersecting circles⟩ **3** : WIDESPREAD 1, GENERAL ⟨facts of *common* knowledge⟩ **4** : occurring or appearing frequently : FAMILIAR ⟨a *common* sight⟩ **5** : not above the average in rank, merit, or social position ⟨a *common* soldier⟩ ⟨of the *common* people⟩ **6 a** : falling below ordinary standards : SECOND-RATE **b** : COARSE 5, VULGAR ⟨*common* manners⟩ — **com·mon·ly** *adv* — **com·mon·ness** \-ən-nəs\ *n*

²common *n* **1** *pl* : the common people **2** : a piece of land that is open to common use especially for pasture — often used in pl. — **in common** : shared together ⟨intersecting lines have one point *in common*⟩

common cold *n* : a contagious virus disease of the structures used in breathing which causes the nose and throat to be sore, swollen, and inflamed and in which there is usually much mucus and coughing and sneezing

common denominator *n* : a common multiple of the denominators of a number of fractions ⟨12 is a *common denominator* of ¼ and ⅓⟩

common divisor *n* : a number that divides two or more numbers without remainder ⟨4 is a *common divisor* of 12, 24, and 36⟩ — called also *common factor*

com·mon·er \'käm-ə-nər\ *n* : one of the common people : a person who is not of noble rank

common law *n* : a group of legal practices and traditions originating in judges' decisions in earlier cases and in social customs and having the same force in most of the U.S. as if passed into law by a legislative body

common multiple *n* : a number that is a multiple of each of two or more numbers ⟨20 is a *common multiple* of 5 and 4⟩

common noun *n* : a noun (as *chair* or *fear*) that names a class of persons or things or any individual of a class

¹com·mon·place \'käm-ən-,plās\ *n* : something that is often seen, heard, or met with

²commonplace *adj* : very common or ordinary

common salt *n* : ¹SALT 1a

common sense *n* : ordinary good sense and judgment — **commonsense** \,käm-ən-,sen(t)s\ *adj*

com·mon·weal \'käm-ən-,wēl\ *n* **1** *archaic* : COMMONWEALTH **2** : the general good

com·mon·wealth \-,welth\ *n* **1** : a political unit (as a nation or state) **2** : a state of the U.S. — used officially of

\ə\ abut		\au̇\ out	\i\ tip	\o̊\ saw	\u̇\ foot	
\ər\ further		\ch\ chin	\ī\ life	\o̊i\ coin	\y\ yet	
\a\ mat		\e\ pet	\j\ job	\th\ thin	\yü\ few	
\ā\ take		\ē\ easy	\ŋ\ sing	\th\ this	\yu̇\ cure	
\ä\ cot, cart		\g\ go	\ō\ bone	\ü\ food	\zh\ vision	

Kentucky, Massachusetts, Pennsylvania, and Virginia

com·mo·tion \kə-'mō-shən\ *n* 1 : disturbed or violent motion : AGITATION 2 : noisy excitement and confusion : TUMULT

com·mu·nal \kə-'myün-ᵊl, 'käm-yən-ᵊl\ *adj* 1 : of or relating to a commune or community 2 : shared or used in common by members of a group or community

¹com·mune \kə-'myün\ *vb* **com·muned; com·mun·ing** 1 : to receive Communion 2 : to be in close communication with someone or something ⟨*commune* with nature⟩

²com·mune \'käm-,yün, kə-'myün\ *n* 1 : the smallest administrative district of many countries especially in Europe 2 : a small group of people that live together and share property and duties

com·mu·ni·ca·ble \kə-'myü-ni-kə-bəl\ *adj* : capable of being transferred or carried from one person or thing to another ⟨*communicable* diseases⟩ — **com·mu·ni·ca·bil·i·ty** \-,myü-ni-kə-'bil-ət-ē\ *n*

com·mu·ni·cant \kə-'myü-ni-kənt\ *n* 1 : a person who takes Communion : a church member 2 : a person who communicates

com·mu·ni·cate \kə-'myü-nə-,kāt\ *vb* **-cat·ed; -cat·ing** 1 **a** : to make known ⟨*communicate* the news⟩ **b** : to pass from one to another : TRANSMIT ⟨*communicate* a disease⟩ 2 : to transmit information, thought, or feeling so that it is satisfactorily received or understood ⟨the pilot *communicated* with the airport⟩ 3 : to open into each other : CONNECT ⟨the rooms *communicate*⟩ — **com·mu·ni·ca·tor** \-,kāt-ər\ *n*

com·mu·ni·ca·tion \kə-,myü-nə-'kā-shən\ *n* 1 : an act or instance of transmitting 2 : information communicated : MESSAGE ⟨received an important *communication*⟩ 3 : an exchange of information 4 *pl* **a** : a system (as of telephones) for sending and receiving messages **b** : a system of routes for moving troops, supplies, and vehicles

com·mu·ni·ca·tive \kə-'myü-nə-,kāt-iv, -ni-kət-iv\ *adj* 1 : tending to communicate : TALKATIVE 2 : of or relating to communication — **com·mu·ni·ca·tive·ness** *n*

com·mu·nion \kə-'myü-nyən\ *n* 1 *cap a* : a Christian sacrament in which bread and wine are partaken of as a commemoration of the last supper of Jesus **b** : the part of the Mass in which the Eucharist is received 2 : friendly communication 3 : a body of Christians having a common faith and discipline

com·mu·ni·qué \kə-'myü-nə-,kā, -,myü-nə-'kā\ *n* : an official communication : BULLETIN [French, literally "something communicated"]

com·mu·nism \'käm-yə-,niz-əm\ *n* 1 : a social system in which property and goods are owned in common; *also* : a theory that favors such a system 2 *cap* : a system of government in which a single party controls state-owned means of production with the aim of establishing a stateless society

com·mu·nist \'käm-yə-nəst\ *n* 1 : a person who believes in communism 2 *cap* : a member or follower of a Communist party or movement — **communist** *adj, often cap* — **com·mu·nis·tic** \,käm-yə-'nis-tik\ *adj, often cap*

com·mu·ni·ty \kə-'myü-nət-ē\ *n, pl* **-ties** 1 **a** : the people living in an area; *also* : the area itself **b** : a group of living things that belong to one or more species, interact ecologically, and are located in one place (as a bog or pond) **c** : a group of people with common interests especially when living together ⟨a *community* of monks⟩ 2 **a** : shared ownership or participation ⟨*community* of goods⟩ **b** : SIMILARITY 1, LIKENESS ⟨a *community* of ideas⟩ **c** : shared activity : FELLOWSHIP

community college *n* : a public junior college that fits its instruction to the community's needs

com·mu·ta·tion \,käm-yə-'tā-shən\ *n* 1 : ¹EXCHANGE 2, REPLACEMENT 2 : a reduction of a legal penalty 3 : an act of commuting 4 : the process of reversing the direction of an electric circuit

com·mu·ta·tive \'käm-yə-,tāt-iv, kə-'myüt-ət-iv\ *adj* : of, relating to, having, or being the property that a given mathematical operation and set have when the result obtained using any two numbers of the set with the operation does not differ with the order in which the numbers are used ⟨addition of the real numbers is *commutative* because $a + b = b + a$ for all real numbers a and b but subtraction is not because $a - b \neq b - a$ if a and b are different real numbers⟩ — **com·mu·ta·tiv·i·ty** \kə-,myüt-ə-'tiv-ət-ē, ,käm-yə-tə-\ *n*

com·mu·ta·tor \'käm-yə-,tāt-ər\ *n* : a device for reversing the direction of an electric current so that the alternating currents made in a dynamo are changed to direct current

com·mute \kə-'myüt\ *vb* **com·mut·ed; com·mut·ing** 1 : ²EXCHANGE, INTERCHANGE; *esp* : to substitute a less severe penalty for a greater one ⟨*commute* a death sentence to life imprisonment⟩ 2 : to travel back and forth regularly — **com·mut·able** \-'myüt-ə-bəl\ *adj* — **com·mut·er** *n*

¹com·pact \kəm-'pakt, 'käm-,pakt\ *adj* 1 : closely united or packed : SOLID, FIRM 2 : arranged so as to save space ⟨a *compact* house⟩ 3 : not wordy : BRIEF [Middle English *compact* "firmly put together", from Latin *compactus* (same meaning), from *compingere* "to join", from *com-* "together" and *pangere* "to fasten"] — **com·pact·ly** *adv* — **com·pact·ness** \kəm-'pak(t)-nəs, 'käm-,pak(t)-\ *n*

²compact *vb* 1 : to draw together : COMBINE, CONSOLIDATE 2 : to make or become compact : COMPRESS — **com·pac·tor** *also* **com·pact·er** \kəm-'pak-tər, 'käm-,pak-\ *n*

³com·pact \'käm-,pakt\ *n* 1 : a small cosmetic case 2 : a somewhat small automobile

⁴com·pact \'käm-,pakt\ *n* : AGREEMENT 2a, CONTRACT [from Latin *compactum* "agreement", derived from *compacisci* "to make an agreement", from *com-* "with, together" and *pacisci* "to agree"]

¹com·pan·ion \kəm-'pan-yən\ *n* 1 : one that often accompanies another : COMRADE 2 **a** : one of a pair of matching things **b** : a person employed to live with and serve another [Middle English *compainoun* "companion", from early French *compagnon* (same meaning), from Latin *companion-, companio* "companion", literally "one who eats with another", from *com-* "with, together" and *panis* "food, bread" — related to ACCOMPANY, COMPANY, PANTRY]

²companion *n* : COMPANIONWAY

com·pan·ion·able \kəm-'pan-yə-nə-bəl\ *adj* : having, showing, or leading to feelings of companionship : FRIENDLY — **com·pan·ion·ably** \-blē\ *adv*

com·pan·ion·ship \kəm-'pan-yən-,ship\ *n* : the fellowship that exists among companions

com·pan·ion·way \-,wā\ *n* : a ship's stairway from one deck to another

com·pa·ny \'kəmp-(ə-)nē\ *n, pl* **-nies** 1 **a** : association with another : FELLOWSHIP **b** : a person's companions or associates ⟨known by the *company* you keep⟩ **c** : guests or visitors especially at one's home ⟨we have *company*⟩ 2 **a** : a group of persons or things **b** : a body of soldiers; *esp* : a unit consisting of two or more platoons **c** : an organization of musical or dramatic performers ⟨opera *company*⟩ **d** : the officers and crew of a ship **e** : a fire-fighting unit 3 **a** : an association of persons carrying on a business **b** : those members of a partnership whose names do not appear in the firm name ⟨Doe and *Company*⟩ [Middle English *companie* "company, fellowship", from early French *compagnie* (same meaning), derived from Latin *companio* "companion" — related to ACCOMPANY, COMPANION]

com·pa·ra·ble \'käm-p(ə-)rə-bəl\ *adj* 1 : capable of being compared 2 : worthy of being compared : SIMILAR ⟨cloth *comparable* to the best⟩ — **com·pa·ra·bly** \-blē\ *adv*

¹com·par·a·tive \kəm-'par-ət-iv\ *adj* 1 : of, relating to, or constituting the degree of grammatical comparison that denotes increase in the quality, quantity, or relation expressed by an adjective or adverb   **2** : measured by comparison : RELATIVE ⟨a *comparative* stranger⟩   **3** : involving the study of things that are alike by comparing them ⟨*comparative* anatomy⟩ — **com·par·a·tive·ly** *adv*

²**comparative** *n* : the comparative degree or a word form expressing it ⟨"taller" is the *comparative* of "tall"⟩

¹**com·pare** \kəm-'pa(ə)r, -'pe(ə)r\ *vb* **com·pared; com·par·ing**   **1** : to describe as similar ⟨*compare* an anthill to a town⟩   **2** : to examine in order to discover likenesses or differences ⟨*compare* two bicycles⟩   **3 a** : to be worthy of comparison ⟨roller-skating does not *compare* with ice-skating⟩   **b** : to appear in comparison to others ⟨*compares* well with the rest of the class⟩   **4** : to inflect or modify (an adjective or adverb) according to the degrees of comparison [Middle English *comparen* "to show to be similar, examine for points of likeness", from early French *comparer* (same meaning), from Latin *comparare* "to couple, compare", from *compar* (adjective) "like, similar", from *com-* "with, together" and *par* "equal" — related to PAIR, PAR, PEER, UMPIRE; see Word History at UMPIRE]

²**compare** *n* : the possibility of comparing ⟨beauty beyond *compare*⟩

com·par·i·son \kəm-'par-ə-sən\ *n*   **1** : the act of comparing : the state of being compared   **2** : change in the form of an adjective or an adverb (as by having *-er* or *-est* added or *more* or *most* prefixed) to show different levels of quality, quantity, or relation

comparison shop *vb* : to compare prices in order to find the best value — **comparison shopper** *n*

com·part·ment \kəm-'pärt-mənt\ *n*   **1** : a separate division or section   **2** : one of the parts into which an enclosed space is divided

¹**com·pass** \'kəm-pəs *also* 'käm-\ *vb*   **1** : to travel entirely around ⟨*compass* the earth⟩   **2** : ACCOMPLISH, ACHIEVE

²**compass** *n*   **1 a** : BOUNDARY, CIRCUMFERENCE   **b** : an enclosed space   **c** : ¹RANGE 6, SCOPE ⟨within the *compass* of my voice⟩   **2 a** : a device for determining directions by means of a magnetic needle pointing to the magnetic north   **b** : any of various other devices that indicate direction   **3** : an instrument for drawing circles or transferring measurements that consists of two pointed branches joined at the top — usually used in pl.

compass 2a

com·pas·sion \kəm-'pash-ən\ *n* : sorrow or pity caused by the suffering or misfortune of another : SYMPATHY — **com·pas·sion·ate** \-'pash-(ə-)nət\ *adj* — **com·pas·sion·ate·ly** *adv*

com·pat·i·ble \kəm-'pat-ə-bəl\ *adj*   **1** : capable of existing together in harmony ⟨*compatible* colors⟩ ⟨*compatible* devices⟩   **2** : able to cross-fertilize freely ⟨*compatible* plants⟩ — **com·pat·i·bil·i·ty** \-,pat-ə-'bil-ət-ē\ *n*

com·pa·tri·ot \kəm-'pā-trē-ət, käm-, -trē-,ät\ *n* : a person from one's own country : COUNTRYMAN

com·pel \kəm-'pel\ *vb* **com·pelled; com·pel·ling**   **1** : to cause to do something by the use of physical, moral, or mental pressure : FORCE ⟨illness *compelled* him to stay in bed⟩   **2** : ¹EXACT, EXTORT ⟨*compel* obedience⟩ — **com·pel·ler** *n* — **com·pel·ling·ly** \-'pel-iŋ-lē\ *adv*

com·pen·di·ous \kəm-'pen-dē-əs\ *adj* : marked by a brief presentation of a broad subject : CONCISE ⟨a *compendious* book⟩

com·pen·sate \'käm-pən-,sāt\ *vb* **-sat·ed; -sat·ing**   **1** : to be equal to in value or effect : COUNTERBALANCE   **2** : to make up for ⟨*compensate* for a rude act⟩   **3** : to make equal return to : PAY ⟨*compensate* workers for their labor⟩ — **com·pen·sa·to·ry** \kəm-'pen(t)-sə-,tōr-ē, -,tòr-\ *adj*

com·pen·sa·tion \,käm-pən-'sā-shən\ *n*   **1** : the act of compensating : the state of being compensated   **2 a** : something that compensates; *esp* : payment to an unemployed or injured worker   **b** : payment in the form of salary or wages

com·pete \kəm-'pēt\ *vb* **com·pet·ed; com·pet·ing** : to strive for something (as a prize or reward) for which another is also striving : CONTEST

com·pe·tence \'käm-pət-ən(t)s\ *n*   **1** : a supply (as of money or property) that is enough to provide for the necessities of life   **2** : the quality or state of being competent

com·pe·ten·cy \'käm-pət-ən-sē\ *n* : COMPETENCE

com·pe·tent \'käm-pət-ənt\ *adj* : having the necessary ability or qualities : CAPABLE ⟨a *competent* musician⟩ — **com·pe·tent·ly** *adv*

com·pe·ti·tion \,käm-pə-'tish-ən\ *n*   **1** : the act or process of competing   **2 a** : a contest between rivals   **b** : RIVALRY   **c** : an individual or group one is competing against ⟨look over the *competition*⟩   **3** : the effort of persons or firms to attract business by offering the most favorable terms   **4** : the active seeking after and use of an environmental resource (as food) in limited supply by two or more plants or animals or kinds of plants and animals

com·pet·i·tive \kəm-'pet-ət-iv\ *adj* : relating to, characterized by, or based on competition ⟨*competitive* sports⟩ ⟨*competitive* bidding⟩ — **com·pet·i·tive·ly** *adv* — **com·pet·i·tive·ness** *n*

com·pet·i·tor \kəm-'pet-ət-ər\ *n* : one that competes especially in the selling of goods or services : RIVAL

com·pi·la·tion \,käm-pə-'lā-shən\ *n*   **1** : the act or process of compiling   **2** : something compiled; *esp* : a book of materials gathered from other books

com·pile \kəm-'pīl\ *vb* **com·piled; com·pil·ing**   **1** : to collect into a volume or list ⟨*compile* a book of poems⟩   **2** : to put together in a new form out of materials from other books or documents ⟨*compile* a history of India⟩   **3** : to translate (as a computer program) with a compiler

com·pil·er \kəm-'pī-lər\ *n*   **1** : one that compiles   **2** : a computer program that automatically translates an entire set of instructions written in a computer programming language (as LOGO) into machine language

com·pla·cence \kəm-'plās-ᵊn(t)s\ *n* : a calm or satisfied feeling about one's self : SELF-SATISFACTION — **com·pla·cent** \kəm-'plās-ᵊnt\ *adj* — **com·pla·cent·ly** *adv*

com·pla·cen·cy \kəm-'plās-ᵊn-sē\ *n* : COMPLACENCE

com·plain \kəm-'plān\ *vb*   **1** : to express grief, pain, or discontent : find fault   **2** : to accuse someone of wrongdoing — **com·plain·er** *n* — **com·plain·ing·ly** \-'plā-niŋ-lē\ *adv*

com·plain·ant \kəm-'plā-nənt\ *n* : one who makes a legal complaint

com·plaint \kəm-'plānt\ *n*   **1** : expression of grief, pain, or resentment   **2 a** : a cause or reason for complaining ⟨the noise was her biggest *complaint*⟩   **b** : a bodily ailment or disease   **3** : a charge of illegal wrongdoing against a person

com·plai·sance \kəm-'plās-ᵊn(t)s, -'plāz-; ,käm-plā-'zan(t)s\ *n* : a desire or willingness to please — **com·plai·sant** \-ᵊnt, -'zant\ *adj*

¹**com·ple·ment** \'käm-plə-mənt\ *n*   **1** : something that fills up, completes, or makes perfect   **2** : full quantity, number, or amount ⟨a ship's *complement* of officers and crew⟩   **3** : the angle that when added to a given angle equals 90 degrees   **4** : an added word or group of words by which the predicate of a sentence is made complete ⟨"president" in "they elected her president" and "to work" in "he wants to work" are different kinds of *complements*⟩   **5** : a heat-

\ə\ abut		\au̇\ out	\i\ tip		\ȯ\ saw		\u̇\ foot
\ər\ further		\ch\ chin	\ī\ life		\ȯi\ coin		\y\ yet
\a\ mat		\e\ pet	\j\ job		\th\ thin		\yü\ few
\ā\ take		\ē\ easy	\ŋ\ sing		\th\ this		\yu̇\ cure
\ä\ cot, cart		\g\ go	\ō\ bone		\ü\ food		\zh\ vision

sensitive substance in normal blood that in combination with antibodies destroys antigens (as bacteria and foreign blood corpuscles) **6** : the set of all elements not included in a given mathematical set

²**com·ple·ment** \'käm-plə-,ment\ *vb* : to form or serve as a complement to ⟨a shirt that *complements* a suit⟩

com·ple·men·ta·ry \,käm-plə-'ment-ə-rē, -'men-trē\ *adj* : forming or serving as a complement

complementary angles *n pl* : two angles whose sum is 90 degrees

complementary colors *n pl* : a pair of colors that when mixed in proper proportions produce a neutral color

¹**com·plete** \kəm-'plēt\ *adj* **com·plet·er; com·plet·est** **1** : possessing all necessary parts : ENTIRE ⟨a *complete* set of books⟩ ⟨a *complete* diet⟩ **2** : brought to an end : having been completed **3** : being such to the fullest degree : THOROUGH, ABSOLUTE ⟨*complete* freedom⟩ ⟨a *complete* failure⟩ — **com·plete·ly** *adv* — **com·plete·ness** *n*

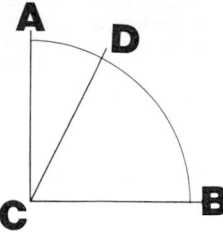

complementary angles: *ACD* and *DCB*

²**complete** *vb* **com·plet·ed; com·plet·ing** **1** : to bring to an end : accomplish or achieve fully ⟨*complete* a job⟩ **2** : to make whole or perfect

complete metamorphosis *n* : insect metamorphosis (as of a butterfly) in which there is a pupal stage between the immature stage and the adult and in which the young insect is very different in form from the adult

complete protein *n* : protein (as in meat, fish, milk, and eggs) supplying all the amino acids that are needed by the human body but cannot be made by it

com·ple·tion \kəm-'plē-shən\ *n* : the act or process of completing : the state of being complete ⟨a job near *completion*⟩

¹**com·plex** \'käm-,pleks\ *n* **1** : a whole made up of many complicated or related parts **2** : a system of thoughts, feelings, and memories that exist in one's mind but of which one is not aware and which influence one's behavior

²**com·plex** \käm-'pleks, kəm-; 'käm-,pleks\ *adj* **1 a** : composed of two or more parts ⟨a *complex* mixture⟩ **b** : consisting of a main clause and one or more subordinate clauses ⟨*complex* sentence⟩ **c** : formed by union of simpler substances **2** : having many parts, details, ideas, or functions often related in a complicated way ⟨a *complex* problem⟩ ⟨a *complex* animal like a human being⟩ — **com·plex·ly** *adv*

complex fraction *n* : a fraction with a fraction or mixed number in the numerator or denominator or both

com·plex·ion \kəm-'plek-shən\ *n* **1** : the hue or appearance of the skin and especially of the face **2** : general appearance : CHARACTER ⟨information that changes the whole *complexion* of a situation⟩ — **com·plex·ioned** \-shənd\ *adj*

com·plex·i·ty \kəm-'plek-sət-ē, käm-\ *n, pl* **-ties** **1** : the quality or state of being complex **2** : something complex ⟨the *complexities* of the English language⟩

com·pli·ance \kəm-'plī-ən(t)s\ *n* **1** : the act or process of complying **2** : a readiness or willingness to yield to others — **in compliance with** : in agreement with : in obedience to ⟨*in compliance with* a court order⟩

com·pli·an·cy \kəm-'plī-ən-sē\ *n* : COMPLIANCE

com·pli·ant \kəm-'plī-ənt\ *adj* : ready or willing to comply : SUBMISSIVE — **com·pli·ant·ly** *adv*

com·pli·cate \'käm-plə-,kāt\ *vb* **-cat·ed; -cat·ing** : to make or become complex or difficult

com·pli·cat·ed \'käm-plə-,kāt-əd\ *adj* **1** : consisting of many combined parts ⟨*complicated* machinery⟩ **2** : diffi-

cult to analyze, understand, or explain : COMPLEX — **com·pli·cat·ed·ly** *adv* — **com·pli·cat·ed·ness** *n*

com·pli·ca·tion \,käm-plə-'kā-shən\ *n* **1 a** : an act or instance of complicating something **b** : a situation or detail of character that complicates a plot **c** : a complex feature or element **d** : something that makes a situation more complicated or difficult ⟨were unable to agree when *complications* arose⟩ **2** : a disease or bodily condition existing at the same time as and affecting the course or severity of another disease or condition

com·plic·i·ty \kəm-'plis-ət-ē\ *n, pl* **-ties** : association or participation in a wrongful act

¹**com·pli·ment** \'käm-plə-mənt\ *n* **1** : an expression of respect, affection, or admiration **2** *pl* : best wishes : REGARDS

syn COMPLIMENT, FLATTERY mean praise directed to someone. COMPLIMENT suggests that one is sincere in admiring someone or giving credit ⟨received many *compliments* on his appearance⟩ FLATTERY is more likely to suggest that one is not sincere but is appealing to a person's vanity especially for selfish reasons ⟨the king received much *flattery* from his servants⟩

²**com·pli·ment** \'käm-plə-,ment\ *vb* : to pay a compliment to

com·pli·men·ta·ry \,käm-plə-'ment-ə-rē, -'men-trē\ *adj* **1** : expressing or containing a compliment ⟨a *complimentary* remark⟩ **2** : given free as a courtesy or favor ⟨*complimentary* tickets⟩

com·ply \kəm-'plī\ *vb* **com·plied; com·ply·ing** : to act in agreement with another's wishes or in obedience to a rule ⟨*comply* with a request⟩ — **com·pli·er** \-'plī(-ə)r\ *n*

¹**com·po·nent** \kəm-'pō-nənt, käm-; 'käm-,pō-nənt\ *n* : a part or element of something ⟨*components* of an electric circuit⟩ ⟨*components* of a meal⟩

²**component** *adj* : being or forming a part : CONSTITUENT

com·port \kəm-'pōrt, -'pȯrt\ *vb* **1** : to be in agreement : ACCORD ⟨acts that *comport* with ideals⟩ **2** : BEHAVE 1, CONDUCT ⟨*comport* yourself with dignity⟩

com·port·ment \kəm-'pōrt-mənt, -'pȯrt-\ *n* : BEHAVIOR 1, BEARING

com·pose \kəm-'pōz\ *vb* **com·posed; com·pos·ing** **1 a** : to form by putting together : FASHION **b** : to form the substance of : CONSTITUTE ⟨a stew *composed* of many ingredients⟩ **c** : to arrange type in order for printing : SET **2** : to create by mental or artistic labor ⟨*compose* a song⟩ **3** : to arrange in proper form **4** : ³QUIET, SETTLE ⟨try to *compose* your feelings⟩

com·posed \kəm-'pōzd\ *adj* : being calm and in control : SELF-POSSESSED — **com·pos·ed·ly** \-'pō-zəd-lē\ *adv*

com·pos·er \kəm-'pō-zər\ *n* : one that composes; *esp* : a person who writes music

¹**com·pos·ite** \käm-'päz-ət, kəm-\ *adj* **1** : made up of various parts or elements ⟨a *composite* photograph⟩ **2** : of or relating to a very large family of dicotyledonous plants (as a daisy or aster) that are characterized by flowers arranged in dense heads that resemble single flowers

²**composite** *n* **1** : something that is made up of different parts : COMPOUND **2** : a composite plant

composite number *n* : a whole number (as 4 or 6) that is a product of two or more whole numbers each greater than 1

com·po·si·tion \,käm-pə-'zish-ən\ *n* **1** : the act or process of composing **2** : the manner in which the parts of a thing are put together : MAKEUP ⟨the *composition* of a painting⟩ **3** : the elements of a compound ⟨the *composition* of rubber⟩ **4** : a product of combining ingredients : COMBINATION ⟨a *composition* made of several different metals⟩ **5** : a literary, musical, or artistic production; *esp* : a short piece of writing done as a school exercise

com·pos·i·tor \kəm-'päz-ət-ər\ *n* : one who arranges type for printing

com·post \'käm-,pōst\ *n* : a mixture largely of decayed organic matter used for fertilizing and conditioning land

com·po·sure \kəm-'pō-zhər\ *n* : calmness especially of mind, manner, or appearance ⟨she never loses her *composure*⟩

com·pote \'käm-,pōt\ *n* **1** : fruits cooked in syrup **2** : a bowl usually with a base and stem from which compotes, fruits, nuts, or sweets are served

¹com·pound \käm-'paůnd, kəm-; 'käm-,paůnd\ *vb* **1** : to put together or be joined to form a whole : COMBINE **2** : to form by combining parts ⟨*compound* a medicine⟩ **3** : to settle or adjust by agreement ⟨*compound* a debt⟩ **4** **a** : to pay in the form of compound interest ⟨interest *compounded* quarterly⟩ **b** : to add to ⟨*compounded* our errors⟩ [Middle English *compounen* "combine, compound", from early French *compondre* (same meaning), from Latin *componere* "compound, combine", from *com-* "with, together" and *ponere* "to place, put" — related to POSITION] — **com·pound·er** *n*

²com·pound \'käm-,paůnd; käm-'paůnd, kəm-\ *adj* **1** : made of or by the union of separate elements or parts ⟨a *compound* substance⟩ **2** : made up of two or more parts that are alike and form a common whole ⟨a *compound* fruit⟩ **3 a** : being a word that is a compound ⟨the *compound* noun "steamboat"⟩ **b** : consisting of two or more main clauses ⟨"I told him to leave and he left" is a *compound* sentence⟩

³com·pound \'käm-,paůnd\ *n* **1** : a word consisting of parts that are words ⟨"rowboat," "high school," and "light-year" are *compounds*⟩ **2** : something formed by a union of elements or parts; *esp* : a distinct substance formed by the union of two or more chemical elements in definite proportion by weight

⁴com·pound \'käm-,paůnd\ *n* : an enclosed area containing a group of buildings [from a word in Malay, the language of the people of the Malay peninsula, *kampong* "enclosure around a building"; both spelling and pronunciation influenced by the more familiar English word *compound*]

compound–complex *adj* : having two or more main clauses and one or more subordinate clauses ⟨*compound-complex* sentence⟩

compound eye *n* : an eye (as of an insect) made up of many separate visual units

compound fracture *n* : a breaking of a bone in such a way as to produce an open wound through which bone fragments stick out

compound interest *n* : interest paid or to be paid both on the principal and on accumulated unpaid interest

compound leaf *n* : a leaf in which the blade is divided to the middle several times forming two or more leaflets

compound microscope *n* : a microscope having an objective and an eyepiece in a tube that can be adjusted in length

compound leaf

com·pre·hend \,käm-pri-'hend\ *vb* **1** : to grasp the meaning of : UNDERSTAND **2** : INCLUDE — **com·pre·hend·ible** \-'hen-də-bəl\ *adj* — **com·pre·hen·si·bil·i·ty** \-,hen(t)-sə-'bil-ət-ē\ *n* — **com·pre·hen·si·ble** \-'hen(t)-sə-bəl\ *adj* — **com·pre·hen·si·bly** \-'hen(t)-sə-blē\ *adv*

com·pre·hen·sion \,käm-pri-'hen-chən\ *n* **1** : the act of comprehending **2** : knowledge gained by comprehending **3** : the capacity for understanding

com·pre·hen·sive \,käm-pri-'hen(t)-siv\ *adj* : including much or all : FULL ⟨a *comprehensive* course of study⟩ ⟨a *comprehensive* list⟩ ⟨*comprehensive* insurance⟩ — **com-**

pre·hen·sive·ness *n*

¹com·press \kəm-'pres\ *vb* **1** : to press or become pressed together **2** : to reduce the volume of by pressure — **com·press·ibil·i·ty** \-,pres-ə-'bil-ət-ē\ *n* — **com·press·ible** \-'pres-ə-bəl\ *adj*

²com·press \'käm-,pres\ *n* **1** : a folded cloth or pad applied so as to press upon a body part ⟨a cold *compress*⟩ **2** : a machine for compressing

com·pressed air \kəm-,prest-\ *n* : air under pressure greater than that of the atmosphere

com·pres·sion \kəm-'presh-ən\ *n* **1** : the act, process, or result of compressing : the state of being compressed **2** : the process of compressing the fuel mixture in the cylinders of an internal-combustion engine — **com·pres·sion·al** \-(ə-)nəl\ *adj*

com·pres·sor \kəm-'pres-ər\ *n* : a person or machine that compresses ⟨air *compressor*⟩

com·prise \kəm-'prīz\ *vb* **com·prised; com·pris·ing** **1** : to include within a scope : CONTAIN ⟨the party's program was *comprised* in its slogan⟩ **2** : to be made up of ⟨the play *comprises* three acts⟩ **3** : COMPOSE 1b, CONSTITUTE ⟨nine players *comprise* a baseball team⟩

¹com·pro·mise \'käm-prə-,mīz\ *n* **1** : a settlement of a dispute by each party giving up some demands **2** : giving up to something that is wrong or degrading : SURRENDER ⟨a *compromise* of one's principles⟩ **3** : the thing agreed upon as a result of a compromise

²compromise *vb* **-mised; -mis·ing** **1** : to adjust or settle differences by means of a compromise **2** : to expose to disgrace, suspicion, or danger ⟨*compromised* his reputation⟩ ⟨*compromise* national security⟩ — **com·pro·mis·er** *n*

comp·trol·ler \kən-'trō-lər, käm(p)-; 'käm(p)-,trō-lər\ *n* : a public official who examines financial accounts

com·pul·sion \kəm-'pəl-shən\ *n* **1** : an act of compelling : the state of being compelled **2** : a force that compels **3** : an irresistible urge ⟨felt a *compulsion* to say something⟩

com·pul·sive \kəm-'pəl-siv\ *adj* : caused by or subject to an irresistible urge ⟨*compulsive* behavior⟩ — **com·pul·sive·ly** *adv*

com·pul·so·ry \kəm-'pəls-(ə-)rē\ *adj* **1** : required by or as if by law ⟨*compulsory* education⟩ **2** : having the power of forcing someone to do something ⟨a *compulsory* law⟩

com·punc·tion \kəm-'pəŋ(k)-shən\ *n* **1** : sharp uneasiness caused by a sense of guilt : REMORSE **2** : a passing feeling of regret for some slight wrong **syn** see QUALM

com·pu·ta·tion \,käm-pyů-'tā-shən\ *n* **1** : the act or action of computing : CALCULATION **2** : a system of calculating especially by mathematical means **3** : an amount computed — **com·pu·ta·tion·al** \-shnəl, -shən-ᵊl\ *adj*

com·pute \kəm-'pyüt\ *vb* **com·put·ed; com·put·ing** : to determine or calculate especially by mathematical means; *also* : to determine or calculate by means of a computer [from Latin *computare* "to count, compute" — related to ACCOUNT, ¹COUNT] — **com·put·able** \-'pyüt-ə-bəl\ *adj*

com·put·er \-'pyüt-ər\ *n* : one that computes; *esp* : an automatic electronic machine that can store, get back again, and work with information to solve problems

com·put·er·ize \kəm-'pyüt-ə-,rīz\ *vb* **-ized; -iz·ing** **1** : to carry out, control, or produce through the use of a computer **2** : to provide with computers **3 a** : to store in a computer **b** : to put into a form that a computer can use

com·rade \'käm-,rad, -rəd\ *n* : a close friend or associate : COMPANION — **com·rade·ly** *adj* — **com·rade·ship** \-,ship\ *n*

\ə\ abut	\aů\ out	\i\ tip	\ò\ saw	\ů\ foot
\ər\ further	\ch\ chin	\ī\ life	\òi\ coin	\y\ yet
\a\ mat	\e\ pet	\j\ job	\th\ thin	\yü\ few
\ā\ take	\ē\ easy	\ŋ\ sing	\t͟h\ this	\yů\ cure
\ä\ cot, cart	\g\ go	\ō\ bone	\ü\ food	\zh\ vision

¹**con** \'kän\ *vb* **conned; con·ning** **1** : MEMORIZE **2** : to study carefully [Middle English *connen* "to know, learn", derived from *can* (auxiliary verb) "to know, know how to"]

²**con** *adv* : on the negative side : in opposition ⟨argue pro and *con*⟩ [Middle English *con* "on the negative side, against", a shortened form of *contra* "against, contrary"]

³**con** *n* : an opposing argument, person, or position ⟨the pros and *cons* of the question⟩

con- — see COM-

con·cat·e·nate \kän-'kat-ə-nāt, kən-\ *vb* **-nat·ed; -nat·ing** : to link together in a series or chain — **con·cat·e·na·tion** \(,)kän-,kat-ə-'nā-shən, kən-\ *n*

con·cave \kän-'kāv, 'kän-,kāv\ *adj* : hollowed or rounded inward like the inside of a bowl ⟨concave lens⟩ — **con·cav·i·ty** \kän-'kav-ət-ē\ *n*

con·ceal \kən-'sē(ə)l\ *vb* **1** : to hide from sight ⟨carry a *concealed* weapon⟩ **2** : to keep secret ⟨conceal a fact⟩ — **con·ceal·able** \-'sē-lə-bəl\ *adj*

con·ceal·ment \kən-'sē(ə)l-mənt\ *n* **1** : the act of hiding : the state of being hidden **2** : a hiding place ⟨attack from *concealment*⟩

con·cede \kən-'sēd\ *vb* **con·ced·ed; con·ced·ing** **1** : to grant as a right or privilege **2** : to admit the truth or existence of something ⟨concede defeat⟩ [from French *concéder* or Latin *concedere*, both meaning "to yield, grant, concede", from Latin *con-, com-* "together, with" and *cedere* "to go" — related to ANCESTOR, NECESSARY, PREDECESSOR, SUCCEED] — **con·ced·er** *n*

con·ceit \kən-'sēt\ *n* **1** : too much pride in one's own worth or virtue **2 a** : an idea showing imagination **b** : a complicated way of expressing something

con·ceit·ed \kən-'sēt-əd\ *adj* : having too high an opinion of oneself — **con·ceit·ed·ly** *adv* — **con·ceit·ed·ness** *n*

con·ceive \kən-'sēv\ *vb* **con·ceived; con·ceiv·ing** **1** : to become pregnant or pregnant with ⟨conceive a child⟩ **2 a** : to take into the mind ⟨conceived a liking for the singer⟩ **b** : to form an idea of : IMAGINE ⟨conceive a new system⟩ **3** : to have an opinion : THINK ⟨conceived of her as a genius⟩ — **con·ceiv·able** \-'sē-və-bəl\ *adj* — **con·ceiv·ably** \-blē\ *adv* — **con·ceiv·er** *n*

¹**con·cen·trate** \'kän(t)-sən-,trāt, -sen-\ *vb* **-trat·ed; -trat·ing** **1 a** : to bring, direct, or come toward or meet in a common center or objective **b** : to gather into one body, mass, or force **2** : to increase the amount of a substance in a space by removing other substances with which it is mixed or in which it is dissolved ⟨concentrate syrup⟩ ⟨concentrate ore⟩ **3** : to fix one's powers, efforts, or attention on one thing ⟨concentrate on a problem⟩ — **con·cen·tra·tor** \-,trāt-ər\ *n*

²**concentrate** *n* : something concentrated ⟨frozen orange juice *concentrate*⟩

con·cen·tra·tion \,kän(t)-sən-'trā-shən, -sen-\ *n* **1** : the act or process of concentrating : the state of being concentrated; *esp* : direction of attention on a single object ⟨don't disturb my *concentration*⟩ **2** : a concentrated mass **3** : the amount of an ingredient or part in relation to that of others : STRENGTH ⟨the *concentration* of salt in a solution⟩

concentration camp *n* : a camp where persons (as prisoners of war, political prisoners, or refugees) are detained

con·cen·tric \kən-'sen-trik, (')kän-\ *adj* : having a common center ⟨concentric circles⟩

con·cept \'kän-,sept\ *n* **1** : something conceived in the mind : THOUGHT, NOTION **2** : a general idea ⟨arrive at the *concept* of a flower by studying many different kinds of flowers⟩ — **con·cep·tu·al** \kən-'sep-chə(-wə)l, -'sepsh-wəl\ *adj*

con·cep·tion \kən-'sep-shən\ *n* **1 a** : the beginning of pregnancy **b** : formation of a zygote **2 a** : the function or process of conceiving ideas **b** : a general idea : CONCEPT ⟨had no *conception* of what he was saying⟩ **3** : the originating of an idea ⟨conception of a new device⟩

¹**con·cern** \kən-'sərn\ *vb* **1** : to relate to : be about ⟨the novel *concerns* three soldiers⟩ **2** : to be the business or affair of ⟨the problem *concerns* us all⟩ **3** : to make worried or disturbed ⟨our mother's illness *concerns* us⟩ **4** : INVOLVE 1, ENGAGE ⟨concerned himself in the matter⟩

²**concern** *n* **1** : something that concerns one : AFFAIR ⟨the *concerns* of the day⟩ **2** : a state of interest and uncertainty : ANXIETY ⟨deep *concern* for their friend's health⟩ ⟨public *concern* over pollution⟩ **3** : a business or manufacturing establishment ⟨a banking *concern*⟩

con·cerned \kən-'sərnd\ *adj* : being worried and disturbed ⟨concerned for our safety⟩

con·cern·ing \kən-'sər-niŋ\ *prep* : relating to : ABOUT ⟨news *concerning* friends⟩

¹**con·cert** \'kän(t)-sərt, 'kän-,sərt\ *n* **1** : agreement in design or plan **2** : a musical performance usually by several voices or instruments or both — **in concert** : TOGETHER 4a

²**con·cert** \kən-'sərt\ *vb* : to plan or arrange together : settle by agreement

con·cert·ed \kən-'sərt-əd\ *adj* **1 a** : mutually planned or agreed on ⟨concerted effort⟩ **b** : performed at the same time ⟨concerted artillery fire⟩ **2** : being music written to be performed by several voices or instruments

con·cer·ti·na \,kän(t)-sər-'tē-nə\ *n* : a small musical instrument resembling an accordion

con·cert·mas·ter \'kän(t)-sərt-,mas-tər\ *or* **con·cert·meis·ter** \-,mī-stər\ *n* : the leader of the first violins and assistant conductor of an orchestra

concertina

con·cer·to \kən-'chert-ō\ *n, pl* **-ti** \-(,)ē\ *or* **-tos** : a piece for one or more soloists and orchestra usually in three movements

con·ces·sion \kən-'sesh-ən\ *n* **1** : the act or an instance of conceding **2** : something conceded or granted **3** : a special right or privilege given by an authority ⟨a *concession* to sell souvenirs⟩ ⟨a mining *concession*⟩

con·ces·sion·aire \kən-,sesh-ə-'na(ə)r, -'ne(ə)r\ *n* : one that has been given a concession (as to sell something)

conch \'käŋk, 'känch\ *n, pl* **conchs** \'käŋks\ *or* **conch·es** \'kän-chəz\ : a large marine gastropod mollusk having a spiral shell; *also* : its shell

con·cil·i·ate \kən-'sil-ē-,āt\ *vb* **-at·ed; -at·ing** **1** : to bring into agreement : RECONCILE **2** : to gain the goodwill or favor of ⟨conciliate the opposition⟩ — **con·cil·i·a·tion** \-,sil-ē-'ā-shən\ *n* — **con·cil·i·a·tor** \-'sil-ē-,āt-ər\ *n* — **con·cil·i·a·to·ry** \-'sil-yə-,tōr-ē, -'sil-ē-ə-, -,tōr-\ *adj*

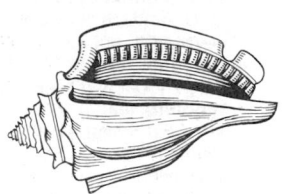
conch

con·cise \kən-'sīs\ *adj* : being brief and to the point ⟨a *concise* review of the year's work⟩ — **con·cise·ly** *adv* — **con·cise·ness** *n*

con·clave \'kän-,klāv\ *n* : a private or secret meeting or assembly

con·clude \kən-'klüd\ *vb* **con·clud·ed; con·clud·ing** **1** : to bring or come to an end : FINISH ⟨conclude a speech⟩ **2** : to form an opinion : decide by reasoning ⟨conclude that they are right⟩ **3** : to bring about as a result : ARRANGE ⟨conclude an agreement⟩ — **con·clud·er** *n*

con·clu·sion \kən-'klü-zhən\ *n* **1** : a final decision reached by reasoning ⟨came to the *conclusion* that we couldn't go⟩ **2 a** : the last part of something : END **b** : a final result : OUTCOME **c** : a final summing up ⟨the *conclusion* of a speech⟩ **3** : an act or instance of concluding

con·clu·sive \kən-'klü-siv, -ziv\ *adj* : DECISIVE 1, CONVINC-ING 〈*conclusive* proof〉 — **con·clu·sive·ly** *adv* — **con·clu·sive·ness** *n*

con·coct \kən-'käkt, kän-\ *vb* **1** : to prepare by combining various ingredients 〈*concoct* a stew〉 **2** : to think up : IN-VENT 〈*concoct* a likely story〉 — **con·coc·tion** \-'käk-shən\ *n*

con·com·i·tant \kən-'käm-ət-ənt, kän-\ *adj* : accompany-ing especially as something of less importance — **con-comitant** *n* — **con·com·i·tant·ly** *adv*

con·cord \'kän-kò(ə)rd, 'kän-\ *n* : a state of agreement : HARMONY

con·cord·ance \kən-'kòrd-ᵊn(t)s, kän-\ *n* **1** : an alphabet-ical index of the principal words in a book or in the works of an author **2** : CONCORD

con·cord·ant \kən-'kòrd-ᵊnt\ *adj* : being in agreement : CONSONANT — **con·cord·ant·ly** *adv*

con·course \'kän-kō(ə)rs, 'kän-, -kò(ə)rs\ *n* **1** : a flocking, moving, or flowing together : GATHERING **2** : a place (as a boulevard, open area, or hall) where many people pass or gather 〈the *concourse* of the bus terminal〉

¹con·crete \(')kän-'krēt, kən-; 'kän-,krēt\ *adj* **1** : naming a real thing or class of things : not abstract 〈"book" is a *concrete* noun but "goodness" is not〉 **2 a** : belonging to or based on actual experience 〈*concrete* examples〉 **b** : ¹MA-TERIAL, REAL 〈*concrete* evidence〉 **3** \'kän-,krēt, kän-'krēt\ : relating to or made of concrete 〈a *concrete* wall〉 — **con·crete·ly** *adv* — **con·crete·ness** *n*

²con·crete \'kän-,krēt, (')kän-'krēt\ *vb* **con·cret·ed; con-cret·ing** **1** : SOLIDIFY **2** : to cover with, form of, or set in concrete

³con·crete \'kän-,krēt, (')kän-'krēt\ *n* : a hard strong build-ing material made by mixing cement, sand, and gravel or broken rock with water

con·cre·tion \kän-'krē-shən, kən-\ *n* **1** : a hard usually inorganic mass formed in a living body **2** : a lump or egg-shaped mass of mineral matter found in rock of different composition

con·cu·bine \'käŋ-kyù-,bīn, 'kän-\ *n* : a woman who lives with a man and among some peoples has a legally recog-nized position in his household less than that of a wife

con·cur \kən-'kər, kän-\ *vb* **con·curred; con·cur·ring** **1** : to happen together : COINCIDE **2** : to act together : COM-BINE 〈several events *concurred* to mark the occasion as special〉 **3** : to be in agreement : ACCORD 〈*concur* with an opinion〉

con·cur·rence \kən-'kər-ən(t)s, -'kə-rən(t)s, kän-\ *n* **1** : agreement in action, opinion, or intent : COOPERATION **2** : ²CONSENT **3** : a coming together : CONJUNCTION

con·cur·rent \kən-'kər-ənt, -'kə-rənt, kän-\ *adj* **1** : oper-ating or occurring at the same time 〈*concurrent* expedi-tions to the Antarctic region〉 **2** : coming together : meet-ing in a point 〈*concurrent* lines〉 **3** : acting together — **con·cur·rent·ly** *adv*

con·cus·sion \kən-'kəsh-ən\ *n* **1** : a violent uneven mo-tion **2** : a hard blow or collision **3** : bodily injury espe-cially of the brain resulting from a sudden sharp jar (as from a blow) — **con·cus·sive** \-'kəs-iv\ *adj*

con·demn \kən-'dem\ *vb* **1** : to declare to be wrong : CEN-SURE 〈*condemned* their behavior〉 **2 a** : to pronounce guilty : CONVICT **b** : ²SENTENCE 1 **3** : to declare to be unfit for use or consumption 〈a *condemned* building〉 — **con·dem·na·tion** \,kän-,dem-'nā-shən, -dəm-\ *n* — **con-demn·er** *or* **con·demn·or** \kən-'dem-ər\ *n*

con·den·sate \'kän-dən-,sāt, -,den-; kən-'den-\ *n* : a prod-uct of condensation 〈steam *condensate*〉

con·den·sa·tion \,kän-,den-'sā-shən, -dən-\ *n* **1** : the act or process of condensing **2** : the quality or state of being condensed **3** : a product of condensing; *esp* : a short-ened literary work

con·dense \kən-'den(t)s\ *vb* **con·densed; con·dens·ing** **1** : to make or become more close, compact, concise, or

dense : CONCENTRATE 〈*condense* a paragraph into a sen-tence〉 **2** : to change from a less dense to a denser form 〈steam *condenses* into water〉

con·densed milk \kən-'den(t)st-\ *n* : evaporated milk with sugar added

con·dens·er \kən-'den(t)-sər\ *n* **1** : one that condenses **2** : CAPACITOR

con·de·scend \,kän-di-'send\ *vb* **1** : to stoop to a level considered less dignified or humbler than one's own **2** : to act in a way that suggests that one considers oneself better than other people — **con·de·scend·ing·ly** \-'sen-diŋ-lē\ *adv*

con·de·scen·sion \,kän-di-'sen-chən\ *n* : the attitude or behavior of a person who condescends

con·di·ment \'kän-də-mənt\ *n* : something used to give food a good taste; *esp* : a tangy seasoning

¹con·di·tion \kən-'dish-ən\ *n* **1** : something on which the carrying out of an agreement depends 〈*conditions* of em-ployment〉 **2** : something essential to the appearance or occurrence of something else **3** : something that limits or restricts : QUALIFICATION **4 a** : a state of being **b** : posi-tion in life 〈people of humble *condition*〉 **c** *pl* : state of affairs **5 a** : a bodily state in which something is wrong 〈a serious heart *condition*〉 **b** : a state of health or fitness 〈an athlete in good *condition*〉

²condition *vb* **-di·tioned; -di·tion·ing** \-'dish-(ə-)niŋ\ **1** : to put into a proper or desired condition **2 a** : to adapt, modify, or mold to respond in a particular way **b** : to change the behavior of (an organism) in such a way that a response to a given stimulus becomes connected with a different and formerly unrelated stimulus 〈dogs can be *conditioned* to salivate at the sound of a bell〉 — **con·di-tion·er** \-'dish-(ə-)nər\ *n*

con·di·tion·al \kən-'dish-nəl, -ən-ᵊl\ *adj* **1** : depending on a condition 〈a *conditional* sale〉 **2** : expressing, contain-ing, or implying something supposed 〈"if we go" is a *con-ditional* clause〉 — **con·di·tion·al·ly** \-nə-lē, -ən-ᵊl-ē\ *adv*

con·di·tioned \kən-'dish-ənd\ *adj* : caused or established by conditioning 〈a *conditioned* response to a stimulus〉

con·dole \kən-'dōl\ *vb* **con·doled; con·dol·ing** : to ex-press sympathetic sorrow 〈*condole* with them in their grief〉 — **con·do·lence** \kən-'dō-lən(t)s, 'kän-də-\ *n*

con·dom \'kən-dəm, 'kän-\ *n* : a flexible sheath worn over the penis during sexual intercourse especially to prevent pregnancy or venereal disease — called also *rubber*

con·do·min·i·um \,kän-də-'min-ē-əm\ *n* : an individually owned unit in a structure (as an apartment building) with many units [derived from Latin *condominium* "joint rule or ownership", from earlier *con-*, *com-* "together" and *domi-nium* "ownership, rule", from *dominus* "master, owner" — related to DOMAIN, DOMINATE]

con·done \kən-'dōn\ *vb* **con·doned; con·don-ing** : to pardon or overlook voluntarily 〈*condones* his friend's faults〉 **syn** see EXCUSE — **con·do·na-tion** \,kän-də-'nā-shən, -dō-\ *n* — **con·don·er** \kən-'dō-nər\ *n*

con·dor \'kän-dər, -,dò(ə)r\ *n* **1** : a very large South American vulture of the high Andes having the head and neck bare and

condor 1

the plumage dull black with a ring of white down behind the head **2** : CALIFORNIA CONDOR

con·duce \kən-'d(y)üs\ *vb* **con·duced; con·duc·ing** : to lead or tend to a usually desirable result — **con·du·cive** \-'d(y)ü-siv\ *adj* — **con·du·cive·ness** *n*

¹con·duct \'kän-(,)dəkt\ *n* **1** : the act, manner, or process of carrying on : MANAGEMENT ⟨the *conduct* of foreign affairs⟩ **2** : personal behavior ⟨scolded for bad *conduct*⟩

²con·duct \kən-'dəkt\ *vb* **1** : ²GUIDE 1, ESCORT **2** : to carry on or direct from a position of command : LEAD ⟨*conduct* a business⟩ ⟨*conduct* a band⟩ **3 a** : to carry in a channel **b** : to act as a substance through which something is carried ⟨copper *conducts* electricity⟩ **4** : to cause (oneself) to act in a particular manner ⟨*conducted* themselves well at the party⟩

con·duc·tance \kən-'dək-tən(t)s\ *n* **1** : conducting power **2** : the readiness with which a conductor carries an electric current : the reciprocal of electrical resistance

con·duc·tion \kən-'dək-shən\ *n* **1** : the act of conducting or conveying **2 a** : passage through a conductor **b** : CONDUCTIVITY **3** : the passage of a reaction to a stimulus through living and especially nerve tissue

con·duc·tive \kən-'dək-tiv\ *adj* : having conductivity : relating to conduction (as of electricity)

con·duc·tiv·i·ty \,kän-,dək-'tiv-ət-ē, kən-\ *n, pl* **-ties** : the quality or power of conducting or transmitting

con·duc·tor \kən-'dək-tər\ *n* **1** : a person who collects fares in a public means of transportation (as a bus or railroad train) **2** : the leader of a musical group **3** : a substance or body that can allow electricity, heat, or sound to pass through it

con·duit \'kän-,d(y)ü-ət *also* -d(w)ət\ *n* **1** : a channel through which water or other fluid is carried **2** : a pipe, tube, or tile for protecting electric wires or cables

cone \'kōn\ *n* **1** : a mass of overlapping woody scales that especially in the pine and related trees are arranged on a structure like a stem and produce seeds between them; *also* : any of several flower or fruit clusters resembling such cones **2 a** : a solid figure formed by rotating a right triangle about one of its legs — called also *right circular cone* **b** : a solid figure that slopes evenly to a point from a usually circular base **3** : something shaped like a cone: as **a** : a sense organ of the retina that functions in color vision **b** : the tip of a volcano **c** : ICE-CREAM CONE

Con·es·to·ga \,kän-ə-'stō-gə\ *n* : a broad-wheeled covered wagon formerly used to carry freight across the prairies — called also *Conestoga wagon* [named for *Conestoga,* town in Pennsylvania where the wagons were first made]

Conestoga

co·ney *or* **cony** \'kō-nē\ *n* **1 a** : RABBIT; *esp* : the common European rabbit **b** : rabbit fur **2** : PIKA

con·fec·tion \kən-'fek-shən\ *n* : a fancy dish or sweet [Middle English *confectioun* "mixture, candy", from early French *confection* "mixture", derived from Latin *confectus,* past participle of *conficere* "to prepare", from *con-, com-* "together" and *-ficere,* from *facere* "to make, do" — related to FASHION]

con·fec·tion·er \kən-'fek-sh(ə-)nər\ *n* : a manufacturer of or dealer in confections

confectioners' sugar *n* : finely powdered sugar

con·fec·tion·ery \kən-'fek-shə-,ner-ē\ *n, pl* **-er·ies** **1** : sweet things to eat (as candy) **2** : a confectioner's art or business **3** : a confectioner's shop

con·fed·er·a·cy \kən-'fed-(ə-)rə-sē\ *n, pl* **-cies** **1** : a league of persons, parties, or states : ALLIANCE **2** *cap*

: the Confederate States of America made up of the 11 southern states that seceded from the U.S. in 1860 and 1861

¹con·fed·er·ate \kən-'fed-(ə-)rət\ *adj* **1** : united in a league : ALLIED **2** *cap* : of or relating to the Confederate States of America ⟨*Confederate* money⟩

²confederate *n* **1** : ²ALLY 2a, ACCOMPLICE **2** *cap* : a soldier, citizen, or supporter of the Confederate States of America

³con·fed·er·ate \kən-'fed-ə-,rāt\ *vb* **-at·ed; -at·ing** : to unite in a confederacy

Confederate Memorial Day *n* : any of several days observed in the South in honor of the soldiers of the Confederacy

con·fed·er·a·tion \kən-,fed-ə-'rā-shən\ *n* **1** : an act of confederating : a state of being confederated : ALLIANCE **2** : ²LEAGUE

con·fer \kən-'fər\ *vb* **con·ferred; con·fer·ring** **1** : to give or grant publicly ⟨*confer* knighthood on him⟩ **2** : to compare views especially in studying a problem ⟨*confer* with the committee⟩ — **con·fer·ral** \-'fər-əl\ *n* — **con·fer·rer** \-'fər-ər\ *n*

con·fer·ee \,kän-fə-'rē\ *n* : one taking part in a conference

con·fer·ence \'kän-f(ə-)rən(t)s, -fərn(t)s\ *n* **1** : a meeting for discussion or exchange of opinions; *also* : the discussion itself **2** : a meeting of members of the two branches of a legislature to settle differences **3** : an association of athletic teams ⟨a football *conference*⟩

con·fess \kən-'fes\ *vb* **1** : to make known (as something wrong) **2 a** : to admit one's sins to God or to a priest **b** : to hear the confession of ⟨the priest *confessed* the penitents⟩ **syn** see ACKNOWLEDGE

con·fessed·ly \kən-'fes-əd-lē, -'fest-lē\ *adv* : by confession : ADMITTEDLY

con·fes·sion \kən-'fesh-ən\ *n* **1** : an act of confessing; *esp* : a telling of one's sins to a priest **2** : a statement admitting guilt ⟨the thief signed a *confession*⟩ **3** : a formal statement of religious beliefs : CREED

con·fes·sion·al \kən-'fesh-(ə-)nəl\ *n* **1** : the enclosed place in which a priest sits and hears confessions **2** : the practice of confessing to a priest

con·fes·sor \kən-'fes-ər\ *n* **1** : one that confesses **2** : a priest who hears confessions

con·fet·ti \kən-'fet-ē\ *n* : small bits of brightly colored paper made for throwing (as at weddings) [from Italian *confetti,* plural of *confetto* "a little candy or bonbon"; so named because the paper bits were originally imitations of the candies thrown at festivals]

con·fi·dant \'kän-fə-,dant, -,dänt\ *n* : a person to whom secrets are entrusted : a close friend

con·fi·dante \'kän-fə-,dant, -,dänt\ *n* : a female confidant

con·fide \kən-'fīd\ *vb* **con·fid·ed; con·fid·ing** **1** : to have confidence : TRUST ⟨*confide* in a doctor's skill⟩ **2** : to show confidence by telling secrets ⟨*confided* in her mother⟩ **3** : to tell in confidence ⟨*confide* a secret to a friend⟩ **4** : ENTRUST 1 ⟨*confide* one's safety to the police⟩ [Middle English *confiden* "to confide, trust", from early French *confider* or Latin *confidere* (both, same meaning), from Latin *con-, com-* "with, together" and *fidere* "to trust" — related to FAITH] — **con·fid·er** *n*

con·fi·dence \'kän-fəd-ən(t)s, -fə-,den(t)s\ *n* **1** : a feeling of trust or belief ⟨had *confidence* in our coach⟩ **2** : a feeling of certainty : ASSURANCE ⟨spoke with great *confidence*⟩ **3 a** : reliance on another's secrecy or loyalty ⟨told us in *confidence*⟩ **b** : legislative support ⟨vote of *confidence*⟩ **4** : something told in confidence : SECRET

confidence game *n* : a swindle in which the swindler takes advantage of the confidence or trust the victim has been persuaded to place in him or her

confidence man *n* : a swindler in a confidence game

con·fi·dent \'kän-fəd-ənt, -fə-,dent\ *adj* : having or showing confidence : SURE, SELF-ASSURED ⟨*confident* of winning⟩ ⟨a *confident* manner⟩ — **con·fi·dent·ly** *adv*

con·fi·den·tial \ˌkän-fə-'den-chəl\ *adj* **1** : [1]SECRET 1a, PRIVATE ⟨*confidential* information⟩ **2** : indicating or suggesting closeness : INTIMATE ⟨a *confidential* tone of voice⟩ **3** : trusted with secret matters ⟨a *confidential* secretary⟩ — **con·fi·den·tial·ly** \-'dench-(ə-)lē\ *adv*

con·fid·ing \kən-'fīd-iŋ\ *adj* : tending to confide : TRUSTFUL — **con·fid·ing·ly** \-iŋ-lē\ *adv*

co·fig·u·ra·tion \kən-ˌfig-(y)ə-'rā-shən, kän-\ *n* : arrangement of parts or the pattern produced by such arrangement

con·fig·ure \kən-'fig-yər\ *vb* **-ured; -ur·ing** : to set up for operation especially in a particular way ⟨ships *configured* for observation⟩

con·fine \kən-'fīn\ *vb* **con·fined; con·fin·ing** **1** : to keep within limits : RESTRICT ⟨*confined* the message to twenty words⟩ **2 a** : to shut up : IMPRISON ⟨*confined* for life⟩ **b** : to keep indoors ⟨*confined* with a cold⟩ — **con·fine·ment** \kən-'fīn-mənt\ *n* — **con·fin·er** *n*

con·fines \'kän-ˌfīnz\ *n pl* : the boundary or limits of something ⟨within the *confines* of the city⟩

con·firm \kən-'fərm\ *vb* **1** : to make firm or firmer (as in a habit, faith, or intention) : STRENGTHEN **2** : APPROVE 2, RATIFY ⟨*confirm* a treaty⟩ **3** : to administer confirmation to **4** : to make sure of the truth of : VERIFY ⟨*confirm* a suspicion⟩ — **con·firm·able** \-'fər-mə-bəl\ *adj*

con·fir·ma·tion \ˌkän-fər-'mā-shən\ *n* **1** : an act or process of confirming **2** : a religious ceremony admitting a person to full privileges in a church or synagogue **3** : something that confirms : PROOF — **con·firm·a·to·ry** \kən-'fər-mə-ˌtōr-ē, -ˌtȯr-\ *adj*

con·firmed \kən-'fərmd\ *adj* **1** : made firm or strong **2** : deeply established ⟨a *confirmed* distrust of change⟩ **3** : unlikely to change : HABITUAL, CHRONIC ⟨a *confirmed* optimist⟩

con·fis·cate \'kän-fə-ˌskāt\ *vb* **-cat·ed; -cat·ing** : to seize by or as if by public authority ⟨smuggled goods may be *confiscated* by the police⟩ — **con·fis·ca·tion** \ˌkän-fə-'skā-shən\ *n* — **con·fis·ca·tor** \'kän-fə-ˌskāt-ər\ *n* — **con·fis·ca·to·ry** \kən-'fis-kə-ˌtōr-ē, -ˌtȯr-\ *adj*

con·fla·gra·tion \ˌkän-flə-'grā-shən\ *n* : a large disastrous fire

[1]con·flict \'kän-ˌflikt\ *n* **1** : an extended struggle : FIGHT, BATTLE **2** : a clashing or sharp disagreement (as between ideas, interests, or purposes)

[2]con·flict \kən-'flikt, 'kän-ˌflikt\ *vb* : to be in opposition : CLASH ⟨duty and desire often *conflict*⟩

con·flu·ence \'kän-ˌflü-ən(t)s, kən-'flü-\ *n* **1** : a coming together to one place **2** : a flowing together or place of meeting especially of streams

con·flu·ent \'kän-ˌflü-ənt, kən-'flü-\ *adj* : flowing or coming together ⟨*confluent* rivers⟩

con·form \kən-'fȯ(ə)rm\ *vb* **1** : to bring into harmony ⟨*conform* my behavior to the circumstances⟩ **2** : to be similar or identical ⟨the data *conform* to the pattern⟩ **3** : to act in obedience or agreement; *esp* : to adapt oneself to accepted standards or customs — **con·form·er** *n* — **con·form·ist** \-'fȯr-məst\ *n*

con·form·able \kən-'fȯr-mə-bəl\ *adj* **1** : similar in form or character ⟨*conformable* to established practice⟩ **2** : SUBMISSIVE, COMPLIANT — **con·form·ably** \-blē\ *adv*

con·for·mal \kən-'fȯr-məl, (')kän-\ *adj* : representing small areas in their true shape ⟨a *conformal* map⟩

con·for·ma·tion \ˌkän-(ˌ)fȯr-'mā-shən, -fər-\ *n* **1** : the act of conforming or producing conformity : ADAPTATION **2** : a shaping or putting into form **3 a** : [1]STRUCTURE 3 **b** : the form or outline especially of an animal

con·for·mi·ty \kən-'fȯr-mət-ē\ *n pl* **-ties** **1** : agreement in form, manner, or character ⟨behaved in *conformity* with their beliefs⟩ **2** : action in accordance with a standard or authority : OBEDIENCE ⟨*conformity* to social custom⟩

con·found \kən-'faund, kän-\ *vb* **1** : [1]DAMN 1 **2** : to throw into disorder : mix up : CONFUSE ⟨our clever tactics *confounded* our opponents⟩ — **con·found·ed·ly** *adv*

con·front \kən-'frənt\ *vb* **1** : to face especially in challenge : OPPOSE ⟨*confront* an enemy⟩ **2** : to bring face-to-face : cause to meet ⟨*confront* them with their accusers⟩ ⟨*confronted* with difficulties⟩ — **con·fron·ta·tion** \ˌkän-(ˌ)frən-'tā-shən\ *n*

Con·fu·cian \kən-'fyü-shən\ *adj* : of or relating to the Chinese philosopher Confucius or his teachings or followers — **Confucian** *n* — **Con·fu·cian·ism** \-shə-ˌniz-əm\ *n* — **Con·fu·cian·ist** \-shə-nəst\ *n or adj*

con·fuse \kən-'fyüz\ *vb* **con·fused; con·fus·ing** **1 a** : to make mentally foggy or uncertain : PERPLEX ⟨a complicated problem *confuses* us⟩ **b** : to cause to be embarrassed or upset : DISCONCERT **2** : to make unclear : BLUR ⟨stop *confusing* the issue⟩ **3** : to make disordered : JUMBLE ⟨his motives were hopelessly *confused*⟩ **4** : to fail to tell apart ⟨teachers always *confused* the twins⟩ — **con·fused·ly** \-'fyüz-(ə)d-lē\ *adv* — **con·fus·ing·ly** \-'fyü-ziŋ-lē\ *adv*

con·fu·sion \kən-'fyü-zhən\ *n* **1** : an act or instance of confusing **2** : the quality or state of being confused ⟨her *confusion* was obvious⟩

con·fute \kən-'fyüt\ *vb* **con·fut·ed; con·fut·ing** : to overwhelm in argument : REFUTE — **con·fu·ta·tion** \ˌkän-fyü-'tā-shən\ *n*

con·ga \'käŋ-gə\ *n* : a Cuban dance of African origin performed by a group usually in single file

con game \'kän-\ *n* : CONFIDENCE GAME

con·geal \kən-'jē(ə)l\ *vb* **1** : to change from a fluid to a solid state by or as if by cold **2** : to make or become stiff, thick, or lumpy : COAGULATE

con·ge·nial \kən-'jē-nyəl\ *adj* **1** : having the same disposition, interests, or tastes **2** : suited to one's nature or tastes : AGREEABLE — **con·ge·ni·al·i·ty** \-ˌjē-nē-'al-ət-ē, -ˌjēn-'yal-\ *n* — **con·ge·nial·ly** \-'jē-nyə-lē\ *adv*

con·gen·i·tal \kən-'jen-ə-tᵊl\ *adj* : existing at or dating from birth but usually not inherited ⟨*congenital* disease⟩

con·gest \kən-'jest\ *vb* **1** : to cause an excessive fullness of the blood vessels of (as an organ) **2** : to block by filling too full : CLOG, OVERCROWD ⟨*congested* streets⟩ — **con·ges·tion** \-'jes-chən, -'jesh-\ *n*

con·ges·tive heart failure \kən-'jes-tiv-\ *n* : heart failure in which the heart is unable to keep enough blood circulating in the tissues or is unable to pump out the blood returned to it by the veins

[1]con·glom·er·ate \kən-'gläm-(ə-)rət\ *adj* : made up of parts from various sources or of various kinds

[2]con·glom·er·ate \kən-'gläm-ə-ˌrāt\ *vb* **-at·ed; -at·ing** : to collect or form into a mass — **con·glom·er·a·tion** \-ˌgläm-ə-'rā-shən, kän-\ *n*

[3]con·glom·er·ate \kən-'gläm-(ə-)rət\ *n* **1** : a composite mass or mixture; *esp* : rock made up of rounded pieces varying from small pebbles to large boulders in a cement (as of hardened clay) **2** : a corporation engaging in many different kinds of business

Con·go red \ˌkäŋ-ˌgō-\ *n* : a dye that is red in alkaline and blue in acid solution [named for *Congo*, territory in Africa]

con·grat·u·late \kən-'grach-ə-ˌlāt\ *vb* **-lat·ed; -lat·ing** : to express pleasure to on account of success or good fortune ⟨*congratulate* the winner⟩ [from Latin *congratulatus* "has wished joy", derived from Latin *con-*, *com-* "with, together" and *gratulari* "to wish joy", from *gratus* "pleasing, agreeable, thankful" — related to GRACE, GRATITUDE]

con·grat·u·la·tion \kən-ˌgrach-ə-'lā-shən\ *n* **1** : the act of congratulating **2** : an expression of joy or pleasure at

\ə\	abut	\au̇\	out	\i\	tip	\ȯ\	saw	\u̇\	foot
\ər\	further	\ch\	chin	\ī\	life	\ȯi\	coin	\y\	yet
\a\	mat	\e\	pet	\j\	job	\th\	thin	\yü\	few
\ā\	take	\ē\	easy	\ŋ\	sing	\th\	this	\yu̇\	cure
\ä\	cot, cart	\g\	go	\ō\	bone	\ü\	food	\zh\	vision

another's success or good fortune — usually used in pl.

con·grat·u·la·to·ry \kən-'grach-(ə-)lə-ˌtōr-ē, -ˌtȯr-\ *adj* : expressing congratulations

con·gre·gate \'käŋ-gri-ˌgät\ *vb* **-gat·ed; -gat·ing** : to come together into a group or crowd [Middle English *congregaten* "to collect or assemble together", derived from Latin *congregare* "to assemble, gather", from *con-, com-* "with, together" and *gregare* "to gather into a flock or herd", from *greg-, grex* "flock, herd" — related to AGGREGATE, GREGARIOUS, SEGREGATE] **syn** see GATHER — **con·gre·ga·tor** \-ˌgāt-ər\ *n*

con·gre·ga·tion \ˌkäŋ-gri-'gā-shən\ *n* **1** : a gathering or collection of persons or things **2 a** : an assembly of persons gathered especially for religious worship **b** : the members of a church or synagogue

con·gre·ga·tion·al \ˌkäŋ-gri-'gā-shnəl, -shən-əl\ *adj* **1** : of or relating to a congregation **2** : of or relating to church government placing final authority in the local congregation — **con·gre·ga·tion·al·ism** \-shnə-ˌliz-əm, -shən-əl-iz-əm\ *n, often cap* — **con·gre·ga·tion·al·ist** \-shnə-ləst, -shən-əl-əst\ *n or adj, often cap*

con·gress \'käŋ-grəs\ *n* **1** : a formal meeting of delegates for discussion and action **2** : the chief lawmaking body of a nation and especially of a republic that in the U.S. is made up of the Senate and the House of Representatives **3** : an association of organizations having a common interest — **con·gres·sion·al** \kən-'gresh-nəl, -ən-əl\ *adj* — **con·gres·sion·al·ly** \-ē\ *adv*

con·gress·man \'käŋ-grəs-mən\ *n* : a member of a congress; *esp* : a member of the U.S. House of Representatives

con·gress·wom·an \-ˌwùm-ən\ *n* : a woman member of a congress; *esp* : a woman member of the U.S. House of Representatives

con·gru·ence \kən-'grü-ən(t)s, 'käŋ-grə-wən(t)s\ *n* : the quality or state of having the same size and shape

con·gru·en·cy \kən-'grü-ən-sē, 'käŋ-grə-wən-sē\ *n* : CONGRUENCE

con·gru·ent \kən-'grü-ənt, 'käŋ-grə-wənt\ *adj* : capable of being placed over another figure so that all points of the one correspond to all points of the other : having the same size and shape ⟨*congruent* triangles⟩ — **con·gru·ent·ly** *adv*

con·gru·ity \kən-'grü-ət-ē, kän-\ *n, pl* **-ities** **1** : the quality or state of being congruous : AGREEMENT **2** : a point of agreement

con·gru·ous \'käŋ-grə-wəs\ *adj* **1** : being in agreement or harmony **2** : SUITABLE 2, APPROPRIATE — **con·gru·ous·ly** *adv*

con·ic \'kän-ik\ *adj* : of, relating to, or shaped like a cone

con·i·cal \'kän-i-kəl\ *adj* : shaped like a cone ⟨a *conical* cap⟩ — **con·i·cal·ly** \-i-k(ə-)lē\ *adv*

conic section *n* : a curve formed by the intersection of a plane and a cone

con·i·fer \'kän-ə-fər *also* 'kō-nə-\ *n* : any of an order of mostly evergreen trees and shrubs including forms (as pines) with true cones

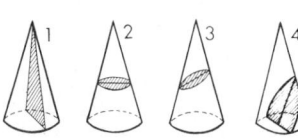

conic section: *1* straight lines, *2* circle, *3* ellipse, *4* parabola

co·nif·er·ous \kō-'nif-(ə-)rəs, kə-\ *adj* **1** : producing cones ⟨*coniferous* trees⟩ **2** : of, relating to, or composed of conifers ⟨*coniferous* wood⟩ ⟨a *coniferous* forest⟩

con·jec·tur·al \kən-'jek-chə-rəl, -'jeksh-rəl\ *adj* : being, involving, or based on conjecture — **con·jec·tur·al·ly** \-rə-lē\ *adv*

¹con·jec·ture \kən-'jek-chər\ *n* : an opinion or judgment based on little or no evidence

²conjecture *vb* **-jec·tured; -jec·tur·ing** \-'jek-chə-riŋ, -'jek-shriŋ\ : GUESS 1 — **con·jec·tur·er** \-'jek-chər-ər\ *n*

con·join \kən-'jȯin, kän-\ *vb* : to join together for a common purpose

con·joint \kən-'jȯint, kän-\ *adj* : made up of or carried on by two or more in combination : JOINT — **con·joint·ly** *adv*

con·ju·gal \'kän-ji-gəl, kən-'jü-\ *adj* : of or relating to marriage — **con·ju·gal·ly** \-gə-lē\ *adv*

¹con·ju·gate \'kän-ji-gət, -jə-ˌgät\ *adj* : joined together especially in pairs : COUPLED

²con·ju·gate \'kän-jə-ˌgät\ *vb* **-gat·ed; -gat·ing** **1** : to give the various forms of a verb in order **2** : to join together **3** : to pair and unite in conjugation

con·ju·ga·tion \ˌkän-jə-'gā-shən\ *n* **1** : the act of conjugating : the state of being conjugated **2** : a class of verbs having the same type of inflectional forms **3 a** : the union of sex cells that are usually of the same size and shape and that in some lower plants (as some algae) serves as a simple form of sexual reproduction **b** : a method of reproduction in ciliated protozoans (as a paramecium) that involves the formation of a bridge of cytoplasm between two individuals, the exchange of material in their nuclei, and the division of each individual after they separate

con·junc·tion \kən-'jəŋ(k)-shən\ *n* **1** : a joining together **2** : a word or expression that joins together sentences, clauses, phrases, or words

con·junc·ti·va \ˌkän-ˌjəŋk-'tī-və, -'tē-\ *n, pl* **-vas** *or* **-vae** \-(ˌ)vē\ : the mucous membrane that lines the inner surface of the eyelids and is continued over the front part of the eyeball

con·junc·tive \kən-'jəŋ(k)-tiv\ *adj* **1** : ¹CONNECTIVE **2** : done or existing in combination : JOINT **3** : being or used like a conjunction ⟨*conjunctive* adverbs such as "however" and "therefore"⟩

con·junc·ti·vi·tis \kən-ˌjəŋ(k)-ti-'vīt-əs\ *n* : inflammation of the conjunctiva

con·ju·ra·tion \ˌkän-jə-'rā-shən, ˌkän-\ *n* **1** : the act of conjuring : INCANTATION **2** : an expression or trick used in conjuring

con·jure \'kän-jər, 'kən-; *in sense 1* kən-'jù(ə)r\ *vb* **conjured; con·jur·ing** **1** : to beg earnestly or solemnly : BESEECH **2 a** : to call forth (as a spirit or a devil) by magical words **b** : to produce as if by magic ⟨her imagination *conjured* up a splendid scene⟩ ⟨managed to *conjure* up something for lunch⟩ **3** : to practice magic or magical tricks — **con·jur·er** *or* **con·ju·ror** \'kän-jər-ər, 'kən-\ *n*

conk \'käŋk, 'kȯŋk\ *vb* : BREAK DOWN 1 — usually used with *out*

con mo·to \kän-'mō-tō, kōn-\ *adv* : with movement : in a spirited manner — used as a direction in music [Italian]

con·nect \kə-'nekt\ *vb* **1** : to join or link together directly or by something coming between : UNITE ⟨towns *connected* by a railroad⟩ ⟨the two bones *connect* at the elbow⟩ **2** : to attach by personal relationship ⟨*connected* by marriage⟩ **3** : to bring together in thought ⟨*connect* the smell of burning leaves with childhood⟩ **4** : to be related ⟨an event *connected* with our success⟩ **syn** see JOIN — **con·nec·tor** *also* **con·nect·er** \-'nek-tər\ *n*

con·nec·tion \kə-'nek-shən\ *n* **1** : the act of connecting **2** : the fact or condition of being connected : RELATIONSHIP ⟨the *connection* between dirt and disease⟩ **3 a** : a thing that connects **b** : a means of continuing a trip (as by train) **4 a** : a person connected with others (as by kinship) **b** : a social, professional, or commercial relationship

¹con·nec·tive \kə-'nek-tiv\ *adj* : connecting or tending to connect

²connective *n* : something that connects; *esp* : a word or expression (as a conjunction or a relative pronoun) that connects words or word groups

connective tissue *n* : a tissue (as bone or cartilage) that forms a supporting framework for the body or its parts and has much fiber-containing material between the cells composing it

conn·ing tower \'kän-iŋ-\ *n* : a raised structure on a submarine used especially for navigation and to direct attacks [from earlier *conn* "to give directions for steering", probably from still earlier *cond* (same meaning), from Middle English *conden* "to conduct"]

conning tower

con·niv·ance \kə-'nī-vən(t)s\ *n* : the act of conniving; *esp* : knowledge that something wrong is going on without trying to stop it

con·nive \kə-'nīv\ *vb* **con·nived; con·niv·ing** : to cooperate secretly or have a secret understanding — **con·niv·er** *n*

con·nois·seur \,kän-ə-'sər, -'sù(ə)r\ *n* : a person qualified to act as a judge in matters of taste and appreciation [from obsolete French *connoisseur* "expert", from early French *connoisseor* (same meaning), derived from *connoistre* "to know", from Latin *cognoscere* "to know" — related to INCOGNITO, RECOGNIZE] — **con·nois·seur·ship** \-,ship\ *n*

con·no·ta·tion \,kän-ə-'tā-shən\ *n* : a meaning suggested by a word or an expression in addition to its exact meaning

con·note \kə-'nōt, kä-\ *vb* **con·not·ed; con·not·ing** : to suggest in addition to the exact meaning

con·nu·bi·al \kə-'n(y)ü-bē-əl\ *adj* : of or relating to marriage — **con·nu·bi·al·ly** \-bē-ə-lē\ *adv*

con·quer \'käŋ-kər\ *vb* **con·quered; con·quer·ing** \-k(ə-)riŋ\ **1** : to get or gain by force of arms ⟨*conquer* a country⟩ **2** : to defeat by force of arms ⟨*conquered* all their enemies⟩ **3** : OVERCOME 1, SUBDUE ⟨*conquer* a habit⟩ **4** : to be victorious — **con·quer·or** \-kər-ər\ *n*
syn CONQUER, VANQUISH, OVERCOME, OVERTHROW mean to defeat by force or planning. CONQUER suggests gaining control over another after a lengthy struggle and then more or less permanently ⟨ancient Rome *conquered* most of southern Europe⟩ VANQUISH stresses a complete overpowering ⟨the *vanquished* people lost many basic rights⟩ OVERCOME suggests defeating with difficulty or after a hard struggle ⟨try to *overcome* your fear of flying⟩ OVERTHROW stresses the bringing down and eventual destruction of those already in power ⟨may use violence to *overthrow* the dictator⟩

con·quest \'kän-,kwest, 'käŋ-\ *n* **1** : the act or process of conquering **2** : something conquered

con·quis·ta·dor \kȯn-'kēs-tə-,dȯ(ə)r, kän-'k(w)is-, kən-\ *n, pl* **con·quis·ta·do·res** \kȯn-,kēs-tə-'dȯr-ēz, -'dȯr-,ās; -'dȯr-; kän-k(w)is-, 'kən-\ *or* **con·quis·ta·dors** : a leader in the Spanish conquest of America in the 16th century [Spanish, from Latin *conquirere* "to search for"]

con·science \'kän-chən(t)s\ *n* : knowledge of right and wrong and a feeling one should do what is right

con·sci·en·tious \,kän-chē-'en-chəs\ *adj* **1** : guided by or agreeing with one's conscience : SCRUPULOUS **2** : using or done with careful attention — **con·sci·en·tious·ly** *adv* — **con·sci·en·tious·ness** *n*

conscientious objector *n* : a person who refuses to serve in the armed forces or to bear arms because of his or her moral or religious beliefs

con·scious \'kän-chəs\ *adj* **1** : aware of facts or feelings ⟨was *conscious* of the cold⟩ **2** : known or felt by one's inner self ⟨*conscious* guilt⟩ **3** : mentally alert or active ⟨became *conscious* again⟩ **4** : done with awareness or purpose ⟨a *conscious* effort to improve⟩ [from Latin *conscius* "knowing or being aware of something, knowing something along with another person", derived from *con-*, *com-* "with" and *scire* "to know" — related to SCIENCE] —

con·scious·ly *adv*
con·scious·ness \'kän-chəs-nəs\ *n* **1** : the condition of being conscious **2** : the normal state of conscious life in contrast to sleep or an insensible state **3** : the part of mental life that involves conscious thought and awareness

[1]con·script \'kän-,skript\ *adj* **1** : enrolled into service by force **2** : made up of conscripted persons
[2]conscript *n* : a conscripted person (as a military recruit)
[3]con·script \kən-'skript\ *vb* : to enroll into service by force : DRAFT ⟨was *conscripted* into the army⟩ — **con·scrip·tion** \kən-'skrip-shən\ *n*

con·se·crate \'kän(t)-sə-,krāt\ *vb* **-crat·ed; -crat·ing** **1** : to set apart to the service of God **2** : to devote to a purpose in a very sincere manner [Middle English *consecraten* "to consecrate", derived from Latin *consecrare* "to make holy", from *con-*, *com-* "together" and *sacrare* "to consecrate", from *sacr-*, *sacer* "sacred" — related to SACRED] **syn** see DEVOTE

con·se·cra·tion \,kän(t)-sə-'krā-shən\ *n* **1** : the act or ceremony of consecrating **2** : the state of being consecrated

con·sec·u·tive \kən-'sek-(y)ət-iv\ *adj* : following one after the other in order [from French *consécutif* "following in a series, consecutive", from Latin *consecutus*, past participle of *consequi* "to follow", from *con-, com-* "with, together" and *sequi* "to follow" — related to SEQUEL] — **con·sec·u·tive·ly** *adv*

con·sen·sus \kən-'sen(t)-səs\ *n, pl* **-sus·es** **1** : general agreement ⟨the *consensus* of opinion⟩ **2** : the judgment arrived at by most of those concerned ⟨the *consensus* was to go ahead⟩

[1]con·sent \kən-'sent\ *vb* : to express willingness or approval : AGREE — **con·sent·er** *n*
[2]consent *n* : approval of what is done or suggested

con·se·quence \'kän(t)-sə-,kwen(t)s, -si-kwen(t)s\ *n* **1** : [2]RESULT 1, EFFECT **2** : importance that comes from the power to produce an effect **syn** see IMPORTANCE

con·se·quent \'kän(t)-si-kwənt, -sə-,kwent\ *adj* : following as a result or effect

con·se·quen·tial \,kän(t)-sə-'kwen-chəl\ *adj* **1** : CONSEQUENT **2** : having important consequences

con·se·quent·ly \'kän(t)-sə-,kwent-lē, -si-kwənt-\ *adv* : as a result : ACCORDINGLY

con·ser·va·tion \,kän(t)-sər-'vā-shən\ *n* : a careful preservation and protection of something; *esp* : planned management of a natural resource to prevent exploitation, pollution, destruction, or neglect

con·ser·va·tion·ist \,kän(t)-sər-'vā-sh(ə-)nəst\ *n* : a person who is in favor of conservation especially of natural resources (as forests)

conservation of energy : a principle in physics that states that energy can neither be created nor destroyed and that the total energy of a system by itself remains constant

conservation of mass : a principle in physics that states that mass can neither be created nor destroyed and that the total mass of any material system is neither increased nor decreased by reactions between the parts — called also *conservation of matter*

con·ser·va·tism \kən-'sər-və-,tiz-əm\ *n* **1** : a political belief supporting established institutions and customs and preferring gradual development to sudden change **2** : a desire to preserve an existing situation or existing ways

[1]con·ser·va·tive \kən-'sər-vət-iv\ *adj* **1** : tending to conserve or preserve **2** : of or relating to conservatism **3** : tending to preserve existing views, conditions, or institutions : TRADITIONAL **4** : CAUTIOUS, MODERATE ⟨a *conser-*

\ə\ abut	\aù\ **out**	\i\ tip	\ȯ\ **saw**	\ù\ **foot**
\ər\ **further**	\ch\ **chin**	\ī\ **life**	\ȯi\ **coin**	\y\ **yet**
\a\ **mat**	\e\ **pet**	\j\ **job**	\th\ **thin**	\yü\ **few**
\ā\ **take**	\ē\ **easy**	\ŋ\ **sing**	\th\ **this**	\yù\ **cure**
\ä\ **cot, cart**	\g\ **go**	\ō\ **bone**	\ü\ **food**	\zh\ **vision**

vative estimate⟩ **5** : being in agreement with the usual standards of taste or manners ⟨a *conservative* suit⟩ ⟨a *conservative* dresser⟩ — **con·ser·va·tive·ly** *adv* — **con·ser·va·tive·ness** *n*

²conservative *n* : a person who is conservative especially in politics

Conservative Judaism *n* : Judaism as practiced especially among some U.S. Jews that keeps to the Torah and Talmud but makes allowance for some changes suitable for differing times and circumstances

con·ser·va·to·ry \kən-'sər-və-ˌtōr-ē, -ˌtȯr-\ *n, pl* **-ries** **1** : a greenhouse for growing or displaying plants **2** : a place of instruction in some special study (as music)

¹con·serve \kən-'sərv\ *vb* **con·served; con·serv·ing** **1 a** : to keep in a safe or sound state **b** : to avoid wasteful or destructive use of : use carefully ⟨*conserve* natural resources⟩ ⟨*conserve* energy⟩ **2** : to preserve with sugar **3** : to keep (a quantity) constant during a process of change (as chemical change) — **con·serv·er** *n*

²con·serve \'kän-ˌsərv\ *n* **1** : a candied fruit **2** : ²PRESERVE 1

con·sid·er \kən-'sid-ər\ *vb* **-ered; -er·ing** \-(ə-)riŋ\ **1 a** : to think about carefully **b** : to think about with the idea of taking some action ⟨we are *considering* you for the job⟩ **2** : to treat in a kind or thoughtful way ⟨you never *consider* my feelings⟩ **3** : to think of in a certain way : BELIEVE ⟨*consider* the price too high⟩ ⟨*consider* careful work to be essential⟩

con·sid·er·able \kən-'sid-ər-(ə-)bəl, -'sid-rə-bəl\ *adj* : large in size, amount, or quantity ⟨a *considerable* number⟩ ⟨was in *considerable* pain⟩ — **con·sid·er·ably** \-blē\ *adv*

con·sid·er·ate \kən-'sid-(ə-)rət\ *adj* **1** : tending to consider things carefully **2** : thoughtful of the rights and feelings of others — **con·sid·er·ate·ly** *adv* — **con·sid·er·ate·ness** *n*

con·sid·er·ation \kən-ˌsid-ə-'rā-shən\ *n* **1** : careful thought : DELIBERATION **2** : thoughtfulness for other people **3** : something that needs to be considered before deciding or acting **4** : a payment made in return for something

con·sid·er·ing \kən-'sid-(ə-)riŋ\ *prep* : in view of : taking into account

con·sign \kən-'sīn\ *vb* **1** : to give over to another's care : ENTRUST **2** : to give, transfer, or deliver to another **3** : to send or address (as goods) to an agent to be cared for or sold

con·sign·ment \kən-'sīn-mənt\ *n* **1** : the act or process of consigning **2** : something consigned especially in a single shipment

con·sist \kən-'sist\ *vb* : to be made up or composed ⟨breakfast *consisted* of cereal, milk, and fruit⟩ ⟨coal *consists* mostly of carbon⟩

con·sis·ten·cy \kən-'sis-tən-sē\ *n, pl* **-cies** **1** : the degree of thickness, firmness, or stickiness ⟨dough of the right *consistency*⟩ **2** : agreement or harmony between parts or elements **3** : a sticking with one way of thinking or acting

con·sis·tent \kən-'sis-tənt\ *adj* **1** : being in agreement or harmony ⟨is *consistent* with our policy⟩ **2** : being unchanging in behavior or beliefs ⟨a *consistent* supporter⟩ — **con·sis·tent·ly** *adv*

con·so·la·tion \ˌkän(t)-sə-'lā-shən\ *n* **1** : the act or an instance of consoling : the state of being consoled **2** : something that consoles — **con·sol·a·to·ry** \kən-'sōl-ə-ˌtōr-ē, -säl-ə-, -ˌtȯr-\ *adj*

¹con·sole \'kän-ˌsōl\ *n* **1 a** : the part of an organ at which the organist sits and which contains the keyboard and controls **b** : a panel or cabinet with dials and switches for controlling an electronic or mechanical device **2** : a cabinet (as for a phonograph or television set) that stands on the floor

²con·sole \kən-'sōl\ *vb* **con·soled; con·sol·ing** : to comfort in times of grief, distress, or suffering

con·sol·i·date \kən-'säl-ə-ˌdāt\ *vb* **-dat·ed; -dat·ing** **1** : to join together into one whole : UNITE **2** : to make firm or safe : STRENGTHEN ⟨*consolidate* a beachhead⟩ — **con·sol·i·da·tion** \kən-ˌsäl-ə-'dā-shən\ *n*

consolidated school *n* : a public school that is formed by joining other schools together

con·som·mé \ˌkän(t)-sə-'mā\ *n* : a clear meat soup [French]

con·so·nance \'kän(t)-s(ə-)nən(t)s\ *n* : harmony or agreement especially of musical tones or speech sounds

¹con·so·nant \'kän(t)-s(ə-)nənt\ *adj* : being in harmony or agreement — **con·so·nant·ly** *adv*

²consonant *n* **1** : a speech sound (as \p\, \n\, or \s\) produced by narrowing or closing the breath channel at one or more points **2** : a letter representing a consonant; *esp* : any letter of the English alphabet except *a, e, i, o,* and *u* — **con·so·nan·tal** \ˌkän(t)-sə-'nant-ᵊl\ *adj*

¹con·sort \'kän-ˌsȯ(ə)rt\ *n* : a wife or husband : SPOUSE

²con·sort \kən-'sȯ(ə)rt\ *vb* : to go together as companions : ASSOCIATE

con·spic·u·ous \kən-'spik-yə-wəs\ *adj* **1** : easily seen **2** : attracting attention : STRIKING **syn** see NOTICEABLE — **con·spic·u·ous·ly** *adv* — **con·spic·u·ous·ness** *n*

con·spir·a·cy \kən-'spir-ə-sē\ *n, pl* **-cies** **1** : the act of conspiring together **2 a** : an agreement among conspirators **b** : a group of conspirators

con·spir·a·tor \kən-'spir-ət-ər\ *n* : a person who conspires

con·spir·a·to·ri·al \kən-ˌspir-ə-'tōr-ē-əl, -'tȯr-\ *adj* : of or relating to a conspiracy — **con·spir·a·to·ri·al·ly** \-ē-ə-lē\ *adv*

con·spire \kən-'spī(ə)r\ *vb* **con·spired; con·spir·ing** **1** : to agree secretly to do an unlawful act : PLOT ⟨*conspiring* to overthrow the dictator⟩ **2** : to act together ⟨measles and the weather *conspired* to spoil our vacation⟩

con·sta·ble \'kän(t)-stə-bəl, 'kən(t)-\ *n* **1** : a high officer of a royal or noble household in the Middle Ages **2** : the person in charge of a royal castle or a town **3** : a police officer usually of a village or small town

> **Word History** A constable in the Middle Ages was a very important official in a court, even though the title meant "officer of the stable". Early French *conestable* came from the Latin phrase *comes stabuli,* meaning "officer of the stable". Being in charge of a ruler's horses in those days was something like being in charge of all the vehicles — tanks, trucks, airplanes, helicopters — of a modern army. As time went on, the title remained, but it came to describe the person in charge of guarding a castle or fortified city. From this idea came the modern sense: "a police officer". [Middle English *conestable* "chief military or police officer of a court or royal domain", from early French *conestable* (same meaning), from Latin *comes stabuli,* literally "officer of the stables", from *comes* "companion, member of a royal court" and *stabuli,* plural of *stabulum* "stable" — related to ³COUNT, ¹STABLE]

con·stab·u·lary \kən-'stab-yə-ˌler-ē\ *n, pl* **-lar·ies** **1** : an organized body of constables or of police officers **2** : a police force organized like the military

con·stan·cy \'kän(t)-stən-sē\ *n, pl* **-cies** **1** : firmness and loyalty in one's beliefs or personal relationships **2** : freedom from change

¹con·stant \'kän(t)-stənt\ *adj* **1** : always faithful and true ⟨*constant* friends⟩ **2** : remaining steady and unchanged ⟨a *constant* temperature⟩ **3** : occurring over and over again ⟨*constant* headaches⟩ — **con·stant·ly** *adv*

²constant *n* : something unchanging; *esp* : a number whose value does not change under given mathematical conditions

con·stel·la·tion \ˌkän(t)-stə-'lā-shən\ *n* : any of 88 groups of stars forming patterns [Middle English *constellacioun* "the position of the stars in the sky at the time of a person's birth", from early French *constellation* (same meaning), derived from Latin *constellatus* "studded with stars", from *con-, com-* "with" and *stella* "star"]

con·ster·na·tion \,kän(t)-stər-'nā-shən\ *n* : amazement, alarm, or disappointment that makes one feel helpless or confused

con·sti·pate \'kän(t)-stə-,pāt\ *vb* **-pat·ed; -pat·ing** : to cause constipation in

con·sti·pa·tion \,kän(t)-stə-'pā-shən\ *n* : abnormally difficult or infrequent bowel movements

con·stit·u·en·cy \kən-'stich-(ə-)wən-sē\ *n, pl* **-cies** **1** : a body of citizens having the right to elect a representative to a legislature **2** : the people living in an electoral district **3** : an electoral district

¹**con·stit·u·ent** \kən-'stich-(ə-)wənt\ *n* **1** : one of the parts of which a thing is made up : ELEMENT, INGREDIENT **2** : any of the voters who elect a person to represent them

²**constituent** *adj* **1** : forming a part of a whole : COMPONENT **2** : having the power to create a government or make or change a constitution ⟨a *constituent* assembly⟩

con·sti·tute \'kän(t)-stə-,t(y)üt\ *vb* **-tut·ed; -tut·ing** **1** : to appoint to an office or duty ⟨*constituted* authorities⟩ **2** : SET UP 4, ESTABLISH ⟨a fund was *constituted* to help needy students⟩ **3** : MAKE UP 2, FORM ⟨twelve months *constitute* a year⟩

con·sti·tu·tion \,kän(t)-stə-'t(y)ü-shən\ *n* **1** : the act of establishing, making, or setting up **2 a** : the physical makeup of an individual **b** : the structure, composition, or basic qualities of something **3 a** : the basic beliefs and laws of a nation, state, or social group that establish the powers and duties of the government and guarantee certain rights to the people in it **b** : a document containing a constitution

¹**con·sti·tu·tion·al** \'kän(t)-stə-'t(y)ü-shnəl, -shən-ᵊl\ *adj* **1** : of or relating to a person's physical or mental makeup **2** : of, relating to, or in agreement with a constitution ⟨a *constitutional* amendment⟩ ⟨*constitutional* rights⟩ — **con·sti·tu·tion·al·ly** \-shnə-lē, -shən-ᵊl-ē\ *adv*

²**constitutional** *n* : exercise (as a walk) taken for one's health

con·sti·tu·tion·al·i·ty \,kän(t)-stə-,t(y)ü-shə-'nal-ət-ē\ *n* : the quality or state of being in agreement with a constitution

con·strain \kən-'strān\ *vb* **1** : COMPEL 1 **2** : CONFINE 1 **3** : RESTRAIN 1

con·straint \kən-'strānt\ *n* **1** : the act of constraining : the state of being constrained **2** : something that constrains : CHECK **3** : a keeping back of one's natural feelings

con·strict \kən-'strikt\ *vb* : to make or become narrower or smaller by drawing together : SQUEEZE, TIGHTEN — **con·stric·tive** \-'strik-tiv\ *adj*

con·stric·tion \kən-'strik-shən\ *n* **1** : an act or instance of constricting **2** : something that constricts : a part that is constricted

con·stric·tor \kən-'strik-tər\ *n* : a snake that suffocates its prey by crushing in its coils

con·struct \kən-'strəkt\ *vb* **1** : to make or form by combining or arranging parts : BUILD **2** : to draw (a geometrical figure) with suitable instruments and under given conditions — **con·struct·ible** \-'strək-tə-bəl\ *adj* — **con·struc·tor** \-'strək-tər\ *n*

con·struc·tion \kən-'strək-shən\ *n* **1** : the arrangement and connection of words or groups of words in a sentence **2** : the process, art, or manner of constructing **3** : something built or put together : STRUCTURE **4** : INTERPRETATION 1 ⟨strict *construction* of the constitution⟩

construction paper *n* : a thick paper available in many colors and used especially for school artwork

con·struc·tive \kən-'strək-tiv\ *adj* : helping to develop or improve something ⟨*constructive* suggestions⟩ — **con·struc·tive·ly** *adv* — **con·struc·tive·ness** *n*

con·strue \kən-'strü\ *vb* **con·strued; con·stru·ing** **1** : to explain the grammatical relationships of the words in a sentence, clause, or phrase **2** : to understand or explain the sense or intention of : INTERPRET — **con·stru·able** \-'strü-ə-bəl\ *adj*

con·sul \'kän(t)-səl\ *n* **1** : either of two chief officials of the ancient Roman republic who were elected each year **2** : an official appointed by a government to live in a foreign country to look after the commercial interests of citizens of the appointing country — **con·sul·ar** \-s(ə-)lər\ *adj* — **con·sul·ship** \-səl-,ship\ *n*

con·sul·ate \'kän(t)-s(ə-)lət\ *n* : the residence or office of a consul

con·sult \kən-'səlt\ *vb* **1** : to seek the opinion or advice of ⟨*consult* a doctor⟩ **2** : to seek information from ⟨*consult* a dictionary⟩ **3** : to talk something over ⟨have to *consult* with my lawyer⟩ — **con·sult·er** *n*

con·sult·ant \kən-'səlt-ᵊnt\ *n* **1** : a person who consults another **2** : a person who gives professional advice or services

con·sul·ta·tion \,kän(t)-səl-'tā-shən\ *n* **1** : a discussion between doctors on a case or its treatment **2** : the act of consulting

con·sume \kən-'süm\ *vb* **con·sumed; con·sum·ing** **1** : to destroy by or as if by fire **2** : USE UP, SPEND ⟨the search *consumed* most of our time⟩ **3** : to eat or drink up ⟨*consumed* a whole gallon of ice cream⟩ **4** : to take up the interest or attention of ⟨was *consumed* with curiosity⟩ **syn** see EAT — **con·sum·able** \-'sü-mə-bəl\ *adj*

con·sum·er \kən-'sü-mər\ *n* **1** : one that consumes; *esp* : a person who buys and uses up goods **2** : a plant or animal that requires complex organic compounds for food which it obtains by preying on other living things or eating particles of organic matter

con·sum·er·ism \kən-'sü-mə-,riz-əm\ *n* : the promotion of the consumer's interests

¹**con·sum·mate** \kən-'səm-ət, 'kän(t)-sə-mət\ *adj* : of the highest degree, quality, or skill ⟨a *consummate* politician⟩ — **con·sum·mate·ly** *adv*

²**con·sum·mate** \'kän(t)-sə-,māt\ *vb* **-mat·ed; -mat·ing** : to make perfect or complete — **con·sum·ma·tion** \,kän(t)-sə-'mā-shən\ *n*

con·sump·tion \kən-'səm(p)-shən\ *n* **1 a** : the act or process of consuming **b** : the amount consumed **2 a** : a gradual and continuous wasting away of the body especially from tuberculosis of the lungs **b** : TUBERCULOSIS

¹**con·sump·tive** \kən-'səm(p)-tiv\ *adj* : of, relating to, or affected with consumption

²**consumptive** *n* : a person who has consumption

¹**con·tact** \'kän-,takt\ *n* **1** : a meeting or touching of surfaces **2** : the connection of two electrical conductors through which a current passes or a part made for such a connection **3** : a person one knows who has influence especially in the business or political world ⟨our *contacts* in Los Angeles may be able to assist you⟩ **4** : an establishing of communication especially with someone or something distant ⟨make *contact* by radio⟩ [from French *contact* or Latin *contactus,* both meaning "a touching of body surfaces", derived from Latin *contingere* "to have contact with, affect, happen", from *con-, com-* "with, together" and *tangere* "to touch" — related to CONTAGIOUS, CONTINGENT, TANGENT, TANGIBLE]

²**con·tact** \'kän-,takt, kən-'takt\ *vb* **1** : to bring or come into contact **2** : to get in touch or communication with ⟨*contact* your local dealer for details⟩

³**con·tact** \'kän-,takt\ *adj* : involving or acting upon contact ⟨football and ice hockey are *contact* sports⟩ ⟨*contact* insecticides⟩

\ə\ abut		\au̇\ out	\i\ tip	\o̅\ saw	\u̇\ foot
\ər\ further		\ch\ chin	\ī\ life	\o̅i\ coin	\y\ yet
\a\ mat		\e\ pet	\j\ job	\th\ thin	\yü\ few
\ā\ take		\ē\ easy	\ŋ\ sing	\t̲h̲\ this	\yu̇\ cure
\ä\ cot, cart		\g\ go	\ō\ bone	\ü\ food	\zh\ vision

con·tact lens \,kän-,tak(t)-\ *n* : a thin lens used to correct bad eyesight and worn right over the cornea of the eye

con·ta·gion \kən-'tā-jən\ *n* **1** : the passing of a disease from one individual to another by direct or indirect contact **2** : CONTAGIOUS DISEASE; *also* : something (as a virus) that causes a contagious disease

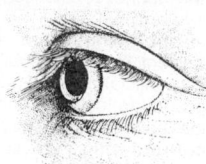

contact lens

con·ta·gious \kən-'tā-jəs\ *adj* **1** : able to be passed on by contact between individuals ⟨colds are *contagious*⟩ **2** : so pleasantly irresistable as to be picked up by one person after another ⟨your enthusiasm is *contagious*⟩ [Middle English *contagious* "likely to be passed on through contact", from early French *contagieus* (same meaning), derived from Latin *contingere* "to have contact with, affect, happen" — related to CONTACT, CONTINGENT]

contagious disease *n* : a disease that can be passed on by contact with a person who has it, his or her bodily discharges, or something that has touched the person or his or her bodily discharges — compare INFECTIOUS DISEASE

con·tain \kən-'tān\ *vb* **1** : to keep within limits : RESTRAIN, CHECK ⟨tried to *contain* my laughter⟩ ⟨the forest fire was finally *contained*⟩ **2** : to have within **3** : to consist of : INCLUDE **4** : to be divisible by especially without a remainder ⟨20 *contains* 5 four times⟩ — **con·tain·ment** \-'tān-mənt\ *n*

　　syn CONTAIN, HOLD, ACCOMMODATE mean to have or be capable of having within. CONTAIN suggests the actual presence of a particular thing or quantity within something ⟨a bottle *containing* a liter of liquid⟩ HOLD suggests the capacity of something or its usual or permanent purpose ⟨that cooler will *hold* 12 cartons of milk⟩ ACCOMMODATE stresses holding without crowding or inconvenience ⟨the ballroom can *accommodate* 500 people easily⟩

con·tain·er \kən-'tā-nər\ *n* : one that contains; *esp* : something into which other things can be put (as for storage)

con·tain·er·ship \kən-'tā-nər-,ship\ *n* : a ship designed or equipped to carry very large containers of cargo

con·tam·i·nant \kən-'tam-ə-nənt\ *n* : something that contaminates

con·tam·i·nate \kən-'tam-ə-,nāt\ *vb* **-nat·ed; -nat·ing** **1** : to soil, stain, or infect by contact or association **2** : to make impure or unfit for use by adding something harmful or unpleasant ⟨wells *contaminated* by chemicals⟩ — **con·tam·i·na·tion** \-,tam-ə-'nā-shən\ *n* — **con·tam·i·na·tor** \-'tam-ə-,nāt-ər\ *n*

con·tem·plate \'känt-əm-,plāt, 'kän-,tem-\ *vb* **-plat·ed; -plat·ing** **1** : to view or consider with careful and thoughtful attention **2** : to have in mind : plan on ⟨*contemplating* a trip to Europe⟩ — **con·tem·pla·tor** \-,plāt-ər\ *n*

con·tem·pla·tion \,känt-əm-'plā-shən, ,kän-,tem-\ *n* **1** : the act of thinking about spiritual things : MEDITATION **2** : the act of looking at or thinking about something steadily **3** : a looking ahead to some future event : ANTICIPATION

con·tem·pla·tive \kən-'tem-plət-iv; 'känt-əm-,plāt-, 'kän-,tem-\ *adj* : involving or devoted to contemplation : MEDITATIVE ⟨the *contemplative* life⟩ — **con·tem·pla·tive·ly** *adv* — **con·tem·pla·tive·ness** *n*

con·tem·po·ra·ne·ous \kən-,tem-pə-'rā-nē-əs\ *adj* : existing, occurring, or beginning during the same time — **con·tem·po·ra·ne·ous·ly** *adv* — **con·tem·po·ra·ne·ous·ness** *n*

¹con·tem·po·rary \kən-'tem-pə-,rer-ē\ *adj* **1** : living or occurring at the same period of time **2** : of the present time : MODERN, CURRENT

²contemporary *n, pl* **-rar·ies** : a person who lives at the same time or is about the same age as another

con·tempt \kən-'tem(p)t\ *n* **1** : the act of despising : the state of mind of one who despises **2** : the state of being despised **3** : disobedience or disrespect to a court, judge, or legislature

con·tempt·ible \kən-'tem(p)-tə-bəl\ *adj* : deserving contempt ⟨a *contemptible* lie⟩ — **con·tempt·ibly** \-blē\ *adv*

con·temp·tu·ous \kən-'tem(p)-ch(ə-w)əs, -'tem(p)sh-wəs\ *adj* : feeling or showing contempt — **con·temp·tu·ous·ly** *adv*

　　syn CONTEMPTUOUS, SCORNFUL, DISDAINFUL mean feeling or showing a lack of respect or concern. CONTEMPTUOUS suggests a lofty attitude toward whatever one hates ⟨*contemptuous* of cowards⟩ SCORNFUL suggests anger and disgust often expressed in mockery ⟨*scornful* of their customs and traditions⟩ DISDAINFUL suggests proudly considering someone or something as not worthy of one's notice ⟨*disdainful* of people who were not as rich as they were⟩

con·tend \kən-'tend\ *vb* **1** : COMPETE **2** : to try hard to deal with ⟨many problems to *contend* with⟩ **3** : to argue or state earnestly ⟨*contend* that my opinion is right⟩ — **con·tend·er** *n*

¹con·tent \kən-'tent\ *adj* : pleased and satisfied with what one has or is

²content *vb* : to make content : SATISFY

³content *n* : CONTENTMENT; *esp* : freedom from care or discomfort

⁴con·tent \'kän-,tent\ *n* **1 a** : something contained — usually used in pl. ⟨the *contents* of a jar⟩ **b** : the subject matter or topics treated (as in a book) ⟨table of *contents*⟩ **2** : the essential meaning ⟨I enjoy the rhythm of the poem but I don't understand its *content*⟩ **3** : an amount that is contained or can be contained ⟨oil with a high *content* of sulfur⟩ ⟨the jug has a *content* of four liters⟩

con·tent·ed \kən-'tent-əd\ *adj* : satisfied with one's possessions or situation in life — **con·tent·ed·ly** *adv* — **con·tent·ed·ness** *n*

con·ten·tion \kən-'ten-chən\ *n* **1** : an act or instance of contending **2** : an idea or point for which a person argues (as in a debate or argument)

con·ten·tious \kən-'ten-chəs\ *adj* : inclined to argue **syn** see BELLIGERENT — **con·ten·tious·ness** *n*

con·tent·ment \kən-'tent-mənt\ *n* : freedom from worry or restlessness : peaceful satisfaction

¹con·test \kən-'test, 'kän-,test\ *vb* : to make (something) a cause of dispute or fighting ⟨*contest* a claim⟩

²con·test \'kän-,test\ *n* : a struggle for victory : COMPETITION

con·test·ant \kən-'tes-tənt *also* 'kän-,tes-\ *n* : a person who takes part in a contest

con·text \'kän-,tekst\ *n* : the parts of something written or spoken that are near a certain word or group of words and that help to explain its meaning — **con·tex·tu·al** \kän-'teks-chə(-wə)l, kən-\ *adj* — **con·tex·tu·al·ly** \-ē\ *adv*

con·ti·gu·ity \,känt-ə-'gyü-ət-ē\ *n* : the quality or state of being contiguous

con·tig·u·ous \kən-'tig-yə-wəs\ *adj* **1** : being in contact : ADJOINING **2** : very near though not in contact **3** : touching or connected in an unbroken series ⟨the 48 *contiguous* states⟩ — **con·tig·u·ous·ly** *adv*

con·ti·nent \'känt-ᵊn-ənt, 'känt-nənt\ *n* **1** : one of the great divisions of land (as North America, South America, Europe, Asia, Africa, Australia, or Antarctica) on the globe **2** *cap* : the continent of Europe

¹con·ti·nen·tal \,känt-ᵊn-'ent-ᵊl\ *adj* **1** : of or relating to a continent ⟨*continental* waters⟩; *esp, often cap* : of or relating to the continent of Europe **2** *often cap* : of or relating to the colonies later forming the U.S. ⟨*Continental* Congress⟩

²continental *n* **1 a** *often cap* : a soldier in the Continental army **b** : a piece of paper money issued by the Continental Congress **2** : EUROPEAN

continental drift *n* : the slow movement that the continents are believed to make on a fluid layer that is located deep within the earth

continental shelf *n* : a shallow submarine plain of varying width forming a border to a continent and typically ending at the continental slope

continental slope *n* : a usually steep slope from a continental shelf to the ocean floor

con·tin·gen·cy \kən-'tin-jən-sē\ *n, pl* **-cies** : something (as an emergency) that might or might not happen or that might happen if something else occurs ⟨prepared for every *contingency*⟩

¹**con·tin·gent** \kən-'tin-jənt\ *adj* : depending on something else ⟨plans *contingent* on the weather⟩ [Middle English *contingent* "touching, connected with", from early French *contingent* (same meaning), derived from Latin *contingere* "to have contact with, affect, happen" — related to CONTACT, CONTAGIOUS] — **con·tin·gent·ly** *adv*

²**contingent** *n* : a number of persons representing or drawn from an area or group

con·tin·u·al \kən-'tin-yə(-wə)l\ *adj* **1** : continuing without interruption ⟨days of *continual* sunshine⟩ **2** : occurring again and again within short intervals ⟨*continual* interruptions⟩ — **con·tin·u·al·ly** \-ē\ *adv*

con·tin·u·ance \kən-'tin-yə-wən(t)s\ *n* **1** : the act of continuing **2** : the extent of continuing : DURATION **3** : postponement of a case in a law court

con·tin·u·a·tion \kən-,tin-yə-'wā-shən\ *n* **1** : the act or fact of continuing in or extending the time of a state or activity **2** : a beginning again after an interruption **3** : a thing or part by which something is continued

con·tin·ue \kən-'tin-yü\ *vb* **-tin·ued; -tin·u·ing 1** : to do or cause to do the same thing without stopping ⟨I *continue* to work hard⟩ ⟨the weather *continued* hot and sunny⟩ **2** : to go on or carry on after an interruption : RESUME ⟨to be *continued* next week⟩ — **con·tin·u·er** \-yə-wər\ *n*

continued fraction *n* : an expression in the form of a fraction whose numerator is an integer and whose denominator is an integer plus a fraction whose numerator is an integer and whose denominator is an integer plus a fraction and so on; thus:

$$\cfrac{a}{a' + \cfrac{b}{b' + \cfrac{c}{c' + \dots}}}$$

con·ti·nu·ity \,känt-ᵊn-'(y)ü-ət-ē\ *n, pl* **-ities 1** : the quality or state of being continuous **2** : something that has or provides continuity

con·tin·u·ous \kən-'tin-yə-wəs\ *adj* : continuing without a stop — **con·tin·u·ous·ly** *adv* — **con·tin·u·ous·ness** *n*

con·tin·u·um \kən-'tin-yə-wəm\ *n, pl* **-ua** \-yə-wə\ *also* **-u·ums** : something that is continuous and the same throughout and that is often thought of as a series of elements or values which differ by only tiny amounts

con·tort \kən-'tȯ(ə)rt\ *vb* : to twist into an unusual appearance or unnatural shape

con·tor·tion \kən-'tȯr-shən\ *n* **1** : a twisting or being twisted out of shape **2** : a contorted shape or thing

con·tor·tion·ist \kən-'tȯr-sh(ə-)nəst\ *n* : an acrobat able to twist the body into unusual positions

¹**con·tour** \'kän-,tu̇(ə)r\ *n* **1** : the outline of a figure, body, or surface **2** : a line or drawing showing an outline

²**contour** *adj* **1** : following contour lines or forming furrows or ridges along them ⟨*contour* farming⟩ ⟨*contour* flooding⟩ **2** : made to fit the contour of something

³**contour** *vb* **1** : to shape the contour of **2** : to shape to fit contours

contour line *n* : a line (as on a map) connecting the points that have the same elevation on a land surface

contra- *prefix* **1** : against : contrary : contrasting **2**

: pitched below normal bass ⟨*contra*bassoon⟩ [derived from Latin *contra* "against, opposite"]

con·tra·band \'kän-trə-,band\ *n* **1** : goods forbidden by law to be owned or to be brought into or out of a country **2** : smuggled goods [from Italian *contrabbando* "smuggling", from Latin *contrabannum*, literally "against the decree or command", from *contra* "against" and *bannum, bannus* "decree"; of Germanic origin] — **contraband** *adj*

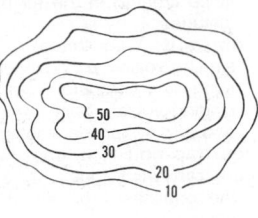

contour line

con·tra·bas·soon \,kän-trə-bə-'sün, -ba-\ *n* : a musical instrument that is similar to a bassoon but has a longer body with more turns and is pitched an octave lower

con·tra·cep·tion \,kän-trə-'sep-shən\ *n* : deliberate prevention of conception and pregnancy especially by using a drug or a device (as a condom)

¹**con·tra·cep·tive** \,kän-trə-'sep-tiv\ *adj* : relating to or used for contraception

²**contraceptive** *n* : a contraceptive drug or device

¹**con·tract** \'kän-,trakt\ *n* **1** : a legally binding agreement between two or more parties **2** : a document stating the terms of a contract **syn** see AGREEMENT

²**con·tract** \kən-'trakt, *sense 2 usually* 'kän-,trakt\ *vb* **1 a** : to bring on oneself ⟨*contract* debts⟩ **b** : to become affected with ⟨*contract* a cold⟩ **2** : to agree by contract ⟨*contract* to build a house⟩ **3 a** : to draw or squeeze together so as to make or become smaller or shorter and broader ⟨brows *contracting* in puzzlement⟩ ⟨*contract* a muscle⟩ **b** : to make or become smaller ⟨metal *contracts* when cold⟩ **4** : to shorten (a word) by leaving out one or more sounds or letters

con·trac·tile \kən-'trak-tᵊl, -,tīl\ *adj* : having the power or property of contracting ⟨a *contractile* cell⟩ ⟨a *contractile* fiber⟩ — **con·trac·til·i·ty** \,kän-,trak-'til-ət-ē\ *n*

contractile vacuole *n* : a vacuole in a single-celled plant or animal that contracts regularly to discharge fluid from the cell

con·trac·tion \kən-'trak-shən\ *n* **1 a** : the act or process of contracting : the state of being contracted **b** : the shortening and thickening of a working muscle or muscle fiber **2 a** : a shortening of a word, syllable, or word group by leaving out a sound or letter **b** : a form (as *don't* or *they've*) produced by such shortening

con·trac·tor \'kän-,trak-tər, kən-'trak-\ *n* : one that enters into a contract; *esp* : a person who contracts to perform work or provide supplies at a certain price or within a certain time ⟨building *contractor*⟩

con·trac·tu·al \kən-'trak-chə(-wə)l, kän-, -'traksh-wəl\ *adj* : of, relating to, or being a contract ⟨*contractual* agreements⟩ — **con·trac·tu·al·ly** \-ē\ *adv*

con·tra·dict \,kän-trə-'dikt\ *vb* **1** : to say the opposite of what someone else has said : deny the truth of **2** : to be opposed or contrary to : go against ⟨your actions *contradict* your words⟩ — **con·tra·dic·tor** \-'dik-tər\ *n*

con·tra·dic·tion \,kän-trə-'dik-shən\ *n* **1** : something (as a statement) that contradicts something else **2** : a condition in which things oppose each other

con·tra·dic·to·ry \,kän-trə-'dik-t(ə-)rē\ *adj* : involving, causing, or being a contradiction ⟨*contradictory* statements⟩ — **con·tra·dic·to·ri·ness** \-t(ə-)rē-nəs\ *n*

\ə\ abut	\au̇\ out	\i\ tip	\ȯ\ saw	\u̇\ foot
\ər\ further	\ch\ chin	\ī\ life	\ȯi\ coin	\y\ yet
\a\ mat	\e\ pet	\j\ job	\th\ thin	\yü\ few
\ā\ take	\ē\ easy	\ŋ\ sing	\th\ this	\yu̇\ cure
\ä\ cot, cart	\g\ go	\ō\ bone	\ü\ food	\zh\ vision

con·trail \'kän-ˌtrāl\ *n* : a stream of visible water or ice particles created in the air by an airplane or rocket at high altitudes

con·tral·to \kən-'tral-tō\ *n, pl* **-tos** **1 a** : the lowest female singing voice **b** : a singer with such a voice **2** : the part sung by a contralto [from Italian *contralto* "lowest female singing voice", from *contra-* "having a lower pitch than" and *alto* "a female singing voice"]

con·trap·tion \kən-'trap-shən\ *n* : DEVICE 1c, GADGET

con·trari·wise \'kän-ˌtrer-ē-ˌwīz, kən-'trer-\ *adv* **1** : just the opposite : on the contrary **2** : VICE VERSA, CONVERSELY

¹con·trary \'kän-ˌtrer-ē\ *n, pl* **-trar·ies** : something opposite or contrary — **on the contrary** : just the opposite

²con·trary \'kän-ˌtrer-ē, sense 4 is often kən-'tre(ə)r-ē\ *adj* **1** : exactly opposite : entirely different ⟨*contrary* opinions⟩ **2** : being against or opposed : in violation ⟨actions *contrary* to the law⟩ **3** : not favorable or helpful ⟨a *contrary* wind⟩ **4** : unwilling to obey or behave well ⟨a *contrary* child⟩ — **con·trar·i·ly** \-ˌtrer-ə-lē, -'trer-\ *adv* — **con·trar·i·ness** \-ˌtrer-ē-nəs, -'trer-\ *n*

¹con·trast \kən-'trast, 'kän-ˌtrast\ *vb* **1** : to show noticeable differences **2** : to compare two persons or things so as to show the differences between them

²con·trast \'kän-ˌtrast\ *n* **1** : a person or thing that shows differences when compared to another **2** : difference or unlikeness (as in color or brightness) between related things especially when very plain

con·trib·ute \kən-'trib-yət, -(ˌ)yüt\ *vb* **-ut·ed; -ut·ing** **1** : to give along with others **2** : to have a part in bringing about something ⟨everybody *contributed* to the success of the show⟩ **3** : to supply (as an article) for publication especially in a magazine — **con·trib·u·tor** \-yət-ər\ *n*

con·tri·bu·tion \ˌkän-trə-'byü-shən\ *n* **1** : the act of contributing **2** : a sum or a thing contributed — **con·trib·u·tive** \kən-'trib-yət-iv\ *adj*

con·trib·u·to·ry \kən-'trib-yə-ˌtōr-ē, -ˌtȯr-ē\ *adj* : serving to contribute; *esp* : helping to accomplish a result

con·trite \'kän-ˌtrīt, kən-'trīt\ *adj* : very sorry for a wrong that one has done — **con·trite·ly** *adv* — **con·trite·ness** *n*

con·tri·tion \kən-'trish-ən\ *n* : the state of being contrite

con·triv·ance \kən-'trī-vən(t)s\ *n* : something (as a scheme or mechanical device) produced with skill and cleverness

con·trive \kən-'trīv\ *vb* **con·trived; con·triv·ing** **1** : ²PLAN 1, PLOT ⟨*contrive* a way to escape⟩ **2** : to form or make in a skillful or clever way : INVENT **3** : BRING ABOUT, MANAGE ⟨*contriving* to make ends meet⟩ — **con·triv·er** *n*

¹con·trol \kən-'trōl\ *vb* **con·trolled; con·trol·ling** **1 a** : to keep within limits : RESTRAIN ⟨*control* your temper⟩ **b** : to direct the action of ⟨*control* a plane⟩ **2** : to have power over : RULE **3** : to reduce the number of individuals or cases especially to a level that is not dangerous ⟨*control* insects⟩ ⟨*control* a disease⟩ — **con·trol·la·ble** \-'trō-lə-bəl\ *adj*

²control *n* **1** : the power or authority to control **2** : ability to control ⟨the car went out of *control*⟩ ⟨keep *control* of a situation⟩ **3 a** : a means for controlling ⟨the *controls* of an airplane⟩ ⟨price *controls*⟩ **b** : an organization that directs a flight beyond the earth's atmosphere ⟨mission *control*⟩ **4 a** : CONTROL EXPERIMENT **b** : an individual or group that is part of a control experiment **5** : reduction in or regulation of the number of individuals or cases in an area ⟨disease *control*⟩

control experiment *n* : an experiment in which the individuals taking part are treated in the same way as those in another experiment except that the procedure or agent being tested is omitted and which is used as a standard to compare with the results of the other experiment

con·trol·ler \kən-'trō-lər, 'kän-ˌtrō-lər\ *n* **1** : the chief accounting officer of a business or institution **2** : a person who controls ⟨an air traffic *controller*⟩

con·tro·ver·sial \ˌkän-trə-'vər-shəl, -'vər-sē-əl\ *adj* : relating to or causing controversy — **con·tro·ver·sial·ly** \-ē\ *adv*

con·tro·ver·sy \'kän-trə-ˌvər-sē\ *n, pl* **-sies** **1** : an often long or heated discussion of something about which there is great difference of opinion : DISPUTE **2** : ¹QUARREL 2, STRIFE [Middle English *controversie* "act or cause of disagreeing, dispute", from Latin *controversia* (same meaning), literally "something turned against or to the contrary", from *contro-, contra-* "against, contrary" and *versus* "turned", from *vertere* "to turn" — related to ANNIVERSARY, CONVERSE, DIVERT, VERSATILE]

con·tu·sion \kən-'t(y)ü-zhən\ *n* : an injury to tissue that usually does not break the skin : BRUISE — **con·tuse** \-'t(y)üz\ *vb*

co·nun·drum \kə-'nən-drəm\ *n* : ¹RIDDLE 1, PUZZLE

con·ur·ba·tion \ˌkän-(ˌ)ər-'bā-shən\ *n* : a number of cities or towns that come one right after the other with no countryside in between

con·va·lesce \ˌkän-və-'les\ *vb* **-lesced; -lesc·ing** : to regain health and strength gradually after illness or weakness

con·va·les·cence \ˌkän-və-'les-ᵊn(t)s\ *n* : the process or period of convalescing

¹con·va·les·cent \ˌkän-və-'les-ᵊnt\ *adj* : going through convalescence

²convalescent *n* : a person who is convalescing

con·vec·tion \kən-'vek-shən\ *n* : motion in a fluid in which the warmer portions rise and the colder portions sink; *also* : the transfer of heat by this motion — **con·vec·tion·al** \-shnəl, -shən-ᵊl\ *adj* — **con·vec·tive** \-'vek-tiv\ *adj*

convection oven *n* : an oven with a fan that circulates hot air evenly and continuously around the food as it cooks

con·vene \kən-'vēn\ *vb* **con·vened; con·ven·ing** **1** : to come together in a group : ASSEMBLE **2** : to cause to convene : call together

¹con·ve·nience \kən-'vēn-yən(t)s\ *n* **1** : the quality or state of being convenient **2** : personal comfort : freedom from trouble **3** : a convenient time : OPPORTUNITY ⟨come at your earliest *convenience*⟩ **4** : something that gives comfort or advantage ⟨a house with all modern *conveniences*⟩

²convenience *adj* : designed for quick and easy preparation ⟨*convenience* foods⟩

convenience store *n* : a small market that is open many hours

con·ve·nient \kən-'vēn-yənt\ *adj* **1** : suited to a person's comfort or easy use ⟨a *convenient* time⟩ ⟨a *convenient* location⟩ **2** : easy to get to ⟨schools, churches, and stores are all *convenient*⟩ — **con·ve·nient·ly** *adv*

con·vent \'kän-vənt, -ˌvent\ *n* **1** : a community of nuns living together **2** : a house or set of buildings occupied by nuns

con·ven·tion \kən-'ven-chən\ *n* **1** : AGREEMENT 2a, COVENANT ⟨an international *convention* banning the spread of nuclear weapons⟩ **2** : a meeting of persons for a common purpose ⟨a constitutional *convention*⟩ ⟨teachers' *convention*⟩ **3** : a custom or a way of acting or doing things that is widely accepted and followed ⟨the *conventions* of punctuation⟩

con·ven·tion·al \kən-'vench-nəl, -'ven-chən-ᵊl\ *adj* : following, agreeing with, or based on convention ⟨*conventional* people⟩ ⟨*conventional* remarks⟩ ⟨a *conventional* detective story⟩ ⟨*conventional* symbols⟩ — **con·ven·tion·al·ly** \-ē\ *adv*

con·ven·tion·al·i·ty \kən-ˌven-chə-'nal-ət-ē\ *n, pl* **-ties** **1** : the quality or state of being conventional **2** : a conventional practice, custom, or rule

con·verge \kən-'vərj\ *vb* **con·verged; con·verg·ing** **1** : to tend or move toward one point or one another **2** : to come together and unite in a common interest

con·ver·gence \kən-'vər-jən(t)s\ *n* : the act or condition of converging

con·ver·gent \kən-'vər-jənt\ *adj* : tending to converge

con·ver·sant \kən-'vərs-ᵊnt\ *adj* : having knowledge or experience : FAMILIAR ⟨*conversant* with the facts of the case⟩

con·ver·sa·tion \ˌkän-vər-'sā-shən\ *n* : talking or a talk between two or more people — **con·ver·sa·tion·al** \-'sā-shnəl, -shən-ᵊl\ *adj* — **con·ver·sa·tion·al·ly** \-ē-\ *adv*

con·ver·sa·tion·al·ist \ˌkän-vər-'sā-shnə-ləst, -shən-ᵊl-əst\ *n* : a person who is fond of or good at conversation

¹con·verse \kən-'vərs\ *vb* **con·versed; con·vers·ing** : to engage in conversation : TALK [Middle English *conversen* "to live or be associated with a certain place, have dealings with", from early French *converser* (same meaning), from Latin *conversari* "to pass one's life, be associated with", derived from *convertere* "to turn around, change", from *con-* "with, together" and *vertere* "to turn" — related to ANNIVERSARY, ³CONVERSE, CONTROVERSY, DIVERT, REVERSE, UNIVERSE, VERTICAL, VERSATILE, VICE VERSA] — **con·vers·er** *n*

²con·verse \'kän-ˌvərs\ *n* : something that is the opposite of something else

³con·verse \kən-'vərs, 'kän-ˌvərs\ *adj* : reversed in order, relation, or action [from Latin *conversus*, past participle of *convertere* "to turn around, change", from *con-* "with, together" and *vertere* "to turn" — related to ¹CONVERSE] — **con·verse·ly** *adv*

con·ver·sion \kən-'vər-zhən\ *n* **1** : the act of converting : the state of being converted **2** : a change in nature, form, or units **3** : a change of religion

¹con·vert \kən-'vərt\ *vb* **1** : to change from one belief, view, or party to another **2 a** : to change from one substance, form, use, or unit to another ⟨*convert* pounds to grams⟩ **b** : to exchange for something equal in value ⟨*convert* francs into dollars⟩ — **con·vert·er** *n*

²con·vert \'kän-ˌvərt\ *n* : a person who has been converted

converted rice \kən-'vərt-əd-\ *n* : rice that has been treated to retain its natural mineral and vitamin content and to keep for a longer time

¹con·vert·ible \kən-'vərt-ə-bəl\ *adj* : capable of being converted : able to be changed in form or use ⟨a sofa *convertible* into a bed⟩ — **con·vert·ibil·i·ty** \-ˌvərt-ə-'bil-ət-ē\ *n*

²convertible *n* **1** : something convertible **2** : an automobile with a top that can be raised, lowered, or removed

con·vex \kän-'veks, kən; 'kän-ˌveks\ *adj* : curved or rounded like the outside of a sphere or circle ⟨a *convex* lens⟩ — **con·vex·i·ty** \kən-'vek-sət-ē, kän-\ *n*

con·vey \kən-'vā\ *vb* **con·veyed; con·vey·ing** **1** : to carry from one place to another : TRANSPORT **2** : to serve as a way of carrying ⟨pipes *convey* water⟩ **3** : to make known : COMMUNICATE ⟨we use words to *convey* meaning⟩

con·vey·ance \kən-'vā-ən(t)s\ *n* **1** : the act of conveying **2** : something used to carry goods or passengers

con·vey·or \kən-'vā-ər\ *n* : a mechanical device for carrying packages or bulk material from place to place (as by an endless moving belt)

¹con·vict \kən-'vikt\ *vb* : to find or prove guilty

²con·vict \'kän-ˌvikt\ *n* : a person serving a prison sentence

con·vic·tion \kən-'vik-shən\ *n* **1** : the act of convicting : the state of being convicted **2 a** : a strong belief or opinion ⟨has deep *convictions*⟩ **b** : the state of mind of a person who is sure that what he or she believes or says is true ⟨spoke with *conviction*⟩ **syn** see OPINION

con·vince \kən-'vin(t)s\ *vb* **con·vinced; con·vinc·ing** : to make a person agree or believe by arguing or showing evidence ⟨*convinced* them to go along⟩ ⟨*convinced* me it was true⟩ — **con·vinc·er** *n*

con·vinc·ing \kən-'vin(t)-siŋ\ *adj* : causing one to believe or agree — **con·vinc·ing·ly** \-siŋ-lē\ *adv*

con·viv·i·al \kən-'viv-yəl, -'viv-ē-əl\ *adj* : of, relating to, or fond of food, drink, merrymaking, and good company — **con·viv·i·al·i·ty** \-ˌviv-ē-'al-ət-ē\ *n* — **con·viv·i·al·ly**

\-'viv-yə-lē, -'viv-ē-ə-lē\ *adv*

con·vo·ca·tion \ˌkän-və-'kā-shən\ *n* : an assembly of persons convoked

con·voke \kən-'vōk\ *vb* **con·voked; con·vok·ing** : to call together to a meeting

con·vo·lut·ed \'kän-və-ˌlüt-əd\ *adj* **1** : folded or curved in twisted windings; *esp* : having convolutions **2** : complicated in form : INTRICATE ⟨*convoluted* phrasing⟩

con·vo·lu·tion \ˌkän-və-'lü-shən\ *n* : one of the uneven ridges on the surface of the brain and especially of the cerebrum of higher mammals

con·vol·vu·lus \kən-'väl-vyə-ləs, -'vȯl-\ *n, pl* **-lus·es** *or* **-li** \-ˌlī, -ˌlē\ : any of a genus of trailing or twining herbs and shrubs that are related to the morning glories

¹con·voy \'kän-ˌvȯi, kən-'vȯi\ *vb* : to go with to protect

²con·voy \'kän-ˌvȯi\ *n* **1** : one that convoys **2** : the act of convoying **3** : a group convoyed

con·vulse \kən-'vəls\ *vb* **con·vulsed; con·vuls·ing** : to shake violently; *esp* : to shake with usually uncontrolled jerky movements ⟨was *convulsed* with laughter⟩

con·vul·sion \kən-'vəl-shən\ *n* **1** : an abnormal violent contraction or series of contractions of the muscles that is not under control of the will **2** : a violent disturbance

con·vul·sive \-'vəl-siv\ *adj* **1 a** : being or producing a convulsion **b** : accompanying or having convulsions **2** : resembling a convulsion especially in being sudden or violent — **con·vul·sive·ly** *adv*

cony *variant of* CONEY

coo \'kü\ *vb* **1** : to make the low soft cry of a dove or pigeon or a similar sound **2** : to talk fondly or lovingly — **coo** *n*

¹cook \'kuk\ *n* : one who prepares food for eating [Middle English *cook* "a person who prepares food", from Old English *cōc* (same meaning), from Latin *coquus* (same meaning), from *coquere* "to cook" — related to KITCHEN; see *Word History* at KITCHEN]

²cook *vb* **1** : to prepare food for eating by the use of heat **2** : to go through the process of being cooked **3** : to think up : DEVISE ⟨*cook* up a scheme⟩

cook·book \'kuk-ˌbuk\ *n* : a book of cooking recipes and cooking directions

cook·er \'kuk-ər\ *n* : one that cooks; *esp* : a utensil, device, or piece of equipment for cooking

cook·ery \'kuk-(ə-)rē\ *n* : the art or practice of cooking

cook·ie *or* **cooky** \'kuk-ē\ *n, pl* **cook·ies** : a small sweet flat or slightly raised cake

cook·out \'kuk-ˌaut\ *n* : an outing at which a meal is cooked and served outdoors

cook·stove \-ˌstōv\ *n* : a stove for cooking

cook·ware \-ˌwa(ə)r, -ˌwe(ə)r\ *n* : utensils used in cooking

¹cool \'kül\ *adj* **1** : somewhat cold : lacking in warmth **2** : not letting in or keeping in heat ⟨*cool* clothes⟩ **3** : marked by steady calmness and self-control **4** : not friendly or interested ⟨was *cool* toward strangers⟩ **5** : producing an impression of being cool ⟨blue is a *cool* color⟩ — **cool·ish** \'kü-lish\ *adj* — **cool·ly** \'kül-(l)ē\ *adv* — **cool·ness** \'kül-nəs\ *n*

²cool *vb* **1** : to make or become cool **2** : to make or become less excited : CALM ⟨allow tempers to *cool*⟩

³cool *n* : a cool time or place ⟨the *cool* of the night⟩

cool·ant \'kü-lənt\ *n* : a usually fluid cooling substance

cool·er \'kü-lər\ *n* : a container for keeping food or drink cool

cool·head·ed \'kül-'hed-əd\ *adj* : not easily excited — **cool·head·ed·ness** \-'hed-əd-nəs\ *n*

coo·lie \'kü-lē\ *n* : a laborer usually in or from the Far East

\ə\ abut	\au\ out	\i\ tip	\o\ saw	\u\ foot
\ər\ further	\ch\ chin	\ī\ life	\oi\ coin	\y\ yet
\a\ mat	\e\ pet	\j\ job	\th\ thin	\yü\ few
\ā\ take	\ē\ easy	\ŋ\ sing	\th\ this	\yu\ cure
\ä\ cot, cart	\g\ go	\ō\ bone	\ü\ food	\zh\ vision

coon \'kün\ *n* : RACCOON

coon·skin \-,skin\ *n* : the fur or pelt of the raccoon

¹coop \'küp, 'kúp\ *n* : a cage or small enclosure or building for housing poultry or small animals

²coop *vb* : to place or keep in or as if in a coop

co—op \'kō-,äp, kō-'äp\ *n* : ²COOPERATIVE

coo·per \'kü-pər, 'kúp-ər\ *n* : a worker who makes or repairs wooden casks, tubs, or barrels

coo·per·age \'kü-p(ə-)rij, 'kúp-(ə-)rij\ *n* **1** : a cooper's work or products **2** : a cooper's place of business

co·op·er·ate \kō-'äp-(ə-),rāt\ *vb* **-at·ed; -at·ing** : to act, work, or associate with others so as to get something done

co·op·er·a·tion \kō-,äp-ə-'rā-shən\ *n* : the act or process of cooperating

¹co·op·er·a·tive \kō-'äp-(ə-)rət-iv, -'äp-ə-,rāt-\ *adj* **1** : willing to cooperate ⟨*cooperative* neighbors⟩ **2** : of, relating to, or organized as a cooperative ⟨a *cooperative* store⟩ ⟨*cooperative* apartments⟩ — **co·op·er·a·tive·ly** *adv* — **co·op·er·a·tive·ness** *n*

²cooperative *n* : an association owned by and operated for the benefit of those using its services

Coo·per's hawk \,kü-pərz-, kúp-ərz-\ *n* : an American hawk that has a rounded tail and is slightly smaller than a crow

Cooper's hawk

¹co·or·di·nate \kō-'órd-nət, -ᵊn-ət\ *adj* **1** : equal in rank **2 a** : being of equal rank in a compound sentence ⟨*coordinate* clauses⟩ **b** : COORDINATING — **co·or·di·nate·ly** *adv*

²co·or·di·nate \kō-'órd-ᵊn-,āt\ *vb* **-nat·ed; -nat·ing** **1** : to make or become coordinate **2** : to work or cause to work together smoothly — **co·or·di·na·tor** \-,āt-ər\ *n*

³co·or·di·nate \kō-'órd-nət, -ᵊn-ət\ *n* **1** : one that is coordinate with another **2** : any of a set of numbers used to locate a point on a line or surface or in space

coordinate axis *n* : a number line (as an x-axis or a y-axis) that is part of a coordinate system and along or parallel to which coordinates are measured

coordinate plane *n* : a plane whose points are labeled by means of coordinates

coordinate system *n* : any of various systems for locating points by means of lines and coordinates; *esp* : one consisting of a plane in which points are located by pairs of coordinates each of which measures the distance of a point from one of two perpendicular number lines along a line parallel to the other

co·or·di·nat·ing *adj* : joining words or word groups of the same grammatical rank ⟨*coordinating* conjunction⟩

co·or·di·na·tion \(,)kō-,órd-ᵊn-'ā-shən\ *n* **1** : the act of coordinating **2** : smooth working together (as of parts) ⟨good muscular *coordination*⟩

coot \'küt\ *n* **1** : a sluggish slow-flying slaty-black bird that somewhat resembles a duck but is related to the rails **2** : any of several North American scoters **3** : a harmless simple person

coo·tie \'küt-ē\ *n* : BODY LOUSE

cop \'käp\ *n* : a police officer

co·pa·cet·ic *or* **co·pa·set·ic** \,kō-pə-'set-ik\ *adj* : very satisfactory

¹cope \'kōp\ *n* : a long vestment that is worn like a cape by a priest or bishop [Old English *-cap* "long vestment, cope", from Latin *cappa* "head covering" — related to ²CAPE]

²cope *vb* **coped; cop·ing** : to struggle or try to manage especially with some success ⟨*cope* with a situation⟩ [from earlier *cope* "strike, fight, engage in a struggle", from Middle English *copen* "strike, fight", from early French *couper* "strike, cut", from earlier *coup* "a blow" — related to COUP,

COUPON]

co·pe·pod \'kō-pə-,päd\ *n* : any of a large group of usually tiny freshwater and marine crustaceans — **copepod** *adj*

Co·per·ni·can \kō-'pər-ni-kən, kə-\ *adj* : of or relating to Copernicus or his theory that the earth rotates daily on its axis and the planets revolve in orbits around the sun

copi·er \'käp-ē-ər\ *n* : one that copies; *esp* : a machine that makes copies (as of letters or drawings)

co·pi·lot \'kō-,pī-lət\ *n* : a pilot who assists the pilot or commander of a flight of an aircraft or spacecraft

cop·ing \'kō-piŋ\ *n* : the top or covering layer of a wall that is usually sloped to carry off water

co·pi·ous \'kō-pē-əs\ *adj* : very plentiful **syn** see PLENTIFUL — **co·pi·ous·ly** *adv* — **co·pi·ous·ness** *n*

co·pol·y·mer \(')kō-'päl-ə-mər\ *n* : a product of copolymerization

co·po·lym·er·iza·tion \,kō-pə-,lim-ə-rə-'zā-shən, ,kō-,päl-ə-mə-rə-\ *n* : the repeated chemical combination of two different molecules to form a usually much larger molecule — **co·po·lym·er·ize** \,kō-pə-'lim-ə-,rīz, ,kō-'päl-ə-mə-\ *vb*

cop–out \'käp-,aút\ *n* **1** : something that provides a way for someone to cop out **2** : a person who cops out **3** : an act or instance of copping out

cop out \(')käp-'aút\ *vb* **1** : to back out of something one does not want to do ⟨said I was *copping out* of the race because I was afraid I'd lose⟩ **2** : to avoid or take the easy way out of something one ought to do ⟨*cop out* on a promise⟩ ⟨*cop out* on a cause⟩

cop·per \'käp-ər\ *n* **1** : a reddish metallic element that is one of the best conductors of heat and electricity — see ELEMENT table **2** : a copper or bronze coin **3** *chiefly British* : a large copper kettle or boiler **4** : any of various small butterflies with usually copper-colored wings — **cop·pery** \'käp-(ə-)rē\ *adj*

cop·per·head \'käp-ər-,hed\ *n* **1** : a common largely coppery brown poisonous snake of the pit viper family that occurs in the eastern U.S. **2** : a person in the northern states who sympathized with the South during the Civil War

copper sulfate *n* : a usually blue crystalline compound that is used to destroy algae and fungi

cop·pice \'käp-əs\ *n* : a thicket, grove, or growth of small trees

co·pra \'kō-prə\ *n* : dried coconut meat

copse \'käps\ *n* : COPPICE

cop·ter \'käp-tər\ *n* : HELICOPTER

cop·u·late \'käp-yə-,lāt\ *vb* **-lat·ed; -lat·ing** : to engage in sexual intercourse — **cop·u·la·tion** \,käp-yə-'lā-shən\ *n* — **cop·u·la·to·ry** \'käp-yə-lə-,tōr-ē, -,tór-\ *adj*

¹copy \'käp-ē\ *n, pl* **cop·ies** **1** : something that is made to look exactly like something else : DUPLICATE ⟨a *copy* of a letter⟩ ⟨a *copy* of a painting⟩ **2** : one of the total number of books, magazines, or papers printed at one time **3** : written or printed material to be set in type

²copy *vb* **cop·ied; copy·ing** **1** : to make a copy : DUPLICATE **2** : IMITATE 1, 3

copy·cat \'käp-ē-,kat\ *n* : one who imitates or adopts the behavior or practices of another

copy·ist \'käp-ē-əst\ *n* **1** : a person who makes copies **2** : one who imitates

copy·read·er \'käp-ē-,rēd-ər\ *n* **1** : a person who edits and writes headlines for newspaper copy **2** : an employee of a publishing house who corrects manuscript copy

¹copy·right \-,rīt\ *n* : the legal right to be the only one to reproduce, publish, and sell the contents and form of a literary, musical, or artistic work — **copyright** *adj*

²copyright *vb* : to get a copyright on

co·que·try \'kō-kə-trē, kō-'ke-trē\ *n, pl* **-tries** : the behavior of a coquette

co·quette \kō-'ket\ *n* : a woman who tries without sincere affection to gain the attention and admiration of men : FLIRT — **co·quett·ish** \-'ket-ish\ *adj* — **co·quett·ish·ly** *adv*

co·qui·na \kō-'kē-nə\ *n* **1** : a soft whitish limestone formed of broken shells and corals cemented together and used for building **2** : a small marine clam used especially to make broth or chowder

cor·a·cle \'kòr-ə-kəl, 'kär-\ *n* : a boat made of hoops covered with horsehide or canvas

cor·al \'kòr-əl, 'kär-\ *n* **1 a** : the stony or horny deposit that is composed of the skeletons of various polyps; *esp* : a richly red material used in jewelry **b** : a polyp or polyp colony together with its membranes and skeleton **2** : a deep pink — **coral** *adj*

coral 1b

coral reef *n* : a reef made up of corals, other organic substances, and limestone

coral snake *n* : any of several poisonous chiefly tropical New World snakes brilliantly banded in red, black, and yellow or white; *also* : any of several harmless snakes resembling the coral snakes

¹cord \'kò(ə)rd\ *n* **1** : material like a small thin rope that is used mostly for tying things **2** : a bodily structure (as a tendon or nerve) resembling a cord **3** : a small flexible insulated electrical cable with a plug at one or both ends used for connecting an appliance to an outlet **4** : an amount of firewood equal to a pile of wood 4 × 4 × 8 feet or 128 cubic feet (about 3.6 cubic meters) **5 a** : a rib like a cord on a fabric **b** : a fabric with such ribs

²cord *vb* **1** : to supply, bind, or connect with a cord **2** : to pile up wood in cords

cord·age \'kòrd-ij\ *n* **1** : ropes or cords; *esp* : the ropes in the rigging of a ship **2** : the number of cords of wood on a specified area

cord·ed \'kòrd-əd\ *adj* **1** : having or drawn into ridges or cords ⟨*corded* muscles⟩ ⟨*corded* cloth⟩ **2** : bound or wound about with cords

¹cor·dial \'kòr-jəl\ *n* **1** : a stimulating medicine or drink **2** : LIQUEUR

²cordial *adj* **1** : tending to refresh or cheer **2** : being warm and friendly [Middle English *cordial* "from the heart, vital", from Latin *cordialis* (same meaning), from earlier *cord-, cor* "heart" — related to COURAGE] **syn** see GRACIOUS — **cor·di·al·i·ty** \,kòr-jē-'al-ət-ē\ *n* — **cor·dial·ly** \'kòrj-(ə-)lē\ *adv*

cord·less \'kòrd-ləs\ *adj* : having no cord; *esp* : powered by a battery ⟨a *cordless* telephone⟩

cor·don \'kòrd-ⁿn, 'kò(ə)r-,dän\ *n* **1** : an ornamental cord used especially on costumes **2** : a line of persons or things around a person or place ⟨a *cordon* of police⟩ **3** : a cord or ribbon worn as a badge or decoration

cor·do·van \'kòrd-ə-vən\ *n* **1** : a soft fine-grained colored leather **2** : thick leather tanned from the inner layer of horsehide — **cordovan** *adj*

cor·du·roy \'kòrd-ə-,ròi\ *n* **1 a** : a strong ribbed usually cotton cloth **b** *pl* : pants of corduroy **2** : a road built of logs laid side by side

cord·wood \'kò(ə)r-,dwùd\ *n* : wood piled or sold in cords

¹core \'kō(ə)r, 'kò(ə)r\ *n* **1** : a central or most important part **2** : the usually inedible central part of some fruits (as a pineapple or apple) **3** : a part removed from the interior of a mass especially to find out the interior composition or a hidden condition ⟨took a *core* of rock⟩ **4 a** : a mass of iron used to concentrate and strengthen the magnetic field resulting from a current in a surrounding coil **b** : a tiny doughnut-shaped piece of magnetic material at one time commonly used in computer memories **c** : a computer

memory made up of strings of cores **d** : the memory of a computer **5** : the central part of the earth having different properties from those of the surrounding parts; *also* : the central part of a heavenly body **6** : a system of studies that brings together material from subjects that are usually taught separately **7** : the place in a nuclear reactor where fission takes place

²core *vb* **cored; cor·ing** : to remove a core from ⟨*core* an apple⟩ — **cor·er** *n*

Co·rin·thi·an \kə-'rin(t)-thē-ən\ *adj* : of or relating to a style of Greek architecture characterized by a bell-shaped capital covered with sculptured leaves [named for *Corinth,* region and city in ancient Greece]

Co·rin·thi·ans \kə-'rin(t)-thē-ənz\ *n* — see BIBLE table

Co·ri·o·lis force \,kòr-ē-,ō-ləs-, ,kòr-, -ē-ə-,lēs-\ *n* : a force that as a result of the earth's rotation acts on a body in motion (as a projectile)

¹cork \'kò(ə)rk\ *n* **1 a** : the elastic tough outer tissue of the cork oak used especially for stoppers and insulation **b** : the tissue of a woody plant making up most of the bark and arising from an inner cambium **2** : a usually cork stopper for a bottle or jug **3** : a fishing float

²cork *vb* **1** : to furnish, fit, or seal with a cork **2** : to blacken with burnt cork

cork·er \'kòr-kər\ *n* **1** : one that corks containers **2** : an outstanding person or thing

cork oak *n* : an oak of southern Europe and northern Africa that is the source of the cork used especially for stoppers and insulation

¹cork·screw \'kòrk-,skrü\ *n* : a pointed spiral tool with a handle for pulling corks from bottles

²corkscrew *adj* : resembling a corkscrew : SPIRAL

corky \'kòr-kē\ *adj* **cork·i·er; -est** : resembling cork especially in dry porous quality

corm \'kòrm\ *n* : a solid bulblike underground part of a stem (as of the crocus or gladiolus) — compare BULB 1a, TUBER 1

cor·mo·rant \'kòrm-(ə-)rənt, 'kòr-mə-,rant\ *n* : any of various dark-colored web-footed seabirds with a long neck, a wedge-shaped tail, a hooked bill, and a patch of bare often brightly colored skin under the mouth

cormorant

¹corn \'kò(ə)rn\ *n* **1 a** : the seeds of a cereal plant and especially of the important cereal crop of a particular region (as in Britain wheat, in Scotland and Ireland oats, and in the New World and Australia Indian corn) **b** : sweet corn served as a vegetable while the kernels are still soft and milky **2** : a plant that produces corn **3** : corny actions or speech [Old English *corn* "seeds of a cereal plant"]

²corn *vb* : to preserve by packing with salt or by soaking in salty water ⟨*corned* beef⟩

³corn *n* : a local hardening and thickening of skin (as on a toe) [Middle English *corne* "thickening of the skin", from early French *corne* "horn, corner", from Latin *cornu* "horn, point" — related to UNICORN]

corn belt *n* : an area (as the central portion of the U.S.) in which more land is used for growing corn than any other single crop

corn borer *n* : any of several insects that bore in corn; *esp*

\ə\ abut	\aủ\ out	\i\ tip	\ò\ saw	\ủ\ foot
\ər\ further	\ch\ chin	\ī\ life	\òi\ coin	\y\ yet
\a\ mat	\e\ pet	\j\ job	\th\ thin	\yü\ few
\ā\ take	\ē\ easy	\ŋ\ sing	\th\ this	\yủ\ cure
\ä\ cot, cart	\g\ go	\ō\ bone	\ü\ food	\zh\ vision

: a moth whose larva is a major pest especially in the stems and the part of the root that joins the stem of Indian corn, dahlias, and potatoes

corn bread *n* : bread made with cornmeal

corn chip *n* : a piece of a dry crisp snack food prepared from a seasoned cornmeal batter

corn·cob \'kȯ(ə)rn-ˌkäb\ *n* : the woody core on which the kernels of Indian corn are arranged

corncob pipe *n* : a tobacco pipe with a bowl made by hollowing out a piece of corncob

corn·crib \-ˌkrib\ *n* : a crib for storing ears of Indian corn

corn dog *n* : a frankfurter dipped in cornmeal batter, fried, and served on a stick

cor·nea \'kȯr-nē-ə\ *n* : the transparent part of the coat of the eyeball that covers the iris and pupil and lets light through to the interior — **cor·ne·al** \-nē-əl\ *adj*

corn ear·worm \-'i(ə)r-ˌwərm\ *n* : a moth whose striped yellow-headed larva is especially destructive to ears of Indian corn

¹cor·ner \'kȯ(r)-nər\ *n* **1 a** : the point or place where edges or sides meet : ANGLE **b** : the place where two streets or roads meet **c** : a piece designed to form, mark, or protect a corner **2** : a place far away from ordinary affairs or life ⟨a quiet *corner* of the town⟩ **3** : a position from which escape or retreat is difficult or impossible ⟨was backed into a *corner*⟩ **4** : control or ownership of enough of the available supply of something to control its price — **cor·nered** \-nərd\ *adj*

²corner *adj* **1** : situated at a corner ⟨the *corner* drugstore⟩ **2** : used or fitted for use in or on a corner ⟨a *corner* cupboard⟩

³corner *vb* **cor·nered; cor·ner·ing** \'kȯ(r)n-(ə-)riŋ\ **1** : to drive into a corner ⟨the police *cornered* the criminal⟩ **2** : to get a corner on ⟨*corner* the wheat market⟩ **3** : to turn a corner ⟨a car that *corners* well⟩

cor·ner·stone \'kȯ(r)nər-ˌstōn\ *n* **1** : a stone forming part of a corner in a wall **2** : something of basic importance ⟨the *cornerstone* of our foreign policy⟩

cor·net \kȯr-'net\ *n* **1** : a brass instrument like the trumpet but having a shorter tube and a softer tone **2** : something shaped like a cone [Middle English *cornet* "cornet", from early French *cornet*, literally "little horn", from Latin *cornu* "horn" — related to ³CORN] — **cor·net·ist** *or* **cor·net·tist** \-'net-əst\ *n*

corn·field \'kȯ(ə)rn-ˌfēld\ *n* : a field in which corn is grown

corn·flakes \-ˌflāks\ *n pl* : toasted flakes made from hulled kernels of corn and used as a breakfast cereal

corn·flow·er \-ˌflaὐ(-ə)r\ *n* : BACHELOR'S BUTTON

cor·nice \'kȯr-nəs\ *n* **1** : the decorative piece that forms the top edge of a building or column and extends beyond it **2** : an ornamental molding where the walls meet the ceiling of a room **3** : a decorative band of metal or wood to conceal curtain fixtures

Cor·nish \'kȯr-nish\ *n* : any of an English breed of sturdy compact chickens

Cor·nish·man \-mən\ *n* : a person born or living in Cornwall, England

corn·meal \'kȯ(ə)rn-ˌmē(ə)l, -ˌmēl\ *n* : meal ground from corn

corn oil *n* : a yellow fatty oil obtained from the germ of corn kernels and used chiefly in salad oil, in soft soap, and in margarine

corn pone *n, Southern & Midland* : corn bread often made without milk or eggs and baked or fried

corn·stalk \'kȯ(ə)rn-ˌstȯk\ *n* : a stalk of Indian corn

corn·starch \-ˌstärch\ *n* : a fine starch made from corn and used in foods for thickening, in making corn syrup and sugars, and in making adhesives and sizes for papers and textiles

corn syrup *n* : a syrup obtained from cornstarch and used in baked goods and candy

cor·nu·co·pia \ˌkȯr-n(y)ə-'kō-pē-ə\ *n* **1** : a horn-shaped container overflowing with fruits and flowers used as a symbol of plenty **2** : a container shaped like a horn or a cone

cornucopia 1

corny \'kȯr-nē\ *adj* **corn·i·er; -est** : tastelessly old-fashioned : tiresomely simple or sentimental ⟨*corny* music⟩ ⟨*corny* jokes⟩

co·rol·la \kə-'räl-ə, -'rōl-\ *n* : the part of a flower that consists of the petals and encloses the stamens and pistil

cor·ol·lary \'kȯr-ə-ˌler-ē, 'kär-\ *n, pl* **-lar·ies** **1** : something that follows directly from something that has been proved **2** : something that naturally follows : RESULT

co·ro·na \kə-'rō-nə\ *n* **1** : a usually colored circle often seen around and close to a shining body (as the sun or moon) **2** : the outermost part of the atmosphere of the sun appearing as a halo around the moon's black disk during a total eclipse of the sun; *also* : a similar part of the atmosphere of a star **3** : a faint glow next to the surface of an electrical conductor at high voltage — **co·ro·nal** \'kȯr-ən-ᵊl, 'kär-; kə-'rōn-\ *adj*

¹cor·o·nary \'kȯr-ə-ˌner-ē, 'kär-\ *adj* : of, relating to, or being the vessels that supply blood to the heart; *also* : of or relating to the heart

²coronary *n, pl* **-nar·ies** **1** : a coronary blood vessel **2** : CORONARY THROMBOSIS

coronary artery *n* : either of the two arteries that arise from the aorta and supply the tissues of the heart

coronary heart disease *n* : a condition (as coronary thrombosis) that reduces the blood flow through the coronary arteries to the heart muscle

coronary occlusion *n* : the partial or complete blocking (as by a thrombus or spasm) of a coronary artery

coronary thrombosis *n* : the blocking of an artery of the heart by a thrombus

cor·o·na·tion \ˌkȯr-ə-'nā-shən, ˌkär-\ *n* : the act or ceremony of crowning a king or queen

cor·o·ner \'kȯr-ə-nər, 'kär-\ *n* : a public officer whose chief duty is to discover the causes of any death possibly not due to natural causes

cor·o·net \ˌkȯr-ə-'net, ˌkär-\ *n* **1** : a small crown worn by a noble **2** : an ornamental wreath or band worn around the head ⟨a *coronet* of flowers⟩

¹cor·po·ral \'kȯr-p(ə-)rəl\ *adj* : of or relating to the body ⟨whipping and other *corporal* punishments⟩ — **cor·po·ral·ly** \-ē\ *adv*

²corporal *n* : a noncommissioned officer in the army or marines with a rank just below that of sergeant

corpora lutea *pl of* CORPUS LUTEUS

cor·po·rate \'kȯr-p(ə-)rət\ *adj* **1 a** : formed into a corporation **b** : of, relating to, or being a corporation ⟨take *corporate* action⟩ **2** : of, relating to, or being a whole composed of individuals ⟨try to change the *corporate* structure⟩ — **cor·po·rate·ly** *adv*

cor·po·ra·tion \ˌkȯr-pə-'rā-shən\ *n* : a group that is authorized by law to carry on an activity (as a business enterprise) with the rights and duties of a single person

cor·po·re·al \kȯr-'pōr-ē-əl, -'pȯr-\ *adj* : having, consisting of, or relating to a physical material body — **cor·po·re·al·ly** \-'pōr-ē-ə-lē, -'pȯr-\ *adv*

corps \'kō(ə)r, 'kȯ(ə)r\ *n, pl* **corps** \'kō(ə)rz, 'kȯ(ə)rz\ **1 a** : an organized branch of the military establishment ⟨Marine *Corps*⟩ ⟨*Corps* of Engineers⟩ **b** : a military unit consisting of two or more divisions **2** : a group of persons acting under one authority ⟨diplomatic *corps*⟩ [from French *corps* "part of a military organization", from Latin *corpus* "body" — related to CORPSE]

corpse \'kȯ(ə)rps\ *n* : a dead body [Middle English *corps* "human body", from early French *corps* (same meaning), from Latin *corpus* "body"]

corps·man \'kō(ə)r(z)-mən, 'kó(ə)r(z)-\ *n* : an enlisted man trained to give first aid

cor·pu·lence \'kòr-pyə-lən(t)s\ *n* : the state of being corpulent : OBESITY

cor·pu·lent \'kòr-pyə-lənt\ *adj* : very fat : OBESE

Cor·pus Chris·ti \,kòr-pəs-'kris-tē\ *n* : the Thursday after Trinity Sunday observed as a Roman Catholic festival in honor of the Eucharist [Middle English *Corpus Christi* "church festival of Corpus Christi", from Latin *Corpus Christi*, literally "body of Christ"]

cor·pus·cle \'kòr-(,)pəs-əl\ *n* 1 : a very small particle 2 : one of the very small cells (as a red blood cell) that float freely in the blood — **cor·pus·cu·lar** \kòr-'pəs-kyə-lər\ *adj*

cor·pus lu·te·um \,kòr-pəs-'lüt-ē-əm\ *n, pl* **cor·po·ra lu·tea** \,kòr-p(ə)rə-'lüt-ē-ə\ : a yellowish mass of tissue formed in a graafian follicle in the ovary of a mammal after the egg is released

¹cor·ral \kə-'ral\ *n* 1 : a pen for keeping or capturing livestock 2 : an enclosure made with wagons for defense of a camp

²corral *vb* **cor·ralled; cor·ral·ling** 1 : to keep in or as if in a corral 2 : ¹SURROUND, CAPTURE 3 : to arrange wagons so as to form a corral

¹cor·rect \kə-'rekt\ *vb* 1 a : to make or set right b : COUNTERACT, NEUTRALIZE c : to alter or adjust so as to bring to some standard or required condition 2 a : ¹REBUKE, PUNISH b : to indicate the faults or errors of and show how they can be made right ⟨*correct* a student's composition⟩ — **cor·rect·able** \-'rek-tə-bəl\ *adj*

   syn CORRECT, RECTIFY, AMEND mean to make right. CORRECT suggests doing something that removes mistakes or merely points them out ⟨teachers *correct* tests⟩ RECTIFY suggests changing something to make it accurate or to bring it under proper control ⟨*rectified* the crowded conditions by building a new school⟩ AMEND suggests improving or restoring by making changes ⟨*amend* the sentence so that it makes sense⟩

²correct *adj* 1 : meeting or agreeing with a particular standard ⟨*correct* behavior⟩ 2 : agreeing with fact or known truth — **cor·rect·ly** \-'rek-(t)lē\ *adv* — **cor·rect·ness** \-'rek(t)-nəs\ *n*

   syn CORRECT, ACCURATE, EXACT, PRECISE mean brought into agreement with truth, a fact, or a standard. CORRECT stresses the notion that something is free from error ⟨a *correct* answer⟩ ACCURATE stresses that great care has been taken to make sure that something agrees with the facts ⟨an *accurate* description of the meeting⟩ EXACT stresses that something agrees very closely with fact or truth ⟨the *exact* number of people present at the meeting⟩ PRECISE suggests an even closer or more careful agreement with fact or with a certain standard ⟨the *precise* measurements of the room⟩

cor·rec·tion \kə-'rek-shən\ *n* 1 : the action or an instance of correcting 2 : a change that makes something right 3 : punishment or scolding intended to correct faults of character or behavior — **cor·rec·tion·al** \-shnəl, -shən-ᵊl\ *adj*

cor·rec·tive \kə-'rek-tiv\ *adj* : serving to correct : having the power of making right, normal, or regular — **corrective** *n*

cor·re·late \'kòr-ə-,lāt, 'kär-\ *vb* **-lat·ed; -lat·ing** : to connect in a systematic way ⟨*correlate* history and literature lessons⟩

cor·re·la·tion \,kòr-ə-'lā-shən, ,kär-\ *n* 1 : the act or process of correlating 2 : the state of being correlated; *esp* : a mutual relation discovered to exist between things ⟨the apparent *correlation* between the degree of poverty in a society and the crime rate⟩ — **cor·re·la·tion·al** \-shnəl, -shən-ᵊl\ *adj*

¹cor·rel·a·tive \kə-'rel-ət-iv\ *adj* 1 : mutually related 2

: having a mutual grammatical relation and regularly used together ⟨"either" and "or" are *correlative* conjunctions⟩ — **cor·rel·a·tive·ly** *adv*

²correlative *n* : either of two correlative things

cor·re·spond \,kòr-ə-'spänd, ,kär-\ *vb* 1 : to be alike 2 a : to be equivalent (as in meaning, position, purpose, or structure) : MATCH b : to be connected by means of a mathematical relationship ⟨point A *corresponds* to the number 1⟩ 3 : to communicate by means of letters — **cor·re·spond·ing·ly** \-'spän-diŋ-lē\ *adv*

cor·re·spon·dence \,kòr-ə-'spän-dən(t)s\ *n* 1 a : agreement between certain things b : a point of similarity c : a relation between sets in which each member of one set is matched to one or more members of the other set 2 a : communication by letters b : the letters exchanged

¹cor·re·spon·dent \,kòr-ə-'spän-dənt\ *adj* 1 : SIMILAR 1 2 : being in agreement : FITTING

²correspondent *n* 1 : something that corresponds to something else 2 a : one who communicates with another by letter b : one who contributes news to a newspaper or newscast often from a distant place

corresponding angle *n* : one of a pair of nonadjacent angles which are on the same side of a line intersected by two lines and of which one angle is inside and the other outside the two lines

C corresponding angle

cor·ri·dor \'kòr-əd-ər, 'kär-, -ə-,dò(ə)r\ *n* 1 : a passageway (as in a school) into which compartments or rooms open 2 : a narrow strip of land especially through territory held by an enemy [from early French *corridor* "passageway", from early Italian *corridore* (same meaning), from *correre* "to run", from Latin *currere* "to run" — related to COURSE, CURRENT]

cor·rob·o·rate \kə-'räb-ə-,rāt\ *vb* **-rat·ed; -rat·ing** : to support with evidence or authority ⟨*corroborated* my brother's story⟩ — **cor·rob·o·ra·tion** \-,räb-ə-'rā-shən\ *n* — **cor·rob·o·ra·tive** \-'räb-ə-,rāt-iv, -'räb-(ə-)rət-iv\ *adj* — **cor·rob·o·ra·tor** \-'räb-ə-,rāt-ər\ *n* — **cor·rob·o·ra·to·ry** \-'räb-(ə-)rə-,tōr-ē, -,tòr-ē, -,tòr-\ *adj*

cor·rode \kə-'rōd\ *vb* **cor·rod·ed; cor·rod·ing** : to eat or be eaten away by degrees as if by gnawing ⟨a bridge *corroded* by rust⟩

cor·ro·sion \kə-'rō-zhən\ *n* : the action, process, or effect of corroding

cor·ro·sive \kə-'rō-siv, -ziv\ *adj* : tending or having the power to corrode ⟨*corrosive* acids⟩ — **corrosive** *n* — **cor·ro·sive·ly** *adv* — **cor·ro·sive·ness** *n*

corrosive sublimate *n* : a poisonous chloride of mercury used to kill germs and fungi and in photography

cor·ru·gate \'kòr-ə-,gāt, 'kär-\ *vb* **-gat·ed; -gat·ing** : to form or shape into wrinkles or folds : FURROW ⟨*corrugated* paper⟩

cor·ru·ga·tion \,kòr-ə-'gā-shən, ,kär-\ *n* 1 : the act of corrugating : the state of being corrugated 2 : a ridge or groove of a corrugated surface

¹cor·rupt \kə-'rəpt\ *vb* 1 : to change from good to bad in morals, manners, or actions; *esp* : to influence a public official improperly 2 : ¹ROT 1a, SPOIL 3 : to change from the original or correct form or version ⟨*corrupt* a text⟩ 4 : to become debased [Middle English *corrupten* "change

\ə\ abut	\aú\ out	\i\ tip	\ò\ saw	\ú\ foot
\ər\ further	\ch\ chin	\ī\ life	\òi\ coin	\y\ yet
\a\ mat	\e\ pet	\j\ job	\th\ thin	\yü\ few
\ā\ take	\ē\ easy	\ŋ\ sing	\th\ this	\yù\ cure
\ä\ cot, cart	\g\ go	\ō\ bone	\ü\ food	\zh\ vision

from good to bad, corrupt", from Latin *corruptus* "corrupted" from *corrumpere* "to corrupt", from *cor-*, *com-* "with" and *rumpere* "to break" — related to ABRUPT, RUPTURE] — **cor·rupt·er** *or* **cor·rup·tor** \-'rəp-tər\ *n*

²**corrupt** *adj* **1** : morally corrupted : DEPRAVED **2** : characterized by improper conduct ⟨a *corrupt* government⟩ — **cor·rupt·ly** \-'rəp(t)-lē\ *adv* — **cor·rupt·ness** \-'rəp(t)-nəs\ *n*

cor·rupt·ible \kə-'rəp-tə-bəl\ *adj* : capable of being corrupted — **cor·rupt·ibil·i·ty** \-,rəp-tə-'bil-ət-ē\ *n*

cor·rup·tion \kə-'rəp-shən\ *n* **1** : physical decay or rotting **2** : dishonest or evil behavior **3** : the causing of someone else to do wrong (as by bribery) **4** : a change for the worse

cor·sage \kòr-'säzh, -'säj; 'kòr-,säzh, -,säj\ *n* : a bouquet of flowers usually worn at the shoulder

cor·sair \'kòr-,sa(ə)r, -,se(ə)r\ *n* : ¹PIRATE

corse \'kò(ə)rs\ *n, archaic* : CORPSE

corse·let *or* **cors·let** \'kòr-slət\ *n* : the body armor worn by a knight especially on the upper part of the body

cor·set \'kòr-sət\ *n* : a tight stiff undergarment worn to support or give shape to waist and hips — **corset** *vb*

cor·tege *also* **cor·tège** \kòr-'tezh, 'kòr-,tezh\ *n* **1** : a group of attendants : RETINUE **2** : PROCESSION 2; *esp* : a funeral procession

cor·tex \'kòr-,teks\ *n, pl* **cor·ti·ces** \'kòrt-ə-,sēz\ *or* **cor·tex·es** : an outer layer of a plant or animal or one of its parts ⟨the *cortex* of the kidney⟩: as **a** : the outer layer of gray matter of the brain **b** : the layer of tissue outside the

corselet

xylem and phloem and inside the corky or epidermal tissues of a vascular plant; *also* : all tissues external to the xylem

cor·ti·sone \'kòrt-ə-,sōn, -,zōn\ *n* : a hormone of the adrenal glands that is used especially in the treatment of arthritis

co·run·dum \kə-'rən-dəm\ *n* : a very hard mineral of aluminum oxide used for grinding, smoothing, or polishing or in some crystalline forms as a gem (as ruby or sapphire)

cor·vette \kòr-'vet\ *n* **1** : an armed naval sailing ship **2** : an armed escort ship that is small and fast

cosily, cosiness *variant of* COZILY, COZINESS

co·sine \'kō-,sīn\ *n* : the ratio between the side next to an acute angle in a right triangle and the hypotenuse

¹**cos·met·ic** \käz-'met-ik\ *n* : a cosmetic preparation (as a cream, lotion, or powder)

²**cosmetic** *adj* : intended to beautify the hair or complexion

cos·me·tol·o·gist \,käz-mə-'täl-ə-jəst\ *n* : one who gives beauty treatments (as to skin and hair) — **cos·me·tol·o·gy** \-jē\ *n*

cos·mic \'käz-mik\ *adj* **1** : of or relating to the cosmos ⟨*cosmic* theories⟩ **2** : extremely vast : GRAND ⟨*cosmic* dimensions⟩

cosmic dust *n* : very fine particles of solid matter found in any part of the universe

cosmic ray *n* : a stream of atomic nuclei of extremely penetrating character that enter the earth's atmosphere from outer space at speeds approaching that of light

cos·mol·o·gy \käz-'mäl-ə-jē\ *n, pl* **-gies** : a branch of astronomy that deals with the beginning, structure, and space-time relationships of the universe — **cos·mol·o·gist** \-jəst\ *n*

cos·mo·naut \'käz-mə-,nòt, -,nät\ *n* : a Soviet astronaut

cos·mo·pol·i·tan \,käz-mə-'päl-ət-ªn\ *adj* **1** : having a worldwide scope or outlook : not limited or narrow ⟨*cosmopolitan* world travelers⟩ **2** : composed of persons or elements from many parts of the world ⟨a *cosmopolitan* city⟩ **3** : found in most parts of the world and in many kinds of ecological conditions ⟨a *cosmopolitan* herb⟩ — **cosmopolitan** *n*

cos·mos \'käz-məs, *senses 1 & 2 also* -,mōs, -,mäs\ *n* **1** : the orderly universe **2** : a complex harmonious system **3** : a tall garden plant that is related to the daisies and has showy white, pink, or rose-colored flower heads with usually yellow centers

cos·sack \'käs-,ak, -ək\ *n* : a member of a group of frontiersmen of southern Russia organized as cavalry in the czarist army

¹**cost** \'kòst\ *n* **1** : the amount paid or charged for something : PRICE **2** : the loss or penalty involved in achieving a goal ⟨won the battle at the *cost* of many lives⟩ **3** *pl* : legal expenses awarded usually to the winning side against the losing side ⟨fined $50 and *costs*⟩

²**cost** *vb* **cost; cost·ing** **1** : to have a price of : require payment of ⟨each ticket *costs* one dollar⟩ **2** : to cause one to pay, spend, or lose ⟨selfishness *cost* him many friends⟩

cos·tal \'käs-tªl\ *adj* : of, relating to, or located near the ribs

cos·ter \'käs-tər\ *n, British* : COSTERMONGER

cos·ter·mon·ger \'käs-tər-,məng-gər, -,mäng-\ *n, British* : a person who sells fruit or vegetables in the street from a stand or cart

cos·tive \'käs-tiv\ *adj* **1** : affected with constipation **2** : causing constipation ⟨a *costive* diet⟩

cost·ly \'kòs(t)-lē\ *adj* **cost·li·er; -est** **1** : of great cost or value ⟨*costly* furs⟩ **2** : gained at great expense or sacrifice ⟨*costly* victory⟩ — **cost·li·ness** *n*

¹**cos·tume** \'käs-,t(y)üm\ *n* **1** : the style of clothing, ornaments, and hair characteristic of a certain period, region, or class ⟨ancient Roman *costume*⟩ ⟨peasant *costume*⟩ **2** : special or fancy dress (as for wear on the stage or at a masquerade party) **3** : a person's outer clothing — **costume** *adj*

²**costume** *vb* **cos·tumed; cos·tum·ing** : to provide with a costume

cos·tum·er \'käs-,t(y)ü-mər\ *n* : one who makes, sells, or rents costumes

cosy *variant of* COZY

¹**cot** \'kät\ *n* : COTTAGE 1 [Old English *cot* "cottage"]

²**cot** *n* : a narrow bed often made of fabric stretched over a folding frame [from Hindi *khāt* "frame of a bed"]

cote \'kōt, 'kät\ *n* : a shed or coop for small domestic animals (as pigeons)

co·te·rie \'kōt-ə-(,)rē, ,kōt-ə-'rē\ *n* : a small close group of people with a shared interest

co·til·lion \kō-'til-yən, kə-\ *n* **1** : a complicated formal dance with frequent changing of partners **2** : a formal ball

cot·tage \'kät-ij\ *n* **1** : a small one-family house **2** : a small house for vacation use

cottage cheese *n* : a very soft cheese made from soured skim milk

cot·tag·er \'kät-ij-ər\ *n* : one who lives in a cottage; *esp* : one occupying a private house at a vacation resort

¹**cot·ter** *or* **cot·tar** \'kät-ər\ *n* : a peasant or farm laborer occupying a cottage usually in return for services

²**cot·ter** \'kät-ər\ *n* : a wedge-shaped piece used to fasten parts together

cotter pin *n* : a half-round metal strip bent into a pin whose ends can be spread apart after insertion through a slot or hole

¹**cot·ton** \'kät-ªn\ *n* **1 a** : a soft usually white fluffy material that is made up of the hairs around the seeds of a tall plant related to the mallows and that is spun into yarn **b** : any plant that produces cotton **2 a** : fabric made of cotton **b**

: yarn spun from cotton —
cotton *adj*

²**cot·ton** *vb* **cot·toned; cot·ton·ing** \'kät-niŋ, -ᵊn-iŋ\
: to take a liking ⟨*cottoned*
to them at our first meet-
ing⟩

cotton candy *n* : a candy
made of spun sugar

cotton gin *n* : a machine
that separates the seeds,
hulls, and foreign material
from cotton

cot·ton·mouth \'kät-ᵊn-
,maùth\ *n* : WATER MOCCASIN

cottonmouth moccasin *n* : WATER MOCCASIN

cot·ton·seed \'kät-ᵊn-,sēd\ *n* : the seed of the cotton plant

cottonseed oil *n* : a pale yellow oil that is obtained from
cottonseed and is used chiefly in salad and cooking oils
and in shortenings and margarine

cot·ton·tail \'kät-ᵊn-,tāl\ *n* : any of several small brownish
gray rabbits with a white fluffy tail

cot·ton·wood \-,wùd\ *n* : a poplar with a small bunch of
cottony hairs on the seed; *esp* : one of the eastern and
central U.S. that grows tall and rapidly and produces many leaves

cot·tony \'kät-nē, -ᵊn-ē\ *adj* **1** : covered with soft hairs
: DOWNY **2** : ¹SOFT 1d

cot·y·le·don \,kät-ᵊl-'ēd-ᵊn\ *n* : the first leaf or one of the
first leaves developed by the embryo of a seed plant that
is usually folded within the seed until germination and
serves as a storehouse of food — called also *seed leaf*

¹**couch** \'kaùch\ *vb* **1** : to lie down for rest or sleep **2** : to
bring down : LOWER ⟨a knight charging with *couched*
lance⟩ **3** : to phrase in a specified manner ⟨a letter
couched in polite terms⟩

²**couch** *n* : a piece of furniture (as a bed or sofa) that one
can sit or lie on

cou·gar \'kü-gər *also*
-,gär\ *n, pl* **cougars**
also **cougar** : a large
powerful brownish
yellow cat formerly
widespread in the
Americas but no
longer found in many
areas — called also
*catamount, moun-
tain lion, panther,
puma*

cougar

¹**cough** \'kóf\ *vb* **1** : to force air from the lungs with a sharp
short noise or series of noises **2** : to get rid of by coughing

²**cough** *n* **1** : a condition marked by repeated or frequent
coughing **2** : an act or sound of coughing

cough drop *n* : a small piece of candy or a tablet that contains medicine and is used to relieve coughing

cough syrup *n* : any of various sweet liquids that contain
medicine and are used to relieve coughing

could \kəd, (')kùd\ *past of* CAN — used as a helping verb in
the past ⟨we found we *could* go⟩ ⟨we said we would go if
we *could*⟩ and as a polite or less forceful alternative to *can*
⟨*could* you do this for me⟩

couldn't \'kùd-ᵊnt\ : could not

couldst \kədst, (')kùdst\ *archaic past 2d sing of* CAN

cou·lee \'kü-lē\ *n* **1 a** : a dry creek bed **b** : a usually
small or shallow ravine **2** : a thick sheet or stream of lava

cou·lomb \'kü-,läm, -,lōm; kü-'läm, -'lōm\ *n* : the practical
meter-kilogram-second unit of electric charge equal to the
quantity of electricity transferred by a current of one ampere in one second [named for Charles-Augustin de *Coulomb* 1736–1806, French scientist]

coun·cil \'kaùn(t)-səl\ *n* **1** : a meeting for consultation **2**

: an advisory or legislative body ⟨governor's *council*⟩ **3**
: an administrative body ⟨city *council*⟩

coun·cil·lor *or* **coun·cil·or** \'kaùn(t)-s(ə-)lər\ *n* : a member of a council

coun·cil·man \'kaùn(t)-səl-mən\ *n* : a member of a council
(as of a town or city)

¹**coun·sel** \'kaùn(t)-səl\ *n* **1** : advice given **2** : DELIBERA-
TION 1, 2, CONSULTATION **3** *pl* **counsel** : a lawyer engaged in the trial or management of a case in court

²**counsel** *vb* **-seled** *or* **-selled; -sel·ing** *or* **-sel·ling**
\-s(ə-)liŋ\ **1** : to give counsel to : ADVISE ⟨*counsel* a student on a choice of studies⟩ **2** : to seek counsel : CON-
SULT ⟨*counsel* with friends⟩

coun·sel·or *or* **coun·sel·lor** \'kaùn(t)-s(ə-)lər\ *n* **1** : a
person who gives counsel ⟨guidance *counselor*⟩ **2** : LAW-
YER **3** : a supervisor of campers or activities at a summer
camp

¹**count** \'kaùnt\ *vb* **1 a** : to add one by one so as to find
the total number of a group of things ⟨*count* the apples in
a box⟩ **b** : to name the consecutive numbers up to and
including ⟨*count* ten⟩ **c** : to recite the numbers one by
one or by groups ⟨*count* to one hundred by fives⟩ **d** : to
include in a tally ⟨forty present, *counting* children⟩ **2**
a : CONSIDER 3 ⟨*count* myself lucky⟩ **b** : to include or
leave out by or as if by counting ⟨*count* me out⟩ **3 a**
: RELY 2, DEPEND ⟨someone you can *count* on⟩ **b** : ²PLAN
1 ⟨*counted* on going⟩ **4** : to have value or importance
⟨every vote *counts*⟩ [Middle English *counten* "to add one
by one", from early French *conter, compter* (same meaning), derived from Latin *computare* "to count, compute" —
related to ACCOUNT, COMPUTE] — **count·able** \-ə-bəl\ *adj*

²**count** *n* **1 a** : the act or process of counting **b** : a total
obtained by counting : TALLY **2** : a charge of wrongdoing;
esp : a separate item in a legal accusation ⟨guilty on all
counts⟩

³**count** *n* : a European nobleman whose rank is equal to that
of a British earl [from early French *conte, comte* "nobleman", derived from Latin *comes* "companion, member of
a royal court", literally "one who goes with another", from
com- "with" and *-es*, a form of *ire* "to go" — related to
COUNTY, ITINERARY]

count·down \'kaùnt-,daùn\ *n* : the process of counting off
backward in fixed units (as seconds) the time remaining
before an event (as the launching of a rocket)

¹**coun·te·nance** \'kaùnt-ᵊn-ənts, 'kaùnt-nənts\ *n* **1 a**
: calm expression **b** : calmness of mind **2** : ¹FACE 1, 3a;
esp : facial expression as a sign of mood, emotion, or
character **3** : a show of approval ⟨gave no *countenance*
to the plan⟩

²**countenance** *vb* **-nanced; -nanc·ing** : TOLERATE 1, EN-
COURAGE ⟨refused to *countenance* their constant lateness⟩

¹**count·er** \'kaùnt-ər\ *n* **1** : a piece (as of metal or plastic)
used in counting or in games **2** : a level surface (as a
table) over which business is done or food is served or on
which goods are displayed [Middle English *countour*
"something used in counting", from early French *comp-
touer* (same meaning), from Latin *computatorium* "a
place for counting or keeping accounts", derived from earlier *computare* "to count, compute" — related to ¹COUNT,
COMPUTE]

²**count·er** *n* : one that counts; *esp* : a device for indicating a
number or amount

³**coun·ter** \'kaùnt-ər\ *vb* **coun·tered; coun·ter·ing**
\'kaùnt-ə-riŋ, 'kaùnt-riŋ\ **1** : to act in opposition to
: OPPOSE ⟨*countering* the claim for damages⟩ **2** : to give
a blow in return ⟨*counter* with a left hook⟩ [Middle English

\ə\ abut	\aù\ out	\i\ tip	\ó\ saw	\ù\ foot
\ər\ further	\ch\ chin	\ī\ life	\ói\ coin	\y\ yet
\a\ mat	\e\ pet	\j\ job	\th\ thin	\yü\ few
\ā\ take	\ē\ easy	\ŋ\ sing	\th\ this	\yù\ cure
\ä\ cot, cart	\g\ go	\ō\ bone	\ü\ food	\zh\ vision

cotton 1a

countren "to oppose", partly from Middle English encountren "to encounter" and partly from early French contre "against" — related to CONTRA-, COUNTER-]

⁴**coun·ter** adv : in another or opposite direction ⟨acting counter to advice⟩

⁵**coun·ter** n **1 a** : the act of giving a return blow **b** : the blow given **2** : a stiffener to give permanent form to a shoe or boot above and around the heel

⁶**coun·ter** adj **1** : moving in an opposite direction ⟨ship slowed by counter tides⟩ **2** : designed to oppose ⟨a counter opinion⟩

coun·ter- prefix **1 a** : contrary : opposite ⟨counter-clockwise⟩ **b** : opposing : retaliatory ⟨counteroffensive⟩ **2** : like : matching ⟨counterpart⟩ [derived from Latin contra "against, opposite" — related to CONTRA-]

coun·ter·act \ˌkaunt-ə-'rakt\ vb : to lessen the force of : OFFSET ⟨a drug that counteracts a poison⟩ — **coun·ter·ac·tion** \-'rak-shən\ n

coun·ter·at·tack \'kaunt-ə-rə-ˌtak\ n : an attack made to counter an enemy's attack — **counterattack** vb

¹**coun·ter·bal·ance** \'kaunt-ər-ˌbal-ən(t)s, ˌkaunt-ər-'bal-\ n **1** : a weight that balances another **2** : a force or influence that checks an opposing force

²**counterbalance** vb : to oppose or balance with an equal weight or force

counter check n : a blank check available at a bank and usually to be cashed only at the bank by the person writing the check

coun·ter·claim \'kaunt-ər-ˌklām\ n : an opposing claim — **counterclaim** vb — **coun·ter·claim·ant** \-ˌklā-mənt\ n

coun·ter·clock·wise \ˌkaunt-ər-'kläk-ˌwīz\ adv : in a direction opposite to that in which the hands of a clock rotate — **counterclockwise** adj

coun·ter·cur·rent \'kaunt-ər-ˌkər-ənt, -ˌkə-rənt\ n : a current flowing in a direction opposite to that of another current

¹**coun·ter·feit** \'kaunt-ər-ˌfit\ vb **1** : to imitate or copy especially in order to deceive ⟨counterfeiting money⟩ **2** : ¹PRETEND 1, FEIGN ⟨counterfeit enthusiasm to mask boredom⟩ — **coun·ter·feit·er** n

²**counterfeit** adj **1** : made in exact imitation of something else with the intention of deceiving : FORGED ⟨counterfeit money⟩ **2** : not sincere : SHAM

³**counterfeit** n : something counterfeit : FORGERY

coun·ter·foil \'kaunt-ər-ˌfoil\ n : a detachable stub (as on a check or ticket) usually serving as a record or receipt

coun·ter·in·tel·li·gence \ˌkaunt-ə-rin-'tel-ə-jən(t)s\ n : activities designed to counter the activities of an enemy's intelligence service by blocking its sources of information and to deceive the enemy through tricks and misinformation

coun·ter·mand \'kaunt-ər-ˌmand, ˌkaunt-ər-'mand\ vb **1** : to cancel a previous command **2** : to recall or order back by a contrary order

coun·ter·march \'kaunt-ər-ˌmärch\ n : a marching back; esp : a maneuver by which a marching unit reverses direction but keeps the same order — **countermarch** vb

coun·ter·mel·o·dy \'kaunt-ər-ˌmel-əd-ē\ n : a secondary melody that goes along with and often contrasts with a main melody

coun·ter·of·fen·sive \'kaunt-ə-rə-ˌfen(t)-siv\ n : a large-scale counterattack

coun·ter·pane \'kaunt-ər-ˌpān\ n : BEDSPREAD

coun·ter·part \'kaunt-ər-ˌpärt\ n **1** : a part or thing that matches another ⟨the left arm is the counterpart of the right⟩ **2** : something that serves to complete something else : COMPLEMENT **3** : a person closely resembling another

coun·ter·point \'kaunt-ər-ˌpoint\ n **1** : one or more independent melodies added as accompaniment to a principal melody **2** : combination of two or more melodies into a harmony in which each keeps its own identity

coun·ter·poise \'kaunt-ər-ˌpoiz\ vb : ²COUNTERBALANCE — **counterpoise** n

coun·ter·rev·o·lu·tion \ˌkaunt-ə(r)-ˌrev-ə-'lü-shən\ n : a revolution intended to overthrow a government established by an earlier revolution — **coun·ter·rev·o·lu·tion·ary** \-'lü-shə-ˌner-ē\ adj or n — **coun·ter·rev·o·lu·tion·ist** \-'lü-sh(ə-)nəst\ n

¹**coun·ter·sign** \'kaunt-ər-ˌsīn\ n : a sign used in reply to another; esp : PASSWORD

²**countersign** vb : to add one's signature to a document after another has already signed it in order to confirm its genuineness — **coun·ter·sig·na·ture** \ˌkaunt-ər-'sig-nə-ˌchu(ə)r, -chər\ n

¹**coun·ter·sink** \'kaunt-ər-ˌsiŋk\ vb **-sunk** \-ˌsəŋk\; **-sinking** **1** : to make a countersink on **2** : to set the head of (as a screw) at or below the surface

²**countersink** n **1** : a bit or drill for making a countersink **2** : a funnel-shaped enlargement at the end of a drilled hole

coun·ter·spy \'kaunt-ər-ˌspī\ n : a spy employed in counterintelligence

coun·ter·ten·or \'kaunt-ər-ˌten-ər\ n : a tenor with an unusually high range

coun·ter·top \'kaunt-ər-ˌtäp\ n : the surface of waist-level kitchen cabinets used as a work area

coun·ter·weight \'kaunt-ər-ˌwāt\ n : ¹COUNTERBALANCE 1

count·ess \'kaunt-əs\ n **1** : the wife or widow of a count or an earl **2** : a woman holding the rank of count or earl

count·ing·house \'kaunt-iŋ-ˌhaus\ n : a building, room, or office used for keeping books and carrying on business

counting number n : NATURAL NUMBER

count·less \'kaunt-ləs\ adj : too numerous to be counted : INNUMERABLE

count noun n : a noun (as bean or sheet) that forms a plural and that can be used with a numeral

coun·tri·fied also **coun·try·fied** \'kən-tri-ˌfīd\ adj : looking or acting like a person from the country : RUSTIC

¹**coun·try** \'kən-trē\ n, pl **countries 1** : an indefinite usually large stretch of land : REGION ⟨hill country⟩ **2 a** : the land of a person's birth, residence, or citizenship **b** : a nation or its territory **3** : the people of a state or district : POPULACE **4** : the open rural area outside of big towns and cities ⟨lives out in the country⟩

²**country** adj : of, relating to, or characteristic of the country : RURAL, RUSTIC

country and western n : COUNTRY MUSIC

country club n : a suburban club for social life and recreation

coun·try·man \'kən-trē-mən, sense 3 is often -ˌman\ n **1** : a person born or living in a particular country **2** : a person born or living in the same country as another **3** : one living in the country or marked by country ways : RUSTIC

country music n : music coming from or imitating the folk style of the Southern U.S. or the Western cowboy

coun·try·seat \ˌkən-trē-'sēt\ n : a mansion or estate in the country

coun·try·side \'kən-trē-ˌsīd\ n : a rural area or its people

coun·ty \'kaunt-ē\ n, pl **counties 1** : the area owned by a count **2** : a division of a state or of a country for local government [Middle English counte "division of the country for the purposes of government", from early French conté "region under control of a count", derived from Latin comes "companion, member of a royal court" — related to ³COUNT]

county agent n : a government agent employed to provide information about agriculture and home economics in rural areas

county seat n : a town that is the seat of county administration

coup \'kü\ n, pl **coups** \'küz\ **1** : a brilliant, sudden, and usually highly successful action **2** : COUP D'ÉTAT [from French coup "blow, stroke"]

coup d'é·tat \ˌküd-(ˌ)ā-'tä, ˌküd-ə-\ n, pl **coups d'é·tat**

\-'tä(z)\ : a sudden overthrowing of a government by a small group [from French *coup d'état,* literally "stroke of state (the government)", from *coup* "blow, stroke" and *de* "of" and *état* "state"]

cou·pé *or* **coupe** \kü-'pā, *sense 2 is often* 'küp\ *n* **1** : a four-wheeled closed carriage pulled by horses for two persons with an outside seat for the driver **2** *usually* **coupe a** : a closed two-door automobile for usually two persons **b** : a usually closed two-door automobile with a full-width rear seat

coupé 1

¹cou·ple \'kəp-əl\ *vb* **cou·pled; cou·pling** \'kəp-(ə-)liŋ\ **1** : to join together : CONNECT **2** : to join in pairs — **cou·pler** \-p(ə-)lər\ *n*

²couple *n* **1** : a man and woman paired or associated together (as by marriage or on a date) **2** : two persons or things paired together **3** : an indefinite small number : FEW ⟨a *couple* of days ago⟩

cou·plet \'kəp-lət\ *n* : two lines of verse that follow in order and form a unit; *esp* : two rhyming lines of the same length

cou·pling \'kəp-liŋ *(usual for sense 2),* -ə-liŋ\ *n* **1** : the act of bringing or coming together **2** : something that connects two parts or things

cou·pon \'k(y)ü-,pän\ *n* **1** : a statement of due interest to be cut from a bond and presented for payment on a stated date **2 a** : one of a series of tickets to be detached and presented as needed **b** : a ticket or form allowing the bearer to purchase rationed articles **c** : a certificate or other evidence of a purchase that may be exchanged for premiums **d** : a part of an advertisement to be cut off to use as an order blank or inquiry form or to obtain a discount on the price of something [from French *coupon* "a part of a bill to be cut off and turned in with payment", from early French *coupon* "a piece (cut off)", from *couper* "to cut" — related to ²COPE, COUP]

cour·age \'kər-ij, 'kə-rij\ *n* : strength of mind to carry on in spite of danger or difficulty [Middle English *corage* "the heart as a source of feelings, spirit, confidence", from early French *corage, curage* (same meaning), from *cuer* "heart", from Latin *cor* "heart" — related to CORDIAL]

syn COURAGE, BRAVERY, VALOR, HEROISM mean greatness of spirit in facing danger or difficulty. COURAGE suggests strength in overcoming fear and carrying on against difficulties ⟨the *courage* of the pioneers⟩ BRAVERY stresses bold and daring defiance of danger ⟨the *bravery* shown by the fire fighters⟩ VALOR applies especially to bravery in fighting a dangerous enemy ⟨honored for *valor* in battle⟩ HEROISM suggests bravery and boldness in accepting risk or sacrifice for a noble or generous purpose ⟨the *heroism* shown by many in the early struggle for women's rights⟩

cou·ra·geous \kə-'rā-jəs\ *adj* : having or marked by courage : BRAVE — **cou·ra·geous·ly** *adv* — **cou·ra·geous·ness** *n*

cou·ri·er \'kùr-ē-ər, 'kər-ē-, 'kə-rē-\ *n* : a messenger especially in the diplomatic service [Middle English *courrier* "a person who carries (runs) messages from one place to another quickly", from early Italian *corriere* (same meaning), derived from Latin *currere* "to run" — related to CURRENT]

¹course \'kō(ə)rs, 'kò(ə)rs\ *n* **1** : the act or action of moving in a path from point to point ⟨during the *course* of a year⟩ **2** : the direction or route of motion or progress ⟨the *course* of a river⟩ ⟨a ship's *course*⟩ **3** : land laid out for golf **4** : normal or accustomed process or procedure ⟨the disease ran its *course*⟩ **5** : manner of proceeding : CON-

DUCT ⟨a wise *course*⟩ **6 a** : an ordered process or series **b** : a series of classes in a subject; *also* : a group of such courses ⟨a four-year *course* in chemistry⟩ **7** : a part of a meal served at one time ⟨had salad for the first *course*⟩ **8** : a layer of brick or other building material in a wall [Middle English *cours, course* "action of moving in a certain path, path of movement, progress", from early French *cors, course* (same meaning), derived from Latin *currere* "to run" — related to CORRIDOR, CURRENT] — **of course** **1** : following the ordinary way or procedure ⟨did it as a matter of course⟩ **2** : as might be expected

²course *vb* **coursed; cours·ing** **1** : to run through or over ⟨buffalo *coursed* the plains⟩ **2** : to move rapidly : RACE ⟨blood *coursing* through the veins⟩

cours·er \'kōr-sər, 'kòr-\ *n* : a swift or spirited horse

¹court \'kō(ə)rt, 'kò(ə)rt\ *n* **1 a** : the residence of a ruler and especially a king or queen **b** : a ruler's formal assembly of advisers and officers as a governing body **c** : the family and followers of a ruler **2 a** : an open space completely or partly surrounded by buildings **b** : a space for playing a ball game ⟨tennis *court*⟩ **c** : a wide alley with only one opening onto a street **3 a** : an assembly for carrying out judicial business **b** : a session of a judicial assembly ⟨*court* is now adjourned⟩ **c** : a building or room where legal cases are heard **d** : a judge in session **4** : attention designed to win favor ⟨pay *court* to the king⟩

²court *vb* **1 a** : to try to gain ⟨*court* favor⟩ **b** : to act so as to invite or provoke ⟨*court* disaster⟩ **2** : to seek the affections or favor of ⟨*courted* a college student⟩ ⟨the candidate *courted* the voters⟩ **3 a** : to engage in social relationships usually leading to marriage **b** : to engage in activity leading to mating ⟨a pair of robins *courting*⟩

cour·te·ous \'kərt-ē-əs\ *adj* **1** : marked by good manners suitable to a court **2** : marked by respect for and consideration of others — **cour·te·ous·ly** *adv* — **cour·te·ous·ness** *n*

cour·te·sy \'kərt-ə-sē\ *n, pl* **-sies** **1** : courtly politeness **2** : a favor courteously performed **3** : a favor as distinguished from a right ⟨a title by *courtesy* only⟩

court·house \'kō(ə)rt-,hàus, 'kò(ə)rt-\ *n* : a building in which courts of law are held or county offices are located

court·ier \'kōrt-ē-ər, 'kòrt-\ *n* **1** : a person in attendance to a ruler at a royal court **2** : a person who practices flattery

court·ly \'kō(ə)rt-lē, 'kò(ə)rt-\ *adj* : suitable to a royal court : ELEGANT ⟨*courtly* manners⟩ — **court·li·ness** *n*

¹court–mar·tial \'kōrt-,mär-shəl, 'kòrt-, -'mär-\ *n, pl* **courts–martial** *also* **court–martials** **1** : a military court **2** : a trial by court-martial

²court–martial *vb* **—mar·tialed** *also* **—mar·tialled; —mar·tial·ing** *also* **—mar·tial·ling** \-,märsh-(ə-)liŋ, -'märsh-\ : to try by court-martial

court plaster *n* : an adhesive plaster especially of silk coated with isinglass and glycerin

court·room \'kō(ə)rt-,rüm, 'kò(ə)rt-, -,rùm\ *n* : a room in which a court of law is held

court·ship \-,ship\ *n* : the act or process of courting

court·yard \-,yärd\ *n* : a court or enclosure next to a building

cous·in \'kəz-ᵊn\ *n* **1 a** : a child of one's uncle or aunt **b** : a relative descended from a common ancestor **2** : a person of a race or people ethnically or culturally related ⟨our English *cousins*⟩

cove \'kōv\ *n* **1** : a small sheltered inlet or bay **2** : a level area sheltered by hills or mountains

cov·en \'kəv-ən\ *n* : a meeting or band of witches

\ə\ **abut**	\au̇\ **out**	\i\ **tip**	\ȯ\ **saw**	\u̇\ **foot**
\ər\ **further**	\ch\ **chin**	\ī\ **life**	\ȯi\ **coin**	\y\ **yet**
\a\ **mat**	\e\ **pet**	\j\ **job**	\th\ **thin**	\yü\ **few**
\ā\ **take**	\ē\ **easy**	\ŋ\ **sing**	\th\ **this**	\yu̇\ **cure**
\ä\ **cot, cart**	\g\ **go**	\ō\ **bone**	\ü\ **food**	\zh\ **vision**

¹cov·e·nant \'kəv-(ə-)nənt\ *n* : a solemn agreement : CON-TRACT

²cov·e·nant \'kəv-(ə-)nənt, -ə-,nant\ *vb* **1** : to promise by a covenant : PLEDGE **2** : to enter into a covenant : CON-TRACT

¹cov·er \'kəv-ər\ *vb* **cov·ered; cov·er·ing** \'kəv-(ə-)riŋ\ **1 a** : to guard from attack **b** : to have within range of one's guns **c** : to provide protection to or against : INSURE ⟨insurance that *covers* the traveler in any accident⟩ ⟨the policy *covered* water damage⟩ **d** : to maintain a check on especially by patrolling ⟨state police *covering* the highways⟩ **2 a** : to hide something from sight or knowledge ⟨*cover* up a scandal⟩ **b** : to conceal something dishonest or embarrassing from notice ⟨*cover* for a friend in an investigation⟩ **c** : to act as a substitute or replacement ⟨*covered* for me during my vacation⟩ **3 a** : to spread or lie over or on ⟨*covered* the child with a blanket⟩ ⟨water *covered* the floor⟩ **b** : to put something protective or concealing over ⟨*cover* the mouth while coughing⟩ **4 a** : to deal with ⟨an exam *covering* a semester's work⟩ **b** : to provide or plan for ⟨plans *covering* an emergency⟩ **5** : to have as one's territory or field of activity ⟨a reporter *covering* the courthouse⟩ **6** : to pass over or through ⟨*cover* long distances every day⟩ — **cov·er·er** \-ər-ər\ *n*

²cover *n* **1** : something that protects, shelters, or conceals (as a natural shelter for an animal or natural features that shelter or conceal) **2** : something that is placed over or about another thing (as the lid of a box or a sheet or blanket on a bed) **b** : a binding or case for a book or the front or back of such a binding **c** : something (as plants or snow) that covers the ground **3** : an envelope or wrapper for mail — **under cover** : under concealment : in secret

cov·er·age \'kəv-(ə-)rij\ *n* **1** : the act or fact of covering or something that covers ⟨insurance *coverage*⟩ ⟨news *coverage* at a political convention⟩ **2** : the number or amount covered : SCOPE

cov·er·all \'kəv-ə-,ról\ *n* : a one-piece outer garment worn to protect clothes — usually used in pl.

cover charge *n* : a charge made by a restaurant or nightclub in addition to the charge for food and drink

cover crop *n* : a crop planted to prevent soil erosion and to provide humus

covered wagon *n* : a wagon with an arched canvas top

cover glass *n* : a piece of very thin transparent material used to cover something mounted on a microscope slide

cov·er·ing \'kəv-(ə-)riŋ\ *n* : something that covers or conceals

cov·er·let \'kəv-ər-lət\ *n* : BEDSPREAD

cov·er·slip \'kəv-ər-,slip\ *n* : COVER GLASS

¹co·vert \'kō-(,)vərt, kō-'vərt, 'kəv-ərt\ *adj* **1** : not openly made or done ⟨a *covert* glance⟩ ⟨*covert* military operations⟩ **2** : covered over : SHELTERED ⟨a *covert* nook⟩ — **cov·ert·ly** *adv* — **cov·ert·ness** *n*

²co·vert \'kəv-ərt, 'kō-vərt\ *n* **1** : hiding place : SHELTER **2** : a thicket giving cover to game

cov·er·up \'kəv-ə-,rəp\ *n* : a planned effort to conceal a wrongful act or situation

cov·et \'kəv-ət\ *vb* : to wish for greatly or with envy ⟨*covet* success⟩ ⟨*covet* a friend's possessions⟩ — **cov·et·er** \-ər\ *n* — **cov·et·ing·ly** \-iŋ-lē\ *adv*

cov·et·ous \'kəv-ət-əs\ *adj* : marked by a too eager desire especially for another's possessions — **cov·et·ous·ly** *adv* — **cov·et·ous·ness** *n*

cov·ey \'kəv-ē\ *n, pl* **coveys** **1** : a small flock (as of quail) **2** : COMPANY 2a, GROUP

¹cow \'kaů\ *n* **1** : an adult female of any of various usually large animals (as elephants, whales, or seals) **2** : any domestic bovine animal regardless of sex or age [Old English *cū* "cow"]

²cow *vb* : to lessen the spirits or courage of : FRIGHTEN ⟨were *cowed* into silence by threats⟩ [probably of Scandinavian origin]

cow·ard \'kaů(-ə)rd\ *n* : one who shows shameful fear or timidity — **coward** *adj*

Word History A frightened animal may put its tail between its hind legs, and if it is very frightened it may run away. In an animal like the hare, the white flash of the fleeing tail is especially obvious. This action gives us the phrase *turn tail,* meaning "to run away, flee". But even tailless animals like people can turn tail and run when frightened. It is in the "tail end" of an army that you might expect to find the cowards. We do not know whether the word *coward* developed from the idea of an animal's tail or an army's, but we do know the word comes from an early French word that meant "tail". [Middle English *coward* "coward", from early French *coart* "coward", from *coe* "tail", from Latin *cauda* "tail" — related to CODA, ²CUE, QUEUE; see *Word History* at QUEUE]

cow·ard·ice \'kaů(-ə)rd-əs\ *n* : lack of courage to face danger : shameful fear

cow·ard·ly \'kaů(-ə)rd-lē\ *adj* **1** : lacking courage : disgracefully timid ⟨a *cowardly* rascal⟩ **2** : characteristic of a coward ⟨a *cowardly* attack from behind⟩ — **cowardly** *adv* — **cow·ard·li·ness** *n*

cow·bell \'kaů-,bel\ *n* : a bell hung about the neck of a cow to indicate its whereabouts

cow·bird \-,bərd\ *n* : a small North American blackbird that lays its eggs in the nests of other birds

cow·boy \-,bói\ *n* : one who tends cattle or horses; *esp* : a mounted cattle-ranch worker

cow·catch·er \-,kach-ər, -,kech-\ *n* : a strong frame on the front of a locomotive for throwing obstacles off the track

cow·er \'kaů-(ə)r\ *vb* : to shrink away or crouch down (as from fear)

cow·girl \'kaů-,gər(-ə)l\ *n* : a girl or woman who tends cattle or horses

cow·hand \-,hand\ *n* : COWBOY

cow·herd \-,hərd\ *n* : one who tends cows

¹cow·hide \-,hīd\ *n* **1** : the hide of a cow or leather made from it **2** : a whip of rawhide or braided leather

²cowhide *vb* **cow·hid·ed; cow·hid·ing** : to whip with a cowhide

cowl \'kaů(ə)l\ *n* **1** : a monk's hood or long hooded cloak **2** : the top part of an automobile body forward of the two front doors to which are attached the windshield and instrument panel **3** : COWLING — **cowled** \'kaůld\ *adj*

cow·lick \'kaů-,lik\ *n* : a lock or bunch of hair that grows in a different direction from the rest of the hair and cannot be made to lie flat

cowl·ing \'kaů-liŋ\ *n* : a removable metal covering for the engine and sometimes a part of the fuselage of an airplane; *also* : a metal cover for an engine

cow·man \'kaů-mən, -,man\ *n* **1** : COWBOY **2** : a cattle owner or rancher

co·work·er \'kō-,wər-kər\ *n* : a fellow worker

C cowl 1

cow·pea \'kaů-,pē\ *n* : BLACK-EYED PEA

Cow·per's gland \,kaů-pərz-, ,kü-pərz-, ,kůp-ərz-\ *n* : either of two small glands that empty into the male urethra

cow·poke \'kaů-,pōk\ *n* : COWBOY

cow pony *n* : a strong and active saddle horse trained for herding cattle

cow·pox \'kaů-,päks\ *n* : a mild disease of the cow that when passed on to human beings produces a temporary rash and protects against smallpox

cow·punch·er \-,pən-chər\ *n* : COWBOY

cow·rie or **cow·ry** \'kau̇(ə)r-ē\ n, pl **cowries** : any of numerous small snails of warm seas with glossy often brightly colored shells

cow·slip \'kau̇-ˌslip\ n : MARSH MARIGOLD

cox \'käks\ n : COXSWAIN 2 — **cox** vb

cox·comb \'käks-ˌkōm\ n : a conceited foolish person

cox·swain \'käk-sən, -ˌswän\ n **1** : a sailor who has charge of a ship's boat and its crew **2** : one who steers a racing shell

coy \'kȯi\ adj **1** : BASHFUL, SHY **2** : pretending shyness — **coy·ly** adv — **coy·ness** n

coy·ote \'kī-ˌōt, kī-'ōt-ē\ n, pl **coyotes** or **coyote** : a mammal related to the domestic dog and the timber wolf that is native to western North America

coy·pu \'kȯi-(ˌ)pü\ n : NUTRIA

coz·en \'kəz-ᵊn\ vb **coz·ened; coz·en·ing** \'kəz-niŋ, -ᵊn-iŋ\ : to deceive by skillful trickery — **coz·en·er** \'kəz-nər, -ᵊn-ər\ n

¹**co·zy** also **co·sy** \'kō-zē\ adj **co·zi·er; -est** : ²SNUG 2, COMFORTABLE — **co·zi·ly** \-zə-lē\ adv — **co·zi·ness** \-zē-nəs\ n

²**cozy** also **cosy** n, pl **cozies** : a padded cover for a teapot to keep the contents hot

¹**crab** \'krab\ n **1** : an invertebrate that belongs to the crustaceans and has a short broad usually flattened shell of chitin, a small abdomen curled forward beneath the body, and a front pair of limbs with strong pincers; also : any of various other crustaceans resembling the true crabs in having an abdomen much reduced in size **2** cap : CANCER 1 **3** : any of various machines for raising or hauling heavy weights **4** pl : the state of being infested with crab lice

²**crab** vb **crabbed; crab·bing** : to fish for crabs — **crab·ber** n

³**crab** vb **crabbed; crab·bing** : to find fault : COMPLAIN

⁴**crab** n **1** : CRAB APPLE **2** : a sour ill-tempered person

crab apple n **1 a** : a small wild sour apple **b** : any of several cultivated varieties of often highly colored sour apple **2** : a tree that produces crab apples

crab·bed \'krab-əd\ adj **1** : ³CROSS 3 **2** : difficult to read or understand ⟨crabbed handwriting⟩ — **crab·bed·ly** adv — **crab·bed·ness** n

crab·by \'krab-ē\ adj **crab·bi·er; -est** : ³CROSS 3, ILL-NATURED

crab·grass \'krab-ˌgras\ n : a weedy grass with creeping or sprawling stems that root freely at the nodes

crab louse n : a louse infesting the human pubic region

¹**crack** \'krak\ vb **1 a** : to break or cause to break with a sudden sharp sound : SNAP **b** : to make or cause to make such a sound ⟨crack a whip⟩ **2** : to break with or without complete separation of parts ⟨the ice cracked in several places⟩ **3** : to tell especially in a clever or witty way ⟨crack jokes⟩ **4 a** : to lose control **b** : to fail in tone ⟨voice cracked⟩ **c** : to give or receive a sharp blow ⟨cracked my head⟩ **5 a** : to puzzle out : SOLVE ⟨crack a code⟩ **b** : to break into or through ⟨crack a safe⟩ ⟨crack the sound barrier⟩ **6 a** : to put hydrocarbons through cracking ⟨crack petroleum⟩ **b** : to produce by cracking ⟨cracked gasoline⟩

²**crack** n **1** : a sudden sharp noise **2** : a sharp witty remark : QUIP **3** : a narrow break or opening ⟨a crack in the glass⟩ ⟨open the window a crack⟩ **4 a** : WEAKNESS 2, FLAW **b** : a broken tone of the voice **5** : the beginning moment ⟨the crack of dawn⟩ **6** : a sharp resounding blow **7** : ²TRY ⟨take a crack at it⟩ **8** : highly purified cocaine in small chips used illegally used for smoking

³**crack** adj : of high quality or ability ⟨crack troops⟩

crack·brain \'krak-ˌbrān\ n : CRACKPOT — **crack·brained** \-ˈbrānd\ adj

crack down \'krak-'dau̇n\ vb : to take strong action especially to control or put down ⟨crack down on crime⟩ — **crack·down** \-ˌdau̇n\ n

cracked \'krakt\ adj **1** : broken into coarse pieces

⟨cracked corn⟩ **2** : mentally disturbed : CRAZY

crack·er \'krak-ər\ n **1** : something (as a firecracker) that makes a cracking noise **2** : a dry thin crisp baked food made of flour and water **3** : the equipment in which cracking (as of petroleum) is carried out

crack·er·jack \'krak-ər-ˌjak\ n : a person or thing of special excellence ⟨she's a crackerjack at solving crossword puzzles⟩ — **crackerjack** adj

crack·ing \'krak-iŋ\ n : a process in which heavy hydrocarbons (as oils from petroleum) are broken up by heat into lighter products (as gasoline)

crack·le \'krak-əl\ vb **crack·led; crack·ling** \-(ə-)liŋ\ : to make small sharp sudden repeated noises — **crackle** n

crack·ling n **1** \'krak-(ə-)liŋ\ : a series of small sharp crackling sounds **2** \'krak-lən, 'krak-liŋ\ : the crisp remainder left after the fat has been separated from the meat or skin (as of pork) — usually used in pl.

crack·pot \'krak-ˌpät\ n : a crazy or very strange person — **crackpot** adj

crack–up \'krak-ˌəp\ n : COLLISION, WRECK

crack up \'krak-'əp\ vb **1** : to cause or have a crack-up ⟨crack up a car⟩ **2** : PRAISE 1 ⟨it's not all it's cracked up to be⟩

¹**cra·dle** \'krād-ᵊl\ n **1** : a bed for a baby usually on rockers **2** : a place of origin **3** : a framework or support resembling a baby's cradle in appearance or use **4** : a tool with rods like fingers attached to a scythe and used formerly for harvesting grain **5** : a rocking tool used in panning for gold **6** : a support for a telephone handset

²**cradle** vb **cra·dled; cra·dling** \'krād-liŋ, -ᵊl-iŋ\ **1 a** : to place or keep in or as if in a cradle **b** : to protect and cherish lovingly **2** : to cut grain with a cradle **3** : to wash in a miner's cradle

¹**craft** \'kraft\ n **1** : skill in planning, making, or doing **2** : an occupation requiring skill in using the hands : TRADE **3** : skill in deceiving to gain an end **4** : the members of a trade **5** pl usually **craft a** : a boat especially of small size **b** : AIRCRAFT **c** : SPACECRAFT

²**craft** vb : to make by or as if by hand ⟨crafted a sculpture⟩ ⟨a carefully crafted story⟩

crafts·man \'kraf(t)-smən\ n **1** : one who practices a trade or handicraft : ARTISAN **2** : a highly skilled worker — **crafts·man·ship** \-ˌship\ n

crafty \'kraf-tē\ adj **craft·i·er; -est** : skillful at deceiving others **syn** see CUNNING — **craft·i·ly** \-tə-lē\ adv — **craft·i·ness** \-tē-nəs\ n

crag \'krag\ n : a steep rugged rock or cliff — **crag·gy** \'krag-ē\ adj

cram \'kram\ vb **crammed; cram·ming** **1** : to stuff or crowd in ⟨cram clothes into a bag⟩ **2** : to fill full ⟨barns crammed with hay⟩ **3** : to study hard just before a test **syn** see PACK — **cram·mer** n

¹**cramp** \'kramp\ n **1** : a sudden painful involuntary tightening of muscle **2** : sharp pain in the abdomen — usually used in pl.

²**cramp** vb **1** : to affect with or as if with cramps **2 a** : to hold back from free movement : CONFINE ⟨felt cramped in the tiny room⟩ **b** : to hold back from free action or expression : HAMPER — used especially in the phrase cramp one's style

cram·pon \'kram-ˌpän\ n : a set of steel spikes that fit on the bottom of a climbing boot to give a better grip on slopes of hard ice or snow — usually used in pl.

cran·ber·ry \'kran-ˌber-ē, -b(ə-)rē\ n : the bright red sour berry of any of several trailing plants related to the blueberry; also : a plant producing these

\ə\ abut	\au̇\ out	\i\ tip	\ȯ\ saw	\u̇\ foot
\ər\ further	\ch\ chin	\ī\ life	\ȯi\ coin	\y\ yet
\a\ mat	\e\ pet	\j\ job	\th\ thin	\yü\ few
\ā\ take	\ē\ easy	\ŋ\ sing	\th\ this	\yu̇\ cure
\ä\ cot, cart	\g\ go	\ō\ bone	\ü\ food	\zh\ vision

¹crane \'krān\ *n* **1** : any of a family of tall wading birds related to the rails **2** : any of several herons **3 a** : a machine with a swinging arm for lifting and carrying heavy weights **b** : a mechanical arm that swings freely from a center and is used to support or carry a weight

²crane *vb* **craned; cran·ing** **1** : to raise or lift by or as if by a crane **2** : to stretch out one's neck to see better

crane fly *n* : any of numerous long-legged slender two-winged flies that resemble large mosquitoes but do not bite

cra·ni·al \'krā-nē-əl\ *adj* **1** : of, relating to, or directed toward the skull or cranium

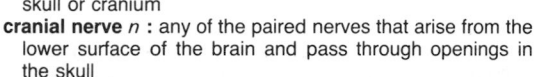

crane 1

cranial nerve *n* : any of the paired nerves that arise from the lower surface of the brain and pass through openings in the skull

cra·ni·um \'krā-nē-əm\ *n, pl* **-ni·ums** *or* **-nia** \-nē-ə\ : SKULL 1; *esp* : the part that encloses the brain

¹crank \'krank\ *n* **1** : a bent part of an axle or shaft or an armlike part at right angles to the end of a shaft that gives or receives circular motion **2 a** : a person with strange ideas **b** : a cross or irritable person

²crank *vb* : to move, run, or start by or as if by turning a crank ⟨*crank* up the window⟩ ⟨you had to *crank* the old car⟩ ⟨the engine isn't *cranking* right⟩

crank·case \'krank-,kās\ *n* : the covering of a crankshaft

crank·shaft \-,shaft\ *n* : a shaft turning or driven by a crank

cranky \'kran-kē\ *adj* **crank·i·er; -est** **1** : easily angered or irritated **2** : hard to handle ⟨a *cranky* boat⟩ — **crank·i·ness** \-kē-nəs\ *n*

cran·ny \'kran-ē\ *n, pl* **crannies** : a small break or slit (as in a cliff)

crape \'krāp\ *n* **1** : CREPE 1 **2** : a band of crepe worn on a hat or sleeve as a sign of mourning

crape myrtle *n* : an East Indian shrub or tree widely grown in warm regions for its showy red, pink, purple or sometimes white flowers

crap·pie \'kräp-ē\ *n* **1** : BLACK CRAPPIE **2** : WHITE CRAPPIE

craps \'kraps\ *n pl* : a gambling game played with two dice

crap·shoot·er \'krap-,shüt-ər\ *n* : a person who plays craps — **crap·shoot·ing** \-,shüt-iŋ\ *n*

¹crash \'krash\ *vb* **1 a** : to break with violence and much noise : SMASH **b** : to damage (an airplane) in landing **2 a** : to make or cause to make a loud noise ⟨*crash* cymbals together⟩ ⟨waves *crashing* on the shore⟩ **b** : to move or force a way roughly or with loud crashing noises ⟨we went *crashing* through the underbrush⟩ **3** : to enter or attend without an invitation or without paying ⟨*crash* a party⟩ ⟨tried to *crash* the gates⟩ **4** : to go bad or go out of order suddenly ⟨the computer system *crashed*⟩ [Middle English *crasschen* "crash"] — **crash·er** *n*

²crash *n* **1** : a loud sound (as of things smashing) **2** : a breaking to pieces by or as if by hitting something : COLLISION, SMASHUP **3** : the crashing of something ⟨was hurt in the *crash*⟩ **4** : a sudden weakening or failure (as of a business or prices) ⟨stock-market *crash*⟩

³crash *adj* : designed to do what it is supposed to do in a big hurry ⟨a *crash* program⟩ ⟨went on a *crash* diet⟩

⁴crash *n* : a coarse fabric used for draperies and clothing [probably from Russian *krashenina* "colored linen"]

crash–land \'krash-'land\ *vb* : to land (an airplane or spacecraft) in an emergency usually with damage to it — **crash landing** *n*

crass \'kras\ *adj* : showing no interest in the finer things : INSENSITIVE — **crass·ly** *adv* — **crass·ness** *n*

¹crate \'krāt\ *n* : a box or frame of wooden slats or boards for packing or protecting something in shipment

²crate *vb* **crat·ed; crat·ing** : to pack in a crate

cra·ter \'krāt-ər\ *n* **1** : a hollow shaped like a bowl around the opening of a volcano **2** : a hole made by the impact of a meteorite or by the explosion of a bomb or shell

cra·vat \krə-'vat\ *n* : NECKTIE

crave \'krāv\ *vb* **craved; crav·ing** **1** : to ask earnestly : BEG ⟨*crave* a person's pardon⟩ **2** : to have a strong desire for ⟨*crave* water⟩ ⟨*crave* affection⟩

¹cra·ven \'krā-vən\ *adj* : COWARDLY — **cra·ven·ly** *adv* — **cra·ven·ness** \-vən-(n)əs\ *n*

²craven *n* : COWARD

crav·ing \'krā-viŋ\ *n* : a great desire or longing

craw \'krò\ *n* **1** : the crop of a bird or insect **2** : the stomach especially of a lower animal

craw·dad \'krò-,dad\ *n, dialect* : CRAYFISH 1

craw·fish \'krò-,fish\ *n* **1** : CRAYFISH 1 **2** : SPINY LOBSTER

¹crawl \'kròl\ *vb* **1** : to move slowly with the body close to the ground : move on hands and knees **2** : to move along slowly ⟨the bus *crawled* along⟩ **3** : to be covered with or have the feeling of being covered with creeping things ⟨the floor was *crawling* with ants⟩ — **crawl·er** *n*

²crawl *n* **1** : the act or motion of crawling **2** : a swimming method in which the swimmer lies facing down in the water and moves with overarm strokes and a thrashing kick

crawl·way \'kròl-,wā\ *n* : a low passage (as in a cave) that one must crawl through

cray·fish \'krā-,fish\ *n* **1** : any of numerous freshwater invertebrates that are crustaceans and are usually much smaller than the related lobsters **2** : SPINY LOBSTER

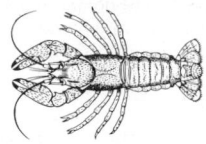

crayfish 1

¹cray·on \'krā-,än, -ən; 'kran\ *n* : a stick of white or colored chalk or of colored wax used for writing or drawing

²crayon *vb* : to draw or color with a crayon

¹craze \'krāz\ *vb* **crazed; craz·ing** **1** : to make or become insane or as if insane **2** : to develop a network of fine cracks

²craze *n* **1** : something that is very popular for a short time **2** : a tiny crack in a surface or coating (as of glaze or enamel)

cra·zy \'krā-zē\ *adj* **cra·zi·er; -est** **1** : having a diseased or abnormal mind : INSANE **2** : not sensible or logical ⟨that's a *crazy* idea⟩ **3** : very excited or pleased ⟨*crazy* about the new car⟩ — **cra·zi·ly** \-zə-lē\ *adv* — **cra·zi·ness** \-zē-nəs\ *n*

crazy bone *n* : FUNNY BONE

crazy quilt *n* : a patchwork quilt without a regular design

creak \'krēk\ *vb* : to make a long scraping or squeaking sound; *also* : to go slowly with or as if with creaking wheels — **creak** *n*

creaky \'krē-kē\ *adj* **creak·i·er; -est** : making or likely to make a creaking sound — **creak·i·ly** \-kə-lē\ *adv*

¹cream \'krēm\ *n* **1** : the yellowish part of milk containing butterfat **2 a** : a food prepared with cream ⟨*cream* soup⟩ **b** : something having about the same thickness as cream ⟨hand *cream*⟩ **3** : the best part ⟨the *cream* of the crop⟩ **4** : a pale yellow

²cream *vb* **1** : to skim the cream from **2** : to put cream into ⟨*cream* tea⟩ **3** : to stir or blend until soft and smooth

cream cheese *n* : a soft white cheese made from whole milk enriched with cream

cream·er \'krē-mər\ *n* **1** : a device for separating cream from milk **2** : a small container for serving cream **3** : a substitute for cream (as in coffee)

cream·ery \'krēm-(ə-)rē\ *n, pl* **-er·ies** : a place where butter and cheese are made or where milk and cream are sold or prepared

cream of tartar : a white salt used especially in baking powder and in some ways to prepare metals

cream puff *n* : a round shell of light pastry filled with whipped cream or a cream filling

creamy \'krē-mē\ *adj* **cream·i·er; -est** **1** : full of or containing cream **2** : resembling cream in appearance, color, or taste — **cream·i·ness** \-mē-nəs\ *n*

1crease \'krēs\ *n* **1** : a line or mark made by or as if by folding or wrinkling **2** : a specially marked area around the goal in various sports (as hockey or lacrosse)

2crease *vb* **creased; creas·ing** **1** : to make a crease in or on **2** : to become creased

cre·ate \krē-'āt, 'krē-,āt\ *vb* **cre·at·ed; cre·at·ing** : to bring into existence : MAKE, PRODUCE

cre·ation \krē-'ā-shən\ *n* **1** : the act of creating; *esp* : the bringing of the world into existence out of nothing **2** : something created **3** : all created things : WORLD

cre·ative \krē-'āt-iv\ *adj* **1** : able to create especially new and original things **2** : showing or requiring imagination ⟨*creative* writing⟩ — **cre·ative·ly** *adv* — **cre·ative·ness** *n* — **cre·ativ·i·ty** \,krē-ā-'tiv-ət-ē, ,krē-ə-\ *n*

cre·ator \krē-'āt-ər\ *n* **1** : one that creates or produces : MAKER **2** *cap* : GOD 1

crea·ture \'krē-chər\ *n* **1** : a created being **2 a** : a lower animal **b** : PERSON 1

crèche \'kresh\ *n* : a scene representing the Nativity in the stable at Bethlehem

cre·dence \'krēd-ᵊn(t)s\ *n* : an accepting in the mind as true or real **syn** see BELIEF

cre·den·tials \kri-'den-chəlz\ *n pl* : documents showing that a person has a right to perform certain official acts [derived from Latin *credentialis* (adjective) "showing one is entitled to credit or confidence", from *credentia* "promise, credit", derived from earlier *credere* "to believe, trust, entrust" — related to CREDIT, CREED, INCREDIBLE]

cred·i·ble \'kred-ə-bəl\ *adj* : offering reasonable grounds for being believed ⟨a *credible* story⟩ — **cred·i·bil·i·ty** \,kred-ə-'bil-ət-ē\ *n* — **cred·i·bly** \'kred-ə-blē\ *adv*

1cred·it \'kred-ət\ *n* **1** : a balance in an account in a person's favor ⟨debits and *credits*⟩ **2** : an amount or sum that a bank or company will let a person use **3 a** : trust given to a customer for future payment for goods purchased ⟨extended them *credit*⟩ ⟨buy on *credit*⟩ **b** : reputation for paying one's bills ⟨check on a person's *credit*⟩ **c** : time given for payment ⟨30 days' *credit*⟩ ⟨long-term *credit*⟩ **4** : CREDENCE, BELIEF ⟨a story that deserves little *credit*⟩ **5** : reputation for honesty or integrity : good name **6** : a source of honor ⟨a *credit* to her school⟩ **7** : something that adds to a person's reputation or honor ⟨got *credit* for the discovery⟩ **8 a** : official certification of the completion of a course of study **b** : a unit of academic work for which such certification is made [from early French *credit* "reputation, permission to buy without paying immediately", from early Italian *credito* (same meaning), from Latin *creditum* "loan", derived from *credere* "to believe, trust, entrust" — related to CREDENTIALS, CREED, INCREDIBLE]

2credit *vb* **1** : BELIEVE 3 **2** : to enter a sum on the credit side of ⟨we'll *credit* your account with $10⟩ **3 a** : to give credit to ⟨they *credit* you with quite a sense of humor⟩ **b** : to give the credit for to somebody or something ⟨*credited* the rescue to her quick thinking⟩

cred·it·able \'kred-ət-ə-bəl\ *adj* : good enough to deserve praise — **cred·it·abil·i·ty** \,kred-ət-ə-'bil-ət-ē\ *n* — **cred·it·ably** \'kred-ət-ə-blē\ *adv*

credit card *n* : a card with which one can buy things on credit

cred·i·tor \'kred-ət-ər\ *n* : a person to whom a debt is owed

credit union *n* : a cooperative association that makes small loans to its members at low interest rates

cre·do \'krēd-ō, 'krād-\ *n, pl* **credos** : CREED

cre·du·li·ty \kri-'d(y)ü-lət-ē\ *n* : a willingness to believe statements especially on little or no evidence

cred·u·lous \'krej-ə-ləs\ *adj* : ready to believe especially on little evidence — **cred·u·lous·ly** *adv* — **cred·u·lous·ness** *n*

Cree \'krē\ *n, pl* **Cree** *or* **Crees** : a member of an American Indian people of Manitoba and Saskatchewan

creed \'krēd\ *n* **1** : a statement of the basic beliefs of a religious faith **2** : a set of guiding principles or beliefs [Middle English *crede* "creed", from early French *crēda* (same meaning), from Latin *credo*, literally "I believe" (used as the first words in many creeds), from *credere* "to believe, trust, entrust" — related to CREDENTIALS, CREDIT, INCREDIBLE]

creek \'krēk, 'krik\ *n* **1** *chiefly British* : a small narrow inlet or bay **2** : a stream of water usually smaller than a river

Creek \'krēk\ *n* : a member of an American Indian tribe that once occupied most of Alabama and Georgia but was removed to Oklahoma in the 1830s

creel \'krē(ə)l\ *n* : a basket for holding a catch of fish

1creep \'krēp\ *vb* **crept** \'krept\; **creep·ing** **1** : to move along with the body close to the ground : move slowly on hands and knees **2** : to advance slowly, timidly, or quietly ⟨the tide *crept* up the beach⟩ **3** : to spread or grow over the ground or a surface ⟨ivy *creeping* up a wall⟩ ⟨a *creeping* vine⟩ **4** : to slip or gradually shift position **5** : to feel as though insects were crawling on the body ⟨the shriek made my flesh *creep*⟩

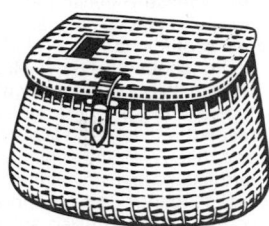
creel

2creep *n* **1** : a creeping movement **2 a** : a sensation like that of insects creeping over one's flesh **b** : a feeling of horror — usually used in pl. **3** : an unpleasant or hateful person

creep·er \'krē-pər\ *n* : one that creeps: as **a** : a creeping plant **b** : a bird that creeps about on trees or bushes searching for insects

creepy \'krē-pē\ *adj* **creep·i·er; -est** : having or producing a sensation as of insects creeping on the skin; *esp* : EERIE — **creep·i·ness** *n*

cre·mate \'krē-,māt, kri-'māt\ *vb* **cre·mat·ed; cre·mat·ing** : to burn (as a dead body) to ashes — **cre·ma·tion** \kri-'mā-shən\ *n*

cre·ma·to·ri·um \,krē-mə-'tōr-ē-əm, ,krem-ə-, -'tòr-\ *n, pl* **-ri·ums** *or* **-ria** \-ē-ə\ : 1CREMATORY

1cre·ma·to·ry \'krē-mə-,tōr-ē, 'krem-ə-, -,tòr-\ *n, pl* **-ries** : a furnace for cremating or a building containing such a furnace

2crematory *adj* : of, relating to, or used in cremation

cren·el·lat·ed \'kren-ᵊl-,āt-əd\ *adj* : having battlements ⟨a *crenellated* tower⟩

cre·ole \'krē-,ōl\ *adj* **1** *often cap* : of or relating to the Creoles or their language **2** : *often cap* : relating to or being the traditional spicy food of the Creoles

Cre·ole \'krē-,ōl\ *n* **1** : a white person descended from early French or Spanish settlers in the U.S. Gulf states **2** : a person of mixed French or Spanish and black descent speaking a dialect of French or Spanish **3 a** : a language evolved from a pidgin based on French that is spoken by blacks in southern Louisiana **b** *not cap* : a language that has evolved from a pidgin and serves as the native language of a group of people

¹**cre·o·sote** \'krē-ə-ˌsōt\ *n* : a brownish oily liquid obtained from coal tar and used especially to preserve wood

²**creosote** *vb* **-sot·ed; -sot·ing** : to treat with creosote

crepe *or* **crêpe** \'krāp\ *n* **1** : a thin crinkled fabric (as of silk or wool) **2** : a small very thin pancake

crepe de chine \ˌkrāp-də-'shēn\ *n* : a soft thin crepe made especially of silk and used for clothing

crepe myrtle *or* **crêpe myrtle** *n* : CRAPE MYRTLE

crepe paper *n* : paper with a crinkled or puckered look and feel

crepe su·zette \ˌkrāp-sù-'zet\ *n, pl* **crepes suzette** \ˌkrāp(s)-sù-'zet\ *or* **crepe suzettes** \ˌkrāp-sù-'zets\ : a crepe rolled or folded in a hot orange-butter sauce that is sprinkled with a liqueur and set ablaze for serving

crept *past and past participle of* CREEP

cre·pus·cu·lar \kri-'pəs-kyə-lər\ *adj* : resembling twilight : DIM ⟨a faint *crepuscular* light⟩

cre·scen·do \kri-'shen-dō\ *n, pl* **-dos** *or* **-does** **1** : a gradual increase especially in the loudness of music **2** : the peak of a gradual increase — **crescendo** *adv or adj*

¹**cres·cent** \'kres-ᵊnt\ *n* **1** : the shape of the visible moon during about the first week after a new moon or the last week before the next new moon **2** : a curved figure that tapers to two points like a crescent moon

²**crescent** *adj* : shaped like a crescent

cress \'kres\ *n* : any of numerous plants related to the mustard and having leaves that are used in salads

¹**crest** \'krest\ *n* **1 a** : a showy growth (as of flesh or feathers) on the head of an animal **b** : an emblem or design on a helmet (as of a knight) or over a coat of arms **2** : an upper part, edge, or limit ⟨the *crest* of a hill⟩ ⟨the *crest* of a wave⟩ — **crest·ed** \'kres-təd\ *adj*

²**crest** *vb* **1** : to give a crest to **2** : to reach the crest of ⟨*crest* the hill⟩ **3** : to rise to a crest ⟨the river *crested* at eight feet⟩

crest·fall·en \'krest-ˌfo-lən\ *adj* : feeling humiliation or disappointment

Cre·ta·ceous \kri-'tā-shəs\ *adj* : of, relating to, or being the latest period of the Mesozoic era of geological history marked by the extinction of the dinosaurs at the close of the period; *also* : relating to the corresponding system of rocks — see GEOLOGIC TIME table — **Cretaceous** *n*

cre·tin \'krēt-ᵊn\ *n* **1** : one having cretinism **2** : DOLT

cre·tin·ism \'krēt-ᵊn-ˌiz-əm\ *n* : an abnormal condition that is usually present from birth, is marked by physical and mental stunting, and is caused by a lack of the secretion of the thyroid gland

cre·tonne \'krē-ˌtän, kri-'tän\ *n* : a cotton or linen cloth

cre·vasse \kri-'vas\ *n* : a deep crevice (as in a glacier)

crev·ice \'krev-əs\ *n* : a narrow opening caused by a split or crack : FISSURE

crew \'krü\ *n* **1** : a group or gathering of people ⟨a happy *crew*⟩ **2** : a group of people working together ⟨the kitchen *crew*⟩ **3** : a group of people who operate a ship, train, or airplane **4** : the rowers and coxswain of a racing shell

crew cut *n* : a very short haircut in which the hair resembles the surface of a brush

crew·el \'krü-əl\ *n* : a loosely twisted wool yarn used for embroidery; *also* : embroidery made with this yarn

crew·man \'krü-mən\ *n* : a member of a crew

¹**crib** \'krib\ *n* **1** : a manger for feeding animals **2** : a small bed frame with high sides for a child **3** : a bin or building for storing grain **4** : the cards discarded in cribbage **5 a** : PONY 2 **b** : something used for cheating on a test

²**crib** *vb* **cribbed; crib·bing** **1** : to copy (as an idea or piece of writing) and use as one's own : PLAGIARIZE **2** : to use a translation or notes dishonestly — **crib·ber** *n*

crib·bage \'krib-ij\ *n* : a card game in which each player tries to form various counting combinations of cards

crick \'krik\ *n* : a painful spasm of muscles (as of the neck or back)

¹**crick·et** \'krik-ət\ *n* : a small leaping insect that has leathery forewings and thin hind wings and is noted for the chirping notes of the males [Middle English *criket* "cricket (insect)", from early French *criquet* (same meaning); probably an imitation of the insect's sound]

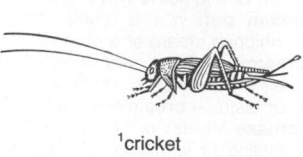

¹cricket

²**cricket** *n* **1** : a game played on a large field with bats, ball, and wickets by two teams of 11 players each **2** : fair play [from early French *criquet* "goal stake in an old bowling game", probably from earlier *criquer* "to crack"; probably an imitation of the sound made by hitting or breaking the stake] — **crick·et·er** *n*

cri·er \'krī-(ə)r\ *n* : one who calls out orders or announcements

crime \'krīm\ *n* **1** : the doing of an act forbidden by law or the failure to do an act required by law especially when serious **2** : criminal activity ⟨the war on *crime*⟩ **3** : an act that is sinful, foolish, or disgraceful ⟨it's a *crime* to waste good food⟩ **syn** see OFFENSE

¹**crim·i·nal** \'krim-ən-ᵊl, 'krim-nəl\ *adj* **1** : being or guilty of a crime ⟨a *criminal* act⟩ **2** : relating to crime or its punishment ⟨*criminal* court⟩ — **crim·i·nal·i·ty** \ˌkrim-ə-'nal-ət-ē\ *n* — **crim·i·nal·ly** \'krim-ən-ᵊl-ē, -nə-lē\ *adv*

²**criminal** *n* : a person who has committed a crime

crim·i·nol·o·gy \ˌkrim-ə-'näl-ə-jē\ *n* : a scientific study of crime, of criminals, and of their punishment or correction — **crim·i·no·log·i·cal** \ˌkrim-ən-ᵊl-'äj-i-kəl\ *adj* — **crim·i·nol·o·gist** \ˌkrim-ə-'näl-ə-jəst\ *n*

¹**crimp** \'krimp\ *vb* : to make wavy or bent

²**crimp** *n* **1** : something produced by or as if by crimping **2** : something that holds back

¹**crim·son** \'krim-zən\ *n* : a deep purplish red — **crimson** *adj*

²**crimson** *vb* : to make or become crimson

cringe \'krinj\ *vb* **cringed; cring·ing** \'krin-jiŋ\ **1** : to shrink in fear : COWER **2** : to behave in a too humble or cowardly way — **cring·er** *n*

¹**crin·kle** \'kriŋ-kəl\ *vb* **crin·kled; crin·kling** \-k(ə-)liŋ\ **1** : to form or cause little waves or wrinkles on the surface **2** : ¹RUSTLE 1

²**crinkle** *n* : ¹WRINKLE 1, RIPPLE — **crin·kly** \-k(ə-)lē\ *adj*

cri·noid \'krī-ˌnoid\ *n* : any of a large class of invertebrates that are echinoderms and usually have a cup-shaped body with five or more feathery arms — **crinoid** *adj*

crin·o·line \'krin-ᵊl-ən\ *n* **1** : a cloth used for stiffening and lining **2** : a full stiff skirt; *esp* : one lined with crinoline **3** : HOOPSKIRT — **crinoline** *adj*

¹**crip·ple** \'krip-əl\ *n* : a lame or disabled person

²**cripple** *vb* **crip·pled; crip·pling** \'krip-(ə-)liŋ\ **1** : to cause to become a cripple ⟨*crippled* by rheumatism⟩ **2** : to make useless or imperfect ⟨loss of power *crippled* the city⟩ — **crip·pler** \-(ə-)lər\ *n*

cri·sis \'krī-səs\ *n, pl* **cri·ses** \'krī-ˌsēz\ **1** : the turning point for better or worse in a disease **2** : a turning point (as in a person's life or in the plot of a story) **3 a** : an unstable or difficult time or state of affairs ⟨a financial *crisis*⟩ **b** : a situation that has become very serious ⟨the energy *crisis*⟩

¹**crisp** \'krisp\ *adj* **1 a** : being thin and hard and easily crumbled ⟨*crisp* crackers⟩ **b** : pleasantly firm and fresh ⟨*crisp* lettuce⟩ **2 a** : having sharp distinct outlines ⟨a *crisp* illustration⟩ **b** : being clear and brief ⟨a *crisp* reply⟩ **c** : fresh and neat ⟨a *crisp* housedress⟩ **d** : being quick and

lively ⟨a *crisp* performance⟩ ⟨a *crisp* tale of adventure⟩ **3** : pleasantly cool and invigorating ⟨a *crisp* autumn day⟩ — **crisp·i·ness** \'kris-pē-nəs\ *n* — **crisp·ly** *adv* — **crisp·ness** *n* — **crispy** \'kris-pē\ *adj*

²crisp *vb* : to make or become crisp — **crisp·er** *n*

³crisp *n* : something crisp or brittle ⟨burned to a *crisp*⟩

¹criss·cross \'kris-,krös\ *n* : a pattern formed by crossed lines — **crisscross** *adj or adv*

²crisscross *vb* **1** : to mark with lines that cross each other **2** : to go or cross back and forth ⟨*crisscrossing* the state⟩

cri·te·ri·on \krī-'tir-ē-ən\ *n, pl* **-ria** \-ē-ə\ : a standard on which a judgment or decision may be based

crit·ic \'krit-ik\ *n* **1** : a person who makes or gives a judgment of the value, worth, beauty, or excellence of something **2** : FAULTFINDER

crit·i·cal \'krit-i-kəl\ *adj* **1 a** : inclined to criticize in an unfavorable way ⟨you're always so *critical*⟩ **b** : consisting of or involving criticism or the judgments of critics ⟨*critical* writings⟩ **c** : using or involving careful judgment ⟨a *critical* examination of a patient⟩ **2 a** : of, relating to, or being a turning point ⟨*critical* phase of a fever⟩; *also* : being at a critical stage of illness ⟨listed the patient as *critical*⟩ **b** : being or relating to a state or point at which a change occurs **c** : CRUCIAL 1 ⟨*critical* test⟩ **3** : INDISPENSABLE, VITAL ⟨provides *critical* services⟩ **4** : of big enough size to keep a chain reaction going — used of a mass of material that can go through fission — **crit·i·cal·ly** \-i-k(ə-)lē\ *adv*

critical temperature *n* : the temperature above which a gas cannot be turned into a liquid no matter how much pressure is applied to it

crit·i·cism \'krit-ə-,siz-əm\ *n* **1** : the act of criticizing and especially of finding fault **2** : a critical remark or comment **3** : a careful judgment or review especially by a critic

crit·i·cize \'krit-ə-,sīz\ *vb* **-cized; -ciz·ing** **1** : to examine and judge as a critic **2** : to find fault with

crit·ter \'krit-ər\ *n* : CREATURE

croak \'krōk\ *vb* **1 a** : to make a deep harsh sound **b** : to speak in a hoarse throaty voice **2** : GRUMBLE 1, COMPLAIN **3** *slang* **a** : ¹DIE 1 **b** : ¹KILL 1 — **croak** *n*

croak·er \'krō-kər\ *n* **1** : one that croaks **2** : any of various fishes that produce croaking or grunting noises

Croat \'krō-,at, 'krō-(ə)t\ *n* : CROATIAN

Cro·atian \krō-'ā-shən\ *n* **1** : a person born or living in Croatia **2** : a Slavic language spoken by the Croatian people — **Croatian** *adj*

croc \'kräk\ *n* : CROCODILE

¹cro·chet \krō-'shā\ *n* : needlework done by forming and weaving loops in a thread with a hooked needle

²crochet *vb* **crocheted; crochet·ing** : to make something of crochet — **cro·chet·er** \-'shā-ər\ *n*

¹crock \'kräk\ *n* : a pot or jar made of baked clay

²crock *n* : one that is broken-down or useless ⟨an old *crock* who needs an afternoon nap⟩

crock·ery \'kräk-(ə-)rē\ *n* : EARTHENWARE

Crock·pot \'kräk-,pät\ *trademark* — used for an electric cooking pot

croc·o·dile \'kräk-ə-,dīl\ *n* : any of several large thick-skinned long-bodied reptiles of tropical and subtropical waters — compare ALLIGATOR

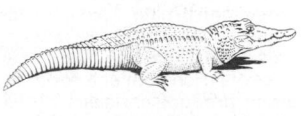
crocodile

Word History The English word *crocodile* can be traced back to the ancient Greek word *krokodilos.* But the word went through a curious spelling change along the way. The Greeks first saw this strange animal in Egypt, where it lived along the Nile river. They named it *krokodilos,* the Greek word for "lizard". *Krokodilos* literally means "pebble worm". It is made up of the Greek words *krokos,* meaning "pebble" and *drilos,* "worm". The first part apparently comes from the habit of lizards of sunning themselves on warm rocks or pebbles. The last part, *drilos,* is the word the Greeks used for any creature that looked like a snake. The Romans borrowed this Greek word into Latin as *crocodilus.* However, later writers misplaced the *r* when they copied it, and it came to be spelled *cocodrillus.* It is the misspelled form that was taken into early French and later into Middle English as *cocodrille.* Later, English scholars reading the earliest Latin books found that the Latin word had originally been spelled *crocodilus* instead of *cocodrillus.* Then they changed the spelling of the English word to match the form it had in Latin and Greek. [from Middle English *cocodrille* "crocodile", from early French *cocodrille* (same meaning), from Latin *cocodrillus* and earlier *crocodilus* "crocodile", from Greek *krokodilos* "crocodile, lizard"]

crocodile tears *n pl* : pretended tears or sorrow

Word History An ancient fable tells of a crocodile that sheds tears while eating its prey. Of course, a crocodile is not really sorry for killing and eating another animal because that's how it survives. So when someone is said to shed *crocodile tears,* it refers to a show of pretended sorrow usually by someone who has done something cruel.

croc·o·dil·ian \,kräk-ə-'dil-ē-ən, -'dil-yən\ *n* : any of an order of reptiles that includes the crocodiles, alligators, and related extinct forms — **crocodilian** *adj*

cro·cus \'krō-kəs\ *n, pl* **cro·cus·es** **1** *pl also* **cro·ci** \-,kē, -,kī, -,sī\ : any of a large genus of small herbs that are related to the iris and have showy solitary long-tubed flowers and slender grasslike leaves **2** : SAFFRON 1

croft \'kröft\ *n* **1** *chiefly British* : a small enclosed field **2** *chiefly British* : a small farm worked by a tenant — **croft·er** *n, chiefly British*

Cro–Mag·non \krō-'mag-nən, -'man-yən\ *n* : any of a tall erect human race known from the remains of skeletons found chiefly in southern France and often placed in the same species as the human beings that live on the earth today [from *Cro-Magnon,* name of a cave in France where the skeletons were found] — **Cro–Magnon** *adj*

crone \'krōn\ *n* : WITCH 2

cro·ny \'krō-nē\ *n, pl* **cronies** : a close companion : PAL

¹crook \'krük\ *vb* : ¹BEND 2, CURVE

²crook *n* **1** : a shepherd's staff with one end curved into a hook **2** : a dishonest person (as a thief or swindler) **3** : a curved or hooked part of a thing : BEND

crook·ed \'krük-əd\ *adj* **1** : having bends and curves ⟨a *crooked* path⟩ **2** : not set or placed straight ⟨the picture is *crooked*⟩ **3** : DISHONEST ⟨a *crooked* card game⟩ — **crook·ed·ly** *adv* — **crook·ed·ness** *n*

crook·neck \'krük-,nek\ *n* : a squash with a long curved neck

croon \'krün\ *vb* : to hum or sing in a low soft voice ⟨*croon* a lullaby⟩ — **croon** *n*

¹crop \'kräp\ *n* **1 a** : the handle of a whip **b** : a short riding whip **2** : an enlargement of the gullet of a bird or insect that forms a pouch to receive food and prepare it for digestion **3 a** : a plant or animal or plant or animal product that can be grown and harvested **b** : the product or yield especially of a harvested crop **c** : BATCH 2, LOT

²crop *vb* **cropped; crop·ping** **1 a** : to remove the upper or outer parts of ⟨*crop* a hedge⟩ ⟨*crop* a dog's ears⟩ **b** : to cut off short : CLIP ⟨*crop* a photograph⟩ **2 a** : to cause

\ə\ abut		\au̇\ out		\i\ tip		\ȯ\ saw		\u̇\ foot
\ər\ **further**		\ch\ **chin**		\ī\ **life**		\ȯi\ **coin**		\y\ **yet**
\a\ **mat**		\e\ **pet**		\j\ **job**		\th\ **thin**		\yü\ **few**
\ā\ **take**		\ē\ **easy**		\ŋ\ **sing**		\th\ **this**		\yu̇\ **cure**
\ä\ **cot, cart**		\g\ **go**		\ō\ **bone**		\ü\ **food**		\zh\ **vision**

land to bear produce   **b** : to grow as a crop ⟨*crop* cotton⟩ **3** : to produce or make a crop ⟨the apple trees *cropped* well⟩   **4** : to come or appear when not expected ⟨problems *crop* up daily⟩

crop·land \'kräp-,land\ *n* : land on which crops are grown

¹crop·per \'kräp-ər\ *n* : one that crops; *esp* : SHARECROP-PER

²cropper *n*   **1** : a severe fall   **2** : a sudden or violent failure or collapse

crop rotation *n* : the practice of growing first one and then another crop on the same land especially to preserve the ability of the soil to produce crops

cro·quet \krō-'kā\ *n* : a game in which the players use mallets to drive wooden balls through a series of wickets set out on a lawn

cro·quette \krō-'ket\ *n* : a roll or ball of hashed meat, fish, or vegetables fried in deep fat

cro·sier *or* **cro·zier** \'krō-zhər\ *n* : a staff like a shepherd's crook carried by bishops and abbots as a symbol of office

crosier

¹cross \'kros\ *n*   **1 a** : a structure consisting of one bar crossing another at right angles   **b** *often cap* : the cross on which Jesus was crucified used as a symbol of Christianity and the Christian religion   **2** : sorrow or suffering as a test of patience or virtue ⟨had their *crosses* to bear⟩   **3** : an object or mark shaped like a cross ⟨a stone *cross*⟩ ⟨put a *cross* next to the name⟩   **4 a** : an act of crossing unlike individuals   **b** : a crossbred individual or kind   **5** : a punch that crosses over an opponent's punch in boxing [Old English *cros,* probably from an early Norse or an early Irish word derived from Latin *crux* "cross" — related to CRUCIAL, CRUISE, CRUSADE, CRUX, EXCRUCIATING]

²cross *vb*   **1 a** : to lie or be situated across ⟨put a nail where the boards *cross* each other⟩   **b** : ¹INTERSECT 1 ⟨where two lines *cross*⟩   **c** : to move, pass, or extend across ⟨a bridge *crossing* the river⟩ ⟨*cross* the street⟩   **2** : to make the sign of the cross on or over (as in prayer)   **3** : to cancel by marking a cross on or drawing a line through ⟨*cross* names off a list⟩ ⟨*cross* out a mistake⟩   **4** : to place one over the other ⟨*cross* the arms⟩   **5** : to act against : OPPOSE ⟨don't *cross* me⟩   **6** : to draw a line across ⟨*cross* your *t's*⟩   **7** : INTERBREED, HYBRIDIZE   **8** : to pass in opposite directions ⟨our letters *crossed* in the mail⟩   **9** : to occur to ⟨it never *crossed* my mind⟩   **10** : to turn (the eyes) inward toward the nose ⟨eyes were *crossed*⟩

³cross *adj*   **1** : lying or moving across ⟨*cross* traffic⟩   **2** : ¹CONTRARY 1   **3** : marked by bad temper : GRUMPY — **cross·ly** *adv* — **cross·ness** *n*

cross·bar \'kros-,bär\ *n* : a bar, piece, or stripe placed crosswise or across something

cross·bill \-,bil\ *n* : any of a genus of finches with the upper and lower parts of the bill curved so that they cross each other when the bill is closed

cross·bones \-,bōnz\ *n pl* : two leg or arm bones placed or pictured as lying across each other ⟨skull and *crossbones*⟩

cross·bow \-,bō\ *n* : a short bow mounted crosswise near the end of a wooden stock that shoots short arrows

cross·bred \'kros-'bred\ *adj* : ²HYBRID; *esp* : produced by crossing two pure but different breeds, strains, or varieties

¹cross·breed \'kros-,brēd, -'brēd\ *vb* **-bred** \-,bred, -'bred\; **-breed·ing** : HYBRIDIZE; *esp* : to cross two varieties or breeds of the same species

²cross·breed \-,brēd\ *n* : ¹HYBRID 1

¹cross–coun·try \'krō-'skən-trē\ *adj*   **1** : extending or moving across a country ⟨a *cross-country* railroad⟩ ⟨a *cross-country* concert tour⟩   **2** : going over the countryside rather than by roads   **3** : dealing with or being racing or skiing over the countryside instead of over a track or run — **cross–country** *adv*

²cross–country *n* : cross-country skiing or racing

¹cross·cut \'krò-,sket, -'sket\ *vb* **-cut; -cut·ting** : to cut or saw across the grain of wood

²crosscut *adj*   **1** : made or used for cutting across the grain of wood ⟨a *crosscut* saw⟩   **2** : cut across

³cross·cut \'krò-,sket\ *n*   **1** : something that cuts across or through   **2** : a crosscut saw

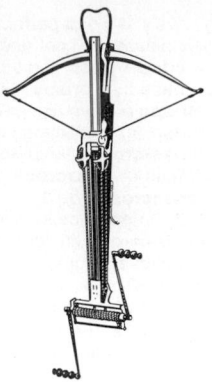

crossbow

cross–ex·am·ine \,krò-sig-'zam-ən\ *vb* : to question (a person) in an effort to show that statements or answers given earlier were false — **cross–ex·am·i·na·tion** \-,zam-ə-'nā-shən\ *n* — **cross–ex·am·in·er** \-'zam-(ə-)nər\ *n*

cross–eyed \'krò-,sīd\ *adj* : having one or both eyes turned inward toward the nose

cross–fer·til·i·za·tion \'kròs-,fərt-ᵊl-ə-'zā-shən\ *n*   **1** : fertilization between sex cells produced by separate individuals or sometimes by individuals of different kinds   **2** : CROSS-POLLINATION — **cross–fer·tile** \-'fərt-ᵊl\ *adj* — **cross–fer·til·ize** \-'fərt-ᵊl-,īz\ *vb*

cross fire *n*   **1** : gunfire from two or more places so that the lines of fire cross   **2** : a rapid or angry exchange (as of words)

cross hair *n* : one of the very thin wires or threads in the eyepiece of an optical instrument (as a microscope) used as a reference line

cross·hatch \'kròs-,hach\ *vb* : to mark with sets of parallel lines that cross — **crosshatch** *n*

cross·ing \'krò-siŋ\ *n*   **1 a** : the act of one that crosses   **b** : a voyage across water   **c** : the act or process of interbreeding or hybridizing   **2** : a place where a street or stream is crossed   **3** : a place where two things (as a street and a railroad track) cross

cross·ing–over \,krò-siŋ-'ō-vər\ *n* : an exchange of genes or chromosome segments between corresponding parts of similar but usually not identical chromosomes during meiosis

cross–legged \'krò-'sleg(-ə)d\ *adv* : with the legs crossed and the knees spread wide

cross–link \'krò-,sliŋk\ *n* : an atom or group of atoms that is a crosswise connection between two long series of atoms of a molecule — **cross–link** *vb*

cross·over \'krò-,sō-vər\ *n* : an instance or product of genetic crossing-over

cross·piece \'krò-,spēs\ *n* : something placed so as to cross something else

cross–pol·li·nate \,krò-'späl-ə-,nāt\ *vb* : to subject to cross-pollination

cross–pol·li·na·tion \,krò-,späl-ə-'nā-shən\ *n* : the transfer of pollen from one flower to the stigma of another

cross product *n* : either of the two products obtained by multiplying together the two means or the two extremes of a proportion

cross–pur·pose \'krò-'spər-pəs\ *n* : a purpose that works against someone else's purpose usually without meaning to ⟨the two were always at *cross-purposes*⟩

cross–ref·er·ence \'kròs-'ref-ərn(t)s, -'ref-(ə-)rən(t)s\ *n* : a reference made from one place to another (as in a dictionary)

cross·road \'kròs-,rōd, -'rōd\ *n*   **1** : a road that crosses a

main road or runs across country between main roads **2**
a : a place where roads cross — usually used in pl. **b**
: a small community at a crossroads **3** : a place or time
at which a decision must be made

cross section *n* **1 a** : a cutting made across something (as
a log or an apple) **b** : a representation of a cross section
⟨a *cross section* of a blood vessel⟩ **2** : a number of persons or things selected from a group to stand for the whole
⟨a *cross section* of society⟩ — **cross·sec·tion·al** \'kròs-
'sek-sh(ə-)nəl\ *adj*

cross–stitch \'kròs-ˌ(s)tich\ *n* : a needlework stitch that
forms an X; *also* : needlework having cross-stitches

cross·tie \'krò-ˌstī\ *n* : a railroad tie

cross·town \'krò-'staùn\ *adj* **1** : being on different sides
of a town ⟨the two schools were *crosstown* rivals in football⟩ **2** : going across a town ⟨a *crosstown* bus⟩ ⟨*crosstown* streets⟩ — **crosstown** *adv*

cross·walk \'krò-ˌswòk\ *n* : a specially paved or marked
path for people walking across a street or road

cross·ways \-ˌswāz\ *adv* : CROSSWISE

cross·wise \-ˌswīz\ *adv* : so as to cross something
: ACROSS ⟨logs laid *crosswise*⟩ — **crosswise** *adj*

cross·word puzzle \ˌkrò-ˌswərd-\ *n* : a puzzle in which
words are filled into a pattern of numbered squares in answer to clues so that they read across and down

crotch \'kräch\ *n* : an angle formed by the spreading apart
of two legs or branches or of a limb from its trunk

crotch·et \'kräch-ət\ *n* : an unusual personal opinion or
habit — **crotch·et·i·ness** \-ət-ē-nəs\ *n* — **crotch·ety**
\-ət-ē\ *adj*

crouch \'kraùch\ *vb* : to stoop or bend low with the arms
and legs close to the body — **crouch** *n*

¹croup \'krüp\ *n* : the rump of a four-footed animal [Middle
English *croupe* "rump", from early French *croupe* (same
meaning); of Germanic origin]

²croup *n* : a laryngitis especially of infants marked by periods of difficult breathing and a hoarse cough [from an English dialect word *croup* "to cry or cough"; probably originally an imitation of the sound] — **croupy** \'krü-pē\ *adj*

crou·pi·er \'krü-pē-ər, -pē-ˌā\ *n* : an employee of a gambling casino who collects and pays bets

crou·ton \'krü-ˌtän, krü-'tän\ *n* : a small cube of bread
toasted or fried crisp

¹crow \'krō\ *n* **1** : any of various large usually entirely
glossy black perching birds related to the jays **2** *cap* : a
member of an American Indian people of Montana — **as
the crow flies** : in a straight line

²crow *vb* **crowed** \'krōd\; **crow·ing** **1** : to make the loud
shrill sound that a rooster makes **2** : to make sounds of
delight **3** : to brag loudly or joyfully **syn** see BOAST

³crow *n* **1** : the cry of the rooster **2** : a cry of triumph

crow·bar \'krō-ˌbär\ *n* : a metal bar used as a lever (as for
prying things apart)

¹crowd \'kraùd\ *vb* **1** : to press forward or close ⟨*crowd*
into an elevator⟩ ⟨*crowded* around the speaker⟩ **2** : to
push or press into a small space ⟨*crowd* clothes into a
closet⟩ **3** : to fill or pack by pressing together ⟨cars
crowded the roads⟩ **4** : to push or force by or as if by a
crowd ⟨we were *crowded* off the sidewalk⟩ ⟨don't let soft
drinks *crowd* milk out of your diet⟩

²crowd *n* **1** : a large number of persons or things crowded
or crowding together **2** : the population as a whole : ordinary people ⟨books that appeal to the *crowd*⟩ **3** : a
large number of things close together **4** : a group of people having a common interest ⟨running around with the
wrong *crowd*⟩ **syn** see MULTITUDE

crowd·ed·ness \'kraùd-əd-nəs\ *n* : the state of being
crowded

¹crown \'kraùn\ *n* **1 a** : a wreath or band for the head
especially as a mark of victory or honor **b** : the title representing a sports championship ⟨the heavyweight *crown*⟩
2 : a royal headdress **3 a** : the top of the head **b** : the

highest part (as of a mountain or tree) **c** : the part of a
hat covering the crown of the head **d** : the part of a tooth
outside of the gum **4** : something resembling a crown **5**
a : royal power or authority **b** *cap* : the executive part of
the British government **6** : any of various coins (as an old
British coin worth five shillings) — **crowned** \'kraùnd\ *adj*
— **crown·like** \'kraùn-ˌlīk\ *adj*

²crown *vb* **1 a** : to place a crown on; *esp* : to make sovereign **b** : to declare officially to be ⟨was *crowned* champion⟩ **2 a** : ²TOP 2 ⟨snow *crowned* the mountain's peak⟩
b : to top a checker with a checker to make a king **3** : to
bring to a successful conclusion : finish off : COMPLETE **4**
of a forest fire : to burn rapidly through the tops of trees

crown glass *n* : a very clear glass that is used for optical
instruments

crown prince *n* : the prince next in line for a crown or throne

crown princess *n* **1** : the wife of a crown prince **2** : the
princess next in line for a crown or throne

crow's–foot \'krōz-ˌfút\ *n, pl* **crow's–feet** \-ˌfēt\ : any of
the wrinkles around the outer corners of the eyes — usually used in pl.

crow's nest *n* : a partly enclosed
platform high on a ship's mast for
use as a lookout

crozier *variant of* CROSIER

cruces *pl of* CRUX

cru·cial \'krü-shəl\ *adj* **1** : being
a final or very important test or
decision : DECISIVE ⟨the *crucial*
game of a series⟩ **2** : very important : SIGNIFICANT ⟨water is a
crucial element in our weather⟩
[from French *crucial* "having the
form of a cross, being or involving a crisis", from Latin *cruc-,
crux* "cross, trouble, torture" —
related to CROSS, CRUCIFY, CRUX]
— **cru·cial·ly** \'krüsh-(ə-)lē\
adv

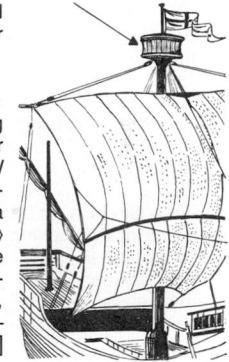
crow's nest

cru·ci·ble \'krü-sə-bəl\ *n* **1** : a
pot made of a substance not easily damaged by fire that
is used for holding something to be treated under great
heat **2** : a severe test

cru·ci·fix \'krü-sə-ˌfiks\ *n* : a cross with a figure of Jesus
crucified on it [Middle English *crucifix* "crucifix", from Latin
crucifixus (same meaning), derived from earlier Latin *crucifigere* "to crucify", from *cruc-, crux* "cross" and *figere*
"to fasten, fix" — related to CROSS, CRUCIFY, FIX]

cru·ci·fix·ion \ˌkrü-sə-'fik-shən\ *n* **1** : an act of crucifying
2 *cap* : the crucifying of Jesus

cru·ci·form \'krü-sə-ˌfòrm\ *adj* : forming or arranged in a
cross

cru·ci·fy \'krü-sə-ˌfī\ *vb* **-fied; -fy·ing** **1** : to put to death
by nailing or binding the hands and feet to a cross **2** : to
treat cruelly : TORTURE, PERSECUTE ⟨were *crucified* in the
newspapers⟩ [Middle English *crucifien* "to crucify", from
early French *crucifier* (same meaning), from Latin *crucifigere* "to crucify", from *cruc-, crux* "cross" and *figere* "to
fasten, fix" — related to CROSS, CRUCIFIX, EXCRUCIATING,
FIX]

¹crude \'krüd\ *adj* **crud·er; crud·est** **1** : being in a natural
state and not changed by cooking or refining : RAW ⟨*crude*
oil⟩ **2** : not having or showing good manners : VULGAR **3**
: planned or done in a rough or unskilled way — **crude·ly**
adv — **crude·ness** *n*

²crude *n* : crude oil

\ə\ abut		\aù\ out		\i\ tip		\ò\ saw	\ù\ foot
\ər\ further		\ch\ chin		\ī\ life		\òi\ coin	\y\ yet
\a\ mat		\e\ pet		\j\ job		\th\ thin	\yü\ few
\ā\ take		\ē\ easy		\ŋ\ sing		\t͟h\ this	\yu̇\ cure
\ä\ cot, cart		\g\ go		\ō\ bone		\ü\ food	\zh\ vision

cru·di·ty \'krüd-ət-ē\ *n, pl* **-ties** **1** : the quality or state of being crude **2** : something that is crude

cru·el \'krü-əl\ *adj* **cru·el·er** *or* **cru·el·ler; cru·el·est** *or* **cru·el·lest** **1** : ready to hurt others **2** : causing or helping to cause suffering — **cru·el·ly** \'krü-ə-lē\ *adv* — **cru·el·ness** *n*

cru·el·ty \'krü-əl-tē\ *n, pl* **-ties** **1** : the quality or state of being cruel **2** : cruel treatment

cru·et \'krü-ət\ *n* : a small glass bottle for holding vinegar, oil, or sauce for use at the table

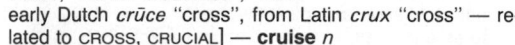

cruet

cruise \'krüz\ *vb* **cruised; cruis·ing** **1** : to travel by boat often stopping at a series of ports **2** : to travel for enjoyment **3** : to travel at the best operating speed ⟨the *cruising* speed of an airplane⟩ [from Dutch *kruisen* "to cruise, move crosswise", from early Dutch *crūce* "cross", from Latin *crux* "cross" — related to CROSS, CRUCIAL] — **cruise** *n*

cruis·er \'krü-zər\ *n* **1** : SQUAD CAR **2** : a large fast warship smaller than a battleship **3** : a motorboat equipped for living aboard

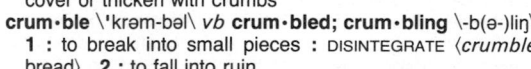

cruiser 3

crul·ler \'krəl-ər\ *n* : a small twisted oblong cake made like a donut

¹crumb \'krəm\ *n* **1** : a small piece especially of bread or cracker **2** : a little bit

²crumb *vb* **1** : to break into crumbs : CRUMBLE **2** : to cover or thicken with crumbs

crum·ble \'krəm-bəl\ *vb* **crum·bled; crum·bling** \-b(ə-)liŋ\ **1** : to break into small pieces : DISINTEGRATE ⟨*crumble* bread⟩ **2** : to fall into ruin

crum·bly \-b(ə-)lē\ *adj* **crum·bli·er; -est** : easily crumbled

crum·pet \'krəm-pət\ *n* : a small round unsweetened bread cooked on a griddle

crum·ple \'krəm-pəl\ *vb* **crum·pled; crum·pling** \-p(ə-)liŋ\ **1** : to press, bend, or crush out of shape ⟨*crumple* paper⟩ **2** : to become crumpled **3** : ¹COLLAPSE 1 ⟨*crumpled* and fell⟩

¹crunch \'krənch\ *vb* **1** : to chew or grind with a crushing noise **2** : to make the sound of being crushed or squeezed ⟨snow *crunching* underfoot⟩

²crunch *n* **1** : an act or sound of crunching **2** : CRISIS 3 ⟨the energy *crunch*⟩

crunchy \'krən-chē\ *adj* **crunch·i·er; -est** : making a crunching sound (as when bitten or chewed) ⟨*crunchy* cereal⟩ ⟨*crunchy* pickles⟩

crup·per \'krəp-ər, 'krùp-\ *n* **1** : a leather strap passing under a horse's tail to keep a saddle or harness in place **2** : the rump of a horse : CROUP

¹cru·sade \krü-'sād\ *n* **1** *cap* : any of the military expeditions made by Christian countries in the 11th, 12th, and 13th centuries to recover the Holy Land from the Muslims **2** : a campaign to get things changed for the better ⟨a *crusade* against crime⟩ [derived from early French *croisade* and Spanish *cruzada*, both meaning literally "an expedition of persons marked with or bearing the sign of the cross" and both derived from Latin *cruc-, crux* "cross" — related to CROSS]

²crusade *vb* **cru·sad·ed; cru·sad·ing** : to take part in a crusade — **cru·sad·er** *n*

cruse \'krüz, 'krüs\ *n* : a jar or pot for holding a liquid

¹crush \'krəsh\ *vb* **1** : to squeeze together so as to break or destroy the natural shape or condition ⟨*crush* grapes⟩ **2** : HUG 1 **3** : to break into fine pieces by pressing, pounding, or grinding ⟨*crush* stone⟩ **4 a** : OVERWHELM 2 ⟨*crushed* the enemy⟩ **b** : OPPRESS 1 — **crush·er** *n*

²crush *n* **1** : an act of crushing **2** : a crowding together of many people **3** : a strong but often temporary liking : INFATUATION ⟨have a *crush* on someone⟩

crust \'krəst\ *n* **1 a** : the hardened outside surface of bread **b** : a piece of dry hard bread **2** : the pastry cover of a pie **3 a** : a hard surface layer ⟨a *crust* of snow⟩ **b** : the outer part of the earth — **crust·al** \'krəs-təl\ *adj*

crus·ta·cea \ˌkrəs-'tā-sh(ē-)ə\ *n pl* : arthropods that are crustaceans

crus·ta·cean \ˌkrəs-'tā-shən\ *n* : any of a large class of mostly water-dwelling arthropods (as lobsters, shrimps, crabs, wood lice, water fleas, and barnacles) having an exoskeleton of chitin or chitin and a compound of calcium — **crustacean** *adj*

crusty \'krəs-tē\ *adj* **crust·i·er; -est** **1** : having or being a crust **2** : ³CROSS 3 — **crust·i·ness** *n*

crutch \'krəch\ *n* **1** : a support usually made with a piece at the top to fit under the armpit for use by a lame or injured person as an aid in walking **2** : something (as a support or prop) like a crutch in shape or use

crux \'krəks, 'krùks\ *n, pl* **crux·es** *also* **cru·ces** \'krü-ˌsēz\ : the most important point ⟨the *crux* of the problem⟩ [from Latin *crux* "cross, torture, trouble" — related to CROSS, CRUCIAL, CRUCIFY]

cru·zei·ro \krü-'ze(ə)r-ō, -ü\ *n, pl* **-ros** **1** : the basic unit of money of Brazil **2** : a coin representing one cruzeiro

¹cry \'krī\ *vb* **cried; cry·ing** **1** : to call loudly : SHOUT **2** : to shed tears often noisily : WEEP, BAWL **3** : to utter a special sound or call **4** : to make known to the public **5** : to suggest strongly a need ⟨the situation *cries* out for action⟩ — **cry havoc** : to sound an alarm — **cry over spilled milk** : to express regret over something that cannot be helped — **cry wolf** : to give alarm without a reason

²cry *n, pl* **cries** **1** : a loud call or shout (as of pain, fear, or joy) **2** : ¹APPEAL 2, PLEA ⟨hear my *cry*⟩ **3** : a fit of weeping ⟨had a good *cry*⟩ **4** : the special sound of an animal (as a bird) **5** : SLOGAN 2 — **a far cry** : a great distance — **in full cry** : in full pursuit

cry·ba·by \'krī-ˌbā-bē\ *n* : a person who cries easily or complains often

cry down *vb* : DISPARAGE 2, BELITTLE

cry·ing \'krī-iŋ\ *adj* **1** : calling for attention and correction ⟨a *crying* need⟩ **2** : NOTORIOUS ⟨a *crying* shame⟩

cryo·gen·ics \ˌkrī-ə-'jen-iks\ *n* : a branch of physics that deals with the production and effects of very low temperatures

cryo·lite \'krī-ə-ˌlīt\ *n* : a mineral consisting of sodium, aluminum, and fluorine that is used especially in making aluminum

crypt \'kript\ *n* : an underground chamber; *also* : a chamber for burial

cryp·tic \'krip-tik\ *adj* **1** : meant to be puzzling or mysterious ⟨a *cryptic* remark⟩ **2** : serving to conceal ⟨*cryptic* coloring of an animal⟩ — **cryp·ti·cal·ly** \-ti-k(ə-)lē\ *adv*

cryp·to·gram \'krip-tə-ˌgram\ *n* : something written in cipher or code

cryp·to·graph \'krip-tə-ˌgraf\ *n* : CRYPTOGRAM — **cryp·to·graph·ic** \ˌkrip-tə-'graf-ik\ *adj*

cryp·tog·ra·phy \krip-'täg-rə-fē\ *n* : the coding and decoding of secret messages — **cryp·tog·ra·pher** \-fər\ *n*

¹crys·tal \'kris-təl\ *n* **1** : a quartz that is transparent or nearly so **2** : something transparent like crystal **3** : a solid form of a substance or mixture that has a regularly repeating internal arrangement of its atoms and often external plane faces ⟨a *crystal* of quartz⟩ ⟨a snow *crystal*⟩ ⟨a salt *crystal*⟩ **4** : a clear colorless glass of very good qual-

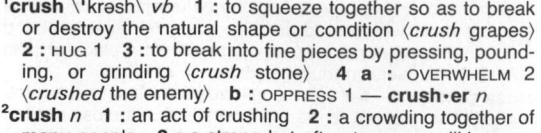

ity; *also* : things made of this glass   **5** : the transparent cover over a watch or clock dial

²**crystal** *adj*   **1** : made of or resembling crystal   **2** : using a crystal as a detector ⟨a *crystal* radio receiver⟩

crystal ball *n* : a clear ball especially of quartz crystal used by a fortune-teller to predict the future

crys·tal·line \'kris-tə-lən\ *adj*   **1** : made of crystal or crystals   **2** : clear and sparkling like crystal ⟨*crystalline* drops of honey⟩   **3** : of or relating to a crystal

crystalline lens *n* : the lens of the vertebrate eye

crys·tal·ize \'kris-tə-ˌlīz\ *vb* **-lized; -liz·ing**   **1 a** : to cause to form crystals or assume crystalline form   **b** : to become crystallized   **2** : to take or cause to take definite form ⟨the plan *crystallized* slowly⟩ ⟨trying to *crystallize* her thoughts⟩ — **crys·tal·li·za·tion** \ˌkris-tə-lə-'zā-shən\ *n*

crys·tal·log·ra·phy \ˌkris-tə-'läg-rə-fē\ *n* : a science that deals with the form and structure of crystals — **crys·tal·log·ra·pher** \-fər\ *n*

crys·tal·loid \'kris-tə-ˌlȯid\ *n* : a substance that forms a true solution and is capable of being crystallized

cub \'kəb\ *n*   **1 a** : a young flesh-eating mammal ⟨bear *cubs*⟩ ⟨lion *cubs*⟩   **b** : a young shark   **2** : a young person   **3** : a person just learning a job : APPRENTICE ⟨a *cub* reporter⟩ ⟨a *cub* pilot⟩   **4** : CUB SCOUT

cub·by·hole \'kəb-ē-ˌhōl\ *n* : a snug place (as for storing things)

¹**cube** \'kyüb\ *n*   **1** : the solid body having six equal square sides   **2** : the product obtained by taking a number three times as a factor ⟨the *cube* of 2 is 8⟩

²**cube** *vb* **cubed; cub·ing**   **1** : to raise to the third power   **2** : to form into a cube   **3** : to cut a checkered pattern into ⟨*cube* a steak⟩

cube root *n* : a number whose cube is a given number ⟨the *cube root* of 27 is 3⟩

cube 1

cu·bic \'kyü-bik\ *also* **cu·bi·cal** \-bi-kəl\ *adj*   **1** : having the form of a cube   **2** : being or having the volume of a cube whose edge is a specified unit ⟨*cubic* centimeter⟩ ⟨*cubic* inch⟩   **3 a** : having length, width, and height   **b** : relating to volume — **cu·bi·cal·ly** \-bi-k(ə-)lē\ *adv*

cu·bi·cle \'kyü-bi-kəl\ *n* : a small separate space (as for sleeping or studying)

cubic measure *n* : a unit (as a cubic inch or cubic centimeter) for measuring volume — see MEASURE table, METRIC SYSTEM table

cub·ism \'kyü-ˌbiz-əm\ *n* : a style of art in which natural forms are broken up into geometric shapes (as squares, triangles, or circles)

cu·bit \'kyü-bət\ *n* : an ancient unit of length based on the length of the forearm from the elbow to the tip of the middle finger and usually equal to about 46 centimeters

cu·boi·dal \kyü-'bȯid-ᵊl\ *adj* : made of parts (as cells) that are shaped somewhat like cubes ⟨*cuboidal* epithelium⟩

Cub Scout *n* : a member of the Boy Scouts of America program for boys of the age range eight to ten

¹**cuck·oo** \'kük-ü, 'kük-\ *n, pl* **cuckoos**   **1** : a largely grayish brown European bird that lays its eggs in the nests of other birds for them to hatch; *also* : any of various related birds   **2** : the call of a cuckoo

²**cuckoo** *adj* : short on sense or intelligence

cuckoo clock *n* : a clock that announces the hours with sounds like a cuckoo's call

cu·cum·ber \'kyü-(ˌ)kəm-bər\ *n* : the long fleshy many-seeded fruit of a vine of the gourd family that is grown as a garden vegetable; *also* : this vine

cud \'kəd, 'kùd\ *n* : food brought up into the mouth by some animals (as a cow) from the rumen to be chewed again

cud·dle \'kəd-ᵊl\ *vb* **cud·dled; cud·dling** \'kəd-liŋ, -ᵊl-iŋ\   **1** : to hold close for warmth or comfort or in affection   **2** : to lie close : NESTLE, SNUGGLE — **cuddle** *n* — **cud·dly** \'kəd-lē, -ᵊl-ē\ *adj*

¹**cud·gel** \'kəj-əl\ *n* : a short heavy club

²**cudgel** *vb* **-geled** *or* **-gelled; -gel·ing** *or* **-gel·ling** \-(ə-)liŋ\ : to beat with or as if with a cudgel — **cudgel one's brains** : to think hard

¹**cue** \'kyü\ *n*   **1** : a word, phrase, or action in a play serving as a signal for the next actor to speak or do something   **2** : something serving as a signal or suggestion : HINT [probably from *q* or *qu*, abbreviations for Latin *quando* "when", formerly used in actors' copies of scripts of plays]

²**cue** *vb* **cued; cu·ing** : to give a cue to

³**cue** *n*   **1** : a tapering rod used in playing billiards or pool   **2** : ¹QUEUE 2 [from French *queue* "pigtail, a line of people", literally "tail", from Latin *cauda* "tail" — related to COWARD, QUEUE, CODA; see *Word History* at COWARD, QUEUE]

cue ball *n* : the ball a player strikes with the cue in billiards or pool

¹**cuff** \'kəf\ *n*   **1** : a part of a sleeve or glove that goes around the wrist   **2** : the turned-back hem of a trouser leg   **3** : a band that is capable of being inflated and is wrapped around an arm or leg to control the flow of blood through the part when measuring blood pressure

²**cuff** *vb* : to strike with or as if with the palm of the hand : SLAP

³**cuff** *n* : a blow with the hand especially when open : SLAP

cuff link *n* : an ornamental device for fastening the cuffs of a shirt

cui·rass \kwi-'ras, kyü-\ *n* : a piece of armor covering the body from neck to waist; *also* : the breastplate of such a piece

cuir·as·sier \ˌkwir-ə-'si(ə)r, ˌkyùr-\ *n* : a mounted soldier wearing a cuirass

cui·sine \kwi-'zēn, kwē-\ *n* : style of cooking ⟨Mexican *cuisine*⟩ ⟨Chinese *cuisine*⟩; *also* : the food cooked

cu·lex \'kyü-ˌleks\ *n* : any of a large genus of mosquitoes that includes the common house mosquito of Europe and North America

cul·i·nary \'kəl-ə-ˌner-ē, 'kyü-lə-\ *adj* : of or relating to the kitchen or cooking ⟨*culinary* workers⟩ ⟨*culinary* skills⟩

¹**cull** \'kəl\ *vb*   **1** : to select from a group : CHOOSE   **2** : to identify and remove the culls from — **cull·er** *n*

²**cull** *n* : something rejected from a group or lot as not as good as the rest

cul·mi·nate \'kəl-mə-ˌnāt\ *vb* **-nat·ed; -nat·ing** : to reach the highest point — **cul·mi·na·tion** \ˌkəl-mə-'nā-shən\ *n*

cu·lotte \'k(y)ü-ˌlät, k(y)ü-'lät\ *n* : a divided skirt or a garment with a divided skirt — often used in pl.

cul·pa·ble \'kəl-pə-bəl\ *adj* : deserving blame — **cul·pa·bil·i·ty** \ˌkəl-pə-'bil-ət-ē\ *n* — **cul·pa·bly** \'kəl-pə-blē\ *adv*

cul·prit \'kəl-prət, -ˌprit\ *n*   **1** : one accused of or charged

cuckoo 1

\ə\ abut	\au̇\ out	\i\ tip	\ȯ\ saw	\u̇\ foot
\ər\ further	\ch\ chin	\ī\ life	\ȯi\ coin	\y\ yet
\a\ mat	\e\ pet	\j\ job	\th\ thin	\yü\ few
\ā\ take	\ē\ easy	\ŋ\ sing	\th\ this	\yu̇\ cure
\ä\ cot, cart	\g\ go	\ō\ bone	\ü\ food	\zh\ vision

with a crime or fault   **2** : one guilty of a crime or fault : OFFENDER

cult \'kəlt\ *n*   **1** : a system of religious worship   **2** : enthusiastic but often temporary devotion to a person, idea, or thing   **3** : a group of persons who belong to or show devotion to a cult — **cult·ist** \'kəl-təst\ *n*

cul·ti·gen \'kəl-tə-jən\ *n* : a cultivated animal or plant (as Indian corn) of a variety or species for which a wild ancestor is unknown

cul·ti·vate \'kəl-tə-ˌvāt\ *vb* **-vat·ed; -vat·ing**   **1 a** : to prepare land for the raising of crops   **b** : to loosen or break up the soil around (growing plants)   **2 a** : to raise or assist the growth of by tilling or by labor and care ⟨*cultivate* vegetables⟩   **b** : ²CULTURE 2   **3** : to improve or develop by careful attention, training, or study : devote time and thought to ⟨*cultivate* one's mind⟩ ⟨*cultivate* the arts⟩   **4** : to seek the company and friendship of

cul·ti·vat·ed *adj*   **1** : raised or produced under cultivation ⟨*cultivated* fruits⟩   **2** : having or showing good education and proper manners

cul·ti·va·tion \ˌkəl-tə-'vā-shən\ *n*   **1** : the act or art of cultivating especially the soil   **2** : REFINEMENT 2

cul·ti·va·tor \'kəl-tə-ˌvāt-ər\ *n* : one that cultivates; *esp* : a tool or machine to loosen the soil while crops are growing

cul·tur·al \'kəlch-(ə-)rəl\ *adj* : of or relating to culture — **cul·tur·al·ly** \-rə-lē\ *adv*

¹cul·ture \'kəl-chər\ *n*   **1** : CULTIVATION 1, TILLAGE   **2** : the raising or development of a product or crop by careful attention ⟨bee *culture*⟩ ⟨the *culture* of grapes⟩   **3** : improvement of the mind, tastes, and manners through careful training   **4** : a particular stage, form, or kind of civilization ⟨ancient Greek *culture*⟩   **5** : cultivation of living material in a special nutrient preparation that often looks like pudding; *also* : a product of such cultivation

²culture *vb* **cul·tured; cul·tur·ing** \'kəlch-(ə-)riŋ\ : to grow in a prepared medium

cul·tured \'kəl-chərd\ *adj*   **1** : CULTIVATED 2   **2** : produced under artificial conditions ⟨*cultured* viruses⟩ ⟨*cultured* pearls⟩

cul·vert \'kəl-vərt\ *n* : a drain or waterway crossing under a road or railroad

cum \(ˌ)kùm, (ˌ)kəm\ *prep* : combined with : along with ⟨worked as cook-*cum*-dishwasher⟩ [from Latin *cum* "with"]

cum·ber·some \'kəm-bər-səm\ *adj* : hard to handle or manage because of size or weight — **cum·ber·some·ly** *adv* — **cum·ber·some·ness** *n*

cum·brous \'kəm-b(ə-)rəs\ *adj* : CUMBERSOME — **cum·brous·ly** *adv*

cum laude \ˌkùm-'laùd-ə, -ə; ˌkəm-'lòd-ē\ *adv or adj* : with distinction : with honors ⟨graduated *cum laude*⟩ [Latin, "with praise"]

cum·mer·bund \'kəm-ər-ˌbənd\ *n* : a wide sash worn around the waist

cu·mu·la·tive \'kyü-myə-lət-iv, -ˌlāt-\ *adj* : increasing (as in force, strength, or amount) by additions one after another ⟨*cumulative* effects⟩ — **cu·mu·la·tive·ly** *adv* — **cu·mu·la·tive·ness** *n*

cu·mu·lo·nim·bus \ˌkyü-myə-lō-'nim-bəs\ *n* : a cumulus cloud often spread out in the shape of an anvil extending to great heights

cu·mu·lo·stra·tus \ˌkyü-myə-lō-'strāt-əs, -'strat-\ *n* : a cumulus cloud whose base extends parallel to the ground as a stratus cloud

cu·mu·lus \'kyü-myə-ləs\ *n, pl* **cu·mu·li** \-ˌlī, -ˌlē\ : a large cloud form having a flat base and rounded outlines often piled up like a mountain

¹cu·ne·i·form \kyü-'nē-ə-ˌfórm, 'kyü-n(ē-)ə-\ *adj*   **1** : having the shape of a wedge   **2** : made up of or written with marks or letters shaped like wedges

²cuneiform *n* : cuneiform writing

cun·ner \'kən-ər\ *n* : a small American food fish that is abundant along the rocky shores of New England

¹cun·ning \'kən-iŋ\ *adj*   **1** : very good or very clever at using special knowledge or skills or at getting something done ⟨*cunning* workers in metal⟩   **2** : marked by especially animal cleverness in gaining ends : ARTFUL   **3** : CUTE 2, PRETTY — **cun·ning·ly** \-iŋ-lē\ *adv*

syn CUNNING, CRAFTY, SLY, WILY mean skillful at trickery. CUNNING suggests cleverness or skill in using sometimes limited intelligence to deal with dangers or difficulties ⟨a *cunning* prisoner making an escape⟩ CRAFTY suggests skill in deceiving with shrewd devices and schemes ⟨a *crafty* peddler known for successful bargaining⟩ SLY often suggests secret or sneaky deceiving ⟨a *sly* thief⟩ WILY suggests cleverness in setting or avoiding traps ⟨the *wily* fox⟩

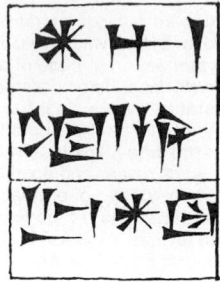

cuneiform

²cunning *n*   **1** : SKILL 1, DEXTERITY   **2** : cleverness in getting what one wants often by tricks or deceiving

¹cup \'kəp\ *n*   **1 a** : something to drink out of in the shape of a bowl usually with a handle ⟨a coffee *cup*⟩   **b** : a similar container used to measure amounts (as in cooking) ⟨a measuring *cup*⟩   **2 a** : the contents of a cup : CUPFUL ⟨drank two *cups* of cocoa⟩   **b** : a half pint : eight ounces (237 milliliters)   **c** : one quarter liter (250 milliliters) ⟨a metric *cup*⟩   **3** : a large ornamental cup offered as a prize   **4** : something (as the corolla of a flower) resembling a cup   **5** : a food served in a cup-shaped container ⟨fruit *cup*⟩ — **cup·like** *adj*

²cup *vb* **cupped; cup·ping**   **1** : to curve into the shape of a cup ⟨*cupped* his hands around his mouth⟩   **2** : to place in or as if in a cup ⟨*cupped* her mouth with her hands and shouted⟩

cup·bear·er \'kəp-ˌbar-ər, -ˌber-\ *n* : a person whose duty is to serve cups of wine

cup·board \'kəb-ərd\ *n* : a closet with shelves for cups, dishes, or food

cup·cake \'kəp-ˌkāk\ *n* : a small cake baked in a cup-shaped mold

cup·ful \'kəp-ˌfúl\ *n, pl* **cup·fuls** \-ˌfúlz\ *also* **cups·ful** \'kəps-ˌfúl\   **1** : the amount held by a cup   **2** : ¹CUP 2b, 2c

cu·pid \'kyü-pəd\ *n* : a picture or statue of Cupid the Roman god of love often as a winged naked child with a bow and arrow

cu·pid·i·ty \kyü-'pid-ət-ē\ *n* : excessive desire for wealth : GREED

cu·po·la \'kyü-pə-lə, -ˌlō\ *n*   **1** : a rounded roof or ceiling : DOME   **2** : a small structure built on top of a roof

cu·prite \'k(y)ü-ˌprīt\ *n* : a mineral that is an oxide of copper and an ore of copper

cur \'kər\ *n*   **1** : a worthless mongrel dog   **2** : ¹HEEL 4, CAD

cur·able \'kyúr-ə-bəl\ *adj* : possible to cure

cu·ra·re \k(y)ü-'rär-ē\ *n* : a dried product in water especially of a tropical American vine used in medicine to relax muscles

cu·rate \'kyúr-ət\ *n* : a member of the clergy who assists the rector, pastor, or vicar of a church [Middle English *curate* "member of the clergy", from Latin *curatus* (same meaning), from *cura* "spiritual charge of souls", from earlier *cura* "care, healing" — related to ACCURATE, CURE]

cu·ra·tive \'kyúr-ət-iv\ *adj* : relating to or used in the cure of diseases

cu·ra·tor \'kyú(ə)r-ˌāt-ər, kyù-'rāt-, 'kyúr-ət-\ *n* : a person in charge of a museum or zoo — **cu·ra·tor·ship** \-ˌship\ *n*

¹curb \'kərb\ *n*   **1** : a chain or strap on a horse's bit used to control the horse by pressing against the lower jaw   **2**

: ¹CHECK 3 ⟨price *curbs*⟩   **3** : an enclosing border (as of stone or concrete) often along the edge of a street

²curb *vb* : to control by or furnish with a curb ⟨legislation to *curb* price and wage increases⟩

curb·ing \'kər-biŋ\ *n*   **1** : the material for a curb   **2** : ¹CURB 3

curd \'kərd\ *n*   **1** : the thickened or solid part of sour or partly digested milk   **2** : something resembling the curd of milk — **curdy** \-ē\ *adj*

cur·dle \'kərd-ᵊl\ *vb* **cur·dled; cur·dling** \'kərd-liŋ, -ᵊl-iŋ\   **1** : to cause curds to form in ⟨too high heat *curdled* the custard⟩   **2** : to form curds : COAGULATE ⟨a ghost story that will make your blood *curdle*⟩

¹cure \'kyu̇(ə)r\ *n*   **1 a** : recovery or relief from a disease   **b** : something that cures a disease : REMEDY   **c** : a method or period of medical treatment   **2** : something that corrects or heals a bad situation ⟨a *cure* for unemployment⟩

Word History In Latin the noun *cura* had the general sense of "the care, concern, or attention given to something or someone". Often it referred to "medical care or healing". The Roman Christians, however, used the word chiefly in regard to "the care of souls", since that was one of their main concerns. The word passed into French as *cure* and then into English with this spiritual sense. The English noun *curate,* meaning "one who takes care of souls, a member of the clergy", developed from this sense. Later the medical senses of *cure* became more common. Latin *cura* was also the basis for the verb *accurare,* meaning "to take care of". This verb became the source of our word *accurate,* which at first meant "done with care". [Middle English *cure* "care of souls", from early French *cure* (same meaning), from Latin *cura* "spiritual charge of souls", from earlier *cura* "care, healing" — related to ACCURATE, CURATE, CURIOUS, SECURE]

²cure *vb* **cured; cur·ing**   **1 a** : to make or become healthy or sound again   **b** : to bring about recovery from   **2** : ²REMEDY   **3 a** : to prepare by a chemical or physical process for use or storage ⟨*cure* bacon⟩   **b** : to go through a curing process ⟨hay *curing* in the sun⟩ — **cur·er** *n*

cure-all \'kyu̇(ə)r-,o̊l\ *n* : a remedy for everything wrong

cu·ret·tage \,kyu̇r-ə-'täzh\ *n* : a surgical cleaning or scraping of a body part (as the uterus)

cur·few \'kər-,fyü\ *n*   **1** : an order or law requiring certain or all people to be off the streets at a stated time   **2** : a signal (as the ringing of a bell) formerly given to announce the beginning of a curfew   **3** : the time when a curfew is sounded

Word History During the Middle Ages, houses in European towns were often made of wood, and they were built very close together. A fire burning out of control could quickly spread from house to house. To prevent this disaster, people were required to put out or cover their hearth fires by a certain time in the evening. A bell was rung as a signal when the time had come. In early French this signal was called *covrefeu,* a compound of *covrir,* meaning "to cover", and *feu,* "fire". Even when hearth fires were no longer regulated, many towns had other rules that called for the ringing of an evening bell, and this signal was still called *covrefeu.* A common *covrefeu* regulation required that certain people be off the streets by a given time. This is the meaning taken when the word *covrefeu* was borrowed from early French into Middle English and the spelling changed to *curfew.* [Middle English *curfew* "an order to be off the streets at a certain time", from early French *covrefeu* "signal to cover a hearth fire, curfew", from *covrir* "to cover" and *feu* "fire"]

cu·rie \'kyu̇(ə)r-(,)ē, kyu̇-'rē\ *n* : a unit of radioactivity equal to 37 billion disintegrations per second

cu·rio \'kyu̇r-ē-,ō\ *n, pl* **cu·ri·os** : an object or article val-

ued because it is strange or rare

cu·ri·os·i·ty \,kyu̇r-ē-'äs-ət-ē\ *n, pl* **-ties**   **1** : an eager desire to learn and often to learn what does not concern one : INQUISITIVENESS   **2 a** : something strange or unusual ⟨the *curiosities* of nature⟩   **b** : CURIO

cu·ri·ous \'kyu̇r-ē-əs\ *adj*   **1** : eager to learn ⟨a cat *curious* about its new surroundings⟩   **2** : INQUISITIVE   2   **3** : attracting attention by being strange or unusual : ODD ⟨a *curious* old coin⟩ ⟨that's *curious* — they were here yesterday⟩ [Middle English *curious* "made carefully, skillful, eager to learn", from early French *curios* (same meaning), from Latin *curiosus* "careful, curious", from *cura* "care, healing" — related to ACCURATE, CURE] — **cu·ri·ous·ly** *adv* — **cu·ri·ous·ness** *n*

> **syn** CURIOUS, INQUISITIVE, PRYING mean interested in what is not one's own business. CURIOUS in general suggests an active desire to learn or to know ⟨children are *curious* about everything⟩ INQUISITIVE suggests annoying and regular curiosity along with steady quizzing ⟨dreaded the visits of their *inquisitive* relatives⟩ PRYING suggests truly bothersome meddling ⟨*prying* neighbors who refuse to mind their own business⟩

cu·ri·um \'kyu̇r-ē-əm\ *n* : a metallic radioactive element artificially produced — see ELEMENT table

¹curl \'kərl\ *vb*   **1** : to form into or grow in coils or ringlets   **2** : to take or move in a curved form ⟨smoke *curling* from the chimney⟩

²curl *n*   **1** : a lock of hair that coils : RINGLET   **2** : a spiral or winding form : COIL   **3** : the state of being curled   **4** : a hollow place under the crest of a breaking wave

curl·er \'kər-lər\ *n*   **1** : one that curls; *esp* : a device for putting a curl into hair   **2** : a player in the game of curling

cur·lew \'kərl-,(y)ü\ *n, pl* **curlews** *or* **curlew** : any of various largely brownish birds which are related to the woodcocks and are distinguished by long legs and a long slender bill that curves downward and most of which migrate

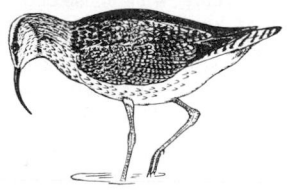

curlew

curli·cue *also* **curly·cue** \'kər-li-,kyü\ *n* : a fancy curve or spiral

curl·ing \'kər-liŋ\ *n* : a game in which two teams of four players slide special stones over ice toward a target circle

curling iron *n* : a rod-shaped device that is heated to curl hair with

curl up *vb* : to arrange oneself in or as if in a curl or ball ⟨*curl up* with a good book⟩

curly \'kər-lē\ *adj* **curl·i·er; -est**   **1** : tending to curl   **2** : having curls — **curl·i·ness** *n*

cur·mud·geon \kər-'məj-ən\ *n* : a grumpy and usually old man

cur·ragh \'kə-rə(k)\ *n* : CORACLE

cur·rant \'kər-ənt, 'kə-rənt\ *n*   **1** : a small seedless raisin used in baking and cooking   **2** : the acid edible fruit of several shrubs related to the gooseberries; *also* : a plant bearing currants [from Middle English *raison of Coraunte,* literally "raisin of Corinth", from *Corinth,* city in Greece from which it was exported]

cur·ren·cy \'kər-ən-sē, 'kə-rən-\ *n, pl* **-cies**   **1** : common use or acceptance   **2** : money in circulation

¹cur·rent \'kər-ənt, 'kə-rənt\ *adj*   **1 a** : now passing ⟨the

\ə\ abut	\au̇\ **out**	\i\ **tip**	\o̊\ **saw**	\u̇\ **foot**
\ər\ **further**	\ch\ **chin**	\ī\ **life**	\o̊i\ **coin**	\y\ **yet**
\a\ **mat**	\e\ **pet**	\j\ **job**	\th\ **thin**	\yü\ **few**
\ā\ **take**	\ē\ **easy**	\ŋ\ **sing**	\th\ **this**	\yu̇\ **cure**
\ä\ **cot, cart**	\g\ **go**	\ō\ **bone**	\ü\ **food**	\zh\ **vision**

current month⟩ **b** : occurring in or belonging to the present time ⟨*current* events⟩ **2** : generally accepted, used, or practiced ⟨*current* customs⟩ [Middle English *curraunt, coraunt* "moving, flowing, running", from early French *corant, curant* "running", derived from Latin *currere* "to run" — related to CORRIDOR, COURIER, COURSE, EXCURSION, INCUR, OCCUR] — **cur·rent·ly** *adv* — **cur·rent·ness** *n*

²**current** *n* **1 a** : the part of a fluid body moving continuously in a certain direction **b** : the swiftest part of a stream **2** : general course or movement : TREND **3** : a stream of electric charge; *also* : the rate of such movement

cur·ric·u·lum \kə-'rik-yə-ləm\ *n, pl* **-la** \-lə\ *also* **-lums** : all the courses of study offered by a school — **cur·ric·u·lar** \-lər\ *adj*

¹**cur·ry** \'kər-ē, 'kə-rē\ *vb* **cur·ried; cur·ry·ing** : to rub and clean the coat of ⟨*curry* a horse⟩ [Middle English *currayen* "to comb the coat of (a horse)", from early French *correer* "to prepare", probably from a Latin word of Germanic origin] — **cur·ri·er** *n* — **curry fa·vor** \-'fā-vər\ : to try to win approval by flattering or doing favors

²**cur·ry** \'kər-ē, 'kə-rē\ *n, pl* **curries** **1** : CURRY POWDER **2** : a food seasoned with curry powder [from *kaṛi*, a word in a native dialect of India, meaning "a spiced dish of food"]

³**curry** *vb* **cur·ried; cur·ry·ing** : to flavor or cook with curry powder

cur·ry·comb \'kər-ē-ˌkōm, 'kə-rē-\ *n* : a comb with rows of metallic teeth or ridges used to curry horses — **currycomb** *vb*

curry powder *n* : a seasoning made of ground spices

¹**curse** \'kərs\ *n* **1** : a calling for harm or injury to come to someone **2** : a word or an expression used in cursing and swearing **3** : evil or misfortune that comes as if in answer to a curse **4** : a cause of great harm or evil

²**curse** *vb* **cursed; curs·ing** **1** : to call upon divine power to send harm or evil upon **2** : SWEAR 5 **3** : to bring unhappiness or evil upon : AFFLICT

cursed \'kər-səd, 'kərst\ *also* **curst** \'kərst\ *adj* : being under or deserving a curse — **cursed·ly** *adv* — **cursed·ness** *n*

cur·sive \'kər-siv\ *adj* : written or formed with the strokes of the letters joined together and the angles rounded ⟨*cursive* handwriting⟩ — **cur·sive·ly** *adv*

cur·sor \'kər-sər\ *n* : a mark (as a bright blinking spot) on a computer display screen that shows the place where the user is working

cur·so·ry \'kərs-(ə)-rē\ *adj* : rapid and usually careless : HASTY ⟨a *cursory* glance⟩ — **cur·so·ri·ly** \-rə-lē\ *adv* — **cur·so·ri·ness** \-rē-nəs\ *n*

curt \'kərt\ *adj* : rudely abrupt or brief in speech ⟨a *curt* reply⟩ **syn** see BLUFF — **curt·ly** *adv* — **curt·ness** *n*

cur·tail \(ˌ)kər-'tā(ə)l\ *vb* : to make less by or as if by cutting off part of — **cur·tail·er** \-'tā-lər\ *n* — **cur·tail·ment** \-'tāl-mənt\ *n*

cur·tain \'kərt-ᵊn\ *n* **1** : a piece of material (as cloth) hung up to darken, hide, divide, or decorate **2** : the opening or closing of the curtain in front of the stage of a theater **3** : something that covers, hides, or separates like a curtain — **curtain** *vb*

curtain call *n* : an appearance by a performer (as after the final curtain of a play) in response to the applause of the audience

¹**curt·sy** *or* **curt·sey** \'kərt-sē\ *n, pl* **curtsies** *or* **curtseys** : a bow made especially by women that consists of a slight lowering of the body and bending of the knees

²**curtsy** *or* **curtsey** *vb* **curt·sied** *or* **curt·seyed; curt·sy·ing** *or* **curt·sey·ing** : to make a curtsy

cur·va·ture \'kər-və-ˌchủ(ə)r, -chər\ *n* **1** : the act of curving : the state of being curved **2** : an abnormal curving ⟨*curvature* of the spine⟩

¹**curve** \'kərv\ *vb* **curved; curv·ing** **1** : to turn or change from a straight line or course ⟨the road *curved* to the left⟩ **2** : to cause to curve

²**curve** *n* **1 a** : a line especially when curved **b** : a line connecting points on a graph or in a coordinate system **2** : something that bends or turns without angles ⟨a *curve* in the road⟩ **3** : a ball thrown so that it moves away from a straight course

¹**cur·vet** \(ˌ)kər-'vet\ *n* : a leap of a horse in which first the forelegs and then the hind are raised so that for an instant all the legs are in the air

²**curvet** *vb* **cur·vet·ted** *or* **cur·vet·ed; cur·vet·ting** *or* **cur·vet·ing** **1** : to make a curvet **2** : ²CAPER, PRANCE

curvet

¹**cush·ion** \'kush-ən\ *n* **1** : a soft pillow or pad to rest on or against **2** : something resembling a cushion in use, shape, or softness **3** : a rubber pad along the inner rim of a billiard table **4** : something serving to lessen the effects of something bad or unpleasant

²**cushion** *vb* **cush·ioned; cush·ion·ing** \-(ə-)niŋ\ **1** : to place on or as if on a cushion **2** : to furnish with a cushion **3** : to soften or lessen the force or shock of

cusp \'kəsp\ *n* : a point or pointed end or part: as **a** : either of the pointed ends of a crescent moon **b** : a point on the grinding surface of a tooth **c** : a fold or flap of a heart valve

cus·pid \'kəs-pəd\ *n* : a canine tooth

cus·pi·dor \'kəs-pə-dò(ə)r\ *n* : SPITTOON

¹**cuss** \'kəs\ *n* **1** : ¹CURSE 2 **2** : ¹FELLOW 4a ⟨an ornery *cuss*⟩

²**cuss** *vb* : SWEAR 5

cus·tard \'kəs-tərd\ *n* : a sweetened mixture of milk and eggs baked, boiled, or frozen

cus·to·di·an \ˌkəs-'tōd-ē-ən\ *n* : one that guards and protects or takes care of something

cus·to·dy \'kəs-təd-ē\ *n* **1** : direct responsibility for care and control **2** : the state of being arrested or held by the police

¹**cus·tom** \'kəs-təm\ *n* **1** : the usual way of doing things : the usual practice of a person or group **2** *pl* : duties or taxes paid on imports or exports **3** : support given a business by its customers **syn** see HABIT

²**custom** *adj* **1** : made or done to order ⟨*custom* clothes⟩ **2** : specializing in custom work ⟨a *custom* tailor⟩

cus·tom·ary \'kəs-tə-ˌmer-ē\ *adj* **1** : based on or established by custom ⟨*customary* rent⟩ **2** : commonly done, observed, or used ⟨my *customary* evening stroll⟩ ⟨*customary* units of weight like the pound⟩ — **cus·tom·ar·i·ly** \ˌkəs-tə-'mer-ə-lē\ *adv*

cus·tom·er \'kəs-tə-mər\ *n* **1** : one that buys a product or service ⟨that company is one of our best *customers*⟩ **2** : PERSON 1, FELLOW

cus·tom·house \'kəs-təm-ˌhaủs\ *also* **cus·toms·house** \-təmz-\ *n* : a building where customs are paid or collected and where ships are entered and cleared at a port

cus·tom·ize \'kəs-tə-ˌmīz\ *vb* **-ized; -iz·ing** : to build, fit, or change to suit a specific customer ⟨a *customized* van⟩

cus·tom–made \ˌkəs-təm-'(m)ād\ *adj* : made for a specific customer

¹**cut** \'kət\ *vb* **cut; cut·ting** **1 a** : to penetrate or divide with or as if with an edged tool (as a knife) ⟨*cut* my finger⟩ ⟨*cutting* and pasting colored paper⟩ ⟨*cut* the pie⟩ **b** : to function as an edged tool ⟨be careful — that glass will *cut*⟩ ⟨this old knife won't *cut* anymore⟩ **c** : to be able to be cut ⟨cheese *cuts* easily⟩ **2** : to experience the growth of through the gum ⟨the baby is *cutting* teeth⟩ **3** : to hurt the feelings of **4 a** : ¹TRIM 3a ⟨*cut* your hair⟩ **b** : ²MOW 1 ⟨*cut* the grass⟩ **c** : DISSOLVE 2 ⟨a detergent *cuts* grease⟩

5 : to make smaller ⟨*cut* costs⟩ **6** : to remove with or as if with a knife ⟨*cut* a piece of ham⟩ ⟨*cut* two players from the team⟩ **7 a** : to go straight rather than around ⟨*cut* across the backyard⟩ **b** : ¹INTERSECT 1, CROSS ⟨lines *cutting* other lines⟩ **c** : to make a quick change of direction ⟨go out 10 steps, then *cut* right and I'll throw you a pass⟩ ⟨the camera *cuts* to the crowd in the street⟩ **8** : to divide a deck of cards **9** : to cause to stop ⟨*cut* the nonsense⟩ ⟨*cut* the engine⟩ — often used with *out* ⟨now *cut* that out⟩ **10** : ¹SNUB 2 ⟨*cut* a former friend⟩ **11** : to fail to attend ⟨*cut* a class⟩ **12 a** : to make or shape with or as if with an edged tool ⟨farmers *cut* clearings out of the wilderness⟩ ⟨*cut* a diamond⟩ **b** : to record sounds on ⟨*cut* a record⟩ **13** : to give the appearance of ⟨*cut* a fine figure⟩ — **cut corners** : to do something the easiest or cheapest way — **cut ice** : to be important ⟨that's not going to *cut* any *ice* with the kids⟩

²cut *n* **1 a** : something cut or cut off ⟨a *cut* of beef⟩ **b** : ¹SHARE 1 ⟨your *cut* of the winnings⟩ **2 a** : a product of cutting **b** : a wound made by something sharp **c** : a passage made by cutting ⟨a railroad *cut*⟩ **d** : a grade or step especially in a social scale ⟨a *cut* above the ordinary⟩ **e** : a pictorial illustration **3 a** : an act or instance of cutting **b** : something done or said that hurts the feelings ⟨an unkind *cut*⟩ **c** : an act of removing a part ⟨a *cut* in pay⟩ **d** : an act or turn of cutting cards ⟨it's your *cut*⟩ **4** : a voluntary absence from a class ⟨too many *cuts* in gym⟩ **5** : a swing by a batter at the ball ⟨took a good *cut*⟩ **6** : a sudden switch from one sound or image to another in movies, radio, or television **7** : the shape and style in which a thing is cut, formed, or made ⟨clothes of the latest *cut*⟩

cut·abil·i·ty \ˌkət-ə-ˈbil-ət-ē\ *n* : the proportion of lean edible meat (as in a side of beef)

cu·ta·ne·ous \kyu̇-ˈtā-nē-əs\ *adj* : of, relating to, or affecting the skin ⟨*cutaneous* infection⟩

¹cut·away \ˈkət-ə-ˌwā\ *adj* : showing the top or outside cut away so the inside parts can be seen ⟨a *cutaway* view of a flower⟩

²cutaway *n* **1** : a coat with skirts cut from the front waistline to form tails at the back **2** : a cutaway illustration

cut·back \ˈkət-ˌbak\ *n* : an act or instance of cutting something back

cut back \ˈkət-ˈbak\ *vb* **1** : ²PRUNE 1, 2a **2** : to reduce something in amount ⟨*cut back* on smoking⟩

cut down *vb* **1** : to make over in a smaller size ⟨*cutting down* an older sister's outfit⟩ **2** : to knock down and kill or wound ⟨the American soldiers *cut* the Hessians *down*⟩ **3** : to reduce something in amount ⟨*cut down* on energy use⟩

cute \ˈkyüt\ *adj* **cut·er; cut·est** **1** : CLEVER 3, SHREWD ⟨they're not *cute* enough to fool me⟩ **2** : attractive especially in looks or actions ⟨a *cute* baby⟩ **3** : acting like a smart aleck ⟨don't get *cute* with me⟩ — **cute·ly** *adv* — **cute·ness** *n*

cut glass *n* : glass ornamented by cutting and polishing

cu·ti·cle \ˈkyüt-i-kəl\ *n* **1** : an outer layer (as of skin or a leaf) often produced by the cells beneath **2** : a dead or horny layer of skin especially around a fingernail

cu·tin \ˈkyüt-ᵊn\ *n* : a substance that contains waxes, fatty acids, soaps, and resins and forms a continuous layer on the outer wall of the epidermis of a plant

cut in *vb* **1** : to join in suddenly ⟨*cut in* on a conversation⟩ **2** : to interrupt a dancing couple and take one partner's place ⟨may I *cut in*?⟩ **3** : to mix with cutting motions ⟨add the shortening to the flour and *cut* it *in*⟩ **4** : to include among those who get a cut ⟨I'll *cut* you *in* on the profits⟩

cut·lass \ˈkət-ləs\ *n* : a short curved sword

cut·ler \ˈkət-lər\ *n* : one who makes, deals in, or repairs cutlery

cut·lery \ˈkət-lə-rē\ *n* **1** : cutting tools (as knives and scissors) **2** : utensils for cutting, serving, and eating food

cut·let \ˈkət-lət\ *n* **1** : a small slice of meat cut for broiling or frying ⟨veal *cutlets*⟩ **2** : a piece of food shaped like a cutlet

cut·off \ˈkət-ˌȯf\ *n* **1** : the action of cutting off **2** : a device for cutting off **3** *pl* : shorts made from jeans with the legs cut off short — **cutoff** *adj*

cut off \ˌkət-ˈȯf\ *vb* **1** : to stop the flow or movement of ⟨earthquake *cut off* our water supply⟩ ⟨trees *cut off* the wind⟩ **2** : ISOLATE ⟨*cut off* from the rest of the world⟩ **3** : DISCONTINUE ⟨*cut off* its relations with its neighbors⟩ **4** : to stop or interrupt while in communication ⟨operator, somebody *cut* me *off*⟩

cut·out \ˈkət-ˌau̇t\ *n* : something cut out or off from something else — **cutout** *adj*

¹cut out \ˌkət-ˈau̇t\ *vb* **1** : to assign through necessity ⟨you've got your work *cut out* for you⟩ **2** : to come to a stop ⟨one by one the engines *cut out*⟩

²cut out *adj* : naturally meant or fitted ⟨not *cut out* to be a lawyer⟩

cut·over \ˌkət-ˌō-vər\ *adj* : having most of its good timber cut ⟨*cutover* land⟩

cut–rate \ˈkət-ˈrāt\ *adj* **1** : selling or offered at reduced prices ⟨a *cut-rate* store⟩ **2** : SECOND-RATE, CHEAP

cut·ter \ˈkət-ər\ *n* **1** : one that cuts ⟨a diamond *cutter*⟩ ⟨a cookie *cutter*⟩ **2 a** : a ship's boat for carrying supplies or passengers **b** : a small sailing boat with one mast **c** : a small armed boat in government service **3** : a small sleigh

¹cut·throat \ˈkət-ˌthrōt\ *n* : a person likely to cut someone's throat

²cutthroat *adj* : RUTHLESS ⟨*cutthroat* competition⟩

¹cut·ting \ˈkət-iŋ\ *n* : something cut or cut off or out; *esp* : a section of a plant or animal capable of developing into a new individual

²cutting *adj* **1** : designed for cutting : SHARP ⟨the *cutting* edge of a knife⟩ **2** : marked by piercing cold ⟨a *cutting* wind⟩ **3** : likely to hurt the feelings ⟨*cutting* remarks⟩ — **cut·ting·ly** \-iŋ-lē\ *adv*

cutting board *n* : a board on which something (as cloth or food) is placed for cutting

cut·tle·bone \ˈkət-ᵊl-ˌbōn\ *n* : the shell of cuttlefishes used for making polishing powder or for supplying birds in cages with calcium and salts

cut·tle·fish \-ˌfish\ *n* : a 10-armed marine mollusk differing from the related squid in having an internal shell composed of compounds of calcium

cut·up \ˈkət-ˌəp\ *n* : a person who clowns or acts noisily

cut up \ˈkət-ˈəp\ *vb* : to act like a clown

cut·worm \ˈkət-ˌwərm\ *n* : any of various smooth-bodied moth caterpillars that usually feed on plants at night and hide by day

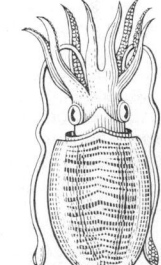

cuttlefish

-cy \sē\ *n suffix, pl* **-cies** **1** : action : practice ⟨occupan*cy*⟩ **2** : rank : office ⟨captain*cy*⟩ **3** : state : quality ⟨accura*cy*⟩ ⟨bankrupt*cy*⟩ ⟨normal*cy*⟩ [derived from Latin *-tia* "action, quality"]

cy·an \ˈsī-ˌan, -ən\ *n* : a greenish blue

¹cy·a·nide \ˈsī-ə-ˌnīd, -nəd\ *n* : a very poisonous compound consisting of carbon and nitrogen with either sodium

\ə\ abut	\au̇\ out	\i\ tip	\ȯ\ saw	\u̇\ foot
\ər\ further	\ch\ chin	\ī\ life	\ȯi\ coin	\y\ yet
\a\ mat	\e\ pet	\j\ job	\th\ thin	\yü\ few
\ā\ take	\ē\ easy	\ŋ\ sing	\th\ this	\yu̇\ cure
\ä\ cot, cart	\g\ go	\ō\ bone	\ü\ food	\zh\ vision

or potassium

²cy·a·nide \-ˌnīd\ *vb* **-nid·ed; -nid·ing** : to prepare with a cyanide

cy·ano·gen \sī-'an-ə-jən\ *n* : a colorless flammable poisonous gas consisting of carbon and nitrogen

cy·ber·net·ics \ˌsī-bər-'net-iks\ *n* : a science concerned especially with studies comparing automatic control systems (as that of the nervous system and brain and mechanical-electrical communication systems) — **cy·ber·net·ic** \-'net-ik\ *adj*

cy·cad \'sī-kəd\ *n* : a tropical palmlike evergreen plant with fernlike leaves

cy·cla·men \'sī-klə-mən, 'sik-lə-\ *n* : any of a genus of plants related to the primroses and often grown in pots for their showy nodding flowers

¹cy·cle \'sī-kəl\ *n* **1** : a period of time taken up by a series of events or actions that repeat themselves regularly and in the same order ⟨the *cycle* of the seasons⟩ **2 a** : a series of events or operations that happen again and again regularly and usually lead back to the starting point ⟨the *cycle* of the blood from the heart, through the blood vessels, and back again⟩ ⟨the drying *cycle* of a dishwasher⟩ **b** : one complete occurrence of a cycle ⟨a *cycle* of alternating current⟩ ⟨the *cycle* of an electromagnetic or sound wave⟩ ⟨the *cycle* of a vibration⟩ **3** : a long period of time : AGE — **cy·clic** \'sī-klik *also* 'sik-lik\ *or* **cy·cli·cal** \'sī-kli-kəl, 'sik-li-\ *adj* — **cy·cli·cal·ly** \-k(ə-)lē\ *adv*

²cy·cle \'sī-kəl, 'sik-əl\ *vb* **cy·cled; cy·cling** \'sī-k(ə-)liŋ, 'sik-(ə-)liŋ\ : to ride a bicycle or motorcycle

cy·clist \'sī-k(ə-)ləst, 'sik-(ə-)ləst\ *n* : a person who rides a bicycle or motorcycle

cy·cloid \'sī-ˌklȯid\ *n* : a curve that is traced by a point on the circumference of a circle that is rolling along a straight line

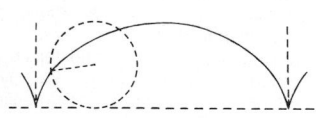

cycloid

cy·clone \'sī-ˌklōn\ *n* **1** : a storm or system of winds that rotates about a center of low atmospheric pressure counterclockwise in the northern hemisphere, advances at a speed of 32 to 48 kilometers an hour, and often brings a great deal of rain **2** : TORNADO — **cy·clon·ic** \sī-'klän-ik\ *adj*

cy·clo·pe·dia *or* **cy·clo·pae·dia** \ˌsī-klə-'pēd-ē-ə\ *n* : ENCYCLOPEDIA — **cy·clo·pe·dic** \-'pēd-ik\ *adj*

cy·clops \'sī-ˌkläps\ *n* **1** *pl* **cy·clo·pes** \sī-'klō-ˌpēz\ *cap* : one of a race of giants in Greek legend with a single eye in the middle of the forehead **2** *pl* **cyclops** : WATER FLEA

cy·clo·tron \'sī-klə-ˌträn\ *n* : a device for giving high speeds to charged particles by means of the combined action of a constant magnetic force and a rapidly oscillating electric force

cyg·net \'sig-nət\ *n* : a young swan

Cyg·nus \'sig-nəs\ *n* : a northern group of stars near Pegasus in the Milky Way [from Latin *cygnus*, literally "swan"]

cyl·in·der \'sil-ən-dər\ *n* **1** : a closed space figure or surface that has two congruent and parallel bases and can be formed by moving a line along the curve bounding one base so that it is always parallel to a certain line fixed in place **2** : a body (as the piston chamber of an engine, the barrel of a pump, or the part of a revolver which turns and holds the cartridges) shaped like a cylinder — **cy·lin·dri·cal** \sə-'lin-dri-kəl\ *adj* — **cy·lin·dri·cal·ly** \-dri-k(ə-)lē\ *adv*

cym·bal \'sim-bəl\ *n* : either of a pair of brass plates that are clashed together to make a sharp ringing sound and that together form a musical percussion instrument — **cym·bal·ist** \-bə-ləst\ *n*

cyn·ic \'sin-ik\ *n* : a person who distrusts people; *esp* : one who believes that people act only in self-interest

Word History In ancient Greece a certain philosopher taught that moral excellence was the only goal in life worth striving for. He and his followers lived a simple life, and they sometimes offended other Greeks with their open scorn of wealth and pleasure. Such a philosopher was called *kynikos*, which literally means "like a dog". One likely reason for this name is that the leader of the group taught at a school with a name that began with the same letters as in the Greek word for dog. It is also likely that many Greeks who used *kynikos* for these philosophers had been bothered by their rudeness. *Cynic* has been used in English since the 16th century for such philosophers. Once the word had appeared in English, it wasn't long before *cynic* was applied to any faultfinding critic. Later it was used chiefly of one who doubts the sincerity of all human motives except selfishness. [from early French *cynique* or Latin *cynicus*, both meaning "cynic", from Greek *kynikos*, literally "like a dog"]

cyn·i·cal \'sin-i-kəl\ *adj* : having or showing the attitude of a cynic : not trusting human nature — **cyn·i·cal·ly** \-k(ə-)lē\ *adv*

cyn·i·cism \'sin-ə-ˌsiz-əm\ *n* : a cynical attitude or quality; *also* : an expression of cynical quality

cy·no·sure \'sī-nə-ˌshu̇(ə)r, 'sin-ə-\ *n* : a center of attraction or attention ⟨the *cynosure* of all eyes⟩

cy·press \'sī-prəs\ *n* **1** : any of a genus of mostly evergreen trees that are related to the pines and have overlapping scalelike leaves **2** : either of two large swamp trees of the southern U.S. with hard red wood used for shingles **3** : the wood of a cypress tree

cyst \'sist\ *n* **1** : a closed pouch or sac of fluid that develops in the body in some diseased conditions **2** : a covering resembling a cyst or a body (as a spore) with such a covering — **cys·tic** \'sis-tik\ *adj*

cystic fibrosis *n* : an inherited glandular disease that appears usually in early childhood and is marked especially by faulty digestion, by difficulty in breathing, and by the loss of much salt in the sweat

cy·to·chrome \'sīt-ə-ˌkrōm\ *n* : any of several iron-containing pigments that are important in oxidation reactions occurring in the living cell

cy·tol·o·gist \sī-'täl-ə-jəst\ *n* : a person who specializes in cytology

cy·tol·o·gy \sī-'täl-ə-jē\ *n* : a branch of biology dealing with cells — **cy·to·log·i·cal** \ˌsīt-ᵊl-'äj-i-kəl\ *or* **cy·to·log·ic** \-'äj-ik\ *adj*

cy·to·plasm \'sīt-ə-ˌplaz-əm\ *n* : the protoplasm of a plant or animal cell except for the nucleus — **cy·to·plas·mic** \ˌsīt-ə-'plaz-mik\ *adj*

cy·to·sine \'sīt-ə-ˌsēn\ *n* : a chemical base that is a pyrimidine and codes genetic information in DNA and RNA — compare ADENINE, GUANINE, THYMINE, URACIL

czar \'zär\ *n* **1** *or* **tsar** *also* **tzar** : the ruler of Russia until the 1917 revolution **2** *also* **tsar** : one having great power or authority ⟨baseball *czar*⟩ [scientific Latin *czar* "czar", from Russian *tsar'* (same meaning), from early Russian *tsĭsarĭ, tsĕsarĭ* "emperor", from a Germanic word *kaisar* "emperor", derived from Latin *Caesar* (title of a line of Roman emperors after Augustus Caesar) — see *Word History* at EMPEROR] — **czar·dom** \'zärd-əm\ *n*

cza·ri·na \zä-'rē-nə\ *n* **1** : the wife of a czar **2** : a woman who has the rank of czar

czar·ist \'zär-əst\ *adj* : of, relating to, or ruled by a czar ⟨*czarist* Russia⟩

Czech \'chek\ *n* **1** : a person born or living in Czechoslovakia; *esp* : one from Bohemia or Moravia **2** : the Slavic language of the Czechs — **Czech** *adj*

Czecho·slo·vak \ˌchek-ə-'slō-ˌväk, -, -ˌvak\ *or* **Czecho·slo·va·ki·an** \-ˌslō-'väk-ē-ən, -'vak-\ *adj* : of, relating to, or characteristic of Czechoslovakia or its people — **Czechoslovak** *or* **Czechoslovakian** *n*

D

d \'dē\ *n, often cap* **1** : the fourth letter of the English alphabet **2** : five hundred in Roman numerals **3** : the musical note referred to by the letter D : the second tone of the C-major scale **4** : a grade rating a student's work as poor

'd \d, əd\ *vb* **1** : HAD **2** : WOULD **3** : DID

¹dab \'dab\ *n* **1** : a quick blow or thrust : POKE **2** : a gentle touch or stroke : PAT

²dab *vb* **dabbed; dab·bing** **1** : to strike or touch lightly ⟨*dabs* at her eyes with a handkerchief⟩ **2** : to apply with quick light strokes : DAUB — **dab·ber** *n*

³dab *n* **1** : ¹SMEAR 1 **2** : a small amount ⟨just a *dab* more ice cream⟩

dab·ble \'dab-əl\ *vb* **dab·bled; dab·bling** \-(ə-)liŋ\ **1** : to wet by splashing : SPATTER **2 a** : to paddle or play in or as if in water **b** : to reach with the bill to the bottom of shallow water to obtain food ⟨ducks *dabbled* in the pond⟩ **3** : to work or concern oneself lightly or without deep involvement ⟨they *dabble* in poetry⟩ — **dab·bler** \-(ə-)lər\ *n*

da ca·po \dä-'käp-ō, də-\ *adv or adj* : from the beginning — used as a direction in music to repeat

dace \'dās\ *n, pl* **dace** : any of various North American freshwater fishes related to the carp

dachs·hund \'däks-ˌhùnt, 'däk-sənt\ *n* : a small dog of a breed of German origin that has a long body, very short legs, and long drooping ears

> **Word History** The dachshund is a dog with short legs and a long history. The breed was developed in Germany more than a thousand years ago to hunt burrowing animals such as badgers. With its short legs and long, powerful body, the dachshund could follow a badger right down into its hole. It could even fight with the badger underground. The German name for the breed was *dachshund*, a compound of *dachs*, meaning "badger", and *hund*, "dog". This German name was borrowed directly into English. [from German *dachshund* "dachshund", literally "badger dog", from *dachs* "badger" and *hund* dog]

dachshund

Da·cron \'dā-ˌkrän, 'dak-ˌrän\ *trademark* — used for a synthetic textile fiber

dac·tyl \'dak-t°l\ *n* : a metrical foot consisting of one accented syllable followed by two unaccented syllables (as in *tenderly*) — **dac·tyl·ic** \dak-'til-ik\ *adj*

dad \'dad\ *n* : ¹FATHER 1a

dad·dy \'dad-ē\ *n, pl* **daddies** : ¹FATHER 1a

dad·dy long·legs \ˌdad-ē-'lóŋ-ˌlegz\ *n* : any of various invertebrates that are arachnids which resemble true spiders but have a small rounded body and very long slender legs — called also *harvestman*

da·do \'dād-ō\ *n, pl* **dadoes** : the part of a pedestal of a column between the base and the top moldings

daemon *variant of* DEMON

daf·fo·dil \'daf-ə-ˌdil\ *n* : any of a genus of herbs that produce long slender leaves and yellow, white, or pinkish flowers from an overwintering bulb in the spring; *esp* : one with petals whose inner parts are arranged to form a trumpet-shaped tube — compare JONQUIL

daf·fy \'daf-ē\ *adj* **daf·fi·er; -est** : silly, odd, or peculiar usually in an amusing way ⟨a *daffy* spy story⟩; *also* : attracted to or fascinated with ⟨*daffy* over cars⟩ ⟨*daffy* about stamp collecting⟩

daft \'daft\ *adj* : DAFFY — **daft·ly** *adv* — **daft·ness** \'daf(t)-nəs\ *n*

dag·ger \'dag-ər\ *n* **1** : a short weapon for stabbing **2** : a symbol † used in printing

da·guerre·o·type \də-'ger-(ē-)ə-ˌtīp\ *n* : an early photograph produced on a metal plate [named for L. J. M. *Daguerre* 1789–1851 French painter and inventor]

dahl·ia \'dal-yə, 'däl-\ *n* : any of a genus of American herbs related to the daisies and having opposite leaves, brightly colored flower heads, and a root that is a tuber

¹dai·ly \'dā-lē\ *adj* **1 a** : occurring, done, produced, or used every day or every weekday ⟨*daily* newspaper⟩ **b** : of or relating to every day ⟨*daily* visitor⟩ **2** : figured in terms of one day ⟨*daily* wages⟩ — **daily** *adv*

²daily *n, pl* **dailies** : a newspaper published every weekday

¹dain·ty \'dānt-ē\ *n, pl* **dainties** : something delicious to the taste : DELICACY

²dainty *adj* **dain·ti·er; -est** **1** : TASTY 1, DELICIOUS **2** : delicately pretty ⟨a *dainty* flower⟩ **3 a** : having or showing delicate or finicky taste **b** : FASTIDIOUS ⟨a *dainty* eater⟩ — **dain·ti·ly** \'dānt-°l-ē\ *adv* — **dain·ti·ness** \'dānt-ē-nəs\ *n*

dai·qui·ri \'dī-kə-rē, 'dak-ə-\ *n* : a cocktail made of rum, lime juice, and sugar

dairy \'de(ə)r-ē, da(ə)r-\ *n, pl* **dair·ies** **1** : a place where milk is kept and butter or cheese is made **2** : a farm devoted to the production of milk **3** : an establishment for the sale or distribution of milk and milk products

dairy cattle *n* : cattle rasied especially to produce milk

dairy·ing \'der-ē-iŋ\ *n* : the business of operating a dairy

dairy·maid \'der-ē-ˌmād\ *n* : a woman employed in a dairy

dairy·man \-mən, -ˌman\ *n* : a person who operates a dairy farm or works in a dairy

da·is \'dā-əs, 'dī-\ *n* : a raised platform (as in a hall)

dai·sy \'dā-zē\ *n, pl* **daisies** **1** : any of numerous composite plants having flower heads with well-developed ray flowers: as **a** : a low-growing European herb with white or pink ray flowers **b** : a tall leafy-stemmed wildflower introduced into America from Europe and having a flower head with a yellow disk in the center surrounded by long white ray flowers **2** : the flower head of a daisy [Old English *dægesēage* "daisy", literally "day's eye", from *dæg* "day" and *ēage* "eye"]

daisy wheel *n* : a disk having spokes with type on the end that is the printing part of a typewriter or printer for a computer

Da·ko·ta \də-'kōt-ə\ *n, pl* **Dakotas** *also* **Dakota** : a member of an American Indian people of the northern Mississippi valley — called also *Sioux*

dale \'dā(ə)l\ *n* : VALLEY

dal·li·ance \'dal-ē-ən(t)s\ *n* **1** : ¹PLAY 2; *esp* : the act of flirting **2** : action lacking in importance or seriousness ⟨a short *dalliance* with politics⟩

dal·ly \'dal-ē\ *vb* **dal·lied; dal·ly·ing** **1** : to act playfully

\ə\ abut	\aú\ out	\i\ tip	\ó\ saw	\ù\ foot
\ər\ further	\ch\ chin	\ī\ life	\ói\ coin	\y\ yet
\a\ mat	\e\ pet	\j\ job	\th\ thin	\yü\ few
\ā\ take	\ē\ easy	\ŋ\ sing	\th\ this	\yù\ cure
\ä\ cot, cart	\g\ go	\ō\ bone	\ü\ food	\zh\ vision

: TRIFLE **2 a** : to waste time ⟨*dally* at one's work⟩ **b** : LINGER 1, DAWDLE ⟨*dally* on the way home⟩ — **dal·li·er** *n*

dal·ma·tion \dal-'mā-shən\ *n, often cap* : one of a breed of dogs that have a white short-haired coat with black or brown spots

dal se·gno \däl-'sän-yō\ *adv* — used as a direction in music to return to the sign that marks the beginning of a passage to be repeated

dalmatian

¹**dam** \'dam\ *n* : a female parent — used especially of a domestic animal [Middle English *dam, dame* "lady, female parent"]

²**dam** *n* **1** : a barrier preventing the flow of water **2** : a body of water held back by a dam [Middle English *dam* "barrier to hold back water"]

³**dam** *vb* **dammed; dam·ming** **1** : to provide or restrain with a dam ⟨*dam* a stream⟩ **2** : to stop up : BLOCK ⟨*dammed*-up feelings⟩

¹**dam·age** \'dam-ij\ *n* **1** : a loss or harm caused by injury to one's person or property **2** *pl* : payment in money ordered by a court for loss or injury ⟨collected *damages* for his broken arm in the accident claim⟩ **syn** see INJURY

²**damage** *vb* **dam·aged; dam·ag·ing** : to cause damage to

dam·ask \'dam-əsk\ *n* **1** : a firm shiny reversible fabric used especially for household linen **2** : a tough steel having decorative wavy lines [Middle English *damaske* "damask", derived from Latin *Damascus*, city in Syria where the fabrics were originally made] — **damask** *adj*

dame \'dām\ *n* : a woman of rank, station, or authority: as **a** *archaic* : the mistress of a household **b** : the wife or daughter of a lord **c** : a female member of an order of knighthood — used as a title prefixed to the given name [Middle English *dame* "a woman of rank or authority, lady", from early French *dame* (same meaning), from Latin *domina* "mistress, lady", feminine form of *dominus* "master, owner" — related to DAMSEL, DOMINATE, ¹DON, MADAM, MADONNA, PRIMA DONNA]

¹**damn** \'dam\ *vb* **1** : to condemn to a punishment or fate; *esp* : to condemn to hell **2** : to condemn as bad or as a failure **3** : to swear at : CURSE

²**damn** *n* **1** : the saying of the word *damn* as a curse **2** : something of little value ⟨not worth a *damn*⟩

dam·na·ble \'dam-nə-bəl\ *adj* **1** : deserving condemnation ⟨*damnable* conduct⟩ **2** : very bad : TERRIBLE ⟨*damnable* weather⟩ — **dam·na·bly** \-blē\ *adv*

dam·na·tion \dam-'nā-shən\ *n* **1** : the act of damning **2** : the state of being damned

¹**damp** \'damp\ *n* **1** : a harmful gas especially in a coal mine **2** : MOISTURE, HUMIDITY **3** : DISCOURAGEMENT 2

²**damp** *vb* : DAMPEN

³**damp** *adj* : slightly wet **syn** see MOIST — **damp·ness** *n*

damp·en \'dam-pən\ *vb* **damp·ened; damp·en·ing** \'damp-(ə-)niŋ\ **1** : to check or lessen in activity or vigor : DEADEN **2** : to make or become damp — **damp·en·er** \'damp-(ə-)nər\ *n*

damp·er \'dam-pər\ *n* : one that damps ⟨put a *damper* on the celebration⟩: as **a** : a valve or plate (as in the flue of a furnace) for regulating the draft **b** : a device (as one of the felt-covered pieces of wood in a piano) used to deaden vibrations or oscillations

dam·sel \'dam-zəl\ *also* **dam·o·sel** *or* **dam·o·zel** \'dam-ə-,zel\ *n* : GIRL 1b, MAIDEN [Middle English *damesel* "damsel", from early French *dameisele* (same meaning), probably from Latin *domnicella* "young lady, young noblewoman", from earlier *domina* "lady, mistress" — related to DAME]

dam·sel·fish \'dam-zəl-,fish\ *n* : any of numerous often brilliantly colored marine fishes that live especially along coral reefs

dam·sel·fly \-,flī\ *n* : any of a group of insects that are closely related to the dragonflies, have eyes which stick out on the sides, and fold the wings above the body when at rest — compare DRAGONFLY

¹**dance** \'dan(t)s\ *vb* **danced; danc·ing** **1** : to engage in or perform a dance **2** : to move quickly up and down or about **3** : to perform or take part in as a dancer — **danc·er** *n*

²**dance** *n* **1** : an act or instance of dancing **2** : a series of rhythmic and patterned bodily movements usually performed to music **3** : a social gathering for dancing **4** : a piece of music by which dancing may be guided **5** : the art of dancing

D & C \,dē-ən(d)-'sē, -an(d)-\ *n* : a surgical procedure that is used to test for cancer of the uterus or to perform an abortion and that involves stretching the opening of the uterus and scraping the inside walls [*d*ilation & *c*urettage]

dan·de·li·on \'dan-d²l-,ī-ən\ *n* **1** : any of a genus of yellow-flowered weedy plants related to chicory; *esp* : one with long deeply toothed stemless leaves sometimes grown as a potherb **2** : a flower of a dandelion

Word History Sometimes plants are named for their resemblance, real or imagined, to animal shapes. The dandelion might not be a plant we would be quick to connect with a lion's teeth. And yet, in early French this common plant with its yellow flowers was called *dent de lion*, meaning literally "tooth of the lion". The dandelion leaves have deep notches along the edges. These make the leaves appear to have a row of sharp triangular teeth. In time the French name came to be spelled and pronounced as one word when it came into English, giving us *dandelion* today. [from early French *dent de lion* "dandelion", literally "tooth of the lion"; *dent* derived from Latin *dens* "tooth" — related to DENTAL]

dan·der \'dan-dər\ *n* : ¹ANGER, TEMPER ⟨the insults got my *dander* up⟩

dan·dle \'dan-d²l\ *vb* **dan·dled; dan·dling** \-dliŋ, -d²l-iŋ\ **1** : to move up and down in one's arms or on one's knee in affectionate play **2** : PAMPER, PET

dan·druff \'dan-drəf\ *n* : a thin whitish flaky crust that forms on the scalp and is shed as scales

¹**dan·dy** \'dan-dē\ *n, pl* **dandies** **1** : a man extremely interested in his clothing and personal appearance **2** : something excellent in its class — **dan·dy·ish** \-dē-ish\ *adj*

²**dandy** *adj* **dan·di·er; -est** : very good : SPLENDID, EXCELLENT

Dane \'dān\ *n* **1** : a person born or living in Denmark **2** : a person of Danish ancestry

dan·ger \'dān-jər\ *n* **1** : the state of not being protected from injury, harm, or evil **2** : something that may cause injury or harm ⟨the *dangers* of the jungle⟩

syn DANGER, HAZARD, PERIL, RISK mean a threat of loss, injury, or death. DANGER suggests possible harm that may or may not be avoided ⟨the *danger* of a new war starting⟩ HAZARD suggests danger from something beyond one's control ⟨the *hazards* of mining coal⟩ PERIL suggests immediate danger and a cause for fear ⟨during the storm their lives were in *peril*⟩ RISK suggests danger that may result from a chance freely taken ⟨willing to take the *risks* that come with flying a plane⟩

dan·ger·ous \'dānj-(ə-)rəs\ *adj* **1** : exposing to or involving danger ⟨a *dangerous* mission⟩ **2** : able or likely to cause injury ⟨*dangerous* weapons⟩ — **dan·ger·ous·ly** *adv* — **dan·ger·ous·ness** *n*

dan·gle \'dan-gəl\ *vb* **dan·gled; dan·gling** \-g(ə-)liŋ\ **1** : to hang loosely especially with a swinging motion **2** : to be left without proper grammatical connection in a sentence ⟨a *dangling* participle⟩ **3** : to cause to dangle

: SWING — **dan·gler** \-g(ə-)lər\ *n*

Dan·iel \'dan-yəl\ *n* — see BIBLE table

¹Dan·ish \'dā-nish\ *adj* : of, relating to, or characteristic of Denmark, the Danes, or Danish

²Danish *n* : the Germanic language of the Danes

Danish pastry *n* : a pastry made of a rich raised dough

dank \'daŋk\ *adj* : unpleasantly moist or wet　**syn** see MOIST — **dank·ly** *adv* — **dank·ness** *n*

dan·seuse \dän-'sə(r)z, -'süz\ *n* : a female ballet dancer

daph·nia \'daf-nē-ə\ *n* : any of a genus of tiny freshwater invertebrates that are classified with the crustaceans

dap·per \'dap-ər\ *adj*　**1** : being neat and trim in dress or appearance : SPRUCE　**2** : being alert and lively in movement and manners

¹dap·ple \'dap-əl\ *n*　**1** : any spot or patch of a dappled pattern　**2** : a dappled state　**3** : a dappled animal

²dapple *vb* **dap·pled; dap·pling** \-(ə-)liŋ\ : to mark or become marked with a dappled pattern ⟨daisies *dappled* the field⟩

dap·pled \'dap-əld\ *also* **dapple** *adj* : marked with numerous usually cloudy and rounded spots or patches of a color or shade different from their background ⟨a *dappled* fawn⟩ ⟨rested in the *dappled* shade⟩

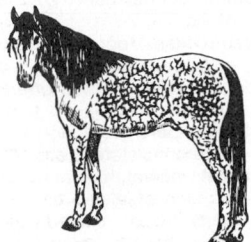

dapple 3

¹dare \'da(ə)r, 'de(ə)r\ *vb* **dared; dar·ing**　**1 a** : to have enough courage : be bold enough to ⟨try it if you *dare*⟩　**b** — used as a helping verb ⟨no one *dared* say a word⟩　**2** : to challenge to perform an action especially as a proof of courage ⟨I *dare* you⟩　**3** : to face boldly ⟨*dared* the dangerous crossing⟩

²dare *n* : an act or instance of daring : CHALLENGE ⟨dived from the bridge on a *dare*⟩

dare·dev·il \'da(ə)r-,dev-əl, 'de(ə)r-\ *n* : a recklessly bold person — **daredevil** *adj*

¹dar·ing \'da(ə)r-iŋ, 'de(ə)r-\ *adj* : ready to take risks　**syn** see ADVENTUROUS — **dar·ing·ly** \-iŋ-lē\ *adv*

²daring *n* : fearless boldness

¹dark \'därk\ *adj*　**1 a** : being without light or without much light ⟨in winter it gets *dark* early⟩　**b** : not giving off light ⟨the *dark* side of the moon⟩　**2** : not light in color ⟨a *dark* suit⟩ ⟨*dark* blue⟩　**3** : not bright and cheerful : GLOOMY ⟨look on the *dark* side of things⟩　**4** : being without knowledge and culture : IGNORANT　**5** : SECRETIVE, SILENT　**6** : not clear to the understanding ⟨the fortune-teller puzzled us with his *dark* sayings⟩ — **dark·ish** \'där-kish\ *adj* — **dark·ly** \-klē\ *adv* — **dark·ness** \'därk-nəs\ *n*

²dark *n*　**1 a** : absence of light : DARKNESS　**b** : a place or time of little or no light : NIGHT, NIGHTFALL ⟨get home before *dark*⟩　**2** : a dark or deep color

Dark Ages *n pl* : the period from about A.D. 476 to about 1000; *also* : MIDDLE AGES

dark·en \'där-kən\ *vb* **dark·ened; dark·en·ing** \'därk-(ə-)niŋ\　**1** : to make or grow dark or darker ⟨the sky *darkened*⟩　**2** : to make or become gloomy or forbidding ⟨her face *darkened* in anger⟩ — **dark·en·er** \'därk-(ə-)nər\ *n*

dark horse *n* : a contestant or a political figure whose abilities and chances as a contender are not known ⟨the convention nominated a *dark horse*⟩

dark lantern *n* : a lantern with an opening that can be closed to hide the light

dark·ling \'där-kliŋ\ *adj*　**1** : ¹DARK 1a ⟨a *darkling* plain⟩　**2** : MYSTERIOUS ⟨*darkling* secrets⟩

dark·room \'därk-,rüm, -,rum\ *n* : a small usually lightproof room used in developing photographic plates and film

dark·some \'därk-səm\ *adj* : gloomily somber : DARK

¹dar·ling \'där-liŋ\ *n*　**1** : a dearly loved person　**2** : ¹FAVORITE 1

²darling *adj*　**1** : dearly loved : FAVORITE　**2** : very pleasing : CHARMING

¹darn \'därn\ *vb* : to mend with interlacing stitches ⟨*darn* socks⟩

²darn *n* : a place that has been darned

³darn *vb* : ¹DAMN 1 — **darn** \'därn\ *or* **darned** \'därn(d)\ *adj or adv*

⁴darn *n* : ²DAMN 2 ⟨not worth a *darn*⟩

darning needle *n*　**1** : a long needle with a large eye for use in darning　**2** : DRAGONFLY, DAMSELFLY

¹dart \'därt\ *n*　**1 a** : a small pointed object that is meant to be thrown　**b** *pl* : a game in which darts are thrown at a target　**2** : something causing a sudden pain　**3** : a stitched fold in a garment　**4** : a quick movement

²dart *vb* : to move or shoot out suddenly and quickly ⟨the toad *darted* its tongue at a fly⟩ ⟨*darted* through the traffic⟩

Dar·win·ian \där-'win-ē-ən\ *adj* : of or relating to Charles Darwin, his theories, or his followers — **Darwinian** *n*

Dar·win·ism \'där-wə-,niz-əm\ *n* : a theory explaining the origin and continued existence of new kinds of animals and plants by means of natural selection acting on chance variations

Dar·win's finches \,där-wənz-\ *n pl* : finches (as the ground finches) of the Galapagos islands that differ strikingly in size and shape of bill among the various species and that were studied by Darwin prior to his discovery of the theory of evolution

¹dash \'dash\ *vb*　**1** : to knock, hurl, or thrust violently ⟨the storm *dashed* the boat against a reef⟩　**2** : to break by striking or knocking ⟨*dashed* a plate against the wall⟩　**3** : ¹SPLASH 1b, SPATTER　**4** : DESTROY 1, RUIN ⟨*dash* one's hopes⟩　**5** : to affect by mixing in something different ⟨the sauce was *dashed* with vinegar⟩　**6** : to perform or finish hastily ⟨*dash* off a letter⟩　**7** : to move with sudden speed ⟨*dashed* upstairs⟩ — **dash·er** *n*

²dash *n*　**1** : a sudden burst or splash ⟨a *dash* of cold water⟩　**2 a** : a stroke of a pen　**b** : a punctuation mark — that is used chiefly to indicate a break in the thought or structure of a sentence　**3** : a small usually special and noticeable addition ⟨add a *dash* of salt⟩　**4** : liveliness in style and action ⟨a leader of *dash* and vigor⟩　**5 a** : a sudden rush or attempt ⟨made a *dash* for the exit⟩　**b** : a short fast race　**6** : a long click or buzz forming a letter or part of a letter (as in Morse code)　**7** : DASHBOARD 2

dash·board \'dash-,bō(ə)rd, -,bó(ə)rd\ *n*　**1** : a screen on the front of a usually horse-pulled vehicle to keep out water, mud, or snow　**2** : a panel across an automobile or airplane below the windshield usually containing dials and controls

dashed \'dasht\ *adj* : made up of a series of dashes

da·shi·ki \də-'shē-kē\ *n* : a usually brightly colored one-piece pullover garment [derived from *danshiki*, a native word for this garment in a language of eastern Africa]

dash·ing \'dash-iŋ\ *adj*　**1** : noticeably bold and forceful ⟨a *dashing* attack⟩　**2** : showy

dashiki

\ə\ abut	\au̇\ **out**	\i\ **tip**	\ȯ\ **saw**	\u̇\ **foot**
\ər\ **further**	\ch\ **chin**	\ī\ **life**	\ȯi\ **coin**	\y\ **yet**
\a\ **mat**	\e\ **pet**	\j\ **job**	\th\ **thin**	\yü\ **few**
\ā\ **take**	\ē\ **easy**	\ŋ\ **sing**	\th\ **this**	\yu̇\ **cure**
\ä\ **cot, cart**	\g\ **go**	\ō\ **bone**	\ü\ **food**	\zh\ **vision**

and stylish especially in dress and manners ⟨made a *dashing* appearance⟩ — **dash·ing·ly** *adv*

das·tard \'das-tərd\ *n* : COWARD; *esp* : one who sneakily commits harmful acts — **das·tard·li·ness** \-lē-nəs\ *n* — **das·tard·ly** \-lē\ *adj*

da·ta \'dāt-ə, 'dat-, 'dät-\ *n sing or pl* 1 : facts about something that can be used in calculating, reasoning, or planning 2 : DATUM

data bank *n* : DATA BASE

data base *n* : a collection of data that is organized especially to be used by a computer

data processing *n* : the action or process of putting data into a computer and having the computer use it to produce a desired result

¹date \'dāt\ *n* 1 : the oblong edible fruit of a tall Old World palm 2 : a tall palm that produces dates — called also *date palm*

Word History The word *date* that means "the fruit of the palm" and the word *date* that means "the time of an event" look alike. They are not related to each other, though. And neither one is related to the word *day*. The word for the fruit can be traced back to the Greek word *daktylos*, originally meaning "finger" and "toe". No one knows just how the fruit came to be called by the word for finger. It may be because of its small size and shape or because of the long slender shape of the palm leaves. Or it may be that this word *daktylos* was the closest Greek word to the sound of a word for the fruit borrowed from another language. The word for "the time of an event" comes to us from Latin, but the Latin word did not mean either "day" or "time". *Date* derives from the Latin phrase *data Romae*, meaning "given at Rome", an expression used just before the date on letters and documents. The word *data* is from the Latin word *dare* "to give". In later Latin, the word *data* came to be used alone to stand for the date, and it came into English as *date*. [Middle English *date* "fruit of the palm", from early French *date* (same meaning), derived from Latin *dactylus* "date", from Greek *daktylos* "date", literally "finger"]

²date *n* 1 **a** : the time at which an event occurs **b** : a statement giving the time of doing or making (as of a coin or check) 2 : DURATION 3 : the period of time to which something belongs 4 **a** : APPOINTMENT 3; *esp* : a social engagement between two persons of opposite sex **b** : a person of the opposite sex with whom one has a social engagement [Middle English *date* "time of an event", from early French *date* (same meaning), derived from Latin *data (Romae)* "given (at Rome)", a phrase used in putting the date on documents, derived from *dare* "to give" — see Word History at ¹DATE] — **to date** : up to the present moment ⟨have received no complaints *to date*⟩

³date *vb* **dat·ed; dat·ing** 1 : to record the date of or on ⟨*date* a letter⟩ 2 : to show or find out the date, age, or period of ⟨the architecture *dates* the house⟩ ⟨*dating* geological periods⟩ 3 : to make or have a date with 4 **a** : to come into existence : ORIGINATE ⟨*dates* from the sixth century⟩ **b** : to go as far back : EXTEND ⟨*dating* back to childhood⟩ 5 : to show qualities typical of a past period ⟨such formality is *dated*⟩ — **dat·able** *or* **date·able** \'dāt-ə-bəl\ *adj* — **dat·er** *n*

date·less \'dāt-ləs\ *adj* 1 : ENDLESS 1 2 : having no date 3 : too ancient to be dated 4 : not restricted to a particular time or date

date line *n* : an imaginary line approximately along the 180th meridian named as the place where each calendar day begins

da·tive \'dāt-iv\ *adj* : of, relating to, or being the grammatical case that marks typically the indirect object of a verb or the object of some prepositions — **dative** *n*

da·tum \'dāt-əm, 'dat-, 'dät-\ *n, pl* **da·ta** \-ə\ *or* **datums** : a single piece of information : FACT

¹daub \'dȯb, 'däb\ *vb* 1 : to cover with soft sticky matter

: PLASTER 2 : ²SMEAR 2a, SMUDGE 3 : to apply coloring material thickly and heavily to — **daub·er** *n*

²daub *n* 1 : something daubed on 2 : a quickly and carelessly done picture

¹daugh·ter \'dȯt-ər\ *n* 1 : a female offspring; *esp* : a human female who is related as a child to its parent 2 : something derived from its origin as if feminine 3 : a form of an element that is the product of the radioactive decay of another element — **daugh·ter·ly** \-lē\ *adj*

²daughter *adj* 1 : having the characteristics or relationship of a daughter ⟨*daughter* cities⟩ 2 : being first generation offspring ⟨*daughter* cells⟩

daugh·ter–in–law \'dȯt-ə-rən-ˌlȯ, -ərn-ˌlȯ\ *n, pl* **daughters–in–law** \-ər-zən-\ : the wife of one's son

daunt \'dȯnt, 'dänt\ *vb* : to lessen the courage of : make afraid

daunt·less \'dȯnt-ləs, 'dänt-\ *adj* : FEARLESS, UNDAUNTED — **daunt·less·ly** *adv* — **daunt·less·ness** *n*

dau·phin \'dȯ-fən\ *n, often cap* : the eldest son of a king of France

dav·en·port \'dav-ən-ˌpō(ə)rt, 'dav-ᵊm-, -pȯ(ə)rt\ *n* : a large upholstered sofa

da·vit \'dā-vət, 'dav-ət\ *n* : one of a pair of posts with curved arms having ropes and pulleys attached and used especially on ships to raise and lower small boats

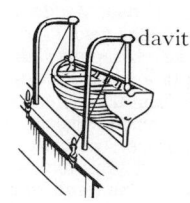

davit

Da·vy Jones's locker \ˌdā-vē-ˌjōnz(-əz)-\ *n* : the bottom of the sea [from *Davy Jones*, a name used by sailors to represent the spirit of the sea]

daw \'dȯ\ *n* : JACKDAW

daw·dle \'dȯd-ᵊl\ *vb* **daw·dled; daw·dling** \'dȯd-liŋ, -ᵊl-iŋ\ 1 : to spend time wastefully or idly : LINGER ⟨*dawdled* over her homework⟩ 2 : LOITER 2 3 : ²IDLE 1 ⟨*dawdle* the time away⟩ — **daw·dler** \'dȯd-lər, -ᵊl-ər\ *n*

¹dawn \'dȯn, 'dän\ *vb* 1 : to begin to grow light as the sun rises ⟨waited for the day to *dawn*⟩ 2 : to begin to appear or develop ⟨a smile *dawned* on her face⟩ 3 : to begin to be understood ⟨the solution *dawned* on him⟩

²dawn *n* 1 : the first appearance of light in the morning 2 : a first appearance : BEGINNING ⟨the *dawn* of a new age⟩

day \'dā\ *n* 1 **a** : the time of light between one night and the next **b** : DAYLIGHT 2 **a** : the time the earth takes to make one turn on its axis **b** : the time required for a heavenly body to turn once on its axis ⟨a lunar *day*⟩ 3 : a period of 24 hours beginning at midnight 4 : a specified day or date ⟨the *day* of the picnic⟩ ⟨their wedding *day*⟩ 5 : a specified time or period : AGE ⟨in grandmother's *day*⟩ 6 : the conflict or dispute of the day ⟨fought hard and carried the *day*⟩ 7 : the time set apart by custom or law for work ⟨the eight-hour *day*⟩

day·bed \'dā-ˌbed\ *n* : a couch with low head and foot pieces

day·break \-ˌbrāk\ *n* : ²DAWN 1

day–care center \'dā-ˌke(ə)r-, -ˌka(ə)r-\ *n* : a place that provides personal care, shelter, food, and play and learning experiences for preschool children during the day

¹day·dream \'dā-ˌdrēm\ *n* : a dreamy sequence of usually happy or pleasant imaginings about oneself or one's future

²daydream *vb* : to have a daydream — **day·dream·er** *n*

day laborer *n* : one who works by the day or for daily wages especially as an unskilled laborer

day·light \'dā-ˌlīt\ *n* 1 : the light of day 2 : DAYTIME 3 : ²DAWN 1 4 : knowledge or understanding of something that has been unclear ⟨began to see *daylight* on the problem⟩

daylight saving time *n* : time usually one hour ahead of standard time

day lily *n* : any of various Eurasian plants that have short-lived flowers resembling lilies and are widespread in cultivation and in the wild after escaping from cultivation

Day of Atonement : YOM KIPPUR

day·time \'dā-,tīm\ *n* : the period of daylight

day–to–day \'dāt-ə-,dā\ *adj* **1** : taking place, made, or done in the course of days following one after another 〈*day-to-day* problems〉 **2** : providing for a day at a time 〈never thought about the future but lived a *day-to-day* life〉

¹daze \'dāz\ *vb* **dazed; daz·ing** **1** : to stun especially by a blow 〈the boxer was *dazed* by blows to the head〉 **2** : to dazzle with light

²daze *n* : the state of being dazed

daz·zle \'daz-əl\ *vb* **daz·zled; daz·zling** \-(ə-)liŋ\ **1** : to overpower with light 〈the desert sunlight *dazzled* us〉 **2** : to impress greatly or confuse with brilliance 〈*dazzled* the crowds with fiery speeches〉 — **dazzle** *n* — **daz·zler** \-(ə-)lər\ *n* — **daz·zling·ly** \-(ə-)liŋ-lē\ *adv*

DDT \,dēd-(,)ē-'tē\ *n* : a colorless odorless insecticide that is poisonous to many higher animals

de- *prefix* **1** : do the opposite of 〈*decode*〉 **2 a** : remove (a specified thing) from 〈*delouse*〉 **b** : remove from (a specified thing) 〈*dethrone*〉 **3** : reduce 〈*demean*〉 [derived from Latin *de-* "from, down, away" and Latin *dis-*, literally "apart"]

dea·con \'dē-kən\ *n* **1** : a member of the clergy next below a priest **2** : a church member in various Christian churches who has special duties

dea·con·ess \'dē-kə-nəs\ *n* : a woman in various Christian churches who is chosen to assist in the church ministry

de·ac·ti·vate \(')dē-'ak-tə-,vāt\ *vb* : to make inactive or ineffective

¹dead \'ded\ *adj* **1** : deprived of life : having died **2 a** : having the appearance of death : DEATHLY 〈in a *dead* faint〉 **b** : ¹NUMB 1 **c** : very tired 〈the trip was really tiring; I'm *dead*〉 **d** : not reacting : INSENSITIVE 〈*dead* to pity〉 **e** : not burning 〈*dead* coals〉 **3 a** : INANIMATE 1, INERT 〈*dead* matter〉 **b** : no longer producing or functioning 〈*dead* battery〉 **4 a** : no longer in use or effect : OBSOLETE 〈*dead* language〉 **b** : no longer active : EXTINCT 〈*dead* volcano〉 **c** : not lively 〈*dead* party〉 **d** : lacking in activity : QUIET **e** : lacking spring 〈*dead* tennis ball〉 **f** : being out of action or out of use 〈a *dead* telephone line〉 **g** : being out of play 〈a *dead* ball〉 **5** : not running or circulating : STAGNANT 〈*dead* air〉 **6 a** : absolutely uniform 〈*dead* level〉 **b** : UNERRING, EXACT 〈a *dead* shot〉 〈*dead* center of the target〉 **c** : being sudden and complete 〈a *dead* stop〉 — **dead·ness** *n*

²dead *n, pl* **dead** **1** *pl* : those that are dead 〈the living and the *dead*〉 **2** : the time of greatest quiet or least activity 〈*dead* of night〉 〈*dead* of winter〉

³dead *adv* **1** : to the highest degree 〈*dead* right〉 **2** : suddenly and completely 〈stopped *dead*〉 **3** : ²STRAIGHT 〈*dead* ahead〉

dead·beat \'ded-,bēt\ *n* : one who fails to pay his debts

dead·en \'ded-ⁿn\ *vb* **dead·ened; dead·en·ing** \'ded-niŋ, -ⁿn-iŋ\ : to reduce or weaken in strength or feeling : DULL 〈*deaden* pain with drugs〉

dead–end \,ded-,end\ *adj* **1** : having no opportunities for advancement 〈a *dead-end* job〉 **2** : ¹TOUGH 6 〈*dead-end* kids〉

dead end *n* : an end (as of a street) without an exit

dead heat *n* : a contest in which two or more competitors tie

dead letter *n* **1** : something that has lost its force or authority without being abolished **2** : a letter that cannot be delivered or returned by the post office

dead·line \'ded-,līn\ *n* : a date or time before which something must be done

dead·lock \-,läk\ *n* : a stopping of action because both sides in a struggle are equally powerful and neither will

give in — **deadlock** *vb*

¹dead·ly \'ded-lē\ *adj* **dead·li·er; -est** **1** : likely to cause or capable of causing death 〈a *deadly* weapon〉 **2 a** : aiming to kill or destroy 〈a *deadly* enemy〉 **b** : very accurate : UNERRING 〈a *deadly* marksman〉 **3** : fatal to spiritual progress 〈a *deadly* sin〉 **4** : very great : EXTREME 〈a *deadly* bore〉 — **dead·li·ness** *n*

    syn DEADLY, MORTAL, FATAL, LETHAL mean causing or likely to cause death. DEADLY applies to known or likely causes of death 〈a *deadly* disease〉 MORTAL suggests that death has occurred or will certainly occur 〈a *mortal* wound〉 FATAL stresses the necessity of what has in fact resulted in death or destruction 〈the *fatal* consequence of their error〉 LETHAL applies especially to something that is bound to cause death or exists for the destruction of life 〈*lethal* gas〉

²deadly *adv* **1** : suggesting death 〈*deadly* pale〉 **2** : to a very great degree 〈*deadly* dull〉

deadly nightshade *n* : BELLADONNA 1

dead march *n* : a solemn march for a funeral

dead pan *n* : a face that shows no emotion — **dead·pan** \'ded-,pan\ *adj or adv*

dead reckoning *n* : calculation of the position of a ship or aircraft from the distance it has covered and the direction it has traveled without taking observations of the sun, stars, or moon

dead·weight \'ded-'wāt\ *n* : the full weight of a mass that is not moving

dead·wood \-,wu̇d\ *n* **1** : wood that is dead on a tree **2** : useless material or unproductive persons

deaf \'def\ *adj* **1** : wholly or partly unable to hear **2** : unwilling to hear or listen 〈*deaf* to all suggestions〉 — **deaf·ness** *n*

deaf·en \'def-ən\ *vb* **deaf·ened; deaf·en·ing** \-(ə-)niŋ\ **1** : to make deaf **2** : to stun with noise — **deaf·en·ing·ly** \-(ə-)niŋ-lē\ *adv*

deaf–mute \'def-,myüt\ *n* : a deaf person who cannot speak or has not been taught to speak

¹deal \'dē(ə)l\ *n* **1 a** : an indefinite amount or extent 〈means a great *deal*〉 **b** : a large quantity **2 a** : the act or right of passing out cards to players in a card game **b** : ¹HAND 11b

²deal *vb* **dealt** \'delt\; **deal·ing** \'dē-liŋ\ **1** : to give as one's portion : DISTRIBUTE 〈*deal* out sandwiches〉 〈*deal* the cards〉 **2** : ¹GIVE 9a 〈*dealt* him a blow〉 **3** : to have to do : TREAT 〈the book *deals* with education〉 **4** : to take action 〈*deal* with offenders〉 **5 a** : to engage in bargaining : TRADE **b** : to sell or distribute something as a business 〈*deals* in insurance〉 — **deal·er** \'dē-lər\ *n*

³deal *n* **1 a** : an act of dealing : TRANSACTION **b** : the result of bargaining : a mutual agreement 〈make a *deal* for a used car〉 **2** : treatment received 〈a dirty *deal*〉 **3** : a secret agreement **4** : a purchase at a fair or very low price : BARGAIN 〈a good *deal* on a new car〉

deal·ing *n* **1** *pl* : friendly or business relations 〈*dealings* with an automobile agency〉 **2** : a way of acting or of doing business 〈fair *dealing*〉

dean \'dēn\ *n* **1** : the head of the chapter of a cathedral church **2 a** : the head of a division, faculty, college, or school of a university **b** : a college or secondary school administrator in charge of students or instruction **3** : the senior member of a group 〈the *dean* of the diplomatic corps〉 — **dean·ship** \-,ship\ *n*

¹dear \'di(ə)r\ *adj* **1** : highly valued : PRECIOUS **2** — used as a form of address in letters and sometimes in speech 〈*Dear* Sir〉 **3** : high-priced : EXPENSIVE **4** : deeply and

\ə\ **abut**	\au̇\ **out**	\i\ **tip**	\ȯ\ **saw**	\u̇\ **foot**	
\ər\ **further**	\ch\ **chin**	\ī\ **life**	\ȯi\ **coin**	\y\ **yet**	
\a\ **mat**	\e\ **pet**	\j\ **job**	\th\ **thin**	\yü\ **few**	
\ā\ **take**	\ē\ **easy**	\ŋ\ **sing**	\th\ **this**	\yu̇\ **cure**	
\ä\ **cot, cart**	\g\ **go**	\ō\ **bone**	\ü\ **food**	\zh\ **vision**	

earnestly felt ⟨my *dearest* wish⟩ — **dear** *adv* — **dear·ly** *adv* — **dear·ness** *n*

²**dear** *n* : a loved one : DARLING

dearth \'dərth\ *n* : SCARCITY, LACK

death \'deth\ *n* **1** : the permanent stopping of all the vital bodily activities (as the beating of the heart and working of the brain) : the end of life **2** : the cause of loss of life ⟨drinking was the *death* of him⟩ **3** *cap* : the destroyer of life represented usually as a skeleton with a scythe **4** : the state of being dead **5** : DESTRUCTION 1, EXTINCTION — **death·like** \-,līk\ *adj*

death·bed \-'bed\ *n* **1** : the bed in which a person dies **2** : the last hours of life

death·blow \-'blō\ *n* : a destructive or killing stroke or event

death cap *n* : a very poisonous mushroom that varies in color from pure white to olive to yellow and has an obvious swollen covering about the base — called also *death cup*

death·less \'deth-ləs\ *adj* : IMMORTAL, IMPERISHABLE ⟨*deathless* fame⟩ — **death·less·ness** *n*

death·ly \'deth-lē\ *adj* **1** : causing death or destruction **2** : of, relating to, or suggestive of death ⟨a *deathly* paleness⟩ — **deathly** *adv*

death rate *n* : the proportion of deaths in a population that is often expressed as the number of individuals that die in a year per thousand individuals in the population at the beginning of the year

death ray *n* : a weapon that generates an intense beam of particles or radiation by which it destroys its target

death's–head \'deths-,hed\ *n* : a human skull representing death

death trap *n* : an object or situation likely to cause death ⟨that old elevator is a *death trap*⟩

¹**death·watch** \'deth-,wäch\ *n* : a small insect (as a beetle) that makes a ticking sound

²**deathwatch** *n* : a watch kept with the dead or dying

deb \'deb\ *n* : DEBUTANTE

de·ba·cle \di-'bäk-əl, -'bak-\ *n* : a great disaster or complete failure ⟨the army's retreat was a *debacle*⟩

de·bar \di-'bär\ *vb* **de·barred; de·bar·ring** : to prevent from having or doing something — **de·bar·ment** \-mənt\ *n*

de·bark \di-'bärk\ *vb* : to go or put ashore from a ship — **de·bar·ka·tion** \,dē-,bär-'kā-shən\ *n*

de·base \di-'bās\ *vb* **de·based; de·bas·ing** : to lower in character, dignity, quality, or value — **de·base·ment** \-mənt\ *n* — **de·bas·er** *n*

de·bat·able \di-'bāt-ə-bəl\ *adj* : open to question or dispute ⟨a *debatable* decision⟩

¹**de·bate** \di-'bāt\ *n* : a verbal argument: as **a** : the discussion of a motion before a legislature **b** : a regulated discussion of a problem between two matched sides

²**debate** *vb* **de·bat·ed; de·bat·ing** **1** : to discuss or examine a question often publicly by presenting and considering arguments on both sides **2** : to take part in a debate **3** : to present or consider the reasons for and against : CONSIDER **syn** see DISCUSS — **de·bat·er** *n*

¹**de·bauch** \di-'bóch, -'bäch\ *vb* : to lead away from virtue or morality : CORRUPT — **de·bauch·er** *n*

²**debauch** *n* : an act, occasion, or period of debauchery

de·bauch·ery \di-'bóch-(ə-)rē, -'bäch-\ *n*, *pl* **-er·ies** : extreme and unreasonable involvement in physical pleasures

de·bil·i·tate \di-'bil-ə-,tāt\ *vb* **-tat·ed; -tat·ing** : to reduce the strength of : WEAKEN — **de·bil·i·ta·tion** \-,bil-ə-'tā-shən\ *n*

de·bil·i·ty \di-'bil-ət-ē\ *n*, *pl* **-ties** : a weakened state

¹**deb·it** \'deb-ət\ *vb* : to enter as a debit : charge with or as a debt

²**debit** *n* : an entry in an account representing an amount paid out or owed

deb·o·nair \,deb-ə-'na(ə)r, -'ne(ə)r\ *adj* : gaily and gracefully charming ⟨a *debonair* manner⟩ [Middle English *debonere* "courteous, debonair", from early French *debon-*

aire (same meaning), from earlier phrase *de bon aire* "of good family"] — **deb·o·nair·ly** *adv* — **deb·o·nair·ness** *n*

de·brief \di-'brēf, 'dē-\ *vb* : to question (as an astronaut) on return from a mission or assignment in order to obtain useful information

de·bris \də-'brē, dā-; 'dā-,brē\ *n*, *pl* **de·bris** \-'brēz, -,brēz\ **1** : the remains of something broken down or destroyed : RUINS **2** : an accumulation of fragments of rock

debt \'det\ *n* **1** : SIN 1, TRESPASS **2** : something owed to another : a thing or amount due ⟨pay a *debt* of $10⟩ **3** : a condition of owing; *esp* : the state of owing money in amounts greater than one can pay ⟨hopelessly in *debt*⟩

debt·or \'det-ər\ *n* **1** : SINNER **2** : one that owes a debt

de·bug \(')dē-'bəg\ *vb* : to remove mistakes from ⟨*debug* a computer program⟩

de·bunk \(')dē-'bəŋk\ *vb* : to expose the falseness in ⟨*debunk* popular myths⟩ — **de·bunk·er** *n*

de·but \'dā-,byü, dā-'byü\ *n* **1** : a first public appearance ⟨my *debut* as a pianist⟩ **2** : a formal entrance into society

deb·u·tante \'deb-yù-,tänt\ *n* : a young woman making her debut

deca- *or* **dec-** *or* **deka-** *or* **dek-** *combining form* : ten [derived from Greek *deka* "ten"]

de·cade \'dek-,ād, -əd; de-'kād; *sense 3 is usually* 'dek-əd\ *n* **1** : a group or set of 10 **2** : a period of 10 years **3** : a part of the rosary devoted to one sacred mystery and made up of ten Hail Marys with the Lord's Prayer before and the Gloria Patri after

dec·a·dence \'dek-əd-ən(t)s *also* di-'kād-°n(t)s\ *n* : a falling off in quality or strength : a sinking to a lower state or level — **dec·a·dent** \'dek-əd-ənt *also* di-'kād-°nt\ *adj* — **dec·adent** *n* — **dec·a·dent·ly** *adv*

de·caf·fein·at·ed \(')dē-'kaf-(ē-)ə-,nāt-əd\ *adj* : having the caffeine removed ⟨*decaffeinated* coffee⟩

deca·gon \'dek-ə-,gän\ *n* : a polygon of 10 angles and 10 sides

deca·gram *variant of* DEKA-GRAM

de·cal \'dē-,kal, di-'kal, 'dek-əl\ *n* : a picture, design, or label made to be transferred (as to glass) from specially prepared paper [a shortened form of earlier *decalcomania* "the art of transferring pictures", from French *décalcomanie* (same meaning), from *décalquer* "to copy by tracing" and *manie* "mania, craze"]

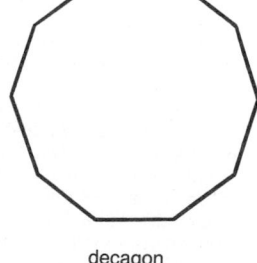

decagon

deca·li·ter *variant of* DEKALITER

dec·a·logue \'dek-ə-,lóg, -,läg\ *n* **1** *cap* : TEN COMMANDMENTS **2** : a basic set of rules that must be obeyed

deca·me·ter *variant of* DEKAMETER

de·camp \di-'kamp\ *vb* **1** : to pack up gear and leave a camp **2** : to depart suddenly : ABSCOND ⟨*decamped* with the funds⟩ — **de·camp·ment** \-mənt\ *n*

de·cant \di-'kant\ *vb* : to pour from one container into another — **de·can·ta·tion** \,dē-,kan-'tā-shən\ *n*

de·cant·er \di-'kant-ər\ *n* : an ornamental glass bottle used especially for serving wine

de·cap·i·tate \di-'kap-ə-,tāt\ *vb* **-tat·ed; -tat·ing** : to cut off the head of : BEHEAD [derived from Latin *decapitare* "to cut off the head of", from *de-* "from, away" and *caput* "head" — related to CAPITAL] — **de·cap·i·ta·tion** \-,kap-ə-'tā-shən\ *n*

de·cath·lon \di-'kath-lən, -,län\ *n* : an athletic contest in which each competitor takes part in each of a series of 10 track-and-field events

¹**de·cay** \di-'kā\ *vb* **1** : to lose soundness, health, strength, or vigor **2** : to go through or cause to go through decom-

position ⟨a radioactive element *decays*⟩ ⟨apples that *decayed* in storage⟩

²**decay** *n* **1** : gradual loss of strength, soundness, health, or vigor **2** : ²ROT 1 **3** : a natural decrease in the number of radioactive atoms in radioactive material

de·cease \di-'sēs\ *n* : DEATH 1 — **decease** *vb*

de·ceased \di-'sēst\ *n, pl* **deceased** : a dead person ⟨the will of the *deceased*⟩

de·ce·dent \di-'sēd-ᵊnt\ *n* : a deceased person

de·ceit \di-'sēt\ *n* **1** : the act or practice of deceiving : DECEPTION **2** : an attempt or device to deceive : TRICK **3** : the quality of being deceitful

de·ceit·ful \di-'sēt-fəl\ *adj* **1** : practicing or tending to practice deceit **2** : showing or containing deceit or fraud : DECEPTIVE ⟨a *deceitful* answer⟩ — **de·ceit·ful·ly** \-fə-lē\ *adv* — **de·ceit·ful·ness** \-fəl-nəs\ *n*

de·ceive \di-'sēv\ *vb* **de·ceived; de·ceiv·ing** **1** : to cause to believe what is untrue : MISLEAD ⟨*deceived* the customer about the condition of the car⟩ **2** : to deal with dishonestly : CHEAT **3** : to use or practice deceit — **de·ceiv·er** *n* — **de·ceiv·ing·ly** \-'sē-viŋ-lē\ *adv*

de·cel·er·ate \(')dē-'sel-ə-ˌrāt\ *vb* **-at·ed; -at·ing** : to move or cause to move at decreasing speed : slow down — **de·cel·er·a·tion** \(ˌ)dē-ˌsel-ə-'rā-shən\ *n* — **de·cel·er·a·tor** \(')dē-'sel-ə-ˌrāt-ər\ *n*

De·cem·ber \di-'sem-bər\ *n* : the 12th month of the year

Word History In the first calendar used by the ancient Romans, the year began with the month of March. The Romans called the tenth month of the year *December*, using the Latin word *decem*, meaning "ten". When the word was borrowed into early French, it became *decembre*. That was also how it was first spelled when it came into Middle English. In time, however, the English word was changed to match the original Latin in spelling and in having a capital letter. [Middle English *Decembre, December* "last month of the year", from early French *decembre* (same meaning), from Latin *December*, literally "tenth month", from *decem* "ten" — related to DECIMAL, DIME]

de·cen·cy \'dēs-ᵊn-sē\ *n, pl* **-cies** **1 a** : the quality or state of being decent : PROPRIETY **b** : agreement with standards of taste, quality, or proper behavior ⟨*decency*, not fear of punishment, made them behave⟩ **2** : a standard of proper behavior ⟨always observed the *decencies* of the formal dance⟩

de·cen·ni·al \di-'sen-ē-əl\ *adj* **1** : consisting of 10 years **2** : happening every 10 years ⟨*decennial* census⟩ — **de·cen·ni·al·ly** \-ē-ə-lē\ *adv*

de·cent \'dēs-ᵊnt\ *adj* **1 a** : agreeing with standards of proper behavior, good taste, or morality **b** : clothed in a proper and suitable manner and style **2** : free from poor taste or bad manners ⟨our conversations were always *decent*, never obscene⟩ **3** : fairly good : ADEQUATE ⟨*decent* housing⟩ — **de·cent·ly** *adv*

de·cen·tral·ize \(')dē-'sen-trə-ˌlīz\ *vb* **1** : to scatter or spread out among various regional or local authorities ⟨*decentralize* the operations of the school system⟩ **2** : to cause to withdraw from urban centers to outlying areas ⟨*decentralize* industries⟩ — **de·cen·tral·iza·tion** \(ˌ)dē-ˌsen-trə-lə-'zā-shən\ *n*

de·cep·tion \di-'sep-shən\ *n* **1 a** : the act of deceiving **b** : the fact or condition of being deceived **2** : something that deceives : TRICK

de·cep·tive \di-'sep-tiv\ *adj* : tending or having power to deceive — **de·cep·tive·ly** *adv* — **de·cep·tive·ness** *n*

deci- *combining form* : tenth part ⟨*deci*gram⟩ [derived from Latin *decimus* "tenth", from *decem* "ten"]

deci·bel \'des-ə-ˌbel, -bəl\ *n* : a unit for measuring the relative loudness of sounds — *abbr. dB*

de·cide \di-'sīd\ *vb* **de·cid·ed; de·cid·ing** **1** : to give a judgment on ⟨*decided* the case in favor of the person accused⟩ **2** : to bring to a final end ⟨one blow *decided* the

fight⟩ **3** : to cause to come to a choice or judgment ⟨their appeals *decided* me to give generously⟩ **4** : to make a choice or judgment ⟨*decided* to go⟩ — **de·cid·able** \-'sīd-ə-bəl\ *adj* — **de·cid·er** *n*

de·cid·ed \di-'sīd-əd\ *adj* **1** : UNMISTAKABLE, CLEAR ⟨a *decided* smell of gas⟩ **2** : ¹FIRM 3 ⟨a *decided* tone of voice⟩ — **de·cid·ed·ly** *adv* — **de·cid·ed·ness** *n*

de·cid·u·ous \di-'sij-ə-wəs\ *adj* **1** : falling off (as at the end of a growing period or stage of development) ⟨antlers are *deciduous*⟩ ⟨*deciduous* leaves⟩ **2** : having deciduous parts or members with deciduous parts ⟨*deciduous* trees⟩ ⟨a *deciduous* forest⟩

deciduous tooth *n* : MILK TOOTH

deci·gram \'des-ə-ˌgram\ *n* — see METRIC SYSTEM table

deci·li·ter \'des-ə-ˌlēt-ər\ *n* — see METRIC SYSTEM table

de·cil·lion \di-'sil-yən\ *n* — see NUMBER table

¹**dec·i·mal** \'des-(ə-)məl\ *adj* **1** : based on the number 10; *esp* : expressed in, used in, or using decimal notation especially with the decimal point ⟨a *decimal* system of writing numerals⟩ ⟨¼ in *decimal* form is .25⟩ **2** : divided into 10th or 100th units ⟨*decimal* coinage⟩ [derived from Latin *decimalis* "of a tenth part", derived from *decimus* "a tenth part", from *decem* "ten" — related to DECEMBER, DIME]

²**decimal** *n* **1** : any real number expressed in base 10 **2** : a fraction (as .25 = $^{25}/_{100}$ or .025 = $^{25}/_{1000}$) or mixed number (as 3.025 = $3^{25}/_{1000}$) in which the denominator is a power of 10 usually expressed by use of the decimal point — called also *decimal fraction*

decimal notation *n* : expression of a number in base 10 by using one of the first nine integers or 0 in each place and letting each place value be a power of 10

decimal place *n* : any of the places to the right of the decimal point in a number expressed in decimal notation ⟨5.732 has three *decimal places*⟩

decimal point *n* : the dot at the left of a decimal (as .678) that is a proper fraction or between the parts of a mixed number (as 3.678) expressed by a whole number and a decimal fraction

dec·i·mate \'des-ə-ˌmāt\ *vb* **-mat·ed; -mat·ing** **1** : to pick by lot and kill every tenth man of ⟨the Roman army would *decimate* a legion for cowardice⟩ **2** : to destroy a large part of ⟨a population *decimated* by an epidemic⟩ — **dec·i·ma·tion** \ˌdes-ə-'mā-shən\ *n*

deci·me·ter \'des-ə-ˌmēt-ər\ *n* — see METRIC SYSTEM table

de·ci·pher \di-'sī-fər\ *vb* **1** : to convert into understandable form; *esp* : DECODE **2** : to make out the meaning of despite lack of clearness ⟨*decipher* sloppy handwriting⟩ — **de·ci·pher·able** \-f(ə-)rə-bəl\ *adj* — **de·ci·pher·ment** \-fər-mənt\ *n*

de·ci·sion \di-'sizh-ən\ *n* **1** : the act or result of deciding ⟨the *decision* of the court⟩ **2** : promptness and firmness in deciding : DETERMINATION ⟨a leader of courage and *decision*⟩

de·ci·sive \di-'sī-siv\ *adj* **1** : having the power to decide ⟨the *decisive* vote⟩ **2** : of such nature as to settle a question or dispute ⟨a *decisive* victory⟩ **3** : marked by or showing decision ⟨a *decisive* manner⟩ — **de·ci·sive·ly** *adv* — **de·ci·sive·ness** *n*

¹**deck** \'dek\ *n* **1** : a platform extending from side to side in a ship and forming a floor **2** : a flat structure resembling the deck of a ship **3** : a pack of playing cards — **on deck** : next in line

²**deck** *vb* **1 a** : to clothe in a fine and impressive way : ARRAY ⟨*decked* out in a new suit⟩ **b** : DECORATE 1 **2** : to provide (as a ship) with a deck

\ə\ abut	\au̇\ out	\i\ tip	\ȯ\ saw	\u̇\ foot
\ər\ further	\ch\ chin	\ī\ life	\ȯi\ coin	\y\ yet
\a\ mat	\e\ pet	\j\ job	\th\ thin	\yü\ few
\ā\ take	\ē\ easy	\ŋ\ sing	\t̲h̲\ this	\yu̇\ cure
\ä\ cot, cart	\g\ go	\ō\ bone	\ü\ food	\zh\ vision

deck·hand \'dek-,hand\ *n* : a sailor who performs manual duties

de·claim \di-'klām\ *vb* : to speak or deliver in the manner of a formal speech — **de·claim·er** *n* — **dec·la·ma·tion** \,dek-lə-'mā-shən\ *n* — **de·clam·a·to·ry** \di-'klam-ə-,tōr-ē, -,tȯr-\ *adj*

dec·la·ra·tion \,dek-lə-'rā-shən\ *n* **1** : the act of declaring : ANNOUNCEMENT **2** : something declared or a document containing such a declaration ⟨the *Declaration* of Independence⟩

de·clar·a·tive \di-'klar-ət-iv, -'kler-\ *adj* : making a declaration or statement ⟨*declarative* sentence⟩

de·clare \di-'kla(ə)r, -'kle(ə)r\ *vb* **de·clared; de·clar·ing** **1** : to make known openly or officially ⟨*declare* war⟩ **2** : to state strongly **3** : to make a full statement of (taxable property or items on which duty must be paid) [Middle English *declaren* "to make clear, make known", from early French *declarer* (same meaning), from Latin *declarare* "to make clear", from *de-* "from" and *clarare* "to make clear", from *clarus* "clear, bright" — related to *clear*] **syn** see ASSERT — **de·clar·a·to·ry** \-'klar-ə-,tōr-ē, -,tȯr-\ *adj* — **de·clar·er** *n*

de·clen·sion \di-'klen-chən\ *n* **1 a** : the giving of noun, adjective, or pronoun inflections especially in a specified order **b** : a class of nouns or adjectives having the same type of inflectional forms **2** : ²DECLINE 1, DETERIORATION **3** : DESCENT 4a, SLOPE — **de·clen·sion·al** \-'klench-nəl, -'klen-chən-ᵊl\ *adj*

dec·li·na·tion \,dek-lə-'nā-shən\ *n* **1** : angular distance north or south from the celestial equator measured along a great circle passing through the celestial poles ⟨the *declination* of a star⟩ **2** : a bending downward : INCLINATION **3** : the angle that the magnetic needle makes with a true north and south line

¹de·cline \di-'klīn\ *vb* **de·clined; de·clin·ing** **1 a** : to slope downward : DESCEND **b** : to bend down ⟨*declined* his head⟩ **2** : to pass toward a lower level : RECEDE **3** : to draw a close : WANE **4** : to show unwillingness to accept, do, engage in, or agree to ⟨*declined* to run for a second term⟩ ⟨*declined* the invitation⟩ **5** : to give the declension of a noun, pronoun, or adjective — **de·clin·able** \-'klī-nə-bəl\

syn DECLINE, REFUSE, REJECT mean to express unwillingness to go along with a demand or request. DECLINE suggests a polite negative response ⟨*decline* an invitation to a party⟩ REFUSE suggests a forceful or absolute denial ⟨*refused* to see him at all⟩ REJECT may suggest an unwillingness even to consider a demand or request ⟨*rejected* her plan before she had finished speaking⟩

²decline *n* **1** : the process of declining : **a** : a gradual sinking and wasting away **b** : a change to a lower state or level **2** : the time when something is approaching its end **3** : a downward slope

de·cliv·i·ty \di-'kliv-ət-ē\ *n, pl* **-ties** **1** : downward inclination **2** : a descending slope

de·code \(')dē-'kōd\ *vb* : to change (as a secret message) from code into ordinary language — **de·cod·er** *n*

de·col·or·ize \(')dē-'kəl-ə-,rīz\ *vb* **-ized; -iz·ing** : to remove color from

de·com·mis·sion \,dē-kə-'mish-ən\ *vb* : to remove (as a ship) from use or service

de·com·pose \,dē-kəm-'pōz\ *vb* **1** : to separate a thing into its parts or into simpler compounds ⟨*decompose* water into hydrogen and oxygen⟩ **2** : to break down through chemical change : ROT — **de·com·pos·able** \-'pō-zə-bəl\ *adj*

de·com·pos·er \,dē-kəm-'pō-zər\ *n* : an organism (as a bacterium or a fungus) that lives on and decomposes dead organisms

de·com·po·si·tion \(,)dē-,käm-pə-'zish-ən\ *n* : the action or process of decomposing: as **a** : the separation of a chemical substance into simpler chemical substances and especially the elements of which it is made up ⟨decom-

position of water into hydrogen and oxygen⟩ **b** : decay of plant or animal matter ⟨*decomposition* of a dead body⟩

de·com·press \,dē-kəm-'pres\ *vb* : to release (as a diver) from pressure or compression — **de·com·pres·sion** \-'presh-ən\ *n*

de·con·tam·i·nate \,dē-kən-'tam-ə-,nāt\ *vb* : to rid of something (as radioactive material) that contaminates — **de·con·tam·i·na·tion** \-,tam-ə-'nā-shən\ *n*

dec·o·rate \'dek-ə-,rāt\ *vb* **-rat·ed; -rat·ing** **1** : to make more attractive by adding something that is beautiful or becoming ⟨*decorate* a room⟩ **2** : to award a decoration of honor to ⟨*decorate* a soldier for bravery⟩ **syn** see ADORN

dec·o·ra·tion \,dek-ə-'rā-shən\ *n* **1** : the act or action of decorating **2** : something that decorates or beautifies : ORNAMENT ⟨holiday *decorations*⟩ **3** : a badge of honor (as a medal, cross, or ribbon)

Decoration Day *n* : MEMORIAL DAY

dec·o·ra·tive \'dek-(ə-)rət-iv, 'dek-ə-,rāt-\ *adj* : serving to decorate : ORNAMENTAL — **dec·o·ra·tive·ly** *adv* — **dec·o·ra·tive·ness** *n*

dec·o·ra·tor \'dek-ə-,rāt-ər\ *n* : one that decorates; *esp* : a person who decorates the interiors of buildings

dec·o·rous \'dek-ə-rəs *also* di-'kōr-əs, -'kȯr-\ *adj* : noticeable for proper behavior and good taste : CORRECT ⟨*decorous* conduct⟩ — **dec·o·rous·ly** *adv* — **dec·o·rous·ness** *n*

de·co·rum \di-'kōr-əm, -'kȯr-\ *n* **1** : agreement with accepted standards of conduct : proper behavior ⟨social *decorum*⟩ **2** : the state or condition of being calm, orderly, and well-regulated ⟨disturb the *decorum* of the meeting⟩

¹de·coy \'dē-,kȯi, di-'kȯi\ *n* **1** : something intended to lure into a trap; *esp* : an artificial bird used to attract live birds within shooting range **2** : a person used to lead another into a trap

²decoy \di-'kȯi, 'dē-,kȯi\ *vb* : to attract by or as if by a decoy : ENTICE

¹de·crease \di-'krēs, 'dē-,krēs\ *vb* **de·creased; de·creas·ing** : to make or become smaller ⟨*decrease* speed⟩ ⟨*decrease* 6 by 2⟩

²de·crease \'dē-,krēs, di-'krēs\ *n* **1** : a process of decreasing ⟨a *decrease* in accidents⟩ **2** : the amount by which a thing decreases ⟨a *decrease* of three dollars in wages⟩

¹de·cree \di-'krē\ *n* : an order or decision given by one in authority

²decree *vb* **de·creed; de·cree·ing** : to command or order by decree

dec·re·ment \'dek-rə-mənt\ *n* : a gradual loss or the amount lost

de·crep·it \di-'krep-ət\ *adj* : broken down with age : WORN-OUT

de·crep·i·tude \di-'krep-ə-,t(y)üd\ *n* : the quality or state of being decrepit : loss of strength or sturdiness especially from old age

¹de·cre·scen·do \,dā-krə-'shen-dō\ *adv or adj* : with diminishing volume — used as a direction in music

²decrescendo *n, pl* **-dos** : a lessening in volume of sound

de·cry \di-'krī\ *vb* **1** : to express disrespect and scorn for : BELITTLE ⟨*decry* a hero's deeds⟩ **2** : to find fault with : CONDEMN ⟨*decried* the waste of resources⟩ — **de·cri·er** \-'krī-(ə)r\ *n*

ded·i·cate \'ded-i-,kāt\ *vb* **-cat·ed; -cat·ing** **1** : to set apart for some purpose and especially a sacred or serious purpose **2** : to address or inscribe as a compliment ⟨*dedicated* her book to her mother⟩ **syn** see DEVOTE — **ded·i·ca·tor** \-,kāt-ər\ *n*

ded·i·ca·tion \,ded-i-'kā-shən\ *n* **1 a** : an act or rite of dedicating to a divine being or to a sacred use **b** : a setting aside for a particular purpose **2** : the inscription dedicating a literary work **3** : self-sacrificing devotion — **ded·i·ca·to·ry** \'ded-i-kə-,tōr-ē, -,tȯr-\ *adj*

de·duce \di-'d(y)üs\ *vb* **de·duced; de·duc·ing** **1** : to trace the course or origin of **2 a** : to draw (a conclusion) necessarily from given information **b** : to determine by reasoning from a general principle — **de·duc·ible** \-'d(y)ü-sə-bəl\ *adj*

de·duct \di-'dəkt\ *vb* : to take away (an amount) from a total : SUBTRACT — **de·duct·ible** \-'dək-tə-bəl\ *adj*

de·duc·tion \di-'dək-shən\ *n* **1** : an act of taking away **2 a** : the drawing of a conclusion by reasoning; *esp* : reasoning in which the conclusion follows necessarily from the given information **b** : a conclusion reached by such reasoning **3** : something that is or may be subtracted ⟨*deductions* from taxable income⟩ — **de·duc·tive** \-'dək-tiv\ *adj* — **de·duc·tive·ly** *adv*

¹deed \'dēd\ *n* **1** : something that is done : ACT ⟨we are judged by our *deeds*⟩ **2** : a legal document by which one person transfers land or buildings to another — **deed·less** \-ləs\ *adj*

²deed *vb* : to transfer by deed

deem \'dēm\ *vb* : to have an opinion : BELIEVE, SUPPOSE ⟨*deemed* it wise to go slow⟩

¹deep \'dēp\ *adj* **1 a** : extending far downward ⟨a *deep* well⟩ : having a great distance between the top and bottom surfaces ⟨*deep* water⟩ : not shallow **b** : extending well inward from an outer or front surface ⟨a *deep* gash⟩ **c** : extending far outward from a center ⟨*deep* space⟩ **d** : occurring or located near the outer limits ⟨*deep* right field⟩ **2** : having a specified extension downward or backward ⟨a shelf 40 centimeters *deep*⟩ **3 a** : difficult to understand ⟨a *deep* book⟩ **b** : MYSTERIOUS, OBSCURE ⟨a *deep* dark secret⟩ **c** : PROFOUND 1 ⟨a *deep* thinker⟩ **d** : completely absorbed ⟨*deep* in thought⟩ **e** : being to an extreme degree : HEAVY ⟨*deep* sleep⟩ **4 a** : dark and rich in color ⟨a *deep* red⟩ **b** : having a low musical pitch or range ⟨a *deep* voice⟩ **5 a** : coming from or located well within ⟨a *deep* sigh⟩ ⟨a house *deep* in the forest⟩ **b** : covered, enclosed, or filled often to a specified degree ⟨knee-*deep* in water⟩ ⟨a road *deep* with snow⟩ — **deep·ly** *adv*

²deep *adv* **1** : to a great depth : DEEPLY **2** : far on : LATE ⟨*deep* in the night⟩

³deep *n* **1 a** : an extremely deep place or part (as of the ocean) **b** : OCEAN 1 **2** : the middle or most intense part ⟨the *deep* of night⟩

deep–dish pie *n* : a pie usually with a fruit filling baked in a deep dish

deep·en \'dē-pən\ *vb* **deep·ened; deep·en·ing** \'dēp-(ə-)niŋ\ : to make or become deep or deeper

deep fat *n* : hot fat or oil in a cooking utensil that is deep enough to cover the food to be fried

deep·root·ed \'dēp-'rüt-əd, -'rüt-\ *adj* : deeply fixed or established ⟨a *deep-rooted* loyalty⟩

deep–sea \,dēp-,sē\ *adj* : of, relating to, or occurring in the deeper parts of the sea

deep–seat·ed \'dēp-'sēt-əd\ *adj* **1** : set or located far below the surface **2** : firmly established ⟨a *deep-seated* tradition⟩

deep–set \-'set\ *adj* : set far in ⟨*deep-set* eyes⟩

deep–wa·ter \,dēp-,wot-ər, -,wät-\ *adj* : of or relating to water of great depth; *esp* : DEEP-SEA ⟨*deepwater* sailors⟩

deer \'di(ə)r\ *n, pl* **deer** : any of a family of cloven-hoofed cud-chewing mammals (as an elk, a reindeer, or a white-tailed deer) of which the males of almost all species have antlers while the females of only a few species do

Word History The meaning of a word often develops from the general to the specific. For instance, *deer* is used in modern English to mean several related forms, including white-tailed deer, mule deer, elk, and moose. The Old English *dēor*, however, could refer to any animal, tame or wild, or to wild animals in general. In time, *deer* came to be used only for wild animals that were hunted and then for the red deer, once widely hunted in England. From that usage the term has spread to related animals, becoming somewhat more general again. [Old English *dēor* "wild animal, beast"]

deer fly *n* : any of numerous small horseflies that are about the size of houseflies and usually have dark spots on the wings

deer mouse *n* : any of numerous North American field and woodland mice related to the hamsters

deer mouse

deer·skin \'di(ə)r-,skin\ *n* **1** : leather made from the skin of a deer **2** : a garment of deerskin

de–es·ca·late \(')dē-'es-kə-,lāt\ *vb* : to decrease in extent, volume, or scope ⟨*de-escalate* the war⟩ — **de–es·ca·la·tion** \(,)dē-,es-kə-'lā-shən\ *n*

de·face \di-'fās\ *vb* : to destroy or damage the face or surface of — **de·face·ment** \-'fās-mənt\ *n* — **de·fac·er** *n*

de·fame \di-'fām\ *vb* **de·famed; de·fam·ing** : to injure or destroy the reputation of : speak evil of : LIBEL — **def·a·ma·tion** \,def-ə-'mā-shən\ *n* — **de·fam·a·to·ry** \di-'fam-ə-,tōr-ē, -,tor-\ *adj* — **de·fam·er** *n*

¹de·fault \di-'folt\ *n* **1** : failure to take action ⟨lost a great opportunity by *default*⟩ ⟨a decision made by *default* — not deciding⟩ **2** : failure to do something required (as make a payment or appear in court) ⟨in *default* on a loan⟩ ⟨lost a court case by *default*⟩ **3** : a selection to be made automatically according to a computer program when the user does not specify a choice

²default *vb* : to fail to carry out a contract, obligation, or duty — **de·fault·er** *n*

¹de·feat \di-'fēt\ *vb* **1** : to destroy the value or effect of ⟨the lawyers *defeated* the will⟩ **2** : to win a victory over ⟨*defeated* their team⟩

²defeat *n* **1** : the act or an instance of making ineffective by prevention of success ⟨*defeat* of the bill by Congress⟩ ⟨*defeat* of one's hopes⟩ **2 a** : an overthrow of an army in battle **b** : loss of a contest (as by a team)

de·feat·ism \di-'fēt-,iz-əm\ *n* : an attitude of expecting defeat or of accepting defeat with the belief that further effort would be useless — **de·feat·ist** \-'fēt-əst\ *n or adj*

def·e·cate \'def-i-,kāt\ *vb* **-cat·ed; -cat·ing** : to expel feces from the bowels — **def·e·ca·tion** \,def-i-'kā-shən\ *n*

¹de·fect \'dē-,fekt, di-'fekt\ *n* : a lack of something necessary for completeness or perfection — compare BIRTH DEFECT **syn** see BLEMISH

²de·fect \di-'fekt\ *vb* : to desert a cause or party often in order to take up another — **de·fec·tion** \-'fek-shən\ *n* — **de·fec·tor** \-'fek-tər\ *n*

¹de·fec·tive \di-'fek-tiv\ *adj* : lacking something essential : FAULTY ⟨*defective* brakes⟩ — **de·fec·tive·ly** *adv* — **de·fec·tive·ness** *n*

²defective *n* : a person who is subnormal physically or mentally

de·fend \di-'fend\ *vb* **1** : to repel danger or attack ⟨were *defending* their own country⟩ **2** : to act as attorney for **3** : to oppose the claim of another in a lawsuit : CONTEST **4** : to uphold against opposition ⟨*defended* the freedom of the press⟩ — **de·fend·er** *n*

de·fend·ant \di-'fen-dənt\ *n* : a person who is being sued or accused in a legal action

de·fense *or* **de·fence** \di-'fen(t)s; *as antonym of* "offense" *often* 'dē-,fen(t)s\ *n* **1** : the act of defending : resistance

\ə\ abut	\au̇\ out	\i\ tip	\ȯ\ saw	\u̇\ foot
\ər\ further	\ch\ chin	\ī\ life	\ȯi\ coin	\y\ yet
\a\ mat	\e\ pet	\j\ job	\th\ thin	\yü\ few
\ā\ take	\ē\ easy	\ŋ\ sing	\th\ this	\yu̇\ cure
\ä\ cot, cart	\g\ go	\ō\ bone	\ü\ food	\zh\ vision

against attack   **2** : capability of resisting attack   **3 a** : means or method of defending   **b** : an argument in support   **4 a** : a defending party or group   **b** : a defensive team   **5** : the answer made by the defendant in a legal action — **de·fense·less** \di-ˈfen(t)s-ləs\ *adj* — **de·fense·less·ly** *adv* — **de·fense·less·ness** *n* — **de·fen·si·bil·i·ty** \di-ˌfen(t)-sə-ˈbil-ət-ē\ *n* — **de·fen·si·ble** \-ˈfen(t)-sə-bəl\ *adj* — **de·fen·si·bly** \-blē\ *adv*

¹**de·fen·sive** \di-ˈfen(t)-siv, ˈdē-ˌfen(t)-\ *adj*   **1** : of or relating to defense : serving or intended to defend or protect ⟨a *defensive* alliance⟩   **2** : of or relating to the attempt to keep an opponent from scoring in a game or contest — **de·fen·sive·ly** *adv* — **de·fen·sive·ness** *n*

²**defensive** *n* : a defensive position ⟨put on the *defensive* by an attack⟩

¹**de·fer** \di-ˈfər\ *vb* **de·ferred; de·fer·ring** : POSTPONE, PUT OFF ⟨*defer* payment⟩ [Middle English *deferren, differren* "to put off, delay", from early French *differer* (same meaning), from Latin *differre* "to put off, be different", from *dif-dis-* "apart" and *ferre* "to bear, carry, yield" — related to ²DEFER, FERTILE, OFFER, REFER, TRANSFER] — **de·fer·ra·ble** \-ˈfər-ə-bəl\ *adj* — **de·fer·rer** *n*

²**defer** *vb* **de·ferred; de·fer·ring** : to give in or yield to another's wish or opinion ⟨*deferred* to their guest's choice of TV shows⟩ [Middle English *deferren, differren* "to entrust to another person", from early French *deferer, defferer* (same meaning), derived from Latin *deferre* "to bring down", from *de-* "down, from, away" and *ferre* "to bear, carry" — related to ¹DEFER]

def·er·ence \ˈdef-(ə-)rən(t)s\ *n* : courteous, respectful, or flattering regard for another's wishes

def·er·en·tial \ˌdef-ə-ˈren-chəl\ *adj* : showing or expressing deference — **def·er·en·tial·ly** \-ˈrench-(ə-)lē\ *adv*

de·fer·ment \di-ˈfər-mənt\ *n* : the act of delaying

de·fi·ance \di-ˈfī-ən(t)s\ *n*   **1** : the act or an instance of defying : CHALLENGE   **2** : a tendency to resist : contempt of opposition

de·fi·ant \di-ˈfī-ənt\ *adj* : full of defiance : IMPUDENT, INSOLENT — **de·fi·ant·ly** *adv*

de·fi·cien·cy \di-ˈfish-ən-sē\ *n, pl* **-cies**   **1** : the quality or state of being deficient   **2** : the quality or state of being inadequate; *esp* : a shortage of substances necessary to health

deficiency disease *n* : a disease (as scurvy or beriberi) caused by a lack of one or more essential substances (as a vitamin or mineral) in the diet

¹**de·fi·cient** \di-ˈfish-ənt\ *adj* : lacking something necessary for completeness : not up to a given or normal standard ⟨a diet *deficient* in proteins⟩ ⟨*deficient* in their knowledge of history⟩ — **de·fi·cient·ly** *adv*

²**deficient** *n* : a person who is deficient

def·i·cit \ˈdef-ə-sət\ *n* : a deficiency in amount; *esp* : an excess of expenses over income

¹**de·file** \di-ˈfī(ə)l\ *vb* **de·filed; de·fil·ing**   **1** : to make filthy : DIRTY ⟨stored grain *defiled* by rats⟩   **2** : to corrupt the purity or perfection of ⟨*defile* buildings with posters⟩   **3** : DESECRATE ⟨a shrine *defiled* by the invaders⟩   **4** : ²DISHONOR 1 ⟨*defiled* our good name⟩ — **de·file·ment** \-ˈfī(ə)l-mənt\ *n* — **de·fil·er** \-ˈfī-lər\ *n*

²**de·file** \di-ˈfī(ə)l, ˈdē-ˌfīl\ *n* : a narrow passage or gorge

de·fine \di-ˈfīn\ *vb* **de·fined; de·fin·ing**   **1 a** : to determine the essential qualities of ⟨*define* the idea of loyalty⟩ ⟨*define* a circle⟩   **b** : to set forth the meaning of ⟨*define* a word⟩   **c** : to specify (as a programming task) for a computer to use ⟨*define* a procedure⟩   **2 a** : to fix or mark the limits of ⟨the boundary was clearly *defined*⟩   **b** : to make distinct in outline ⟨the tree was well *defined* against the sky⟩ [Middle English *definen* "to define, mark the limits of", from early French *definer* and Latin *definire* (both same meaning), from Latin *de-* "from, away" and *finire* "to limit", from *finis* "end, limit" — related to FINAL, FINISH, INFINITY] — **de·fin·able** \-ˈfī-nə-bəl\ *adj* — **de·fin·er** *n*

def·i·nite \ˈdef-(ə-)nət\ *adj*   **1** : having certain or distinct limits : FIXED ⟨a *definite* period of time⟩   **2 a** : clear in meaning : EXPLICIT, EXACT ⟨a *definite* answer⟩   **b** : UNQUESTIONABLE ⟨a *definite* improvement⟩   **3** : typically designating an identified or immediately identifiable person or thing ⟨the *definite* article "the"⟩ — **def·i·nite·ly** *adv* — **def·i·nite·ness** *n*

def·i·ni·tion \ˌdef-ə-ˈnish-ən\ *n*   **1** : an act of determining or settling the limits   **2 a** : a statement of the meaning of a word or word group or a sign or symbol   **b** : the action or process of defining   **3 a** : the action or the power of making definite and clear   **b** : CLARITY, DISTINCTNESS — **def·i·ni·tion·al** \-ˈnish-nəl, -ən-°l\ *adj*

de·fin·i·tive \di-ˈfin-ət-iv\ *adj*   **1** : serving to provide a final solution : DECISIVE ⟨a *definitive* victory⟩   **2** : being the most accurate and apparently thorough ⟨the *definitive* book on the subject⟩   **3** : serving to define or specify precisely ⟨*definitive* laws⟩ — **de·fin·i·tive·ly** *adv* — **de·fin·i·tive·ness** *n*

de·flate \di-ˈflāt, ˈdē-\ *vb* **de·flat·ed; de·flat·ing**   **1** : to release air or gas from   **2** : to cause to move from a higher to a lower level : reduce from a state of inflation ⟨*deflate* the national economy⟩   **3** : to become deflated : COLLAPSE — **de·fla·tor** \-ˈflāt-ər\ *n*

de·fla·tion \di-ˈflā-shən, ˈdē-\ *n*   **1** : an act or instance of deflating : the state of being deflated   **2** : a reduction in the volume of available money or credit resulting in a decline of the general price level — **de·fla·tion·ary** \-shə-ˌner-ē\ *adj*

de·flect \di-ˈflekt\ *vb* : to turn or cause to turn aside (as from a course, direction, or position) ⟨a bullet *deflected* by striking a wall⟩ — **de·flec·tion** \-ˈflek-shən\ *n*

de·fo·li·ant \(ˈ)dē-ˈfō-lē-ənt\ *n* : a chemical that is applied to plants and causes their leaves to drop off

de·fo·li·ate \(ˈ)dē-ˈfō-lē-ˌāt\ *vb* **-at·ed; -at·ing** : to deprive of leaves — **de·fo·li·a·tion** \(ˌ)dē-ˌfō-lē-ˈā-shən\ *n* — **de·fo·li·a·tor** \(ˈ)dē-ˈfō-lē-ˌāt-ər\ *n*

de·for·es·ta·tion \(ˌ)dē-ˌfȯr-ə-ˈstā-shən, -ˌfär-\ *n* : the action or process of clearing an area of forests; *also* : the state of having been cleared of forests — **de·for·est** \(ˈ)dē-ˈfȯr-əst, -ˈfär-\ *vb*

de·form \di-ˈfȯ(ə)rm, ˈdē-\ *vb* : to make or become misshapen or changed in shape — **de·for·ma·tion** \ˌdē-ˌfȯr-ˈmā-shən, ˌdef-ər-\ *n*

de·formed *adj* : distorted in form : MISSHAPEN

de·for·mi·ty \di-ˈfȯr-mət-ē\ *n, pl* **-ties**   **1** : the state of being deformed   **2** : a physical blemish or twisting out of a natural shape or condition   **3** : a morally disgusting or artistically ugly imperfection

de·fraud \di-ˈfrȯd\ *vb* : to deprive of something by trickery, deception, or fraud — **de·fraud·er** \di-ˈfrȯd-ər\ *n*

de·fray \di-ˈfrā\ *vb* : to pay or provide for the payment of ⟨more money to *defray* expenses⟩

de·frost \di-ˈfrȯst, ˈdē-\ *vb*   **1** : to free from a frozen state : thaw out ⟨*defrost* meat⟩   **2** : to free from ice ⟨*defrost* a refrigerator⟩

deft \ˈdeft\ *adj* : quick and neat in action : SKILLFUL ⟨knitting with *deft* fingers⟩ — **deft·ly** *adv* — **deft·ness** \ˈdef(t)-nəs\ *n*

de·funct \di-ˈfəŋ(k)t\ *adj* : having finished the course of life or existence : DEAD, EXTINCT ⟨a *defunct* organization⟩

de·fy \di-ˈfī\ *vb* **de·fied; de·fy·ing**   **1** : to challenge to do something considered impossible : DARE ⟨the magician *defied* the audience to explain the trick⟩   **2** : to refuse boldly to obey or to yield to : DISREGARD ⟨*defy* public opinion⟩   **3** : to resist attempts at : WITHSTAND, BAFFLE ⟨a scene that *defies* description⟩ — **de·fi·er** \-ˈfī-(ə)r\ *n*

de·gas \(ˈ)dē-ˈgas\ *vb* : to free from gas

de·gen·er·a·cy \di-ˈjen-(ə-)rə-sē\ *n, pl* **-cies** : the state of being or process of becoming degenerate : DEGRADATION, DEBASEMENT

¹**de·gen·er·ate** \di-ˈjen-(ə-)rət\ *adj* : having degenerated

: DEBASED, DEGRADED — **de·gen·er·ate·ly** *adv*

²**degenerate** *n* : a degenerate person

³**de·gen·er·ate** \di-'jen-ə-ˌrāt\ *vb* **1** : to pass from a higher to a lower type or condition : DETERIORATE ⟨*degenerate* from the ancestral stock⟩ **2** : to undergo evolution toward an earlier or less highly organized biological form

de·gen·er·a·tion \di-ˌjen-ə-'rā-shən, ˌdē-\ *n* **1** : a lowering of power, vitality, or essential quality to a feebler and poorer kind or state **2 a** : a change in a tissue or an organ resulting in diminished activity or usefulness ⟨kidney *degeneration* in old age⟩ **b** : a condition marked by degeneration and by loss of organs present in related forms ⟨tapeworms exhibit extreme *degeneration*⟩

de·gen·er·a·tive \di-'jen-ə-ˌrāt-iv, -'jen-(ə)rət-iv\ *adj* : of, relating to, or tending to cause degeneration ⟨a *degenerative* disease⟩

deg·ra·da·tion \ˌdeg-rə-'dā-shən\ *n* **1 a** : a reduction in rank, dignity, or standing **b** : removal from office **2** : loss of honor or reputation **3** : DEGENERATION 1, DETERIORATION

de·grade \di-'grād\ *vb* **1** : to reduce from a higher to a lower rank or degree : deprive of an office or position **2** : to lower the character of : DEBASE **3** : to reduce the complexity of a chemical compound : DECOMPOSE — **de·grad·able** \-'grād-ə-bəl\ *adj* — **de·grad·er** *n*

de·gree \di-'grē\ *n* **1** : a step or stage in a process or series ⟨advance by *degrees*⟩ **2 a** : the intensity of something as measured by degrees ⟨murder in the first *degree*⟩ **b** : one of the forms used in the comparison of an adjective or adverb **3** : a rank or grade of official or social position ⟨persons of high *degree*⟩ **4 a** : a grade of membership in an order or society **b** : a title given a student by a college, university, or professional school upon completion of a program of study ⟨a *degree* of doctor of medicine⟩ **c** : an academic title granted to honor a person who is not a student **5** : one of the divisions marked on a measuring instrument (as a thermometer) **6** : a unit of measure for angles and arcs that for angles is equal to an angle with its vertex at the center of a circle and its sides cutting off ¹⁄₃₆₀ of the circumference and that for an arc of a circle is equal to ¹⁄₃₆₀ of the circumference **7 a** : a line or space of the musical staff **b** : a step, note, or tone of a musical scale — **to a degree 1** : to a remarkable extent **2** : in a small way

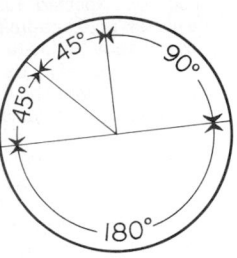

degree 6

de·hu·mid·i·fy \ˌdē-hyü-'mid-ə-ˌfī, ˌdē-yü-\ *vb* : to remove moisture from (as the air) — **de·hu·mid·i·fi·er** \-ˌfī(-ə)r\ *n*

de·hy·drate \(')dē-'hī-ˌdrāt\ *vb* **1** : to remove water from (as foods) **2** : to lose water or body fluids — **de·hy·dra·tion** \ˌdē-ˌhī-'drā-shən\ *n*

de·hy·dro·ge·nase \ˌdē-(ˌ)hī-'dräj-ə-ˌnās, (')dē-'hī-drə-jə-\ *n* : an enzyme that speeds up the removal and transfer of hydrogen

de·hy·dro·ge·na·tion \ˌdē-(ˌ)hī-ˌdräj-ə-'nā-shən, (ˌ)dē-ˌhī-drə-jə-\ *n* : the process of removing hydrogen from a chemical compound

de·ice \(')dē-'īs\ *vb* : to keep free or rid of ice — **de·ic·er** *n*

de·i·fy \'dē-ə-ˌfī\ *vb* **-fied; -fy·ing 1 a** : to make a god of ⟨Roman emperors were often *deified*⟩ **b** : to take as an object of worship ⟨Druids *deified* oak trees⟩ **2** : to glorify as of supreme worth ⟨*deify* money⟩ — **de·i·fi·ca·tion** \ˌdē-ə-fə-'kā-shən\ *n*

deign \'dān\ *vb* : to think proper to one's dignity ⟨did not *deign* to reply to the rude remark⟩

de·ion·ize \(')dē-'ī-ə-ˌnīz\ *vb* : to remove ions from

de·i·ty \'dē-ət-ē\ *n, pl* **-ties 1 a** : DIVINITY 1 **b** *cap* : GOD 1 ⟨the *Deity*⟩ **2 a** : GOD 2 **b** : GODDESS 1 [Middle English *deitee* "the nature of being divine", from early French *deité* (same meaning), derived from Latin *deus, Deus* "god" — related to ADIEU, ADIOS]

de·ject·ed \di-'jek-təd\ *adj* : low in spirits : SAD, DEPRESSED — **de·ject·ed·ly** *adv* — **de·ject·ed·ness** *n*

de·jec·tion \di-'jek-shən\ *n* : lowness of spirits

deka- *or* **dek-** — see DECA-

deka·gram *or* **deca·gram** \'dek-ə-ˌgram\ *n* — see METRIC SYSTEM table

deka·li·ter *or* **deca·li·ter** \'dek-ə-ˌlēt-ər\ *n* — see METRIC SYSTEM table

deka·me·ter *or* **deca·me·ter** \'dek-ə-ˌmēt-ər\ *n* — see METRIC SYSTEM table

Del·a·ware \'del-ə-ˌwa(ə)r, -ˌwe(ə)r, -wər\ *n* : a member of an American Indian people originally of the Delaware river valley

¹**de·lay** \di-'lā\ *n* **1** : the act of delaying : the state of being delayed **2** : the time during which something is delayed

²**delay** *vb* **1** : POSTPONE, PUT OFF **2** : to stop, detain, or hinder for a time ⟨*delayed* by a storm⟩ **3** : to move or act slowly — **delay·er** *n*

de·lec·ta·ble \di-'lek-tə-bəl\ *adj* **1** : highly pleasing : DELIGHTFUL **2** : DELICIOUS — **de·lec·ta·bly** \-blē\ *adv*

de·lec·ta·tion \ˌdē-ˌlek-'tā-shən, di-; ˌdel-ək-\ *n* **1** : ¹DELIGHT 1 **2** : something that gives pleasure : DIVERSION

¹**del·e·gate** \'del-i-gət, -ˌgāt\ *n* : a person sent with power to act for another : REPRESENTATIVE

²**del·e·gate** \'del-i-ˌgāt\ *vb* **-gat·ed; -gat·ing 1** : to entrust to another ⟨*delegate* authority⟩ **2** : to appoint as one's delegate

del·e·ga·tion \ˌdel-i-'gā-shən\ *n* **1** : the act of delegating power or authority to another **2** : one or more persons chosen to represent others

de·lete \di-'lēt\ *vb* **de·let·ed; de·let·ing** : to eliminate especially by blotting out, cutting out, or erasing — **de·le·tion** \di-'lē-shən\ *n*

del·e·te·ri·ous \ˌdel-ə-'tir-ē-əs\ *adj* : HARMFUL, NOXIOUS — **del·e·te·ri·ous·ly** *adv* — **del·e·te·ri·ous·ness** *n*

delft \'delft\ *n* : a Dutch pottery with a white glaze and blue decoration [named for *Delft,* an area in the Netherlands where the pottery was first made]

delft·ware \'delft-ˌtwa(ə)r, -ˌtwe(ə)r\ *n* : DELFT

deli \'del-ē\ *n, pl* **del·is** : DELICATESSEN 2

¹**de·lib·er·ate** \di-'lib-ə-ˌrāt\ *vb* **-at·ed; -at·ing** : to think about deliberately : consider problems and decisions carefully ⟨*deliberate* before answering⟩

Word History To weigh a decision is to think about it carefully, comparing one fact or idea with another as if by balancing them on a scale. The notion that slow and careful thought is like using a scale has given us the word *deliberate. Deliberate* can be traced back to the Latin verb *deliberare* meaning "to weigh in the mind". The core of this word is the noun *libra,* meaning "a scale". A deliberate decision, therefore, is one that has been carefully weighed. [from Latin *deliberatus,* past participle of *deliberare* "to weigh in the mind", derived from *de-* "from, away" and *libra* "scale, pound" — related to EQUILIBRIUM, LIBRA]

²**de·lib·er·ate** \di-'lib-(ə-)rət\ *adj* **1** : decided on as a result of careful thought : carefully considered ⟨a *deliberate* judgment⟩ **2** : done or said on purpose ⟨a *deliberate* lie⟩ **3** : considering facts and arguments carefully : careful and

\ə\ abut	\au̇\ **out**	\i\ **tip**	\ȯ\ **saw**	\u̇\ **foot**
\ər\ **further**	\ch\ **chin**	\ī\ **life**	\ȯi\ **coin**	\y\ **yet**
\a\ **mat**	\e\ **pet**	\j\ **job**	\th\ **thin**	\yü\ **few**
\ā\ **take**	\ē\ **easy**	\ŋ\ **sing**	\th\ **this**	\yu̇\ **cure**
\ä\ **cot, cart**	\g\ **go**	\ō\ **bone**	\ü\ **food**	\zh\ **vision**

slow in deciding ⟨a *deliberate* speaker⟩ **4** : slow in action : not hurried ⟨*deliberate* movements⟩ **syn** see VOLUNTARY — **de·lib·er·ate·ly** *adv* — **de·lib·er·ate·ness** *n*

de·lib·er·a·tion \di-ˌlib-ə-'rā-shən\ *n* **1** : the act of deliberating **2** : a discussion and consideration of the reasons for and against something **3** : the quality of being deliberate : DELIBERATENESS

de·lib·er·a·tive \di-'lib-ə-ˌrāt-iv, -'lib-(ə-)rət-iv\ *adj* : of, relating to, or engaged in deliberation

del·i·ca·cy \'del-i-kə-sē\ *n, pl* **-cies** **1** : something pleasing to eat because it is rare or a luxury **2 a** : fineness of structure : DAINTINESS ⟨lace of great *delicacy*⟩ **b** : weakness of body : FRAILTY **3** : the ability to express very slight degrees of feeling (as in painting or music) **4** : consideration for the feelings of others **5** : the ability to sense or indicate very slight differences : PRECISION **6** : the tendency to be or state of being squeamish **7** : the quality or state of requiring careful treatment ⟨the *delicacy* of a situation⟩

del·i·cate \'del-i-kət\ *adj* **1** : satisfying or pleasing because of fineness or mildness ⟨a *delicate* flavor⟩ ⟨*delicate* blossoms⟩ **2** : FASTIDIOUS **3** : able to sense or indicate very slight differences ⟨a *delicate* instrument⟩ **4** : easily unsettled or upset ⟨a *delicate* balance⟩ **5** : having fineness of structure, workmanship, or texture ⟨*delicate* lace⟩ **6** : easily torn or hurt; *also* : WEAK 1, SICKLY ⟨was too *delicate* to play football⟩ **7** : resulting from or requiring skill or careful treatment ⟨*delicate* handling of a difficult situation⟩ ⟨a *delicate* operation⟩ — **del·i·cate·ly** *adv* — **del·i·cate·ness** *n*

del·i·ca·tes·sen \ˌdel-i-kə-'tes-ᵊn\ *n pl* **1** : ready-to-eat food products (as cooked meats and prepared salads) **2** *sing, pl* **delicatessens** : a store where delicatessen are sold

Word History We owe both the word *delicatessen* and the special food it represents to the German immigrants who came to this country toward the end of the 19th century. But although the food was originally German, the word was not. The Germans borrowed the word from the French. The obsolete German word *delicatessen* is a plural form of *delicatesse* and means "delicacies, ready-to-eat foods". This word was borrowed from the French word *délicatesse,* meaning "delicacy". In English, *delicatessen* originally meant only the specially-prepared food. In time, the delicatessen store where this food was sold came to be called a *delicatessen,* and a new meaning for the word was born. Now the word is often shortened to *deli.* [from obsolete German *delicatessen* (now spelled *delikatessen*) "specially prepared ready-to-eat foods", plural of *delicatesse* "delicacy", from French *délicatesse* (same meaning), derived from Latin *delicatus* "delicate"]

de·li·cious \di-'lish-əs\ *adj* : giving great pleasure : DELIGHTFUL; *esp* : very pleasing to the taste — **de·li·cious·ly** *adv* — **de·li·cious·ness** *n*

De·li·cious \di-'lish-əs\ *n, pl* **De·li·cious·es** *or* **Delicious** : an important red or yellow market apple of American origin that has five bumps arranged around the end opposite the stem

¹de·light \di-'līt\ *n* **1** : extreme pleasure or satisfaction : JOY **2** : something that gives great pleasure

²delight *vb* **1** : to take great pleasure **2** : to give joy or satisfaction to : please greatly

de·light·ed \di-'līt-əd\ *adj* : highly pleased : GRATIFIED, JOYOUS — **de·light·ed·ly** *adv* — **de·light·ed·ness** *n*

de·light·ful \di-'līt-fəl\ *adj* : highly pleasing : giving delight — **de·light·ful·ly** \-fə-lē\ *adv* — **de·light·ful·ness** *n*

de·lim·it \di-'lim-ət\ *vb* : to fix or mark the limits of : BOUND — **de·lim·i·ta·tion** \-ˌlim-ə-'tā-shən\ *n*

de·lin·eate \di-'lin-ē-ˌāt\ *vb* **-eat·ed; -eat·ing** **1** : to indicate by lines : SKETCH **2** : to describe in sharp or vivid detail ⟨*delineate* the characters in a story⟩ — **de·lin·ea-**

tion \-ˌlin-ē-'ā-shən\ *n* — **de·lin·ea·tor** \-'lin-ē-ˌāt-ər\ *n*

¹de·lin·quent \di-'liŋ-kwənt\ *n* : a delinquent person

²delinquent *adj* **1** : offending by neglect or violation of duty or of law **2** : being overdue in payment ⟨a *delinquent* charge account⟩ — **de·lin·quen·cy** \-kwən-sē\ *n* — **de·lin·quent·ly** *adv*

del·i·quesce \ˌdel-ə-'kwes\ *vb* **-quesced; -quesc·ing** : to dissolve or melt away; *esp* : to exhibit the behavior of a deliquescent substance

del·i·ques·cent \ˌdel-ə-'kwes-ᵊnt\ *adj* **1** : tending to melt or dissolve; *esp* : tending to dissolve gradually by absorbing moisture from the air **2** : having repeated division into branches ⟨elms are *deliquescent* trees⟩ — **del·i·ques·cence** \-ᵊn(t)s\ *n*

de·lir·i·ous \di-'lir-ē-əs\ *adj* **1** : marked by delirium **2** : wildly excited — **de·lir·i·ous·ly** *adv*

de·lir·i·um \di-'lir-ē-əm\ *n* **1** : a mental disturbance marked by confusion, disturbed speech, and hallucinations **2** : wild excitement

de·liv·er \di-'liv-ər\ *vb* **de·liv·ered; de·liv·er·ing** \-(ə-)riŋ\ **1** : to set free : SAVE ⟨*deliver* us from evil⟩ **2** : HAND OVER, TRANSFER ⟨*deliver* a letter⟩ **3** : to assist in giving birth; *also* : to aid in the birth of **4** : ²UTTER 2 ⟨*deliver* a speech⟩ **5** : to send to an intended target or destination ⟨*deliver* a pitch⟩ **6** : to produce the promised, desired, or expected results ⟨*deliver* on a promise⟩ — **de·liv·er·able** \-(ə-)rə-bəl\ *adj* — **de·liv·er·er** \-ər-ər\ *n*

de·liv·er·ance \di-'liv-(ə-)rən(t)s\ *n* **1** : an act of delivering or the state of being delivered; *esp* : SALVATION 3, RESCUE ⟨*deliverance* from the hands of the enemy⟩ **2** : something delivered or communicated; *esp* : a publicly expressed opinion or decision

de·liv·ery \di-'liv-(ə-)rē\ *n, pl* **-er·ies** **1** : a delivering from something that restricts or burdens **2 a** : the act of handing over **b** : a legal transfer of right or title **c** : something delivered at one time or in one unit **3** : the action of giving birth **4** : a delivering especially of a speech **5** : manner or style of delivering

de·liv·ery·man \di-'liv-(ə-)rē-mən, -ˌman\ *n* : a person who delivers goods to customers usually over a regular local route

dell \'del\ *n* : a secluded small valley

de·louse \(')dē-'laus, -'lauz\ *vb* **de·loused; de·lous·ing** : to remove lice from

del·phin·i·um \del-'fin-ē-əm\ *n* : any of a large genus of erect branching herbs related to the buttercups and producing flowers in showy spikes

del·ta \'del-tə\ *n* **1** : the 4th letter of the Greek alphabet — Δ or δ **2** : something shaped like a capital Δ; *esp* : the triangular or fan-shaped piece of land made by deposits of mud and sand at the mouth of a river — **del·ta·ic** \del-'tā-ik\ *adj*

de·lude \di-'lüd\ *vb* **de·lud·ed; de·lud·ing** : to lead into error : mislead the judgment of : DECEIVE, TRICK ⟨*deluded* by false promises⟩ — **de·lud·er** *n*

¹del·uge \'del-yüj\ *n* **1 a** : an overflowing of the land by water : FLOOD **b** : a drenching rain **2** : an overwhelming amount or number ⟨a *deluge* of Christmas mail⟩

²deluge *vb* **del·uged; del·ug·ing** **1** : to overflow with water : INUNDATE, FLOOD **2** : to overwhelm as if with a deluge ⟨*deluged* with inquiries⟩

de·lu·sion \di-'lü-zhən\ *n* **1** : the act of deluding : the state of being deluded **2 a** : a mistaken or misleading belief **b** : a false belief that persists despite the facts and occurs especially in some mentally disturbed states — **de·lu·sion·al** \-'lüzh-nəl, -ən-ᵊl\ *adj*

de·lu·sive \di-'lü-siv, -ziv\ *adj* : deluding or likely to delude — **de·lu·sive·ly** *adv*

de·lu·so·ry \di-'lü-sə-rē, -zə-\ *adj* : DECEPTIVE, DELUSIVE

de·luxe \di-'lùks, -'ləks, -'lüks\ *adj* : very luxurious or elegant ⟨a *deluxe* edition⟩

delve \'delv\ *vb* **delved; delv·ing** **1** : to dig or labor with a spade   **2** : to make a careful or thorough search for information — **delv·er** n

de·mag·ne·tize \(')dē-'mag-nə-,tīz\ vb : to cause to lose magnetic properties — **de·mag·ne·ti·za·tion** \(,)dē-,mag-nət-ə-'zā-shən\ n

dem·a·gogue or **dem·a·gog** \'dem-ə-,gäg\ n : a person who appeals to the emotions and prejudices of people in order to arouse discontent and advance his or her own political purposes — **dem·a·gog·ic** \,dem-ə-'gäg-ik also -'gäj-\ adj — **dem·a·gogu·ery** \'dem-ə-,gäg-(ə-)rē\ n — **dem·a·gogy** \-,gäg-ē, -,gäj-, -,gō-jē\ n

¹de·mand \di-'mand\ n   **1 a** : an act of demanding   **b** : something claimed as due   **2 a** : an expressed desire   **b** : the ability and desire to purchase goods or services at a specified time and price   **c** : the quantity of an article or service that is wanted at a specified price   **3** : a seeking or state of being sought after ⟨tickets are in great *demand*⟩   **4** : an urgent need or requirement ⟨*demands* on her energy⟩ — **on demand** : upon request for payment

²demand vb   **1** : to ask or call for with authority : claim as one's right ⟨*demand* payment of a debt⟩ ⟨*demand* an apology⟩   **2** : to ask earnestly or in the manner of a command ⟨the guard *demanded* the password⟩   **3** : ²NEED 2, REQUIRE ⟨an illness that *demands* constant care⟩ — **de·mand·able** \-'man-də-bəl\ adj — **de·mand·er** n

de·mand·ing \di-'man-diŋ\ adj : making many or difficult demands : EXACTING ⟨a *demanding* job⟩ — **de·mand·ing·ly** adv

de·mar·cate \di-'mär-,kāt, 'dē-,mär-\ vb **-cat·ed; -cat·ing**   **1** : to mark the limits or boundaries of   **2** : to set apart : SEPARATE — **de·mar·ca·tion** \,dē-,mär-'kā-shən\ n

¹de·mean \di-'mēn\ vb **de·meaned; de·mean·ing** : to conduct or behave (oneself) usually in a proper manner ⟨he *demeans* himself like a true gentleman⟩

²demean vb **de·meaned; de·mean·ing** : DEGRADE 2, DEBASE ⟨*demeaned* themselves by dishonesty⟩

de·mean·or \di-'mē-nər\ n : outward manner or behavior : CONDUCT, BEARING

de·ment·ed \di-'ment-əd\ adj : MAD 1, INSANE — **de·ment·ed·ly** adv

de·men·tia \di-'men-chə\ n : INSANITY 2

de·mer·it \di-'mer-ət\ n   **1** : a quality that deserves blame : FAULT   **2** : a mark placed against a person's record for some fault or offense

de·mesne \di-'mān, -'mēn\ n   **1** : REALM 2, DOMAIN   **2** : land actually possessed by the lord of an estate and not held by tenants   **3 a** : the land attached to a mansion   **b** : property that is land : ESTATE   **c** : REGION 2a, TERRITORY

demi- prefix : one that partly belongs to (a specified type or class) ⟨*demi*god⟩ [derived from Latin *dimidius* "half"]

demi·god \'dem-i-,gäd\ n   **1** : one who is partly divine and partly human   **2** : an outstanding person who seems godlike

demi·john \dem-i-,jän\ n : a large bottle of glass or stoneware enclosed in a basket of the same shape

de·mil·i·ta·rize \(')dē-'mil-ə-tə-,rīz\ vb : to strip of military forces, weapons, or fortification ⟨a *demilitarized* zone⟩ — **de·mil·i·ta·ri·za·tion** \(,)dē-,mil-ə-tə-rə-'zā-shən\ n

de·mise \di-'mīz\ n   **1** : DEATH 1   **2** : an ending of existence or activity ⟨the *demise* of a newspaper⟩

demi·tasse \'dem-i-,tas, -,täs\ n : a small cup of black coffee; also : the cup used to serve it

demo \'dem-ō\ n, pl **dem·os** : DEMONSTRATOR 2

de·mo·bi·lize \di-'mō-bə-,līz, (')dē-\ vb   **1** : to dismiss

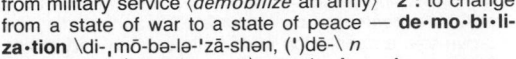

demijohn

from military service ⟨*demobilize* an army⟩   **2** : to change from a state of war to a state of peace — **de·mo·bi·li·za·tion** \di-,mō-bə-lə-'zā-shən, (')dē-\ n

de·moc·ra·cy \di-'mäk-rə-sē\ n, pl **-cies**   **1 a** : government by the people; esp : rule of the majority   **b** : government in which the supreme power is held by the people and used by them directly or indirectly through representation   **2** : a political unit (as a nation) that has a democratic government   **3** : belief in or practice of the idea that all people are socially equal [from early French *democratie* "democracy", from Latin *democratia* (same meaning), from Greek *demokratia* "democracy", from *dēmos* "people, the masses" and *-kratia* "rule, government", from *kratos* "strength, power, authority" — related to EPIDEMIC]

dem·o·crat \'dem-ə-,krat\ n   **1** : one who believes in or practices democracy   **2** cap : a member of the Democratic party of the U.S.

dem·o·crat·ic \,dem-ə-'krat-ik\ adj   **1** : of, relating to, or favoring political, social, or economic democracy   **2** cap : of or relating to a major U.S. political party associated with policies of helping the common people and encouraging cooperation between nations   **3** : of, relating to, or appealing to the common people   **4** : favoring social equality : not snobbish — **dem·o·crat·i·cal·ly** \-i-k(ə-)lē\ adv

Democratic–Republican adj : of or relating to an early 19th century American political party preferring strict interpretation of the constitution and emphasizing states' rights

de·moc·ra·tize \di-'mäk-rə-,tīz\ vb **-tized; -tiz·ing** : to make democratic — **de·moc·ra·ti·za·tion** \-,mäk-rət-ə-'zā-shən\ n

de·mod·u·late \(')dē-'mäj-ə-,lāt\ vb : to get the information meaning from (a modulated radio, laser, or computer signal)

de·mog·ra·phy \di-'mäg-rə-fē\ n : the statistical study of human populations — **de·mog·ra·pher** \-fər\ n — **de·mo·graph·ic** \,dē-mə-'graf-ik, ,dem-ə-\ adj

de·mol·ish \di-'mäl-ish\ vb   **1 a** : TEAR DOWN, RAZE   **b** : to break to pieces : SMASH   **2** : to do away with : put an end to — **de·mol·ish·er** n — **de·mol·ish·ment** \-ish-mənt\ n

de·mo·li·tion \,dem-ə-'lish-ən, ,dē-mə-\ n : the act of demolishing; esp : destruction by means of explosives

de·mon or **dae·mon** \'dē-mən\ n   **1** : an evil spirit   **2** usually **daemon** : an accompanying power or spirit : GENIUS   **3** usually **daemon** : DEMIGOD 1   **4** : one that has a lot of energy   **5** : a word that is frequently misspelled — **de·mon·ic** \di-'män-ik\ adj

¹de·mo·ni·ac \di-'mō-nē-,ak\ also **de·mo·ni·a·cal** \,dē-mə-'nī-ə-kəl\ adj   **1** : possessed or influenced by a demon   **2** : of, relating to, or suggestive of a demon : DEVILISH, FIENDISH ⟨*demoniac* cruelty⟩ — **de·mo·ni·a·cal·ly** \,dē-mə-'nī-ə-k(ə-)lē\ adv

²demoniac n : one possessed by a demon

de·mon·stra·ble \di-'män(t)-strə-bəl\ adj : capable of being demonstrated or proved — **de·mon·stra·bly** \-blē\ adv

dem·on·strate \'dem-ən-,strāt\ vb **-strat·ed; -strat·ing**   **1** : to show clearly   **2 a** : to prove or make clear by reasoning or evidence   **b** : to illustrate and explain especially with examples   **3** : to show publicly the good qualities of a product ⟨*demonstrate* a new car⟩   **4** : to make a public display (as of feeling or military force) ⟨citizens *demonstrated* in protest⟩

dem·on·stra·tion \,dem-ən-'strā-shən\ n   **1** : an act, process, or means of demonstrating the truth of something:

\ə\ abut	\au̇\ out	\i\ tip	\ȯ\ saw	\u̇\ foot
\ər\ further	\ch\ chin	\ī\ life	\ȯi\ coin	\y\ yet
\a\ mat	\e\ pet	\j\ job	\th\ thin	\yü\ few
\ā\ take	\ē\ easy	\ŋ\ sing	\t̲h̲\ this	\yu̇\ cure
\ä\ cot, cart	\g\ go	\ō\ bone	\ü\ food	\zh\ vision

a : convincing evidence   **b** : an explanation (as of a theory) by experiment   **c** : a course of reasoning intended to prove that a conclusion must be true when certain conditions are accepted   **d** : a showing or using of a product for sale to display its good points   **2** : an outward expression or display ⟨a *demonstration* of joy⟩   **3** : a show of armed force   **4** : a public display of group feelings toward a person or cause

¹de·mon·stra·tive \di-'män(t)-strət-iv\ *adj*   **1** : characterized or established by demonstration ⟨*demonstrative* reasoning⟩   **2** : indicating the one referred to and pointing it out from others of the same kind ⟨the *demonstrative* pronoun "this" in "this is my hat"⟩ ⟨the *demonstrative* adjective "that" in "that book"⟩   **3** : showing feeling freely ⟨a *demonstrative* greeting⟩ — **de·mon·stra·tive·ly** *adv*

²demonstrative *n* : a demonstrative word; *esp* : a demonstrative pronoun

dem·on·stra·tor \'dem-ən-,strāt-ər\ *n*   **1** : a person who makes or takes part in a demonstration   **2** : a manufactured article (as an automobile) used for purposes of demonstration

de·mor·al·ize \di-'mȯr-ə-,līz, -'mär-\ *vb*   **1** : to make bad or evil   **2** : to weaken in spirit or discipline ⟨fear *demoralized* the army⟩ — **de·mor·al·i·za·tion** \-,mȯr-ə-lə-'zā-shən, -,mär-\ *n* — **de·mor·al·iz·er** \-'mȯr-ə-,lī-zər, -'mär-\ *n*

de·mote \di-'mōt, 'dē-\ *vb* **de·mot·ed; de·mot·ing** : to reduce to a lower grade or rank — **de·mo·tion** \di-'mō-shən, 'dē-\ *n*

de·mount \(')dē-'mau̇nt\ *vb*   **1** : to remove from an attached position   **2** : to take apart : DISASSEMBLE — **de·mount·able** \-ə-bəl\ *adj*

¹de·mur \di-'mər\ *vb* **de·murred; de·mur·ring** : ²OBJECT 2

²demur *n* : the act of objecting : PROTEST ⟨accepted without *demur*⟩

de·mure \di-'myu̇(ə)r\ *adj*   **1** : MODEST 1   **2** : falsely modest, reserved, or serious : COY — **de·mure·ly** *adv* — **de·mure·ness** *n*

den \'den\ *n*   **1** : the shelter or resting place of a wild animal   **2** : a hiding place (as for thieves)   **3** : a dirty run-down place in which people live or gather ⟨*dens* of misery⟩   **4** : a comfortable room set apart for reading and relaxation   **5** : a division of a Cub Scout pack

de·na·ture \(')dē-'nā-chər\ *vb* **de·na·tured; de·na·tur·ing** \-'nāch-(ə-)riŋ\ : to remove the natural qualities of: as **a** : to make (alcohol) unfit for drinking without taking away usefulness for other purposes   **b** : to modify the structure of (as an enzyme) so that the original properties are removed or diminished — **de·na·tur·ation** \(,)dē-,nā-chə-'rā-shən\ *n*

den·drite \'den-,drīt\ *n*   **1** : a branching figure (as in a mineral or stone) resembling a tree   **2** : any of the usually branching protoplasmic extensions of a nerve cell over which impulses travel toward the cell body — compare AXON — **den·drit·ic** \den-'drit-ik\ *adj*

den·drol·o·gy \den-'dräl-ə-jē\ *n* : the study of trees

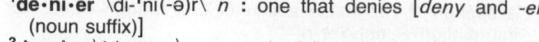

dendrite 1

Den·eb \'den-,eb, -əb\ *n* : the brightest star in the group of stars of Cygnus

de·ni·al \di-'nī(-ə)l\ *n*   **1** : a refusal to grant something asked for   **2** : a refusal to admit the truth of a statement : CONTRADICTION ⟨a flat *denial* of the charges⟩   **3** : a refusal to admit the truth of a statement   **4** : a refusal to accept or believe in something ⟨make a public *denial* of political beliefs once held⟩   **5** : a cutting down or limiting of a person's own desires or activity ⟨*denial* of one's appetite⟩

¹de·ni·er \di-'nī(-ə)r\ *n* : one that denies [*deny* and -*er* (noun suffix)]

²den·ier \'den-yər\ *n* : a unit of fineness for silk, rayon, or nylon yarn [Middle English *denere* "small silver coin formerly used in Europe", from early French *denier* (same meaning), from Latin *denarius* "coin valued at 10 asses", derived from *deni* "ten each", from *decem* "ten"]

den·im \'den-əm\ *n*   **1** : a firm durable twilled usually cotton fabric   **2** *pl* : overalls or trousers of denim

Word History Many fabrics have been named for the places where they were once made. *Denim* gets its name from Nimes, a city in France famous for its textiles. But the name came about in an unusual way. The fabric, a heavy serge, was originally called *serge de Nimes*, literally "serge from Nimes". The "s" on *Nimes* is not pronounced in French, so when the name of the fabric came into English, it was often written *serge de Nim* and later *serge denim*. In time this was shortened to simply *denim*. [from French *(serge) de Nimes* "serge (fabric) from Nimes (city in France)"]

de·ni·tri·fi·ca·tion \(,)dē-,nī-trə-fə-'kā-shən\ *n* : a process by which various nitrogen compounds are changed or broken down and which is usually brought about (as in the soil or in sewage) by denitrifying bacteria with formation of free nitrogen

de·ni·tri·fy \(')dē-'nī-trə-,fī\ *vb* : to change a nitrogen compound to free nitrogen or to a different state especially as a step in the nitrogen cycle

de·ni·tri·fy·ing bacteria \(')dē-'nī-trə-,fī-iŋ-\ *n pl* : bacteria that bring about denitrification especially with the formation of nitrogen gas

den·i·zen \'den-ə-zən\ *n* : INHABITANT; *esp* : a person, animal, or plant found in a particular region or environment

den mother *n* : a female adult leader of a Cub Scout den

de·nom·i·nate \di-'näm-ə-,nāt\ *vb* : to give a name to : DESIGNATE

de·nom·i·nate number \di-,näm-ə-nət-\ *n* : a number (as 7 in *7 meters*) that specifies a quantity in terms of a unit of measurement

de·nom·i·na·tion \di-,näm-ə-'nā-shən\ *n*   **1** : an act of denominating   **2** : one of a series of related values each having a special name ⟨a $5 bill and a $10 bill represent two *denominations* of U.S. money⟩   **3** : ¹NAME 1, DESIGNATION; *esp* : a general name for a class of things   **4** : a religious body made up of a number of congregations with similar beliefs — **de·nom·i·na·tion·al** \-shnəl, -shən-ᵊl\ *adj*

de·nom·i·na·tor \di-'näm-ə-,nāt-ər\ *n* : the part of a fraction that is below the line indicating division and that in fractions with 1 as the numerator indicates into how many parts the unit is divided : DIVISOR

de·no·ta·tion \,dē-nō-'tā-shən\ *n*   **1** : an act or process of denoting   **2** : ¹MEANING 1a; *esp* : a direct specific meaning as distinct from connotations   **3** : a term or label that indicates something : NAME, SIGN — **de·no·ta·tive** \'dē-nō-,tāt-iv, di-'nōt-ət-iv\ *adj*

de·note \di-'nōt\ *vb*   **1** : to mark out plainly : point out : INDICATE ⟨the hands of a clock *denote* the time⟩   **2** : to make known : SHOW ⟨smiled to *denote* pleasure⟩   **3** : to have the meaning of : MEAN, NAME ⟨the word "derby" can *denote* a horse race or a kind of hat⟩

de·noue·ment \,dā-nü-'mäṅ, dā-'nü-,\ *n*   **1** : the final solution or untangling of the conflicts or difficulties that make up the plot of a literary work   **2** : a solution or working out especially of a complicated or difficult situation

de·nounce \di-'nau̇n(t)s\ *vb* **de·nounced; de·nounc·ing**   **1** : to point out as deserving blame or punishment   **2** : to inform against : ACCUSE   **3** : to announce formally the ending of (as a treaty) — **de·nounce·ment** \-mənt\ *n* — **de·nounc·er** *n*

dense \'den(t)s\ *adj* **dens·er; dens·est**   **1** : marked by closeness or crowding together of parts ⟨a *dense* forest⟩

2 : mentally dull   3 : ¹THICK 4 ⟨*dense* fog⟩   4 : having between any two mathematical elements at least one element ⟨the set of rational numbers is *dense*⟩ — **dense·ly** *adv* — **dense·ness** *n*

den·si·ty \'den(t)-sət-ē\ *n, pl* **-ties**   1 : the quality or state of being dense   2 : the quantity of something per unit volume, unit area, or unit length: as   **a** : the mass of a substance per unit volume ⟨*density* expressed in grams per cubic centimeter⟩   **b** : the average number of individuals or units in a unit of area or volume ⟨population *density*⟩   3 : STUPIDITY 1

¹dent \'dent\ *vb*   1 : to make a dent in or on   2 : to become marked by a dent

²dent *n*   1 : a notch or hollow made by a blow or by pressure   2 **a** : an impression or effect made usually against resistance ⟨that purchase made a big *dent* in our savings⟩   **b** : noticeable progress ⟨made a *dent* in our pile of work⟩

den·tal \'dent-ᵊl\ *adj* : of or relating the teeth or dentistry [from Latin *dentalis* "relating to the teeth", from *dent-, dens* "tooth" — related to DANDELION, INDENT, TRIDENT]

dental floss *n* : a usually flattened thread used to clean between the teeth

dental hygienist *n* : a person who assists a dentist especially in cleaning teeth

den·ti·frice \'dent-ə-frəs\ *n* : a powder, paste, or liquid for cleaning the teeth

den·tin \'dent-ᵊn\ *or* **den·tine** \'den-,tēn, den-'tēn\ *n* : a bonelike material that contains lime salts and makes up the principal mass of a tooth — **den·tin·al** \den-'tēn-ᵊl, 'dent-ən-ᵊl\ *adj*

den·tist \'dent-əst\ *n* : a professional person who is trained in the care, treatment, and repair of the teeth and the fitting of artificial teeth

den·tist·ry \'dent-ə-strē\ *n* : the profession or practice of a dentist

den·ti·tion \den-'tish-ən\ *n* : the number, kind, and arrangement of teeth (as of a person or animal)

den·ture \'den-chər\ *n* : a set of teeth; *esp* : a partial or complete set of false teeth

de·nude \di-'n(y)üd\ *vb* **de·nud·ed; de·nud·ing** : to strip of covering : lay bare ⟨erosion that *denudes* the rocks of soil⟩ — **de·nu·da·tion** \,dē-(,)n(y)ü-'dā-shən, ,den-yù-\ *n*

de·nun·ci·a·tion \di-,nən(t)-sē-'ā-shən\ *n* : the act of denouncing; *esp* : a public charge of wrongdoing ⟨publish a *denunciation* of an official⟩ — **de·nun·ci·a·to·ry** \-'nən(t)-sē-ə-,tōr-ē, -,tòr-\ *adj*

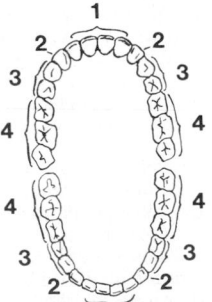

dentition: *top* upper jaw, *bottom* lower jaw, *1* incisors, *2* canines, *3* premolars, *4* molars

de·ny \di-'nī\ *vb* **de·nied; de·ny·ing**   1 : to declare not to be true : CONTRADICT ⟨*deny* a report⟩   2 : to refuse to grant ⟨*deny* a request⟩   3 : to refuse to accept the existence or truth of

de·odor·ant \dē-'ōd-ə-rənt\ *n* : a preparation that destroys or masks unpleasant odors — **deodorant** *adj*

de·odor·ize \dē-'ōd-ə-,rīz\ *vb* **-ized; -iz·ing** : to eliminate or prevent the unpleasant odor of — **de·odor·iz·er** *n*

de·ox·i·dize \(')dē-'äk-sə-,dīz\ *vb* : to remove oxygen from

de·oxy·ri·bo·nu·cle·ic acid \(,)dē-,äk-sē-,rī-bō-n(y)ù-,klē-ik-, -,klā-\ *n* : DNA

de·oxy·ri·bose \dē-,äk-sē-'rī-,bōs\ *n* : a sugar that has five carbon atoms and four oxygen atoms in each molecule and is part of DNA — compare RIBOSE

de·part \di-'pärt\ *vb*   1 **a** : to go away or go away from

: LEAVE   **b** : ¹DIE 1   2 : to turn aside : DEVIATE

de·part·ed *adj*   1 : BYGONE   2 : no longer living

de·part·ment \di-'pärt-mənt\ *n*   1 : a distinct area of interest or activity ⟨taking care of the cat is not my *department*⟩   2 **a** : a major administrative division of a government or business   **b** : a major territorial administrative division   **c** : a division of a college or school giving instruction in a particular subject   **d** : a section of a department store — **de·part·men·tal** \di-,pärt-'ment-ᵊl, ,dē-\ *adj* — **de·part·men·tal·ly** \-ᵊl-ē\ *adv*

department store *n* : a store having separate departments for a wide variety of goods

de·par·ture \di-'pär-chər\ *n*   1 : the act of going away   2 : a setting out (as on a new course)   3 : DIVERGENCE 3

de·pend \di-'pend\ *vb*   1 : to be determined by or based on ⟨success of the picnic will *depend* on the weather⟩   2 : ²TRUST 1a, RELY ⟨a person you can *depend* on⟩   3 : to rely for support ⟨children *depend* on their parents⟩   4 : to hang down ⟨a vine *depending* from a tree⟩ [Middle English *dependen* "to exist or result from some other condition, hang down", from early French *dependre* (same meaning), derived from Latin *dependēre* "to hang down, hang from", from *de-* "from, down" and *pendēre* "to hang" — related to PENDULUM, PERPENDICULAR]

de·pend·able \di-'pen-də-bəl\ *adj* : capable of being depended on : TRUSTWORTHY, RELIABLE — **de·pend·abil·i·ty** \-,pen-də-'bil-ət-ē\ *n* — **de·pend·ably** \-'pen-də-blē\ *adv*

de·pend·ence \di-'pen-dən(t)s\ *n*   1 : the quality or state of being dependent; *esp* : the quality or state of being influenced by or subject to another   2 : RELIANCE 2, TRUST   3 : something on which one relies

de·pend·en·cy \di-'pen-dən-sē\ *n, pl* **-cies**   1 : DEPENDENCE 1   2 : a territory under the authority of a nation but not formally a part of it

¹de·pend·ent \di-'pen-dənt\ *adj*   1 : hanging down   2 **a** : determined by something else   **b** : relying on another for support ⟨*dependent* children⟩   **c** : being under another's authority ⟨a *dependent* territory⟩   3 : ¹SUBORDINATE 3a ⟨a *dependent* clause⟩ — **de·pend·ent·ly** *adv*

²dependent *also* **de·pend·ant** \-dənt\ *n* : a person who relies on another for support

dependent variable *n* : a variable whose value can be found from one or more other variables whose value is known first — compare INDEPENDENT VARIABLE

de·pict \di-'pikt\ *vb*   1 : to represent by a picture   2 : to describe in words — **de·pic·tion** \-'pik-shən\ *n*

de·pil·a·to·ry \di-'pil-ə-,tōr-ē, -,tòr-\ *n, pl* **-ries** : a preparation for removing hair, wool, or bristles

de·plete \di-'plēt\ *vb* **de·plet·ed; de·plet·ing** : to reduce in amount by using up : exhaust especially of strength or resources ⟨soil *depleted* of minerals⟩ ⟨a *depleted* treasury⟩ — **de·ple·tion** \-'plē-shən\ *n*

de·plor·able \di-'plōr-ə-bəl, -'plòr-\ *adj*   1 : deserving to be deplored : LAMENTABLE ⟨a *deplorable* accident⟩   2 : very bad : WRETCHED ⟨*deplorable* conditions⟩ — **de·plor·able·ness** *n* — **de·plor·ably** \-blē\ *adv*

de·plore \di-'plō(ə)r, -'plò(ə)r\ *vb* **de·plored; de·plor·ing**   1 **a** : to feel or express grief for   **b** : to regret strongly   2 : to consider unfortunate or deserving of disapproval — **de·plor·er** *n* — **de·plor·ing·ly** \-iŋ-lē\ *adv*

de·ploy \di-'plòi\ *vb* : to spread out or place in position for some purpose ⟨troops *deployed* for battle⟩ ⟨*deploy* police to prevent a riot⟩ — **de·ploy·ment** \-mənt\ *n*

de·po·nent \di-'pō-nənt\ *n* : a person who gives evidence

de·pop·u·late \(')dē-'päp-yə-,lāt\ *vb* : to reduce greatly

\ə\ abut		\aú\ out	\i\ tip	\ò\ saw	\ú\ foot
\ər\ further		\ch\ chin	\ī\ life	\òi\ coin	\y\ yet
\a\ mat		\e\ pet	\j\ job	\th\ thin	\yü\ few
\ā\ take		\ē\ easy	\ŋ\ sing	\th\ this	\yù\ cure
\ä\ cot, cart		\g\ go	\ō\ bone	\ü\ food	\zh\ vision

the population of (as a city or region) by destroying or driving away the inhabitants ⟨*depopulated* by plague⟩ — **de·pop·u·la·tion** \(ˌ)dē-ˌpäp-yə-'lā-shən\ *n*

de·port \di-'pō(ə)rt, -'pó(ə)rt\ *vb* **1** : to cause (oneself) to act in a certain way : CONDUCT ⟨*deported* themselves well in public⟩ **2** : to force (a person who is not a citizen) to leave a country — **de·por·ta·tion** \ˌdē-ˌpōr-'tā-shən, -ˌpòr-\ *n* — **de·por·tee** \ˌdē-ˌpōr-'tē, -ˌpòr-\ *n*

de·port·ment \di-'pōrt-mənt, -'pòrt-\ *n* : manner of conducting oneself : BEHAVIOR

de·pose \di-'pōz\ *vb* **de·posed; de·pos·ing** **1** : to remove from a high office ⟨*deposed* the king⟩ **2** : to testify under oath or by a sworn written statement

¹**de·pos·it** \di-'päz-ət\ *vb* **1** : to place for safekeeping; *esp* : to put money in a bank **2** : to give as a pledge that a purchase will be made or a service used ⟨*deposit* $10 on a new bicycle⟩ **3** : to lay down : PLACE, PUT ⟨*deposit* a parcel on a table⟩ **4** : to let fall or sink ⟨silt *deposited* by a flood⟩ — **de·pos·i·tor** \-'päz-ət-ər, -'päz-tər\ *n*

²**deposit** *n* **1** : the state of being deposited ⟨money on *deposit*⟩ **2 a** : something placed for safekeeping; *esp* : money deposited in a bank **b** : money given as a pledge or down payment **3** : an act of depositing **4** : something laid or thrown down ⟨a *deposit* of silt left by the flood⟩ **5** : an accumulation of mineral matter (as ore, oil, or gas) in nature

de·po·si·tion \ˌdep-ə-'zish-ən, ˌdē-pə-\ *n* **1** : the act of removing a person from high office ⟨the *deposition* of the king⟩ **2** : a statement especially in writing made under oath **3** : the action or process of depositing ⟨the *deposition* of silt by a stream⟩ **4** : something deposited : DEPOSIT — **de·po·si·tion·al** \-'zish-nəl, -ən-ºl\ *adj*

de·pos·i·to·ry \di-'päz-ə-ˌtōr-ē, -ˌtòr-\ *n, pl* **-ries** : a place where something is deposited especially for safekeeping

de·pot *senses 1 & 2 are* 'dep-ˌō *also* 'dē-ˌpō, *sense 3 is* 'dē-ˌpō *sometimes* 'dep-ˌō\ *n* **1** : a place of deposit for goods : STOREHOUSE **2** : a place where military supplies are kept or where troops are assembled and trained **3** : a building for railroad or bus passengers or freight : STATION

de·prave \di-'prāv\ *vb* **de·praved; de·prav·ing** : to make evil : PERVERT — **de·praved·ly** \-'prā-vəd-lē, -'prāvd-lē\ *adv* — **de·praved·ness** \-'prā-vəd-nəs, -'prāvd-nəs\ *n*

de·prav·i·ty \di-'prav-ət-ē\ *n, pl* **-ties** **1** : the quality or state of being depraved **2** : a corrupt act or practice

dep·re·cate \'dep-ri-ˌkāt\ *vb* **-cat·ed; -cat·ing** **1** : to express disapproval of **2** : to represent as of little value : DEPRECIATE — **dep·re·cat·ing·ly** \-ˌkāt-iŋ-lē\ *adv* — **dep·re·ca·tion** \ˌdep-ri-'kā-shən\ *n*

dep·re·ca·to·ry \'dep-ri-kə-ˌtōr-ē, -ˌtòr-\ *adj* : seeking to avoid disapproval : APOLOGETIC

de·pre·ci·ate \di-'prē-shē-ˌāt\ *vb* **-at·ed; -at·ing** **1** : to lower the price or value of ⟨*depreciate* the currency⟩ **2** : to represent as of little value : DISPARAGE **3** : to fall in value ⟨new cars *depreciate* rapidly⟩ — **de·pre·cia·tive** \-'prē-shət-iv, -shē-ˌāt-iv\ *adj* — **de·pre·cia·to·ry** \-shə-ˌtōr-ē, -ˌtòr-\ *adj*

de·pre·ci·a·tion \di-ˌprē-shē-'ā-shən\ *n* **1** : a decline in the purchasing power or exchange value of money **2** : the act of making a person or a thing seem little or unimportant : DISPARAGEMENT **3** : a decline (as from age or wear and tear) in the value of something

dep·re·da·tion \ˌdep-rə-'dā-shən\ *n* : the action or an act of looting or laying waste

de·press \di-'pres\ *vb* **1 a** : to press down **b** : to cause to sink to a lower position **2** : to lessen the activity or strength of **3** : SADDEN, DISCOURAGE **4** : to lessen in price or value : DEPRECIATE — **de·press·ible** \-ə-bəl\ *adj* — **de·press·ing·ly** \-iŋ-lē\ *n*

de·pres·sant \di-'pres-ºnt\ *n* : a chemical substance (as a drug) that reduces the activity of bodily systems — **depressant** *adj*

de·pressed *adj* **1 a** : low in spirits : SAD **b** : suffering from mental depression **2** : suffering from economic depression

de·pres·sion \di-'presh-ən\ *n* **1** : an act of depressing : a state of being depressed: as **a** : a pressing down : LOWERING **b** : a state of feeling sad : DEJECTION; *also* : a mental disorder marked by sadness, inactivity, and loss of a sense of one's own worth **c** : a reduction in activity, amount, quality, or force **2** : a depressed place or part : HOLLOW **3** : a period of low general economic activity with widespread unemployment

de·pres·sor \di-'pres-ər\ *n* : one that depresses; *esp* : a device for pressing a part (as the tongue) down or aside

de·pres·sur·ize \(')dē-'presh-ə-ˌrīz\ *vb* : to release (as an aircraft with near-normal atmospheric pressure) from pressure

de·prive \di-'prīv\ *vb* **de·prived; de·priv·ing** **1** : to take something away from ⟨*deprive* a ruler of power⟩ **2** : to stop from having something ⟨*deprived* of sleep by street noises⟩ — **dep·ri·va·tion** \ˌdep-rə-'vā-shən\ *n*

de·prived *adj* : kept from having the necessities of life or a healthful environment ⟨culturally *deprived* families⟩

depth \'depth\ *n* **1 a** : something that is deep : a deep place or part (as of a body of water) **b** : a part that is far from the outside or surface ⟨the *depths* of the woods⟩ **c** : ABYSS **2 a** : the middle of a time ⟨the *depth* of winter⟩ **b** : an extreme state (as of despair) **3** : distance from top to bottom or from front to back **4** : the quality of being deep ⟨*depth* of understanding⟩ **5** : degree of intensity ⟨the *depth* of a color⟩ — **depth·less** \-ləs\ *adj*

depth charge *n* : an explosive device for underwater use especially against submarines that is designed to detonate at a predetermined depth

dep·u·ta·tion \ˌdep-yə-'tā-shən\ *n* **1** : the act of appointing a deputy **2** : a group of people appointed to represent others

de·pute \di-'pyüt\ *vb* **de·put·ed; de·put·ing** : ²DELEGATE

dep·u·tize \'dep-yə-ˌtīz\ *vb* **-tized; -tiz·ing** **1** : to appoint as deputy **2** : to act as deputy

dep·u·ty \'dep-yət-ē\ *n, pl* **-ties** **1** : a person appointed to act for or in place of another **2** : an assistant who usually takes charge when his or her superior is absent — **deputy** *adj*

de·rail \di-'rā(ə)l\ *vb* : to cause to run off the rails ⟨a train *derailed* by heavy snow⟩ — **de·rail·ment** \-mənt\ *n*

de·rail·leur \di-'rā-lər\ *n* : a device for shifting gears on a bicycle that operates by moving the chain from one set of exposed gears to another [from French *dérailleur* "gear changing device", from *dérailler* "to derail"]

de·range \di-'rānj\ *vb* **de·ranged; de·rang·ing** **1** : to put out of order : DISARRANGE, UPSET ⟨hair *deranged* by the wind⟩ **2** : to make insane — **de·range·ment** \-mənt\ *n*

der·by \'dər-bē, *especially British* 'där-bē\ *n, pl* **derbies** **1** : a horse race usually for three-year-olds held annually **2** : a race or contest open to all comers ⟨fishing *derby*⟩ **3** : a stiff felt hat with dome-shaped top and narrow brim

derby 3

Word History The original derby is a horse race held every year on a racetrack not far from London. The race got its name from the man who started it back in 1780, Edward Stanley, the 12th earl of *Derby*. Stanley's title comes from the name of an English county and town. In time, the derby became the most important horse race in England.

Later, people started using the word *derby* for the most important horse race in other countries and then for a race or contest of any kind. Just how the man's dome-shaped hat came to be called a derby is not known. But it probably started when men began to wear this hat on sporting occasions, such as to the races. [named for Edward Stanley, 12th earl of *Derby* (a county and town in England)]

¹der·e·lict \'der-ə-ˌlikt\ *adj* **1** : abandoned by the owner or occupant ⟨a *derelict* ship⟩ **2** : NEGLIGENT 2, NEGLECTFUL ⟨*derelict* in one's duty⟩

²derelict *n* **1** : something voluntarily abandoned; *esp* : a ship abandoned on the high seas **2** : a person without apparent means of support : BUM

der·e·lic·tion \ˌder-ə-'lik-shən\ *n* **1** : the act of abandoning : the state of being abandoned ⟨the *dereliction* of a cause by its leaders⟩ **2** : neglect of one's duty

de·ride \di-'rīd\ *vb* **de·rid·ed; de·rid·ing** : to laugh at scornfully : make fun of — **de·rid·er** *n* — **de·rid·ing·ly** \-'rīd-iŋ-lē\ *adv*

de·ri·sion \di-'rizh-ən\ *n* **1** : scornful ridicule **2** : an object of ridicule — **de·ri·sive** \-'rī-siv\ *adj* — **de·ri·sive·ly** *adv* — **de·ri·sive·ness** *n* — **de·ri·so·ry** \-'rī-sə-rē, -zə-\ *adj*

der·i·va·tion \ˌder-ə-'vā-shən\ *n* **1 a** : the formation (as by the addition of a prefix or suffix) of a word from another word or root **b** : an act of finding out or stating how a word was formed **c** : ETYMOLOGY **2 a** : a point of origin : SOURCE **b** : development from a source : DESCENT **c** : an act or process of deriving — **der·i·va·tion·al** \-shnəl, -shən-ᵊl\ *adj*

¹de·riv·a·tive \di-'riv-ət-iv\ *n* **1** : a word formed by derivation ⟨the word "kindness" is a *derivative* of "kind"⟩ **2** : something derived **3** : a substance that can be made from another substance in one or more steps ⟨a *derivative* of coal tar⟩

²derivative *adj* **1** : formed by derivation **2** : made up of or having elements derived from something else ⟨*derivative* poetry⟩

de·rive \di-'rīv\ *vb* **de·rived; de·riv·ing** **1** : to receive or obtain from a source **2** : to arrive at by reasoning and observation : INFER, DEDUCE **3** : to trace the origin, descent, or derivation of **4** : to come from a certain source or basis ⟨the lumen *derives* from the candela⟩ — **de·riv·able** \-'rī-və-bəl\ *adj*

der·mal \'dər-məl\ *adj* : of or relating to the dermis or epidermis : CUTANEOUS

der·ma·ti·tis \ˌdər-mə-'tīt-əs\ *n* : inflammation of the skin

der·ma·tol·o·gist \ˌdər-mə-'täl-ə-jəst\ *n* : a physician who specializes in dermatology and especially in the treatment of the diseases of the skin

der·ma·tol·o·gy \ˌdər-mə-'täl-ə-jē\ *n* : a branch of medical science concerned with the structure, functions, and diseases of the skin

der·mis \'dər-məs\ *n* : the layer of skin directly under the epidermis

de·rog·a·to·ry \di-'räg-ə-ˌtōr-ē, -ˌtȯr-\ *adj* **1** : intended to lower the reputation of a person or thing **2** : expressing a low opinion ⟨*derogatory* remarks⟩ — **de·rog·a·to·ri·ly** \-ˌräg-ə-'tōr-ə-lē, -'tȯr-\ *adv*

der·rick \'der-ik\ *n* **1** : any of various machines for moving or hoisting heavy weights by means of a long beam fitted with pulleys and cables **2** : a framework or tower over a deep drill hole (as of an oil well) for supporting machinery

derrick 2

der·ring–do \ˌder-iŋ-'dü\ *n* : dar-

ing action : DARING

der·vish \'dər-vish\ *n* : a member of a Muslim religious group noted for its customs (as bodily movements leading to a trance)

de·sa·li·nate \(')dē-'sal-ə-ˌnāt *also* -'sä-lə-\ *vb* **-nat·ed; -nat·ing** : DESALT — **de·sa·li·na·tion** \(ˌ)dē-ˌsal-ə-'nā-shən *also* -ˌsä-lə-\ *n*

de·sal·i·ni·za·tion \(ˌ)dē-ˌsal-ə-nə-'zā-shən\ *n* : removal of salt (as from seawater)

de·salt \(')dē-'sȯlt\ *vb* : to remove salt from (as seawater)

¹des·cant \'des-ˌkant\ *n* **1** : a melody sung or played usually above a principal melody **2** : a discussion or comment on a subject

²des·cant \'des-ˌkant, des-'kant\ *vb* **1** : ¹SING 1a, 2 **2** : to talk or write at length ⟨*descanted* on foreign films⟩

de·scend \di-'send\ *vb* **1 a** : to pass from a higher to a lower place or level **b** : to pass, move, or climb down or down along **2 a** : to come down from a source : DERIVE ⟨*descended* from an ancient family⟩ **b** : to be handed down to an heir or from an earlier time ⟨the mansion *descended* to a son⟩ ⟨a custom *descended* from ancient times⟩ **3** : to incline, lead, or extend downward ⟨the road *descends* to the river⟩ **4** : to make a sudden attack by or as if by swooping down **5** : to sink in status, dignity, or condition

¹de·scend·ant *or* **de·scend·ent** \di-'sen-dənt\ *adj* **1** : moving or directed downward **2** : proceeding from an ancestor or source

²descendant *or* **descendent** *n* **1** : one descended from another or from a common stock **2** : one coming directly from an earlier and usually similar type or individual

de·scent \di-'sent\ *n* **1** : one's line of ancestors : BIRTH, LINEAGE **2** : the act or process of descending **3** : a downward step (as in station or value) : DECLINE **4 a** : a downward slant : SLOPE **b** : a descending way (as a stairway) **5** : a sudden raid or assault

de·scribe \di-'skrīb\ *vb* **des·cribed; des·crib·ing** **1** : to represent or give an account of in words **2** : to trace the outline of ⟨*describe* a circle⟩ — **de·scrib·able** \-'skrī-bə-bəl\ *adj* — **de·scrib·er** *n*

de·scrip·tion \di-'skrip-shən\ *n* **1** : an account of something; *esp* : an account that presents a picture to a person who reads or hears it **2** : ¹SORT 1a, KIND ⟨people of every *description*⟩ [Middle English *descripcioun* "description", from early French *description* and Latin *description-*, *descriptio* (both, same meaning), from Latin *descriptus*, past participle of *describere* "to describe", from *de-* "down" and *scribere* "to write" — related to SCRIBE]

de·scrip·tive \di-'skrip-tiv\ *adj* : serving to describe ⟨*descriptive* account⟩ ⟨*descriptive* adjective⟩ — **de·scrip·tive·ly** *adv* — **de·scrip·tive·ness** *n*

de·scry \di-'skrī\ *vb* **de·scried; de·scry·ing** **1** : to catch sight of **2** : to discover or detect by observation or investigation

des·e·crate \'des-i-ˌkrāt\ *vb* **-crat·ed; -crat·ing** : to treat a sacred place or sacred object shamefully or with great disrespect — **des·e·crat·er** *or* **des·e·cra·tor** \-ˌkrāt-ər\ *n* — **des·e·cra·tion** \ˌdes-i-'krā-shən\ *n*

de·seg·re·gate \(')dē-'seg-ri-ˌgāt\ *vb* : to eliminate segregation in; *esp* : to end by law the isolation of members of a particular race in separate units ⟨*desegregate* city schools⟩ — **de·seg·re·ga·tion** \(ˌ)dē-ˌseg-ri-'gā-shən\ *n*

¹des·ert \'dez-ərt\ *n* **1** : dry land with few plants and little rainfall **2** : a cheerless or discouraging area ⟨lost in a *desert* of doubt⟩ [Middle English *desert* "barren land", from early French *desert* (same meaning), derived from

\ə\ abut	\au̇\ out	\i\ tip	\ȯ\ saw	\u̇\ foot
\ər\ further	\ch\ chin	\ī\ life	\ȯi\ coin	\y\ yet
\a\ mat	\e\ pet	\j\ job	\th\ thin	\yü\ few
\ā\ take	\ē\ easy	\ŋ\ sing	\th\ this	\yu̇\ cure
\ä\ cot, cart	\g\ go	\ō\ bone	\ü\ food	\zh\ vision

Latin *deserere* "to desert, abandon", from *de-* "from, away" and *serere* "to join together"]

²des·ert \'dez-ərt\ *adj* : of, relating to, or resembling a desert; *esp* : being barren and without life ⟨a *desert* island⟩

³de·sert \di-'zərt\ *n* **1** : worthiness of reward or punishment ⟨rewarded according to their *deserts*⟩ **2** : a deserved reward or punishment ⟨got your just *deserts*⟩ [Middle English *deserte* "quality of being worthy of a reward or punishment", from early French *desert* (same meaning), from *deservir* "to deserve"]

⁴de·sert \di-'zərt\ *vb* **1** : to withdraw from : LEAVE ⟨the town was *deserted*⟩ **2** : to leave someone or something one should stay with ⟨*deserted* a friend in trouble⟩ **3** : to fail one in time of need ⟨my courage *deserted* me⟩ **4** : to quit one's post without permission especially with the intention of remaining away permanently [from French *déserter* "to desert, abandon", from Latin *desertare* (same meaning), derived from earlier *deserere* "to desert, abandon" — related to ¹DESERT] **syn** see ABANDON — **de·sert·er** *n* — **de·ser·tion** \di-'zər-shən\ *n*

de·serve \di-'zərv\ *vb* **de·served; de·serv·ing** : to be worthy of : MERIT ⟨*deserves* another chance⟩

de·serv·ed·ly \di-'zər-vəd-lē\ *adv* : as one deserves ⟨*deservedly* praised⟩ ⟨*deservedly* punished⟩

de·serv·ing \di-'zər-viŋ\ *adj* : ¹WORTHY 2; *esp* : worthy of financial help ⟨aid for *deserving* families⟩

de·sex \(')dē-'seks\ *vb* : CASTRATE, SPAY ⟨capons are *desexed* male chickens⟩

des·ic·ca·tor \'des-i-ˌkāt-ər\ *n* : a container for drying substances and keeping them free of moisture

¹de·sign \di-'zīn\ *vb* **1 a** : to think up and plan out in the mind ⟨*designed* the perfect crime⟩ **b** : to have as a purpose : INTEND ⟨*designed* to become a lawyer⟩ **c** : to create for a specific function or end ⟨*design* a training program for auto mechanics⟩ **2 a** : to make a pattern or sketch of ⟨*design* new fashions⟩ **b** : to think up and draw the plans for ⟨*design* an airplane⟩

²design *n* **1** : a project or scheme in which means to an end are laid down **2** : deliberate planning : a planned intention ⟨happened by accident rather than by *design*⟩ **3** : a secret project or scheme : PLOT — often used in pl. with *on* or *against* ⟨had *designs* on the money⟩ ⟨has no *designs* against friendly governments⟩ **4** : a preliminary sketch, model, or plan **5** : the arrangement of elements that make up a structure or a work of art **6** : a decorative pattern **syn** see INTENTION

des·ig·nate \'dez-ig-ˌnāt\ *vb* **-nat·ed; -nat·ing** **1** : to appoint or choose by name for a special purpose ⟨*designate* someone as team captain⟩ **2** : to mark or point out : INDICATE **3** : to call by name or title [from Latin *designatus*, past participle of *designare* "to design", from *de-* "down, from" and *signare* "to mark, mark out, sign, stamp with a seal", from *signum* "mark, sign, image" — related to SIGN] — **des·ig·na·tive** \-ˌnāt-iv\ *adj* — **des·ig·na·tor** \-ˌnāt-ər\ *n*

des·ig·na·tion \ˌdez-ig-'nā-shən\ *n* **1** : the act of indicating or identifying **2** : appointment to or selection for an office, post, or service **3** : a name, sign, or title that identifies something

de·sign·ed·ly \di-'zī-nəd-lē\ *adv* : PURPOSELY

¹de·sign·er \di-'zī-nər\ *n* : one who designs; *esp* : one who creates and manufactures a new product style

²designer *adj* : relating to or produced by a designer and often displaying the name of the designer ⟨*designer* jeans⟩

de·sign·ing \di-'zī-niŋ\ *adj* : CRAFTY, SCHEMING

de·sir·able \di-'zī-rə-bəl\ *adj* **1** : having pleasing qualities or properties : ATTRACTIVE ⟨a *desirable* location⟩ **2** : worth having, seeking, or doing : ADVISABLE ⟨*desirable* legislation⟩ — **de·sir·abil·i·ty** \-ˌzī-rə-'bil-ət-ē\ *n* — **de·sir·able·ness** \-'zī-rə-bəl-nəs\ *n* — **de·sir·ably** \-blē\ *adv*

¹de·sire \di-'zī(ə)r\ *vb* **de·sired; de·sir·ing** **1** : to long for

: wish earnestly ⟨*desire* wealth⟩ ⟨*desire* peace⟩ **2** : to call for : express a wish for : REQUEST ⟨the librarian *desires* us to return all overdue books⟩

²desire *n* **1** : a strong wish : LONGING; *also* : the mental power or ability to experience desires **2** : an expressed wish : REQUEST **3** : something desired

de·sir·ous \di-'zī(ə)r-əs\ *adj* : eagerly wishing ⟨*desirous* of an invitation⟩ — **de·sir·ous·ly** *adv* — **de·sir·ous·ness** *n*

de·sist \di-'zist, -'sist\ *vb* : to stop something one is doing

desk \'desk\ *n* **1 a** : a table, frame, or case with a flat or sloping surface especially for writing and reading **b** : a counter at which a person works **2 a** : a specialized division of an organization (as a newspaper) ⟨city *desk*⟩ **b** : a seating position according to rank in an orchestra

desk·top \'desk-ˌtäp\ *adj* : of a size that is suitable for use on a desk or table ⟨a *desktop* computer⟩

des·mid \'dez-məd\ *n* : any of numerous single-celled colonial green algae

¹des·o·late \'des-ə-lət, 'dez-\ *adj* **1** : ABANDONED **2** : having no companionship : LONELY **3 a** : showing the results of abandonment and neglect : DILAPIDATED **b** : lacking signs of life : BARREN ⟨a *desolate* landscape⟩ **c** : CHEERLESS ⟨*desolate* thoughts⟩ [Middle English *desolat* "having no inhabitants or visitors, deserted", from Latin *desolatus*, past participle of *desolare* "to abandon", from *de-* "from, away" and *solus* "alone" — related to ⁴SOLE, SOLITUDE, SOLO] — **des·o·late·ly** *adv* — **des·o·late·ness** *n*

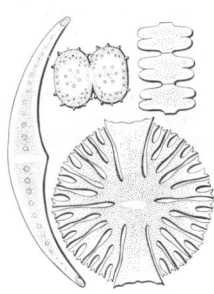

desmid

²des·o·late \'des-ə-ˌlāt, 'dez-\ *vb* **-lat·ed; -lat·ing** : to make or leave desolate

des·o·la·tion \ˌdes-ə-'lā-shən, ˌdez-\ *n* **1** : the action of desolating **2** : sadness resulting from grief or loneliness **3** : the condition of being desolated : RUIN **4** : lifeless land

des·oxy·ri·bo·nu·cle·ic acid \de-ˌzäk-sē-ˌrī-bō-n(y)ù-ˌklē-ik-, -ˌklā-\ *n* : DNA

¹de·spair \di-'spa(ə)r, -'spe(ə)r\ *vb* : to lose all hope or confidence — **de·spair·ing** *adj* — **de·spair·ing·ly** \-iŋ-lē\ *adv*

²despair *n* **1** : utter loss of hope : feeling of complete hopelessness **2** : a cause of hopelessness

despatch *variant of* DISPATCH

des·per·a·do \ˌdes-pə-'räd-ō, -'rād-\ *n, pl* **-does** *or* **-dos** : a bold or reckless criminal

des·per·ate \'des-p(ə-)rət\ *adj* **1** : being beyond or almost beyond hope ⟨a *desperate* illness⟩ **2** : reckless because of despair : RASH ⟨a *desperate* attempt⟩ — **des·per·ate·ly** *adv* — **des·per·ate·ness** *n*

des·per·a·tion \ˌdes-pə-'rā-shən\ *n* **1** : a loss of hope and surrender to misery or dread **2** : a state of hopelessness leading to extreme recklessness

de·spi·ca·ble \di-'spik-ə-bəl, 'des-(ˌ)pik-\ *adj* : deserving to be despised ⟨*despicable* traitor⟩ — **de·spi·ca·ble·ness** *n* — **de·spi·ca·bly** \-blē\ *adv*

de·spise \di-'spīz\ *vb* **de·spised; de·spis·ing** : to consider as beneath one's notice or respect : feel scorn and dislike for — **de·spis·er** *n* — **de·spis·ing·ly** *adv*

¹de·spite \di-'spīt\ *n* **1** : CONTEMPT 1 : SPITE, MALICE **3 a** : an act showing scorn and disrespect **b** : DETRIMENT — **in despite of** : in spite of

²despite *prep* : in spite of ⟨ran *despite* an injury⟩

de·spite·ful \di-'spīt-fəl\ *adj* : expressing hate or the wish to harm — **de·spite·ful·ly** \-fə-lē\ *adv* — **de·spite·ful·ness** *n*

de·spoil \di-'spȯil\ *vb* : to strip of belongings, possessions, or value : PLUNDER, PILLAGE — **de·spoil·er** n — **de·spoil·ment** \-'spoi(ə)l-mənt\ n

de·spo·li·a·tion \di-,spō-lē-'ā-shən\ n : the act of despoiling : the state of being despoiled

de·spond \di-'spänd\ vb : to become discouraged

de·spond·en·cy \di-'spän-dən-sē\ n : the state of being despondent : DEJECTION, DISCOURAGEMENT

de·spond·ent \di-'spän-dənt\ adj : feeling quite discouraged or depressed : being in very low spirits — **de·spond·ent·ly** adv

des·pot \'des-pət, -,pät\ n **1** : a ruler with absolute power and authority **2** : a person who uses power in a cruel, unjust, or harmful way — **des·pot·ic** \des-'pät-ik\ adj — **des·pot·i·cal·ly** \-i-k(ə-)lē\ adv

des·po·tism \'des-pə-,tiz-əm\ n **1** : rule by a despot : TYRANNY **2** : a state or a system of government in which the ruler has unlimited power

des·sert \di-'zərt\ n : a course of sweet food, fruit, or cheese served at the close of a meal

des·ti·na·tion \,des-tə-'nā-shən\ n **1** : the purpose for which something is destined **2** : an act of appointing, setting aside for a purpose, or deciding beforehand **3** : a place which is the goal of a journey or to which something is sent

des·tine \'des-tən\ vb **des·tined; des·tin·ing** **1** : to settle in advance ⟨a plan *destined* to fail⟩ **2** : to choose, assign, or dedicate in advance ⟨*destined* their child for the study of law⟩ **3** : to be bound or directed ⟨a ship *destined* for New York⟩

des·ti·ny \'des-tə-nē\ n, pl **-nies** **1** : something to which a person or thing is destined : FORTUNE **2** : the course of events held to be arranged by a superhuman power

    syn DESTINY, FATE, LOT, DOOM mean a state or end that has been decided beforehand. DESTINY suggests something that has been ordered in advance and often suggests a great or noble course ⟨the *destiny* of this great country⟩ FATE suggests an unavoidable and usually unfortunate ending ⟨his *fate* was to die unhappy⟩ LOT suggests that chance alone decides the handing out of success or happiness ⟨it was not their *lot* to have children⟩ DOOM suggests an unhappy judgment or end ⟨a sense of *doom* hung over the starving city⟩

des·ti·tute \'des-tə-,t(y)üt\ adj **1** : lacking something needed or desirable ⟨*destitute* of the necessities of life⟩ **2** : extremely poor : suffering great want — **des·ti·tu·tion** \,des-tə-'t(y)ü-shən\ n

de·stroy \di-'stroi\ vb **1** : to put an end to : do away with : RUIN **2** : ¹KILL 1, SLAUGHTER

de·stroy·er \di-'stroi(-ə)r\ n **1** : one that destroys **2** : a small fast warship armed with guns, depth charges, torpedoes, and sometimes guided missiles

de·struct \di-'strəkt\ n : the deliberate destruction of a rocket after launching

de·struc·ti·ble \di-'strək-tə-bəl\ adj : capable of being destroyed — **de·struc·ti·bil·i·ty** \-,strək-tə-'bil-ət-ē\ n

de·struc·tion \di-'strək-shən\ n **1** : the state or fact of being destroyed : RUIN **2** : the action or process of destroying something

de·struc·tive \di-'strək-tiv\ adj **1** : causing destruction : RUINOUS ⟨*destructive* storm⟩ **2** : designed or tending to destroy ⟨*destructive* criticism⟩ ⟨*destructive* interference of light waves⟩ — **de·struc·tive·ly** adv — **de·struc·tive·ness** n

destructive distillation n : the breakup of a substance (as coal, oil, or wood) by heat in a closed container and collection of the volatile products produced

des·ul·to·ry \'des-əl-,tōr-ē, -,tor-\ adj : passing aimlessly from one thing or subject to another ⟨*desultory* conversation⟩ — **des·ul·to·ri·ly** \,des-əl-'tōr-ə-lē, -'tor-\ adv — **des·ul·to·ri·ness** \'des-əl-,tōr-ē-nəs, -,tor-\ n

de·tach \di-'tach\ vb : to separate especially from a larger mass and usually without violence or damage — **de·tach·able** \-'tach-ə-bəl\ adj — **de·tach·ably** \-blē\ adv

de·tached \di-'tacht\ adj **1** : not joined or connected : SEPARATE ⟨a *detached* house⟩ **2** : ²ALOOF, UNCONCERNED, IMPARTIAL ⟨a *detached* attitude⟩ — **de·tached·ly** \-'tach-əd-lē, -'tach-tlē\ adv — **de·tached·ness** \-'tach-əd-nəs, -'tach(t)-nəs\ n

de·tach·ment \di-'tach-mənt\ n **1** : the action or process of detaching : SEPARATION **2 a** : the sending out of a body of troops or part of a fleet from the main body **b** : a small military unit with a special task or function **3 a** : a lack of interest in worldly concerns **b** : freedom from the influence of emotions : IMPARTIALITY

¹de·tail \di-'tā(ə)l, 'dē-,tāl\ n **1 a** : a dealing with something item by item ⟨go into *detail* about an event⟩ **b** : a small part or feature : ITEM ⟨the *details* of a story⟩ **2 a** : selection (as of a group of soldiers) for some special service **b** : a soldier or group of soldiers appointed for special duty — **in detail** : item by item leaving out nothing : THOROUGHLY ⟨explain *in detail*⟩

²detail vb **1** : to report in detail : SPECIFY **2** : to assign to a task — **de·tail·er** n

de·tailed \di-'tā(ə)ld, 'dē-,tāld\ adj **1** : including many details ⟨a *detailed* report⟩ **2** : furnished with finely finished details ⟨beautifully *detailed* hats⟩ — **de·tailed·ly** \di-'tā(-ə)d-lē, 'dē-,tāld-\ adv — **de·tailed·ness** \di-'tā-ləd-nəs, -'tāl(d)-nəs, 'dē-,tāld-\ n

de·tain \di-'tān\ vb **1** : to hold or keep in or as if in prison **2** : to prevent from proceeding : STOP — **de·tain·ment** \-mənt\ n

de·tect \di-'tekt\ vb : to discover the nature, existence, presence, or fact of ⟨*detect* the approach of an airplane⟩ — **de·tect·able** \-'tek-tə-bəl\ adj — **de·tec·tion** \-'tek-shən\ n

¹de·tec·tive \di-'tek-tiv\ adj : of or relating to detectives or their work ⟨a *detective* story⟩

²detective n : a person whose business is solving crimes and catching criminals or gathering information that is not easy to get

de·tec·tor \di-'tek-tər\ n **1** : one that detects or warns ⟨a smoke *detector*⟩ **2** : a device in a radio receiver for changing the high-frequency current of radio waves into current that can vibrate a loudspeaker to reproduce the original sound

de·ten·tion \di-'ten-chən\ n : the act of detaining : the state of being detained: as **a** : temporary custody before a trial **b** : the punishment of being kept in after school

de·ter \di-'tər\ vb **de·terred; de·ter·ring** **1** : to turn aside, discourage, or prevent from acting ⟨wasn't *deterred* by the threats⟩ **2** : INHIBIT 2 ⟨painting to *deter* rust⟩ — **de·ter·ment** \-'tər-mənt\ n

¹de·ter·gent \di-'tər-jənt\ adj : able to clean : used in cleansing ⟨*detergent* oil for engines⟩

²detergent n : a substance that cleanses; *esp* : a chemical product that is like soap in its ability to cleanse

de·te·ri·o·rate \di-'tir-ē-ə-,rāt\ vb **-rat·ed; -rat·ing** : to make or become worse or of less value : DEGENERATE — **de·te·ri·o·ra·tion** \-,tir-ē-ə-'rā-shən\ n — **de·te·ri·o·ra·tive** \-'tir-ē-ə-,rāt-iv\ adj

de·ter·mi·nant \di-'tərm-(ə-)nənt\ n : something that determines or influences

de·ter·mi·nate \di-'tərm-(ə-)nət\ adj **1** : having fixed limits : DEFINITE **2** : definitely settled ⟨arranged in a *determinate* order⟩ — **de·ter·mi·nate·ly** adv — **de·ter·mi·nate·ness** n

de·ter·mi·na·tion \di-,tər-mə-'nā-shən\ n **1** : the act of coming to a decision; *also* : the decision or conclusion

\ə\ abut	\au̇\ out	\i\ tip	\ȯ\ saw	\u̇\ foot
\ər\ further	\ch\ chin	\ī\ life	\oi\ coin	\y\ yet
\a\ mat	\e\ pet	\j\ job	\th\ thin	\yü\ few
\ā\ take	\ē\ easy	\ŋ\ sing	\th\ this	\yu̇\ cure
\ä\ cot, cart	\g\ go	\ō\ bone	\ü\ food	\zh\ vision

reached **2** : a settling or making sure of the position, size, or nature of something ⟨*determination* of the position of a ship⟩ **3** : accurate measurement (as of length or volume) **4** : firm or fixed intention : FIRMNESS

de·ter·mine \di-'tər-mən\ *vb* **de·ter·mined; de·ter·min·ing** \-'tərm-(ə-)niŋ\ **1 a** : to fix exactly or with authority ⟨*determine* who will be president⟩ **b** : to have a strong influence on : GOVERN ⟨demand *determines* the price⟩ **2** : to come to a decision : SETTLE, RESOLVE ⟨*determine* to learn to spell⟩ **3** : to gain definite knowledge about : FIND OUT ⟨*determine* the size of a room⟩ **4** : to be the cause of or reason for ⟨a pupil's work *determines* his mark⟩

de·ter·mined \di-'tər-mənd\ *adj* **1** : having reached a decision : RESOLVED **2** : not weak or uncertain ⟨a very *determined* opponent⟩ — **de·ter·mined·ly** \-mən-dlē, -mə-nəd-lē\ *adv* — **de·ter·mined·ness** \-mən(d)-nəs\ *n*

de·ter·min·er \di-'tər-mə-nər\ *n* : a word belonging to a group of noun modifiers that can occur before descriptive adjectives modifying the same noun ⟨"the" in "the red house" is a *determiner*⟩

de·ter·rence \di-'tər-ən(t)s, -'ter-\ *n* : the act, process, or capability of deterring

de·ter·rent \di-'tər-ənt, -'ter-\ *adj* : able or acting to deter — **deterrent** *n*

de·test \di-'test\ *vb* : to dislike very strongly **syn** see HATE — **de·test·er** *n*

de·test·able \di-'tes-tə-bəl\ *adj* : arousing or deserving strong dislike : ABOMINABLE — **de·test·able·ness** *n* — **de·test·ably** \-blē\ *adv*

de·throne \di-'thrōn\ *vb* **de·throned; de·thron·ing** : to remove from a throne — **de·throne·ment** \-mənt\ *n*

det·o·nate \'det-ᵊn-,āt, 'det-ə-,nāt\ *vb* **-nat·ed; -nat·ing** : to explode or cause to explode with sudden violence — **det·o·na·tion** \,det-ᵊn-'ā-shən, ,det-ə-'nā-\ *n*

det·o·na·tor \'det-ᵊn-,āt-ər, -ə-,nāt-\ *n* : a device or small quantity of explosive used for detonating another explosive

¹de·tour \'dē-,tu̇(ə)r *also* di-'tu̇(ə)r\ *n* : a departure from a direct course or the usual procedure; *esp* : a roundabout way temporarily replacing a regular route

²detour *vb* : to send or proceed by a detour

de·tract \di-'trakt\ *vb* : to take away some of the value or importance ⟨*detract* from a person's reputation⟩ — **de·trac·tion** \-'trak-shən\ *n* — **de·trac·tive** \-'trak-tiv\ *adj* — **de·trac·tive·ly** *adv* — **de·trac·tor** \-'trak-tər\ *n*

det·ri·ment \'de-trə-mənt\ *n* : injury or damage or its cause

det·ri·men·tal \,de-trə-'ment-ᵊl\ *adj* : HARMFUL ⟨*detrimental* effects of drug abuse⟩ — **det·ri·men·tal·ly** \-ᵊl-ē\ *adv*

de·tri·tus \di-'trīt-əs\ *n, pl* **detritus** \-'trīt-əs, -'trī-tüs\ **1** : loose material that results directly from the natural breaking up of rocks **2** : a product of disintegration or wearing away

deuce \'d(y)üs\ *n* **1 a** : the face of dice that bears two spots **b** : a playing card bearing the number two **c** : a throw of dice resulting in two points **2** : a tie in tennis after each side has scored 40 **3** : ¹DEVIL 1, DICKENS — used chiefly as a mild oath [from early French *deus* "two", from Latin *duos* (same meaning), from *duo* "two" — related to DUAL]

deu·te·ri·um \d(y)ü-'tir-ē-əm\ *n* : the hydrogen isotope that is twice the mass of ordinary hydrogen — called also *heavy hydrogen*

Deu·ter·on·o·my \,d(y)üt-ə-'rän-ə-mē\ *n* — see BIBLE table

deut·sche mark \,dȯich(-ə)-'märk\ *n* **1** : the basic unit of money of Germany and formerly of West Germany **2** : a coin or bill representing one deutsche mark

dev·as·tate \'dev-ə-,stāt\ *vb* **-tat·ed; -tat·ing** **1** : to reduce to ruin : lay waste **2** : OVERWHELM 2, OVERPOWER — **dev·as·tat·ing·ly** \-,stāt-iŋ-lē\ *adv* — **dev·as·ta·tion** \,dev-ə-'stā-shən\ *n*

de·vel·op \di-'vel-əp\ *vb* **1 a** : to make or become clear gradually or in detail ⟨as the story *developed*⟩ **b** : to ap-

ply chemicals to exposed photographic material (as a film) in order to bring out the picture **c** : to make (a musical theme) more complicated by varying the rhythm and harmony **2** : to bring to a more advanced or more nearly perfect state ⟨exercise *develops* one's muscles⟩ **3** : to make more available or usable ⟨*develop* land⟩ **4** : to acquire gradually ⟨*developed* a taste for olives⟩ **5** : to go through a process of natural growth or evolution in a series of stages ⟨a blossom *develops* from a bud⟩ — **de·vel·op·able** \-'vel-ə-pə-bəl\ *adj*

de·vel·oped \di-'vel-əpt\ *adj* : having a relatively high level of industrialization and standard of living

de·vel·op·er \di-'vel-ə-pər\ *n* : one that develops: as **a** : a chemical used to develop exposed photographic materials **b** : a person who develops real estate; *esp* : one who divides land and builds and sells houses on it

de·vel·op·ing \di-,vel-ə-piŋ\ *adj* : UNDERDEVELOPED 2

de·vel·op·ment \di-'vel-əp-mənt\ *n* **1** : the act, process, or result of developing **2** : the state of being developed **3** : a developed piece of land; *esp* : one that has houses built on it

de·vel·op·men·tal \-,vel-əp-'ment-əl\ *adj* : of or relating to development — **de·vel·op·men·tal·ly** \-əl-ē\ *adv*

developmentally disabled *adj* : having a physical or mental handicap (as mental retardation) that slows down or prevents normal development

de·vi·ance \'dē-vē-ən(t)s\ *n* : quality, state, or behavior that differs from what is normal or accepted

¹de·vi·ant \'dē-vē-ənt\ *adj* : deviating especially from some accepted standard of behavior or morals

²deviant *n* : a person whose behavior or morals differs from accepted or normal standards

de·vi·ate \'dē-vē-,āt\ *vb* **-at·ed; -at·ing** : to turn aside from a course, principle, standard, or topic

de·vi·a·tion \,dē-vē-'ā-shən\ *n* : an act or instance of deviating: as **a** : the difference found by subtracting some fixed number (as the arithmetic mean) from any of a series of values **b** : noticeable difference from accepted standards (as of behavior or morals)

de·vice \di-'vīs\ *n* **1 a** : a scheme to deceive : STRATAGEM **b** : something in a written work designed to achieve a particular artistic effect **c** : a piece of equipment to serve a special purpose **2** *pl* : a preferred way of doing or acting : INCLINATION ⟨left to her own *devices*⟩ **3** : a design that is an emblem; *esp* : one used in a coat of arms

¹dev·il \'dev-əl\ *n* **1** *often cap* : the personal supreme spirit of evil often represented as the ruler of hell — often used with *the* as a mild oath or expression of surprise, irritation, or emphasis **2** : DEMON 2 **3 a** : a person who is wicked, mischievous, reckless, or lively **b** : PERSON 1 — usually used in the phrases *poor devil* and *lucky devil*

²devil *vb* **dev·iled** *or* **dev·illed; dev·il·ing** *or* **dev·il·ling** \'dev-(ə-)liŋ\ **1** : to chop fine and season highly ⟨*deviled* eggs⟩ **2** : ¹TEASE 2a, ANNOY

dev·il·fish \'dev-əl-,fish\ *n* **1** : any of several extremely large rays widely distributed in warm seas — called also *manta, manta ray, sea devil* **2** : OCTOPUS 1

dev·il·ish \'dev-(ə-)lish\ *adj* **1** : characteristic of or resembling the devil ⟨*devilish* tricks⟩ **2** : ¹EXTREME 1, EXCESSIVE ⟨in a *devilish* hurry⟩ — **devilish** *adv* — **dev·il·ish·ly** *adv* — **dev·il·ish·ness** *n*

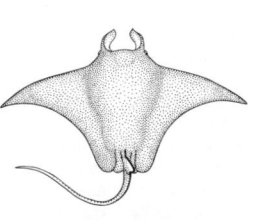

devilfish 1

dev·il–may–care \,dev-əl-(,)mā-'ke(ə)r, -'ka(ə)r\ *adj* : EASYGOING, CAREFREE

dev·il·ment \'dev-əl-mənt, -,ment\ *n* : DEVILRY

devil ray *n* : DEVILFISH 1

dev·il·ry \'dev-əl-rē\ *or* **dev·il·try** \-əl-trē\ *n, pl* **-ries** *or* **-tries**   **1** : wicked or cruel behavior   **2** : MISCHIEF 3

devil's advocate *n*   **1** : a Roman Catholic official whose duty is to point out faults in the evidence when someone is proposed for sainthood   **2** : a person who supports the less accepted or approved cause for the sake of argument

devil's darning needle *n*   **1** : DRAGONFLY   **2** : DAMSELFLY

dev·il's food cake \'dev-əlz-ˌfüd-ˌkāk\ *n* : a rich chocolate cake

devil's paintbrush *n* : any of various hawkweeds found in the eastern U.S.

de·vi·ous \'dē-vē-əs\ *adj*   **1** : straying from a straight course : ROUNDABOUT ⟨the *devious* trail that wound along the creek⟩ ⟨leading through *devious* mazes⟩   **2** : SNEAKY, DECEPTIVE ⟨*devious* conduct⟩ ⟨got it by *devious* means⟩ — **de·vi·ous·ly** *adv* — **de·vi·ous·ness** *n*

de·vise \di-'vīz\ *vb* **de·vised; de·vis·ing**   **1** : to form in the mind by new combinations or applications of ideas or principles : INVENT   **2** : to give (real estate) by will — **de·vis·er** *n*

de·void \di-'vȯid\ *adj* : not having a usual or expected quality ⟨a book *devoid* of interest⟩

De·vo·ni·an \di-'vō-nē-ən\ *adj* : of, relating to, or being a period of the Paleozoic era of geological history or the corresponding system of rocks — see GEOLOGIC TIME table — **Devonian** *n*

de·vote \di-'vōt\ *vb* **de·vot·ed; de·vot·ing**   **1** : to set apart for a special purpose ⟨*devote* an hour to worship⟩   **2** : to give (oneself) up to ⟨*devoted* herself to her career⟩
    syn DEVOTE, DEDICATE, CONSECRATE mean to set apart for a special and often higher purpose. DEVOTE is likely to suggest strong reasons and often a long-term goal ⟨*devoted* her evenings to studying law⟩ DEDICATE suggests a solemn devotion to a serious or sacred purpose ⟨*dedicated* his life to helping the poor⟩ CONSECRATE suggests the giving of a solemn or sacred quality to something ⟨*consecrate* a church to the worship of God⟩

de·vot·ed *adj* : having strong love, affection, or dedication ⟨his *devoted* wife⟩ ⟨her grandchildren were *devoted* to her⟩ ⟨a rock singer's *devoted* admirers⟩ — **de·vot·ed·ly** *adv* — **de·vot·ed·ness** *n*

dev·o·tee \ˌdev-ə-'tē, -'tā\ *n* : a keen or earnest follower, supporter, or enthusiast

de·vo·tion \di-'vō-shən\ *n*   **1 a** : strong religious feeling   **b** : a religious exercise or practice other than the regular worship of a congregation   **2 a** : the act of devoting or the quality of being devoted   **b** : strong love, affection, or dedication — **de·vo·tion·al** \-shnəl, -shən-ᵊl\ *adj* — **de·vo·tion·al·ly** \-ē\ *adv*

de·vour \di-'vaù(ə)r\ *vb*   **1** : to eat up greedily or hungrily   **2** : to swallow up or destroy as if by eating   **3** : to enjoy eagerly ⟨*devour* a book⟩   **syn** see EAT

de·vout \di-'vaùt\ *adj*   **1** : devoted to religion or to religious duties or exercises   **2** : expressing devotion   **3** : ²EARNEST 1, SINCERE ⟨gave them *devout* thanks⟩ — **de·vout·ly** *adv* — **de·vout·ness** *n*

dew \'d(y)ü\ *n*   **1** : moisture that collects on the surfaces of cool bodies at night   **2** : something resembling dew in purity, freshness, or power to refresh — **dewy** \'d(y)ü-ē\ *adj*

Dew·ar flask \ˌd(y)ü-ər-\ *n* : VACUUM BOTTLE [named for Sir James *Dewar* 1842–1923 Scottish scientist]

dew·ber·ry \'d(y)ü-ˌber-ē\ *n*   **1** : any of several blackberries with trailing stems that root at the joints or tip   **2** : the small purplish fruit of a dewberry

dew·drop \'d(y)ü-ˌdräp\ *n* : a drop of dew

Dew·ey decimal system \ˌd(y)ü-ē-\ *n* : a system of library classification in which publications are assigned a number from 0 to 999 according to subject [named for Melvil *Dewey* 1851–1931 American librarian]

dew·lap \'d(y)ü-ˌlap\ *n* : loose skin hanging under the neck of various animals (as dogs or cattle of some breeds)

dew point *n* : the temperature at which the moisture in the air begins to collect on surfaces

dex·ter·i·ty \dek-'ster-ət-ē\ *n, pl* **-ties**   **1** : mental skill or quickness   **2** : ease and grace in physical activity; *esp* : skill and ease in using the hands

dex·ter·ous *or* **dex·trous** \'dek-st(ə-)rəs\ *adj*   **1** : mentally skillful and clever : EXPERT   **2** : done with skill   **3** : skillful with the hands — **dex·ter·ous·ly** *adv*

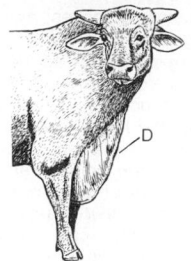

D dewlap

dex·trose \'dek-ˌstrōs\ *n* : the naturally occurring form of glucose found in plants, fruits, and blood — called also *grape sugar*

di- *combining form*   **1** : twice : twofold : double   **2** : containing two atoms, radicals, or groups ⟨*di*chloride⟩ [derived from Latin *di-* "twice, containing two", from Greek *di-* (same meaning)]

di·a·be·tes \ˌdī-ə-'bēt-ēz, -'bēt-əs\ *n* : any of various bodily conditions in which abnormally large amounts of urine are produced; *esp* : DIABETES MELLITUS

diabetes mel·li·tus \-'mel-ət-əs\ *n* : an abnormal bodily condition in which less than the normal amount of insulin is produced, greater than normal amounts of urine are produced, and large amounts of sugar are contained in the blood and urine and which is marked especially by thirst, hunger, and loss of weight

¹di·a·bet·ic \ˌdī-ə-'bet-ik\ *adj* : of, relating to, or having diabetes ⟨a *diabetic* person⟩

²diabetic *n* : a person who has diabetes

di·a·bol·ic \ˌdī-ə-'bäl-ik\ *adj* : of, relating to, or characteristic of the devil : FIENDISH — **di·a·bol·i·cal** \-'bäl-i-kəl\ *adj* — **di·a·bol·i·cal·ly** \-i-k(ə-)lē\ *adv* — **di·a·bol·i·cal·ness** \-i-kəl-nəs\ *n*

di·a·crit·ic \ˌdī-ə-'krit-ik\ *n* : DIACRITICAL MARK

di·a·crit·i·cal mark \ˌdī-ə-ˌkrit-i-kəl-\ *n* : a mark used with a letter or group of letters and indicating a sound value different from that given the unmarked or otherwise marked letter or combination of letters

di·a·dem \'dī-ə-ˌdem, -əd-əm\ *n* : a headband worn especially as a symbol of royalty

di·aer·e·sis *also* **di·er·e·sis** \dī-'er-ə-səs\ *n, pl* **di·aer·e·ses** *also* **di·er·e·ses** \-'er-ə-ˌsēz\ : a mark ¨ placed over a vowel to show that it is pronounced in a separate syllable (as in *naïve* or *Brontë*)

di·ag·nose \'dī-ig-ˌnōs, -ˌnōz; ˌdī-ig-'nōs, -'nōz\ *vb* **-nosed; -nos·ing** : to recognize by signs and symptoms : make a diagnosis ⟨*diagnose* a disease⟩ ⟨*diagnose* a play in football⟩

di·ag·no·sis \ˌdī-ig-'nō-səs\ *n, pl* **-no·ses** \-'nō-ˌsēz\   **1 a** : the art or act of identifying a disease from its signs and symptoms   **b** : the decision reached by diagnosis   **2 a** : a careful study of something especially to determine its nature or importance   **b** : the conclusion reached after a study or examination

di·ag·nos·tic \ˌdī-ig-'näs-tik\ *adj*   **1** : of, relating to, or used in diagnosis ⟨a *diagnostic* test for cancer⟩   **2** : testing knowledge in a particular subject especially to find out what is not known or not understood ⟨a *diagnostic* arithmetic test⟩

di·ag·nos·ti·cian \ˌdī-ig-(ˌ)näs-'tish-ən\ *n* : a person who

\ə\ abut	\aù\ out	\i\ tip	\ȯ\ saw	\ù\ foot	
\ər\ further	\ch\ chin	\ī\ life	\ȯi\ coin	\y\ yet	
\a\ mat	\e\ pet	\j\ job	\th\ thin	\yü\ few	
\ā\ take	\ē\ easy	\ŋ\ sing	\th\ this	\yù\ cure	
\ä\ cot, cart	\g\ go	\ō\ bone	\ü\ food	\zh\ vision	

makes diagnoses; *esp* : a specialist in making medical diagnoses

¹di·ag·o·nal \dī-'ag-ən-ᵊl, -'ag-nəl\ *adj* **1** : joining two opposite corners of a four-sided figure **2** : running in a slanting direction — **di·ag·o·nal·ly** \-ən-ᵊl-ē, -nə-lē\ *adv*

²diagonal *n* **1** : a diagonal line or direction **2** : a diagonal row, arrangement, or pattern

¹di·a·gram \'dī-ə-ˌgram\ *n* : a drawing, sketch, plan, or chart that makes something clearer or easier to understand — **di·a·gram·mat·ic** \ˌdī-ə-grə-'mat-ik\ *also* **di·a·gram·mat·i·cal** \-'mat-i-kəl\ *adj* — **di·a·gram·mat·i·cal·ly** \-'mat-i-k(ə-)lē\ *adv*

²diagram *vb* **-gramed** *or* **-grammed** \-ˌgramd\; **-gram·ing** *or* **-gram·ming** \-ˌgram-iŋ\ : to represent by or put into the form of a diagram ⟨*diagram* a sentence⟩

¹di·al \'dī(-ə)l\ *n* **1 a** : SUNDIAL **b** : the face of a watch or clock **2 a** : a face or scale on which some measurement is registered usually by means of numbers and a pointer **b** : a disk usually with a knob or slots that may be turned to make electrical connections (as on a telephone) or to regulate the operation of a device (as a radio)

²dial *vb* **di·aled** *or* **di·alled; di·al·ing** *or* **di·al·ling** **1** : to turn a dial so as to operate, regulate, or select **2** : to make a telephone call or connection

di·a·lect \'dī-ə-ˌlekt\ *n* **1** : a regional variety of a language differing from the standard language **2** : a variety of a language used by the members of a particular group or class ⟨peasant *dialect*⟩ — **dialect** *or* **di·a·lec·tal** \ˌdī-ə-'lek-tᵊl\ *adj* — **di·a·lec·tal·ly** \-tᵊl-ē\ *adv* — **di·a·lec·ti·cal** \ˌdī-ə-'lek-ti-kəl\ *adj*

di·a·logue *or* **di·a·log** \'dī-ə-ˌlóg, -ˌläg\ *n* **1** : a conversation between two or more persons **2** : conversation given in a written story or play

di·al·y·sis \dī-'al-ə-səs\ *n, pl* **-y·ses** \-ə-ˌsēz\ : the separation of substances in solution by means of their unequal diffusion through membranes with pores of a specified maximum size; *esp* : such a separation of colloids from dissolved substances

di·am·e·ter \dī-'am-ət-ər\ *n* **1** : a straight line passing through the center of a figure or body; *esp* : a line segment through the center of a circle with its endpoints on the circumference **2** : the length of a diameter

diameter 1

di·a·met·ric \ˌdī-ə-'me-trik\ *or* **di·a·met·ri·cal** \-'me-tri-kəl\ *adj* **1** : of or relating to a diameter **2** : completely opposed or opposite — **di·a·met·ri·cal·ly** \-tri-k(ə-)lē\ *adv*

di·a·mond \'dī-(ə-)mənd\ *n* **1 a** : a very hard stone of crystallized carbon that is used as a precious gem and industrially as a powder for grinding, smoothing, or polishing and in cutting tools **b** : a piece of this stone especially when cut and polished **2** : a figure that is formed by four equal straight lines and has two opposite acute angles and two opposite obtuse angles **3** : a red diamond-shaped figure used to mark one of the four kinds of playing cards; *also* : a card of the kind bearing diamonds **4 a** : INFIELD 1a **b** : the entire playing field in baseball or softball

    Word History Diamond, the hardest substance found in nature, was known to the ancient Greeks. They called the gemstone *adamas,* using the same word they used for any unbreakable or indestructible substance, such as the hardest metal, or for anything unmovable. They spelled the stem of this word *adamant-.* Later, Latin writers borrowed these Greek words, sometimes spelling them *adamant-, adamas* and sometimes *adimant-, adimas.* The spellings *adamant-, adamas* in time gave us the English noun *adamant,* meaning "an imaginary

stone of great hardness", and the adjective *adamant,* meaning "firmly fixed or decided". The "i" spellings in Latin were later changed from *adimant-, adimas* to *diamant-, diamas* and came to be used only for the gemstone which we now call *diamond.* [Middle English *diamaunde* "diamond", from early French *diamant* (same meaning), derived from Latin *diamant-, diamas,* an altered form of *adimant-, adimas* and *adamant-, adamas* "the hardest metal, diamond", from Greek *adamant-, adamas* (same meaning) — related to ADAMANT]

di·a·mond·back \'dī-(ə-)mən(d)-ˌbak\ *adj* : having marks like diamonds on the back

diamondback rattlesnake *n* : a large and deadly rattlesnake of the southern U.S. — called also *diamondback, diamondback rattler*

diamondback terrapin *n* : any of several edible terrapins of coastal salt marshes of the southeastern U.S.

dia·pause \'dī-ə-ˌpóz\ *n* : a period (as in some insects) in which development slows down or in which bodily activities are decreased

¹di·a·per \'dī-(ə-)pər\ *n* **1** : a usually white linen or cotton fabric woven in a pattern formed by the repetition of a simple design; *also* : the design on such cloth **2** : a garment for infants consisting of a piece of absorbent material drawn up between the legs and fastened about the waist by pins or tape

²diaper *vb* **di·a·pered; di·a·per·ing** \-p(ə-)riŋ\ **1** : to decorate with diaper designs **2** : to put a diaper on ⟨*diaper* a baby⟩

di·a·phragm \'dī-ə-ˌfram\ *n* **1** : a sheet of muscle that separates the cavities of the chest and abdomen in mammals **2** : a device that limits the size of an opening in order to control the amount of light passing through a lens (as of a camera or microscope) **3** : a thin flexible disk that vibrates (as in a microphone) **4** : a cup-shaped device usually of thin rubber that fits over the cervix of the uterus and acts to prevent pregnancy by keeping sperm from reaching the egg — **di·a·phrag·mat·ic** \ˌdī-ə-frə(g)-'mat-ik, -ˌfrag-\ *adj*

di·ar·rhea *or* **di·ar·rhoea** \ˌdī-ə-'rē-ə\ *n* : abnormally frequent and watery bowel movements

di·a·ry \'dī-(ə)rē\ *n, pl* **-ries** : a daily record especially of personal experiences and thoughts; *also* : a book for keeping such a record [from Latin *diarium* "a record of business dealings or activities during the day", from *dies* "day" — related to MERIDIAN, SUNDAY; see *Word History* at SUNDAY]

di·a·stase \'dī-ə-ˌstās\ *n* : AMYLASE

di·as·to·le \dī-'as-tə-(ˌ)lē\ *n* : the stretching of the cavities of the heart during which they fill with blood

di·a·stol·ic \ˌdī-ə-'stäl-ik\ *adj* : of, relating to, or occurring during diastole

diastolic pressure *n* : the lowest blood pressure in the arteries during the cycle from one heartbeat to the next that occurs during diastole

di·as·tro·phism \dī-'as-trə-ˌfiz-əm\ *n* : a changing of shape in the earth's crust to form continents and ocean basins, plateaus and mountains, and faults — **di·a·stroph·ic** \ˌdī-ə-'sträf-ik\ *adj*

di·a·tom \'dī-ə-ˌtäm\ *n* : any of a class of minute floating single-celled or colonial algae that are common in fresh and salt water and in soil and have a cell wall of silica that remains as a skeleton after death — **di·a·to·ma·ceous** \ˌdī-ət-ə-'mā-shəs\ *adj*

di·atom·ic \ˌdī-ə-'täm-ik\ *adj* : having two atoms in the molecule

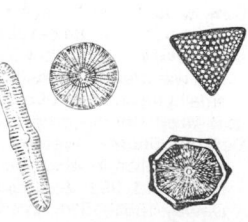
diatom

di·at·o·mite \dī-'at-ə-ˌmīt\ *n* : a light crumbly silica-containing material that comes chiefly from diatom remains and is used especially as a filter

dia·ton·ic \ˌdī-ə-'tän-ik\ *adj* : relating to or being a standard major or minor scale of eight tones to the octave — **dia·ton·i·cal·ly** \-'tän-i-k(ə-)lē\ *adv*

di·a·tribe \'dī-ə-ˌtrīb\ *n* : a bitter or angry attack in speech or writing

dib·ble \'dib-əl\ *n* : a small hand tool for making holes in the ground for plants, seeds, or bulbs

¹dice \'dīs\ *n, pl* **dice** **1** : a small cube marked on each side with one to six spots and used usually in pairs in various games **2** : a gambling game played with dice

²dice *vb* **diced; dic·ing** **1** : to cut into small cubes ⟨*diced* carrots⟩ **2** : to play games with dice — **dic·er** *n*

di·chlo·ride \(')dī-'klō(ə)r-ˌīd, -'klȯ(ə)r-\ *n* : a compound containing two atoms of chlorine combined with an element or group of atoms

di·chot·o·mous key \dī-'kät-ə-məs-\ *n* : a series of pairs of phrases or descriptions which are used to classify a group of living things by making choices between the sets of traits and characters described in each pair

dick·ens \'dik-ənz\ *n* : ¹DEVIL 1, DEUCE — used chiefly as a mild oath ⟨what the *dickens* do you mean?⟩

dick·er \'dik-ər\ *vb* **dick·ered; dick·er·ing** \'dik-(ə-)riŋ\ : ²BARGAIN, HAGGLE — **dicker** *n*

dick·ey *or* **dicky** \'dik-ē\ *n, pl* **dick·eys** *or* **dick·ies** **1** : any of various articles of clothing: as **a** : a separate or detachable front of a shirt **b** : a small cloth insert worn to fill in the neckline **2** : a small bird

Dick test \'dik-\ *n* : a test that tells whether one can get scarlet fever and is made by an injection of scarlet fever toxin [named for George F. *Dick* 1881–1967 and Gladys H. *Dick* 1881–1963 American doctors]

di·cot \'dī-ˌkät\ *n* : DICOTYLEDON

di·cot·y·le·don \ˌdī-ˌkät-ᵊl-'ēd-ᵊn\ *n* : any of a group of flowering plants (as an aster, an oak, or a cabbage) having an embryo with two cotyledons, leaves with veins that usually branch and interlace to form a network, and flower parts that do not occur in groups of three

di·cot·y·le·don·ous \ˌdī-ˌkät-ᵊl-'ēd-ᵊn-əs\ *adj* : of, relating to, or being plants that are dicotyledons

¹dic·tate \'dik-ˌtāt, dik-'tāt\ *vb* **dic·tat·ed; dic·tat·ing** **1** : to speak or read for a person to write down or for a machine to record ⟨*dictate* a letter to a secretary⟩ **2** : to say or state with authority or power : give orders ⟨*dictate* terms of surrender⟩ ⟨few people enjoy being *dictated* to⟩ [from Latin *dictatus,* past participle of *dictare* "to assert, dictate," derived from *dicere* "to say" — related to DICTIONARY, PREDICT, VERDICT]

²dictate \'dik-ˌtāt\ *n* : an order or direction given with authority : COMMAND ⟨the *dictates* of conscience⟩

dic·ta·tion \dik-'tā-shən\ *n* **1** : the act or process of giving commands **2 a** : the dictating of words ⟨write from *dictation*⟩ **b** : something that is dictated or is taken down from dictation

dic·ta·tor \'dik-ˌtāt-ər, dik-'tāt-ər\ *n* **1** : a person who rules with total authority and often in a cruel or brutal manner **2** : one that dictates — **dic·ta·to·ri·al** \ˌdik-tə-'tōr-ē-əl, -'tȯr-\ *adj* — **dic·ta·to·ri·al·ly** \-ē-ə-lē\ *adv* — **dic·ta·to·ri·al·ness** *n*

dic·ta·tor·ship \dik-'tāt-ər-ˌship, 'dik-ˌtāt-\ *n* **1** : the office or term of office of a dictator **2** : rule, control, or leadership by one person with total power **3** : a government or country in which total power is held by a dictator or a small group

dic·tion \'dik-shən\ *n* **1** : choice of words especially with regard to correctness, clearness, or effectiveness : WORDING ⟨careless *diction* in the student's essay⟩ **2** : quality of vocal expression : ENUNCIATION ⟨a good singer with excellent *diction*⟩

dic·tio·nary \'dik-shə-ˌner-ē\ *n, pl* **-nar·ies** **1** : a reference book giving information about the meanings, forms, pronunciations, uses, and origins of words listed in alphabetical order **2** : a reference book that lists in alphabetical order terms or names important to a particular subject along with explanations of their meanings and uses ⟨a law *dictionary*⟩ **3** : a reference book giving words of one language and their meanings in another ⟨an English-French *dictionary*⟩ [from Latin *dictionarium* "dictionary", from earlier *diction-, dictio-* "words, speaking", derived from *dicere* "to say" — related to DICTATE]

dic·tum \'dik-təm\ *n, pl* **dic·ta** \-tə\ *also* **dic·tums** : a statement made with authority : PRONOUNCEMENT

did *past of* DO

di·dac·tic \dī-'dak-tik, də-\ *adj* **1** : intended primarily to instruct rather than to entertain; *esp* : intended to teach a moral lesson ⟨*didactic* literature⟩ **2** : having or showing a fondness for instructing or lecturing others ⟨a *didactic* manner⟩ — **di·dac·ti·cal** \-ti-kəl\ *adj* — **di·dac·ti·cal·ly** \-ti-k(ə-)lē\ *adv* — **di·dac·ti·cism** \-tə-ˌsiz-əm\ *n*

didn't \'did-ᵊnt\ : did not

didst \(')didst\ *archaic past 2d sing of* DO

¹die \'dī\ *vb* **died; dy·ing** \'dī-iŋ\ **1** : to stop living : EXPIRE ⟨*died* of old age⟩ **2 a** : to pass out of existence ⟨a *dying* race⟩ **b** : to disappear or lessen gradually ⟨the wind *died* down⟩ **3** : to wish eagerly or desperately ⟨*dying* to go⟩ **4** : ¹STOP 7b ⟨the motor sputtered and *died*⟩ [Middle English *dien* "to die"; of Norse origin]

²die \'dī\ *n* **1** *pl* **dice** \'dīs\ : ¹DICE 1 **2** *pl* **dies** \'dīz\ : any of various devices used for cutting, shaping, or stamping a material or object [Middle English *dee* "small cube marked with spots and thrown in gambling, dice", from early French *dé* (same meaning)]

dieresis *variant of* DIAERESIS

die·sel \'dē-zəl, -səl\ *n* **1** : DIESEL ENGINE **2** : a vehicle (as a truck or train) driven by a diesel engine [named for Rudolf *Diesel* 1858–1913 German engineer]

diesel engine *n* : an internal-combustion engine in which air is compressed to make enough heat to ignite the oil in the cylinder

¹di·et \'dī-ət\ *n* **1** : the food and drink that a person, animal, or group usually takes ⟨many birds live on a *diet* of insects⟩ **2** : the kind and amount of food selected for a person or animal for a special reason (as being in ill health or overweight) ⟨a high-protein *diet*⟩ [Middle English *diete* "regular food, diet", from early French *diete* (same meaning), derived from Greek *diaita,* literally "manner of living"]

²diet *vb* : to eat or cause to eat less or according to special rules

³diet *adj* : reduced in calories ⟨a *diet* soft drink⟩

⁴diet *n* : a body of lawmakers : LEGISLATURE [from Latin *dieta* "assembly, day's work", from earlier *dies* "day"]

di·etary \'dī-ə-ˌter-ē\ *adj* : of or relating to a diet or to the rules of diet

di·et·er \'dī-ət-ər\ *n* : a person who is on a diet

di·etet·ic \ˌdī-ə-'tet-ik\ *adj* : of or relating to diet or dietetics

di·etet·ics \ˌdī-ə-'tet-iks\ *n* : the science of applying the principles of nutrition to feeding

di·eti·tian *or* **di·eti·cian** \ˌdī-ə-'tish-ən\ *n* : a specialist in dietetics

dif·fer \'dif-ər\ *vb* **dif·fered; dif·fer·ing** \'dif-(ə-)riŋ\ **1** : to be not the same : be unlike ⟨brothers who *differ* in looks⟩ **2** : DISAGREE 2

dif·fer·ence \'dif-ərn(t)s, 'dif-(ə-)rən(t)s\ *n* **1** : the quality or state of being different ⟨the striking *difference* in the sisters' looks⟩ **2** : the degree or amount by which things differ; *esp* : the number that is obtained by subtracting one

\ə\ abut	\au̇\ out	\i\ tip	\ȯ\ saw	\u̇\ foot
\ər\ further	\ch\ chin	\ī\ life	\ȯi\ coin	\y\ yet
\a\ mat	\e\ pet	\j\ job	\th\ thin	\yü\ few
\ā\ take	\ē\ easy	\ŋ\ sing	\th\ this	\yu̇\ cure
\ä\ cot, cart	\g\ go	\ō\ bone	\ü\ food	\zh\ vision

number from another 〈the *difference* between 4 and 6 is 2〉   **3** : a disagreement in opinion : DISPUTE 〈persons unable to settle their *differences*〉   **4** : an important change 〈the weather didn't make any *difference* in our plans〉

dif·fer·ent \'dif-ərnt, 'dif-(ə-)rənt\ *adj*   **1** : not of the same kind : partly or totally unlike another 〈this apple is *different* from the others in size and color〉   **2** : not the same : OTHER, SEPARATE 〈see the same person at *different* times〉 — **dif·fer·ent·ly** *adv*

¹dif·fer·en·tial \,dif-ə-'ren-chəl\ *adj*   **1 a** : of, relating to, or being a difference   **b** : treating some individuals or classes differently from others : DISCRIMINATORY   **2** : acting or proceeding differently or at a different rate with respect to different individuals or substances 〈*differential* diffusion through a membrane〉 — **dif·fer·en·tial·ly** \-'rench-(ə-)lē\ *adv*

²differential *n* : DIFFERENTIAL GEAR

differential gear *n* : an arrangement of gears in an automobile that allows one wheel to turn faster than another (as in going around a curve)

dif·fer·en·ti·ate \,dif-ə-'ren-chē-,āt\ *vb* **-at·ed; -at·ing**   **1** : to make or become different in some way 〈the color of their eyes *differentiates* the twins〉   **2** : to undergo or cause to undergo differentiation in the course of development   **3** : to see or state the difference or differences 〈*differentiate* between two plants〉

dif·fer·en·ti·a·tion \,dif-ə-,ren-chē-'ā-shən\ *n*   **1** : the act or process of differentiating   **2** : the processes by which cells, tissues, and structures develop their specialized adult form and function; *also* : the result of these processes

dif·fi·cult \'dif-i-(,)kəlt\ *adj*   **1** : hard to do, make, or carry out : ARDUOUS 〈a *difficult* climb〉   **2 a** : hard to deal with, manage, or overcome 〈a *difficult* child〉   **b** : hard to understand : PUZZLING 〈*difficult* reading〉 — **dif·fi·cult·ly** *adv*

dif·fi·cul·ty \'dif-ə-(,)kəl-tē\ *n, pl* **-ties**   **1** : difficult nature 〈slowed up by the *difficulty* of a task〉   **2** : great effort 〈accomplish a task with *difficulty*〉   **3** : something that is hard to do : OBSTACLE 〈overcome *difficulties*〉   **4** : a difficult or trying situation : TROUBLE 〈in financial *difficulties*〉   **5** : a disagreement in opinion 〈the partners ironed out their *difficulties*〉

dif·fi·dent \'dif-əd-ənt, -ə-,dent\ *adj*   **1** : lacking confidence : TIMID   **2** : RESERVED 1, UNASSERTIVE   **syn** see SHY — **dif·fi·dence** \-əd-ən(t)s, -ə-,den(t)s\ *n* — **dif·fi·dent·ly** *adv*

dif·fract \dif-'rakt\ *vb* : to cause to go through diffraction

dif·frac·tion \dif-'rak-shən\ *n* : the bending or spreading of a beam of light especially when passing through a narrow opening or when reflected from a ruled surface; *also* : similar changes in other waves (as sound waves)

diffraction grating *n* : GRATING 2

¹dif·fuse \dif-'yüs\ *adj*   **1** : using too many words : VERBOSE 〈a *diffuse* writer〉   **2** : poured or spread out : not concentrated 〈*diffuse* daylight〉 — **dif·fuse·ly** *adv* — **dif·fuse·ness** *n*

²dif·fuse \dif-'yüz\ *vb* **dif·fused; dif·fus·ing**   **1** : to pour out and permit or cause to spread freely   **2** : to go through or cause to go through diffusion   **3** : to break up (light) by reflection (as from a rough surface)

dif·fu·sion \dif-'yü-zhən\ *n*   **1** : a diffusing or a being diffused   **2** : the mixing of particles of liquids, gases, or solids so that they move from a region of high concentration to one of lower concentration   **3** : the reflection of light from a rough surface or the passage of light through a translucent material (as frosted glass)

¹dig \'dig\ *vb* **dug** \'dəg\; **dig·ging**   **1 a** : to turn up the soil (as with a spade or hoe)   **b** : to hollow out or form by removing earth 〈*dig* a hole〉 〈*dig* a cellar〉   **2** : to uncover or search for or as if by turning up earth 〈*dig* potatoes〉 〈*dig* for gold〉 〈*dig* through books for information〉   **3** : FIND OUT

〈*dig* up the facts〉   **4** : ¹PROD 1, POKE 〈*dig* a person in the ribs〉   **5** *slang* **a** : to pay attention to 〈*dig* that hat〉   **b** : UNDERSTAND 1a 〈you *dig* me?〉   **c** : ¹LIKE 1 〈really *digs* rock music〉 — **dig·ger** *n*

²dig *n*   **1** : ³POKE, THRUST   **2** : a harsh remark : GIBE   **3** : a place where scientists (as archaeologists or paleontologists) try to recover buried objects by digging; *also* : the process of digging for such objects

¹di·gest \'dī-,jest\ *n* : a body of information or a literary work in shortened form 〈a *digest* of the laws〉

²di·gest \dī-'jest, də-\ *vb*   **1** : to think over and arrange in the mind 〈*digest* the news〉   **2** : to convert food into simpler forms that can be taken in and used by the body   **3** : SUMMARIZE 1   **4** : to become digested

di·gest·ible \dī-'jes-tə-bəl, də-\ *adj* : capable of being digested — **di·gest·ibil·i·ty** \-,jes-tə-'bil-ət-ē\ *n*

di·ges·tion \dī-'jes-chən, də-\ *n* : the process or power of digesting something and especially food

di·ges·tive \dī-'jes-tiv, də-\ *adj*   **1** : of or relating to digestion 〈the *digestive* system of the body〉   **2** : having the power to cause or help digestion 〈*digestive* enzymes〉

dig·ger wasp \'dig-ər-\ *n* : a burrowing wasp; *esp* : one that digs nests in the soil and stocks them with insects or spiders paralyzed by stinging

dig·gings \'dig-iŋz\ *n pl*   **1** : a place where ore, metals, or gems are dug   **2** : LODGING 2

dig in *vb*   **1** : to dig and take position in a trench 〈the soldiers *dug in*〉   **2 a** : to go to work   **b** : to begin eating

dig·it \'dij-ət\ *n*   **1 a** : any of the arabic numerals 1 to 9 and usually the symbol 0   **b** : one of the elements that are used to form numbers in a system other than the decimal system   **2** : ¹FINGER 1, TOE   **3** : a unit of length based on the width of a finger and equal in the English system to about ¾ inch (about 1.90 centimeters) [Middle English *digit* "numeral," from Latin *digitus* "finger, toe"; so called because the earliest counting was done on the fingers]

dig·i·tal \'dij-ət-ᵊl\ *adj*   **1** : of, relating to, or done with a finger or toe   **2** : of, relating to, or using calculation directly with digits rather than through measurable physical quantities   **3** : providing displayed or recorded information in numerical digits from an automatic device 〈a *digital* watch〉 — **dig·i·tal·ly** \-ᵊl-ē\ *adv*

digital computer *n* : a computer that operates with numbers expressed as digits (as in the binary system) — compare ANALOG COMPUTER

dig·i·tal·is \,dij-ə-'tal-əs *also* -'tāl-\ *n* : a powerful drug used to stimulate the heart and prepared from the dried leaves of the common foxglove

dig·i·tize \'dij-ə-,tīz\ *vb* **-tized; -tiz·ing** : to change (as data or an image) to digital form — **dig·i·tiz·er** *n*

dig·ni·fied \'dig-nə-,fīd\ *adj* : having or showing dignity 〈a *dignified* butler〉

dig·ni·fy \'dig-nə-,fī\ *vb* **-fied; -fy·ing** : to give dignity or importance to : HONOR

dig·ni·tary \'dig-nə-,ter-ē\ *n, pl* **-tar·ies** : a person of high position or honor 〈*dignitaries* of the church〉

dig·ni·ty \'dig-nət-ē\ *n, pl* **-ties**   **1** : the quality or state of being worthy, honored, or respected   **2** : high rank, office, or position   **3** : a look or way of behaving that suggests seriousness and self-control

di·gress \dī-'gres, də-\ *vb* : to turn aside especially from the main subject in writing or speaking — **di·gres·sion** \-'gresh-ən\ *n* — **di·gres·sive** \-'gres-iv\ *adj*

di·he·dral angle \(')dī-,hē-drəl-\ *n* : the angle between two intersecting planes

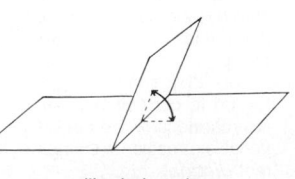

dihedral angle

¹di·hy·brid \(ˌ)dī-ˈhī-brəd\ *n* : an individual that is hybrid with respect to two different traits or pairs of genes

²dihybrid *adj* : being, involving, or producing individuals that are hybrid with respect to two different traits or pairs of genes

¹dike *or* **dyke** \ˈdīk\ *n* **1** : a channel dug in the earth to carry water : DITCH **2** : a bank of earth constructed to control water : LEVEE **3** : a long body of igneous rock that has been forced while melted into a narrow opening or crack

²dike *or* **dyke** *vb* **diked** *or* **dyked; dik·ing** *or* **dyk·ing** **1** : to surround or protect with a dike **2** : to drain by a dike — **dik·er** *n*

di·lap·i·dat·ed \də-ˈlap-ə-ˌdāt-əd\ *adj* : partly ruined or decayed from age or lack of care ⟨a *dilapidated* old house⟩

di·lap·i·da·tion \də-ˌlap-ə-ˈdā-shən\ *n* : a dilapidated condition : partial ruin

di·la·ta·tion \ˌdil-ə-ˈtā-shən, ˌdī-lə-\ *n* : DILATION 2

di·late \dī-ˈlāt, ˈdī-ˌlāt\ *vb* **di·lat·ed; di·lat·ing** : to make or grow larger or wider ⟨lungs *dilated* with air⟩ **syn** *see* EXPAND

di·la·tion \dī-ˈlā-shən\ *n* **1** : the act of dilating : the state of being dilated : EXPANSION **2** : the action of stretching or enlarging an organ or part of the body

dil·a·to·ry \ˈdil-ə-ˌtōr-ē, -ˌtȯr-\ *adj* **1** : tending or intended to cause delay ⟨*dilatory* tactics⟩ **2** : tending to be late : TARDY — **dil·a·to·ri·ly** \ˌdil-ə-ˈtōr-ə-lē, -ˈtȯr-\ *adv* — **dil·a·to·ri·ness** \ˈdil-ə-ˌtōr-ē-nəs, -ˌtȯr-\ *n*

di·lem·ma \də-ˈlem-ə *also* dī-\ *n* : a situation in which one has to choose between two or more things, ways, or plans that are equally unsatisfactory : a difficult choice

dil·et·tante \ˈdil-ə-ˌtänt, -ˌtant, ˌdil-ə-ˈtänt(-ē), -ˈtant(-ē)\ *n, pl* **-tantes** *or* **-tan·ti** \-ˈtänt-ē, -ˈtant-ē\ **1** : an admirer or lover of the arts **2** : a person who has a shallow interest in an art or area of knowledge — **dilettante** *adj* — **dil·et·tan·tism** \-ˌtän-ˌtiz-əm, -ˌtan-\ *n*

dil·i·gence \ˈdil-ə-jən(t)s\ *n* : careful and continued work : INDUSTRY

dil·i·gent \ˈdil-ə-jənt\ *adj* : showing steady and earnest care and effort : PAINSTAKING ⟨a *diligent* search⟩ ⟨a *diligent* worker⟩ **syn** *see* BUSY — **dil·i·gent·ly** *adv*

dill \ˈdil\ *n* : an herb with aromatic foliage and with seeds used in flavoring pickles

dill pickle *n* : a pickle seasoned with dill or dill juice

dil·ly·dal·ly \ˈdil-ē-ˌdal-ē\ *vb* : to waste time : DAWDLE

¹di·lute \dī-ˈlüt, də-\ *vb* **di·lut·ed; di·lut·ing** : to make thinner or more liquid by adding in and mixing something

²dilute *adj* : lacking normal strength especially as a result of being diluted

di·lu·tion \dī-ˈlü-shən, də-\ *n* **1** : the action of diluting : the state of being diluted **2** : something (as a solution) that is diluted

¹dim \ˈdim\ *adj* **dim·mer; dim·mest** **1** : not bright or clear : OBSCURE, FAINT ⟨a *dim* light⟩ **2** : being without luster : DULL **3 a** : not seeing or understanding clearly ⟨*dim* eyes⟩ **b** : not seen or understood clearly — **dim·ly** *adv* — **dim·ness** *n*

²dim *vb* **dimmed; dim·ming** **1** : to make or become dim **2** : to reduce the light from headlights by switching to the low beam

dime \ˈdīm\ *n* : a U.S. coin worth ¹⁄₁₀ dollar [Middle English *dime* "a tenth part", from early French *dime* (same meaning), derived from Latin *decimus* "a tenth part", from *decem* "ten" — related to DECEMBER, DECIMAL, DOZEN]

dime novel *n* : a cheap novel with usually much adventure or romance

di·men·sion \də-ˈmen-chən *also* dī-\ *n* **1 a** : extension in one direction **b** : measure of extension in one direction or in all directions : SIZE **2** : the range over which something extends : SCOPE — usually used in pl. [Middle English *dimensioun* "dimension", from early French *dimen-*

sion (same meaning), derived from Latin *dimensus*, past participle of *dimetiri* "to measure out", from *di-*, *dis-* "apart" and *metiri* "to measure" — related to IMMENSE, MEASURE] — **di·men·sion·al** \-ˈmench-nəl, -ˈmen-chən-əl\ *adj* — **di·men·sion·al·ly** \-ˈmench-nə-lē, -ˈmen-chən-əl-ē\ *adv* — **di·men·sion·less** \-ˈmen-chən-ləs\ *adj*

dime store *n* : a store that sells mainly inexpensive goods

di·min·ish \də-ˈmin-ish\ *vb* **1 a** : to make less or cause to appear less **b** : to reduce by subtracting ⟨8 *diminished* by 5⟩ **2** : BELITTLE **3** : to become gradually less : DWINDLE — **di·min·ish·ment** \-mənt\ *n*

di·min·u·en·do \də-ˌmin-(y)ə-ˈwen-dō\ *adv or adj* : ¹DECRESCENDO — **diminuendo** *n*

dim·i·nu·tion \ˌdim-ə-ˈn(y)ü-shən\ *n* : the act, process, or an instance of diminishing : DECREASE

¹di·min·u·tive \də-ˈmin-yət-iv\ *n* **1** : a diminutive word or affix **2** : a diminutive object or individual

²diminutive *adj* **1** : indicating small size and sometimes the state or quality of being lovable or pitiful ⟨the *diminutive* suffixes "-ette" and "-ling"⟩ ⟨the *diminutive* noun "duckling"⟩ **2** : extremely small : TINY — **di·min·u·tive·ly** *adv* — **di·min·u·tive·ness** *n*

dim·i·ty \ˈdim-ət-ē\ *n, pl* **-ties** : a usually corded cotton fabric in checks or stripes

dim·mer \ˈdim-ər\ *n* : a device for controlling the amount of light from an electric lighting unit (as the headlights of an automobile or the lights of a room)

¹dim·ple \ˈdim-pəl\ *n* **1** : a slight natural hollow in the surface of some part of the human body **2** : a slight hollow ⟨the *dimples* on a golf ball⟩

²dimple *vb* **dim·pled; dim·pling** \-p(ə-)liŋ\ : to mark with or form dimples

¹din \ˈdin\ *n* : a loud confused mixture of noises

²din *vb* **dinned; din·ning** **1** : to make a din **2** : to repeat again and again in order to impress on someone's mind ⟨*dinned* in our ears the consequences of failure⟩

dine \ˈdīn\ *vb* **dined; din·ing** **1** : to eat dinner ⟨*dine* out⟩ **2** : to give a dinner to : FEED ⟨wined and *dined* their friends⟩

din·er \ˈdī-nər\ *n* **1** : one that dines **2 a** : DINING CAR **b** : a restaurant in the shape of a railroad car

di·nette \dī-ˈnet\ *n* : a separate area or small room used for dining

ding \ˈdiŋ\ *vb* : to make a ringing sound : CLANG

ding·dong \ˈdiŋ-ˌdȯŋ, -ˌdäŋ\ *n* : the ringing sound made by repeated strokes especially on a bell

din·ghy \ˈdiŋ-ē, -gē\ *n, pl* **dinghies** **1** : a small rowboat or sailboat; *esp* : one carried on a larger boat **2** : a rubber life raft

din·gle \ˈdiŋ-gəl\ *n* : a small wooded valley

din·go \ˈdiŋ-gō\ *n, pl* **dingoes** : a reddish brown bushy-tailed wild dog of Australia

din·gy \ˈdin-jē\ *adj* **din·gi·er; -est** : rather dark and dirty : not fresh or clean ⟨a *dingy* room⟩ ⟨*dingy* colors⟩ — **din·gi·ly** \-jə-lē\ *adv* — **din·gi·ness** \-jē-nəs\ *n*

dingo

din·ing car \ˈdī-niŋ-\ *n* : a railroad car in which meals are served

din·ky \ˈdiŋ-kē\ *adj* **din·ki·er; -est** : very small and unimpressive ⟨a *dinky* room⟩

\ə\ abut	\au̇\ out	\i\ tip	\ȯ\ saw	\u̇\ foot
\ər\ further	\ch\ chin	\ī\ life	\ȯi\ coin	\y\ yet
\a\ mat	\e\ pet	\j\ job	\th\ thin	\yü\ few
\ā\ take	\ē\ easy	\ŋ\ sing	\t̠h\ this	\yu̇\ cure
\ä\ cot, cart	\g\ go	\ō\ bone	\ü\ food	\zh\ vision

din·ner \'din-ər\ *n* **1** : the main meal of the day **2** : ¹BANQUET

din·ner·time \-ˌtīm\ *n* : the usual time for dinner

din·ner·ware \-ˌwa(ə)r, -ˌwe(ə)r\ *n* : utensils (as dishes and glasses) used at the dinner table

di·no·flag·el·late \ˌdī-nō-'flaj-ə-lət, -ˌlāt\ *n* : any of an order of chiefly marine floating organisms that resemble both algae and protozoa and are important in marine food chains

di·no·saur \'dī-nə-ˌsȯr\ *n* : any of a group of extinct mostly land-dwelling reptiles with long tails and limbs used for walking [derived from Greek *deinos* "terrible" and Greek *sauros* "lizard"]

¹**dint** \'dint\ *n* **1** : the force or power of something — used chiefly in the phrase *by dint of* ⟨succeeded by *dint* of hard work⟩ **2** : ²DENT 1

²**dint** *vb* : ¹DENT 1

¹**di·oc·e·san** \dī-'äs-ə-sən\ *adj* : of or relating to a diocese

²**diocesan** *n* : a bishop having authority over a diocese

di·o·cese \'dī-ə-səs, -ˌsēz, -ˌsēs\ *n, pl* **-ces·es** \'dī-ə-ˌsēz, -ˌsē-zēz, -sə-səz\ : the district over which a bishop has authority

di·ode \'dī-ˌōd\ *n* **1** : a two-electrode electron tube having a cathode and an anode **2** : a semiconductor device for changing alternating current into direct current

di·o·rama \ˌdī-ə-'ram-ə, -'räm-\ *n* : a scenic representation in which lifelike sculptured figures and surrounding details are realistically set against a painted background

di·ox·ide \(')dī-'äk-ˌsīd\ *n* : an oxide containing two atoms of oxygen in the molecule

¹**dip** \'dip\ *vb* **dipped; dip·ping** **1** : to sink or push briefly into or as if into a liquid ⟨*dip* a towel in water⟩ ⟨*dips* a hand into his pocket⟩ **2** : to lift out with something that holds liquid : LADLE ⟨*dip* water from a pail⟩ **3** : to lower and then raise again ⟨*dip* a flag in salute⟩ **4 a** : to drop down into a liquid and quickly come out ⟨oars *dipping* rhythmically⟩ **b** : to put something for treatment under the surface of a liquid **5 a** : to drop down or out of sight ⟨the road *dipped* below the crest⟩ **b** : to decrease somewhat usually for a short time ⟨prices *dipped*⟩ **6** : to reach down inside or as if inside especially to take out a part of the contents ⟨*dipped* into their savings⟩ **7** : to look at or consider something briefly; *esp* : to read a little of something ⟨*dip* into a book⟩

²**dip** *n* **1** : an act of dipping; *esp* : a brief plunge into the water for sport or exercise **2 a** : a downward slope **b** : a sharp or slight downward course : DROP ⟨a *dip* in prices⟩ **3** : the angle formed with the horizon by a magnetic needle free to rotate in a vertical plane **4** : something obtained by or used in dipping ⟨a *dip* of ice cream⟩ **5** : a sauce or soft mixture into which food (as raw vegetables) may be dipped **6** : a liquid into which an object may be dipped (as for cleansing or coloring)

diph·the·ria \dif-'thir-ē-ə, dip-\ *n* : a contagious bacterial disease with fever in which the air passages become coated with a membranous layer that often obstructs breathing — **diph·the·rit·ic** \ˌdif-thə-'rit-ik, ˌdip-\ *adj*

diph·thong \'dif-ˌthȯŋ, 'dip-\ *n* : a two-element speech sound that begins with the tongue position for one vowel and ends with the tongue position for another all within one syllable ⟨the sounds of "ou" in "out" and of "oy" in "boy" are *diphthongs*⟩

dip·lo·coc·cus \ˌdip-lō-'käk-əs\ *n, pl* **-coc·ci** \-'käk-ˌ(s)ī, -ˌ(s)ē\ : any of various bacteria that occur usually in pairs in a capsule and include some that cause serious diseases

di·plod·o·cus \də-'pläd-ə-kəs, dī-\ *n* : any of a genus of very large plant-eating dinosaurs from what are now Colorado and Wyoming

di·plo·ma \də-'plō-mə\ *n* : a document granting a special right, honor, or power; *esp* : a document that shows a person has finished a course or graduated from a school

di·plo·ma·cy \də-'plō-mə-sē\ *n* **1** : the work of keeping up relations between the governments of different countries **2** : skill in dealing with others without causing bad feelings : TACT

dip·lo·mat \'dip-lə-ˌmat\ *n* : a person employed or skilled in diplomacy

dip·lo·mat·ic \ˌdip-lə-'mat-ik\ *adj* **1** : of, relating to, or concerned with diplomacy or diplomats ⟨*diplomatic* credentials⟩ **2** : TACTFUL ⟨found a *diplomatic* way to say no⟩ — **dip·lo·mat·i·cal·ly** \-'mat-i-k(ə-)lē\ *adv*

di·plo·ma·tist \də-'plō-mət-əst\ *n* : DIPLOMAT

dip·lo·pod \'dip-lə-ˌpäd\ *n* : MILLIPEDE

dip net *n* : a small bag-shaped net with a handle that is used especially to scoop small fish from the water

di·pole \'dī-ˌpōl\ *n* : a pair of equal and opposite electric charges or magnetic poles of opposite sign separated especially by a small distance

dip·per \'dip-ər\ *n* **1** : any of several birds skilled in diving — called also *water ouzel* **2** : one that dips; *esp* : something (as a long-handled cup) used for dipping **3** *cap* **a** : the seven major stars of Ursa Major arranged in a form resembling a dipper — called also *Big Dipper* **b** : the seven major stars in Ursa Minor similarly arranged with the North Star forming the outer end of the handle — called also *Little Dipper* — **dipperful** \-ˌfül\ *n*

dip·stick \'dip-ˌstik\ *n* : a rod with marks for indicating depth (as of the oil in an automobile)

¹**dip·ter·an** \'dip-tə-rən\ *adj* : of, relating to, or being a two-winged fly

²**dipteran** *n* : TWO-WINGED FLY

dip·ter·ous \'dip-tə-rəs\ *adj* : DIPTERAN

dire \'dī(ə)r\ *adj* **dir·er; dir·est** **1** : causing horror : DREADFUL **2** : warning of disaster ⟨a *dire* forecast⟩ **3** : ¹EXTREME 1 ⟨*dire* need⟩ — **dire·ly** *adv* — **dire·ness** *n*

¹**di·rect** \də-'rekt, dī-\ *vb* **1** : to mark with a name and address ⟨*direct* a letter⟩ **2** : to cause to turn, move, or point or to follow a straight course **3** : to point in a specified line, course, or direction **4** : to show or point out the way for ⟨the signs *directed* us to the museum⟩ **5** : to guide the activities or course of ⟨*direct* the project⟩ ⟨*direct* a play⟩ **6** : to request or instruct with authority ⟨the court *directed* the jury to acquit them⟩ **syn** see COMMAND

²**direct** *adj* **1** : proceeding from one point to another in time or space without turning or stopping : STRAIGHT **2 a** : coming immediately from a source, cause, or reason ⟨*direct* result⟩ **b** : done or working without something else coming in between ⟨*direct* action⟩ ⟨*direct* printing⟩ **c** : being in an unbroken family line : LINEAL ⟨*direct* ancestor⟩ **3** : ¹NATURAL 8, STRAIGHTFORWARD ⟨*direct* manner⟩ **4** : consisting of or reproducing the exact words of a speaker ⟨*direct* quotation⟩ — **direct** *adv* — **di·rect·ness** \-'rek(t)-nəs\ *n*

direct current *n* : an electric current flowing in one direction only — abbr. *DC*

directed number *n* : a number with a plus or minus sign in front of it

di·rec·tion \də-'rek-shən, dī-\ *n* **1** : guidance of action or conduct : MANAGEMENT ⟨many people working under my *direction*⟩ ⟨*direction* of a play⟩ **2** : an instruction, indication, or order given with authority ⟨follow *directions*⟩ **3** : the line or course along which something moves, lies, or points ⟨headed in a northern *direction*⟩ **4** : TENDENCY 1, TREND — **di·rec·tion·less** \-ləs\ *adj*

di·rec·tion·al \də-'rek-sh(ə-)nəl, dī-\ *adj* **1** : relating to or indicating direction ⟨*directional* signal lights on an automobile⟩ **2** : relating to direction or guidance especially of thought or effort

di·rec·tive \də-'rek-tiv, dī-\ *n* : something that guides or directs; *esp* : a general instruction from a high-level body or official

¹**di·rect·ly** \də-'rek-(t)lē, dī-, *in sense 2 also* 'drek-lē\ *adv* **1** : in a direct manner ⟨she spoke *directly*⟩ **2** : without delay : IMMEDIATELY ⟨we'll be leaving *directly*⟩ **3** : in the

manner of direct variation ⟨the perimeter *P* of a square varies *directly* with the length of a side *s* since $P = 4s$⟩

²**di·rect·ly** \də-'rek-(t)lē, dī-; 'drek-lē\ *conj, chiefly British* : AS SOON AS

directly proportional *adj* : related by direct variation ⟨the earnings of a newspaper carrier are *directly proportional* to the number of papers delivered⟩ — compare INVERSELY PROPORTIONAL

direct object *n* : a grammatical object that is the main goal or the result of the action of its verb ⟨*me* in "he touched me" and *house* in "we built a house" are *direct objects*⟩

di·rec·tor \də-'rek-tər, dī-\ *n* : one that directs: as **a** : one of a group of persons who direct the business of an organized body (as a corporation) ⟨the board of *directors*⟩ **b** : one that guides the making of a show (as for stage or screen) **c** : CONDUCTOR 2 — **di·rec·to·ri·al** \də-,rek-'tōr-ē-əl, (,)dī-, -'tòr-\ *adj* — **di·rec·tor·ship** \də-'rek-tər-,ship, dī-\ *n*

di·rec·to·ry \də-'rek-t(ə-)rē, dī-\ *n, pl* **-ries** : an alphabetical list containing names and addresses

direct variation *n* **1** : mathematical relationship between two variables which can be expressed by an equation in which one variable is equal to a constant times the other ⟨the relation between the total amount earned *T* and the amount paid per hour *h* is that of *direct variation* if the number of hours worked *k* stays the same since $T = k h$⟩ **2** : an equation or function expressing direct variation — compare INVERSE VARIATION 2

dire·ful \'dī(ə)r-fəl\ *adj* : DIRE 1, 2 — **dire·ful·ly** \-fə-lē\ *adv*

dirge \'dərj\ *n* : a song or hymn of mourning; *esp* : one intended for funeral or memorial ceremonies

> **Word History** The meaning of English *dirge* is not directly related to the meaning of the Latin word it comes from. *Dirge* and its earlier form *dirige*, meaning "a song or hymn of mourning", come from the first word of a Latin chant used in the church service for the dead: "Dirige, Domine deus meus, in conspectu tuo viam meam" (Direct, O Lord my God, my way in thy sight). Because hymns and chants were often referred to by their first words, *dirge* became the common word for this chant. Later it was used for a slow, solemn hymn of mourning. [Middle English *dirige* "service performed when someone dies", from Latin *dirige* "direct", first word in a prayer for the dead, from earlier *dirigere* "to direct"]

¹**dir·i·gi·ble** \'dir-ə-jə-bəl, də-'rij-ə-\ *adj* : capable of being steered

²**dirigible** *n* : AIRSHIP

dirk \'dərk\ *n* : a long dagger with a straight blade — **dirk** *vb*

dirndl \'dərn-dᵊl\ *n* : a full skirt with a tight waistband [a shortened form of German *dirndlkleid*, literally "girl's dress", from *dirndl* "girl" and *kleid* "dress"]

dirt \'dərt\ *n* **1** : a filthy or soiling substance (as mud, dust, or grime) **2** : loose or packed earth : SOIL **3 a** : CORRUPTION 2 **b** : indecent language : OBSCENITY **4** : harmful gossip

dirt bike *n* : a motorcycle designed to be used off the road

¹**dirty** \'dərt-ē\ *adj* **dirt·i·er; -est 1** : not clean ⟨*dirty* clothes⟩ ⟨*dirty* air⟩ **2** : UNFAIR 1, BASE ⟨a *dirty* trick⟩ **3** : INDECENT, SMUTTY ⟨*dirty* talk⟩ **4** : STORMY 1 ⟨*dirty* weather⟩ **5** : not clear in color : DULL ⟨a *dirty* red⟩ **6** : showing dislike or anger ⟨a *dirty* look⟩ —
dirt·i·ly \'dərt-ᵊl-ē\ *adv* — **dirt·i·ness** \'dərt-ē-nəs\ *n*

dirndl

syn DIRTY, FILTHY, FOUL, SQUALID mean being especially unclean. DIRTY is a general word used to describe anything covered with dirt ⟨children who were *dirty* after playing⟩ FILTHY stresses the fact that the dirt has been building up and is really unpleasant ⟨a *filthy* kitchen floor covered with grease⟩ FOUL adds to FILTHY the idea that something is rotten or stinking ⟨a *foul* garbage dump⟩ SQUALID suggests that the dirtiness is the result of carelessness and neglect ⟨*squalid* slums⟩

²**dirty** *vb* **dirt·ied; dirty·ing** : to make or become dirty

dis- *prefix* **1 a** : do the opposite of ⟨*disagree*⟩ **b** : deprive of ⟨*disarm*⟩ **c** : exclude or expel from ⟨*disbar*⟩ **2** : opposite or absence of ⟨*disaffection*⟩ ⟨*disfavor*⟩ **3** : not ⟨*discourteous*⟩ [derived from Latin *dis-*, literally "apart"]

dis·abil·i·ty \,dis-ə-'bil-ət-ē\ *n, pl* **-ties 1** : the condition of being disabled : lack of ability, power, or fitness to do something **2** : something that disables (as a physical injury)

dis·able \dis-'ā-bəl\ *vb* **dis·abled; dis·abling** \-b(ə-)liŋ\ **1** : to disqualify legally **2** : to cause to be unable to do or act; *esp* : to deprive of physical or moral strength : CRIPPLE ⟨*disable* a computer key⟩ ⟨a *disabling* illness⟩ — **dis·able·ment** \-bəl-mənt\ *n*

dis·abled *adj* : deprived of the power to perform one or more natural bodily activities (as running or seeing) by illness, injury, or wounds

dis·abuse \,dis-ə-'byüz\ *vb* : to free from mistakes or false beliefs ⟨*disabuse* us of our errors⟩

di·sac·cha·ride \(')dī-'sak-ə-,rīd\ *n* : any of a class of sugars (as sucrose) that can be separated into two monosaccharide molecules — called also *double sugar*

¹**dis·ad·van·tage** \,dis-əd-'vant-ij\ *n* **1** : loss or damage especially to one's good name or finances ⟨the deal worked to our *disadvantage*⟩ **2 a** : a state or condition that favors someone else ⟨was at a *disadvantage* in educated company⟩ **b** : something not helpful : a cause of difficulty

²**disadvantage** *vb* **-taged; -tag·ing** : to place at a disadvantage : HARM

dis·ad·van·ta·geous \(,)dis-,ad-,van-'tā-jəs, -vən-\ *adj* : making it harder for a person to succeed or do something ⟨in a *disadvantageous* position⟩ — **dis·ad·van·ta·geous·ly** *adv* — **dis·ad·van·ta·geous·ness** *n*

dis·af·fect \,dis-ə-'fekt\ *vb* : to lose the affection or loyalty of : cause discontent in ⟨the troops were *disaffected*⟩ — **dis·af·fec·tion** \-'fek-shən\ *n*

dis·agree \,dis-ə-'grē\ *vb* **1** : to fail to agree ⟨the two stories *disagree*⟩ **2** : to differ in opinion ⟨*disagree* over the price⟩ **3** : to have an unpleasant effect ⟨fried foods *disagree* with me⟩

dis·agree·able \,dis-ə-'grē-ə-bəl\ *adj* **1** : causing discomfort : UNPLEASANT, OFFENSIVE ⟨a *disagreeable* taste⟩ **2** : having a bad disposition : PEEVISH ⟨a *disagreeable* person⟩ — **dis·agree·able·ness** *n* — **dis·agree·ably** \-blē\ *adv*

dis·agree·ment \,dis-ə-'grē-mənt\ *n* **1** : the act of disagreeing **2 a** : the state of being different **b** : a difference of opinion : QUARREL

dis·al·low \,dis-ə-'laù\ *vb* : to refuse to admit or allow : REJECT ⟨*disallow* a claim⟩ — **dis·al·low·ance** \-'laù-ən(t)s\ *n*

dis·ap·pear \,dis-ə-'pi(ə)r\ *vb* **1** : to cease to be visible : pass out of sight : VANISH ⟨the moon *disappeared* behind a cloud⟩ **2** : to cease to be ⟨the dinosaur *disappeared* ages ago⟩ — **dis·ap·pear·ance** \-'pir-ən(t)s\ *n*

dis·ap·point \,dis-ə-'pòint\ *vb* : to fail to satisfy the expec-

\ə\ abut	\aù\ out	\i\ tip	\ò\ saw	\ù\ foot	
\ər\ further	\ch\ chin	\ī\ life	\òi\ coin	\y\ yet	
\a\ mat	\e\ pet	\j\ job	\th\ thin	\yü\ few	
\ā\ take	\ē\ easy	\ŋ\ sing	\th\ this	\yù\ cure	
\ä\ cot, cart	\g\ go	\ō\ bone	\ü\ food	\zh\ vision	

tation or hope of ⟨the show *disappointed* them⟩

dis·ap·point·ed *adj* : defeated in expectation or hope ⟨we were *disappointed* that they couldn't go⟩

dis·ap·point·ment \,dis-ə-'pȯint-mənt\ *n* 1 : the act or an instance of disappointing : the state or emotion of being disappointed 2 : one that disappoints ⟨the play was a *disappointment*⟩

dis·ap·pro·ba·tion \(,)dis-,ap-rə-'bā-shən\ *n* : DISAPPROVAL

dis·ap·prov·al \,dis-ə-'prü-vəl\ *n* 1 : the act of disapproving : the state of being disapproved 2 : ¹CENSURE 1, CRITICISM ⟨the plan met with *disapproval*⟩

dis·ap·prove \,dis-ə-'prüv\ *vb* 1 : to dislike or be against someone or something ⟨*disapproved* the child's conduct⟩ ⟨*disapproves* of smoking⟩ 2 : to refuse to give approval to : REJECT ⟨*disapproved* the architect's plans⟩ — **dis·ap·prov·ing·ly** \-'prü-viŋ-lē\ *adv*

dis·arm \(')dis-'ärm\ *vb* 1 : to take weapons from ⟨*disarm* a prisoner⟩ 2 : to reduce the size and strength of the armed forces of a country 3 : to make harmless, peaceable, or friendly : remove dislike or suspicion ⟨a *disarming* smile⟩ — **dis·ar·ma·ment** \-'är-mə-mənt\ *n*

dis·ar·range \,dis-ə-'rānj\ *vb* : to disturb the arrangement or order of ⟨the wind *disarranged* my hair⟩ — **dis·ar·range·ment** \-mənt\ *n*

¹**dis·ar·ray** \,dis-ə-'rā\ *n* 1 : a lack of order : CONFUSION, DISORDER ⟨the room was in *disarray*⟩ 2 : disorderly dress

²**disarray** *vb* : to throw into disorder

dis·as·sem·ble \,dis-ə-'sem-bəl\ *vb* : to take apart ⟨*disassemble* an engine⟩ — **dis·as·sem·bly** \-'sem-blē\ *n*

di·sas·ter \diz-'as-tər, dis-\ *n* : something (as a flood or tornado) that happens suddenly and causes much suffering or loss — **di·sas·trous** \-'as-trəs\ *adj* — **di·sas·trous·ly** *adv*

> **Word History** People who have bad luck are sometimes said to be "star-crossed". This expression comes from the old belief that the positions of the stars and planets can have a direct influence on earthly events. The origins of the word *disaster* can be traced to this belief. *Disaster* comes from *disastro*, an old Italian word formed by combining the negative prefix *dis-* and the noun *astro*, meaning "star". *Disaster* at first meant "an unfavorable position of a star or planet". In time it came to be applied to the kind of terrible misfortune which such a position was thought to cause. [from early French *desastre* and early Italian *disastro*, both meaning "an unfavorable position of a star", from early Italian *dis-* (negative prefix) and *astro* "star", from Latin *astrum* "star"]

dis·avow \,dis-ə-'vaȯ\ *vb* : to deny having, knowing, or being responsible for ⟨will *disavow* any knowledge of your activities⟩ — **dis·avow·al** \-'vaȯ(-ə)l\ *n*

dis·band \dis-'band\ *vb* : to break up the organization of a group : DISPERSE ⟨*disband* the club⟩ — **dis·band·ment** \-'ban(d)-mənt\ *n*

dis·bar \dis-'bär\ *vb* **dis·barred; dis·bar·ring** : to deprive (a lawyer) of the right to work in the legal profession — **dis·bar·ment** \-'bär-mənt\ *n*

dis·be·lief \,dis-bə-'lēf\ *n* : the act or state of disbelieving : rejection of a statement as untrue

dis·be·lieve \,dis-bə-'lēv\ *vb* : to think not to be true or real : fail to believe ⟨*disbelieved* the witness's testimony⟩ — **dis·be·liev·er** *n*

dis·bur·den \(')dis-'bərd-ᵊn\ *vb* : UNBURDEN — **dis·bur·den·ment** \-mənt\ *n*

dis·burse \dis-'bərs\ *vb* **dis·bursed; dis·burs·ing** : to pay out : EXPEND [from early French *desbourser* "to pay out money", from *des-* "do the opposite" and *bourser* "to get money", from *borse* "a purse", from Latin *bursa* "a small leather bag" — related to PURSE, REIMBURSE] — **dis·burs·er** *n*

dis·burse·ment \dis-'bər-smənt\ *n* : the act of disbursing;

also : funds paid out

disc *variant of* DISK

¹**dis·card** \dis-'kärd, 'dis-,kärd\ *vb* 1 : to let go a playing card from one's hand 2 : to get rid of as useless or unwanted ⟨*discard* an old hat⟩ — **dis·card·able** \-ə-bəl\ *adj*

²**dis·card** \'dis-,kärd\ *n* 1 : the act of discarding 2 : a person or thing cast off or rejected

disc brake *n* : a brake that operates by the friction of two plates pressing against the sides of a rotating disc

dis·cern \dis-'ərn, diz-\ *vb* 1 : to detect with the eyes : DISTINGUISH ⟨*discern* an airplane in the clouds⟩ 2 : to come to know, recognize, or understand ⟨*discern* the basic issue⟩ ⟨*discern* right from wrong⟩ — **dis·cern·ible** \-'ər-nə-bəl\ *adj* — **dis·cern·ibly** \-blē\ *adv*

dis·cern·ing *adj* : seeing and understanding clearly and intelligently ⟨a *discerning* critic⟩ — **dis·cern·ing·ly** \-'ər-niŋ-lē\ *adv*

dis·cern·ment \dis-'ərn-mənt, diz-\ *n* : the quality of being able to understand clearly

¹**dis·charge** \dis-'chärj, 'dis-,chärj\ *vb* 1 : to relieve of a load or burden : UNLOAD 2 : ¹SHOOT 1a, b; FIRE ⟨*discharge* a gun⟩ 3 : to set free ⟨*discharge* a prisoner⟩ 4 : to dismiss from service or employment ⟨*discharge* a soldier⟩ 5 : to let go or let off ⟨*discharge* passengers⟩ 6 : to give forth fluid or other contents ⟨this river *discharges* into the ocean⟩ 7 : to get rid of by paying or doing ⟨*discharge* a debt⟩ ⟨*discharge* a function⟩ — **dis·charg·er** *n*

²**dis·charge** \'dis-,chärj, dis-'chärj\ *n* 1 a : the act of discharging b : something that discharges; *esp* : a certification of release or payment 2 : a firing off 3 a : a flowing out; *also* : a rate of flow b : something that is given forth ⟨a *discharge* of pus from a wound⟩ 4 a : release or dismissal especially from an office or employment b : complete separation from military service ⟨was given an honorable *discharge*⟩ 5 : a flow of electricity (as in lightning or through a gas)

discharge tube *n* : an electron tube which contains gas or vapor at low pressure and through which electrical conduction takes place when a high voltage is applied

dis·ci·ple \dis-'ī-pəl\ *n* 1 : a person who accepts and helps to spread the teachings of another 2 : APOSTLE 1a [Middle English *disciple* "one who follows and spreads the teaching of another", from Old English *discipul* and early French *desciple* (both, same meaning), from Latin *discipulus* "one of Jesus' apostles", from earlier *discipulus* "pupil"] — **dis·ci·ple·ship** \-,ship\ *n*

dis·ci·pli·nar·i·an \,dis-ə-plə-'ner-ē-ən\ *n* : one who disciplines or enforces order — **disciplinarian** *adj*

dis·ci·plin·ary \'dis-ə-plə-,ner-ē\ *adj* : of or relating to discipline : CORRECTIVE ⟨take *disciplinary* action⟩

¹**dis·ci·pline** \'dis-ə-plən\ *n* 1 : a field of study : SUBJECT 2 : strict training that corrects or strengthens 3 : PUNISHMENT 1 4 : control gained by enforcing obedience or order ⟨trying to maintain *discipline*⟩ 5 : a system of rules

²**discipline** *vb* **-plined; -plin·ing** 1 : to punish or penalize for the sake of discipline 2 : to train or develop by instruction and exercise especially in self-control 3 : to bring under control ⟨*discipline* troops⟩ **syn** *see* PUNISH — **dis·ci·plin·er** *n*

disc jockey *n* : one who conducts and announces a radio show of popular recorded music

dis·claim \dis-'klām\ *vb* : to deny being a part of or responsible for : DISOWN ⟨the prisoner *disclaimed* any part in the prank⟩

dis·claim·er \dis-'klā-mər\ *n* : an act of disclaiming : a statement that disclaims : DENIAL

disclike *variant of* DISKLIKE

dis·close \dis-'klōz\ *vb* : to make known ⟨*disclose* secrets⟩ **syn** *see* REVEAL — **dis·clos·er** *n*

dis·clos·ing \dis-'klō-ziŋ\ *adj* : being a substance (as a tablet or liquid) containing a usually red dye that is used to stain and make visible dental plaque so as to remove it completely by brushing

dis·clo·sure \dis-'klō-zhər\ *n* **1** : the act or an instance of disclosing : EXPOSURE ⟨full *disclosure* of the facts⟩ **2** : something that is disclosed : REVELATION

dis·co \'dis-kō\ *n, pl* **dis·cos** : DISCOTHEQUE

dis·col·or \(')dis-'kəl-ər\ *vb* : to change in color especially for the worse ⟨the stain *discolored* the rug⟩ — **dis·col·or·a·tion** \(,)dis-,kəl-ə-'rā-shən\ *n*

dis·com·fit \dis-'kəm(p)-fət, *especially Southern* ,dis-kəm-'fit\ *vb* : to make confused or upset ⟨the speaker was *discomfited* by the embarrassing question⟩ — **dis·com·fi·ture** \dis-'kəm(p)-fə-,chú(ə)r, -fə-chər\ *n*

dis·com·fort \dis-'kəm(p)-fərt\ *vb* : to make uncomfortable or uneasy : DISTRESS — **discomfort** *n*

dis·com·mode \,dis-kə-'mōd\ *vb* **-mod·ed; -mod·ing** : to make things difficult for : TROUBLE

dis·com·pose \,dis-kəm-'pōz\ *vb* **1** : to disturb the calmness or peace of : AGITATE ⟨*discomposed* by the bad news⟩ **2** : DISARRANGE ⟨hair *discomposed* by the wind⟩ — **dis·com·po·sure** \-'pō-zhər\ *n*

dis·con·cert \,dis-kən-'sərt\ *vb* **1** : to disturb the arrangement of : UPSET ⟨the unexpected event *disconcerted* their plans⟩ **2** : to disturb the self-control of ⟨your frank stare *disconcerted* me⟩ **syn** see EMBARRASS — **dis·con·cert·ing·ly** \-iŋ-lē\ *adv*

dis·con·nect \,dis-kə-'nekt\ *vb* : to undo or break the connection of ⟨*disconnect* two pipes⟩ ⟨*disconnect* a telephone⟩ — **dis·con·nec·tion** \-'nek-shən\ *n*

dis·con·nect·ed *adj* **1** : not connected : SEPARATE **2** : INCOHERENT 2 ⟨a *disconnected* speech⟩ — **dis·con·nect·ed·ly** *adv* — **dis·con·nect·ed·ness** *n*

dis·con·so·late \dis-'kän(t)-sə-lət\ *adj* : very sad : DEJECTED — **dis·con·so·late·ly** *adv* — **dis·con·so·late·ness** *n*

¹dis·con·tent \,dis-kən-'tent\ *adj* : DISCONTENTED

²discontent *vb* : to make discontented — **dis·con·tent·ment** \-mənt\ *n*

³discontent *n* : the condition of being dissatisfied

dis·con·tent·ed *adj* : not contented or pleased — **dis·con·tent·ed·ly** *adv* — **dis·con·tent·ed·ness** *n*

dis·con·tin·ue \,dis-kən-'tin-yü\ *vb* : to bring or come to an end : STOP — **dis·con·tin·u·ance** \-'tin-yə-wən(t)s\ *n*

dis·con·tin·u·ous \,dis-kən-'tin-yə-wəs\ *adj* : not continuous : having interruptions or gaps : BROKEN ⟨*discontinuous* sleep⟩ — **dis·con·ti·nu·i·ty** \(,)dis-,känt-ᵊn-'(y)ü-ət-ē\ *n* — **dis·con·tin·u·ous·ly** \,dis-kən-'tin-yə-wəs-lē\ *adv*

dis·cord \'dis-,kò(ə)rd\ *n* **1** : lack of agreement or harmony : CONFLICT ⟨*discord* between political parties⟩ **2 a** : a harsh combination of musical sounds **b** : a harsh or unpleasant sound

dis·cord·ance \dis-'kòrd-ᵊn(t)s\ *n* **1** : the state or an instance of being discordant **2** : discordant sounds or noise

dis·cord·ant \dis-'kòrd-ᵊnt\ *adj* **1 a** : not being in agreement **b** : QUARRELSOME **2** : relating to or producing a discord ⟨*discordant* music⟩ — **dis·cord·ant·ly** *adv*

dis·co·theque \'dis-kə-,tek, ,dis-kə-'tek\ *n* : a nightclub for dancing to recorded music [from French *discothèque* "nightclub with music for dancing", from *disque* "phonograph record, disk" and *thèque* (the same ending as in French *bibliothèque* "library")]

¹dis·count \'dis-,kaúnt\ *n* : an amount taken off a regular price ⟨two percent *discount* for paying with cash⟩

²dis·count \'dis-,kaúnt, dis-'kaúnt\ *vb* **1 a** : to lower the amount of a bill, debt, or charge **b** : to sell or offer for sale at a lowered price **2 a** : MINIMIZE 2 ⟨shouldn't *discount* the importance of studying⟩ **b** : to believe only partly : view with doubt — **dis·count·able** \-ə-bəl\ *adj*

dis·coun·te·nance \dis-'kaúnt-ᵊn-ən(t)s, -'kaúnt-nən(t)s\ *vb* **1** : EMBARRASS 2, DISCONCERT **2** : to look with disfavor on

dis·cour·age \dis-'kər-ij, -'kə-rij\ *vb* **-aged; -ag·ing** **1** : to lessen the courage or confidence of : DISHEARTEN ⟨didn't let losing *discourage* me⟩ **2 a** : to make less likely or appealing : DETER ⟨laws that *discourage* speeding⟩ **b** : to advise against a course of action : DISSUADE ⟨*discouraged* their child from becoming a musician⟩ — **dis·cour·ag·ing·ly** \-iŋ-lē\ *adv*

dis·cour·age·ment \dis-'kər-ij-mənt, -'kə-rij-\ *n* **1** : an act of discouraging : the state of being discouraged **2** : something that discourages

¹dis·course \'dis-,kō(ə)rs, -,kò(ə)rs, dis-'\ *n* **1** : CONVERSATION **2** : a long talk or composition about a subject

²dis·course \dis-'kō(ə)rs, -'kò(ə)rs, 'dis-,\ *vb* **dis·coursed; dis·cours·ing** : to talk especially for a long time

dis·cour·te·ous \(')dis-'kərt-ē-əs\ *adj* : not polite : UNCIVIL, RUDE — **dis·cour·te·ous·ly** *adv* — **dis·cour·te·ous·ness** *n*

dis·cour·te·sy \dis-'kərt-ə-sē\ *n, pl* **-sies** **1** : rude behavior **2** : a rude act

dis·cov·er \dis-'kəv-ər\ *vb* **dis·cov·ered; dis·cov·er·ing** \-'kəv-(ə-)riŋ\ **1** : to make known or visible **2 a** : to obtain sight or knowledge of for the first time ⟨*discovered* America⟩ ⟨*discovered* the law of gravity⟩ **b** : to detect the presence of : FIND ⟨*discovered* arsenic in the victim's coffee⟩ **c** : FIND OUT ⟨was surprised to *discover* that I had lost my keys⟩ — **dis·cov·er·able** \-'kəv-(ə-)rə-bəl\ *adj* — **dis·cov·er·er** \-'kəv-ər-ər\ *n*

dis·cov·ery \dis-'kəv-(ə-)rē\ *n, pl* **-er·ies** **1** : the act or process of discovering **2** : something discovered

¹dis·cred·it \(')dis-'kred-ət\ *vb* **1** : to refuse to accept as true or correct : DISBELIEVE ⟨*discredit* a rumor⟩ **2** : to cause to seem dishonest or untrue ⟨*discredit* a witness⟩; *also* : ¹DISGRACE ⟨involvement in the scandal *discredited* them⟩ — **dis·cred·it·able** \-ə-bəl\ *adj* — **dis·cred·it·ably** \-blē\ *adv*

²discredit *n* **1** : loss of good name or respect ⟨brought *discredit* on their family⟩ **2** : lack or loss of belief or confidence ⟨bring a story into *discredit*⟩

dis·creet \dis-'krēt\ *adj* : having or showing good judgment especially in conduct or speech — **dis·creet·ly** *adv* — **dis·creet·ness** *n*

dis·crep·an·cy \dis-'krep-ən-sē\ *n, pl* **-cies** **1** : the quality or state of being different : DISAGREEMENT **2** : something that is different or that disagrees ⟨*discrepancies* in the firm's financial statements⟩

dis·crep·ant \dis-'krep-ənt\ *adj* : not being in agreement ⟨*discrepant* statements⟩ — **dis·crep·ant·ly** *adv*

dis·crete \dis-'krēt, 'dis-,krēt\ *adj* : DISTINCT 1, SEPARATE — **dis·crete·ly** *adv* — **dis·crete·ness** *n*

dis·cre·tion \dis-'kresh-ən\ *n* **1** : the quality of being discreet : PRUDENCE **2 a** : individual choice or judgment ⟨left the decision to your *discretion*⟩ **b** : power of free decision ⟨reached the age of *discretion*⟩ — **dis·cre·tion·ary** \-'kresh-ə-,ner-ē\ *adj*

dis·crim·i·nant \dis-'krim-(ə-)nənt\ *n* : the expression $b^2 - 4ac$ which is used to find out how many solutions exist for a quadratic equation of the general form $ax^2 + bx + c = 0$ and which indicates that two real solutions exist when it is positive, one solution exists when it is equal to zero, and no solutions exist when it is less than zero

dis·crim·i·nate \dis-'krim-ə-,nāt\ *vb* **-nat·ed; -nat·ing** **1 a** : to see the special features of **b** : DISTINGUISH 1, DIFFERENTIATE ⟨*discriminate* hundreds of colors⟩ **2** : to be able to tell the difference especially between similar things ⟨*discriminate* between a tree and a bush⟩ **3** : to treat some people better than others without any fair or proper reason ⟨*discriminated* against because of their race⟩ —

\ə\ **abut**		\aú\ **out**	\i\ **tip**		\ò\ **saw**		\ú\ **foot**
\ər\ **further**		\ch\ **chin**	\ī\ **life**		\òi\ **coin**		\y\ **yet**
\a\ **mat**		\e\ **pet**	\j\ **job**		\th\ **thin**		\yü\ **few**
\ā\ **take**		\ē\ **easy**	\ŋ\ **sing**		\th\ **this**		\yú\ **cure**
\ä\ **cot, cart**		\g\ **go**	\ō\ **bone**		\ü\ **food**		\zh\ **vision**

dis·crim·i·na·ble \-ə-nə-bəl\ *adj*

dis·crim·i·nat·ing \dis-'krim-ə-,nāt-iŋ\ *adj* **1** : DISCERNING, JUDICIOUS ⟨a *discriminating* taste⟩ **2** : DISCRIMINATORY — **dis·crim·i·nat·ing·ly** *adv*

dis·crim·i·na·tion \dis-,krim-ə-'nā-shən\ *n* **1** : the act of perceiving distinctions **2** : the ability to make fine distinctions **3** : the treating of some people better than others without any fair or proper reason ⟨laws to end racial *discrimination*⟩ — **dis·crim·i·na·tion·al** \-shnəl, -shən-ᵊl\ *adj*

dis·crim·i·na·tive \dis-'krim-ə-,nāt-iv, -'krim-(ə-)nə-tiv\ *adj* **1** : seeing the differences between things **2** : DISCRIMINATORY — **dis·crim·i·na·tive·ly** *adv*

dis·crim·i·na·to·ry \dis-'krim-(ə-)nə-,tōr-ē, -,tôr-\ *adj* : showing discrimination : being unfair ⟨*discriminatory* treatment⟩

dis·cur·sive \dis-'kər-siv\ *adj* : passing from one topic to another ⟨a *discursive* speech⟩ — **dis·cur·sive·ly** *adv* — **dis·cur·sive·ness** *n*

dis·cus \'dis-kəs\ *n, pl* **dis·cus·es** : a heavy disk that is hurled for distance in a track-and-field event

dis·cuss \dis-'kəs\ *vb* **1** : to consider carefully and openly by reasoning or argument ⟨*discuss* a proposal⟩ **2** : to talk about ⟨*discuss* the weather⟩

syn DISCUSS, ARGUE, DEBATE mean to talk about something with the intention of reaching agreement or merely of putting forth different points of view. DISCUSS suggests a lively expression of differing opinions in order to clarify a problem ⟨*discuss* plans for a new road⟩ ARGUE suggests an exchange of opinions by people who disagree often strongly ⟨*argued* over who was to blame⟩ DEBATE suggests an often public contest between persons taking opposite sides of a question ⟨the candidates will *debate* the need for new taxes⟩

discus

dis·cus·sion \dis-'kəsh-ən\ *n* : conversation or debate for the purpose of understanding a question or subject

¹**dis·dain** \dis-'dān\ *n* : a feeling of scorn for something regarded as beneath oneself

²**disdain** *vb* **1** : to look with scorn on ⟨*disdained* us for being afraid⟩ **2** : to reject or refuse because of disdain ⟨*disdained* to answer⟩

dis·dain·ful \dis-'dān-fəl\ *adj* : full of or expressing disdain **syn** see CONTEMPTUOUS — **dis·dain·ful·ly** \-fə-lē\ *adv*

dis·ease \diz-'ēz\ *n* : an abnormal bodily condition of a living plant or animal that interferes with functioning and can usually be recognized by signs and symptoms : ILLNESS — **dis·eased** \-'ēzd\ *adj*

dis·em·bark \,dis-əm-'bärk\ *vb* : to go or put ashore from a ship ⟨the passengers *disembarked*⟩ — **dis·em·bar·ka·tion** \(,)dis-,em-,bär-'kā-shən, -bər-\ *n*

dis·em·body \,dis-əm-'bäd-ē\ *vb* : to deprive of bodily existence ⟨*disembodied* spirits⟩

dis·em·bow·el \,dis-əm-'bau̇-(ə)l\ *vb* **-eled** *or* **-elled; -eling** *or* **-el·ling** : to take out the bowels of — **dis·em·bow·el·ment** \-mənt\ *n*

dis·en·chant \,dis-ᵊn-'chant\ *vb* : DISILLUSION — **dis·en·chant·ment** \-mənt\ *n*

dis·en·cum·ber \,dis-ᵊn-'kəm-bər\ *vb* : to free from a burden

dis·en·fran·chise \,dis-ᵊn-'fran-,chīz\ *vb* : DISFRANCHISE — **dis·en·fran·chise·ment** \-,chīz-mənt, -chəz-\ *n*

dis·en·gage \,dis-ᵊn-'gāj\ *vb* : to free or release from an engagement, entanglement, or burden : EXTRICATE, DISENTANGLE ⟨*disengage* a clutch⟩ — **dis·en·gage·ment** \-mənt\ *n*

dis·en·tan·gle \,dis-ᵊn-'taŋ-gəl\ *vb* : to straighten out : UNTANGLE — **dis·en·tan·gle·ment** \-mənt\ *n*

¹**dis·fa·vor** \(')dis-'fā-vər\ *n* **1** : ²DISLIKE, DISAPPROVAL ⟨practices looked upon with *disfavor*⟩ **2** : the state or fact of being disliked or disapproved ⟨fell into *disfavor*⟩

²**disfavor** *vb* : ¹DISLIKE, DISAPPROVE

dis·fig·ure \dis-'fig-yər, *especially British* -'fig-ər\ *vb* : to spoil the appearance of ⟨*disfigured* by a scar⟩ — **dis·fig·ure·ment** \-mənt\ *n*

dis·fran·chise \(')dis-'fran-,chīz\ *vb* **-chised; -chis·ing** : to deprive of a legal right; *esp* : to deprive of the right to vote — **dis·fran·chise·ment** \-,chīz-mənt, -chəz-\ *n*

dis·gorge \(')dis-'gȯ(ə)rj\ *vb* **1** : ²VOMIT 1 **2** : to cause to come out violently or forcefully ⟨the volcano *disgorged* lava⟩

¹**dis·grace** \dis-'grās\ *vb* **dis·graced; dis·grac·ing** : to bring shame to — **dis·grac·er** *n*

²**disgrace** *n* **1** : the condition of being looked down on : loss of respect ⟨in *disgrace* with one's schoolmates⟩ **2** : ¹DISHONOR 1, SHAME ⟨the *disgrace* of being a coward⟩ **3** : a cause of shame ⟨that person's manners are a *disgrace*⟩ — **dis·grace·ful** \dis-'grās-fəl\ *adj* — **dis·grace·ful·ly** \-fə-lē\ *adv* — **dis·grace·ful·ness** *n*

dis·grun·tle \dis-'grənt-ᵊl\ *vb* **dis·grun·tled; dis·grun·tling** \-'grənt-liŋ, -ᵊl-iŋ\ : to put in a bad mood — **dis·grun·tle·ment** \-ᵊl-mənt\ *n*

¹**dis·guise** \dis-'gīz\ *vb* **dis·guised; dis·guis·ing** **1** : to change the dress or looks of so as to conceal identity ⟨spies *disguised* as tourists⟩ **2 a** : to keep from showing : HIDE ⟨*disguised* their true feelings⟩ **b** : to make different in order to fool someone ⟨tried to *disguise* her voice⟩ — **dis·guised·ly** \-'gīz-(ə)d-lē\ *adv* — **dis·guis·er** *n*

²**disguise** *n* **1** : clothing put on to hide one's true identity or imitate another's **2** : an outward appearance that hides what something really is ⟨a blessing in *disguise*⟩

¹**dis·gust** \dis-'gəst\ *n* : a strong feeling of dislike caused especially by something sickening or evil

²**disgust** *vb* : to cause to feel disgust — **dis·gust·ed** *adj* — **dis·gust·ed·ly** *adv*

dis·gust·ing \dis-'gəs-tiŋ\ *adj* : causing disgust ⟨*disgusting* behavior⟩ — **dis·gust·ing·ly** *adv*

¹**dish** \'dish\ *n* **1 a** : a shallow usually circular vessel for serving food **b** : the food served in a dish ⟨a *dish* of strawberries⟩ **2** : food prepared in a particular way **3 a** : something that is shaped like a dish **b** : a directional receiver having a concave reflector; *esp* : one used as a microwave antenna

²**dish** *vb* **1** : to put into a dish or dishes ⟨*dish* up some soup⟩ **2** : to shape something like a dish

dish·cloth \'dish-,klȯth\ *n* : a cloth for washing dishes

dis·heart·en \(')dis-'härt-ᵊn\ *vb* : to deprive of courage and hope : DISCOURAGE — **dis·heart·en·ing** \-'härt-niŋ, -ᵊn-iŋ\ *adj* — **dis·heart·en·ing·ly** \-lē\ *adv* — **dis·heart·en·ment** \-'härt-ᵊn-mənt\ *n*

di·shev·el \dish-'ev-əl\ *vb* **di·shev·eled** *or* **di·shev·elled; di·shev·el·ing** *or* **di·shev·el·ling** \-'ev-(ə-)liŋ\ : to let hang or fall loosely in disorder : make untidy

dis·hon·est \(')dis-'än-əst\ *adj* : not honest or trustworthy : DECEITFUL — **dis·hon·est·ly** *adv*

dis·hon·es·ty \(')dis-'än-ə-stē\ *n* : lack of honesty : the quality of being dishonest

¹**dis·hon·or** \(')dis-'än-ər\ *n* **1** : loss of honor or good name **2** : the state of one who has lost honor **3** : a cause of disgrace — **dis·hon·or·able** \(')dis-'än-(ə-)rə-bəl, -'än-ər-bəl\ *adj* — **dis·hon·or·ably** \-blē\ *adv*

²**dishonor** *vb* **1** : to bring shame on : DISGRACE **2** : to refuse to accept or pay (as a check) — **dis·hon·or·er** *n*

dish·wash·er \'dish-,wȯsh-ər, -,wäsh-\ *n* : a person or a machine that washes dishes — **dish·wash·ing** \-,wȯsh-iŋ,

-wäsh- *n or adj*

dish·wa·ter \-,wȯt-ər, -,wät-\ *n* : water in which dishes have been or are to be washed

dis·il·lu·sion \,dis-ə-'lü-zhən\ *vb* **dis·il·lu·sioned; dis·il·lu·sion·ing** \-'lüzh-(ə-)niŋ\ : to free from mistaken beliefs or foolish hopes — **dis·il·lu·sion·ment** \-'lü-zhən-mənt\ *n*

dis·in·cline \,dis-ᵊn-'klīn\ *vb* : to make or be unwilling 〈was *disinclined* to go〉 — **dis·in·cli·na·tion** \(,)dis-,in-klə-'nā-shən, -,iŋ-\ *n*

dis·in·fect \,dis-ᵊn-'fekt\ *vb* : to cleanse of germs that might cause disease — **dis·in·fec·tion** \-'fek-shən\ *n*

dis·in·fect·ant \,dis-ᵊn-'fek-tənt\ *n* : something (as a chemical) that is able to destroy harmful germs but not ordinarily spores of bacteria — **disinfectant** *adj*

dis·in·her·it \,dis-ᵊn-'her-ət\ *vb* : to deprive of the right to inherit

dis·in·te·grate \(')dis-'int-ə-,grāt\ *vb* **1** : to break or decompose into the elements, parts, or small particles making up something **2** : to go through a change in composition 〈an atomic nucleus that *disintegrates* because of radioactivity〉 — **dis·in·te·gra·tor** \-,grāt-ər\ *n*

dis·in·te·gra·tion \(,)dis-,int-ə-'grā-shən\ *n* : the act or process of disintegrating : the state of being disintegrated

dis·in·ter \,dis-ᵊn-'tər\ *vb* **1** : to take out of the grave or tomb **2** : DISCLOSE, UNEARTH — **dis·in·ter·ment** \-mənt\ *n*

dis·in·ter·est·ed \dis-'int-ə-res-təd, 'dis-; -'in-trəs-, -,tres-; -'int-ərs-, -'int-ə-rəs-\ *adj* **1** : not interested 〈was *disinterested* in sports〉 **2** : free from selfish interest : UNBIASED 〈a *disinterested* decision〉 — **dis·in·ter·est·ed·ly** *adv* — **dis·in·ter·est·ed·ness** *n*

dis·join \(')dis-'jȯin\ *vb* : to end the union of : become separated

¹dis·joint \(')dis-'jȯint\ *adj* : completely separate; *esp* : having no members in common 〈*disjoint* mathematical sets〉

²disjoint *vb* **1** : to separate the parts of **2** : to take apart at the joints

dis·joint·ed *adj* **1** : separated at or as if at the joint **2** : not clear and orderly : INCOHERENT 〈*disjointed* conversation〉 — **dis·joint·ed·ly** *adv* — **dis·joint·ed·ness** *n*

¹disk *or* **disc** \'disk\ *n* **1 a** : the central part of the flower head of a typical composite plant (as a daisy or aster) made up of closely packed tube‑shaped disk flowers **b** : any of various rounded and flattened animal anatomical structures **2 a** : a thin circular object **b** *usually* **disc** : a phonograph record **c** : a round flat plate coated with a magnetic substance on which data for a computer is stored **3** *usually* **disc** : a tilling implement (as a harrow) with sharp-edged circular cutting blades; *also* : one of these blades — **disk·like** *or* **disc·like** \-,līk\ *adj*

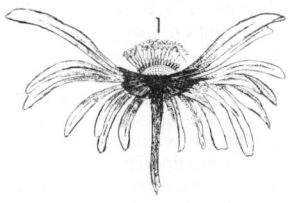

1 disk 1a

²disk *or* **disc** *vb* : to cultivate (land) with a disc

dis·kette \'dis-,ket, ,dis-'ket\ *n* : FLOPPY DISK

disk flower *n* : any of the tube-shaped flowers in the disk of a composite plant (as a daisy or aster)

¹dis·like \(')dis-'līk\ *vb* : to feel dislike for

²dislike *n* : a strong feeling of not liking or approving

dis·lo·cate \'dis-lō-,kāt, (')dis-'lō-\ *vb* **1** : to put out of place; *esp* : to displace (a bone) from normal connections with another bone **2** : DISRUPT

dis·lo·ca·tion \,dis-(,)lō-'kā-shən\ *n* : the act of dislocating : the state of being dislocated; *esp* : displacement of one or more bones at a joint

dis·lodge \(')dis-'läj\ *vb* : to force out of a place especially of rest, hiding, or defense

dis·loy·al \(')dis-'lȯi(-ə)l\ *adj* : lacking in loyalty — **dis·loy·al·ly** \-'lȯi-ə-lē\ *adv* — **dis·loy·al·ty** \-'lȯi(-ə)l-tē\ *n*

dis·mal \'diz-məl\ *adj* : very gloomy and depressing : DREARY 〈*dismal* weather〉 — **dis·mal·ly** \-mə-lē\ *adv*

Word History In the Middle Ages calendars marked two days in every month as *dies mali* or "evil days". These were thought to be unlucky. Astronomers of ancient Egypt were thought to have discovered their evil nature. At first, English *dismal* was a noun meaning "the set of evil days". By the 15th century *dismal* was often used as an adjective. A "dismal day" was one of the 24 days each year that belonged to the dismal, the group of unlucky days. Before long the word was being used as a more general adjective, meaning at first "unlucky" and then "gloomy" or "depressing". [Middle English *dismal* "days marked on a calendar as unlucky", derived from Latin *dies mali,* literally "evil days"]

dis·man·tle \(')dis-'mant-ᵊl\ *vb* **dis·man·tled; dis·man·tling** \-'mant-liŋ, -ᵊl-iŋ\ **1** : to take to pieces : take apart 〈*dismantled* the engine to repair it〉 **2** : to strip of furniture and equipment 〈*dismantle* an office〉 — **dis·man·tle·ment** \-'mant-ᵊl-mənt\ *n*

¹dis·may \dis-'mā, diz-\ *vb* : to cause to lose courage or to feel concern : DAUNT 〈*dismayed* by their opponent's size〉 — **dis·may·ing·ly** \-iŋ-lē\ *adv*

²dismay *n* **1** : loss of courage or determination from alarm or fear **2** : a feeling of alarm or disappointment

dis·mem·ber \(')dis-'mem-bər\ *vb* **dis·mem·bered; dis·mem·ber·ing** \-b(ə-)riŋ\ **1** : to cut off or separate the limbs or parts of **2** : to break up or tear into pieces — **dis·mem·ber·ment** \-bər-mənt\ *n*

dis·miss \dis-'mis\ *vb* **1** : to send away : cause or allow to go 〈*dismiss* a messenger〉 **2** : to discharge from office, service, or employment **3** : to put aside or out of mind 〈*dismiss* the thought〉 **4** : to refuse further judicial hearing or consideration to 〈the judge *dismissed* the charge〉 [derived from Latin *dismissus,* past participle of *dimittere* "to send away", from *di-, dis-* "away, apart", and *mittere* "to send, throw" — related to EMIT] — **dis·miss·al** \-'mis-əl\ *n*

dis·mount \(')dis-'maùnt\ *vb* **1** : to get down from something (as a horse) **2** : to cause to fall off or get off especially from a horse **3** : to take (as a cannon) off a support — **dismount** *n*

dis·obe·di·ence \,dis-ə-'bēd-ē-ən(t)s\ *n* : failure or refusal to obey — **dis·obe·di·ent** \-ənt\ *adj* — **dis·obe·di·ent·ly** *adv*

dis·obey \,dis-ə-'bā\ *vb* : to refuse, neglect, or fail to obey

dis·oblige \,dis-ə-'blīj\ *vb* **1** : to go against the wishes of **2** : ²INCONVENIENCE

¹dis·or·der \(')dis-'ȯrd-ər\ *vb* **1** : to disturb the order of **2** : to disturb the regular or normal functions of

²disorder *n* **1** : lack of order : a state or condition without order 〈clothes in *disorder*〉 **2** : an abnormal physical or mental condition : AILMENT

dis·or·dered *adj* **1** : marked by disorder **2** : not functioning in a normal orderly healthy way

dis·or·der·ly \(')dis-ȯrd-ər-lē\ *adj* **1** : not behaving quietly or well : upsetting public order : UNRULY 〈*disorderly* persons〉 〈*disorderly* conduct〉 **2** : not neat or orderly 〈a *disorderly* mass of papers〉 — **dis·or·der·li·ness** *n*

dis·or·ga·nize \(')dis-'ȯr-gə-,nīz\ *vb* : to break up the regular arrangement of : CONFUSE, DISORDER — **dis·or·ga·ni·za·tion** \(,)dis-,ȯrg-(ə-)nə-'zā-shən\ *n*

\ə\ abut	\aù\ out	\i\ tip	\ȯ\ saw	\ù\ foot
\ər\ further	\ch\ chin	\ī\ life	\ȯi\ coin	\y\ yet
\a\ mat	\e\ pet	\j\ job	\th\ thin	\yü\ few
\ā\ take	\ē\ easy	\ŋ\ sing	\th\ this	\yù\ cure
\ä\ cot, cart	\g\ go	\ō\ bone	\ü\ food	\zh\ vision

dis·ori·ent \(')dis-'ōr-ē-,ent, -'ȯr-\ *vb* : to cause to be confused or lost

dis·own \(')dis-'ōn\ *vb* : to refuse to accept any longer as one's own : RENOUNCE, DISCLAIM

dis·par·age \dis-'par-ij\ *vb* **-aged; -ag·ing** **1** : to lower in rank : DEGRADE **2** : to speak of as unimportant or not much good : BELITTLE ⟨*disparaged* the performance⟩ — **dis·par·age·ment** \-mənt\ *n* — **dis·par·ag·ing·ly** \-ij-iŋ-lē\ *adv*

dis·par·ate \dis-'par-ət, 'dis-p(ə-)rət\ *adj* : very different : individual in quality or character — **dis·par·ate·ly** *adv* — **dis·par·ate·ness** *n* — **dis·par·i·ty** \dis-'par-ət-ē\ *n*

dis·pas·sion·ate \(')dis-'pash-(ə-)nət\ *adj* : not influenced by strong feeling : CALM, IMPARTIAL ⟨a *dispassionate* judge⟩ — **dis·pas·sion·ate·ly** *adv*

¹dis·patch *or* **des·patch** \dis-'pach\ *vb* **1** : to send away quickly to a particular place or for a particular purpose ⟨*dispatch* a messenger⟩ ⟨*dispatch* a train⟩ **2** : to put to death : KILL **3** : to get done speedily ⟨*dispatch* business⟩ — **dis·patch·er** *n*

²dispatch *or* **despatch** *n* **1 a** : the sending of a message or messenger **b** : the shipment of goods **2** : MESSAGE 1; *esp* : an important official message **3** : the act of killing **4** : a news story sent in to a newspaper **5** : promptness in performing a task ⟨did our homework with *dispatch*⟩

dis·pel \dis-'pel\ *vb* **dis·pelled; dis·pel·ling** : to drive away by or as if by scattering : DISSIPATE

dis·pens·able \dis-'pen(t)-sə-bəl\ *adj* : not necessary : NONESSENTIAL — **dis·pens·abil·i·ty** \-,pen(t)-sə-'bil-ət-ē\ *n*

dis·pen·sa·ry \dis-'pen(t)s-(ə-)rē\ *n, pl* **-ries** : a place where medical or dental aid is given

dis·pen·sa·tion \,dis-pən-'sā-shən, -,pen-\ *n* **1 a** : a system of rules for ordering affairs **b** : a particular arrangement especially of nature **2** : release from a rule or from a vow or oath **3 a** : the act of dispensing **b** : something dispensed or distributed — **dis·pen·sa·tion·al** \-shnəl, -shən-ᵊl\ *adj*

dis·pense \dis-'pen(t)s\ *vb* **dis·pensed; dis·pens·ing** **1 a** : to give out in shares ⟨*dispense* charity⟩ **b** : ADMINISTER ⟨*dispense* justice⟩ **2** : to prepare and give out (medicines) **syn** *see* DISTRIBUTE — **dispense with** : to do or get along without

dis·pens·er \dis-'pen(t)-sər\ *n* : one that dispenses; *esp* : a container that gives out something a little at a time ⟨soap *dispenser*⟩

dis·pers·al \dis-'pər-səl\ *n* : the act or result of dispersing

dis·perse \dis-'pərs\ *vb* **dis·persed; dis·pers·ing** **1** : to cause to become spread widely : SCATTER ⟨police *dispersed* the crowd⟩ **2** : to subject (as light) to dispersion **3** : to move in different directions ⟨the clouds *dispersed*⟩

dispenser

dis·per·sion \dis-'pər-zhən\ *n* **1** : the act or process of dispersing : the state of being dispersed **2** : the separation of light (as by a prism) into a series of colors — **dis·per·sive** \-'pər-siv, -ziv\ *adj*

dispir·it \(')dis-'pir-ət\ *vb* : to deprive of cheerful spirit : DISHEARTEN — **dispir·it·ed·ly** *adv* — **dispir·it·ed·ness** *n*

dis·place \dis-'plās\ *vb* **1** : to remove from a usual or proper place; *esp* : to expel or force to flee from home or homeland ⟨*displaced* persons⟩ **2 a** : to remove physically out of position ⟨water *displaced* by a floating object⟩ **b** : to take the place of : REPLACE — **dis·place·able** \-ə-bəl\ *adj*

dis·place·ment \-'plā-smənt\ *n* **1** : the act of displacing : the state of being displaced **2 a** : the volume or weight of a fluid (as water) displaced by a floating body (as a ship) of equal weight **b** : the difference between the first position of an object and any later position **c** : the volume displaced by a piston (as in a pump or engine) in a single stroke; *also* : the total volume displaced in this way by all the pistons in an internal-combustion engine (as of an automobile)

¹dis·play \dis-'plā\ *vb* **1** : to put in plain view ⟨*display* the flag⟩ ⟨the results *displayed* on a computer screen⟩ ⟨*display* toys in a store window⟩ **2** : to make clear the existence or presence of : make a display of ⟨*display* anger⟩ **syn** *see* SHOW

²display *n* **1 a** : a showing of something **b** : an electronic device (as a cathode-ray tube in a computer or radar receiver) that gives information in visual form; *also* : the visual information **2** : overdone or unnecessary show **3** : an attractive exhibition

dis·please \(')dis-'plēz\ *vb* : to cause to feel disapproval, dislike, or annoyance ⟨was *displeased* by the delay⟩

dis·plea·sure \(')dis-'plezh-ər, -'plāzh-\ *n* : a feeling of dislike and irritation : DISSATISFACTION

dis·port \dis-'pō(ə)rt, -'pȯ(ə)rt\ *vb* **1 a** : AMUSE 1, DIVERT ⟨*disporting* themselves on the beach⟩ **b** : ²FROLIC **2** : ¹DISPLAY 2

dis·pos·able \dis-'pō-zə-bəl\ *adj* : made to be thrown away after use ⟨a *disposable* bottle⟩ ⟨*disposable* diapers⟩

dis·pos·al \dis-'pō-zəl\ *n* **1** : the right or power to use or control something : COMMAND ⟨funds at our *disposal*⟩ **2** : an orderly arrangement ⟨the *disposal* of troops for battle⟩ **3** : a getting rid of or putting out of the way ⟨trash *disposal*⟩ **4** : MANAGEMENT 1, ADMINISTRATION **5** : the transfer of something to a new owner ⟨a *disposal* of property⟩

dis·pose \dis-'pōz\ *vb* **dis·posed; dis·pos·ing** **1** : to make ready and willing ⟨I was not *disposed* to go to the meeting⟩ **2** : to put in place : ARRANGE ⟨you'll need more room to *dispose* your legs comfortably⟩ — **dis·pos·er** *n* — **dispose of** **1** : to settle or decide the future, condition, or use of ⟨King James claimed the right to *dispose of* the whole American continent⟩ **2** : to get rid of : put out of the way : DISCARD ⟨how to *dispose of* radioactive waste⟩ **3** : to take care of : deal with ⟨I have some business to *dispose of* first⟩

dis·po·si·tion \,dis-pə-'zish-ən\ *n* **1** : the act or power of disposing : DISPOSAL **2** : ARRANGEMENT 1 ⟨the *disposition* of furniture in a room⟩ **3 a** : one's usual attitude or mood ⟨a cheerful *disposition*⟩ **b** : a leaning toward a particular way of thinking or acting : TENDENCY, INCLINATION ⟨neither showed a *disposition* to retreat⟩

dis·pos·sess \,dis-pə-'zes\ *vb* : to take away the possession of or the right to occupy land or houses — **dis·pos·ses·sion** \-'zesh-ən\ *n*

dis·proof \(')dis-'prüf\ *n* **1** : the action of disproving **2** : evidence that disproves

dis·pro·por·tion \,dis-prə-'pōr-shən, -'pȯr-\ *n* : lack of proportion, balance, or proper relation; *also* : an instance of this

dis·pro·por·tion·ate \,dis-prə-'pōr-sh(ə-)nət, -'pȯr-\ *adj* : being out of proportion — **dis·pro·por·tion·ate·ly** *adv*

dis·prove \(')dis-'prüv\ *vb* : to prove to be false

dis·put·able \dis-'pyüt-ə-bəl, 'dis-pyət-\ *adj* : not yet proved : DEBATABLE — **dis·put·ably** \-blē\ *adv*

dis·pu·tant \dis-'pyüt-ᵊnt, 'dis-pyət-\ *n* : a person who takes part in a dispute

dis·pu·ta·tion \,dis-pyə-'tā-shən\ *n* : the act of disputing : DEBATE

dis·pu·ta·tious \,dis-pyə-'tā-shəs\ *adj* : likely to dispute or cause dispute; *also* : marked by disputation — **dis·pu·ta·tious·ness** *n*

¹dis·pute \dis-'pyüt\ *vb* **dis·put·ed; dis·put·ing** **1** : to engage in argument : DEBATE **2** : to quarrel angrily : WRANGLE **3** : to question the truth or rightness of ⟨dis-

pute a statement⟩ **4** : to fight over : CONTEST ⟨the two nations *disputed* the territory⟩ — **dis·put·er** *n*

²**dispute** *n* **1** : ARGUMENT 1b, DEBATE **2** : an angry difference of opinion : QUARREL

dis·qual·i·fi·ca·tion \(ˌ)dis-ˌkwäl-ə-fə-'kā-shən\ *n* **1** : something that disqualifies **2** : the act of disqualifying : the state of being disqualified

dis·qual·i·fy \(')dis-'kwäl-ə-ˌfī\ *vb* **-fied; -fy·ing** : to make or declare unfit or not qualified

¹**dis·qui·et** \(')dis-'kwī-ət\ *vb* : to make uneasy or restless : DISTURB — **dis·qui·et·ing·ly** \-iŋ-lē\ *adv*

²**disquiet** *n* : an uneasy feeling

¹**dis·re·gard** \ˌdis-ri-'gärd\ *vb* : to pay no attention to : treat as unworthy of regard or notice   **syn** see NEGLECT

²**disregard** *n* : the act of disregarding : the state of being disregarded — **dis·re·gard·ful** \-fəl\ *adj*

dis·re·pair \ˌdis-ri-'pa(ə)r, -'pe(ə)r\ *n* : the condition of needing repair

dis·rep·u·ta·ble \(')dis-'rep-yət-ə-bəl\ *adj* : not respectable : having a bad reputation — **dis·rep·u·ta·ble·ness** *n* — **dis·rep·u·ta·bly** \-blē\ *adv*

dis·re·pute \ˌdis-ri-'pyüt\ *n* : loss or lack of good reputation : DISGRACE

dis·re·spect \ˌdis-ri-'spekt\ *n* : lack of respect : DISCOURTESY — **dis·re·spect·ful** \-fəl\ *adj* — **dis·re·spect·ful·ly** \-fə-lē\ *adv*

dis·robe \(')dis-'rōb\ *vb* : ¹UNDRESS

dis·rupt \dis-'rəpt\ *vb* : to throw into disorder ⟨*disrupted* the class⟩ — **dis·rupt·er** *n* — **dis·rup·tion** \-'rəp-shən\ *n* — **dis·rup·tive** \-'rəp-tiv\ *adj* — **dis·rup·tive·ly** *adv* — **dis·rup·tive·ness** *n*

dis·sat·is·fac·tion \(ˌ)dis-ˌ(s)at-əs-'fak-shən\ *n* : the quality or state of being dissatisfied

dis·sat·is·fy \(')dis-'(s)at-əs-ˌfī\ *vb* : to fail to satisfy : DISPLEASE

dis·sect \dis-'ekt; dī-'sekt, 'dī-ˌsekt\ *vb* **1** : to cut up (as a plant or animal) into separate parts for examination and study **2** : to make a careful examination of [from Latin *dissectus*, past participle of *dissecare* "to cut apart", from *dis-* "apart" and *secare* "to cut" — related to INSECT, SECTION]

dis·sec·tion \dis-'ek-shən; dī-'sek-, 'dī-ˌsek-\ *n* **1** : the act or process of dissecting : the state of being dissected **2** : a plant or animal or a part of one that has been dissected for anatomy

dis·sem·ble \dis-'em-bəl\ *vb* **-bled; -bling** \-b(ə-)liŋ\ : to hide one's true feelings : put on a false appearance — **dis·sem·bler** \-b(ə-)lər\ *n*

dis·sem·i·nate \dis-'em-ə-ˌnāt\ *vb* **-nat·ed; -nat·ing** : to spread around as if sowing seed ⟨*disseminate* ideas⟩ — **dis·sem·i·na·tion** \-ˌem-ə-'nā-shən\ *n* — **dis·sem·i·na·tor** \-'em-ə-ˌnāt-ər\ *n*

dis·sen·sion \dis-'en-chən\ *n* : disagreement in opinion : DISCORD

¹**dis·sent** \dis-'ent\ *vb* : to differ in opinion : DISAGREE

²**dissent** *n* : difference of opinion

dis·sent·er \dis-'ent-ər\ *n* **1** : one that dissents **2** *cap* : an English Protestant who is not in agreement with the rules or beliefs of the Church of England

dis·sen·tient \dis-'en-chənt\ *adj* : expressing dissent ⟨a *dissentient* opinion⟩

dis·ser·ta·tion \ˌdis-ər-'tā-shən\ *n* : a long usually written treatment of a subject

dis·ser·vice \(')dis-'(s)ər-vəs\ *n* : HARM 1, INJURY; *also* : a harmful act

dis·sev·er \dis-'ev-ər\ *vb* : to separate completely

dis·si·dence \'dis-əd-ən(t)s\ *n* : DISSENT, DISAGREEMENT

dis·si·dent \'dis-əd-ənt\ *adj* : disagreeing with an opinion or a group — **dissident** *n*

dis·sim·i·lar \(')dis-'(s)im-ə-lər\ *adj* : DIFFERENT 1, UNLIKE — **dis·sim·i·lar·i·ty** \(ˌ)dis-ˌ(s)im-ə-'lar-ət-ē\ *n* — **dis·sim·i·lar·ly** \(')dis-'(s)im-ə-lər-lē\ *adv*

dis·sim·u·late \(')dis-'im-yə-ˌlāt\ *vb* **-lat·ed; -lat·ing** : DISSEMBLE — **dis·sim·u·la·tion** \(ˌ)dis-ˌim-yə-'lā-shən\ *n* — **dis·sim·u·la·tor** \(')dis-'im-yə-ˌlāt-ər\ *n*

dis·si·pate \'dis-ə-ˌpāt\ *vb* **-pat·ed; -pat·ing** **1** : to cause to spread out to the point of vanishing : DISSOLVE ⟨the breeze *dissipated* the fog⟩ **2** : to use up wastefully or foolishly : SQUANDER ⟨*dissipated* his fortune⟩ **3** : to separate into parts and scatter or vanish **4** : to be unreasonable or uncontrollable in the pursuit of pleasure; *esp* : to drink alcoholic beverages to excess

dis·si·pat·ed *adj* : affected by or showing the effects of dissipation : DISSOLUTE — **dis·si·pat·ed·ly** *adv* — **dis·si·pat·ed·ness** *n*

dis·si·pa·tion \ˌdis-ə-'pā-shən\ *n* : the act of dissipating : the state of being dissipated

dis·so·ci·ate \(')dis-'ō-sē-ˌāt, -shē-\ *vb* **-at·ed; -at·ing** **1** : to separate from association or union with another **2** : ¹DIVIDE 1

dis·so·ci·a·tion \(ˌ)dis-ˌō-sē-'ā-shən, -shē-\ *n* : the act or process of dissociating : the state of being dissociated; *esp* : the process by which a chemical combination breaks up into simpler substances of which it is made

dis·so·lute \'dis-ə-ˌlüt\ *adj* : having or showing bad morals or behavior — **dis·so·lute·ly** *adv* — **dis·so·lute·ness** *n*

dis·so·lu·tion \ˌdis-ə-'lü-shən\ *n* **1** : the action or process of dissolving **2** : the ending or breaking up of an assembly or a partnership or corporation

dis·solve \diz-'älv, -'olv\ *vb* **dis·solved; dis·solv·ing** **1** : to mix or cause to mix with a liquid so that the result is a liquid that is the same throughout ⟨sugar *dissolves* in water⟩ **2** : to bring to an end : TERMINATE ⟨*dissolved* their partnership⟩ **3** : to fade away as if by breaking up or melting ⟨his courage *dissolved* in the face of danger⟩ **4** : to be overcome by a strong feeling ⟨*dissolved* into tears⟩ **5** : to appear or fade out gradually so that one scene is replaced by another (as in movies or television) — **dis·solv·er** *n*

dis·so·nance \'dis-ə-nən(t)s\ *n* : an unpleasant combination of musical sounds

dis·so·nant \'dis-ə-nənt\ *adj* : marked by dissonance — **dis·so·nant·ly** *adv*

dis·suade \dis-'wād\ *vb* **dis·suad·ed; dis·suad·ing** : to persuade or advise not to do something

¹**dis·taff** \'dis-ˌtaf\ *n, pl* **distaffs** \-ˌtafs, -ˌtavz\ **1** : a staff for holding the flax or wool in spinning **2** : the female branch or side of a family

distaff 1

Word History Before the invention of the spinning wheel, the spinning of yarn or thread was traditionally done by women using a spindle and a distaff. A spindle was a long spool to hold and spin the yarn. A distaff was a short rod with an opening or branches at the top for holding the flax or wool. The word *distæf* in Old English meant literally "flax staff", from *dis-* "a bunch of flax" and *stæf* "staff". Because women usually did the spinning, the distaff came to be a symbol for women's work. The word *distaff* in time took on the meaning "women's work" and later "woman". The noun *distaff* is rarely used in this way today, but the female members of a family are still referred to as the distaff side. [from earlier *distaff* (noun)

\ə\ abut	\au̇\ out	\i\ tip	\ȯ\ saw	\u̇\ foot	
\ər\ further	\ch\ chin	\ī\ life	\ȯi\ coin	\y\ yet	
\a\ mat	\e\ pet	\j\ job	\th\ thin	\yü\ few	
\ā\ take	\ē\ easy	\ŋ\ sing	\th\ this	\yu̇\ cure	
\ä\ cot, cart	\g\ go	\ō\ bone	\ü\ food	\zh\ vision	

"a staff for holding flax or wool for spinning", from Old English *distæf* (same meaning), from *dis-* "bunch of flax" and *stæf* "staff"]

²distaff *adj* : of, relating to, or being a woman ⟨the *distaff* side of the family⟩ ⟨*distaff* skiers⟩

¹dis·tance \'dis-tən(t)s\ *n* **1 a** : separation in time **b** : the space or amount of space between two points, lines, surfaces, or objects **c** : the full length ⟨go the *distance*⟩ **2** : the quality or state of being not friendly : RESERVE **3** : a distant point or place ⟨a light seen in the *distance*⟩

²distance *vb* **dis·tanced; dis·tanc·ing** : to leave far behind

dis·tant \'dis-tənt\ *adj* **1 a** : separated in space or time : AWAY **b** : being at a great distance : FAR-OFF ⟨*distant* countries⟩ **2** : not close in relationship ⟨*distant* cousin⟩ **3** : ¹COLD 2, UNFRIENDLY — **dis·tant·ly** *adv* — **dis·tant·ness** *n*

dis·taste \(')dis-'tāst\ *n* : a strong dislike : AVERSION ⟨a *distaste* for work⟩

dis·taste·ful \dis-'tāst-fəl\ *adj* : causing displeasure : UNPLEASANT, DISAGREEABLE — **dis·taste·ful·ly** \-fə-lē\ *adv* — **dis·taste·ful·ness** *n*

dis·tem·per \dis-'tem-pər\ *n* : a highly contagious virus disease especially of dogs marked by fever and by respiratory and sometimes nervous symptoms

dis·tend \dis-'tend\ *vb* : to stretch or bulge out in all directions : SWELL

dis·ten·sion *or* **dis·ten·tion** \dis-'ten-chən\ *n* : the act of distending or the state of being distended

dis·till *also* **dis·til** \dis-'til\ *vb* **dis·tilled; dis·till·ing** : to obtain or purify by distillation

dis·til·late \'dis-tə-,lāt, -lət; dis-'til-ət\ *n* : a liquid product cooled from vapor during distillation

dis·til·la·tion \,dis-tə-'lā-shən\ *n* **1** : a process of heating a liquid or solid until it sends off a vapor and then cooling the vapor until it becomes liquid **2** : something obtained by or as if by distilling : ESSENCE

dis·till·er \dis-'til-ər\ *n* : one that distills especially alcoholic liquors

dis·till·ery \dis-'til-(ə-)rē\ *n, pl* **-er·ies** : a place where distilling especially of alchoholic liquors is done

dis·tinct \dis-'tiŋ(k)t\ *adj* **1** : real and different from each other ⟨five *distinct* varieties⟩ ⟨pears as *distinct* from apples⟩ **2** : clearly seen, heard, or understood : PLAIN, UNMISTAKABLE ⟨speaks with a *distinct* accent⟩ ⟨a *distinct* possibility⟩ — **dis·tinct·ly** *adv* — **dis·tinct·ness** *n*

dis·tinc·tion \dis-'tiŋ(k)-shən\ *n* **1 a** : the seeing or pointing out of a difference **b** : DIFFERENCE 1 ⟨the *distinction* between good and evil⟩ **2** : something that makes a person or thing special or different ⟨the *distinction* of being the oldest house in the city⟩ **3 a** : ¹HONOR 5b ⟨served with *distinction*⟩ **b** : ¹HONOR 4b

dis·tinc·tive \dis-'tiŋ(k)-tiv\ *adj* **1** : clearly marking a person or a thing as different from others ⟨a *distinctive* walk⟩ **2** : having or giving a special look or way ⟨*distinctive* clothes⟩ — **dis·tinc·tive·ly** *adv* — **dis·tinc·tive·ness** *n*

dis·tin·guish \dis-'tiŋ-(g)wish\ *vb* **1** : to recognize one thing from others by some mark or quality ⟨*distinguish* the sound of a piano in an orchestra⟩ **2** : to hear or see clearly : MAKE OUT, DISCERN ⟨*distinguish* a light in the distance⟩ **3** : to know or point out the difference ⟨*distinguish* between right and wrong⟩ **4** : to set apart as different or special ⟨*distinguished* themselves by heroic actions⟩ — **dis·tin·guish·able** \-ə-bəl\ *adj* — **dis·tin·guish·ably** \-blē\ *adv*

dis·tin·guished *adj* : widely known and admired for excellence ⟨a *distinguished* scientist⟩

dis·tort \dis-'tȯ(ə)rt\ *vb* **1** : to tell in a way that is misleading : MISREPRESENT ⟨*distorted* the facts⟩ **2** : to twist out of a natural, normal, or original shape or condition [from Latin *distortus*, past participle of *distorquēre* "to distort, twist out of proper meaning", from *dis-* "reverse, apart" and *torquēre* "to twist" — related to EXTORT, RETORT, TOR-

TURE] — **dis·tort·er** *n*

dis·tor·tion \dis-'tȯr-shən\ *n* **1** : the act of distorting **2** : the condition of being distorted or a product of distortion — **dis·tor·tion·al** \-shnəl, -shən-°l\ *adj*

dis·tract \dis-'trakt\ *vb* **1** : to draw the attention or mind to something else **2** : to upset or trouble in mind to the point of confusion

dis·trac·tion \dis-'trak-shən\ *n* **1** : the act of distracting : the state of being distracted; *esp* : mental confusion **2 a** : something that makes it hard to pay attention **b** : AMUSEMENT 1 — **dis·trac·tive** \-'trak-tiv\ *adj*

dis·trait \di-'strā\ *adj* : unaware of one's surroundings or action

dis·traught \dis-'trȯt\ *adj* **1** : disturbed with doubt or painful feelings **2** : INSANE 1 — **dis·traught·ly** *adv*

¹dis·tress \dis-'tres\ *n* **1** : great suffering of body or mind : PAIN, ANGUISH **2** : MISFORTUNE 1, TROUBLE, SORROW **3** : a condition of danger or desperate need ⟨a ship in *distress*⟩

²distress *vb* **1** : to cause to experience painful difficulties **2** : to cause to worry or be troubled : UPSET — **dis·tress·ing·ly** \-iŋ-lē\ *adv*

dis·tress·ful \dis-'tres-fəl\ *adj* : causing distress : full of distress — **dis·tress·ful·ly** \-fə-lē\ *adv* — **dis·tress·ful·ness** *n*

dis·trib·u·tary \dis-'trib-yə-,ter-ē\ *n, pl* **-tar·ies** : a river branch flowing away from the main stream

dis·trib·ute \dis-'trib-yət\ *vb* **-ut·ed; -ut·ing** **1** : to divide among several or many **2** : to spread out so as to cover something : SCATTER **3** : to divide or separate especially into kinds

syn DISTRIBUTE, DISPENSE, DIVIDE, DOLE mean to give out usually in shares to each member of a group. DISTRIBUTE suggests the giving out of something by separating it into parts, units, or amounts ⟨*distributed* the art supplies to the class⟩ DISPENSE suggests the giving of a carefully measured portion ⟨*dispensed* the medicine to the suffering people⟩ DIVIDE stresses the separation of a whole into usually equal parts ⟨*divided* the money that they had earned together⟩ DOLE suggests a carefully measured portion that is often barely enough or too little ⟨slowly *doled* out the last of the food⟩

dis·tri·bu·tion \,dis-trə-'byü-shən\ *n* **1** : the act or process of distributing **2 a** : the position, arrangement, or numbers (as of the members of a group) **b** : the natural geographic range of a living thing ⟨the *distribution* of human beings⟩ **3 a** : something distributed **b** : FREQUENCY DISTRIBUTION ⟨population age *distribution*⟩ **4** : the marketing of goods — **dis·tri·bu·tion·al** \-shnəl, -shən-°l\ *adj*

dis·trib·u·tive \dis-'trib-yət-iv\ *adj* **1** : of or relating to distribution : serving to distribute **2 a** : being an operation (as multiplication in $a(b + c) = ab + ac$) that produces the same result when operating on the whole mathematical expression as when operating on each part and collecting the results **b** : being or relating to a rule or property concerning a distributive operation ⟨the *distributive* property of multiplication with respect to addition⟩ — **dis·trib·u·tive·ly** *adv*

dis·trib·u·tor \dis-'trib-yət-ər\ *n* **1** : one that distributes **2** : an agent or agency for marketing goods **3** : a device that sends electric current to the spark plugs of an engine so that they fire in the proper order

¹dis·trict \'dis-(,)trikt\ *n* **1** : an area or section (as of a city or nation) set apart for some purpose ⟨school *district*⟩ ⟨judicial *district*⟩ **2** : an area or region having some special feature ⟨a coal-mining *district*⟩

²district *vb* : to divide or organize into districts

district attorney *n* : the prosecuting officer of a judicial district

¹dis·trust \(')dis-'trəst\ *vb* : to have no trust or confidence in

²distrust *n* : a lack of trust or confidence **syn** see DOUBT — **dis·trust·ful** \-fəl\ *adj* — **dis·trust·ful·ly** \-fə-lē\ *adv* — **dis·trust·ful·ness** *n*

dis·turb \dis-'tərb\ *vb* **1 a** : to interfere with : INTERRUPT **b** : to change the position, arrangement, or stability of **2 a** : to trouble the mind of : make uneasy **b** : to throw into confusion or disorder **c** : to cause bother to — **dis·turb·er** *n*

dis·turb·ance \dis-'tər-bən(t)s\ *n* **1** : the act of disturbing **2** : mental confusion : UPSET **3** : public commotion : DISORDER

dis·turbed \dis-'tərbd\ *adj* : showing signs of mental or emotional illness

di·sul·fide \(')dī-'səl-,fīd\ *n* : a compound containing two atoms of sulfur combined with an element or chemical group

dis·union \dish-'ü-nyən, (')dis-'yü-\ *n* : the ending of union : SEPARATION

dis·unite \,dish-ü-'nīt, ,dis-yü-\ *vb* : ¹DIVIDE 1, SEPARATE

dis·uni·ty \dish-'ü-nət-ē, (')dis-'yü-\ *n* : lack of unity; *esp* : DISSENSION

¹dis·use \dish-'üz, (')dis-'yüz\ *vb* : to end the use or practice of

²dis·use \dish-'üs, (')dis-'yüs\ *n* : lack of use

¹ditch \'dich\ *n* : a long narrow channel or trench dug in the earth

²ditch *vb* **1** : to dig a ditch in or around **2** : to get rid of : DISCARD **3** : to make a forced landing of (an airplane) on water

dith·er \'dith-ər\ *n* : a highly nervous or excited state — **dith·ery** \-ə-rē\ *adj*

dit·to \'dit-ō\ *n, pl* **dittos** **1** : another of the same thing mentioned before or above — used to avoid repeating a word ⟨lost: one shirt (white); *ditto* (blue)⟩ **2** : a mark composed of a pair of quotation marks or apostrophes used as a symbol for the word *ditto*

dit·ty \'dit-ē\ *n, pl* **ditties** : a short simple song

di·uret·ic \,dī-(y)ə-'ret-ik\ *n* : a substance that increases the amount of urine produced by the body — **diuretic** *adj*

di·ur·nal \dī-'ərn-ᵊl\ *adj* **1** : occurring every day : DAILY ⟨*diurnal* task⟩ **2 a** : of, relating to, or occurring in the daytime ⟨the city's *diurnal* noises⟩ **b** : active chiefly in the daytime ⟨*diurnal* animals⟩ — **di·ur·nal·ly** \-'ərn-ᵊl-ē\ *adv*

di·van \di-'van, 'dī-,van\ *n* : a large couch often with no back or arms

¹dive \'dīv\ *vb* **dived** \'dīvd\ *or* **dove** \'dōv\; **div·ing** **1 a** : to plunge into water headfirst **b** : SUBMERGE 1 **2 a** : to fall fast **b** : to descend in an airplane at a very steep angle **3 a** : to plunge into some matter or activity **b** : to thrust oneself forward suddenly : LUNGE ⟨*dived* for cover⟩ — **div·er** *n*

²dive *n* **1** : the act or an instance of diving: as **a** : a plunge into water done in a specified manner **b** : a steep downward movement of a submarine or an airplane **c** : a sharp drop (as in prices) **2** : a bar that is not respectable **3** : a faked knockout in boxing

di·verge \də-'vərj, dī-\ *vb* **di·verged; di·verg·ing** : to move or extend in different directions from a common point : draw apart ⟨*diverging* rays of light⟩ ⟨two roads *diverged*⟩

di·ver·gence \də-'vər-jən(t)s, dī-\ *n* : the state of diverging : a drawing apart (as of lines extending from a common center)

di·ver·gent \də-'vər-jənt, dī-\ *adj* : diverging from each other — **di·ver·gent·ly** *adv*

di·vers \'dī-vərz\ *adj* : VARIOUS 4

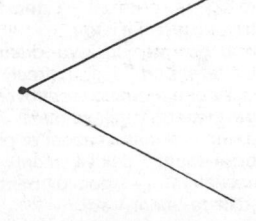

divergence

di·verse \dī-'vərs, də-, 'dī-,vərs\ *adj* : differing from one another : UNLIKE — **di·verse·ly** *adv* — **di·verse·ness** *n*

di·ver·si·fy \də-'vər-sə-,fī, dī-\ *vb* **-fied; -fy·ing** **1** : to make diverse : give variety to **2** : to increase the variety of products of — **di·ver·si·fi·ca·tion** \-,vər-sə-fə-'kā-shən\ *n*

di·ver·sion \də-'vər-zhən, dī-\ *n* **1** : the act or an instance of diverting or turning aside **2** : something that relaxes, amuses, or entertains — **di·ver·sion·ary** \-zhə-,ner-ē\ *adj*

di·ver·si·ty \də-'vər-sət-ē, dī-\ *n, pl* **-ties** **1** : the condition of being different **2** : an instance or a point of difference

di·vert \də-'vərt, dī-\ *vb* **1 a** : to turn aside : turn from one course or use to another **b** : to turn the attention away : DISTRACT **2** : to give pleasure to by causing the time to pass pleasantly [Middle English *diverten* "to turn aside from a course", from early French *divertir* "to divert" and Latin *divertere* "to turn aside, go different ways", from *di-, dis-* "away, apart" and *vertere* "to turn" — related to CONVERSE, REVERSE, VERSATILE] **syn** see AMUSE

di·vest \dī-'vest, də-\ *vb* : to take something off or away from ⟨*divested* myself of my heavy backpack⟩

¹di·vide \də-'vīd\ *vb* **di·vid·ed; di·vid·ing** **1 a** : to separate into two or more parts or pieces **b** : to separate into classes or categories **c** : ²CLEAVE, PART **2 a** : to give out in shares **b** : to own or use in common : SHARE **3** : to cause to be separate, different, or apart from one another **4 a** : to perform or use in mathematical division **b** : to subject (a number) to the operation of finding how many times it contains another number ⟨*divide* 42 by 14⟩ **c** : to use as a divisor ⟨*divide* 14 into 42⟩ **5 a** : to undergo cell division ⟨the cell *divides*⟩ **b** : ²BRANCH 2, FORK **syn** see DISTRIBUTE, SEPARATE

²divide *n* : a dividing ridge between drainage areas : WATERSHED

di·vid·ed *adj* **1 a** : separated into parts or pieces **b** : having a barrier (as a guardrail) to separate lanes of traffic going in opposite directions ⟨a *divided* highway⟩ **2** : disagreeing with each other

div·i·dend \'div-ə-,dend, -əd-ənd\ *n* **1** : a sum to be divided and given out **2** : BONUS **3** : a number to be divided by another

di·vid·er \də-'vīd-ər\ *n* **1** : something that divides ⟨a room *divider*⟩ **2** *pl* : an instrument for measuring or marking

div·i·na·tion \,div-ə-'nā-shən\ *n* : the art or practice of using omens or magic powers to foretell the future

¹di·vine \də-'vīn\ *adj* **1 a** : of, relating to, or coming directly from God or a god **b** : being God or a god ⟨the *divine* Savior⟩ **c** : directed to God or a god ⟨*divine* worship⟩ **2 a** : extremely good : SUPERB **b** : having godlike qualities — **di·vine·ly** *adv*

²divine *n* : a member of the clergy

³divine *vb* **di·vined; di·vin·ing** **1** : to discover or understand something without reasoning **2** : to practice divination : PROPHESY — **di·vin·er** *n*

diving bell *n* : a diving device consisting of a container open only at the bottom and supplied with compressed air by a hose

diving board *n* : a flexible board fastened at one end and used for diving into water

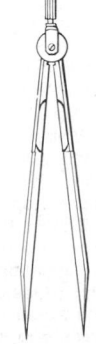

divider 2

\ə\ abut	\au̇\ **out**	\i\ **tip**	\ȯ\ **saw**	\u̇\ **foot**
\ər\ **further**	\ch\ **chin**	\ī\ **life**	\ȯi\ **coin**	\y\ **yet**
\a\ **mat**	\e\ **pet**	\j\ **job**	\th\ **thin**	\yü\ **few**
\ā\ **take**	\ē\ **easy**	\ŋ\ **sing**	\th\ **this**	\yu̇\ **cure**
\ä\ **cot, cart**	\g\ **go**	\ō\ **bone**	\ü\ **food**	\zh\ **vision**

divining rod *n* : a forked rod believed to reveal the presence of water or minerals by dipping downward when held over a vein

di·vin·i·ty \də-'vin-ət-ē\ *n, pl* **-ties** **1** : the quality or state of being divine : GODHEAD **2 a** *often cap* : GOD 1 **b** : GOD 2 **c** : GODDESS 1 **d** : DEMIGOD 1 **3** : THEOLOGY 1

di·vis·i·ble \də-'viz-ə-bəl\ *adj* : capable of being divided — **di·vis·i·bil·i·ty** \-,viz-ə-'bil-ət-ē\ *n*

di·vi·sion \də-'vizh-ən\ *n* **1 a** : the act or process of dividing : the state of being divided **b** : DISTRIBUTION 1 **c** : CELL DIVISION **2** : a part or portion of a whole **3** : something that divides, separates, or marks off **4** : a large military unit **5** : a large unit of a governmental, business, or educational organization **6** : difference in opinion or interest : DISAGREEMENT **7** : the mathematical operation of finding out how many times one number is contained in another **8** : a phylum in most classifications of the plant kingdom — **di·vi·sion·al** \-'vizh-(ə-)nəl\ *adj*

di·vi·sor \də-'vī-zər\ *n* : the number by which a dividend is divided

¹di·vorce \də-'vōrs, -'vòrs\ *n* **1** : a complete legal ending of a marriage **2** : complete separation

²divorce *vb* **di·vorced; di·vorc·ing** **1 a** : to end marriage with one's spouse by divorce **b** : to cancel the marriage contract between two spouses **2** : to make or keep separate : SEPARATE, DISUNITE — **di·vorce·ment** \-mənt\ *n*

di·vor·cé \də-,vōr-'sā, -,vòr-, -'sē\ *n* : a divorced man

di·vor·cée \də-,vōr-'sā, -,vòr-, -'sē\ *n* : a divorced woman

di·vulge \də-'vəlj, dī-\ *vb* **di·vulged; di·vulg·ing** : to make public : DISCLOSE — **di·vul·gence** \-'vəl-jən(t)s\ *n*

dix·ie·land \'dik-sē-,land\ *n* : lively jazz music in a style developed in New Orleans

diz·zy \'diz-ē\ *adj* **diz·zi·er; -est** **1 a** : having a feeling of whirling **b** : mentally confused **2 a** : causing or caused by a whirling sensation **b** : extremely rapid — **diz·zi·ly** \'diz-ə-lē\ *adv* — **diz·zi·ness** \'diz-ē-nəs\ *n*

D layer *n* : a layer that may exist within the part of the ionosphere occurring approximately between 50 and 90 kilometers above the earth's surface; *also* : the lowest part of the ionosphere between 50 and 90 kilometers

DMT \,dē-,em-'tē\ *n* : a fast-acting drug that causes hallucinations

DNA \,dē-,en-'ā\ *n* : any of various nucleic acids that are located especially in cell nuclei and are the chemical basis of heredity

DNA fingerprinting *n* : a method of identification (as for forensic purposes) by determining the unique pattern of a person's DNA — **DNA fingerprint** *n*

¹do \(')dü\ *vb* **did** \(')did\; **done** \'dən\; **do·ing** \'dü-iŋ\; **does** \(')dəz\ **1 a** : to cause (an act or action) to happen : CARRY OUT, PERFORM ⟨*do* me a favor⟩ **b** : ²ACT 3, BEHAVE ⟨*do* as I say⟩ **2 a** : to work at ⟨what one *does* for a living⟩ **b** : to take suitable action on ⟨*do* your homework⟩ ⟨*do* the dishes⟩ **c** : ¹SET 11 ⟨have my hair *done*⟩ **d** : DECORATE 1 ⟨*did* the bedroom in blue⟩ **3** : to make progress ⟨*does* well in school⟩ **4** : to act so as to bring : RENDER ⟨sleep will *do* you good⟩ **5** : to come to the end of : FINISH ⟨turn out the light when you are *done*⟩ **6** : to put forth : EXERT ⟨*did* your best to win⟩ **7 a** : to travel a distance of ⟨*did* 500 miles that day⟩ **b** : to travel at a speed of ⟨*doing* 55 on the turnpike⟩ **8** : ¹SERVE 1d ⟨*did* five years for robbery⟩ **9 a** : to serve the purpose ⟨half of that will *do*⟩ **b** : to be fitting or proper ⟨it won't *do* to be late⟩ **10** — used as a helping verb (1) before the subject in an interrogative sentence ⟨*do* you play the piano?⟩, (2) in a negative statement ⟨I *do* not know⟩, (3) for emphasis ⟨you *do* know⟩, and (4) as a substitute for a preceding verb ⟨you work harder than I *do*⟩ [Old English *dōn* "cause to happen, perform"] — **do away with** **1** : to put an end to : get rid of : ABOLISH **2** : ¹KILL 1

²do \'dō\ *n* : the first note of the musical scale [Italian]

do·able \'dü-ə-bəl\ *adj* : capable of being done

Do·ber·man pin·scher \,dō-bər-mən-'pin-chər\ *n* : a short-haired medium-sized dog of a breed of German origin [from German *Dobermann-pinscher* (breed of dog), from Ludwig *Dobermann*, German dog breeder, and *pinscher* "breed of hunting dog"]

dob·son·fly \'däb-sən-,flī\ *n* : a large-eyed winged insect with a large flesh-eating water-dwelling larva

Doberman pinscher

doc·ile \'däs-əl\ *adj* : easily taught, led, or managed [from Latin *docilis* "easily taught", from *docēre* "to teach" — related to DOCTOR, DOCTRINE] — **doc·ile·ly** \'däs-ə(l)-lē\ *adv* — **do·cil·i·ty** \dä-'sil-ət-ē, dō-\ *n*

¹dock \'däk\ *n* : any of a genus of coarse weedy plants which are related to the buckwheat and some of which are cooked for food [Old English *docce* "the dock plant"]

²dock *vb* **1** : to cut off the end of : cut short **2** : to take away a part of : make a deduction from **3** : to deprive of something due because of a fault ⟨was *docked* for being late⟩ [Middle English *docken* "to cut off the end of a tail", from *dok, docke* "end of an animal's tail"]

³dock *n* **1** : a usually artificial basin to receive ships that has gates to control the water height **2** : ²SLIP 1b **3** : a wharf or platform for loading and unloading [probably from early Dutch *docke* "ditch, dock", from Latin *ductio* "act of conducting" — related to DUCT]

⁴dock *vb* **1** : to bring or come into a dock **2** : to join (as two spacecraft) mechanically while in space

⁵dock *n* : the place in a court where a prisoner stands or sits during trial [from a Dutch dialect word *docke* "cage"]

¹dock·et \'däk-ət\ *n* **1** : a list of legal cases to be tried **2** : a list of items to be acted on : AGENDA

²docket *vb* : to place on the docket for legal action

dock·side \'däk-,sīd\ *n* : the shore or area next to a dock

dock·work·er \-,wər-kər\ *n* : LONGSHOREMAN

dock·yard \-,yärd\ *n* : SHIPYARD

¹doc·tor \'däk-tər\ *n* **1** : a person holding one of the highest degrees (as a PhD) given by a university **2** : a person (as a physician, dentist, or veterinarian) skilled and specializing in the art of healing [Middle English *doctour* "doctor, teacher", from early French *doctour* and Latin *doctor* (both, same meaning), from earlier Latin *doctor* "teacher", derived from *docēre* "to teach" — related to DOCILE, DOCTRINE] — **doc·tor·al** \-t(ə-)rəl\ *adj*

²doctor *vb* **doc·tored; doc·tor·ing** \-t(ə-)riŋ\ **1 a** : to give medical treatment to **b** : to practice medicine **c** : to bring back to good condition : REPAIR ⟨*doctor* an old clock⟩ **2** : to tamper with ⟨*doctored* the election returns⟩

doc·tor·ate \'däk-t(ə-)rət\ *n* : the degree, title, or rank of a doctor

doc·trine \'däk-trən\ *n* **1** : something that is taught **2** : a principle or the principles in a system of belief [Middle English *doctrine* "instruction", from early French *doctrine* and Latin *doctrina* (both, same meaning), from earlier Latin *doctor* "teacher", from *docēre* "to teach" — related to DOCILE, DOCTOR] — **doc·tri·nal** \-trən-ᵊl\ *adj* — **doc·tri·nal·ly** \-ᵊl-ē\ *adv*

do·cu·dra·ma \'däk-yə-,dräm-ə -,dram-\ *n* : a drama (as for television) dealing freely with historical events especially of a recent or controversial nature

¹doc·u·ment \'däk-yə-mənt\ *n* : a written or printed paper giving information about or proof of something

²doc·u·ment \'däk-yə-,ment\ *vb* : to give evidence of by a document — **doc·u·ment·able** \'däk-yə-,ment-ə-bəl, ,däk-yə-'ment-\ *adj*

¹doc·u·men·ta·ry \,däk-yə-'ment-ə-rē, -'men-trē\ *adj* **1** : consisting of documents; *also* : being in writing ⟨*docu-*

mentary proof⟩ **2** : presenting actual events or facts about something ⟨a *documentary* film⟩ — **doc·u·men·tar·i·ly** \-mən-'ter-ə-lē, -,men-\ *adv*

²**documentary** *n, pl* **-ries** : a documentary presentation (as a film)

doc·u·men·ta·tion \,däk-yə-mən-'tā-shən, -,men-\ *n* **1** : the providing of documents as proof **2** : evidence in the form of documents **3** : written instructions for using a computer or computer program

dod·der \'däd-ər\ *vb* **dod·dered; dod·der·ing** \-(ə-)riŋ\ **1** : to tremble or shake from weakness or age **2** : to go in a shaky or feeble way

dod·der·ing *adj* : showing signs of old age

do·deca·he·dron \(,)dō-,dek-ə-'hē-drən\ *n, pl* **-drons** *or* **-dra** \-drə\ : a solid that has 12 plane faces

¹**dodge** \'däj\ *vb* **dodged; dodg·ing 1 a** : to move suddenly aside or to and fro ⟨*dodging* through the crowd⟩ **b** : to avoid by moving quickly aside ⟨*dodge* a blow⟩ **2** : EVADE 1 ⟨*dodged* the question⟩

²**dodge** *n* **1** : an act of avoiding by sudden bodily movement **2** : a sly means of avoiding, deceiving, or tricking ⟨just another *dodge* to get out of working⟩ — **dodg·er** *n*

dodge·ball \'däj-,bȯl\ *n* : a game in which players stand in a circle and try to hit other players within the circle with a large inflated ball

do·do \'dōd-ō\ *n, pl* **do·does** *or* **dodos 1** : a large heavy flightless extinct bird related to the pigeons and formerly found on some of the islands of the Indian ocean **2 a** : a person who is hopelessly behind the times **b** : a stupid person [from Portuguese *doudo*, name given by Portuguese sailors to the bird, from *doudo* (adjective) "silly, stupid"]

dodo 1

doe \'dō\ *n, pl* **does** *or* **doe** : the female especially of an adult mammal (as a deer, an antelope, or a rabbit) of which the male is called *buck*

do·er \'dü-ər\ *n* : one that does

does *present third sing of* DO

doe·skin \'dō-,skin\ *n* **1** : the skin of does or leather made of it; *also* : soft leather from sheepskins or lambskins **2** : a soft smooth firm cloth

doesn't \'dəz-ᵊnt\ : does not

doff \'däf, 'dȯf\ *vb* : to take off (as one's hat as an act of politeness) [Middle English *doffen* "to take off", from *don* "to do" and *of* "off"]

¹**dog** \'dȯg\ *n* **1 a** : a domestic mammal that eats meat and is related to the wolves and foxes **b** : any animal of the family to which the dog belongs **c** : a male dog **2 a** : any of various devices for holding, gripping, or fastening that consist of a spike, rod, or bar **b** : ANDIRON **3** : a show of being stylish or rich ⟨put on the *dog*⟩ **4** *pl* : FEET — **dog·like** \-,līk\ *adj*

²**dog** *vb* **dogged; dog·ging** : to hunt, track, or follow like a hound

dog·cart \'dȯg-,kärt\ *n* **1** : a cart drawn by a dog **2** : a light one-horse carriage with two seats back to back

dog days *n pl* : the hot and humid period of summer between early July and early September

Word History The "dog" in the expression *dog days* is not a real animal but a star in the sky. *Dog days* is a translation of the Latin phrase *dies caniculares*. The ancient Romans applied this phrase to the hottest days of the summer when the star Sirius, the brightest star in the sky, comes up over the horizon at about the same time as the sun. Sirius got its name from an ancient Greek word meaning "burning" or "scorching". The Romans of-

ten referred to Sirius as *canicula*, literally "little dog", because it is the principal star in the star group known as Canis Major ("greater dog"), which was thought to have the shape of a dog. [translation of Latin *dies caniculares*, from *canicula*, literally "little dog", from *canis* "dog"; so called from the fact that they begin at the time when the Dog Star rises with or near the sun — related to CANINE]

doge \'dōj\ *n* : the chief magistrate in the former republics of Venice and Genoa

dog–ear \'dȯg-,gi(ə)r\ *n* : the turned-down corner of a leaf of a book — **dog–ear** *vb*

dog–eared \'dȯg-,gi(ə)rd\ *adj* **1** : having dog-ears **2** : worn-out from too much use

dog·face \'dȯg-,fās\ *n* : an infantry soldier

dog·fight \-,fīt\ *n* : a fight at close range between fighter planes

dog·fish \-,fish\ *n* : any of various small sharks that hunt in schools near shore

dog·ged \'dȯg-gəd\ *adj* : stubbornly determined : TENACIOUS ⟨in *dogged* pursuit of power⟩ **syn** *see* OBSTINATE — **dog·ged·ly** *adv* — **dog·ged·ness** *n*

dog·gie bag \'dȯg-gē-\ *n* : a bag used for carrying home leftover food and especially meat from a meal eaten at a restaurant

dog·gy *or* **dog·gie** \'dȯg-gē\ *n, pl* **dog·gies** : a small or young dog

dog·house \'dȯg-,haús\ *n* : a shelter for a dog — **in the doghouse** : in a state of disfavor

do·gie \'dō-gē\ *n, chiefly West* : a motherless calf in a range herd

dog·ma \'dȯg-mə, 'däg-\ *n, pl* **dog·mas** *also* **dog·ma·ta** \-mət-ə\ **1** : something considered as an established opinion **2** : a belief or body of beliefs concerning faith or morals laid down by a church

dog·mat·ic \dȯg-'mat-ik, däg-\ *adj* **1** : expressing opinions very strongly or positively as if they were facts **2** : of or relating to dogma — **dog·mat·i·cal·ly** \-'mat-i-k(ə-)lē\ *adv*

dog·ma·tism \'dȯg-mə-,tiz-əm, 'däg-\ *n* : positiveness in expressing one's opinions especially when no supporting evidence is given — **dog·ma·tist** \-mət-əst\ *n*

dog paddle *n* : a simple swimming stroke in which the arms paddle in the water and the legs make a kicking motion

dog·sled \'dȯg-,sled\ *n* : a sled drawn by dogs

Dog Star *n* : SIRIUS

dog·tooth violet \'dȯg-,tüth-\ *n* : any of a genus of wild herbs that are related to the lilies, grow from bulbs, and produce flowers in the spring — called also *adder's-tongue*

dog·trot \-,trät\ *n* : a gentle trot — **dogtrot** *vb*

dog watch *n* : a watch on a ship from 4 to 6 or from 6 to 8 p.m.

dog·wood \'dȯg-,wúd\ *n* : any of a group of trees and shrubs having clusters of small flowers often surrounded by four showy leaves that look like petals

doi·ly \'dȯi-lē\ *n, pl* **doilies 1** : a small napkin **2** : a small often decorative cloth or paper used to protect the surface of furniture

do in *vb* **1** : to bring about the defeat or destruction of : RUIN **2** : ¹KILL 1 **3** : to bring almost to the point of exhaustion : WEAR OUT ⟨*done in* at the end of the day⟩

do·ing \'dü-iŋ\ *n* **1** : the act of performing or carrying out : ACTION ⟨it will take some *doing* to beat us⟩ **2** *pl* **a** : things that are done or that occur ⟨everyday *doings*⟩ **b** : social activities ⟨big *doings* tonight⟩

\ə\ **abut**	\aú\ **out**	\i\ **tip**	\ȯ\ **saw**	\ú\ **foot**
\ər\ **further**	\ch\ **chin**	\ī\ **life**	\ȯi\ **coin**	\y\ **yet**
\a\ **mat**	\e\ **pet**	\j\ **job**	\th\ **thin**	\yü\ **few**
\ā\ **take**	\ē\ **easy**	\ŋ\ **sing**	\th\ **this**	\yú\ **cure**
\ä\ **cot, cart**	\g\ **go**	\ō\ **bone**	\ü\ **food**	\zh\ **vision**

do-it-your-self \ˌdü-ə-chər-'self\ *adj* : of, relating to, or designed for a person without professional training or help to use — **do-it-your-self-er** \-'sel-fər\ *n*

dol-drums \'dōl-drəmz, 'däl-, 'dȯl-\ *n pl* 1 : a spell of low spirits 2 : a part of the ocean near the equator known for its calms 3 : a state in which nothing seems to be going on ⟨business is in the *doldrums*⟩

¹dole \'dōl\ *n* 1 : a giving out of food, money, or clothing to the needy 2 : something given out as charity

²dole *vb* **doled; dol-ing** 1 : to give out as charity 2 : to give or deliver in small portions : PARCEL — usually used with *out* **syn** see DISTRIBUTE

dole-ful \'dōl-fəl\ *adj* 1 : full of grief : SAD 2 : expressing grief — **dole-ful-ly** \-fə-lē\ *adv* — **dole-ful-ness** *n*

doll \'däl, 'dȯl\ *n* 1 : a small figure of a human being used especially as a child's plaything 2 a : a pretty young woman b : an attractive person

dol-lar \'däl-ər\ *n* 1 : a coin (as a Spanish piece of eight) similar to an earlier German silver coin 2 a : a basic unit of money (as of the U.S. and Canada) b : a coin or bill representing one dollar [from Dutch *daler* "silver coin formerly used in Germany", from German *taler* (same meaning), shortened from *joachimstaler* "a coin made in *Sankt Joachimstad* (Saint Joachim's Valley) in Bohemia (a former kingdom in Europe)"]

dollar sign *n* : a mark $ or $ placed before a number to indicate that it stands for dollars

doll up *vb* : to dress in fine stylish clothing

dolly \'däl-ē, 'dȯl-ē\ *n, pl* **doll-ies** 1 : DOLL 1 2 : a platform on a roller or on wheels for moving heavy objects; *esp* : a wheeled platform for a television or motion-picture camera

dol-man sleeve \ˌdōl-mən-, ˌdȯl-, ˌdäl-\ *n* : a sleeve that is very wide at the armhole and tight at the wrist [from French *doliman* "a woman's coat with dolman sleeves", from Turkish *dolama* "a robe (in the Turkish style)"]

do-lo-mite \'dō-lə-ˌmīt, 'däl-ə-\ *n* : a mineral found in broad layers as a compact limestone

do-lor \'dō-lər, 'däl-ər\ *n* : ¹SORROW 1a

do-lor-ous \'dō-lə-rəs, 'däl-ə-\ *adj* : causing, marked by, or expressing sorrow — **do-lor-ous-ly** *adv*

dol-phin \'däl-fən, 'dȯl-\ *n*
1 a : any of various small whales with teeth and a long nose b : PORPOISE 1
2 : either of two active spiny-finned marine food fishes noted for their brilliant coloring when dying out of water

dolt \'dōlt\ *n* : a stupid person — **dolt-ish** \'dōl-tish\ *adj* — **dolt-ish-ly** *adv* — **dolt-ish-ness** *n*

dolphin 1a

-dom \dəm\ *n suffix* 1 : realm : jurisdiction ⟨sheik*dom*⟩ 2 : state or fact of being ⟨free*dom*⟩ 3 : those having a (specified) office, occupation, interest, or character ⟨official*dom*⟩ [Old English *-dōm* "office, high position or rank, area of authority"]

do-main \dō-'mān, də-\ *n* 1 : a territory over which control is exercised 2 : an area of influence, knowledge, or activity 3 : a small region of a magnetic substance that contains atoms all lined up in the same direction and behaving like a single tiny magnet [from early French *demaine, domaine* "land one owns", from Latin *dominium* "rule, ownership", from *dominus* "master, owner" — related to CONDOMINIUM, DOMINATE, DOMINION]

¹dome \'dōm\ *n* 1 : a large rounded roof or ceiling shaped like half of a ball 2 : a structure or natural formation that resembles the dome of a building ⟨rock *domes*⟩ [from French *dôme* "mansion, cathedral" and Italian *duomo* "cathedral" and Latin *domus* "church", from earlier Latin

domus "house" — related to DOMESTIC, DOMICILE]

²dome *vb* **domed; dom-ing** 1 : to cover with or as if with a dome 2 : to form into or swell upward or outward like a dome

¹do-mes-tic \də-'mes-tik\ *adj* 1 a : living near or about the places where human beings live ⟨*domestic* vermin⟩ b : living with or under the care of human beings : TAME 2 : of, relating to, made in, or done in one's own country 3 : of or relating to a household or family [from early French *domestique* "living around humans, domestic", from Latin *domesticus* (same meaning), from *domus* "house" — related to DOME, DOMICILE] — **do-mes-ti-cal-ly** \-ti-k(ə-)lē\ *adv*

²domestic *n* : a household servant

domestic animal *n* : any of various domesticated animals (as the horse or sheep)

do-mes-ti-cate \də-'mes-ti-ˌkāt\ *vb* **-cat-ed; -cat-ing** 1 : to bring into domestic use : ADOPT ⟨European customs *domesticated* in America⟩ 2 : to adapt to living with human beings and to serving their purposes — **do-mes-ti-ca-tion** \-ˌmes-ti-'kā-shən\ *n*

do-mes-tic-i-ty \ˌdō-ˌmes-'tis-ət-ē, -məs-, də-\ *n* : the quality or state of being domestic or domesticated

domestic science *n* : instruction and training in household management and arts (as cooking and sewing)

¹dom-i-cile \'däm-ə-ˌsīl, 'dō-mə-; 'däm-ə-səl\ *n* : a place to live : HOME [from early French *domicile* "place where one lives, home", from Latin *domicilium* (same meaning), from *domus* "house" — related to DOME, DOMESTIC]

²domicile *vb* **-ciled; -cil-ing** : to establish in or provide with a place to live

do-mi-cil-i-ate \ˌdäm-ə-'sil-ē-ˌāt, ˌdō-mə-\ *vb* **-at-ed; -at-ing** : ²DOMICILE

dom-i-nance \'däm-ə-nən(t)s\ *n* : the fact or state of being dominant: as a : the relative position of an individual in a series of social ranks or levels b : the property of a genetic dominant that prevents expression of a genetic recessive c : the control or influence over the environment of an ecological community that a dominant has d : greater activity and usage of one of a pair of bodily structures (as the right hand compared to the left hand)

¹dom-i-nant \'däm-(ə-)nənt\ *adj* 1 : commanding, controlling, or having great influence over all others ⟨a *dominant* political type⟩ 2 : rising high above the surroundings 3 : PREDOMINANT, OUTSTANDING 4 : expressed as a bodily characteristic in a living thing when a contrasting recessive gene or a gene for a contrasting recessive characteristic is present ⟨a *dominant* gene⟩ ⟨*dominant* traits in peas⟩ 5 : of, relating to, or being an ecological dominant — **dom-i-nant-ly** *adv*

²dominant *n* 1 a : a dominant gene or a character which it controls b : a kind of living thing (as a species) that has a major influence on the environment of an ecological community 2 : the fifth note of the musical scale

dom-i-nate \'däm-ə-ˌnāt\ *vb* **-nat-ed; -nat-ing** 1 : to have a commanding position or controlling power over 2 : to seem to command by rising high above ⟨a volcano *dominates* the island⟩ ⟨the statue *dominates* the square⟩ [derived from Latin *dominari* "to rule, govern, control", from *dominus* "master, owner" — related to CONDOMINIUM, DAME, DOMAIN, DOMINION, ¹DON] — **dom-i-na-tion** \ˌdäm-ə-'nā-shən\ *n* — **dom-i-na-tive** \'däm-ə-ˌnāt-iv\ *adj* — **dom-i-na-tor** \-ˌnāt-ər\ *n*

dom-i-neer \ˌdäm-ə-'ni(ə)r\ *vb* : to rule or behave in a bossy way — **dom-i-neer-ing** *adj*

Do-min-i-can \də-'min-i-kən\ *n* : a member of a Roman Catholic order of preaching friars founded in 1215 — **Dominican** *adj*

do-mi-nie *sense 1 usually* 'däm-ə-nē, *sense 2 usually* 'dō-mə-\ *n* 1 *chiefly Scottish* : SCHOOLMASTER 2 : a member of the clergy

do-min-ion \də-'min-yən\ *n* 1 : supreme authority : SOV-

EREIGNTY **2** : DOMAIN 1 **3** *often cap* : a self-governing nation of the Commonwealth other than the United Kingdom that accepts the British monarch as chief of state [Middle English *dominioun* "control, rule", from early French *dominion* (same meaning), from Latin *dominium* "rule, ownership", from *dominus* "master, owner" — related to DOMINION, DOMINATE]

Dominion Day *n* : July 1 observed in Canada as a legal holiday in honor of the formation of the Dominion of Canada in 1867

dom·i·no \'däm-ə-ˌnō\ *n, pl* **-noes** *or* **-nos** **1** : a long loose hooded cloak usually worn with a half mask as a masquerade costume **2 a** : a flat rectangular block whose face is divided into two equal parts that are blank or bear dots **b** *pl* : any of several games played with dominoes

domino theory *n* **1** : a theory that if one nation becomes Communist-controlled the neighboring nations will also become Communist-controlled **2** : the theory that if one act or event is allowed to take place a series of similar acts or events will follow

¹don \'dän\ *n* **1** : a Spanish nobleman or gentleman — used as a title **2** : a teacher in a college or university [from Spanish *don* "a nobleman or gentleman", from Latin *dominus* "master, owner" — related to DAME, DOMINATE]

²don *vb* **donned; don·ning** : to dress oneself in : PUT ON [from a contraction of *do on*]

do·nate \'dō-ˌnāt, dō-'nāt\ *vb* **do·nat·ed; do·nat·ing** : to make a gift of : CONTRIBUTE ⟨*donate* blood⟩ **syn** see GIVE — **do·na·tor** \-ˌnāt-ər, -'nāt-\ *n*

do·na·tion \dō-'nā-shən\ *n* : a giving of something without charge; *also* : the thing given (as to charity)

done *past participle of* DO

done·ness \'dən-nəs\ *n* : the condition of being cooked

don·jon \'dän-jən, 'dən-\ *n* : the main inner tower in a castle [Middle English *donjon* "inner tower of a castle", from early French *donjon* (same meaning) — related to DUNGEON; see *Word History* at DUNGEON]

1 donjon

don·key \'däŋ-kē, 'dəŋ-, 'dòŋ-\ *n, pl* **donkeys** **1** : a sturdy and patient domestic mammal that is classified with the asses and is used especially to carry things **2** : a stupid or stubborn person

do·nor \'dō-nər, -ˌnòr\ *n* **1** : one that donates **2** : one used as a source of bodily parts ⟨a blood *donor*⟩

don't \(')dōnt\ : do not

¹doo·dle \'düd-ᵊl\ *vb* **doo·dled; doo·dling** \'düd-liŋ, -ᵊl-iŋ\ : to make a doodle — **doo·dler** \-lər, -ᵊl-ər\ *n*

²doodle *n* : a scribble, design, or sketch done while thinking of something else

doo·dle·bug \'düd-ᵊl-ˌbəg\ *n* : the larva of an ant lion

¹doom \'düm\ *n* **1** : a decision made by a court : SENTENCE **2 a** : a usually unhappy end **b** : DEATH 1, RUIN **syn** see DESTINY

²doom *vb* **1** : CONDEMN 2 **2** : to set on a fixed course to an unhappy end ⟨the plan was *doomed* to failure⟩

dooms·day \'dümz-ˌdā\ *n* : JUDGMENT DAY

domino 2a

door \'dō(ə)r, 'dò(ə)r\ *n* **1** : a barrier by which an entry is closed and opened; *also* : a similar part of a piece of furniture **2** : DOORWAY 1

door·bell \-ˌbel\ *n* : a bell, gong, or set of chimes to be rung usually by a push button at an outside door

door·frame \-ˌfrām\ *n* : a structure that encloses a doorway and usually supports a door

door·jamb \-ˌjam\ *n* : a vertical piece that forms a side of a doorway

door·keep·er \-ˌkē-pər\ *n* : a person who tends a door

door·knob \-ˌnäb\ *n* : a knob that when turned releases a door latch

door·man \-ˌman, -mən\ *n* : a person who tends a door (as of a hotel) and assists people (as by calling taxis)

door·mat \-ˌmat\ *n* : a mat placed before or inside a door for wiping dirt from the shoes

door·post \-ˌpōst\ *n* : DOORJAMB

door·step \-ˌstep\ *n* : a step or series of steps before an outer door

door–to–door \ˌdōrt-ə-'dō(ə)r, ˌdòrt-ə-'dò(ə)r\ *adj* : being or making a call (as to sell something) at every residence in an area — **door–to–door** *adv*

door·way \-ˌwā\ *n* **1** : the opening or passage that a door closes **2** : a means of reaching or gaining something ⟨the *doorway* to success⟩

door·yard \-ˌyärd\ *n* : a yard right outside the door of a house

¹dope \'dōp\ *n* **1** : a thick sticky material (as one used to make pipe joints tight) **2** : a drug preparation especially when narcotic or addictive and used illegally **3** : a stupid person **4** : information especially from a reliable source

²dope *vb* **doped; dop·ing** **1** : to treat or affect with dope; *esp* : to give a narcotic to **2** : FIND OUT — usually used with *out*

dop·er \'dō-pər\ *n* : a person who regularly uses drugs especially illegally

dop·ey \'dō-pē\ *adj* **dop·i·er; -est** **1** : dulled by or as if by alcohol or a narcotic **2** : STUPID 1, 3, 4 ⟨your *dopey* friends⟩ ⟨a *dopey* TV show⟩ —**dop·i·ness** *n*

Dopp·ler effect \'däp-lər-\ *n* : a change in the frequency with which waves (as of sound or light) from a source reach an observer when the source and the observer are moving rapidly toward or away from each other [named for Christian J. *Doppler* 1803–1853 Austrian physicist]

Doppler radar *n* : a radar system using the Doppler effect for measuring speed

Dor·ic \'dòr-ik, 'där-\ *adj* : belonging to the simplest Greek architectural order [derived from Greek *Dōris*, name of a kingdom in ancient Greece]

dork \'dòrk\ *n, slang* : JERK 3

dorky \'dòr-kē\ *adj* **dork·i·er; -est** *slang* : foolishly stupid

dorm \'dò(ə)rm\ *n* : DORMITORY

dor·man·cy \'dòr-mən-sē\ *n* : the quality or state of being dormant

dor·mant \'dòr-mənt\ *adj* **1** : not active but capable of becoming active ⟨*dormant* volcano⟩ **2 a** : sleeping or appearing to be asleep : SLUGGISH **b** : having growth or other biological activity much reduced or suspended ⟨a *dormant* bud⟩ **3** : of, relating to, or used during a period of no or greatly reduced activity or growth ⟨*dormant* spray for fruit trees⟩

dor·mer \'dòr-mər\ *n* : a window placed upright in a sloping roof; *also* : the structure containing a dormer window

dor·mi·to·ry \'dòr-mə-ˌtōr-ē, -ˌtòr-\ *n, pl* **-ries** **1** : a sleeping room especially for several people **2** : a residence hall having many sleeping rooms

\ə\ abut		\au̇\ out	\i\ tip	\ȯ\ saw	\u̇\ foot
\ər\ further		\ch\ chin	\ī\ life	\ȯi\ coin	\y\ yet
\a\ mat		\e\ pet	\j\ job	\th\ thin	\yü\ few
\ā\ take		\ē\ easy	\ŋ\ sing	\th\ this	\yu̇\ cure
\ä\ cot, cart		\g\ go	\ō\ bone	\ü\ food	\zh\ vision

dor·mouse \'dȯ(ə)r-,maus\ *n, pl* **dor·mice** \-,mīs\ : any of numerous Old World rodents that resemble small squirrels

dor·sal \'dȯr-səl\ *adj* : relating to or situated near or on the back (as of an animal) — **dor·sal·ly** \-sə-lē\ *adv*

dorsal fin *n* : a fin on the ridge along the middle of the back of a fish or sea mammal (as a whale)

do·ry \'dōr-ē, 'dȯr-\ *n, pl* **dories** : a boat with a flat bottom, high sides that curve upward and outward, and a sharp bow

dos·age \'dō-sij\ *n* **1 a** : the giving of medicine in doses **b** : the amount of a single dose **2** : the addition or application of a substance in a measured dose

dormouse

¹dose \'dōs\ *n* **1 a** : the measured amount of a medicine to be taken at one time **b** : the quantity of radiation given or absorbed **2** : a portion of a substance added during a process **3** : an experience to which one is exposed ⟨a *dose* of hard work⟩

²dose *vb* **dosed; dos·ing** **1** : to give medicine to **2** : to treat with something

do·sim·e·ter \dō-'sim-ət-ər\ *n* : an instrument for measuring doses of X rays or of radioactivity

dos·sier \'dȯs-,yā, 'dȯs-ē-,ā, 'däs-\ *n* : a file of papers containing a detailed report

dost \(')dəst\ *archaic present second sing of* DO

¹dot \'dät\ *n* **1** : a small spot : SPECK **2** : a small mark made with or as if with a pen: as **a** : a point after a note or rest in music indicating increase of the time value by one half **b** : DECIMAL POINT **c** : a centered dot · used as a sign of multiplication **3** : an exact point in time or space ⟨arrived on the *dot*⟩ **4** : a short click or buzz forming a letter or part of a letter (as in the Morse code)

²dot *vb* **dot·ted; dot·ting** **1** : to mark with a dot ⟨*dot* an "i"⟩ **2** : to cover with or as if with dots ⟨green buds *dotted* the branches⟩ — **dot·ter** *n*

dote \'dōt\ *vb* **dot·ed; dot·ing** : to be foolishly fond ⟨*doted* on their grandchild⟩ — **dot·ing·ly** \'dōt-iŋ-lē\ *adv*

doth \(')dəth\ *archaic present third sing of* DO

dot matrix *n* : a rectangular arrangement of dots from which letters, numbers, and symbols can be formed (as by a computer printer or on a display screen)

dot·ty \'dät-ē\ *adj* **dot·ti·er; -est** : a little crazy

Dou·ay Version \dü-'ā-\ *n* : an English translation of the Vulgate used by Roman Catholics [named for *Douay,* city in France where part of this translation was published in 1609–1610]

¹dou·ble \'dəb-əl\ *adj* **1** : DUAL 1 ⟨a *double* role⟩ **2** : consisting of two members or parts ⟨an egg with a *double* yolk⟩ **3** : being twice as great or as many **4** : folded in two **5** : having more than the usual number of floral parts and especially petals ⟨*double* roses⟩ [Middle English *double* "double, dual", from early French *double* (same meaning), from Latin *duplus* "double", from *duo* "two" and *-plus* "multiplied by" — related to DUAL] — **dou·ble·ness** *n*

²double *vb* **dou·bled; dou·bling** \'dəb-(ə-)liŋ\ **1** : to make, be, or become twice as great or as many **2 a** : to make of two thicknesses : FOLD **b** : to close tightly the fingers of : CLENCH ⟨*doubled* his fist⟩ **c** : to cause to bend at the waist **d** : to become bent or folded usually in the middle **3** : to have an additional use or job ⟨the cook *doubles* as dishwasher⟩ **4** : to make a double **5** : to turn sharply and go back on the same path first taken

³double *adv* **1** : DOUBLY 1 **2** : two together ⟨sleep *double*⟩

⁴double *n* **1 a** : something twice another ⟨12 is the *double*

of 6⟩ **b** : a hit in baseball that allows a batter to reach second base **2** : ³DUPLICATE; *esp* : a person who closely resembles another **3** : a sharp turn : REVERSAL **4** : ⁴FOLD 2 **5** *pl* : a game between two pairs of players ⟨tennis *doubles*⟩

double bass *n* : the largest instrument of the violin family

double boiler *n* : a kitchen utensil consisting of two saucepans fitting together so that the contents of the upper can be cooked or heated by boiling water in the lower

double bond *n* : a chemical bond in which two atoms in a molecule share two pairs of electrons — compare SINGLE BOND, TRIPLE BOND

dou·ble–breast·ed \,dəb-əl-'bres-təd\ *adj* : having one half of the front lapped over the other and usually two rows of buttons ⟨*double-breasted* jacket⟩

dou·ble–check \,dəb-əl-'chek, 'dəb-əl-,chek\ *vb* : to make a careful check (as for accuracy) of something already checked — **double check** *n*

double cross *n* : an act of betraying or cheating especially an associate — **dou·ble–cross** \,dəb-əl-'krȯs\ *vb* — **dou·ble–cross·er** *n*

dou·ble–deal·ing \,dəb-əl-'dē-liŋ\ *n* : DUPLICITY — **dou·ble–deal·er** *n* — **double–dealing** *adj*

dou·ble–deck·er \,dəb-əl-'dek-ər\ *n* : something (as a ship, bus, or bed) having two decks

dou·ble–head·er \,dəb-əl-'hed-ər\ *n* : two games played one after the other on the same day

double helix *n* : a helix or spiral consisting of two strands in the surface of a cylinder which coil around its axis; *esp* : the arrangement in space of the chemical bases and nucleotides that make up DNA

double hyphen *n* : a punctuation mark ⸗ that is used in place of a hyphen in a word divided at the end of a line to show that the word is usually hyphenated at that place

dou·ble–joint·ed \,dəb-əl-'jȯint-əd\ *adj* : having one or more joints that permit the parts joined to be bent freely to unusual angles ⟨a *double-jointed* finger⟩

double knit *n* : a knitted fabric made with a double set of needles to produce a double thickness of fabric with each thickness joined by interlocking stitches; *also* : an article of clothing made of such fabric

double negative *n* : a substandard grammatical construction that contains two negatives and is intended to have a negative meaning (as in "I didn't hear nothing" instead of "I didn't hear anything")

double play *n* : a play in baseball in which two base runners are put out

double pneumonia *n* : pneumonia involving both lungs

dou·ble–space \,dəb-əl-'spās\ *vb* : to type something leaving every other line blank

double star *n* : two stars very near to each other but generally seen with a telescope as separate

double sugar *n* : DISACCHARIDE

dou·blet \'dəb-lət\ *n* **1** : a close-fitting jacket worn by men of western Europe chiefly in the 16th century **2** : one of two similar or identical things

dou·ble take \'dəb-əl-,tāk\ *n* : a delayed reaction to a surprising or unusual situation after first failing to notice anything unusual

dou·ble–talk \'dəb-əl-,tȯk\ *n* : language that seems to make sense but is actually a mixture of sense and nonsense

double time *n* **1** : a marching rate of 180 steps per minute **2** : payment of a worker at twice the regular wage rate

dou·ble–time \'dəb-əl-,tīm\ *vb* : to move at double time

double vision *n* : vision in which an object is seen as double

D doublet 1

because of unequal action of the eye muscles

dou·bloon \,də-'blün\ *n* : an old gold coin of Spain and Spanish America [from Spanish *doblón* "doubloon"]

dou·bly \'dəb-lē\ *adv* : to twice the amount or degree

¹doubt \'daút\ *vb* **1** : to be uncertain about **2** : to lack confidence in **3** : to consider unlikely — **doubt·able** \-ə-bəl\ *adj* — **doubt·er** *n* — **doubt·ing·ly** \-iŋ-lē\ *adv*

²doubt *n* **1** : uncertainty of belief or opinion **2** : the state of being uncertain ⟨the outcome is in *doubt*⟩ **3 a** : a lack of confidence **b** : an inclination not to believe or accept
syn DOUBT, UNCERTAINTY, DISTRUST, SUSPICION mean a feeling that one is not sure about someone or something. DOUBT may suggest a lack of certainty that results in an inability to make a decision ⟨so filled with *doubt* that she didn't know what to do⟩ UNCERTAINTY may range from a feeling just short of certainty to almost complete lack of knowledge about something ⟨there is still *uncertainty* about what causes cancer⟩ DISTRUST suggests lack of trust or confidence on vague or general grounds ⟨an unthinking *distrust* of foreigners⟩ SUSPICION stresses lack of faith in the truth, reality, fairness, or reliability of someone or something ⟨my *suspicion* is that he is lying⟩

doubt·ful \'daút-fəl\ *adj* **1** : not clear or certain as to fact ⟨a *doubtful* claim⟩ **2** : QUESTIONABLE 2 ⟨*doubtful* intentions⟩ **3** : undecided in opinion **4** : not certain in outcome — **doubt·ful·ly** \-fə-lē\ *adv* — **doubt·ful·ness** *n*

¹doubt·less \'daút-ləs\ *adv* **1** : without doubt : CERTAINLY **2** : in all probability

²doubtless *adj* : free from doubt : CERTAIN

douche \'düsh\ *n* **1 a** : a jet of fluid (as water) directed against a part or into a cavity of the body **b** : a cleansing with a douche **2** : a device for giving douches — **douche** *vb*

dough \'dō\ *n* **1 a** : a soft mass of moistened flour or meal thick enough to knead or roll **b** : any similar soft mass **2** : MONEY 1a — **doughy** \'dō-ē\ *adj*

dough·boy \'dō-,bói\ *n* : an American infantryman especially in World War I

dough·nut *or* **do·nut** \-(,)nət\ *n* **1** : a small ring of sweet dough fried in fat **2** : something resembling a doughnut especially in shape

dough·ty \'daút-ē\ *adj* **dough·ti·er; -est** : very strong and brave — **dough·ti·ly** \'daút-°l-ē\ *adv* — **dough·ti·ness** \'daút-ē-nəs\ *n*

Doug·las fir \,dəg-ləs-\ *n* : a tall evergreen cone-bearing timber tree of the western U.S.

dour \'dù(ə)r, 'daù(ə)r\ *adj* : looking or being stern or sullen — **dour·ly** *adv* — **dour·ness** *n*

douse \'daús *also* 'daúz\ *vb* **doused; dous·ing** **1 a** : to stick into water **b** : to throw a liquid on **2** : EXTINGUISH 1 ⟨*douse* the lights⟩

¹dove \'dəv\ *n* **1** : any of numerous pigeons; *esp* : a small wild pigeon **2** : a person who opposes war or warlike policies — **dov·ish** \-ish\ *adj*

²dove \'dōv\ *past and past participle of* DIVE

dove·cote \'dəv-,kōt, -,kät\ *also* **dove·cot** \-,kät\ *n* : a small raised house or box with compartments for domestic pigeons

¹dove·tail \-,tāl\ *n* : something shaped like a dove's tail; *esp* : a joint between two pieces (as of wood) formed by a wedge-shaped part that sticks out from one piece fitting tightly into a wedge-shaped slot in the other piece

²dovetail *vb* **1 a** : to join by means of dovetails **b** : to cut to a dovetail **2** : to fit skillfully together to form a whole

dow·a·ger \'daú-i-jər\ *n* : a dignified elderly woman

dowdy \'daúd-ē\ *adj* **dowd·i·er; -est** **1** : not neatly or well dressed or cared for **2** : not stylish — **dowd·i·ly** \'daúd-°l-ē\ *adv* — **dowd·i·ness** \'daúd-ē-nəs\ *n*

¹dow·el \'daú(-ə)l\ *n* : a pin or peg used for fastening together two pieces of wood

²dowel *vb* **-eled** *or* **-elled; -el·ing** *or* **-el·ling** : to fasten by dowels

¹down \'daún\ *n* : a rolling grassy upland — usually used in pl. [Old English *dūn* "hill"]

²down *adv* **1 a** : toward or in a lower position **b** : to a lying or sitting position **c** : toward or to the ground, floor, or bottom **2** : as a down payment ⟨paid $10 *down*⟩ **3** : in a direction opposite to up ⟨add the numbers across and *down*⟩ **4** : to or in a lower or worse condition ⟨Parliament could tax them *down* to their last penny⟩ **5** : from a past time ⟨heirlooms that have been handed *down*⟩ **6** : to or in a state of less activity ⟨excitement died *down*⟩ [Old English *dune* "down", shortened from *adūne*, literally "off the hill", from a- "off" and *dūne*, form of *dūn* "hill"]

³down *adj* **1 a** : being in a low position; *esp* : lying on the ground **b** : directed or going downward ⟨a *down* escalator⟩ **c** : being at a lower level ⟨sales are *down*⟩ **2 a** : low in spirits : DOWNCAST **b** : SICK 1a ⟨*down* with flu⟩ **3** : being finished, completed, or come to an end ⟨eight *down* and two to go⟩ — **down on** : having a low opinion of or dislike for

⁴down *prep* : down along : down through : down toward : down in : down into : down on ⟨*down* the road⟩

⁵down *n* **1** : a low or falling period ⟨the ups and *downs* of life⟩ **2** : one of a series of four plays that a football team gets to advance the ball ten yards

⁶down *vb* **1** : to go or cause to go or come down **2** : ²SWALLOW 1a **3** : to cause (a football) to be out of play

⁷down *n* **1** : a covering of soft fluffy feathers **2** : something soft and fluffy like down [Middle English *doun* "down, feathers"; of Norse origin]

down·beat \'daún-,bēt\ *n* : the downward stroke of a conductor indicating the principally accented note of a measure of music

down·cast \-,kast\ *adj* **1** : being in a state of lowered confidence or courage : DEJECTED **2** : directed down ⟨a *downcast* glance⟩

down·draft \-,draft, -,dràft\ *n* : a downward current of gas (as air in a chimney or during a thunderstorm)

down·er \'daún-ər\ *n* **1** : a depressant drug; *esp* : BARBITURATE **2** : something that is depressing

down·fall \'daún-,fól\ *n* : a sudden fall (as from power, happiness, or high position) or a cause of such a fall — **down·fall·en** \-,fó-lən\ *adj*

¹down·grade \-,grād\ *n* **1** : a downward slope **2** : a lowering toward a worse condition ⟨a neighborhood on the *downgrade*⟩ — **downgrade** *adv*

²downgrade *vb* : to lower in grade, rank, or standing

down·heart·ed \'daún-'härt-əd\ *adj* : DOWNCAST 1 — **down·heart·ed·ly** *adv* — **down·heart·ed·ness** *n*

down·hill \-'hil\ *adv* : toward the bottom of a hill — **down·hill** \-,hil\ *adj*

down·load \'daún-,lōd\ *vb* : to transfer (data) from a usually large computer to the memory of another device (as a smaller computer) — **down·load·able** \-,lōd-ə-bəl\ *adj*

down payment *n* : a part of the full price paid at the time of purchase or delivery with the remainder to be paid later

down·pour \-,pōr, -,pór\ *n* : a heavy rain

¹down·right \-,rīt\ *adv* : in a complete and absolute manner ⟨that was *downright* stupid⟩

²downright *adj* **1** : ABSOLUTE 3, UTTER ⟨a *downright* lie⟩ **2** : OUTSPOKEN, BLUNT ⟨*downright* country people⟩ — **down·right·ly** *adv* — **down·right·ness** *n*

Down's syndrome \'daún(z)-\ *n* : a birth defect characterized by slanting eyes, a broad short skull, broad hands with short fingers, mental deficiency, and the presence of three of the chromosomes numbered 21 in human beings — called also *mongolism* [named for J. L. H. Down

\ə\ abut	\aú\ out	\i\ tip	\ó\ saw	\ú\ foot
\ər\ further	\ch\ chin	\ī\ life	\ói\ coin	\y\ yet
\a\ mat	\e\ pet	\j\ job	\th\ thin	\yü\ few
\ā\ take	\ē\ easy	\ŋ\ sing	\th\ this	\yú\ cure
\ä\ cot, cart	\g\ go	\ō\ bone	\ü\ food	\zh\ vision

1828–1896 English doctor]

down·stage \'daủn-'stāj\ *adv or adj* : toward or at the part of a theatrical stage or set closest to the audience or the motion-picture or television camera

¹down·stairs \'daủn-'sta(ə)rz, -'ste(ə)rz\ *adv* : down the stairs : on or to a lower floor

²down·stairs \-,sta(ə)rz, -,ste(ə)rz\ *adj* : situated on a lower level or on the main or first floor

³down·stairs \'daủn-'sta(ə)rz, -'ste(ə)rz, -,sta(ə)rz, -,ste(ə)rz\ *n sing or pl* : the lower floor of a building

down·stream \'daủn-'strēm\ *adv or adj* : in the direction a stream is flowing

down·stroke \-,strōk\ *n* : a downward stroke

down–to–earth \,daủn-tə-'(w)ərth\ *adj* : PRACTICAL 4, REALISTIC

¹down·town \,daủn-'taủn\ *adv* : to, toward, or in the main business district

²downtown \-,taủn\ *adj* : situated downtown

down·trod·den \'daủn-'träd-°n\ *adj* : crushed by superior power

¹down·ward \'daủn-wərd\ *also* **down·wards** \-wərdz\ *adv* **1** : from a higher place or condition to a lower one **2** : from an earlier time

²downward *adj* : moving or reaching down

down·wind \'daủn-'wind\ *adv or adj* : in the direction that the wind is blowing

downy \'daủ-nē\ *adj* **down·i·er; -est** **1** : resembling a bird's down **2** : covered with or made of down

downy woodpecker *n* : a small black-and-white woodpecker of North America that has a white back and is smaller than the hairy woodpecker

dow·ry \'daủ(ə)r-ē\ *n, pl* **dowries** : the property that a woman brings to her husband in marriage

dox·ol·o·gy \däk-'säl-ə-jē\ *n, pl* **-gies** : an expression of praise to God

doze \'dōz\ *vb* **dozed; doz·ing** : to sleep lightly — **doze** *n* — **doz·er** *n*

doz·en \'dəz-°n\ *n, pl* **dozens** *or* **dozen** **1** : a group of twelve **2 dozens** *pl* : a game that consists of exchanging insults usually about the opponent's family [Middle English *dozeine* "dozen", from early French *dozaine* (same meaning), derived from Latin *duodecim* "twelve", from *duo* "two" and *decem* "ten" — related to DECIMAL, DIME, DUAL] — **dozen** *adj* — **doz·enth** \-°n(t)th\ *adj*

DP \(')dē-'pē\ *n* : a displaced person

¹drab \'drab\ *n* : a light olive brown

²drab *adj* **drab·ber; drab·best** **1** : of the color drab **2** : lacking variety and interest : DULL 〈a *drab* life〉 — **drab·ly** *adv* — **drab·ness** *n*

dra·cae·na \drə-'sē-nə\ *n* : any of a genus of trees or shrubs that are related to the lilies, have branches with bunches of sword-shaped leaves at the ends, and bear clusters of small greenish white flowers

drach·ma \'drak-mə\ *n, pl* **drach·mas** *or* **drach·mai** \-,mī\ *or* **drach·mae** \-(,)mē, -,mī\ **1** : any of various ancient Greek units of weight **2 a** : an ancient Greek silver coin **b** : the basic unit of money of Greece; *also* : a coin representing this unit

Dra·co \'drā-kō\ *n* : a group of stars between the Big Dipper and Little Dipper [from Latin *Draco*, literally "dragon"]

¹draft \'draft, 'dråft\ *n* **1 a** : the act of pulling or hauling **b** : the thing or amount pulled **2** : the act or an instance of drinking or inhaling; *also* : the portion drunk or inhaled at one time **3 a** : something represented in words or lines : DESIGN, PLAN **b** : a quick sketch, outline, or version from which a final work is produced **4 a** : the act of drawing out liquid (as from a barrel) **b** : a portion of liquid drawn out **5** : the depth of water required for a ship to float when loaded **6** : a picking of persons for required military service **7** : an order issued by one party to another to pay money to a third party **8 a** : a current of air **b** : a device to regulate an air supply (as in a stove) — **on draft** : ready

to be drawn from a container

²draft *adj* **1** : used for pulling loads 〈*draft* animals〉 **2** : being a version to be finished later 〈a *draft* treaty〉 **3** : being or having been on draft 〈*draft* beer〉

³draft *vb* **1** : to pick especially for required military service **2 a** : to make a draft of : OUTLINE **b** : COMPOSE 2, PREPARE — **draft·er** *n*

draft·ee \draf-'tē, dråf-\ *n* : a person who is drafted especially into the armed forces

drafts·man \'draf(t)s-mən, 'dråf(t)s-\ *n* : a person who draws plans (as for machinery) — **drafts·man·ship** \-,ship\ *n*

drafty \'draf-tē, 'dråf-\ *adj* **draf·ti·er; -est** : exposed to a draft or current of air 〈a *drafty* hall〉 — **draft·i·ly** \-tə-lē\ *adv* — **draft·i·ness** \-tē-nəs\ *n*

¹drag \'drag\ *n* **1** : a device for dragging under water to detect or gather objects **2** : something without wheels (as a sledge for carrying heavy loads) that is dragged, pulled, or drawn along or over a surface **3 a** : the act or an instance of dragging or drawing **b** : a draw on a pipe, cigarette, or cigar : PUFF; *also* : a drink of liquid **4 a** : something that slows

drag 1

down motion **b** : the force acting on a body (as an airplane) to slow it down as the body moves through a fluid (as air) **c** : something that hinders or obstructs progress **5** : someone or something boring **6** : STREET 1, ROAD 〈the main *drag*〉

²drag *vb* **dragged; drag·ging** **1 a** : to haul slowly or heavily 〈*dragging* the trunk across the room〉 **b** : to move with painful slowness or difficulty **c** : to pass or cause to pass slowly 〈the day *dragged* on〉 **2** : to hang or lag behind **3** : to trail along on the ground **4** : to search or fish with a drag **5** : to take part in a drag race — **drag·ger** *n*

drag·gle \'drag-əl\ *vb* **drag·gled; drag·gling** \-(ə-)liŋ\ **1** : to make or become wet and dirty by dragging **2** : to follow slowly : STRAGGLE

drag·net \'drag-,net\ *n* **1** : a net dragged along the bottom of a body of water **2** : a series of planned actions for catching a criminal

drag·on \'drag-ən\ *n* **1** : an imaginary animal usually pictured as a huge serpent or lizard with wings and large claws **2** *cap* : DRACO [Middle English *dragon* "dragon", from early French *dragon* (same meaning), from Latin *dracon-, draco* "serpent, dragon", from Greek *drakōn* "serpent, dragon" — related to RANKLE]

drag·on·fly \-,flī\ *n* : any of a group of large harmless insects that have four long wings held horizontal and sticking out instead of folded to the side next to the body when at rest and that feed especially on flies, gnats, and mosquitoes — compare DAMSELFLY

¹dra·goon \drə-'gün, dra-\ *n* : a mounted infantry soldier

²dragoon *vb* : to get (someone) to do something by force

dragonfly

drag race *n* : a race between two vehicles to see which can accelerate faster — **drag racer** *n* — **drag racing** *n*

drag·ster \'drag-stər\ *n* : a vehicle (as an automobile) made for drag racing

drag strip *n* : a place for drag races that is paved and usually at least a quarter mile long

¹**drain** \'drān\ *vb* **1 a** : to draw off or flow off gradually or completely ⟨*drain* water from a tank⟩ **b** : to exhaust physically or emotionally **2 a** : to make or become gradually dry or empty ⟨*drain* a swamp⟩ **b** : to empty a little at a time — **drain·er** *n*

²**drain** *n* **1** : a means (as a pipe, channel, or sewer) of draining **2 a** : the act of draining **b** : a gradual using up **3** : something that causes a using up ⟨a *drain* on our resources⟩ — **down the drain** : to a state of being wasted or lost

drain·age \'drā-nij\ *n* **1 a** : the act of draining **b** : something drained off **2** : a method of draining; *also* : a system of drains

drain·pipe \'drān-,pīp\ *n* : a pipe for drainage

drake \'drāk\ *n* : a male duck

dram \'dram\ *n* — see MEASURE table

dra·ma \'dräm-ə, 'dram-\ *n* **1** : a written work that tells a story through action and speech and is meant to be acted on a stage : PLAY **2** : dramatic art, literature, or affairs **3** : an exciting event or series of events

dra·mat·ic \drə-'mat-ik\ *adj* **1** : of or relating to the drama **2 a** : suitable to or resembling that of the drama **b** : catching the attention ⟨made a *dramatic* entrance⟩ — **dra·mat·i·cal·ly** \-'mat-i-k(ə-)lē\ *adv*

dra·mat·ics \drə-'mat-iks\ *n sing or pl* **1** : the study or practice of theatrical arts **2** : dramatic behavior or expression

dra·ma·tis per·so·nae \,dram-ət-əs-pər-'sō-(,)nē, ,dräm-, -,nī\ *n pl* : the characters or actors in a play [modern Latin]

dram·a·tist \'dram-ət-əst, 'dräm-\ *n* : PLAYWRIGHT

dram·a·tize \'dram-ə-,tīz, 'dräm-\ *vb* **1** : to make into a drama **2** : to present or represent in a dramatic manner — **dram·a·ti·za·tion** \,dram-ət-ə-'zā-shən, ,dräm-\ *n*

drank *past of* DRINK

¹**drape** \'drāp\ *n* **1** *pl* : DRAPERY 2 **2** : arrangement in or of folds **3** : the cut or hang of clothing

²**drape** *vb* **draped; drap·ing** **1** : to cover or decorate with or as if with folds of cloth **2** : to arrange in flowing lines

drap·er \'drā-pər\ *n, British* : a dealer in cloth and sometimes also in clothing and dry goods

drap·ery \'drā-p(ə-)rē\ *n, pl* **-er·ies** **1** : a decorative fabric hung in loose folds **2** : curtains of heavy fabric often used over thinner curtains

dras·tic \'dras-tik\ *adj* **1** : acting rapidly or violently **2** : severe in effect : HARSH ⟨had to take *drastic* measures⟩ — **dras·ti·cal·ly** \-ti-k(ə-)lē\ *adv*

draught \'draft, 'dråft\ *chiefly British variant of* DRAFT

¹**draw** \'dro\ *vb* **drew** \'drü\; **drawn** \'dron\; **draw·ing** **1 a** : to cause to move by pulling : cause to follow **b** : to pull up or to one side ⟨*draw* the drapes⟩ **c** : to pull up or out ⟨*draw* a gun⟩ **d** : to cause to come out of a container ⟨*draw* water for a bath⟩ **2** : to move or go steadily or gradually ⟨day was *drawing* to a close⟩ **3 a** : ATTRACT, ENTICE ⟨*drew* a crowd⟩ **b** : PROVOKE 2 ⟨*drew* criticism⟩ **c** : to bring on as a response ⟨*drew* cheers from the crowd⟩ **4** : INHALE 1 ⟨*drew* a deep breath⟩ **5 a** : to cause (as the contents or essence) to come forth ⟨brine *draws* moisture and sugars from the cucumbers⟩ **b** : EVISCERATE ⟨*drawn* and plucked chickens⟩ **6** : to need (a specified depth) to float in ⟨the boat *draws* three feet of water⟩ **7 a** : ACCUMULATE 1, GAIN ⟨*draw* interest⟩ **b** : to take money from a place of deposit : WITHDRAW **c** : to receive regularly from a source ⟨*draw* a salary⟩ **8** : to receive or take at random ⟨*drew* a winning number⟩ ⟨*draw* a card — any card⟩ **9** : to bend (a bow) by pulling back the string **10** : to cause to shrink or pucker **11** : to leave (a contest) undecided : TIE **12 a** : to produce a likeness of by making

lines on a surface ⟨*draw* a picture⟩ ⟨the computer can *draw* a graph on the screen⟩ **b** : to write out in proper form ⟨*draw* a will⟩ — often used with *up* ⟨*draw* up a deed⟩ **c** : to describe in words **13** : DEDUCE 2a ⟨*draw* a conclusion⟩ **14** : to stretch or spread by or as if by pulling ⟨some metals can be *drawn* out to form wire⟩ **15** : to produce a draft of air ⟨the chimney *draws* well⟩ — **draw on** *or* **draw upon** : to use as a source of supply ⟨what experiences can you *draw on* for a story⟩

²**draw** *n* **1** : the act or result of drawing **2** : a tie contest or game **3** : something that draws attention **4** : a gully shallower than a ravine

draw·back \'dro-,bak\ *n* : ¹DISADVANTAGE 2b

draw·bar \-,bär\ *n* : a beam across the rear of a tractor to which tools are hitched

draw·bridge \-,brij\ *n* : a bridge made to be wholly or partly raised up, let down, or drawn aside so as to permit or prevent passage

draw·er \'dro(-ə)r\ *n* **1** : one that draws **2** : a sliding boxlike compartment (as in a desk) **3** *pl* : an undergarment for the lower part of the body

draw·ing \'dro-iŋ\ *n* **1** : an act or instance of drawing lots **2** : the act or art of making a figure, plan, or sketch by means of lines **3** : a picture made by drawing

drawbridge

drawing board *n* : a board on which paper for drawing can be fastened

drawing room *n* : a formal room for entertaining company [shortened from *withdrawing room* "a room one can go to to be alone"]

¹**drawl** \'drol\ *vb* : to speak slowly with vowels drawn out beyond their usual length

²**drawl** *n* : a drawling way of speaking

drawn butter \'dron-\ *n* : melted butter

draw on *vb* : to come closer : APPROACH ⟨as night *drew on*⟩

draw out *vb* **1** : to cause to last longer than usual **2** : to cause or encourage to speak freely ⟨tried to *draw* the shy child *out*⟩

draw·string \'dro-,striŋ\ *n* : a string, cord, or tape used to close a bag, control fullness in clothes, or open or close curtains

draw up *vb* **1** : to arrange (as a body of troops) in order **2** : to straighten (oneself) to an erect posture **3** : to bring or come to a stop

dray \'drā\ *n* : a strong low cart or wagon without sides for hauling heavy loads

¹**dread** \'dred\ *vb* **1** : to fear greatly **2** : to be very unwilling to meet or face

²**dread** *n* **1 a** : great fear especially in the face of approaching harm **b** *archaic* : ¹AWE **2** : one causing fear or awe **syn** see FEAR

³**dread** *adj* : causing great fear or anxiety ⟨a *dread* disease⟩

dread·ful \'dred-fəl\ *adj* **1** : causing dread or awe **2** : very disagreeable, unpleasant, or shocking ⟨a *dreadful* cold⟩ ⟨such *dreadful* manners⟩ — **dread·ful·ly** \-f(ə-)lē\ *adv* — **dread·ful·ness** \-fəl-nəs\ *n*

dread·nought \'dred-,not, -,nät\ *n* : a battleship armed with big guns of the same caliber

¹**dream** \'drēm\ *n* **1** : a series of thoughts, pictures, or feel-

\ə\ abut	\aů\ out	\i\ tip	\ò\ saw	\ů\ foot
\ər\ further	\ch\ chin	\ī\ life	\òi\ coin	\y\ yet
\a\ mat	\e\ pet	\j\ job	\th\ thin	\yü\ few
\ā\ take	\ē\ easy	\ŋ\ sing	\th\ this	\yů\ cure
\ä\ cot, cart	\g\ go	\ō\ bone	\ü\ food	\zh\ vision

ings occurring during sleep **2** : a vision created in the imagination : DAYDREAM **3** : something notable for its beauty or pleasing quality **4** : a goal that is longed for : IDEAL — **dream·like** \-,līk\ adj

²**dream** \'drēm\ vb **dreamed** \'drem(p)t, 'drēmd\ or **dreamt** \'drem(p)t\; **dream·ing** \'drē-miŋ\ **1** : to have a dream **2** : to spend time having daydreams **3** : think of as happening or possible : IMAGINE ⟨dreamed of success⟩ — **dream·er** n

dream·land \'drēm-,land\ n : an unreal delightful country existing only in imagination or in dreams

dream·less \'drēm-ləs\ adj : having no dreams ⟨a dreamless sleep⟩ — **dream·less·ly** adv — **dream·less·ness** n

dreamy \'drē-mē\ adj **dream·i·er; -est** **1** : full of dreams **2** : tending to spend time in dreaming **3 a** : suggesting a dream **b** : being quiet and soothing ⟨dreamy music⟩ **c** : DELIGHTFUL, PLEASING — **dream·i·ly** \-mə-lē\ adv — **dream·i·ness** \-mē-nəs\ n

drear \'dri(ə)r\ adj : DREARY

drea·ry \'dri(ə)r-ē\ adj **drea·ri·er** \'drir-ē-ər\; **-est** : having nothing likely to provide cheer, comfort, or interest : DISMAL, GLOOMY — **drea·ri·ly** \'drir-ə-lē\ adv — **drea·ri·ness** \'drir-ē-nəs\ n

¹**dredge** \'drej\ vb **dredged; dredg·ing** **1 a** : to dig, gather, or pull out with or as if with a dredge — often used with up **b** : to deepen (as a waterway) with a dredge **2** : to search with or as if with a dredge

²**dredge** n **1** : an iron frame with an attached net used especially to catch fish or shellfish **2** : a machine for removing earth usually by buckets on a continuous chain or by a suction tube [probably from a Scottish word element *dreg-* "dredge" that may be from Old English *dragan* "to pull, drag"]

¹dresser

³**dredge** vb **dredged; dredg·ing** : to coat (food) by sprinkling (as with flour) [from obsolete *dredge* (noun) "a candied fruit", derived from early French *dragie* (same meaning), from Latin *tragemata* (plural) "candied fruits", from Greek *tragēmata* (same meaning), derived from *trōgein* "to gnaw"]

dregs \'dregz\ n pl **1** : sediment contained in a liquid or precipitated from it : LEES **2** : the most undesirable part ⟨the *dregs* of humanity⟩

drench \'drench\ vb : to wet thoroughly **syn** see SOAK

¹**dress** \'dres\ vb **1** : to make or set straight (as soldiers on parade) **2 a** : to put clothes on **b** : to provide with clothing **c** : to put on or wear formal or fancy clothes **3** : to trim or decorate for display **4** : to put in order **5 a** : to apply dressings or medicine to ⟨*dress* a wound⟩ **b** : to arrange (the hair) by combing, brushing, or curling **c** : ²GROOM 1 **d** : to kill and prepare for market ⟨*dress* a chicken⟩ **e** : to apply manure or fertilizer to **6** : ²SMOOTH 1, FINISH

²**dress** n **1** : CLOTHING 1 **2** : an outer garment with a skirt for a woman or child **3** : clothing appropriate to a particular time or occasion ⟨Roman *dress*⟩ ⟨evening *dress*⟩

³**dress** adj **1** : relating to or used for a dress ⟨*dress* goods⟩ **2** : suitable or required for a formal occasion ⟨*dress* clothes⟩ ⟨a *dress* uniform⟩

dress down vb : to reprove severely — **dressing down** n

¹**dress·er** \'dres-ər\ n : a piece of furniture (as a chest or bureau) with a mirror

²**dresser** n : one that dresses

dress·ing \'dres-iŋ\ n **1 a** : the act or process of one that dresses **b** : an instance of dressing **2 a** : a sauce for adding to a dish **b** : a seasoned mixture used as a stuff-

ing (as for poultry) or baked and served separately **3 a** : material used to cover an injury **b** : fertilizing material (as manure or compost)

dressing gown n : a loose robe worn indoors

dressing room n : a room (as in a theater) used for dressing

dressing table n : a table often with drawers and a mirror in front of which one sits while dressing and grooming oneself

dress·mak·ing \'dres-,mā-kiŋ\ n : the process or occupation of making dresses — **dress·mak·er** \-kər\ n

dress rehearsal n : a rehearsal of a play in costume and with stage properties shortly before the first performance

dress up vb **1** : to put on one's best or formal clothes **2** : to put on strange or fancy clothes ⟨*dress up* for Halloween⟩

dressy \'dres-ē\ adj **dress·i·er; -est** **1** : showy in dress **2** : suitable for formal occasions

drew past of DRAW

¹**drib·ble** \'drib-əl\ vb **drib·bled; drib·bling** \-(ə-)liŋ\ **1** : to fall or flow or let fall in small drops : TRICKLE **2** : DROOL **3** : to move forward by tapping, bouncing, or kicking ⟨*dribble* a basketball⟩ — **drib·bler** \-(ə-)lər\ n

²**dribble** n **1** : a small trickling flow **2** : an act or instance of dribbling a ball or puck

drib·let \'drib-lət\ n **1** : a small amount **2** : a falling drop

¹**drier** comparative of DRY

²**dri·er** also **dry·er** \'drī-(ə)r\ n **1** : something that dries **2** : a substance used (as in paints or varnishes) to speed up drying **3** usually **dryer** : a device for drying something by heat or air

driest superlative of DRY

¹**drift** \'drift\ n **1 a** : a drifting motion or course **b** : the flow or the velocity of a river or ocean stream **2 a** : wind-driven snow, rain, cloud, dust, or smoke usually near the ground **b** : a mass of matter (as sand) deposited by or as if by wind or water **c** : a deposit of clay, sand, gravel, and boulders transported by a glacier or by running water from a glacier **3 a** : a course something appears to be taking **b** : the meaning of something said or implied

²**drift** vb **1** : to become or cause to be driven or carried along by a current of water, wind, or air **2** : to move along without effort **3** : to be piled up in heaps by wind or water — **drift·ing·ly** \'drif-tiŋ-lē\ adv

drift·er \'drif-tər\ n : one that drifts; esp : a person who travels about without purpose

drift·wood \'drift-,wùd\ n : wood drifted or floated by water

¹**drill** \'dril\ n **1** : a tool for making holes in hard substances **2** : the training of soldiers in military skill and discipline **3** : a physical or mental exercise regularly practiced **4** : a marine snail that bores through oyster shells and feeds on the soft parts [probably from Dutch *dril* "a tool for drilling holes", derived from early Dutch *drillen* (verb) "to drill"]

²**drill** vb **1** : to instruct or train by repetition ⟨*drill* a child in arithmetic⟩ ⟨*drill* troops⟩ **2** : to bore or make a hole in with or as if with a drill ⟨*drill* a tooth⟩ ⟨*drill* a hole⟩ — **drill·er** n

³**drill** n **1** : a shallow furrow or trench into which seed is sown **2** : a planting machine that makes holes or furrows, drops in seed, and covers it with earth [perhaps from earlier *drill* "a trickling stream"]

⁴**drill** vb : to sow with or as if with a drill

⁵**drill** n : a strong cotton fabric in twill weave [shortened from *drilling* "heavy cotton fabric", from German *drillich* (same meaning)]

dril·ling \'dril-iŋ\ n : ⁵DRILL

drill·mas·ter \'dril-,mas-tər\ n : an instructor in military drill

drily variant of DRYLY

¹**drink** \'driŋk\ vb **drank** \'draŋk\; **drunk** \'drəŋk\ or **drank**; **drink·ing** **1 a** : to swallow liquid **b** : ABSORB 1 **c** : to take in through the senses ⟨*drink* in the scenery⟩ **2** : to drink alcoholic beverages — **drink·able** \'driŋ-kə-bəl\ adj — **drink·er** n

²**drink** n **1 a** : BEVERAGE **b** : alcoholic liquor **2** : a draft

or portion of liquid

¹drip \'drip\ *vb* **dripped; drip·ping** **1** : to fall or let fall in or as if in drops **2** : to let fall drops of liquid ⟨a *dripping* faucet⟩ — **drip·per** *n*

²drip *n* **1 a** : a falling in drops **b** : liquid that drips **2** : the sound made by drops

drip–dry \'drip-'drī\ *vb* : to dry with few or no wrinkles when hung dripping wet — **drip–dry** \-,drī\ *adj*

drip·pings \'drip-iŋz\ *n pl* : fat and juices drawn from meat during cooking

¹drive \'drīv\ *vb* **drove** \'drōv\; **driv·en** \'driv-ən\; **driv·ing** \'drī-viŋ\ **1 a** : to urge, push, or force onward **b** : to cause to penetrate with force ⟨*drive* a nail⟩ **2 a** : to direct the movement or course of (as a vehicle or animals drawing a vehicle) **b** : to move or transport in a vehicle **3** : to set or keep in motion ⟨*drive* machinery by electricity⟩ **4** : to carry through strongly ⟨*drive* a bargain⟩ **5 a** : to force to act ⟨*driven* by hunger to steal⟩ **b** : to project, inject, or impress forcefully ⟨*drove* the lesson home⟩ **6** : to bring into a specified condition ⟨noise enough to *drive* a person crazy⟩ **7** : to force (a passage) by pressing or digging **8** : to rush and press with violence ⟨the police *drove* into the mob⟩

²drive *n* **1** : an act of driving: as **a** : a trip in a carriage or automobile **b** : a driving together of animals **c** : the guiding of logs downstream to a mill **d** : the act of driving a ball **e** : the flight of a ball **2 a** : DRIVEWAY **b** : a public road (as in a park) for driving **3** : a long or forceful campaign ⟨an armored *drive* into the enemy stronghold⟩ ⟨a *drive* for charity⟩ **4 a** : an urgent or basic need or longing **b** : energetic quality ⟨full of *drive*⟩ **5 a** : the means for giving motion to a machine or machine part ⟨a chain *drive*⟩ **b** : the means by which the movement of an automotive vehicle is controlled and directed ⟨front wheel *drive*⟩ **6** : a device for reading and writing on a magnetic substance (as on magnetic tape or disks)

drive–in \'drī-,vin\ *adj* : designed and equipped to serve customers while they remain in their automobiles ⟨a *drive-in* bank⟩ — **drive–in** *n*

¹driv·el \'driv-əl\ *vb* **driv·eled** *or* **driv·elled; driv·el·ing** *or* **driv·el·ling** \-(ə-)liŋ\ **1** : to let saliva dribble from the mouth : SLOBBER **2** : to talk or utter stupidly — **driv·el·er** *or* **driv·el·ler** \-(ə-)lər\ *n*

²drivel *n* : NONSENSE 1

driv·er \'drī-vər\ *n* **1** : one that drives: as **a** : the operator of a motor vehicle **b** : a tool for driving ⟨a nail *driver*⟩ **c** : a golf club having a usually wooden head with a nearly straight face

drive shaft *n* : a shaft that transmits mechanical power

drive·way \'drīv-,wā\ *n* : a short private road from the street to a house, garage, or parking lot

¹driz·zle \'driz-əl\ *vb* **driz·zled; driz·zling** \-(ə-)liŋ\ : to rain in very small drops

²drizzle *n* : a fine misty rain — **driz·zly** \'driz-(ə-)lē\ *adj*

drogue \'drōg\ *n* : a parachute for slowing down or stabilizing something (as an astronaut's capsule) or for pulling out a larger parachute

droll \'drōl\ *adj* : having an odd or amusing quality — **droll·ness** *n* — **drol·ly** \'drō(l)-lē\ *adv*

-drome \,drōm\ *n combining form* : racecourse : large specially prepared place ⟨aerodrome⟩ [derived from Greek *dromos* "course for running"]

drom·e·dary \'dräm-ə-,der-ē *also* 'drəm-\ *n, pl* **-dar·ies** : the one-humped camel of western Asia and northern Africa — called also

Arabian camel

drogue

¹drone \'drōn\ *n* **1** : a male bee (as of the honeybee) that does not have a sting and gathers no honey **2** : a lazy person **3** : an airplane, helicopter, or ship without a pilot that is controlled by radio signals

²drone *vb* **droned; dron·ing** : to make or speak with a low dull monotonous humming sound

³drone *n* **1** : one of the pipes on a bagpipe that sound fixed continuous tones **2** : a deep monotonous sound : HUM

drool \'drül\ *vb* **1** : to water at the mouth **2** : to let saliva or some other substance flow from the mouth : DRIVEL

¹droop \'drüp\ *vb* **1** : to sink, bend, or hang down **2** : to become depressed or weak — **droop·ing·ly** \'drü-piŋ-lē\ *adv* — **droopy** \'drü-pē\ *adj*

²droop *n* : the condition or appearance of drooping

¹drop \'dräp\ *n* **1 a** (1) : the quantity of fluid that falls naturally in one rounded mass (2) *pl* : a dose of medicine measured by drops **b** : a small quantity of drink **c** : the smallest practical unit of liquid measure **2** : something (as a hanging ornament on jewelry or a round candy) shaped like a drop **3 a** : the act or an instance of dropping : FALL **b** : a decline in quantity or quality ⟨a *drop* in water pressure⟩ ⟨a *drop* in prices⟩ **c** : a descent by parachute **d** : a place where something (as mail or goods) is left to be picked up **4** : the distance through which something drops **5** : an unframed piece of cloth scenery in a theater **6** : ADVANTAGE 1 ⟨we've got the *drop* on them⟩

²drop *vb* **dropped; drop·ping** **1** : to fall or let fall in drops **2 a** : to let fall **b** : to reduce to a lower level or stage **3** : SEND 1 ⟨*drop* me a line⟩ **4** : to stop doing, using, or considering ⟨*drop* the subject⟩ ⟨*dropped* everything and ran to the door⟩ ⟨you can *drop* that idea⟩ **5** : to knock or shoot down : cause to fall **6** : to go lower ⟨prices *dropped*⟩ **7** : to make a brief visit ⟨*drop* in for a chat⟩ **8** : to pass into a less active state ⟨*drop* off to sleep⟩ **9** : to move downward or with a current **10** : to leave (a letter standing for a speech sound) unsounded ⟨*drop* the "g" in "running"⟩ **11** : to give birth to ⟨the cow *dropped* her calf⟩

drop·kick \'dräp-'kik\ *n* : a kick made by dropping a ball to the ground and kicking it as it bounces — **drop–kick** *vb* — **drop–kick·er** *n*

drop·let \'dräp-lət\ *n* : a very small drop

drop·out \'dräp-,aút\ *n* : a person who drops out especially from a school or a training program

drop out \dräp-'aút\ *vb* : to withdraw from taking part or membership : QUIT ⟨*dropped out* of school⟩

drop·per \'dräp-ər\ *n* **1** : one that drops **2** : a short glass or plastic tube with a rubber bulb used to measure out liquids by drops — called also *medicine dropper* — **drop·per·ful** \-,fúl\ *n*

dropping bottle *n* : a bottle designed to supply liquid in drops; *esp* : a bottle with a dropper

drop·pings \'dräp-iŋz\ *n pl* : DUNG

drop·sy \'dräp-sē\ *n* : EDEMA — **drop·si·cal** \-si-kəl\ *adj*

dro·soph·i·la \drō-'säf-ə-lə\ *n* : any of a genus of small two-winged flies used especially in genetics — called also *vinegar fly*

dross \'dräs, 'dròs\ *n* **1** : the scum that forms on molten metal **2** : waste or foreign matter

drought *also* **drouth** \'draút, 'draúth\ *n* **1** : lack of rain or water **2** : a long period of dry weather — **droughty** \-ē\ *adj*

¹drove \'drōv\ *n* **1** : a group of animals driven or moving in a body **2** : a crowd of people moving or acting together [Old English *drāf* "group of animals moving together", from *drīfan* "to drive"]

\ə\ abut	\aú\ out	\i\ tip	\ó\ saw	\ú\ foot
\ər\ further	\ch\ chin	\ī\ life	\ói\ coin	\y\ yet
\a\ mat	\e\ pet	\j\ job	\th\ thin	\yü\ few
\ā\ take	\ē\ easy	\ŋ\ sing	\th\ this	\yú\ cure
\ä\ cot, cart	\g\ go	\ō\ bone	\ü\ food	\zh\ vision

²drove *past of* DRIVE

drov·er \'drō-vər\ *n* : a person who drives cattle or sheep

drown \'draůn\ *vb* **1 a** : to suffocate in a liquid and especially in water **b** : to become drowned **2** : to cover with water : INUNDATE **3** : to overpower especially with noise

drowse \'draůz\ *vb* **drowsed; drows·ing** : DOZE — **drowse** *n*

drowsy \'draů-zē\ *adj* **drows·i·er; -est** **1** : ready to fall asleep **2** : making one sleepy ⟨a *drowsy* afternoon⟩ **syn** *see* SLEEPY — **drows·i·ly** \-zə-lē\ *adv* — **drows·i·ness** \-zē-nəs\ *n*

drub \'drəb\ *vb* **drubbed; drub·bing** **1** : to beat severely **2** : to defeat completely

¹drudge \'drəj\ *vb* **drudged; drudg·ing** : to do hard or dull work — **drudg·er** *n*

²drudge *n* : a person who drudges

drudg·ery \'drəj-(ə-)rē\ *n, pl* **-er·ies** : hard or dull work

¹drug \'drəg\ *n* **1** : a substance used as a medicine or in making medicines **2** : something for which there is no demand ⟨a *drug* on the market⟩ **3** : a substance (as heroin, LSD, or marijuana) that affects bodily activities often in a harmful way and is taken for other than medical reasons

²drug *vb* **drugged; drug·ging** **1** : to affect or treat with a drug; *esp* : to make dull or numb by a drug **2** : to lull or make dull or numb as if with a drug

drug·gist \'drəg-əst\ *n* : a person who sells drugs and medicines; *also* : PHARMACIST

drug·store \'drəg-,stō(ə)r, -,stȯ(ə)r\ *n* : a retail store where medicines and miscellaneous articles are sold

dru·id \'drü-əd\ *n, often cap* : a member of an ancient Celtic priesthood — **dru·id·ic** \drü-'id-ik\ *or* **dru·id·i·cal** \-i-kəl\ *adj, often cap* — **dru·id·ism** \'drü-ə-,diz-əm\ *n, often cap*

¹drum \'drəm\ *n* **1** : a musical percussion instrument usually consisting of a hollow cylinder with a thin layer of skin or plastic stretched over one or both ends that is sounded by hitting the skin with a stick or with the hands **2** : the sound of a drum; *also* : a similar sound **3** : a drum-shaped object: as **a** : a cylindrical mechanical device or part **b** : a cylindrical container ⟨oil *drums*⟩ **c** : a disk-shaped ammunition container that may be attached to a firearm

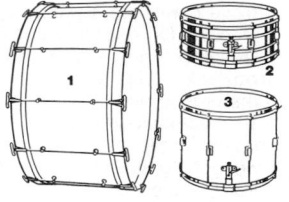

drum 1: *1* bass, *2* snare (orchestra), *3* snare (parade)

²drum *vb* **drummed; drum·ming** **1** : to beat or play on or as if on a drum **2** : to sound rhythmically : THROB, BEAT **3** : to call or gather together by or as if by beating a drum ⟨*drum* up business⟩ **4** : to dismiss in shame : EXPEL ⟨*drummed* out of the army⟩ **5** : to drive or force by steady effort or repetition ⟨*drummed* the lesson into their heads⟩

drum·beat \'drəm-,bēt\ *n* : a stroke on a drum or its sound

drum·lin \'drəm-lən\ *n* : a long or oval hill of material left by a glacier

drum major *n* : the marching leader of a band or drum corps

drum ma·jor·ette \,drəm-,mā-jə-'ret\ *n* : a girl or woman marching leader of a band or drum corps

drum·mer \'drəm-ər\ *n* **1** : one that plays a drum **2** : TRAVELING SALESMAN

drum·stick \'drəm-,stik\ *n* **1** : a stick for beating a drum **2** : the lower part of a fowl's leg

¹drunk *past participle of* DRINK

²drunk \'drəŋk\ *adj* **1** : being so much under the influence of alcohol that normal thinking or acting becomes difficult or impossible **2** : controlled by some feeling as if under the influence of alcohol ⟨*drunk* with power⟩

³drunk *n* **1 a** : a person who is drunk **b** : DRUNKARD **2** : a period of drinking too much : SPREE

drunk·ard \'drəŋ-kərd\ *n* : a person who makes a habit of getting drunk

drunk·en \'drəŋ-kən\ *adj* **1 a** : ²DRUNK 1 **b** : having a habit of drinking too much alcohol **2** : resulting from being drunk — **drunk·en·ly** *adv* — **drunk·en·ness** \-kən-nəs\ *n*

drupe \'drüp\ *n* : a fleshy fruit (as the plum, cherry, or peach) having one seed enclosed in a hard bony stone

¹dry \'drī\ *adj* **dri·er** \'drī(-ə)r\; **dri·est** \'drī-əst\ **1** : free or nearly free from liquid and especially water ⟨*dry* weight⟩ ⟨*dry* steam⟩ **2** : characterized by loss or lack of water: as **a** : lacking precipitation and humidity ⟨a *dry* climate⟩ **b** : lacking freshness : STALE **c** : low in or deprived of natural juices or moisture ⟨*dry* hay⟩ ⟨a *dry* fruit⟩ **3** : not being in or under water ⟨*dry* land⟩ **4 a** : THIRSTY 1 **b** : marked by the absence of alcoholic beverages ⟨a *dry* party⟩ **c** : no longer damp or sticky ⟨the paint is *dry*⟩ **5** : containing or using no liquid (as water) ⟨a *dry* creek⟩ ⟨*dry* heat⟩ **6** : not giving milk ⟨a *dry* cow⟩ **7** : not producing phlegm ⟨*dry* cough⟩ **8** : not producing or yielding what is expected or wanted ⟨a *dry* oil well⟩ **9** : marked by a matter-of-fact, ironic, or terse manner of expression ⟨*dry* humor⟩ **10** : failing to arouse interest or enthusiasm ⟨a *dry* lecture⟩ **11** : not sweet ⟨*dry* wines⟩ **12** : relating to, favoring, or practicing prohibition of alcoholic beverages ⟨a *dry* county⟩ — **dry·ly** *adv* — **dry·ness** *n*

²dry *vb* **dried; dry·ing** : to make or become dry

³dry *n, pl* **drys** \'drīz\ : PROHIBITIONIST

dry·ad \'drī-əd, -,ad\ *n* : a nymph living in woods

dry cell *n* : a small cell producing electricity by the reaction of chemicals that cannot be spilled ⟨a *dry cell* for a flashlight⟩

dry–clean \'drī-,klēn\ *vb* : to clean (fabrics) with chemical solvents — **dry–clean·able** \-'klē-nə-bəl\ *adj* — **dry cleaner** *n* — **dry cleaning** *n*

dry dock \'drī-,däk\ *n* : a dock that can be kept dry during the construction or repair of ships

dryer *variant of* DRIER

dry farmer *n* : a person who engages in dry farming

dry farming *n* : farming on dry land without irrigation using moisture-conserving methods and drought-resistant crops — **dry–farm** *vb* — **dry farm** *n*

dry fly *n* : a fishing fly designed to float upon the surface of the water

dry goods \'drī-,gůdz\ *n pl* : cloth goods (as fabrics, lace, and ribbon)

dry ice *n* : solid carbon dioxide usually in the form of blocks that at −78.5°C changes directly to a gas and that is used chiefly as a refrigerant

dry land *n* : solid land as opposed to bodies of water

dry measure *n* : a series of units of capacity for dry products — *see* MEASURE table, METRIC SYSTEM table

dry·point \'drī-,pȯint\ *n* : a picture made by engraving a metal plate with a tool and not using acid

dry rot *n* : decay of dried timber in which the cellulose of wood is used for food by fungi leaving a soft skeleton that easily crumbles to powder

dry run *n* **1** : a practice firing without ammunition **2** : a practice exercise

dry–shod \'drī-'shäd\ *adj* : having dry shoes or feet

dry·wall \'drī-,wȯl\ *n* : PLASTERBOARD

du·al \'d(y)ü-əl\ *adj* **1** : consisting of two parts or elements : having two parts alike **2** : having a double character or nature ⟨*dual* personality⟩ ⟨*dual* citizenship⟩ [from Latin *dualis* "dual", from *duo* "two" — related to DEUCE, DOUBLE, DOZEN] — **du·al·i·ty** \d(y)ü-'al-ət-ē\ *n* — **du·al·ly** \'d(y)ü-ə-lē\ *adv*

¹dub \'dəb\ *vb* **dubbed; dub·bing** **1** : to make a knight of **2** : ²NAME 1

²dub *vb* **dubbed; dub·bing** : to add sound effects to a film or broadcast

du·bi·ous \'d(y)ü-bē-əs\ *adj* **1** : causing doubt : UNCERTAIN ⟨a *dubious* honor⟩ **2** : feeling doubt : UNDECIDED ⟨*dubious* about our chances in the race⟩ **3** : of uncertain outcome ⟨a *dubious* struggle⟩ **4** : questionable in value, quality, or origin ⟨won by *dubious* means⟩ — **du·bi·ous·ly** *adv* — **du·bi·ous·ness** *n*

du·cal \'d(y)ü-kəl\ *adj* : of or relating to a duke or duchy

duc·at \'dək-ət\ *n* : a former gold coin of various European countries

duch·ess \'dəch-əs\ *n* **1** : the wife or widow of a duke **2** : a woman holding the rank of duke

duchy \'dəch-ē\ *n, pl* **duch·ies** : the territory of a duke or duchess

¹duck \'dək\ *n, pl* **duck** or **ducks** : any of various swimming birds with the neck and legs short, the body heavy, the bill often broad and flat, and the sexes almost always different from each other in the color and form of their feathers [Old English *dūce* "duck"]

¹duck

²duck *vb* **1** : to thrust or plunge under water **2** : to lower the head or body suddenly **3** : ¹DODGE 1, EVADE [Middle English *douken* "thrust under water"] — **duck·er** *n*

³duck *n* **1** : a coarse usually cotton cloth rather like canvas **2** *pl* : clothes made of duck [from Dutch *doek* "cloth"]

⁴duck *n* : an amphibious truck [altered form of *DUKW*, military code name for this vehicle]

duck·bill \'dək-,bil\ *n* : PLATYPUS — called also *duck-billed platypus* \,dək-,bil(d)-\

duck·ling \'dək-liŋ\ *n* : a young duck

duck soup *n* : something easy to do : CINCH

duck·weed \'dək-,wēd\ *n* : a tiny stemless plant that floats without attachment on the surface of a body of still water (as a pond)

duct \'dəkt\ *n* **1** : a tube or vessel carrying a bodily fluid (as the secretion of a gland) **2** : a pipe, tube, or channel through which a fluid (as air or water) flows [from scientific Latin *ductus* "tube or vessel from a gland", from Latin *ductus* "aqueduct", from earlier *ductus* "act of conducting" — related to AQUEDUCT, ³DOCK] — **duct·less** \'dək-tləs\ *adj*

duc·tile \'dək-t³l, -,tīl\ *adj* : capable of being drawn out (as into a wire) or hammered thin ⟨*ductile* metal⟩ — **duc·til·i·ty** \,dək-'til-ət-ē\ *n*

ductless gland *n* : ENDOCRINE GLAND

dud \'dəd\ *n* **1** *pl* **a** : CLOTHES 1 **b** : personal belongings **2** : a complete failure **3** : a missile (as a bomb or shell) that fails to explode

dude \'d(y)üd\ *n* **1** : a man who pays excessive attention to his dress : DANDY **2** : an Easterner in the West **3** : ¹MAN 1a, GUY — **dud·ish** \'d(y)üd-ish\ *adj*

dude ranch *n* : a vacation resort offering horseback riding and other activities typical of western ranches

dud·geon \'dəj-ən\ *n* : ill humor ⟨stomped off in high *dudgeon*⟩

¹due \'d(y)ü\ *adj* **1** : owed or owing as a debt or right ⟨respect *due* to the court⟩ **2** : ²APPROPRIATE, FITTING ⟨treat the judge with *due* respect⟩ **3 a** : SUFFICIENT, ADEQUATE ⟨arrived in *due* time⟩ **b** : ¹REGULAR 2a, LAWFUL ⟨due process of law⟩ **4** : being a result — used with *to* ⟨accidents *due* to carelessness⟩ **5** : having reached the date at which payment is required **6** : required or expected to happen ⟨*due* to arrive any minute now⟩

²due *n* **1** : something owed : DEBT **2** *pl* : a regular or legal charge or fee ⟨membership *dues*⟩

³due *adv* : ¹DIRECTLY 1, EXACTLY ⟨*due* north⟩

¹du·el \'d(y)ü-əl\ *n* **1** : a combat between two persons; *esp* : one fought with weapons in the presence of witnesses **2** : a conflict between two opponents [from Latin *duellum* "duel", from an archaic form of earlier *bellum* "war"; revived in the Middle Ages to mean combat between two persons because the *du-* suggested Latin *duo* "two"]

²duel *vb* **du·eled** or **du·elled; du·el·ing** or **du·el·ling** : to fight in a duel — **du·el·er** *n* — **du·el·ist** \'d(y)ü-ə-ləst\ *n*

du·en·na \d(y)ü-'en-ə\ *n* **1** : an elderly woman in charge of the younger ladies in a Spanish or Portuguese family **2** : ¹CHAPERON

du·et \d(y)ü-'et\ *n* : a composition for two performers

due to *prep* : because of

duff \'dəf\ *n* : the partly decayed plant and animal matter on the floor of a forest

duf·fel \'dəf-əl\ *n* : an outfit of supplies (as for camping) : KIT

duffel bag *n* : a large cylindrical fabric bag for personal belongings

dug *past and past participle of* DIG

du·gong \'dü-,gäng, -,gòng\ *n* : a mammal that lives in water, eats plants, and is related to the manatees but has a two-lobed tail and tusks in the male

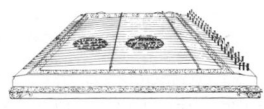
dugong

dug·out \'dəg-,aut\ *n* **1** : a boat made by hollowing out a log **2** : a shelter dug in a hillside or in the ground **3** : a low shelter facing a baseball diamond and containing the players' bench

dui·ker \'dī-kər\ *n* : any of several small African antelopes

duke \'d(y)ük\ *n* **1** : a supreme and independent ruler of a duchy **2** : a nobleman of the highest rank especially of the British nobility

duke·dom \'d(y)ük-dəm\ *n* : DUCHY

dul·cet \'dəl-sət\ *adj* : sweet to the ear : MELODIOUS

dul·ci·mer \'dəl-sə-mər\ *n* **1** : a stringed instrument played with light hammers held in the hands **2** : an American folk instrument with three or four strings held on the lap and played by plucking or strumming

dulcimer 1

¹dull \'dəl\ *adj* **1** : mentally slow : STUPID **2** : LISTLESS **3** : slow in action : SLUGGISH **4** : lacking sharpness of edge or point **5** : lacking brilliance or luster **6** : not ringing, sharp, or intense ⟨a *dull* roar⟩ **7** : CLOUDY 2, OVERCAST **8** : TEDIOUS, UNINTERESTING ⟨a *dull* lecture⟩ **9** : slightly grayish ⟨a *dull* blue⟩ — **dull·ness** or **dul·ness** \'dəl-nəs\ *n* — **dul·ly** \'dəl-(l)ē\ *adv*

²dull *vb* : to make or become dull

du·ly \'d(y)ü-lē\ *adv* : in a due manner, time, or degree

dumb \'dəm\ *adj* **1 a** : lacking the normal power of speech **b** : naturally incapable of speech ⟨*dumb* animals⟩ **2** : not willing to speak **3** : STUPID 1a, UNTHINKING — **dumb·ly**

\ə\ abut	\aů\ out	\i\ tip	\ȯ\ saw	\ů\ foot	
\ər\ further	\ch\ chin	\ī\ life	\ȯi\ coin	\y\ yet	
\a\ mat	\e\ pet	\j\ job	\th\ thin	\yü\ few	
\ā\ take	\ē\ easy	\ŋ\ sing	\th\ this	\yů\ cure	
\ä\ cot, cart	\g\ go	\ō\ bone	\ü\ food	\zh\ vision	

\'dəm-lē\ *adv* — **dumb·ness** *n*

dumb·bell \'dəm-ˌbel\ *n* **1** : a bar with weights at the ends that is usually used for exercise or building strength **2** : a stupid person

dumb·found *or* **dum·found** \ˌdəm-'faůnd\ *vb* : to cause to become speechless with astonishment : AMAZE

dumb·wait·er \'dəm-ˌwāt-ər\ *n* : a small elevator for carrying food or goods from one story to another

¹dum·my \'dəm-ē\ *n, pl* **dummies** **1** : a person who lacks or seems to lack the power of speech **2** : a stupid person **3** : an imitation used as a substitute for something ⟨*dummies* in a store window⟩ **4 a** : the bridge hand of the partner of the player who wins the bid that is placed face up and played by the bid winner **b** : a bridge player whose hand is a dummy

²dummy *adj* **1** : having the appearance of being real but lacking ability to function ⟨*dummy* hinges for ornament⟩ **2** : existing in name only : FICTITIOUS ⟨a *dummy* corporation⟩

¹dump \'dəmp\ *vb* **1** : to let fall in a heap or mass ⟨*dump* the coats on the bed⟩ **2** : to get rid of quickly or without concern ⟨*dumped* their friends at the party and went home⟩ **3** : to dump trash or garbage ⟨no *dumping* allowed⟩ **4** : to place a copy of (data in a computer's internal storage) in external storage (as a tape or disk); *also* : to make a printing of (data) from a computer's internal storage — **dump·er** *n*

²dump *n* **1** : a place where discarded materials (as trash) are dumped **2** : a place where reserve military supplies are stored **3** : the dumping of data stored in a computer

dump·ling \'dəm-pliŋ\ *n* **1** : a portion of dough cooked by boiling or steaming **2** : a dessert of fruit baked in biscuit dough

dumps \'dəm(p)s\ *n pl* : a dull gloomy state of mind : low spirits ⟨in the *dumps*⟩

dump truck *n* : a truck for carrying and dumping loose material

dumpy \'dəm-pē\ *adj* **dump·i·er; -est** : short and thick in build : SQUAT — **dump·i·ness** *n*

¹dun \'dən\ *n* **1** : a light tan horse with a black mane and tail **2** : a slightly brownish dark gray [Old English *dunn* (adjective) "having the color of brownish dark gray"] — **dun** *adj*

²dun *vb* **dunned; dun·ning** : to make repeated demands upon for payment [origin unknown]

³dun *n* **1** : a person who duns another **2** : a demand for payment

dunce \'dən(t)s\ *n* : a mentally dull person [an altered form of earlier *duns,* from the name John *Duns* Scotus 1266?–1308 a Scottish religious teacher whose writings came to be ridiculed in the 16th century]

dune \'d(y)ün\ *n* : a hill or ridge of sand piled up by the wind

dune buggy *n* : a motor vehicle with oversize tires for use on sand

dung \'dəŋ\ *n* : waste matter of an animal : MANURE

dun·ga·ree \ˌdəŋ-gə-'rē\ *n* **1** : blue denim **2** *pl* : trousers or work clothes made of blue denim

dung beetle *n* : a beetle (as a tumblebug) that rolls balls of dung in which to lay eggs and on which the larvae feed

dun·geon \'dən-jən\ *n* **1** : DONJON **2** : a dark usually underground prison

Word History The English words for two different parts of a castle both come from the same source. The word *dungeon,* meaning "a dark usually underground prison", comes from the early French word *donjon.* This French word also gives us our English word *donjon,* meaning "an inner tower in a castle". *Dungeon* was first used in English in the 14th century for the strong tower in the protected inner part of the castle. Residents and defenders could retreat to this tower if attackers managed to get inside the castle walls. Part of the tower usually included an underground room. This dark, damp dungeon room was usually used as a cell for prisoners.

Throughout its history, the word *dungeon* has had many spellings. Sometimes it was spelled *donjon* like the early French word it comes from, and sometimes in other ways. In time the spelling *donjon* came to be used mostly for the castle tower. The spelling *dungeon* came to be used mostly for the underground room or prison. [Middle English *donjon* "tower in a castle, dungeon", from early French *donjon* "castle tower" — related to DONJON]

dung·hill \'dəŋ-ˌhil\ *n* : a manure pile

dunk \'dəŋk\ *vb* **1** : to dip (as a doughnut) into liquid (as coffee) **2** : to plunge oneself into water

dunk shot *n* : a shot in basketball made by jumping high in the air and throwing the ball down through the basket

duo \'d(y)ü-ō\ *n, pl* **du·os** **1** : DUET; *esp* : a duet for two performers at two pianos **2** : ¹PAIR 1

¹duo·dec·i·mal \ˌd(y)ü-ə-'des-ə-məl\ *adj* : of, relating to, or being a system of numbers with a base of 12

²duodecimal *n* : a number or digit in the duodecimal system of numbers

du·o·de·num \ˌd(y)ü-ə-'dē-nəm, d(y)ů-'äd-ᵉn-əm\ *n, pl* **-de·na** \-'dē-nə, -ᵉn-ə\ *or* **-denums** : the first part of the small intenstine extending from the opening from the stomach into the small intestine to the jejunum — **du·o·de·nal** \-'dēn-ᵉl, -ᵉn-əl\ *adj*

¹dupe \'d(y)üp\ *n* : one who is easily deceived or cheated

²dupe *vb* **duped; dup·ing** : DECEIVE 1, CHEAT — **dup·er** *n*

du·ple \'d(y)ü-pəl\ *adj* **1** : taken by twos : TWOFOLD **2** : having two beats or a multiple of two beats to the measure ⟨*duple* time⟩

¹du·plex \'d(y)ü-ˌpleks\ *adj* **1** : being or consisting of two parts : TWOFOLD **2** : allowing communication at a distance (as by telephone or television) in opposite directions at the same time

²duplex *n* : something duplex: as **a** : a two-family house **b** : an apartment with rooms on two floors

¹du·pli·cate \'d(y)ü-pli-kət\ *adj* **1** : having two parts exactly the same or alike **2** : being the same as another

²du·pli·cate \'d(y)ü-pli-ˌkāt\ *vb* **-cat·ed; -cat·ing** **1** : to make double **2** : to make a duplicate of — **du·pli·ca·tive** \-ˌkāt-iv\ *adj*

³duplicate \'d(y)ü-pli-kət\ *n* : a thing that is exactly like another

du·pli·ca·tion \ˌd(y)ü-pli-'kā-shən\ *n* **1 a** : an act or process of duplicating **b** : the state of being duplicated **2** : ³DUPLICATE

du·pli·ca·tor \'d(y)ü-pli-ˌkāt-ər\ *n* : one that duplicates; *esp* : COPIER

du·plic·i·ty \d(y)ü-'plis-ət-ē\ *n, pl* **-ties** : deception by pretending to feel and act one way while acting another

du·ra·ble \'d(y)ůr-ə-bəl\ *adj* : able to last a long time ⟨*durable* clothing⟩ ⟨*durable* goods⟩ **syn** see LASTING — **du·ra·bil·i·ty** \ˌd(y)ůr-ə-'bil-ət-ē\ *n* — **du·ra·bly** \'d(y)ůr-ə-blē\ *adv*

durable press *n* : PERMANENT PRESS

du·ral·u·min \d(y)ů-'ral-yə-mən\ *n* : a light strong alloy of aluminum, copper, manganese, and magnesium

du·rance \'d(y)ůr-ən(t)s\ *n* : the state of being restrained by or as if by physical force

du·ra·tion \d(y)ů-'rā-shən\ *n* : the time during which something exists or lasts

du·ress \d(y)ů-'res\ *n* : the use of force or threats

dur·ing \ˌd(y)ůr-iŋ\ *prep* **1** : throughout the course of ⟨swims every day *during* the summer⟩ **2** : at some time in the course of ⟨you may call me *during* the day⟩

dur·ra \'důr-ə\ *n* : any of several sorghums widely grown for their grain in warm dry regions

du·rum wheat \ˌd(y)ůr-əm-\ *n* : a hard wheat that yields a flour used especially in pasta

dusk \'dəsk\ *n* **1** : the darker part of twilight especially at night **2** : partial darkness

dusky \'dəs-kē\ *adj* **dusk·i·er; -est** **1** : somewhat dark in color 2 : somewhat dark : DIM — **dusk·i·ly** \-kə-lē\ *adv* — **dusk·i·ness** \-kē-nəs\ *n*

¹dust \'dəst\ *n* **1 a** : fine dry powdery particles (as of earth) **b** : a fine powder **2** : the powdery remains of bodies once alive **3** : the surface of the ground **4** : something worthless

²dust *vb* **1** : to make free of dust : brush or wipe away dust **2** : to sprinkle with dust or as a dust ⟨*dust* a pan with flour⟩ ⟨*dust* insecticide on plants⟩

dust bowl *n* : a region that suffers from long droughts and dust storms

dust devil *n* : a small whirlwind containing sand or dust

dust·er \'dəs-tər\ *n* **1** : one that dusts **2** : a short housecoat

dust jacket *n* : a removable usually decorative paper cover for a book

dust·pan \'dəs(t)-,pan\ *n* : a pan shaped like a shovel for sweepings

dust storm *n* : a violent wind carrying dust across a dry region

dusty \'dəs-tē\ *adj* **dust·i·er; -est** **1** : filled or covered with dust **2** : resembling dust — **dust·i·ly** \-tə-lē\ *adv* — **dust·i·ness** \-tē-nəs\ *n*

¹Dutch \'dəch\ *adj* : of or relating to the Netherlands, its inhabitants, or their language

²Dutch *n* **1** : the Germanic language of the Netherlands **2 Dutch** *pl* : the people of the Netherlands **3** : ¹DISFAVOR 2 ⟨was in *Dutch* with the teacher⟩

Dutch door *n* : a door divided so that the lower part can be shut while the upper part remains open

Dutch elm disease *n* : a disease of elms caused by a fungus carried from one tree to another by bark beetles and marked by yellowing of the foliage, loss of leaves, and death

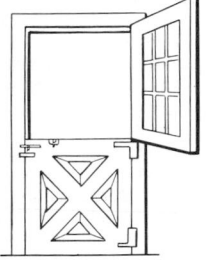

Dutch door

Dutch·man \'dəch-mən\ *n* **1** : a person born or living in the Netherlands **2** : a person of Dutch ancestry

Dutch·man's–breech·es \,dəch-mənz-'brich-əz\ *n pl* : a delicate spring-flowering herb of the eastern U.S. resembling the related bleeding heart but having cream-white flowers with two spurs

Dutch oven *n* **1** : a brick oven for cooking **2 a** : a kettle with a tight cover used for baking in an open fire **b** : a large pot

Dutch treat *n* : a treat for which each person pays his or her own way

du·ti·able \'d(y)üt-ē-ə-bəl\ *adj* : subject to a tax

du·ti·ful \'d(y)üt-i-fəl\ *adj* : having or showing a sense of duty — **du·ti·ful·ly** \-f(ə-)lē\ *adv* — **du·ti·ful·ness** \-fəl-nəs\ *n*

du·ty \'d(y)üt-ē\ *n, pl* **duties** **1** : conduct due to parents and superiors : RESPECT **2** : the action required by one's position or occupation **3 a** : a moral or legal obligation **b** : the force of moral obligation **4** : ²TAX 1; *esp* : a tax on imports **5** : the service required (as of an electric machine) ⟨stand heavy *duty*⟩ **syn** see TASK

¹dwarf \'dwȯ(ə)rf\ *n, pl* **dwarfs** \'dwȯ(ə)rfs\ *also* **dwarves** \'dwȯ(ə)rvz\ **1** : a person, animal, or plant much below

normal size **2** : a small legendary being usually pictured as a deformed and ugly person **3** : a star (as the sun) that in comparison to other stars gives off an ordinary or small amount of energy and has small mass and size — **dwarf** *adj* — **dwarf·ish** \'dwȯr-fish\ *adj* — **dwarf·ness** *n*

²dwarf *vb* **1** : to restrict the growth or development of : STUNT **2** : to cause to appear smaller

dwell \'dwel\ *vb* **dwelt** \'dwelt\ *or* **dwelled** \'dweld, 'dwelt\; **dwell·ing** **1** : to stay for a while **2** : to live in a place : RESIDE **3** : to keep the attention directed ⟨*dwelt* on their mistakes⟩ — **dwell·er** *n*

dwell·ing \'dwel-iŋ\ *n* : a shelter in which people live : HOUSE

dwin·dle \'dwin-dᵊl\ *vb* **dwin·dled; dwin·dling** \'dwin-dliŋ, -dᵊliŋ\ : to make or become less

¹dye \'dī\ *n* **1** : color produced by dyeing **2** : a material used for dyeing or staining

²dye *vb* **dyed; dye·ing** : to stain or color usually permanently — **dy·er** \'dī-(ə)r\ *n*

dye·stuff \'dī-,stəf\ *n* : ¹DYE 2

dying *present participle of* DIE

dyke *variant of* DIKE

dy·nam·ic \dī-'nam-ik\ *also* **dy·nam·i·cal** \-'nam-i-kəl\ *adj* **1 a** : of or relating to physical force or energy **b** : of or relating to dynamics : ACTIVE **2 a** : marked by continuous usually productive activity or change **b** : marked by energy : FORCEFUL — **dy·nam·i·cal·ly** \-'nam-i-k(ə-)lē\ *adv*

dy·nam·ics \dī-'nam-iks\ *n sing or pl* **1** : the science of the motion of bodies and the action of forces in producing or changing their motion **2** : physical, moral, or intellectual forces or the laws relating to them **3** : the pattern of change or growth **4** : variation in force or intensity (as in music)

¹dy·na·mite \'dī-nə-,mīt\ *n* : a blasting explosive that is made chiefly of nitroglycerin absorbed in another substance; *also* : a blasting explosive that contains no nitroglycerin

²dynamite *vb* **-mit·ed; -mit·ing** : to blow up with dynamite — **dy·na·mit·er** *n*

dy·na·mo \'dī-nə-,mō\ *n, pl* **-mos** : GENERATOR 3

dy·nas·ty \'dī-nə-stē *also* -,nas-tē\ *n, pl* **-ties** : a succession of rulers of the same line of descent — **dy·nas·tic** \dī-'nas-tik\ *adj* — **dy·nas·ti·cal·ly** \-ti-k(ə-)lē\ *adv*

dyne \'dīn\ *n* : the unit of force in the centimeter-gram-second system equal to the force that would give a free mass of one gram an acceleration of one centimeter per second squared

dys·en·tery \'dis-ən-,ter-ē\ *n* **1** : a disease characterized by severe diarrhea with passage of mucus and blood from the bowels **2** : DIARRHEA

dys·lex·ia \dis-'lek-sē-ə\ *n* : a disturbance of the ability to read

¹dys·lex·ic \dis-'lek-sik\ *adj* : having dyslexia

²dyslexic *n* : a person who has dyslexia

dys·pep·sia \dis-'pep-shə, -sē-ə\ *n* : INDIGESTION

¹dys·pep·tic \dis-'pep-tik\ *adj* **1** : relating to or having indigestion **2** : showing or having a sour disposition — **dys·pep·ti·cal·ly** \-ti-k(ə-)lē\ *adv*

²dyspeptic *n* : a person having indigestion

dys·pnea \'dis(p)-nē-ə\ *n* : difficult or labored breathing

dys·pnoea \'dis(p)-nē-ə\ *chiefly British variant of* DYSPNEA

dys·pro·si·um \dis-'prō-zē-əm, -zh(ē-)əm\ *n* : a chemical element that forms very magnetic compounds — see ELEMENT table

\ə\ abut	\au̇\ out	\i\ tip	\o̧\ saw	\u̇\ foot
\ər\ further	\ch\ chin	\ī\ life	\o̧i\ coin	\y\ yet
\a\ mat	\e\ pet	\j\ job	\th\ thin	\yü\ few
\ā\ take	\ē\ easy	\ŋ\ sing	\th\ this	\yu̇\ cure
\ä\ cot, cart	\g\ go	\ō\ bone	\ü\ food	\zh\ vision

E

e \'ē\ *n, often cap* **1** : the fifth letter of the English alphabet **2** : the musical note referred to by the letter E **:** the third tone of a C-major scale **3** : a grade rating a student's work as poor or failing

¹each \'ēch\ *adj* : being one of two or more individuals

²each *pron* : each one ⟨*each* of us took a turn⟩

³each *adv* : to or for each : APIECE ⟨50 cents *each*⟩

each other *pron* : each of two or more in a shared action or relation ⟨looked at *each other*⟩

ea·ger \'ē-gər\ *adj* : having or showing an impatient or enthusiastic desire or interest ⟨was *eager* to get going⟩ ⟨were *eager* for news of old friends⟩ [Middle English *egre* "sharp, sour, eager", from early French *aigre* (same meaning), from Latin *acer* "sharp, sour, spirited" — related to VINEGAR] — **ea·ger·ly** *adv* — **ea·ger·ness** *n*

syn EAGER, KEEN, ANXIOUS mean moved by a strong and urgent desire or interest. EAGER suggests great enthusiasm and sometimes impatience at delay or restriction ⟨*eager* passengers waiting for the tour to start⟩ KEEN suggests strong interest and readiness to act ⟨the new members are *keen* and willing to learn⟩ ANXIOUS stresses fear of failure or disappointment ⟨I'm *anxious* to see the test scores⟩

ea·gle \'ē-gəl\ *n* **1** : any of various large day-flying sharp-eyed birds with a powerful flight that prey on other animals and are related to the hawks **2** : a seal or standard bearing an eagle **3** : a 10-dollar gold coin of the U.S. **4** : a golf score of two strokes less than par on a hole

ea·glet \'ē-glət\ *n* : a young eagle

-ean — see ²-AN

¹ear \'i(ə)r\ *n* **1 a** : the organ of hearing and balance of vertebrates that in the typical mammal consists of a sound-collecting outer ear separated by an eardrum from a sound-carrying middle ear that in turn is separated from an inner ear containing nerve cells that receive sound and send nerve impulses to the brain **b** : OUTER EAR **2** : an ability to understand and appreciate something heard ⟨a good *ear* for music⟩ ⟨an *ear* for languages⟩ **3** : willing or sympathetic attention ⟨give *ear* to a request⟩ ⟨lend an *ear*⟩ **4** : something resembling an ear in shape or position [Old English *ēare* "organ of hearing"] — **eared** \'i(ə)rd\ *adj* — **ear·less** \'i(ə)r-ləs\ *adj* — **by ear** : relying on what one has heard rather than reading music ⟨play a song by *ear*⟩

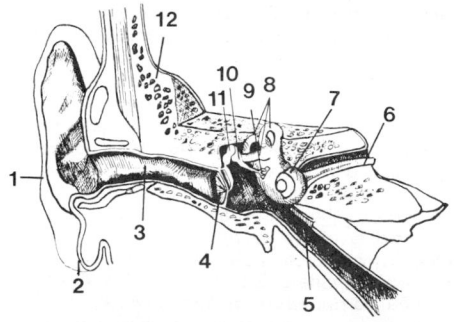

¹ear 1a: *1* pinna, *2* lobe, *3* auditory canal, *4* eardrum, *5* eustachian tube, *6* auditory nerve, *7* cochlea, *8* semicircular canals, *9* stirrup, *10* anvil, *11* malleus, *12* bones of skull

²ear *n* : the seed-bearing head of a cereal (as Indian corn) including both the seeds and protective structures [Old English *ēar* "seed part of a plant"] — **ear** *vb*

ear·ache \'i(ə)r-,āk\ *n* : an ache or pain in the ear

ear·drum \-,drəm\ *n* : the thin membrane that separates the outer and middle ear and carries sound waves as vibrations to the chain of tiny bones in the middle ear — called also *tympanic membrane, tympanum;* compare TYMPANUM 2

eared seal \,i(ə)rd-\ *n* : any of a family of seals including the sea lions and fur seals and having small well-developed ears on the outside of the head

earl \'ərl\ *n* : a member of the British nobility ranking below a marquess and above a viscount [Old English *eorl* "warrior"] — **earl·dom** \-dəm\ *n*

ear·less seal \,i(ə)r-ləs-\ *n* : HAIR SEAL

ear·lobe \'i(ə)r-,lōb\ *n* : a part hanging down from the ear of human beings and some fowls

¹ear·ly \'ər-lē\ *adv* **ear·li·er; -est 1** : near the beginning of a period of time or of a process or series **2** : before the usual time ⟨arrived *early*⟩

²early *adj* **ear·li·er; -est 1** : of, relating to, or occurring near the beginning of a period or of a process or series **2 a** : occurring before the usual time ⟨had an *early* spring this year⟩ **b** : maturing or producing sooner than related forms ⟨an *early* peach⟩ — **ear·li·ness** *n*

¹ear·mark \'i(ə)r-,märk\ *n* **1** : a mark of identification on the ear of an animal **2** : a mark or quality by which something can be known ⟨the *earmarks* of success⟩

²earmark *vb* **1** : to mark with or as if with an earmark **2** : to set aside for a special purpose ⟨money *earmarked* for a vacation⟩

ear·muff \'i(ə)r-,məf\ *n* : one of a pair of pads joined by a flexible band and worn to protect the ears against cold or noise

earn \'ərn\ *vb* **1** : to get for services given ⟨*earn* a good salary⟩ **2** : to deserve as a result of labor or service ⟨*earned* every cent we were paid⟩ — **earn·er** *n*

¹ear·nest \'ər-nəst\ *n* : a serious state of mind

²earnest *adj* **1** : having or showing a serious attitude : not light or playful ⟨made an *earnest* request⟩ **2** : IMPORTANT 1 **syn** see SERIOUS — **ear·nest·ly** *adv* — **ear·nest·ness** \-nəs(t)-nəs\ *n*

earn·ings \'ər-niŋz\ *n pl* : something earned; *esp* : money received as wages or gained as profit

ear·phone \'i(ə)r-,fōn\ *n* : a device that changes electrical energy into sound waves and is worn over or inserted into the ear

ear·piece \-,pēs\ *n* : a part of an instrument (as a telephone) that is placed against or in the ear; *esp* : EARPHONE

ear·ring \-,riŋ\ *n* : an ornament for the earlobe

ear·shot \-,shät\ *n* : the range within which the unaided voice may be heard

ear·split·ting \-,split-iŋ\ *adj* : unbearably loud or shrill

earth \'ərth\ *n* **1** : the soft or granular material composing part of the surface of the globe; *esp* : soil that can be cultivated **2** : the place of mortal life as distinguished from heaven and hell **3** : land as distinguished from sea and air **:** GROUND **4** *often cap* : the planet on which we live — see PLANET table **5** : any of several metallic oxides (as alumina)

earth·en \'ər-thən, -thən\ *adj* : made of earth or of baked clay ⟨an *earthen* floor⟩ ⟨*earthen* dishes⟩

earth·en·ware \-,wa(ə)r, -,we(ə)r\ *n* : articles (as dishes or ornaments) made of baked clay

earth·light \'ərth-,līt\ *n* : EARTHSHINE

earth·ling \'ərth-liŋ\ *n* : an inhabitant of the earth

earth·ly \'ərth-lē\ *adj* **1** : belonging to or having to do with the earth ⟨*earthly* joys⟩ **2** : IMAGINABLE, POSSIBLE ⟨that tool is of no *earthly* use⟩ — **earth·li·ness** *n*

earth·quake \'ərth-,kwāk\ *n* : a shaking or trembling of a portion of the earth

earth science *n* : any of the sciences (as geology, meteorology, or oceanography) that deal with the earth or with one or more of its parts — **earth scientist** *n*

earth·shine \'ərth-,shīn\ *n* : sunlight reflected by the earth that lights up the dark part of the moon

earth·work \-,wərk\ *n* : something (as a raised bank or wall) constructed of earth especially for protection

earth·worm \-,wərm\ *n* : a long slender worm with a segmented body that lives in damp earth and moves with the aid of bristles

earthy \'ər-thē, -thē\ *adj* **earth·i·er; -est** **1** : consisting of or resembling earth ⟨an *earthy* flavor⟩ **2 a** : PRACTICAL 4 **b** : not polite : CRUDE ⟨*earthy* humor⟩ — **earth·i·ness** *n*

ear·wax \'i(ə)r-,waks\ *n* : a brownish yellow or orange waxlike substance produced by the glands of the external ear

ear·wig \-,wig\ *n* : any of numerous insects with slender many-jointed antennae and a large forcepslike organ at the end of the body

    Word History Centuries ago it was thought that a certain insect, whose body ended in what looked like a pair of pincers, crawled into people's ears. The Old English name for this insect was *ēarwicga*, a compound of *ēare*, meaning "ear", and *wicga*, meaning "insect". *Earwig*, our modern English name for the insect, comes from the Old English word, even though we know that the old belief is not true. [Old English *ēarwicga*, from *ēare* "ear" and *wicga* "insect"]

¹ease \'ēz\ *n* **1** : freedom from pain or trouble : comfort of body or mind ⟨a life of *ease*⟩ **2** : freedom from any feeling of difficulty or embarrassment ⟨speak with *ease*⟩ **3** : looseness that provides free movement in a garment — **at ease** : free from pain, discomfort, or difficulty

²ease *vb* **eased; eas·ing** **1** : to free from discomfort or worry : RELIEVE ⟨*ease* one's pain⟩ **2** : to make less tight : LOOSEN **3** : to move slowly or gently **4** : to sew a garment so that the longer and shorter parts fit together smoothly

ea·sel \'ē-zəl\ *n* : a frame for supporting something (as an artist's canvas)

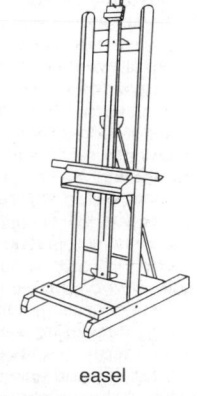

    Word History An easel is a frame for holding up such things as an artist's painting or a chalkboard. In the 17th century the Dutch had become famous throughout Europe for their oil painting. Thus it was their word *ezel*, which they used to refer to this piece of equipment, that was borrowed into English at that time. This sense of *ezel* was an extension of the original meaning "donkey", probably because an easel, like a beast of burden, is used to hold things. [from Dutch *ezel* "a frame to hold an artist's canvas", literally "donkey", from Latin *asinus* "donkey, ass"]

easel

eas·i·ly \'ēz-(ə-)lē\ *adv* **1** : in an easy manner ⟨won the game *easily*⟩ **2** : by far ⟨*easily* the best player⟩

¹east \'ēst\ *adv* : to or toward the east

²east *adj* **1** : situated toward or at the east **2** : coming from the east ⟨an *east* wind⟩

³east *n* **1 a** : the general direction of sunrise **b** : the compass point directly opposite to west **2** *cap* : regions or countries east of a specified or implied point

east·bound \'ēs(t)-,baund\ *adj* : going east

Eas·ter \'ē-stər\ *n* : a Christian church festival celebrating Christ's resurrection that is observed on the first Sunday following the first full moon on or after March 21

Easter lily *n* : any of several white cultivated lilies that bloom in early spring

east·er·ly \'ē-stər-lē\ *adv or adj* **1** : toward the east ⟨they sailed *easterly*⟩ **2** : from the east ⟨an *easterly* storm⟩

east·ern \'ē-stərn\ *adj* **1** *often cap* : of, relating to, or like that of the East ⟨*Eastern* philosophy⟩ **2** : lying toward or coming from the east — **east·ern·most** \-,mōst\ *adj*

East·ern·er \'ē-stə(r)-nər\ *n* : a person born or living in the East (as of the U.S.)

eastern hemisphere *n, often cap E&H* : the half of the earth to the east of the Atlantic ocean including Europe, Asia, and Africa

Eastern Orthodox *adj* : of or consisting of the Christian churches that originated in the church of the Eastern Roman Empire and that do not recognize the authority of the pope

eastern time *n, often cap E* : the time of the fifth time zone west of Greenwich that includes the eastern U.S.

¹east·ward \'ēs-twərd\ *adv or adj* : toward the east — **east·ward·ly** *adv or adj* — **east·wards** \-twərdz\ *adv*

²eastward *n* : eastward direction or part

¹easy \'ē-zē\ *adj* **eas·i·er; -est** **1** : not hard to do or get : not difficult ⟨an *easy* lesson⟩ **2 a** : not hard to please : LENIENT ⟨an *easy* teacher⟩ **b** : not steep ⟨*easy* slopes⟩ **3 a** : free from pain, trouble, or worry ⟨rest *easy*⟩ **b** : not hurried : LEISURELY ⟨an *easy* pace⟩ **4** : not false or strained : NATURAL ⟨an *easy* manner⟩ **5** : giving ease and comfort ⟨an *easy* chair⟩ — **eas·i·ness** *n*

²easy *adv* **eas·i·er; -est** **1** : EASILY 1 ⟨take life *easy*⟩ **2** : with slow care : CAUTIOUSLY ⟨go *easy*⟩

easy·go·ing \,ē-zē-'gō-iŋ\ *adj* : taking life easy : CAREFREE — **easy·go·ing·ness** *n*

eat \'ēt\ *vb* **ate** \'āt\; **eat·en** \'ēt-ᵊn\; **eat·ing** **1** : to take into the mouth and swallow food : chew and swallow in turn **2** : to take a meal ⟨*eat* at home⟩ **3** : to destroy as if by eating : wear away ⟨rocks *eaten* away by waves⟩ **4** : to affect something by destroying or using up bit by bit ⟨termites *eating* away at a house⟩ ⟨acid *eating* into metal⟩ — **eat·er** *n*

    syn EAT, CONSUME, DEVOUR mean to swallow usually after chewing. EAT is a general word that can apply to any manner of taking in food ⟨*eat* your dinner⟩ CONSUME suggests eating up something completely ⟨by noon they had *consumed* all of their food supplies⟩ DEVOUR suggests eating quickly and greedily ⟨the hungry children *devoured* the grapes⟩

¹eat·able \'ēt-ə-bəl\ *adj* : fit to be eaten

²eatable *n* **1** : something to eat **2** *pl* : FOOD 3

eaves \'ēvz\ *n sing or pl* : the lower edge of a roof that sticks out beyond the wall of a building

eaves·drop \'ēvz-,dräp\ *vb* : to listen secretly to private conversation — **eaves·drop·per** *n*

eaves trough *n* : GUTTER 1a

¹ebb \'eb\ *n* **1** : the flowing back from the shore of water brought in by the tide **2** : a passing from a high to a low point; *also* : the time of such a passing

²ebb *vb* **1** : to recede from the flood state **2** : ¹DECLINE 2, WEAKEN

ebb tide *n* **1** : the tide while ebbing **2** : ¹EBB 2

EBCDIC \'eps-ə-,dik, 'ebs-\ *n* : a computer code for expressing numerals, letters of the alphabet, and symbols [*e*xtended *b*inary *c*oded *d*ecimal *i*nterchange *c*ode]

eb·on \'eb-ən\ *adj* : ²EBONY

¹eb·o·ny \'eb-ə-nē\ *n, pl* **-nies** **1** : a hard heavy wood of various Old World tropical trees related to the persimmon **2** : a tree that produces ebony

²ebony *adj* **1** : made of or resembling ebony **2** : ¹BLACK 1

\ə\ abut	\au̇\ out	\i\ tip	\ȯ\ saw	\u̇\ foot	
\ər\ further	\ch\ chin	\ī\ life	\ȯi\ coin	\y\ yet	
\a\ mat	\e\ pet	\j\ job	\th\ thin	\yü\ few	
\ā\ take	\ē\ easy	\ŋ\ sing	\th\ this	\yu̇\ cure	
\ä\ cot, cart	\g\ go	\ō\ bone	\ü\ food	\zh\ vision	

¹**ec·cen·tric** \ik-'sen-trik, ek-\ *adj* **1** : not having the same center ⟨*eccentric* spheres⟩ **2 a** : acting or thinking in an unusual way ⟨an *eccentric* person⟩ **b** : not of the usual or normal kind ⟨*eccentric* behavior⟩ **3** : not following a truly circular path ⟨an *eccentric* orbit⟩ — **ec·cen·tri·cal·ly** \-tri-k(ə-)lē\ *adv*

²**eccentric** *n* : an eccentric person

ec·cen·tric·i·ty \,ek-,sen-'tris-ət-ē\ *n, pl* **-ties 1 a** : the quality or state of being eccentric **b** : something that is eccentric; *esp* : unusual behavior **2** : the amount by which a nearly circular path is eccentric ⟨a planet's *eccentricity*⟩

Ec·cle·si·as·tes \ik-,lē-zē-'as-(,)tēz, e-,klē-\ *n* — see BIBLE table

ec·cle·si·as·tic \ik-,lē-zē-'as-tik, e-,klē-\ *n* : CLERGYMAN

ec·cle·si·as·ti·cal \ik-,lē-zē-'as-ti-kəl, e-,klē-\ *or* **ec·cle·si·as·tic** \-tik\ *adj* : of or relating to a church ⟨*ecclesiastical* history⟩ — **ec·cle·si·as·ti·cal·ly** \-ti-k(ə-)lē\ *adv*

Ec·cle·si·as·ti·cus \ik-,lē-zē-'as-ti-kəs, e-,klē-\ *n* — see BIBLE table

ech·e·lon \'esh-ə-,län\ *n* **1** : a formation of units (as troops or airplanes) resembling a series of steps; *also* : a unit in such a formation **2** : one of a series of levels especially of authority; *also* : the people who are at such a level

echid·na \i-'kid-nə\ *n* : a spiny-coated toothless burrowing egg-laying mammal of Australia with a tapering snout and long tongue for eating ants — called also *spiny anteater*

echidna

echi·no·derm \i-'kī-nə-,dərm\ *n* : any of a phylum of marine animals (as starfishes and sea urchins) that have a number of similar body parts (as the arms of a starfish) arranged around a central axis, often a calcium-containing outer skeleton, and a water-vascular system

¹**echo** \'ek-ō\ *n, pl* **ech·oes 1** : the repeating of a sound caused by reflection of sound waves **2 a** : a repetition or imitation of another **b** : REPERCUSSION 2, RESULT **3** : one who closely imitates or repeats another — **echo·ic** \i-'kō-ik, e-\ *adj*

²**echo** *vb* **ech·oed; echo·ing 1** : to be filled with echoes ⟨the stadium *echoed* with cheers⟩ **2** : to produce an echo : send back or repeat a sound **3** : ¹REPEAT 1c, IMITATE ⟨*echoing* the teacher's words⟩

echo·lo·ca·tion \,ek-ō-lō-'kā-shən\ *n* : a process for locating distant or invisible objects by means of sound waves reflected back to the sender by the objects

echo sounder *n* : an instrument used to find out the depth of a body of water or of an object below the surface by means of sound waves

éclair \ā-'kla(ə)r, i-, -'kle(ə)r; 'ā-,kla(ə)r, ,klā(ə)r, 'ē-\ *n* : an oblong pastry with whipped cream or custard filling

> **Word History** The English word *éclair* comes directly from a French word whose chief meaning is "lightning" or "flash of lightning". No one is sure why a pastry was named after lightning. Some say the lightness of the cream puff and its soft filling is the reason for the name. Others say that the frosting often used to decorate an éclair looks a bit like a bolt of lightning. Perhaps the éclair is named after lightning because it is likely to be eaten in a flash. [French, literally "lightning"]

¹**eclipse** \i-'klips\ *n* **1 a** : the total or partial hiding of one heavenly body by another **b** : the passing into the shadow of a heavenly body **2** : a falling into disgrace or out of use or public favor

²**eclipse** *vb* **eclipsed; eclips·ing 1** : to cause an eclipse of **2 a** : to reduce in importance **b** : to do or be much

better than : OUTSHINE

eclip·tic \i-'klip-tik\ *n* : the great circle of the celestial sphere on which the sun appears to move among the stars

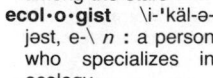

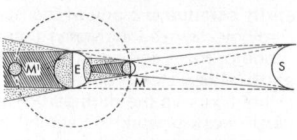

eclipse 1a and b: *S* sun, *E* earth, *M* moon in solar eclipse, *M*¹ moon in lunar eclipse

ecol·o·gist \i-'käl-ə-jəst, e-\ *n* : a person who specializes in ecology

ecol·o·gy \i-'käl-ə-jē, e-\ *n* **1** : a branch of science concerned with the relationships between living things and their environment **2** : the pattern of relationships between a group of living things and their environment [from German *ökologie* "ecology", from *ök-* "home, habitat" and *-o-* (added for ease in pronouncing) and *-logie* "science, study"; *ök-* derived from Greek *oikos* "house" and *-logie* derived from Greek *logos* "word, reason"] — **eco·log·i·cal** \,ē-kə-'läj-i-kəl, ,ek-ə-\ *also* **eco·log·ic** \-'läj-ik\ *adj* — **eco·log·i·cal·ly** \-'läj-i-k(ə-)lē\ *adv*

ec·o·nom·ic \,ek-ə-'näm-ik, ,ē-kə-\ *adj* **1 a** : of or relating to the science of economics **b** : of, relating to, or based on the production, distribution, and consumption of goods and services **2** : having practical or industrial uses : affecting material resources ⟨*economic* pests⟩

ec·o·nom·i·cal \,ek-ə-'näm-i-kəl, ,ē-kə-\ *adj* **1** : managing one's resources with care and without waste **2** : operating with little waste or at a saving ⟨an *economical* car⟩ **syn** see FRUGAL — **ec·o·nom·i·cal·ly** \-i-k(ə-)lē\ *adv*

ec·o·nom·ics \,ek-ə-'näm-iks, ,ē-kə-\ *n* **1** : a social science concerned with description and analysis of the production, distribution, and consumption of goods and services **2** : financial considerations ⟨the *economics* of buying a house⟩ — **econ·o·mist** \i-'kän-ə-məst\ *n*

econ·o·mize \i-'kän-ə-,mīz\ *vb* **-mized; -miz·ing 1** : to practice economy : be thrifty ⟨*economize* on fuel⟩ **2** : to use less of : SAVE ⟨*economize* fuel⟩ — **econ·o·miz·er** *n*

econ·o·my \i-'kän-ə-mē\ *n, pl* **-mies 1** : careful use of money and goods : THRIFT **2** : a special arrangement or system : ORGANIZATION **3** : the way an economic system (as of a country or a period in history) is arranged

eco·sys·tem \'ē-kō-,sis-təm, 'ek-ō-\ *n* : a system made up of an ecological community and its environment especially under natural conditions

ec·ru \'ek-rü, 'ā-krü\ *adj* : of the color beige

ec·sta·sy \'ek-stə-sē\ *n, pl* **-sies 1** : a state of being beyond reason and self-control **2** : a state of overwhelming emotion ⟨an *ecstasy* of fear⟩; *esp* : very great joy — **ec·stat·ic** \ek-'stat-ik, ik-\ *adj* — **ec·stat·i·cal·ly** \-i-k(ə-)lē\ *adv*

ecto- *combining form* : outside : outer ⟨*ecto*derm⟩ [scientific Latin *ect-, ecto-* "outside", from Greek *ekto-* (same meaning), derived from *ex* "out"]

ec·to·derm \'ek-tə-,dərm\ *n* **1** : the outer layer of cells of a two-layered animal (as a jellyfish) **2** : the outermost of the three basic layers of an embryo from which skin, nerves, and certain other structures develop — **ec·to·der·mal** \,ek-tə-'dər-məl\ *adj*

ec·to·plasm \'ek-tə-,plaz-əm\ *n* : the firm outer layer of the cytoplasm of a cell

ec·u·men·i·cal \,ek-yə-'men-i-kəl\ *adj* **1** : of, relating to, or representing the whole of a body of churches **2** : leading toward agreement or cooperation among Christians [from Latin *oecumenicus* "worldwide", derived from Greek *oikoumenē* "the inhabited world", derived from *oikein* "to inhabit", from *oikos* "house"] — **ec·u·men·i·cal·ly** \-i-k(ə-)lē\ *adv*

ec·ze·ma \ig-'zē-mə, 'eg-zə-mə, 'ek-sə-\ *n* : a skin disease marked by redness, itching, and scaly or crusty lesions

¹**-ed** \d *after a vowel or* b, g, j, l, m, n, ŋ, r, th, v, z, zh; əd,

id *after* d, t; t *after other sounds; exceptions are pro-nounced at their subentries or entries\ vb suffix or adj suffix* **1** — used to form the past participle of regular weak verbs ⟨end*ed*⟩ ⟨fad*ed*⟩ ⟨tri*ed*⟩ ⟨patt*ed*⟩ **2 a** : having : characterized by ⟨cultur*ed*⟩ ⟨two-legg*ed*⟩ **b** : having the characteristics of ⟨dogg*ed*⟩ [Old English *-ed, -od, -ad* (mark of the past participle of certain verbs)]

²-ed *vb suffix* — used to form the past tense of regular weak verbs ⟨judg*ed*⟩ ⟨deni*ed*⟩ ⟨dropp*ed*⟩ [Old English *-de, -ede, -ode, -ade* (mark of the past tense of certain verbs)]

Edam \'ēd-əm, 'ē-,dam\ *n* : a Dutch cheese of yellow color and mild flavor [named for *Edam*, seaport in the Nether-lands, where the cheese was first sold]

edaph·ic \i-'daf-ik\ *adj* : of, relating to, or influenced by the soil

¹ed·dy \'ed-ē\ *n, pl* **eddies** : a current of air or water run-ning against the main current or in a circle

²eddy *vb* **ed·died; ed·dy·ing** : to move in an eddy or so as to form an eddy

eddy current *n* : a electric current caused by an alternating magnetic field

edel·weiss \'ād-°l-,wīs\ *n* : a small woolly herb that is re-lated to the thistles and grows high in the Alps

ede·ma \i-'dē-mə\ *n* **1** : an abnormal collection of watery fluid in a bodily tissue or cavity **2** : an illness marked by edema

Eden \'ēd-°n\ *n* **1** : the garden where according to the Bi-ble Adam and Eve first lived **2** : PARADISE 3

eden·tate \(')ē-'den-,tāt\ *n* : any of a group of mammals having few or no teeth and including the sloths, armadillos, and New World anteaters — **edentate** *adj*

¹edge \'ej\ *n* **1 a** : the cutting side of a blade **b** : the sharpness of a blade **c** : a harsh or sharp quality ⟨his voice had a sarcastic *edge*⟩ **2 a** : the line where an object or surface begins or ends; *also* : the narrow part next to it **b** : a line segment that is the intersection of two plane faces of a solid ⟨*edge* of a prism⟩ **3** : ADVANTAGE 3 ⟨our experience gave us an *edge*⟩ **syn** see BORDER — **edged** \'ejd\ *adj* — **on edge** : ANXIOUS 1, NERVOUS

²edge *vb* **edged; edg·ing** **1** : to give an edge to ⟨*edge* a sleeve with lace⟩ **2** : to advance slowly or by short moves ⟨*edged* my chair closer⟩

edge·ways \'ej-,wāz\ *or* **edge·wise** \-,wīz\ *adv* : with the edge in front : SIDEWAYS

edg·ing \'ej-iŋ\ *n* : something that forms an edge or border ⟨a lace *edging*⟩

edgy \'ej-ē\ *adj* **edg·i·er; -est** **1** : having an edge : SHARP **2** : ²TENSE 2, IRRITABLE — **edg·i·ly** \'ej-ə-lē\ *adv* — **edg·i·ness** \'ej-ē-nəs\ *n*

ed·i·ble \'ed-ə-bəl\ *adj* : fit or safe to be eaten ⟨*edible* fruit⟩ — **ed·i·bil·i·ty** \,ed-ə-'bil-ət-ē\ *n* — **edible** *n*

edict \'ē-,dikt\ *n* : a law or order made or given by an au-thority (as a ruler) — **edic·tal** \i-'dik-t°l\ *adj*

ed·i·fice \'ed-ə-fəs\ *n* : BUILDING 1; *esp* : a large or impres-sive building (as a church)

ed·i·fy \'ed-ə-,fī\ *vb* **-fied; -fy·ing** : to instruct and improve especially in moral and religious knowledge ⟨an *edifying* sermon⟩ — **ed·i·fi·ca·tion** \,ed-ə-fə-'kā-shən\ *n*

ed·it \'ed-ət\ *vb* **1 a** : to correct, revise, and prepare for publication ⟨*edit* a book of poems⟩ **b** : to assemble (as a film or tape recording) by cutting and rearranging **2** : to direct the publication of ⟨*edit* a daily newspaper⟩

edi·tion \i-'dish-ən\ *n* **1** : the form in which a book is pub-lished ⟨an illustrated *edition*⟩ **2** : the whole number of copies printed or published at one time ⟨a third *edition*⟩ **3** : one of the several issues of a newspaper for a single day ⟨the late *edition*⟩

ed·i·tor \'ed-ət-ər\ *n* **1** : a person who edits especially as an occupation **2** : a computer program that permits the user to create or change a program in a computer system — **ed·i·tor·ship** \-,ship\ *n*

¹ed·i·to·ri·al \,ed-ə-'tōr-ē-əl, -'tòr-\ *adj* **1** : of or relating to an editor ⟨an *editorial* office⟩ **2** : being or resembling an editorial ⟨an *editorial* statement⟩ — **ed·i·to·ri·al·ly** \-ē-ə-lē\ *adv*

²editorial *n* : a newspaper or magazine article that gives the opinions of its editors or publishers

ed·u·ca·ble \'ej-ə-kə-bəl\ *adj* : capable of being educated

ed·u·cate \'ej-ə-,kāt\ *vb* **-cat·ed; -cat·ing** **1** : to provide schooling for **2 a** : to develop the mind and morals of especially by instruction **b** : ²TRAIN 2a — **ed·u·ca·tor** \-,kāt-ər\ *n*

ed·u·cat·ed *adj* **1** : having an education; *esp* : having an education beyond the average **2** : showing education ⟨*educated* speech⟩ **3** : based on some knowledge of fact ⟨an *educated* guess⟩

ed·u·ca·tion \,ej-ə-'kā-shən\ *n* **1 a** : the action or process of educating or of being educated **b** : knowledge, skill, and development gained from study or practice **2** : the field of study that deals mainly with methods and problems of teaching — **ed·u·ca·tion·al** \-shnəl, -shən-°l\ *adj* — **ed·u·ca·tion·al·ly** \-ē\ *adv*

syn EDUCATION, TRAINING mean an action or process of learning. EDUCATION suggests a general course of in-struction in a school with the stress on mental develop-ment ⟨much *education* is needed in order to become a lawyer⟩ TRAINING suggests practical and usually specific instruction for learning certain skills (as in a craft or trade) ⟨six months of *training* for a clerk⟩

ed·u·ca·tive \'ej-ə-,kāt-iv\ *adj* : helping to educate : IN-STRUCTIVE

educe \i-'d(y)üs\ *vb* **educed; educ·ing** : to draw forth : ELICIT ⟨*educe* a response⟩ — **educ·i·ble** \-'d(y)ü-sə-bəl\ *adj*

¹-ee \'ē, (,)ē\ *n suffix* **1** : one that receives or benefits from (a specified action or thing) ⟨appoint*ee*⟩ ⟨grant*ee*⟩ ⟨paten-t*ee*⟩ **2** : a person who does (a specified action) ⟨stand*ee*⟩ [derived from Latin *-atus* (past participle ending of certain verbs)]

²-ee *n suffix* **1** : a particular especially small kind of ⟨boo-t*ee*⟩ **2** : one resembling or suggestive of ⟨goat*ee*⟩ [prob-ably an altered form of *-y* (noun suffix)]

eel \'ē(ə)l\ *n, pl* **eels** *or* **eel** : any of nu-merous long snake-like fishes that have a smooth slimy skin and the fins in the middle of the back and bottom continu-ous around the tail — **eel·like** \'ē(ə)l-,līk\ *adj*

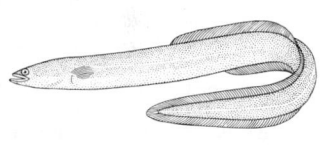
eel

eel·grass \'ē(ə)l-,gras\ *n* : a plant that is a monocotyledon, grows underwater, and has long ribbonlike leaves

e'en \(')ēn\ *adv* : ³EVEN

-eer \'i(ə)r\ *n suffix* : one who is connected with or who op-erates or produces ⟨auction*eer*⟩ ⟨puppet*eer*⟩ ⟨pamphlet*eer*⟩ [derived from Latin *-arius* (noun suffix)]

e'er \(')e(ə)r, (')a(ə)r\ *adv* : EVER

ee·rie *also* **ee·ry** \'i(ə)r-ē\ *adj* **ee·ri·er; -est** : causing fear or uneasiness because of strangeness or gloominess ⟨an *eerie* shadow⟩ — **ee·ri·ly** \'ir-ə-lē\ *adv* — **ee·ri·ness** \'ir-ē-nəs\ *n*

ef·face \i-'fās, e-\ *vb* **ef·faced; ef·fac·ing** **1** : WIPE OUT, OBLITERATE **2** : to make unclear by or as if by rubbing out — **ef·face·able** \-'fā-sə-bəl\ *adj* — **ef·face·ment** \-'fās-

\ə\ abut	\aů\ out	\i\ tip	\ò\ saw	\ů\ foot
\ər\ further	\ch\ chin	\ī\ life	\òi\ coin	\y\ yet
\a\ mat	\e\ pet	\j\ job	\th\ thin	\yü\ few
\ā\ take	\ē\ easy	\ŋ\ sing	\th\ this	\yů\ cure
\ä\ cot, cart	\g\ go	\ō\ bone	\ü\ food	\zh\ vision

mənt\ *n* — **ef·fac·er** *n*

¹ef·fect \i-'fekt\ *n* **1** : an event, condition, or state of affairs that is produced by a cause **2** : REALITY 1, FACT ⟨the suggestion was in *effect* an order⟩ **3** : the act of making a particular impression ⟨talked merely for *effect*⟩ **4** : ¹INFLUENCE 1 ⟨the *effect* of climate on growth⟩ **5** *pl* : personal property or possessions ⟨household *effects*⟩ **6** : EXECUTION 1, OPERATION ⟨the law went into *effect* today⟩

²effect *vb* : BRING ABOUT, ACCOMPLISH ⟨*effect* a change⟩ — **ef·fect·er** *n*

ef·fec·tive \i-'fek-tiv\ *adj* **1 a** : producing or able to produce a desired effect ⟨*effective* treatment of a disease⟩ **b** : IMPRESSIVE, STRIKING ⟨an *effective* performance⟩ **2** : being in actual operation ⟨the law becomes *effective* next year⟩ **3** : being or determined by a rate of interest equal to the rate of simple interest that gives the same increase in one dollar when the interest is paid once at the end of the interest period (as a year) as a given rate of interest does at compound interest over the same period ⟨the *effective* rate of interest equivalent to an interest rate of 7% per year compounded daily by a bank is slightly more than 7.25%⟩ — **ef·fec·tive·ly** *adv* — **ef·fec·tive·ness** *n*

ef·fec·tor \i-'fek-tər, -,tȯ(ə)r\ *n* : a bodily organ (as a gland or muscle) that becomes active in response to stimulation (as by a nerve)

ef·fec·tu·al \i-'fek-chə(-wə)l, -'feksh-wəl\ *adj* : EFFECTIVE 1a ⟨an *effectual* remedy⟩ — **ef·fec·tu·al·ly** \-ē\ *adv* — **ef·fec·tu·al·ness** *n*

ef·fec·tu·ate \i-'fek-chə-,wāt\ *vb* **-at·ed; -at·ing** : BRING ABOUT

ef·fem·i·na·cy \ə-'fem-ə-nə-sē\ *n* : the quality of being effeminate

ef·fem·i·nate \ə-'fem-ə-nət\ *adj* : having or showing qualities that are considered more suited to women than to men : not manly — **ef·fem·i·nate·ly** *adv* — **ef·fem·i·nate·ness** *n*

ef·fer·ent \'ef-ə-rənt; 'ef-,er-ənt, 'ē-,fer-\ *adj* : conducting outward from a part or organ; *esp* : conveying nervous impulses to an effector ⟨*efferent* nerve fibers⟩

ef·fer·vesce \,ef-ər-'ves\ *vb* **-vesced; -vesc·ing 1** : to bubble, hiss, and foam as gas escapes **2** : to show liveliness or excitement — **ef·fer·ves·cence** \-'ves-ᵊn(t)s\ *n* — **ef·fer·ves·cent** \-ᵊnt\ *adj* — **ef·fer·ves·cent·ly** *adv*

ef·fete \e-'fēt, i-\ *adj* **1** : no longer productive **2 a** : WORN-OUT, 2, EXHAUSTED **b** : having lost strength, courage, or spirit : DECADENT ⟨*effete* snobs⟩ — **ef·fete·ly** *adv* — **ef·fete·ness** *n*

ef·fi·ca·cious \,ef-ə-'kā-shəs\ *adj* : having the power to produce a desired result ⟨an *efficacious* remedy⟩ — **ef·fi·ca·cious·ly** *adv* — **ef·fi·ca·cious·ness** *n*

ef·fi·ca·cy \'ef-i-kə-sē\ *n, pl* **-cies** : the power to produce a desired result

ef·fi·cien·cy \i-'fish-ən-sē\ *n, pl* **-cies 1** : the quality or degree of being efficient **2** : efficient operation **3** : the ratio of the useful energy delivered by a machine to the energy supplied to it

ef·fi·cient \i-'fish-ənt\ *adj* : capable of producing desired results especially without waste (as of time or energy) ⟨an *efficient* worker⟩ ⟨*efficient* machinery⟩ — **ef·fi·cient·ly** *adv*

ef·fi·gy \'ef-ə-jē\ *n, pl* **-gies** : a likeness especially of a person: as **a** : a sculpture of a person on a tomb **b** : a crude figure meant to represent a hated person ⟨hanged their cruel ruler in *effigy*⟩

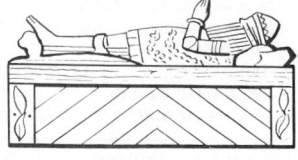

effigy a

ef·flu·ent \'ef-,lü-ənt; e-'flü-, ə-\ *n* : liquid (as sewage or industrial by-products) discharged as waste — **effluent** *adj*

ef·fort \'ef-ərt, -,ȯrt\ *n* **1** : hard work of mind or body **2** : a serious attempt : TRY ⟨made a good *effort*⟩ **3** : something produced by work ⟨this painting was one of my best *efforts*⟩ **4** : the force applied to a simple machine (as a lever) in contrast to the force applied by it against a load

ef·fort·less \'ef-ərt-ləs\ *adj* : showing or requiring little or no effort : EASY — **ef·fort·less·ly** *adv* — **ef·fort·less·ness** *n*

ef·fron·tery \i-'frənt-ə-rē, e-\ *n, pl* **-ter·ies** : NERVE 3c ⟨had the *effrontery* to deny any guilt⟩

ef·ful·gence \i-'fùl-jən(t)s, e-, -'fəl-\ *n* : shining brightness — **ef·ful·gent** \-jənt\ *adj*

ef·fu·sion \i-'fyü-zhən, e-\ *n* **1** : free expression of words or feelings **2 a** : escape of a fluid from containing vessels **b** : the fluid that escapes

ef·fu·sive \i-'fyü-siv, e-, -ziv\ *adj* : expressing or showing much emotion ⟨*effusive* thanks for their anniversary present⟩ — **ef·fu·sive·ly** *adv* — **ef·fu·sive·ness** *n*

eft \'eft\ *n* : NEWT

eft·soons \eft-'sünz\ *or* **eft·soon** \-'sün\ *adv, archaic* : soon afterward; *also* : AGAIN 2, OFTEN

egad \i-'gad\ *interj* — used as a mild oath

¹egg \'eg\ *vb* : INCITE, URGE — usually used with *on* ⟨*egged* us on to fight⟩ [Middle English *eggen* "to stir up to action, incite", from early Norse *eggja* (same meaning)]

²egg *n* **1 a** : a hard-shelled reproductive body produced by a bird and especially by domestic poultry **b** : a reproductive body produced by an animal and consisting of an ovum with its food-containing and protecting envelopes and being capable of development into a new individual **c** : a germ cell produced by a female — called also *ovum* **2** : something shaped like an egg ⟨darning *egg*⟩ [Middle English *egge* "egg", from early Norse *egg* (same meaning)]

egg·beat·er \'eg-,bēt-ər\ *n* : a device used for beating eggs or liquids (as cream)

egg case *n* : a case that encloses and protects eggs (as of an insect)

egg cell *n* : ²EGG 1c

egg·head \'eg-,hed\ *n* : HIGHBROW, INTELLECTUAL

egg·nog \-,näg\ *n* : a drink made of eggs beaten with sugar, milk or cream, and often alcoholic liquor

egg·plant \-,plant\ *n* **1** : a widely cultivated herb that is related to the potato and yields edible fruit **2** : the usually glossy purple egg-shaped fruit of an eggplant

¹egg·shell \-,shel\ *n* : the shell of an egg

²eggshell *adj* **1** : being thin and fragile ⟨*eggshell* china⟩ **2** : slightly glossy

egg white *n* : the clear fluid mass of material surrounding the yolk of an egg

eg·lan·tine \'eg-lən-,tīn, -,tēn\ *n* : SWEETBRIER

ego \'ē-gō\ *n, pl* **egos 1** : ²SELF 1; *esp* : the conscious self **2 a** : CONCEIT 1 **b** : SELF-RESPECT 1 ⟨winning was good for our *egos*⟩

ego·cen·tric \,ē-gō-'sen-trik\ *adj* : overly concerned with oneself : SELF-CENTERED

ego·ism \'ē-gə-,wiz-əm\ *n* **1** : excessive interest in oneself : a self-centered attitude **2** : EGOTISM 2 — **ego·ist** \-wəst\ *n* — **ego·is·tic** \,ē-gə-'wis-tik\ *adj* — **ego·is·ti·cal·ly** \-'wis-ti-k(ə-)lē\ *adv*

ego·tism \'ē-gə-,tiz-əm\ *n* **1** : the practice of talking about oneself too much **2** : an overly high opinion of one's own importance : CONCEIT — **ego·tist** \-təst\ *n* — **ego·tis·tic** \,ē-gə-'tis-tik\ *or* **ego·tis·ti·cal** \-'tis-ti-kəl\ *adj* — **ego·tis·ti·cal·ly** \-'tis-ti-k(ə)lē\ *adv*

egre·gious \i-'grē-jəs\ *adj* : very noticeable : GLARING ⟨*egregious* errors⟩ — **egre·gious·ly** *adv* — **egre·gious·ness** *n*

egress \'ē-,gres\ *n* **1** : the act or right of going or coming out **2** : a way out : EXIT

egret \'ē-grət, i-'gret, 'ē-,gret, 'eg-rət\ *n* : any of various herons that bear long plumes during the breeding season

Egyp·tian \i-'jip-shən\ *n* **1** : a person born or living in Egypt **2** : the language spoken by the ancient Egyptians — **Egyptian** *adj*

ei·der \'īd-ər\ *n* **1** : a large duck that is found in northern coastal regions, is mostly white above and black below, and has very soft down — called also *eider duck* **2** : EIDERDOWN 1

egret

ei·der·down \-,daūn\ *n* **1** : the down of the eider **2** : a quilt filled with eiderdown

eight \'āt\ *n* **1** — see NUMBER table **2** : the eighth in a set or series **3** : something having eight units or members — **eight** *adj or pron*

eigh·teen \(,)ā(t)-'tēn\ *n* — see NUMBER table — **eighteen** *adj or pron* — **eigh·teenth** \-'tēn(t)th\ *adj or n*

eighth \'ātth\ *n, pl* **eighths** \'āt(th)s\ — see NUMBER table — **eighth** *adj or adv*

eighth note *n* : a musical note equal in time to ⅛ of a whole note

eighty \'āt-ē\ *n, pl* **eight·ies** — see NUMBER table — **eight·i·eth** \-ē-əth\ *adj or n* — **eighty** *adj or pron*

ein·stei·ni·um \īn-'stī-nē-əm\ *n* : a radioactive element produced artificially — see ELEMENT table

¹ei·ther \'ē-thər *also* 'ī-\ *adj* **1** : the one and the other of two : EACH ⟨flowers blooming on *either* side of the walk⟩ **2** : the one or the other of two ⟨take *either* road⟩

²either *pron* : the one or the other

³either *conj* — used before the first of two or more words or word groups the last of which follows *or* to show that they are choices or possibilities ⟨a statement is *either* true or false⟩

⁴either *adv* **1** : LIKEWISE 2, MOREOVER — used after a negative ⟨not wise or handsome *either*⟩ **2** : so far as that is concerned — used after a choice or possibility following a question or conditional clause ⟨if your father had come or your mother *either* all would have gone well⟩

ejac·u·late \i-'jak-yə-,lāt\ *vb* **-lat·ed; -lat·ing** **1** : to eject a fluid and especially semen **2** : to utter suddenly and forcefully — **ejac·u·la·to·ry** \-yə-lə-,tōr-ē, -,tȯr-\ *adj*

ejac·u·la·tion \i-,jak-yə-'lā-shən\ *n* **1** : an act of ejaculating; *esp* : a sudden emptying of a fluid from a duct **2** : something ejaculated; *esp* : a short sudden exclamation

eject \i-'jekt\ *vb* **1 a** : to drive out especially by physical force **b** : to force off property **2** : to throw out or off from within — **ejec·tion** \-'jek-shən\ *n* — **ejec·tor** \-'jek-tər\ *n*

eke out \'ēk-\ *vb* **1 a** : ²SUPPLEMENT ⟨*eked* out their small income by working for neighbors⟩ **b** : to make (a supply) last by careful use **2** : to get with great difficulty ⟨*eked* out a living from the poor soil of the family's farm⟩

el \'el\ *n, often cap* : ELEVATED RAILROAD

¹elab·o·rate \i-'lab-(ə-)rət\ *adj* : made or done with great care or with much detail ⟨*elaborate* preparations⟩ ⟨an *elaborate* design⟩ — **elab·o·rate·ly** *adv* — **elab·o·rate·ness** *n*

²elab·o·rate \i-'lab-ə-,rāt\ *vb* **-rat·ed; -rat·ing** **1** : to work out in detail : DEVELOP ⟨*elaborate* an idea⟩ **2** : to give more details ⟨*elaborate* on a story⟩ — **elab·o·ra·tion** \-,lab-ə-'rā-shən\ *n* — **elab·o·ra·tive** \-'lab-ə-,rāt-iv\ *adj* — **elab·o·ra·tor** \-,rāt-ər\ *n*

eland \'ē-lənd, -,land\ *n* : either of two large African antelopes resembling oxen and having short spirally twisted horns in both sexes

elapse \i-'laps\ *vb* **elapsed; elaps·ing** : to slip or glide away : PASS ⟨weeks *elapsed* before I got around to writing

to my parents⟩

¹elas·tic \i-'las-tik\ *adj* **1 a** : capable of returning to original shape or size after being stretched, pressed, or squeezed together ⟨sponges are *elastic*⟩ **b** : capable of indefinite expansion ⟨gases are *elastic* substances⟩ **2** : able to recover quickly especially from sadness or disappointment ⟨youthful, *elastic* spirit⟩ **3** : capable of being changed : FLEXIBLE ⟨an *elastic* plan⟩ — **elas·tic·i·ty** \i-,las-'tis-ət-ē, ,ē-,las-\ *n*

eland

²elastic *n* **1 a** : an elastic fabric usually made of yarns containing rubber **b** : something made from elastic fabric **2** : RUBBER BAND

elas·tin \i-'las-tən\ *n* : a protein that is similar to collagen and helps make up the fibers of connective tissue

elate \i-'lāt\ *vb* **elat·ed; elat·ing** : to fill with joy or pride ⟨*elated* over the team's victory⟩ — **elat·ed·ly** *adv* — **elat·ed·ness** *n*

el·a·ter \'el-ət-ər\ *n* : CLICK BEETLE

ela·tion \i-'lā-shən\ *n* : the quality or state of being elated

E layer *n* : a layer of the ionosphere that occurs at about 110 kilometers above the earth's surface during daylight hours and is capable of reflecting radio waves

¹el·bow \'el-,bō\ *n* **1 a** : the joint of the arm; *also* : the outer curve of a bent arm **b** : a corresponding joint in the front limb of an animal **2** : a part (as of a pipe) bent like an elbow

²elbow *vb* **1** : to push or shove with the elbow : JOSTLE **2** : to advance by or as if by pushing with the elbow ⟨*elbowed* their way through the crowd⟩

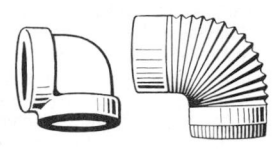

elbow 2

elbow grease *n* : forceful effort in doing physical labor

el·bow·room \'el-,bō-,rüm, -,rûm\ *n* **1** : room for moving the elbows freely **2** : enough space for work or operation

eld \'eld\ *n* **1** *archaic* : old age **2** *archaic* : ancient times : ANTIQUITY

¹el·der \'el-dər\ *n* : ELDERBERRY 2 [Old English *ellærn* "elder tree"]

²elder *adj* : of greater age ⟨the *elder* cousin⟩ [Old English *ieldra*, comparative form of *eald* "old"]

³elder *n* **1** : one who is older : SENIOR **2** : a person having authority because of age and experience ⟨the village *elders*⟩ **3** : any of various church officers — **el·der·ship** \-,ship\ *n*

el·der·ber·ry \'el-də(r)-,ber-ē\ *n* **1** : the edible black or red fruit of any of a genus of shrubs or trees of the same family as the honeysuckles that produce flat clusters of small white or pink flowers **2** : any tree or shrub that produces elderberries

el·der·ly \'el-dər-lē\ *adj* **1** : somewhat old; *esp* : past middle age **2** : of or relating to later life or elderly persons — **el·der·li·ness** *n*

elder statesman *n* : a respected older member of a group

\ə\ **abut**	\aū\ **out**	\i\ **tip**	\ȯ\ **saw**	\ü\ **foot**
\ər\ **further**	\ch\ **chin**	\ī\ **life**	\ȯi\ **coin**	\y\ **yet**
\a\ **mat**	\e\ **pet**	\j\ **job**	\th\ **thin**	\yü\ **few**
\ā\ **take**	\ē\ **easy**	\ŋ\ **sing**	\th\ **this**	\yû\ **cure**
\ä\ **cot, cart**	\g\ **go**	\ō\ **bone**	\ü\ **food**	\zh\ **vision**

or organization; *esp* : a retired statesman who gives advice to current leaders

el·dest \'el-dəst\ *adj* : of the greatest age

¹elect \i-'lekt\ *adj* **1** : carefully selected **2** : chosen for office but not yet holding office ⟨president-*elect*⟩

²elect *n pl* : a carefully chosen group — used with *the*

³elect *vb* **1** : to select by vote for an office, position, or membership ⟨*elect* a senator⟩ **2** : ²SELECT, CHOOSE ⟨we *elected* to stay home⟩

elec·tion \i-'lek-shən\ *n* **1** : an act or process of electing; *esp* : the process of voting to choose a person for office **2** : the fact of being elected

elec·tion·eer \i-,lek-shə-'ni(ə)r\ *vb* : to work for a candidate or party in an election

¹elec·tive \i-'lek-tiv\ *adj* **1** : chosen by election ⟨an *elective* official⟩ **2** : held by a person who is elected ⟨the presidency is an *elective* office⟩ **3** : followed or taken by choice : not required ⟨an *elective* subject in school⟩ — **elec·tive·ly** *adv* — **elec·tive·ness** *n*

²elective *n* : an elective course or subject in school

elec·tor \i-'lek-tər, -,tȯ(ə)r\ *n* **1** : one qualified to vote in an election **2** : a member of the electoral college in the U.S.

elec·tor·al \i-'lek-t(ə-)rəl\ *adj* : of or relating to an election or electors

electoral college *n* : a body of electors; *esp* : one that elects the president and vice president of the U.S.

elec·tor·ate \i-'lek-t(ə-)rət\ *n* : a body of people entitled to vote

electr- *or* **electro-** *combining form* : electricity : electric [from scientific Latin *electricus* "produced from amber by friction"]

¹elec·tric \i-'lek-trik\ *adj* **1** *or* **elec·tri·cal** \-tri-kəl\ : of, relating to, operated by, or produced by electricity **2** : having a thrilling effect ⟨an *electric* performance⟩ [from scientific Latin *electricus* "produced from amber by friction", derived from earlier Latin *electrum* "the resin amber", derived from Greek *ēlektron* (same meaning); so called because static electricity was first discovered by the friction produced by rubbing a piece of amber] — **elec·tri·cal·ly** \-tri-k(ə-)lē\ *adv* — **elec·tri·cal·ness** \-kəl-nəs\ *n*

²electric *n* : something (as a light, automobile, or train) operated by electricity

electrical engineering *n* : engineering that deals with the practical applications of electricity — **electrical engineer** *n*

electrical storm *n* : THUNDERSTORM — called also *electric storm*

electric charge *n* : a quantity of electricity

electric eel *n* : a large South American eel-shaped fish able to give a severe electric shock

electric eye *n* : PHOTOELECTRIC CELL

elec·tri·cian \i-,lek-'trish-ən\ *n* : one who installs, operates, or repairs electrical equipment

elec·tric·i·ty \i-,lek-'tris-ət-ē, -'tris-tē\ *n* **1** : a form of energy that is found in nature but that can be artificially produced by rubbing together two unlike things (as glass and silk), by the action of chemicals, or by means of a generator **2** : electric current

electric ray *n* : any of various round-bodied short-tailed rays of warm seas able to give a severe electric shock

elec·tri·fy \i-'lek-trə-,fī\ *vb* **-fied; -fy·ing 1 a** : to charge with electricity **b** : to equip for use of electric power or supply with electric power **2** : to cause to feel great or sudden excitement : THRILL — **elec·tri·fi·ca·tion** \-,lek-trə-fə-'kā-shən\ *n*

elec·tro·chem·i·cal \i-,lek-trō-'kem-i-kəl\ *adj* : of or relating to electrochemistry ⟨an *electrochemical* cell⟩

elec·tro·chem·is·try \i-,lek-trō-'kem-ə-strē\ *n* : a science that deals with the relation of electricity to chemical changes and with the change of chemical to electrical en-

ergy or vice versa

elec·tro·cute \i-'lek-trə-,kyüt\ *vb* **-cut·ed; -cut·ing** : to kill by electric shock; *esp* : to execute (a criminal) in this way — **elec·tro·cu·tion** \-,lek-trə-'kyü-shən\ *n*

elec·trode \i-'lek-,trōd\ *n* : a conductor (as a metal or carbon) used to make electrical contact with a part of an electrical circuit that is not metallic

elec·tro·en·ceph·a·lo·gram \i-,lek-trō-en-'sef-ə-lə-,gram\ *n* : the tracing of brain waves that is made by an electroencephalograph

elec·tro·en·ceph·a·lo·graph \i-,lek-trō-en-'sef-ə-lə-,graf\ *n* : an apparatus for detecting and recording brain waves — **elec·tro·en·ceph·a·lo·graph·ic** \-en-,sef-ə-lə-'graf-ik\ *adj* — **elec·tro·en·ceph·a·log·ra·phy** \-,sef-ə-'läg-rə-fē\ *n*

elec·trol·y·sis \i-,lek-'träl-ə-səs\ *n* **1** : the producing of chemical changes by passage of an electric current through an electrolyte **2** : the destruction of hair roots with an electric current

elec·tro·lyte \i-'lek-trə-,līt\ *n* **1** : a conductor in which electric current is carried by the movement of ions that are not metallic **2** : a substance that when dissolved in water or when melted becomes an ionic conductor

elec·tro·lyt·ic \i-,lek-trə-'lit-ik\ *adj* : of or relating to electrolysis or an electrolyte — **elec·tro·lyt·i·cal·ly** \-'lit-i-k(ə-)lē\ *adv*

elec·tro·mag·net \i-,lek-trō-'mag-nət\ *n* : a core of magnetic material (as soft iron) surrounded by a coil of wire through which an electric current is passed to magnetize the core

elec·tro·mag·net·ic \i-,lek-trō-mag-'net-ik\ *adj* : of, relating to, or produced by electromagnetism

electromagnetic spectrum *n* : the entire range of wavelengths or frequencies of electromagnetic waves extending from gamma rays to the longest radio waves and including visible light

electromagnetic wave *n* : a wave (as a radio wave, wave of visible light, or X ray) that consists of an associated electric and magnetic effect and travels at the speed of light

electromagnet

elec·tro·mag·ne·tism \i-,lek-trō-'mag-nə-,tiz-əm\ *n* : magnetism developed by a current of electricity

elec·tro·me·chan·i·cal \i-,lek-trō-mə-'kan-i-kəl\ *adj* : of, relating to, or being a mechanical process or device put into motion or controlled electrically

elec·tro·mo·tive force \i-,lek-trə-,mōt-iv-\ *n* : the work per unit charge required to carry a positive charge around a closed circuit in an electric field — *abbr.* emf

elec·tron \i-'lek-,trän\ *n* : an elementary particle that has a negative charge of electricity and travels around the nucleus of an atom

electron gun *n* : the part of a cathode-ray tube that produces, accelerates, and focuses a stream of electrons

¹elec·tron·ic \i-,lek-'trän-ik\ *adj* **1** : of or relating to electrons **2** : of, relating to, or using devices constructed or working by principles of electronics — **elec·tron·i·cal·ly** \-'trän-i-k(ə-)lē\ *adv*

²electronic *n* : an electronic circuit or device

electronic mail *n* : messages sent and received electronically (as between computer terminals linked by telephone lines)

elec·tron·ics \i-lek-'trän-iks\ *n* : a branch of physics that deals with the giving off, action, and effects of electrons in vacuums, gases, and semiconductors and with electronic devices

electron microscope *n* : an instrument in which a beam of electrons is used to produce an enlarged image of a very small object on a fluorescent screen or a photographic plate in a way similar to that in which light is used to form the image in an ordinary microscope

electron tube *n* : a device in which conduction of electricity by electrons takes place through a vacuum or a gas within a sealed glass or metal container and which has various common uses (as in radio and television)

elec·tro·plate \i-'lek-trə-ˌplāt\ *vb* : to cover with a coating (as of metal or rubber) by means of electrolysis

elec·tro·scope \i-'lek-trə-ˌskōp\ *n* : any of various instruments for detecting the presence of an electric charge on a body, for finding out whether the charge is positive or negative, or for indicating and measuring intensity of radiation

elec·tro·stat·ic \i-ˌlek-trə-'stat-ik\ *adj* : of or relating to static electricity or electrostatics

electrostatic generator *n* : a device for the production of electrical discharges at high voltage commonly consisting of an insulated hollow conducting sphere that builds up large quantities of electric charge

electrostatic precipitator *n* : an electrostatic device in chimneys that removes particles from escaping gases

elec·tro·stat·ics \i-ˌlek-trə-'stat-iks\ *n* : physics that deals with happenings resulting from attractions or repulsions of electric charges but not dependent on their motion

elec·trum \i-'lek-trəm\ *n* : a natural pale yellow alloy of gold and silver

el·e·gance \'el-i-gən(t)s\ *n* **1** : gracefulness of style or movement **2** : decoration or design that is rich but in good taste

el·e·gan·cy \'el-i-gən-sē\ *n, pl* **-cies** : ELEGANCE

el·e·gant \'el-i-gənt\ *adj* **1** : having or showing elegance **2** : of excellent quality : SPLENDID — **el·e·gant·ly** *adv*

el·e·gy \'el-ə-jē\ *n, pl* **-gies** **1** : a poem expressing sorrow for one who is dead **2** : a poem that is mournful in spirit — **el·e·gi·ac** \ˌel-ə-'jī-ək\ *adj* — **el·e·gize** \'el-ə-ˌjīz\ *vb*

el·e·ment \'el-ə-mənt\ *n* **1 a** : one of the four substances air, water, fire, or earth formerly believed to make up the physical universe **b** *pl* : forces of nature; *esp* : stormy or cold weather **c** : the state or place natural or suited to a person or thing ⟨at school she was in her *element*⟩ **2** : one of the parts of which something is made up: as **a** *pl* : the simplest principles of a subject of study **b** : one of the basic individual things that belong to a mathematical set or class — called also *member* **c** : any of more than 100 fundamental substances that consist of atoms of only one kind and that cannot be separated by ordinary chemical means into simpler substances **3** *pl* : the bread and wine used in the sacrament of Communion

CHEMICAL ELEMENTS

ELEMENT	SYMBOL	ATOMIC NUMBER	ATOMIC WEIGHT (C = 12)
actinium	Ac	89	227.0278
aluminum	Al	13	26.98154
americium	Am	95	
antimony	Sb	51	121.75
argon	Ar	18	39.948
arsenic	As	33	74.9216
astatine	At	85	
barium	Ba	56	137.33
berkelium	Bk	97	
beryllium	Be	4	9.01218
bismuth	Bi	83	208.9804
boron	B	5	10.81
bromine	Br	35	79.904
cadmium	Cd	48	112.41
calcium	Ca	20	40.08
californium	Cf	98	
carbon	C	6	12.011
cerium	Ce	58	140.12
cesium	Cs	55	132.9054
chlorine	Cl	17	35.453
chromium	Cr	24	51.996
cobalt	Co	27	58.9332
copper	Cu	29	63.546
curium	Cm	96	
dysprosium	Dy	66	162.50
einsteinium	Es	99	
erbium	Er	68	167.26
europium	Eu	63	151.96
fermium	Fm	100	
fluorine	F	9	18.998403
francium	Fr	87	
gadolinium	Gd	64	157.25
gallium	Ga	31	69.72
germanium	Ge	32	72.59
gold	Au	79	196.9665
hafnium	Hf	72	178.49
helium	He	2	4.00260
holmium	Ho	67	164.9304
hydrogen	H	1	1.0079
indium	In	49	114.82
iodine	I	53	126.9045
iridium	Ir	77	192.22
iron	Fe	26	55.847
krypton	Kr	36	83.80
lanthanum	La	57	138.9055
lawrencium	Lr	103	
lead	Pb	82	207.2
lithium	Li	3	6.941
lutetium	Lu	71	174.967
magnesium	Mg	12	24.305
manganese	Mn	25	54.9380
mendelevium	Md	101	
mercury	Hg	80	200.59
molybdenum	Mo	42	95.94
neodymium	Nd	60	144.24
neon	Ne	10	20.179
neptunium	Np	93	237.0482
nickel	Ni	28	58.69
niobium	Nb	41	92.9064
nitrogen	N	7	14.0067
nobelium	No	102	
osmium	Os	76	190.2
oxygen	O	8	15.9994
palladium	Pd	46	106.42
phosphorus	P	15	30.97376
platinum	Pt	78	195.08
plutonium	Pu	94	
polonium	Po	84	
potassium	K	19	39.0983
praseodymium	Pr	59	140.9077
promethium	Pm	61	
protactinium	Pa	91	231.0359
radium	Ra	88	226.0254
radon	Rn	86	
rhenium	Re	75	186.207
rhodium	Rh	45	102.9055
rubidium	Rb	37	85.4678
ruthenium	Ru	44	101.07
samarium	Sm	62	150.36
scandium	Sc	21	44.9559
selenium	Se	34	78.96

\ə\ **abut**	\aú\ **out**	\i\ **tip**	\ó\ **saw**	\ú\ **foot**
\ər\ **further**	\ch\ **chin**	\ī\ **life**	\ói\ **coin**	\y\ **yet**
\a\ **mat**	\e\ **pet**	\j\ **job**	\th\ **thin**	\yü\ **few**
\ā\ **take**	\ē\ **easy**	\ŋ\ **sing**	\th\ **this**	\yú\ **cure**
\ä\ **cot, cart**	\g\ **go**	\ō\ **bone**	\ü\ **food**	\zh\ **vision**

ELEMENT	SYMBOL	ATOMIC NUMBER	ATOMIC WEIGHT (C = 12)
silicon	Si	14	28.0855
silver	Ag	47	107.868
sodium	Na	11	22.98977
strontium	Sr	38	87.62
sulfur	S	16	32.06
tantalum	Ta	73	180.9479
technetium	Tc	43	
tellurium	Te	52	127.60
terbium	Tb	65	158.9254
thallium	Tl	81	204.383
thorium	Th	90	232.0381
thulium	Tm	69	168.9342
tin	Sn	50	118.69
titanium	Ti	22	47.88
tungsten	W	74	183.85
unnilhexium	Unh	106	
unnilpentium	Unp	105	
unnilquadium	Unq	104	
uranium	U	92	238.0289
vanadium	V	23	50.9415
xenon	Xe	54	131.29
ytterbium	Yb	70	173.04
yttrium	Y	39	88.9059
zinc	Zn	30	65.38
zirconium	Zr	40	91.22

el·e·men·tal \‚el-ə-'ment-ªl\ *adj* **1 a** : of, relating to, or being an element; *esp* : existing as an uncombined chemical element **b** : ELEMENTARY 1 **2** : of, relating to, or resembling a force of nature — **el·e·men·tal·ly** \-'mentªl-ē\ *adv*

el·e·men·ta·ry \‚el-ə-'ment-ə-rē, -'men-trē\ *adj* **1** : of or relating to the simplest principles of a subject **2** : of, relating to, or teaching the basic subjects of education ⟨*elementary* school⟩

elementary particle *n* : any of the particles (as electrons or photons) of matter and energy that are smaller than atoms and do not appear to be made up of a combination of more basic things

el·e·phant \'el-ə-fənt\ *n* : any of a family of huge thickset nearly hairless mammals that have the snout lengthened into a trunk and two incisors in the upper jaw developed into long outward-curving pointed tusks which furnish ivory and that include two living forms and various extinct relatives

elephant: *left* African, *right* Indian

elephant grass *n* : an Old World cattail used especially in making baskets

el·e·phan·ti·a·sis \‚el-ə-fən-'tī-ə-səs, -‚fan-\ *n* : the enormous enlargment of an arm or a leg or of the scrotum that is caused by blocking of the lymphatics by nematode worms

el·e·phan·tine \‚el-ə-'fan-‚tēn, -‚tīn, 'el-ə-fən-\ *adj* **1 a** : very big : HUGE, MASSIVE **b** : CLUMSY 1a, PONDEROUS **2** : of or relating to an elephant

el·e·vate \'el-ə-‚vāt\ *vb* **-vat·ed; -vat·ing** **1** : to lift up : RAISE **2** : to raise in rank or importance **3** : to improve the mind or spirits of [Middle English *elevaten* "lift up", from Latin *elevatus,* past participle of *elevare* "to lift up", from e- "away" and *levare* "to raise" — related to LEVER]

¹**el·e·vat·ed** \'el-ə-‚vāt-əd\ *adj* **1** : raised especially above the ground ⟨*elevated* highway⟩ **2 a** : being on a high level ⟨an *elevated* mind⟩ **b** : DIGNIFIED, FORMAL ⟨*elevated* language⟩

²**elevated** *n* : ELEVATED RAILROAD

elevated railroad *n* : a railroad operating chiefly on elevated tracks

el·e·va·tion \‚el-ə-'vā-shən\ *n* **1 a** the height to which something is elevated **b** : the height above sea level : ALTITUDE **2** : an act or instance of elevating **3** : an elevated place (as a hill) **4** : the quality or state of being elevated **syn** see HEIGHT

el·e·va·tor \'el-ə-‚vāt-ər\ *n* **1 a** : a continuous belt or chain conveyor for raising material **b** : a cage or platform and its hoisting machinery for carrying something to different levels **c** : a building for elevating, storing, unloading, and sometimes grinding grain — called also *grain elevator* **2** : a movable device shaped like a wing that is usually attached to the level tail surfaces of an airplane for producing motion up or down

elev·en \i-'lev-ən\ *n* **1** — see NUMBER table **2** : the eleventh in a set or series **3** : something having 11 units or members — **eleven** *adj or pron* — **elev·enth** \-ən(t)th\ *n* — **eleventh** *adj or adv*

elf \'elf\ *n, pl* **elves** \'elvz\ : a small and often mischievous fairy — **elf·ish** \'el-fish\ *adj* — **elf·ish·ly** *adv*

elf·in \'el-fən\ *adj* **1** : of or relating to elves **2** : resembling an elf; *esp* : having a strange beauty or charm

elf owl *n* : a very small insect-eating owl living in or about the giant cacti of desert areas of the southwestern U.S. and northern Mexico

elic·it \i-'lis-ət\ *vb* : to draw out often by skillful questioning or discussion ⟨*elicit* the truth from an unwilling witness⟩

el·i·gi·ble \'el-ə-jə-bəl\ *adj* **1** : qualified to be chosen ⟨*eligible* to be president⟩ **2** : having a right to something ⟨*eligible* to retire⟩ — **el·i·gi·bil·i·ty** \‚el-ə-jə-'bil-ət-ē\ *n* — **eligible** *n* — **el·i·gi·bly** \'el-ə-jə-blē\ *adv*

elim·i·nate \i-'lim-ə-‚nāt\ *vb* **-nat·ed; -nat·ing** **1** : to get rid of : REMOVE ⟨*eliminate* the causes of an epidemic⟩ **2** : to expel from the living body — **elim·i·na·tive** \-‚nāt-iv\ *adj*

elim·i·na·tion \i-‚lim-ə-'nā-shən\ *n* : the act or process of eliminating or emptying: as **a** : the act of excreting or emptying waste products from the body **b** : the act or process of excluding from a match, game, or contest the losers of any round or heat

elite \ā-'lēt, i-\ *n* **1 a** : the part or group having the highest quality or importance **b** : a small powerful group of people **2** : a typewriter type providing 12 characters to the inch — **elite** *adj*

elix·ir \i-'lik-sər\ *n* **1 a** : a substance held to be capable of changing metals into gold **b** : a substance held to be capable of extending life **c** : CURE-ALL **2** : a sweetened usually alcoholic liquid containing medicinal agents

Eliz·a·be·than \i-‚liz-ə-'bē-thən\ *adj* : of, relating to, or suggesting Elizabeth I of England or her time — **Elizabethan** *n*

elk \'elk\ *n, pl* **elk** *or* **elks** **1** : the largest existing deer of Europe and Asia related to the American moose and having broad spreading antlers **2** : a large North American deer with curved antlers having many branches — called also *wapiti*

elk 2

¹**ell** \'el\ *n* : a former English unit of length for cloth equal to 45 inches (1.1 meters)

²**ell** *n* : a part of a building that extends at right angles to the main part

el·lipse \i-'lips, e-\ *n* : a closed plane curve that is a conic section of oval shape

el·lip·sis \i-'lip-səs, e-\ *n, pl* **-lip·ses** \-'lip-,sēz\ **1** : the leaving out of one or more words that are not necessary for a phrase to be understood ("begin when ready" for "begin when you are ready" is an example of *ellipsis*) **2** : marks or a mark (as . . . or . . . .) used to indicate that something (as words) has been left out

el·lip·tic \i-'lip-tik, e-\ *or* **el·lip·ti·cal** \-ti-kəl\ *adj* **1** : ²OVAL **2** : of, relating to, or marked by ellipsis — **el·lip·ti·cal·ly** \-ti-k(ə-)lē\ *adv*

elm \'elm\ *n* **1** : any of a genus of large graceful trees that have toothed leaves, small flowers without petals, and nearly circular one-seeded winged fruits and are often grown as shade trees; *esp* : AMERICAN ELM **2** : the wood of an elm

El Ni·ño \el-'nē-nyō\ *n, pl* **El Niños** : an irregularly occurring flow of usually warm surface water along the western coast of South America that is accompanied by abnormally high rainfall in usually dry areas and a decline in the regional fish population [Spanish, "the child" (referring to the Christ child); from the appearance of the flow at the Christmas season]

el·o·cu·tion \,el-ə-'kyü-shən\ *n* **1** : the art of effective public speaking **2** : a style of speaking especially in public — **el·o·cu·tion·ary** \-shə-,ner-ē\ *adj* — **el·o·cu·tion·ist** \-sh(ə-)nəst\ *n*

elo·dea \i-'lōd-ē-ə\ *n* : any of a small genus of American herbs with leafy stems that live underwater

elon·gate \i-'lȯŋ-,gāt\ *vb* **-gat·ed; -gat·ing** : to make or grow longer — **elon·ga·tion** \(,)ē-,lȯŋ-'gā-shən\ *n*

elon·gat·ed \i-'lȯŋ-,gāt-əd\ *adj* : stretched out; *esp* : being much greater in length than in width

elope \i-'lōp\ *vb* **eloped; elop·ing** : to run away secretly especially to get married without parental consent — **elope·ment** \-mənt\ *n* — **elop·er** *n*

el·o·quence \'el-ə-kwən(t)s\ *n* : speech or writing that is forceful and convincing; *also* : the art or power of speaking or writing in a forceful and convincing way

el·o·quent \'el-ə-kwənt\ *adj* **1** : having or showing clear and forceful expression ⟨an *eloquent* speaker⟩ ⟨an *eloquent* essay⟩ **2** : clearly showing some feeling or meaning ⟨an *eloquent* look⟩ — **el·o·quent·ly** *adv*

¹**else** \'els\ *adv* **1** : in a different or additional manner or place or at a different time ⟨how *else* could it be done⟩ ⟨where *else* can we meet⟩ **2** : if the facts are or were different : if not : OTHERWISE

²**else** *adj* **1** : being different in identity ⟨somebody *else*⟩ **2** : being in addition ⟨what *else*⟩

else·where \'els-,(h)we(ə)r, -,(h)wa(ə)r\ *adv* : in or to another place

elu·ci·date \i-'lü-sə-,dāt\ *vb* **-dat·ed; -dat·ing** : to make clear or plain : EXPLAIN — **elu·ci·da·tion** \i-,lü-sə-'dā-shən\ *n* — **elu·ci·da·tive** \i-'lü-sə-,dāt-iv\ *adj* — **elu·ci·da·tor** \-,dāt-ər\ *n*

elude \ē-'lüd\ *vb* **elud·ed; elud·ing** : to avoid or escape by being quick, skillful, or tricky

elu·sive \ē-'lü-siv, -ziv\ *adj* **1** : hard to find or capture : EVASIVE **2** : hard to understand or define ⟨an *elusive* idea⟩ — **elu·sive·ly** *adv* — **elu·sive·ness** *n*

el·ver \'el-vər\ *n* : a young eel

elves *pl of* ELF

elv·ish \'el-vish\ *adj* : MISCHIEVOUS 2, 3

Ely·si·um \i-'lizh-ē-əm, -'liz-\ *n* : a place or condition of ideal happiness : PARADISE [derived from Greek *Ēlysion*, name in mythology of a place for the dead] — **Ely·sian** \-'lizh-ən\ *adj*

el·y·tron \'el-ə-,trän\ *also* **el·y·trum** \-trəm\ *n, pl* **-tra** \-trə\ : one of the thick modified front wings in beetles and some other insects that protect the hind pair of wings that are used for flying

em- — see EN-

ema·ci·ate \i-'mā-shē-,āt\ *vb* **-at·ed; -at·ing** : to cause to lose flesh so as to become very thin — **ema·ci·a·tion** \-,mā-shē-'ā-shən, -sē-\ *n*

E–mail \'ē-,māl\ *n* : ELECTRONIC MAIL

em·a·nate \'em-ə-,nāt\ *vb* **-nat·ed; -nat·ing** **1** : to come out from a source **2** : EMIT 1a, GIVE OUT — **em·a·na·tion** \,em-ə-'nā-shən\ *n* — **em·a·na·tion·al** \-shnəl, -shən-ᵊl\ *adj* — **em·a·na·tive** \'em-ə-,nāt-iv\ *adj*

eman·ci·pate \i-'man(t)-sə-,pāt\ *vb* **-pat·ed; -pat·ing** : to free from someone else's control or power; *esp* : to free from slavery — **eman·ci·pa·tion** \-,man(t)-sə-'pā-shən\ *n* — **eman·ci·pa·tor** \-'man(t)-sə-,pāt-ər\ *n*

emas·cu·late \i-'mas-kyə-,lāt\ *vb* **-lat·ed; -lat·ing** **1** : CASTRATE **2** : to deprive of masculine strength or spirit : WEAKEN — **emas·cu·la·tion** \-,mas-kyə-'lā-shən\ *n* — **emas·cu·la·tor** \-'mas-kyə-,lāt-ər\ *n*

em·balm \im-'bä(l)m\ *vb* : to treat a dead body with special preparations to preserve it from decay — **em·balm·er** *n* — **em·balm·ment** \-mənt\ *n*

em·bank \im-'baŋk\ *vb* : to enclose by an embankment

em·bank·ment \im-'baŋk-mənt\ *n* : a raised bank or wall to carry a roadway, prevent floods, or hold back water

em·bar·go \im-'bär-gō\ *n, pl* **-goes** **1** : an order of a government prohibiting commercial ships from leaving its ports **2** : legal prohibition or restriction of trade **3** : STOPPAGE, IMPEDIMENT; *esp* : PROHIBITION 2 — **embargo** *vb*

em·bark \im-'bärk\ *vb* **1** : to go or put on board a ship or airplane **2** : to begin some task or project ⟨*embark* on a career⟩ — **em·bar·ka·tion** \,em-,bär-'kā-shən\ *n* — **em·bark·ment** \im-'bärk-mənt\ *n*

em·bar·rass \im-'bar-əs\ *vb* **1** : to cause to feel confused or distressed ⟨unexpected laughter *embarrassed* the speaker⟩ **2** : to restrict the movement of : HINDER, IMPEDE **3** : to involve in financial difficulties — **em·bar·rass·ing·ly** \-'bar-ə-siŋ-lē\ *adv*

syn EMBARRASS, DISCONCERT, ABASH mean to make upset, uncomfortable, or confused in one's emotions. EMBARRASS suggests a feeling of uneasiness or discomfort ⟨*embarrassed* to see my relatives in the audience⟩ DISCONCERT suggests emotional upset or confusion from a strong and direct source ⟨street noises *disconcert* me during piano practice⟩ ABASH suggests a complete loss of self-control (as from feelings of guilt or inferiority) ⟨was *abashed* by their haughty behavior⟩

em·bar·rass·ment \im-'bar-əs-mənt\ *n* **1** : the state of being embarrassed **2 a** : something that embarrasses : IMPEDIMENT **b** : an overly large quantity from which to select — used especially in the phrase *embarrassment of riches*

em·bas·sy \'em-bə-sē\ *n, pl* **-sies** **1** : the position, role, or business of an ambassador **2** : a group of representatives headed by an ambassador **3** : the residence or office of an ambassador

em·bat·tle \im-'bat-ᵊl\ *vb* **em·bat·tled; em·bat·tling**

\ə\ abut	\au̇\ out	\i\ tip	\ȯ\ saw	\u̇\ foot
\ər\ further	\ch\ chin	\ī\ life	\ȯi\ coin	\y\ yet
\a\ mat	\e\ pet	\j\ job	\th\ thin	\yü\ few
\ā\ take	\ē\ easy	\ŋ\ sing	\th\ this	\yu̇\ cure
\ä\ cot, cart	\g\ go	\ō\ bone	\ü\ food	\zh\ vision

\-'bat-liŋ, -ᵊl-iŋ\ **1** : to arrange in order of battle : prepare for battle **2** : FORTIFY a

em·bat·tled *adj* : engaged in battle or conflict

em·bed *or* **im·bed** \im-'bed\ *vb* **em·bed·ded** *or* **im·bed·ded; em·bed·ding** *or* **im·bed·ding** **1** : to enclose in or as if in a surrounding mass : set solidly in or as if in a bed ⟨*embed* a post in concrete⟩ **2** : to prepare (material for use under a microscope) for sectioning by infiltrating with and enclosing in a supporting substance (as paraffin)

em·bel·lish \im-'bel-ish\ *vb* : to make beautiful with ornamentation : add ornamental details to   **syn** see ADORN — **em·bel·lish·ment** \-mənt\ *n*

em·ber \'em-bər\ *n* : a glowing piece of coal or wood from a fire; *esp* : such a piece smoldering in ashes

em·bez·zle \im-'bez-əl\ *vb* **-bez·zled; -bez·zling** \-(ə-)liŋ\ : to take (property entrusted to one's care) dishonestly for one's own use — **em·bez·zle·ment** \-əl-mənt\ *n* — **em·bez·zler** \-(ə-)lər\ *n*

em·bit·ter \im-'bit-ər\ *vb* : to make bitter; *esp* : to cause bitter feeling in — **em·bit·ter·ment** \-mənt\ *n*

em·bla·zon \im-'blāz-ᵊn\ *vb* **1** : to inscribe or decorate with markings or emblems used in heraldry **2 a** : to decorate in bright colors **b** : CELEBRATE 3, EXTOL ⟨a name *emblazoned* in history⟩

em·blem \'em-bləm\ *n* **1** : an object or likeness used to suggest a thing that cannot be pictured ⟨the flag is the *emblem* of one's country⟩ **2** : a device, symbol, design, or figure used as an identifying mark

    syn EMBLEM, TOKEN, SYMBOL mean a sign for something else. EMBLEM applies to an object or picture that is commonly understood to stand for an idea ⟨the bald eagle is an *emblem* of the United States⟩ TOKEN applies to an act, gesture, or object that is taken as a sign of sentiment ⟨please accept this watch as a *token* of our appreciation⟩ SYMBOL applies to anything that is understood as a sign of something else ⟨the lion is the *symbol* of courage⟩

em·blem·at·ic \,em-blə-'mat-ik\ *also* **em·blem·at·i·cal** \-'mat-i-kəl\ *adj* : of, relating to, or serving as an emblem : SYMBOLIC

em·bod·i·ment \im-'bäd-i-mənt\ *n* **1** : the act of embodying : the state of being embodied **2** : one that embodies something

em·body \im-'bäd-ē\ *vb* **-bod·ied; -body·ing** **1** : to bring together so as to form a body or system ⟨the Constitution *embodies* the fundamental laws of the United States⟩ **2** : to make a part of a body or system **3** : to give definite form to ⟨*embodied* her ideas in suitable words⟩ **4** : to represent in visible form ⟨a leader who *embodies* courage⟩ — **em·bod·i·er** *n*

em·bold·en \im-'bōl-dən\ *vb* : to make bold

em·bo·lism \'em-bə-,liz-əm\ *n* **1** : the sudden blocking of a blood vessel by an embolus **2** : EMBOLUS

em·bo·lus \'em-bə-ləs\ *n, pl* **-li** \-,lī\ : an abnormal particle (as an air bubble) circulating in the blood — compare THROMBUS

em·bo·som \im-'buz-əm\ *vb* : to shelter closely : ENCLOSE

em·boss \im-'bäs, -'bos\ *vb* : to decorate with a raised pattern or design — **em·boss·er** *n* — **em·boss·ment** \-mənt\ *n*

em·bow·er \im-'bau̇(-ə)r\ *vb* : to shelter or enclose in or as if in a bower

¹em·brace \im-'brās\ *vb* **em·braced; em·brac·ing** **1** : to clasp in the arms : HUG **2** : to enclose on all sides ⟨low hills *embraced* the valley⟩ **3 a** : to take up readily or gladly ⟨*embrace* a cause⟩ **b** : to make use of : WELCOME ⟨*embrace* an opportunity⟩ **4** : TAKE IN 4, INCLUDE — **em·brace·able** \-'brā-sə-bəl\ *adj* — **em·brac·er** *n*

    Word History One of the meanings of the English word *brace* is "two of a kind", as in "a brace of quail". In early French, however, the word *brace,* from which we get our English words *brace* and *embrace,* had a more limited

meaning of "two arms". The early French *brace* came from the plural form of the Latin word *bracchium,* meaning "arm". When combined with the early French prefix *em-,* meaning "to put into", the word formed the verb *embracier,* which meant literally "to put into the two arms"; in other words, "to hug". In time the word was borrowed into English and became *embrace.* [Middle English *embracen* "hug, embrace", from early French *embracer* (same meaning), from earlier *embracier,* literally "to put into the two arms", from *em-* "to put into" and *brace* "two arms", derived from Latin *bracchium* "arm" — related to ¹BRACE, BRACELET]

²embrace *n* : a close encircling with the arms

em·bra·sure \im-'brā-zhər\ *n* **1** : an opening in a wall for a door or window **2** : an opening with sides slanting outward in a wall or parapet for the firing of cannon

em·broi·der \im-'brȯid-ər\ *vb* **em·broi·dered; em·broi·der·ing** \-(ə-)riŋ\ **1** : to make or fill in a design with needlework **2** : to decorate with needlework **3** : to add to the interest of (as a story) with details or by exaggerating — **em·broi·der·er** \-ər-ər\ *n*

E embrasure 1

em·broi·dery \im-'brȯid-(ə-)rē\ *n, pl* **-der·ies** **1** : the process or art of embroidering **2** : needlework done to decorate cloth

em·broil \im-'brȯi(ə)l\ *vb* **1** : to throw into disorder or confusion **2** : to involve in conflict or difficulties ⟨*embroiled* in a complicated lawsuit⟩ — **em·broil·ment** \-mənt\ *n*

em·bryo \'em-brē-,ō\ *n, pl* **-bry·os** **1** : an animal in the early stages of development that are marked by cleavage, the laying down of the basic tissues, and the formation of primitive organs and organ systems — compare FETUS **2** : a tiny young plant within a seed **3** : a beginning or undeveloped stage — used especially in the phrase *in embryo*

em·bry·ol·o·gist \,em-brē-'äl-ə-jəst\ *n* : a person who specializes in embryology

em·bry·ol·o·gy \,em-brē-'äl-ə-jē\ *n* **1** : a branch of biology dealing with embryos and their development **2** : the facts and events characteristic of the development of an embryo — **em·bry·o·log·i·cal** \,em-brē-ə-'läj-i-kəl\ *adj* — **em·bry·o·log·i·cal·ly** \-i-k(ə-)lē\ *adv*

em·bry·on·ic \,em-brē-'än-ik\ *adj* **1** : of or relating to an embryo **2** : being in an early or undeveloped stage : being in embryo ⟨an *embryonic* plan⟩ — **em·bry·on·i·cal·ly** \-i-k(ə-)lē\ *adv*

embryo sac *n* : the individual that produces female germ cells in the sexually reproducing generation of a seed plant and that consists of a thin-walled sac containing the egg nucleus and other nuclei which form tissue used for food upon fertilization

¹em·cee \'em-'sē\ *n* : MASTER OF CEREMONIES [an altered form of *M.C.,* from *m*aster of *c*eremonies]

²emcee *vb* **em·ceed; em·cee·ing** : to act as master of ceremonies for something ⟨*emcee* a television show⟩

emend \ē-'mend\ *vb* : to correct usually by changing the wording of ⟨*emend* a text⟩ — **emen·da·tion** \,ē-,men-'dā-shən, ,em-ən-\ *n*

¹em·er·ald \'em-(ə-)rəld\ *n* : a rich green gem

²emerald *adj* : brightly or richly green

emerge \i-'mərj\ *vb* **emerged; emerg·ing** **1** : to become known or apparent ⟨the facts *emerged*⟩ **2** : to rise from or as if from a fluid : come out into view

emer·gence \i-'mər-jən(t)s\ *n* : the act or an instance of emerging

emer·gen·cy \i-'mər-jən-sē\ *n, pl* **-cies** **1** : an unexpected situation that calls for immediate action **2** : an urgent need for help ⟨a state of *emergency*⟩

emer·i·tus \i-'mer-ət-əs\ *adj* : retired with an honorary title from an office or position ⟨professor *emeritus*⟩ — **emeritus** *n*

em·ery \'em-(ə-)rē\ *n, pl* **em·er·ies** : a dark mineral used in the form of powder or grains for polishing and grinding

emery board *n* : a nail file made of cardboard covered with powdered emery

emet·ic \i-'met-ik\ *n* : something (as a chemical) that causes vomiting — **emetic** *adj*

em·i·grant \'em-i-grənt\ *n* **1** : one that emigrates **2** : a migrant plant or animal — **emigrant** *adj*

em·i·grate \'em-ə-,grāt\ *vb* **-grat·ed; -grat·ing** : to leave a country or region to live elsewhere — **em·i·gra·tion** \,em-ə-'grā-shən\ *n*

émi·gré *also* **emi·gré** \'em-i-,grā, ,em-i-'grā\ *n* : EMIGRANT 1; *esp* : a person forced to emigrate for political reasons [French]

em·i·nence \'em-ə-nən(t)s\ *n* **1** : the condition of being eminent **2 a** : a person of high rank or achievements — used as a title for a cardinal **b** : an area of high ground : HEIGHT

em·i·nent \'em-i-nənt\ *adj* : standing above others especially in rank, worth, or achievement ⟨an *eminent* physician⟩ — **em·i·nent·ly** *adv*

eminent domain *n* : a right of a government to take private property for public use

emir \i-'mi(ə)r, ā-\ *n* : a ruler, chief, or commander in Islamic countries [from Arabic *amīr* "commander"]

emir·ate \'em-ə-rət, -,rāt\ *n* : the state or jurisdiction of an emir

em·is·sary \'em-ə-,ser-ē\ *n, pl* **-sar·ies** : a person sent on a mission to represent another

emis·sion \ē-'mish-ən\ *n* **1** : an act or instance of emitting **2** : something emitted : DISCHARGE — **emis·sive** \ē-'mis-iv\ *adj*

emit \ē-'mit\ *vb* **emit·ted; emit·ting** **1 a** : to throw or give off or out ⟨*emit* light⟩ **b** : to send out : EJECT **2** : ²UTTER 1 ⟨*emit* a groan⟩ [from Latin *emittere* "to send out", from *e-, ex-* "out, forth" and *mittere* "to send, throw" — related to DISMISS, MESSAGE, MISSILE, TRANSMIT]

em·mer \'em-ər\ *n* : a hard red wheat having spikelets with two kernels

emol·u·ment \i-'mäl-yə-mənt\ *n* : profit from one's job or from an office held : SALARY, WAGES

emote \i-'mōt\ *vb* **emot·ed; emot·ing** : to give expression to emotion in or as if in a play

emo·tion \i-'mō-shən\ *n* **1** : strong feeling (as of anger, joy, hate, or fear) that causes a mental or physical effect **2** : a mental and bodily reaction marked by strong feeling

emo·tion·al \i-'mō-shnəl, -shən-ᵊl\ *adj* **1** : of or relating to the emotions ⟨an *emotional* upset⟩ **2** : likely to show or express emotion : easily moved ⟨an *emotional* person⟩ **3** : causing one to feel emotion ⟨an *emotional* speech⟩ — **emo·tion·al·ly** \-ē\ *adv*

em·pa·thy \'em-pə-thē\ *n* : a being aware of and sharing another person's feelings, experiences, and emotions; *also* : the ability for this

em·per·or \'em-pər-ər, -prər\ *n* : the ruler of an empire
  Word History The word *emperor* is a general word for a ruler having total control of a country or region. There are similar words for such all-powerful rulers in various countries: the *Caesars* in ancient Rome, the *czars* in Russia, the *kaisers* in Germany. All these terms go back to one source: the first of the emperors of the Roman lands, known as Imperator Caesar Augustus. Augustus (whose name was really a title, meaning "majesty") was the adopted son of the great Roman general and ruler Julius Caesar. Augustus took the family name Caesar as part of his official name. Later emperors of Rome also used the name *Caesar* to show that they were heirs to the throne. This is how the word *Caesar* came to be used to mean "an emperor of Rome". The word *Caesar* was spelled *kaisar* and later *kaiser* in the Germanic languages of Europe. It is from this word that we got our English word *kaiser* for "a ruler in Germany". Through the Russian word *tsar'*, which also came from the Germanic word *kaiser*, we got our English word *czar*, meaning "a ruler in Russia". Use of the word *emperor* itself can also be traced back to Imperator Caesar Augustus. The Latin word *imperator* was originally a title given to great Roman generals. The word meant "commander", and it was derived from the verb *imperare* "to command". It is because Augustus, the first Roman emperor, used *imperator* as a title that we use *emperor* as we do today. [Middle English *emperour* "emperor", from early French *empereor* (same meaning), from Latin *imperator* "commander" (title assumed by Caesar Augustus), from *imperare* "to command"]

em·pha·sis \'em(p)-fə-səs\ *n, pl* **-pha·ses** \-fə-,sēz\ **1 a** : forcefulness of expression ⟨spoke with *emphasis*⟩ **b** : the act or fact of giving stress to a word or syllable when speaking **2** : special note made of or importance given to something

em·pha·size \'em(p)-fə-,sīz\ *vb* **-sized; -siz·ing** : to place emphasis on : stress as being important or so as to stand out

em·phat·ic \im-'fat-ik, em-\ *adj* **1** : uttered with or marked by emphasis **2** : tending to express oneself in forceful speech or action **3** : attracting special attention ⟨an *emphatic* design⟩ — **em·phat·i·cal·ly** \-'fat-i-k(ə-)lē\ *adv*

em·phy·se·ma \,em(p)-fə-'zē-mə, -'sē-\ *n* : a condition marked especially by abnormal expansion of the air spaces of the lungs and often by faulty heart action

em·pire \'em-,pī(ə)r\ *n* **1 a** : a major political unit with a large territory or a number of territories or peoples under one ruler with total authority; *esp* : one having an emperor as chief of state **b** : the territory of such a unit **c** : something resembling an empire; *esp* : a large group of businesses under one control **2** : the state of being under or of having complete rule or control

em·pir·i·cal \im-'pir-i-kəl, em-\ *also* **em·pir·ic** \-'pir-ik\ *adj* **1** : relying on experience or observation usually without regard for a system and theory ⟨*empirical* medicine⟩ **2** : based on observation or experience ⟨*empirical* data⟩ **3** : capable of being proved or disproved by observation or experiment ⟨*empirical* laws⟩ — **em·pir·i·cal·ly** \-'pir-i-k(ə-)lē\ *adv*

empirical formula *n* : a chemical formula showing the simplest ratio of elements in a compound rather than the total number of atoms in the molecule

em·pir·i·cism \im-'pir-ə-,siz-əm, em-\ *n* **1** : the practice of relying on observation and experiment in the natural sciences **2** : a theory that knowledge begins with experience — **em·pir·i·cist** \-səst\ *n*

em·place \im-'plās\ *vb* : to put into place

em·place·ment \im-'plās-mənt\ *n* **1** : a prepared position for weapons **2** : a putting into position : PLACEMENT

¹em·ploy \im-'ploi\ *vb* **1** : to make use of : USE **2 a** : to use or obtain the services of ⟨*employ* a lawyer to draw up a will⟩ **b** : to provide with a job that pays wages or a salary ⟨*employ* a staff of twenty⟩ **3** : to use or direct toward a particular goal ⟨*employ* all of your energies to getting the job done⟩ — **em·ploy·able** \-ə-bəl\ *adj*

²employ *n* : employment especially for wages or a salary ⟨generous to people in their *employ*⟩

\ə\ **abut**	\au̇\ **out**	\i\ **tip**	\ȯ\ **saw**	\u̇\ **foot**
\ər\ **further**	\ch\ **chin**	\ī\ **life**	\ȯi\ **coin**	\y\ **yet**
\a\ **mat**	\e\ **pet**	\j\ **job**	\th\ **thin**	\yü\ **few**
\ā\ **take**	\ē\ **easy**	\ŋ\ **sing**	\t̲h̲\ **this**	\yu̇\ **cure**
\ä\ **cot, cart**	\g\ **go**	\ō\ **bone**	\ü\ **food**	\zh\ **vision**

em·ploy·ee *or* **em·ploye** \im-,plòi-'ē, (,)em-; im-'plòi-,ē, em-\ *n* : one who works for another for wages or a salary

em·ploy·er \im-'plòi-(ə)r\ *n* : one that employs others

em·ploy·ment \im-'plòi-mənt\ *n* **1** : ¹USE 1a, PURPOSE; *also* : the act of using **2 a** : the act of hiring a person for work **b** : the job for which one is hired : OCCUPATION **c** : the state of being employed ⟨*employment* in the machine trade⟩ **d** : the relative number of persons in a labor force who are employed ⟨*employment* is high⟩

employment agency *n* : a company whose business is to find jobs for certain people and to find people suitable for certain jobs

em·po·ri·um \im-'pōr-ē-əm, em-, -'pòr-\ *n, pl* **-ri·ums** *also* **-ria** \-ē-ə\ **1 a** : MARKETPLACE **b** : a center of business activity **2** : a store carrying a wide variety of merchandise

em·pow·er \im-'pau̇-(ə)r\ *vb* : to give official authority or legal power to

em·press \'em-prəs\ *n* **1** : the wife or widow of an emperor **2** : a woman who is the ruler of an empire

¹emp·ty \'em(p)-tē\ *adj* **emp·ti·er; -est** **1** : containing nothing ⟨an *empty* box⟩ **2** : not being lived in ⟨an *empty* house⟩ **3** : having no reality or importance ⟨*empty* dreams⟩ **4** : lacking in value, sense, effect, or sincerity ⟨*empty* threats⟩ **5** : HUNGRY 1 ⟨feel *empty* before dinner⟩ **6** : NULL 2 — **emp·ti·ly** \-tə-lē\ *adv* — **emp·ti·ness** \-tē-nəs\ *n*

²empty *vb* **emp·tied; emp·ty·ing** **1** : to make empty : remove the contents of ⟨*empty* a barrel⟩ **2** : to remove all of from a container ⟨*empty* flour from a bag⟩ **3** : to become empty **4** : to give forth contents (as fluid) : DISCHARGE ⟨the river *empties* into the ocean⟩

³empty *n, pl* **emp·ties** : an empty container

emp·ty–hand·ed \,em(p)-tē-'han-dəd\ *adj* **1** : having nothing in the hands **2** : having acquired or gained nothing

em·pur·ple \im-'pər-pəl\ *vb* **em·pur·pled; em·pur·pling** \-'pər-p(ə-)liŋ\ : to tinge or color purple

em·py·re·an \,em-,pī-'rē-ən, -pə-; em-'pir-ē-ən, -'pī-rē-ən\ *n* **1** : the highest heaven or heavenly sphere **2** : SKY 1, HEAVENS — **em·py·re·al** \-əl\ *adj* — **empyrean** *adj*

emu \'ē-myü\ *n* : a swift-running Australian bird with undeveloped wings that is related to but smaller than the ostrich

em·u·late \'em-yə-,lāt\ *vb* **-lat·ed; -lat·ing** : to try to be like or better than — **em·u·la·tor** \-,lāt-ər\ *n*

em·u·la·tion \,em-yə-'lā-shən\ *n* : the ambition or effort to emulate — **em·u·la·tive** \'em-yə-,lāt-iv\ *adj*

em·u·lous \'em-yə-ləs\ *adj* : eager or ambitious to emulate someone or something — **em·u·lous·ly** *adv* — **em·u·lous·ness** *n*

emul·si·fi·er \i-'məl-sə-,fī(-ə)r\ *n* : a substance (as a soap) that helps to form and stabilize an emulsion

emul·si·fy \i-'məl-sə-,fī\ *vb* **-fied; -fy·ing** : to change (as an oil) into an emulsion — **emul·si·fi·ca·tion** \i-,məl-sə-fə-'kā-shən\ *n*

emul·sion \i-'məl-shən\ *n* : a material consisting of a mixture of liquids that do not dissolve in each other and having droplets of one liquid scattered throughout the other ⟨an *emulsion* of oil in water⟩

en- *also* **em-** \e *also* occurs in these prefixes although only* i *may be shown as in "engage"*\ *prefix* **1** : put into or onto ⟨encode⟩ ⟨enthrone⟩ : go into or onto ⟨enplane⟩ **2** : cause to be ⟨enslave⟩ **3** : provide with ⟨empower⟩ **4** : so as to cover ⟨enwrap⟩ : thoroughly ⟨entangle⟩ — in all senses usually **em-** before *b, m,* or *p* [derived from Latin

in- "in, into, put into"]

¹-en \ən\ *also* **-n** \n\ *adj suffix* : made of : consisting of ⟨earth*en*⟩ ⟨wool*en*⟩ [Old English *-en* (adjective suffix)]

²-en *vb suffix* **1** : become or cause to be ⟨sharp*en*⟩ **2** : cause or come to have ⟨length*en*⟩ [Old English *-nian* (verb suffix)]

en·able \in-'ā-bəl\ *vb* **en·abled; en·abling** \-b(ə-)liŋ\ **1 a** : to make able ⟨glasses *enable* you to read⟩ **b** : to make possible, practical, or easy **2** : to give legal power or permission to

en·act \in-'akt\ *vb* **1** : to make (as a bill) into law ⟨*enact* legislation⟩ **2** : to act out ⟨*enact* a scene from a play⟩ — **en·ac·tor** \-'ak-tər\ *n*

en·act·ment \in-'ak(t)-mənt\ *n* **1** : the act of enacting : the state of being enacted **2** : LAW 1a, STATUTE

¹enam·el \in-'am-əl\ *vb* **-eled** *or* **-elled; -el·ing** *or* **-el·ling** \-'am-(ə-)liŋ\ : to cover or decorate with enamel

²enamel *n* **1** : a glassy substance used to coat the surface of metal, glass, or pottery **2** : a surface that resembles enamel **3** : a very hard outer layer covering the crown of a tooth **4** : a paint that flows out to a smooth hard coat when applied and dries with a glossy appearance

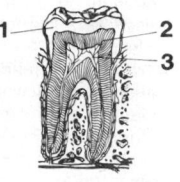
enamel 3:
*1 enamel, 2 dentin,
3 pulp*

enam·el·ware \in-'am-əl-,wa(ə)r, -,we(ə)r\ *n* : metal utensils (as pots and pans) coated with enamel

en·am·or \in-'am-ər\ *vb* **-ored; or·ing** \-(ə-)riŋ\ : to cause to feel love

en·camp \in-'kamp\ *vb* **1** : to set up and occupy a camp : CAMP **2** : to place or establish in a camp ⟨*encamp* troops⟩

en·camp·ment \in-'kamp-mənt\ *n* **1** : the act of encamping : the state of being encamped **2** : the site of a camp

en·cap·su·late \in-'kap-sə-,lāt\ *vb* **-lat·ed; -lat·ing** **1** : to enclose in a capsule **2** : to condense (as a report) into a few words — **en·cap·su·la·tion** \-,kap-sə-'lā-shən\ *n*

en·case \in-'kās\ *vb* : to enclose in or as if in a case — **en·case·ment** \-mənt\ *n*

-ence \ən(t)s, ⁿn(t)s\ *n suffix* **1** : action or process ⟨emerg*ence*⟩ : instance of an action or process ⟨refer*ence*⟩ **2** : quality or state ⟨evanesc*ence*⟩ [derived from Latin *-entia* "action or process"]

encephal- *or* **encephalo-** *combining form* : brain ⟨enceph*al*itis⟩ [derived from Greek *enkephal-* "brain", derived from *en-* "in" and *kephalē* "head"]

en·ceph·a·li·tis \in-,sef-ə-'līt-əs, (,)en-\ *n* : any of several infectious or contagious diseases (as sleeping sickness) marked by inflammation of the brain

en·chain \in-'chān\ *vb* : to bind with or as if with chains — **en·chain·ment** \-mənt\ *n*

en·chant \in-'chant\ *vb* **1** : to influence by charms and magic : BEWITCH **2** : ¹THRILL 1, FASCINATE

en·chant·ed *adj* : being or appearing to be under a magic spell ⟨an *enchanted* forest⟩

en·chant·er \in-'chant-ər\ *n* : one that enchants; *esp* : SORCERER

en·chant·ing \in-'chant-iŋ\ *adj* : having great charm and attraction — **en·chant·ing·ly** *adv*

en·chant·ment \in-'chant-mənt\ *n* **1** : the act or art of enchanting : the state of being enchanted **2** : something that enchants : SPELL

en·chant·ress \in-'chan-trəs\ *n* **1** : a woman who practices magic : SORCERESS **2** : a fascinating woman

en·chi·la·da \,en-chə-'läd-ə\ *n* : a tortilla spread with a meat or cheese filling, rolled up, and covered with a chili sauce [American Spanish, derived from earlier *enchilar* "to season with chili"]

emu

en·ci·pher \in-'sī-fər, en-\ *vb* : to change (a message) from ordinary language into cipher

en·cir·cle \in-'sər-kəl\ *vb* **1** : to form a circle around : SURROUND **2** : to pass completely around — **en·cir·cle·ment** \-mənt\ *n*

en·clave \'en-ˌklāv, 'än-, 'äŋ-\ *n* : a region or community (as within a country or city) made up of people of a different race or cultural background [from French *enclave* "enclave", derived from early French *enclaver* "to enclose"]

en·close *or* **in·close** \in-'klōz\ *vb* **1 a** : to close in : SURROUND ⟨*enclose* a porch with glass⟩ **b** : to hold in : CONFINE ⟨*enclose* animals in a pen⟩ **2** : to place in a parcel or envelope ⟨*enclose* a card with the present⟩

en·clo·sure *or* **in·clo·sure** \in-'klō-zhər\ *n* **1** : the act of enclosing : the state of being enclosed **2** : an enclosed space **3** : something (as a fence) that encloses **4** : something enclosed ⟨a letter with two *enclosures*⟩

en·code \in-'kōd, en-\ *vb* : to change (as a body of information) from one system of communication into another; *esp* : to change (a message) into code — **en·cod·er** *n*

en·co·mi·um \en-'kō-mē-əm\ *n, pl* **-mi·ums** *or* **-mia** \-mē-ə\ : warm or high praise especially when formally expressed : EULOGY

en·com·pass \in-'kəm-pəs, -'käm-\ *vb* **1** : to form a circle about : SURROUND **2 a** : to cover or surround especially so as to conceal or protect **b** : to take in as a part : INCLUDE — **en·com·pass·ment** \-mənt\ *n*

¹en·core \'än-ˌkō(ə)r, -ˌkȯ(ə)r\ *n* : a demand made by an audience for a repeat or an additional performance; *also* : a further performance in response to such a demand

²encore *vb* **en·cored; en·cor·ing** : to call (as by clapping) for a further performance or appearance of or by

¹en·coun·ter \in-'kaunt-ər\ *vb* **en·coun·tered; en·coun·ter·ing** \-'kaunt-ə-riŋ, -'kaun-triŋ\ **1** : to engage in a struggle with as an enemy or rival **2** : to come upon face-to-face : MEET **3** : to come upon unexpectedly ⟨*encountered* problems⟩

²encounter *n* **1** : a clash between enemies or rivals; *also* : a very unfriendly meeting ⟨had an *encounter* with the boss⟩ **2 a** : a chance meeting **b** : a meeting face-to-face

en·cour·age \in-'kər-ij, -'kə-rij\ *vb* **-aged; -ag·ing** **1** : to cause to feel courage, spirit, or hope **2** : to spur on : STIMULATE **3** : to give help to ⟨government grants to *encourage* young artists⟩ ⟨warm weather *encourages* plant growth⟩ — **en·cour·age·ment** \-mənt\ *n* — **en·cour·ag·ing·ly** \-ij-iŋ-lē, -rij-\ *adv*

en·croach \in-'krōch\ *vb* **1** : to enter or force oneself on another's property or rights little by little **2** : to advance beyond the usual or desirable limits ⟨the *encroaching* sea⟩ — **en·croach·ment** \-mənt\ *n*

en·crust *also* **in·crust** \in-'krəst\ *vb* **1** : to cover with a crust **2** : to form a crust

en·crus·ta·tion \(ˌ)in-ˌkrəs-'tā-shən, ˌen-\ *variant of* INCRUSTATION

en·cum·ber \in-'kəm-bər\ *vb* **en·cum·bered; en·cum·ber·ing** \-b(ə-)riŋ\ **1** : to place an excessive burden on **2** : to create difficulty for the work or activity of

en·cum·brance \in-'kəm-brən(t)s\ *n* **1** : something that encumbers : BURDEN **2** : a legal claim (as a mortgage) against property

-en·cy \ən-sē, ᵊn-\ *n suffix, pl* **-encies** : quality or state (despondency) [derived from Latin *-entia* (noun suffix)]

en·cyc·li·cal \in-'sik-li-kəl, en-\ *n* : a document usually in the form of a letter stating a rule or official opinion; *esp* : a letter from the pope to the bishops of the church as a whole or to those in one country on a matter of church teaching or religious belief — **encyclical** *adj*

en·cy·clo·pe·dia *also* **en·cy·clo·pae·dia** \in-ˌsī-klə-'pēd-ē-ə\ *n* : a work that contains information on all subjects or one that covers a certain subject thoroughly usually with articles arranged alphabetically [from Latin *encyclopedia* "course of general education", from Greek *enkyklios* "general, all-around", literally "circular" and Greek *paideia* "education, child rearing"]

en·cy·clo·pe·dic *also* **en·cy·clo·pae·dic** \in-ˌsī-klə-'pēd-ik\ *adj* **1** : of or relating to an encyclopedia **2** : covering a wide range of subjects ⟨*encyclopedic* knowledge⟩ — **en·cy·clo·pe·di·cal·ly** \-'pēd-i-k(ə)lē\ *adv*

en·cyst \in-'sist, en-\ *vb* : to form or become enclosed in a cyst — **en·cyst·ment** \-'sis(t)-mənt\ *n*

¹end \'end\ *n* **1 a** : the part at the boundary of an area **b** : a point that marks the limit of something or the point where something no longer exists ⟨there is no *end* to your generosity⟩ ⟨the *end* of the month⟩ **c** : the last part lengthwise : TIP **2 a** : the stopping of a process or activity **b** : DEATH 1, DESTRUCTION ⟨came to a horrible *end*⟩ **3** : something left over : REMNANT **4** : GOAL 2, PURPOSE **5** : a football lineman whose position is at the end of the line **6** : a phase of an undertaking ⟨the advertising *end* of the business⟩ — **end·ed** \'en-dəd\ *adj* — **on end** : without interruption

²end *vb* : to bring or come to an end : STOP

end- *or* **endo-** *combining form* **1** : within : inside ⟨*endo*skeleton⟩ — compare EXO- **2** : taking in ⟨*endo*thermic⟩ [derived from Greek *end-*, *endo-* "inside, within"]

en·dan·ger \in-'dān-jər\ *vb* **en·dan·gered; en·dan·ger·ing** \-'dānj-(ə-)riŋ\ : to bring into danger or peril — **en·dan·ger·ment** \-mənt\ *n*

en·dan·gered *adj* : threatened with extinction ⟨an *endangered* species⟩

en·dear \in-'di(ə)r\ *vb* : to cause to become dear or beloved

en·dear·ment \in-'di(ə)r-mənt\ *n* : a word or an act (as a caress) showing love or affection

en·deav·or *or* \in-'dev-ər\ *vb* **en·deav·ored; en·deav·or·ing** \-(ə-)riŋ\ **1** : to make an effort : TRY **2** : to work for a particular goal or result — **endeavor** *n*

en·dem·ic \en-'dem-ik, in-\ *adj* : originating or growing or found especially and often only in a certain locality or region ⟨*endemic* diseases⟩ ⟨an *endemic* plant⟩

end·ing \'en-diŋ\ *n* : the final part : CONCLUSION, END ⟨a novel with a happy *ending*⟩

en·dive \'en-ˌdīv\ *n* **1** : an herb closely related to chicory and widely grown as a salad plant — called also *escarole* **2** : the developing shoot of chicory when it is made pale or white by growing in the dark for use in salads

endive 1

end·less \'en-(d)ləs\ *adj* **1** : being or seeming to be without end **2** : joined at the ends : CONTINUOUS ⟨an *endless* belt⟩ — **end·less·ly** *adv* — **end·less·ness** *n*

end line *n* : a line marking an end or boundary (as on a playing field)

end·most \'en(d)-ˌmōst\ *adj* : situated at the very end

en·do·crine \'en-də-krən, -ˌkrīn, -ˌkrēn\ *adj* **1** : producing secretions that are distributed in the body by way of the bloodstream **2** : of, relating to, or resembling that of an endocrine gland **3** : HORMONAL

endocrine gland *n* : any of various glands that have no duct and pour their secretions directly into the lymph or blood circulating through them — called also *ductless gland*

en·do·derm \'en-də-ˌdərm\ *n* **1** : the innermost of the

\ə\ abut	\au̇\ out	\i\ tip	\ȯ\ saw	\u̇\ foot	
\ər\ further	\ch\ chin	\ī\ life	\ȯi\ coin	\y\ yet	
\a\ mat	\e\ pet	\j\ job	\th\ thin	\yü\ few	
\ā\ take	\ē\ easy	\ŋ\ sing	\th\ this	\yu̇\ cure	
\ä\ cot, cart	\g\ go	\ō\ bone	\ü\ food	\zh\ vision	

three basic layers of an embryo that forms the epithelium of the digestive tract and the parts of the body formed from it   **2** : the inner layer of cells of an animal (as a jellyfish or hydra) whose body is composed of two layers of cells — **en·do·der·mal** \,en-də-'dər-məl\ *adj*

en·do·me·tri·um \,en-dō-'mē-trē-əm\ *n, pl* **-tria** \-trē-ə\ : the mucous membrane lining the uterus

en·do·plasm \'en-də-,plaz-əm\ *n* : the inner relatively fluid part of the cytoplasm

en·do·plas·mic reticulum \,en-də-'plaz-mik-\ *n* : a system of cavities and minute connecting canals that occupy much of the cytoplasm of the cell

en·dorse \in-'dȯ(ə)rs\ *vb* **en·dorsed; en·dors·ing**   **1** : to sign the back of (a check, bank note, or bill) especially to receive payment, to indicate method of payment, or to transfer to someone else   **2** : to give one's support to ⟨*endorse* a candidate⟩ — **en·dors·er** *n*

en·dorse·ment \in-'dȯr-smənt\ *n*   **1** : the act or process of endorsing   **2** : a signature often with additional writing endorsing a check or note   **3** : official approval and support : SANCTION

en·do·skel·e·ton \,en-dō-'skel-ət-°n\ *n* : an inside skeleton or supporting framework in an animal

en·do·sperm \'en-də-,spərm\ *n* : a food-containing tissue formed within the seed in seed plants

en·do·ther·mic \,en-də-'thər-mik\ *adj* : characterized by or formed with absorption of heat ⟨*endothermic* chemical reactions⟩

en·dow \in-'daů\ *vb*   **1** : to provide with money for a regular income ⟨*endow* a hospital⟩   **2** : to furnish with something freely or naturally ⟨human beings are *endowed* with reason⟩

en·dow·ment \in-'daů-mənt\ *n*   **1** : the providing of a permanent fund for support or the fund provided ⟨a college with a large *endowment*⟩   **2** : a person's natural ability or talent

end·point \'en(d)-,pȯint\ *n* : either of two points that mark the ends of a line segment or a point that marks the end of a ray

end rhyme *n* : a rhyme of the last word or the last syllable of two or more lines of verse

end run *n* : a football play in which the ballcarrier attempts to run wide around the end

end table *n* : a small table used beside a sofa or chair

en·due \in-'d(y)ü\ *vb* **en·dued; en·du·ing** : to provide with a quality or power ⟨*endued* with grace⟩

en·dur·ance \in-'d(y)ůr-ən(t)s\ *n*   **1** : the quality of lasting or of being permanent   **2** : the ability to withstand hardship, adversity, or stress ⟨athletes need to develop *endurance*⟩   **3** : SUFFERING 1 ⟨*endurance* of many hardships⟩

en·dure \in-'d(y)ů(ə)r\ *vb* **en·dured; en·dur·ing**   **1** : to continue in the same state : LAST   **2** : to bear patiently : SUFFER   **3** : to allow to happen or continue : TOLERATE — **en·dur·able** \-'d(y)ůr-ə-bəl\ *adj* — **en·dur·ing** \in-'d(y)ůr-iŋ\ *adj* — **en·dur·ing·ly** *adv*

end user *n* : the ultimate consumer of a finished product

end·ways \'en-,dwāz\ *or* **end·wise** \-,dwīz\ *adv or adj*   **1** : with the end forward   **2** : LENGTHWISE

end zone *n* : the area where points are scored beyond the goal line at each end of a football field

-ene \,ēn\ *n suffix* : unsaturated carbon compound ⟨benzene⟩; *esp* : carbon compound with one double bond ⟨ethylene⟩ [derived from Greek *-ēnos* (adjective suffix)]

en·e·ma \'en-ə-mə\ *n* : the injection of liquid into the rectum by way of the anus usually to cause the bowels to empty; *also* : the material injected

en·e·my \'en-ə-mē\ *n, pl* **-mies**   **1** : one that tries to hurt or overthrow or that seeks the failure of another   **2** : something that harms   **3 a** : a nation with which a country is at war   **b** : a military force, a ship, or a person belonging to such a nation [Middle English *enemi* "enemy", from early French *enemi* (same meaning), from Latin *in-*

imicus (same meaning), from *in-* "not" and *amicus* "friend"]

en·er·get·ic \,en-ər-'jet-ik\ *adj* : having or showing energy : ACTIVE, FORCEFUL ⟨an *energetic* salesperson⟩   **syn** see VIGOROUS — **en·er·get·i·cal·ly** \-'jet-i-k(ə-)lē\ *adv*

en·er·gize \'en-ər-,jīz\ *vb* **-gized; -giz·ing**   **1** : to put forth energy : ACT   **2 a** : to give energy to   **b** : to make energetic   **3** : to apply voltage to — **en·er·giz·er** *n*

en·er·gy \'en-ər-jē\ *n, pl* **-gies**   **1** : power or ability to be active : strength of body or mind to do things or to work ⟨a teacher of great intellectual *energy*⟩   **2** : natural power vigorously exerted : vigorous action ⟨work with *energy*⟩   **3** : the capacity (as of heat, light, or running water) for doing work   **4 a** : usable power (as heat or electricity)   **b** : a source of energy; *esp* : a resource (as oil) used to provide energy ⟨develop a long-range plan for conserving *energy*⟩   **syn** see POWER

energy level *n* : one of the stable states of constant energy that may be assumed by a physical system — used especially of the states of electrons in atoms

en·er·vate \'en-ər-,vāt\ *vb* **-vat·ed; -vat·ing** : to cause to decline in strength or vigor : WEAKEN — **en·er·va·tion** \,en-ər-'vā-shən\ *n*

en·fee·ble \in-'fē-bəl\ *vb* **en·fee·bled; en·fee·bling** \-b(ə-)liŋ\ : to make feeble — **en·fee·ble·ment** \-bəl-mənt\ *n*

en·fold \in-'fōld\ *vb*   **1** : to cover with folds : enclose in the folds of something   **2** : to clasp within the arms : EMBRACE

en·force \in-'fō(ə)rs, -'fȯ(ə)rs\ *vb*   **1** : to bring about by force : COMPEL ⟨*enforce* obedience⟩   **2** : to carry out effectively ⟨*enforce* the law⟩ — **en·force·able** \-'fōr-sə-bəl, -fȯr-\ *adj* — **en·force·ment** \-'fōr-smənt, -fȯr-\ *n* — **en·forc·er** *n*

en·fran·chise \in-'fran-,chīz\ *vb* **-chised; -chis·ing**   **1** : to set free (as from slavery)   **2** : to give full privileges of citizenship to; *esp* : to give the right to vote — **en·fran·chise·ment** \-,chīz-mənt, -chəz-\ *n*

en·gage \in-'gāj\ *vb* **en·gaged; en·gag·ing**   **1** : to bind oneself to do something; *esp* : to bind by a pledge to marry   **2 a** : to arrange for the use or services of : HIRE ⟨*engage* a lawyer⟩   **b** : to keep fixed or concentrated ⟨the task *engaged* our attention⟩   **3 a** : to cause to take part ⟨*engaged* the stranger in conversation⟩   **b** : PARTICIPATE ⟨*engaged* in sports⟩   **4** : to enter into contest with ⟨*engage* the enemy⟩   **5** : to come together or cause to come together and mesh ⟨the gears *engaged*⟩

en·gaged \in-'gājd\ *adj*   **1** : being occupied with some activity ⟨*engaged* in conversation⟩   **2** : pledged to be married : BETROTHED ⟨an *engaged* couple⟩

en·gage·ment \in-'gāj-mənt\ *n*   **1 a** : a promise to be present at a specified place and time   **b** : employment especially for a stated time ⟨the band had *engagements* in different towns⟩   **2** : ¹PLEDGE 5, OBLIGATION   **3 a** : the act of engaging : the state of being engaged   **b** : the act or fact of becoming pledged for marriage   **4** : the state of being meshed into a working arrangement in which one part drives another   **5** : the state of being in conflict, opposition, or battle

en·gag·ing \in-'gā-jiŋ\ *adj* : having a very pleasing appearance or manner : ATTRACTIVE — **en·gag·ing·ly** *adv*

en·gen·der \in-'jen-dər\ *vb* **-dered; -der·ing** \-d(ə-)riŋ\   **1** : to reproduce offspring   **2** : to be the source or cause of : PRODUCE ⟨tensions that *engender* emotional conflicts⟩

en·gine \'en-jən\ *n*   **1** : a mechanical device   **2** : a machine that changes energy (as heat from burning fuel) into mechanical motion   **3** : a railroad locomotive [Middle English *engin* "natural talent or skill, mechanical device", from early French *engin* (same meaning), from Latin *ingenium* "natural ability or desire to do something, inborn ability", from *in* "in" and *-genium*, from *gignere* "to father, beget" — related to GENIUS, ¹GIN, INGENIOUS]

¹en·gi·neer \,en-jə-'ni(ə)r\ *n*   **1** : a member of a military group devoted to engineering work   **2 a** : a designer or builder of engines   **b** : a person who is trained in or follows as a profession a branch of engineering   **3** : a person who runs or has charge of an engine or technical machinery

²engineer *vb*   **1** : to plan, build, or manage as an engineer   **2** : to guide the course of ⟨*engineer* a fund-raising campaign⟩

en·gi·neer·ing \,en-jə-'ni(ə)r-iŋ\ *n* : the science or profession of developing and using nature's power and resources in ways that are useful to people (as in designing and building roads, bridges, dams, or machines and in creating new products)

¹En·glish \'iŋ-glish\ *adj*   **1** : of, relating to, or characteristic of England, the English people, or the English language   **2** : of, relating to, or being the English system of measurement [Old English *englisc* "English", from *Engle* "the Angles (Germanic people who invaded England in the 5th century along with the Saxons and with them formed the Anglo-Saxon peoples)"]

²English *n*   **1 a** : the language of the people of England and the U.S. and many areas now or formerly under British control   **b** : English language, literature, or writing technique that is a subject of study   **2 English** *pl* : the people of England   **3** : a sideways spin given to a ball when it is struck or bowled

English horn *n* : a woodwind instrument similar to the oboe but lower in pitch

English ivy *n* : IVY 1

En·glish·man \'iŋ-glish-mən\ *n* : a person born or living in England

English saddle *n* : a rather flat saddle without a horn and high seat back

English setter *n* : any of a breed of bird dogs with a flat silky coat of white with flecks or patches of black or brown

English sonnet *n* : a sonnet in which the rhyme pattern is in three groups of four lines each and one group of two lines

English horn

English   sparrow   *n* : HOUSE SPARROW

English springer spaniel *n* : any of a breed of compact bird dogs with a flat silky coat of white with large patches of usually black or brown

English system *n* : a system of weights and measures in which the foot is the principal unit of length and the pound is the principal unit of weight

En·glish·wom·an \'iŋ-glish-,wum-ən\ *n* : a woman born or living in England

en·gorge \in-'gȯ(ə)rj\ *vb*   **1** : to eat greedily : GORGE   **2** : to fill with blood : CONGEST — **en·gorge·ment** \-mənt\ *n*

en·grave \in-'grāv\ *vb* **en·graved; en·grav·ing**   **1 a** : to cut or carve (as letters or designs) on a hard surface   **b** : to cut lines, letters, figures, or designs on or into (a hard surface) often for use in printing   **c** : to print from a cut surface ⟨an *engraved* wedding invitation⟩   **2** : to impress deeply ⟨the incident was *engraved* in my memory⟩ — **en·grav·er** *n*

en·grav·ing \in-'grā-viŋ\ *n*   **1** : the art of cutting something especially into the surface of wood, stone, or metal   **2** : a print made from an engraved surface

en·gross \in-'grōs\ *vb* : to take up the whole interest or attention of : ABSORB — **en·gross·er** *n* — **en·gross·ment** \-mənt\ *n*

en·gulf \in-'gəlf\ *vb* : to flow over and enclose — **en·gulf·ment** \-mənt\ *n*

en·hance \in-'han(t)s\ *vb* **en·hanced; en·hanc·ing** : to increase or improve in value, desirability, or attractiveness

— **en·hance·ment** \-mənt\ *n* — **en·hanc·er** *n*

enig·ma \i-'nig-mə\ *n* : something hard to understand or explain   **syn** see MYSTERY — **en·ig·mat·ic** \,en-ig-'mat-ik, ,ē-nig-\ *also* **en·ig·mat·i·cal** \-'mat-i-kəl\ *adj* — **en·ig·mat·i·cal·ly** \-i-k(ə-)lē\ *adv*

en·join \in-'jȯin\ *vb*   **1** : to direct or demand (an action) by authoritative order (as from a court of law)   **2** : FORBID 1, PROHIBIT

en·joy \in-'jȯi\ *vb*   **1** : to have or experience as a benefit or for one's use ⟨*enjoy* great success⟩ ⟨*enjoying* the freedom to pursue one's interests⟩   **2** : to take pleasure from ⟨I didn't *enjoy* the movie⟩ — **en·joy·able** \-ə-bəl\ *adj* — **en·joy·able·ness** *n* — **en·joy·ably** \-blē\ *adv*

en·joy·ment \in-'jȯi-mənt\ *n*   **1** : the condition of enjoying something : possession and use of something with satisfaction ⟨the *enjoyment* of good health⟩   **2** : satisfaction taken in something ⟨find *enjoyment* in skating⟩   **3** : something that gives pleasure   **syn** see PLEASURE

en·large \in-'lärj\ *vb* **en·larged; en·larg·ing**   **1** : to make or grow larger : INCREASE, EXPAND   **2** : to give more details : ELABORATE ⟨*enlarge* on a story⟩ — **en·larg·er** *n*

en·large·ment \in-'lärj-mənt\ *n*   **1** : an act or instance of enlarging : the state of being enlarged   **2** : a photographic print made larger than the negative

en·light·en \in-'līt-ᵊn\ *vb* **en·light·ened; en·light·en·ing** \-'līt-niŋ, -ᵊn-iŋ\ : to give knowledge or understanding to : INSTRUCT — **en·light·en·ment** \-ᵊn-mənt\ *n*

en·list \in-'list\ *vb*   **1 a** : to enroll for military or naval service; *esp* : to join one of the armed services voluntarily   **b** : to participate heartily (as in a cause or drive)   **2** : to obtain the help or support of ⟨*enlisted* their friends in the campaign⟩ — **en·list·ment** \-'lis(t)-mənt\ *n*

en·list·ed \in-'lis-təd\ *adj* : of, relating to, or forming the part of a military or naval force in the ranks below commissioned or warrant officers

en·liv·en \in-'lī-vən\ *vb* : to give life, action, or spirit to : ANIMATE

en masse \än-'mas\ *adv* : in a body : as a whole

en·mesh \in-'mesh\ *vb* : to entangle in or as if in meshes ⟨was *enmeshed* in a series of disputes⟩

en·mi·ty \'en-mət-ē\ *n, pl* **-ties** : a very deep unfriendly feeling : HATRED

en·no·ble \in-'ō-bəl\ *vb* **-bled; -bling** \-b(ə-)liŋ\   **1** : to make noble : ELEVATE   **2** : to raise to the rank of nobility — **en·no·ble·ment** \-bəl-mənt\ *n*

en·nui \'än-'wē\ *n* : a lack of spirit, enthusiasm, or satisfaction : BOREDOM

enor·mi·ty \i-'nȯr-mət-ē\ *n, pl* **-ties**   **1** : the quality of being overly or shockingly large and troublesome ⟨had not been aware of the *enormity* of the job⟩ ⟨the *enormity* of the offense⟩   **2** : an outrageous act or offense

enor·mous \i-'nȯr-məs\ *adj* : extraordinarily great in size, number, or degree — **enor·mous·ly** *adv* — **enor·mous·ness** *n*

　　syn ENORMOUS, IMMENSE, HUGE, VAST mean unusually large. ENORMOUS suggests going beyond the usual limits in size, amount, or degree ⟨the *enormous* cost of the new building⟩ IMMENSE suggests size far beyond ordinary measurements or ideas ⟨an *immense* waste of our natural resources⟩ HUGE suggests greatness of bulk, size, or capacity ⟨*huge* barrels of oil⟩ VAST suggests greatness or broadness of extent ⟨*vast* stretches of desert⟩

¹enough \i-'nəf\ *adj* : equal to the demands or needs : SUFFICIENT

²enough *adv*   **1** : in sufficient amount or degree : SUFFI-

\ə\ abut		\au̇\ **out**	\i\ **tip**	\ȯ\ **saw**	\u̇\ **foot**
\ər\ **further**		\ch\ **chin**	\ī\ **life**	\ȯi\ **coin**	\y\ **yet**
\a\ **mat**		\e\ **pet**	\j\ **job**	\th\ **thin**	\yü\ **few**
\ā\ **take**		\ē\ **easy**	\ŋ\ **sing**	\t͟h\ **this**	\yu̇\ **cure**
\ä\ **cot, cart**		\g\ **go**	\ō\ **bone**	\ü\ **food**	\zh\ **vision**

CIENTLY ⟨ran fast *enough*⟩ **2** : FULLY 1, QUITE ⟨ready *enough* to blame someone else for your mistakes⟩ **3** : so as to be moderately good : TOLERABLY ⟨sang well *enough*⟩

³**enough** *n* : a sufficient quantity ⟨*enough* to meet our needs⟩

enow \i-ʹnaů\ *adv or adj, archaic* : ENOUGH

en·plane \in-ʹplān\ *vb* : to board an airplane

enquire, enquiry *variant of* INQUIRE, INQUIRY

en·rage \in-ʹrāj\ *vb* : to fill with rage : MADDEN

en·rap·ture \in-ʹrap-chər\ *vb* **en·rap·tured; en·rap·tur·ing** \-ʹrap-chə-riŋ, -ʹrap-shriŋ\ : to fill with delight

en·rich \in-ʹrich\ *vb* **1** : to make rich or richer ⟨*enrich* the mind⟩ **2** : ADORN, ORNAMENT **3 a** : to make (soil) more fertile **b** : to improve the value of (food) for nutrition by adding vitamins and minerals in processing **c** : to increase the proportion of a desirable ingredient ⟨*enriched* uranium⟩ ⟨*enriched* natural gas⟩ — **en·rich·ment** \-mənt\ *n*

en·roll *or* **en·rol** \in-ʹrōl\ *vb* **en·rolled; en·roll·ing** **1** : to enter in a list or roll : REGISTER **2 a** : to take into membership **b** : to become a member : JOIN, ENTER ⟨*enroll* in the army⟩ ⟨*enroll* in school⟩ — **en·roll·ment** \-mənt\ *n*

en route \än-ʹrüt, en-, in-\ *adv* : on or along the way

en·sconce \in-ʹskän(t)s\ *vb* **en·sconced; en·sconc·ing** **1** : to place or hide securely : CONCEAL ⟨*ensconced* myself behind a tree⟩ **2** : to establish comfortably : settle snugly

en·sem·ble \än-ʹsäm-bəl\ *n* : a group of people or things making up a complete unit: as **a** : musicians that perform music in several parts; *also* : the music itself **b** : a set of clothes that look nice together [from French *ensemble* "group, ensemble", from *ensemble* (adjective) "together", from Latin *insimul* (same meaning), from *in-* "in, into" and *simul* "at the same time, together" — related to ASSEMBLE, SIMULTANEOUS]

en·shrine \in-ʹshrīn\ *vb* **en·shrined; en·shrin·ing** **1** : to enclose in or as if in a shrine **2** : to preserve or cherish as sacred

en·shroud \in-ʹshraůd\ *vb* : to cover or enclose with or as if with a shroud

en·sign \ʹen(t)-sən, *in senses 1 & 2 also* ʹen-ˌsīn\ *n* **1** : a flag flown as the symbol of nationality (as on a ship) **2** : a badge of office, rank, or power **3** : a naval commissioned officer of the lowest rank

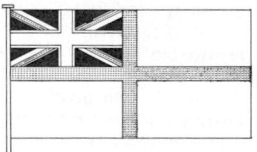

ensign 1

en·si·lage \ʹen(t)-sə-lij\ : the process of converting feed crops into silage; *also* : SILAGE

en·slave \in-ʹslāv\ *vb* : to make a slave of — **en·slave·ment** \-mənt\ *n* — **en·slav·er** *n*

en·snare \in-ʹsna(ə)r, -ʹsne(ə)r\ *vb* : ²SNARE 1, ENTRAP

en·sue \in-ʹsü\ *vb* **en·sued; en·su·ing** : to come at a later time or as a result : FOLLOW ⟨*ensuing* effects⟩

en·sure \in-ʹshů(ə)r\ *vb* **en·sured; en·sur·ing** : to make sure, certain, or safe : GUARANTEE

¹**en·tail** \in-ʹtā(ə)l\ *vb* **1** : to limit the inheritance of (property) to the owner's direct descendants or to a certain group of them **2** : to have as a necessary step or result — **en·tail·ment** \-mənt\ *n*

²**en·tail** \ʹen-ˌtāl, in-ʹtā(ə)l\ *n* **1 a** : an entailing especially of lands **b** : an entailed estate **2** : the rule fixing descent by entailment

en·tan·gle \in-ʹtaŋ-gəl\ *vb* **1** : ¹TANGLE 2, CONFUSE **2** : to involve in a tangle or a confused or difficult situation — **en·tan·gle·ment** \-mənt\ *n*

en·ter \ʹent-ər\ *vb* **en·tered; en·ter·ing** \ʹent-ə-riŋ, ʹen-triŋ\ **1** : to go or come in or into ⟨*enter* a room⟩ **2** : PENETRATE 1b, PIERCE ⟨the needle *enters* the skin at an

angle⟩ **3** : to cause to be admitted to ⟨*enter* a child in kindergarten⟩ **4** : to become a member of : JOIN **5** : to make a beginning ⟨*enter* into business⟩ **6** : to take part or play a part ⟨*enter* into a discussion⟩ ⟨*entered* the competition⟩ **7** : to take possession ⟨*entered* upon their inheritance⟩ **8 a** : to set down in a book or list ⟨*entered* my name on the roster⟩ **b** : to put in or into : INSERT ⟨*enter* the number 23 in a computer⟩ **9** : to place formally before a legal authority (as a court) ⟨*enter* a complaint⟩ — **en·ter·able** \ʹent-ə-rə-bəl, ʹen-trə-\ *adj*

en·ter·i·tis \ˌent-ə-ʹrīt-əs\ *n* : inflammation of the intestines; *also* : a disease marked by this

en·ter·prise \ʹent-ə(r)-ˌprīz\ *n* **1** : a difficult, complicated, or risky project or undertaking **2** : a business organization **3** : readiness to engage in daring or difficult action — **en·ter·pris·er** \-ˌprī-zər\ *n*

en·ter·pris·ing \ʹent-ə(r)-ˌprī-ziŋ\ *adj* : bold, active, and energetic in undertaking or experimenting

en·ter·tain \ˌent-ər-ʹtān\ *vb* **1** : to receive and provide for as host : have as a guest ⟨*entertain* friends over the weekend⟩ **2 a** : to provide entertainment **b** : to be a source of entertainment for ⟨*entertain* us with stories⟩ **3** : to have in mind : CONSIDER ⟨*entertained* thoughts of quitting⟩ **syn** *see* AMUSE

en·ter·tain·er \ˌent-ər-ʹtā-nər\ *n* : one that entertains; *esp* : one who gives or takes part in public entertainments

en·ter·tain·ing \ˌent-ər-ʹtān-iŋ\ *adj* : providing amusement, diversion, or recreation ⟨an *entertaining* book⟩ — **en·ter·tain·ing·ly** *adv*

en·ter·tain·ment \ˌent-ər-ʹtān-mənt\ *n* **1** : the act or process of providing pleasure, recreation, or amusement **2** : a means of amusement or recreation; *esp* : a public performance

en·thrall *or* **en·thral** \in-ʹthrol\ *vb* **en·thralled; en·thrall·ing** : to hold by or as if by a spell : CHARM — **en·thrall·ment** \-mənt\ *n*

en·throne \in-ʹthrōn\ *vb* **en·throned; en·thron·ing** **1 a** : to seat formally on a throne **b** : to install in office or in a position of authority **2** : to place high value on : EXALT — **en·throne·ment** \-mənt\ *n*

en·thuse \in-ʹth(y)üz\ *vb* **en·thused; en·thus·ing** **1** : to make enthusiastic **2** : to show enthusiasm

en·thu·si·asm \in-ʹth(y)ü-zē-ˌaz-əm\ *n* **1** : strong excitement and active interest **2** : something causing a feeling of excitement and active interest

en·thu·si·ast \in-ʹth(y)ü-zē-ˌast, -əst\ *n* : a person filled with enthusiasm

en·thu·si·as·tic \in-ˌth(y)ü-zē-ʹas-tik\ *adj* : filled with or marked by enthusiasm — **en·thu·si·as·ti·cal·ly** \-ti-k(ə-)lē\ *adv*

en·tice \in-ʹtīs\ *vb* **en·ticed; en·tic·ing** : to attract by arousing hope or desire : TEMPT — **en·tice·ment** \-mənt\ *n* — **en·tic·ing·ly** \-iŋ-lē\ *adv*

en·tire \in-ʹtī(ə)r, ʹen-ˌtī(ə)r\ *adj* **1** : having no element or part left out : COMPLETE **2** : being to the fullest degree : TOTAL ⟨her *entire* devotion⟩ **3** : having the margin continuous and free from indentations ⟨an *entire* leaf⟩ — **en·tire** *adv* — **en·tire·ly** *adv* — **en·tire·ness** *n*

en·tire·ty \in-ʹtī-rət-ē, -ʹtī(ə)rt-ē\ *n* : the state of being entire or complete — **in its entirety** : taking or involving the whole of something

en·ti·tle \in-ʹtīt-ᵊl\ *vb* **en·ti·tled; en·ti·tling** \-ʹtīt-liŋ, -ᵊl-iŋ\ **1** : to give a title to **2** : to give a right to : QUALIFY ⟨the card *entitles* us to a discount⟩ — **en·ti·tle·ment** \-ᵊl-mənt\ *n*

en·ti·ty \ʹent-ət-ē\ *n, pl* **-ties** : something existing or thought of as existing as a separate and independent thing

en·tomb \in-ʹtüm\ *vb* : to place in a tomb : BURY — **en·tomb·ment** \-ʹtüm-mənt\ *n*

en·to·mol·o·gist \ˌent-ə-ʹmäl-ə-jəst\ *n* : a person who specializes in entomology

en·to·mol·o·gy \ˌent-ə-ʹmäl-ə-jē\ *n* : a branch of zoology that deals with insects — **en·to·mo·log·i·cal** \-'läj-i-kəl\ *adj*

en·trails \'en-trəlz, -ˌtrālz\ *n pl* : internal organs : VISCERA; *esp* : the part of the digestive system composed of the intestines

en·train \in-'trān\ *vb* : to put or go aboard a train

¹en·trance \'en-trən(t)s\ *n*   **1** : the act of entering ⟨made an *entrance*⟩   **2 a** : the means or place of entry   **b** : a point in a play where a character comes on stage ⟨watch for your *entrance*⟩   **3** : the right to enter : ADMISSION ⟨gained *entrance* to the club⟩ ⟨an *entrance* exam⟩

²en·trance \in-'tran(t)s\ *vb* **en·tranced; en·tranc·ing**   **1** : to put into a trance   **2** : to fill with delight, wonder, or overwhelming emotion — **en·trance·ment** \-mənt\ *n*

en·trant \'en-trənt\ *n* : one that enters; *esp* : one that enters a contest

en·trap \in-'trap\ *vb* : to catch in or as if in a trap — **en·trap·ment** \-mənt\ *n*

en·treat \in-'trēt\ *vb* : to ask in a serious and urgent manner : PLEAD, BEG — **en·treat·ing·ly** \-iŋ-lē\ *adv*

en·treaty \in-'trēt-ē\ *n, pl* **-treat·ies** : earnest request : APPEAL, PLEA

en·trée *or* **en·tree** \'än-ˌtrā\ *n*   **1** : the principal dish of the meal   **2** : ¹ENTRANCE 1, 3 [from French *entrée* "act or manner of entering"]

en·trench \in-'trench\ *vb*   **1 a** : to dig, place within, surround with, or occupy a trench especially for defense   **b** : to establish solidly   **2** : ENCROACH 1 — used with *on* or *upon*

en·trench·ment \in-'trench-mənt\ *n*   **1** : the act of entrenching : the state of being entrenched   **2** : DEFENSE 3a; *esp* : a defensive work consisting of a trench and a wall of earth

en·trust \in-'trəst\ *vb*   **1** : to give into the care of another ⟨*entrust* your savings to a bank⟩   **2** : to give custody, care, or charge of something to ⟨*entrust* a bank with your savings⟩ — **en·trust·ment** \-'trəs(t)-mənt\ *n*

en·try \'en-trē\ *n, pl* **entries**   **1** : the act or opportunity of entering : ENTRANCE ⟨gained *entry* through a back window⟩   **2** : a place through which entrance is made : HALL, VESTIBULE   **3 a** : the act of making a written record of something (as in a book or list) or of putting data into a calculator or computer   **b** : the thing recorded (as in a book or list) ⟨dictionary *entries*⟩

en·try·way \'en-trē-ˌwā\ *n* : ENTRY 2

entry word *n* : a word entered in a list or book; *esp* : a word in boldface type that is being explained in a dictionary

en·twine \in-'twīn\ *vb* : to twine together or around

enu·mer·ate \i-'n(y)ü-mə-ˌrāt\ *vb* **-at·ed; -at·ing**   **1** : to find out the number of : COUNT   **2** : to list one after another — **enu·mer·a·tion** \-ˌn(y)ü-mə-'rā-shən\ *n*

enun·ci·ate \ē-'nən(t)-sē-ˌāt\ *vb* **-at·ed; -at·ing**   **1** : ANNOUNCE 1, PROCLAIM   **2** : to pronounce clearly : ARTICULATE — **enun·ci·a·tion** \-ˌnən(t)-sē-'ā-shən\ *n* — **enun·ci·a·tor** \-'nən(t)-sē-ˌāt-ər\ *n*

en·vel·op \in-'vel-əp\ *vb* : to surround and enclose completely with or as if with a covering — **en·vel·op·ment** \-mənt\ *n*

en·ve·lope \'en-və-ˌlōp, 'än-\ *n*   **1** : something that envelops   **2** : a flat usually paper container (as for a letter)   **3** : the bag containing the gas or hot air in a balloon or airship   **4** : a natural enclosing covering (as a membrane)

en·ven·om \in-'ven-əm\ *vb*   **1** : to poison with venom   **2** : to cause to feel bitterness or hatred

en·vi·able \'en-vē-ə-bəl\ *adj* : likely to be the object of envy : highly desirable — **en·vi·able·ness** *n* — **en·vi·ably** \-blē\ *adv*

en·vi·ous \'en-vē-əs\ *adj* : feeling or showing envy ⟨*envious* of a neighbor's good luck⟩ ⟨an *envious* look⟩ — **en·vi·ous·ly** *adv* — **en·vi·ous·ness** *n*

en·vi·ron \in-'vī-rən, -'vī(-ə)rn\ *vb* : ENCIRCLE 1, SURROUND

en·vi·ron·ment \in-'vī-rən-mənt, -'vī(-ə)rn-\ *n*   **1** : SURROUNDINGS ⟨their home was in a comfortable rural *environment*⟩   **2** : the surrounding conditions or forces that influence or modify: as   **a** : the whole complex of factors (as soil, climate, and living things) that influence the form and the ability to survive of a plant or animal or ecological community   **b** : the social and cultural conditions that influence the life of a person or human community ⟨an unhappy home *environment*⟩ — **en·vi·ron·men·tal** \-ˌvī-rən-'ment-ᵊl, -ˌvī(-ə)rn-\ *adj* — **en·vi·ron·men·tal·ly** \-ᵊl-ē\ *adv*

en·vi·rons \in-'vī-rənz, -'vī(-ə)rnz\ *n pl*   **1** : the districts around a city   **2** : SURROUNDINGS

en·vis·age \in-'viz-ij\ *vb* **-aged; -ag·ing** : to have a mental picture of : VISUALIZE

en·voy \'en-ˌvȯi, 'än-\ *n*   **1 a** : a diplomatic representative who ranks between an ambassador and a minister   **b** : a representative sent by one government to another ⟨ambassadors and other *envoys*⟩   **2** : ²REPRESENTATIVE 2, AGENT

¹en·vy \'en-vē\ *n, pl* **envies**   **1** : painful or resentful awareness of an advantage or possession enjoyed by another joined with a desire to possess the same thing   **2** : an object of envy ⟨she was the *envy* of all her friends⟩

²envy *vb* **en·vied; en·vy·ing** : to feel envy toward or on account of — **en·vi·er** *n* — **en·vy·ing·ly** \-iŋ-lē\ *adv*

en·wrap \in-'rap\ *vb* : ENFOLD 1, ENVELOP

en·zyme \'en-ˌzīm\ *n* : any of various complex proteins produced by living cells that bring about or accelerate reaction (as in the digestion of food) at body temperatures without being permanently altered — **en·zy·mat·ic** \ˌen-zə-'matik\ *adj* — **en·zy·mat·i·cal·ly** \-'mat-i-k(ə-)lē\ *adv*

Eo·cene \'ē-ə-ˌsēn\ *adj* : of, relating to, or being an epoch of the Tertiary period of geological history or the corresponding system of rocks — see GEOLOGIC TIME table — **Eocene** *n*

eo·hip·pus \ˌē-ō-'hip-əs\ *n* : any of a genus of small primitive four-toed horses from the Eocene epoch of the western U.S.

eo·lian \ē-'ō-lē-ən, -'ōl-yən\ *adj* : carried, deposited, produced, or eroded by the wind ⟨*eolian* sand⟩

Eo·lith·ic \ˌē-ə-'lith-ik\ *adj* : of or relating to the earliest period of the Stone Age marked by the use of very crudely chipped flint tools

eon \'ē-ən, 'ē-ˌän\ *variant of* AEON

eo·sin·o·phil \ˌē-ə-'sin-ə-ˌfil\ *n* : a cell and especially a white blood cell with a granule-containing cytoplasm that takes up a special dye

-eous *adj suffix* : resembling : being : having the form or qualities of ⟨gas*eous*⟩ [from Latin *-eus* (adjective suffix)]

ep·au·let *also* **ep·au·lette** \ˌep-ə-'let, 'ep-ə-ˌlet\ *n* : a shoulder ornament on a uniform especially of a military or naval officer

ephed·rine \i-'fed-rən\ *n* : a basic substance obtained from Chinese woody plants or made artificially and used as a salt in relieving hay fever, asthma, and nasal congestion

ephem·er·al \i-'fem-(ə-)rəl\ *adj*   **1** : lasting one day only   **2** : lasting a very short time — **ephem·er·al·ly** \-rə-lē\ *adv*

E epaulet

Ephe·sians \i-'fē-zhənz\ *n* — see BIBLE table

epi- *prefix* : over : upon ⟨*epi*phyte⟩ [derived from Greek *epi*

\ə\ abut	\au̇\ out	\i\ tip	\ȯ\ saw	\u̇\ foot
\ər\ further	\ch\ chin	\ī\ life	\ȯi\ coin	\y\ yet
\a\ mat	\e\ pet	\j\ job	\th\ thin	\yü\ few
\ā\ take	\ē\ easy	\ŋ\ sing	\th\ this	\yu̇\ cure
\ä\ cot, cart	\g\ go	\ō\ bone	\ü\ food	\zh\ vision

"on, at"]

ep·ic \'ep-ik\ *n* : a long poem telling of the deeds of a hero and often centering on the ideals of a nation or culture — **epic** *adj*

epi·cen·ter \'ep-i-,sent-ər\ *n* : the part of the earth's surface directly above the starting point of an earthquake

ep·i·cure \'ep-i-,kyů(ə)r\ *n* : a person with carefully improved tastes in food or wine [named for *Epicurus*, an ancient Greek philosopher who believed pleasure to be the chief aim of life] — **ep·i·cu·re·an** \,ep-i-kyů-'rē-ən, -'kyůr-ē-\ *adj or n*

epi·cy·cle \'ep-ə-,sī-kəl\ *n* : a circle according to an early astronomy theory in which a planet moves and which has a center that is itself carried around at the same time on the circumference of a larger circle

¹ep·i·dem·ic \,ep-ə-'dem-ik\ *adj* : spreading widely and affecting many individuals at one time [from French *épidémique* (adjective) "epidemic", derived from early French *epidemie* (noun) "an epidemic", from Latin *epidemia* (same meaning), from Greek *epidēmia* "an epidemic, visit", derived from *epi-* "on, at" and *dēmos* "people, the masses" — related to DEMOCRACY]

²epidemic *n* **1** : an outbreak of epidemic disease **2** : a sudden rapidly spreading outbreak or growth ⟨a crime *epidemic*⟩

ep·i·de·mi·ol·o·gist \,ep-ə-,dē-mē-'äl-ə-jəst\ *n* : a person who specializes in epidemiology

ep·i·de·mi·ol·o·gy \,ep-ə-,dē-mē-'äl-ə-jē\ *n* **1** : a branch of medical science that deals with the occurrence, distribution, and control of disease in a population **2** : the sum of the factors controlling the presence or absence of a particular disease — **ep·i·de·mi·o·log·i·cal** \-mē-ə-'läj-i-kəl\ *also* **ep·i·de·mi·o·log·ic** \-'läj-ik\ *adj*

epi·der·mal \,ep-ə-'dər-məl\ *adj* : of, relating to, or arising from the epidermis ⟨*epidermal* tissues⟩

epi·der·mis \,ep-ə-'dər-məs\ *n* **1** : the thin outer layer of the animal body that in vertebrates forms an insensitive covering over the dermis **2** : a thin surface layer of protecting cells in seed plants and ferns

ep·i·did·y·mis \,ep-ə-'did-ə-məs\ *n, pl* **-did·y·mi·des** \-'did-ə-mə-,dēz\ : a mass at the back of the testis composed of coiled tubes in which sperms are stored

epi·glot·tis \,ep-ə-'glät-əs\ *n* : a thin plate of flexible cartilage in front of the glottis that folds back over and protects the glottis during swallowing — **epi·glot·tal** \-'glät-ºl\ *adj*

ep·i·gram \'ep-ə-,gram\ *n* **1** : a short poem ending with a clever or witty expression **2** : a brief witty saying — **ep·i·gram·ma·tist** \,ep-ə-'gram-ət-əst\ *n*

ep·i·gram·mat·ic \,ep-ə-grə-'mat-ik\ *adj* **1** : of, relating to, or resembling an epigram **2** : given to the use of epigrams — **ep·i·gram·mat·i·cal** \-'mat-i-kəl\ *adj* — **ep·i·gram·mat·i·cal·ly** \-i-k(ə-)lē\ *adv*

ep·i·lep·sy \'ep-ə-,lep-sē\ *n* : a disorder marked by disturbed electrical rhythms of the central nervous system, by attacks of convulsions, and by loss of consciousness

¹ep·i·lep·tic \,ep-ə-'lep-tik\ *adj* : of, relating to, or having epilepsy ⟨an *epileptic* seizure⟩

²epileptic *n* : a person who has epilepsy

ep·i·logue *also* **ep·i·log** \'ep-ə-,lòg, -,läg\ *n* **1** : a final section that brings to an end and summarizes or comments on the action or characters of a story **2** : a speech often in verse addressed to the audience by an actor at the end of a play

ep·i·neph·rine \,ep-ə-'nef-rən\ *n* : a hormone of the adrenal gland acting especially on smooth muscle, causing narrowing of blood vessels, and raising blood pressure — called also *adrenaline*

Epiph·a·ny \i-'pif-ə-nē\ *n* : January 6 observed as a Christian festival in honor of the coming of the three kings to the infant Jesus or in the Eastern church in celebration of Christ's baptism

ep·i·phyte \'ep-ə-,fīt\ *n* : a plant that gets moisture and the materials needed to make its food from the air and rain and that usually grows on another plant

ep·i·phyt·ic \,ep-ə-'fit-ik\ *adj* **1** : of, relating to, or being an epiphyte **2** : living on the surface of plants

epis·co·pa·cy \i-'pis-kə-pə-sē\ *n, pl* **-cies** **1** : government of a church by bishops **2** : EPISCOPATE 2

epis·co·pal \i-'pis-kə-pəl\ *adj* **1** : of or relating to a bishop or episcopacy **2** *cap* : of or relating to the Protestant Episcopal Church [Middle English *episcopal* "relating to a bishop", from Latin *episcopalis* (same meaning), from *episcopus* "bishop", from Greek *episkopos*, literally "overseer", from *epi-* "over" and *skopos* "watcher, goal, object" — related to BISHOP, HOROSCOPE, SCOPE; see *Word History* at BISHOP] — **epis·co·pal·ly** \-p(ə-)lē\ *adv*

Epis·co·pa·lian \i-,pis-kə-'pāl-yən\ *n* : a member of the Protestant Episcopal Church — **Episcopalian** *adj* — **Epis·co·pa·lian·ism** \-yə-,niz-əm\ *n*

epis·co·pate \i-'pis-kə-pət\ *n* **1** : the rank, office, or term of office of a bishop **2** : the whole body of bishops

epis·i·ot·o·my \i-,piz-ē-'ät-ə-mē\ *n, pl* **-mies** : an operation to enlarge the opening of the external female genitalia at the time of childbirth to make delivery easier

ep·i·sode \'ep-ə-,sōd\ *n* : an event that is part of a longer story or of history or a life but which is viewed as complete by itself — **ep·i·sod·ic** \,ep-ə-'säd-ik\ *adj*

epis·tle \i-'pis-əl\ *n* **1** *cap* : any of the letters to the early Christians that are part of the New Testament **2** : a formal letter

epis·to·lary \i-'pis-tə-,ler-ē\ *adj* : of, relating to, or suitable to a letter

ep·i·taph \'ep-ə-,taf\ *n* : something written (as on a gravestone) in memory of a dead person

ep·i·the·li·um \,ep-ə-'thē-lē-əm\ *n, pl* **-lia** \-lē-ə\ **1** : a tissue like a membrane that is made up of cells and covers a free surface or lines a tube or cavity of an animal body **2** : a usually thin layer of cells of a plant that is part of the parenchyma and lines a cavity or tube — **ep·i·the·li·al** \-lē-əl\ *adj*

ep·i·thet \'ep-ə-,thet\ *n* **1** : a word or phrase (as *Lion-Hearted* in "Richard the Lion-Hearted") that expresses a quality thought to be characteristic of a person or thing; *also* : a word or name used as a term of abuse **2** : the part of a taxonomic name identifying a subordinate unit within a genus — **ep·i·thet·ic** \,ep-ə-'thet-ik\ *or* **ep·i·thet·i·cal** \-'thet-i-kəl\ *adj*

epit·o·me \i-'pit-ə-mē\ *n* **1** : ²SUMMARY, ABSTRACT **2** : something thought to represent a basic quality or an ideal example ⟨your response was the *epitome* of good sense⟩

epit·o·mize \i-'pit-ə-,mīz\ *vb* **-mized; -miz·ing** : to make or serve as an epitome of

ep·och \'ep-ək, -,äk *also* 'ē-,päk\ *n* **1** : an event or a time that begins a new period of development **2** : a memorable event, date, or period **3** : a division of geologic time less than a period and greater than an age — **ep·och·al** \-əl\ *adj* — **ep·och·al·ly** \-ə-lē\ *adv*

ep·oxy \i-'päk-sē\ *n, pl* **epoxies** : EPOXY RESIN

epoxy resin *n* : a synthetic resin used chiefly in coatings and adhesives

ep·si·lon \'ep-sə-,län, -lən\ *n* : the 5th letter of the Greek alphabet — E or ε

Ep·som salt \,ep-səm-\ *n* : a bitter colorless or white salt of magnesium used especially as a strong laxative — usually used in pl.

equa·ble \'ek-wə-bəl, 'ē-kwə-\ *adj* : ¹UNIFORM 1; *esp* : free from extremes or sudden or harsh changes ⟨an *equable* temper⟩ ⟨an *equable* climate⟩ — **eq·ua·bly** \-blē\ *adv*

¹equal \'ē-kwəl\ *adj* **1 a** : exactly the same in number, amount, degree, rank, or quality ⟨an *equal* number of apples and oranges⟩ ⟨officers of *equal* rank⟩ ⟨of *equal* importance⟩ **b** : identical in mathematical value : EQUIVALENT **2** : not varying from one person or part to another ⟨*equal* job opportunities⟩ ⟨*equal* pressure throughout the system⟩

3 : IMPARTIAL ⟨*equal* laws⟩   **4** : capable of meeting requirements : SUFFICIENT ⟨*equal* to the task⟩   **syn** see SAME — **equal·ly** *adv*

²equal *n*   **1** : one that is equal ⟨has no *equal* at chess⟩   **2** : an equal quantity

³equal *vb* **equaled** *or* **equalled; equal·ing** *or* **equal·ling**   **1** : to be equal to   **2** : to produce something equal to : MATCH ⟨see if you can *equal* that!⟩

equal·i·ty \i-'kwäl-ət-ē\ *n, pl* **-ties** : the quality, fact, or state of being equal

equal·ize \'ē-kwə-,līz\ *vb* **-ized; -iz·ing**   **1** : to make equal   **2** : to make uniform; *esp* : to distribute evenly — **equal·iza·tion** \,ē-kwə-lə-'zā-shən\ *n* — **equal·iz·er** \'ē-kwə-,lī-zər\ *n*

equal sign *n* : a sign = indicating mathmetical or logical equivalence — called also *equality sign, equals sign*

equa·nim·i·ty \,ē-kwə-'nim-ət-ē, ,ek-wə-\ *n, pl* **-ties** : evenness of emotions or temper : COMPOSURE ⟨accept misfortunes with *equanimity*⟩

equate \i-'kwāt\ *vb* **equat·ed; equat·ing** : to make or treat as equal or equivalent

equa·tion \i-'kwā-zhən *also* -shən\ *n*   **1** : the act or process of equating : the state of being equated   **2 a** : a statement of the equality of two mathematical expressions   **b** : an expression involving chemical symbols for a chemical reaction

equa·tor \i-'kwāt-ər, 'ē-,kwāt-\ *n* : an imaginary circle around the earth everywhere equally distant from the north pole and the south pole

equa·to·ri·al \,ē-kwə-'tōr-ē-əl, ,ek-wə-, -'tór-\ *adj*   **1** : of, relating to, or located at the equator   **2** : of, originating in, or suggesting the region around the equator ⟨*equatorial* heat⟩

equer·ry \'ek-wə-rē, i-'kwer-ē\ *n, pl* **equerries**   **1** : an officer in charge of the horses of a prince or nobleman   **2** : a personal attendant of a member of the British royal family

¹eques·tri·an \i-'kwes-trē-ən\ *adj*   **1** : of or relating to horses, horseback riding, or people who ride horses   **2** : mounted on horseback ⟨*equestrian* troops⟩

²equestrian *n* : one who rides on horseback

eques·tri·enne \i-,kwes-trē-'en\ *n* : a girl or woman who is an equestrian

equi- *combining form* : equal ⟨*equi*poise⟩ : equally ⟨*equi*angular⟩ [derived from Latin *aequi-* "equal"]

equi·an·gu·lar \,ē-kwi-'aŋ-gyə-lər, ,ek-wi-\ *adj* : having all or corresponding angles equal

equi·dis·tant \,ē-kwə-'dis-tənt, ,ek-wə-\ *adj* : equally distant

equi·lat·er·al \,ē-kwə-'lat-ə-rəl, ,ek-wə-, -'la-trəl\ *adj* : having all sides or faces equal ⟨an *equilateral* triangle⟩

equi·lib·ri·um \,ē-kwə-'lib-rē-əm, ,ek-wə-\ *n, pl* **-ri·ums** *or* **-ria** \-rē-ə\   **1** : a state of balance between opposing forces or actions   **2** : the normal balanced state of the body of an animal that is maintained in relation to the forces (as gravity) acting on it and to things in the environment (as the surface on which life is lived) and that is sensed and checked by the inner ear of vertebrates including human beings [from Latin *aequilibrium* "state of being in balance", derived from *aequus* "equal" and *libra* "weight, balance, scales" — related to DELIBERATE, LIBRA]

equine \'ē-,kwīn, 'ek-,wīn\ *adj* : of, relating to, or resembling a horse or a closely related animal — **equine** *n*

equi·noc·tial \,ē-kwə-'näk-shəl, ,ek-wə-\ *adj*   **1** : of, relating to, or occurring at or near an equinox   **2** : of or relating to the regions or climate near the equator : EQUATORIAL

equi·nox \'ē-kwə-,näks, 'ek-wə-\ *n* : either of the two times each year about March 21 and September 23 when the sun appears overhead at the equator and day and night are everywhere of equal length [Middle English *equinox* "equinox", from early French *equinoxe* or Latin *equinoxium* (both, same meaning), derived from earlier Latin *aequi-* "equal" and *noct-, nox* "night" — related to NOCTURNAL]

equip \i-'kwip\ *vb* **equipped; equip·ping** : to provide with the necessary materials or supplies for service or action; *also* : PREPARE 1

eq·ui·page \'ek-wə-pij\ *n*   **1** : things that serve as equipment   **2** : a horse-drawn carriage with or without attendants

equip·ment \i-'kwip-mənt\ *n*   **1 a** : the act of equipping a person or thing   **b** : the state of being equipped   **2** : the articles serving to equip a person or thing

equi·poise \'ek-wə-,póiz, 'ē-kwə-\ *n*   **1** : a state of balance : EQUILIBRIUM   **2** : a weight used to balance another weight

eq·ui·se·tum \,ek-wə-'sēt-əm\ *n, pl* **-se·tums** *or* **-se·ta** \-'sēt-ə\ : any of a genus of primitive plants that produce spores and have hollow stems with joints and leaves reduced to sheaths about the joints — called also *horsetail, scouring rush*

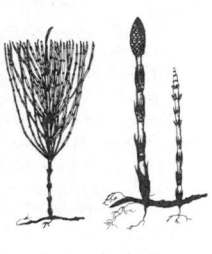

equisetum

eq·ui·ta·ble \'ek-wət-ə-bəl\ *adj* : being fair or just ⟨reached an *equitable* settlement of their dispute⟩ — **eq·ui·ta·ble·ness** *n* — **eq·ui·ta·bly** \-blē\ *adv*

eq·ui·ta·tion \,ek-wə-'tā-shən\ *n* : the action or art of riding on horseback

eq·ui·ty \'ek-wət-ē\ *n, pl* **-ties**   **1** : fairness or justice in dealings between persons   **2** : a system of law that is a more flexible addition to ordinary common and statute law and is designed to protect rights and achieve just settlements in cases where ordinary legal settlements may be too strict   **3** : the value of an owner's interest in a property in excess of claims against it (as the amount of a mortgage)

equiv·a·lence \i-'kwiv-(ə-)lən(t)s\ *n* : the quality or state of being equivalent

equiv·a·len·cy \i-'kwiv-(ə-)lən-sē\ *n, pl* **-cies** : EQUIVALENCE

¹equiv·a·lent \i-'kwiv-(ə-)lənt\ *adj*   **1 a** : alike or equal in number, value, or meaning   **b** : having the same numerical value ⟨*equivalent* fractions⟩ ⟨*equivalent* numerals⟩   **c** : having the same solution set ⟨y = 2 and 2y = 4 are *equivalent* equations⟩   **2** : having the same effect or function ⟨*equivalent* statements⟩   **3** : capable of being placed in a one-to-one correspondence ⟨*equivalent* sets⟩   **syn** see IDENTICAL — **equiv·a·lent·ly** *adv*

²equivalent *n* : one that is equivalent; *esp* : a number (as a decimal) that is equivalent to another (as a fraction written as the quotient of two integers) ⟨a table of fractional *equivalents*⟩

equiv·o·cal \i-'kwiv-ə-kəl\ *adj*   **1** : having two or more possible meanings : AMBIGUOUS ⟨an *equivocal* answer⟩   **2** : not easily or definitely understood : UNCERTAIN, DOUBTFUL ⟨an *equivocal* result⟩   **3** : SUSPICIOUS 1, QUESTIONABLE ⟨*equivocal* behavior⟩ — **equiv·o·cal·ly** \-k(ə-)lē\ *adv* — **equiv·o·cal·ness** \-kəl-nəs\ *n*

equiv·o·cate \i-'kwiv-ə-,kāt\ *vb* **-cat·ed; -cat·ing** : to use equivocal language especially in order to deceive; *also* : to avoid giving a definite answer — **equiv·o·ca·tion** \-,kwiv-ə-'kā-shən\ *n* — **equiv·o·ca·tor** \-'kwiv-ə-,kāt-ər\ *n*

¹-er \ər; *after some vowels, often* r; *after* ŋ, *usually* gər\ *adj suffix or adv suffix* — used to form the comparative degree of adjectives and adverbs of one syllable ⟨hott*er*⟩

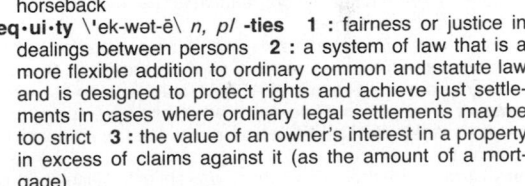

\ə\ abut	\aù\ out	\i\ tip	\ó\ saw	\ù\ foot
\ər\ further	\ch\ chin	\ī\ life	\ói\ coin	\y\ yet
\a\ mat	\e\ pet	\j\ job	\th\ thin	\yü\ few
\ā\ take	\ē\ easy	\ŋ\ sing	\th\ this	\yù\ cure
\ä\ cot, cart	\g\ go	\ō\ bone	\ü\ food	\zh\ vision

⟨dri*er*⟩ and of some adjectives and adverbs of two or more syllables ⟨complet*er*⟩ [Old English *-ra* (adjective suffix) or Old English *-or* (adverb suffix)]

²-er \ər; *after some vowels, often* r\ *also* **-ier** \ē-ər, yər\ *or* **-yer** \yər\ *n suffix* **1 a** : person connected with a particular job or occupation ⟨hatt*er*⟩ ⟨furri*er*⟩ ⟨law*yer*⟩ **b** : person or thing belonging to or associated with ⟨old-tim*er*⟩ **c** : native of : resident of ⟨New York*er*⟩ ⟨cottag*er*⟩ **d** : one that has ⟨double-deck*er*⟩ **e** : one that produces or yields ⟨pork*er*⟩ **2 a** : one that does or performs (a specified action) ⟨report*er*⟩ **b** : one that is a suitable object of (a specified action) ⟨broil*er*⟩ **3** : one that is ⟨foreign*er*⟩ [derived from Old English *-ere* and Latin *-arius* (both noun suffixes)]

era \'ir-ə, 'er-ə, 'ē-rə\ *n* **1** : a period of time beginning with some special date or event ⟨the Christian *era*⟩ **2** : an important or outstanding period of history ⟨the Revolutionary *era*⟩ **3** : one of the five major divisions of geologic time ⟨Paleozoic *era*⟩ **syn** see PERIOD

erad·i·cate \i-'rad-ə-ˌkāt\ *vb* **-cat·ed; -cat·ing** : to remove by or as if by uprooting : ELIMINATE, DESTROY ⟨*eradicate* weeds⟩ ⟨*eradicating* a disease⟩ [from Latin *eradicatus*, past participle of *eradicare* "to root out, pull up by the roots", from *e-, ex-* "out, forth" and *radic-, radix* "root" — related to RADICAL, RADISH; see *Word History* at RADICAL] — **erad·i·ca·tion** \-ˌrad-ə-'kā-shən\ *n*

erad·i·ca·tor \i-'rad-ə-ˌkāt-ər\ *n* : something that eradicates; *esp* : a chemical preparation for removing ink marks or stains by bleaching

erase \i-'rās\ *vb* **erased; eras·ing** **1** : to rub out (as something written) **2** : to remove as if by erasing ⟨*erase* an event from one's memory⟩ — **eras·able** \-'rā-sə-bəl\ *adj*

eras·er \i-'rā-sər\ *n* : one that erases; *esp* : a piece of rubber or a felt pad used to erase marks (as from a pencil or chalk)

era·sure \i-'rā-shər *also* -zhər\ *n* : an act or instance of erasing

er·bi·um \'ər-bē-əm\ *n* : a metallic element that occurs with yttrium — see ELEMENT table

¹ere \(ˌ)e(ə)r, (ˌ)a(ə)r\ *prep* : ²BEFORE 3

²ere *conj* : ³BEFORE 2

¹erect \i-'rekt\ *adj* **1** : straight up and down : UPRIGHT ⟨an *erect* pole⟩ ⟨*erect* poplars⟩ **2** : straight in posture ⟨sit *erect*⟩ **3** : directed upward : RAISED ⟨a tree with *erect* branches⟩ **4** : being in a state of physiological erection — **erect·ly** \-'rek-(t)lē\ *adv* — **erect·ness** \-'rek(t)-nəs\ *n*

²erect *vb* **1** : to put up or together by fitting together materials : BUILD, ASSEMBLE ⟨*erect* a building⟩ ⟨*erect* a playground slide⟩ **2** : to set upright ⟨*erect* a flagpole⟩ **3** : to construct (as a perpendicular) on a given base — **erec·tor** \i-'rek-tər\ *n*

erec·tile \i-'rek-tᵊl, -ˌtīl\ *adj* : capable of becoming erect ⟨*erectile* tissue⟩ ⟨*erectile* feathers of a bird⟩ — compare CAVERNOUS 3

erec·tion \i-'rek-shən\ *n* **1** : the process of erecting : the state of being erected **2 a** : the state marked by firm swollen form and erect position of a previously limp or flabby bodily part whose tissue becomes dilated with blood **b** : an occurrence of such a state in the penis or clitoris **3** : something erected

ere·long \e(ə)r-'lȯŋ, a(ə)r-\ *adv* : before long : SOON

er·e·mite \'er-ə-ˌmīt\ *n* : HERMIT 1; *esp* : a religious hermit

erep·sin \i-'rep-sən\ *n* : a mixture of peptidases from the intestinal juice

erg \'ərg\ *n* : a centimeter-gram-second unit of work equal to the work done by a force of one dyne acting through a distance of one centimeter and equal to one ten-millionth joule

er·go \'e(ə)r-gō, 'ər-\ *adv* : THEREFORE, HENCE

Er·len·mey·er flask \ˌər-lən-ˌmī(-ə)r-, ˌer-lən-\ *n* : a flat-bottomed laboratory flask that tapers upward to a straight neck [named for Emil *Erlenmeyer* 1825–1909 German

chemist]

er·mine \'ər-mən\ *n, pl* **ermine** *or* **ermines** **1** : any of several weasels with black on the tail and a brown coat of fur which usually becomes white in the winter **2** : the white fur of an ermine

erne *or* **ern** \'ərn, 'e(ə)rn\ *n* : EAGLE 1; *esp* : one with a white tail

erode \i-'rōd\ *vb* **erod·ed; erod·ing** **1 a** : to destroy gradually by chemical means : CORRODE **b** : to wear away by or as if by the action of water, wind, or glacial ice **2** : to undergo erosion [from Latin *erodere* "to eat away", from *e-* "away" and *rodere* "to gnaw" — related to RODENT]

ermine 1

ero·sion \i-'rō-zhən\ *n* : the action or process of eroding : the state of being eroded — **ero·sion·al** \-'rōzh-nəl, -'rō-zhən-ᵊl\ *adj*

ero·sive \i-'rō-siv, -ziv\ *adj* : tending to erode or to bring about or permit erosion ⟨the *erosive* effect of water⟩ — **ero·sive·ness** *n*

erot·ic \i-'rät-ik\ *adj* : of, relating to, or marked by sexual love or desire — **erot·i·cal·ly** \-'rät-i-k(ə-)lē\ *adv* — **erot·i·cism** \-'rät-ə-ˌsiz-əm\ *n*

err \'e(ə)r, 'ər\ *vb* **1** : to make a mistake ⟨*erred* in my calculations⟩ **2** : to do wrong : SIN

er·rand \'er-ənd\ *n* : a short trip taken to do or get something especially for someone else; *also* : the object or purpose of such a trip

er·rant \'er-ənt\ *adj* **1 a** : moving around from place to place without apparent purpose or goal **b** : wandering in search of adventure ⟨an *errant* knight⟩ **2 a** : straying outside proper bounds ⟨an *errant* calf⟩ **b** : behaving or having behaved badly or wrongfully — **er·rant·ry** \-ən-trē\ *n*

er·rat·ic \ir-'at-ik\ *adj* : marked by lack of consistency or regularity : ECCENTRIC ⟨*erratic* behavior⟩ — **er·rat·i·cal·ly** \-'at-i-k(ə-)lē\ *adv*

er·ro·ne·ous \ir-'ō-nē-əs, e-'rō-\ *adj* : being wrong or inaccurate; *esp* : being or containing an error ⟨an *erroneous* report⟩ — **er·ro·ne·ous·ly** *adv* — **er·ro·ne·ous·ness** *n*

er·ror \'er-ər\ *n* **1 a** : departure from a code of behavior ⟨the *error* of their ways⟩ **b** : an unintentional departure from truth, accuracy, or a goal ⟨made an *error* in my addition⟩ **c** : a misplay made by a fielder in baseball **2** : the quality or state of erring **3** : a false belief or a set of false beliefs **4** : something produced by mistake **5** : the difference between an observed or calculated value and a true value; *esp* : variation in measurements, calculations, or observations of a quantity as a result of mistakes or uncontrollable conditions **6** : the amount of error — **er·ror·less** \-ləs\ *adj*

syn ERROR, MISTAKE, BLUNDER mean a failure to speak or act according to truth, accuracy, or good judgment. ERROR suggests that one fails to follow a model correctly ⟨an *error* in addition⟩ MISTAKE suggests that one misunderstands something and does not mean to do wrong ⟨took someone else's coat by *mistake*⟩ BLUNDER suggests a bad mistake made because of a lack of knowledge, intelligence, caution, or care ⟨the actors made several *blunders* during the play⟩

erst·while \'ərst-ˌ(h)wīl\ *adv* : in the past : ONCE, FORMERLY — **erstwhile** *adj*

er·u·dite \'er-(y)ə-ˌdīt\ *adj* : having or showing erudition — **er·u·dite·ly** *adv*

er·u·di·tion \ˌer-(y)ə-'dish-ən\ *n* : wide knowledge gained chiefly from books : LEARNING

erupt \i-'rəpt\ *vb* **1** : to burst forth or cause to burst forth : EXPLODE **2** : to break through a surface ⟨teeth *erupting* from the gum⟩　**3** : BREAK OUT 2 — **erup·tive** \-'rəp-tiv\ *adj*

erup·tion \i-'rəp-shən\ *n*　**1** : an act, process, or instance of erupting　**2** : a product (as a skin rash) of erupting

-ery \(ə-)rē\ *n suffix, pl* **-er·ies**　**1** : qualities considered as a group : character ⟨snobb*ery*⟩　**2** : place of doing, keeping, producing, or selling (the thing specified) ⟨fish*ery*⟩ ⟨bak*ery*⟩　**3** : collection : aggregate ⟨fin*ery*⟩　**4** : state or condition ⟨slav*ery*⟩ [derived from early French *-erie* (noun suffix)]

eryth·ro·blas·to·sis \i-,rith-rə-,blas-'tō-səs\ *n* : the abnormal presence of immature red blood cells in the circulating blood; *esp* : ERYTHROBLASTOSIS FETALIS

erythroblastosis fe·ta·lis \-fi-'tal-əs\ *n* : a disease of fetuses and newborn babies that occurs when the system of an Rh-negative mother produces antibodies against an antigen in the blood of an Rh-positive fetus which cross the placenta and destroy the red blood cells of the fetus and that is marked by an increase in circulating immature red blood cells and by jaundice

eryth·ro·cyte \i-'rith-rə-,sīt\ *n* : RED BLOOD CELL

[1]es \əz, iz *after* s, z, sh, ch; z *after* v *or a vowel*\ *n pl suffix* — used to form the plural of most nouns that end in *s* ⟨glass*es*⟩, *z* ⟨fuzz*es*⟩, *sh* ⟨bush*es*⟩, *ch* ⟨peach*es*⟩, or a final *y* that changes to *i* ⟨lad*ies*⟩ and of some nouns ending in *f* that changes to *v* ⟨loav*es*⟩ [derived from Old English *-as* (plural suffix)]

[2]es *adv suffix* : [2]-S

[3]es *vb suffix* — used to form the third person singular present of most verbs that end in *s* ⟨bless*es*⟩, *z* ⟨fizz*es*⟩, *sh* ⟨hush*es*⟩, *ch* ⟨catch*es*⟩, or a final *y* that changes to *i* ⟨defi*es*⟩ [derived from Old English *-es, -as* (verb suffix)]

es·ca·late \'es-kə-,lāt\ *vb* **-lat·ed; -lat·ing** : to increase in extent, volume, or scope : EXPAND ⟨*escalate* prices⟩ — **es·ca·la·tion** \,es-kə-'lā-shən\ *n*

es·ca·la·tor \'es-kə-,lāt-ər\ *n* : a moving set of stairs arranged like a continuous belt

escallop *variant of* SCALLOP

es·ca·pade \'es-kə-,pād\ *n* : a mischievous adventure : PRANK

[1]es·cape \is-'kāp\ *vb* **es·caped; es·cap·ing**　**1 a** : GET AWAY ⟨*escape* from the routine⟩ ⟨*escape* from a burning building⟩　**b** : to leak out from some enclosed place ⟨gas is *escaping*⟩　**c** : to grow in the wild after being in cultivation　**2** : to get out of the way of : AVOID ⟨*escape* punishment⟩　**3** : to fail to be noticed or recalled by ⟨the name *escapes* me⟩　**4** : to come out from or be uttered by unexpectedly or almost uncontrollably ⟨a sigh of relief *escaped* us⟩ — **es·cap·er** *n*

Word History If you were being held captive by someone gripping the coat or cloak you were wearing, you might be able to get away by slipping out of it. This is the idea on which the word *escape* is based. *Escape* is made up of the Latin prefix *ex-*, which means "out of", and the Latin word *cappa*, which means "head covering" or "cloak". [Middle English *escapen* "escape", from early French *escaper* (same meaning), probably from Latin *escappare* "escape", from earlier *ex-* "out, out of" and *cappa* "head covering, cloak" — related to [2]CAPE]

[2]escape *n*　**1** : an act or instance of escaping　**2** : a means of escaping　**3** : a cultivated plant growing in the wild

escape velocity *n* : the lowest velocity that a moving body (as a rocket) must have to escape from the field of gravity of the earth or of a heavenly body and move outward into space

es·cap·ism \is-'kā-,piz-əm\ *n* : a habit of thinking about purely imaginary things in order to escape from reality or everyday matters — **es·cap·ist** \-pəst\ *adj or n*

es·ca·role \'es-kə-,rōl\ *n* : ENDIVE 1

es·carp·ment \is-'kärp-mənt\ *n*　**1** : a steep slope in front of a fort or defensive area　**2** : a long cliff

es·chew \is-'chü\ *vb* : SHUN, AVOID

[1]es·cort \'es-,kȯ(ə)rt\ *n*　**1** : a person or group of persons accompanying another to give protection or show courtesy　**2** : the man who goes on a date with a woman　**3** : a protective screen of vehicles, warships, or planes ⟨motorcycle *escort*⟩ ⟨fighter *escort*⟩

[2]es·cort \is-'kȯ(ə)rt, es-', es-, \ *vb* : to go along with as an escort **syn** see ACCOMPANY

es·cu·do \is-'küd-ō\ *n, pl* **-dos**　**1** : the basic unit of money of Portugal　**2** : a coin representing one escudo [Portuguese, literally "shield"]

es·cu·lent \'es-kyə-lənt\ *adj* : fit to eat

es·cutch·eon \is-'kəch-ən\ *n* : the shield-shaped surface on which a coat of arms is shown

Es·dras \'ez-drəs\ *n* — see BIBLE table

[1]ese \'ēz, 'ēs\ *adj suffix* : of, relating to, or originating in (a specified place or country) ⟨Japan*ese*⟩ [derived from Latin *-ensis* (adjective suffix)]

[2]ese *n suffix, pl* **-ese**　**1** : one born or living in (a specified place or country) ⟨Chin*ese*⟩　**2 a** : language of (a specified place, country, or nationality) ⟨Vietnam*ese*⟩　**b** : speech or literary style of (a specified place, person, or group) ⟨journal*ese*⟩ [from [1]-ese]

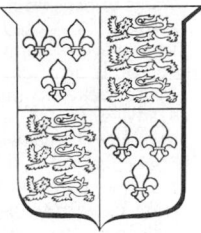

escutcheon

es·ker \'es-kər\ *n* : a long narrow mound of material (as sand or gravel) deposited by a stream flowing on, within, or beneath a melting glacier

Es·ki·mo \'es-kə-,mō\ *n, pl* **Eskimo** *or* **Eskimos**　**1** : a member of a group of peoples of northern North America and eastern Siberia　**2** : the language of the Eskimo people — **Es·ki·mo·an** \,es-kə-'mō-ən\ *adj*

Eskimo dog *n* : a sled dog of American origin

esoph·a·gus \i-'säf-ə-gəs\ *n, pl* **-gi** \-,gī, -,jī\ : a muscular tube that leads from the cavity behind the mouth to the stomach — **esoph·a·ge·al** \-,säf-ə-'jē-əl\ *adj*

es·o·ter·ic \,es-ə-'ter-ik\ *adj*　**1** : taught to or understood by members of a special group ⟨*esoteric* knowledge⟩　**2** : hard to understand ⟨*esoteric* subjects⟩　**3** : of special or unusual interest ⟨*esoteric* colors⟩ — **es·o·ter·i·cal·ly** \-'ter-i-k(ə-)lē\ *adv*

es·pa·drille \'es-pə-,dril\ *n* : a lightweight shoe with a cloth upper and flexible sole often with a rope braid around the edge

es·pal·ier \is-'pal-yər, -,yā\ *n* : a plant (as a fruit tree) trained to grow flat against a support (as a wall or trellis) — **espalier** *vb*

es·par·to \is-'pärt-ō\ *n, pl* **-tos** : either of two Spanish and Algerian grasses from which rope, shoes, baskets, and paper are made — called also *esparto grass*

es·pe·cial \is-'pesh-əl\ *adj*　**1** : UNUSUAL, NOTABLE ⟨put *especial* emphasis on this point⟩　**2** : relating to or unique to a certain person or thing : PARTICULAR ⟨each has its own *especial* qualities⟩ — **es·pe·cial·ly** \-'pesh-(ə-)lē\ *adv*

es·pi·o·nage \'es-pē-ə-,näzh, -,näj, -,nij\ *n* : the practice of spying : the use of spies

es·pla·nade \'es-plə-,näd, ,es-plə-'\ *n* : a level open stretch or area; *esp* : one for walking or driving along a shore

es·pous·al \is-'pau̇-zəl *also* -səl\ *n*　**1 a** : WEDDING　**b** : the act of becoming engaged : state of being engaged　**2** : a taking up of a cause or belief as a supporter

es·pouse \is-'pau̇z, -'pau̇s\ *vb* **es·poused; es·pous·ing**

\ə\ abut	\au̇\ out	\i\ tip	\ȯ\ saw	\u̇\ foot
\ər\ further	\ch\ chin	\ī\ life	\ȯi\ coin	\y\ yet
\a\ mat	\e\ pet	\j\ job	\th\ thin	\yü\ few
\ā\ take	\ē\ easy	\ŋ\ sing	\th\ this	\yu̇\ cure
\ä\ cot, cart	\g\ go	\ō\ bone	\ü\ food	\zh\ vision

1 : ¹MARRY 2, 3   2 : to take up the cause of : SUPPORT — **es·pous·er** *n*

espres·so \e-'spres-ō\ *n, pl* **-sos** : coffee brewed by forcing steam through finely ground darkly roasted coffee beans

es·prit \is-'prē\ *n* : lively cleverness or wit [from French *esprit*, literally "spirit"]

es·prit de corps \is-,prēd-ə-'kō(ə)r, -'kȯ(ə)r\ *n* : enthusiastic devotion of members to a group and strong regard for the honor of the group

es·py \is-'pī\ *vb* **es·pied; es·py·ing** : to catch sight of

es·quire \'es-,kwī(ə)r, is-'-\ *n* 1 : a member of the English gentry ranking immediately below a knight   2 : one who wants to become a knight and who works as a servant to a knight   3 — used as a title of courtesy usually placed in its abbreviated form after the surname 〈John Smith, *Esq.*〉

-ess \əs, is *also* ,es\ *n suffix* : female 〈priest*ess*〉 [derived from Greek *-issa* (feminine noun suffix)]

¹**es·say** \e-'sā, 'es-,ā\ *vb* : ¹ATTEMPT 1, TRY 〈again *essayed* to ride on the camel〉

²**es·say** \'es-,ā, *in sense 1 also* e-'sā\ *n* 1 : ²ATTEMPT 1, TRY; *esp* : an uncertain or hesitant effort   2 : a usually short written work giving a personal view or opinion on a subject

es·say·ist \'es-,ā-əst\ *n* : a writer of essays

es·sence \'es-ən(t)s\ *n* 1 : the basic nature of a thing : the quality or qualities that make a thing what it is 〈the *essence* of love is unselfishness〉   2 : a substance physically or chemically separated from another substance (as a plant or drug) and having the special qualities (as odor) of the original substance 〈*essence* of peppermint〉   3 : ¹PERFUME 1, SCENT

¹**es·sen·tial** \i-'sen-chəl\ *adj* 1 : forming or belonging to the essence 〈free speech is an *essential* right of citizenship〉   2 : containing or having the character of an easily evaporated essence 〈*essential* oils〉   3 : important in the highest degree : NECESSARY 〈food is *essential* to life〉 — **es·sen·ti·al·i·ty** \-,sen-chē-'al-ət-ē\ *n* — **es·sen·tial·ly** \-'sench-(ə-)lē\ *adv* — **es·sen·tial·ness** \-'sen-chəl-nəs\ *n*

²**essential** *n* : something basic, necessary, or indispensable 〈the *essentials* for success〉

essential amino acid *n* : an amino acid that is necessary for proper growth of the animal body and that cannot be made by the body unassisted but must be obtained from food containing proteins

¹**-est** \əst, ist\ *adj suffix or adv suffix* — used to form the superlative degree of adjectives and adverbs of one syllable 〈fatt*est*〉 〈lat*est*〉 and of some adjectives and adverbs of two or more syllables 〈lucki*est*〉 〈often*est*〉 [Old English *-est, -ost* (adjective or adverb suffix)]

²**-est** \əst, ist\ *or* **-st** \st\ *suffix* — used to form the archaic second person singular of verbs (with *thou*) 〈gett*est*〉 〈did*st*〉 [Old English *-est, -ast* (verb suffix)]

es·tab·lish \is-'tab-lish\ *vb* 1 : to put securely in place or cause to have a firm and lasting position 〈*established* a home in the community〉   2 : to make a permanent part of a nation's laws 〈*establish* a constitution〉   3 a : to bring into existence : FOUND 〈*establish* a republic〉 〈*establish* a school〉   b : to cause to exist : BRING ABOUT 〈*establish* a good relationship〉 〈*establish* radio contact〉   4 : to set on a firm basis 〈*establish* their children in business〉   5 : to gain full recognition or acceptance of 〈*establish* a claim〉 〈*established* new ideas〉 〈*established* their innocence〉 — **es·tab·lish·er** *n*

established church *n* : a church recognized by law as the official church of a nation

es·tab·lish·ment \is-'tab-lish-mənt\ *n* 1 a : the act of establishing : the state or fact of being established   b : the granting of a privileged position 〈*establishment* of a church〉   2 : a place for residence or business 〈a dry⸗ cleaning *establishment*〉   3 : an established order of society; *also* : the social, economic, and political leaders of such an order 〈rebelling against the *establishment*〉

es·tate \is-'tāt\ *n* 1 : the condition or circumstances of one's existence   2 : a social or political class   3 a : the possessions or property of a person; *esp* : a person's property in land   b : the assets and liabilities left by a person at death   c : a large country house on a large piece of land

¹**es·teem** \is-'tēm\ *n* : the degree of respect or liking one has for something or someone; *esp* : a very favorable opinion

²**esteem** *vb* 1 : to think of in a particular way : CONSIDER 〈*esteem* it a privilege〉   2 : to think very highly or favorably of

es·ter \'es-tər\ *n* : an organic compound formed by the reaction between an acid and an alcohol

Es·ther \'es-tər\ — see BIBLE table

esthetic, esthetics *variant of* AESTHETIC, AESTHETICS

¹**es·ti·mate** \'es-tə-,māt\ *vb* **-mat·ed; -mat·ing** 1 : to judge the approximate value, size, or cost of on the basis of experience rather than actual measurement 〈*estimate* the distance〉 〈*estimate* a painting job〉   2 : CONCLUDE 2, DETERMINE 〈*estimated* that the fire started in the kitchen〉 — **es·ti·ma·tor** \-,māt-ər\ *n*

²**es·ti·mate** \'es-tə-mət\ *n* 1 : the act of estimating   2 : an opinion or judgment of the nature, character, or quality of a thing   3 : a rough or approximate calculation   4 : a statement by a contractor of the probable cost for a job

es·ti·ma·tion \,es-tə-'mā-shən\ *n* 1 : JUDGMENT 3, OPINION   2 : ²ESTIMATE 3   3 : ¹ESTEEM

es·ti·vate *or* **aes·ti·vate** \'es-tə-,vāt\ *vb* **-vat·ed; -vat·ing** : to pass the summer in an inactive or resting state — **es·ti·va·tion** *or* **aes·ti·va·tion** \,es-tə-'vā-shən\ *n*

Es·to·nian \e-'stō-nē-ən, -nyən\ *n* 1 : a member of a Caucasian people chiefly of Estonia   2 : the language of the Estonians — **Estonian** *adj*

es·trange \is-'trānj\ *vb* **es·tranged; es·trang·ing** : to cause to change from friendly or loving to unfriendly or uncaring : ALIENATE 〈*estranged* from their children〉 — **es·trange·ment** \-mənt\ *n*

es·tro·gen \'es-trə-jən\ *n* : a substance (as a sex hormone) that tends to cause estrus and the development of secondary sex characteristics in the female — **es·tro·gen·ic** \,es-trə-'jen-ik\ *adj*

estrous cycle *n* : the cycle of changes in the endocrine and reproductive systems of a female mammal from the beginning of one period of estrus to the beginning of the next

es·trus \'es-trəs\ *n* 1 : a periodic state of sexual excitability during which the female of most mammals is willing to mate with the male and is capable of becoming pregnant : HEAT   2 : ESTROUS CYCLE — **es·trous** \-trəs\ *adj*

es·tu·ary \'es-chə-,wer-ē\ *n, pl* **-ar·ies** : a passage where the tide meets a river current; *esp* : an arm of the sea at the lower end of a river — **es·tu·a·rine** \'es-chə-wə-,rīn\ *adj*

-et \'et, ,et, ət, it\ *n suffix* 1 : small one : lesser one 〈fresh*et*〉   2 : group 〈oct*et*〉 [derived from Latin *-itus, -ita* (noun suffix) "small one"]

eta \'āt-ə\ *n* : the seventh letter of the Greek alphabet — H or η

éta·gère *or* **eta·gere** \,ā-,tä-'zhe(ə)r, ,āt-ə-\ *n* : a piece of furniture that consists of a set of open shelves [French]

et cet·era \et-'set-ə-rə, -'se-trə\ : and others especially of the same kind : and so forth [Latin]

etch \'ech\ *vb* 1 a : to produce (as a pattern or design) on a hard material by lines eaten into the material's surface (as by acid or laser beam)   b : to produce a pattern or design on by such etching 〈*etched* glass〉 〈an *etched* silicon chip〉   2 : to outline or impress clearly 〈migrating ducks *etched* against the sky〉 — **etch·er** *n*

etch·ing *n* 1 a : the act or process of etching a hard material   b : the art of printing from an etched metal plate   2 a : a product of etching   b : a print made from an etched metal plate

eter·nal \i-'tərn-ᵊl\ *adj* **1** : having no beginning and no end : lasting forever **2** : continuing without interruption — **eter·nal·ly** \-ᵊl-ē\ *adv* — **eter·nal·ness** *n*

eter·ni·ty \i-'tər-nət-ē\ *n, pl* **-ties** **1** : the quality or state of being eternal **2** : endless time **3** : the state after death : IMMORTALITY **4** : time that seems to be endless

¹**-eth** \əth, ith\ *or* **-th** \th\ *vb suffix* — used to form the archaic third person singular present of verbs ⟨do*th*⟩ [Old English *-eth, -ath, -th* (verb suffix)]

²**-eth** — see ²-TH

eth·ane \'eth-,ān\ *n* : a colorless odorless gas that consists of carbon and hydrogen, is found in natural gas, and is used especially as a fuel

eth·a·nol \'eth-ə-,nȯl, -,nōl\ *n* : ALCOHOL 1a

eth·ene \'eth-,ēn\ *n* : ETHYLENE

ether \'ē-thər\ *n* **1 a** : an invisible substance once believed to fill the upper regions of space **b** : the upper regions of space : HEAVENS **2** : an easily evaporated flammable liquid used chiefly to dissolve other substances

ethe·re·al \i-'thir-ē-əl\ *adj* : being light and airy : DELICATE — **ethe·re·al·ly** \-ē-ə-lē\ *adv* — **ethe·re·al·ness** *n*

ether·ize \'ē-thə-,rīz\ *vb* **-ized; -iz·ing** : to treat or anesthetize with ether

eth·i·cal \'eth-i-kəl\ *adj* **1** : of or relating to ethics **2 a** : following accepted rules of conduct **b** : following professional standards of conduct **3** : sold only on a doctor's prescription ⟨*ethical* drugs⟩ — **eth·i·cal·ly** \-i-k(ə-)lē\ *adv*

eth·ics \'eth-iks\ *n sing or pl* **1** : a branch of philosophy dealing with what is good and bad and with moral duty and obligation **2** : the rules of moral conduct governing an individual or a group

Ethi·op·ic \,ē-thē-'äp-ik, -'ō-pik\ *n* : a language formerly spoken in Ethiopia and still used in church services there

¹**eth·nic** \'eth-nik\ *n* : a member of an ethnic group; *esp* : a member of a minority group who keeps customs, language, or social ideas of the group

²**ethnic** *adj* **1** : of or relating to races or large groups of people classed according to common traits and customs ⟨*ethnic* minorities⟩ **2** : of or relating to ethnics ⟨*ethnic* neighborhoods⟩ — **eth·ni·cal·ly** \-ni-k(ə-)lē\ *adv*

eth·no·cen·tric \,eth-nō-'sen-trik\ *adj* : favoring one's own ethnic group

eth·nol·o·gist \eth-'näl-ə-jəst\ *n* : a specialist in the science or study of ethnology

eth·nol·o·gy \eth-'näl-ə-jē\ *n* **1** : a science that deals with human races **2** : a study that compares human cultures — **eth·no·log·i·cal** \,eth-nə-'läj-i-kəl\ *adj*

ethol·o·gist \ē-'thäl-ə-jəst\ *n* : a specialist in ethology

ethol·o·gy \ē-'thäl-ə-jē\ *n* : the scientific study of animal behavior

ethyl alcohol *n* : ALCOHOL 1a

eth·yl·ene \'eth-ə-,lēn\ *n* : a colorless flammable gas found in coal gas or obtained from petroleum and used to ripen fruits or as an anesthetic

ethylene gly·col \-'glī-,kȯl, -,kōl\ *n* : a thick liquid alcohol used especially as an antifreeze and in making polyester fibers

eth·yne \'ē-,thīn, e-'thīn\ *n* : ACETYLENE

eti·o·lat·ed \,ēt-ē-ə-'lāt-əd\ *adj* : bleached because of having grown in the absence of light ⟨*etiolated* bean seedlings⟩

et·i·quette \'et-i-kət, -,ket\ *n* : the rules governing the proper way to behave [from French *étiquette* "etiquette", literally "ticket", from earlier *etiquet* "ticket"—related to TICKET]

Etrus·can \i-'trəs-kən\ *n* **1** : a person born or living in ancient Etruria **2** : the language of the Etruscans — **Etruscan** *adj*

-ette \'et, ,et, ət, it\ *n suffix* **1** : little one ⟨kitchen*ette*⟩ **2** : female ⟨major*ette*⟩ [derived from early French *-ette*, feminine form of *-et* "small one"]

étude \'ā-,t(y)üd\ *n* : a piece of music for practice [from French *étude*, literally "study"]

et·y·mol·o·gy \,et-ə-'mäl-ə-jē\ *n, pl* **-gies** : the history of a word shown by tracing it or its parts back to the earliest known forms and meanings both in its own language and any other language from which it or its parts may have been taken [Middle English *ethimologie* "etymology", from Latin *etymologia* (same meaning), from Greek *etymon* "true meaning of a word" and Greek *-logia* "study, science", from *etymos* "true" and *logos* "word, reason"] — **et·y·mo·log·i·cal** \-mə-'läj-i-kəl\ *adj* — **et·y·mo·log·i·cal·ly** \-'läj-i-k(ə-)lē\ *adv* — **et·y·mol·o·gist** \-'mäl-ə-jəst\ *n*

eu·ca·lypt \'yü-kə-,lipt\ *n* : EUCALYPTUS

eu·ca·lyp·tus \,yü-kə-'lip-təs\ *n, pl* **-ti** \-,tī, -,tē\ *or* **-tus·es** : any of a genus of mostly Australian evergreen trees that are related to the myrtle and include many that are widely cultivated for their gums, resins, oils, and useful woods

Eu·cha·rist \'yü-k(ə-)rəst\ *n* : COMMUNION 1a [Middle English *eukarist* "Eucharist", from early French *euchariste* (same meaning), derived from Greek *eucharistia* "Eucharist, gratitude", from *eu-* "good" and *charizesthai* "to show favor or gratitude"] — **eu·cha·ris·tic** \,yü-kə-'ris-tik\ *adj*, *often cap*

Eu·clid·e·an algorithm \yü-'klid-ē-ən-\ *n* : a method of finding the greatest common divisor of two numbers by dividing the larger by the smaller, the smaller by the remainder, the first remainder by the second remainder, and so on until division without a remainder occurs when the greatest common divisor is the divisor leaving no remainder [named for *Euclid* Greek mathematician around 300 B.C.]

eu·di·om·e·ter \,yüd-ē-'äm-ət-ər\ *n* : an instrument used to analyze and measure the volume of gases

eu·gen·ic \yü-'jen-ik\ *adj* **1** : relating to or fitted for the production of good offspring **2** : of or relating to eugenics

eu·gen·ics \yü-'jen-iks\ *n* : a science that deals with the improvement of inherited qualities of a race or breed and especially of human beings

eu·gle·na \yü-'glē-nə\ *n* : any of a large genus of green freshwater flagellates often classified with the algae

eu·gle·noid \yü-'glē-,nȯid\ *n* : any of a group of varied flagellates that are typically green or colorless, live alone, and have one or two flagella coming out of a food-intake opening — **euglenoid** *adj*

euglenoid movement *n* : wriggly movement typical of some euglenoid flagellates

eu·lo·gize \'yü-lə-,jīz\ *vb* **-gized; -giz·ing** : to speak or write high praise of — **eu·lo·gist** \-jəst\ *n* — **eu·lo·gis·tic** \,yü-lə-'jis-tik\ *adj* — **eu·lo·gis·ti·cal·ly** \-ti-k(ə-)lē\ *adv*

eu·lo·gy \'yü-lə-jē\ *n, pl* **-gies** **1** : a formal speech in praise especially of a dead person **2** : high praise

euglena

eu·phe·mism \'yü-fə-,miz-əm\ *n* : the substitution of a mild or pleasant expression for one that is too strong or unpleasant; *also* : a mild or pleasant expression so substituted — **eu·phe·mis·tic** \,yü-fə-'mis-tik\ *adj* — **eu·phe·mis·ti·cal·ly** \-ti-k(ə-)lē\ *adv*

\ə\ abut	\aù\ out	\i\ tip	\ȯ\ saw	\ù\ foot
\ər\ further	\ch\ chin	\ī\ life	\ȯi\ coin	\y\ yet
\a\ mat	\e\ pet	\j\ job	\th\ thin	\yü\ few
\ā\ take	\ē\ easy	\ŋ\ sing	\th\ this	\yù\ cure
\ä\ cot, cart	\g\ go	\ō\ bone	\ü\ food	\zh\ vision

eu·pho·ni·um \yü-'fō-nē-əm\ *n* : a brass musical instrument resembling a tuba but playing in a higher pitch range

eu·pho·ny \'yü-fə-nē\ *n, pl* **-nies** : pleasing or sweet sound; *esp* : the pleasant sound of words combined [from French *euphonie* "pleasing sound", from Latin *euphonia* (same meaning), derived from Greek *eu-* "good" and Greek *phōnē* "voice, sound" — related to PHONETIC, SYMPHONY] — **eu·pho·ni·ous** \yü-'fō-nē-əs\ *adj*

euphonium

eu·pho·ria \yü-'fōr-ē-ə, -'fôr-\ *n* : a strong feeling of happiness — **eu·phor·ic** \-'fôr-ik, -'fär-\ *adj*

Eur·asian \yü-'rā-zhən, -shən\ *adj* **1** : of or relating to Eurasia **2** : of mixed European and Asian origin — **Eurasian** *n*

eu·re·ka \yü-'rē-kə\ *interj* — used to express the thrill of discovery [from Greek *heurēka* "I have found it"]

Eu·ro·pe·an \,yür-ə-'pē-ən\ *n* **1** : a person born or living in Europe **2** : a person of European ancestry — **European** *adj*

eu·ro·pi·um \yü-'rō-pē-əm\ *n* : a metallic chemical element found in a sand — see ELEMENT table

eu·sta·chian tube \yü-,stā-sh(ē)ən-, -,stā-kē-ən-\ *n, often cap E* : a tube connecting the middle ear with the throat and equalizing air pressure on both sides of the eardrum

eu·tha·na·sia \,yü-thə-'nā-zh(ē-)ə\ *n* : MERCY KILLING

evac·u·ate \i-'vak-yə-,wāt\ *vb* **-at·ed; -at·ing** **1** : to make empty **2** : to discharge waste matter from the body **3** : to remove something (as a gas) from especially by pumping **4** : to remove troops or people from a place of danger — **evac·u·a·tion** \-,vak-yə-'wā-shən\ *n*

evac·u·ee \i-,vak-yə-'wē\ *n* : a person who has been evacuated from a place

evade \i-'vād\ *vb* **evad·ed; evad·ing** **1** : to get away from or avoid by skill or trickery ⟨*evade* a question⟩ ⟨*evade* capture⟩ **2** : to escape the understanding of ⟨the meaning of the message *evaded* them⟩ — **evad·able** \-'vād-ə-bəl\ *adj* — **evad·er** *n*

eval·u·ate \i-'val-yə-,wāt\ *vb* **-at·ed; -at·ing** **1** : to find the value of ⟨*evaluate* a mathematical expression⟩ **2** : to decide the value or worth of after study ⟨*evaluate* a job training program⟩ — **eval·u·a·tion** \-,val-yə-'wā-shən\ *n* — **eval·u·a·tive** \-'val-yə-,wāt-iv\ *adj* — **eval·u·a·tor** \-,wāt-ər\ *n*

ev·a·nesce \,ev-ə-'nes\ *vb* **-nesced; -nesc·ing** : to vanish like vapor

ev·a·nes·cence \,ev-ə-'nes-ⁿ(t)s\ *n* : evanescent quality

ev·a·nes·cent \,ev-ə-'nes-ⁿnt\ *adj* : tending to vanish like vapor : not lasting

evan·gel·i·cal \,ē-,van-'jel-i-kəl, ,ev-ən-\ *adj* **1** : of, relating to, or being in agreement with the Christian gospel especially as given in the four Gospels **2** : stressing salvation by faith in Jesus, the authority of the Bible, and the importance of preaching

evan·ge·lism \i-'van-jə-,liz-əm\ *n* : the winning or reawakening of personal pledges to Jesus — **evan·ge·lis·tic** \-,van-jə-'lis-tik\ *adj*

evan·ge·list \i-'van-jə-ləst\ *n* : a Christian preacher who goes about from place to place trying to change or increase people's religious feelings [Middle English *evangelist* "one of the writers of the four Gospels", from early French and Latin *evangelista* (same meaning), derived from Greek *euangelizein* "to preach the gospel", derived from *euangelion* "good news, gospel", derived from *eu-* "good" and *angelos* "messenger, angel"]

evap·o·rate \i-'vap-ə-,rāt\ *vb* **-rat·ed; -rat·ing** **1** : to pass off or cause to pass off into vapor from a liquid state **2** : to pass off or away : DISAPPEAR **3** : to remove some of the water from (as by heating) — **evap·o·ra·tor** \-,rāt-ər\ *n*

evaporated milk *n* : unsweetened canned milk from which much of the water has been evaporated

evap·o·ra·tion \i-,vap-ə-'rā-shən\ *n* : the process of evaporating

evap·o·rite \i-'vap-ə-,rīt\ *n* : a sedimentary rock (as gypsum) that forms from evaporation of seawater in an enclosed basin

eva·sion \i-'vā-zhən\ *n* **1** : the act or an instance of evading ⟨tax *evasion*⟩ **2** : a means of evading

eva·sive \i-'vā-siv, -ziv\ *adj* : tending or meant to evade ⟨gave an *evasive* answer⟩ — **eva·sive·ly** *adv* — **eva·sive·ness** *n*

eve \'ēv\ *n* **1** : EVENING **2** : the evening or the day before a special day ⟨New Year's *Eve*⟩ **3** : the period just before an important event

¹even \'ē-vən\ *n, archaic* : EVENING

²even *adj* **1 a** : having a horizontal surface : FLAT **b** : being without breaks or bumps : SMOOTH **c** : being on the same line or level **2 a** : equal in size, number, or amount ⟨*even* distances apart⟩ **b** : staying the same over a period of time ⟨*even* breathing⟩ **3 a** : without advantage on either side : FAIR ⟨start out *even*⟩ ⟨an *even* trade⟩ **b** : leaving nothing due on either side ⟨now we're *even*⟩ **c** : showing neither profit nor loss **4 a** : being any of the natural numbers beginning with two and counting by twos ⟨2, 4, 6, 8, . . . are *even* numbers⟩ **b** : marked by an even number ⟨an *even* page of a book⟩ **5** : being whole or exact without a remainder or fractional part ⟨an *even* dollar⟩ ⟨an *even* dozen⟩ **syn** see LEVEL — **even·ly** *adv* — **even·ness** \-vən-nəs\ *n*

³even *adv* **1** : at the very same time ⟨*even* as the clock struck⟩ **2** : INDEED 1 ⟨willing, *even* eager, to help⟩ **3** — used to stress an extreme or highly unlikely condition or instance ⟨so simple *even* a child can do it⟩ **4** : to a greater extent or degree ⟨*even* better⟩ **5** — used to stress the smallness of an amount or effort ⟨didn't *even* offer to help⟩ ⟨gave it not *even* a glance⟩

⁴even *vb* **evened; even·ing** \'ēv-(ə-)niŋ\ : to make or become even — **even·er** \'ēv-(ə-)nər\ *n*

even·hand·ed \,ē-vən-'han-dəd\ *adj* : not favoring one over another : FAIR, IMPARTIAL

eve·ning \'ēv-niŋ\ *n* **1** : the final part of the day and early part of the night **2** : a late part ⟨the *evening* of life⟩

evening primrose *n* **1** : a coarse herb that lives two years and produces yellow flowers that open in the evening **2** : any of several plants related to the evening primrose

evening star *n* : a bright planet (as Venus) seen especially in the western sky at or after sunset

even·song \'ē-vən-,sòŋ\ *n, often cap* : VESPERS

event \i-'vent\ *n* **1 a** : something usually of importance that happens **b** : a social occasion or activity (as a party) **2** : EVENTUALITY ⟨in the *event* of rain the ceremony will be held indoors⟩ **3** : any of the contests in a program of sports ⟨track-and-field *events*⟩ **4** : a subset of the possible outcomes of an experiment in probability or statistics ⟨7 is an *event* in the throwing of two dice⟩

event·ful \i-'vent-fəl\ *adj* **1** : full of events ⟨an *eventful* day⟩ **2** : very important : MOMENTOUS — **event·ful·ly** \-fə-lē\ *adv* — **event·ful·ness** *n*

even·tide \'ē-vən-,tīd\ *n* : EVENING 1

even·tu·al \i-'vench-(ə-)wəl, -'ven-chəl\ *adj* : coming at some later time : ULTIMATE ⟨our *eventual* success⟩

even·tu·al·i·ty \i-,ven-chə-'wal-ət-ē\ *n, pl* **-ties** : something that might happen : POSSIBILITY

even·tu·al·ly \i-'vench-(ə-)wəl-ē, -'ven-chəl-ē\ *adv* : at some later time : in the end

ev·er \'ev-ər\ *adv* **1** : at all times : ALWAYS ⟨*ever* faithful⟩

2 a : at any time ⟨has this *ever* been done before⟩ **b :** in any way : AT ALL ⟨how can I *ever* thank you⟩ **3** — used especially with *so* to give more force to a word ⟨thank you *ever* so much⟩

ev·er·glade \'ev-ər-ˌglād\ *n* : a low-lying tract of swampy or marshy land

¹ev·er·green \'ev-ər-ˌgrēn\ *adj* : having leaves that remain green and functional through more than one growing season ⟨most conifers are *evergreen* trees⟩ — compare DECIDUOUS

²evergreen *n* **1 :** an evergreen plant; *also* : CONIFER **2** *pl* : twigs and branches of evergreen plants used for decoration

¹ev·er·last·ing \ˌev-ər-'las-tiŋ\ *adj* **1 :** lasting forever : ETERNAL **2 a :** going on for a long time or for too long ⟨*everlasting* complaints⟩ **b :** keeping form or color for a long time when dried ⟨*everlasting* flowers⟩ — **ev·er·last·ing·ly** \-tiŋ-lē\ *adv* — **ev·er·last·ing·ness** *n*

²everlasting *n* **1 :** a plant with everlasting flowers **2 :** an everlasting flower

ev·er·more \ˌev-ər-'mō(ə)r, -'mȯ(ə)r\ *adv* : FOREVER 1

ev·ery \'ev-rē\ *adj* **1 :** being each one of a group or series without leaving out any ⟨heard *every* word you said⟩ **2** : ¹COMPLETE 1 ⟨have *every* confidence in you⟩

ev·ery·body \'ev-ri-ˌbäd-ē, -ˌbəd-ē\ *pron* : every person

ev·ery·day \ˌev-rē-ˌdā\ *adj* : used, suitable for, or seen everyday : ORDINARY ⟨*everyday* clothes⟩ ⟨*everyday* people⟩

ev·ery·one \'ev-rē-(ˌ)wən\ *pron* : EVERYBODY

ev·ery·place \-ˌplās\ *adv* : EVERYWHERE

ev·ery·thing \-ˌthiŋ\ *pron* **1 a :** every thing there is : ALL **b :** all that relates to the subject ⟨tell *everything*⟩ **2 :** the most important thing ⟨to some people money is *everything*⟩

ev·ery·where \-ˌ(h)we(ə)r, -ˌ(h)wa(ə)r\ *adv* : in or to every place

evict \i-'vikt\ *vb* : to put (a person) out from property by legal action — **evic·tion** \-'vik-shən\ *n* — **evic·tor** \-'vik-tər\ *n*

¹ev·i·dence \'ev-əd-ən(t)s, -ə-ˌden(t)s\ *n* **1 :** an outward sign : INDICATION ⟨*evidence* of the life of ancient people⟩ ⟨gave no *evidence* that he was going to bunt⟩ **2 :** material presented to a court to help find the truth in a matter — **in evidence :** to be easily seen : CONSPICUOUS

²evidence *vb* **-denced; -denc·ing :** to be or give evidence of

ev·i·dent \'ev-əd-ənt, -ə-ˌdent\ *adj* : clear to the sight or mind : PLAIN [Middle English *evident* "clearly seen or understood", from early French *evident* (same meaning), from Latin *evident-, evidens* (same meaning), from *e-, ex-* "out, away" and *vident-, videns,* a form of *vidēre* "to see" — related to VISION]

ev·i·dent·ly \'ev-əd-ənt-lē, -ə-ˌdent-; ˌev-ə-'dent-lē\ *adv* : it is evident ⟨*evidently* nobody saw them leave⟩

¹evil \'ē-vəl\ *adj* **evil·er** *or* **evil·ler; evil·est** *or* **evil·lest** **1** : morally bad : WICKED **2 a :** causing harm : tending to injure **b :** marked by misfortune ⟨fall on *evil* days⟩ — **evil·ly** \-vəl-(l)ē\ *adv*

²evil *n* **1 :** something that brings sorrow, trouble, or destruction **2 :** the fact of suffering or wrongdoing

evil·do·er \ˌē-vəl-'dü-ər\ *n* : a person who does evil — **evil·do·ing** \-'dü-iŋ\ *n*

evil eye *n* : an eye or glance thought to be able to do harm

evil–mind·ed \ˌē-vəl-'mīn-dəd\ *adj* : having an evil disposition or evil thoughts

evince \i-'vin(t)s\ *vb* **evinced; evinc·ing :** to give evidence of : show clearly ⟨*evinced* an interest in puppets at an early age⟩

evis·cer·ate \i-'vis-ə-ˌrāt\ *vb* **-at·ed; -at·ing :** to take out the internal organs of — **evis·cer·a·tion** \-ˌvis-ə-'rā-shən\ *n*

evo·ca·tion \ˌē-vō-'kā-shən, ˌev-ə-\ *n* : an act or instance of evoking

evoc·a·tive \i-'väk-ət-iv\ *adj* : having the power to evoke

evoke \i-'vōk\ *vb* **evoked; evok·ing :** to call forth or up : SUMMON ⟨the old house *evoked* memories of days gone by⟩

ev·o·lu·tion \ˌev-ə-'lü-shən, ˌē-və-\ *n* **1 a :** a process of change especially from a lower or simple to a higher or complex state : GROWTH **b :** something evolved **2 :** one of a set of prescribed movements **3 :** the process of working out or developing **4 a :** the history of the development of a biological group (as a race or species) **b :** a theory that the various kinds of plants and animals are descended from other kinds that lived in earlier times and that the differences are due to inherited changes that took place over many generations — **ev·o·lu·tion·ary** \-shə-ˌner-ē\ *adj*

ev·ol·u·tion·ist \ˌev-ə-'lü-sh(ə-)nəst\ *n* : a student of or a follower of a theory of evolution

evolve \i-'välv, -'vȯlv\ *vb* **evolved; evolv·ing 1 :** to develop or work out from something else ⟨*evolved* a new plan⟩ ⟨*evolved* a safer design from the old one⟩ **2 :** to produce by a process of evolution **3 :** to change by a process of evolution

ewe \'yü\ *n* : a female of the sheep or a related animal especially when mature

ew·er \'yü-ər, 'yu̇-(ə)r\ *n* : a vase-shaped pitcher or jug

¹ex- \(ˌ)eks, 'eks\ *prefix* : former ⟨*ex*-president⟩ ⟨*ex*-child actor⟩ [from earlier *ex-* (prefix), from Latin *ex-* "out of, from"]

²ex- — see EXO-

¹ex·act \ig-'zakt\ *vb* : to demand and get by force or threat ⟨*exacted* a heavy tribute from the weaker nation⟩ — **ex·ac·tion** \-'zak-shən\ *n*

²exact *adj* **1 :** fully and completely in agreement with fact, a standard, or an original ⟨the *exact* time⟩ ⟨an *exact* rhyme⟩ ⟨an *exact* replica⟩ **2 :** providing great accuracy ⟨*exact* instruments⟩ **syn** see CORRECT — **exact·ness** \-'zak(t)-nəs\ *n*

ewer

ex·act·ing \ig-'zak-tiŋ\ *adj* : making many or difficult demands upon a person ⟨an *exacting* task⟩ ⟨an *exacting* teacher⟩ — **ex·act·ing·ly** \-tiŋ-lē\ *adv* — **ex·act·ing·ness** *n*

ex·ac·ti·tude \ig-'zak-tə-ˌt(y)üd\ *n* : the quality or state of being exact

ex·act·ly \ig-'zak-(t)lē\ *adv* **1 a :** in an exact manner ⟨do *exactly* as you're told⟩ **b :** so as to match fact or a state ⟨at *exactly* three o'clock⟩ ⟨*exactly* the same size⟩ **c :** in every way : ALTOGETHER ⟨that was *exactly* the wrong thing to do⟩ ⟨not *exactly* what I had in mind⟩ **2 :** quite so : just as you say — used to express agreement

ex·ag·ger·ate \ig-'zaj-ə-ˌrāt\ *vb* **-at·ed; -at·ing :** to enlarge a fact or statement beyond what is actual or true [from Latin *exaggeratus* "exaggerate", from *exaggerare,* literally "to heap up"] — **ex·ag·ger·at·ed·ly** \-ˌrāt-əd-lē\ *adv* — **ex·ag·ger·a·tion** \-ˌzaj-ə-'rā-shən\ *n* — **ex·ag·ger·a·tor** \-'zaj-ə-ˌrāt-ər\ *n*

ex·alt \ig-'zȯlt\ *vb* **1 :** to raise high especially in rank or power **2 :** GLORIFY 2, 3 — **ex·alt·er** *n*

ex·al·ta·tion \ˌeg-ˌzȯl-'tā-shən\ *n* **1 :** the act of exalting

: the state of being exalted   **2** : a greatly heightened sense of personal well-being, power, or importance

ex·am \ig-'zam\ *n* : EXAMINATION

ex·am·i·na·tion \ig-,zam-ə-'nā-shən\ *n*   **1** : the act or process of examining : the state of being examined   **2** : a test to determine progress, fitness, or knowledge

ex·am·ine \ig-'zam-ən\ *vb* **-ined; -in·ing**   **1** : to look at or check carefully ⟨*examine* a company's books⟩ ⟨have your eyes *examined*⟩   **2** : to question closely ⟨*examine* a witness⟩ — **ex·am·in·er** *n*

ex·am·ple \ig-'zam-pəl\ *n*   **1** : one that serves as a pattern to be followed ⟨a bad *example*⟩ ⟨set a good *example*⟩   **2 a** : punishment given to someone as a warning to others   **b** : the person so punished ⟨we'll make an *example* of you⟩   **3** : one of a group or collection that shows what the whole is like : SAMPLE ⟨a fine *example* of the silversmith's art⟩   **4** : a problem to be solved to show how a rule works ⟨*examples* in arithmetic⟩   **syn** see PATTERN — **for example** : as an example

ex·as·per·ate \ig-'zas-pə-,rāt\ *vb* **-at·ed; -at·ing** : to make angry : ANNOY, IRRITATE

ex·as·per·a·tion \ig-,zas-pə-'rā-shən\ *n*   **1** : extreme annoyance : ANGER   **2** : a source of annoyance

Ex·cal·i·bur \ek-'skal-ə-bər\ *n* : King Arthur's sword

ex·ca·vate \'ek-skə-,vāt\ *vb* **-vat·ed; -vat·ing**   **1** : to hollow out : form a hole in ⟨*excavate* the side of a hill⟩   **2** : to make by hollowing out ⟨*excavate* a tunnel⟩   **3** : to dig out and remove ⟨*excavate* sand⟩   **4** : to uncover by digging away covering earth ⟨*excavate* an ancient city⟩ — **ex·ca·va·tor** \-,vāt-ər\ *n*

ex·ca·va·tion \,ek-skə-'vā-shən\ *n*   **1** : the act or process of excavating   **2** : a hollowed-out place formed by excavating

ex·ceed \ik-'sēd\ *vb*   **1** : to be greater than ⟨the cost must not *exceed* ten dollars⟩   **2** : to go or be beyond the limit   **syn** EXCEED, SURPASS, EXCEL, OUTDO mean to go beyond a certain limit, measure, or degree. EXCEED suggests going beyond a limit set by authority, custom, or earlier achievement ⟨*exceed* the speed limit⟩ SURPASS suggests being greater in worth, merit, or skill ⟨the book *surpassed* our hopes⟩ EXCEL suggests supremacy in achievement or value ⟨*excels* in science⟩ OUTDO suggests bettering one's previous work ⟨the chef really *outdid* herself this time⟩

ex·ceed·ing \ *adj* : EXCEPTIONAL 2, EXTRAORDINARY ⟨*exceeding* darkness⟩

ex·ceed·ing·ly \ik-'sēd-iŋ-lē\ *or* **ex·ceed·ing** *adv* : to a very great degree : EXTREMELY ⟨an *exceedingly* fine job⟩ ⟨I am *exceedingly* cold⟩

ex·cel \ik-'sel\ *vb* **ex·celled; ex·cel·ling** : to do or be better than others : SURPASS ⟨a student who *excels* in sports⟩ ⟨*excels* her brother at tennis⟩   **syn** see EXCEED

ex·cel·lence \'ek-s(ə-)lən(t)s\ *n*   **1** : high quality   **2** : an excellent quality : VIRTUE

ex·cel·len·cy \'ek-s(ə-)lən-sē\ *n, pl* **-cies**   **1** : EXCELLENCE   **2** — used as a title for some high government and church officials ⟨your *Excellency*⟩

ex·cel·lent \'ek-s(ə-)lənt\ *adj* : very good of its kind — **ex·cel·lent·ly** *adv*

ex·cel·si·or \ik-'sel-sē-ər\ *n* : fine curled wood shavings used especially for packing fragile items

¹**ex·cept** \ik-'sept\ *vb* : to leave out from a number or a whole : EXCLUDE [Middle English *excepten* "to take or leave out", from early French *excepter* (same meaning), derived from Latin *excipere* "to take out", from *ex-* "out" and *capere* "to take" — related to ACCEPT, CAPTURE, INTERCEPT]

²**except** *also* **ex·cept·ing** *prep*   **1** : not including ⟨daily *except* Sundays⟩   **2** : other than ⟨take no orders *except* from me⟩

³**except** *also* **excepting** *conj* : if it were not for the fact that : ONLY ⟨I'd go, *except* it's too far⟩

except for *prep* : with the exception of : but for ⟨all A's *except for* a B in Latin⟩

ex·cep·tion \ik-'sep-shən\ *n*   **1** : the act of excepting ⟨it's all here, with the *exception* of the sweater⟩   **2** : a case where a rule does not apply ⟨we'll make an *exception* this time⟩   **3** : an objection or a ground for objection ⟨took *exception* to the remark⟩

ex·cep·tion·able \ik-'sep-sh(ə-)nə-bəl\ *adj* : OBJECTIONABLE — **ex·cep·tion·ably** \-blē\ *adv*

ex·cep·tion·al \ik-'sep-shnəl, -shən-ᵊl\ *adj*   **1** : forming an exception ⟨an *exceptional* amount of rain⟩   **2** : better than average : SUPERIOR ⟨an *exceptional* student in math⟩ — **ex·cep·tion·al·ly** \-ē\ *adv* — **ex·cep·tion·al·ness** *n*

¹**ex·cerpt** \ek-'sərpt, eg-'zərpt; 'ek-,sərpt, 'eg-,zərpt\ *vb* : to select for quoting

²**ex·cerpt** \'ek-,sərpt, 'eg-,zərpt\ *n* : a part taken from a longer work ⟨read an *excerpt* from the play⟩

¹**ex·cess** \ik-'ses, 'ek-,ses\ *n*   **1** : a state of being more than enough   **2 a** : an amount beyond what is usual, needed, or asked   **b** : the amount by which one thing or quantity exceeds another

²**excess** *adj* : more than is usual, acceptable, or needed ⟨*excess* baggage⟩ ⟨an outlet for their *excess* energy⟩

ex·ces·sive \ik-'ses-iv\ *adj* : showing excess : too much — **ex·ces·sive·ly** *adv* — **ex·ces·sive·ness** *n*

¹**ex·change** \iks-'chānj, 'eks-,chānj\ *n*   **1** : a giving or taking of one thing in return for another : TRADE   **2** : the act of substituting one thing for another   **3** : the act of giving and receiving between two groups ⟨the *exchange* of students between two countries⟩   **4 a** : a place where things or services are exchanged ⟨a *stock* exchange⟩   **b** : a central office in which telephone lines are connected to permit communication

²**exchange** *vb* **ex·changed; ex·chang·ing** : to give in exchange : TRADE, SWAP — **ex·change·abil·i·ty** \iks-,chānjə-'bil-ət-ē\ *n* — **ex·change·able** \iks-'chān-jə-bəl\ *adj* — **ex·chang·er** *n*

exchange student *n* : a student from one country received into a school in another in exchange for one sent to the first country

ex·che·quer \'eks-,chek-ər, iks-'chek-\ *n*   **1** : a department of the British Government concerned with funds to run the government   **2** : money available : FUNDS

¹**ex·cise** \'ek-,sīz, -,sīs\ *n* : a tax on the manufacture, sale, or use of certain goods with a country [from obsolete Dutch *excijs* "tax", probably derived from early French *assise* "assessment"]

²**ex·cise** \ek-'sīz\ *vb* **ex·cised; ex·cis·ing** : to remove by cutting out [from Latin *excisus,* past participle of *excidere* "to cut out", from *ex-* "out, out of" and *caedere* "to cut"] — **ex·ci·sion** \-'sizh-ən\ *n*

ex·cit·able \ik-'sīt-ə-bəl\ *adj*   **1** : easily excited   **2** : capable of being excited — **ex·cit·abil·i·ty** \-,sīt-ə-'bil-ət-ē\ *n*

ex·ci·ta·tion \,ek-,sī-'tā-shən, ,ek-sə-\ *n* : EXCITEMENT 1; *esp* : the process by which protoplasm becomes active in response to a stimulus or the state resulting from this

ex·cite \ik-'sīt\ *vb* **ex·cit·ed; ex·cit·ing**   **1** : to stir up feeling in : ROUSE ⟨the ideas that *excite* young people⟩   **2** : to cause to be felt or done ⟨*excite* admiration⟩ ⟨posters *excited* much interest in the show⟩   **3 a** : ENERGIZE 2a   **b** : to produce a magnetic field in   **4** : to increase the activity of (as nervous tissue) : STIMULATE   **5** : to raise (as an atom) to a higher energy level   **syn** see PROVOKE — **ex·cit·er** *n*

ex·cit·ed *adj* : having or showing strong feeling ⟨*excited* about the trip⟩ — **ex·cit·ed·ly** *adv*

ex·cite·ment \ik-'sīt-mənt\ *n*   **1** : something that excites   **2** : the state of being excited : AGITATION

ex·cit·ing \ik-'sīt-iŋ\ *adj* : causing excitement — **ex·cit·ing·ly** \-iŋ-lē\ *adv*

ex·claim \iks-'klām\ *vb* : to cry out or speak suddenly or with strong feeling ⟨"I won!" she *exclaimed*⟩

ex·cla·ma·tion \ˌeks-klə-'mā-shən\ *n* **1** : a sharp or sudden cry of strong feeling **2** : a strong expression of anger or complaint

exclamation mark *n* : EXCLAMATION POINT

exclamation point *n* : a punctuation mark ! used chiefly after an exclamation to show a forceful way of speaking or a strong feeling

ex·clam·a·to·ry \iks-'klam-ə-ˌtōr-ē, -ˌtȯr-\ *adj* : containing or using exclamation ⟨an *exclamatory* sentence⟩

ex·clude \iks-'klüd\ *vb* **ex·clud·ed; ex·clud·ing** : to shut or keep out — **ex·clud·able** \-'klüd-ə-bəl\ *adj* — **ex·clu·sion** \-'klü-zhən\ *n*

ex·clu·sive \iks-'klü-siv, -ziv\ *adj* **1** : excluding or trying to exclude others ⟨an *exclusive* neighborhood⟩ **2** : ⁴SOLE 2a ⟨we have *exclusive* use of the beach⟩ **3** : ¹FULL 2c, COMPLETE ⟨gave their *exclusive* attention to the job⟩ **4** : not including ⟨for five days *exclusive* of today⟩ — **ex·clu·sive·ly** *adv* — **ex·clu·sive·ness** *n*

ex·clu·siv·i·ty \ˌeks-ˌklü-'siv-ət-ē, iks-, -'ziv-\ *n, pl* **-ties** **1** : the quality or state of being exclusive **2** : exclusive rights or services

ex·com·mu·ni·cate \ˌeks-kə-'myü-nə-ˌkāt\ *vb* **-cat·ed; -cat·ing** : to shut off officially from the rights of church membership — **ex·com·mu·ni·ca·tion** \-ˌmyü-nə-'kā-shən\ *n* — **ex·com·mu·ni·ca·tor** \-'myü-nə-ˌkāt-ər\ *n*

ex·co·ri·ate \ek-'skōr-ē-ˌāt, -'skȯr-\ *vb* **-at·ed; -at·ing** : to criticize most severely — **ex·co·ri·a·tion** \(ˌ)ek-ˌskōr-ē-'ā-shən, -ˌskȯr-\ *n*

ex·cre·ment \'ek-skrə-mənt\ *n* : waste matter discharged from the body and especially from the alimentary canal

ex·cres·cence \ek-'skres-ᵊn(t)s\ *n* : OUTGROWTH 1; *esp* : an abnormal outgrowth (as a wart) on the body

ex·cre·ta \ek-'skrēt-ə\ *n pl* : waste matter eliminated or separated from a living thing

ex·crete \ik-'skrēt\ *vb* **ex·cret·ed; ex·cret·ing** : to separate and eliminate (waste) from the blood or tissues or from the active protoplasm usually in the form of sweat or urine

ex·cre·tion \ik-'skrē-shən\ *n* **1** : the act or process of excreting **2** : excreted matter

ex·cre·to·ry \'ek-skrə-ˌtōr-ē, -ˌtȯr-\ *adj* : of, relating to, or functioning in excretion

ex·cru·ci·at·ing \ik-'skrü-shē-ˌāt-iŋ\ *adj* **1** : causing great mental or physical pain : AGONIZING ⟨*excruciating* torture⟩ ⟨an *excruciating* moment of embarrassment⟩ **2** : very severe ⟨*excruciating* pain) [derived from Latin *excruciatus*, past participle of *excruciare* "to torture", from *ex-* "out of, from " and *cruciare* "to torment, crucify", from *cruc-, crux* "cross" — related to CROSS, CRUCIAL, CRUCIFY] — **ex·cru·ci·at·ing·ly** \-iŋ-lē\ *adv*

ex·cul·pate \'ek-(ˌ)skəl-ˌpāt, ek-'skəl-\ *vb* **-pat·ed; -pat·ing** : to clear from a charge of fault or guilt — **ex·cul·pa·tion** \ˌek-(ˌ)skəl-'pā-shən\ *n* — **ex·cul·pa·to·ry** \ek-'skəl-pə-ˌtōr-ē, -ˌtȯr-\ *adj*

ex·cur·rent \ek-'skər-ənt, -'skə-rənt\ *adj* : marked by a current that flows outward ⟨*excurrent* canals of a sponge⟩

ex·cur·sion \ik-'skər-zhən\ *n* **1 a** : a short trip for pleasure **b** : a trip at special reduced rates **2** : a wandering off from the subject : DIGRESSION [from Latin *excursio, excursion-* "a going out", from *excursus* past participle of *excurrere* "to run out, make an excursion, extend", from *ex-* "out, forth" and *currere* "to run" — related to CURRENT]

ex·cur·sion·ist \ik-'skərzh-(ə-)nəst\ *n* : a person who goes on an excursion

¹ex·cuse \ik-'skyüz\ *vb* **ex·cused; ex·cus·ing** **1** : to make apology for ⟨*excused* myself for being late⟩ **2** : to overlook or dismiss as of little importance ⟨*excuse* a mistake⟩ **3** : to let off from doing something ⟨*excused* the class from homework⟩ **4** : to be an acceptable reason for : JUSTIFY ⟨nothing *excuses* bad manners⟩ — **ex·cus·able** \-'skyü-zə-bəl\ *adj* — **ex·cus·ably** \-blē\ *adv* — **ex·cus·er** *n*

syn EXCUSE, CONDONE, PARDON, FORGIVE mean to demand neither punishment nor payment in return for a loss or wrong. EXCUSE suggests overlooking a fault or error by not criticizing or punishing the one responsible ⟨*excused* them for being late⟩ CONDONE suggests accepting without protest a blameworthy act or condition ⟨does not *condone* cheating on taxes⟩ PARDON suggests the freeing from a penalty that is due ⟨the governor *pardoned* the convicted criminals⟩ FORGIVE suggests giving up feelings of resentment and the desire for revenge ⟨*forgave* the students who had been mean to us⟩

²ex·cuse \ik-'skyüs\ *n* **1** : the act of excusing **2** : something offered as a reason for being excused **3** : something that excuses or is a reason for excusing

ex·e·cra·ble \'ek-si-krə-bəl\ *adj* : very bad ⟨living conditions in the slums were *execrable*⟩ — **ex·e·cra·ble·ness** *n* — **ex·e·cra·bly** \-blē\ *adv*

ex·e·crate \'ek-sə-ˌkrāt\ *vb* **-crat·ed; -crat·ing** **1** : to declare to be evil **2** : to dislike very strongly : ABHOR — **ex·e·cra·tion** \ˌek-sə-'krā-shən\ *n*

ex·e·cute \'ek-sə-ˌkyüt\ *vb* **-cut·ed; -cut·ing** **1** : to put into effect : CARRY OUT, PERFORM ⟨*execute* a plan⟩ ⟨*execute* a dance step⟩ **2** : to do what is required by ⟨the computer *executed* the first line of the program⟩ **3** : to put to death according to a legal order **4** : to make or produce by carrying out a design ⟨a statue *executed* in bronze⟩

ex·e·cu·tion \ˌek-sə-'kyü-shən\ *n* **1** : the act or process of executing : a carrying through of something to its finish ⟨put a plan into *execution*⟩ **2** : a putting to death as a legal penalty **3** : the way in which something is executed

ex·e·cu·tion·er \ˌek-sə-'kyü-sh(ə-)nər\ *n* : a person who carries out a sentence of death

¹ex·ec·u·tive \ig-'zek-(y)ət-iv\ *adj* **1** : fitted for or relating to the managing or directing of things ⟨*executive* skills⟩ ⟨an *executive* program for a computer⟩ **2** : of or relating to the carrying out of laws and the conduct of public affairs ⟨the *executive* branch of government⟩ **3** : of or relating to an executive ⟨the *executive* dining room⟩

²executive *n* **1** : the executive branch of a government **2** : a person who manages or directs

ex·ec·u·tor \ig-'zek-(y)ət-ər, *in sense 1 also* 'ek-sə-ˌkyüt-\ *n* **1** : a person who executes something **2** : the person named in a will to carry it out

ex·ec·u·trix \ig-'zek-(y)ə-(ˌ)triks\ *n, pl* **ex·ec·u·trix·es** *or* **ex·ec·u·tri·ces** \-ˌzek-(y)ə-'trī-ˌsēz\ : a woman who is an executor

ex·em·plar \ig-'zem-ˌplär, -plər\ *n* **1** : one that serves as a model or pattern; *esp* : an ideal model **2** : a typical example

ex·em·pla·ry \ig-'zem-plə-rē\ *adj* : deserving to be imitated : COMMENDABLE — **ex·em·plar·i·ly** \ˌeg-ˌzem-'pler-ə-lē\ *adv*

ex·em·pli·fy \ig-'zem-plə-ˌfī\ *vb* **-fied; -fy·ing** **1** : to show by example **2** : to serve as an example of — **ex·em·pli·fi·ca·tion** \-ˌzem-plə-fə-'kā-shən\ *n*

ex·em·plum \ig-'zem-pləm\ *n, pl* **-pla** \-plə\ : a story used to point out a moral or support an argument

¹ex·empt \ig-'zem(p)t\ *adj* : free or released from some condition or requirement that others must meet or deal with

²exempt *vb* : to make exempt

ex·emp·tion \ig-'zem(p)-shən\ *n* **1** : the act of exempting : the state of being exempt **2** : something that is exempted

¹ex·er·cise \'ek-sər-ˌsīz\ *n* **1** : the act of putting into use, action, or practice ⟨the *exercise* of power⟩ **2** : bodily ac-

\ə\	abut	\au̇\	out	\i\	tip	\ȯ\	saw	\u̇\	foot
\ər\	further	\ch\	chin	\ī\	life	\ȯi\	coin	\y\	yet
\a\	mat	\e\	pet	\j\	job	\th\	thin	\yü\	few
\ā\	take	\ē\	easy	\ŋ\	sing	\th\	this	\yu̇\	cure
\ä\	cot, cart	\g\	go	\ō\	bone	\ü\	food	\zh\	vision

tivity for the sake of physical fitness ⟨get plenty of fresh air and *exercise*⟩ **3** : something done to develop skill ⟨arithmetic *exercises*⟩ ⟨finger *exercises*⟩ **4** *pl* : a program of songs, speeches, and announcements of awards and honors ⟨graduation *exercises*⟩

²exercise *vb* **-cised; -cis·ing** **1** : to put into use : EXERT ⟨*exercise* patience⟩ ⟨*exercise* authority⟩ **2 a** : to use again and again in order to strengthen or develop ⟨*exercise* a muscle⟩ **b** : to put through exercises : give exercise to ⟨*exercise* the dog⟩ **3** : to worry, alarm, or annoy about something ⟨the people were *exercised* about pollution⟩ **4** : to take exercise ⟨*exercises* every day⟩ — **ex·er·cis·able** \-ˌsī-zə-bəl\ *adj* — **ex·er·cis·er** *n*

ex·ert \ig-ˈzərt\ *vb* **1** : to put forth (as strength) : bring into play ⟨the force *exerted* by a machine⟩ ⟨*exert* influence⟩ **2** : to put (oneself) into action or to tiring effort ⟨don't *exert* yourself too much⟩

ex·er·tion \ig-ˈzər-shən\ *n* : the act or an instance of exerting

ex·e·unt \ˈek-sē-(ˌ)ənt\ — used as a stage direction that all or some characters leave the stage

ex·fo·li·a·tion \(ˌ)eks-ˌfō-lē-ˈā-shən\ *n* : the action or process of shedding or removing in thin layers or scales; *esp* : the phase of weathering of rock in which thin pieces break loose — **ex·fo·li·ate** \(ˈ)eks-ˈfō-lē-ˌāt\ *vb*

ex·ha·la·tion \ˌeks-(h)ə-ˈlā-shən\ *n* : something exhaled or given off

ex·hale \eks-ˈhāl\ *vb* **ex·haled; ex·hal·ing** **1** : to breathe out **2** : to send forth (as gas or odor)

¹ex·haust \ig-ˈzȯst\ *vb* **1 a** : to use up completely ⟨*exhausted* our funds⟩ **b** : to use up all of the mental or physical energy of **2 a** : to draw off or let out completely ⟨*exhaust* the air from the jar⟩ **b** : to empty by drawing something from **3** : to try out all of ⟨they *exhausted* all possibilities⟩ **syn** see TIRE — **ex·haust·er** *n* — **ex·haust·ibil·i·ty** \-ˌzȯ-stə-ˈbil-ət-ē\ *n* — **ex·haust·ible** \-ˈzȯ-stə-bəl\ *adj*

²exhaust *n* **1** : the gas that escapes from an engine **2** : a system of pipes through which exhaust escapes

ex·haus·tion \ig-ˈzȯs-chən\ *n* **1** : the act of exhausting **2** : the state of being exhausted

ex·haus·tive \ig-ˈzȯ-stiv\ *adj* : trying all possibilities : THOROUGH ⟨an *exhaustive* search⟩ — **ex·haus·tive·ly** *adv* — **ex·haus·tive·ness** *n*

¹ex·hib·it \ig-ˈzib-ət\ *vb* **1** : to show by outward signs : REVEAL ⟨*exhibit* an interest in music⟩ **2** : to put on display ⟨*exhibit* a collection of paintings⟩ **syn** see SHOW — **ex·hib·i·tor** \-ət-ər\ *n*

²exhibit *n* **1** : an article or a collection shown in an exhibition **2** : an article shown as evidence in a law court

ex·hi·bi·tion \ˌek-sə-ˈbish-ən\ *n* **1** : an act or instance of exhibiting **2** : a public showing (as of works of art, manufactured goods, or athletic skill)

ex·hil·a·rate \ig-ˈzil-ə-ˌrāt\ *vb* **-rat·ed; -rat·ing** : to cause to feel cheerful or lively : put into high spirits — **ex·hil·a·ra·tive** \-ˌrāt-iv\ *adj*

ex·hil·a·ra·tion \ig-ˌzil-ə-ˈrā-shən\ *n* **1** : the action of exhilarating **2** : the state or the feeling of being exhilarated : high spirits

ex·hort \ig-ˈzȯrt\ *vb* : to try to influence by words or advice : urge strongly — **ex·hort·er** *n*

ex·hor·ta·tion \ˌeks-ȯr-ˈtā-shən, ˌegz-\ *n* : an act or instance of exhorting

ex·hume \igz-ˈ(y)üm, iks-ˈ(h)yüm\ *vb* **ex·humed; ex·hum·ing** : to remove from a place of burial — **ex·hu·ma·tion** \ˌeks-(h)yü-ˈmā-shən, ˌegz-(y)ü-\ *n*

ex·i·gence \ˈek-sə-jən(t)s\ *n* : EXIGENCY

ex·i·gen·cy \ˈek-sə-jən-sē, ig-ˈzij-ən-\ *n, pl* **-cies** : a situation requiring immediate action

¹ex·ile \ˈeg-ˌzīl, ˈek-ˌsīl\ *n* **1 a** : an act or instance of being forced to leave one's country or home; *also* : voluntary absence from one's country or home **b** : the state of one

so absent **2** : a person who is in exile

²exile *vb* **ex·iled; ex·il·ing** : to force to leave one's own country or home

ex·ist \ig-ˈzist\ *vb* **1** : to have actual being : be real ⟨do unicorns *exist*⟩ **2** : to continue to be ⟨as long as doubt *exists*⟩ **3** : to continue to live : stay alive ⟨earned barely enough to *exist* on⟩

ex·ist·ence \ig-ˈzis-tən(t)s\ *n* **1** : the fact or the state of having being or of being real ⟨the largest animal in *existence*⟩ **2** : the state of being alive : LIFE ⟨owed my *existence* to a doctor's skill⟩

ex·ist·ent \ig-ˈzis-tənt\ *adj* **1** : having being **2** : existing now : EXTANT

¹ex·it \ˈeg-zət, ˈek-sət\ — used as a stage direction to indicate who goes offstage [from Latin *exit* "he goes out", from *exire* "to go out", from *ex-* "out of, from" and *ire* "to go" — related to ISSUE, ITINERARY]

²exit *n* **1** : a departure from a stage **2** : the act of going out or going away **3** : a way to go out of a place

³exit *vb* : to go out : LEAVE, DEPART

exo- *or* **ex-** *combining form* : outside : outer ⟨*exo*skeleton⟩ ⟨*ex*urb⟩ — compare END- 1 [from Greek *exō* "out, outside"]

exo·crine \ˈek-sə-krən, -ˌkrīn, -ˌkrēn\ *adj* : producing, being, or relating to a secretion that is released outside its source ⟨*exocrine* cells of the pancreas⟩

exocrine gland *n* : a gland (as a sweat gland or a kidney) that releases a secretion outside of or at the surface of an organ by means of a duct or canal

ex·o·dus \ˈek-səd-əs\ *n* **1** *cap* — see BIBLE table **2** : a mass departure [from Latin *Exodus* "a book of the Bible", derived from Greek *exodos* "a road or journey out", from *ex-* "out" and *hodos* "road"]

ex of·fi·cio \ˌeks-ə-ˈfish-ē-ˌō, -ˈfis-\ *adv or adj* : because of an office ⟨the Vice President serves *ex officio* as president of the Senate⟩

ex·on·er·ate \ig-ˈzän-ə-ˌrāt\ *vb* **-at·ed; -at·ing** : to clear from a charge of wrongdoing or from blame — **ex·on·er·a·tion** \ig-ˌzän-ə-ˈrā-shən\ *n*

ex·or·bi·tant \ig-ˈzȯr-bət-ənt\ *adj* : going beyond the limits of what is fair, reasonable, or expected ⟨*exorbitant* prices⟩ — **ex·or·bi·tant·ly** *adv*

ex·or·cise \ˈek-ˌsȯr-ˌsīz, -ˌsər-\ *vb* **-cised; -cis·ing** : to drive (as an evil spirit) off by calling upon some holy name or by spells

ex·or·cism \ˈek-ˌsȯr-ˌsiz-əm, -ˌsər-\ *n* : the act or practice of exorcising — **ex·or·cist** \-ˌsist, -ˌsəst\ *n*

exo·skel·e·ton \ˌek-sō-ˈskel-ət-ᵊn\ *n* : a hard supporting or protective structure (as of an insect, spider, or crustacean) on the outside of the body

exo·sphere \ˈek-sō-ˌsfi(ə)r\ *n* : the outermost region of the atmosphere of the earth or a planet

exo·ther·mic \ˌek-sō-ˈthər-mik\ *adj* : characterized by or formed by the giving off of heat ⟨an *exothermic* chemical reaction⟩

¹ex·ot·ic \ig-ˈzät-ik\ *adj* **1** : introduced from another country ⟨*exotic* plants⟩ **2** : very different or unusual ⟨*exotic* colors⟩ — **ex·ot·i·cal·ly** \-ˈzät-i-k(ə-)lē\ *adv* — **ex·ot·ic·ness** \-ik-nəs\ *n*

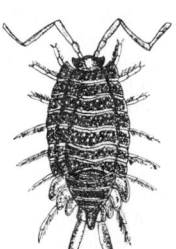

exoskeleton

²exotic *n* : something (as a plant) that is exotic

ex·pand \ik-ˈspand\ *vb* **1** : to open wide : UNFOLD ⟨a bird with wings *expanded*⟩ **2** : to increase in size, number, or amount ⟨substances *expand* when heated⟩ ⟨the *expanding* universe⟩ ⟨their work *expanded*⟩ **3** : to work out in greater detail ⟨*expand* an argument⟩ **4** : to state in enlarged form or in a series : write out in full ⟨*expand* a binomial raised to a power⟩ — **ex·pand·able** \-ˈspan-də-bəl\ *adj* — **ex·pand·er** *n*

  syn EXPAND, SWELL, INFLATE, DILATE mean to increase in size or volume. EXPAND may apply to increases coming from both inside and outside ⟨bread *expands* as it bakes⟩ ⟨*expanded* the size of the house by adding a room⟩ SWELL suggests a gradual enlargement beyond the original or normal limits of a thing ⟨the injury caused her leg to *swell*⟩ INFLATE suggests expanding by the addition of air or something that lacks substance ⟨*inflate* a tire⟩ DILATE applies especially to the expansion of an outer boundary ⟨the pupils of your eyes will *dilate* in dim light⟩

expanded notation *n* : the writing of a number in terms of powers of the base in which it is expressed ⟨123 in base 10 when written in *expanded notation* is $1(10^2)$ + $2(10^1)$ + $3(10^0)$⟩

ex·panse \ik-'span(t)s\ *n* : a wide space, area, or stretch ⟨the vast *expanse* of the ocean⟩

ex·pan·sion \ik-'span-chən\ *n* **1** : the act of expanding or the state of being expanded **2** : something expanded or a result of expanding **3** : the result of an indicated operation ⟨the *expansion* of $(a + b)^2$ is $a^2 + 2ab + b^2$⟩

ex·pan·sive \ik-'span(t)-siv\ *adj* **1** : having a capacity or a tendency to expand ⟨gases are *expansive*⟩ **2** : causing or tending to cause expansion ⟨an *expansive* force⟩ **3** : being in a good or talkative mood **4** : having considerable extent : BROAD — **ex·pan·sive·ly** *adv* — **ex·pan·sive·ness** *n*

ex·pa·ti·ate \ek-'spā-shē-,āt\ *vb* **-at·ed; -at·ing** : to speak or write in a full or lengthy manner — **ex·pa·ti·a·tion** \(,)ek-,spā-shē-'ā-shən\ *n*

¹ex·pa·tri·ate \ek-'spā-trē-,āt\ *vb* **-at·ed; -at·ing** : ²EXILE — **ex·pa·tri·a·tion** \(,)ek-,spā-trē-'ā-shən\ *n*

²ex·pa·tri·ate \ek-'spā-trē-,āt, -trē-ət\ *adj* : living in a foreign country

³ex·pa·tri·ate \ek-'spā-trē-,āt, -trē-ət\ *n* : a person living in a foreign country; *esp* : one who has given up his or her original country

ex·pect \ik-'spekt\ *vb* **1** : SUPPOSE 3, THINK ⟨who do you *expect* will win⟩ **2** : to believe that something will occur and wait for it to happen ⟨*expect* rain⟩ ⟨*expect* her home soon⟩ **3 a** : to consider reasonable, due, or necessary ⟨*expect* an honest day's work⟩ **b** : to consider to be obliged ⟨*expected* you to pay your debts⟩ [from Latin *expectare, exspectare* "to look forward to", from *ex-* "out, forth" and *spectare* "to watch, look at", derived from *specere* "to look, look at" — related to AUSPICE, SPECTACLE] — **ex·pect·able** \-'spek-tə-bəl\ *adj*

ex·pect·an·cy \ik-'spek-tən-sē\ *n, pl* **-cies** **1** : EXPECTATION 1 **2** : the expected amount (as of years of life) based on statistical probability ⟨life *expectancy*⟩

ex·pect·ant \ik-'spek-tənt\ *adj* **1** : characterized by or being in a state of expectation **2** : expecting the birth of a child — **ex·pect·ant·ly** *adv*

ex·pec·ta·tion \,ek-,spek-'tā-shən, ik-\ *n* **1** : the act or state of expecting : a looking forward to or waiting for something **2** : chances of good or bad fortune — usually used in pl. **3** : something expected

ex·pec·to·rate \ik-'spek-tə-,rāt\ *vb* **-rat·ed; -rat·ing** : to discharge (as phlegm) from the throat or lungs by coughing and spitting; *also* : ²SPIT 1a — **ex·pec·to·ra·tion** \-,spek-tə-'rā-shən\ *n*

ex·pe·di·ence \ik-'spēd-ē-ən(t)s\ *n* : EXPEDIENCY

ex·pe·di·en·cy \ik-'spēd-ē-ən-sē\ *n, pl* **-cies** : the use of expedient means and methods

¹ex·pe·di·ent \ik-'spēd-ē-ənt\ *adj* : suitable for bringing about a desired result often without regard to what is fair or right — **ex·pe·di·ent·ly** *adv*

²expedient *n* : a means to accomplish an end; *esp* : one used in place of a better means that is not available

ex·pe·dite \'ek-spə-,dīt\ *vb* **-dit·ed; -dit·ing** : to speed up the process or progress of

ex·pe·di·tion \,ek-spə-'dish-ən\ *n* **1 a** : a journey or trip undertaken for a specific purpose (as war or exploring) **b** : a group making such a journey **2** : prompt handling of what needs to be done

ex·pe·di·tion·ary \ek-spə-'dish-ə-,ner-ē\ *adj* : sent on military service abroad ⟨an *expeditionary* force⟩

ex·pe·di·tious \,ek-spə-'dish-əs\ *adj* : marked by or acting with promptness — **ex·pe·di·tious·ly** *adv* — **ex·pe·di·tious·ness** *n*

ex·pel \ik-'spel\ *vb* **ex·pelled; ex·pel·ling** **1** : to drive or force out ⟨*expel* air from the lungs⟩ **2** : to force to leave usually by official action ⟨*expelled* from school⟩

ex·pend \ik-'spend\ *vb* **1** : to pay out : SPEND **2** : USE UP

ex·pend·able \ik-'spen-də-bəl\ *adj* : normally used up in service ⟨*expendable* supplies like pencils and paper⟩ — **ex·pend·abil·i·ty** \-,spen-də-'bil-ət-ē\ *n* — **expendable** *n* — **ex·pend·ably** \-'spen-də-blē\ *adv*

ex·pen·di·ture \ik-'spen-di-chər, -də-,chu̇(ə)r\ *n* **1** : the act of spending (as money, time, or energy) **2** : something that is spent

ex·pense \ik-'spen(t)s\ *n* **1** : something spent or required to be spent : COST **2** : a cause of spending ⟨a car is a great *expense*⟩

expense account *n* : an account of expenses for which an employer will repay an employee

ex·pen·sive \ik-'spen(t)-siv\ *adj* **1** : COSTLY **2** ⟨an *expensive* mistake⟩ **2 a** : having a high price ⟨*expensive* gifts⟩ **b** : marked by high prices ⟨*expensive* shops⟩ — **ex·pen·sive·ly** *adv* — **ex·pen·sive·ness** *n*

¹ex·pe·ri·ence \ik-'spir-ē-ən(t)s\ *n* **1** : the actual living through an event or series of events ⟨learn by *experience*⟩ **2 a** : skill or knowledge gained by actually doing or feeling a thing ⟨a job that requires someone with *experience*⟩ ⟨had gained a lot of *experience* by the end of the season⟩ **b** : the amount of such skill or knowledge ⟨has five years' *experience*⟩ **3** : something one has actually done or lived through ⟨my *experiences* as a riverboat pilot⟩

²experience *vb* **-enced; -enc·ing** : to have experience of : UNDERGO

ex·pe·ri·enced \ik-'spir-ē-ən(t)st\ *adj* : made skillful or wise through experience ⟨an *experienced* driver⟩

¹ex·per·i·ment \ik-'sper-ə-mənt\ *n* : ¹TEST 1, TRIAL; *esp* : a procedure or operation carried out under controlled conditions in order to discover something, to test a hypothesis, or to serve as an example

²ex·per·i·ment \ik-'sper-ə-,ment\ *vb* : to make experiments — **ex·per·i·men·ta·tion** \ik-,sper-ə-mən-'tā-shən, -,men-\ *n*

¹ex·per·i·men·tal \ik-,sper-ə-'ment-ᵊl\ *adj* **1 a** : of, relating to, or based on experience or experiment ⟨*experimental* evidence⟩ **b** : subjected to the condition that is different from normal for a factor being tested in an experiment ⟨the *experimental* group⟩ **2** : relating to or having the characteristics of experiment : TENTATIVE — **ex·per·i·men·tal·ly** \-ᵊl-ē\ *adv*

²experimental *n* : a plant or animal actually made to experience the experimental conditions of an experiment as contrasted to one kept for a control

ex·per·i·ment·er \ik-'sper-ə-,ment-ər\ *n* : a person who experiments or conducts an experiment

experiment station *n* : an establishment for scientific research (as in agriculture) especially of practical importance and for the giving out of information

¹ex·pert \'ek-,spərt, ik-'spərt\ *adj* : showing special skill or knowledge gained from training or experience **syn** see SKILLFUL — **ex·pert·ly** *adv* — **ex·pert·ness** *n*

\ə\ abut	\au̇\ **out**	\i\ tip	\ȯ\ **saw**	\u̇\ **foot**	
\ər\ **further**	\ch\ **chin**	\ī\ **life**	\ȯi\ **coin**	\y\ **yet**	
\a\ **mat**	\e\ **pet**	\j\ **job**	\th\ **thin**	\yü\ **few**	
\ā\ **take**	\ē\ **easy**	\ŋ\ **sing**	\th\ **this**	\yu̇\ **cure**	
\ä\ **cot, cart**	\g\ **go**	\ō\ **bone**	\ü\ **food**	\zh\ **vision**	

²**ex·pert** \'ek-ˌspərt\ *n* : a person with special skill in or knowledge of a subject

ex·per·tise \ˌek-(ˌ)spər-'tēz, -'tēs\ *n* : the skill of an expert

ex·pi·ate \'ek-spē-ˌāt\ *vb* **-at·ed; -at·ing** : to make up for : ATONE — **ex·pi·a·tion** \ˌek-spē-'ā-shən\ *n*

ex·pi·ra·tion \ˌek-spə-'rā-shən\ *n* **1 a** : the expelling of air from the lungs in breathing **b** : air or vapor expelled from the lungs **2** : the fact of coming to an end

expiration date *n* **1** : the date on which something expires ⟨the *expiration date* of a credit card⟩ **2** : the last date on which a product can be safely used ⟨the *expiration date* on a box of cereal⟩

ex·pi·ra·to·ry \ik-'spī-rə-ˌtōr-ē, ek-, -ˌtòr-; 'ek-sp(ə)rə-\ *adj* : of, relating to, or used in breathing air out of the lungs

ex·pire \ik-'spī(ə)r, *oftenest for sense 3* ek-\ *vb* **ex·pired; ex·pir·ing** **1** : to breathe one's last breath : DIE **2** : to come to an end : be no longer in force ⟨this offer *expires* March 1⟩ ⟨my driver's license has *expired*⟩ **3 a** : to let the breath out **b** : to breathe out from or as if from the lungs

ex·plain \ik-'splān\ *vb* **1** : to make plain or understandable **2** : to give the reason for or cause of — **ex·plain·able** \-'splā-nə-bəl\ *adj* — **ex·plain·er** *n*

explain away *vb* : to cause to seem less important by explaining

ex·pla·na·tion \ˌek-splə-'nā-shən\ *n* **1** : the act or process of explaining **2** : a statement that makes something clear

ex·plan·a·to·ry \ik-'splan-ə-ˌtōr-ē, -ˌtòr-\ *adj* : serving to explain — **ex·plan·a·to·ri·ly** \-ˌsplan-ə-'tòr-ə-lē, -'tōr-\ *adv*

ex·ple·tive \'ek-splət-iv\ *n* : an exclamatory word or phrase; *esp* : SWEARWORD

ex·pli·ca·ble \ek-'splik-ə-bəl, 'ek-(ˌ)splik-\ *adj* : able to be explained — **ex·pli·ca·bly** \-blē\ *adv*

ex·pli·cate \'ek-splə-ˌkāt\ *vb* **-cat·ed; -cat·ing** : to give a complete explanation of — **ex·pli·ca·tion** \ˌek-splə-'kā-shən\ *n*

ex·plic·it \ik-'splis-ət\ *adj* : so clear in statement that there is no doubt about the meaning — **ex·plic·it·ly** *adv* — **ex·plic·it·ness** *n*

ex·plode \ik-'splōd\ *vb* **ex·plod·ed; ex·plod·ing** **1** : to cause to be given up or rejected ⟨science has *exploded* many old theories⟩ **2 a** : to burst or cause to burst with violence and noise ⟨the boiler *exploded*⟩ **b** : to go through a rapid chemical or nuclear reaction with the production of noise, heat, and violent expansion of gases **3** : to burst forth ⟨*exploded* with laughter⟩ ⟨zoomed out of the alley and *exploded* into the street⟩ ⟨talk *exploded* around them⟩

Word History Theatergoers in ancient Rome could be noisy in showing both their enjoyment and their dislike of a performance. One of the ways they made noise was by clapping their hands loudly. The Latin verb *plaudere* meant "to make a noise by loud clapping". When the Romans were showing their approval of a performance, the word used was *applaudere*, from which we get our English word *applaud*. When the Romans did not like a performance, they often drove the performer from the stage by loud claps. The word for this was *explaudere*, from the prefix *ex-*, meaning "out, away", and *plaudere*. It is from this word that we get our English word *explode*. In the beginning, the English word *explode* had the meaning "to drive from the stage by a noisy expression of dislike". But this sense has all but disappeared. Other meanings that have either the idea of disapproval or the idea of violent noise have since come into wide use. [from Latin *explaudere* "to drive off the stage by clapping", from *ex-* "out, away" and *plaudere* "to clap" — related to APPLAUD, PLAUDIT, PLAUSIBLE; see *Word History* at PLAUSIBLE]

ex·plod·ed *adj* : showing the parts separated but in correct relationship to each other ⟨an *exploded* view of a machine⟩

¹**ex·ploit** \'ek-ˌsplòit, ik-'splòit\ *n* : a brave or daring act

²**ex·ploit** \ik-'splòit, 'ek-ˌsplòit\ *vb* **1** : to get value or use from ⟨*exploit* your talents⟩ ⟨*exploit* an opponent's weaknesses⟩ **2** : to make use of unfairly for one's own advantage — **ex·ploit·able** \-ə-bəl\ *adj* — **ex·ploi·ta·tion** \ˌek-ˌsplòi-'tā-shən\ *n* — **ex·ploit·er** \ik-'splòit-ər, 'ek-ˌsplòit-\ *n*

ex·plo·ra·tion \ˌek-splə-'rā-shən\ *n* : the act or an instance of exploring

ex·plor·a·to·ry \ik-'splòr-ə-ˌtōr-ē, -ˌtòr-\ *adj* : of, relating to, or being exploration ⟨*exploratory* drilling for oil⟩ ⟨an *exploratory* trip⟩ ⟨*exploratory* surgery⟩

ex·plore \ik-'splō(ə)r, -'splò(ə)r\ *vb* **ex·plored; ex·plor·ing** **1 a** : to search through : look into ⟨*exploring* new ideas⟩ **b** : to go into or range over for purposes of discovery ⟨*explore* a cave⟩ ⟨*explore* the moon⟩ **c** : to examine carefully and in detail especially in order to make a diagnosis ⟨*explore* a wound⟩ **2** : to make a careful search ⟨*explore* for oil⟩

ex·plor·er \ik-'splòr-ər, -'splòr-\ *n* **1** : one that explores ⟨a vehicle called the lunar *explorer*⟩; *esp* : a person who travels in search of new geographical or scientific information **2** *cap* : a member of the scouting program of the Boy Scouts of America for young people 14 to 20 years old

ex·plo·sion \ik-'splō-zhən\ *n* **1** : the act or an instance of exploding **2** : a violent outburst of feeling

¹**ex·plo·sive** \ik-'splō-siv, -ziv\ *adj* **1** : able to cause explosion ⟨the *explosive* power of gunpowder⟩ **2** : likely to explode ⟨an *explosive* temper⟩ — **ex·plo·sive·ly** *adv* — **ex·plo·sive·ness** *n*

²**explosive** *n* : an explosive substance

ex·po·nent \ik-'spō-nənt, 'ek-ˌspō-\ *n* **1** : a symbol written above and to the right of a mathematical expression to indicate how many times the expression is to be repeated as a factor ⟨in the expression a^3, the *exponent* 3 indicates that the product with *a* used three times as a factor is to be found⟩ **2** : a person who supports or favors a cause

ex·po·nen·tial \ˌek-spə-'nen-chəl\ *adj* : of, relating to, or involving an exponent ⟨*xn* is an *exponential* expression⟩ — **ex·po·nen·tial·ly** \-'nench-(ə-)lē\ *adv*

ex·po·nen·ti·a·tion \ˌek-spə-ˌnen-chē-'ā-shən\ *n* : the mathematical operation of raising a quantity to a power

¹**ex·port** \ek-'spō(ə)rt, -'spò(ə)rt, 'ek-ˌspō(ə)rt, 'ek-ˌspò(ə)rt\ *vb* : to carry or send abroad especially for sale in another country — **ex·port·able** \-'spòrt-ə-bəl, -'spōrt-\ *adj* — **ex·por·ta·tion** \ˌek-ˌspòr-'tā-shən, -ˌspōr-, -spòr-, -spər-\ *n* — **ex·port·er** \ek-'spōrt-ər, -'spòrt-, 'ek-ˌ\ *n*

²**ex·port** \'ek-ˌspō(ə)rt, -ˌspò(ə)rt\ *n* **1** : something that is exported **2** : an act of exporting — **export** *adj*

ex·pose \ik-'spōz\ *vb* **ex·posed; ex·pos·ing** **1 a** : to leave without shelter, protection, or care **b** : to lay open to an action or influence ⟨*expose* students to good books⟩ ⟨had been *exposed* to measles⟩; *esp* : to let light fall on ⟨photographic film⟩ **2** : to put on display **3** : to make known ⟨*expose* a dishonest scheme⟩ — **ex·pos·er** *n*

ex·po·sé \ˌek-spō-'zā\ *n* : an exposing of something disgraceful

ex·po·si·tion \ˌek-spə-'zish-ən\ *n* **1** : an explaining of something **2 a** : a piece of writing that explains **b** : a kind of writing that explains **3** : a public exhibition **4** : the first part of a piece of music in which the theme is presented — **ex·pos·i·tor** \ik-'späz-ət-ər\ *n* — **ex·pos·i·to·ry** \ik-'späz-ə-ˌtōr-ē, -ˌtòr-\ *adj*

ex post fac·to \ˌek-ˌspōst-'fak-tō\ *adv or adj* : after the fact [Latin, literally "from a thing done afterward"]

ex·pos·tu·late \ik-'späs-chə-ˌlāt\ *vb* **-lat·ed; -lat·ing** : REMONSTRATE — **ex·pos·tu·la·tion** \-ˌspäs-chə-'lā-shən\ *n*

ex·po·sure \ik-'spō-zhər\ *n* **1** : the fact or condition of being exposed ⟨*exposure* to cold⟩ **2 a** : the act or an instance of exposing **b** : the act of letting light expose photographic film; *also* : the amount or length of time of such exposure **3** : a position with respect to direction ⟨a southern *exposure*⟩ **4** : a section of a film for a single picture

ex·pound \ik-'spaúnd\ *vb* **1** : to make known (as one's ideas or beliefs) : set forth **2** : to explain clearly : INTERPRET — **ex·pound·er** *n*

¹**ex·press** \ik-'spres\ *adj* **1** : EXPLICIT ⟨my *express* orders⟩ ⟨*express* written consent⟩ **2** : of a particular sort : SPECIFIC ⟨came for that *express* purpose⟩ **3** : sent or traveling at high speed ⟨*express* mail⟩; *esp* : making few or no stops ⟨an *express* train⟩

²**express** *adv* : by express ⟨send a package *express*⟩

³**express** *n* **1 a** : a system for the special transportation of goods **b** : a company operating such a service **c** : the goods or shipments so transported **2** : an express vehicle (as an elevator or train)

⁴**express** *vb* **1 a** : to represent or give expression to especially in words : STATE **b** : to make one's opinions, feelings, or abilities known **c** : SYMBOLIZE **2** : to press or squeeze out **3** : to send by express — **ex·press·er** *n* — **ex·press·ible** \-ə-bəl\ *adj*

ex·pres·sion \ik-'spresh-ən\ *n* **1** : the act or process of expressing especially in words **2 a** : a meaningful word or phrase **b** : a mathematical symbol or a combination of symbols and signs representing a quantity or operation **3** : a way of speaking or singing or of playing an instrument so as to show mood or feeling ⟨sing with *expression*⟩ **4** : the way one's face looks or one's voice sounds that shows one's feelings ⟨a pleased *expression*⟩ **5** : the detectable effect of a gene — **ex·pres·sion·less** \-ləs\ *adj* — **ex·pres·sion·less·ly** *adv*

ex·pres·sive \ik-'spres-iv\ *adj* **1** : full of expression; *also* : openly expressing one's feelings **2** : serving to express **3** : of or relating to expression — **ex·pres·sive·ly** *adv* — **ex·pres·sive·ness** *n*

ex·press·ly \ik-'spres-lē\ *adv* **1** : so as to be absolutely clear : EXPLICITLY ⟨was *express*ly forbidden to smoke⟩ **2** : for the express purpose : ESPECIALLY ⟨came *express*ly to congratulate her⟩

ex·press·way \ik-'spres-,wā\ *n* : a divided superhighway that may be entered and left only at special places

ex·pro·pri·ate \ek-'sprō-prē-,āt\ *vb* **-at·ed; -at·ing** **1** : to deprive of ownership or the right of ownership **2** : to take over the property of another especially by government action — **ex·pro·pri·a·tion** \(,)ek-,sprō-prē-'ā-shən\ *n*

ex·pul·sion \ik-'spəl-shən\ *n* : the act of expelling : the state of being expelled

ex·punge \ik-'spənj\ *vb* **ex·punged; ex·pung·ing** : to blot or rub out : ERASE — **ex·pung·er** *n*

ex·pur·gate \'ek-spər-,gāt\ *vb* **-gat·ed; -gat·ing** : to remove objectionable parts from (as a book) — **ex·pur·ga·tion** \,ek-spər-'gā-shən\ *n* — **ex·pur·ga·tor** \'ek-spər-,gāt-ər\ *n*

ex·quis·ite \ek-'skwiz-ət, 'ek-(,)skwiz-\ *adj* **1** : finely done or made ⟨an *exquisite* lacy handkerchief⟩ ⟨*exquisite* artistry⟩ **2** : very appreciative ⟨*exquisite* taste⟩ **3** : pleasing through beauty, fitness, or perfection ⟨*exquisite* flowers⟩ **4** : very severe : INTENSE ⟨*exquisite* pain⟩ — **ex·quis·ite·ly** *adv* — **ex·quis·ite·ness** *n*

ex·tant \'ek-stənt, ek-'stant\ *adj* : existing at the present time : not destroyed or lost

ex·tem·po·ra·ne·ous \(,)ek-,stem-pə-'rā-nē-əs\ *adj* : made up or done on the spur of the moment : IMPROMPTU — **ex·tem·po·ra·ne·ous·ly** *adv* — **ex·tem·po·ra·ne·ous·ness** *n*

ex·tem·po·re \ik-'stem-pə-(,)rē\ *adv* : in an extemporaneous manner — **extempore** *adj*

ex·tem·po·rize \ik-'stem-pə-,rīz\ *vb* **-rized; -riz·ing** : to do, make, or speak extempore : IMPROVISE

ex·tend \ik-'stend\ *vb* **1** : to straighten out or stretch forth ⟨*extended* both arms⟩ **2 a** : to offer to someone ⟨*extend* an apology⟩ **b** : to make available ⟨*extend* credit⟩ **3 a** : to stretch out : make longer ⟨*extend* a visit⟩ ⟨an *ex-*

tended metaphor⟩ **b** : to make larger ⟨*extend* the meaning of a word⟩ **4** : to stretch out or reach across a distance, space, or time ⟨the woods *extend* for miles to the west⟩ ⟨the bridge *extends* across the river⟩ — **ex·tend·able** *or* **ex·tend·ible** \-'sten-də-bəl\ *adj*

extended family *n* : a family that includes parents and children and other relatives (as grandparents, aunts, or uncles) in the same household

ex·tend·er \ik-'sten-dər\ *n* : something added to something else especially to make it go farther ⟨meat *extenders*⟩

ex·ten·si·ble \ik-'sten(t)-sə-bəl\ *adj* : able to be extended — **ex·ten·si·bil·i·ty** \-,sten(t)-sə-'bil-ət-ē\ *n*

ex·ten·sion \ik-'sten-chən\ *n* **1** : the act of extending : the state of being extended **2** : a granting of extra time **3** : education by special programs at a distance from a school **4 a** : a part forming an addition or increase **b** : an extra telephone connected to the main line

extension agent *n* : COUNTY AGENT

ex·ten·sive \ik-'sten(t)-siv\ *adj* : having wide or large extent — **ex·ten·sive·ly** *adv* — **ex·ten·sive·ness** *n*

ex·ten·sor \ik-'sten(t)-sər\ *n* : a muscle serving to extend a bodily part (as a limb)

ex·tent \ik-'stent\ *n* **1** : the range, distance, or space over or through which something extends **2** : the point, degree, or limit to which something extends

ex·ten·u·ate \ik-'sten-yə-,wāt\ *vb* **-at·ed; -at·ing** : to try to make less serious by partial excuses — **ex·ten·u·a·tion** \-,sten-yə-'wā-shən\ *n*

¹**ex·te·ri·or** \ek-'stir-ē-ər\ *adj* : EXTERNAL 1, 2 ⟨an *exterior* surface⟩ ⟨*exterior* paint⟩ — **ex·te·ri·or·ly** *adv*

²**exterior** *n* : an exterior part or surface

exterior angle *n* : an angle formed by a transversal cutting two lines and lying outside the latter

ex·ter·mi·nate \ik-'stər-mə-,nāt\ *vb* **-nat·ed; -nat·ing** : to get rid of completely ⟨*exterminate* termites⟩ — **ex·ter·mi·na·tion** \-,stər-mə-'nā-shən\ *n* — **ex·ter·mi·na·tor** \-'stər-mə-,nāt-ər\ *n*

¹**ex·ter·nal** \ek-'stərn-ᵊl\ *adj* **1** : outwardly visible ⟨*external* signs⟩ **2 a** : of, relating to, or connected

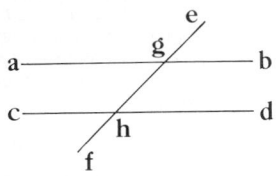

exterior angle:
ega, egb, fhc, fhd

with the outside or an outer part **b** : applied or applicable to the outside ⟨for *external* use only⟩ **3** : arising or acting from outside ⟨*external* pressures⟩ **4** : of or relating to relationships with foreign countries ⟨*external* affairs⟩ — **ex·ter·nal·ly** \-ᵊl-ē\ *adv*

²**external** *n* : something external — usually used in pl.

external–combustion engine *n* : a heat engine (as a steam engine) that gets its heat from fuel burned outside the engine cylinder

external ear *n* : the outer part of the ear consisting of the projecting sound-collecting part composed of cartilage and the canal leading from this to the eardrum

ex·tinct \ik-'stiŋ(k)t, 'ek-,\ *adj* **1** : no longer active ⟨an *extinct* volcano⟩ **2** : no longer existing ⟨an *extinct* species of animal⟩

ex·tinc·tion \ik-'stiŋ(k)-shən\ *n* **1** : an act of extinguishing or an instance of being extinguished **2 a** : the state of being extinct **b** : the process of becoming extinct **3** : the process of eliminating or reducing a conditioned response

\ə\ **abut**	\aú\ **out**	\i\ **tip**	\ó\ **saw**	\ú\ **foot**	
\ər\ **further**	\ch\ **chin**	\ī\ **life**	\ói\ **coin**	\y\ **yet**	
\a\ **mat**	\e\ **pet**	\j\ **job**	\th\ **thin**	\yü\ **few**	
\ā\ **take**	\ē\ **easy**	\ŋ\ **sing**	\<u>th</u>\ **this**	\yů\ **cure**	
\ä\ **cot, cart**	\g\ **go**	\ō\ **bone**	\ü\ **food**	\zh\ **vision**	

by not providing the stimulus with which it has become associated by conditioning

ex·tin·guish \ik-'stiŋ-gwish\ *vb* **1** : to cause to stop burning **2** : to cause to die out — **ex·tin·guish·able** \-ə-bəl\ *adj* — **ex·tin·guish·er** *n*

ex·tir·pate \'ek-stər-,pāt\ *vb* **-pat·ed; -pat·ing** **1** : to pull up by the roots **2** : to destroy completely — **ex·tir·pa·tion** \,ek-(,)stər-'pā-shən\ *n*

ex·tol *also* **ex·toll** \ik-'stōl\ *vb* **ex·tolled; ex·tol·ling** : to praise highly — **ex·tol·ler** *n* — **ex·tol·ment** \-mənt\ *n*

ex·tort \ik-'stò(ə)rt\ *vb* : to get (as money) from a person by the use of force or threats [from Latin *extortus,* past participle of *extorquēre* "to twist out, extort", from *ex-* "out, away" and *torquēre* "to twist" — related to DISTORT, RETORT, TORTURE] — **ex·tort·er** *n*

ex·tor·tion \ik-'stòr-shən\ *n* : the practice or crime of extorting (as money) — **ex·tor·tion·er** \-sh(ə-)nər\ *n* — **ex·tor·tion·ist** \-sh(ə-)nəst\ *n*

ex·tor·tion·ate \ik-'stòr-sh(ə-)nət\ *adj* **1** : marked by extortion **2** : extremely high : EXORBITANT ⟨*extortionate* prices⟩ — **ex·tor·tion·ate·ly** *adv*

¹**ex·tra** \'ek-strə\ *adj* : more than is due, usual, or necessary

²**extra** *n* : something extra: as **a** : a special edition of a newspaper **b** : a person hired to act in a group scene (as in a movie)

³**extra** *adv* : beyond the usual size, extent, or degree ⟨*extra* long⟩ ⟨*extra* large eggs⟩

extra- *prefix* : outside : beyond ⟨*extra*curricular⟩ [derived from Latin *extra* "outside, beyond" — related to STRANGE]

ex·tra·cel·lu·lar \,ek-strə-'sel-yə-lər\ *adj* : situated or occurring outside a cell or the cells of the body

¹**ex·tract** \ik-'strakt, *oftenest in sense 4* ek-,strakt\ *vb* **1** : to remove by pulling ⟨*extract* a tooth⟩ **2** : to get out by pressing, distilling, or by a chemical process ⟨*extract* juice from apples⟩ **3** : to calculate a mathematical root **4** : to choose and take out for separate use ⟨*extract* a few lines from a poem⟩ — **ex·tract·able** \ik-'strak-tə-bəl, 'ek-,\ *adj* — **ex·trac·tor** \-tər\ *n*

²**ex·tract** \'ek-,strakt\ *n* **1** : a selection from a writing **2** : a product obtained by extracting ⟨vanilla *extract*⟩

ex·trac·tion \ik-'strak-shən\ *n* **1** : the act or process of extracting **2** : the origin of a person ⟨of Italian *extraction*⟩

ex·tra·cur·ric·u·lar \,ek-strə-kə-'rik-yə-lər\ *adj* : of or relating to those activities (as athletics) that are offered by a school but are not part of the course of study

ex·tra·dite \'ek-strə-,dīt\ *vb* **-dit·ed; -dit·ing** : to cause to be delivered by extradition — **ex·tra·dit·able** \-,dīt-ə-bəl\ *adj*

ex·tra·di·tion \,ek-strə-'dish-ən\ *n* : the delivery of an accused criminal from one place (as a U.S. state) to another where the trial will be held

ex·tra·mar·i·tal \,ek-strə-'mar-ət-ᵊl\ *adj* : of or relating to sexual intercourse by a married person with someone other than his or her spouse

ex·tra·ne·ous \ek-'strā-nē-əs\ *adj* **1** : not forming a necessary part **2** : IRRELEVANT — **ex·tra·ne·ous·ly** *adv* — **ex·tra·ne·ous·ness** *n*

ex·traor·di·nary \ik-'strórd-ᵊn-,er-ē, ,ek-strə-'órd-\ *adj* : so unusual as to be remarkable — **ex·traor·di·nar·i·ly** \ik-,strórd-ᵊn-'er-ə-lē, ,ek-strə-,órd-\ *adv* — **ex·traor·di·nar·i·ness** \ik-'strórd-ᵊn-,er-ē-nəs, ,ek-strə-'órd-\ *n*

extra point *n* : a point scored in football after a touchdown by kicking the ball between the goalposts or advancing it a short distance into the end zone

ex·trap·o·late \ik-'strap-ə-,lāt\ *vb* **-lat·ed; -lat·ing** : to work out unknown facts from known facts — **ex·trap·o·la·tion** \-,strap-ə-'lā-shən\ *n* — **ex·trap·o·la·tor** \-'strap-ə-,lāt-ər\ *n*

ex·tra·sen·so·ry \,ek-strə-'sen(t)s-(ə-)rē\ *adj* : not acting or occurring through use of the known senses ⟨*extrasensory* experience⟩

extrasensory perception *n* : an awareness of events or

facts that cannot be explained by communication using any of the known senses

ex·tra·ter·res·tri·al \,ek-strə-tə-'res-trē-əl\ *adj* : coming from or existing outside the earth or its atmosphere ⟨*extraterrestrial* life⟩ — **extraterrestrial** *n*

ex·trav·a·gance \ik-'strav-i-gən(t)s\ *n* **1 a** : the wasteful or careless spending of money **b** : something that is extravagant **2** : the quality or fact of being extravagant

ex·trav·a·gant \ik-'strav-i-gənt\ *adj* **1** : going beyond what is reasonable or suitable ⟨*extravagant* praise⟩ **2** : wasteful especially of money [Middle English *extravagaunt* "wandering away, going beyond the usual limits", from early French *extravagant* (same meaning), from Latin *extravagant-, extravagans* (same meaning), from earlier *extra-* "outside, beyond" and *vagari* "to wander away" — related to VAGABOND] — **ex·trav·a·gant·ly** *adv*

ex·trav·a·gan·za \ik-,strav-ə-'gan-zə\ *n* : a spectacular show

ex·tra·ve·hic·u·lar \,ek-strə-vē-'hik-yə-lər\ *adj* : taking place outside a vehicle (as a spacecraft)

¹**ex·treme** \ik-'strēm\ *adj* **1** : existing to a very great degree ⟨*extreme* heat⟩ ⟨*extreme* poverty⟩ **2** : farthest from a center — **ex·treme·ly** *adv* — **ex·treme·ness** *n*

²**extreme** *n* **1** : something situated as far away as possible from another ⟨*extremes* of heat and cold⟩ **2** : the first term or the last term of a mathematical proportion ⟨in the proportion

$$\frac{a}{b} = \frac{c}{d}$$

a and *d* are the *extremes*⟩

ex·trem·ism \ik-'strē-,miz-əm\ *n* : belief in and support for extreme political ideas — **ex·trem·ist** \-məst\ *n or adj*

ex·trem·i·ty \ik-'strem-ət-ē\ *n, pl* **-ties** **1** : the farthest limit, point, or part **2** : an end part of a limb of the body (as a hand or foot) **3** : an extreme degree (as of emotion or pain)

ex·tri·cate \'ek-strə-,kāt\ *vb* **-cat·ed; -cat·ing** : to free from entanglement or difficulty — **ex·tri·ca·ble** \ek-'strik-ə-bəl, 'ek-(,)strik-\ *adj* — **ex·tri·ca·tion** \,ek-strə-'kā-shən\ *n*

ex·trin·sic \ek-'strin-zik, -'strin(t)-sik\ *adj* : not being part of or belonging to a thing : EXTRANEOUS — **ex·trin·si·cal·ly** \-zi-k(ə-)lē, -si-\ *adv*

ex·tro·ver·sion *or* **ex·tra·ver·sion** \,ek-strə-'vər-zhən, -shən\ *n* : the act, state, or habit of being concerned mostly with what is going on in the world outside oneself

ex·tro·vert *or* **ex·tra·vert** \'ek-strə-,vərt\ *n* : a person who is interested only or mostly in things outside the self — **ex·tro·vert·ed** *or* **ex·tra·vert·ed** \'ek-strə-,vərt-əd\ *adj*

ex·trude \ik-'strüd\ *vb* **ex·trud·ed; ex·trud·ing** **1** : to force, press, or push out **2** : to shape by forcing through a die

ex·tru·sion \ik-'strü-zhən\ *n* : the act or process of extruding; *also* : a form or product produced by this process

ex·tru·sive \ik-'strü-siv, -ziv\ *adj* : relating to or formed by geological extrusion from the earth in a melted state or as volcanic ash ⟨*extrusive* rock⟩

ex·u·ber·ant \ig-'zü-b(ə-)rənt\ *adj* : joyfully enthusiastic — **ex·u·ber·ance** \-b(ə-)rən(t)s\ *n* — **ex·u·ber·ant·ly** *adv*

ex·ude \ig-'züd\ *vb* **ex·ud·ed; ex·ud·ing** **1** : to discharge slowly through pores or cuts : OOZE ⟨*exude* sweat⟩ **2** : to give forth ⟨brown eyes *exuding* confidence⟩

ex·ult \ig-'zəlt\ *vb* : to be very joyful : REJOICE — **ex·ult·ing·ly** \-'zəl-tiŋ-lē\ *adv*

ex·ult·ant \ig-'zəlt-ᵊnt\ *adj* : full of or expressing joy or triumph — **ex·ult·ant·ly** *adv*

ex·ul·ta·tion \,ek-(,)səl-'tā-shən, ,eg-(,)zəl-\ *n* : the act of exulting : the state of being exultant

ex·urb \'ek-,sərb, 'eg-,zərb\ *n* : a region or district outside a city and its suburbs where many well-to-do people live

ex·ur·ban·ite \ek-'sər-bə-,nīt, eg-'zər-\ n : a person living in an exurb

ex·ur·bia \ek-'sər-bē-ə, eg-'zər-\ n : the region of exurbs

-ey — see ¹-Y

¹**eye** \'ī\ n 1 : an organ of sight; esp : a rounded hollow organ lined with a sensitive retina and located in a bone-lined cavity in the skull of a vertebrate 2 a : ability to see or appreciate ⟨a good eye for painting⟩ b : ²GLANCE 3b ⟨it took my eye⟩ c : close attention ⟨keep an eye on it⟩ d : JUDGMENT 1 ⟨guilty in the eyes of the law⟩ 3 : something like or suggestive of an eye: as a : the hole through the head of a needle b : a loop to catch or receive a hook c : an undeveloped bud (as on a potato) d : a device (as a photoelectric cell) that functions somewhat like human vision 4 : the center of something ⟨the eye of a hurricane⟩ — **eyed** \'īd\ adj — **eye·less** \'ī-ləs\ adj — **eye·like** \-,līk\ adj

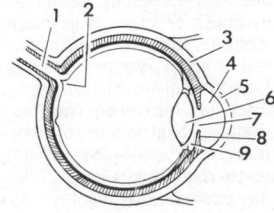

eye 1: 1 optic nerve, 2 blind spot, 3 sclera, 4 anterior chamber, 5 cornea, 6 lens, 7 pupil, 8 iris, 9 posterior chamber

²**eye** vb **eyed**; **eye·ing** or **ey·ing** : to watch closely

eye·ball \'ī-,bòl\ n : the eye of a vertebrate

eye bank n : a place for the storage of human corneas taken from the eyes of people who have died and kept for use as transplants into the eyes of persons who are partly or wholly blind because of defects in their corneas

eye·brow \'ī-,braù\ n : the ridge over the eye or hair growing on it

eye–catching \'ī-,kach-iŋ, -,kech-\ adj : attractive to the eye

eye contact n : the act of looking another person straight in the eye

eye·cup \'ī-,kəp\ n : a small oval cup with a rim curved to fit the orbit of the eye used for applying liquid medicine to the eyes

eye·drop·per \'ī-,dräp-ər\ n : DROPPER 2

eye·ful \-,fùl\ n : something attractive to look at

eye·glass \-,glas\ n 1 : a glass lens used to help one see clearly 2 pl : ¹GLASS 2b

eye·hole \-,hōl\ n : EYELET 1

eye·lash \-,lash\ n : a single hair of the fringe on the eyelid

eye lens n : the lens nearest the eye in an eyepiece

eye·let \'ī-lət\ n 1 : a small hole (as in cloth or leather) for a lace or rope 2 : GROMMET

eye·lid \'ī-,lid\ n : one of the movable lids of skin and muscle that can be closed over the eyeball

eye–open·ing \'ī-,ōp(-ə)-niŋ\ adj : being surprising or startling

eye·piece \'ī-,pēs\ n : the lens or combination of lenses at the eye end of an optical instrument (as a microscope or telescope)

eye shadow n : a colored cosmetic applied to the eyelids

eye·sight \'ī-,sīt\ n : ¹SIGHT 3, VISION ⟨keen eyesight⟩

eye socket n : ¹ORBIT

eye·sore \'ī-,sōr, -,sòr\ n : something displeasing to the sight

eye·spot \-,spät\ n 1 a : a simple organ for vision or the detection of light b : a small body in various single-celled algae that contains pigment 2 : a spot of color

eye·stalk \-,stòk\ n : a movable stalk bearing an eye at the tip in a crustacean

eye·strain \-,strān\ n : weariness or a strained state of the eye

eye·tooth \-'tüth\ n : a canine tooth of the upper jaw

eye·wash \-,wòsh, -,wäsh\ n : an eye lotion

eye·wit·ness \-'wit-nəs\ n : a person who sees an occurrence and is able to give a report of it

ey·rie \'ī(ə)r-ē, or like AERIE\ variant of AERIE

Eze·chiel \i-'zē-kyəl, -kē-əl\ n — see BIBLE table

Eze·kiel \i-'zē-kyəl, -kē-əl\ n — see BIBLE table

Ez·ra \'ez-rə\ n — see BIBLE table

F

f \'ef\ n, often cap 1 : the sixth letter of the English alphabet 2 : a musical note referred to by the letter F : the fourth tone of a C-major scale 3 : a grade rating a student's work as failing

fa \'fä\ n : the fourth note of the musical scale

fa·ble \'fā-bəl\ n : a short fictitious story; esp : one intended to teach a lesson and in which animals speak and act like human beings

fa·bled \'fā-bəld\ adj : told about in fable ⟨a fabled mountain of gold⟩

fab·ric \'fab-rik\ n 1 : the basic structure ⟨the fabric of society⟩ 2 : CLOTH 1

fab·ri·cate \'fab-ri-,kāt\ vb **-cat·ed**; **-cat·ing** 1 : CONSTRUCT 1, MANUFACTURE 2 : INVENT 2, CREATE 3 : to make up in order to deceive — **fab·ri·ca·tion** \,fab-ri-'kā-shən\ n — **fab·ri·ca·tor** \'fab-ri-,kāt-ər\ n

fab·u·lous \'fab-yə-ləs\ adj 1 a : resembling a fable especially in being marvelous or beyond belief ⟨fabulous wealth⟩ b : very good : MARVELOUS ⟨had a fabulous time⟩ 2 : told in or based on fable ⟨fabulous animals⟩ — **fab·u·lous·ly** adv — **fab·u·lous·ness** n

fa·cade also **fa·çade** \fə-'säd\ n 1 : the face or front of a building 2 : a false or misleading appearance

¹**face** \'fās\ n 1 : the front part of the head 2 : PRESENCE 1 ⟨in the face of danger⟩ 3 a : an expression of the face ⟨put a brave face on⟩ b : GRIMACE ⟨make a face⟩ 4 a : outward appearance ⟨on the face of it⟩ b : DIGNITY 1, PRESTIGE ⟨lose face⟩ 5 a : a front, upper, or outer surface ⟨the face of a cliff⟩ b : any of the plane surfaces that form the boundary of a solid in geometry c : a surface or side that is marked or specially prepared ⟨the face of a certificate⟩ 6 : the end (as of a mine tunnel) at which work is going on — **faced** \'fāst\ adj

facade 1

²**face** vb **faced**; **fac·ing** 1 a : to line near the edge especially with a different material ⟨face a hem⟩ b : to cover the front or surface of ⟨faced the building with marble⟩ 2

\ə\ abut		\aù\ out	\i\ tip	\ò\ saw	\ù\ foot	
\ər\ further		\ch\ chin	\ī\ life	\òi\ coin	\y\ yet	
\a\ mat		\e\ pet	\j\ job	\th\ thin	\yü\ few	
\ā\ take		\ē\ easy	\ŋ\ sing	\th\ this	\yù\ cure	
\ä\ cot, cart		\g\ go	\ō\ bone	\ü\ food	\zh\ vision	

: to bring face-to-face ⟨*faced* them with the evidence⟩ **3 a** : to stand or sit with the face toward ⟨*face* the class⟩ **b** : to front on ⟨a house *facing* the park⟩ **4 a** : to meet directly so as to deal with ⟨*face* facts⟩ **b** : to oppose firmly ⟨*face* danger⟩ **5** : to turn toward ⟨*face* the east⟩ — **face the music** : to meet something unpleasant (as punishment) or danger

face card *n* : a king, queen, or jack in a deck of cards

face·down \'fās-'daún\ *adv* : with the face down ⟨floated *facedown*⟩

face·less \'fās-ləs\ *adj* **1** : lacking a face **2** : not able to be identified

face·lift·ing \'fā-,slif-tiŋ\ *n* **1** : plastic surgery for removal of facial defects (as wrinkles or sagging) **2** : a changing or remodeling intended to modernize

face·off \'fā-,sóf\ *n* **1** : a method of putting a puck in play in ice hockey by dropping it between two opposing players **2** : a meeting of opposing forces : CONFRONTATION

face·plate \'fā-splāt\ *n* : a cover for protecting the face (as of a diver)

fac·et \'fas-ət\ *n* **1** : a small plane surface (as on a cut gem) **2** : ASPECT 2, PHASE **3** : the surface of a functional unit of vision of a compound eye — **fac·et·ed** \'fas-ət-əd\ *adj*

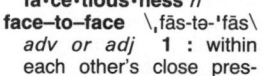

facet 1

fa·ce·tious \fə-'sē-shəs\ *adj* **1** : intended or trying to be funny **2** : FLIPPANT — **fa·ce·tious·ly** *adv* — **fa·ce·tious·ness** *n*

face–to–face \,fās-tə-'fās\ *adv or adj* **1** : within each other's close presence ⟨met *face-to-face*⟩ **2** : having to make a decision or to take action ⟨*face-to-face* with an emergency⟩

face·up \'fā-'səp\ *adv* : with the face up ⟨the card fell *faceup*⟩

face value *n* : the value indicated on the face of something (as a coin, bill, bond, or insurance policy)

¹fa·cial \'fā-shəl\ *adj* : of or relating to the face — **fa·cial·ly** \-shə-lē\ *adv*

²facial *n* : a treatment for the face

fac·ile \'fas-əl\ *adj* **1 a** : easily done, handled, or achieved **b** : ¹SHALLOW 2 **c** : easily displayed and often insincere **2** : working, moving, or performing with skill and ease : FLUENT ⟨a *facile* writer⟩ — **fac·ile·ly** \-ə(l)-lē\ *adv*

fa·cil·i·tate \fə-'sil-ə-,tāt\ *vb* **-tat·ed; -tat·ing** : to make easier — **fa·cil·i·ta·tion** \-,sil-ə-'tā-shən\ *n*

fa·cil·i·ty \fə-'sil-ət-ē\ *n, pl* **-ties 1** : freedom from difficulty : EASE ⟨handled with *facility*⟩ **2** : skill and ease in doing something ⟨a great *facility* for writing well⟩ **3 a** : something that makes an action, operation, or activity easier — usually used in pl. ⟨gym *facilities*⟩ **b** : something (as a hospital) that is put up for a particular purpose

fac·ing \'fā-siŋ\ *n* **1** : a lining at the edge especially of a garment **2** : an ornamental or protective layer ⟨a house with brick *facing*⟩ **3** : material for facing

fac·sim·i·le \fak-'sim-ə-lē\ *n* **1** : an exact copy **2** : a system of transmitting and reproducing printed matter or pictures by means of signals sent over telephone lines

fact \'fakt\ *n* **1** : a thing done; *esp* : CRIME 1 ⟨accessory after the *fact*⟩ **2** : the quality of being actual **3 a** : something that actually exists or occurs ⟨space travel is now a *fact*⟩ **b** : an occurrence, quality, or relation that can be experienced or inferred ⟨a number *fact*⟩ **c** : a piece of information about a fact ⟨a book filled with *facts*⟩

fac·tion \'fak-shən\ *n* : a group acting together within a larger body : CLIQUE — **fac·tion·al** \-shnəl, -shən-əl\ *adj* — **fac·tion·al·ism** \-,iz-əm\ *n*

fac·ti·tious \fak-'tish-əs\ *adj* : not natural or genuine : AR-

TIFICIAL — **fac·ti·tious·ly** *adv* — **fac·ti·tious·ness** *n*

¹fac·tor \'fak-tər\ *n* **1** : one that buys or sells property for another : AGENT **2** : something that contributes to the production of a result : INGREDIENT **3** : GENE **4** : any of the numbers or symbols in mathematics that when multiplied together form a product; *esp* : any of the integers that divide a given integer without a remainder usually excluding 1 and the given integer itself

²factor *vb* **fac·tored; fac·tor·ing** \-t(ə-)riŋ\ : to find the mathematical factors of and especially the prime mathematical factors — **fac·tor·able** \-t(ə-)rə-bəl\ *adj*

¹fac·to·ri·al \fak-'tōr-ē-əl, -'tòr-\ *n* **1** : the product of all the positive integers from 1 to n — symbol $n!$ **2** : the quantity $0!$ that is defined as equal to 1

²factorial *adj* : of, relating to, or being a factor or factorial

fac·tor·iza·tion \,fak-tə-rə-'zā-shən\ *n* : the act or process or an instance of factoring

factor tree *n* : a branching diagram which is used to factor a composite number and in which the original number is placed at the base point, two factors whose product equals the number are placed at the end of lines diverging from it, two other factors whose product equals one of these factors if it is a composite number are placed at the end of lines diverging from it, and so on until all the numbers from which no lines diverge are prime

fac·to·ry \'fak-t(ə-)rē\ *n, pl* **-ries** : a building or set of buildings equipped for manufacturing [from early French *factorie* "a place where business is carried on", derived from Latin *factor* "one that does or makes", from *factus*, past participle of *facere* "to make, do" — related to FASHION, MANUFACTURE]

fac·tu·al \'fak-chə(-wə)l, 'faksh-wəl\ *adj* **1** : of or relating to facts **2** : restricted to or based on fact — **fac·tu·al·i·ty** \,fak-chə-'wal-ət-ē\ *n* — **fac·tu·al·ly** \'fak-chə(-wə)-lē, 'faksh-wə-lē\ *adv* — **fac·tu·al·ness** *n*

fac·ul·ty \'fak-əl-tē\ *n, pl* **-ties 1** : ability to do something : TALENT ⟨a *faculty* for making friends⟩ **2** : one of the powers of the mind or body ⟨the *faculty* of hearing⟩ **3** : the teachers in a school or college

fad \'fad\ *n* : a practice or interest followed for a time with exaggerated zeal : CRAZE — **fad·dish** \'fad-ish\ *adj* — **fad·dist** \'fad-əst\ *n*

¹fade \'fād\ *vb* **fad·ed; fad·ing 1** : to lose freshness or health **2** : to lose or cause to lose brilliance of color **3** : to disappear gradually **4** : to change gradually in loudness or visibility — used of a motion-picture image or of an electronics signal and usually with *in* or *out*

²fade *n* : a gradual changing of one picture to another in a motion-picture or television sequence

fa·er·ie *also* **fa·ery** \'fā-(ə-)rē, 'fa(ə)r-ē, 'fe(ə)r-ē\ *n, pl* **fa·er·ies** : FAIRY — **faery** *adj*

¹fag \'fag\ *vb* **fagged; fag·ging 1** : ¹DRUDGE **2** : to act as a fag in an English public school **3** : to tire by hard work [from obsolete *fag* "to droop"]

²fag *n* **1** : an English public-school boy who acts as servant to another **2** : ²DRUDGE

³fag *n* : CIGARETTE [from *fag end*]

fag end *n* **1 a** : the last part or coarser end of a piece of cloth **b** : the untwisted end of a rope **2 a** : a poor or worn-out end : REMNANT **b** : the extreme end

fag·ot *or* **fag·got** \'fag-ət\ *n* : a bundle of sticks or twigs

fag·ot·ing *or* **fag·got·ing** \'fag-ət-iŋ\ *n* : embroidery done by tying threads in hourglass-shaped bunches

Fahr·en·heit \'far-ən-,hīt\ *adj* : relating or conforming to or having a thermometer scale on which under

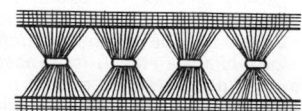

fagoting

standard atmospheric pressure the boiling point of water is at 212 degrees above the zero of the scale and the freezing point is at 32 degrees above zero — abbr. *F* [named for Gabriel *Fahrenheit* 1686–1736 German physicist]

¹fail \'fā(ə)l\ *vb* **1 a** : to lose strength : WEAKEN   **b** : to stop functioning ⟨the engine *failed*⟩   **2 a** : to fall short ⟨*failed* in their duty⟩   **b** : to become absent or lacking ⟨the power *failed*⟩   **c** : to be unsuccessful (as in passing an examination)   **d** : to grade as not passing ⟨*fail* a student⟩   **e** : to become bankrupt   **3** : DISAPPOINT, DESERT ⟨*fail* a friend in need⟩   **4 a** : to become unable to do or perform something ⟨the light *failed* to go on⟩   **b** : ¹NEGLECT 2 ⟨*fail* to answer the telephone⟩

²fail *n* : FAILURE 1 — usually used in the phrase *without fail*

¹fail·ing \'fā-liŋ\ *n* : WEAKNESS 2, SHORTCOMING

²failing *prep* : in the absence or lack of

fail·ure \'fā(ə)l-yər\ *n* **1 a** : a failing to do or perform   **b** : neglect of an assigned or expected action   **c** : inability to perform a normal function adequately ⟨heart *failure*⟩   **2 a** : a lack of success   **b** : BANKRUPTCY   **3 a** : a falling short : DEFICIENCY ⟨crop *failure*⟩   **b** : a breaking down ⟨a *failure* of memory⟩   **4** : one that has failed ⟨the scheme was a complete *failure*⟩

¹fain \'fān\ *adj* **1** *archaic* : GLAD 1c   **2** *archaic* : DESIROUS   **3** *archaic* : FORCED 1

²fain *adv* **1** *archaic* : in a willing manner : GLADLY   **2** *archaic* : RATHER 1

¹faint \'fānt\ *adj* **1** : TIMID, COWARDLY ⟨*faint* heart⟩   **2** : being weak, dizzy, and likely to collapse ⟨feel *faint*⟩   **3** : lacking strength : WEAK ⟨*faint* cries for help⟩   **4** : not clear or plain : DIM — **faint·ly** *adv* — **faint·ness** *n*

²faint *vb* : to lose consciousness

³faint *n* : an act or condition of fainting

faint·heart·ed \'fānt-'härt-əd\ *adj* : TIMID — **faint·heart·ed·ly** *adv* — **faint·heart·ed·ness** *n*

¹fair \'fa(ə)r, 'fe(ə)r\ *adj* **1** : attractive in appearance : BEAUTIFUL ⟨our *fair* city⟩   **2 a** : ¹CLEAN 2, PURE ⟨my *fair* name⟩   **b** : ¹CLEAR 3, LEGIBLE ⟨make a *fair* copy⟩   **3** : not stormy or cloudy ⟨*fair* weather⟩   **4 a** : UNBIASED, JUST ⟨wanted *fair* treatment⟩   **b** : observing the rules : ALLOWED ⟨*fair* play⟩   **c** : open to lawful pursuit or attack ⟨*fair* game⟩   **5 a** : PROMISING, LIKELY ⟨a *fair* chance of winning⟩   **b** : favorable to a ship's course ⟨a *fair* wind⟩   **6** : not dark : BLOND   **7** : neither good nor bad ⟨did a *fair* job⟩ [Old English *fæger* "pleasing to the eye or mind"] — **fair·ness** *n*

²fair *adv* **1** : in a fair manner   **2** : so as to be a fair ball

³fair *n* **1** : a gathering of buyers and sellers for trade   **2** : an exhibition (as of farm products) usually with accompanying entertainment, amusements, and competitions   **3** : a sale of articles usually for a charitable purpose [Middle English *feire* "a gathering of buyers and sellers", from early French *feire* (same meaning), from Latin *feria* "weekday, fair", derived from earlier *feriae* (plural) "holidays"]

fair ball *n* : a batted baseball that lands within the foul lines or that is within the foul lines when bounding to the outfield past first or third base or when going beyond the outfield for a home run

fair·ground \'fa(ə)r-,graůnd, 'fe(ə)r-\ *n* : an area set aside for fairs, circuses, and exhibitions

fair·ly \'fa(ə)r-lē, 'fe(ə)r-\ *adv* **1** : in a favorable manner ⟨*fairly* situated⟩   **2** : in a manner of speaking : QUITE ⟨*fairly* bursting with pride⟩   **3** : in a fair manner : JUSTLY ⟨treat each person *fairly*⟩   **4** : for the most part : RATHER ⟨a *fairly* easy job⟩

fair·way \'fa(ə)r-,wā, 'fe(ə)r-\ *n* : the mowed part of a golf course between a tee and a green

fairy \'fa(ə)r-ē, 'fe(ə)r-\ *n, pl* **fair·ies** : an imaginary being usually having a small human form and magic powers — **fairy** *adj* — **fairy·like** \-ē-,līk\ *adj*

fairy·land \-,land\ *n* **1** : the land of fairies   **2** : a place of delicate beauty or magical charm

fairy ring *n* : a ring of mushrooms in a lawn or meadow that is produced at the edge of a body of mycelium which is growing outward from a central point

fairy shrimp *n* : any of several delicate transparent freshwater crustaceans

fairy tale *n* **1** : a simple children's story about fairies — called also *fairy story*   **2** : FIB

faith \'fāth\ *n* **1 a** : allegiance to duty or a person : LOYALTY   **b** : the quality of being true to one's promises   **2 a** : belief and trust in and loyalty to God   **b** : belief in the doctrines of a religion   **c** : firm belief even in the absence of proof   **d** : complete confidence   **3** : something that is firmly believed; *esp* : a system of religious beliefs [Middle English *feith* "loyalty", from early French *feid, foi* (same meaning), from Latin *fides* "faith", from *fidere* "to trust" — related to BONA FIDE, CONFIDE, FIANCÉ]   **syn** see BELIEF

¹faith·ful \'fāth-fəl\ *adj* **1** : full of faith especially in God   **2** : firm in keeping promises or in fulfilling duties ⟨a *faithful* worker⟩   **3** : LOYAL 1b ⟨a *faithful* friend⟩   **4** : true to the facts : ACCURATE ⟨*faithful* copy⟩ — **faith·ful·ly** \-fə-lē\ *adv* — **faith·ful·ness** *n*

    syn FAITHFUL, LOYAL, STAUNCH, STEADFAST mean firm in one's allegiance to someone or something. FAITHFUL suggests that one has a firm and constant allegiance that is based on or as if on a pledge ⟨always be *faithful* to your duty⟩ LOYAL suggests that one firmly refuses to desert or betray ⟨citizens who are *loyal* to their country⟩ STAUNCH suggests courage and determination in one's allegiance ⟨*staunch* supporters of the senator⟩ STEADFAST suggests a steady and unfailing course in love, allegiance, or deeply held belief ⟨a *steadfast* fighter for civil rights⟩

²faithful *n, pl* **faithful** *or* **faithfuls** : one that is faithful

faith·less \'fāth-ləs\ *adj* **1** : not having faith   **2** : not worthy of trust : DISLOYAL — **faith·less·ly** *adv* — **faith·less·ness** *n*

¹fake \'fāk\ *vb* **faked; fak·ing** **1** : to treat so as to make false ⟨*faked* the results⟩   **2** : ¹COUNTERFEIT 1 ⟨*fake* a rare first edition⟩   **3** : ¹PRETEND 1, SIMULATE ⟨*fake* surprise⟩ — **fak·er** *n* — **fak·ery** \'fā-k(ə-)rē\ *n*

²fake *n* **1** : an imitation that is passed off as genuine : COUNTERFEIT   **2** : IMPOSTOR, CHARLATAN — **fake** *adj*

fa·kir \fə-'ki(ə)r, fä-, fa-; 'fā-kər\ *n* **1** : DERVISH   **2** : a wandering Hindu holy man who performs feats of magic [from Arabic *faqir*, literally "poor man"]

fal·con \'fal-kən, 'fȯl- *also* 'fȯ-kən\ *n* **1** : a hawk trained for use in falconry   **2** : any of various swift long-winged dark-eyed hawks having a notch and tooth on the upper jaw

fal·con·er \'fal-kə-nər, 'fȯl- *also* 'fȯ-\ *n* : one who hunts with hawks or trains hawks for hunting

fal·con·ry \'fal-kən-rē, 'fȯl- *also* 'fȯ-\ *n* **1** : the art of training hawks to hunt in cooperation with a person   **2** : the sport of hunting with hawks

¹fall \'fȯl\ *vb* **fell** \'fel\; **fall·en** \'fȯ-lən\; **fall·ing** **1 a** : to come or go down freely by the force of gravity   **b** : to hang freely   **c** : to drop oneself to a lower position   **d** : to come as if by dropping down ⟨night *fell*⟩   **2 a** : to become of lower degree or level ⟨the temperature

falcon 1

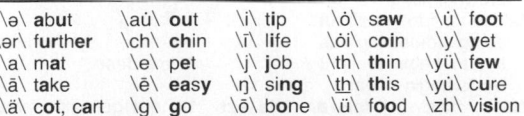

\ə\ abut	\aů\ out	\i\ tip	\ȯ\ saw	\ů\ foot
\ər\ further	\ch\ chin	\ī\ life	\ȯi\ coin	\y\ yet
\a\ mat	\e\ pet	\j\ job	\th\ thin	\yü\ few
\ā\ take	\ē\ easy	\ŋ\ sing	\th\ this	\yů\ cure
\ä\ cot, cart	\g\ go	\ō\ bone	\ü\ food	\zh\ vision

fell 10°⟩ **b** : to become lowered **3 a** : to topple from an upright position suddenly **b** : to enter blindly : STRAY ⟨*fell* into a trap⟩ **c** : to drop down wounded or dead **d** : to become captured or defeated ⟨the fortress *fell*⟩ **e** : to experience ruin or failure **4** : to fail to live up to a standard of conduct **5 a** : to move or extend downward ⟨the ground *falls* away to the east⟩ **b** : SUBSIDE 3, ABATE ⟨the tide is *falling*⟩ **c** : to become less in quality, activity, quantity, or value **d** : to take on a look of shame or low spirits **6 a** : to occur at a certain time **b** : to come by chance **c** : to pass (as a responsibility) from one person to another **d** : to have the proper place or station ⟨the accent *falls* on the second syllable⟩ **7** : to come within the range of something **8** : to pass from one condition of body or mind to another ⟨*fall* ill⟩ ⟨*fall* asleep⟩ **9** : to set about with enthusiasm or activity ⟨*fell* to work⟩ — **fall flat** : to produce no response or result — **fall for 1** : to fall in love with **2** : to become a victim of ⟨we *fell for* the trick⟩ — **fall foul** : to have a quarrel : CLASH — **fall from grace** : to lapse morally : SIN, BACKSLIDE — **fall short 1** : to be lacking **2** : to fail to reach a desired goal

²**fall** *n* **1** : the act of falling by the force of gravity ⟨a *fall* from a horse⟩ **2 a** : a falling out, off, or away ⟨the *fall* of the leaves⟩ **b** : AUTUMN 1 **c** : a thing or quantity that falls or has fallen ⟨a heavy *fall* of snow⟩ **3 a** : loss of greatness : COLLAPSE **b** : the surrender or capture of a place under attack **c** : departure from innocence or goodness **4 a** : ³SLOPE 2 **b** : WATERFALL — usually used in pl. **5** : a decrease in size, quantity, degree, activity, or value **6** : the distance which something falls **7** : an act of forcing a wrestler's shoulders to the mat

¹**fal·la·cious** \fə-'lā-shəs\ *adj* **1** : containing a fallacy **2** : leading in a wrong direction or into a mistaken action or belief — **fal·la·cious·ly** *adv* — **fal·la·cious·ness** *n*

fal·la·cy \'fal-ə-sē\ *n, pl* **-cies 1** : a false or mistaken idea **2** : the quality or state of being false

fall back *vb* : ²RETREAT 1 — **fall back on** : to turn for help to

fall guy *n* **1** : one who is easily cheated or deceived **2** : a person on whom something is blamed : SCAPEGOAT

fal·li·ble \'fal-ə-bəl\ *adj* : capable of making a mistake or being wrong — **fal·li·bil·i·ty** \,fal-ə-'bil-ət-ē\ *n* — **fal·li·bly** \'fal-ə-blē\ *adv*

fall·ing–out \,fó-liŋ-'aút\ *n, pl* **fallings–out** *or* **falling–outs** : ¹QUARREL 2

falling star *n* : METEOR

fal·lo·pi·an tube \fə-,lō-pē-ən-\ *n, often cap F* : either of the pair of tubes that carry eggs from the ovary to the uterus

fall·out \'fó-,laút\ *n* : the often radioactive particles that are stirred up by or result from a nuclear explosion and descend through the atmosphere

fall out \(')fó-'laút\ *vb* **1** : HAPPEN 1 **2** : to have a quarrel

¹**fal·low** \'fal-ō\ *n* **1** : land for crops allowed to lie idle during the growing season **2** : the tilling of land without sowing it for a season

²**fallow** *vb* : to till (land) without seeding

³**fallow** *adj* **1** : left untilled or unsown **2** : DORMANT 1, INACTIVE

fallow deer *n* : a small European deer with broad antlers and a pale yellow coat spotted white in the summer [from earlier *fallow* "a pale yellowish brown color"]

fallow deer

fall to *vb* : to set about doing something: as **a** : to begin to fight **b** : to begin to eat

false \'fóls\ *adj* **fals·er; fals·est 1** : not genuine ⟨false documents⟩ ⟨*false* teeth⟩ **2 a** : intentionally untrue ⟨*false* testimony⟩ **b** : intended or tending to mislead ⟨*false* promise⟩ **3** : not true : INCORRECT **4** : not faithful or loyal : TREACHEROUS **5** : not necessary to structure ⟨*false* ceiling⟩ **6** : inaccurate in pitch ⟨a *false* note⟩ **7** : based on mistaken ideas ⟨*false* pride⟩ — **false·ly** *adv* — **false·ness** *n*

false·hood \'fóls-,húd\ *n* **1** : an untrue statement : LIE **2** : the habit of lying

fal·set·to \fól-'set-ō\ *n, pl* **-tos** : an artificially high voice

fal·si·fy \'fól-sə-,fī\ *vb* **-fied; -fy·ing** : to make false : change so as to deceive ⟨*falsify* financial accounts⟩ — **fal·si·fi·ca·tion** \,fól-sə-fə-'kā-shən\ *n* — **fal·si·fi·er** \'fól-sə-,fī(-ə)r\ *n*

fal·si·ty \'fól-sət-ē\ *n, pl* **-ties 1** : something false : LIE **2** : the quality or state of being false

fal·ter \'fól-tər\ *vb* **fal·tered; fal·ter·ing** \'fól-t(ə-)riŋ\ **1** : to move unsteadily : WAVER **2** : ¹STAMMER **3** : to hesitate in purpose or action — **falter** *n* — **fal·ter·er** \-tər-ər\ *n* — **fal·ter·ing·ly** \-t(ə-)riŋ-lē\ *adv*

fame \'fām\ *n* : the fact or condition of being known to the public : RENOWN — **famed** \'fāmd\ *adj*

fa·mil·ial \fə-'mil-yəl\ *adj* : of, relating to, or typical of a family

¹**fa·mil·iar** \fə-'mil-yər\ *n* **1** : a close associate : COMPANION **2** : a spirit believed to serve or guard a person — called also *familiar spirit*

²**familiar** *adj* **1** : closely acquainted : INTIMATE **2 a** : INFORMAL 1 ⟨spoke in a *familiar* way⟩ **b** : too friendly or bold : PRESUMPTUOUS **3 a** : frequently seen or experienced **b** : of everyday occurrence **4** : having a good knowledge — **fa·mil·iar·ly** *adv*

fa·mil·iar·i·ty \fə-,mil-'yar-ət-ē, -,mil-ē-'ar-\ *n, pl* **-ties 1** : close friendship : INTIMACY **2** : close acquaintance with or knowledge of something **3** : lack of formality : freedom and ease in personal relations **4** : an overly bold act or expression

fa·mil·iar·ize \fə-'mil-yə-,rīz\ *vb* **-ized; -iz·ing** : to make familiar — **fa·mil·iar·iza·tion** \-,mil-yə-rə-'zā-shən\ *n*

fam·i·ly \'fam-(ə-)lē\ *n, pl* **-lies 1** : a group of persons who come from the same ancestor **2** : a group of individuals living under one roof and under one head **3** : a group of things having common characteristics; *esp* : a closely related series of elements or chemical compounds **4** : a social group composed of one or two parents and their children **5** : a group of related plants or animals ranking in biological classification above a genus and below an order

family name : SURNAME 2

family planning *n* : planning that is intended to fix the number and spacing of one's children by using effective methods of birth control

family tree *n* **1** : GENEALOGY 1 **2** : a diagram showing genealogical relationships

fam·ine \'fam-ən\ *n* **1** : an extreme general shortage of food **2** : a great shortage

fam·ish \'fam-ish\ *vb* **1** : STARVE 1 **2** : to suffer or cause to suffer from a lack of something necessary — **fam·ish·ment** \-mənt\ *n*

fa·mous \'fā-məs\ *adj* **1** : much talked about : very well-known ⟨*famous* explorer⟩ **2** : deserving to be remembered : EXCELLENT

syn FAMOUS, RENOWNED, CELEBRATED, NOTORIOUS mean known far and wide. FAMOUS suggests simply that one is popularly known and sometimes only for a short time ⟨a *famous* actor⟩ RENOWNED stresses glory and honor ⟨heroes *renowned* in story and song⟩ CELEBRATED stresses frequent public notice and mention especially in print ⟨a *celebrated* murder trial⟩ NOTORIOUS suggests that one is famous for wrongdoing ⟨one of the most *notorious* traitors in history⟩

fa·mous·ly \'fā-məs-lē\ *adv* : in a splendid or excellent

manner ⟨got along *famously* together⟩

¹fan \'fan\ *n* **1** : an instrument for producing a current of air: as **a** : a device that is often in the shape of a section of a circle and is waved back and forth by hand **b** : a device with a set of rotating blades driven by a motor **2** : something shaped like a hand fan [Old English *fann* "fan", from Latin *vannus* "fan"] — **fan·like** \-,līk\ *adj*

²fan *vb* **fanned; fan·ning** **1** : to move air with a fan **2 a** : to direct a current of air upon with a fan **b** : to stir up to activity as if by fanning **3** : to spread out or move like a fan **4** : to strike out in baseball — **fan·ner** *n*

³fan *n* : an enthusiastic follower or admirer [probably a shortened form of *fanatic*]

fa·nat·ic \fə-'nat-ik\ *or* **fa·nat·i·cal** \-'nat-i-kəl\ *adj* : overly enthusiastic or devoted — **fanatic** *n* — **fa·nat·i·cal·ly** \-i-k(ə-)lē\ *adv* — **fa·nat·i·cism** \-'nat-ə-,siz-əm\ *n*

fan·ci·er \'fan(t)-sē-ər\ *n* : a person with a special liking or interest ⟨a cat *fancier*⟩

fan·ci·ful \'fan(t)-si-fəl\ *adj* **1** : showing free use of the imagination ⟨a *fanciful* tale⟩ **2** : coming from the fancy rather than from reason ⟨a *fanciful* scheme⟩ — **fan·ci·ful·ly** \-f(ə-)lē\ *adv* — **fan·ci·ful·ness** \-fəl-nəs\ *n*

¹fan·cy \'fan(t)-sē\ *n, pl* **fancies** **1** : LIKING ⟨took a *fancy* to the stray dog⟩ **2** : NOTION, WHIM ⟨a passing *fancy*⟩ **3** : IMAGINATION

²fancy *vb* **fan·cied; fan·cy·ing** **1** : to have a fancy for : LIKE **2** : to form a mental image of : IMAGINE

³fancy *adj* **fan·ci·er; -est** **1** : based on fancy : WHIMSICAL **2 a** : not plain : ORNAMENTAL **b** : of particular excellence **c** : bred especially for a showy appearance **3** : done with great skill and grace ⟨*fancy* diving⟩ — **fan·ci·ly** \'fan(t)-sə-lē\ *adv* — **fan·ci·ness** \-sē-nəs\ *n*

fan·cy–free \'fan(t)-sē-'frē\ *adj* : not centering the attention on any one person or thing

fan·cy·work \-,wərk\ *n* : ornamental needlework (as embroidery)

fan·dan·go \fan-'daŋ-gō\ *n, pl* **-gos** : a lively Spanish or Spanish-American dance

fan·fare \'fan-,fa(ə)r, -,fe(ə)r\ *n* : a short stirring tune played by trumpets

fang \'faŋ\ *n* **1 a** : one of the long sharp teeth which are used by an animal to seize, hold, and tear apart its prey **b** : one of the long hollow or grooved teeth of a poisonous snake **2** : a root of a tooth — **fanged** \'faŋd\ *adj*

fan·light \'fan-,līt\ *n* : a semicircular window having bars extending from the center that is placed over a door or window

1 fang 1b

fan·ny \'fan-ē\ *n, pl* **fannies** : BUTTOCKS

fan·ta·sia \fan-'tā-zhə, ,fant-ə-'zē-ə\ *n* : a musical composition written without following a particular style

fan·tas·tic \fan-'tas-tik, fən-\ *also* **fan·tas·ti·cal** \-ti-kəl\ *adj* **1** : produced by the fancy or like something produced by the fancy ⟨a *fantastic* scheme⟩ **2** : hardly believable ⟨*fantastic* speeds⟩ — **fan·tas·ti·cal·ly** \-ti-k(ə-)lē\ *adv* — **fan·tas·ti·cal·ness** \-kəl-nəs\ *n*

fan·ta·sy *or* **phan·ta·sy** \'fant-ə-sē, -ə-zē\ *n, pl* **-sies** **1** : IMAGINATION 3, FANCY **2** : something imagined; *esp* : ILLUSION 2 **3** : FANTASIA **4** : a work of literature set in an unreal world often with superhuman characters and monsters

¹far \'fär\ *adv* **far·ther** \-thər\ *or* **fur·ther** \'fər-\; **far·thest** *or* **fur·thest** \-thəst\ **1** : at or to a great distance in space or time ⟨*far* from home⟩ **2** : to a great extent : MUCH ⟨*far* better⟩ **3** : to or at a definite distance, point, or degree ⟨as *far* as I know⟩ **4** : to an advanced point or extent : a long way ⟨a smart student can go *far*⟩ — **by far** : by a great

extent or degree : GREATLY — **far and away** : by far

²far *adj* **farther** *or* **further; farthest** *or* **furthest** **1** : very distant in space or time **2** : ¹LONG 3 ⟨a *far* journey⟩ **3** : the more distant of two ⟨the *far* side of the lake⟩

far·away \,fär-ə-,wä\ *adj* **1** : REMOTE 1, DISTANT ⟨*faraway* lands⟩ **2** : PREOCCUPIED 1, ABSTRACTED ⟨a *faraway* look⟩

farce \'färs\ *n* **1** : a play about ridiculous situations and happenings that is intended to make people laugh **2** : humor characteristic of a farce **3** : something that is ridiculous — **far·ci·cal** \'fär-si-kəl\ *adj*

¹fare \'fa(ə)r, 'fe(ə)r\ *vb* **fared; far·ing** **1** : ¹GO 1, TRAVEL **2** : to proceed toward a goal **3** : EAT 1, DINE

²fare *n* **1** : the money a person pays to travel by public transportation (as a bus) **2** : a person paying a fare : PASSENGER **3** : FOOD 1

¹fare·well \fa(ə)r-'wel, fe(ə)r-\ *imperative verb* : get along well — used to or by one departing

²farewell *n* **1** : an expression of good wishes at parting : GOOD-BYE **2** : an act of departure

³fare·well \,fa(ə)r-,wel, ,fe(ə)r-\ *adj* : of or relating to a time or act of leaving : FINAL ⟨a *farewell* concert⟩

far·fetched \'fär-'fecht\ *adj* : not easily or naturally thought of : IMPROBABLE

far–flung \'fär-'fləŋ\ *adj* : covering great areas : having wide range

fa·ri·na \fə-'rē-nə\ *n* : a fine meal made chiefly from cereal grains

¹farm \'färm\ *n* **1 a** : a piece of land used for growing crops or raising livestock **b** : a body of water used for the cultivation of aquatic animals **2** : a minor-league baseball team

²farm *vb* **1** : to turn over for performance or use usually on contract or for an agreed payment — usually used with *out* ⟨*farm* out the electrical work⟩ **2 a** : to devote to agriculture or the cultivation of aquatic animals ⟨*farm* 60 acres⟩ ⟨*farm* the sea⟩ **b** : to engage in raising crops or livestock

farm·er \'fär-mər\ *n* : a person who cultivates land or crops or raises animals or fish

farm·hand \'färm-,hand\ *n* : a farm laborer

farm·house \-,haús\ *n* : a dwelling on a farm

farm·ing \'fär-miŋ\ *n* : the occupation or business of a person who farms

farm·land \'färm-,land\ *n* : land used or suitable for farming

farm·stead \-,sted\ *n* : the buildings and nearby service areas of a farm

farm·yard \-,yärd\ *n* : space around or enclosed by farm buildings

far–off \'fär-'òf\ *adj* : remote in time or space

far–out \-'aút\ *adj* : very strange or unusual

far–reach·ing \-'rē-chiŋ\ *adj* : having a wide range, influence, or effect ⟨a *far-reaching* decision⟩

¹far·row \'far-ō\ *vb* : to give birth to pigs

²farrow *n* : a litter of pigs

Far·si \'fär-sē\ *n* : PERSIAN 2

far·sight·ed \'fär-'sīt-əd\ *adj* **1** : able to see distant things more clearly than near ones **2** : having foresight — **far·sight·ed·ly** *adv*

far·sight·ed·ness \-'sīt-əd-nəs\ *n* **1** : the condition of having foresight **2** : a visual condition in which the image focuses behind the retina

¹far·ther \'fär-thər\ *adv* **1** : at or to a greater distance or more advanced point **2** : more completely

²farther *adj* **1** : more distant : REMOTER **2** : ²FURTHER 2

far·ther·most \-thər-,mōst\ *adj* : ¹FARTHEST

¹far·thest \'fär-thəst\ *adj* : most distant in space or time

²farthest *adv* **1** : to or at the greatest distance in space or

\ə\ abut		\aú\ out	\i\ tip	\ò\ saw	\ú\ foot	
\ər\ further		\ch\ chin	\ī\ life	\òi\ coin	\y\ yet	
\a\ mat		\e\ pet	\j\ job	\th\ thin	\yü\ few	
\ā\ take		\ē\ easy	\ŋ\ sing	\th\ this	\yú\ cure	
\ä\ cot, cart		\g\ go	\ō\ bone	\ü\ food	\zh\ vision	

time : REMOTEST   **2** : to the most advanced point   **3** : by the greatest degree or extent : MOST

far·thing \'fär-thin\ *n* : a former British unit of money equal to ¼ of a penny; *also* : a coin representing this unit

fas·ci·nate \'fas-ᵊn-‚āt\ *vb* **-nat·ed; -nat·ing**   **1** : to grip the attention of especially so as to take away the power to move, act, or think for oneself   **2** : to attract and hold by charming qualities — **fas·ci·na·tion** \‚fas-ᵊn-'ā-shən\ *n* — **fas·ci·na·tor** \'fas-ᵊn-‚āt-ər\ *n*

fas·ci·nat·ing \'fas-ə-‚nāt-in\ *adj* : extremely interesting or charming — **fas·ci·nat·ing·ly** *adv*

fas·cism \'fash-‚iz-əm\ *n, often cap* : a political system headed by a dictator in which the government controls business and labor and opposition is not permitted — **fas·cist** \'fash-əst\ *n or adj, often cap*

¹fash·ion \'fash-ən\ *n*   **1** : the shape or form of something   **2** : MANNER 2, WAY ⟨behave in a strange *fashion*⟩   **3** : a common style especially of dress during a particular time or among a certain group ⟨an idea that is out of *fashion*⟩ [Middle English *facioun* "shape, manner", from early French *façon* (same meaning), from Latin *faction-, factio* "action of making", from *factus*, past participle of *facere* "to make, do" — related to ARTIFICIAL, BENEFIT, CONFECTION, FACTORY, MANUFACTURE, PERFECT, SATISFY]

²fashion *vb* **fash·ioned; fash·ion·ing** \'fash-(ə-)nin\ : to give shape or form to — **fash·ion·er** \-(ə-)nər\ *n*

fash·ion·able \'fash-(ə-)nə-bəl\ *adj*   **1 a** : following the fashion : STYLISH ⟨*fashionable* clothes⟩   **b** : dressing according to fashion ⟨*fashionable* people⟩   **2** : popular among those who set fashions ⟨*fashionable* stores⟩ — **fash·ion·able·ness** *n* — **fash·ion·ably** \-blē\ *adv*

¹fast \'fast\ *adj*   **1 a** : firmly fixed or bound   **b** : tightly shut   **c** : sticking firmly   **d** : UNCHANGEABLE   **2** : firmly loyal : STAUNCH   **3 a** : moving or able to move rapidly   **b** : taking a short time   **c** : giving quickness of motion (as to a thrown ball)   **d** : favorable to speed ⟨the *faster* route⟩   **4** : indicating ahead of the correct time ⟨my clock is *fast*⟩   **5** : tricky and unfair ⟨pulled a *fast* one⟩   **6** : not likely to fade ⟨*fast* colors⟩ [Old English *fæst* "firmly fixed"]

syn FAST, RAPID, SWIFT, HASTY mean moving, proceeding, or acting with great speed. FAST usually applies to things that move ⟨a *fast* horse⟩ RAPID usually applies to the movement itself ⟨a river with a *rapid* current⟩ SWIFT suggests great rapidity combined with ease of movement ⟨returned the ball with one *swift* stroke⟩ HASTY suggests rashness and often carelessness ⟨a *hasty* inspection of the damage⟩

²fast *adv*   **1** : in a fixed manner ⟨stuck *fast*⟩   **2** : in a complete manner : SOUNDLY, DEEPLY ⟨*fast* asleep⟩   **3** : with great speed ⟨a building *fast* going to ruin⟩

³fast *vb*   **1** : to go without eating   **2** : to eat in small amounts or only certain foods [Old English *fæstan* "to go without eating"]

⁴fast *n*   **1** : the act of fasting   **2** : a time of fasting

fast·back \'fas(t)-‚bak\ *n*   **1** : an automobile roof with a long curving downward slope to the rear   **2** : an automobile having a fastback

fas·ten \'fas-ᵊn\ *vb* **fas·tened; fas·ten·ing** \'fas-nin, -ᵊn-in\   **1** : to attach or join by or as if by pinning, tying, or nailing ⟨*fasten* clothes on a line⟩   **2** : to make fast : fix securely ⟨*fasten* a door⟩   **3** : to fix or set steadily ⟨*fastened* their eyes on the distant ship⟩   **4** : to become fixed or joined — **fas·ten·er** \'fas-nər, -ᵊn-ər\ *n*

fas·ten·ing *n* : something that fastens

fast–food \‚fas(t)-‚füd\ *adj* : specializing in food that can be prepared and served quickly ⟨a *fast-food* restaurant⟩

¹fast–for·ward \‚fast-'fȯr-wərd\ *n*   **1** : a function of a tape recorder that advances a tape at a speed that is higher than normal   **2** : a state of rapid advancement

²fast–forward *vb*   **1** : to advance (a tape) at a high speed   **2** : to advance rapidly especially in time

fas·tid·i·ous \fa-'stid-ē-əs\ *adj* : hard to please : very par-

ticular — **fas·tid·i·ous·ly** *adv* — **fas·tid·i·ous·ness** *n*

fast·ness \'fas(t)-nəs\ *n*   **1** : the quality or state of being fast   **2** : a fortified or secure place

¹fat \'fat\ *adj* **fat·ter; fat·test**   **1 a** : ⁵PLUMP, FLESHY   **b** : OILY 1, GREASY   **2 a** : ¹THICK 1 ⟨a *fat* book⟩   **b** : well stocked : ABUNDANT   **3** : PROFITABLE ⟨accepted a *fat* contract⟩   **4** : PRODUCTIVE 1, FERTILE   **5** : containing minerals that cause a greasy feel ⟨*fat* soil⟩   **6** : being swollen ⟨got a *fat* lip in the fight⟩ — **fat·ness** *n*

²fat *n*   **1** : animal tissue consisting chiefly of cells containing much greasy or oily matter   **2 a** : any of numerous compounds of carbon, hydrogen, and oxygen that make up most of plant and animal fat, are a major class of energy-rich food, and can be dissolved by ether but not by water   **b** : a solid or semisolid fat (as lard) as distinguished from an oil   **3** : the best or richest part ⟨the *fat* of the land⟩   **4** : an amount beyond what is usual or needed : EXCESS

³fat *vb* **fat·ted; fat·ting** : to make fat : FATTEN

fa·tal \'fāt-ᵊl\ *adj*   **1** : deciding one's fate : FATEFUL ⟨on that *fatal* day⟩   **2** : causing death or ruin ⟨a *fatal* accident⟩   **syn** see DEADLY — **fa·tal·ly** \-ᵊl-ē\ *adv*

fa·tal·ism \'fāt-ᵊl-‚iz-əm\ *n* : the belief or attitude that events are decided in advance by powers beyond one's control — **fa·tal·ist** \-əst\ *n* — **fa·tal·is·tic** \‚fāt-ᵊl-'is-tik\ *adj* — **fa·tal·is·ti·cal·ly** \-ti-k(ə-)lē\ *adv*

fa·tal·i·ty \fā-'tal-ət-ē, fə-\ *n, pl* **-ties** : a death resulting from a disaster or accident

fat·back \'fat-‚bak\ *n* : the strip of fat from the back of a hog carcass

fat cell *n* : any of the fat-containing cells that make up the connective tissue in which bodily fat is stored

¹fate \'fāt\ *n*   **1** : a power beyond one's control that is believed to decide what happens   **2** : something that happens as though decided by fate   **3** : a final result   **4** *pl, cap* : the three goddesses in classical mythology who decide the course of human life   **syn** see DESTINY

²fate *vb* **fat·ed; fat·ing**   **1** : DESTINE 1   **2** : ²DOOM 2

fate·ful \'fāt-fəl\ *adj*   **1** : having serious results : IMPORTANT ⟨a *fateful* decision⟩   **2** : ¹DEADLY 1, DESTRUCTIVE — **fate·ful·ly** \-fə-lē\ *adv* — **fate·ful·ness** *n*

fat·head \'fat-‚hed\ *n* : a stupid person

¹fa·ther \'fäth-ər, 'fȧth-\ *n*   **1 a** : a male parent   **b** *cap* : GOD 1   **c** *cap* : the first person of the Trinity   **2** : ANCESTOR 1   **3 a** : one who cares for another as a father might   **b** : one deserving the respect and love given to a father ⟨the founding *fathers*⟩   **4** : a person who invents or begins something ⟨the *father* of modern science⟩   **5** : PRIEST — used especially as a title — **fa·ther·hood** \-‚hu̇d\ *n* — **fa·ther·less** \-ləs\ *adj*

²father *vb* **fa·thered; fa·ther·ing** \'fäth-(ə-)rin, 'fȧth-\   **1 a** : BEGET 1   **b** : to be the founder, producer, or author of   **2** : to treat or care for as a father

fa·ther–in–law \'fäth-(ə-)rən-‚lȯ, 'fȧth-, -ərn-‚lȯ\ *n, pl* **fa·thers–in–law** \'fäth-ər-zən-, 'fȧth-\ : the father of one's husband or wife

fa·ther·land \'fäth-ər-‚land, 'fȧth-\ *n*   **1** : one's native land   **2** : the native land of one's ancestors

fa·ther·ly \'fäth-ər-lē, 'fȧth-\ *adj*   **1** : of or resembling a father   **2** : showing the affection or concern of a father ⟨*fatherly* advice⟩ — **fa·ther·li·ness** *n*

Fa·ther's Day \'fäth-ərz-, 'fȧth-\ *n* : the third Sunday in June set aside for the honoring of fathers

¹fath·om \'fath-əm\ *n* : a unit of length equal to six feet (about 1.8 meters) used especially for measuring the depth of water

²fathom *vb*   **1** : to measure by a sounding line   **2** : to come to understand — **fath·om·able** \'fath-ə-mə-bəl\ *adj*

¹fa·tigue \fə-'tēg\ *n*   **1 a** : weariness from labor or exertion   **b** : the condition of a part of the body (as a sense organ or gland) that temporarily loses the power to respond after a long period of stimulation   **2** *pl* : the uniform worn by members of the armed forces for physical labor   **3** : the tendency of a material (as metal) to break under repeated stress (as bending)

²**fatigue** *vb* **fa·tigued; fa·tigu·ing** **1** : to cause to become very tired **2** : to cause a condition of fatigue in   **syn** *see* TIRE

fat·ten \'fat-ⁿn\ *vb* **fat·tened; fat·ten·ing** \'fat-niŋ, -ⁿn-iŋ\ : to make or become fat — **fat·ten·er** \-(ə-)nər\ *n*

fat·ty \'fat-ē\ *adj* **fat·ti·er; -est** **1** : containing fat especially in unusual amounts **2** : GREASY 2 — **fat·ti·ness** *n*

fatty acid *n* : any of numerous acids that contain only carbon, hydrogen, and oxygen and occur naturally in fats and various oils

fa·tu·ity \fə-'t(y)ü-ət-ē, fa-\ *n, pl* **-ities** **1** : something foolish or stupid **2** : STUPIDITY 1

fat·u·ous \'fach-(ə-)wəs\ *adj* : FOOLISH, STUPID — **fat·u·ous·ly** *adv*

fau·cet \'fo-sət, 'fäs-ət\ *n* : a fixture for controlling the flow of a liquid (as from a pipe or cask)

¹**fault** \'folt\ *n* **1 a** : a weakness in character **b** : FAILING **b** : FLAW, IMPERFECTION **2 a** : a wrongful act **b** : ²MISTAKE 2 **3** : responsibility for wrongdoing or failure ⟨it's all my *fault*⟩ **4** : a break in the earth's crust accompanied by a displace-

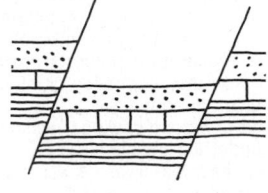

fault 4

ment of rock masses parallel to the break — **fault·less** \-ləs\ *adj* — **fault·less·ly** *adv* — **fault·less·ness** *n* — **at fault** : deserving blame : RESPONSIBLE — **to a fault** : to the point of being or doing too much ⟨generous *to a fault*⟩

²**fault** *vb* **1** : to fracture so as to produce a geologic fault **2** : to find a fault in

fault·find·er \'folt-,fīn-dər\ *n* : a person who tends to find fault — **fault·find·ing** \-diŋ\ *n or adj*

faulty \'fol-tē\ *adj* **fault·i·er; -est** : having a fault, blemish, or weakness : IMPERFECT — **fault·i·ly** \-tə-lē\ *adv* — **fault·i·ness** \-tē-nəs\ *n*

faun \'fon, 'fän\ *n* : a Roman god of country life represented as part goat and part man

fau·na \'fon-ə, 'fän-\ *n, pl* **faunas** *also* **fau·nae** \-,ē, -,ī\ : animals or animal life especially of a region, period, or environment — **fau·nal** \-ⁿl\ *adj*

¹**fa·vor** \'fā-vər\ *n* **1 a** : friendly regard shown toward another **b** : APPROVAL, APPROBATION ⟨look with *favor* on a project⟩ **c** : PARTIALITY 1 **d** : the quality or state of being popular ⟨lose *favor*⟩ **2** : an act of kindness ⟨do a friend a *favor*⟩ **3** : a small gift given out at a party — **in favor of 1** : in agreement or sympathy with **2** : in support of

²**favor** *vb* **fa·vored; fa·vor·ing** \'fāv-(ə-)riŋ\ **1 a** : to look upon or treat with favor **b** : to do a kindness for : OBLIGE **c** : to treat gently or carefully : SPARE ⟨*favor* a sore leg⟩ **2** : PREFER 1 **3** : to make possible or easy : help to succeed ⟨darkness *favored* the attack⟩ **4** : to look like : RESEMBLE ⟨*favors* his mother⟩ — **fa·vor·er** \'fā-vər-ər\ *n*

fa·vor·able \'fāv-(ə-)rə-bəl, 'fā-vər-bəl\ *adj* **1** : showing favor : APPROVING **2** : PROMISING, ADVANTAGEOUS — **fa·vor·able·ness** *n* — **fa·vor·ably** \-blē\ *adv*

¹**fa·vor·ite** \'fāv-(ə-)rət\ *n* **1** : a person or a thing that is favored **2** : the contestant considered as having the best chance to win

²**favorite** *adj* : being a favorite

fa·vor·it·ism \'fāv-(ə-)rət-,iz-əm\ *n* : unfairly favorable treatment of some to the neglect of others

¹**fawn** \'fon, 'fän\ *vb* **1** : to show affection — used especially of a dog **2** : to try to win favor by behavior that shows lack of self-respect — **fawn·er** *n* — **fawn·ing·ly** \-iŋ-lē\ *adv*

²**fawn** *n* **1** : a young deer; *esp* : one in its first year **2** : a

light grayish brown

fax \'faks\ *n* **1** : FACSIMILE 2 **2** : a machine used to send or receive facsimile communications **3** : a facsimile communication — **fax** *vb*

fay \'fā\ *n* : FAIRY, ELF — **fay** *adj*

faze \'fāz\ *vb* **fazed; faz·ing** : to disturb the self-control or courage of : DAUNT

fe·al·ty \'fē(-ə)l-tē\ *n, pl* **-ties** : LOYALTY, ALLEGIANCE

¹**fear** \'fi(ə)r\ *n* **1 a** : an unpleasant often strong emotion caused by expectation or awareness of danger **b** : an instance of fear or a state marked by fear **2** : concern about what may happen : WORRY **3** : ¹AWE

syn FEAR, DREAD, ALARM, FRIGHT mean painful emotion experienced in the presence or expectation of danger. FEAR is the most general word and suggests a continuing emotional state ⟨people living in *fear* of violent crimes⟩ DREAD suggests strong unwillingness to face something ⟨the *dread* felt by people awaiting bad news⟩ ALARM may suggest strong emotional upset caused by an unexpected or immediate danger ⟨viewed the worsening food shortage with *alarm*⟩ FRIGHT suggests the shock of something startling and often suggests a short-lived emotion ⟨the creaking door caused them *fright*⟩

²**fear** *vb* **1** : to feel great awe of ⟨*fear* God⟩ **2** : to be afraid of : have fear **3** : to be worried — **fearer** *n*

fear·ful \'fi(ə)r-fəl\ *adj* **1** : causing fear ⟨the *fearful* roar of a lion⟩ **2** : filled with fear ⟨*fearful* of danger⟩ **3** : showing or caused by fear ⟨a *fearful* glance⟩ **4** : extremely bad, large, or intense ⟨*fearful* cold⟩ — **fear·ful·ly** \-fə-lē\ *adv* — **fear·ful·ness** *n*

fear·less \'fi(ə)r-ləs\ *adj* : free from fear : BRAVE — **fear·less·ly** *adv* — **fear·less·ness** *n*

fear·some \'fi(ə)r-səm\ *adj* **1** : causing fear **2** : TIMID — **fear·some·ly** *adv* — **fear·some·ness** *n*

fea·si·ble \'fē-zə-bəl\ *adj* : possible to do or carry out — **fea·si·bil·i·ty** \,fē-zə-'bil-ət-ē\ *n* — **fea·si·ble·ness** \'fē-zə-bəl-nəs\ *n* — **fea·si·bly** \-blē\ *adv*

¹**feast** \'fēst\ *n* **1** : a meal with plenty of food and drink : BANQUET **2** : a day on which a religious festival falls [Middle English *feste* "feast, festival", from early French *feste* (same meaning), from Latin *festa*, plural of *festum* "festival, feast" — related to FESTIVAL, FIESTA]

²**feast** *vb* **1** : to eat plentifully : take part in a feast **2** : to entertain with a feast **3** : ²DELIGHT 2 — **feast·er** *n*

feat \'fēt\ *n* **1** : ¹ACT 1, DEED **2 a** : a deed notable especially for courage **b** : an act or product of skill, strength, or cleverness

¹**feath·er** \'feth-ər\ *n* **1** : one of the light horny growths that make up the outer covering of the body of a bird **2 a** : ¹KIND 1, NATURE ⟨birds of a *feather*⟩ **b** : CLOTHING 1, DRESS ⟨in full *feather*⟩ **c** : ¹CONDITION 5b, MOOD ⟨in fine *feather*⟩ — **feath·ered** \-ərd\ *adj* — **feath·er·less** \-ər-ləs\ *adj* — **feath·ery** \-(ə-)rē\ *adj* — **a feather in one's cap** : an accomplishment deserving praise

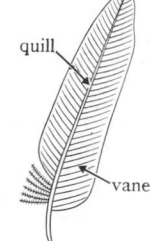

quill

vane

feather 1

²**feather** *vb* **feath·ered; feath·er·ing** \'feth-(ə-)riŋ\ **1 a** : to furnish (as an arrow) with a feather **b** : to cover, clothe, or adorn with feathers **2 a** : to turn (an oar blade) parallel to the water when lifting from the water at the end of a stroke **b** : to change the

\ə\ abut	\aů\ out	\i\ tip	\ȯ\ saw	\ů\ foot
\ər\ further	\ch\ chin	\ī\ life	\ȯi\ coin	\y\ yet
\a\ mat	\e\ pet	\j\ job	\th\ thin	\yü\ few
\ā\ take	\ē\ easy	\ŋ\ sing	\th\ this	\yů\ cure
\ä\ cot, cart	\g\ go	\ō\ bone	\ü\ food	\zh\ vision

angle of (airplane propeller blades) toward the line of flight; *also* : to change the angle of airplane propeller blades of (an engine) in such a manner **3** : to grow feathers **4** : to move, spread, or grow like feathers — **feather one's nest** : to provide for one's own comfort

feather bed *n* : a mattress filled with feathers; *also* : a bed with such a mattress

feath·er·brain \'feth-ər-,brān\ *n* : a foolish scatterbrained person — **feath·er·brained** \-,brānd\ *adj*

feath·er·weight \-,wāt\ *n* **1** : a very light weight **2** : one that weighs little; *esp* : a boxer in a weight division having the approximate range of 54 to 57 kilograms

¹fea·ture \'fē-chər\ *n* **1 a** : the shape or appearance of the face **b** : a single part of the face (as the nose or the mouth) **2** : a part or detail that stands out **3 a** : the principal motion picture on a program **b** : a special column or section in a newspaper or magazine **syn** see CHARACTERISTIC — **fea·ture·less** \-ləs\ *adj*

²feature *vb* **fea·tured; fea·tur·ing** \'fēch-(ə-)riŋ\ **1** : to be a feature of something **2** : to have as a feature; *esp* : to make a feature of

Feb·ru·ary \'feb-(y)ə-,wer-ē, 'feb-rə-\ *n* : the second month of the year

> **Word History** In the winter of each year the ancient Romans would celebrate a festival of spiritual cleansing. The name of the festival was *Februa*. Because of its importance the Romans named the month in which it fell *Februarius*, which means "of Februa". The English name *February* comes from the Latin *Februarius*. [Old English *Februarius* "February", from Latin *Februarius* "February", literally "of Februa", from *Februa* "feast of cleansing"]

fe·ces \'fē-(,)sēz\ *n pl* : bodily waste discharged through the anus : EXCREMENT — **fe·cal** \'fē-kəl\ *adj*

fe·cund \'fek-ənd, 'fē-kənd\ *adj* **1** : producing many offspring or much vegetation : PROLIFIC **2** : mentally productive or inventive — **fe·cun·di·ty** \fi-'kən-dət-ē\ *n*

fed·er·al \'fed-(ə-)rəl\ *adj* **1 a** : formed by an agreement between political units that surrender supreme authority to a central authority but keep certain powers **b** : of or being a form of government in which power is distributed between a central authority and individual units **2** *often cap* : of, relating to, or loyal to the federal government of the U.S. especially in the Civil War — **fed·er·al·ly** \-rə-lē\ *adv*

Fed·er·al \'fed-(ə-)rəl\ *n* **1** : a supporter of the government of the U.S. in the Civil War; *esp* : a soldier in the federal armies **2** : a federal agent or officer

fed·er·al·ist \'fed-(ə-)rə-ləst\ *n* **1** : a supporter of federal government; *esp, often cap* : a supporter of the adoption of the U.S. Constitution **2** *cap* : a member of a major political party in the early years of the U.S. favoring a strong central national government — **fed·er·al·ism** \-,liz-əm\ *n, often cap* — **federalist** *adj, often cap*

fed·er·al·ize \'fed-(ə-)rə-,līz\ *vb* **-ized; -iz·ing** : to unite in or under a federal system of authority — **fed·er·al·iza·tion** \,fed-(ə-)rə-lə-'zā-shən\ *n*

fed·er·ate \'fed-ə-,rāt\ *vb* **-at·ed; -at·ing** : to join in a federation

fed·er·a·tion \,fed-ə-'rā-shən\ *n* **1** : the act of federating **2** : something formed by federation

fe·do·ra \fi-'dōr-ə, -'dȯr-\ *n* : a low soft felt hat with the crown creased lengthwise

fed up *adj* : exhausted of patience

fee \'fē\ *n* **1** : a fixed charge ⟨admission *fee*⟩ ⟨license *fee*⟩ **2** : a charge for a professional service ⟨a doctor's *fees*⟩ **syn**

fedora

see PRICE

fee·ble \'fē-bəl\ *adj* **fee·bler** \-b(ə-)lər\; **-blest** \-b(ə-)ləst\ **1** : lacking in strength or endurance **2** : not forceful or loud ⟨a *feeble* cry⟩ ⟨a *feeble* attempt⟩ **syn** see WEAK — **fee·ble·ness** \-bəl-nəs\ *n* — **fee·bly** \-blē\ *adv*

fee·ble·mind·ed \,fē-bəl-'mīn-dəd\ *adj* : not having normal intelligence : mentally deficient — **fee·ble·mind·ed·ness** *n*

¹feed \'fēd\ *vb* **fed** \'fed\; **feed·ing** **1 a** : to give food to **b** : to give as food **c** : EAT 1 **d** : ²PREY 1a — used with *on, upon,* or *off* **2 a** : to furnish with something necessary **b** : to supply (material to be operated on) to a machine **c** : to nourish or become nourished as if by food **3 a** : to supply (as material) for use **b** : to supply (a signal) to an electronic circuit

²feed *n* **1** : ¹MEAL; *esp* : a large meal **2** : food for livestock **3** : a mechanism by which feeding is carried out

feed·back \'fēd-,bak\ *n* **1** : the return to the input of a part of the output of a machine, system, or process **2** : the giving or sending of information or of something from which information can be obtained about the value, effect, or result of an action or process to the controlling source; *also* : the information or information-containing material so given or sent

feed dog *n* : a sewing-machine device that moves the fabric under the needle

feed·er \'fēd-ər\ *n* **1 a** : a device for supplying food ⟨bird *feeder*⟩ **b** : ²FEED 3 **c** : a branch (as of a river or a transportation system) that supplies another **2 a** : one that eats **b** : an animal being fattened or suitable for fattening

feed·lot \'fēd-,lät\ *n* : a plot of land on which livestock are fattened for market

feed·stuff \-,stəf\ *n* : ²FEED 2

¹feel \'fēl\ *vb* **felt** \'felt\; **feel·ing** **1 a** : to sense through direct contact; *esp* : ¹TOUCH 1 **b** : to examine or test by touching : HANDLE **2 a** : ²EXPERIENCE **b** : to suffer from **3** : to discover by cautious trial — often used with *out* **4 a** : to be aware of ⟨*feel* trouble brewing⟩ **b** : to be conscious of a physical or mental state ⟨*feel* happy⟩ ⟨*feel* sick⟩ **c** : BELIEVE 5, THINK **5** : to search for something with the fingers **6** : to seem especially to the touch ⟨*feels* like wool⟩ **7** : to have sympathy or pity ⟨I *feel* for you⟩

²feel *n* **1** : the sense of touch **2** : SENSATION 1c, FEELING **3** : the quality of a thing as indicated through touch

feel·er \'fē-lər\ *n* **1** : one that feels; *esp* : a movable organ (as an antenna) of an animal that is usually an organ of touch **2** : a suggestion or remark made to find out the views of other people

¹feel·ing \'fē-liŋ\ *n* **1 a** : a sense by which the hardness or softness, hotness or coldness, or heaviness or lightness of things is found out; *esp* : ²TOUCH 3 **b** : a sensation experienced through this sense **2 a** : a state of mind ⟨a *feeling* of loneliness⟩ **b** : such a state with regard to something ⟨a *feeling* of dislike⟩ **c** *pl* : general emotional condition : SENSIBILITIES ⟨hurt their *feelings*⟩ **3** : the quality of one's awareness **4** : an opinion or belief especially when not based on evidence ⟨a *feeling* that it will rain⟩ **5** : SYMPATHY 3

²feeling *adj* : SENSITIVE 2 — **feel·ing·ly** \'fē-liŋ-lē\ *adv* — **feel·ing·ness** *n*

feet *pl of* FOOT

feet-first \'fēt-'fərst\ *adv* : with both feet or all four feet

Feh·ling's solution \'fā-liŋ(z)-\ *n* : a blue solution prepared by mixing solutions of Rochelle salt and copper sulfate and used especially in a test for sugars

feign \'fān\ *vb* **1** : to represent by a false appearance of : FAKE ⟨*feign* illness⟩ **2** : to state as if true ⟨*feign* an excuse⟩ — **feign·er** *n*

feint \'fānt\ *n* : a pretended blow or attack at one point in order to distract attention from the point one really intends to attack — **feint** *vb*

feld·spar \'fel(d)-ˌspär\ *n* : any of a group of crystalline minerals that consist of silicates of aluminum with potassium, sodium, calcium, or barium and that are a basic part of nearly all crystalline rocks

fe·lic·i·tate \fi-'lis-ə-ˌtāt\ *vb* **-tat·ed; -tat·ing** : CONGRATULATE — **fe·lic·i·ta·tion** \-ˌlis-ə-'tā-shən\ *n*

fe·lic·i·tous \fi-'lis-ət-əs\ *adj* **1** : very well suited or expressed ⟨*felicitous* wording⟩ **2** : PLEASANT 1, DELIGHTFUL — **fe·lic·i·tous·ly** *adv* — **fe·lic·i·tous·ness** *n*

fe·lic·i·ty \fi-'lis-ət-ē\ *n, pl* **-ties** **1** : great happiness : BLISS **2** : something that causes happiness **3** : a talent for apt expression **4** : an apt expression

¹fe·line \'fē-ˌlīn\ *adj* **1 a** : belonging to the family of flesh‑eating mammals with soft fur that includes the cats, lions, tigers, leopards, pumas, and lynxes **b** : of or resembling a cat : characteristic of cats **2** : SLY 1, STEALTHY

²feline *n* : a feline animal : CAT

¹fell \'fel\ *vb* **1 a** : to cut, beat, or knock down ⟨*fell* trees for lumber⟩ **b** : ¹KILL 1 **2** : to sew (a seam) by folding one edge under the other [Old English *fellan* "to knock down"]

²fell *past of* ¹FALL

³fell *adj* : FIERCE 1, CRUEL; *also* : ¹DEADLY 1, 2a [Middle English *fel* "fierce, terrible", from early French *fel* (same meaning), from Latin *fellon-, fello* "villain, evildoer" — related to FELON]

fel·lah \'fel-ə, fə-'lä\ *n, pl* **fel·la·hin** \ˌfel-ə-'hēn, fə-ˌlä-'hēn\ : a peasant or agricultural laborer in Arab countries (as Egypt or Syria)

¹fel·low \'fel-ō\ *n* **1** : COMRADE, ASSOCIATE **2 a** : an equal in rank, power, or character : PEER **b** : one of a pair : MATE **3** : a person holding any of various positions at a university **4 a** : a male person **b** : BOYFRIEND 2 **5** : a person granted funds for advanced study

²fellow *adj* : being a companion, mate, or associate

fel·low·man \ˌfel-ō-'man\ *n* : a human being of similar nature

fel·low·ship \'fel-ō-ˌship\ *n* **1** : the condition of friendly relationship existing among persons **2** : a sharing of interest or feeling **3** : a group with similar interests **4 a** : the position of a fellow (as of a university) **b** : the funds granted a fellow

fel·on \'fel-ən\ *n* : ²CRIMINAL; *esp* : one who has committed a felony [Middle English *felon* "one who has committed a felony", from early French *felon* (same meaning), from Latin *fellon-, fello* "villain, evildoer" — related to ³FELL]

fel·o·ny \'fel-ə-nē\ *n, pl* **-nies** : a serious crime punishable by a heavy sentence — **fe·lo·ni·ous** \fə-'lō-nē-əs\ *adj* — **fe·lo·ni·ous·ly** *adv*

¹felt \'felt\ *n* : a heavy material made by rolling and pressing fibers (as of wool) together

²felt *vb* **1** : to mat together **2** : to make into felt

³felt *past of* FEEL

¹fe·male \'fē-ˌmāl\ *n* : a female plant or animal

> **Word History** In the 14th century, *female* appeared in English with such spellings as *femel, femelle,* and *female.* The word comes from the Latin *femella,* meaning "young woman, girl", which in turn is based on *femina,* meaning "woman". In English, the similarity in form and sound between the words *female* and *male* led people to use only the *female* spelling. This closeness also led to the belief that *female* comes from or is somehow related to *male.* However, apart from the influence of *male* on the modern spelling of *female,* there is no link between the origins of the two words. [Middle English *female* "a girl or woman", an altered form of *femel, femelle* (same meaning), from early French *femelle* and Latin *femella,* both meaning "a girl or woman", from earlier Latin *femella* "a young woman, girl", from *femina* "woman" — related to FEMININE]

²female *adj* **1 a** : of, relating to, or being the sex that bears young **b** : having only seed-producing flowers ⟨a *female*

holly⟩ **2 a** : of, relating to, or characteristic of the female sex **b** : made up of females — **fe·male·ness** *n*

¹fem·i·nine \'fem-ə-nən\ *adj* **1** : ²FEMALE 1a **2** : characteristic of or belonging to women : WOMANLY **3** : of, relating to, or making up the class of words that ordinarily includes most of those referring to females ⟨a *feminine* noun in Latin⟩ ⟨the *feminine* gender⟩ [Middle English *feminine* "female", from early French *feminin* (same meaning), derived from Latin *femina* "woman" — related to FEMALE; see *Word History* at FEMALE] — **fem·i·nin·i·ty** \ˌfem-ə-'nin-ət-ē\ *n*

²feminine *n* **1** : a word or form of the feminine gender **2** : the feminine gender

fem·i·nism \'fem-ə-ˌniz-əm\ *n* **1** : the theory of the political, economic, and social equality of the sexes **2** : organized activity on behalf of women's rights and interests — **fem·i·nist** \-nəst\ *n or adj* — **fem·i·nis·tic** \ˌfem-ə-'nis-tik\ *adj*

fe·mur \'fē-mər\ *n, pl* **fe·murs** *or* **fem·o·ra** \'fem-(ə-)rə\ **1** : the long bone of the hind or lower limb extending from the hip to the knee and supporting the thigh — called also *thighbone* **2** : the segment of an insect's leg that is third from the body — **fem·o·ral** \'fem-(ə-)rəl\ *adj*

fen \'fen\ *n* : low land covered wholly or partly by water

¹fence \'fen(t)s\ *n* **1** : a barrier (as of wood or wire) to prevent escape or entry or to mark a boundary **2** : a person who receives stolen goods — **fence·less** \-ləs\ *adj* — **on the fence** : not having one's mind made up

²fence *vb* **fenced; fenc·ing** **1 a** : to enclose with a fence **b** : to keep in or out with a fence **2** : to practice fencing **3** : to sell (stolen property) to a fence — **fenc·er** *n*

fence rider *n* : a ranch worker who inspects and repairs fences

fenc·ing *n* **1** : the art or practice of attack and defense with a sword **2** : material for fences

fend \'fend\ *vb* **1** : REPEL 1 ⟨*fend* off an attack⟩ **2** : to try to get along without help ⟨had to *fend* for themselves⟩

fend·er \'fen-dər\ *n* : a device that protects: as **a** : a frame in front of a locomotive or streetcar to catch or throw off anything that is hit **b** : a guard over a wheel of an automobile, motorcycle, or bicycle **c** : a low metal frame or screen placed on the hearth before an open fireplace

fen·nec \'fen-ik\ *n* : a small African fox with large ears

fen·nel \'fen-ᵊl\ *n* : a garden plant related to the carrot that is grown for its seeds, stems, and fine needle‑shaped leaflets

fennec

fe·ral \'fir-əl, 'fer-\ *adj* : having escaped from domestication and become wild

fer–de–lance \ˌferd-ᵊl-'an(t)s, -'än(t)s\ *n, pl* **fer–de–lance** : a large extremely poisonous pit viper of Central and South America [from French *fer-de-lance,* literally "iron (point) of a lance (spear)"]

¹fer·ment \(ˌ)fər-'ment\ *vb* **1** : to undergo or cause to undergo fermentation **2** : to be or cause to be in a state of unrest or excitement

²fer·ment \'fər-ˌment\ *n* **1** : an agent that is capable of causing fermentation **2** : a state of unrest or excitement

fer·men·ta·tion \ˌfər-mən-'tā-shən, -ˌmen-\ *n* : chemical breaking down of an organic substance (as in the souring of milk or the formation of alcohol from sugar) produced by an enzyme and often accompanied by the formation of a gas — **fer·men·ta·tive** \(,)fər-'ment-ət-iv\ *adj*

fer·mi·um \'fer-mē-əm, 'fər-\ *n* : a radioactive metallic element artificially produced (as by bombardment of plutonium with neutrons) — see ELEMENT table

fern \'fərn\ *n* : any of an order of vascular plants resembling seed plants in having root, stem, and leaflike fronds but reproducing by spores instead of by flowers and seeds — **fern·like** \-,līk\ *adj* — **ferny** \'fər-nē\ *adj*

fe·ro·cious \fə-'rō-shəs\ *adj* **1** : FIERCE 1, SAVAGE **2** : very great : EXTREME — **fe·ro·cious·ly** *adv* — **fe·ro·cious·ness** *n* — **fe·roc·i·ty** \fə-'räs-ət-ē\ *n*

fern

¹fer·ret \'fer-ət\ *n* : a partially domesticated usually albino European mammal related to the weasel and used especially for hunting rodents

²ferret *vb* **1** : to drive out of a hiding place **2** : to find and bring to light by searching — usually used with *out*

fer·ric \'fer-ik\ *adj* : of, relating to, or containing iron

ferric oxide *n* : the red or black oxide of iron found in nature as hematite and as rust

Fer·ris wheel \'fer-əs-\ *n* : an amusement device consisting of a large vertical wheel that is driven by a motor and has seats around its rim [named for G. W. G. *Ferris* 1859–1896 American engineer]

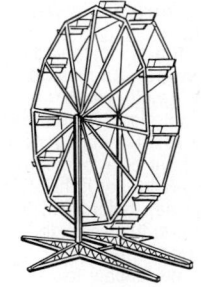

Ferris wheel

fer·ro·mag·net·ic \,fer-ō-mag-'net-ik\ *adj* : of or relating to substances (as iron and nickel) that are easily magnetized

fer·rous \'fer-əs\ *adj* : of, relating to, or containing iron

ferrous sulfate *n* : a salt that consists of iron, sulfur, and oxygen and is used in treating industrial wastes and in medicine

fer·rule \'fer-əl\ *n* : a metal ring or cap placed around the end of a wooden shaft or handle to prevent splitting or to provide a strong joint

¹fer·ry \'fer-ē\ *vb* **fer·ried; fer·ry·ing** **1 a** : to carry by boat over a body of water **b** : to cross by a ferry **2 a** : to carry (as by aircraft or motor vehicle) from one place to another **b** : to deliver an airplane under its own power

²ferry *n, pl* **ferries** **1** : a place where persons or things are ferried **2** : FERRYBOAT

fer·ry·boat \'fer-ē-,bōt\ *n* : a boat used to ferry passengers, vehicles, or goods

fer·tile \'fərt-ºl\ *adj* **1** : producing vegetation or crops plentifully : RICH ⟨*fertile* farmland⟩ **2** : producing abundantly ⟨a *fertile* mind⟩ **3 a** : capable of growing and developing ⟨a *fertile* seed⟩ **b** : capable of reproducing or of producing reproductive cells ⟨a *fertile* bull⟩ ⟨*fertile* fungous hyphae⟩ [Middle English *fertile* "bearing in abundance, productive", from early French *fertile* and Latin *fertilis* (both same meaning), from Latin *ferre* "to bear, carry, yield, produce" — related to ¹DEFER, TRANSFER] — **fer·til·i·ty** \(,)fər-'til-ət-ē\ *n*

syn FERTILE, FRUITFUL, PROLIFIC mean producing or ca-pable of producing offspring or fruit. FERTILE suggests having the power to reproduce or helping in reproduction and growth ⟨the *fertile* soil of the farm states⟩ FRUITFUL stresses the yielding of desirable or useful results ⟨*fruitful* methods of increasing the corn harvest⟩ PROLIFIC stresses the power to reproduce and spread rapidly ⟨rabbits are *prolific* animals⟩

fer·til·iza·tion \,fərt-ºl-ə-'zā-shən\ *n* **1** : an act or process of making fertile; *esp* : the application of fertilizer **2** : the union of male and female germ cells to form a zygote

fer·til·ize \'fərt-ºl-,īz\ *vb* **-ized; -iz·ing** : to make fertile: as **a** : to cause the fertilization of; *also* : to unite with in the process of fertilization ⟨a sperm *fertilizes* an egg⟩ **b** : to apply a fertilizer to

fer·til·iz·er \'fərt-ºl-,ī-zər\ *n* : a substance (as manure or a chemical) used to make soil produce larger or more plant life

fer·vent \'fər-vənt\ *adj* : having or expressing great warmth or depth of feeling ⟨a *fervent* hope⟩ — **fer·ven·cy** \-vən-sē\ *n* — **fer·vent·ly** *adv*

fer·vid \'fər-vəd\ *adj* : filled with passion or eagerness — **fer·vid·ly** *adv* — **fer·vid·ness** *n*

fer·vor \'fər-vər\ *n* : strength of feeling

fes·cue \'fes-(,)kyü\ *n* : a tufted perennial grass

fes·tal \'fest-ºl\ *adj* : FESTIVE 1 — **fes·tal·ly** \-ºl-ē\ *adv*

¹fes·ter \'fes-tər\ *n* : a pus-filled sore

²fester *vb* **fes·tered; fes·ter·ing** \-t(ə-)riŋ\ **1** : to form pus **2** : to become painful and inflamed **3** : ¹ROT 1a

fes·ti·val \'fes-tə-vəl\ *n* **1** : a time of celebration in honor of a special occasion **2** : a program of cultural events or entertainment [from earlier *festival* (adjective), derived from early French *festival* "festive", from Latin *festivus* "festive", from *festum* (noun) "festival, feast" — related to FEAST, FIESTA] — **festival** *adj*

fes·tive \'fes-tiv\ *adj* **1** : of, relating to, or suitable for a feast or festival **2** : JOYOUS, GAY — **fes·tive·ly** *adv* — **fes·tive·ness** *n*

fes·tiv·i·ty \fes-'tiv-ət-ē\ *n, pl* **-ties** **1** : FESTIVAL 1 **2** : ¹JOY 1, GAIETY **3** : festive activity

¹fes·toon \fes-'tün\ *n* : a decorative chain or strip hanging between two points

²festoon *vb* : to hang or form festoons on

fe·ta \'fet-ə, 'fe-,tä\ *n* : a white Greek cheese made from sheep's or goat's milk and cured in brine [from modern Greek *pheta* "slice (of cheese)"]

fe·tal \'fēt-ºl\ *adj* : of, relating to, or being a fetus

fetal alcohol syndrome *n* : a variable group of birth defects including deficient mental and physical growth that tend to occur in the infants of women who drink large amounts of alcohol during pregnancy

fetal membrane *n* : any of the structures that are formed from a fertilized egg but do not make up part of the embryo itself; *esp* : any of three membranes that surround and protect the developing embryo or fetus and are shed as part of the afterbirth

fetch \'fech\ *vb* **1** : to go after and bring back **2** : to cause to come : bring forth **3** : to bring as a price : sell for — **fetch·er** *n*

fetch·ing \'fech-iŋ\ *adj* : ATTRACTIVE, PLEASING — **fetch·ing·ly** *adv*

fetch up *vb* : to come to or bring to a stop

¹fete *or* **fête** \'fāt\ *n* **1** : FESTIVAL 1 **2** : a fancy entertainment or party

²fete *or* **fête** *vb* **fet·ed** *or* **fêt·ed; fet·ing** *or* **fêt·ing** **1** : to honor with a fete **2** : to pay high honor to

fet·id \'fet-əd\ *adj* : having a strong unpleasant smell — **fet·id·ly** *adv* — **fet·id·ness** *n*

fe·tish *also* **fe·tich** \'fet-ish *also* 'fēt-\ *n* **1** : an object (as an idol or image) believed to have supernatural or magical powers **2** : an object of unreasonable devotion or concern — **fe·tish·ism** \-,iz-əm\ *n*

fet·lock \'fet-,läk\ *n* **1** : a projection with a bunch of hair on the back of a horse's leg above the hoof **2** : the bunch of hair growing out of the fetlock

fet·ter \'fet-ər\ *n* **1** : a chain for the feet **2** : something that restricts : RESTRAINT — **fetter** *vb*

fet·tle \'fet-ᵊl\ *n* : a state of fitness or order : CONDITION ⟨in fine *fettle*⟩

fe·tus \'fēt-əs\ *n, pl* **fe·tus·es** : a young animal while in the body of its mother or in the egg especially in the later stages of development; *esp* : a developing human being in the uterus from usually three months after pregnancy occurs to birth — compare EMBRYO 1

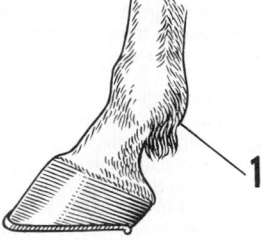

1 fetlock 1

feud \'fyüd\ *n* : a long quarrel; *esp* : a lasting conflict between families or clans usually having acts of violence and revenge — **feud** *vb*

feu·dal \'fyüd-ᵊl\ *adj* : of or relating to feudalism

feu·dal·ism \'fyüd-ᵊl-,iz-əm\ *n* : a system of political organization (as in Europe during the Middle Ages) in which a vassal served a lord and received protection and land in return — **feu·dal·is·tic** \,fyüd-ᵊl-'is-tik\ *adj*

fe·ver \'fē-vər\ *n* **1 a** : a rise of body temperature above the normal **b** : a disease of which fever is an important symptom **2** : a state of excited emotion or activity

fever blister *n* : COLD SORE

fe·ver·ish \'fēv-(ə-)rish\ *adj* **1 a** : marked by fever **b** : of, relating to, or being fever **c** : tending to cause fever **2** : showing great emotion or activity : HECTIC — **fe·ver·ish·ly** *adv* — **fe·ver·ish·ness** *n*

fever thermometer *n* : CLINICAL THERMOMETER

¹few \'fyü\ *pron* : not many persons or things

²few *adj* **1** : amounting to only a small number ⟨one of my *few* pleasures⟩ **2** : not many but some ⟨caught a *few* fish⟩ — **few·ness** *n*

³few *n* **1** : a small number of units or individuals ⟨a *few* of them⟩ **2** : a special limited number ⟨the select *few*⟩

¹few·er \'fyü-ər\ *adj* : not so many : a smaller number of

²fewer *pron* : a smaller number of persons or things ⟨*fewer* came than were expected⟩

fez \'fez\ *n, pl* **fez·zes** : a round red felt hat that has a flat top and a tassel but no brim

fi·an·cé \,fē-,än-'sā, fē-'än-,sā\ *n* : a man engaged to be married [from French *fiancé* "man engaged to be married", derived from early French *fiancé*, past participle of *fiancer* "to promise", derived from Latin *fidere* "to trust" — related to FAITH]

fi·an·cée \,fē-,än-'sā, fē-'än-,sā\ *n* : a woman engaged to be married

fez

fi·as·co \fē-'as-kō\ *n, pl* **-coes** : a complete failure

fi·at \'fē-ət, -,at, -,ät; 'fī-ət, -,at\ *n* : an order from someone in charge

fib \'fib\ *n* : an unimportant lie — **fib** *vb* — **fib·ber** *n*

fi·ber *or* **fi·bre** \'fī-bər\ *n* **1** : a thread or a structure or object resembling a thread: as **a** : a slender root (as of a grass) **b** : a long tapering thick-walled plant cell especially of vascular tissue **c** : a muscle cell **d** : AXON, DENDRITE **e** : a slender and very long natural or synthetic unit of material (as wool, cotton, asbestos, gold, glass, or rayon) usually able to be spun into yarn **f** : ROUGHAGE **2** : material made of fibers; *esp* : a tough substance made from cellulose fibers and used for luggage, electrical insulation, and boxes **3** : basic toughness : STRENGTH ⟨moral *fiber*⟩

fi·ber·board \'fī-bər-,bōrd, -,bȯrd\ *n* : a material made by pressing fibers (as of wood) into stiff sheets; *also* : PAPERBOARD

fi·ber·fill \-,fil\ *n* : synthetic fibers used as a filling material (as for pillows)

fi·ber·glass \-,glas\ *n* : glass in the form of fibers used in making various products (as yarn, insulation, or boats)

fiber optics *n* **1** *pl* : thin transparent enclosed fibers of glass or plastic that carry light by internal reflections; *also* : a bundle of such fibers used in an instrument **2** : the technique of the use of fiber optics

Fi·bo·nac·ci number \,fē-bə-'näch-ē-, ,fib-ə-\ *n* : any of the integers in the infinite sequence 1, 1, 2, 3, 5, 8, 13 . . . of which the first two terms are 1 and 1 and each following term is the sum of the two just before it [named for Leonardo *Fibonacci* about 1170–about 1240 Italian mathematician]

Fibonacci sequence *n* : a mathematical sequence composed of the Fibonacci numbers in order

fi·brin \'fī-brən\ *n* : a white fibrous substance that is difficult to dissolve and is formed in the clotting of the blood

fi·brin·o·gen \fī-'brin-ə-jən\ *n* : a protein that is produced in the liver, is difficult to dissolve, is present especially in blood plasma, and is changed into fibrin during the clotting of blood

fi·bro·sis \fī-'brō-səs\ *n* : an abnormal bodily condition in which increased amounts of fibrous tissue form in other tissues — compare CYSTIC FIBROSIS

fi·brous \'fī-brəs\ *adj* **1** : containing, consisting of, or resembling fibers **2** : ¹TOUGH 1b, STRINGY

fibrous root *n* : a root (as in most grasses) that is one of many similar slender roots branching directly from the base of the stem of a plant — compare TAPROOT

fi·bro·vas·cu·lar bundle \,fib-rō-,vas-kyə-lər-, ,fib-\ *n* : VASCULAR BUNDLE

fib·u·la \'fib-yə-lə\ *n, pl* **-lae** \-,lē, -,lī\ *or* **-las** : the outer and usually the smaller of the two bones of the hind limb below the knee — **fib·u·lar** \-lər\ *adj*

fick·le \'fik-əl\ *adj* : likely to change frequently without good reason : INCONSTANT ⟨*fickle* friends⟩ — **fick·le·ness** *n*

fic·tion \'fik-shən\ *n* **1** : something told or written that is not fact **2** : a made-up story — **fic·tion·al** \-shnəl, -shən-ᵊl\ *adj* — **fic·tion·al·ly** \-shnə-lē, -shən-ᵊl-ē\ *adv*

fic·tion·al·ize \'fik-shnə-,līz, -shən-ᵊl-,īz\ *vb* **-ized; -iz·ing** : to make into fiction — **fic·tion·al·iza·tion** \,fik-shnə-lə-'zā-shən, -shən-ᵊl-ə-\ *n*

fic·tion·ize \'fik-shə-,nīz\ *vb* **-ized; -iz·ing** : FICTIONALIZE

fic·ti·tious \fik-'tish-əs\ *adj* : not real : MADE-UP, IMAGINARY ⟨a *fictitious* story⟩ — **fic·ti·tious·ly** *adv* — **fic·ti·tious·ness** *n*

¹fid·dle \'fid-ᵊl\ *n* : VIOLIN 1

²fiddle *vb* **fid·dled; fid·dling** \'fid-liŋ, -ᵊl-iŋ\ **1** : to play on a fiddle **2 a** : to move the hands or fingers restlessly **b** : to spend time in aimless activity **c** : MEDDLE, TAMPER — **fid·dler** \'fid-lər, -ᵊl-ər\ *n*

fid·dle·head \'fid-ᵊl-,hed\ *n* : one of the young tightly coiled leaves of some ferns that are often eaten as greens

fiddler crab *n* : a burrowing crab of which the male has one claw much larger than the other

fid·dle·stick \'fid-ᵊl-,stik\ *n* **1** : a violin bow **2** *pl* : NONSENSE 1 — used as an interjection

fi·del·i·ty \fə-'del-ət-ē, fī-\ *n, pl* **-ties** **1 a** : the quality or state of being faithful **b** : exactness in details **2** : the

\ə\ abut	\au̇\ out	\i\ tip	\ȯ\ saw	\u̇\ foot	
\ər\ further	\ch\ chin	\ī\ life	\ȯi\ coin	\y\ yet	
\a\ mat	\e\ pet	\j\ job	\th\ thin	\yü\ few	
\ā\ take	\ē\ easy	\ŋ\ sing	\th\ this	\yu̇\ cure	
\ä\ cot, cart	\g\ go	\ō\ bone	\ü\ food	\zh\ vision	

degree to which an electronic device (as a record player, radio, or television) correctly reproduces its effect (as sound or a picture)

¹fidg·et \'fij-ət\ *n* **1** *pl* : restlessness as shown by nervous movements **2** : one that fidgets — **fidg·ety** \-ət-ē\ *adj*

²fidget *vb* : to move or cause to move or act nervously or restlessly

fie \'fī\ *interj* — used to express slight shock or disapproval

fief \'fēf\ *n* : a feudal estate

¹field \'fē(ə)ld\ *n* **1 a** : open country — usually used in pl. **b** : a piece of open land **c** : a piece of land put to some special use or yielding some special product ⟨athletic *field*⟩ ⟨gas *field*⟩ **d** : a place in which military operations are carried on **e** : an open space **2 a** : an area of activity or influence ⟨the *field* of science⟩ **b** : the area of practical activity outside a laboratory, office, or factory ⟨earth scientists working in the *field*⟩ **3** : a background on which something is drawn, painted, or mounted ⟨the American flag has white stars on a blue *field*⟩ **4** : the individuals that make up all or part of a sports activity ⟨a race with a large *field* of runners⟩ **5** : a region or space in which an effect (as gravity, electricity, or magnetism) exists **6** : the area visible through the lens of an optical instrument

²field *vb* : to catch or stop and throw a ball as a fielder ⟨the shortstop *fielded* the ground ball⟩

³field *adj* : of or relating to a field

field corn *n* : an Indian corn with starchy kernels grown for feeding livestock or for market grain — compare SWEET CORN

field day *n* **1** : a day of outdoor sports and athletic competition **2** : a time of unusual pleasure or unexpected success ⟨newspapers had a *field day* with the story⟩

field·er \'fēl-dər\ *n* : one that fields; *esp* : a baseball player stationed in the field while the opposing team is at bat

field event *n* : an event in a track meet other than a race

field glass *n* : a hand-held instrument for seeing at a distance that consists of two telescopes usually without prisms on a single frame — usually used in pl.

field goal *n* **1** : a score of three points in football made by kicking the ball over the crossbar during ordinary play **2** : BASKET 3b

field hockey *n* : a game played on a field in which each team uses curved sticks to try to knock a ball into the other team's goal

field magnet *n* : a magnet for producing and maintaining a magnetic field especially in a generator or electric motor

field marshal *n* : an officer (as in the British army) of the highest rank

field mouse *n* : any of various mice that inhabit open fields

field of view : ¹FIELD 6

field of vision : VISUAL FIELD

field·stone \'fē(ə)ld-,stōn\ *n* : stone (as in building) in usually unchanged form as taken from the field

field trip *n* : a visit (as to a factory, farm, or museum) made by students and usually a teacher for purposes of firsthand observation

fiend \'fēnd\ *n* **1** : DEMON 1, DEVIL **2** : an extremely wicked or cruel person **3 a** : a person enthusiastically devoted to something **b** : ²ADDICT — **fiend·ish** \'fēn-dish\ *adj* — **fiend·ish·ly** *adv* — **fiend·ish·ness** *n*

fierce \'fi(ə)rs\ *adj* **fierc·er**; **fierc·est 1 a** : violently unfriendly or aggressive in disposition **b** : eager to fight or kill **2** : expressed with extreme force or anger : INTENSE ⟨a *fierce* argument⟩ **3** : furiously active or determined ⟨a *fierce* effort⟩ **4** : wild or threatening in appearance — **fierce·ly** *adv* — **fierce·ness** *n*

fi·ery \'fī-(ə-)rē\ *adj* **fi·er·i·er**; **-est 1** : being on fire : BLAZING **2** : hot or glowing like a fire **3 a** : full of spirit ⟨a *fiery* speech⟩ **b** : easily set off ⟨a *fiery* temper⟩ — **fi·er·i·ness** *n*

fi·es·ta \fē-'es-tə\ *n* : FESTIVAL 1; *esp* : a saint's day celebrated in Spain and Latin America with parades and dances [from Spanish *fiesta* "a festival, a religious celebration", from Latin *festa,* plural of *festum* "festival, feast" — related to FEAST, FESTIVAL]

fife \'fīf\ *n* : a small shrill musical instrument resembling a flute

fif·teen \(')fif-'tēn\ *n* — see NUMBER table — **fifteen** *adj or pron* — **fif·teenth** \-'tēn(t)th\ *adj or n*

fifth \'fith, 'fif(t)th\ *n* **1** — see NUMBER table **2** : the difference in pitch between the first tone and the fifth tone of a scale — **fifth** *adj or adv* — **fifth·ly** *adv*

fif·ty \'fif-tē\ *n, pl* **fifties** — see NUMBER table — **fif·ti·eth** \-tē-əth\ *adj or n* — **fifty** *adj or pron*

fif·ty–fif·ty \,fif-tē-'fif-tē\ *adj* **1** : shared equally **2** : half favorable and half unfavorable ⟨a *fifty-fifty* chance to live⟩ — **fifty–fifty** *adv*

fig \'fig\ *n* : an edible fruit that is oblong or shaped like a pear and grows on a tree related to the mulberries; *also* : a tree bearing figs

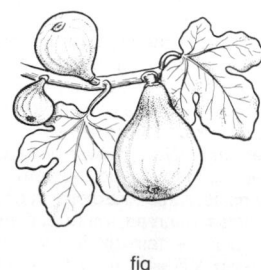

fig

¹fight \'fīt\ *vb* **fought** \'fȯt\; **fight·ing 1 a** : to struggle against another in battle or physical combat **b** : ⁵BOX 2 **2** : to try hard ⟨*fighting* to stay awake⟩ **3 a** : to act for or against : STRUGGLE, CONTEND ⟨*fight* for the right⟩ ⟨*fight* a fire⟩ ⟨*fight* discrimination⟩ **b** : to attempt to prevent the success or effectiveness of ⟨*fight* off a cold⟩

²fight *n* **1 a** : a violent struggle between opposing forces : COMBAT, BATTLE **b** : a boxing match **c** : a verbal disagreement **2** : a struggle for a goal or an objective ⟨in a *fight* for their lives⟩ **3** : strength or disposition for fighting ⟨full of *fight*⟩

fight·er \'fīt-ər\ *n* : one that fights: **a** : WARRIOR, SOLDIER **b** : ¹BOXER **c** : a fast airplane armed with weapons for destroying enemy aircraft

fig·ment \'fig-mənt\ *n* : something imagined or made up

fig·u·ra·tive \'fig-(y)ə-rət-iv\ *adj* : expressing one thing in terms normally used for another : METAPHORICAL ⟨the *figurative* use of "foot" in "the foot of the mountain"⟩ — **fig·u·ra·tive·ly** *adv*

¹fig·ure \'fig-yər, *British and often US* 'fig-ər\ *n* **1 a** : NUMERAL 1 **b** *pl* : ARITHMETIC 2 ⟨a good head for *figures*⟩ **c** : ¹PRICE 1 **2 a** : the shape or outline of something **b** : bodily shape or form especially of a person **3 a** : something that represents a form especially of a person **b** : a diagram or pictorial illustration **c** : a combination of points, lines, or surfaces in geometry ⟨a circle is a closed plane *figure*⟩ **4** : ¹PATTERN 3, DESIGN **5** : PERSONALITY 4, PERSONAGE — **fig·ured** \-(y)ərd\ *adj*

²figure *vb* **fig·ured; fig·ur·ing** \'fig-yə-riŋ, 'fig-(ə-)\ **1** : to decorate with a pattern **2** : BELIEVE 5, DECIDE ⟨*figured* we might win⟩ **3** : to be or appear important ⟨*figure* in the news⟩ **4** : COMPUTE, CALCULATE — **fig·ur·er** \-(y)ər-ər\ *n* — **figure on 1** : to take into consideration **2** : to rely on **3** : ²PLAN 2

fig·ure·head \'fig-(y)ər-hed\ *n* **1** : a figure, statue, or bust on the bow of a ship **2** : a person who has the title but not the powers of the head of something

figurehead 1

figure of speech : a form of expression (as a simile or metaphor) that uses words other than in a plain or literal way

figure out *vb* **1** : FIND OUT, DISCOVER ⟨try to *figure out* a way to do it⟩ **2** : SOLVE ⟨*figure out* a problem⟩

figure skating *n* : skating in which the skaters move in exact patterns and also perform various jumps and turns

fig·u·rine \,fig-(y)ə-'rēn\ *n* : a small carved or molded figure

fig·wort \'fig-,wərt, -,wȯ(ə)rt\ *n* : any of a genus of chiefly coarse upright herbs with toothed leaves and flowers in clusters

fil·a·ment \'fil-ə-mənt\ *n* : a single thread or a thin flexible threadlike object, process, or part: as **a** : a wire (as in a light bulb) that is made to glow by the passage of an electric current **b** : a long thin slender part of a gill that is the place where gas exchange occurs between water and the blood of a water-dwelling animal that breathes by gills **c** : the anther-bearing stalk of a plant stamen — **fil·a·men·tous** \,fil-ə-'ment-əs\ *adj*

fil·bert \'fil-bərt\ *n* **1** : either of two European hazels; *also* : the sweet thick-shelled nut of a filbert **2** : HAZELNUT
> **Word History** Hazel trees are common in England, and their sweet nuts become ripe in late summer. The feast day of a French saint named Philibert was celebrated during the time that people picked these nuts. In the form of French spoken in England after the Normans conquered it in 1066, the nut of the hazel tree was called *philber,* after the saint. English borrowed the word as *filbert.* [Middle English *filbert* "filbert", from *philber,* name for the nut in the French language used in England after 1066; named for Saint *Philibert,* French abbot who has a feast day at the time when the nuts ripen]

filch \'filch\ *vb* : to steal something slyly : PILFER

¹file \'fīl\ *n* : a usually steel tool with sharp ridges or teeth on its surface for smoothing or rubbing down hard substances [Old English *fēol* "tool for smoothing rough edges"]

²file *vb* **filed; fil·ing** : to rub, smooth, or cut away with a file

³file *vb* **filed; fil·ing** **1** : to arrange in order for keeping or reference **2** : to enter or record as required by law [Middle English *filen* "to arrange (documents) in order", from early French *filer* "to thread documents on a string", from *fil* "thread", derived from Latin *filum* "thread" — related to ⁵FILE]

⁴file *n* **1** : a device (as a folder, case, or cabinet) for keeping papers or records in order **2 a** : a collection of papers or records arranged in order **b** : a collection of related quantities of data considered as units for a computer

⁵file *n* : a row of persons, animals, or things arranged one behind the other [from early French *file* "a row of things", from *filer* (verb) "to spin", derived from Latin *filum* "thread" — related to ³FILE]

⁶file *vb* **filed; fil·ing** : to march or proceed in file

file·fish \'fī(ə)l-,fish\ *n* : any of various fishes with rough leathery skins

fi·let mi·gnon \,fil-(,)ā-mēn-'yän, fi-,lā-\ *n, pl* **filets mignons** \-mēn-'yänz\ : a thick slice of beef cut from the narrow end of a tenderloin [French, literally "dainty fillet"]

fil·i·al \'fil-ē-əl, 'fil-yəl\ *adj* **1** : of, relating to, or befitting a son or daughter ⟨*filial* obedience⟩ **2** : being or having the relation of offspring

¹fil·i·bus·ter \'fil-ə-,bəs-tər\ *n* : the use of delaying tactics (as long speeches) to put off or prevent action especially in a legislative assembly; *also* : an instance of this practice
> **Word History** One Dutch word has given us two different English words. The Dutch word *vrijbuiter* referred to a person who robbed openly and with force in wartime especially for personal gain. The English borrowed this word in the 16th century, translating it as *freebooter.* The word was later picked up by the Spanish, who kept the same meaning but spelled it *filibustero.* Both words stayed in the realm of history until the middle of the 19th

century. Then soldiers of fortune went out from the U.S. to try to cause uprisings in Central American countries. The governments there accused these Americans of wanting personal gain more than justice and called them *filibusteros.* English-speaking journalists wrote this word as *filibuster,* making it sound more like an English word. The filibusters used hit-and-run and other delaying tactics, since they never had enough fighters for a regular battle. Later in the 19th century, members of Congress who delayed passage of laws by means such as long speeches were compared to the adventurers of Central America. *Filibuster* then came to mean "the use of delaying tactics to put off or prevent the passage of laws". [from Spanish *filibustero,* literally "freebooter", probably derived from English *freebooter*]

²filibuster *vb* **-tered; -ter·ing** \-t(ə-)riŋ\ : to engage in a filibuster — **fil·i·bus·ter·er** \-tər-ər\ *n*

fil·i·gree \'fil-ə-,grē\ *n* **1** : ornamental work especially of fine wire applied chiefly to gold and silver surfaces **2 a** : ornamental work of delicate or complicated design done so as to show openings through the material **b** : a pattern or design resembling such work

fil·ing \'fī-liŋ\ *n* : a small piece scraped off in filing ⟨iron *filings*⟩

Fil·i·pi·no \,fil-ə-'pē-nō\ *n, pl* **-nos** : a person born or living in the Philippines [Spanish] — **Filipino** *adj*

¹fill \'fil\ *vb* **1** : to put into as much as can be held or contained ⟨*fill* one's plate⟩ **2** : to become full **3** : SATISFY 1a ⟨*fill* all requirements⟩ **4** : to occupy fully : take up whatever space there is ⟨clothes *filled* the closet⟩ **5** : to spread through ⟨laughter *filled* the room⟩ **6** : to stop up (as holes) : PLUG ⟨*fill* a crack with putty⟩ ⟨*fill* a tooth⟩ **7 a** : to perform the duties of : OCCUPY ⟨*fill* the office of president⟩ **b** : to put a person in ⟨*filled* several vacancies⟩ **8** : to supply according to directions ⟨*fill* a prescription⟩ — **fill one's shoes** : to take one's place or position

²fill *n* **1** : a full supply; *esp* : a quantity that satisfies ⟨eat one's *fill*⟩ **2** : material used to fill a container, cavity, passage, or low place

fill·er \'fil-ər\ *n* : one that fills: as **a** : a substance added to a product (as to increase size or weight) **b** : a pack of paper to put in a binder **c** : a sound, word, or phrase used to fill pauses in speaking

¹fil·let \'fil-ət *also* fi-'lā, 'fil-(,)ā\ *also* **fi·let** \fi-'lā, 'fil-(,)ā\ *n* : a piece or slice of boneless meat or fish

²fillet *vb* : to cut into fillets

fill in *vb* **1** : to furnish with specified information ⟨*fill in* an application⟩ ⟨*filled* us *in* on the latest news⟩ **2** : to fill a vacancy usually temporarily : SUBSTITUTE ⟨*filled in* during the emergency⟩

fill·ing \'fil-iŋ\ *n* **1** : material that is used to fill something ⟨a *filling* for a tooth⟩ **2** : something that completes: as **a** : the yarn crossing over and under the warp in a fabric **b** : a food mixture used to fill pastry or sandwiches

fil·lip \'fil-əp\ *n* : a feature added to attract interest

fill out *vb* **1** : to put on flesh **2** : to complete by filling in blanks ⟨*fill out* an application⟩

fil·ly \'fil-ē\ *n, pl* **fillies** : a young female horse usually less than four years old

¹film \'film\ *n* **1** : a thin skin or membrane **2** : a thin coating or layer **3** : a roll or strip of thin flexible transparent material coated with a chemical substance sensitive to light and used in taking pictures **4** : MOTION PICTURE

²film *vb* **1** : to cover or become covered with film **2** : to make a motion picture of or from

film·strip \'film-,strip\ *n* : a strip of film for projecting still

\ə\ abut	\au̇\ out	\i\ tip	\ȯ\ saw	\u̇\ foot
\ər\ further	\ch\ chin	\ī\ life	\ȯi\ coin	\y\ yet
\a\ mat	\e\ pet	\j\ job	\th\ thin	\yü\ few
\ā\ take	\ē\ easy	\ŋ\ sing	\th\ this	\yu̇\ cure
\ä\ cot, cart	\g\ go	\ō\ bone	\ü\ food	\zh\ vision

pictures on a screen

filmy \'fil-mē\ *adj* **film·i·er; -est** : of, resembling, suggesting, or made of film — **film·i·ness** *n*

¹fil·ter \'fil-tər\ *n* **1** : a substance with pores through which a gas or liquid is passed to separate out floating matter **2** : a device containing a filter **3** : a transparent material (as colored glass) that absorbs light of some wavelengths and is used to change light (as in photography)

²filter *vb* **fil·tered; fil·ter·ing** \-t(ə-)riŋ\ **1** : to expose to the action of a filter **2** : to remove by means of a filter **3** : to pass through or as if through a filter

fil·ter·able *also* **fil·tra·ble** \'fil-t(ə-)rə-bəl\ *adj* : capable of being separated by or of passing through a filter — **fil·ter·abil·i·ty** \,fil-t(ə-)rə-'bil-ət-ē\ *n*

filterable virus *n* : any of the infectious agents that remain infectious after passing through a filter of diatomite or unglazed porcelain and that include the agents and microbes now classified as viruses as well as various other groups (as the rickettsias) which were once considered viruses before they were known to be cells

filter bed *n* : a bed of sand or gravel for filtering water or sewage

filter paper *n* : porous paper used especially for filtering

filth \'filth\ *n* **1** : disgusting dirt **2** : something that tends to disgust, offend, or dirty

filthy \'fil-thē\ *adj* **filth·i·er; -est** **1** : covered with or containing filth : disgustingly dirty **2 a** : ²UNDERHAND 1, VILE **b** : OBSCENE 2 **syn** see DIRTY — **filth·i·ly** \-thə-lē\ *adv* — **filth·i·ness** \-thē-nəs\ *n*

fil·trate \'fil-,trāt\ *n* : the fluid that has passed through a filter

fil·tra·tion \fil-'trā-shən\ *n* : the act or process of filtering

fin \'fin\ *n* **1** : a thin process on the outside of an aquatic animal (as a fish or whale) used in propelling or guiding the body **2** : something shaped like a fin — **fin·like** \-,līk\ *adj* — **finned** \'find\ *adj*

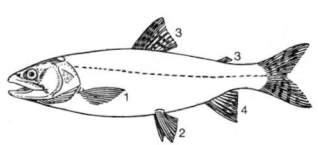

fin 1: *1* pectoral, *2* pelvic, *3* dorsal, *4* anal

fi·na·gle \fə-'nā-gəl\ *vb* **-gled; -gling** \-g(ə-)liŋ\ : to use trickery to get what one wants — **fi·na·gler** \-g(ə-)lər\ *n*

¹fi·nal \'fīn-°l\ *adj* **1** : not to be changed or undone ⟨my *final* offer⟩ **2** : relating to or occurring at the end or conclusion : ULTIMATE ⟨the *final* act of the play⟩ [Middle English *final* "perfect, final, not to be changed", from early French *final* (same meaning), from Latin *finalis* "final, relating to the end" — related to DEFINE, FINISH, INFINITY] — **fi·nal·ly** \'fīn-°l-ē, -lē\ *adv*

²final *n* : something final: as **a** : the last match or game of a tournament — usually used in pl. **b** : the last examination in a course

fi·na·le \fə-'nal-ē, fi-'näl-\ *n* : the close or end of something (as a musical work)

fi·nal·ist \'fīn-°l-əst\ *n* : a contestant in the finals of a competition

fi·nal·i·ty \fī-'nal-ət-ē, fə-\ *n, pl* **-ties** **1** : the character or state of being final, settled, or complete **2** : something final

fi·nal·ize \'fīn-°l-īz\ *vb* **-ized; -iz·ing** : to put in final or finished form

¹fi·nance \fə-'nan(t)s, 'fī-,nan(t)s, fī-'nan(t)s\ *n* **1** *pl* : resources (as money) available especially to a government or business **2** : the obtaining or providing of funds or capital **3** : the system that includes the circulation of money, the providing of banks and credit, and the making of investments — **fi·nan·cial** \fə-'nan-chəl, fī-\ *adj* — **fi·nan·cial·ly** \-'nanch-(ə-)lē\ *adv*

²finance *vb* **fi·nanced; fi·nanc·ing** : to provide money for ⟨*finance* a trip⟩

finance charge *n* : a charge for credit that is generally a percentage of the amount of credit given

finance company *n* : a company that specializes in making small loans usually to individuals

fin·an·cier \,fin-ən-'si(ə)r, fə-,nan-, ,fī-nan-\ *n* : a person who specializes in finance and especially in the financing of businesses

fin·back \'fin-,bak\ *n* : a common whalebone whale of the Atlantic coast of the U.S. that attains a length of over 20 meters

finch \'finch\ *n* : any of numerous songbirds (as the sparrows, grosbeaks, crossbills, goldfinches, linnets, and buntings) that have a short stout bill adapted for crushing seeds

¹find \'fīnd\ *vb* **found** \'faúnd\; **find·ing** **1** : to meet with someone or something by chance ⟨*found* a dime⟩ **2** : to come upon by searching, study, or effort ⟨finally *found* the answer⟩ **3** : to obtain by effort or management ⟨*find* time to do it⟩ **4** : to make a decision ⟨*find* a verdict⟩ **5** : to know by experience ⟨people *found* it useful⟩ **6** : to gain or regain the use of ⟨*found* my voice again⟩ — **find fault** : to discover real or imaginary faults : CRITICIZE, COMPLAIN

²find *n* : something found; *esp* : a valuable item found

find·er \'fīn-dər\ *n* : one that finds: as **a** : a small telescope attached to a larger one for finding an object **b** : a device on a camera that shows the view being photographed by the camera

find·ing \'fīn-diŋ\ *n* : the result of a judicial proceeding or inquiry

find out *vb* : to learn by study, observation, or search : DISCOVER

¹fine \'fīn\ *n* : a sum of money to be paid as a punishment [from earlier *fine* "a final agreement to settle a lawsuit", from Middle English *fine* "end, conclusion", from early French *fin* (same meaning), from Latin *finis* "end, limit" — related to FINAL]

²fine *vb* **fined; fin·ing** : to punish by a fine

³fine *adj* **fin·er; fin·est** **1** : free from impurity **2 a** : not thick, coarse, or dull ⟨*fine* thread⟩ ⟨*fine* sand⟩ **b** : ¹SMALL 1 ⟨*fine* print⟩ **c** : DELICATE 5 ⟨*fine* china⟩ **d** : done with extreme care and accuracy ⟨*fine* measurement⟩ **3** : SUBTLE 1b ⟨a *fine* distinction⟩ **4** : excellent in quality or appearance ⟨a *fine* spring day⟩ **5** : to one's liking : AGREEABLE ⟨that's *fine* with me⟩ [Middle English *fin* "pure, brought to perfection", from early French *fin* (same meaning), from Latin *finis* (noun) "end, limit" as in *finis honorum* "the height of honor, the highest honor"] — **fine·ly** *adv* — **fine·ness** \'fīn-nəs\ *n*

⁴fine *adv* **1** : in a fine manner **2** : very well ⟨did *fine* on the test⟩ ⟨I liked it *fine*⟩

⁵fi·ne \'fē-(,)nā\ *n* : ¹END 1b — used as a direction in music to mark the closing point after a repeat [Italian, from Latin *finis* "end, limit"]

fine art *n* : art or an art (as painting, sculpture, or music) concerned primarily with the creation of beautiful objects — usually used in pl.

fin·ery \'fīn-(ə-)rē\ *n, pl* **-er·ies** : showy clothing and jewels

¹fi·nesse \fə-'nes\ *n* : skillful or delicate handling or artistry

²finesse *vb* **fi·nessed; fi·ness·ing** : to bring about a result by finesse

fin·fish \'fin-,fish\ *n* : ¹FISH 1b — compare SHELLFISH

¹fin·ger \'fiŋ-gər\ *n* **1** : one of the five divisions of the end of the hand; *esp* : one other than the thumb **2 a** : something that resembles or does the work of a finger **b** : a part of a glove into which a finger is inserted **3** : the width of a finger — **fin·gered** \-gərd\ *adj* — **fin·ger·like** \-gər-,līk\ *adj*

²finger *vb* **fin·gered; fin·ger·ing** \-g(ə-)riŋ\ **1** : to touch with the fingers : HANDLE **2** : to perform with the fingers or with a certain fingering

fin·ger·board \'fiŋ-gər-,bō(ə)rd, -,bȯ(ə)rd\ *n* : the part of a stringed instrument against which the fingers press the strings to vary the pitch

finger bowl *n* : a small bowl of water for rinsing the fingers at the table

finger food *n* : a food (as a radish or carrot stick) that is meant to be picked up with the fingers and eaten

fingerboard

finger hole *n* : a hole in the tube of a wind instrument that may be covered with the finger or left open to change the tone

fin·ger·ing \'fiŋ-g(ə-)riŋ\ *n* **1** : the act or process of handling or touching with fingers **2 a** : the method of using the fingers in playing an instrument **b** : the marking on a piece of music that shows what fingers are to be used

fin·ger·nail \'fiŋ-gər-,nāl, ,fiŋ-gər-'nā(ə)l\ *n* : the nail of a finger

finger painting *n* **1** : a method of spreading paint on wet paper chiefly with the fingers **2** : a picture produced by finger painting

fin·ger·print \'fiŋ-gər-,print\ *n* : the pattern of marks made by pressing the tip of a finger on a surface; *esp* : a pattern of marks in ink of the lines on the tip of a finger taken for the purpose of identification — **fingerprint** *vb* — **fin·ger·print·ing** \-,prin-tiŋ\ *n*

fin·ger·tip \-,tip\ *n* : the tip of a finger

fin·icky \'fin-i-kē\ *adj* : very hard to please : FUSSY — **fin·ick·i·ness** *n*

fin·is \'fin-əs, 'fī-nəs\ *n* : ¹END 2a, CONCLUSION

¹fin·ish \'fin-ish\ *vb* **1** : to bring or come to an end : TERMINATE **2** : to bring to completion : PERFECT **3** : to put a final coat or surface on **4** : to sew or trim edges of a garment so as to prevent the fabric from separating **5** : to come to the end of a course, task, or undertaking [Middle English *finisshen* "to finish, bring to an end", from early French *finiss-, finir* (same meaning), derived from Latin *finis* "end, limit" — related to DEFINE, FINAL, INFINITY] — **fin·ish·er** *n*

²finish *n* **1** : ¹END 2a, CONCLUSION **2** : the final treatment or coating of a surface or the appearance given by finishing

finishing nail *n* : a wire nail with a small head

finish line *n* : a line marking the end of a racecourse

fi·nite \'fī-,nīt\ *adj* **1** : having certain limits : limited in scope or nature : not infinite **2** : showing differences in grammatical person and number ⟨a *finite* verb⟩ — **fi·nite·ly** *adv* — **fi·nite·ness** *n*

Finn \'fin\ *n* : a person born or living in Finland

fin·nan had·die \,fin-ən-'had-ē\ *n* : smoked haddock

¹Finn·ish \'fin-ish\ *adj* : of, relating to, or characteristic of Finland, the Finns, or Finnish

²Finnish *n* : a language of the Finns

fin·ny \'fin-ē\ *adj* : resembling or having fins

fin whale *n* : FINBACK

fiord *variant of* FJORD

fir \'fər\ *n* **1** : any of various usually large evergreen trees related to the pines some of which yield useful lumber or resins **2** : the wood of a fir

¹fire \'fī(ə)r\ *n* **1** : the light and heat and especially the flame produced by burning **2** : fuel that is burning (as in a fireplace or stove) **3** : the destructive burning of something (as a building or a forest) **4** : eager liveliness : ENTHUSIASM **5** : the shooting of guns — **on fire** **1** : in the process of burning **2** : ARDENT, EAGER — **under fire** **1** : exposed to the firing of enemy guns **2** : under attack

²fire *vb* **fired; fir·ing** **1 a** : to set on fire : KINDLE, IGNITE **b**

: ¹STIR 3, ENLIVEN ⟨a story to *fire* the imagination⟩ ⟨all *fired* up⟩ **2** : to dismiss from employment **3** : to cause to explode ⟨*fire* dynamite⟩ **4 a** : to cause to be driven from or as if from a gun : LAUNCH ⟨*fire* an arrow⟩ ⟨*fire* a rocket⟩ **b** : to throw with speed : HURL ⟨*fired* the ball to first base⟩ **c** : to shoot off a firearm : DISCHARGE **5 a** : to subject to great heat ⟨*fire* pottery⟩ **b** : to feed the fire of ⟨*fire* a furnace⟩ **6 a** : to begin to burn **b** : to have fuel (as in a cylinder of an engine) ignite at the proper time — **fir·er** *n*

fire alarm *n* : an alarm sounded to signal the outbreak of a fire; *also* : a device for sounding such an alarm

fire ant *n* : any of a genus of fiercely stinging ants; *esp* : IMPORTED FIRE ANT

fire·arm \'fī(ə)r-,ärm\ *n* : a weapon from which a shot is discharged by gunpowder — usually used only of small arms

fire·ball \-,bȯl\ *n* **1** : a ball of fire **2** : a very bright meteor **3** : the glowing cloud of vapor and dust created by a nuclear explosion

fire·boat \-,bōt\ *n* : a boat equipped for fighting fires

fire·box \-,bäks\ *n* **1** : a chamber (as of a furnace) that contains a fire **2** : a box containing a fire alarm

fire·brand \-,brand\ *n* **1** : a piece of burning wood **2** : AGITATOR 1

fire·break \-,brāk\ *n* : a barrier of cleared or plowed land intended to stop the spread of a forest or grass fire

fire·brick \-,brik\ *n* : a brick capable of resisting great heat and used for lining furnaces or fireplaces

fire·bug \-,bəg\ *n* : a person who deliberately sets destructive fires : ARSONIST

fire·clay \-,klā\ *n* : clay capable of resisting high temperatures that is used especially for firebrick or heat-resistant containers

fire·crack·er \-,krak-ər\ *n* : a paper tube containing an explosive and usually set off for amusement

fire·damp \-,damp\ *n* : a flammable mine gas that consists chiefly of methane; *also* : the explosive mixture of this gas with air

fire·dog \-,dȯg\ *n* : ANDIRON

fire drill *n* : a practice drill in putting out fires or in getting out of a building in case of fire

fire engine *n* : a motortruck having equipment for pumping and directing water or chemicals to put out fires

fire escape *n* : a stairway or ladder that provides a means of escape from a building in case of fire

fire extinguisher *n* : something used to put out a fire; *esp* : a portable or wheeled device for putting out small fires by spraying fire-extinguishing chemicals

fire fighter *n* : a member of a company organized to fight fires — **fire fighting** *n*

fire·fly \'fī(ə)r-,flī\ *n* : any of numerous night-flying beetles that produce a bright soft flashing light for courtship purposes

fire·house \-,haůs\ *n* : FIRE STATION

fire irons *n pl* : tools for tending a fire in a fireplace

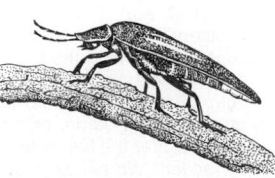

firefly

fire lane *n* : FIREBREAK

fire·light \'fī(ə)r-,līt\ *n* : the light of a fire and especially of one in a fireplace

fire·lock \-,läk\ *n* : MUZZLE-LOADER

fire·man \-mən\ *n* **1** : FIRE FIGHTER **2** : a person who

\ə\ abut	\aů\ out	\i\ tip	\ȯ\ saw	\ů\ foot
\ər\ further	\ch\ chin	\ī\ life	\ȯi\ coin	\y\ yet
\a\ mat	\e\ pet	\j\ job	\th\ thin	\yü\ few
\ā\ take	\ē\ easy	\ŋ\ sing	\th\ this	\yů\ cure
\ä\ cot, cart	\g\ go	\ō\ bone	\ü\ food	\zh\ vision

tends fires : STOKER

fire·place \-,plās\ *n* **1** : a framed opening in a chimney to hold an open fire **2** : an outdoor structure of brick, stone, or metal for an open fire

fire·plug \-,pləg\ *n* : HYDRANT

fire·pow·er \-,paù(-ə)r\ *n* : the ability to deliver gunfire or warheads on a target

[1]fire·proof \-'prüf\ *adj* : not easily burned : made safe against fire

[2]fireproof *vb* : to make fireproof

fire ship *n* : a ship carrying flammable materials or explosives that is sent among the enemy's ships and set on fire to destroy them

fire·side \'fī(ə)r-,sīd\ *n* **1** : a place near the hearth **2** : [1]HOME 1a

fire station *n* : a building housing fire engines and usually fire fighters

fire tower *n* : a tower (as in a forest) from which a watch for fires is kept

fire·trap \'fī(ə)r-,trap\ *n* : a building or place that is apt to catch on fire or is difficult to escape from in case of fire

fire wall *n* : a wall for preventing the spread of fire

fire·weed \'fī(ə)r-,wēd\ *n* : a plant with pinkish purple flowers that grows especially in clearings or burned areas

fire·wood \-,wùd\ *n* : wood cut for fuel

fire·work \-,wərk\ *n* **1** : a device that makes a display of light or noise by the burning of explosive or flammable materials **2** *pl* : a display of fireworks **3** *pl* : a display of temper

fir·ing squad \'fī(ə)r-iŋ-\ *n* **1** : a military unit assigned to fire shots over the grave of one buried with military honors **2** : a military unit assigned to carry out a sentence of death by shooting

fir·kin \'fər-kən\ *n* : a small wooden container or barrel

[1]firm \'fərm\ *adj* **1 a** : solidly fixed in place **b** : not weak or uncertain : VIGOROUS **c** : having a solid or compact texture **2 a** : not likely to be changed ⟨a *firm* offer⟩ **b** : not easily moved or disturbed : STEADFAST ⟨a *firm* believer⟩ **3** : indicating firmness or determination [Middle English *ferm* "firm, secure", from early French *ferm* (same meaning), from Latin *firmus* "firm, secure, solid"] **syn** see HARD — **firm** *vb* — **firm·ly** *adv* — **firm·ness** *n*

[2]firm *n* : a business organization ⟨law *firm*⟩ [from German *firma* "the name or sign under which a company does business", from Italian *firma* "signature", derived from Latin *firmare* "to make firm, to approve, to sign", from *firmus* "firm, secure"]

fir·ma·ment \'fər-mə-mənt\ *n* : the arch of the sky

firm·ware \'fərm-,wa(ə)r, -,we(ə)r\ *n* : computer programs contained permanently in a hardware device (as ROM)

[1]first \'fərst\ *adj* **1** — see NUMBER table **2** : coming before all others in time, order, or importance: as **a** : being the earliest **b** : being the lowest forward gear or speed of a motor vehicle **c** : having or playing the principal part of a group of instruments ⟨*first* oboe⟩

[2]first *adv* **1 a** : before any other in time, space, or importance **b** : for the first time **2** : rather than something else ⟨surrender? We will die *first*⟩

[3]first *n* **1** — see NUMBER table **2 a** : the first forward gear or speed of a motor vehicle **b** : the winning place in a competition or contest — **at first** : in the beginning

first aid *n* : emergency treatment given to an ill or injured person

first base *n* : the base that must be touched first by a base runner in baseball; *also* : the position of the player defending the area around first base

first baseman *n* : the player defending the area around first base

first·born \'fərs(t)-'bò(ə)rn\ *adj* : born first : ELDEST — **firstborn** *n*

first class *n* : the best or highest group in a classification — **first-class** *adj*

first cousin *n* : COUSIN 1a

first–degree burn *n* : a mild burn marked by heat, pain, and reddening of the burned surface but not showing blistering or charring of tissues

first·hand \'fərst-'hand\ *adj* : coming directly from the original source — **firsthand** *adv*

first lady *n, often cap F&L* : the wife or hostess of the male chief executive of a state or nation

first lieutenant *n* : a military commissioned officer with a rank just below that of captain

first·ling \'fərst-liŋ\ *n* : one that comes or is produced first

first·ly \'fərst-lē\ *adv* : in the first place

first person *n* **1** : a set of words or forms (as pronouns or verb forms) referring to the person speaking or writing them **2** : a writing style making use of pronouns and verbs of the first person

first–rate \'fər-'strāt\ *adj* : of the first order of size, importance, or quality — **first–rate** *adv*

first sergeant *n* **1** : a noncommissioned officer who is the chief assistant to a military commander **2** : a noncommissioned officer with the rank just below sergeant major in the army and the marines

firth \'fərth\ *n* : a narrow arm of the sea

fis·cal \'fis-kəl\ *adj* **1** : of or relating to public finances **2** : of or relating to financial matters — **fis·cal·ly** \-kə-lē\ *adv*

[1]fish \'fish\ *n, pl* **fish** *or* **fish·es** **1 a** : a water-dwelling animal — usually used in combination ⟨star*fish*⟩ ⟨cuttle*fish*⟩ **b** : a cold-blooded vertebrate animal with a typically long scaly tapering body, limbs developed as fins, and a vertical tail fin that lives and breathes in water **2** : the flesh of fish used as food — **fish·like** \-,līk\ *adj*

[2]fish *vb* **1** : to catch or try to catch fish **2** : to catch or try to catch fish in ⟨*fish* the stream⟩ **3** : to seek something by or as if by groping or feeling ⟨*fished* for compliments⟩

fish·er \'fish-ər\ *n* **1** : one that fishes **2** : a large dark brown North American flesh-eating mammal related to the weasels; *also* : its valuable fur or pelt

fish·er·man \'fish-ər-mən\ *n* **1** : a person who fishes **2** : a ship used in commercial fishing

fisher 2

fish·ery \'fish-(ə-)rē\ *n, pl* **-er·ies** **1** : the activity or business of fishing **2** : a place or establishment for catching fish

fish hawk *n* : OSPREY

fish·hook \'fish-,hùk\ *n* : a usually barbed hook for catching fish

fishing banks *n pl* : a plateau at a shallow depth under the sea where fish frequently gather in schools

fish ladder *n* : an arrangement of pools by which fish can pass around a dam

fish–liver oil *n* : a fatty oil from fish livers (as of cod, halibut, and sharks) used as a source of vitamin A and formerly of vitamin D

fish·net \'fish-,net\ *n* : a net for catching fish

fish·pond \-,pänd\ *n* : a pond stocked with fish

fish protein concentrate *n* : a nearly colorless and tasteless powder that is obtained from ground whole fish, is rich in protein, and is added to food

fishy \'fish-ē\ *adj* **fish·i·er; -est** **1** : of, relating to, or resembling fish ⟨a *fishy* odor⟩ **2** : arousing doubt or suspicion : QUESTIONABLE ⟨the story sounds *fishy* to me⟩

[1]fis·sion \'fish-ən *also* 'fizh-\ *n* **1** : a splitting or breaking up into parts **2** : a method of reproduction in which a living cell or body divides into two or more parts each of which grows into a whole new individual   **3** : the splitting of an atomic nucleus resulting in the release of large amounts of energy

²**fission** *vb* **fis·sioned; fis·sion·ing** \'fish-(ə-)niŋ, 'fizh-\ : to go through or cause to go through fission

fis·sion·able \'fish-(ə-)nə-bəl, 'fizh-\ *adj* : capable of going through fission ⟨*fissionable* material⟩

fission bomb *n* : ATOM BOMB 1

fis·sure \'fish-ər\ *n*   **1** : a narrow opening or crack ⟨a *fissure* in rock⟩   **2** : a narrow natural space between body parts (as bones of the skull) or in the material making up an organ — **fissure** *vb*

fist \'fist\ *n*   **1** : the hand clenched with fingers doubled into the palm   **2** : ¹INDEX 4

fist·i·cuffs \'fis-ti-,kəfs\ *n pl* : a fight with fists

fis·tu·la \'fis-chə-lə\ *n, pl* **-las** *or* **-lae** \-,lē, -,lī\ : an abnormal passage leading from an abscess or hollow organ

¹**fit** \'fit\ *n*   **1** : a sudden violent attack of a disease or condition (as epilepsy) especially when marked by convulsions or loss of consciousness   **2** : a sudden outburst (as of laughter) [Old English *fitt* "a sudden attack of a disease or physical condition"]

²**fit** *adj* **fit·ter; fit·test**   **1** : suitable for a particular purpose ⟨water *fit* for drinking⟩; *esp* : so adapted to the environment as to be capable of surviving — often used in the phrase *survival of the fittest*   **2** : acceptable from a particular point of view : PROPER   **3** : ¹READY 1, PREPARED ⟨get the ship *fit* for sea⟩   **4** : QUALIFIED 1, COMPETENT   **5** : sound physically and mentally : HEALTHY [Middle English *fit* "suitable to a particular purpose"] — **fit·ness** *n*

> **syn** FIT, PROPER, SUITABLE, APPROPRIATE mean right with respect to the nature, condition, or use of the thing referred to. FIT suggests that something has been made right or is qualified for use or action ⟨a rebuilt bike now *fit* for riding⟩ PROPER suggests that something is right because of its basic nature ⟨a *proper* diet⟩ or because it agrees with some custom or rule ⟨*proper* dress is required⟩ SUITABLE suggests that something meets the requirements of the situation ⟨find a *suitable* container for the mixture⟩ APPROPRIATE suggests that something is unusually or especially suitable for the purpose ⟨furniture that would be *appropriate* in a large living room⟩

³**fit** *vb* **fit·ted; fit·ting**   **1** : to be suitable for or to : BEFIT   **2 a** : to be of the right size and shape ⟨the suit *fits*⟩   **b** : to insert or adjust until correctly in place   **c** : to make a place or room for   **3** : to be in agreement with ⟨*fit* the facts⟩   **4 a** : to make ready : PREPARE   **b** : to bring to a required form and size : ADJUST   **5** : to supply what is needed for : EQUIP ⟨*fit* out an expedition⟩   **6** : to be in harmony or agreement : BELONG — often used with *in*

⁴**fit** *n*   **1** : the way something fits ⟨a tight *fit*⟩   **2** : a piece of clothing that fits

fit·ful \'fit-fəl\ *adj* : not regular : RESTLESS ⟨*fitful* sleep⟩ — **fit·ful·ly** \-fə-lē\ *adv* — **fit·ful·ness** *n*

fit·ter \'fit-ər\ *n* : one that fits; *esp* : a person who adjusts articles of clothing being tried on by a customer

¹**fit·ting** \'fit-iŋ\ *adj* : ²APPROPRIATE, SUITABLE — **fit·ting·ly** *adv* — **fit·ting·ness** *n*

²**fitting** *n*   **1** : a trying on of clothes being made or altered   **2** : a small accessory part ⟨a pipe *fitting*⟩

five \'fīv\ *n*   **1** — see NUMBER table   **2** : the fifth in a set or series   **3** : something having five units or members; *esp* : a basketball team — **five** *adj or pron*

five–and–ten \,fī-vən-'ten\ *also* **five–and–dime** \-vən-'dīm\ *n* : a store selling inexpensive articles

¹**fix** \'fiks\ *vb*   **1 a** : to make firm, stable, or fast   **b** : to give a permanent or final form to   **c** : to change into a stable or useful form ⟨bacteria that *fix* nitrogen⟩   **d** : ¹AFFIX 1, ATTACH   **2** : to set or place definitely : ESTABLISH ⟨*fix* the date of a meeting⟩   **3** : to get ready : PREPARE ⟨*fix* dinner⟩   **4** : ²REPAIR 1   **5 a** : to get even with   **b** : to influence the outcome of (as a sports contest) dishonestly [Middle En-

glish *fixen* "to fix, make firm", from Latin *fixus*, past participle of *figere* "to fasten, fix" — related to CRUCIFIX, CRUCIFY] — **fix·able** \'fik-sə-bəl\ *adj*

²**fix** *n*   **1** : a position of difficulty or embarrassment : PREDICAMENT   **2** : the position (as of a ship) decided upon by calculations and compass, observations, or radio; *also* : a deciding upon of one's position   **3 a** : an act of bribery or fraud   **b** : a sports contest whose outcome has been arranged in advance   **4** : a shot of a narcotic

fix·a·tion \fik-'sā-shən\ *n*   **1** : the act, process, or result of fixing   **2** : a state of concern or attachment especially when abnormal and lasting for a long time

fix·a·tive \'fik-sət-iv\ *n* : something that fixes or sets

fixed \'fikst\ *adj*   **1 a** : firmly placed or fastened ⟨a *fixed* gaze⟩   **b** : not changing : SETTLED ⟨a *fixed* income⟩   **2** : supplied with a definite amount of something needed ⟨well *fixed* for food⟩ — **fix·ed·ly** \'fik-səd-lē\ *adv* — **fix·ed·ness** \'fik-səd-nəs\ *n*

fixed star *n* : a star so distant that its motion can be measured only by very exact observations over long periods

fix·er \'fik-sər\ *n*   **1** : one that fixes   **2** : SODIUM THIOSULFATE

fix·ing \'fik-siŋ, *sense 2 is often* -sənz\ *n*   **1** : a putting in permanent form   **2** *pl* : something that decorates or completes ⟨turkey with all the *fixings*⟩

fix·i·ty \'fik-sət-ē\ *n, pl* **-ties**   **1** : the quality or state of being fixed   **2** : something that is fixed

fix·ture \'fiks-chər\ *n*   **1** : the act of fixing : the state of being fixed   **2** : something attached as a permanent part ⟨bathroom *fixtures*⟩   **3** : one firmly established in a place

¹**fizz** \'fiz\ *vb* : to make a hissing or sputtering sound

²**fizz** *n*   **1** : a hissing sound   **2** : a bubbling drink — **fizzy** \'fiz-ē\ *adj*

fiz·zle \'fiz-əl\ *vb* **fiz·zled; fiz·zling** \-(ə-)liŋ\ : to fail after a good start — **fizzle** *n*

fjord *or* **fiord** \fē-'ȯrd\ *n* : a narrow inlet of the sea between cliffs or steep slopes [Norwegian]

flab·ber·gast \'flab-ər-,gast\ *vb* : ASTONISH, DUMBFOUND

flab·by \'flab-ē\ *adj* **flab·bi·er; -est** : not hard and firm : SOFT — **flab·bi·ly** \'flab-ə-lē\ *adv* — **flab·bi·ness** \'flab-ē-nəs\ *n*

flac·cid \'flas-əd, 'flak-səd\ *adj* : not firm or stiff

fjord

¹**flag** \'flag\ *n* : any of various irises; *esp* : a wild iris [Middle English *flagge* "reed"]

²**flag** *n*   **1** : a piece of cloth with a special design that is used as a symbol (as of a nation) or for signaling   **2** : something used like a flag to signal or attract attention [perhaps derived from *flag* "iris"]

³**flag** *vb* **flagged; flag·ging** : to signal with or as if with a flag; *esp* : to signal to stop ⟨*flag* a taxi⟩

⁴**flag** *vb* **flagged; flag·ging**   **1** : to be limp : DROOP   **2** : to become weak ⟨their interest *flagged*⟩ [origin unknown]

⁵**flag** *n*   **1** : a hard stone that easily splits into flat pieces   **2** : a piece of flag used for paving [Middle English *flagge* "a piece of turf, a flat paving stone", from an ancient Norse word meaning "slab"]

⁶**flag** *vb* **flagged; flag·ging** : to pave (as a walk) with flags

Flag Day *n* : June 14 observed in some states as the anniversary of the adoption of the U.S. flag in 1777

\ə\ abut	\au̇\ out	\i\ tip	\ȯ\ saw	\u̇\ foot
\ər\ further	\ch\ chin	\ī\ life	\ȯi\ coin	\y\ yet
\a\ mat	\e\ pet	\j\ job	\th\ thin	\yü\ few
\ā\ take	\ē\ easy	\ŋ\ sing	\t͟h\ this	\yu̇\ cure
\ä\ cot, cart	\g\ go	\ō\ bone	\ü\ food	\zh\ vision

¹flag·el·late \'flaj-ə-ˌlāt\ vb **-lat·ed; -lat·ing** : ¹WHIP 2 — **flag·el·la·tion** \ˌflaj-ə-'lā-shən\ n

²flag·el·late \'flaj-ə-lət, -ˌlāt; flə-'jel-ət\ adj **1 a** or **flag·el·lat·ed** \'flaj-ə-ˌlāt-əd\ : having flagella **b** : shaped like a flagellum **2** : of, relating to, or caused by flagellates

³flagellate \like ²\ n : a protozoan or alga having flagella

fla·gel·lum \flə-'jel-əm\ n, pl **-gel·la** \-'jel-ə\ also **-gellums** : a long whiplike structure by which some tiny plants and animals move — **fla·gel·lar** \-'jel-ər\ adj

fla·geo·let \ˌflaj-ə-'let\ n : a musical instrument resembling a flute but with a whistle mouthpiece

flag·ging \'flag-iŋ\ n : a pavement of flagstones

flag·man \'flag-mən\ n : a person who signals with or as if with a flag

flag·on \'flag-ən\ n : a container for liquids usually having a handle, spout, and lid

flag·pole \'flag-ˌpōl\ n : a pole from which a flag flies

flag rank n : any of the ranks in the navy above a captain

fla·grant \'flā-grənt\ adj : so bad as to be impossible to overlook : OUTRAGEOUS ⟨a flagrant violation of the rules⟩ — **fla·grant·ly** adv

flag·ship \'flag-ˌship\ n : the ship carrying the commander of a group of ships and flying the flag that tells the commander's rank

flag·staff \-ˌstaf\ n : FLAGPOLE

flag·stone \-ˌstōn\ n : ⁵FLAG 2

¹flail \'flā(ə)l\ n : a tool for threshing grain by hand

²flail vb **1** : to strike with or as if with a flail **2** : to move or wave about as if swinging a flail ⟨flailed their arms to drive away the insects⟩

flair \'fla(ə)r, 'fle(ə)r\ n : natural ability

flak \'flak\ n : antiaircraft guns or the bursting shells fired from them [derived from the German word for "antiaircraft guns", from the first letters of flieger "flier" and abwehr "defense" and kanonen "cannons"]

¹flake \'flāk\ n : a small thin flat usually loose piece : CHIP

²flake vb **flaked; flak·ing** : to form or separate into flakes

flaky \'flā-kē\ adj **flak·i·er; -est 1** : consisting of flakes **2** : tending to flake ⟨pie with a crisp flaky crust⟩ **3** : odd or strange in behavior — **flak·i·ly** \-kə-lē\ adv — **flak·i·ness** \-kē-nəs\ n

flam·beau \'flam-ˌbō\ n, pl **flam·beaux** \-ˌbōz\ or **flam·beaus** : a flaming torch

flam·boy·ance \flam-'bȯi-ən(t)s\ n : the quality or state of being flamboyant

flam·boy·ant \flam-'bȯi-ənt\ adj : tending to make a dashing display : SHOWY — **flam·boy·ant·ly** adv

¹flame \'flām\ n **1** : the glowing gas that makes up part of a fire **2** : a state of burning brightly ⟨burst into flame⟩ ⟨a building in flames⟩ **3** : a condition or appearance suggesting a flame **4** : the person one is in love with : SWEETHEART ⟨an old flame⟩

²flame vb **flamed; flam·ing 1** : to burn with a flame : BLAZE **2** : to burst or break out violently **3** : to shine brightly **4** : to treat or affect by flame or fire; esp : to sterilize by a flame

fla·min·go \flə-'miŋ-gō\ n, pl **-gos** also **-goes** : any of several rosy-white birds

flamingo

flagon

with scarlet wings, a very long neck and legs, and a broad bill bent down at the end that are often found wading in shallow water

Word History Most flamingos are a pale pink. When they are standing at rest or wading in search of food, there would seem to be nothing about them to suggest a flame. Yet in its origin the word flamingo means "flame". English borrowed the word flamingo from Portuguese, which in turn had taken the word from Spanish flamenco. This flamenco means "flamingo", but it came from Latin flamma, meaning "flame". When flamingos take flight, their scarlet wing feathers are suddenly revealed. The vivid red flash is indeed like a burst of flame. [from Portuguese flamingo "flamingo", from Spanish flamenco "flamingo", derived from Latin flamma "flame"; so called from the fiery red feathers on the underside of the wings]

flam·ma·ble \'flam-ə-bəl\ adj : capable of being easily set on fire and of burning rapidly ⟨a flammable liquid⟩ — **flam·ma·bil·i·ty** \ˌflam-ə-'bil-ət-ē\ n — **flammable** n

flange \'flanj\ n : a rib or rim used for strength, for guiding, or for attachment to another object ⟨the flange on a locomotive wheel⟩ — **flanged** \'flanjd\ adj

¹flank \'flaŋk\ n **1 a** : the fleshy part of the side between the ribs and the hip **b** : a cut of meat from this part of an animal **2 a** : ¹SIDE 2 **b** : the right or left of a military formation

²flank vb **1 a** : to attack or threaten the flank of **b** : to pass around the flank of **2** : to be located at the side of : BORDER

flank·er \'flaŋ-kər\ n **1** : one that flanks **2** : a football player stationed wide of the formation especially as a pass receiver

flan·nel \'flan-ᵊl\ n **1** : a soft cloth made of wool or cotton **2** pl : flannel underwear or trousers

flan·nel·ette \ˌflan-ᵊl-'et\ n : a cotton flannel

¹flap \'flap\ n **1** : ¹SLAP 1 **2** : a broad and limber and flat piece that hangs loose (as on a pocket or envelope) **3** : the motion or sound of a flap **4** : a movable part of an airplane wing that is attached to the trailing edge of the wing and that is used to increase lift

²flap vb **flapped; flap·ping 1** : ²SLAP 1a **2** : to move or cause to move with a beating motion ⟨birds flapping their wings⟩

flap·jack \'flap-ˌjak\ n : PANCAKE

¹flare \'fla(ə)r, 'fle(ə)r\ vb **flared; flar·ing 1** : to burn with an unsteady flame **2 a** : to shine or blaze suddenly **b** : to become suddenly excited or angry ⟨flare up⟩ **3** : to open or spread outward

²flare n **1** : an unsteady glaring light **2** : a fire or blaze of light used to signal, light up something, or attract attention; also : a device or material that produces such a flare **3** : FLARE-UP **4** : a spreading outward; also : a place or part that spreads **5** pl : bell-bottom trousers

flare–up \'fla(ə)r-ˌəp, 'fle(ə)r-\ n : a sudden burst (as of flame or anger)

¹flash \'flash\ vb **1** : to shine in or like a sudden flame ⟨lightning flashed⟩ ⟨her eyes flashed with excitement⟩ **2** : to send out in or as if in flashes ⟨flash a message⟩ **3** : to appear or pass very suddenly ⟨a car flashed by⟩ **4** : to gleam or glow in sudden bursts **5** : to expose to view briefly ⟨flash a badge⟩

²flash n **1 a** : a sudden burst of light, flame, or heat **b** : a movement of a flag or light in signaling **2** : a sudden and brilliant burst ⟨a flash of wit⟩ **3** : a brief time **4** : one that attracts notice **esp** : an outstanding athlete **5** : a device for producing a brief and very bright flash of light for taking photographs

³flash adj : beginning suddenly and lasting only a short time ⟨a flash fire⟩

flash·back \'flash-ˌbak\ n : the introduction of a past event into a story or motion picture; also : this past event

flash·bulb \-,bəlb\ *n* : an electric bulb in which metal foil or wire is burned to produce a brief and very bright flash of light for taking photographs

flash card *n* : a card having words, numbers, or pictures that is held up briefly by a teacher to a class during drills (as in spelling or arithmetic)

flash·cube \'flash-,kyüb\ *n* : a device in the form of a cube that has four flashbulbs

flash·er \'flash-ər\ *n* : BLINKER 1

flash·light \'flash-,līt\ *n* : a small battery-operated portable electric light

flashy \'flash-ē\ *adj* **flash·i·er; -est** : GAUDY, SHOWY — **flash·i·ly** \'flash-ə-lē\ *adv* — **flash·i·ness** \'flash-ē-nəs\ *n*

flask \'flask\ *n* : a container shaped like a flattened bottle

¹flat \'flat\ *n* **1** : a level surface of land : PLAIN **2** : a flat part or surface **3 a** : a musical tone one half step lower than a specified tone **b** : a character ♭ before a note indicating that it is to be a flat **4** : a shallow box in which seedlings are started **5** : a shoe or slipper having a flat heel or no heel **6** : an apartment on one floor **7** : a deflated tire

²flat *adj* **flat·ter; flat·test 1** : having a smooth level surface ⟨*flat* ground⟩ **2** : having a smooth even surface **3** : spread out on or along a surface ⟨was *flat* on the ground⟩ **4** : having a broad smooth surface and little thickness **5** : ABSOLUTE 3, DOWNRIGHT ⟨a *flat* refusal⟩ **6** : FIXED 1b, UNCHANGING ⟨charge a *flat* rate⟩ **7** : ²EXACT 1 ⟨in two minutes *flat*⟩ **8** : lacking in interest or flavor : DULL, INSIPID ⟨a *flat* story⟩ ⟨the stew tastes *flat*⟩ **9** : being deflated — used of tires **10 a** : lower than the true pitch **b** : lower by a half step ⟨tone of A *flat*⟩ **11** : free from gloss ⟨*flat* paint⟩ **syn** see LEVEL — **flat·ly** *adv* — **flat·ness** *n*

³flat *adv* **1** : on or against a flat surface ⟨lie *flat*⟩ **2** : as much as possible : COMPLETELY ⟨was *flat* broke⟩ **3** : below the true musical pitch

⁴flat *vb* **flat·ted; flat·ting** : to lower in pitch especially by a half step

flat·bed \'flat-,bed\ *n* : a truck or trailer with a body in the form of a platform or shallow box

flat·boat \-,bōt\ *n* : a boat with a flat bottom and square ends used on rivers for carrying freight

flatboat

flat·car \-,kär\ *n* : a railroad freight car without sides or roof

flat·fish \-,fish\ *n* : any of a group of marine fishes (as halibuts, flounders, or soles) that as adults swim on one side of the flattened body and have both eyes on the upper side

flat·foot \-,fút, -'fút\ *n, pl* **flat·feet** \-,fēt, -'fēt\ **1** : a condition in which the main arch of the foot is so flattened that the entire sole rests upon the ground **2** : a foot affected with flatfoot — **flat–foot·ed** \-,fút-əd, -'fút-əd\ *adj*

flat·iron \-,ī-(ə)rn\ *n* : ¹IRON 2c

flat·ten \'flat-ᵊn\ *vb* **flat·tened; flat·ten·ing** \'flat-niŋ, -ᵊn-iŋ\ : to make or become flat

flat·ter \'flat-ər\ *vb* **1** : to praise too much and not sincerely **2** : to represent too attractively ⟨a picture that *flatters* me⟩ **3** : to judge oneself as better than another ⟨I *flatter* myself on my skill in dancing⟩ — **flat·ter·er** \-ər-ər\ *n* — **flat·ter·ing·ly** \-ə-riŋ-lē\ *adv*

flat·tery \'flat-ə-rē\ *n, pl* **-ter·ies 1** : the act of flattering **2** : praise that is excessive or not sincere **syn** see COMPLIMENT

flat·top \'flat-,täp\ *n* : AIRCRAFT CARRIER

flat·u·lence \'flach-ə-lən(t)s\ *n* : the presence of too much gas or air in the stomach or intestine

flat·ware \'flat-,wa(ə)r, -,we(ə)r\ *n* : eating and serving utensils (as forks, spoons, and knives)

flat·worm \-,wərm\ *n* : any of a phylum of worms (as trematodes and tapeworms) that have a flat body undivided into segments, lack a body cavity, are mostly parasitic, and have bilateral symmetry

flaunt \'flönt, 'flänt\ *vb* **1** : to wave or flutter in a showy way ⟨a flag *flaunting* in the breeze⟩ **2** : to make a big show of : PARADE ⟨*flaunting* their knowledge⟩

flau·tist \'flöt-əst, 'flaut-\ *n* : FLUTIST

fla·vor \'flā-vər\ *n* **1 a** : the quality of something that affects the sense of taste : SAVOR **b** : the blend of taste and smell sensations caused by a substance in the mouth **2** : a substance added to food or drink to give it a desired taste **3** : characteristic or most noticeable quality — **fla·vor** *vb* — **fla·vored** \-vərd\ *adj* — **fla·vor·ful** \-vər-fəl\ *adj* — **fla·vor·less** \-ləs\ *adj*

fla·vor·ing *n* : FLAVOR 2

flaw \'flö\ *n* : a small often hidden defect **syn** see BLEMISH — **flaw** *vb* — **flaw·less** \-ləs\ *adj* — **flaw·less·ly** *adv* — **flaw·less·ness** *n*

flax \'flaks\ *n* : a slender plant with blue flowers that is grown for its fiber from which linen is made and for its seed from which oil and livestock feed are obtained; *also* : its fiber

flax·en \'flak-sən\ *adj* **1** : made of flax **2** : of a pale yellow color ⟨*flaxen* hair⟩

flax·seed \'flak(s)-,sēd\ *n* : the seed of flax used as a source of linseed oil and in medicine

flay \'flā\ *vb* **1** : to strip off the skin or surface of : SKIN **2** : to scold severely

F layer *n* : the highest and most highly charged layer of the ionosphere occurring at night within a region that extends in altitude from 130 kilometers to more than 500 kilometers

flea \'flē\ *n* : any of an order of small wingless bloodsucking insects with a hard body and legs used for leaping

flea·bane \'flē-,bān\ *n* : any of various plants related to the daisies

flea collar *n* : a collar for dogs and cats that contains insecticide to kill fleas

flea market *n* : a usually outdoor market for secondhand articles and antiques

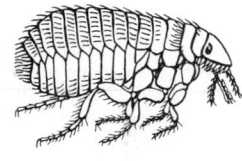

flea

¹fleck \'flek\ *vb* : ²STREAK 1, SPOT

²fleck *n* **1** : ¹SPOT 2a, MARK **2** : ¹FLAKE, PARTICLE

fledge \'flej\ *vb* **fledged; fledg·ing 1** : to develop the feathers necessary for flying **2** : to provide with feathers ⟨*fledge* an arrow⟩

fledg·ling \'flej-liŋ\ *n* **1** : a young bird just fledged **2** : an immature or inexperienced person

flee \'flē\ *vb* **fled** \'fled\; **flee·ing 1 a** : to run away often from danger or evil : FLY **b** : to run away from : SHUN **2** : to pass away swiftly : VANISH ⟨the mist *fled* before the rising sun⟩

¹fleece \'flēs\ *n* : the woolly coat of an animal (as a sheep) — **fleecy** \'flē-sē\ *adj*

²fleece *vb* **fleeced; fleec·ing 1** : to remove the fleece from : SHEAR **2** : to rob by trickery

¹fleet \'flēt\ *n* **1** : a group of warships under one command **2** : a group of ships or vehicles that move together or are under one management ⟨a *fleet* of taxis⟩ ⟨a fishing *fleet*⟩

\ə\ abut	\aú\ out	\i\ tip	\ò\ saw	\ú\ foot
\ər\ further	\ch\ chin	\ī\ life	\òi\ coin	\y\ yet
\a\ mat	\e\ pet	\j\ job	\th\ thin	\yü\ few
\ā\ take	\ē\ easy	\ŋ\ sing	\t̲h̲\ this	\yú\ cure
\ä\ cot, cart	\g\ go	\ō\ bone	\ü\ food	\zh\ vision

²fleet *adj* : very swift ⟨*fleet* of foot⟩ — **fleet·ly** *adv* — **fleet·ness** *n*

fleet admiral *n* : an admiral of the highest rank in the navy

fleet–foot·ed \'flēt-'fut-əd\ *adj* : able to run fast

fleet·ing \'flēt-iŋ\ *adj* : not lasting : passing swiftly **syn** see TRANSIENT

Flem·ing \'flem-iŋ\ *n* : a member of a people living in northern Belgium

Flem·ish \'flem-ish\ *n* **1** : the Germanic language of the Flemings **2 Flemish** *pl* : FLEMINGS — **Flemish** *adj*

¹flesh \'flesh\ *n* **1 a** : the soft parts of the body of an animal and especially the muscular parts **b** : sleek plump condition of body **2** : parts of an animal used as food **3** : the physical being of a person as distinguished from the soul **4** : a fleshy plant part (as the pulp of a fruit) — **fleshed** \'flesht\ *adj* — **in the flesh** : in person

²flesh *vb* : to give substance to ⟨*flesh* out a story with details⟩

flesh·ly \'flesh-lē\ *adj* **1** : CORPOREAL, BODILY **2** : SENSUAL, WORLDLY

fleshy \'flesh-ē\ *adj* **flesh·i·er; -est 1 a** : resembling or consisting of flesh **b** : ⁵PLUMP, FAT **2** : ¹SUCCULENT 1b, PULPY — **flesh·i·ness** *n*

fleshy fruit *n* : a fruit (as a berry, drupe, or pome) consisting largely of soft juicy flesh

fleur–de–lis *or* **fleur–de–lys** \,flərd-ᵊl-'ē, ,flurd-\ *n, pl* **fleurs–de–lis** *or* **fleur–de–lis** *or* **fleurs–de–lys** *or* **fleur–de–lys** \,flərd-ᵊl-'ē(z), ,flurd-\ **1** : IRIS 2 **2** : a simple drawing of an iris used in art and heraldry [Middle English *flourdelis* "fleur-de-lis", from early French *flor de lis,* literally "flower of the lily"]

fleur-de-lis 2

flew *past of* ¹FLY

flex \'fleks\ *vb* : to bend especially over and over

flex·a·gon \'flek-sə-,gän\ *n* : a folded paper figure that can be made to expose various arrangements of its faces by flexing along its folds

flex·i·ble \'flek-sə-bəl\ *adj* **1** : capable of being bent : PLIANT **2** : readily changed or changing : ADAPTABLE — **flex·i·bil·i·ty** \,flek-sə-'bil-ət-ē\ *n* — **flex·i·bly** \'flek-sə-blē\ *adv*

flex·ion \'flek-shən\ *n* : muscular movement that lessens the angle between bones or parts; *also* : the resulting state or relation of parts

flex·or \'flek-sər, -,sȯ(ə)r\ *n* : a muscle that produces flexion

flex·ure \'flek-shər\ *n* **1** : the quality or state of being flexed **2** : ²TURN 2b, FOLD

¹flick \'flik\ *n* **1** : a light sharp jerky stroke or movement **2** : a sound produced by a flick **3** : BLOTCH 2, SPOT

²flick *vb* **1** : to strike lightly with a quick sharp motion **2** : ¹FLICKER 1

¹flick·er \'flik-ər\ *vb* **flick·ered; flick·er·ing** \-(ə-)riŋ\ **1** : to move irregularly or unsteadily : FLUTTER **2** : to burn unsteadily or with a constantly changing light ⟨a *flickering* candle⟩

²flicker *n* : a large insect-eating North American woodpecker with a black crescent on the breast and yellow or red on the underside of the wings and tail

³flicker *n* **1** : an act of flickering **2** : a flickering light **3** : a brief stirring ⟨a *flicker* of interest⟩ — **flick·ery** \'flik-(ə-)rē\ *adj*

fli·er *or* **fly·er** \'flī-(ə)r\ *n* **1** : one that flies; *esp* : ¹PILOT 3 **2** : an undertaking (as in business) that involves much risk **3** : an advertising circular

¹flight \'flīt\ *n* **1** : an act or instance of passing through the air by the use of wings ⟨a *flight* in a plane⟩ ⟨the *flight* of birds⟩ **2 a** : a passing through the air or through outer space ⟨the *flight* of a bullet⟩ ⟨the *flight* of a rocket to the moon⟩ **b** : the distance covered in a flight **3** : a scheduled airplane trip **4** : a group of similar things flying through the air together ⟨a *flight* of ducks⟩ **5** : a brilliant, imaginative, or uncontrolled exercise or display ⟨a *flight* of fancy⟩ **6** : a continuous series of stairs from one landing or floor to another

²flight *n* : an act or instance of running away

flight attendant *n* : a person who provides service to passengers on an airplane

flight control *n* : the control from a ground station of an airplane or spacecraft especially by radio

flight engineer *n* : a crew member of an airplane responsible for mechanical operation

flight·less \'flīt-ləs\ *adj* : unable to fly ⟨*flightless* birds⟩

flight path *n* : the path in the air or space made or followed by something (as a particle, an airplane, or a spacecraft) in flight

flighty \'flīt-ē\ *adj* **flight·i·er; -est 1** : easily excited : SKITTISH ⟨*flighty* horses⟩ **2** : SILLY 3, FRIVOLOUS — **flight·i·ly** \'flīt-ᵊl-ē\ *adv* — **flight·i·ness** \'flīt-ē-nəs\ *n*

flim·sy \'flim-zē\ *adj* **flim·si·er; -est 1** : not strong or solid ⟨*flimsy* clothes⟩ ⟨a *flimsy* old car⟩ **2** : not likely to convincing ⟨a *flimsy* excuse⟩ ⟨a movie with a *flimsy* plot⟩ — **flim·si·ly** \-zə-lē\ *adv* — **flim·si·ness** \-zē-nəs\ *n*

flinch \'flinch\ *vb* : to draw back from or as if from physical pain — **flinch** *n* — **flinch·er** *n*

¹fling \'fliŋ\ *vb* **flung** \'fləŋ\; **fling·ing** \'fliŋ-iŋ\ **1** : to move in an abrupt or headlong manner ⟨*flung* out of the room in a huff⟩ **2** : to kick or plunge vigorously **3 a** : to throw or swing with force **b** : to cast aside : DISCARD **4** : to put suddenly and unexpectedly into a state or condition ⟨*flung* into confusion⟩ **syn** see THROW — **fling·er** \'fliŋ-ər\ *n*

²fling *n* **1** : an act or instance of flinging **2** : a casual try **3** : a time of freedom for pleasure

flint \'flint\ *n* **1** : a hard quartz that produces a spark when struck by steel **2** : an alloy (as of iron and cerium) used for producing a spark in lighters **3** : something very hard ⟨a heart of *flint*⟩ — **flint·i·ly** \'flint-ᵊl-ē\ *adv* — **flint·i·ness** \'flint-ē-nəs\ *n* — **flinty** \-ē\ *adj*

flint glass *n* : heavy glass that contains an oxide of lead and is used for optical structures (as lenses)

flint·lock \'flint-,läk\ *n* : a muzzle-loader with a firing mechanism having a flint in the hammer for striking a spark to ignite the priming powder

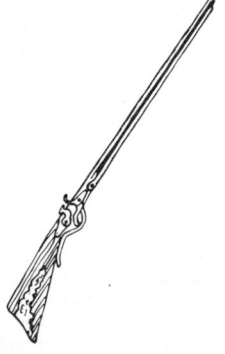

¹flip \'flip\ *vb* **flipped; flip·ping 1** : to turn by tossing ⟨*flip* a coin⟩ **2** : to turn over quickly ⟨*flip* the pages of a magazine⟩ **3** : ²FLICK 1 ⟨*flip* a switch⟩ **4** : to get excited or angry ⟨you'll *flip* when you hear this⟩

²flip *n* : an act or instance of flipping

³flip *adj* : FLIPPANT

flip·pan·cy \'flip-ən-sē\ *n, pl* **-cies** : an act or instance of being flippant

flip·pant \'flip-ənt\ *adj* : treating lightly something serious or worthy of respect — **flip·pant·ly** *adv*

flintlock

flip·per \'flip-ər\ *n* **1** : a broad flat limb (as of a seal or whale) used for swimming **2** : a flat rubber shoe with the front widened into a paddle for use in skin diving

¹flirt \'flərt\ *vb* **1** : to show a liking for someone of the opposite sex just for fun **2** : ²TOY ⟨*flirted* with the idea⟩

— **flir·ta·tion** \ˌflər-ˈtā-shən\ *n* — **flir·ta·tious** \-shəs\ *adj* — **flir·ta·tious·ness** *n* — **flirt·er** \ˈflərt-ər\ *n*

²**flirt** *n* **1** : an act or instance of flirting **2** : a person who flirts a lot

flit \ˈflit\ *vb* **flit·ted; flit·ting** : to move or progress in quick irregular darts — **flit** *n*

fliv·ver \ˈfliv-ər\ *n* : a small cheap old automobile

¹**float** \ˈflōt\ *n* **1** : an act or instance of floating **2** : something that floats: as **a** : a cork or bob that holds up the baited end of a fishing line **b** : a floating platform anchored near a shoreline for use by swimmers or boats **c** : a hollow ball that controls the flow or level of the liquid it floats on (as in a tank) **d** : a watertight structure that holds up an airplane on water **3 a** : a vehicle with a platform used to carry an exhibit in a parade **b** : the vehicle and exhibit together **4** : a drink consisting of ice cream floating in a beverage

²**float** *vb* **1** : to rest on the surface of a fluid **2** : to drift on or through or as if on or through a fluid ⟨dust *floating* through the air⟩ **3** : to cause to float ⟨*float* logs down a river⟩ — **float·er** *n*

floating–point *adj* : involving or being a mathematical notation (as scientific notation) in which a quantity is expressed by a number multiplied by the base of the system in which the numbers are written ⟨999.9 can be expressed in a *floating-point* system as 9.999×10^2⟩

floating rib *n* : a rib (as one of the two bottom pairs in human beings) that has no attachment to the sternum

¹**flock** \ˈfläk\ *n* **1** : a group of birds or mammals assembled or herded together **2** : a group someone keeps watch over **3** : a large number

²**flock** *vb* : to gather or move in a crowd ⟨they *flocked* to the beach⟩

floe \ˈflō\ *n* : a sheet or mass of floating ice

flog \ˈfläg\ *vb* **flogged; flog·ging** : to beat severely with or as if with a rod or whip — **flog·ger** *n*

¹**flood** \ˈfləd\ *n* **1 a** : a great flow of water that rises and spreads over the land **b** *cap* : a flood described in the Bible as covering the earth in the time of Noah **2** : the flowing in of the tide **3** : an overwhelming quantity or volume ⟨a *flood* of mail⟩

²**flood** *vb* **1** : to cover or become filled with a flood **2** : to fill as if with a flood ⟨a room *flooded* with light⟩ ⟨*flood* a carburetor⟩ **3** : to pour forth, go, or come in a flood

flood·gate \ˈfləd-ˌgāt\ *n* : a gate (as in a canal) for controlling a body of water : SLUICE

flood·light \-ˌlīt\ *n* **1** : artificial light in a broad beam **2** : a light that gives a broad beam — **floodlight** *vb*

flood·plain \-ˌplān\ *n* **1** : low flat land along a stream or river that may flood **2** : a plain built up from earth left by floodwaters

flood tide *n* **1** : a rising tide **2 a** : an overwhelming quantity **b** : a high point : PEAK ⟨our success was at *flood tide*⟩

flood·wa·ter \ˈfləd-ˌwȯt-ər, -ˌwät-\ *n* : the water of a flood

¹**floor** \ˈflō(ə)r, ˈflȯ(ə)r\ *n* **1** : the part of a room on which one stands **2 a** : the lower inside surface of a hollow structure ⟨the *floor* of a car⟩ **b** : a ground surface ⟨the ocean *floor*⟩ **3** : a story of a building ⟨lives on the second *floor*⟩

²**floor** *vb* **1** : to cover with a floor or flooring **2 a** : to knock to the floor **b** : ³SHOCK 1, OVERWHELM

floor·ing \ˈflōr-iŋ, ˈflȯr-\ *n* **1** : ¹FLOOR 1 **2** : material for floors

floor·walk·er \ˈflōr-ˌwȯ-kər, ˈflȯr-\ *n* : an employee of a retail store who oversees the salespeople and aids customers

¹**flop** \ˈfläp\ *vb* **flopped; flop·ping** **1** : to swing or bounce loosely : flap about ⟨a hat brim *flopping* in the wind⟩ **2 a** : to throw oneself down in a heavy, clumsy, or relaxed manner ⟨*flopped* into the chair with a sigh⟩ **b** : to throw or drop suddenly and heavily or noisily ⟨*flopped* the bundles onto the table with a thud⟩ **3** : to fail completely ⟨the

play *flopped*⟩

²**flop** *n* **1** : an act or sound of flopping **2** : a complete failure : DUD

flop·py \ˈfläp-ē\ *adj* **flop·pi·er; -est** : being soft and flexible

floppy disk *n* : a small flexible disk with a magnetic coating on which data for a computer can be stored

flo·ra \ˈflōr-ə, ˈflȯr-\ *n, pl* **floras** *also* **flo·rae** \ˈflō(ə)r-ˌē, ˈflȯ(ə)r-, -ˌī\ : plants or plant life especially of a region, period, or environment

flo·ral \ˈflōr-əl, ˈflȯr-\ *adj* : of or relating to flowers or a flora ⟨a *floral* pattern in wallpaper⟩

Flor·ence flask \ˌflȯr-ən(t)s-, ˌflär-\ *n* : a round usually flat-bottomed glass laboratory container with a long neck [named for *Florence,* city in Italy; so called from the fact that at one time some Italian wines were sold in bottles of this shape]

flo·ret \ˈflōr-ət, ˈflȯr-\ *n* : a small flower; *esp* : one of the small flowers forming the head of a composite plant (as a daisy)

flor·id \ˈflȯr-əd, ˈflär-\ *adj* **1** : FLOWERY 2, ORNATE ⟨*florid* writing⟩ **2** : tinged with red : RUDDY ⟨a *florid* complexion⟩ [from Latin *floridus* "blooming, flowery", from *florēre* "to blossom, flourish", from *flor-, flos* "a flower, blossom" — related to FLOUR, FLOURISH, FLOWER] — **flor·id·ly** *adv*

flor·in \ˈflȯr-ən, ˈflär-\ *n* **1** : an old gold coin first made in Florence in 1252 **2** : any of various coins patterned after the florin

flo·rist \ˈflōr-əst, ˈflȯr-, ˈflär-\ *n* : a person who sells flowers and ornamental plants

¹**floss** \ˈfläs, ˈflȯs\ *n* **1** : soft silk or cotton thread used for embroidery **2** : fluffy material full of fibers

²**floss** *vb* : to use dental floss on (one's teeth)

flo·ta·tion \flō-ˈtā-shən\ *n* **1** : the act, process, or state of floating **2** : the separation of the particles of a mass of ground ore according to how they compare in ability to float on a liquid

flo·til·la \flō-ˈtil-ə\ *n* : ¹FLEET 1; *esp* : a fleet of small ships

flot·sam \ˈflät-səm\ *n* : floating wreckage of a ship or its cargo

¹**flounce** \ˈflaún(t)s\ *vb* **flounced; flounc·ing** **1** : to move with exaggerated jerky motions **2** : to go with sudden determination ⟨*flounced* out of the room in anger⟩ [perhaps of Scandinavian origin]

²**flounce** *n* : an act or instance of flouncing

³**flounce** *vb* **flounced; flounc·ing** : to trim with flounces [an altered form of earlier *frounce* "to trim with ruffles", from Middle English *frouncen* "to curl"]

⁴**flounce** *n* : a strip of fabric attached by the upper edge

¹**floun·der** \ˈflaún-dər\ *n, pl* **flounder** *or* **flounders** : FLATFISH; *esp* : any of various important marine food fishes [Middle English *flounder* "a flatfish"; of Scandinavian origin]

²**flounder** *vb* **floun·dered; floun·der·ing** \-d(ə-)riŋ\ : to struggle or go clumsily ⟨*floundering* through the deep snow⟩ [probably an altered form of *founder* "to go lame, collapse"]

¹**flour** \ˈflaú(ə)r\ *n* **1** : finely ground powdery meal of wheat or of any cereal grain or edible seed **2** : a fine soft powder [Middle English *flour* "finely ground wheat meal", from earlier *flour* "best part, flower", from early French *flor, flour* "flower", from Latin *flor-, flow* "flower, blossom" — related to FLORID, FLOURISH, FLOWER]

²**flour** *vb* : to coat with flour

flour beetle *n* : any of several usually flattened brown beetles that are pests especially in flour or meal

¹**flour·ish** \ˈflər-ish, ˈflə-rish\ *vb* **1** : to grow well : THRIVE

\ə\ abut	\aú\ out	\i\ tip	\ȯ\ saw	\ú\ foot
\ər\ further	\ch\ chin	\ī\ life	\ȯi\ coin	\y\ yet
\a\ mat	\e\ pet	\j\ job	\th\ thin	\yü\ few
\ā\ take	\ē\ easy	\ŋ\ sing	\th\ this	\yu̇\ cure
\ä\ cot, cart	\g\ go	\ō\ bone	\ü\ food	\zh\ vision

2 a : PROSPER 1, SUCCEED **b** : to be active ⟨*flourished* around 1850⟩ **3** : to make bold sweeping gestures **4** : to shake or wave around ⟨*flourish* a sword⟩ [Middle English *florisshen* "to flourish, thrive", from early French *floriss-, florir* (same meaning), derived from Latin *florēre* "to blossom, flourish", from *flor-, flos* "a flower, blossom" — related to FLORID, FLOUR, FLOWER]

²flourish *n* **1** : a fancy bit of decoration added to something (as handwriting) **2** : a sweeping motion **3** : FANFARE

floury \'flaú(ə)r-ē\ *adj* **1** : of, relating to, or resembling flour **2** : covered with flour

flout \'flaút\ *vb* : to ignore in a disrespectful way ⟨*flouting* the rules⟩ — **flout·er** *n*

¹flow \'flō\ *vb* **1** : to move in a stream **2** : ¹RISE 5a ⟨the tide ebbs and *flows*⟩ **3** : to glide or pass smoothly and readily **4** : to hang loose and waving — **flow·ing·ly** \-iŋ-lē\ *adv*

²flow *n* **1** : an act of flowing **2** : ¹FLOOD 1, 2 **3 a** : a smooth even movement **b** : a mass of matter that has flowed when melted ⟨a lava *flow*⟩ **4** : the quantity that flows in a certain time ⟨the *flow* of water over a dam⟩

flow·chart \'flō-,chärt\ *n* : a diagram that shows step-by-step progression through a process or system by using special symbols and connecting lines

¹flow·er \'flaú(-ə)r\ *n* **1 a** : ¹BLOSSOM 1, INFLORESCENCE **b** : a shoot of a higher plant that is specialized for reproduction and bears modified leaves (as petals) **c** : a plant cultivated or outstanding for its blossoms **2 a** : the best part or example **b** : a state or time of thriving ⟨when knighthood was in *flower*⟩ [Middle English *flour* "flower, best part", from early French *flor, flour* (same meaning), from Latin *flor-, flos* "flower, blossom" — related to FLORID, FLOUR, FLOURISH] — **flow·er·less** \-ləs\ *adj* — **flow·er·like** \-,līk\ *adj*

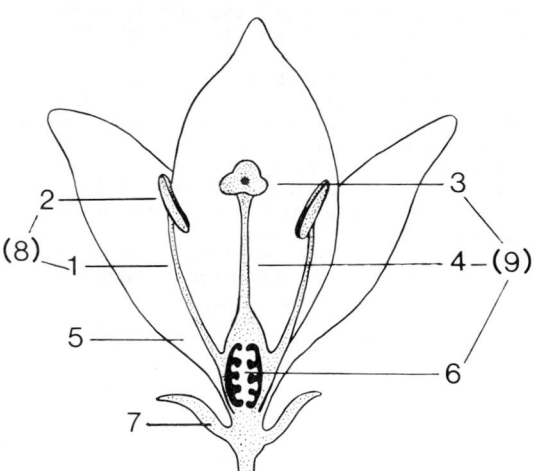

flower 1b: *1* filament, *2* anther, *3* stigma, *4* style, *5* petal, *6* ovary, *7* sepal, *8* stamen, *9* pistil

²flower *vb* **1** : to produce flowers : BLOOM **2** : ¹FLOURISH 1

flow·ered \'flaú(-ə)rd\ *adj* **1** : having or bearing flowers **2** : decorated with flowers or flowerlike figures ⟨*flowered* silk⟩

flower head *n* : a tight cluster of small flowers without stems that are arranged so that the whole looks like a single flower

flowering plant *n* : any of a major group of higher plants

that produce flowers, fruits, and seeds — compare SEED PLANT

flow·er·pot \'flaú(-ə)r-,pät\ *n* : a pot in which to grow plants

flow·ery \'flaú(-ə)r-ē\ *adj* **flow·er·i·er; -est** **1** : full of or covered with flowers **2** : full of fine words or phrases ⟨*flowery* language⟩ — **flow·er·i·ness** *n*

flown *past participle of* ¹FLY

flu \'flü\ *n* **1** : INFLUENZA 1 **2** : any of several virus diseases that are something like a cold

flub \'fləb\ *vb* **flubbed; flub·bing** : BOTCH, BUNGLE — **flub** *n*

fluc·tu·ate \'flək-chə-,wāt\ *vb* **-at·ed; -at·ing** **1** : to move up and down or back and forth like a wave **2** : to be constantly changing especially up and down — **fluc·tu·a·tion** \,flək-chə-'wā-shən\ *n*

flue \'flü\ *n* : an enclosed passageway for directing a current; *esp* : a channel in a chimney for carrying flame and smoke to the outer air

flu·en·cy \'flü-ən-sē\ *n* : the quality or state of being fluent

flu·ent \'flü-ənt\ *adj* **1** : ¹FLUID 1a **2 a** : able to speak easily and smoothly ⟨*fluent* in Spanish⟩ **b** : done in a smooth easy way [from Latin *fluent-, fluens*, present participle of *fluere* "to flow" — related to FLUID] — **flu·ent·ly** *adv*

¹fluff \'fləf\ *n* **1** : ³NAP, DOWN **2** : something fluffy

²fluff *vb* : to make or become fluffy

fluffy \'fləf-ē\ *adj* **fluff·i·er; -est** **1** : having, covered with, or resembling fluff or down ⟨the *fluffy* fur of a kitten⟩ **2** : being light and soft or airy ⟨a *fluffy* omelet⟩ — **fluff·i·ness** *n*

¹flu·id \'flü-əd\ *adj* **1 a** : capable of flowing like a liquid or gas **b** : likely or tending to change or move **2** : showing a smooth easy style ⟨*fluid* movements⟩ [from French *fluide* or Latin *fluidus*, both meaning "fluid, able to flow", from Latin *fluere* "to flow" — related to AFFLUENT, FLUENT, ²FLUSH, INFLUENCE, SUPERFLUOUS] — **flu·id·ly** *adv*

²fluid *n* : a substance tending to flow or take the shape of its container ⟨liquids and gases are *fluids*⟩

flu·id·i·ty \flü-'id-ət-ē\ *n* : the quality or state of being fluid

fluid mechanics *n* : a branch of science that deals with the special properties of liquids and gases

flu·id·ounce \,flü-əd-'aún(t)s\ *n* : a unit of liquid capacity equal to 1/16 pint (about 29.6 milliliters) — see MEASURE table

flu·idram \,flü-ə(d)-'dram\ *n* : a unit of liquid capacity equal to 1/8 fluidounce — see MEASURE table

¹fluke \'flük\ *n* : any of various trematode flatworms — compare LIVER FLUKE

²fluke *n* **1** : the part of an anchor that digs into the ground **2** : a barbed head (as of a harpoon) **3** : one of the lobes of a whale's tail

³fluke *n* : a stroke of good luck ⟨won by a *fluke*⟩ — **fluky** \'flü-kē\ *adj*

flume \'flüm\ *n* **1** : a sloping channel for carrying water (as for power) **2** : a ravine or gorge with a stream running through it

flung *past and past participle of* FLING

flunk \'fləŋk\ *vb* **1** : ¹FAIL 2c ⟨*flunk* a test⟩ **2** : to give a failing grade to — **flunk** *n*

flunk out *vb* : to dismiss or be dismissed from a school for failing

flun·ky *or* **flun·key** \'flən-kē\ *n, pl* **flunkies** *or* **flunkeys** **1 a** : a servant in livery **b** : a person who has simple or unskilled duties **2** : a person who flatters or constantly agrees with another in the hope of receiving favors

flu·o·resce \,flü(-ə)r-'es\ *vb* **-resced; -resc·ing** : to produce, exhibit, or be exposed to fluorescence

flu·o·res·cence \,flü(-ə)r-'es-ᵊn(t)s\ *n* : the giving off or the property of a substance of giving off radiation usually as visible light when exposed to radiation from another source (as ultraviolet light); *also* : the radiation given off — **flu·o·res·cent** \-ənt\ *adj*

fluorescent lamp *n* : an electric lamp in the form of a tube in which light is produced on the inside fluorescent coating by the action of ultraviolet light

flu·o·ri·date \'flùr-ə-ˌdāt\ *vb* **-dat·ed; -dat·ing** : to add a fluoride to (as drinking water) in order to reduce tooth decay — **flu·o·ri·da·tion** \ˌflùr-ə-'dā-shən\ *n*

flu·o·ride \'flù(-ə)r-ˌīd\ *n* : a compound of fluorine with another element or chemical group

flu·o·ri·nate \'flùr-ə-ˌnāt\ *vb* **-at·ed; -at·ing** : to treat or cause to combine with fluorine or a compound of fluorine — **flu·o·ri·na·tion** \ˌflùr-ə-'nā-shən\ *n*

flu·o·rine \'flù(-ə)r-ˌēn, -ən\ *n* : a nonmetallic element that is normally found alone as a pale yellowish flammable irritating poisonous gas having two atoms per molecule — see ELEMENT table

flu·o·rite \'flù(-ə)r-ˌīt\ *n* : a transparent or nearly transparent mineral of different colors that consists of a fluoride of calcium and is used as a flux and in making glass

flu·o·ro·car·bon \ˌflù(-ə)r-ō-'kär-bən\ *n* : any of various compounds of carbon and fluorine used chiefly as lubricants, refrigerants, nonstick coatings, in making plastics, and formerly as the driving force in aerosol cans

¹**flu·o·ro·scope** \'flùr-ə-ˌskōp\ *n* : an instrument that is used for observing with X rays the inner structure of objects (as the living body) through which light cannot pass — **flu·o·ro·scop·ic** \ˌflùr-ə-'skäp-ik\ *adj* — **flu·o·ros·co·py** \ˌflù(-ə)r-'äs-kə-pē\ *n*

²**fluoroscope** *vb* **-scoped; -scop·ing** : to examine by fluoroscopy

flu·or·spar \'flù(-ə)r-ˌspär\ *n* : FLUORITE

flur·ry \'flər-ē, 'flə-rē\ *n, pl* **flurries** **1 a** : a gust of wind **b** : a brief light snowfall **2** : a sudden commotion ⟨a *flurry* of publicity⟩ **3** : a brief outburst of activity ⟨a *flurry* of trading in the stock exchange⟩ — **flurry** *vb*

¹**flush** \'fləsh\ *vb* : to take flight or cause to take flight suddenly ⟨*flushed* several quail⟩ [Middle English *flusshen* "to fly up suddenly"]

²**flush** *n* **1** : a sudden flow (as of water) **2** : a sudden increase (as of emotion) ⟨a *flush* of triumph⟩ **3 a** : ²BLUSH **2** **b** : a fresh and vigorous state ⟨the *flush* of youth⟩ **4** : a brief sensation of heat [perhaps from Latin *fluxus,* past participle of *fluere* "to flow" — related to FLUID]

³**flush** *vb* **1** : ¹BLUSH **1** **2** : to pour liquid over or through; *esp* : to wash out with a rush of liquid ⟨*flush* a car radiator⟩ **3** : to make red or hot

⁴**flush** *adj* **1 a** : filled to overflowing **b** : well supplied especially with money **2 a** : full of life and vigor : LUSTY **b** : of a healthy reddish color **3 a** : having an unbroken surface ⟨*flush* paneling⟩ **b** : even with the neighboring surface ⟨a river *flush* with the top of its bank⟩ — **flush·ness** *n*

⁵**flush** *adv* **1** : so as to be flush **2** : so as to make solid contact ⟨a blow *flush* on the chin⟩

flus·ter \'fləs-tər\ *vb* **flus·tered; flus·ter·ing** \-t(ə-)riŋ\ : to make nervous and unsure : UPSET ⟨*flustered* by their rudeness⟩ — **fluster** *n*

¹**flute** \'flüt\ *n* **1** : a woodwind instrument played by blowing across a hole near the closed end **2** : a rounded groove; *esp* : one on an architectural column — **flute·like** \-ˌlīk\ *adj*

²**flute** *vb* **flut·ed; flut·ing** **1** : to play a flute **2** : to make a sound like that of a flute **3** : to form flutes in ⟨*fluted* columns⟩

flut·ing \'flüt-iŋ\ *n* : fluted decoration

flut·ist \'flüt-əst\ *n* : a flute player

¹**flut·ter** \'flət-ər\ *vb* **1** : to move

flute 1

or cause the wings to move rapidly without flying or in short flights ⟨butterflies *flutter*⟩ **2** : to move with quick wavering or flapping motions ⟨flags *fluttered* in the breeze⟩ **3** : to move about or behave in an excited aimless manner — **flut·tery** \'flət-ə-rē\ *adj*

²**flutter** *n* **1** : an act of fluttering **2** : FLURRY 2, COMMOTION **3** : an unsteadiness of pitch in reproduced sound

¹**flux** \'fləks\ *n* **1 a** : a flowing in ⟨*flux* of the tide⟩ **b** : a series of changes : a state of continuous change **2** : a substance used to aid the melting or joining (as by removing impurities) of metals or minerals

²**flux** *vb* **1** : to become or cause to become fluid : FUSE **2** : to treat with a flux

¹**fly** \'flī\ *vb* **flew** \'flü\; **flown** \'flōn\; **fly·ing** **1 a** : to move in or pass through the air with wings **b** : to move through the air or with the wind; *also* : to move through outer space **c** : to float or cause to float, wave, or soar in the air ⟨flags *flying*⟩ ⟨*fly* a kite⟩ **2** : to take flight : FLEE **3** : to move or pass swiftly ⟨time *flies*⟩ **4 a** : to operate or travel in an aircraft or spacecraft **b** : to journey over or through by flying ⟨*fly* the Atlantic⟩ **c** : to transport by aircraft or spacecraft [Old English *flēogan* "to move through the air, fly"] — **fly at** : to attack suddenly and violently

²**fly** *n, pl* **flies** **1 a** : a garment closing concealed by a fold of cloth **b** : the outer fabric of a tent with a double top **c** : the length of an extended flag; *also* : the loose end of a flag **2** : a baseball hit high into the air — **on the fly** : in motion especially while still in the air

³**fly** *vb* **flied; fly·ing** : to hit a fly in baseball

⁴**fly** *n, pl* **flies** **1** : a winged insect **2** : TWO-WINGED FLY; *esp* : one (as a housefly) that is large and has a stout body in comparison with others (as a mosquito) **3** : a fishhook covered to look like an insect [Old English *flēoge* "flying insect"] — **fly in the ointment** : an unpleasant feature in something otherwise pleasant

fly ash *n* : fine solid particles of ashes, dust, and soot carried out from burning fuel (as coal or oil) by the draft

fly ball *n* : ²FLY 2

fly-blown \'flī-ˌblōn\ *adj* : not pure : TAINTED, CORRUPT

fly·by \-ˌbī\ *n* **1** : a usually low-altitude flight past a chosen place by one or more aircraft **2 a** : a flight of a spacecraft past a heavenly body (as Mars) close enough to obtain scientific information **b** : a spacecraft that makes a flyby

fly·catch·er \-ˌkach-ər, -ˌkech-\ *n* : a small bird that feeds on insects that it captures in the air

flyer *variant of* FLIER

fly·ing \'flī-iŋ\ *adj* **1 a** : rapidly moving **b** : HASTY 1a ⟨a *flying* visit⟩ **2** : ready to move or act quickly ⟨a *flying* squad⟩

flying boat *n* : a seaplane with a hull designed for floating

flying buttress *n* : an arched structure that extends beyond a wall or building and supports it

flying fish *n* : any of numerous sea fishes having long fins that look like wings and are used to glide some distance through the air

flying fox *n* : FRUIT BAT

flying machine *n* : AIRCRAFT

flying saucer *n* : any of various unidentified flying objects often reported to be saucer-shaped or disk‡shaped

flying squirrel *n* : a squirrel

1 flying buttress

\ə\ **abut**	\au̇\ **out**	\i\ **tip**	\ȯ\ **saw**	\u̇\ **foot**
\ər\ **further**	\ch\ **chin**	\ī\ **life**	\ȯi\ **coin**	\y\ **yet**
\a\ **mat**	\e\ **pet**	\j\ **job**	\th\ **thin**	\yü\ **few**
\ā\ **take**	\ē\ **easy**	\ŋ\ **sing**	\t̲h̲\ **this**	\yu̇\ **cure**
\ä\ **cot, cart**	\g\ **go**	\ō\ **bone**	\ü\ **food**	\zh\ **vision**

with folds of skin connecting the forelegs and hind legs and enabling it to make long gliding leaps

fly·leaf \'flī-,lēf\ *n* : a blank leaf at the beginning or end of a book

fly·pa·per \-,pā-pər\ *n* : paper coated with a sticky often poisonous substance for killing flies

fly·speck \-,spek\ *n* **1** : a speck of waste matter of a fly **2** : something small and of little importance — **flyspeck** *vb*

fly·way \-,wā\ *n* : an established air route of birds that migrate

fly·weight \-,wāt\ *n* : a boxer in a weight division having the approximate range of 48 to 51 kilograms

fly·wheel \-,hwēl, -,wēl\ *n* : a heavy wheel for regulating the speed of machinery

FM \'ef-,em\ *n* : a system of broadcasting using frequency modulation; *also* : a receiver of radio waves broadcast by such a system — **FM** *adj*

¹foal \'fōl\ *n* : a young animal of the horse family; *esp* : one under one year

²foal *vb* : to give birth to a foal

¹foam \'fōm\ *n* **1** : a light mass of fine bubbles formed in or on a liquid **2** : a mass of fine bubbles formed (as by a horse) in producing saliva or sweating **3** : a long-lasting mass of bubbles produced chemically and used especially in fighting oil fires **4** : a material (as rubber) in a lightweight cellular form resulting from the presence of gas bubbles during manufacture — **foam·i·ly** \'fō-mə-lē\ *adv* — **foam·i·ness** \'fō-mē-nəs\ *n* — **foamy** \-mē\ *adj*

²foam *vb* **1** : to produce or form foam : FROTH **2** : to be angry

foam rubber *n* : rubber prepared in the form of a spongy foam

fob \'fäb\ *n* **1** : a short strap, ribbon, or chain attached especially to a pocket watch **2** : a small ornament worn on a watch chain

fo·cal \'fō-kəl\ *adj* : of, relating to, or having a focus — **fo·cal·ly** \-kə-lē\ *adv*

focal length *n* : the distance of a focus from the surface of a lens or inwardly-curved mirror

focal point *n* : ¹FOCUS 1

fo'c'sle *variant of* FORECASTLE

¹fo·cus \'fō-kəs\ *n, pl* **fo·ci** \-,sī\ *also* **fo·cus·es** **1** : a point at which rays (as of light, heat, or sound) meet or from which they draw apart or appear to draw apart; *esp* : the point at which an image is formed by a mirror, lens, or optical system **2 a** : FOCAL LENGTH **b** : adjustment (as of the eye or binoculars) for clear vision 〈bring into *focus*〉 **3** : a center of activity or interest **4** : one of the two points within an ellipse the sum of whose distances from any point on the ellipse is a constant number **5** : the starting point of an earthquake

²focus *vb* **fo·cused** *also* **fo·cussed; fo·cus·ing** *also* **fo·cus·sing** **1** : to bring to a focus 〈*focus* rays of light〉 **2** : to cause to be concentrated 〈*focus* public attention on a problem〉 **3 a** : to adjust the focus of 〈*focus* the eyes〉 〈*focus* a telescope〉 **b** : to bring into focus **4** : to come to a focus **5** : to adjust one's eye or a camera to a certain range

fod·der \'fäd-ər\ *n* : coarse dry food (as cornstalks) for livestock

foe \'fō\ *n* **1** : one who hates another : ENEMY **2** : an enemy in war

foehn \'fə(r)n, 'fān\ *n* : a warm dry wind blowing down the side of a mountain

foe·tal \'fēt-ºl\, **foe·tus** \'fēt-əs\ *chiefly British variant of* FETAL, FETUS

¹fog \'fȯg, 'fäg\ *n* **1 a** : fine particles of water floating in the atmosphere near the ground **b** : a fine spray or a foam for fire fighting **2** : a gloomy condition of the atmosphere or a substance causing it **3** : a state of mental confusion

²fog *vb* **fogged; fog·ging** **1** : to cover or become covered

with or as if with fog **2** : to make confused

fog·gy \'fȯg-ē, 'fäg-\ *adj* **fog·gi·er; -est** **1** : filled with fog **2** : VAGUE 2 — **fog·gi·ly** \-ə-lē\ *adv* — **fog·gi·ness** \-ē-nəs\ *n*

fog·horn \'fȯg-,hȯ(ə)rn, 'fäg-\ *n* : a horn (as on a ship) sounded in foggy weather to give warning

fo·gy *also* **fo·gey** \'fō-gē\ *n, pl* **fogies** *also* **fogeys** : a person with old-fashioned ideas — usually used with *old*

foi·ble \'fȯi-bəl\ *n* : a minor fault in personal character or behavior : WEAKNESS

¹foil \'fȯi(ə)l\ *vb* : to prevent from achieving a goal : DEFEAT 〈*foil* a plot〉 [Middle English *foilen* "to trample underfoot", from early French *fouler* (same meaning), from Latin *fullare* "to trample, to shrink and thicken cloth"] **syn** see FRUSTRATE

²foil *n* : a fencing weapon having a light flexible blade with a blunt point

³foil *n* **1** : a very thin sheet of metal 〈tin or aluminum *foil*〉 **2** : one that serves as a contrast to another 〈acted as a *foil* for the comedian〉 [Middle English *foil* "leaf", from early French *foille, foil* (same meaning), derived from Latin *folium* "leaf" — related to FOLIAGE]

foist \'fȯist\ *vb* : to pass off (something false) as genuine

fo·la·cin \'fō-lə-sən\ *n* : FOLIC ACID

¹fold \'fōld\ *n* **1** : a pen for sheep **2** : a group of people with a common faith or interest [Old English *falod* "pen for sheep"]

²fold *vb* : to shut up in a fold

³fold *vb* **1** : to lay one part over or against another part 〈*fold* a letter〉 〈birds *folding* their wings〉 **2** : to clasp together 〈*fold* the hands〉 **3** : ¹EMBRACE **4** : to bend (as a layer of rock) into folds **5** : to add (a food ingredient) to a mixture by gently and repeatedly lifting one part over another **6** : to become doubled or pleated **7** : to fail completely 〈the business *folded*〉 [Old English *fealdan* "to fold, make double thickness"]

⁴fold *n* **1** : a doubling or folding over **2** : a part doubled or laid over another part **3** : a bend produced in rock

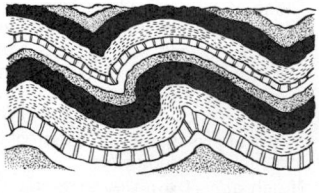

⁴fold 3

-fold \,fōld, 'fōld\ *suffix* **1** : multiplied by (a specified number) : times — in adjectives 〈a twelve*fold* increase〉 and adverbs 〈repay you ten*fold*〉 **2** : having (so many) parts 〈a three*fold* problem〉 [Old English *-feald* (suffix) "being increased (so many) times"]

fold·er \'fōl-dər\ *n* **1** : one that folds **2** : a printed circular of folded sheets **3** : a folded cover or large envelope for holding loose papers

fo·li·age \'fō-l(ē-)ij *also* 'fōl-yij\ *n* : the mass of leaves of a plant [an altered form of earlier *foillage* "a mass of leaves", from early French *fuellage* (same meaning), from *fuelle, foille* "leaf", derived from Latin *folium* "leaf" — related to ³FOIL, PORTFOLIO] — **fo·li·aged** \-l(ē-)ijd *also* -yijd\ *adj*

fo·li·at·ed \'fō-lē-,āt-əd\ *adj* : composed of or capable of being separated into layers 〈*foliated* metamorphic rocks〉

fo·lic acid \,fō-lik-\ *n* : a crystalline vitamin of the B complex used especially in the treatment of nutritional anemias

fo·lio \'fō-lē-,ō\ *n, pl* **fo·li·os** **1** : a leaf of a manuscript or book **2 a** : a book made up of sheets of paper that have been folded to produce two leaves **b** : a very large book

¹folk \'fōk\ *n, pl* **folk** *or* **folks** **1** : a group of people forming a tribe or nation **2** *pl* : a certain kind or class of people **3** *folks pl* : people in general **4** *folks pl* : the persons of one's own family 〈visit my *folks*〉

²folk *adj* : of, relating to, or originating among the common people of a country or region 〈*folk* customs〉 〈*folk* songs〉

folk·lore \'fōk-,lō(ə)r, -,lȯ(ə)r\ *n* : customs, beliefs, stories, and sayings of a people handed down from generation to generation — **folk·lor·ist** \-,lȯr-əst, -,lōr-\ *n*

folk·sing·er \-,sing-ər\ *n* : a singer of folk songs

folk·tale \-,tāl\ *n* : a story made up and handed down by the common people

fol·li·cle \'fäl-i-kəl\ *n* **1 a** : a small cavity or a deep bodily depression with a narrow mouth (as one from which a hair grows) **b** : GRAAFIAN FOLLICLE **2** : a dry one-celled fruit (as in the peony, larkspur, or milkweed) that develops from a single ovary and splits open by one seam when ripe — **fol·lic·u·lar** \fə-'lik-yə-lər, fä-\ *adj*

follicle–stimulating hormone *n* : a hormone from the front part of the pituitary gland that causes the graafian follicle to grow in females and makes sperm-forming cells active in males

¹follow \'fäl-ō\ *vb* **1** : to go or come after or behind **2** : to be guided by : OBEY 〈*follow* your conscience〉 〈*follow* instructions〉 **3** : to go after or on the track of 〈*follow* a clue〉 **4** : to go along 〈*follow* a path〉 **5** : to work in or at something as a business or way of life 〈*follow* the sea〉 **6** : to come after in order of rank or natural sequence 〈two *follows* one〉 **7** : to keep one's attention fixed on 〈*follow* a speech〉 **8** : to result from something 〈fame *followed* the captain's success〉 〈from the evidence given, it *follows* that the accused is guilty〉 **syn** see CHASE — **follow suit** : to play a card of the same suit as the card led

²follow *n* : the act or process of following

fol·low·er \'fäl-ə-wər\ *n* **1** : ²ATTENDANT 1 **2** : SUPPORTER, ADHERENT **3** : DISCIPLE 1

¹fol·low·ing \'fäl-ə-wiŋ\ *adj* **1** : next after 〈the *following* day〉 **2** : that immediately follows 〈trains will leave at the *following* times〉

²following *n* : a group of followers

³following *prep* : immediately after 〈*following* the lecture refreshments were served〉

follow through *vb* **1** : to complete a stroke or swing **2** : to continue in an activity or process especially to a conclusion — **fol·low–through** \'fäl-ō-,thrü, ,fäl-ō-'thrü, -ə-\ *n*

fol·low–up \'fäl-ə-,wəp\ *n* **1** : the act or an instance of following up **2** : something that follows up — **follow–up** *adj*

follow up \,fäl-ə-'wəp\ *vb* **1** : to follow with something similar, related, or additional 〈*follow up* an idea with action〉 **2** : to seek more details about 〈the police *follow up* leads〉

fol·ly \'fäl-ē\ *n, pl* **follies** **1** : lack of good sense or judgment **2 a** : a foolish act or idea **b** : foolish actions or conduct

fo·ment \'fō-,ment, fō-'mənt\ *vb* : to stir up : ROUSE, INSTIGATE 〈*foment* rebellion〉 — **fo·ment·er** *n*

fo·men·ta·tion \,fō-mən-'tā-shen, -,men-\ *n* **1** : a warm or hot moist material (as a hot damp cloth) applied to the body to ease pain **2** : the act of fomenting : INSTIGATION

fond \'fänd\ *adj* **1** : having a liking or love 〈*fond* of praise〉 〈*fond* of music〉 **2** : LOVING, AFFECTIONATE 〈a *fond* family〉 〈a *fond* farewell〉 **3** : cherished with great affection 〈their *fondest* hopes〉 — **fond·ly** \'fän-(d)lē\ *adv* — **fond·ness** \'fän(d)-nəs\ *n*

fon·dant \'fän-dənt\ *n* **1** : a creamy preparation of sugar used as a basis for candies or icings **2** : a candy consisting chiefly of fondant

fon·dle \'fän-dᵊl\ *vb* **fon·dled; fon·dling** \-(d)liŋ, -dᵊl-iŋ\ : to touch or handle in a tender or loving manner : CARESS, PET — **fon·dler** \-(d)lər, -dᵊl-ər\ *n*

fon·due \fän-'d(y)ü\ *n* : a preparation of melted cheese and flavorings

F₁ layer \'ef-'wən-\ *n* : a layer of the ionosphere that occurs during the day from 130 to 200 kilometers in altitude

¹font \'fänt\ *n* **1** : a basin for baptismal or holy water **2** : FOUNTAIN 2 [Old English *font* "basin for holy water", de-

rived from Latin *font-, fons* "fountain, spring" — related to FOUNTAIN]

²font *n* : an assortment of type all of one size and style [from early French *fonte* "act of casting metal", derived from Latin *fundere* "to pour melted metal into a mold" — related to ³FOUND, ³FOUNDER]

food \'füd\ *n* **1** : material containing or consisting of carbohydrates, fats, and proteins used in the body of an animal to sustain growth, repair, and vital processes and to furnish energy; *also* : such material together with extra substances (as vitamins and minerals) **2 a** : organic substances taken in by green plants and used to build organic nutrients **b** : organic material produced by green plants and used by them as building material and as a source of energy **3** : nourishment in solid form **4** : something that nourishes, supports, or supplies 〈*food* for thought〉

food chain *n* : a series of organisms in which each uses the next usually lower member of the series as a food source

food poisoning *n* : a digestive sickness caused by bacteria or by chemicals in food

food processor *n* : an electric kitchen appliance that has blades that turn inside a container and is used for cutting and blending food

food pyramid *n* : a series of levels of ecological food relationships especially when expressed in measured amounts (as of mass, numbers, or energy) in which the chief predator is at the top, each level preys on the next lower level, and green plants are usually at the bottom

food stamp *n* : a coupon issued by the government that is sold or given to low-income persons to be exchanged for food

food·stuff \'füd-,stəf\ *n* : a substance with food value; *esp* : a specific nutrient (as protein or fat)

food vacuole *n* : a vacuole (as in an amoeba) in which ingested food is digested

food web *n* : the whole group of interacting food chains in an ecological community

¹fool \'fül\ *n* **1** : a person who lacks good sense or judgment **2** : a person formerly kept in a noble or royal household to amuse with jests and pranks

²fool *vb* **1 a** : to spend time idly 〈just *fooling* around〉 **b** : to meddle or tamper thoughtlessly or ignorantly 〈don't *fool* with that dial〉 **2** : to speak or act in fun : JOKE 〈I was only *fooling*〉 **3** : to make a fool of : TRICK 〈I *fooled* you〉

fool·ery \'fül-(ə)rē\ *n, pl* **-er·ies** **1** : foolish behavior **2** : a foolish act : HORSEPLAY

fool·har·dy \'fül-,härd-ē\ *adj* : foolishly adventurous or bold — **fool·har·di·ly** \-,härd-ᵊl-ē\ *adv* — **fool·har·di·ness** \-,härd-ē-nəs\ *n*

fool·ish \'fü-lish\ *adj* : lacking in good sense or judgment : SENSELESS, SILLY — **fool·ish·ly** *adv* — **fool·ish·ness** *n*

fool·proof \'fül-'prüf\ *adj* : done, made, or planned so well that nothing can go wrong 〈*foolproof* directions〉 〈a *foolproof* plan〉

fool's gold *n* **1** : PYRITE **2** : CHALCOPYRITE

¹foot \'fut\ *n, pl* **feet** \'fēt\ *also* **foot** **1 a** : the end part of the leg below the ankle of a vertebrate animal **b** : an organ upon which an invertebrate animal stands or moves; *esp* : a bottom muscular part of a mollusk **2** : a unit of length equal to ⅓ yard (0.3048 meter) or 12 inches 〈a 10⁼ *foot* pole〉 〈six *feet* tall〉 — see MEASURE table **3** : the basic unit of verse meter made up of a group of accented and unaccented syllables **4** : something resembling an animal's foot in position or use or in being opposite the head 〈the *foot* of a mountain〉 〈the *foot* of a bed〉 — **on foot** **1** : by walking 〈went *on foot*〉 **2** : UNDER WAY 2 〈an

\ə\ abut	\aú\ out	\i\ tip	\ȯ\ saw	\ú\ foot
\ər\ further	\ch\ chin	\ī\ life	\ȯi\ coin	\y\ yet
\a\ mat	\e\ pet	\j\ job	\th\ thin	\yü\ few
\ā\ take	\ē\ easy	\ŋ\ sing	\t͟h\ this	\yu̇\ cure
\ä\ cot, cart	\g\ go	\ō\ bone	\ü\ food	\zh\ vision

investigation was set *on foot*⟩

²**foot** *vb* **1 a :** ¹DANCE 1 **b :** ¹WALK 1 **c :** ¹RUN 1a **2 a** : to add up **b :** to pay or provide for paying ⟨*foot* the bill⟩

foot–and–mouth disease *n* : a virus disease especially of cattle that is marked by fever and by ulcers in the mouth, about the hooves, and on the udder — called also *hoof= and-mouth disease*

foot·ball \'fût-,bȯl\ *n* **1 :** any of several games in which two teams try to advance a ball to the goals at each end of a large rectangular field **: as a** *British* : SOCCER **b** *British* : RUGBY **c :** an American game played between two teams of 11 players each in which the ball is advanced by running or passing **2 :** the ball used in football

foot·board \-,bō(ə)rd, -,bȯ(ə)rd\ *n* : a board forming the foot of a bed

foot·bridge \-,brij\ *n* : a bridge for pedestrians

foot·can·dle \-'kan-d'l\ *n* : a unit for measuring illumination that equals the illumination on the inner surface of a sphere with a radius of one foot from a light source of one candle at the center of the sphere and that amounts to about 10.76 lux

foot·ed \'fût-əd\ *adj* : having a foot or feet especially of a certain kind or number ⟨flat-*footed*⟩ ⟨a four-*footed* animal⟩

foot·fall \'fût-,fȯl\ *n* : the sound of a footstep

foot·gear \-,gi(ə)r\ *n* : FOOTWEAR

foot·hill \-,hil\ *n* : a hill at the foot of higher hills or mountains

foot·hold \-,hōld\ *n* **1 :** a hold for the feet : FOOTING **2** : a position usable as a base for further advance

foot·ing \'fût-iŋ\ *n* **1 a :** the placing of one's feet in a position to secure a firm or safe stand **b :** a place for the foot to rest securely **2 a :** position with respect to one another : STATUS ⟨nations on a friendly *footing*⟩ **b :** BASIS ⟨put the business on a firm *footing*⟩

foot·lights \'fût-,līts\ *n pl* **1 :** a row of lights set across the front of a stage floor **2 :** acting on the stage as a profession

foot·lock·er \-,läk-ər\ *n* : a small trunk designed to be placed at the foot of a bed

foot·loose \-,lüs\ *adj* : having no ties : free to roam

foot·man \-mən\ *n* **1 :** an infantry soldier **2 :** a male servant who lets in visitors and waits on the table

foot·note \-,nōt\ *n* : a note of reference, explanation, or comment placed below the text on a printed page — **foot·note** *vb*

foot·pad \-,pad\ *n* : a somewhat flat foot on the leg of a spacecraft for distributing weight to decrease sinking into a surface (as on the moon)

foot·path \-,path, -,păth\ *n* : a narrow path for pedestrians

foot–pound \-'pau̇nd\ *n, pl* **foot–pounds** : a unit of work that equals the work done by a force of one pound acting through a distance of one foot and that is equal to about 1.36 joules

F footpad

foot–pound–second *adj* : being or relating to a system of units based upon the foot as the unit of length, the pound as the unit of weight, and the second as the unit of time — abbr. *fps*

foot·print \'fût-,print\ *n* : a track left by the foot

foot·race \-,rās\ *n* : a race run on foot

foot·rest \-,rest\ *n* : a support for the feet

foot soldier *n* : INFANTRYMAN

foot·sore \'fût-,sō(ə)r, -,sȯ(ə)r\ *adj* : having sore or tender feet (as from much walking)

foot·step \-,step\ *n* **1 a :** a step of the foot **b :** the dis-

tance covered by a step : PACE **2 a :** the mark of the foot **b :** the sound of a footstep **3 :** a step on which to go up or down

foot·stool \-,stül\ *n* : a low stool to support the feet

foot·wear \-,wa(ə)r, -,we(ə)r\ *n* : covering (as shoes) for the feet

foot·work \-,wərk\ *n* : the movement of the feet (as in boxing)

foo·zle \'fü-zəl\ *vb* **foo·zled; foo·zling** \'füz-(ə-)liŋ\ *n* : BUNGLE — **foozle** *n*

fop \'fäp\ *n* : ¹DANDY 1 — **fop·pish** \'fäp-ish\ *adj*

¹**for** \fər, (')fȯ(ə)r\ *prep* **1** — used to indicate a purpose ⟨money *for* lunch⟩, an intended goal ⟨left *for* work⟩, or an object of one's desire ⟨now *for* a good rest⟩ **2 :** as being ⟨do you take me *for* a fool⟩ ⟨eggs *for* breakfast⟩ **3 :** because of ⟨cried *for* joy⟩ **4 a :** in support of ⟨fighting *for* their country⟩ **b** — used to indicate suitability or fitness ⟨it's not *for* me to say⟩ ⟨medicine *for* an illness⟩ **c :** so as to bring about a certain state ⟨shouted the news *for* all to hear⟩ **5 a :** in place of ⟨Doe batting *for* Roe⟩ **b :** as the equal or equivalent of in an exchange or loan ⟨paid $10 *for* a hat⟩ **6 :** in spite of ⟨unconvinced *for* all the clever arguments⟩ **7 :** CONCERNING ⟨had an eye *for* news⟩ **8** — used to indicate equality or proportion ⟨point *for* point⟩ ⟨tall *for* your age⟩ **9** — used to indicate length of time or extent of space ⟨waited *for* several hours⟩ **10 :** ²AFTER 3a ⟨named *for* my grandmother⟩

²**for** *conj* : for the reason that : on this ground : BECAUSE ⟨they were certainly there, *for* I saw them⟩

fora *pl of* FORUM

¹**for·age** \'fȯr-ij, 'fär-\ *n* **1 :** food (as pasture) for browsing or grazing animals **2 :** a search for food or supplies

²**forage** *vb* **for·aged; for·ag·ing** **1 :** ¹BROWSE 1, GRAZE **2** : to make a search especially for food or supplies ⟨*forage* for grain⟩ ⟨*forage* for firewood⟩ **3 :** to get by foraging — **for·ag·er** *n*

for·a·min·i·fer \,fȯr-ə-'min-ə-fər, ,fär-\ *n* : any of an order of large chiefly marine protozoans that resemble amebas, usually have perforated shells, and are important sources of chalk and limestone

fo·ra·min·if·era \fə-,ram-ə-'nif-(ə-)rə, ,fȯr-ə-mə-'nif-, ,fär-\ *n pl* : protozoans that are foraminifers

for·ay \'fȯr-,ā\ *vb* : to raid especially in order to steal : PILLAGE — **foray** *n*

¹**for·bear** \fȯr-'ba(ə)r, fər-, -'be(ə)r\ *vb* **-bore** \-'bō(ə)r, -'bȯ(ə)r\; **-borne** \-'bō(ə)rn, -'bȯ(ə)rn\; **-bear·ing** **1 :** to hold back or keep from : ABSTAIN **2 :** to be patient when annoyed — **for·bear·er** *n*

²**forbear** *variant of* FOREBEAR

for·bear·ance \fȯr-'bar-ən(t)s, fər-, -'ber-\ *n* **1 :** the act of forbearing **2 :** the quality of being forbearing : PATIENCE

for·bid \fər-'bid, fȯr-\ *vb* **-bade** \-'bad, -'bād\ *or* **-bad** \-'bad\; **-bid·den** \-'bid-ᵊn\; **-bid·ding** : to order not to do or to be done or used ⟨I *forbid* you to go⟩ ⟨cameras are *forbidden*⟩ — **for·bid·der** *n*

for·bid·ding *adj* : tending to frighten or discourage — **for·bid·ding·ly** \-iŋ-lē\ *adv*

forbode *variant of* FOREBODE

¹**force** \'fō(ə)rs, 'fȯ(ə)rs\ *n* **1 a :** strength or energy put forth : active power ⟨*forces* of nature⟩ **b :** capacity to persuade or convince ⟨the *force* of this argument⟩ **c :** the state of existing and being enforced : EFFECT ⟨that law is still in *force*⟩ **2 :** a group of persons trained and available for action ⟨a police *force*⟩ ⟨the nation's labor *force*⟩ **3** : violence or power used on a person or thing ⟨open a door by *force*⟩ **4 :** an influence (as a push or pull) that tends to produce a change in the speed or direction of motion of something ⟨the *force* of gravity⟩ — **force·less** \-ləs\ *adj*

²**force** *vb* **forced; forc·ing** **1 :** to make (as a person) do something ⟨*forced* them to work⟩ **2 a :** to get or make by using force ⟨*forced* their way into the room⟩ **b :** to break open or through ⟨*force* a lock⟩ **3 :** to produce with effort

⟨*forced* a weak smile⟩ **4** : to speed up the development of ⟨*force* flowers⟩ — **forc·er** *n*

forced \'fō(ə)rst, 'fò(ə)rst\ *adj* **1** : caused or brought about by force or by circumstances : INVOLUNTARY ⟨made a *forced* landing⟩ **2** : done or produced with effort ⟨a *forced* laugh⟩

force·ful \'fōrs-fəl, 'fòrs-\ *adj* : having or done with much force : VIGOROUS ⟨a *forceful* speech⟩ — **force·ful·ly** \-fə-lē\ *adv* — **force·ful·ness** *n*

for·ceps \'fòr-səps, -ˌseps\ *n, pl* **forceps** : an instrument for grasping or holding objects especially in delicate operations (as by a jeweler or surgeon) — **for·ceps·like** \-ˌlīk\ *adj*

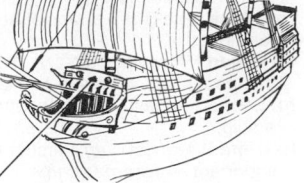

forceps

forc·i·ble \'fōr-sə-bəl, 'fòr-\ *adj* **1** : got, made, or done by force or violence ⟨a *forcible* entrance⟩ **2** : FORCEFUL — **forc·i·bly** \-blē\ *adv*

¹ford \'fō(ə)rd, 'fò(ə)rd\ *n* : a shallow part of a body of water that may be crossed by wading

²ford *vb* : to cross (a body of water) by wading — **ford·able** \-ə-bəl\ *adj*

¹fore \'fō(ə), 'fò(ə)r\ *adv* : in, toward, or near the front : FORWARD

²fore *adj* : being or coming before in time, order, or space

³fore *n* : a front place or position ⟨came to the *fore*⟩

⁴fore *interj* — used by a golfer to warn anyone within range of a hit ball

fore- *combining form* **1 a** : earlier : beforehand ⟨*foresee*⟩ **b** : occurring earlier : occurring beforehand **2 a** : situated at the front : in front ⟨*foreleg*⟩ **b** : front part of (something specified) ⟨*forearm*⟩ [Old English *fore-* "earlier, beforehand"]

fore–and–aft \ˌfōr-ə-'naft, ˌfòr-\ *adj* **1** : lying, running, or acting along the length of a structure (as of a ship) ⟨*fore-and-aft* sails⟩ **2** : having no square sails

fore–and–aft rig *n* : a sailing-ship rig in which most or all of the sails are set lengthwise along the centerline of the ship rather than across it — **fore–and–aft rigged** *adj*

¹fore·arm \(')fōr-ˌärm, (')fòr-\ *vb* : to arm in advance : PREPARE

²fore·arm \'fōr-ˌärm, 'fòr-\ *n* : the part of the arm between the elbow and the wrist

fore-and-aft rig

fore·bear *or* **for·bear** \'fōr-ˌba(ə)r, -ˌbe(ə)r\ *n* : ANCESTOR 1, FOREFATHER

fore·bode *also* **for·bode** \fōr-'bōd, fòr-\ *vb* **1** : FORETELL, PORTEND ⟨the heavy air *forebodes* a storm⟩ **2** : to have a feeling that something especially unfortunate is going to happen — **fore·bod·er** *n* — **fore·bod·ing** \-'bōd-iŋ\ *n* — **fore·bod·ing·ly** \-iŋ-lē\ *adv*

fore·brain \'fō(ə)r-ˌbrān, 'fò(ə)r-\ *n* : the front division of the embryonic brain of an animal with a backbone or the parts developed from it

¹fore·cast \'fō(ə)r-ˌkast, 'fò(ə)r-\ *vb* **forecast** *also* **fore·cast·ed; fore·cast·ing** : to calculate or predict (a future event or state) usually by study and examination of data ⟨*forecast* the weather⟩ **syn** see FORETELL — **fore·cast·er** *n*

²forecast *n* : an estimate or prediction of a future happening or condition ⟨weather *forecasts*⟩

fore·cas·tle \'fōk-səl; 'fōr-ˌkas-əl, 'fòr-\ *or* **fo'·c'sle** \'fōk-səl\ *n* **1** : the forward part of the upper deck of a ship **2** : the living area for the crew in the front part of a ship

forecastle 1

fore·close \(')fōr-'klōz, (')fòr-\ *vb* : to take legal measures to end a mortgage and take possession of the mortgaged property because the conditions of the mortgage have not been met — **fore·clo·sure** \-'klō-zhər\ *n*

fore·deck \'fō(ə)r-ˌdek, 'fò(ə)r-\ *n* : the front part of a ship's main deck

fore·doom \(')fōr-'düm, (')fòr-\ *vb* : to doom beforehand

fore·fa·ther \'fō(ə)r-ˌfäth-ər, 'fò(ə)r-, -ˌfäth-\ *n* **1** : ANCESTOR 1 **2** : a person of an earlier period and similar culture

fore·fin·ger \-ˌfiŋ-gər\ *n* : the finger next to the thumb — called also *index finger*

fore·foot \-ˌfùt\ *n* : one of the front feet of a four-footed animal

fore·front \-ˌfrənt\ *n* : the most important part or place

foregather *variant of* FORGATHER

¹fore·go \fōr-'gō, fòr-\ *vb* **-went** \-'went\; **-gone** \-'gòn *also* -'gän\ **-go·ing** \-'gō-iŋ\ : to go before : PRECEDE — **fore·go·er** \-'gō-(ə)r\ *n*

²forego *variant of* FORGO

fore·go·ing \fōr-'gō-iŋ, fòr-\ *adj* : going before : PRECEDING

fore·gone \ˌfōr-ˌgòn, fòr- *also* -ˌgän\ *adj* : settled in advance ⟨a *foregone* conclusion⟩

fore·ground \'fō(ə)r-ˌgraùnd, 'fò(ə)r-\ *n* : the part of a scene or picture that is nearest to and in front of the viewer

fore·hand \-ˌhand\ *n* : a stroke made with the palm of the hand turned in the direction in which the hand is moving — **forehand** *adv or adj*

fore·hand·ed \fōr-'han-dəd, fòr-\ *adj* : thinking of future needs : THRIFTY — **fore·hand·ed·ly** *adv*

fore·head \'fär-əd, 'fòr-; 'fō(ə)r-ˌhed, 'fò(ə)r-\ *n* : the part of the face above the eyes

forehand

for·eign \'fòr-ən, 'fär-\ *adj* **1** : located outside a place or country and especially outside one's own country ⟨*foreign* nations⟩ **2** : born in, belonging to, or characteristic of a place or country other than the one under consideration ⟨*foreign* language⟩ ⟨*foreign* customs⟩ **3** : related to or dealing with other nations ⟨*foreign* affairs⟩ ⟨*foreign* office⟩ **4** : not normally found in an area or part ⟨a *foreign* body in the eye⟩ — **for·eign·ness** \-ən-nəs\ *n*

for·eign·er \'fòr-ə-nər, 'fär-\ *n* : a person who is from a foreign country

foreign minister *n* : a government minister for foreign affairs

fore·know \(')fōr-'nō, (')fòr-\ *vb* **-knew** \-'n(y)ü\; **-known** \-'nōn\; **-know·ing** : to have earlier knowledge of : know beforehand — **fore·knowl·edge** \-'näl-ij\ *n*

fore·leg \'fōr-ˌleg, 'fòr-\ *n* : a front leg

fore·limb \-ˌlim\ *n* : an arm, fin, wing, or leg that is a foreleg

\ə\ abut	\aú\ out	\i\ tip	\ò\ saw	\ù\ foot	
\ər\ further	\ch\ chin	\ī\ life	\òi\ coin	\y\ yet	
\a\ mat	\e\ pet	\j\ job	\th\ thin	\yü\ few	
\ā\ take	\ē\ easy	\ŋ\ sing	\th\ this	\yù\ cure	
\ä\ cot, cart	\g\ go	\ō\ bone	\ü\ food	\zh\ vision	

or corresponds to one

fore·lock \-,läk\ *n* : a lock of hair growing from the front of the head

fore·man \'fōr-mən, 'fȯr-\ *n* **1** : a member of a jury who is the leader **2** : a person in charge of a group of workers

fore·mast \-,mast, -məst\ *n* : the mast nearest the bow of a ship

fore·most \-,mōst\ *adj* : first in time, place, or order : most important — **foremost** *adv*

fore·name \-,nām\ *n* : a first name

fore·noon \-,nün\ *n* : the early part of the day ending with noon : MORNING

fo·ren·sic \fə-'ren(t)-sik, -'ren-zik\ *adj* : belonging to, used in, or suitable to courts of law or to public discussion and debate [from Latin *forensis* "of a forum, public", from *forum* "market, place of public discussion, court"] — **fo·ren·si·cal·ly** \-si-k(ə-)lē, -zi-\ *adv*

fore·or·dain \,fōr-ȯr-'dān, ,fȯr-\ *vb* : to determine in advance : PREDESTINE

fore·part \'fō(ə)r-,pärt, 'fȯ(ə)r-\ *n* : the part most advanced or first in place or in time

fore·paw \-,pȯ\ *n* : the paw of a foreleg

fore·quar·ter \-,kwȯ(r)t-ər\ *n* : the left or right half of a front half of the body of a four-footed animal

fore·run·ner \-,rən-ər\ *n* **1** : one going or sent before to give notice of the approach of others : HARBINGER **2** : PREDECESSOR, ANCESTOR

fore·sail \-,sāl, -səl\ *n* : the lowest and largest sail on the foremast of a square-rigged ship or schooner

fore·see \fōr-'sē, fȯr-\ *vb* **-saw** \-'sȯ\; **-seen** \-'sēn\; **-see·ing** : to see or realize beforehand : EXPECT — **fore·see·able** \-'sē-ə-bəl\ *adj* — **fore·se·er** \-'sē-ər\ *n*

fore·shad·ow \-'shad-ō\ *vb* : to give a hint or suggestion of beforehand — **fore·shad·ow·er** *n*

fore·short·en \-'shȯrt-ə n\ *vb* : to shorten (a detail) in a drawing or painting so that it appears to have depth

fore·sight \'fō(ə)r-,sīt, 'fȯ(ə)r-\ *n* **1** : the act or power of foreseeing **2** : care or preparation for the future — **fore·sight·ed** \-,sīt-əd\ *adj* — **fore·sight·ed·ly** *adv* — **fore·sight·ed·ness** *n*

fore·skin \-,skin\ *n* : a fold of skin that covers the end of the penis — called also *prepuce*

for·est \'fȯr-əst, 'fär-\ *n* : a dense growth of trees and underbrush covering a large area

fore·stall \fȯr-'stȯl, fȯr-\ *vb* : to keep out, interfere with, or prevent by steps taken in advance — **fore·stall·er** *n* — **fore·stall·ment** \-'stȯl-mənt\ *n*

for·es·ta·tion \,fȯr-ə-'stā-shən, ,fär-\ *n* : the planting and care of a forest

for·est·ed \'fȯr-ə-stəd, 'fär-\ *adj* : covered with trees or forests : WOODED

for·est·er \'fȯr-ə-stər, 'fär-\ *n* : a person who practices or is trained in forestry

forest fire *n* : an uncontrolled fire in a wooded area

forest floor *n* : the upper layer of mixed soil and decayed or decaying organic material typical of forested land

forest ranger *n* : a person in charge of the management and protection of a forest

for·est·ry \'fȯr-ə-strē, 'fär-\ *n* : the science and practice of caring for forests

foreswear *variant of* FORSWEAR

fore·taste \'fō(ə)r-,tāst, 'fȯ(ə)r-\ *n* : a sample or partial experience of something that will not be fully experienced until later ⟨the cold day was a *foretaste* of winter⟩

fore·tell \fōr-'tel, fȯr-\ *vb* **-told** \-'tōld\; **-tell·ing** : to tell of or describe beforehand — **fore·tell·er** *n*

syn FORETELL, PREDICT, FORECAST mean to tell beforehand. FORETELL applies to the coming of a future event especially through mysterious powers ⟨wizards *foretold* battles in the sky⟩ PREDICT may suggest an exact statement that is the result of the gathering of information and the use of scientific methods ⟨scientists can sometimes *predict* the course of a hurricane⟩ FORECAST suggests the gathering of evidence and a statement of what is most likely to happen ⟨the weather bureau *forecast* that it would snow⟩

fore·thought \'fō(ə)r-,thȯt, 'fȯ(ə)r-\ *n* : thought or care taken in advance — **fore·thought·ful** \-fəl\ *adj*

fore·top \'fō(ə)r-,täp, 'fȯ(ə)r-; 'fōrt-əp, 'fȯrt-\ *n* : a platform near the top of a ship's foremast

for·ev·er \fə-'rev-ər, fȯ-\ *adv* **1** : for a limitless time : EVERLASTINGLY **2** : ALWAYS 1, CONSTANTLY ⟨a dog that was *forever* chasing cars⟩

for·ev·er·more \fə-,rev-ə(r)-'mō(ə)r, -'mȯ(ə)r, fȯ-\ *adv* : FOREVER 1

fore·warn \fōr-'wȯ(ə)rn, fȯr-\ *vb* : to warn in advance ⟨*forewarned* of danger⟩

forewent *past of* [1]FOREGO

fore·wing \'fō(ə)r-,wiŋ, 'fȯ(ə)r-\ *n* : either of the front wings of a four-winged insect

fore·word \'fōr-(,)wərd, 'fȯr-\ *n* : [1]PREFACE

[1]for·feit \'fȯr-fət\ *n* : something forfeited : PENALTY, FINE

[2]forfeit *vb* : to lose or lose the right to as a punishment for an error, offense, or crime — **for·feit·er** *n*

for·fei·ture \'fȯr-fə-,chú(ə)r, -chər\ *n* **1** : the act of forfeiting **2** : something forfeited : PENALTY

for·gath·er *or* **fore·gath·er** \fȯr-'gath-ər, fōr-\ *vb* : to come together : ASSEMBLE, MEET

[1]forge \'fō(ə)rj, 'fȯ(ə)rj\ *n* : a furnace or a shop with its furnace where metal is shaped and worked by heating and hammering [Middle English *forge* "workshop where metal is heated and shaped", from early French *forge* (same meaning), from Latin *fabrica* "workshop for making things of metal"]

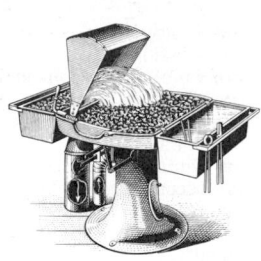

forge

[2]forge *vb* **forged; forg·ing** **1 a** : to form (as metal) by heating and hammering **b** : to form (metal) by a press **2** : to form or shape in any way : FASHION ⟨*forged* an agreement⟩ **3** : to make or imitate falsely especially with intent to deceive : COUNTERFEIT ⟨*forge* a check⟩ ⟨*forge* a signature⟩ — **forg·er** *n*

[3]forge *vb* **forged; forg·ing** : to move forward steadily but gradually ⟨*forged* through the snow⟩ [origin unknown]

forg·ery \'fȯrj-(ə-)rē, 'fȯrj-\ *n, pl* **-er·ies** **1** : the crime of falsely making or changing a written paper or signing someone else's name **2** : something (as a signature) that has been forged

for·get \fər-'get, fȯr-\ *vb* **-got** \-'gät\; **-got·ten** \-'gät-ə n\ *or* **-got; -get·ting** **1** : to be unable to think of or recall ⟨*forgot* the address⟩ **2 a** : to fail to remember to do something ⟨*forgot* to turn off the light⟩ ⟨*forgot* about paying the bill⟩ **b** : [1]NEGLECT 1 ⟨*forget* old friends⟩ — **for·get·ter** *n* — **forget oneself** : to lose one's temper or self-control

for·get·ful \fər-'get-fəl, fȯr-\ *adj* : forgetting easily — **for·get·ful·ly** \-fə-lē\ *adv* — **for·get·ful·ness** *n*

for·get—me—not \fər-'get-mē-,nät, fȯr-\ *n* : any of a genus of small herbs with bright blue or white flowers

forg·ing \'fȯr-jiŋ, 'fȯr-\ *n* : a piece of forged work ⟨aluminum *forgings*⟩

for·give \fər-'giv, fȯr-\ *vb* **-gave** \-'gāv\; **-giv·en** \-'giv-ən\; **-giv·ing** **1** : to stop feeling resentment against (an offender) ⟨*forgive* your enemies⟩ **2 a** : to give up resentment of or claim to revenge for ⟨*forgive* an insult⟩ **b** : to relieve a debtor of the duty to repay ⟨*forgive* a debt⟩ **syn** see EXCUSE — **for·giv·able** \-'giv-ə-bəl\ *adj* — **for·giv·er** *n*

for·give·ness \fər-'giv-nəs, fȯr-\ *n* : the act of forgiving : PARDON

for·giv·ing \fər-'giv-iŋ, fȯr-\ *adj* **1** : showing forgiveness : inclined or ready to forgive ⟨a person with a *forgiving* nature⟩ **2** : allowing for human error or weakness ⟨a tennis racket designed to be *forgiving*⟩ — **for·giv·ing·ly** *adv* — **for·giv·ing·ness** *n*

for·go *or* **fore·go** \fȯr-'gō, fōr-\ *vb* **-went** \-'went\; **-gone** \-'gȯn *also* -'gän\; **-go·ing** \-'gō-iŋ\ : to let pass : go without ⟨*forgo* lunch⟩ ⟨*forgo* an opportunity⟩

¹fork \'fȯ(ə)rk\ *n* **1** : a tool with two or more prongs used especially for taking up (as in eating), pitching, or digging **2** : a forked part or tool **3 a** : a dividing into branches or the place where something divides into branches ⟨a *fork* in the road⟩ **b** : a branch of a fork ⟨take the left *fork*⟩

²fork *vb* **1** : to divide into two or more branches ⟨the road *forks*⟩ **2** : to raise or pitch with a fork ⟨*fork* hay⟩ — **fork·er** *n*

forked \'fȯ(ə)rkt, 'fȯr-kəd\ *adj* : having a fork : shaped like a fork

fork·ful \'fȯ(ə)rk-,fu̇l\ *n, pl* **forkfuls** *or* **forks·ful** \'fȯ(ə)rks-,fu̇l\ : as much as a fork will hold

fork·lift \'fȯr-,klift\ *n* : a machine for lifting heavy objects by means of steel fingers inserted under the load

for·lorn \fər-'lȯrn, fȯr-\ *adj* **1** : feeling sad and lonely especially because of being left alone **2** : nearly hopeless ⟨a *forlorn* cause⟩ — **for·lorn·ly** *adv* — **for·lorn·ness** \-'lȯrn-nəs\ *n*

¹form \'fȯ(ə)rm\ *n* **1 a** : the shape and structure of something as distinguished from its material **b** : a body (as of a person) especially in its outward appearance or as distinguished from the face **2** : an established manner of doing or saying something ⟨a *form* of worship⟩ **3** : a document with blank spaces for inserting information ⟨a tax *form*⟩ **4 a** : conduct determined by custom : CEREMONY, CONVENTION; *also* : display without meaning **b** : manner of behaving according to recognized standards ⟨it's bad *form* not to wait for your turn⟩ **5** : a long seat : BENCH **6 a** : a model of the human figure used for displaying clothes **b** : a mold in which concrete is placed to set **7** : one of the different varieties of a particular thing or substance ⟨coal is a *form* of carbon⟩ **8 a** : orderly method of arrangement; *also* : a kind or instance of such arrangement ⟨painting is an art *form*⟩ **b** : the structural element, plan, or design of a work of art **9** : a bounded surface or volume **10** : a grade in a British secondary school or in some American private schools **11 a** : ability as shown by past performance **b** : condition for performing ⟨in top *form*⟩ **12** : any of the different pronunciations or spellings a word may take in inflection or compounding **13** : a special way of stating a mathematical expression ⟨the number 2.5 can be written in fractional *form* as ⁵⁄₂⟩

²form *vb* **1** : to give form or shape to : FASHION, MAKE ⟨*form* the letter A⟩ **2** : INSTRUCT 1, TRAIN ⟨education *forms* the mind⟩ **3** : DEVELOP 4, ACQUIRE ⟨*form* a habit⟩ **4** : MAKE UP 2, CONSTITUTE ⟨a hat *formed* of feathers⟩ **5** : to arrange in order ⟨*form* a line⟩ **6** : to take form : ARISE ⟨fog *forms* in the valleys⟩ **7** : to take a definite form, shape, or arrangement ⟨the customers *formed* in line⟩ **syn** *see* MAKE — **form·er** *n*

¹for·mal \'fȯr-məl\ *adj* **1** : of, relating to, or being the form of something rather than content **2 a** : following or agreeing with established form, custom, or rule **b** : relating to, suitable for, or being an event requiring elegant dress and manners ⟨a *formal* ball⟩ ⟨*formal* dress⟩ **3** : done in due or lawful form ⟨a *formal* contract⟩ — **for·mal·ly** \-mə-lē\ *adv*

²formal *n* : something (as a dance) formal in nature

form·al·de·hyde \fȯr-'mal-də-,hīd, fər-\ *n* : a colorless gas that consists of carbon, hydrogen, and oxygen, has a sharp irritating odor, and when dissolved in water is used to disinfect or to prevent decay

for·mal·ism \'fȯr-mə-,liz-əm\ *n* : the strict observance of forms or customs — **for·mal·ist** \-ləst\ *n* — **for·mal·is-**

tic \,fȯr-mə-'lis-tik\ *adj* — **for·mal·is·ti·cal·ly** \-ti-k(ə-)lē\ *adv*

for·mal·i·ty \fȯr-'mal-ət-ē\ *n, pl* **-ties** **1** : the quality or state of being formal **2** : a going along with formal or customary rules : CEREMONY **3** : an established form that is required or usual

for·mal·ize \'fȯr-mə-,līz\ *vb* **-ized; -iz·ing** **1** : to make formal **2** : to give formal rank or approval to — **for·mal·iz·er** *n*

¹for·mat \'fȯ(ə)r-,mat\ *n* : the general organization or arrangement of something

²format *vb* **for·mat·ted; for·mat·ting** : to produce in a particular format

for·ma·tion \fȯr-'mā-shən\ *n* **1** : a forming of something **2** : something formed **3** : the manner in which a thing is formed : STRUCTURE, SHAPE **4** : a bed of rocks or series of beds recognizable as a unit **5** : an arrangement or grouping of persons, ships, or airplanes

for·ma·tive \'fȯr-mət-iv\ *adj* **1** : giving or able to give form ⟨a *formative* influence⟩ **2** : of, relating to, or characterized by important growth or formation ⟨*formative* years⟩ — **for·ma·tive·ly** *adv* — **for·ma·tive·ness** *n*

for·mer \'fȯr-mər\ *adj* **1** : coming before in time **2** : first mentioned or first of two things mentioned or understood ⟨of the two choices the *former* is better⟩ **3** : having once been ⟨a *former* big-league ballplayer⟩

for·mer·ly \'fȯr-mər-lē\ *adv* : at an earlier time : PREVIOUSLY

for·mic acid \,fȯr-mik-\ *n* : a colorless strong-smelling acid that irritates the skin, is found in insects (as ants) and in many plants, and is used chiefly in dyeing and finishing woven fabrics

for·mi·da·ble \'fȯr-məd-ə-bəl *also* fȯr-'mid-\ *adj* **1** : causing fear or dread ⟨a *formidable* foe⟩ **2** : offering serious difficulties ⟨the mountains were a *formidable* barrier⟩ **3** : very impressive ⟨had won a *formidable* number of medals⟩ — **for·mi·da·ble·ness** *n* — **for·mi·da·bly** \-blē\ *adv*

form·less \'fȯrm-ləs\ *adj* : having no regular form or shape — **form·less·ly** *adv* — **form·less·ness** *n*

for·mu·la \'fȯr-myə-lə\ *n, pl* **-las** *or* **-lae** \-,lē, -,lī\ **1** : a set form of words for use in a ceremony or ritual **2 a** : RECIPE 3, PRESCRIPTION ⟨my *formula* for happiness⟩ **b** : a milk mixture or substitute for feeding a baby **3 a** : a general fact or rule expressed in symbols and especially mathematical symbols **b** : an expression in symbols of the composition of a substance ⟨the *formula* for water is H_2O⟩ **4** : a required or set form or method — **for·mu·la·ic** \,fȯr-myə-'lā-ik\ *adj* — **for·mu·la·ical·ly** \-'lā-ə-k(ə-)lē\ *adv*

for·mu·late \'fȯr-myə-,lāt\ *vb* **-lat·ed; -lat·ing** **1** : to express in a formula **2** : to put in systematic form : state definitely and clearly ⟨*formulate* a plan⟩ — **for·mu·la·tion** \,fȯr-myə-'lā-shən\ *n* — **for·mu·la·tor** \'fȯr-myə-,lāt-ər\ *n*

for·ni·ca·tion \,fȯr-nə-'kā-shən\ *n* : sexual intercourse between unmarried people

for·ni·cate \'fȯr-nə-,kāt\ *vb* **-cat·ed; -cat·ing** : to commit fornication — **for·ni·ca·tor** \-,kāt-ər\ *n*

for·sake \fər-'sāk, fȯr-\ *vb* **for·sook** \-'su̇k\; **for·sak·en** \-'sā-kən\; **for·sak·ing** : to give up or leave entirely **syn** *see* ABANDON

for·sooth \fər-'süth\ *adv* : in truth : INDEED

for·swear *or* **fore·swear** \fȯr-'swa(ə)r, fōr-, -'swe(ə)r\ *vb* **-swore** \-'swō(ə)r, -'swȯ(ə)r\; **-sworn** \-'swō(ə)rn, -'swȯ(ə)rn\; **-swear·ing** : to swear falsely : commit perjury

\ə\ abut	\au̇\ out	\i\ tip	\ȯ\ saw	\u̇\ foot
\ər\ further	\ch\ chin	\ī\ life	\ȯi\ coin	\y\ yet
\a\ mat	\e\ pet	\j\ job	\th\ thin	\yü\ few
\ā\ take	\ē\ easy	\ŋ\ sing	\th\ this	\yu̇\ cure
\ä\ cot, cart	\g\ go	\ō\ bone	\ü\ food	\zh\ vision

for·syth·ia \fər-'sith-ē-ə\ *n*
: any of a genus of shrubs related to the olive and having yellow bell-shaped flowers appearing before the leaves in early spring

fort \'fō(ə)rt, 'fó(ə)rt\ *n* **1** : a strong or fortified place **2** : a permanent army post

forsythia

¹forte \'fō(ə)rt, 'fó(ə)rt, 'fór-,tā\ *n* : something in which a person shows special ability : a strong point ⟨drawing was always your *forte*⟩ [from earlier *fort* "the thing a person does very well, strong point", from early French *fort* (same meaning), derived from Latin *fortis* "strong"]

²for·te \'fór-,tā, 'fort-ē\ *adv or adj* : in a loud manner — used as a direction in music [from Italian *forte* "strongly, loudly", from *forte* (adjective) "strong, loud", from Latin *fortis* "strong"]

forth \'fō(ə)rth, 'fó(ə)rth\ *adv* **1** : ²FORWARD, ONWARD ⟨from that time *forth*⟩ ⟨back and *forth*⟩ **2** : out into view ⟨plants putting *forth* leaves⟩

forth·com·ing \(')fōrth-'kəm-iŋ, (')fórth-\ *adj* **1** : being about to appear : APPROACHING ⟨the *forthcoming* holidays⟩ **2** : readily available ⟨supplies will be *forthcoming* soon⟩

forth·right \'fōrth-,rīt, 'fórth-\ *adj* : going straight to the point clearly and firmly ⟨a *forthright* answer⟩ — **forth·right·ly** *adv* — **forth·right·ness** *n*

forth·with \(')fōrth-'with, (')fórth-, -'with\ *adv* : IMMEDIATELY 2

for·ti·fi·ca·tion \,fórt-ə-fə-'kā-shən\ *n* **1** : the act of fortifying **2** : a construction built for defense

for·ti·fy \'fórt-ə-,fī\ *vb* **-fied; -fy·ing** : to make strong: as **a** : to strengthen by military defenses ⟨*fortify* a town⟩ **b** : to give strength or endurance to ⟨*fortify* the body against illness⟩ **c** : to add material to for strengthening or improving : ENRICH ⟨*fortify* a soil with fertilizer⟩ ⟨milk *fortified* with vitamin D⟩ — **for·ti·fi·er** \-,fī-(ə)r\ *n*

for·tis·si·mo \fór-'tis-ə-,mō\ *adv or adj* : very loudly — used as a direction in music

for·ti·tude \'fórt-ə-,t(y)üd\ *n* : strength of mind that enables a person to meet danger or bear pain or hardship with courage

fort·night \'fórt-,nīt, 'fórt-\ *n* : a period of 14 days : two weeks [Old English *fēowertȳne niht* "fourteen nights"] — **fort·night·ly** \-lē\ *adv or adj*

FOR·TRAN *or* **For·tran** \'fō(ə)r-,tran\ *n* : a language for programming a computer especially to solve mathematical, scientific, and engineering problems [*for*mula *tran*slation]

for·tress \'fór-trəs\ *n* : a fortified place

for·tu·i·tous \fór-'t(y)ü-ət-əs, fər-\ *adj* **1** : occurring by chance **2** : FORTUNATE 1 — **for·tu·i·tous·ly** *adv* — **for·tu·i·tous·ness** *n*

for·tu·nate \'fórch-(ə-)nət\ *adj* **1** : coming or happening by good luck : bringing good that was not expected **2** : receiving some unexpected or unearned good : LUCKY — **for·tu·nate·ness** *n*

for·tun·ate·ly \'fórch-(ə-)nət-lē\ *adv* : it is fortunate : LUCKILY ⟨*fortunately* it landed right side up⟩

for·tune \'fór-chən\ *n* **1 a** : favorable results that come partly by chance : good luck **b** : what happens to a person : good or bad luck ⟨follows the *fortunes* of two families through the years⟩ **2** : what is to happen to one in the future ⟨had my *fortune* told⟩ **3 a** : the possession of material goods : WEALTH **b** : a store of material possessions : RICHES ⟨the family *fortune*⟩ **c** : a large sum of money

for·tune–tell·er \-,tel-ər\ *n* : a person who claims to foretell future events — **for·tune–tell·ing** \-,tel-iŋ\ *n or adj*

for·ty \'fórt-ē\ *n, pl* **forties** — see NUMBER table — **for·ti·eth** \-ē-əth\ *adj or n* — **forty** *adj or pron*

for·ty–five \,fórt-ē-'fīv\ *n* : a 45 caliber pistol — usually written .45

for·ty–nin·er \,fórt-ē-'nī-nər\ *n* : a person who went to California in the gold rush of 1849

forty winks *n sing or pl* : a short sleep : NAP

fo·rum \'fōr-əm, 'fór-\ *n, pl* **forums** *also* **fo·ra** \-ə\ **1** : the marketplace or public place of an ancient Roman city serving as the center of public business **2** : a means (as a newspaper or television) of open discussion or expression of ideas **3** : a meeting or program involving discussion

¹for·ward \'fór-wərd\ *adj* **1** : near, being at, or belonging to the front part **2** : lacking proper modesty or reserve **3** : moving, tending, or leading to a position in front — **for·ward·ly** *adv* — **for·ward·ness** *n*

²forward *adv* : to or toward what is in front

³forward *vb* **1** : to help onward : PROMOTE ⟨*forward* a friend's career⟩ **2** : to send on or forward ⟨*forward* a letter⟩

⁴forward *n* : a player at or near the front of the team or near the opponent's goal

for·ward·er \'fór-wərd-ər\ *n* : one that forwards

forward pass *n* : a pass in football thrown in the direction of the opponents' goal

for·wards \'fór-wərdz\ *adv* : ²FORWARD

forwent *past of* FORGO

¹fos·sil \'fäs-əl\ *adj* : being or resembling a fossil

²fossil *n* **1** : a trace or print or the remains of a plant or animal of a past age preserved in earth or rock **2 a** : a person whose ideas are out-of-date **b** : something that has become fixed and cannot be changed

fossil fuel *n* : a fuel (as coal, oil, or natural gas) that is formed in the earth from plant or animal remains

fos·sil·ize \'fäs-ə-,līz\ *vb* **-ized; -iz·ing** : to change or become changed into a fossil — **fos·sil·iza·tion** \,fäs-ə-lə-'zā-shən\ *n*

¹fos·ter \'fós-tər, 'fäs-\ *adj* : giving, receiving, or sharing parental care even though not related by blood or legal ties ⟨*foster* parent⟩ ⟨*foster* child⟩ ⟨a *foster* home⟩

²foster *vb* **fos·tered; fos·ter·ing** \-t(ə-)riŋ\ **1** : to give parental care to **2** : to help the growth or development of — **fos·ter·er** \-tər-ər\ *n*

Fou·cault pendulum \,fü-,kō-\ *n* : a device that consists of a heavy weight hung by a long wire and that swings in a constant direction which appears to change showing that the earth rotates

fought *past and past participle of* FIGHT

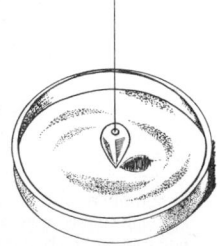

Foucault pendulum

¹foul \'faù(ə)l\ *adj* **1 a** : disgusting in looks, taste, or smell **b** : full of or covered with dirt **2** : being vulgar or insulting ⟨*foul* language⟩ **3** : being wet and stormy ⟨*foul* weather⟩ **4 a** : very unfair ⟨fair means or *foul*⟩ **b** : breaking a rule in a game or sport ⟨a *foul* blow in boxing⟩ **5** : being outside the foul lines in baseball ⟨a *foul* grounder⟩ **syn** see DIRTY — **foul** *adv* — **foul·ly** \'faù(l)-lē\ *adv* — **foul·ness** \'faù(ə)l-nəs\ *n*

²foul *n* **1** : an entanglement or collision in fishing or sailing **2 a** : a breaking of the rules in a game or sport **b** : FREE THROW **3** : FOUL BALL

³foul *vb* **1** : to make or become foul or filthy ⟨*foul* the air⟩ ⟨*foul* a stream⟩ **2 a** : to make a foul in a game or sport **b** : to hit a foul ball **3** : to become or cause to become entangled

⁴foul *adv* : so as to be foul

foul ball *n* : a baseball batted into foul territory

foul line *n* **1** : either of two straight lines running from the rear corner of home plate through first and third base on to the boundary of a baseball field **2** : a line across which a player must not step (as when bowling or shooting a free throw)

foul out *vb* : to be put out of a basketball game for making too many fouls ⟨three of our players *fouled out*⟩

foul play *n* : unfair dealing : dishonest conduct; *esp* : VIOLENCE 1 ⟨a victim of *foul play*⟩

foul shot *n* : a free throw in basketball

foul–up \'fau̇-,ləp\ *n* : an instance of fouling up : a state of being fouled up

foul up \(')fau̇-'ləp\ *vb* : to spoil by bad work or stupidity : BOTCH

¹found \'fau̇nd\ *past and past participle of* FIND

²found *vb* : ESTABLISH 3a ⟨*found* a colony⟩ ⟨*founded* the company in 1847⟩ ⟨*found* a museum⟩ [Middle English *founden* "found, establish", from early French *fondre* (same meaning), from Latin *fundare* (same meaning), from *fundus* "bottom, base" — related to ¹FOUNDER, ²FOUNDER, FUND, FUNDAMENTAL]

³found *vb* : to melt (metal) and pour into a mold [from early French *fondre* "to mix, melt", from Latin *fundere* "to pour melted metal into a mold" — related to ²FONT, ³FOUNDER]

foun·da·tion \fau̇n-'dā-shən\ *n* **1** : the act of founding **2** : the support upon which something rests ⟨a house with a cinder-block *foundation*⟩ ⟨suspicions with no *foundation* in fact⟩ **3** : funds given for the permanent support of an institution; *also* : an institution supported by such funds — **foun·da·tion·al** \-shnəl, -shən-ᵊl\ *adj*

¹found·er \'fau̇n-dər\ *n* : one that founds or establishes [Middle English *foundere* "one who establishes or builds", from early French *fondeor* (same meaning), derived from Latin *fundatus*, past participle of *fundare* "to found", from *fundus* "bottom, base" — related to ²FOUND, ²FOUNDER, FUND, FUNDAMENTAL]

²foun·der \'fau̇n-dər\ *vb* **foun·dered; foun·der·ing** \-d(ə-)riŋ\ **1** : to become lame ⟨the horse *foundered*⟩ **2** : to sink below the surface of the water ⟨a *foundering* ship⟩ [Middle English *foundren* "to knock down to the ground", from early French *fondrer* "to fall on the ground, send to the bottom (of water)", derived from Latin *fundus* "bottom" — related to ²FOUND, ¹FOUNDER, FUND, FUNDAMENTAL]

³found·er *n* : one that founds metal [Middle English *foundour, founder* "one that founds metal", derived from early French *fondre* "to mix, melt", from Latin *fundere* "to pour melted metal into a mold" — related to ²FONT, ³FOUND]

found·ling \'fau̇n-(d)liŋ\ *n* : an infant found after being abandoned by unknown parents

found·ry \'fau̇n-drē\ *n, pl* **foundries** : a building or factory where metals are cast

fount \'fau̇nt\ *n* : FOUNTAIN 2

foun·tain \'fau̇nt-ᵊn\ *n* **1** : a spring of water coming from the earth **2** : the source from which something comes ⟨a *fountain* of knowledge⟩ **3** : an artificial stream or spray of water (as for drinking or ornament); *also* : the device from which such a stream or spray rises [Middle English *fountain* "fountain", from early French *fontaine* (same meaning), derived from Latin *font-, fons* "fountain, spring" — related to ¹FONT]

foun·tain·head \'fau̇nt-ᵊn-,hed\ *n* **1** : a spring that is the source of a stream **2** : an original or primary source : ORIGIN ⟨the *fountainhead* of our liberties⟩ ⟨a *fountainhead* of wisdom⟩

fountain pen *n* : a pen with ink inside that is fed to the writing point as needed

four \'fō(ə)r, 'fȯ(ə)r\ *n* **1** — see NUMBER table **2** : the fourth in a set or series **3** : something having four units or members — **four** *adj or pron*

four–flush·er \'fōr-'fləsh-ər, 'fȯr-\ *n* : one who tries to bluff others : PRETENDER, PHONY

four·fold \-,fōld, -'fōld\ *adj* : being four times as great or as many

four–foot·ed \-'fu̇t-əd\ *adj* : having four feet : QUADRUPED

4–H \'fō(ə)r-'āch, 'fȯ(ə)r-\ *adj* : of or relating to a program supported in the U.S. by the U.S. Department of Agriculture to instruct young people in useful skills (as in agriculture) and in good citizenship ⟨*4-H* club⟩ [so called from the goal of improving a person in *head, heart, hands,* and *health*]

four–in–hand \'fōr-ən-,hand, 'fȯr-\ *n* : a necktie tied in a slipknot so that the ends overlap and hang down in front

four–o'clock \'fōr-ə-,kläk, 'fȯr-\ *n* : an American herb with fragrant yellow, red, or white flowers that open late in the afternoon

four–post·er \-'pō-stər\ *n* : a bed with tall posts at each corner

four·score \'fōr-'skō(ə)r, 'fȯr-'skȯ(ə)r\ *adj* : being four times twenty : EIGHTY

four·some \'fōr-səm, 'fȯr-\ *n* **1** : a group of four persons or things **2** : a golf match between two pairs of partners

four·square \'fōr-'skwa(ə)r, -'skwe(ə)r, 'fȯr-\ *adj* **1** : ²SQUARE 1a **2** : marked by boldness and firmness : FORTHRIGHT — **foursquare** *adv*

four·teen \(')fōr(t)-'tēn, (')fȯr(t)-\ *n* — see NUMBER table — **fourteen** *adj or pron* — **four·teenth** \-'tēn(t)th\ *adj or n*

fourth \'fō(ə)rth, 'fȯ(ə)rth\ *n* **1** — see NUMBER table **2** : the difference in pitch between the first tone and the fourth tone of a scale — **fourth** *adj or adv* — **fourth·ly** *adv*

fourth estate *n, often cap F & E* : the journalists of a country

Fourth of July : INDEPENDENCE DAY

four–wheel \-,fōr-,hwēl, -fȯr-,wēl\ *or* **four–wheeled** \'fōr-'hwē(ə)ld, 'fȯr-, -'wē(ə)ld\ *adj* **1** : having four wheels **2** : acting on or by means of four wheels ⟨a car with *four-wheel* drive⟩

fo·vea \'fō-vē-ə\ *n, pl* **fo·ve·ae** \-vē-,ē, -vē-,ī\ : an area in the middle of the retina that gives the sharpest vision of any part of the retina and contains only cones

¹fowl \'fau̇(ə)l\ *n, pl* **fowl** *or* **fowls** **1** : ¹BIRD 1: as **a** : a domestic cock or hen; *esp* : a full-grown hen **b** : any of several domesticated or wild birds related to the common domestic chicken **2** : the meat of fowl used as food

²fowl *vb* : to hunt, catch, or kill wildfowl — **fowl·er** *n*

fowling piece *n* : a light shotgun for shooting birds or small animals

¹fox \'fäks\ *n, pl* **fox·es** *also* **fox** **1 a** : any of various alert flesh-eating mammals related to the wolves but smaller and with shorter legs and a more pointed muzzle **b** : the fur of a fox **2** : a clever tricky person

²fox *vb* : OUTWIT

fox fire *n* : an eerie glow seen at night in woods and bogs that is caused by a fungus in decaying wood

fox·glove \'fäks-,gləv\ *n* : any of a genus of upright herbs related to the snapdragon; *esp* : a tall herb with showy dotted white or purple tube-shaped flowers that is a source of digitalis

fox·hole \-,hōl\ *n* : a pit dug usually in a hurry for individual cover against enemy fire

fox·hound \-,hau̇nd\ *n* : a large swift powerful hound of any of several breeds often trained to hunt foxes

fox·tail \-,tāl\ *n* **1** : the tail of a fox **2** : any of several grasses with spikes that resemble brushes

\ə\ **abut**		\au̇\ **out**		\i\ **tip**		\ȯ\ **saw**	\u̇\ **foot**
\ər\ **further**		\ch\ **chin**		\ī\ **life**		\ȯi\ **coin**	\y\ **yet**
\a\ **mat**		\e\ **pet**		\j\ **job**		\th\ **thin**	\yü\ **few**
\ā\ **take**		\ē\ **easy**		\ŋ\ **sing**		\th\ **this**	\yu̇\ **cure**
\ä\ **cot, cart**		\g\ **go**		\ō\ **bone**		\ü\ **food**	\zh\ **vision**

fox terrier *n* : a small lively terrier formerly used to dig out foxes and existing in smooth-haired and wire-haired varieties

fox terrier

foxy \'fäk-sē\ *adj* **fox·i·er; -est** **1** : resembling a fox in appearance **2** : cunning and careful in planning and action — **fox·i·ly** \-sə-lē\ *adv* — **fox·i·ness** \-sē-nəs\ *n*

foy·er \'fȯi(-ə)r, 'fȯi-,(y)ā\ *n* **1** : a lobby especially in a theater **2** : an entrance hall

fra·cas \'frā-kəs, 'frak-əs\ *n* : a noisy quarrel or fight

frac·tion \'frak-shən\ *n* **1** : a number (as ½ or ¾) that indicates one or more equal parts or the division of one number by another; *also* : a number (as 3.323) consisting of a whole number and a decimal **2** : a part of a whole

frac·tion·al \'frak-shnəl, -shən-ᵊl\ *adj* **1** : of, relating to, or being a fraction ⟨*fractional* equivalents of percentages⟩ **2** : fairly small — **frac·tion·al·ly** \-ē\ *adv*

frac·tion·ate \'frak-shə-,nāt\ *vb* **-at·ed; -at·ing** : to separate into different portions — **frac·tion·ation** \,frak-shə-'nā-shən\ *n*

frac·ture \'frak-chər, -shər\ *n* **1** : the act or process of breaking : the state of being broken; *esp* : the breaking of a bone **2** : the result of fracturing; *esp* : an injury resulting from fracture of a bone — **fracture** *vb*

frag·ile \'fraj-əl, -,īl\ *adj* : easily broken or destroyed : DELICATE — **fra·gil·i·ty** \frə-'jil-ət-ē\ *n*

frag·ment \'frag-mənt\ *n* **1** : a part that is broken off or incomplete **2** : SENTENCE FRAGMENT **syn** see PART — **frag·ment** \-,ment\ *vb*

frag·men·tal \frag-'ment-ᵊl\ *adj* : FRAGMENTARY

frag·men·tary \'frag-mən-,ter-ē\ *adj* : made up of fragments : INCOMPLETE

fra·grance \'frā-grən(t)s\ *n* : a sweet, pleasant, and often flowery or fruity smell

fra·grant \'frā-grənt\ *adj* : sweet or agreeable in smell — **fra·grant·ly** *adv*

frail \'frā(ə)l\ *adj* **1** : easily led into evil ⟨*frail* humanity⟩ **2** : FRAGILE **3** : not having normal strength or force **syn** see WEAK — **frail·ly** \'frā(ə)l-lē\ *adv* — **frail·ness** *n*

frail·ty \'frā(-ə)l-tē\ *n, pl* **frailties** **1** : the quality or state of being frail **2** : a weakness of character

¹frame \'frām\ *vb* **framed; fram·ing** **1 a** : ²PLAN 1 **b** : to give expression to ⟨*frame* a reply⟩ **c** : ¹SHAPE 1, CONSTRUCT **2** : to enclose in a frame ⟨*frame* a picture⟩ **3** : to make (an innocent person) appear guilty — **fram·er** *n*

²frame *n* **1** : the bodily structure of an animal and especially a human being : PHYSIQUE **2 a** : an arrangement of parts that gives form or support to something ⟨the *frame* of a house⟩ **b** : an open case or structure for holding or enclosing something ⟨a picture *frame*⟩ ⟨a window *frame*⟩ **c** : one picture of the series on a length of film or in a television transmission **3** : a particular state or mood ⟨in a good *frame* of mind⟩

³frame *adj* : having a wood frame ⟨*frame* houses⟩

frame–up \'frā-,məp\ *n* : a scheme to cause an innocent person to be accused of a crime

frame·work \'frām-,wərk\ *n* : a basic supporting part or structure

franc \'fraŋk\ *n* **1** : the basic unit of money of any of several countries (as France, Belgium, or Switzerland) **2** : a coin representing one franc

fran·chise \'fran-,chīz\ *n* **1** : the right to vote **2** : the right to sell a company's goods or services in a particular territory

fran·ci·um \'fran(t)-sē-əm\ *n* : a radioactive element obtained artificially by the bombardment of thorium with protons — see ELEMENT table

Franco- \'fran-kō\ *combining form* : French and ⟨*Franco*-German⟩ [derived from Latin *Francus* "Frenchman, Frank"]

fran·gi·pa·ni *also* **fran·gi·pan·ni** \,fran-jə-'pan-ē, -'pän-\ *n, pl* **-pani** *or* **-pani** *also* **-panis** *or* **-pannis** : any of several shrubs or small trees that have thick fleshy branches and large fragrant waxy-looking white, yellow, red, or pink twisted flowers and are native to the American tropics but are introduced elsewhere

frank \'fraŋk\ *adj* : free in speaking one's feelings and opinions — **frank·ness** *n*

Frank \'fraŋk\ *n* : a member of a people living in ancient Gaul — **Frank·ish** \'fraŋ-kish\ *adj*

frank·furt·er \'fraŋk-fə(r)t-ər\ *n* : a seasoned beef or beef and pork sausage [named for *Frankfurt am Main*, city in West Germany]

frank·in·cense \'fraŋ-kən-,sen(t)s\ *n* : a fragrant gum resin from African or Arabian trees that is burned as incense

Frank·lin stove \,fraŋ-klən-\ *n* : a metal heating stove that looks like a fireplace when its doors are open and is made to be set out in a room [named for Benjamin *Franklin* 1706–1790 American inventor]

frank·ly \'fraŋ-klē\ *adv* **1** : in a frank manner ⟨you can speak *frankly* to us⟩ **2** : to tell the truth ⟨*frankly*, I don't think it's wise⟩

fran·tic \'frant-ik\ *adj* **1** : wildly excited ⟨*frantic* cries for help⟩ ⟨was *frantic* with fear⟩ **2** : marked by wild and hurried activity ⟨a *frantic* search for the missing child⟩ — **fran·ti·cal·ly** \-i-k(ə-)lē\ *adv* — **fran·tic·ly** \-i-klē\ *adv*

fra·ter·nal \frə-'tərn-ᵊl\ *adj* **1 a** : of or relating to brothers **b** : of, relating to, or being a fraternity **2** : ¹KINDLY 2, FRIENDLY — **fra·ter·nal·ly** \-ᵊl-ē\ *adv*

fraternal twin *n* : either of a pair of twins that are produced from different fertilized eggs and may not have the same sex, appearance, or disposition

fra·ter·ni·ty \frə-'tər-nət-ē\ *n, pl* **-ties** **1** : a social, honorary, or professional organization; *esp* : a social club of male college students **2** : BROTHERHOOD 1, BROTHERLINESS

frat·er·nize \'frat-ər-,nīz\ *vb* **-nized; -niz·ing** : to associate as friends — **frat·er·ni·za·tion** \,frat-ər-nə-'zā-shən\ *n* — **frat·er·niz·er** \'frat-ər-,nī-zər\ *n*

fraud \'frȯd\ *n* **1 a** : TRICKERY, DECEIT; *esp* : the use of dishonest methods to cheat another person of something valuable **b** : an act of deceiving : TRICK **2** : a person who pretends to be what he or she is not

fraud·u·lent \'frȯ-jə-lənt\ *adj* : based on or done by fraud — **fraud·u·lent·ly** *adv* — **fraud·u·lent·ness** *n*

fraught \'frȯt\ *adj* : full of something specified ⟨*fraught* with danger⟩

¹fray \'frā\ *n* : ²FIGHT 1a, 1c, 2 [from earlier *fray* "fright", from *affray* "quarrel, fight", derived from early French *affreer* "to frighten" — related to AFRAID]

²fray *vb* **1 a** : to wear (as an edge of cloth) by or as if by rubbing **b** : to separate the threads at the edge of ⟨cutoff jeans with *frayed* edges⟩ **2** : to show or cause to show signs of strain ⟨nerves were beginning to *fray*⟩ [Middle English *fraien* "to fray", from early French *froyer*, *frayer* "to rub", from Latin *fricare* "to rub" — related to FRICTION]

fraz·zle \'fraz-əl\ *n* : a tired or nervous condition ⟨worn to a *frazzle*⟩

¹freak \'frēk\ *n* **1 a** : a sudden strange idea : WHIM **b** : a strange, abnormal, or unusual person, thing, or event **2** : ENTHUSIAST ⟨a movie *freak*⟩ — **freak·ish** \'frē-kish\ *adj* — **freak·ish·ly** *adv* — **freak·ish·ness** *n*

²freak *adj* : being or suggesting a freak : IMPROBABLE ⟨a *freak* accident⟩

³freak *vb* : to disturb one's calmness of mind : UPSET — usually used with *out* ⟨it *freaks* me out to think they would do that⟩

¹freck·le \'frek-əl\ *n* : a small brownish spot in the skin — **freck·ly** \-(ə-)lē\ *adv*

²freckle *vb* **freck·led; freck·ling** \'frek-(ə-)liŋ\ : to mark or become marked with freckles

¹free \'frē\ *adj* **fre·er** \'frē-ər\; **fre·est** \'frē-əst\ **1 a** : having liberty : not being a slave ⟨*free* citizens⟩ **b** : not controlled by others : INDEPENDENT ⟨a *free* country⟩ ⟨a *free* press⟩ **2 a** : released or not suffering from something unpleasant or painful ⟨*free* from worry⟩ ⟨*free* from disease⟩ **b** : not bound or contained by or as if by force ⟨you are *free* to leave⟩ **3** : having nothing that must be done instead ⟨I'm *free* tomorrow night⟩ **4 a** : not blocked : CLEAR **b** : not being used or occupied ⟨*free* time⟩ ⟨*free* memory in the computer⟩ **5** : not fastened ⟨put the *free* end of the tube in the water⟩ **6** : not cheap : GENEROUS ⟨a *free* spender⟩ **7** : not costing or charging anything ⟨*free* tickets⟩ **8** : not held back by fear or distrust : OPEN ⟨*free* expression of opinion⟩ **9** : not combined with something else ⟨*free* oxygen⟩ **10** : able to be used alone as a meaningful unit of language ⟨the word "hats" is a *free* form⟩ **11** : not restricted by or limited to the usual forms ⟨children are *freer* and more imaginative than adults in writing⟩ ⟨speech is *freer* than writing⟩ — **free·ly** *adv*

²free *adv* **1** : in a free manner **2** : without charge

³free *vb* **freed; free·ing** : to make or set free

free·bie *or* **free·bee** \'frē-bē\ *n* : something given or received without charge

free·board \'frē-,bō(ə)rd, -,bȯ(ə)rd\ *n* : the distance between the waterline and the upper edge of the side of a ship or boat

free·boo·ter \'frē-,büt-ər\ *n* : ¹PIRATE [partial translation (influenced by English *booty*) of Dutch *vrijbuiter* "one who robs people openly and with force", from *vrijbuit* "to rob openly especially with force", from *vrij* "free" and *buit* "stolen property, booty" — related to FILIBUSTER; see *Word History* at FILIBUSTER]

free·born \'frē-'bȯrn\ *adj* : not born in slavery

freed·man \'frēd-mən, -,man\ *n* : a person freed from slavery

free·dom \'frēd-əm\ *n* **1 a** : the state of being free : LIBERTY, INDEPENDENCE **b** : ability to move or act freely **c** : the state of being released from something unpleasant ⟨*freedom* from care⟩ **d** : the quality of being frank or open **e** : use without restriction ⟨has the *freedom* of the house⟩ **2** : a political right

free enterprise *n* : freedom of private business to operate with little regulation by the government

free–fall \'frē-'fȯl\ *n* : a condition of falling freely (as before opening one's parachute)

free–for–all \'frē-fə-,rȯl\ *n* : a competition or fight open to all comers usually without rules — **free–for–all** *adj*

free·hand \'frē-,hand\ *adj* : done without mechanical aids or devices ⟨*freehand* drawing⟩ — **freehand** *adv*

free hand *n* : freedom to act or decide

free·hand·ed \'frē-'han-dəd\ *adj* : GENEROUS 1

free–lance \'frē-,lan(t)s\ *adj* : working wherever jobs can be found rather than for one steady employer ⟨a *free-lance* writer⟩

free·man \'frē-mən, -,man\ *n* : a free person : one who is not a slave

free market *n* : an economic market operating by free competition

free on board *adv or adj* : delivered without charge onto a means of transportation

free–spo·ken \'frē-'spō-kən\ *adj* : speaking freely : OUTSPOKEN

free·stand·ing \-'stan-diŋ\ *adj* : standing alone on its own foundation free of attachment or support

free·stone \-,stōn\ *adj* : having or being a fruit stone to which the flesh does not stick when the fruit is split open ⟨*freestone* peaches⟩ — **freestone** *n*

free·style \-,stīl\ *n* : a competition (as a swimming race) in which the competitors are not restricted to a certain way of performing

free–swim·ming \-,swim-iŋ\ *adj* : able to swim about : not attached

free throw *n* : a basketball shot worth one point that must be made from behind a special line and is given because of a foul by an opponent

free trade *n* : trade between nations without restrictions (as high taxes on imports)

free verse *n* : verse whose rhythm is not smooth and even

free·way \'frē-,wā\ *n* : an expressway that can be used without paying tolls

free·wheel·ing \-'hwē(ə)l-iŋ, -'wē(ə)l-iŋ\ *adj* : not held back by rules, duties, or worries ⟨*freewheeling* adventures⟩ ⟨led a *freewheeling* life in the big city⟩

free·will \,frē-'wil\ *adj* : of or done by one's own free will : VOLUNTARY ⟨a *freewill* offering⟩

free will \'frē-'wil\ *n* : one's own choice or decision

¹freeze \'frēz\ *vb* **froze** \'frōz\; **fro·zen** \'frōz-ᵊn\; **freez·ing** **1** : to harden into or be hardened into a solid (as ice) by loss of heat ⟨the river *froze* over⟩ ⟨*freeze* the stew for dinner next week⟩ **2** : to be or become uncomfortably cold ⟨turn up the heat — I'm *freezing*⟩ **3 a** : to damage or kill by frost ⟨*froze* the tomato plants⟩ **b** : to anesthetize by cold **4** : to stick by or as if by freezing ⟨the clothes *froze* to the line⟩ ⟨fear *froze* the driver's hands to the wheel⟩ **5** : to clog or become clogged with ice ⟨the water pipes *froze*⟩ **6** : to make or become fixed or motionless ⟨the engine *froze*⟩ ⟨*froze* in their tracks⟩ **7** : to fix at a certain stage or level ⟨*freeze* prices⟩

²freeze *n* **1** : a state of weather marked by low temperature **2 a** : an act or instance of freezing ⟨a wage *freeze*⟩ **b** : the state of being frozen

freeze–dry \'frēz-'drī\ *vb* : to dry in a vacuum while frozen in order to preserve ⟨*freeze-dried* foods⟩

freez·er \'frē-zər\ *n* : a compartment, device, or room for freezing food or keeping it frozen

freezer burn *n* : a dried-out spot on frozen food (as meat) that has been frozen that results from improper wrapping

freezing point *n* : the temperature at which a liquid becomes solid

¹freight \'frāt\ *n* **1** : the amount paid (as to a shipping company) for carrying goods **2 a** : goods or cargo carried by ship, train, truck, or airplane **b** : the carrying of goods from one place to another by vehicle ⟨ship the order by *freight*⟩ **3** : a train that carries freight

²freight *vb* **1** : to load for transportation **2** : to ship by freight

freight·er \'frāt-ər\ *n* **1** : a person who carries or ships freight **2** : a ship or airplane used chiefly to carry freight

¹French \'french\ *adj* : of or relating to France, its people, or their language

²French *n* **1** : the Romance language of the French **2** **French** *pl* : the people of France

French bread *n* : a crusty bread usually baked in long thin loaves

French Canadian *n* : a person whose ancestors were

French settlers in what is now the province of Quebec — **French–Canadian** *adj*

French cuff *n* : a shirt cuff that folds over and is fastened by cuff links

French door *n* : a door with small panes of glass extending the full length

French dressing *n* **1** : a thin salad dressing usually made of vinegar and oil with spices **2** : a creamy salad dressing flavored with tomatoes

¹french fry *vb, often cap 1st F* : to fry in deep fat until brown

²french fry *n, often cap 1st F* : a strip of potato fried in deep fat

French horn *n* : a circular brass musical instrument with a large opening at one end and a mouthpiece shaped like a small funnel

French·man \'french-mən\ *n* : a person who is French

French provincial *n, often cap P* : a style (as of furniture) based on styles popular in the French provinces in the 17th and 18th centuries

French horn

French toast *n* : bread dipped in a mixture of eggs and milk and fried at low heat

French window *n* : a pair of windows with small panes that reach to the floor and open in the middle like doors

French·wom·an \'french-ˌwu̇m-ən\ *n* : a woman who is French

fre·net·ic \fri-'net-ik\ *adj* : FRENZIED, FRANTIC — **fre·net·i·cal·ly** \-'net-i-k(ə-)lē\ *adv*

fren·zied \'fren-zēd\ *adj* : very excited or upset — **fren·zied·ly** *adv*

fren·zy \'fren-zē\ *n, pl* **frenzies** : great and often wild or disorderly activity

Fre·on \'frē-ˌän\ *trademark* — used for any of various chlorofluorocarbons

fre·quen·cy \'frē-kwən-sē\ *n, pl* **-cies** **1** : the fact or condition of happening often **2** : how often something happens : rate of repetition **3** : the number of repetitions of a periodic process in a unit of time: as **a** : the number of times per second that an electric current flowing in one direction changes direction then changes back ⟨a current having a *frequency* of 60 hertz⟩ **b** : the number of waves (as of sound or electromagnetic energy) that pass a fixed point each second ⟨a sound having a *frequency* of 1500 hertz⟩ ⟨the *frequency* of yellow light⟩ **4** : the number or proportion of items in a class especially in relation to the whole ⟨the *frequency* of the birth of twins⟩

frequency distribution *n* : an arrangement of statistical data that shows the frequency of the occurrence of the values of a variable

frequency modulation *n* : variation of the frequency of the carrier wave according to the strength of the audio or video signal; *also* : the system of broadcasting using this method of modulation

¹fre·quent \'frē-kwənt\ *adj* **1** : happening often ⟨made *frequent* trips to town⟩ **2** : ¹REGULAR 3b, HABITUAL ⟨a *frequent* visitor to the museum⟩ — **fre·quent·ly** *adv* — **fre·quent·ness** *n*

²fre·quent \frē-'kwent, 'frē-kwənt\ *vb* : to visit, associate with, or go to often ⟨*frequents* the library⟩ — **fre·quent·er** *n*

fres·co \'fres-kō\ *n, pl* **frescoes** **1** : the art of painting on freshly spread moist plaster **2** : a painting done in fresco [Italian, from *fresco* "fresh"]

fresh \'fresh\ *adj* **1 a** : not salt ⟨*fresh* water⟩ **b** : ¹PURE 1, INVIGORATING ⟨*fresh* air⟩ **c** : fairly strong : BRISK ⟨*fresh* breeze⟩ **2 a** : not frozen, canned, or pickled ⟨*fresh* fish⟩ **b** : not stale, sour, or spoiled ⟨*fresh* bread⟩ **c** : not worn, dirty, or rumpled ⟨a *fresh* shirt⟩ **3 a** : newly made or received ⟨a *fresh* wound⟩ **b** : ¹NEW 6 ⟨make a *fresh* start⟩ **c** : remaining clear or vivid ⟨*fresh* in my mind⟩ **4** : IMPUDENT **syn** see NEW — **fresh·ly** *adv* — **fresh·ness** *n*

fresh·en \'fresh-ən\ *vb* **fresh·ened**; **fresh·en·ing** \-(ə-)niŋ\ **1** : to make or become fresh : REFRESH ⟨*freshen* up with a shower⟩ **2** : to become brisk or strong ⟨the wind *freshened*⟩ **3** : to brighten in appearance ⟨*freshen* up a room with a spot of color⟩ — **fresh·en·er** \-(ə-)nər\ *n*

fresh·et \'fresh-ət\ *n* : a sudden overflowing of a stream

fresh·man \'fresh-mən\ *n* **1** : BEGINNER, NEWCOMER **2** : a student in the first year (as of college)

fresh·wa·ter \ˌfresh-ˌwȯt-ər, -ˌwät-\ *adj* : of, relating to, or living in fresh water

¹fret \'fret\ *vb* **fret·ted**; **fret·ting** **1** : to make or become worried ⟨*fret* over a problem⟩ **2** : to eat into or wear away ⟨adobe *fretted* clean by wind and sand⟩ [Old English *fretan* "to devour"]

²fret *n* : an irritated or worried state ⟨in a *fret*⟩

³fret *n* : an ornamental design of short lines or bars [Middle English *fret* "an ornamental design, fret", from early French *frete* "an interwoven design"]

⁴fret *n* : one of a series of ridges fixed across the fingerboard of a stringed musical instrument — **fret·less** \'fret-ləs\ *adj* — **fret·ted** \'fret-əd\ *adj*

³fret

fret·ful \'fret-fəl\ *adj* : likely to fret : IRRITABLE — **fret·ful·ly** \-fə-lē\ *adv* — **fret·ful·ness** *n*

fret·work \'fret-ˌwərk\ *n* : decoration consisting of frets

fri·a·ble \'frī-ə-bəl\ *adj* : easily crumbled or broken up — **fri·a·bil·i·ty** \ˌfrī-ə-'bil-ət-ē\ *n*

fri·ar \'frī(-ə)r\ *n* : a member of a Roman Catholic religious order for men

fri·ary \'frī-(ə-)rē\ *n, pl* **-ar·ies** : a monastery of friars

¹fric·as·see \'frik-ə-ˌsē, ˌfrik-ə-'\ *n* : a dish of meat (as chicken) cut into pieces and stewed in a gravy

²fricassee *vb* **-seed**; **-see·ing** : to cook as a fricassee

fric·tion \'frik-shən\ *n* **1 a** : the rubbing of one thing against another **b** : the force that resists motion between bodies in contact ⟨the *friction* of a box sliding along the floor⟩ ⟨lubrication reduces *friction*⟩ **2** : disagreement between persons or groups [Middle English *friction* "a rubbing of two things together, friction", from early French *friction* or Latin *friction-, frictio* (both same meaning), derived from Latin *fricare* "to rub" — related to ²FRAY] — **fric·tion·al** \-shnəl, -shən-°l\ *adj* — **fric·tion·al·ly** \-ē\ *adv* — **fric·tion·less** \-ləs\ *adj*

Fri·day \'frīd-ē\ *n* : the sixth day of the week

Word History The Germanic people of northern Europe worshiped many gods and goddesses in ancient times. Their most important goddess was one who is now usually known as *Frigga*. Her name in Old English was *Frig*, and the sixth day of the week was called *frīgedæg*, meaning "day of Frig", in her honor. The modern English *Friday* comes from the Old English *frīgedæg*. [Old English *frīgedæg*, literally, "day of Frig"]

friend \'frend\ *n* **1** : a person who has a strong liking for and trust in another **2** : a person who is not an enemy ⟨are you *friend* or foe⟩ **3** : a person who aids or favors something **4** *cap* : a member of a Christian group that stresses Inner Light, rejects sacraments and an ordained ministry, and opposes war — **friend·less** \-ləs\ *adj* —

friend·less·ness n

¹**friend·ly** \'fren-dlē\ adj **friend·li·er; -est** : of, relating to, or right for a friend: as **a** : showing kindly interest and goodwill ⟨a *friendly* gesture⟩ **b** : not being an enemy **c** : HELPFUL, FAVORABLE ⟨a *friendly* breeze⟩ **d** : bringing comfort or cheer ⟨the *friendly* glow of the fire⟩ — **friend·li·ness** n

²**friendly** n, pl **friend·lies** : a person who is friendly or cooperative

friend·ship \'fren(d)-,ship\ n : the state of being friends

frier variant of FRYER

frieze \'frēz\ n : a sculptured or ornamental band (as around a building)

frig·ate \'frig-ət\ n **1** : a medium-sized square-rigged warship **2** : a warship that is smaller than a destroyer and that is used for escort and patrol duties

frigate bird n : any of several seabirds noted for their power of flight and the habit of robbing other birds of fish — called also man-o'-war bird

frieze

fright \'frīt\ n **1** : fear caused by sudden danger : sudden terror ⟨cry out in *fright*⟩ **2** : something that is strange, ugly, or shocking ⟨your hair looks a *fright*⟩ **syn** see FEAR

fright·en \'frīt-ᵊn\ vb **fright·ened; fright·en·ing** \'frīt-niŋ, -ᵊn-iŋ\ **1** : to make afraid : TERRIFY **2** : to drive away or out by frightening **3** : to become frightened — **fright·en·ing·ly** \-niŋ-lē, -ᵊn-iŋ-\ adv

fright·ful \'frīt-fəl\ adj **1** : causing fear or alarm **2** : causing shock or horror ⟨the *frightful* cost of war⟩ **3** : very strong ⟨a *frightful* thirst⟩ — **fright·ful·ly** \-fə-lē\ adv — **fright·ful·ness** n

frig·id \'frij-əd\ adj **1** : freezing cold **2** : not friendly — **fri·gid·i·ty** \frij-'id-ət-ē\ n — **frig·id·ly** \'frij-əd-lē\ adv — **frig·id·ness** n

frigid zone n : the area or region between the arctic circle and the north pole or between the antarctic circle and the south pole — compare TEMPERATE ZONE, TORRID ZONE

fri·jo·le \frē-'hō-lē\ n : any of various beans used in Mexican-style cooking [American Spanish, from Spanish *frijol* "bean"]

frill \'fril\ n **1** : ²RUFFLE 2a **2** : something added mostly for show **3** : a thick fringe of hair or feathers about the neck of an animal

frilly \'fril-ē\ adj **frill·i·er; -est** : having or resembling frills

¹**fringe** \'frinj\ n **1** : an ornamental border consisting of hanging threads or strips **2** : something suggesting a fringe ⟨lived on the *fringe* of the forest⟩

²**fringe** vb **fringed; fring·ing** **1** : to provide or decorate with a fringe ⟨*fringed* a buckskin jacket⟩ **2** : to serve as a fringe for : BORDER ⟨a jungle *fringed* the shore⟩

fringe benefit n : a benefit (as vacation, health insurance, or pension plan) given by an employer to employees in addition to pay

fringy \'frin-jē\ adj : decorated with fringes

frip·pery \'frip-(ə-)rē\ n, pl **-per·ies** **1** : showy or frilly clothing **2** : something that is not necessary, not serious, or not important

Fris·bee \'friz-bē\ trademark — used for a plastic disc sailed between players by a flip of the wrist

frisk \'frisk\ vb **1** : to move around in a lively or playful way **2** : to search (a person) quickly especially for concealed weapons — **frisk·er** n

frisky \'fris-kē\ adj **frisk·i·er; -est** : tending to frisk : PLAYFUL, LIVELY — **frisk·i·ly** \-kə-lē\ adv — **frisk·i·ness** \-kē-nəs\ n

frit·il·lary \'frit-ᵊl-,er-ē\ n, pl **-laries** : any of numerous but-terflies that are usually orange with black spots on the upper side of both wings and silver spotted on the underside of the hind wing

¹**frit·ter** \'frit-ər\ n : a small lump of fried batter often containing fruit or meat

²**fritter** vb : to spend or use up bit by bit especially on worthless things — usually used with *away* — **frit·ter·er** \-ər-ər\ n

friv·ol \'friv-əl\ vb **-oled** or **-olled; -ol·ing** or **-ol·ling** \-(ə-)liŋ\ : ²TRIFLE 1b

fri·vol·i·ty \friv-'äl-ət-ē\ n, pl **-ties** **1** : the quality or state of being frivolous **2** : a frivolous act or thing

friv·o·lous \'friv-(ə-)ləs\ adj **1** : of little importance : TRIVIAL **2** : lacking in seriousness : PLAYFUL — **friv·o·lous·ly** adv — **friv·o·lous·ness** n

friz·zle \'friz-əl\ vb **friz·zled; friz·zling** \-(ə-)liŋ\ : to fry until crisp and curled

frizzy \'friz-ē\ adj **frizz·i·er; -est** : tightly curled

fro \'frō\ adv : in a direction away — used in the phrase *to and fro*

frock \'fräk\ n **1** : a long outer garment worn by monks and friars **2** : a woman's or girl's dress

frock coat n : a man's long overcoat

frog \'frȯg, 'fräg\ n **1 a** : any of various tailless animals with smooth skin and webbed feet that are classified as amphibians and spend more of their time in the water than the related toads **b** : a hoarse condition ⟨have a *frog* in one's throat⟩ **2** : an ornamental fastening for a garment (as a jacket)

frog 2

frog·man \-,man, -mən\ n : a swimmer equipped to work underwater for long periods of time

¹**frol·ic** \'fräl-ik\ n **1** : a playful or mischievous action **2** : a good time : FUN

²**frolic** vb **frol·icked; frol·ick·ing** : to play about happily : ROMP

frol·ic·some \'fräl-ik-səm\ adj : full of high spirits : given to frolic : PLAYFUL, FRISKY

from \(')frəm, 'främ\ prep **1** — used to show a starting point ⟨came here *from* the city⟩ ⟨a letter *from* home⟩ ⟨a farmer *from* way back⟩ **2** — used to show removal or separation ⟨the dictator fell *from* power⟩ ⟨subtract 3 *from* 9⟩ ⟨far *from* safe⟩ **3** — used to show a material, source, or cause ⟨a doll made *from* rags⟩ ⟨reading aloud *from* a book⟩ ⟨suffering *from* a cold⟩

frond \'fränd\ n : a large leaf especially of a fern or palm tree that often has many divisions

¹**front** \'frənt\ n **1** : outer often pretended appearance ⟨put up a good *front*⟩ **2** : a region in which active warfare is taking place **3** : the forward part or surface ⟨the *front* of a shirt⟩ ⟨the *front* of the house⟩ **4** : the boundary between two dissimilar air masses **5** : someone or something that hides the true identity of those who are in control ⟨a *front* for organized crime⟩ — **in front of** : directly ahead of ⟨the car *in front of* ours⟩

²**front** vb : to have the front or face toward ⟨the cottage *fronts* on the lake⟩ ⟨the house *fronts* the street⟩

³**front** adj : of, relating to, or situated at the front

front·age \'frənt-ij\ n : the front boundary line of a lot or its

\ə\ abut	\au\ out	\i\ tip	\ȯ\ saw	\u̇\ foot
\ər\ further	\ch\ chin	\ī\ life	\ȯi\ coin	\y\ yet
\a\ mat	\e\ pet	\j\ job	\th\ thin	\yü\ few
\ā\ take	\ē\ easy	\ŋ\ sing	\th\ this	\yu̇\ cure
\ä\ cot, cart	\g\ go	\ō\ bone	\ü\ food	\zh\ vision

length

front·al \'frɔnt-ᵊl\ *adj* **1** : of, relating to, or next to the forehead **2** : of, relating to, or directed at the front ⟨a *frontal* attack⟩ — **fron·tal·ly** \-ᵊl-ē\ *adv*

fron·tier \ˌfrən-'ti(ə)r, frän-\ *n* **1** : a border between two countries **2 a** : a region that forms the edge of the settled part of a country **b** : the outer limits of knowledge or achievement ⟨the *frontiers* of science⟩ — **frontier** *adj*

fron·tiers·man \ˌfrən-'ti(ə)rz-mən, frän-\ *n* : a person living on the frontier

fron·tis·piece \'frənt-ə-ˌspēs\ *n* : an illustration facing the title page of a book

¹frost \'frȯst\ *n* **1** : the temperature that causes freezing **2** : a covering of tiny ice crystals on a cold surface

²frost *vb* **1 a** : to cover with or as if with frost; *esp* : to put icing on (as cake) **b** : to give a surface that looks like frost to **2** : to injure or kill by frost : FREEZE

¹frost·bite \'frȯs(t)-ˌbīt\ *vb* **-bit** \-ˌbit\; **-bit·ten** \-ˌbit-ᵊn\; **-bit·ing** \-ˌbīt-iŋ\ : to injure by frost or frostbite

²frostbite *n* : the freezing or the local effect of a partial freezing of some part of the body

frost·free \ˌfrȯs(t)-ˌfrē\ *adj* : needing no defrosting ⟨a *frost-free* refrigerator⟩

frost·ing \'frȯ-stiŋ\ *n* **1** : ICING **2** : a dull finish on metal or glass

frost·work \'frȯs-ˌtwərk\ *n* : the design made by moisture freezing on a surface (as a window)

frosty \'frȯ-stē\ *adj* **frost·i·er; -est** **1** : cold enough to produce frost ⟨a *frosty* night⟩ **2** : covered or appearing to be covered with frost ⟨a *frosty* glass⟩ **3** : cool in manner — **frost·i·ly** \-stə-lē\ *adv* — **frost·i·ness** \-stē-nəs\ *n*

¹froth \'frȯth\ *n* **1 a** : bubbles formed in or on a liquid **b** : the foam produced by saliva in certain diseases or nervous excitement **2** : something of little value — **froth·i·ly** \'frȯ-thə-lē\ *adv* — **froth·i·ness** \-thē-nəs\ *n* — **frothy** \-thē\ *adj*

²froth \'frȯth, 'frȯth\ *vb* **1** : to foam at the mouth **2** : to produce or form froth

fro·ward \'frō-(w)ərd\ *adj* : likely to disobey and oppose : WILLFUL — **fro·ward·ly** *adv* — **fro·ward·ness** *n*

¹frown \'fraun\ *vb* **1** : to wrinkle the forehead (as in anger or thought) **2** : to look with disapproval ⟨*frowns* on rudeness⟩ — **frown·er** *n* — **frown·ing·ly** \'frau-niŋ-lē\ *adv*

²frown *n* : a wrinkling of the brow in displeasure or thought

frow·sy *or* **frow·zy** \'frau-zē\ *adj* **frow·si·er** *or* **frow·zi·er; -est** : having an untidy appearance

froze *past of* ¹FREEZE

frozen *past participle of* ¹FREEZE

fruc·tose \'frək-ˌtōs, 'frük-\ *n* : a very sweet sugar that dissolves easily and occurs especially in fruit juices and honey — called also *levulose*

fru·gal \'frü-gəl\ *adj* : careful in spending or using resources — **fru·gal·i·ty** \frü-'gal-ət-ē\ *n* — **fru·gal·ly** \'frü-gə-lē\ *adv*

> **syn** FRUGAL, THRIFTY, ECONOMICAL mean careful with money and other resources. FRUGAL suggests a simple lifestyle that is lacking in luxuries ⟨a *frugal* woman who seldom allowed herself even small pleasures⟩ THRIFTY suggests a habit of saving and an avoidance of wastefulness ⟨*thrifty* shoppers looking for bargains⟩ ECONOMICAL suggests the wise management of one's resources ⟨*economical* cooks use everything and waste nothing⟩

¹fruit \'früt\ *n* **1** : a usually useful product of plant growth ⟨*fruits* of the earth⟩ **2 a** : the usually edible reproductive body of a seed plant; *esp* : one (as a strawberry or apple) having a sweet pulp **b** : a juicy plant part (as of the rhubarb or strawberry) used chiefly as a dessert or sweet course **3** : a product of fertilization in a plant with its coverings or associated parts; *esp* : the ripened ovary of a plant (as the pod of a pea, a nut, a grain, or a berry) with or without the attached parts **4** : ²RESULT 1, PRODUCT ⟨the *fruits* of our labors⟩ — **fruit·ed** \-əd\ *adj*

²fruit *vb* : to bear or cause to bear fruit

fruit bat *n* : any of numerous large Old World fruit-eating bats of warm regions — called also *flying fox*

fruit·cake \'früt-ˌkāk\ *n* : a rich cake containing nuts, dried or candied fruits, and spices

fruit fly *n* : any of various small two-winged flies whose larvae feed on fruit or decaying vegetable matter

fruit·ful \'früt-fəl\ *adj* **1** : yielding or producing fruit **2 a** : very productive ⟨a *fruitful* soil⟩ **b** : bringing results ⟨a *fruitful* idea⟩ **syn** see FERTILE — **fruit·ful·ly** \-fə-lē\ *adv* — **fruit·ful·ness** *n*

fruiting body *n* : a plant organ specialized for producing spores

fru·i·tion \frü-'ish-ən\ *n* **1** : the state of bearing fruit **2** : the state of being real or complete : REALIZATION, ACCOMPLISHMENT ⟨brought her dreams to *fruition*⟩

fruit·less \'früt-ləs\ *adj* **1** : not bearing fruit **2** : producing no good results : UNSUCCESSFUL ⟨a *fruitless* attempt⟩ — **fruit·less·ly** *adv* — **fruit·less·ness** *n*

fruit sugar *n* : FRUCTOSE

fruity \'früt-ē\ *adj* **fruit·i·er; -est** : relating to or suggesting fruit ⟨a *fruity* smell⟩

frus·trate \'frəs-ˌtrāt\ *vb* **frus·trat·ed; frus·trat·ing** **1** : to prevent from carrying out a purpose ⟨tried to *frustrate* his opponents in their efforts⟩ **2** : to bring to nothing ⟨the accident *frustrated* the plan⟩

> **syn** FRUSTRATE, THWART, FOIL, OUTWIT mean to check or defeat another's plan or prevent achievement of a goal. FRUSTRATE suggests the causing of failure despite determined or repeated efforts ⟨lack of education *frustrated* him in his attempt to find a job⟩ THWART suggests checking another's plan by deliberately opposing it ⟨at every turn they were *thwarted* by the enemy⟩ FOIL suggests checking or defeating that discourages further attempts ⟨went out of business after every effort to raise money was *foiled* by poor credit⟩ OUTWIT suggests the use of slyness or cunning to defeat others ⟨*outwitted* the waiting reporters by leaving from the roof in a helicopter⟩

frus·trat·ing *adj* : producing frustration

frus·tra·tion \(ˌ)frəs-'trā-shən\ *n* **1 a** : an act of frustrating **b** : a state or an instance of being frustrated **2** : a feeling of being unable to get anything done **3** : something that frustrates

¹fry \'frī\ *vb* **fried; fry·ing** : to cook in fat or oil [Middle English *frien* "to fry", from early French *frire* (same meaning), from Latin *frigere* "to fry"]

²fry *n, pl* **fries** **1** : something fried; *esp* : ²FRENCH FRY — usually used in pl. ⟨steak and *fries*⟩ **2** : a get-together where fried food is eaten ⟨a fish *fry*⟩

³fry *n, pl* **fry** **1 a** : recently hatched fish **b** : the young of animals other than fish **2** : very small adult fish **3** : members of a group or class : INDIVIDUALS ⟨small *fry*⟩ [Middle English *fry* "recently hatched fish"; probably of Norse origin]

fry bread *n* : quick bread cooked in deep fat

fry·er *also* **fri·er** \'frī(-ə)r\ *n* **1** : something (as a young chicken) suitable for frying **2** : a deep utensil for frying foods

frying pan *n* : a metal pan with a handle for frying foods

fry pan *n* : FRYING PAN

F₂ layer \'ef-ˌtü-\ *n* : a layer of the ionosphere that occurs during the day from 200 to more than 500 kilometers in altitude

fuch·sia \'fyü-shə\ *n* **1** : any of a genus of shrubs related to the evening primrose and having showy nodding flowers usually in deep pinks, reds, and purples **2** : a vivid reddish purple

fuch·sin *or* **fuch·sine** \'fyük-sən, -ˌsēn\ *n* : a synthetic dye that yields a brilliant bluish red

fu·cus \'fyü-kəs\ *n* : any of various brown algae common along rocky shores

fud·dy–dud·dy \'fəd-ē-ˌdəd-ē\ *n, pl* **-dies** : a person who is old-fashioned, very cautious, or fussy [probably from *fuddy,* a word in Scottish dialect meaning "short-tailed animal" and *duddy* (a word to rhyme with *fuddy*)]

¹fudge \'fəj\ *vb* **fudged; fudg·ing**   **1** : to go beyond proper limits : cheat a little ⟨*fudged* on the rules⟩ ⟨*fudged* the figures⟩   **2** : to avoid being open or direct : HEDGE ⟨politicians *fudging* on the issues⟩

²fudge *n*   **1** : foolish nonsense   **2** : a soft creamy candy often containing nuts

¹fu·el \'fyü(-ə)l\ *n*   **1 a** : a material used to produce heat or power by burning   **b** : a material from which atomic energy can be produced especially in a reactor   **2** : a source of energy

²fuel *vb* **-eled** *or* **-elled; -el·ing** *or* **-el·ling** : to supply with or take in fuel

fuel cell *n* : a device that continuously changes the chemical energy of a fuel (as hydrogen) into electrical energy

fuel oil *n* : an oil that is used for fuel and that usually ignites at a higher temperature than kerosene

¹fu·gi·tive \'fyü-jət-,iv\ *n* : one who is running away [Middle English *fugitif, fugitive* "one who is running away", from early French *fugitif* and Latin *fugitivus* (both, same meaning), from Latin *fugitus,* past participle of *fugere* "to run away, flee" — related to CENTRIFUGAL, REFUGEE]

²fugitive *adj*   **1** : running away or trying to run away ⟨a *fugitive* slave⟩   **2** : likely to vanish suddenly : not fixed or lasting ⟨*fugitive* thoughts⟩ — **fu·gi·tive·ly** *adv* — **fu·gi·tive·ness** *n*

fugue \'fyüg\ *n*   **1** : a musical composition in which themes are introduced and then developed and interwoven through different instrumental parts   **2** : a disturbed state of mind in which a person does things of which he or she seems to be aware but does not remember upon return to the normal state — **fu·gal** \'fyü-gəl\ *adj*

¹-ful \fəl\ *adj suffix*   **1** : full of ⟨joy*ful*⟩   **2** : characterized by ⟨peace*ful*⟩   **3** : having the qualities of ⟨master*ful*⟩   **4** : tending, given, or liable to ⟨mourn*ful*⟩ [Old English *-ful* "full"]

²-ful \,fúl\ *n suffix* : number or quantity that fills or would fill ⟨room*ful*⟩

ful·crum \'fúl-krəm, 'fəl-\ *n, pl* **fulcrums** *or* **ful·cra** \-krə\ : the support about which a lever turns

F fulcrum

ful·fill *or* **ful·fil** \fúl-'fil\ *vb* **ful·filled; ful·fill·ing**   **1** : ACCOMPLISH ⟨fulfill a promise⟩   **2** : to measure up to : SATISFY ⟨fulfill requirements⟩ — **ful·fill·er** *n* — **ful·fill·ment** \-mənt\ *n*

¹full \'fúl\ *adj*   **1** : containing as much or as many as possible or normal ⟨a bottle *full* of milk⟩ ⟨when the disk is *full* and will take no more data⟩   **2 a** : complete in number, amount, or duration ⟨a *full* set of dishes⟩ ⟨for a *full* hour⟩   **b** : not missing any essentials   **c** : being at the highest or greatest degree ⟨in *full* bloom⟩ ⟨at *full* power⟩ ⟨*full* strength⟩   **3 a** : plump and rounded in outline ⟨a *full* face⟩   **b** : having much material ⟨a *full* skirt⟩   **4** : possessing or containing a great number or amount ⟨a room *full* of pictures⟩ ⟨*full* of hope⟩   **5** : satisfied especially with food or drink   **6** : having the same parents ⟨*full* sisters⟩   **7** : completely taken up especially with a thought or plan ⟨*full* of one's own concerns⟩ ⟨*full* of oneself⟩   **8** : having a rich quality ⟨a *full* voice⟩ — **full·ness** *n* — **full of it** : not to be believed

²full *adv*   **1 a** : ²VERY 1, EXTREMELY ⟨knew *full* well who they were⟩   **b** : all the way : ENTIRELY ⟨filled *full*⟩   **2** : ⁵SMACK, SQUARELY ⟨was hit *full* in the face⟩

³full *n*   **1** : the highest state, extent, or degree   **2** : the complete amount ⟨paid in *full*⟩

full·back \'fúl-,bak\ *n* : a football back who usually lines up between the halfbacks

full blast *adv* : with all power or resources being used ⟨a sawmill running *full blast*⟩ ⟨the stereo was going *full blast*⟩

full–blood·ed \'fúl-'bləd-əd\ *adj* : of pure ancestry

full–blown \-'blōn\ *adj*   **1** : being at the height of bloom   **2** : fully mature or developed

full–bod·ied \-'bäd-ēd\ *adj* : having a rich strong flavor

full dress *n* : the style of dress required on certain special occasions

full·er's earth \'fúl-ərz-\ *n* : an earthy substance used for filtering and as an absorbent

full–fledged \'fúl-'flejd\ *adj* : fully developed : MATURE

full–grown \-'grōn\ *adj* : having reached full growth or development : MATURE

full–length \-'len(k)th\ *adj*   **1** : made to fit the full length of the human figure ⟨a *full-length* dress⟩   **2** : having a length that is normal for things of its kind ⟨a *full-length* play⟩

full moon *n* : the moon with its whole disk lighted

full–scale \'fúl-'skā(ə)l\ *adj*   **1** : identical to an original in size   **2** : having all available resources in use ⟨a *full-scale* war⟩

full–ser·vice \-'sər-vəs\ *adj* : offering all services of a certain kind ⟨a *full-service* bank⟩

full steam ahead *adv* : at full power or speed

full tilt *adv* : at high speed : very fast ⟨running *full tilt*⟩

full–time \'fúl-'tīm\ *adj* : working or involving the full number of hours considered normal or standard ⟨a *full-time* job⟩ ⟨*full-time* employees⟩

ful·ly \'fúl-(l)ē\ *adv*   **1** : in a full manner : in every way or detail : COMPLETELY   **2** : at least ⟨*fully* 90 percent of us⟩

ful·mi·nate \'fúl-mə-,nāt, 'fəl-\ *vb* **-nat·ed; -nat·ing** : to utter loud or forceful complaints or strong or violent language — **ful·mi·na·tion** \,fúl-mə-'nā-shən, ,fəl-\ *n* — **ful·mi·na·tor** \'fúl-mə-,nāt-ər, 'fəl-\ *n*

ful·some \'fúl-səm\ *adj*   **1** : very full or complete ⟨described in *fulsome* detail⟩   **2** : very or overly flattering ⟨praised the boss in *fulsome* terms⟩ — **ful·some·ly** *adv* — **ful·some·ness** *n*

fum·ble \'fəm-bəl\ *vb* **fum·bled; fum·bling** \-b(ə-)liŋ\ : to feel about for or handle something clumsily — **fumble** *n* — **fum·bler** \-b(ə-)lər\ *n*

¹fume \'fyüm\ *n* : a disagreeable smoke, vapor, or gas — usually used in pl. ⟨automobile exhaust *fumes*⟩ ⟨acid *fumes*⟩ — **fumy** \'fyü-mē\ *adj*

²fume *vb* **fumed; fum·ing**   **1** : to expose to or treat with fumes   **2** : to give off fumes   **3** : to show bad temper or anger

fu·mi·gant \'fyü-mi-gənt\ *n* : a substance used in fumigating

fu·mi·gate \'fyü-mə-,gāt\ *vb* **-gat·ed; -gat·ing** : to apply smoke, vapor, or gas to especially for the purpose of disinfecting or of destroying pests — **fu·mi·ga·tion** \,fyü-mə-'gā-shən\ *n* — **fu·mi·ga·tor** \'fyü-mə-,gāt-ər\ *n*

¹fun \'fən\ *n*   **1** : someone or something that provides amusement or enjoyment ⟨the twins were *fun* to have around⟩ ⟨picnics are great *fun*⟩   **2** : a good time : AMUSEMENT, ENJOYMENT ⟨have *fun*⟩ ⟨plays cards just for *fun*⟩   **3** : words or actions that make someone or something an object of unkind laughter ⟨kids making *fun* of me⟩

²fun *vb* **funned; fun·ning** : to engage in joking or play ⟨I was only *funning*⟩

³fun *adj* : providing fun ⟨vacation is a *fun* time⟩ ⟨a *fun* person⟩ ⟨a *fun* place to go⟩

¹func·tion \'fəŋ(k)-shən\ *n*   **1** : professional job or duties

\ə\ abut	\aú\ out	\i\ tip	\ó\ saw	\ú\ foot
\ər\ further	\ch\ chin	\ī\ life	\ói\ coin	\y\ yet
\a\ mat	\e\ pet	\j\ job	\th\ thin	\yü\ few
\ā\ take	\ē\ easy	\ŋ\ sing	\th\ this	\yú\ cure
\ä\ cot, cart	\g\ go	\ō\ bone	\ü\ food	\zh\ vision

: OCCUPATION **2 a** : the particular purpose for which a person or thing is specially fitted or used or for which a thing exists ⟨the *function* of a knife is cutting⟩ **b** : the natural or proper action of a bodily part in a living thing ⟨the *function* of the heart⟩ **3** : a large important ceremony or social affair **4 a** : a mathematical relationship that assigns to each element of a set one and only one element of the same or another set **b** : a variable (as a quality, trait, or measurement) that depends on and varies with another ⟨height is a *function* of age in children⟩ — **func·tion·less** \-ləs\ *adj*

²**function** *vb* **func·tioned; func·tion·ing** \-sh(ə-)niŋ\ : to serve a certain purpose : WORK

func·tion·al \'fuŋ(k)-shnəl, -shən-ᵊl\ *adj* **1 a** : of, connected with, or being a function **b** : affecting bodily functions but not structure ⟨*functional* heart disease⟩ **2** : designed or developed chiefly from the point of view of use ⟨*functional* clothes⟩ ⟨*functional* writing⟩ **3** : performing or able to perform a regular function — **func·tion·al·ly** \-shnə-lē, -shən-ᵊl-ē\ *adv*

func·tion·ary \'fəŋ(k)-shə-,ner-ē\ *n, pl* **-ar·ies** : a person who has a certain job; *esp* : a political or governmental official

function word *n* : a word expressing primarily grammatical relationship

¹**fund** \'fənd\ *n* **1** : a quantity of available resources : STOCK, SUPPLY ⟨a large *fund* of jokes⟩ **2 a** : a sum of money for a special purpose ⟨the book *fund*⟩ **b** : available money — usually used in pl. [derived from Latin *fundus* "bottom, piece of land owned as property" — related to ²FOUND, ¹FOUNDER, ²FOUNDER, FUNDAMENTAL]

²**fund** *vb* : to supply funds for ⟨a program *funded* by the state⟩

¹**fun·da·men·tal** \,fən-də-'ment-ᵊl\ *adj* **1** : being or forming a foundation : BASIC, ESSENTIAL ⟨a discovery *fundamental* to modern science⟩ ⟨our *fundamental* rights⟩ **2** : of or relating to essential structure or function : RADICAL ⟨*fundamental* change⟩ **3** : of, relating to, or produced by the lowest part of a complex vibration **4** : of central importance : PRINCIPAL ⟨*fundamental* purpose⟩ [Middle English *fundamental* "serving as a base or source of support", from Latin *fundamentalis* "of a foundation", from *fundamentum* "foundation", derived from *fundus* "bottom, base" — related to ²FOUND, ¹FOUNDER, ²FOUNDER, FUND] — **fun·da·men·tal·ly** \-ᵊl-ē\ *adv*

²**fundamental** *n* **1** : something fundamental : a basic part ⟨*fundamentals* of arithmetic⟩ **2** : the part of a complex wave that has the lowest frequency and commonly the greatest amplitude

fu·ner·al \'fyün-(ə-)rəl\ *n* : the ceremonies held for a dead person (as before burial) — **funeral** *adj*

funeral director *n* : a person whose profession is the managing of funerals and the preparation of the dead for burial or cremation

funeral home *n* : a place where the dead are prepared for burial or cremation and funerals are held

fu·ne·re·al \fyù-'nir-ē-əl\ *adj* : suggesting a funeral ⟨*funereal* gloom⟩ — **fu·ne·re·al·ly** \-ē-ə-lē\ *adv*

fun·gal \'fəŋ-gəl\ *adj* **1** : of, relating to, or resembling fungi **2** : caused by a fungus

fun·gi·cide \'fən-jə-,sīd, 'fəŋ-gə-\ *n* : a substance that destroys fungi — **fun·gi·cid·al** \,fən-jə-'sīd-ᵊl, ,fəŋ-gə-\ *adj*

fun·gous \'fəŋ-gəs\ *adj* : FUNGAL

fun·gus \'fəŋ-gəs\ *n, pl* **fun·gi** \'fən-,jī, 'fəŋ-,gī\ *also* **fun·gus·es** **1** : any of a major group of flowerless plants (as molds, rusts, mildews, smuts, and mushrooms) that lack chlorophyll and are parasitic or live on dead or decaying organic matter **2** : infection with a fungus — **fungus** *adj*

fu·nic·u·lar \fyù-'nik-yə-lər, fə-\ *n* : a cable railway going up a mountain

¹**fun·nel** \'fən-ᵊl\ *n* **1** : a utensil usually shaped like a hollow cone with a tube extending from the point and used to catch and direct a downward flow (as of liquid) **2** : something shaped like a funnel ⟨the *funnel* cloud of a tornado⟩ **3** : a large pipe for the escape of smoke or for ventilation (as on a ship)

²**funnel** *vb* **-neled** *also* **-nelled; -nel·ing** *also* **-nel·ling** : to move or cause to move to a central point or into a central channel

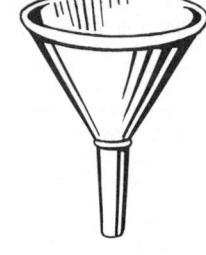

funnel 1

¹**fun·ny** \'fən-ē\ *adj* **fun·ni·er; -est** **1** : causing or intended to cause laughter ⟨a *funny* story⟩ **2** : different from ordinary in a way that is odd, curious, or suspicious ⟨it's *funny* you should ask⟩ ⟨that's *funny* — they were here yesterday⟩ ⟨there's something *funny* going on⟩ **3** : involving trickery ⟨don't try anything *funny*⟩ — **fun·ni·ly** \'fən-ᵊl-ē\ *adv* — **fun·ni·ness** \'fən-ē-nəs\ *n* — **funny** *adv*

²**funny** *n, pl* **funnies** : a comic strip or comic section of a newspaper — usually used in pl.

funny bone *n* **1** : a place at the back of the elbow where a blow causes a painful tingling sensation — called also *crazy bone* **2** : a sense of humor ⟨it tickled my *funny bone*⟩

funny paper *n* : the comic section of a newspaper — usually used in pl.

fur \'fər\ *n* **1** : a piece of the pelt of an animal **2** : an article of clothing made with fur **3** : the hairy coat of a mammal especially when fine, soft, and thick **4** : a coating (as on the tongue) resembling fur — **fur·less** \-ləs\ *adj* — **furred** \'fərd\ *adj*

Word History When the word *fur* first came into English, it was a verb that meant "to line a person's garment with the soft hair of an animal". The noun developed from the verb. First the noun referred to the animal hair that was used for lining and trimming a garment. Then it came to refer to the hairy coat on the animal itself. The verb, not much used anymore, was taken from the early French verb *fourrer*, meaning "to line a garment". This verb came from an earlier verb meaning "to line, encase". It was formed from a still earlier French word meaning "a sheath". Thus our word *fur* for the hairy coat that covers or encases an animal traces back to a word for a sheath that encases a knife or

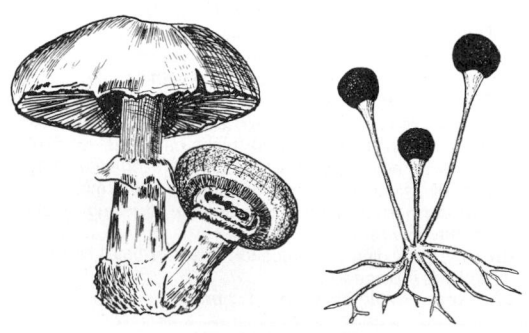

fungus 1

sword. [Middle English *furre* "a piece of animal skin used to line a garment", from *furrer* (verb) "to line a garment with fur", from early French *fourrer* "to line a garment", derived from earlier *fuerre* "sheath"; of Germanic origin]

fur·bear·er \'fər-,bar-ər, -,ber-\ *n* : an animal that bears fur

fur·be·low \'fər-bə-,lō\ *n* **1** : [4]FLOUNCE, RUFFLE **2** : something suggesting a furbelow

fu·ri·ous \'fyūr-ē-əs\ *adj* **1** : very angry **2** : very active : VIOLENT ⟨a *furious* storm⟩ — **fu·ri·ous·ly** *adv*

[1]furl \'fər(ə)l\ *vb* : to wrap or roll (as a sail or a flag) close to or around something

[2]furl *n* **1** : a furled coil **2** : the act of furling

fur·long \'fər-,lȯŋ\ *n* : a unit of distance equal to 220 yards (about 201.2 meters)

[1]fur·lough \'fər-lō\ *n* : a leave of absence from duty granted especially to a soldier

[2]furlough *vb* **1** : to grant a furlough to **2** : to lay off from work

fur·nace \'fər-nəs\ *n* : an enclosed structure in which heat is produced (as for heating a house or melting metals)

fur·nish \'fər-nish\ *vb* **1** : to provide with what is needed ⟨the cave *furnished* us with some shelter⟩; *esp* : to provide with furniture **2** : to supply or give to someone or something ⟨we'll *furnish* the food for the guests⟩ — **fur·nish·er** *n*

fur·nish·ings \'fər-nish-iŋz\ *n pl* : articles of furniture for a room or building

fur·ni·ture \'fər-ni-chər\ *n* : movable articles (as chairs, tables, or beds) used in making a room ready for use

fu·ror \'fyūr-,ȯr, -,ȯr\ *n* **1** : FURY 1, RAGE **2** : an outburst of excitement : UPROAR

fu·rore \'fyūr-,ȯr, -,ȯr\ *n* : FUROR 2

fur·ri·er \'fər-ē-ər\ *n* : a person who deals in furs

[1]fur·row \'fər-ō, 'fə-rō\ *n* **1** : a trench in the earth made by or as if by a plow **2** : a narrow groove or wrinkle

[2]furrow *vb* : to make furrows, grooves, wrinkles, or lines in

fur·ry \'fər-ē\ *adj* **fur·ri·er; -est** **1** : made of or resembling fur **2** : covered with fur

fur seal *n* : any of various seals with a valuable dense soft undercoat

[1]fur·ther \'fər-thər\ *adv* **1** : [1]FARTHER 1 **2** : in addition : BESIDES, ALSO **3** : to a greater degree or extent

[2]further *adj* **1** : [2]FARTHER 1 **2** : going or extending beyond : ADDITIONAL ⟨*further* study is needed⟩

[3]further *vb* **fur·thered; further·ing** \'fərth-(ə-)riŋ\ : to help forward : PROMOTE — **fur·ther·er** \'fər-thər-ər\ *n*

fur seal

fur·ther·ance \'fərth-(ə-)rən(t)s\ *n* : the act of furthering : ADVANCEMENT

fur·ther·more \'fər-thə(r)-,mō(ə)r, -,mȯ(ə)r\ *adv* : in addition to what precedes : MOREOVER

fur·ther·most \'fər-thə(r)-,mōst\ *adj* : most distant : FARTHEST

fur·thest \'fər-thəst\ *adv or adj* : FARTHEST

fur·tive \'fərt-iv\ *adj* : done in a sneaky or sly manner ⟨a *furtive* look⟩ — **fur·tive·ly** *adv* — **fur·tive·ness** *n*

fu·ry \'fyū(ə)r-ē\ *n, pl* **furies** **1** : violent anger **2 a** *cap* : one of the avenging spirits of classical mythology **b** : a violently angry person **3** : wild and dangerous force ⟨the *fury* of the storm⟩ **syn** see ANGER

furze \'fərz\ *n* : GORSE

[1]fuse \'fyūz\ *n* **1** : a cord or cable that is set afire to ignite an explosive charge by carrying fire to it **2** *usually* **fuze** : a mechanical or electrical device for setting off the explo-

sive charge of an artillery shell, bomb, or torpedo [from Italian *fuso* "a slender tapering rod used for twisting yarn, spindle", from Latin *fusus* "spindle"]

[2]fuse *or* **fuze** *vb* **fused** *or* **fuzed; fus·ing** *or* **fuz·ing** : to equip with a fuse

[3]fuse *vb* **fused; fus·ing** **1** : to change into a liquid or plastic state by heat **2** : to become fluid with heat **3** : to unite by or as if by melting together [from Latin *fusus* past participle of *fundere* "to pour melted metal into a mold" — related to [3]FOUND]

[4]fuse *n* : an electrical safety device having a metal wire or strip that melts and interrupts the circuit when the current becomes too strong

fu·se·lage \'fyü-sə-,läzh, 'fyü-zə-\ *n* : the central body portion of an airplane that holds the crew, passengers, and cargo

fus·ible \'fyü-zə-bəl\ *adj* : capable of being fused and especially melted by heat — **fus·ibil·i·ty** \,fyü-zə-'bil-ət-ē\ *n*

fu·sil·lade \'fyü-sə-,läd, -,lȧd, -zə-; ,fyü-sə-'läd, -'lȧd, -zə-\ *n* **1** : a number of shots fired at the same time or rapidly one after another **2** : something like a fusillade of shots

fu·sion \'fyü-zhən\ *n* **1** : the act or process of melting or making fluid by heat **2** : union by or as if by melting **3** : the union of light atomic nuclei to form heavier nuclei resulting in the release of enormous quantities of energy

[1]fuss \'fəs\ *n* **1** : unnecessary activity or excitement often over something unimportant **2** : [1]PROTEST **3** : a great show of interest ⟨made a *fuss* over the baby⟩

[2]fuss *vb* : to make a fuss — **fuss·er** *n*

fussy \'fəs-ē\ *adj* **fuss·i·er; -est** **1** : inclined to complain or whine ⟨a *fussy* child⟩ **2 a** : needing or giving much attention to details ⟨a *fussy* job⟩ **b** : hard to please ⟨*fussy* about food⟩ — **fuss·i·ly** \'fəs-ə-lē\ *adv* — **fuss·i·ness** \'fəs-ē-nəs\ *n*

fus·tic \'fəs-tik\ *n* : the wood of a tropical American tree that is related to the mulberries and is the source of a yellow dye; *also* : a tree that produces this wood

fus·ty \'fəs-tē\ *adj* **fus·ti·er; -est** **1** : full of dust and stale odors : MUSTY **2** : very old-fashioned — **fus·ti·ly** \-tə-lē\ *adv* — **fus·ti·ness** \-tē-nəs\ *n*

fu·tile \'fyüt-ᵊl, 'fyü-,tīl\ *adj* : having no result or effect : USELESS ⟨all our efforts proved *futile*⟩ ⟨a *futile* and foolish gesture⟩ — **fu·tile·ly** \-ᵊl-(l)ē, -,tīl-lē\ *adv*

fu·til·i·ty \fyū-'til-ət-ē\ *n, pl* **-ties** **1** : the quality or state of being futile **2** : a useless act

[1]fu·ture \'fyü-chər\ *adj* **1** : coming after the present ⟨*future* events⟩ **2** : of, relating to, or being a verb form in the future tense [Middle English *future* "future", from early French *futur* (same meaning) and Latin *futurus* "about to be", from the Latin verb *esse* "to be"]

[2]future *n* **1 a** : time that is to come ⟨sometime in the *future*⟩ **b** : what is going to happen ⟨predict the *future*⟩ **2** : expectation of future success ⟨a promising *future*⟩ **3 a** : FUTURE TENSE **b** : a verb form in the future tense

fu·ture·less \'fyü-chər-ləs\ *adj* : having no expectation of future success

future perfect tense *n* : a verb tense formed in English with *will have* and *shall have* and expressing completion of an action by a specified time that is yet to come

future tense *n* : a verb tense formed in English with *will* or *shall* and expressing an action or state in time yet to come

fu·tur·ist \'fyü-chə-rəst\ *n* : a person who tries to tell what the future will be like by studying current trends

fu·tur·is·tic \,fyü-chə-'ris-tik\ *adj* : being or resembling the style or type predicted for the future ⟨*futuristic* furniture⟩

\ə\ abut	\au̇\ out	\i\ tip	\ȯ\ saw	\u̇\ foot
\ər\ further	\ch\ chin	\ī\ life	\ȯi\ coin	\y\ yet
\a\ mat	\e\ pet	\j\ job	\th\ thin	\yü\ few
\ā\ take	\ē\ easy	\ŋ\ sing	\th\ this	\yu̇\ cure
\ä\ cot, cart	\g\ go	\ō\ bone	\ü\ food	\zh\ vision

— **fu·tur·is·ti·cal·ly** \-ti-k(ə-)lē\ *adv*
fu·tu·ri·ty \fyu̇-'t(y)u̇r-ət-ē, -'chu̇r-\ *n, pl* **-ties** **1** : ²FUTURE 1 **2** : the quality or state of being future **3** *pl* : future events or possibilities
fuze *variant of* FUSE
fuzz \'fəz\ *n* : fine light particles or fibers (as of down or fluff)
fuzzy \'fəz-ē\ *adj* **fuzz·i·er; -est** **1** : covered with or re-

sembling fuzz **2** : not clear : INDISTINCT — **fuzz·i·ly** \'fəz-ə-lē\ *adv* — **fuzz·i·ness** \'fəz-ē-nəs\ *n*
-fy \,fī\ *vb suffix* **-fied; -fy·ing** **1** : cause to become ⟨beautify⟩ **2** : gain or cause to gain qualities related to ⟨citify⟩ [derived from Latin *-ficare* (suffix), from *facere* "to make, do"]

G

g \'jē\ *n, pl* **g's** *or* **gs** *often cap* **1** : the seventh letter of the English alphabet **2** : the musical note referred to by the letter G : the fifth tone of a C-major scale **3** : the acceleration that a body experiences at the earth's surface due to the pull of gravity; *also* : a unit of force equal to the weight of a body on which the force acts ⟨an astronaut experiences 10 *g's* during lift-off⟩
G *trademark* — used to certify that a motion picture is of such a nature that persons of all ages may be allowed admission
gab \'gab\ *vb* **gabbed; gab·bing** : to talk idly : CHATTER — **gab** *n*
gab·ar·dine \'gab-ər-,dēn\ *n* **1** : a firm cloth with diagonal ribs and a hard smooth finish **2** : a garment of gabardine
gab·ble \'gab-əl\ *vb* **gab·bled; gab·bling** \'gab-(ə-)liŋ\ : ¹JABBER, BABBLE — **gabble** *n* — **gab·bler** \'gab-(ə-)lər\ *n*
gab·by \'gab-ē\ *adj* **gab·bi·er; -est** : TALKATIVE
gab·fest \'gab-,fest\ *n* : a time spent in talking
ga·ble \'gā-bəl\ *n* **1** : the triangular part of an outside wall of a building that is formed by the sides of the roof sloping down from the ridgepole to the eaves **2** : a triangular structure (as over a door or window) — **ga·bled** \-bəld\ *adj*

1 gable 1

gable roof *n* : a roof having two sides sloping from a ridge and forming a gable at each end
¹gad \'gad\ *vb* **gad·ded; gad·ding** : to roam to little purpose — usually used with *about*
²gad *interj* — used as a mild oath
gad·about \'gad-ə-,bau̇t\ *n* : a person who goes from place to place without much reason — **gadabout** *adj*
gad·fly \'gad-,flī\ *n* **1** : any of various flies (as a horsefly or botfly) that are pests especially of livestock **2** : a person who is an annoying pest
gad·get \'gaj-ət\ *n* : an interesting, unfamiliar, or unusual device — **gad·get·ry** \'gaj-ə-trē\ *n*
gad·o·lin·i·um \,gad-ºl-'in-ē-əm\ *n* : a magnetic metallic chemical element — see ELEMENT table
Gael \'gā(ə)l\ *n* **1** : a Scottish Highlander **2** : a Celtic especially Gaelic-speaking person born or living in Ireland, Scotland, or the Isle of Man
Gael·ic \'gāl-ik, 'gal-, 'gäl-\ *adj* **1** : of or relating to the Gaels and especially the Celtic Highlanders of Scotland **2** : of, relating to, or being the Celtic speech of persons born or living in Ireland, the Isle of Man, and the Scottish Highlands — **Gaelic** *n*
gaff \'gaf\ *n* **1** : a spear or hook for lifting heavy fish **2** : a pole that extends from the back of a mast to support the top of a sail **3** : something hard to take ⟨couldn't stand the *gaff*⟩ — **gaff** *vb*

¹gag \'gag\ *vb* **gagged; gag·ging** **1** : to prevent from speaking or crying out by or as if by stopping up the mouth **2 a** : to vomit or cause to feel like vomiting **b** : ¹CHOKE 2 **3** : to be unable to endure something : BALK
²gag *n* **1 a** : something thrust into the mouth especially to prevent speech or outcry **b** : a check to free speech **2** : something said or done to cause laughter
¹gage \'gāj\ *n* **1** : a glove or cap thrown on the ground as a challenge to combat **2** : something deposited as a pledge : SECURITY
²gage *variant of* GAUGE
gag·gle \'gag-əl\ *n* : ¹FLOCK 1; *esp* : a flock of geese when not in flight
gai·ety *or* **gay·ety** \'gā-ət-ē\ *n, pl* **-eties** **1** : MERRYMAKING 1 **2** : gay spirits or manner **3** : ELEGANCE 2, FINERY
gai·ly *or* **gay·ly** \'gā-lē\ *adv* **1** : in a merry or lively way **2** : in a bright or showy way ⟨*gaily* dressed crowds⟩
¹gain \'gān\ *n* **1** : advantage gained or increased : PROFIT ⟨financial *gains*⟩ **2** : an increase in amount, size, or degree ⟨a *gain* in weight⟩
²gain *vb* **1 a** : to get possession of often by effort : EARN ⟨*gain* an advantage⟩ **b** : to win in competition or conflict ⟨*gain* a victory⟩ **c** : to get by a natural development or process ⟨*gain* strength⟩ **d** : to arrive at ⟨the swimmer *gained* the shore⟩ **2** : to win to one's side : PERSUADE **3** : to increase in ⟨*gain* momentum⟩ **4** : to run fast ⟨my watch *gains* a minute a day⟩ **5** : to get advantage : PROFIT ⟨hoped to *gain* from the deal⟩ **6 a** : ¹INCREASE 1 ⟨the day was *gaining* in warmth⟩ **b** : to increase in weight **c** : to improve in health — **gain·er** *n* — **gain ground** : to make progress
gain·ful \'gān-fəl\ *adj* : producing gain : making money ⟨*gainful* employment⟩ — **gain·ful·ly** \-fə-lē\ *adv* — **gain·ful·ness** *n*
gain·say \gān-'sā\ *vb* **gain·said** \-'sād, -'sed\; **gain·say·ing** \-'sā-iŋ\ **1** : DENY 1, DISPUTE **2** : CONTRADICT 3 — **gain·say·er** *n*
gait \'gāt\ *n* : manner of moving on foot; *also* : a particular style of such movement — **gait·ed** \-əd\ *adj*
gai·ter \'gāt-ər\ *n* : a leg covering reaching from the instep to above the ankle or to mid-calf or knee
gal \'gal\ *n* : GIRL
ga·la \'gā-lə, 'gal-ə\ *n* : a gay celebration : FESTIVITY — **gala** *adj*
ga·lac·tic \gə-'lak-tik\ *adj* : of or relating to a galaxy
ga·lac·tose \gə-'lak-,tōs\ *n* : a sugar that is less easily dissolved and is less sweet than glucose
Ga·la·tians \gə-'lā-shənz\ *n* — see BIBLE table
gal·axy \'gal-ək-sē\ *n, pl* **gal·ax·ies** **1** : MILKY WAY GALAXY **2** : one of billions of systems of stars, gas, and dust that make up the universe [Middle English *galaxie* "the Milky Way", from Latin *galaxias* (same meaning), from Greek *galaxias* "Milky Way", from *galakt-, gala* "milk"]
gale \'gā(ə)l\ *n* **1** : a strong current of air; *esp* : a wind of from 51 to 101 kilometers per hour **2** : an emotional outburst ⟨*gales* of laughter⟩
ga·le·na \gə-'lē-nə\ *n* : a bluish gray mineral with metallic

luster that consists of sulfide of lead and that is the principal ore of lead

¹gall \'gȯl\ *n* **1 a** : BILE 1 **b** : something bitter to endure **c** : bitterness of spirit **2** : NERVE 3c [Old English *gealla* "bile"]

²gall *n* : a skin sore (as on a horse's back) caused by repeated irritation (as from rubbing by a saddle) [Old English *gealla* "skin sore," from Latin *galla* "plant gall"]

³gall *vb* **1** : to make or become sore or worn by rubbing **2** : IRRITATE 1, VEX ⟨sarcasm *galls* her⟩

⁴gall *n* : a swelling or growth of plant tissue usually due to fungi or insect parasites [Middle English *galle* "a swelling on a plant, plant gall," from early French *galle* (same meaning), from Latin *galla* "plant gall"]

¹gal·lant \gə-'lant, gȧ-'länt, 'gal-ənt\ *n* **1** : a young man of fashion **2 a** : a man who likes the company of women and is attentive to them **b** : SUITOR 3

²gal·lant \'gal-ənt *(usually in sense 2b);* gə-'lant, gȧ-'länt *(usually in sense 3)*\ *adj* **1** : showy in dress or bearing **2 a** : SPLENDID 2, STATELY ⟨a *gallant* ship⟩ **b** : SPIRITED, BRAVE ⟨made a *gallant* stand⟩ **c** : CHIVALROUS 2a, NOBLE ⟨a *gallant* knight⟩ **3** : polite and attentive to women — **gal·lant·ly** *adv*

gal·lant·ry \'gal-ən-trē\ *n, pl* **-ries** **1** : courteous attention to a woman **2** : conspicuous bravery

gall·blad·der \'gȯl-,blad-ər\ *n* : a muscular sac in which bile from the liver is stored

gal·le·on \'gal-ē-ən\ *n* : a large sailing ship with square sails used especially by the Spanish at the time of Columbus and later

gal·lery \'gal-(ə-)rē\ *n, pl* **gal·ler·ies** **1** : an outdoor balcony **2 a** : a long narrow room, hall, or passage **b** : an underground passageway (as in a mine or cave) **c** : a passage (as in earth or wood) made by an animal and especially an insect **3 a** : a room or building devoted to the exhibition of works of art **b** : a business dealing in works of art **4** : a balcony in an auditorium; *esp* : the highest balcony in a theater or the people who sit there ⟨play to the *gallery*⟩ **5** : a photographer's studio

galleon

gal·ley \'gal-ē\ *n, pl* **galleys** **1** : a large low ship of olden times moved by oars and sails **2** : the kitchen especially of a ship or airplane

gall·fly \'gȯl-,flī\ *n* : an insect that deposits its eggs in plants and causes galls in which the larvae feed

Gal·lic \'gal-ik\ *adj* : of or relating to Gaul or France : FRENCH

gall·ing \'gȯ-liŋ\ *adj* : very irritating : VEXING

gal·li·nule \'gal-ə-,n(y)ü(ə)l\ *n* : any of several birds related to the rails that are usually found in or near water

gal·li·um \'gal-ē-əm\ *n* : a bluish white metallic element — see ELEMENT table

gal·li·vant \'gal-ə-,vant\ *vb* : to travel or roam about for pleasure

gal·lon \'gal-ən\ *n* — see MEASURE table

¹gal·lop \'gal-əp\ *vb* **1** : to go or cause to go at a gallop **2** : to run fast — **gal·lop·er** *n*

²gallop *n* **1** : a fast bounding gait of a four-footed animal; *esp* : a fast gait of the horse with a three-beat rhythm **2** : a ride or run at a gallop

gal·lows \'gal-(,)ōz, -əz\ *n, pl* **gallows** *or* **gal·lows·es** : a structure from which criminals are hanged

gall·stone \'gȯl-,stōn\ *n* : a hard mass like a pebble that is formed in the gallbladder or bile passages

gall wasp *n* : a wasp that is a gallfly

ga·lore \gə-'lō(ə)r, -'lȯ(ə)r\ *adj* : ABUNDANT, PLENTIFUL — used after the word it modifies ⟨has charm *galore*⟩

ga·losh \gə-'läsh\ *n* : a high overshoe worn especially in snow and slush

gal·va·nize \'gal-və-,nīz\ *vb* **-nized; -niz·ing** **1 a** : to subject to the action of an electric current ⟨*galvanize* a muscle⟩ **b** : to stimulate or excite as if by an electric shock ⟨an issue that *galvanized* the public⟩ **2** : to coat (as iron) with zinc for protection — **gal·va·ni·za·tion** \,gal-və-nə-'zā-shən\ *n*

gal·va·nom·e·ter \,gal-və-'näm-ət-ər\ *n* : an instrument for detecting or measuring a small electric current

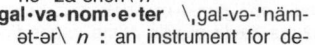

gallows

¹gam·ble \'gam-bəl\ *vb* **gam·bled; gam·bling** \-b(ə-)liŋ\ **1 a** : to play a game for money or property **b** : to bet on an uncertain outcome **2** : to bet something on the chance of gain : take a chance ⟨we *gambled* on not being seen⟩ **3** : ²RISK 1, HAZARD — **gam·bler** \-blər\ *n*

²gamble *n* : a risky undertaking

gam·bol \'gam-bəl\ *vb* **-boled** *or* **-bolled; -bol·ing** *or* **-bol·ling** \-bə-liŋ *also* -bliŋ\ : to run or skip about in play : FRISK — **gambol** *n*

gam·brel roof \,gam-brəl-\ *n* : a roof with a lower steeper slope and an upper flatter one on each side

¹game \'gām\ *n* **1 a** : AMUSEMENT 1, DIVERSION **b** : ¹FUN 1, SPORT ⟨make *game* of a nervous player⟩ **2 a** : ¹PLAN 2, STRATAGEM **b** : a line of work : PROFESSION **3 a** : a contest carried on following set rules for amusement, exercise, or reward **b** : a division of a larger contest **c** : the number of points necessary to win **d** : the manner of playing in a contest **4 a** : animals pursued or taken by hunting **b** : the flesh of game animals **c** : an object of ridicule or attack — often used in the phrase *fair game*

²game *vb* **gamed; gam·ing** : ¹GAMBLE 1a

³game *adj* **gam·er; gam·est** **1** : full of spirit or eagerness : DETERMINED **2** : of or relating to animals that are hunted — **game·ly** *adv* — **game·ness** *n*

⁴game *adj* : ¹LAME 1b ⟨a *game* leg⟩

game·cock \'gām-,käk\ *n* : a rooster trained for fighting

game fish *n* : a fish regularly sought by anglers

game·keep·er \'gām-,kē-pər\ *n* : a person in charge of the breeding and protection of game animals or birds on private land

game show *n* : a television program in which contestants compete for prizes in a game (as a quiz)

ga·mete \gə-'mēt, 'gam-,ēt\ *n* : a mature sex cell that usually has half of the normal number of chromosomes and is capable of uniting with a gamete of the opposite sex to begin the formation of a new individual — **ga·met·ic** \gə-'met-ik\ *adj* — **ga·met·i·cal·ly** \-'met-i-k(ə-)lē\ *adv*

ga·me·to·phyte \gə-'mēt-ə-,fīt\ *n* : the individual or generation of plants with alternating sexual and asexual generations that produces sperm and eggs — compare SPOROPHYTE — **ga·me·to·phyt·ic** \-,mēt-ə-'fit-ik\ *adj*

gam·in \'gam-ən\ *n* **1** : a boy who hangs out on the streets **2** : GAMINE 2

ga·mine \ga-'mēn\ *n* **1** : a girl who hangs out on the streets **2** : a girl of typically slight build and elfish charm

\ə\ abut	\au̇\ out	\i\ tip	\ȯ\ saw	\u̇\ foot
\ər\ further	\ch\ chin	\ī\ life	\ȯi\ coin	\y\ yet
\a\ mat	\e\ pet	\j\ job	\th\ thin	\yü\ few
\ā\ take	\ē\ easy	\ŋ\ sing	\th\ this	\yu̇\ cure
\ä\ cot, cart	\g\ go	\ō\ bone	\ü\ food	\zh\ vision

gam·ing \'gā-miŋ\ *n* : the practice of gambling

gam·ma \'gam-ə\ *n* : the third letter of the Greek alphabet — Γ or γ

gamma globulin *n* **1 a** : a part of blood plasma that is rich in antibodies **b** : a solution of gamma globulin made by mixing blood from human blood donors and given to provide immunity against some infectious diseases (as measles and German measles) **2** : any of numerous globulins of blood plasma or serum that include most antibodies

gamma rays *n pl* : very penetrating rays that are like X rays but of shorter wavelength and are given off by radioactive atomic nuclei — called also *gamma radiation*

gam·ut \'gam-ət\ *n* : an entire range or series [probably a contraction of *gamma ut*, a Latin expression in the Middle Ages for "the full range of notes in music", from *gamma* "the lowest note on the staff" and *ut* "the first note of the scale"]

gamy *or* **gam·ey** \'gā-mē\ *adj* **gam·i·er; -est** **1** : ³GAME 1, PLUCKY **2** : having the flavor of wild game especially when slightly spoiled ⟨*gamy* meat⟩ — **gam·i·ly** \'gā-mə-lē\ *adv* — **gam·i·ness** \'gā-mē-nəs\ *n*

¹gan·der \'gan-dər\ *n* : a male goose

²gander *n* : ²GLANCE 3b

¹gang \'gaŋ\ *n* **1** : two or more tools or devices arranged to work together **2** : a group of persons working or going about together **3** : a group of persons associated together to do something illegal

²gang *vb* **1** : to attack in a gang — usually used with *up* **2** : to form into or move or act as a gang

gang·land \'gaŋ-,land, -lənd\ *n* : the world of organized crime

gan·gling \'gaŋ-gliŋ, -glən\ *adj* : loosely and awkwardly built : LANKY

gan·gly \'gaŋ-glē\ *adj* **gan·gli·er; -est** : GANGLING

gan·gli·on \'gaŋ-glē-ən\ *n, pl* **-glia** \-glē-ə\ *also* **-gli·ons** : a mass of nerve tissue lying outside the brain or spinal cord and containing nerve cells; *also* : NUCLEUS c — **gan·gli·on·ic** \,gaŋ-glē-'än-ik\ *adj*

gang·plank \'gaŋ-,plaŋk\ *n* : a movable bridge from a ship to the shore

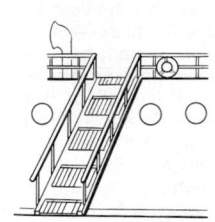
gangplank

¹gan·grene \'gaŋ-,grēn, 'gan-; gaŋ-'grēn, gan-\ *n* : the death of soft tissues in a local area of the body due to loss of the blood supply — **gan·gre·nous** \'gaŋ-grə-nəs\ *adj*

²gangrene *vb* **gan·grened; gan·gren·ing** : to make or become diseased with gangrene

gang·ster \'gaŋ-stər\ *n* : a member of a gang of criminals : RACKETEER — **gang·ster·ism** \-stə-,riz-əm\ *n*

gang·way \'gaŋ-,wā\ *n* **1** : a passage into, through, or out of an enclosed place **2** : GANGPLANK **3** : a clear passage through a crowd — often used as an interjection

gan·net \'gan-ət\ *n, pl* **gannets** *also* **gannet** : any of several large fish-eating seabirds that breed chiefly on offshore islands

gantlet *variant of* GAUNTLET

gan·try \'gan-trē\ *n, pl* **gantries** **1** : a platform made to carry a traveling crane and supported by towers running on parallel tracks **2** : a movable structure used for erecting and servicing rockets before launching **3** : a structure spanning several railroad tracks and displaying signals

gaol \'jā(ə)l\, **gaol·er** \'jā-lər\ *chiefly British variant of* JAIL, JAILER

gap \'gap\ *n* **1** : an opening made by a break or a parting **2** : a mountain pass **3** : a break in continuity ⟨unexplained *gaps* in your story⟩ **4** : the distance between two electrodes (as in a spark plug)

¹gape \'gāp\ *vb* **gaped; gap·ing** **1 a** : to open the mouth wide **b** : to open or part widely **2** : to stare with mouth open in surprise or wonder **3** : ¹YAWN 2 **syn** see GAZE — **gap·er** *n* — **gap·ing·ly** \'gā-piŋ-lē\ *adv*

²gape *n* : an act or instance of gaping

gar \'gär\ *n* : any of various fishes with a long body like that of a pike and long narrow jaws

¹ga·rage \gə-'räzh, -'räj\ *n* : a shelter or repair shop for automotive vehicles

²garage *vb* **ga·raged; ga·rag·ing** : to keep or put in a garage

ga·rage·man \gə-'räzh-,man, -'räj-\ *n* : a person who works in a garage

garage sale *n* : a sale of used household or personal items (as furniture or clothing) held at the seller's home

garb \'gärb\ *n* **1** : style of dress **2** : outward form : APPEARANCE — **garb** *vb*

gar·bage \'gär-bij\ *n* : food waste : REFUSE

gar·bage·man \'gär-bij-,man\ *n* : a person who collects and hauls away garbage

gar·ban·zo \gär-'bän-zō\ *n, pl* **-zos** : CHICK-PEA — called also *garbanzo bean*

gar·ble \'gär-bəl\ *vb* **gar·bled; gar·bling** \-b(ə-)liŋ\ : to change or twist the meaning or sound of — **gar·bler** \-b(ə-)lər\ *n*

¹gar·den \'gärd-ᵊn\ *n* **1** : a plot of ground where herbs, fruits, flowers, or vegetables are grown **2 a** : a public recreation area or park usually ornamented with plants and trees ⟨a botanical *garden*⟩ **b** : an open-air eating or drinking place

²garden *vb* **gar·dened; gar·den·ing** \'gärd-niŋ, -ᵊn-iŋ\ **1** : to lay out or work in a garden **2** : to make into a garden

³garden *adj* **1** : of, relating to, or frequenting gardens **2** : of a kind grown under cultivation especially in the open **3** : ²ORDINARY 2, COMMONPLACE

gar·den·er \'gärd-nər, -ᵊn-ər\ *n* : a person who gardens especially for pay

gar·de·nia \gär-'dē-nyə\ *n* : any of various Old World tropical trees and shrubs with leathery leaves and fragrant white or yellow flowers; *also* : one of the flowers

¹gar·gle \'gär-gəl\ *vb* **gar·gled; gar·gling** \-g(ə-)liŋ\ : to rinse the throat with a liquid kept in motion by air forced through it from the lungs

²gargle *n* **1** : a liquid used in gargling **2** : a gargling sound

gar·goyle \'gär-,gòil\ *n* : a waterspout in the form of a strange or frightening human or animal figure sticking out at the roof or eaves of a building

gar·ish \'ga(ə)r-ish, 'ge(ə)r-\ *adj* : too bright or showy : GAUDY — **gar·ish·ly** *adv* — **gar·ish·ness** *n*

¹gar·land \'gär-lənd\ *n* : a wreath or rope of leaves or flowers

²garland *vb* : to form into or decorate with a garland

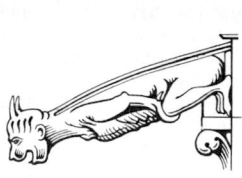
gargoyle

gar·lic \'gär-lik\ *n* : a European herb related to onion and grown for its bulbs that have a strong smell and taste and are used to flavor foods; *also* : one of the bulbs — **gar·licky** \-li-kē\ *adj*

garlic salt *n* : a seasoning made of ground dried garlic and salt

gar·ment \'gär-mənt\ *n* : an article of clothing — **garment** *vb*

gar·ner \'gär-nər\ *vb* **1** : to gather in and store **2 a** : to acquire by effort : EARN **b** : ACCUMULATE 1, COLLECT

gar·net \'gär-nət\ *n* **1** : a transparent deep red mineral that is used as a gem **2** : a deep red color

Word History The garnet owes its name to its color.

The deep red color of this gemstone reminded the French of a red-skinned fruit. In early French the fruit was called *pomme grenate,* which means "seedy apple". This later became *pomegranate* in English. The early French word *grenate,* meaning "seedy", is the source of the adjective *grenat,* meaning "red like a pomegranate". This word was then used as a noun to refer to the deep-red gemstone. When borrowed into English, *grenat* became *garnet.* [Middle English *grenat* "garnet", from early French *grenat* (same meaning), from *grenat* (adjective) "red like a pomegranate", from *pomme grenate* "pomegranate", literally "seedy apple"; *pomme* from earlier *pome* "apple" and *grenate* derived from Latin *granum* "grain, seed" — related to GRAIN, GRENADE, POMEGRANATE]

garnet paper *n* : a paper that has crushed garnet glued on one side and is used for smoothing and polishing

gar·nish \'gär-nish\ *vb* **1** : DECORATE 1, EMBELLISH **2** : to add decorations or seasonings to (food) — **garnish** *n* — **gar·nish·ment** \-mənt\ *n*

gar·ret \'gar-ət\ *n* : a room or unfinished part of a house just under the roof

¹gar·ri·son \'gar-ə-sən\ *n* **1** : a military post; *esp* : a permanent military installation **2** : the troops stationed at a garrison

²garrison *vb* **gar·ri·soned; gar·ri·son·ing** \'gar-ə-s(ə-)niŋ\ **1** : to station troops in **2** : to send (troops) to a garrison

¹gar·rote *or* **ga·rotte** \gə-'rät, -'rōt; 'gar-ət\ *n* **1 a** : a method of execution by strangling **b** : the apparatus used **2** : an implement (as a wire with a handle at each end) for strangling

²garrote *or* **garotte** *vb* **gar·rot·ed** *or* **ga·rott·ed; gar·rot·ing** *or* **ga·rott·ing** : to strangle with or as if with a garrote — **gar·rot·er** *n*

gar·ru·lous \'gar-ə-ləs\ *adj* : overly talkative   **syn** see TALKATIVE — **gar·ru·lous·ly** *adv* — **gar·ru·lous·ness** *n*

gar·ter \'gärt-ər\ *n* : a band worn to hold up a stocking or sock

garter snake *n* : any of numerous harmless American snakes with stripes along the back

¹gas \'gas\ *n, pl* **gas·es** *also* **gas·ses** **1** : a fluid (as hydrogen or air) that has no fixed shape and tends to expand without limit **2 a** : a gas or mixture of gases used as a fuel or as an anesthetic **b** : a fluid substance (as tear gas) that can be used to produce a poisonous or suffocating atmosphere **3** : unimportant talk : BOMBAST **4** : GASOLINE **5** *slang* : something appealing or enjoyable ⟨the party was a *gas*⟩

²gas *vb* **gassed; gas·sing** **1** : to supply with gas **2 a** : to treat with gas **b** : to poison with gas **3** : to talk idly

gas·eous \'gas-ē-əs, 'gash-əs\ *adj* **1** : having the form of or being gas **2** : of or relating to gas

gas–guz·zler \'gas-ˌgəz(-ə)-lər\ *n* : a usually large automobile that gets low gas mileage — **gas–guz·zling** \-ˌgəz(-ə)-liŋ\ *adj*

¹gash \'gash\ *n* : a long deep cut

²gash *vb* : to make a long deep cut in

gas·ket \'gas-kət\ *n* **1** : a line or band used to lash a furled sail **2** : material (as asbestos, rubber, or metal) used to prevent a joint from leaking

gas·light \'gas-ˌlīt, -'līt\ *n* **1** : light made by burning gas **2 a** : a gas flame **b** : a gas lighting fixture — **gas·light·ing** \-iŋ\ *n* — **gas·lit** \-ˌlit, -'lit\ *adj*

gas mask *n* : a mask connected to a chemical air filter and used to protect the face and lungs against poison gases

garter snake

gas·o·hol \'gas-ə-ˌhȯl\ *n* : a fuel consisting of 10 percent ethyl alcohol and 90 percent gasoline [from *gas*oline and alco*hol*]

gas·o·line \'gas-ə-ˌlēn, ˌgas-ə-'lēn\ *n* : a flammable liquid produced usually by blending products from natural gas and petroleum and used especially as a fuel for engines

gasp \'gasp\ *vb* **1** : to breathe with difficulty : PANT **2** : to utter with quick difficult breaths — **gasp** *n*

gas station *n* : SERVICE STATION

gas·sy \'gas-ē\ *adj* **gas·si·er; -est** **1** : full of or containing gas **2** : having the characteristics of gas — **gas·si·ness** *n*

gas·tric \'gas-trik\ *adj* : of, relating to, or located near the stomach ⟨*gastric* ulcers⟩

gastric juice *n* : a watery acid fluid that helps in digestion and is secreted by glands in the walls of the stomach

gas·tri·tis \ga-'strīt-əs\ *n* : inflammation of the stomach and especially of its mucous membrane

gas·troc·ne·mi·us \ˌgas-(ˌ)träk-'nē-mē-əs, -trək-\ *n, pl* **-mii** \-ˌmē-ˌī\ : the largest muscle of the calf of the leg that points the toe, flexes the leg, and tends to rotate the foot

gas·tron·o·my \ga-'strän-ə-mē\ *n* : the art of appreciating fine food — **gas·tro·nom·ic** \ˌgas-trə-'näm-ik\ *also* **gas·tro·nom·i·cal** \-'näm-i-kəl\ *adj*

gas·tro·pod \'gas-trə-ˌpäd\ *n* : any of a large class of mollusks (as snails) that have a muscular foot at the bottom and usually both a distinct head bearing sense organs and a spiral shell into which the body can be withdrawn — **gas·tropod** *adj*

gas·tro·trich \'gas-trə-ˌtrik\ *n* : any of a small group of tiny freshwater animals made up of many cells

gas·tru·la \'gas-trə-lə\ *n, pl* **-las** *or* **-lae** \-ˌlē, -ˌlī\ : an early embryo usually consisting of a double cup-shaped layer of cells produced by a folding in of the wall of the blastula

gas·tru·la·tion \ˌgas-trə-'lā-shən\ *n* : the process of becoming or forming a gastrula

gas turbine *n* : an engine in which gases produced by burning fuel are used to spin blades connected to a drive shaft

gas·works \'gas-ˌwərks\ *n, pl* : a plant for manufacturing gas

gat \'gat\ *n, slang* : HANDGUN

gate \'gāt\ *n* **1** : an opening in a wall or fence **2** : a city or castle entrance often with defensive structures **3** : the frame or door that closes a gate **4** : a means of entrance or exit **5** : a door, valve, or other device for controlling the passage of fluid **6** : the total admission receipts or the number of spectators especially at a sports event

gate·keep·er \-ˌkē-pər\ *n* : a person who tends or guards a gate

gate·way \-ˌwā\ *n* **1** : an opening for a gate **2** : a passage into or out of a place or state ⟨knowledge is the *gateway* to wisdom⟩

¹gath·er \'gath-ər, 'geth-\ *vb* **gath·ered; gath·er·ing** \'gath-(ə-)riŋ\ **1** : to bring together : COLLECT **2** : ¹PICK 2b, HARVEST **3** : to gain by gradual increase ⟨gather speed⟩ **4** : to prepare (as oneself) by calling on strength ⟨*gather* courage to dive⟩ **5** : to draw about or close to something **6** : to pull (cloth) along a line of stitching so as to draw into puckers **7** : GUESS 1, DEDUCE **8** : to come together in a body or around a center of attraction ⟨a crowd *gathered* round⟩ — **gath·er·er** \ər-ər\ *n*

syn GATHER, COLLECT, ASSEMBLE, CONGREGATE mean to come or bring together into a group, mass, or unit. GATHER applies broadly to the coming or bringing together of things from a spread-out or scattered state

\ə\ abut		\au̇\ out	\i\ tip	\ȯ\ saw	\u̇\ foot
\ər\ further		\ch\ chin	\ī\ life	\ȯi\ coin	\y\ yet
\a\ mat		\e\ pet	\j\ job	\th\ thin	\yü\ few
\ā\ take		\ē\ easy	\ŋ\ sing	\t͟h\ this	\yu̇\ cure
\ä\ cot, cart		\g\ go	\ō\ bone	\ü\ food	\zh\ vision

⟨farmers from all over *gathered* at the fair⟩ COLLECT often suggests careful selection or orderly arrangement ⟨she likes to *collect* stamps⟩ ASSEMBLE suggests an ordered gathering or organization of persons or things usually for a purpose ⟨all students will *assemble* in the auditorium to hear the speaker⟩ CONGREGATE suggests an unplanned coming together into a crowd or huddle ⟨people began to *congregate* on street corners⟩

²**gather** *n* : the result of gathering cloth : PUCKER

gath·er·ing *n* **1** : ASSEMBLY 1, MEETING **2** : a pus-filled swelling (as an abscess) **3** : the collecting of food and raw materials from the wild **4** : COLLECTION 2a **5** : a gather in cloth

ga·tor \'gāt-ər\ *n* : ALLIGATOR

gauche \'gōsh\ *adj* : lacking social experience or grace [French, literally "left, on the left hand"; probably so called because for most people the left hand is more awkward to use than the right] — **gauche·ness** *n*

gau·cho \'gaù-chō\ *n, pl* **gauchos** : a cowboy of the South American grass-covered plains

gaud \'gòd, 'gäd\ *n* : ¹ORNAMENT 1, TRINKET

gaudy \'gòd-ē, 'gäd-\ *adj* **gaud·i·er; -est** : too showy — **gaud·i·ly** \'gòd-ᵊl-ē, 'gäd-\ *adv* — **gaud·i·ness** \-ē-nəs\ *n*

¹**gauge** *or* **gage** \'gāj\ *n* **1** : measurement according to some standard or system **2** *usually* **gage** : an instrument for measuring, testing, or registering **3** : the distance between the rails of a railroad **4** : the size of a shotgun expressed as the number of lead balls of the same size as the interior diameter of the barrel required to make a pound ⟨a 12-*gauge* shotgun⟩ **5** : the thickness of sheet metal or the diameter of wire or a screw **6** : the fineness of a knitted fabric in loops per 1½ inch

²**gauge** *or* **gage** *vb* **gauged** *or* **gaged; gaug·ing** *or* **gag·ing 1 a** : to measure exactly **b** : to find out the capacity or contents of **2** : ¹ESTIMATE 1, JUDGE — **gauge·able** \'gā-jə-bəl\ *adj* — **gaug·er** *n*

gaunt \'gònt, 'gänt\ *adj* **1** : being thin and bony (as from hunger or suffering) **2** : grim and forbidding : BARREN, DESOLATE ⟨*gaunt*, leafless trees⟩ — **gaunt·ly** *adv* — **gaunt·ness** *n*

¹**gaunt·let** \'gònt-lət, 'gänt-\ *n* **1** : a protective glove worn with a suit of armor **2** : a protective glove used in industry — **gaunt·let·ed** \-lət-əd\ *adj*

²**gauntlet** *or* **gant·let** *n* : a double file of men armed with weapons (as clubs) with which to strike at a person who is made to run between them

gauze \'gòz\ *n* **1** : a thin often transparent fabric **2** : a loosely woven cotton surgical bandage **3** : a woven fabric of fine metal or plastic wires — **gauzy** \'gò-zē\ *adj*

gave *past of* GIVE

gav·el \'gav-əl\ *n* : the mallet of an officer in charge of a meeting or of an auctioneer

ga·votte \gə-'vät\ *n* : a French peasant dance in moderately quick 4/4 time — **gavotte** *vb*

¹**gawk** \'gòk\ *n* : a clumsy stupid peson : LOUT [probably from a dialect word *gawk* "left-handed"]

²**gawk** *vb* : to stare stupidly [probably an altered form of obsolete *gaw* "to stare"; of Norse origin]

gawky \'gò-kē\ *adj* **gawk·i·er; -est** : AWKWARD 2, CLUMSY — **gawk·i·ly** \-kə-lē\ *adv* — **gawk·i·ness** \-kē-nəs\ *n*

gay \'gā\ *adj* **gay·er; gay·est 1** : happily excited : MERRY **2 a** : CHEERFUL 1a, LIVELY **b** : brilliant in color **3** : given to social pleasures **4** : ¹HOMOSEXUAL — **gay** *adv* — **gay·ness** *n*

gayety *variant of* GAIETY

gayly *variant of* GAILY

gaze \'gāz\ *vb* **gazed; gaz·ing** : to fix the eyes in a steady intent look — **gaze** *n* — **gaz·er** *n*

syn GAZE, GAPE STARE, GLARE mean to fix one's eyes on something for a long time. GAZE suggests looking steadily at something in wonder, admiration, or absentmind-

edness ⟨*gazing* at the moon⟩ GAPE suggests an open-mouthed, often stupid, wonder ⟨toddlers *gaping* at strangers⟩ STARE suggests a wide-eyed, often curious, rude, or vacant, gaze ⟨people were *staring* at the couple who were arguing⟩ GLARE suggests fierce or angry staring ⟨the speaker *glared* at the people talking⟩

ga·zelle \gə-'zel\ *n, pl* **ga·zelles** *also* **gazelle** : any of numerous small graceful swift antelopes with soft bright eyes

ga·zette \gə-'zet\ *n* **1** : NEWSPAPER **2** : an official journal

gaz·et·teer \,gaz-ə-'ti(ə)r\ *n* : a geographical dictionary

gaz·pa·cho \gəz-'päch-ō, gəs-\ *n, pl* **-chos** : a spicy soup that is usually made from chopped vegetables (as tomato and cucumber) and is served cold [Spanish]

gazelle

ge- *or* **geo-** *combining form* : earth : ground : soil ⟨*geo*logy⟩ [derived from Greek *gē* "earth, land"]

¹**gear** \'gi(ə)r\ *n* **1** : EQUIPMENT **2** ⟨fishing *gear*⟩ ⟨camping *gear*⟩ ⟨electronic *gear*⟩ **2 a** : a mechanism that performs a specific function in a machine ⟨steering *gear*⟩ **b** : a toothed wheel : COGWHEEL **3 a** : working relation or adjustment ⟨in *gear*⟩ **b** : one of the adjustments of a motor-vehicle transmission that determine the direction of travel and the relative speed of the engine and the vehicle — **gear·less** \-ləs\ *adj*

²**gear** *vb* **1** : to provide or connect with gearing **2** : to prepare for operation ⟨*gear* up for production⟩ **3** : to make suitable ⟨a book *geared* for children⟩

gear·box \'gi(ə)r-,bäks\ *n* : TRANSMISSION 3

gear·ing \'gi(ə)r-iŋ\ *n* **1** : the act or process of providing or fitting with gears **2** : the parts by which motion is transmitted from one portion of machinery to another

gear·shift \'gi(ə)r-,shift\ *n* : a mechanism by which transmission gears are connected and disconnected

gear wheel *n* : COGWHEEL

gecko \'gek-ō\ *n, pl* **geck·os** *or* **geck·oes** : any of numerous small harmless chiefly tropical lizards that eat insects and are active at night

¹**gee** \'jē\ *imperative verb* — used as a direction to turn to the right or move ahead

²**gee** *interj* — used to show surprise or enthusiasm

geese *pl of* GOOSE

Gei·ger counter \,gī-gər-\ *or* **Geiger–Mül·ler counter** \-'myül-ər-, -'mil-, -'məl-\ *n* : an instrument for detecting the presence of cosmic rays or radioactive substances

gei·sha \'gā-shə, 'gē-\ *n, pl* **geisha** *or* **geishas** : a Japanese girl who is trained to provide entertaining company for men [Japanese, from *gei* "art" and *-sha* "person"]

¹**gel** \'jel\ *n* : a solid jellylike colloid (as gelatin dessert)

²**gel** *vb* **gelled; gel·ling** : to change into or take on the form of a gel

gel·a·tin *also* **gel·a·tine** \'jel-ət-ᵊn\ *n* **1** : gummy or sticky protein obtained by boiling animal tissues and used as food, in photography, and in medicine **2** : an edible jelly formed with gelatin **3** : a thin colored transparent sheet used to color a stage light — **gel·a·tin·like** \-,līk\ *adj*

ge·lat·i·nous \jə-'lat-nəs, -ᵊn-əs\ *adj* **1** : resembling gelatin or jelly **2** : of, relating to, or containing gelatin

geld \'geld\ *vb* : CASTRATE; *also* : SPAY

geld·ing \'gel-diŋ\ *n* : a castrated animal; *esp* : a castrated male horse

gem \'jem\ *n* **1 a** : ¹JEWEL 3 **b** : a usually valuable stone cut and polished for ornament **2** : something prized as being beautiful or perfect — **gem** *vb*

Gem·i·ni \'jem-ə-(,)nē, -,nī; 'gem-ə-,nē\ *n* **1** : a group of stars between Taurus and Cancer usually pictured as twins sitting together   **2 a** : the third sign of the zodiac — see ZODIAC table   **b** : a person whose sign of the zodiac is Gemini

> **Word History** Among the gods worshiped by the ancient Greeks and Romans was a set of twins named Castor and Pollux. They were believed to be sons of Zeus and Leda. These twins spent most of their lives together, and after their deaths, Zeus allowed them to spend eternity together in the sky as stars. They were worshiped as protectors of athletes and sailors. The two of them are usually pictured together in the constellation called *Gemini*, the Latin word for "twins". [Latin, literally "the twins" (Castor and Pollux)]

gem·stone \'jem-,stōn\ *n* : a mineral that when cut and polished can be used in jewelry

gen·darme \'zhän-,därm *also* 'jän-\ *n* : a member of an armed national police force especially in France [from French *gendarme* "policeman", derived as a singular form from earlier *gendarmes, gens d'armes,* literally "men of arms (weapons)"]

gen·der \'jen-dər\ *n*   **1** : SEX 1   **2** : any of two or more classes of words (as nouns or pronouns) or of forms of words (as adjectives) that are partly based on sex and that determine agreement with other words or grammatical forms

gene \'jēn\ *n* : a part of DNA or sometimes RNA that contains chemical information needed to make a particular protein (as an enzyme) controlling or influencing an inherited bodily trait or activity (as eye color, height, or metabolism) or that influences or controls the activity of another gene or genes and that is usually located in a chromosome in the cell nucleus

ge·ne·al·o·gy \,jē-nē-'äl-ə-jē, ,jen-ē-, -'al-\ *n, pl* **-gies**   **1** : the line of ancestors of a person or family or a history of such a line of ancestors   **2** : the study of family lines of ancestors — **ge·ne·a·log·i·cal** \,jē-nē-ə-'läj-i-kəl, ,jen-ē-\ *adj* — **ge·ne·al·o·gist** \-'äl-ə-jəst, -'al-\ *n*

gene mutation *n* : mutation due to a chemical change in a gene

genera *pl of* GENUS

¹**gen·er·al** \'jen-(ə-)rəl\ *adj*   **1** : of, relating to, or influencing the whole : not local or partial (a *general* election)   **2** : taken as a whole (the *general* body of citizens)   **3** : relating to or covering all instances (a *general* conclusion)   **4** : not specific or in detail (a *general* outline)   **5** : common to many (the *general* custom here)   **6** : not special : not specialized (a *general* store)   **7** : of top rank (*general* manager) (inspector *general*)

²**general** *n* : a military officer with a rank above that of a colonel; *esp* : an officer with the rank just above that of a lieutenant general — **in general** : for the most part

gen·er·a·lis·si·mo \,jen-(ə-)rə-'lis-ə-,mō\ *n, pl* **-mos** : the commander in chief of an army [Italian]

gen·er·al·ist \'jen-(ə-)rə-ləst\ *n* : a person whose skills or interests extend to several different fields

gen·er·al·i·ty \,jen-ə-'ral-ət-ē\ *n, pl* **-ties**   **1** : the quality or state of being general   **2 a** : GENERALIZATION 2   **b** : a statement that is unclear or that does not give enough information   **3** : the greatest part : BULK

gen·er·al·iza·tion \,jen-(ə-)rə-lə-'zā-shən\ *n*   **1** : the act or process of generalizing   **2** : a general statement

gen·er·al·ize \'jen-(ə-)rə-,līz\ *vb* **-ized; -iz·ing** : to put in the form of a general rule : draw or state a general conclusion from a number of items or instances

gen·er·al·ly \'jen-(ə-)rə-lē, 'jen-ər-lē\ *adv*   **1** : for the most part (*generally* speaking)   **2** : as a rule : USUALLY

general of the air force : a general of the highest rank in the air force

general of the army : a general of the highest rank in the army

general practitioner *n* : a physician or veterinarian whose

practice is not limited to a specialty

gen·er·ate \'jen-ə-,rāt\ *vb* **-at·ed; -at·ing** : to bring into existence — **gen·er·a·tive** \-ə-,rāt-iv, -(ə-)rət-\ *adj*

gen·er·a·tion \,jen-ə-'rā-shən\ *n*   **1 a** : those having the same parents and being a step in a line from one ancestor (a family that has lived in the same house for four *generations*)   **b** : a group of individuals born and living at the same time   **c** : a type or class of objects developed from an earlier type (third *generation* computers)   **2** : the average length of time between the birth of parents and that of their offspring   **3** : the action or process of generating

gen·er·a·tor \'jen-ə-,rāt-ər\ *n*   **1** : one that generates   **2** : a piece of laboratory equipment in which vapor or gas is formed   **3** : a machine by which mechanical energy is changed into electrical energy

ge·ner·ic \jə-'ner-ik\ *adj*   **1 a** : of, relating to, or characteristic of a whole group or class : GENERAL   **b** : not protected by a trademark registration (*generic* drugs)   **2** : of, relating to, or ranking as a biological genus — **ge·ner·i·cal·ly** \-ner-i-k(ə-)lē\ *adv*

gen·er·os·i·ty \,jen-ə-'räs-ət-ē\ *n, pl* **-ties**   **1** : freedom in spirit or act; *esp* : readiness in giving   **2** : a generous act

gen·er·ous \'jen-(ə-)rəs\ *adj*   **1** : free in giving or sharing   **2** : ¹NOBLE 5, HIGH-MINDED   **3** : ABUNDANT (a *generous* supply) — **gen·er·ous·ly** *adv* — **gen·er·ous·ness** *n*

gen·e·sis \'jen-ə-səs\ *n, pl* **-e·ses** \-ə-,sēz\ : the origin or coming into being of something

Genesis — see BIBLE table

ge·net·ic \jə-'net-ik\ *also* **ge·net·i·cal** \-i-kəl\ *adj* : of, relating to, or involving genetics (*genetic* counseling about the chances of having a child with a birth defect) — **ge·net·i·cal·ly** \-i-k(ə-)lē\ *adv*

genetic code *n* : the chemical code that is the basis of genetic inheritance and consists of triplets of three linked chemical groups which specify particular kinds of amino acids used to make proteins or which start or stop the process of making proteins

genetic engineering *n* : the alteration of genetic material by intervention in genetic processes — **genetically engineered** *adj* — **genetic engineer** *n*

ge·net·i·cist \jə-'net-ə-səst\ *n* : a person who specializes in genetics

ge·net·ics \jə-'net-iks\ *n* : a branch of biology that deals with the inherited traits and variation of organisms

ge·nial \'jēn-yəl\ *adj*   **1** : favoring growth or comfort (a *genial* climate)   **2** : being cheerful and pleasant   **syn** see GRACIOUS — **ge·nial·i·ty** \,jē-nē-'al-ət-ē, jēn-'yal-\ *n* — **ge·nial·ly** \'jē-nyə-lē\ *adv* — **ge·nial·ness** *n*

ge·nie \'jē-nē\ *n* : a magic spirit believed to take human form and serve the person who calls it

gen·i·tal \'jen-ə-t⁰l\ *adj* : of or relating to reproduction or the sexual organs

genital herpes *n* : herpes simplex of the type typically affecting the genitalia

gen·i·ta·lia \,jen-ə-'tāl-yə\ *n pl* : reproductive organs; *esp* : the genital organs on the outside of the body — **gen·i·ta·lic** \-'tal-ik, -'tāl-\ *adj*

gen·i·tals \'jen-ə-t⁰lz\ *n pl* : GENITALIA

gen·i·tive \'jen-ət-iv\ *adj* : of, relating to, or being a grammatical case marking typically possession or source — compare POSSESSIVE — **gen·i·ti·val** \,jen-ə-'tī-vəl\ *adj* — **genitive** *n*

gen·i·to·uri·nary \,jen-ə-tō-'yur-ə-,ner-ē\ *adj* : of or relating to the genital and urinary organs or functions

ge·nius \'jēn-yəs, 'jē-nē-əs\ *n, pl* **ge·nius·es** *or* **ge·nii** \-ē-,ī, -nē-,ī\   **1** *pl* **genii** : an accompanying spirit of a

\ə\ abut	\au̇\ **out**	\i\ **tip**	\ȯ\ **saw**	\u̇\ **foot**
\ər\ **further**	\ch\ **chin**	\ī\ **life**	\ȯi\ **coin**	\y\ **yet**
\a\ **mat**	\e\ **pet**	\j\ **job**	\th\ **thin**	\yü\ **few**
\ā\ **take**	\ē\ **easy**	\ŋ\ **sing**	\th\ **this**	\yu̇\ **cure**
\ä\ **cot, cart**	\g\ **go**	\ō\ **bone**	\ü\ **food**	\zh\ **vision**

person or place **2** : a strong leaning or inclination ⟨a *genius* for getting into trouble⟩ **3** : a peculiar, distinctive, or identifying character ⟨the *genius* of a nation⟩ **4** *pl usually* **geniuses** **a** : a marked aptitude **b** : great natural ability **c** : a very gifted person

Word History The ancient Romans believed in special beings or spirits that were not gods or humans but something in between. They believed that from birth each person had one of these spirits to act as a protector. The Latin name for this spirit was *genius,* which came from *gignere,* meaning "to be the father of, beget". This sense came into English in the early 15th century. Part of such a genius's role was to protect a person's moral character. From this idea in the 16th century came the sense of *genius* meaning "an identifying character". This led to the sense of "a marked aptitude". In time *genius* came to mean "very great intellectual power" and to be applied to people who have such power. [from Latin *genius* "special guardian spirit", from *gignere* "to father, beget" — related to ENGINE, ¹GIN, INGENIOUS]

geno·cide \'jen-ə-ˌsīd\ *n* : the deliberate destruction of a racial, political, or cultural group — **geno·cid·al** \ˌjen-ə-'sīd-ᵊl\ *adj*

ge·no·type \'jē-nə-ˌtīp, 'jen-ə-\ *n* : the whole set of genes of an individual or group — **ge·no·typ·ic** \ˌjē-nə-'tip-ik, ˌjen-ə-\ *adj*

genre \'zhän-rə, 'zhäⁿ-, 'jän-rə\ *n* : a particular type or category of literary or artistic composition [French]

gent \'jent\ *n* : ¹MAN 1a, FELLOW

gen·teel \jen-'tē(ə)l\ *adj* **1** : or or relating to the upper classes **2** : ELEGANT 1, GRACEFUL **3** : free from bad manners or bad taste — **gen·teel·ly** \-'tē(ə)l-lē\ *adv* — **gen·teel·ness** *n*

gen·tian \'jen-chən\ *n* : any of various herbs that produce showy bell-shaped or funnel‡ shaped usually blue flowers in the fall and have smooth leaves arranged in pairs with one of each pair on opposite sides of the stem

gentian violet *n* : a violet dye used as a stain in biology and in a cream or liquid as an antiseptic in some infections caused by bacteria and fungi

gen·tile \'jen-ˌtīl\ *n* **1** *often cap* : a person who is not Jewish **2** : a person who does not follow the God of the Bible : HEATHEN, PAGAN **3** *often cap* : a person who is not a Mormon [Middle English *gentil, gentile* "one who is not Jewish", derived from Latin *gentilis* "a member of the same family, clan, or nation", from *gent-, gens* "clan, family, race"; from the fact that the early Christians used the Latin word *genes,* plural of *gens,* as a translation of the Hebrew *gōyīm,* literally "the nations", used to refer to all non-Jewish people] — **gentile** *adj*

gen·til·i·ty \jen-'til-ət-ē\ *n, pl* **-ties** **1** : good birth and family **2** : the qualities of a well-bred person **3** : good manners

gen·tle \'jent-ᵊl\ *adj* **gen·tler** \'jent-lər, -ᵊl-ər\; **gen·tlest** \'jent-ləst, -ᵊl-əst\ **1** : belonging or suitable to a family of high social rank **2 a** : easily handled : DOCILE **b** : not harsh or stern : MILD **3** : ¹SOFT 1, SOOTHING ⟨a *gentle* murmur⟩ **4** : ¹MODERATE 2a ⟨*gentle* slopes⟩ — **gentle** *vb* — **gen·tle·ness** *n* — **gent·ly** \'jent-lē\ *adv*

gen·tle·folk \'jent-ᵊl-ˌfōk\ *also* **gen·tle·folks** \-ˌfōks\ *n pl* : persons of gentle or good family and breeding

gen·tle·man \'jen(t)-ᵊl-mən\ *n* **1** : a man of good birth and

gentian

position **2** : a man of good education and social position **3** : a man with very good manners **4** *pl* — used as a form of address in speaking to a group of men — **gen·tle·man·li·ness** \-lē-nəs\ *n* — **gen·tle·man·ly** \-lē\ *adj*

gen·tle·wom·an \'jent-ᵊl-ˌwùm-ən\ *n* **1 a** : a woman of good birth and position **b** : a woman attending a lady of rank **2** : a woman with very good manners : LADY

gen·try \'jen-trē\ *n, pl* **gentries** **1** : people of good birth, breeding, and education : ARISTOCRACY **2** : the class of English people between the nobility and the yeomanry

gen·u·flect \'jen-yə-ˌflekt\ *vb* : to kneel on one knee and then rise again as an act of deep respect

gen·u·ine \'jen-yə-wən, -(ˌ)win\ *adj* **1** : being actually what it seems to be : REAL ⟨*genuine* gold⟩ **2** : not pretended : SINCERE, HONEST ⟨a *genuine* interest⟩ — **gen·u·ine·ly** *adv* — **gen·u·ine·ness** \-wən-(n)əs\ *n*

ge·nus \'jē-nəs\ *n, pl* **gen·era** \'jen-ə-rə\ : a category of classification in biology that ranks between the family and the species, contains related species, and is named by a capitalized noun formed in Latin

geo- — see GE-

geo·cen·tric \ˌjē-ō-'sen-trik\ *adj* **1** : relating to or measured from the earth's center **2** : having or relating to the earth as a center

geo·chem·is·try \ˌjē-ō-'kem-ə-strē\ *n* : a science that deals with the chemical composition of and chemical changes in the crust of the earth — **geo·chem·i·cal** \-'kem-i-kəl\ *adj* — **geo·chem·ist** \-'kem-əst\ *n*

ge·ode \'jē-ˌōd\ *n* : a section of stone having a cavity lined with crystals or mineral matter

geo·de·sic \ˌjē-ə-'des-ik, -'dēs-, -'dez-, -'dēz-\ *adj* : made of light short straight structural elements ⟨a *geodesic* dome⟩

geo·det·ic survey \ˌjē-ə-'det-ik-\ *n* : a survey of a large land area in which corrections are made for the curving of the earth's surface

geographical mile *n* : NAUTICAL MILE

ge·og·ra·phy \jē-'äg-rə-fē\ *n, pl* **-phies** **1** : a science that deals with the location of living and nonliving things on earth and the way they affect one another **2** : the natural parts of an area ⟨the *geography* of the western United States⟩ — **ge·og·ra·pher** \-fər\ *n* — **geo·graph·ic** \ˌjē-ə-'graf-ik\ *or* **geo·graph·i·cal** \-i-kəl\ *adj* — **geo·graph·i·cal·ly** \-i-k(ə-)lē\ *adv*

geologic time *n* : the long period of time marked by events in the earth's geological history

ge·ol·o·gy \jē-'äl-ə-jē\ *n, pl* **-gies** **1 a** : a science that deals with the history of the earth and its life especially as recorded in rocks **b** : a study of the features of a heavenly body (as the moon) **2** : the geologic features (as mountains or plains) of an area — **geo·log·ic** \ˌjē-ə-'läj-ik\ *or* **geo·log·i·cal** \-i-kəl\ *adj* — **geo·log·i·cal·ly** \-i-k(ə-)lē\ *adv* — **ge·ol·o·gist** \jē-'äl-ə-jəst\ *n*

geo·mag·net·ic \ˌjē-ō-mag-'net-ik\ *adj* : of or relating to the magnetism of the earth — **geo·mag·ne·tism** \-'mag-nə-ˌtiz-əm\ *n*

ge·om·e·ter \jē-'äm-ət-ər\ *n* : a person who specializes in geometry

geo·met·ric \ˌjē-ə-'me-trik\ *also* **geo·met·ri·cal** \-'me-tri-kəl\ *adj* : of, relating to, or based on geometry and especially on the methods or principles of geometry — **geo·met·ri·cal·ly** \-tri-k(ə-)lē\ *adv*

ge·om·e·try \jē-'äm-ə-trē\ *n, pl* **-tries** **1** : a branch of mathematics that deals with points, lines, angles, surfaces, and solids **2** : ²SHAPE 1 ⟨the *geometry* of a crystal⟩

Geor·gian \'jòr-jən\ *adj* : of, relating to, or characteristic of the reigns of the first four British kings named George ⟨*Georgian* architecture⟩

geo·tax·is \ˌjē-ō-'tak-səs\ *n, pl* **-tax·es** \-'tak-sēz\ : a taxis in which the force of gravity is the cause of the movement

geo·ther·mal \ˌjē-ō-'thər-məl\ *also* **geo·ther·mic** \-mik\ *adj* : of, relating to, or using the heat of the earth's interior;

GEOLOGIC TIME

EON	ERA	PERIOD	EPOCH	APPROXIMATE NUMBER OF YEARS AGO	BIOLOGICAL FORMS
Phanerozoic	Cenozoic	Quaternary	Holocene	10,000	
			Pleistocene	1,600,000	Earliest humans
		Tertiary	Pliocene	5,000,000	
			Miocene	24,000,000	Earliest hominids
			Oligocene	37,000,000	
			Eocene	58,000,000	Earliest grasses
			Paleocene	65,000,000	
	Mesozoic	Cretaceous		144,000,000	Extinction of dinosaurs at end of period Earliest flowering plants
		Jurassic		208,000,000	Earliest birds & mammals
		Triassic		245,000,000	Age of dinosaurs begins
	Paleozoic	Permian		286,000,000	
		Carboniferous			
		Pennsylvanian		320,000,000	Earliest reptiles
		Mississippian		360,000,000	
		Devonian		408,000,000	Earliest amphibians & ferns
		Silurian		438,000,000	Earliest insects & land plants
		Ordovician		505,000,000	
		Cambrian		570,000,000	Earliest fish
Proterozoic				2,500,000,000	Earliest soft-bodied invertebrates
Archean				4,000,000,000	Life appears: earliest algae & primitive bacteria

also : produced by such heat

ge·ot·ro·pism \jē-'ä-trə-,piz-əm\ *n* : a tropism involving turning or movement toward the earth — **geo·tro·pic** \,jē-ə-'trō-pik, -'träp-ik\ *adj*

ge·ra·ni·um \jə-'rā-nē-əm\ *n* **1** : any of a genus of herbs with usually deeply cut leaves, flowers in which glands alternate with the petals, and long slender dry fruits **2** : any of a genus of herbs that have clusters of scarlet, pink, or white flowers with the sepals joined at the base into a hollow tube closed at one end

  Word History Many of the plants in the geranium family have long, thin, pointed seedpods or fruits that look like the bills of birds. The ancient Greeks noticed this resemblance. They named the wild geranium *geranion*, literally meaning "little crane", for the long-legged, long-billed wading bird. English borrowed the Latin form *geranium*. English also borrowed the idea that the geranium's seedpod looks like a bird's bill. The common English name of the wild geranium is *cranesbill*. [from Latin *geranium* "geranium", from Greek *geranion*, literally "little crane", from *geranos* "crane"]

ger·bil \'jer-bəl\ *n* : any of several Old World desert rodents with long hind legs

ge·ri·at·ric \,jer-ē-'a-trik, ,jir-\ *adj* : of or relating to geri-

\ə\ **abut**	\au̇\ **out**	\i\ **tip**	\ȯ\ **saw**	\u̇\ **foot**
\ər\ **further**	\ch\ **chin**	\ī\ **life**	\ȯi\ **coin**	\y\ **yet**
\a\ **mat**	\e\ **pet**	\j\ **job**	\th\ **thin**	\yü\ **few**
\ā\ **take**	\ē\ **easy**	\ŋ\ **sing**	\th\ **this**	\yu̇\ **cure**
\ä\ **cot, cart**	\g\ **go**	\ō\ **bone**	\ü\ **food**	\zh\ **vision**

atrics, the aged, or the process of aging

ge·ri·at·rics \,jer-ē-'a-triks, ,jir-\ *n* : a branch of medicine that deals with the problems and diseases of old age and aging people

germ \'jərm\ *n* **1 a** : a small mass of living substance capable of developing into a whole individual or one of its parts **b** : the embryo in the seed of a cereal (as corn or wheat) together with its cotyledon that is usually separated from the starchy part of the seed during milling **2** : something that serves as an origin ⟨the *germ* of an idea⟩ **3** : a microscopic living thing; *esp* : one that causes disease

Ger·man \'jər-mən\ *n* **1** : a person born or living in Germany, East Germany, or West Germany **2** : the Germanic language of Germany, Austria, and parts of Switzerland — **German** *adj*

German cockroach *n* : a small active cockroach with wings that is probably of African origin but is now common in many city buildings in the U.S.

ger·mane \(,)jər-'mān\ *adj* : having a close relationship : FITTING ⟨her comment was *germane* to the discussion⟩ — **ger·mane·ly** *adv*

¹Ger·man·ic \(,)jər-'man-ik\ *adj* **1** : of, relating to, or characteristic of the peoples speaking Germanic languages **2** : of or relating to Germanic

²Germanic *n* : a branch of the Indo-European language family containing English, German, Dutch, and the Scandinavian languages

ger·ma·ni·um \(,)jər-'mā-nē-əm\ *n* : a grayish white hard brittle element used as a semiconductor — see ELEMENT table

German measles *n sing or pl* : a contagious virus disease that is like the usual kind of measles but is milder and that may cause birth defects or the death of the fetus when it occurs in a pregnant woman — called also *rubella*

German shepherd *n* : a large erect-eared intelligent dog of a breed originating in northern Europe that is often used in police work and as a guide dog for the blind

German silver *n* : a silver-white blend of copper, zinc, and nickel

germ cell *n* : an egg or sperm or one of the cells reserved by the body for forming eggs and sperms

germ·free \'jərm-,frē\ *adj* : free of germs

ger·mi·cid·al \,jər-mə-'sīd-ᵊl\ *adj* : of or relating to a germicide; *also* : destroying germs

gerrymander

ger·mi·cide \'jər-mə-,sīd\ *n* : a substance that destroys germs

ger·mi·nate \'jər-mə-,nāt\ *vb* **-nat·ed; -nat·ing** **1** : to cause to sprout or develop **2** : to begin to grow : SPROUT **3** : to come into being : EVOLVE — **ger·mi·na·tion** \,jər-mə-'nā-shən\ *n*

germ theory *n* **1** : the theory that living things can be produced only by development from living parts (as a fertilized egg produced by combination of egg and sperm) from other living things **2** : the theory that infectious and contagious disease results from the action of living things

¹ger·ry·man·der \,jer-ē-'man-dər, 'jer-ē-,man-dər *also* ,ger-, 'ger-\ *n* : the act or result of gerrymandering [from Elbridge *Gerry*, former governor of Massachusetts, and sala*mander*; so called from the shape of an election district formed during Gerry's term in office]

²gerrymander *vb* **-dered; -der·ing** \-d(ə-)riŋ\ : to divide (as a state) into election districts so as to give one political party an advantage

ger·und \'jer-ənd\ *n* : an English noun formed from a verb by the addition of *-ing* that is capable of taking adverbial modifiers and having an object

ges·so \'jes-ō\ *n* : a material like plaster used in art (as for modeling)

ges·ta·tion \je-'stā-shən\ *n* : the carrying of young in the uterus : PREGNANCY

ges·tic·u·late \je-'stik-yə-,lāt\ *vb* **-lat·ed; -lat·ing** : to make gestures especially when speaking — **ges·tic·u·la·tion** \-,stik-yə-'lā-shən\ *n*

¹ges·ture \'jes-chər, 'jesh-\ *n* **1** : a movement of the body or limbs that expresses or emphasizes an idea or a feeling **2** : something said or done by way of courtesy or for its effect on other people ⟨a political *gesture*⟩

²gesture *vb* **ges·tured; ges·tur·ing** : to make or direct with a gesture

get \(')get, *especially when unemphatic also* git\ *vb* **got** \(')gät\; **got** *or* **got·ten** \'gät-ᵊn\; **get·ting** **1** : to gain possession of (as by receiving, acquiring, earning, buying, or winning) ⟨*get* a present⟩ ⟨*got* first prize⟩ ⟨*get* a dog⟩ **2 a** : to obtain by request or as a favor ⟨*get* your mother's permission⟩ **b** : to come to have ⟨*get* a good night's sleep⟩ **c** : to come down with (an illness) : CATCH ⟨*get* the measles⟩ **3 a** : to succeed in coming or going ⟨*got* out⟩ ⟨*got* home early⟩ **b** : to cause to come or go ⟨*got* the car to the gas station⟩ **4** : to become the father of : BEGET **5 a** : to cause to be in a certain condition ⟨*got* his hair cut⟩ ⟨*got* her feet wet⟩ **b** : BECOME 1 ⟨*get* sick⟩ ⟨*get* better⟩ ⟨it's *getting* warmer⟩ **c** : PREPARE 2 ⟨started *getting* dinner⟩ **6 a** : ¹BAFFLE 1, PUZZLE ⟨the third question *got* everybody⟩ **b** : IRRITATE 1 ⟨don't let it *get* you⟩ **c** : ¹HIT 1c ⟨*got* him in the leg⟩ **d** : ¹KILL 1 ⟨swore to *get* them⟩ **7 a** : to be subjected to or experience ⟨*get* a broken nose⟩ **b** : to receive as punishment ⟨*got* six months for larceny⟩ **8 a** : to find out by calculation ⟨*got* the right answer⟩ **b** : to hear correctly ⟨I didn't *get* your name⟩ **c** : UNDERSTAND 1a ⟨now I've *got* it⟩ ⟨I *get* you⟩ **9** : PERSUADE, INDUCE ⟨couldn't *get* her to agree⟩ **10 a** : ¹HAVE 1 — used in the present perfect form with present meaning ⟨I've *got* no time⟩ **b** : to have to : MUST — used in the present perfect form with present meaning ⟨has *got* to come⟩ **11** : DELIVER 6 ⟨the car *gets* 20 miles to the gallon⟩

syn GET, OBTAIN, PROCURE, SECURE mean to bring into one's possession. GET applies broadly to any manner of gaining possession ⟨*get* me another pencil⟩ OBTAIN may suggest getting by planning or effort ⟨forms must be completed to *obtain* a loan from the bank⟩ PROCURE may suggest getting something through a formal or set procedure ⟨*procured* new desks for the workers⟩ SECURE may suggest safe or lasting possession ⟨*secured* rights to publish the book⟩

— **get across** : to make clear ⟨*got* the point *across*⟩ — **get ahead** : to achieve success (as in business) — **get around** **1** : to get the better of **2** : EVADE 1 — **get at** **1** : to reach effectively **2** : to try to prove or make clear ⟨what is he *getting at*?⟩ — **get away with** : to avoid criticism or punishment for (as a bad action) — **get back at** : to get even with — **get even** : to get revenge — **get even with** : to repay in kind — **get into** : to become strongly involved in — **get into the act** : to get involved in a situation — **get it** : to receive a scolding or punishment — **get one's goat** : to make one angry or annoyed — **get over** : to recover from (as an illness) — **get through** : to reach the end of — **get to** **1** : BEGIN 1 ⟨*gets* to worrying very easily⟩ **2** : to be ready to deal with ⟨I'll *get to* my homework after dinner⟩ **3** : to have an effect on : INFLUENCE — **get together** **1** : to bring or come together : ASSEMBLE **2** : to reach agreement — **get wind of** : to become aware of — **get with it** : to become alert or aware

get along *vb* **1 a** : ²PROGRESS 2 **b** : to approach old age ⟨*getting along* in years⟩ **2** : MANAGE 4 ⟨*get along* on a small pension⟩ **3** : to be or remain on pleasant terms ⟨easy to *get along* with⟩

get·away \'get-ə-,wā\ *n* **1** : ²ESCAPE 1 **2** : the action of starting

get away *vb* **1** : to get free from a trap or a limiting or dangerous situation   **2** : to move off from a starting point (as to begin a trip)

get by *vb* **1** : MANAGE 4   **2** : to succeed with the least possible effort or accomplishment ⟨barely *got by*⟩

get off *vb* **1** : SET OUT 2 ⟨*got off* on their camping trip⟩   **2** : to escape or help to escape punishment or harm ⟨*got off* with just a warning⟩

get on *vb* **1** : GET ALONG 1, 3 ⟨was *getting on* in years⟩ ⟨*got on* well with the boss⟩ ⟨*get on* with the game⟩

get out *vb* **1** : PUBLISH 2a   **2** : to escape or help to escape   **3** : to become known : leak out ⟨their secret *got out*⟩

get–to·geth·er \'get-tə-,geth-ər\ *n* : MEETING 2; *esp* : an informal social gathering

get·up \'get-,əp\ *n* : ¹OUTFIT 1, COSTUME

get up \get-'əp, git-\ *vb* **1 a** : to arise from bed   **b** : to rise to one's feet   **2** : PREPARE 2, ORGANIZE ⟨*get up* a petition⟩

gew·gaw \'g(y)ü-gò\ *n* : a thing of little worth : TRINKET

gey·ser \'gī-zər\ *n* : a spring that now and then shoots out hot water and steam [from Icelandic *geysir* "gusher"; of Norse origin]

ghast·ly \'gast-lē\ *adj* **ghast·li·er**; **-est** : HORRIBLE 1, SHOCKING ⟨a *ghastly* crime⟩ — **ghast·li·ness** *n* — **ghastly** *adv*

gher·kin \'gər-kən\ *n* : a small young cucumber used to make pickles; *also* : a small prickly fruit of a vine related to the cucumber that is used for the same purpose

ghet·to \'get-ō\ *n, pl* **ghettos** *or* **ghettoes** **1** : a part of a city in which Jews were formerly required to live   **2** : a part of a city in which members of a minority group live especially because of social, legal, or economic pressure

ghost \'gōst\ *n* : the soul of a dead person thought of as living in an unseen world or as appearing to living people

ghost·ly \'gōst-lē\ *adj* **ghost·li·er**; **-est** : of, relating to, or having the characteristics of a ghost — **ghost·li·ness** *n*

ghost town *n* : a town deserted because some nearby natural resource has been used up

ghost·write \'gō-,strīt\ *vb* **-wrote** \-,strōt\; **-writ·ten** \-,strit-ᵊn\; **-writ·ing** \-,strīt-iŋ\ : to write for and in the name of another — **ghost·writ·er** *n*

ghoul \'gül\ *n* **1** : an evil being of legend that robs graves and feeds on corpses   **2** : a person (as a grave robber) whose activities suggest those of a ghoul — **ghoul·ish** \'gü-lish\ *adj* — **ghoul·ish·ly** *adv* — **ghoul·ish·ness** *n*

¹GI \(')jē-'ī\ *adj* : of, relating to, or characteristic of U.S. military forces [from the abbreviation for *galvanized iron* used in listing such articles as garbage cans, but mistaken as standing for *government issue*]

²GI *n, pl* **GI's** *or* **GIs** : a member or former member of the U.S. armed forces

¹gi·ant \'jī-ənt\ *n* **1** : a being of legend of great size and strength   **2** : a person or thing that is very large or powerful

²giant *adj* : much larger or more powerful than ordinary

giant cactus *n* : SAGUARO

giant sequoia *n* : BIG TREE

giant squid *n* : any of a group of very large squids that include the largest mollusks known with some being 12 meters long including the long arms

giant star *n* : a very bright star of large mass

giant tortoise *n* : any of numerous large plant-eating tortoises that were formerly common on the islands of the western Indian ocean and on the Galapagos islands but are now much reduced in numbers

gib·ber \'jib-ər\ *vb* **gib·bered**; **gib·ber·ing** \-(ə-)riŋ\ : to speak rapidly and often foolishly — **gib·ber** *n*

gib·ber·el·lin \,jib-ə-'rel-ən\ *n* : any of several chemical substances that regulate the growth of plants and in low concentrations cause shoots to grow

gib·ber·ish \'jib-(ə-)rish, 'gib-\ *n* : confused meaningless talk

gib·bet \'jib-ət\ *n* : GALLOWS

gib·bon \'gib-ən\ *n* : any of several tailless apes of southeastern Asia and the East Indies that are smaller and spend more time in trees than the gorilla, chimpanzee, and orangutan

gib·bous \'jib-əs, 'gib-\ *adj* : seen with more than half but not all of the disk lighted ⟨*gibbous* moon⟩

gibbon

gibe *or* **jibe** \'jīb\ *vb* **gibed** *or* **jibed**; **gib·ing** *or* **jib·ing** : JEER — **gibe** *or* **jibe** *n* — **gib·er** *n*

gib·let \'jib-lət *also* 'gib-\ *n* : an edible inner organ (as the heart or liver) of a fowl — usually used in pl.

gid·dap \gid-'ap, -'əp\ *imperative verb* — used as a command to a horse to go ahead or go faster

gid·dy \'gid-ē\ *adj* **gid·di·er**; **-est** **1** : having a feeling of whirling or spinning about : DIZZY   **2** : causing dizziness   **3** : SILLY 3 — **gid·di·ly** \'gid-ᵊl-ē\ *adv* — **gid·di·ness** \'gid-ē-nəs\ *n*

gift \'gift\ *n* **1** : a special ability : TALENT   **2** : something given : PRESENT — **gift·ed** \'gif-təd\ *adj*

gig \'gig\ *n* **1** : a long light ship's boat   **2** : a light two=wheeled one-horse carriage

giga- \'jig-ə, 'gig-ə\ *combining form* : billion ⟨*giga*byte⟩ [derived from Greek *gigas* "giant"]

giga·byte \-,bīt\ *n* : 1,073,741,824 bytes

gi·gan·tic \jī-'gant-ik\ *adj* : being beyond the ordinary or expected (as in size, weight, or strength)

gig·gle \'gig-əl\ *vb* **gig·gled**; **gig·gling** \-(ə-)liŋ\ : to laugh with repeated short high sounds — **giggle** *n*

Gi·la monster \,hē-lə-\ *n* : a large orange and black poisonous lizard of the southwestern U.S.; *also* : a related Mexican lizard [from *Gila*, name of a river in Arizona]

Gila monster

¹gild \'gild\ *vb* **gild·ed** \'gil-dəd\ *or* **gilt** \'gilt\; **gild·ing** : to cover with or as if with a coating of gold — **gilder** *n*

²gild *variant of* GUILD

¹gill \'jil\ *n* — see MEASURE table

²gill \'gil\ *n* **1** : an organ (as of a fish) of thin plates or threadlike processes for obtaining oxygen from water   **2** : the flesh under or about the chin or jaws — usually used in pl.   **3** : one of the plates arranged in a circle and forming the undersurface of the cap of a mushroom

gill arch *n* **1** : one of the several bars of bone or cartilage that occur in pairs with one of each pair on each side of the throat and that support the gills of fishes and amphibians   **2** : one of the undeveloped ridges that occur in the embryos of all higher vertebrates and correspond to the gill arches

gill filament *n* : one of the threadlike processes making up a gill

gill raker *n* : one of the bony spines that lie in front of the gills of a fish and that prevent solid particles from entering the gills

gill slit *n* **1** : any of the openings or clefts which occur in vertebrates with gills and through which water taken in at the mouth moves to the outside bathing the gills   **2** : a gill slit in an early stage that occurs at some time in the de-

\ə\ abut	\au̇\ out	\i\ tip	\ȯ\ saw	\u̇\ foot
\ər\ further	\ch\ chin	\ī\ life	\ȯi\ coin	\y\ yet
\a\ mat	\e\ pet	\j\ job	\th\ thin	\yü\ few
\ā\ take	\ē\ easy	\ŋ\ sing	\t͟h\ this	\yu̇\ cure
\ä\ cot, cart	\g\ go	\ō\ bone	\ü\ food	\zh\ vision

velopment of the embryos of all vertebrates

¹gilt \\'gilt\\ *adj* : of the color of gold

²gilt *n* : gold or something like gold laid on a surface

gim·let \\'gim-lət\\ *n* : a small tool with a screw point and cross handle for boring holes

gim·mick \\'gim-ik\\ *n*　**1** : an ingenious scheme or device　**2** : an important feature that is not immediately apparent — **gim·micky** \\-i-kē\\ *adj*

¹gin \\'jin\\ *n* : COTTON GIN [Middle English *gin* "a mechanical device, skill, trick", from early French *engin* (same meaning), from Latin *ingenium* "natural ability or desire to do something, inborn ability", from *in* "in" and *-genium*, from *gignere* "to father, beget" — related to ENGINE, GENIUS, INGENIOUS]

²gin *vb* **ginned; gin·ning** : to separate (cotton fiber) from seeds and waste material — **gin·ner** *n*

³gin *n* : a clear strong alcoholic liquor flavored with juniper berries [an altered form of earlier *geneva* "gin (liquor)", from obsolete Dutch *genever*, literally "juniper"]

gin·ger \\'jin-jər\\ *n*　**1 a** : a thick underground plant stem that is used to make a spice and sometimes in medicine　**b** : a spice prepared by drying and grinding ginger　**2** : any of a genus of Old World herbs that have thick underground stems and include one supplying most of the ginger used as a spice and in medicine　**3** : high spirit : PEP — **gin·gery** \\'jinj-(ə-)rē\\ *adj*

ginger ale *n* : a soft drink flavored with ginger

gin·ger·bread \\'jin-jər-ˌbred\\ *n*　**1** : a cake made with molasses and flavored with ginger　**2** : showy ornamentation especially in architecture — **gingerbread** *adj*

gin·ger·ly \\'jin-jər-lē\\ *adj* : very cautious or careful — **gingerly** *adv*

gin·ger·root \\'jin-jər-ˌ(r)üt, -ˌ(r)u̇t\\ *n* : GINGER 1a

gin·ger·snap \\'jin-jər-ˌsnap\\ *n* : a thin brittle cookie flavored with ginger

ging·ham \\'giŋ-əm\\ *n* : a cotton clothing fabric in plain weave

gin·gi·vi·tis \\ˌjin-jə-'vīt-əs\\ *n* : inflammation of the gums

gink·go *also* **ging·ko** \\'giŋ-kō *also* 'giŋk-gō\\ *n, pl* **gink·goes** *or* **ginkgos** : a large Chinese tree with fan-shaped leaves and bad-smelling fruit that is often grown as a shade tree

gin·seng \\'jin-ˌsaŋ, -ˌseŋ, -ˌ(ˌ)siŋ\\ *n*　**1** : a forked fragrant root of a Chinese or North American herb that is used especially in oriental medicine　**2** : either the Chinese or the North American herb that is the source of ginseng

Gipsy *variant of* GYPSY

gi·raffe \\'jə-'raf\\ *n, pl* **giraffe** *or* **giraffes** : a large swift cud-chewing spotted African mammal with a very long neck that is the tallest of living four-footed animals

gird \\'gərd\\ *vb* **gird·ed** \\'gərd-əd\\ *or* **girt** \\'gərt\\; **gird·ing**　**1** : to encircle or fasten with or as if with a belt or cord　**2** : to provide especially with the sword of knighthood

gird·er \\'gərd-ər\\ *n* : a horizontal main supporting beam

¹gir·dle \\'gərd-ᵊl\\ *n*　**1** : a belt or sash encircling the waist　**2** : a light corset worn below the waist　**3** : a bony arch that supports an arm or leg

²girdle *vb* **gir·dled; gir·dling** \\'gərd-liŋ, -ᵊl-iŋ\\　**1** : to bind or encircle with or as if with a girdle : CIRCLE　**2** : to cut away the bark and cambium in a ring around (a plant) usually in order to kill by stopping the circulation of water and food

girl \\'gər(-ə)l\\ *n*　**1 a** : a female child　**b** : a young woman　**2** : a female servant　**3** : SWEETHEART [Middle English

giraffe

gurle, girle "a young person of either sex"] — **girl·hood** \\-ˌhu̇d\\ *n* — **girl·ish** \\'gər-lish\\ *adj* — **girl·ish·ness** *n*

girl·friend \\'gər(-ə)l-ˌfrend\\ *n*　**1** : a female friend　**2** : a frequent or regular female companion of a boy or man

Girl Scout *n* : a member of the Girl Scouts of the United States of America

girt \\'gərt\\ *vb*　**1** : GIRD　**2** : to fasten by means of a girth

girth \\'gərth\\ *n*　**1** : a band around the body of an animal to fasten something (as a saddle) upon its back　**2** : a measure around a body ⟨a person of large *girth*⟩ ⟨the *girth* of a tree trunk⟩ — **girth** *vb*

gist \\'jist\\ *n* : the main point of a subject : DRIFT

¹give \\'giv\\ *vb* **gave** \\'gāv\\; **giv·en** \\'giv-ən\\; **giv·ing**　**1** : to make a present of or to ⟨*gave* me a book⟩　**2 a** : ¹GRANT 2, BESTOW　**b** : to make a donation ⟨*give* blood⟩ ⟨we already *gave* at the office⟩　**c** : to grant or yield to another ⟨*gave* her trust to her friend⟩　**3 a** : to put into the possession or keeping of another ⟨*give* me the letter to mail⟩　**b** : to offer to another : PROFFER ⟨*gave* his hand to the visitor⟩　**c** : HAND OVER, DELIVER; *esp* : to deliver in exchange ⟨*gave* loyalty in return for protection⟩　**d** : ¹PAY 1 ⟨wouldn't *give* a penny for that bike⟩　**4 a** : to present in public performance ⟨*give* a concert⟩　**b** : to present to view ⟨*gave* the signal to start⟩　**5** : to provide by way of entertainment ⟨*give* a party⟩　**6** : to point out or set aside as a share or portion ⟨*gave* their daughter half of their estate⟩　**7** : to indicate the source or cause of ⟨*give* all the glory to her mother⟩　**8** : to form, make, or yield as a product or result ⟨cows *give* milk⟩ ⟨84 divided by 12 *gives* 7⟩　**9 a** : to deliver by some bodily action ⟨*gave* me a push⟩　**b** : to carry out a movement : PERFORM ⟨*gave* a sudden leap⟩　**c** : ²UTTER 2 ⟨*give* judgment⟩　**10** : to offer for consideration or acceptance ⟨*gives* no reason for his absence⟩　**11** : to apply fully : DEVOTE ⟨*gave* herself to the cause⟩　**12** : to cause to have ⟨*gave* pleasure to the reader⟩　**13** : to yield or collapse under force or pressure ⟨the box *gave* under his foot⟩ — **giv·er** *n*

　　syn GIVE, PRESENT, DONATE mean to hand over to someone without expecting something in return. GIVE can be used of anything that is delivered in any way ⟨*give* me those cups⟩ ⟨*give* a gift to a friend⟩ PRESENT suggests that something is given with some ceremony ⟨*presented* a trophy to the winner⟩ DONATE suggests giving to a charity or for the public good ⟨*donated* new uniforms for the school band⟩

— **give birth** : to have a baby — **give birth to** : to bring forth : BEAR — **give it to** : to attack vigorously ⟨*gave it to* him right between the eyes⟩ — **give rise to** : to be the cause or source of : PRODUCE — **give the lie to** : to show to be false — **give way**　**1** : ²RETREAT 1　**2** : to lose control of oneself ⟨*gave way* to tears at the sad news⟩　**3** : ¹COLLAPSE 3

²give *n*　**1** : tendency to yield to force or strain　**2** : the quality or state of being springy

give–and–take \\ˌgiv-ən-'tāk\\ *n*　**1** : the practice of all sides in a dispute settling for less than they want　**2** : good-natured exchange of ideas

give·away \\'giv-ə-ˌwā\\ *n*　**1** : an unintentional act of revealing or betraying ⟨his expression was a dead *giveaway* of his guilt⟩　**2** : something that is given away free　**3** : a radio or television program on which prizes are given away

give away \\ˌgiv-ə-'wā\\ *vb*　**1** : to present (a bride) to the bridegroom at a wedding　**2 a** : to show unintentionally　**b** : DISCLOSE, REVEAL

give in *vb* : to yield to demands or pleading ⟨*gave in* to the children's cries for a treat⟩

giv·en \\'giv-ən\\ *adj*　**1** : PRONE 1 ⟨*given* to swearing⟩　**2** : FIXED 1b ⟨at a *given* time⟩　**3** : granted as true ⟨*given* that we are all equal⟩

given name *n* : FORENAME

give off *vb* : EMIT 1a

give out *vb*　**1** : EMIT 1b　**2** : to become exhausted : COL-

LAPSE **3** : BREAK DOWN 1

give up vb **1** : ¹SURRENDER 1   **2** : to abandon (oneself) to a feeling, influence, or activity   **3** : ¹STOP 7a

giz·mo or **gis·mo** \'giz-mō\ n, pl **gizmos** or **gismos** : GADGET

giz·zard \'giz-ərd\ n : a large muscular part of the digestive tube (as of a bird) which has a horny lining and in which food is churned and ground into small pieces

gla·cial \'glā-shəl\ adj **1 a** : extremely cold : FRIGID   **b** : lacking warmth of feeling   **2 a** : of, relating to, or produced by glaciers   **b** : of, relating to, or being any of those parts of geologic time when a large portion of the earth was covered by glaciers   **c** cap : PLEISTOCENE

gla·ci·ate \'glā-shē-ˌāt\ vb **-at·ed; -at·ing 1** : to cover with a glacier   **2** : to expose to glacial action; also : to produce glacial effects in or on — **gla·ci·a·tion** \ˌglā-shē-'ā-shən, -sē-\ n

gla·cier \'glā-shər\ n : a large body of ice moving slowly down a slope or valley or spreading outward on a land surface

glad \'glad\ adj **glad·der; glad·dest 1 a** : experiencing pleasure, joy, or delight : made happy   **b** : satisfied in hope, desire, conscience, or vanity ⟨glad you could come⟩ ⟨glad things turned out well⟩   **c** : very willing ⟨glad to do it⟩   **2** : causing happiness and joy : PLEASANT ⟨glad tidings⟩   **3** : full of brightness and cheerfulness ⟨a glad spring morning⟩ — **glad·ly** adv — **glad·ness** n

glad·den \'glad-ən\ vb **glad·dened; glad·den·ing** \-(ə-)niŋ\ : to make glad

glade \'glād\ n : a grassy open space in a forest

glad·i·a·tor \'glad-ē-ˌāt-ər\ n **1** : a person engaged in a fight to the death for public entertainment in ancient Rome   **2** : a person engaging in a fierce fight or controversy [from Latin gladiator, literally "swordsman", from gladius "sword" — related to GLADIOLUS] — **glad·i·a·to·ri·al** \ˌglad-ē-ə-'tōr-ē-əl, -'tòr-\ adj

glad·i·o·lus \ˌglad-ē-'ō-ləs\ n, pl **-o·li** \-'ō-(ˌ)lē, -'ō-ˌlī\ or **-o·lus** or **-o·lus·es** : any of a genus of chiefly African plants related to the irises and having erect sword-shaped leaves and stalks of brilliantly colored flowers [from Latin gladiolus, literally "little sword", from gladius "sword" — related to GLADIATOR]

gladiolus

glad·some \'glad-səm\ adj : giving or showing joy : CHEERFUL ⟨gladsome looks and cheerful voice⟩ — **glad·some·ly** adv — **glad·some·ness** n

glam·or·ize also **glam·our·ize** \'glam-ə-ˌrīz\ vb **-ized; -iz·ing 1** : to make glamorous   **2** : to present so as to seem glamorous

glam·or·ous also **glam·our·ous** \'glam-(ə-)rəs\ adj : full of glamour — **glam·or·ous·ly** adv — **glam·or·ous·ness** n

glam·our or **glam·or** \'glam-ər\ n : romantic, exciting, and often misleading attractiveness

¹glance \'glan(t)s\ vb **glanced; glanc·ing 1** : to strike and fly off at an angle ⟨the arrow glanced off the shield⟩   **2** : to give a quick or hasty look ⟨glanced at my watch⟩ ⟨glanced up from a book⟩   **3** : GLINT a — **glanc·ing·ly** \'glan(t)-siŋ-lē\ adv

²glance n **1** : a quick flash or gleam that comes and goes   **2** : an impact or blow that is turned aside   **3 a** : a swift movement of the eyes   **b** : a quick or hasty look

gland \'gland\ n : a cell or group of cells that makes and secretes a product (as saliva, sweat, bile, or shell) for further use in or for elimination from the plant or animal body

glan·ders \'glan-dərz\ n sing or pl : a destructive bacterial disease especially of horses

glan·du·lar \'glan-jə-lər\ adj **1** : of, relating to, or involving glands, gland cells, or their products ⟨glandular activity⟩   **2** : having the traits or activities of a gland ⟨glandular tissue⟩ — **glan·du·lar·ly** adv

glans \'glanz\ n, pl **glan·des** \'glan-ˌdēz\ : a cone-shaped vascular body forming the end of the penis or clitoris

glare \'gla(ə)r, 'gle(ə)r\ vb **glared; glar·ing 1 a** : to shine with a harsh uncomfortably brilliant light   **b** : to stand out annoyingly   **2** : to stare angrily or fiercely   **syn** see GAZE — **glare** n — **glary** \'gla(ə)r-ē, 'gle(ə)r-\ adj

glar·ing \'gla(ə)r-iŋ, 'gle(ə)r-\ adj : painfully obvious ⟨a glaring mistake⟩ — **glar·ing·ly** adv — **glar·ing·ness** n

¹glass \'glas\ n **1** : a hard brittle usually transparent substance commonly formed by melting a mixture of sand and chemicals and cooling to hardness   **2 a** : something (as a water tumbler, lens, mirror, barometer, or telescope) that is made of glass or has a glass lens   **b** pl : a pair of glass lenses used to help one see clearly   **3** : the quantity held by a glass — **glass·ful** \-ˌfůl\ n

²glass vb : to fit or protect with glass

glass·blow·ing \-ˌblō-iŋ\ n : the art of shaping a mass of hot glass by blowing air into it through a tube — **glass·blow·er** \-ˌblō(-ə)r\ n

glass·mak·er \-ˌmā-kər\ n : a person who makes glass

glass snake n : a limbless lizard of the southern U.S. resembling a snake and having a fragile tail that easily breaks into pieces

glass·ware \'glas-ˌwa(ə)r, -ˌwe(ə)r\ n : articles of glass

glassy \'glas-ē\ adj **glass·i·er; -est 1** : resembling glass   **2** : not shiny or bright ⟨glassy eyes⟩ — **glass·i·ly** \'glas-ə-lē\ adv — **glass·i·ness** \'glas-ē-nəs\ n

glau·co·ma \glau̇-'kō-mə, glȯ-\ n : an abnormal condition of the eye marked by increased pressure inside the eye that causes damage to the retina and gradual loss of vision

¹glaze \'glāz\ vb **glazed; glaz·ing 1** : to set glass in ⟨glaze a window⟩   **2** : to cover with a glassy surface ⟨glaze pottery⟩   **3** : to become shiny or glassy in appearance — **glaz·er** n

²glaze n : a glassy surface or coating

gla·zier \'glā-zhər, -zē-ər\ n : a person who sets glass in window frames

gleam \'glēm\ n **1** : a small briefly visible light : GLINT   **2** : a brief or faint appearance : TRACE ⟨gleam of hope⟩ — **gleam** vb

glean \'glēn\ vb **1** : to gather from a field or vineyard what has been left (as by reapers)   **2** : to gather little by little ⟨glean knowledge from books⟩ — **glean·er** n

glean·ings \'glē-niŋz\ n pl : things acquired by gleaning

glee \'glē\ n **1** : high-spirited joy   **2** : an unaccompanied song for three or more voices — **glee·ful** \-fəl\ adj — **glee·ful·ly** \-fə-lē\ adv — **glee·ful·ness** n

glee club n : a chorus organized for singing usually short choral pieces

glen \'glen\ n : a narrow hidden valley

gli·a·din \'glī-əd-ən\ n : a simple protein that can be obtained from gluten from wheat or rye

glib \'glib\ adj **glib·ber; glib·best** : speaking or spoken with careless ease and often with little regard for truth ⟨a glib excuse⟩ — **glib·ly** adv — **glib·ness** n

glide \'glīd\ vb **glid·ed; glid·ing 1** : to move smoothly, silently, and effortlessly   **2** : to descend gradually without enough engine power for level flight ⟨glide in an airplane⟩ — **glide** n

glid·er \'glīd-ər\ n **1** : an aircraft without an engine that glides on air currents   **2** : a porch seat suspended from a frame by short chains or straps

\ə\ abut	\au̇\ out	\i\ tip	\ȯ\ saw	\ů\ foot
\ər\ further	\ch\ chin	\ī\ life	\ȯi\ coin	\y\ yet
\a\ mat	\e\ pet	\j\ job	\th\ thin	\yü\ few
\ā\ take	\ē\ easy	\ŋ\ sing	\th\ this	\yů\ cure
\ä\ cot, cart	\g\ go	\ō\ bone	\ü\ food	\zh\ vision

glim·mer \'glim-ər\ *n* **1 a** : a feeble or unsteady light **b** : a soft shimmer **2 a** : a faint idea : INKLING **b** : a small amount : BIT — **glimmer** *vb*

¹glimpse \'glim(p)s\ *vb* **glimpsed; glimps·ing** : to take a brief look : see momentarily or incompletely 〈*glimpsed* the deer running through the underbrush〉 — **glimps·er** *n*

²glimpse *n* **1** : a short hurried view 〈catch a *glimpse* of something rushing by〉 **2** : a faint idea : GLIMMER

glint \'glint\ *vb* : to shine by reflection: **a** : to shine with small bright flashes **b** : ¹GLITTER 1 **c** : to shine briefly — **glint** *n*

glis·san·do \gli-'sän-dō\ *n, pl* **-di** \-(ˌ)dē\ *or* **-dos** : a rapid sliding up or down the musical scale

glis·ten \'glis-ᵊn\ *vb* **glis·tened; glis·ten·ing** \'glis-niŋ, -ᵊn-iŋ\ : to shine by reflection with a soft luster or sparkle — **glisten** *n*

glis·ter \'glis-tər\ *vb* **glis·tered; glis·ter·ing** \-t(ə-)riŋ\ : GLISTEN — **glister** *n*

¹glit·ter \'glit-ər\ *vb* **1** : to shine with brilliant or metallic luster 〈*glittering* sequins〉 **2** : ¹SPARKLE 1b **3** : to shine with a hard cold brilliance 〈eyes *glittered* cruelly〉

²glitter *n* **1** : sparkling brilliancy **2** : small glittering objects used for ornamentation — **glit·tery** \'glit-ə-rē\ *adj*

gloam·ing \'glō-miŋ\ *n* : TWILIGHT, DUSK

gloat \'glōt\ *vb* : to gaze at or think about something with great satisfaction or joy 〈*gloating* over their enemy's loss〉 — **gloat·er** *n*

glob \'gläb\ *n* : a small drop : BLOB

glob·al \'glō-bəl\ *adj* **1** : SPHERICAL **2** : WORLDWIDE 〈*global* war〉 **3** : of, relating to, or applying to the whole of something (as a computer program) 〈a *global* search through the data〉 — **glob·al·ly** \-bə-lē\ *adv*

globe \'glōb\ *n* : a round object: as **a** : a model of the earth or heavens **b** : EARTH 4 — usually with *the* — **glob·u·lar** \'gläb-yə-lər\ *adj*

glob·ule \'gläb-(ˌ)yü(ə-)l\ *n* : a tiny globe or ball 〈*globules* of fat〉

glob·u·lin \'gläb-yə-lən\ *n* : any of a class of simple proteins that cannot be dissolved in pure water but can be dissolved in weak salt solutions and that occur widely in plant and animal tissues

glock·en·spiel \'gläk-ən-ˌshpēl, -ˌspēl\ *n* : a portable musical instrument consisting of a series of metal bars played with two hammers [German, from *glocke* "bell" and *spiel* "play"]

¹gloom \'glüm\ *vb* **1** : to look sullen, discouraged, or depressed **2** : to be or become overcast

²gloom *n* **1** : partial or total darkness **2** : a sad mood — **gloom·i·ly** \'glü-mə-lē\ *adv* — **gloom·i·ness** \-mē-nəs\ *n* — **gloomy** \-mē\ *adj*

Glo·ria Pa·tri \ˌglōr-ē-ə-'pä-(ˌ)trē, ˌglȯr-\ *n* : a Christian hymn of praise to God beginning "Glory be to the Father"

glockenspiel

glo·ri·fy \'glōr-ə-ˌfī, 'glȯr-\ *vb* **-fied; -fy·ing** **1** : ²WORSHIP 1, ADORE **2** : to praise highly **3** : to present in a highly often overly favorable light 〈*glorify* war〉 — **glo·ri·fi·ca·tion** \ˌglōr-ə-fə-'kā-shən, ˌglȯr-\ *n* — **glo·ri·fi·er** \'glōr-ə-fī(-ə)r, 'glȯr-\ *n*

glo·ri·ous \'glōr-ē-əs, 'glȯr-\ *adj* **1 a** : possessing or deserving glory : ILLUSTRIOUS **b** : bringing glory 〈*glorious* victory〉 **2** : having great beauty or splendor 〈a *glorious* sunset〉 **3** : DELIGHTFUL **syn** see SPLENDID — **glo·ri·ous·ly** *adv* — **glo·ri·ous·ness** *n*

¹glo·ry \'glōr-ē, 'glȯr-\ *n, pl* **glories** **1 a** : praise, honor, or distinction extended by common consent **b** : worshipful praise, honor, and thanksgiving **2 a** : something that brings praise or renown **b** : a distinguished quality or brilliant asset 〈the *glory* of the town was its fountain〉 **3 a** : SPLENDOR 2 **b** : the splendor and bliss of heaven **4** : a height of prosperity or achievement

²glory *vb* **glo·ried; glo·ry·ing** : to rejoice proudly : EXULT

¹gloss \'gläs, 'glȯs\ *n* **1** : brightness from a smooth surface : LUSTER, SHEEN **2** : a falsely attractive appearance 〈a thin *gloss* of good manners〉

²gloss *vb* **1** : to give a gloss to **2** : to smooth over : explain away 〈*gloss* over one's mistakes〉

glos·sa·ry \'gläs-(ə-)rē, 'glȯs-\ *n, pl* **-ries** **1** : a list of the hard or unusual words found in a book **2** : a dictionary of the special terms in a particular field

glossy \'gläs-ē, 'glȯs-\ *adj* **gloss·i·er; -est** : having a surface luster or brightness — **gloss·i·ness** *n*

glot·tis \'glät-əs\ *n, pl* **glot·tis·es** *or* **glot·ti·des** \'glät-ə-ˌdēz\ : the long opening between the vocal cords in the larynx — **glot·tal** \'glät-ᵊl\ *adj*

glove \'gləv\ *n* **1** : a covering for the hand having separate sections for each finger **2 a** : a padded leather covering for the hand used in baseball **b** : BOXING GLOVE — **gloved** \'gləvd\ *adj*

glove compartment *n* : a small storage cabinet in the dashboard of an automobile

¹glow \'glō\ *vb* **1** : to shine with or as if with great heat : give off light without flame 〈*glowing* coals〉 **2** : to have a rich warm usually reddish color **3** : to be or look warm and flushed (as from exercise or excitement) 〈*glow* with pride〉

²glow *n* **1** : brightness or warmth of color 〈a rosy *glow* of health〉 **2 a** : warmth of feeling **b** : a feeling of physical warmth **3** : light such as that given off by something that is very hot but not flaming

glow·er \'glaù(-ə)r\ *vb* : to stare angrily : SCOWL — **glower** *n*

glow·worm \'glō-ˌwərm\ *n* : any of various insect larvae or adults that give off light

glox·in·ia \gläk-'sin-ē-ə\ *n* : any of a genus of Brazilian herbs related to the African violets; *esp* : one often grown for its showy bell-shaped or slipper-shaped flowers

gloze \'glōz\ *vb* **glozed; gloz·ing** : to make appear right or acceptable : GLOSS 〈*gloze* over a person's faults〉

glu·cose \'glü-ˌkōs\ *n* : a sugar known in three different forms; *esp* : a naturally occurring form that is found in plants, fruits, and blood and is a source of energy for living things

¹glue \'glü\ *n* : a substance used to stick things tightly together — **glu·ey** \'glü-ē\ *adj*

²glue *vb* **glued; glu·ing** *also* **glue·ing** : to stick with or as if with glue

glum \'gləm\ *adj* **glum·mer; glum·mest** **1** : SULLEN 1a **2** : seeming gloomy and sad 〈a *glum* expression〉 — **glum·ly** *adv* — **glum·ness** *n*

¹glut \'glət\ *vb* **glut·ted; glut·ting** **1** : to fill with food to the point of discomfort : STUFF **2** : to flood with more goods than are needed 〈the market was *glutted* with fruit〉

²glut *n* : too much of something

glu·tam·ic acid \(ˌ)glü-ˌtam-ik-\ *n* : an amino acid found in many plant and animal proteins and used in the form of a sodium salt as a seasoning

glu·ten \'glüt-ᵊn\ *n* : a tough elastic protein substance in flour especially from wheat that holds together dough and makes it sticky

glu·te·us max·i·mus \ˌglüt-ē-əs-'mak-sə-məs, glü-'tē-\ *n, pl* **gluteus max·i·mi** \-'mak-sə-ˌmī\ : the largest and outermost of the three major muscles in each of the human buttocks that extends the thigh and rotates it to the side

glu·ti·nous \'glüt-nəs, -ᵊn-əs\ *adj* : resembling glue : STICKY — **glu·ti·nous·ly** *adv*

glut·ton \'glət-ᵊn\ *n* **1** : one that eats too much **2** : WOLVERINE; *esp* : one found in the Old World — **glut·ton·ous**

\\'glət-nəs, -ᵊn-əs\\ *adj* — **glut·ton·ous·ly** *adv*

glut·tony \\'glət-nē, -ᵊn-ē\\ *n, pl* **-ton·ies** : the act or habit of eating or drinking too much

glyc·er·in *or* **glyc·er·ine** \\'glis-(ə-)rən\\ *n* : GLYCEROL

glyc·er·ol \\'glis-ə-,ról, -,rōl\\ *n* : a sweet colorless syrupy alcohol usually obtained from fats and oils and used especially to dissolve things

gly·co·gen \\'glī-kə-jən\\ *n* : a white tasteless substance that is the chief form in which carbohydrate is stored in animals

G-man \\'jē-,man\\ *n* : a special agent of the Federal Bureau of Investigation [probably a shortened form of *government man*]

gnarl \\'när(-ə)l\\ *n* : a large or hard knot in wood or on a tree — **gnarled** \\'när(-ə)ld\\ *adj* — **gnarly** \\'när-lē\\ *adj*

gnash \\'nash\\ *vb* : to strike or grind (as the teeth) together ⟨*gnash* the car's gears⟩

gnat \\'nat\\ *n* : any of various small usually biting two-winged flies

gnaw \\'nó\\ *vb* **1 a** : to bite or chew with the teeth; *esp* : to wear away by repeated biting or nibbling ⟨dog *gnawing* a bone⟩ **b** : to make by gnawing ⟨rats *gnawed* a hole⟩ **2 a** : ANNOY, IRRITATE ⟨worry *gnawed* at me day and night⟩ **b** : to affect like gnawing ⟨*gnawing* hunger⟩ — **gnaw·er** \\'nó-(ə)r\\ *n*

gneiss \\'nīs\\ *n* : a rock in layers that is similar in composition to granite

gnome \\'nōm\\ *n* : a dwarf of folklore living inside the earth and guarding precious ore or treasure — **gnom·ish** \\'nō-mish\\ *adj*

gno·mon \\'nō-mən, -,män\\ *n* : an object (as on a sundial) that by the position or length of its shadow serves to indicate the hour of the day

gnu \\'n(y)ü\\ *n, pl* **gnu** *or* **gnus** : any of several large African antelopes with a head like that of an ox, a short mane, a long tail, and horns in both sexes that curve downward and outward — called also *wildebeeste*

gnu

¹go \\'gō\\ *vb* **went** \\'went\\; **gone** \\'gòn\\ *also* \\'gän\\; **go·ing** \\'gō-iŋ\\; **goes** \\'gōz\\ **1** : to move on a course : PROCEED ⟨*go* slow⟩ ⟨*go* by way of Dubuque⟩ **2 a** : to move away from one point to or toward another : LEAVE, DEPART **b** : ¹FOLLOW 4, TRAVERSE ⟨*go* the whole route⟩ ⟨*go* my way⟩ **c** : to leave a stated or suggested place (as one's home) ⟨*gone* for the day⟩ ⟨just *going* out⟩ **3 a** : to pass by a process like journeying ⟨the message *went* by wire⟩ ⟨the prize *went* to the winnner⟩ **b** : EXTEND 4, RUN ⟨our land *goes* to the river⟩ **c** : ¹LEAD 1d ⟨that door *goes* to the cellar⟩ **4** : to be habitually in a certain state ⟨*goes* bareheaded⟩ **5 a** : to become lost, consumed, or spent ⟨funds *going* for research⟩ **b** : to slip away : ELAPSE ⟨where did the time *go*⟩ **c** : to pass by sale ⟨*went* for a good price⟩ **d** : to become damaged or weakened ⟨my hearing started to *go*⟩ **e** : to give way under force or pressure : BREAK ⟨the dam *went*⟩ **6 a** : to take place : HAPPEN ⟨what's *going* on⟩ **b** : to be in general or on an average ⟨cheap, as yachts *go*⟩ **c** : to become especially as the result of a contest ⟨decision *went* against us⟩ **7** : to put or subject oneself ⟨*go* to great expense⟩ **8** : to make use of to settle a dispute : RESORT ⟨*go* to court to recover damages⟩ **9 a** : to begin or continue an action or motion ⟨*go* when the light turns⟩ ⟨drums *going* strong⟩ **b** : to function properly ⟨get the motor to *go*⟩ **10** : to pass from one to another : be widely known ⟨the report *goes*⟩ **11** : to be or act in agreement ⟨a good rule to *go* by⟩ **12** : to contribute to a result ⟨qualities that *go* to make a hero⟩ **13 a** : to be

about, intending, or expecting ⟨is *going* to leave town⟩ **b** : to come or arrive at a certain state or condition ⟨*go* to sleep⟩ **c** : to come to be ⟨the tire *went* flat⟩ **14 a** : to be able to be placed ⟨these clothes will *go* in your suitcase⟩ **b** : to have a usual or proper place ⟨these books *go* on the top shelf⟩ **c** : to be capable of being contained in another quantity ⟨5 *goes* into 60 12 times⟩ **15** : to be likely : TEND ⟨*goes* to show they can be trusted⟩ **16** : to be acceptable : DO ⟨any kind of dress *goes*⟩ **17** : ²BET 1, BID ⟨willing to *go* $50⟩ — **go at** **1** : ¹ATTACK 1, 2 **2** : to set to work on — **go back on** : BETRAY 2 — **go for** **1** : to pass for or serve as **2** : to have an interest in or liking for — **go in** : to share costs or expenses ⟨*went in* with his friends on a used car⟩ — **go in for** : to take part in out of interest or liking ⟨*go in for* stamp collecting⟩ — **go one better** : EXCEL, SURPASS ⟨*went* him *one better*⟩ — **go over** **1** : ²STUDY 2, REVIEW **2** : to look over in order to correct or improve ⟨*went over* my term paper twice⟩ — **go places** : to be on the way to success — **go steady** : to have frequent dates with only one person ⟨she's not *going steady* anymore⟩ — **go through** **1** : EXAMINE 1, STUDY **2** : ²EXPERIENCE, UNDERGO **3** : CARRY OUT, PERFORM ⟨*went through* his act perfectly⟩ — **to go** **1** : remaining to pass or be done ⟨five minutes *to go*⟩ **2** : to be taken from a restaurant ⟨ham sandwich *to go*⟩

²go *n, pl* **goes** **1** : the height of fashion ⟨that dress is all the *go*⟩ **2** : ENERGY 1, VIGOR ⟨full of *go*⟩ **3 a** : ²ATTEMPT 1, TRY ⟨have a *go* at it⟩ **b** : a spell of activity ⟨did it in one *go*⟩ **c** : SUCCESS 1c ⟨make a *go* of a business⟩ — **no go** : of no help : USELESS — **on the go** : constantly or restlessly active

³go *adj* : ready to go : fully prepared ⟨everything is *go* for launch⟩

goad \\'gōd\\ *n* **1** : a pointed rod used to urge an animal on **2** : something that urges : SPUR — **goad** *vb*

goal \\'gōl\\ *n* **1 a** : the ending point of a race **b** : an area to be reached safely in children's games **2** : the object toward which effort is directed **3 a** : an area or object into which a ball or puck must be driven to score points in various games **b** : the score resulting from driving a ball or puck into a goal

goal·ie \\'gō-lē\\ *n* : GOALKEEPER

goal·keep·er \\'gōl-,kē-pər\\ *n* : a player who defends the goal in various games

goal line *n* : a line at the end of a playing area that marks the goal

goal·post \\'gōl-,pōst\\ *n* : one of two upright posts that with a crossbar serve as the goal in various games

goal·tend·er \\-,ten-dər\\ *n* : GOALKEEPER

goat \\'gōt\\ *n, pl* **goat** *or* **goats** **1** : any of various cud-chewing mammals having hollow horns that curve backward, a short tail, and usually straight hair and related to the sheep but of lighter build **2** : SCAPEGOAT — **goat·like** \\-,līk\\ *adj*

goa·tee \\gō-'tē\\ *n* : a small trim pointed or tufted beard on a man's chin

goat·herd \\'gōt-,hərd\\ *n* : a person who tends goats

goat·skin \\-,skin\\ *n* : the skin of a goat or a leather made from it

goatee

\\ə\\ **abut**	\\aù\\ **out**	\\i\\ **tip**	\\ò\\ **saw**	\\ù\\ **foot**
\\ər\\ **further**	\\ch\\ **chin**	\\ī\\ **life**	\\òi\\ **coin**	\\y\\ **yet**
\\a\\ **mat**	\\e\\ **pet**	\\j\\ **job**	\\th\\ **thin**	\\yü\\ **few**
\\ā\\ **take**	\\ē\\ **easy**	\\ŋ\\ **sing**	\\th\\ **this**	\\yù\\ **cure**
\\ä\\ **cot, cart**	\\g\\ **go**	\\ō\\ **bone**	\\ü\\ **food**	\\zh\\ **vision**

¹gob \'gäb\ *n* **1** : ¹LUMP 1, MASS **2** : a large amount — usually used in pl. ⟨*gobs* of money⟩

²gob *n* : SAILOR

gob·bet \'gäb-ət\ *n* : ¹LUMP 1, MASS

¹gob·ble \'gäb-əl\ *vb* **gob·bled; gob·bling** \-(ə-)liŋ\ **1** : to swallow or eat greedily **2** : to take eagerly : GRAB ⟨the small country was *gobbled* up by its neighbor⟩

²gobble *vb* : to make the natural noise of a male turkey — **gobble** *n*

gob·ble·dy·gook *or* **gob·ble·de·gook** \,gäb-əl-dē-'gúk\ *n* : wordy and generally meaningless jargon [a playful expansion of *gobble* (noun) "a noise like that of a turkey"]

gob·bler \'gäb-lər\ *n* : a male turkey — called also *turkey-cock*

go–be·tween \'gō-bə-,twēn\ *n* : a person who acts as a messenger or a peacemaker between two persons or groups

gob·let \'gäb-lət\ *n* : a drinking glass with a foot and stem

gob·lin \'gäb-lən\ *n* : an ugly, evil, or mischievous elf

go·by \'gō-bē\ *n, pl* **gobies** *also* **goby** : any of numerous spiny-finned fishes that often have the pelvic fins united to form a sucking disk

god \'gäd *also* 'gòd\ *n* **1** *cap* : the supreme or almighty reality; *esp* : the Being perfect in power, wisdom, and goodness whom people worship as creator and ruler of the universe **2** : a being believed to have more than human powers ⟨ancient peoples worshiped many *gods*⟩ **3** : a physical object (as an image or idol) worshiped as divine **4** : something held to be the most important thing in existence ⟨make a *god* of money⟩ — **god·hood** \-,húd\ *n* — **god·like** \-,līk\ *adj*

god·child \-,chīld\ *n* : a person for whom another person acts as sponsor at baptism

god·daugh·ter \-,dòt-ər\ *n* : a female person for whom another person acts as sponsor at baptism

god·dess \'gäd-əs\ *n* **1** : a female god **2** : a woman of great charm or beauty

god·fa·ther \'gäd-,fäth-ər *also* 'gòd-\ *n* : a male sponsor at baptism

god·for·sak·en \-fər-,sā-kən\ *adj* : REMOTE 1, DESOLATE ⟨the most *godforsaken* place in the world⟩

god·head \-,hed\ *n* **1** : divine nature : DIVINITY **2** *cap* : GOD 1

god·less \'gäd-ləs *also* 'gòd-\ *adj* : not believing in God or a god — **god·less·ness** *n*

god·ly \'gäd-lē *also* 'gòd-\ *adj* **god·li·er; -est** : PIOUS 1, DEVOUT ⟨a *godly* person⟩ — **god·li·ness** *n*

god·moth·er \'gäd-,məth-ər *also* 'gòd-\ *n* : a female sponsor at baptism

god·par·ent \-,par-ənt, -,per-\ *n* : a sponsor at baptism

god·send \-,send\ *n* : a desirable or needed thing or event that comes unexpectedly

god·son \-,sən\ *n* : a male person for whom another person acts as sponsor at baptism

God·speed \-'spēd\ *n* : a wish for success given to a person on parting

go·er \'gō-(-ə)r\ *n* : one that goes

goes *present third sing of* ¹GO, *pl of* ²GO

go–get·ter \'gō-,get-ər\ *n* : an ambitious person who eagerly goes after what is desired — **go–get·ting** \-,get-iŋ\ *adj or n*

¹gog·gle \'gäg-əl\ *vb* **gog·gled; gog·gling** \-(ə-)liŋ\ : to stare with goggle eyes — **gog·gler** \-(ə-)lər\ *n*

²goggle *adj* : being bulging ⟨*goggle* eyes⟩ — **gog·gly** \'gäg-(ə-)lē\ *adj* — **gog·gle–eyed** \,gäg-ə-'līd\ *adj*

gog·gles \'gäg-əlz\ *n pl* : protective eyeglasses set in a flexible frame that fits snugly against the face

¹go·ing \'gō-iŋ\ *n* **1** : DEPARTURE 1 **2** : the condition of the ground especially for walking or driving **3** : advance toward an objective : PROGRESS

²going *adj* **1** : being in existence : ALIVE ⟨best novelist *going*⟩ **2** : ¹CURRENT 1b, PREVAILING ⟨*going* price⟩ **3** : being successful and likely to continue successful ⟨a *going* concern⟩

go·ings–on \,gō-iŋz-'zòn, -'än\ *n pl* : actions or events that are taking place

goi·ter \'gòit-ər\ *n* : a swelling on the front of the neck caused by enlargement of the thyroid gland

goi·tre \'gòit-ər\ *chiefly British variant of* GOITER

gold \'gōld\ *n* **1** : a soft yellow metallic element that is used especially in coins and jewelry — see ELEMENT table **2 a** : gold coins **b** : MONEY 1a **3** : a deep yellow — **gold** *adj*

gold·brick \'gōl(d)-,brik\ *n* : a person (as a soldier) who avoids assigned work — **goldbrick** *vb*

gold·en \'gōl-dən\ *adj* **1** : consisting of, relating to, or containing gold **2** : having the color of gold ⟨*golden* hair⟩ **3** : PROSPEROUS ⟨a *golden* age⟩ **4** : FAVORABLE 2 ⟨a *golden* opportunity⟩ **5** : MELLOW 4, RESONANT ⟨a smooth *golden* tenor⟩

gold·en·ag·er \'gōl-də-,nā-jər\ *n* : an elderly and often retired person

golden eagle *n* : a large and powerful eagle of the northern hemisphere that has brownish yellow tips on head and neck feathers

Golden Fleece *n* : a treasure in the form of a fleece of gold placed in a grove guarded by dragons and sought and recovered by Jason and the Argonauts

golden hamster *n* : a small brownish yellow hamster that is native to Asia Minor but is kept as a pet or used as a lab animal elsewhere

golden mean *n* : the medium between extremes

golden plover *n* : either of two plovers which migrate and which in their summer coat of feathers

golden eagle

are speckled golden-yellow and white above with the lower parts being black; *esp* : one that breeds in arctic America and Siberia and winters in Hawaii and the southern hemisphere

golden retriever *n* : any of a breed of medium-sized retrievers that have a coat of golden hair of medium length

gold·en·rod \'gōl-dən-,räd\ *n* : any of numerous chiefly North American plants that are related to the asters and have tall stiff stems topped with rows of tiny yellow or sometimes white flowers on slender branches

golden rule *n* : a rule that one should treat others as one would like to be treated

gold–filled \'gōl(d)-'fild\ *adj* : covered with a layer of gold ⟨a *gold-filled* bracelet⟩

gold·finch \-,finch\ *n* **1** : a small largely red, black, and yellow European finch often kept in a cage **2** : any of several small American finches of which the males in their summer coat of feathers are usually yellow with black wings, tail, and top of the head

gold·fish \-,fish\ *n* : a small usually yellow or orange carp that is often kept in aquariums or ponds

gold leaf *n* : a very thin sheet of gold used especially for gilding

gold·smith \'gōl(d)-,smith\ *n* : one who makes articles of gold

golf \'gälf, 'gòlf, 'gäf, 'gòf\ *n* : a game in which the player uses specialized clubs to try to hit a small ball with as few strokes as possible into each of 9 or 18 holes — **golf** *vb* — **golf·er** *n*

Gol·gi apparatus \'gòl-(,)jē-\ *n* : a part of the cytoplasm of a cell that consists of parallel membranes without ribosomes and is active in the formation and secretion of cell products — called also *Golgi complex*

Golgi body *n* : any particle that is part of the Golgi apparatus

-gon \‚gän *also* -gən\ *n combining form* : figure having (so many) angles ⟨deca*gon*⟩ [derived from Greek *gōnia* "angle"]

go·nad \'gō-‚nad\ *n* : a sperm- or egg-producing gland : TESTIS, OVARY — called also *sex gland*

go·nad·o·tro·pin \gō-‚nad-ə-'trō-pən\ *or* **go·nad·o·tro·phin** \-fən\ *n* : a hormone that acts on or stimulates the gonads

gon·do·la \'gän-də-lə *(usual for sense 1)*, gän-'dō-\ *n* **1** : a long narrow boat with a high prow and stern used on the canals of Venice **2** : a railroad car with low sides and no top used for hauling loose freight **3** : an enclosure that hangs from something: as **a** : the part of a balloon in which passengers or instruments are carried **b** : a car that hangs from a cable and is used especially as a lift for skiers

gon·do·lier \‚gän-də-'li(ər)\ *n* : one who drives a gondola

gone \'gȯn *also* 'gän\ *adj* **1** : ¹DEAD 1 **2 a** : being advanced, involved, or absorbed ⟨far *gone* in grief⟩ **b** : being infatuated ⟨*gone* on each other⟩

gon·er \'gȯn-ər *also* 'gän-\ *n* : one whose case is hopeless

gong \'gäŋ, 'gȯŋ\ *n* **1** : a metallic disk that makes a deep ringing sound when struck **2** : a flat saucer-shaped bell

gono·coc·cus \‚gän-ə-'käk-əs\ *n, pl* **-coc·ci** \-'käk-‚(s)ī, -'käk-(‚)(s)ē\ : a pus-producing bacterium that causes gonorrhea

gon·or·rhea \‚gän-ə-'rē-ə\ *n* : a contagious inflammatory venereal disease of the genital and urinary organs that is caused by the gonococcus — called also *clap* — **gon·or·rhe·al** \-'rē-əl\ *adj*

goo \'gü\ *n* : sticky substance [perhaps an altered form of *glue*] — **goo·ey** \'gü-ē\ *adj*

goo·ber \'gü-bər, 'gub-ər\ *n, dialect* : PEANUT 1

¹good \'gu̇d\ *adj* **bet·ter** \'bet-ər\; **best** \'best\ **1 a** : of a favorable character or tendency ⟨*good* news⟩ **b** : FERTILE 1 ⟨*good* land⟩ **c** : HANDSOME 3, ATTRACTIVE ⟨*good* looks⟩ **d** : AGREEABLE 1, PLEASANT ⟨a *good* place to live⟩ **e** : SUITABLE 1, FIT ⟨*good* to eat⟩ ⟨a remedy *good* for a cold⟩ **f** : RELIABLE ⟨a *good* friend in a pinch⟩ **g** : ¹SOUND 1a, WHOLE ⟨one *good* arm⟩ **2 a** : certain to last or live ⟨*good* for another year⟩ **b** : certain to provide or produce ⟨always *good* for a laugh⟩ **3 a** : of a noticeably large size or quantity ⟨present in *good* numbers⟩ **b** : ¹FULL 2a ⟨*good* measure⟩ **4 a** : based on sound reasoning, information, judgment, or grounds ⟨*good* reasons⟩ **b** : ¹TRUE 3 ⟨holds *good* for society as a whole⟩ **c** : recognized or valid especially in law ⟨member in *good* standing⟩ ⟨has a *good* title⟩ **5 a** : ADEQUATE 1, SATISFACTORY ⟨*good* care⟩ **b** : conforming to a standard ⟨*good* English⟩ **c** : DISCERNING, DISCRIMINATING ⟨*good* taste⟩ **6 a** : VIRTUOUS, JUST ⟨a *good* person⟩ **b** : ¹RIGHT 2 ⟨*good* conduct⟩ **c** : ²KIND 1, BENEVOLENT ⟨*good* intentions⟩ **d** : being of the upper class ⟨of *good* family⟩ **e** : SKILLFUL 1 ⟨a *good* doctor⟩ **f** : LOYAL 2 ⟨a *good* party member⟩ — **good·ness** *n* — **as good as** : in effect : VIRTUALLY ⟨as *good* as dead⟩ — **good and** : ²VERY 1, ENTIRELY ⟨was *good and* mad⟩

²good *n* **1** : something good, useful, or desirable ⟨health and prosperity are *goods*⟩ **2** : ¹BENEFIT 1a, WELFARE ⟨the *good* of the community⟩ **3** *pl* : CLOTH 1 **4** *pl* : manufactured articles or products of art or craft **5** *pl* : good persons — used with *the* **6** *pl* : proof of wrongdoing ⟨got the *goods* on them⟩

³good *adv* : ³WELL 1

good book *n, often cap G & B* : BIBLE 1a

good–bye *or* **good–by** \gu̇d-'bī, gəd-, gə-\ *n* : a concluding remark at parting — often used interjectionally [a shortened and altered form of *God be with you*]

good faith *n* : honesty or lawfulness of purpose ⟨bargained in *good faith*⟩

Good Friday *n* : the Friday before Easter observed by Christians as the anniversary of the crucifixion of Christ

good–heart·ed \'gu̇d-'härt-əd\ *adj* : having a kindly generous disposition — **good–heart·ed·ly** *adv* — **good–heart·ed·ness** *n*

good–hu·mored \-'hyü-mərd, -'yü-\ *adj* : GOOD-NATURED, CHEERFUL — **good–hu·mored·ly** *adv* — **good–hu·mored·ness** *n*

good·ish \'gu̇d-ish\ *adj* : fairly good

good·ly \'gu̇d-lē\ *adj* **good·li·er; -est** **1** : of pleasing appearance **2** : LARGE, CONSIDERABLE ⟨a *goodly* number⟩

good·man \'gu̇d-mən\ *n* **1** *archaic* : the master of a household : HUSBAND **2** *archaic* : MR. 1

good–na·tured \'gu̇d-'nā-chərd\ *adj* : of a pleasant cheerful disposition — **good–na·tured·ly** *adv* — **good–na·tured·ness** *n*

good–sized \-'sīzd\ *adj* : fairly large

good–tem·pered \-'tem-pərd\ *adj* : having an even temper — **good–tem·pered·ly** *adv* — **good–tem·pered·ness** *n*

good–wife \-‚wīf\ *n* **1** *archaic* : the mistress of a household **2** *archaic* : MRS.

good·will \-'wil\ *n* **1** : kindly feeling : BENEVOLENCE **2** : the value of the trade a business has built up **3 a** : cheerful consent **b** : willing effort

goody \'gu̇d-ē\ *n, pl* **good·ies** : something that is particularly good to eat or otherwise attractive

goody–goody \‚gu̇d-ē-'gu̇d-ē\ *adj* : pretending to be good in order to impress people — **goody–goody** *n*

goof \'güf\ *vb* : ¹BLUNDER 2 — **goof** *n*

go off *vb* **1** : EXPLODE 2b **2** : to burst forth or break out suddenly or noisily **3** : to take place : PROCEED ⟨the dance *went off* as planned⟩

goofy \'gü-fē\ *adj* **goof·i·er; -est** : CRAZY 2, SILLY — **goof·i·ly** \-fə-lē\ *adv* — **goof·i·ness** \-fē-nəs\ *n*

goo·gol \'gü-‚gȯl\ *n* : a very large number that is expressed in numerals as 1 followed by one hundred 0's

Word History The term *googol* was invented by a nine-year-old boy. In the late 1930s an American mathematician, Edward Kasner, asked his nephew, Milton Sirotta, to think up a word for a very big number, in particular, the number 1 followed by 100 zeros. The boy came up with the word *googol.* The term was then used by Kasner and other mathematicians and scientists. Such people needed this word, and so it became part of the language. [coined by Milton Sirotta, age 9, and first used by his uncle Edward Kasner 1878-1955 American mathematician]

goon \'gün\ *n* **1** : a stupid person **2** : a person hired to terrorize or beat up or kill opponents : THUG

Word History Some comic strips have had a lasting effect on culture. One such strip, first drawn in the 1920s by Elzie Segar and now known as "Popeye", apparently was responsible for adding the word *goon* to the everyday language. One of the characters Segar created for the comic strip looked a bit like an overgrown pear with legs. This creature, which was not really human, had a big nose, a bald head, and hairy arms and legs. It was called "Alice the goon". Alice was basically good-hearted but not very smart. As a result of the popularity of the comic strip and of Alice, people began to use the word *goon* in the meaning "a stupid person" or "a person with not much common sense". Later, when thugs and criminals were hired to terrorize workers during labor troubles in the 1930s, these thugs, whose actions weren't very "human", were also called *goons.* But even though Alice may have been responsible for making the word *goon* popular, the word may not have started with the comic strip. The word can be traced back to an En-

\ə\ abut		\au̇\ out	\i\ tip	\ȯ\ saw	\u̇\ foot		
\ər\ further		\ch\ chin	\ī\ life	\ȯi\ coin	\y\ yet		
\a\ mat		\e\ pet	\j\ job	\th\ thin	\yü\ few		
\ā\ take		\ē\ easy	\ŋ\ sing	\th\ this	\yu̇\ cure		
\ä\ cot, cart		\g\ go	\ō\ bone	\ü\ food	\zh\ vision		

glish dialect word *gooney,* first used in the 16th century, meaning "a person lacking in common sense, simpleton". [probably a shortened form of a dialect word *gooney* "simpleton"]

goose \'güs\ *n, pl* **geese** \'gēs\ **1 a :** any of numerous birds with long necks that are larger than the related ducks and smaller than swans **b :** a female goose in contrast to a gander **2 :** a person lacking in common sense **3** *pl* **goos·es :** an iron with a gooseneck handle used by tailors for smoothing clothes

goose·ber·ry \'güs-,ber-ē, 'güz-\ *n :* the acid usually prickly fruit of any of several shrubs related to the currant

goose egg *n :* ¹ZERO 1, NOTHING

goose·flesh \'güs-,flesh\ *n :* a roughening of the skin caused usually by cold or fear

goose·foot \-,fút\ *n, pl* **goose·foots :** any of numerous mostly woody smooth herbs with branched clusters of small greenish or whitish flowers without petals

goose·neck \'gü-,snek\ *n :* something (as a flexible jointed metal pipe) curved like the neck of a goose or U-shaped — **goose·necked** \-,snekt\ *adj*

goose pimples *n pl :* GOOSEFLESH

goose step *n :* a straight-legged stiff-kneed step used by troops of some armies on parade — **goose–step** \'güs-'step\ *vb*

go out *vb* **1 :** to leave one's home **2 :** to stop working **3 :** to stop burning or glowing **4 :** to become a candiate ⟨*went out* for the football team⟩

go over *vb :* to be favorably received : SUCCEED ⟨the joke *went over* very well⟩

go·pher \'gō-fər\ *n* **1** : a burrowing American land tortoise **2 a :** any of several burrowing American rodents (as a pocket gopher) with large cheek pouches **b** : a small striped ground squirrel of the prairie region of the U.S.

gopher 2a

gopher snake *n :* BULL SNAKE

¹**gore** \'gō(ə)r, 'gó(ə)r\ *n :* ¹BLOOD 1a; *esp :* clotted blood [Old English *gor* "filth"]

²**gore** *n :* a tapering or triangular piece of cloth (as in a skirt) [Old English *gāre* "triangular piece of land"]

³**gore** *vb* **gored; gor·ing** **1 :** to cut into a tapering triangular form **2 :** to provide with a gore

⁴**gore** *vb* **gored; gor·ing :** to pierce or wound with something pointed (as a tusk or horn) [Middle English *goren* "pierce, gore"]

¹**gorge** \'gó(ə)rj\ *n :* a narrow passage (as between two mountains)

²**gorge** *vb* **gorged; gorg·ing :** to eat greedily : stuff oneself — **gorg·er** *n*

gor·geous \'gór-jəs\ *adj :* having an impressive beauty ⟨*gorgeous* sunset⟩ **syn** see SPLENDID — **gor·geous·ly** *adv* — **gor·geous·ness** *n*

Word History In the late Middle Ages many women wore a type of headdress — called a *wimple* in English — that surrounded the neck and head, leaving only the face uncovered. The word *gorgias,* from *gorge,* meaning "throat", was then the French name for the part of the headdress that covered the throat and shoulders. In time it also came to be used as a name for the entire garment. A beautiful headdress was so much the mark of a fashionable lady that *gorgias* then became an adjective meaning "elegant" or "fond of dress". Borrowed into English as *gorgayse* and then *gorgeous,* the word gradually took on the meaning of "beautiful" which it has today. [Middle English *gorgayse* "very showy, splen-

did", from early French *gorgias* "elegant", from *gorgias* "headdress, wimple", from *gorge* "part of the wimple covering the throat, throat"]

Gor·gon \'gór-gən\ *n :* any of three snaky-haired sisters in Greek mythology capable of turning to stone anyone who looked at them

Gor·gon·zo·la \,gór-gən-'zō-lə\ *n :* a cheese of Italian origin ripened by veins of greenish blue mold [named for *Gorgonzola,* town in Italy where the cheese was first made]

go·ril·la \gə-'ril-ə\ *n :* an ape of west equatorial Africa that is the largest member of the group of higher apes now living that is most nearly related to human beings and is the member closest to human beings in structure [derived from Greek *Gorillai,* a name used by ancient Greek explorers for what they thought was a tribe of hairy women in Africa]

gorilla

gor·man·dize \'gór-mən-,dīz\ *vb* **-dized; -diz·ing :** to eat greedily — **gor·man·diz·er** *n*

gorse \'gó(ə)rs\ *n :* a prickly mostly leafless evergreen shrub of the legume family that has yellow flowers — called also *furze*

gory \'gō(ə)r-ē, 'gó(ə)r-\ *adj* **gor·i·er; -est** **1 :** covered with gore : BLOODSTAINED **2 :** BLOODCURDLING

gos·hawk \'gäs-,hók\ *n :* any of several hawks that have a long tail and short wings and are noted for their powerful flight, activity, and vigor

gos·ling \'gäz-liŋ, 'góz-, -lən\ *n :* a young goose

¹**gos·pel** \'gäs-pəl\ *n* **1 a** *often cap :* the Christian message concerning Christ, the kingdom of God, and salvation **b** *cap :* one of the first four New Testament books telling of the life, death, and resurrection of Jesus Christ **2 :** something accepted as the truth or as a guiding principle [Old English *gōdspel,* a translation of Greek *euangelion* "gospel", literally "good tidings, good news"; *gōdspel* from *gōd* "good" and *spell* "talk, tale"]

²**gospel** *adj* **1 :** relating to or in accordance with the gospel : EVANGELICAL **2 :** of or relating to the winning or revival of personal devotion to Christ ⟨a *gospel* team⟩ **3 :** of or relating to religious songs associated with evangelism ⟨a *gospel* singer⟩

gos·sa·mer \'gäs-ə-mər *also* 'gäz(-ə)-mər\ *n* **1 :** a film of cobwebs floating in air **2 :** something light or very delicate — **gossamer** *adj* — **gos·sa·mery** \-mə-rē\ *adj*

gos·sip \'gäs-əp\ *n* **1 :** a person who reveals personal or sensational facts **2 a :** rumor or report of a personal nature **b :** chatty talk — **gossip** *vb* — **gos·sip·er** *n* — **gos·sipy** \-ə-pē\ *adj*

got *past and past participle of* GET

Goth·ic \'gäth-ik\ *adj :* relating to or being an old style of architecture (as for churches) having pointed arches and thinner and taller walls and more and larger windows than Romanesque architecture

gotten *past participle of* GET

¹**gouge** \'gaúj\ *n* **1 :** a chisel with a curved blade for scooping or cutting holes **2 :** a hole or groove made with or as if with a gouge

²**gouge** *vb* **gouged; goug·ing** **1 :** to cut holes or grooves in with or as if with a gouge **2 :** to force out (an eye) with the thumb **3 :** OVERCHARGE 1 — **goug·er** *n*

gou·lash \'gü-,läsh, -,lash\ *n :* a beef stew with onion, paprika, and caraway [from Hungarian *gulyás* "stew eaten by cattle herdsmen, a cattle herdsman", from *gulya* "herd of cattle"]

gourd \'gō(ə)rd, 'gó(ə)rd, 'gú(ə)rd\ *n* **1 :** any of a family of tendril-bearing vines (as the cucumber, melon, squash, and pumpkin) **2 :** the hard-shelled many-seeded fruit of a

gourd — **gourd·like** \-,līk\ *adj*

gour·mand \'gu̇(ə)r-,mänd\ *n* **1** : GLUTTON 1 **2** : GOURMET — **gour·mand·ism** \'gu̇(ə)r-,män-,diz-əm, -mən-\ *n*

gour·met \'gu̇(ə)r-,mā, gu̇r-'mā\ *n* : a person who can enjoy and appreciate fine eating and drinking

gout \'gau̇t\ *n* : a disease marked by a painful inflammation and swelling of the joints and by the deposit of salts of uric acid in and around the joints — **gouty** \-ē\ *adj*

gourd 2

gov·ern \'gəv-ərn\ *vb* **1** : to exercise authority over : RULE ⟨the queen *governed* wisely⟩ **2** : to control the speed of by automatic means **3 a** : to control, direct, or strongly influence the actions and conduct of ⟨*governed* by his emotions⟩ **b** : to hold in check : RESTRAIN ⟨our income *governs* our spending⟩ **4** : to require a word to be in a certain case or mood ⟨in English a transitive verb *governs* a pronoun in the objective case⟩ **5** : to serve as a rule or law for ⟨etiquette *governing* their behavior⟩ — **gov·ern·able** \-ər-nə-bəl\ *adj*

syn GOVERN, RULE mean to use power or authority in controlling others. GOVERN suggests the aim of keeping something running smoothly for the good of both the individual and the whole group ⟨*governed* the country wisely⟩ RULE stresses the laying down of laws and the giving of commands and often suggests the harsh use of power ⟨the king *ruled* firmly and would not allow any disobedience⟩

gov·er·nance \'gəv-ər-nən(t)s\ *n* : the exercise of control : GOVERNMENT

gov·ern·ess \'gəv-ər-nəs\ *n* : a woman who teaches and trains a child in a private home

gov·ern·ment \'gəv-ər(n)-mənt, 'gəb-ᵊm-ənt, 'gəv-mənt\ *n* **1 a** : the act or process of governing; *esp* : direction of a political unit **b** : the making of policy as distinguished from the administration of policy decisions **2 a** : the agency through which a political unit exercises authority **b** : manner of governing : the institutions, laws, and customs through which a political unit is governed ⟨republican *government*⟩ **3 a** : the officials making up the governing body of a political unit **b** *cap* : the executive branch of the U.S. federal government **4** : POLITICAL SCIENCE — **gov·ernment** *adj* — **gov·ern·men·tal** \,gəv-ər(n)-'ment-ᵊl\ *adj* — **gov·ern·men·tal·ly** \-ᵊl-ē\ *adv*

gov·er·nor \'gəv-(ə)-nər *also* 'gəv-ər-nər\ *n* **1** : one that governs; *esp* : an official elected or appointed to act as ruler, chief executive, or head of a political unit (as a colony, state, or province) **2** : an attachment to a machine for automatic control of speed — **gov·er·nor·ship** \-,ship\ *n*

gown \'gau̇n\ *n* **1** : an official robe worn especially by a judge, a member of the clergy, or a teacher **2** : a woman's dress; *esp* : one suitable for afternoon or evening wear **3** : a loose robe (as a dressing gown or a nightgown) — **gown** *vb*

graaf·ian follicle \,gräf-ē-ən-, ,graf-\ *n* : a small fluid-filled cavity in the ovary of a mammal that encloses a developing egg

¹grab \'grab\ *vb* **grabbed; grab·bing** : to take hastily : CLUTCH, SNATCH — **grab·ber** *n*

²grab *n* **1 a** : a sudden snatch **b** : an unlawful or forceful taking of something ⟨land *grab*⟩ **c** : something grabbed **2** : a device for clutching an object

¹grace \'grās\ *n* **1 a** : help given to people by God in overcoming temptation **b** : a state of freedom from sin enjoyed through divine grace **2** : a short prayer at a meal

3 a : KINDNESS 1, FAVOR **b** : a temporary delay granted from the performance of an obligation (as the payment of a debt) **c** : APPROVAL, ACCEPTANCE ⟨stayed in the boss's good *graces*⟩ **4 a** : a charming trait or quality **b** : ease of movement ⟨walks with *grace*⟩ **5** — used as a title for a duke, a duchess, or an archbishop [Middle English *grace* "help from God", from early French *grace* (same meaning), from Latin *gratia* "favor, charm, thanks", from *gratus* "pleasing, thankful, agreeable" — related to AGREE, CONGRATULATE, GRACIOUS, GRATITUDE] — **grace·ful** \-fəl\ *adj* — **grace·ful·ly** \-fə-lē\ *adv* — **grace·ful·ness** *n*

²grace *vb* **graced; grac·ing** **1** : ²HONOR 1b ⟨deeds that *graced* the town⟩ **2** : ADORN, EMBELLISH

grace·less \'grā-sləs\ *adj* : having no grace, charm, or elegance; *esp* : showing lack of feeling for what is fitting ⟨*graceless* behavior⟩ — **grace·less·ly** *adv* — **grace·less·ness** *n*

grace note *n* : a short musical note added before another as an ornament

gra·cious \'grā-shəs\ *adj* **1** : marked by kindness and courtesy **2** : pleasing or attractive in motion or form ⟨*gracious* ballet steps⟩ **3** : characterized by charm, good taste, and politeness ⟨*gracious* living⟩ [Middle English *gracious* "having received divine grace", from early French *gracieus* (same meaning), from Latin *gratiosus* "enjoying favor, agreeable", from *gratia* "favor, thanks", from *gratus* "pleasing, agreeable, thankful" — related to GRACE, GRATITUDE] — **gra·cious·ly** *adv* — **gra·cious·ness** *n*

syn GRACIOUS, CORDIAL, AFFABLE, GENIAL mean very pleasant and relaxed in social situations. GRACIOUS suggests courtesy and kindly consideration ⟨a *gracious* host makes his guests feel comfortable⟩ CORDIAL stresses warmth and heartiness ⟨the *cordial* innkeeper welcomed us⟩ AFFABLE suggests ease and readiness in responding pleasantly to conversation or requests ⟨a principal who is *affable* and friendly⟩ GENIAL stresses cheerfulness and even joyfulness ⟨a *genial* woman with a nice sense of humor⟩

grack·le \'grak-əl\ *n* : any of several rather large American blackbirds with glossy black feathers showing changeable green, purple, and bronze colors

gra·da·tion \grā-'dā-shən, grə-\ *n* **1 a** : a series of grades **b** : ²GRADE 1 **2** : the act or process of grading — **gra·da·tion·al** \-shnəl, -shən-ᵊl\ *adj* — **gra·da·tion·al·ly** \-ē\ *adv*

¹grade \'grād\ *vb* **grad·ed; grad·ing** **1** : to arrange in grades : SORT ⟨*grade* apples⟩ **2** : to make level or evenly sloping ⟨*grade* a highway⟩ **3** : to give a grade to ⟨*grade* a student's performance⟩ **4** : to assign to a grade **5** : to form a series having only slight differences ⟨colors that *grade* into one another⟩

²grade *n* **1** : a stage, step, or degree in a series, order, or ranking **2** : position in a scale of rank, quality, or order ⟨the *grade* of sergeant⟩ ⟨leather of the highest *grade*⟩ **3** : a class of things that are of the same rank, quality, or order **4 a** : a division of the school course representing a year's work ⟨finish the fourth *grade*⟩ **b** : the pupils in a school division **c** *pl* : the elementary school system ⟨teach in the *grades*⟩ **5** : a mark or rating especially of accomplishment in school ⟨a *grade* of 90 in a test⟩ **6** : a standard of quality ⟨government *grades* for meat⟩ **7** : the degree of slope (as of a road or railroad track)

grade crossing *n* : a crossing (as of highways, railroad tracks, or pedestrian walks) on the same level

grad·er \'grād-ər\ *n* **1** : one that grades **2** : a machine for leveling earth **3** : a pupil in a school grade ⟨a group of

\ə\ abut		\au̇\ out	\i\ tip	\ȯ\ saw	\u̇\ foot
\ər\ further		\ch\ chin	\ī\ life	\ȯi\ coin	\y\ yet
\a\ mat		\e\ pet	\j\ job	\th\ thin	\yü\ few
\ā\ take		\ē\ easy	\ŋ\ sing	\t͟h\ this	\yu̇\ cure
\ä\ cot, cart		\g\ go	\ō\ bone	\ü\ food	\zh\ vision

sixth *graders*⟩

grade school *n* : a public school including the first six or the first eight grades

gra·di·ent \'grād-ē-ənt\ *n* **1** : ³SLOPE 2, GRADE **2** : a continuous graded change in measure, activity, or substance ⟨vertical temperature *gradient* in a lake⟩ ⟨a *gradient* in developmental activity in a seedling⟩

grad·u·al \'graj-(ə-)wəl, 'graj-əl\ *adj* **1** : proceeding by steps or degrees **2** : moving or changing by slight degrees — **grad·u·al·ly** *adv* — **grad·u·al·ness** *n*

grad·u·al·ism \'graj-(ə-)wəl-,iz-əm, 'graj-əl-\ *n* : the policy of approaching a desired goal by gradual stages — **grad·u·al·ist** \-əst\ *n or adj*

¹grad·u·ate \'graj-(ə-)wət, -ə-,wāt\ *n* **1** : a holder of an academic degree or diploma **2** : a graduated cup, cylinder, or flask for measuring

²graduate *adj* **1** : holding an academic degree or diploma **2** : of or relating to studies beyond the bachelor's degree

³grad·u·ate \'graj-ə-,wāt\ *vb* **-at·ed; -at·ing** **1** : to grant or receive an academic degree or diploma **2** : to divide into grades, classes, or intervals ⟨*graduated* thermometer⟩ — **grad·u·a·tor** \-,wāt-ər\ *n*

graduated cylinder *n* : a tall narrow container with a volume scale used especially for measuring liquids

grad·u·a·tion \,graj-ə-'wā-shən\ *n* **1** : a mark or the marks on an instrument or container indicating degrees or quantity **2 a** : an act or process of graduating **b** : the ceremony marking the completion by a student of a course of study at a school or college : COMMENCEMENT **3** : arrangement in degrees or ranks

graf·fi·to \gra-'fēt-ō\ *n, pl* **-ti** \-(,)ē\ : a writing or drawing made on a public surface (as a wall or rock) [Italian, literally "little scratch", from *graffio* "scratch", derived from Latin *graphium* "pointed device for writing on wax tablets", derived from Greek *graphein* "to write" — related to -GRAM, GRAMMAR, -GRAPH]

¹graft \'graft\ *vb* **1 a** : to insert a twig or bud from one plant into another plant so that they are joined and grow together **b** : to join one thing to another as if by grafting ⟨*graft* skin over a scar⟩ **2** : to gain money or advantage by graft — **graft·er** *n*

²graft *n* **1 a** : a grafted plant **b** : the point in a plant where a part that is being grafted is inserted **2** : the act of grafting **3** : something used in grafting: as **a** : SCION 1 **b** : living tissue used in surgical grafting **4 a** : the getting of money or advantage by dishonest means through misuse of an official position ⟨exposed *graft* in the city government⟩ **b** : the money or advantage gained ⟨accused of taking *graft*⟩

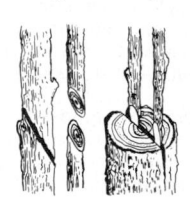

graft 1b

gra·ham cracker \,grā-əm-, ,gra-(ə)m-\ *n* : a slightly sweet cracker made chiefly of whole wheat flour

¹grain \'grān\ *n* **1 a** : the edible seed or seedlike fruit of grasses that are cereals (as wheat, Indian corn, or oats) and of a few other plants (as buckwheat) **b** : the threshed seed or fruits of various food plants (as cereal grasses, flax, peas, or sugarcane) **c** : plants producing grain **2** : a small hard particle ⟨*grain* of sand⟩ **3** : a unit of weight based on the weight of a grain of wheat — see MEASURE table **4 a** : the arrangement of fibers in wood **b** : appearance or feel due to the particles or fibers of which something is composed ⟨the *grain* of a rock⟩ **c** : the direction of threads in cloth **5** : natural disposition : TEMPER ⟨making excuses goes against my *grain*⟩ [Middle English *grain, grein* "kernel, seed", from early French *grain* "cereal plant" and early French *graine* "seed", both derived from Latin *granum* "grain, seed" — related to GARNET,

GRENADE, POMEGRANATE; see *Word History* at GARNET] — **grained** \'grānd\ *adj* — **grainy** \'grā-nē\ *adj* — **with a grain of salt** : with a doubtful attitude : SKEPTICALLY ⟨take his predictions *with a grain of salt*⟩

²grain *vb* : to paint in imitation of the grain of wood or stone — **grain·er** *n*

grain alcohol *n* : ALCOHOL 1a

grain elevator *n* : ELEVATOR 1c

grain·field \'grān-,fēld\ *n* : a field where grain is grown

grain sorghum *n* : any of several sorghums cultivated primarily for grain

gram \'gram\ *n* : a metric unit of mass equal to ¹/₁₀₀₀ kilogram and nearly equal to the mass of one cubic centimeter of water at its maximum density — see METRIC SYSTEM table

-gram \,gram\ *n combining form* : drawing : writing : record ⟨tele*gram*⟩ [from Latin *-gramma* "piece of writing, record", derived from Greek *gramma* "letter", derived from *graphein* "to write" — related to GRAFFITO, GRAMMAR, -GRAPH]

grama \'gram-ə\ *n* : any of several pasture grasses of the western U.S. — called also *grama grass*

gra·mer·cy \grə-'mər-sē\ *interj, archaic* — used to express gratitude or astonishment

gram·mar \'gram-ər\ *n* **1** : the study of the classes of words, their inflections, and their functions and relations in a language **2** : the facts of language with which grammar deals **3 a** : a grammar textbook **b** : speech or writing evaluated according to its conformity to grammatical rules ⟨"Him and I went" is bad *grammar*⟩ [Middle English *gramere, grammer* "study of how words are used and related in a sentence", from early French *gramaire* (same meaning), from Latin *grammatica* (same meaning), derived from Greek *gramma* "letter, piece of writing", derived from *graphein* "to write" — related to GRAFFITO, -GRAM, -GRAPH]

gram·mar·i·an \grə-'mer-ē-ən, -'mar-\ *n* : a specialist in or a teacher of grammar

grammar school *n* : an elementary school

gram·mat·i·cal \grə-'mat-i-kəl\ *adj* **1** : of or relating to grammar **2** : conforming to the rules of grammar — **gram·mat·i·cal·i·ty** \-,mat-ə-'kal-ət-ē\ *n* — **gram·mat·i·cal·ly** \-'mat-i-k(ə-)lē\ *adv* — **gram·mat·i·cal·ness** \-kəl-nəs\ *n*

grana *pl of* GRANUM

gra·na·ry \'grān-(ə-)rē, 'gran-\ *n, pl* **-ries** **1** : a storehouse for grain **2** : a region producing plenty of grain

¹grand \'grand\ *adj* **1** : higher in rank than others of the same class : FOREMOST, PRINCIPAL ⟨*grand* champion⟩ ⟨*grand* prize⟩ **2** : great in size **3** : including all things being considered : COMPLETE ⟨a *grand* total⟩ **4 a** : marked by magnificence : SPLENDID ⟨a *grand* coronation ceremony⟩ **b** : showing wealth or high social standing ⟨the airs of a *grand* lady⟩ **5** : IMPRESSIVE, STATELY, ADMIRABLE ⟨a *grand* old man⟩ **6** : very good : FINE ⟨*grand* weather⟩ ⟨have a *grand* time⟩ — **grand·ly** \'gran-(d)lē\ *adv* — **grand·ness** \'gran(d)-nəs\ *n*

syn GRAND, MAGNIFICENT, MAJESTIC, GRANDIOSE mean large and impressive. GRAND suggests handsomeness and dignity ⟨the royal wedding was a *grand* affair⟩ MAGNIFICENT suggests an appropriate greatness of size that remains dignified and in good taste ⟨a *magnificent* palace⟩ MAJESTIC suggests awe-inspiring grandeur or great size ⟨a *majestic* waterfall⟩ GRANDIOSE may suggest largeness or greatness but is usually applied to something that is foolishly exaggerated or showy ⟨*grandiose* plans for world conquest⟩

²grand *n* : GRAND PIANO

gran·dam \'gran-,dam, -dəm\ *or* **gran·dame** \-,dām, -dəm\ *n* **1** : GRANDMOTHER **2** : an old woman

grand·aunt \'gran-'dant, -'dànt\ *n* : an aunt of one's father or mother

grand·child \'gran(d)-,chīld\ *n* : a child of one's son or daughter

grand·daugh·ter \'gran-ˌdȯt-ər\ *n* : a daughter of one's son or daughter

gran·dee \gran-'dē\ *n* : a man of elevated rank or station; *esp* : a high-ranking Spanish or Portuguese nobleman

gran·deur \'gran-jər\ *n* **1** : the quality or state of being grand : awe-inspiring magnificence **2** : something that is grand

grand·fa·ther \'gran(d)-ˌfäth-ər\ *n* : the father of one's father or mother; *also* : ANCESTOR 1

grandfather clock *n* : a tall clock standing directly on the floor

gran·dil·o·quence \gran-'dil-ə-kwən(t)s\ *n* : high-sounding or overly impressive language in speech or writing : BOMBAST — **gran·dil·o·quent** \-kwənt\ *adj* — **gran·dil·o·quent·ly** *adv*

gran·di·ose \'gran-dē-ˌōs\ *adj* **1** : impressive because of uncommon largeness, scope, effect, or grandeur **2** : characterized by deliberately assumed grandeur or splendor or by absurd exaggeration ⟨*grandiose* schemes⟩ **syn** see GRAND — **gran·di·ose·ly** *adv* — **gran·di·os·i·ty** \ˌgran-dē-'äs-ət-ē\ *n*

grand jury *n* : a jury that chiefly examines accusations of crime made against persons and if the evidence warrants makes formal charges on which the accused persons are later tried

grandfather clock

grand·moth·er \'gran(d)-ˌməth-ər\ *n* : the mother of one's father or mother; *also* : a female ancestor

grand·neph·ew \-'nef-(ˌ)yü\ *n* : a grandson of one's brother or sister

grand·niece \-'nēs\ *n* : a granddaughter of one's brother or sister

grand opera *n* : a serious opera in which the entire text is sung

grand·par·ent \'gran(d)-ˌpar-ənt, -ˌper-\ *n* : a parent of one's father or mother

grand piano *n* : a piano in which the frame and strings are in a horizontal rather than an upright position

grand·sire \'gran(d)-ˌsī(ə)r\ *or* **grand·sir** \'gran(t)-sər\ *n* **1** *dialect* : GRANDFATHER **2** *archaic* : an aged man

grand slam *n* : a home run hit with three runners on base

grand·son \'gran(d)-ˌsən\ *n* : a son of one's son or daughter

grand·stand \-ˌstand\ *n* : a usually roofed stand for spectators at a racecourse or stadium

grand·un·cle \'gran-'dəŋ-kəl\ *n* : an uncle of one's father or mother

grange \'grānj\ *n* **1** : ¹FARM 1a; *esp* : a farmhouse with its various buildings **2** *cap* : one of the lodges of a national association of farmers; *also* : the association itself

grang·er \'grān-jər\ *n* : a member of a Grange

gran·ite \'gran-ət\ *n* **1** : a very hard rock that can be polished and is used in buildings and monuments **2** : unyielding firmness (as of character, will, or opinion)

gran·ny *or* **gran·nie** \'gran-ē\ *n, pl* **grannies 1** : GRANDMOTHER **2** : an ankle-length dress usually with long sleeves and a high waist

granny glasses *n pl* : metal-rimmed eyeglasses with small lenses

granny knot *n* : an insecure knot often made instead of a square knot

gra·no·la \grə-'nō-lə\ *n* : a mixture of oats and other ingredients (as brown sugar, raisins, coconut, or nuts) that is eaten especially for breakfast

¹grant \'grant\ *vb* **1 a** : to consent to : PERMIT ⟨*grant* your request⟩ **b** : to permit as a right, privilege, or favor **2**

: to give the possession or benefit of formally or legally ⟨the king *granted* land to the settlers⟩ **3** : to admit something not yet proved to be true ⟨*granted* you are right, you must still pay for the damage⟩ — **grant·er** \-ər\ *n* — **grant·or** \'grant-ər, grant-'ȯr\ *n*

²grant *n* **1** : the act of granting **2** : something granted: as **a** : a gift for a particular purpose ⟨a study *grant*⟩ **b** : an area of land granted by a government

grant·ee \grant-'ē\ *n* : one to whom a grant is made

gran·u·lar \'gran-yə-lər\ *adj* **1** : consisting of grains **2** : having a grainy structure, feel, or appearance — **gran·u·lar·i·ty** \ˌgran-yə-'lar-ət-ē\ *n*

gran·u·late \'gran-yə-ˌlāt\ *vb* **-lat·ed; -lat·ing** : to form or crystallize into grains or granules

gran·u·la·tion \ˌgran-yə-'lā-shən\ *n* **1** : the act or process of granulating or the condition of being granulated **2** : one of the small raised places of a granulated surface

gran·ule \'gran-yü(ə)l\ *n* **1** : a small grain or particle ⟨*granules* of sugar⟩ **2** : one of the short-lived brilliant spots on the sun

gra·num \'grā-nəm\ *n, pl* **gra·na** \-nə\ : one of the stacks of chlorophyll-containing material in plant chloroplasts

grape \'grāp\ *n* **1** : a smooth-skinned juicy greenish white, deep red, or purple berry eaten dried or fresh as a fruit or fermented to produce wine **2** : any of numerous woody vines widely grown for their bunches of grapes **3** : GRAPESHOT — **grapy** \'grā-pē\ *adj*

grape·fruit \'grāp-ˌfrüt\ *n* **1** : a large citrus fruit with a bitter yellow rind and a highly flavored somewhat acid juicy pulp **2** : a tree that bears grapefruit

grape hyacinth *n* : any of several small herbs related to the lilies that produce usually blue flowers in the spring

grape·shot \'grāp-ˌshät\ *n* : small iron balls formerly fired at short range from cannon against people (as soldiers or rioters)

grape sugar *n* : DEXTROSE

grape·vine \'grāp-ˌvīn\ *n* **1** : GRAPE 2 **2** : an unofficial means of spreading information or gossip from person to person

grape 1

¹graph \'graf\ *n* **1** : a diagram that shows change in one variable factor in comparison with that of one or more other factors **2** : a pictorial diagram (as a line or curve) representing the solution set of an equation or a given set of points

²graph *vb* : to represent by or plot on a graph ⟨*graph* each equation⟩

-graph \ˌgraf\ *n combining form* : something written ⟨homo*graph*⟩ [derived from Greek -*graphon* "something written", from -*graphos* "writing", from *graphein* "to write" — related to GRAFFITO, -GRAM]

¹graph·ic \'graf-ik\ *also* **graph·i·cal** \-i-kəl\ *adj* **1** : clearly and impressively told or described **2** : of, relating to, or being arts such as painting, engraving, printing, or photography **3** : of, relating to, or represented by a graph — **graph·i·cal·ly** \-i-k(ə-)lē\ *adv*

syn GRAPHIC, VIVID, PICTURESQUE mean presenting a picture of something in words. GRAPHIC suggests that the picture is sharp and lifelike ⟨a *graphic* report on hunger in the world⟩ VIVID suggests giving a strong and lasting

\ə\ abut		\au̇\ out	\i\ tip	\ȯ\ saw	\u̇\ foot
\ər\ further		\ch\ chin	\ī\ life	\ȯi\ coin	\y\ yet
\a\ mat		\e\ pet	\j\ job	\th\ thin	\yü\ few
\ā\ take		\ē\ easy	\ŋ\ sing	\th\ this	\yu̇\ cure
\ä\ cot, cart		\g\ go	\ō\ bone	\ü\ food	\zh\ vision

impression of reality ⟨a *vivid* story about heroes⟩ PIC-TURESQUE suggests an impressive or effective picture that is the product of many separate pleasing or clear details ⟨a *picturesque* tale about growing up on a farm⟩

²graphic *n* **1** : a picture, map, or graph used for illustration **2** *pl* : a display (as of pictures or graphs) generated by a computer on a screen, printer, or plotter

graphics tablet *n* : a device by which pictures, graphs, or maps are put into a computer in a manner similar to drawing

graph·ite \'graf-ˌīt\ *n* : a soft shiny black carbon that is used in making lead pencils and as a dry lubricant

gra·phol·o·gy \gra-'fäl-ə-jē\ *n* : the study of handwriting especially for the purpose of analyzing the writer's personality — **gra·phol·o·gist** \-jəst\ *n*

graph paper *n* : paper ruled (as into small squares) for drawing graphs or making diagrams

-g·ra·phy \g-rə-fē\ *n combining form, pl* **-graphies** : writing or representation in a (specified) manner or by a (specified) means or of a (specified) object ⟨photo*graphy*⟩ ⟨tele*graphy*⟩ [derived from Latin *-graphia* "writing", from Greek *graphein* "to write"]

grap·nel \'grap-nᵊl\ *n* : a small anchor with pointed hooks or claws used in dragging or grappling

¹grap·ple \'grap-əl\ *n* **1** : the act of grappling : GRIP, HOLD **2** : an instrument for grappling

²grapple *vb* **grap·pled; grap·pling** \'grap-(ə-)liŋ\ **1** : to seize or hold with or as if with a hooked instrument **2** : to seize and struggle with one another **3** : to attempt to deal : COPE ⟨*grappled* with a problem⟩ — **grap·pler** \-(ə-)lər\ *n*

¹grasp \'grasp\ *vb* **1** : to make the motion of seizing : CLUTCH ⟨*grasp* at straws⟩ **2** : to clasp or embrace with or as if with the fingers or arms **3** : to lay hold of with the mind : COMPREHEND ⟨failed to *grasp* its importance⟩ — **grasp·able** \'gras-pə-bəl\ *adj* — **grasp·er** *n*

²grasp *n* **1** : ²EMBRACE **2** : ²CONTROL 1, HOLD ⟨land in the *grasp* of a tyrant⟩ **3 a** : the reach of the arms ⟨the limb was beyond my *grasp*⟩ **b** : the power of seizing and holding **4** : COMPREHENSION 3, UNDERSTANDING

grasp·ing \'gras-piŋ\ *adj* : GREEDY 3, AVARICIOUS — **grasp·ing·ly** *adv* — **grasp·ing·ness** *n*

¹grass \'gras\ *n* **1** : herbs suitable for or eaten by grazing animals **2** : any of a large family of green plants (as wheat, Indian corn, bamboo, or sugarcane) with jointed usually hollow stems, long slender leaves, and small dry one-seeded fruits often in groups **3** : grass-covered land; *esp* : ²LAWN **4** *slang* : MARIJUANA — **grass·like** \-ˌlīk\ *adj* — **grassy** \'gras-ē\ *adj*

²grass *vb* **1** : to seed with grass **2** : to furnish with pasture or with grass for food

grass·hop·per \'gras-ˌhäp-ər\ *n* : any of numerous plant-eating insects that have long hind legs used for leaping

grass·land \-ˌland\ *n* : land covered with herbs (as grasses and clover) rather than shrubs and trees

grass roots *n pl* : society at the local and popular level especially in areas away from political or cultural centers

grasshopper

¹grate \'grāt\ *n* **1** : GRATING 1 **2** : a frame or basket of iron bars for holding burning fuel (as in a furnace or a fireplace)

²grate *vb* **grat·ed; grat·ing** **1** : to make into small particles by rubbing against something rough ⟨*grate* cheese⟩ **2** : to grind or rub against something with a scratching noise **3** : to have a harsh or irritating effect — **grat·er** *n*

grate·ful \'grāt-fəl\ *adj* **1 a** : appreciative of benefits re-

ceived **b** : expressing gratitude **2** : giving pleasure or contentment : PLEASING — **grate·ful·ly** \-fə-lē\ *adv* — **grate·ful·ness** *n*

grat·i·fy \'grat-ə-ˌfī\ *vb* **-fied; -fy·ing** **1** : to give or be a source of pleasure or satisfaction to **2** : to grant a favor to : INDULGE — **grat·i·fi·ca·tion** \ˌgrat-ə-fə-'kā-shən\ *n*

grat·ing \'grāt-iŋ\ *n* **1** : a frame of parallel bars or cross-bars **2** : a transparent surface that is ruled with a series of very closely spaced parallel lines or bars and is used to produce spectra by the diffraction of light

gra·tis \'grat-əs, 'grāt-\ *adv or adj* : without charge : FREE

grat·i·tude \'grat-ə-ˌt(y)üd\ *n* : the state of being grateful [Middle English *gratitude* "gratitude", derived from Latin *gratitudo* (same meaning), from *gratus* "pleasing, thankful, agreeable" — related to CONGRATULATE, GRACE]

gra·tu·i·tous \grə-'t(y)ü-ət-əs\ *adj* **1** : done or provided freely with nothing expected in return **2** : not called for by the circumstances : UNWARRANTED ⟨a *gratuitous* insult⟩ — **gra·tu·i·tous·ly** *adv* — **gra·tu·i·tous·ness** *n*

gra·tu·i·ty \grə-'t(y)ü-ət-ē\ *n, pl* **-ties** : something given freely; *esp* : ¹⁰TIP

¹grave \'grāv\ *vb* **graved; grav·en** \'grā-vən\ *or* **graved; grav·ing** **1** : CARVE 1, SCULPTURE **2** : ENGRAVE 1a [Old English *grafan* "dig, carve"]

²grave *n* **1** : a hole dug to bury a body in **2** : TOMB 2

³grave \'grāv, *in sense 3 often* 'gräv\ *adj* **1 a** : deserving serious consideration : IMPORTANT ⟨a *grave* matter⟩ **b** : threatening great harm or danger ⟨received a *grave* injury⟩ **2** : dignified in appearance or manner : SOLEMN, SERIOUS **3** : of, marked by, or being an accent mark having the form ` [from early French *grave* "important, serious, weighty", from Latin *gravis* "heavy, serious" — related to AGGRAVATE, GRAVITY, GRIEVE] — **grave·ly** *adv* — **grave·ness** *n*

⁴gra·ve \'gräv-(ˌ)ā\ *adv or adj* : in a slow and solemn manner — used as a direction in music

¹grav·el \'grav-əl\ *n* : small pieces of rock and pebbles larger than grains of sand

²gravel *adj* : GRAVELLY 2

³gravel *vb* **grav·eled** *or* **grav·elled; grav·el·ing** *or* **grav·el·ling** \'grav-(ə-)liŋ\ : to cover or spread with gravel

grav·el·ly \'grav-(ə-)lē\ *adj* **1** : of, containing, or covered with gravel ⟨*gravelly* soil⟩ **2** : having a harsh scratchy sound ⟨a *gravelly* voice⟩

grave·stone \'grāv-ˌstōn\ *n* : a burial monument

grave·yard \-ˌyärd\ *n* : CEMETERY

grav·id \'grav-əd\ *adj* : PREGNANT 1

gra·vi·me·ter \gra-'vim-ət-ər, 'grav-ə-ˌmēt-\ *n* : an instrument for measuring differences in the force of gravity at different places

grav·i·tate \'grav-ə-ˌtāt\ *vb* **-tat·ed; -tat·ing** : to move or tend to move toward something

grav·i·ta·tion \ˌgrav-ə-'tā-shən\ *n* **1** : a force of attraction that tends to draw particles or bodies together **2** : the action or process of gravitating — **grav·i·ta·tion·al** \-shnəl, -shən-ᵊl\ *adj* — **grav·i·ta·tion·al·ly** \-ē\ *adv* — **grav·i·ta·tive** \'grav-ə-ˌtāt-iv\ *adj*

grav·i·ty \'grav-ət-ē\ *n, pl* **-ties** **1 a** : the quality or state of being dignified and proper **b** : the quality or state of being important or serious **2** : ²MASS 2 — used chiefly in the phrase *center of gravity* **3 a** : the gravitational attraction of the mass of a heavenly body (as the earth) for bodies at or near its surface **b** : GRAVITATION 1 **c** : ACCELERATION OF GRAVITY [from early French *gravité* or Latin *gravitas*, both meaning "the quality or state of being serious or dignified, the quality of being weighty", from Latin *gravis* "heavy, serious" — related to AGGRAVATE, ³GRAVE, GRIEVE]

gra·vy \'grā-vē\ *n, pl* **gravies** **1** : a sauce made from the thickened and seasoned juices of cooked meat **2** : something that is over and above what is ordinarily earned or expected

¹gray \\'grā\\ *adj* **1** : of the color gray; *also* : dull in color **2** : having gray hair **3** : lacking cheer or brightness : DISMAL ⟨a *gray* day⟩ — **gray·ness** *n*

²gray *n* **1** : one of the series of neutral colors ranging between black and white **2** : something gray — **gray** *vb* — **gray·ish** \\'grā-ish\\ *adj*

gray·beard \\'grā-,bi(ə)rd\\ *n* : an old man

gray fox *n* : a fox with coarse gray hair and white underparts that is found from southern Canada to northern South America

gray·ling \\'grā-liŋ\\ *n, pl* **grayling** *also* **graylings** **1** : any of several freshwater fishes related to the trouts and valued for food and sport **2** : any of various gray and brown butterflies

gray matter *n* **1** : nerve tissue especially of the brain and spinal cord that has a brownish gray color **2** : INTELLIGENCE 1

gray squirrel *n* : a common light gray to black squirrel native to eastern North America and introduced into Europe

gray whale *n* : a rather large whalebone whale of the northern Pacific

gray wolf *n* : TIMBER WOLF

¹graze \\'grāz\\ *vb* **grazed; graz·ing** **1** : to feed on growing grass or herbs **2** : to feed or put cattle to feed on grass or herbs

²graze *vb* **grazed; graz·ing** **1** : to rub or touch lightly in passing : touch against and quickly move away from ⟨the car's wheel *grazed* the curb⟩ **2** : to scratch or scrape by rubbing against something ⟨*grazed* her knee when she fell⟩

³graze *n* : an act or result of grazing; *esp* : a skin injury caused by grazing : SCRAPE

¹grease \\'grēs\\ *n* **1** : melted animal fat **2** : oily matter **3** : a thick lubricant

²grease \\'grēs, 'grēz\\ *vb* **greased; greas·ing** **1** : to smear with grease **2** : to lubricate with grease — **greas·er** *n*

grease·paint \\'grē-,spānt\\ *n* : theatrical makeup

grease pencil *n* : a pencil with lead like a soft crayon for marking on hard surfaces (as glass)

grease·wood \\'grē-,swu̇d\\ *n* : a low stiff shrub that is related to the goosefoots and is common in salty soils in the western U.S.

greasy \\'grē-sē, -zē\\ *adj* **greas·i·er; -est** **1** : smeared with grease **2** : containing grease ⟨*greasy* food⟩ **3** : resembling grease or oil : SMOOTH, SLIPPERY — **greas·i·ly** \\-sə-lē, -zə-\\ *adv* — **greas·i·ness** \\-sē-nəs, -zē-\\ *n*

great \\'grāt\\ *adj, in South also* **'gre(ə)t**\\ *adj* **1** : large in size : not small or little **2** : large in number : NUMEROUS ⟨a *great* crowd⟩ **3** : long continued ⟨a *great* while⟩ **4** : beyond the average or ordinary ⟨a *great* weight⟩ ⟨in no *great* rush⟩ ⟨in *great* pain⟩ **5** : DISTINGUISHED, PROMINENT ⟨a *great* artist⟩ **6** : more distant in relationship by one generation ⟨*great*-grandchildren⟩ **7** : superior in quality or character ⟨*great* of heart⟩ **8** : remarkable in skill ⟨*great* at tennis⟩ **9** — used as a term of general approval ⟨had a *great* time⟩ — **great·ly** *adv* — **great·ness** *n*

great ape *n* : any of several large tailless apes that exist at the present time and include the gibbon, chimpanzee, gorilla, and orangutan

great auk *n* : an extinct large auk that was unable to fly and was formerly common along North Atlantic coasts

great–aunt *n* : GRANDAUNT

Great Bear *n* : URSA MAJOR

great blue heron *n* : a large grayish blue American heron with a crest of dark feathers pointing backward on its head

great circle *n* : a circle on the surface of a sphere that has the same center as the sphere; *esp* : one on the surface of the earth a portion of which Is the shortest travel distance between two points

great·coat \\'grāt-,kōt\\ *n* : a heavy overcoat

Great Dane *n* : any of a breed of very tall powerful smooth‑coated dogs

great divide *n* : a watershed located between major drain-

age systems

greatest common divisor *n* : the largest integer that is an exact divisor of each of two or more integers — called also *greatest common factor*

great·heart·ed \\'grāt-'härt-əd\\ *adj* **1** : COURAGEOUS **2** : nobly generous — **great·heart·ed·ly** *adv* — **great·heart·ed·ness** *n*

great horned owl *n* : an American owl with two bunches of feathers resembling ears or horns at the top of the head

great–nephew *n* : GRANDNEPHEW

great–niece *n* : GRANDNIECE

great power *n* : one of the nations that have the greatest influence, resources, and military strength in the world

great–uncle *n* : GRANDUNCLE

great white shark *n* : WHITE SHARK

grebe \\'grēb\\ *n* : any of a family of swimming and diving birds closely related to the loons

Gre·cian \\'grē-shən\\ *adj* : GREEK — **Gre·cian** *n*

greed \\'grēd\\ *n* : selfish desire for food, money, or possessions over and above one's needs

greedy \\'grēd-ē\\ *adj* **greed·i·er; -est** **1** : having a keen appetite **2** : having an eager and often selfish desire or longing ⟨*greedy* for praise⟩ **3** : wanting more than one needs or more than one's fair share (as of food) — **greed·i·ly** \\'grēd-ºl-ē\\ *adv* — **greed·i·ness** \\'grēd-ē-nəs\\ *n*

Greek \\'grēk\\ *n* **1 a** : a person born or living in Greece **b** : a person of Greek ancestry **2** : the Indo-European language of the Greeks — **Greek** *adj*

¹green \\'grēn\\ *adj* **1** : of the color green **2 a** : covered by green leaves or herbs **b** : consisting of green plants or of the leafy part of a plant ⟨a *green* salad⟩ **3** : not fully grown or ripe **4** : marked by a sickly appearance ⟨*green* with envy⟩ **5** : lacking training, knowledge, or experience ⟨*green* troops⟩ — **green·ish** \\'grē-nish\\ *adj* — **green·ly** \\'grēn-lē\\ *adv* — **green·ness** \\'grēn-nəs\\ *n*

²green *n* **1** : a color (as that of growing fresh grass or of the emerald) that ranges between blue and yellow **2 a** : green vegetation **b** *pl* : leafy parts of plants used for some purpose (as ornament or food) ⟨turnip *greens*⟩ **3** : a grassy plain or plot; *esp* : a smooth grassy area around the hole into which the ball must be played in golf

green alga *n* : an alga in which the chlorophyll is not masked by other pigments

green·back \\'grēn-,bak\\ *n* : a piece of U.S. paper money

green bean *n* : a kidney bean with the pods green when ready for harvest

green·belt \\'grēn-,belt\\ *n* : a belt of landscaped roads, parks, or farmlands that encircles a community

green·ery \\'grēn-(ə-)rē\\ *n, pl* **-er·ies** : green leaves or plants : VERDURE

green·gro·cer \\'grēn-,grō-sər\\ *n, chiefly British* : a person who sells fresh vegetables and fruit to the public — **green·gro·cery** \\-,grōs-(ə-)rē\\ *n*

green·horn \\-,hȯrn\\ *n* : an inexperienced person; *esp* : one easily tricked or cheated

¹green·house \\-,hau̇s\\ *n* : a glassed enclosure for cultivation of plants

²greenhouse *adj* : of, relating to, or caused by the greenhouse effect ⟨*greenhouse* warming⟩

greenhouse effect *n* : the warming effect on the earth's atmosphere that occurs when the sun's radiation of short wavelength passes through the atmosphere, is absorbed by the earth, and is given off as radiation of longer wavelength that can be absorbed by carbon dioxide and water vapor in the atmosphere

green manure *n* : a crop of plants (as clover) that is plowed

\\ə\\ abut	\\au̇\\ out	\\i\\ tip	\\ȯ\\ saw	\\u̇\\ foot
\\ər\\ further	\\ch\\ chin	\\ī\\ life	\\ȯi\\ coin	\\y\\ yet
\\a\\ mat	\\e\\ pet	\\j\\ job	\\th\\ thin	\\yü\\ few
\\ā\\ take	\\ē\\ easy	\\ŋ\\ sing	\\th\\ this	\\yu̇\\ cure
\\ä\\ cot, cart	\\g\\ go	\\ō\\ bone	\\ü\\ food	\\zh\\ vision

under while green to enrich the soil

green mold *n* : a mold (as a penicillium) that is green or produces green spores

green onion *n* : a young onion that is pulled from the ground before the bulb has become large and is used especially in salads

green pepper *n* : a sweet pepper before it turns red at maturity

green snake *n* : either of two bright green harmless largely insect-eating snakes of North America

green soap *n* : a soft soap made from vegetable oils and used especially to treat skin diseases

green·sward \'grēn-,swȯ(ə)rd\ *n* : turf green with growing grass

green thumb *n* : an unusual ability to make plants grow — **green–thumbed** \'grēn-'thəmd\ *adj*

green turtle *n* : a large edible sea turtle with a smooth greenish shell

green vegetable *n* : a vegetable that has the edible parts rich in chlorophyll and is an important source of vitamins

Green·wich time \'grin-ij-, 'gren-, -ich-\ *n* : the time of the meridian of Greenwich used as the basis of standard time throughout the world

green·wood \'grēn-,wu̇d\ *n* : a forest green with leaves

greet \'grēt\ *vb* **1** : to address upon arrival or meeting with expressions of kind wishes **2** : to meet or react to in a specified manner ⟨*greeted* with cheers⟩ **3** : to appear or present itself to — **greet·er** *n*

greet·ing *n* **1** : SALUTATION **2** : an expression of good wishes : REGARDS — usually used in pl.

greeting card *n* : a decorated card with a message of goodwill that is sent to or received by a person usually on a special occasion

gre·gar·i·ous \gri-'gar-ē-əs, -'ger-\ *adj* **1** : tending to associate with others of one's kind : SOCIABLE **2** : tending to live or move with others of one's own kind : tending to flock together [from Latin *gregarius* "relating to a herd or flock", from *greg-, grex* "flock, herd" — related to CONGREGATE] — **gre·gar·i·ous·ly** *adv* — **gre·gar·i·ous·ness** *n*

Gre·go·ri·an calendar \gri-,gȯr-ē-ən-, -,gȯr-\ *n* : a calendar introduced by Pope Gregory XIII in 1582 and adopted in Great Britain and the American colonies in 1752 — compare JULIAN CALENDAR

Gregorian chant *n* : a simple tune with no regular rhythm that is sung in unison and without accompaniment in services of the Roman Catholic Church

grem·lin \'grem-lən\ *n* : a small mischievous or troublesome creature

gre·nade \grə-'nād\ *n* : a small bomb designed to be thrown by hand or launched (as by a rifle) [from early French *grenade, granade* "pomegranate, grenade", from Latin *granata* "pomegranate", derived from Latin *granatus* "seedy", from *granum* "grain, seed" — related to GARNET, GRAIN, POMEGRANATE; see *Word History* at GARNET]

gren·a·dier \,gren-ə-'di(ə)r\ *n* : a soldier of a European regiment formerly armed with grenades

grew *past of* GROW

grey *variant of* GRAY

grey·hound \'grā-,hau̇nd\ *n* : a tall slender swift dog with a smooth coat and narrow head

greyhound

grid \'grid\ *n* **1** : GRATING 1 **2** : a metal plate used as a conductor in a storage battery **3** : an element of an electron tube consisting of a network of fine wire **4** : a network of horizontal and perpendicular lines (as for locating points on a map by means of coordinates or for counting a sample of particles or tiny living things on a microscope slide)

grid·dle \'grid-ᵊl\ *n* : a flat surface or pan on which food is cooked

griddle cake *n* : PANCAKE

grid·iron \'grid-,ī(-ə)rn\ *n* **1** : a grate for broiling food **2** : something consisting of or covered with a grid **3** : a football field

grief \'grēf\ *n* **1 a** : deep sorrow : SADNESS **b** : a cause of sorrow **2 a** : things that cause problems ⟨enough *grief* for one day⟩ **b** : an unfortunate happening ⟨the boat came to *grief* on the rocks⟩ **syn** see SORROW

griev·ance \'grē-vən(t)s\ *n* **1** : a cause of distress giving reason for complaint **2** : the formal expression of a grievance : COMPLAINT

grieve \'grēv\ *vb* **grieved; griev·ing** **1** : to cause grief or suffering to : DISTRESS **2** : to feel or express grief [Middle English *greven* "distress, grieve", from early French *grever* (same meaning), from Latin *gravare* "to burden", from *gravis* "heavy, serious" — related to AGGRAVATE, ³GRAVE, GRAVITY] — **griev·er** *n*

griev·ous \'grē-vəs\ *adj* **1** : ¹HEAVY 2, SEVERE ⟨the *grievous* cost of war⟩ **2** : causing pain, suffering, or sorrow ⟨a *grievous* wound⟩ **3** : SERIOUS 4, GRAVE ⟨*grievous* fault⟩ — **griev·ous·ly** *adv* — **griev·ous·ness** *n*

grif·fin *or* **grif·fon** *also* **gryph·on** \'grif-ən\ *n* : an imaginary animal that is half eagle and half lion

¹grill \'gril\ *vb* **1** : to broil on a grill **2 a** : to torment as if by broiling **b** : to question with repeated questions

²grill *n* **1** : a grate on which food is broiled **2** : broiled food **3** : a restaurant that serves broiled foods

grille *also* **grill** \'gril\ *n* **1** : a grating forming a barrier or screen **2** : an opening covered with a grille

grim \'grim\ *adj* **grim·mer; grim·mest** **1** : CRUEL 2, FIERCE **2 a** : harsh in appearance **b** : FRIGHTFUL 1 **3** : UNFLINCHING, UNYIELDING ⟨*grim* determination⟩ — **grim·ly** *adv* — **grim·ness** *n*

grim·ace \'grim-əs, grim-'ās\ *n* : a twisting of the face or features (as in disgust or disapproval) — **grimace** *vb*

grime \'grīm\ *n* : dirt rubbed into or covering a surface; *also* : accumulated dirtiness and disorder — **grime** *vb* — **grim·i·ness** \'grī-mē-nəs\ *n* — **grimy** \'grī-mē\ *adj*

grin \'grin\ *vb* **grinned; grin·ning** : to draw back the lips so as to show the teeth especially in laughter — **grin** *n*

¹grind \'grīnd\ *vb* **ground** \'grau̇nd\; **grind·ing** **1** : to reduce to powder or pieces by friction (as in a mill or with the teeth) **2** : to wear down, polish, or sharpen by friction : WHET **3** : to press with a scraping noise : GRIT **4** : OPPRESS 1, HARASS **5 a** : to operate or produce by turning a crank **b** : to produce by steady hard work ⟨*grind* out a composition⟩ **6** : to move with difficulty or friction especially so as to make a scraping noise ⟨*grind* the gears⟩

²grind *n* **1 a** : an act of grinding **b** : the sound of grinding **2 a** : steady hard work; *esp* : study that takes much effort **b** : a student who studies too much **3** : the result of grinding; *esp* : the size of particle obtained by grinding

grind·er \'grīn-dər\ *n* **1** : one that grinds **2** : ²SUBMARINE 2

grind·stone \'grīn-,stōn\ *n* : a stone disk that turns on an axle and is used for grinding or sharpening

gri·ot \'grē-,ō\ *n* : any of a class of musician-entertainers of western Africa whose performances include tribal histories and genealogies

¹grip \'grip\ *vb* **gripped; grip·ping** **1** : to seize firmly **2** : to hold strongly the interest of ⟨the story *grips* the reader⟩

²grip *n* **1 a** : a firm grasp **b** : strength in gripping **c** : a way of clasping the hand by which

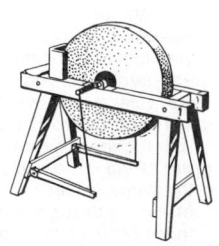

grindstone

members of a secret society recognize or greet one an-other **2 a** : ²CONTROL 1, MASTERY ⟨in the *grip* of a blizzard⟩ **b** : COMPREHENSION 3, UNDERSTANDING **3** : a part or de-vice for gripping or by which something is grasped; *esp* : ¹HANDLE 1 **4** : SUITCASE

¹**gripe** \'grīp\ *vb* **griped; grip·ing** **1** : to seize firmly : GRIP **2 a** : AFFLICT, DISTRESS **b** : IRRITATE 1, VEX ⟨laziness *gripes* our teacher⟩ **3** : to cause or experience spasms of pain in the bowels **4** : COMPLAIN 1 — **grip·er** *n*

·²**gripe** *n* **1** : ²GRIP 1 **2 a** : AFFLICTION 1 **b** : COMPLAINT 1 **3** : a spasm of pain in the bowels

grippe \'grip\ *n* : a virus disease that is the same as or very much like influenza — **grippy** \'grip-ē\ *adj*

gris·ly \'griz-lē\ *adj* **gris·li·er; -est** : HORRIBLE, GRUESOME — **gris·li·ness** *n*

grist \'grist\ *n* : grain to be ground or already ground

gris·tle \'gris-əl\ *n* : tough chewy matter in meat served as food that is composed of cartilage, tendons, and fibers — **gris·tly** \'gris-(ə-)lē\ *adj*

grist·mill \'grist-,mil\ *n* : a mill for grinding grain

¹**grit** \'grit\ *n* **1 a** : a small hard sharp particle (as of sand) **b** : material (as an abrasive) composed of grits **2** : firm-ness of mind or spirit : unyielding courage — **grit·ty** \'grit-ē\ *adj*

²**grit** *vb* **grit·ted; grit·ting** : to grind or cause to grind : GRATE ⟨*grit* one's teeth⟩

grits \'grits\ *n pl* : coarsely ground hulled grain ⟨hominy *grits*⟩

griz·zled \'griz-əld\ *adj* : sprinkled, streaked, or mixed with gray

¹**griz·zly** \'griz-lē\ *adj* **griz·zli·er; -est** : GRIZZLED

²**grizzly** *n, pl* **grizzlies** : GRIZZLY BEAR

grizzly bear *n* : a large powerful usually brown-ish yellow bear of west-ern North America — called also *grizzly*

groan \'grōn\ *vb* **1** : to utter a deep moan of pain, grief, or irritation **2** : to make a harsh sound under strain ⟨the chair *groaned* under my weight⟩ — **groan** *n* — **groan·er** *n*

grizzly bear

¹**groat** \'grōt\ *n* **1** : hulled grain broken into frag-ments larger than grits — usually used in pl. ⟨buckwheat *groats*⟩ **2** : a grain (as of oats) without the hull [Old En-glish *grotan,* plural of *grot* "particle"]

²**groat** *n* : a former British coin worth four pennies [Middle English *groot* "coin"; of Dutch origin]

gro·cer \'grō-sər\ *n* : a dealer in food and household sup-plies

gro·cery \'grōs-(ə-)rē\ *n, pl* **-cer·ies** **1** *pl* : food sold by a grocer ⟨went out to buy the *groceries*⟩ **2** : a grocer's store

grog \'gräg\ *n* : alcoholic liquor; *esp* : liquor (as rum) weak-ened with water — **grog·gery** \'gräg-ə-rē\ *n* — **grog-shop** \'gräg-,shäp\ *n*

grog·gy \-'gräg-ē\ *adj* **grog·gi·er; -est** : weak and un-steady on the feet or in action — **grog·gi·ly** \'gräg-ə-lē\ *adv* — **grog·gi·ness** \'gräg-ē-nəs\ *n*

¹**groin** \'groin\ *n* **1** : the junction of the lower abdomen and inner part of the thigh or the part of the body around this junction **2** : the curved line or rib on a ceiling along which two vaults meet

²**groin** *vb* : to build or equip with groins

grom·met \'gräm-ət, 'grəm-\ *n* : an eyelet of firm material to strengthen or protect an opening

¹**groom** \'grüm, 'grum\ *n* **1 a** : a male servant **b** : a per-son in charge of horses **2** : BRIDEGROOM

²**groom** *vb* **1** : to clean and care for (an animal) **2** : to

make neat, attractive, or acceptable

grooms·man \'grümz-mən, 'grumz-\ *n* : a male friend who accompanies a bridegroom at his wedding

¹**groove** \'grüv\ *n* **1** : a long narrow channel made in a surface **2** : a fixed routine : RUT **3** : top form

²**groove** *vb* **grooved; groov·ing** **1** : to form a groove in **b** : to become grooved **2** : to enjoy very much

groovy \'grü-vē\ *adj* **groov·i·er; -est** : very good : EXCEL-LENT

grope \'grōp\ *vb* **groped; grop·ing** **1** : to seek by or as if by feeling around uncertainly ⟨*groped* for the light switch⟩ ⟨*grope* for the right word⟩ **2** : to feel one's way by groping ⟨*grope* along a wall⟩

gros·beak \'grōs-,bēk\ *n* : any of several finches (as the rose-breasted grosbeak) of Europe or America having large stout cone-shaped bills

gro·schen \'grō-shən, 'grȯ-\ *n, pl* **groschen** **1** : a unit of value equal to ¹⁄₁₀₀ schilling **2** : a coin representing one groschen

¹**gross** \'grōs\ *adj* **1 a** : very obvious : GLARING ⟨a *gross* error⟩ **b** : SHAMEFUL 1 ⟨*gross* injustice⟩ **2** : ¹BIG 2a, BULKY; *esp* : excessively fat **3** : consisting of a whole before any deductions ⟨*gross* earnings⟩ **4** : COARSE 5, VULGAR ⟨*gross* language⟩ [Middle English *gros, gross* "large, thick, easy to see or understand", from early French *gros* "thick, coarse", from Latin *grossus* (same meaing)] — **gross·ly** *adv* — **gross·ness** *n*

²**gross** *n* : a whole before any deductions

³**gross** *vb* : to earn before deductions ⟨*grossed* $50,000 be-fore taxes⟩

⁴**gross** *n, pl* **gross** : 12 dozen ⟨a *gross* of pencils⟩ [Middle English *groce* "a group of 12 dozen", from early French *grosse* (same meaning), derived from *gros* "thick"]

gross national product *n* : the total value of the goods and services produced in a nation during a year

grot \'grät\ *n* : GROTTO

gro·tesque \grō-'tesk\ *adj* **1** : combining (as in a painting or poem) details not found together in nature **2** : unnatu-rally odd or ugly — **gro·tesque·ly** *adv* — **gro-tesque·ness** *n*

> **Word History** When the Italians were digging among the ruins of ancient Rome, they found strange paintings on the walls of some of the rooms. These paintings were of human and animal forms mixed with those of strange fruits and flowers. The Italians called such a painting *pit-tura grottesca,* which means "cave painting". The Ital-ian adjective *grottesca* came from *grotta,* meaning "cave". We also get English *grotto* from this word. The Italian word *grotta* in turn came from the Latin *crypta,* which meant "cavern, crypt". The French borrowed the word *grottesca* from Italian and spelled it *grotesque.* This is the form in which it came into English. At first the adjective was used to describe pictures having strange combinations of things not normally found together. Later it came to be used for anything that looked weird or unnatural. [from French *grotesque* "relating to or being a style of art with unusual designs and combina-tions of figures of animals, humans, and plants", from Italian *(pittura) grottesca* "cave painting", from *grot-tesca* "of a cave", from *grotta, grotto* "cave", from Latin *crypta* "cavern, crypt" — related to GROTTO]

grot·to \'grät-ō\ *n, pl* **grottoes** *also* **grottos** **1** : ¹CAVE **2** : an artifical structure made to resemble a natural cave [from Italian *grotta, grotto* "cave", from Latin *crypta* "cav-ern, crypt" — related to GROTESQUE]

grouch \'grauch\ *n* **1** : a sudden outburst of bad temper

\ə\ abut	\au\ out	\i\ tip	\ȯ\ saw	\u̇\ foot
\ər\ further	\ch\ chin	\ī\ life	\ȯi\ coin	\y\ yet
\a\ mat	\e\ pet	\j\ job	\th\ thin	\yü\ few
\ā\ take	\ē\ easy	\ŋ\ sing	\th\ this	\yu̇\ cure
\ä\ cot, cart	\g\ go	\ō\ bone	\ü\ food	\zh\ vision

2 : an irritable or complaining person — **grouch** *vb* — **grouch·i·ly** \'graú-chə-lē\ *adv* — **grouch·i·ness** \-chē-nəs\ *n* — **grouchy** \-chē\ *adj*

¹**ground** \'graúnd\ *n* **1 a** : the bottom of a body of water ⟨the boat struck *ground*⟩ **b** *pl* : SEDIMENT 1, LEES **2** : BASIS, FOUNDATION ⟨*grounds* for divorce⟩ **3** : a surrounding area : BACKGROUND ⟨a picture on a gray *ground*⟩ **4 a** : the surface of the earth **b** : an area used for a particular purpose ⟨parade *ground*⟩ ⟨fishing *grounds*⟩ **c** *pl* : the area around and belonging to a building ⟨the capitol *grounds*⟩ **5** : ³SOIL 1, EARTH **6** : an area to be won or defended in or as if in battle ⟨gaining *ground* on the other runners⟩ **7 a** : an object that makes an electrical connection with the earth **b** : a large conducting body (as the earth) used as a common return for an electric circuit

²**ground** *vb* **1** : to bring to or place on the ground **2 a** : to provide a reason for **b** : to instruct in fundamentals ⟨well *grounded* in mathematics⟩ **3** : to connect electrically with a ground **4** : to restrict to the ground ⟨*ground* a pilot⟩ **5** : to run aground ⟨the ship *grounded* on a reef⟩ **6** : to hit a ground ball ⟨*grounded* to the shortstop⟩

³**ground** *past and past participle of* GRIND

ground ball *n* : a batted baseball that rolls or bounces along the ground

ground crew *n* : the mechanics and technicians who maintain and service an aircraft

ground·er \'graún-dər\ *n* : GROUND BALL

ground finch *n* : any of several dull-colored finches with large bills that are found in the Galápagos islands

ground·hog \'graúnd-ˌhòg, -ˌhäg\ *n* : WOODCHUCK 1

Groundhog Day *n* : February 2 when according to tradition the groundhog comes out of its burrow and if it sees its shadow and is frightened back underground there will be six more weeks of winter

ground·less \'graún-(d)ləs\ *adj* : not justified : having no real basis ⟨*groundless* fears⟩ — **ground·less·ly** *adv* — **ground·less·ness** *n*

ground·ling \'graún-(d)liŋ\ *n* : a spectator who stood in the part of a theater in Shakespeare's time where there were no seats

ground·nut \'graún(d)-ˌnət\ *n, chiefly British* : PEANUT 1

ground pine *n* : any of several club mosses with long creeping stems and upright branches

ground plan *n* **1** : a plan of a floor of a building **2** : a first or basic plan

ground rule *n* : a rule set up for a specified activity

ground squirrel *n* : any of numerous burrowing rodents (as gophers and chipmunks) that differ from true squirrels in having cheek pouches and shorter fur

ground state *n* : the energy level of a physical system (as an atom) having the least energy of all its possible states

ground swell *n* : a broad deep ocean swell caused by a distant storm or earthquake

ground·wa·ter \'graún-ˌdwòt-ər, -ˌdwät-\ *n* : water within the earth that supplies wells and springs

ground·work \'graún-ˌdwərk\ *n* : FOUNDATION 2, BASIS

¹**group** \'grüp\ *n* **1** : a number of objects or persons considered as a unit **2 a** : a number of living things having some natural relationship **b** : a combination of atoms commmonly found together in a molecule ⟨a methyl *group*⟩ **3** : a small band : COMBO ⟨a rock *group*⟩

²**group** *vb* : to arrange or combine in a group ⟨*group* children by ages⟩

grou·per \'grü-pər\ *n, pl* **groupers** *also* **grouper** : any of numerous mostly large fishes that live at the bottom of warm seas and are related to the sea basses

group·ie \'grü-pē\ *n* : a fan of a rock group who usually follows the group around on concert tours

¹**grouse** \'graús\ *n, pl* **grouse** *or* **grouses** : any of numerous plump-bodied game birds that are usually less brilliant in the colors of their feathers than the related pheasants

²**grouse** *vb* **groused; grous·ing** : COMPLAIN 1, GRUMBLE —

grous·er *n*

grove \'grōv\ *n* : a small wood; *esp* : a group of trees without underbrush ⟨an orange *grove*⟩

grov·el \'gräv-əl, 'grəv-\ *vb* **-eled** *or* **-elled; -el·ing** *or* **-el·ling** \-(ə-)liŋ\ **1** : to creep or lie face down on the ground (as in fear) **2** : to degrade oneself by behaving like a fearful slave : CRINGE — **grov·el·er** *or* **grov·el·ler** \-(ə-)lər\ *n*

grow \'grō\ *vb* **grew** \'grü\; **grown** \'grōn\; **grow·ing** **1 a** : to spring up and develop to maturity **b** : to be able to grow in some place or situation ⟨rice *grows* in water⟩ **c** : to take on some relation through or as if through growth ⟨a tree with limbs *grown* together⟩ **2** : ¹INCREASE 1, EXPAND ⟨the city is *growing* rapidly⟩ ⟨*grows* in wisdom⟩ **3** : ORIGINATE 2 ⟨the project *grew* out of a mere suggestion⟩ **4 a** : to pass into a condition : BECOME ⟨*grew* pale⟩ **b** : to have an increasing influence ⟨habits *grow* on you⟩ **5** : to cause to grow : CULTIVATE, RAISE ⟨*grow* wheat⟩ — **grow·er** \'grō-(ə)r\ *n*

grouse

growing point *n* : the tip of a plant shoot from which additional shoot tissues develop

growing season *n* : the period of the year that is warm enough for growth especially of cultivated plants; *esp* : the period between the last killing frost in the spring and the first one in the fall

growl \'graú(ə)l\ *vb* **1 a** : ¹RUMBLE **b** : to utter a deep threatening sound ⟨the dog *growled*⟩ **2** : COMPLAIN 1 — **growl** *n* — **growl·er** \'graú-lər\ *n*

grown \'grōn\ *adj* : fully grown : MATURE ⟨a job for a *grown* man⟩

grown–up \'grō-ˌnəp\ *adj* : ¹ADULT 2 — **grown–up** *n*

growth \'grōth\ *n* **1 a** : stage or condition reached in growing : SIZE ⟨the dog hasn't reached full *growth*⟩ **b** : a process of growing especially through orderly increase in amount of protoplasm or inorganic substance ⟨*growth* of a crystal⟩ **c** : a process of developing ⟨the *growth* of civilization⟩; *also* : ²INCREASE 1 ⟨*growth* of wealth⟩ **2** : a result or product of growing ⟨covered with a *growth* of mold⟩ ⟨a thick *growth* of underbrush⟩ **3** : an abnormal mass of tissue (as a tumor or wart)

growth hormone *n* : a hormone in plants or animals that regulates growth; *esp* : one produced by the pituitary gland

grow up *vb* : to grow toward or reach full mental and physical growth

¹**grub** \'grəb\ *vb* **grubbed; grub·bing** **1** : to clear or root out by digging ⟨*grub* up roots⟩ ⟨*grub* for potatoes⟩ **2** : to work hard : DRUDGE — **grub·ber** *n*

²**grub** *n* **1** : a soft thick wormlike larva of an insect **2** : ²DRUDGE **3** : FOOD 1

grub·by \'grəb-ē\ *adj* **grub·bi·er; -est** : ¹DIRTY 1, SLOVENLY — **grub·bi·ly** \'grəb-ə-lē\ *adv* — **grub·bi·ness** \'grəb-ē-nəs\ *n*

grub·stake \'grəb-ˌstāk\ *n* : supplies or funds given to a mining prospector in return for a promise of a share in his finds — **grubstake** *vb* — **grub·stak·er** *n*

¹**grudge** \'grəj\ *vb* **grudged; grudg·ing** : BEGRUDGE — **grudg·er** *n* — **grudg·ing·ly** \-iŋ-lē\ *adv*

²**grudge** *n* : a strong lasting feeling of resentment toward someone for a real or imagined wrong

gru·el \'grü-əl\ *n* : a thin food made by boiling cereal (as oatmeal or cornmeal) in water or milk

gru·el·ing *or* **gru·el·ling** \'grü-ə-liŋ\ *adj* : requiring extreme effort : EXHAUSTING

grue·some \'grü-səm\ *adj* : causing horror or disgust : GRISLY — **grue·some·ly** *adv* — **grue·some·ness** *n*

gruff \'grəf\ *adj* **1** : rough or stern in manner, speech, or look ⟨a *gruff* reply⟩ **2** : being deep and harsh : HOARSE ⟨a *gruff* voice⟩ — **gruff·ly** *adv* — **gruff·ness** *n*

grum·ble \'grəm-bəl\ *vb* **grum·bled; grum·bling** \-b(ə-)liŋ\ **1** : to mutter in discontent **2** : ¹RUMBLE — **grumble** *n* — **grum·bler** \-b(ə-)lər\ *n* — **grum·bling·ly** \-,b(ə-)liŋ-lē\ *adv*

grump \'grəmp\ *n* : GROUCH 2 — **grump·i·ly** \'grəm-pə-lē\ *adv* — **grump·i·ness** \-pē-nəs\ *n* — **grumpy** \-pē\ *adj*

grun·gy \'grən-jē\ *adj* **grun·gi·er; -est** : being in a shabby or dirty condition

grunt \'grənt\ *n* **1 a** : the deep short sound made by a hog **b** : a similar sound **2** : any of numerous marine fishes related to the snappers — **grunt** *vb* — **grunt·er** *n*

Gru·yère \grü-'ye(ə)r, grē-'(y)e(ə)r\ *n* : a firm cheese of Switzerland that has a nutty flavor [named for *Gruyère*, district in Switzerland where the cheese was first made]

gryphon *variant of* GRIFFIN

G suit *n* : a suit designed to counteract the effects of acceleration on an aviator or astronaut [*gravity*]

gua·ca·mo·le \,gwäk-ə-'mō-lē\ *n* : mashed avocado that is mixed with chopped tomatoes and onion, seasoned, and often served as a spread or dip

gua·na·co \gwə-'näk-ō\ *n, pl* **-cos** : a South American mammal that has a soft thick light grayish brown coat and is related to the camels

gua·nine \'gwän-,ēn\ *n* : a purine base that codes genetic information in DNA and RNA — compare ADENINE, CYTOSINE, THYMINE

gua·no \'gwän-ō\ *n* : a substance composed chiefly of the bodily waste matter of seabirds and used as a fertilizer

¹guar·an·tee \,gar-ən-'tē, ,gär-\ *n* **1** : GUARANTOR **2** : an agreement by which a person or firm guarantees something or someone **3** : something given as security : PLEDGE

²guarantee *vb* **-teed; -tee·ing** **1** : to promise to answer for the debt, failure to perform, or faulty performance of another **2** : to promise that some condition holds or will be fulfilled ⟨*guarantee* a car against defects for one year⟩ ⟨*guaranteed* annual wage⟩ **3** : to give security : SECURE

guar·an·tor \,gar-ən-'tò(ə)r, 'gar-ən-tər, ,gär-, 'gär-\ *n* : a person who gives a guarantee

guar·an·ty \'gar-ən-tē, 'gär-\ *n, pl* **-ties** : ¹GUARANTEE 2, 3 — **guaranty** *vb*

¹guard \'gärd\ *n* **1** : an attitude of defense **2** : the act or duty of protecting or defending **3 a** : a person who guards or group of persons who guard **b** *pl* : a body of troops whose duties include guarding a head of state **4 a** : a football player who lines up next to the center **b** : either of two players stationed usually away from the basket in basketball **5** : a protective or safety device (as on a machine) — **on guard** : WATCHFUL, ALERT

²guard *vb* **1** : to protect from danger : DEFEND **2** : to watch over so as to restrict, control, or check ⟨*guard* a prisoner⟩ ⟨a closely *guarded* secret⟩ ⟨*guard* one's tongue⟩ **3** : to try to keep (an opponent) from scoring **4** : to be on guard : take precautions ⟨*guard* against infection⟩

guard cell *n* : one of two crescent-shaped cells that form the margin of a stoma in the epidermis of a leaf and serve to open and close it

guard·ed \'gärd-əd\ *adj* : CAUTIOUS, NONCOMMITTAL ⟨a *guarded* answer⟩ — **guard·ed·ly** *adv*

guard·house \'gärd-,haus\ *n* **1** : a building occupied by a guard or used as a headquarters by soldiers on guard duty **2** : a military jail

guard·i·an \'gärd-ē-ən\ *n* **1** : one that guards : CUSTODIAN **2** : one who legally has the care of the person or property of another — **guard·i·an·ship** \-,ship\ *n*

guard·rail \'gär-,drāl\ *n* : a protective railing placed along dangerous areas (as of a road)

guard·room \'gär-,drüm, -,drum\ *n* **1** : a room used by a military guard while on duty **2** : a room where military prisoners are kept

guards·man \'gärdz-mən\ *n* : a member of a military body called *guard* or *guards*

gua·va \'gwäv-ə\ *n* : the sweet acid yellow fruit of a shrubby tropical American tree of the myrtle family that is used especially for making jelly and jam; *also* : a tree that produces guavas and is widely grown in cultivation

gua·yu·le \(g)wī-'ü-lē\ *n* : a low shrubby plant of the composite family that is found in Mexico and the southwestern United States and has been grown as a source of rubber

gu·ber·na·to·ri·al \,güb-ə(r)-nə-'tōr-ē-əl, ,gyüb-, -'tòr-\ *adj* : of or relating to a govenor

guern·sey \'gərn-zē\ *n, pl* **guernseys** : any of a breed of light brown and white dairy cattle that are larger than jerseys and produce rich yellowish milk

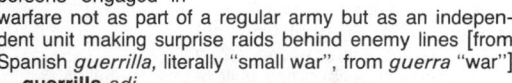

guernsey

guer·ril·la *or* **gue·ril·la** \gə-'ril-ə\ *n* : a member of a band of persons engaged in warfare not as part of a regular army but as an independent unit making surprise raids behind enemy lines [from Spanish *guerrilla*, literally "small war", from *guerra* "war"] — **guerrilla** *adj*

guess \'ges\ *vb* **1** : to form an opinion from little or no evidence **2** : to solve correctly by or as if by chance ⟨we *guessed* the riddle⟩ **3** : BELIEVE 5, SUPPOSE ⟨I *guess* you're right⟩ — **guess** *n* — **guess·er** *n*

guess·work \-,wərk\ *n* : work performed or results gotten by guessing

guest \'gest\ *n* **1** : a person entertained in one's house **2** : a person to whom hospitality is given ⟨*guests* at a school banquet⟩ **3** : a customer at a hotel, motel, inn, or restaurant **4** : a usually well-known person who appears or performs on a program by invitation ⟨*guests* on a TV show⟩

guf·faw \(,)gə-'fò\ *n* : a loud burst of laughter — **guffaw** *vb*

guid·ance \'gīd-ᵊn(t)s\ *n* **1** : the act or process of guiding **2** : advice given to students to help them make educational or personal decisions **3** : the process of controlling the course (as of a missile) by built-in equipment ⟨*guidance* system⟩

¹guide \'gīd\ *n* **1 a** : one who leads or directs another on a course **b** : one who shows and explains points of interest (as on a tour) **c** : something that provides guiding information ⟨a street *guide*⟩ **2** : a device or organ for steadying or directing the motion of something

²guide *vb* **guid·ed; guid·ing** **1** : to act as a guide : CONDUCT ⟨*guide* a group on a tour⟩ **2 a** : MANAGE 1, DIRECT ⟨*guide* a boat through the rapids⟩ **b** : ²COUNSEL 1, INSTRUCT — **guid·able** \'gīd-ə-bəl\ *adj*

guide·book \'gīd-,buk\ *n* : a book of information for travelers

guided missile *n* : a missile whose course may be changed during flight

guide·line \'gīd-,līn\ *n* **1** : a means of identification (as a number) or location (as a line) by which one is guided **2** : an outline of standards for future policy or action

guide·post \-,pōst\ *n* **1** : a post (as at the fork of a road) with directions for travelers **2** : INDICATION 2, SIGN

guide word *n* : either of the terms at the head of a page of an alphabetical reference work (as a dictionary) indicating the alphabetically first and last entries on the page

\ə\ **abut**	\au̇\ **out**	\i\ **tip**	\ȯ\ **saw**	\u̇\ **foot**
\ər\ **further**	\ch\ **chin**	\ī\ **life**	\ȯi\ **coin**	\y\ **yet**
\a\ **mat**	\e\ **pet**	\j\ **job**	\th\ **thin**	\yü\ **few**
\ā\ **take**	\ē\ **easy**	\ŋ\ **sing**	\th\ **this**	\yu̇\ **cure**
\ä\ **cot, cart**	\g\ **go**	\ō\ **bone**	\ü\ **food**	\zh\ **vision**

gui·don \'gīd-,än, -°n\ *n* : a small flag (as of a military unit)

guild *also* **gild** \'gild\ *n* : an association of persons with common interests or aims; *esp* : an association of merchants or craftsmen in the Middle Ages

guile \'gī(ə)l\ *n* : sly trickery : DUPLICITY — **guile·ful** \-fəl\ *adj*

guile·less \'gī(ə)l-ləs\ *adj* : not sly or tricky : INNOCENT, NAÏVE ⟨a *guileless* person⟩ ⟨a *guileless* smile⟩ — **guile·less·ly** *adv* — **guile·less·ness** *n*

guil·lo·tine \'gil-ə-,tēn, ,gē-(y)ə-'tēn, 'gē-(y)ə,-tēn\ *n* : a machine for cutting off a person's head by means of a heavy blade sliding in two upright grooved posts [named for Joseph *Guillotin* 1738-1814 French doctor and public official] — **guillotine** *vb*

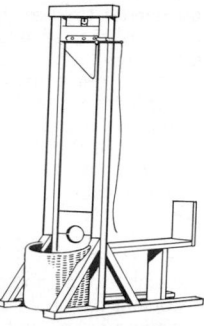

guillotine

guilt \'gilt\ *n* **1** : the fact of having done something wrong and especially something that is punishable by law **2** : the state of one who has done something wrong : BLAMEWORTHINESS **3** : a feeling of responsibility for wrongdoing — **guilt·less** \-ləs\ *adj*

guilty \'gil-tē\ *adj* **guilt·i·er; -est** **1** : having done wrong **2 a** : suggesting or involving guilt ⟨a *guilty* manner⟩ **b** : aware of or suffering from guilt — **guilt·i·ly** \-tə-lē\ *adv* — **guilt·i·ness** \-tē-nəs\ *n*

guin·ea \'gin-ē\ *n* **1** : a British gold coin no longer issued worth 21 shillings **2** : a former unit of value equal to 21 shillings

guin·ea fowl \'gin-ē-\ *n* : a gray and white spotted African bird related to the pheasants that has a bare neck and head and is widely raised for food

guinea hen *n* : GUINEA FOWL; *esp* : a female guinea fowl

guinea pig *n* **1** : a small stocky rodent with short ears and a very short tail that is often kept as a pet and is used in biological research **2** : a person or thing experimented on

guise \'gīz\ *n* **1** : a form or style of dress : COSTUME ⟨in the *guise* of a shepherd⟩ **2** : outer or disguised appearance : SEMBLANCE ⟨swindled people under the *guise* of friendship⟩

gui·tar \gə-'tär\ *n* : a stringed instrument with a flat body, a long neck with frets, and usually six strings that are plucked with the fingers or with a pick [from French *guitare* "guitar", derived from Arabic *qītār* (same meaning)] — **gui·tar·ist** \-əst\ *n*

gulch \'gəlch\ *n* : RAVINE

gul·den \'gül-dən, 'gùl-\ *n* **1** : the basic unit of money of the Netherlands **2** : a coin or bill representing one gulden

gulf \'gəlf\ *n* **1** : a part of an ocean or sea extending into the land **2** : a deep hollow in the earth : CHASM, ABYSS **3** : a wide separation or gap

¹gull \'gəl\ *n* : any of numerous mostly white or gray birds with long wings, webbed feet, and a hooked bill that are associated with water [Middle English *gull* "gull"; of Celtic origin]

²gull *vb* : DECEIVE 1, CHEAT [from obsolete English *gull* "gullet"]

³gull *n* : a person easily deceived or cheated : DUPE

gul·let \'gəl-ət\ *n* **1 a** : the tube that leads from the back of the mouth to the stomach : ESOPHAGUS **b** : THROAT 1 **2** : a tubular folding-in of the protoplasm of various protozoans (as a paramecium) that is sometimes used to take in food

gull·ible \'gəl-ə-bəl\ *adj* : easily deceived or cheated — **gull·ibil·i·ty** \,gəl-ə-'bil-ət-ē\ *n* — **gull·ibly** \'gəl-ə-blē\ *adv*

gul·ly \'gəl-ē\ *n, pl* **gullies** : a trench worn in the earth by

running water after rains — **gully** *vb*

gully erosion *n* : soil erosion produced by running water

gulp \'gəlp\ *vb* **1** : to swallow hurriedly or greedily or in one swallow **2** : to keep back as if by swallowing ⟨*gulp* down a sob⟩ **3** : to catch the breath as if in taking a long drink — **gulp** *n* — **gulp·er** *n*

¹gum \'gəm\ *n* : the tissue along the jaws of animals that surrounds the necks of the teeth [Old English *gōma* "roof of the mouth, palate"]

²gum *n* **1** : any of numerous complex sticky colloidal substances (as gum arabic) that are obtained from plants, harden on drying, and are either soluble in water or swell up in contact with water and that are used in preparing some drugs, for adhesives, as food thickeners, and in inks; *also* : any of various gummy plant substances including natural resins, rubber, and rubberlike substances **2** : a substance resembling a plant gum (as in stickiness) **3** : a tree that yields a gum **4** : CHEWING GUM [Middle English *gomme* "plant gum", from early French *gomme* (same meaning), from Latin *cummi, gummi* (same meaning), derived from Egyptian *qmy.t* "plant gum"]

³gum *vb* **gummed; gum·ming** **1** : to smear, seal, or clog with or as if with gum **2** : to cause not to work properly ⟨*gum* up the works⟩

gum arabic *n* : a gum that can be dissolved in water, is obtained from several acacias, and is used especially in making adhesives, drugs, and candy

gum·bo \'gəm-bō\ *n, pl* **gumbos** **1** : a soup thickened with okra pods **2** : any of various silty soils that become very sticky when wet

gum·boil \'gəm-,bòil\ *n* : an abscess in the gums

gum·drop \-,dräp\ *n* : a candy made usually from corn syrup with gelatin or gum arabic and coated with sugar crystals

gum·my \'gəm-ē\ *adj* **gum·mi·er; -est** **1** : consisting of, containing, or covered with gum **2** : VISCOUS 1, STICKY — **gum·mi·ness** *n*

gump·tion \'gəm(p)-shən\ *n* : COURAGE, SPUNK

¹gun \'gən\ *n* **1 a** : an artillery piece with a usually long barrel and firing shot or shells in a somewhat flattened curve **b** : a portable firearm (as a rifle or pistol) **2 a** : a firing of a gun ⟨a 21-*gun* salute⟩ **b** : a signal marking a beginning or ending ⟨the opening *gun* of the campaign⟩ **3** : something suggesting a gun in shape or use ⟨grease *gun*⟩ **4** : ²THROTTLE 1 — **gunned** \'gənd\ *adj*

²gun *vb* **gunned; gun·ning** **1** : to hunt or shoot with a gun ⟨*gunning* for rabbits⟩ **2** : to open up the throttle of so as to increase speed ⟨*gun* the engine⟩

gun·boat \'gən-,bōt\ *n* : a small lightly armed ship for use in shallow waters

gun·fight \-,fīt\ *n* : a fight fought with guns — **gun·fight·er** *n*

gun·fire \-,fī(ə)r\ *n* : the firing of guns

gung ho \'gən-'hō\ *adj* : extremely enthusiastic

   Word History Since the war was not going well for the United States in 1942, Marine Lt. Col. Evans F. Carlson needed something special to make his troops feel hopeful and excited. He was organizing the Second Raider Battalion in Asia and told his men their motto would be *gung ho*. This, he told them, was Chinese for "work together". Since there was a Chinese Industrial Cooperatives Society known as *gung ho* and since *gung* does mean "work", and *ho* does mean "together", what he said seemed to make sense. But *gung* and *ho* cannot be put together in Chinese to mean "work together". The organization known as *gung ho* was, in full, *chung-kuo kung-yeh ho-tso she*. The Chinese themselves shortened it to *gung ho* just as we abbreviate long names and titles in English. But in English *gung ho* stuck as a motto and went on to become an adjective meaning "extremely enthusiastic". [*Gung ho!* motto (thought to mean "work together") of United States Marine battalion in World War II, from the Chinese (Pekingese dialect) phrase *chung-kuo kung-yeh ho-tso she* "Chinese Industrial Cooperatives Society"]

gun·lock \-ˌläk\ *n* : the firing mechanism in a muzzle-loader or the firing mechanism together with the breech-closing device in a firearm loaded at the breech

gun·man \-mən\ *n* : a person armed with a gun; *esp* : an armed criminal

gun·ner \'gən-ər\ *n* **1** : one who operates or aims a gun **2** : one who hunts with a gun

gun·nery \'gən-(ə-)rē\ *n* : the use of guns

gunnery sergeant *n* : a noncommissioned officer in the marines with a rank just below that of master sergeant

gun·ny \'gən-ē\ *n, pl* **gunnies** **1** : coarse jute material for sacks **2** : BURLAP

gun·ny·sack \-ˌsak\ *n* : a sack made of gunny

gun·point \'gən-ˌpȯint\ *n* : the point of a gun — **at gun-point** : under a threat of death by being shot

gun·pow·der \-ˌpaȯd-ər\ *n* : an explosive mixture used in guns and blasting

gun·ship \-ˌship\ *n* : an aircraft armed with rockets and machine guns for protection of ground troops or helicopters carrying them

gun·shot \-ˌshät\ *n* **1** : shot fired from a gun **2** : the range of a gun ⟨within *gunshot*⟩

gun·sling·er \-ˌsliŋ-ər\ *n* : a person known for speed and skill in handling and shooting a gun especially in the American West

gun·smith \-ˌsmith\ *n* : one whose business is the making and repair of firearms

gun·wale *also* **gun·nel** \'gən-ᵊl\ *n* : the upper edge of a ship's side

gup·py \'gəp-ē\ *n, pl* **gup-pies** : a small tropical minnow often kept in aquariums

gur·gle \'gər-gəl\ *vb* **gur-gled; gur·gling** \'gər-g(ə-)liŋ\ **1** : to flow in a broken bubbling current **2** : to make a sound like that of a gurgling liquid — **gur-gle** *n*

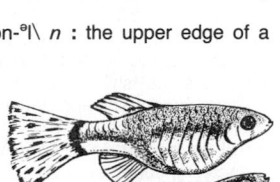

guppy: *top* female, *bottom* male

gu·ru \gə-'rü, 'gu̇(ə)r-ü\ *n* : a personal religious teacher and spiritual guide in Hinduism [from *gurū*, a word in Hindi (the major language in India) meaning "Hindu teacher or spiritual guide", derived from Sanskrit *guru* (adjective) "worthy of respect"]

¹gush \'gəsh\ *vb* **1** : to flow out or pour forth in great quantities or violently : SPOUT ⟨oil *gushed* from the new well⟩ **2** : to make an exaggerated display of affection or enthusiasm ⟨*gushed* about their favorite rock star⟩

²gush *n* **1** : a sudden outpouring **2** : an exaggerated display of affection or enthusiasm

gush·er \'gəsh-ər\ *n* : one that gushes; *esp* : an oil well with a very plentiful natural flow

gus·set \'gəs-ət\ *n* : a usually triangular or diamond-shaped insert (as in a glove) to give width or strength

gust \'gəst\ *n* **1** : a sudden brief rush of wind **2** : a sudden outburst : SURGE ⟨a *gust* of anger⟩ — **gusty** \'gəs-tē\ *adj*

gus·ta·to·ry \'gəs-tə-ˌtōr-ē, -ˌtȯr-\ *adj* : relating to, associated with, or being the sense or sensation of taste

gus·to \'gəs-tō\ *n* : keen enjoyment or appreciation ⟨eat with *gusto*⟩

¹gut \'gət\ *n* **1 a** : ENTRAILS, VISCERA — usually used in pl. **b** : the digestive tube or part of it; *esp* : the intestine of an animal prepared for some special use (as stringing tennis rackets) **c** : ABDOMEN 1, BELLY **2** *pl* : the inner essential parts **3** *pl* : COURAGE

²gut *vb* **gut·ted; gut·ting** **1** : to remove the entrails from ⟨scale and *gut* a fish⟩ **2** : to destroy the inside of ⟨fire *gutted* the building⟩

gutsy \'gət-sē\ *adj* **guts·i·er; -est** : aggressively tough : COURAGEOUS

¹gut·ter \'gət-ər\ *n* **1 a** : a trough along the eaves of a house to catch and carry off water **b** : a low area (as at a roadside) to carry off surface water **2** : a narrow channel or groove

²gutter *vb* **1** : to form gutters in **2 a** : to flow in small streams **b** : to melt away by having wax stream down in channels ⟨a *guttering* candle⟩ **3** : to flicker in a draft

gut·tur·al \'gət-ə-rəl\ *adj* **1** : formed or pronounced in the throat ⟨*guttural* sounds⟩ **2** : formed with the back of the tongue touching or near the palate — **guttural** *n* — **gut-tur·al·ly** \-rə-lē\ *adv*

¹guy \'gī\ *n* : a rope, chain, rod, or wire attached to something as a brace or guide [probably from Dutch *gei* "a rope used to control a sail"]

²guy *vb* : to steady or strengthen with a guy

³guy *n* **1** : ¹MAN 1a, FELLOW **2** : PERSON 1
Word History November 5 is a holiday in England, and people celebrate it by setting off fireworks and lighting bonfires. Human likenesses made of tattered clothes stuffed with hay or rags are burned on the bonfires. The holiday is called Guy Fawkes Day for a 17th century man who played a leading role in a plot to blow up the British Parliament buildings. Fawkes managed to hide 20 barrels of gunpowder in the cellars of the buildings. However, the plot was discovered before Fawkes could carry out his plans. He was seized and later put to death. The human likenesses burned to celebrate the failure of Guy Fawkes's plot came to be called *guys*. The use of the word was extended to similar figures and then to a person of strange appearance or dress. In the United States the word came to mean simply "man" or "fellow" and in time came to be used for a person of either sex. [named for *Guy Fawkes* 1570–1606 English criminal]

guz·zle \'gəz-əl\ *vb* **guz·zled; guz·zling** \-(ə-)liŋ\ : to drink greedily — **guz·zler** \-(ə-)lər\ *n*

gybe *variant of* ¹JIBE

gym \'jim\ *n* **1** : GYMNASIUM **2** : PHYSICAL EDUCATION

gym·na·si·um \jim-'nā-zē-əm, -zhəm\ *n, pl* **-si·ums** *or* **-sia** \-zē-ə, -zhə\ : a room or building for sports activities [from Latin *gymnasium* "exercise ground, school", from Greek *gymnasion* (same meaning), from *gymnazein* "to exercise naked", from *gymnos* "naked"]

gym·nast \'jim-ˌnast, -nəst\ *n* : a person who is skilled in gymnastics

gym·nas·tics \jim-'nas-tiks\ *n sing or pl* : physical exercises for developing skill, strength, and control in the use of the body; *also* : a sport in which such exercises are performed — **gym·nas·tic** \-tik\ *adj*

gym·no·sperm \'jim-nə-ˌspərm\ *n* : any of a group of woody vascular plants that produce naked seeds not enclosed in a true fruit

gy·ne·col·o·gist \ˌgīn-i-'käl-ə-jəst, ˌjin-\ *n* : a physician who specializes in gynecology

gy·ne·col·o·gy \ˌgīn-i-'käl-ə-jē, ˌjin-\ *n* : a branch of medicine that is concerned with women, their diseases, and their hygiene

¹gyp \'jip\ *n* **1** : ²CHEAT 2, SWINDLER **2** : ²SWINDLE, FRAUD

²gyp *vb* **gypped; gyp·ping** : ¹CHEAT 1, SWINDLE

gyp·sum \'jip-səm\ *n* : a colorless mineral that consists of calcium sulfate occurring in crystals or masses and that is

\ə\ **abut**	\au̇\ **out**	\i\ **tip**	\ȯ\ **saw**	\u̇\ **foot**
\ər\ **further**	\ch\ **chin**	\ī\ **life**	\ȯi\ **coin**	\y\ **yet**
\a\ **mat**	\e\ **pet**	\j\ **job**	\th\ **thin**	\yü\ **few**
\ā\ **take**	\ē\ **easy**	\ŋ\ **sing**	\th\ **this**	\yu̇\ **cure**
\ä\ **cot, cart**	\g\ **go**	\ō\ **bone**	\ü\ **food**	\zh\ **vision**

used especially as a soil improver and in making plaster of paris

Gyp·sy *or* **Gip·sy** \'jip-sē\ *n, pl* **Gypsies** *or* **Gipsies** **1** : one of a dark Caucasian people coming originally from India to Europe in the 14th or 15th century and living and maintaining a wandering way of life **2** : ROMANY 2 [a shortened and altered form of *Egyptian;* so called because Gypsies were once believed to have come from Egypt]

gypsy moth *n* : an Old World moth introduced about 1869 into the U.S. and having a grayish hairy caterpillar that is marked with spots and does great damage to trees (as oaks) by eating the leaves

gy·rate \'jī-,rāt\ *vb* **gy·rat·ed; gy·rat·ing** **1** : to rotate around a point or axis **2** : [1]SPIN 13, WHIRL — **gy·ra·tion** \jī-'rā-shən\ *n* — **gy·ra·tion·al** \-shnəl, -shən-ᵊl\ *adj*

gy·rene \jī-'rēn\ *n, slang* : a U.S. marine

gyr·fal·con \'jər-,fal-kən, -,fȯl-; -,fô-kən\ *n* : an arctic falcon that is the largest of all falcons, is more powerful though less active than the peregrine falcon, and occurs in several forms

gy·ro \'jī-rō\ *n, pl* **gyros** **1** : GYROSCOPE **2** : GYROCOMPASS

gy·ro·com·pass \'jī-rō-,kəm-pəs *also* -,käm-\ *n* : a compass consisting of a constantly spinning gyroscope whose spin axis is always parallel to the earth's axis of rotation so that the compass always points to true north

gy·ro·scope \'jī-rə-,skōp\ *n* : a wheel or disk mounted to spin rapidly about an axis that is free to turn in various directions — **gy·ro·scop·ic** \,jī-rə-'skäp-ik\ *adj*

gyrfalcon

H

h \'āch\ *n, often cap* : the eighth letter of the English alphabet

ha \'hä\ *interj* — used to express surprise or joy

Ha·ba·cuc \'hab-ə-,kək, hə-'bak-ək\ *n* — see BIBLE table

Hab·ak·kuk \'hab-ə-,kək, hə-'bak-ək\ *n* — see BIBLE table

ha·be·as cor·pus \,hā-bē-ə-'skȯr-pəs\ *n* **1** : a legal order for an inquiry to determine whether a person has been lawfully imprisoned **2** : the right of a citizen to obtain a writ of habeas corpus as a protection against illegal imprisonment [derived from the Latin phrase, meaning literally "you should have the body", used as the opening words of a legal order to jailers to bring the prisoner to court]

hab·er·dash·er \'hab-ə(r)-,dash-ər\ *n* : a dealer in men's clothing and accessories

hab·er·dash·ery \'hab-ə(r)-,dash-(ə-)rē\ *n, pl* **-er·ies** **1** : goods sold by a haberdasher **2** : a haberdasher's shop

ha·bil·i·ment \hə-'bil-ə-mənt\ *n* : CLOTHING 1 — usually used in pl.

hab·it \'hab-ət\ *n* **1** : a costume characteristic of an occupation, rank, or function (riding *habit*) **2** : a usual manner of behavior or thinking **3** : a way of behaving that has become fixed by being repeated often — compare [1]REFLEX 1 **4** : characteristic way of growing or occurring (elms have a spreading *habit*)

syn HABIT, PRACTICE, USAGE, CUSTOM mean a way of acting that has become fixed through repetition. HABIT suggests doing something without thinking about it because one has done it so often (put the keys in his pocket out of *habit*) PRACTICE suggests an act performed regularly and usually by choice (our *practice* is to go to the park every Sunday) USAGE suggests a practice followed by so many that it becomes the accepted practice of society (what a word means in common *usage*) CUSTOM applies to an act so long and continuously associated with an individual or group that in effect it becomes an unofficial rule (the *custom* of many is to eat turkey on Thanksgiving)

hab·it·able \'hab-ət-ə-bəl\ *adj* : suitable or fit to live in (a *habitable* cave) — **hab·it·abil·i·ty** \,hab-ət-ə-'bil-ət-ē\ *n*

hab·i·tant \'hab-ət-ənt\ *n* : INHABITANT, RESIDENT

hab·i·tat \'hab-ə-,tat\ *n* : the place or type of place where a plant or animal naturally or normally lives or grows

hab·i·ta·tion \,hab-ə-'tā-shən\ *n* **1** : the act of inhabiting : OCCUPANCY **2** : a dwelling place : RESIDENCE

hab·it–form·ing \'hab-ət-,fȯr-miŋ\ *adj* : causing an addiction (heroin is a *habit-forming* drug)

ha·bit·u·al \hə-'bich-(ə-)wəl, ha-\ *adj* **1** : being or done by habit (*habitual* tardiness) **2** : doing or acting out of habit (*habitual* talker) **3** : REGULAR 3b (*habitual* evening walk) — **ha·bit·u·al·ly** \-ē\ *adv* — **ha·bit·u·al·ness** *n*

ha·bit·u·ate \hə-'bich-ə-,wāt, ha-\ *vb* **-at·ed; -at·ing** : to make used to — **ha·bit·u·a·tion** \-,bich-ə-'wā-shən\ *n*

ha·chure \ha-'shù(ə)r\ *n* : a short line used in drawing and engraving for shading or especially to show different levels or slopes on a map

ha·ci·en·da \,(h)äs-ē-'en-də\ *n* : a large estate in Spanish-speaking countries

[1]**hack** \'hak\ *vb* **1** : to cut or sever with repeated irregular or unskillful blows **2** : to cough in a short dry manner [Old English *-haccian* "to cut with repeated blows"]

[2]**hack** *n* **1** : [1]NICK 1, NOTCH **2** : a short dry cough

[3]**hack** *n* **1 a** : a horse that can be hired for use by the public **b** : a horse used in all kinds of work **c** : a worn-out horse **d** : a light saddle horse **2 a** : [1]HACKNEY 2 **b** : TAXICAB **c** : a driver of a taxicab **3 a** : a writer who works mainly for hire **b** : one who serves a cause merely for reward (political *hacks*) [a shortened form of *hackney*]

[4]**hack** *adj* **1** : working for hire **2** : done by or characteristic of a hack (*hack* writing)

[5]**hack** *vb* **1** : to ride or drive at an ordinary pace or over the roads rather than across country **2** : to operate a taxicab

hack·ber·ry \'hak-,ber-ē\ *n* **1** : any of a genus of trees and shrubs that are related to the elm and have small often edible berries **2** : the wood of a hackberry

hack·er \'hak-ər\ *n* **1** : one that hacks **2** : a person who is unskilled at a particular activity **3** : an expert at programming and solving problems with a computer **4** : a person who illegally gains access to information in a computer system

hack·le \'hak-əl\ *n* **1** : a comb for smoothing fibers (as flax or hemp) **2** : one of the long narrow feathers on the neck or lower back of a bird **3** : hairs along the neck and back especially of a dog that can be made to stand up

[1]**hack·ney** \'hak-nē\ *n, pl* **hackneys** **1** : any of a breed of

hackney 1

compact high-stepping English horses **2** : a carriage or automobile kept for hire

²**hackney** *adj* **1** : kept for public hire **2** : HACKNEYED

hack·neyed \'hak-nēd\ *adj* : worn out from too long or too much use : COMMONPLACE ⟨a *hackneyed* expression⟩

hack·saw \'hak-,só\ *n* : a saw used for cutting hard materials (as metal) that consists of a frame and a blade with small teeth

had *past and past participle of* HAVE

had·dock \'had-ək\ *n, pl* **haddock** *also* **haddocks** : an important food fish of the Atlantic that is usually smaller than the related common cod

ha·des \'hād-(,)ēz\ *n* **1** *cap* : the abode of the dead in Greek mythology **2** : HELL 1

hadn't \'had-ᵊnt\ : had not

hadst \(')hadst, (h)ədst\ *archaic past 2d sing of* HAVE

hae \(')hā\ *chiefly Scottish variant of* HAVE

haf·ni·um \'haf-nē-əm\ *n* : a gray metallic element that is useful because of its ready absorption of neutrons — see ELEMENT table

haft \'haft\ *n* : the handle of a weapon or tool

hag \'hag\ *n* **1** : an ugly or evil old woman **2** : WITCH 1

Hag·gai \'hag-ē-,ī, 'hag-,ī\ *n* — see BIBLE table

hag·gard \'hag-ərd\ *adj* : very thin especially from great hunger, worry, or pain

hag·gle \'hag-əl\ *vb* **hag·gled; hag·gling** \-(ə-)liŋ\ : to dispute or argue especially in bargaining — **haggle** *n* — **hag·gler** \-(ə-)lər\ *n*

Hag·i·og·ra·pha \,hag-ē-'äg-rə-fə, ,hā-jē-\ *n sing or pl* : the third part of the Jewish scriptures — compare LAW 2, PROPHETS

hai·ku \'hī-(,)kü\ *n, pl* **haiku** : a verse form of Japanese origin having three lines containing five, seven, and five syllables respectively; *also* : a poem written in this form

¹**hail** \'hā(ə)l\ *n* **1** : small lumps of ice that fall from clouds sometimes during thunderstorms **2** : something that gives the effect of falling hail ⟨a *hail* of bullets⟩ [Old English *hægl* "lumps of ice, hail"]

²**hail** *vb* **1** : to fall as hail **2** : to pour down like hail

³**hail** *interj* **1** — used to express enthusiastic approval **2** *archaic* — used as a greeting [Middle English *hail* (an interjection of approval or greeting), derived from early Norse *heill* "healthy" — related to ¹HALE, WASSAIL]

⁴**hail** *vb* **1 a** : GREET 1 **b** : to greet with enthusiastic approval : ACCLAIM ⟨*hailed* them as heroes⟩ **2** : to summon by calling ⟨*hail* a taxi⟩ **3** : to call out to ⟨*hail* a passing ship⟩ — **hail from** : to come from ⟨he *hails from* New York⟩

⁵**hail** *n* **1** : an act or instance of hailing **2** : hailing distance ⟨within *hail*⟩

Hail Mary \-'me(ə)r-ē, -'ma(ə)r-ē, -'mä-rē\ *n* : a prayer to the Virgin Mary as the mother of God

hail·stone \'hā(ə)l-,stōn\ *n* : a small lump of hail

hail·storm \-,stó(ə)rm\ *n* : a storm accompanied by hail

hair \'ha(ə)r, 'he(ə)r\ *n* **1 a** : a slender threadlike growth from the skin of an animal; *esp* : one that usually contains pigment and forms part of the characteristic coat of a mammal **b** : a covering or growth of hairs of an animal or a body part **2** : a tiny distance or amount ⟨won by a *hair*⟩ **3** : a threadlike structure that resembles hair ⟨leaf *hair*⟩ — **haired** \'ha(ə)rd, 'he(ə)rd\ *adj* — **hair·less** \'ha(ə)r-ləs, 'he(ə)r-\ *adj* — **hair·like** \-,līk\ *adj*

hair·breadth \'ha(ə)r-,bretth, 'he(ə)r-, -,bredth\ *or* **hairs·breadth** \'ha(ə)rz-, 'he(ə)rz-\ *n* : a very small distance or margin — **hairbreadth** *adj*

hair·brush \'ha(ə)r-,brəsh, 'he(ə)r-\ *n* : a brush for the hair

hair·cloth \-,klóth\ *n* : any of various stiff wiry fabrics especially of horsehair or camel hair used for upholstery or stiffening in garments

hair·cut \-,kət\ *n* : the act, process, or style of cutting and shaping the hair — **hair·cut·ter** \-,kət-ər\ *n* — **hair·cut·ting** \-,kət-iŋ\ *n*

hair·do \-,dü\ *n, pl* **hairdos** : a way of dressing a person's hair : COIFFURE ⟨the very latest in *hairdos*⟩

hair·dress·er \-,dres-ər\ *n* : one who dresses or cuts hair — **hair·dress·ing** \-,dres-iŋ\ *n*

hair follicle *n* : the tube-shaped sheath surrounding the lower part of a hair shaft

hair hygrometer *n* : a hygrometer that uses one or more strands of human hair that expand with increasing humidity and contract with decreasing humidity and are connected to a pointer on a scale

hair·line \'ha(ə)r-,līn, 'he(ə)r-\ *n* **1** : a very slender line **2** : the outline of the hair on the head and especially on the forehead — **hair·line** *adj*

hair·pin \-,pin\ *n* **1** : a two-pronged U-shaped pin to hold the hair in place **2** : something shaped like a hairpin; *esp* : an extremely sharp turn in a road — **hairpin** *adj*

hair–rais·ing \-,rā-ziŋ\ *adj* : causing terror, excitement, or astonishment ⟨a *hair-raising* story⟩ — **hair–rais·ing·ly** \-ziŋ-lē\ *adv*

hair seal *n* : any of a family of seals with hairy coats and no ears on the outside of the head — called also *earless seal, true seal*

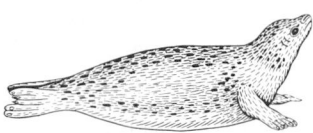
hair seal

hair·split·ter \'ha(ə)r-,split-ər\ *n* : a person who argues about differences too small to be important — **hair·split·ting** \-,split-iŋ\ *adj or n*

hair·spring \-,spriŋ\ *n* : a slender coiled spring that regulates the motion of the balance wheel in a timepiece

hair·streak \-,strēk\ *n* : any of various small usually dark butterflies with hairlike tails sticking out from the hind wings

hair trigger *n* : a trigger so adjusted as to permit a firearm to be fired by a very slight pressure

hair·worm \'ha(ə)r-,wərm, 'he(ə)r-\ *n* : any of various very long slender worms (as a horsehair worm)

hairy \'ha(ə)r-ē, 'he(ə)r-\ *adj* **hair·i·er; -est** **1** : bearing or covered with or as if with hair **2** : made of or resembling hair — **hair·i·ness** *n*

hairy woodpecker *n* : a common North American woodpecker closely resembling but larger than the downy woodpecker

hake \'hāk\ *n* : any of several marine food fishes related to the cod

hal·berd \'hal-bərd, 'hól-\ *or* **hal·bert** \-bərt\ *n* : a long-handled weapon used both as a spear and as a battle-ax especially in the 15th and 16th centuries

hal·berd·ier \,hal-bər-'di(ə)r, ,hól-\ *n* : a person armed with a halberd

¹**hal·cy·on** \'hal-sē-ən\ *n* **1** : a bird identified with the kingfisher and believed in ancient legend to nest at sea in December and calm the waves **2** : KINGFISHER

Word History According to ancient legend, fourteen days of good weather occurred every year around December 22. This time of clear skies and calm seas was thought to be the result of a magical bird's concern for her nest. The legend explained that the female kingfisher built a floating nest on the sea during this period. She calmed the waves and winds to keep her nest safe. The Greek name for the kingfisher was *halkyōn*. English borrowed the Latin spelling of the bird's name, and today we call any quiet, peaceful period *halcyon days*. [Middle

\ə\ abut		\au̇\ out	\i\ tip		\ó\ saw	\u̇\ foot
\ər\ further		\ch\ chin	\ī\ life		\ói\ coin	\y\ yet
\a\ mat		\e\ pet	\j\ job		\th\ thin	\yü\ few
\ā\ take		\ē\ easy	\ŋ\ sing		\th\ this	\yu̇\ cure
\ä\ cot, cart		\g\ go	\ō\ bone		\ü\ food	\zh\ vision

English *alceon* "kingfisher", from Latin *halcyon* (same meaning), from Greek *halkyōn* "legendary bird that builds a nest at sea"]

²**halcyon** *adj* : ¹CALM 2, PEACEFUL ⟨*halcyon* days⟩

¹**hale** \'hā(ə)l\ *adj* : ¹SOUND 1a, HEALTHY ⟨grandmother was still *hale* and hearty at eighty⟩ [partly from Middle English *hale* "healthy, unhurt", from Old English *hāl* (same meaning) and partly from Middle English *hail* (an interjection of approval or greeting), derived from early Norse *heill* "healthy" — related to ³HAIL, HEALTH, WASSAIL, WHOLE]

²**hale** *vb* **haled; hal·ing** **1** : ¹HAUL 1, PULL **2** : to force to go ⟨*haled* them into court⟩ [Middle English *halen* "to pull", from early French *haler* (same meaning); of Germanic origin — related to HAUL]

¹**half** \'haf, 'håf\ *n, pl* **halves** \'havz, 'håvz\ **1** : one of two equal or nearly equal parts into which a thing is divisible **2** : one of a pair; *esp* : one of the two equal periods that make up the playing time of some games (as football) — **in half** : into two halves

²**half** *adj* **1** : being one of two halves **2** : of half the usual size or extent — **half·ness** *n*

³**half** *adv* **1 a** : to the extent of half ⟨*half* full⟩ **b** : to some degree ⟨*half* persuaded⟩ **2** : by any means : AT ALL ⟨the song wasn't *half* bad⟩

half·back \'haf-,bak, 'håf-\ *n* **1** : a football back who lines up toward the right or left side of the formation **2** : a player positioned behind the forward line in some games (as soccer or field hockey)

half–breed \-,brēd\ *n* : the offspring of parents of different races; *esp* : the offspring of an American Indian and a white person — **half–breed** *adj*

half brother *n* : a brother by one parent only

half–caste \'haf-,kast, 'håf-\ *n* : HALF-BREED — **half–caste** *adj*

half–cocked \-'käkt\ *adj* : lacking preparation or planning ⟨went off *half-cocked*⟩

half–dol·lar \-'däl-ər\ *n* **1** : a coin representing one half of a dollar **2** : the sum of fifty cents

half·heart·ed \-'härt-əd\ *adj* : lacking spirit or interest — **half·heart·ed·ly** *adv* — **half·heart·ed·ness** *n*

half hitch *n* : a simple knot so made as to be easily unfastened

half hour *n* **1** : thirty minutes **2** : the middle point of an hour — **half–hour·ly** \'haf-'aů(ə)r-lē, 'håf-\ *adv or adj*

half–knot \'haf-,nät, 'håf-\ *n* : a knot joining the ends of two cords and used in tying other knots

half–life \-,līf\ *n* : the time required for half of the atoms of a radioactive substance to change composition

half line *n* : a straight line extending from a point in one direction only

half–mast \'haf-'mast, 'håf-\ *n* : a point about halfway down below the top of a mast or staff ⟨flags hanging at *half‑mast*⟩

half–moon \-,mün\ *n* : the moon when half its disk appears lighted

half note *n* : a musical note equal in time to ½ of a whole note

half·pen·ny \'hāp-(ə)nē US also 'haf-,-pen-ē, 'håf-\ *n, pl* **half·pence** \'hā-pən(t)s, US also 'haf-,pen(t)s, 'håf-\ *or* **halfpennies** : a former British coin representing one half of a penny

half plane *n* : the part of a plane on one side of a straight line drawn in it that extends forever in both directions

half sister *n* : a sister by one parent only

half sole *n* : a shoe sole extending from the shank forward — **half–sole** \'haf-'sōl, 'håf-\ *vb*

half step *n* : the pitch interval between any two adjacent tones on a keyboard instrument — called also *semitone*

half·tone \'haf-,tōn, 'håf-\ *n* : a medium tint or tone in a painting, engraving, or photograph

half–track \-,trak\ *n* **1** : an endless-chain track used in place of a rear wheel on a heavy-duty vehicle **2** : a motor vehicle moved by half-tracks

half–truth \-,trüth\ *n* : a statement that is only partly true; *esp* : one that deliberately mixes truth and falsehood

half·way \-'wā\ *adj* **1** : midway between two points ⟨stop at the *halfway* mark⟩ **2** : PARTIAL 3 ⟨*halfway* measures⟩ — **halfway** *adv*

halfway house *n* : a place that provides living quarters and usually counseling to persons who have left an institution (as a prison or mental hospital) but are not ready to live in the community

half–wit \'haf-,wit, 'håf-\ *n* : a foolish or unintelligent person — **half–wit·ted** \-'wit-əd\ *adj*

hal·i·but \'hal-ə-bət, 'häl-\ *n, pl* **halibut** *also* **halibuts** : a marine food fish that is the largest flatfish, may reach a weight of several hundred pounds in the female, and is now usually classified into a species in the Atlantic ocean and one in the Pacific ocean

> **Word History** Among the different kinds of fish found in the world's oceans is a group called the flatfish. Flatfish are well named, for they have flattened bodies with both eyes on the upper side of the head. In Middle English the word for flatfish was *butte*. Many of the flatfish are good to eat, and the largest of the flatfish got its name because it was popular as food. During the Middle Ages fish was often eaten on holy days in place of meat. The most popular fish for the holy days was the largest variety of flatfish, or "butte". Thus, this particular fish came to be called in Middle English *halybutte*, meaning literally "holy flatfish", from *haly*, a form of *holy*, and *butte*. In Modern English the spelling has been changed to *halibut*. [Middle English *halybutte*, literally "holy flatfish", from *haly* "holy" and *butte* "flatfish"; so called from the fact it was regularly eaten on holy days]

hal·ite \'hal-,īt, 'hā-,līt\ *n* : ROCK SALT

hall \'hól\ *n* **1 a** : a large or impressive residence or public building ⟨city *hall*⟩ **b** : one of the buildings of a college or university ⟨Science *Hall*⟩ ⟨residence *halls*⟩ **2 a** : the entrance room of a building : LOBBY **b** : a corridor or passage in a building **3** : a large room for assembly : AUDITORIUM **4** : a place used for public entertainment

¹**hal·le·lu·jah** \,hal-ə-'lü-yə\ *interj* — used to express praise, joy, or thanks

²**hallelujah** *n* : a shout or song of praise or thanksgiving

hall·mark \'hól-,märk\ *n* **1** : an official mark stamped on gold and silver articles in England to certify their purity **2** : a mark or indication of excellence, quality, or purity ⟨bears the *hallmarks* of genius⟩ [named for Goldsmith's *Hall* in London, England, where gold and silver articles formerly were tested for purity and stamped] — **hallmark** *vb*

hal·low \'hal-ō\ *vb* **1** : to make holy or set apart for holy use : CONSECRATE **2** : to respect greatly : VENERATE — **hal·lowed** \'hal-ōd, *in the Lord's Prayer also* 'hal-ə-wəd\ *adj*

Hal·low·een \,hal-ə-'wēn, ,häl-\ *n* : October 31 celebrated with merrymaking (as the wearing of costumes or trick-or‑treating)

> **Word History** Modern-day Christians know the first of November as All Saints' Day. In the Middle Ages it was called All Hallow Day. This was a hallowed or holy day celebrated in honor of all the saints in heaven. Since November 1 was a special holy day with a special name, the day before it had a special name as well. October 31 was called All Hallow Eve or All Hallow Even. The words *eve* and *even* were used both for the evening and the day before a special day. This name was sometimes written *All Hallow E'en* and later shortened to *Halloween*. [an altered form of *All Hallow Even*, the eve of All Saints' Day]

hal·lu·ci·nate \hə-'lüs-ə-,nāt\ *vb* **-nat·ed; -nat·ing** : to have hallucinations or experience as an hallucination

hal·lu·ci·na·tion \hə-,lüs-ə-'nā-shən\ *n* : the awareness of something (as a visual image, a sound, or a smell) that seems to be experienced through one of the senses but is not real, cannot be sensed by someone else, and is usually the result of mental disorder or the effect of a drug; *also* : something of which one is aware but which is not real

hal·lu·ci·na·to·ry \hə-'lü-sə-nə-‚tōr-ē, -‚tȯr-\ *adj* **1** : tending to produce hallucinations **2** : resembling, involving, or being an hallucination

hal·lu·ci·no·gen \hə-'lü-sə-nə-jən\ *n* : a drug that causes hallucinations — **hal·lu·ci·no·gen·ic** \-‚lü-sə-nə-'jen-ik\ *adj*

hall·way \'hȯl-‚wā\ *n* **1** : an entrance hall **2** : CORRIDOR 1

ha·lo \'hā-lō\ *n, pl* **halos** *or* **haloes** **1** : a circle of light around the sun or moon caused by the presence of tiny ice crystals in the air **2** : NIMBUS 1, 2 **3** : the atmosphere of glory or sentiment surrounding a person or thing considered perfect

hal·o·gen \'hal-ə-jən\ *n* : any of the elements fluorine, chlorine, bromine, iodine, and astatine

¹halt \'hȯlt\ *adj* : ¹LAME 1a [Old English *healt* "lame"]

²halt *vb* **1** : ¹LIMP 1 **2** : to move unsteadily — **halt·ing·ly** \'hȯl-tiŋ-lē\ *adv*

³halt *n* : the ending of movement, progress, or action ⟨call a *halt*⟩ [from German *halt* "stop", derived from earlier *halten* "to hold"]

⁴halt *vb* **1** : to stop marching or journeying **2** : to bring to a stop : END

hal·ter \'hȯl-tər\ *n* **1 a** : a rope or strap for leading or tying an animal **b** : a set of straps enclosing an animal's head to which a lead may be attached **2** : a rope for hanging criminals : NOOSE **3** : a woman's article of clothing that covers the upper body, that is held in place by straps, and that leaves the back, arms, and midriff bare — **halter** *vb*

halter 1b

hal·tere \'hȯl-‚ti(ə)r, 'hal-\ *n, pl* **hal·teres** \hȯl-'ti(ə)r-(‚)ēz, 'hȯl-‚ti(ə)rz\ : one of a pair of club-shaped organs that are the modified second pair of wings of a two-winged fly and serve to maintain balance in flight

halve \'hav, 'hȧv\ *vb* **halved; halv·ing** **1** : to divide into two halves **2** : to reduce to one half ⟨*halving* the cost⟩

halves *pl of* HALF

hal·yard *or* **hal·liard** \'hal-yərd\ *n* : a rope or tackle for raising and lowering (as a sail)

¹ham \'ham\ *n* **1** : a buttock with its associated thigh — usually used in pl. **2** : a cut of meat consisting of a thigh; *esp* : one from a hog **3 a** : an unskillful but showy performer **b** : an operator of an amateur radio station — **ham** *adj*

¹ham *vb* **hammed; ham·ming** : to act with exaggerated speech or gestures

ham·burg·er \'ham-‚bər-gər\ *or* **ham·burg** \-‚bərg\ *n* **1 a** : ground beef **b** : a cooked patty of ground beef **2** : a sandwich consisting of a patty of hamburger in a split round bun

Word History It may seem odd that there isn't any ham in a hamburger. The origins of the word *hamburger*, however, have nothing to do with a type of meat. The word really comes from the name of the German city Hamburg. *Hamburger*, when capitalized, means "of Hamburg". Fried, flat cakes of ground beef were a popular food in Hamburg in the 19th century, and so they became known in English as *Hamburger steaks*. The name was later shortened to *hamburger*. Most people no longer associate the word *hamburger* with the city of

Hamburg, since the hamburger is now usually thought of as an American food. [German *Hamburger* (adjective) "of Hamburg", city in Germany]

ham·let \'ham-lət\ *n* : a small village

¹ham·mer \'ham-ər\ *n* **1 a** : a hand tool that consists of a solid head set crosswise on a handle and is used for pounding (as in driving nails) **b** : a power tool for pounding **2** : something that resembles a hammer in shape or action (as the part of a gun whose striking action causes explosion of the charge) **3** : MALLEUS **4** : a heavy metal ball with a flexible handle that is thrown for distance in a track-and-field contest

²hammer *vb* **ham·mered; ham·mer·ing** \'ham-(ə-)riŋ\ **1** : to strike blows with or as if with a hammer : POUND **2** : to make repeated efforts ⟨*hammer* away at one's lessons⟩ **3** : to fasten, build, or shape with or as if with a hammer ⟨*hammer* out a policy⟩ — **ham·mer·er** \'ham-ər-ər\ *n*

ham·mer·head \'ham-ər-‚hed\ *n* : any of various active sharks of medium size that have the eyes at the ends of sideward extensions of the flattened head

hammerhead

ham·mock \'ham-ək\ *n* : a swinging couch or bed usually made of netting or canvas and slung by cords from supports at each end

¹ham·per \'ham-pər\ *vb* **ham·pered; ham·per·ing** \-p(ə-)riŋ\ : to restrict or interfere with the movement or operation of : IMPEDE ⟨muddy ground *hampered* their walk⟩

²hamper *n* : a large basket usually with a cover ⟨a clothes *hamper*⟩

ham·ster \'ham(p)-stər\ *n* : any of various stocky Old World rodents with a short tail and large cheek pouches

¹ham·string \'ham-‚striŋ\ *n* : either of two groups of tendons at the back of the human knee

²hamstring *vb* **-strung** \-‚strəŋ\; **-string·ing** \-‚striŋ-iŋ\ **1** : to cripple by cutting the leg tendons **2** : to make ineffective or powerless : CRIPPLE ⟨*hamstrung* by restrictions⟩

¹hand \'hand\ *n* **1 a** : the free end part of the arm or forelimb when fitted (as in man) for handling, grasping, and holding **b** : any of various bodily parts (as the hind foot of an ape or the pincers of a crab) that are like the hand in structure or function **2** : something resembling a hand: as **a** : a pointer on a dial **b** : a figure of a hand with forefinger extended to point something out **c** : a bunch of bananas **3** : personal possession : CONTROL ⟨in the *hands* of the enemy⟩ **4 a** : ¹SIDE 2, DIRECTION ⟨fighting on either *hand*⟩ **b** : a side or point of view in an issue or argument ⟨on the one *hand* . . . on the other *hand*⟩ **5** : a pledge especially of marriage ⟨asked for her *hand*⟩ **6** : HANDWRITING 1, 2 **7 a** : SKILL 1, ABILITY ⟨try one's *hand* at chess⟩ **b** : a part or share in doing something ⟨take a *hand* in the work⟩ **c** : one that supplies information ⟨learn at first *hand*⟩ **9** : a unit of measure equal to 4 inches (about 10.16 centimeters) used especially for the height of horses **10** : a round of applause ⟨give him a *hand*⟩ **11 a** : the cards or pieces held by a player in a game **b** : a single round in a game **12 a** : one who performs or produces a work ⟨two portraits by the same *hand*⟩ **b** : a hired worker **c** : a member of a ship's crew ⟨all *hands* on deck⟩

\ə\ abut	\au̇\ out	\i\ tip	\ȯ\ saw	\u̇\ foot
\ər\ further	\ch\ chin	\ī\ life	\ȯi\ coin	\y\ yet
\a\ mat	\e\ pet	\j\ job	\th\ thin	\yü\ few
\ā\ take	\ē\ easy	\ŋ\ sing	\th\ this	\yu̇\ cure
\ä\ cot, cart	\g\ go	\ō\ bone	\ü\ food	\zh\ vision

d : one skilled in a particular activity or field ⟨an old *hand* at foreign affairs⟩ **13** : WORKMANSHIP 2 ⟨the *hand* of a master⟩ — **at hand** : ¹NEAR 1 — **by hand** : with the hands — **in hand** **1** : in one's possession or control **2** : in preparation — **on hand** **1** : in present possession ⟨goods *on hand*⟩ **2** : in attendance : PRESENT — **out of hand** : out of control — **out of one's hands** : out of one's control

²hand *vb* **1** : to guide or assist with the hand **2** : to give or pass with or as if with the hand ⟨*hand* a person a letter⟩

hand·bag \'han(d)-,bag\ *n* **1** : TRAVELING BAG **2** : a woman's bag for carrying small personal articles and money

hand·ball \-,bȯl\ *n* **1** : a game played in a walled court or against a single wall or board by two or four players who use their hands to strike a ball **2** : the ball used in handball

hand·bill \-,bil\ *n* : a printed sheet to be distributed by hand

hand·book \-,bu̇k\ *n* : a small book of facts or useful information usually about a particular subject : MANUAL

hand·car \'han(d)-,kär\ *n* : a small railroad car powered by hand or by a small motor

¹hand·craft \-,kraft\ *n* : HANDICRAFT

²handcraft *vb* : to make by handicraft

hand·cuff \'han(d)-,kəf\ *n* : a metal fastening locking around a wrist and usually connected by a chain or bar with another such fastening — usually used in pl. — **handcuff** *vb*

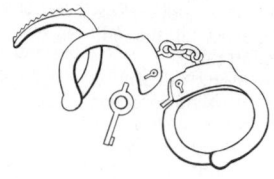

handcuff

hand down *vb* **1** : to pass down from older to younger (as from parent to child) **2** : to form and express a judicial decision

hand·ed \'han-dəd\ *adj* : having or using such or so many hands ⟨a right-*handed* person⟩ — **hand·ed·ness** *n*

hand·ful \'han(d)-,fu̇l\ *n, pl* **handfuls** \-,fu̇lz\ *also* **handsful** \'han(d)z-,fu̇l\ **1** : as much or as many as the hand will grasp **2** : a small quantity or number **3** : as much as one can control or manage

hand·gun \'han(d)-,gən\ *n* : a firearm designed to be held and fired with one hand

¹hand·i·cap \'han-di-,kap\ *n* **1** : a race or contest in which competitors with different levels of ability are given an artificial advantage or disadvantage to equalize their chances of winning; *also* : the advantage or disadvantage given **2** : a disadvantage that makes progress or success difficult ⟨being overweight was a *handicap*⟩

²handicap *vb* **-capped; -cap·ping** **1** : to give a handicap to **2** : to put at a disadvantage ⟨*handicapped* by poor health⟩

hand·i·craft \'han-di-,kraft\ *n* **1** : an occupation (as weaving or pottery making) requiring skill with the hands **2** : articles made by one working at a handicraft — **hand·i·craft·er** \-,kraf-tər\ *n*

hand·i·ly \'han-də-lē\ *adv* **1** : in a skillful manner **2** : EASILY 1 ⟨won *handily*⟩

hand·i·ness \'han-dē-nəs\ *n* : the quality or state of being handy

hand·i·work \'han-di-,wərk\ *n* : work done by the hands or by oneself

hand·ker·chief \'haŋ-kər-chəf, -(,)chif, -,chēf\ *n, pl* **-chiefs** *also* **-chieves** \-chəfs, -(,)chifs, -,chēvz, -,chēfs, -,chəvz, -,chivz\ **1** : a small piece of cloth used for wiping the face, nose, or eyes **2** : KERCHIEF 1

¹han·dle \'han-dᵊl\ *n* **1** : a part that is designed to be grasped by the hand **2** : ¹NAME 1, TITLE — **han·dled** \-dᵊld\ *adj* — **off the handle** : into a state of sudden and violent anger ⟨flew *off the handle* and yelled at my friend⟩

²handle *vb* **han·dled; han·dling** \'han-(d)liŋ, -dᵊl-iŋ\ **1 a** : to touch, feel, hold, or move with the hand **b** : to man-

age with the hands ⟨*handle* a horse⟩ **2 a** : to deal with **b** : ¹CONTROL 1b, DIRECT **3** : to deal or trade in ⟨a store that *handles* rugs⟩ **4** : to act, behave, or feel in a certain way when managed or directed ⟨a car that *handles* well⟩ — **han·dler** \'han-(d)lər, -dᵊl-ər\ *n*

syn HANDLE, MANIPULATE, WIELD mean to manage skillfully or efficiently. HANDLE suggests applying an acquired skill in order to accomplish something ⟨knows how to *handle* her bike well⟩ MANIPULATE suggests using special skills in order to accomplish a complicated or difficult task ⟨surgeons must be able to *manipulate* delicate instruments⟩ WIELD suggests handling a tool or weapon with power or authority ⟨*wielded* the sword with all his might⟩

han·dle·bar \'han-dᵊl-,bär\ *n* : a bar with a handle (as for steering a bicycle) at each end — usually used in pl.

hand lens *n* : a magnifying glass to be held in the hand

hand·made \'han(d)-'mād\ *adj* : made by hand or with hand tools

hand·maid·en \-,mād-ᵊn\ *or* **hand·maid** \-,mād\ *n* : a female servant or attendant

hand–me–down \'han(d)-mē-,dau̇n\ *adj* : USED 2, SECONDHAND — **hand–me–down** *n*

hand·off \'han-,dȯf\ *n* : the act of handing the ball to a teammate (as in football)

hand organ *n* : a barrel organ operated by a hand crank

hand·out \'han-,dau̇t\ *n* **1** : food, clothing, or money given to a beggar **2** : an information sheet for free distribution **3** : a prepared statement released to the press

hand over *vb* : to yield control of

hand·pick \'han(d)-'pik\ *vb* : to select personally ⟨a *handpicked* successor⟩

hand·rail \'han-,drāl\ *n* : a narrow rail for grasping as a support (as on a staircase)

hand·saw \'han(d)-,sȯ\ *n* : a saw designed to be used with one hand

hand·shake \-,shāk\ *n* : a clasping of hands by two people especially in greeting or farewell

hand·some \'han(t)-səm\ *adj* **1** : fairly large : SIZABLE ⟨a *handsome* fortune⟩ **2** : GENEROUS 1, GRACIOUS ⟨a *handsome* tribute⟩ **3** : having a pleasing and usually impressive or dignified appearance **syn** see BEAUTIFUL — **hand·some·ly** *adv* — **hand·some·ness** *n*

hand·spring \'han(d)-,spriŋ\ *n* : a tumbling feat in which the body turns in a full circle from a standing position and lands first on the hands and then on the feet

hand–to–hand \,han-tə-'hand\ *adj* : involving physical contact ⟨*hand-to-hand* combat⟩

hand–to–mouth \-tə-'mau̇th\ *adj* : having or providing nothing to spare ⟨a *hand-to-mouth* existence⟩

hand·work \'han-,dwərk\ *n* : work done with the hands and not by machine

hand·writ·ing \'han-,drīt-iŋ\ *n* **1** : writing done by hand **2** : the form of a particular person's writing **3** : ²MANUSCRIPT 2

hand·writ·ten \'han-,drit-ᵊn\ *adj* : written by hand

handy \'han-dē\ *adj* **hand·i·er; -est** **1 a** : conveniently near **b** : easily handled or used ⟨a *handy* sloop⟩ ⟨a *handy* reference book⟩ **2** : clever in using the hands : DEXTEROUS ⟨*handy* with a needle⟩

handy·man \-,man\ *n* : a person who does various small jobs

¹hang \'haŋ\ *vb* **hung** \'həŋ\ *also* **hanged** \'haŋd\; **hang·ing** \'haŋ-iŋ\ **1 a** : to fasten or be fastened to an elevated point without support from below : SUSPEND, DANGLE **b** : to kill or be killed by hanging from a rope tied round the neck ⟨sentenced to be *hanged*⟩ **c** : to fasten so as to allow free motion forward and backward ⟨*hang* a door⟩ **2** : to cover, decorate, or furnish by hanging pictures, trophies, or drapery **3** : ¹DROOP 1 ⟨*hung* my head in shame⟩ **4** : to fasten to a wall ⟨*hang* wallpaper⟩ **5** : to display pictures in a gallery **6** : HOVER 1b ⟨clouds *hanging* low overhead⟩ **7** : to stay steadily **8** : DEPEND 1 ⟨election *hangs* on one vote⟩ **9 a** : to take hold for support : CLING ⟨the children *hung* on his arm⟩ **b** : to be hard to bear ⟨time *hangs* on her hands⟩ **10** : to be uncertain ⟨the decision is still *hanging*⟩ **11** : to be in a state of close attention ⟨*hung* on my every word⟩ **12** : LINGER 1, LOITER — **hang·able** \'haŋ-ə-bəl\ *adj*

²hang *n* **1** : the manner in which a thing hangs ⟨the *hang* of a skirt⟩ **2 a** : ¹MEANING 1b ⟨the *hang* of an argument⟩ **b** : a special method : KNACK ⟨get the *hang* of driving⟩ — **give a hang** *or* **care a hang** : to be concerned or worried

hang·ar \'haŋ-ər, 'haŋ-gər\ *n* : a shelter for housing and repairing aircraft [from French *hangar* "shed", probably derived from Latin *angarium* "shed for shoeing horses"]

hang around *vb* **1** : to remain in an area for no obvious reason **2** : to spend time in company ⟨*hangs around* with older kids⟩

hang back *vb* **1** : to linger behind others **2** : to be unwilling to do something : HESITATE ⟨always *hangs back* when everyone else is dancing⟩

hang·dog \'haŋ-,dȯg\ *adj* **1** : ASHAMED 1, GUILTY ⟨a *hangdog* look⟩ **2** : DEJECTED, COWED

hang·er \'haŋ-ər\ *n* **1** : one that hangs **2** : a device by which something hangs; *esp* : a device for hanging a garment from a hook or rod

hang·er–on \'haŋ-ə-,rȯn, -,rän\ *n, pl* **hangers–on** : one that hangs around a person, place, or institution in hope of personal gain

hang glider *n* : a glider which resembles a kite and from which a rider hangs while gliding down from a cliff or hill — **hang gliding** *n*

hang in *vb* : to refuse to be discouraged or frightened ⟨*hang in* there, kid! Don't quit⟩

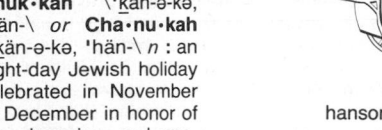

hang glider

¹hang·ing \'haŋ-iŋ\ *n* **1** : an execution by strangling or breaking the neck by a suspended noose **2** : something hung (as a curtain or tapestry) — usually used in pl.

²hanging *adj* **1** : located on steeply sloping ground ⟨*hanging* gardens⟩ **2 a** : sticking out ⟨*hanging* rocks⟩ **b** : supported only by the wall on one side ⟨a *hanging* staircase⟩ **3** : suitable for holding a hanging object **4** : punishable by hanging ⟨a *hanging* offense⟩

hang·man \'haŋ-mən\ *n* : a person who hangs condemned criminals

hang·nail \-,nāl\ *n* : a bit of skin hanging loose at the side or base of a fingernail

hang on *vb* **1** : to keep hold or possession especially tightly ⟨*hang on* or you'll fall⟩ ⟨*hang on* to your money⟩ **2** : to continue stubbornly ⟨a cold that *hung on* all spring⟩

hang·out \'haŋ-,aút\ *n* : a place in which a person hangs out

hang out \(')haŋ-'aút\ *vb* : to spend one's time idly or in loitering around ⟨*hangs out* at the corner store⟩

hang·over \'haŋ-,ō-vər\ *n* **1** : something (as a surviving custom) that remains from what is past **2** : a sick uncomfortable state that comes from drinking too many drinks of alcoholic beverage

hang·tag \-,tag\ *n* : a tag attached to an article of merchandise giving information about its material and proper care

hang–up \'haŋ-,əp\ *n* : a source of mental or emotional difficulty

hang up \(')haŋ-'əp\ *vb* **1 a** : to place on a hook or hanger ⟨*hang up* your coat⟩ **b** : to replace a telephone receiver on the cradle so that the connection is broken; *also* : to end a telephone conversation **2** : to snag or cause to

snag so as to be immovable ⟨the ship *hung up* on a sandbar⟩

hank \'haŋk\ *n* : ²COIL 1a, SKEIN; *esp* : a coil of yarn

han·ker \'haŋ-kər\ *vb* **han·kered; han·ker·ing** \-k(ə-)riŋ\ : to have an eager or continual desire ⟨*hanker* after fame⟩ — **han·ker·er** \-kər-ər\ *n*

han·ky–pan·ky \,haŋ-kē-'paŋ-kē\ *n* : questionable or sneaky activity : TRICKERY

Han·sen's disease \'han(t)-sənz-\ *n* : LEPROSY

han·som \'han(t)-səm\ *n* : a light two-wheeled carriage with the driver's seat elevated behind

Ha·nuk·kah \'känə-kə, 'hän-\ *or* **Cha·nu·kah** \'kän-ə-kə, 'hän-\ *n* : an eight-day Jewish holiday celebrated in November or December in honor of the cleansing and second dedication of the Temple after the Syrians were driven out of Jerusalem in 165 B.C.

hansom

hap \'hap\ *n* **1** : something that happens : OCCURRENCE **2** : something that happens unexpectedly without intention or observable cause — **hap** *vb* — **hap·ly** \-lē\ *adv*

hap·haz·ard \(')hap-'haz-ərd\ *adj* : marked by lack of plan, order, or direction — **haphazard** *adv* — **hap·haz·ard·ly** *adv* — **hap·haz·ard·ness** *n*

hap·less \'hap-ləs\ *adj* : having no luck : UNFORTUNATE — **hap·less·ly** *adv* — **hap·less·ness** *n*

hap·pen \'hap-ən, 'hap-ᵊm\ *vb* **hap·pened; hap·pen·ing** \'hap-(ə-)niŋ\ **1** : to occur or come about by chance **2** : to take place : OCCUR **3** : to have occasion or opportunity ⟨*happened* to overhear⟩ **4 a** : to meet or find something by chance ⟨*happened* on the right answer⟩ **b** : to appear casually or by chance ⟨*happened* into the room just as the music started⟩ **5** : to come by way of injury or harm ⟨I promise nothing will *happen* to you⟩ [Middle English *happenen* "to occur by chance", from *hap* "chance, chance occurrence" — related to HAPPY, MISHAP, PERHAPS]

hap·pen·ing *n* **1** : EVENT 1a, OCCURRENCE **2** : an event that is especially interesting, entertaining, or important

hap·pi·ly \'hap-ə-lē\ *adv* **1** : in a fortunate or lucky manner ⟨*happily*, no one was injured⟩ **2** : in a happy manner or state ⟨lived *happily* ever after⟩ **3** : in a fitting, effective, or successful manner ⟨his remarks were *happily* worded⟩

hap·pi·ness \'hap-i-nəs\ *n* : a state of well-being and contentment : JOY

hap·py \'hap-ē\ *adj* **hap·pi·er; -est** **1** : FORTUNATE 1, LUCKY **2** : SUITABLE 1 ⟨a *happy* choice for governor⟩ **3 a** : enjoying well-being and contentment ⟨*happy* in my work⟩ **b** : expressing or suggestive of happiness ⟨*happy* laughter⟩ **c** : being pleased or glad ⟨*happy* to accept an invitation⟩ [Middle English *happy* "having or being good luck", a specialized sense of *hap* "chance, chance occurrence" — related to HAPPEN, MISHAP, PERHAPS]

hap·py–go–lucky \,hap-ē-gō-'lək-ē\ *adj* : cheerfully unconcerned : CAREFREE

ha·rangue \hə-'raŋ\ *n* **1** : a speech addressed to a public assembly **2** : a forceful or scolding speech or writing — **harangue** *vb* — **ha·rangu·er** \-'raŋ-ər\ *n*

ha·rass \hə-'ras, 'har-əs\ *vb* **1** : to tire out by continual efforts **2** : to worry or annoy with repeated attacks — **ha·rass·ment** \-mənt\ *n*

\ə\ abut	\aú\ **out**	\i\ tip	\ȯ\ **saw**	\ú\ **foot**
\ər\ **further**	\ch\ **chin**	\ī\ life	\ȯi\ **coin**	\y\ **yet**
\a\ **mat**	\e\ **pet**	\j\ **job**	\th\ **thin**	\yü\ **few**
\ā\ **take**	\ē\ **easy**	\ŋ\ **sing**	\th\ **this**	\yú\ **cure**
\ä\ **cot, cart**	\g\ **go**	\ō\ **bone**	\ü\ **food**	\zh\ **vision**

har·bin·ger \'här-bən-jər\ *n* : one that announces or shows what is coming : FORERUNNER ⟨warm rains that come as *harbingers* of spring⟩ — **harbinger** *vb*

¹**har·bor** \'här-bər\ *n* **1** : a place of safety and comfort : REFUGE **2** : a part of a body of water protected and deep enough to be a place of safety for ships : PORT — **har·bor·less** \-ləs\ *adj*

²**harbor** *vb* **har·bored; har·bor·ing** \-b(ə-)riŋ\ **1** : to give shelter to ⟨*harbor* an escaped convict⟩ **2** : to hold a thought or feeling of ⟨*harbor* a grudge⟩ **3** : to take shelter in or as if in a harbor — **har·bor·er** *n*

har·bor·age \'här-bə-rij\ *n* : ¹SHELTER 1, HARBOR

¹**hard** \'härd\ *adj* **1** : not easily penetrated, cut, or divided into parts : not soft **2 a** : high in alcoholic content ⟨*hard* cider⟩ **b** : containing substances that prevent lathering with soap ⟨*hard* water⟩ **3** : stable and high in value and often convertible into gold ⟨*hard* currency⟩ **4 a** : physically fit **b** : HARDY 2, 3 **5 a** : ¹FIRM 2a, DEFINITE ⟨*hard* agreement⟩ **b** : based on clear fact ⟨*hard* evidence⟩ **c** : being thorough, intense, and searching ⟨*hard* look⟩ **d** : lacking sympathy or tender feelings **5** : difficult to endure : HARSH, SEVERE ⟨*hard* words⟩ ⟨a *hard* winter⟩ ⟨*hard* times⟩ **b** : RESENTFUL 2 ⟨*hard* feelings⟩ **c** : STRICT 1, UNRELENTING ⟨drives a *hard* bargain⟩ **d** : physically or mentally difficult ⟨a *hard* problem⟩ ⟨*hard* work⟩ **7** : DILIGENT, ENERGETIC ⟨a *hard* worker⟩ **8 a** : sharply or harshly defined or outlined ⟨*hard* shadows⟩ **b** : sounding as in *cold* and *geese* respectively — used of *c* and *g* — **hard up 1** : short of money : POOR **2** : poorly provided ⟨*hard* up for friends⟩

syn HARD, FIRM, SOLID mean having a structure that can stand up against pressure. HARD is used of something that does not easily bend, stretch, or dent ⟨steel is *hard*⟩ FIRM is used of something that is flexible but also tough or compact ⟨*firm* muscles⟩ ⟨a *firm* mattress⟩ SOLID is used of something that has a fixed structure and is heavy and compact all the way through ⟨a *solid* wall of bricks⟩

²**hard** *adv* **1 a** : with great effort or energy ⟨work *hard*⟩ ⟨try *hard*⟩ **b** : as far as possible ⟨turn the wheel *hard* left⟩ **2 a** : in such a manner as to cause hardship, bitterness, or pain **b** : with bitterness or grief ⟨took the defeat *hard*⟩ **3** : in a tight or firm manner ⟨hold *hard* to something⟩ **4** : to the point of hardness ⟨dry *hard*⟩ **5** : ⁴CLOSE 6 ⟨the school stood *hard* by a church⟩

hard–and–fast \,härd-ᵊn-'fast\ *adj* : not be changed : FIXED ⟨a *hard-and-fast* rule⟩

hard·back \'härd-,bak\ *n* : a book bound in hard covers

hard·ball \-,bȯl\ *n* : BASEBALL

hard–bit·en \-'bit-ᵊn\ *adj* : TOUGH 3 ⟨*hard-bitten* veterans⟩

hard–boiled \-'bȯild\ *adj* **1** : boiled until both white and yolk have become solid ⟨*hard-boiled* eggs⟩ **2** : lacking tender feelings : TOUGH ⟨a *hard-boiled* prison guard⟩

hard coal *n* : ANTHRACITE

hard copy *n* : a copy of information (as words, numbers, or pictures) on paper in normal size ⟨a *hard copy* of a picture on the computer display screen⟩

hard core *n* **1** : an unchanging and lasting central part **2** : a small number of aggressive members of a group — **hard–core** *adj*

hard·en \'härd-ᵊn\ *vb* **hard·ened; hard·en·ing** \'härd-niŋ, -ᵊn-iŋ\ **1** : to make or become hard or harder **2** : to make or become hardy or strong ⟨muscles *hardened* by exercise⟩ **3 a** : to make or become stubborn, unfeeling, or unsympathetic **b** : to become set in one's ways ⟨a *hardened* criminal⟩ **4** : to protect from blast, heat, or radiation (as by a thick barrier or by placing underground) ⟨*hardened* missile sites⟩ — **hard·en·er** \'härd-nər, -ᵊn-ər\ *n*

hard·en·ing *n* : SCLEROSIS ⟨*hardening* of the arteries⟩

hard·hack \'härd-,hak\ *n* : a shrubby American spirea with rusty hairy leaves and dense bunches of pink or occasion-

ally white flowers at the top of a straight woody stem

hard hat *n* **1** : a protective helmet worn especially by construction workers **2** : a construction worker

hard·head·ed \'härd-'hed-əd\ *adj* **1** : STUBBORN 1 **2** : marked by sound judgment : REALISTIC ⟨a *hardheaded* judgment⟩ — **hard·head·ed·ly** *adv* — **hard·head·ed·ness** *n*

hard·heart·ed \-'härt-əd\ *adj* : UNFEELING 2, PITILESS — **hard·heart·ed·ly** *adv* — **hard·heart·ed·ness** *n*

har·di·hood \'härd-ē-,hu̇d\ *n* **1** : BRAVERY 2 **2** : VIGOR 1, ROBUSTNESS

hard·ly \'härd-lē\ *adv* **1** : in a severe or harsh manner ⟨deal *hardly* with them⟩ **2** : with difficulty ⟨a *hardly* won victory⟩ **3** : only just : BARELY, SCARCELY ⟨we *hardly* knew them⟩ **4** : certainly not ⟨that news is *hardly* surprising⟩

hard·ness \'härd-nəs\ *n* **1** : the quality or state of being hard **2** : the ability of a substance (as a mineral) to scratch another substance or be itself scratched

hard–of–hearing \,härd-ə(v)-'hi(ə)r-iŋ\ *adj* **1** : partly deaf **2** : of or relating to partial deafness

hard palate *n* : the bony front part of the roof of the mouth

hard put *adj* : barely able ⟨*hard put* to find an explanation⟩

hard rubber *n* : a firm rubber or rubber product

hard–shell crab \,härd-,shel-\ *n* : a crab that has not recently shed its shell — called also *hard-shelled crab* \-,shel(d)-\

hard–shelled \'härd-'sheld\ *adj* : having a hard shell

hard·ship \'härd-,ship\ *n* **1** : ¹PAIN 2a, PRIVATION **2** : something that causes pain or loss

hard·tack \-,tak\ *n* : a hard biscuit or bread made of flour and water without salt

hard·top \-'täp\ *n* : an automobile having a permanent rigid top

hard·ware \'här-,dwa(ə)r, -,dwe(ə)r\ *n* **1** : articles (as fittings, cutlery, tools, utensils, or parts of machines) made of metal **2** : the equipment used for a particular purpose ⟨computer *hardware*⟩ ⟨military *hardware*⟩

hard wheat *n* : a wheat with hard flinty kernels that is used to make a flour especially suitable for bread and macaroni

¹**hard·wood** \'här-,dwu̇d\ *n* **1** : the wood of a tree (as an oak or maple) producing enclosed seeds as compared to those of a tree bearing cones **2** : a tree that yields hardwood

²**hardwood** *adj* **1** : having or made of hardwood ⟨*hardwood* floors⟩ **2** : consisting of mature woody tissue ⟨a *hardwood* cutting⟩

har·dy \'härd-ē\ *adj* **har·di·er; -est 1** : BOLD 1a, BRAVE **2** : able to stand fatigue or hardships : ROBUST **3** : able to survive unfavorable conditions (as of weather) ⟨a *hardy* rose⟩ — **har·di·ly** \'härd-ᵊl-ē\ *adv* — **har·di·ness** \'härd-ē-nəs\ *n*

hare \'ha(ə)r, 'he(ə)r\ *n, pl* **hare** or **hares** : any of various swift timid animals that are like the related rabbits but have young born with open eyes and a furry coat

hare·bell \-,bel\ *n* : a slender herb with bright blue bell-shaped flowers

hare·brained \-'brānd\ *adj* : SILLY 1, GIDDY

hare·lip \-'lip\ *n* : a deformity in which the upper lip is split like that of a hare — **hare·lipped** \-'lipt\ *adj*

har·em \'har-əm, 'her-\ *n* **1 a** : the rooms assigned to the women in a Muslim household **b** : the women of a Muslim household **2** : a group of females controlled by and usually mating with one male — used of polygamous animals

hare

hark \'härk\ *vb* : LISTEN 1

hark back *vb* : to recall or cause to recall something earlier ⟨*hark back* to the good old days⟩

har·le·quin \'här-li-k(w)ən\ *n* **1** : ¹CLOWN 2 **2** : a pattern of usually diamond-shaped figures of different colors — **harlequin** *adj*

har·lot \'här-lət\ *n* : ²PROSTITUTE

har·lot·ry \'här-lə-trē\ *n* : PROSTITUTION 1

harm \'härm\ *n* **1** : physical or mental damage : INJURY **2** : MISCHIEF 3, HURT **syn** see INJURY — **harm** *vb*

harm·ful \'härm-fəl\ *adj* : causing damage : INJURIOUS — **harm·ful·ly** \-fə-lē\ *adv* — **harm·ful·ness** *n*

harm·less \'härm-ləs\ *adj* **1** : free from harm **2** : unable to harm ⟨a *harmless* joke⟩ — **harm·less·ly** *adv* — **harm·less·ness** *n*

¹har·mon·ic \här-'män-ik\ *adj* : of or relating to musical harmony as opposed to melody or rhythm — **har·mon·i·cal·ly** \-'män-i-k(ə-)lē\ *adv*

²harmonic *n* : OVERTONE 1

har·mon·i·ca \här-'män-i-kə\ *n* : a small musical instrument that is held in the hand and played by the mouth and that produces a sound through metal reeds which vibrate as air is blown or drawn past them

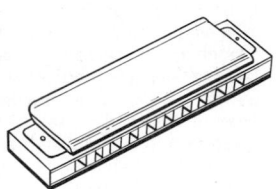
harmonica

har·mo·ni·ous \här-'mō-nē-əs\ *adj* **1** : having a pleasing mixture of notes ⟨a *harmonious* song⟩ ⟨*harmonious* voices⟩ **2** : having the parts agreeably related ⟨decorated in *harmonious* colors⟩ **3** : marked by agreement in feeling or action ⟨a *harmonious* family⟩ — **har·mo·ni·ous·ly** *adv* — **har·mo·ni·ous·ness** *n*

har·mo·nize \'här-mə-,nīz\ *vb* **-nized; -niz·ing** **1** : to play or sing in harmony **2** : to be in harmony **3** : to bring into harmony **4** : to provide or accompany with harmony — **har·mo·ni·za·tion** \,här-mə-nə-'zā-shən\ *n* — **har·mo·niz·er** \'här-mə-,nī-zər\ *n*

har·mo·ny \'här-mə-nē\ *n, pl* **-nies** **1 a** : the combination of musical notes played together as chords **b** : the structure of music with respect to the way it is written and to the way notes are grouped as chords **c** : the science of harmony **2 a** : pleasing or suitable arrangement of parts **b** : AGREEMENT 1b, ACCORD ⟨lives in *harmony* with her neighbors⟩

¹har·ness \'här-nəs\ *n* **1** : the straps and fastenings by which an animal pulls a load **2** : an arrangement that resembles a harness

²harness *vb* **1** : to put a harness on **2** : to tie together : YOKE **3** : to put to work : UTILIZE ⟨*harness* the sun's energy to heat homes⟩

harness racing *n* : the sport of racing horses that are harnessed to two-wheeled vehicles

¹harp \'härp\ *n* : a musical instrument that has strings stretched across a large open triangular frame and that is plucked with the fingers — **harp·ist** \'här-pəst\ *n*

²harp *vb* **1** : to play on a harp **2** : to dwell on a subject tiresomely ⟨always *harping* on his shortcomings⟩ — **harp·er** *n*

¹har·poon \här-'pün\ *n* : a barbed spear used especially in hunting large fish or whales

²harpoon *vb* : to strike with a harpoon — **har·poon·er** *n*

harp·si·chord \'härp-si-,kȯ(ə)rd\ *n* : a keyboard instrument similar to a piano but with strings that are plucked rather than struck

har·py \'här-pē\ *n, pl* **harpies** **1** *cap* : a foul creature of Greek mythology that is part woman and part bird **2 a** : a greedy person **b** : an evil-tempered woman

har·que·bus \'här-kwi-(,)bəs\ *or* **ar·que·bus** \'är-\ *n* : a portable firearm of the 15th and 16th centuries later replaced by the musket

¹har·ri·er \'har-ē-ər\ *n* : a hunting dog like a large beagle used especially for hunting rabbits

²harrier *n* **1** : one that harries **2** : any of various slender long-legged hawks (as the marsh hawk)

¹har·row \'har-ō\ *n* : a cultivating tool that has spikes, teeth, or disks and is used for breaking up and smoothing the soil

²harrow *vb* **1** : to cultivate with a harrow **2** : ²TORMENT, VEX — **har·row·er** *n*

har·ry \'har-ē\ *vb* **har·ried; har·ry·ing** **1** : ²RAID, PILLAGE **2** : ²TORMENT 2, WORRY

harsh \'härsh\ *adj* **1** : disagreeable to the touch **2** : causing discomfort or pain **3** : making many or difficult demands : SEVERE ⟨*harsh* discipline⟩ **4** : jarring to the artistic sense ⟨*harsh* colors⟩ **syn** see ROUGH — **harsh·ly** *adv* — **harsh·ness** *n*

hart \'härt\ *n, chiefly British* : a male red deer especially over five years old : STAG

harte·beest \'härt-(ə-),bēst\ *n* : either of two large African antelopes with a long head, ringed horns, and the top of the body above the front legs higher than the top part above the hind legs resulting in a sloping back

hartebeest

har·um–scar·um \,har-əm-'skar-əm, ,her-əm-'sker-\ *adj* : RECKLESS, IRRESPONSIBLE — **harum–scarum** *adv*

¹har·vest \'här-vəst\ *n* **1** : the season when crops are gathered **2** : the gathering of a crop **3** : a ripe crop (as of grain or fruit); *also* : the quantity of a crop gathered in a single season

²harvest *vb* **1** : to gather in a crop : REAP **2** : to gather as if by harvesting ⟨*harvest* timber⟩

har·vest·er \'här-vəs-tər\ *n* **1** : a person who gathers by or as if by harvesting **2** : a machine for harvesting field crops

har·vest·man \'här-vəs(t)-mən\ *n* : DADDY LONGLEGS

harvest moon *n* : the full moon nearest the time of the September equinox

has *present 3d sing of* HAVE

has–been \'haz-,bin\ *n* : one that has passed the peak of ability, power, or popularity

¹hash \'hash\ *vb* **1 a** : to chop into small pieces **b** : CONFUSE 3, MUDDLE **2** : to talk about : DISCUSS ⟨*hashed* over the problem⟩ [from French *hacher* "to chop up into small pieces", from early French *hachier* (same meaning), from *hache* "battle-ax"; of Germanic origin — related to ⁴HATCH, HATCHET]

²hash *n* **1** : chopped meat mixed with potatoes and browned **2** : a mixture of many different things

³hash *n* : HASHISH [a shortened form of *hashish*]

hash·ish \'hash-,ēsh, ha-'shēsh\ *n* : a drug prepared from hemp that is smoked, chewed, or drunk for its intoxicating effect — compare CANNABIS, MARIJUANA

hasn't \'haz-ᵊnt\ : has not

hasp \'hasp\ *n* : a fastener especially for a door or lid consisting of a hinged metal strap that fits over a staple and is held by a pin or padlock

\ə\ **abut**	\au̇\ **out**	\i\ **tip**	\ȯ\ **saw**	\u̇\ **foot**	
\ər\ **further**	\ch\ **chin**	\ī\ **life**	\ȯi\ **coin**	\y\ **yet**	
\a\ **mat**	\e\ **pet**	\j\ **job**	\th\ **thin**	\yü\ **few**	
\ā\ **take**	\ē\ **easy**	\ŋ\ **sing**	\th\ **this**	\yu̇\ **cure**	
\ä\ **cot, cart**	\g\ **go**	\ō\ **bone**	\ü\ **food**	\zh\ **vision**	

¹has·sle \'has-əl\ *vb* **has·sled; has·sling** \-(ə-)liŋ\ **1** : ARGUE 2, DISPUTE ⟨*hassled* with the umpire⟩ **2** : ANNOY, HARASS

²hassle *n* **1** : ARGUMENT 2 **2** : ²FIGHT 1a **3** : something that is annoying or troublesome

has·sock \'has-ək\ *n* **1** : TUSSOCK **2 a** : a cushion to kneel on in prayer **b** : a cushion that serves as a seat or as a leg rest

hast \(')həst, (h)əst\ *archaic present 2d sing of* HAVE

has·tate \'has-,tāt\ *adj* : shaped like an arrowhead with flaring barbs ⟨*hastate* leaf⟩

¹haste \'hāst\ *n* **1** : rapidity of motion or action **2** : reckless action **3** : eagerness to act that is not proper or suitable

²haste *vb* **hast·ed; hast·ing** : HASTEN

has·ten \'hā-sᵊn\ *vb* **has·tened; has·ten·ing** \'hās-niŋ, -ᵊn-iŋ\ **1** : to urge on **2** : to speed up : ACCELERATE ⟨*hastened* my steps⟩ **3** : to move or act quickly : HURRY — **has·ten·er** \'hās-nər, -ᵊn-ər\ *n*

hasty \'hā-stē\ *adj* **hast·i·er; -est** **1 a** : done or made in a hurry ⟨made a *hasty* sketch of the scene⟩ **b** : fast and often not thorough ⟨made a *hasty* survey of the problem⟩ **2** : acting or done without forethought : RASH **3** : quick to anger : IRRITABLE ⟨a *hasty* temper⟩ **syn** see FAST — **hast·i·ly** \-stə-lē\ *adv* — **hast·i·ness** \-stē-nəs\ *n*

hasty pudding *n* **1** *British* : a porridge of oatmeal or flour boiled in water **2** *New England* : cornmeal mush

hat \'hat\ *n* : a covering for the head usually having a shaped crown and brim

hat·box \'hat-,bäks\ *n* : a round piece of luggage for carrying hats

¹hatch \'hach\ *n* **1** : an opening in a deck, floor, or roof **2** : a small door or opening (as in an airplane) **3** : the covering for a hatch [Old English *hæc* "small door or opening"]

²hatch *vb* **1 a** : to produce from eggs **b** : INCUBATE 1 **2** : to bring into being : ORIGINATE; *esp* : to organize or put together in secret ⟨*hatch* a plot⟩ **3 a** : to come forth from an egg, pupa, or chrysalis **b** : to give forth young or adults [Middle English *hacchen* "to cause to be born out of an egg"]

³hatch *n* **1** : an act or instance of hatching **2** : a brood of hatched young

⁴hatch *vb* : to mark (as the shading in a picture) with hatching [Middle English *hachen* "to mark with a pattern of fine lines", from early French *hacher* "to inlay, chop up", derived from earlier *hache* "battle-ax"; of Germanic origin — related to ¹HASH, HATCHET]

hatch·back \'hach-,bak\ *n* **1** : a back on an automobile having an upward-opening hatch **2** : an automobile having a hatchback

hatch·ery \'hach-(ə-)rē\ *n, pl* **-er·ies** : a place for hatching eggs

hatch·et \'hach-ət\ *n* : a small ax with a short handle [Middle English *hachet* "small ax, hatchet", from early French *hachette*, literally "small battle-ax", from *hache* "battle-ax"; of Germanic origin — related to ¹HASH, ⁴HATCH]

hatch·ing \'hach-iŋ\ *n* : the engraving or drawing of fine lines close together chiefly to give an effect of shading; *also* : the pattern so created

hatch·ling \'hach-liŋ\ *n* : a recently hatched animal

hatch·way \'hach-,wā\ *n* : a hatch usually with a ladder or stairs

¹hate \'hāt\ *n* **1** : strong dislike and ill will **2** : something or someone that is hated

²hate *vb* **hat·ed; hat·ing** **1** : to feel strong dislike toward ⟨*hates* his country's enemies⟩ **2 a** : to have a strong feeling of disgust for ⟨*hate* hypocrisy⟩ **b** : to find distasteful : DISLIKE ⟨*hates* cold weather⟩ — **hat·er** *n*

syn HATE, DETEST, ABHOR, LOATHE mean to have strong feelings against. HATE suggests deep dislike and the wishing of harm to another ⟨they *hated* their enemies⟩ DETEST suggests violent feelings against something or someone but without the desire for harm ⟨I *detest* lying and cheating⟩ ABHOR suggests strong distaste ⟨*abhorred* sentimental poetry⟩ LOATHE suggests complete disgust or rejection ⟨*loathed* the thought of having to move again⟩

hate·ful \'hāt-fəl\ *adj* **1** : full of hate : MALICIOUS ⟨*hateful* enemies⟩ **2** : causing or deserving hate ⟨a *hateful* crime⟩ — **hate·ful·ly** \-fə-lē\ *adv* — **hate·ful·ness** *n*

hath \(')hath, (h)əth\ *archaic present 3d sing of* HAVE

ha·tred \'hā-trəd\ *n* : ¹HATE 1

hat·ter \'hat-ər\ *n* : one that makes, sells, or cleans and repairs hats

hau·berk \'hò-(,)bərk\ *n* : a tunic of chain mail worn as defensive armor from the 12th to the 14th century

haugh·ty \'hòt-ē, 'hät-\ *adj* **haugh·ti·er; -est** : rudely proud in a manner that expresses scorn for others : ARROGANT — **haugh·ti·ly** \'hòt-ə-lē, 'hät-\ *adv* — **haugh·ti·ness** \'hòt-ē-nəs, 'hät-\ *n*

¹haul \'hòl\ *vb* **1** : to pull or drag with effort : DRAW ⟨*haul* a cart⟩ **2** : to obtain or move by hauling **3** : to transport in a vehicle [Middle English *halen* "to pull", from early French *haler* (same meaning); of Germanic origin — related to ²HALE] — **haul·er** *n*

²haul *n* **1** : the act or process of hauling : PULL **2 a** : an amount collected : TAKE ⟨a burglar's *haul*⟩ **b** : the fish taken in a single drawing of a net **3** : the distance over which a load is hauled ⟨a long *haul*⟩

haunch \'hònch, 'hänch\ *n* **1 a** : ²HIP **b** : HINDQUARTER 2 — usually used in pl. **2** : HINDQUARTER 1

¹haunt \'hònt, 'hänt\ *vb* **1** : to visit often : FREQUENT ⟨they *haunted* the antique shops⟩ **2** : to come back to the mind of again and again ⟨the tune *haunted* me all day⟩ **3** : to visit or live in as a ghost ⟨spirits *haunted* the house⟩ — **haunt·ing·ly** \-iŋ-lē\ *adv*

²haunt \'hònt, 'hänt\ *n* : a place repeatedly visited ⟨favorite *haunts* of birds⟩

haut·bois *or* **haut·boy** \'(h)ō-,bói\ *n, pl* **hautbois** \-,bóiz\ *or* **hautboys** : OBOE

¹have \(')hav, (h)əv, v; *in "have to" meaning "must" usually* 'haf\ *vb, past & past participle* **had** \(')had, (h)əd, d\; *present participle* **hav·ing** \'hav-iŋ\; *present 3d sing* **has** \(')haz, (h)əz, z, s; *in "have to" meaning "must" usually* 'has\ **1 a** : POSSESS 1, OWN ⟨*have* a dog⟩ ⟨*have* the right to vote⟩ **b** : to consist of ⟨April *has* 30 days⟩ **2** : to be forced by duty or conscience in regard to : MUST ⟨*have* to go⟩ ⟨*have* a letter to write⟩ **3** : to stand in relationship to ⟨*have* enemies⟩ **4 a** : OBTAIN 1, GET ⟨best to be *had*⟩ **b** : RECEIVE 1 ⟨*had* news of the war⟩ **c** : ACCEPT 1a; *esp* : to accept in marriage ⟨she wouldn't *have* him⟩ **5 a** : to be marked or characterized by ⟨*have* red hair⟩ **b** : REVEAL 1 ⟨*had* the courage to refuse⟩ **c** : ²USE 3a, EXERCISE ⟨*have* mercy⟩ **6 a** : ²EXPERIENCE, UNDERGO ⟨*have* a good time⟩ ⟨*have* a cold⟩ **b** : to carry on : PERFORM ⟨*have* a look at that cut⟩ ⟨*have* a fight⟩ **c** : to hold in the mind ⟨*have* an opinion⟩ ⟨*have* doubts⟩ **7 a** : to cause to do or be done ⟨*had* my hair cut⟩ ⟨please *have* the children stay⟩ **b** : to cause to be ⟨*has* everyone confused⟩ **8** : ¹PERMIT 1 ⟨we'll *have* no more of that⟩ **9 a** : to hold an advantage over ⟨we *have* them now⟩ **b** : ²TRICK 1, FOOL ⟨been *had* by a partner⟩ **10** : BEGET 1, BEAR ⟨*have* a baby⟩ **11** : to partake of ⟨*have* dinner⟩ **12** : ²BRIBE ⟨can be *had* for a price⟩ **13** — used as a helping verb with the past participle of another verb ⟨*has* gone home⟩ ⟨*had* already eaten⟩ ⟨will *have* finished dinner by then⟩ — **have at** : to go at or deal with : ATTACK — **have done** : ¹FINISH 1, STOP — **have it in for** : to intend to do harm to — **have to do with** **1** : to deal with ⟨the book *has* to do with fish⟩ **2** : to have a specified relationship with or effect on

²have \'hav\ *n* : one that has much material wealth

ha·ven \'hā-vən\ *n* **1** : ¹HARBOR 2, PORT **2** : a place of safety : SHELTER

have–not \'hav-ˌnät, -'nät\ *n* : one that is poor in material wealth

haven't \'hav-ənt\ : have not

hav·er·sack \'hav-ər-ˌsak\ *n* : a bag similar to a knapsack but worn over one shoulder

hav·oc \'hav-ək\ *n* **1** : wide and general destruction ⟨*havoc* caused by a tornado⟩ **2** : great confusion and disorder

haversack

¹haw \'hȯ\ *vb* **1** : to make a sound (as \ə\) during a pause in speaking which is usually written as *haw* ⟨hemmed and *hawed* before answering⟩ **2** : to hesitate in speaking

²haw *n* : a pause in speaking filled by the sound which is usually written as *haw*

³haw *imperative verb* — used as a direction to turn left

Ha·waii–Aleu·tian time \hə-'wä-(y)ē-ə-'lü-shən-, -'wī-, -'wȯ-\ *n* : the time of the 11th time zone west of Greenwich that includes the Hawaiian islands and the Aleutian islands west of the Fox group

Ha·wai·ian \hə-'wä-yən, -'wī(y)ən, -'wȯ-yən\ *n* **1** : a person born or living in Hawaii; *esp* : one of Polynesian ancestry **2** : the Polynesian language of the Hawaiians — **Hawaiian** *adj*

¹hawk \'hȯk\ *n* **1** : any of numerous birds of prey that have a strong hooked bill and sharp curved claws and are smaller than most eagles **2** : a person who supports war or warlike policies [Old English *hafoc* "hawk"] — **hawk·ish** \'hȯ-kish\ *adj*

²hawk *vb* : to hunt birds by means of a trained hawk — **hawk·er** *n*

³hawk *vb* : to offer for sale by calling out in the street ⟨*hawk* vegetables⟩ [from English *hawker* "one who sells goods by calling out in the street", from German *höker* "peddler"] — **hawk·er** *n*

⁴hawk *vb* **1** : to make a harsh coughing sound in or as if in clearing the throat **2** : to raise by hawking ⟨*hawk* up phlegm⟩

hawk·moth \'hȯk-ˌmȯth\ *n* : any of numerous moths with a stout body, long strong narrow pointed front wings, and small hind wings

hawk·weed \'hȯ-ˌkwēd\ *n* : any of several plants that are related to the daisies and usually have flower heads with red or orange ray flowers

haw·ser \'hȯ-zər\ *n* : a large rope for towing or tying up a ship

haw·thorn \'hȯ-ˌthȯ(ə)rn\ *n* : any of a genus of thorny shrubs or small trees that are related to the rose and have glossy leaves, white or pink fragrant flowers that bloom in the spring, and small red fruits

¹hay \'hā\ *n* : any of various herbs (as grasses) cut and dried for use as fodder

²hay *vb* **1** : to cut, cure, and store plants for hay **2** : to feed with hay — **hay·er** *n*

hay·cock \'hā-ˌkäk\ *n* : a cone-shaped pile of hay

hay fever *n* : a sickness like a cold usually affecting people sensitive to plant pollen

hay·field \'hā-ˌfēld\ *n* : a field where grass is grown for hay

hay·fork \-ˌfȯrk\ *n* **1** : PITCHFORK **2** : a mechanically operated fork for loading or unloading hay

hay·loft \-ˌlȯft\ *n* : the upper part of a barn where hay is stored

hay·mow \-ˌmaủ\ *n* : HAYLOFT

hay·rack \-ˌrak\ *n* : a frame mounted on a wagon and used especially in hauling hay or straw; *also* : the wagon and frame

hay·rick \-ˌrik\ *n* : a large sometimes thatched outdoor stack of hay

hay·stack \-ˌstak\ *n* : a stack of hay

hay·wire \-ˌwī(ə)r\ *adj* **1** : being out of order : not working ⟨the radio went *haywire*⟩ **2** : CRAZY 1

¹haz·ard \'haz-ərd\ *n* **1** : a game of chance played with dice **2** : ¹CHANCE 1, ACCIDENT **3** : a source of danger ⟨a fire *hazard*⟩ **4** : an obstacle on a golf course **syn** see DANGER

Word History *Hazard* was at first a game of chance played with dice. The English word comes from an early form of French, in which the game was called *hasard*. This French word was probably borrowed during the time of the Crusades from Arabic *az-zahr,* meaning "the dice" or "one of the dice". The game was borrowed from the French by the English, and within a few centuries what had been a chance taken on the outcome of a throw of the dice could be any venture or risk. Now "chance" or "venture" and "risk" or "peril" are the usual meanings of *hazard*. [Middle English *hazard* "game of chance", from early French *hasard* (same meaning), from Arabic *az-zahr* "the dice"]

²hazard *vb* : ¹VENTURE 1, RISK ⟨*hazard* a guess⟩

haz·ard·ous \'haz-ərd-əs\ *adj* : DANGEROUS 1, RISKY ⟨a *hazardous* voyage⟩ — **haz·ard·ous·ly** *adv* — **haz·ard·ous·ness** *n*

¹haze \'hāz\ *n* **1** : fine dust, smoke, or light vapor causing lack of transparency in the air **2** : unclearness of mind or perception : DAZE [from *hazy*]

²haze *vb* **hazed; haz·ing** : to make or become hazy or cloudy

³haze *vb* **hazed; haz·ing** : to play unpleasant and humiliating tricks on (as new members of a college fraternity) or force to perform humiliating tasks or stunts [origin unknown] — **haz·er** *n*

ha·zel \'hā-zəl\ *n* **1** : any of a genus of shrubs or small trees related to birches and bearing edible nuts enclosed in a leafy case **2** : a light brown to a strong yellowish brown — **hazel** *adj*

ha·zel·nut \-ˌnət\ *n* : the nut of a hazel

hazy \'hā-zē\ *adj* **haz·i·er; -est** **1** : partly hidden or darkened by or as if by haze ⟨*hazy* weather⟩ **2** : VAGUE 2, INDEFINITE ⟨a *hazy* idea⟩ — **haz·i·ly** \-zə-lē\ *adv* — **haz·i·ness** \-zē-nəs\ *n*

H–bomb \'āch-ˌbäm\ *n* : HYDROGEN BOMB

he \(')hē, ē\ *pron* **1** : that male one who is neither speaker nor hearer ⟨*he* is my father⟩ **2** — used in a general sense or when the sex of the person is unknown ⟨everyone should do the best *he* can⟩ ⟨tell whoever is in there that *he* had better come out⟩

¹head \'hed\ *n* **1** : the upper or front part of the body (as of a human being or an insect) that contains the brain, the chief sense organs, and the mouth **2 a** : ¹MIND 2, UNDERSTANDING ⟨a good *head* for figures⟩ **b** : control of the mind or feelings ⟨kept a level *head* in time of danger⟩ **3** : the side of a coin bearing a head or the major design **4 a** : each one among a number : INDIVIDUAL **b** *pl* **head** : one of a number (as of livestock) ⟨100 *head* of cattle⟩ **5 a** : the end that is upper or higher or opposite the foot ⟨the *head* of the bed⟩ **b** : the front part ⟨*head* of the column⟩ **c** : the uppermost part : TOP **d** : a skin or something like a thin piece of skin stretched across one or both ends of a drum **6** : HEADMASTER **7** : a compact mass of plant parts (as leaves or flowers) ⟨a *head* of cabbage⟩ **8 a** : the place where a stream begins **b** : the difference in elevation between two points in a body of fluid **c** : the resulting pressure at the lower point; *also* : pressure of a fluid ⟨a *head* of steam⟩ **9 a** : the place of leadership or command ⟨the

\ə\	abut	\aủ\	out	\i\	tip	\ȯ\	saw	\ủ\	foot
\ər\	further	\ch\	chin	\ī\	life	\ȯi\	coin	\y\	yet
\a\	mat	\e\	pet	\j\	job	\th\	thin	\yü\	few
\ā\	take	\ē\	easy	\ŋ\	sing	\th\	this	\yủ\	cure
\ä\	cot, cart	\g\	go	\ō\	bone	\ü\	food	\zh\	vision

person at the *head* of the group⟩ **b** : a person in this place : CHIEF, LEADER **10** : the foam that rises on a foaming liquid **11 a** : the part of a boil, pimple, or abscess at which it is likely to break **b** : CRISIS **2** ⟨events came to a *head*⟩ **12** : a part of a machine, tool, or weapon that performs the main function ⟨*head* of a lance⟩ ⟨a machine with a grinding *head*⟩ ⟨the record *head* of a tape recorder⟩ — **head·ship** \'hed-,ship\ *n* — **out of one's head** : DELIRIOUS 1 — **over one's head** **1** : beyond one's understanding **2** : so as to bypass one in a higher position ⟨went over the principal's *head* to complain to the school board⟩

²**head** *adj* **1** : PRINCIPAL, CHIEF ⟨*head* cook⟩ **2** : placed at the head ⟨sat at the *head* table at the banquet⟩ **3** : coming from in front ⟨*head* sea⟩

³**head** *vb* **1** : to form a head ⟨this cabbage *heads* early⟩ **2** : to be or put oneself at the head of : LEAD ⟨*head* a revolt⟩ ⟨*head* the list of heroes⟩ **3 a** : to get in front of so as to hinder, stop, or turn back ⟨*head* them off at the pass⟩ **b** : to take a lead over (as in a race) **4** : to go or point in a specified course ⟨*head* for home⟩ ⟨*head* the ship north⟩

head·ache \'hed-,āk\ *n* **1** : pain in the head **2** : an annoying or baffling situation or problem — **head·achy** \-,ā-kē\ *adj*

head·band \-,band\ *n* : a band worn on or around the head

head·board \-,bō(ə)rd, -,bȯ(ə)rd\ *n* : a board forming the head (as of a bed)

head cold *n* : a common cold centered in the nasal passages and nearby mucous tissues

head·dress \'hed-,dres\ *n* : a covering or ornament for the head

head·ed \'hed-əd\ *adj* : having such a head or so many heads ⟨curly-*headed*⟩ ⟨two-*headed* ax⟩

head·er \'hed-ər\ *n* : a fall or dive headfirst ⟨took a *header* downstairs⟩

head·first \'hed-'fərst\ *adv* : with the head foremost — **headfirst** *adj*

head·gear \-,gi(ə)r\ *n* **1** : a covering (as a hat or helmet) for the head **2** : harness for a horse's head

head·hunt·ing \-,hənt-iŋ\ *n* : the practice of cutting off and preserving the heads of enemies — **head·hunt·er** *n*

head·ing \'hed-iŋ\ *n* **1** : the direction in which a ship or aircraft points **2** : something (as a title or an address) at the top or beginning (as of a letter or chapter)

head·land \'hed-lənd, -,land\ *n* : a point of land sticking out into the sea : PROMONTORY

head·less \'hed-ləs\ *adj* **1** : having no head **2** : having no chief **3** : lacking good sense or prudence : FOOLISH — **head·less·ness** *n*

head·light \'hed-,līt\ *n* : a light on the front of a vehicle

¹**head·line** \-,līn\ *n* **1** : a line at the top of a page (as in a book) giving a heading **2** : the title over an item or article in a newspaper

²**headline** *vb* **1** : to provide with a headline **2** : to publicize highly

¹**head·long** \'hed-'lȯŋ\ *adv* **1** : HEADFIRST **2** : without careful thought : RECKLESSLY

²**headlong** *adj* **1** : lacking in calmness or restraint : RASH ⟨*headlong* flight⟩ **2** : plunging headfirst ⟨a *headlong* dive⟩

head louse *n* : a louse that lives on the human scalp

head·man \'hed-'man, -,man\ *n* : one who is a leader (as of a tribe, clan, or village) : CHIEF

head·mas·ter \-,mas-tər, -'mas-\ *n* : a male head of a private school

head·mis·tress \-,mis-trəs, -'mis-\ *n* : a female head of a private school

head-on \-'ȯn, -'än\ *adj* : having the head or front facing forward : front to front ⟨a *head-on* collision⟩

head over heels *adv* **1** : in or as if in a somersault ⟨fell *head over heels* down the hill⟩ **2** : very much : DEEPLY ⟨*head over heels* in love⟩

head·phone \'hed-,fōn\ *n* : an earphone held over the ear by a band worn on the head

head·piece \-,pēs\ *n* : a protective covering for the head

head·pin \-,pin\ *n* : a pin that stands at the front in a triangular arrangement of bowling pins

head·quar·ters \'hed-,kwȯ(r)t-ərz, (')hed-'kwȯ(r)t-ərz\ *n sing or pl* **1** : a place from which a commander exercises command **2** : the governing and directing center of an organization

head·rest \'hed-,rest\ *n* : a support for the head

head·set \-,set\ *n* : a pair of headphones

head·shrink·er \-,shriŋk-ər\ *n* : a doctor who practices psychiatry

heads·man \'hedz-mən\ *n* : one that beheads

head·stand \'hed-,stand\ *n* : the acrobatic feat of standing on one's head usually with support from the hands

head start *n* **1** : an advantage given to a contestant at the beginning of a race ⟨a five-minute *head start*⟩ **2** : a favorable or promising beginning

head·stone \-,stōn\ *n* : a memorial stone placed at the head of a grave

head·strong \-,strȯŋ\ *adj* **1** : not easily controlled : wanting one's own way ⟨a *headstrong* child⟩ **2** : directed by uncontrollable will ⟨violent *headstrong* actions⟩ **syn** see UNRULY

head·wait·er \-'wāt-ər\ *n* : the head of the dining-room staff of a restaurant or hotel

head·wa·ters \-,wȯt-ərz, -,wät-\ *n pl* : the beginning and upper part of a stream

head·way \-,wā\ *n* **1** : motion forward **2** : ¹PROGRESS 2

head wind *n* : a wind blowing in a direction opposite to a course especially of a ship or aircraft

head·work \'hed-,wərk\ *n* : mental work : clever thinking

heady \'hed-ē\ *adj* **head·i·er; -est** **1** : WILLFUL 1, RASH **2** : likely to make one dizzy ⟨*heady* wine⟩ ⟨a *heady* height⟩ — **head·i·ly** \'hed-ə-lē\ *adv* — **head·i·ness** \'hed-ē-nəs\ *n*

heal \'hē(ə)l\ *vb* : to make or become healthy or whole ⟨*heal* the sick⟩ ⟨a cut that *heals* slowly⟩

heal·er \'hē-lər\ *n* : one that heals

health \'helth\ *n* **1 a** : the condition of being sound in body, mind, or spirit; *esp* : freedom from disease **b** : the overall condition of the body ⟨in poor *health*⟩ **2** : flourishing condition **3** : a toast to someone's health or success ⟨drink a *health*⟩ [Old English *hælth* "health", from *hāl* "healthy" — related to ¹HALE]

health food *n* : a food that is said to be especially good for one's health

health·ful \'helth-fəl\ *adj* **1** : good for the health of the body or mind ⟨*healthful* exercise⟩ **2** : HEALTHY 1 — **health·ful·ly** \-fə-lē\ *adv* — **health·ful·ness** *n*

 syn HEALTHFUL, WHOLESOME mean good for the health of the body or mind. HEALTHFUL suggests a positive contribution to a healthy condition ⟨a *healthful* diet⟩ WHOLESOME applies to whatever benefits, builds up, or maintains one's physical, mental, or spiritual health ⟨*wholesome* foods⟩ ⟨*wholesome* family entertainment⟩

healthy \'hel-thē\ *adj* **health·i·er; -est** **1 a** : being in good health : WELL **b** : indicating good health ⟨*healthy* complexion⟩ **2** : HEALTHFUL 1 **3 a** : enjoying vigorous and rapid growth ⟨a *healthy* economy⟩ **b** : not small or feeble : CONSIDERABLE ⟨a *healthy* crowd in attendance⟩ — **health·i·ly** \-thə-lē\ *adv* — **health·i·ness** \-thē-nəs\ *n*

¹**heap** \'hēp\ *n* **1** : a collection of things thrown one on another : PILE ⟨a rubbish *heap*⟩ **2** : a great number or large quantity : LOT ⟨*heaps* of money⟩ ⟨a *heap* of fun⟩

²**heap** *vb* **1** : to throw or lay in a heap : AMASS, PILE ⟨*heap* up leaves⟩ **2** : to toss or give in large quantities ⟨*heaped*

headphone

scorn on our efforts⟩ **3** : to fill to capacity ⟨heaped the plate with food⟩

hear \'hi(ə)r\ vb **heard** \'hərd\; **hear·ing** \'hi(ə)r-iŋ\ **1** : to take in through the ear ⟨hear music⟩; also : to have the power of taking in sound ⟨doesn't hear well⟩ **2** : to gain knowledge of by hearing : LEARN ⟨heard you're leaving⟩ **3** : to listen to : HEED ⟨hear me out⟩ **4 a** : to give a legal hearing to ⟨hear a case⟩ **b** : to take testimony from ⟨hear witnesses⟩ **5 a** : to get news ⟨heard from them yesterday⟩ **b** : to have knowledge ⟨never heard of such a thing⟩ **6** : to consider the idea ⟨wouldn't hear of it⟩ — **hear·er** \'hir-ər\ n

hear·ing n **1 a** : the process or power of taking in sound : the sense by which a person hears **b** : the range within which the normal voice may be heard ⟨stay within hearing⟩ **2 a** : a chance to present one's case ⟨demanded a hearing⟩ **b** : a listening to arguments or testimony **c** : a session in which testimony is heard ⟨held public hearings on the bill⟩

hearing aid n : an electronic device usually worn by a partly deaf person to make sounds louder

hear·ken \'här-kən\ vb **hear·kened; hear·ken·ing** \'härk-(ə-)niŋ\ : LISTEN 1, ATTEND

hear·say \'hi(ə)r-,sā\ n **1** : something heard from another : RUMOR **2** : evidence based not on a witness's personal knowledge but on matters told him or her by another

hearse \'hərs\ n : a vehicle for conveying the dead to the grave

> **Word History** An early form of French used the word herce for a harrow, a farm tool used to break up and smooth the soil. Herce was also applied to a triangular frame that was similar in shape to the frame of a harrow and was used for holding candles. Herce was borrowed into English as hearse, and both the literal sense of "harrow" and the extended sense of "a frame for holding candles" were kept. In those days a large and decorative framework might be raised over the tomb or coffin of an honored person. Because this framework was often decorated with candles, the word hearse was applied to it. A series of slightly changed meanings led to the use of hearse for a platform for a corpse or coffin, and from that to a vehicle to carry the dead to the grave. [Middle English herse "a triangular frame for holding candles", from early French herce "frame for holding candles, harrow"]

heart \'härt\ n **1 a** : a hollow muscular organ of vertebrates that expands and contracts to move blood through the arteries, veins, and capillaries **b** : a structure in an invertebrate that serves a purpose like that of the heart of a vertebrate **2** : the central or most important part ⟨the heart of a forest⟩ ⟨the heart of the argument⟩ **3 a** : something

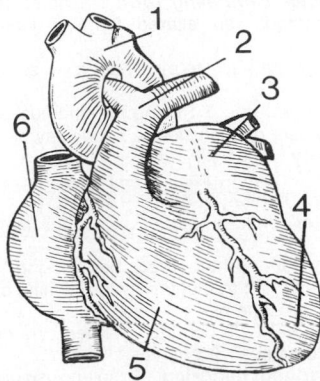

heart 1a: 1 aorta, 2 pulmonary artery, 3 left atrium, 4 left ventricle, 5 right ventricle, 6 right atrium

resembling a heart in shape **b** : a playing card marked with red simplified patterns of hearts **c** pl : a card game whose object is to avoid taking tricks with hearts **4 a** : human feelings : AFFECTION, KINDNESS ⟨a ruler without heart⟩ **b** : COURAGE, SPIRIT ⟨take heart⟩ **c** : ¹MOOD 1 ⟨a light heart⟩ **5** : MEMORY 1 ⟨learn by heart⟩ **6** : PERSON 1 ⟨dear heart⟩ ⟨a crew of stout hearts⟩ — **heart·ed** \-əd\ adj — **to heart** : with deep concern

heart·ache \'härt-,āk\ n : ¹SORROW 1a, ANGUISH

heart attack n : a sudden severe occurrence of heart disease caused by too little blood going to the heart muscle especially when due to the blocking of a coronary artery (as by a thrombus)

heart·beat \'härt-,bēt\ n : a single contracting and expanding of the heart

heart·break \-,brāk\ n : crushing grief, anguish, or distress — **heart·break·ing** \-,brā-kiŋ\ adj — **heart·break·ing·ly** adv — **heart·bro·ken** \-,brō-kən\ adj

heart·burn \-,bərn\ n : a burning discomfort seeming to occur in the area of the heart and usually related to spasms of the lower esophagus or the upper stomach

heart disease n : an abnormal condition of the heart or of the heart and circulation

heart·en \'härt-ᵊn\ vb **heart·ened; heart·en·ing** \'härt-niŋ, -ᵊn-iŋ\ : to cheer up : ENCOURAGE

heart·felt \'härt-,felt\ adj : deeply felt : EARNEST ⟨heartfelt thanks⟩

hearth \'härth\ n **1 a** : the area in front of a fireplace **b** : the floor of a fireplace **c** : the lowest section of a blast furnace **2** : ¹HOME 1a

hearth·stone \-,stōn\ n **1** : stone forming a hearth **2** : ¹HOME 1a

heart·i·ly \'härt-ᵊl-ē\ adv **1** : with sincerity, goodwill, or enthusiasm ⟨set to work heartily⟩ ⟨eat heartily⟩ **2** : in a cheerful manner ⟨make a guest heartily welcome⟩ **3** : in a complete or thorough manner ⟨heartily sick of their complaints⟩

heart·land \'härt-,land\ n : a central land area; esp : one of great economic and military importance

heart·less \'härt-ləs\ adj : PITILESS, CRUEL — **heart·less·ly** adv — **heart·less·ness** n

heart murmur n : MURMUR 3

heart·rend·ing \'härt-,ren-diŋ\ adj : causing heartbreak ⟨a heartrending tragedy⟩

heart·sick \-,sik\ adj : very sad and discouraged : DEPRESSED — **heart·sick·ness** n

heart·sore \-,sō(ə)r, -,sȯ(ə)r\ adj : HEARTSICK

heart·string \-,striŋ\ n : the deepest emotions or affections ⟨touched the heartstrings of the audience⟩

heart–to–heart \,härt-tə-,härt\ adj : FRANK, SINCERE ⟨a heart-to-heart talk⟩

heart·warm·ing \'härt-,wȯr-miŋ\ adj : making one feel good inside : cheering to one's emotions

heart·wood \-,wu̇d\ n : the older harder nonliving and usually darker wood of the central part of a tree trunk — compare SAPWOOD

¹hearty \'härt-ē\ adj **heart·i·er; -est 1 a** : WHOLEHEARTED, SINCERE ⟨hearty agreement⟩ **b** : enthusiastically friendly ⟨a hearty welcome⟩ **c** : UNRESTRAINED 2 ⟨hearty laughter⟩ **2 a** : exhibiting very good health ⟨hale and hearty⟩ **b** : having a good appetite ⟨a hearty eater⟩ **c** : being plentiful and satisfying ⟨a hearty meal⟩ **d** : NOURISHING ⟨hearty soup⟩ **3** : ENERGETIC, VIGOROUS ⟨gave a hearty pull⟩ — **heart·i·ness** n

²hearty n, pl **heart·ies** : COMRADE; also : SAILOR

¹heat \'hēt\ vb **1** : to make or become warm or hot **2** : to

\ə\ abut	\au̇\ out	\i\ tip	\ȯ\ saw	\u̇\ foot
\ər\ further	\ch\ chin	\ī\ life	\ȯi\ coin	\y\ yet
\a\ mat	\e\ pet	\j\ job	\th\ thin	\yü\ few
\ā\ take	\ē\ easy	\ŋ\ sing	\th\ this	\yu̇\ cure
\ä\ cot, cart	\g\ go	\ō\ bone	\ü\ food	\zh\ vision

make or become excited or angry

²heat n **1 a** : a condition of being hot : WARMTH **b** : a high degree of hotness **c** : a hot place or period ⟨the *heat* of the day⟩ **d** : a form of energy that causes substances to rise in temperature or to go through associated changes (as melting, evaporation, or expansion) **2 a** : strength of feeling; *esp* : ¹ANGER ⟨answered with some *heat*⟩ **b** : the height of an action or condition ⟨the *heat* of battle⟩ **c** : sexual excitement especially in a female mammal; *esp* : ESTRUS 1 **3** : a single race in a contest made up of two or more races — **heat·less** \'hēt-ləs\ *adj* — **heat·proof** \-'prüf\ *adj*

heat·ed \'hēt-əd\ *adj* **1** : HOT 1 ⟨a *heated* engine⟩ **2** : marked by excited or angry feelings ⟨a *heated* debate⟩ — **heat·ed·ly** *adv*

heat·er \'hēt-ər\ *n* : a device that heats or holds something to be heated

heat exchanger *n* : a device (as an automobile radiator) for transferring heat from one fluid to another without allowing them to mix

heat exhaustion *n* : a condition marked by weakness, nausea, dizziness, and much sweating that results from physical exertion in a hot environment — called also *heat prostration*

heath \'hēth\ *n* **1** : any of a family of shrubby often evergreen plants that grow well on open barren usually acid and poorly drained soil; *esp* : a low evergreen shrub with needlelike leaves and clusters of small flowers **2** : a usually level area of land overgrown with low shrubs — **heathy** \'hē-thē\ *adj*

hea·then \'hē-thən\ *n, pl* **heathens** *or* **heathen 1** : a person who does not know about and worship the God of the Bible : PAGAN **2** : an uncivilized person — **heathen** *adj* — **hea·then·dom** \-dəm\ *n* — **hea·then·ish** \-thə-nish\ *adj* — **hea·then·ism** \-,niz-əm\ *n*

heath·er \'heth-ər\ *n* : HEATH 1; *esp* : a common evergreen heath of northern and alpine regions with small stemless leaves and tiny usually purplish pink flowers — **heath·ery** \-(ə-)rē\ *adj*

heath hen *n* : an extinct grouse of the northeastern U.S. related to the prairie chicken

heat lightning *n* : flashes of lightning without thunder seen near the horizon

heat pump *n* : a device for heating or cooling a building by transferring heat contained in a fluid to or from the building

heat rash *n* : PRICKLY HEAT

heat shield *n* : a barrier of insulation to protect a space capsule from heat on its return to earth

heat·stroke \'hēt-,strōk\ *n* : a condition marked especially by the stopping of sweating, a high body temperature, and exhaustion that results from exposure to high temperature for a long time — compare SUNSTROKE

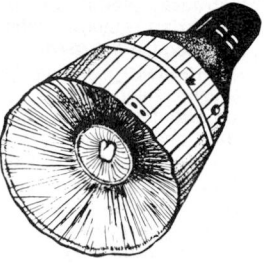

heat shield

heat wave *n* : a period of hot weather

¹heave \'hēv\ *vb* **heaved** *or* **hove** \'hōv\; **heav·ing 1** : to raise with effort ⟨*heave* a trunk onto a truck⟩ **2** : ¹THROW 1a, CAST, HURL ⟨*heave* a rock⟩ **3** : to utter with effort ⟨*heave* a sigh⟩ **4** : to rise and fall repeatedly ⟨the runner's chest was *heaving*⟩ **5** : to be thrown up or raised ⟨the ground *heaved* during the earthquake⟩ **6** : ²VOMIT 1 **syn** see RAISE — **heav·er** *n* — **heave to** : to bring a ship to a stop

²heave *n* **1 a** : an effort to heave or raise **b** : a forceful throw : CAST **2** : a rhythmic rising (as of the chest in breathing)

heav·en \'hev-ən\ *n* **1** : SKY 1 — usually used in pl. **2** *often cap* : the dwelling place of God and of the blessed dead **3** : a place or condition of complete happiness

heav·en·ly \'hev-ən-lē\ *adj* **1** : of or relating to heaven or the heavens ⟨*heavenly* bodies such as the stars⟩ **2** : ¹DIVINE 1a, SACRED, BLESSED ⟨*heavenly* grace⟩ **3** : completely delightful ⟨a *heavenly* day⟩ — **heav·en·li·ness** *n*

heav·en·ward \'hev-ən-wərd\ *adv or adj* : toward heaven

¹heavy \'hev-ē\ *adj* **heavi·er; -est 1 a** : having great weight or greater than usual weight **b** : weighty in proportion to bulk : having a high density ⟨gold is a *heavy* metal⟩ **c** : having or being atoms of greater than normal mass ⟨*heavy* isotopes⟩ **2** : very hard to deal with : GRIEVOUS ⟨a *heavy* sorrow⟩ **3 a** : of weighty importance : SERIOUS ⟨words *heavy* with meaning⟩ **b** : INTENSE 2 **4** : lacking life, gaiety, or charm : DULL **5** : DROWSY 1 **6** : greater in volume or force than the average ⟨*heavy* traffic⟩ ⟨*heavy* seas⟩ **7** : ²OVERCAST ⟨a *heavy* sky⟩ **8** : ¹THICK 3a ⟨a *heavy* growth of timber⟩ **9** : LABORIOUS 2, LABORED ⟨*heavy* breathing⟩ **10** : using or consuming much ⟨a *heavy* eater⟩ **11** : rich and not easily digested ⟨*heavy* desserts⟩ **12** : producing goods (as coal or steel) used in the production of other goods ⟨*heavy* industry⟩ **13** : heavily armed or armored ⟨*heavy* infantry⟩ — **heavi·ly** \'hev-ə-lē\ *adv* — **heavi·ness** \'hev-ē-nəs\ *n*

²heavy *adv* : in a heavy manner : HEAVILY ⟨time hung *heavy* on their hands⟩

³heavy *n, pl* **heav·ies 1** : HEAVYWEIGHT 2 **2 a** : a theatrical role or an actor representing a dignified or impressive person **b** : VILLAIN 2

heavy–du·ty \,hev-ē-'d(y)üt-ē\ *adj* : able or designed to take hard use or great strain ⟨*heavy-duty* vehicles⟩

heavy–hand·ed \,hev-ē-'han-dəd\ *adj* **1** : CLUMSY 1 **2** : severe or harsh in dealing with others

heavy hydrogen *n* : DEUTERIUM

heavy·set \,hev-ē-'set\ *adj* : STOCKY; *also* : ¹STOUT 4

heavy water *n* : water containing more than the usual amount of heavy isotopes; *esp* : water enriched in deuterium

heavy·weight \'hev-ē-,wāt\ *n* **1** : one above average in weight **2** : one in the heaviest class of contestants; *esp* : a boxer weighing usually more than 81 kilograms

He·brew \'hē-,brü\ *n* **1** : a member of one of a group of northern Semitic peoples including the Israelites; *esp* : ISRAELITE **2** : the Semitic language of the Hebrews — **He·bra·ic** \hi-'brā-ik\ *adj* — **Hebrew** *adj*

He·brews \'hē-,brüz\ *n* — see BIBLE table

heck·le \'hek-əl\ *vb* **heck·led; heck·ling** \-(ə-)liŋ\ : to interrupt with questions or comments usually with the intention of annoying or hindering ⟨were *heckling* the speaker⟩ — **heck·ler** \-(ə-)lər\ *n*

hect- *or* **hecto-** *combining form* : hundred [from French *hect-* "hundred", an altered form of Greek *hekaton* "hundred"]

hect·are \'hek-,ta(ə)r, -,te(ə)r, -,tär\ *n* — see METRIC SYSTEM table

hec·tic \'hek-tik\ *adj* **1** : being hot and flushed **2** : filled with excitement or confusion ⟨a *hectic* day of shopping⟩ — **hec·ti·cal·ly** \-ti-k(ə-)lē\ *adv*

hec·to·gram \'hek-tə-,gram\ *n* — see METRIC SYSTEM table

hec·to·li·ter \'hek-tə-,lēt-ər\ *n* — see METRIC SYSTEM table

hec·to·me·ter \'hek-tə-,mēt-ər\ *n* — see METRIC SYSTEM table

hec·tor \'hek-tər\ *vb* **hec·tored; hec·tor·ing** \-t(ə-)riŋ\ **1** : ¹SWAGGER 1 **2** : to frighten by threatening or bullying

he'd \(,)hēd, ēd\ : he had : he would

¹hedge \'hej\ *n* **1** : a boundary formed by a dense row of shrubs or low trees **2** : BARRIER 1, LIMIT

²hedge *vb* **hedged; hedg·ing 1** : to enclose or protect with or as if with a hedge **2** : to block with or as if with a barrier ⟨*hedged* in by restrictions⟩ **3** : to avoid giving a direct or exact answer or promise ⟨*hedged* when asked to

support the campaign⟩ — **hedg·er** *n*

hedge·hog \'hej-,hòg, -,häg\ *n* **1** : an Old World mammal that eats insects, has sharp spines mixed with the hair on its back, and is able to roll itself up into a spiny ball **2** : PORCUPINE

hedgehog 1

hedge·hop \-,häp\ *vb* : to fly an airplane so low that it is necessary to climb to avoid obstacles (as trees) — **hedge·hop·per** *n*

hedge·row \-,rō\ *n* : a row of shrubs or trees forming the boundary of or separating fields

¹heed \'hēd\ *vb* **1** : to pay attention **2** : to take notice of : MIND

²heed *n* : ATTENTION 1, NOTICE

heed·ful \'hēd-fəl\ *adj* : taking heed : CAREFUL — **heed·ful·ly** \-fə-lē\ *adv* — **heed·ful·ness** *n*

heed·less \'hēd-ləs\ *adj* : not taking heed : CARELESS — **heed·less·ly** *adv* — **heed·less·ness** *n*

¹heel \'hē(ə)l\ *n* **1 a** : the back part of the human foot behind the arch and below the ankle; *also* : the corresponding part of a lower vertebrate **b** : the part of the palm of the hand nearest the wrist **2** : a part (as of a shoe) that covers or supports the human heel **3** : a lower, back, or end part; *esp* : one of the crusty ends of a loaf of bread **4** : CAD [Old English *hēla* "back part of the foot"] — **heel·less** \'hē(ə)l-ləs\ *adj* — **on the heels of** : close behind

²heel *vb* : to provide with a heel — **heel·er** \'hē-lər\ *n*

³heel *vb* : to tilt to one side : LIST [Old English *hieldan* "to lean to one side"]

⁴heel *n* : a tilt to one side

¹heft \'heft\ *n* : ¹WEIGHT 1a, HEAVINESS

²heft *vb* **1** : to heave up : LIFT **2** : to test the weight of by lifting

hefty \'hef-tē\ *adj* **heft·i·er**; **-est** : ¹HEAVY 1a, BULKY — **heft·i·ly** \-tə-lē\ *adv* — **heft·i·ness** \-tē-nəs\ *n*

heif·er \'hef-ər\ *n* : a young cow; *esp* : one that has not had a calf

height \'hīt, 'hītth\ *n* **1 a** : the highest part or point : SUMMIT, CLIMAX **b** : the most advanced or extreme point ⟨the *height* of stupidity⟩ **2 a** : the distance from bottom to top **b** : the distance above a level **3** : the condition of being tall or high **4 a** : a landmass rising above the surrounding country **b** : a high point or position

> **syn** HEIGHT, ALTITUDE, ELEVATION mean distance upward. HEIGHT may be used in measuring something from bottom to top ⟨a wall that is three meters in *height*⟩ ALTITUDE is used in measuring the distance of an object above a fixed level ⟨a plane flying at a low *altitude*⟩ ELEVATION is used in measuring the height to which something is raised ⟨the *elevation* of the tower is 90 meters⟩ or vertical height on land especially above sea level ⟨Denver is situated at a high *elevation*⟩

height·en \'hīt-ᵊn\ *vb* **height·ened**; **height·en·ing** \'hīt-niŋ, -ᵊn-iŋ\ **1** : to make or become brighter or greater ⟨*heightened* the citizens' awareness⟩ **2** : to raise high or higher : ELEVATE

hei·nous \'hā-nəs\ *adj* : shockingly evil : ABOMINABLE — **hei·nous·ly** *adv* — **hei·nous·ness** *n*

heir \'a(ə)r, 'e(ə)r\ *n* **1** : a person who inherits or has the right to inherit property **2** : a person who has legal claim to a title or a throne when the person holding it dies — **heir·ship** \-,ship\ *n*

heir apparent *n, pl* **heirs apparent** : an heir whose right to succeed (as to a throne) cannot be taken away if he or she outlives the present holder

heir·ess \'ar-əs, 'er-\ *n* : a girl or woman who is an heir

heir·loom \'a(ə)r-,lüm, 'e(ə)r-\ *n* : a piece of personal property handed down from generation to generation

held *past of* HOLD

he·li·cop·ter \'hel-ə-,käp-tər, 'hē-lə-\ *n* : an aircraft that is supported in the air by propellers revolving on a vertical axis

he·lio·cen·tric \,hē-lē-ō-'sen-trik\ *adj* **1** : referred to or measured from the sun's center or appearing as if seen from it **2** : having or relating to the sun as a center

he·lio·trope \'hē-lē-ə-,trōp, 'hel-yə-\ *n* : any of a genus of herbs or shrubs having small white or purple flowers

he·li·ot·ro·pism \,hē-lē-'ä-trə-,piz-əm\ *n* : a turning or curving (as of a sunflower head) toward the sunlight

he·li·port \'hel-ə-,pō(ə)rt, 'hē-lə-, -,pò(ə)rt\ *n* : a landing and takeoff place for a helicopter

he·li·um \'hē-lē-əm\ *n* : a light colorless nonflammable element that is found in various natural gases and is used especially to blow up balloons — see ELEMENT table

he·lix \'hē-liks\ *n, pl* **he·li·ces** \'hel-ə-,sēz, 'hē-lə-\ *also* **he·lix·es** \'hē-lik-səz\ : a curve in space traced by a point rotating around an axis and moving forward in a direction parallel to the axis — compare DOUBLE HELIX — **he·li·cal** \'hel-i-kəl, 'hē-li-\ *adj*

heliotrope

hell \'hel\ *n* **1** : a place where souls are believed to survive after death **2** : the place or state of punishment for the wicked after death : the home of evil spirits **3** : a place or condition of misery or wickedness **4** : a place or state of great confusion, disorder, or destruction : HAVOC, PANDEMONIUM **5** : something that causes torment; *esp* : a severe scolding

he'll \(,)hē(ə)l, hil, əl, il\ : he shall : he will

hell·ben·der \'hel-,ben-dər\ *n* : a large water-dwelling salamander of the Ohio valley

hell–bent \-,bent\ *adj* : stubbornly and often recklessly determined ⟨*hell-bent* on revenge⟩

hel·le·bore \'hel-ə-,bō(ə)r, -,bò(ə)r\ *n* **1** : any of a genus of herbs related to the buttercup and having white, greenish, or purplish flowers; *also* : its dried root formerly used in medicine **2** : a poisonous herb related to the lily; *also* : its dried root or a product of this containing chemical substances used in medicine and insecticides

Hel·lene \'hel-,ēn\ *n* : GREEK 1 — **Hel·len·ic** \he-'len-ik, hə-\ *adj*

Hel·le·nis·tic \,hel-ə-'nis-tik\ *adj* : of or relating to the widespread Greek-based culture that developed after the conquests of Alexander the Great

hell·gram·mite \'hel-grə-,mīt\ *n* : the flesh-eating larva of a dobsonfly that lives in water and is much used as fish bait

hell·ion \'hel-yən\ *n* : a troublesome or mischievous person

hell·ish \'hel-ish\ *adj* : of, resembling, or suitable to hell : INFERNAL — **hell·ish·ly** *adv* — **hell·ish·ness** *n*

hel·lo \hə-'lō, he-\ *n, pl* **hellos** : an expression or gesture of greeting — used in greeting, in answering the telephone, or to express surprise

¹helm \'helm\ *n* : HELMET 1

²helm *n* **1** : a lever or wheel controlling the rudder of a ship; *also* : the steering equipment of a ship **2** : a position of control : HEAD

\ə\ abut	\au̇\ **out**	\i\ tip	\o̊\ **saw**	\u̇\ **foot**
\ər\ **further**	\ch\ **chin**	\ī\ life	\o̊i\ **coin**	\y\ **yet**
\a\ **mat**	\e\ **pet**	\j\ job	\th\ **thin**	\yü\ **few**
\ā\ **take**	\ē\ **easy**	\ŋ\ **sing**	\th\ **this**	\yu̇\ **cure**
\ä\ **cot, cart**	\g\ **go**	\ō\ **bone**	\ü\ **food**	\zh\ **vision**

hel·met \'hel-mət\ *n* **1** : a covering or enclosing headpiece of armor **2** : any of various protective head coverings usually made of a hard material — **hel·met·like** \-ˌlīk\ *adj*

helms·man \'helmz-mən\ *n* : the person at the helm

hel·ot \'hel-ət\ *n* : SERF, SLAVE

¹help \'help\ *vb* **1** : to provide with what is useful in achieving an end : AID, ASSIST ⟨*helped* me get a job⟩ **2** : ²REMEDY, RELIEVE ⟨rest *helps* a cold⟩ **3 a** : to keep from ⟨couldn't *help* laughing⟩ **b** : PREVENT 1 ⟨it couldn't be *helped*⟩ **4** : to serve with food or drink ⟨*help* yourself⟩

²help *n* **1** : an act or instance of helping : AID, ASSISTANCE ⟨give *help*⟩ ⟨thanked us for our *help*⟩ **2** : the state of being helped : RELIEF ⟨a situation beyond *help*⟩ **3** : a person or a thing that helps ⟨a *help* in time of trouble⟩ **4** : a hired helper or a body of hired helpers ⟨hire additional *help*⟩

help·er \'hel-pər\ *n* : one that helps; *esp* : a person who helps a more skilled person

helper T cell *n* : a T cell that plays an important part in producing a normal immune response and that is greatly reduced in numbers in AIDS — called also *helper cell*

help·ful \'help-fəl\ *adj* : providing help ⟨a *helpful* neighbor⟩ — **help·ful·ly** \-fə-lē\ *adv* — **help·ful·ness** *n*

help·ing \'hel-piŋ\ *n* : a portion of food : SERVING

helping verb *n* : a verb (as *have, be, may, do, shall, will, can, must*) that is used with another verb and expresses such things as person, number, mood, or tense — called also *auxiliary verb*

help·less \'hel-pləs\ *adj* **1** : being without defense **2** : POWERLESS — **help·less·ly** *adv* — **help·less·ness** *n*

help·mate \'help-ˌmāt\ *n* : one that is a companion and helper; *esp* : WIFE 2

help·meet \-ˌmēt\ *n* : HELPMATE

hel·ter–skel·ter \ˌhel-tər-'skel-tər\ *adv* **1** : in a confused and reckless manner : PELL-MELL ⟨ran *helter-skelter* down the hill⟩ **2** : in no particular order : HAPHAZARDLY ⟨clothes strewn *helter-skelter* about the room⟩ — **helter–skelter** *adj*

¹hem \'hem\ *n* : a border of a garment or cloth; *esp* : one made by folding back an edge and sewing it down [Old English *hem* "border on a garment"]

²hem *vb* **hemmed**; **hem·ming** **1** : to finish with or make a hem in sewing **2** : to surround in a confining manner ⟨a town *hemmed* in by mountains⟩ — **hem·mer** *n*

³hem *vb* **hemmed**; **hem·ming** **1** : to make a sound during a pause in speaking which is usually written as *hem* **2** : to hesitate in speaking

⁴hem *a throat-clearing sound; often read as* 'hem\ *interj* — often used to indicate a pause in speaking [an imitation of the throat-clearing sound]

hem- *or* **hemo-** *combining form* : blood [derived from Greek *haima* "blood"]

he–man \'hē-'man\ *n* : a strong active man

he·ma·tite \'hē-mə-ˌtīt\ *n* : a mineral that consists of an oxide of iron, is an important iron ore, and is found in crystals or in a red earthy form

he·ma·tol·o·gist \ˌhē-mə-'täl-ə-jəst\ *n* : a person who specializes in the study of blood and the blood-forming organs

he·ma·tox·y·lin \ˌhē-mə-'täk-sə-lən\ *n* : a compound found in the wood of a tropical American tree and used chiefly as a biological stain

heme \'hēm\ *n* : a deep red pigment that contains iron and is obtained from hemoglobin

hemi- *prefix* : half [derived from Greek *hēmi-* "half"]

he·mip·ter·an \hi-'mip-tə-rən\ *n* : any of a large order of insects including the true bugs (as the bedbug and chinch bug) and related forms (as plant lice) and having flattened bodies, two pairs of wings, and heads with piercing and sucking organs

hemi·sphere \'hem-ə-ˌsfi(ə)r\ *n* **1** : one of the halves of the earth as divided by the equator or by a meridian **2** : one of two halves of a sphere **3** : CEREBRAL HEMISPHERE

hemi·spher·ic \ˌhem-ə-'sfi(ə)r-ik, -'sfer-\ *or* **hemi·spher·i·cal** \-'sfir-i-kəl, -'sfer-\ *adj* : of or relating to a hemisphere

hem·line \'hem-ˌlīn\ *n* : the line formed by the hem of a dress, skirt, or coat

hem·lock \'hem-ˌläk\ *n* **1** : any of several poisonous herbs related to the carrot and having finely divided leaves and small white flowers **2** : any of a genus of evergreen trees related to the pine; *also* : the soft light splintery wood of a hemlock

hemo- — see HEM-

he·mo·glo·bin \'hē-mə-ˌglō-bən\ *n* : a protein that contains iron, is the chief means of transporting oxygen in the body of vertebrate animals, occurs in the red blood cells, and is able to combine loosely with oxygen in regions (as the lungs) where it is in high concentration and release it in regions (as the tissues of the internal organs) where it is in low concentration

he·mo·phil·ia \ˌhē-mə-'fil-ē-ə\ *n* : an inherited blood defect that is sex-linked, is found almost always in males, and is marked by delayed clotting of blood and a resulting difficulty in stopping bleeding

he·mo·phil·i·ac \ˌhē-mə-'fil-ē-ˌak\ *n* : a person who has hemophilia

¹hem·or·rhage \'hem-(ə-)rij\ *n* : a great loss of blood from the blood vessels especially when caused by injury — **hem·or·rhag·ic** \ˌhem-ə-'raj-ik\ *adj*

²hemorrhage *vb* **-rhaged**; **-rhag·ing** : to bleed heavily or uncontrollably

hem·or·rhoid \'hem-(ə-)ˌroid\ *n* **1** : a swollen mass of veins located at or just within the anus **2** *pl* : the condition of a person who has hemorrhoids — called also *piles*

hemp \'hemp\ *n* **1** : a tall Asian herb related to the mulberry and widely grown for its tough woody fiber that is used to make rope and for its flowers and leaves from which are obtained various drugs (as hashish and marijuana) that affect the mind or behavior **2** : the fiber of hemp

hemp·en \'hem-pən\ *adj* : of, relating to, or resembling hemp

hemp 1

¹hem·stitch \'hem-ˌstich\ *vb* : to embroider fabric by drawing out parallel threads and stitching the exposed threads in groups to form designs — **hem·stitch·er** *n*

²hemstitch *n* **1** : decorative needlework **2** : a stitch used in hemstitching

hen \'hen\ *n* **1** : a female domestic chicken especially over a year old **2** : a female of any bird

hence \'hen(t)s\ *adv* **1** : from this place or time ⟨a week *hence*⟩ **2** : CONSEQUENTLY, THEREFORE ⟨was a newcomer and *hence* had no close friends in the city⟩

hence·forth \'hen(t)s-ˌfō(ə)rth, -ˌfo(ə)rth; hen(t)s-'fō(ə)rth, -'fo(ə)rth\ *adv* : from this point on

hence·for·ward \hen(t)s-'for-wərd\ *adv* : HENCEFORTH

hench·man \'hench-mən\ *n* : a trusted follower or supporter

hen·e·quen \'hen-i-kən, ˌhen-i-'ken\ *n* : a strong hard fiber obtained from the leaves of a tropical American agave and used to make twine; *also* : a plant that produces henequen

hen·house \'hen-ˌhaůs\ *n* : a house or shelter for fowl and especially for domestic chickens

¹hen·na \'hen-ə\ *n* : a reddish brown dye obtained from the leaves of an Old World tropical shrub and used especially on hair

²henna *vb* **hen·naed** \'hen-əd\; **hen·na·ing** : to dye or tint with henna

hen party *n* : a party for women only

hen·peck \'hen-,pek\ *vb* : to nag and boss one's husband

he·pat·ic \hi-'pat-ik\ *adj* : of, relating to, or resembling the liver

he·pat·i·ca \hi-'pat-i-kə\ *n* : any of a genus of herbs related to the buttercup and having leaves with three lobes and delicate white, pink, or bluish flowers

hep·a·ti·tis \,hep-ə-'tīt-əs\ *n, pl* **-tit·i·des** \-'tit-ə-,dēz\ : inflammation of the liver; *also* : a virus disease marked by hepatitis, jaundice, and fever

hep·ta·gon \'hep-tə-,gän\ *n* : a polygon of seven angles and seven sides — **hep·tag·o·nal** \hep-'tag-ən-ᵊl\ *adj*

heptagon

¹**her** \(h)ər, ,hər\ *adj* : of, relating to, or belonging to her or herself ⟨*her* house⟩ ⟨*her* success⟩

²**her** \ər, (')hər\ *pron,* objective case of SHE

¹**her·ald** \'her-əld\ *n* **1** : an official announcer or messenger **2** : an officer responsible for granting and registering coats of arms **3** : HARBINGER

²**herald** *vb* **1** : to give notice of : ANNOUNCE **2** : to greet with enthusiasm : HAIL

he·ral·dic \he-'ral-dik, hə-\ *adj* : of or relating to heralds or heraldry — **he·ral·di·cal·ly** \-di-k(ə-)lē\ *adv*

her·ald·ry \'her-əl-drē\ *n, pl* **-ries** **1** : the science of tracing a person's family and finding out the family's coat of arms **2** : COAT OF ARMS

herb \'ərb *also* 'hərb\ *n* **1** : a seed plant that does not develop long-lived woody tissue but dies down at the end of a growing season **2** : a plant or plant part used for making medicine and seasonings

her·ba·ceous \,(h)ər-'bā-shəs\ *adj* **1** : of, relating to, or resembling an herb **2** : being a stem with little or no woody tissue and lasting usually only for a single growing season

herb·age \'(h)ər-bij\ *n* **1** : vegetation (as grass) composed of herbs especially when used for grazing **2** : the juicy parts of herbs or plants that resemble herbs

herb·al \'(h)ər-bəl\ *adj* : of, relating to, or made of herbs

her·bar·i·um \,(h)ər-'bar-ē-əm, -'ber-\ *n, pl* **-ia** \-ē-ə\ **1** : a collection of dried plant specimens **2** : a place that houses an herbarium

her·bi·cide \'(h)ər-bə-,sīd\ *n* : a chemical substance used to destroy or stop plant growth — **her·bi·cid·al** \,(h)ər-bə-'sīd-ᵊl\ *adj*

her·bi·vore \'(h)ər-bə-,vō(ə)r, -,vȯ(ə)r\ *n* : a plant-eating animal; *esp* : ²UNGULATE

her·biv·o·rous \,(h)ər-'biv-ə-rəs\ *adj* : eating or living on plants

her·cu·le·an \,hər-kyə-'lē-ən, ,hər-'kyü-lē-\ *adj* **1** *cap* : of, relating to, or characteristic of Hercules **2** : of great power, size, or difficulty ⟨a *herculean* task⟩

¹**herd** \'hərd\ *n* **1** : a number of animals of one kind kept or living together **2** : the common people

²**herd** *vb* **1** : to assemble or come together into a herd or group **2** : to gather, lead, or drive a herd ⟨*herd* cattle⟩ — **herd·er** *n*

herds·man \'hərdz-mən\ *n* : a manager, breeder, or tender of livestock

¹**here** \'hi(ə)r\ *adv* **1** : in or at this place ⟨turn *here*⟩ **2** : at this point ⟨*here* we agree⟩ **3** : to or into this place ⟨come *here*⟩

²**here** *n* : this place ⟨get away from *here*⟩

here·abouts \'hi(ə)r-ə-,bauts\ *or* **here·about** \-,baut\ *adv* : near or around this place : in this vicinity

¹**here·af·ter** \hi(ə)r-'af-tər\ *adv* **1** : after this **2** : in some future time or state

²**hereafter** *n* **1** : ²FUTURE 1a **2** : life after death ⟨belief in the *hereafter*⟩

here and there *adv* : in one place and another

here·by \hi(ə)r-'bī, 'hi(ə)r-,bī\ *adv* : by means of this

he·red·i·tary \hə-'red-ə-,ter-ē\ *adj* **1** : genetically passed or capable of being passed from parent to offspring ⟨*hereditary* traits⟩ **2 a** : received or passing by inheritance ⟨*hereditary* rank⟩ **b** : having title or possession through inheritance ⟨*hereditary* ruler⟩ **3** : of or relating to inheritance or heredity

he·red·i·ty \hə-'red-ət-ē\ *n, pl* **-ties** **1** : the genes and the genetic traits whose expression they control that are passed on from one's parents **2** : the passing on of genes and genetic traits from parent to offspring

Her·e·ford \'hər-fərd\ *n* : any of an English breed of hardy red white-faced cattle widely raised in the western U.S. for beef

here·in \hi(ə)r-'in\ *adv* : in this

here·of \-'əv, -'äv\ *adv* : of this

here·on \-'ȯn, -'än\ *adv* : on this

her·e·sy \'her-ə-sē\ *n, pl* **-sies** **1** : religious opinion that is opposed to the doctrines of a church **2** : opinion that is opposed to a generally accepted belief

her·e·tic \'her-ə-,tik\ *n* : a person who believes or teaches something opposed to accepted beliefs

he·ret·i·cal \hə-'ret-i-kəl\ *adj* : of, relating to, or characterized by heresy : UNORTHODOX — **he·ret·i·cal·ly** \-i-k(ə-)lē\ *adv*

here·to·fore \'hi(ə)rt-ə-,fō(ə)r, -,fȯ(ə)r; ,hirt-ə-'fō(ə)r, -'fȯ(ə)r\ *adv* : up to this time

here·un·to \hi(ə)r-'ən-tü\ *adv* : to this; *esp* : to this document

here·up·on \'hi(ə)r-ə-,pȯn, -,pän; ,hir-ə-'pȯn, -'pän\ *adv* : on this : immediately after this

here·with \hi(ə)r-'with, -'with\ *adv* : with this : enclosed in this

her·i·ta·ble \'her-ət-ə-bəl\ *adj* : HEREDITARY 1 ⟨*heritable* differences in structure⟩

her·i·tage \'her-ət-ij\ *n* **1** : property that is handed down to an heir **2** : something acquired from the past ⟨a rich *heritage* of folklore⟩

her·maph·ro·dite \(,)hər-'maf-rə-,dīt\ *n* : a hermaphroditic plant or animal

her·maph·ro·dit·ic \(,)hər-,maf-rə-'dit-ik\ *adj* : having both male and female reproductive organs — **her·maph·ro·dit·ism** \-'maf-rə-,dit-,iz-əm\ *n*

her·met·ic \(,)hər-'met-ik\ *adj* : AIRTIGHT 1 — **her·met·i·cal·ly** \-i-k(ə-)lē\ *adv*

her·mit \'hər-mət\ *n* **1** : one that lives apart from others especially for religious reasons : RECLUSE **2** : a spiced molasses cookie

her·mit·age \'hər-mət-ij\ *n* : a hermit's home; *also* : a residence screened or hidden from view : RETREAT

hermit crab *n* : any of various crabs having soft abdomens and occupying empty mollusk shells

her·nia \'hər-nē-ə\ *n, pl* **her·ni·as** *or* **her·ni·ae** \-nē-,ē, -nē-,ī\ : a sticking out of an organ or part through connective tissue or through a wall of the cavity in which it is normally enclosed — called also *rupture*

he·ro \'hē-rō, 'hi(ə)r-ō\ *n, pl* **heroes** **1 a** : a mythological or legendary figure of great strength or ability **b** : an outstanding warrior or soldier **c** : a person admired for achievements and qualities **d** : one that shows great courage ⟨the *hero* of a rescue⟩ **2** : the chief male figure in a literary work or in an event or period **3** *pl* **heros** : ²SUBMARINE 2

\ə\ abut	\au̇\ out	\i\ tip	\ȯ\ saw	\u̇\ foot
\ər\ further	\ch\ chin	\ī\ life	\ȯi\ coin	\y\ yet
\a\ mat	\e\ pet	\j\ job	\th\ thin	\yü\ few
\ā\ take	\ē\ easy	\ŋ\ sing	\th\ this	\yu̇\ cure
\ä\ cot, cart	\g\ go	\ō\ bone	\ü\ food	\zh\ vision

he·ro·ic \hi-'rō-ik *also* her-'ō- *or* hē-'rō-\ *adj* **1** : of or relating to heroes especially of ancient times ⟨the *heroic* age⟩ ⟨*heroic* legends⟩ **2** : COURAGEOUS, DARING ⟨a *heroic* rescue⟩ **3** : large or impressive in size or range : GRAND — **he·ro·i·cal·ly** \-i-k(ə-)lē\ *adv*

he·ro·ics \hi-'rō-iks *also* her-'ō- *or* hē-'rō-\ *n pl* : exaggerated display of heroic attitudes in action or expression

her·o·in \'her-ə-wən\ *n* : a strongly addictive drug made from the opium poppy and stronger than morphine

her·o·ine \'her-ə-wən\ *n* **1** : a woman of courage and daring **2** : a woman admired for her achievements and qualities **3** : the chief female figure in a literary work or in an event or period

her·o·ism \'her-ə-,wiz-əm *also* 'hir-\ *n* : heroic conduct or qualities **syn** see COURAGE

her·on \'her-ən\ *n, pl* **herons** *also* **heron** : any of various wading birds with a long neck, a long thin bill, large wings, and a soft covering of feathers

her·pes \'hər-(,)pēz\ *n* : any of several virus diseases (as herpes simplex) marked by the formation of blisters on the skin or mucous membranes and caused by herpesviruses — compare COLD SORE

heron

her·pes gen·i·tal·is \'hər-(,)pēz-,jen-ə-'tal-əs\ *n* : the form of herpes simplex marked by the formation of watery blisters on the skin and mucous membranes of the sex organs

herpes sim·plex \-'sim-,pleks\ *n* : either of two kinds of herpes marked in one case by groups of watery blisters on the skin and mucous membranes (as of the mouth and lips) above the waist and in the other by such blisters on the sex organs

her·pes·vi·rus \,hər-(,)pēz-'vī-rəs\ *n* : any of a group of viruses that contain DNA, reproduce in cell nuclei, and cause herpes

her·pe·tol·o·gist \,hər-pə-'täl-ə-jəst\ *n* : a person who specializes in herpetology

her·pe·tol·o·gy \,hər-pə-'täl-ə-jē\ *n* : a branch of zoology dealing with reptiles and amphibians

her·ring \'her-iŋ\ *n, pl* **herring** *or* **herrings** : a valuable food fish that is very common in the north Atlantic ocean; *also* : any of various fishes like this one or related to it

her·ring·bone \'her-iŋ-,bōn\ *n* **1** : a pattern of rows of parallel lines with every other row slanting in the opposite direction **2** : a fabric with a herringbone pattern

herring gull *n* : a common large gull of the northern hemisphere that as an adult is largely white and gray with dark wing tips

hers \'hərz\ *pron* : her one : her ones ⟨the book is *hers*⟩

her·self \(h)ər-'self\ *pron* **1** : that identical female one — used for emphasis or to show that the subject and object of the verb are the same ⟨she considers *herself* lucky⟩ ⟨she *herself* did it⟩ **2** : her normal, healthy, or sane self ⟨was *herself* again after a good night's sleep⟩

hertz \'he(ə)rts, 'hərts\ *n* : a unit of frequency equal to one cycle per second — abbr. *Hz*

he's \(,)hēz, ēz\ : he is : he has

hes·i·tance \'hez-ə-tən(t)s\ *n* : HESITANCY

hes·i·tan·cy \'hez-ə-tən-sē\ *n, pl* **-cies** **1** : a tendency to hesitate **2** : an act or instance of hesitating

hes·i·tant \'hez-ə-tənt\ *adj* : feeling or showing hesitation — **hes·i·tant·ly** *adv*

hes·i·tate \'hez-ə-,tāt\ *vb* **-tat·ed; -tat·ing** **1** : to stop or pause because of forgetfulness, uncertainty, or indecision ⟨*hesitate* before answering⟩ **2** : to be unwilling ⟨*hesitate* to ask a favor⟩ **3** : ¹STAMMER — **hes·i·tat·er** *n* — **hes·i·tat·ing·ly** \-,tāt-iŋ-lē\ *adv* — **hes·i·ta·tion** \,hez-ə-'tā-shən\ *n*

Hes·sian \'hesh-ən\ *n* : a German soldier serving in the British forces during the American Revolution [from *Hesse*, a region in Germany]

Hessian fly *n* : a small two-winged fly destructive to wheat in America

heter- *or* **hetero-** *combining form* : other : different ⟨*hetero*sexual⟩ [derived from Greek *heteros* "different, other"]

het·ero·dox \'het-ə-rə-,däks\ *adj* **1** : opposed to established opinions, beliefs, or standards; *esp* : UNORTHODOX **2** : holding or expressing unaccepted beliefs or opinions

het·ero·doxy \'het-ə-rə-,däk-sē\ *n, pl* **-dox·ies** **1** : the quality or state of being heterodox **2** : a heterodox opinion or belief

het·er·o·ge·neous \,het-ə-rə-'jē-nē-əs, -nyəs\ *adj* : differing in kind : consisting of dissimilar parts : MIXED ⟨a *heterogeneous* population⟩ — **het·er·o·ge·neous·ly** *adv* — **het·er·o·ge·neous·ness** *n*

¹het·ero·sex·u·al \,het-ə-rō-'seksh-(ə-)wəl, -'sek-shəl\ *adj* : of, relating to, or marked by sexual interest in members of the opposite sex — **het·ero·sex·u·al·i·ty** \-,sek-shə-'wal-ət-ē\ *n*

²heterosexual *n* : a heterosexual individual

het·ero·troph \'het-ə-rə-,trōf, -,träf\ *n* : a heterotrophic organism

het·ero·tro·phic \,het-ə-rə-'trōf-ik\ *adj* : unable to live and grow without complex organic compounds of nitrogen and carbon

het·ero·zy·gos·i·ty \,het-ə-rō-(,)zī-'gäs-ət-ē\ *n* : the state of being heterozygous

het·ero·zy·gote \,het-ə-rō-'zī-,gōt\ *n* : a heterozygous individual

het·ero·zy·gous \,het-ə-rō-'zī-,gəs\ *adj* : having the two genes at a given place on a pair of chromosomes different for one or more places

het up \'het-'əp\ *adj* : highly excited : UPSET

hew \'hyü\ *vb* **hewed; hewed** *or* **hewn** \'hyün\; **hew·ing** **1** : to chop down ⟨*hew* trees⟩ **2** : to make or shape by cutting with an ax ⟨a cabin built of rough-*hewn* logs⟩ **3** : to stick close to : ADHERE ⟨*hew* to the established rules⟩ — **hew·er** *n*

¹hex \'heks\ *vb* **1** : to put a hex on **2** : to affect as if by an evil spell : JINX — **hex·er** *n*

²hex *n* **1** : ¹SPELL 1b, JINX **2** : WITCH 1

³hex *n* : a hexadecimal number system

hexa- *or* **hex-** *combining form* : six [derived from Greek *hex* "six"]

hexa·dec·i·mal \,hek-sə-'des-(ə-)məl\ *adj* : of, relating to, or being a number system with a base of 16 ⟨*hexadecimal* numbers⟩ ⟨*hexadecimal* notation⟩ — **hexadecimal** *n*

hexa·gon \'hek-sə-,gän\ *n* : a polygon of six angles and six sides

hex·ag·o·nal \hek-'sag-ən-ᵊl\ *adj* **1** : having six angles and six sides **2** : having a hexagon for a base or for a section made by a plane ⟨a *hexagonal* prism⟩

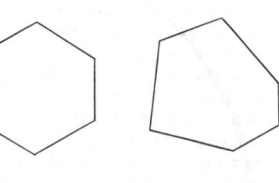
hexagon

hex·am·e·ter \hek-'sam-ət-ər\ *n* : a line of verse consisting of six metrical feet

hex·ose \'hek-,sōs\ *n* : a sugar containing six carbon atoms in a molecule

hey \'hā\ *interj* — used especially to call attention or to express surprise or joy

hey·day \'hā-,dā\ *n* : the time of greatest strength or vigor

hi \'hī(-ē)\ *interj* — used especially as a greeting

hi·a·tus \hī-'āt-əs\ *n, pl* **-tus·es** : a gap in space or time; *esp* : a break where a part is missing

hi·ba·chi \hi-'bäch-ē\ *n* : a charcoal grill

hi·ber·nate \'hī-bər-ˌnāt\ *vb* **-nat·ed; -nat·ing** : to pass the winter in a sleeping or resting state — **hi·ber·na·tion** \ˌhī-bər-'nā-shən\ *n* — **hi·ber·na·tor** \'hī-bər-ˌnāt-ər\ *n*

hi·bis·cus \hī-'bis-kəs, hə-\ *n, pl* **-cus·es** : any of a large genus of herbs, shrubs, or small trees related to the mallow and having toothed leaves and large showy flowers

¹hic·cup *also* **hic·cough** \'hik-(ˌ)əp\ *n* : a sudden drawing in of breath that is followed and stopped by sudden closure of the glottis and accompanied by a gulping sound

²hiccup *also* **hiccough** *vb* **hic·cuped** *also* **hic·cupped; hic·cup·ing** *also* **hic·cup·ping** : to make a hiccup or be affected with hiccups

hick \'hik\ *n* : an awkward or simple person especially from a small town or the country

hick·o·ry \'hik-(ə-)rē\ *n, pl* **-ries** 1 : any of a genus of North American hardwood trees related to the walnut and having an edible nut with a hard shell 2 : the usually tough pale wood of a hickory

hi·dal·go \hid-'al-gō, ē-'thäl-\ *n, pl* **-gos** : a member of the lower nobility of Spain [Spanish contraction of earlier *hijo de algo, fijo de algo* "a person born into wealth", literally "son of something"]

¹hide \'hīd\ *vb* **hid** \'hid\; **hid·den** \'hid-ᵊn\ *or* **hid; hid·ing** \'hīd-iŋ\ 1 : to put or get out of sight : CONCEAL ⟨*hide* a treasure⟩ ⟨*hid* in a closet⟩ 2 : to keep secret ⟨*hide* one's grief⟩ 3 : to screen from view ⟨a house *hidden* by trees⟩ ⟨clouds *hid* the sun⟩ 4 : to seek protection or avoid responsibility [Old English *hȳdan* "to get out of sight"] — **hid·er** \'hīd-ər\ *n*

²hide *n* : the skin of an animal whether raw or dressed [Old English *hȳd* "skin of an animal"]

³hide *vb* **hid·ed; hid·ing** : to give a beating to

hide–go–seek \ˌhīd-ᵊn-ˌgō-'sēk\ *n* : HIDE-AND-SEEK

hide–and–seek \ˌhīd-ᵊn-'sēk\ *n* : a children's game in which everyone hides from one player who tries to find them

hide·away \'hīd-ə-ˌwā\ *n* : ¹RETREAT 2, HIDEOUT

hide·bound \-ˌbaȯnd\ *adj* 1 : having a dry skin adhering closely to the underlying flesh ⟨a *hidebound* horse⟩ 2 : stubbornly unwilling to change

hid·eous \'hid-ē-əs\ *adj* : horribly ugly or disgusting : FRIGHTFUL — **hid·eous·ly** *adv* — **hid·eous·ness** *n*

hide·out \'hī-ˌdaȯt\ *n* : a secret place for hiding (as from the police)

¹hid·ing \'hīd-iŋ\ *n* : a state or place of concealment

²hiding *n* : a severe beating or whipping

hie \'hī\ *vb* **hied; hy·ing** *or* **hie·ing** : ¹HURRY 1, HASTEN

hi·er·ar·chi·cal \ˌhī-(ə-)'rär-ki-kəl\ *or* **hi·er·ar·chic** \-kik\ *adj* : of, relating to, or arranged in a hierarchy — **hi·er·ar·chi·cal·ly** \-'rär-ki-k(ə-)lē\ *adv*

hi·er·ar·chy \'hī-(ə-)ˌrär-kē\ *n, pl* **-chies** 1 : a ruling body especially of clergy organized into ranks 2 a : an arrangement into a series according to rank b : persons or things arranged in ranks or classes

hi·ero·glyph \'hī-(ə-)rə-ˌglif\ *n* : a character used in hieroglyphic writing

hi·ero·glyph·ic \ˌhī-(ə-)rə-'glif-ik\ *n* 1 : HIEROGLYPH 2 : a system of writing mainly in pictorial characters; *esp* : the picture script of the ancient Egyptian priesthood 3 : unclear or unreadable signs or writing [derived from early French *hiéroglyphique* (adjective) "relating to or being

hieroglyphic 2

writing that consists of pictures or symbols rather than words", derived from Greek *hieroglyphikos* (same meaning), from *hieros* "sacred, holy" and *glyphikos* "of carving"; so called because it referred to the system of carvings used on ancient Egyptian temples] — **hieroglyphic** *adj*

hi–fi \'hī-'fī\ *n* 1 : HIGH FIDELITY 2 : equipment for reproduction of sound with high fidelity

hig·gle·dy–pig·gle·dy \ˌhig-əl-dē-'pig-əl-dē\ *adv* : in confusion : TOPSY-TURVY — **higgledy–piggledy** *adj*

¹high \'hī\ *adj* 1 a : extending to a great distance upward : having greater height than average or usual ⟨rooms with *high* ceilings⟩ b : having a specified elevation ⟨six feet *high*⟩ 2 : advanced toward fullness ⟨*high* summer⟩ 3 : ²SHRILL, SHARP ⟨*high* note⟩ 4 : far from the equator ⟨*high* latitude⟩ 5 : ¹NOBLE 5 ⟨a writer of *high* purpose⟩ 6 : of greater degree, size, amount, or content than average or ordinary ⟨*high* pressure⟩ ⟨*high* power of a microscope⟩ 7 : of relatively great importance: as a : first in rank or standing ⟨*high* society⟩ b : SERIOUS 4, GRAVE ⟨*high* crimes⟩ 8 : STRONG 7 ⟨*high* winds⟩ 9 a : showing joy or excitement ⟨*high* spirits⟩ b : ²DRUNK 1; *also* : excited or stupefied by a drug (as marijuana or heroin) 10 : COSTLY 1, DEAR ⟨everything's *high* nowadays⟩ 11 : very advanced or complex especially in content, structure, or development ⟨*higher* mathematics⟩ ⟨*higher* animals including human beings⟩

syn HIGH, TALL, LOFTY mean being above the usual level in height. HIGH is used of height that is measured from the ground or some other standard ⟨a *high* fence surrounded the house⟩ TALL is used of what is considered high when compared to others of the same kind ⟨a *tall* youngster for that age⟩ LOFTY is used of something that rises to a grand or impressive height ⟨*lofty* mountains⟩

²high *adv* 1 : at or to a high place, altitude, or degree 2 : RICHLY 1, LUXURIOUSLY ⟨living *high*⟩

³high *n* 1 a : ¹HILL 1, KNOLL b : SKY 1 ⟨watched the birds on *high*⟩ c : HEAVEN 2 ⟨a judgment from on *high*⟩ 2 : a region of high barometric pressure : ANTICYCLONE 3 a : a high point or level : HEIGHT ⟨prices reached a new *high*⟩ b : the arrangement of gears (as in an automobile) that gives the highest speed and consequently the highest speed of travel 4 : a state of good feeling or excitement; *esp* : one induced by drugs

high·ball \'hī-ˌbȯl\ *n* : a drink of alcoholic liquor with water or a carbonated beverage served in a tall glass

high beam *n* : the point of aim of a vehicle headlight for long distances

high blood pressure *n* 1 : blood pressure that is abnormally high especially in the arteries 2 : the condition resulting from high blood pressure that is marked by nervousness, dizziness, and headache

high·born \'hī-'bȯ(ə)rn\ *adj* : of noble birth

high·boy \-ˌbȯi\ *n* : a high chest of drawers set on a base with long legs

high·brow \-ˌbraȯ\ *n* : a person who has or pretends to have more learning or culture than others : INTELLECTUAL — **highbrow** *adj*

high chair *n* : a child's chair with long legs, a feeding tray, and a footrest

higher education *n* : education provided by a college or university

high·fa·lu·tin \ˌhī-fə-'lüt-ᵊn\ *adj* : PRETENTIOUS, POMPOUS ⟨*highfalutin* talk⟩ ⟨*highfalutin* people⟩

high fidelity *n* : the reproduction of sound with a high degree of faithfulness to the original

\ə\ **abut**	\aȯ\ **out**	\i\ **tip**	\ȯ\ **saw**	\ȯ\ **foot**
\ər\ **further**	\ch\ **chin**	\ī\ **life**	\ȯi\ **coin**	\y\ **yet**
\a\ **mat**	\e\ **pet**	\j\ **job**	\th\ **thin**	\yü\ **few**
\ā\ **take**	\ē\ **easy**	\ŋ\ **sing**	\th\ **this**	\yu̇\ **cure**
\ä\ **cot, cart**	\g\ **go**	\ō\ **bone**	\ü\ **food**	\zh\ **vision**

high–flown \'hī-'flōn\ *adj* : not plain or simple : FLOWERY, EXTRAVAGANT ⟨*high-flown* language⟩

high frequency *n* : a radio frequency in the range between 3 and 30 megahertz — abbr. *HF*

high–grade \'hī-'grād\ *adj* : of a better grade or quality

high–hand·ed \-'han-dəd\ *adj* : having or showing no regard for the rights, concerns, or feelings of others — **high–hand·ed·ly** *adv* — **high–hand·ed·ness** *n*

¹high–hat \-'hat\ *adj* : having the attitude or manner of a snob

²high–hat *vb* **–hat·ted; –hat·ting** : to treat in a high-hat manner

high jinks \'hī-,jiŋks\ *n pl* : wild or rowdy behavior

high jump *n* : a track-and-field event in which competitors try to jump over a high crossbar — **high jumper** *n*

¹high·land \'hī-lənd\ *n* : elevated or mountainous land

²highland *adj* **1** : of or relating to a highland **2** *cap* : of or relating to the Highlands of Scotland

high·land·er \-lən-dər\ *n* **1** : an inhabitant of a highland **2** *cap* : an inhabitant of the Highlands of Scotland

Highland fling *n* : a lively Scottish folk dance

high–lev·el \'hī-'lev-əl\ *adj* : being of high importance or rank

¹high·light \'hī-,līt\ *n* **1 a** : one of the spots or areas on an object that reflect the most light **b** : the brightest spot (as in a painting or drawing) **2** : an event or scene of major interest

²highlight *vb* **-light·ed; -light·ing** **1** : to throw a strong light on **2 a** : to center attention on : EMPHASIZE **b** : to be a highlight of

high·ly \'hī-lē\ *adv* **1** : ²VERY 1, EXTREMELY ⟨*highly* pleased⟩ **2** : with approval ⟨speaks *highly* of you⟩

high–mind·ed \'hī-'mīn-dəd\ *adj* : having or expressing noble ideas and feelings — **high–mind·ed·ly** *adv* — **high–mind·ed·ness** *n*

high·ness \'hī-nəs\ *n* **1** : the quality or state of being high **2** — used as a title for persons (as a king or queen) of high rank ⟨Your Royal *Highness*⟩

high noon *n* : exactly noon

high–octane *adj* : having a high octane number and therefore good antiknock properties ⟨*high-octane* gasoline⟩

high–pitched \'hī-'picht\ *adj* : having a high pitch ⟨a *high-pitched* voice⟩

¹high–pressure *adj* **1 a** : having or involving a high pressure especially much higher than that of the atmosphere **b** : having a high atmospheric pressure **2** : using or involving very aggressive sales techniques

²high–pressure *vb* : to sell or influence by high-pressure methods

high–rise \'hī-'rīz\ *adj* **1** : having several stories and being equipped with elevators ⟨*high-rise* apartments⟩ **2** : of, relating to, or being extra-high bicycle handlebars — **high rise** *n*

high·road \-,rōd\ *n* : HIGHWAY

high school *n* : a secondary school usually including the 9th to 12th or 10th to 12th years of study

high seas *n pl* : the open part of a sea or ocean especially outside territorial waters

high–sound·ing \'hī-'saun-diŋ\ *adj* : POMPOUS 1, IMPOSING

high–speed \-'spēd\ *adj* : going or made for operation at high speed

high–spir·it·ed \-'spir-ət-əd\ *adj* : characterized by a bold or lively spirit : EXUBERANT — **high–spir·it·ed·ly** *adv* — **high–spir·it·ed·ness** *n*

high–strung \-'strəŋ\ *adj* : very nervous or sensitive

high–tension *adj* **1** : having a high voltage **2** : relating to or being equipment to be used at high voltage

high–test *adj* : meeting a high standard; *esp* : HIGH-OCTANE

high tide *n* : the tide when the water is at its greatest height

high–top \'hī-,täp\ *adj* : extending up over the ankle ⟨*high-top* sneakers⟩ — **high–tops** \-,täps\ *n pl*

high treason *n* : TREASON 2

high–water mark *n* : the highest point of development : PEAK

high·way \'hī-,wā\ *n* : a public road; *esp* : a main direct road

high·way·man \-mən\ *n* : a person who robs travelers on a highway

hi·jack *also* **high–jack** \'hī-,jak\ *vb* **1** : to stop and steal from a moving vehicle ⟨*hijack* a truck⟩ ⟨*hijack* a load of furs⟩ **2** : to force a pilot to fly an aircraft where one wants ⟨*hijack* an airliner to Iran⟩ — **hi·jack·er** *n*

¹hike \'hīk\ *vb* **hiked; hik·ing** **1** : to move or raise up ⟨*hike* rents⟩ **2** : to go on a long walk — **hik·er** *n*

²hike *n* **1** : a long walk especially for pleasure or exercise **2** : an upward movement : RISE ⟨a price *hike*⟩

hi·lar·i·ous \hil-'ar-ē-əs, -'er-; hī-'lar-, -'ler-\ *adj* : causing hilarity : wildly funny — **hi·lar·i·ous·ly** *adv* — **hi·lar·i·ous·ness** *n*

hi·lar·i·ty \hil-'ar-ət-ē, -'er-; hī-'lar-, -'ler-\ *n* : noisy fun

¹hill \'hil\ *n* **1** : a usually rounded height of land lower than a mountain **2** : an artificial heap or mound (as of earth) **3** : several seeds or plants planted in a group rather than a row ⟨a *hill* of beans⟩

²hill *vb* **1** : to form into a heap **2** : to draw earth around the roots or base of

hill·bil·ly \'hil-,bil-ē\ *n, pl* **-lies** : a person from a mountainous backwoods area

hillbilly music *n* : COUNTRY MUSIC

hill·ock \'hil-ək\ *n* : a small hill — **hill·ocky** \-ə-kē\ *adj*

hill·side \'hil-,sīd\ *n* : the side of a hill

hill·top \-,täp\ *n* : the highest part of a hill

hilly \'hil-ē\ *adj* **hill·i·er; -est** **1** : having many hills ⟨a *hilly* city⟩ **2** : ¹STEEP 1

hilt \'hilt\ *n* : a handle especially of a sword or dagger — **to the hilt** : COMPLETELY

hi·lum \'hī-ləm\ *n, pl* **hi·la** \-lə\ : a scar on a seed at the point of attachment of the ovule

him \im, (')him\ *pron, objective case of* HE

¹Hi·ma·la·yan \,him-ə-'lā-ən, him-'äl-(ə-)yən\ *adj* : of, relating to, or characteristic of the Himalaya mountains or the people living there

²Himalayan *n* : any of a breed of stocky blue-eyed domestic cats that have a long thick coat and a pale body with darker ears, paws, tail, and face

Himalayan

him·self \(h)im-'self\ *pron* **1** : that identical male one : that identical one whose sex is unknown or immaterial — used for emphasis or to show that the subject and object of the verb are the same ⟨considers *himself* lucky⟩ ⟨he *himself* did it⟩ **2** : his normal, healthy, or sane self ⟨he's *himself* again⟩

¹hind \'hīnd\ *n, pl* **hinds** *also* **hind** : a female of the common deer of temperate Europe and Asia [Old English *hind* "female red deer"]

²hind *adj* : located behind : REAR ⟨*hind* legs⟩ [probably from Old English *hinder* (adverb) "behind"]

hind·brain \'hīn(d)-,brān\ *n* : the third and most posterior division of the embryonic vertebrate brain or the parts that develop from it

hin·der \'hin-dər\ *vb* **hin·dered; hin·der·ing** \-d(ə-)riŋ\ **1** : to make slow or difficult : HAMPER ⟨progress was *hindered* by bad weather⟩ **2** : to hold back : CHECK ⟨*hindered* by lack of energy⟩ — **hin·der·er** \-dər-ər\ *n*

Hin·di \'hin-(,)dē\ *n* : an official language of northern India — **Hindi** *adj*

hind·most \'hīn(d)-,mōst\ *adj* : farthest to the rear

hind·quar·ter \-,kwȯ(r)t-ər\ *n*   **1** : the back half of a side half of the body or carcass of a four-footed animal ⟨a *hindquarter* of beef⟩   **2** *pl* : the part of a four-footed animal behind the attachment of the hind legs to the trunk

hin·drance \'hin-drən(t)s\ *n*   **1** : the state of being hindered   **2** : the action of hindering   **3** : something that hinders : IMPEDIMENT

hind·sight \'hīn(d)-,sīt\ *n*   **1** : a rear sight of a firearm   **2** : realization of the meaning or importance of an event only after it has happened

Hin·du \'hin-(,)dü\ *n*   **1** : a follower of Hinduism   **2** : a person born or living in India — **Hindu** *adj*

Hindu–Arabic *adj* : relating to, being, or composed of Arabic numerals ⟨the *Hindu-Arabic* numeration system⟩

Hin·du·ism \'hin-(,)dü-,iz-əm\ *n* : a body of social, cultural, and religious beliefs and practices native to the Indian subcontinent

Hin·du·stani \,hin-dú-'stan-ē, -'stän-ē\ *n* : a group of Indic dialects of northern India

hind wing *n* : a wing behind a forewing of a four-winged insect

¹hinge \'hinj\ *n*   **1** : a jointed piece on which a door, lid, or other swinging part turns   **2** : the joint between valves of a bivalve's shell

²hinge *vb* **hinged; hing·ing**   **1** : to attach by or provide with hinges   **2** : to hang or turn as if on a hinge : DEPEND

hinge joint *n* : a joint between bones (as at the elbow) that permits motion in only one plane

hin·ny \'hin-ē\ *n, pl* **hinnies** : a hybrid between a male horse and a female donkey

¹hint \'hint\ *n*   **1** : a slight mention : a suggestion or reminder ⟨a *hint* of winter in the air⟩   **2** : a very small amount : TRACE ⟨a *hint* of garlic⟩

²hint *vb* : to bring to mind by or give a hint — **hint·er** *n*

hin·ter·land \'hint-ər-,land\ *n*   **1** : a region lying inland from a coast   **2** : a region far from cities and towns

¹hip \'hip\ *n* : the fruit of a rose [Old English *hēope* "fruit of a rose"]

²hip *n* : the part of the body that curves outward below the waist on each side and is formed by the side part of the pelvis and the upper part of the thigh [Old English *hype* "hip of the body"] — **hipped** \'hipt\ *adj*

³hip *adj* **hip·per; hip·pest**   **1** : keenly aware of or interested in the newest developments   **2** : ²WISE 2, ALERT [an altered form of *hep* "keenly aware of and interested in the newest developments"; of unknown origin]

hip·bone \'hip-'bōn, -,bōn\ *n* : either of two large bones that make up the side halves of the pelvis in mammals, provide points of attachment for the skeleton of the leg, and unite in front and with the backbone in the rear to form a closed bony ring which supports the lower part of the trunk and the organs of the abdomen

hip girdle *n* : PELVIC GIRDLE

hip·po \'hip-ō\ *n, pl* **hippos** : HIPPOPOTAMUS

hip·po·drome \'hip-ə-,drōm\ *n*   **1** : an oval stadium for horse and chariot races in ancient Greece   **2** : an arena for spectacles (as horse shows or circuses)

hip·po·pot·a·mus \,hip-ə-'pät-ə-məs\ *n, pl* **-mus·es** *or* **-mi** \-,mī, -(,)mē\ : any of several large African mammals that spend most of their time in the water, feed on plants, have an extremely large head and mouth, very thick hairless skin, and short legs with four toes on each foot, and are related to pigs

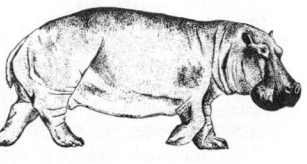

hippopotamus

Word History The ancient Greeks gave the name *hip-*

popotamos to a big, barrel-shaped animal they saw in Africa. English, using the Latin spelling *hippopotamus*, has kept this name. It is a combination of the Greek words *hippos*, meaning "horse" and *potamos*, meaning "river". In fact, the hippopotamus is more closely related to the hog than to the horse. However, the "river" in the name is certainly right for an animal that always lives near water and spends most of its time in it. The eyes, ears, and nostrils of a hippopotamus are placed so that the animal can see, hear, and breathe even if most of its head is underwater. [from Latin *hippopotamus* "hippopotamus", from Greek *hippopotamos* (same meaning), literally "river horse", from *hippos* "horse" and *potamos* "river"]

hip·py \'hip-ē\ *adj* **hip·pi·er; -est** : having large hips

¹hire \'hī(ə)r\ *n*   **1 a** : payment for temporary use   **b** : payment for services : WAGES   **2 a** : the act of hiring   **b** : the state of being hired : EMPLOYMENT

²hire *vb* **hired; hir·ing**   **1** : ¹EMPLOY 2 ⟨*hire* a new crew⟩   **2** : to get the temporary use of for a set sum ⟨*hire* a hall⟩   **3** : to take a job ⟨*hired* out as a cook⟩ — **hir·er** *n*

hire·ling \'hī(ə)r-lin\ *n* : a person who works for wages and usually for no other reason

hir·sute \'hər-,süt, 'hi(ə)r-\ *adj* : very hairy especially with coarse stiff hairs

¹his \(h)iz, ,hiz\ *adj* : of, relating to, or belonging to him or himself ⟨*his* house⟩ ⟨*his* writings⟩

²his \'hiz\ *pron* : his one : his ones ⟨the book is *his*⟩

His·pan·ic \his-'pan-ik\ *adj* : of or relating to the people, speech, or culture of Spain, Portugal, or Latin America — **Hispanic** *n*

hiss \'his\ *vb* : to make a long sharp sound like that of the speech sound \s\ or that made by an alarmed animal (as a snake or cat) usually as a sign of disapproval ⟨*hissed* them off the stage⟩ — **hiss** *n* — **hiss·er** *n*

hist \s *often prolonged and usually with* p *preceding and* t *following; often read as* 'hist\ *interj* — used to attract attention

his·ta·mine \'his-tə-,mēn, -mən\ *n* : a compound that occurs in many animal tissues and is believed to play an important part in allergic reactions (as in hives, asthma, and hay fever)

his·to·gram \'his-tə-,gram\ *n* : a representation of a frequency distribution using rectangles in which the different values included in a given class are represented by the width of the rectangle and the number of items in the class are represented by its height if the rectangles all have the same width or by its area if the rectangles do not all have the same width

his·tol·o·gist \his-'täl-ə-jəst\ *n* : a person who specializes in histology

his·tol·o·gy \his-'täl-ə-jē\ *n, pl* **-gies**   **1** : a branch of anatomy that deals with the structure of animal and plant tissues as seen under a microscope   **2** : tissue structure or organization

his·to·ri·an \his-'tōr-ē-ən, -'tȯr-, -'tär-\ *n* : a student or writer of history

his·tor·ic \his-'tȯr-ik, -'tär-\ *adj*   **1** : HISTORICAL 1   **2** : famous in history ⟨*historic* events⟩

his·tor·i·cal \his-'tȯr-i-kəl, -'tär-\ *adj*   **1 a** : of, relating to, or having the character of history; *esp* : known to be true ⟨*historical* fact⟩   **b** : based on history ⟨*historical* novels⟩   **c** : of, relating to, or exhibiting objects from the past ⟨a *historical* museum⟩   **2** : HISTORIC 2   **3** : CHRONOLOGICAL ⟨in *historical* order⟩ — **his·tor·i·cal·ly** \-i-k(ə-)lē\ *adv* — **his·tor·i·cal·ness** \-i-kəl-nəs\ *n*

\ə\ **abut**	\au̇\ **out**	\i\ **tip**	\ȯ\ **saw**	\u̇\ **foot**
\ər\ **further**	\ch\ **chin**	\ī\ **life**	\ȯi\ **coin**	\y\ **yet**
\a\ **mat**	\e\ **pet**	\j\ **job**	\th\ **thin**	\yü\ **few**
\ā\ **take**	\ē\ **easy**	\ŋ\ **sing**	\th\ **this**	\yu̇\ **cure**
\ä\ **cot, cart**	\g\ **go**	\ō\ **bone**	\ü\ **food**	\zh\ **vision**

his·to·ry \'his-t(ə-)rē\ *n, pl* **-ries** **1** : a story of real or imaginary events **2 a** : a written record of important events and their causes **b** : a branch of knowledge that records and explains past events **c** : events that form the topics of a history

his·tri·on·ic \,his-trē-'än-ik\ *adj* : of or relating to actors, acting, or the theater — **his·tri·on·i·cal·ly** \-'än-i-k(ə-)lē\ *adv*

his·tri·on·ics \,his-trē-'än-iks\ *n pl* **1** : theatrical performances **2** : exaggerated display of feeling

¹hit \'hit\ *vb* **hit; hit·ting** **1 a** : to strike usually with force ⟨*hit* a ball⟩ ⟨the ball *hit* the house⟩ **b** : to make or bring into contact with something ⟨tipped over and *hit* hard⟩ **c** : to strike something aimed at ⟨*hit* the bull's-eye⟩ **2 a** : ¹ATTACK 1 **b** : to affect as if by a blow **3** : OCCUR 2, HAPPEN ⟨the storm *hit* just at sundown⟩ **4 a** : to come upon : DISCOVER ⟨*hit* upon the answer accidentally⟩ **b** : to get to : REACH ⟨*hit* town that night⟩ **c** : to reflect accurately ⟨*hits* the right note⟩ **5** : to fire the charge in the cylinders — **hit·ter** *n* — **hit it off** : to get along well

²hit *n* **1 a** : a blow striking an object aimed at **b** : ⁴BLOW 1, COLLISION **2 a** : a stroke of luck **b** : a great success ⟨the show was a *hit*⟩ **3** : BASE HIT **4** : a single dose of a narcotic drug

hit–and–miss \,hit-³n-'mis\ *adj* : sometimes successful and sometimes not : HAPHAZARD

hit–and–run \-'rən\ *adj* **1** : being or involving a motor vehicle driver who does not stop after having an accident **2** : involving or intended for quick action or results

¹hitch \'hich\ *vb* **1** : to move by jerks **2** : to catch, fasten, or connect by or as if by a hook or knot ⟨*hitch* a horse to a rail⟩ **3** : HITCHHIKE — **hitch·er** *n*

²hitch *n* **1** : a jerky movement or pull **2** : an unexpected stop or obstacle ⟨the plan went off without a *hitch*⟩ **3** : the connection between something towed (as a plow or trailer) and its mover (as a tractor, automobile, or animal) **4** : a knot used for a temporary fastening **5** : a period usually of military service ⟨do a *hitch* in the army⟩

hitch·hike \'hich-,hīk\ *vb* : to travel by or secure free rides — **hitch·hik·er** *n*

¹hith·er \'hith-ər\ *adv* : to this place ⟨come *hither*⟩

²hither *adj* : ³NEAR 3, NEARER ⟨the *hither* side of the hill⟩

hith·er·to \'hith-ər-,tü\ *adv* : up to this time ⟨*hitherto* unknown facts⟩

hit or miss *adv* : without plan, order, or direction : HAPHAZARDLY — **hit–or–miss** \,hit-ər-'mis\ *adj*

HIV \,āch-,ī-'vē\ *n* : any of a group of viruses that infect and destroy helper T cells causing the marked reduction in their numbers that is diagnostic of AIDS

¹hive \'hīv\ *n* **1 a** : a container for housing honeybees **b** : a colony of bees **2** : a place swarming with busy occupants

²hive *vb* **hived; hiv·ing** **1 a** : to collect into a hive ⟨*hive* bees⟩ **b** : to enter and take over a hive or nesting place **2** : to live or gather in close association

hive 1a

hives \'hīvz\ *n sing or pl* : an allergic condition in which the skin or mucous membrane breaks out in large red itching patches

ho \'hō\ *interj* — used especially to attract attention ⟨land ho⟩

hoa·gie \'hō-gē\ *n* : ²SUBMARINE 2

¹hoar \'hō(ə)r, 'hò(ə)r\ *adj* : HOARY

²hoar *n* : ¹FROST 2

hoard \'hō(ə)rd, 'hò(ə)rd\ *n* : a hidden supply or fund stored up — **hoard** *vb* — **hoard·er** *n*

hoar·frost \'hō(ə)r-,fròst, 'hò(ə)r-\ *n* : ¹FROST 2

hoarse \'hō(ə)rs, 'hò(ə)rs\ *adj* **hoars·er; hoars·est** **1** : harsh in sound **2** : having a rough voice ⟨a cold made me *hoarse*⟩ — **hoarse·ly** *adv* — **hoarse·ness** *n*

hoary \'hō(ə)r-ē, 'hò(ə)r-\ *adj* **hoar·i·er; -est** **1** : grayish or whitish especially from age ⟨bowed his *hoary* head⟩ **2** : very old : ANCIENT ⟨*hoary* legends⟩ — **hoar·i·ness** *n*

hoax \'hōks\ *n* **1** : an act intended to trick or deceive **2** : something false passed off or accepted as genuine — **hoax** *vb* — **hoax·er** *n*

hob \'häb\ *n* : ²TROUBLE 1b, MISCHIEF ⟨raise *hob*⟩

¹hob·ble \'häb-əl\ *vb* **hob·bled; hob·bling** \-(ə-)liŋ\ **1 a** : to walk with difficulty : LIMP ⟨*hobble* along on crutches⟩ **b** : to make lame : CRIPPLE ⟨*hobbled* by an ankle injury⟩ **2 a** : to keep from straying by tying two legs together ⟨*hobble* a horse⟩ **b** : ¹HAMPER, IMPEDE

²hobble *n* **1** : a hobbling walk **2** : something used to hobble an animal

hob·ble·de·hoy \'häb-əl-di-,hòi\ *n* : an awkward youth

hob·by \'häb-ē\ *n, pl* **hobbies** : an interest or activity to which a person devotes time for pleasure — **hob·by·ist** \-ē-əst\ *n*

hob·by·horse \-,hò(ə)rs\ *n* **1** : a stick with an imitation horse's head at one end that a child pretends to ride **2** : ROCKING HORSE **3** : a toy horse hung by springs from a frame

hob·gob·lin \'häb-,gäb-lən\ *n* **1** : a mischievous elf or goblin **2** : BOGEY 2

hob·nail \'häb-,nāl\ *n* : a large-headed nail driven into the soles of heavy shoes as a protection against wear — **hob·nailed** \-,nāld\ *adj*

hob·nob \'häb-,näb\ *vb* **hob·nobbed; hob·nob·bing** : to associate in a friendly manner — **hob·nob·ber** *n*

ho·bo \'hō-bō\ *n, pl* **hoboes** *also* **hobos** : ²TRAMP 1 — **hobo** *vb*

¹hock \'häk\ *n* **1** : the region in the hind limb of a four-footed animal (as the horse) that corresponds to the human ankle **2** : a small cut of meat from either the front or hind leg just above the foot especially of a pig ⟨ham *hock*s⟩ [Old English *hōh* "heel"]

²hock *vb* : ³PAWN

³hock *n* : ²PAWN 2 [from Dutch *hok* "pen, prison"]

hock·ey \'häk-ē\ *n* **1** : FIELD HOCKEY **2** : ICE HOCKEY

ho·cus–po·cus \,hō-kə-'spō-kəs\ *n* **1** : a set form of words used by magicians **2** : nonsense used to deceive

hod \'häd\ *n* **1** : a long-handled tray used to carry mortar or bricks on the shoulder **2** : a bucket for holding or carrying coal

hodge·podge \'häj-,päj\ *n* : a confused mixture : JUMBLE

Word History *Hodgepodge* and its older form *hotchpotch* are part of a group of words that rhyme all by themselves. *Hobnob* and *willy-nilly* are others. In the case of *hodgepodge* and *hotchpotch*, the rhyme is not an accident. These words came to English from early French in the form *hochepot*. The spelling was changed to make the second half of the word rhyme with the first. In French *hochepot* was a stew of many foods cooked together in a pot. Perhaps the pot was shaken instead of stirred since *hochepot* was formed from *hochier*, meaning "to shake", and *pot*, which had the same meaning in early French as it does in English now. Before long *hotchpotch* and *hodgepodge* were used not just for a mixture of foods cooking in a pot but for any mixture of different things. [an altered form of *hotchpotch*, from Middle English *hochepot* "mixed stew", derived from early French *hochepot* (same meaning), from *hochier* "to shake" and *pot* "pot, container"]

¹hoe \'hō\ *n* : a farm or garden tool with a thin flat blade at nearly a right angle to a long handle that is used for weeding and loosening the earth

²hoe *vb* **hoed; hoe·ing** : to use or work with a hoe

hoe·cake \'hō-,kāk\ *n* : a small cornmeal cake

¹hog \'hȯg, 'häg\ *n, pl* **hogs** *also* **hog**   **1 a** : a domestic swine especially when weighing more than 54 kilograms   **b** : any of various animals related to the domestic swine   **2** : a selfish, greedy, or filthy person — **hog·gish** \'hȯg-ish, 'häg-\ *adj* — **hog·gish·ly** *adv* — **hog·gish·ness** *n*

²hog *vb* **hogged; hog·ging** : to take more than one's share

ho·gan \'hō-ˌgän\ *n* : an earth-covered dwelling of the Navajo Indians

hog cholera *n* : a highly infectious often fatal virus disease of swine

hog·nose snake \ˌhȯg-ˌnōz-, ˌhäg-\ *n* : any of several rather small harmless North American snakes that have stout bodies and hiss when disturbed — called also *hogⁱ nosed snake* \-ˌnōzd-\, *puff adder*

hogan

hogs·head \'hȯgz-ˌhed, 'hägz-\ *n*   **1** : a large cask or barrel; *esp* : one containing from 63 to 140 gallons (about 238 to 530 liters)   **2** : a U.S. measure for liquids equal to 63 gallons (about 238 liters)

hog·wash \'hȯg-ˌwȯsh, 'häg-, -ˌwäsh\ *n*   **1** : ²SWILL 1   **2** : NONSENSE 1

¹hoist \'hȯist\ *vb* : to raise or become raised into position especially by mechanical means   **syn** see RAISE — **hoist·er** *n*

²hoist *n*   **1** : an act of hoisting : LIFT   **2** : a machine for hoisting heavy loads

hol- *or* **holo-** *combining form* : complete : total [derived from Greek *holos* "whole"]

¹hold \'hōld\ *vb* **held** \'held\; **hold·ing**   **1 a** : to keep in one's possession : POSSESS, HAVE ⟨*hold* this for me⟩   **b** : to have by right ⟨*hold* property⟩ ⟨*hold* a bachelor's degree⟩ ⟨*hold* elective office⟩   **2 a** : to keep or restrict by force ⟨the troops *held* the bridge⟩   **b** : ²DELAY 2 ⟨*held* the train⟩   **c** : to make accept a legal or moral duty ⟨I'll *hold* you to your word⟩   **3 a** : to have or keep in the grasp ⟨*hold* the pen upright⟩   **b** : to fix or keep in a place, position, or situation ⟨*hold* the ladder steady⟩   **c** : to remain fastened ⟨the anchor *held*⟩   **d** : ¹SUPPORT 4a, SUSTAIN ⟨the floor will *hold* 10 metric tons⟩   **e** : to keep as or as if a captive ⟨*held* without bail⟩   **4** : to bear or keep oneself ⟨please *hold* still⟩   **5 a** : to keep in being or action ⟨*hold* silence⟩   **b** : to keep the interest or devotion of ⟨the play *held* the audience⟩   **6** : to receive and keep ⟨the bottle *holds* two liters⟩   **7 a** : to have in mind : ENTERTAIN ⟨*hold* a theory⟩   **b** : CONSIDER 3, JUDGE ⟨was *held* to be the best⟩   **8** : to carry on as a group ⟨*hold* a meeting⟩   **9** : to be or stand in ⟨each digit *holds* a place⟩   **10 a** : to maintain position ⟨the line *held* under attack⟩   **b** : to continue unchanged : LAST ⟨their interest *held* up⟩ ⟨hope the weather *holds*⟩   **11** : to be true : APPLY ⟨the rule *holds* in most cases⟩   **12** : to refrain from an act : HALT, PAUSE [Old English *healdan* "to hold, own"]   **syn** see CONTAIN — **hold forth** : to preach or speak in public usually for a long time — **hold good** : to remain true ⟨the rule *holds good* in this case⟩ — **hold one's own** : to maintain one's place or condition especially against opposition — **hold one's tongue** : to keep silent — **hold the bag**   **1** : to be left empty-handed   **2** : to get the blame that should be shared by others — **hold water** : to stand up under criticism or examination ⟨your story doesn't *hold water*⟩ — **hold with** : to agree with : approve of

²hold *n*   **1** : FORTRESS, STRONGHOLD   **2** : something that holds, secures, or fastens   **3** : the act or manner of holding : GRIP, GRASP ⟨have a *hold* on the rope⟩   **4** : full or immediate control ⟨get *hold* of yourself⟩   **5** : a manner of grasping the opponent in wrestling   **6** : authority to take or

keep : POWER ⟨the law has no *hold* over this person⟩   **7** : something that may be grasped or held   **8** : a note or rest in music that is continued longer than usual   **9** : an order or indication that something is to be reserved or delayed   **10** : STOPPAGE, HALT ⟨a *hold* in a rocket countdown⟩ — **on hold** : in a state of interruption

³hold *n*   **1** : the interior of a ship below decks; *esp* : the cargo deck of a ship   **2** : the cargo compartment of an airplane [an altered form of *hole*]

hold back *vb* : to make difficult the progress or achievement of

hold·er \'hōl-dər\ *n*   **1** : a person that holds; *esp* : a legal owner   **2** : a device that holds

hold·fast \'hōl(d)-ˌfast\ *n* : a part by which a plant (as a seaweed) or animal clings (as to a flat surface or the body of a host)

hold in *vb* : RESTRAIN 1, CHECK

hold·ing \'hōl-diŋ\ *n*   **1** : land or property (as bonds or stocks) owned   **2** : a ruling of a court

holding pattern *n* : the course flown (as over an airport) by an aircraft waiting for permission to land

hold off *vb*   **1** : to keep away : WITHSTAND ⟨*held off* the attack⟩   **2 a** : POSTPONE, DELAY ⟨decided to *hold off* on the decision⟩   **b** : ¹REFRAIN

hold on *vb*   **1** : to keep a hold   **2** : to go on : CONTINUE   **3** : ¹WAIT 1a

hold out \(')hōl-'daut\ *vb*   **1** : to remain in being : LAST ⟨hope the food *holds out*⟩   **2** : to remain unyielding : refuse to surrender or give in ⟨*held out* until help arrived⟩ — **hold·out** \'hōl-ˌdaut\ *n* — **hold out on** : to keep a fair share from

hold over \(')hōl-'dō-vər\ *vb* : to continue beyond a normal or planned time ⟨the movie was *held over* for three weeks⟩ — **hold·over** \'hōl-ˌdō-vər\ *n*

hold·up \'hōl-ˌdəp\ *n*   **1** : a robbery at gunpoint   **2** : ¹DELAY 1

hold up \(')hōl-'dəp\ *vb*   **1** : ²DELAY 2, IMPEDE   **2** : to rob at gunpoint

hole \'hōl\ *n*   **1** : an opening into or through a thing   **2 a** : a hollow place (as a pit or cave)   **b** : a deep place in a body of water ⟨trout *holes*⟩   **3** : an underground habitation : BURROW   **4** : FLAW, FAULT   **5 a** : the shallow cup into which the ball is played in golf   **b** : a part of a golf course from the tee to the hole   **6** : a shabby or dingy place   **7** : an awkward position : FIX — **hole** *vb* — **hol·ey** \'hō-lē\ *adj* — **in the hole** : in a position of owing or losing money

holed \'hōld\ *adj* : having one or more holes — often used in combination ⟨two-*holed* stopper⟩

hole up *vb* : to take shelter in or as if in a hole or cave

hol·i·day \'häl-ə-ˌdā\ *n*   **1** : HOLY DAY   **2** : a day of freedom from work; *esp* : a day of celebration or remembrance fixed by law   **3** : a period of relaxation : VACATION — **holiday** *vb* — **hol·i·day·er** *n*

ho·li·ness \'hō-lē-nəs\ *n*   **1** : the quality or state of being holy   **2** *cap* — used as a title for various high religious officials ⟨His *Holiness* the Pope⟩

hol·ler \'häl-ər\ *vb* **hol·lered; hol·ler·ing** \-(ə-)riŋ\   **1** : to cry or call out : SHOUT   **2** : COMPLAIN 1 — **holler** *n*

¹hol·low \'häl-ō\ *adj*   **1** : curved inward : SUNKEN ⟨*hollow* cheeks⟩   **2** : having a hole inside : not solid throughout ⟨*hollow* tree⟩   **3** : lacking value or meaning ⟨*hollow* victory⟩   **4** : being like a sound made in or by beating on a large empty enclosure : MUFFLED ⟨a *hollow* roar⟩   **5** : INSINCERE ⟨*hollow* promises⟩ — **hollow** *vb* — **hol·low·ly** \'häl-ō-lē, -ə-lē\ *adv* — **hol·low·ness** *n*

²hollow *n*   **1** : a low spot in a surface; *esp* : VALLEY   **2** : an

\ə\ abut		\au̇\ out	\i\ tip	\ȯ\ saw	\u̇\ foot
\ər\ further		\ch\ chin	\ī\ life	\ȯi\ coin	\y\ yet
\a\ mat		\e\ pet	\j\ job	\th\ thin	\yü\ few
\ā\ take		\ē\ easy	\ŋ\ sing	\th\ this	\yu̇\ cure
\ä\ cot, cart		\g\ go	\ō\ bone	\ü\ food	\zh\ vision

empty space within something : HOLE

hol·ly \'häl-ē\ *n, pl* **hollies** **1** : either of two trees or shrubs of which one is found in the eastern U.S. and the other in Eurasia and which have evergreen leaves with spiny margins and usually bright red berries often used for Christmas decorations **2** : the leaves, berries, and branches of the holly

hol·ly·hock \'häl-ē-ˌhäk, -ˌhòk\ *n* : a widely grown Chinese herb related to the mallow and having large coarse rounded leaves and tall stalks bearing showy flowers

hol·mi·um \'hō(l)-mē-əm\ *n* : a metallic element that occurs with yttrium and forms highly magnetic compounds — see ELEMENT table

holo- — see HOL-

holly 2

ho·lo·caust \'hò-lə-ˌkòst, 'häl-ə- *also* -ˌkäst *or* 'hò-lə-ˌkòst\ *n* **1** : a sacrifice destroyed by fire **2** : a thorough destruction especially by fire **3** *often cap* : the killing of European Jews by the Nazis during World War II

Ho·lo·cene \'hō-lə-ˌsēn, 'häl-ə-\ *adj* : of, relating to, or being the present epoch of geological history — see GEOLOGIC TIME table — **Holocene** *n*

ho·lo·gram \'hō-lə-ˌgram, 'häl-ə-\ *n* : a three-dimensional picture made by laser light reflected from an object onto photographic film without camera or lenses

ho·lo·graph \'hō-lə-ˌgraf, 'häl-ə-\ *n* : a document entirely in the handwriting of the author — **holograph** *or* **ho·lo·graph·ic** \ˌhō-lə-'graf-ik, ˌhäl-ə-\ *adj*

ho·log·ra·phy \hō-'läg-rə-fē\ *n* : the process of making or using a hologram

hol·stein \'hōl-ˌstēn, -ˌstīn\ *n* : any of a breed of large black-and-white dairy cattle producing large quantities of milk that is low in fat compared to the milk of other breeds

hol·stein–frie·sian \-'frē-zhən\ *n* : HOLSTEIN

hol·ster \'hōl(t)-stər\ *n* : a usually leather case for carrying a pistol

holstein

ho·ly \'hō-lē\ *adj* **ho·li·er; -est** **1** : set apart to the service of God or a god : SACRED **2** : worthy of complete devotion and trust **3** : DIVINE **4** : respected as sacred

holy day *n* : a day observed as a religious feast

Holy Ghost *n* : HOLY SPIRIT

Holy Grail \-'grā(ə)l\ *n* : the cup or platter which according to legend was used by Christ and was sought after by knights during the Middle Ages

Holy Saturday *n* : the Saturday before Easter

Holy Spirit *n* : the third person of the Trinity

ho·ly·stone \'hō-lē-ˌstōn\ *n* : a soft sandstone used to scrub a ship's decks — **holystone** *vb*

Holy Thursday *n* : MAUNDY THURSDAY

holy war *n* : a war carried on for what is considered a holy purpose

holy water *n* : water blessed by a priest and used to purify

Holy Week *n* : the week before Easter

Holy Writ *n* : BIBLE 1

hom- *or* **homo-** *combining form* : similar : alike ⟨*homo*graph⟩ [derived from Greek *homos* "same"]

hom·age \'(h)äm-ij\ *n* **1** : a ceremony in which a person pledged allegiance to a lord and became his vassal **2**

: something done or given in fulfilling a vassal's duty to a lord **3** : ¹RESPECT 2a, HONOR

hom·bre \'äm-brē, 'əm-, -, brā\ *n* : ¹MAN 1a, FELLOW [from Spanish *hombre* "man", from Latin *homin-, homo* "man"]

hom·burg \'häm-ˌbərg\ *n* : a man's felt hat with a stiff curled brim and a high crown creased lengthwise

¹home \'hōm\ *n* **1 a** : the house in which a person or family lives **b** : ¹HOUSE 1 **2** : a family living together in one dwelling **3** : the place where something is usually or naturally found : HABITAT ⟨the *home* of the elephant⟩ **4 a** : a starting point **b** : the country or place where one lives or where one's ancestors lived **5** : a place for the care of persons unable to care for themselves ⟨old people's *home*⟩ **6** : the goal or point to be reached in some games — **home·like** \-ˌlīk\ *adj* — **at home** : relaxed and comfortable

²home *adv* **1** : to or at home ⟨went *home*⟩ **2** : to a final, closed, or standard position ⟨drive a nail *home*⟩ **3** : deeply and meaningfully ⟨the truth struck *home*⟩

³home *vb* **homed; hom·ing** **1** : to go or return home **2** : to send to or provide with a home

home- *or* **homeo-** *combining form* : like : similar ⟨*homeo*stasis⟩ [derived from Greek *homoios* "like, similar", from *homos* "same"]

home·body \'hōm-ˌbäd-ē\ *n* : one whose life centers in the home

home·boy \-ˌbòi\ *n* **1** : a boy or man from one's neighborhood, hometown, or region **2** : a fellow member of a youth gang

home computer *n* : a small inexpensive microcomputer

home economics *n* : the study of the care and management of a household — **home economist** *n*

home·land \'hōm-ˌland\ *n* : native land : FATHERLAND

home·less \-ləs\ *adj* : having no home or permanent residence

home·ly \'hōm-lē\ *adj* **home·li·er; -est** **1** : characteristic of home life : PLAIN, SIMPLE ⟨*homely* meals⟩ **2** : not pretty or handsome ⟨a *homely* person⟩ — **home·li·ness** *n*

home·made \'hōm-'(m)ād\ *adj* : made in the home

home·mak·er \'hōm-ˌmā-kər\ *n* : one who manages a household especially as a wife and mother — **home·mak·ing** \-kiŋ\ *n or adj*

ho·meo·sta·sis \ˌhō-mē-ō-'stā-səs\ *n* : a tendency for the conditions inside the body of a higher animal (as a mammal) to stay pretty much the same even when outside environmental conditions (as temperature) change — **ho·meo·stat·ic** \-'stat-ik\ *adj*

home·own·er \'hōm-ˌō-nər\ *n* : one that owns a home

home plate *n* : the base where a baseball batter stands and which a base runner must touch in order to score

hom·er \'hō-mər\ *n* **1** : HOMING PIGEON **2** : HOME RUN

home·room \'hōm-ˌrüm, -ˌrùm\ *n* : a classroom where pupils report at the beginning of each school day

home rule *n* : self-government in local affairs by the citizens of a local political unit

home run *n* : a hit in baseball that allows the batter to go completely around the bases and score a run

home·sick \'hōm-ˌsik\ *adj* : longing for home and family while away from them — **home·sick·ness** *n*

home·spun \-ˌspən\ *n* : a loosely woven usually woolen or linen fabric — **homespun** *adj*

¹home·stead \-ˌsted\ *n* **1** : a home and surrounding land **2** : a piece of land acquired from U.S. public lands by living on and cultivating it

²homestead *vb* : to acquire or settle on public land for use as a homestead — **home·stead·er** \-ˌsted-ər\ *n*

home·stretch \'hōm-'strech\ *n* **1** : the part of a racetrack between the final turn and the finish line **2** : a final stage

home·town \-'taùn\ *n* : the city or town where one was born or grew up

home·ward \'hōm-wərd\ *or* **home·wards** \-wərdz\ *adv* : toward or in the direction of home — **homeward** *adj*

home·work \'hōm-ˌwərk\ *n* : work and especially school

lessons to be done outside the regular class period

hom·ey \'hō-mē\ *adj* **hom·i·er; -est** : resembling or suggestive of a home : COZY — **hom·ey·ness** *or* **hom·i·ness** *n*

ho·mi·cid·al \ˌhäm-ə-'sīd-°l, ˌhō-mə-\ *adj* : having or showing tendencies toward the killing of another person : MURDEROUS — **ho·mi·cid·al·ly** \-'sīd-°l-ē\ *adv*

ho·mi·cide \'häm-ə-ˌsīd, 'hō-mə-\ *n* : a killing of one human being by another [Middle English *homicide* "the killing of a person", from early French *homicide* (same meaning), from Latin *homicidium* "the act of killing a man", from *homo* "man" and *-cidium* "the act of killing", from *caedere* "to kill, cut"]

hom·i·ly \'häm-ə-lē\ *n, pl* **-lies** : SERMON 1

¹hom·ing \'hō-miŋ\ *n* : an accurate return of an animal (as a pigeon or salmon) to a known place

²homing *adj* **1** : returning by habit to a known place **2** : guiding or being guided to a goal

homing pigeon *n* : a racing pigeon trained to return home

hom·i·nid \'häm-ə-nəd, -ˌnid\ *n* : any of a family of two-footed primate mammals that include the human beings who have lived since the Pleistocene, their ancestors, and related extinct forms — **hominid** *adj*

hom·i·ny \'häm-ə-nē\ *n* : kernels of dried corn from which the hulls have been removed by soaking and boiling in water containing lye

ho·mo \'hō-mō\ *n, pl* **homos** : any of a genus of primate mammals that includes all human beings alive today and various related species no longer living

homo- — see HOM-

ho·mog·e·nate \hō-'mäj-ə-ˌnāt\ *n* : a product of homogenizing

ho·mo·ge·neous \ˌhō-mə-'jē-nē-əs, -nyəs\ *adj* **1** : of the same or a similar kind or nature **2** : being the same throughout — **ho·mo·ge·ne·ity** \-jə-'nē-ət-ē\ *n* — **ho·mo·ge·neous·ly** \-'jē-nē-əs-lē\ *adv*

ho·mog·e·nize \hō-'mäj-ə-ˌnīz, hə-\ *vb* **-nized; -niz·ing** **1** : to make homogeneous **2 a** : to reduce to small particles of uniform size and distribute evenly ⟨*homogenize* peanut butter⟩ ⟨*homogenize* paint⟩ **b** : to break up the fat of (milk) into very fine particles especially by forcing through minute openings — **ho·mog·e·ni·za·tion** \-ˌmäj-ə-nə-'zā-shən\ *n* — **ho·mog·e·niz·er** \-'mäj-ə-ˌnī-zər\ *n*

ho·mo·graph \'häm-ə-ˌgraf, 'hō-mə-\ *n* : one of two or more words alike in spelling but different in origin or meaning or pronunciation ⟨"row" of seats and "row" (a fight) are *homographs,* as are "fair" (market) and "fair" (beautiful)⟩

ho·mol·o·gous \hō-'mäl-ə-gəs, hə-\ *adj* **1** : showing biological homology **2** : having the same or allelic genes usually arranged in the same order ⟨a pair of *homologous* chromosomes⟩

ho·mo·logue *or* **ho·mo·log** \'hō-mə-ˌlòg, 'häm-ə-, -ˌläg\ *n* : either chromosome of a homologous pair

ho·mol·o·gy \hō-'mäl-ə-jē, hə-\ *n, pl* **-gies** : a likeness often due to common origin: as **a** : structural likeness between corresponding parts of different plants or animals due to evolution from a common ancestor in the distant past **b** : structural likeness between different parts of the same individual

hom·onym \'häm-ə-ˌnim, 'hō-mə-\ *n* **1** : HOMOPHONE **2** : HOMOGRAPH **3** : one of two or more words spelled and pronounced alike but different in meaning ⟨the noun "bear" and the verb "bear" are *homonyms*⟩ [from Latin *homonymum* "homonym", derived from Greek *homonymos* (adjective) "having the same name", from *hom-, homos* "same" and *onyma, onoma* "name"] — **hom·onym·ic** \ˌhäm-ə-'nim-ik, ˌhō-mə-\ *adj*

ho·mo·phone \'häm-ə-ˌfōn, 'hō-mə-\ *n* : one of two or more words pronounced alike but different in meaning, origin, or spelling ⟨"to," "too," and "two" are *homophones*⟩ — **ho·moph·o·nous** \hō-'mäf-ə-nəs\ *adj*

ho·moph·o·ny \hō-'mäf-ə-nē\ *n* : music having a single accompanied melodic line — **ho·mo·phon·ic** \ˌhäm-ə-'fän-ik, ˌhō-mə-\ *adj*

Ho·mo sa·pi·ens \ˌhō-mō-'sap-ē-ənz, -'sä-pē-ˌenz\ *n* : MANKIND 1 [scientific Latin, derived from *homo* "man" and *sapiens* "wise, intelligent"]

¹ho·mo·sex·u·al \ˌhō-mə-'seksh-(ə-)wəl, -'sek-shəl\ *adj* : of, relating to, or showing sexual desire toward another of the same sex as one's self

²homosexual *n* : a homosexual individual

ho·mo·sex·u·al·i·ty \ˌhō-mə-ˌsek-shə-'wal-ət-ē\ *n* : the quality or state of being homosexual

ho·mo·zy·gos·i·ty \ˌhō-mə-zī-'gäs-ət-ē\ *n* : the state of being homozygous

ho·mo·zy·gote \ˌhō-mə-'zī-ˌgōt\ *n* : a homozygous individual

ho·mo·zy·gous \ˌhō-mə-'zī-gəs\ *adj* : having the two genes at a given place on a pair of homologous chromosomes the same at one or more places ⟨a plant *homozygous* for yellow seed⟩

hone \'hōn\ *vb* **honed; hon·ing** : to sharpen with or as if with a fine abrasive stone

¹hon·est \'än-əst\ *adj* **1** : free from fraud or trickery : TRUTHFUL ⟨an *honest* plea⟩ **2** : being just what is indicated : GENUINE, REAL ⟨made an *honest* mistake⟩ **3** : not given to cheating, stealing, or lying ⟨poor but *honest* people⟩ **4** : TRUSTWORTHY **5** : FRANK, OPEN **syn** see UPRIGHT

²honest *adv* : to tell the truth : I mean it ⟨I didn't do it — *honest* I didn't⟩

hon·est·ly \'än-əst-lē\ *adv* **1** : in an honest manner: as **a** : without cheating ⟨counted the votes *honestly*⟩ **b** : in fact : ACTUALLY, GENUINELY ⟨was *honestly* scared⟩ ⟨I can *honestly* say⟩ **2** : to be honest : to tell the truth ⟨*honestly,* I don't know how you do it⟩

hon·es·ty \'än-ə-stē\ *n* : the quality or state of being honest

hon·ey \'hən-ē\ *n, pl* **honeys** **1** : a thick sugary material prepared by bees from the nectar of flowers and stored by them in a honeycomb for food **2 a** : SWEETHEART, DEAR — often used as a term of affection **b** : something very good ⟨a *honey* of a play⟩ **3** : the quality or state of being sweet — **honey** *adj*

hon·ey·bee \-ˌbē\ *n* : a bee that produces honey and lives in colonies; *esp* : a European bee widely kept for its honey and wax

¹hon·ey·comb \-ˌkōm\ *n* **1** : a mass of six-sided wax cells built by honeybees in their nest to contain young bees and stores of honey **2** : something that resembles a honeycomb in structure or appearance

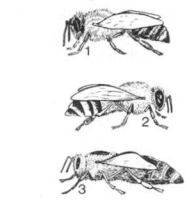

honeybee: *1* worker, *2* drone, *3* queen

²honeycomb *vb* : to make or become full of holes like a honeycomb

hon·ey·dew \'hən-ē-ˌd(y)ü\ *n* : a sugary substance deposited on the leaves of plants usually by aphids or scale insects but sometimes by a fungus

honeydew melon *n* : a pale smooth-skinned muskmelon with greenish sweet flesh

hon·ey·moon \'hən-ē-ˌmün\ *n* **1** : the time immediately after marriage **2** : the holiday spent by a newly-married couple — **honeymoon** *vb* — **hon·ey·moon·er** *n*

\ə\ **abut**	\aů\ **out**	\i\ tip	\ò\ **saw**	\ů\ **foot**
\ər\ **further**	\ch\ **chin**	\ī\ **life**	\òi\ **coin**	\y\ **yet**
\a\ **mat**	\e\ **pet**	\j\ **job**	\th\ **thin**	\yü\ **few**
\ā\ **take**	\ē\ **easy**	\ŋ\ **sing**	\th\ **this**	\yů\ **cure**
\ä\ **cot, cart**	\g\ **go**	\ō\ **bone**	\ü\ **food**	\zh\ **vision**

hon·ey·suck·le \-ˌsək-əl\ *n* : any of a genus of shrubs having leaves arranged in pairs on opposite sides of the stem and often showy flowers rich in nectar

honk \'häŋk, 'hȯŋk\ *n* : the cry of a goose; *also* : a similar sound (as of a horn) — **honk** *vb*

¹hon·or \'än-ər\ *n* **1 a** : a good name : public admiration : REPUTATION **b** : a showing of respect : RECOGNITION ⟨a dinner in *honor* of a new coach⟩ **2** : ¹PRIVILEGE ⟨whom have I the *honor* of addressing⟩ **3 a** *cap* — used especially as a title for an official of high rank (as a judge) ⟨if your *Honor* please⟩ **b** : one whose worth brings respect or fame : CREDIT ⟨an *honor* to your profession⟩ **4 a** : evidence or a symbol of great respect (as a title or medal) **b** *pl* : special credit or recognition given to graduating students for high achievement **5 a** : CHASTITY, PURITY **b** : high moral standards of behavior : INTEGRITY ⟨a person of *honor*⟩ **6** *pl* : courteous actions of a host or hostess ⟨did the *honors* at the table⟩

²honor *vb* **hon·ored; hon·or·ing** \'än-(ə-)riŋ\ **1 a** : to treat with honor : RESPECT ⟨*honor* your parents⟩ **b** : to give an honor to **2** : to fulfill the terms of ⟨*honored* the contract⟩

hon·or·able \'än-(ə-)rə-bəl, 'än-ər-bəl\ *adj* **1** : deserving of honor **2** : performed or accompanied with marks of honor ⟨an *honorable* burial⟩ **3** — used as a title especially for various government officials **4** : doing credit to the possessor ⟨*honorable* wounds⟩ **5** : characterized by honesty : ETHICAL — **hon·or·ably** \-blē\ *adv*

hon·or·ary \'än-ə-ˌrer-ē\ *adj* **1** : given or done as a sign of honor ⟨an *honorary* degree⟩ **2** : ¹VOLUNTARY 1, UNPAID ⟨*honorary* president⟩ — **hon·or·ari·ly** \ˌän-ə-ˈrer-ə-lē\ *adv*

honor guard *n* : a guard assigned to a ceremonial duty

¹hood \'hu̇d\ *n* **1** : a soft covering for the head and neck often attached to a coat or cape **2** : a marking, crest, or fold on the head of an animal **3 a** : something resembling a hood in form or use **b** : a cover for parts of mechanisms; *esp* : the movable metal covering over the engine of an automobile **c** : an enclosure provided with a draft for carrying off disagreeable or harmful fumes, sprays, or dust — **hood·ed** \-əd\ *adj* — **hood·like** \-ˌlīk\ *adj*

²hood \'hu̇d, 'hüd\ *n* : HOODLUM

-hood \ˌhu̇d\ *n suffix* **1** : state : condition : quality ⟨child*hood*⟩ ⟨hardi*hood*⟩ **2** : instance of a state or quality ⟨false*hood*⟩ **3** : individuals sharing a state or character ⟨brother*hood*⟩ [Old English *hād* "condition, quality"]

hood·lum \'hüd-ləm\ *n* **1** : MOBSTER, THUG **2** : a young ruffian

hoo·doo \'hüd-ü\ *n, pl* **hoodoos** **1** : VOODOOISM 1 **2** : something that brings bad luck [of African origin] — **hoodoo** *vb* — **hoo·doo·ism** \-ˌiz-əm\ *n*

hood·wink \'hu̇d-ˌwiŋk\ *vb* : to deceive by false appearance : TRICK

¹hoof \'hu̇f, 'hüf\ *n, pl* **hooves** \'hu̇vz, 'hüvz\ *or* **hoofs** **1** : a covering of horn that protects the front of or encloses the ends of the toes of some mammals (as horses, oxen, and pigs) and that corresponds to a nail or claw **2** : a hoofed foot especially of a horse — **hoofed** \'hu̇ft, 'hüft, 'hu̇vd, 'hüvd\ *adj* — **on the hoof** : LIVING 1a ⟨meat animals bought *on the hoof*⟩

²hoof *vb* **1** : to move or travel on foot : WALK **2** : ¹DANCE 1, 3 — **hoof·er** *n*

hoof–and–mouth disease *n* : FOOT-AND-MOUTH DISEASE

hoof·beat \'hu̇f-ˌbēt, 'hüf-\ *n* : the sound of a hoof striking a hard surface (as the ground)

hoof·print \-ˌprint\ *n* : a mark or hollow made by a hoof

¹hook \'hu̇k\ *n* **1** : a curved or bent tool for catching, holding, or pulling **2** : something curved or bent **3** : the flight of a ball curving to the left when hit or thrown by a right-hander or to the right when hit or thrown by a left-hander **4** : a short sweeping punch made with the elbow bent — **by hook or by crook** : by any means — **off the hook**

: out of trouble — **on one's own hook** : by oneself : INDEPENDENTLY

²hook *vb* **1** : to form into a hook : CROOK, CURVE **2 a** : to seize, make fast, or connect by or as if by a hook **b** : to become secured or connected by or as if by a hook **3** : PILFER, STEAL **4** : to strike or pierce as if with a hook **5** : to make by drawing loops of thread, yarn, or cloth through a coarse fabric with a hook ⟨*hook* a rug⟩ **6** : to hit or throw a ball so that a hook results

hook and eye *n* : a clothing fastener made up of a small hook that catches over a bar or into a loop

hooked \'hu̇kt\ *adj* **1** : shaped like or provided with a hook **2 a** : addicted to narcotics **b** : fascinated by or fond of something ⟨*hooked* on skiing⟩

hook·up \'hu̇k-ˌəp\ *n* **1 a** : an arrangement (as of circuits) used for a specific purpose (as in radio) **b** : the diagram of such an arrangement **2** : an arrangement of mechanical parts **3** : CONNECTION 2, ALLIANCE ⟨a *hookup* between two countries⟩

hook·worm \-ˌwərm\ *n* **1** : a parasitic nematode worm having strong hooks or plates about the mouth **2** : a diseased state marked by blood loss, paleness, and weakness due to hookworms in the intestine — called also **hookworm disease**

hooky *or* **hook·ey** \'hu̇k-ē\ *n, pl* **hook·ies** *or* **hookeys** : TRUANT

hoop \'hu̇p, 'hüp\ *n* **1** : a circular band used for holding together the strips that make up the sides of a barrel; *also* : a similar band used as a toy **2** : a circular figure or object : RING **3** : a circle or series of circles of flexible material used for spreading out a woman's full skirt — **hoop** *vb*

hoop·skirt \-ˈskərt\ *n* : a skirt stiffened with or as if with hoops

hooray *variant of* HURRAH

hoose·gow \'hüs-ˌgau̇\ *n, slang* : PRISON 2 [from Spanish *juzgado* "panel of judges, courtroom", derived from *juzgar* "to judge", from Latin *judicare* "to judge" — related to JUDGE]

hoopskirt

¹hoot \'hüt\ *vb* **1** : to utter a loud shout usually of scorn **2** : to make the characteristic call of an owl or a similar sound **3** : to drive out by hooting — **hoot·er** *n*

²hoot *n* **1** : a sound of hooting; *esp* : the call of an owl **2** : a very small amount ⟨don't care a *hoot*⟩

hoo·te·nan·ny \'hüt-ᵊn-ˌan-ē\ *n, pl* **-nies** : a gathering at which folksingers entertain

¹hop \'häp\ *vb* **hopped; hop·ping** **1** : to move by a quick springy leap or series of leaps; *esp* : to jump on one foot **2** : to jump over ⟨*hop* a puddle⟩ **3** : to get aboard by or as if by hopping ⟨*hop* a train⟩ **4** : to make a quick trip especially by air [Old English *hoppian* "to leap, hop"]

²hop *n* **1 a** : a short brisk leap especially on one leg **b** : ²BOUNCE 1b **2** : ²DANCE 3, BALL ⟨the junior *hop*⟩ **3 a** : a flight in an airplane **b** : a short trip

³hop *n* **1** : a twining vine related to the mulberry and having leaves with lobes and flowers in cone-shaped catkins **2** *pl* : the ripe dried catkins of a hop used especially to give a bitter flavor to malt liquors [Middle English *hoppe* "the hop vine"; of Dutch origin]

⁴hop *vb* **hopped; hop·ping** **1** : to flavor with hops **2** : to increase the power of ⟨*hop* up an engine⟩

¹hope \'hōp\ *vb* **hoped; hop·ing** : to desire something and expect that it will happen or be obtained ⟨*hope* to succeed⟩ ⟨*hope* for an invitation⟩ ⟨*hope* for a bicycle⟩

²hope *n* **1** : ¹TRUST 1a, RELIANCE ⟨our *hope* is in the president⟩ **2 a :** desire accompanied by expectation of fulfillment ⟨in *hope* of an early recovery⟩ **b :** someone or something on which hopes are centered ⟨a home run was the only *hope* for victory⟩ **c :** something hoped for

¹**hope·ful** \'hōp-fəl\ *adj* **1 :** full of or inclined to hope **2 :** having qualities which inspire hope — **hope·ful·ness** *n*

²**hopeful** *n* **:** a person who has hopes or is considered promising

hope·ful·ly \'hōp-fə-lē\ *adv* **1 :** in a hopeful manner ⟨a dog looking *hopefully* for a tidbit⟩ **2 :** I hope : we hope ⟨*hopefully* it won't rain tomorrow⟩

hope·less \'hō-pləs\ *adj* **1 a :** having no expectation of good or success **b :** giving no reason for hope : DESPERATE ⟨a *hopeless* situation⟩ **2 a :** INCURABLE **b :** incapable of solution or accomplishment : IMPOSSIBLE ⟨a *hopeless* task⟩ — **hope·less·ly** *adv* — **hope·less·ness** *n*

Ho·pi \'hō-pē\ *n* **:** a member of a Pueblo American Indian people of northeastern Arizona

hop·per \'häp-ər\ *n* **1 a :** one that hops **b :** a leaping insect; *esp* **:** a young hopping form of an insect **2 a :** a usually funnel-shaped container for delivering material (as grain) **b :** a tank with a device for releasing its liquid through a pipe

hop·scotch \'häp-,skäch\ *n* **:** a child's game in which a player hops through a figure drawn on the ground

horde \'hō(ə)rd, 'ho(ə)rd\ *n* **1 :** a wandering people or tribe **2 :** a great multitude : THRONG, SWARM ⟨*hordes* of tourists⟩

ho·ri·zon \hə-'rīz-ᵊn\ *n* **1 :** the line where the earth or sea seems to meet the sky **2 :** the limit or range of a person's outlook or experience ⟨reading broadens our *horizons*⟩ **3 :** a distinct layer of soil or its underlying material in a vertical section of land — **ho·ri·zon·al** \-'rīz-nəl, -ᵊn-əl\ *adj*

¹**hor·i·zon·tal** \,hȯr-ə-'zänt-ᵊl, ,här-\ *adj* **1 :** of or relating to the horizon **2 :** parallel to the horizon : LEVEL **3 :** being on the same level — **hor·i·zon·tal·ly** \-ᵊl-ē\ *adv*

²**horizontal** *n* **:** a horizontal line or plane

hor·mon·al \hȯr-'mōn-ᵊl\ *adj* **:** of, relating to, or brought about by hormones

hor·mone \'hȯr-,mōn\ *n* **:** a product of living cells that circulates in body fluids or sap and produces a specific and usually stimulating effect at a distance from the place where it is made

horn \'hȯ(ə)rn\ *n* **1 :** one of the hard bony growths on the head of many hoofed animals (as cattle, goats, or sheep) **2 :** a part like an animal's horn **3 :** the material of which horns are composed or a similar material **4 :** a hollow horn used to hold something ⟨powder *horn*⟩ **5 :** something resembling a horn ⟨saddle *horn*⟩ ⟨*horns* of the crescent moon⟩ **6 a :** a brass wind instrument (as a trumpet or French horn) **b :** a device that makes a noise like that of a horn ⟨an automobile *horn*⟩ — **horned** \'hȯ(ə)rnd\ *adj* — **horn·less** \'hȯ(ə)rn-ləs\ *adj* — **horn·like** \-,līk\ *adj*

horn·beam \-,bēm\ *n* **:** any of a genus of trees related to the birch and having smooth gray bark and hard white wood

horn·bill \-,bil\ *n* **:** any of a family of large Old World birds having enormous bills

horn·blende \-,blend\ *n* **:** a dark mineral commonly found as a kind of rock

horned owl *n* **:** any of several owls with two bunches of feathers on the head that look like ears

hornbill

horned pout *n* **:** a common bullhead of the eastern U.S.

horned toad *n* **:** any of several small harmless insect-eating lizards of the western U.S. and Mexico having hornlike spines

hor·net \'hȯr-nət\ *n* **:** any of the larger wasps that live in colonies

horn·fels \'hȯ(ə)rn-,felz\ *n* **:** a fine-grained rock formed by the action of heat

horn of plenty *n* **:** CORNUCOPIA

horn·pipe \'hȯ(ə)rn-,pīp\ *n* **1 :** a wind instrument made up of a wooden or bone pipe and a bell usually of horn **2 :** a lively folk dance originally accompanied by hornpipe playing

horn·wort \-,wȯrt, -,wȯ(ə)rt\ *n* **:** any of an order of plants that usually live in water and are related to the liverworts

horny \'hȯr-nē\ *adj* **horn·i·er; -est** **1 :** made of horn or of something resembling horn **2 :** ¹HARD 1, CALLOUS ⟨*horny* hands⟩

horo·scope \'hȯr-ə-,skōp, 'här-\ *n* **1 :** a diagram of the positions of planets and signs of the zodiac used by astrologers to foretell events of a person's life **2 :** an astrological forecast [Middle English *oruscope* "horoscope", from early French *horoscope* (same meaning), from Latin *horoscopus* (same meaning), from Greek *hōroskopos*, literally "hour watcher", from *hōra* "hour" and *skopos* "watcher" — related to BISHOP, EPISCOPAL, SCOPE; see *Word History* at BISHOP]

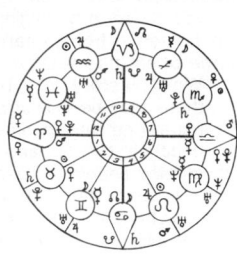

horoscope 1

hor·ren·dous \hȯ-'ren-dəs, hä-, hə-\ *adj* **:** DREADFUL, HORRIBLE — **hor·ren·dous·ly** *adv*

hor·ri·ble \'hȯr-ə-bəl, 'här-\ *adj* **1 :** marked by or arousing horror **2 :** extremely unpleasant or disagreeable — **hor·ri·bly** \-blē\ *adv*

hor·rid \'hȯr-əd, 'här-\ *adj* **1 :** HIDEOUS, SHOCKING **2 :** REPULSIVE, OFFENSIVE — **hor·rid·ly** *adv* — **hor·rid·ness** *n*

hor·ri·fy \'hȯr-ə-,fī, 'här-\ *vb* **-fied; -fy·ing :** to cause to feel horror

hor·ror \'hȯr-ər, 'här-\ *n* **1 :** strong fear, dread, or dislike **2 :** the quality of inspiring horror **3 :** something horrible — **horror** *adj*

hors d'oeuvre \ȯr-'dərv\ *n, pl* **hors d'oeuvres** *also* **hors d'oeuvre** \-'dərv(z)\ **:** any of various tasty foods usually served as appetizers [from French *hors-d'œuvre* "something extra", from the phrase *hors d'œuvre* "nonessential", literally "outside of work"]

¹**horse** \'hȯ(ə)rs\ *n, pl* **hors·es** *also* **horse** **1 a :** a large hoofed grazing domestic mammal that is used to carry or draw loads and for riding **b :** a male horse : STALLION **2 a :** a frame that supports something (as wood while being cut) **b :** a piece of gymnasium equipment used for balancing and swinging movements or for vaulting exercises **3** *horse pl* **:** CAVALRY **4** *slang* **:** HEROIN — **horse** *adj*

²**horse** *vb* **horsed; hors·ing** **1 :** to provide with a horse **2 :** to engage in horseplay : FOOL ⟨was *horsing* around instead of studying⟩

¹**horse·back** \'hȯrs-,bak\ *n* **:** the back of a horse

²**horseback** *adv* **:** on horseback

horse·car \'hȯrs-,kär\ *n* **:** a streetcar drawn by horses

horse chestnut *n* **1 :** a large Asian tree with leaves divided into fingerlike parts and large flower clusters that is widely grown as an ornamental and shade tree **2 :** the large glossy brown seed of a horse chestnut

horse·fly \'hȯrs-,flī\ *n* **:** any of a family of swift usually large two-winged flies with bloodsucking females

\ə\ **abut**	\au̇\ **out**	\i\ **tip**	\ȯ\ **saw**	\u̇\ **foot**
\ər\ **further**	\ch\ **chin**	\ī\ **life**	\ȯi\ **coin**	\y\ **yet**
\a\ **mat**	\e\ **pet**	\j\ **job**	\th\ **thin**	\yü\ **cure**
\ā\ **take**	\ē\ **easy**	\ŋ\ **sing**	\t̲h̲\ **this**	\yu̇\ **cure**
\ä\ **cot, cart**	\g\ **go**	\ō\ **bone**	\ü\ **food**	\zh\ **vision**

horse·hair \-,ha(ə)r, -,he(ə)r\ *n* **1** : hair of a horse especially from the mane or tail **2** : cloth made from horsehair — **horsehair** *adj*

horsehair worm *n* : any of various long slender worms that are related to nematodes but have a true body cavity and a reduced digestive tract in the adult and are parasites on arthropods as larvae — called also *horsehair snake*

horse·hide \'hòrs-,hīd\ *n* : a horse's hide or leather made from it

horse latitudes *n pl* : either of two regions in the neighborhoods of 30° N. and 30° S. latitude having high pressure, calms, and light changeable winds

horse·laugh \'hòr-,slaf, -,slàf\ *n* : a loud laugh : GUFFAW

horse·man \'hòr-smən\ *n* **1 a** : a rider on horseback **b** : one skilled in managing horses **2** : a breeder or raiser of horses — **horse·man·ship** \-,ship\ *n*

horse opera *n* : ²WESTERN

> **Word History** You have probably noticed that while there may be lots of horses in a cowboy film, there is usually no singing. The word OPERA is used in this term because the exciting stories and the overacting reminded people of operas. *Horse opera,* in reference to a western, dates from the late 1920s. About ten years later the term *soap opera* came to be used for a radio and still later for a television drama that was frequently sponsored by a soap manufacturer. By the late 1940s the term *space opera* came into use for a drama involving space travelers and beings on other planets.

horse·play \'hòr-,splā\ *n* : rough or loud play

horse·pow·er \'hòr-,spaù(-ə)r\ *n* : a unit of power equal in the U.S. to 746 watts and nearly equal to the English unit of the same name that equals 550 foot-pounds of work per second

horse·rad·ish \'hòrs-,rad-ish, -,red-\ *n* **1 a** : a tall coarse white-flowered herb related to the mustard **b** : the sharp tasting root of the horseradish **2** : a strong seasoning made from the root of the horseradish

horse sense *n* : COMMON SENSE

horse·shoe \'hòrs-,shü, 'hòrsh-\ *n* **1** : a usually U-shaped band of iron shaped and nailed to the rim of a horse's hoof **2** : something shaped like a horseshoe **3** *pl* : a game in which horseshoes are tossed at a stake in the ground — **horseshoe** *vb* — **horse·sho·er** *n*

horseshoe crab *n* : any of an order of arthropods that have a broad crescent shaped united head and thorax with a pair of compound eyes and a pair of simple eyes, a small abdomen, and a movable stiff tail spine

horse·tail \'hòr-,stāl\ *n* : EQUISETUM

horse trade *n* : bargaining marked by clever careful dealing by both sides — **horse–trade** *vb* — **horse trader** *n*

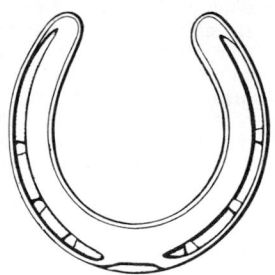

horseshoe 1

horse·whip \'hòr-,swip, 'hòrs-,hwip\ *vb* : to beat with or as if with a whip made to be used on a horse

horse·wom·an \'hòr-,swùm-ən\ *n* **1** : a woman horseback rider **2** : a woman skilled in caring for or managing horses

hors·ey *or* **horsy** \'hòr-sē\ *adj* **hors·i·er; -est** **1** : of, relating to, or suggesting a horse, horses, or horse racing **2** : characteristic of horsemen or horsewomen — **hors·i·ness** *n*

hor·ti·cul·ture \'hòrt-ə-,kəl-chər\ *n* : the science of growing fruits, vegetables, flowers, or ornamental plants — **hor·ti·cul·tur·al** \,hòrt-ə-'kəlch-(ə-)rəl\ *adj*

hor·ti·cul·tur·ist \,hòrt-ə-'kəlch-(ə-)rəst\ *n* : a person who specializes in horticulture

ho·san·na \hō-'zan-ə\ *interj* — used as a cry of praise and adoration

¹**hose** \'hōz\ *n* **1** *pl* **hose a** : STOCKING, SOCK **b** : a close-fitting garment covering the legs and waist worn by men about 1600 **c** : short pants reaching to the knee **2** *pl* **hose** *or* **hos·es** : a flexible tube for carrying fluid

²**hose** *vb* **hosed; hos·ing** : to spray, water, or wash with a hose

Ho·sea \hō-'zā-ə, -'zē-\ *n* — see BIBLE table

ho·siery \'hōzh(-ə)-rē, 'hōz(-ə)-\ *n* : stockings or socks in general

hos·pice \'häs-pəs\ *n* **1** : an inn for travelers; *esp* : one kept by a religious order **2** : a place or program for caring for dying persons

hos·pi·ta·ble \hä-'spit-ə-bəl, 'häs-(,)pit-\ *adj* **1** : generous and friendly in entertaining guests **2 a** : PLEASANT 2, INVITING **b** : offering a pleasant or healthful environment ⟨a *hospitable* climate⟩ **3** : ¹OPEN 7 ⟨*hospitable* to new ideas⟩ — **hos·pi·ta·bly** \-blē\ *adv*

hos·pi·tal \'häs-,pit-ⁿl\ *n* : an institution where the sick or injured are given medical or surgical care [Middle English *hospital* "a stopping place for travelers, a place that cares for people too old, sick, or poor to care for themselves", from early French *hospital* (same meaning), derived from Latin *hospitale* "bedroom, guest room", from *hospitalis* "of a guest, showing hospitality", from *hospit-, hospes* "host, stranger, guest", from *hostis* "stranger, enemy" — related to HOSPITALITY, ¹HOST, ²HOST, HOSTILE, HOTEL]

hos·pi·tal·i·ty \,häs-pə-'tal-ət-ē\ *n, pl* **-ties** : hospitable treatment of visitors and guests [Middle English *hospitalite* "hospitality", from early French *hospitalité* (same meaning), derived from Latin *hospitale* "of a guest, showing hospitality", from *hospit-, hospes* "host, stranger, guest" — related to HOSPITAL, ²HOST, HOTEL]

hos·pi·tal·ize \'häs-,pit-ⁿl-,īz\ *vb* **-ized; -iz·ing** : to place in a hospital for care and treatment — **hos·pi·tal·iza·tion** \,häs-,pit-ⁿl-ə-'zā-shən\ *n*

¹**host** \'hōst\ *n* **1** : ARMY 1a **2** : a great number [Middle English *host* "army", from early French *hoste* (same meaning), from Latin *hostis* (same meaning), from earlier *hostis* "stranger, enemy" — related to HOSPITAL, HOSTILE]

²**host** *n* **1** : one who receives or entertains guests socially or as a business **2** : a living animal or plant that serves as a place to live for another plant or animal and is a source of food or protection for it [Middle English *hoste* "host, guest", from early French *hoste* (same meaning), derived from Latin *hospit-, hospes* "host, stranger, guest" — related to HOSPITAL, HOSPITALITY] — **host** *vb*

³**host** *n, often cap* : a round thin piece of bread used in the Eucharist

hos·tage \'häs-tij\ *n* : a person held captive as a pledge that promises will be kept or terms met by another

hos·tel \'häs-tⁿl\ *n* **1** : INN **2** : an inexpensive lodging for usually young travelers — called also *youth hostel*

hos·tel·er \'häs-tə-lər\ *n* **1** : one who lodges paying guests **2** : a young traveler who stays in hostels

hos·tel·ry \'häs-tⁿl-rē\ *n, pl* **-ries** : INN, HOTEL

host·ess \'hō-stəs\ *n* : a woman who acts as host; *esp* : one who greets and provides service for diners in a restaurant or passengers on an airplane or ship

hos·tile \'häs-tⁿl, -,tīl\ *adj* **1** : of or relating to an enemy ⟨*hostile* troops⟩ **2** : showing ill will : UNFRIENDLY **3** : not hospitable : FORBIDDING ⟨a *hostile* environment⟩ [from early French *hostile* or Latin *hostilis,* both meaning "hostile", from Latin *hostis* "stranger, enemy" — related to HOSPITAL, ¹HOST] — **hos·tile·ly** \-tⁿl-(l)ē, -tīl-lē\ *adv*

hos·til·i·ty \hä-'stil-ət-ē\ *n, pl* **-ties** **1** : a hostile state, attitude, or action **2** *pl* : acts of warfare

hos·tler \'äs-lər, 'häs-\ *also* **ost·ler** \'äs-\ *n* : one who takes care of horses or mules

hot \'hät\ *adj* **hot·ter; hot·test** **1** : having a high temperature **2 a** : easily excited : ARDENT, FIERY ⟨*hot* temper⟩

b : VIOLENT 1, RAGING   **c** : EAGER ⟨*hot* for reform⟩   **d** : exciting in rhythm and mood ⟨*hot* music⟩   **3** : feeling or causing an uncomfortable degree of body heat ⟨my forehead is *hot*⟩   **4** : newly made : FRESH ⟨*hot* scent⟩; *also* : close to something sought ⟨you're getting *hotter*⟩   **5** : suggestive of heat or of burning or glowing objects ⟨*hot* spicy foods⟩ ⟨*hot* colors⟩   **6 a** : temporarily capable of unusual performance (as in a sport)   **b** : currently popular ⟨a *hot* topic of conversation⟩   **7 a** : carrying electric current   **b** : RADIOACTIVE   **c** : dealing with radioactive material   **8 a** : recently stolen ⟨*hot* jewels⟩   **b** : wanted by the police — **hot** *adv* — **hot·ly** *adv* — **hot·ness** *n*

hot air *n* : empty talk

hot·bed \'hät-ˌbed\ *n*   **1** : a heated bed of soil enclosed in glass and used for growing seedlings   **2** : an environment that favors rapid growth or development ⟨a *hotbed* of crime⟩

hot–blood·ed \-'bləd-əd\ *adj* : easily excited : PASSIONATE — **hot–blood·ed·ness** *n*

hot·box \-ˌbäks\ *n* : a bearing (as of a railroad car) overheated by friction

hot·cake \-ˌkāk\ *n* : PANCAKE

hotch·potch \'häch-ˌpäch\ *n* : HODGEPODGE [Middle English *hochepot* "mixed stew", derived from early French *hochepot* (same meaning), from *hochier* "to shake" and *pot* "pot, container" — see *Word History* at HODGEPODGE]

hot dog \'hät-ˌdȯg\ *n* : FRANKFURTER; *esp* : a cooked frankfurter served in a long split roll

ho·tel \hō-'tel\ *n* : an establishment that provides lodging and usually meals, entertainment, and personal services for its guests [from French *hotel* "hotel", from early French *hostel* "a place for young travelers to spend the night", derived from Latin *hospitalis* "of a guest, showing hospitality", from *hospit-, hospes* "host, stranger, guest" — related to HOSPITAL, HOSPITALITY]

¹hot·foot \'hät-ˌfût\ *adv* : in haste

²hotfoot *vb* : to go quickly : HURRY ⟨*hotfoot* it home⟩

hot·head \'hät-ˌhed\ *n* : a hotheaded person

hot·head·ed \-'hed-əd\ *adj* : RASH, FIERY — **hot·head·ed·ly** *adv* — **hot·head·ed·ness** *n*

hot·house \-ˌhaús\ *n* : a heated glass-enclosed house for raising plants — **hothouse** *adj*

hot line *n* : a telephone line for direct emergency use (as between heads of governments or to a counseling service)

hot pepper *n*   **1** : an often thin-walled and small pepper with a sharp or biting taste   **2** : a pepper plant related to the potato that bears hot peppers

hot plate *n* : a small portable appliance for heating or cooking

hot rod *n* : an automobile rebuilt or changed for high speed and fast acceleration — **hot–rod·der** \'hät-'räd-ər\ *n*

hot·shot \'hät-ˌshät\ *n* : a showily skillful person

hot spring *n* : a spring whose water flows out at a temperature higher than the average temperature of the place where the spring is located; *esp* : a spring with a water temperature higher than 37°C

hot war *n* : a conflict involving actual fighting

hot water *n* : a distressing situation : DIFFICULTY ⟨in *hot water* for not doing my chores⟩

¹hound \'haúnd\ *n*   **1** : ¹DOG 1a   **2** : a dog of any of various hunting breeds having large drooping ears and a deep voice and following their prey by scent

²hound *vb* : to pursue with or as if with hounds

hour \'aú(ə)r\ *n*   **1** : one of the 24 divisions of a day : 60 minutes   **2** : the time of day   **3** : a fixed or particular time ⟨lunch *hour*⟩ ⟨an *hour* of need⟩   **4** : the distance traveled in an hour ⟨lives two *hours* away⟩   **5** : a class session ⟨a 50-minute *hour*⟩ — **after hours** : after the regular hours of work or operation

hour·glass \'aú(ə)r-ˌglas\ *n* : an instrument for measuring time in which sand, water, or mercury runs from the upper part to the lower part of a glass container in an hour —

hour·glass *adj*

hour·ly \'aú(ə)r-lē\ *adj*   **1** : occurring every hour ⟨*hourly* bus service⟩   **2** : figured in terms of one hour ⟨*hourly* wages⟩ — **hourly** *adv*

¹house \'haús\ *n, pl* **hous·es** \'haú-zəz\   **1** : a building in which one or more families live   **2 a** : something (as a nest or den) used by an animal for shelter   **b** : a building in which something is stored ⟨carriage *house*⟩   **3 a** : one of the 12 equal sections into which the celestial sphere is divided in astrology   **b** : a sign of the zodiac that is the seat of a planet's greatest influence   **4 a** : ¹HOUSEHOLD   **b** : FAMILY 1; *esp* : a royal or noble family   **5** : a residence for a religious community or for students   **6** : a body of persons assembled to make and discuss laws   **7 a** : a place of business or entertainment   **b** : a business firm   **c** : the audience in a theater or concert hall [Old English *hūs* "house, home" — related to HUSBAND]

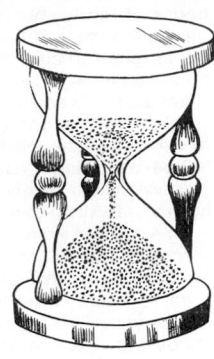

hourglass

²house \'haúz\ *vb* **housed; hous·ing**   **1 a** : to provide with living quarters or shelter   **b** : to store in a house   **2** : to encase or enclose for protection   **3** : to take shelter : LODGE

house·boat \'haús-ˌbōt\ *n* : a roomy pleasure boat equipped for use as a dwelling or for cruising

house·boy \-ˌbȯi\ *n* : a boy or man hired as a general household servant

house·break \-ˌbrāk\ *vb* **-broke; -bro·ken; -break·ing** : to make housebroken

house·break·ing \-ˌbrā-kiŋ\ *n* : the act of breaking into a person's house with the intention of committing a crime — **house·break·er** \-kər\ *n*

house·bro·ken \-ˌbrō-kən\ *adj* : trained in habits of eliminating bodily waste that are acceptable in indoor living

house cat *n* : CAT 1a

house·clean·ing \'haús-ˌklē-niŋ\ *n* : the cleaning of a house and its furniture

house·coat \'haú-ˌskōt\ *n* : a woman's loose and often long garment for wear around the house

house·dress \'haús-ˌdres\ *n* : a dress that is suitable for housework

house·fly \-ˌflī\ *n* : a two-winged fly that is common about human living places and spreads diseases (as typhoid fever)

¹house·hold \'haús-ˌhōld, 'haú-ˌsōld\ *n* : those who live as a family in one house

²household *adj*   **1** : of or relating to a household : DOMESTIC   **2** : ²FAMILIAR 3a, COMMON ⟨a *household* word⟩

house·hold·er \'haús-ˌhōl-dər, 'haú-ˌsōl-\ *n* : one who lives in a dwelling alone or as the head of a household

house·keep·er \'haú-ˌskē-pər\ *n* : a person employed to take care of a house

house·keep·ing \'haú-ˌskē-piŋ\ *n* : the care and management of a house and home affairs

house·maid \'haú-ˌsmād\ *n* : a female servant who does housework

housemaid's knee *n* : a swelling over the knee in front of the kneecap

House of Commons : the lower house of the British and Canadian parliaments

\ə\ abut		\aú\ out	\i\ tip	\ȯ\ saw	\ú\ foot
\ər\ further		\ch\ chin	\ī\ life	\ȯi\ coin	\y\ yet
\a\ mat		\e\ pet	\j\ job	\th\ thin	\yü\ few
\ā\ take		\ē\ easy	\ŋ\ sing	\th\ this	\yú\ cure
\ä\ cot, cart		\g\ go	\ō\ bone	\ü\ food	\zh\ vision

House of Lords : the upper house of the British Parliament

house of representatives : the lower house of a legislative body (as the U.S. Congress)

house·plant \'haù-,splant\ *n* : a plant grown or kept indoors

house sparrow *n* : an Old World sparrow that has been introduced into and now occurs widely in the New World — called also *English sparrow*

house·top \'haù-,stäp\ *n* : ¹ROOF 1a

house·warm·ing \'haù-swȯr-miŋ\ *n* : a party to celebrate moving into a new home

house·wife \'haù-,swīf, *sense 2 is often* 'həz-əf, 'həs-əf\ *n* **1** : a married woman who manages her own home **2** : a small container for small articles (as thread) — **house·wife·li·ness** \'haù-,swī-flē-nəs\ *n* — **house·wife·ly** \-flē\ *adj* — **house·wif·ery** \'haù-,swī-fə-rē, -frē\ *n*

house·work \-,swərk\ *n* : the work of housekeeping

¹hous·ing \'haù-ziŋ\ *n* **1 a** : SHELTER, LODGING **b** : dwellings provided for people ⟨*housing* for the elderly⟩ **2 a** : something that covers or protects **b** : a support (as a frame) for mechanical parts

²housing *n* : CAPARISON 1

hove *past and past participle of* HEAVE

hov·el \'həv-əl, 'häv-\ *n* **1** : an open shed or shelter **2** : a small poorly built house : HUT

hov·er \'həv-ər, 'häv-\ *vb* **hov·ered; hov·er·ing** \-(ə-)riŋ\ **1 a** : to hang fluttering in the air or on the wing **b** : to remain floating over a place or object **2 a** : to move to and fro near a place ⟨waiters *hovered* about⟩ **b** : to be in an undecided or uncertain state ⟨*hovering* between life and death⟩ — **hover** *n* — **hov·er·er** \-ər-ər\ *n*

hov·er·craft \-,kraft\ *n* : a vehicle supported above the surface of land or water by a cushion of air produced by fans blowing downward

¹how \(')haù\ *adv* **1** : in what manner or way ⟨study *how* plants grow⟩ ⟨*how* was it done⟩ **2** : for what reason : WHY ⟨*how* could you say that⟩ **3** : to what degree or extent ⟨*how* far is Denver⟩ **4** : in what state or condition ⟨*how* are you⟩ — **how about** : what do you say to or think of ⟨*how about* another game⟩

²how *conj* : in what manner or condition ⟨remember *how* they fought⟩ ⟨asked *how* they were⟩

¹how·be·it \haù-'bē-ət\ *adv* : NEVERTHELESS

²howbeit *conj* : ALTHOUGH

how·dah \'haùd-ə\ *n* : a seat or covered platform on the back of an elephant or camel

¹how·ev·er \haù-'ev-ər\ *conj* : in whatever way or manner ⟨do it *however* you like⟩

²however *adv* **1 a** : to whatever degree or extent **b** : in whatever manner or way **2** : in spite of that : on the other hand : BUT ⟨I'd like to go; *however*, I'd better not⟩

how·it·zer \'haù-ət-sər\ *n* : an artillery piece capable of firing a shell in a high arc [from Dutch *houwitser* "howitzer", derived from a Czechoslovakian word for "catapult"]

howl \'haù(ə)l\ *vb* **1** : to make a long loud mournful sound like that of a dog **2** : to cry out loudly (as with pain, grief, or rage) **3** : to make or bring about with an outcry ⟨*howled* in protest⟩ ⟨*howled* down the opposition⟩ — **howl** *n*

howdah

howl·er \'haù-lər\ *n* **1** : one that howls **2** : a stupid and ridiculous blunder

how·so·ev·er \,haù-sə-'wev-ər\ *adv* **1** : in whatever manner **2** : to whatever degree or extent

hoy·den \'hȯid-ᵊn\ *n* : a bold rowdy girl : TOMBOY — **hoy·den·ish** \-ish\ *adj*

hua·ra·che \wə-'räch-ē, hə-\ *n* : a sandal made of leather

thongs woven together [Mexican Spanish]

hub \'həb\ *n* **1** : the central part of a wheel, propeller, or fan **2** : a center of activity

Hub·bard squash \'həb-ərd-\ *n* : any of various large dark green to orange winter squashes with a somewhat oval shape and warty skin — called also *Hubbard*

hub·bub \'həb-,əb\ *n* : UPROAR, TURMOIL

hub·cap \'həb-,kap\ *n* : a removable metal covering on the tire of a car or truck

huck·le·ber·ry \'hək-əl-,ber-ē\ *n* **1 a** : an American shrub related to the blueberry **b** : the edible dark blue to black usually acid berry of a huckleberry **2** : BLUEBERRY

huck·ster \'hək-stər\ *n* **1** : one that peddles : HAWKER, PEDDLER **2** : a writer of advertising especially for radio or television

¹hud·dle \'həd-ᵊl\ *vb* **hud·dled; hud·dling** \'həd-liŋ, ᵊl-iŋ\ **1** : to crowd, push, or pile together ⟨people *huddled* in a doorway⟩ **2** : to gather in a huddle in football **3** : CURL UP, CROUCH ⟨a child *huddled* in its crib⟩ — **hud·dler** \'həd-lər, -ᵊl-ər\ *n*

²huddle *n* **1** : a close-packed group : BUNCH **2 a** : CONFERENCE 1 **b** : a brief gathering of football players away from the line of scrimmage to hear instructions for the next play

hue \'hyü\ *n* **1** : ¹COLOR 1a **2** : a particular variety of a color : SHADE **3** : a color other than white, gray, and black

hue and cry \,hyü-\ *n* **1** : a loud outcry formerly used in the pursuit of someone suspected of a crime **2** : a loud noise of alarm or protest

¹huff \'həf\ *vb* : ¹PUFF 1a

²huff *n* : a fit of anger or irritation

huffy \'həf-ē\ *adj* **huff·i·er; -est** : easily offended : TOUCHY — **huff·i·ly** \'həf-ə-lē\ *adv* — **huff·i·ness** \'həf-ē-nəs\ *n*

hug \'həg\ *vb* **hugged; hug·ging** **1** : to press tightly especially in the arms : EMBRACE **2** : to stay close to ⟨drives along *hugging* the curb⟩ — **hug** *n*

huge \'hyüj, 'yüj\ *adj* **1** : of great size or area **2** : of great scale or degree **3** : of limitless range or character **syn** see ENORMOUS — **huge·ly** *adv* — **huge·ness** *n*

hug·ger-mug·ger \'həg-ər-,məg-ər\ *n* **1** : SECRECY 2 **2** : a disorderly jumble — **hugger-mugger** *adj*

hu·la \'hü-lə\ *or* **hu·la-hu·la** \,hü-lə-'hü-lə\ *n* : a Polynesian dance composed of slow rhythmic body movements usually accompanied by chants and drumming [a native word in Hawaii]

¹hulk \'həlk\ *n* **1** : a heavy clumsy ship **2** : the body of an old ship unfit for service or of an abandoned wreck **3** : a bulky or clumsy person or thing

²hulk *vb* : to appear impressively large : BULK — **hulk·ing** \'həl-kiŋ\ *adj*

¹hull \'həl\ *n* **1 a** : the outer covering of a fruit or seed **b** : the remains of the flower that cling to the base of some fruits **2** : the frame or body of a ship, flying boat, or airship

²hull *vb* : to remove the hulls of ⟨*hulling* strawberries⟩ — **hull·er** *n*

hul·la·ba·loo \'həl-ə-bə-,lü\ *n, pl* **-loos** : UPROAR, DIN

hum \'həm\ *vb* **hummed; hum·ming** **1 a** : to utter a continuous \m\ sound **b** : to make the natural buzzing noise of an insect in motion : DRONE **c** : to give forth a low continuous blend of sound **2** : to produce musical tones while keeping the lips closed **3** : to be busily active ⟨the place was *humming*⟩ — **hum** *n* — **hum·mer** *n*

¹hu·man \'hyü-mən, 'yü-\ *adj* **1** : relating to or characteristic of human beings; *esp* : showing qualities typical of human beings ⟨a *human* failing⟩ **2** : consisting of human beings ⟨the *human* race⟩ **3** : having human form or characteristics ⟨the dog's expression was almost *human*⟩ — **hu·man·ness** \-mən-nəs\ *n*

²human *n* : a human being — **hu·man·like** \-,līk\ *adj*

hu·mane \hyü-'mān, yü-\ *adj* : marked by sympathy or consideration for others — **hu·mane·ly** *adv* — **hu·mane-**

ness \-'mān-nəs\ *n*

human im·mu·no·de·fi·cien·cy virus \-,im-yə-nō-di-'fish-ən(t)-sē-, -im-,yü-nō-\ *n* : HIV

hu·man·i·tar·i·an \hyü-,man-ə-'ter-ē-ən, yü-\ *n* : a person devoted to or working for the health and happiness of other people — **humanitarian** *adj* — **hu·man·i·tar·i·an·ism** \-ē-ə-,niz-əm\ *n*

hu·man·i·ty \hyü-'man-ət-ē, yü-\ *n, pl* **-ties** **1** : the quality or state of being human or of being humane **2** *pl* : studies (as literature, history, and art) concerned primarily with human culture **3** : the whole collection of human beings both past and present

hu·man·ize \'hyü-mə-,nīz, 'yü-\ *vb* **-ized; -iz·ing** **1** : to make suitable for human nature or use **2** : to make humane : CIVILIZE, REFINE — **hu·man·iza·tion** \,hyü-mə-nə-'zā-shən, ,yü-\ *n*

hu·man·kind \'hyü-mən-,kīnd, 'yü-\ *n* : HUMANITY 3

hu·man·ly \'hyü-mən-lē, 'yü-\ *adv* **1** : within the range of human ability ⟨a task not *humanly* possible⟩ **2** : in a human manner

human nature *n* : the nature of human beings; *esp* : the ways of thinking, acting, and reacting that are common to most or all human beings or that are learned in social situations

hu·man·oid \'hyü-mə-,nȯid, 'yü-\ *adj* : having human form or characteristics — **humanoid** *n*

¹hum·ble \'həm-bəl, 'əm-\ *adj* **hum·bler** \-b(ə-)lər\; **hum·blest** \-b(ə-)ləst\ **1** : modest or meek in spirit or manner : not proud or bold ⟨*humble* apology⟩ **2** : low in rank or status ⟨a *humble* position⟩ — **hum·bly** \-blē\ *adv*

²humble *vb* **hum·bled; hum·bling** \-b(ə-)liŋ\ **1** : to make humble in spirit or manner **2** : to destroy the power or influence of ⟨*humbled* the enemy with a crushing attack⟩ — **hum·bler** \-b(ə-)lər\ *n*

hum·bug \'həm-,bəg\ *n* **1** : a false or deceiving person or thing : FRAUD **2** : NONSENSE 1, DRIVEL — **hum·bug** *vb* — **hum·bug·gery** \-,bəg-(ə-)rē\ *n*

hum·drum \'həm-,drəm\ *adj* : MONOTONOUS 2, DULL

hu·mer·us \'hyüm-(ə-)rəs\ *n, pl* **hu·meri** \'hyü-mə-,rī, -,rē\ : the long bone of the upper arm or forelimb that extends from the shoulder to the elbow

hu·mid \'hyü-məd, 'yü-\ *adj* : ³DAMP, MOIST ⟨a *humid* climate⟩ — **hu·mid·ly** *adv*

hu·mid·i·fy \hyü-'mid-ə-,fī, yü-\ *vb* **-fied; -fy·ing** : to make (as the air of a room) more moist : MOISTEN — **hu·mid·i·fi·ca·tion** \-,mid-ə-fə-'kā-shən\ *n* — **hu·mid·i·fi·er** \-'mid-ə-,fī-(ə)r\ *n*

hu·mid·i·ty \hyü-'mid-ət-ē, yü-\ *n, pl* **-ties** : MOISTURE, DAMPNESS; *esp* : the amount of moisture in the air

hu·mi·dor \'hyü-mə-,dȯr, 'yü-\ *n* : a case in which the air is kept properly humidified for storing cigars or tobacco

hu·mil·i·ate \hyü-'mil-ē-,āt, yü-\ *vb* **-at·ed; -at·ing** : to cause a loss of pride or self-respect : HUMBLE — **hu·mil·i·a·tion** \-,mil-ē-'ā-shən\ *n*

Word History In modern English we sometimes say that a person who has been criticized or humiliated has been *put down.* We speak as though the person had actually been forced to the ground or made to bow down in front of someone else. The origins of the word *humiliate* itself also suggest the idea of physically putting someone down to the ground. *Humiliate* can be be traced back to the Latin *humus,* meaning "earth, ground". From *humus* came the Latin adjective *humilis,* meaning "low, humble", which later gave rise to the verb *humiliare,* meaning "to make low or humble". The English *humiliate* derives from Latin *humiliare.* [from Latin *humiliatus* "to cause to lose pride or self-respect", from earlier *humiliare* "to make low or humble", from *humilis* "low, humble", from *humus* "earth"]

hu·mil·i·ty \hyü-'mil-ət-ē, yü-\ *n* : the quality or state of being humble

hum·ming·bird \'həm-iŋ-,bərd\ *n* : any of numerous tiny brightly colored American birds related to the swifts and having narrow swiftly beating wings, a slender bill, and a long tongue for sipping nectar

hummingbird

hum·mock \'həm-ək\ *n* **1** : a rounded mound of earth : KNOLL **2** : a ridge or pile of ice — **hum·mocky** \-ə-kē\ *adj*

¹hu·mor \'hyü-mər, 'yü-\ *n* **1** : a changeable state of mind often influenced by circumstances ⟨in a bad *humor*⟩ **2** : the amusing quality of things ⟨the *humor* of a situation⟩ **3** : the power to see or tell about the amusing or comic side of things **4** : humorous writings or entertainment — **hu·mor·less** \-ləs\ *adj* — **hu·mor·less·ness** *n*

Word History In the Middle Ages it was believed that a person's health and disposition were the result of a balance or imbalance of four fluids in the body. These fluids were called "humors", from the Latin word *humor,* meaning "moisture". These fluids were blood, phlegm, yellow bile, and black bile. If a person had a cheerful, confident disposition, it was said to be a result of an excess of blood. Such a person was called "sanguine", from the Latin word *sanguis,* meaning "blood". A sluggish disposition was said to be the result of an excess of phlegm. A person having such a disposition was called "phlegmatic", from the Greek word *phlegma,* meaning "flame, phlegm". A fiery, hot-tempered disposition was said to be caused by an excess of yellow bile. A person with this disposition was said to be "choleric", from the Greek word *cholē,* meaning "bile". The disposition of a gloomy, depressed person was said to be the result of an excess of black bile. Such a person was called "melancholy", from the Greek words *melan-,* meaning "black", and *cholē,* meaning "bile". In time the word *humor* came to be used as a general term for "disposition or temperament". From this developed the sense of "a changeable state of mind" or "mood". More recently *humor* has come to refer to something that is funny. [Middle English *humour* "one of the four bodily fluids thought to affect a person's health", from early French *humeur* (same meaning), derived from Latin *humor* "moisture"]

²humor *vb* **hu·mored; hu·mor·ing** \'hyüm-(ə-)riŋ, 'yüm-\ : to go along with the wishes or mood of ⟨*humor* a sick person⟩

hu·mor·ist \'hyüm-(ə-)rəst, 'yüm-\ *n* : a person specializing in or noted for humor

hu·mor·ous \'hyüm-(ə-)rəs, 'yüm-\ *adj* : full of, characterized by, or expressing humor : DROLL ⟨a *humorous* story⟩ — **hu·mor·ous·ly** *adv* — **hu·mor·ous·ness** *n*

¹hump \'həmp\ *n* **1** : a rounded bulge or lump (as on the back of a camel) **2** : a difficult part (as of a task) — **humped** \'həm(p)t\ *adj*

²hump *vb* **1** : to move or work energetically : HUSTLE **2** : to make hump-shaped : HUNCH

hump·back \'həmp-,bak\ *n* **1** : a humped or crooked back **2** : HUNCHBACK 2 **3** : HUMPBACK WHALE — **hump·backed** \-'bakt\ *adj*

humpback whale *n* : a large whalebone whale with very long flippers

\ə\ **abut**	\au̇\ **out**	\i\ **tip**	\ȯ\ **saw**	\u̇\ **foot**
\ər\ **further**	\ch\ **chin**	\ī\ **life**	\ȯi\ **coin**	\y\ **yet**
\a\ **mat**	\e\ **pet**	\j\ **job**	\th\ **thin**	\yü\ **few**
\ā\ **take**	\ē\ **easy**	\ŋ\ **sing**	\th\ **this**	\yu̇\ **cure**
\ä\ **cot, cart**	\g\ **go**	\ō\ **bone**	\ü\ **food**	\zh\ **vision**

hu·mus \'hyü-məs, 'yü-\ *n* : a brown or black product of partial decay of plant or animal matter that forms the organic portion of soil

Hun \'hən\ *n* : a member of a warlike Asian people gaining control of a large part of Europe about A.D. 450

¹**hunch** \'hənch\ *vb* **1** : to push oneself forward by jerks ⟨*hunch* nearer the fire⟩ **2** : to bend one's body into an arch or hump ⟨were *hunched* over the table⟩ **3** : to draw up close together or into an arch ⟨*hunched* my shoulders⟩

²**hunch** *n* **1** : ¹HUMP 1 **2** : a strong feeling about what will happen : INTUITION

hunch·back \'hənch-,bak\ *n* **1** : HUMPBACK 1 **2** : a person with a humpback — **hunch·backed** \-'bakt\ *adj*

hun·dred \'hən-drəd, -dərd\ *n, pl* **hundreds** *or* **hun·dred** **1** — see NUMBER table **2** : a very large number ⟨*hundreds* of times⟩ — **hundred** *adj*

hundreds digit *n* : the numeral (as 4 in 456) in the hundreds place

hundreds place *n* : the place three to the left of the decimal point in a number expressed in the Arabic system of writing numbers

hun·dredth \'hən-drədth, -drətth\ *n* **1** : one of 100 equal parts of something **2** — see NUMBER table — **hundredth** *adj*

hun·dredths place \'hən-drədths-, -drətths-\ *n* : the second place to the right of a decimal point in a number expressed in the Arabic system of writing numbers

hun·dred·weight \'hən-drə-,dwāt, -dər-,dwāt\ *n, pl* **-weight** *or* **-weights** **1** : a unit of weight equal to 100 pounds (about 45.6 kilograms) — called also *short hundredweight;* see MEASURE table **2** *British* : a unit of weight equal to 112 pounds (about 50.8 kilograms) — called also *long hundredweight*

hung *past and past participle of* HANG

Hun·gar·i·an \,hən-'ger-ē-ən, -'gar-\ *n* **1 a** : a person born or living in Hungary : MAGYAR **b** : a person of Hungarian descent **2** : MAGYAR 2 — **Hungarian** *adj*

¹**hun·ger** \'hən-gər\ *n* **1 a** : a desire or a need for food **b** : an uneasy feeling or weakened condition resulting from lack of food **2** : a strong desire : CRAVING ⟨a *hunger* for praise⟩ — **hunger** *adj*

²**hunger** *vb* **hun·gered; hun·ger·ing** \-g(ə-)riŋ\ **1** : to feel or suffer hunger **2** : to have an eager desire ⟨*hungered* for affection⟩

hunger strike *n* : refusal (as by a prisoner) to eat enough to stay alive

hung jury *n* : a jury that is unable to reach a verdict on which everyone agrees

hun·gry \'həŋ-grē\ *adj* **hun·gri·er; -est** **1** : feeling or showing hunger **2** : EAGER, AVID ⟨*hungry* for all the details⟩ — **hun·gri·ly** \-grə-lē\ *adv*

hung up *adj* **1** : delayed or detained for a time **2** : anxiously nervous **3** : much involved or concerned with ⟨*hung up* on winning⟩

hunk \'həŋk\ *n* : a large lump or piece

¹**hunt** \'hənt\ *vb* **1 a** : to seek out and chase (game) for food or sport ⟨*hunt* squirrel⟩ **b** : to use in hunting game ⟨*hunts* a pack of dogs⟩ **2 a** : to chase in order to capture **b** : to search out : look for : SEEK ⟨*hunting* for my gloves⟩; *also* : to find by hunting ⟨*hunting* bargains⟩ **3** : to drive or chase especially by repeated attacks ⟨*hunt* a criminal out of town⟩ **4** : to search through looking for prey ⟨*hunts* the woods⟩ **syn** see SEEK

²**hunt** *n* **1** : the action, the practice, or an instance of hunting **2** : a group of hunters; *esp* : persons with horses and dogs engaged in hunting (as foxes)

hunt·er \'hənt-ər\ *n* **1** : a person who hunts; *esp* : one who hunts game **2** : a dog or horse used or trained for hunting

hunt·er–gath·er·er \-'gath-ər-ər, -'geth-\ *n* : a member of a culture in which food is gotten by hunting, fishing, and gathering rather than by agriculture

hunt·ing *n* : the action of one that hunts; *esp* : the chasing of game

Hun·ting·ton's cho·rea \,hənt-iŋ-tənz-kə-'rē-ə\ *n* : an inherited nervous disorder that develops in adult life and leads to a form of insanity

hunt·ress \'hən-trəs\ *n* : a woman who hunts game

hunts·man \'hən(t)-smən\ *n* **1** : a person who hunts game **2** : a person who manages a hunt and looks after the hounds

¹**hur·dle** \'hərd-ᵊl\ *n* **1** : a movable panel used as a fence **2 a** : a barrier to be jumped in a race **b** : a race in which such barriers must be jumped **3** : OBSTACLE

²**hurdle** *vb* **hur·dled; hur·dling** \'hərd-liŋ, -ᵊl-iŋ\ **1** : to leap over while running ⟨the horse *hurdled* the fence⟩ **2** : OVERCOME 1, SURMOUNT — **hur·dler** \'hərd-lər, -ᵊl-ər\ *n*

hur·dy–gur·dy \,hərd-ē-'gərd-ē\ *n, pl* **–gur·dies** : a musical instrument in which the sound is produced by turning a crank; *esp* : BARREL ORGAN

hurdle 2a

hurl \'hər(-ə)l\ *vb* **hurled; hurl·ing** \'hər-liŋ\ **1** : to throw violently or powerfully **2** : ³PITCH 2, 5a **syn** see THROW — **hurl·er** \'hər-lər\ *n*

hur·ly–bur·ly \,hər-lē-'bər-lē\ *n, pl* **–bur·lies** : TUMULT

hur·rah \hù-'rò, -'rä\ *or* **hoo·ray** \-'rā\ *also* **hur·ray** \-'rā\ *interj* — used to express joy, approval, or encouragement

hur·ri·cane \'hər-ə-,kān, -i-kən, 'hə-rə-, 'hə-ri-\ *n* : a cyclone formed in the tropics with winds of 117 kilometers per hour or greater usually accompanied by rain, thunder, and lightning

hur·ried \'hər-ēd, 'hə-rēd\ *adj* **1** : going or working with speed ⟨a *hurried* waitress⟩ **2** : done in a hurry ⟨a *hurried* meal⟩ — **hur·ried·ly** \'hər-əd-lē, 'hə-rəd-\ *adv*

¹**hur·ry** \'hər-ē, 'hə-rē\ *vb* **hur·ried; hur·ry·ing** **1 a** : to carry or cause to go with haste ⟨*hurry* the child to the hospital⟩ **b** : to move or act with haste ⟨had to *hurry* to arrive in time⟩ **2 a** : to urge on to greater speed : PROD **b** : to hasten the doing of ⟨*hurry* a repair job⟩ — **hur·ri·er** *n*

²**hurry** *n, pl* **hurries** **1** : great speed; *esp* : unnecessary haste **2** : a state of eagerness or urgency : RUSH — **in a hurry** : without delay ⟨wanted their tickets *in a hurry*⟩

¹**hurt** \'hərt\ *vb* **hurt; hurt·ing** **1 a** : to cause physical pain to **b** : to do harm to : DAMAGE **2 a** : to cause mental suffering to : OFFEND **b** : ¹HAMPER ⟨losing that game *hurt* our chances for the championship⟩ **3** : to feel or cause pain ⟨my tooth *hurts*⟩ — **hurt·er** *n*

²**hurt** *n* **1** : a cause of injury or damage **2** : a physical injury or wound **3 a** : physical pain **b** : mental distress : SUFFERING **4** : ¹WRONG 1, HARM

hurt·ful \'hərt-fəl\ *adj* : causing injury or suffering : DAMAGING — **hurt·ful·ly** \-fə-lē\ *adv* — **hurt·ful·ness** *n*

hur·tle \'hərt-ᵊl\ *vb* **hur·tled; hur·tling** \'hərt-liŋ, -ᵊl-iŋ\ **1** : to move suddenly or violently ⟨boulders *hurtled* down the hill⟩ **2** : HURL 1, FLING

¹**hus·band** \'həz-bənd\ *n* : a married man [Old English *hūsbonda* "master of a house", from early Norse *hūsbondi*, literally "house owner" — related to HOUSE]

²**husband** *vb* : to manage carefully and economically : CONSERVE ⟨*husbanded* their resources⟩ — **hus·band·er** *n*

hus·band·man \'həz-bən(d)-mən\ *n* : one that plows and cultivates land : FARMER

hus·band·ry \'həz-bən-drē\ *n* **1** : wise management of resources : ECONOMY **2** : FARMING, AGRICULTURE

¹**hush** \'həsh\ *vb* **1** : to make quiet, calm, or still : SOOTHE ⟨*hush* a baby⟩ **2** : to become quiet **3** : to keep from public knowledge : SUPPRESS ⟨*hush* up the crime⟩

²**hush** *n* : a silence or calm especially following noise : QUIET

¹husk \'həsk\ n　**1** : a usually thin dry outer covering of a seed or fruit　**2** : an outer layer : SHELL

²husk vb : to strip the husk from — **husk·er** n

¹hus·ky \'həs-kē\ adj **hus·ki·er; -est** : HOARSE 2 [probably derived from an obsolete sense of husk, meaning "to have a dry cough"] — **hus·ki·ly** \'həs-kə-lē\ adv — **hus·ki·ness** \-kē-nəs\ n

²hus·ky n, pl **huskies** : a heavy-coated working dog especially of the New World arctic region [probably an altered form of Eskimo]

³hus·ky adj **hus·ki·er; -est** : BURLY, ROBUST [probably from husk "a hard outer covering"]

hus·sar \(,)hə-'zär, -'sär\ n : a member of any of various European originally cavalry military units

hus·sy \'həs-ē, 'həz-\ n, pl **hussies**　**1** : an immoral woman　**2** : a disrespectful or mischievous girl

hus·tings \'həs-tiŋz\ n pl : a place where political campaign speeches are made [Old English hūsting "local court or assembly", from early Norse hūsthing "an assembly of the king's council", literally "house assembly", from hūs "house" and thing "assembly"]

hus·tle \'həs-əl\ vb **hus·tled; hus·tling** \'həs-(ə-)liŋ\　**1** : to push, crowd, or force forward roughly ⟨hustled the prisoner to jail⟩　**2** : to move or work rapidly and tirelessly　**3** : to sell something to or get something from by energetic and especially dishonest activity — **hustle** n — **hus·tler** \'həs-lər\ n

hut \'hət\ n : a small and often temporary dwelling or shelter : SHACK

hutch \'həch\ n　**1 a** : a chest or compartment for storage　**b** : a low cupboard topped by usually open shelves　**2** : a pen or coop for an animal　**3** : SHANTY, SHACK

huz·zah or **huz·za** \(,)hə-'zä\ interj — used to express joy or approval

hy·a·cinth \'hī-ə-(,)sin(t)th\ n　**1** : a red or brownish gem　**2** : any of a genus of herbs related to the lily that grow from bulbs; esp : a common garden plant widely grown for the beauty and fragrance of its bell-shaped flowers that have six lobes and grow in a thick spike

¹hy·brid \'hī-brəd\ n　**1** : an offspring of parents with different genes especially when of different races, breeds, species, or genera　**2** : something of mixed origin or composition

²hybrid adj : of or relating to a hybrid : of mixed origin

hybrid corn n　**1** : the grain of Indian corn developed by hybridizing two or more inbred strains　**2** : the plant grown from hybrid corn

hy·brid·ize \'hī-brə-,dīz\ vb **-ized; -iz·ing** : to produce or cause to produce hybrids : INTERBREED — **hy·brid·iza·tion** \,hī-brəd-ə-'zā-shən\ n — **hy·brid·iz·er** \'hī-brə-,dī-zər\ n

hybrid vigor n : unusual vigor or capacity for growth often shown by hybrid plants or animals

hydr- or **hydro-** combining form　**1** : water ⟨hydrous⟩ ⟨hydroelectricity⟩　**2** : hydrogen : containing or combined with hydrogen ⟨hydrocarbon⟩ [derived from Greek hydr-, hydōr "water"]

hy·dra \'hī-drə\ n : any of numerous small tube-shaped freshwater animals related to the jellyfishes and having a mouth surrounded by tentacles at one end

hy·dran·gea \hī-'drān-jə\ n : any of a genus of shrubby or woody plants with showy clusters of usually sterile white, pink, or blue flowers

hy·drant \'hī-drənt\ n : a pipe with a valve and spout at which water may be drawn from the main pipes

¹hy·drate \'hī-,drāt\ n : a compound formed by the union of water with some other substance ⟨a hydrate of copper sulfate⟩

²hydrate vb **hy·drat·ed; hy·drat·ing** : to cause to take up or combine with water or the elements of water — **hy·dra·tion** \hī-'drā-shən\ n

hy·drau·lic \hī-'drò-lik\ adj　**1** : operated, moved, or brought about by means of water　**2** : of or relating to hydraulics ⟨hydraulic engineer⟩　**3** : operated by pressure transmitted when a quantity of liquid is forced through a small hole or through a tube ⟨hydraulic brakes⟩　**4** : hardening or setting under water ⟨hydraulic cement⟩ — **hy·drau·li·cal·ly** \-'drò-li-k(ə-)lē\ adv

hy·drau·lics \hī-'drò-liks\ n : a science that deals with uses of liquid (as water) in motion

hy·dra·zine \'hī-drə-,zēn\ n : a colorless fuming liquid used especially in fuels for rocket engines

hy·dro \'hī-drō\ adj : HYDROELECTRIC ⟨hydro energy⟩

hy·dro·bro·mic acid \,hī-drə-,brō-mik-\ n : a strong acid formed by dissolving the bromide of hydrogen in water

hy·dro·car·bon \,hī-drə-'kär-bən\ n : a compound containing only carbon and hydrogen

hy·dro·ceph·a·lus \,hī-drō-'sef-ə-ləs\ also **hy·dro·ceph·a·ly** \-'sef-ə-lē\ n : an abnormal condition in which an increased amount of cerebrospinal fluid causes an increase in the size of the ventricles of the brain and the size of the skull and the wasting away of the brain

hy·dro·chlo·ric acid \,hī-drə-,klōr-ik-, -,klòr-\ n : a strong acid formed by dissolving hydrogen chloride in water that is widely used in industry and in the laboratory

hy·dro·elec·tric \,hī-drō-i-'lek-trik\ adj : of or relating to production of electricity by waterpower — **hy·dro·elec·tric·i·ty** \-,lek-'tris-ət-ē, -,lek-'tris-tē\ n

hy·dro·flu·or·ic acid \,hī-drō-flū-,òr-ik-, -flū-,är-ik-\ n : a weak poisonous acid that is formed by dissolving hydrogen fluoride in water

hy·dro·foil \'hī-drə-,fòil\ n : a boat that has fins attached to the bottom by braces for lifting the hull clear of the water to allow faster speeds

hydrofoil

hy·dro·gen \'hī-drə-jən\ n : a chemical element that is the simplest and lightest of all chemical elements and is normally found alone as a colorless odorless highly flammable gas having two atoms per molecule — see ELEMENT table [from French hydrogène "hydrogen", from hydr- "water" and -gène "producer"; so called because when hydrogen gas burns, it combines with oxygen to produce water] — **hy·drog·e·nous** \hī-'dräj-ə-nəs\ adj

hy·dro·ge·nate \hī-'dräj-ə-,nāt, 'hī-drə-jə-\ vb **-nat·ed; -nat·ing** : to combine or treat with hydrogen; esp : to add hydrogen to a molecule of ⟨hydrogenate a vegetable oil to form a fat⟩ — **hy·dro·ge·na·tion** \hī-,dräj-ə-'nā-shən, ,hī-drə-jə-\ n

hydrogen bomb n : a bomb whose violent explosive power is due to the sudden release of atomic energy when hydrogen nuclei unite

hydrogen chloride n : a colorless sharp-smelling poisonous gas that is made up of hydrogen and chlorine and produces hydrochloric acid when dissolved in water

hydrogen fluoride n : a colorless poisonous gas that is made up of hydrogen and fluorine and produces hydrofluoric acid when dissolved in water

hydrogen ion n : the positive ion of acids that consists of a hydrogen atom whose electron has been transferred to the negative ion of the acid and that most often consists of a single proton

hydrogen peroxide n : an unstable liquid compound con-

\ə\ abut	\au̇\ out	\i\ tip	\ò\ saw	\u̇\ foot
\ər\ further	\ch\ chin	\ī\ life	\òi\ coin	\y\ yet
\a\ mat	\e\ pet	\j\ job	\th\ thin	\yü\ few
\ā\ take	\ē\ easy	\ŋ\ sing	\t̲h̲\ this	\yu̇\ cure
\ä\ cot, cart	\g\ go	\ō\ bone	\ü\ food	\zh\ vision

taining hydrogen and oxygen and used especially for bleaching and as an antiseptic

hydrogen sulfide *n* : a flammable poisonous gas with a disagreeable odor suggestive of rotten eggs

hy·drog·ra·phy \hī-'dräg-rə-fē\ *n* **1** : the study of bodies of water (as seas, lakes, and rivers) especially in relation to their use by people **2** : the mapping of bodies of water — **hy·drog·ra·pher** \-fər\ *n* — **hy·dro·graph·ic** \,hī-drə-'graf-ik\ *adj*

¹hy·droid \'hī-,drȯid\ *adj* : of or relating to the hydrozoans; *esp* : resembling a hydra

²hydroid *n* : HYDROZOAN; *esp* : a hydrozoan polyp in contrast to a hydrozoan jellyfish

hy·dro·log·ic cycle \,hī-drə-,läj-ik-\ *n* : the series of conditions through which water naturally passes from water vapor in the atmosphere through precipitation upon land or water surfaces and finally back into the atmosphere as a result of evaporation and transpiration

hy·drol·o·gist \hī-'dräl-ə-jəst\ *n* : a person who specializes in hydrology

hy·drol·o·gy \hī-'dräl-ə-jē\ *n* : a science dealing with the characteristics, distribution, and circulation of water on and below the surface of the land and in the atmosphere — **hy·dro·log·ic** \,hī-drə-'läj-ik\ *adj*

hy·drol·y·sis \hī-'dräl-ə-səs\ *n* : a process of breaking down a chemical compound that involves splitting a bond and adding the elements of water to the resulting molecular fragments

hy·dro·lyze \'hī-drə-,līz\ *vb* **-lyzed; -lyz·ing** : to go through or cause to go through hydrolysis

hy·drom·e·ter \hī-'dräm-ət-ər\ *n* : an instrument for finding out the strength of a liquid (as battery acid or an alcohol solution) by measuring its specific gravity

hy·dro·ni·um \hī-'drō-nē-əm\ *n* : an ion formed by the combination of a hydrogen ion with a water molecule

hy·dro·pho·bia \,hī-drə-'fō-bē-ə\ *n* **1** : an abnormal fear of water **2** : RABIES — **hy·dro·pho·bic** \-'fō-bik, -'fäb-ik\ *adj*

hy·dro·phone \'hī-drə-,fōn\ *n* : an instrument for listening to sound transmitted through water

hy·dro·phyte \'hī-drə-,fīt\ *n* : a plant growing in water or in waterlogged soil

hy·dro·plane \'hī-drə-,plān\ *n* **1** : a speedboat whose hull is completely or partly out of the water as it skims the water **2** : SEAPLANE

hydrometer

hy·dro·pon·ics \,hī-drə-'pän-iks\ *n* : the growing of plants in nutrient solutions — **hy·dro·pon·ic** \-ik\ *adj*

hy·dro·pow·er \'hī-drə-,pau̇(-ə)r\ *n* : hydroelectric power

hy·dro·sphere \'hī-drə-,sfi(ə)r\ *n* : the surface waters of the earth and the water vapor in the atmosphere

hy·drot·ro·pism \hī-'drä-trə-,piz-əm\ *n* : a tropism (as in plant roots) in which water or water vapor causes the movement — **hy·dro·tro·pic** \,hī-drə-'trō-pik, -'träp-ik\ *adj*

hy·drox·ide \hī-'dräk-,sīd\ *n* : a negatively charged ion consisting of one atom of oxygen and one atom of hydrogen

hy·drox·yl \hī-'dräk-səl\ *n* : a chemical group or ion that consists of one atom of hydrogen and one of oxygen and is positively charged or neutral

hy·dro·zo·an \,hī-drə-'zō-ən\ *n* : any of a class of coelenterates including the hydras and various polyps and jellyfishes — **hydrozoan** *adj*

hy·e·na \hī-'ē-nə\ *n* : any of several large strong Old World mammals that eat flesh and are active at night

Word History Many pigs have manes of stiff hair that extend down their necks. When the ancient Greeks first saw hyenas, they thought the animals' manes looked like the manes of pigs. They called these strange animals *hyaina*, which comes from the Greek word *hys*, meaning "hog, pig". *Hyaena* is the Latin form, which was borrowed into English and spelled *hyena*. [Middle English *hyene* "hyena", from Latin *hyaena* (same meaning), from Greek *hyaina* (same meaning), from *hys* "hog, pig"]

hyena

hy·giene \'hī-,jēn\ *n* **1** : a science that deals with the bringing about and keeping up of good health in individuals and groups **2** : conditions or practices (as of cleanliness) that are aids to good health

hy·gien·ic \,hī-jē-'en-ik, hī-'jen-, hī-'jēn-\ *adj* : of, relating to, or leading toward good health or hygiene — **hy·gien·i·cal·ly** \-i-k(ə-)lē\ *adv*

hy·gien·ist \hī-'jēn-əst, 'hī-,jēn-, hī-'jen-\ *n* : a person skilled in hygiene; *esp* : DENTAL HYGIENIST

hy·gro·graph \'hī-grə-,graf\ *n* : an instrument for automatic recording of changes in the amount of moisture in the air

hy·grom·e·ter \hī-'gräm-ət-ər\ *n* : an instrument for measuring the amount of moisture in the air

hying *present participle of* HIE

hy·men \'hī-mən\ *n* : a fold of mucous membrane partly closing the opening of the vagina — **hy·men·al** \-əl\ *adj*

hy·me·nop·tera \,hī-mə-'näp-tə-rə\ *n pl* : insects that are hymenopterans

hy·me·nop·ter·an \,hī-mə-'näp-tə-rən\ *n* : any of an order of highly specialized and often colonial insects (as bees, wasps, and ants) that have usually four thin transparent wings and the abdomen on a slender stalk — **hymenopteran** *adj* — **hy·me·nop·ter·ous** \-rəs\ *adj*

hymn \'him\ *n* **1** : a song of praise especially to God **2** : a religious song

hym·nal \'him-nəl\ *n* : a book of hymns

hymn·book \'him-,bu̇k\ *n* : HYMNAL

hyp- — see HYPO-

hyper- *prefix* **1** : above : beyond : SUPER- **2 a** : excessively ⟨*hyper*sensitive⟩ **b** : excessive [derived from Greek *hyper* "over"]

hy·per·acid·i·ty \,hī-pə-rə-'sid-ət-ē\ *n* : the condition of containing more than the normal amount of acid — **hy·per·ac·id** \,hī-pə-'ras-əd\ *adj*

hy·per·ac·tive \,hī-pər-'ak-tiv\ *adj* : very active especially to an abnormal amount — **hy·per·ac·tiv·i·ty** \-ak-'tiv-ət-ē\ *n*

hy·per·bo·le \hī-'pər-bə-(,)lē\ *n* : extravagant exaggeration used to emphasize a point ⟨"an apple a day keeps the doctor away" is an example of *hyperbole*⟩ — **hy·per·bol·ic** \,hī-pər-'bäl-ik\ *adj*

hy·per·crit·i·cal \,hī-pər-'krit-i-kəl\ *adj* : too critical — **hy·per·crit·i·cal·ly** \-k(ə-)lē\ *adv*

hy·per·sen·si·tive \,hī-pər-'sen(t)-sət-iv, -'sen(t)-stiv\ *adj* : very sensitive especially to an abnormal amount — **hy·per·sen·si·tive·ness** *n*

hy·per·sen·si·tiv·i·ty \,hī-pər-,sen(t)-sə-'tiv-ət-ē\ *n* : the state of being hypersensitive; *esp* : an abnormal bodily state in which certain substances (as a particular pollen or food) cause a reaction and physical distress (as sneezing, hives, or asthma)

hy·per·ten·sion \'hī-pər-,ten-chən\ *n* : HIGH BLOOD PRESSURE

hy·per·ten·sive \,hī-pər-'ten(t)-siv\ *adj* : having or marked by high blood pressure

hy·per·thy·roid·ism \,hī-pər-'thī-,rȯid-,iz-əm, -rəd-\ *n* : abnormally high activity of the thyroid gland; *also* : the resulting abnormal state of health — **hy·per·thy·roid** \-,ròid\ *adj*

hy·per·ven·ti·la·tion \,hī-pər-,vent-ᵊl-'ā-shən\ *n* : breathing that is very fast and deep and leads to abnormal loss of carbon dioxide from the blood — **hy·per·ven·ti·late** \-'vent-ᵊl-,āt\ *vb*

hy·pha \'hī-fə\ *n, pl* **hy·phae** \-(,)fē\ : one of the threads that make up the mycelium of a fungus — **hy·phal** \-fəl\ *adj*

¹hy·phen \'hī-fən\ *n* : a punctuation mark - used to divide or to compound words or word elements

²hyphen *vb* : HYPHENATE

hy·phen·ate \'hī-fə-,nāt\ *vb* **-at·ed; -at·ing** : to connect or mark with a hyphen

hyp·no·sis \hip-'nō-səs\ *n, pl* **-no·ses** \-'nō-,sēz\ : a state which resembles sleep but in which the person responds to suggestions of the hypnotist [scientific Latin *hypnosis* "hypnosis", derived from Greek *hypnos* "sleep", from *Hypnos* "the Greek god of sleep"]

¹hyp·not·ic \hip-'nät-ik\ *adj* **1** : tending to cause sleep **2** : of or relating to hypnosis or hypnotism — **hyp·not·i·cal·ly** \-i-k(ə-)lē\ *adv*

²hypnotic *n* : an agent (as a drug) that causes or tends to cause sleep

hyp·no·tism \'hip-nə-,tiz-əm\ *n* **1** : the study of or act of causing hypnosis **2** : HYPNOSIS

hyp·no·tist \'hip-nə-təst\ *n* : a person who practices hypnotism

hyp·no·tize \'hip-nə-,tīz\ *vb* **-tized; -tiz·ing** **1** : to cause hypnosis in **2** : to deaden judgment or resistance by or as if by hypnotic suggestion — **hyp·no·tiz·able** \-,tī-zə-bəl\ *adj*

¹hy·po \'hī-pō\ *n* : SODIUM THIOSULFATE

²hypo *n, pl* **hypos** : a hypodermic syringe or injection

hypo- *or* **hyp-** *prefix* **1** : under : beneath : down ⟨*hypo*dermic⟩ **2** : less than normal or normally ⟨*hypo*tension⟩ [derived from Greek *hypo* "under"]

hy·po·chon·dria \,hī-pə-'kän-drē-ə\ *n* : serious mental depression often accompanied by a false belief that one has a physical disease or abnormal condition

hy·po·chon·dri·ac \,hī-pə-'kän-drē-,ak\ *n* : a person who has hypochondria

hy·po·cot·yl \'hī-pə-,kät-ᵊl\ *n* : the part of the axis of a plant embryo or seedling below the cotyledons

hy·poc·ri·sy \hip-'äk-rə-sē\ *n, pl* **-sies** : a pretending to be what one is not or to believe what one does not; *esp* : a pretending to be more virtuous or religious than one really is

hyp·o·crite \'hip-ə-,krit\ *n* : a person who pretends to have virtues or qualities that he or she does not have — **hyp·o·crit·i·cal** \,hip-ə-'krit-i-kəl\ *adj* — **hyp·o·crit·i·cal·ly** \-i-k(ə-)lē\ *adv*

¹hy·po·der·mic \,hī-pə-'dər-mik\ *adj* : of, relating to, or injected into the parts beneath the skin — **hy·po·der·mi·cal·ly** \-mi-k(ə-)lē\ *adv*

²hypodermic *n* **1** : HYPODERMIC INJECTION **2** : HYPODERMIC SYRINGE

hypodermic injection *n* : an injection made into the tissues beneath the skin

hypodermic needle *n* **1** : ¹NEEDLE 1c **2** : a hypodermic syringe complete with needle

hypodermic syringe *n* : a small syringe used with a hollow needle for injection of material into or beneath the skin

hy·poph·y·sis \hī-'päf-ə-səs\ *n, pl* **-y·ses** \-ə-,sēz\ : PITUITARY GLAND

hy·po·ten·sion \'hī-pō-,ten-chən\ *n* : LOW BLOOD PRESSURE

hy·pot·e·nuse \hī-'pät-ᵊn-,(y)üs, -,(y)üz\ *n* : the side opposite the right angle of a triangle having a right angle

hy·po·thal·a·mus \,hī-pō-'thal-ə-məs\ *n* : a part of the brain that lies beneath the thalamus, produces hormones which pass to the front part of the pituitary gland, and is important in the activities of the autonomic nervous system

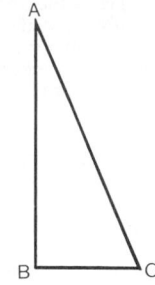

AC hypotenuse

hy·po·ther·mia \,hī-pō-'thər-mē-ə\ *n* : reduction of the body temperature to an abnormally low level

hy·poth·e·sis \hī-'päth-ə-səs\ *n, pl* **-e·ses** \-ə-,sēz\ : something not proved but assumed to be true for purposes of argument or further study or investigation

hy·poth·e·size \hī-'päth-ə-,sīz\ *vb* **-sized; -siz·ing** **1** : to make a hypothesis **2** : to adopt as a hypothesis

hy·po·thet·i·cal \,hi-pə-'thet-i-kəl\ *adj* **1** : involving a hypothesis or the making of assumptions : ASSUMED **2** : imagined for purposes of example ⟨a *hypothetical* case⟩ — **hy·po·thet·i·cal·ly** \-i-k(ə-)lē\ *adv*

hy·po·thy·roid·ism \,hī-pō-'thī-,ròid-,iz-əm\ *n* : too little activity of the thyroid gland; *also* : the bodily condition that results from this and is marked especially by a lowered metabolic rate and loss of vigor — **hy·po·thy·roid** \-,ròid\ *adj*

hy·rax \'hī-,raks\ *n, pl* **hy·rax·es** \-,rak-səz\ *also* **hy·ra·ces** \-rə-,sēz\ : any of several small mammals of Africa, Syria, Israel, Sinai, and Arabia that have a thickset body with short ears, legs, and tail and feet with soft pads and broad nails

hyrax

hys·te·ria \his-'ter-ē-ə, -'tir-\ *n* **1** : a nervous disorder marked by excitability of the emotions **2** : unmanageable fear or outburst of emotion — **hys·ter·i·cal** \-'ter-i-kəl\ *adj* — **hys·ter·i·cal·ly** \-i-k(ə-)lē\ *adv*

hys·ter·ics \his-'ter-iks\ *n sing or pl* : a fit of uncontrollable laughter or crying

\ə\ **abut**	\au̇\ **out**	\i\ **tip**	\ò\ **saw**	\u̇\ **foot**
\ər\ **further**	\ch\ **chin**	\ī\ **life**	\ȯi\ **coin**	\y\ **yet**
\a\ **mat**	\e\ **pet**	\j\ **job**	\th\ **thin**	\yü\ **few**
\ā\ **take**	\ē\ **easy**	\ŋ\ **sing**	\t̲h̲\ **this**	\yu̇\ **cure**
\ä\ **cot, cart**	\g\ **go**	\ō\ **bone**	\ü\ **food**	\zh\ **vision**

I

i \ˈī\ *n, often cap* **1** : the ninth letter of the English alphabet **2** : one in Roman numerals **3** : a grade rating a student's work as incomplete

I \(ˈ)ī, ə\ *pron* : the person speaking or writing ⟨*I* feel fine⟩

-ial *adj suffix* : ¹-AL ⟨financ*ial*⟩

iamb \ˈī-ˌam(b)\ *n* : a metrical foot consisting of one unaccented syllable followed by one accented syllable (as in *away*) — **iam·bic** \ī-ˈam-bik\ *adj*

-ian — see -AN

i·a·sis \ˈī-ə-səs\ *n suffix, pl* **-i·a·ses** \-ˌsēz\ : disease produced by (something specified) ⟨ameb*iasis*⟩ [derived from Greek *-iasis* (noun suffix)]

ibex \ˈī-ˌbeks\ *n, pl* **ibex** or **ibex·es** : any of several wild goats living chiefly in high mountain areas of the Old World and having large horns that curve backward

-ibility — see -ABILITY

ibis \ˈī-bəs\ *n, pl* **ibis** or **ibis·es** : any of several wading birds that differ from the related herons in having a long slender bill that curves downward

ibex

-ible — see -ABLE

IC \(ˈ)ī-ˈsē\ *n* : INTEGRATED CIRCUIT

-ic \ik\ *adj suffix* **1 a** : resembling in form or manner ⟨cherub*ic*⟩ **b** : made up of ⟨run*ic*⟩ **2 a** : of or relating to ⟨chivalr*ic*⟩ **b** : derived from or containing ⟨alcohol*ic*⟩ **3** : in the manner of ⟨autocrat*ic*⟩ **4** : making use of ⟨electron*ic*⟩ **5 a** : marked by ⟨nostalg*ic*⟩ **b** : affected with ⟨allerg*ic*⟩ **6** : caused by ⟨amoeb*ic*⟩ [derived from Latin *-icus* (adjective suffix)]

-i·cal \i-kəl\ *adj suffix* : -IC ⟨symmetr*ical*⟩ ⟨geolog*ical*⟩

ICBM \ˌī-ˌsē-(ˌ)bē-ˈem\ *n* : an intercontinental ballistic missile

¹ice \ˈīs\ *n* **1 a** : frozen water **b** : a sheet of frozen water ⟨skating on the *ice*⟩ **2** : a state of coldness (as in personal behavior) **3** : a substance resembling ice **4** : a frozen dessert usually made with sweetened fruit juice — **on ice** : set aside for use when needed : in reserve — **on thin ice** : in a dangerous situation

²ice *vb* **iced; ic·ing** **1 a** : to coat or become coated with ice **b** : to chill with ice **2** : to cover with icing

ice age *n* : a time of widespread glaciation; *esp, cap I & A* : the most recent such period in the earth's past

ice·berg \ˈīs-ˌbərg\ *n* : a large floating mass of ice detached from a glacier

ice·boat \-ˌbōt\ *n* : a boat-like frame driven by sails and gliding over the ice on runners

ice·bound \-ˌbaund\ *adj* : surrounded or blocked by ice

ice·box \-ˌbäks\ *n* : REFRIGERATOR

ice·break·er \-ˌbrā-kər\ *n* : a ship equipped to make and keep open a channel through ice

ice cap *n* : a large glacier forming on level land and flowing outward from its center

ice–cold \ˈī-ˈskōld\ *adj* : very cold

ice cream \(ˈ)ī-ˈskrēm, ˈī-ˌskrēm\ *n* : a frozen food containing sweetened and flavored cream or butterfat

ice–cream cone *n* : a crisp cone-shaped wafer for holding ice cream; *also* : one filled with ice cream

ice field *n* : ICE CAP

ice hockey *n* : a game played on an ice rink in which two teams of skating players use curved sticks to try to shoot a puck into the opponent's goal

ice·house \ˈīs-ˌhaus\ *n* : a building in which ice is made or stored

Ice·land·er \ˈī-ˌslan-dər, ˈī-ˌslən-\ *n* : a person born or living in Iceland

¹Ice·lan·dic \ī-ˈslan-dik\ *adj* : of, relating to, or characteristic of Iceland, the Icelanders, or Icelandic

²Icelandic *n* : the Germanic language of the Icelandic people

ice·man \ˈī-ˌsman\ *n* : one who sells or delivers ice

ice milk *n* : a sweetened frozen food made of skim milk

ice pack *n* : a large area of pack ice

ice pick *n* : a hand tool ending in a spike for chipping ice

ice sheet *n* : ICE CAP

ice show *n* : a show consisting of exhibitions by ice skaters usually with music

ice–skate \ˈī(s)-ˌskāt\ *vb* : to skate on ice — **ice skater** *n*

ice skate *n* : a shoe with a metal runner attached to the sole for ice-skating

ice storm *n* : a storm in which falling rain freezes as it lands

ice water *n* : chilled or iced water especially for drinking

ich·neu·mon fly \ik-ˈn(y)ü-mən-\ *n* : any of a large group of insects that are related to wasps and whose larvae are usually internal parasites of other insect larvae

ichor \ˈī-ˌkȯ(ə)r, -kər\ *n* : a fluid taking the place of blood in the veins of the gods and goddesses of Greek mythology

ich·thy·ol·o·gist \ˌik-thē-ˈäl-ə-jəst\ *n* : a person who specializes in ichthyology

ich·thy·ol·o·gy \ˌik-thē-ˈäl-ə-jē\ *n* : a branch of zoology that deals with fishes

ich·thyo·saur \ˈik-thē-ə-ˌsȯ(ə)r\ *n* : any of an order of extinct marine reptiles with a fish-shaped body and a long snout

ichthyosaur

-i·cian \ˈish-ən\ *n suffix* : one who practices or specializes in a particular field ⟨beau*tician*⟩ ⟨techn*ician*⟩ [derived from Latin *-ica* (noun suffix) and early French *-ien* (noun suffix)]

ici·cle \ˈī-ˌsik-əl\ *n* : a hanging mass of ice formed by the freezing of dripping water

ic·ing \ˈī-siŋ\ *n* : a sweet coating for baked goods (as cakes)

icon \ˈī-ˌkän\ *n* : a religious image usually painted on a small wooden panel

-ics \(ˌ)iks\ *n sing or pl suffix* **1** : study : knowledge : skill : practice ⟨electron*ics*⟩ **2** : characteristic actions or qualities ⟨acrobat*ics*⟩ [derived from Greek *-ika* "study, skill"]

icy \ˈī-sē\ *adj* **ic·i·er; -est** **1 a** : covered with, full of, or consisting of ice ⟨*icy* roads⟩ **b** : very cold ⟨*icy* weather⟩ **2** : UNFRIENDLY 1 ⟨an *icy* stare⟩ — **ic·i·ly** \-sə-lē\ *adv* — **ic·i·ness** \-sē-nəs\ *n*

I'd \(ˌ)īd\ : I had : I should : I would

-ide \ˌīd\ *also* **-id** \əd, (ˌ)id\ *n suffix* : negatively charged atom or chemical group that is usually part of a compound ⟨hydrogen sulf*ide*⟩ [derived from French *-ide* (noun suffix) "atom or part of a chemical compound"]

idea \ī-ˈdē-ə, ˈīd-(ˌ)ē-ə\ *n* **1** : a plan of action : INTENTION ⟨my *idea* is to study law⟩ **2** : something imagined or pictured in the mind : NOTION ⟨form an *idea* of a place from reading⟩ **3** : a central meaning or purpose ⟨the *idea* of the game is to keep from getting caught⟩ — **idea·less** \ī-ˈdē-ə-ləs\ *adj*

¹**ide·al** \ī-ˈdē-(ə)l, ˈī-ˌdē(ə)l\ *adj* **1** : existing only in the mind : not real ⟨a purely *ideal* conception of society⟩ **2** : having no flaw : PERFECT ⟨*ideal* weather⟩

²**ideal** *n* **1** : a standard of perfection, beauty, or excellence **2** : a perfect type : a model for imitation **syn** see PATTERN

ide·al·ism \ī-ˈdē-(ə-)ˌliz-əm, ˈī-(ˌ)dē-\ *n* : the practice of forming ideals or living under their influence — **ide·al·ist** \-(ə-)ləst\ *n* — **ide·al·is·tic** \(ˌ)ī-ˌdē-(ə-)ˈlis-tik, ˌī-dē-\ *adj* — **ide·al·is·ti·cal·ly** \-ti-k(ə-)lē\ *adv*

ide·al·ize \ī-ˈdē-(ə-)ˌlīz\ *vb* **-ized; -iz·ing** : to think of or represent persons or things as one believes they should be rather than as they are — **ide·al·iza·tion** \-ˌdē-(ə-)lə-ˈzā-shən\ *n* — **ide·al·iz·er** \-ˈdē-(ə-)ˌlī-zər\ *n*

ide·al·ly \ī-ˈdē-ə-lē, -ˈdē-(ə)l-lē\ *adv* **1** : in agreement with an ideal : PERFECTLY ⟨*ideally* suited to the job⟩ **2** : for best results ⟨*ideally*, each student should be taught individually⟩

idée fixe \(ˌ)ē-ˌdā-ˈfēks\ *n, pl* **idées fixes** \-ˈfēks(-əz)\ : an idea that takes over a person's mind [French, literally "fixed idea"]

iden·ti·cal \ī-ˈdent-i-kəl, ə-ˈdent-\ *adj* **1** : being one and the same ⟨the *identical* place we stopped at last year⟩ **2** : exactly alike or equal ⟨wearing *identical* coats⟩ **syn** see SAME — **iden·ti·cal·ly** \-i-k(ə-)lē\ *adv* — **iden·ti·cal·ness** \-kəl-nəs\ *n*

identical twin *n* : either member of a pair of twins that are produced from a single fertilized egg and usually have identical genes

iden·ti·fi·ca·tion \ī-ˌdent-ə-fə-ˈkā-shən, ə-ˌdent-\ *n* **1** : an act of identifying : the state of being identified **2** : evidence of identity ⟨carry *identification* at all times⟩

iden·ti·fy \ī-ˈdent-ə-ˌfī, ə-ˈdent-\ *vb* **-fied; -fy·ing** **1** : to think of as united (as in spirit or principle) ⟨groups *identified* with conservation⟩ **2** : to find out or show the identity of ⟨*identified* the dog as her lost pet⟩ **3** : to think of oneself as having the same problems and feelings as someone else ⟨*identify* with a character in a story⟩ — **iden·ti·fi·able** \-ˌfī-ə-bəl\ *adj* — **iden·ti·fi·ably** \-blē\ *adv* — **iden·ti·fi·er** \-ˌfī-(ə)r\ *n*

iden·ti·ty \ī-ˈden(t)-ət-ē, ə-ˈden(t)-\ *n, pl* **-ties** **1** : the condition of being exactly alike : SAMENESS **2** : INDIVIDUALITY 1 **3** : the fact of being the same person or thing as claimed ⟨prove one's *identity*⟩ **4** : IDENTITY ELEMENT

identity element *n* : an element (as 0 in the set of integers under addition or 1 in the same set under multiplication) that leaves any element of the set to which it belongs unchanged when combined with it by a specified operation (as addition or multiplication)

ideo·gram \ˈīd-ē-ə-ˌgram, ˈid-\ *n* **1** : a picture or symbol used in a system of writing to represent a thing or an idea but not a particular word or phrase **2** : a character or symbol (as *3*) used in a system of writing to represent an entire word but not its individual sounds

ideo·graph \ˈīd-ē-ə-ˌgraf, ˈid-\ *n* : IDEOGRAM — **ideo·graph·ic** \ˌīd-ē-ə-ˈgraf-ik, ˌid-\ *adj* — **ideo·graph·i·cal·ly** \-ˈgraf-i-k(ə-)lē\ *adv*

ide·ol·o·gy \ˌīd-ē-ˈäl-ə-jē, ˌid-\ *n, pl* **-gies** : ideas characteristic of a person, group, or political party — **ideo·log·i·cal** \-ē-ə-ˈläj-i-kəl\ *adj* — **ideo·log·i·cal·ly** \-i-k(ə-)lē\ *adv* — **ide·ol·o·gist** \-ˈäl-ə-jəst\ *n*

ides \ˈīdz\ *n pl* : the 15th day of March, May, July, or October or the 13th day of any other month in the ancient Roman calendar

id·i·o·cy \ˈid-ē-ə-sē\ *n, pl* **-cies** **1** : extremely low intelligence commonly due to incomplete or abnormal development of the brain **2** : something stupid or foolish

id·i·om \ˈid-ē-əm\ *n* **1** : the choice of words and the way they are combined that is characteristic of a language **2** : an expression that cannot be understood from the meanings of its separate words but must be learned as a whole ⟨the expression "give way," meaning "retreat," is an *idiom*⟩ — **id·i·om·at·ic** \ˌid-ē-ə-ˈmat-ik\ *adj* — **id·i·om-**

at·i·cal·ly \-i-k(ə-)lē\ *adv*

id·io·syn·cra·sy \ˌid-ē-ə-ˈsiŋ-krə-sē\ *n, pl* **-sies** : a way of behaving or thinking that is characteristic of a person — **id·io·syn·crat·ic** \ˌid-ē-ō-(ˌ)sin-ˈkrat-ik\ *adj* — **id·io·syn·crat·i·cal·ly** \-ˈkrat-i-k(ə-)lē\ *adv*

id·i·ot \ˈid-ē-ət\ *n* **1** : a person affected with idiocy; *esp* : one who has a level of intelligence no greater than that of a three-year-old child and who requires complete care **2** : a silly or foolish person — **idiot** *adj*

id·i·ot·ic \ˌid-ē-ˈät-ik\ *adj* **1** : marked by idiocy **2** : showing complete lack of thought or common sense : FOOLISH — **id·i·ot·i·cal·ly** \-ˈät-i-k(ə-)lē\ *adv*

¹**idle** \ˈīd-ᵊl\ *adj* **idler** \ˈīd-lər, -ᵊl-ər\; **idlest** \ˈīd-ləst, -ᵊl-əst\ **1** : having no worth or basis ⟨*idle* rumors⟩ ⟨it is *idle* to want what you cannot have⟩ **2** : not being used or employed ⟨*idle* workers⟩ ⟨*idle* factories⟩ ⟨*idle* hours⟩ **3** : LAZY 1 — **idle·ness** \ˈīd-ᵊl-nəs\ *n* — **idly** \ˈīd-lē, -ᵊl-ē\ *adv*

²**idle** *vb* **idled; idling** \ˈīd-liŋ, -ᵊl-iŋ\ **1** : to spend time doing nothing **2** : to run without being connected for doing useful work ⟨left the engine *idling*⟩ — **idler** \ˈīd-lər, -ᵊl-ər\ *n*

idol \ˈīd-ᵊl\ *n* **1** : an image worshiped as a god **2** : a greatly loved and admired person or thing

idol·a·ter *or* **idol·a·tor** \ī-ˈdäl-ət-ər\ *n* **1** : a worshiper of idols **2** : a person who admires or loves greatly

idol·a·trous \ī-ˈdäl-ə-trəs\ *adj* **1** : of or relating to idolatry **2** : given to idolatry — **idol·a·trous·ly** *adv*

idol·a·try \ī-ˈdäl-ə-trē\ *n, pl* **-tries** **1** : the worship of an idol as a god **2** : too great attachment or devotion to something

idol·ize \ˈīd-ᵊl-ˌīz\ *vb* **-ized; -iz·ing** : to worship as an idol : love or admire too much — **idol·iza·tion** \ˌīd-ᵊl-ə-ˈzā-shən\ *n* — **idol·iz·er** \ˈīd-ᵊl-ˌī-zər\ *n*

idyll *or* **idyl** \ˈīd-ᵊl\ *n* **1** : a simple poetic or prose work that describes peaceful country life **2** : a scene or event one might write an idyll about

idyl·lic \ī-ˈdil-ik\ *adj* : simple and charming like an idyll

-ie *also* **-y** \ē\ *n suffix, pl* **-ies** **1** : little one ⟨sonn*y*⟩ ⟨pant*ie*⟩ **2** : one having such a quality ⟨smart*y*⟩ [Middle English *-ie* "little one"]

-ier — see ²-ER

if \(ˌ)if, əf\ *conj* **1** : in the event that ⟨come *if* you can⟩ **2** : whether it is or was true that ⟨asked *if* the mail had come⟩ **3** — used to introduce a wish ⟨*if* it would only rain⟩ **4** : even though : BUT ⟨an interesting *if* unbelievable excuse⟩

if·fy \ˈif-ē\ *adj* : full of uncertain or unknown conditions ⟨an *iffy* situation⟩

-i·fy \ə-ˌfī\ *vb suffix* **-i·fied; -i·fy·ing** : -FY

ig·loo \ˈig-lü\ *n, pl* **ig-loos** : an Eskimo house usually made of wood, sod, or stone when permanent or of blocks of snow or ice in the form of a dome when built for temporary use

igloo

ig·ne·ous \ˈig-nē-əs\ *adj* : formed by hardening of melted earth ⟨*igneous* rock⟩ — compare METAMORPHIC, SEDIMENTARY 2

ig·nite \ig-ˈnīt\ *vb* **ig·nit·ed; ig·nit·ing** **1 a** : to set on fire : LIGHT **b** : to cause (a fuel mixture) to burn **2** : to catch fire — **ig·nit·able** \-ˈnīt-ə-bəl\ *adj* — **ig·nit·er** *or* **ig·ni·tor** \-ˈnīt-ər\ *n*

ig·ni·tion \ig-ˈnish-ən\ *n* **1** : the act of igniting **2** : the

\ə\ abut	\au̇\ out	\i\ tip	\ȯ\ saw	\u̇\ foot
\ər\ further	\ch\ chin	\ī\ life	\ȯi\ coin	\y\ yet
\a\ mat	\e\ pet	\j\ job	\th\ thin	\yü\ few
\ā\ take	\ē\ easy	\ŋ\ sing	\th\ this	\yu̇\ cure
\ä\ cot, cart	\g\ go	\ō\ bone	\ü\ food	\zh\ vision

process or means (as an electric spark) of igniting a fuel mixture

ig·no·ble \ig-'nō-bəl\ *adj* **1** : not of noble birth **2** : not noble or honorable ⟨*ignoble* thoughts⟩ ⟨*ignoble* conduct⟩ — **ig·no·bly** \-blē\ *adv*

ig·no·min·i·ous \,ig-nə-'min-ē-əs\ *adj* : causing disgrace or shame ⟨an *ignominious* defeat⟩ — **ig·no·min·i·ous·ly** *adv*

ig·no·mi·ny \'ig-nə-,min-ē, ig-'näm-ə-nē\ *n, pl* **-nies** : deep humiliation and disgrace

ig·no·ra·mus \,ig-nə-'rā-məs\ *n, pl* **-mus·es** : an ignorant person [from *Ignoramus,* name of a character in a play]

ig·no·rance \'ig-nə-rən(t)s\ *n* : the state or fact of being ignorant

ig·no·rant \'ig-nə-rənt\ *adj* **1 a** : having no knowledge or education **b** : having no knowledge or understanding of a certain thing ⟨*ignorant* of mathematics⟩ **2** : not informed : UNAWARE ⟨*ignorant* of the facts⟩ **3** : resulting from or showing lack of knowledge ⟨an *ignorant* mistake⟩ — **ig·no·rant·ly** *adv*

syn IGNORANT, UNEDUCATED, UNLETTERED, ILLITERATE mean not having the kind of knowledge gained from education. IGNORANT suggests a lack of knowledge either in general or in some particular field ⟨*ignorant* about computers⟩ UNEDUCATED suggests a general lack of formal education ⟨there are few jobs for *uneducated* people⟩ UNLETTERED suggests a lack of the kind of knowledge gained from wide reading ⟨*unlettered* people would not appreciate the play⟩ ILLITERATE suggests either a total or major inability to read and write ⟨countries having large numbers of *illiterate* people⟩

ig·nore \ig-'nō(ə)r, -'nó(ə)r\ *vb* **ig·nored; ig·nor·ing** : to refuse to notice : pay no attention to **syn** see NEGLECT — **ig·nor·er** *n*

igua·na \i-'gwän-ə\ *n* : any of various large plant-eating tropical American lizards that have a ridge of tall scales along the middle of the back and that are used as human food

iguana

ike·ba·na \,ik-ā-'bän-ə, ,ik-i-, ,ēk-\ *n* : a Japanese art of flower arranging [Japanese, from *ikeru* "to keep alive, arrange" and *hana* "flower"]

il- — see IN-

il·e·um \'il-ē-əm\ *n, pl* **il·ea** \-ē-ə\ : the part of the small intestine between the jejunum and the large intestine — **il·e·al** \-ē-əl\ *adj*

il·i·ac \'il-ē-,ak\ *adj* : of, relating to, or located on the ilium ⟨an *iliac* spine⟩

Il·i·ad \'il-ē-əd, -ē-,ad\ *n* : an ancient Greek epic poem about the Trojan War that is believed to have been composed by Homer

il·i·um \'il-ē-əm\ *n, pl* **il·ia** \-ē-ə\ : the upper one of the three bones composing either side of the pelvis

ilk \'ilk\ *n* : ¹SORT 1a, KIND ⟨it's even worse than other films of that *ilk*⟩

¹ill \'il\ *adj* **worse** \'wərs\; **worst** \'wərst\ **1** : meant to do harm or evil ⟨*ill* deeds⟩ **2 a** : causing suffering or distress ⟨*ill* weather⟩ **b** : not normal or sound ⟨*ill* health⟩ **c** : not being in good health ⟨had been *ill* for some years⟩ **d** : affected by nausea **3** : not helpful to one : UNLUCKY ⟨an *ill* omen⟩ **4** : not right or proper ⟨*ill* manners⟩ **5** : not kind or friendly ⟨*ill* feeling⟩ ⟨never said an *ill* word⟩

²ill *adv* **worse; worst** **1 a** : with displeasure or anger ⟨the remark was *ill* received⟩ **b** : in a harsh manner ⟨treated me *ill*⟩ **2** : in a way that deserves blame ⟨an *ill*-spent youth⟩ ⟨*ill*-gotten gains⟩ **3** : HARDLY 3, SCARCELY ⟨can *ill*

afford it⟩ **4** : in a faulty way : BADLY, POORLY ⟨*ill*-prepared to face the winter⟩

³ill *n* **1** : the opposite of good : EVIL **2 a** : SICKNESS 2, AILMENT ⟨childhood *ills*⟩ **b** : ²TROUBLE 1a ⟨the *ills* of society⟩

I'll \(,)ī(ə)l\ : I shall : I will

ill–ad·vised \,il-əd-'vīzd\ *adj* : showing bad advice or too little thinking ahead ⟨an *ill-advised* decision⟩ — **ill–ad·vis·ed·ly** \-'vī-zəd-lē\ *adv*

ill at ease *adj* : feeling uncomfortable

ill–bred \'il-'bred\ *adj* : badly brought up : IMPOLITE

il·le·gal \(')il-'(l)ē-gəl\ *adj* : contrary to the laws or rules : UNLAWFUL — **il·le·gal·i·ty** \,il-i-'gal-ət-ē\ *n* — **il·le·gal·ly** \(')il-'(l)ē-gə-lē\ *adv*

il·leg·i·ble \(')il-'(l)ej-ə-bəl\ *adj* : impossible or very hard to read ⟨*illegible* handwriting⟩ — **il·leg·i·bly** \(')il-'(l)ej-ə-blē\ *adv*

il·le·git·i·ma·cy \,il-i-'jit-ə-mə-sē\ *n* : the quality or state of being illegitimate

il·le·git·i·mate \,il-i-'jit-ə-mət\ *adj* **1** : born of a father and mother who are not married **2** : ILLEGAL — **il·le·git·i·mate·ly** *adv*

ill–fat·ed \'il-'fāt-əd\ *adj* : doomed to disaster ⟨an *ill-fated* expedition⟩

ill–fa·vored \'il-'fā-vərd\ *adj* : not pretty or handsome : having an ugly face

ill–hu·mored \'il-'hyü-mərd, 'il-'yü-\ *adj* : being in a bad mood : IRRITABLE, CROSS — **ill–hu·mored·ly** *adv*

il·lic·it \(')il-'(l)is-ət\ *adj* : ILLEGAL ⟨*illicit* drug traffic⟩ — **il·lic·it·ly** *adv*

il·lim·it·able \(')il-'(l)im-ət-ə-bəl\ *adj* : not able to be limited or measured

il·lit·er·a·cy \(')il-'(l)it-ə-rə-sē, -'(l)i-trə-sē\ *n, pl* **-cies** **1** : the quality or state of being illiterate; *esp* : inability to read or write **2** : a mistake made by or typical of an illiterate person

il·lit·er·ate \(')il-'(l)it-ə-rət, -'(l)i-trət\ *adj* **1** : having little or no education; *esp* : unable to read or write **2** : showing lack of education **syn** see IGNORANT — **illiterate** *n* — **il·lit·er·ate·ly** *adv*

ill–man·nered \'il-'man-ərd\ *adj* : showing bad manners : RUDE

ill–na·tured \'il-'nā-chərd\ *adj* : having a bad disposition : SURLY ⟨is usually *ill-natured* in the morning until after breakfast⟩ — **ill–na·tured·ly** *adv*

ill·ness \'il-nəs\ *n* **1** : an unhealthy condition of body or mind **2** : SICKNESS 2

il·log·i·cal \(')il-'(l)äj-i-kəl\ *adj* : not using or following good reasoning — **il·log·i·cal·ly** \-i-k(ə-)lē\ *adv*

ill–starred \'il-'stärd\ *adj* : ILL-FATED, UNLUCKY ⟨*ill-starred* lovers⟩

ill–tem·pered \'il-'tem-pərd\ *adj* : having or showing a bad temper : ILL-NATURED ⟨an *ill-tempered* neighbor⟩ ⟨wrote an *ill-tempered* reply⟩ — **ill–tem·pered·ly** *adv*

ill–treat \'il-'trēt\ *vb* : to treat in a cruel or improper way : MALTREAT ⟨punished for *ill-treating* the neighbor's cat⟩ — **ill–treat·ment** \-mənt\ *n*

il·lu·mi·nate \il-'ü-mə-,nāt\ *vb* **-nat·ed; -nat·ing** **1** : to supply with light : light up ⟨*illuminate* a room⟩ ⟨the part of the moon *illuminated* by the sun⟩ **2** : to make clear : EXPLAIN ⟨*illuminated* the point with good examples⟩ **3** : to decorate with designs or pictures in gold or colors ⟨*illuminate* a manuscript⟩ — **il·lu·mi·na·tive** \-,nāt-iv\ *adj* — **il·lu·mi·na·tor** \-,nāt-ər\ *n*

il·lu·mi·na·tion \il-,ü-mə-'nā-shən\ *n* **1 a** : the action of illuminating or state of being illuminated **b** : amount of light **2** : gold or colored decoration in a manuscript

il·lu·mine \il-'ü-mən\ *vb* **-mined; -min·ing** : ILLUMINATE 1

ill–use \'il-'yüz\ *vb* : ILL-TREAT, MALTREAT — **ill–us·age** \-'yü-sij, -'yü-zij\ *n*

il·lu·sion \il-'ü-zhən\ *n* **1** : a misleading image presented to the eye **2** : the state or fact of being led to accept as

true something un-
real or imagined **3**
: a mistaken idea
il·lu·sive \il-'ü-siv, -'ü-
ziv\ *adj* : ILLUSORY —
il·lu·sive·ly *adj*
il·lu·so·ry \il-'üs-
(ə-)rē, -'üz-\ *adj*
: based on or produc-
ing illusion
il·lus·trate \'il-əs-ˌtrāt,
il-'əs-\ *vb* **-trat·ed;**
-trat·ing **1** : to

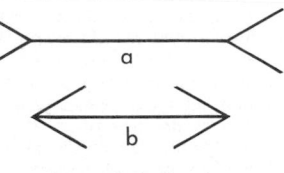

illusion 1: *a* equals *b*
in length

make clear by using examples **2 a** : to provide with pictures or diagrams intended to explain or decorate **b** : to
serve as an illustration — **il·lus·tra·tor** \-ˌtrāt-ər\ *n*
il·lus·tra·tion \ˌil-əs-'trā-shən\ *n* **1** : the action of illustrating : the condition of being illustrated **2** : an example or
instance used to make something clear **3** : a picture or
diagram that explains or decorates
il·lus·tra·tive \il-'əs-trət-iv\ *adj* : serving or meant to illustrate 〈*illustrative* examples〉
il·lus·tri·ous \il-'əs-trē-əs\ *adj* : very outstanding : EMINENT
— **il·lus·tri·ous·ly** *adv*
ill will *n* : unfriendly feeling
il·ly \'il-(l)ē\ *adv* : ²ILL, BADLY
im- — see IN-
I'm \(ˌ)īm\ : I am
¹**im·age** \'im-ij\ *n* **1** : something (as a statue) made to look
like a person or thing **2** : a picture of an object formed by
a device (as a mirror, lens, or electronic system) **3** : a
person who looks very much like another **4 a** : a mental
picture of something not actually present **b** : a mental
picture created by words **c** : a popular idea of what
something or someone is that is created especially by advertising and publicity
²**image** *vb* **im·aged; im·ag·ing** **1** : to describe in words or
pictures **2** : REFLECT 2, MIRROR
im·ag·ery \'im-ij-(ə-)rē\ *n, pl* **-er·ies** **1** : images that can
be seen or that are imagined **2** : language that suggests
how someone or something looks, sounds, feels, smells,
or tastes
imag·in·able \im-'aj-(ə-)nə-bəl\ *adj* : possible to imagine —
imag·in·ably \-blē\ *adv*
imag·i·nary \im-'aj-ə-ˌner-ē\ *adj* : existing only in imagination : not real
imag·i·na·tion \im-ˌaj-ə-'nā-shən\ *n* **1** : the act, process,
or power of forming a mental picture of something not
present and especially of something one has not known or
experienced **2** : creative ability **3** : a creation of the
mind
imag·i·na·tive \im-'aj-(ə-)nət-iv, -'aj-ə-ˌnāt-\ *adj* **1** : of, relating to, or showing imagination **2** : having a lively imagination — **imag·i·na·tive·ly** *adv* — **imag·i·na·tive·ness**
n
imag·ine \im-'aj-ən\ *vb* **imag·ined; imag·in·ing** \-'aj-
(ə-)niŋ\ **1** : to form a mental picture of : use the imagination **2** : THINK 2, SUPPOSE 〈I *imagine* it will snow〉
im·ag·ing \'im-ij-iŋ\ *n* : the action or process of producing
an image especially by means (as ultrasound) other than
visible light
ima·go \im-'ā-gō, -'äg-ō\ *n, pl* **imagoes** *or* **ima·gi·nes**
\-'ā-gə-ˌnēz, -'äg-ə-\ : an insect in its final adult, sexually
mature, and usually winged state — **ima·gi·nal** \-'ā-gən-
əl, -ˌäg-ən-\ *adj*
im·bal·ance \(ˌ)im-'bal-ən(t)s\ *n* : the state of being out of
balance or out of proportion
¹**im·be·cile** \'im-bə-səl, -ˌsil\ *or* **im·be·cil·ic** \ˌim-bə-'sil-
ik\ *adj* : of very low intelligence : very stupid
²**imbecile** *n* : a person of very low intelligence; *esp* : a feebleminded person who needs help in performing routine
daily tasks of caring for himself or herself

im·be·cil·i·ty \ˌim-bə-'sil-ət-ē\ *n, pl* **-ties** **1** : the quality
or state of being imbecile or an imbecile **2** : something
very foolish
imbed *variant of* EMBED
im·bibe \im-'bīb\ *vb* **im·bibed; im·bib·ing** **1** : to receive
into the mind and retain 〈*imbibe* knowledge〉 **2 a** : ¹DRINK
1a **b** : ABSORB 1 — **im·bib·er** *n*
im·bue \im-'byü\ *vb* **im·bued; im·bu·ing** : to influence
deeply as if by dyeing
im·i·ta·ble \'im-ət-ə-bəl\ *adj* : able to be imitated or worth
imitating
im·i·tate \'im-ə-ˌtāt\ *vb* **-tat·ed; -tat·ing** **1** : to follow as a
pattern, model, or example **2** : to be or appear similar to
3 : to copy exactly — **im·i·ta·tor** \-ˌtāt-ər\ *n*
    syn IMITATE, APE, MIMIC, MOCK mean to follow the ex-
ample of another. IMITATE suggests using someone that
one admires as a model or pattern 〈children *imitating*
their parents〉 APE suggests a close and often clumsy imitation of an admired example 〈some teenagers try to
ape the behavior of rock singers〉 MIMIC may suggest imitation of another's personal manner often for humor 〈the
comedian *mimicked* a popular actor〉 MOCK suggests
making fun of someone by imitating that person in his or
her presence 〈*mocked* the dictator's swaggering walk〉
¹**im·i·ta·tion** \ˌim-ə-'tā-shən\ *n* **1** : an act of imitating **2**
: something produced as a copy
²**imitation** *adj* : resembling something else especially of better quality 〈*imitation* pearls〉 〈*imitation* leather〉
im·i·ta·tive \'im-ə-ˌtāt-iv\ *adj* **1** : involving imitation **2**
: given to imitating **3** : imitating something better — **im-
i·ta·tive·ly** *adv*
im·mac·u·late \im-'ak-yə-lət\ *adj* **1** : having no stain or
blemish : PURE 〈an *immaculate* record of service〉 **2**
: perfectly clean 〈*immaculate* linen〉 — **im·mac·u·late·ly**
adv — **im·mac·u·late·ness** *n*
Immaculate Conception *n* : December 8 observed as a Roman Catholic festival in honor of the conception of the Virgin Mary as free from original sin
im·ma·te·ri·al \ˌim-ə-'tir-ē-əl\ *adj* **1** : not consisting of
matter **2** : not important : INSIGNIFICANT
im·ma·ture \ˌim-ə-'t(y)ù(ə)r\ *adj* : not mature or fully developed : YOUNG, UNRIPE 〈*immature* animals〉 〈*immature*
fruit〉 — **im·ma·ture·ly** *adv*
im·ma·tu·ri·ty \ˌim-ə-'t(y)ùr-ət-ē\ *n* : the state or quality of
being immature
im·mea·sur·able \(ˌ)im-'(m)ezh-(ə-)rə-bəl, -'(m)ezh-ər-bəl,
-'(m)āzh-\ *adj* : impossible to measure : VAST, BOUNDLESS
— **im·mea·sur·ably** \-blē\ *adv*
im·me·di·a·cy \im-'ēd-ē-ə-sē\ *n, pl* **-cies** **1** : the quality
or state of being immediate **2** : something that is of immediate importance 〈*immediacies* of daily life〉
im·me·di·ate \im-'ēd-ē-ət\ *adj* **1** : acting or being without
anything else coming between 〈the *immediate* cause of
disease〉 **2** : being next in line or nearest in relationship
〈my *immediate* family〉 **3** : closest in importance 〈our *immediate* needs〉 **4** : acting or being without delay 〈needs
immediate help〉 **5** : not far away in time or space
im·me·di·ate·ly \im-'ēd-ē-ət-lē\ *adv* **1** : with nothing between : DIRECTLY 〈the person *immediately* to my left〉 **2**
: right away : at once 〈do it *immediately*〉
im·me·mo·ri·al \ˌim-ə-'mōr-ē-əl, -'mòr-\ *adj* : going back
beyond the reach of memory or record : very ancient 〈from
time *immemorial*〉 — **im·me·mo·ri·al·ly** \-ē-ə-lē\ *adv*
im·mense \im-'en(t)s\ *adj* : very great in size or amount
[from early French *immense* "immense, huge", from Latin
immensus "boundless, too great to be measured", from

\ə\ abut	\au̇\ out	\i\ tip	\ȯ\ saw	\u̇\ foot
\ər\ further	\ch\ chin	\ī\ life	\ȯi\ coin	\y\ yet
\a\ mat	\e\ pet	\j\ job	\th\ thin	\yü\ few
\ā\ take	\ē\ easy	\ŋ\ sing	\th\ this	\yu̇\ cure
\ä\ cot, cart	\g\ go	\ō\ bone	\ü\ food	\zh\ vision

im-, in- "not" and *mensus,* past participle of *metiri* "to measure" — related to DIMENSION, MEASURE] **syn** see ENORMOUS — **im·mense·ly** *adv* — **im·mense·ness** *n*

im·men·si·ty \im-'en(t)-sət-ē\ *n, pl* **-ties** **1** : the quality or state of being immense **2** : something immense

im·merse \im-'ərs\ *vb* **im·mersed; im·mers·ing** **1** : to plunge into something (as a fluid) that surrounds or covers **2** : to become completely involved in ⟨*immersed* in a good book⟩ — **im·mer·sion** \-'ər-zhən, -shən\ *n*

im·mers·ible \im-'ər-sə-bəl\ *adj* : able to be completely put under water without damage to the heating element ⟨an *immersible* electric frying pan⟩

immersion heater *n* : an electric unit for heating the liquid it is immersed in

im·mi·grant \'im-i-grənt\ *n* **1** : a person who comes to a country to live there **2** : a plant or animal that becomes established in an area where it did not occur previously — **immigrant** *adj*

im·mi·grate \'im-ə-ˌgrāt\ *vb* **-grat·ed; -grat·ing** : to come into a foreign country to live — **im·mi·gra·tion** \ˌim-ə-'grā-shən\ *n*

im·mi·nence \'im-ə-nən(t)s\ *n* : the quality or state of being imminent

im·mi·nent \'im-ə-nənt\ *adj* : being about to happen ⟨in *imminent* danger⟩ — **im·mi·nent·ly** *adv*

im·mo·bile \(')im-'(m)ō-bəl, -ˌbēl, -ˌbīl\ *adj* : unable to move or be moved — **im·mo·bil·i·ty** \ˌim-(ˌ)ō-'bil-ət-ē\ *n*

im·mo·bi·lize \im-'ō-bə-ˌlīz\ *vb* **-lized; -liz·ing** : to fix in place : make immobile — **im·mo·bi·li·za·tion** \im-ˌō-bə-lə-'zā-shən\ *n* — **im·mo·bi·liz·er** \im-'ō-bə-ˌlī-zər\ *n*

im·mod·er·a·cy \(')im-'(m)äd-(ə-)rə-sē\ *n* : the quality or state of being immoderate

im·mod·er·ate \(')im-'(m)äd-(ə-)rət\ *adj* : going too far or asking too much : EXCESSIVE — **im·mod·er·ate·ly** *adv*

im·mod·est \(')im-'(m)äd-əst\ *adj* : not modest — **im·mod·est·ly** *adv* — **im·mod·es·ty** \-ə-stē\ *n*

im·mo·late \'im-ə-ˌlāt\ *vb* **-lat·ed; -lat·ing** : to kill as a sacrifice — **im·mo·la·tion** \ˌim-ə-'lā-shən\ *n* — **im·mo·la·tor** \'im-ə-ˌlāt-ər\ *n*

im·mor·al \(')im-'(m)òr-əl, -'(m)är-\ *adj* : not moral : WICKED, BAD — **im·mor·al·ly** \-ə-lē\ *adv*

im·mo·ral·i·ty \ˌim-(ˌ)ò-'ral-ət-ē, ˌim-ə-'ral-\ *n, pl* **-ties** **1** : the quality or state of being immoral **2** : an immoral act or custom

¹im·mor·tal \(')im-'òrt-ᵊl\ *adj* : living or lasting forever — **im·mor·tal·ly** \-ᵊl-ē\ *adv*

²immortal *n* **1** : an immortal being **2** : a person whose fame is lasting ⟨baseball *immortals*⟩

im·mor·tal·i·ty \ˌim-,ór-'tal-ət-ē\ *n* : the quality or state of being immortal: **a** : endless life **b** : lasting fame or glory

im·mor·tal·ize \im-'òrt-ᵊl-ˌīz\ *vb* **-ized; -iz·ing** : to make immortal ⟨the battle was *immortalized* in a famous poem⟩ — **im·mor·tal·iza·tion** \-ˌòrt-ᵊl-ə-'zā-shən\ *n*

im·mov·able \(')im-'(m)ü-və-bəl\ *adj* **1 a** : not able to be moved **b** : not moving : STATIONARY **2** : STEADFAST 1b — **im·mov·abil·i·ty** \(ˌ)im-ˌ(m)ü-və-'bil-ət-ē\ *n* — **im·mov·ably** \(')im-'(m)ü-və-blē\ *adv*

im·mune \im-'yün\ *adj* **1** : ¹EXEMPT ⟨*immune* from punishment⟩ **2 a** : not influenced by something ⟨*immune* to persuasion⟩ **b** : having a high level of natural or acquired resistance ⟨*immune* to diphtheria⟩ **3** : containing or producing antibodies

immune response *n* : a bodily response to a foreign substance, cell, or tissue that involves the formation of antibodies and cells capable of reacting with it and rendering it harmless — called also *immune reaction*

immune system *n* : the bodily system that protects the body from foreign substances, cells, and tissues by producing the immune response and that includes especially the thymus, spleen, lymph nodes, lymphocytes, and antibodies

im·mu·ni·ty \im-'yü-nət-ē\ *n, pl* **-ties** **1** : EXEMPTION 1 **2**

: bodily power to resist an infectious disease that usually results from vaccination or inoculation, a previous attack of the disease, or a natural resistance

im·mu·ni·za·tion \ˌim-yə-nə-'zā-shən\ *n* : treatment (as with a vaccine) to produce immunity to a disease

im·mu·nize \'im-yə-ˌnīz\ *vb* **-nized; -niz·ing** : to make immune ⟨have been *immunized* against polio⟩

im·mu·no·de·fi·cien·cy \ˌim-yə-(ˌ)nō-də-'fish-ən-sē, (ˌ)im-'yü-nō-\ *n* : inability to produce the normal number of antibodies or T cells capable of acting in an immune system

im·mu·nol·o·gist \ˌim-yə-'näl-ə-jəst\ *n* : a person who specializes in immunology

im·mu·nol·o·gy \ˌim-yə-'näl-ə-jē\ *n* : a science that deals with immunity to disease — **im·mu·no·log·ic** \-yən-ᵊl-'äj-ik\ *or* **im·mu·no·log·i·cal** \-'äj-i-kəl\ *adj*

im·mure \im-'yü(ə)r\ *vb* **im·mured; im·mur·ing** : to enclose within or as if within walls : IMPRISON — **im·mure·ment** \-mənt\ *n*

im·mu·ta·ble \(')im-'(m)yüt-ə-bəl\ *adj* : impossible to change — **im·mu·ta·bil·i·ty** \(ˌ)im-ˌ(m)yüt-ə-'bil-ət-ē\ *n* — **im·mu·ta·bly** \(')im-'(m)yüt-ə-blē\ *adv*

imp \'imp\ *n* **1** : a small demon **2** : a mischievous child

¹im·pact \im-'pakt\ *vb* **1** : to have a strong effect on **2** : to hit or cause to hit with force

²im·pact \'im-ˌpakt\ *n* **1** : a striking together of two bodies : COLLISION **2** : a forceful effect

im·pact·ed \im-'pak-təd\ *adj* **1** : wedged between the jawbone and another tooth **2** : packed or wedged in

im·pac·tion \im-'pak-shən\ *n* : the act of becoming or the state of being impacted

im·pair \im-'pa(ə)r, -'pe(ə)r\ *vb* : to damage or make worse by or as if by making smaller, less, or weaker ⟨smoking can *impair* one's health⟩ — **im·pair·ment** \-mənt\ *n*

im·pa·la \im-'pal-ə, -'päl-\ *n* : a large brownish African antelope that in the male has slender curving horns [a native name in an African language]

im·pale \im-'pā(ə)l\ *vb* **im·paled; im·pal·ing** : to pierce with or as if with something pointed

im·pal·pa·ble \(')im-'pal-pə-bəl\ *adj* **1** : unable to be felt by touch **2** : not easily seen or understood

im·pan·el \im-'pan-ᵊl\ *vb* **-eled** *or* **-elled; -el·ing** *or* **-el·ling** : to enroll in or on a panel ⟨*impanel* a jury⟩

im·part \im-'pärt\ *vb* **1** : to give or grant from or as if from a store ⟨schools *impart* knowledge⟩ **2** : to make known : DISCLOSE ⟨I have a bit of news to *impart*⟩

im·par·tial \(')im-'pär-shəl\ *adj* : treating all equally : not partial — **im·par·tial·i·ty** \(ˌ)im-ˌpär-shē-'al-ət-ē, -ˌpär-'shal-\ *n* — **im·par·tial·ly** \(')im-'pärsh-(ə-)lē\ *adv*

im·pass·able \(')im-'pas-ə-bəl\ *adj* : impossible to pass, cross, or travel over ⟨roads made *impassable* by the hurricane⟩ — **im·pass·abil·i·ty** \(ˌ)im-ˌpas-ə-'bil-ət-ē\ *n*

im·passe \'im-ˌpas, im-'pas\ *n* : a situation from which it seems impossible to escape; *esp* : DEADLOCK

im·pas·sioned \im-'pash-ənd\ *adj* : showing very strong feeling

im·pas·sive \(')im-'pas-iv\ *adj* : not feeling or not showing emotion — **im·pas·sive·ly** *adv* — **im·pas·siv·i·ty** \ˌim-ˌpas-'iv-ət-ē\ *n*

im·pa·tience \(')im-'pā-shən(t)s\ *n* **1** : lack of patience **2** : restless or eager desire

im·pa·tiens \im-'pā-shənz, -shən(t)s\ *n* : any of a large genus of juicy annual herbs that produce often brightly colored flowers — called also *jewelweed, touch-me-not*

im·pa·tient \(')im-'pā-shənt\ *adj* **1** : not patient ⟨an *impatient* disposition⟩ **2** : showing or coming from impatience ⟨an *impatient* answer⟩ **3** : restless and eager ⟨*impatient* to get going⟩ — **im·pa·tient·ly** *adv*

im·peach \im-'pēch\ *vb* **1** : to charge a public official formally with misconduct in office **2** : to cast doubt on ⟨*impeached* the witness's testimony⟩ — **im·peach·able** \-'pē-chə-bəl\ *adj* — **im·peach·ment** \-'pēch-mənt\ *n*

im·pec·ca·ble \(')im-'pek-ə-bəl\ *adj* : free from fault or blame — **im·pec·ca·bil·i·ty** \(,)im-,pek-ə-'bil-ət-ē\ *n* — **im·pec·ca·bly** \(')im-'pek-ə-blē\ *adv*

im·pe·cu·nious \,im-pi-'kyü-nyəs, -nē-əs\ *adj* : having little or no money — **im·pe·cu·nious·ness** *n*

im·pede \im-'pēd\ *vb* **im·ped·ed; im·ped·ing** : to interfere with the movement or progress of [from Latin *impedire* "to hinder, get in the way of", literally "to bind or hold the feet of", derived from *im-, in-* "in, into" and *ped-, pes* "foot" — related to PEDESTRIAN] — **im·ped·er** *n*

im·ped·i·ment \im-'ped-ə-mənt\ *n* **1** : something that impedes **2** : a defect in speech

im·ped·i·men·ta \(,)im-,ped-ə-'ment-ə\ *n pl* : things (as baggage or equipment) that keep one from moving freely

im·pel \im-'pel\ *vb* **im·pelled; im·pel·ling** : to urge or drive forward or into action — **im·pel·ler** \-'pel-ər\ *n*

im·pend \im-'pend\ *vb* **1** : to threaten to occur immediately ⟨*impending* danger⟩ **2** : to be about to happen ⟨an *impending* trip⟩ **3** *archaic* : to hang out or over

im·pen·e·tra·ble \(')im-'pen-ə-trə-bəl\ *adj* **1** : impossible to get through or into ⟨*impenetrable* walls⟩ ⟨*impenetrable* jungle⟩ **2** : impossible to understand ⟨an *impenetrable* mystery⟩ — **im·pen·e·tra·bil·i·ty** \(,)im-,pen-ə-trə-'bil-ət-ē\ *n* — **im·pen·e·tra·bly** \(')im-'pen-ə-trə-blē\ *adv*

im·pen·i·tence \(')im-'pen-ə-tən(t)s\ *n* : the quality or state of being impenitent

im·pen·i·tent \(')im-'pen-ə-tənt\ *adj* : not sorry for having done wrong — **im·pen·i·tent·ly** *adv*

¹**im·per·a·tive** \im-'per-ət-iv\ *adj* **1 a** : of, relating to, or being the grammatical mood that expresses a command, request, or encouragement **b** : expressing a command, request, or strong encouragement ⟨an *imperative* sentence⟩ **2** : impossible to avoid or ignore : URGENT — **im·per·a·tive·ly** *adv* — **im·per·a·tive·ness** *n*

²**imperative** *n* **1** : the imperative mood of a verb or a verb in this mood **2** : something that is imperative

im·pe·ra·tor \,im-pə-'rät-ər, -'rä-,tò(ə)r\ *n* : a commander in chief or emperor of the ancient Romans

im·per·cep·ti·ble \,im-pər-'sep-tə-bəl\ *adj* **1** : not noticeable : not perceptible by a sense or by the mind ⟨one whose beauty was *imperceptible* to others⟩ **2** : hardly noticeable : very small or gradual ⟨an *imperceptible* smile⟩ — **im·per·cep·ti·bly** \-blē\ *adv*

¹**im·per·fect** \(')im-'pər-fikt\ *adj* **1** : not perfect: **a** : ¹DEFECTIVE ⟨*imperfect* clothing⟩ **b** : having stamens or pistils but not being a flower with both **2** : of, relating to, or being a verb tense used to express a continuing state or an incomplete action especially in the past — **im·per·fect·ly** \-fik-(t)lē\ *adv*

²**imperfect** *n* : the imperfect tense of a verb or a verb in this tense

im·per·fec·tion \,im-pər-'fek-shən\ *n* **1** : the quality or state of being imperfect **2** : FLAW, FAULT

¹**im·pe·ri·al** \im-'pir-ē-əl\ *adj* : of, relating to, or fine enough for an empire or an emperor — **im·pe·ri·al·ly** \-ē-ə-lē\ *adv*

²**imperial** *n* : a pointed beard growing below the lower lip

im·pe·ri·al·ism \im-'pir-ē-ə-,liz-əm\ *n* : the actions by which one nation is able to control other usually smaller or weaker nations — **im·pe·ri·al·ist** \-ē-ə-ləst\ *n or adj* — **im·pe·ri·al·is·tic** \im-,pir-ē-ə-'lis-tik\ *adj* — **im·pe·ri·al·is·ti·cal·ly** \-ti-k(ə)lē\ *adv*

imperial

im·per·il \im-'per-əl\ *vb* **-iled** *or* **-illed; il·ing** *or* **-il·ling** : to place in great danger : ENDANGER — **im·per·il·ment** \-əl-mənt\ *n*

im·pe·ri·ous \im-'pir-ē-əs\ *adj* **1** : behaving like someone who is a supreme ruler **2** : ¹IMPERATIVE 2, URGENT ⟨the *imperious* problems of a new age⟩ — **im·pe·ri·ous·ly** *adv* — **im·pe·ri·ous·ness** *n*

im·per·ish·able \(')im-'per-ish-ə-bəl\ *adj* : INDESTRUCTIBLE — **im·per·ish·abil·i·ty** \(,)im-,per-ish-ə-'bil-ət-ē\ *n* — **im·per·ish·ably** \(')im-'per-ish-ə-blē\ *adv*

im·per·ma·nence \(')im-'pərm-(ə)-nən(t)s\ *n* : the quality or state of being impermanent

im·per·ma·nent \(')im-'pərm-(ə)-nənt\ *adj* : not permanent : not lasting long — **im·per·ma·nent·ly** *adv*

im·per·me·able \(')im-'pər-mē-ə-bəl\ *adj* : not permitting passage (as of a fluid) through the material of which it is made — **im·per·me·abil·i·ty** \(,)im-,pər-mē-ə-'bil-ət-ē\ *n*

im·per·mis·si·ble \,im-pər-'mis-ə-bəl\ *adj* : not permissible

im·per·son·al \(')im-'pərs-nəl, -ᵊn-əl\ *adj* **1** : having no expressed subject or no subject other than "it" ⟨"rained" in "it rained" is an *impersonal* verb⟩ **2** : not personal: **a** : not showing or involving personal feelings : DETACHED ⟨an *impersonal* professional attitude⟩ **b** : not caring about individual persons or their feelings ⟨cold *impersonal* cities⟩ ⟨a giant *impersonal* corporation⟩ — **im·per·son·al·i·ty** \(,)im-,pərs-ᵊn-'al-ət-ē\ *n* — **im·per·son·al·ly** \(')im-'pərs-nə-lē, -ᵊn-ə-lē\ *adv*

im·per·son·ate \im-'pərs-ᵊn-,āt\ *vb* **-at·ed; -at·ing** : to pretend to be some other person ⟨*impersonate* a police officer⟩ — **im·per·son·ation** \-,pərs-ᵊn-'ā-shən\ *n* — **im·per·son·ator** \-'pərs-ᵊn-,āt-ər\ *n*

im·per·ti·nence \(')im-'pərt-ᵊn-ən(t)s, -'pərt-nən(t)s\ *n* **1** : the quality or state of being impertinent **2** : a rude act or remark

im·per·ti·nent \(')im-'pərt-ᵊn-ənt, -'pərt-nənt\ *adj* : INSOLENT, RUDE — **im·per·ti·nent·ly** *adv*

im·per·turb·able \,im-pər-'tər-bə-bəl\ *adj* : hard to disturb or upset — **im·per·turb·abil·i·ty** \-,tər-bə-'bil-ət-ē\ *n* — **im·per·turb·ably** \-'tər-bə-blē\ *adv*

im·per·vi·ous \(')im-'pər-vē-əs\ *adj* **1** : not letting something enter or pass through ⟨a coat *impervious* to rain⟩ **2** : not disturbed or upset ⟨*impervious* to criticism⟩ — **im·per·vi·ous·ness** *n*

im·pe·ti·go \,im-pə-'tē-gō, -'tī-\ *n* : a contagious skin disease marked by pimples, blisters, and yellowish crusts

im·pet·u·os·i·ty \im-,pech-ə-'wäs-ət-ē\ *n, pl* **-ties** **1** : the quality or state of being impetuous : RASHNESS **2** : an impetuous act

im·pet·u·ous \im-'pech-(ə-)wəs\ *adj* **1** : IMPULSIVE, RASH **2** : marked by force of action or movement — **im·pet·u·ous·ly** *adv* — **im·pet·u·ous·ness** *n*

im·pe·tus \'im-pət-əs\ *n* **1 a** : a driving force : IMPULSE **b** : INCENTIVE **2** : MOMENTUM 1

im·pi·ety \(')im-'pī-ət-ē\ *n, pl* **-ties** **1** : the quality or state of being impious **2** : an impious act

im·pinge \im-'pinj\ *vb* **im·pinged; im·ping·ing** **1** : to strike or dash especially with a sharp collision ⟨sound waves *impinge* on the eardrums⟩ **2** : ENCROACH 1, INFRINGE ⟨*impinge* on another's rights⟩ —**im·pinge·ment** \-mənt\ *n*

im·pi·ous \'im-pē-əs, (')im-'pī-\ *adj* : not pious : IRREVERENT — **im·pi·ous·ly** *adv*

imp·ish \'im-pish\ *adj* : MISCHIEVOUS 3 — **imp·ish·ly** *adv* — **imp·ish·ness** *n*

im·pla·ca·ble \(')im-'plak-ə-bəl, -'plā-kə-\ *adj* : not possible to please, satisfy, or change ⟨an *implacable* enemy⟩ — **im·pla·ca·bly** \-blē\ *adv*

\ə\ abut		\au̇\ out	\i\ tip	\ȯ\ saw	\u̇\ foot
\ər\ further		\ch\ chin	\ī\ life	\ȯi\ coin	\y\ yet
\a\ mat		\e\ pet	\j\ job	\th\ thin	\yü\ few
\ā\ take		\ē\ easy	\ŋ\ sing	\th\ this	\yu̇\ cure
\ä\ cot, cart		\g\ go	\ō\ bone	\ü\ food	\zh\ vision

im·plant \im-'plant\ vb **1** : to fix or set securely or deeply **2** : to insert in a living site for growth or absorption — **im·plant·able** \-ə-bəl\ adj

im·plan·ta·tion \,im-,plan-'tā-shən\ n **1** : the act of implanting something **2** : the process of becoming implanted or the resulting state

im·plau·si·ble \(')im-'plò-zə-bəl\ adj : causing disbelief : not plausible — **im·plau·si·bil·i·ty** \(,)im-,plò-zə-'bil-ət-ē\ n — **im·plau·si·bly** \(')im-'plò-zə-blē\ adv

¹im·ple·ment \'im-plə-mənt\ n : an article intended for use in work

syn IMPLEMENT, TOOL, INSTRUMENT, UTENSIL mean a device for doing work. IMPLEMENT may apply to anything needed to complete a task ⟨gardening *implements* such as rakes and hoes⟩ TOOL suggests a device designed for a specific job that may require some skill on the user's part ⟨carpenter's *tools*⟩ INSTRUMENT suggests a device that can be used for delicate or precise work ⟨one needs great skill to handle the *instruments* of a surgeon⟩ UTENSIL suggests a fairly simple device for jobs around the house ⟨kitchen *utensils* include knives and ladles⟩

²im·ple·ment \'im-plə-,ment\ vb : to take steps to put into practice : CARRY OUT ⟨*implement* the terms of a treaty⟩ — **im·ple·men·ta·tion** \,im-plə-mən-'tā-shən, -,men-\ n

im·pli·cate \'im-plə-,kāt\ vb **-cat·ed; -cat·ing** : to show to be connected or involved

im·pli·ca·tion \,im-plə-'kā-shən\ n **1** : the act of implicating : the state of being implicated **2 a** : the act of implying : the state of being implied **b** : something implied

im·plic·it \im-'plis-ət\ adj **1** : understood though not put clearly into words ⟨an *implicit* agreement⟩ **2** : being without doubt : ABSOLUTE, COMPLETE ⟨*implicit* trust⟩ — **im·plic·it·ly** adv — **im·plic·it·ness** n

im·plode \im-'plōd\ vb **im·plod·ed; im·plod·ing** : to burst inward

im·plore \im-'plō(ə)r, -'plò(ə)r\ vb **im·plored; im·plor·ing** : to call upon with a humble request : BESEECH ⟨*implored* the manager to give her more responsibility⟩ — **im·plor·ing·ly** adv

im·plo·sion \im-'plō-zhən\ n : the action of imploding — **im·plo·sive** \-'plō-siv, -ziv\ adj

im·ply \im-'plī\ vb **im·plied; im·ply·ing** **1** : to include or involve as a natural or necessary part even though not put clearly into words ⟨rights *imply* obligations⟩ ⟨an *implied* warranty⟩ **2** : to express indirectly : suggest rather than say plainly ⟨your remark *implies* that I am wrong⟩

im·po·lite \,im-pə-'līt\ adj : not polite : RUDE — **im·po·lite·ly** adv — **im·po·lite·ness** n

im·pon·der·a·ble \(')im-'pän-d(ə-)rə-bəl\ adj : not able to have the importance, strength, or value figured out — **im·ponderable** n

¹im·port \im-'pō(ə)rt, -'pò(ə)rt; 'im-,pō(ə)rt, -,pò(ə)rt\ vb **1** : ²MEAN 2 **2** : to be important : MATTER **3** : to bring (as goods) into a country usually for selling ⟨*imports* coffee⟩ ⟨*imported* cars⟩ — **im·port·er** n

²im·port \'im-,pō(ə)rt, -,pò(ə)rt\ n **1** : ¹MEANING 1 **2** : IMPORTANCE **3** : something brought into a country

im·por·tance \im-'pòrt-ᵊn(t)s, -ᵊn(t)s\ n : the quality or state of being important

syn IMPORTANCE, CONSEQUENCE, SIGNIFICANCE mean a quality or condition of something that makes people believe it to be of great value or influence. IMPORTANCE suggests the making of a value judgment regarding something's superior worth ⟨he said nothing of *importance*⟩ CONSEQUENCE suggests that a thing's importance comes from its possible or likely outcome, effects, or results ⟨choosing the right courses will be of great *consequence* for your college career⟩ SIGNIFICANCE may apply to some aspect of a thing that makes it important but may not be immediately obvious ⟨at first people did not realize the *significance* of the invention⟩

im·por·tant \im-'pòrt-ᵊnt, -ᵊnt\ adj **1** : having great mean-

ing or influence : SIGNIFICANT ⟨an *important* day to remember⟩ ⟨our most *important* product⟩ ⟨an *important* change⟩ **2** : having power or authority ⟨an *important* leader⟩ **3** : believing or acting as if one's importance is greater than it really is — **im·por·tant·ly** adv

im·por·ta·tion \,im-,pōr-'tā-shən, -,pòr-, -pər-\ n **1** : the act or practice of importing **2** : something imported : IMPORT

imported fire ant n : either of two small South American fire ants that are pests in the southeastern U.S. especially in fields used to grow crops

im·por·tu·nate \im-'pòrch-(ə-)nət\ adj : making a nuisance of oneself with requests or demands — **im·por·tu·nate·ly** adv

im·por·tune \,im-pər-'t(y)ün, im-'pòr-chən\ vb **-tuned; -tun·ing** : to beg or urge so much as to be a nuisance — **im·por·tun·er** n

im·por·tu·ni·ty \,im-pər-'t(y)ü-nət-ē\ n, pl **-ties** : the quality or state of being importunate

im·pose \im-'pōz\ vb **im·posed; im·pos·ing** **1 a** : to establish or apply as a charge or penalty ⟨*impose* a fine⟩ ⟨*impose* a tax⟩ **b** : to force somebody to accept or put up with ⟨*impose* one's will on another⟩ **2** : to take unfair advantage ⟨*impose* on a friend's good nature⟩ — **im·pos·er** n

im·pos·ing \im-'pō-ziŋ\ adj : impressive in size, dignity, or magnificence — **im·pos·ing·ly** adv

im·po·si·tion \,im-pə-'zish-ən\ n **1** : the act of imposing **2 a** : something (as a tax) that is imposed **b** : a demand or request that is very troublesome

im·pos·si·bil·i·ty \(,)im-,päs-ə-'bil-ət-ē\ n, pl **-ties** **1** : the quality or state of being impossible **2** : something impossible

im·pos·si·ble \(')im-'päs-ə-bəl\ adj **1 a** : incapable of being or of occurring **b** : felt to be too difficult : HOPELESS ⟨an *impossible* situation⟩ **2** : very bad or unpleasant ⟨an *impossible* person to deal with⟩ — **im·pos·si·bly** \-blē\ adv

im·post \'im-,pōst\ n : ²TAX 1

im·pos·tor or **im·pos·ter** \im-'päs-tər\ n : a person who pretends to be someone else in order to deceive

im·pos·ture \im-'päs-chər\ n : the act or conduct of an impostor

im·po·tence \'im-pət-ən(t)s\ n : the quality or state of being impotent

im·po·tent \'im-pət-ənt\ adj **1** : lacking in power or strength **2** : unable to copulate; *also* : STERILE 1 — usually used of males — **im·po·tent·ly** adv

im·pound \im-'paùnd\ vb **1** : to shut up in or as if in an enclosed place **2** : to seize and hold in the hands of the law ⟨*impound* evidence for a trial⟩ — **im·pound·ment** \-'paùn(d)-mənt\ n

im·pov·er·ish \im-'päv-(ə-)rish\ vb **1** : to make poor **2** : to use up the strength or richness of ⟨*impoverished* soil⟩ — **im·pov·er·ish·ment** \-mənt\ n

im·prac·ti·ca·ble \(')im-'prak-ti-kə-bəl\ adj : difficult to put into practice or use ⟨an *impracticable* plan⟩ — **im·prac·ti·ca·bil·i·ty** \(,)im-,prak-ti-kə-'bil-ət-ē\ n

im·prac·ti·cal \(')im-'prak-ti-kəl\ adj : not practical — **im·prac·ti·cal·i·ty** \,im-,prak-ti-'kal-ət-ē\ n — **im·prac·ti·cal·ly** \(')im-'prak-ti-k(ə-)lē\ adv

im·pre·cate \'im-pri-,kāt\ vb **-cat·ed; -cat·ing** : ²CURSE 1

im·pre·ca·tion \,im-pri-'kā-shən\ n : ¹CURSE 1, 2

im·pre·cise \,im-pri-'sīs\ adj : not precise — **im·pre·cise·ly** adv — **im·pre·cise·ness** n — **im·pre·ci·sion** \-'sizh-ən\ n

im·preg·na·ble \im-'preg-nə-bəl\ adj : not able to be captured by assault : UNCONQUERABLE — **im·preg·na·bly** \-blē\ adv

im·preg·nate \im-'preg-,nāt\ vb **-nat·ed; -nat·ing** **1 a** : to make pregnant **b** : to introduce sperm cells into **c** : to make fertile or fruitful **2** : to cause (a material) to be filled or soaked with something — **im·preg·na·tion** \(ˌ)im-ˌpreg-ˈnā-shən\ *n* — **im·preg·na·tor** \im-ˈpreg-ˌnāt-ər\ *n*

im·pre·sa·rio \ˌim-prə-ˈsär-ē-ˌō, -ˈsar-, -ˈzär-\ *n, pl* **-ri·os** : a person who puts on an entertainment (as a concert)

¹im·press \im-ˈpres\ *vb* **1** : to produce by stamping, pressing, or printing **2 a** : to fix in or on one's mind : produce a vivid impression of ⟨the lesson was *impressed* on their minds⟩ **b** : to move or affect strongly ⟨I am *impressed* by what you've done⟩ ⟨tries to *impress* people⟩

²im·press \ˈim-ˌpres\ *n* **1** : the act of impressing **2** : a mark made by pressure **3** : a characteristic or special mark **4** : IMPRESSION 2b

³im·press \im-ˈpres\ *vb* : to force into naval service — **im·press·ment** \-mənt\ *n*

im·pres·sion \im-ˈpresh-ən\ *n* **1** : the act or process of impressing **2 a** : something (as a design or a footprint) made by pressing or stamping **b** : something that impresses or is impressed on one's mind ⟨those words made a strong *impression*⟩ ⟨the candidate made a good *impression*⟩ **3** : a memory or belief that is vague or uncertain ⟨it's my *impression* that you don't have to go⟩ **4** : an imitation of a famous person done for entertainment

im·pres·sion·able \im-ˈpresh-(ə-)nə-bəl\ *adj* : easy to impress or influence — **im·pres·sion·abil·i·ty** \-ˌpresh-(ə-)nə-ˈbil-ət-ē\ *n*

im·pres·sion·ism \im-ˈpresh-ə-ˌniz-əm\ *n* **1** *often cap* : a style of painting beginning in France around 1870 in which dabs or strokes of primary colors are used to give the effect of light actually reflected from things **2** : a style of musical composition designed to create moods through rich and varied harmonies

im·pres·sion·ist \im-ˈpresh-(ə-)nəst\ *n* **1** *often cap* : a person (as a painter) who practices impressionism **2** : an entertainer who does impressions

im·pres·sion·is·tic \(ˌ)im-ˌpresh-ə-ˈnis-tik\ *adj* **1** *or* **im·pres·sion·ist** \im-ˈpresh-(ə-)nəst\ : of or relating to impressionism **2** : involving one's impressions rather than knowledge or facts — **im·pres·sion·is·ti·cal·ly** \(ˌ)im-ˌpresh-ə-ˈnis-ti-k(ə-)lē\ *adv*

im·pres·sive \im-ˈpres-iv\ *adj* : having the power to impress the mind or feelings ⟨an *impressive* speech⟩ — **im·pres·sive·ly** *adv* — **im·pres·sive·ness** *n*

im·pri·ma·tur \ˌim-prə-ˈmä-tů(ə)r\ *n* : official approval (as to print or publish)

¹im·print \im-ˈprint, ˈim-ˌ\ *vb* **1** : to mark by or as if by pressure : STAMP **2** : to fix firmly (as on the memory) **3** : to go through the process of imprinting

²im·print \ˈim-ˌprint\ *n* **1** : something imprinted or printed : IMPRESSION ⟨the *imprint* of a hippo's foot⟩ **2** : a publisher's name on the title page of a book

im·print·ing \ˈim-ˌprint-iŋ, im-ˈprint-\ *n* : a rapid learning process that takes place early in the life of a social animal (as a goose) and that results in the formation of a special way of behaving (as knowing and being attracted to one's own kind)

im·pris·on \im-ˈpriz-ᵊn\ *vb* **-pris·oned; -pris·on·ing** \-ˈpriz-(ə-)niŋ\ : to put in or as if in prison — **im·pris·on·ment** \-ˈpriz-ən-mənt\ *n*

im·prob·a·ble \(ˈ)im-ˈpräb-(ə-)bəl\ *adj* : not probable : unlikely to be true or to occur — **im·prob·a·bil·i·ty** \(ˌ)im-ˌpräb-ə-ˈbil-ət-ē\ *n* — **im·prob·a·bly** \(ˈ)im-ˈpräb-(ə-)blē\ *adv*

im·promp·tu \im-ˈpräm(p)-t(y)ü\ *adj* : not prepared ahead of time : EXTEMPORANEOUS ⟨an *impromptu* speech⟩ — **im·promp·tu** *adv or n*

im·prop·er \(ˈ)im-ˈpräp-ər\ *adj* : not proper, right, or suitable — **im·prop·er·ly** *adv*

improper fraction *n* : a fraction whose numerator is equal to or larger than the denominator

im·pro·pri·ety \ˌim-prə-ˈprī-ət-ē\ *n, pl* **-ties** **1** : the quality or state of being improper **2** : an improper act or remark

im·prove \im-ˈprüv\ *vb* **im·proved; im·prov·ing** **1** : to make or become better ⟨genetics helps us *improve* plants⟩ ⟨when economic conditions *improve*⟩ **2** : to increase the value of (land or property) by making improvements **3** : to make good use of ⟨*improved* their time by studying programming⟩ **4** : to make useful additions or changes — **im·prov·able** \-ˈprü-və-bəl\ *adj* — **im·prov·er** *n*

im·prove·ment \im-ˈprüv-mənt\ *n* **1** : the act or process of improving **2 a** : increased value or excellence **b** : something that adds to the value or appearance (as of a house)

im·prov·i·dence \(ˈ)im-ˈpräv-əd-ən(t)s, -ə-ˌden(t)s\ *n* : the quality or state of being improvident

im·prov·i·dent \(ˈ)im-ˈpräv-əd-ənt, -ə-ˌdent\ *adj* : not providing or saving up for the future — **im·prov·i·dent·ly** *adv*

im·pro·vi·sa·tion \(ˌ)im-ˌpräv-ə-ˈzā-shən, ˌim-prə-və-\ *n* **1** : the act or art of improvising **2** : something that is improvised — **im·pro·vi·sa·tion·al** \-shnəl, -shən-ᵊl\ *adj*

im·pro·vise \ˈim-prə-ˌvīz, ˌim-prə-ˌvīz\ *vb* **-vised; -vis·ing** **1** : to compose, recite, play, or sing without preparation **2** : to make, invent, or arrange with whatever is at hand — **im·pro·vis·er** *or* **im·pro·vis·or** \-ˈvī-zər, -ˌvī-\ *n*

im·pru·dence \(ˈ)im-ˈprüd-ᵊn(t)s\ *n* : the quality or state of being imprudent

im·pru·dent \(ˈ)im-ˈprüd-ᵊnt\ *adj* : not prudent : RASH, UNWISE — **im·pru·dent·ly** *adv*

im·pu·dence \ˈim-pyəd-ən(t)s\ *n* : impudent behavior or speech : INSOLENCE, DISRESPECT

im·pu·dent \ˈim-pyəd-ənt\ *adj* : showing scorn for or disregard of others : INSOLENT, DISRESPECTFUL — **im·pu·dent·ly** *adv*

im·pugn \im-ˈpyün\ *vb* : to attack as false or not to be trusted ⟨*impugn* the honesty of an opponent⟩

im·pulse \ˈim-ˌpəls\ *n* **1 a** : a force that starts a body into motion **b** : the motion produced by an impulse **2** : a sudden stirring up of the mind and spirit to do something ⟨an *impulse* to run away⟩ ⟨buy something on *impulse*⟩ **3** : an information-carrying signal that is carried by living material and especially by nerves and muscle and that results in a change in the activity of a bodily part **4** : ²PULSE 3a

impulse buying *n* : the buying on impulse of something not really needed

im·pul·sive \im-ˈpəl-siv\ *adj* **1** : acting or tending to act on impulse **2** : resulting from a sudden impulse — **im·pul·sive·ly** *adv* — **im·pul·sive·ness** *n*

im·pu·ni·ty \im-ˈpyü-nət-ē\ *n* : freedom from punishment, harm, or loss

im·pure \(ˈ)im-ˈpyů(ə)r\ *adj* **1** : not pure : UNCLEAN, DIRTY **2** : mixed with something else that is usually not as good ⟨an *impure* chemical⟩ — **im·pure·ly** *adv*

im·pu·ri·ty \(ˈ)im-ˈpyůr-ət-ē\ *n, pl* **-ties** **1** : the quality or state of being impure **2** : something that is impure or that makes impure ⟨remove *impurities* from water⟩

im·pu·ta·tion \ˌim-pyə-ˈtā-shən\ *n* : the act or an instance of imputing

im·pute \im-ˈpyüt\ *vb* **im·put·ed; im·put·ing** : to give the blame or credit for to some person or cause — **im·put·able** \-ˈpyüt-ə-bəl\ *adj*

¹in \(ˈ)in, ən, ᵊn\ *prep* **1 a** — used to show enclosing, including, or placing within limits ⟨*in* the lake⟩ ⟨wounded *in* the leg⟩ ⟨*in* the summer⟩ ⟨*in* a minute⟩ **b** : INTO 1a ⟨went *in* the house⟩ ⟨don't come *in* here with those muddy feet⟩ **2** — used to show means or medium ⟨written *in* pencil⟩ ⟨works *in* plastics⟩ ⟨photographs *in* color⟩ **3 a** — used to show a state or condition ⟨we're *in* trouble⟩ ⟨is made *in*

\ə\ abut	\au̇\ out	\i\ tip	\ȯ\ saw	\u̇\ foot	
\ər\ further	\ch\ chin	\ī\ life	\ȯi\ coin	\y\ yet	
\a\ mat	\e\ pet	\j\ job	\th\ thin	\yü\ few	
\ā\ take	\ē\ easy	\ŋ\ sing	\th\ this	\yu̇\ cure	
\ä\ cot, cart	\g\ go	\ō\ bone	\ü\ food	\zh\ vision	

three sizes⟩ ⟨*in* power⟩ ⟨*in* love⟩   **b** : INTO 2a ⟨broke *in* pieces⟩   **4** — used to show manner or purpose ⟨said *in* reply⟩   **5** — used to show the larger member of a ratio ⟨one *in* five⟩

²**in** \'in\ *adv*   **1 a** : to or toward the inside ⟨went *in* and closed the door⟩   **b** : to or toward a place ⟨flew *in* yesterday⟩   **c** : so as to be or seem near ⟨play close *in*⟩   **d** : into the midst of something ⟨mix *in* the flour⟩   **e** : to or at its proper place ⟨fit a piece *in*⟩   **f** : so as to be in agreement ⟨fell *in* with our plans⟩   **2 a** : on the inner side : WITHIN ⟨everyone is *in*⟩   **b** : on good terms ⟨*in* with the right people⟩   **c** : in fashion ⟨boots are *in* this year⟩   **d** : at hand : on hand ⟨the evidence was *in*⟩ ⟨harvests are *in*⟩ — **in for** : sure to experience ⟨*in for* a surprise⟩

³**in** \'in\ *adj*   **1 a** : being inside or within ⟨the *in* part⟩   **b** : being in power ⟨the *in* party⟩   **2** : directed or bound inward : INCOMING ⟨the *in* train⟩   **3** : very fashionable ⟨the *in* thing to do⟩ ⟨the *in* place to go⟩

¹**in-** *or* **il-** *or* **im-** *or* **ir-** *prefix* : not : NON-, UN- — usually *il-* before *l* ⟨*il*logical⟩ and *im-* before *b, m,* or *p* ⟨*im*balance⟩ ⟨*im*moral⟩ ⟨*im*practical⟩ and *ir-* before *r* ⟨*ir*reducible⟩ and *in-* before other sounds ⟨*in*conclusive⟩ [derived from Latin *in-* "not"]

²**in-** *or* **il-** *or* **im-** *or* **ir-** *prefix*   **1** : in : within : into : toward : on — usually *il-* before *l, im-* before *b, m,* or *p, ir-* before *r,* and *in-* before other sounds   **2** : EN- 2 ⟨*im*peril⟩ [derived from Latin *in* "in, into"]

-in \ən\ *n suffix* : chemical compound ⟨stear*in*⟩ ⟨insul*in*⟩ ⟨niac*in*⟩ [derived from Latin *-ina, -inus* (adjective suffixes)]

in·abil·i·ty \,in-ə-'bil-ət-ē\ *n* : the condition of being unable : lack of ability, power, or means

in·ac·ces·si·ble \,in-ik-'ses-ə-bəl, (,)in-,ak-\ *adj* : hard or impossible to get to or get at — **in·ac·ces·si·bil·i·ty** \-,ses-ə-'bil-ət-ē\ *n*

in·ac·cu·ra·cy \(')in-'ak-yə-rə-sē\ *n, pl* **-cies**   **1** : the quality or state of being inaccurate   **2** : ERROR 1b, MISTAKE

in·ac·cu·rate \(')in-'ak-yə-rət\ *adj* : not accurate : not right or correct : not exact — **in·ac·cu·rate·ly** *adv*

in·ac·tion \(')in-'ak-shən\ *n* : lack of action or activity : IDLENESS

in·ac·ti·vate \(')in-'ak-tə-,vāt\ *vb* : to make inactive — **in·ac·ti·va·tion** \(,)in-,ak-tə-'vā-shən\ *n*

in·ac·tive \(')in-'ak-tiv\ *adj* : not active: as   **a** : slow to move or act : SLUGGISH   **b** : being out of use or activity ⟨an *inactive* mine⟩ ⟨an *inactive* volcano⟩   **c** : INERT ⟨argon is chemically *inactive*⟩ — **in·ac·tive·ly** *adv*

in·ac·tiv·i·ty \(,)in-,ak-'tiv-ət-ē\ *n* : the state of being inactive

in·ad·e·qua·cy \(')in-'ad-i-kwə-sē\ *n, pl* **-cies**   **1** : the quality or state of being inadequate   **2 a** : an inadequate amount   **b** : a failure to come up to expectations ⟨feelings of *inadequacy*⟩ ⟨aware of my own *inadequacies*⟩

in·ad·e·quate \(')in-'ad-i-kwət\ *adj* : not adequate : not enough or not good enough — **in·ad·e·quate·ly** *adv*

in·ad·mis·si·ble \,in-əd-'mis-ə-bəl\ *adj* : not admissible — **in·ad·mis·si·bil·i·ty** \-,mis-ə-'bil-ət-ē\ *n*

in·ad·ver·tence \,in-əd-'vərt-ᵊn(t)s\ *n*   **1** : INATTENTION   **2** : a result of not paying attention : OVERSIGHT

in·ad·ver·ten·cy \,in-əd-'vərt-ᵊn-sē\ *n, pl* **-cies** : INADVERTENCE

in·ad·ver·tent \,in-əd-'vərt-ᵊnt\ *adj*   **1** : not paying attention : INATTENTIVE   **2** : not meant, sought, or intended : UNINTENTIONAL ⟨an *inadvertent* violation of the law⟩ — **in·ad·ver·tent·ly** *adv*

in·ad·vis·able \,in-əd-'vī-zə-bəl\ *adj* : not wise to do : not advisable : UNWISE — **in·ad·vis·abil·i·ty** \-,vī-zə-'bil-ət-ē\ *n*

in·alien·able \(')in-'āl-yə-nə-bəl, -'ā-lē-ə-nə-\ *adj* : impossible to take away or give up ⟨*inalienable* rights⟩ — **in·alien·ably** \-blē\ *adv*

inane \in-'ān\ *adj* : lacking meaning or point : SILLY ⟨*inane* remarks about the weather⟩ — **inane·ly** *adv* — **inane-**

ness \-'ān-nəs\ *n*

in·an·i·mate \(')in-'an-ə-mət\ *adj*   **1** : not having life ⟨stones are *inanimate*⟩ ⟨an *inanimate* object⟩   **2** : not animated or lively : DULL — **in·an·i·mate·ly** *adv*

inan·i·ty \in-'an-ət-ē\ *n, pl* **-ties**   **1** : the quality or state of being inane   **2** : something inane

in·ap·pli·ca·ble \(')in-'ap-li-kə-bəl *also* ,in-ə-'plik-ə-\ *adj* : not applicable : IRRELEVANT — **in·ap·pli·ca·bil·i·ty** \(,)in-,ap-li-kə-'bil-ət-ē *also* ,in-ə-,plik-ə-\ *n*

in·ap·pre·cia·ble \,in-ə-'prē-shə-bəl\ *adj* : very small or slight

in·ap·pro·pri·ate \,in-ə-'prō-prē-ət\ *adj* : not appropriate : UNSUITABLE ⟨certain language is *inappropriate* in the classroom⟩ — **in·ap·pro·pri·ate·ly** *adv* — **in·ap·pro·pri·ate·ness** *n*

in·apt \(')in-'apt\ *adj* : not apt — **in·apt·ly** \-'ap-(t)lē\ *adv* — **in·apt·ness** \-'ap(t)-nəs\ *n*

in·ap·ti·tude \(')in-'ap-tə-,t(y)üd\ *n* : lack of aptitude

in·ar·tic·u·late \,in-(,)är-'tik-yə-lət\ *adj*   **1 a** : not understandable as spoken words ⟨*inarticulate* cries⟩ ⟨*inarticulate* murmurs⟩   **b** : not able to speak : MUTE   **c** : not able to be expressed ⟨*inarticulate* longings⟩   **2** : not able to give clear expression to ideas or feelings   **3** : not jointed or segmented — **in·ar·tic·u·late·ly** *adv* — **in·ar·tic·u·late·ness** *n*

in·ar·tis·tic \,in-är-'tis-tik\ *adj* : not artistic — **in·ar·tis·ti·cal·ly** \-ti-k(ə-)lē\ *adv*

in·as·much as \,in-əz-,məch-əz\ *conj* : considering that : ³SINCE 3

in·at·ten·tion \,in-ə-'ten-chən\ *n* : failure to pay attention — **in·at·ten·tive** \-'tent-iv\ *adj* — **in·at·ten·tive·ly** *adv* — **in·at·ten·tive·ness** *n*

in·au·di·ble \(')in-'od-ə-bəl\ *adj* : impossible to hear : not audible — **in·au·di·bil·i·ty** \(,)in-,od-ə-'bil-ət-ē\ *n* — **in·au·di·bly** \(')in-'od-ə-blē\ *adv*

¹**in·au·gu·ral** \in-'o-gyə-rəl, -g(ə-)rəl\ *adj*   **1** : of or relating to an inauguration ⟨the *inaugural* address⟩ ⟨an *inaugural* ball⟩   **2** : marking a beginning ⟨the *inaugural* run of a new high-speed train⟩

²**inaugural** *n*   **1** : an inaugural address   **2** : INAUGURATION

in·au·gu·rate \in-'o-g(y)ə-,rāt\ *vb* **-rat·ed; -rat·ing**   **1** : to introduce into office with suitable ceremonies : INSTALL ⟨*inaugurate* a president⟩   **2** : to celebrate the opening of ⟨*inaugurate* a new gym⟩   **3** : to bring into being or action ⟨*inaugurate* a new plan⟩ — **in·au·gu·ra·tor** \-,rāt-ər\ *n*

in·au·gu·ra·tion \in-,o-g(y)ə-'rā-shən\ *n* : an act or ceremony of inaugurating

in·aus·pi·cious \,in-o-'spish-əs\ *adj* : not auspicious : not looking good for future success — **in·aus·pi·cious·ly** *adv* — **in·aus·pi·cious·ness** *n*

in·board \'in-,bō(ə)rd, -,bo(ə)rd\ *adv or adj*   **1** : inside the hull of a ship or boat   **2** : close or closest to the center line of an aircraft or ship

in·born \'in-'bo(ə)rn\ *adj*   **1** : born in one : not acquired by training or experience : NATURAL, INSTINCTIVE   **2** : HEREDITARY 1, INHERITED ⟨an *inborn* tendency toward mental illness⟩

in·bound \'in-,baund\ *adj* : inward bound ⟨*inbound* traffic⟩

in·bred \'in-'bred\ *adj*   **1** : deeply rooted in a person ⟨an *inbred* love of freedom⟩   **2** : subjected to or produced by inbreeding

in·breed \'in-'brēd\ *vb* **in·bred** \-'bred\; **in·breed·ing** : to subject to or engage in inbreeding

in·breed·ing \'in-,brēd-iŋ\ *n* : the interbreeding of closely related individuals especially to improve or keep up the quality of a stock

In·ca \'iŋ-kə\ *n*   **1** : a noble or a member of the Indian peoples of Peru maintaining an empire until the Spanish conquest   **2** : a member of any people under Inca influence — **In·can** \-kən\ *adj*

in·cal·cu·la·ble \(')in-'kal-kyə-lə-bəl\ *adj* : not able to be calculated: as   **a** : very great   **b** : not able to be predicted —

in·cal·cu·la·bil·i·ty \(,)in-,kal-kyə-lə-'bil-ət-ē\ *n* — **in·cal·cu·la·bly** \(')in-'kal-kyə-lə-blē\ *adv*

in·can·des·cence \,in-kən-'des-ᵊn(t)s\ *n* : the glowing of a substance due to its high temperature

in·can·des·cent \,in-kən-'des-ᵊnt\ *adj* : white or glowing with great heat — **in·can·des·cent·ly** *adv*

incandescent lamp *n* : a lamp whose light is produced by the glow of a wire heated by an electric current

in·can·ta·tion \,in-,kan-'tā-shən\ *n* : a series of words used to produce a magic spell

in·ca·pa·ble \(')in-'kā-pə-bəl\ *adj* : not able to do something — **in·ca·pa·bil·i·ty** \(,)in-,kā-pə-'bil-ət-ē\ *n*

in·ca·pac·i·tate \,in-kə-'pas-ə-,tāt\ *vb* **-tat·ed; -tat·ing** : to make incapable : DISABLE — **in·ca·pac·i·ta·tion** \-,pas-ə-'tā-shən\ *n*

in·ca·pac·i·ty \,in-kə-'pas-ət-ē, -'pas-tē\ *n, pl* **-ties** : lack of ability or power

in·car·cer·ate \in-'kär-sə-,rāt\ *vb* **-at·ed; -at·ing** : to put in prison : CONFINE — **in·car·cer·a·tion** \(,)in-,kär-sə-'rā-shən\ *n*

¹**in·car·nate** \in-'kär-nət, -,nāt\ *adj* : given bodily or actual form ⟨the devil *incarnate*⟩ ⟨a little tornado *incarnate*⟩

²**in·car·nate** \in-'kär-,nāt, 'in-,kär-,nāt\ *vb* **-nat·ed; -nat·ing** : to make incarnate

in·car·na·tion \,in-,kär-'nā-shən\ *n* **1** : the appearance of a god or spirit in an earthly form **2** *cap* : the union of divine and human natures in Jesus Christ **3** : an actual instance of a quality or concept ⟨she was the *incarnation* of goodness⟩

in·cau·tious \(')in-'kȯ-shəs\ *adj* : not cautious : RASH — **in·cau·tious·ly** *adv* — **in·cau·tious·ness** *n*

¹**in·cen·di·ary** \in-'sen-dē-,er-ē\ *n, pl* **-ar·ies** **1** : a person who deliberately sets fire to property (as a building) **2** : a person who excites quarrels : AGITATOR

²**incendiary** *adj* **1** : of, relating to, or involving the deliberate burning of property **2** : tending to excite quarrels : INFLAMMATORY **3** : containing chemicals that burst into flame on contact ⟨an *incendiary* bomb⟩

¹**in·cense** \'in-,sen(t)s\ *n* **1 a** : material used to produce a fragrant odor when burned **b** : the odor so produced **2** : a pleasing scent

²**in·cense** \in-'sen(t)s\ *vb* **in·censed; in·cens·ing** : to make very angry

in·cen·ter \'in-,sent-ər\ *n* : the one and only point in a triangle that is passed through by each of the three lines that divide one of the three angles of the triangle into two equal parts

in·cen·tive \in-'sent-iv\ *n* : something that makes a person try or work hard or harder

in·cep·tion \in-'sep-shən\ *n* : an act or instance of beginning

in·cer·ti·tude \(')in-'sərt-ə-,t(y)üd\ *n* : UNCERTAINTY

in·ces·sant \(')in-'ses-ᵊnt\ *adj* : going on and on : not stopping or letting up — **in·ces·sant·ly** *adv*

in·cest \'in-,sest\ *n* : sexual intercourse between persons so closely related that they are forbidden by law to marry

in·ces·tu·ous \in-'ses-chə-wəs\ *adj* **1** : being or involving incest **2** : guilty of incest — **in·ces·tu·ous·ly** *adv*

¹**inch** \'inch\ *n* **1** : a unit of length equal to ¹/₃₆ yard (2.54 centimeters) — SEE MEASURE table **2** : a small amount, distance, or degree ⟨won't budge an *inch*⟩ [Old English *ynce* "inch", from Latin *uncia* "a 12th part, ounce", from *unus* "one" — related to OUNCE, UNITE; see *Word History* at OUNCE]

²**inch** *vb* : to move a little bit at a time

Inch·worm \'inch-,wərm\ *n* : LOOPER 1

in·ci·dence \'in(t)-səd-ən(t)s, -sə-,den(t)s\ *n* **1** : rate of occurrence ⟨the *incidence* of skin cancer⟩ **2** : ANGLE OF INCIDENCE

¹**in·ci·dent** \'in(t)-səd-ənt, -sə-,dent\ *n* : an often unimportant happening that may form part of a larger event

²**incident** *adj* **1** : ¹INCIDENTAL **2** : falling or striking on something ⟨*incident* light rays⟩

¹**in·ci·den·tal** \,in(t)-sə-'dent-ᵊl\ *adj* **1** : happening by chance **2** : of minor importance

²**incidental** *n* : something that is incidental

in·ci·den·tal·ly \,in(t)-sə-'dent-ᵊl-ē, *especially for sense 2* -'dent-lē\ *adv* **1** : in an incidental manner ⟨discusses the problem only *incidentally*⟩ **2** : BY THE WAY ⟨a one-room school — still standing, *incidentally* — which was painted red⟩

in·cin·er·ate \in-'sin-ə-,rāt\ *vb* **-at·ed; -at·ing** : to burn to ashes — **in·cin·er·a·tion** \-,sin-ə-'rā-shən\ *n*

in·cin·er·a·tor \in-'sin-ə-,rāt-ər\ *n* : a furnace or a container for burning waste materials

in·cip·i·en·cy \in-'sip-ē-ən-sē\ *n* : the fact or state of being incipient

in·cip·i·ent \in-'sip-ē-ənt\ *adj* : beginning to come into being or to become apparent — **in·cip·i·ent·ly** *adv*

in·cise \in-'sīz\ *vb* **in·cised; in·cis·ing** : to cut into : CARVE, ENGRAVE

in·ci·sion \in-'sizh-ən\ *n* **1** : a cut or gash made in something; *esp* : a surgical cut made into the body ⟨removed the diseased appendix through a small *incision*⟩ **2** : an act of cutting into something ⟨watched the surgeon's skillful *incision*⟩

in·ci·sive \in-'sī-siv\ *adj* : impressively clear and direct ⟨an *incisive* argument⟩ — **in·ci·sive·ly** *adv* — **in·ci·sive·ness** *n*

in·ci·sor \in-'sī-zər\ *n* : a tooth for cutting; *esp* : one of the cutting teeth in front of the canines of a mammal

in·cite \in-'sīt\ *vb* **in·cit·ed; in·cit·ing** : to move to action : stir up — **in·cit·er** *n*

in·cite·ment \in-'sīt-mənt\ *n* **1** : the act of inciting : the state of being incited **2** : something that incites

in·ci·vil·i·ty \,in(t)-sə-'vil-ət-ē\ *n, pl* **-ties** **1** : the quality or state of being impolite **2** : a rude or discourteous act

in·clem·ent \(')in-'klem-ənt\ *adj* : STORMY 1 ⟨*inclement* weather⟩ — **in·clem·ent·ly** *adv*

in·cli·na·tion \,in-klə-'nā-shən, iŋ-\ *n* **1** : a feeling of liking or of wanting to do something ⟨an *inclination* for sleeping late⟩ **2** : an act or the action of bending or tilting **3 a** : a departure from the true vertical or horizontal : SLANT ⟨the *inclination* of the earth's axis⟩ **b** : the amount of such departure **c** : an inclined surface : SLOPE **4** : a quality which leads to some state or action ⟨the door has an *inclination* to stick⟩ — **in·cli·na·tion·al** \-shnəl, -shən-ᵊl\ *adj*

¹**in·cline** \in-'klīn\ *vb* **in·clined; in·clin·ing** **1** : to bend the head or body forward : BOW **2** : to be drawn to an opinion or course of action ⟨*inclined* to go swimming⟩ **3** : to turn or move from a line, direction, or course : LEAN, SLOPE **4** : to cause to bend or bow **5** : to have influence on : PERSUADE ⟨a teacher's example *inclined* me to become a teacher too⟩ — **in·clin·able** \in-'klī-nə-bəl\ *adj*

²**in·cline** \'in-,klīn\ *n* : ³SLOPE 2

in·clined *adj* : having an inclination

inclined plane *n* : a flat surface that makes an angle with the plane of the horizon

in·cli·nom·e·ter \,in-klə-'näm-ət-ər, ,iŋ-\ *n* : an instrument for indicating the angle to the horizontal of an axis of an aircraft or ship

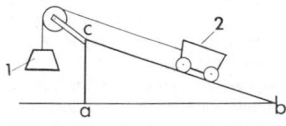

inclined plane: *ab* base, *ac* height, *cb* inclined plane, *1* force, *2* resistance

inclose, inclosure *variant of* ENCLOSE, ENCLOSURE

\ə\ abut		\au̇\ out	\i\ tip	\ȯ\ saw	\u̇\ foot
\ər\ further		\ch\ chin	\ī\ life	\ȯi\ coin	\y\ yet
\a\ mat		\e\ pet	\j\ job	\th\ thin	\yü\ few
\ā\ take		\ē\ easy	\ŋ\ sing	\th\ this	\yu̇\ cure
\ä\ cot, cart		\g\ go	\ō\ bone	\ü\ food	\zh\ vision

in·clude \in-'klüd\ *vb* **in·clud·ed; in·clud·ing** : to take in or have as part of a whole ⟨the recipe *included* many ingredients⟩ — **in·clud·able** *or* **in·clud·ible** \-'klüd-ə-bəl\ *adj*

in·clu·sion \in-'klü-zhən\ *n* **1** : the act of including : the state of being included **2** : something that is included

in·clu·sive \in-'klü-siv, -ziv\ *adj* **1** : including the stated limits and everything in between ⟨pages 10 to 20 *inclusive*⟩ **2** : covering everything or all important points ⟨an *inclusive* tour⟩ ⟨an *inclusive* insurance policy⟩ — **in·clu·sive·ly** *adv* — **in·clu·sive·ness** *n*

in·cog·ni·to \,in-,käg-'nēt-ō, in-'käg-nə-,tō\ *adv or adj* : with one's identity concealed (as by a false name or title) ⟨was traveling *incognito*⟩ [from Italian *incognito* "so as not to be known or recognized", from Latin *incognitus* "unknown", from *in-* "not" and *cognitus*, past participle of *cognoscere* "to know" — related to CONNOISSEUR, RECOGNIZE]

in·co·her·ence \,in-kō-'hir-ən(t)s, -'her-\ *n* **1** : the quality or state of being incoherent **2** : something that is incoherent

in·co·her·ent \,in-kō-'hir-ənt, -'her-\ *adj* **1** : not sticking closely or compactly together : LOOSE **2** : not clearly or logically connected ⟨told an *incoherent* story⟩ — **in·co·her·ent·ly** *adv*

in·com·bus·ti·ble \,in-kəm-'bəs-tə-bəl\ *adj* : incapable of being burned

in·come \'in-,kəm\ *n* : a gain usually measured in money that comes in from labor, business, or property

income tax \'in-(,)kəm-\ *n* : a tax on the income of a person or business

in·com·ing \'in-,kəm-iŋ\ *adj* : coming in: as **a** : taking a place formerly held by another ⟨the *incoming* president⟩ **b** : arriving at a destination ⟨*incoming* mail⟩ **c** : just starting or beginning ⟨the *incoming* class⟩

in·com·men·su·rate \,in-kə-'men(t)s-(ə-)rət, -'mench-(ə-)rət\ *adj* : not commensurate; *esp* : not adequate : not enough to satisfy ⟨funds *incommensurate* with need⟩

in·com·mode \,in-kə-'mōd\ *vb* **-mod·ed; -mod·ing** : ²INCONVENIENCE

in·com·mu·ni·ca·ble \,in-kə-'myü-ni-kə-bəl\ *adj* : not capable of being communicated

in·com·mu·ni·ca·do \,in-kə-,myü-nə-'käd-ō\ *adv or adj* : without being able to communicate with others ⟨a prisoner held *incommunicado*⟩

in·com·pa·ra·ble \(')in-'käm-p(ə-)rə-bəl\ *adj* **1** : better than any other : MATCHLESS **2** : not suited for comparison — **in·com·pa·ra·bil·i·ty** \(,)in-,käm-p(ə-)rə-'bil-ət-ē\ *n* — **in·com·pa·ra·bly** \(')in-'käm-p(ə-)rə-blē\ *adv*

in·com·pat·i·bil·i·ty \,in-kəm-,pat-ə-'bil-ət-ē\ *n, pl* **-ties** : the quality or state of being incompatible

in·com·pat·i·ble \,in-kəm-'pat-ə-bəl\ *adj* **1** : not able to be brought together in harmony ⟨their personalities were *incompatible*⟩ ⟨*incompatible* colors⟩ **2** : unsuitable for use in blood transfusion because of an unfavorable reaction occurring when mixed with the blood of the one who receives it ⟨*incompatible* blood types⟩ — **in·com·pat·i·bly** \-blē\ *adv*

in·com·pe·tence \(')in-'käm-pət-ən(t)s\ *n* : the quality, state, or fact of being incompetent

in·com·pe·ten·cy \(')in-'käm-pət-ən-sē\ *n, pl* **-cies** : INCOMPETENCE

¹in·com·pe·tent \(')in-'käm-pət-ənt\ *adj* **1** : not legally qualified **2** : lacking qualities (as knowledge, skill, or ability) needed to do something well ⟨an *incompetent* writer⟩ — **in·com·pe·tent·ly** *adv*

²incompetent *n* : an incompetent person

in·com·plete \,in-kəm-'plēt\ *adj* : not complete : lacking some part ⟨handed in an *incomplete* assignment⟩ — **in·com·plete·ly** *adv* — **in·com·plete·ness** *n*

incomplete metamorphosis *n* : insect metamorphosis (as of a grasshopper) in which there is no pupal stage between the immature stage and the adult and in which the young insect usually resembles the adult — compare COMPLETE METAMORPHOSIS

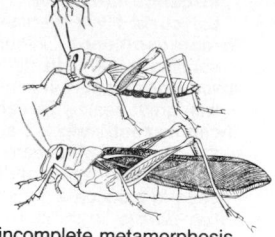

incomplete metamorphosis

in·com·pre·hen·si·ble \(,)in-,käm-pri-'hen(t)-sə-bəl\ *adj* : impossible to understand ⟨found their behavior *incomprehensible*⟩ — **in·com·pre·hen·si·bil·i·ty** \-,hen(t)-sə-'bil-ət-ē\ *n* — **in·com·pre·hen·si·bly** \-'hen(t)-sə-blē\ *adv*

in·com·pre·hen·sion \(,)in-,käm-pri-'hen-chən\ *n* : lack of understanding

in·com·press·ible \,in-kəm-'pres-ə-bəl\ *adj* : impossible or difficult to compress — **in·com·press·ibil·i·ty** \-,pres-ə-'bil-ət-ē\ *n*

in·con·ceiv·able \,in-kən-'sē-və-bəl\ *adj* : impossible to imagine or believe — **in·con·ceiv·ably** \-blē\ *adv*

in·con·clu·sive \,in-kən-'klü-siv, -ziv\ *adj* : not leading to a definite conclusion or result ⟨*inconclusive* evidence⟩ — **in·con·clu·sive·ly** *adv* — **in·con·clu·sive·ness** *n*

in·con·gru·ous \(')in-'käŋ-grə-wəs\ *adj* : not harmonious, suitable, or proper ⟨*incongruous* colors⟩ — **in·con·gru·ity** \,in-kən-'grü-ət-ē, -,kän-\ *n* — **in·con·gru·ous·ly** \(')in-'kaŋ-grə-wəs-lē\ *adv* — **in·con·gru·ous·ness** *n*

in·con·se·quen·tial \(,)in-,kän(t)-sə-'kwen-chəl\ *adj* : not important

in·con·sid·er·able \,in-kən-'sid-ər-(ə-)bəl, -'sid-rə-bəl\ *adj* : not worth considering : SLIGHT, TRIVIAL

in·con·sid·er·ate \,in-kən-'sid-(ə-)rət\ *adj* : careless of the rights or feelings of others ⟨an *inconsiderate* remark⟩ — **in·con·sid·er·ate·ly** *adv* — **in·con·sid·er·ation** \-,sid-ə-'rā-shən\ *n*

in·con·sis·ten·cy \,in-kən-'sis-tən-sē\ *n, pl* **-cies** **1** : the quality or state of being inconsistent **2** : an example of being inconsistent

in·con·sis·tent \,in-kən-'sis-tənt\ *adj* **1** : not being in agreement or harmony : INCOMPATIBLE ⟨an explanation *inconsistent* with the facts⟩ **2** : not logical or regular in thought or actions : CHANGEABLE ⟨a very *inconsistent* person⟩ — **in·con·sis·tent·ly** *adv*

in·con·sol·able \,in-kən-'sō-lə-bəl\ *adj* : incapable of being comforted : DISCONSOLATE — **in·con·sol·ably** \-blē\ *adv*

in·con·spic·u·ous \,in-kən-'spik-yə-wəs\ *adj* : not easily seen or noticed — **in·con·spic·u·ous·ly** *adv* — **in·con·spic·u·ous·ness** *n*

in·con·stan·cy \(')in-'kän(t)-stən-sē\ *n, pl* **-cies** : the quality or state of being inconstant

in·con·stant \(')in-'kän(t)-stənt\ *adj* : likely to change frequently without apparent reason : CHANGEABLE

in·con·test·able \,in-kən-'tes-tə-bəl\ *adj* : not open to doubt : UNQUESTIONABLE — **in·con·test·ably** \-'tes-tə-blē\ *adv*

in·con·ti·nence \(')in-'känt-ᵊn-ən(t)s\ *n* : the quality or state of being incontinent

in·con·ti·nent \(')in-'känt-ᵊn-ənt\ *adj* : having or showing a lack of self-restraint or control — **in·con·ti·nent·ly** *adv*

in·con·tro·vert·ible \(,)in-,kän-trə-'vərt-ə-bəl\ *adj* : INDISPUTABLE ⟨*incontrovertible* evidence⟩ — **in·con·tro·vert·ibly** \-blē\ *adv*

¹in·con·ve·nience \,in-kən-'vē-nyən(t)s\ *n* **1** : something that is inconvenient **2** : the quality or state of being inconvenient

²inconvenience *vb* **-nienced; -nienc·ing** : to cause discomfort to : put to trouble ⟨*inconvenienced* by the bad weather⟩

in·con·ve·nient \,in-kən-'vē-nyənt\ *adj* : not convenient

: causing difficulty, discomfort, or annoyance ⟨an *inconvenient* delay⟩ — **in·con·ve·nient·ly** *adv*

in·cor·po·rate \in-'kȯr-pə-ˌrāt\ *vb* **-rat·ed; -rat·ing** **1** : to unite or combine to form a single whole : BLEND **2** : to give form to : EMBODY **3** : to form, make into, or become a corporation ⟨*incorporate* a company⟩ — **in·cor·po·ra·tion** \-ˌkȯr-pə-'rā-shən\ *n* — **in·cor·po·ra·tor** \-'kȯr-pə-ˌrāt-ər\ *n*

in·cor·po·re·al \ˌin-(ˌ)kȯr-'pōr-ē-əl, -'pȯr-\ *adj* : having no material body or form : IMMATERIAL

in·cor·rect \ˌin-kə-'rekt\ *adj* : not correct: as **a** : INACCURATE, FAULTY ⟨an *incorrect* copy⟩ **b** : not true : WRONG ⟨an *incorrect* answer⟩ **c** : not proper ⟨*incorrect* behavior⟩ — **in·cor·rect·ly** \-'rek-(t)lē\ *adv* — **in·cor·rect·ness** \-'rek(t)-nəs\ *n*

¹in·cor·ri·gi·ble \(')in-'kȯr-ə-jə-bəl, -'kär-\ *adj* : not able to be corrected or reformed ⟨an *incorrigible* gambler⟩

²incorrigible *n* : an incorrigible person

in·cor·rupt·ible \ˌin-kə-'rəp-tə-bəl\ *adj* **1** : not subject to decay **2** : incapable of being corrupted : HONEST — **in·cor·rupt·ibil·i·ty** \-ˌrəp-tə-'bil-ət-ē\ *n* — **in·cor·rupt·ibly** \-'rəp-tə-blē\ *adv*

¹in·crease \in-'krēs, 'in-ˌkrēs\ *vb* **in·creased; in·creas·ing** **1** : to make or become greater ⟨increase speed⟩ ⟨skill *increases* with practice⟩ **2** : to become more numerous by the production of young

²in·crease \'in-ˌkrēs, in-'krēs\ *n* **1** : the act of increasing **2** : something added (as by growth)

in·creas·ing·ly \in-'krē-siŋ-lē, 'in-ˌkrē-\ *adv* : to an increasing degree : more and more ⟨the work became *increasingly* difficult⟩

in·cred·i·ble \(')in-'kred-ə-bəl\ *adj* : UNBELIEVABLE [Middle English *incredible* "too unusual to be believed", from Latin *incredibilis* (same meaning), from *in-* "not" and *credibilis* "believable", from *credere* "to believe, trust, entrust" — related to CREDENTIALS, CREDIT, CREED] — **in·cred·ibil·i·ty** \(ˌ)in-ˌkred-ə-'bil-ət-ē\ *n* — **in·cred·i·bly** \(')in-'kred-ə-blē\ *adv*

in·cre·du·li·ty \ˌin-kri-'d(y)ü-lət-ē\ *n* : the quality or state of being incredulous : DISBELIEF

in·cred·u·lous \(')in-'krej-ə-ləs\ *adj* : feeling or showing an inability to believe something : SKEPTICAL ⟨listened with an *incredulous* smile⟩ — **in·cred·u·lous·ly** *adv*

in·cre·ment \'iŋ-krə-mənt, 'in-\ *n* **1** : a growth especially in quantity or value : INCREASE **2 a** : something gained or added — **in·cre·men·tal** \ˌiŋ-krə-'ment-ᵊl, ˌin-\ *adj*

in·crim·i·nate \in-'krim-ə-ˌnāt\ *vb* **-nat·ed; -nat·ing** : to charge with or involve in a crime or fault : ACCUSE — **in·crim·i·na·tion** \(ˌ)in-ˌkrim-ə-'nā-shən\ *n* — **in·crim·i·na·to·ry** \in-'krim-(ə-)nə-ˌtōr-ē, -ˌtȯr-\ *adj*

incrust *variant of* ENCRUST

in·crus·ta·tion \ˌin-ˌkrəs-'tā-shən\ *n* **1** : the act of encrusting : the state of being encrusted **2** : a hard coating : CRUST

in·cu·bate \'iŋ-kyə-ˌbāt, 'in-\ *vb* **-bat·ed; -bat·ing** **1** : to sit on eggs to hatch them by warmth **2** : to maintain (as bacteria or a chemically active system) under conditions good for development or reaction **3** : to go through the process of incubation

in·cu·ba·tion \ˌiŋ-kyə-'bā-shən, ˌin-\ *n* **1** : the act or process of incubating **2** : INCUBATION PERIOD

incubation period *n* **1** : the period of brooding or incubating required to bring an egg to hatching **2** : the period between infection with a germ and the appearance of the disease it causes

in·cu·ba·tor \'iŋ-kyə-ˌbāt-ər, 'in-\ *n* : one that incubates; *esp* : a piece of equipment providing suitable conditions (as of warmth and moisture) for incubating something ⟨an *incubator* for premature babies⟩

in·cu·bus \'iŋ-kyə-bəs, 'in-\ *n, pl* **-bi** \-ˌbī, -ˌbē\ *also* **-bus·es** **1** : an evil spirit once believed to lie upon persons in their sleep **2** : NIGHTMARE 1

incubator

in·cul·cate \in-'kəl-ˌkāt, 'in-(ˌ)kəl-\ *vb* **-cat·ed; -cat·ing** : to teach by frequent repetition ⟨childhood training *inculcated* a deep sense of responsibility⟩ — **in·cul·ca·tion** \ˌin-(ˌ)kəl-'kā-shən\ *n*

in·cum·ben·cy \in-'kəm-bən-sē\ *n, pl* **-cies** : the time during which a person holds an office or position

¹in·cum·bent \in-'kəm-bənt\ *n* : the holder of an office or position

²incumbent *adj* **1** : lying or resting on something else **2** : given as a duty : OBLIGATORY **3** : being an incumbent

in·cur \in-'kər\ *vb* **in·curred; in·cur·ring** **1** : to meet with (as an inconvenience) ⟨*incur* expenses⟩ **2** : to bring upon oneself ⟨*incur* punishment⟩ [from Latin *incurrere* "to meet with", literally "to run into", from *in-* "in, into" and *currere* "to run" — related to CURRENT, OCCUR]

in·cur·able \(')in-'kyur-ə-bəl\ *adj* : not capable of being cured — **in·cur·ably** \-blē\ *adv*

in·cu·ri·ous \(')in-'kyur-ē-əs\ *adj* : showing no interest or concern : INDIFFERENT — **in·cu·ri·ous·ly** *adv*

in·cur·sion \in-'kər-zhən\ *n* : a sudden usually temporary invasion : RAID

in·cus \'iŋ-kəs\ *n, pl* **in·cu·des** \iŋ-'kyüd-(ˌ)ēz\ : ANVIL 2

in·debt·ed \in-'det-əd\ *adj* : being in debt : owing something (as money or gratitude)

in·debt·ed·ness *n* **1** : the condition of being indebted **2** : something that is owed

in·de·cen·cy \(')in-'dēs-ən-sē\ *n, pl* **-cies** **1** : lack of decency **2** : an indecent act or word

in·de·cent \(')in-'dēs-ənt\ *adj* : not decent or proper : COARSE, VULGAR ⟨*indecent* language⟩ — **in·de·cent·ly** *adv*

in·de·ci·sion \ˌin-di-'sizh-ən\ *n* : slowness or trouble in making up one's mind

in·de·ci·sive \ˌin-di-'sī-siv\ *adj* **1** : not decisive or final ⟨an *indecisive* battle⟩ **2** : finding it hard to make decisions ⟨an *indecisive* person⟩ — **in·de·ci·sive·ly** *adv* — **in·de·ci·sive·ness** *n*

in·de·co·rous \(')in-'dek-ə-rəs; ˌin-di-'kōr-əs, -'kȯr-\ *adj* : not proper or in good taste : UNBECOMING — **in·de·co·rous·ly** *adv*

in·deed \in-'dēd\ *adv* : without any question : TRULY, CERTAINLY — often used interjectionally to express disbelief or surprise

in·de·fat·i·ga·ble \ˌin-di-'fat-i-gə-bəl\ *adj* : capable of working a long time without tiring : TIRELESS — **in·de·fat·i·ga·bly** \-blē\ *adv*

in·de·fea·si·ble \ˌin-di-'fē-zə-bəl\ *adj* : impossible to abolish ⟨*indefeasible* rights⟩ — **in·de·fea·si·bly** \-'fē-zə-blē\ *adv*

in·de·fen·si·ble \ˌin-di-'fen(t)-sə-bəl\ *adj* : impossible to defend ⟨an *indefensible* position⟩

in·de·fin·able \ˌin-di-'fī-nə-bəl\ *adj* : incapable of being exactly described or analyzed — **in·de·fin·ably** \-blē\ *adv*

in·def·i·nite \(')in-'def-(ə-)nət\ *adj* **1** : not clear or fixed in meaning or details : VAGUE ⟨an *indefinite* answer⟩ **2** : not certain or limited (as in amount or length) ⟨an *indefinite* period⟩ **3** : typically designating a person or thing that is

\ə\ abut	\au̇\ **out**	\i\ tip	\ȯ\ **saw**	\u̇\ **foot**
\ər\ **further**	\ch\ **chin**	\ī\ life	\ȯi\ **coin**	\y\ **yet**
\a\ mat	\e\ **pet**	\j\ **job**	\th\ **thin**	\yü\ **few**
\ā\ take	\ē\ **easy**	\ŋ\ **sing**	\th\ **this**	\yu̇\ **cure**
\ä\ cot, cart	\g\ **go**	\ō\ **bone**	\ü\ **food**	\zh\ **vision**

unidentified or cannot be immediately identified ⟨the *indefinite* articles "a" and "an"⟩ — **indefinite** *n* — **in·def·i·nite·ly** *adv* — **in·def·i·nite·ness** *n*

in·del·i·ble \in-'del-ə-bəl\ *adj* **1** : impossible to erase, remove, or blot out ⟨an *indelible* impression⟩ **2** : making or leaving marks not easily erased ⟨an *indelible* pencil⟩ ⟨*indelible* ink⟩ — **in·del·i·bly** \-blē\ *adv*

in·del·i·ca·cy \(')in-'del-i-kə-sē\ *n, pl* **-cies** **1** : the quality or state of being indelicate : COARSENESS **2** : something (as an act or word) that is indelicate

in·del·i·cate \(')in-'del-i-kət\ *adj* : having or showing bad manners or taste : IMMODEST, COARSE — **in·del·i·cate·ly** *adv* — **in·del·i·cate·ness** *n*

in·dem·ni·fy \in-'dem-nə-ˌfī\ *vb* **-fied; -fy·ing** **1** : to insure or protect against loss, damage, or injury **2** : to give something in order to make up for loss, damage, or injury ⟨*indemnify* victims of a disaster⟩ — **in·dem·ni·fi·ca·tion** \-ˌdem-nə-fə-'kā-shən\ *n*

in·dem·ni·ty \in-'dem-nət-ē\ *n, pl* **-ties** **1** : protection from loss, damage, or injury : INSURANCE **2** : freedom from penalty for past offenses **3** : something given to make up for loss, damage, or injury

¹in·dent \in-'dent\ *vb* **1** : to notch the edge of : make jagged ⟨*indented* leaves⟩ **2** : to set in from the margin ⟨*indent* the first line of a paragraph⟩ [Middle English *indenten* "indent", from early French *endenter* (same meaning), derived from earlier *en-* "to provide with" and *dent* "tooth", from Latin *dent-, dens* "tooth" — related to DENTAL]

²indent *vb* : to form a dent in — **in·dent·er** *n*

in·den·ta·tion \ˌin-ˌden-'tā-shən\ *n* **1 a** : an angular cut in an edge : NOTCH **b** : a deep recess (as in a coastline) **2 a** : the action of indenting : the state of being indented **b** : a blank or empty space produced by indenting **3** : ²DENT 1

in·den·tion \in-'den-chən\ *n* : INDENTATION 2b

¹in·den·ture \in-'den-chər\ *n* **1** : a written agreement : CONTRACT **2** : a contract by which one person is made to work for another for a stated period — usually used in pl.

²indenture *vb* **-tured; -tur·ing** : to bind by indentures ⟨*indenture* an apprentice⟩

in·de·pen·dence \ˌin-də-'pen-dən(t)s\ *n* : the quality or state of being independent : freedom from outside control or support

Independence Day *n* : July 4 observed as a legal holiday in honor of the adoption of the Declaration of Independence in 1776; *also* : a holiday celebrating the beginnings of national independence in another country

¹in·de·pen·dent \ˌin-də-'pen-dənt\ *adj* **1** : not being controlled or ruled by another : FREE ⟨an *independent* nation⟩ **2** : not having connections with another : SEPARATE ⟨the same story told by *independent* witnesses⟩ **3** : having or providing enough money to live on without anyone else's help; *also* : not having to work for a living ⟨a person of *independent* means⟩ **4** : not easily influenced ⟨an *independent* mind⟩ **5** : having full meaning in itself and capable of standing alone as a simple sentence : MAIN ⟨*independent* clause⟩ **6** : not belonging to a political party **7** : having probabilities such that whether or not one event takes place does not influence whether or not another event takes place ⟨the outcomes of the tossing of two dice are *independent*⟩ — **in·de·pen·dent·ly** *adv*

²independent *n* : one that is independent; *esp* : a voter who doesn't belong to a political party

independent variable *n* : a variable whose values are specified first or before an experiment is performed and are used to find values of an expression, another variable, or a function that depends on the first variable — compare DEPENDENT VARIABLE

in–depth \(ˌ)in-ˌdepth\ *adj* : covering many or all important points : THOROUGH ⟨an *in-depth* investigation⟩

in·de·scrib·able \ˌin-di-'skrī-bə-bəl\ *adj* : impossible to describe ⟨*indescribable* beauty⟩ — **in·de·scrib·ably** \-bə-blē\ *adv*

in·de·struc·ti·ble \ˌin-di-'strək-tə-bəl\ *adj* : impossible to destroy — **in·de·struc·ti·bil·i·ty** \-ˌstrək-tə-'bil-ət-ē\ *n* — **in·de·struc·ti·ble·ness** \-'strək-tə-bəl-nəs\ *n* — **in·de·struc·ti·bly** \-blē\ *adv*

in·de·ter·min·able \ˌin-di-'tərm-(ə-)nə-bəl\ *adj* : impossible to decide or find out — **in·de·ter·min·ably** \-blē\ *adv*

in·de·ter·mi·na·cy \ˌin-di-'tərm-(ə-)nə-sē\ *n* : the quality or state of being indeterminate

in·de·ter·mi·nate \ˌin-di-'tərm-(ə-)nət\ *adj* **1** : not clearly or exactly decided : VAGUE ⟨*indeterminate* plans⟩ **2** : not leading to a clear end or result — **in·de·ter·mi·nate·ly** *adv* — **in·de·ter·mi·nate·ness** *n*

¹in·dex \'in-ˌdeks\ *n, pl* **in·dex·es** \-ˌdek-səz\ *or* **in·di·ces** \-də-ˌsēz\ **1 a** : a device used to indicate something : POINTER ⟨the *index* on a scale⟩ **b** : INDICATION 2 ⟨the price of goods is an *index* of business conditions⟩ **2** : an alphabetical list in a printed work that gives with each item listed the page number where it may be found **3** *pl usually indices* : a mathematical figure, letter, or expression (as the exponent 3 in a^3) showing a power or root of another **4** : a symbol ☞ used to direct attention

²index *vb* **1 a** : to provide with an index ⟨*index* a book⟩ **b** : to list in an index **2** : to serve as an index of — **in·dex·er** *n*

index finger *n* : FOREFINGER

index fossil *n* : a fossil that is found over a relatively short span of geological time and can be used in dating formations in which it is found

index of refraction *n* : the ratio of the speed of light in the first of two media to the speed of light in the second as it passes from one into the other

in·dia ink \ˌin-dē-ə-\ *n, often cap 1st I* **1** : a black pigment (as lampblack) used in drawing and lettering **2** : a fluid made from india ink

In·di·an \'in-dē-ən\ *n* **1** : a person born or living in the country of India, the subcontinent of India, or the East Indies **2 a** : AMERICAN INDIAN **b** : an American Indian language — **Indian** *adj*

> **Word History** Once the name India was applied not only to the region we now call India, but also to China, the East Indies, and Japan. Trade with the distant East brought valuable gold, gems, spices, and silk back to Europe. However, the overland journey to the Orient by way of the caravan routes was long and difficult. Christopher Columbus, in the late 15th century, believed that he knew an easier way of reaching the wealth of the East. According to his calculations, the westward distance by sea was less than one-third of the eastward overland route. Columbus was able to test his theory in 1492. He was delighted to find land just about where he had said it would be. He decided that he must have reached the outer islands of "India", although in fact he had landed in the Bahamas. Because of Columbus's mistake, the newly discovered lands were called *India* or the *Indies*. They were still called this even after people realized that they were not the same as the *India* or *Indies* of Asia. Later the islands in the New World came to be called the West Indies in order to tell them apart from the East Indies. But *Indian,* the incorrect name given to the people living in the new "India", remained. [sense 2a so called because of Columbus's belief that the lands he discovered were part of India]

Indian corn *n* **1** : a tall widely cultivated American cereal-producing plant of the grass family bearing seeds on long ears which are used as food or for feeding livestock **2** : the ears of Indian corn; *also* : its edible seeds

Indian elephant *n* : an elephant of the forests of southeastern Asia that has relatively small ears

Indian paintbrush *n* **1** : any of a large genus of American and northeast Asian herbs that have dense spikes of flowers with brightly colored bracts **2** : ORANGE HAWKWEED

Indian pipe *n* : a waxy white leafless woodland herb with a single nodding bell-shaped flower on each stem that does not make its own food but lives on dead or decaying organic matter

Indian pudding *n* : a pudding made chiefly of cornmeal, milk, and molasses

Indian summer *n* : a period of mild weather in late autumn or early winter

In·dia paper \,in-dē-ə-\ *n* : a thin tough printing paper

india rubber *n, often cap I* **1** : ¹RUBBER 2a **2** : something made of rubber

In·dic \'in-dik\ *adj* : of, relating to, or being the Indian branch of the Indo-European languages

Indian pipe

in·di·cate \'in-də-,kāt\ *vb* **-cat·ed; -cat·ing** **1 a** : to point out or point to **b** : to be a sign of ⟨flowers *indicating* the arrival of spring⟩ **2** : to state or express briefly : SUGGEST

in·di·ca·tion \,in-də-'kā-shən\ *n* **1** : the action of indicating **2** : something that indicates : SIGN, SUGGESTION

¹in·dic·a·tive \in-'dik-ət-iv\ *adj* **1** : of, relating to, or being the grammatical mood that represents an act or state as a fact that can be known or proved ⟨in "I am here," the verb "am" is in the *indicative* mood⟩ **2** : indicating something ⟨remarks *indicative* of jealousy⟩ — **in·dic·a·tive·ly** *adv*

²indicative *n* : the indicative mood of a verb or a verb in this mood

in·di·ca·tor \'in-də-,kāt-ər\ *n* **1** : one that indicates: as **a** : a pointer on a dial or scale **b** : ¹GAUGE 2 **2** : a substance used to show visually (as by change of color) the presence of acid or base in a solution

indices *pl of* INDEX

in·dict \in-'dīt\ *vb* : to charge with an offense or crime : ACCUSE — **in·dict·able** \-ə-bəl\ *adj*

in·dict·ment \in-'dīt-mənt\ *n* **1** : the act or process of indicting **2** : an official written statement charging a person with a crime

in·dif·fer·ence \in-'dif-ərn(t)s, -'dif-(ə-)rən(t)s\ *n* **1** : lack of feeling for or against something **2** : lack of importance ⟨a matter of *indifference* to them⟩

in·dif·fer·ent \in-'dif-ərnt, -'dif-(ə-)rənt\ *adj* **1 a** : having or showing no special liking for or dislike of something ⟨the audience was *indifferent*⟩ **b** : not interested or concerned ⟨*indifferent* to the troubles of others⟩ **2** : neither good nor bad : MEDIOCRE ⟨*indifferent* health⟩ **3** : of no special influence or value : not important — **in·dif·fer·ent·ly** *adv*

in·di·gence \'in-di-jən(t)s\ *n* : POVERTY 1

in·dig·e·nous \in-'dij-ə-nəs\ *adj* : produced, growing, or living naturally in a particular region or environment — **in·dig·e·nous·ly** *adv*

in·di·gent \'in-di-jənt\ *adj* : ¹POOR 1, NEEDY

in·di·gest·ible \,in-dī-'jes-tə-bəl, -də-\ *adj* : not digestible or easily digested

in·di·ges·tion \,in-dī-'jes-chən, -də-\ *n* **1** : inability to digest or difficulty in digesting something **2** : a case or attack of indigestion

in·dig·nant \in-'dig-nənt\ *adj* : filled with or expressing indignation — **in·dig·nant·ly** *adv*

in·dig·na·tion \,in-dig-'nā-shən\ *n* : anger caused by something unjust, unworthy, or mean

in·dig·ni·ty \in-'dig-nət-ē\ *n, pl* **-ties** **1** : an act that injures a person's dignity or self-respect : INSULT **2** : humiliating treatment

in·di·go \'in-di-,gō\ *n, pl* **-gos** *or* **-goes** **1** : a blue dye

made artificially and formerly obtained from plants and especially indigo plants **2** : a dark grayish blue [from an Italian dialect word *indigo* "a blue dye from indigo plants", from Latin *indicum* (same meaning), derived from Greek *indikos* (adjective) "of or relating to India"; so called because the plant dye was first widely produced in India]

indigo plant *n* : any of a genus of plants of the legume family that are a source of indigo

indigo snake *n* : a large harmless blue-black snake of the southern U.S.

in·di·rect \,in-də-'rekt, -dī-\ *adj* **1** : not straight or direct ⟨an *indirect* route⟩ **2** : not straightforward ⟨*indirect* methods⟩ ⟨an *indirect* answer⟩ **3** : not having a plainly seen connection ⟨an *indirect* cause⟩ **4** : stating what an original speaker said with changes in wording that make the statement fit grammatically with the rest of the sentence ("that he would call" in "He said that he would call" is in *indirect* discourse) — **in·di·rect·ly** *adv* — **in·di·rect·ness** \-'rek(t)-nəs\ *n*

indirect object *n* : a grammatical object representing the secondary goal of the action of its verb ⟨"me" in "gave me the book" is an *indirect object*⟩

in·dis·creet \,in-dis-'krēt\ *adj* : not discreet : IMPRUDENT — **in·dis·creet·ly** *adv*

in·dis·cre·tion \,in-dis-'kresh-ən\ *n* **1** : lack of discretion : IMPRUDENCE **2** : an indiscreet act or remark

in·dis·crim·i·nate \,in-dis-'krim-(ə-)nət\ *adj* : showing lack of discrimination : not choosing carefully ⟨an *indiscriminate* reader⟩ ⟨*indiscriminate* enthusiasm⟩ — **in·dis·crim·i·nate·ly** *adv*

in·dis·pens·able \,in-dis-'pen(t)-sə-bəl\ *adj* : absolutely necessary : ESSENTIAL ⟨an *indispensable* employee⟩ — **in·dis·pens·abil·i·ty** \-,pen(t)-sə-'bil-ət-ē\ *n*

in·dis·posed \,in-dis-'pōzd\ *adj* **1** : slightly ill **2** : UNWILLING ⟨was *indisposed* to help⟩

in·dis·po·si·tion \(,)in-,dis-pə-'zish-ən\ *n* **1** : a slight illness **2** : lack of willingness

in·dis·put·able \,in-dis-'pyüt-ə-bəl, (')in-'dis-pyət-\ *adj* : not disputable : UNQUESTIONABLE ⟨*indisputable* proof⟩ — **in·dis·put·ably** \-blē\ *adv*

in·dis·sol·u·ble \,in-dis-'äl-yə-bəl\ *adj* : impossible to dissolve, do away with, break up, or decompose ⟨an *indissoluble* contract⟩ — **in·dis·sol·u·bil·i·ty** \-dis-,äl-yə-'bil-ət-ē\ *n* — **in·dis·sol·u·bly** \-dis-'äl-yə-blē\ *adv*

in·dis·tinct \,in-dis-'tiŋ(k)t\ *adj* : not distinct or clear ⟨*indistinct* figures in the fog⟩ ⟨a far-off *indistinct* light⟩ — **in·dis·tinct·ly** *adv* — **in·dis·tinct·ness** *n*

in·dis·tin·guish·able \,in-dis-'tiŋ-gwish-ə-bəl\ *adj* : impossible to distinguish clearly

in·di·um \'in-dē-əm\ *n* : a soft silvery metallic element — see ELEMENT table

¹in·di·vid·u·al \,in-də-'vij-(ə-)wəl, -'vij-əl\ *adj* **1** : of or relating to an individual ⟨*individual* traits⟩ **2** : intended for one person ⟨*individual* servings⟩ **3** : ¹PARTICULAR 1, SEPARATE ⟨*individual* copies⟩ **4** : having a special quality : DISTINCT ⟨an *individual* style⟩ — **in·di·vid·u·al·ly** \-ē\ *adv*

²individual *n* **1** : a single member of a class, species, or collection **2** : a single human being

in·di·vid·u·al·ism \,in-də-'vij(ə)wə-,liz-əm, -'vij-ə-,liz-\ *n* **1** : a belief that the interests of the individual are of the greatest importance **2** : a belief that the individual has political or economic rights with which the state must not interfere

in·di·vid·u·al·ist \,in-də-'vij-(ə)wə-ləst, -'vij-əl-əst\ *n* **1** : a person who thinks or behaves in an individual or inde-

\ə\ **abut**	\au̇\ **out**	\i\ **tip**	\o̊\ **saw**	\u̇\ **foot**
\ər\ **further**	\ch\ **chin**	\ī\ **life**	\o̊i\ **coin**	\y\ **yet**
\a\ **mat**	\e\ **pet**	\j\ **job**	\th\ **thin**	\yü\ **few**
\ā\ **take**	\ē\ **easy**	\ŋ\ **sing**	\th\ **this**	\yu̇\ **cure**
\ä\ **cot, cart**	\g\ **go**	\ō\ **bone**	\ü\ **food**	\zh\ **vision**

pendent way **2** : a supporter of individualism — **in·di·vid·u·al·is·tic** \-ˌvij-(ə)wə-'lis-tik, -ˌvij-ə-'lis-tik\ adj

in·di·vid·u·al·i·ty \ˌin-də-ˌvij-ə-'wal-ət-ē\ n, pl **-ties 1** : the qualities that make one person or thing different from all others **2** : the quality or state of being an individual

in·di·vid·u·al·ize \ˌin-də-'vij-(ə)wə-ˌlīz, -'vij-ə-ˌliz\ vb **-ized; -iz·ing 1** : to make individual in character **2** : to treat or notice individually **3** : to change to fit the needs of an individual — **in·di·vid·u·al·iza·tion** \-ˌvij-(ə)wə-lə-'zā-shən, -ˌvij-ə-lə-\ n

in·di·vis·i·ble \ˌin-də-'viz-ə-bəl\ adj : impossible to divide or separate — **in·di·vis·i·bly** \-blē\ adv

in·doc·tri·nate \in-'däk-trə-ˌnāt\ vb **-nat·ed; -nat·ing 1** : INSTRUCT 1, TEACH **2** : to teach the ideas, opinions, or beliefs of a particular group — **in·doc·tri·na·tion** \(ˌ)in-ˌdäk-trə-'nā-shən\ n — **in·doc·tri·na·tor** \in-'däk-trə-ˌnāt-ər\ n

¹In·do–Eu·ro·pe·an \ˌin-dō-ˌyùr-ə-'pē-ən\ adj : of, relating to, or being a family of languages including those spoken in most of Europe, in the parts of the world colonized by Europeans, and in parts of Asia

²Indo–European n **1** : the Indo-European languages **2** : a member of a people who originally spoke an Indo-European language

in·dole·ace·tic acid \'in-ˌdōl-ə-ˌsēt-ik-\ n : a plant hormone that promotes growth and rooting of plants

in·do·lence \'in-də-lən(t)s\ n : the quality or state of being indolent : LAZINESS

in·do·lent \'in-də-lənt\ adj : disliking effort or activity : LAZY ⟨felt indolent every spring⟩ — **in·do·lent·ly** adv

in·dom·i·ta·ble \in-'däm-ət-ə-bəl\ adj : UNCONQUERABLE ⟨indomitable courage⟩ — **in·dom·i·ta·bil·i·ty** \(ˌ)in-ˌdäm-ət-ə-'bil-ət-ē\ n — **in·dom·i·ta·ble·ness** \in-'däm-ət-ə-bəl-nəs\ n — **in·dom·i·ta·bly** \-blē\ adv

In·do·ne·sian \ˌin-də-'nē-zhən, -shən\ n **1** : a person born or living in Indonesia **2** : the language based on Malay that is the national language of Indonesia — **Indonesian** adj

in·door \ˌin-ˌdō(ə)r, -ˌdȯ(ə)r\ adj **1** : of or relating to the interior of a building **2** : done, living, used, or belonging within a building ⟨an indoor sport⟩

in·doors \(')in-'dō(ə)rz, -'dȯ(ə)rz\ adv : in or into a building ⟨games to be played indoors⟩

in·du·bi·ta·ble \(')in-'d(y)ü-bət-ə-bəl\ adj : impossible to doubt : beyond question — **in·du·bi·ta·bly** \-blē\ adv

in·duce \in-'d(y)üs\ vb **in·duced; in·duc·ing 1** : to lead on to do something : PERSUADE **2** : BRING ABOUT, CAUSE ⟨an illness induced by overwork⟩ **3** : to reach (a general conclusion) based on particular facts or examples **4** : to produce (as an electric current) by induction — **in·duc·er** n — **in·duc·ible** \-'d(y)ü-sə-bəl\ adj

in·duce·ment \in-'d(y)ü-smənt\ n **1** : the act of inducing **2** : something that induces ⟨a money-back guarantee is an inducement to buy⟩

in·duct \in-'dəkt\ vb **1** : to place in office : INSTALL **2** : to draft into military service — **in·duct·ee** \(ˌ)in-ˌdək-'tē\ n

in·duc·tion \in-'dək-shən\ n **1 a** : the act or process of inducting (as into office) **b** : a first experience of something : INITIATION **c** : the procedure by which a civilian is inducted into military service **2** : reasoning from particular examples to a general conclusion **3 a** : the act of causing or bringing on or about **b** : the process of producing an electrical or magnetic effect through the influence of a nearby magnet, electric current, or electrically charged body

induction coil n : a device that changes a low steady voltage into a repeating high voltage by induction

induction coil: 1 primary coil, 2 interrupter, 3 secondary coil

in·duc·tive \in-'dək-tiv\ adj : relating to, using, or based on induction — **in·duc·tive·ly** adv

in·duc·tor \in-'dək-tər\ n **1** : one that inducts **2** : a part of an electrical device that acts upon another or is itself acted upon by induction

in·dulge \in-'dəlj\ vb **in·dulged; in·dulg·ing 1** : to give in to one's own or another's desires : HUMOR ⟨indulged their grandchildren's whims⟩ **2** : to allow oneself the pleasure of having or doing something ⟨decided to indulge in a hamburger⟩ — **in·dulg·er** n

in·dul·gence \in-'dəl-jən(t)s\ n **1** : the act of indulging : the state of being indulgent **2** : an indulgent act **3** : something indulged in

in·dul·gent \in-'dəl-jənt\ adj : indulging or showing indulgence : LENIENT ⟨an indulgent parent⟩ — **in·dul·gent·ly** adv

in·du·rat·ed \'in-d(y)ə-ˌrāt-əd\ adj : having become firm or hard ⟨indurated tissue⟩

in·dus·tri·al \in-'dəs-trē-əl\ adj **1** : of, relating to, or engaged in industry **2** : having highly developed industries ⟨an industrial nation⟩ **3** : coming from or used in industry ⟨industrial diamonds⟩ — **in·dus·tri·al·ly** \-trē-ə-lē\ adv

industrial arts n sing or pl : a subject taught in elementary and secondary schools that aims at developing skills necessary for working with tools and machines

industrial engineering n : engineering that deals with the design, improvement, and installation of systems of people, materials, equipment, and energy — **industrial engineer** n

in·dus·tri·al·ist \in-'dəs-trē-ə-ləst\ n : an owner or manager of an industry : MANUFACTURER

in·dus·tri·al·ize \in-'dəs-trē-ə-ˌlīz\ vb **-ized; -iz·ing** : to make or become industrial ⟨industrialize an agricultural region⟩ — **in·dus·tri·al·iza·tion** \-ˌdəs-trē-ə-lə-'zā-shən\ n

industrial revolution n : a rapid major change in an economy (as in England in the late 18th century) marked by the general introduction of power-driven machinery

in·dus·tri·ous \in-'dəs-trē-əs\ adj : constantly or regularly occupied **syn** see BUSY — **in·dus·tri·ous·ly** adv — **in·dus·tri·ous·ness** n

in·dus·try \'in-(ˌ)dəs-trē\ n, pl **-tries 1** : the habit of working hard and steadily : DILIGENCE **2** : steady labor ⟨lived by their own industry⟩ **3 a** : the businesses that provide a particular product or service ⟨the steel industry⟩ ⟨the tourist industry⟩ **b** : manufacturing activity ⟨commerce and industry⟩

¹ine·bri·ate \in-'ē-brē-ət\ n : a person who is intoxicated especially as a habit

²ine·bri·ate \in-'ē-brē-ət, -ˌāt\ adj : INEBRIATED

ine·bri·at·ed \in-'ē-brē-ˌāt-əd\ adj : affected by or as if by alcohol : being intoxicated — **ine·bri·a·tion** \-ˌē-brē-'ā-shən\ n

in·ed·i·ble \(')in-'ed-ə-bəl\ adj : not fit or safe for eating ⟨inedible mushrooms⟩

in·ef·fa·ble \(')in-'ef-ə-bəl\ adj : impossible to express : INEXPRESSIBLE — **in·ef·fa·bil·i·ty** \(ˌ)in-ˌef-ə-'bil-ət-ē\ n — **in·ef·fa·bly** \(')in-'ef-ə-blē\ adv

in·ef·fec·tive \ˌin-ə-'fek-tiv\ adj : not producing the desired effect ⟨an ineffective law⟩ ⟨an ineffective leader⟩ — **in·ef·fec·tive·ly** adv — **in·ef·fec·tive·ness** n

in·ef·fec·tu·al \ˌin-ə-'fek-chə-(wə)l, -'feksh-wəl\ adj : not producing the proper or usual effect — **in·ef·fec·tu·al·ly** \-'fek-chə-(wə)-lē, -'feksh-wə-\ adv — **in·ef·fec·tu·al·ness** n

in·ef·fi·cien·cy \ˌin-ə-'fish-ən-sē\ n, pl **-cies 1** : the quality or state of being inefficient **2** : something that is inefficient

in·ef·fi·cient \ˌin-ə-'fish-ənt\ adj **1** : INEFFECTUAL **2** : not able or willing to do something well ⟨an inefficient worker⟩ — **in·ef·fi·cient·ly** adv

in·elas·tic \ˌin-ə-'las-tik\ adj : not elastic : slow to respond to changing conditions — **in·elas·tic·i·ty** \ˌin-i-

,las-'tis-ət-ē\ *n*

in·el·e·gant \(')in-'el-i-gənt\ *adj* : lacking in grace or good taste — **in·el·e·gant·ly** *adv*

in·el·i·gi·ble \(')in-'el-ə-jə-bəl\ *adj* : not qualified to be chosen or used — **in·el·i·gi·bil·i·ty** \(,)in-,el-ə-jə-'bil-ət-ē\ *n* — **ineligible** *n*

in·ept \in-'ept\ *adj* **1** : not suited for the occasion : INAPPROPRIATE ⟨an *inept* remark⟩ **2** : lacking in skill or ability : INCOMPETENT — **in·ep·ti·tude** \-'ep-tə-,t(y)üd\ *n* — **in·ept·ly** \-'ep-(t)lē\ *adv* — **in·ept·ness** \-'ep(t)-nəs\ *n*

in·equal·i·ty \,in-i-'kwäl-ət-ē\ *n, pl* **-ties 1** : the quality of being unequal **2** : an instance of being unequal (as an irregularity in a surface) **3** : a statement of inequality in mathematics or logic between two quantities usually separated by a special sign (as $<$, $>$, or $\neq$ meaning in the order named *is less than*, *is greater than*, and *is not equal to*)

in·eq·ui·ta·ble \(')in-'ek-wət-ə-bəl\ *adj* : not equitable : UNFAIR — **in·eq·ui·ta·bly** \-blē\ *adv*

in·eq·ui·ty \(')in-'ek-wət-ē\ *n, pl* **-ties 1** : INJUSTICE 1, UNFAIRNESS **2** : an instance of injustice or unfairness

in·ert \in-'ərt\ *adj* : unable or slow to move, act, or react ⟨*inert* ingredients in cough medicine⟩ ⟨*inert* gas⟩ — **in·ert·ly** *adv* — **in·ert·ness** *n*

in·er·tia \in-'ər-shə, -shē-ə\ *n* **1** : a property of matter by which it remains at rest or in unchanging motion unless acted on by some external force **2** : a tendency not to move or change — **in·er·tial** \-shəl\ *adj*

inertial guidance *n* : guidance (as of an aircraft) by automatic devices that respond to changes in speed or direction

in·es·cap·able \,in-ə-'skā-pə-bəl\ *adj* : impossible to escape or avoid — **in·es·cap·ably** \-blē\ *adv*

in·es·ti·ma·ble \(')in-'es-tə-mə-bəl\ *adj* **1** : impossible to estimate ⟨did *inestimable* damage⟩ **2** : too valuable or excellent to be measured or appreciated — **in·es·ti·ma·bly** \-blē\ *adv*

in·ev·i·ta·ble \in-'ev-ət-ə-bəl\ *adj* : impossible to avoid or evade : sure to happen : CERTAIN ⟨the *inevitable* result⟩ — **in·ev·i·ta·bil·i·ty** \(,)in-,ev-ət-ə-'bil-ət-ē\ *n* — **in·ev·i·ta·ble·ness** \(')in-'ev-ət-ə-bəl-nəs\ *n* — **in·ev·i·ta·bly** \-blē\ *adv*

in·ex·act \,in-ig-'zakt\ *adj* : not exactly correct or true : INACCURATE — **in·ex·act·ly** \-'zak-(t)lē\ *adv* — **in·ex·act·ness** \-'zak(t)-nəs\ *n*

in·ex·cus·able \,in-ik-'skyü-zə-bəl\ *adj* : too bad to be excused : not justifiable ⟨*inexcusable* rudeness⟩ — **in·ex·cus·ably** \-blē\ *adv*

in·ex·haust·ible \,in-ig-'zȯ-stə-bəl\ *adj* **1** : impossible to use up ⟨an *inexhaustible* supply⟩ **2** : impossible to tire out ⟨an *inexhaustible* worker⟩ — **in·ex·haust·ibil·i·ty** \-,zȯ-stə-'bil-ət-ē\ *n* — **in·ex·haust·ibly** \-'zȯ-stə-blē\ *adv*

in·ex·o·ra·ble \(')in-'eks-(ə-)rə-bəl\ *adj* : RELENTLESS — **in·ex·o·ra·bil·i·ty** \(,)in-,eks-(ə-)rə-'bil-ət-ē\ *n* — **in·ex·o·ra·ble·ness** \(')in-'eks-(ə-)rə-bəl-nəs\ *n* — **in·ex·o·ra·bly** \-blē\ *adv*

in·ex·pe·di·ent \,in-ik-'spēd-ē-ənt\ *adj* : not suited to bring about a desired result : UNWISE ⟨an *inexpedient* decision⟩ — **in·ex·pe·di·ent·ly** *adv*

in·ex·pen·sive \,in-ik-'spen(t)-siv\ *adj* : not high in price : CHEAP — **in·ex·pen·sive·ly** *adv* — **in·ex·pen·sive·ness** *n*

in·ex·pe·ri·ence \,in-ik-'spir-ē-ən(t)s\ *n* : lack of experience — **in·ex·pe·ri·enced** \-ən(t)st\ *adj*

in·ex·pert \(')in-'ek-,spərt, ,in-ik-'spərt\ *adj* : not expert : UNSKILLED — **in·ex·pert·ly** *adv* — **in·ex·pert·ness** *n*

in·ex·pli·ca·ble \,in-ik-'splik-ə-bəl, (')in-'ek-(,)splik-\ *adj* : impossible to explain ⟨an *inexplicable* mystery⟩ — **in·ex·pli·ca·bil·i·ty** \,in-ik-,splik-ə-'bil-ət-ē, (,)in-,ek-(,)splik-\ *n* — **in·ex·pli·ca·bly** \-blē\ *adv*

in·ex·press·ible \,in-ik-'spres-ə-bəl\ *adj* : impossible to express : INDESCRIBABLE ⟨*inexpressible* joy⟩ — **in·ex·press·ibly** \-blē\ *adv*

in·ex·pres·sive \,in-ik-'spres-iv\ *adj* : not expressive ⟨an *inexpressive* face⟩ — **in·ex·pres·sive·ly** *adv*

in·ex·tin·guish·able \,in-ik-'stiŋ-(g)wish-ə-bəl\ *adj* : impossible to extinguish

in·ex·tri·ca·ble \,in-ik-'strik-ə-bəl, (')in-'ek-(,)strik-\ *adj* : impossible to untangle or to get free from ⟨an *inextricable* knot⟩ — **in·ex·tri·ca·bly** \-blē\ *adv*

in·fal·li·ble \(')in-'fal-ə-bəl\ *adj* **1** : not capable of being wrong : UNERRING **2** : not likely to fail : SURE ⟨an *infallible* remedy⟩ — **in·fal·li·bil·i·ty** \(,)in-,fal-ə-'bil-ət-ē\ *n* — **in·fal·li·bly** \(')in-'fal-ə-blē\ *adv*

in·fa·mous \'in-fə-məs\ *adj* **1** : having an evil reputation ⟨an *infamous* traitor⟩ **2** : causing or bringing an evil reputation : DETESTABLE ⟨an *infamous* crime⟩ — **in·fa·mous·ly** *adv*

in·fa·my \'in-fə-mē\ *n, pl* **-mies 1** : an evil reputation **2 a** : an infamous act **b** : the state of being infamous

in·fan·cy \'in-fən-sē\ *n, pl* **-cies 1** : early childhood **2** : a beginning or early period of existence

in·fant \'in-fənt\ *n* : a child in the first period of life — **infant** *adj*

in·fan·tile \'in-fən-,tīl, -t*ə*l, -,tēl\ *adj* : of, relating to, or resembling infants or infancy : CHILDISH

infantile paralysis *n* : POLIOMYELITIS

in·fan·til·ism \'in-fən-,tīl-,iz-əm, -tə-,liz-; in-'fan-t*ə*l-,iz-\ *n* : childish qualities or behavior in an adult

in·fan·try \'in-fən-trē\ *n, pl* **-tries** : a branch of an army made up of soldiers trained, armed, and equipped to fight on foot

> **Word History** In the Middle Ages in France, a young soldier from a good family who was not yet a knight was called *enfant*, which means "child". Likewise, in Italy a soldier moving on foot behind a knight riding a horse was an *infante*. Later, Italian foot soldiers as a group became known as *infanteria*, which was borrowed into French as *infanterie* and into English as *infantry*. [from early French *infanterie* and early Italian *infanteria*, both meaning "infantry", from early Italian *infante* "infant, boy, foot soldier", from Latin *infans* "infant"]

in·fan·try·man \-mən\ *n* : a soldier of the infantry

in·fat·u·ate \in-'fach-ə-,wāt\ *vb* **-at·ed; -at·ing** : to fill with a foolish or excessive love or admiration — **in·fat·u·a·tion** \in-,fach-ə-'wā-shən\ *n*

in·fect \in-'fekt\ *vb* **1** : to contaminate with a disease-producing substance or germ ⟨*infected* bedding⟩ **2 a** : to communicate a germ or disease to ⟨coughing people who *infect* others⟩ **b** : to enter and cause disease in ⟨bacteria that *infect* wounds⟩ **3** : to cause to share one's feelings ⟨*infected* everyone with his enthusiasm⟩ — **in·fec·tor** \-'fek-tər\ *n*

in·fec·tion \in-'fek-shən\ *n* **1** : an act or process of infecting **2 a** : the state produced by something infectious (as a germ or parasite) living in or on a suitable host **b** : a disease resulting from infection : INFECTIOUS DISEASE **3 a** : something infectious **b** : material contaminated with something infectious

in·fec·tious \in-'fek-shəs\ *adj* **1 a** : capable of causing infection **b** : capable of being spread by infection **2** : capable of being easily spread ⟨*infectious* laughter⟩ — **in·fec·tious·ly** *adv*

infectious disease *n* : a disease caused by the presence, growth, and increase in numbers of germs in the body — compare CONTAGIOUS DISEASE

in·fec·tive \in-'fek-tiv\ *adj* : producing or able to produce

\ə\ abut		\au̇\ out	\i\ tip	\ȯ\ saw	\u̇\ foot
\ər\ further		\ch\ chin	\ī\ life	\ȯi\ coin	\y\ yet
\a\ mat		\e\ pet	\j\ job	\th\ thin	\yü\ few
\ā\ take		\ē\ easy	\ŋ\ sing	\th\ this	\yu̇\ cure
\ä\ cot, cart		\g\ go	\ō\ bone	\ü\ food	\zh\ vision

infection — **in·fec·tiv·i·ty** \(,)in-,fek-'tiv-ət-ē\ *n*

in·fe·lic·i·tous \,in-fi-'lis-ət-əs\ *adj* : not appropriate : not suitably chosen for the occasion ⟨an *infelicitous* remark⟩ — **in·fe·lic·i·tous·ly** *adv*

in·fe·lic·i·ty \,in-fi-'lis-ət-ē\ *n, pl* **-ties** 1 : a lack of suitability 2 : an inappropriate act or expression

in·fer \in-'fər\ *vb* **in·ferred; in·fer·ring** 1 : to arrive at as a conclusion 2 : ¹GUESS 1, SURMISE 3 : IMPLY 2 — **in·fer·able** \-ə-bəl\ *adj*

in·fer·ence \'in-f(ə-)rən(t)s\ *n* 1 : the act or process of inferring 2 : something inferred

¹**in·fe·ri·or** \in-'fir-ē-ər\ *adj* 1 : situated lower down 2 : of low or lower degree or rank 3 : of little or less importance, value, or merit

²**inferior** *n* : an inferior person or thing

in·fe·ri·or·i·ty \(,)in-,fir-ē-'ȯr-ət-ē, -'är-\ *n, pl* **-ties** 1 : the state of being inferior 2 : a sense of being inferior

inferiority complex *n* : a personal sense of being inferior that may be expressed by behavior that is either timid or aggressive

inferior vena cava *n* : a large vein that is a branch of the vena cava and returns blood to the heart from the lower parts of the body including the inside organs below the lungs and the lower limbs

in·fer·nal \in-'fərn-ᵊl\ *adj* 1 : of or relating to hell 2 : very bad or unpleasant ⟨an *infernal* nuisance⟩ — **in·fer·nal·ly** \-ᵊl-ē\ *adv*

in·fer·no \in-'fər-nō\ *n, pl* **-nos** : a place or state that resembles or suggests hell especially in great heat or raging fire [from Italian *inferno* "underworld, hell", from Latin *infernus* (same meaning), from earlier *infernus* (adjective) "lying beneath, in the lower regions"]

in·fer·tile \(')in-'fərt-ᵊl\ *adj* : not fertile or productive : BARREN — **in·fer·til·i·ty** \,in-(,)fər-'til-ət-ē\ *n*

in·fest \in-'fest\ *vb* 1 : to spread or swarm in or over in a troublesome manner 2 : to live in or on as a parasite — **in·fes·ta·tion** \,in-,fes-'tā-shən\ *n*

in·fi·del \'in-fəd-ᵊl, -fə-,del\ *n* : a person who does not believe in a particular religion — **infidel** *adj*

in·fi·del·i·ty \,in-fə-'del-ət-ē, -(,)fī-\ *n, pl* **-ties** 1 : lack of faith in a religion 2 : unfaithfulness especially to one's husband or wife

in·field \'in-,fēld\ *n* 1 a : the part of a baseball field enclosed by and around the three bases and home plate b : the players positioned in the infield 2 : the area enclosed by a racetrack or running track — **in·field·er** \-,fēl-dər\ *n*

in·fil·trate \in-'fil-,trāt, 'in-(,)fil-\ *vb* **-trat·ed; -trat·ing** 1 : to pass into or through by filtering 2 : to enter or become established gradually or secretly — **in·fil·tra·tion** \,in-(,)fil-'trā-shən\ *n* — **in·fil·tra·tor** \in-'fil-,trāt-ər, 'in-(,)fil-\ *n*

infield 1a

¹**in·fi·nite** \'in-fə-nət\ *adj* 1 : being without limits of any kind : ENDLESS ⟨*infinite* space⟩ 2 : seeming to be without limits : VAST ⟨*infinite* patience⟩ ⟨*infinite* wealth⟩ 3 a : lying or being beyond or being larger than any number no matter how large ⟨the number of positive integers is *infinite*⟩ b : having an infinite number of elements or terms ⟨an *infinite* set⟩ — **in·fi·nite·ly** *adv*

²**infinite** *n* : something that is infinite (as in number)

in·fin·i·tes·i·mal \(,)in-,fin-ə-'tes-ə-məl\ *adj* : too small to be measurable — **in·fin·i·tes·i·mal·ly** \-mə-lē\ *adv*

in·fin·i·tive \in-'fin-ət-iv\ *n* : a verb form serving as a noun or as a modifier and at the same time taking objects and adverbial modifiers ⟨"carry" in "help them carry it" and "to

do" in "they have nothing to do" are *infinitives*⟩ — **infinitive** *adj*

in·fin·i·ty \in-'fin-ət-ē\ *n, pl* **-ties** 1 a : the quality of being infinite b : a space, quantity, or period of time that is without limit 2 : an indefinitely great number or amount 3 : a point infinitely far away [Middle English *infinite* "the quality of having no limit", from early French *infinité* (same meaning), derived from Latin *infinitus* (adjective) "having no limit", from *in-* "not" and *finitus*, past participle of *finire* "to limit, bring to an end", from *finis* "end, limit" — related to DEFINE, FINAL, FINISH]

in·firm \in-'fərm\ *adj* : weak or frail in body (as from age or disease)

in·fir·ma·ry \in-'fərm-(ə-)rē\ *n, pl* **-ries** : a place for the care and housing of infirm or sick people

in·fir·mi·ty \in-'fər-mət-ē\ *n, pl* **-ties** 1 : the quality or state of being infirm 2 : AILMENT, DISEASE

in·flame \in-'flām\ *vb* **in·flamed; in·flam·ing** 1 : to set on fire : KINDLE 2 : to excite to too much action or feeling 3 : to cause to redden or grow hot from anger or excitement 4 : to cause inflammation in (bodily tissue) 5 : to become affected with inflammation

in·flam·ma·ble \in-'flam-ə-bəl\ *adj* 1 : FLAMMABLE 2 : easily inflamed : EXCITABLE — **in·flam·ma·bil·i·ty** \-,flam-ə-'bil-ət-ē\ *n* — **in·flam·ma·bly** \-'flam-ə-blē\ *adv*

in·flam·ma·tion \,in-flə-'mā-shən\ *n* 1 : the act of inflaming : the state of being inflamed 2 : a bodily response to injury in which heat, redness, pain, swelling, and more than the usual amount of blood are present in the area affected

in·flam·ma·to·ry \in-'flam-ə-,tōr-ē, -,tȯr-\ *adj* 1 : stirring up anger, disorder, or rebellion ⟨*inflammatory* speeches⟩ 2 : causing or accompanied by inflammation ⟨*inflammatory* diseases⟩

in·flate \in-'flāt\ *vb* **in·flat·ed; in·flat·ing** 1 : to swell or fill with air or gas ⟨*inflate* a balloon⟩ 2 : to increase abnormally ⟨*inflated* prices⟩ **syn** see EXPAND — **in·flat·able** \-ə-bəl\ *adj*

in·flat·ed \in-'flāt-əd\ *adj* : hollow and stretched or swelled ⟨*inflated* pods of a plant⟩

in·fla·tion \in-'flā-shən\ *n* 1 : an act of inflating : the state of being inflated 2 : a continual increase in the price of goods and services

in·fla·tion·ary \in-'flā-shə-,ner-ē\ *adj* : of, relating to, or causing inflation

in·flect \in-'flekt\ *vb* 1 : to change a word by inflection 2 : to change the pitch of the voice

in·flec·tion \in-'flek-shən\ *n* 1 : a change in the pitch or tone of a person's voice 2 : the change in the form of a word showing its case, gender, number, person, tense, mood, voice, or comparison — **in·flec·tion·al** \-shnəl, -shən-ᵊl\ *adj*

in·flex·i·ble \(')in-'flek-sə-bəl\ *adj* 1 : not easily bent or twisted : RIGID, STIFF 2 : not easily influenced or persuaded : FIRM ⟨an *inflexible* judge⟩ 3 : incapable of change : UNALTERABLE ⟨*inflexible* laws⟩ — **in·flex·i·bil·i·ty** \(,)in-,flek-sə-'bil-ət-ē\ *n* — **in·flex·i·bly** \(')in-'flek-sə-blē\ *adv*

in·flict \in-'flikt\ *vb* 1 : to give by or as if by striking ⟨*inflict* a wound⟩ 2 : to cause (something damaging or painful) to be endured ⟨*inflict* punishment⟩ — **in·flic·tion** \-'flik-shən\ *n*

in·flo·res·cence \,in-flə-'res-ᵊn(t)s\ *n* 1 a : the pattern of development and arrangement of flowers on a stalk b : a flow-

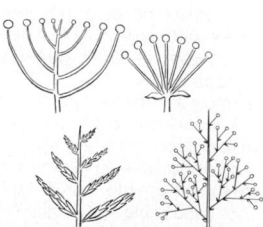

inflorescence 1a

ering stalk with all its parts; *also* : a flower cluster or sometimes a flower that grows alone   **2** : the forming and unfolding of blossoms

in·flow \'in-,flō\ *n*   **1** : the act of flowing in   **2** : something that flows in

¹in·flu·ence \'in-,flü-ən(t)s\ *n*   **1** : the act or power of producing an effect indirectly or without apparent use of force or exercise of command   **2** : dishonest interference with authority for personal gain   **3** : a person or thing that influences [Middle English *influence* "a fluid formerly believed to flow from the stars to cause people to act a certain way", from early French *influence* (same meaning), derived from Latin *influere* "to flow in", from *in-* "in" and *fluere* "to flow" — related to FLUID] — **under the influence** : affected by liquor

²influence *vb* **-enced; -enc·ing** : to have an influence on : affect by influence — **in·flu·enc·er** *n*

in·flu·en·tial \,in-(,)flü-'en-chəl\ *adj* : having influence — **in·flu·en·tial·ly** \-'ench-(ə-)lē\ *adv*

in·flu·en·za \,in-(,)flü-'en-zə\ *n*   **1** : a very contagious virus disease with fever, exhaustion, severe aches and pains, and inflammation of the respiratory tract   **2** : any of various diseases of human beings or domestic animals that are usually caused by viruses, are marked by fever and usually by respiratory symptoms and inflammation, and often affect the body as a whole

Word History Originally the Italian word *influenza* meant what the similar-sounding word in English, *influence,* means: "the act or power of producing an effect indirectly". But it also had the Latin meaning of "an invisible fluid through which the stars and planets control and direct the earth and things and people on it". When epidemics raged through Europe, no one knew what the real cause was. People blamed them on evil stars working through the invisible fluid, or influence. For this reason the Italians called the disease *influenza*. In 1743 an epidemic very much like our modern flu began in Rome and spread. That was when the Italian word was borrowed into English. *Flu* is a shortened form of *influenza*. [from Italian *influenza*, literally "influence", from Latin *influentia* "influence", derived from earlier *influere* "to flow in", from *in-* "in, into" and *fluere* "to flow"]

in·flux \'in-,fləks\ *n* : a flowing or coming in : INFLOW

in·form \in-'fò(ə)rm\ *vb*   **1** : to let a person know something : TELL   **2** : to give information so as to accuse or cause suspicion ⟨*inform* against them to the police⟩

in·for·mal \(')in-'fòr-məl\ *adj*   **1** : not formal ⟨an *informal* party⟩   **2** : suited for ordinary or everyday use ⟨*informal* clothes⟩ — **in·for·mal·i·ty** \,in-(,)fòr-'mal-ət-ē, -fər-\ *n* — **in·for·mal·ly** \(')in-'fòr-mə-lē\ *adv*

in·for·mant \in-'fòr-mənt\ *n* : INFORMER

in·for·ma·tion \,in-fər-'mā-shən\ *n*   **1** : the giving or receiving of knowledge or intelligence   **2 a** : knowledge obtained from investigation, study, or instruction   **b** : knowledge of a particular event or situation : NEWS   **c** : a characteristic or quality (as of DNA or a computer program) that stands for, expresses, or tells about one group of things or ways of doing things instead of others   **3** : the quality of something (as DNA or a computer program) that represents a specific choice between a number of possible choices — **in·for·ma·tion·al** \-shnəl, -shən-°l\ *adj*

in·for·ma·tive \in-'fòr-mət-iv\ *adj* : providing knowledge : INSTRUCTIVE — **in·for·ma·tive·ly** *adv* — **in·for·ma·tive·ness** *n*

in·formed \in-'fò(ə)rmd\ *adj* : having or based on information ⟨*informed* sources⟩ ⟨an *informed* decision⟩

in·form·er \in-'fòr-mər\ *n* : someone who informs; *esp* : a person who informs against someone else

infra- *prefix* : below in a scale or series ⟨*infra*red⟩ [from Latin *infra* "below, underneath"]

in·frac·tion \in-'frak-shən\ *n* : an act of violating something : VIOLATION

in·fra·red \,in-frə-'red, -(,)frä-\ *adj* : being, relating to, producing, or using rays like light but lying outside the visible spectrum at its red end ⟨*infrared* radiation⟩ ⟨*infrared* photography⟩ — **infrared** *n*

in·fre·quent \(')in-'frē-kwənt\ *adj*   **1** : seldom happening or occurring : RARE   **2** : not placed, made, or done at frequent intervals ⟨made *infrequent* stops⟩ — **in·fre·quent·ly** *adv*

in·fringe \in-'frinj\ *vb* **in·fringed; in·fring·ing**   **1** : to fail to obey or act in agreement with : VIOLATE ⟨*infringe* a treaty⟩   **2** : ENCROACH 1 ⟨*infringe* on a person's rights⟩ — **in·fringe·ment** \-mənt\ *n* — **in·fring·er** *n*

in·fu·ri·ate \in-'fyùr-ē-,āt\ *vb* **-at·ed; -at·ing** : to make furious : ENRAGE — **in·fu·ri·at·ing·ly** \-,āt-iŋ-lē\ *adv* — **in·fu·ri·a·tion** \-,fyùr-ē-'ā-shən\ *n*

in·fuse \in-'fyüz\ *vb* **in·fused; in·fus·ing**   **1** : to put in as if by pouring ⟨*infused* courage into her followers⟩   **2** : to steep without boiling ⟨*infuse* tea⟩

in·fu·sion \in-'fyü-zhən\ *n*   **1** : the act or process of infusing   **2** : a product obtained by infusing ⟨a strong *infusion* of tea⟩   **3** : a watery mixture of decaying organic matter ⟨culturing protozoans in a hay *infusion*⟩

¹-ing \iŋ, ēŋ; *in some dialects usually & in other dialects informally* in, ēn, ən\ *vb suffix or adj suffix* — used to form the present participle ⟨sail*ing*⟩ and sometimes to form an adjective not derived from a verb ⟨hulk*ing*⟩ [Old English *-ende* (verb suffix)]

²-ing *n suffix*   **1** : action or process ⟨runn*ing*⟩ ⟨sleep*ing*⟩ ⟨meet*ing*⟩   **2** : product or result of an action or process ⟨an engrav*ing*⟩ ⟨earn*ings*⟩   **3** : something used in or connected with making or doing ⟨bedd*ing*⟩ ⟨roof*ing*⟩ [Old English *-ing, -ung* "one belonging to or of a (specified) kind"]

in·ge·nious \in-'jēn-yəs\ *adj* : having or showing ingenuity : very clever ⟨an *ingenious* plan⟩ [from early French *ingenieux* "calling for or showing special intelligence or cleverness", from Latin *ingeniosus* (same meaning), from *ingenium* "natural ability or desire to do something, inborn ability", from *in* "in" and *-genium,* from *gignere* "to father, beget" — related to ENGINE, GENIUS, ¹GIN] — **in·ge·nious·ly** *adv* — **in·ge·nious·ness** *n*

in·ge·nue *or* **in·gé·nue** \'an-jə-,nü, 'än-\ *n* : an innocent girl or young woman or an actor playing such a person

in·ge·nu·ity \,in-jə-'n(y)ü-ət-ē\ *n, pl* **-ities**   **1** : skill or cleverness in discovering, inventing, or planning   **2** : an ingenious device

in·gen·u·ous \in-'jen-yə-wəs\ *adj* : showing innocent or childlike simplicity and straightforwardness — **in·gen·u·ous·ly** *adv* — **in·gen·u·ous·ness** *n*

in·gest \in-'jest\ *vb* : to take in for digestion — **in·ges·tion** \-'jes-chən\ *n*

in·gle·nook \'iŋ-(g)əl-,nùk\ *n* : a corner by the fire or chimney

in·glo·ri·ous \(')in-'glōr-ē-əs, -'glòr-\ *adj*   **1** : not glorious : not bringing honor or glory   **2** : bringing disgrace : SHAMEFUL ⟨*inglorious* defeat⟩ — **in·glo·ri·ous·ly** *adv*

in·got \'iŋ-gət\ *n* : a mass of metal cast into a shape that is easy to handle or store

inglenook

¹in·grain \(')in-'grān\ *vb* : to work deeply into the texture of something or into the

\ə\ abut	\aú\ out	\i\ tip	\ò\ saw	\ù\ foot
\ər\ further	\ch\ chin	\ī\ life	\òi\ coin	\y\ yet
\a\ mat	\e\ pet	\j\ job	\th\ thin	\yü\ few
\ā\ take	\ē\ easy	\ŋ\ sing	\th\ this	\yù\ cure
\ä\ cot, cart	\g\ go	\ō\ bone	\ü\ food	\zh\ vision

mental or moral nature of someone ⟨an *ingrained* habit⟩

²in·grain \'in-,grān\ *adj* **1** : made of fiber that is dyed before being spun into yarn **2** : made of yarn that is dyed before being woven or knitted ⟨*ingrain* carpet⟩ — **ingrain** *n*

in·grate \'in-,grāt\ *n* : an ungrateful person

in·gra·ti·ate \in-'grā-shē-,āt\ *vb* **-at·ed; -at·ing** : to gain favor or acceptance for by deliberate effort ⟨quickly *ingratiated* herself with her new pupils⟩ — **in·gra·ti·a·tion** \-,grā-shē-'ā-shən\ *n*

in·gra·ti·at·ing \in-'grā-shē-,āt-iŋ\ *adj* **1** : PLEASING ⟨an *ingratiating* smile⟩ **2** : intended to gain favor ⟨*ingratiating* manners⟩ — **in·gra·ti·at·ing·ly** *adv*

in·grat·i·tude \(')in-'grat-ə-,t(y)üd\ *n* : lack of gratitude

in·gre·di·ent \in-'grēd-ē-ənt\ *n* : one of the substances that make up a mixture ⟨*ingredients* of a salad⟩

in·gress \'in-,gres\ *n* **1** : the act of entering **2** : the power or liberty of entering

in·grown \'in-,grōn\ *adj* : grown in; *esp* : having the free tip or edge grown back into the flesh ⟨an *ingrown* toenail⟩

in·hab·it \in-'hab-ət\ *vb* : to live or dwell in — **in·hab·it·able** \-ət-ə-bəl\ *adj*

in·hab·it·ant \in-'hab-ət-ənt\ *n* : one who lives permanently in a place

in·hal·ant \in-'hā-lənt\ *n* : something (as a medicine-containing spray) that is inhaled — **inhalant** *adj*

in·ha·la·tor \'in-(h)ə-,lāt-ər, 'in-ᵊl-,āt-\ *n* : a device used in inhaling something (as a mixture of oxygen and carbon dioxide)

in·hale \in-'hā(ə)l\ *vb* **in·haled; in·hal·ing** **1** : to draw in by breathing **2** : to breath in — **in·ha·la·tion** \,in-(h)ə-'lā-shən, ,in-ᵊl-'ā-\ *n*

in·hal·er \in-'hā-lər\ *n* : INHALATOR

in·har·mo·ni·ous \,in-(,)här-'mō-nē-əs\ *adj* : not harmonious : DISCORDANT

in·here \in-'hi(ə)r\ *vb* **in·hered; in·her·ing** : to be inherent : BELONG

in·her·ent \in-'hir-ənt, -'her-\ *adj* : belonging to or being a part of the nature of a person or thing ⟨an *inherent* sense of fair play⟩ ⟨fluidity is an *inherent* quality of gas⟩ — **in·her·ent·ly** *adv*

in·her·it \in-'her-ət\ *vb* **1** : to receive by legal right from a person at the person's death **2** : to receive by genetic transmission ⟨*inherit* red hair⟩ **3** : to have handed on to one by someone else ⟨*inherit* a job⟩ — **in·her·it·able** \-ət-ə-bəl\ *adj* — **in·her·i·tor** \-ət-ər\ *n*

in·her·i·tance \in-'her-ət-ən(t)s\ *n* **1** : the act of inheriting **2** : something that is or may be inherited

in·hib·it \in-'hib-ət\ *vb* **1** : to prevent or hold back from doing something : RESTRAIN, REPRESS ⟨fear can *inhibit* the natural expression of feelings⟩ **2** : to prevent or slow down the activity or occurrence of ⟨oil *inhibits* rust⟩ ⟨a drug which *inhibits* an infection⟩ — **in·hib·i·tor** \-ət-ər\ *n* — **in·hib·i·to·ry** \-ə-,tōr-ē, -,tor-\ *adj*

in·hib·it·ed \in-'hib-ət-əd\ *adj* : finding it hard to show desires, feelings, and thoughts

in·hi·bi·tion \,in-(h)ə-'bish-ən\ *n* **1 a** : the act of inhibiting : the state of being inhibited **b** : something that inhibits **2** : an inner force that prevents or makes difficult the free expression of thoughts, emotions, or desires

in·hos·pi·ta·ble \,in-(,)häs-'pit-ə-bəl, (')in-'häs-(,)pit-\ *adj* **1** : not friendly or generous : not showing hospitality **2** : providing no shelter or food : BARREN ⟨an *inhospitable* desert⟩ — **in·hos·pi·ta·bly** \-blē\ *adv* — **in·hos·pi·tal·i·ty** \(,)in-,häs-pə-'tal-ət-ē\ *n*

in·hu·man \(')in-'hyü-mən, -'yü-\ *adj* **1 a** : lacking pity or kindness : SAVAGE **b** : lacking human warmth : IMPERSONAL **c** : not fit for human needs ⟨*inhuman* conditions⟩ **2** : unlike what is typically human ⟨an *inhuman* cry⟩ — **in·hu·man·ly** *adv*

in·hu·mane \,in-(,)hyü-'mān, -(,)yü-\ *adj* : not humane : INHUMAN 1 ⟨*inhumane* treatment of prisoners⟩ — **in·hu-**

mane·ly *adv*

in·hu·man·i·ty \,in-(,)hyü-'man-ət-ē, -(,)yü-\ *n, pl* **-ties** : a cruel or barbarous act or attitude

in·im·i·cal \in-'im-i-kəl\ *adj* **1** : not friendly : HOSTILE **2** : having a harmful effect ⟨habits *inimical* to health⟩

in·im·i·ta·ble \(')in-'im-ət-ə-bəl\ *adj* : not capable of being imitated : MATCHLESS

in·iq·ui·tous \in-'ik-wət-əs\ *adj* : UNJUST, WICKED

in·iq·ui·ty \in-'ik-wət-ē\ *n, pl* **-ties** **1** : complete injustice or wickedness **2** : something that is unjust or wicked : SIN

¹ini·tial \in-'ish-əl\ *adj* **1** : of, relating to, or existing at the beginning : EARLIEST ⟨*initial* stages of a disease⟩ **2** : placed or standing at the beginning : FIRST ⟨*initial* letter of a word⟩ — **ini·tial·ly** \-'ish-(ə-)lē\ *adv*

²initial *n* **1** : a first letter of a name **2** : a large letter beginning a text or paragraph

³initial *vb* **ini·tialed** *or* **ini·tialled; ini·tial·ing** *or* **ini·tial·ling** \-'ish-(ə-)liŋ\ : to mark with initials or an initial ⟨*initial* a handkerchief⟩

¹ini·ti·ate \in-'ish-ē-,āt\ *vb* **-at·ed; -at·ing** **1** : to set going : BEGIN ⟨*initiate* a new policy⟩ **2** : to instruct in the basics of something : INTRODUCE ⟨*initiate* tourists into the local customs⟩ **3** : to admit into membership by special ceremonies [from Latin *initiatus,* past participle of *initiare* "to begin" — related to COMMENCE] — **ini·ti·a·tor** \-,āt-ər\ *n* — **ini·tia·to·ry** \-'ish-(ē-)ə-,tōr-ē, -,tor-\ *adj*

²ini·ti·ate \in-'ish-(ē-)ət\ *n* **1** : a person who is undergoing or has passed an initiation **2** : an expert in a special field

ini·ti·a·tion \in-,ish-ē-'ā-shən\ *n* **1** : the act of initiating : the process of being initiated : INTRODUCTION **2** : the ceremonies with which a person is made a member of a club or society

ini·tia·tive \in-'ish-ət-iv\ *n* **1** : a first step or movement ⟨take the *initiative* in becoming acquainted⟩ **2** : energy shown in initiating something : ENTERPRISE ⟨has ability but lacks *initiative*⟩

in·ject \in-'jekt\ *vb* **1 a** : to throw, drive, or force into something ⟨*inject* fuel into an engine⟩ **b** : to force a fluid into (a part of the body) especially for medical reasons **2** : to introduce as an additional element ⟨*injected* humor into her speech⟩ — **in·ject·able** \-'jek-tə-bəl\ *adj* — **in·jec·tor** \-'jek-tər\ *n*

in·jec·tion \in-'jek-shən\ *n* **1** : an act or instance of injecting **2** : something (as a medical drug) that is injected

in·ju·di·cious \,in-jü-'dish-əs\ *adj* : not judicious : UNWISE — **in·ju·di·cious·ly** *adv*

in·junc·tion \in-'jəŋ(k)-shən\ *n* : a court order commanding or forbidding the doing of some act ⟨an *injunction* against the strike⟩

in·jure \'in-jər\ *vb* **in·jured; in·jur·ing** \'inj-(ə-)riŋ\ **1** : to do an injustice to : WRONG **2** : to cause pain or harm to ⟨*injured* her arm⟩ ⟨*injured* his pride⟩ **3** : to cause to suffer damage or loss ⟨a tax that *injured* business⟩

in·ju·ri·ous \in-'jur-ē-əs\ *adj* : causing injury : HARMFUL — **in·ju·ri·ous·ly** *adv*

in·ju·ry \'inj-(ə-)rē\ *n, pl* **-ries** **1** : an act that damages or hurts : WRONG **2** : hurt, damage, or loss received

 syn INJURY, HARM, DAMAGE mean an act that causes loss or pain. INJURY suggests an act that results in the loss or lessening of one's rights, health, freedom, property, or success ⟨the accident caused both physical and emotional *injuries*⟩ HARM applies to any evil that injures and often suggests suffering, pain, or bother ⟨promised that no one would receive *harm* of any kind⟩ DAMAGE applies especially to an injury that results in a loss ⟨the pests did much *damage* to the crop⟩

in·jus·tice \(')in-'jəs-təs\ *n* **1** : violation of the rights of another : UNFAIRNESS **2** : an unjust act

¹ink \'iŋk\ *n* **1** : a usually liquid material for writing or printing **2** : the black protective secretion of a cephalopod

²ink *vb* **1** : to put ink on **2** : to write or draw in ink — **ink·er** *n*

ink·horn \'iŋk-,hȯ(ə)rn\ *n* : a portable container for ink

in·kling \'iŋ-kliŋ\ *n* : a vague notion : HINT ⟨didn't have an *inkling* of what it all meant⟩

ink·stand \'iŋk-,stand\ *n* : INKWELL

ink·well \'iŋ-,kwel\ *n* : a container for ink

inky \'iŋ-kē\ *adj* **ink·i·er; -est** **1** : consisting of or resembling ink ⟨*inky* blackness of the sea⟩ **2** : soiled with ink ⟨*inky* hands⟩

in·laid \'in-'lād\ *adj* **1** : set into a surface in a decorative design; *also* : decorated with an inlaid design **2** : having a design that goes all the way through ⟨*inlaid* linoleum⟩

¹in·land \'in-,land, -lənd\ *adj* : of or relating to the part of a country away from the coast or boundaries

²inland *n* : the part of a country away from the coast or boundaries : INTERIOR — **in·land·er** \-,lan-dər, -lən-\ *n*

³inland *adv* : into or toward the area away from a coast ⟨traveled *inland*⟩

in—law \'in-,lȯ\ *n* : a relative by marriage

¹in·lay \(')in-'lā\ *vb* **in·laid** \-'lād\; **in·lay·ing** : to set into a surface for decoration or strengthening — **in·lay·er** *n*

²in·lay \'in-,lā\ *n* **1** : inlaid work or material used in inlaying **2** : a tooth filling shaped to fit a cavity and then cemented into place

in·let \'in-,let, -lət\ *n* **1** : a small or narrow bay **2** : an opening for intake especially of fluids

in·mate \'in-,māt\ *n* : a member of a group living in a single residence; *esp* : a person kept in an institution (as an asylum or prison)

in·most \'in-,mōst\ *adj* : INNERMOST

inn \'in\ *n* : a public house that provides lodging and food for travelers : HOTEL

in·nards \'in-ərdz\ *n pl* **1** : the internal organs of a human being or animal; *esp* : VISCERA **2** : the internal parts of a structure or machine

in·nate \in-'āt, 'in-,āt\ *adj* **1** : existing in or belonging to an individual from birth ⟨an *innate* ability⟩ **2** : INHERENT ⟨*innate* defects in the plan⟩ [Middle English *innat* "belonging from birth", from Latin *innatus*, past participle of *innasci* "to be born in, be a native", from *in-* "in" and *nasci* "to be born" — related to NATIVE, NATURE] — **in·nate·ly** *adv* — **in·nate·ness** *n*

in·ner \'in-ər\ *adj* **1 a** : situated farther in ⟨*inner* room⟩ **b** : being near a center especially of influence ⟨an *inner* circle of advisors⟩ **2** : of or relating to the mind or spirit ⟨*inner* peace⟩ — **in·ner·ly** *adv*

inner city *n* : the usually older and more heavily populated central section of a city — **inner–city** *adj*

inner ear *n* : the part of the ear that is most important for hearing, is located in a cavity in the temporal bone, and contains the ends of the nerves used for hearing and for sensing one's position in space

inner light *n, often cap I & L* : a divine presence held (as in Quaker doctrine) to enlighten and guide the soul

in·ner·most \'in-ər-,mōst\ *adj* : farthest inward

inner tube *n* : TUBE 3

in·ning \'in-iŋ\ *n* : a baseball team's turn at bat; *also* : a division of a baseball game consisting of a turn at bat for each team

inn·keep·er \'in-,kē-pər\ *n* : the person who runs an inn

in·no·cence \'in-ə-sən(t)s\ *n* : the quality or state of being innocent

in·no·cent \'in-ə-sənt\ *adj* **1** : free from sin : PURE **2** : free from guilt or blame : GUILTLESS ⟨*innocent* of the crime⟩ **3** : free from harmful influence or effect : HARMLESS ⟨*innocent* fun⟩ **4** : NAIVE 1, UNSOPHISTICATED — **innocent** *n* — **in·no·cent·ly** *adv*

in·noc·u·ous \in-'äk-yə-wəs\ *adj* **1** : producing no injury : HARMLESS ⟨treatment to make sewage *innocuous*⟩ **2** : not likely to bother anyone : INOFFENSIVE ⟨made a few *innocuous* jokes⟩ — **in·noc·u·ous·ly** *adv* — **in·noc·u·ous·ness** *n*

in·no·vate \'in-ə-,vāt\ *vb* **-vat·ed; -vat·ing** : to introduce

something new : do something in a new way — **in·no·va·tive** \-,vāt-iv\ *adj* — **in·no·va·tor** \-,vāt-ər\ *n*

in·no·va·tion \,in-ə-'vā-shən\ *n* **1** : the introduction of something new **2** : a new idea, method, or device : NOVELTY

in·nu·en·do \,in-yə-'wen-dō\ *n, pl* **-dos** *or* **-does** : a slight suggestion or hint; *esp* : a suggestion that hurts someone's reputation

in·nu·mer·a·ble \in-'(y)üm-(ə-)rə-bəl\ *adj* : too many to be numbered : COUNTLESS — **in·nu·mer·a·bly** \-blē\ *adv*

in·oc·u·late \in-'äk-yə-,lāt\ *vb* **-lat·ed; -lat·ing** **1** : to introduce a microscopic living thing into ⟨beans *inoculated* with nitrogen-fixing bacteria⟩ **2** : to inject a serum, vaccine, or weakened germ into to protect against or treat a disease ⟨*inoculate* children against diphtheria⟩ — **in·oc·u·la·tor** \-,lāt-ər\ *n*

in·oc·u·la·tion \in-,äk-yə-'lā-shən\ *n* **1** : the act or an instance of inoculating **2** : material used in inoculating

in·of·fen·sive \,in-ə-'fen(t)-siv\ *adj* : not offensive or harmful — **in·of·fen·sive·ly** *adv*

in·op·er·a·ble \(')in-'äp-(ə-)rə-bəl\ *adj* **1** : not suitable for surgery **2** : not in working order

in·op·er·a·tive \(')in-'äp-(ə-)rət-iv, -'äp-ə-,rāt-\ *adj* : not functioning : producing no effect ⟨an *inoperative* law⟩

in·op·por·tune \(,)in-,äp-ər-'t(y)ün\ *adj* : INCONVENIENT ⟨an *inopportune* time⟩ — **in·op·por·tune·ly** *adv*

in order that *conj* : ³THAT 2

in·or·di·nate \in-'ȯrd-ᵊn-ət, -'ȯrd-nət\ *adj* : going beyond reasonable limits : IMMODERATE ⟨an *inordinate* curiosity⟩ — **in·or·di·nate·ly** *adv*

in·or·gan·ic \,in-,ȯr-'gan-ik\ *adj* **1** : being or composed of matter that does not come from plants or animals either alive or dead : MINERAL **2** : of or relating to a branch of chemistry concerned with substances that contain little or no carbon — **in·or·gan·i·cal·ly** \-i-k(ə-)lē\ *adv*

in·pa·tient \'in-,pā-shənt\ *n* : a hospital patient who receives lodging and food as well as treatment — compare OUTPATIENT

¹in·put \'in-,pút\ *n* **1** : power, energy, a signal, or information put into a machine or system **2** : a point at which an input is put in **3** : the act or process of putting in

²input *vb* **in·put·ted** *or* **input; in·put·ting** : to enter (as data) into a computer

in·quest \'in-,kwest\ *n* : a judicial or official investigation

in·quire *also* **en·quire** \in-'kwī(ə)r\ *vb* **in·quired; in·quir·ing** **1** : to ask about ⟨*inquired* the way to the station⟩ **2** : to make an investigation **3** : to ask a question ⟨*inquired* about the weather⟩ — **in·quir·er** *n* — **in·quir·ing·ly** \-'kwī-riŋ-lē\ *adv*

in·qui·ry *also* **en·qui·ry** \in-'kwī(ə)r-ē, 'in-,kwī(ə)r-; 'in-kwə-rē, 'iŋ-; 'in-,kwi(ə)r-ē\ *n, pl* **-ries** **1 a** : the act of inquiring ⟨learn by *inquiry*⟩ **b** : a request for information ⟨make *inquiries* at the station⟩ **2** : a search for truth or knowledge : INVESTIGATION

in·qui·si·tion \,in-kwə-'zish-ən\ *n* **1** : the act of inquiring **2** : INQUEST **3 a** *cap* : a former Roman Catholic court for the discovery and punishment of heresy **b** : an investigation conducted with little concern for individual rights **c** : a severe questioning — **in·qui·si·tion·al** \-'zish-nəl, -ən-ᵊl\ *adj*

in·quis·i·tive \in-'kwiz-ət-iv\ *adj* **1** : tending to inquire or investigate **2** : asking many questions; *esp* : too curious about other people's affairs **syn** see CURIOUS — **in·quis·i·tive·ly** *adv* — **in·quis·i·tive·ness** *n*

in·quis·i·tor \in-'kwiz-ət-ər\ *n* : one who conducts an inquisition — **in·quis·i·to·ri·al** \-,kwiz-ə-'tȯr-ē-əl, -'tȯr-\ *adj*

\ə\ abut	\aú\ out	\i\ tip	\ȯ\ saw	\ú\ foot
\ər\ further	\ch\ chin	\ī\ life	\ȯi\ coin	\y\ yet
\a\ mat	\e\ pet	\j\ job	\th\ thin	\yü\ few
\ā\ take	\ē\ easy	\ŋ\ sing	\t̲h̲\ this	\yú\ cure
\ä\ cot, cart	\g\ go	\ō\ bone	\ü\ food	\zh\ vision

in·road \'in-ˌrōd\ *n* **1** : a sudden hostile invasion : RAID **2** : an important advance often at the expense of someone or something ⟨making *inroads* against the competition⟩

in·rush \'in-ˌrəsh\ *n* : a crowding or flooding in ⟨the discovery of gold brought an *inrush* of miners⟩

in·sane \(')in-'sān\ *adj* **1** : having or showing a very abnormal and very sick state of mind : not sane ⟨an *insane* person⟩ ⟨an *insane* look⟩ **2** : used by or for the insane ⟨an *insane* ward in a hospital⟩ **3** : extremely foolish or unreasonable ⟨an *insane* attempt⟩ — **in·sane·ly** *adv*

in·san·i·tary \(')in-'san-ə-ˌter-ē\ *adj* : so unclean as to endanger health : UNHEALTHY

in·san·i·ty \in-'san-ət-ē\ *n, pl* **-ties** **1** : the condition of being insane especially when serious enough to keep one from being convicted of a crime or from performing duties required by law **2** : a mental illness or disorder **3 a** : extreme foolishness or unreasonableness **b** : senseless conduct

in·sa·tia·ble \(')in-'sā-shə-bəl\ *adj* : impossible to satisfy ⟨*insatiable* thirst⟩ ⟨an *insatiable* desire for knowledge⟩ — **in·sa·tia·bly** \-blē\ *adv*

in·scribe \in-'skrīb\ *vb* **in·scribed; in·scrib·ing** **1 a** : to write, engrave, or print as a lasting record ⟨*inscribe* a name on a monument⟩ **b** : to enter on a list : ENROLL **2** : to write, engrave, or print something on or in ⟨*inscribe* a book⟩ **3** : to stamp deeply : IMPRESS ⟨a scene *inscribed* on my memory⟩ **4** : to dedicate to someone ⟨*inscribe* a poem⟩ **5** : to draw within a figure so as to touch in as many places as possible — **in·scrib·er** *n*

in·scrip·tion \in-'skrip-shən\ *n* : something that is inscribed

in·scru·ta·ble \in-'skrüt-ə-bəl\ *adj* : not easily understood : MYSTERIOUS ⟨an *inscrutable* expression⟩ — **in·scru·ta·bly** \-blē\ *adv*

in·seam \'in-ˌsēm\ *n* : the seam on the inside of the leg of a pair of pants; *also* : the length of this seam

in·sect \'in-ˌsekt\ *n* **1** : any of numerous small invertebrate animals (as spiders or centipedes) that are more or less obviously made up of segments **2** : any of a class of arthropods (as butterflies, true bugs, two-winged flies, bees, and grasshoppers) with the body clearly divided into a head, thorax, and abdomen, with three pairs of jointed legs, and usually with one or two pairs of wings

Word History The bodies of insects have segments, or divisions. Thus they seem to have a series of notches cut into them. This appearance led the Greek philosopher Aristotle to give insects the name *entomon* "a thing cut into". *Entomon* comes from the prefix *en-* "in", combined with the verb *temnein* "to cut". Later, when the Romans wanted a word for this kind of creature, they did not simply borrow the Greek word. Instead they translated it into the Latin word *insectum*, from the verb *insecare* "to cut into". *Insectum* was borrowed into English as *insect*. [from Latin *insectum* "insect", derived from *insecare* "to cut into", from *in-* "in" and *secare* "to cut" — related to DISSECT, SECTION]

in·sec·ti·cide \in-'sek-tə-ˌsīd\ *n* : a chemical used to kill insects — **in·sec·ti·cid·al** \(ˌ)in-ˌsek-tə-'sīd-ᵊl\ *adj*

in·sec·ti·vore \in-'sek-tə-ˌvō(ə)r, -ˌvȯ(ə)r\ *n* **1** : any of an order of mammals (as the moles, shrews, and hedgehogs) that are mostly small, insect-eating, and active at night **2** : an insect-eating plant or animal

in·sec·tiv·o·rous \ˌin-ˌsek-'tiv-(ə-)rəs\ *adj* : depending on insects as food

in·se·cure \ˌin(t)-si-'kyu̇(ə)r\ *adj* **1** : not confident or sure **2** : not well protected : not safe ⟨*insecure* property⟩ **3** : not firmly fastened : LOOSE ⟨an *insecure* hinge⟩ **4** : lacking self-assurance ⟨*insecure* people⟩ — **in·se·cure·ly** *adv* — **in·se·cu·ri·ty** \-'kyu̇r-ət-ē\ *n*

in·sem·i·nate \in-'sem-ə-ˌnāt\ *vb* **-nat·ed; -nat·ing** : to introduce semen into the genital tract of (a female) — **in·sem·i·na·tion** \-ˌsem-ə-'nā-shən\ *n*

in·sen·sate \(')in-'sen-ˌsāt\ *adj* **1** : lacking awareness or sensation : INANIMATE **2** : lacking sense or understanding **3** : lacking humane feelings : BRUTAL — **in·sen·sate·ly** *adv*

in·sen·si·bil·i·ty \(ˌ)in-ˌsen(t)-sə-'bil-ət-ē\ *n* : the quality or state of being insensible

in·sen·si·ble \(')in-'sen(t)-sə-bəl\ *adj* **1** : IMPERCEPTIBLE 1 ⟨*insensible* motion⟩ **2 a** : INANIMATE 1 **b** : ¹UNCONSCIOUS 2 **c** : not able to feel or be aware of using a sense or senses ⟨*insensible* to pain⟩ **3** : not aware of or caring about something ⟨*insensible* to fear⟩ ⟨*insensible* of their danger⟩ — **in·sen·si·bly** \-blē\ *adv*

in·sen·si·tive \(')in-'sen(t)-sət-iv, -'sen(t)-stiv\ *adj* : not sensitive; *esp* : lacking feeling — **in·sen·si·tive·ly** *adv* — **in·sen·si·tiv·i·ty** \(ˌ)in-ˌsen(t)-sə-'tiv-ət-ē\ *n*

in·sep·a·ra·ble \(')in-'sep-(ə-)rə-bəl\ *adj* : impossible to separate ⟨*inseparable* friends⟩ — **in·sep·a·ra·bil·i·ty** \(ˌ)in-ˌsep-(ə-)rə-'bil-ət-ē\ *n* — **in·sep·a·ra·bly** \(')in-'sep-(ə-)rə-blē\ *adv*

¹in·sert \in-'sərt\ *vb* **1** : to put or place in ⟨*inserted* the key in the lock⟩ ⟨*insert* a word in a sentence⟩ **2** : to set in and make fast — **in·sert·er** *n*

²in·sert \'in-ˌsərt\ *n* : something that is or is meant to be inserted; *esp* : printed material inserted (as in a newspaper)

in·ser·tion \in-'sər-shən\ *n* **1** : the act or process of inserting **2 a** : something inserted; *esp* : the part of a muscle that is attached to a part to be moved **b** : the mode or place of attachment of an organ or part

¹in·set \'in-ˌset\ *n* : something that is inset: as **a** : a small map or picture set within a larger one **b** : a piece of cloth set into a garment for decoration

²in·set \'in-ˌset, in-'set\ *vb* **inset** *or* **in·set·ted; in·set·ting** : ¹INSERT 2

¹in·shore \'in-'shō(ə)r, -'shȯ(ə)r\ *adj* **1** : situated or carried on near shore ⟨*inshore* fishing⟩ **2** : moving toward shore ⟨an *inshore* wind⟩

²inshore *adv* : to or toward shore

¹in·side \(')in-'sīd, 'in-ˌsīd\ *n* **1** : an inner side or surface **2 a** : an interior or internal part **b** : inward nature, thoughts, or feeling **c** : ENTRAILS — usually used in pl.

²inside *adj* **1** : of, relating to, or being on or near the inside ⟨an *inside* wall⟩ **2** : relating or known to a special group of people ⟨*inside* information⟩

³inside *prep* **1 a** : in or into the interior of ⟨they are *inside* the house⟩ **b** : on the inner side of ⟨put the dot *inside* the curve⟩ **2** : before the end of : WITHIN ⟨*inside* an hour⟩

⁴inside *adv* **1** : on the inner side ⟨cleaned my car *inside* and out⟩ **2** : in or into the interior ⟨went *inside*⟩

inside of *prep* : ³INSIDE

inside out *adv* : in such a way that the inner surface becomes the outer

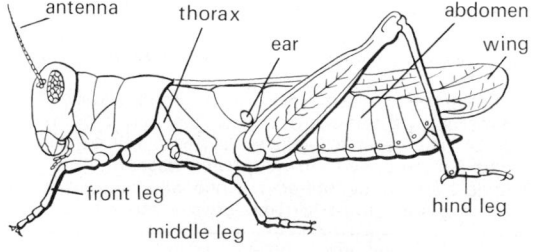

antenna   thorax   abdomen   ear   wing   front leg   hind leg   middle leg

insect 2

in·sid·er \(')in-'sīd-ər\ *n* : a person who is a member of a special group or organization

in·sid·i·ous \in-'sid-ē-əs\ *adj* **1 a** : awaiting a chance to trap : TREACHEROUS **b** : harmful but attractive **2** : having a more harmful effect than is apparent ⟨an *insidious* disease⟩ — **in·sid·i·ous·ly** *adv* — **in·sid·i·ous·ness** *n*

in·sight \'in-,sīt\ *n* : the power or act of seeing into or understanding a situation

in·sig·nia \in-'sig-nē-ə\ *or* **in·sig·ne** \-nē\ *n, pl* **-nia** *or* **-ni·as** : an emblem of a special authority, office, or honor : BADGE

insignia

in·sig·nif·i·cance \,in(t)-sig-'nif-i-kən(t)s\ *n* : the quality or state of being insignificant

in·sig·nif·i·cant \,in(t)-sig-'nif-i-kənt\ *adj* : not significant : UNIMPORTANT — **in·sig·nif·i·cant·ly** *adv*

in·sin·cere \,in(t)-sin-'si(ə)r\ *adj* : not sincere : HYPOCRITICAL — **in·sin·cere·ly** *adv* — **in·sin·cer·i·ty** \-'ser-ət-ē *also* -'sir-\ *n*

in·sin·u·ate \in-'sin-yə-,wāt\ *vb* **-at·ed; -at·ing** **1** : to introduce in a gradual, secret, or clever way ⟨*insinuated* herself into his confidence⟩ **2** : ²HINT, IMPLY ⟨*insinuated* that I had cheated⟩ — **in·sin·u·a·tion** \(,)in-,sin-yə-'wā-shən\ *n* — **in·sin·u·a·tor** \in-'sin-yə-,wāt-ər\ *n*

in·sip·id \in-'sip-əd\ *adj* **1** : lacking taste or flavor : TASTELESS **2** : not interesting or exciting : DULL, FLAT ⟨*insipid* fiction⟩ [from French *insipide* and Latin *insipidus,* both meaning "insipid, tasteless", from earlier Latin *in-* "not" and *sipidus* "having good flavor", from *sapere* "to have flavor, be wise" — related to ¹SAGE, SAVANT] — **in·si·pid·i·ty** \,in(t)-sə-'pid-ət-ē\ *n* — **in·sip·id·ly** \in-'sip-əd-lē\ *adv*

in·sist \in-'sist\ *vb* **1** : to place special stress or great importance ⟨*insists* on punctuality⟩ **2** : to make a demand : request urgently ⟨*insisted* that I come⟩

in·sis·tence \in-'sis-tən(t)s\ *n* **1** : the act or an instance of insisting **2** : the quality or state of being insistent

in·sis·tent \in-'sis-tənt\ *adj* : demanding attention : PERSISTENT — **in·sis·tent·ly** *adv*

in si·tu \(')in-'sī-t(y)ü, -'si-\ *adv or adj* : in the natural or original position ⟨the cancer cells remained *in situ*⟩ [Latin, "in position"]

in·so·far as \,in(t)-sə-,fär-əz\ *conj* : to the extent or degree that ⟨helped us *insofar as* she was able⟩

in·so·la·tion \,in(t)-(,)sō-'lā-shən\ *n* : solar radiation that has been received (as by the earth)

in·sole \'in-,sōl\ *n* **1** : an inside sole of a shoe **2** : a loose thin strip placed inside a shoe for warmth or comfort

in·so·lence \'in(t)-s(ə-)lən(t)s\ *n* **1** : the quality or state of being insolent **2** : an instance of insolent conduct or treatment

in·so·lent \'in(t)-s(ə-)lənt\ *adj* **1** : disrespectful or rude in speech or conduct ⟨an *insolent* child⟩ **2** : showing boldness or rudeness ⟨an *insolent* act⟩ — **in·so·lent·ly** *adv*

in·sol·u·bil·i·ty \(,)in-,säl-yə-'bil-ət-ē\ *n* : the quality or state of being insoluble

in·sol·u·ble \(')in-'säl-yə-bəl\ *adj* **1** : impossible to solve ⟨an *insoluble* problem⟩ **2** : impossible or difficult to dissolve ⟨a substance *insoluble* in water⟩

in·sol·ven·cy \(')in-'säl-vən-sē\ *n, pl* **-cies** : the quality or state of being insolvent

in·sol·vent \(')in-'säl-vənt\ *adj* : not having or providing enough money to pay debts ⟨an *insolvent* company⟩ ⟨an *insolvent* estate⟩

in·som·nia \in-'säm-nē-ə\ *n* : prolonged inability to sleep : SLEEPLESSNESS

in·som·ni·ac \in-'säm-nē-,ak\ *n* : a person who has insomnia

in·sou·ci·ance \in-'sü-sē-ən(t)s\ *n* : a lighthearted lack of concern — **in·sou·ci·ant** \-ənt\ *adj*

in·spect \in-'spekt\ *vb* **1** : to examine closely (as for judging quality or condition) ⟨*inspect* meat⟩ **2** : to view and examine officially ⟨*inspect* the troops⟩

in·spec·tion \in-'spek-shən\ *n* : the act or an instance of inspecting

in·spec·tor \in-'spek-tər\ *n* **1** : a person who makes inspections ⟨meat *inspector*⟩ **2** : a police officer ranking just below a superintendent or deputy superintendent — **in·spec·tor·ship** \-,ship\ *n*

in·spi·ra·tion \,in(t)-spə-'rā-shən\ *n* **1** : the drawing of air into the lungs in breathing **2 a** : the act or power of moving the mind or the emotions ⟨the *inspiration* of music⟩ **b** : the quality or state of being inspired ⟨the artist's *inspiration* came from many sources⟩ **c** : something that is inspired ⟨a scheme that was an *inspiration*⟩ **d** : someone or something that inspires ⟨his wife was his greatest *inspiration*⟩ — **in·spi·ra·tion·al** \-shnəl, -shən-ᵊl\ *adj* — **in·spi·ra·tion·al·ly** \-ē\ *adv*

in·spire \in-'spī(ə)r\ *vb* **in·spired; in·spir·ing** **1** : to move or guide by divine influence ⟨prophets *inspired* by God⟩ **2 a** : to give spirit to : make spirited ⟨*inspired* by his parents⟩ **b** : to cause to have a particular thought or feeling ⟨a childhood that *inspired* her with a desire for education⟩ **c** : to cause a feeling of : AROUSE ⟨*inspires* confidence in her followers⟩ **3** : INHALE **4** : BRING ABOUT ⟨studies that *inspired* several inventions⟩ — **in·spir·er** *n*

in·sta·bil·i·ty \,in(t)-stə-'bil-ət-ē\ *n* : the quality or state of being unstable

in·stall *or* **in·stal** \in-'stöl\ *vb* **in·stalled; in·stall·ing** **1** : to place in an office or rank ⟨*installed* the new president⟩ **2** : to put in an indicated place or condition ⟨*installed* himself in the best chair⟩ **3** : to set up for use or service ⟨*install* a TV set⟩ — **in·stall·er** *n*

in·stal·la·tion \,in(t)-stə-'lā-shən\ *n* **1** : the act of installing : the state of being installed **2** : something installed for use **3** : a military base

¹in·stall·ment *or* **in·stal·ment** \in-'stöl-mənt\ *n* : INSTALLATION 1

²installment *also* **instalment** *n* **1** : one of the parts into which a debt is divided when payment is made little by little over a period of time **2** : one of several parts (as of a publication) presented over a period of time — **installment** *adj*

installment plan *n* : a system of paying for goods or services in installments

¹in·stance \'in(t)-stən(t)s\ *n* **1** : ¹REQUEST 1 ⟨entered the writing contest at the *instance* of her teacher⟩ **2** : EXAMPLE 1 ⟨an *instance* of rare courage⟩ **3** : a particular point or step in an action or process ⟨in the first *instance*⟩ — **for instance** : as an example

²instance *vb* **in·stanced; in·stanc·ing** : to mention as an example : CITE

¹in·stant \'in(t)-stənt\ *n* : a very small space of time : MOMENT

²instant *adj* **1** : PRESSING, URGENT ⟨in *instant* need⟩ **2** : happening or done at once ⟨an *instant* response⟩ **3** : partially prepared by the manufacturer to make final preparation easy ⟨*instant* cake mix⟩; *esp* : made to dissolve quickly in water ⟨*instant* coffee⟩

in·stan·ta·neous \,in(t)-stən-'tā-nē-əs, -nyəs\ *adj* **1** : happening in an instant **2** : done without delay — **in·stan·ta·neous·ly** *adv* — **in·stan·ta·neous·ness** *n*

in·stan·ter \in-'stant-ər\ *adv* : IMMEDIATELY 2

in·stant·ly \'in(t)-stənt-lē\ *adv* : without delay : IMMEDIATELY

\ə\ abut	\au̇\ **out**	\i\ **tip**	\ȯ\ **saw**	\u̇\ **foot**
\ər\ **further**	\ch\ **chin**	\ī\ **life**	\ȯi\ **coin**	\y\ **yet**
\a\ **mat**	\e\ **pet**	\j\ **job**	\th\ **thin**	\yü\ **few**
\ā\ **take**	\ē\ **easy**	\ŋ\ **sing**	\th\ **this**	\yu̇\ **cure**
\ä\ **cot, cart**	\g\ **go**	\ō\ **bone**	\ü\ **food**	\zh\ **vision**

in·state \in-'stāt\ *vb* **in·stat·ed; in·stat·ing** : to install in a rank or office

in·stead \in-'sted\ *adv* : as a substitute ⟨was going to write but called *instead*⟩

instead of \in-,sted-ə(v), -,stid-\ *prep* : as a substitute for : rather than ⟨had milk *instead of* juice⟩

in·step \'in-,step\ *n* **1** : the arched middle part of the human foot **2** : the part of a shoe or stocking over the instep

instep 1

in·sti·gate \'in(t)-stə-,gāt\ *vb* **-gat·ed; -gat·ing** : INCITE, PROVOKE — **in·sti·ga·tion** \,in(t)-stə-'gā-shən\ *n* — **in·sti·ga·tor** \'in(t)-stə-,gāt-ər\ *n*

in·still *also* **in·stil** \in-'stil\ *vb* **in·stilled; in·still·ing** : to gradually cause to feel or have ⟨*instill* a love of music⟩ — **in·stil·la·tion** \,in(t)-stə-'lā-shən\ *n*

in·stinct \'in-,stiŋ(k)t\ *n* **1** : a natural ability or desire **2 a** : an act or course of action in response to a stimulus that is usually inherited and is automatic rather than learned **b** : behavior that is based on automatic actions

in·stinc·tive \in-'stiŋ(k)-tiv\ *adj* **1** : of, relating to, or being instinct **2** : resulting from or caused by instinct — **in·stinc·tive·ly** *adv*

in·stinc·tu·al \in-'stiŋ(k)-chə(-wə)l, -'stiŋ(k)sh-wəl\ *adj* : of, relating to, or based on instinct : INSTINCTIVE ⟨*instinctual* behavior⟩

¹in·sti·tute \'in(t)-stə-,t(y)üt\ *vb* **-tut·ed; -tut·ing** **1** : ESTABLISH 3a, FOUND ⟨*institute* a society⟩ **2** : to set going : BEGIN ⟨*institute* an investigation⟩ — **in·sti·tut·er** *or* **in·sti·tu·tor** \-,t(y)üt-ər\ *n*

²institute *n* **1** : something that is instituted **2 a** : an organization for the support of a cause : ASSOCIATION ⟨an *institute* for mental health⟩ **b** : a place for study usually in a special field ⟨an art *institute*⟩

in·sti·tu·tion \,in(t)-stə-'t(y)ü-shən\ *n* **1** : the act of instituting : ESTABLISHMENT **2** : an established custom, practice, or law ⟨family visits are a Thanksgiving *institution*⟩ **3 a** : an established society or organization; *esp* : a public one ⟨educational *institutions*⟩ ⟨a financial *institution*⟩ **b** : the building used by such an organization — **in·sti·tu·tion·al** \-shnəl, -shən-ᵊl\ *adj* — **in·sti·tu·tion·al·ly** \-ē\ *adv*

in·sti·tu·tion·al·ize \,in(t)-stə-'t(y)ü-shnə-,līz, -shən-ᵊl-,īz\ *vb* **-ized; -iz·ing** **1** : to make into or treat like an institution ⟨*institutionalized* housing⟩ **2** : to put into an institution

in·struct \in-'strəkt\ *vb* **1** : to give knowledge to : TEACH **2** : to give information to : INFORM **3** : to give directions or commands to **syn** see COMMAND

in·struc·tion \in-'strək-shən\ *n* **1 a** : PRECEPT **b** : ²COMMAND 2, ORDER **c** *pl* : an outline or set of procedures to be followed : DIRECTIONS **d** : a code that tells a computer to perform a particular operation **2** : the action or practice of an instructor or teacher — **in·struc·tion·al** \-shnəl, -shən-ᵊl\ *adj*

in·struc·tive \in-'strək-tiv\ *adj* : giving knowledge : helping to instruct or inform ⟨an *instructive* experience⟩ — **in·struc·tive·ly** *adv*

in·struc·tor \in-'strək-tər\ *n* : one that instructs : TEACHER — **in·struc·tor·ship** \-,ship\ *n*

in·stru·ment \'in(t)-strə-mənt\ *n* **1** : a device used to produce music **2** : a way of getting something done **3** : a tool or implement designed especially for precision work ⟨a surgical *instrument*⟩ **4** : an official legal document (as a deed, bond, or agreement) **5 a** : a measuring device for finding out the present value of a quantity under observa-

tion **b** : an electrical or mechanical device used in navigating an airplane; *esp* : such a device used as the only way of navigating **syn** see IMPLEMENT

in·stru·men·tal \,in(t)-strə-'ment-ᵊl\ *adj* **1** : acting as an instrument or means ⟨was *instrumental* in organizing the club⟩ **2** : relating to, composed for, or performed on a musical instrument **3** : of, relating to, or done with an instrument ⟨*instrumental* error⟩ — **in·stru·men·tal·ly** \-ᵊl-ē\ *adv*

in·stru·men·tal·ist \,in(t)-strə-'ment-ᵊl-əst\ *n* : a person who plays a musical instrument

in·stru·men·tal·i·ty \,in(t)-strə-mən-'tal-ət-ē, -,men-\ *n, pl* **-ties** **1** : the quality or state of being instrumental **2** : AGENCY 1

in·stru·men·ta·tion \,in(t)-strə-mən-'tā-shən, -,men-\ *n* **1** : the arrangement or composition of music for instruments **2** : instruments for a particular purpose ⟨the *instrumentation* of an aircraft⟩

instrument panel *n* : DASHBOARD 2

in·sub·or·di·nate \,in(t)-sə-'bórd-ᵊn-ət, -'bórd-nət\ *adj* : not obeying authority : DISOBEDIENT — **in·sub·or·di·nate·ly** *adv* — **in·sub·or·di·na·tion** \-,bórd-ᵊn-'ā-shən\ *n*

in·sub·stan·tial \,in(t)-səb-'stan-chəl\ *adj* **1** : not real : IMAGINARY **2** : not firm or solid — **in·sub·stan·ti·al·i·ty** \-,stan-chē-'al-ət-ē\ *n*

in·suf·fer·able \(')in-'səf-(ə)rə-bəl\ *adj* : impossible to endure : INTOLERABLE ⟨*insufferable* boredom⟩ — **in·suf·fer·able·ness** *n* — **in·suf·fer·ably** \-blē\ *adv*

in·suf·fi·cien·cy \,in(t)-sə-'fish-ən-sē\ *n, pl* **-cies** **1** : the quality or state of being insufficient **2** : a lack of something : DEFICIENCY

in·suf·fi·cient \,in(t)-sə-'fish-ənt\ *adj* : not sufficient : INADEQUATE — **in·suf·fi·cient·ly** *adv*

in·su·lar \'in(t)s-(y)ə-lər, 'in-shə-lər\ *adj* **1** : of, relating to, or forming an island **2** : being isolated or detached ⟨an *insular* building⟩ **3** : not open to new or different ideas : NARROW ⟨an *insular* viewpoint⟩ — **in·su·lar·i·ty** \,in(t)s-(y)ə-'lar-ət-ē, ,in-shə-'lar-\ *n*

in·su·late \'in(t)-sə-,lāt\ *vb* **-lat·ed; -lat·ing** : to place in a detached situation : ISOLATE; *esp* : to separate from conducting bodies by means of nonconductors so as to prevent transfer of electricity, heat, or sound [from Latin *insula* "island" — related to ISLE, ISOLATE, PENINSULA]

in·su·la·tion \,in(t)-sə-'lā-shən\ *n* **1** : the act of insulating : the state of being insulated **2** : material used in insulating

in·su·la·tor \'in(t)-sə-,lāt-ər\ *n* : one that insulates; *esp* : a material that is a poor conductor of heat or electricity or a device made of such material

in·su·lin \'in(t)-s(ə-)lən\ *n* : a hormone that is produced by the pancreas and is necessary for the normal use of sugar by the body

insulin shock *n* : a condition of too little blood sugar associated with too much insulin in the system and marked by coma

¹in·sult \in-'səlt\ *vb* : to treat or speak to with disrespect or scorn — **in·sult·er** *n*

Word History The phrase "to jump on" is used informally today to mean "to criticize or insult severely". The origin of the word *insult* also suggests the idea of jumping. *Insult* comes from the Latin verb *insultare*, literally meaning "to leap upon". It is made up of the prefix *in-*, meaning "on, upon", and a form of the verb *salire* "to leap". One of the first meanings of *insult* in English was "to make a military attack". That sense became obsolete, and *insult* now means to attack or "jump on" someone only with words of scorn or disrespect rather than with weapons. [from early French *insulter* "to insult", from Latin *insultare* "insult, attack", literally "to leap upon", derived from *in-* "on, upon" and *salire* "to leap, spring" — related to ASSAULT, RESILIENT]

²**in·sult** \'in-ˌsəlt\ *n* : an act or expression showing disrespect or scorn

in·su·per·a·ble \(')in-'sü-p(ə-)rə-bəl\ *adj* : impossible to overcome ⟨*insuperable* difficulties⟩ — **in·su·per·a·bly** \-blē\ *adv*

in·sup·port·a·ble \ˌin(t)-sə-'pōrt-ə-bəl, -'pòrt-\ *adj* : impossible to support; *esp* : too bad to be endured

in·sur·a·ble \in-'shür-ə-bəl\ *adj* : capable of being insured — **in·sur·a·bil·i·ty** \-ˌshür-ə-'bil-ət-ē\ *n*

in·sur·ance \in-'shür-ən(t)s\ *n* **1** : the act of insuring : the state of being insured **2 a** : the business of insuring persons or property **b** : a contract by which someone guarantees for a fee to pay someone else for the value of property if it is lost or damaged (as through theft or fire) or to pay usually a specified amount for injury or death **c** : the amount for which something is insured

in·sure \in-'shü(ə)r\ *vb* **in·sured; in·sur·ing 1** : to give or get insurance on or for **2** : to make certain : ENSURE — **in·sur·er** \in-'shür-ər\ *n*

in·sur·gen·cy \in-'sər-jən-sē\ *n, pl* **-cies** : REBELLION 2

¹**in·sur·gent** \in-'sər-jənt\ *n* : a person who revolts : REBEL

²**insurgent** *adj* : REBELLIOUS 1

in·sur·mount·able \ˌin(t)-sər-'maůnt-ə-bəl\ *adj* : incapable of being surmounted

in·sur·rec·tion \ˌin(t)-sə-'rek-shən\ *n* : REBELLION 2 — **in·sur·rec·tion·ary** \-shə-ˌner-ē\ *adj or n* — **in·sur·rec·tion·ist** \-sh(ə-)nəst\ *n*

in·tact \in-'takt\ *adj* : untouched especially by anything that harms : not damaged or lessened

in·ta·glio \in-'tal-yō, -'tag-lē-ˌō\ *n, pl* **-glios** : an engraving cut deeply into the surface of a hard material (as stone)

in·take \'in-ˌtāk\ *n* **1** : a place where liquid or air is taken into something (as a pump) **2** : the act of taking in **3** : something taken in ⟨food *intake*⟩

in·tan·gi·ble \(')in-'tan-jə-bəl\ *adj* **1** : impossible to touch ⟨light is *intangible*⟩ **2** : impossible to think of as matter or substance ⟨goodwill is an *intangible* asset⟩ — **in·tan·gi·bil·i·ty** \(ˌ)in-ˌtan-jə-'bil-ət-ē\ *n* — **intangible** *n* — **in·tan·gi·ble·ness** \(')in-'tan-jə-bəl-nəs\ *n* — **in·tan·gi·bly** \-blē\ *adv*

in·te·ger \'int-i-jər\ *n* : a number that is a natural number (as 1, 2, or 3), the negative of a natural number, or 0 — called also *whole number*

in·te·gral \'int-i-grəl *(usually so in mathematics)*; in-'teg-rəl *also* -'tēg-\ *adj* **1** : needed for completeness **2** : of or relating to an integer **3** : composed of integral parts **4** : ENTIRE 1, COMPLETE, WHOLE — **in·te·gral·ly** \'int-i-grə-lē; in-'teg-rə- *also* -'tēg-\ *adv*

in·te·grate \'int-ə-ˌgrāt\ *vb* **-grat·ed; -grat·ing 1** : to form or unite into a whole **2** : to form or unite into a larger unit; *esp* : to end the segregation of and bring into common and equal membership in society **3** : DESEGREGATE ⟨*integrate* school districts⟩ **4** : to become integrated

integrated circuit *n* : a tiny group of electronic devices and their connections that is produced in or on a small slice of material (as silicon)

in·te·gra·tion \ˌint-ə-'grā-shən\ *n* : the act, the process, or an instance of integrating; *esp* : acceptance as equals into society of persons from different races

in·te·gra·tion·ist \ˌint-ə-'grā-sh(ə-)nəst\ *n* : a person who favors integration

in·teg·ri·ty \in-'teg-rət-ē\ *n* **1** : the condition of being free from damage or defect **2** : total honesty and sincerity **3** : the quality or state of being complete or undivided

in·teg·u·ment \in-'teg-yə-mənt\ *n* : something that covers or encloses; *esp* : an outer enclosing layer (as a skin, membrane, or husk) of a living thing or one of its parts — **in·teg·u·men·ta·ry** \(ˌ)in-ˌteg-yə-'ment-ə-rē, -'men-trē\ *adj*

in·tel·lect \'int-ᵊl-ˌekt\ *n* **1 a** : the power of knowing **b** : the capacity for thought especially when highly developed **2** : a person of notable intellect

¹**in·tel·lec·tu·al** \ˌint-ᵊl-'ek-ch(ə-w)əl\ *adj* **1** : relating to the intellect or understanding **2** : having intellect to a high degree : engaged in or given to learning and thinking ⟨*intellectual* person⟩ **3** : requiring study and thought ⟨*intellectual* work⟩ — **in·tel·lec·tu·al·i·ty** \-ˌek-chə-'wal-ət-ē\ *n* — **in·tel·lec·tu·al·ly** \-'ek-chə-(wə-)lē\ *adv*

²**intellectual** *n* : an intellectual person

in·tel·li·gence \in-'tel-ə-jən(t)s\ *n* **1** : the ability to learn and understand or to deal with problems : REASON **2 a** : NEWS 1 **b** : information concerning an enemy or possible enemy; *also* : an agency engaged in obtaining such information

intelligence quotient *n* : a number that is often used as a measure of a person's intelligence and is found by dividing the mental age of the person as given by a score on a special test by the age in years since birth and multiplying by 100

intelligence test *n* : a test designed to measure a person's intelligence compared to others

in·tel·li·gent \in-'tel-ə-jənt\ *adj* **1** : having or showing intelligence or intellect ⟨an *intelligent* person⟩ ⟨an *intelligent* answer⟩ **2** : able to perform computing tasks ⟨an *intelligent* terminal⟩ — **in·tel·li·gent·ly** *adv*

  syn INTELLIGENT, CLEVER, ALERT, QUICK-WITTED mean having a sharp mind. INTELLIGENT stresses the ability to deal with new situations and solve problems ⟨*intelligent* people are needed for police work⟩ CLEVER suggests a natural ability to find solutions but it may also suggest shallow thinking ⟨*clever* enough to get by without studying⟩ ALERT stresses quickness in seeing and understanding something ⟨an *alert* student saw that there was a catch to the question⟩ QUICK-WITTED suggests coming up with quick replies in conversation or finding solutions in emergencies ⟨a *quick-witted* debater⟩ ⟨a *quick-witted* baby-sitter put out the fire⟩

in·tel·li·gen·tsia \in-ˌtel-ə-'jen(t)-sē-ə, -'gen(t)-\ *n* : intellectuals as a group : educated people

in·tel·li·gi·ble \in-'tel-ə-jə-bəl\ *adj* : able to be understood — **in·tel·li·gi·bil·i·ty** \-ˌtel-ə-jə-'bil-ət-ē\ *n* — **in·tel·li·gi·ble·ness** \-'tel-ə-jə-bəl-nəs\ *n* — **in·tel·li·gi·bly** \-blē\ *adv*

in·tem·per·ance \(')in-'tem-p(ə-)rən(t)s\ *n* : lack of moderation or self-restraint; *esp* : excessive use of alcoholic beverages

in·tem·per·ate \(ˌ)in-'tem-p(ə-)rət\ *adj* **1** : not moderate or mild : SEVERE ⟨*intemperate* weather⟩ **2** : lacking or showing lack of restraint ⟨*intemperate* language⟩ **3** : being in the habit of drinking alcoholic beverages too much — **in·tem·per·ate·ly** *adv* — **in·tem·per·ate·ness** *n*

in·tend \in-'tend\ *vb* : to have in mind as a purpose or aim

¹**in·tend·ed** \in-'ten-dəd\ *adj* **1** : expected to be such in the future ⟨your *intended* career⟩ **2** : INTENTIONAL ⟨an *intended* insult⟩

²**intended** *n* : a person engaged to be married

in·tense \in-'ten(t)s\ *adj* **1** : existing in an extreme degree ⟨an *intense* light⟩ **2** : very earnest or intent ⟨*intense* study⟩ **3** : feeling deeply ⟨an *intense* person⟩ — **in·tense·ly** *adv* — **in·tense·ness** *n*

in·ten·si·fy \in-'ten(t)s-ə-ˌfī\ *vb* **-fied; -fy·ing** : to make or

intaglio

\ə\ abut	\aů\ out	\i\ tip	\ò\ saw	\ů\ foot
\ər\ further	\ch\ chin	\ī\ life	\òi\ coin	\y\ yet
\a\ mat	\e\ pet	\j\ job	\th\ thin	\yü\ few
\ā\ take	\ē\ easy	\ŋ\ sing	\t͟h\ this	\yů\ cure
\ä\ cot, cart	\g\ go	\ō\ bone	\ü\ food	\zh\ vision

become intense or more intensive — **in·ten·si·fi·ca·tion** \-,ten(t)-sə-fə-'kā-shən\ *n* — **in·ten·si·fi·er** \-'ten(t)-sə-,fī(-ə)r\ *n*

in·ten·si·ty \in-'ten(t)-sət-ē\ *n, pl* **-ties** **1** : the quality or state of being intense; *esp* : extreme strength or force **2** : the degree or amount of a quality or condition ⟨the *intensity* of an electric field⟩

¹in·ten·sive \in-'ten(t)-siv\ *adj* **1** : marked by special effort ⟨an *intensive* campaign⟩ **2** : serving to give emphasis ⟨an *intensive* pronoun⟩ — **in·ten·sive·ly** *adv* — **in·ten·sive·ness** *n*

²intensive *n* : an intensive word

intensive care *n* : special medical equipment and services for taking care of seriously ill patients ⟨heart patients in *intensive care*⟩ ⟨an *intensive care* unit⟩

¹in·tent \in-'tent\ *n* **1** : PURPOSE 1, INTENTION ⟨with *intent* to kill⟩ **2** : ¹MEANING 1a ⟨the *intent* of the law⟩

²intent *adj* **1** : directed with strained or eager attention ⟨an *intent* gaze⟩ **2 a** : having the mind, attention, or will concentrated on something **b** : set on some end or purpose ⟨*intent* on going⟩ — **in·tent·ly** *adv* — **in·tent·ness** *n*

in·ten·tion \in-'ten-chən\ *n* **1** : a determination to act in a certain way **2** : an intended goal : AIM **3** : a person or purpose that is especially prayed for **4** : ¹MEANING 3, SIGNIFICANCE

syn INTENTION, PURPOSE, DESIGN, OBJECTIVE mean what one will try to accomplish or reach. INTENTION suggests only that one has something in mind to do ⟨our *intention* to visit Alaska someday⟩ PURPOSE suggests a fixed determination to accomplish something ⟨have the finding of happiness as one's *purpose* in life⟩ DESIGN suggests a carefully calculated plan ⟨a coach with great *designs* for her star athlete⟩ OBJECTIVE stresses a definite goal and one that is within reach ⟨our *objective* is to cross the river before dark⟩

in·ten·tion·al \in-'tench-nəl, -'ten-chən-ºl\ *adj* : done by intention : not accidental **syn** see VOLUNTARY — **in·ten·tion·al·ly** \-'tench-nə-lē, -'ten-chən-ºl-ē\ *adv*

in·ter \in-'tər\ *vb* **in·terred; in·ter·ring** : BURY 1 [from the Latin phrase *in terra* "in the earth"]

inter- *prefix* **1** : between : among : in the midst ⟨*inter*lock⟩ ⟨*inter*stellar⟩ **2** : reciprocal ⟨*inter*relate⟩ : reciprocally ⟨*inter*act⟩ **3** : located or occurring between ⟨*inter*lining⟩ **4** : carried on between ⟨*inter*national⟩ **5** : shared by or involving two or more [derived from Latin *inter* "between, among"]

in·ter·act \,int-ə-'rakt\ *vb* : to act on one another

in·ter·ac·tion \,int-ə-'rak-shən\ *n* : the action or influence of people, groups, or things on one another — **in·ter·ac·tion·al** \-shnəl, -shən-ºl\ *adj*

in·ter·ac·tive \,int-ə-'rak-tiv\ *adj* **1** : active between people, groups, or things **2** : allowing two-way electronic communications (as between a person and a computer) — **in·ter·ac·tive·ly** *adv*

in·ter·atom·ic \,int-ə-rə-'täm-ik\ *adj* : located or acting between atoms

in·ter·breed \,int-ər-'brēd\ *vb* **-bred** \-'bred\; **-breed·ing** : to breed or cause to breed together: as **a** : HYBRIDIZE **b** : to breed within a population

in·ter·cede \,int-ər-'sēd\ *vb* **-ced·ed; -ced·ing** **1** : to act as a go-between for hostile parties **2** : to plead in behalf of another

in·ter·cel·lu·lar \,int-ər-'sel-yə-lər\ *adj* : lying between cells ⟨*intercellular* spaces⟩

¹in·ter·cept \,int-ər-'sept\ *vb* **1** : to take or seize on the way to or before arrival ⟨*intercept* a letter⟩ ⟨*intercept* a pass⟩ **2** : to include (part of a line, surface, or solid) between two points, curves, or surfaces ⟨a line *intercepted* between points A and B⟩ [from Latin *interceptus,* past participle of *intercipere* "to take or hinder in the course of", from *inter-* "between, in the course of" and *cipere,* a form of *capere* "to take, seize" — related to CAPTURE, EXCEPT]

— **in·ter·cep·tion** \-'sep-shən\ *n*

²in·ter·cept \'int-ər-,sept\ *n* : the distance from the origin to a point where a graph crosses a coordinate axis

in·ter·cep·tor \,int-ər-'sep-tər\ *n* : one that intercepts; *esp* : a fast fighter plane designed for defense against bombers

in·ter·ces·sion \,int-ər-'sesh-ən\ *n* : the act of interceding — **in·ter·ces·sor** \-'ses-ər\ *n*

¹in·ter·change \,int-ər-'chānj\ *vb* **1** : to put each in the place of the other **2** : ²EXCHANGE **3** : to change places mutually — **in·ter·change·abil·i·ty** \-,chān-jə-'bil-ət-ē\ *n* — **in·ter·change·able** \-'chān-jə-bəl\ *adj* — **in·ter·change·ably** \-blē\ *adv* — **in·ter·chang·er** *n*

²in·ter·change \'int-ər-,chānj\ *n* **1** : the act or process or an instance of interchanging **2** : a joining of two or more highways by a system of separate levels that permit streams of traffic to pass from one to another without crossing

in·ter·col·le·giate \,int-ər-kə-'lē-j(ē-)ət\ *adj* : existing or carried on between colleges

in·ter·com \'int-ər-,käm\ *n* : INTERCOMMUNICATION SYSTEM

in·ter·com·mu·ni·cate \,int-ər-kə-'myü-nə-,kāt\ *vb* : to exchange communication with one another — **in·ter·com·mu·ni·ca·tion** \-,myü-nə-'kā-shən\ *n*

intercommunication system *n* : a two-way communication system with microphone and loudspeaker at each end

in·ter·con·nect \,int-ər-kə-'nekt\ *vb* : to connect with one another — **in·ter·con·nec·ted** *adj* — **in·ter·con·nec·tion** \-'nek-shən\ *n*

in·ter·con·ti·nen·tal \,int-ər-,känt-ºn-'ent-ºl\ *adj* **1** : extending among or carried on between continents ⟨*intercontinental* trade⟩ **2** : capable of traveling from one continent to another ⟨an *intercontinental* ballistic missile⟩

in·ter·con·vert·ible \,int-ər-kən-'vərt-ə-bəl\ *adj* : capable of being interchanged

in·ter·course \'int-ər-,kō(ə)rs, -,ko(ə)rs\ *n* **1** : dealings between persons or groups : RELATIONS **2** : physical sexual contact between individuals that involves the genitalia of at least one individual; *esp* : SEXUAL INTERCOURSE

in·ter·crop \,int-ər-'kräp\ *vb* : to grow two or more crops at one time on the same piece of land

in·ter·de·pend \,int-ər-di-'pend\ *vb* : to depend on one another — **in·ter·de·pen·dence** \-'pen-dən(t)s\ — **in·ter·de·pen·den·cy** \-dən-sē\ *n* — **in·ter·de·pen·dent** \-dənt\ *adj* — **in·ter·de·pen·dent·ly** *adv*

¹in·ter·dict \'int-ər-,dikt\ *n* **1** : a Roman Catholic ecclesiastical withdrawal of sacraments and Christian burial from a person or district **2** : PROHIBITION 2

²in·ter·dict \,int-ər-'dikt\ *vb* : to prohibit or forbid especially by an interdict — **in·ter·dic·tion** \-'dik-shən\ *n*

¹in·ter·est \'in-trəst; 'int-ə-,rest, -ə-rəst, 'int-ərst; 'in-,trest\ *n* **1** : a right, title, or legal share in something **2** : WELFARE 1, BENEFIT; *esp* : SELF-INTEREST 2 **3 a** : a charge for borrowed money that is generally a percentage of the amount borrowed **b** : the profit in goods or money that is made on invested capital **4 a** : readiness to be concerned with or moved by something **b** : a quality that arouses interest

²interest *vb* **1** : to involve the interest of : AFFECT, CONCERN **2** : to persuade to participate or take part **3** : to arouse or hold the interest of

in·ter·est·ing \'in-trəst-iŋ; 'int-ə-,rest-iŋ, -ə-rəst-, -ərst-\ *adj* : holding the attention : arousing interest

in·ter·est·ing·ly \'in-trəst-iŋ-lē; 'int-ə-,rest-iŋ-le, -ə-rəst-, -ərst-\ *adv* **1** : in an interesting manner ⟨a story *interestingly* told⟩ **2** : it is interesting ⟨*interestingly* enough, that was the first one⟩

¹in·ter·face \'int-ər-,fās\ *n* **1** : a surface forming a common boundary of two bodies, spaces, or phases ⟨an *interface* between oil and water⟩ **2 a** : the place at which independent systems meet and act on or communicate with each other **b** : the ways by which interaction or communication is brought about at an interface — **in·ter·fa·cial**

\,int-ər-'fā-shəl\ *adj*

²**interface** *vb* **1** : to connect or become connected through an interface **2** : to serve as an interface for

in·ter·fere \,int-ə(r)-'fi(ə)r\ *vb* **-fered; -fer·ing** **1** : to come in collision or be in opposition : CLASH **2** : to take part in the concerns of others **3** : to act on one another ⟨*interfering* light waves⟩ — **syn** see MEDDLE — **in·ter·fer·er** *n*

in·ter·fer·ence \,int-ə(r)-'fir-ən(t)s\ *n* **1 a** : the act or process of interfering **b** : something that interferes **2** : the shared effect on meeting of two waves (as of light or sound) whereby the waves cancel each other at some points and strengthen each other at other points **3 a** : the act of legally blocking an opponent in football **b** : the act of illegally hitting or getting in the way of an opponent in sports **4 a** : confusion of received radio signals due to undesired signals **b** : something that produces such confusion

in·ter·fer·om·e·ter \,int-ə(r)-fə-'räm-ət-ər, -,fir-'äm-\ *n* : an instrument that uses the interference of waves (as of light) for making exact measurements (as of wavelength)

in·ter·fer·on \,int-ə(r)-'fi(ə)r-,än\ *n* : any of a group of proteins produced by cells that keep viruses attacking the cells from multiplying

in·ter·ga·lac·tic \,int-ər-gə-'lak-tik\ *adj* : located in or relating to the spaces between galaxies

¹**in·ter·gla·cial** \,int-ər-'glā-shəl\ *adj* : occurring or relating to the time between glaciations

²**interglacial** *n* : a period of time of warm climate between glaciations

in·ter·im \'in-tə-rəm\ *n* : a time intervening : INTERVAL — **interim** *adj*

¹**in·te·ri·or** \in-'tir-ē-ər\ *adj* **1** : existing or occurring within the limits : INNER **2** : remote from the border or shore — **in·te·ri·or·ly** *adv*

²**interior** *n* **1** : the internal or inner part ⟨the *interior* of a house⟩ **2** : ²INLAND **3** : the internal affairs of a state or nation ⟨secretary of the *Interior*⟩

interior angle *n* : any of the four angles formed in the area between a pair of lines when a third line cuts them

interior decoration *n* : the art of decorating and furnishing the interior of a building

in·ter·ject \,int-ər-'jekt\ *vb* : to throw in between or among other things ⟨*interject* a remark⟩ — **in·ter·jec·tor** \-'jek-tər\ *n* — **in·ter·jec·to·ry** \-t(ə-)rē\ *adj*

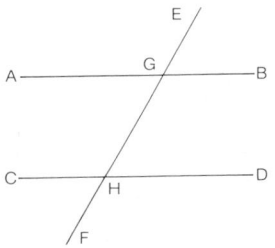

interior angle:
agh, bgh, ghd, ghc

in·ter·jec·tion \,int-ər-'jek-shən\ *n* **1** : an interjecting of something **2** : something interjected **3** : a word or cry expressing sudden or strong feeling — **in·ter·jec·tion·al** \-shnəl, -shən-ᵊl\ *adj* — **in·ter·jec·tion·al·ly** \-shnəl-ē, -shən-ᵊl-ē\ *adv*

in·ter·lace \,int-ər-'lās\ *vb* : to unite or cross by or as if by lacing together : INTERWEAVE ⟨*interlaced* fibers⟩ ⟨*interlacing* branches⟩ — **in·ter·lace·ment** \-'lā-smənt\ *n*

¹**in·ter·line** \,int-ər-'līn\ *vb* : to write between lines already written

²**interline** *vb* : to provide a garment with an interlining

in·ter·lin·ear \,int-ər-'lin-ē-ər\ *adj* **1** : written between lines already written or printed **2** : printed in different languages in alternate lines ⟨an *interlinear* translation⟩ — **in·ter·lin·ear·ly** *adv*

in·ter·lin·ing \'int-ər-,lī-niŋ\ *n* : a lining between the ordinary lining and the outside fabric

in·ter·lock \,int-ər-'läk\ *vb* : to lock together : interlace firmly

in·ter·lop·er \,int-ər-'lō-pər, 'int-ər-,lō-pər\ *n* : a person who interferes wrongly or meddlesomely

in·ter·lude \'int-ər-,lüd\ *n* **1** : a performance between the acts of a play **2** : an intervening period, space, or event : INTERVAL **3** : a musical composition inserted between the parts of a longer one, a drama, or a religious service

in·ter·mar·riage \,int-ər-'mar-ij\ *n* : marriage between members of different racial, social, or religious groups

in·ter·mar·ry \,int-ər-'mar-ē\ *vb* **1** : to marry each other **2** : to become connected by intermarriage

in·ter·me·di·ary \,int-ər-'mēd-ē-,er-ē\ *adj* **1** : INTERMEDIATE ⟨an *intermediary* stage⟩ **2** : acting as a mediator ⟨*intermediary* agent⟩ — **intermediary** *n*

in·ter·me·di·ate \,int-ər-'mēd-ē-ət\ *adj* : being or occurring in the middle or between [Middle Latin *intermediatus* "intermediate", derived from Latin *inter-* "among, in the midst" and *medius* "middle" — related to ¹MEDIAN] — **intermediate** *n* — **in·ter·me·di·ate·ly** *adv*

intermediate host *n* : a host that is normally used by a parasite in the course of its life cycle and that may actively carry it from one living thing to another

in·ter·ment \in-'tər-mənt\ *n* : BURIAL

in·ter·mesh \,int-ər-'mesh\ *vb* : to mesh with one another

in·ter·mez·zo \,int-ər-'mets-ō, -'medz-ō\ *n, pl* **-zi** \-ē\ *or* **-zos** **1** : a short light piece between the acts of a serious drama or opera **2 a** : a short movement connecting parts of a longer musical work **b** : a short independent instrumental composition **3** : an instrumental work often suggesting a particular mood

in·ter·mi·na·ble \(')in-'tərm-(ə-)nə-bəl\ *adj* : having or seeming to have no end; *esp* : tiresomely long — **in·ter·mi·na·ble·ness** *n* — **in·ter·mi·na·bly** \-blē\ *adv*

in·ter·min·gle \,int-ər-'miŋ-gəl\ *vb* : INTERMIX

in·ter·mis·sion \,int-ər-'mish-ən\ *n* **1** : ¹PAUSE 1, INTERRUPTION **2** : a pause or interval especially between the acts of a play

in·ter·mit \,int-ər-'mit\ *vb* **-mit·ted; -mit·ting** : to stop for a time and then continue

in·ter·mit·tence \,int-ər-'mit-ᵊn(t)s\ *n* : the quality or state of being intermittent

in·ter·mit·tent \,int-ər-'mit-ᵊnt\ *adj* : starting, stopping, and starting again ⟨an *intermittent* fever⟩ — **in·ter·mit·tent·ly** *adv*

in·ter·mix \,int-ər-'miks\ *vb* : to mix together — **in·ter·mix·ture** \-'miks-chər\ *n*

in·ter·mo·lec·u·lar \,int-ər-mə-'lek-yə-lər\ *adj* : existing or acting between molecules

¹**in·tern** \'in-,tərn, in-'tərn\ *vb* : to confine especially during a war ⟨*interned* enemy aliens⟩

²**in·tern** *or* **in·terne** \'in-,tərn\ *n* : an advanced student or graduate in a special field (as medicine or teaching) who is gaining supervised practical experience (as in a hospital or classroom) — **in·tern·ship** \-,ship\ *n*

³**in·tern** \'in-,tərn\ *vb* : to act as an intern

in·ter·nal \in-'tərn-ᵊl\ *adj* **1** : existing or lying within : INNER ⟨*internal* structure⟩ **2** : relating to, occurring, or located in the interior of the body ⟨*internal* medicine⟩ ⟨*internal* fertilization⟩ **3** : of or relating to the domestic affairs of a state ⟨*internal* revenue⟩ — **in·ter·nal·ly** \-ē\ *adv*

internal–combustion engine *n* : an engine in which the fuel is ignited within the engine cylinder

internal rhyme *n* : a rhyme between a word within a line and another either at the end of the same line or within another line

internal secretion *n* : HORMONE

¹**in·ter·na·tion·al** \,int-ər-'nash-nəl, -ən-ᵊl\ *adj* : of, relating

\ə\ abut		\aú\ **out**	\i\ tip		\ó\ **saw**		\ú\ **foot**
\ər\ further		\ch\ **chin**	\ī\ life		\ói\ **coin**		\y\ **yet**
\a\ mat		\e\ **pet**	\j\ **job**		\th\ **thin**		\yü\ **few**
\ā\ take		\ē\ **easy**	\ŋ\ **sing**		\th̲\ **this**		\yü\ **cure**
\ä\ cot, cart		\g\ **go**	\ō\ **bone**		\ü\ **food**		\zh\ **vision**

to, affecting, or involving two or more nations ⟨*international* trade⟩ — **in·ter·na·tion·al·iza·tion** \-,nash-nǝl-ǝ-'zā-shǝn, -ǝn-ᵊl-\ *n* — **in·ter·na·tion·al·ize** \-'nash-nǝl-,īz, -ǝn-ᵊl-\ *vb* — **in·ter·na·tion·al·ly** \-'nash-nǝ-lē, -ǝn-ᵊl-ē\ *adv*

²**international** *n* : an organization having branches in more than one country

international date line *n* : DATE LINE

in·ter·na·tion·al·ism \,int-ǝr-'nash-nǝl-,iz-ǝm, -'nash-ǝn-ᵊl-\ *n* : a policy of cooperation among nations or an attitude favoring such a policy — **in·ter·na·tion·al·ist** \-ǝst\ *n or adj*

International System *n* : METRIC SYSTEM

in·ter·ne·cine \'int-ǝr-'nes-,ēn, -'nē-,sīn; in-'tǝr-nǝ-,sēn\ *adj* **1** : marked by slaughter : DEADLY **2** : of, relating to, or involving conflict within a group ⟨*internecine* feuds⟩

in·tern·ee \(,)in-,tǝr-'nē\ *n* : an interned person

in·ter·neu·ron \,int-ǝr-'n(y)ü-,rän, -'n(y)ú(ǝ)r-,än\ *n* : a nerve cell that carries a nerve impulse from one nerve cell to another

in·ter·nist \'in-,tǝr-nǝst\ *n* : a physician who specializes in internal medicine

in·tern·ment \in-'tǝrn-mǝnt, 'in-,tǝrn-\ *n* : the act of interning : the state of being interned

in·ter·node \'int-ǝr-,nōd\ *n* : a part between two nodes (as of a plant stem)

in·ter·nun·ci·al neuron \,int-ǝr-'nǝn(t)-sē-ǝl-, -'nùn(t)-\ *n* : a neuron in the central nervous system that is part of the pathway connecting a sensory and motor neuron — called also *association neuron*

in·ter·pen·e·trate \,int-ǝr-'pen-ǝ-,trāt\ *vb* **1** : to penetrate between, within, or throughout **2** : to penetrate mutually — **in·ter·pen·e·tra·tion** \-,pen-ǝ-'trā-shǝn\ *n*

in·ter·phase \'int-ǝr-,fāz\ *n* : the period between the end of one mitotic cell division and the beginning of the next

in·ter·plan·e·tary \,int-ǝr-'plan-ǝ-,ter-ē\ *adj* : existing, carried on, or operating between planets ⟨*interplanetary* travel⟩

in·ter·play \'int-ǝr-,plā\ *n* : mutual action or influence : INTERACTION — **in·ter·play** \,int-ǝr-'plā, 'int-ǝr-,plā\ *vb*

in·ter·po·late \in-'tǝr-pǝ-,lāt\ *vb* **-lat·ed; -lat·ing** **1** : to alter by inserting new matter **2** : to insert between other things or parts — **in·ter·po·la·tion** \-,tǝr-pǝ-'lā-shǝn\ *n* — **in·ter·po·la·tive** \-'tǝr-pǝ-,lāt-iv\ *adj* — **in·ter·po·la·tor** \-,lāt-ǝr\ *n*

in·ter·pose \,int-ǝr-'pōz\ *vb* **-posed; -pos·ing** **1 a** : to place in an intervening position **b** : INTRUDE 1, INTERRUPT **2** : to introduce in between the parts of a conversation or argument **3** : to be or come between; *esp* : to step in between opposing parties — **in·ter·pos·er** *n* — **in·ter·po·si·tion** \-pǝ-'zish-ǝn\ *n*

in·ter·pret \in-'tǝr-prǝt\ *vb* **1** : to explain the meaning of ⟨*interpret* a dream⟩ **2** : to understand according to one's own belief, judgment, or interest ⟨*interpret* an action as unfriendly⟩ **3** : to bring out the meaning or significance of by performing ⟨an actor *interprets* a role⟩ **4** : to translate for speakers of different languages — **in·ter·pret·able** \-prǝt-ǝ-bǝl\ *adj*

in·ter·pre·ta·tion \in-,tǝr-prǝ-'tā-shǝn\ *n* **1** : the act or the result of interpreting : EXPLANATION **2** : an instance of artistic interpretation in performance or adaptation — **in·ter·pre·ta·tive** \-'tǝr-prǝ-,tāt-iv\ *adj*

in·ter·pret·er \in-'tǝr-prǝt-ǝr\ *n* **1** : one that interprets; *esp* : a person who translates orally for people speaking different languages **2** : a computer program that translates an instruction into machine language and executes it before going to the next instruction

in·ter·pre·tive \in-'tǝr-prǝt-iv\ *adj* **1** : of or relating to interpretation **2** : of, relating to, or using an interpreter — **in·ter·pre·tive·ly** *adv*

in·ter·ra·cial \,int-ǝr-'rā-shǝl\ *adj* : of, involving, or designed for members of different races

in·ter·reg·num \,int-ǝ-'reg-nǝm\ *n, pl* **-nums** *or* **-na** \-nǝ\ : a period between two reigns or regimes

in·ter·re·late \,int-ǝ(r)-ri-'lāt\ *vb* : to bring into or have a shared relationship — **in·ter·re·la·tion** \-'lā-shǝn\ *n* — **in·ter·re·la·tion·ship** \-,ship\ *n*

in·ter·ro·gate \in-'ter-ǝ-,gāt\ *vb* **-gat·ed; -gat·ing** : to question thoroughly and according to established methods ⟨*interrogate* a prisoner of war⟩ — **in·ter·ro·ga·tion** \-,ter-ǝ-'gā-shǝn\ *n* — **in·ter·ro·ga·tor** \-'ter-ǝ-,gāt-ǝr\ *n*

interrogation point *n* : QUESTION MARK

¹**in·ter·rog·a·tive** \,int-ǝ-'räg-ǝt-iv\ *adj* **1** : having the form or force of a question ⟨an *interrogative* phrase⟩ **2** : used in a question ⟨an *interrogative* pronoun⟩ — **in·ter·rog·a·tive·ly** *adv*

²**interrogative** *n* : a word used in asking questions

in·ter·rog·a·to·ry \,int-ǝ-'räg-ǝ-,tōr-ē, -,tòr-\ *adj* : containing, expressing, or implying a question

in·ter·rupt \,int-ǝ-'rǝpt\ *vb* **1** : to stop or hinder by breaking in ⟨*interrupt* a conversation⟩ **2** : to break the sameness of or connection between [Middle English *interrupten* "to interrupt", from Latin *interruptus,* past participle of *interrumpere* "to interrupt", from *inter-* "between, among" and *rumpere* "to break" — related to RUPTURE] — **in·ter·rupt·er** *n* — **in·ter·rup·tion** \-'rǝp-shǝn\ *n* — **in·ter·rup·tive** \-'rǝp-tiv\ *adj*

in·ter·scho·las·tic \,int-ǝr-skǝ-'las-tik\ *adj* : existing or carried on between schools

¹**in·ter·sect** \,int-ǝr-'sekt\ *vb* **1** : to divide by passing through or across : CROSS ⟨one line *intersecting* another⟩ **2** : to meet and cross at one or more points ⟨lines *intersecting* at right angles⟩ ⟨*intersecting* circles *intersect* at two points⟩

²**intersect** *n* : INTERSECTION 3

in·ter·sec·tion \,int-ǝr-'sek-shǝn\ *n* **1** : the act or process of intersecting **2** : the place or point where two or more things and especially streets intersect ⟨a busy *intersection*⟩ **3** : the set of mathematical elements common to two or more sets; *esp* : the set of points common to two geometric figures

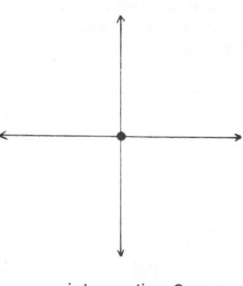

intersection 3

in·ter·sex \'int-ǝr-,seks\ *n* : an individual that is intermediate in sex between a normal male and a normal female

¹**in·ter·space** \'int-ǝr-,spās\ *n* : an intervening space

²**in·ter·space** \,int-ǝr-'spās\ *vb* : to separate by spaces

in·ter·spe·cif·ic \,int-ǝr-spi-'sif-ik\ *or* **in·ter·spe·cies** \-'spē-(,)shēz, -(,)sēz\ *adj* : existing or arising between species ⟨*interspecific* hybrid⟩

in·ter·sperse \,int-ǝr-'spǝrs\ *vb* **-spersed; -spers·ing** **1** : to set here and there among other things **2** : to vary with things inserted here and there — **in·ter·sper·sion** \-'spǝr-zhǝn\ *n*

¹**in·ter·state** \,int-ǝr-'stāt\ *adj* : of, connecting, or existing between states especially of the U.S. ⟨*interstate* highways⟩

²**in·ter·state** \'int-ǝr-,stāt\ *n* : an interstate highway

in·ter·stel·lar \,int-ǝr-'stel-ǝr\ *adj* : located or taking place among the stars ⟨*interstellar* space⟩

in·ter·ster·ile \,int-ǝr-'ster-ǝl\ *adj* : unable to pollinate one another

in·ter·stice \in-'tǝr-stǝs\ *n, pl* **in·ter·stic·es** \-stǝ-,sēz, -stǝ-sǝz\ : a little space between two things

in·ter·sti·tial \,int-ǝr-'stish-ǝl\ *adj* : relating to or located in the interstices — **in·ter·sti·tial·ly** \-'stish-ǝ-lē\ *adv*

in·ter·tid·al \,int-ǝr-'tīd-ᵊl\ *adj* : of, relating to, or being the area that is above low-tide mark but exposed to flooding by the tide

in·ter·twine \,int-ər-'twīn\ *vb* : to twine or cause to twine about one another : INTERLACE

in·ter·ur·ban \,int-ər-'ər-bən\ *adj* : connecting cities or towns ⟨*interurban* transportation⟩

in·ter·val \'int-ər-vəl\ *n* **1** : a period of time between events or states : PAUSE ⟨a three-month *interval*⟩ **2** : a space between things ⟨the *interval* between two desks⟩ **3** : difference in pitch between tones

in·ter·vene \,int-ər-'vēn\ *vb* **-vened; -ven·ing** **1** : to happen as an unrelated event **2** : to come between points of time or between events **3** : to come between in order to stop, settle, or change **4** : to be or lie between — **in·ter·ven·tion** \-'ven-chən\ *n*

in·ter·view \'int-ər-,vyü\ *n* **1** : a meeting face to face especially for the purpose of talking or consulting **2** : a meeting between a journalist and another person in order to get news or an article; *also* : the account of such a meeting — **interview** *vb* — **in·ter·view·er** *n*

in·ter·weave \,int-ər-'wēv\ *vb* **1** : to weave together **2** : to blend or cause to blend together — **in·ter·wo·ven** \-'wō-vən\ *adj*

in·tes·tate \in-'tes-,tāt, -'tes-tət\ *adj* **1** : not having made a will ⟨he died *intestate*⟩ **2** : not disposed of by will — **in·tes·ta·cy** \-'tes-tə-sē\ *n*

in·tes·ti·nal \in-'tes-tən-ᵊl\ *adj* **1** : of or relating to the intestine **2** : affecting or occurring in the intestine — **in·tes·ti·nal·ly** \-ē\ *adv*

in·tes·tine \in-'tes-tən\ *n* : the part of the alimentary canal that is a long tube composed of the small intestine and the large intestine, that extends from the stomach to the anus, that helps to digest food and absorb nutrients, and that carries waste matter to be discharged

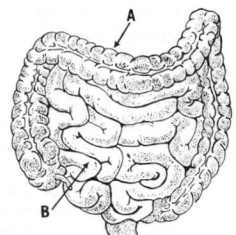

in·ti·ma·cy \'int-ə-mə-sē\ *n, pl* **-cies** **1** : the state of being intimate **2** : an instance of being intimate

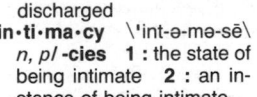

intestine: *A* large intestine, *B* small intestine

¹**in·ti·mate** \'int-ə-,māt\ *vb* **-mat·ed; -mat·ing** **1** : ANNOUNCE **2** : to communicate indirectly : HINT — **in·ti·mat·er** *n* — **in·ti·ma·tion** \,int-ə-'mā-shən\ *n*

²**in·ti·mate** \'int-ə-mət\ *adj* **1** : belonging to or characterizing one's deepest nature **2** : marked by very close association or contact **3 a** : marked by a warm friendship developing through long association ⟨on *intimate* terms⟩ **b** : suggesting informal warmth or privacy ⟨*intimate* clubs⟩ **4** : of a very personal or private nature — **in·ti·mate·ly** *adv* — **in·ti·mate·ness** *n*

³**in·ti·mate** \'int-ə-mət\ *n* : an intimate friend : CONFIDANT

in·tim·i·date \in-'tim-ə-,dāt\ *vb* **-dat·ed; -dat·ing** : to make timid or fearful by or as if by threats — **in·tim·i·da·tion** \-,tim-ə-'dā-shən\ *n* — **in·tim·i·da·tor** \-'tim-ə-,dāt-ər\ *n*

in·to \'in-tə, -tü\ *prep* **1 a** : to the inside of ⟨came *into* the room⟩ **b** — used to indicate entry, introduction, or inclusion ⟨enter *into* an agreement⟩ **2 a** : to the state, condition, or form of ⟨came *into* being⟩ ⟨divide *into* four parts⟩ **b** : to the occupation, action, or possession of ⟨go *into* farming⟩ **3** : AGAINST **4** ⟨ran *into* a wall⟩ **4** : engaged in or involved with ⟨was never *into* drugs⟩

in·tol·er·a·ble \(')in-'täl-(ə-)rə-bəl, -'täl-ər-bəl\ *adj* : not tolerable : UNBEARABLE — **in·tol·er·a·bil·i·ty** \(,)in-,täl-(ə-)rə-'bil-ət-ē\ *n* — **in·tol·er·a·bly** \(')in-'täl-(ə-)rə-blē, -'täl-ər-blē\ *adv*

in·tol·er·ance \(')in-'täl-(ə-)rən(t)s\ *n* **1** : the quality or state of being intolerant **2** : exceptional sensitivity (as to a drug or food)

in·tol·er·ant \(')in-'täl-(ə-)rənt\ *adj* **1** : unable or unwilling to endure **2** : unwilling to grant equality, freedom, or other social rights : BIGOTED — **in·tol·er·ant·ly** *adv*

in·to·na·tion \,in-tə-'nā-shən\ *n* **1** : the act of intoning; *also* : something intoned **2** : the act of singing or playing music in tune **3** : the rise and fall in pitch of the voice in speech — **in·to·na·tion·al** \-shnəl, -shən-ᵊl\ *adj*

in·tone \in-'tōn\ *vb* **in·toned; in·ton·ing** : to utter in musical or prolonged tones : CHANT — **in·ton·er** *n*

in·tox·i·cant \in-'täk-si-kənt\ *n* : something that intoxicates; *esp* : an alcoholic drink — **intoxicant** *adj*

in·tox·i·cate \in-'täk-sə-,kāt\ *vb* **-cat·ed; -cat·ing** **1** : to affect by alcohol or a drug especially to the point where physical and mental control is much reduced **2** : to excite to enthusiasm or frenzy

Word History The Greek word *toxon* means "bow" or "arrow". From this came the Greek *toxikon*, meaning "a poison in which arrows are dipped". *Toxikon* was borrowed into Latin as *toxicum*, which gave rise to the Latin verb *intoxicare* "to poison". The English word *intoxicate* comes from this Latin verb. *Intoxicate* originally meant "to poison" in English, but now it is almost never used with this meaning. It is related to the words *toxic*, meaning "poisonous", and *toxin*, meaning "a poison". Both of these words can also be traced to the Greek *toxon*. [from Latin *intoxicatus*, past participle of *intoxicare* "to poison", from earlier *in-* "put into" and *toxicum* "poison", from Greek *toxikon* "arrow poison", from *toxon* "bow, arrow" — related to TOXIC, TOXIN]

in·tox·i·ca·tion \in-,täk-sə-'kā-shən\ *n* **1 a** : an unhealthy state that is or is like a poisoning ⟨intestinal *intoxication*⟩ **b** : the condition of being drunk **2** : a strong excitement or elation

in·tra- \,in-trə, ,in-(,)trä\ *prefix* **1** : within ⟨*intra*mural⟩ **2** : into ⟨*intra*venous⟩ [derived from Latin *intra* "within, between"]

in·tra·cel·lu·lar \,in-trə-'sel-yə-lər\ *adj* : being or occurring within a cell — **in·tra·cel·lu·lar·ly** *adv*

in·trac·ta·ble \(')in-'trak-tə-bəl\ *adj* **1** : not easily managed or controlled ⟨an *intractable* child⟩ **2** : not easily relieved or cured ⟨*intractable* pain⟩ — **in·trac·ta·bil·i·ty** \(,)in-,trak-tə-'bil-ət-ē\ *n* — **in·trac·ta·bly** \(')in-'trak-tə-blē\ *adv*

in·tra·der·mal \,in-trə-'dər-məl, ,in-(,)trä-\ *adj* : situated or done within or between the layers of the skin — **in·tra·der·mal·ly** \-mə-lē\ *adv*

in·tra·mu·ral \,in-trə-'myŭr-əl, ,in-(,)trä-\ *adj* : being, occurring, or undertaken within the limits usually of a school ⟨*intramural* sports⟩

in·tra·mus·cu·lar \,in-trə-'məs-kyə-lər, ,in-(,)trä-\ *adj* : located in, occurring in, or injected into a muscle

in·tran·si·tive \(')in-'tran(t)s-ət-iv, -'tranz-\ *adj* : not transitive; *esp* : not having or containing a direct object ⟨an *intransitive* verb⟩ — **in·tran·si·tive·ly** *adv*

in·tra·spe·cif·ic \,in-trə-spi-'sif-ik\ *adj* : occurring within a species or involving members of one species ⟨*intraspecific* variation⟩

in·tra·state \,in-trə-'stāt\ *adj* : existing or occurring within a state

in·tra·uter·ine \,in-trə-'yüt-ə-rən, -,rīn\ *adj* : located, used, or occurring within the uterus ⟨*intrauterine* growth⟩

intrauterine device : a device (as a spiral of plastic or a ring of stainless steel) inserted in the uterus and left there to prevent pregnancy — called also *IUD*

in·tra·ve·nous \,in-trə-'vē-nəs\ *adj* : being within or entering by way of the veins ⟨*intravenous* feeding⟩ — **in·tra·**

\ə\ **abut**	\aů\ **out**	\i\ **tip**	\ȯ\ **saw**	\ů\ **foot**	
\ər\ **further**	\ch\ **chin**	\ī\ **life**	\ȯi\ **coin**	\y\ **yet**	
\a\ **mat**	\e\ **pet**	\j\ **job**	\th\ **thin**	\yü\ **few**	
\ā\ **take**	\ē\ **easy**	\ŋ\ **sing**	\th\ **this**	\yů\ **cure**	
\ä\ **cot, cart**	\g\ **go**	\ō\ **bone**	\ü\ **food**	\zh\ **vision**	

ve·nous·ly adv

in·trep·id \in-'trep-əd\ adj : feeling no fear : BOLD — **in·tre·pid·i·ty** \,in-trə-'pid-ət-ē\ n — **in·trep·id·ly** \-'trep-əd-lē\ adj — **in·trep·id·ness** n

in·tri·ca·cy \'in-tri-kə-sē\ n, pl **-cies** 1 : the quality or state of being intricate 2 : something intricate

in·tri·cate \'in-tri-kət\ adj : difficult to follow, understand, or analyze — **in·tri·cate·ly** adv — **in·tri·cate·ness** n

¹**in·trigue** \in-'trēg\ vb **in·trigued; in·trigu·ing** 1 : to make or accomplish by secret plotting 2 : ²PLOT 2, SCHEME 3 : to arouse the interest or curiosity of 〈intrigued by the tale〉 — **in·trigu·er** n

²**in·trigue** \'in-,trēg, in-'trēg\ n 1 : a secret and complicated scheme : PLOT 2 : a secret love affair

in·trin·sic \in-'trin-zik, -'trin(t)-sik\ adj : belonging to the essential nature of a thing 〈intrinsic value of a gem〉 〈intrinsic brightness of light〉 — **in·trin·si·cal·ly** \-k(ə-)lē\ adv

in·tro- \-,in-trə, ,in-(,)trō\ prefix : inward 〈introvert〉 [derived from Latin intro "inside"]

in·tro·duce \,in-trə-'d(y)üs\ vb **-duced; -duc·ing** 1 : to bring into practice or use 2 : to lead or bring in 〈introduce birds from other countries〉 3 a : to cause to become acquainted b : to present or announce officially 〈introduce a legislative bill〉 c : to make preliminary remarks about 4 : to present or bring forward for discussion 5 : to put in : INSERT — **in·tro·duc·er** n

in·tro·duc·tion \,in-trə-'dək-shən\ n 1 a : the action of introducing b : something introduced 2 : the part of a book that leads up to and explains what will be found in the main part 3 : a book for beginners in a subject

in·tro·duc·to·ry \,in-trə-'dək-t(ə-)rē\ adj : serving to introduce — **in·tro·duc·to·ri·ly** \-t(ə-)rə-lē\ adv

in·tro·spec·tion \,in-trə-'spek-shən\ n : an examination of one's own thoughts or feelings — **in·tro·spec·tive** \-'spek-tiv\ adj — **in·tro·spec·tive·ly** adv

in·tro·ver·sion \,in-trə-'ver-zhən, -shən\ n : the state of being mainly concerned with or interested in one's own thoughts and ideas

in·tro·vert \'in-trə-,vərt\ n 1 : one that is or can be turned in or inward on itself 2 : a person whose personality is characterized by introversion — **introvert** adj — **in·tro·vert·ed** \-,vərt-əd\ adj

in·trude \in-'trüd\ vb **in·trud·ed; in·trud·ing** 1 : to bring or force in unasked 2 : to come or go in without invitation — **in·trud·er** n

in·tru·sion \in-'trü-zhən\ n 1 : the act of intruding : the state of being intruded 2 : the entry by force of melted rock into or between other rock formations

in·tru·sive \in-'trü-siv, -ziv\ adj 1 : characterized by intrusion; esp : intruding where one is not welcome or invited 2 : having been forced while in a melted state into cavities or between layers 〈intrusive rocks〉 — **intrusive** n — **in·tru·sive·ly** adv — **in·tru·sive·ness** n

in·tu·ition \,in-t(y)ü-'ish-ən\ n 1 : the power of knowing immediately and without conscious reasoning 2 : something known or understood at once — **in·tu·ition·al** \-'ish-nəl, -ən-ᵊl\ adj

in·tu·itive \in-'t(y)ü-ət-iv\ adj 1 : knowing or understanding by intuition 〈an intuitive person〉 2 : having or characterized by intuition 〈an intuitive mind〉 3 : known or understood by intuition 〈intuitive knowledge〉 — **in·tu·itive·ly** adj — **in·tu·itive·ness** n

in·un·date \'in-(,)ən-,dāt\ vb **-dat·ed; -dat·ing** : to cover with a flood — **in·un·da·tion** \,in-(,)ən-'dā-shən\ n

Inu·pi·at \in-'ü-pē-,ät, in-'yü-\ n, pl **Inupiat** or **Inupiats** : a member of the Eskimo people of northern Alaska 2 : the language of the Inupiat people

in·ure \in-'(y)u̇(ə)r\ vb **in·ured; in·ur·ing** 1 : to make less sensitive : HARDEN 〈inured to cold〉 2 : ACCRUE 1

in·vade \in-'vād\ vb **in·vad·ed; in·vad·ing** 1 : to enter for conquest or plunder 〈invade a country〉 2 : to disturb or intrude upon 〈invaded their privacy〉 3 : to spread over

or into usually harmfully 〈bacteria invading tissue〉 — **in·vad·er** n

¹**in·val·id** \(')in-'val-əd\ adj : having no force or effect : not valid [from earlier invalid "not having a sound basis in fact or reason, not valid", from Latin invalidus "not strong, not adequate"] — **in·va·lid·i·ty** \,in-və-'lid-ət-ē\ n — **in·val·id·ly** \(')in-'val-əd-lē\ adv

²**in·va·lid** \'in-və-ləd\ adj 1 : suffering from disease or disability : SICKLY 2 : of, relating to, or suited to an invalid [from French invalide "suffering from a disease, sickly", from Latin invalidus "not strong, not adequate"]

³**invalid** \like²\ n : one that is sickly or disabled

⁴**in·va·lid** \'in-və-ləd, -,lid\ vb : to make sickly or disabled

in·val·i·date \(')in-'val-ə-,dāt\ vb : to weaken or destroy the effect of — **in·val·i·da·tion** \(,)in-,val-ə-'dā-shən\ n

in·valu·able \(')in-'val-yə(-wə)-bəl\ adj : having value too great to be estimated — **in·valu·ably** \-blē\ adv

in·vari·able \(')in-'ver-ē-ə-bəl, -'var-\ adj : not changing or capable of change 〈an invariable routine〉 — **in·vari·abil·i·ty** \(,)in-,ver-ē-ə-'bil-ət-ē, -,var-\ n — **invariable** n — **in·vari·ably** \(')in-'ver-ē-ə-blē, -'var-\ adv

in·vari·ant \(')in-'ver-ē-ənt, -'var-\ adj : not changing or altering — **invariant** n

in·va·sion \in-'vā-zhən\ n : an act of invading; esp : entrance of an army into a country for conquest

in·va·sive \in-'vā-siv, -ziv\ adj : tending to spread especially to healthy tissue 〈invasive cancer cells〉

in·vec·tive \in-'vek-tiv\ n : harsh or insulting words

in·veigh \in-'vā\ vb : to protest or complain bitterly

in·vei·gle \in-'vā-gəl\ vb **in·vei·gled; in·vei·gling** \-g(ə-)liŋ\ 1 : to win over by flattery : ENTICE 2 : to acquire by cleverness or flattery

in·vent \in-'vent\ vb 1 : to think up : MAKE UP 〈invent an excuse〉 2 : to create or produce for the first time — **in·ven·tor** \-'vent-ər\ n

in·ven·tion \in-'ven-chən\ n 1 : something invented; esp : an original device or process 2 : an imaginary story 3 : the act, process, or power of inventing

in·ven·tive \in-'vent-iv\ adj : gifted with the skill and imagination to invent — **in·ven·tive·ly** adv — **in·ven·tive·ness** n

¹**in·ven·to·ry** \'in-vən-,tōr-ē, -,tȯr-\ n, pl **-ries** 1 : a complete list of items (as of goods on hand) 2 : the stock of goods on hand 3 : the act or process of making an inventory

²**inventory** vb **-ried; -ry·ing** : to make an inventory of

¹**in·verse** \(')in-'vərs, 'in-vərs\ adj : opposite in order, nature, or effect; esp : being a mathematical operation opposite in effect to another 〈addition and subtraction are inverse operations〉

²**in·verse** \'in-,vərs, (')in-'vərs\ n : something inverse or resulting in or from inversion

in·verse·ly \'in-,vərs-lē, (')in-'vərs-lē\ adv 1 : in an inverse order or manner 2 : in the manner of inverse variation

inversely proportional adj : related by inverse variation

inverse square law n : a statement in physics: a physical quantity (as illumination) varies as the reciprocal of the square of the distance of the quantity from its source

inverse variation n 1 : mathematical relationship between two variables which can be expressed by an equation in which the product of two variables is equal to a constant 2 : an equation or function expressing inverse variation — compare DIRECT VARIATION 2

in·ver·sion \in-'vər-zhən, -shən\ n 1 : a reversal of position, order, or relationship 2 : the act or process of inverting 3 : increase of temperature of the air with increasing altitude

in·vert \in-'vərt\ vb 1 : to reverse the position, order, or relationship of 2 a : to turn inside out or upside down b : to turn inward

in·ver·te·brate \(')in-'vərt-ə-brət, -,brāt\ adj : lacking a backbone; *also* : of or relating to invertebrate animals — **invertebrate** *n*

¹**in·vest** \in-ˈvest\ *vb* **1 a** : INSTALL 1 **b** : to furnish with power or authority **2** : to cover completely **3** : CLOTHE 1a, ADORN **4** : to surround with troops or ships : BESIEGE **5** : to supply with a quality or characteristic

²**invest** *vb* **1** : to commit money so as to return a profit ⟨*invest* in real estate⟩ **2** : to expend for future benefits or advantages ⟨*invest* in a project⟩ ⟨*invest* time in education⟩ — **in·ves·tor** \-ˈves-tər\ *n*

in·ves·ti·gate \in-ˈves-tə-ˌgāt\ *vb* **-gat·ed; -gat·ing** : to study by close examination and systematic inquiry — **in·ves·ti·ga·tion** \-ˌves-tə-ˈgā-shən\ *n* — **in·ves·ti·ga·tive** \-ˈves-tə-ˌgāt-iv\ *adj* — **in·ves·ti·ga·tor** \-ˌgāt-ər\ *n* — **in·ves·ti·ga·to·ry** \-ˈves-ti-gə-ˌtōr-ē, -ˌtȯr-\ *adj*

Word History A detective investigating a crime may find the criminal by following clues. In much the same way, a hunter may find game by following tracks. The origins of the word *investigate* show how fitting it is to compare the detective to the hunter. The Latin word *vestigium* meant "footprint, track". Joined with the prefix *in-*, the noun *vestigium* gave rise to the verb *investigare*. This word meant both "to track or trace by footprints" and "to study or examine closely". Only the second meaning was kept when the verb was borrowed into English as *investigate*. [from Latin *investigare* "to track, investigate", from *in-* "in, toward" and *vestigium* "footprint" — related to VESTIGE]

in·ves·ti·ture \in-ˈves-tə-ˌchúr, -chər\ *n* **1** : the act of establishing in office **2** : CLOTHING 1, APPAREL

¹**in·vest·ment** \in-ˈves(t)-mənt\ *n* **1** : INVESTITURE 1 **2** : BLOCKADE, SIEGE

²**investment** *n* **1** : the outlay of money for income or profit **2** : a sum of money invested or a property purchased

in·vet·er·ate \in-ˈvet-ə-rət, -ˈve-trət\ *adj* **1** : firmly established by age or by long continuation **2** : HABITUAL 2 — **in·vet·er·ate·ly** *adv*

in·vid·i·ous \in-ˈvid-ē-əs\ *adj* **1** : of an unpleasant or objectionable kind ⟨*invidious* criticism⟩ **2** : of a kind to cause resentment ⟨an *invidious* comparison⟩ — **in·vid·i·ous·ly** *adv* — **in·vid·i·ous·ness** *n*

in·vig·o·rate \in-ˈvig-ə-ˌrāt\ *vb* **-rat·ed; -rat·ing** : to give life and energy to — **in·vig·o·ra·tion** \-ˌvig-ə-ˈrā-shən\ *n* — **in·vig·o·ra·tor** \-ˈvig-ə-ˌrāt-ər\ *n*

in·vin·ci·ble \(ˈ)in-ˈvin(t)-sə-bəl\ *adj* : incapable of being defeated, overcome, or subdued ⟨an *invincible* army⟩ — **in·vin·ci·bil·i·ty** \(ˌ)in-ˌvin(t)-sə-ˈbil-ət-ē\ *n* — **in·vin·ci·bly** \(ˈ)in-ˈvin(t)-sə-blē\ *adv*

in·vi·o·la·ble \(ˈ)in-ˈvī-ə-lə-bəl\ *adj* **1** : too sacred to be violated ⟨an *inviolable* oath⟩ **2** : incapable of being harmed or destroyed by violence — **in·vi·o·la·bil·i·ty** \(ˌ)in-ˌvī-ə-lə-ˈbil-ət-ē\ *n* — **in·vi·o·la·bly** \(ˈ)in-ˈvī-ə-lə-blē\ *adv*

in·vi·o·late \(ˈ)in-ˈvī-ə-lət\ *adj* : not violated; *esp* : PURE — **in·vi·o·late·ly** *adv* — **in·vi·o·late·ness** *n*

in·vis·i·ble \(ˈ)in-ˈviz-ə-bəl\ *adj* **1** : impossible to see ⟨sound is *invisible*⟩ **2** : being so small or slight as to be hardly noticeable — **in·vis·i·bil·i·ty** \(ˌ)in-ˌviz-ə-ˈbil-ət-ē\ *n* — **in·vis·i·bly** \(ˈ)in-ˈviz-ə-blē\ *adv*

in·vi·ta·tion \ˌin-və-ˈtā-shən\ *n* **1** : the act of inviting **2** : the written, printed, or spoken expression by which a person is invited — **in·vi·ta·tion·al** \-shnəl, -shən-ᵊl\ *adj*

¹**in·vite** \in-ˈvīt\ *vb* **in·vit·ed; in·vit·ing** **1** : to make more likely ⟨behavior that *invites* criticism⟩ ⟨*invite* disaster by speeding⟩ **2 a** : to request the presence or participation of **b** : to request formally or politely — **in·vit·er** *n*

²**in·vite** \ˈin-ˌvīt\ *n* : INVITATION

in·vit·ing \in-ˈvīt-iŋ\ *adj* : ATTRACTIVE, TEMPTING ⟨an *inviting* prospect⟩ — **in·vit·ing·ly** \-iŋ-lē\ *adv*

in·vo·ca·tion \ˌin-və-ˈkā-shən\ *n* **1 a** : the act or process of asking for help or support **b** : a prayer for blessing or guidance (as at the beginning of a religious service) **2**

: a formula for calling forth spirits or performing magic : INCANTATION — **in·vo·ca·tion·al** \-shnəl, -shən-ᵊl\ *adj*

¹**in·voice** \ˈin-ˌvȯis\ *n* : an itemized statement of goods or services with their prices and the terms of sale

²**invoice** *vb* **in·voiced; in·voic·ing** : to submit an invoice for : BILL

in·voke \in-ˈvōk\ *vb* **in·voked; in·vok·ing** **1** : to call on for aid or protection (as in prayer) **2** : to call forth by magic : CONJURE **3** : to appeal to as an authority or for support

in·vol·un·tary \(ˈ)in-ˈväl-ən-ˌter-ē\ *adj* **1** : not made or done willingly or from choice : UNWILLING **2** : being enforced or required : MANDATORY **3** : not normally under the control of the will ⟨an *involuntary* response to a stimulus⟩ — **in·vol·un·tari·ly** \(ˌ)in-ˌväl-ən-ˈter-ə-lē\ *adv*

involuntary muscle *n* : SMOOTH MUSCLE

in·vo·lu·tion \ˌin-və-ˈlü-shən\ *n* : INTRICACY, COMPLEXITY

in·volve \in-ˈvälv, -ˈvȯlv\ *vb* **in·volved; in·volv·ing** **1** : to take part in as a participant ⟨*involved* in bird watching⟩ **2** : to occupy absorbingly **3** : to have within or as a part ⟨one problem *involves* others⟩ **4** : to call for : REQUIRE ⟨the job *involved* building 10 bridges⟩ **5** : ²AFFECT a — **in·volve·ment** \-mənt\ *n* — **in·volv·er** *n*

in·volved *adj* : very complicated ⟨a long and *involved* story⟩

in·vul·ner·a·ble \(ˈ)in-ˈvəln-(ə)rə-bəl, -ˈvəl-nər-bəl\ *adj* **1** : impossible to wound, injure, or damage **2** : immune to or proof against attack : IMPREGNABLE — **in·vul·ner·a·bil·i·ty** \(ˌ)in-ˌvəln-(ə)rə-ˈbil-ət-ē\ *n* — **in·vul·ner·a·bly** \-ˈvəln-(ə)rə-blē, -ˈvəl-nər-blē\ *adv*

¹**in·ward** \ˈin-wərd\ *adj* **1** : situated on the inside : INNER **2 a** : MENTAL 1a **b** : ¹SPIRITUAL 1 **3** : directed toward the interior ⟨an *inward* flow⟩

²**inward** *or* **in·wards** \ˈin-wərdz\ *adv* **1** : toward the inside, center, or interior **2** : toward the mind or spirit

in·ward·ly \ˈin-wərd-lē\ *adv* **1** : in the mind or spirit **2 a** : on the inside ⟨bled *inwardly*⟩ **b** : to oneself : PRIVATELY ⟨chuckled *inwardly*⟩ **3** : toward the inside ⟨curving *inwardly*⟩

in–your–face \ˌin-yər-ˌfās\ *adj* : characterized by bold and often arrogant aggressiveness ⟨*in-your-face* basketball⟩

io·dide \ˈī-ə-ˌdīd\ *n* : a compound of iodine with another element or chemical group

io·dine \ˈī-ə-ˌdīn, -əd-ᵊn, -ə-ˌdēn\ *also* **io·din** \ˈī-əd-ᵊn\ *n* **1** : a nonmetallic element that is obtained usually as heavy shining blackish gray crystals and is used especially in medicine and photography — see ELEMENT table **2** : a solution of iodine in alcohol used to kill germs

io·dize \ˈī-ə-ˌdīz\ *vb* **io·dized; io·diz·ing** : to treat with iodine or an iodide ⟨*iodized* salt⟩

io moth \ˈī-ō-\ *n* : a large yellowish American moth with a large spot on each hind wing

ion \ˈī-ən, ˈī-ˌän\ *n* : an atom or group of atoms that carries a positive or negative electric charge as a result of having lost or gained one or more electrons

io moth

-ion *n suffix* **1 a** : act or process ⟨valida*tion*⟩ **b** : result of an act or process ⟨regula*tion*⟩ **2** : state or condition ⟨hydra*tion*⟩ [derived from Latin *-ion-* (suffix) "act or process"]

\ə\	**abut**	\aú\	**out**	\i\	tip	\ȯ\	saw	\ú\	**foot**
\ər\	**further**	\ch\	**chin**	\ī\	life	\ȯi\	**coin**	\y\	**yet**
\a\	**mat**	\e\	**pet**	\j\	**job**	\th\	**thin**	\yü\	**few**
\ā\	**take**	\ē\	**easy**	\ŋ\	**sing**	\th\	**this**	\yú\	**cure**
\ä\	**cot, cart**	\g\	**go**	\ō\	**bone**	\ü\	**food**	\zh\	**vision**

ion·ic \ī-'än-ik\ *adj* : of, relating to, or existing in the form of ions

Ion·ic \ī-'än-ik\ *adj* : belonging to or resembling a style of Greek architecture characterized especially by the scroll≈like decoration of the capital of a column

ionic bond *n* : a chemical bond formed between ions of opposite charge

ion·ize \'ī-ə-,nīz\ *vb* **ion·ized; ion·iz·ing** **1** : to convert wholly or partly into ions **2** : to become ionized — **ion·iz·able** \-,nī-zə-bəl\ *adj* — **ion·iza·tion** \,ī-ə-nə-'zā-shən\ *n*

ion·o·sphere \ī-'än-ə-,sfi(ə)r\ *n* : the part of the earth's atmosphere beginning at an altitude of about 40 kilometers, extending outward more than 400 kilometers, and containing free electrically charged particles — **ion·o·spher·ic** \ī-,än-ə-'sfi(ə)r-ik, -'sfer-\ *adj*

io·ta \ī-'ōt-ə\ *n* **1** : the ninth letter of the Greek alphabet — I or ι **2** : a tiny amount : JOT

IOU \,ī-(,)ō-'yü\ *n* : a paper that has on it the letters IOU, a stated sum, and a signature and that is given to acknowledge a debt

-ious *adj suffix* : -OUS ⟨capac*ious*⟩ [derived from Latin *-iosus* and *-ius* (adjective suffixes)]

ip·e·cac \'ip-i-,kak\ *or* **ipe·ca·cu·a·nha** \ē-,pek-ə-kú-'an-yə\ *n* : a South American creeping plant related to the madder; *also* : its dried roots or rhizome or a concentrated preparation of these used especially formerly to cause vomiting or as a strong laxative

IQ \'ī-'kyü\ *n* : INTELLIGENCE QUOTIENT

ir- — see IN-

Ira·ni·an \ir-'ā-nē-ən\ *n* **1** : a person born or living in Iran **2** : a branch of the Indo-European family of languages that includes Persian — **Iranian** *adj*

iras·ci·ble \ir-'as-ə-bəl\ *adj* : having a hot temper and easily angered — **iras·ci·bil·i·ty** \ir-,as-ə-'bil-ət-ē\ *n* — **iras·ci·bly** \ir-'as-ə-blē\ *adv*

irate \ī-'rāt\ *adj* : ANGRY 1a — **irate·ly** *adv* — **irate·ness** *n*

ire \'ī(ə)r\ *n* : ¹ANGER — **ire** *vb* — **ire·ful** \-fəl\ *adj* — **ire·ful·ly** \-fə-lē\ *adv*

ir·i·des·cence \,ir-ə-'des-ᵊn(t)s\ *n* : a play of colors producing rainbow effects (as in a soap bubble)

ir·i·des·cent \,ir-ə-'des-ᵊnt\ *adj* : having or showing iridescence — **ir·i·des·cent·ly** *adv*

irid·i·um \ir-'id-ē-əm\ *n* : a silver-white hard brittle very heavy metallic element — see ELEMENT table

iris \'ī-rəs\ *n, pl* **iris·es** \-rə-səz\ *or* **iri·des** \'ī-rə-,dēz, 'ir-ə-\ **1** : the colored part around the pupil of the eye that varies in size to control the amount of light entering the pupil **2** *or pl* **iris** : any of a large genus of plants with long pointed leaves and large usually brightly colored flowers **3** : IRIS DIAPHRAGM

iris diaphragm *n* : an adjustable diaphragm of thin plates used for changing the diameter of a central opening to control the amount of light passing (as into a microscope or camera)

Irish \'ī(ə)r-ish\ *n* **1** Irish *pl* : the people of Ireland **2** : the Celtic language of Ireland — **Irish** *adj*

iris 2

Irish·man \'ī-rish-mən\ *n* : a person born or living in Ireland

Irish moss *n* **1** : the dried and bleached plants of two red algae used especially in cooking and pharmacy **2** : either of the two red algae that are the source of Irish moss

Irish potato *n* : POTATO 2b

Irish setter *n* : any of a breed of bird dogs having a mahogany-red coat

Irish terrier *n* : any of a breed of active medium-sized terriers developed in Ireland and having a dense close usually reddish stiff coat

Irish wolfhound *n* : any of a breed of very tall heavily-built hounds having a rough stiff coat

Irish·wom·an \'ī-rish-,wùm-ən\ *n* : a woman born or living in Ireland

irk \'ərk\ *vb* : to make weary, irritated, or bored : ANNOY

irk·some \'ərk-səm\ *adj* : annoying because of length or dullness ⟨an *irksome* task⟩ — **irk·some·ly** *adv* — **irk·some·ness** *n*

¹iron \'ī(-ə)rn\ *n* **1** : a heavy magnetic silver-white metallic element that quickly rusts in moist air, occurs in meteorites and rocks, and is easily shaped — see ELEMENT table **2** : something made of iron: as **a** *pl* : handcuffs or chains used to bind or hinder movement **b** : a heated metal tool used for branding **c** : a household device with a flat metal base that is heated to smooth or press cloth **3** : STRENGTH 1, HARDNESS ⟨muscles of *iron*⟩

²iron *adj* **1** : of, relating to, or made of iron **2** : resembling iron **3** : being strong and healthy : ROBUST ⟨an *iron* constitution⟩ **4** : INFLEXIBLE 3, UNRELENTING ⟨*iron* determination⟩

³iron *vb* : to smooth or press clothes with a heated iron ⟨*iron* a shirt⟩ — **iron·er** *n*

Iron Age *n* : the period of human culture characterized by the smelting and use of iron and beginning somewhat before 1000 B.C. in western Asia and Egypt

iron·bound \'ī(-ə)rn-'baund\ *adj* **1** : RUGGED 1 ⟨*ironbound* coasts⟩ **2** : ¹STERN 1a ⟨*ironbound* traditions⟩

¹iron·clad \-'klad\ *adj* **1** : covered by iron armor **2** : RIGOROUS 1, EXACTING ⟨*ironclad* laws⟩

²iron·clad \-,klad\ *n* : an armored naval vessel

iron curtain *n* : a political and military barrier that isolates an area from outside contact

iron horse *n* : ²LOCOMOTIVE

iron·ic \'ī-'rän-ik\ *or* **iron·i·cal** \-i-kəl\ *adj* : relating to, containing, or being irony ⟨an *ironic* turn of events⟩ ⟨an *ironic* laugh⟩ — **iron·i·cal·ly** \-i-k(ə-)lē\ *adv*

iron lung *n* : a device for artificial respiration in which the air pressure in a chamber surrounding a patient's chest changes in a rhythm and forces air into and out of the lungs

iron out **1** : to make smooth or flat by or as if by ironing **2** : to work out a solution to ⟨*ironed out* their differences⟩

iron oxide *n* : any of the oxides of iron; *esp* : FERRIC OXIDE

iron·stone \'ī(-ə)rn-,stōn\ *n* : a hard white pottery first made in England — called also *ironstone china*

iron sulfide *n* : a compound (as a pyrite) of iron and sulfur

iron·ware \'ī(-ə)rn-,wa(ə)r, -,we(ə)r\ *n* : articles made of iron

iron·weed \-,wēd\ *n* : any of several mostly weedy American plants related to the asters and bearing clusters of red or purple flowers at the end of a stalk

iron·wood \-,wùd\ *n* **1** : any of numerous trees and shrubs with very tough hard wood **2** : the wood of an ironwood

iron·work \-,wərk\ *n* **1** : work in iron **2** *pl* : a mill or building where iron or steel is smelted or heavy iron or steel products are made — **iron·work·er** \-,wər-kər\ *n*

iro·ny \'ī-rə-nē\ *n, pl* **-nies** **1 a** : the use of words that mean the opposite of what one really intends **b** : an ironic expression or utterance **2 a** : a big difference between an actual and an expected result of a sequence of events **b** : a result marked by this incongruity **3** : the contradiction between the situation developed in a drama and the words or actions of the characters that is understood by the audience but not by the characters themselves

Ir·o·quois \'ir-ə-,kwói\ *n, pl* **Iroquois** \-,kwói(z)\ : a member of any of the peoples of an American Indian confederacy that existed originally in central New York state

ir·ra·di·ate \ir-'ād-ē-,āt\ *vb* **-at·ed; -at·ing** **1 a** : to cast rays of light on : ILLUMINATE **b** : to affect or treat by exposure to radiation (as of ultraviolet light, X rays, or gamma rays) **2** : to give off like rays of light : RADIATE — **ir·ra·di·a·tion** \-ˌād-ē-'ā-shən\ n

ir·ra·tio·nal \(')ir-'(r)ash-nəl, -ən-ᵊl\ adj **1** : unable to reason ⟨*irrational* beasts⟩ ⟨*irrational* from fever⟩ **2** : not based on reason ⟨*irrational* fear⟩ **3** : being an irrational number ⟨an *irrational* root of an equation⟩ — **ir·ra·tio·nal·i·ty** \(ˌ)ir-ˌ(r)ash-ə-'nal-ət-ē\ n — **ir·ra·tio·nal·ly** \(')ir-'(r)ash-nə-lē, -ən-ᵊl-ē\ adv

irrational number n : a number that can be expressed as a decimal with an infinite number of digits to the right of the decimal point and with no set of consecutive digits repeating itself indefinitely but cannot be expressed as the quotient of two integers

ir·rec·on·cil·able \(ˌ)ir-ˌ(r)ek-ən-'sī-lə-bəl, (')ir-'(r)ek-ən-ˌsī-\ adj : impossible to reconcile, adjust, or harmonize ⟨ended the partnership because of *irreconcilable* differences⟩ — **ir·rec·on·cil·ably** \-blē\ adv

ir·re·cov·er·able \ˌir-i-'kəv-(ə)rə-bəl\ adj : not capable of being recovered or made right — **ir·re·cov·er·ably** \-blē\ adv

ir·re·deem·able \ˌir-i-'dē-mə-bəl\ adj **1** : not redeemable **2** : being beyond remedy : HOPELESS — **ir·re·deem·ably** \-blē\ adv

ir·re·duc·ible \ˌir-i-'d(y)ü-sə-bəl\ adj : not reducible — **ir·re·duc·ibil·i·ty** \-ˌd(y)ü-sə-'bil-ət-ē\ n — **ir·re·duc·ibly** \-'d(y)ü-sə-blē\ adv

ir·re·fut·able \ˌir-i-'fyüt-ə-bəl, (')ir-'(r)ef-yət-\ adj : not capable of being proved wrong : INDISPUTABLE — **ir·re·fut·ably** \-blē\ adv

¹ir·reg·u·lar \(')ir-'(r)eg-yə-lər\ adj **1 a** : not following custom or rule **b** : not belonging to a recognized or organized body ⟨*irregular* troops⟩ **2 a** : not following the normal or usual manner of inflection ⟨the *irregular* verb "sell"⟩ **b** : STRONG 12 ⟨the *irregular* verb "write"⟩ **3 a** : having one or more like parts unequal in size, form, or the way they are joined so that the whole structure has bilateral symmetry instead of radial symmetry ⟨*irregular* flowers⟩ **b** : UNEVEN **4** : not continuous or regular in occurrence ⟨at *irregular* intervals⟩ — **ir·reg·u·lar·ly** adv

²irregular n **1** : an irregular soldier **2** : merchandise that is slightly imperfect

ir·reg·u·lar·i·ty \(ˌ)ir-ˌ(r)eg-yə-'lar-ət-ē\ n, pl **-ties** **1** : the quality or state of being irregular **2** : something (as dishonest conduct) that is irregular

ir·rel·e·vant \(')ir-'(r)el-ə-vənt\ adj : not relevant : not applicable or pertinent ⟨the evidence presented was judged *irrelevant* to the case⟩ — **ir·rel·e·vance** \-vən(t)s\ or **ir·rel·e·van·cy** \-vən-sē\ n — **ir·rel·e·vant·ly** adv

ir·re·li·gious \ˌir-i-'lij-əs\ adj : lacking religious emotions, principles, or practices — **ir·re·li·gious·ly** adv

ir·re·me·di·a·ble \ˌir-i-'mēd-ē-ə-bəl\ adj : not remediable; esp : INCURABLE — **ir·re·me·di·a·bly** \-blē\ adv

ir·re·mov·able \ˌir-i-'mü-və-bəl\ adj : not removable — **ir·re·mov·abil·i·ty** \-ˌmü-və-'bil-ət-ē\ n — **ir·re·mov·ably** \-'mü-və-blē\ adv

ir·rep·a·ra·ble \(')ir-'(r)ep-(ə-)rə-bəl\ adj : not capable of being repaired or regained ⟨an *irreparable* loss⟩ — **ir·rep·a·ra·bly** \-blē\ adv

ir·re·place·able \ˌir-i-'plā-sə-bəl\ adj : not replaceable ⟨a museum full of *irreplaceable* works of art⟩

ir·re·press·ible \ˌir-i-'pres-ə-bəl\ adj : impossible to repress or control ⟨*irrepressible* curiosity⟩ — **ir·re·press·ibil·i·ty** \-ˌpres-ə-'bil-ət-ē\ n — **ir·re·press·ibly** \-'pres-ə-blē\ adv

ir·re·proach·able \ˌir-i-'prō-chə-bəl\ adj : not reproachable : BLAMELESS — **ir·re·proach·ably** \-blē\ adv

ir·re·sist·ible \ˌir-i-'zis-tə-bəl\ adj : impossible to resist ⟨an *irresistible* attraction⟩ — **ir·re·sist·ibil·i·ty** \-ˌzis-tə-'bil-ət-ē\ adj — **ir·re·sist·ibly** \-'zis-tə-blē\ adv

ir·res·o·lute \(')ir-'(r)ez-ə-ˌlüt, -lət\ adj : not resolute : HESITANT — **ir·res·o·lute·ly** adv — **ir·res·o·lute·ness** n —

ir·res·o·lu·tion \(ˌ)ir-ˌ(r)ez-ə-'lü-shən\ n

ir·re·spec·tive of \ˌir-i-'spek-tiv-\ prep : without regard to

ir·re·spon·si·ble \ˌir-i-'spän(t)-sə-bəl\ adj **1** : not legally responsible **2** : having or showing no sense of responsibility **3** : unable to bear responsibility — **ir·re·spon·si·bil·i·ty** \-ˌspän(t)-sə-'bil-ət-ē\ n — **ir·re·spon·si·bly** \-'spän(t)-sə-blē\ adv

ir·re·triev·able \ˌir-i-'trē-və-bəl\ adj : not capable of being recovered, regained, or remedied — **ir·re·triev·ably** \-blē\ adv

ir·rev·er·ent \(')ir-'(r)ev-(ə-)rənt, -ərnt\ adj : showing lack of reverence ⟨*irreverent* joking and giggling in church⟩ — **ir·rev·er·ence** \-'(r)ev-(ə-)rən(t)s, -'(r)ev-ərn(t)s\ n — **ir·rev·er·ent·ly** adv

ir·re·vers·ible \ˌir-i-'vər-sə-bəl\ adj : impossible to reverse ⟨an *irreversible* chemical reaction⟩ ⟨*irreversible* damage⟩ — **ir·re·vers·ibil·i·ty** \-ˌvər-sə-'bil-ət-ē\ n — **ir·re·vers·ibly** \-'vər-sə-blē\ adv

ir·rev·o·ca·ble \(')ir-'(r)ev-ə-kə-bəl\ adj : not capable of being revoked ⟨an *irrevocable* decision⟩ — **ir·rev·o·ca·bil·i·ty** \(ˌ)ir-ˌ(r)ev-ə-kə-'bil-ət-ē\ n — **ir·rev·o·ca·bly** \(')ir-'(r)ev-ə-kə-blē\ adv

ir·ri·gate \'ir-ə-ˌgāt\ vb **-gat·ed; -gat·ing** **1** : to supply with water by artificial means ⟨*irrigate* a field⟩ ⟨*irrigate* crops⟩ **2** : to flush with a liquid ⟨*irrigate* a wound⟩

ir·ri·ga·tion \ˌir-ə-'gā-shən\ n : an act or process of irrigating

ir·ri·ta·bil·i·ty \ˌir-ət-ə-'bil-ət-ē\ n, pl **-ties** **1** : the quality or state of being irritable; esp : readiness to become annoyed or angry **2** : the property of protoplasm and of living things that permits them to react to stimuli

ir·ri·ta·ble \'ir-ət-ə-bəl\ adj : capable of being irritated; esp : easily irritated — **ir·ri·ta·ble·ness** n — **ir·ri·ta·bly** \-blē\ adv

¹ir·ri·tant \'ir-ə-tənt\ adj : tending to produce anger, annoyance, impatience, soreness, or inflammation; esp : tending to produce physical irritation

²irritant n : something that irritates

ir·ri·tate \'ir-ə-ˌtāt\ vb **-tat·ed; -tat·ing** **1** : to excite impatience, anger, or displeasure in : ANNOY ⟨were *irritated* by the child's rudeness⟩ **2** : to make sore or inflamed ⟨harsh soaps can *irritate* the skin⟩

ir·ri·ta·tion \ˌir-ə-'tā-shən\ n **1** : the act of irritating : the state of being irritated **2** : ²IRRITANT

ir·rupt \(')i(ə)r-'(r)əpt\ vb : to rush in violently : burst in — **ir·rup·tion** \-'(r)əp-shən\ n

is present 3d sing of BE

is- or **iso-** combining form : equal : uniform ⟨*iso*bar⟩ [derived from Greek *isos* "equal"]

Isa·iah \ī-'zā-ə\ n — see BIBLE table

Isa·ias \ī-'zā-əs\ n — see BIBLE table

is·chi·um \'is-kē-əm\ n, pl **-chia** \-kē-ə\ : the one of the three bones making up each side of the pelvis that is uppermost and in back

-ish \ish\ adj suffix **1** : of, relating to, or being ⟨Finn*ish*⟩ **2 a** : characteristic of ⟨boy*ish*⟩ ⟨mul*ish*⟩ **b** : somewhat ⟨purpl*ish*⟩ **c** : having the approximate age of ⟨forty*ish*⟩ **d** : being or occurring at the approximate time of ⟨arrive around eight*ish*⟩ [Old English *-isc* (adjective suffix)]

isin·glass \'iz-ᵊn-ˌglas, 'ī-ziŋ-\ n : mica in thin sheets

Is·lam \is-'läm, iz-, -'lam; 'is-ˌläm, 'iz-ˌläm, -ˌlam\ n **1** : a religion marked by belief in Allah as the sole deity, in Muhammad as his prophet, and in the Koran **2 a** : the civilization erected upon Islamic faith **b** : the modern nations in which Islam is the dominant religion — **Is·lam·ic** \is-'läm-ik, iz-, -'lam-\ adj

\ə\ abut	\au̇\ out	\i\ tip	\ȯ\ saw	\u̇\ foot
\ər\ further	\ch\ chin	\ī\ life	\ȯi\ coin	\y\ yet
\a\ mat	\e\ pet	\j\ job	\th\ thin	\yü\ few
\ā\ take	\ē\ easy	\ŋ\ sing	\t͟h\ this	\yu̇\ cure
\ä\ cot, cart	\g\ go	\ō\ bone	\ü\ food	\zh\ vision

is·land \'ī-lənd\ *n* **1** : an area of land surrounded by water and smaller than a continent **2** : something suggestive of an island in its isolation [an altered form of earlier *iland* "island", derived from Old English *īgland* "island"; the spelling *island* was influenced by the word *isle,* which is not related]

is·land·er \'ī-lən-dər\ *n* : a person born or living on an island

island of Langerhans : ISLET OF LANGERHANS

island universe *n* : a galaxy other than the Milky Way

isle \'ī(ə)l\ *n* : ISLAND 1; *esp* : ISLET [from early French *isle* "isle, island", from Latin *insula* "island" — related to IN-SULATE, ISOLATE, PENINSULA]

is·let \'ī-lət\ *n* : a little island

islet of Lang·er·hans \-'läŋ-ər-,hänz, -,hän(t)s\ : any of the groups of small endocrine cells in the pancreas that produce and give off insulin

ism \'iz-əm\ *n* : a distinctive belief, cause, or theory

-ism \,iz-əm\ *n suffix* **1 a** : act : practice : process ⟨criti*cism*⟩ ⟨plagiar*ism*⟩ **b** : manner of action or behavior ⟨hero*ism*⟩ **2 a** : state : condition : property ⟨skeptic*ism*⟩ **b** : abnormal state or condition ⟨alcohol*ism*⟩ ⟨mongol*ism*⟩ **3** : doctrine : theory : cult ⟨Buddh*ism*⟩ ⟨social*ism*⟩ **4** : characteristic or peculiar feature ⟨colloquial*ism*⟩ [derived from Greek *-isma* and Greek *-ismos* (noun suffixes)]

isn't \'iz-ᵊnt\ : is not

iso·bar \'ī-sə-,bär\ *n* : a line drawn on a map to indicate areas having the same atmospheric pressure at a given time or for a given period — **iso·bar·ic** \,ī-sə-'bär-ik, -'bar-\ *adj*

iso·late \'ī-sə-,lāt *also* 'is-ə-\ *vb* **-lat·ed; -lat·ing** : to set or keep apart from others [derived from French *isolé* (adjective) "isolated, set off from others", from Italian *isola* "island", from Latin *insula* "island" — related to INSULATE, ISLE, PENINSULA]

isobar

iso·la·tion \,ī-sə-'lā-shən *also* ,is-ə-\ *n* **1** : the act of isolating : the condition of being isolated **2** : separation of a population of living things from related forms in such a manner as to prevent crossbreeding

iso·la·tion·ism \,ī-sə-'lā-shə-,niz-əm\ *n* : a national policy of avoiding international political and economic relations — **iso·la·tion·ist** \-sh(ə-)nəst\ *n or adj*

iso·mer \'ī-sə-mər\ *n* : one of two or more chemical compounds or groups that have the same numbers of atoms of the same elements but differ in structure — **iso·mer·ic** \,ī-sə-'mer-ik\ *adj* — **isom·er·ism** \ī-'säm-ə-,riz-əm\ *n*

iso·met·ric \,ī-sə-'me-trik\ *adj* : of, relating to, or being muscular contraction of the kind that takes place in doing isometrics

iso·met·rics \,ī-sə-'me-triks\ *n sing or pl* : exercise or a system of exercises in which opposing muscles are contracted in such a way that there is little shortening but great increase in the tone of the muscle fibers involved

iso·pod \'ī-sə-,päd\ *n* : any of a large order of small crustaceans (as a wood louse) with a thorax made up of seven segments of which each bears a pair of legs — **isopod** *adj*

iso·prene \'ī-sə-,prēn\ *n* : a compound used especially in making synthetic rubber

iso·pro·pyl alcohol \,ī-sə-'prō-pəl-\ *n* : a flammable liquid used especially to dissolve things and as rubbing alcohol

isos·ce·les \ī-,säs-(ə-),lēz\ *adj* **1** : being a triangle with two equal sides **2** : being a trapezoid whose two nonparallel sides are equal

isos·ta·sy \ī-'säs-tə-sē\ *n* : the state of balance that exists

between the earth's crust and the denser rock material beneath — **iso·stat·ic** \,ī-sə-'stat-ik\ *adj*

iso·therm \'ī-sə-,thərm\ *n* : a line on a map connecting points having the same temperature

iso·tope \'ī-sə-,tōp\ *n* : any of the forms of an element that differ in the number of neutrons in an atom — **iso·top·ic** \,ī-sə-'täp-ik, -'tō-pik\ *adj* — **iso·top·i·cal·ly** \-'täp-i-k(ə-)lē, -'tō-pi-\ *adv*

Is·rae·li \iz-'rā-lē\ *adj* : of, relating to, or characteristic of the republic of Israel or its people — **Israeli** *n*

Is·ra·el·ite \'iz-r(ē-)ə-,līt\ *n* : a descendant of the Hebrew patriarch Jacob; *esp* : a person born or living in the ancient kingdom of Israel — **Israelite** *adj*

is·su·ance \'ish-ù-wən(t)s\ *n* : the act of issuing especially officially

¹is·sue \'ish-ü\ *n* **1** : the action of going, coming, or flowing out **2** : a means or place of going out : EXIT, OUTLET **3** : OFFSPRING, PROGENY **4** : final outcome : RESULT **5** : a point of debate or controversy **6** : a giving off (as of blood) from the body **7** : something issued or issuing; *esp* : the copies of a publication published at one time

²issue *vb* **is·sued; is·su·ing** **1** : to go, come, or flow out : EMERGE ⟨water *issuing* from a pipe⟩ **2 a** : to cause to come forth **b** : to distribute officially **c** : to send out for sale or circulation : PUBLISH **3** : to come as an effect : RESULT [Middle English *issuen* "to go out, flow out", derived from early French *issir* "to come or go out", from Latin *exire* "go out", from *ex-* "out of, from" and *ire* "to go" — related to EXIT, ITINERARY, TRANSIT] — **is·su·er** *n*

-ist \əst\ *n suffix* **1 a** : one that performs a (specified) action ⟨cycl*ist*⟩ : one that makes or produces ⟨novel*ist*⟩ **b** : one that plays a (specified) musical instrument ⟨harp*ist*⟩ **c** : one that operates a (specified) machine ⟨automobil*ist*⟩ **2** : one that specializes in a (specified) art or science or skill ⟨geolog*ist*⟩ **3** : one that believes in or favors a (specified) doctrine or system or code of behavior ⟨social*ist*⟩ or that of a (specified) individual ⟨Buddh*ist*⟩ [derived from Greek *-istēs* (noun suffix)]

isth·mus \'is-məs\ *n* : a narrow strip of land connecting two larger land areas

-is·tic \'is-tik\ *or* **-is·ti·cal** \'is-ti-kəl\ *adj suffix* : of, relating to, or characteristic of [derived from Greek *-istikos* (adjective suffix), from *-istēs* (noun suffix) "-ist"]

¹it \(')it, ət\ *pron* **1** : that one — used usually to refer to a lifeless thing ⟨caught the ball and threw *it* back⟩, a living thing whose sex is unknown or disregarded ⟨don't know who *it* is⟩, a group, or an abstract entity **2** — used as subject of a verb that expresses a condition or action without a doer ⟨*it* is raining⟩ **3 a** — used in the usual place of a noun, phrase, or clause not in its ordinary place ⟨*it* is necessary to repeat the whole thing⟩ ⟨*it* was here that I lost my way⟩ **b** — used as a direct object with little or no meaning ⟨footed *it* back to camp⟩ **4** : the general state of affairs ⟨how is *it* going⟩

²it \'it\ *n* : the player in a game (as tag) who has to catch the others

Ital·ian \ə-'tal-yən, i-\ *n* **1 a** : a person born or living in Italy **b** : a person of Italian ancestry **2** : the Romance language of the Italians — **Italian** *adj*

Italian sandwich *n* : ²SUBMARINE 2

¹ital·ic \ə-'tal-ik, i-, ī-\ *adj* **1** *cap* : of or relating to ancient Italy, its peoples, or their Indo-European languages **2** : of, relating to, or being a type style with characters that slant upward to the right (as in *"these words are italic"*)

²italic *n* : an italic character or type

ital·i·cize \ə-'tal-ə-,sīz, i-, ī-\ *vb* **-cized; -ciz·ing** : to print in italics or underline with a single line

¹itch \'ich\ *vb* **1** : to have or produce an itch **2** : to cause to itch **3** : to have a strong desire ⟨*itching* to get going⟩

²itch *n* **1 a** : an uneasy irritating feeling in the skin usually held to result from exciting cells or groups of cells which sense pain **b** : a skin disorder accompanied by an itch;

esp : SCABIES **2** : a restless usually constant desire — **itch·i·ness** \'ich-ē-nəs\ *n* — **itchy** \-ē\ *adj*

it'd \'it-əd\ : it had : it would

-ite \,īt\ *n suffix* **1 a** : one who is from or lives in a (specified) area ⟨suburban*ite*⟩ ⟨New Jersey*ite*⟩ **b** : descendant ⟨Israel*ite*⟩ **2** : product **3** : fossil ⟨ammon*ite*⟩ **4** : mineral ⟨hal*ite*⟩ : rock ⟨quartz*ite*⟩ [derived from Greek *-ītēs* (noun and adjective suffix)]

item \'īt-əm\ *n* **1** : a separate part in a list, account, or series **2** : a brief piece of news or an article reporting it

item·ize \'īt-ə-,mīz\ *vb* **-ized; -iz·ing** : to set down one by one : LIST ⟨*itemize* expenses⟩ — **item·iza·tion** \,īt-ə-mə-'zā-shən\ *n*

it·er·a·tion \,it-ə-'rā-shən\ *n* : REPETITION; *esp* : a computational process in which a series of operations is repeated a number of times

itin·er·ant \ī-'tin-ə-rənt, ə-'tin-\ *adj* : traveling from place to place ⟨an *itinerant* preacher⟩

itin·er·ary \ī-'tin-ə-,rer-ē, ə-\ *n, pl* **-ar·ies** **1** : the route of a journey **2** : a travel diary **3** : a traveler's guidebook [Middle English *itinerarie* "route of a journey", from Latin *itinerarium* (same meaning), derived from earlier *itiner-, iter* "journey, passage", from *ire* "to go" — related to EXIT, ISSUE, TRANSIT] — **itinerary** *adj*

-i·tis \'īt-əs\ *n suffix, pl* **-i·tis·es** \'īt-ə-səz\ *also* **-it·i·des** \'it-ə-,dēz\ *or* **-i·tes** \'īt-(,)ēz, 'ēt-\ : inflamed state of or disorder with inflammation of ⟨bronch*itis*⟩ [derived from Greek *-itis* (noun and adjective suffix)]

it'll \,it-ᵊl\ : it shall : it will

its \(,)its, əts\ *adj* : of or relating to it or itself especially as possessor ⟨*its* kennel⟩, agent ⟨a child proud of *its* first drawings⟩, or object of an action ⟨*its* enactment into law⟩

it's \(,)its, əts\ **1** : it is **2** : it has

it·self \it-'self, ət-\ *pron* **1** : that identical one — used to show that the subject and object of the verb are the same ⟨the cat gave *itself* a bath⟩ or for emphasis ⟨the letter *itself* was missing⟩ **2** : its normal, healthy, or sane self

-ity \ət-ē\ *n suffix, pl* **-ities** : quality : state : degree ⟨alkalin*ity*⟩ [derived from Latin *-itat-, -itas* "quality, state"]

IUD \,ī-,yü-'dē\ *n* : INTRAUTERINE DEVICE

-ive \iv\ *adj suffix* : that performs or tends toward an indicated action ⟨exhaust*ive*⟩ [derived from Latin *-ivus* (adjective suffix)]

I've \(,)īv\ : I have

ivied \'ī-vēd\ *adj* : covered with ivy

ivo·ry \'īv-(ə-)rē\ *n, pl* **-ries** **1** : the hard creamy-white substance of which the tusks of a tusked mammal (as an elephant) are formed **2** : a pale whitish yellow

ivo·ry–billed woodpecker \,īv-(ə-)rē-,bild-\ *n* : a large nearly extinct woodpecker with glossy black feathers, a large ivory-white bill, and in the male a large pointed bunch of scarlet feathers on the head

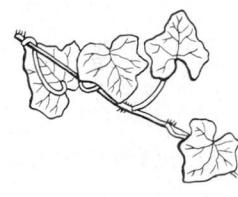

ivory-billed woodpecker

ivy \'ī-vē\ *n, pl* **ivies** **1** : a climbing woody vine with glossy evergreen leaves, small yellowish flowers, and black berries that is often grown on the outside of buildings — called also *English ivy* **2** : any of several plants (as Virginia creeper) resembling ivy

-ize \,īz\ *vb suffix* **1** : cause to be or conform to or resemble ⟨american*ize*⟩ : form or cause to be formed into ⟨crystal*ize*⟩ ⟨union*ize*⟩ **2 a** : subject to a specified action ⟨satir*ize*⟩ **b** : saturate, treat, or combine with ⟨oxid*ize*⟩ ⟨macadam*ize*⟩ **3** : treat like ⟨idol*ize*⟩ **4** : engage in a (specified) activity ⟨philosoph*ize*⟩ [derived from Greek *-izein* (verb suffix)]

ivy 1

J

j \'jā\ *n, often cap* : the 10th letter of the English alphabet

jab \'jab\ *vb* **jabbed; jab·bing** : to poke quickly or suddenly with or as if with something sharp — **jab** *n*

¹jab·ber \'jab-ər\ *vb* **jab·bered; jab·ber·ing** \-(ə-)riŋ\ : to talk or speak too fast or not clearly enough to be understood — **jab·ber·er** \'jab-ər-ər\ *n*

²jabber *n* : GIBBERISH, CHATTER

jab·ber·wocky \'jab-ər-,wäk-ē\ *n* : meaningless speech or writing

ja·bot \zha-'bō, 'jab-,ō\ *n* : a ruffle of cloth or lace that falls from the collar down the front of a dress or shirt

¹jack \'jak\ *n* **1 a** : ¹MAN 1a **b** *often cap* : SAILOR **2 a** : a device for turning a spit (as in roasting meat) **b** : any of various portable devices for applying pressure or lifting a heavy body (as an automobile or a building) a short distance **3** : any of various animals: as **a** : a male donkey **b** : JACKRABBIT **4 a** : a small national flag flown by a ship **b** : a small six-pointed metal object used in a game **c** *pl* : a game played with jacks **5** : a playing card bearing the figure of a soldier or servant **6** *slang* : MONEY 1a **7** : a socket used with a plug to connect one electric circuit with another

²jack *vb* **1** : to move or lift by or as if by a jack **2** : ¹INCREASE 1, RAISE ⟨*jack* up prices⟩ — **jack·er** *n*

jack·al \'jak-əl, -,ȯl\ *n* : any of several Old World wild dogs like but smaller than the related wolves

jack·ass \'jak-,as\ *n* **1** : DONKEY 1; *esp* : a male donkey **2** : a stupid person : FOOL

jackal

jack·boot \-,büt\ *n* : a heavy military boot; *esp* : one reaching above the knee

\ə\ abut	\au̇\ **out**	\i\ **tip**	\ȯ\ **saw**	\u̇\ **foot**	
\ər\ **further**	\ch\ **chin**	\ī\ **life**	\ȯi\ **coin**	\y\ **yet**	
\a\ **mat**	\e\ **pet**	\j\ **job**	\th\ **thin**	\yü\ **few**	
\ā\ **take**	\ē\ **easy**	\ŋ\ **sing**	\th\ **this**	\yu̇\ **cure**	
\ä\ **cot, cart**	\g\ **go**	\ō\ **bone**	\ü\ **food**	\zh\ **vi**sion	

jack·daw \-,dȯ\ *n* : a common black and gray Eurasian bird related to but smaller than the crows

jack·et \'jak-ət\ *n* **1** : a garment for the upper body usually having a front opening, collar, and sleeves **2** : an outer covering or casing: as **a** : a tough metal covering on a bullet or projectile **b** : a coating or covering of a nonconducting material used to prevent heat radiation **c** : an outer paper wrapper on a bound book — **jack·et·ed** \-ət-əd\ *adj*

jack·ham·mer \'jak-,ham-ər\ *n* : a tool driven by compressed air that is used for drilling or breaking up hard substances (as rock or pavement) by a repeated pounding action

jack–in–the–box \'jak-ən-thə-,bäks\ *n, pl* **jack–in–the–box·es** *or* **jacks–in–the–box** : a small box out of which a figure (as of a clown's head) springs when the lid is raised

jack–in–the–pul·pit \,jak-ən-thə-'pùl-,pit\ *n, pl* **jack–in–the–pulpits** *or* **jacks–in–the–pulpit** *n* : an American spring-flowering herb that grows in moist shady places and bears an upright club-shaped flower cluster over which arches a green and purple bract like a hood

¹**jack·knife** \'jak-,nïf\ *n* **1** : a large strong pocketknife **2** : a dive in which the diver bends from the waist and touches the ankles before straightening out

²**jackknife** *vb* : to double up like a jackknife ⟨the trailer truck *jackknifed*⟩

jack–of–all–trades \,jak-ə-'vȯl-,trādz\ *n, pl* **jacks–of–all–trades** : a person who can work at various trades

jack–o'–lan·tern \'jak-ə-,lant-ərn\ *n* : a lantern made of a pumpkin cut to look like a face

jack pine *n* : a North American pine with pairs of stout twisted needles and wood used especially to make pulp for paper

jack·pot \'jak-,pät\ *n* **1** : a large poker pot formed by the accumulation of stakes from previous play **2 a** : a combination on a slot machine that wins a top prize or all the coins in the machine **b** : the sum so won **3** : a great often unexpected success or reward

jack·rab·bit \-,rab-ət\ *n* : any of several large hares of western North America with very long ears and long hind legs

jack·screw \-,skrü\ *n* : a jack operated by a screw for lifting or for applying pressure

jack·stone \-,stōn\ *n* **1** : ¹JACK 4b **2** *pl* : ¹JACK 4c

jack·straw \-,strȯ\ *n* **1** : one of the pieces used in the game jackstraws **2** *pl* : a game in which straws or thin strips are let fall in a heap and each player in turn tries to remove one at a time without disturbing the rest

jack–tar \-'tär\ *n, often cap* : SAILOR

¹**jade** \'jād\ *n* : a broken-down, bad-tempered, or worthless horse [Middle English *jade* "a broken-down or worthless horse"]

²**jade** *vb* **jad·ed; jad·ing** **1 a** : WEAR OUT 1, TIRE **b** : to become weary **2** : to make dull or uninterested by too much of something

³**jade** *n* : a tough usually green gemstone that takes a high polish

> **Word History** Gemstones were once thought to cure sickness as well as to work magic. Jade was supposed to be especially good at curing kidney problems. Many Indians of the Americas treasured jade and used the stone to make beautiful objects. In the 16th century the Spanish brought some of this jade back home from the New World. They named the gemstone *piedra de la ijada*, because of their belief that jade could cure kidney disease. Spain was not the only country to value this gemstone. Jade became popular throughout western Europe both for wearing as jewelry and for curing or preventing disease. Our English word comes from French, which had borrowed the last word in the Spanish name, spelling it *jade*. [from French *jade* "the gemstone jade", from obsolete Spanish *(piedra de la) ijada*,

literally "stone of the loin"; *ijada* derived from Latin *ileum* "groin, ileum"]

jade green *n* : a light bluish green

¹**jag** \'jag\ *n* : a sharp pointed part

²**jag** *n* : SPREE ⟨a crying *jag*⟩

jag·ged \'jag-əd\ *adj* : having a sharp uneven edge or surface — **jag·ged·ly** *adv* — **jag·ged·ness** *n*

jag·uar \'jag(-yə)-,wär\ *n* : a large yellowish brown black-spotted cat of tropical America that is larger and has a more solid build than the leopard

jaguar

jai alai \'hī-,lī, ,hī-ə-'lī\ *n* : a court game somewhat like handball played by two or four players using a ball and a long curved basket strapped to the wrist

jail \'jā(ə)l\ *n* : PRISON — **jail** *vb*

jail·bird \-,bərd\ *n* : a person who is or is often in jail

jail·break \-,brāk\ *n* : an escape from jail by use of force

jail·er *or* **jail·or** \'jā-lər\ *n* : a keeper of a jail

ja·lopy \jə-'läp-ē\ *n, pl* **-lop·ies** : a worn-out old automobile

jal·ou·sie \'jal-ə-sē\ *n* **1** : a blind with adjustable horizontal strips (as of wood, plastic, or glass) to admit light and air and shut out sun and rain **2** : a window made of adjustable glass louvers

¹**jam** \'jam\ *vb* **jammed; jam·ming** **1 a** : to press or push into a close or tight position ⟨*jam* a book into a bookcase⟩ **b** : to be or cause to be wedged so as to be unworkable ⟨*jam* the typewriter keys⟩ **c** : to crowd into : PACK ⟨2000 people *jammed* the hall⟩ **2** : to push suddenly and with force ⟨*jam* on the brakes⟩ **3** : to squeeze or crush painfully ⟨*jammed* my finger in the door⟩ **4** : to make impossible to understand by sending out interfering signals or messages ⟨*jam* a radio broadcast⟩ **5** : to take part in a jam session — **jam·mer** *n*

²**jam** *n* **1 a** : an act or instance of jamming **b** : a crowded mass that slows or prevents movement ⟨traffic *jam*⟩ **2** : a difficult state of affairs

³**jam** *n* : a food made of fruit and sugar thickened by boiling

jamb \'jam\ *n* : an upright piece forming the side of an opening (as of a door)

jam·ba·laya \,jəm-bə-'lī-ə\ *n* : rice cooked with ham, sausage, chicken, shrimp, or oysters and seasoned with herbs

jam·bo·ree \,jam-bə-'rē\ *n* **1** : a large festive gathering **2** : a national or international camping assembly of Boy Scouts

jam–pack \'jam-'pak\ *vb* : to pack tightly : CRAM

James \'jāmz\ *n* — see BIBLE table

jam session *n* : an informal performance by a group of musicians (as jazz musicians) who often invite visitors to join in

jan·gle \'jaŋ-gəl\ *vb* **jan·gled; jan·gling** \-g(ə-)liŋ\ **1** : to make or cause to make a harsh ringing sound **2** : to excite to tense irritation ⟨*jangled* nerves⟩ — **jangle** *n*

jan·i·tor \'jan-ət-ər\ *n* **1** : DOORKEEPER **2** : a person who has the care of a building — **jan·i·to·ri·al** \,jan-ə-'tōr-ē-əl, -'tȯr-\ *adj*

Jan·u·ary \'jan-yə-,wer-ē\ *n* : the first month of the year

> **Word History** Among the many gods worshiped by the ancient Romans was one named Janus. He was believed to have two faces, one looking forward and one

looking back. Janus was associated with doors, gates, and all beginnings. Because of that, when the Romans changed their calendar and added two months to the beginning of the year, they named the first one *Januarius* to honor Janus. The English *January* comes from Latin *Januarius.* [from Latin *Januarius* "first month of the year", from *Janus,* a Roman god]

Jap·a·nese \,jap-ə-'nēz, -'nēs\ *n, pl* **Japanese 1 a :** a person born or living in Japan   **b :** a person of Japanese ancestry   **2 :** the language of the Japanese — **Japanese** *adj*

Japanese beetle *n* : a small glossy green and brown Asian beetle introduced into America where it is a harmful pest whose larvae feed on the roots of grasses and on decaying vegetation and whose adults eat leaves, flowers, and fruits

Japanese lantern *n* : CHINESE LANTERN

Japanese quince *n* : a hardy Chinese ornamental shrub of the rose family with scarlet flowers

ja·pon·i·ca \jə-'pän-i-kə\ *n* : JAPANESE QUINCE

¹jar \'jär\ *vb* **jarred; jar·ring 1 a :** to make a harsh or disagreeable sound   **b :** to have a harsh or disagreeable effect 〈noise that *jars* the nerves〉   **2 :** to cause to vibrate : SHAKE   **3 :** ¹CLASH 2b, CONFLICT 〈*jarring* opinions〉 [probably an imitation of the sound made]

²jar *n*   **1 :** a harsh sound   **2 :** ²JOLT   **3 :** ¹QUARREL 2, DISPUTE   **4 :** a painful effect : SHOCK

³jar *n*   **1 :** a usually glass or pottery container having a wide mouth   **2 :** the quantity held by a jar [from early French *jarre* "a container with a wide mouth", derived from Arabic *jarrah* "a pottery water container"]

jar·di·niere \,järd-ᵊn-'i(ə)r\ *n* : an ornamental stand or pot for plants or flowers

jar·gon \'jär-gən, -,gän\ *n*   **1 :** a mixed language used for communication between peoples whose native languages are different   **2 :** the special language of a particular activity or group 〈legal *jargon*〉   **3 :** language that is not clear and is full of long important-sounding words

jas·mine \'jaz-mən\ *or* **jes·sa·mine** \'jes-(ə-)mən\ *n* : any of numerous often climbing shrubs that are related to the olive and have extremely fragrant flowers; *also* : any of various plants noted for sweet-scented flowers

jas·per \'jas-pər\ *n* : an opaque usually red, green, yellow, or brown stone used for making ornamental objects (as vases); *esp* : green chalcedony — **jas·pery** \-pə-rē\ *adj*

jaun·dice \'jȯn-dəs, 'jän-\ *n*   **1** : yellowish discoloring of the skin,

jasmine

tissues, and body fluids caused by the presence of coloring matter from the bile; *also* : a disease or abnormal condition marked by jaundice   **2 :** a state or attitude marked by envy, dislike, or hostility

jaun·diced \'jȯn-dəst\ *adj*   **1 :** affected with or as if with jaundice   **2 :** showing or influenced by envy, dislike, or hostility 〈a *jaundiced* eye〉

jaunt \'jȯnt, 'jänt\ *n* : a short trip for pleasure — **jaunt** *vb*

jaun·ty \'jȯnt-ē, 'jänt-\ *adj* **jaun·ti·er; -est** : perky in manner or appearance : LIVELY 〈*jaunty* marching tunes〉 — **jaun·ti·ly** \'jȯnt-ᵊl-ē, 'jänt-\ *adv* — **jaun·ti·ness** \'jȯnt-ē-nəs, 'jänt-\ *n*

Ja·va man \,jäv-ə-, ,jav-\ *n* : a small-brained prehistoric human being known chiefly from parts of skeletons found in Java and now classified with the pithecanthropines

jav·e·lin \'jav-(ə-)lən\ *n*   **1 :** a light spear   **2 :** a slender usually metal shaft that is thrown for distance in a track-and-field event

¹jaw \'jȯ\ *n*   **1 a :** either of two structures of bone or carti-

lage of vertebrate animals that support the soft parts enclosing the mouth and usually bear teeth   **b :** the parts making up the walls of the mouth and serving to open and close it — usually used in pl.   **c :** any of various organs of invertebrate animals that serve the same purpose as the jaws of vertebrate animals   **2 :** something resembling the jaw of an animal in form or action; *esp* : one of a set of opposing parts that open and close for holding or crushing something between them — **jawed** \'jȯd\ *adj*

²jaw *vb*   **1 :** to talk for a long time   **2 :** ²SCOLD 1

jaw·bone \'jȯ-'bōn, -,bōn\ *n* : ¹JAW 1a

jaw·break·er \-,brā-kər\ *n* : a round hard candy

jaw·less fish \,jȯ-ləs-\ *n* : any of a group of primitive vertebrate animals that do not have jaws and include the lampreys and their relatives

jay \'jā\ *n* : any of several noisy birds that are related to the crow but are smaller and usually more brightly colored

jay·walk \'jā-,wȯk\ *vb* : to cross a street carelessly without paying attention to traffic regulations — **jay·walk·er** *n*

¹jazz \'jaz\ *n*   **1 :** American music marked by lively rhythms with unusual accents and often by melodies made up by musicians as they play   **2 :** empty talk 〈don't give me any of that *jazz*〉   **3 :** similar but unspecified things : STUFF

²jazz *vb*   **1 :** ENLIVEN — usually used with *up*   **2 :** to play in the manner of jazz

jazzy \'jaz-ē\ *adj* **jazz·i·er; -est**   **1 :** resembling jazz   **2** : LIVELY 3, FLASHY — **jazz·i·ness** \'jaz-ē-nəs\ *n*

jeal·ous \'jel-əs\ *adj*   **1 :** demanding complete devotion   **2** : feeling mean resentment toward a rival or competitor   **3** : fearful of the loss of a loved one's devotion   **4 :** WATCHFUL, CAREFUL — **jeal·ous·ly** *adv*

jeal·ou·sy \'jel-ə-sē\ *n, pl* **-sies** : a jealous disposition, attitude, or feeling

jean \'jēn\ *n*   **1 :** a heavy cotton cloth used especially for sportswear and work clothes   **2** *pl* : pants made of jean, denim, or corduroy [a shortened form of earlier *jean fustian,* literally "a fustian (heavy cotton cloth) from Genoa", from Middle English *Jene, Gene* "Genoa, Italy"]

jeep \'jēp\ *n* : a small general-purpose motor vehicle with four-wheel drive used by the U.S. Army in World War II

Word History In March 1936 in newspapers across the country, Popeye's girlfriend, Olive Oyl, was delivered a box labeled "Eugene the Jeep". The contents of the box turned out to be a friendly little animal that made the sound "jeep". Elzie Segar, the creator of the comic strip, went on with the story of Eugene the Jeep through much of 1936. In 1937 work began on the development of an all-purpose vehicle for the military. When this vehicle was ready for use, it was apparently called *g.p.* for "general purpose". Probably because of the popularity of Eugene the Jeep, the pronunciation of *g.p.* was shortened to one syllable, and the spelling *jeep* became normal. [an altered form of *g.p.,* an abbreviation for "general purpose", influenced by the name Eugene the Jeep, a comic strip character]

jeer \'ji(ə)r\ *vb* : to speak or cry out in scorn : MOCK — **jeer** *n*

Je·ho·vah \ji-'hō-və\ *n* : GOD 1

je·ju·num \ji-'jü-nəm\ *n* : the section of the small intestine between the duodenum and the ileum

jell \'jel\ *vb*   **1 :** to make or become jelly   **2 :** to take shape : FORM 〈an idea *jelled*〉

¹jel·ly \'jel-ē\ *n, pl* **jellies**   **1 :** a food with a soft elastic consistency due usually to gelatin or pectin; *esp* : a fruit product made by boiling sugar and the juice of fruit   **2 :** a substance resembling jelly — **jel·ly·like** \-ē-,līk\ *adj*

\ə\ abut	\au̇\ out	\i\ tip	\ȯ\ saw	\u̇\ foot
\ər\ further	\ch\ chin	\ī\ life	\ȯi\ coin	\y\ yet
\a\ mat	\e\ pet	\j\ job	\th\ thin	\yü\ few
\ā\ take	\ē\ easy	\ŋ\ sing	\th\ this	\yu̇\ cure
\ä\ cot, cart	\g\ go	\ō\ bone	\ü\ food	\zh\ vision

²**jelly** *vb* **jel·lied; jel·ly·ing** : JELL 1

jel·ly·fish \'jel-ē-ˌfish\ *n* **1** : any of numerous free-swimming coelenterate animals that reproduce sexually and have a jellylike, saucer-shaped, and usually nearly transparent body **2** : any of various sea animals that resemble jellyfish

jen·net \'jen-ət\ *n* : a small Spanish horse

jen·ny \'jen-ē\ *n, pl* **jennies** **1 a** : a female bird ⟨*jenny* wren⟩ **b** : a female donkey **2** : SPINNING JENNY

jeop·ar·dize \'jep-ər-ˌdīz\ *vb* **-dized; -diz·ing** : to expose to danger

jeop·ar·dy \'jep-ərd-ē\ *n* : DANGER 1

jer·boa \jər-'bō-ə\ *n* : any of several social Old World jumping rodents with long hind legs and a long tail that are active at night

Jer·e·mi·ah \ˌjer-ə-'mī-ə\ *n* — see BIBLE table

Jer·e·mi·as \ˌjer-ə-'mī-əs\ *n* — see BIBLE table

jerboa

¹**jerk** \'jərk\ *n* **1** : a short quick pull or twist : TWITCH **2** : an involuntary muscular movement or spasm **3** : a stupid or foolish person

²**jerk** *vb* **1** : to give a short quick push, pull, or twist to **2** : to move in jerks or with a jerk [probably an altered form of earlier *yerk* "to beat or thrash"]

³**jerk** *vb* : to preserve in long strips dried in the sun [from ¹*jerky*]

jer·kin \'jər-kən\ *n* : a close-fitting hip-length sleeveless jacket

jerk·wa·ter \'jər-ˌkwòt-ər, -ˌkwät-\ *adj* : small, rural, and unimportant ⟨*jerkwater* towns⟩

¹**jer·ky** \'jər-kē\ *n* : jerked meat [from Spanish *charqui* "jerky"]

²**jerky** \'jər-kē\ *adj* **jerk·i·er; -est** **1** : marked by jerks ⟨a *jerky* ride on a dirt road⟩ **2** : being stupid or foolish [*jerk* (noun) and *-y* (adjective suffix)] — **jerk·i·ly** \-kə-lē\ *adv* — **jerk·i·ness** \-kē-nəs\ *n*

jer·sey \'jər-zē\ *n, pl* **jerseys** **1** : a plain knitted fabric **2** : a close-fitting knitted garment (as a shirt) **3** : any of a breed of small usually light tan dairy cattle noted for their rich milk

jessamine *variant of* JASMINE

jest \'jest\ *n* **1** : a comic act or remark : JOKE **2** : a playful mood or manner ⟨spoken in *jest*⟩ — **jest** *vb*

jest·er \'jes-tər\ *n* **1** : ¹FOOL 2 ⟨court *jester*⟩ **2** : a person given to jests

¹**jet** \'jet\ *n* **1** : a compact black mineral that takes a good polish and is often used for jewelry **2** : a very dark black [Middle English *jet* "black mineral", from early French *jaiet* (same meaning), derived from Greek *gagatēs* (same meaning), from *Gagas,* a town and river in Asia Minor]

²**jet** *vb* **jet·ted; jet·ting** : ¹SPOUT 1, SPURT [from early French *jeter,* literally "to throw", from Latin *jactare* "to throw"]

³**jet** *n* **1 a** : a forceful rush of liquid, gas, or vapor through a narrow opening or a nozzle **b** : a nozzle for a jet of fluid (as gas or water) **2 a** : JET ENGINE **b** : JET AIRPLANE

⁴**jet** *vb* **jet·ted; jet·ting** : to travel by jet airplane

jet airplane *n* : an airplane powered by

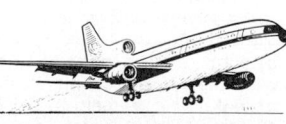

jet airplane

one or more jet engines — called also *jet plane*

jet engine *n* : an engine that produces motion as a result of the rearward discharge of a jet of fluid; *esp* : an aircraft engine that uses atmospheric oxygen to burn fuel and produces a rearward discharge of heated air and exhaust gases

jet lag *n* : a condition that is marked by physical and mental symptoms (as tiredness and bad temper) and occurs following a long flight through several time zones

jet–pro·pelled \ˌjet-prə-'peld\ *adj* : propelled by a jet engine

jet propulsion *n* : forward motion of a body produced by the forces resulting from the rearward discharge of a jet of fluid; *esp* : propulsion of an airplane by jet engines

jet·sam \'jet-səm\ *n* : goods thrown overboard to lighten a ship in distress; *esp* : such goods when washed ashore

jet set *n* : an international group of wealthy people who often travel to fashionable resorts

jet stream *n* : a long narrow wandering current of high-speed winds blowing from a generally westerly direction several kilometers above the earth's surface

jet·ti·son \'jet-ə-sən, -ə-zən\ *vb* **1** : to throw goods overboard from a ship or airplane especially to lighten it in distress **2** : ¹DISCARD 2 — **jettison** *n*

jet·ty \'jet-ē\ *n, pl* **jetties** **1** : a pier built out into the water to influence the current or protect a harbor **2** : a landing wharf

Jew \'jü\ *n* **1** : one of the ancient Hebrews or a descendant of the ancient Hebrews **2** : one whose religion is Judaism — **Jew·ish** \'jü-ish\ *adj*

¹**jew·el** \'jü-əl, 'jül\ *n* **1** : an ornament of precious metal often set with stones and worn as an accessory of dress **2** : one that is highly valued or prized **3** : a precious stone : GEM **4** : a bearing in a watch made of a crystal or a precious stone

²**jewel** *vb* **-eled** *or* **-elled; -el·ing** *or* **-el·ling** : to adorn or equip with jewels

jew·el·er *or* **jew·el·ler** \'jü-ə-lər, 'jü-lər\ *n* : a person who makes or deals in jewelry and related articles

jew·el·ry \'jü-əl-rē, 'jül-rē\ *n* : ornamental pieces (as rings and necklaces) worn on the person : JEWELS

jew·el·weed \'jü-əl-ˌwēd, 'jül-\ *n* : IMPATIENS

Jew·ry \'jü(ə)r-ē, 'jü-rē\ *n* **1** *pl* **Jewries** : a district in which Jews lived : GHETTO **2** : the Jewish people

Jew's harp *or* **Jews' harp** \'jüz-ˌhärp\ *n* : a small simple musical instrument that consists of a flexible metal strip attached at one end to a flat pear-shaped frame and that is played by plucking the strip while holding the frame between the teeth

jib \'jib\ *n* : a triangular sail set on a line running from the bow to the head of the foremast

¹**jibe** *or* **gybe** *vb* **jibed** *or* **gybed; jib·ing** *or* **gyb·ing** **1** : to shift suddenly from one side to the other **2** : to cause a sail to jibe [perhaps a modified form of Dutch *gijben* "to shift suddenly from one side to another"]

J jib

²**jibe** *variant of* GIBE

³**jibe** *vb* **jibed; jib·ing** : to be in agreement ⟨the two reports *jibed*⟩ [origin unknown]

jif·fy \'jif-ē\ *n, pl* **jiffies** : MOMENT 1, INSTANT ⟨in a *jiffy*⟩

¹**jig** \'jig\ *n* **1** : a lively springy dance **2** : ¹TRICK 1, GAME — used chiefly in the phrase *the jig is up*

²**jig** *vb* **jigged; jig·ging** **1** : to dance a jig **2** : to jerk up and down or to and fro

¹**jig·ger** \'jig-ər\ *n* **1** : one that jigs **2** : DEVICE 1c, GADGET **3** : a measure used in mixing drinks that usually holds 1½

ounces (about 44 milliliters) [*jig* (verb) and *-er* (noun suffix)]

²jig·ger *n* : CHIGGER [of African origin]

jig·gle \'jig-əl\ *vb* **jig·gled; jig·gling** \-(ə-)liŋ\ : to move or cause to move with quick little jerks — **jiggle** *n*

jig·saw \'jig-ˌsȯ\ *n* : a machine saw with a narrow blade for cutting curved and irregular lines

jigsaw puzzle *n* : a puzzle consisting of small pieces of various shapes that are to be fitted together to form a picture

¹jilt \'jilt\ *vb* : to cast a lover aside unfeelingly

²jilt *n* : a person who jilts a lover

jim crow \'jim-'krō\ *n, often cap J & C* : discrimination against black Americans

jim–dan·dy \'jim-'dan-dē\ *n* : something very good — **jim–dandy** *adj*

¹jim·my \'jim-ē\ *n, pl* **jimmies** : a short crowbar used by burglars

²jimmy *vb* **jim·mied; jim·my·ing** : to force open with or as if with a jimmy

jim·son·weed \'jim(p)-sən-ˌwēd\ *n, often cap* : a coarse poisonous weed that is related to the potato and has bad-smelling leaves and large white or violet trumpet-shaped flowers

¹jin·gle \'jiŋ-gəl\ *vb* **jin·gled; jin·gling** \-g(ə-)liŋ\ : to make or cause to make a light clinking sound ⟨coins *jingled* in their pockets⟩ — **jin·gler** \-g(ə-)lər\ *n*

²jingle *n* **1** : a light clinking sound **2** : a catchy repetition of sounds in a poem **3** : a verse or song marked by catchy repetition — **jin·gly** \-g(ə-)lē\ *adj*

jin·go \'jiŋ-gō\ *n, pl* **jingoes** : a person who favors a warlike policy toward other countries — **jin·go·ism** \-ˌiz-əm\ *n* — **jin·go·is·tic** \ˌjiŋ-gō-'is-tik\ *adj*

jin·ni \'jē-'nē, 'jin-ē, jə-'nē\ *or* **jinn** \'jin\ *n, pl* **jinn** *or* **jinns** : GENIE

jin·rik·i·sha \jin-'rik-ˌshȯ\ *n* : RICKSHA

¹jinx \'jiŋ(k)s\ *n* : someone or something that brings bad luck

²jinx *vb* : to bring bad luck to

jit·ney \'jit-nē\ *n, pl* **jitneys** : a small bus that carries passengers over a regular route

jit·ter·bug \'jit-ər-ˌbəg\ *n* **1** : a dance in which couples swing, balance, and twirl with lively acrobatics **2** : a person who dances the jitterbug — **jitterbug** *vb*

jit·ters \'jit-ərz\ *n pl* : extreme nervousness — **jit·tery** \-ə-rē\ *adj*

jiujitsu *or* **jiujutsu** *variant of* JUJITSU

¹jive \'jīv\ *n* **1** : swing music or dancing performed to it **2 a** : glib, deceptive, or foolish talk **b** : a special jargon of difficult or slang terms

²jive *vb* **jived; jiv·ing** **1** : ²KID **2** : to dance or play jive

job \'jäb\ *n* **1 a** : a piece of work; *esp* : one done at a specified rate **b** : something produced by or as if by work ⟨did a good *job*⟩ **2** : a special duty or function : TASK ⟨your *job* is to mow the lawn⟩ **3** : a position at which one regularly works for pay ⟨lost my *job*⟩ **syn** see TASK — **job·less** \-ləs\ *adj* — **job·less·ness** *n*

Job \'jōb\ *n* — see BIBLE table

job·ber \'jäb-ər\ *n* : a person who buys goods and then sells them to usually smaller dealers

job·hold·er \'jäb-ˌhōl-dər\ *n* : one having a regular job

¹jock \'jäk\ *n* **1** : ¹JOCKEY **2** : DISC JOCKEY

²jock *n* **1** : ATHLETIC SUPPORTER **2** : ATHLETE

¹jock·ey \'jäk-ē\ *n, pl* **jockeys** **1** : one who rides a horse especially as a professional in a race **2** : one who operates something ⟨a gas-pump *jockey*⟩

²jockey *vb* **jock·eyed; jock·ey·ing** **1** : to ride a horse as a jockey **2** : to move or manage skillfully or cleverly or so as to gain advantage ⟨*jockey* a truck into position⟩ ⟨*jockeying* for position⟩

jo·cose \jō-'kōs\ *adj* : MERRY 1, MIRTHFUL — **jo·cose·ly** *adv* — **jo·cose·ness** *n*

joc·u·lar \'jäk-yə-lər\ *adj* **1** : fond of jesting **2** : said or

done in jest — **joc·u·lar·i·ty** \ˌjäk-yə-'lar-ət-ē\ *n* — **joc·u·lar·ly** \'jäk-yə-lər-lē\ *adv*

jo·cund \'jäk-ənd *also* 'jōk-(ˌ)ənd\ *adj* : feeling, exhibiting, or characteristic of good cheer : CHEERFUL, JOLLY — **jo·cund·ly** *adv*

jodh·pur \'jäd-pər\ *n* **1** *pl* : riding breeches loose above the knee and tight-fitting below **2** : an ankle-high boot fastened with a strap that is buckled at the side

jodhpur 1

Jo·el \'jō-əl\ *n* — see BIBLE table

¹jog \'jäg, 'jȯg\ *vb* **jogged; jog·ging** **1** : to give a slight shake or push to : NUDGE **2** : ¹ROUSE 3, STIR ⟨*jog* one's memory⟩ **3** : to move up and down or about with a short heavy motion **4 a** : to go or cause to go at a jog **b** : to run at a slow pace especially for exercise [probably an altered form of a dialect word *shog* "jolt, jostle"] — **jog·ger** *n*

²jog *n* **1** : a slight shake : PUSH **2** : a slow steady jolting gait especially of a horse **3** : an instance of jogging

³jog *n* **1** : an unevenness (as a bulge or a dent) in a line or surface **2** : a short change in direction [probably an altered form of *jag* "a sharp projecting edge"]

jog·gle \'jäg-əl\ *vb* **jog·gled; jog·gling** \-(ə-)liŋ\ : to shake slightly

John \'jän\ *n* — see BIBLE table

John Doe \'jän-'dō\ *n* : a person in legal proceedings whose true name is unknown

john·ny·cake \'jän-ē-ˌkāk\ *n* : a bread made with cornmeal, flour, eggs, and milk

John·ny–jump–up \ˌjän-ē-'jəm-ˌpəp\ *n* : any of various pansies or violets with small flowers

join \'jȯin\ *vb* **1 a** : to bring or fasten together in close contact ⟨*join* hands⟩ **b** : to connect (as points) by a line **c** : to become joined ⟨place where two roads *join*⟩ **2** : to come or bring into close association ⟨*join* a club⟩ ⟨*join* in marriage⟩ **3** : to come into the company of ⟨*join* friends for lunch⟩ **4** : ADJOIN 2 ⟨the two farms *join*⟩ **5** : to take part with others in an activity ⟨*join* in singing⟩ — **join·able** \'jȯi-nə-bəl\ *adj*

    syn JOIN, CONNECT, COMBINE, UNITE mean to bring or come together into some kind of union. JOIN suggests an actual touching or meeting of two or more things ⟨*join* the ends with glue⟩ CONNECT suggests a loose or outside attachment ⟨*connect* the two poles with a piece of rope⟩ COMBINE suggests some blending of the things coming together and some loss of separate identity ⟨*combining* the ingredients for a salad⟩ UNITE suggests an even more complete coming together that turns two or more things into one ⟨*united* the two metal bars by welding⟩

join·er \'jȯi-nər\ *n* **1** : a woodworker who constructs articles by joining pieces of wood **2** : a person who joins many organizations

¹joint \'jȯint\ *n* **1 a** : the point of contact of two bones in the animal body often including the surrounding and supporting parts **b** : NODE 2 **c** : a part of space included between two joints, knots, or nodes ⟨the upper *joint* of the arm⟩ **2** : a large piece of meat for roasting **3** : a place where two things or parts are joined ⟨a *joint* in a pipe⟩ **4 a** : a cheap or shabby place of entertainment **b** : ¹PLACE 2b, ESTABLISHMENT **5** : a marijuana cigarette — **joint·ed** \-əd\ *adj* — **out of joint** **1** : being a dislocated bone with its head slipped from its socket **2** : out of harmony : in an

\ə\ **abut**		\au̇\ **out**	\i\ **tip**	\ȯ\ **saw**	\u̇\ **foot**	
\ər\ **further**		\ch\ **chin**	\ī\ **life**	\ȯi\ **coin**	\y\ **yet**	
\a\ **mat**		\e\ **pet**	\j\ **job**	\th\ **thin**	\yü\ **few**	
\ā\ **take**		\ē\ **easy**	\ŋ\ **sing**	\th\ **this**	\yu̇\ **cure**	
\ä\ **cot, cart**		\g\ **go**	\ō\ **bone**	\ü\ **food**	\zh\ **vision**	

unsuitable relationship or arrangement **3** : in bad humor : DISGRUNTLED

²**joint** *adj* **1** : UNITED 1, COMBINED ⟨a *joint* effort⟩ **2** : done by or shared by two or more persons ⟨a *joint* account⟩ **3** : sharing with another ⟨*joint* owner⟩ — **joint·ly** *adv*

³**joint** *vb* **1 a** : to fit together **b** : to provide with a joint **2** : to separate the joints of — **joint·er** *n*

joist \'joist\ *n* : a small beam laid crosswise to support a floor or ceiling

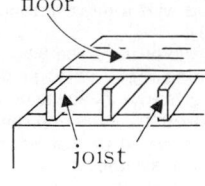
floor

joist

¹**joke** \'jōk\ *n* **1 a** : something said or done to cause laughter; *esp* : a brief story with a humorous twist **b** : the humorous element in something **c** : good-natured kidding ⟨can't take a *joke*⟩ **2** : something not to be taken seriously ⟨that exam was a *joke*⟩

²**joke** *vb* **joked; jok·ing** : to make jokes : JEST — **jok·ing·ly** \'jō-kiŋ-lē\ *adv*

jok·er \'jō-kər\ *n* **1** : a person who jokes **2** : an extra card used in some card games **3** : a hidden or misleading part of an agreement that works to one party's disadvantage : CATCH **4** : PERSON 1, FELLOW; *esp* : ¹JERK 3

joke·ster \'jōk-stər\ *n* : JOKER 1

jol·li·fi·ca·tion \,jäl-i-fə-'kā-shən\ *n* : MERRYMAKING 1

jol·li·ty \'jäl-ət-ē\ *n, pl* **-ties** : MERRYMAKING 1, GAIETY

¹**jol·ly** \'jäl-ē\ *adj* **jol·li·er; -est** **1 a** : MERRY 1, CHEERFUL **b** : JOVIAL **2** : very pleasant or agreeable : SPLENDID

²**jolly** *adv* : ²VERY 1 ⟨a *jolly* good time⟩

Jol·ly Rog·er \,jäl-ē-'räj-ər\ *n* : a black flag with a white skull and crossbones formerly used by pirates

¹**jolt** \'jōlt\ *vb* **1** : to give a quick hard blow to : JAR **2** : to move jerkily — **jolt·er** *n*

²**jolt** *n* **1** : a sudden jarring blow or movement **2** : a sudden shock or surprise

Jo·nah \'jō-nə\ *n* — see BIBLE table

Jo·nas \'jō-nəs\ *n* — see BIBLE table

Jon·a·than \'jän-ə-thən\ *n* : any of a variety of red-skinned apple

jon·quil \'jän-kwəl, 'jäŋ-\ *n* : a Mediterranean plant that is related to the daffodil but bears clusters of fragrant yellow or white flowers having a short central tube — compare NARCISSUS

josh \'jäsh\ *vb* : to joke with : TEASE

Josh·ua \'jäsh(ə-)wə\ *n* — see BIBLE table

Joshua tree *n* : a tall branched yucca of the southwestern U.S. with short leaves and clusters of greenish white flowers

¹**jos·tle** \'jäs-əl\ *vb* **jos·tled; jos·tling** \-(ə-)liŋ\ **1** : to run or knock against so as to jar : push roughly **2** : to make one's way by jostling

²**jostle** *n* : a jostling blow : SHOVE

Jos·ue \'jäsh-ə-wē\ *n* — see BIBLE table

Joshua tree

¹**jot** \'jät\ *n* : the least bit

²**jot** *vb* **jot·ted; jot·ting** : to make a brief note of ⟨*jot* this down⟩

joule \'jü(ə)l\ *n* : a unit of work or energy equal to the work done by a force of one newton acting through a distance of one meter

jounce \'jaun(t)s\ *vb* **jounced; jounc·ing** : to move or cause to move in an up-and-down manner — **jounce** *n*

jour·nal \'jərn-ᵊl\ *n* **1 a** : a brief account of daily events

: DIARY **b** : a record of the happenings of a conference or a legislative body **2 a** : a daily newspaper **b** : a magazine that reports on things of special interest to a particular group [Middle English *journal* "a daily record of a journey, record of daily transactions", from early French *journal* (same meaning), from *journal* (adjective) "daily", derived from Latin *diurnus* "of the day, daily", from *dies* "day" — related to DIARY, JOURNEY; see *Word History* at JOURNEY]

jour·nal·ese \,jərn-ᵊl-'ēz, -'ēs\ *n* : a way of writing said to be similar to that of newspapers

jour·nal·ism \'jərn-ᵊl-,iz-əm\ *n* **1** : the collecting and editing of news to be presented in newspapers or magazines or over television or radio **2** : writing designed for or characteristic of newspapers or magazines — **jour·nal·is·tic** \,jərn-ᵊl-'is-tik\ *adj*

jour·nal·ist \'jərn-ᵊl-əst\ *n* : an editor of or writer for a newspaper or magazine or radio and television news

¹**jour·ney** \'jər-nē\ *n, pl* **journeys** : travel from one place to another

Word History The Latin word *dies* means "day", and *diurnus* means "of a day". From these two Latin words came the early French *jour*, meaning "day", and *journee*, meaning "a day's work, a day's travel". *Journee* was borrowed into Middle English with both of its meanings, but only the second one, "a day's travel", came into widespread use. The modern form *journey* now refers to travel without regard to the amount of time taken. The English word *journal* can also be traced back to the Latin *dies*. From the adjective *diurnus*, the word *diurnalis*, meaning "daily", was formed. This was taken into French as *journal*. In this form it was borrowed into Middle English. It was at first also used to mean "daily", but it is now found only as a noun in English. [Middle English *journey* "a trip, travel", from early French *journee* "day's work, day's journey", from *jour* "day", derived from Latin *diurnus* "of a day, daily", from *dies* "day" — related to DIARY, JOURNAL]

syn JOURNEY, TRIP, TOUR mean travel from one place to another. JOURNEY usually suggests that one travels a long distance and often that the traveling may be dangerous or difficult ⟨the long *journey* across the desert⟩ TRIP suggests that the traveling is brief, swift, or ordinary ⟨our weekly *trip* to the supermarket⟩ TOUR suggests a circular journey with several stopping places and an end at the place where one began ⟨the sightseers took a *tour* of the city⟩

²**journey** *vb* **jour·neyed; jour·ney·ing** : to go on a journey — **jour·ney·er** *n*

jour·ney·man \'jər-nē-mən\ *n* **1** : a worker who has learned a trade and works for another person usually by the day **2** : an experienced reliable worker

joust \'jaust\ *n* : a combat on horseback between two knights with lances especially as part of a tournament — **joust** *vb* — **joust·er** *n*

jo·vi·al \'jō-vē-əl\ *adj* : full of or expressing good humor — **jo·vi·al·i·ty** \,jō-vē-'al-ət-ē\ *n* — **jo·vi·al·ly** \'jō-vē-ə-lē\ *adv*

¹**jowl** \'jau(ə)l\ *n* **1** : ¹JAW 1; *esp* : the lower jaw **2** : CHEEK 1

²**jowl** *n* : loose flesh associated with the cheeks, lower jaw, or throat — **jowly** \'jau-lē\ *adj*

¹**joy** \'joi\ *n* **1** : a feeling of great pleasure or happiness that comes from success, good fortune, or a sense of well-being : GLADNESS **2** : something that gives joy ⟨a *joy* to behold⟩ **syn** see PLEASURE — **joy·less** \-ləs\ *adj* — **joy·less·ness** *n*

²**joy** *vb* : to experience joy : REJOICE

joy·ful \'joi-fəl\ *adj* : feeling, causing, or showing joy ⟨a *joyful* family reunion⟩ — **joy·ful·ly** \-fə-lē\ *adv* — **joy·ful·ness** *n*

joy·ous \'joi-əs\ *adj* : feeling, causing, or showing joy : JOYFUL — **joy·ous·ly** *adv* — **joy·ous·ness** *n*

joy·ride \'joi-,rīd\ *n* : a ride taken for pleasure and often marked by reckless driving — **joy·rid·er** \-,rīd-or\ *n*

joy·stick \-,stik\ *n* : a control lever for a device (as a computer display) that allows motion in two or more directions

ju·bi·lant \'jü-bə-lənt\ *adj* : feeling or expressing great joy : EXULTANT ⟨*jubilant* teammates celebrating their victory⟩ — **ju·bi·lant·ly** *adv*

ju·bi·la·tion \,jü-bə-'lā-shən\ *n* : an act of rejoicing : the state of being jubilant

ju·bi·lee \'jü-bə-,lē, ,jü-bə-'lē\ *n* **1** : a special anniversary; *esp* : a 50th anniversary **2** : a celebration especially of an anniversary

Ju·da·ism \'jüd-ə-,iz-əm, 'jüd-ē-\ *n* **1** : a religion developed among the ancient Hebrews that stresses belief in one God and faithfulness to the laws of the Old Testament **2** : the beliefs and practices of the Jews — **Ju·da·ic** \jü-'dā-ik\ *adj*

Jude \'jüd\ *n* — see BIBLE table

¹judge \'jəj\ *vb* **judged; judg·ing** **1** : to form an opinion after careful consideration **2** : to decide as a judge : TRY **3** : to reach a conclusion about something : THINK [Middle English *juggen* "to judge", from early French *jugier* (same meaning), from Latin *judicare* "to judge", from *judic-, judex* "judge", from *jus* "right, law", and *dicere* "to say" — related to HOOSEGOW, JURY, JUST, PREJUDICE]

²judge *n* **1** : a public official having authority to decide questions brought before a court **2** : a person appointed to decide in a contest or competition : UMPIRE **3** : a person who is qualified to give an opinion : CRITIC — **judge·ship** \-,ship\ *n*

Judg·es \'jəj-əz\ *n* — see BIBLE table

judg·ment *or* **judge·ment** \'jəj-mənt\ *n* **1** : the act of judging **2** : a decision given by a court **3 a** : the process of forming an opinion by examining and comparing **b** : an opinion so formed **4** : the ability to judge : DISCERNMENT

Judgment Day *n* : the day of the final judging of all human beings by God

ju·di·cial \jü-'dish-əl\ *adj* **1** : of or relating to courts or judges **2** : ordered or enforced by a court ⟨a *judicial* decision⟩ — **ju·di·cial·ly** \-(ə-)lē\ *adv*

ju·di·cia·ry \jü-'dish-ē-,er-ē, -'dish-ə-rē\ *n* **1 a** : a system of courts of law **b** : the judges of these courts **2** : a branch of government in which judicial power is vested — **judiciary** *adj*

ju·di·cious \jü-'dish-əs\ *adj* : having, exercising, or characterized by sound judgment : DISCREET — **ju·di·cious·ly** *adv*

Ju·dith \'jüd-əth\ *n* — see BIBLE table

ju·do \'jüd-ō\ *n, pl* **judos** : a sport developed from jujitsu in which opponents attempt to throw each other by using quick movements and leverage

¹jug \'jəg\ *n* **1 a** : a large deep container with a narrow mouth and a handle **b** : the amount held by a jug **2** : PRISON 2, JAIL

²jug *vb* **jugged; jug·ging** : IMPRISON

jug·ful \'jəg-,ful\ *n* : ¹JUG 1b

jug·gle \'jəg-əl\ *vb* **jug·gled; jug·gling** \-(ə-)lin\ **1** : to keep several objects in motion in the air at the same time **2** : to work things so as to accomplish something desired ⟨*juggle* an account to hide a loss⟩ **3** : to hold or balance insecurely — **jug·gler** \-(ə-)lər\ *n*

jug·glery \'jəg-lə-rē\ *n, pl* **-gler·ies** **1** : the art or practice of a juggler **2** : TRICKERY

jug·u·lar \'jəg-yə-lər\ *adj* **1** : of, relating to, or situated in or on the throat or neck **2** : of or relating to the jugular vein

jugular vein *n* : a large vein on each side of the neck or any of several veins that drain blood into it from the head — called also *jugular*

juice \'jüs\ *n* **1 a** : the liquid part that can be squeezed out of vegetables and fruits **b** : the fluid part of meat **2 a** : the natural fluids (as blood, lymph, and secretions) of an

animal body **b** : the liquid or moisture contained in something **3** : something (as electricity or gasoline) that supplies power — **juiced** \'jüst\ *adj*

juicy \'jü-sē\ *adj* **juic·i·er; -est** **1** : having much juice : SUCCULENT **2 a** : rich in interest : COLORFUL **b** : ¹RACY **2** ⟨a *juicy* scandal⟩ — **juic·i·ly** \-sə-lē\ *adv* — **juic·i·ness** \-sē-nəs\ *n*

ju·jit·su *or* **ju·jut·su** *or* **jiu·jit·su** *or* **jiu·jut·su** \jü-'jit-sü\ *n* : the Japanese art of unarmed fighting using holds, throws, and paralyzing blows

juke·box \'jük-,bäks\ *n* : a coin-operated phonograph

ju·lep \'jü-ləp\ *n* : a drink of bourbon, sugar, and mint served with crushed ice

Ju·lian calendar \,jül-yən-\ *n* : a calendar introduced in Rome in 46 B.C. establishing the 12-month year of 365 days with each fourth year having 366 days and the months each having 31 or 30 days except for February which has 28 or in leap years 29 days — compare GREGORIAN CALENDAR

Ju·ly \jü-'lī\ *n* : the seventh month of the year

Word History The first ancient Roman calendar began the year with March. The original name of the fifth month of the year was *Quinctilis,* a Latin word meaning "fifth". In order to honor the statesman Gaius Julius Caesar, however, the Roman senate changed *Quinctilis* to *Julius.* The name *Julius* was borrowed into Old English and eventually became the Modern English *July.* [Old English *Julius* "July", from Latin *Julius* "the fifth month of the old Roman calendar", named for Gaius *Julius* Caesar 100–44 B.C]

jum·ble \'jəm-bəl\ *vb* **jum·bled; jum·bling** \-b(ə-)lin\ : to mix in a confused mass — **jumble** *n*

jum·bo \'jəm-bō\ *n, pl* **jumbos** : something very large of its kind [from *Jumbo,* name of a huge elephant shown by circus owner P. T. Barnum]— **jumbo** *adj*

¹jump \'jəmp\ *vb* **1 a** : to spring into the air : LEAP **b** : to give a sudden movement : START **c** : to begin to move — usually used with *off* **2** : to rise or raise suddenly in rank, status, or condition ⟨prices *jumped*⟩ **3** : to make a sudden attack ⟨*jumped* on us for being late⟩ **4** : to become lively with activity ⟨the woods were *jumping*⟩ **5 a** : to pass over or cause to pass over by a leap ⟨*jump* a hurdle⟩ **b** : ²BYPASS ⟨*jump* electrical connections⟩ **c** : to leap aboard ⟨*jump* a freight⟩ **6** : to run away and hide while at liberty under (bail) **7** : to depart from a normal course ⟨*jump* the track⟩ **8** : to occupy illegally ⟨*jump* a mining claim⟩ — **jump the gun** : to start too soon

²jump *n* **1 a** : an act of jumping : LEAP **b** : any of several sports competitions that involve jumping **c** : a space covered by a leap **d** : a sudden involuntary movement : START **e** : a move made in a board game by jumping **2 a** : a sharp sudden increase **b** : one in a series of moves ⟨keep one *jump* ahead⟩ **3** : an advantage at the start

¹jump·er \'jəm-pər\ *n* **1** : one that jumps **2** : JUMP SHOT

²jum·per \'jəm-pər\ *n* **1** : a loose blouse or jacket worn by workers **2** : a sleeveless dress worn usually with a blouse

jumping bean *n* : a seed of any of several Mexican shrubs that tumbles about because of the movements of the larva of a small moth inside it

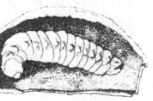

jumping bean

jumping jack *n* **1** : a toy figure of a man jointed and made to jump or dance by means of strings or a sliding stick **2** : a training exercise that involves jumping in place

jump shot *n* : a basketball shot made while jumping

jump·suit \'jəmp-,süt\ *n* **1** : a uniform worn by parachutists for jumping **2** : a one-piece garment consisting of a blouse or shirt with attached trousers or shorts

jumpy \'jəm-pē\ *adj* **jump·i·er; -est** : NERVOUS 2a, JITTERY ⟨after a long restless night, the soldiers were *jumpy*⟩ — **jump·i·ness** *n*

jun·co \'jəŋ-kō\ *n, pl* **juncos** *or* **juncoes** : any of a genus of small American finches usually with a pink bill, ashy gray head and back, and white tail feathers

junc·tion \'jəŋ(k)-shən\ *n* **1** : an act of joining : the state of being joined **2** : a place or point of meeting ⟨a railroad *junction*⟩

junc·ture \'jəŋ(k)-chər\ *n* **1** : an instance of joining : UNION **2** : [1]JOINT 3a, CONNECTION **3** : an important point of time ⟨they feel they must make a decision at this *juncture*⟩ — **junc·tur·al** \-chə-rəl\ *adj*

June \'jün\ *n* : the sixth month of the year

> **Word History** The English word *June* comes from the Latin *Junius,* the name given to the first month of summer by the ancient Romans. It isn't known for certain why the Romans named it as they did. *Junius* was also the name of a large Roman family group, and maybe the month was named in honor of the family. Or perhaps it was named for the Roman goddess *Juno.* [from Latin *Junius,* probably from *Junius,* name of a family group, or from *Juno,* a Roman goddess]

june beetle *n, often cap J* : any of various large leaf-eating beetles which fly chiefly in late spring and whose larvae are white grubs that live in soil and feed on roots — called also *june bug*

June·ber·ry \'jün-,ber-ē\ *n* : SERVICEBERRY; *also* : its fruit

jun·gle \'jəŋ-gəl\ *n* **1** : a thick tangled mass of tropical vegetation **2** : an area overgrown with jungle or other rank vegetation

jungle gym *n* : a structure of upright and crosswise bars for use by children at play

[1]ju·nior \'jün-yər\ *adj* **1 a** : being the younger one — used chiefly to distinguish a son with the same given name as his father **b** : designed for young teenagers **2** : lower in standing or rank ⟨*junior* partner⟩ **3** : of or relating to juniors in a school

[2]junior *n* **1** : a person who is younger or of lower rank than another **2** : a student in the next-to-last year in a high school, college, or university

junior college *n* : a school that offers two years of studies similar to those in the first two years of a four-year college

junior high school *n* : a school usually including the seventh, eighth, and ninth grades

junior varsity *n* : a team for players who lack the experience or qualifications for the varsity

ju·ni·per \'jü-nə-pər\ *n* **1** : any of a genus of evergreen shrubs and trees that are related to the pines but produce tiny berrylike fruits; *esp* : one with a low spreading or shrubby manner of growth **2** : any of various evergreen trees resembling true junipers

[1]junk \'jəŋk\ *n* **1** : old iron, glass, paper, or waste : discarded articles **2** : something of poor quality : TRASH **3** *slang* : [1]NARCOTIC 1; *esp* : HEROIN [Middle English *jonke* "piece of old or worn-out rope"] — **junky** \'jəŋ-kē\ *adj*

[3]junk

[2]junk *vb* : to get rid of as worthless : SCRAP

[3]junk *n* : a ship of eastern

Asia with a high stern and four-cornered sails [from Portuguese *junco* "a Chinese ship"]

[1]jun·ket \'jəŋ-kət\ *n* **1** : a dessert of sweetened flavored milk set in a jelly **2** : [1]TRIP 2a; *esp* : a trip made by an official at public expense

[2]junket *vb* **1** : [2]FEAST 1, BANQUET **2** : to go on a junket

junk food *n* : food that is high in calories but low in nutritional value

junk·ie *or* **junky** \'jəŋ-kē\ *n, pl* **junk·ies** *slang* : a narcotics peddler or addict

junk mail *n* : mail that consists mostly of advertising circulars and is often addressed to "occupant" or "resident"

jun·ta \'hün-tə, 'jənt-ə, 'hən-tə\ *n* **1** : a group of persons controlling a government especially after a revolution **2** : JUNTO

jun·to \'jənt-ō\ *n, pl* **juntos** : a group of persons joined for a common purpose

Ju·pi·ter \'jü-pət-ər\ *n* : the largest of the planets and fifth in order of distance from the sun — see PLANET table

Ju·ras·sic \jü-'ras-ik\ *adj* : of, relating to, or being a period of the Mesozoic era of geological history marked by the presence of dinosaurs and the first appearance of birds; *also* : relating to the corresponding system of rocks — see GEOLOGIC TIME table — **Jurassic** *n*

ju·ris·dic·tion \,jür-əs-'dik-shən\ *n* **1** : the power, right, or authority to interpret and apply the law **2** : the authority of a sovereign power to govern or legislate **3** : the limits or territory within which authority may be exercised

ju·ris·pru·dence \,jür-ə-'sprüd-ᵊn(t)s\ *n* **1** : a system of laws **2** : the science of law **3** : a department of law ⟨medical *jurisprudence*⟩

ju·rist \'jú(ə)r-əst\ *n* : one (as a lawyer or judge) having a thorough knowledge of law

ju·ris·tic \jú-'ris-tik\ *adj* **1** : of or relating to a jurist or jurisprudence **2** : relating to law

ju·ror \'júr-ər, -,ór\ *n* : a member of a jury

ju·ry \'jú(ə)r-ē\ *n, pl* **juries** **1** : a body of persons sworn to inquire into a matter of fact and give their verdict **2** : a committee that judges and awards prizes at an exhibition or contest [Middle English *jure* "jury", derived from early French *jurer* "to swear", from Latin *jurare* (same meaning), from *jur-, jus* "right, law" — related to JUDGE, JUST]

[1]just \'jəst\ *adj* **1 a** : WELL-FOUNDED, REASONABLE ⟨a *just* comment⟩ **b** : being in agreement with a standard of correctness : PROPER ⟨a *just* price⟩ **2 a** : morally right or good : RIGHTEOUS ⟨a *just* cause for war⟩ **b** : being deserved ⟨*just* punishment⟩ **3** : legally right ⟨a *just* title⟩ [Middle English *just* "reasonable, proper", from early French *juste* and Latin *justus* (same meaning), from Latin *jus* "right, law" — related to JUDGE, JURY, PREJUDICE] **syn** see UPRIGHT — **just·ly** *adv*

[2]just \(,)jəst, (,)jist, (,)jest\ *adv* **1 a** : EXACTLY 1, PRECISELY ⟨*just* right⟩ **b** : very recently ⟨the bell *just* rang⟩ **2 a** : by a small amount : BARELY ⟨*just* over the line⟩ **b** : IMMEDIATELY 1, DIRECTLY ⟨*just* west of here⟩ **3 a** : nothing more than : ONLY ⟨*just* a note⟩ **b** : QUITE 1, VERY ⟨*just* wonderful⟩

jus·tice \'jəs-təs\ *n* **1** : just conduct, management, or treatment ⟨do *justice* to a book⟩ **2 a** : [2]JUDGE 1 **b** : the administration of law ⟨received *justice* in court⟩ **3 a** : the quality of being fair or just **b** : basis in morality, the right, or the law

justice of the peace : a local official having the authority to try minor cases, to administer oaths, and to perform marriages

jus·ti·fi·ca·tion \,jəs-tə-fə-'kā-shən\ *n* **1** : the act or an instance of justifying or of being justified **2** : something that justifies : DEFENSE

jus·ti·fy \'jəs-tə-,fī\ *vb* **-fied; -fy·ing** **1** : to prove or show to be just, right, legal, or reasonable **2** : to release from the guilt of sin — **jus·ti·fi·able** \,jəs-tə-,fī-ə-bəl\ *adj* — **jus·ti·fi·ably** \-blē\ *adv* — **jus·ti·fi·er** \-,fī(-ə)r\ *n*

jut \\'jət\ *vb* **jut·ted; jut·ting** : to stick out, up, or forward : PROJECT — **jut** *n*

jute \\'jüt\ *n* : a glossy fiber from either of two East Indian plants that is used chiefly for making sacks and twine

Jute \\'jüt\ *n* : a member of a Germanic people invading England from Jutland and settling in Kent in the 5th century A.D.

¹**ju·ve·nile** \\'jü-və-ˌnīl, -vən-ᵊl\ *adj* **1** : showing incomplete development : IMMATURE, CHILDISH **2** : of, relating to, or characteristic of children or young people — **ju·ve·nil·i·ty** \ˌjü-və-'nil-ət-ē\ *n*

²**juvenile** *n* **1** : a young person, animal, or plant **2** : a book for young people **3** : an actor who plays youthful parts

juvenile delinquency *n* : violation of the law (as stealing) or antisocial behavior (as playing hooky from school) by a young person

juvenile delinquent *n* : a person whose behavior or conduct is considered juvenile delinquency

jux·ta·pose \\'jək-stə-ˌpōz\ *vb* **-posed; -pos·ing** : to place side by side — **jux·ta·po·si·tion** \ˌjək-stə-pə-'zish-ən\ *n*

K

k \\'kā\ *n, often cap* **1** : the 11th letter of the English alphabet **2 a** : THOUSAND **b** : a unit of computer memory equal to 1024 bytes

Kaa·ba \\'käb-ə\ *n* : a small stone building in the court of the Great Mosque at Mecca that contains a sacred black stone and is the point toward which Muslims turn in praying

Ka·bu·ki \kə-'bü-kē, 'käb-ù-(ˌ)kē\ *n* : traditional popular Japanese drama with singing and dancing

kaftan *variant of* CAFTAN

kai·ser \\'kī-zər\ *n* : the ruler of Germany from 1871 to 1918 [Middle English *keiser* "emperor" and German *kaiser* (title of a German ruler), both derived from a Germanic word *kaisar* "emperor", derived from Latin *Caesar* (title of a line of Roman emperors after Caesar Augustus) — see *Word History* at EMPEROR]

kale \\'kā(ə)l\ *n* : a hardy cabbage with wrinkled leaves that do not form a head

ka·lei·do·scope \kə-'līd-ə-ˌskōp\ *n* **1** : a tube containing loose bits of colored glass or plastic and two mirrors at one end that shows many different patterns as it is turned **2** : a changing pattern or scene [from Greek *kalos* "beautiful" and Greek *eidos* "form, shape" and English *-scope* (combining form)] — **ka·lei·do·scop·ic** \-ˌlīd-ə-'skäp-ik\ *adj* — **ka·lei·do·scop·i·cal·ly** \-'skäp-i-k(ə-)lē\ *adv*

kame \\'kām\ *n* : a short ridge or mound of material deposited by water from a melting glacier

kan·ga·roo \ˌkaŋ-gə-'rü\ *n, pl* **-roos** : any of numerous leaping marsupial mammals of Australia, New Guinea, and adjacent islands that feed on plants and have a small head, long powerful hind legs, a long thick tail used as a support in standing or walking, and in the female a pouch on the abdomen in which the young are carried

kangaroo court *n* : a court that uses unfair methods or is not a proper court of law

kangaroo rat *n* : a pouched burrowing rodent of dry regions of the western U.S.

ka·olin \\'kā-ə-lən\ *n* : a fine usually white clay used in making porcelain, in paper, and in medicines that treat diarrhea

ka·olin·ite \\'kā-ə-lə-ˌnīt\ *n* : a mineral that consists of the silicate of aluminum and is the principal mineral in kaolin

ka·pok \\'kā-ˌpäk\ *n* : a mass of silky fibers that clothe the seeds of a large tropical tree and are used as a filling for mattresses, life preservers, and sleeping bags

kap·pa \\'kap-ə\ *n* : the 10th letter of the Greek alphabet — K or κ

kangaroo

kar·a·kul \\'kar-ə-kəl\ *n* **1** : any of a breed of hardy Asian sheep with coarse fur **2** : the tightly curled glossy black coat of the newborn lamb of a karakul valued as fur

kar·a·o·ke \ˌkar-ē-ˌō-kē, kə-'rō-kē\ *n* : a device that plays music to which the user sings along and that records the user's singing with the music

kar·at *or* **car·at** \\'kar-ət\ *n* : a unit of fineness for gold equal to ¹⁄₂₄ part of pure gold in a blend with one or more other metals

ka·ra·te \kə-'rät-ē\ *n* : a Japanese art of self-defense without a weapon [from Japanese *karate,* literally "empty hand"]

Kashmir *variant of* CASHMERE

ka·ty·did \\'kät-ē-ˌdid\ *n* : any of several large green American long-horned grasshoppers with males that make a shrill noise using sound-producing organs on the forewings

> **Word History** Some animal names have been created through imitation of the sounds the animals make. The name *katydid* is an example of this process. These insects were given this name because the noise they make was thought of as sounding like "Katy-did, Katy-didn't" repeated over and over [imitation]

kay·ak \\'kī-ˌak\ *n* **1** : an Eskimo canoe made of a frame covered with skins except for a small opening in the center **2** : a small canvas-covered canoe resembling a kayak

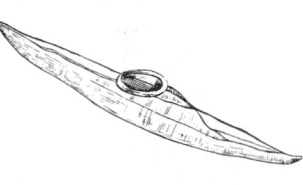
kayak 1

¹**kayo** \(ˌ)kā-'ō, 'kā-ō\ *n, pl* **kay·os** : KNOCKOUT 1

²**kayo** *vb* **kay·oed; kayo·ing** : KNOCK OUT

ka·zoo \kə-'zü\ *n, pl* **kazoos** : a toy musical instrument containing a membrane which produces a buzzing tone when one hums into the mouth hole

¹**keel** \\'kē(ə)l\ *n* **1** : a timber or plate running lengthwise along the center of the bottom of a ship and usually sticking out from the bottom **2** : something (as the breastbone of a bird or the lower two petals of a pea flower) that is like a ship's keel in form or use

²**keel** *vb* : to turn (a ship or boat) over

keel·boat \\'kē(ə)l-ˌbōt\ *n* : a shallow covered riverboat with a keel that is usually rowed, poled, or towed and is used to carry freight

keel·haul \-ˌhȯl\ *vb* **1** : to haul under the keel of a ship as

\ə\ abut	\aù\ out	\i\ tip	\ȯ\ saw	\ù\ foot
\ər\ further	\ch\ chin	\ī\ life	\ȯi\ coin	\y\ yet
\a\ mat	\e\ pet	\j\ job	\th\ thin	\yü\ few
\ā\ take	\ē\ easy	\ŋ\ sing	\th\ this	\yù\ cure
\ä\ cot, cart	\g\ go	\ō\ bone	\ü\ food	\zh\ vision

punishment or torture **2** : to scold severely

keel over *vb* : to fall suddenly (as in a faint)

¹keen \'kēn\ *adj* **1** : having a sharp edge or point ⟨a *keen* knife⟩ **2** : seeming to cut or sting ⟨a *keen* wind⟩ **3** : full of enthusiasm ⟨*keen* about baseball⟩ **4 a** : having or showing mental sharpness ⟨a *keen* mind⟩ **b** : very sensitive (as in seeing or hearing) ⟨*keen* eyesight⟩ **5** : very nice : WONDERFUL ⟨gee, that's *keen*⟩ **syn** see EAGER, SHARP — **keen·ly** *adv* — **keen·ness** \'kēn-nəs\ *n*

²keen *vb* : to mourn in a loud wailing voice

³keen *n* : a mourning for the dead with loud wails

¹keep \'kēp\ *vb* **kept** \'kept\; **keep·ing** **1 a** : to be faithful to : FULFILL ⟨*keep* a promise⟩ **b** : to act properly in relation to ⟨*keep* the Sabbath⟩ **2 a** : PROTECT ⟨*keep* us from harm⟩ **b** : to take care of : TEND ⟨*keep* a garden⟩ **3** : to continue doing something : MAINTAIN ⟨*keep* silence⟩ ⟨*keep* on working⟩ ⟨*keep* that up and you'll get into trouble⟩ **4** : to have in one's service or at one's disposal ⟨*keep* a car⟩ **5** : to preserve a record in ⟨*keep* a diary⟩ **6** : to have on hand regularly for sale ⟨*keep* neckties⟩ **7** : to continue to have in one's possession or power ⟨*kept* the marbles I won⟩ **8 a** : to prevent from leaving : DETAIN ⟨*keep* a person in jail⟩ ⟨was *kept* after school⟩ **b** : to place for storage ⟨*keeps* the catsup in the refrigerator⟩ ⟨*keep* my socks in a drawer⟩ **9** : to hold back ⟨*keep* a secret⟩ **10 a** : to remain or cause to remain in a place, situation, or condition ⟨*keep* off the grass⟩ ⟨*keep* him waiting⟩ **b** : to continue in an unspoiled condition ⟨food that *keeps* well⟩ **11** : ¹REFRAIN ⟨*keep* from talking⟩ **12** : to take charge of (as a business) : MANAGE ⟨*keep* a boardinghouse⟩ ⟨*kept* an inn⟩

> **syn** KEEP, OBSERVE, CELEBRATE, COMMEMORATE mean to notice or honor a day, occasion, or deed. KEEP stresses the idea of not neglecting or violating ⟨*keep* the Sabbath⟩ OBSERVE is likely to suggest the holding of formal ceremonies ⟨not all holidays are *observed* across the nation⟩ CELEBRATE suggests honoring an occasion by festivity ⟨*celebrate* Independence Day with a parade⟩ COMMEMORATE suggests having customs or ceremonies that call to mind what the occasion means ⟨*commemorate* Memorial Day with the laying of wreaths on gravestones⟩

²keep *n* **1** : the strongest part of a castle in the Middle Ages **2** : the necessities of life ⟨earn one's *keep*⟩ — **for keeps 1** : with the understanding that one may keep what is won ⟨play marbles *for keeps*⟩ **2** : for a long time : PERMANENTLY

keep·er \'kē-pər\ *n* : one that keeps ⟨they are *keepers* of their word⟩; *esp* : a person who watches, guards, or takes care of something or someone

keep·ing \'kē-pin\ *n* **1** : watchful attention : CARE **2** : a proper or fitting relationship : HARMONY ⟨in *keeping* with good taste⟩

keep·sake \'kēp-,sāk\ *n* : something kept or given to be kept in memory of a person, place, or happening

keep up *vb* **1** : MAINTAIN 1 ⟨*keep* standards *up*⟩ **2** : to stay well informed about something ⟨*keep up* on the news⟩ **3** : to continue without interruption ⟨rain *kept up* all night⟩ **4** : to stay even with others (as in a race) ⟨found it difficult to *keep up* with the rest of the class⟩

keg \'keg, 'kag, 'kāg\ *n* **1** : a small cask or barrel holding about 114 liters **2** : the contents of a keg

kelp \'kelp\ *n* : any of various large brown seaweeds; *also* : a mass of these

kel·vin \'kel-vən\ *n* : a unit of temperature equal to ¹⁄₂₇₃.₁₆ of the Kelvin scale temperature of the triple point of water and equal to the Celsius degree in size — *abbr. K*

Kelvin scale *n* : a temperature scale that is based on absolute zero (−273.15°C), has the kelvin as its unit of measurement, and according to which water freezes at 273.15K and boils at 373.15K

¹ken \'ken\ *vb* **kenned; ken·ning** *chiefly Scottish* : ¹KNOW

²ken *n* **1** : range of vision : SIGHT **2** : range of understanding ⟨miracles beyond human *ken*⟩

¹ken·nel \'ken-ᵊl\ *n* **1** : a shelter for a dog **2** : a place where dogs are bred or housed

²kennel *vb* **-neled** *or* **-nelled; -nel·ing** *or* **-nel·ling** : to put or keep in a kennel

Ken·tucky bluegrass \kən-,tək-ē-\ *n* : a valuable pasture, lawn, and meadow grass that has tall stalks and slender bright green leaves and is found in both Europe and America

ker·a·tin \'ker-ət-ᵊn\ *n* : a sulfur-containing protein that makes up hair and horny tissues

ker·chief \'kər-chəf, -,chēf\ *n, pl* **ker·chiefs** \-chəfs, -,chēfs\ *also* **ker·chieves** \-,chēvz\ **1** : a square of cloth worn as a head covering or as a scarf **2** : HANDKERCHIEF 1

kerf \'kərf\ *n* : a slit or notch made by a saw or a cutting torch

ker·nel \'kərn-ᵊl\ *n* **1 a** : the inner softer part of a seed, fruit stone, or nut **b** : a whole grain or seed of a cereal (as wheat or corn) **2** : a central or basic part ⟨a *kernel* of truth in what they say⟩

Kentucky bluegrass

ker·o·sene *or* **ker·o·sine** \'ker-ə-,sēn, ker-ə-'sēn, 'kar-, ,kar-\ *n* : a thin oil obtained from petroleum and used as a fuel and solvent

Ker·ry blue terrier \,ker-ē-\ *n* : any of an Irish breed of medium-sized terriers with a long head, deep chest, and silky bluish coat

ketch \'kech\ *n* : a two-masted fore-and-aft-rigged ship

ketchup *variant of* CATSUP

ket·tle \'ket-ᵊl\ *n* **1** : a pot for boiling liquids **2** : TEAKETTLE

ket·tle·drum \-,drəm\ *n* : a large brass or copper drum that has a rounded bottom and can be varied in pitch

ketch

¹key \'kē\ *n, pl* **keys** **1 a** : an instrument by which the bolt of a lock is turned **b** : a device having the form or function of a key ⟨a *key* for opening a can of meat⟩ ⟨a *key* for winding a clock⟩ **2** : a means of gaining or preventing entrance, possession, or control **3 a** : something that provides an explanation, solution, or means of identifying ⟨the *key* to a riddle⟩ **b** : a series of numbered or lettered phrases or statements usually arranged in pairs of which the members describe characteristics by which plants or animals of a particular group differ, give either a number or a reference to another pair, and are used for identification by making choices between pairs one after another until a name is obtained **c** : a map legend **4** : one of the levers with a flat surface that is pressed by a finger in operating a machine or playing an instrument **5** : a system of seven musical tones arranged in relation to a keynote from which the system is named ⟨the *key* of C⟩ **6** : a characteristic way (as of thought) **7** : a small switch for opening or closing an electric circuit [Old English *cǣg* "key"]

²key *vb* **keyed; key·ing** **1** : to adjust the musical pitch of **2** : to bring into harmony **3** : to make nervous, tense, or excited — usually used with *up* ⟨all *keyed* up about the test⟩ **4** : to record by operating the keys of a machine ⟨*key* each price into the cash register⟩

³key *adj* : of great importance ⟨the *key* people in the organization⟩ ⟨the *key* question is "Can we afford it?"⟩ ⟨use *key*

words in an outline〉

⁴key n : a low island or reef 〈the Florida *Keys*〉 [from Spanish *cayo* "a low island or reef"]

key·board \'kē-,bō(ə)rd, -,bȯ(ə)rd\ n **1** : a row or set of keys by which a musical instrument (as a piano) is played **2** : the whole arrangement of keys by which a machine (as a typewriter or computer) is operated

key deer n, often cap K : any of a race of very small rare white-tailed deer native to the Florida Keys

key·hole \'kē-,hōl\ n : a hole for receiving a key

keyhole saw n : a narrow pointed handsaw

¹key·note \'kē-,nōt\ n **1** : the first and harmonically fundamental tone of a scale **2** : the fundamental or central fact, idea, or mood 〈humor is the *keynote* of the play〉

²keynote vb **1** : to set the keynote of **2** : to give the keynote address at 〈*keynoted* the convention〉 — **key·not·er** n

keynote address n : the main speech given at a gathering (as a political convention)

key·pad \'kē-,pad\ n : a small keyboard (as on a pocket calculator)

key·punch \-,pənch\ n : a machine with a keyboard for punching cards to be used in data processing — **key·punch** vb

key signature n : the sharps or flats placed after a clef in music to indicate the key

key·stone \'kē-,stōn\ n **1** : the wedge-shaped piece at the top of an arch that locks the other pieces in place **2** : something on which other things depend

key·stroke \-,strōk\ n : the act or an instance of pushing down a key on a keyboard

kha·ki \'kak-ē, 'käk-\ n **1** : a light yellowish brown **2** : a light yellowish brown cloth often used for military uniforms

> **Word History** In northern India a language known as Hindi gave the name *khākī* to a certain kind of strong cloth. This Hindi name meant "dust-colored," because the cloth was a light yellowish brown. When the British spent time in India, they discovered that the strong brown material made good military uniforms. Now the word *khaki* is used in English for a uniform, as well as for the cloth used to make it. [from Hindi *khākī* "dust-colored," from *khāk* "dust"; of Persian origin]

khan \'kän, 'kan\ n **1** : a Mongolian leader **2** : a local chieftain or man of rank in some countries of central Asia

khe·dive \kə-'dēv\ n : a governor of Egypt from 1867 to 1914

Khmer \kə-'me(ə)r\ n : a member of a native people of Cambodia

kib·butz \kib-'ůts, -'üts\ n, pl **kib·but·zim** \-,ůt-'sēm, -,üt-\ : a farming settlement in Israel that is owned and shared equally by the people who live there and run it

ki·bitz·er \'kib-ət-sər, kə-'bit-\ n : a person who looks on and often offers unwanted advice especially at a card game — **ki·bitz** \'kib-əts, kə-'bits\ vb

ki·bosh \'kī-,bäsh\ n : ¹END 2a, STOP — used in the phrase *put the kibosh on*

¹kick \'kik\ vb **1** : to strike out or hit with the foot **2** : to object strongly : PROTEST 〈*kicked* about their low grades〉 **3** : to spring back 〈a shotgun *kicks* when fired〉 **4** : to be full of pep and energy 〈still alive and *kicking*〉 **5** : to score by kicking a ball 〈*kick* a field goal〉 **6** slang : to free oneself of 〈*kick* the habit〉 — **kick·er** n — **kick up one's heels** : to have a good lively time

²kick n **1 a** : a blow with the foot **b** : the movement of the legs in swimming **2 a** : a sudden moving (as of a ball) with the foot **b** : the sudden move backward of a gun when fired **3** : a feeling of or cause for objection **4** : a feeling or source of pleasure

kick·back \'kik-,bak\ n : a secret return of part of a sum of money received

kick·ball \-,bȯl\ n : a game resembling baseball played with a large rubber ball that is kicked instead of hit with a bat

kick in vb : CONTRIBUTE 1

kick·off \'kik-,ȯf\ n : a kick that puts the ball into play (as in soccer or football)

kick off \(')kik-'ȯf\ vb **1** : to make a kickoff **2** : BEGIN 1

¹kid \'kid\ n **1** : the young of a goat or of a related animal **2 a** : the flesh, fur, or skin of a kid **b** : something (as leather) made of kid **3** : a young person : CHILD, YOUNGSTER — **kid·dish** \'kid-ish\ adj

²kid vb **kid·ded; kid·ding 1** : to deceive or trick as a joke **2** : ¹TEASE 2a — **kid·der** n

kid·nap \'kid-,nap\ vb **kid·napped** or **kid·naped** \-,napt\; **kid·nap·ping** or **kid·nap·ing** \-,nap-iŋ\ : to carry away a person by unlawful force or by fraud and against his or her will — **kid·nap·per** or **kid·nap·er** \-,nap-ər\ n

kid·ney \'kid-nē\ n, pl **kidneys 1** : either of a pair of oval to bean-shaped organs located in the back part of the abdomen near the spine that give off waste products in the form of urine **2** : an organ of an invertebrate animal that gives off waste

kidney bean n : an edible seed and especially a large red bean seed of any of several varieties of bean plants grown for their large seeds and belonging to the species commonly cultivated in gardens; *also* : a plant that produces kidney beans

kid·skin \'kid-,skin\ n : the skin of a kid or leather made from or resembling it

¹kill \'kil\ vb **1** : to deprive of life : put to death **2 a** : to put an end to : RUIN 〈that *killed* our chances〉 **b** : ¹DEFEAT 1 〈the committee *killed* the bill〉 **c** : to stop the use or functioning of 〈*kill* the lights〉 〈*killed* the engine〉 **d** : DELETE 〈*kill* a line of text〉 **3** : to cause to pass 〈just *killing* time〉 **4** : to use up completely 〈*killed* two cartons of milk〉

> **syn** KILL, MURDER, ASSASSINATE mean to take the life of. KILL suggests nothing about the manner of death and can apply to the death of anything 〈the early frost *killed* the crops〉 〈a person *killed* in an accident〉 MURDER applies to the deliberate and unlawful killing of a person. ASSASSINATE usually suggests the murder of an important person often for political reasons.

²kill n **1** : an act of killing **2** : an animal killed 〈a lion devouring its *kill*〉

kill·deer \'kil-,di(ə)r\ n, pl **killdeers** or **killdeer** : a North American plover that is grayish brown on the upper side, has two black bands on its white breast, and has a shrill mournful cry

> **Word History** Killdeers are not vicious birds. They have no special hatred of deer, and they do not eat venison. This attractive, dark-eyed bird has a loud, rather sad cry that to some people sounds like "Kill deer! Kill deer!" So the killdeer is an animal that got its name from human interpretation of its call. [imitation]

¹killer \'kil-ər\ n : one that kills

²killer adj **1** : strikingly impressive or effective 〈a *killer* smile〉 **2** : extremely difficult 〈a *killer* exam〉; *also* : causing death or devastation 〈a *killer* tornado〉

kill·er whale \'kil-ər-\ n : a fierce flesh-eating largely black whale 5 to 10 meters long that travels in groups — called also *killer*

killer whale

kill·ing \'kil-iŋ\ n : a sudden large profit

kill·joy \'kil-,jȯi\ n : a

\ə\ abut	\aů\ out	\i\ tip	\ȯ\ saw	\ů\ foot	
\ər\ further	\ch\ chin	\ī\ life	\ȯi\ coin	\y\ yet	
\a\ mat	\e\ pet	\j\ job	\th\ thin	\yü\ few	
\ā\ take	\ē\ easy	\ŋ\ sing	\th\ this	\yů\ cure	
\ä\ cot, cart	\g\ go	\ō\ bone	\ü\ food	\zh\ vision	

person who spoils the pleasure of others

kiln \'kiln, 'kil\ *n* : an oven or furnace for hardening, burning, or drying something ⟨brick *kilns*⟩ ⟨a *kiln* for rapid drying of lumber⟩ — **kiln** *vb*

ki·lo \'kē-(,)lō\ *n, pl* **kilos** : KILOGRAM

kilo- *combining form* : thousand ⟨*kilo*ton⟩ [derived from Greek *chilioi* "thousand"]

ki·lo·byte \'kē-lə-,bīt, 'kil-ə-\ *n* : 1024 bytes

ki·lo·cal·o·rie \'kē-lə-,kal-(ə-)rē, 'kil-ə-\ *n* : CALORIE 1b

kilo·cy·cle \'kil-ə-,sī-kəl\ *n* : 1000 cycles; *esp* : KILOHERTZ

ki·lo·gram \'kē-lə-,gram, 'kil-ə-\ *n*   **1** : the basic metric unit of mass equal to 1000 grams   **2** : the weight of a kilogram mass that is under a gravitational attraction equal to that of the earth — see METRIC SYSTEM table

ki·lo·hertz \'kil-ə-,hərts, 'kē-lə-, -,he(ə)rts\ : 1000 hertz

kilo·joule \'kil-ə-,jül\ *n* : 1000 joules

kilo·li·ter \'kil-ə-,lēt-ər\ *n* — see METRIC SYSTEM table

ki·lo·me·ter \kə-'läm-ət-ər, kil-'äm-; 'kil-ə-,mēt-ər\ *n* — see METRIC SYSTEM table

kilo·pas·cal \'kil-ə-pas-'kal\ *n* : 1000 pascals

ki·lo·ton \'kil-ə-,tən, 'kē-lə- *also* -,tän\ *n*   **1** : 1000 tons (about 907 metric tons)   **2** : an explosive force equivalent to that of 1000 tons of TNT

ki·lo·volt \'kē-lə-,vōlt, 'kil-ə-\ *n* : 1000 volts

kilo·watt \'kil-ə-,wät\ *n* : 1000 watts

kilowatt–hour *n* : a unit of work or energy equal to that expended by one kilowatt in one hour and equal to 3.6 million joules

kilt \'kilt\ *n* : a knee-length pleated skirt usually of tartan worn by men in Scotland — **kilt·ed** \'kil-təd\ *adj*

kil·ter \'kil-tər\ *n* : proper condition ⟨the TV is out of *kilter*⟩

ki·mo·no \kə-'mō-nə\ *n, pl* **-nos**   **1** : a loose robe with wide sleeves that is traditionally worn with a broad sash as an outer garment by the Japanese   **2** : a loose dressing gown worn chiefly by women

¹kin \'kin\ *n*   **1** : a person's relatives   **2** : KINSMAN

²kin *adj* : being related : KINDRED

-kin \kən\ *also* **-kins** \kənz\ *n suffix* : little — often used in affectionate nicknames ⟨ba-by*kins*⟩ [Middle English *-kin* "little", from early Dutch *-kin* "little"]

¹kind \'kīnd\ *n*   **1 a** : a group united by common traits or interests : CATEGORY ⟨hawks and other birds of their *kind*⟩   **b** : VARIETY 3a ⟨all *kinds* of people⟩ ⟨what *kind* of car do you have⟩   **c** : one that is barely a member of a category ⟨a *kind* of gray⟩   **2** : essential quality or character ⟨differences in *kind*⟩   **3 a** : goods as distinguished from money ⟨payment in *kind* rather than in cash⟩   **b** : something equal to what has been offered or received ⟨returned the favor in *kind*⟩

²kind *adj*   **1** : wanting and liking to do good and to bring happiness to others   **2** : showing or growing out of gentleness or goodness of heart ⟨a *kind* act⟩

kin·der·gar·ten \'kin-də(r)-,gärt-ᵊn, -,gärd-\ *n* : a school or class for very young children [from German *kindergarten* "a school for very young children", from *kinder* "children" and *garten* "garden"]

kin·der·gart·ner \'kin-der-,gärt-nər, -,gärd-\ *n* : a kindergarten pupil

kind·heart·ed \'kīnd-'härt-əd\ *adj* : having or showing a kind and sympathetic nature — **kind·heart·ed·ly** *adv* — **kind·heart·ed·ness** *n*

kin·dle \'kin-dᵊl\ *vb* **kin·dled; kin·dling** \-(d)liŋ, -dᵊl-iŋ\   **1** : to set on fire or take fire : LIGHT   **2** : to stir up : EXCITE ⟨trying to *kindle* their interest⟩

kin·dling \'kin-(d)liŋ\ *n* : material that burns easily and is used to start a fire

¹kind·ly \'kīn-(d)lē\ *adj* **kind·li·er; -est**   **1** : pleasant or wholesome in nature ⟨a *kindly* climate⟩   **2** : of a sympathetic or generous nature ⟨*kindly* people⟩ — **kind·li·ness** *n*

²kindly *adv*   **1** : in a willing manner ⟨does not take *kindly* to criticism⟩   **2 a** : in a kind manner ⟨treat animals *kindly*⟩   **b** : in an appreciative manner ⟨I would take it *kindly* if you would put in a good word for us⟩   **c** : in an obliging manner ⟨they *kindly* asked us to go along⟩   **d** : as a matter of courtesy : PLEASE ⟨*kindly* pass the salt⟩

kind·ness \'kīn(d)-nəs\ *n*   **1** : a kind deed : FAVOR   **2** : the quality or state of being kind

kind of \,kīn-də(v)\ *adv* : to a moderate degree : SOMEWHAT ⟨it's *kind of* cold in here⟩ ⟨I think he *kind of* likes me⟩

¹kin·dred \'kin-drəd\ *n*   **1** : a group of related individuals   **2** : a person's relatives

²kindred *adj* : alike in nature or character

kine \'kīn\ *archaic pl of* COW

ki·ne·sics \kə-'nē-siks, kī-, -ziks\ *n* : the study of body motions (as blushes, shrugs, or eye movement) that communicate

ki·net·ic \kə-'net-ik, kī-\ *adj* : of or relating to the motions of material bodies and the forces and energy associated with them [from Greek *kinētikos* "relating to motion", derived from *kinein* "to move" — related to CINEMA]

kinetic energy *n* : energy associated with motion

kinetic theory *n* : a theory that states that all matter is composed of particles in motion and that the rate of motion varies directly with the temperature

kin·folk \'kin-,fōk\ *n pl* : ¹KINDRED 2

king \'kiŋ\ *n*   **1** : a male ruler of a country who usually inherits his position and rules for life   **2** : a chief among competitors ⟨an oil *king*⟩   **3** : the chief piece in the game of chess   **4** : a playing card bearing the figure of a king   **5** : a piece in the game of checkers that has reached the opponent's back row and has been crowned

king·bird \-,bərd\ *n* : any of several American tyrant flycatchers

king cobra *n* : a large very poisonous snake of southeastern Asia and the Philippines

king crab   **1** : HORSESHOE CRAB   **2** : any of several very large crabs

king·dom \'kiŋ-dəm\ *n*   **1** : a country whose ruler is a king or queen   **2** : a region in which something or someone has very strong influence ⟨the cotton *kingdom*⟩   **3 a** : one of the three primary divisions into which natural objects are classified — compare ANIMAL KINGDOM, MINERAL KINGDOM, PLANT KINGDOM   **b** : a major category in the scientific classification of living things that ranks above the phylum and is the highest and broadest group

kingdom come *n* : the next world (as heaven)

king·fish \'kiŋ-,fish\ *n* : any of various sea fishes; *esp* : a large sport and food fish of the warm western Atlantic

king·fish·er \-,fish-ər\ *n* : any of a family of bright-colored birds with a short tail, a long stout sharp bill, and usually a bunch of feathers on the head

King James Version \kiŋ-'jāmz-\ *n* : AUTHORIZED VERSION

king·let \'kiŋ-lət\ *n* : any of several small birds that resemble warblers but have some of the habits of titmice

king·ly \'kiŋ-lē\ *adj* **king·li·er; -est**   **1** : having royal rank   **2** : of, relating to, or worthy of a king — **king·li·ness** *n* — **kingly** *adv*

king·pin \'kiŋ-,pin\ *n*   **1** : a pin that stands in the middle of a triangular arrangement of bowling pins; *also* : HEADPIN   **2** : the chief person in a group or undertaking

kimono 1

kingfisher

Kings \'kiŋz\ *n* — see BIBLE table

king·ship \'kiŋ-,ship\ *n* **1** : the position, office, or dignity of a king **2** : the personality of a king : MAJESTY **3** : government by a king

king–size \'kiŋ-,sīz\ *or* **king–sized** \-,sīzd\ *adj* : unusually long or large

king snake *n* : any of numerous harmless brightly marked snakes of the southern and central U.S. that feed on rodents

king's ransom *n* : a very large sum of money

¹kink \'kiŋk\ *n* **1** : a short tight twist or curl (as in a thread, rope, or hose) **2** : ¹CRAMP 1 ⟨a *kink* in my back⟩ **3** : an imperfection that makes something hard to use or work

²kink *vb* : to form or cause to form a kink

kin·ka·jou \'kiŋ-kə-,jü\ *n* : a slender long-tailed mammal of Central and South America that is related to the raccoon, is about one meter long, and has large eyes and soft woolly yellowish brown fur

kinkajou

kinky \'kiŋ-kē\ *adj* **kink·i·er; -est 1** : tightly twisted or curled **2** : very strange or odd — **kink·i·ness** *n*

-kins — see -KIN

kins·folk \'kinz-,fōk\ *n pl* : ¹KINDRED 2

kin·ship \'kin-,ship\ *n* : the quality or state of being kin : RELATIONSHIP

kins·man \'kinz-mən\ *n* : a relative usually by birth

kins·wom·an \'kinz-,wùm-ən\ *n* : a woman who is a relative usually by birth

ki·osk \'kē-,äsk, kē-'äsk\ *n* : a small light structure with one or more open sides

Ki·o·wa \'kī-ə-,wò, -,wä\ *n* : a member of an American Indian people of what are now Colorado, Kansas, New Mexico, Oklahoma, and Texas

¹kip·per \'kip-ər\ *n* : a kippered herring or salmon

²kipper *vb* **kip·pered; kip·per·ing** \-(ə-)riŋ\ : to cure by splitting, cleaning, salting, and smoking

kirk \'ki(ə)rk, 'kərk\ *n, chiefly Scottish* : CHURCH 1

¹kiss \'kis\ *vb* **1** : to touch with the lips as a mark of love or greeting **2** : to touch gently or lightly — **kiss·able** \-ə-bəl\ *adj*

²kiss *n* **1** : a loving touch with the lips **2** : a gentle touch or contact **3 a** : a small cookie made of meringue **b** : a bite-size candy ⟨a chocolate *kiss*⟩

kiss·er \'kis-ər\ *n* **1** : one that kisses **2** *slang* **a** : ¹MOUTH 1a **b** : ¹FACE 1

¹kit \'kit\ *n* **1 a** : a collection of articles for personal use ⟨a shaving *kit*⟩ **b** : a set of tools or supplies ⟨a first-aid *kit*⟩ **c** : a set of parts to be put together ⟨model-airplane *kit*⟩ **2** : a container (as a bag or case) for a kit **3** : a group of persons or things — used in the phrase *the whole kit and kaboodle* [Middle English *kit* "a wooden tub"]

²kit *n* : a small narrow violin [origin unknown]

³kit *n* **1** : KITTEN **2** : a young or small fur-bearing animal (as a fox) [a shortened form of *kitten*]

kitch·en \'kich-ən\ *n* : a place (as a room) in which cooking is done

Word History Although a room where food is cooked is called a kitchen, the words *cook* and *kitchen* are so different that it is surprising to learn that they both come from the same source. Both words can be traced to the Latin verb *coquere*, meaning "to cook". The connection between *coquere* and *cook* is easy to see, but *kitchen* has a more involved history. From the verb *coquere* came the later Latin noun *coquina*, meaning "a kitchen". With some changes in spelling and pronuncia-

tion, *coquina* came into Old English as *cycene*. Further changes over the course of many years gave us *kichene* and finally the Modern English *kitchen*. [Middle English *kichene* "kitchen", from Old English *cycene* (same meaning), from Latin *coquina* "a place where food is cooked", from earlier *coquere* "to cook" — related to COOK]

kitch·en·ette \,kich-ə-'net\ *n* : a small kitchen

kitchen garden *n* : a piece of land where vegetables are grown for household use

kitchen police *n* : KP

kitch·en·ware \'kich-ən-,wa(ə)r, -,we(ə)r\ *n* : utensils and appliances for use in a kitchen

kite \'kīt\ *n* **1** : any of various hawks with long narrow wings, a deeply forked tail, and feet used for catching insects and small reptiles as prey **2** : a light covered frame for flying in the air at the end of a long string

kith \'kith\ *n* : familiar friends and neighbors or relatives ⟨*kith* and kin⟩

kit·ten \'kit-ᵊn\ *n* : a young cat; *also* : a young individual of various other small mammals

kit·ten·ish \'kit-nish, -ᵊn-ish\ *adj* : resembling a kitten — **kit·ten·ish·ly** *adv* — **kit·ten·ish·ness** *n*

kit·ti·wake \'kit-ē-,wāk\ *n* : any of several gulls having the hind toe short

¹kit·ty \'kit-ē\ *n, pl* **kitties** : CAT 1a; *esp* : KITTEN

²kitty *n, pl* **kitties** : a sum of money often made up of small contributions

kitty–corner *or* **kitty–cornered** *variant of* CATERCORNER

ki·va \'kē-və\ *n* : a Pueblo Indian ceremonial structure that is usually round and partly underground

ki·wi \'kē-(,)wē\ *n* : a flightless New Zealand bird with weak and undeveloped wings, stout legs, a long bill, and grayish brown hairlike feathers

Klee·nex \'klē-,neks\ *trademark* — used for a cleansing tissue

klep·to·ma·nia \,klep-tə-'mā-nē-ə, -nyə\ *n* : a continuous abnormal desire to steal

klep·to·ma·ni·ac \,klep-tə-'mā-nē-,ak\ *n* : a person who exhibits kleptomania

kiwi

klieg light *or* **kleig light** \'klēg-\ *n* : a very bright lamp used in taking motion pictures

knack \'nak\ *n* **1** : a clever or skillful way of doing something : TRICK **2** : a natural ability : TALENT ⟨has a *knack* for making friends⟩

knap·sack \'nap-,sak\ *n* : a carrying case or pouch slung from the shoulders over the back

knave \'nāv\ *n* **1** : RASCAL 1 **2** : ¹JACK 5 [from earlier *knave* "a boy servant, a person of humble birth", from Old English *cnafa* "boy"] — **knav·ish** \'nā-vish\ *adj* — **knav·ish·ly** *adv*

knav·ery \'nāv-(ə-)rē\ *n, pl* **-er·ies** : the practices of a knave : RASCALITY

knead \'nēd\ *vb* **1** : to work and press into a mass with or as if with the hands **2** : to treat as if by kneading : MASSAGE — **knead·er** *n*

¹knee \'nē\ *n* **1** : the joint or region in the middle part of the human leg in which the femur, tibia, and kneecap come together; *also* : a corresponding part of a four-footed mammal **2** : something resembling the knee; *esp* : a cone-shaped upward growth from the roots of a few swamp-growing trees (as a cypress of the southern U.S.)

\ə\ **abut**	\aù\ **out**	\i\ **tip**	\ò\ **saw**	\ù\ **foot**	
\ər\ **further**	\ch\ **chin**	\ī\ **life**	\òi\ **coin**	\y\ **yet**	
\a\ **mat**	\e\ **pet**	\j\ **job**	\th\ **thin**	\yü\ **few**	
\ā\ **take**	\ē\ **easy**	\ŋ\ **sing**	\th\ **this**	\yù\ **cure**	
\ä\ **cot, cart**	\g\ **go**	\ō\ **bone**	\ü\ **food**	\zh\ **vision**	

that extends above the surrounding water **3** : the part of a garment covering the knee — **kneed** \'nēd\ *adj*

²**knee** *vb* **kneed; knee·ing** : to strike with the knee

knee·cap \'nē-,kap\ *n* : a thick flat movable bone forming the front part of the knee — called also *patella*

knee–deep \-'dēp\ *adj* : being up to one's knees ⟨*knee-deep* in mud⟩ ⟨*knee-deep* snowdrifts⟩

knee·hole \-,hōl\ *n* : a space (as under a desk) for the knees

knee jerk *n* : an involuntary forward kick produced by a light blow on the tendon below the kneecap

kneel \'nē(ə)l\ *vb* **knelt** \'nelt\ *or* **kneeled** \'nē(ə)ld\; **kneel·ing** : to bend the knee : support oneself on the knees — **kneel·er** *n*

¹**knell** \'nel\ *vb* **1** : to ring slowly and solemnly : TOLL **2** : to summon, announce, or warn by a knell

²**knell** *n* **1** : a stroke or sound of a bell especially when rung slowly for a death, funeral, or disaster **2** : an indication (as a sound) of the end or failure of something

knew *past of* KNOW

knick·er·bock·ers \'nik-ə(r)-,bäk-ərz\ *n pl* : KNICKERS [named for Diedrich *Knickerbocker,* made-up name used as the author of *History of New York,* which was really written by Washington Irving]

knick·ers \'nik-ərz\ *n pl* : loose-fitting short pants gathered just below the knee

knick·knack \'nik-,nak\ *n* : a small ornamental object

¹**knife** \'nīf\ *n, pl* **knives** \'nīvz\ **1** : a cutting instrument consisting of a sharp blade fastened to a handle **2** : a cutting blade in a machine

²**knife** *vb* **knifed; knif·ing** **1** : to stab, slash, or wound with a knife **2** : to move like a knife ⟨ships *knifing* through the sea⟩

knife–edge \'nī-,fej\ *n* : a sharp wedge usually of steel used as a support for a lever beam in a very exact instrument (as a balance)

knife switch *n* : an electric switch in which contact is made by pushing one or more flat blades between the jaws of clips

¹**knight** \'nīt\ *n* **1 a** : a warrior of olden times who fought on horseback, served a king, held a special military rank, and swore to behave in a noble way **b** : a man honored by a sovereign for merit and in Great Britain ranking below a baronet **2** : a chess piece that makes an L-shaped move [Old English *cniht* "youth, military follower"] — **knight·ly** \-lē\ *adj or adv*

²**knight** *vb* : to make a knight of

knight–er·rant \'nīt-'er-ənt\ *n, pl* **knights–errant** : a knight traveling in search of adventures — **knight–er·rant·ry** \'nīt-'er-ən-trē\ *n*

knight·hood \'nīt-,hùd\ *n* **1** : the rank, dignity, or profession of a knight **2** : the qualities that a knight should have **3** : knights as a class or body

knish \kə-'nish\ *n* : a small round or square piece of dough stuffed with a filling and baked or fried [Yiddish]

¹**knit** \'nit\ *vb* **knit** *or* **knit·ted; knit·ting** **1** : to form a fabric or garment by interlacing yarn or thread in connected loops with needles ⟨*knit* a sweater⟩ **2** : to draw or come together closely as if knitted : unite firmly ⟨wait for a broken bone to *knit*⟩ **3** : ²WRINKLE ⟨*knit* her brow⟩ — **knit·ter** *n*

²**knit** *n* : a knit fabric or garment

knit·ting *n* **1** : the action or method of one that knits **2** : work done or being done by one that knits

knitting needle *n* : a slender rod (as of metal or plastic) with one or both ends pointed that is used for knitting by hand

knit·wear \'nit-,wa(ə)r, -,we(ə)r\ *n* : knitted clothing

knob \'näb\ *n* **1 a** : a rounded lump **b** : a small rounded handle **2** : a rounded hill — **knobbed** \'näbd\ *adj* — **knob·by** \'näb-ē\ *adj*

¹**knock** \'näk\ *vb* **1 a** : to strike with a sharp blow **b** : to set in motion with a sharp blow **2** : to bump against something **3** : WANDER 1 ⟨*knocked* about the country last summer⟩ **4** : to have engine knock **5** : to find fault with ⟨don't *knock* it — there are worse jobs⟩ — **knock cold** : KNOCK OUT — **knock for a loop** : to cause to be overwhelmed : SHOCK, BEWILDER — **knock together** : to make or build hastily or carelessly

²**knock** *n* **1** : a sharp blow **2** : a severe misfortune or hardship **3 a** : a pounding noise ⟨heard a *knock* on the door⟩ **b** : a sharp rattling noise caused by abnormal ignition in an automobile engine

knock·about \'näk-ə-,baùt\ *adj* : being noisy and rough : BOISTEROUS

knock down *vb* **1** : to sell to the highest bidder at an auction **2** : to take or come apart

knock·er \'näk-ər\ *n* : a device made like a hinge and fastened to a door for use in knocking

knock–kneed \'näk-'nēd\ *adj* : having the legs bowed inward

knock–knock joke \'näk-'näk-\ *n* : a punning joke beginning with the lines "Knock, knock." "Who's there?"

knock off *vb* : to stop doing something

knock·out \'näk-,aùt\ *n* **1** : the act of knocking out : the condition of being knocked out **2** : something very striking or attractive — **knockout** *adj*

knock out \'näk-'aùt, näk-'aùt\ *vb* : to make unconscious

knock·wurst \'näk-(,)wərst\ *n* : a short thick sausage [from German *knackwurst* "knockwurst", from *knacken* "to crackle (when being fried)" and *wurst* "sausage"]

knoll \'nōl\ *n* : a small round hill

¹**knot** \'nät\ *n* **1** : an interlacing (as of string or ribbon) that forms a lump or knob **2** : something hard to solve : PROBLEM **3** : a bond of union **4 a** : a lump or swelling in bodily tissue **b** : the base of a woody branch enclosed in the stem from which it arises; *also* : a section of a knot in lumber **5** : a cluster of persons or things **6** : one nautical mile per hour (about two kilometers per hour)

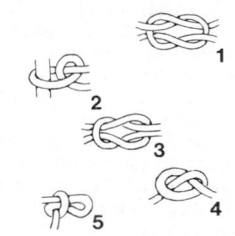

knot 1: *1* granny, *2* half hitch, *3* square, *4* overhand, *5* slipknot

²**knot** *vb* **knot·ted; knot·ting** **1** : to tie in or with a knot **2** : to unite closely

knot·head \'nät-,hed\ *n* : a stupid person : BLOCKHEAD

knot·hole \-,hōl\ *n* : a hole in a board or tree trunk where a knot has come out

knot·ted \'nät-əd\ *adj* **1** : tied in or with a knot **2** : KNOTTY

knot·ty \'nät-ē\ *adj* **knot·ti·er; -est** **1** : full of knots ⟨*knotty* wood⟩ **2** : DIFFICULT 2b ⟨a *knotty* problem⟩

knout \'naùt, 'nüt\ *n* : a whip for beating criminals as punishment

¹**know** \'nō\ *vb* **knew** \'n(y)ü\; **known** \'nōn\; **know·ing** **1 a** : to have understanding of ⟨*know* yourself⟩ **b** : to recognize the nature of ⟨*knew* them to be honest⟩ **2 a** : to recognize the identity of ⟨*knew* me by my walk⟩ **b** : to be acquainted or familiar with ⟨*knows* the city very well⟩ **3 a** : to be aware of the truth of ⟨*know* that the earth is round⟩ **b** : to have a practical understanding of ⟨*knows* how to write⟩ **4** : to have information or knowledge ⟨ask someone who *knows*⟩ **5** : to be or become aware ⟨*knew* about the problem⟩ — **know·able** \'nō-ə-bəl\ *adj* — **know·er** \'nō-(ə)r\ *n*

²**know** *n* : the fact of knowing : KNOWLEDGE — **in the know**

knickers

: well-informed

know–how \'nō-,haù\ *n* : knowledge of how to get things done : EXPERTISE

know·ing \'nō-iŋ\ *adj* **1** : having or showing special knowledge **2** : shrewdly and keenly alert **3** : INTENTIONAL — **know·ing·ly** *adv*

know–it–all \'nō-ət-,ȯl\ *n* : a person who always claims to know everything

knowl·edge \'näl-ij\ *n* **1** : understanding or skill gained by experience ⟨a *knowledge* of carpentry⟩ **2 a** : the state of being aware of something or of having information **b** : the range of one's information or understanding ⟨answered to the best of my *knowledge*⟩ **3** : something learned and kept in the mind : LEARNING ⟨has a vast *knowledge* of history⟩

   syn KNOWLEDGE, LEARNING, SCHOLARSHIP mean what is known or can be known by a person or by human beings in general. KNOWLEDGE applies to facts or ideas acquired by study, observation, or experience ⟨gained a *knowledge* of horses in growing up on a ranch⟩ LEARNING applies to knowledge gained usually through formal schooling especially at an advanced level ⟨a college professor of great *learning*⟩ SCHOLARSHIP suggests the learning of an advanced scholar in a specialized field of study ⟨a history book that shows much *scholarship* on the part of the author⟩

knowl·edge·able \'näl-ij-ə-bəl\ *adj* : having or showing knowledge or intelligence

known \'nōn\ *adj* : generally recognized ⟨a *known* expert on art⟩

know–noth·ing \'nō-,nəth-iŋ\ *n* : a person who is ignorant : IGNORAMUS

¹knuck·le \'nək-əl\ *n* **1** : the rounded lump formed by the ends of two bones (as of a finger) where they come together in a joint **2** : any of several parts (as the hock or shank or a tarsal joint) of the leg of a four-footed animal as used for food

²knuckle *vb* **knuck·led; knuck·ling** \'nək-(ə-)liŋ\ : to place the knuckles on the ground in shooting a marble

knuck·le·ball \'nək-əl-,bȯl\ *n* : a baseball pitch gripped with the knuckles or fingertips and thrown with very little spin

knuckle down *vb* : to apply oneself in an earnest manner

knuckle under *vb* : SUBMIT 4, GIVE IN

¹KO \(')kā-'ō, 'kā-ō\ *n, pl* **KO's** : a knockout in boxing

²KO *vb* **KO'd** \kā-'ōd, 'kā-ōd\; **KO'·ing** \-'ō-iŋ, -ō-\ : to knock out in boxing

ko·ala \kō-'äl-ə, kə-'wäl-ə\ *n* : an Australian tree-dwelling marsupial mammal that has large hairy ears, thick gray fur, sharp claws for climbing, and no tail and feeds on eucalyptus leaves

koala

Koch's postulates \'kȯks-\ *n pl* : a statement of the steps required to identify a germ as the cause of a disease: (1) it must be found in all cases of the disease; (2) it must be found in the individual with the disease and grown in pure culture; (3) it must produce the disease when a healthy individual capable of getting the disease is infected with it; (4) it must be found in the individual that is experimentally infected

kohl \'kōl\ *n* : a cosmetic used by women especially in Arabia and Egypt to darken the edges of the eyelids

kohl·ra·bi \kōl-'räb-ē\ *n, pl* **-bies** : a cabbage that does not form a head but has a swollen fleshy edible stem

ko·la nut \'kō-lə-\ *n* : the bitter seed of an African tree containing much caffeine and used in beverages and medicine for its stimulating effect

koodoo *variant of* KUDU

kook \'kük\ *n* : a person who acts in a strange or insane way : NUT — **kooky** \'kü-kē\ *adj*

kook·a·bur·ra \'kùk-ə-,bər-ə, 'kùk-, -,bə-rə\ *n* : an Australian kingfisher that is about the size of a crow and has a call resembling loud laughter — called also *laughing jackass*

ko·peck *or* **ko·pek** \'kō-,pek\ *n* **1** : a unit of money equal to ¹⁄₁₀₀ ruble **2** : a coin representing one kopeck

Ko·ran \kə-'ran, -'rän; 'kȯ(ə)r-,an, 'kō(ə)r-\ *n* : a book of sacred writings accepted by Muslims as revealed to Muhammad by Allah

Ko·re·an \kə-'rē-ən\ *n* **1** : a person born or living in Korea **2** : the language of the Korean people — **Korean** *adj*

ko·sher \'kō-shər\ *adj* **1 a** : accepted by Jewish law; *esp* : ritually fit for use ⟨*kosher* corned beef⟩ **b** : selling or serving food ritually fit according to Jewish law ⟨a *kosher* restaurant⟩ **2** : PROPER 5

kow·tow \'kaù-'taù, 'kaù-,taù\ *vb* : to show overly respectful attention [from Chinese *k'o t'on,* literally "to bump the head (in bowing to the ground)"]

KP \(')kā-'pē\ *n* **1** : the military duty of helping to prepare, serve, and clean up after meals **2** : a person on KP

kraal \'krȯl, 'kräl\ *n* **1** : a village of southern African natives **2** : an enclosure for tame animals in southern Africa

krait \'krīt\ *n* : any of several brightly banded extremely poisonous Asian snakes

kra·ken \'kräk-ən\ *n* : a sea monster of Scandinavian legend

Krebs cycle \'krebz-\ *n* : a series of chemical reactions in living things in which acetic acid or a related substance is oxidized to produce energy which is stored in phosphate bonds

krill \'kril\ *n* : small living things (as crustaceans and larvae) that make up plankton and form a major food of whales

¹kro·na \'krō-nə\ *n, pl* **kro·nor** \-,nȯ(ə)r, -nər\ **1** : the basic unit of money of Sweden **2** : a coin representing one krona

²kro·na \'krō-nə\ *n, pl* **kro·nur** \-nər\ **1** : the basic unit of money of Iceland **2** : a coin representing one krona

¹kro·ne \'krō-nə\ *n, pl* **kro·ner** \-nər\ **1** : the basic unit of money of Denmark and Norway **2** : a coin representing one krone

²kro·ne \'krō-nə\ *n, pl* **kro·nen** \-nən\ **1** : the basic unit of money of Austria from 1892 to 1925 **2** : a coin representing one krone

kryp·ton \'krip-,tän\ *n* : a colorless gaseous element found in air and used especially in electric lamps — see ELEMENT table

ku·du *also* **koo·doo** \'küd-(,)ü\ *n* : a large grayish brown African antelope with large twisted horns

kud·zu \'kùd-zü\ *n* : a trailing Asian vine that is related to the pea and is used widely for hay, for grazing, and for erosion control

kum·quat \'kəm-,kwät\ *n* **1** : a small citrus fruit with sweet spongy skin and somewhat acid pulp used especially for preserves **2** : a tree or shrub that bears kumquats

kudu

\ə\ **abut**	\aù\ **out**	\i\ **tip**	\ȯ\ **saw**	\ù\ **foot**
\ər\ **further**	\ch\ **chin**	\ī\ **life**	\ȯi\ **coin**	\y\ **yet**
\a\ **mat**	\e\ **pet**	\j\ **job**	\th\ **thin**	\yü\ **few**
\ā\ **take**	\ē\ **easy**	\ŋ\ **sing**	\th\ **this**	\yù\ **cure**
\ä\ **cot, cart**	\g\ **go**	\ō\ **bone**	\ü\ **food**	\zh\ **vision**

kung fu \,kən-'fü, ,kün-\ *n* : a Chinese art of self-defense resembling karate

Kurd \'kü(ə)rd, 'kərd\ *n* : a member of a nomadic people who live in a region that is partly in Turkey, Iran, Iraq, Syria, and Soviet Armenia and Azerbaijan — **Kurd·ish** \-ish\ *adj*

kwash·i·or·kor \,kwäsh-ē-ē-'òr-kər\ *n* : a disease of young children resulting from not getting enough protein to eat

L

l \'el\ *n, often cap* **1** : the 12th letter of the English alphabet **2** : fifty in Roman numerals

la \'lä\ *n* : the sixth note of the musical scale

lab \'lab\ *n* : LABORATORY

¹la·bel \'lā-bəl\ *n* **1** : a slip (as of paper or cloth) that is attached to something to identify or describe it **2 a** : a descriptive or identifying word or phrase **b** : the brand name of a commercial product

²label *vb* **la·beled** *or* **la·belled; la·bel·ing** *or* **la·bel·ling** \-b(ə-)liŋ\ **1** : to attach a label to **2** : to name or describe with or as if with a label **3** : to make (a chemical element) traceable (as through the steps of a biochemical process) by substitution of a detectable isotope

la·bi·al \'lā-bē-əl\ *adj* : of or relating to the lips or labia

la·bi·um \'lā-bē-əm\ *n, pl* **-bia** \-bē-ə\ **1** : any of the folds at the margin of the vulva **2** : the lower lip of an insect

¹la·bor \'lā-bər\ *n* **1** : physical or mental effort especially when hard or required : TOIL, WORK **2 a** : the services performed by workers for wages **b** : those who do labor for wages **3** : the physical efforts and pain of giving birth; *also* : the period of such labor **4** : something that requires work : TASK

²labor *vb* **la·bored; la·bor·ing** \-b(ə-)riŋ\ **1 a** : to work hard **b** : to work for wages in production of goods or services **2** : to move with great effort **syn** *see* WORK

lab·o·ra·to·ry \'lab-(ə-)rə-,tòr-ē, -,tòr-\ *n, pl* **-ries** : a place equipped for making scientific experiments and tests

Labor Day *n* : the first Monday in September observed as a legal holiday in honor of working people

la·bored \'lā-bərd\ *adj* : produced or done with labor ⟨*labored* breathing⟩

la·bor·er \'lā-bər-ər\ *n* : one that works; *esp* : a person who does unskilled physical work for wages

la·bo·ri·ous \lə-'bòr-ē-əs, -'bòr-\ *adj* **1** : INDUSTRIOUS **2** : requiring hard effort — **la·bo·ri·ous·ly** *adv* — **la·bo·ri·ous·ness** *n*

la·bor·sav·ing \'lā-bər-,sā-viŋ\ *adj* : designed to replace or decrease human labor and especially physical labor

labor union *n* : an organization of workers formed to protect the rights and advance the interests of its members concerning wages, benefits, and working conditions

Lab·ra·dor retriever \,lab-rə-,dòr-\ *n* : any of a breed of strongly built retrievers having a broad head and a short dense coat

la·brum \'lā-brəm\ *n* : the upper lip of an arthropod in front of or above the mandibles

lab·y·rinth \'lab-ə-,rin(t)th\ *n* **1** : a place full of passageways and blind alleys so arranged as to make it difficult to find one's way around : MAZE **2** : something extremely complicated or twisting ⟨the cockpit was a *labyrinth* of instruments and controls⟩ **3** : the internal ear or its bony or membranous part — **lab·y·rin·thine** \,lab-ə-'rin(t)-thən\ *adj*

Labrador retriever

lac \'lak\ *n* : a substance given off by a scale insect and used in the manufacture of shellac, lacquers, and sealing wax

¹lace \'lās\ *vb* **laced; lac·ing** **1** : to fasten or join with or as if with a lace **2** : to adorn with lace **3** : INTERTWINE **4** : ¹BEAT 1a, LASH

²lace *n* **1** : a cord or string for drawing together two edges (as of a shoe) **2** : an ornamental braid for trimming coats or uniforms **3** : a fine open-worked fabric of thread or cord used chiefly for ornament of dress — **laced** \'lāst\ *adj* — **lace·like** \'lā-,slīk\ *adj*

Word History When the ancient Romans wanted to trap a small animal, such as a rabbit, they used a loop of light rope laid on the ground in its path. A triggering device was used to tighten the loop around the animal. They called such a loop or noose *laqueus,* which became *laz* in early French. The English borrowed it as *las* in the 14th century. They used it to refer to a cord that holds something together by weaving, as a shoelace. Finally, it came to mean the delicate fabric made by weaving and knotting thin strands of material. [Middle English *las, lace* "a string used to draw together two edges of material", from early French *laz* (same meaning), from Latin *laqueus* "noose, snare" — related to ³LASH, ¹LASSO]

lac·er·ate \'las-ə-,rāt\ *vb* **-at·ed; -at·ing** : to tear roughly : injure by tearing

lac·er·a·tion \,las-ə-'rā-shən\ *n* **1** : an act or instance of lacerating **2** : a torn and ragged wound

lace·wing \'lā-,swiŋ\ *n* : any of various insects that have delicate lacy wings, long antennae, and bright eyes

lach·ry·mal *or* **lac·ri·mal** \'lak-rə-məl\ *adj* : of, relating to, or being the glands that produce tears

lach·ry·mose \'lak-rə-,mōs\ *adj* **1** : tending to weep : TEARFUL **2** : tending to cause tears : MOURNFUL ⟨*lachrymose* songs about dying heroes⟩ — **lach·ry·mose·ly** *adv*

lac·ing \'lā-siŋ\ *n* **1** : the action of one that laces **2** : ²LACE

¹lack \'lak\ *vb* **1** : to be missing **2** : to need, want, or be short of ⟨*lacks* money⟩

²lack *n* **1** : the fact or state of being absent or in short supply **2** : something that is lacking or is needed

lack·a·dai·si·cal \,lak-ə-'dā-zi-kəl\ *adj* : lacking spirit or enthusiasm : LANGUID, LISTLESS — **lack·a·dai·si·cal·ly** \-k(ə-)lē\ *adv*

lack·ey \'lak-ē\ *n, pl* **lackeys** **1** : FOOTMAN 2 **2** : an overly respectful follower : TOADY

lack·lus·ter \'lak-,ləs-tər\ *adj* : lacking in brightness, radiance, or interest : DULL ⟨a *lackluster* performance⟩

la·con·ic \lə-'kän-ik\ *adj* : using few words : TERSE ⟨a *laconic* reply⟩ — **la·con·i·cal·ly** \-'kän-i-k(ə-)lē\ *adv*

lac·quer \'lak-ər\ *n* : a material like varnish that dries quickly into a shiny layer (as on wood or metal) — **lacquer** *vb*

la·crosse \lə-'kròs\ *n* : a game played on a field in which players use long-handled sticks with shallow nets for catching, throwing, and carrying the ball

Word History The game of lacrosse was invented many centuries ago by American Indians, who called it *baggataway.* It was given the name *lacrosse* by French settlers in Canada. *La crosse* in French means "the cro-sier", a long staff that looks like a hooked shepherd's staff but is carried by bishops and abbots as a symbol of their office. Because the long-handled stick used in lacrosse is curved over at the top and looks somewhat like a crosier, the French Canadians called it *la crosse*. The term *la crosse* later came to be used as a name for the game itself. The two words in time became the sin-gle word *lacrosse*. [from Canadian French *la crosse*, lit-erally "the crosier"]

lac·tase \'lak-ˌtās\ *n* : an enzyme that breaks down lactose and related compounds and occurs especially in the intes-tines of young mammals and in yeasts

lac·tate \'lak-ˌtāt\ *vb* **lac·tat·ed; lac·tat·ing** : to give off milk — **lac·ta·tion** \lak-'tā-shən\ *n*

lac·te·al \'lak-tē-əl\ *n* : one of the lymphatic vessels that arise from the villi of the small intestine and carry chyle

lac·tic acid \ˌlak-tik-\ *n* : an organic acid present in cells and especially muscle, made from carbohydrate, and used especially in food and medicine

lac·tose \'lak-ˌtōs\ *n* : a sugar present in milk that breaks down to give glucose and galactose and on fermentation gives especially lactic acid — called also *milk sugar*

la·cus·trine \lə-'kəs-trən\ *adj* : of, relating to, formed in, or growing in lakes

lacy \'lā-sē\ *adj* **lac·i·er; -est** : resembling or consisting of lace

lad \'lad\ *n* **1** : BOY 1, YOUTH **2** : ¹FELLOW 4a, CHAP

lad·der \'lad-ər\ *n* **1** : a structure for climbing that consists of two long parallel pieces (as of wood, rope, or metal) joined at short distances by crosspieces on which one may step **2** : something that suggests a ladder in form or use **3** : a series of steps or stages : SCALE

lad·die \'lad-ē\ *n* : a young lad

lade \'lād\ *vb* **lad·ed; lad·ed** *or* **lad·en** \'lād-ᵊn\; **lad·ing** **1** : ²LOAD 1a ⟨*lade* a ship⟩ ⟨a truck *laden* with gravel⟩ **2** : to burden heavily ⟨*laden* with cares⟩ **3** : ²LADLE

¹la·dle \'lād-ᵊl\ *n* : a spoon or dipper with a long handle and a deep bowl used for dipping

²ladle *vb* **la·dled; la·dling** \'lād-liŋ, -ᵊl-iŋ\ : to take up and carry in or as if in a ladle

la·dy \'lād-ē\ *n, pl* **ladies 1** : a woman of property, rank, or authority; *esp* : one having a standing equivalent to that of a lord — used as a title **2** *cap* : VIRGIN MARY — usually used with *Our* **3** : a woman of high social position **4** : WOMAN 1 **5** : WIFE 2

Word History The word *lady* is nowadays generally used as a polite term for a woman. In the past, however, *lady* was used primarily for "a woman of a high social class". The Old English ancestor of *lady* was *hlæfdige*, which came from two other words. One was *hlāf*, mean-ing "loaf of bread". The other was *-dīge*, a form of an ancient root word meaning "to knead dough". But the word *hlæfdige* was not used in Old English for an actual bread maker. It was used instead to refer to the woman in charge of maids and of a household. Only very rich and powerful women, members of the nobility, had maids and large households, so a lady was owed much respect. The title *lady* is still used in Great Britain for a woman who is a member of the nobility. [Old English *hlæfdige*, from *hlāf* "loaf of bread" and *-dīge*, a form of an ancient root word mean-ing "to knead dough" — re-lated to LOAF, LORD; see *Word History* at LORD]

lady beetle *n* : LADYBUG

la·dy·bird \'lād-ē-ˌbərd\ *n* : LADYBUG

la·dy·bug \-ˌbəg\ *n* : any of

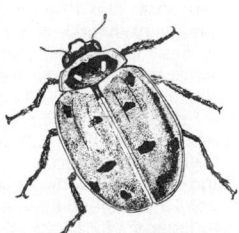

ladybug

numerous small roundish-backed often brightly colored beetles that usually feed both when young and adult on other insects

la·dy–in–wait·ing \ˌlād-ē-in-'wāt-iŋ\ *n, pl* **ladies–in–wait·ing** : a lady appointed to attend or wait on a queen or princess

la·dy·like \'lād-ē-ˌlīk\ *adj* **1** : resembling a lady in appear-ance or manners **2** : suitable to a lady ⟨*ladylike* behavior⟩

la·dy·love \'lād-ē-ˌləv, ˌlād-ē-'ləv\ *n* : a woman with whom one is in love : SWEETHEART

la·dy·ship \'lād-ē-ˌship\ *n* : the rank or dignity of a lady — used as a title ⟨her *Ladyship* is not at home⟩

lady's slipper *or* **lady slipper** \'lād-ē(z)-ˌslip-ər\ *n* : any of sev-eral temperate-zone orchids whose large drooping flowers suggest a slipper in shape

lady's slipper

¹lag \'lag\ *n* **1** : the action or con-dition of lagging **2 a** : amount of lagging **b** : a time during which lagging continues

²lag *vb* **lagged; lag·ging 1** : to stay or fall behind **2** : to hang back : LINGER, LOITER **3** : to move, function, or develop too slowly ⟨production *lagged* behind schedule⟩ **4** : to slacken little by little : FLAG **syn** see LINGER — **lag·ger** *n*

lag·gard \'lag-ərd\ *adj* : lagging or tending to lag : SLOW — **laggard** *n* — **lag·gard·ly** *adv or adj*

la·gniappe \'lan-ˌyap, lan-'yap\ *n* : something given free especially with a customer's purchase [American French]

lago·morph \'lag-ə-ˌmȯrf\ *n* : any of an order of gnawing mammals having two pairs of upper incisor teeth one be-hind the other and including the rabbits, hares, and pikas — compare RODENT

la·goon \lə-'gün\ *n* : a shallow channel or pond near or con-nected with a larger body of water

laid *past and past participle of* LAY

laid–back \'lād-'bak\ *adj* : relaxed in style or manner

lain *past participle of* ¹LIE

lair \'la(ə)r, 'le(ə)r\ *n* : the den or resting place of a wild animal; *also* : REFUGE 1, HIDEAWAY

laird \'la(ə)rd, 'le(ə)rd\ *n* : a Scottish landowner

lais·sez–faire \ˌle-ˌsā-'fa(ə)r, ˌlā-, -ˌzā-, -'fe(ə)r\ *n* : a doc-trine opposing governmental interference in economic af-fairs [from the French phrase *laissez faire* "let (people) do (as they choose)"] — **laissez–faire** *adj*

la·ity \'lā-ət-ē\ *n, pl* **-ties 1** : the people of a religious faith who are not members of its clergy **2** : persons not of a particular profession

lake \'lāk\ *n* : a large inland body of standing water; *also* : a pool of liquid (as oil or pitch)

lake trout *n* : any of several lake fishes; *esp* : a large dark American trout that is an important sport and commercial fish in northern lakes

¹lam \'lam\ *vb* **lammed; lam·ming 1** : ¹STRIKE 2a, THRASH **2** : to flee hastily

²lam *n* : a sudden or hurried flight especially from the law ⟨on the *lam*⟩

la·ma \'läm-ə\ *n* : a Lamaist monk

La·ma·ism \'läm-ə-ˌiz-əm\ *n* : the Buddhism of Tibet and Mongolia having a ruling body of monks organized into ranks — **La·ma·ist** \'läm-ə-əst\ *n or adj* — **La·ma·is·tic**

\ə\ abut	\au̇\ **out**	\i\ **tip**	\ȯ\ **saw**	\u̇\ **foot**
\ər\ **further**	\ch\ **chin**	\ī\ **life**	\ȯi\ **coin**	\y\ **yet**
\a\ **mat**	\e\ **pet**	\j\ **job**	\th\ **thin**	\yü\ **few**
\ā\ **take**	\ē\ **easy**	\ŋ\ **sing**	\t͟h\ **this**	\yu̇\ **cure**
\ä\ **cot, cart**	\g\ **go**	\ō\ **bone**	\ü\ **food**	\zh\ **vision**

\,läm-ə-'is-tik\ *adj*

La·marck·ian \lə-'mär-kē-ən\ *adj* : of or relating to a theory of organic evolution holding that changes in the environment cause changes in the structure of animals and plants that are passed on to offspring

la·ma·sery \'läm-ə-,ser-ē\ *n, pl* **-ser·ies** : a monastery of lamas

¹**lamb** \'lam\ *n* **1 a** : a young sheep especially less than one year old or without permanent teeth **b** : the flesh of a lamb used as food **2** : an innocent, weak, or gentle person

²**lamb** *vb* : to give birth to a lamb

lam·baste *or* **lam·bast** \(')lam-'bāst, -'bast\ *vb* **lam·bast·ed; lam·bast·ing** **1** : ¹STRIKE 2a, BEAT **2** : to scold roughly

lamb·da \'lam-də\ *n* : the eleventh letter of the Greek alphabet — Λ or λ

lam·bent \'lam-bənt\ *adj* **1** : playing lightly over a surface : FLICKERING **2** : softly radiant

lamb·kin \'lam-kən\ *n* : a little lamb

lamb·skin \'lam-,skin\ *n* : a lamb's skin or a small fine-grade sheepskin or leather made from either

lamb's-quar·ters \'lamz-,kwȯ(r)t-ərz\ *n sing or pl* : a goosefoot with leaves that are sometimes used as greens

¹**lame** \'lām\ *adj* **lam·er; lam·est** **1 a** : having a body part and especially an arm or a leg crippled enough so as to be unable to get around without pain or difficulty **b** : being stiff and sore ⟨a *lame* shoulder⟩ **2** : not very convincing : WEAK ⟨a *lame* excuse⟩ — **lame·ly** *adv* — **lame·ness** *n*

²**lame** *vb* **lamed; lam·ing** : to make lame : CRIPPLE

lame duck *n* : an elected official continuing to hold office until a successor takes office

la·mel·la \lə-'mel-ə\ *n, pl* **-mel·lae** \-'mel-(,)ē, -,ī\ *also* **-mellas** : a thin flat scale, layer, or membrane

¹**la·ment** \lə-'ment\ *vb* **1** : to mourn aloud : WAIL **2** : to express sorrow for : BEWAIL — **lam·en·ta·tion** \,lam-ən-'tā-shən\ *n*

²**lament** *n* **1** : a crying out in grief **2** : a mournful song or poem

la·men·ta·ble \'lam-ən-tə-bəl, lə-'ment-ə-\ *adj* **1** : that is to be regretted or lamented **2** : SORROWFUL 2 — **la·men·ta·ble·ness** *n* — **la·men·ta·bly** \-blē\ *adv*

Lam·en·ta·tions \,lam-ən-'tā-shənz\ *n* — see BIBLE table

lam·i·na \'lam-ə-nə\ *n, pl* **-nae** \-,nē, -,nī\ *or* **-nas** : a thin plate or scale

lam·i·nar·ia \,lam-ə-'ner-ē-ə, -'nar-\ *n* : any of various large kelps with an unbranched cylinder-shaped or flattened stalk and a smooth or wavy blade

lam·i·nate \'lam-ə-,nāt\ *vb* **-nat·ed; -nat·ing** **1** : to roll or compress into a thin plate **2** : to make by uniting layers of one or more materials — **lam·i·nate** \-nət, -,nāt\ *n* — **lam·i·na·tion** \,lam-ə-'nā-shən\ *n* — **lam·i·na·tor** \'lam-ə-,nāt-ər\ *n*

lamp \'lamp\ *n* : a device for producing light or heat

lamp·black \-,blak\ *n* : a fine black soot made by incomplete burning of carbon-containing material and used to color things black

lamp·light \'lam-,plīt\ *n* : the light of a lamp

lamp·light·er \'lamp-,plīt-ər\ *n* : one that lights a lamp; *esp* : a person employed to light gas streetlights

¹**lam·poon** \lam-'pün\ *n* : a writing or drawing that makes fun of a person

²**lampoon** *vb* : to make fun of by a lampoon : RIDICULE — **lampoon·er** *n*

lamp·post \'lam(p)-,pōst\ *n* : a post supporting a usually outdoor lamp or lantern

lam·prey \'lam-prē, -,prā\ *n, pl* **lampreys** : any of an order of jawless fishes that resemble eels but have a large sucking mouth with no jaws

lamprey

lamp·shell \'lamp-,shel\ *n* : BRACHIOPOD

¹**lance** \'lan(t)s\ *n* **1** : a weapon consisting of a long shaft with a sharp steel head that was used by knights on horseback **2** : a sharp instrument; *esp* : LANCET

²**lance** *vb* **lanced; lanc·ing** : to pierce or cut with a lance or lancet

lance corporal *n* : an enlisted person with a rank just below that of corporal in the marines

lance·let \'lan(t)-slət\ *n* : any of various small marine animals related to the vertebrates — called also *amphioxus*

lanc·er \'lan(t)-sər\ *n* : one who carries a lance; *esp* : a light cavalryman armed with a lance

lan·cet \'lan(t)-sət\ *n* : a sharp-pointed and usually two-edged surgical instrument

¹**land** \'land\ *n* **1** : the solid part of the surface of the earth **2** : a portion of the earth's surface ⟨fenced *land*⟩ ⟨marshy *land*⟩ **3** : ¹COUNTRY 2b, NATION **4** : REAL ESTATE ⟨owns *land* in Alaska⟩ — **land·less** \'lan-dləs\ *adj*

²**land** *vb* **1 a** : to set or go ashore from a ship : DISEMBARK **b** : to stop at or near a place on shore **2** : to come down or bring down and settle on a surface ⟨*land* a plane⟩ **3** : to bring to or arrive at a destination or a position or condition ⟨*land* in jail⟩ ⟨*landed* in trouble⟩ **4 a** : to catch and bring in ⟨*land* a fish⟩ **b** : ²GAIN 1a,b, SECURE ⟨*land* a job⟩ — **land·er** *n*

land breeze *n* : a breeze blowing toward the sea

land·ed \'lan-dəd\ *adj* **1** : owning land **2** : consisting of real estate

land·fall \'lan(d)-,fȯl\ *n* **1** : a sighting or making of land after a voyage or flight **2** : the land first sighted on a voyage or flight

land·fill \-,fil\ *n* **1** : a system of trash and garbage disposal in which the waste is buried between layers of earth **2** : an area built up by landfill

land·form \-,fȯrm\ *n* : a natural feature of a land surface

land·hold·er \'land-,hōl-dər\ *n* : LANDOWNER — **land·hold·ing** \-diŋ\ *n*

land·ing \'lan-diŋ\ *n* **1** : the action of one that lands **2** : a place (as a wharf) for unloading or taking on passengers and cargo **3** : the level part of a staircase (as between flights of stairs)

landing craft *n* : any of numerous naval craft designed for putting troops and equipment ashore

landing field *n* : a field where aircraft may land and take off

landing gear *n* : the part that supports the weight of an aircraft or spacecraft when on the ground

landing strip *n* : AIRSTRIP

land·la·dy \'lan-,(d)lād-ē\ *n* **1** : a woman who owns land or houses that she rents **2** : a woman who runs an inn or rooming house

land·locked \-(d)läkt\ *adj* **1** : enclosed or nearly enclosed by land ⟨a *landlocked* country⟩ **2** : kept from leaving fresh water by some barrier ⟨*landlocked* salmon⟩

land·lord \-,(d)lȯ(ə)rd\ *n* **1** : the owner of land or houses that is rented to another **2** : a person who runs an inn or rooming house

land·lub·ber \-,(d)ləb-ər\ *n* : LANDSMAN

land·mark \'lan(d)-,märk\ *n* **1** : an object that marks the boundary of land **2 a** : a usually large object on land that is easy to see and can help a person find the way to a place near it **b** : an important building or monument ⟨historical *landmarks*⟩ **3** : an event that marks a turning point

land·mass \-,mas\ *n* : a large area of land

land·own·er \'lan-,dō-nər\ *n* : an owner of land — **land·own·ing** \-niŋ\ *adj*

¹**land·scape** \'lan(d)-,skāp\ *n* **1** : a picture of natural scenery **2** : the land that can be seen in one glance

²**landscape** *vb* **land·scaped; land·scap·ing** : to improve the natural beauties of a piece of land by grading, clearing, or gardening

land·slide \'lan(d)-ˌslīd\ *n* **1** : the slipping down of a mass of rocks or earth on a steep slope; *also* : the mass of material that slides **2** : an overwhelming victory especially in a political contest ⟨won by a *landslide*⟩

lands·man \'lan(d)z-mən\ *n* : a person who lives or works on land; *esp* : one who knows little or nothing of the sea and ships

land·ward \'lan-dwərd\ *adj or adv* : lying or being toward the land or on the side toward the land

lane \'lān\ *n* **1** : a narrow way or road usually between fences, hedges, or buildings **2** : a somewhat narrow way or track: as **a** : an ocean route for ships; *also* : AIR LANE **b** : a strip of roadway for a single line of vehicles **c** : a bowling alley **d** : a passageway alongside a cashier's counter (as in a supermarket)

lan·guage \'laŋ-gwij\ *n* **1 a** : the words, their pronunciation, and the methods of combining them used and understood by a large group of people **b** : a means of communicating ideas ⟨sign *language*⟩ **2** : the means by which animals communicate or are thought to communicate with each other ⟨*language* of the bees⟩ **3** : a system of signs and symbols and rules for using them that is used to carry information ⟨BASIC is a computer *language*⟩ **4** : the way in which words are used ⟨strong *language*⟩ **5** : the words and expressions of a particular group or field ⟨the *language* of medicine⟩ **6** : the study of language

    Word History The tongue plays an important part in human speech. Different sounds are made by moving the tongue in different ways. The tongue and speech are so closely connected that in many languages the word that means "tongue" also means "language". This is true in English, as when we say "she spoke a foreign tongue". It was also true in Latin, where the word *lingua* meant both "tongue" and "language". From the Latin *lingua* came the early French *langue*, meaning "tongue, language", which gave rise to the early French word *language*. The English word *language* comes directly from this early French word. [Middle English *language* "language", from early French *language* (same meaning), from *langue* "language, tongue", from Latin *lingua* "tongue, language"]

language arts *n pl* : the subjects (as reading, spelling, and composition) that aim at developing the student's understanding and skills for using language

lan·guid \'laŋ-gwəd\ *adj* **1** : weak from or as if from exhaustion **2** : lacking spirit : LISTLESS **3** : lacking force or quickness of movement : SLOW — **lan·guid·ly** *adv*

lan·guish \'laŋ-gwish\ *vb* **1** : to become weak or languid : waste away ⟨*languish* in prison⟩ **2** : to become weak with longing : PINE — **lan·guish·ing·ly** \-iŋ-lē\ *adv* — **lan·guish·ment** \-mənt\ *n*

lan·guor \'laŋ-(g)ər\ *n* **1** : weakness or weariness of body or mind **2** : a state of dreamy idleness — **lan·guor·ous** \-(g)ə-rəs\ *adj* — **lan·guor·ous·ly** *adv*

lank \'laŋk\ *adj* **1** : not well filled out : THIN ⟨*lank* cattle⟩ **2** : hanging straight and limp without spring or curl ⟨*lank* hair⟩ — **lank·ly** *adv* — **lank·ness** *n*

lanky \'laŋ-kē\ *adj* **lank·i·er; -est** : being tall, thin, and usually loose-jointed ⟨a *lanky* teenager⟩ — **lank·i·ly** \-kə-lē\ *adv* — **lank·i·ness** \-kē-nəs\ *n*

lan·o·lin \'lan-ᵊl-ən\ *n* : the fatty coating of sheep's wool especially when purified for use in ointments and cosmetics

lan·ta·na \lan-'tän-ə\ *n* : any of a genus of tropical shrubs that have showy heads of small bright flowers

lan·tern \'lant-ərn\ *n* **1** : a usually portable light with a protective covering **2** : PROJECTOR

lantern fish *n* : any of numerous small fishes mostly of deep seas that have a large mouth, large eyes, and usually shining spots or glands on the body

lantern fly *n* : any of several large brightly marked insects that are related to the cicadas and aphids and have the front of the head lengthened into a hollow structure

lan·tha·num \'lan(t)-thə-nəm\ *n* : a white soft metallic element — see ELEMENT table

lantern 1

lan·yard \'lan-yərd\ *n* **1** : a rope or line for fastening something in ships **2** : a cord worn around the neck or shoulder to hold a knife, whistle, or pistol **3** : a strong cord used in firing cannon

Lao \'laů\ *n* **1** : a member of a Buddhist people living in Laos and northeastern Thailand **2** : the Thai language of the Lao people — **Lao** *adj*

Lao·tian \lā-'ō-shən, 'laů-shən\ *n or adj* : LAO

¹lap \'lap\ *n* **1** : a loose panel in a garment : FLAP **2 a** : the clothing that lies on the knees and thighs when one sits **b** : the front part of a person between the waist and the knees when seated [Old English *læppa* "flap of a garment"]

²lap *vb* **lapped; lap·ping** **1** : ³FOLD 1 **2** : ¹WRAP 1a **3** : to lay or lie over or near something else so as to partly cover it ⟨*lap* one shingle over another⟩

³lap *n* **1 a** : the amount by which one object overlaps another **b** : the part of an object that overlaps another **2 a** : one time around a racetrack **b** : one part of a journey

⁴lap *vb* **lapped; lap·ping** **1** : to scoop up food or drink with the tongue or a part like the tongue **2** : to wash or splash gently [Old English *lapian* "to take into the mouth by means of the tongue"]

⁵lap *n* : an act or sound of lapping

lap·dog \'lap-ˌdóg\ *n* : a dog small enough to be held in the lap

la·pel \lə-'pel\ *n* : the fold of the front of a coat that is usually a part of the collar

lap·i·dary \'lap-ə-ˌder-ē\ *n, pl* **-dar·ies** : a person who cuts and polishes precious stones — **lapidary** *adj*

la·pis la·zu·li \ˌlap-ə-'slazh-ə-lē, -'slaz-\ *n* : a deep blue gemstone

Lapp \'lap\ *n* : a member of a people of northern Scandinavia, Finland, and the Kola peninsula of the U.S.S.R.

¹lapse \'laps\ *n* **1 a** : a slight error or slip ⟨*lapse* of memory⟩ **b** : a temporary fall especially from a higher to a lower state ⟨*lapse* into bad habits⟩ **2** : the ending of a right or privilege through failure to meet requirements **3** : a passage of time; *also* : INTERVAL 1

²lapse *vb* **lapsed; laps·ing** **1** : to slip, pass, or fall gradually ⟨*lapse* into silence⟩ **2** : to become little used ⟨a custom that had *lapsed*⟩ **3** : to come to an end : CEASE

lar·board \'lär-bərd\ *n* : ³PORT [Middle English *ladeborde* "the side of a ship on which it is loaded and unloaded", derived from Old English *hladen* (verb) "to load" and Old English *bord* "the side of a ship" — see *Word History* at STARBOARD] — **larboard** *adj*

lar·ce·ny \'lärs-nē, -ᵊn-ē\ *n, pl* **-nies** : the unlawful taking of personal property with the intention of depriving the rightful owner of it permanently : THEFT — **lar·ce·nous** \-nəs, -ᵊn-əs\ *adj*

larch \'lärch\ *n* : any of a genus of trees related to the pines that shed their needles each fall

¹lard \'lärd\ *vb* **1** : to insert strips of usually pork fat into meat before cooking **2** : to smear with lard, fat, or grease **3** : to add to; *esp* : ENRICH 1

\ə\ abut	\aů\ out	\i\ tip	\ó\ saw	\ů\ foot
\ər\ further	\ch\ chin	\ī\ life	\ói\ coin	\y\ yet
\a\ mat	\e\ pet	\j\ job	\th\ thin	\yü\ few
\ā\ take	\ē\ easy	\ŋ\ sing	\th\ this	\yů\ cure
\ä\ cot, cart	\g\ go	\ō\ bone	\ü\ food	\zh\ vision

²lard *n* : a soft white fat from the fatty tissue of the hog

lar·der \'lärd-ər\ *n* : a place where foods are kept

large \'lärj\ *adj* **larg·er; larg·est** : greater, bigger, more extended, or more powerful than usual — **large·ness** *n* — **at large** **1** : not locked up : FREE ⟨the criminal is still *at large*⟩ **2** : as a whole ⟨the public *at large*⟩ **3** : representing a whole state or area rather than one of its divisions ⟨delegate-*at-large*⟩

large calorie *n* : CALORIE 1b

large intestine *n* : the lower or last part of the intestine which is wider and shorter than the small intestine, which consists of the cecum, colon, and rectum, and which absorbs water from the material left over from digestion and prepares the feces for release from the body

large·ly \'lärj-lē\ *adv* **1** : GENERALLY 1 ⟨the story is *largely* true⟩ **2** : in a great amount ⟨tipped the waiter *largely*⟩

large·mouth bass \,lärj-,maúth-\ *n* : a large bass of warm slow-moving waters that is blackish green above and lighter or whitish below — called also *largemouth black bass*

large–scale integration \'lärj-'skāl-\ *n* : the process of placing a large number of circuits on a small chip

lar·gess *or* **lar·gesse** \lär-'zhes, lär-'jes\ *n* **1** : generous giving **2** : a generous gift

larg·ish \'lär-jish\ *adj* : rather large

¹lar·go \'lär-gō\ *adv or adj* : in a very slow and broad manner — used as a direction in music

²largo *n, pl* **largos** : a largo movement

lar·i·at \'lar-ē-ət\ *n* : a rope with a noose used to catch livestock or to tie up grazing animals : LASSO

¹lark \'lärk\ *n* **1** : any of numerous Old World singing birds; *esp* : ¹SKYLARK **2** : any of various birds (as the meadowlark) that are mostly dull-colored and usually live on the ground

²lark *n* : something done just for fun or adventure — **lark** *vb*

lark·spur \'lärk-,spər\ *n* : DELPHINIUM; *esp* : a cultivated delphinium grown for its stalks of showy blue, pink, or white flowers

lar·va \'lär-və\ *n, pl* **lar·vae** \-(,)vē, -,vī\ *also* **larvas** **1** : a young wingless often wormlike form (as a grub or caterpillar) that hatches from the egg of many insects **2** : an early form of any animal that at birth or hatching is very different from its parents ⟨the tadpole is the *larva* of the frog⟩ — **lar·val** \-vəl\ *adj*

lar·vi·cide \'lär-və-,sīd\ *n* : a chemical substance used for killing larvae that are pests

lar·yn·gi·tis \,lar-ən-'jīt-əs\ *n* : inflammation of the larynx

lar·ynx \'lar-iŋ(k)s\ *n, pl* **la·ryn·ges** \lə-'rin-(,)jēz\ *or* **lar·ynx·es** : the upper part of the windpipe that in human beings and most mammals contains the vocal cords — called also *voice box*

la·sa·gna \lə-'zän-yə\ *n* : broad flat noodles baked with a sauce usually of tomatoes, cheese, and meat

larynx: *1* epiglottis, *2* glottis, *3* pharynx, *4* larynx, *5* vocal cords, *6* trachea, *7* esophagus

las·civ·i·ous \lə-'siv-ē-əs\ *adj* : LEWD 1, LUSTFUL — **las·civ·i·ous·ly** *adv* — **las·civ·i·ous·ness** *n*

la·ser \'lā-zər\ *n* : a device that uses the natural vibrations of atoms or molecules to generate a beam of light having only one frequency [*l*ight *a*mplification by *s*timulated *e*mission of *r*adiation]

¹lash \'lash\ *vb* **1** : to move violently or suddenly **2** : to strike with or as if with a whip **3** : to attack with strong language [Middle English *lassen* "to move violently or suddenly"]

²lash *n* **1 a** : a stroke with a whip or switch **b** : the flexible part of a whip; *also* : ²WHIP 1 **2** : a sudden swinging blow **3** : EYELASH

³lash *vb* : to tie down with a rope, cord, or chain [Middle English *lasschen* "to lace", from early French *lacier* (same meaning), derived from Latin *laqueare* "to snare, catch in a noose", from *laqueus* "noose, snare" — related to LACE, ¹LASSO; see *Word History* at LACE] — **lash·er** *n*

lash·ing \'lash-iŋ\ *n* : something used for tying, wrapping, or fastening

lass \'las\ *n* : a young woman : GIRL

lass·ie \'las-ē\ *n* : LASS, GIRL

las·si·tude \'las-ə-,t(y)üd\ *n* **1** : a condition of weariness : FATIGUE **2** : a state of dreamy idleness : LANGUOR

¹las·so \'las-ō, la-'sü\ *n, pl* **lassos** *or* **lassoes** : a rope or long leather thong with a noose used especially for catching livestock [from Spanish *lazo* "lasso", from Latin *laqueus* "noose, snare" — related to LACE, ²LASH; see *Word History* at LACE]

²lasso *vb* : to catch with a lasso

¹last \'last\ *vb* **1** : to continue in being or operation ⟨*lasted* three hours⟩ **2** : to be enough for the needs of ⟨supplies to *last* a week⟩ [Old English *læstan* "to last, follow"]

²last *n* : a form which is shaped like the human foot and on which a shoe is shaped or repaired [Old English *læste* "footprint"]

³last *vb* : to shape with a last

⁴last *adj* **1 a** : following all the rest in time, place, or rank ⟨*last* one out⟩ **b** : being the only remaining ⟨*last* dollar⟩ **2** : belonging to the final stage **3** : next before the present : LATEST ⟨*last* week⟩ **4** : least likely ⟨the *last* thing we'd want⟩ [Old English *latost* "latest", from *læt* "late" — related to ¹LATE]

⁵last *adv* **1** : at the end ⟨ran *last*⟩ **2** : most lately ⟨saw them *last* at school⟩ **3** : in conclusion ⟨and *last,* I'd like to talk about our success⟩

⁶last *n* : something that is last — **at last** : at the end of a period of time : FINALLY

last·ing \'las-tiŋ\ *adj* : existing or continuing a long while — **last·ing·ly** *adv* — **last·ing·ness** *n*
   syn LASTING, PERMANENT, DURABLE mean going on for so long as to seem fixed. LASTING suggests an ability to continue endlessly ⟨a book that left a *lasting* impression on me⟩ PERMANENT usually adds the suggestion of being intended to stand or continue without limit ⟨a *permanent* living arrangement⟩ DURABLE suggests the ability to withstand forces that tend to wear down or destroy ⟨*durable* furniture⟩

last·ly \'last-lē\ *adv* : in conclusion : in the last place

last straw *n* : the last of a series (as of events or troubles) that causes one to give up or lose patience

Last Supper *n* : the supper eaten by Jesus and his disciples on the night of his betrayal

last word *n* **1** : the final remark in a discussion **2** : the power of final decision **3** : the most modern or fashionable one of its kind ⟨the *last word* in sportswear⟩

¹latch \'lach\ *vb* **1** : to get hold **2** : to attach oneself

²latch *n* : a catch (as a spring bolt) that holds a door or gate closed

³latch *vb* : to catch or fasten by means of a latch

latch·key \'lach-,kē\ *n* : a key for opening a door latch

¹late \'lāt\ *adj* **lat·er; lat·est** **1 a** : coming or remaining after the due, usual, or proper time ⟨*late* spring⟩ **b** : far advanced toward the close especially of the day or night ⟨*late* hours⟩ **2 a** : having died or held an office ⟨the *late* president⟩ **b** : RECENT 1b ⟨a *late* discovery⟩ [Old English *læt* "late, slow" — related to ⁴LAST] — **late·ness** *n*

²late *adv* **lat·er; lat·est** **1 a** : after the usual or proper time ⟨came in *late*⟩ **b** : at or to an advanced point in time ⟨*later* in the day⟩ **2** : not long ago : RECENTLY ⟨a musician *late* of Chicago⟩ — **of late** : during a recent period : LATELY

late·com·er \'lāt-,kəm-ər\ *n* : one who arrives late; *also* : one who has recently arrived

la·teen \lə-'tēn\ *adj* : of, relating to, or being a sailing rig of the Mediterranean having a triangular sail extended by a long pole attached to a short mast

late·ly \'lāt-lē\ *adv* : not long ago

la·tent \'lāt-ᵊnt\ *adj* : present but not visible or active ⟨*latent* abilities⟩ ⟨*latent* infection⟩ — **la·ten·cy** \-ᵊn-sē\ *n* — **la·tent·ly** *adv*

¹lat·er·al \'lat-ə-rəl, 'la-trəl\ *adj* 1 : of or relating to the side : located on, directed toward, or coming from the side 2 : of, relating to, or being part of a geometric solid that is not part of the base ⟨*lateral* area of a cylinder⟩ — **lat·er·al·ly** \-ē\ *adv*

²lateral *n* : a pass in football thrown to the side or to the rear

la·tex \'lā-,teks\ *n, pl* **la·ti·ces** \'lāt-ə-,sēz, 'lat-\ *or* **la·tex·es** 1 : a milky juice produced by the cells of various plants (as milkweeds, poppies, and the rubber tree) 2 : a mixture of water and fine particles of rubber or plastic used especially in paints and adhesives

lath \'lath *also* 'lath\ *n, pl* **laths** *or* **lath** : a thin narrow strip of wood used especially as a base for plaster — **lath** *vb*

lathe \'lāth\ *n* : a machine in which a piece of material is held and turned while being shaped by a tool

¹lath·er \'lath-ər\ *n* 1 a : foam formed when a detergent is stirred or shaken in water b : foam from sweating (as on a horse) 2 : a highly nervous or excited state : DITHER — **lath·ery** \-(ə-)rē\ *adj*

²lather *vb* **lath·ered; lath·er·ing** \'lath-(ə-)riŋ\ 1 : to spread lather over 2 : to form lather or a froth like lather

¹Lat·in \'lat-ᵊn\ *adj* 1 a : of, relating to, or composed in Latin ⟨*Latin* grammar⟩ b : ROMANCE ⟨*Latin* languages⟩ 2 : of or relating to that part of the Catholic Church that formerly used a Latin rite 3 : of, relating to, or characteristic of the countries or peoples of Latin America

²Latin *n* 1 : the Italic language of ancient Rome 2 : an ancient Roman 3 : a member of one of the peoples speaking Romance languages; *esp* : a person born or living in Latin America

la·ti·no \la-'tē-,nō\ *n, pl* **-nos** *often cap* : a person born or living in Latin America

lat·ish \'lāt-ish\ *adj or adv* : somewhat late

lat·i·tude \'lat-ə-,t(y)üd\ *n* 1 a : distance north or south from the equator measured in degrees b : a region or locality as marked by its latitude 2 : freedom from narrow restrictions — **lat·i·tu·di·nal** \,lat-ə-'t(y)üd-nəl, -ᵊn-əl\ *adj* — **lat·i·tu·di·nal·ly** \-ē\ *adv*

la·trine \lə-'trēn\ *n* 1 : a receptacle (as a pit in the earth) for use as a toilet 2 : BATHROOM, TOILET

lat·ter \'lat-ər\ *adj* 1 a : more recent : LATER b : of or relating to the end : FINAL 2 : of, relating to, or being the second of two things referred to

latitude 1a: hemisphere marked with parallels of latitude

lat·ter·ly \'lat-ər-lē\ *adv* : during a recent period

lat·tice \'lat-əs\ *n* 1 a : a framework or structure of crossed wood or metal strips b : a window, door, or gate having a lattice 2 : an arrangement of points or objects that is evenly spaced over an area or throughout a volume ⟨the *lattice* of atoms in a crystal⟩ — **lat·ticed** \-əst\ *adj*

¹Lat·vi·an \'lat-vē-ən\ *adj* : of, relating to, or characteristic of Latvia, the Latvians, or Latvian

²Latvian *n* 1 : a person born or living in Latvia 2 : the Baltic language of the Latvian people

laud \'lȯd\ *vb* : PRAISE 1

laud·able \'lȯd-ə-bəl\ *adj* : PRAISEWORTHY — **laud·abil·i·ty** \,lȯd-ə-'bil-ət-ē\ *n* — **laud·ably** \'lȯd-ə-blē\ *adv*

lau·da·num \'lȯd-nəm, -ᵊn-əm\ *n* : a formerly used preparation of opium

lau·da·to·ry \'lȯd-ə-,tōr-ē, -,tȯr-\ *adj* : expressing praise

¹laugh \'laf, 'laf\ *vb* 1 a : to show mirth, joy, or scorn with a smile and chuckle or explosive sound b : to become amused 2 : to utter with a laugh — **laugh·er** *n*

²laugh *n* 1 : the act or sound of laughing 2 a : something funny b : something deserving scorn

laugh·able \'laf-ə-bəl, 'laf-\ *adj* : causing laughter or scorn : RIDICULOUS — **laugh·able·ness** *n* — **laugh·ably** \-blē\ *adv*

laughing gas *n* : NITROUS OXIDE

laughing jackass *n* : KOOKABURRA

laugh·ing·ly \'laf-iŋ-lē, 'laf-\ *adv* : with laughter

laugh·ing·stock \'laf-iŋ-,stäk, 'laf-\ *n* : a person or thing that is made fun of

laugh·ter \'laf-tər, 'laf-\ *n* : the action or sound of laughing

¹launch \'lȯnch, 'länch\ *vb* 1 a : to throw or spring forward : HURL ⟨*launch* a spear⟩ b : to send off an object especially with force ⟨*launch* a rocket⟩ c : to set a ship afloat 2 a : to put in operation : BEGIN ⟨*launch* an attack⟩ b : to give a person a start c : to make a start especially energetically [Middle English *launchen* "to launch, hurl", from an early French dialect word *launcher* (same meaning), from Latin *lanceare* "to use a lance"] — **launch·er** *n*

²launch *n* : an act of launching

³launch *n* : a small motorboat used for pleasure or short-distance transportation [from Spanish or Portuguese *lancha* "a boat used to go to and from a large ship"]

launch·pad \'lȯnch-,pad, 'länch-\ *n* : a nonflammable platform from which a rocket can be launched — called also *launching pad*

laun·der \'lȯn-dər, 'län-\ *vb* **laun·dered; laun·der·ing** \-d(ə-)riŋ\ 1 : to wash or wash and iron clothing or household linens 2 : to undergo washing and ironing — **laun·der·er** \-dər-ər\ *n*

Laun·dro·mat \'lȯn-drə-,mat, 'län-\ *service mark* — used for a self-service laundry

laun·dry \'lȯn-drē, 'län-\ *n, pl* **-dries** 1 : clothes or linens that have been or are to be laundered 2 : a place where laundering is done [from an obsolete word *launder* (noun) "one who washes clothes", derived from early French *lavandier* (or *lavandiere*) "a man (or woman) who washes clothes", from Latin *lavandus* "needing to be washed", from *lavare* "to wash" — related to LAVATORY, LAVISH, LOTION]

lau·re·ate \'lȯr-ē-ət, 'lär-\ *n* : a person honored for achievement in an art or science; *esp* : POET LAUREATE — **laureate** *adj*

lau·rel \'lȯr-əl, 'lär-\ *n* 1 : any of a genus of trees or shrubs related to the sassafras and cinnamon; *esp* : a small evergreen tree of southern Europe with shiny pointed leaves used by the ancient Greeks to crown victors in various contests 2 : a tree or shrub (as a mountain laurel) that resembles the true laurel 3 a : a crown of laurel b : ¹HONOR 1, FAME — usually used in pl.

laurel 1

la·va \'läv-ə, 'lav-\ *n* : melted rock coming from a volcano; *also* : such rock that has cooled and hardened

\ə\ **abut**	\au̇\ **out**	\i\ **tip**	\ȯ\ **saw**	\u̇\ **foot**
\ər\ **further**	\ch\ **chin**	\ī\ **life**	\ȯi\ **coin**	\y\ **yet**
\a\ **mat**	\e\ **pet**	\j\ **job**	\th\ **thin**	\yü\ **few**
\ā\ **take**	\ē\ **easy**	\ŋ\ **sing**	\th\ **this**	\yu̇\ **cure**
\ä\ **cot, cart**	\g\ **go**	\ō\ **bone**	\ü\ **food**	\zh\ **vision**

la·va·liere or **la·val·liere** \,läv-ə-'li(ə)r, ,lav-\ n : an ornament hanging from a chain that is worn around the neck

lav·a·to·ry \'lav-ə-,tōr-ē, -,tȯr-\ n, pl **-ries** 1 : a basin for washing; esp : a small sink with running water and drainpipe 2 : a room with lavatories and usually with toilets 3 : TOILET 2b [Middle English lavatorie "basin for washing", from Latin lavatorium (same meaning), derived from earlier lavare "to wash" — related to LAUNDRY, LAVISH, LOTION]

lave \'lāv\ vb **laved; lav·ing** 1 a : ¹WASH 1 b archaic : to wash oneself : BATHE 2 : to flow along or against

lav·en·der \'lav-ən-dər\ n 1 a : a Mediterranean mint widely cultivated for its narrow somewhat woolly leaves and stalks of small sweet-smelling pale violet flowers — compare SEA LAVENDER b : the dried leaves and flowers of lavender used to perfume clothes and bed linen 2 : a pale purple

¹lav·ish \'lav-ish\ adj 1 : spending or giving more than is necessary : EXTRAVAGANT ⟨lavish with praise⟩ 2 : spent, produced, or given freely ⟨lavish gifts⟩ [Middle English lavas "an abundance", from early French lavasse, lavache "a downpour of rain", derived from Latin lavare "to wash" — related to LAUNDRY, LAVATORY, LOTION] — **lav·ish·ly** adv — **lav·ish·ness** n

²lavish vb : to spend or give freely

law \'lȯ\ n 1 a : a rule of conduct or action laid down and enforced by the supreme governing authority (as the legislature) of a community or established by custom b : the whole collection of such rules ⟨the law of the land⟩ c : the control brought about by enforcing rules ⟨forces of law and order⟩ d : trial in a court to decide what is just and right according to the laws ⟨go to law⟩ e : an agent or agency for enforcing laws 2 cap : the first part of the Jewish scriptures — compare HAGIOGRAPHA, PROPHETS 3 : a basic rule or principle ⟨the laws of poetry⟩ 4 a : the profession of a lawyer b : lawyers as a group c : the branch of knowledge that deals with laws and their interpretation and application ⟨study law⟩ 5 : a rule or principle stating something that always works in the same way under the same conditions ⟨the law of gravity⟩

law–abid·ing \'lȯ-ə-,bīd-iŋ\ adj : obedient to the law

law·break·er \'lȯ-,brā-kər\ n : a person who breaks the law — **law·break·ing** \-kiŋ\ adj or n

law·ful \'lȯ-fəl\ adj 1 : permitted by law ⟨lawful conduct⟩ 2 : recognized by law : RIGHTFUL ⟨the lawful owner⟩ — **law·ful·ly** \-f(ə-)lē\ adv — **law·ful·ness** \-fəl-nəs\ n

law·giv·er \'lȯ-,giv-ər\ n 1 : one who gives a code of laws to a people 2 : LEGISLATOR

law·less \'lȯ-ləs\ adj 1 : having no laws : not based on or regulated by law ⟨the lawless society of the frontier⟩ 2 : not controlled by law : UNRULY, DISORDERLY ⟨lawless mob⟩ — **law·less·ly** adv — **law·less·ness** n

law·mak·er \'lȯ-,mā-kər\ n : LEGISLATOR — **law·mak·ing** \-kiŋ\ adj or n

¹lawn \'lȯn, 'län\ n : ground covered with grass that is kept mowed [Middle English launde "an open space between woods", from early French lande "land overgrown with shrubs"; of Celtic origin]

²lawn n : a fine sheer linen or cotton fabric [Middle English lawn "a sheer fabric", from Laon, a town in France where linen was made]

lawn bowling n : a game played on a green in which balls are rolled at a small target ball

lawn mower n : a machine for cutting grass on lawns

law of definite proportions : a law of chemistry that states that every definite compound always contains the same elements in the same proportions by mass

law of dominance : MENDEL'S LAW 3

law of independent assortment : MENDEL'S LAW 2

law of segregation : MENDEL'S LAW 1

law·ren·ci·um \lȯ-'ren(t)-sē-əm\ n : a short-lived radioactive element produced from californium — see ELEMENT table

law·suit \'lȯ-,süt\ n : a suit in law : a case before a court

law·yer \'lȯ-yər, 'lȯi-ər\ n : a person whose profession is to conduct lawsuits for clients or to advise about legal rights and obligations

lax \'laks\ adj 1 : not firm or tight : LOOSE 2 : not strict — **lax·ly** adv — **lax·ness** n

¹lax·a·tive \'lak-sət-iv\ adj : tending to relieve constipation

²laxative n : a usually mild drug that helps relieve constipation — compare PURGATIVE

lax·ity \'lak-sət-ē\ n : the quality or state of being lax

¹lay \'lā\ vb **laid** \'lād\; **lay·ing** 1 : to beat or strike down ⟨wheat laid flat by the wind and rain⟩ 2 a : to put or set on or against a surface or in order ⟨lay the book on the table⟩ ⟨lay bricks⟩ b : to place for rest or sleep; also : BURY 1 3 : to produce and deposit eggs 4 nonstandard : ¹LIE 5 : to cause to settle ⟨a shower laid the dust⟩; also : to make calm : ALLAY ⟨laid his fears⟩ 6 : to spread over a surface ⟨lay plaster⟩ 7 : to make ready : PREPARE ⟨lay plans⟩ ⟨lay a table⟩ 8 : to deposit as a wager : BET ⟨I'll lay you $10 on that⟩ 9 : IMPOSE 1a ⟨lay a tax⟩ ⟨lay blame⟩ 10 : to place or assign in one's scheme of things ⟨lays great stress on manners⟩ 11 : to bring to a specified condition ⟨lay waste to the land⟩ 12 : to put forward : SUBMIT ⟨lay claim to an estate⟩ [Old English lecgan "beat down"] — **lay eyes on** : to catch sight of : SEE — **lay for** : to lie in wait to attack — **lay hold of** : ¹GRASP, SEIZE

²lay n : the way in which a thing lies in relation to something else ⟨lay of the land⟩

³lay past of ¹LIE

⁴lay n 1 : a simple poem that tells a story : BALLAD 2 : MELODY 2, SONG [Middle English lay "ballad", from early French lai (same meaning)]

⁵lay adj : of or relating to laymen or the laity [Middle English lay "of the people other than priests and clergy", from early French lai (same meaning), from Latin laicus "of the people", derived from Greek laos "people"]

lay·away \'lā-ə-,wā\ n : a purchasing agreement by which a seller agrees to hold merchandise on which a deposit has been made until the price is paid in full by the buyer

lay away \'lā-ə-'wā\ vb : to put aside for future use or delivery

lay down vb 1 : ESTABLISH 2, PRESCRIBE ⟨lay down standards⟩ 2 : to state or declare forcefully ⟨lay down the law⟩

¹lay·er \'lā-ər, 'le(-ə)r\ n 1 : one that lays ⟨their hens were poor layers⟩ 2 : one thickness or fold over or under another ⟨a layer or rock⟩ — **lay·ered** \'lā-ərd, 'le(-ə)rd\ adj

²layer vb 1 : to separate into layers 2 : to form by adding layers

lay·er·ing \'lā-ə-riŋ, 'le(-ə)-riŋ\ n : a method of treating a shoot or branch of a plant to cause rooting (as by bending to the ground and covering with soil) while it is still attached to the parent plant

lay·ette \lā-'et\ n : an outfit of clothing and equipment for a newborn infant

lay·man \'lā-mən\ n : a person who is not a member of the clergy or a member of a particular profession

lay·off \'lā-,ȯf\ n 1 : the act of laying off an employee or a work force 2 : a period during which there is no activity

lay off \'(')lā-'ȯf\ vb 1 : to mark or measure off 2 : to stop employing (a person) usually temporarily ⟨lay off workers⟩ 3 : to stop doing or taking something ⟨lay off of that stuff⟩

lay on vb : ¹ATTACK 1, BEAT

lay·out \'lā-,aút\ n 1 : ¹PLAN 1, ARRANGEMENT 2 : something laid out 3 : a set or outfit especially of tools

lay out \'(')lā-'aút\ vb 1 : ²PLAN 1 ⟨lay out a campaign⟩ 2 : to arrange for display or for working on ⟨lay out an exhibit⟩ 3 : SPEND 1

lay·over \'lā-,ō-vər\ n : STOPOVER 1

lay over \'(')lā-'ō-vər\ vb : to make a temporary halt or stop

lay–up \'lā-ˌəp\ *n* : a basketball shot made from near the basket usually by bouncing the ball off the backboard

lay up \(')lā-'əp\ *vb* **1** : to store up **2** : to disable or confine with illness or injury **3** : to take out of active service

la·zy \'lā-zē\ *adj* **la·zi·er; -est 1** : not willing to act or work : INDOLENT **2** : moving slowly : SLUGGISH ⟨a *lazy* stream⟩ — **la·zi·ly** \-zə-lē\ *adv* — **la·zi·ness** \-zē-nəs\ *n*

la·zy·bones \-ˌbōnz\ *n* : a lazy person

la·zy·ish \'lā-zē-ish\ *adj* : somewhat lazy

lea \'lē, lā\ *n* : MEADOW, PASTURE

leach \'lēch\ *vb* : to pass a liquid through to carry off the soluble components; *also* : to dissolve out by such means ⟨*leach* minerals from rocks⟩

¹lead \'lēd\ *vb* **led** \'led\; **lead·ing** \'lēd-iŋ\ **1 a** : to guide especially by going in advance : CONDUCT **b** : to direct on a course or in a direction **c** : to serve as a channel for **d** : to lie, go, or open in a specified direction ⟨the path *leads* uphill⟩ ⟨study *leading* to a degree⟩ **2** : to go through : LIVE ⟨*lead* a quiet life⟩ **3 a** : to direct the activity of : MANAGE, DIRECT ⟨*lead* an orchestra⟩ ⟨*lead* a campaign⟩ **b** : to be first or best in ⟨*lead* the league⟩; *also* : BEGIN 1, OPEN **c** : to be ahead of ⟨*led* their opponents by 20 points at the end of the third quarter⟩ [Old English *lǣdan* "to lead"]

²lead *n* **1 a** : position at the front : LEADERSHIP **b** : EXAMPLE 1, PRECEDENT **c** : an amount or distance ahead **2** : INDICATION 2, CLUE **3** : a principal role in a play; *also* : one who plays such a role **4** : a beginning section of a news story; *also* : a news story of chief importance **5** : the first in a series; *also* : the right to be first **6** : an insulated electrical conductor **7** : a position taken by a base runner off a base toward the next

³lead *adj* : acting or serving as a lead or leader ⟨*lead* guitarist⟩

⁴lead \'led\ *n* **1** : a heavy soft bluish white metallic element that is found mostly in combination with other elements, is easily shaped, and is used especially in pipes, cable coverings, and for type in printing — see ELEMENT table **2 a** : a mass of lead used on a line for finding the depth of water (as in the ocean) **b** *pl* : lead framing for glass (as in windows) **3** : a thin stick of marking substance (as graphite) in or for a pencil **4** : bullets in quantity **5** : TETRAETHYL LEAD [Old English *lēad* "the metal lead"]

⁵lead \'led\ *vb* **lead·ed; lead·ing 1** : to cover, line, or weight with lead **2** : to fix (window glass) in position with lead **3** : to treat or mix with lead or a lead compound ⟨*leaded* gasoline⟩

lead·en \'led-ᵊn\ *adj* **1 a** : made of lead **b** : of the color of lead : dull gray **2** : low in quality : POOR **3 a** : heavy and difficult to move ⟨*leaden* feet⟩ **b** : lacking spirit : DULL

lead·er \'lēd-ər\ *n* **1** : something that leads: as **a** : a short line for attaching the end of a fishing line to a lure or hook **b** : a pipe for conducting fluid **2** : a person that leads: as **a** : ¹GUIDE 1a **b** : COMMANDER 1 **c** : CONDUCTOR 2 **d** : a person in charge or in control : BOSS, CHIEF **3** : a horse placed in front of the other horses of a team — **lead·er·less** \-ləs\ *adj* — **lead·er·ship** \-ˌship\ *n*

lead–in \'lēd-ˌin\ *n* : something that leads in; *esp* : the part of a radio antenna that runs to the transmitting or receiving set — **lead–in** *adj*

lead·ing \'lēd-iŋ\ *adj* **1** : coming or ranking first or among the first : FOREMOST **2** : exercising leadership **3** : providing direction or guidance ⟨a *leading* question⟩

leading lady *n* : an actress who plays the leading female role in a play or movie

leading man *n* : an actor who plays the leading male role in a play or movie

leading tone *n* : the seventh musical degree of a major or minor scale — called also *subtonic*

lead·off \'lēd-ˌof\ *n* **1** : a beginning action **2** : one that begins something — **leadoff** *adj*

lead on *vb* : to persuade to proceed in a course especially when unwise or mistaken

lead pencil \'led-\ *n* : a pencil using graphite as the marking material

lead up \(')lēd-'əp\ *vb* : to make a gradual approach to a topic

¹leaf \'lēf\ *n, pl* **leaves** \'lēvz\ **1 a** : one of the green usually flat parts that grow from a stem or twig of a plant, make up the foliage, and have the primary purpose of making food by photosynthesis **b** : FOLIAGE **2 a** : a part of a book or folded sheet containing a page on each side **b** : a part (as of window shutters) that slides or is hinged **c** : the movable or additional part of a table top **d** : a thin sheet (as of metal) — **leaf·less** \'lē-fləs\ *adj* — **leaf·like** \'lē-ˌflīk\ *adj*

leaf 1a: *1* petiole, *2* stipule, *3* leaflet

²leaf *vb* **1** : to produce leaves **2** : to turn the pages of a book

leaf·age \'lē-fij\ *n* : FOLIAGE

leaf bud *n* : a bud that develops into a leafy shoot and does not produce flowers

leaf·hop·per \'lēf-ˌhäp-ər\ *n* : any of numerous small leaping insects that are related to the cicadas and suck the juices of plants

leaf·let \'lē-flət\ *n* **1 a** : one of the divisions of a compound leaf — see LEAF illustration **b** : a small or young leaf **2** : PAMPHLET

leaf miner *n* : any of various small insects that as larvae burrow in and eat the tissue of leaves

leaf mold *n* : a compost or layer composed chiefly of decayed vegetable matter

leaf·stalk \'lēf-ˌstok\ *n* : PETIOLE

leafy \'lē-fē\ *adj* **leaf·i·er; -est 1 a** : having or full of leaves ⟨*leafy* woodlands⟩ **b** : consisting mostly of leaves ⟨*leafy* vegetables⟩ **2** : resembling a leaf

¹league \'lēg\ *n* : any of various units of distance from about 2.4 to 4.6 statute miles (3.9 to 7.4 kilometers)

²league *n* **1** : an association or alliance of nations **2** : an association of persons or groups united for common interests or goals ⟨a softball *league*⟩ — **league** *vb*

leagu·er \'lē-gər\ *n* : a member of a league

¹leak \'lēk\ *vb* **1** : to enter or escape or permit to enter or escape accidentally or by mistake ⟨fumes *leaked* in⟩ ⟨the secret *leaked* out⟩ **2** : to give out information secretly ⟨*leaked* the story to the press⟩

²leak *n* **1** : something and especially a crack or hole that lets something in or out usually accidentally **2** : LEAKAGE

leak·age \'lē-kij\ *n* **1 a** : the act, process, or an instance of leaking **b** : loss of electricity due especially to faulty insulation **2** : something or the amount that is lost in a leak

leaky \'lē-kē\ *adj* **leak·i·er; -est** : permitting fluid to leak in or out ⟨a *leaky* boat⟩ — **leak·i·ness** *n*

¹lean \'lēn\ *vb* **leaned** \'lēnd, *chiefly Brit* 'lent\; **lean·ing** \'lē-niŋ\ **1 a** : to slant or cause to slant or bend from an upright position ⟨the tree *leans* to one side⟩ ⟨*lean* a ladder against a wall⟩ **b** : to cast one's weight to one side for support ⟨*lean* on me⟩ **2** : to depend for support ⟨*lean* on one's family in a crisis⟩ **3** : to tend in opinion, taste, or desire ⟨*lean* toward simplicity⟩ [Old English *hleonian* "to slant to one side"]

\ə\ abut	\aù\ out	\i\ tip	\ò\ saw	\ù\ foot
\ər\ further	\ch\ chin	\ī\ life	\òi\ coin	\y\ yet
\a\ mat	\e\ pet	\j\ job	\th\ thin	\yü\ few
\ā\ take	\ē\ easy	\ŋ\ sing	\t̲h̲\ this	\yù\ cure
\ä\ cot, cart	\g\ go	\ō\ bone	\ü\ food	\zh\ vision

²lean n : the act or an instance of leaning

³lean adj **1 a :** having little body fat ⟨*lean* cattle⟩ **b :** containing little or no fat ⟨*lean* meat⟩ **2 :** lacking richness or fullness ⟨a *lean* fuel-air mixture⟩ [Old English *hlǣne* "having very little body flesh"] — **lean·ness** \'lēn-nəs\ n

> **syn** LEAN, THIN, SKINNY mean not having a great amount of flesh. LEAN suggests a lack of unnecessary flesh and may also suggest the tough muscular frame of an athlete ⟨the hard *lean* body of a runner⟩ THIN applies to a person having not much flesh or fat and often having an amount less than is desirable for good health ⟨a *thin* and sickly child⟩ SKINNY suggests a bony, noticeably thin appearance that may indicate a lack of proper nourishment ⟨*skinny* and malnourished⟩

⁴lean n : the part of meat that consists mainly of fat-free muscle

lean·ing \'lē-niŋ\ n : TENDENCY 2, INCLINATION

¹lean–to \'lēn-,tü\ n, pl **lean–tos** **1 :** a wing of a building having a lean-to roof **2 :** a rough shed or shelter having a lean-to roof

²lean–to adj : having only one slope or pitch ⟨*lean-to* roof⟩

¹leap \'lēp\ vb **leapt** \'lēpt also 'lept\ or **leaped;** **leap·ing** \'lē-piŋ\ **1 :** to spring or cause to spring free from or as if from the ground : JUMP ⟨*leap* over a fence⟩ **2 a :** to pass suddenly from one state or topic to another **b :** to act hastily ⟨I'd *leap* at the chance⟩ — **leap·er** \'lē-pər\ n

²leap n **1 a :** an act of leaping : SPRING, BOUND **b :** a place leaped over or from **c :** the distance covered by a leap **2 :** a sudden change of state — **by leaps and bounds** : very rapidly

leap·frog \'lēp-,frȯg, -,fräg\ n : a game in which the first player bends down and another leaps over

leap year n : a year in the Gregorian calendar containing 366 days with February 29 as the extra day

learn \'lərn\ vb **learned** \'lərnd, 'lərnt\; **learn·ing** **1 :** to gain knowledge or understanding of or skill in by study, instruction, or experience **2 :** MEMORIZE ⟨*learn* the lines of a play⟩ **3 a :** to come to be able to ⟨*learn* to swim⟩ **b :** to come to realize **4** substandard : to cause to learn : TEACH **5 :** FIND OUT, ASCERTAIN **6 :** to acquire knowledge ⟨never too late to *learn*⟩ — **learn·able** \'lər-nə-bəl\ adj — **learn·er** n

learn·ed \'lər-nəd\ adj : having or showing learning : SCHOLARLY — **learn·ed·ly** adv — **learn·ed·ness** n

learn·ing \'lər-niŋ\ n **1 :** the act or experience of one that learns **2 :** knowledge or skill acquired by instruction or study **syn** see KNOWLEDGE

learning disabled adj : having difficulty in learning a basic scholastic skill because of a disorder (as dyslexia) that interferes with the learning process — **learning disability** n

¹lease \'lēs\ n **1 :** an agreement to hand over real estate for a period of time usually for a specified rent; also : the act of leasing real estate **2 :** property that is leased

²lease vb **leased; leas·ing** **1 :** to grant by lease : LET **2 :** to hold under a lease

leash \'lēsh\ n : a line for leading or controlling an animal — **leash** vb

¹least \'lēst\ adj **1 :** lowest in importance or position **2 :** smallest in size or degree

²least n : one that is least : something of the lowest possible value or importance — **at least** **1 :** at the minimum **2 :** in any case

³least adv : in the smallest or lowest degree

least common denominator n : the least common multiple of the denominators of two or more fractions — called also *lowest common denominator*

least common multiple n : the smallest number that is a multiple of each of two or more numbers — called also *lowest common multiple*

least·ways \'lēs-,twāz\ adv, dialect : at least

least·wise \'lēs-,twīz\ adv : at least

leath·er \'leth-ər\ n **1 :** animal skin prepared for use **2 :** something entirely or partly made of leather

leath·ern \'leth-ərn\ adj : made of or resembling leather

leath·er·neck \'leth-ər-,nek\ n : a member of the U.S. Marine Corps

leath·ery \'leth-(ə-)rē\ adj : resembling leather in appearance or quality : TOUGH

¹leave \'lēv\ vb **left** \'left\; **leav·ing** **1 :** to allow or cause to remain behind ⟨*leave* your books at home⟩ **2 :** HAND OVER, DELIVER ⟨the letter carrier *left* a package⟩ **3 :** to have remaining ⟨taking 7 from 10 *leaves* 3⟩ **4 :** to give by will : BEQUEATH **5 :** to let stay without interference ⟨*leave* someone alone⟩ **6** substandard : ²LET 3, 4 **7 :** to go away from a place ⟨*leave* at 10 o'clock⟩ **8 :** to end association with ⟨*left* school and got a job⟩ [Old English *lǣfan* "to give to one's heirs"]

²leave n **1 a :** PERMISSION **2** **b :** authorized absence from duty or employment **2 :** an act of leaving [Old English *lēaf* "permission"]

³leave vb **leaved; leav·ing** : ²LEAF 1 [Middle English *leven* "to produce leaves," from *leef* "a leaf"]

leaved \'lēvd\ adj : having leaves ⟨broad-*leaved*⟩

¹leav·en \'lev-ən\ n **1 a :** a substance (as yeast) used to produce a gaseous fermentation (as in dough) **b :** a material (as baking powder) used to produce a gas that makes dough or batter rise and become light **2 :** something that changes slightly or lightens a mass or whole

²leaven vb **leav·ened; leav·en·ing** \'lev-(ə-)niŋ\ **1 :** to raise (dough) with a leaven **2 :** to mix or spread throughout with leaven

leave off vb : ¹STOP 7a, CEASE

leaves pl of LEAF

leave–tak·ing \'lēv-,tā-kiŋ\ n : an act of going away : FAREWELL

leav·ings \'lē-viŋz\ n pl : things remaining

lec·tern \'lek-tərn\ n : a desk to read from while standing; esp : one from which scripture lessons are read in a church service

¹lec·ture \'lek-chər, -shər\ n **1 :** a talk given before an audience or class especially for instruction **2 :** ¹REPRIMAND, SCOLDING

²lecture vb **lec·tured; lec·tur·ing** \'lek-chə-riŋ, 'lek-shriŋ\ **1 :** to give a lecture or a series of lectures **2 :** to instruct by lectures **3 :** ²REPRIMAND, SCOLD — **lec·tur·er** \-chər-ər, -shrər\ n

led past and past participle of LEAD

ledge \'lej\ n **1 :** a projecting ridge or raised edge along a surface **2 :** an underwater ridge or reef especially near the shore **3 :** a narrow flat surface or shelf; esp : one that sticks out from a wall of rock

led·ger \'lej-ər\ n : a book in which accounts are kept in final form

ledger line n : a short line added above or below a musical staff for notes that are too high or too low to be placed on the staff

¹lee \'lē\ n **1 :** protecting shelter **2 :** the side (as of a ship) that is sheltered (as from the wind)

²lee adj : of or relating to the lee

leech \'lēch\ n **1 :** any of numerous flesh-eating or bloodsucking usually flattened worms that are made up of segments and have a sucker at each end **2 :** a person who clings like a leech to another person for advantage or gain : PARASITE

> **Word History** In the early days of medicine, a physician, known in Old English as a *lǣce*, often drew blood from patients. These doctors acted in the belief that good

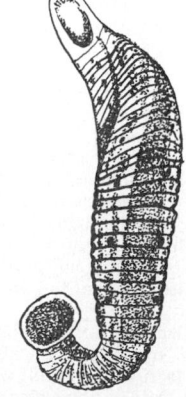

leech 1

health depended on a balance of four controlling fluids in the body. These four fluids were called *humors,* and one of them was blood. In those days physicians believed that a person became ill if there was too much blood or too little of any of the other humors in the body. Thus they used a controlled bleeding of the patient, or *bloodletting* as it was called, to balance the humors. An easy way to do this was to attach bloodsucking worms to the body. These worms are common in all parts of the world and especially in marshes and swamps. Today we call these sucking worms *leeches,* taking the name from those ancient doctors who used them so often. [Old English *lǣce* "doctor, physician"]

leek \'lēk\ *n* : a garden herb closely related to the onion and grown for its mildly sharp-tasting leaves and thick stalk

leer \'li(ə)r\ *vb* : to give a nasty or sexually suggestive look — **leer** *n*

leery \'li(ə)r-ē\ *adj* : SUSPICIOUS 2, WARY

lees \'lēz\ *n pl* : the settlings of liquor (as wine) during fermentation and aging : DREGS

¹**lee·ward** \'lē-wərd, *especially among sailors* 'lü-ərd\ *n* : the lee side

²**leeward** *adj* : located away from the wind : DOWNWIND

lee·way \'lē-,wā\ *n* **1** : sideways movement of a ship when under way **2** : an extra amount (as of room or time) that allows some freedom or variation

¹**left** \'left\ *adj* **1** : of, relating to, or being the side of the body in which the heart is mostly located ⟨the *left* leg⟩ **2** : located nearer to the left side of the body than to the right ⟨the *left* arm of a chair⟩ — **left** *adv*

²**left** *n* **1** : the left side or the part on the left side **2** : the members of a European legislative body sitting to the left of the presiding officer and holding more radical views than other members **3** *cap* : political liberals or radicals; *also* : their beliefs

³**left** *past and past participle of* LEAVE

left field *n* **1** : the part of the baseball outfield to the left looking out from home plate **2** : the position of the player defending left field — **left fielder** *n*

left–hand \',left-,hand\ *adj* **1** : located on the left **2** : LEFT-HANDED 1, 2

left–hand·ed \'left-'han-dəd\ *adj* **1** : using the left hand more easily than the right **2** : relating to, designed for, or done with the left hand **3** : BACKHANDED 2 **4** : going in or involving a counterclockwise direction ⟨a *left-handed* screw⟩ — **left–handed** *adv* — **left–hand·ed·ly** *adv* — **left–hand·ed·ness** *n* — **left–hand·er** \-'han-dər\ *n*

left·ist \'lef-təst\ *n* : a liberal or radical in politics — **leftist** *adj*

left·over \'lef-,tō-vər\ *n* : something remaining; *esp* : food left over from one meal and served at another — **leftover** *adj*

left·ward \'lef-twərd\ *adv or adj* : toward or on the left

¹**leg** \'leg\ *n* **1** : a limb of an animal used especially for supporting the body and for walking and running; *esp* : the part of a leg of a vertebrate animal between the knee and the foot **2** : something resembling an animal leg in shape or use ⟨*legs* of a table⟩ **3** : the part of an article of clothing that covers the leg **4** : either side of a triangle as compared to the base or hypotenuse **5 a** : a portion of a trip : STAGE **b** : one section of a relay race

²**leg** *vb* **legged; leg·ging** : to use the legs in walking or especially in running

leg·a·cy \'leg-ə-sē\ *n, pl* **-cies** : something left to a person by or as if by will

le·gal \'lē-gəl\ *adj* **1** : of or relating to law or lawyers **2** : based on law ⟨a *legal* right⟩ **3** : permitted by law or established rules — **le·gal·ly** \-gə-lē\ *adv*

legal holiday *n* : a holiday established by legal authority

le·gal·i·ty \li-'gal-ət-ē\ *n, pl* **-ties 1** : the quality or state of being legal : LAWFULNESS **2** : something that is required

by law

le·gal·ize \'lē-gə-,līz\ *vb* **-ized; -iz·ing** : to make legal ⟨wanted to *legalize* gambling in their city⟩ — **le·gal·iza·tion** \,lē-gə-lə-'zā-shən\ *n*

legal tender *n* : money that the law authorizes for paying debts

leg·ate \'leg-ət\ *n* : an official representative (as an ambassador or envoy)

leg·a·tee \,leg-ə-'tē\ *n* : a person to whom a legacy is left

le·ga·tion \li-'gā-shən\ *n* **1** : a group of representatives sent to a foreign country; *esp* : one headed by a minister **2** : the official residence and office of such a group

le·ga·to \li-'gät-ō\ *adv or adj* : in a manner that is smooth and connected — used as a direction in music

leg·end \'lej-ənd\ *n* **1** : a story coming down from the past whose truth is popularly accepted but cannot be checked **2 a** : writing or a title on an object **b** : CAPTION 2 **c** : an explanatory list of the symbols on a map or chart

Word History The Latin verb *legere* originally meant "to gather". In time the verb came to mean "to gather with the eye, to see", and that led to the sense "to read". From this verb came the Latin noun *legenda,* used in the Middle Ages to mean "a thing to be read". *Legenda* was used to refer in particular to stories about the lives of saints. Many such stories were written in the Middle Ages, and they often included fiction along with fact. Because of that, when *legenda* was borrowed into English as *legend,* it came to mean "a story coming down from the past which may or may not be entirely true". [Middle English *legende* "a legend", derived from Latin *legenda* "something to be read", derived from earlier *legere* "to gather, read"]

leg·end·ary \'lej-ən-,der-ē\ *adj* **1** : of or resembling a legend **2** : WELL-KNOWN, FAMOUS

leg·er·de·main \,lej-ərd-ə-'mān\ *n* **1** : SLEIGHT OF HAND **2** : a display of trickery

legged \'leg-əd, 'legd\ *adj* : having legs ⟨four-*legged*⟩

leg·ging *or* **leg·gin** \'leg-ən, 'leg-in\ *n* : a covering for the leg

leg·horn \'leg-,(h)ò(ə)rn, 'leg-ərn\ *n* **1 a** : a fine plaited straw made from an Italian wheat **b** : a hat of this straw **2** : any of a Mediterranean breed of small hardy domestic chickens noted for their ability to produce many white eggs

leg·i·ble \'lej-ə-bəl\ *adj* : capable of being read : PLAIN — **leg·i·bil·i·ty** \,lej-ə-'bil-ət-ē\ *n* — **leg·i·bly** \'lej-ə-blē\ *adv*

le·gion \'lē-jən\ *n* **1** : the chief unit of the Roman army consisting of 3000 to 6000 foot soldiers with cavalry **2** : ARMY 1a **3** : a very large number : MULTITUDE

¹**le·gion·ary** \'lē-jə-,ner-ē\ *adj* : of, relating to, or forming a legion

²**legionary** *n, pl* **-ar·ies** : LEGIONNAIRE

le·gion·naire \,lē-jə-'na(ə)r, -'ne(ə)r\ *n* : a member of a legion

leg·is·late \'lej-ə-,slāt\ *vb* **-lat·ed; -lat·ing 1** : to make laws **2** : to cause, create, or bring about by legislation

leg·is·la·tion \,lej-ə-'slā-shən\ *n* **1** : the action of making laws **2** : the laws made by a legislator or legislative body

leg·is·la·tive \'lej-ə-,slāt-iv\ *adj* **1** : having the power of legislating ⟨the *legislative* branch⟩ **2** : of or relating to a legislature or legislation — **leg·is·la·tive·ly** *adv*

leg·is·la·tor \'lej-ə-,slā-,tó(ə)r, -,slāt-ər\ *n* : a person who makes laws; *esp* : a member of a legislature

leg·is·la·ture \'lej-ə-,slā-chər\ *n* : an organized body of persons having the authority to make laws

le·git·i·ma·cy \li-'jit-ə-mə-sē\ *n* : the quality or state of

\ə\ abut	\au̇\ out	\i\ tip	\ȯ\ saw	\u̇\ foot
\ər\ further	\ch\ chin	\ī\ life	\ȯi\ coin	\y\ yet
\a\ mat	\e\ pet	\j\ job	\th\ thin	\yü\ few
\ā\ take	\ē\ easy	\ŋ\ sing	\th\ this	\yu̇\ cure
\ä\ cot, cart	\g\ go	\ō\ bone	\ü\ food	\zh\ vision

being legitimate

¹le·git·i·mate \li-'jit-ə-mət\ *adj* **1** : born of parents who are married ⟨*legitimate* children⟩ **2** : LAWFUL ⟨a *legitimate* claim⟩ **3** : being in keeping with what is right or with standards ⟨a *legitimate* excuse⟩ — **le·git·i·mate·ly** *adv*

²le·git·i·mate \li-'jit-ə-ˌmāt\ *vb* **-mat·ed; -mat·ing** : to make lawful or legal — **le·git·i·ma·tion** \-ˌjit-ə-'mā-shən\ *n*

le·git·i·mize \li-'jit-ə-ˌmīz\ *vb* **-mized; -miz·ing** : ²LEGITIMATE

leg·less \'leg-ləs\ *adj* : having no legs

leg·man \'leg-ˌman\ *n* **1** : a reporter assigned usually to gather information **2** : an assistant who gathers information and runs errands

leg·ume \'leg-ˌyüm, li-'gyüm\ *n* **1 a** : any of a large family of herbs, shrubs, and trees belonging to the dicotyledons, having fruits that are dry single-celled pods and split into two pieces when ripe, bearing nodules on the roots that contain nitrogen-fixing bacteria, and including important food plants (as peas, beans, or clovers) **b** : the part (as seeds or pods) of a legume used as food **2** : the pod of a legume

le·gu·mi·nous \li-'gyü-mə-nəs, le-\ *adj* : of, relating to, or consisting of plants that are legumes

leg·work \'leg-ˌwərk\ *n* : the work involved in gathering information

lei \'lā, 'lä-ˌē\ *n* : a wreath or necklace usually of flowers [Hawaiian]

lei·sure \'lēzh-ər, 'lezh-, 'lāzh-\ *n* **1** : freedom from work or duties **2** : ¹EASE 1 **3** : time at one's command : CONVENIENCE — **leisure** *adj*

lei·sure·ly \'lēzh-ər-lē, 'lezh-, 'lāzh-\ *adj* : characterized by leisure : UNHURRIED — **lei·sure·li·ness** *n* — **leisurely** *adv*

lem·ming \'lem-iŋ\ *n* : any of several small short-tailed northern rodents with furry feet and small ears; *esp* : a European rodent that takes part in periodic mass migrations which often continue into the sea where large numbers are drowned

lemming

lem·on \'lem-ən\ *n* **1 a** : a yellow oblong citrus fruit with acid juice and a thick skin from which a fragrant oil is obtained **b** : the stout thorny citrus tree that bears lemons **2** : the color of ripe lemons **3** : one that turns out to be unsatisfactory or disappointing ⟨our new car is a *lemon*⟩ — **lemon** *adj*

lem·on·ade \ˌlem-ə-'nād\ *n* : a drink made of lemon juice, sugar, and water

lemon shark *n* : a dangerous medium-sized shark of the warm Atlantic that is yellowish brown to gray above with yellow or greenish sides

le·mur \'lē-mər\ *n* : any of numerous tree-dwelling mammals that are active at night, and are related to the monkeys, and usually have a muzzle like a fox, large eyes, very soft woolly fur, and a long furry tail

Word History The large island of Madagascar off the southeast coast of Africa is home to many unusual animals. Some of these animals live in trees and are active at night. Their big eyes give them an eerie

lemur

look, especially when the animals are moving through the trees at night. When 18th-century scientists saw these mammals for the first time, they thought the creatures looked like ghosts. They named the animals *lemurs*. This name comes from the Latin word *lemures*, meaning "ghosts". In Roman legend *lemures* were the spirits of people left unburied, who returned by night from the dead to haunt the living. [from Latin *lemures* (plural) "ghosts"]

lend \'lend\ *vb* **lent** \'lent\; **lend·ing** **1 a** : to give to another for temporary use with the understanding that it or a like thing will be returned ⟨*lend* a book⟩ **b** : to let out (money) for temporary use with the understanding that it will be paid back with interest ⟨banks and other *lending* institutions⟩ **2** : to give usually for a time ⟨*lend* assistance⟩ **3** : to have the quality or nature that makes suitable ⟨a voice that *lends* itself to singing in opera⟩ — **lend·er** *n*

length \'leŋ(k)th, 'len(t)th\ *n* **1 a** : the measured distance from one end to the other of the longer or longest side of an object; *also* : any measured distance **b** : the quality or state of being long **2 a** : the amount of time something takes ⟨the *length* of a visit⟩ **b** : the sound of a vowel or syllable as it is affected by the time needed to pronounce it **3** : a piece of something long ⟨a *length* of pipe⟩ **4** : the distance from top to bottom of an article of clothing — **at length** **1** : very fully ⟨discussed my shortcomings *at length*⟩ **2** : at the end : FINALLY ⟨*at length* we decided to join⟩

length·en \'leŋ(k)-thən, 'len(t)-\ *vb* **length·ened; length·en·ing** \'leŋ(k)th-(ə-)niŋ, 'len(t)th-\ : to make or become longer — **length·en·er** \'leŋ(k)th-(ə-)nər, 'len(t)th-\ *n*

length·ways \'leŋ(k)th-ˌwāz, 'len(t)th-\ *adv* : in the direction of the length

length·wise \'leŋ(k)th-ˌwīz, 'len(t)th-\ *adv or adj* : in the direction of the length ⟨fold the paper *lengthwise*⟩ ⟨a *lengthwise* crease⟩

lengthy \'leŋ(k)th-ē, 'len(t)-\ *adj* **length·i·er; -est** : very long — **length·i·ly** \-thə-lē\ *adv* — **length·i·ness** \-thē-nəs\ *n*

le·nience \'lē-nyən(t)s, -nē-ən(t)s\ *n* : LENIENCY

le·nien·cy \'lē-nē-ən-sē, -nyən-sē\ *n* : the quality or state of being lenient **syn** see MERCY

le·nient \'lē-nē-ənt, -nyənt\ *adj* : being kind and patient — **le·nient·ly** *adv*

len·i·ty \'len-ət-ē\ *n* : LENIENCY

lens \'lenz\ *n* **1** : a clear curved piece of material (as glass) used to bend rays of light to form an image **2** : a clear part of the eye that focuses rays of light so as to form an image (as upon the retina)

Lent \'lent\ *n* : a period of fasting and regret for one's sins that is observed on the 40 weekdays from Ash Wednesday to Easter by many churches — **Lent·en** \'lent-ᵊn\ *adj*

len·ti·cel \'lent-ə-ˌsel\ *n* : a pore in a stem of a woody plant through which gases are exchanged between the atmosphere and the stem tissues

len·til \'lent-ᵊl\ *n* : a Eurasian plant of the legume family widely grown for its flattened edible seeds and leafy stalks used as food for cattle; *also* : its seed

len·to \'len-ˌtō\ *adv or adj* : in a slow manner — used as a direction in music

Leo \'lē-ō\ *n* **1** : a group of stars between Cancer and Virgo usually pictured as a lion **2 a** : the fifth sign of the zodiac — see ZODIAC table **b** : a person whose sign of the zodiac is Leo

le·o·nine \'lē-ə-ˌnīn\ *adj* : of, relating to, or resembling a lion

leop·ard \'lep-ərd\ *n* : a large strong cat of southern Asia and Africa that has a brownish buff coat with black spots arranged in broken rings —

called also *panther*

leop·ard·ess \'lep-ərd-əs\ *n* : a female leopard

leopard frog *n* : a common spotted frog of the eastern U.S.

le·o·tard \'lē-ə-ˌtärd\ *n* : a tight one-piece garment worn especially by dancers, gymnasts, and acrobats

leopard

lep·er \'lep-ər\ *n* : a person who has leprosy

lep·i·dop·tera \ˌlep-ə-'däp-tə-rə\ *n pl* : insects that are lepidopterans

lep·i·dop·ter·an \ˌlep-ə-'däp-tə-rən\ *n* : any of a large order of insects that include the butterflies, moths, and skippers and that as adults have four wings usually covered with minute overlapping often brightly colored scales and as larvae are caterpillars — **lepidopteran** *adj* — **lep·i·dop·ter·ous** \-tə-rəs\ *adj*

lep·re·chaun \'lep-rə-ˌkän, -ˌkȯn\ *n* : a mischievous elf of Irish folklore that some believe will reveal where treasure is hidden if caught

lep·ro·sy \'lep-rə-sē\ *n* : a disease caused by a bacterium and marked by slow-growing spreading swellings accompanied by loss of sensation, weight, and strength and by deformities — called also *Hansen's disease*

lep·rous \'lep-rəs\ *adj* : infected with, relating to, or resembling leprosy

les·bi·an \'lez-bē-ən\ *n, often cap* : a female homosexual — **lesbian** *adj, often cap* — **les·bi·an·ism** \-bē-ə-ˌniz-əm\ *n*

le·sion \'lē-zhən\ *n* : a change in the structure of a bodily organ or part due to injury or disease; *esp* : an injured or diseased spot or area clearly marked off from healthy tissue around it

les·pe·de·za \ˌles-pə-'dē-zə\ *n* : any of a genus of plants of the legume family including some widely used to improve soil and for hay

¹less \'les\ *adj* **1** : being a smaller number : FEWER ⟨8 times 2 is *less* than 6 times 3⟩ ⟨*less* than six hours⟩ **2** : of lower rank, degree, or importance ⟨no *less* a person than the president⟩ **3** : not so much : being a smaller amount ⟨we need *less* talk and more work⟩ ⟨finished in *less* time⟩

²less *adv* : not so much or so well ⟨*less* difficult⟩ ⟨liked the second book *less*⟩

³less *prep* : ¹MINUS 1 ⟨the regular price *less* a discount⟩

⁴less *n, pl* **less** **1** : a smaller number or amount ⟨we have *less* this year than last⟩ **2** : something that is poorer or less important than another ⟨could have been arrested for *less*⟩

-less \ləs\ *adj suffix* **1** : not having ⟨child*less*⟩ **2** : not able to be acted on or to act in a specified way ⟨cease*less*⟩ [Old English *-lēas* (suffix) "not having", from *lēas* "false"]

les·see \le-'sē\ *n* : a person holding or occupying property under a lease

less·en \'les-ᵊn\ *vb* **less·ened; less·en·ing** \'les-niŋ, -ᵊn-iŋ\ : to make or become less

¹less·er \'les-ər\ *adj* : of smaller size or importance

²lesser *adv* : ²LESS

lesser celandine *n* : CELANDINE 2

les·son \'les-ᵊn\ *n* **1** : a part of the Scripture read in a church service **2 a** : a reading or exercise assigned to be studied **b** : something learned by study or experience

les·sor \'les-ˌȯ(ə)r, le-'sȯ(ə)r\ *n* : one that leases property to another

lest \(ˌ)lest\ *conj* : for fear that ⟨tied the dog *lest* it should escape⟩

¹let \'let\ *n* : something that interferes : OBSTACLE ⟨without *let* or hindrance⟩

²let *vb* **let; let·ting** **1** : to cause to : MAKE ⟨*let* it be known⟩

2 : to give use of in return for payment ⟨rooms to *let*⟩ **3 a** : to allow or permit to ⟨*let* them go⟩ **b** — used to introduce a request ⟨*let* us hope for the best⟩ **4** : to allow to go or pass ⟨*let* them through⟩

-let \lət\ *n suffix* **1** : small one ⟨book*let*⟩ **2** : something worn on ⟨ank*let*⟩ [derived from early French *-elet* "small one", from *-el* and *-et*, both suffixes meaning "small"]

let·down \'let-ˌdau̇n\ *n* **1** : DISAPPOINTMENT 2 **2** : a slackening of effort

let down \(')let-'dau̇n\ *vb* **1** : to fail to help or support ⟨*let down* a friend in a crisis⟩ **2** : to fail to come up to expectations : DISAPPOINT ⟨the end of the story *lets* the reader *down*⟩

¹le·thal \'lē-thəl\ *adj* : causing or capable of causing death **syn** see DEADLY — **le·thal·ly** \'lē-thə-lē\ *adv*

²lethal *n* : LETHAL GENE

lethal gene *n* : a gene capable of preventing development or causing the death of a living thing or its germ cells

leth·ar·gy \'leth-ər-jē\ *n* **1** : abnormal drowsiness **2** : the quality or state of being slow, lazy, or not caring — **le·thar·gic** \lə-'thär-jik, le-\ *adj*

let on *vb* **1** : ADMIT 1b, REVEAL ⟨don't *let on* that I told you⟩ **2** : ¹PRETEND ⟨she *let on* that she was more surprised than she really was⟩

let's \(ˌ)lets, (ˌ)les\ : let us

Lett \'let\ *n* : a member of a people closely related to the Lithuanians and mainly living in Latvia

¹let·ter \'let-ər\ *n* **1** : one of the marks that are symbols for speech sounds in writing or print and that make up the alphabet **2** : a written or printed communication **3** *pl* : LITERATURE 2a **4** : the strict or outward meaning ⟨the *letter* of the law⟩ **5** : the initial of a school awarded to a student especially for athletic achievement

²letter *vb* : to mark with letters — **let·ter·er** \-ər-ər\ *n*

letter carrier *n* : a person who delivers mail

let·ter·head \'let-ər-ˌhed\ *n* : stationery having a printed or engraved heading; *also* : the heading itself

let·ter·ing \'let-ə-riŋ\ *n* : letters used in an inscription

let·ter–per·fect \ˌlet-ər-'pər-fikt\ *adj* : correct to the smallest point

Lett·ish \'let-ish\ *adj* : of or relating to the Latvians or their language — **Lettish** *n*

let·tuce \'let-əs\ *n* : a common garden vegetable related to the daisies that has crisp juicy leaves used especially in salads

let·up \'let-ˌəp\ *n* **1** : a slackening of effort or force **2** : a break in bad weather ⟨rained three days without a *letup*⟩

let up \(')let-'əp\ *vb* **1** : to slow down : SLACKEN **2** : to come to a stop : CEASE ⟨the rain *let up*⟩ **3** : to ease off : be less severe — used with *on*

leu·cine \'lü-ˌsēn\ *n* : an amino acid that is very important in the nutrition of human beings

leu·co·plast \'lü-kə-ˌplast\ *n* : a colorless plastid of a plant cell usually concerned with starch formation and storage

leu·ke·mia \lü-'kē-mē-ə\ *n* : a disease of warm-blooded animals including human beings that is a kind of cancer in which leukocytes increase abnormally in the tissues and often in the blood — **leu·ke·mic** \-mik\ *adj*

leu·ko·cyte *also* **leu·co·cyte** \'lü-kə-ˌsīt\ *n* : a white or colorless blood cell having a nucleus

le·va·tor \li-'vāt-ər\ *n, pl* **lev·a·to·res** \ˌlev-ə-'tōr-(ˌ)ēz\ *or* **le·va·tors** \li-'vāt-ərz\ : a muscle that serves to raise a body part

lev·ee \'lev-ē\ *n* **1** : a bank built along a river to prevent flooding **2** : a landing place along a river

¹lev·el \'lev-əl\ *n* **1** : a device used (as by a carpenter) to

\ə\ abut	\au̇\ out	\i\ tip	\ȯ\ saw	\u̇\ foot
\ər\ further	\ch\ chin	\ī\ life	\ȯi\ coin	\y\ yet
\a\ mat	\e\ pet	\j\ job	\th\ thin	\yü\ few
\ā\ take	\ē\ easy	\ŋ\ sing	\th\ this	\yu̇\ cure
\ä\ cot, cart	\g\ go	\ō\ bone	\ü\ food	\zh\ vision

establish a horizontal line or surface **2** : a horizontal line or surface usually at a named height ⟨placed at eye *level*⟩ **3** : a step or stage in height, position, or rank ⟨rose to the *level* of manager⟩ **4** : a horizontal passage in a mine **5 a** : an amount of something especially in comparison with something else ⟨production is at a low *level* this year⟩ **b** : the amount of a substance especially per unit volume of a body fluid (as blood) ⟨high *level* of sugar in the blood⟩ — **on the level** : BONA FIDE 1a, HONEST ⟨find out if the offer is *on the level*⟩

²**level** *vb* **lev·eled** *or* **lev·elled; lev·el·ing** *or* **lev·el·ing** \'lev-(ə-)liŋ\ **1** : to make or become horizontal, flat, or even **2** : ¹AIM 1, DIRECT **3** : to knock flat ⟨the explosion *leveled* the house⟩ **4** : to reach or come to a level ⟨the plane *leveled* off at 5000 meters⟩ — **lev·el·er** *or* **lev·el·ler** \-(ə-)lər\ *n*

³**level** *adj* **1** : having a flat even surface ⟨a *level* lawn⟩ **2** : being on a line with the horizon : HORIZONTAL ⟨in a *level* position⟩ **3** : of the same height or rank : EVEN ⟨the water is *level* with my waist⟩ **4** : steady and cool in judgment ⟨a *level* head⟩ — **lev·el·ly** *adv* — **lev·el·ness** *n*

syn LEVEL, FLAT, EVEN mean having a surface without bends, curves, or interruptions. LEVEL applies especially to a surface or a line that does not slant up or down ⟨a *level* road between two hills⟩ FLAT applies to a surface that is free from curves or bumps or hollows but may not be parallel to the ground ⟨a room with *flat* walls⟩ EVEN stresses the lack of breaks or bumps in a line or surface but need not suggest that the object is level or straight ⟨trimmed the top of the hedge to make it *even*⟩

— **level best** : very best

lev·el·head·ed \,lev-əl-'hed-əd\ *adj* : having sound judgment : SENSIBLE — **lev·el·head·ed·ness** *n*

¹**le·ver** \'lev-ər, 'lē-vər\ *n* **1** : a bar used to pry or move something **2** : a stiff bar for applying a force (as for lifting a weight) at one point of its length by effort at a second point and turning at a third point on a fulcrum **3** : a bar or rod used to

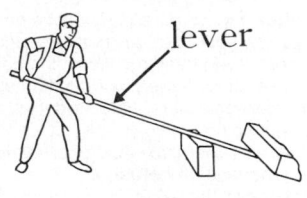

lever

lever 2

run or adjust something ⟨a gearshift *lever*⟩ [Middle English *lever* "bar for prying", from early French *levier* (same meaning), from *lever* (verb) "to raise", from Latin *levare* "to raise" — related to ELEVATE]

²**lever** *vb* **le·vered; le·ver·ing** \'lev-(ə-)riŋ, 'lēv-\ : to pry, raise, or move with a lever

le·ver·age \'lev-(ə-)rij, 'lēv-\ *n* : the action of a lever or the increase in force gained by using a lever

le·vi·a·than \li-'vī-ə-thən\ *n* **1** *often cap* : a sea monster often standing for evil in the Old Testament and Christian literature **2** : something very large or powerful of its kind

Le·vi's \'lē-,vīz\ *trademark* — used especially for blue denim jeans

lev·i·ta·tion \,lev-ə-'tā-shən\ *n* : the rising or lifting of a person or thing as if by magic

Le·vit·i·cus \li-'vit-i-kəs\ *n* — see BIBLE table

lev·i·ty \'lev-ət-ē\ *n, pl* **-ties** : a lack of seriousness often at an improper time : FRIVOLITY

lev·u·lose \'lev-yə-,lōs\ *n* : FRUCTOSE

¹**levy** \'lev-ē\ *n, pl* **lev·ies** **1 a** : the laying or collection especially of a tax **b** : an amount levied **2** : the calling of troops into service

²**levy** *vb* **lev·ied; levy·ing** **1** : to establish or collect by legal authority ⟨*levy* a tax⟩ ⟨*levy* a fine⟩ **2** : to raise or collect troops for military service

lewd \'lüd\ *adj* **1** : overly concerned with sex ⟨*lewd* behavior⟩ **2** : INDECENT ⟨*lewd* remarks⟩ — **lewd·ly** *adv* —

lewd·ness *n*

lex·i·cal \'lek-si-kəl\ *adj* : of or relating to words, a vocabulary, or a dictionary

lex·i·cog·ra·pher \,lek-sə-'käg-rə-fər\ *n* : an author or editor of a dictionary

lex·i·cog·ra·phy \,lek-sə-'käg-rə-fē\ *n* : the editing or making of a dictionary — **lex·i·co·graph·i·cal** \-kō-'graf-i-kəl\ *or* **lex·i·co·graph·ic** \-'graf-ik\ *adj*

lex·i·con \'lek-sə-,kän, -si-kən\ *n* : DICTIONARY 1

Ley·den jar \,līd-ᵊn-\ *n* : a device for storing electric charge consisting of a glass jar coated inside and outside with metal foil and having the inner coating connected to a conducting rod passed through the insulating stopper

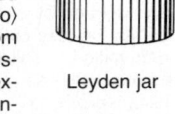

Leyden jar

li·a·bil·i·ty \,lī-ə-'bil-ət-ē\ *n, pl* **-ties** **1** : the state of being liable ⟨*liability* for his debts⟩ ⟨*liability* to disease⟩ **2** *pl* : that for which a person is liable : DEBTS **3** : something that works as a disadvantage : DRAWBACK

li·a·ble \'lī-ə-bəl, *especially in senses 2 & 3* 'lī-bəl\ *adj* **1** : forced by law or by what is right to make good ⟨we are *liable* for damage that we do⟩ **2** : not sheltered or protected (as from danger or accident) ⟨*liable* to diseases⟩ **3** : exposed to or likely to experience something that usually is undesirable ⟨you're *liable* to slip there⟩ ⟨it's *liable* to rain before we're done⟩

li·ai·son \'lē-ə-,zän, lē-'ā-\ *n* **1** : a close connection **2** : communication especially between parts of an armed force **3** : a person who sets up or keeps up liaison

li·a·na \lē-'än-ə, -'an-ə\ *n* : a climbing leafy or woody vine especially of a tropical forest that roots in the ground

li·ar \'lī(-ə)r\ *n* : a person who tells lies

lib \'lib\ *n* : LIBERATION 2

li·ba·tion \lī-'bā-shən\ *n* **1 a** : the act of pouring a liquid in honor of a god **b** : a liquid (as wine) poured as a libation **2** : a drink poured or taken as if to honor a god

¹**li·bel** \'lī-bəl\ *n* **1** : something spoken, written, or drawn that injures a person's good name **2** : the act or crime of publishing a libel

Word History The Latin word for book was *liber*. This was the same word used for the inner bark of a tree on which the early books were written. When the suffix *-ellus* was added to the root of the word, *libellus,* meaning "a little book," was created. In English the word became *libel,* and at first it had the meaning "little book", just as the Latin word had. But little books and pamphlets became a popular way to spread gossip and interesting but untrue stories about famous people. The writers and publishers of such books were often sued for their libels. Before long the spreading of untrue stories that damage a person's reputation came to be called *libel*. [Middle English *libel* "a written statement, little book" from early French *libel* (same meaning), from Latin *libellus,* "little book", from *liber* "book" — related to LIBRARY]

²**libel** *vb* **li·beled** *or* **li·belled; li·bel·ing** *or* **li·bel·ling** : to hurt by a libel — **li·bel·er** *or* **li·bel·ler** \-b(ə-)lər\ *n*

li·bel·ous *or* **li·bel·lous** \'lī-b(ə-)ləs\ *adj* : being a libel

¹**lib·er·al** \'lib-(ə-)rəl\ *adj* **1** : of, relating to, or based on the liberal arts ⟨a *liberal* education⟩ **2 a** : not stingy : GENEROUS ⟨a *liberal* giver⟩ **b** : more than enough ⟨a *liberal* allowance⟩ **3** : not strict; *esp* : not bound by traditional forms or beliefs **4** : of or relating to liberalism : not conservative — **lib·er·al·ly** \-rə-lē\ *adv*

²**liberal** *n* : a person who is liberal especially in politics

liberal arts *n pl* : the studies (as literature, philosophy, languages, or history) in a college or university intended to develop the mind in a general way rather than give professional or vocational skills

lib·er·al·ism \'lib-(ə)-rə-ˌliz-əm\ *n* : a political belief stressing progress, the essential goodness of humankind, and individual freedom

lib·er·al·i·ty \ˌlib-ə-'ral-ət-ē\ *n, pl* **-ties** **1** : the quality or state of being liberal **2** : a generous act

lib·er·al·ize \'lib-(ə)-rə-ˌlīz\ *vb* **-ized; -iz·ing** : to make or become liberal or more liberal — **lib·er·al·iza·tion** \ˌlib-(ə)-rə-lə-'zā-shən\ *n*

lib·er·ate \'lib-ə-ˌrāt\ *vb* **-at·ed; -at·ing** : to set free — **lib·er·a·tor** \-ˌrāt-ər\ *n*

lib·er·at·ed *adj* : freed from or opposed to traditional social and sexual attitudes or roles

lib·er·a·tion \ˌlib-ə-'rā-shən\ *n* **1** : the act of liberating : the state of being liberated **2** : a movement seeking equal rights for a group

lib·er·tar·i·an \ˌlib-ər-'ter-ē-ən\ *n* : a person who believes in liberty of thought and action — **libertarian** *adj* — **lib·er·tar·i·an·ism** \-ē-ə-ˌniz-əm\ *n*

lib·er·tine \'lib-ər-ˌtēn\ *n* : a person who leads an immoral life — **libertine** *adj*

lib·er·ty \'lib-ərt-ē\ *n, pl* **-ties** **1** : the condition of those who are free and independent : FREEDOM **2** : power to do what one pleases ⟨give a child some *liberty*⟩ **3** : the act of a person who goes beyond proper behavior or good sense ⟨took *liberties* with the truth⟩ ⟨take foolish *liberties* with one's health⟩ **4** : permission to be absent from naval duty for a short time — **at liberty** **1** : not held back : FREE ⟨you are *at liberty* to go or stay⟩ **2** : at leisure : not busy ⟨I'm *at liberty* this afternoon⟩

Li·bra \'lē-brə, 'lī-\ *n* **1** : a group of stars between Virgo and Scorpio usually pictured as a balance scale **2 a** : the seventh sign of the zodiac — see ZODIAC table **b** : a person whose sign of the zodiac is Libra [Middle English *Libra* "sign of the zodiac", from Latin *libra,* literally "balance, scales" — related to DELIBERATE, EQUILIBRIUM]

li·brar·i·an \lī-'brer-ē-ən\ *n* : a person in charge of a library — **li·brar·i·an·ship** \-ˌship\ *n*

li·brary \'lī-ˌbrer-ē\ *n, pl* **-brar·ies** **1 a** : a place where books, magazines, and records are kept for use but not for sale **b** : a collection of books, magazines, or records **2** : a collection resembling or suggesting a library ⟨a *library* of computer programs⟩ [Middle English *library, librarie* "a place where books are kept", from Latin *librarium* (same meaning), from earlier *librarius* "of books", from *liber* "book" — related to LIBEL; see *Word History* at LIBEL]

library paste *n* : a thick white adhesive paste

li·bret·tist \lə-'bret-əst\ *n* : the writer of a libretto

li·bret·to \lə-'bret-ō\ *n, pl* **-tos** *or* **-ti** \-ē\ : the text of an opera or musical

lice *pl of* LOUSE

¹li·cense *or* **li·cence** \'līs-ᵊn(t)s\ *n* **1 a** : permission granted by qualified authority to do something **b** : a document, plate, or tag showing that such permission has been granted **2** : liberty of action that is carried too far

²license *also* **licence** *vb* **li·censed; li·cens·ing** : to permit or authorize by license — **li·cens·able** \'līs-ᵊn-sə-bəl\ *adj*

licensed practical nurse *n* : a person who has been trained and has been given a license (as by a state) to perform routine care of the sick — called also *LPN*

license plate *n* : a plate or tag (as of metal) showing that a license has been gotten and usually bearing a registration number

li·cen·tious \lī-'sen-chəs\ *adj* : marked by immoral or lawless behavior — **li·cen·tious·ly** *adv* — **li·cen·tious·ness** *n*

lichee *variant of* LITCHI

li·chen \'lī-kən\ *n* : any of numerous complex plants made up of an alga and a fungus growing together on a solid surface (as a rock)

¹lick \'lik\ *vb* **1 a** : to pass the tongue over ⟨*licked* the

bowl⟩ **b** : to touch or pass over like a tongue ⟨flames were already *licking* the ceiling⟩ **2** : to take up with the tongue ⟨kittens *licking* milk⟩ **3 a** : to hit again and again : BEAT **b** : to get the better of — **lick·ing** *n*

lichen

²lick *n* **1 a** : an act or instance of licking **b** : a small amount : BIT ⟨hasn't done a *lick* of work⟩ **c** : a hasty careless effort **2** : a sharp hit : BLOW ⟨got in a few *licks* of my own⟩ **3** : a place (as a spring) having a deposit of salt that animals regularly lick — called also *salt lick*

lic·o·rice \'lik-(ə)-rish, -rəs\ *n* : a candy made from a preparation of the dried root of a European plant of the legume family; *also* : the plant, its dried root, or the preparation from it [Middle English *licorice* "licorice", from early French *licorice* (same meaning), from Latin *liquiritia* (same meaning), derived from Greek *glykyrrhiza,* literally "sweet root"]

lid \'lid\ *n* **1** : a movable cover (as for a box or jar) **2** : EYELID **3** *slang* : HAT **4** : a force that holds back ⟨tried to keep a *lid* on the news⟩ — **lid·ded** \'lid-əd\ *adj*

¹lie \'lī\ *vb* **lay** \'lā\; **lain** \'lān\; **ly·ing** \'lī-iŋ\ **1 a** : to be in, stay in, or take up a horizontal position ⟨*lay* fast asleep⟩ ⟨*lie* down⟩ **b** : to stay in hiding or in ambush ⟨*lie* low⟩ ⟨*lie* in wait⟩ **2** : to be spread flat so as to cover ⟨snow *lying* on the ground⟩ **3** : to have direction : EXTEND ⟨our route *lay* to the west⟩ **4** : to be located ⟨Ohio *lies* east of Indiana⟩ [Old English *liegan* "to get into or be in a horizontal position"]

²lie *n* **1** : the position in which something lies **2** *chiefly British* : ²LAY

³lie *vb* **lied; ly·ing** \'lī-iŋ\ **1** : to make a statement one knows to be untrue **2** : to give a false idea ⟨statistics sometimes *lie*⟩ [Old English *lēogan* "to say something that is not true"]

⁴lie *n* : something said or done in the hope of deceiving

lie detector *n* : an instrument for detecting physical signs of the tension that goes with lying

lief \'lēv, 'lēf\ *adv* : SOON 4, WILLINGLY ⟨I had as *lief* go as not⟩

¹liege \'lēj\ *adj* **1** : having the right to receive service and loyalty ⟨*liege* lord⟩ **2** : owing or giving service to a lord

²liege *n* **1** : VASSAL **2** : a feudal lord

lien \'lēn, 'lē-ən\ *n* : a legal claim on the property of another person until he or she has met a certain obligation (as a debt)

lieu \'lü\ *n, archaic* : ¹PLACE 7b, STEAD — **in lieu of** : in the place of : INSTEAD OF

lieu·ten·an·cy \lü-'ten-ən-sē\ *n, pl* **-cies** : the office, rank, or commission of a lieutenant

lieu·ten·ant \lü-'ten-ənt\ *n* **1** : an official who acts for a higher official **2 a** : FIRST LIEUTENANT **b** : SECOND LIEUTENANT **c** : a naval commissioned officer with a rank just below that of lieutenant commander **d** : a fire or police department officer ranking below a captain

Word History The phrase *in lieu of* means the same thing as *in place of* or *instead of.* The word *lieu* came into English from early French, in which it meant "place, position, function". Another English word that came from early French is *tenant.* In early French, this word was an adjective meaning "holding". Joined together, these two

\ə\	**abut**	\aú\	**out**	\i\	**tip**	\ó\	**saw**	\ù\	**foot**
\ər\	**further**	\ch\	**chin**	\ī\	**life**	\ói\	**coin**	\y\	**yet**
\a\	**mat**	\e\	**pet**	\j\	**job**	\th\	**thin**	\yü\	**few**
\ā\	**take**	\ē\	**easy**	\ŋ\	**sing**	\th\	**this**	\yù\	**cure**
\ä\	**cot, cart**	\g\	**go**	\ō\	**bone**	\ü\	**food**	\zh\	**vision**

words gave the early French word *lieutenant.* It originally meant "a person holding another person's place" or "a person acting in place of another". In English, *lieutenant* is best known as a military title, but the word is still sometimes used in its original meaning to refer to a person who acts in *lieu* of someone else. [Middle English *lieutenant* "lieutenant", from early French *lieutenant* (same meaning), literally "one holding the place for another", from *lieu* "place, position" and *tenant* "holding"]

lieutenant colonel *n* : a military commissioned officer with a rank just below that of colonel

lieutenant commander *n* : a naval commissioned officer with a rank just below that of commander

lieutenant general *n* : a military commissioned officer with a rank just below that of general

lieutenant governor *n*   **1** : an elected official serving as deputy to the governor of an American state   **2** : the formal head of the government of a Canadian province appointed to represent the crown

lieutenant junior grade *n* : a naval commissioned officer with a rank just below that of lieutenant

¹life \'līf\ *n, pl* **lives** \'līvz\   **1 a** : the quality that separates plants and animals from such things as water or rock : the quality that plants and animals lose when they die   **b** : a state of a living thing marked especially by capacity for metabolism, growth, reaction to stimuli, and reproduction   **2 a** : all the experiences that make up the existence of a person ⟨never heard of such a thing in all my *life*⟩   **b** : BIOGRAPHY   **3 a** : the period during which a person, animal, or plant lives   **b** : a specific part of living ⟨adult *life*⟩   **c** : the period from an event until death ⟨remained friends for *life*⟩   **4** : a way or manner of living ⟨the *life* of the ant⟩   **5** : a living being ⟨many *lives* were saved⟩   **6** : energy or spirit in action or expression ⟨eyes full of *life*⟩ ⟨still some *life* left in the coals⟩   **7** : the form or pattern of something that exists in actual fact ⟨painted from *life*⟩ ⟨looks larger than *life*⟩   **8** : the period of usefulness, popularity, or existence of something ⟨battery *life*⟩ ⟨the *life* of an insurance policy⟩   **9** : living beings ⟨as of a kind or place⟩ ⟨forest *life*⟩   **10** : living activity and movement ⟨stirrings of *life*⟩ ⟨streets humming with *life*⟩   **11** : one providing interest and vigor ⟨the *life* of the party⟩

²life *adj*   **1** : of or relating to living existence ⟨the *life* force⟩   **2** : LIFELONG ⟨a *life* member⟩

life–and–death *adj* : ending in life or death : deciding which will survive ⟨a *life-and-death* struggle⟩

life belt *n* : a life preserver worn like a belt

life·blood \'līf-'bləd\ *n* : something that gives strength and energy

life·boat \-,bōt\ *n* : a strong boat designed for use in saving lives at sea

life buoy *n* : a float consisting of a ring of very light material to hold up a person who has fallen into the water

life cycle *n*   **1** : the series of stages of form and activity through which a living thing passes from a beginning stage in one individual to the same stage in its offspring   **2** : LIFE HISTORY 1

life expectancy *n* : the number of years that an individual or group of a certain age can expect to live on the average based on experience in the past for individuals or groups of the same kind

life·guard \'līf-,gärd\ *n* : a usually expert swimmer employed at a beach or swimming pool to protect swimmers from drowning

life history *n*   **1** : a history of the changes through which a living thing passes in its development from the first stage to its natural death   **2** : LIFE CYCLE 1

life insurance *n* : insurance providing for a specified sum to be paid when the insured person dies

life jacket *n* : a life preserver that is worn like a jacket or vest

life·less \'līf-fləs\ *adj* : having no life — **life·less·ly** *adv* — **lifeless·ness** *n*

life·like \'lī-,flīk\ *adj* : showing or looking like real life — **life·likeness** *n*

life·line \'lī-,flīn\ *n*   **1** : a line persons may hang on to for safety or rescue   **2** : something suggesting a lifeline in its being considered necessary for survival

life·long \'lī-,flȯŋ\ *adj* : continuing or lasting through life ⟨a *lifelong* love for trees⟩ ⟨a *lifelong* friendship⟩

life jacket

life plant *n* : BRYOPHYLLUM

life preserver *n* : a device designed to save a person from drowning by holding up the body while in the water

life raft *n* : a raft designed for use by people forced into the water

life·sav·er \'līf-,sā-vər\ *n*   **1** : a person trained to save the lives of drowning persons   **2** : something that relieves distress when most needed

¹life·sav·ing \'līf-,sā-viŋ\ *adj* : designed for or used in saving lives

²lifesaving *n* : the methods that can be used to save lives especially of drowning persons

life science *n* : a branch of science (as biology, medicine, anthropology, or sociology) that deals with living things and life processes — usually used in pl.

life scientist *n* : a person who specializes in one or more of the life sciences

life–size \'līf-'sīz\ *or* **life–sized** \-'sīzd\ *adj* : of natural size : having the same size as the original

life span *n* : the average length of life of a living thing or of the persistence of a material object under specified circumstances or in a particular environment

life·style \'līf-'stī(ə)l\ *n* : the usual way of life of a person, group, or society : the way we live

life–support system *n* : a system that provides all or some of the items (as oxygen, food, water, proper temperature and air pressure, elimination of carbon dioxide and body wastes) necessary for maintaining life or health

life·time \'līf-,tīm\ *n*   **1** : ¹LIFE 3a   **2** : ¹LIFE 8

life·work \-'wərk\ *n* : the entire or chief work of one's lifetime

¹lift \'lift\ *vb*   **1** : to move to a higher position, rate, or amount   **2** : to rise from the ground ⟨planes *lifting* from the runway⟩ ⟨the rocket *lifted* off⟩   **3** : to stop or remove often temporarily ⟨*lift* a blockade⟩ ⟨*lift* a ban⟩   **4** : to move upward and disappear or become scattered ⟨when the fog *lifts*⟩   *syn* see RAISE — **lift·er** *n*

²lift *n*   **1** : the amount that may be lifted at one time : LOAD   **2** : the action or an instance of lifting   **3** : help especially in the form of a ride ⟨can I give you a *lift*?⟩   **4 a** : *British* : ELEVATOR 1b   **b** : a device for carrying people up or down a mountain   **5** : a raising of the spirits ⟨their visit gave me a *lift*⟩   **b** : an upward force (as on an airplane wing) that opposes the pull of gravity

lift–off \'lif-,tȯf\ *n* : a vertical takeoff (as by a rocket)

lig·a·ment \'lig-ə-mənt\ *n* : a tough band of tissue that holds bones together or keeps an organ in place in the body [Middle English *ligament* "connecting tissue, ligament", derived from Latin *ligamentum* "band, something used for tying", from *ligare* "to bind, tie" — related to *ally*]

li·ga·tion \lī-'gā-shən\ *n* : the act of tying a bodily part (as a fallopian tube) with a ligature

lig·a·ture \'lig-ə-,chù(ə)r-, -chər\ *n*   **1** : a binding or tying of something   **2** : something that binds or connects : BAND, BOND   **3** : a thread used in surgery especially for tying blood vessels

¹light \'līt\ *n*   **1 a** : something that makes vision possible   **b**

: the sensation aroused by stimulation of the visual sense organs **c** : an electromagnetic radiation in the wavelength range including infrared, visible, ultraviolet, and X rays and traveling in a vacuum with a speed of about 300,000 kilometers per second; *esp* : the part of this range that is visible to the human eye **2** : DAYLIGHT 1 ⟨by dawn's early *light*⟩ **3** : a source (as a lamp) of light ⟨turn on the *light*⟩ **4 a** : public knowledge ⟨facts brought to *light*⟩ **b** : a particular appearance presented to view ⟨were shown in a bad *light* by the lawyer⟩ ⟨I see the matter in a different *light* now⟩ **5** : a particular illumination ⟨by the *light* of the moon⟩ **6** : something that helps one to know or understand ⟨shed *light* on a problem⟩ **7** : a noted person ⟨one of the leading *lights* of the city⟩ **8 a** : LIGHTHOUSE, BEACON **b** : TRAFFIC SIGNAL ⟨turn left at the next *light*⟩ **9** : a flame for lighting something [Old English *lēoht* "light, that which makes seeing possible"] — **in light of** : with respect to ⟨consider their advice *in light of* your own needs⟩

²**light** *adj* **1** : having light : BRIGHT ⟨a *light* room⟩ **2** : not dark or deep in color : PALE ⟨*light* blue⟩ — **light·ness** *n*

³**light** *vb* **light·ed** *or* **lit** \'lit\; **light·ing** **1** : to make or become bright — often used with *up* **2** : to cause to burn or begin to burn — often used with *up* **3** : to lead with a light ⟨*light* a guest up the stairs⟩

⁴**light** *adj* **1 a** : having little or less than usual weight : not heavy **b** : designed to carry a small load ⟨*light* truck⟩ **2 a** : of little importance **b** : not abundant : SCANTY ⟨*light* rain⟩ **c** : not strong or violent : MODERATE ⟨*light* breezes⟩ **3 a** : easily disturbed ⟨a *light* sleeper⟩ **b** : putting forth little force or pressure : GENTLE ⟨a *light* touch⟩ **4** : not hard to bear, do, pay, or digest ⟨*light* punishment⟩ ⟨*light* exercise⟩ ⟨*light* food⟩ **5** : capable of moving swiftly or nimbly ⟨*light* on one's feet⟩ **6** : intended chiefly to entertain ⟨*light* reading⟩ ⟨*light* verse⟩ **7** : having a spongy or fluffy quality ⟨*light* pastry⟩ **8** : producing goods that will be sold to the people who use them rather than to another manufacturer ⟨*light* industry⟩ [Old English *lēoht* "not heavy"] — **light·ly** *adv* — **light·ness** *n*

⁵**light** *adv* **1** : in a light manner **2** : with little baggage ⟨traveling *light*⟩

⁶**light** *vb* **light·ed** *or* **lit** \'lit\; **light·ing** **1** : to come down out of the air and settle : ALIGHT ⟨birds *lit* on the lawn⟩ **2** : to come by chance ⟨*lit* upon a solution⟩ [Old English *līhtan* "to come down off something or out of the air"]

light bulb *n* : INCANDESCENT LAMP

¹**light·en** \'līt-°n\ *vb* **light·ened**; **light·en·ing** \'līt-niŋ, -°n-iŋ\ **1** : to make or become light, lighter, or clear : BRIGHTEN **2** : to give out flashes of lightning — **light·en·er** \'līt-nər, -°n-ər\ *n*

²**lighten** *vb* **light·ened**; **light·en·ing** \'līt-niŋ, -°n-iŋ\ : to make or become less heavy or less difficult ⟨*lighten* a load⟩ ⟨*lightened* her duties⟩ — **light·en·er** \'līt-nər, -°n-ər\ *n*

¹**ligh·ter** \'līt-ər\ *n* : a large barge used especially in unloading or loading ships [Middle English *lighter* "boat"; of Dutch origin]

²**lighter** *vb* : to carry by a lighter

³**light·er** \'līt-ər\ *n* : one that lights; *esp* : a device for lighting ⟨a cigarette *lighter*⟩ [from ³*light* and *-er*]

lighter–than–air *adj* : able to fly by the use of a gas (as helium or hot air) less dense than the air that would occupy the same amount of space

light·face \'līt-ˌfās\ *n* : the style of printing type used for ordinary text (as in books) — **light·faced** \-'fāst\ *adj*

light–foot·ed \-'fút-əd\ *adj* : having a light and springy step or movement

light–head·ed \-'hed-əd\ *adj* **1** : feeling confused or dizzy **2** : not showing maturity or seriousness : FRIVOLOUS — **light–head·ed·ness** *n*

light–heart·ed \-'härt-əd\ *adj* : free from worry — **light–heart·ed·ly** *adv* — **light–heart·ed·ness** *n*

light heavyweight *n* : a boxer in a weight division having the approximate range of 75 to 81 kilograms

light·house \-ˌhaùs\ *n* : a tower with a powerful light at the top that is built on or near the shore to guide sailors at night

light·ing \'līt-iŋ\ *n* **1** : supply of light : ILLUMINATION **2** : artificial light (as for a play) or the apparatus providing it

light meter *n* **1** : a small portable device for measuring the amount of light in an area **2** : a device for indicating correct photographic exposure for varying amounts of light

light microscope *n* : MICROSCOPE 1

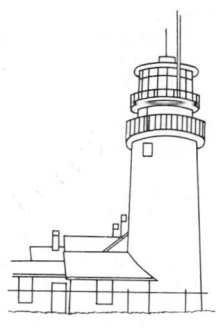

lighthouse

¹**light·ning** \'līt-niŋ\ *n* : the flashing of light produced by a discharge of atmospheric electricity from one cloud to another or between a cloud and the earth; *also* : the discharge itself

²**lightning** *adj* : moving or done with or as if with the speed of lightning

lightning arrester *n* : a device for protecting electrical equipment from damage by lightning

lightning bug *n* : FIREFLY

lightning rod *n* : a metal rod set up on a building or a ship and connected with the earth or water below to decrease the chances of damage from lightning

light opera *n* : OPERETTA

light out *vb* : to leave in a hurry ⟨*lit out* for home⟩

light pen *n* : a pen-shaped device that senses light signals and is used to work with information on a computer display screen

light·proof \'līt-'prüf\ *adj* : not letting in light

light·ship \-ˌship\ *n* : a ship equipped to work like a lighthouse and anchored at a place dangerous to sailors

light·some \'līt-səm\ *adj* **1** : free from care : CHEERFUL **2** : marked by a light or springy quality

light trap *n* : a device for collecting or destroying insects by attracting them to a light and trapping or killing them

¹**light·weight** \'līt-ˌwāt\ *n* **1** : one of less than average weight; *esp* : a boxer in a weight division having the approximate range of 57 to 60 kilograms **2** : a person of little importance

²**lightweight** *adj* : having less than the usual or expected weight

light–year \'līt-ˌyi(ə)r\ *n* **1** : a unit of length in astronomy equal to the distance that light travels in one year or 9,458,000,000,000 kilometers **2** : a very great distance especially in progress ⟨*light-years* ahead in design⟩

lig·nin \'lig-nən\ *n* : a substance related to cellulose that occurs in the woody cell walls of plants and in the cementing material between them

lig·nite \'lig-ˌnīt\ *n* : a usually brownish black coal between peat and bituminous coal in age and heating ability; *esp* : one in which the texture of the original wood is distinct

lik·able *or* **like·able** \'lī-kə-bəl\ *adj* : easily liked — **lik·able·ness** *n*

¹**like** \'līk\ *vb* **liked**; **lik·ing** **1** : to have a liking for : ENJOY ⟨*likes* baseball⟩ **2** : to feel toward : REGARD ⟨how do you *like* this weather?⟩ **3** : to wish to have : WANT ⟨would *like* a drink⟩ **4** : to feel inclined : CHOOSE ⟨you can leave any time you *like*⟩ [Old English *līcian* "to take pleasure in"]

²**like** *n* : LIKING, PREFERENCE ⟨my *likes* and dislikes⟩

\ə\ abut	\aù\ out	\i\ tip	\ò\ saw	\ù\ foot
\ər\ further	\ch\ chin	\ī\ life	\òi\ coin	\y\ yet
\a\ mat	\e\ pet	\j\ job	\th\ thin	\yü\ few
\ā\ take	\ē\ easy	\ŋ\ sing	\th\ this	\yù\ cure
\ä\ cot, cart	\g\ go	\ō\ bone	\ü\ food	\zh\ vision

³like *adj* : being the same or very nearly the same ⟨two *like* magnetic poles⟩ ⟨suits of *like* design⟩ [Old English *gelīc* "alike"]

⁴like *prep* **1 a** : similar to ⟨the house looks *like* a barn⟩ **b** : typical of ⟨it would be just *like* you to do that⟩ **2** : similarly to ⟨acting *like* a fool⟩ ⟨blow it up *like* a balloon⟩ **3** : likely to ⟨looks *like* rain⟩ **4** : such as ⟨a subject *like* physics⟩

⁵like *n* : ²EQUAL 1 ⟨may never see its *like* again⟩; *also* : ¹KIND 1a ⟨I'd keep him and his *like* from causing any more trouble⟩

⁶like *adv* **1** : ²LIKELY, PROBABLY ⟨*like* enough, you will⟩ ⟨*like* as not the cat's under the porch⟩ **2** : in some amount : SOMEWHAT, SEEMINGLY ⟨it moves stiff *like*⟩ **3** : close to : within a little : NEARER ⟨the rate is more *like* 18 percent⟩

⁷like *conj* **1** : AS IF ⟨the plane looked *like* it would crash⟩ ⟨pedaling *like* mad⟩ **2** : in the same way that : AS ⟨you sound just *like* I do⟩ ⟨does it look *like* it did when you began?⟩

⁸like *or* **liked** \'līkt\ *helping verb, chiefly dialect* : came near : was near ⟨I *like* to have died laughing⟩

-like *adj combining form* : resembling or characteristic of ⟨bell-*like*⟩ ⟨lady*like*⟩

like·li·hood \'lī-klē-,hud\ *n* : PROBABILITY 1

like·li·ness \'lī-klē-nəs\ *n* : PROBABILITY 1

¹like·ly \'lī-klē\ *adj* **like·li·er; -est** **1** : very possibly going to happen ⟨that bomb is *likely* to expode any time⟩ **2** : seeming to be the truth : BELIEVABLE ⟨a *likely* story⟩ **3** : giving hope of turning out well : PROMISING ⟨a *likely* spot for a picnic⟩ ⟨a *likely* looking customer⟩

²likely *adv* : without great doubt : PROBABLY ⟨the first loaves of bread people made were *likely* hard and flat⟩

lik·en \'lī-kən\ *vb* **lik·ened; lik·en·ing** \'līk-(ə-)niŋ\ : ¹COMPARE 1

like·ness \'līk-nəs\ *n* **1** : a picture especially of a person : PORTRAIT **2** : the quality or state of being like : RESEMBLANCE

like·wise \'lī-,kwīz\ *adv* **1** : in like manner : SIMILARLY **2** : in addition : ALSO

lik·ing \'lī-kiŋ\ *n* : a being pleased with someone or something : FONDNESS, TASTE

li·lac \'lī-lək, -,lak, -,läk\ *n* **1** : any of a genus of shrubs and trees related to the olive; *esp* : a European shrub widely grown for its showy clusters of fragrant grayish pink, purple, or white flowers **2** : a medium purple

¹lilt \'lilt\ *vb* : to sing or play in a lively cheerful manner — **lilt·ing·ly** \'lil-tiŋ-lē\ *adv*

²lilt *n* : a lively and cheerful sound or expression ⟨a tune with a *lilt*⟩ ⟨a *lilt* in her voice⟩

lily \'lil-ē\ *n, pl* **lil·ies** : any of a genus of herbs with leafy stems that grow from bulbs and have funnel-shaped flowers; *also* : any of various related plants

lily–liv·ered \,lil-ē-'liv-ərd\ *adj* : COWARDLY 1

Word History In the Middle Ages the study of anatomy, or the cutting up and examining of human corpses, was illegal. Most of what was thought about the body thus was based on the theory of humors. The humor, or body fluid, that was supposed to control anger, spirit, and courage was bile, produced by the liver. A person who lacked courage was supposed to have a white liver, because it had no yellow bile to color it. Thus a cowardly person was called *white-livered* or, more poetically, *lily-livered*.

lily of the valley

lily of the valley : a low herb that is related to the lilies and has usually two large oblong leaves and a stalk of fragrant flowers shaped like bells

lily pad *n* : a floating leaf of a water lily

lily–white \,lil-ē-'hwīt, -'wīt\ *adj* **1** : white as a lily **2** : free from fault or blame : FAULTLESS, PURE

li·ma bean \,lī-mə-\ *n* : any of various beans widely grown for their flat edible usually pale green or whitish seeds; *also* : this seed

¹limb \'lim\ *n* **1** : any of the paired parts (as an arm, wing, or leg) of an animal that stick out from the body and are used mostly in moving and grasping; *esp* : a leg or arm of a human being **2** : a large branch of a tree — **limb·less** \'lim-ləs\ *adj*

²limb *vb* : to cut off the limbs of ⟨a felled tree⟩

¹lim·ber \'lim-bər\ *adj* : bending easily : FLEXIBLE, SUPPLE — **lim·ber·ly** *adv* — **lim·ber·ness** *n*

²limber *vb* **lim·bered; lim·ber·ing** \'lim-b(ə-)riŋ\ : to make or become limber ⟨*limbered* up with exercises⟩

¹lim·bo \'lim-bō\ *n, pl* **limbos** **1** *often cap* : a place for souls (as of unbaptized infants) believed to be barred from heaven through no fault of their own **2 a** : a place or state of being held or forgotten **b** : a middle place or state [Middle English *limbo* "a place for souls", derived from Latin *limbus* (same meaning), from earlier *limbus* "border"]

²limbo *n* : a West Indian dance that involves bending backward and passing under a horizontal pole [a native name for the dance in the West Indies]

¹lime \'līm\ *n* **1** : a white substance that is primarily an oxide of calcium, is made by heating limestone or shells, and is used in making plaster and cement and in farming **2** : a dry white powder consisting chiefly of the hydroxide of calcium that is made by treating lime with water [Old English *līm* "substance from limestone"]

²lime *vb* **limed; lim·ing** : to treat or cover with lime ⟨*lime* a garden⟩

³lime *adj* : of, relating to, or containing lime or limestone

⁴lime *n* : a European linden tree [Old English *lind* "linden tree"]

⁵lime *n* : a fruit like the lemon but smaller and with a greenish yellow skin; *also* : the citrus tree that bears it [from French *lime* "the fruit lime"; of Arabic origin]

lime·light \'līm-,līt\ *n* : the center of public attention

lim·er·ick \'lim-(ə-)rik\ *n* : a humorous poem five lines long in which the first, second, and fifth lines have one rhyme and the third and fourth another

lime·stone \'līm-,stōn\ *n* : a rock that is formed chiefly from animal remains (as shells or coral), consists mainly of calcium carbonate, is used in building, and gives lime when burned

lime·wa·ter \-,wot-ər, -,wät-\ *n* : a colorless alkaline water solution of the hydroxide of calcium that turns white on contact with carbon dioxide

¹lim·it \'lim-ət\ *n* **1** : a boundary line ⟨within the city *limits*⟩ **2** : a point beyond which a person or thing cannot go — **lim·it·less** \-ləs\ *adj*

²limit *vb* : to set limits to : keep within limits ⟨*limit* expenses⟩ ⟨management reserves the right to *limit* quantities⟩ ⟨an adjective *limits* the meaning of a noun⟩

lim·i·ta·tion \,lim-ə-'tā-shən\ *n* **1** : the act or an instance of limiting **2** : the quality or state of being limited **3** : something that limits

lim·it·ed *adj* **1** : held within limits **2** : having constitutional limitations placed on the exercise of power ⟨a *limited* monarchy⟩ — **lim·it·ed·ly** *adv* — **lim·it·ed·ness** *n*

limited war *n* : a war whose goal is less than the total defeat of the enemy

lim·it·ing *adj* : being an environmental factor (as food) that limits the size of a population of living things

li·mo·nite \'lī-mə-,nīt\ *n* : an ore of iron consisting of oxides of iron — **li·mo·nit·ic** \,lī-mə-'nit-ik\ *adj*

lim·ou·sine \'lim-ə-,zēn, ,lim-ə-'zēn\ *n* **1** : a large luxurious automobile often driven by a chauffeur   **2** : a large vehicle for passengers going to and from an airport

¹limp \'limp\ *vb*   **1** : to walk lamely   **2** : to go slowly or with difficulty

²limp *n* : a limping movement or gait

³limp *adj*   **1** : not firm or stiff   **2** : ¹WEARY 1, EXHAUSTED — **limp·ly** *adv* — **limp·ness** *n*

lim·pet \'lim-pət\ *n* : a marine mollusk that has a low cone-shaped shell, moves over rocks or timbers feeding on food found there, and clings very tightly when disturbed

lim·pid \'lim-pəd\ *adj* : perfectly clear : TRANSPARENT ⟨*limpid* streams⟩ — **lim·pid·i·ty** \lim-'pid-ət-ē\ *n* — **lim·pid·ly** \'lim-pəd-lē\ *adv* — **lim·pid·ness** *n*

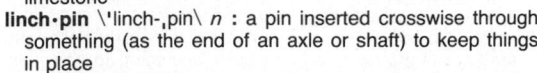

limpet

limy \'lī-mē\ *adj* **lim·i·er;** **-est** : containing lime or limestone

linch·pin \'linch-,pin\ *n* : a pin inserted crosswise through something (as the end of an axle or shaft) to keep things in place

Lin·coln's Birthday \,liŋ-kənz-\ *n* : February 12 or the first Monday in February observed as a legal holiday in many of the states of the U.S.

lin·den \'lin-dən\ *n*   **1** : any of a genus of trees with large heart-shaped leaves, drooping clusters of yellowish flowers rich in nectar, and hard pea-shaped fruits   **2** : the light white wood of a linden

¹line \'līn\ *vb* **lined; lin·ing** : to cover the inner surface of ⟨*line* a box with paper⟩ ⟨tapestries *lined* the walls⟩ [Old English *līn* "flax"]

²line *n*   **1** : a long thin cord ⟨a fishing *line*⟩   **2** : a cord, wire, or tape used in measuring and leveling   **3 a** : a pipe for carrying a fluid ⟨gas *line*⟩ ⟨water *line*⟩ ⟨steam *line*⟩   **b** : a wire or set of wires carrying electricity ⟨a power *line*⟩ ⟨telegraph *lines*⟩ ⟨a telephone *line*⟩   **4 a** : a row of words, letters, numbers, or symbols that are written, printed, or displayed (as on a page or TV screen); *also* : space for such a line   **b** : a structural unit of something written (as a poem or a computer program)   **c** : a short letter : NOTE ⟨drop me a *line*⟩   **d** *pl* : the words of a part in a play ⟨forgot her *lines*⟩   **5 a** : something (as a ridge, seam, or wrinkle) that is long and narrow   **b** : the direction followed by something in motion ⟨the *line* of flight of a bullet⟩   **c** : the boundary or limit of a place or lot ⟨town *line*⟩ ⟨property *line*⟩   **d** : the track of a railway   **6** : a state of agreement ⟨the red one is more in *line* with what I had in mind⟩   **7 a** : a course of behavior or thinking ⟨a conservative political *line*⟩   **b** : what one does or is interested in ⟨is medicine your *line*?⟩   **c** : smooth or interesting talk that is often insincere ⟨has a nice *line* of gab⟩   **8** : FAMILY 1 ⟨descended from a royal *line*⟩   **9 a** : the position of military forces facing the enemy ⟨on the front and behind the *lines*⟩ ⟨our first *line* of defense⟩   **b** : an arrangement of persons or things in a series ⟨waiting in *line*⟩   **10** : goods for sale of one general kind ⟨a *line* of clothing⟩   **11** : a system of transportation or the route over which it travels ⟨a bus *line*⟩ ⟨a steamship *line*⟩ ⟨military supply *lines*⟩   **12 a** : a long narrow mark (as one made by a pencil)   **b** : one of the horizontal lines on a music staff   **c** : the football players whose positions are along the line of scrimmage   **13** : a geometric element that is formed by a moving point and that has length but no width or thickness; *esp* : STRAIGHT LINE   **14 a** : ¹OUTLINE 1, CONTOUR ⟨a ship's *lines*⟩ ⟨the *lines* of a coat⟩   **b** : a general plan ⟨a story along these *lines*⟩ [Middle English *line* "thread", partly from Old English *līne* (same meaning) and partly from early French *ligne* (same mean-

ing), derived from Latin *linum* "flax"] — **between the lines** : in such a way as to learn or reveal something not expressed openly ⟨read *between the lines*⟩ — **in line for** : due to receive — **on the line**   **1** : to be kept or lost depending on what happens ⟨the champ's title is *on the line*⟩   **2** : IMMEDIATELY 2 ⟨pay cash *on the line*⟩ — **out of line** : beyond what is reasonable to put up with ⟨your behavior is getting *out of line*⟩ ⟨these prices are way *out of line*⟩

³line *vb* **lined; lin·ing**   **1** : to mark with a line or lines   **2** : to place or form a line along   **3** : to form a line : form into lines   **4** : to hit a line drive

lin·eage \'lin-ē-ij\ *n*   **1** : the ancestors from whom a person is descended   **2** : the people descended from the same ancestor

lin·eal \'lin-ē-əl\ *adj*   **1** : LINEAR ⟨*lineal* measure⟩   **2 a** : consisting of or being in a direct line of descent   **b** : HEREDITARY 3 — **lin·eal·ly** \-ē-ə-lē\ *adv*

lin·ea·ment \'lin-ē-ə-mənt\ *n* : a line of a body or figure and especially of the face

lin·ear \'lin-ē-ər\ *adj*   **1 a** : relating to, consisting of, or resembling a line : STRAIGHT   **b** : involving a single dimension   **c** : of, relating to, based on, or being linear equations or linear functions   **2** : long and uniformly narrow ⟨*linear* leaf of the hyacinth⟩ — **lin·ear·i·ty** \,lin-ē-'ar-ət-ē\ *n* — **lin·ear·ly** \'lin-ē-ər-lē\ *adv*

linear accelerator *n* : a device in which charged particles are accelerated in a straight line by successive pushes from a series of electric fields

linear equation *n* : an equation in which each term is either a constant or contains only one variable, in which each variable has an exponent of 1, and which always has a straight line as a graph ⟨$y = mx + b$ is the general form of a *linear equation* where *m* and *b* are any real numbers⟩

linear function *n* : a function whose graph is a straight line and which is represented by an equation of the form $y = ax + b$ where *a* and *b* are constants with $a \neq 0$ and *x* is any real number

linear measure *n*   **1** : a measure of length   **2** : a system of measures of length

linear programming *n* : a mathematical method for solving practical problems that often has the object of finding some best, largest, worst, or least value and that uses functions that are often sums of many variables each of which is in a separate term with or without a coefficient, has an exponent of 1, and may be restricted in the values it can take on

line·back·er \'līn-,bak-ər\ *n* : a football player on the defending team whose usual position is a short distance in back of the line of scrimmage

line drive *n* : a batted baseball hit not far above the ground in a nearly straight line

line graph *n* : a graph composed of line segments with each segment drawn between one point representing a specific value and the next point

line graph

line·man \'līn-mən\ *n*   **1** : one who sets up or repairs power or telephone lines   **2** : a football player whose position is on the line of scrimmage

lin·en \'lin-ən\ *n*   **1** : smooth strong cloth or yarn made from flax   **2**

\ə\ **abut**	\au̇\ **out**	\i\ **tip**	\ȯ\ **saw**	\u̇\ **foot**
\ər\ **further**	\ch\ **chin**	\ī\ **life**	\ȯi\ **coin**	\y\ **yet**
\a\ **mat**	\e\ **pet**	\j\ **job**	\th\ **thin**	\yü\ **few**
\ā\ **take**	\ē\ **easy**	\ŋ\ **sing**	\th\ **this**	\yu̇\ **cure**
\ä\ **cot, cart**	\g\ **go**	\ō\ **bone**	\ü\ **food**	\zh\ **vision**

: household articles (as tablecloths or sheets) or clothing (as shirts or underwear) that were once often made of linen — **linen** *adj*

line of force : an imaginary line that shows the direction in space in which force (as from a magnetic or electric field) acts

line of scrimmage : an imaginary line in football parallel to the goal lines and running through the place the ball is laid before each play begins

line printer *n* : a very fast printing machine for a computer that prints whole lines at once instead of one letter at a time

¹lin·er \'lī-nər\ *n* **1** : a ship or airplane of a regular transportation line ⟨an ocean *liner*⟩ **2** : something with which lines are made or drawn ⟨use a cosmetic *liner* to make the eyes more attractive⟩

²liner *n* : one that lines or is used to line something

line segment *n* : ¹SEGMENT 2b

lines·man \'līnz-mən\ *n* : an official who assists a referee in a game (as football or hockey)

line·up \'lī-,nəp\ *n* **1** : a line of persons arranged especially for identification by police **2** : a list of players taking part in a game (as baseball)

line up \(')lī-'nəp\ *vb* **1** : to come together or arrange in a line or rows ⟨*line up* for inspection⟩ **2** : to put into alignment ⟨*line up* the edges so they are even⟩ ⟨*line up* the decimal points before adding or subtracting⟩ **3** : to arrange for ⟨*lined up* support for the candidate⟩ ⟨*lined up* a summer job⟩

-ling \-liŋ\ *n suffix* **1** : one connected with or having the quality of ⟨hire*ling*⟩ **2** : young, small, or minor one ⟨duck*ling*⟩ [Old English *-ling* (noun suffix) "one having the quality of . . ."]

lin·ger \'liŋ-gər\ *vb* **lin·gered; lin·ger·ing** \-g(ə-)riŋ\ **1** : to be slow in quitting a place or activity ⟨*lingered* in bed⟩ **2** : to be slow to act — **lin·ger·er** \-gər-ər\ *n* — **lin·ger·ing·ly** \-g(ə-)riŋ-lē\ *adv*

syn LINGER, LOITER, LAG mean to pause often without good reason or explanation. LINGER suggests an unwillingness to leave a pleasant place ⟨*lingered* in the park after the concert⟩ LOITER suggests aimless wandering or waiting in a place ⟨restless youths *loitering* in the town square⟩ LAG suggests an inability or unwillingness to keep up with others ⟨two of the hikers *lagged* behind the rest of us⟩

lin·ge·rie \,län-jə-'rā, ,lan-zhə-, -'rē\ *n* : women's nightclothes or underwear [French, derived from early French *linge* "linen"]

lin·go \'liŋ-gō\ *n, pl* **lingoes** : language that is strange or hard to understand

lin·gual \'liŋ-g(yə-)wəl\ *adj* **1** : of, relating to, or resembling a tongue **2** : produced by the tongue ⟨*lingual* sounds such as \t\ or \l\⟩ — **lin·gual·ly** \-ē\ *adv*

lin·guist \'liŋ-gwəst\ *n* **1** : a person skilled in languages **2** : a person who specializes in linguistics

lin·guis·tic \liŋ-'gwis-tik\ *adj* : of or relating to language or linguistics — **lin·guis·ti·cal·ly** \-ti-k(ə-)lē\ *adv*

linguistic form *n* : a meaningful unit of speech (as a part of a word, a word, or a sentence)

lin·guis·tics \liŋ-'gwis-tiks\ *n* : the study of human speech including the units, nature, structure, and development of language, languages, or a language

lin·i·ment \'lin-ə-mənt\ *n* : a liquid medicine rubbed on the skin (as to relieve pain)

lin·ing \'lī-niŋ\ *n* : something that lines an inner surface

¹link \'liŋk\ *vb* : to join by or as if by a link — **link·er** *n*

²link *n* **1** : a connecting structure: as **a** : a single ring of a chain **b** : a usually ornamental device for fastening a shirt cuff **c** : ¹BOND 2b **d** : an intermediate rod or piece for transmitting force or motion **2** : something resembling a link of chain: as **a** : a piece of sausage in a series of connected pieces **b** : ¹BOND 3

link·age \'liŋ-kij\ *n* **1** : the manner or style of being united: as **a** : the manner in which atoms or radicals are linked in a molecule **b** : ¹BOND 2b **2** : the quality or state of being linked; *esp* : the occurring together of genes on the same chromosome with the result that the traits they control are not inherited independently of each other but tend to be found together **3** : a system of links; *esp* : a system of links or bars jointed together by means of which lines or curves may be traced

linked \'liŋ(k)t\ *adj* : exhibiting genetic linkage : tending to be inherited together

linking verb *n* : an intransitive verb (as *be* or *seem*) that links a subject with a word or words in the predicate ("look" in "you look happy" and "are" in "my favorite fruits are apples and oranges" are *linking verbs*) — compare ACTION VERB

links \'liŋ(k)s\ *n pl* : a golf course

link·up \'liŋ-,kəp\ *n* **1** : a getting together : MEETING ⟨the *linkup* of two spacecraft⟩ **2** : something that serves as a link

Lin·nae·an *or* **Lin·ne·an** \lə-'nē-ən, -'nā-; 'lin-ē-\ *adj* : of, relating to, or following the method of the Swedish botanist Linné who established the system of binomial nomenclature used in classifying plants and animals

lin·net \'lin-ət\ *n* : a common small old-world finch with feathers that vary greatly in color according to age, sex, and season

Word History Many birds eat seeds. One small songbird, known as the linnet, seems especially fond of seeds of the flax plant, a fondness that appears to have earned the bird its name. The Latin word for flax is *linum,* which is also the source of the English word *linen,* a cloth made from flax. When *linum* was borrowed from Latin into early French, it became *lin.* The songbird that feeds on the flax seeds came to be called *linette* in early French and later *linnet* in English. [from early French *linette* "linnet", from *lin* "flax", from Latin *linum* "flax"]

li·no·leum \lə-'nō-lē-əm, -'nōl-yəm\ *n* : a floor covering with a canvas back and a surface of hardened linseed oil and usually cork dust

Li·no·type \'lī-nə-,tīp\ *trademark* — used for a machine that sets type in whole lines on a solid piece of metal

lin·seed \'lin-,sēd\ *n* : FLAXSEED

linseed oil *n* : a yellowish oil obtained from flaxseed and used especially in paint, varnish, printing ink, and linoleum

lin·sey–wool·sey \,lin-zē-'wùl-zē\ *n* : a coarse fabric made of wool and linen or cotton

lint \'lint\ *n* **1** : loose fibers or bits of thread **2** : ¹COTTON 1a — **lint·less** \-ləs\ *adj* — **linty** \-ē-\ *adj*

lin·tel \'lint-ᵊl\ *n* : a horizontal piece across the top of an opening (as of a door) that carries the weight of the structure above it

li·on \'lī-ən\ *n, pl* **lion** *or* **lions** : a large flesh-eating mammal of the cat family that has a brownish buff coat, a tufted tail, and in the male a shaggy mane and that lives in open or rocky areas of Africa and formerly southern Asia — **li·on·like** \-,līk\ *adj*

lion

li·on·ess \'lī-ə-nəs\ *n* : a female lion

li·on·heart·ed \'lī-ən-,härt-əd\ *adj* : COURAGEOUS, BRAVE

lion's share *n* : the largest portion

¹lip \'lip\ *n* **1** : either of the two fleshy folds that surround the mouth **2 a** : a fleshy edge or margin ⟨*lips* of a wound⟩ **b** : the labium of an insect; *also* : the part around the edge of an insect's labium or labrum   **3** : the edge of a hollow container especially where it is slightly spread out — **lip·less** \-ləs\ *adj* — **lip·like** \-ˌlīk\ *adj* — **lipped** \ˈlipt\ *adj*

²lip *adj* : spoken with the lips only : not sincere ⟨*lip* service⟩

li·pase \ˈlī-ˌpās, -ˌpāz\ *n* : an enzyme that speeds up a chemical reaction making or breaking down fats or one breaking down fatty proteins

lip·id \ˈlip-əd\ *n* : any of various substances (as fats and waxes) that with proteins and carbohydrates make up the principal structural parts of living cells

lip–read \ˈlip-ˌrēd\ *vb* **–read** \-ˌred\; **–read·ing** \-ˌrēd-iŋ\ : to use lipreading to understand a speaker's words — **lip–read·er** \-ˌrēd-ər\ *n*

lip·read·ing \-ˌrēd-iŋ\ *n* : the getting of the meaning of a speaker's words without hearing the voice by watching lip and face movements

lip·stick \-ˌstik\ *n* : a waxy solid colored cosmetic for the lips usually in stick form

liquefied petroleum gas *n* : a compressed gas consisting of flammable light hydrocarbons and used especially as fuel or as a starting material for making other chemicals

liq·ue·fy \ˈlik-wə-ˌfī\ *vb* **-fied; -fy·ing** : to make or become liquid — **liq·ue·fi·able** \-ˌfī-ə-bəl\ *adj*

li·queur \li-ˈkər, -ˈk(y)u̇(ə)r\ *n* : a flavored and usually sweetened alcoholic beverage

¹liq·uid \ˈlik-wəd\ *adj* **1** : flowing freely like water   **2** : neither solid nor gaseous ⟨*liquid* mercury⟩   **3** : resembling liquid in clearness or smoothness ⟨large *liquid* eyes⟩ ⟨*liquid* notes of a bird⟩   **4** : being without friction and like a vowel ⟨the *liquid* consonant \l\⟩   **5** : made up of or easily changed into cash ⟨*liquid* assets⟩ — **li·quid·i·ty** \lik-ˈwid-ət-ē\ *n* — **liq·uid·ly** \ˈlik-wəd-lē\ *adv*

²liquid *n* **1** : a liquid consonant   **2** : a liquid substance

liquid air *n* : air in the liquid state used chiefly as a refrigerant

liq·ui·date \ˈlik-wə-ˌdāt\ *vb* **-dat·ed; -dat·ing** **1** : PAY OFF **1** ⟨*liquidate* a debt⟩   **2** : to put an end to : do away with — **liq·ui·da·tion** \ˌlik-wə-ˈdā-shən\ *n*

liquid measure *n* : a unit or series of units for measuring liquid capacity — see MEASURE table, METRIC SYSTEM table

li·quor \ˈlik-ər\ *n* **1** : a liquid substance or solution ⟨dye *liquor*⟩   **2** : a strong alcoholic beverage

li·ra \ˈlir-ə\ *n* **1** *pl* **li·re** \ˈlē-ˌrā\ *or* **liras** : the basic unit of money of Italy   **2** *pl* **liras** *also* **lire** : the basic unit of money of Turkey   **3** : a coin or bill representing one lira

lisle \ˈlī(ə)l\ *n* : a smooth tightly twisted thread usually made of cotton

¹lisp \ˈlisp\ *vb* : to pronounce the sounds \s\ and \z\ as \th\ and \ṯẖ\ — **lisp·er** *n*

²lisp *n* : the act or habit of lisping

lis·some *also* **lis·som** \ˈlis-əm\ *adj* **1** : bending easily : FLEXIBLE, LITHE   **2** : quick and light in action : NIMBLE

¹list \ˈlist\ *vb, archaic* : CHOOSE 3 [Old English *lystan* "to please, suit, be desirable"]

²list *vb, archaic* : to listen to : HEAR [Old English *hlystan* "to listen"]

³list *n* **1** : a band or strip of material   **2** *pl* **a** : an arena for jousting   **b** : a field of competition or dispute [Old English *līste* "strip"]

⁴list *n* : a record or catalog of names or items ⟨guest *list*⟩ ⟨grocery *list*⟩ [from French *liste* "a series of names or numbers", from Italian *lista* (same meaning); of Germanic origin]

⁵list *vb* **1** : to make a list of   **2** : to put on a list   **3** : to have a list price ⟨a car that *lists* at $9000⟩

⁶list *vb* : to lean to one side : TILT ⟨a *listing* ship⟩ [origin unknown]

⁷list *n* : a leaning to one side : TILT

lis·ten \ˈlis-ᵊn\ *vb* **lis·tened; lis·ten·ing** \ˈlis-niŋ, -ᵊn-iŋ\ **1** : to pay attention in order to hear ⟨*listen* for a signal⟩ ⟨*listen* to a new record⟩   **2** : to give heed : follow advice ⟨*listen* to a warning⟩ — **lis·ten·er** \ˈlis-nər, -ᵊn-ər\ *n*

listen in *vb* **1** : to listen to a broadcast   **2** : EAVESDROP

list·ing *n* **1** : ⁴LIST   **2** : something listed

list·less \ˈlist-ləs\ *adj* : too tired or too little interested to want to do things [Middle English *listles* "having a lack of desire to act or move", from earlier *list* "desire, liking"] — **list·less·ly** *adv* — **list·less·ness** *n*

list price *n* : the retail price of an item as published in a catalog, price list, or advertisement

lit *past and past participle of* LIGHT

lit·a·ny \ˈlit-ᵊn-ē, ˈlit-nē\ *n, pl* **-nies** : a prayer consisting of a series of lines spoken alternately by a leader and the congregation

li·tchi *or* **li·chee** \ˈlī-(ˌ)chē, ˈlē-\ *n* : the oval fruit of an Asian tree having a hard outer covering and a seed surrounded by sweetish edible flesh that when dried is firm and black; *also* : the tree bearing this fruit

litchi

li·ter *or* **li·tre** \ˈlēt-ər\ *n* : a metric unit of capacity equal to one cubic decimeter — see METRIC SYSTEM table

lit·er·a·cy \ˈlit-ə-rə-sē, ˈli-trə-sē\ *n* : the quality or state of being literate ⟨computer *literacy*⟩; *esp* : ability to read and write

lit·er·al \ˈlit-ə-rəl, ˈli-trəl\ *adj* **1 a** : following the ordinary or usual meaning of the words ⟨*literal* and figurative meanings⟩   **b** : true to fact : PLAIN, UNADORNED ⟨took the television drama to be the *literal* truth⟩   **c** : concerned mainly with facts ⟨a *literal*-minded person⟩   **2** : of, relating to, or expressed in letters ⟨*literal* equations⟩   **3** : done word for word : EXACT, VERBATIM ⟨a *literal* translation⟩ — **lit·er·al·ness** *n*

lit·er·al·ly \ˈlit-ər-(ə)lē, ˈli-trə-lē\ *adv* **1** : in a literal sense or manner : ACTUALLY ⟨the flying machine *literally* never got off the ground⟩   **2** : PRACTICALLY 2, VIRTUALLY ⟨*literally* poured out new ideas⟩

lit·er·ary \ˈlit-ə-ˌrer-ē\ *adj* **1 a** : of or relating to literature   **b** : BOOKISH 2   **2** : of or relating to writers or writing as a profession — **lit·er·ari·ly** \ˌlit-ə-ˈrer-ə-lē\ *adv* — **lit·er·ari·ness** \ˈlit-ə-ˌrer-ē-nəs\ *n*

¹lit·er·ate \ˈlit-ə-rət, ˈli-trət\ *adj* **1** : EDUCATED 1, CULTURED   **2** : able to read and write   **3** : having knowledge or experience in a particular area ⟨computer *literate*⟩ — **lit·er·ate·ly** *adv*

²literate *n* **1** : an educated person   **2** : a person who can read and write

lit·er·a·ture \ˈlit-ə-rə-ˌchu̇(ə)r, ˈli-trə-, -chər\ *n* **1** : written works having excellence of form or expression and ideas of lasting and widespread interest   **2** : written material (as of a period or on a subject)

-lith \ˌlith\ *n combining form* : structure or implement of stone [derived from Greek *lithos* "stone"]

lithe \ˈlīṯẖ, ˈlīth\ *adj* **1** : easily bent : FLEXIBLE ⟨long *lithe* stems⟩   **2** : light and graceful in movement ⟨*lithe* dancers⟩ — **lithe·ly** *adv* — **lithe·ness** *n*

lithe·some \ˈlīṯẖ-səm, ˈlīth-\ *adj* : LITHE 2

lith·i·um \ˈlith-ē-əm\ *n* : a soft silver-white element that is the lightest metal known — see ELEMENT table

litho- *combining form* : stone ⟨*litho*logy⟩ [derived from Greek *lithos* "stone"]

¹litho·graph \ˈlith-ə-ˌgraf\ *vb* : to print by lithography —

\ə\	abut	\au̇\	out	\i\	tip	\ȯ\	saw	\u̇\	foot
\ər\	further	\ch\	chin	\ī\	life	\ȯi\	coin	\y\	yet
\a\	mat	\e\	pet	\j\	job	\th\	thin	\yü\	few
\ā\	take	\ē\	easy	\ŋ\	sing	\ṯẖ\	this	\yu̇\	cure
\ä\	cot, cart	\g\	go	\ō\	bone	\ü\	food	\zh\	vision

litho·gra·pher \lith-'äg-rə-fər, 'lith-ə-,graf-ər\ *n*

²lithograph *n* : a print made by lithography — **litho·graph·ic** \,lith-ə-'graf-ik\ *adj* — **litho·graph·i·cal·ly** \-'graf-i-k(ə-)lē\ *adv*

li·thog·ra·phy \lith-'äg-rə-fē\ *n* : a method of printing from a flat surface (as a smooth stone or metal plate) that has been prepared in such a way that only the areas meant to print will take ink

li·thol·o·gy \lith-'äl-ə-jē\ *n* : the study of rocks

litho·sphere \'lith-ə-,sfi(ə)r\ *n* : the outer part of the solid earth

Lith·u·a·nian \,lith-(y)ə-'wā-nē-ən, -nyən\ *n* **1** : a person born or living in Lithuania **2** : the language of the Lithuanian people — **Lithuanian** *adj*

lit·i·gant \'lit-i-gənt\ *n* : a person taking part in a lawsuit

lit·i·gate \'lit-ə-,gāt\ *vb* **-gat·ed; -gat·ing** : to carry on a lawsuit — **lit·i·ga·tion** \,lit-ə-'gā-shən\ *n*

lit·mus paper \'lit-məs-\ *n* : paper treated with coloring matter that turns red in acid solutions and blue in alkaline solutions

litre *variant of* LITER

¹lit·ter \'lit-ər\ *n* **1 a** : a covered and curtained couch with poles to use for handles that is used for carrying a single passenger **b** : a device (as a stretcher) for carrying a sick or injured person **2** : material spread in areas where farm animals (as cows or chickens) are kept especially to absorb their urine and feces **3** : the young born to an animal at a single time **4** : a messy collection of things scattered about : RUBBISH

²litter *vb* **1** : to give birth to young **2 a** : to cover with litter **b** : to scatter about in disorder **c** : to lie about in disorder

lit·ter·bug \'lit-ər-,bəg\ *n* : a person who litters a public area

lit·ter·mate \-,māt\ *n* : one of a litter of offspring considered in relation to the other members of the litter

¹lit·tle \'lit-ⁿl\ *adj* **lit·tler** \'lit-ⁿl-ər, 'lit-lər\ *or* **less** \'les\ *or* **less·er** \'les-ər\; **lit·tlest** \'lit-ⁿl-əst, 'lit-ləst\ *or* **least** \'lēst\ **1 a** : small in size **b** : small in comparison with related forms ⟨*little* blue heron⟩ ⟨*little* celandine⟩ **c** : ¹NARROW 3, MEAN ⟨people with *little* minds⟩ **2 a** : small in quantity ⟨there was *little* food to feed them⟩ **b** : short in duration ⟨*little* time left⟩ **3** : small in importance ⟨life's *little* problems⟩ **4** : being younger ⟨my *little* brother⟩ — **lit·tle·ness** \'lit-ⁿl-nəs\ *n*

²little *adv* **less** \'les\; **least** \'lēst\ **1** : in a very small quantity or degree : SLIGHTLY ⟨had *little* more than we needed⟩ ⟨a *little* known fact⟩ **2** : not very often ⟨travels *little*⟩

³little *n* **1** : a small amount or quantity **2** : a short time or distance

Little Bear *n* : URSA MINOR

little by little *adv* : by small steps or amounts : GRADUALLY

Little Dipper *n* : DIPPER 3b

little finger *n* : the fourth finger of the hand counting the finger next to the thumb as one

¹lit·to·ral \'lit-ə-rəl; ,lit-ə-'ral, -'räl\ *adj* : of, relating to, or situated or growing on or near a shore (as of the sea)

²littoral *n* : a coastal region

lit·ur·gy \'lit-ər-jē\ *n, pl* **-gies** : a religious rite or body of rites — **li·tur·gi·cal** \lə-'tər-ji-kəl, li-\ *adj*

liv·able *also* **live·able** \'liv-ə-bəl\ *adj* : suitable for living in or with — **liv·able·ness** *n*

¹live \'liv\ *vb* **lived; liv·ing** **1 a** : to be alive **b** : to continue alive **2** : to keep oneself alive : SUBSIST ⟨*lived* on berries the whole time⟩ ⟨courtiers *living* off the king⟩ **3** : to have a home : DWELL ⟨*lives* next door⟩ **4** : to pass one's life ⟨*live* peacefully⟩ — **live it up** : to carry on an activity or one's life with great enthusiasm and excitement — **live up to** : to act in keeping with : KEEP ⟨*live up to* one's promises⟩

²live \'līv\ *adj* **1** : having life : LIVING **2 a** : burning usually without flame ⟨*live* coals⟩ **b** : carrying an electric current ⟨a *live* wire⟩ **c** : not exploded ⟨a *live* bomb⟩ **3** : of pres-

ent or continuing interest ⟨a *live* issue⟩ **4 a** : being present at the performance ⟨a *live* audience⟩ **b** : broadcast at the time of production ⟨a *live* television program⟩

live–bear·er \'līv-,bar-ər, -,ber-\ *n* : a fish that brings forth living young rather than eggs; *esp* : any of a family of numerous small fishes that feed at the surface of the water

-lived \'līvd, 'livd\ *adj combining form* : having a life of a specified kind or length ⟨long-*lived*⟩ [Middle English *-lived* "having life", from *lif* "life"]

live down *vb* : to live so as to wipe out the memory of ⟨*live down* a mistake⟩

live·li·hood \'līv-lē-,hůd\ *n* : ²LIVING 3

live·long \,liv-,lȯŋ\ *adj* : during the whole of : ENTIRE ⟨worked all the *livelong* day⟩

live·ly \'līv-lē\ *adj* **live·li·er; -est** **1** : full of life : ACTIVE ⟨a *lively* puppy⟩ **2** : ¹KEEN 3 ⟨a *lively* interest⟩ **3** : full of spirit or feeling ⟨a *lively* debate⟩ **4** : showing activity or spirit ⟨a *lively* manner⟩ — **live·li·ness** *n* — **lively** *adv*
syn LIVELY, ANIMATED, VIVACIOUS mean very much alive and spirited. LIVELY suggests briskness, alertness, or energy ⟨a *lively* kitten⟩ ANIMATED suggests great spirit and sparkle ⟨an *animated* discussion of current events⟩ VIVACIOUS suggests attractive cheerfulness and a quick wit ⟨a *vivacious* singer⟩

liv·en \'lī-vən\ *vb* **liv·ened; liv·en·ing** \'līv-(ə-)niŋ\ : to make or become lively — often used with *up*

live oak \'lī-,vōk\ *n* : any of several American oaks with evergreen leaves and hard durable wood; *esp* : one found in the southeastern states, cultivated for its shelter and shade, and formerly much used in building ships

live oak

¹liv·er \'liv-ər\ *n* **1 a** : a large glandular organ of vertebrates (as fishes and human beings) that secretes bile and causes changes in the blood (as by changing sugars into glycogen and by forming urea) **b** : any of various large probably digestive glands of invertebrate animals **2** : the tissue of the liver (as of a calf or pig) eaten as food

²liv·er \'liv-ər\ *n* : one that lives especially in a specified way

-liv·ered \'liv-ərd\ *adj combining form* : expressing courage or spirit that suggests a person having (such) a liver ⟨lily-*livered*⟩

liver fluke *n* : any of various trematode worms that invade the liver of mammals

liv·er·ied \'liv-(ə-)rēd\ *adj* : wearing a livery

liv·er·wort \'liv-ər-,wərt, -,wȯ(ə)rt\ *n* : any of a class of flowerless plants related to and resembling the mosses but differing especially in their reproduction and development

liv·er·wurst \'liv-ə(r)-,wərst, -,wů(ə)rst; 'livər-,wůst\ *n* : a sausage made chiefly of cooked liver

liv·ery \'liv-(ə-)rē\ *n, pl* **-er·ies** **1** : a special uniform worn by the servants of a wealthy household ⟨a footman in *livery*⟩ **2** : the clothing worn to distinguish an association of persons ⟨the *livery* of a school⟩ **3 a** : the feeding, care, and stabling of horses for pay **b** : the keeping of horses and vehicles for hire **c** : LIVERY STABLE

livery stable *n* : a stable where horses and vehicles are kept for hire and where horses may be stabled

lives *pl of* LIFE

live·stock \'līv-,stäk\ *n* : animals kept or raised; *esp* : farm animals kept for use and profit

live wire *n* : an alert active forceful person

liv·id \'liv-əd\ *adj* **1** : discolored by bruising **2** : pale as ashes ⟨*livid* with rage⟩ — **liv·id·ly** *adv*

¹liv·ing \'liv-iŋ\ *adj* **1 a** : not dead : ALIVE ⟨*living* authors⟩ **b** : ACTIVE 4b ⟨a *living* faith⟩ **2** : naturally giving life ⟨liv-

ing waters⟩   **3** : true to life ⟨the *living* image of your mother⟩

²living *n*   **1** : the condition of being alive   **2** : conduct or manner of life   **3** : what one has to have to meet one's needs ⟨earned a *living* as a cook⟩

living fossil *n* : an animal or plant (as the horseshoe crab or the ginkgo tree) that has remained almost unchanged from earlier geologic times and whose near relatives are nearly all extinct

living room *n* : a room in a house for general family use

liz·ard \'liz-ərd\ *n* : any of a group of reptiles that can be told apart from the related snakes by their lower jaw which has the two halves joined and inseparable, by their ears which are outside the body, by eyes with movable lids, and usually by two pairs of well-formed limbs which function in movement

'll \l, əl, ᵊl\ *vb* : WILL ⟨you'll be late⟩

lla·ma \'läm-ə\ *n* : any of several wild and domesticated South American hoofed mammals that chew the cud and are related to the camels but smaller and without a hump

lla·no \'län-ō, 'lan-\ *n, pl* **llanos** : an open grassy plain in Spanish America or the southwestern U.S.

lo \'lō\ *interj* — used to call attention or show wonder or surprise

'load \'lōd\ *n*   **1 a** : something taken up and carried   **b** : the amount that can be carried at one time ⟨10 *loads* of sand⟩ — often used in combination ⟨a boat*load* of tourists⟩   **2** : a mass or weight supported by something ⟨the *load* on a column⟩   **3** : something that depresses the mind or spirits ⟨a *load* of care⟩   **4** : a large quantity : LOT — usually used in pl. ⟨had *loads* of fun⟩   **5** : a charge for a firearm   **6 a** : amount of work done or expected to be done   **b** : the demand upon the ability of a system to produce what it is meant to produce ⟨the *load* on an engine⟩   **7** *slang* : a good look : a full view — used in the phrase *get a load of*

²load *vb*   **1 a** : to put a load in or on ⟨*load* a truck⟩ ⟨*load* a gun⟩ ⟨arms *loaded* with books⟩   **b** : to place a weight or burden on ⟨vines *loaded* down with grapes⟩ ⟨I'm *loaded* with work⟩   **c** : to supply abundantly ⟨*load* a person with honors⟩   **d** : to put runners on (first, second, and third base) in baseball ⟨the bases were *loaded*⟩   **e** : to fill with an often unfair appeal to the emotions ⟨*load* a question⟩ ⟨*loaded* words⟩   **f** : to put something like a load into ⟨*load* a camera with film⟩ ⟨*load* a disk drive⟩   **2 a** : to put or place in, on, or into something as or as if a load ⟨*load* wood on a truck⟩ ⟨*load* film into a camera⟩   **b** : to enter into a computer ⟨*load* a program⟩ — **load·er** *n*

load·ed \'lōd-əd\ *adj* **1** *slang* : ²DRUNK 1   **2** : WEALTHY 1, RICH

load line *n* : a line on a ship showing the depth to which it sinks in the water when properly loaded

loadstar *variant of* LODESTAR

loadstone *variant of* LODESTONE

'loaf \'lōf\ *n, pl* **loaves** \'lōvz\   **1** : a usually oblong mass of dough   **2** : a dish (as of meat) baked in the form of a loaf [Old English *hlāf* "loaf of bread" — related to LADY, LORD; see *Word Histories* at LADY, LORD]

²loaf *vb* : to spend time idly or lazily

loaf·er \'lō-fər\ *n* : a person who loafs

Loaf·er \'lō-fər\ *trademark* — used for a low shoe with no laces

loam \'lōm\ *n* : ³SOIL 2; *esp* : a soil consisting of a loose easily crumbled mixture of varying amounts of clay, silt, and sand — **loamy** \'lō-mē\ *adj*

'loan \'lōn\ *n*   **1** : money lent at interest   **2** : permission to use something for a time

²loan *vb* : LEND 1

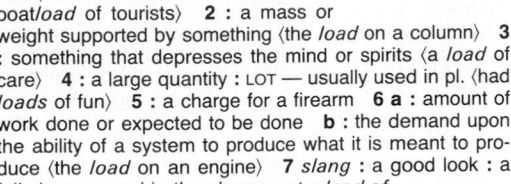

llama

loan shark *n* : a person who lends money at very high rates of interest

loan·word \'lōn-,wərd\ *n* : a word that is taken into one language from another

loath *or* **loth** \'lōth, 'lōth\ *adj* : unwilling to do something : RELUCTANT

loathe \'lōth\ *vb* **loathed; loath·ing** : to feel extreme disgust for or at ⟨*loathe* the smell of burning rubber⟩   **syn** see HATE

loath·ing \'lō-thiŋ\ *n* : very great dislike : extreme disgust

loath·some \'lōth-səm, 'lōth-\ *adj* : very unpleasant : OFFENSIVE — **loath·some·ly** *adv* — **loath·some·ness** *n*

'lob \'läb\ *vb* **lobbed; lob·bing** : to send (as a ball) in a high arc by hitting or throwing easily

²lob *n* : a lobbed throw or shot (as in tennis)

'lob·by \'läb-ē\ *n, pl* **lobbies**   **1** : a hall or entry especially when large enough to serve as a waiting room ⟨a hotel *lobby*⟩   **2** : a group of persons engaged in lobbying ⟨the oil *lobby*⟩

²lobby *vb* **lob·bied; lob·by·ing** : to try to influence public officials and especially members of a legislative body — **lob·by·ist** \'läb-ē-əst\ *n*

lobe \'lōb\ *n* : a curved or rounded part; *esp* : one that is part of a bodily organ or part — **lobed** \'lōbd\ *adj*

lobe–fin \'lōb-,fin\ *n* : LOBE-FINNED FISH — **lobe–finned** \-'find\ *adj*

lobe–finned fish *n* : any of a group of mostly extinct fishes that have paired fins suggesting limbs and may be closely related to or closely resemble the ancestors of the land-dwelling vertebrates

lo·be·lia \lō-'bēl-yə\ *n* : any of a genus of widely distributed herbs (as the cardinal flower) often grown for their clusters of showy flowers

lob·lol·ly pine \,läb-,läl-ē-\ *n* : a pine of the southern U.S. with thick flaky bark, long needles in groups of three, and spiny-tipped cones; *also* : its coarse-grained wood — called also *lob·lol·ly* \'läb-\

lob·ster \'läb-stər\ *n* : any of several large edible marine crustaceans with stalked eyes, a pair of large claws, and a long abdomen; *also* : SPINY LOBSTER

lobster pot *n* : a trap for catching lobsters

lobster

'lo·cal \'lō-kəl\ *adj*   **1** : of or relating to position in space   **2** : relating to a particular place ⟨*local* news⟩ ⟨a *local* custom⟩   **3** : serving the needs of a certain district ⟨*local* government⟩   **4** : involving or affecting only a small part of the body ⟨a *local* infection⟩ — **lo·cal·ly** \-kə-lē\ *adv*

²local *n*   **1** : a public vehicle (as a bus or train) that makes all of the stops or most of the stops along its route   **2** : a local branch (as of a lodge or labor union)

local color *n* : the presentation in a story or play of the peculiarities of a particular place and the people who live there

lo·cale \lō-'kal\ *n* : a place where something happens or is supposed to happen ⟨the *locale* of the accident⟩ ⟨the *locale* of a play⟩

lo·cal·ism \'lō-kə-,liz-əm\ *n* : a local peculiarity of speech or acting

lo·cal·i·ty \lō-'kal-ət-ē\ *n, pl* **-ties** : a place and its surroundings

\ə\ abut	\au̇\ out	\i\ tip	\o̅\ saw	\u̇\ foot
\ər\ further	\ch\ chin	\ī\ life	\o̅i\ coin	\y\ yet
\a\ mat	\e\ pet	\j\ job	\th\ thin	\yü\ few
\ā\ take	\ē\ easy	\ŋ\ sing	\t̲h̲\ this	\yu̇\ cure
\ä\ cot, cart	\g\ go	\ō\ bone	\ü\ food	\zh\ vision

lo·cal·ize \'lō-kə-,līz\ *vb* **-ized; -iz·ing** **1** : to assign to or keep in a definite place or locality **2** : to be restricted to or accumulate in a limited area ⟨pain *localized* in a joint⟩ — **lo·cal·iza·tion** \,lō-kə-lə-'zā-shən\ *n*

lo·cate \'lō-,kāt, lō-'kāt\ *vb* **lo·cat·ed; lo·cat·ing** **1** : to set oneself or one's business up in a particular place **2** : to state and fix exactly the place, limits, or position of ⟨*locate* property lines⟩ ⟨*locate* point B⟩ **3 a** : to look for and find the position ⟨trying to *locate* the problem with the engine⟩ **b** : to find or fix the place of in a series ⟨*locate* an event in history⟩

lo·ca·tion \lō-'kā-shən\ *n* **1 a** : a place fit for or having some particular use ⟨a lovely *location* for a house⟩ ⟨each *location* in a computer memory has its own address⟩ **b** : a place outside a studio where a motion picture is filmed ⟨on *location* in the desert⟩ **2** : the act or process of locating

lo·ca·tor *also* **lo·cat·er** \'lō-,kāt-ər, lō-'kāt-\ *n* : one (as a person or device) that locates something

loch \'läk, 'läḵ\ *n* **1** *Scottish* : LAKE **2** *Scottish* : an arm of the sea especially when it is nearly surrounded by land

loci *pl of* LOCUS

¹lock \'läk\ *n* : a small bunch of hair or fiber (as cotton or wool) [Old English *locc* "small bunch of hair"]

²lock *n* **1 a** : a fastening (as for a door) in which a bolt is operated (as by a key) **b** : a device for exploding the charge or cartridge of a firearm **2** : an enclosure (as in a canal) with gates at each end used in raising or lowering boats as they pass from level to level **3** : a wrestling hold that prevents any movement of the part of the body that is being held ⟨a leg *lock*⟩ [Old English *loc* "fastener"]

³lock *vb* **1** : to fasten with or as if with a lock ⟨*lock* up the house⟩ ⟨the door *locks* from the inside⟩ **2 a** : to shut in or out or make secure by or as if by means of a lock ⟨*locked* up my bike⟩ ⟨*locked* in jail⟩ **b** : to make or become fast or motionless ⟨pump the brake pedal to keep the wheels from *locking*⟩ **3** : to make fast by the linking of parts together ⟨*lock* arms⟩

lock·er \'läk-ər\ *n* : a cabinet, compartment, or chest for personal use or for storing food at a low temperature

locker room *n* : a room for changing clothes and for storing clothes and equipment in lockers

lock·et \'läk-ət\ *n* : a small ornamental case usually worn on a chain

lock·jaw \'läk-,jȯ\ *n* : a symptom of tetanus marked by spasms of the jaw muscles and inability to open the jaws; *also* : TETANUS 1

lock·out \-,aút\ *n* : the stopping of work or closing of a plant by an employer during a labor dispute in order to make the employees come to terms

lock·smith \-,smith\ *n* : a worker who makes or repairs locks

lock·step \-,step\ *n* : a way of marching in step in which the marchers are very close one behind the other

lock·stitch \-,stich\ *n* : a sewing machine stitch in which a thread on the bottom of the material is looped over a thread pushed through from the top and then both are pulled tight

lock·up \-,əp\ *n* : PRISON 2, JAIL

lo·co \'lō-kō\ *adj, slang* : not sane : CRAZY

lo·co·mo·tion \,lō-kə-'mō-shən\ *n* : the act or power of moving from place to place

¹lo·co·mo·tive \,lō-kə-'mōt-iv\ *adj* **1** : of or relating to locomotion **2** : of, relating to, or being a locomotive

²locomotive *n* : an engine that moves under its own power; *esp* : one that hauls cars on a railroad

lo·co·mo·tor \,lō-kə-'mōt-ər\ *adj* : of, relating to, or used in locomotion

lo·co·weed \'lō-kō-,wēd\ *n* : any of several plants of the legume family that occur in western North America and cause poisoning in livestock

lo·cus \'lō-kəs\ *n, pl* **lo·ci** \'lō-,sī, -,kī, -,kē\ **1** : ¹PLACE

3a, LOCALITY **2** : the set of all points whose location is fixed by stated conditions

lo·cust \'lō-kəst\ *n* **1 a** : SHORT-HORNED GRASSHOP-PER; *esp* : a grasshopper that often migrates in vast swarms and eats up the plants in its course **b** : CICADA **2 a** : any of various trees of the legume family with hard wood **b** : the wood of a locust

lo·cu·tion \lō-'kyü-shən\ *n* **1** : a particular form of expression ⟨complicated *locutions* in legal documents⟩ **2** : style of expression or speaking

locoweed

lode \'lōd\ *n* **1** : a mass or strip of a mineral (as gold or copper ore) that fills a crack in rock **2** : a mass of ore in the earth or among rocks

lode·star *or* **load·star** \'lōd-,stär\ *n* : a star that leads or guides; *esp* : NORTH STAR

lode·stone *or* **load·stone** \'lōd-,stōn\ *n* **1** : a rock having magnetic properties **2** : something that strongly attracts

¹lodge \'läj\ *vb* **lodged; lodg·ing** **1 a** : to provide or serve as especially temporary quarters for ⟨*lodged* their guests overnight⟩ **b** : to establish or settle oneself in a place **c** : to settle or live in as a residence **d** : to rent lodgings **2** : to serve as a receptacle for : CONTAIN **3** : to bring or come to a rest and remain ⟨the bone *lodged* in my throat⟩ ⟨the bullet *lodged* in a tree⟩ **4** : to lay before a proper authority : FILE ⟨*lodge* a complaint⟩

²lodge *n* **1 a** : a house set apart for residence in a special season ⟨hunting *lodge*⟩ **b** : a resort hotel ⟨ski *lodge*⟩ **c** : a house for an employee on an estate ⟨gamekeeper's *lodge*⟩ **2** : a den or lair of wild animals **3** : the meeting place of a branch (as of a fraternal organization); *also* : the members of such a branch **4 a** : WIGWAM **b** : a family of North American Indians

lodge·pole pine \,läj-,pōl-\ *n* : either of two western North American pines with needles in pairs and short cones

lodg·er \'läj-ər\ *n* : one that lodges; *esp* : one that occupies a rented room in another's house

lodg·ing \'läj-iŋ\ *n* **1** : DWELLING; *esp* : a temporary dwelling or sleeping place **2** : a room or suite of rooms in another's house rented as a dwelling — usually used in pl.

lodging house *n* : ROOMING HOUSE

lodg·ment *or* **lodge·ment** \'läj-mənt\ *n* **1 a** : a lodging place : SHELTER **b** : LODGING 2 **2** : the act, fact, or manner of lodging; *esp* : a placing, depositing, or coming to rest **3** : an accumulation of something deposited in a place ⟨a *lodgment* of leaves in a gutter⟩

loess \'les, 'lə(r)s, 'lō-əs\ *n* : a fine usually yellowish brown soil found in North America, Europe, and Asia and believed to be chiefly deposited by the wind

¹loft \'lȯft\ *n* **1** : ATTIC **2 a** : a gallery in a church or hall ⟨organ *loft*⟩ **b** : an upper floor of a warehouse or business building when not partitioned **c** : HAYLOFT **3** : the backward slant of the face of a golf-club head

²loft *vb* **1** : to place, house, or store in a loft **2** : to strike or throw a ball so that it rises high in the air ⟨*lofted* a high fly to center field⟩

lofty \'lȯf-tē\ *adj* **loft·i·er; -est** **1** : PROUD 1a, HAUGHTY ⟨a *lofty* air⟩ **2 a** : of high, noble, or excellent quality ⟨*lofty* ideals⟩ **b** : of high rank : SUPERIOR **3** : rising to a great height ⟨*lofty* redwood trees⟩ **syn** see HIGH — **loft·i·ly** \-tə-lē\ *adv* — **loft·i·ness** \-tē-nəs\ *n*

¹log \'lȯg, 'läg\ *n* **1** : a large piece of rough timber; *esp* : a long piece of a tree trunk trimmed and ready for sawing **2** : a device for measuring the speed of a ship **3 a** : the daily record of a ship's speed and progress **b** : the full record of a ship's voyage or of an aircraft's flight **4 a** : a record of how something (as a piece of equipment) works in actual use   **b** : a record of work done (as the flying time of a pilot)

²log *vb* **logged; log·ging**   **1** : to cut trees for lumber or to clear land of trees in lumbering   **2** : to put details of or about in a log   **3 a** : to move a distance or reach a speed as noted in a log   **b** : to sail a ship or fly an aircraft for an indicated distance or time ⟨the pilot *logged* thousands of miles and hundreds of hours⟩

³log *n* : LOGARITHM

lo·gan·ber·ry \'lō-gən-,ber-ē\ *n* : a blackberry that grows upright and produces red fruit; *also* : its berry

log·a·rithm \'lòg-ə-,rith-əm, 'läg-\ *n* : the exponent that indicates the power to which a number is raised to produce a given number ⟨the *logarithm* of 100 to the base 10 is 2⟩ — **log·a·rith·mic** \,lòg-ə-'rith-mik, ,läg-\ *adj*

log·book \'lòg-,bùk, 'läg-\ *n* : ¹LOG 3, 4

loge \'lōzh\ *n*   **1** : a box in a theater   **2** : the forward section of a theater mezzanine

log·ger \'lòg-ər, 'läg-\ *n* : one whose work is logging

log·ger·head \'lòg-ər-,hed, 'läg-\ *n* : any of various very large turtles; *esp* : a flesh-eating sea turtle of the warmer parts of the western Atlantic — **at loggerheads** : in or into a state of quarrelsome disagreement

loggerhead

log·ic \'läj-ik\ *n*   **1** : the study of the rules and tests of sound reasoning   **2** : REASONING 1; *esp* : sound reasoning ⟨no *logic* in that remark⟩   **3** : connection (as of facts or events) in a way that seems reasonable ⟨the *logic* of a situation⟩   **4** : the arrangement of circuit elements (as in a computer) needed for computation

log·i·cal \'läj-i-kəl\ *adj*   **1** : of or relating to logic : used in logic   **2** : according to the rules of logic ⟨a *logical* argument⟩   **3** : skilled in logic ⟨a *logical* thinker⟩   **4** : being in agreement with what may be reasonably expected ⟨a *logical* result of an action⟩ — **log·i·cal·ly** \-k(ə-)lē\ *adv* — **log·i·cal·ness** \-kəl-nəs\ *n*

lo·gi·cian \lō-'jish-ən\ *n* : a person who is skilled in logic

lo·gis·tics \lō-'jis-tiks\ *n sing or pl* : a branch of military science that deals with the transportation, housing, and supplying of troops — **lo·gis·tic** \-tik\ *or* **lo·gis·ti·cal** \-ti-kəl\ *adj*

logo \'lō-gō; 'lòg-ō, 'läg-\ *n, pl* **log·os** \-gōz, -ōz\ : an identifying symbol or motto ⟨T-shirts with company *logos*⟩

LO·GO *or* **Lo·go** \'lō-gō\ *n* : a simplified language for programming and communicating with a computer that uses drawing on a display screen as a tool for teaching programming principles

log·roll·ing \'lòg-,rō-liŋ, 'läg-\ *n*   **1** : the rolling of logs in water by treading   **2** : the trading of votes by two legislators to secure favorable action on projects of interest to each

log·wood \'lòg-,wùd, 'läg-\ *n* : a Central American and West Indian tree of the legume family that has hard brown or brownish red heartwood used in dyeing; *also* : the heartwood or a preparation made from it

lo·gy \'lō-gē\ *adj* **lo·gi·er; -est** : SLUGGISH, TIRED — **lo·gi·ness** \-gē-nəs\ *n*

-l·o·gy \-ə-jē\ *n combining form* : doctrine : theory : science ⟨bio*logy*⟩ [derived from Greek *logos* "word"]

loin \'lòin\ *n*   **1 a** : the part of the body on each side of the spinal column between the hip and the lower ribs   **b** : a cut of meat (as beef) from the loin of an animal   **2** *pl* **a** : the pubic region   **b** : the organs of reproduction

loin·cloth \-,klòth\ *n* : a cloth worn as a garment about the loins

loi·ter \'lòit-ər\ *vb*   **1** : to interrupt or delay an errand or a journey with pointless stops   **2 a** : to remain in an area for no good reason   **b** : to lag behind   **syn** see LINGER — **loi·ter·er** *n*

loll \'läl\ *vb*   **1** : to hang or let hang loosely : DROOP   **2** : to recline, lean, or move in a loose or lazy manner : LOUNGE ⟨*loll* around in the sun⟩

lol·li·pop *or* **lol·ly·pop** \'läl-i-,päp\ *n* : a lump of hard candy on the end of a stick

lone \'lōn\ *adj*   **1** : having no company : SOLITARY ⟨a *lone* traveler⟩   **2** : situated by itself ⟨a *lone* outpost⟩

lone·ly \'lōn-lē\ *adj* **lone·li·er; -est**   **1** : LONE 1   **2** : not visited by human beings : DESOLATE ⟨a *lonely* spot⟩   **3** : LONESOME 1 ⟨feeling *lonely*⟩ — **lone·li·ness** *n*

lon·er \'lō-nər\ *n* : one that avoids others; *esp* : INDIVIDUALIST 1

lone·some \'lōn(t)-səm\ *adj*   **1** : sad from lack of companionship or separation from others   **2** : not often visited or traveled over ⟨a *lonesome* highway⟩ ⟨the *lonesome* frontier⟩ — **lone·some·ness** *n*

lone wolf *n* : a person who prefers to act, live, or work alone : LONER

¹long \'lòŋ\ *adj* **lon·ger** \'lòŋ-gər\; **lon·gest** \'lòŋ-gəst\   **1** : of great extent from end to end : not short   **2 a** : having a specified length ⟨a meter *long*⟩   **b** : forming the chief linear dimension ⟨the *long* side of the table⟩   **3** : lasting for a considerable or specified time ⟨a *long* friendship⟩   **4** : overly long   **5** : containing many or a specified number of units ⟨a *long* series of wins⟩   **6** : being a syllable or speech sound of relatively great duration   **7** : extending far into the future ⟨take a *long* view of things⟩   **8** : strong in or well supplied with something ⟨*long* on golf⟩ ⟨*long* on wisdom⟩ [Old English *long, lang* "extending a great distance"] — **at long last** : after a long wait : FINALLY

²long *adv*   **1** : for or during a long time   **2** : for the length of a specified period ⟨all summer *long*⟩   **3** : at a distant point of time ⟨*long* before we arrived⟩ — **as long as** *or* **so long as**   **1** : in view of the fact that : SINCE   **2** : provided that : IF — **so long** : GOOD-BYE

³long *vb* **longed; long·ing** \'lòŋ-iŋ\ : to feel a strong desire or wish [Old English *langian* "to feel a strong desire for something"]   **syn** see YEARN

long·boat \'lòŋ-,bōt\ *n* : a large boat carried on a ship

long bone *n* : one of the bones supporting a limb of a vertebrate and consisting of a long nearly cylinder-shaped shaft that contains marrow and has enlarged ends

long·bow \'lòŋ-,bō\ *n* : a wooden bow drawn by hand and usually about 1¾ meters long

¹long–dis·tance \-'dis-tən(t)s\ *adj* : of or relating to telephone communication with a distant point

²long–distance *adv* : by long-distance telephone

long distance *n*   **1** : communication by long-distance telephone   **2** : a telephone operator or exchange that gives long-distance connections

long division *n* : arithmetical division in which the several steps corresponding to the division of parts of the dividend by the divisor are shown in detail

lon·gev·i·ty \län-'jev-ət-ē, lòn-\ *n*   **1** : long life   **2** : length of life

long·hand \'lòŋ-,hand\ *n* : the characters or words written out fully by hand

long·horn \-,hò(ə)rn\ *n* : any of the cattle with long horns that were formerly common in the southwestern U.S.

long–horned grasshopper \-,lòŋ-,hòrn(d)-\ *n* : any of various grasshoppers that have very long antennae

long·house \-,haus\ *n* : a long dwelling especially of the Iroquois for several families

\ə\ abut	\au̇\ out	\i\ tip	\ȯ\ saw	\u̇\ foot
\ər\ further	\ch\ chin	\ī\ life	\ȯi\ coin	\y\ yet
\a\ mat	\e\ pet	\j\ job	\th\ thin	\yü\ few
\ā\ take	\ē\ easy	\ŋ\ sing	\t͟h\ this	\yu̇\ cure
\ä\ cot, cart	\g\ go	\ō\ bone	\ü\ food	\zh\ vision

long hundredweight *n* : HUNDREDWEIGHT 2

long·ing \'lȯṅ-iṅ\ *n* : an eager desire : CRAVING — **long-ing·ly** \-iṅ-lē\ *adv*

long·ish \'lȯṅ-ish\ *adj* : somewhat long

lon·gi·tude \'län-jə-,t(y)üd\ *n* : distance measured by degrees or time east or west from the prime meridian ⟨the *longitude* of New York is 74 degrees or about five hours west of Greenwich⟩

lon·gi·tu·di·nal \,län-jə-'t(y)üd-nəl, -ᵊn-əl\ *adj* **1** : of or relating to length **2** : placed or running lengthwise — **lon·gi·tu·di·nal·ly** \-ē\ *adv*

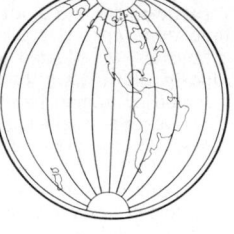

longitude: hemisphere marked with meridians of longitude

long johns \'lȯṅ-,jänz\ *n pl* : long underwear

long jump *n* : a jump for distance in track-and-field competition — **long jumper** *n*

long·leaf pine \,lȯṅ-,lēf-\ *n* : a large pine of the southern U.S. that has clusters of very long dark green needles and long cones and is a major timber tree; *also* : its tough coarse-grained wood

long–leaved pine \,lȯṅ-,lēv(d)-\ *n* : LONGLEAF PINE

long–lived \'lȯṅ-'līvd, -'livd\ *adj* : living or lasting long

long–play·ing \'lȯṅ-'plā-iṅ\ *adj* : of, relating to, or being a phonograph record designed to be played at 33⅓ revolutions per minute

long–range \-'rānj\ *adj* **1** : capable of traveling or shooting over great distances ⟨a *long-range* gun⟩ **2** : LONG-TERM ⟨*long-range* planning⟩

long·shore·man \'lȯṅ-'shōr-mən, -'shȯr-\ *n* : one who loads and unloads ships at a port : STEVEDORE

long shot \'lȯṅ-,shät\ *n* : an entry (as in a horse race) given little chance of winning

long–suf·fer·ing \-'səf(-ə)-riṅ\ *n* : long and patient bearing of hardship — **long–suffering** *adj*

long–term \-'tərm\ *adj* : extending over or involving a long period of time

long–wind·ed \'lȯṅ-'win-dəd\ *adj* : boringly long in speaking or writing — **long–wind·ed·ly** *adv* — **long–wind·ed·ness** *n*

¹look \'lu̇k\ *vb* **1** : to exercise the power of vision : SEE **2** : to express by the eyes or by an expression of the face **3 a** : to have an appearance that is suitable for ⟨*looks* her age⟩ **b** : SEEM 1 ⟨it *looks* dangerous⟩ **4** : to direct one's attention or eyes ⟨*look* in the mirror⟩ **5** : ²POINT 4, FACE ⟨the house *looks* east⟩ — **look after** : to attend to — **look daggers** : to look threateningly — **look down on** : to treat as an inferior : DISDAIN — **look for 1** : EXPECT 2 **2** : to search for : SEEK — **look forward to** : to expect with pleasure — **look into** : to examine carefully — **look on** *or* **look upon** : CONSIDER 3, REGARD ⟨*looked upon* me as a friend⟩ — **look out for 1** : to be on guard against ⟨*look out for* the trains⟩ **2** : to care for : PROTECT ⟨*look out for* our interests⟩ — **look to 1** : to direct one's attention to **2** : to take care of **3** : to rely on

²look *n* **1 a** : the action of looking **b** : ²GLANCE 3 **2 a** : the expression of the face **b** : physical appearance; *esp* : attractive physical appearance — usually used in pl. **3** : the state or form in which something appears : ASPECT

look·er–on \,lu̇k-ə-'rȯn, -'rän\ *n, pl* **lookers–on** : SPECTATOR, ONLOOKER

looking glass *n* : ¹MIRROR 1

look·out \'lu̇k-,au̇t\ *n* **1** : a person who keeps watch **2** : a high place or structure from which a wide view is possible **3** : a careful looking or watching **4** : OUTLOOK 1b **5** : a matter of care or concern ⟨the plants are wilting, but that's not my *lookout*⟩

look over *vb* : to inspect or examine usually in a hurried or shallow way

look up *vb* : to seek for or out ⟨*look up* a word in the dictionary⟩ ⟨*look up* a friend⟩

¹loom \'lüm\ *n* : a frame or machine for weaving threads or yarns to produce cloth

²loom *vb* **1** : to appear suddenly and often with a large, dim, or strange form ⟨*loomed* out of the fog⟩ **2** : to be about to happen

loon \'lün\ *n* : any of several diving birds that eat fish and have webbed feet, a black head, and a black back spotted with white

loon

loo·ny *or* **loo·ney** \'lü-nē\ *adj* **loo·ni·er; -est** : CRAZY, FOOLISH [an altered form of *lunatic* (adjective)] — **loony** *n*

¹loop \'lüp\ *n* **1** : a fold or doubling of a line through which another line can be passed or into which a hook may be hooked **2** : a loop-shaped ornament, figure, bend, course, or device ⟨a *loop* in a river⟩ **3** : a circular airplane maneuver involving flying upside down **4** : a complete electric circuit **5** : a piece of motion-picture film or magnetic tape whose ends are joined together to project or play back the same things continuously **6** : a series of instructions (as for a computer) that is repeated usually until a requirement for ending is met — **for a loop** : into a state of amazement, confusion, or distress ⟨the news knocked me *for a loop*⟩

²loop *vb* **1** : to make or form a loop **2 a** : to make a loop in, on, or about **b** : to fasten with a loop **3** : to perform a loop in an airplane

loop·er \'lü-pər\ *n* **1** : any of numerous small caterpillars that are mostly larvae of moths, move with a looping movement, and have little or no hair — called also *inchworm, measuring worm* **2** : one that loops

loop·hole \'lüp-,hōl\ *n* **1** : a small opening; *esp* : one in a wall through which firearms may be discharged **2** : a way of escaping something; *esp* : a way of avoiding a law or regulation

¹loose \'lüs\ *adj* **loos·er; loos·est** **1 a** : not firmly fastened or securely attached **b** : no longer attached ⟨a boat *loose* from its moorings⟩ **c** : not tight-fitting **2 a** : not shut in, tied up, or held back ⟨a lion *loose* in the streets⟩ **b** : not brought together in a bundle, container, or binding ⟨*loose* sheets of pages⟩ **3** : not dense or compact ⟨*loose* dirt⟩ ⟨cloth of *loose* weave⟩ **4** : not respectable : IMMORAL ⟨*loose* conduct⟩ **5** : not tightly drawn or stretched : SLACK **6** : not exact or careful ⟨a *loose* guess⟩ — **loose** *adv* — **loose·ly** *adv* — **loose·ness** *n*

²loose *vb* **loosed; loos·ing** **1** : LOOSEN 1 **2** : ¹SHOOT 1, FIRE ⟨*loose* a volley⟩

loose–joint·ed \'lüs-'jȯint-əd\ *adj* : moving with unusual freedom or ease

loose–leaf \'lü-'slēf\ *adj* : designed so that sheets (as of paper) can be removed or inserted by opening a locking device ⟨*loose-leaf* notebook⟩

loos·en \'lüs-ᵊn\ *vb* **loos·ened; loos·en·ing** \'lüs-niṅ, -ᵊn-iṅ\ **1** : to set free **2** : to make or become loose or looser **3** : to cause or permit to become less strict

loose·strife \'lü(s)-,strīf\ *n* **1** : any of a genus of plants that are related to the primrose and have leafy stems and yellow or white flowers **2** : any of a genus of herbs including some with showy spikes of purple flowers

¹loot \'lüt\ *n* : something stolen or taken by force

²loot *vb* : PLUNDER, STEAL — **loot·er** *n*

lop \'läp\ *vb* **lopped; lop·ping** **1** : to cut branches or twigs from a tree **2** : to remove unnecessary or undesirable parts from something — usually used with *off* — **lop·per** *n*

lope \'lōp\ *n* : an easy leaping way of moving — **lope** *vb* — **lop·er** *n*

lop–eared \'läp-ˌi(ə)rd\ *adj* : having ears that droop

lop·sid·ed \'läp-ˌsīd-əd\ *adj* : leaning to one side : UNBALANCED — **lop·sid·ed·ness** *n*

lo·qua·cious \lō-'kwā-shəs\ *adj* : very talkative **syn** see TALKATIVE — **lo·qua·cious·ly** *adv* — **lo·qua·cious·ness** *n* — **lo·quac·i·ty** \-'kwas-ət-ē\ *n*

¹lord \'lò(ə)rd\ *n* **1 a** : a person who has power and authority; *esp* : a ruler to whom service and obedience are due **b** : a person from whom a feudal estate is held **2** *cap* **a** : GOD 1 **b** : JESUS **3** : a man of rank or high position: as **a** : a feudal tenant holding his estate directly from the king **b** : a British nobleman or a bishop entitled to sit in the House of Lords — used as a title **c** *pl, cap* : HOUSE OF LORDS

> **Word History** The word *lord* comes from the Old English word *hlāford.* This word was formed from the words *hlāf,* meaning "loaf of bread", and *weard,* meaning "keeper, guard". This "bread keeper", however, actually had no more to do with bread than our modern "breadwinner". The hlāford was much more important than his title suggests. He was the head of a great household and had power and authority over many people. The related word *lady* developed in much the same way. [Old English *hlāford* "lord", literally "bread keeper", from *hlāf* "loaf of bread" and *weard* "keeper, guard" — related to LADY, LOAF; see *Word History* at LADY]

²lord *vb* : to act as if having the rank or power of a lord : DOMINEER — used with *it* ⟨*lording* it over her younger brothers⟩

lord·ly \'lò(ə)rd-lē\ *adj* **lord·li·er; -est 1** : of, relating to, or having the characteristics of a lord : NOBLE **2** : PROUD 1a, HAUGHTY — **lord·li·ness** *n* — **lordly** *adv*

lor·do·sis \lòr-'dō-səs\ *n* : abnormal curving of the spine forward

lord·ship \'lò(ə)rd-ˌship\ *n* **1** : the rank or dignity of a lord — used as a title ⟨his *lordship* is not at home⟩ **2** : the authority, power, or territory of a lord

Lord's Prayer *n* : the prayer in Matthew 6 : 9–13 that Jesus taught his disciples

Lord's Supper *n* : COMMUNION 1a

lore \'lō(ə)r, 'lò(ə)r\ *n* : KNOWLEDGE 1; *esp* : a particular body of knowledge or tradition ⟨forest *lore*⟩

lo·ris \'lōr-əs, 'lòr-\ *n* : either of two small slow-moving lemurs that are active at night

lorn \'lòr(ə)rn\ *adj* : having been abandoned or forsaken

lor·ry \ \'lòr-ē, 'lär-\ *n, pl* **lorries** *chiefly British* : a large open truck

lose \'lüz\ *vb* **lost** \'lòst\; **los·ing** \'lü-ziŋ\ **1** : ²RUIN 1, DESTROY ⟨ship was *lost* on the reef⟩ **2** : to be unable to find or have at hand : MISLAY ⟨*lose* a billfold⟩ **3** : to become deprived of especially accidentally or by death ⟨*lose* his eyesight⟩ ⟨*lost* her son by drowning⟩ **4 a** : to fail to use to advantage : WASTE **b** : to fail to win, gain, or obtain ⟨*lose* a contest⟩ **c** : to fail to catch with the senses or the mind ⟨*lost* part of what was said⟩ **5** : to cause the loss of ⟨one careless statement *lost* her the election⟩ **6** : to fail to keep, sustain, or maintain ⟨*lost* his balance⟩ **7 a** : to miss or cause to miss one's way or bearings ⟨*lost* herself in the woods⟩ **b** : to make uncon-

loris

scious ⟨*lost* himself in daydreams⟩ **8** : to leave behind by going faster or farther ⟨*lost* their pursuers⟩ **9** : to free oneself from : get rid of ⟨dieting to *lose* some weight⟩ — **los·er** *n* — **lose ground** : to fail to advance or improve — **lose one's heart** : to fall in love

loss \'lòs\ *n* **1 a** : the act or an instance of losing ⟨the *loss* of a ship⟩ **b** : the harm or distress resulting from losing ⟨her death was a *loss* to the community⟩ **2 a** : a person, thing, or amount lost **b** *pl* : killed, wounded, or captured soldiers **3** : failure to gain, win, obtain or use; *esp* : an amount by which the cost of an article is above the selling price **4** : decrease in amount, size, or degree

lost \'lòst\ *adj* **1** : not used, won, or claimed ⟨*lost* opportunities⟩ **2** : no longer possessed or known ⟨a long *lost* uncle⟩ **3** : ruined or destroyed physically or morally **4** : unable to find the way ⟨a *lost* puppy⟩ **5** : having the mind absorbed and not aware of surroundings ⟨*lost* in daydreams⟩

lot \'lät\ *n* **1** : an object used as a counter in determining a question by chance **2 a** : the use of lots as a means of deciding something ⟨choose by *lot*⟩ **b** : the choice resulting from deciding by lot **3 a** : something that comes to one by or as if by lot **b** : one's course in life especially as decided by chance **4 a** : a piece or plot of land ⟨owns the corner *lot*⟩ ⟨a building *lot*⟩ **b** : a motion-picture studio and its surrounding property **5** : a number of articles offered (as at an auction) for sale as one item **6** : a number of associated persons : SET ⟨the *lot* that hangs around the arcade⟩ **7** : a large amount, quantity, or number ⟨a *lot* of space⟩ ⟨a *lot* of books⟩ ⟨*lots* of food⟩ ⟨had been there *lots* of times⟩ **syn** see DESTINY

loth *variant of* LOATH

lo·tion \'lō-shən\ *n* : a liquid preparation for use as a cosmetic or as a medicine on the outside of the body [from Latin *lotion-, lotio* "act of washing", from *lotus,* past participle of *lavare* "to wash" — related to LAUNDRY, LAVATORY, LAVISH]

lots \'läts\ *adv* : MUCH ⟨feeling *lots* better⟩

lot·tery \'lät-ə-rē, 'lä-trē\ *n, pl* **-ter·ies** : a drawing of lots in which prizes are given to the winning names or numbers

lo·tus \'lōt-əs\ *n* : any of various water lilies including several represented in ancient Egyptian and Hindu art

loud \'laud\ *adj* **1 a** : marked by a high volume of sound **b** : producing a loud sound **2** : NOISY 1 **3** : unpleasantly bold or bright in color or pattern ⟨a *loud* plaid⟩ — **loud** *adv* — **loud·ly** *adv* — **loud·ness** *n*

lotus

loud·mouth \-ˌmauth\ *n* : a person given to loud unpleasant talk — **loud·mouthed** \-'mauthd, -'mautht\ *adj*

loud·speak·er \-'spē-kər\ *n* : a device that changes electrical signals into sound

¹lounge \'launj\ *vb* **lounged; loung·ing 1** : to move or act in a lazy, slow, or tired way : LOAF **2** : to stand, sit, or lie in a lazy relaxed manner — **loung·er** *n*

²lounge *n* **1 a** : a room with comfortable furniture for lounging **b** : a room in a public building or vehicle furnished for lounging and often with toilets and smoking facilities **2** : a long couch

lour, louring *variant of* ¹LOWER, ²LOWER, LOWERING

\ə\ abut		\au̇\ out	\i\ tip		\ȯ\ saw		\u̇\ foot
\ər\ further		\ch\ chin	\ī\ life		\ȯi\ coin		\y\ yet
\a\ mat		\e\ pet	\j\ job		\th\ thin		\yü\ few
\ā\ take		\ē\ easy	\ŋ\ sing		\th\ this		\yu̇\ cure
\ä\ cot, cart		\g\ go	\ō\ bone		\ü\ food		\zh\ vision

louse \'laůs\ *n* **1** *pl* **lice** \'līs\ **a** : any of various small wingless usually flat insects that live as parasites on the bodies of warm-blooded animals **b** : any of several small arthropods (as a book louse or wood louse) that are not parasites **2** *pl* **lous·es** \'laů-səz\ : a mean person

louse up \('))laů-'səp\ *vb* : BUNGLE

lousy \'laů-zē\ *adj* **lous·i·er; -est 1** : infested with lice **2 a** : totally disgusting : CONTEMPTIBLE **b** : of very poor quality **c** : well supplied ⟨*lousy* with money⟩ — **lous·i·ness** \-zē-nəs\ *n*

lout \'laůt\ *n* : a stupid, rude, or awkward person — **lout·ish** \-ish\ *adj* — **lout·ish·ly** *adv* — **lout·ish·ness** *n*

lou·ver *or* **lou·vre** \'lü-vər\ *n* **1** : an opening provided with one or more slanted strips to allow flow of air or light but to exclude rain or sun or to provide privacy **2** : one of the slanted strips of a louver — **lou·vered** \-vərd\ *adj*

lov·able \'ləv-ə-bəl\ *adj* : having qualities that tend to make one loved — **lov·able·ness** *n* — **lov·ably** \-blē\ *adv*

¹love \'ləv\ *n* **1** : a quality or feeling of strong or constant affection for and dedication to another ⟨motherly *love*⟩ **2 a** : attraction based on sexual desire : the strong affection and tenderness felt by lovers **b** : a beloved person : DARLING **3 a** : warm attachment, enthusiasm, or devotion ⟨*love* of the sea⟩ **b** : the object of attachment or devotion **4** : a score of zero in tennis — **in love** : feeling love for and devotion toward someone

²love *vb* **loved; lov·ing 1** : to hold dear : CHERISH **2 a** : to feel a lover's passion, devotion, or tenderness for **b** : to touch or stroke lightly **3** : to like or desire actively : take pleasure in ⟨*loved* to play the violin⟩ **4** : to grow well in ⟨the rose *loves* sunlight⟩

love affair *n* : a romantic relationship or incident between lovers

love·bird \'ləv-,bərd\ *n* : any of various small usually gray or green parrots that are noted for the expression of caring behavior for their mates

love knot *n* : a decorative knot sometimes used as an emblem of love

love·lorn \'ləv-,lȯ(ə)rn\ *adj* : deserted by one's lover

love·ly \'ləv-lē\ *adj* **love·li·er; -est 1** : gracefully or delicately attractive ⟨a *lovely* dress⟩ **2** : beautiful in character **3** : highly pleasing : FINE ⟨a *lovely* view⟩ **syn** see BEAUTIFUL — **love·li·ness** *n*

lov·er \'ləv-ər\ *n* **1 a** : a person in love **b** *pl* : two persons in love with each other **2** : one that loves ⟨a *lover* of music⟩ **3** : a partner in a sexual relationship other than that of husband and wife

love seat *n* : a sofa for two persons

love·sick \'ləv-,sik\ *adj* **1** : weak with love **2** : expressing a lover's desire ⟨*lovesick* poems⟩ — **love·sick·ness** *n*

lov·ing \'ləv-iŋ\ *adj* : feeling or showing love : AFFECTIONATE ⟨*loving* care⟩ ⟨a *loving* glance⟩ — **lov·ing·ly** *adv*

¹low \'lō\ *n* : the deep sound of a cow — **low** *vb*

²low \'lō\ *adj* **low·er** \'lō(-ə)r\; **low·est** \'lō-əst\ **1 a** : not high or tall ⟨*low* wall⟩ ⟨*low* bridge⟩ **b** : cut far down at the neck **c** : not extending as high as the ankle **2 a** : placed or passing below the normal level ⟨*low* ground⟩ **b** : marking a bottom ⟨*low* point of his career⟩ **3** : STRICKEN 2, PROSTRATE ⟨laid *low*⟩ **4 a** : not loud : SOFT ⟨a *low* whisper⟩ **b** : deep in pitch ⟨a *low* note⟩ **5 a** : being near the equator ⟨*low* northern latitudes⟩ **b** : being near the horizon ⟨the sun is *low*⟩ **6** : ¹POOR 1, LOWER-CLASS ⟨*low* birth⟩ **7 a** : FEEBLE 1, WEAK ⟨*low* with fever⟩ **b** : not cheerful or lively ⟨in *low* spirits⟩ **8** : less than usual (as in number, amount, degree, or rank) ⟨*low* price⟩ ⟨*low* pressure⟩ **9 a** : lacking dignity ⟨*low* style of writing⟩ **b** : morally deserving of criticism : BASE ⟨*low* trick⟩ **c** : COARSE 5, VULGAR

⟨*low* language⟩ **10** : being less complex in structure and development than others ⟨*low* animals⟩ **11** : not favorable ⟨a *low* opinion of their work⟩ — **low** *adv* — **low·ness** *n*

³low *n* **1** : something low; *esp* : a region of low barometric pressure **2** : the arrangement of gears in an automobile that gives the lowest speed of travel

low beam *n* : the point of aim of a vehicle headlight for short distances

low blood pressure *n* : blood pressure that is abnormally low especially in the arteries

low·boy \'lō-,bȯi\ *n* : a chest of drawers about one meter high with long legs

lowboy

low-bred \-'bred\ *adj* : disgusting in manner or action : RUDE, VULGAR

low·brow \-,braů\ *n* : a person without intellectual interests or culture — **lowbrow** *adj*

low·down \'lō-,daůn\ *n* : reliable information

¹low·er *or* **lour** \'laů(-ə)r\ *vb* **1** : to look angry or threatening : FROWN **2** : to become dark, gloomy, and threatening [Middle English *louren* "frown"]

²lower *or* **lour** *n* : a wrinkling of the brow in displeasure

³low·er \'lō(-ə)r\ *adj* **1** : being below another or others in position, rank, or order ⟨*lower* court⟩ ⟨the *lower* house of Congress⟩ **2** : less advanced in the scale of development through evolution ⟨*lower* animals⟩ **3** *cap* : of, relating to, or being an earlier geologic period or formation ⟨*Lower* Cretaceous⟩ [comparative form of *low*]

⁴low·er \'lō(ə)r\ *vb* **1** : ²DROP 2b, DIMINISH ⟨*lowered* my voice⟩ **2 a** : to let fall ⟨*lower* a flag⟩ **b** : to make the aim or goal lower ⟨*lowered* the sights⟩ **c** : to reduce the height of ⟨*lower* a wall⟩ **3 a** : to reduce in value or amount ⟨*lower* the price⟩ **b** : to bring down : DEGRADE ⟨*lowered* himself by lying⟩ **c** : to reduce in rank or position : HUMBLE

low·er·case \,lō-(ə)r-'kās\ *adj* : being a letter having as its typical form a, b, c rather than A, B, C — **lowercase** *n*

low·er–class \-'klas\ *adj* : of, relating to, or being the social class ranking below the middle class

low·er·ing *or* **lour·ing** \'laů-(ə-)riŋ\ *adj* **1** : looking angry or threatening **2** : ²OVERCAST, GLOOMY ⟨a *lowering* sky⟩

low·er·most \'lō(-ə)r-,mōst\ *adj* : being the lowest

lowest common denominator *n* : LEAST COMMON DENOMINATOR

lowest common multiple *n* : LEAST COMMON MULTIPLE

lowest terms *n pl* : the form of a fraction in which the numerator and denominator have no factor in common except 1 — called also *simplest form*

low frequency *n* : a radio frequency in the range between 30 and 300 kilohertz — abbr. *LF*

Low German *n* : the German dialects of northern Germany especially since the end of the Middle Ages

low–grade \'lō-'grād\ *adj* **1** : of poor grade or quality **2** : being near that end of a range which is lowest, weakest, or least able ⟨a *low-grade* fever⟩

low·land \-lənd, -,land\ *n* : low and usually level country — **lowland** *adj*

low·land·er \-lən-dər, -,lan-\ *n* : a person born or living in a lowland region

¹low·ly \'lō-lē\ *adv* : in a humble or meek manner

²lowly *adj* **low·li·er; -est 1** : ¹HUMBLE 1, MEEK **2** : of rank or position — **low·li·ness** *n*

low-ly·ing \'lō-'lī-iŋ\ *adj* : having little upward extension or elevation

low–pres·sure \'lō-'presh-ər\ *adj* **1** : having or operating under a relatively small pressure **2** : EASYGOING

low–spir·it·ed \-'spir-ət-əd\ *adj* : DEJECTED, DEPRESSED

low tide *n* : the tide when the water is at its lowest point

¹lox \'läks\ *n* : liquid oxygen [*l*iquid *ox*ygen]

²lox *n, pl* **lox** *or* **lox·es** : smoked salmon [from Yiddish *laks* "lox", from an old German word *lahs*, meaning "salmon"]

loy·al \'lȯi(-ə)l\ *adj* **1 a** : a faithful to one's lawful government **b** : faithful to a person to whom allegiance or affection is due **2** : faithful to a cause or ideal **syn** see FAITHFUL — **loy·al·ly** \'lȯi-ə-lē\ *adv*

loy·al·ist \'lȯi-ə-ləst\ *n* : one who is or remains loyal to a political cause, government, or sovereign especially in times of revolt

loy·al·ty \'lȯi-(ə)l-tē\ *n, pl* **-ties** : the quality or state of being loyal

loz·enge \'läz-°nj\ *n* **1** : a diamond-shaped figure **2 a** : something shaped like a lozenge **b** : a small disk or tablet that usually contains medicine

LP \'el-'pē\ *n* : a phonograph record designed to be played at 33⅓ revolutions per minute [*l*ong-*p*laying]

LPN \,el-,pē-'en\ *n* : LICENSED PRACTICAL NURSE

LSD \,el-,es-'dē\ *n* : a drug that causes hallucinations and can produce symptoms like those of severe mental illness

lu·au \'lü-,aů\ *n* : a Hawaiian feast

lub·ber \'ləb-ər\ *n* **1** : a big clumsy person **2** : an unskilled seaman — **lub·ber·ly** \-lē\ *adj or adv*

lube \'lüb\ *n* : LUBRICANT

lu·bri·cant \'lü-bri-kənt\ *n* : something (as a grease or oil) capable of reducing friction when applied between moving parts — **lubricant** *adj*

lu·bri·cate \'lü-brə-,kāt\ *vb* **-cat·ed; -cat·ing** **1** : to make smooth or slippery **2** : to apply a lubricant to ⟨*lubricate* a car⟩ **3** : to act as a lubricant — **lu·bri·ca·tion** \,lü-brə-'kā-shən\ *n* — **lu·bri·ca·tor** \'lü-brə-,kāt-ər\ *n*

lu·cent \'lüs-°nt\ *adj* **1** : LUMINOUS 1, BRIGHT **2** : ¹CLEAR 2b, LUCID

lu·cid \'lü-səd\ *adj* **1 a** : bright with light : LUMINOUS **b** : TRANSLUCENT 2 **2** : having full use of one's reasoning ability : clear-minded **3** : clear to the understanding : PLAIN — **lu·cid·i·ty** \lü-'sid-ət-ē\ *n* — **lu·cid·ly** \'lü-səd-lē\ *adv* — **lu·cid·ness** *n*

Lu·ci·fer \'lü-sə-fər\ *n* : ¹DEVIL 1

Word History What we sometimes call "the morning star" is really the planet Venus. The Romans called it *Lucifer,* meaning "bearer of light", because it appeared in the sky just before sunrise. So when, in the Old Testament, the prophet Isaiah says, in describing the downfall of the king of Babylon, "How are you fallen from heaven, O Morning Star, son of dawn", the "Morning Star" became *Lucifer* in the Latin translation. Early Christians thought that Isaiah was also referring to the devil, who had likewise "fallen from heaven". Thus the word *Lucifer* came to be applied to the devil. [Old English *Lucifer* "the morning star, a fallen angel, the Devil", from Latin *Lucifer* "the morning star, bearer of light", derived from *luc-, lux* "light" and *-fer* "bearing"]

luck \'lək\ *n* **1** : whatever happens to a person apparently by chance ⟨have good *luck* fishing⟩ **2** : the accidental way events occur ⟨happening by pure *luck*⟩ **3** : good fortune : SUCCESS ⟨have *luck*⟩ ⟨be out of *luck*⟩ — **luck·less** \-ləs\ *adj*

luck·i·ly \'lək-ə-lē\ *adv* : by good luck ⟨*luckily* no one was hurt⟩

lucky \'lək-ē\ *adj* **luck·i·er; -est** **1** : favored by luck : FORTUNATE **2** : producing a good result apparently by chance ⟨a *lucky* hit⟩ **3** : seeming to bring good luck ⟨a *lucky* coin⟩ — **luck·i·ness** *n*

lu·cra·tive \'lü-krət-iv\ *adj* : producing wealth : PROFITABLE — **lu·cra·tive·ly** *adv* — **lu·cra·tive·ness** *n*

lu·cre \'lü-kər\ *n* : gain in money : PROFIT; *also* : MONEY 1a

lu·di·crous \'lüd-ə-krəs\ *adj* : laughable because of being ridiculous — **lu·di·crous·ly** *adv* — **lu·di·crous·ness** *n*

luff \'ləf\ *vb* : to sail toward the wind — **luff** *n*

¹lug \'ləg\ *vb* **lugged; lug·ging** : to pull or carry especially with great effort

²lug *n* **1** : a part (as a handle) that projects like an ear **2** : a heavy nut used with a bolt **3** : BLOCKHEAD, LOUT

lug·gage \'ləg-ij\ *n* : something that is lugged; *esp* : suitcases or traveling bags for a traveler's belongings : BAGGAGE

lug·ger \'ləg-ər\ *n* : a boat that carries one or more lugsails

Lu·gol's solution \'lü-,gȯlz-, -,gälz-\ *n* : any of several deep brown solutions of iodine and the iodide of potassium in water or alcohol that are used in medicine or as microscopic stains — called also *Lugol's iodine solution*

lugger

lug·sail \'ləg-,sāl, -səl\ *n* : a four-sided sail fastened at the top to a yard that hangs at a slant and is raised and lowered with the sail

lu·gu·bri·ous \lů-'gü-brē-əs *also* -'gyü-\ *adj* : MOURNFUL 1; *esp* : exaggeratedly or insincerely mournful — **lu·gu·bri·ous·ly** *adv* — **lu·gu·bri·ous·ness** *n*

Luke \'lük\ *n* — see BIBLE table

luke·warm \'lü-kwȯ(ə)rm\ *adj* **1** : mildly warm : TEPID ⟨*lukewarm* bath⟩ **2** : not enthusiastic : INDIFFERENT ⟨our plan got a *lukewarm* reception⟩ — **luke·warm·ly** *adv* — **luke·warm·ness** *n*

¹lull \'ləl\ *vb* **1** : to cause to sleep or rest **2** : to cause to relax vigilance

²lull *n* **1** : a temporary calm before or during a storm **2** : a temporary drop in activity

lul·la·by \'ləl-ə-,bī\ *n, pl* **-bies** : a song to quiet children or lull them to sleep

lum·ba·go \,ləm-'bā-gō\ *n* : usually painful muscular rheumatism involving the lower part of the back

lum·bar \'ləm-bər, -,bär\ *adj* : of, relating to, or near the loins or the bony regions of the lower spinal column ⟨*lumbar* region⟩

¹lum·ber \'ləm-bər\ *vb* **lum·bered; lum·ber·ing** \-b(ə-)riŋ\ : to move heavily or clumsily; *also* : ¹RUMBLE [Middle English *lomeren* "to move heavily or clumsily"] — **lum·ber·ing·ly** *adv*

²lumber *n* **1** : extra or unused household articles that are stored **2** : timber or logs especially when sawed and trimmed for use [perhaps derived from the name *Lombard*, originally associated with bankers and pawnbrokers, and so called from the use of pawnshops for storing unwanted or excess property]

³lumber *vb* **lum·bered; lum·ber·ing** \-b(ə-)riŋ\ **1** : ¹CLUTTER, ENCUMBER **2 a** : to cut logs **b** : to saw logs into lumber — **lum·ber·er** \-bər-ər\ *n*

lum·ber·jack \'ləm-bər-,jak\ *n* : LOGGER

lum·ber·man \-mən\ *n* : a person involved in the business of cutting, trimming, and selling lumber

lum·ber·yard \-,yärd\ *n* : a place where lumber is kept for sale

lu·men \'lü-mən\ *n, pl* **lu·mi·na** \-mə-nə\ *or* **lumens** : a unit of light quantity equal to the light on a unit surface all points of which are at a unit distance from a point source of light having a strength of one candle

lumin- *combining form* : light ⟨*lumin*escence⟩ [derived from Latin *lumen* "light"]

lu·mi·nary \'lü-mə-,ner-ē\ *n, pl* **-nar·ies** **1** : a very fa-

\ə\ abut	\aů\ out	\i\ tip	\ȯ\ saw	\ů\ foot	
\ər\ further	\ch\ chin	\ī\ life	\ȯi\ coin	\y\ yet	
\a\ mat	\e\ pet	\j\ job	\th\ thin	\yü\ few	
\ā\ take	\ē\ easy	\ŋ\ sing	\th\ this	\yů\ cure	
\ä\ cot, cart	\g\ go	\ō\ bone	\ü\ food	\zh\ vision	

mous person **2** : a source of light; *esp* : one of the heavenly bodies — **luminary** *adj*

lu·mi·nes·cence \ˌlü-mə-'nes-°n(t)s\ *n* : the giving off of light at low temperatures especially as part of a chemical process (as of the body); *also* : such light

lu·mi·nes·cent \ˌlü-mə-'nes-°nt\ *adj* : relating to, exhibiting, or suitable for the production of luminescence ⟨*luminescent* paint⟩

lu·mi·nos·i·ty \ˌlü-mə-'näs-ət-ē\ *n, pl* **-ties** **1** : the quality or state of being luminous : BRIGHTNESS **2** : something luminous

lu·mi·nous \'lü-mə-nəs\ *adj* **1** : giving off light : SHINING **2** : being lighted ⟨a public square *luminous* with sunlight⟩ **3** : ¹CLEAR 3 — **lu·mi·nous·ly** *adv* — **lu·mi·nous·ness** *n*

¹lump \'ləmp\ *n* **1** : a small uneven mass **2** : a collection or sum of units or parts : TOTAL **3** : an abnormal swelling or growth

²lump *adj* : not divided into parts : WHOLE ⟨*lump* sum⟩

³lump *vb* **1** : to group together **2** : to move noisily and clumsily **3** : to form into a lump

lump·ish \'ləm-pish\ *adj* **1** : ¹DULL 1, STUPID **2** : ¹HEAVY 1a, AWKWARD — **lump·ish·ly** *adv* — **lump·ish·ness** *n*

lumpy \'ləm-pē\ *adj* **lump·i·er; -est** : having or full of lumps — **lump·i·ness** *n*

lu·na·cy \'lü-nə-sē\ *n, pl* **-cies** : INSANITY

lu·na moth \ˌlü-nə-\ *n* : a large mostly pale green American moth with long tails on the hind wings

lu·nar \'lü-nər\ *adj* **1** : of or relating to the moon **2** : measured by the moon's revolution ⟨*lunar* month⟩

lunar eclipse *n* : an eclipse in which the moon passes partially or entirely through the umbra of the earth's shadow

lunar module *n* : a part of a space vehicle designed to carry astronauts from the command module to the surface of the moon and back — called also *lunar excursion module*

¹lu·na·tic \'lü-nə-ˌtik\ *adj* **1 a** : INSANE 1 **b** : designed for insane persons ⟨*lunatic* asylum⟩ **2** : wildly foolish

²lunatic *n* : an insane person

luna moth

Word History A lunatic now tends to be thought of as a person who usually acts in an insane or wild manner. But until the middle of the 19th century, the word *lunatic* was used for people who were insane some of the time yet had periods of normal behavior. This was a common meaning of the term in courts of law until recent times. The ancient belief was that changes in the moon affected such people. They were thought to be at their worst during a full moon but normal during a new moon. The Latin word for such a person was *lunaticus*, which was based on the noun *luna*, meaning "moon". *Lunaticus* came into Middle English as *lunatik*. Then it passed into Modern English as *lunatic*, meaning "one driven mad by the moon". [Middle English *lunatik* "a person driven mad by the changes in the moon", derived from Latin *lunaticus* (same meaning), from earlier *luna* "moon"]

lunch \'lənch\ *n* **1** : a light meal; *esp* : one eaten in the middle of the day **2** : the food prepared for a lunch — **lunch** *vb*

lun·cheon \'lən-chən\ *n* : a light meal at midday; *esp* : a formal lunch

lun·cheon·ette \ˌlən-chə-'net\ *n* : a place where light lunches are sold

lunch·room \'lənch-ˌrüm, -ˌrum\ *n* **1** : LUNCHEONETTE **2** : a room (as in a school) where lunches may be eaten

lung \'ləŋ\ *n* **1 a** : one of the usually paired organs forming the special breathing structure of vertebrates (as lions or human beings) that breathe air **b** : of various respiratory organs of invertebrates **2** : a device (as an iron lung) to promote breathing and make it easier

¹lunge \'lənj\ *n* **1** : a sudden stretching thrust or pass (as with a sword) **2** : a sudden forward rush or reach

²lunge *vb* **lunged; lung·ing** **1** : to move with or as if with a lunge **2** : to make a lunge (as with a sword)

lung·fish \'ləŋ-ˌfish\ *n* : any of various fishes that breathe with structures resembling lungs as well as with gills

lu·pine *also* **lu·pin** \'lü-pən\ *n* : any of a genus of herbs of the legume family that have white, yellow, blue, or pink flowers in long upright clusters and flat pods with kidney-shaped seeds

¹lurch \'lərch\ *n* : an overwhelming defeat in a game (as cribbage) — **in the lurch** : in a helpless or defenseless position

²lurch *n* **1** : a sudden roll of a ship to one side **2** : a sudden swaying or tipping movement ⟨the car gave a *lurch*⟩; *also* : a staggering gait

³lurch *vb* : to move with a lurch

¹lure \'lu̇(ə)r\ *n* **1 a** : something that persuades one to perform an action for pleasure or gain : TEMPTATION **b** : ¹APPEAL 3, ATTRACTION **2** : a decoy for attracting animals to capture; *esp* : an artificial bait used for catching fish

²lure *vb* **lured; lur·ing** : to tempt or lead away by offering some pleasure or advantage : ENTICE

lu·rid \'lu̇r-əd\ *adj* **1** : lifelessly pale : WAN **2** : shining with the red glow of fire seen through smoke **3 a** : causing horror or disgust : GRUESOME ⟨*lurid* tales of murder⟩ **b** : SENSATIONAL 2 ⟨*lurid* book jackets⟩ — **lu·rid·ly** *adv* — **lu·rid·ness** *n*

lurk \'lərk\ *vb* **1 a** : to stay in or about a place secretly **b** : to move quietly and secretly **2** : to lie concealed; *esp* : to be a hidden threat — **lurk·er** *n*

syn LURK, SKULK, SNEAK mean to move or act so as not to be noticed. LURK suggests lying in wait usually with the intention of attacking ⟨a fox *lurked* in the woods⟩ SKULK strongly suggests moving about quietly often with an evil intention but sometimes in fear ⟨a suspicious-looking person *skulking* about the grounds⟩ SNEAK suggests moving into or out of a place in such a way as to avoid detection ⟨*sneaked* into the kitchen and grabbed an apple⟩

lus·cious \'ləsh-əs\ *adj* **1** : having a delicious taste or smell ⟨*luscious* berries⟩ **2** : appealing to the senses : DELIGHTFUL — **lus·cious·ly** *adv* — **lus·cious·ness** *n*

lush \'ləsh\ *adj* **1** : being juicy and fresh ⟨*lush* grass⟩ **2** : covered with thick healthy growth ⟨*lush* pastures⟩ — **lush·ly** *adv* — **lush·ness** *n*

¹lust \'ləst\ *n* **1** : sexual desire especially if strong or uncontrolled **2** : a strong longing : CRAVING

²lust *vb* : to have a strong desire : CRAVE; *esp* : to have a strong sexual desire

lus·ter *or* **lus·tre** \'ləs-tər\ *n* **1** : a shine or sheen especially from reflected light : GLOSS **2** : sparkling brilliance **3** : ¹GLORY 1a, SPLENDOR ⟨the *luster* of a famous name⟩ — **lus·ter·less** \-tər-ləs\ *adj* — **lus·trous** \-trəs\ *adj*

lust·ful \'ləst-fəl\ *adj* : excited by lust — **lust·ful·ly** \-fə-lē\ *adv* — **lust·ful·ness** *n*

lusty \'ləs-tē\ *adj* **lust·i·er; -est** : full of vitality : VIGOROUS, ROBUST — **lust·i·ly** \-tə-lē\ *adv* — **lust·i·ness** \-tē-nəs\ *n*

lute \'lüt\ *n* : a musical instru-

lute

ment resembling a guitar but with a pear-shaped body

lu·tein·iz·ing hormone \'lüt-ē-ə-,nī-ziŋ-\ *n* : a hormone of the pituitary gland that in the female stimulates the development of the corpora lutea and in the male the development of a certain tissue in the testis

lu·te·tium *also* **lu·te·cium** \lü-'tē-sh(ē-)əm\ *n* : a soft metallic chemical element — see ELEMENT table

Lu·ther·an \'lü-th(ə-)rən\ *adj* **1** : of or relating to Martin Luther or his religious doctrines **2** : of or relating to the Protestant churches following Lutheran doctrines — **Lu·ther·an** *n* — **Lu·ther·an·ism** \-,iz-əm\ *n*

lux \'ləks\ *n, pl* **lux** *or* **lux·es** : a unit that is used for measuring the amount of light falling on a surface and that is equal to one lumen per square meter

lux·u·ri·ant \(,)ləg-'zhùr-ē-ənt, (,)lək-'shùr-\ *adj* **1 a** : producing large crops ⟨*luxuriant* valleys⟩ **b** : characterized by heavy growth : LUSH **2** : ¹LAVISH 2 — **lux·u·ri·ance** \-ē-ən(t)s\ *n* — **lux·u·ri·ant·ly** *adv*

lux·u·ri·ate \(,)ləg-'zhùr-ē-,āt, (,)lək-'shùr-\ *vb* **-at·ed; -at·ing 1** : to grow in great numbers or quantity **2** : to enjoy oneself in a luxurious manner

lux·u·ri·ous \(,)ləg-'zhùr-ē-əs, (,)lək-'shùr-\ *adj* **1** : fond of luxury **2** : of, relating to, or marked by luxury — **lux·u·ri·ous·ly** *adv* — **lux·u·ri·ous·ness** *n*

lux·u·ry \'ləksh-(ə-)rē, 'ləgzh-\ *n, pl* **-ries 1 a** : free use or possession of costly food, dress, or anything that pleases a person **b** : great ease or comfort : rich surroundings ⟨live in *luxury*⟩ **2 a** : something desirable but costly or hard to get **b** : something adding to pleasure or comfort but not absolutely necessary — **luxury** *adj*

¹-ly \lē\ *adj suffix* **1** : resembling in appearance, manner, or nature : having the characteristics of ⟨queen*ly*⟩ ⟨father*ly*⟩ **2** : happening in a regular pattern at (specified) time periods ⟨hour*ly*⟩ [Old English *-līc, -lic* "like"]

²-ly *adv suffix* **1** : in a (specified) manner ⟨slow*ly*⟩ **2** : from a (specified) point of view ⟨grammatical*ly*⟩ [Old English *-līce, -lice* "in a (specified) manner", from *-līc* "like"]

ly·ce·um \lī-'sē-əm, 'lī-sē-\ *n* **1** : a hall for public lectures or discussions **2** : an association providing public lectures, concerts, and entertainments

ly·co·po·di·um \,lī-kə-'pōd-ē-əm\ *n* : any of a large genus of club mosses with evergreen leaves that grow upward or creep on the ground

lye \'lī\ *n* **1** : a strong alkaline liquid obtained from wood ashes and used especially in making soap and in washing **2** : any of various strong alkaline liquids; *esp* : SODIUM HYDROXIDE **3** : a solid compound (as caustic soda) that causes chemical burns

¹ly·ing \'lī-iŋ\ *present participle of* LIE

²lying *adj* : UNTRUTHFUL, FALSE

Lyme disease \'līm-\ *n* : a serious disease that is caused by a bacterium transmitted by some ticks, that is often characterized at first by a spreading red patch on the skin,

and that may result in disorders of the heart and nervous system

lymph \'lim(p)f\ *n* : a pale colorless fluid that circulates in lymphatic vessels, bathes the cells of the body, and consists of white blood cells and a liquid portion resembling blood plasma

¹lym·phat·ic \lim-'fat-ik\ *adj* **1** : of, relating to, or produced by lymph **2** : lacking physical or mental energy

²lymphatic *n* : a vessel that contains or transports lymph — called also *lymph vessel*

lymph node *n* : one of the rounded masses of tissue that are associated with the lymphatics and give rise to the lymphocytes — called also *lymph gland*

lym·pho·cyte \'lim(p)-fə-,sīt\ *n* : any of the colorless cells that are produced in the tissue of the lymph nodes, are capable of weak motion, are the most common cells in the lymph, are important in immunity, and make up 20 to 30 percent of the leukocytes of normal human blood

lym·pho·ma \lim-'fō-mə\ *n, pl* **-mas** *or* **-ma·ta** \-mət-ə\ : a tumor composed of tissue making up lymph nodes

lynch \'linch\ *vb* : to put to death by mob action without legal authority — **lynch·er** *n*

lynx \'liŋ(k)s\ *n, pl* **lynx** *or* **lynx·es 1** : a large North American cat with rather long legs, a short stubby tail, a coat marked with spots and blotches, soft fur, ears with small bunches of long fur at the tip, and large padded feet — called also *Canada lynx* **2** : any of several wildcats resembling the lynx

lynx–eyed \'liŋ(k)-'sīd\ *adj* : having sharp sight

lyre \'lī(ə)r\ *n* : a small harp held in the hands for playing

lyre·bird \-,bərd\ *n* : either of two Australian birds of which the males have very long tail feathers displayed during courtship in the shape of a lyre

¹lyr·ic \'lir-ik\ *n* **1** : a lyric poem or song **2** *pl* : the words of a song

²lyric *adj* **1 a** : resembling a song in form, feeling, or literary quality **b** : expressing a poet's own feeling : not narrative or dramatic ⟨*lyric* poetry⟩ **2** : having or involving a light singing style

lyre

lyr·i·cal \'lir-i-kəl\ *adj* : ²LYRIC — **lyr·i·cal·ly** \-i-k(ə-)lē\ *adv*

ly·sine \'lī-,sēn\ *n* : an essential amino acid obtained from various proteins

ly·sis \'lī-səs\ *n, pl* **ly·ses** \'lī-,sēz\ : a process of breaking up especially of cells

\ə\ abut	\aů\ out	\i\ tip	\ȯ\ saw	\ů\ foot
\ər\ further	\ch\ chin	\ī\ life	\ȯi\ coin	\y\ yet
\a\ mat	\e\ pet	\j\ job	\th\ thin	\yü\ few
\ā\ take	\ē\ easy	\ŋ\ sing	\th\ this	\yů\ cure
\ä\ cot, cart	\g\ go	\ō\ bone	\ü\ food	\zh\ vision

M

m \'em\ *n, often cap* **1** : the 13th letter of the English alphabet **2** : one thousand in Roman numerals

'm \m\ *vb* : AM ⟨I'm going⟩

ma \'mä, 'mȯ\ *n, pl* **mas** : MOTHER

ma'am \'mam, *after "yes" often* əm\ *n* : MADAM

ma·ca·bre \mə-'käb(-rə), -'käb-ər, -'käbrᵉ\ *adj* **1** : having death as a subject **2** : marked by or arousing horror

mac·ad·am \mə-'kad-əm\ *n* **1** : a roadway or pavement of small closely packed broken stone **2** : the broken stone used in macadamizing [named for John L. *McAdam* 1756–1836 Scottish engineer who invented the paving process] — **mac·ad·am·ize** \-ə-,mīz\ *vb*

mac·a·ro·ni \,mak-ə-'rō-nē\ *n* : a food made chiefly of wheat flour paste dried in the form of slender tubes

mac·a·roon \,mak-ə-'rün\ *n* : a cookie or small cake made of egg whites, sugar, and ground almonds or coconut

ma·caw \mə-'kȯ\ *n* : any of numerous parrots of South and Central America that have a long tail, a harsh voice, and bright feathers

Mac·ca·bees \'mak-ə-bēz\ *n* — see BIBLE table

¹**mace** \'mās\ *n* **1** : a heavy spiked club used as a weapon in the Middle Ages **2** : an ornamental staff carried as a symbol of authority [Middle English *mace* "a heavy spiked club", from early French *mace* (same meaning); probably of Latin origin]

²**mace** *n* : a spice made from the dried outer covering of the nutmeg [Middle English *mace* "the spice mace", from early French *macis* (same meaning), from Latin *macir* "an East Indian spice", from Greek *makir* (same meaning)]

macaw

Mach \'mäk\ *n* : MACH NUMBER

Mach·a·bees \'mak-ə-bēz\ *n* — see BIBLE table

ma·chete \mə-'shet-ē, -'chet-ē; mə-'shet\ *n* : a large heavy knife used especially for cutting sugarcane and underbrush and as a weapon

Ma·chi·a·vel·lian \,mak-ē-ə-'vel-ē-ən, -'vel-yən\ *adj* **1** : of or relating to the belief that a ruler is justified in using any means to stay in power **2** : characterized by dishonesty or trickery [named for Niccolo *Machiavelli* 1469–1527 an Italian political leader] — **Machiavellian** *n* — **Ma·chi·a·vel·lian·ism** \-,iz-əm\ *n*

mach·i·nate \'mak-ə-,nāt, 'mash-ə-\ *vb* **-nat·ed; -nat·ing** : ²PLOT 2; *esp* : to scheme to do harm — **mach·i·na·tion** \,mak-ə-'nā-shən, ,mash-ə-\ *n* — **mach·i·na·tor** \'mak-ə-,nāt-ər, 'mash-\ *n*

¹**ma·chine** \mə-'shēn\ *n* **1 a** : VEHICLE 2; *esp* : ²AUTOMOBILE **b** : a combination of parts that transmit forces, motion, and energy to do some desired work ⟨a sewing *machine*⟩ **c** : an instrument (as a lever or pulley) designed to transmit or change slightly the application of power, force, or motion **2** : an organized group that controls a political party — **ma·chine·like** \-,līk\ *adj*

²**machine** *vb* **ma·chined; ma·chin·ing** : to shape or finish by machine-operated tools — **ma·chin·able** \mə-'shē-nə-bəl\ *adj*

machine gun *n* : an automatic gun capable of continuous firing — **machine–gun** *vb* — **machine gunner** *n*

machine language *n* **1** : the set of symbolic instruction codes used to represent operations and data in a machine (as a computer) that are usually expressed in binary form **2** : ASSEMBLY LANGUAGE

ma·chine–read·able *adj* : directly usable by a computer ⟨*machine-readable* text⟩

ma·chin·ery \mə-'shēn-(ə-)rē\ *n, pl* **-er·ies** **1** : machines in general **2** : the working parts of a machine or instrument **3** : the organization or system by which something is done or carried on ⟨*machinery* of government⟩

machine shop *n* : a workshop in which metal articles are machined and assembled

machine tool *n* : a machine (as a lathe or drill) that is driven by power and is designed for shaping solid work

ma·chin·ist \mə-'shē-nəst\ *n* : a person who makes or works on machines and engines

Mach number \'mäk-\ *n* : a number representing the comparison of the speed of a body to the speed of sound in the surrounding atmosphere ⟨a *Mach number* of 2 indicates a speed that is twice the speed of sound⟩

mack·er·el \'mak-(ə-)rəl\ *n, pl* **-el** *or* **-els** **1** : a North Atlantic food fish that is green with blue bars above and silvery below **2** : any of various usually small or medium-sized fishes related to the mackerel

mackerel sky *n* : a sky covered with rows of clouds resembling the patterns on a mackerel's back

mack·i·naw \'mak-ə-,nȯ\ *n* : a short heavy woolen often plaid coat

mack·in·tosh *or* **mac·in·tosh** \'mak-ən-,täsh\ *n, chiefly British* : RAINCOAT

mac·ra·mé *also* **mac·ra·me** \'mak-rə-,mā\ *n* : a coarse lace or fringe made by knotting threads or cords; *also* : the art of tying knots in patterns

mac·ro \'mak-rō\ *n, pl* **macros** : a single computer instruction that represents a series of operations

mac·ro·cosm \'mak-rə-,käz-əm\ *n* : the world as a whole : UNIVERSE

ma·cron \'mäk-,rän, 'mak-, -rən\ *n* : a mark ⁻ placed over a vowel (as in \māk\) to show that the vowel is long

mac·ro·scop·ic \,mak-rə-'skäp-ik\ *adj* : large enough to be observed by the naked eye ⟨*macroscopic* animals⟩

mad \'mad\ *adj* **mad·der; mad·dest** **1** : disordered in mind : INSANE **2** : done or made without thinking ⟨a *mad* promise⟩ **3 a** : extremely angry : FURIOUS ⟨make a bull *mad*⟩ **b** : very displeased **4** : ENTHUSIASTIC ⟨*mad* about dancing⟩ **5** : RABID 3 ⟨a *mad* dog⟩ **6** : wildly festive ⟨a *mad* party⟩ **7** : wildly excited : FRANTIC — **mad·ly** *adv* — **mad·ness** *n* — **like mad** : at a high rate

mad·am \'mad-əm\ *n, pl* **mes·dames** \mā-'däm, -'dam\ **1** — used as a form of polite address to a woman **2** *cap* — used as a title especially before the name of rank or office of a high-ranking woman ⟨*Madam* President⟩ [Middle English *madam* "woman of rank or authority, lady", from early French *ma dame*, literally "my lady", from Latin *domina* "mistress, lady", feminine form of *dominus* "master, owner" — related to DAME, DOMINATE, MADONNA]

ma·dame \mə-'dam, ma-'dam, *before a surname also* ,mad-əm\ *n, pl* **mes·dames** \mā-'däm, -'dam\ — used as a title equivalent to *Mrs.* for a married woman not of English-speaking nationality

mad·cap \'mad-,kap\ *adj* : RECKLESS, WILD — **madcap** *n*

mad·den \'mad-ᵉn\ *vb* : to make mad : ENRAGE

mad·den·ing \'mad-niŋ, -ᵉn-iŋ\ *adj* : that irritates or angers ⟨a *maddening* habit⟩ — **mad·den·ing·ly** *adv*

mad·der \'mad-ər\ *n* **1 a** : a Eurasian herb with spear-shaped leaves, small yellowish flowers followed by berries, and red fleshy roots used to make a dye **b** : any of several plants related to the madder **2** : the root of a madder or a dye prepared from it

made *past and past participle of* MAKE

ma·de·moi·selle \,mad-(ə-)mə-'zel, -mwə-'zel; mam-'zel\

n, pl **ma·de·moi·selles** \-'zelz\ *or* **mes·de·moi·selles** \ˌmād-(ə)mə-'zel, -mwə-'zel\ — used by or to French‑speaking people as a title equivalent to *Miss*

made–up \'mā-'dəp\ *adj* **1** : created from the imagination ⟨a *made-up* story⟩ **2** : marked by the use of makeup ⟨*made-up* eyelids⟩

mad·house \'mad-ˌhaus\ *n* **1** : a place where insane persons are kept **2** : a place of uproar or confusion

mad·man \'mad-ˌman, -mən\ *n* : a man who is or who acts as if insane

Ma·don·na \mə-'dän-ə\ *n* **1** : the Virgin Mary **2** : a painting or statue representing the Virgin Mary [from Italian *madonna* "lady, Virgin Mary", from earlier *ma donna*, literally "my lady", from Latin *domina* "mistress, lady", feminine form of *dominus* "master, owner" — related to DAME, DOMINATE, MADAM]

ma·dras \'mad-rəs; mə-'dras, -'dräs\ *n* : a fine plain-woven fabric usually of cotton with various designs (as plaid)

mad·ri·gal \'mad-ri-gəl\ *n* **1** : a short poem common in the Middle Ages **2 a** : a complex vocal piece developed especially in the 16th and 17th centuries **b** : a song usually not accompanied by musical instruments and consisting of two or more voice parts : PART-SONG — **mad·ri·gal·ist** \-gə-ləst\ *n*

mad·wom·an \'mad-ˌwùm-ən\ *n* : a woman who is or who acts as if insane

mael·strom \'mā(ə)l-strəm, -ˌsträm\ *n* **1** : a strong violent whirlpool dangerous to ships **2** : a great confusion ⟨a *maelstrom* of emotions⟩

mae·sto·so \mī-'stō-sō, -zō\ *adv or adj* : so as to be majestic and stately — used as a direction in music

mae·stro \'mī-strō\ *n, pl* **maestros** *or* **mae·stri** \-ˌstrē\ : a master of an art and especially of music [from Italian *maestro*, literally "master", from Latin *magister* "master, one who holds a higher political office" — related to MAGISTRATE, MASTER]

Ma·fia \'mäf-ē-ə, 'maf-\ *n* **1** : a secret society of political terrorists **2** : a secret criminal organization held to control illegal activities (as gambling) throughout the world

ma·fi·o·so \ˌmäf-ē-'ō-sō, ˌmaf-, -zō\ *n, pl* **-si** \-sē, -zē\ : a member of the Mafia

mag·a·zine \'mag-ə-ˌzēn, ˌmag-ə-'zēn\ *n* **1** : a storehouse or warehouse especially for military supplies **2** : a place for keeping explosives in a fort or ship **3** : a publication containing different pieces (as stories, articles, or poems) and issued at regular intervals (as weekly or monthly) **4** : a supply chamber: as **a** : a container in a gun for holding cartridges **b** : a container for film on a camera or motion-picture projector

Word History *Magazine* originally meant "storehouse" or "granary" or "cellar". It came into an early French dialect and then English from the Arabic word *makhzan* (plural *makhāzin*). *Makhzan* had all these meanings. In military and naval use *magazine* came to mean a storage place for gunpowder or weapons or a place on a warship where the powder was kept. Later it came to mean either a place where valuable things were stored or the stored things themselves. A new sense of *magazine* appeared in 1731 with the first issue of a monthly publication called *The Gentleman's Magazine.* This was a collection or storehouse of short stories and articles about things of interest to the general reader. This use of *magazine* caught on and was used for similar publications. [from early French *magazine* "storehouse, warehouse", derived from Arabic *makhāzin*, plural of *makhzan* "storehouse, granary, cellar"]

ma·gen·ta \mə-'jent-ə\ *n* **1** : a deep red dye **2** : a deep purplish red

mag·got \'mag-ət\ *n* : a soft-bodied legless larva of a two‑winged fly (as the housefly)

mag·goty \'mag-ət-ē\ *adj* : infested with maggots

ma·gi \'mā-ˌjī\ *n pl, often cap* : the three wise men from the East who paid respect to the infant Jesus [from Latin *magi*, plural of *magus* "Persian priest or wise man", from Greek *magos* "Persian priest, sorcerer" — related to MAGIC]

mag·ic \'maj-ik\ *n* **1** : the power to control natural forces that is possessed by certain persons (as wizards and witches) in folktales and fiction **2 a** : a power that seems mysterious ⟨the *magic* of a great name⟩ **b** : something that charms ⟨the *magic* of their singing⟩ **3** : the art or skill of performing tricks or illusions as if by magic for entertainment [Middle English *magik* "use of supernatural powers", from early French *magique* (same meaning), from Latin *magice* (same meaning), derived from Greek *magikos* "magical, relating to magi", from *magos* "Persian priest, sorcerer" — related to MAGI] — **magic** *adj* — **mag·i·cal** \'maj-i-kəl\ *adj* — **mag·i·cal·ly** \-i-k(ə-)lē\ *adv*

ma·gi·cian \mə-'jish-ən\ *n* **1** : a person skilled in magic; *esp* : SORCERER **2** : a performer of tricks of illusion

magic lantern *n* : an early type of slide projector

magic square *n* : a square containing a number of integers arranged so that the sum of the numbers in each row, column, and diagonal is the same

4	9	2
3	5	7
8	1	6

6	3	10	15
9	16	5	4
7	2	11	14
12	13	8	1

magic square

mag·is·te·ri·al \ˌmaj-ə-'stir-ē-əl\ *adj* **1** : AUTHORITATIVE **2** : of or relating to a magistrate or the office or duties of a magistrate — **mag·is·te·ri·al·ly** \-ē-ə-lē\ *adv*

mag·is·tra·cy \'maj-ə-strə-sē\ *n, pl* **-cies** **1** : the state of being a magistrate **2** : the office, power, or dignity of a magistrate **3** : a body of magistrates

mag·is·trate \'maj-ə-ˌstrāt, -strət\ *n* **1** : a chief officer of government (as over a nation) ⟨the president is the chief *magistrate*⟩ **2** : a local official with some judicial power [Middle English *magistrat* "magistrate", from Latin *magistratus* (same meaning), from *magister* "master, one who holds a higher political office" — related to MAESTRO, MASTER]

mag·ma \'mag-mə\ *n* : molten rock material within the earth — **mag·mat·ic** \mag-'mat-ik\ *adj*

mag·na cum lau·de \ˌmäg-nə-(ˌ)kùm-'laud-ə, -'laud-ē; ˌmag-nə-ˌkəm-'lôd-ē\ *adv* : with great distinction : with great honors ⟨graduated *magna cum laude*⟩ [Latin]

mag·na·nim·i·ty \ˌmag-nə-'nim-ət-ē\ *n, pl* **-ties** **1** : nobility of character : HIGH-MINDEDNESS **2** : a magnanimous act

mag·nan·i·mous \mag-'nan-ə-məs\ *adj* **1** : having or showing a noble and courageous spirit **2** : being generous and forgiving — **mag·nan·i·mous·ly** *adv*

mag·nate \'mag-ˌnāt, -nət\ *n* : a person of rank, power, or influence (as in an industry)

mag·ne·sia \mag-'nē-shə, -'nē-zhə\ *n* : a white earthy solid that consists of magnesium and oxygen and is used in fertilizers and rubber, as a mild laxative, and against acid in the stomach

mag·ne·sium \mag-'nē-zē-əm, -zhəm\ *n* : a silver-white metallic element that is lighter than aluminum, is easily worked, burns with a dazzling light, and is used in making lightweight alloys — see ELEMENT table

magnesium chloride *n* : a bitter salt that occurs dissolved in seawaters and salty underground water and is used in producing magnesium metal

\ə\ **abut**		\au̇\ **out**	\i\ **tip**	\ȯ\ **saw**	\ü\ **foot**
\ər\ **further**	\ch\ **chin**		\ī\ **life**	\ȯi\ **coin**	\y\ **yet**
\a\ **mat**	\e\ **pet**		\j\ **job**	\th\ **thin**	\yü\ **few**
\ā\ **take**	\ē\ **easy**		\ŋ\ **sing**	\th\ **this**	\yu̇\ **cure**
\ä\ **cot, cart**	\g\ **go**		\ō\ **bone**	\ü\ **food**	\zh\ **vision**

magnesium hydroxide *n* : a weak alkaline compound used especially as a laxative and against acid in the stomach

magnesium sulfate *n* : any of several sulfates of magnesium; *esp* : EPSOM SALT

mag·net \'mag-nət\ *n* **1** : a piece of some material (as the mineral iron oxide) that is able to attract iron; *esp* : a mass of iron or steel so treated that it has this property **2** : something that attracts ⟨the *magnet* of fame⟩

mag·net·ic \mag-'net-ik\ *adj* **1** : having great power to attract ⟨a *magnetic* personality⟩ **2 a** : of or relating to a magnet or magnetism **b** : of or relating to the earth's magnetism ⟨the *magnetic* meridian⟩ **c** : capable of being magnetized **d** : working by magnetic attraction or repulsion — **mag·net·i·cal·ly** \-i-k(ə-)lē\ *adv*

magnetic bottle *n* : a magnetic field used to contain a controlled nuclear fusion reaction

magnetic disk *n* : ¹DISK 2c

magnetic field *n* : the portion of space near a magnetic body or a body carrying an electric current within which magnetic forces due to the body or current can be detected

magnetic needle *n* : a narrow strip of magnetized steel that is free to turn to show the direction of a magnetic field in which it is placed

magnetic north *n* : the northerly direction in the earth's magnetic field indicated by the north-seeking pole of the horizontal magnetic needle

magnetic pole *n* **1** : either of two small regions of the earth which are located near the North and South Poles and toward which a compass needle points **2** : either of the poles of a magnet

magnetic tape *n* : a thin ribbon (as of plastic) coated with a magnetic material on which information (as sound or television images) may be stored

mag·ne·tism \'mag-nə-,tiz-əm\ *n* **1 a** : the property of attracting certain metals or producing a magnetic field as shown by a magnet, a magnetized material, or a conductor carrying an electric current **b** : the science that deals with magnetic occurrences or conditions **2** : the power to attract or charm others

mag·ne·tite \'mag-nə-,tīt\ *n* : a black mineral that is an oxide of iron, is strongly attracted by a magnet, and is an important iron ore

mag·ne·tize \'mag-nə-,tīz\ *vb* **-tized; -tiz·ing** **1** : to cause to be magnetic **2** : to attract like a magnet : CHARM — **mag·ne·tiz·able** \-,tī-zə-bəl\ *adj* — **mag·ne·ti·za·tion** \,mag-nət-ə-'zā-shən\ *n*

mag·ne·to \mag-'nēt-ō\ *n, pl* **-tos** : a small electric generator using permanent magnets; *esp* : one used to produce sparks in an internal-combustion engine

mag·ne·tom·e·ter \,mag-nə-'täm-ət-ər\ *n* : an instrument used to detect the presence of a metallic object or to measure the strength of a magnetic field

mag·ne·to·sphere \mag-'nēt-ə-,sfi(ə)r, -'net-\ *n* : a region of the upper atmosphere that extends out for thousands of kilometers and in which charged particles are trapped by the earth's magnetic field

mag·ni·fi·ca·tion \,mag-nə-fə-'kā-shən\ *n* **1** : the act of magnifying **2 a** : the state of being magnified **b** : the apparent enlargement of an object by an optical instrument — called also *power;* compare RESOLUTION 2

mag·nif·i·cence \mag-'nif-ə-sən(t)s\ *n* : the quality or state of being magnificent

mag·nif·i·cent \mag-'nif-ə-sənt\ *adj* **1** : having impressive beauty ⟨the *magnificent* cathedrals of Europe⟩ **2** : ¹NOBLE 5 ⟨a *magnificent* character⟩ **syn** see GRAND — **mag·nif·i·cent·ly** *adv*

mag·ni·fy \'mag-nə-,fī\ *vb* **-fied; -fy·ing** **1** : EXTOL, PRAISE **2 a** : to increase in importance **b** : EXAGGERATE **3** : to enlarge in fact or in appearance ⟨a microscope *magnifies* an object seen through it⟩ — **mag·ni·fi·er** \-,fī(-ə)r\ *n*

mag·ni·fy·ing glass *n* : a lens that magnifies an object seen through it

mag·ni·tude \'mag-nə-,t(y)üd\ *n* **1 a** : great size or extent : BIGNESS **b** : ¹SIZE 1 **2** : the importance of something in influence or effect **3** : degree of brightness; *esp* : a number representing the brightness of a star

mag·no·lia \mag-'nōl-yə\ *n* : any of a genus of North American and Asian trees or tall shrubs having usually showy white, yellow, rose, or purple flowers that appear before or sometimes with the leaves in the spring

mag·num opus \,mag-nə-'mō-pəs\ *n* : a great work and especially the greatest achievement of an artist or writer

mag·pie \'mag-,pī\ *n* **1** : any of numerous noisy birds related to the jays but having a long tail and black-and-white feathers **2** : a person who chatters constantly

magpie 1

ma·guey \mə-'gā\ *n, pl* **magueys** **1** : any of various agaves with fleshy leaves; *also* : a related plant **2** : any of several hard fibers obtained from magueys

Mag·yar \'mag-,yär, 'mäg-; 'mäj-,är\ *n* **1** : a member of the dominant people of Hungary **2** : the language of the Magyars — **Magyar** *adj*

ma·ha·ra·ja *or* **ma·ha·ra·jah** \,mä-hə-'räj-ə, -'räzh-ə\ *n* : a Hindu prince ranking above a raja [from Sanskrit (ancient language of India) *mahārāja* "maharaja", from *mahā* "great" and *rāja* "king, raja"]

ma·ha·ra·ni *or* **ma·ha·ra·nee** \,mä-hə-'rän-ē\ *n* **1** : the wife of a maharaja **2** : a Hindu princess ranking above a rani

ma·hat·ma \mə-'hät-mə, -'hat-\ *n* : a person respected for being noble, wise, and unselfish — used as a title of honor especially by Hindus [from Sanskrit (ancient language of India) *mahātman* "great-souled", from *mahā* "great" and *atman* "self, soul"]

ma·hog·a·ny \mə-'häg-ə-nē\ *n, pl* **-nies** **1** : the wood of any of various chiefly tropical trees: as **a** : the strong usually reddish brown and heavy wood of a West Indian tree that is widely used to make furniture **b** : any of several African woods that vary in color from pinkish to deep reddish brown **2** : any of various woods resembling or substituted for true mahogany **3** : a tree from which mahogany is obtained **4** : a moderate reddish brown

maid \'mād\ *n* **1** : an unmarried girl or woman; *esp* : ¹MAIDEN **2** : a female servant

¹maid·en \'mād-ᵊn\ *n* : a young unmarried girl or woman — **maid·en·hood** \-,hùd\ *n* — **maid·en·ly** \-lē\ *adj*

²maiden *adj* **1 a** : not married ⟨*maiden* aunt⟩ **b** : ²VIRGIN 1 **2** : of or relating to a maiden **3** : coming before all others : FIRST, EARLIEST ⟨*maiden* voyage⟩

maid·en·hair \'mād-ᵊn-,ha(ə)r, -,he(ə)r\ *n* : any of a genus of ferns with slender stems and delicate much-divided often feathery leaves

maiden name *n* : a woman's family name before she is married

maid of honor **1** : an unmarried woman usually of noble birth who attends a queen or princess **2** : a bride's principal unmarried wedding attendant

maid·ser·vant \'mād-,sər-vənt\ *n* : a female servant

¹mail \'mā(ə)l\ *n* **1** : letters or parcels sent under public authority from one person to another through the post office **2** : something that comes in the mail and especially in a single delivery **3** : a vehicle (as a train, truck, or boat) that carries mail **4** : the system used in the public sending and delivery of letters and parcels ⟨do business by *mail*⟩ [Middle English *male* "a wallet or traveling bag", from early French *male* (same meaning); of Germanic origin]

²mail *vb* : to send by mail : POST — **mail·able** \'mā-lə-bəl\

adj — **mail·er** *n*

³**mail** *n* : armor made of small metal links or sometimes plates ⟨a coat of *mail*⟩ [Middle English *maile, maille* "metal plates used on armor", from early French *maille* (same meaning), derived from Latin *macula* "spot, mesh of a net"] — **mailed** \'mā(ə)ld\ *adj*

mail·box \'mā(ə)l-,bäks\ *n* **1** : a public box in which to place outgoing mail **2** : a private box (as on a house) for the delivery of incoming mail

mail carrier *n* : LETTER CARRIER

mailing tube *n* : a paperboard tube often with a screw cap in which small objects or rolled items (as calendars) are mailed

mail·man \'mā(ə)l-,man\ *n* : LETTER CARRIER

³mail

mail order *n* : an order for goods that is received and filled by mail — **mail–order** *adj*

maim \'mām\ *vb* : to injure badly or cripple by violence

¹**main** \'mān\ *n* **1** : physical strength : FORCE — used in the phrase *with might and main* **2 a** : MAINLAND **b** : HIGH SEAS **3** : the chief part : essential point ⟨they are in the *main* well trained⟩ **4** : a principal pipe or circuit of a utility system ⟨gas *main*⟩ ⟨water *main*⟩

²**main** *adj* **1** : ²CHIEF 2, PRINCIPAL ⟨the *main* idea⟩ **2** : PURE 3, SHEER ⟨by *main* force⟩ **3** : being a clause that is capable of standing alone as a simple sentence but is part of a larger sentence that includes a subordinate clause or another main clause — **main·ly** *adv*

main·frame \'mān-,frām\ *n* : a large fast computer that can do many jobs at once

main·land \'mān-,land, -lənd\ *n* : a continent or the main part of a continent as distinguished from an offshore island or sometimes from a cape or peninsula — **main·land·er** *n*

main·line \-'līn\ *vb* **-lined; -lin·ing** *slang* : to inject a drug directly into a principal vein

main·mast \'mān-,mast, -məst\ *n* : the principal mast of a sailing ship

main·sail \'mān-,sāl, 'mān(t)-səl\ *n* : the principal sail on the mainmast

main·spring \'mān-,spriŋ\ *n* **1** : the principal spring in a mechanical device (as a watch or clock) **2** : the chief or most powerful motive or cause

main·stay \-,stā\ *n* **1** : a large strong rope running from the maintop of a ship usually to the foot of the foremast **2** : a chief support ⟨the *mainstay* of the family⟩

main·stream \-,strēm\ *n* : the principal current or direction of activity or influence

main·tain \mān-'tān, mən-\ *vb* **1** : to keep in an existing state; *esp* : to keep in good condition ⟨*maintain* one's health⟩ ⟨*maintain* machinery⟩ **2** : to defend by argument ⟨*maintain* a position⟩ **3** : to continue in : CARRY ON, KEEP UP ⟨*maintain* your balance⟩ ⟨*maintain* a correspondence⟩ **4** : to provide for : SUPPORT ⟨*maintain* my family by working⟩ **5** : to insist to be true ⟨*maintained* that all men are equal⟩ — **main·tain·able** \-'tā-nə-bəl\ *adj* — **main·tain·er** *n*

main·te·nance \'mānt-nən(t)s, -ᵊn-ən(t)s\ *n* **1** : the act of maintaining : the state of being maintained ⟨*maintenance* of law and order⟩ ⟨money for the family's *maintenance*⟩ **2** : something that maintains **3** : the care of property or equipment ⟨workers in charge of *maintenance*⟩

main·top \'mān-,täp\ *n* : a platform at the head of the mainmast of a square-rigged ship

maize \'māz\ *n* : INDIAN CORN

ma·jes·tic \mə-'jes-tik\ *adj* : being stately and dignified

: NOBLE **syn** see GRAND — **ma·jes·ti·cal·ly** \-ti-k(ə-)lē\ *adv*

maj·es·ty \'maj-ə-stē\ *n, pl* **-ties** **1** : royal power, authority, or dignity **2** — used as a title for a king, queen, emperor, or empress ⟨Your *Majesty*⟩ **3 a** : royal manner or quality **b** : greatness of quality or character

¹**ma·jor** \'mā-jər\ *adj* **1 a** : greater in dignity, rank, or importance ⟨a *major* poet⟩ **b** : greater in number, quantity, or extent ⟨received the *major* part of the blame⟩ **2** : of or relating to an academic major **3 a** : having half steps between the third and fourth and the seventh and eighth degrees ⟨*major* scale⟩ **b** : based on a major scale ⟨*major* key⟩ ⟨*major* chord⟩

²**major** *n* **1** : a military commissioned officer with a rank just below that of lieutenant colonel **2 a** : the chief subject studied by a student ⟨chose history as his *major*⟩ **b** : a student specializing in a field ⟨a French *major*⟩

³**major** *vb* **ma·jored; ma·jor·ing** \'māj-(ə-)riŋ\ : to study an academic major ⟨*major* in English⟩

ma·jor·do·mo \,mā-jər-'dō-mō\ *n, pl* **-mos** : a person in charge of a great and especially of a royal household

ma·jor·ette \,mā-jə-'ret\ *n* : DRUM MAJORETTE

major general *n* : a military commissioned officer with a rank just below that of lieutenant general

ma·jor·i·ty \mə-'jȯr-ət-ē, -'jär-\ *n, pl* **-ties** **1 a** : the age at which one is given full civil rights **b** : the status of one who has reached this age **2 a** : a number greater than half of a total **b** : the amount by which such a number exceeds the smaller number ⟨won by a *majority* of seven⟩ **3** : the group or party that makes up the greater part of a whole body of persons ⟨the *majority* in the senate⟩ **4** : the military office or rank of a major

major league *n* : a league in the highest class of U.S. professional sports

¹**make** \'māk\ *vb* **made** \'mād\; **mak·ing** **1 a** : to seem to begin an action ⟨she *made* as if to go⟩ **b** : to act so as to appear ⟨*make* merry⟩ **2** : to cause to exist or occur : CREATE ⟨*make* a noise⟩ ⟨*make* trouble⟩ ⟨she was *made* to be a surgeon⟩ **3 a** : to form or shape out of material or parts : FASHION, CONSTRUCT ⟨*make* a dress⟩ ⟨*make* a chair⟩ **b** : to combine to produce ⟨2 and 2 *make* 4⟩ **4** : to frame in the mind ⟨*make* plans⟩ **5** : to put together from parts ⟨houses *made* of stone⟩ **6** : to estimate to be : COMPUTE ⟨I *make* it an even $5⟩ **7** : to set in order : PREPARE ⟨*make* a bed⟩ **8** : to cut and spread for drying ⟨*make* hay⟩ **9** : to cause to be or become ⟨*made* herself useful⟩ **10 a** : EXACT 1, ESTABLISH ⟨*make* laws⟩ **b** : to prepare in an appropriate manner ⟨*make* a will⟩ **11 a** : UNDERSTAND 1a ⟨unable to *make* anything of the story⟩ **b** : to regard as being : CONSIDER ⟨he is not the fool you *make* him⟩ **12** : ¹DO 1a, PERFORM ⟨*make* war⟩ ⟨*make* a bow⟩ **13** : to produce or acquire by or as if by action or effort ⟨*made* a mess of the job⟩ ⟨*make* good money⟩ ⟨*make* friends⟩ **14** : to force to act in some manner ⟨*made* her return home⟩ **15** : to cause or assure the success of ⟨the first case *made* the new lawyer⟩ **16 a** : ¹REACH 2c, ATTAIN ⟨the ship *makes* port tonight⟩ ⟨he *made* corporal in 10 months⟩ ⟨they *made* it to the other side of the bridge⟩ **b** : to gain a place on or in ⟨*made* the track team⟩ **17** : ¹CATCH 7b ⟨*make* the train⟩ **18** : to set out in pursuit ⟨*made* after the fox⟩ **19** : to provide the most satisfying experience of ⟨meeting the star of the show really *made* our day⟩

syn MAKE, FORM, MANUFACTURE mean to cause to come into being. MAKE is a word that can be used of many kinds of creation ⟨*make* soup⟩ ⟨*made* many friends⟩ FORM suggests that the thing brought into being has a

\ə\ abut	\au̇\ out	\i\ tip	\ȯ\ saw	\u̇\ foot
\ər\ further	\ch\ chin	\ī\ life	\ȯi\ coin	\y\ yet
\a\ mat	\e\ pet	\j\ job	\th\ thin	\yü\ few
\ā\ take	\ē\ easy	\ŋ\ sing	\th\ this	\yu̇\ cure
\ä\ cot, cart	\g\ go	\ō\ bone	\ü\ food	\zh\ vision

design or structure 〈the colonies *formed* a new nation〉 MANUFACTURE suggests making something in a fixed way and usually nowadays by machinery 〈a company that *manufactures* cars〉

— **make away with** : to carry off — **make believe** : to act as if something known to be imaginary is real or true : PRETEND — **make ends meet** : to keep one's expenses within one's income — **make fun of** : to make the target of one's laughter : RIDICULE 〈*made fun of* the way they talked〉 — **make good** **1** : to make complete : FULFILL 〈*make good* a promise〉 **2** : to make up for a deficiency 〈*make good* the loss〉 **3** : SUCCEED 2 〈*make good* as a reporter〉 — **make it** : to be successful 〈tried to *make it* in the world of sports〉 — **make love** : WOO 1, COURT — **make sail** **1** : to raise or spread sail **2** : to set out on a voyage — **make shift** : to manage with difficulty — **make time** : to travel fast 〈can really *make time* on the new highway〉 — **make use of** : to put to use : EMPLOY — **make way** : to open a path or passage 〈the crowd *made way* for the injured person〉

²**make** *n* **1** : the way in which a thing is made : STRUCTURE **2** : a particular kind of manufactured goods : BRAND 〈looked at several *makes* of car before deciding〉

¹**make–be·lieve** \'māk-bə-ˌlēv\ *n* : a pretending to be another person or character (as in the play of children)

²**make–believe** *adj* : IMAGINARY 〈was only a *make-believe* lion〉

make out *vb* **1** : to draw up in writing 〈*make out* a shopping list〉 **2** : UNDERSTAND 1a 〈how do you *make* that *out*〉 **3** : to represent as being 〈*made* her *out* a hero〉 **4** : to see and identify with difficulty 〈*make out* a form in the fog〉 **5** : SUCCEED 2 〈*make out* well in business〉 **6** : to engage in kissing and petting

make over *vb* **1** : to transfer the title of 〈*made* the estate *over* to his sister〉 **2** : REMAKE, REMODEL 〈*made* the whole house *over*〉

mak·er \'mā-kər\ *n* : one that makes: as **a** *cap* : GOD 1 **b** : a person who signs a promissory note

make·shift \'māk-ˌshift\ *n* : a temporary replacement : SUBSTITUTE — **makeshift** *adj*

make·up \'mā-ˌkəp\ *n* **1** : the way the parts or elements of something are put together : COMPOSITION 〈the *makeup* of a newspaper〉 **2 a** : any of various cosmetics (as lipstick or powder) **b** : materials (as wigs or cosmetics) used in making up 〈put on *makeup* for a play〉 〈too young to wear *makeup*〉

make up \(ˈ)mā-ˈkəp\ *vb* **1** : to form by fitting together or assembling 〈*make up* a suit〉 〈*make up* a train〉 **2** : COMPOSE 1b 〈chapters *make up* a book〉 **3** : to make good for something lacking or for a loss or injury **4** : DECIDE 3, SETTLE 〈*made up* my mind to go〉 **5 a** : to create from the imagination : INVENT 〈*make up* a story〉 **b** : to set in order 〈rooms are *made up* daily〉 **6** : to become friendly again 〈they fought and *made up*〉 **7 a** : to put on costumes or makeup (as for a play) 〈*made up* as a clown〉 **b** : to apply cosmetics

mak·ing \'mā-kiŋ\ *n* **1** : the act of forming, causing, doing, or coming into being 〈spots problems in the *making*〉 **2** : a process or means of advancement or success **3** : material from which something can be developed : POTENTIALITY 〈there is the *making* of a racehorse in this colt〉 — often used in pl. 〈has the *makings* of a great quarterback〉 **4** *pl* : the materials from which something can be made

mal- *combining form* **1 a** : bad 〈*mal*practice〉 **b** : badly 〈*mal*odorous〉 **2 a** : abnormal 〈*mal*formation〉 **b** : abnormally 〈*mal*formed〉 [derived from Latin *malus* "bad, evil"]

Mal·a·chi \'mal-ə-ˌkī\ *n* — see BIBLE table

mal·a·chite \'mal-ə-ˌkīt\ *n* : a green mineral that contains copper and is used as an ore of copper and for ornamental objects

mal·ad·just·ed \ˌmal-ə-'jəs-təd\ *adj* : not well adjusted especially to one's environment 〈socially *maladjusted* persons〉

mal·ad·just·ment \ˌmal-ə-'jəs(t)-mənt\ *n* : poor or faulty adjustment

mal·adroit \ˌmal-ə-'drȯit\ *adj* : AWKWARD 2, CLUMSY — **mal·adroit·ly** *adv* — **mal·adroit·ness** *n*

mal·a·dy \'mal-əd-ē\ *n, pl* **-dies** : a disease or disorder of the body or mind : AILMENT

Mal·a·gasy \ˌmal-ə-'gas-ē\ *n, pl* **-gasy** *also* **-gas·ies** **1** : a person born or living in Madagascar **2** : the language of the Malagasy people — **Malagasy** *adj*

mal·aise \mə-'lāz, ma-, -'lez\ *n* : a hazy feeling of not being well

mal·a·mute *or* **mal·e·mute** \'mal-ə-ˌmyüt\ *n* : a sled dog of northern North America; *esp* : ALASKAN MALAMUTE

ma·lar·ia \mə-'ler-ē-ə\ *n* : a disease caused by protozoan parasites in the red blood cells, passed from one individual to another by the bite of mosquitoes, and marked by periodic attacks of chills and fever — **ma·lar·i·al** \-ē-əl\ *adj*

mal·a·thi·on \ˌmal-ə-'thī-ən, -ˌän\ *n* : a poisonous insecticide that is broken down in nature

Ma·lay \mə-'lā, 'mā-ˌlā\ *n, pl* **Malays** **1** : a member of a people of the Malay peninsula and neighboring islands **2** : the language of the Malay people — **Malay** *adj* — **Ma·lay·an** \mə-'lā-ən, 'mā-ˌlā-\ *adj or n*

mal·con·tent \ˌmal-kən-'tent\ *adj* : not satisfied with the existing state of affairs : DISCONTENTED — **malcontent** *n*

¹**male** \'mā(ə)l\ *adj* **1 a** : of, relating to, or being the sex that fathers young **b** : bearing only stamens; *esp* : having only stamens and not producing fruit or seeds 〈a *male* holly〉 **2** : made up or consisting of males 〈a *male* choir〉 — **male·ness** *n*

²**male** *n* : a male individual

male·dic·tion \ˌmal-ə-'dik-shən\ *n* : a prayer for harm to come to someone : CURSE

male·fac·tion \ˌmal-ə-'fak-shən\ *n* : an evil deed : CRIME

male·fac·tor \'mal-ə-ˌfak-tər\ *n* **1** : one who is guilty of a crime or offense **2** : one who does evil

ma·lev·o·lence \mə-'lev-ə-lən(t)s\ *n* **1** : the quality or state of being malevolent **2** : malevolent behavior

ma·lev·o·lent \mə-'lev-ə-lənt\ *adj* : having or showing ill will : SPITEFUL — **ma·lev·o·lent·ly** *adv*

mal·fea·sance \(ˈ)mal-'fēz-ᵊn(t)s\ *n* : wrongful conduct especially by a public official

mal·for·ma·tion \ˌmal-fȯr-'mā-shən, -fər-\ *n* : a misshapen, abnormal, or faulty formation or structure 〈physical and psychological *malformations*〉

mal·formed \(ˈ)mal-'fȯ(ə)rmd\ *adj* : marked by malformation : badly or imperfectly formed : MISSHAPEN

mal·func·tion \(ˈ)mal-'fəŋ(k)-shən\ *vb* : to fail to function or operate properly — **malfunction** *n*

mal·ice \'mal-əs\ *n* : ILL WILL; *esp* : the intention of doing harm for the satisfaction of doing it

ma·li·cious \mə-'lish-əs\ *adj* **1** : doing mean things for pleasure **2** : just to be mean 〈*malicious* gossip〉 — **ma·li·cious·ly** *adv* — **ma·li·cious·ness** *n*

¹**ma·lign** \mə-'līn\ *adj* **1** : evil in influence or effect **2** : showing strong ill will : MALEVOLENT

²**malign** *vb* : to say evil things about : SLANDER

ma·lig·nan·cy \mə-'lig-nən-sē\ *n, pl* **-cies** **1** : the quality or state of being malignant **2** : a malignant tumor

ma·lig·nant \mə-'lig-nənt\ *adj* **1** : evil in influence or effect : INJURIOUS **2** : MALICIOUS 1 **3** : tending or likely to produce death 〈*malignant* tumor〉 — **ma·lig·nant·ly** *adv*

ma·lig·ni·ty \mə-'lig-nət-ē\ *n, pl* **-ties** **1** : the quality or state of being malignant **2** : something that is malignant

ma·lin·ger \mə-'liŋ-gər\ *vb* **-gered; -ger·ing** \-g(ə-)riŋ\ : to pretend to be sick or injured so as to avoid duty or work — **ma·lin·ger·er** \-gər-ər\ *n*

mall \'mȯl\ *n* **1** : a shaded walk : PROMENADE **2** : a usually paved or grassy strip between two roadways **3** : a group of stores arranged about an often covered way for

pedestrians

Word History The word *mall* was a short form of the name of a game played in England in the 17th century. The full name was *pall-mall*, which literally means "ball-mallet". The object of this game was to drive a wooden ball with a mallet through an iron ring hanging at the end of an alley. The player doing so with the fewest strokes won. In time, the alley on which the game was played was called a *mall*. Even after the game was no longer popular, the word *mall* continued to be used for such alleys, many of which became walks or streets. One of these walks, called "The Mall", was located in St. James's Park, London. It was landscaped with trees and flowers and became a fashionable place to walk. Other such places also were called *malls*. Later, the word was applied to the grassy strip separating roadways. Nowadays a *mall* commonly refers to an enclosed walkway arranged with stores for the convenience of shoppers [a shortened form of *pall-mall* "a game similar to croquet formerly played in England", literally "ball-mallet"]

mal·lard \'mal-ərd\ *n, pl* **mallard** *or* **mallards** : a common and widely distributed wild duck of the northern hemisphere that is the source from which the domestic duck has been obtained by breeding

mallard

mal·lea·ble \'mal-ē-ə-bəl, 'mal-(y)ə-bəl\ *adj* **1** : capable of being extended or shaped by beating with a hammer or by the pressure of rollers ⟨a *malleable* metal⟩ **2** : capable of being changed so as to fit new uses or situations : FLEXIBLE, ADAPTABLE — **mal·lea·bil·i·ty** \,mal-ē-ə-'bil-ət-ē, ,mal-(y)ə-'bil-\ *n*

mal·let \'mal-ət\ *n* **1** : a hammer usually with a barrel-shaped head of soft material (as wood); *esp* : one with a large head used for driving a tool (as a chisel) or for striking a surface without damaging it **2** : a club for striking a ball (as in croquet or polo)

mal·le·us \'mal-ē-əs\ *n, pl* **mal·lei** \'mal-ē-,ī, -ē-,ē\ : the outermost bone of the three small bones of the ear of a mammal

mal·low \'mal-ō\ *n* : any of a group of herbs with lobed leaves, usually showy flowers, and a disk-shaped fruit

mal·nour·ished \(')mal-'nər-isht, -'nə-risht\ *adj* : poorly nourished

mal·nu·tri·tion \,mal-n(y)ù-'trish-ən\ *n* : faulty and especially inadequate nutrition

mal·odor·ous \(')mal-'ōd-ə-rəs\ *adj* : bad-smelling — **mal·odor·ous·ly** *adv* — **mal·odor·ous·ness** *n*

Mal·pi·ghi·an tubule \mal-,pig-ē-ən-, -,pē-gē-ən-\ *n* : any of a group of long vessels opening into the intestine in various arthropods (as insects) and functioning in excretion

mal·prac·tice \(')mal-'prak-təs\ *n* : violation of professional standards especially by carelessness or improper conduct

¹malt \'mòlt\ *n* **1** : grain and especially barley steeped in water and used chiefly in brewing and distilling **2** : MALTED MILK 2 — **malt** *adj*

²malt *vb* **1** : to convert into malt **2** : to make or treat with malt or malt extract

malt·ase \'mòl-,tās\ *n* : an enzyme that accelerates the breakdown of maltose to glucose

malted milk *n* **1** : a soluble powder prepared from dried milk and malted cereals **2** : a beverage made by dissolving malted milk in a liquid (as milk)

Mal·tese \mòl-'tēz\ *n, pl* **Maltese** **1** : a person born or living in Malta **2** : the Semitic language of the Maltese people — **Maltese** *adj*

Maltese cat *n* : a bluish gray domestic short-haired cat

Maltese cross *n* : a cross with four arms of equal size that increase in width toward the ends

malt liquor *n* : a fermented liquor (as beer) made with malt

malt·ose \'mòl-,tōs\ *n* : a sugar formed especially from starch by the action of enzymes and used in brewing and distilling

mal·treat \(')mal-'trēt\ *vb* : to treat unkindly or roughly : ABUSE — **mal·treat·ment** \-mənt\ *n*

ma·ma *or* **mam·ma** *also* **mom·ma** \'mäm-ə\ *n* : ¹MOTHER 1a

mam·ba \'mäm-bə, 'mam-\ *n* : any of several African poisonous snakes related to the cobras but lacking a hood

mam·bo \'mäm-bō\ *n, pl* **mambos** : a dance of Haitian origin related to the rumba — **mambo** *vb*

mam·mal \'mam-əl\ *n* : any of a class of warm-blooded vertebrates that include human beings and all other animals that nourish their young with milk produced by mammary glands and have the skin usually more or less covered with hair

mam·ma·li·an \mə-'mā-lē-ən, ma-'mā-\ *adj* : of, relating to, or characteristic of mammals

mam·ma·ry \'mam-ə-rē\ *adj* : of, relating to, lying near, or affecting the mammary glands

mammary gland *n* : one of the large glands that in female mammals produce milk and in males are usually underdeveloped, are located in pairs on the abdominal side of the animal body, and usually end in a nipple

¹mam·moth \'mam-əth\ *n* **1** : any of numerous large hairy extinct elephants with very long tusks that curve upward **2** : something very large of its kind ⟨a company that is a *mammoth* of the industry⟩

²mammoth *adj* : very large : HUGE

mam·my \'mam-ē\ *n, pl* **mammies** **1** : ¹MOTHER 1a **2** : a black woman serving as a nurse to white children especially in the past in the southern states of the U.S.

mammoth 1

¹man \'man\ *n, pl* **men** \'men\ **1 a** : a human being; *esp* : an adult male human **b** : the human race : MANKIND **c** : ¹HUSBAND, LOVER **d** : any member of the family in biological classification that includes both human beings and extinct related forms known only from fossils **e** — used as an interjection to express strong feeling ⟨*man,* what a game⟩ **2 a** : a tenant in the Middle Ages : VASSAL **b** : an adult male servant **c** *pl* : workers as a group **3** : ²INDIVIDUAL 2, PERSON ⟨a *man* could be killed there⟩ **4** : one of the pieces in a game (as chess) [Old English *man* "person"]

²man *vb* **manned; man·ning** **1** : to supply with men ⟨*man* a ship⟩ **2** : to station members of a ship's crew at ⟨*man* the ropes⟩

man·a·cle \'man-i-kəl\ *n* **1** : a shackle for the hand or wrist : HANDCUFF **2** : something that prevents free action — **manacle** *vb*

man·age \'man-ij\ *vb* **man·aged; man·ag·ing** **1** : to look after and make decisions about : DIRECT ⟨*manage* a factory⟩ **2** : to make and keep under one's control : HANDLE ⟨*manages* her skis well⟩ ⟨skill in *managing* horses⟩ **3** : to treat with care : HUSBAND ⟨there's enough food if it's *managed* well⟩ **4** : to succeed in one's purpose : GET

\ə\ abut		\aù\ out		\i\ tip		\ò\ saw	\ù\ foot
\ər\ further		\ch\ chin		\ī\ life		\òi\ coin	\y\ yet
\a\ mat		\e\ pet		\j\ job		\th\ thin	\yü\ few
\ā\ take		\ē\ easy		\ŋ\ sing		\th\ this	\yù\ cure
\ä\ cot, cart		\g\ go		\ō\ bone		\ü\ food	\zh\ vision

ALONG ⟨*manages* despite a handicap⟩ ⟨always *manages* to win somehow⟩ [from Italian *maneggiare* "to handle, direct, manage", from *mano* "hand", from Latin *manus* "hand" — related to MANEUVER, MANUAL, MANUFACTURE; see *Word History* at MANEUVER] — **man·age·abil·i·ty** \,man-ij-ə-'bil-ət-ē\ *n* — **man·age·able** \'man-ij-ə-bəl\ *adj*

man·age·ment \'man-ij-mənt\ *n* **1** : the act or art of managing : CONTROL, DIRECTION **2** : skill in managing **3** : the people who manage ⟨*management* and labor could not agree⟩

man·ag·er \'man-ij-ər\ *n* **1** : a person who manages especially a business or household affairs **2** : a person who directs a team or an athlete — **man·a·ge·ri·al** \,man-ə-'jir-ē-əl\ *adj*

man–at–arms \,man-ət-'ärmz\ *n, pl* **men–at–arms** \,men-\ : ¹SOLDIER 1; *esp* : a heavily armed mounted soldier

man·a·tee \'man-ə-,tē\ *n* : any of several chiefly tropical water-dwelling mammals that eat plants and differ from the related dugong especially in having the tail broad and rounded

Man·chu \'man-chü, man-'chü\ *n* **1** : a member of the native Mongolian race of Manchuria that conquered China in 1644 **2** : the language of the Manchu people — **Manchu** *adj*

man·da·rin \'man-d(ə-)rən\ *n* **1** : a public official under the Chinese Empire **2** *cap* : the chief dialect of China centering about Peking **3** : a small spiny Chinese orange tree with yellow to reddish orange fruits having loose skins; *also* : its fruit

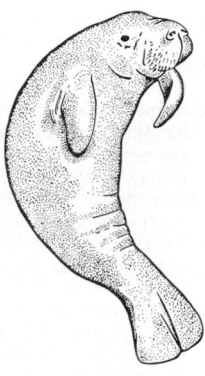

manatee

mandarin orange *n* : MANDARIN 3

¹**man·date** \'man-,dāt\ *n* **1** : an order from a higher court to a lower court **2** : authorization or approval given to a representative especially by voters ⟨accepted the *mandate* of the people⟩ **3 a** : a commission granted by the League of Nations to a member nation to administer a territory on its behalf **b** : a mandated territory

²**mandate** *vb* **man·dat·ed; man·dat·ing** : to administer or assign a territory under a mandate

man·da·to·ry \'man-də-,tōr-ē, -,tȯr-\ *adj* **1** : containing or constituting a command : OBLIGATORY ⟨the assembly was *mandatory* for all students⟩ **2** : of, relating to, or holding a League of Nations mandate

man·di·ble \'man-də-bəl\ *n* **1 a** : a lower jaw of a vertebrate consisting of a single bone or of bones that are completely united **c** : the lower jaw with its surrounding soft parts **c** : either the upper or lower part of the bill of a bird **2** : either of the first pair of mouthparts of some invertebrates and especially arthropods (as an insect or crustacean) that often form biting organs

man·do·lin \,man-də-'lin, 'man-dᵊl-ən\ *also* **man·do·line** \,man-də-'lēn, 'man-dᵊl-ən\ *n* : a stringed instrument with a pear-shaped body and four to six pairs of strings played by plucking

man·drake \'man-,drāk\ *n* **1** : a Mediterranean herb that is related to the potato and has a large forked root having special medical powers according to some superstitious beliefs; *also* : the root itself **2** : MAYAPPLE

mane \'mān\ *n* **1** : long heavy hair growing about the neck of some mammals (as a horse) **2** : long heavy hair on a person's head — **maned** \'mānd\ *adj*

man–eat·er \'man-,ēt-ər\ *n* : one (as a cannibal, shark, or tiger) that has or is thought to have an appetite for human flesh — **man–eat·ing** \-,ēt-iŋ\ *adj*

¹**ma·neu·ver** \mə-'n(y)ü-vər\ *n* **1 a** : a planned movement

of troops or ships **b** : a training exercise by armed forces **2** : a clever or skillful move or action ⟨avoided an accident by a quick *maneuver*⟩

Word History The word *maneuvre* was first used in early French to refer to "work done by hand". It was borrowed from the Latin noun *manuopera*, used in the Middle Ages with the same meaning. The Latin word was formed from the phrase *manu operari*, meaning "to work by hand". In time, the French came to use the spelling *manœuvre* for "a military exercise involving the movement of soldiers or ships". In the 18th century, when French military influence was strong in Europe, *manœuvre* was borrowed into English. Americans later came to spell it *maneuver*. The military sense has remained and has given rise to the more general sense of "a clever move or action". [from French *manœuvre* "a military exercise", from early French *maneuvre* "work done by hand", from Latin *manuopera* (same meaning), derived from earlier *manu operari* "to work by hand", from *manu*, a form of *manus* "hand", and *operari* "to work" — related to MANAGE, MANUAL, OPERATE]

²**maneuver** *vb* **ma·neu·vered; ma·neu·ver·ing** \-'n(y)üv-(ə-)riŋ\ **1** : to move (as troops or ships) in a maneuver **2** : to perform a maneuver **3** : to manage skillfully **4** : to use trickery : SCHEME — **ma·neu·ver·abil·i·ty** \-,n(y)üv-(ə-)rə-'bil-ət-ē\ *n* — **ma·neu·ver·able** \-'n(y)üv-(ə-)rə-bəl\ *adj*

man·ful \'man-fəl\ *adj* : having or showing courage : BRAVE, RESOLUTE — **man·ful·ly** \-fə-lē\ *adv* — **man·ful·ness** *n*

man·ga·nese \'maŋ-gə-,nēz, -,nēs\ *n* : a grayish white usually hard and brittle metallic element that resembles iron but is not magnetic — see ELEMENT table

manganese dioxide *n* : a brown or gray-black insoluble compound of manganese and oxygen that is used in making glass and ceramics

mange \'mānj\ *n* : any of several contagious skin diseases of domestic animals and sometimes human beings that are marked especially by itching and loss of hair; *esp* : one caused by a minute mite

man·ger \'mān-jər\ *n* : a trough or open box in which food for farm animals is placed

¹**man·gle** \'maŋ-gəl\ *vb* **man·gled; man·gling** \-g(ə-)liŋ\ **1** : to cut, bruise, or hack with repeated blows or strokes **2** : to spoil or injure in making or performing : BOTCH ⟨*mangle* a speech⟩ — **man·gler** \-g(ə-)lər\ *n*

²**mangle** *n* : a machine for ironing laundry by passing it between heated rollers

³**mangle** *vb* **man·gled; man·gling** \-g(ə-)liŋ\ : to press or smooth with a mangle — **man·gler** \-g(ə-)lər\ *n*

man·go \'maŋ-gō\ *n, pl* **mangoes** *or* **mangos** : a yellowish red tropical fruit with a firm skin, hard central stony seed, and juicy mildly acid pulp; *also* : an evergreen tree related to the sumacs that bears this fruit

man·grove \'man-,grōv, 'maŋ-\ *n* : any of various tropical trees or shrubs that grow many prop roots and form dense masses in somewhat salty marshes or shallow salt water

mangy \'mān-jē\ *adj* **mang·i·er; -est** **1** : affected with or resulting from mange **2** : SHABBY 1, SEEDY ⟨a *mangy* old rug⟩ — **mang·i·ness** \'mān-jē-nəs\ *n*

man·han·dle \'man-,han-dᵊl\ *vb* **1** : to handle roughly **2** : to move or manage by human force

man·hat·tan \man-'hat-ᵊn, mən-\ *n, often cap* : a cocktail consisting of vermouth and whiskey

man·hole \'man-,hōl\ *n* : a covered hole (as in a pavement, tank, or boiler) through which a worker may go

man·hood \'man-,hủd\ *n* **1** : COURAGE, MANLINESS **2** : the condition of being an adult male **3** : adult human males ⟨the *manhood* of a nation⟩

man–hour \'man-,aủ(-ə)r\ *n* : a unit of one hour's work by one worker used especially as a basis for wages and in accounting

man·hunt \-,hənt\ *n* : an organized hunt for a person and especially for one charged with a crime

ma·nia \'mā-nē-ə, -nyə\ *n* **1** : the state of being mad; *esp* : insanity marked by uncontrollable emotion or excitement **2** : excessive enthusiasm : CRAZE ⟨had a *mania* for saving things⟩

ma·ni·ac \'mā-nē-,ak\ *n* **1** : MADMAN, LUNATIC **2** : a person wildly enthusiastic about something

ma·ni·a·cal \mə-'nī-ə-kəl\ *also* **ma·ni·ac** \'mā-nē-,ak\ *adj* : affected with or suggestive of madness — **ma·ni·a·cal·ly** \mə-'nī-ə-k(ə-)lē\ *adv*

man·i·cot·ti \,man-ə-'kät-ē\ *n, pl* **manicotti** : pasta in the shape of tubes often stuffed with meat or cheese

¹man·i·cure \'man-ə-,kyu̇(ə)r\ *n* **1** : MANICURIST **2** : a beauty treatment for the hands and nails [from French *manicure* "one who gives a beauty treatment for the hands", derived from Latin *manus* "hand" and Latin *cura* "care"]

²manicure *vb* **-cured; -cur·ing** **1** : to give a manicure to **2** : to trim closely and evenly ⟨*manicured* their lawn⟩

man·i·cur·ist \'man-ə-,kyu̇r-əst\ *n* : a person who gives manicures

¹man·i·fest \'man-ə-,fest\ *adj* : clear to the senses or mind : OBVIOUS ⟨their relief was *manifest*⟩ — **man·i·fest·ly** *adv*

²manifest *vb* : to show plainly : DISPLAY

³manifest *n* : a list of cargo or passengers especially for a ship or plane

man·i·fes·ta·tion \,man-ə-fə-'stā-shən, -,fes-'tā-\ *n* **1 a** : the act or an instance of manifesting : EXPRESSION **b** : something that manifests : EVIDENCE **2** : a public demonstration of power and purpose

man·i·fes·to \,man-ə-'fes-tō\ *n, pl* **-tos** *or* **-toes** : a public declaration of intentions or views

¹man·i·fold \'man-ə-,fōld\ *adj* **1** : of many and various kinds ⟨*manifold* excuses⟩ **2** : including or uniting various features ⟨a *manifold* personality⟩ **3** : consisting of or operating many of one kind joined together ⟨a *manifold* pipe⟩ — **man·i·fold·ly** \-,fōl-(d)lē\ *adv*

²manifold *n* : something manifold; *esp* : a pipe fitting having several outlets for connecting one pipe with others

³manifold *vb* : to make several copies ⟨*manifold* a manuscript⟩

man·i·kin *or* **man·ni·kin** \'man-i-kən\ *n* : MANNEQUIN

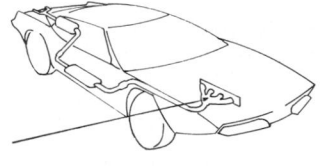

manifold

ma·nila \mə-'nil-ə\ *adj, often cap* : made of manila paper or from Manila hemp ⟨*manila* folder⟩ ⟨*manila* rope⟩

Manila hemp *n* : ABACA

manila paper *n, often cap M* : a tough brownish paper made originally from Manila hemp and used especially as a wrapping paper

man·i·oc \'man-ē-,äk\ *n* : CASSAVA

ma·nip·u·late \mə-'nip-yə-,lāt\ *vb* **-lat·ed; -lat·ing** **1** : to treat or operate with the hands or by mechanical means especially with skill ⟨*manipulate* the TV dials⟩ **2** : to manage or use skillfully ⟨*manipulate* masses of statistics⟩ **3** : to manage especially with intent to deceive ⟨*manipulate* accounts⟩ ⟨*manipulate* public opinion⟩ **syn** see HANDLE — **ma·nip·u·la·tion** \-,nip-yə-'lā-shən\ *n* — **ma·nip·u·la·tor** \-'nip-yə-,lāt-ər\ *n*

man·kind *n* **1** \'man-'kīnd, -,kīnd\ : the human race : all human beings **2** \-,kīnd\ : men as distinguished from women

man·like \'man-,līk\ *adj* : resembling or characteristic of a man : MANNISH

man·ly \'man-lē\ *adj* **man·li·er; -est** **1** : having qualities generally associated with a man : STRONG **2** : appropriate in character to a man ⟨*manly* sports⟩ — **man·li·ness** *n*

man–made \'man-'mād\ *adj* : made by people rather than nature ⟨*man-made* satellites⟩; *esp* : ¹SYNTHETIC 2 ⟨*man-made* fibers⟩

man·na \'man-ə\ *n* **1** : food miraculously supplied to the Israelites in the wilderness **2** : a usually sudden and unexpected source of pleasure or gain

manned \'mand\ *adj* : carrying or performed by a person ⟨*manned* spaceflight⟩

man·ne·quin \'man-i-kən\ *n* **1** : an artist's, tailor's, or dressmaker's jointed figure of the human body **2** : a form representing the human figure used especially for displaying clothes **3** : a person employed to model clothing : MODEL

man·ner \'man-ər\ *n* **1 a** : ¹SORT 1a, KIND ⟨what *manner* of fools are they⟩ **b** : various kinds — usually used in the phrase *all manner of* **2 a** : normal behavior : HABIT, CUSTOM ⟨spoke bluntly as was her *manner*⟩ **b** : a way of acting or proceeding ⟨worked in a brisk *manner*⟩ **c** : ¹STYLE 1 ⟨painted in the artist's early *manner*⟩ **3** *pl* **a** : social conduct or rules of conduct as shown in the prevailing customs **b** : characteristic or habitual conduct : BEHAVIOR ⟨taught the child good *manners*⟩; *esp* : polite behavior

man·nered \'man-ərd\ *adj* : having manners of a specified kind ⟨well-*mannered*⟩ ⟨mild-*mannered*⟩

man·ner·ism \'man-ə-,riz-əm\ *n* : a characteristic and often unconscious way of acting ⟨the *mannerism* of constantly adjusting her glasses⟩

man·ner·ly \'man-ər-lē\ *adj* : showing good manners : POLITE — **man·ner·li·ness** *n* — **mannerly** *adv*

manning *present participle of* MAN

man·nish \'man-ish\ *adj* : resembling, suggesting, suitable to, or characteristic of a man rather than a woman ⟨a *mannish* voice⟩ ⟨her *mannish* clothes⟩ — **man·nish·ly** *adv* — **man·nish·ness** *n*

ma·noeu·vre \mə-'n(y)ü-vər\ *chiefly British variant of* MANEUVER

man of the world : a practical or worldly man of much experience

man–of–war \,man-ə(v)-'wȯ(ə)r\ *n, pl* **men–of–war** \,men-\ : WARSHIP

ma·nom·e·ter \mə-'näm-ət-ər\ *n* : an instrument for measuring pressure (as of gases and vapors)

man·or \'man-ər\ *n* : a usually large estate; *esp* : one granted to a feudal lord — **ma·no·ri·al** \mə-'nōr-ē-əl, -'nȯr-\ *adj*

manor house *n* : the house of the lord of a manor

man–o'–war bird \,man-ə-'wȯr-\ *n* : FRIGATE BIRD

man power *n* **1** : power available from or supplied by the physical effort of human beings **2** *usually* **man·pow·er** : the total supply of persons available and fitted for service ⟨military *manpower*⟩

man·sard \'man-,särd, -sərd\ *n* : a roof having two slopes on all sides with the lower slope steeper than the upper one

manse \'man(t)s\ *n* : the residence of a member of the clergy : PARSONAGE

man·ser·vant \'man-,sər-vənt\ *n, pl* **men·ser·vants** \'men-,sər-vən(t)s\ : a male servant

man·sion \'man-chən\ *n* : a large impressive residence

man–size \'man-,sīz\ *or* **man–sized** \-,sīzd\ *adj* : suitable for or requiring a man ⟨a *man-sized* job⟩

man·slaugh·ter \'man-,slȯt-ər\ *n* : the unlawful killing of a person without the intention to do so

man·ta \'mant-ə\ *n* : DEVILFISH 1

manta ray *n* : DEVILFISH 1

\ə\ abut	\au̇\ out	\i\ tip	\ȯ\ saw	\u̇\ foot
\ər\ further	\ch\ chin	\ī\ life	\ȯi\ coin	\y\ yet
\a\ mat	\e\ pet	\j\ job	\th\ thin	\yü\ few
\ā\ take	\ē\ easy	\ŋ\ sing	\th\ this	\yu̇\ cure
\ä\ cot, cart	\g\ go	\ō\ bone	\ü\ food	\zh\ vision

man·tel \'mant-əl\ *n* : the beam, stone, arch, or shelf above a fireplace

man·tel·piece \-ˌpēs\ *n* **1** : a mantel with its side elements **2** : the shelf of a mantel

man·tid \'mant-əd\ *n* : MANTIS

man·til·la \man-'tē-(y)ə, -'til-ə\ *n* **1** : a light scarf worn over the head and shoulders especially by Spanish and Latin American women **2** : a short light cape or cloak

man·tis \'mant-əs\ *n, pl* **man·tis·es** *or* **man·tes** \'man-ˌtēz\ : any of various insects related to the grasshoppers and roaches that feed upon other insects and hold their prey in the stout spiny first pair of legs

mantis

¹man·tle \'mant-əl\ *n* **1** : a loose sleeveless garment worn over other clothes : CLOAK **2 a** : something that covers or surrounds ⟨a *mantle* of snow⟩ ⟨a *mantle* of secrecy⟩ **b** : a fold or lobe or pair of lobes of the body wall of a mollusk or brachiopod that lines and produces the shell **3** : the portion of the earth lying between the crust and the core

²mantle *vb* **man·tled; man·tling** \'mant-liŋ, -əl-iŋ\ : to cover or surround with or as if with a mantle

¹man·u·al \'man-yə(-wə)l\ *adj* **1** : of, relating to, or involving the hands ⟨*manual* skill⟩ **2** : worked or operated by hand ⟨a car with a *manual* transmission⟩ **3** : requiring or using physical skill and energy ⟨*manual* labor⟩ [Middle English *manuel* "relating to the hands, manual", from early French *manuel* (same meaning), from Latin *manualis* (same meaning), from *manus* "hand" — related to MANAGE, MANEUVER, MANUFACTURE; see *Word History* at MANEUVER] — **man·u·al·ly** \-ē\ *adv*

²manual *n* **1** : a small book; *esp* : HANDBOOK **2** : the set movements in the handling of a weapon during a military drill ⟨the *manual* of arms⟩

manual training *n* : training to develop skill in using the hands (as in woodworking)

man·u·fac·to·ry \ˌman-(y)ə-'fak-t(ə-)rē\ *n, pl* **-ries** : FACTORY

¹man·u·fac·ture \ˌman-(y)ə-'fak-chər\ *n* **1** : something made from raw materials **2** : the making of products by hand or machinery **3** : PRODUCTION 2 ⟨the *manufacture* of blood in the body⟩ [from early French *manufacture* "something made", from Latin *manufactus* "made by hand", from earlier *manu* "by hand" (from *manus* "hand") and *factus*, past participle of *facere* "to make, do" — related to FACTORY, FASHION, MANAGE, MANUAL]

²manufacture *vb* **-tured; -tur·ing** \-'fak-chə-riŋ, -'fak-shriŋ\ **1** : to make into a product suitable for use ⟨*manufacture* wool⟩ **2** : to make from raw materials by hand or by machinery **3** : to make up sometimes with the intention of misleading **syn** see MAKE — **man·u·fac·tur·ing** *n*

man·u·fac·tur·er \ˌman-(y)ə-'fak-chər-ər\ *n* : one that manufactures; *esp* : an employer of workers in manufacturing

man·u·mis·sion \ˌman-yə-'mish-ən\ *n* : a setting free from slavery : EMANCIPATION

man·u·mit \ˌman-yə-'mit\ *vb* **-mit·ted; -mit·ting** : to set free; *esp* : to release from slavery

¹ma·nure \mə-'n(y)ù(ə)r\ *vb* **ma·nured; ma·nur·ing** : to enrich by applying manure ⟨*manure* a field⟩

²manure *n* : material that fertilizes land; *esp* : bodily waste from birds and animals in stables and barnyards with or without litter

¹manu·script \'man-yə-ˌskript\ *adj* : written by hand or typed ⟨*manuscript* letters⟩

²manuscript *n* **1** : a written or typewritten composition or document **2** : writing as opposed to print

Manx cat \'maŋ(k)s-\ *n* : a domestic cat with short hair and no tail visible on the outside

Manx cat

¹many \'men-ē\ *adj* **more** \'mō(ə)r, 'mo(ə)r\; **most** \'mōst\ **1** : amounting to a large number ⟨worked for *many* years⟩ **2** : being one of a large but indefinite number ⟨told *many* a tale⟩ — **as many** : the same in number ⟨saw three plays in *as many* days⟩

²many *pron* : a large number ⟨*many* of the students were late⟩

³many *n* : a large but indefinite number ⟨a good *many* of them⟩

man·za·ni·ta \ˌman-zə-'nēt-ə\ *n* : any of various evergreen shrubs of western North America that belong to the heath family

Mao·ri \'maù(ə)r-ē\ *n, pl* **Maori** *or* **Maoris** **1** : a member of a Polynesian people native to New Zealand **2** : the language of the Maori

¹map \'map\ *n* **1** : a drawing or picture showing selected features of an area (as the surface of the earth or the moon or a section of the brain) and usually drawn to a given scale **2** : a drawing or picture of the sky showing the position of stars and planets [from Latin *mappa* "map", from earlier *mappa* "napkin" — related to APRON, NAPKIN]

²map *vb* **mapped; map·ping** **1** : to make a map of ⟨*map* the heavens⟩ **2** : to chart the course of : plan in detail — often used with *out* ⟨*map* out a campaign⟩ — **map·per** *n*

ma·ple \'mā-pəl\ *n* : any of a group of trees having deeply notched opposite leaves, fruits with two wings, and hard light-colored wood and including some from which maple syrup and maple sugar are obtained; *also* : the wood of a maple

maple sugar *n* : a brown sugar made by boiling maple syrup

maple syrup *n* : syrup made by thickening the sap of maples and especially the sugar maple by boiling

map·mak·er \'map-ˌmā-kər\ *n* : CARTOGRAPHER

mar \'mär\ *vb* **marred; mar·ring** : to make a blemish on : SPOIL

ma·ra·ca \mə-'räk-ə, -'rak-\ *n* : a dried gourd or a rattle like a gourd that contains dried seeds or pebbles and is used as a musical rhythm instrument usually played in pairs by shaking

mar·a·schi·no \ˌmar-ə-'skē-nō, -'shē-\ *n, pl* **-nos** *often cap* **1** : a sweet alcoholic drink made from the juice of a bitter wild cherry **2** : a cherry preserved in true or imitation maraschino

mar·a·thon \'mar-ə-ˌthän\ *n* **1 a** : a long-distance footrace of 42.2 kilometers (26 miles 385 yards) that is run on an open course **b** : a race other than a footrace (as for swimmers) marked especially by great distance **2** : a long hard contest ⟨a dance *marathon*⟩ — **marathon** *adj*

    Word History *Marathon* is the name of a plain in Greece located about 42 kilometers (26 miles) from the city of Athens. It was the scene of a great victory by the Greeks over the Persians in 490 B.C. According to legend a Greek soldier named Pheidippides ran all the way from the battlefield to Athens to deliver the news. He reached the city, gasped out his message, and fell dead. When the modern Olympic Games began in 1896, one of the events was a footrace of 42.2 kilometers (26 miles 385 yards), called a *marathon*, in honor of the legendary run by Pheidippides. [named for *Marathon*, site of a battlefield in ancient Greece]

mar·a·thon·er \'mar-ə-ˌthän-ər\ *n* : one (as a runner) who takes part in a marathon

ma·raud \mə-'rȯd\ *vb* : to roam about and raid in search of things to steal — **ma·raud·er** *n*

¹mar·ble \'mär-bəl\ *n* **1 a** : a limestone that takes a high polish and is used in architecture and sculpture **b** : something made from marble; *esp* : a piece of sculpture **2 a** : a little ball (as of glass) used in various games **b** *pl* : a children's game played with these little balls — **marble** *adj*

²marble *vb* **mar·bled; mar·bling** \'mär-b(ə-)liŋ\ : to give a streaked, spotted, or blotched appearance to (as by staining) ⟨*marble* the edges of a book⟩

mar·bling *n* : a mixture of fat and lean in a cut of meat

¹march \'märch\ *n* **1** : a border region : FRONTIER **2** : a district originally set up to defend a boundary — usually used in pl. ⟨the Welsh *marches*⟩

²march *vb* **1** : to move along with a steady regular stride especially in step with others **2** : to move in a direct purposeful manner : PROGRESS — **march·er** *n*

³march *n* **1 a** : the action of marching **b** : the distance covered within a period of time by marching **c** : a regular even step used in marching **2** : forward movement : PROGRESS ⟨the *march* of time⟩ **3** : a musical piece with a strong regular rhythm that is suitable to march to

March \'märch\ *n* : the third month of the year

> **Word History** One of the gods worshiped by the ancient Romans was a war god named Mars. In his honor they named one of the months of the year *martius*, which means "of Mars" or "belonging to Mars". The Latin *martius* later became *march* in early French, and it was from early French that the word came into English. [Middle English *March* "the third month", from early French *march* (same meaning), derived from Latin *martius* "of (the god) Mars"]

mar·chio·ness \'mär-sh(ə-)nəs\ *n* **1** : the wife or widow of a marquess **2** : a woman holding the rank of marquess

Mar·di Gras \'märd-ē-,grä\ *n* : the Tuesday before Ash Wednesday often observed with parades and merrymaking

> **Word History** The Christian period of fasting known as Lent begins every year on Ash Wednesday. The day before Lent begins is a time of celebration and feasting in many places. One of the original reasons for such feasting was probably to use up the last supplies of foods, such as meat and fat, which were not eaten during Lent. The eating of such foods may be why the day became known in France as *Mardi Gras*, which means "fat Tuesday." It is also possible that the name comes from a former custom of parading a fattened ox through Paris on this day. [French, literally "fat Tuesday"]

¹mare \'ma(ə)r, 'me(ə)r\ *n* : an adult female of the horse or a related animal (as a zebra or donkey) [Old English *mere* "a mature female horse"]

²ma·re \'mär-ā\ *n, pl* **ma·ria** \'mär-ē-ə\ : any of several large dark areas on the surface of the moon or Mars [scientific Latin, from Latin *mare* "sea"]

mar·ga·rine \'märj-(ə-)rən, 'märj-ə-,rēn\ *n* : a food product made from usually vegetable oils and skim milk and used as a spread and a cooking fat

¹mar·gin \'mär-jən\ *n* **1** : the part of a page outside the main body of printed or written matter **2** : boundary area **3** : an extra amount (as of time) allowed for use if needed **syn** see BORDER — **mar·gined** \-jənd\ *adj*

²margin *vb* **1** : to provide with a margin **2** : to form a margin to : BORDER

mar·gin·al \'märj-nəl, -ən-ᵊl\ *adj* **1** : written or printed in the margin ⟨*marginal* notes⟩ **2** : of, relating to, or situated at a margin or border **3** : close to the lower limit of quality ⟨*marginal* ability⟩ ⟨*marginal* land⟩ — **mar·gin·al·ly** \-nə-lē, -ən-ᵊl-ē\ *adv*

mar·gin·al·ize \'märj-nəl-,īz, -ən-ᵊl-\ *vb* **-ized; -iz·ing** : to remove or keep in a position without influence in a society or group — **mar·gin·al·i·za·tion** \,märj-nəl-ə-'zā-shən, -ən-ᵊl-\ *n*

mari·gold \'mar-ə-,gōld, 'mer-\ *n* : any of a genus of tropical American herbs related to the daisies and grown for their showy yellow or red and yellow flower heads

mar·i·jua·na *also* **mar·i·hua·na** \,mar-ə-'wän-ə *also* -'hwän-\ *n* : any of various preparations of the dried leaves and flowering tops of the female hemp plant that are used as a drug usually illegally especially by smoking

ma·rim·ba \mə-'rim-bə\ *n* : a musical instrument resembling a xylophone but with tubes under each bar to help increase the sound

ma·ri·na \mə-'rē-nə\ *n* : a dock or basin providing a place to anchor motorboats and yachts

¹mar·i·nade \,mar-ə-'nād\ *n* : a sauce in which meat or fish is soaked to enrich its flavor

²marinade *vb* **-nad·ed; -nad·ing** : MARINATE

mar·i·nate \'mar-ə-,nāt\ *vb* **-nat·ed; -nat·ing** : to soak in a marinade

¹ma·rine \mə-'rēn\ *adj* **1 a** : of or relating to the sea ⟨*marine* life⟩ **b** : of or relating to the navigation of the sea : NAUTICAL, MARITIME ⟨a *marine* chart⟩ ⟨*marine* insurance⟩ **2** : of or relating to marines ⟨*marine* barracks⟩

²marine *n* **1** : the commercial and naval shipping of a country **2** : one of a class of soldiers serving aboard ship or in association with a naval force; *esp* : a member of the U.S. Marine Corps

mar·i·ner \'mar-ə-nər\ *n* : one who navigates or assists in navigating a ship : SAILOR

mar·i·o·nette \,mar-ē-ə-'net, ,mer-\ *n* : a puppet moved by attached strings or wires

mar·i·tal \'mar-ət-ᵊl\ *adj* : of or relating to marriage : CONJUGAL — **mar·i·tal·ly** \-ət-ᵊl-ē\ *adv*

mar·i·time \'mar-ə-,tīm\ *adj* **1** : of, relating to, or bordering on the sea ⟨*maritime* nations⟩ **2** : of or relating to navigation or commerce on the sea ⟨*maritime* law⟩

mar·jo·ram \'märj-(ə-)rəm\ *n* : any of various usually fragrant mints sometimes used in cookery

¹mark \'märk\ *n* **1 a** : a noticeable object serving as a guide for travelers **b** : something (as a line, notch, or fixed object) designed to record position ⟨high-water *mark*⟩ **c** : something aimed at : TARGET **d** : the starting line or position in a track event **e** : an object of ridicule **f** : a standard of performance, quality, or condition ⟨not up to the *mark*⟩ **2 a** : something that gives evidence of something else : SIGN, INDICATION ⟨a *mark* of friendship⟩ **b** : an impression (as a scar, scratch, or stain) made on a surface **c** : a characteristic or distinguishing trait or quality **d** : a cross made in place of a signature **e** : a written or printed symbol **f** : a symbol (as a brand or label) used for identification (as of ownership or quality) **g** : a symbol (as a number or letter) representing a teacher's estimation of the quality of work or conduct : GRADE **3 a** : IMPORTANCE, DISTINCTION ⟨stands out as a person of *mark*⟩ **b** : a lasting or strong impression ⟨worked at several jobs but didn't make much of a *mark*⟩ [Old English *meare* "boundary"]

²mark *vb* **1 a** : to fix or trace out the bounds of by or as if by a mark **b** : to set apart by a boundary ⟨*mark* off a tennis court⟩ **2 a** : to designate as if by a mark ⟨*marked* for greatness⟩ **b** : to make a mark or notation on **c** : to furnish with natural marks ⟨wings *marked* with white⟩ **d** : to label so as to indicate price or quality **3 a** : to make note of in writing : JOT ⟨*marking* the date in a journal⟩ **b** : to indicate by a mark or symbol ⟨*mark* an accent⟩ **c** : to determine the value of by means of marks : GRADE ⟨*mark* exam papers⟩ **4** : to be an important characteristic of : CHARACTERIZE, DISTINGUISH ⟨a disease *marked* by fever⟩ **5** : to take notice of : OBSERVE ⟨*mark* my words⟩ — **mark**

\ə\ abut	\au̇\ out	\i\ tip	\ȯ\ saw	\u̇\ foot
\ər\ further	\ch\ chin	\ī\ life	\ȯi\ coin	\y\ yet
\a\ mat	\e\ pet	\j\ job	\th\ thin	\yü\ few
\ā\ take	\ē\ easy	\ŋ\ sing	\t̲h̲\ this	\yu̇\ cure
\ä\ cot, cart	\g\ go	\ō\ bone	\ü\ food	\zh\ vision

time 1 : to keep the time of a marching step by moving the feet one after another without advancing 2 : to function or operate without making progress

³**mark** *n* : DEUTSCHE MARK [Old English *marc* "a unit of weight"; probably of Scandinavian origin]

Mark \ˈmärk\ *n* — see BIBLE table

mark·down \ˈmärk-ˌdaun\ *n* 1 : a lowering of price 2 : the amount by which an original selling price is reduced

mark down \(ˈ)märk-ˈdaun\ *vb* : to put a lower price on ⟨*marked down* all the books for the sale⟩

marked \ˈmärkt\ *adj* 1 : having an identifying mark ⟨a *marked* card⟩ 2 : NOTICEABLE, CONSPICUOUS ⟨speaks with a *marked* accent⟩ 3 a : being a person on whom attention is focused b : being an object of attack or suspicion ⟨a *marked* man⟩ — **mark·ed·ly** \ˈmär-kəd-lē\ *adv*

mark·er \ˈmär-kər\ *n* 1 : one that marks 2 : something used for marking

¹**mar·ket** \ˈmär-kət\ *n* 1 a : a meeting together of people to buy and sell b : the people at such a meeting c : a public place where a market is held; *esp* : a place where provisions are sold at wholesale 2 : a store where foods are sold to the public ⟨a meat *market*⟩ 3 a : a geographic region in which things may be sold ⟨*markets* for American cotton⟩ b : a particular category of people who might buy ⟨the youth *market*⟩ 4 : an opportunity for selling ⟨a good *market* for used cars⟩ [Middle English *market* "market", from early French *market* (same meaning), from Latin *mercatus* "trade, marketplace", derived from *mercari* "to trade", from *merc-, merx* "merchandise" — related to COMMERCE, MERCHANT]

²**market** *vb* 1 : to deal in a market 2 : to offer for sale in a market : SELL — **mar·ket·ing** \-iŋ\ *n*

mar·ket·able \ˈmär-kət-ə-bəl\ *adj* 1 : fit to be offered for sale ⟨food that has gone bad is not *marketable*⟩ 2 : wanted by purchasers or employers ⟨*marketable* skills⟩ — **mar·ket·abil·i·ty** \ˌmär-kət-ə-ˈbil-ət-ē\ *n*

mar·ket·place \ˈmär-kət-ˌplās\ *n* 1 : an open square or place in a town where markets are held 2 : the world of trade

market value *n* : a price at which both buyers and sellers are willing to do business

mark·ing \ˈmär-kiŋ\ *n* 1 : the act, process, or an instance of making or giving a mark ⟨the teacher's *marking* was considered to be fair⟩ 2 : a mark made 3 : an arrangement or pattern of marks ⟨as on the coat of an animal⟩

mark·ka \ˈmär-ˌkä\ *n* 1 : the basic unit of money of Finland 2 : a coin representing one markka

marks·man \ˈmärk-smən\ *n* : a person skilled in shooting at a mark or target — **marks·man·ship** \-ˌship\ *n*

mark·up \ˈmär-ˌkəp\ *n* : an amount added to the cost price of an article to set the selling price

mark up \(ˈ)mär-ˈkəp\ *vb* : to put a higher price on

marl \ˈmär(-ə)l\ *n* : a crumbling earthy deposit that consists of clay and calcium carbonate and is used to improve soils lacking lime

mar·lin \ˈmär-lən\ *n* : any of several large saltwater sport fishes related to sailfishes

mar·ma·lade \ˈmär-mə-ˌlād\ *n* : a clear jelly containing pieces of fruit and fruit rind ⟨orange *marmalade*⟩

    Word History Many of us have eaten orange marmalade, but marmalade can be made from any of several fruits. The Portuguese made such a jelly from the quince, a fruit that looks a bit like a yellow apple. The Portuguese word for the quince is *marmelo*, which is based on the Latin word *melimelum*, meaning "a sweet apple". The Portuguese called the jelly they made from the quince *marmelada*. English borrowed this word as *marmalade*. [from Portuguese *marmelada* "jelly made from quince", from *marmelo* "quince", from Latin *melimelum* "sweet apple", from Greek *melimēlon* (same meaning), from *meli* "honey" and *mēlon* "apple"]

mar·mo·set \ˈmär-mə-ˌset, -mə-ˌzet\ *n* : any of numerous South and Central American monkeys that have soft fur, a bushy tail, and claws instead of nails except on the big toe

mar·mot \ˈmär-mət\ *n* : any of a genus of burrowing rodents with a stout body, short legs, coarse fur, a short bushy tail, and very small ears — compare WOODCHUCK

marmoset

¹**ma·roon** \mə-ˈrün\ *vb* 1 : to put ashore and abandon on a lonely island or coast 2 : to leave isolated and helpless

²**maroon** *n* : a dark red

mar·quee \mär-ˈkē\ *n* 1 : a large tent set up for an outdoor party or exhibition 2 : a rooflike structure sticking out over an entrance ⟨a theater *marquee*⟩

mar·quess \ˈmär-kwəs\ *n* 1 : a nobleman of hereditary rank in Europe and Japan 2 : a British nobleman ranking below a duke and above an earl

mar·quis \ˈmär-kwəs, mär-ˈkē\ *n, pl* **mar·quis·es** \-kwə-səz, -ˈkēz\ : MARQUESS 2

mar·quise \mär-ˈkēz\ *n, pl* **mar·quises** \-ˈkēz(-əz)\ : MARCHIONESS

mar·qui·sette \ˌmär-k(w)ə-ˈzet\ *n* : a sheer meshed fabric used for clothing, curtains, and mosquito nets

marred *past and past participle of* MAR

mar·riage \ˈmar-ij\ *n* 1 a : the state of being married : WEDLOCK b : the legal relationship into which a man and a woman enter for the purpose of making a home and usually raising a family 2 : an act of marrying; *esp* : a wedding ceremony 3 : a close union — **mar·riage·able** \-ə-bəl\ *adj*

¹**mar·ried** \ˈmar-ēd\ *adj* 1 : united in marriage ⟨a *married* couple⟩ 2 : of or relating to marriage

²**married** *n, pl* **marrieds** *or* **married** : a married person ⟨young *marrieds* starting their first home⟩

marring *present participle of* MAR

mar·row \ˈmar-ō\ *n* 1 a : a soft tissue rich in fat and blood vessels that fills the cavities of most bones b : the substance of the spinal cord 2 : the innermost, best, or essential part : CORE

¹**mar·ry** \ˈmar-ē\ *vb* **mar·ried; mar·ry·ing** 1 : to join as husband and wife according to law or custom ⟨they were *married* by a priest⟩ 2 : to give in marriage ⟨*married* their children off⟩ 3 : to take as husband or wife ⟨*married* a singer⟩ 4 : to enter into a marriage relationship : WED ⟨decided to *marry*⟩ 5 : to enter into a close union ⟨working long hours, she is *married* to her job⟩ [Middle English *marien* "to marry", from early French *marier* (same meaning), derived from Latin *maritus* "married"]

²**marry** *interj, archaic* — used to express amused or surprised agreement [Middle English *marie,* an interjection, from *Marie* "the Virgin Mary"]

Mars \ˈmärz\ *n* : the planet fourth in order from the sun — see PLANET table

marsh \ˈmärsh\ *n* : an area of soft wet land usually overgrown by grasses and sedges — **marshy** \ˈmär-shē\ *adj*

¹**mar·shal** \ˈmär-shəl\ *n* 1 a : a high official in a royal household in the Middle Ages b : a person who arranges and directs ceremonies or parades 2 : an officer of the highest rank in some military forces 3 a : a federal official having duties similar to those of a sheriff b : the head of a division of a city government ⟨fire *marshal*⟩

    Word History Although most French words come from Latin, some are the result of the Germanic occupation of France in the third century A.D. In early French the word *mareschal*, literally meaning "horse servant", was such a word. By the Middle English period, a mareschal in French was a high royal official. English borrowed the word to name a similar position in England. Much later, *marshal* was used in England as the title of a high-ranking military officer. It is because of this use that many people think the word is related to the word *martial*, meaning "relating to military affairs". But *martial* derives from the Latin name *Mars*, the god of war. It is only an accident that these two words came to be linked many centuries after they had entered English from different languages. [Middle English *marshal* "a high officer in the king's household", from early French *mareschal* (same meaning), literally "horse servant"; of Germanic origin.]

²mar·shal *vb* **-shaled** *or* **-shalled; -shal·ing** *or* **-shal·ling** \'märsh-(ə-)liŋ\ **1** : to arrange in order ⟨*marshal* troops⟩ **2** : to lead with ceremony : USHER ⟨*marshaling* the group of children down the street⟩

marsh gas *n* : METHANE

marsh hawk *n* : a common American hawk with a white patch on the upper side near the base of the tail

marsh·land \'märsh-,land\ : a marshy area : MARSH

marsh·mal·low \'märsh-,mel-ō, -,mal-\ **1** : a pink-flowered herb related to the mallow that has a root sometimes used in sweets and in medicine **2** : a soft spongy sweet formerly made from the root of the marshmallow but now usually prepared from corn syrup, sugar, albumen, and gelatin

marsh marigold *n* : a swamp herb related to the buttercups and having bright yellow flowers and round shiny leaves — called also *cowslip*

¹mar·su·pi·al \mär-'sü-pē-əl\ *adj* : of, relating to, or being a marsupial

²marsupial *n* : any of an order of lower mammals (as kangaroos and opossums) that have a pouch on the abdomen of the female containing the teats and serving to carry the young

mart \'märt\ *n* : a trading place : MARKET

mar·ten \'märt-ᵊn\ *n, pl* **marten** *or* **martens** : a slender flesh-eating mammal that is larger than the related weasels and is sought for its soft gray or brown fur; *also* : its fur

mar·tial \'mär-shəl\ *adj* **1** : of, relating to, or suited for war or a warrior ⟨*martial* music⟩ **2** : of or relating to an army or to military life ⟨*martial* discipline⟩ [Middle English *martial* "relating to or suited for war", from Latin *martialis* "of Mars", from *Mars* "god of war"] — **mar·tial·ly** \-shə-lē\ *adv*

marten

martial law *n* : the law applied by military forces in occupied territory or in an emergency

Mar·tian \'mär-shən\ *adj* : of or relating to the planet Mars or its supposed inhabitants — **Martian** *n*

mar·tin \'märt-ᵊn\ *n* : a small European swallow with a forked tail, bluish black head and back, a white underside, and a large white patch on the back at the base of the tail; *also* : any of various swallows and flycatchers

mar·ti·net \,märt-ᵊn-'et\ *n* : a person who demands strict obedience

mar·ti·ni \mär-'tē-nē\ *n* : a cocktail consisting of gin and dry vermouth

Mar·tin·mas \'märt-ᵊn-məs, -,mas\ *n* : November 11

¹mar·tyr \'märt-ər\ *n* **1** : a person who suffers death rather than give up his or her religion **2** : one who sacrifices life or something of great value for a principle or cause **3** : a person who suffers greatly

²martyr *vb* **1** : to put to death for refusing to give up a belief **2** : ²TORTURE

mar·tyr·dom \'märt-ərd-əm\ *n* **1** : the sufferings and death of a martyr **2** : ¹TORMENT 1

¹mar·vel \'mär-vəl\ *n* : something that causes wonder or astonishment

²marvel *vb* **mar·veled** *or* **mar·velled; mar·vel·ing** *or* **mar·vel·ling** \'märv-(ə-)liŋ\ : to become filled with surprise or astonishment ⟨*marveled* at the magician's skill⟩

mar·vel·ous *or* **mar·vel·lous** \'märv-(ə-)ləs\ *adj* **1** : causing wonder or astonishment **2** : having the characteristics of a miracle **3** : of the highest kind or quality : SPLENDID ⟨we had a *marvelous* time⟩ — **mar·vel·ous·ly** *adv* — **mar·vel·ous·ness** *n*

mar·zi·pan \'märt-sə-,pän, 'mär-zə-,pan\ *n* : a candy or icing of almond paste, sugar, and whites of eggs

mas·cara \ma-'skar-ə\ *n* : a cosmetic especially for darkening the eyelashes

mas·cot \'mas-,kät *also* -kət\ *n* : a person, animal, or object supposed to bring good luck

Word History The word *mascot* is an example of words that come to have a more pleasant meaning as they develop through the years and through many languages. The ancestor of *mascot* is the Latin word *masca*, used in the Middle Ages to mean "witch". *Masca* was borrowed into a dialect of southern France as *masco*. Later it became *mascoto*, literally meaning "little witch" but actually used to mean "charm" or "magic spell". A magic spell can be used for good as well as bad. Already, then, we have the beginnings of a change to a nicer idea in the basic use of the word. The dialect word *mascoto* came to be *mascotte* in modern French, meaning a "good luck charm". It was made popular by the operetta *La Mascotte* in 1880. In this operetta "la mascotte" is the lovely young woman Bettina, whose influence brings victories to the army of the prince of Pisa. English later borrowed the word as *mascot*, with the meaning "a person or thing thought to bring good luck". Today the word is often used to refer to an animal chosen by a school or college as a good luck symbol for its sports teams. [from French *mascotte* "mascot", from a dialect word *mascoto* "charm", literally "little witch", from *masco* "witch", from Latin *masca* "witch"]

¹mas·cu·line \'mas-kyə-lən\ *adj* **1** : of the male sex **2** : characteristic of or belonging to men : MANLY ⟨a *masculine* voice⟩ **3** : of, relating to, or making up the class of words that ordinarily includes most of those referring to males ⟨a *masculine* noun⟩ ⟨*masculine* gender⟩ — **mas·cu·lin·i·ty** \,mas-kyə-'lin-ət-ē\ *n*

²masculine *n* **1** : a word or form of the masculine gender **2** : the masculine gender

ma·ser \'mā-zər\ *n* : a device that uses the natural vibrations of atoms or molecules for generating electromagnetic radiation at a single microwave frequency

¹mash \'mash\ *n* **1** : crushed malt or grain meal soaked and stirred in hot water **2** : a mixture of ground feeds for livestock **3** : a soft pulpy mass

²mash *vb* **1** : to make into a soft pulpy mass by beating or pressure **2** : to expose crushed malt to the action of water with heating and stirring — **mash·er** *n*

¹mask \'mask\ *n* **1 a** : a cover or partial cover for the face used for disguise ⟨a Halloween *mask*⟩ **b** : MASKER **c** : a sculptured face made by a mold in plaster or wax ⟨a death *mask*⟩ **2** : something that disguises or conceals : CLOAK **3 a** : a covering used to protect the face ⟨a baseball catch-

\ə\ **abut**	\au̇\ **out**	\i\ **tip**	\ȯ\ **saw**	\u̇\ **foot**	
\ər\ **further**	\ch\ **chin**	\ī\ **life**	\ȯi\ **coin**	\y\ **yet**	
\a\ **mat**	\e\ **pet**	\j\ **job**	\th\ **thin**	\yü\ **few**	
\ā\ **take**	\ē\ **easy**	\ŋ\ **sing**	\th\ **this**	\yu̇\ **cure**	
\ä\ **cot, cart**	\g\ **go**	\ō\ **bone**	\ü\ **food**	\zh\ **vision**	

er's *mask*⟩ **b** : GAS MASK **c** : a device covering the nose and mouth to make it easier to inhale something **d** : a covering (as of gauze) over the nose and mouth to prevent infectious droplets from being exhaled into the air **4** : the head or face of a mammal (as a fox or dog) **5** : MASQUE 2

²**mask** *vb* **1** : to put on or wear a mask **2** : CONCEAL, DISGUISE ⟨*masked* their real purpose⟩ **3** : to cover for protection

masked \'maskt\ *adj* : marked by the use of masks ⟨a *masked* ball⟩

mask·er \'mas-kər\ *n* : a person who wears a mask; *esp* : one taking part in a masquerade

ma·son \'mās-ᵊn\ *n* : a skilled worker who builds or works with stone, brick, or cement

ma·son·ry \'mās-ᵊn-rē\ *n, pl* **-ries** **1** : something built of stone, brick, or concrete **2** : the art, trade, or occupation of a mason **3** : the work done by a mason

masque \'mask\ *n* **1** : ¹MASQUERADE 1 **2** : an old type of play performed by masked actors

masqu·er \'mas-kər\ *n* : MASKER

¹**mas·quer·ade** \,mas-kə-'rād\ *n* **1** : a party (as a dance) at which people wear masks and often fantastic costumes **2** : an appearance that is only a disguise or outward show : POSE

²**masquerade** *vb* **-ad·ed; -ad·ing** **1** : to take part in a masquerade **2** : to assume the appearance of something one is not : POSE — **mas·quer·ad·er** *n*

¹**mass** \'mas\ *n* **1** *cap* : a series of prayers and ceremonies forming the eucharistic service especially of the Roman Catholic Church **2** *often cap* : a celebration of the Eucharist **3** : a musical setting for parts of the Mass [Old English *mæsse* "religious service", probably from Latin *messa*, literally "dismissal at the end of a religious service", derived from earlier *missus*, past participle of *mittere* "to send"]

²**mass** *n* **1 a** : a quantity of matter or the form of matter that holds or clings together in one body ⟨a *mass* of metal⟩ **b** : large size : BULK **c** : the principal part : main body **2** : the quantity of matter in a body as measured by its inertia ⟨weight is the force on a *mass* due to gravity⟩ **3** : a large amount or number **4** *pl* : the common people [Middle English *masse* "a large body or quantity of material", from early French *masse* (same meaning), from Latin *massa* (same meaning), from Greek *maza* "mass"]

³**mass** *vb* : to form or collect into a mass

⁴**mass** *adj* **1** : of, relating to, or designed for the mass of the people ⟨*mass* market⟩ ⟨television is a *mass* medium⟩ **2** : participated in by or affecting a large number of individuals ⟨*mass* demonstrations⟩

¹**mas·sa·cre** \'mas-i-kər\ *vb* **-cred; -cring** \-k(ə-)riŋ\ : to kill in a massacre : SLAUGHTER — **mas·sa·crer** \-i-kər-ər, -i-krər\ *n*

²**massacre** *n* : the violent and cruel killing of a number of persons

¹**mas·sage** \mə-'säzh, -'säj\ *n* : treatment (as of the body) by rubbing, stroking, kneading, or tapping

²**massage** *vb* **mas·saged; mas·sag·ing** : to give massage to

mas·sa·sau·ga \,mas-ə-'so-gə\ *n* : any of several small rattlesnakes

mas·seur \ma-'sər, mə-\ *n* : a man who practices massage

mas·seuse \ma-'sə(r)z, mə-, -'süz\ *n* : a woman who practices massage

mas·sive \'mas-iv\ *adj* **1** : WEIGHTY 1, HEAVY ⟨*massive* walls⟩ **2 a** : large, solid, or heavy in structure ⟨a *massive*

jaw⟩ **b** : large in extent or degree ⟨a *massive* effort⟩ — **mas·sive·ly** *adv* — **mas·sive·ness** *n*

mass noun *n* : a noun (as *sand, butter,* or *accuracy*) that indicates something that can not be counted, that is used in English only in the singular, and that usually has *some* before it rather than *a* or *an*

mass number *n* : a whole number that expresses the mass of an atom in terms of the number of protons and neutrons in the atom

mass–pro·duce \,mas-prə-'d(y)üs\ *vb* : to produce in quantity usually by machinery — **mass production** *n*

massy \'mas-ē\ *adj* **mass·i·er; -est** : MASSIVE 2a

mast \'mast\ *n* **1** : a long pole that rises from the bottom of a ship or boat and supports the sails and rigging **2** : an upright tall pole (as on a crane) — **mast·ed** \'mas-təd\ *adj* — **before the mast** : as a common sailor

¹**mas·ter** \'mas-tər\ *n* **1 a** : a male teacher **b** : a person holding an academic degree between a bachelor's and a doctor's **2 a** : an independent skilled worker; *esp* : one qualified to teach apprentices **b** : an artist or performer of great skill **3 a** : one having authority : RULER **b** : one that conquers or masters **c** : the captain of a merchant ship **d** : an owner especially of a slave or animal **e** : the employer especially of a servant **4** — used as a title for a boy too young to be called *mister* **5** : a master machine or device [Middle English *master* "master", from Old English *magister* and early French *maistre*, both meaning "master" and both from Latin *magister* "master, one who holds higher political office" — related to MAESTRO, MAGISTRATE, MISTRESS] — **mas·ter·ship** \-,ship\ *n*

²**master** *adj* **1** : being a master ⟨a *master* carpenter⟩ **2** : being the main or guiding one ⟨a *master* plan⟩ **3** : controlling the operation of other devices ⟨a *master* clock⟩

³**master** *vb* **mas·tered; mas·ter·ing** \-t(ə-)riŋ\ **1** : OVERCOME 1, SUBDUE ⟨*master* an enemy⟩ ⟨*master* a desire⟩ **2** : to become skilled at ⟨*master* arithmetic⟩

master chief petty officer *n* : a petty officer of the highest rank in the navy or coast guard

master chief petty officer of the coast guard *n* : a master chief petty officer in the coast guard who advises the senior commanding officer of the coast guard

master chief petty officer of the navy *n* : a master chief petty officer in the navy who advises the senior commanding officer of the navy

mas·ter·ful \'mas-tər-fəl\ *adj* **1** : inclined to take control or dominate **2** : having or showing the technical or artistic skill of a master — **mas·ter·ful·ly** \-fə-lē\ *adv* — **mas·ter·ful·ness** *n*

master gunnery sergeant *n* : a noncommissioned officer of the highest rank in the marines

mas·ter·ly \'mas-tər-lē\ *adj* : suitable to or resembling a master especially in superior knowledge or skill — **masterly** *adv*

mas·ter·mind \'mas-tər-,mīnd, ,mas-tər-'mīnd\ *n* : a person who invents or directs a project — **mastermind** *vb*

master of ceremonies : a person who acts as host at a formal event or on an entertainment program (as on television)

mas·ter·piece \'mas-tər-,pēs\ *n* : a work done with great skill; *esp* : a supreme intellectual or artistic achievement

master sergeant *n* : a military noncommissioned officer with the rank just below that of sergeant major in the army, below that of master gunnery sergeant in the marines, and below that of senior master sergeant in the air force

mas·tery \'mas-t(ə-)rē\ *n, pl* **-ter·ies** **1** : the position or authority of a master **2** : VICTORY **3** : skill or knowledge that makes one master of something : COMMAND ⟨a *mastery* of French⟩

mast·head \'mast-,hed\ *n* **1** : the top of a mast **2** : the name of a newspaper displayed on the top of the first page

mas·tic \'mas-tik\ *n* : a yellow or greenish substance that oozes from cuts in the bark of a southern European tree

mask 1a

and is used in varnish

mas·ti·cate \'mas-tə-ˌkāt\ vb **-cat·ed; -cat·ing** : to grind or crush with the teeth before swallowing : CHEW — **mas·ti·ca·tion** \ˌmas-tə-'kā-shən\ n

mas·tiff \'mas-təf\ n : any of a breed of large powerful smooth-coated dogs used chiefly as watchdogs and guard dogs

mastiff

mast·odon \'mas-tə-ˌdän, -dən\ n : any of numerous huge extinct mammals related to the mammoths and existing elephants

¹**mas·toid** \'mas-ˌtóid\ adj : of, relating to, or being the mastoid process; also : occurring in the region of the mastoid process

²**mastoid** n : a mastoid bone or process

mastoid process n : a somewhat cone-shaped part of a bone of the skull that points downward behind the ear

mas·tur·ba·tion \ˌmas-tər-'bā-shən\ n : sexual stimulation of the genital organs apart from sexual intercourse and especially by use of one's own hand — **mas·tur·bate** \'mas-tər-ˌbāt\ vb

¹**mat** \'mat\ n **1 a** : a piece of coarse fabric of rush, straw, or wool **b** : a piece of material in front of a door to wipe dirty shoe soles on **c** : a decorative piece of material used under a dish or vase **d** : a pad or cushion for gymnastics or wrestling **2** : something made up of many tangled strands ⟨a thick mat of vegetation⟩ [Old English meatte "mat", from Latin matta (same meaning); of Semitic origin]

²**mat** vb **mat·ted; mat·ting 1** : to provide with a mat or matting **2** : to form into a tangled mass

³**mat** or **matt** or **matte** \'mat\ vb **mat·ted; mat·ting 1** : to give a dull effect to **2** : to border (a picture) with a mat

⁴**mat** or **matt** or **matte** adj : lacking luster or gloss [French mat "having a dull finish", from early French mat "defeated", from Latin mattus "drunk"]

⁵**mat** n **1** : a border of stiff paper (as cardboard) going around a picture between picture and frame or serving as the frame **2** : a dull finish

mat·a·dor \'mat-ə-ˌdò(ə)r\ n : the bullfighter who plays the major human part in a bullfight [Spanish, literally "killer"]

¹**match** \'mach\ n **1 a** : a person or thing that is equal or similar to or exactly like another **b** : one that can compete or fight successfully with another ⟨a match for the enemy⟩ **2** : two persons or things that go well together ⟨curtains and carpet are a good match⟩ **3** : a contest between two or more parties ⟨a tennis match⟩ **4 a** : MARRIAGE 1b **b** : a person to be considered as a marriage partner [Old English mǣcca "match"]

²**match** vb **1** : to meet successfully as a competitor **2 a** : to place in competition ⟨matched my strength with my friend's⟩ **b** : to provide with a worthy competitor **3** : to join or give in marriage **4 a** : to make or find the equal or the like of **b** : to make correspond **c** : to be the same as or suitable to one another ⟨do these colors match?⟩ **5** : to flip or toss coins and compare upper surfaces — **match·er** n

³**match** n **1** : an evenly burning wick or cord formerly used to ignite a charge of powder **2** : a short slender piece of material (as wood) tipped with a mixture that ignites when scratched against something else [Middle English macche "a wick", from early French meiche (same meaning)]

match·book \'mach-ˌbùk\ n : a small folder containing rows of paper matches

match·box \-ˌbäks\ n : a box for matches

match·less \'mach-ləs\ adj : having no equal : better than any other — **match·less·ly** adv

match·lock \'mach-ˌläk\ n : a firearm in which the charge is ignited by a slow match in a movable holder attached to the breech

match·mak·er \-ˌmā-kər\ n : one that arranges marriages — **match·mak·ing** \-kiŋ\ n

¹**mate** \'māt\ n **1 a** : ²ASSOCIATE 1, COMPANION **b** : an assistant worker : HELPER ⟨plumber's mate⟩ **2** : a deck officer on a merchant ship ranking below the captain **3 a** : either member of a married couple **b** : one of a breeding pair of animals **c** : either of two matched objects ⟨the mate to a glove⟩

²**mate** vb **mat·ed; mat·ing 1** : to join or fit together **2 a** : to bring or come together as mates; esp : ¹MARRY 1 **b** : to provide a mate for **3** : COPULATE — **mate with** : to take as a mate

ma·té or **ma·te** \'mä-ˌtā\ n : a fragrant beverage made from the leaves and shoots of a South American shrub or tree of the same genus as the hollies; also : these leaves and shoots

¹**ma·te·ri·al** \mə-'tir-ē-əl\ adj **1** : relating to or consisting of matter : PHYSICAL ⟨the material world⟩ ⟨material comforts⟩ **2 a** : IMPORTANT 1 ⟨food is material to health⟩ **b** : RELEVANT ⟨is that information material to the problem?⟩ **3** : physical rather than spiritual or intellectual ⟨material needs⟩ — **ma·te·ri·al·i·ty** \-ˌtir-ē-'al-ət-ē\ n — **ma·te·ri·al·ly** \-'tir-ē-ə-lē\ adv

²**material** n **1** : the elements or substance of which something is made or can be made ⟨building materials⟩ **2** : equipment and supplies for doing or making something ⟨writing materials⟩

ma·te·ri·al·ism \mə-'tir-ē-ə-ˌliz-əm\ n **1** : a theory that everything can be explained as being or coming from matter **2** : a tendency to attach too much importance to physical comfort and well-being — **ma·te·ri·al·ist** \-ē-ə-ləst\ n or adj — **ma·te·ri·al·is·tic** \-ˌtir-ē-ə-'lis-tik\ adj

ma·te·ri·al·ize \mə-'tir-ē-ə-ˌlīz\ vb **-ized; -iz·ing 1** : to give material form and substance to **2** : to assume or cause to assume bodily form ⟨a ghost materialized out of nowhere⟩ **3 a** : to come into existence ⟨a promise that never materialized⟩ **b** : to appear suddenly

ma·té·ri·el or **ma·te·ri·el** \mə-ˌtir-ē-'el\ n : equipment and supplies used by a group or organization [French]

ma·ter·nal \mə-'tərn-ᵊl\ adj **1** : of or relating to a mother : MOTHERLY **2 a** : related through a mother ⟨maternal grandparents⟩ **b** : obtained or received from a female parent ⟨maternal chromosomes⟩ [Middle English maternal "maternal, of or like a mother", from early French maternel (same meaning), from Latin maternus "maternal", from mater "mother" — related to ALMA MATER] — **ma·ter·nal·ly** \-ᵊl-ē\ adv

ma·ter·ni·ty \mə-'tər-nət-ē\ n, pl **-ties 1** : the state of being a mother : MOTHERHOOD **2** : motherly character or qualities : MOTHERLINESS

math \'math\ n : MATHEMATICS

math·e·mat·i·cal \ˌmath-ə-'mat-i-kəl, math-'mat-\ adj **1** : of, relating to, or according with mathematics **2** : very exact ⟨mathematical precision⟩ — **math·e·mat·i·cal·ly** \-i-k(ə-)lē\ adv

math·e·ma·ti·cian \ˌmath-(ə-)mə-'tish-ən\ n : a specialist in mathematics

math·e·mat·ics \ˌmath-ə-'mat-iks, math-'mat-\ n : the science that is concerned with numbers and their properties, relations, and operations and with shapes in space and their structure and measurement

mat·i·nee or **mat·i·née** \ˌmat-ᵊn-'ā\ n : a theatrical performance held in the daytime and especially in the afternoon

\ə\ abut	\aù\ out	\i\ tip	\ó\ saw	\ù\ foot
\ər\ further	\ch\ chin	\ī\ life	\ói\ coin	\y\ yet
\a\ mat	\e\ pet	\j\ job	\th\ thin	\yü\ few
\ā\ take	\ē\ easy	\ŋ\ sing	\t͟h\ this	\yù\ cure
\ä\ cot, cart	\g\ go	\ō\ bone	\ü\ food	\zh\ vision

mat·ins \'mat-ºnz\ *n pl, often cap* **1** : special prayers said between midnight and 4 a.m. **2** : a service of morning prayer

ma·tri·arch \'mā-trē-ˌärk\ *n* : a woman who rules a family, group, or state; *esp* : a mother who is head of her family and descendants — **ma·tri·ar·chal** \ˌmā-trē-'är-kəl\ *adj*

ma·tri·ar·chy \'mā-trē-ˌär-kē\ *n, pl* **-chies** **1** : a family, group, or state headed by a matriarch **2** : a system of social organization in which descent and inheritance are traced through the female line

ma·tri·cide \'ma-trə-ˌsīd, 'mā-\ *n* **1** : murder of a mother by her child **2** : one that murders his or her mother — **ma·tri·cid·al** \ˌma-trə-'sīd-ºl, ˌmā-\ *adj*

ma·tric·u·late \mə-'trik-yə-ˌlāt\ *vb* **-lat·ed; -lat·ing** : to enroll especially in a college or university — **ma·tric·u·la·tion** \-ˌtrik-yə-'lā-shən\ *n*

mat·ri·mo·ny \'ma-trə-ˌmō-nē\ *n, pl* **-nies** : MARRIAGE 1b — **mat·ri·mo·nial** \ˌma-trə-'mō-nē-əl, -nyəl\ *adj* — **mat·ri·mo·nial·ly** \-ē\ *adv*

ma·trix \'mā-triks\ *n, pl* **ma·tri·ces** \'mā-trə-ˌsēz, 'ma-\ *or* **ma·trix·es** \'mā-trik-səz\ : something (as a mold) that gives form, foundation, or origin to something else enclosed in it

ma·tron \'mā-trən\ *n* **1** : a usually mature and dignified married woman **2** : a woman in charge of the household affairs of an institution **3** : a woman who supervises women prisoners in a police station or jail

ma·tron·ly \'mā-trən-lē\ *adj* : of, resembling, or suitable for a matron

matron of honor : a married woman serving as the principal wedding attendant of a bride

matt *or* **matte** *variant of* MAT

matted *past and past participle of* MAT

¹mat·ter \'mat-ər\ *n* **1 a** : a subject of interest or concern ⟨a *matter* of dispute⟩ **b** : something to be dealt with : AFFAIR ⟨personal *matters* to take care of⟩ **c** : a condition affecting a person or thing unfavorably ⟨what's the *matter* with you?⟩ **2 a** : the substance of the universe : something that occupies space and has mass **b** : material substance of a particular kind or function ⟨vegetable *matter*⟩ **c** : PUS **3** : a more or less definite amount or quantity ⟨cooks in a *matter* of minutes⟩ **4** : something written or printed **5** : ¹MAIL 1 ⟨first-class *matter*⟩ — **for that matter** : so far as that is concerned — **no matter** : without regard to ⟨do it *no matter* how unpleasant it seems⟩

²matter *vb* : to be of importance : SIGNIFY

matter of course : something that may be expected as a result of something else

mat·ter-of-fact \ˌmat-ə-rə(v)-'fakt\ *adj* : sticking to fact; *esp* : not fanciful : PRACTICAL, COMMONPLACE — **mat·ter-of-fact·ly** \-'fak-(t)lē\ *adv*

Mat·thew \'math-yü\ *n* — *see* BIBLE table

mat·ting \'mat-iŋ\ *n* : material for mats; *also* : mats or a supply of mats

mat·tock \'mat-ək\ *n* : a tool for digging made of a long wooden handle and a steel head one end of which comes to a point or to a cutting edge

mat·tress \'ma-trəs\ *n* **1** : a fabric case filled with springy material used as a bed or on a bedstead **2** : a sack that can be filled with air or water and used as a mattress

mat·u·ra·tion \ˌmach-ə-'rā-shən\ *n* **1** : the process of becoming mature **2** : the process involving meiosis by which body cells having two sets of chromosomes form gametes with one set of chromosomes

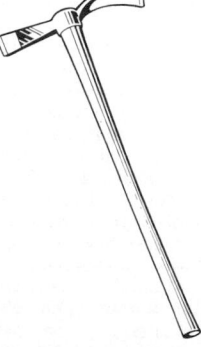

mattock

¹ma·ture \mə-'t(y)ù(ə)r\ *adj* **ma·tur·er; -est** **1** : fully thought out ⟨a *mature* plan⟩ **2 a** : fully grown or developed : ADULT, RIPE ⟨*mature* fruit⟩ **b** : having reached a final or desired state ⟨*mature* wine⟩ **3** : of or relating to a condition of full development ⟨a *mature* outlook⟩ **4** : due for payment ⟨the note becomes *mature* in 90 days⟩ — **ma·ture·ly** *adv*

²mature *vb* **ma·tured; ma·tur·ing** **1** : to bring to maturity or completion ⟨*matured* my plans⟩ **2** : to become fully developed or ripe

ma·tu·ri·ty \mə-'t(y)ùr-ət-ē\ *n* **1** : the quality or state of being mature; *esp* : full development **2** : the date when a note becomes due

mat·zo \'mät-sə, -ˌsō\ *n, pl* **mat·zoth** \-ˌsōth, -ˌsōt, -ˌsōs\ *or* **mat·zos** \-səz, -səs, -ˌsōz\ : unleavened bread eaten at the Passover

maud·lin \'mòd-lən\ *adj* **1** : drunk enough to be tearfully silly **2** : weakly and overly sentimental

Word History The word *maudlin* can be traced back to the name of a town in ancient Palestine, *Magdala*. But the meaning of *maudlin* is associated with a person in the Bible. In the Gospels, Mary Magdalene was so called because she was thought to have come from Magdala. She was a devoted follower of Jesus and was present at his crucifixion. Yet her name was not always spelled as it is today. Our modern English translations of the Bible have gone back to the Latin text for the spelling *Magdalene*. But in early French translations, the *g* dropped out, and the Latin spelling became *Madalaine*. When the name was taken into Middle English from the early French texts, it became *Maudeleyn* and later *Maudlin*. In the Middle Ages, religious artists painting scenes of the crucifixion and burial of Jesus showed Mary as weeping. In time her name became an adjective for a tearful show of emotion and later especially for an exaggerated display of emotion from a drunken person. [Middle English *Maudlin, Maudeleyn* "Mary Magdalene", from early French *Madalaine* (same meaning), from Latin *Magdalene* (same meaning), from Greek *Magdalēnē* "(Mary) of Magdala (town on the Sea of Galilee)"; so called because Mary was frequently shown in religious paintings as weeping]

¹maul \'mòl\ *n* : a heavy hammer often with a wooden head used especially for driving wedges or posts

²maul *vb* **1** : to beat and bruise severely **2** : to handle roughly — **maul·er** *n*

maun·der \'mòn-dər, 'män-\ *vb* **maun·dered; maun·der·ing** \-d(ə-)riŋ\ **1** : to wander slowly and idly **2** : to speak in a disconnected or aimless way — **maun·der·er** \-dər-ər\ *n*

Maun·dy Thursday \ˌmòn-dē-, ˌmän-\ *n* : the Thursday before Easter [Middle English *maunde* "ceremony of washing the feet of the poor on the Thursday before Easter", from early French *mandé* (same meaning), from Latin *mandatum* "command"; so called from Jesus' words "A new Commandment I give to you . . ." in John 13:34 (RSV) after he washed the feet of his disciples at the Last Supper]

mau·so·le·um \ˌmò-sə-'lē-əm, ˌmò-zə-\ *n, pl* **-le·ums** *or* **-lea** \-'lē-ə\ : a large or fancy tomb [from Latin *mausoleum* "a large tomb", from Greek *Mausōleion* "the magnificent tomb of Mausolus (ruler of Caria, an ancient country in Asia Minor)", considered one of the seven wonders of the ancient world]

mauve \'mōv, 'mòv\ *n* : a medium purple, violet, or lilac

mav·er·ick \'mav-(ə-)rik\ *n* **1** : an unbranded range animal; *esp* : a motherless calf **2** : an independent person who refuses to follow the usual standards or customs of the group

Word History A lawyer named Samuel A. Maverick lived in southern Texas in the middle of the 19th century. He was once given 400 cattle instead of money to settle a $1200 debt. Maverick had no use for the cattle, so he left them in the care of one of his workers. The cattle were never branded and were left to roam free. Eventually, the term *maverick* came to be used to name any unbranded cattle. Now *maverick* is most often used to speak of a person who acts in an individual way and refuses to be "branded" as a member of any particular group. [named for Samuel A. *Maverick* 1803–1870 American pioneer]

maw \'mȯ\ *n*   **1** : an organ (as a stomach or a crop) that receives swallowed food   **2** : the throat, gullet, or jaws especially of a flesh-eating animal

mawk·ish \'mȯ-kish\ *adj*   **1** : having a weak often unpleasant taste   **2** : MAUDLIN 2 — **mawk·ish·ly** *adv* — **mawk·ish·ness** *n*

maxi \'mak-sē\ *n* : a long skirt, dress, or coat

max·il·la \mak-'sil-ə\ *n, pl* **max·il·lae** \-'sil-ē, -'sil-ˌī\ *or* **maxillas**   **1 a** : an upper jaw especially of a mammal in which the bony parts are closely united   **b** : either of the two bones of the upper jaw in higher vertebrates including human beings that bear most of the teeth   **2** : one of the first or second pair of mouth appendages behind the mandibles in various arthropods — **max·il·lary** \'mak-sə-ˌler-ē\ *adj or n*

max·im \ˌmak-səm\ *n*   **1** : a general truth or rule of conduct   **2** : a proverbial saying

max·i·mize \'mak-sə-ˌmīz\ *vb* **-mized; -miz·ing**   **1** : to increase to a maximum   **2** : to make the most of

max·i·mum \'mak-s(ə-)məm\ *n, pl* **max·i·ma** \-sə-mə\ *or* **maximums**   **1** : the highest quantity, value, or development   **2** : an upper limit allowed by authority — **maximum** *adj*

may \(')mā\ *helping verb, past* **might** \(')mīt\; *present sing & pl* **may**   **1 a** : have permission to ⟨you *may* go now⟩   **b** : be in some degree likely to ⟨you *may* be right⟩   **2** — used to express a wish ⟨long *may* she reign⟩   **3** — used to express purpose ⟨we exercise so that we *may* be strong⟩ or possibility of happening ⟨he'll do his duty come what *may*⟩

May \'mā\ *n* : the fifth month of the year

Word History Among the gods and goddesses worshiped by the ancient Romans was one known as Maia, a goddess of spring. In spring the Romans would make offerings to her on the first day of a month they called *Maius*, meaning "of Maia". The name of the Roman month was borrowed into early French as *mai* and later into English as *May*. For the early Romans Maius was the third month of the year; but after January and February were added, May became the fifth month. [from Middle English *May* (fifth month), from early French *mai* (same meaning), from Latin *Maius*, originally "third month", from *Maia*, "Roman goddess of spring"]

Ma·ya \'mī-ə\ *n, pl* **Maya** *or* **Mayas** : a member of a group of Indian peoples of the Yucatán peninsula and neighboring areas — **Ma·yan** \'mī-ən\ *adj*

may·ap·ple \'mā-ˌap-əl\ *n* : a North American large-leaved woodland herb related to the barberries that produces a single large waxy white flower followed by a yellow egg-shaped berry; *also* : its edible fruit

may·be \'mā-bē, 'meb-ē\ *adv* : PERHAPS

May·day \mā-'dā, 'mā-ˌdā\ — an international radio signal word used as a distress call

May Day \'mā-ˌdā\ *n* : May 1 celebrated as a springtime festival and in some countries as Labor Day

may·flow·er \'mā-ˌflaú(-ə)r\ *n* : any of various spring-blooming plants (as the trailing arbutus, hepatica, and several North American anemones)

may·fly \-ˌflī\ *n* : any of a group of insects that as adults live only a short time and have fragile wings

may·hap \'mā-ˌhap, mā-'hap\ *adv* : PERHAPS

may·hem \'mā-ˌhem, 'mā-əm\ *n* : deliberate permanent crippling or injury of any part of the body

mayn't \'mā-ənt, (')mānt\ : may not

may·on·naise \'mā-ə-ˌnāz, ˌmā-ə-'nāz\ *n* : a dressing (as for salads) consisting chiefly of egg yolk, vegetable oil, and vinegar or lemon juice

may·or \'mā-ər, 'me(-)ər\ *n* : an official elected to act as head of a city or borough — **may·or·al** \'mā-ə-rəl, 'me-ə-\ *adj*

may·or·al·ty \'mā-ə-rəl-tē, 'mer-əl-\ *n, pl* **-ties** : the office or term of office of a mayor

may·pole \'mā-ˌpōl\ *n, often cap* : a tall pole decorated with ribbons and flowers that forms a center for May Day sports and dances

maze \'māz\ *n* : a confusing complicated network of passages

ma·zur·ka \mə-'zər-kə, -'zúr-\ *n*   **1** : a fast Polish folk dance   **2** : music for the mazurka

mazy \'mā-zē\ *adj* **maz·i·er; -est** : resembling a maze in confusing turns and windings

me \(')mē\ *pron, objective case of* I

maze

¹mead \'mēd\ *n* : an alcoholic drink made of water, honey, malt, and yeast [Old English *medu* "the beverage mead"]

²mead *n, archaic* : MEADOW [Old English *mæd* "meadow"]

mead·ow \'med-ō\ *n* : an area of moist low usually level grassland

mead·ow·lark \-ˌlärk\ *n* : any of several North American songbirds that are largely brown and buff above with a yellow breast having a black V-shaped mark across it

mea·ger *or* **mea·gre** \'mē-gər\ *adj*   **1** : having little flesh : THIN   **2** : lacking in richness or plenty ⟨a *meager* harvest⟩ — **mea·ger·ly** *adv* — **mea·ger·ness** *n*

syn MEAGER, SCANTY, SPARSE mean falling short of what is normal, necessary, or desirable. MEAGER suggests a lack of fullness, richness, or plenty ⟨a *meager* diet⟩ SCANTY stresses that something is not enough in amount, degree, or range ⟨a *scanty* supply of fuel⟩ SPARSE suggests a scattering of a small number of units ⟨a big country with a *sparse* population⟩

¹meal \'mēl\ *n*   **1** : the food eaten or prepared for eating at one time   **2** : the act or time of eating a meal [Old English *mæl* "food eaten at one sitting"]

²meal *n*   **1** : ground seeds of a cereal grass; *esp* : CORNMEAL   **2** : something like meal especially in texture [Old English *melu* "ground grain"]

meal·time \'mēl-ˌtīm\ *n* : the usual time at which a meal is served

meal·worm \-ˌwərm\ *n* : any of various small brownish beetle larvae that live in grain products and are often raised as food for insect-eating animals

mealy \'mē-lē\ *adj* **meal·i·er; -est**   **1** : being soft, dry, and crumbly   **2** : containing meal   **3** : covered with fine grains or with flecks (as of color)   **4** : MEALYMOUTHED

mealy·bug \'mē-lē-ˌbəg\ *n* : any of numerous destructive scale insects with a white powdery covering

mealy·mouthed \ˌmē-lē-'maúthd, -'maútht\ *adj* : not plain and sincere in speech ⟨a *mealymouthed* speaker⟩

¹mean \'mēn\ *adj*   **1** : of low birth or station : HUMBLE   **2** : ¹POOR 7, SHABBY ⟨live in *mean* surroundings⟩   **3** : worthy of little regard : INFERIOR ⟨a person of no *mean* ability⟩   **4** : deliberately unkind   **5** : STINGY 1, MISERLY   **6** : SPITEFUL,

\ə\ abut	\aú\ out	\i\ tip	\ȯ\ saw	\ú\ foot
\ər\ further	\ch\ chin	\ī\ life	\ȯi\ coin	\y\ yet
\a\ mat	\e\ pet	\j\ job	\th\ thin	\yü\ few
\ā\ take	\ē\ easy	\ŋ\ sing	\th\ this	\yú\ cure
\ä\ cot, cart	\g\ go	\ō\ bone	\ü\ food	\zh\ vision

MEASURES AND WEIGHTS[1]

UNIT	ABBREVIATION OR SYMBOL	EQUIVALENTS IN OTHER UNITS OF SAME SYSTEM	APPROXIMATE METRIC EQUIVALENT
LENGTH			
mile	mi	5280 feet, 320 rods, 1760 yards	1.609 kilometers
rod	rd	5.50 yards, 16.5 feet	5.029 meters
yard	yd	3 feet, 36 inches	0.9144 meter
foot	ft *or* '	12 inches, 0.333 yard	30.48 centimeters
inch	in *or* "	0.083 foot, 0.028 yard	2.54 centimeters
AREA			
square mile	sq mi *or* mi²	640 acres, 102,400 square rods	2.590 square kilometers
acre		4840 square yards, 43,560 square feet	4047 square meters
square rod	sq rd *or* rd²	30.25 square yards, 0.00625 acre	25.293 square meters
square yard	sq yd *or* yd²	1296 square inches, 9 square feet	0.836 square meter
square foot	sq ft *or* ft²	144 square inches, 0.111 square yard	0.093 square meter
square inch	sq in *or* in²	0.0069 square foot, 0.00077 square yard	6.452 square centimeters
VOLUME			
cubic yard	cu yd *or* yd³	27 cubic feet, 46,656 cubic inches	0.765 cubic meter
cubic foot	cu ft *or* ft³	1728 cubic inches, 0.0370 cubic yard	0.028 cubic meter
cubic inch	cu in *or* in³	0.00058 cubic foot, 0.000021 cubic yard	16.387 cubic centimeters
WEIGHT			
avoirdupois			
ton			
short ton		20 short hundredweight, 2000 pounds	0.907 metric ton
long ton		20 long hundredweight, 2240 pounds	1.016 metric tons
hundredweight	cwt		
short hundred-weight		100 pounds, 0.05 short ton	45.359 kilograms
long hundred-weight		112 pounds, 0.05 long ton	50.802 kilograms
pound	lb *or* lb avdp *also* #	16 ounces, 7000 grains	0.454 kilogram
ounce	oz *or* oz avdp	16 drams, 437.5 grains	28.350 grams
dram	dr *or* dr avdp	27.344 grains, 0.0625 ounce	1.772 grams
grain	gr	0.037 dram, 0.002286 ounce	0.0648 gram
troy			
pound	lb t	12 ounces, 240 pennyweight, 5760 grains	0.373 kilogram
ounce	oz t	20 pennyweight, 480 grains	31.103 grams
pennyweight	dwt *also* pwt	24 grains, 0.05 ounce	1.555 grams
grain	gr	0.042 pennyweight, 0.002083 ounce	0.0648 gram
apothecaries'			
pound	lb ap	12 ounces, 5760 grains	0.373 kilogram
ounce	oz ap *or* ℥	8 drams, 480 grains	31.103 grams
dram	dr ap *or* ℨ	3 scruples, 60 grains	3.888 grams
scruple	s ap *or* ℈	20 grains, 0.333 dram	1.296 grams
grain	gr	0.05 scruple, 0.002083 ounce, 0.0166 dram	0.0648 gram
CAPACITY			
United States liquid measure			
gallon	gal	4 quarts (231 cubic inches)	3.785 liters
quart	qt	2 pints (57.75 cubic inches)	0.946 liter
pint	pt	4 gills (28.875 cubic inches)	0.473 liter
gill	gi	4 fluidounces (7.219 cubic inches)	118.294 milliliters
fluidounce	fl oz *or* f ℥	8 fluidrams (1.805 cubic inches)	29.573 milliliters
fluidram	fl dr *or* f ℨ	60 minims (0.226 cubic inch)	3.697 milliliters
minim	min *or* ♏	1/60 fluidram (0.003760 cubic inch)	0.061610 milliliter
United States dry measure			
bushel	bu	4 pecks (2150.42 cubic inches)	35.239 liters
peck	pk	8 quarts (537.605 cubic inches)	8.810 liters
quart	qt	2 pints (67.201 cubic inches)	1.101 liters
pint	pt	½ quart (33.600 cubic inches)	0.551 liter

[1]For United States equivalents of metric units see Metric System table

MALICIOUS ⟨a *mean* remark⟩ **7** : causing trouble or bother ⟨a *mean* horse⟩ **8** : EXCELLENT ⟨plays a *mean* trumpet⟩ [Old English *gemǣne* "humblc"] — **mean·ly** *adv* — **mean·ness** \'mēn-nəs\ *n*

²mean \'mēn\ *vb* **meant** \'ment\; **mean·ing** \'mē-niŋ\ **1 a** : to have as a purpose : INTEND ⟨I *mean* to go⟩ **b** : to intend for a particular purpose or use ⟨a book *meant* for children⟩ **2** : to serve to communicate, show, or indicate : SIGNIFY ⟨what do these words *mean*⟩ ⟨those clouds *mean* rain⟩ **3** : to be important to a specified degree ⟨health *means* everything to us⟩ [Old English *mǣnan* "to have in mind, intend"] — **mean business** : to be in earnest

³mean *adj* **1** : holding a middle position : INTERMEDIATE **2 a** : lying about midway between extremes **b** : being the mean of a set of values : AVERAGE ⟨*mean* temperature⟩ [Middle English *mene* "being in a middle position", from early French *meien* (same meaning), from Latin *medianus* "being in the middle" — related to ¹MEDIAN]

⁴mean *n* **1** : a middle point between extremes **2 a** : a value that represents a range of values; *esp* : ARITHMETIC MEAN **b** : either of the middle two terms of a proportion **3** *pl* : something by which a desired result is achieved or furthered ⟨*means* of production⟩ ⟨use any *means* you can⟩ **4** *pl* : WEALTH 1 ⟨a person of *means*⟩ — **by all means** : without fail : CERTAINLY — **by any means** : in any way : at all — **by means of** : through the use of — **by no means** : not at all : certainly not

¹me·an·der \mē-'an-dər\ *n* **1** : a turn or winding of a stream **2** : a winding path or course

²meander *vb* **-dered; -der·ing** \-d(ə-)riŋ\ **1** : to follow a winding or complicated course **2** : to wander without a goal or purpose **syn** see WANDER

¹mean·ing \'mē-niŋ\ *n* **1 a** : the sense one intends to communicate especially by language ⟨do not mistake my *meaning*⟩ **b** : the sense that is communicated ⟨the poem's *meaning* is clear⟩ **2** : PURPOSE 1, INTENTION **3** : intent to communicate information : SIGNIFICANCE ⟨a glance full of *meaning*⟩

²meaning *adj* : MEANINGFUL, EXPRESSIVE ⟨a *meaning* look⟩

mean·ing·ful \'mē-niŋ-fəl\ *adj* : having a meaning or purpose; *esp* : SIGNIFICANT 1 ⟨a *meaningful* experience⟩ — **mean·ing·ful·ly** \-fə-lē\ *adv*

mean·ing·less \'mē-niŋ-ləs\ *adj* **1** : having no meaning **2** : lacking motive — **mean·ing·less·ly** *adv* — **mean·ing·less·ness** *n*

¹mean·time \'mēn-,tīm\ *n* : the time between two events

²meantime *adv* : in the meantime

¹mean·while \'mēn-,hwīl, -,wīl\ *n* : ¹MEANTIME

²meanwhile *adv* **1** : ²MEANTIME **2** : at the same time

mea·sles \'mē-zəlz\ *n sing or pl* : a contagious disease caused by a virus and marked by fever and red spots on the skin; *also* : any of several diseases (as German measles) that resemble measles

mea·sly \'mēz-(ə-)lē\ *adj* **mea·sli·er; -est** : so small or unimportant as to deserve scorn ⟨left a *measly* dime for a tip⟩

mea·sur·able \'mezh-(ə-)rə-bəl, 'māzh-\ *adj* : capable of being measured — **mea·sur·ably** \-blē\ *adv*

¹mea·sure \'mezh-ər, 'māzh-\ *n* **1 a** : an adequate, fixed, or suitable limit or amount ⟨surprised beyond *measure*⟩ **b** : ²AMOUNT, EXTENT, DEGREE ⟨gained a large *measure* of freedom⟩ **2 a** : the size, capacity, or quantity of something as fixed by measuring ⟨give full *measure*⟩ **b** : something (as a meterstick or cup) used in measuring **c** : a unit used in measuring ⟨the

measure 2b

meter is a *measure* of length⟩ **d** : a system of measuring ⟨metric *measure*⟩ **3** : the act or process of measuring **4 a** : ²DANCE 2; *esp* : a stately dance **b** : rhythm or movement in music or poetry : METER, CADENCE **c** : the part of a musical staff between two bars or the group of beats between these bars **5** : an action planned or taken to achieve a desired result; *esp* : a legislative bill or act [Middle English *mesure* "measure", from early French *mesure* (same meaning), from Latin *mensura* "measure", from *mensus*, past participle of *metiri* "to measure" — related to DIMENSION, IMMENSE]

²measure *vb* **mea·sured; mea·sur·ing** \'mezh-(ə-)riŋ, 'māzh-\ **1** : to mark or fix in multiples of a specific unit ⟨*measure* off five centimeters⟩ ⟨*measure* out two liters⟩ **2** : to find out the size, extent, or amount of ⟨*measure* the piece of paper⟩ **3** : ¹ESTIMATE 1 ⟨*measured* the distance with my eye⟩ **4** : to bring into comparison ⟨*measure* your skill against an opponent's⟩ **5** : to serve as a measure of ⟨a thermometer *measures* temperature⟩ **6** : to have as its measurement ⟨the cloth *measures* 3 meters⟩ — **mea·sur·er** \-ər-ər\ *n*

mea·sured \'mezh-ərd, 'māzh-\ *adj* **1 a** : regulated or determined by a standard **b** : marked by rhythm : EVEN ⟨walk with *measured* steps⟩ **2** : ²DELIBERATE 1, CALCULATED ⟨speak with *measured* rudeness⟩

mea·sure·less \'mezh-ər-ləs, 'māzh-\ *adj* : being without or beyond measure : IMMEASURABLE

mea·sure·ment \'mezh-ər-mənt, 'māzh-\ *n* **1** : the act or process of measuring **2** : a figure, extent, or amount obtained by measuring **3** : a system of measures

measure up *vb* **1** : to have necessary or fitting qualifications **2** : to be the equal (as in ability) — used with *to*

measuring worm *n* : LOOPER 1

meat \'mēt\ *n* **1 a** : FOOD 1, 2; *esp* : solid food as distinguished from drink **b** : the edible part of something as distinguished from the covering (as a shell or husk) **2** : animal and especially mammal tissue used as food

meat·ball \-,bȯl\ *n* : a small ball of chopped or ground meat

meat loaf *n* : ground meat seasoned and baked in the form of a loaf

meaty \'mēt-ē\ *adj* **meat·i·er; -est** **1** : full of meat : FLESHY **2** : rich in matter for thought : SUBSTANTIAL ⟨a *meaty* book⟩ — **meat·i·ness** *n*

mec·ca \'mek-ə\ *n, often cap* : a place that attracts especially a particular group of people ⟨a *mecca* for tourists⟩ [named for *Mecca*, city in Arabia, the birthplace of Muhammad and the goal of Muslim pilgrimages]

¹me·chan·ic \mi-'kan-ik\ *adj* : of or relating to work performed by hand or skill at such work ⟨*mechanic* arts⟩

²mechanic *n* : a person who works with his or her hands; *esp* : a repairer of machines

me·chan·i·cal \mi-'kan-i-kəl\ *adj* **1 a** : of or relating to machinery ⟨*mechanical* engineering⟩ **b** : made or operated by a machine or machinery ⟨a *mechanical* toy⟩ **2** : done as if by machine : IMPERSONAL ⟨gave a *mechanical* reply⟩ **3** : relating to or according with the principles of mechanics — **me·chan·i·cal·ly** \-i-k(ə-)lē\ *adv*

mechanical advantage *n* : the ratio of the force that performs the useful work of a machine to the force that is applied to the machine

mechanical drawing *n* **1** : drawing done with the aid of instruments (as compasses and squares) **2** : a drawing made with instruments

me·chan·ics \mi-'kan-iks\ *n sing or pl* **1** : a science that deals with energy and forces and their effect on bodies **2** : the application of mechanics to the making or operation

\ə\ abut	\au̇\ out	\i\ tip	\ȯ\ saw	\u̇\ foot
\ər\ further	\ch\ chin	\ī\ life	\ȯi\ coin	\y\ yet
\a\ mat	\e\ pet	\j\ job	\th\ thin	\yü\ few
\ā\ take	\ē\ easy	\ŋ\ sing	\th\ this	\yu̇\ cure
\ä\ cot, cart	\g\ go	\ō\ bone	\ü\ food	\zh\ vision

of machines **3** : the details of the way something works or is done ⟨the *mechanics* of running⟩ ⟨the *mechanics* of writing plays⟩

mech·a·nism \'mek-ə-ˌniz-əm\ *n* **1** : a piece of machinery **2 a** : the parts by which a machine operates **b** : the steps that make up a process or activity ⟨the *mechanism* of government⟩ **3** : the processes involved in or responsible for a natural occurrence (as evolution or an action or reaction)

mech·a·nize \'mek-ə-ˌnīz\ *vb* **-nized; -niz·ing** **1** : to make mechanical; *esp* : to make automatic **2 a** : to equip with machinery especially to replace human or animal labor **b** : to equip with armed and armored motor vehicles ⟨*mechanized* infantry⟩ — **mech·a·ni·za·tion** \ˌmek-ə-nə-'zā-shən\ *n* — **mech·a·niz·er** \'mek-ə-ˌnī-zər\ *n*

med·al \'med-ᵊl\ *n* : a piece of metal often in the form of a coin with design and words in honor of a special event, a person, or an achievement

med·al·ist *or* **med·al·list** \'med-ᵊl-əst\ *n* : a person who receives a medal

medal

me·dal·lion \mə-'dal-yən\ *n* **1** : a large medal **2** : something resembling a large medal (as in shape)

med·dle \'med-ᵊl\ *vb* **med·dled; med·dling** \'med-liŋ, -ᵊl-iŋ\ : to interest oneself in what is not one's concern ⟨*meddle* in another's business⟩ — **med·dler** \'med-lər, -ᵊl-ər\ *n*

syn MEDDLE, INTERFERE, TAMPER mean to concern oneself with something that is not one's own business. MEDDLE stresses intruding in a thoughtless and annoying fashion ⟨*meddling* in a friend's personal problems⟩ IN- TERFERE suggests getting in the way of or disturbing someone or something whether intentionally or not ⟨building the dam *interfered* with nature⟩ ⟨your noise is *interfering* with my studying⟩ TAMPER suggests intruding or experimenting that is wrong or uncalled-for and likely to be harmful ⟨*tampered* with the lock while trying to get into the building⟩

med·dle·some \'med-ᵊl-səm\ *adj* : inclined to meddle — **med·dle·some·ly** *adv*

media *pl of* MEDIUM

mediaeval *variant of* MEDIEVAL

me·di·al \'mēd-ē-əl\ *adj* **1** : ²MEDIAN 1 **2** : ²ORDINARY 2, AVERAGE — **me·di·al·ly** \-ə-lē\ *adv*

¹me·di·an \'mēd-ē-ən\ *n* **1** : a value in a series arranged from smallest to largest below and above which there are an equal number of values **2** : a line drawn from the vertex of a triangle to the midpoint of the opposite side [from early French *mediane* "median vein (a large vein in the arm)", derived from Latin *medianus* "being in the middle", from *medius* "middle" — related to INTERMEDIATE, ³MEAN, MERIDIAN]

²median *adj* **1** : being in the middle or in an intermediate position **2** : relating to or making up a median

me·di·ant \'mēd-ē-ənt\ *n* : the third tone above the tonic

me·di·ate \'mēd-ē-ˌāt\ *vb* **-at·ed; -at·ing** **1** : to work with opposing sides in an argument in order to bring about an agreement ⟨*mediate* a settlement⟩ ⟨*mediate* a dispute⟩ **2** : to pass on or act as a mechanism or agency that is between others — **me·di·a·tion** \ˌmēd-ē-'ā-shən\ *n*

me·di·a·tor \'mēd-ē-ˌāt-ər\ *n* : one that mediates — **me·di·a·to·ry** \-ē-ə-ˌtōr-ē, -ˌtȯr-\ *adj*

med·ic \'med-ik\ *n* : a person engaged in medical work

med·ic·aid \'med-i-ˌkād\ *n, often cap* : a program of medical aid designed for those unable to afford regular medical service and paid for by the state and federal governments

med·i·cal \'med-i-kəl\ *adj* : of or relating to the science or practice of medicine — **med·i·cal·ly** \-k(ə-)lē\ *adv*

medi·care \'med-i-ˌke(ə)r, -ˌka(ə)r\ *n, often cap* : a government program of medical care especially for the aged

med·i·cat·ed \'med-ə-ˌkāt-əd\ *adj* : treated with or containing a medicine ⟨*medicated* soap⟩

med·i·ca·tion \ˌmed-ə-'kā-shən\ *n* : MEDICINE 1

me·dic·i·nal \mə-'dis-nəl, -ᵊn-əl\ *adj* : tending or used to relieve or cure disease or pain — **me·dic·i·nal·ly** \-ē\ *adv*

med·i·cine \'med-ə-sən\ *n* **1** : a substance or preparation used in treating disease **2** : a science or art that deals with the prevention, cure, or easing of disease; *esp* : the practice of the physician as it differs from that of the surgeon **3** : an object, power, or ceremony held to give control over natural or magical forces

medicine ball *n* : a heavy stuffed leather-covered ball used for strengthening exercises

medicine dropper *n* : DROPPER 2

medicine man *n* : a person among primitive peoples believed to have magic powers that can cure illnesses and keep away evil spirits by potions and charms

medicine show *n* : a traveling show using entertainers to attract a crowd that may buy cures, remedies, and medicines whose benefits are often much exaggerated

me·di·eval *or* **me·di·ae·val** \ˌmēd-ē-'ē-vəl, ˌmed-, ˌmid-; mē-'dē-vəl, mid-'ē-, med-'ē-\ *adj* : of, relating to, or characteristic of the Middle Ages

me·di·o·cre \ˌmēd-ē-'ō-kər\ *adj* : of medium or low quality : ORDINARY

me·di·oc·ri·ty \ˌmēd-ē-'äk-rət-ē\ *n, pl* **-ties** **1** : the quality or state of being mediocre **2** : a mediocre person

med·i·tate \'med-ə-ˌtāt\ *vb* **-tat·ed; -tat·ing** **1 a** : to consider or think over carefully : CONTEMPLATE **b** : to spend time in quiet thinking : REFLECT **2** : INTEND, PLAN ⟨*meditate* a trip abroad⟩

med·i·ta·tion \ˌmed-ə-'tā-shən\ *n* : the act or an instance of meditating

med·i·ta·tive \'med-ə-ˌtāt-iv\ *adj* : having the habit of meditating — **med·i·ta·tive·ly** *adv*

Med·i·ter·ra·nean \ˌmed-ə-tə-'rā-nē-ən, -'rā-nyən\ *adj* : of or relating to the Mediterranean sea or to the lands or peoples around it

Mediterranean fruit fly *n* : a widely distributed two-winged fly with black-and-white markings and a larva destructive to ripening fruit

¹me·di·um \'mēd-ē-əm\ *n, pl* **mediums** *or* **me·dia** \'mēd-ē-ə\ **1 a** : something that is between or in the middle **b** : a middle condition or degree **2** : the thing by which or through which something is done ⟨money is a *medium* of exchange⟩; *esp* : a substance through which a force acts or by which something is carried ⟨air is the common *medium* of sound⟩ **3** *pl usually* **media** : a form or system (as newspapers, radio, or television) of communication **4** *pl* **mediums** : a person through whom others seek to communicate with the spirits of the dead **5** : a surrounding substance or condition : ENVIRONMENT ⟨marine fish live in a *medium* of salt water⟩ **6** *pl* **media a** : a nourishing system for the artificial cultivation of microorganisms (as bacteria) or cells **b** : a fluid or solid in which plant or animal structures are placed (as for mounting or preserving)

²medium *adj* : intermediate in amount, quality, position, or degree

med·ley \'med-lē\ *n, pl* **medleys** **1** : MIXTURE 2; *esp* : a confused mixture **2** : a musical composition made up of a series of songs or short musical pieces

me·dul·la \mə-'dəl-ə\ *n, pl* **-dul·las** *or* **-dul·lae** \-'dəl-ē, -ˌī\ **1** : MEDULLA OBLONGATA **2** : the inner or deep part of an animal or plant structure (as the adrenal gland or kidney) — **med·ul·lary** \'med-ᵊl-ˌer-ē, 'mej-ə-ˌler-ē\ *adj*

medulla ob·lon·ga·ta \-ˌäb-ˌlȯŋ-'gät-ə\ *n* : the somewhat pyramid-shaped bottom part of the vertebrate brain that joins the spinal cord and is concerned with the control of involuntary activities (as breathing and beating of the

heart)

me·du·sa \mi-'d(y)ü-sə, -zə\ *n, pl* **-sae** \-,sē, -,zē\ *or* **-sas**
: JELLYFISH

meek \'mēk\ *adj* **1** : putting up with wrongs patiently and
without complaint : MILD **2** : lacking spirit or self-assurance : HUMBLE — **meek·ly** *adv* — **meek·ness** *n*

meer·schaum \'mi(ə)r-shəm, -,shóm\ *n* **1** : a soft white
lightweight mineral resembling a very fine clay used especially for tobacco pipes **2** : a tobacco pipe made of meer-
schaum [German, literally "sea foam"]

¹meet \'mēt\ *vb* **met** \'met\; **meet·ing** **1** : to come by
chance into the presence of : ENCOUNTER ⟨met an old
friend⟩ **2 a** : to approach from the opposite direction
⟨when you *meet* another car, keep to the right⟩ **b** : to
touch and join or cross ⟨a fork where two roads *meet*⟩ **3**
: to go where a person or thing is or will be ⟨agreed to
meet me at school⟩ **4 a** : to become acquainted ⟨the couple *met* at a dance⟩ **b** : to make the acquaintance of ⟨*met*
interesting people there⟩ **5 a** : to come together as opponents ⟨the teams *met* in the finals⟩ **b** : to struggle
against : OPPOSE ⟨was chosen to *meet* the champion⟩ **6**
: ²MATCH 4a ⟨tries to *meet* the competitor's price⟩ **7** : EN-
DURE 2 ⟨*meet* defeat bravely⟩ **8** : to come together : AS-
SEMBLE ⟨*meet* for discussion⟩ **9** : to become noticed by
⟨sounds that *meet* the ears⟩ **10 a** : to fulfill the requirements of : SATISFY ⟨*met* all our demands⟩ **b** : to pay fully
: DISCHARGE ⟨*meet* a financial obligation⟩ [Old English *mē-
tan* "to meet"] — **meet with** : ¹ENCOUNTER 2

²meet *n* : a meeting for sports competition ⟨a track *meet*⟩

³meet *adj* : SUITABLE 2, PROPER [Old English *gemǣte*
"proper"] — **meet·ly** *adv*

meet·ing \'mēt-iŋ\ *n* **1** : the act of persons or things that meet
⟨a chance *meeting*⟩ **2** : a coming together of a number of
persons for a definite purpose ⟨the club *meeting*⟩ **3** : an assembly for religious worship ⟨a Quaker *meeting*⟩ **4** : the
place where two things come together : JUNCTION

meet·ing·house \-,haús\ *n* : a building used for public assembly and especially for Protestant worship

mega- *combining form* **1** : great : large ⟨*mega*spore⟩ **2**
: million : multiplied by one million ⟨*mega*hertz⟩ [derived
from Greek *megas* "large"]

mega·byte \'meg-ə-,bīt\ *n* : one million bytes

mega·cy·cle \'meg-ə-,sī-kəl\ *n* : one million cycles; *esp*
: MEGAHERTZ

mega·hertz \'meg-ə-,hərts, -,he(ə)rts\ *n* : a unit of frequency equal to one million hertz

mega·hit \'meg-ə-,hit\ *n* : something (as a movie) that is
extremely successful

meg·a·lop·o·lis \,meg-ə-'läp-ə-ləs\ *n* **1** : a very large city
2 : a thickly populated region centering in a large city or
including several large cities

mega·phone \'meg-ə-,fōn\
n : a cone-shaped device
used to direct the voice
and increase its loudness

mega·spore \'meg-ə-
,spō(ə)r, -,spò(ə)r\ *n* : a
plant spore that produces
a female gametophyte

mega·ton \'meg-ə-,tən\ *n*
: an explosive force equal
to that of one million tons
of TNT

megaphone

mei·o·sis \mī-'ō-səs\ *n, pl*
-o·ses \-'ō-,sēz\ : the
process by which the
number of chromosomes in a cell that produces sex cells
is reduced to one half — **mei·ot·ic** \mī-'ät-ik\ *adj* —
mei·ot·i·cal·ly \-'ät-i-k(ə-)lē\ *adv*

mel·an·cho·lia \,mel-ən-'kō-lē-ə\ *n* : a mental disorder
marked by extreme depression, real or imagined physical
symptoms, and often hallucinations and delusions

¹mel·an·choly \'mel-ən-,käl-ē\ *n, pl* **-chol·ies** : a sad or
gloomy mood or condition [Middle English *malencolie*
"melancholy", from early French *melancolie* (same meaning), from Latin *melancholia* (same meaning), from Greek
melancholia "melancholy", literally "black bile", from
melan-, melas "black" and *cholē* "bile"; so called from the
ancient belief that the condition was caused by an excess
of what was thought to be black bile in the body — related
to CHOLERIC, MELANIN; see *Word History* at HUMOR]

²melancholy *adj* **1** : depressed in spirits : DEJECTED, SAD
2 : seriously thoughtful **3** : causing sadness : DISMAL

Mel·a·ne·sian \,mel-ə-'nē-zhən, -shən\ *n* : a member of
the most numerous native group of Melanesia — **Melane-
sian** *adj*

mé·lange \mā-'länzh, -'länj\ *n* : a mixture often of dissimilar
elements

mel·a·nin \'mel-ə-nən\ *n* : a dark brown or black animal or
plant pigment that in human beings is responsible for black
or brown skins [derived from Greek *melan-, melas* "black"
— related to MELANCHOLY]

mel·a·nism \'mel-ə-,niz-əm\ *n* : an exceptionally dark coloring (as of skin, feathers, or hair) of an individual or kind
of living thing

me·la·no·cyte \mə-'lan-ə-,sīt, 'mel-ə-nō-\ *n* : a body cell
(as in the skin) that produces or contains melanin

mel·a·no·ma \,mel-ə-'nō-mə\ *n, pl* **-mas** *also* **-ma·ta**
\-,mət-ə\ : a usually malignant tumor containing dark pigment

me·lee \'mā-,lā, mā-'lā\ *n* : a confused struggle; *esp* : a
hand-to-hand fight among several people

me·lio·rate \'mēl-yə-,rāt, 'mē-lē-ə-\ *vb* **-rat·ed; -rat·ing**
: to make or become better : IMPROVE — **me·lio·ra·tion**
\,mēl-yə-'rā-shən, ,mē-lē-ə-\ *n* — **me·lio·ra·tive** \'mēl-
yə-,rāt-iv, 'mē-lē-ə-\ *adj*

mel·lif·lu·ous \me-'lif-lə-wəs, mə-\ *adj* : smoothly flowing
⟨*mellifluous* speech⟩ — **mel·lif·lu·ous·ly** *adv* — **mel·
lif·lu·ous·ness** *n*

mel·lo·phone \'mel-ə-,fōn\ *n* : an althorn in circular form

¹mel·low \'mel-ō\ *adj* **1 a** : tender and sweet because of
ripeness ⟨*mellow* peaches⟩ **b** : well aged and pleasingly
mild ⟨a *mellow* wine⟩ **2** : made gentle by age or experience ⟨a *mellow* disposition⟩ **3** : being soft and crumbly
⟨*mellow* soil⟩ **4** : being clear, full, and pure ⟨spoke in
mellow tones⟩ — **mel·low·ly** *adv* — **mel·low·ness** *n*

²mellow *vb* : to make or become mellow ⟨old houses,
weather-beaten and *mellowed* by time⟩

me·lo·de·on \mə-'lōd-ē-ən\ *n* : a small reed organ in which
a bellows draws air inward through the reeds

me·lod·ic \mə-'läd-ik\ *adj* : of or relating to melody : MELO-
DIOUS — **me·lod·i·cal·ly** \-i-k(ə-)lē\ *adv*

me·lo·di·ous \mə-'lōd-ē-əs\ *adj* **1** : pleasing to the ear
because of melody **2** : of, relating to, or producing melody ⟨*melodious* birds⟩ — **me·lo·di·ous·ly** *adv* — **me·
lo·di·ous·ness** *n*

melo·dra·ma \'mel-ə-,dräm-ə, -,dram-\ *n* **1 a** : a work (as
a movie or play) marked by the exaggerated emotions of
the characters and the importance of action and plot **b**
: such works as a group **2** : melodramatic events or behavior

melo·dra·mat·ic \,mel-ə-drə-'mat-ik\ *adj* **1** : of or relating
to melodrama **2** : resembling or suitable for melodrama
: SENSATIONAL — **melo·dra·mat·i·cal·ly** \-i-k(ə-)lē\ *adv*

mel·o·dy \'mel-əd-ē\ *n, pl* **-dies** **1** : a pleasing succession
of sounds **2** : a series of musical tones arranged to give
a pleasing effect **3** : the leading part in a musical composition involving harmony

\ə\ abut	\aú\ out	\i\ tip	\ò\ saw	\ú\ foot
\ər\ further	\ch\ chin	\ī\ life	\òi\ coin	\y\ yet
\a\ mat	\e\ pet	\j\ job	\th\ thin	\yü\ few
\ā\ take	\ē\ easy	\ŋ\ sing	\th\ this	\yú\ cure
\ä\ cot, cart	\g\ go	\ō\ bone	\ü\ food	\zh\ vision

mel·on \'mel-ən\ *n* : any of various fruits (as a muskmelon or watermelon) that have juicy and usually sweet flesh and a firm skin, are eaten raw, grow on a vine, and are related to the gourds

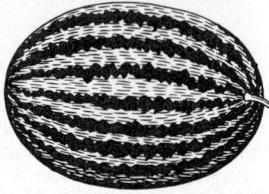

melon

¹**melt** \'melt\ *vb* **1** : to change from a solid to a liquid state usually through heat ⟨*melt* butter⟩ ⟨snow *melts*⟩ **2** : DISSOLVE 1 ⟨sugar *melts* in the mouth⟩ **3** : to grow less : DISAPPEAR ⟨clouds *melting* away⟩ **4** : to make or become gentle : SOFTEN ⟨a warm smile *melts* the heart⟩ **5** : to lose clear outline or shape : BLEND, MERGE — **melt·er** *n*

²**melt** *n* : a melted substance

melt·down \'melt-,daún\ *n* **1** : the accidental melting of the core of a nuclear reactor **2** : a rapid or disastrous decline or collapse

melting point *n* : the temperature at which a solid melts

melting pot *n* **1** : a container in which something is melted : CRUCIBLE **2** : a place (as a city or country) in which various nationalities or races live together and gradually blend into one community

mel·ton \'melt-ᵊn\ *n* : a smooth heavy woolen cloth used for overcoats

melt·wa·ter \'melt-,wòt-ər, -,wät-\ *n* : water that comes from the melting of ice and snow

mem·ber \'mem-bər\ *n* **1** : a part (as an arm, leg, leaf, or branch) of an animal or plant **2** : one of the individuals or units of a group or organization ⟨a club *member*⟩ ⟨UN *members*⟩ **3** : a part of a whole and especially of a structure ⟨a horizontal *member* of a bridge⟩ **4 a** : either of the parts on opposite sides of the equal sign in a mathematical equation **b** : ELEMENT 2b

mem·ber·ship \'mem-bər-,ship\ *n* **1** : the state or status of being a member **2** : all the members of an organization

mem·brane \'mem-,brān\ *n* : a thin soft flexible sheet or layer especially of a plant or animal part (as a cell, tissue, or organ) — **mem·bra·nous** \'mem-brə-nəs\ *adj*

me·men·to \mi-'ment-ō\ *n, pl* **-tos** *or* **-toes** : SOUVENIR

memo \'mem-ō\ *n, pl* **mem·os** : MEMORANDUM

mem·oir \'mem-,wär, -,wò(ə)r\ *n* **1 a** : a story of a personal experience **b** : AUTOBIOGRAPHY — usually used in pl. **c** : BIOGRAPHY **2** : ¹REPORT 2

mem·o·ra·bil·ia \,mem-ə-rə-'bil-ē-ə, -'bil-yə\ *n pl* : things worth remembering; *also* : a collection of souvenirs

mem·o·ra·ble \'mem-(ə)rə-bəl\ *adj* : worth remembering : NOTABLE — **mem·o·ra·bly** \-blē\ *adv*

mem·o·ran·dum \,mem-ə-'ran-dəm\ *n, pl* **-dums** *or* **-da** \-də\ **1** : an informal record or communication **2** : a brief written reminder

¹**me·mo·ri·al** \mə-'mōr-ē-əl, -'mòr-\ *adj* : serving to preserve the memory of a person or an event ⟨a *memorial* service⟩ — **me·mo·ri·al·ly** \-ē-ə-lē\ *adv*

²**memorial** *n* : something that keeps alive the memory of a person or event; *esp* : MONUMENT 1

Memorial Day *n* **1** : May 30 once observed as a legal holiday in honor of those who died in war **2** : the last Monday in May observed as a legal holiday in most states of the U.S. **3** : CONFEDERATE MEMORIAL DAY

me·mo·ri·al·ize \mə-'mōr-ē-ə-,līz, -'mòr-\ *vb* **-ized; -iz·ing** : COMMEMORATE 1

mem·o·rize \'mem-ə-,rīz\ *vb* **-rized; -riz·ing** : to learn by heart — **mem·o·ri·za·tion** \,mem-(ə)rə-'zā-shən\ *n*

mem·o·ry \'mem-(ə)rē\ *n, pl* **-ries** **1 a** : the power or process of recalling what has been learned **b** : the store of things learned and kept in the mind ⟨recite from *memory*⟩ **2** : COMMEMORATION 1 ⟨a monument in *memory* of a hero⟩ **3** : something remembered ⟨has pleasant *memories* of the trip⟩ **4** : the time within which past events can be remembered ⟨within the *memory* of people living today⟩ **5 a** : a device (as in a computer) into which information can be inserted and stored and from which it may be taken when needed **b** : capacity for storing information ⟨a computer with 64K bytes of *memory*⟩

syn MEMORY, REMEMBRANCE, RECOLLECTION, REMINISCENCE mean something remembered. MEMORY suggests always keeping in mind or treasuring something personal ⟨had many fond *memories* of her grandfather⟩ REMEMBRANCE stresses the pleasantness with which something is brought back to mind ⟨a vivid *remembrance* of their wedding day⟩ RECOLLECTION suggests that something is deliberately brought back to mind and often with some effort ⟨to the best of my *recollection* he never said that⟩ REMINISCENCE suggests the remembering of events and especially people from long ago ⟨the author's *reminiscences* of a childhood in Scotland⟩

men *pl of* MAN

¹**men·ace** \'men-əs\ *n* **1** : DANGER 2 **2** : NUISANCE

²**menace** *vb* **men·aced; men·ac·ing** **1** : THREATEN 1 **2** : ENDANGER — **men·ac·ing·ly** \'men-ə-siŋ-lē\ *adv*

mé·nage \mā-'näzh\ *n* : ¹HOUSEHOLD

me·nag·er·ie \mə-'naj-(ə)rē *also* -'nazh-\ *n* **1** : a place where animals are kept and trained especially for exhibition **2** : a collection of wild animals kept especially for exhibition

¹**mend** \'mend\ *vb* **1** : to improve in manners or morals : REFORM **2** : to put into good shape or working order again **3** : to improve in health; *also* : HEAL — **mend·er** *n*

syn MEND, PATCH, REPAIR mean to take something that has been damaged and make it usable again. MEND suggests making something that has been broken or damaged once again whole or fit for use ⟨*mend* a piece of china⟩ PATCH refers to mending a hole or tear by using the same or similar material ⟨*patched* my pants with scraps of cloth⟩ and it may also suggest a hurried careless job ⟨just *patch* the roof for now⟩ REPAIR suggests a skillful mending of a complicated thing that has been damaged considerably ⟨the mechanic *repaired* our car⟩

²**mend** *n* **1** : an act of mending : REPAIR **2** : a mended place — **on the mend** : getting better (as in health)

men·da·cious \men-'dā-shəs\ *adj* : apt to tell lies — **men·da·cious·ly** *adv* — **men·dac·i·ty** \men-'das-ət-ē\ *n*

men·de·le·vi·um \,men-də-'lē-vē-əm\ *n* : a radioactive element that is artificially produced — see ELEMENT table

Men·de·lian \men-'dē-lē-ən, -'dēl-yən\ *adj* : of, relating to, or according with Mendel's laws or the operation of Mendel's laws — **Mendelian** *n*

Men·del's law \,men-dᵊlz-\ *n* **1** : a principle in genetics: paired inherited units that control the expression of a character (as height or seed color) separate during germ cell formation so that each sperm or egg receives only one member of each pair — called also *law of segregation* **2** : a principle in genetics that has to be changed in cases where two or more genes occur on the same chromosome: the members of two or more different pairs of inherited units are passed on to a germ cell independently of each other and the various sperms and eggs unite according to the laws of chance sometimes resulting in new combinations of inherited units and of the characters they control — called also *law of independent assortment* **3** : a principle in genetics that has many exceptions: when the two members of a pair of inherited units are different, the dominant one controls the expression of the character — called also *law of dominance*

men·di·cant \'men-di-kənt\ *n* **1** : one who lives by begging **2** : a member of a religious order originally owning neither personal nor community property and living mostly on charitable donations : FRIAR — **men·di·can·cy** \-kən-sē\ *n* — **mendicant** *adj*

men·folk \'men-ˌfōk\ *or* **men·folks** \-ˌfōks\ *n pl* **1** : men in general **2** : the men of a family or community

men·ha·den \men-'hād-ᵉn, mən-\ *n, pl* **-den** *also* **-dens** : a fish of the Atlantic coast of the U.S. that is related to the herrings and is a source of oil and fertilizer

¹me·nial \'mē-nē-əl, -nyəl\ *adj* : of, relating to, or suitable for servants — **me·nial·ly** \-ē\ *adv*

²menial *n* : SERVANT

men·in·gi·tis \ˌmen-ən-'jīt-əs\ *n* : a disease in which a membrane of the brain or spinal cord becomes inflamed

me·ninx \'mē-niŋ(k)s, 'men-iŋ(k)s\ *n, pl* **me·nin·ges** \mə-'nin-jēz\ : any of the three membranes surrounding the brain and spinal cord

me·nis·cus \mə-'nis-kəs\ *n, pl* **me·nis·ci** \-'nis-,(k)ī, -,kē\ *also* **me·nis·cus·es** : the curved upper surface of a liquid column

Men·no·nite \'men-ə-ˌnīt\ *n* : a member of one of the Protestant groups founded in Holland in the 16th century and noted for dressing plainly and living simply

meno·pause \'men-ə-ˌpȯz\ *n* : the period of life when menstruation stops naturally that usually occurs between the ages of 45 and 50 — **meno·paus·al** \ˌmen-ə-'pȯ-zəl\ *adj*

me·no·rah \mə-'nōr-ə, -'nȯr-\ *n* : a holder for candles used in Jewish worship

menservants *pl of* MANSERVANT

men·ses \'men-ˌsēz\ *n pl* : the menstrual flow

men·stru·al \'men(t)-strə-(wə)l\ *adj* : of or relating to menstruation

menstrual cycle *n* : the whole cycle of bodily changes from the beginning of one menstrual period to the beginning of the next

men·stru·ate \'men(t)-strə-ˌwāt, 'men-ˌsträt\ *vb* : to experience menstruation

men·stru·a·tion \ˌmen(t)-strə-'wā-shən, men-'strā-shən\ *n* : a discharging of blood, secretions, and tissue debris from the uterus at periods of approximately one month in female primates of breeding age that are not pregnant; *also* : PERIOD 3c

men·su·ra·tion \ˌmen(t)-sə-'rā-shən, ˌmen-chə-\ *n* **1** : the process or art of measuring **2** : the branch of mathematics that deals with the measurement of lengths, areas, and volumes

-ment \mənt\ *n suffix* **1** : result, object, or means of a (specified) action ⟨attach*ment*⟩ ⟨govern*ment*⟩ ⟨entertain*ment*⟩ **2 a** : action : process ⟨improve*ment*⟩ ⟨develop*ment*⟩ **b** : place of a (specified) action ⟨encamp*ment*⟩ **3** : state : condition ⟨amaze*ment*⟩ [derived from Latin *-mentum* (noun suffix)]

men·tal \'ment-ᵊl\ *adj* **1 a** : of or relating to the mind ⟨*mental* powers⟩ **b** : carried on in the mind ⟨*mental* arithmetic⟩ **2 a** : relating to or affected by a disorder of the mind ⟨a *mental* patient⟩ **b** : intended for the care of persons affected by mental disorders ⟨*mental* hospital⟩ — **men·tal·ly** \-ᵊl-ē\ *adv*

mental age *n* : a measure of a child's mental development in terms of the number of years from birth it takes an average child to reach the same level

men·tal·i·ty \men-'tal-ət-ē\ *n, pl* **-ties** : mental power : INTELLIGENCE

men·thol \'men-ˌthȯl, -ˌthōl\ *n* : a white soothing substance from oils of mint

¹men·tion \'men-chən\ *n* : a brief or passing reference to something

²mention *vb* **men·tioned; men·tion·ing** \'mench-(ə-)niŋ\ : to refer to or speak about briefly — **men·tion·able**

\'mench-(ə-)nə-bəl\ *adj*

¹men·tor \'men-ˌtȯ(ə)r, 'ment-ər\ *n* : a wise and faithful adviser or teacher

²mentor *vb* : to serve as a mentor for

menu \'men-yü, 'mān-\ *n* **1** : a list of dishes served at or available for a meal; *also* : a similar list of offerings ⟨a *menu* of TV programs⟩ **2** : the dishes served at a meal

Word History Many restaurants boast of having large menus, but the origin of the word *menu* actually suggests the idea of smallness. *Menu* can be traced to the Latin adjective *minutus*, meaning "small". *Minutus* is also the source of our word *minute*. From *minutus* came the French adjective *menu*, which has several meanings including "small" and "detailed". The use of *menu* as a noun meaning "a list of food" probably came from the "detailed" sense of the adjective, since a menu is most often a detailed list. [from French *menu* "a list of food dishes", from *menu* (adjective) "small, detailed", derived from Latin *minutus* "small" — related to MINUTE]

me·ow \mē-'aú\ *n* : the characteristic sound of a cat — **meow** *vb*

mer·can·tile \'mər-kən-ˌtēl, -ˌtīl\ *adj* : of or relating to merchants, trade, or commerce

¹mer·ce·nary \'mərs-ᵊn-ˌer-ē\ *n, pl* **-nar·ies** : one that serves only for wages; *esp* : a soldier hired by a foreign country to fight in its army

²mercenary *adj* **1** : serving only for the pay or reward **2** : greedy for money

mer·cer \'mər-sər\ *n, British* : a dealer in textile fabrics

mer·cer·ize \'mər-sə-ˌrīz\ *vb* **-ized; -iz·ing** : to treat cotton fiber or fabrics with a chemical so that the fibers are strengthened, take dyes better, and often acquire a soft shine — **mer·cer·iza·tion** \ˌmərs-(ə-)rə-'zā-shən\ *n*

¹mer·chan·dise \'mər-chən-ˌdīz, -ˌdīs\ *n* : the goods that are bought and sold in trade

²merchandise \'mər-chən-ˌdīz\ *vb* **-dised; -dis·ing** : to buy and sell : TRADE; *esp* : to try to improve sales of goods or services by attractive presentation and publicity — **mer·chan·dis·er** *n*

¹mer·chant \'mər-chənt\ *n* **1** : a buyer and seller of goods for profit; *esp* : one who carries on trade on a large scale or with foreign countries **2** : STOREKEEPER 2 [Middle English *marchant* "merchant", from early French *marcheant* (same meaning), derived from Latin *mercari* "to trade" from *merc-, merx* "merchandise" — related to COMMERCE, MARKET]

²merchant *adj* **1** : of, relating to, or used in trade ⟨*merchant* ship⟩ **2** : of or relating to a merchant marine

mer·chant·man \'mər-chənt-mən\ *n* : a ship used in trade

merchant marine *n* **1** : the commercial ships of a nation **2** : the persons who work in a merchant marine

merchant ship *n* : MERCHANTMAN

mer·ci·ful \'mər-si-fəl\ *adj* : having or showing mercy : COMPASSIONATE — **mer·ci·ful·ly** \-f(ə-)lē\ *adv* — **mer·ci·ful·ness** \-fəl-nəs\ *n*

mer·ci·less \'mər-si-ləs\ *adj* : having no mercy : PITILESS ⟨*merciless* slaughter⟩ — **mer·ci·less·ly** *adv* — **mer·ci·less·ness** *n*

mer·cu·ri·al \(ˌ)mər-'kyúr-ē-əl\ *adj* **1** : characterized by rapid and unpredictable change of mood **2** : MERCURIC — **mer·cu·ri·al·ly** \-ē-ə-lē\ *adv*

mer·cu·ric \(ˌ)mər-'kyú(ə)r-ik\ *adj* : of, relating to, or containing mercury

Mer·cu·ro·chrome \(ˌ)mər-'kyúr-ə-ˌkrōm\ *trademark* — used for a red solution of a local antiseptic and germicide

mer·cu·ry \'mər-kyə-rē, -k(ə-)rē\ *n* **1 a** : a heavy

meniscus

silver-white poisonous metallic element that is liquid at ordinary temperatures — called also *quicksilver*; see ELEMENT table   **b** : the column of mercury in a thermometer or barometer   **2** *cap* : the planet nearest the sun — see PLANET table

mer·cy \'mər-sē\ *n, pl* **mercies**   **1 a** : kind and gentle treatment of someone (as a wrongdoer or opponent) having no right to it   **b** : a disposition to show mercy   **2 a** : a blessing as an act of divine love ⟨the *mercies* of God⟩   **b** : a fortunate happening ⟨it's a *mercy* the weather cooled off⟩   **3** : kindness shown to victims of misfortune

Word History To the ancient Romans, the Latin word *merces* meant "price paid for something, wages, reward". The early Christians of Rome used the word in a slightly different way. For them it meant the spiritual reward one receives for doing a kindness in response to an unkindness. The word came into early French as *mercit* or *merci* with much the same meaning as was later passed on to our Modern English word *mercy*. But while *mercy* in English now has the meaning "kindness or pity shown to someone", the word *merci* in French has lost much of that meaning and is chiefly used today to mean "thank you". [Middle English *merci, mercy* "mercy", from early French *merci, mercit* (same meaning), derived from Latin *merces* "price paid for something, wages, reward"]

syn MERCY, CLEMENCY, LENIENCY mean the disposition not to be harsh in one's dealings with others. MERCY suggests feeling pity and withholding punishment even when justice demands it ⟨pleaded guilty and asked for *mercy* from the court⟩ CLEMENCY suggests a mild or merciful disposition in the person having the power to punish ⟨a brutal ruler not known for *clemency*⟩ LENIENCY suggests the repeated overlooking of mistakes by one not inclined to be severe ⟨their parents' *leniency* was well-known among the children⟩

mercy killing *n* : the act or practice of killing or permitting the death of hopelessly sick or injured individuals (as persons or domestic animals) with as little pain as possible for reasons of mercy — called also *euthanasia*

¹mere \'mi(ə)r\ *n* : a sheet of still water : POOL [Old English *mere* "lake, pool"]

²mere *adj, superlative* **mer·est** : being only this and nothing else : nothing more than ⟨a *mere* whisper⟩ ⟨a *mere* child⟩ [Middle English *mere* "nothing more or less than", from Latin *merus* "pure"] — **mere·ly** *adv*

mer·e·tri·cious \,mer-ə-'trish-əs\ *adj* : falsely attractive — **mer·e·tri·cious·ly** *adv* — **mer·e·tri·cious·ness** *n*

mer·gan·ser \(,)mər-'gan(t)-sər\ *n, pl* **-sers** *or* **-ser** : any of various fish-eating wild ducks with a slender hooked beak and usually with a bunch of feathers on the head that point backward

merge \'mərj\ *vb* **merged; merg·ing**   **1** : to be or cause to be swallowed up or absorbed in something else : MINGLE, BLEND ⟨*merging* traffic⟩   **2** : COMBINE 3a, UNITE ⟨*merge* two business firms into one⟩

merg·er \'mər-jər\ *n* : the combination of two or more businesses into one

me·rid·i·an \mə-'rid-ē-ən\ *n*   **1** : the highest point reached   **2 a** : an imaginary circle on the earth's surface passing through the north and south poles   **b** : the half of such a circle included between the poles   **c** : a line on a globe or map representing such a circle or half circle and numbered by degrees of longitude [Middle English *meridien* "midday", from early French *meridien* (same meaning), derived from Latin *meridies* "noon", from *meri-* (a form of *medius* "middle") and *dies* "day" — related to DIARY, ¹MEDIAN]

me·ringue \mə-'raŋ\ *n*   **1** : a mixture of beaten egg white and sugar put on pies or cakes and browned   **2** : a shell of baked meringue filled with fruit or ice cream

me·ri·no \mə-'rē-nō\ *n, pl* **-nos**   **1** : any of a breed of sheep that produce a heavy fleece of fine white wool   **2** : a fine soft wool or wool and cotton fabric resembling cashmere   **3** : a fine wool and cotton yarn — **merino** *adj*

mer·i·stem \'mer-ə-,stem\ *n* : a plant tissue made up of cells that are not specialized for a particular purpose, are capable of dividing any number of times, and can produce cells that specialize to form the fully developed plant tissues and organs — **mer·i·ste·mat·ic** \,mer-ə-stə-'mat-ik\ *adj*

¹mer·it \'mer-ət\ *n*   **1** : the condition or fact of deserving well or ill ⟨were rewarded according to *merit*⟩   **2** : a quality worthy of praise : VIRTUE ⟨the *merit* of honesty⟩   **3** : ²WORTH 2, VALUE ⟨your idea has great *merit*⟩

²merit *vb* : to earn by service or performance : DESERVE

mer·i·to·ri·ous \,mer-ə-'tōr-ē-əs, -'tòr-\ *adj* : deserving reward or honor : PRAISEWORTHY — **mer·i·to·ri·ous·ly** *adv* — **mer·i·to·ri·ous·ness** *n*

mer·maid \'mər-,mād\ *n* : an imaginary sea creature usually represented with a woman's body and a fish's tail [Middle English *mermayde* "mermaid", from *mere* "lake, pool, sea" and *mayde* "maid"]

mer·man \'mər-,man, -mən\ *n, pl* **mer·men** \-,men, -mən\ : an imaginary sea creature usually represented with a man's body and a fish's tail

mer·ri·ment \'mer-i-mənt\ *n* : MIRTH, FUN

mer·ry \'mer-ē\ *adj* **mer·ri·er; -est**   **1** : full of good humor and good spirits : MIRTHFUL   **2** : marked by gaiety or festivity ⟨a *merry* Christmas⟩ — **mer·ri·ly** \'mer-ə-lē\ *adv* — **mer·ri·ness** \'mer-ē-nəs\ *n*

mer·ry-go-round \'mer-ē-gō-,raùnd, -gə-\ *n*   **1** : a circular revolving platform fitted with seats and figures of animals on which people sit for a ride   **2** : a rapid round of activities : WHIRL ⟨a *merry-go-round* of parties⟩

mer·ry·mak·ing \'mer-ē-,mā-kiŋ\ *n*   **1** : gay or festive activity : MERRIMENT   **2** : a festive occasion — **mer·ry·mak·er** \-kər\ *n*

me·sa \'mā-sə\ *n* : a flat-topped hill or small plateau with steep sides [Spanish, literally "table"]

mes·cal \me-'skal, mə-\ *n*   **1** : a small spineless cactus that is the source of a stimulant used by Mexican Indians   **2 a** : a usually colorless Mexican liquor distilled especially from the central leaves of agave plants   **b** : a plant from which this liquor is produced

mes·ca·line \'mes-kə-lən, -,lēn\ *n* : a mind-altering chemical that is the active part of the mescal cactus producing its stimulating effects and is sometimes used as a drug

mescal 1

mesdames *pl of* MADAM *or of* MADAME *or of* MRS.

mesdemoiselles *pl of* MADEMOISELLE

me·seems \mi-'sēmz\ *impersonal verb, past* **me·seemed** \-'sēmd\ *archaic* : it seems to me

mes·en·tery \'mez-ᵊn-,ter-ē, 'mes-\ *n, pl* **-ter·ies** : membranous tissue or one of the membranes that enclose the organs (as the intestines) making up the guts and connect them to the wall of the abdominal cavity

¹mesh \'mesh\ *n*   **1** : one of the spaces formed by the threads of a net or the wires of a sieve or screen   **2 a** : a loosely woven fabric with evenly spaced holes   **b** : ¹NET 1   **3** : an arrangement of elements that are linked together : NETWORK   **4** : the coming or fitting together of the teeth of two gears — **meshed** \'mesht\ *adj*

²mesh *vb*   **1** : to catch in or as if in a mesh : ENTANGLE   **2** : to fit together : INTERLOCK ⟨*mesh* gears⟩

mes·mer·ism \'mez-mə-,riz-əm *also* 'mes-\ *n* : HYPNOTISM

mes·mer·ize \'mez-mə-,rīz *also* 'mes-\ *vb* **-ized; -iz·ing**

1 : HYPNOTIZE   2 : FASCINATE 1, SPELLBIND

me·so·derm \'mez-ə-,dərm, 'mēz-, 'mēs-, 'mes-\ *n* : the middle layer of cells of an embryonic animal from which most of the muscular, skeletal, and connective tissues develop; *also* : tissue derived from this layer — **me·so·der·mal** \,mez-ə-'dər-məl, ,mēz-, ,mēs-, ,mes-\ *adj*

me·son \'mez-,än, 'mes-; 'mā-,zän, 'mes-, -,sän\ *n* : any of a group of elementary particles that act strongly on one another and are among the products of nuclear collisions

me·so·pause \'mez-ə-,póz, 'mēz-, 'mēs-, 'mes-\ *n* : the upper boundary of the mesosphere at which the temperature of the atmosphere reaches its lowest point

me·so·phyll \'mez-ə-,fil, 'mēz-, 'mēs-, 'mes-\ *n* : the tissue of a leaf that lies between the surface layers and contains cells used for storage and carrying on photosynthesis — **me·so·phyl·lic** \,mez-ə-'fil-ik, ,mes-\ *adj*

me·so·sphere \'mez-ə-,sfi(ə)r, 'mēz-, 'mēs-, 'mes-\ *n* : a layer of the atmosphere extending from the top of the stratosphere to an altitude of about 90 kilometers

me·so·tho·rax \,mez-ə-'thō(ə)r-,aks, ,mēz-, ,mēs-, ,mes-, -'thô(ə)r-\ *n* : the middle of the three segments of the thorax of an insect

Me·so·zo·ic \,mez-ə-'zō-ik, ,mēz-, ,mēs-, ,mes-\ *adj* : of, relating to, or being an era of geological history between the Paleozoic and Cenozoic eras or the corresponding system of rocks — see GEOLOGIC TIME table — **Mesozoic** *n*

mes·quite \mə-'skēt, me-\ *n* : a thorny deep-rooted tree or shrub of the southwestern U.S. and Mexico that belongs to the legume family, produces pods rich in sugar, and is important as food for livestock

mesquite

¹**mess** \'mes\ *n* **1 a** : a quantity of food   **b** : a dish of soft food ⟨a *mess* of porridge⟩   **2 a** : a group of people who regularly eat together   **b** : the meal they eat   **c** : the place where they eat ⟨an officers' *mess*⟩   **3** : a state of confusion or disorder or unpleasantness ⟨left things in a *mess*⟩; *also* : something that is in such a state

²**mess** *vb* **1 a** : to supply with meals   **b** : to take meals with a mess   **2 a** : to make dirty or untidy : DISARRANGE   **b** : BUNGLE ⟨*messed* up the job⟩   **3** : INTERFERE 2, MEDDLE ⟨don't *mess* with me⟩   **4** : to work without a serious goal : PUTTER ⟨likes to *mess* around with paints⟩

mes·sage \'mes-ij\ *n* **1** : a communication in writing, in speech, or by signals   **2** : a messenger's errand or function   **3** : an underlying theme or idea [Middle English *message* "job or function of a messenger", from early French *message* (same meaning), from Latin *missaticum* "something given to a messenger to deliver", from earlier *missus* (past participle of *mittere* "to send, throw") and *-aticum* "action, result" — related to EMIT, MISSION, PROMISE, SUBMISSIVE]

messeigneurs *pl of* MONSEIGNEUR

mes·sen·ger \'mes-ⁿn-jər\ *n* : one that carries a message or does an errand

messenger RNA *n* : an RNA that carries the code for a particular protein from DNA in the nucleus to the ribosome and that acts as a pattern or mold for the formation of that protein

mes·si·ah \mə-'sī-ə\ *n* **1** *cap* **a** : the expected king and deliverer of the Jews   **b** : Jesus   **2** : a leader of some hope or cause : DELIVERER

messieurs *pl of* MONSIEUR

mess·mate \'mes-,māt\ *n* : a member of a mess (as on a ship)

Messrs. \,mes-ərz\ *pl of* MR.

messy \'mes-ē\ *adj* **mess·i·er; -est** **1** : marked by confusion, disorder, or dirt : UNTIDY   **2** : extremely unpleasant or trying ⟨*messy* lawsuits⟩ — **mess·i·ly** \'mes-ə-lē\ *adv* — **mess·i·ness** \'mes-ē-nəs\ *n*

mes·ti·zo \me-'stē-zō\ *n, pl* **-zos** : a person having mixed European and American Indian ancestors

met *past and past participle of* MEET

met·a·bol·ic \,met-ə-'bäl-ik\ *adj* : of, relating to, or based on metabolism — **met·a·bol·i·cal·ly** \-i-k(ə-)lē\ *adv*

me·tab·o·lism \mə-'tab-ə-,liz-əm\ *n* **1** : the processes by which the living protoplasm in a living thing is built up or broken down   **2** : the processes by which a particular substance (as iodine) is handled in the living body

me·tab·o·lize \mə-'tab-ə-,līz\ *vb* **-lized; -liz·ing** : to break down by metabolism ⟨food is *metabolized* by the body⟩

¹**meta·car·pal** \,met-ə-'kär-pəl\ *adj* : of, relating to, or being the part of the hand or front foot or a bone of this part that is between the carpal bones and the phalanges

²**metacarpal** *n* : a metacarpal bone

met·al \'met-ᵊl\ *n* **1** : any of various substances (as gold, tin, or copper) that have a more or less shiny appearance, are good conductors of electricity and heat, can be melted, and are usually capable of being shaped; *esp* : one that is a chemical element rather than an alloy   **2** : METTLE 2 — **metal** *adj*

me·tal·lic \mə-'tal-ik\ *adj* **1** : of, relating to, or being a metal   **2** : containing or made of metal   **3** : having a harsh or rasping sound ⟨a *metallic* voice⟩

met·al·loid \'met-ᵊl-,óid\ *n* : an element that has some characteristics of metals and some of nonmetals — **metalloid** *adj*

met·al·lur·gy \'met-ᵊl-,ər-jē\ *n* : the science of obtaining metals from their ores and preparing them for use — **met·al·lur·gi·cal** \,met-ᵊl-'ər-ji-kəl\ *adj* — **met·al·lur·gist** \'met-ᵊl-,ər-jəst\ *n*

met·al·work \'met-ᵊl-,wərk\ *n* : the product of metalworking — **met·al·work·er** \-,wər-kər\ *n*

met·al·work·ing \'met-ᵊl-,wər-kiŋ\ *n* : the act or process of shaping things out of metal

meta·mor·phic \,met-ə-'mor-fik\ *adj* : changed into a more compact form by the action of pressure, heat, and water ⟨a *metamorphic* rock⟩ — compare IGNEOUS, SEDIMENTARY 2

meta·mor·phose \,met-ə-'mor-,fōz, -,fōs\ *vb* **-phosed; -phos·ing** : to change or cause to change in form : go through metamorphosis

meta·mor·pho·sis \,met-ə-'mor-fə-səs\ *n, pl* **-pho·ses** \-fə-,sēz\   **1** : a change of form, structure, or substance especially by witchcraft or magic   **2** : an extraordinary change in appearance, character, or circumstances   **3** : the process of basic and usually rather sudden change in the form and habits of some animals during transformation from an immature stage (as a tadpole or a caterpillar) to an adult stage (as a frog or a butterfly)

meta·phase \'met-ə-,fāz\ *n* : the stage of mitosis or meiosis in which the chromosomes are arranged in the center of the dividing cell prior to their separation or splitting and movement to the poles of the cell

met·a·phor \'met-ə-,fó(ə)r *also* -fər\ *n* : a figure of speech in which a word or phrase meaning one kind of object or idea is used in place of another to suggest a similarity between them (as in *the ship plows the sea*) — compare SIMILE — **met·a·phor·i·cal** \,met-ə-'fór-i-kəl, -'fär-\ *adj* — **met·a·phor·i·cal·ly** \-i-k(ə-)lē\ *adv*

meta·phys·i·cal \,met-ə-'fiz-i-kəl\ *adj* **1** : of, relating to, or based on metaphysics   **2** : SUPERNATURAL 1   **3** : difficult to understand : ABSTRACT — **meta·phys·i·cal·ly** \-i-

\ə\ abut	\au̇\ out	\i\ tip	\ȯ\ saw	\u̇\ foot
\ər\ further	\ch\ chin	\ī\ life	\ȯi\ coin	\y\ yet
\a\ mat	\e\ pet	\j\ job	\th\ thin	\yü\ few
\ā\ take	\ē\ easy	\ŋ\ sing	\th\ this	\yu̇\ cure
\ä\ cot, cart	\g\ go	\ō\ bone	\ü\ food	\zh\ vision

k(ə-)lē\ *adv*

meta·phys·ics \,met-ə-'fiz-iks\ *n* : the part of philosophy concerned with the ultimate causes and basic nature of things [from Latin *Metaphysica,* title given to a work by Aristotle on the subject, from Greek *(ta) meta (ta) physika,* literally "the (works) after the physical (works)"; so called because this section came after the section on physics and physical nature in a book of Aristotle's collected writings]

me·tas·ta·sis \mə-'tas-tə-səs\ *n, pl* **-ta·ses** \-,sēz\ **1** : the transfer of something that produces disease (as cancer cells) from the location of disease to another part of the body **2** : a growth of a malignant tumor in another part of the body from the location of the original tumor

¹meta·tar·sal \,met-ə-'tär-səl\ *adj* : of, relating to, or being the part of the foot in human beings or of the hind foot in a four-footed animal that is located between the tarsal bones and the phalanges

²metatarsal *n* : any of the metatarsal bones of which there are five in human beings

meta·tho·rax \,met-ə-'thō(ə)r-,aks, -'thō(ə)r-\ *n* : the one of the three segments in the thorax of an insect that is next to the abdomen

meta·zo·an \,met-ə-'zō-ən\ *n* : any of the great group of animals with a body composed of cells forming tissues and organs — **metazoan** *adj*

mete \'mēt\ *vb* **met·ed; met·ing** : to distribute in a fair or proper manner ⟨*mete* out rewards⟩

me·te·or \'mēt-ē-ər, -ē-,ò(ə)r\ *n* : one of the small bodies of matter in the solar system observable when it falls into the earth's atmosphere where the heat of friction may cause it to glow brightly for a short time; *also* : the streak of light produced by the passage of a meteor

me·te·or·ic \,mēt-ē-'òr-ik, -'är-\ *adj* **1** : of or relating to a meteor ⟨a *meteoric* shower⟩ **2** : resembling a meteor in speed or in sudden and temporary brilliance ⟨a *meteoric* rise to fame⟩ — **me·te·or·i·cal·ly** \-i-k(ə-)lē\ *adv*

me·te·or·ite \'mēt-ē-ə-,rīt\ *n* : a meteor that reaches the surface of the earth

me·te·or·oid \'mēt-ē-ə-,ròid\ *n* : a meteor revolving around the sun

me·te·o·rol·o·gy \,mēt-ē-ə-'räl-ə-jē\ *n* : a science that deals with the atmosphere, weather, and weather forcasting — **me·te·o·ro·log·ic** \,mēt-ē-ə-rə-'läj-ik\ *or* **me·te·o·ro·log·i·cal** \-'läj-i-kəl\ *adj* — **me·te·o·rol·o·gist** \-'räl-ə-jəst\ *n*

¹me·ter \'mēt-ər\ *n* **1** : a systematic rhythm in poetry that is usually repeated **2** : the repeated pattern of musical beats in a measure

²meter *n* : the basic unit of length of the metric system — see METRIC SYSTEM table

³meter *n* : an instrument for measuring and sometimes recording the amount of something ⟨a gas *meter*⟩

meter–kilogram–second *adj* : MKS

me·ter·stick \'mēt-ər-,stik\ *n* : a measuring stick one meter long that is marked off in centimeters and usually millimeters

meth·a·done \'meth-ə-,dōn\ *also* **meth·a·don** \-,dän\ *n* : a narcotic drug that is used to replace heroin in the treatment of heroin addiction

meth·ane \'meth-,ān\ *n* : a colorless odorless flammable gas that consists of carbon and hydrogen and is produced by decay of organic matter

meth·a·nol \'meth-ə-,nòl, -,nōl\ *n* : a light flammable poisonous liquid alcohol that consists of carbon, hydrogen, and oxygen and is used especially as antifreeze and to dissolve things

meth·aqua·lone \me-'thak-wə-,lōn\ *n* : a habit-forming drug that tends to calm nervousness and produce sleep and is not a barbiturate

me·thinks \mi-'thiŋ(k)s\ *impersonal verb, past* **methought** \-'thòt\ *archaic* : it seems to me

meth·od \'meth-əd\ *n* **1** : a way, plan, or procedure for doing something **2** : orderly arrangement

me·thod·i·cal \mə-'thäd-i-kəl\ *adj* **1** : marked by or performed or arranged by method or order ⟨a *methodical* search⟩ **2** : being in the habit of following a method : SYSTEMATIC ⟨a *methodical* teacher⟩ — **me·thod·i·cal·ly** \-i-k(ə-)lē\ *adv* — **me·thod·i·cal·ness** \-i-kəl-nəs\ *n*

Meth·od·ist \'meth-əd-əst\ *adj* : of or relating to any of several Protestant denominations following the teachings of John Wesley — **Meth·od·ism** \-ə-,diz-əm\ *n* — **Methodist** *n*

meth·yl \'meth-əl\ *n* : a chemical group consisting of carbon and hydrogen

methyl alcohol *n* : METHANOL

meth·y·lene blue \,meth-ə-,lēn-\ *n* : a dye used as a biological stain and to reverse the effects of cyanide poisoning

methyl orange *n* : an alkaline liquid mixture used as a dye that is usually orange but that turns red in the presence of acid

me·tic·u·lous \mə-'tik-yə-ləs\ *adj* : extremely or overly careful in small details — **me·tic·u·lous·ly** *adv* — **me·tic·u·lous·ness** *n*

me·tre \'mēt-ər\ *chiefly British variant of* METER

met·ric \'me-trik\ *adj* **1** : of or relating to measurement; *esp* : of, relating to, or based on the metric system **2** : METRICAL 1

met·ri·cal \'me-tri-kəl\ *adj* **1** : of, relating to, or arranged in meter **2** : METRIC 1 — **met·ri·cal·ly** \-k(ə-)lē\ *adv*

met·ri·cize \'me-trə-,sīz\ *vb* **-cized; -ciz·ing** : to change into or express in the metric system

metric system *n* : a system of weights and measures based on the meter and on the kilogram

metric ton *n* — see METRIC SYSTEM table

met·ro·nome \'me-trə-,nōm\ *n* : an instrument that ticks regularly to help a music student play in exact time

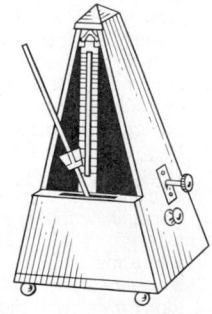

me·trop·o·lis \mə-'träp-(ə-)ləs\ *n* **1** : the chief or capital city of a country, state, or region **2** : a large or important city

¹met·ro·pol·i·tan \,me-trə-'päl-ət-ᵊn\ *n* **1** : the head of a church province **2** : one who lives in a metropolis or who has metropolitan manners or customs

²metropolitan *adj* **1** : of, relating to, or characteristic of a metropolis **2** : of or relating to a city and the densely populated surrounding areas

metronome

met·tle \'met-ᵊl\ *n* **1** : quality or temperament or disposition **2** : strength of spirit **3** : ability to keep going : STAYING POWER — **on one's mettle** : aroused to do one's best

met·tle·some \'met-ᵊl-səm\ *adj* : full of mettle : SPIRITED

¹mew \'myü\ *n* : ¹GULL; *esp* : a common European gull [Old English *mæw* "gull"]

²mew *n* : MEOW [Middle English *mewen* (verb) "meow"; a word imitating the sound of a meow] — **mew** *vb*

³mew *n* **1** : a cage for hawks **2** *pl, chiefly British* : stables usually with living quarters built around a court [Middle English *mewe* "a cage for hawks", from early French *mue* (same meaning), from *muer* "to shed feathers, molt", from Latin *mutare* "to change"]

mewl \'myü(ə)l\ *vb* : to cry weakly : WHIMPER

Mex·i·can \'mek-si-kən\ *n* **1** : a person born or living in Mexico **2** : a person of Mexican ancestry — **Mexican** *adj*

Mexican bean beetle *n* : a spotted ladybug that feeds on the leaves of beans

mez·za·nine \'mez-ᵊn-,ēn, ,mez-ᵊn-'ēn\ *n* **1** : a story between two main stories of a building often in the form of a balcony **2** : the lowest balcony in a theater or its first few

METRIC SYSTEM[1]

LENGTH

unit	abbreviation	number of meters	approximate U.S. equivalent
kilometer	km	1,000	0.62 mile
hectometer	hm	100	109.36 yards
dekameter	dam	10	32.81 feet
meter	m	1	39.37 inches
decimeter	dm	0.1	3.94 inches
centimeter	cm	0.01	0.39 inch
millimeter	mm	0.001	0.039 inch

AREA

unit	abbreviation	number of square meters	approximate U.S. equivalent
square kilometer	sq km *or* km^2	1,000,000	0.3861 square mile
hectare	ha	10,000	2.47 acres
are	a	100	119.60 square yards
square centimeter	sq cm *or* cm^2	0.0001	0.155 square inch

VOLUME

unit	abbreviation	number of cubic meters	approximate U.S. equivalent
cubic meter	m^3	1	1.307 cubic yards
cubic decimeter	dm^3	0.001	61.023 cubic inches
cubic centimeter	cu cm *or* cm^3 *also* cc	0.000001	0.061 cubic inch

CAPACITY

unit	abbreviation	number of liters	approximate U.S. equivalent		
			cubic	*dry*	*liquid*
kiloliter	kl	1,000	1.31 cubic yards		
hectoliter	hl	100	3.53 cubic feet	2.84 bushels	
dekaliter	dal	10	0.35 cubic foot	1.14 pecks	2.64 gallons
liter	l	1	61.02 cubic inches	0.908 quart	1.057 quarts
cubic decimeter	dm^3	1	61.02 cubic inches	0.908 quart	1.057 quarts
deciliter	dl	0.1	6.1 cubic inches	0.18 pint	0.21 pint
centiliter	cl	0.01	0.61 cubic inch		0.338 fluidounce
milliliter	ml	0.001	0.061 cubic inch		0.27 fluidram

MASS AND WEIGHT

unit	abbreviation	number of grams	approximate U.S. equivalent
metric ton	t	1,000,000	1.102 short tons
kilogram	kg	1,000	2.2046 pounds
hectogram	hg	100	3.527 ounces
dekagram	dag	10	0.353 ounce
gram	g	1	0.035 ounce
decigram	dg	0.1	1.543 grains
centigram	cg	0.01	0.154 grain
milligram	mg	0.001	0.015 grain

[1]For metric equivalents of U.S. units see Measures and Weights table

rows

mez·zo for·te \,met-sō-'fȯr-,tā, ,med-zō-, -'fȯrt-ē\ *adj or adv* : played or sung with medium loudness — used as a direction in music [Italian, from *mezzo* "half, medium" and *forte* "strong"]

mez·zo·so·pra·no \,met-sō-sə-'pran-ō, ,med-zō-, -'prän-\ *n* : a woman's voice between that of the soprano and contralto; *also* : a singer having such a voice

mi \mē\ *n* : the third note of the musical scale

mi·as·ma \mī-'az-mə, mē-\ *n, pl* **-mas** *or* **-ma·ta** \-mət-ə\ **1** : a vapor from a swamp formerly believed to cause disease **2** : a harmful influence or atmosphere — **mi·as·mal** \-məl\ *adj* — **mi·as·mat·ic** \,mī-əz-'mat-ik\ *adj*

mi·ca \'mī-kə\ *n* : any of various minerals that contain silicon and can be separated easily into thin often transparent sheets

Mi·cah \'mī-kə\ *n* — see BIBLE table

mice *pl of* MOUSE

Mich·ael·mas \'mik-əl-məs\ *n* : September 29 celebrated as the feast of St. Michael the Archangel

Mi·che·as \'mī-kē-əs, mī-'kē-\ *n* — see BIBLE table

micr- *or* **micro-** *combining form* **1 a** : small : minute ⟨*micro*film⟩ **b** : making a sound, image, or signal larger or stronger ⟨*micro*phone⟩ **2** : one millionth part of a (specified) unit ⟨*micro*second⟩ [derived from Greek *mikros* "small, short"]

[1]mi·cro \'mī-krō\ *adj* : MICROSCOPIC 3

[2]micro *n, pl* **micros** : MICROCOMPUTER

mi·crobe \'mī-,krōb\ *n* : MICROORGANISM, GERM — **mi·cro·bi·al** \mī-'krō-bē-əl\ *also* **mi·cro·bic** \-bik\ *adj*

mi·cro·bi·ol·o·gist \,mī-krō-bī-'äl-ə-jəst\ *n* : a specialist in microbiology

mi·cro·bi·ol·o·gy \,mī-krō-bī-'äl-ə-jē\ *n* : a branch of biology concerned especially with microscopic forms of life (as

\ə\ abut	\au̇\ out	\i\ tip	\ȯ\ saw	\u̇\ foot
\ər\ further	\ch\ chin	\ī\ life	\ȯi\ coin	\y\ yet
\a\ mat	\e\ pet	\j\ job	\th\ thin	\yü\ few
\ā\ take	\ē\ easy	\ŋ\ sing	\t̶h̶\ this	\yu̇\ cure
\ä\ cot, cart	\g\ go	\ō\ bone	\ü\ food	\zh\ vision

bacteria, protozoans, and viruses) — **mi·cro·bi·o·log·i·cal** \ˈmī-krō-ˌbī-ə-ˈläj-i-kəl\ also **mi·cro·bi·o·log·ic** \-ˈläj-ik\ adj — **mi·cro·bi·o·log·i·cal·ly** \-i-k(ə-)lē\ adv

mi·cro·cas·sette \ˌmī-krō-kə-ˈset\ n : a small cassette of magnetic tape that is used especially for dictation

mi·cro·chip \ˈmī-krō-ˌchip\ n : INTEGRATED CIRCUIT

mi·cro·coc·cus \ˌmī-krō-ˈkäk-əs\ n : a small bacterium that is shaped like a ball

mi·cro·com·put·er \ˈmī-krō-kəm-ˌpyüt-ər\ n : a very small computer that uses a microprocessor to handle information

mi·cro·cosm \ˈmī-krə-ˌkäz-əm\ n : an individual or community thought of as a miniature universe or a world in itself

mi·cro·fiche \ˈmī-krō-ˌfēsh, -ˌfish\ n : a sheet of microfilm containing rows of images usually of printed pages

mi·cro·film \ˈmī-krə-ˌfilm\ n : a film carrying a photographic record (as of printing or a drawing) on a reduced scale — **microfilm** vb

mi·cro·me·te·or·ite \ˌmī-krō-ˈmēt-ē-ə-ˌrīt\ n : a very small particle in space

mi·crom·e·ter \mī-ˈkräm-ət-ər\ n 1 : an instrument used with a telescope or microscope for measuring very small distances 2 : MICROMETER CALIPER — **mi·crom·e·try** \-ˈkräm-ə-trē\ n

micrometer caliper n : a caliper having a spindle moved by a finely threaded screw for making precise measurements

mi·cro·min·ia·ture \ˌmī-krō-ˈmin-ē-ə-ˌchů(ə)r, -ˈmin-i-ˌchů(ə)r, -ˈmin-yə-, -chər\ adj : reduced to or produced in a very small size and especially in a size smaller than one considered miniature

mi·cron \ˈmī-ˌkrän\ n : one millionth of a meter

micrometer caliper

mi·cro·or·gan·ism \ˌmī-krō-ˈȯr-gə-ˌniz-əm\ n : an organism (as a bacterium) of microscopic or less than microscopic size

mi·cro·phone \ˈmī-krə-ˌfōn\ n : an instrument in which sound energy is changed into electrical energy usually for the purpose of transmitting or recording sound (as speech or music)

mi·cro·pho·to·graph \ˌmī-krō-ˈfōt-ə-ˌgraf\ n : PHOTOMICROGRAPH

mi·cro·pro·ces·sor \ˌmī-krō-ˈpräs-ˌes-ər, -ˈprōs-\ n : a computer processor contained on an integrated-circuit chip

mi·cro·scope \ˈmī-krə-ˌskōp\ n 1 : an optical instrument consisting of a lens or a combination of lenses for making enlarged or magnified images of minute objects — called also *light microscope* 2 : an instrument using radiation other than light for making enlarged images of minute objects

mi·cro·scop·ic \ˌmī-krə-ˈskäp-ik\ or **mi·cro·scop·i·cal** \-ˈskäp-i-kəl\ adj 1 : of, relating to, or conducted with the microscope or microscopy ⟨a *microscopic* examination⟩ 2 : resembling a microscope : able to see very tiny objects ⟨some insects have *microscopic* vision⟩ 3 : able to be seen only through a microscope : very small ⟨a *microscopic* plant⟩ — **mi·cro·scop·i·cal·ly** \-i-k(ə-)lē\ adv

mi·cros·co·py \mī-ˈkräs-kə-pē\ n : the use of the microscope : investigation with the microscope — **mi·cros·co·pist** \-pəst\ n

mi·cro·sec·ond \ˌmī-krō-ˈsek-ənd, -ənt\ n : one millionth of a second

¹**mi·cro·wave** \ˈmī-krō-ˌwāv\ n 1 : a radio wave between one millimeter and one meter in wavelength 2 : MICROWAVE OVEN

²**microwave** vb : to cook or heat in a microwave oven — **mi·cro·wav·able** or **mi·cro·wave·able** \ˌmī-krə-ˈwā-və-bəl\ adj

microwave oven n : an oven in which food is cooked by the heat produced from microwave penetration of the food

¹**mid** \ˈmid\ adj 1 : being the part in the middle or midst ⟨in *mid* ocean⟩ ⟨*mid*-August⟩ 2 : occupying a middle position

²**mid** \(ˌ)mid\ prep : AMID

mid·af·ter·noon \ˈmid-ˌaf-tər-ˈnün\ n : the middle part of the afternoon — **midafternoon** adj

mid·air \ˈmid-ˈa(ə)r, -ˈe(ə)r\ n : a point or region in the air not very close to the ground ⟨planes collided in *midair*⟩

mid·brain \ˈmid-ˌbrān\ n : the middle division of the three primary divisions of the developing brain of a vertebrate or the parts of the adult brain that develop from it

mid·day \ˈmid-ˌdā, -ˈdā\ n : NOON — **midday** adj

¹**mid·dle** \ˈmid-ᵊl\ adj 1 : equally distant from the ends or sides 2 : being at neither extreme : INTERMEDIATE ⟨of *middle* size⟩ 3 cap : constituting an intermediate division or period ⟨*Middle* Paleozoic⟩

²**middle** n 1 : a middle part, point, or position : CENTER 2 : WAIST 1a

middle age n : the period of life from about 40 to about 60 — **mid·dle-aged** \ˌmid-ᵊl-ˈājd\ adj

Middle Ages n pl : the period of European history from about A.D. 500 to about 1500

middle C n : a note that is printed on a line midway between the treble staff and the bass staff in written music; *also* : the tone made in playing this note

middle class n : a social class that occupies a position between the upper class and the lower class and is composed mainly of business and professional people, government officials, farmers, and skilled workers — **middle-class** adj

middle ear n : a small cavity that is lined with membrane and separated from the outer ear by the eardrum and that carries sound waves from the eardrum to the part separating the middle and inner ears through a chain of tiny bones

Middle English n : the English language of the 12th to 15th centuries

middle finger n : the third finger of the hand if the thumb is counted as the first

mid·dle·man \ˈmid-ᵊl-ˌman\ n : GO-BETWEEN; *esp* : a dealer between the producer of goods and the consumer

mid·dle·most \ˈmid-ᵊl-ˌmōst\ adj : MIDMOST

mid·dle-of-the-road \ˌmid-ᵊl-əv-thə-ˈrōd\ adj : standing for or following a course of action midway between extremes; *esp* : being neither liberal nor conservative in politics — **mid·dle-of-the-road·er** \-ˈrōd-ər\ n

middle school n : a school usually including grades 5 to 8 or 6 to 8

mid·dle·weight \ˈmid-ᵊl-ˌwāt\ n : one of average weight; *esp* : a boxer in a weight division having the approximate range of 67 to 75 kilograms

¹**mid·dling** \ˈmid-liŋ, -lən\ adj : of medium size, degree, or quality — **middling** adv

²**middling** n 1 : any of various products of medium quality or size 2 pl : a product produced by milling grain; *esp* : a product of wheat milling that is used in animal feeds

mid·dy \ˈmid-ē\ n, pl **mid·dies** 1 : MIDSHIPMAN 2 : a loose blouse for women and children with a wide collar

midge \ˈmij\ n : a very small fly : GNAT

midg·et \ˈmij-ət\ n : an individual much smaller than usual or normal — **midget** adj

mid·land \ˈmid-lənd, -ˌland\ n : the central region of a country — **midland** adj

midddy 2

mid·line \ˈmid-ˌlīn\ n : a line through the middle of something; *esp* : a line through a body or one of its parts that lies in a plane dividing it into halves that are mirror images of each other

mid·most \'mid-ˌmōst\ *adj* **1** : being in the exact middle **2** : INNERMOST — **midmost** *adv or n*

mid·night \'mid-ˌnīt\ *n* : 12 o'clock at night — **midnight** *adj*

mid·point \'mid-ˌpȯint\ *n* : a point at or near the center or middle

mid·rib \'mid-ˌrib\ *n* : the central vein or ridge of a leaf or a leaflike part

mid·riff \'mid-ˌrif\ *n* : the middle region of the human body

mid·ship·man \'mid-ˌship-mən, (')mid-'ship-\ *n* : a student naval officer

mid·ships \'mid-ˌships\ *adv* : AMIDSHIPS

¹midst \'midst\ *n* **1** : the middle part or period ⟨in the *midst* of the forest⟩ **2** : a condition of being near or among the members of a group ⟨a traitor in our *midst*⟩ **3** : the condition of being surrounded ⟨in the *midst* of our troubles⟩

²midst \(ˌ)midst\ *prep* : AMID

mid·stream \'mid-'strēm\ *n* : the middle of a stream

mid·sum·mer \'mid-'səm-ər\ *n* **1** : the middle of summer **2** : the summer solstice

¹mid·way \'mid-ˌwā, -'wā\ *adv or adj* : in the middle of the way or distance : HALFWAY

²mid·way \'mid-ˌwā\ *n* : an avenue at a fair, carnival, or amusement park for food stands, games of chance or skill, and amusement rides

mid·week \'mid-ˌwēk\ *n* : the middle of the week — **mid-week** *adj*

mid·wife \'mid-ˌwīf\ *n* : a woman who helps other women in childbirth

mid·wife·ry \ˌmid-'wif-(ə-)rē, -'wīf-; 'mid-ˌwīf-\ *n* : the art or act of assisting at childbirth; *also* : OBSTETRICS

mid·win·ter \'mid-'wint-ər\ *n* **1** : the middle of winter **2** : the winter solstice

mid·year \'mid-ˌyi(ə)r\ *n* **1** : the middle of a calendar year or academic year **2** : a midyear examination — **midyear** *adj*

mien \'mēn\ *n* : look, appearance, or manner especially as showing mood or personality ⟨a kindly *mien*⟩

¹might \(')mīt\ *past of* MAY — used as a helping verb to express permission ⟨asked if I *might* leave⟩, possibility ⟨we *might* go, if asked⟩ ⟨thought you *might* try⟩, or a present condition that does not in fact exist ⟨if you were older, you *might* understand⟩ [Old English *meahte, mihte* (an auxiliary verb)]

²might \'mīt\ *n* : power to do something : FORCE ⟨with all my *might*⟩ [Old English *miht* "power, might"]

might·i·ly \'mīt-ᵊl-ē\ *adv* **1** : in a mighty manner : VIGOROUSLY ⟨fought *mightily*⟩ **2** : very much ⟨contributed *mightily* to the cause⟩

mightn't \'mīt-ᵊnt\ : might not

¹mighty \'mīt-ē\ *adj* **might·i·er; -est 1** : having might : POWERFUL, STRONG ⟨a *mighty* army⟩ **2** : done by might : showing great power ⟨*mighty* deeds⟩ **3** : very great ⟨a *mighty* famine⟩ — **might·i·ness** *n*

²mighty *adv* : ²VERY 1, EXTREMELY ⟨*mighty* proud of you⟩

mi·graine \'mī-ˌgrān\ *n* : a severe headache often restricted to one side of the head and accompanied by sickness in the stomach and throwing up

mi·grant \'mī-grənt\ *n* : a person, animal, or plant that migrates — **migrant** *adj*

mi·grate \'mī-ˌgrāt\ *vb* **mi·grat·ed; mi·grat·ing 1** : to move from one country, place, or locality to another **2** : to pass from one region or climate to another usually on a regular schedule for feeding or breeding **3** : to expand the habitat gradually from an old into a new region

mi·gra·tion \mī-'grā-shən\ *n* **1** : the act or an instance of migrating **2** : a group of individuals that are migrating

mi·gra·to·ry \'mī-grə-ˌtȯr-ē, -ˌtȯr-\ *adj* : having a way of life that includes making migrations ⟨*migratory* workers⟩

mi·ka·do \mə-'käd-ō\ *n, pl* **-dos** : an emperor of Japan

mike \'mīk\ *n* : MICROPHONE

milch \'milk, 'milch, 'milks\ *adj* : ³MILK

mild \'mī(ə)ld\ *adj* **1** : gentle in nature or behavior ⟨a *mild*

person⟩ **2** : not strong in action or effect ⟨a *mild* drug⟩ **3** : TEMPERATE **5** ⟨*mild* weather⟩ — **mild·ly** \'mī(ə)l-(d)lē\ *adv* — **mild·ness** \'mī(ə)l(d)-nəs\ *n*

¹mil·dew \'mil-ˌd(y)ü\ *n* : a usually whitish growth produced on decaying material or living plants by fungi; *also* : a fungus producing mildew — **mil·dewy** \-ˌd(y)ü-ē\ *adj*

²mildew *vb* : to affect with or become affected with mildew

mile \'mī(ə)l\ *n* **1** : a unit of measure equal to 5280 feet (about 1609 meters) — called also *statute mile;* see MEASURE table **2** : NAUTICAL MILE

mile·age \'mī-lij\ *n* **1** : an allowance for traveling expenses at a certain rate per mile **2** : distance or distance covered in miles **3** : the number of miles that something (as a tire) will travel before wearing out **4** : the average number of miles a vehicle will travel on a gallon of gasoline

mile·post \'mī(ə)l-ˌpōst\ *n* : a post indicating the distance in miles to a stated place

mil·er \'mī-lər\ *n* : one that competes in races a mile long

mile·stone \'mī(ə)l-ˌstōn\ *n* **1** : a milepost made of stone **2** : an important point in progress or development

mi·lieu \mēl-'yə(r), -'yü; 'mēl-ˌyü\ *n* : SURROUNDINGS, SETTING

mil·i·tan·cy \'mil-ə-tən-sē\ *n* : the quality or state of being militant

mil·i·tant \'mil-ə-tənt\ *adj* **1** : being at war **2** : aggressively active especially in a cause ⟨*militant* protesters⟩ — **militant** *n* — **mil·i·tant·ly** *adv* — **mil·i·tant·ness** *n*

milestone 1

mil·i·tari·ly \ˌmil-ə-'ter-ə-lē\ *adv* **1** : in a military manner **2** : from a military standpoint

mil·i·ta·rism \'mil-ə-tə-ˌriz-əm\ *n* **1** : control or rule by a military class **2** : extreme admiration and praise of military virtues and ideals **3** : a policy of aggressive military readiness — **mil·i·ta·rist** \-rəst\ *n* — **mil·i·ta·ris·tic** \ˌmil-ə-tə-'ris-tik\ *adj*

mil·i·ta·rize \'mil-ə-tə-ˌrīz\ *vb* **-rized; -riz·ing 1** : to equip with military forces and defenses **2** : to give a military character to — **mil·i·ta·ri·za·tion** \ˌmil-ə-t(ə-)rə-'zā-shən\ *n*

¹mil·i·tary \'mil-ə-ˌter-ē\ *adj* **1** : of, relating to, or characteristic of soldiers, arms, or war ⟨*military* discipline⟩ **2** : carried on or supported by armed force ⟨a *military* government⟩ **3** : of or relating to the army ⟨*military* and naval affairs⟩

²military *n, pl* **military 1** : ARMED FORCES **2** : military persons; *esp* : army officers

military police *n* : a branch of an army that exercises guard and police functions

mil·i·tate \'mil-ə-ˌtāt\ *vb* **-tat·ed; -tat·ing** : to have weight or effect : OPERATE ⟨factors *militating* against success⟩

mi·li·tia \mə-'lish-ə\ *n* : a body of citizens with some military training who are called to active duty only in an emergency

mi·li·tia·man \mə-'lish-ə-mən\ *n* : a member of a militia

¹milk \'milk\ *n* **1** : a whitish liquid secreted by the mammary glands of female mammals as food for their young **2** : a liquid (as a plant juice) like milk

²milk *vb* **1** : to draw milk from the breasts or udder of (as by pressing or sucking) ⟨*milk* a cow⟩ **2** : to draw or yield milk **3** : to draw something from as if by milking — **milk·er** *n*

\ə\ abut	\au̇\ out	\i\ tip	\ȯ\ saw	\u̇\ foot
\ər\ further	\ch\ chin	\ī\ life	\ȯi\ coin	\y\ yet
\a\ mat	\e\ pet	\j\ job	\th\ thin	\yü\ few
\ā\ take	\ē\ easy	\ŋ\ sing	\th\ this	\yu̇\ cure
\ä\ cot, cart	\g\ go	\ō\ bone	\ü\ food	\zh\ vision

³**milk** *adj* : giving milk; *esp* : bred for milk production ⟨a *milk* cow⟩

milk·maid \'milk-,mād\ *n* : DAIRYMAID

milk·man \-,man, -mən\ *n* : a person who sells or delivers milk

milk of magnesia : a milk-white liquid preparation of magnesium hydroxide in water used as a laxative and as a medicine

milk shake *n* : a thoroughly shaken or blended drink made of milk, a flavoring syrup, and often ice cream

milk snake *n* : a common harmless gray or tan snake with black-bordered blotches and an arrow-shaped spot on the head; *also* : KING SNAKE

milk sugar *n* : LACTOSE

milk tooth *n* : one of the first temporary teeth of a young mammal that in human beings number 20 — called also *baby tooth, deciduous tooth*

milk·weed \'mil-,kwēd\ *n* : any of a group of herbs and shrubs with milky juice and flowers usually in dense clusters

milky \'mil-kē\ *adj* **milk·i·er; -est** **1** : resembling milk especially in color **2** : consisting of or containing milk — **milk·i·ness** *n*

Milky Way *n* **1** : a broad band of light that stretches across the sky and is caused by the light of a very great number of faint stars **2** : MILKY WAY GALAXY

Milky Way galaxy *n* : the galaxy of which the solar system is a part and which contains the stars that make up the Milky Way

¹**mill** \'mil\ *n* **1** : a building with machinery for grinding grain into flour **2** : a machine used in treating (as by grinding, crushing, stamping, cutting, or finishing) raw material **3** : FACTORY [Old English *mylen* "mill, factory", from Latin *molina* (same meaning), derived from earlier *mola* "mill, millstone" — related to MOLAR; see *Word History* at MOLAR]

²**mill** *vb* **1** : to process in a mill (as by grinding into flour, meal, or powder or by shaping with a cutter) **2** : to give a raised rim or a grooved edge to ⟨*mill* a coin⟩ **3** : to move in a circle or in a moving mass ⟨people were *milling* about all over the yard⟩

³**mill** *n* : one tenth of a cent [from Latin *mille* "thousand"; so called because it is one one-thousandth of a dollar]

mill·dam \'mil-,dam\ *n* **1** : the dam of a millpond **2** : MILL-POND

mil·len·ni·um \mə-'len-ē-əm\ *n, pl* **-nia** \-ē-ə\ *or* **-ni·ums** **1 a** : a period of 1000 years **b** : a 1000th anniversary or its celebration **2 a** : the thousand years mentioned in Revelation 20 during which holiness is to be triumphant and Jesus is to reign on earth **b** : a period of great happiness — **mil·len·ni·al** \-ē-əl\ *adj*

mill·er \'mil-ər\ *n* **1** : a person who operates a mill; *esp* : a person who grinds grain into flour **2** : a moth whose wings have scales like powdery dust

mil·let \'mil-ət\ *n* **1** : a grass cultivated for its grain and used as human and bird food and in the U.S. sometimes grown for hay **2** : the seed of a millet

milli- *combining form* : thousandth ⟨*milli*meter⟩ [derived from Latin *mille* "thousand"]

mil·li·am·pere \,mil-ē-'am-,pi(ə)r\ *n* : one thousandth of an ampere

mil·liard \'mil-,yärd, 'mil-ē-,ärd\ *n, British* : a thousand millions — see NUMBER table

mil·li·bar \'mil-ə-,bär\ *n* : a unit used in measuring atmospheric pressure equal to a force of 100 newtons per square meter

mil·li·gram \'mil-ə-,gram\ *n* : a weight equal to ¹/₁₀₀₀ gram — see METRIC SYSTEM table

mil·li·li·ter \'mil-ə-,lēt-ər\ *n* : a measure of capacity equal to ¹/₁₀₀₀ liter — see METRIC SYSTEM table

mil·li·me·ter \'mil-ə-,mēt-ər\ *n* : a measure of length equal to ¹/₁₀₀₀ meter — see METRIC SYSTEM table

mil·li·ner \'mil-ə-nər\ *n* : a person who designs, makes, trims, or sells women's hats

mil·li·nery \'mil-ə-,ner-ē\ *n* **1** : women's hats **2** : the business or work of a milliner

mil·lion \'mil-yən\ *n, pl* **millions** *or* **million** **1** — see NUMBER table **2** : a very great number ⟨*millions* of mosquitoes⟩ — **million** *adj* — **mil·lionth** \-yən(t)th\ *adj or n*

mil·lion·aire \,mil-yə-'na(ə)r, 'mil-yə-,na(ə)r, -,ne(ə)r\ *n* : one whose wealth is estimated at a million or more (as of dollars)

mil·li·pede \'mil-ə-,pēd\ *n* : any of a class of numerous arthropods related to the centipedes and having a long segmented body with a hard covering, two pairs of legs on most segments, and no poison fangs — compare CENTIPEDE [from Latin *millepeda* "a small crawling animal", literally "a thousand-footed animal", from *mille* "thousand" and *ped-, pes* "foot"]

mill·pond \'mil-,pänd\ *n* : a pond that supplies water for running a mill

mill·race \-,rās\ *n* **1** : a canal in which water flows to and from a mill wheel **2** : the current that drives a mill wheel

mill·stone \-,stōn\ *n* **1** : either of two circular stones used for grinding a substance (as grain) **2** : a heavy burden

mill·stream \-,strēm\ *n* **1** : a stream whose flow is used to run a mill **2** : the stream in a mill-race

mill wheel *n* : a waterwheel that drives a mill

mill·wright \'mil-,rīt\ *n* : one who builds mills or sets up their machinery

milt \'milt\ *n* : the male sex glands of fishes when filled with sperm-containing liquid; *also* : the sperm-containing liquid

¹**mime** \'mīm, 'mēm\ *n* **1 a** : an actor in a mime **b** : a person who practices mime **2** : MIMIC 2 **3** : an ancient play or skit representing scenes from life usually in a ridiculous manner **4** : the art of showing a character or telling a story by body movements

²**mime** *vb* **mimed; mim·ing** **1** : to act in a mime **2** : to imitate closely : MIMIC **3** : to act out in the manner of a mime

mim·eo·graph \'mim-ē-ə-,graf\ *n* : a machine for making copies of typewritten or written matter using a stencil — **mimeograph** *vb*

mi·met·ic \mə-'met-ik, mī-\ *adj* : relating to, characterized by, or exhibiting mimicry ⟨*mimetic* coloring of a butterfly⟩

¹**mim·ic** \'mim-ik\ *n* **1** : ¹MIME 1 **2** : one that mimics

²**mimic** *adj* **1** : IMITATIVE 2 **2** : ²IMITATION, MOCK

³**mimic** *vb* **mim·icked** \'mim-ikt\; **mim·ick·ing** **1** : to imitate closely **2** : to make fun of by imitating **3** : to resemble by biological mimicry ⟨a butterfly that *mimics* a leaf⟩ **syn** see IMITATE

mim·ic·ry \'mim-i-krē\ *n, pl* **-ries** **1** : the action, art, or an instance of mimicking **2** : a resemblance of one living thing to another or to natural objects among which it lives that gives it an advantage (as concealment or protection)

mi·mo·sa \mə-'mō-sə, mī-, -zə\ *n* : any of a genus of trees, shrubs, and herbs of the legume family that are found in warm regions and have small white or pink flowers in ball-shaped heads

min·a·ret \,min-ə-'ret,

millstone 1

minaret

'min-ə-ˌret\ *n* : a tall slender tower of a mosque with a balcony from which the people are called to prayer

¹**mince** \'min(t)s\ *vb* **minced; minc·ing** **1** : to cut into very small pieces **2** : to act, walk, or speak in an unnaturally dainty way ⟨*mince* no words⟩ — **minc·ing·ly** \'min(t)-siŋ-lē\ *adv*

²**mince** *n* : small bits into which something is chopped; *esp* : MINCEMEAT

mince·meat \'min(t)-ˌsmēt\ *n* **1** : minced meat **2** : a finely chopped mixture (as of raisins, apples, or spices) with or without meat

¹**mind** \'mīnd\ *n* **1** : the state of remembering or of being remembered : MEMORY, RECOLLECTION ⟨call to *mind*⟩ **2** : the part of a person that feels, perceives, thinks, wills, and especially reasons **3** : INTENTION 1, DESIRE ⟨changed my *mind*⟩ **4** : the normal or healthy condition of the mental abilities ⟨lose one's *mind*⟩ **5** : OPINION 1, 2, VIEW ⟨speak one's *mind*⟩

²**mind** *vb* **1** *chiefly dialect* : REMEMBER 1 **2** : to pay attention to : HEED ⟨*mind* what you're doing⟩ ⟨*mind* your own business⟩ **3** : OBEY 1 ⟨*mind* one's parents⟩ **4** : to be bothered by ⟨never *mind* your mistake⟩ ⟨doesn't *mind* the cold⟩ **5** : to be careful about : watch out for ⟨*mind* the broken glass⟩ **6** : to take charge of ⟨*minding* the children⟩

mind·ed \'mīn-dəd\ *adj* **1** : having a specified kind of mind ⟨narrow-*minded*⟩ **2** : greatly interested in something specified ⟨bargain-*minded* customers⟩

mind·ful \'mīn(d)-fəl\ *adj* : keeping in mind : AWARE, HEEDFUL ⟨*mindful* of the needs of others⟩ — **mind·ful·ly** \-fə-lē\ *adv*

mind·less \'mīn-(d)ləs\ *adj* **1 a** : lacking the ability to think, feel, or respond ⟨a *mindless* killer⟩ **b** : showing no use of the intelligence ⟨*mindless* violence⟩ **2** : not mindful : HEEDLESS ⟨*mindless* of danger⟩ — **mind·less·ly** *adv* — **mind·less·ness** *n*

¹**mine** \(')mīn\ *adj, archaic* : MY — used before a word beginning with a vowel or *h* or after a noun [Middle English *min* "my"]

²**mine** \'mīn\ *pron* : my one : my ones

³**mine** \'mīn\ *n* **1** : a pit or tunnel from which minerals (as coal, gold, or diamonds) are taken **2** : a deposit of ore **3** : an underground passage dug beneath an enemy position **4** : an explosive device placed in the ground or water and set to explode when disturbed **5** : a rich source ⟨a *mine* of information⟩ [Middle English *mine* "a pit or tunnel for digging out coal, gold, or diamonds", from early French *mine* (same meaning)]

⁴**mine** \'mīn\ *vb* **mined; min·ing** **1** : to dig or form mines under a place **2** : to obtain from a mine ⟨*mine* coal⟩ **3** : to lay military mines in or under ⟨*mine* a harbor⟩ **4** : to work in a mine — **min·er** *n*

¹**min·er·al** \'min-(ə-)rəl\ *n* **1** : a solid chemical element or compound (as diamond or quartz) that occurs naturally in the form of crystals and results from processes not involving living or once-living matter **2** : a naturally occurring substance (as ore, petroleum, or water) obtained usually from the ground

²**mineral** *adj* **1** : of, relating to, or having the characteristics of a mineral : INORGANIC **2** : containing mineral salts or gases ⟨*mineral* water⟩

mineral kingdom *n* : the one of the three or sometimes four groups of natural objects that includes inorganic objects — compare ANIMAL KINGDOM, PLANT KINGDOM, PROTIST

min·er·al·o·gy \ˌmin-ə-'räl-ə-jē, -'ral-\ *n* : a science dealing with the characteristics and classification of minerals — **min·er·al·og·i·cal** \ˌmin-(ə)rə-'läj-i-kəl\ *adj* — **min·er·al·o·gist** \ˌmin-ə-'räl-ə-jəst, -'ral-\ *n*

mineral oil *n* : an oil (as petroleum) of mineral origin; *esp* : a purified petroleum oil having no color, odor, or taste that is used as a laxative

min·e·stro·ne \ˌmin-ə-'strō-nē, -'strōn\ *n* : a rich thick veg-

etable soup usually made with dried beans and macaroni

mine·sweep·er \'mīn-ˌswē-pər\ *n* : a warship designed for removing or destroying mines

min·gle \'miŋ-gəl\ *vb* **min·gled; min·gling** \-g(ə-)liŋ\ **1** : to bring or combine together or with something else ⟨*mingled* fact with fiction⟩ **2** : to come in contact : ASSOCIATE ⟨*mingles* with all sorts of people⟩ **syn** see MIX

mini \'min-ē\ *n* : something small of its kind: as **a** : MINISKIRT **b** : MINICOMPUTER

mini- *combining form* : very small or short : MINIATURE ⟨*mini*bike⟩ ⟨*mini*skirt⟩ [derived by shortening from *miniature*]

¹**min·ia·ture** \'min-ē-ə-ˌchů(ə)r, 'min-i-ˌchů(ə)r, 'min-yə-, -chər\ *n* **1** : something much smaller than the usual size; *esp* : a copy on a much reduced scale **2** : a very small portrait or painting (as on ivory) **3** : the art of painting miniatures [from Italian *miniatura* "a fancy big letter or small picture used to decorate a page of a book copied by hand", derived from Latin *miniatus,* past participle of *miniare* "to color with red pigment"; so called because the first fancy letters on books were done in red to stand out from the black ink of the rest of the page] — **min·ia·tur·ist** \-ˌchůr-əst, -chər-\ *n*

²**miniature** *adj* : very small : represented on a small scale ⟨collects *miniature* books⟩

min·ia·tur·ize \'min-ē-ə-chə-ˌrīz, 'min-i-chə-, 'min-yə-chə-\ *vb* **-ized; -iz·ing** : to design or construct in small size — **min·ia·tur·iza·tion** \ˌmin-ē-ə-ˌchůr-ə-'zā-shən, ˌmin-i-, ˌmin-yə-, -chər-\ *n*

mini·bike \'min-i-ˌbīk\ *n* : a small one-passenger motorcycle having a low frame and raised handlebars

mini·bus \'min-i-ˌbəs\ *n* : a small bus

mini·com·put·er \ˌmin-i-kəm-'pyüt-ər\ *n* : a small computer that is between a mainframe and a microcomputer in size and speed

mini·course \'min-ē-ˌkō(ə)rs, -ˌkȯ(ə)rs\ *n* : a short course of study usually lasting less than a semester

min·im \'min-əm\ *n* — see MEASURE table

min·i·mal \'min-ə-məl\ *adj* : relating to or being a minimum : LEAST — **min·i·mal·ly** \-mə-lē\ *adv*

min·i·mize \'min-ə-ˌmīz\ *vb* **-mized; -miz·ing** **1** : to make as small as possible ⟨*minimize* the chance of error⟩ **2 a** : to place a low estimate on ⟨*minimized* their losses⟩ **b** : to make (something) seem little or unimportant : BELITTLE, DISPARAGE ⟨*minimized* their opponent's victory⟩

min·i·mum \'min-ə-məm\ *n, pl* **-i·ma** \-ə-mə\ *or* **-i·mums** **1** : the least quantity possible or allowable **2** : the lowest degree or amount reached or recorded — **minimum** *adj*

minimum wage *n* : a wage fixed (as by law) as the least that may be paid to employed persons

min·ing \'mī-niŋ\ *n* : the process or business of working mines

min·ion \'min-yən\ *n* **1** : a person who obediently serves or works for a usually powerful person or organization **2** : ¹FAVORITE 1

mini·skirt \'min-i-ˌskərt\ *n* : a woman's very short skirt

¹**min·is·ter** \'min-ə-stər\ *n* **1 a** : one who performs religious ceremonies in church services **b** : a member of the clergy of a Protestant church **2** : a high official who heads a department of the government **3** : a government representative in a foreign country

²**minister** *vb* **-tered; -ter·ing** \-st(ə-)riŋ\ : to give aid : SERVE ⟨*minister* to the sick⟩ — **min·is·tra·tion** \ˌmin-ə-'strā-shən\ *n*

min·is·te·ri·al \ˌmin-ə-'stir-ē-əl\ *adj* : of or relating to a minister or ministry

\ə\ abut	\au̇\ **out**	\i\ **tip**	\ȯ\ **saw**	\u̇\ **foot**
\ər\ **further**	\ch\ **chin**	\ī\ **life**	\ȯi\ **coin**	\y\ **yet**
\a\ **mat**	\e\ **pet**	\j\ **job**	\th\ **thin**	\yü\ **few**
\ā\ **take**	\ē\ **easy**	\ŋ\ **sing**	\th\ **this**	\yu̇\ **cure**
\ä\ **cot, cart**	\g\ **go**	\ō\ **bone**	\ü\ **food**	\zh\ **vision**

min·is·try \'min-ə-strē\ *n, pl* **-tries** **1** : the action of ministering **2** : the office, duties, or work of a minister **3** **a** : the body of ministers governing a nation or state **b** : a government department headed by a minister **c** : the building in which a ministry is housed

mink \'miŋk\ *n, pl* **mink** *or* **minks** : any of several mammals that resemble the related weasels, have a slender body, partly webbed feet, and a somewhat bushy tail, and live near water; *also* : the soft normally dark brown fur of a mink

mink

min·now \'min-ō\ *n, pl* **minnows** *or* **min·now** : any of various small freshwater fishes (as a dace or shiner) related to the carps; *also* : any of various small fishes that resemble minnows

¹mi·nor \'mī-nər\ *adj* **1** : less in size, importance, or value ⟨a *minor* poet⟩ ⟨a *minor* injury⟩ **2** : not having reached the age to have full civil rights **3 a** : relating to or being a musical scale in which the third tone is lowered a half step **b** : based on a minor scale ⟨*minor* key⟩

²minor *n* : a person who has not reached the age to have full civil rights

mi·nor·i·ty \mə-'nòr-ət-ē, mī-, -'när-\ *n, pl* **-ties** **1** : the state or period of being a legal minor **2** : the smaller number; *esp* : a group having less than the number of votes necessary for control **3** : a part of a population that differs from other groups in some characteristics and is often given unfair treatment

minor league *n* : a professional sports league (as in baseball) that is not one of the major leagues

min·strel \'min(t)-strəl\ *n* **1** : a medieval musical entertainer; *esp* : a singer of verses accompanied by music **2 a** : MUSICIAN **b** : POET **3 a** : one of a group of performers giving a program of black American melodies and jokes usually with blackened faces **b** : a performance by a group of minstrels

min·strel·sy \'min(t)-strəl-sē\ *n, pl* **-sies** **1** : the singing and playing of a minstrel **2** : a body of minstrels **3** : a collection of songs or verse

¹mint \'mint\ *n* **1** : any of a family of herbs and shrubs (as basil or rosemary) with square stems and opposite leaves; *esp* : one (as peppermint or spearmint) that is fragrant and is the source of a flavoring oil **2** : a mint-flavored piece of candy [Old English *minte* "the herb mint", from Latin *mentha, menta* "mint"]

²mint *n* **1** : a place where coins, medals, and tokens are made **2** : a great amount [Middle English *mynt* "coin, money", from early French *mynet* (same meaning), from Latin *moneta* "coin, place where coins are made", from *Moneta* "a special name for the goddess Juno"; so called because the ancient Romans made coins at the temple of Juno Moneta — related to MONEY; see *Word History* at MONEY]

³mint *vb* : to make (as coins) out of metal — **mint·er** *n*

min·u·end \'min-yə-,wend\ *n* : a number from which another number is to be subtracted

min·u·et \,min-yə-'wet\ *n* **1** : a slow graceful dance **2** : music for or in the rhythm of a minuet

¹mi·nus \'mī-nəs\ *prep* **1** : with the subtraction of : LESS ⟨7 *minus* 4 is 3⟩ **2** : ¹WITHOUT 2a ⟨*minus* his hat⟩

²minus *n* **1** : a negative quantity **2** : ²LACK 2, DEFECT

³minus *adj* **1** : mathematically negative ⟨4 plus *minus* 3⟩ **2** : falling low in a specified range ⟨a grade of C *minus*⟩

minus sign *n* : a sign − used especially to indicate subtraction (as in 8 − 6 = 2) or a quantity less than zero (as in −10°)

¹min·ute \'min-ət\ *n* **1** : the 60th part of an hour of time or of a degree : sixty seconds **2** : the distance one can cover in a minute **3** : MOMENT 1 **4** *pl* : a brief record of what went on in a meeting [Middle English *minute* "1/60 part of an hour", from early French *minute* (same meaning), from Latin *minuta* (same meaning), from *minutus* "small" — related to MENU; see *Word History* at MENU]

²mi·nute \mī-'n(y)üt, mə-\ *adj* **1** : very small : TINY **2** : of small importance : PETTY **3** : marked by close attention to details — **mi·nute·ly** *adv* — **mi·nute·ness** *n*

min·ute·man \'min-ət-,man\ *n* : a member of an armed group pledged to take the field at a minute's notice during and immediately before the American Revolution

Mio·cene \'mī-ə-,sēn\ *adj* : of, relating to, or being an epoch of the Tertiary period of geological history or the corresponding system of rocks — see GEOLOGICAL TIME table — **Miocene** *n*

mir·a·cle \'mir-i-kəl\ *n* **1** : an extraordinary event taken as a sign of the supernatural power of God **2** : an extremely outstanding or unusual event, thing, or accomplishment [Middle English *miracle* "a miracle", from early French *miracle* (same meaning), derived from Latin *miraculum* "a wonder", from *mirari* "to wonder" — related to ADMIRE]

miracle drug *n* : a usually newly discovered drug capable of producing a marked and favorable change in a patient's condition — called also *wonder drug*

miracle play *n* **1** : MYSTERY PLAY **2** : a medieval play showing events from the life of a saint or martyr

mi·rac·u·lous \mə-'rak-yə-ləs\ *adj* **1** : of the nature of a miracle : SUPERNATURAL **2** : suggesting a miracle : MARVELOUS **3** : working or able to work miracles — **mi·rac·u·lous·ly** *adv*

mi·rage \mə-'räzh\ *n* : an illusion that gives the appearance of a pool of water or a mirror in which distant objects are seen inverted, that is sometimes seen at sea, in the desert, or over a hot pavement, and that is caused by the bending or reflection of light passing through layers of air having different temperatures

Mi·ran·da \mə-'ran-da\ *adj* : of, relating to, or being the legal rights of an arrested person to have an attorney and to remain silent so as to avoid self-incrimination ⟨the suspect was given a *Miranda* warning⟩

¹mire \'mī(ə)r\ *n* **1** : MARSH, BOG **2** : heavy often deep mud or slush — **miry** \'mī(ə)r-ē\ *adj*

²mire *vb* **mired; mir·ing** **1 a** : to sink or stick fast in mire **b** : ENTANGLE 2, INVOLVE **2** : to soil with mud or slush

¹mir·ror \'mir-ər\ *n* **1** : a smooth or polished surface (as of glass) that forms images by reflection **2** : something that gives a true likeness or description

²mirror *vb* : to reflect in or as if in a mirror

mirror image *n* : something that has its parts joined together in much the same way as those of something else except that each part and each part of a part of one thing is directly opposite to the corresponding part of the other thing and located on the opposite side of, the same distance away from, and facing in the same way toward or away from an axis or plane between the two things ⟨the two sides of an animal with bilateral symmetry are *mirror images* of each other⟩

mirth \'mərth\ *n* : gaiety accompanied by laughter

mirth·ful \'mərth-fəl\ *adj* : full of, expressing, or producing mirth — **mirth·ful·ly** \-fə-lē\ *adv* — **mirth·ful·ness** *n*

mis- *prefix* **1** : badly : wrongly ⟨*mis*judge⟩ **2** : bad : wrong ⟨*mis*deed⟩ **3** : opposite or lack of ⟨*mis*trust⟩ [partly from Old English *mis-* "badly, wrongly" and partly from early French *mes-* (same meaning)]

mis·ad·ven·ture \,mis-əd-'ven-chər\ *n* : MISFORTUNE 2

mis·an·thrope \'mis-ᵊn-,thrōp\ *n* : a person who dislikes and distrusts mankind

mis·an·thro·py \mis-'an(t)-thrə-pē\ *n* : a dislike or hatred of all human beings — **mis·an·throp·ic** \,mis-ᵊn-'thräp-ik\ *adj* — **mis·an·throp·i·cal·ly** \-'thräp-i-k(ə-)lē\ *adv*

mis·ap·ply \,mis-ə-'plī\ *vb* : to apply wrongly — **mis·ap·pli·ca·tion** \,mis-,ap-lə-'kā-shən\ *n*

mis·ap·pre·hend \(,)mis-,ap-ri-'hend\ *vb* : MISUNDERSTAND — **mis·ap·pre·hen·sion** \-'hen-chən\ *n*

mis·ap·pro·pri·ate \,mis-ə-'prō-prē-,āt\ *vb* : to appropriate wrongly; *esp* : to take dishonestly for one's own use — **mis·ap·pro·pri·a·tion** \-,prō-prē-'ā-shən\ *n*

mis·be·got·ten \,mis-bi-'gät-ᵊn\ *adj* **1** : ILLEGITIMATE 1 **2** : wrongfully or improperly created

mis·be·have \,mis-bi-'hāv\ *vb* : to behave badly — **mis·be·hav·ior** \-'hā-vyər\ *n*

mis·be·lief \,mis-bə-'lēf\ *n* : a mistaken or false belief — **mis·be·liev·er** \-'lē-vər\ *n*

mis·cal·cu·late \(')mis-'kal-kyə-,lāt\ *vb* : to calculate wrongly — **mis·cal·cu·la·tion** \,mis-,kal-kyə-'lā-shən\ *n*

mis·call \(')mis-'kȯl\ *vb* : to call by a wrong name

mis·car·riage \mis-'kar-ij\ *n* **1** : bad management; *esp* : a failure in the administration of justice **2** : the accidental separation of an unborn child from the body of its mother before it is capable of living independently : loss of a child through premature birth — compare ABORTION 1

mis·car·ry \(')mis-'kar-ē\ *vb* **1** : to have a miscarriage : give birth prematurely **2** : to go wrong ⟨the plan *miscarried*⟩

mis·cast \(')mis-'kast\ *vb* : to cast in an unsuitable role

mis·ce·ge·na·tion \(,)mis-,ej-ə-'nā-shən, ,mis-i-jə-'nā-\ *n* : marriage or interbreeding between persons of different races

mis·cel·la·neous \,mis-ə-'lā-ne-əs, -nyəs\ *adj* : consisting of many things of different sorts — **mis·cel·la·neous·ly** *adv* — **mis·cel·la·neous·ness** *n*

mis·cel·la·ny \'mis-ə-,lā-nē\ *n, pl* **-nies** **1** : a mixture of various things **2** : a collection of writings

mis·chance \(')mis-'chan(t)s\ *n* **1** : bad luck that is not of a serious nature **2** : a piece of bad luck : MISHAP **syn** see MISFORTUNE

mis·chief \'mis-chəf, 'mish-\ *n* **1** : INJURY 2, HARM **2** : a person or animal who causes mischief **3** : mischievous conduct or quality ⟨a child gets into *mischief*⟩ ⟨had *mischief* in their eyes⟩

mis·chie·vous \'mis-chə-vəs, 'mish-\ *adj* **1** : harming or intended to do harm ⟨*mischievous* gossip⟩ **2** : causing or tending to cause minor injury or annoyance ⟨a *mischievous* puppy⟩ **3** : showing a spirit of mischief ⟨*mischievous* behavior⟩ — **mis·chie·vous·ly** *adv* — **mis·chie·vous·ness** *n*

mis·con·ceive \,mis-kən-'sēv\ *vb* : to form a wrong or mistaken idea of

mis·con·cep·tion \,mis-kən-'sep-shən\ *n* : a wrong or mistaken idea

mis·con·duct \(')mis-'kän-(,)dəkt\ *n* **1** : bad management **2** : improper or unlawful behavior — **mis·con·duct** \,mis-kən-'dəkt\ *vb*

mis·con·struc·tion \,mis-kən-'strək-shən\ *n* : the act, process, or an instance of misconstruing

mis·con·strue \,mis-kən-'strü\ *vb* : to construe wrongly : MISINTERPRET

mis·count \(')mis-'kaunt\ *vb* : to count incorrectly — **mis·count** *n*

mis·cre·ant \'mis-krē-ənt\ *n* : VILLAIN 2, SCOUNDREL — **miscreant** *adj*

¹mis·cue \(')mis-'kyü\ *n* **1** : a faulty stroke in billiards in which the cue slips **2** : ²MISTAKE 2, SLIP

²miscue *vb* **1** : to make a miscue **2 a** : to miss a stage cue **b** : to answer a wrong cue

mis·deal \(')mis-'dē(ə)l\ *vb* **-dealt** \-'delt\; **-deal·ing** \-'dē-liŋ\ : to deal cards incorrectly — **misdeal** *n*

mis·deed \(')mis-'dēd\ *n* : an evil or illegal deed

mis·de·mean·or \,mis-di-'mē-nər\ *n* **1** : a crime less serious than a felony **2** : MISDEED

mis·di·rect \,mis-də-'rekt, -(,)dī-\ *vb* : to direct incorrectly — **mis·di·rec·tion** \-'rek-shən\ *n*

mis·do·ing \(')mis-'dü-iŋ\ *n* : MISDEED — **mis·do·er** \-'dü-ər\ *n*

mi·ser \'mī-zər\ *n* : a mean grasping person; *esp* : one who lives poorly in order to store away money

mis·er·a·ble \'miz-ər-bəl, 'miz-(ə)rə-bəl\ *adj* **1 a** : shabby in condition or quality ⟨a *miserable* place to live⟩ **b** : causing great discomfort or unhappiness ⟨a *miserable* cold⟩ **2** : extremely poor or unhappy : WRETCHED **3** : PITIFUL 1, LAMENTABLE — **mis·er·a·ble·ness** *n* — **mis·er·a·bly** \-blē\ *adv*

mi·ser·ly \'mī-zər-lē\ *adj* : of, relating to, or characteristic of a miser — **mi·ser·li·ness** *n*

mis·ery \'miz-(ə)rē\ *n, pl* **-er·ies** **1** : a state of great suffering and want due to poverty or misfortune **2** : a source of misery **3** : a state of unhappiness

mis·file \(')mis-'fī(ə)l\ *vb* : to file in an incorrect place

mis·fire \(')mis-'fī(ə)r\ *vb* **1** : to have the explosive or driving charge fail to ignite at the proper time ⟨the engine *misfired*⟩ **2** : to fail to fire ⟨the gun *misfired*⟩ **3** : to miss an intended effect ⟨the plan *misfired*⟩ — **misfire** *n*

mis·fit \'mis-,fit, (')mis-'fit\ *n* **1** : something that fits badly **2** : a person poorly adjusted to his or her environment

mis·for·tune \(')mis-'fȯr-chən\ *n* **1** : bad luck especially for a long period of time **2** : an unfortunate condition or event : DISASTER

> **syn** MISFORTUNE, MISCHANCE, MISHAP mean an unlucky turn of events. MISFORTUNE stresses the state of unhappiness that follows an unlucky event ⟨it was her *misfortune* to change jobs unwisely⟩ MISCHANCE usually suggests a situation involving no more than a minor trouble or bother ⟨by *mischance* he took the wrong road⟩ MISHAP suggests an example of bad luck of no real importance ⟨in one of the show's *mishaps* the winner's name was mispronounced⟩

mis·give \(')mis-'giv\ *vb* **-gave** \-'gāv\; **-giv·en** \-'giv-ən\; **-giv·ing** \(')mis-'giv-iŋ\ : to suggest doubt or fear to

mis·giv·ing \(')mis-'giv-iŋ\ *n* : a feeling of doubt or suspicion especially concerning a future event

mis·gov·ern \(')mis-'gəv-ərn\ *vb* : to govern badly — **mis·gov·ern·ment** \-'gəv-ər(n)-mənt, -ə-mənt; 'gəb-ᵊm-ənt, 'gəv-\ *n*

mis·guide \(')mis-'gīd\ *vb* : to lead astray : MISLEAD — **mis·guid·ance** \-'gīd-ᵊn(t)s\ *n*

mis·han·dle \(')mis-'han-dᵊl\ *vb* **1** : to treat roughly : MALTREAT **2** : to manage wrongly

mis·hap \'mis-,hap, mis-'hap\ *n* **1** *archaic* : bad luck **2** : an unfortunate accident [Middle English *mishap* "bad luck", from *mis-* "bad, unfavorable" and *hap* "chance, chance occurrence" — related to HAPPEN, HAPPY, PERHAPS] **syn** see MISFORTUNE

mish·mash \'mish-,mash, -,mäsh\ *n* : HODGEPODGE, JUMBLE

mis·in·form \,mis-ən-'fȯ(ə)rm\ *vb* : to give false or misleading information to — **mis·in·for·ma·tion** \,mis-,in-fər-'mā-shən\ *n*

mis·in·ter·pret \,mis-ᵊn-'tər-prət, -pət\ *vb* : to understand or explain wrongly — **mis·in·ter·pre·ta·tion** \-,tər-prə-'tā-shən, -pə-'tā-\ *n*

mis·judge \(')mis-'jəj\ *vb* : to judge wrongly or unfairly — **mis·judg·ment** \-'jəj-mənt\ *n*

mis·lay \(')mis-'lā\ *vb* **-laid** \-'lād\; **-lay·ing** : to put in a place later forgotten : LOSE

mis·lead \(')mis-'lēd\ *vb* **-led** \-'led\; **-lead·ing** : to lead in a wrong direction or into a mistaken action or belief — **misleading** *adj*

mis·man·age \(')mis-'man-ij\ *vb* : to manage badly or im-

\ə\ abut	\au\ **out**	\i\ tip	\ȯ\ **saw**	\u̇\ **foot**	
\ər\ further	\ch\ **chin**	\ī\ life	\ȯi\ **coin**	\y\ **yet**	
\a\ mat	\e\ **pet**	\j\ **job**	\th\ **thin**	\yü\ **few**	
\ā\ take	\ē\ **easy**	\ŋ\ **sing**	\t̲h̲\ **this**	\yu̇\ **cure**	
\ä\ cot, cart	\g\ **go**	\ō\ **bone**	\ü\ **food**	\zh\ **vision**	

properly — **mis·man·age·ment** \-mənt\ *n*

mis·match \(')mis-'mach\ *vb* : to match unsuitably or badly — **mismatch** *n*

mis·mate \(')mis-'māt\ *vb* : to mate unsuitably

mis·name \(')mis-'nām\ *vb* : to name incorrectly : MISCALL

mis·no·mer \(')mis-'nō-mər\ *n* : a wrong or unsuitable name

mi·sog·a·mist \mə-'säg-ə-məst\ *n* : one who hates marriage — **mi·sog·a·my** \-'säg-ə-mē\ *n*

mi·sog·y·nist \mə-'säj-ə-nəst\ *n* : one who hates or distrusts women — **mi·sog·y·ny** \-ə-nē\ *n*

mis·place \(')mis-'plās\ *vb* **1** : to put in a wrong place **2** : MISLAY — **mis·place·ment** *n*

mis·play \(')mis-'plā\ *n* : a wrong or unskillful play — **mis·play** \(')mis-'plā, 'mis-,plā\ *vb*

mis·print \(')mis-'print\ *vb* : to print incorrectly — **mis·print** \'mis-,print, (')mis-'print\ *n*

mis·pro·nounce \,mis-prə-'naủn(t)s\ *vb* : to pronounce in a way considered incorrect

mis·pro·nun·ci·a·tion \,mis-prə-,nən(t)-sē-'ā-shən\ *n* : an act or an instance of mispronouncing

mis·quote \(')mis-'kwōt\ *vb* : to quote incorrectly — **mis·quo·ta·tion** \,mis-kwō-'tā-shən\ *n*

mis·read \(')mis-'rēd\ *vb* **-read** \-'red\; **-read·ing** \-'rēd-iŋ\ **1** : to read incorrectly **2** : to misinterpret in or as if in reading

mis·rep·re·sent \,(,)mis-,rep-ri-'zent\ *vb* : to give a false or misleading idea of — **mis·rep·re·sen·ta·tion** \,(,)mis-,rep-ri-,zen-'tā-shən\ *n*

¹mis·rule \(')mis-'rül\ *vb* : to rule or govern badly

²misrule *n* **1** : the action of misruling : the state of being misruled **2** : ²DISORDER 1, ANARCHY

¹miss \'mis\ *vb* **1** : to fail to hit, catch, reach, or get ⟨*miss* a target⟩ ⟨*miss* the ball⟩ **2** : ¹ESCAPE 2, AVOID ⟨just *missed* being hurt⟩ **3 a** : to leave out : OMIT ⟨*missed* their lunch⟩ **b** : to fail to attend ⟨*missed* three days of school⟩ **4** : to discover or feel the absence of ⟨*missed* our old friends⟩ **5** : to fail to understand, sense, or experience ⟨*missed* the main point of the story⟩ **6** : MISFIRE 1 ⟨the engine *missed*⟩ [Old English *missan* "to fail to reach or get"]

²miss *n* **1** : a failure to reach a desired goal or result **2** : a failure to fire

³miss *sense 1 is* (,)mis, məs; *sense 2 is* 'mis\ *n* **1 a** — used as a title before the name of an unmarried woman or girl **b** — used to form a title for a girl who represents the thing indicated ⟨*Miss* America⟩ **2** : a young woman or girl ⟨*misses'* dresses⟩ — used as a term of address [a shortened form of *mistress*]

mis·sal \'mis-əl\ *n* : a book containing the prayers to be said or sung in the Mass during the year

mis·send \(')mis-'send\ *vb* **-sent** \-'sent\; **-send·ing** : to send to the wrong place

mis·shap·en \(')mis-'shā-pən, (')mish-\ *adj* : badly shaped : having an ugly shape

mis·sile \'mis-əl\ *n* : an object (as a stone, arrow, artillery shell, bullet, or rocket) that is thrown, shot, or launched usually so as to strike something at a distance [from Latin *missile* "a weapon that is thrown or shot rather than held in the hand", derived from *missus*, past participle of *mittere* "to send, throw" — related to EMIT]

miss·ing \'mis-iŋ\ *adj* : ¹ABSENT 1, LOST ⟨*missing* persons⟩ ⟨*missing* in action⟩

missing link *n* : a form of animal between human beings and the apes in characteristics that is thought to have existed but has not been discovered in the fossil record

mis·sion \'mish-ən\ *n* **1 a** : a group of missionaries **b** : the work of a missionary **c** : a place where a mission or missionary works **2 a** : a group sent to a foreign country to carry on discussions or to provide training or assistance ⟨trade *mission*⟩ ⟨military *mission*⟩ **b** : a group of diplomats who stay in a foreign country **3 a** : a task or job that

is assigned ⟨our *mission* was to recover the stolen plans⟩ **b** : a definite military, naval, or aerospace task ⟨a space *mission*⟩ [from modern Latin *mission-, missio* "a group sent out by a religious organization", derived from earlier Latin *missus*, past participle of *mittere* "to send, throw" — related to MESSAGE]

¹mis·sion·ary \'mish-ə-,ner-ē\ *adj* **1** : relating to, engaged in, or devoted to missions **2** : characteristic of a missionary : ZEALOUS

²missionary *n, pl* **-ar·ies** : one sent to spread a religious faith among unbelievers or to engage in charitable work with religious support

Mis·sis·sip·pi·an \,mis-(ə-)'sip-ē-ən\ *adj* **1** : of or relating to Mississippi, its people, or the Mississippi river **2** : of, relating to, or being the earlier part of the Carboniferous period of the Paleozoic era of geological history in North America or the corresponding system of rocks — see GEOLOGIC TIME table — **Mississippian** *n*

mis·sive \'mis-iv\ *n* : ¹LETTER 2, MESSAGE

mis·spell \(')mis-'spel\ *vb* : to spell incorrectly

mis·spell·ing \(')mis-'spel-iŋ\ *n* : an incorrect spelling

mis·spend \(')mis-'spend\ *vb* **-spent** \-'spent\; **-spend·ing** : ²WASTE 3, SQUANDER ⟨a *misspent* youth⟩

mis·state \(')mis-'stāt\ *vb* : to state incorrectly — **mis·state·ment** \-mənt\ *n*

mis·step \(')mis-'step\ *n* **1** : a wrong step **2** : ²MISTAKE 2, BLUNDER

¹mist \'mist\ *n* **1** : water in the form of particles floating in the air or falling as fine rain **2** : something that keeps one from seeing or understanding clearly

²mist *vb* **1** : to be or become misty **2** : to become dim or blurred **3** : to cover with a mist

¹mis·take \mə-'stāk\ *vb* **mis·took** \-'stủk\; **mis·tak·en** \-'stā-kən\; **mis·tak·ing** **1** : to understand wrongly : MISINTERPRET ⟨*mistook* my meaning⟩ **2** : to estimate incorrectly ⟨*mistook* the strength of the enemy⟩ **3** : to identify wrongly ⟨*mistook* me for her⟩ — **mis·tak·en·ly** *adv*

²mistake *n* **1** : a wrong judgment : MISUNDERSTANDING **2** : a wrong action or statement **syn** see ERROR

mis·ter \'mis-tər, *for sense 1* ,mis-tər\ *n* **1** — used sometimes in writing instead of *Mr.* **2** : SIR 2 — used as a conventional term of address to a man [an altered form of *master*]

mis·time \(')mis-'tīm\ *vb* : to time wrongly

mis·tle·toe \'mis-əl-,tō\ *n* : a European green plant with yellowish flowers and waxy white berries that grows on the branches and trunks of trees; *also* : any of various plants of the same family that resemble the mistletoe

mis·treat \(')mis-'trēt\ *vb* : to treat badly : ABUSE — **mis·treat·ment** \-mənt\ *n*

mis·tress \'mis-trəs\ *n* **1** : a woman who has control or authority like that of

mistletoe

a master ⟨the *mistress* of the household⟩ **2** : something considered as a female that rules or directs **3** : a woman to whom a man is not married and with whom he has a sexual relationship **4** — used formerly as a title before the name of a woman [Middle English *maistresse* "mistress", from early French *maistresse* (same meaning), a feminine form of *maistre* "master" — related to MASTER]

mis·tri·al \'mis-,trī(-ə)l\ *n* : a trial that is cancelled because of an error in the proceedings

¹mis·trust \(')mis-'trəst\ *n* : ²DISTRUST — **mis·trust·ful** \-fəl\ *adj* — **mis·trust·ful·ly** \-fə-lē\ *adv* — **mis·trust·ful·ness** *n*

²mistrust *vb* : ¹DISTRUST

misty \'mis-tē\ *adj* **mist·i·er; -est** **1** : full of mist ⟨a *misty* valley⟩ **2** : VAGUE 3, INDISTINCT ⟨a *misty* memory⟩ — **mist·i·ly** \-tə-lē\ *adv* — **mist·i·ness** \-tē-nəs\ *n*

mis·un·der·stand \(,)mis-,ən-dər-'stand\ *vb* **-stood** \-'stůd\; **-stand·ing** **1** : to fail to understand **2** : to interpret incorrectly

mis·un·der·stand·ing \(,)mis-,ən-dər-'stan-diŋ\ *n* **1** : a failure to understand **2** : DISAGREEMENT 2b, QUARREL

¹mis·use \mish-'üz, (')mish-'yüz, (')mis-'yüz\ *vb* **1** : to use incorrectly : MISAPPLY **2** : ¹ABUSE 2, MISTREAT — **mis·us·age** \-'(y)ü-sij, -zij\ *n*

²mis·use \mish-'üs, (')mish-'yüs, (')mis-'yüs\ *n* : incorrect or improper use

mite \'mīt\ *n* **1** : any of various tiny arthropod animals that are related to the ticks and spiders, often live on plants, animals, and stored foods, and include important carriers of disease **2** : a very small coin or sum of money **3 a** : a very little amount : BIT **b** : a very small object or creature

¹mi·ter *or* **mi·tre** \'mīt-ər\ *n* **1** : a high pointed headdress worn by a bishop or abbot in church ceremonies **2** : MITER JOINT

²miter *or* **mitre** *vb* **mi·tered** *or* **mi·tred; mi·ter·ing** *or* **mi·tring** \'mīt-ə-riŋ\ : to match or fit together in a miter joint

miter joint *n* : the joint or corner made by cutting the edges of two boards at an angle and fitting them together

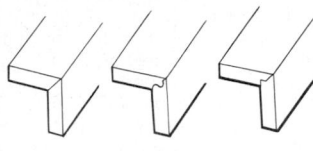

miter joint

mit·i·gate \'mit-ə-,gāt\ *vb* **-gat·ed; -gat·ing** : to make less severe ⟨*mitigate* a punishment⟩ — **mit·i·ga·tion** \,mit-ə-'gā-shən\ *n*

mi·to·chon·dri·on \,mīt-ə-'kän-drē-ən\ *n, pl* **-dria** \-drē-ə\ : one of the round or long bodies found in cells that are rich in fats, proteins, and enzymes and are important centers of metabolic processes (as the breakdown and manufacture of carbohydrates, fats, and amino acids)

mi·to·sis \mī-'tō-səs\ *n, pl* **-to·ses** \-'tō-,sēz\ **1** : a process that takes place in the nucleus of a dividing cell and that results in the formation of two new nuclei with the same number of chromosomes as the parent nucleus **2** : a cell division in which mitosis occurs — **mi·tot·ic** \-'tät-ik\ *adj*

mitt \'mit\ *n* **1** : MITTEN **2** : a baseball catcher's or first baseman's glove

mit·ten \'mit-ᵊn\ *n* : a covering for the hand and wrist having a separate section for the thumb only — **mit·tened** \'mit-ᵊnd\ *adj*

¹mix \'miks\ *vb* **1** : to make into one mass by stirring together : BLEND **2** : to make by combining different things **3** : to become one mass through blending ⟨oil will not *mix* with water⟩ **4** : to associate with others on friendly terms ⟨*mixes* well in any company⟩ **5** : CONFUSE 3 ⟨*mix* up facts⟩

    syn MIX, MINGLE, BLEND, COALESCE mean to combine into a whole that is more or less the same throughout. MIX suggests a fairly complete combining in which the elements may or may not lose their individual identities ⟨*mix* several vegetables for a salad⟩ ⟨*mix* water and frozen orange juice⟩ MINGLE suggests that the different elements can still be identified to some degree ⟨the author *mingled* comic and tragic events in her story⟩ BLEND suggests a complete uniting of things so that the original parts cannot be separated or recognized ⟨*blend* milk and canned tomato soup⟩ COALESCE stresses the action or process of similar things growing into a natural union ⟨after several years the two smaller groups *coalesced*⟩

into one large organization⟩

²mix *n* : MIXTURE; *esp* : a prepared mixture of ingredients for use in preparing foods ⟨a muffin *mix*⟩

mixed \'mikst\ *adj* **1 a** : made of mingled or blended elements ⟨*mixed* nuts⟩ **b** : combining features of more than one kind ⟨a *mixed* economy⟩ **2 a** : involving persons differing in race, national origin, or religion ⟨a *mixed* marriage⟩ **b** : made up of or involving individuals of both sexes ⟨*mixed* company⟩ ⟨a *mixed* chorus⟩ **3** : including or accompanied by different or opposing elements ⟨a *mixed* blessing⟩ ⟨a *mixed* reaction⟩ **4** : resulting from the crossing or breeding of individuals of different races or breeds ⟨a stallion of *mixed* blood⟩

mixed nerve *n* : a nerve that carries nerve impulses toward the central nervous system from a sense organ and also away from the central nervous system to cause movement in muscles

mixed number *n* : a number (as 5⅔) composed of an integer and a fraction — called also *mixed numeral*

mix·er \'mik-sər\ *n* **1** : one that mixes; *esp* : a device or machine for mixing **2** : a party to give members of a group an opportunity to get acquainted

mix·ture \'miks-chər\ *n* **1** : the act or process or an instance of mixing **2 a** : something mixed or being mixed ⟨add eggs to the *mixture*⟩ **b** : a preparation consisting of two or more ingredients or kinds **3** : two or more substances that are mixed together but not chemically combined and that may vary in proportion

mix–up \'mik-,səp\ *n* : an instance of confusion

¹miz·zen *or* **miz·en** \'miz-ᵊn\ *n* **1** : a fore-and-aft sail set on the mizzenmast **2** : MIZZENMAST

²mizzen *or* **mizen** *adj* : of or relating to the mizzenmast

miz·zen·mast \'miz-ᵊn-,mast, -məst\ *n* : the mast just behind the mainmast in a ship

mks \,em-,kā-,es\ *adj* : of, relating to, or being a system of units based on the meter as the unit of length, the kilogram as the unit of mass, and the second as the unit of time

mne·mon·ic \ni-'män-ik\ *adj* : assisting or intended to assist memory

¹moan \'mōn\ *n* **1** : a long low sound indicating pain or grief **2** : a sound like a moan

²moan *vb* **1** : to utter a moan **2** : COMPLAIN 1 **3** : to utter with moans

moat \'mōt\ *n* : a deep wide trench around the walls of a castle or fortress that is usually filled with water

¹mob \'mäb\ *n* **1** : the common people : MASSES **2** : a large rowdy crowd : RABBLE **3** : a criminal gang **syn** see MULTITUDE

²mob *vb* **mobbed; mob·bing** : to crowd about and attack or annoy

¹mo·bile \'mō-bəl, -,bēl, -,bīl\ *adj* **1** : ¹MOVABLE 1 **2** : changing quickly in expression ⟨a *mobile* face⟩ **3** : easily moved ⟨*mobile* troops⟩ **4** : MIGRATORY ⟨*mobile* workers⟩ **5** : characterized by movement from one social class to another ⟨a *mobile* society⟩ — **mo·bil·i·ty** \mō-'bil-ət-ē\ *n*

moat

²mo·bile \'mō-,bēl\ *n* : an artistic structure that is moved easily or that has parts easily moved (as by a current of air)

mobile home *n* : a trailer that is used as a permanent dwelling

mo·bi·lize \'mō-bə-,līz\ *vb* **-lized; -liz·ing** : to assemble and make ready for action : MARSHAL — **mo·bi·li·za·tion** \,mō-bə-lə-'zā-shən\ *n*

Mö·bi·us strip \,mə(r)-bē-əs-, ,mō-\ *n* : a continuous surface constructed by holding one end of a rectangle fixed, rotating the opposite end through 180 degrees, and joining it to the first end

mob·ster \'mäb-stər\ *n* : a member of a criminal gang

moc·ca·sin \'mäk-ə-sən\ *n*
1 a : a soft leather shoe without a heel and with the sole and sides made of one piece **b** : a similar shoe with a separate sole **2** : WATER MOCCASIN

moccasin flower *n* : any of several lady's slippers; *esp* : a woodland orchid of eastern North America with usually pink flowers

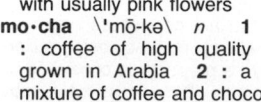

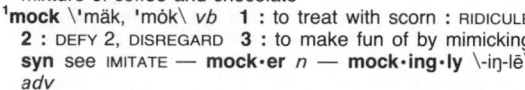

mockingbird

mo·cha \'mō-kə\ *n* **1** : coffee of high quality grown in Arabia **2** : a mixture of coffee and chocolate

¹mock \'mäk, 'mȯk\ *vb* **1** : to treat with scorn : RIDICULE **2** : DEFY 2, DISREGARD **3** : to make fun of by mimicking **syn** see IMITATE — **mock·er** *n* — **mock·ing·ly** \-iŋ-lē\ *adv*

²mock *n* **1** : an act of mocking : JEER **2** : someone or something that is made fun of

³mock *adj* : not real : SHAM

mock·ery \'mäk-(ə-)rē, 'mȯk-\ *n, pl* **-er·ies** **1** : insulting action or speech **2** : someone or something that is laughed at **3** : a ridiculous or poor imitation

mock·ing·bird \'mäk-iŋ-,bərd, 'mȯk-\ *n* : a songbird of the southern U.S. that is closely related to the catbirds and thrashers and is noted for the sweetness of its song and for its imitations of the notes of other birds

mock orange *n* : SYRINGA

mock–up \'mäk-,əp, 'mȯk-\ *n* : a full-sized structural copy built for study, testing, or display ⟨a *mock-up* of an airplane⟩

mod \'mäd\ *adj* : MODERN

mod·acryl·ic fiber \,mäd-ə-,kril-ik-\ *n* : a synthetic fiber used for clothing that dries quickly and resists burning

mod·al \'mōd-ᵊl\ *adj* : relating to or being a modal auxiliary

modal auxiliary *n* : a verb (as *can, must, might, should*) that is typically used with another verb to indicate that the state or action expressed is something other than a simple fact (as a possibility or a necessity) ⟨in "we may go tomorrow" "may" is a *modal auxiliary*⟩

¹mode \'mōd\ *n* **1** : ²MOOD **2** : a form or manner of expression or acting : WAY ⟨a *mode* of travel⟩ **3** : a particular operating arrangement or condition **4** : the most frequent value of a set of values (as data)

²mode *n* : a popular fashion or style

¹mod·el \'mäd-ᵊl\ *n* **1 a** : a small but exact copy of something ⟨a ship *model*⟩ **b** : a pattern or figure of something to be made ⟨clay *models* for a statue⟩ **2** : a person who sets a good example ⟨a *model* of politeness⟩ **3 a** : a person or thing that serves as an artist's pattern; *esp* : a person who poses for an artist or photographer **b** : a person who wears in the presence of customers garments that are for sale or who poses for ads for merchandise (as clothes) **4** : ¹TYPE 2b, KIND ⟨our car is a late *model*⟩ **5** : a description or construction used to help form a picture of something (as an atom) that cannot be seen directly ⟨a *model* of a DNA molecule⟩ **syn** see PATTERN

²model *vb* **mod·eled** *or* **mod·elled; mod·el·ing** *or* **mod·el·ling** \'mäd-liŋ, -ᵊl-iŋ\ **1** : to plan or shape after a pattern **2** : to make a model : MOLD **3** : to act or serve as a model — **mod·el·er** *or* **mod·el·ler** \'mäd-lər, -ᵊl-ər\ *n*

³model *adj* **1** : serving as or worthy of being a pattern ⟨a *model* student⟩ **2** : being a miniature copy of something ⟨a *model* airplane⟩

mo·dem \'mō-,dem\ *n* : a device that changes signals from one form to a form which can be used by another kind of equipment ⟨computer information is sent over telephone lines using a *modem*⟩

¹mod·er·ate \'mäd-(ə-)rət\ *adj* **1 a** : avoiding extremes in behavior or expression ⟨a *moderate* eater⟩ **b** : ¹CALM 2, TEMPERATE **2 a** : neither very much nor very little : average in size or amount ⟨a *moderate* rain⟩ **b** : neither very good nor very bad : MEDIOCRE ⟨met with only *moderate* success⟩ **3** : opposed to major social change or extreme political ideas ⟨a *moderate* candidate⟩ **4** : not expensive : reasonable or low in price ⟨*moderate* rates⟩ — **mod·er·ate·ly** *adv* — **mod·er·ate·ness** *n*

²mod·er·ate \'mäd-ə-,rāt\ *vb* **-at·ed; -at·ing** **1** : to make or become less violent, severe, or intense **2** : to guide a discussion or act as chairperson of a meeting

³mod·er·ate \'mäd-(ə-)rət\ *n* : one who holds moderate views or belongs to a moderate group (as in politics)

mod·er·a·tion \,mäd-ə-'rā-shən\ *n* **1** : the action of moderating **2** : the quality or state of being moderate : avoidance of extremes ⟨does everything in *moderation*⟩

mo·der·a·to \,mäd-ə-'rät-ō\ *adv or adj* : at a moderate tempo — used as a direction in music

mod·er·a·tor \'mäd-ə-,rāt-ər\ *n* **1** : one that moderates: as **a** : the leader of a Presbyterian governing body **b** : the chairperson of a town meeting **c** : the chairperson of a discussion group (as on television) **2** : a substance (as graphite) used for slowing down neutrons in a nuclear reactor

¹mod·ern \'mäd-ərn\ *adj* **1** : of, relating to, or characteristic of the present or the recent past : CONTEMPORARY **2** : of or relating to the period from about 1500 to the present ⟨*modern* history⟩ ⟨*Modern* English⟩ — **mo·der·ni·ty** \mə-'dər-nət-ē, mä-\ *n* — **mod·ern·ness** \'mäd-ərn-nəs\ *n*

²modern *n* : a person of modern times or with modern ideas

mod·ern·ism \'mäd-ər-,niz-əm\ *n* : a modern custom, expression, style, or idea — **mod·ern·ist** \-nəst\ *n or adj* — **mod·ern·is·tic** \,mäd-ər-'nis-tik\ *adj*

mod·ern·ize \'mäd-ər-,nīz\ *vb* **-ized; -iz·ing** : to make or become modern; *esp* : to change to suit present styles, tastes, or needs ⟨*modernize* an old house⟩ — **mod·ern·iza·tion** \,mäd-ər-nə-'zā-shən\ *n* — **mod·ern·iz·er** \'mäd-ər-,nī-zər\ *n*

mod·est \'mäd-əst\ *adj* **1 a** : having a limited and not overly high opinion of oneself and one's abilities **b** : not boastful : somewhat shy ⟨a *modest* winner⟩ **2** : moderate in amount, size, or extent ⟨a *modest* request⟩ ⟨a *modest* cottage⟩ **3** : clean and proper in thought, conduct, and dress : DECENT — **mod·est·ly** *adv*

mod·es·ty \'mäd-ə-stē\ *n* : the quality of being modest

mo·di·cum \'mäd-i-kəm, 'mōd-\ *n* : a small amount ⟨anyone with a *modicum* of intelligence would understand⟩

mod·i·fi·ca·tion \,mäd-ə-fə-'kā-shən\ *n* **1 a** : the act of modifying **b** : the state of being modified **2** : the limiting of a statement : QUALIFICATION **3** : the result of modifying : partial change ⟨*modification* of plans⟩

mod·i·fi·er \'mäd-ə-,fī(-ə)r\ *n* : a word (as an adjective or adverb) or group of words (as a phrase or clause) used with another word or group of words to limit its meaning

mod·i·fy \'mäd-ə-,fī\ *vb* **-fied; -fy·ing** **1** : to make changes in : ALTER ⟨*modify* a plan⟩ **2** : to lower or reduce in amount or degree : MODERATE **3** : to limit in meaning : QUALIFY ⟨in the phrase "green gloves" "green" *modifies* "gloves"⟩ — **mod·i·fi·able** \-,fī-ə-bəl\ *adj*

mod·ish \'mōd-ish\ *adj* : FASHIONABLE 1, STYLISH — **mod·ish·ly** *adv* — **mod·ish·ness** *n*

mod·u·lar \'mäj-ə-lər\ *adj* **1** : of, relating to, or based on a module or modulus **2** : constructed in similar sizes or with similar units for flexibility and variety in use

modular arithmetic *n* : arithmetic that deals with whole numbers where the numbers are replaced by their remainders after division by a fixed number ⟨in a *modular arithmetic* with modulus 5, 3 multiplied by 4 would be 2⟩ ⟨5 hours after 10 o'clock is 3 o'clock because clocks follow a *modular arithmetic* with modulus 12⟩

mod·u·late \'mäj-ə-ˌlāt\ *vb* **-lat·ed; -lat·ing** **1** : to tune to a key or pitch **2** : to adjust or regulate to the proper proportion; *esp* : to tone down : SOFTEN ⟨*modulated* his voice⟩ **3** : to vary a quality (as frequency or amplitude) of an electromagnetic wave for the transmission of information (as by radio) — **mod·u·la·tor** \-ˌlāt-ər\ *n* — **mod·u·la·to·ry** \-lə-ˌtōr-ē, -ˌtȯr-\ *adj*

mod·u·la·tion \ˌmäj-ə-'lā-shən\ *n* **1** : an action of modulating **2** : the extent or degree by which something is modulated **3** : a change from one musical key to another by using a chord that is found in both keys **4** : the process of modulating a carrier wave or signal (as in radio); *also* : the result of this process

mod·ule \'mäj-ü(ə)l\ *n* **1 a** : any in a series of similar units for use together **b** : a usually packaged collection of parts (as for an electronic device) **2** : an independent unit of a space vehicle ⟨a propulsion *module*⟩

mod·u·lo \'mäj-ə-ˌlō\ *prep* : with respect to a modulus of

mod·u·lus \'mäj-ə-ləs\ *n, pl* **-li** \-ˌlī, -ˌlē\ : a whole number that is equal to the number of different numbers in a particular system of modular arithmetic and is the fixed number used to obtain the remainders

¹mo·gul \'mō-(ˌ)gəl, mō-'gəl\ *n* **1** *or* **mo·ghul** *cap* : an Indian Muslim of or descended from a family of Turkish and Mongolian origin that ruled India from the 16th to the 18th century **2** : an important person : MAGNATE [of Persian and Mongolian origin] — **mogul** *adj, often cap*

²mo·gul \'mō-gəl\ *n* : a bump on a ski slope [of Scandinavian origin]

mo·hair \'mō-ˌha(ə)r, -ˌhe(ə)r\ *n* : a fabric or yarn made of or with the long silky hair of the Angora goat; *also* : the hair of the Angora goat

Mohammedan *variant of* MUHAMMADAN

Mo·hawk \'mō-ˌhȯk\ *n* : a member of an American Indian people of the Mohawk river valley in New York state

Mo·hi·can \mō-'hē-kən, mə-\ *n* **1** : a member of an American Indian people of the upper Hudson river valley **2** *or* **Mo·he·gan** \-'hē-gən\ : a member of an American Indian people of southeastern Connecticut

moi·ety \'mȯi-ət-ē\ *n, pl* **-eties** **1** : one of two equal or approximately equal parts : HALF **2** : one of the parts making up something

moil \'mȯi(ə)l\ *vb* : to work hard : DRUDGE

moi·ré \mȯ-'rā, mwä-\ *or* **moire** *same, or* 'mȯi(-ə)r, 'mȯ(ə)r, 'mwär\ *n* : a fabric (as silk) that has a shiny wavy patterned surface — **moiré** *adj*

moist \'mȯist\ *adj* **1** : slightly or moderately wet ⟨*moist* earth⟩ **2** : characterized by high humidity — **moist·ly** *adv* — **moist·ness** \'mȯis(t)-nəs\ *n*

  syn MOIST, DAMP, DANK mean somewhat wet. MOIST suggests a wetness that is just noticeable ⟨grass just *moist* with dew⟩ DAMP suggests that something is wet to the point where it is disagreeable to touch ⟨those clothes are too *damp* to wear⟩ DANK suggests a cold unpleasant wetness that may be unhealthful ⟨a *dank* cellar⟩

moist·en \'mȯis-ᵊn\ *vb* **moist·ened; moist·en·ing** \'mȯisn-iŋ, -ᵊn-iŋ\ : to make or become moist — **moist·en·er** \'mȯis-nər, -ᵊn-ər\ *n*

mois·ture \'mȯish-chər, 'mȯis-\ *n* : a small amount of liquid that causes moistness : DAMPNESS

mois·tur·ize \'mȯish-chə-ˌrīz, 'mȯis-\ *vb* **-ized; -iz·ing** : to add moisture to ⟨*moisturize* the air⟩ — **mois·tur·iz·er** *n*

mo·jo \'mō-jō\ *n, pl* **mojoes** *or* **mojos** : a magic spell, hex, or charm; *also* : magical power [probably of African origin]

¹mo·lar \'mō-lər\ *n* : a tooth with a rounded or flattened surface adapted for grinding; *esp* : one behind the premolars of a mammal

  Word History Food is crushed in the mouth by the grinding of teeth, especially the molars. In much the same manner, grain may be ground into flour between two rough circular millstones. The Latin word for millstone is *mola,* and it seemed fitting to the English in the late Middle Ages that a tooth which acted like a millstone be called a *molar.* [from Latin *molaris* "a grinding tooth", from *mola* "millstone" — related to ¹MILL]

²molar *adj* **1** : adapted for grinding **2** : of or relating to a molar

mo·las·ses \mə-'las-əz\ *n* : a thick brown syrup that is separated from raw sugar in sugar manufacture

¹mold *or* **mould** \'mōld\ *n* : light rich crumbly earth that contains decaying matter (as leaves) [Old English *molde* "rich soil"]

²mold *or* **mould** *n* **1** : the frame on, around, or in which something is constructed or shaped ⟨a candle *mold*⟩ **2** : something shaped in a mold ⟨a *mold* of gelatin⟩ [Middle English *mold* "special nature of something, frame on which something is formed", from early French *modle* (same meaning), from Latin *modulus* "form, measure"]

³mold *or* **mould** *vb* **1** : to work and press into shape ⟨*mold* loaves of bread⟩ **2** : to form in a mold **3** : to determine or influence the character of ⟨*mold* a child's mind⟩ — **mold·er** *n*

⁴mold *also* **mould** *vb* : to become moldy [Middle English *moulen* "to become moldy"]

⁵mold *also* **mould** *n* : an often fuzzy surface growth of fungus especially on damp or decaying matter; *also* : a fungus that produces mold

mold·er \'mōl-dər\ *vb* **mold·ered; mold·er·ing** \-d(ə-)riŋ\ : to crumble to bits by slow decay : DECAY

mold·ing \'mōl-diŋ\ *n* **1 a** : the act or work of a person who molds **b** : an object produced by molding **2** : a strip of material having a shaped surface and used as a decoration (as on a wall or the edge of a table)

moldy \'mōl-dē\ *adj* **mold·i·er; -est** : resembling, containing, or covered with mold — **mold·i·ness** *n*

¹mole \'mōl\ *n* : a small usually brown and sometimes slightly raised permanent spot on the skin [Old English *māl* "spot on the skin"]

²mole *n* : any of numerous burrowing mammals with tiny eyes, concealed ears, and soft fur that eat insects [Middle English *mole* "burrowing animal"]

²mole

³mole *n* : a pier made of heavy solid material (as concrete or stone) that protects a harbor from rough seas [from early French *mole* "stone pier", from early Italian *molo* (same meaning), derived from Latin *moles,* literally "a mass"]

mo·lec·u·lar \mə-'lek-yə-lər\ *adj* : of, relating to, or produced by molecules

molecular formula *n* : a chemical formula that gives the total number of atoms of each element present in a molecule

molecular mass *n* : the mass of a molecule that is equal to the sum of the masses of all the atoms contained in the molecule's formula

molecular weight *n* : the weight of a molecule equal to the

\ə\ abut	\au̇\ out	\i\ tip	\ȯ\ saw	\u̇\ foot
\ər\ further	\ch\ chin	\ī\ life	\ȯi\ coin	\y\ yet
\a\ mat	\e\ pet	\j\ job	\th\ thin	\yü\ few
\ā\ take	\ē\ easy	\ŋ\ sing	\th\ this	\yu̇\ cure
\ä\ cot, cart	\g\ go	\ō\ bone	\ü\ food	\zh\ vision

sum of the weights of the atoms contained in it

mol·e·cule \'mäl-i-ˌkyü(ə)l\ *n* **1** : the smallest particle of a substance having all the characteristics of the substance ⟨a *molecule* of water⟩ ⟨a *molecule* of oxygen⟩ **2** : a very small bit : PARTICLE

mole·hill \'mōl-ˌhil\ *n* **1** : a small mound or ridge of earth pushed up by a burrowing mole **2** : an unimportant obstacle or difficulty ⟨make a mountain out of a *molehill*⟩

mo·lest \mə-'lest\ *vb* **1** : to injure or disturb by interfering : ANNOY **2** : to make unwelcome sexual advances to — **mo·les·ta·tion** \ˌmōl-ˌes-'tā-shən, ˌmōl-əs-, ˌmäl-, es-\ *n* — **mo·lest·er** \mə-'les-tər\ *n*

mol·li·fy \'mäl-ə-ˌfī\ *vb* **-fied; -fy·ing** **1** : to reduce the harshness or violence of **2** : to soothe in temper or disposition : CONCILIATE **syn** see PACIFY — **mol·li·fi·ca·tion** \ˌmäl-ə-fə-'kā-shən\ *n*

mol·lusk *or* **mol·lusc** \'mäl-əsk\ *n* : any of a large phylum of invertebrate animals (as snails, clams, and octopuses) with a soft body lacking segments and usually enclosed in a shell containing calcium — **mol·lus·can** *also* **mol·lus·kan** \mə-'ləs-kən, mä-\ *adj*

¹mol·ly·cod·dle \'mäl-ē-ˌkäd-ᵊl\ *n* : a person whose character has been weakened because of excessive pampering : SISSY

²mollycoddle *vb* **-cod·dled; -cod·dling** \-ˌkäd-liŋ, -ᵊl-iŋ\ : CODDLE 2, PAMPER

¹molt *or* **moult** \'mōlt\ *vb* : to shed hair, feathers, outer skin, or horns with the cast-off parts being replaced by a new growth

²molt *or* **moult** *n* : the act, process, or period of molting

mol·ten \'mōlt-ᵊn\ *adj* : melted especially by very great heat

mol·to \'mōl-tō, 'mȯl-\ *adv* : ²MUCH 1, VERY — used in music directions

mo·lyb·de·num \mə-'lib-də-nəm\ *n* : a metallic element used in steel alloys to give greater strength and hardness — see ELEMENT table

mom \'mäm, 'məm\ *n* : ¹MOTHER 1a

mo·ment \'mō-mənt\ *n* **1** : a brief portion of time : INSTANT **2 a** : present time ⟨at the *moment* she is working on a novel⟩ **b** : a time of importance or success ⟨he has his *moments*⟩ **3** : IMPORTANCE, CONSEQUENCE ⟨an event of great *moment*⟩

mo·men·tar·i·ly \ˌmō-mən-'ter-ə-lē\ *adv* **1** : for a moment ⟨the pain eased *momentarily*⟩ **2** : INSTANTLY ⟨was stunned but recovered *momentarily*⟩ **3** : at any moment ⟨we expect them *momentarily*⟩

mo·men·tary \'mō-mən-ˌter-ē\ *adj* : lasting only a moment **syn** see TRANSIENT

mo·ment·ly \'mō-mənt-lē\ *adv* : MOMENTARILY

mo·men·tous \mō-'ment-əs\ *adj* : very important ⟨a *momentous* decision⟩ — **mo·men·tous·ly** *adv*

mo·men·tum \mō-'ment-əm\ *n, pl* **-men·ta** \-'ment-ə\ *or* **-mentums** **1** : the characteristic of a moving body that is caused by its mass and its motion **2** : IMPETUS 1

momma *variant of* MAMA

mon- *or* **mono-** *combining form* **1** : one : single : alone ⟨*mono*tone⟩ **2** : one atom or group ⟨*mono*xide⟩ [derived from Greek *monos* "alone, single"]

mon·arch \'män-ərk, -ˌärk\ *n* **1** : a person who reigns over a kingdom or empire: as **a** : a ruler who has total power ⟨absolute *monarch*⟩ **b** : someone who acts primarily as chief of state and who has only limited powers ⟨constitutional *monarch*⟩ **2** : someone or something like a monarch ⟨the oak is the *monarch* of the forest⟩ — **mo·nar·chal** \mə-'när-kəl, mä-\ *or* **mo·nar·chi·al** \-kē-əl\ *adj*

monarch butterfly *n* : a large orange and black American butterfly that migrates in large numbers in the spring and fall — called also *monarch*

mo·nar·chi·cal \mə-'när-ki-kəl, mä-\ *also* **mo·nar·chic** \-'när-kik\ *adj* : of or relating to a monarch or monarchy ⟨*monarchical* government⟩

mon·ar·chism \'män-ər-ˌkiz-əm\ *n* : the laws of monarchi-cal government; *also* : belief in or support of these laws — **mon·ar·chist** \-kəst\ *n*

mon·ar·chy \'män-ər-kē\ *n, pl* **-chies** **1** : total rule by one person **2** : a nation or country ruled by a monarch **3** : a form of government having a chief of state who inherits the position, rules for life, and holds powers varying from very limited to total

monarch butterfly

mon·as·tery \'män-ə-ˌster-ē\ *n, pl* **-ter·ies** : a place where a community of monks or nuns live and work — **mon·as·te·ri·al** \ˌmän-ə-'stir-ē-əl\ *adj*

mo·nas·tic \mə-'nas-tik\ *adj* **1** : of or relating to monks or monasteries **2** : resembling life in a monastery — **mo·nastic** *n* — **mo·nas·ti·cal·ly** \-ti-k(ə-)lē\ *adv* — **mo·nas·ti·cism** \-tə-ˌsiz-əm\ *n*

Mon·day \'mən-dē\ *n* : the second day of the week

Word History In ancient times, it was believed that there were seven "planets", one of which was the moon. The seven days of the week were named after the seven "planets" in Latin. One of the days was named *dies Lunae,* which means "day of the moon". The Latin name was later translated into other languages. In Old English, *dies Lunae* became *mōnandæg.* The word *Monday* comes from the Old English *mōnandæg.* [Old English *mōnandæg* "Monday", literally "the moon's day", a translation of Latin *dies Lunae* "day of the moon"]

Mo·nel Metal \mō-ˌnel-\ *trademark* — used for an alloy primarily of nickel and copper

mon·e·tary \'män-ə-ˌter-ē *also* 'mən-\ *adj* : of or relating to money ⟨this administration's *monetary* policy⟩

mon·e·tize \'män-ə-ˌtīz *also* 'mən-\ *vb* **-tized; -tiz·ing** : to accept and set up (as gold) as money in its role of measuring the value of other kinds of money (as paper bills) — **mon·e·ti·za·tion** \ˌmän-ət-ə-'zā-shən *also* ˌmən-\ *n*

mon·ey \'mən-ē\ *n, pl* **moneys** *or* **mon·ies** \-ēz\ **1 a** : something (as coins or bills) generally accepted as a way of measuring value, as a way to trade value, and as a way to pay for goods and services **b** : an amount of money **2** : wealth calculated in terms of money **3** : the first, second, and third place winners in a horse or dog race — usually used in the phrase *in the money*

Word History The wife of the Roman god Jupiter was Juno, but she was also known by several other names. One of them was *Moneta.* The Romans made coins at a temple that was dedicated to this goddess. For that reason the name *Moneta* came to mean "a place where coins are made", and later simply "coin" or "money". The Latin *Moneta* became *moneie* in early French. This early French word was borrowed into Middle English as *moneye.* From it we get the Modern English *money.* [Middle English *moneye* "money", from early French *moneie* (same meaning), from Latin *moneta* "coin, place where coins are made", from *Moneta* "a special name for the goddess Juno"; so called because the ancient Romans made coins at the temple of Juno Moneta — related to ²MINT]

— **for one's money** : according to one's choice or opinion

mon·ey·bags \'mən-ē-ˌbagz\ *n sing or pl* : a wealthy person

money changer *n* : one whose business is the exchanging of one kind of money for the amount of other kinds of money that is equal in value

mon·eyed *or* **mon·ied** \'mən-ēd\ *adj* : having money : WEALTHY

mon·ey·lend·er \'mən-ē-ˌlen-dər\ *n* : one whose business is lending money; *esp* : PAWNBROKER

money order *n* : a written order purchased for a fee to a bank, post office, or express company to pay the person named on it a sum equal to that deposited by the purchaser

Mon·gol \'mäŋ-gəl, 'män-, -ˌgōl\ *n* **1** : a member of one of the Mongoloid peoples of Mongolia **2** : MONGOLIAN 2

Mon·go·lian \män-'gōl-yən, mäŋ-, -'gō-lē-ən\ *n* **1** : a person born or living in Mongolia **2** : the language of the Mongol people — **Mongolian** *adj*

mon·gol·ism \'mäŋ-gə-ˌliz-əm\ *n* : DOWN'S SYNDROME

Mon·gol·oid \'mäŋ-gə-ˌloid\ *adj* **1** : of or relating to peoples of northern and eastern Asia and Malaysia and the Eskimos and often the American Indians **2** *often not cap* : affected with Down's syndrome — **Mongoloid** *n*

mon·goose \'mäŋ-ˌgüs, 'män-\ *n, pl* **mon·goos·es** : a small quick-moving Indian mammal that is related to the civet cats and feeds on snakes and rodents; *also* : any of various related Asian and African mammals

mongoose

¹mon·grel \'məŋ-grəl, 'mäŋ-\ *n* **1** : the offspring of parents of different breeds (as of dogs); *esp* : one whose ancestors are unknown **2** : a person or thing of mixed origin

²mongrel *adj* : of mixed or uncertain kind or origin

¹mon·i·tor \'män-ət-ər\ *n* **1 a** : a student appointed to assist a teacher **b** : a person that warns or instructs **c** : one that monitors or is used in monitoring; *esp* : a video screen used for display (as of television pictures or computer information) **2** : any of various large tropical Old World lizards closely related to the iguanas — called also *monitor lizard* **3 a** : a heavily armored warship having low sides and revolving guns that was used against shipping in harbors and in river patrol **b** : a gunboat used to bombard coastal areas and riverbanks

²monitor *vb* **mon·i·tored; mon·i·tor·ing** \'män-ət-ə-riŋ, 'män-ə-triŋ\ : to watch, observe, or check for a special purpose ⟨*monitor* a broadcast for sound quality⟩

monk \'məŋk\ *n* : a member of a religious community made up of men who agree to give up worldly life, remain poor and unmarried, and obey all laws of their community — **monk·ish** \'məŋ-kish\ *adj*

¹mon·key \'məŋ-kē\ *n, pl* **monkeys** **1** : any of a group of mostly tropical furry animals that are like human beings in many ways and are the closest relatives of human beings in the animal kingdom — used especially of the smaller ones with long tails rather than the apes **2 a** : a mischievous child : IMP **b** : ¹FOOL 1 — **mon·key·ish** \-kē-ish\ *adj*

²monkey *vb* **mon·keyed; mon·key·ing** **1** : to act in a playful or mischievous manner **2** : MEDDLE, TAMPER ⟨don't *monkey* with the lawn mower⟩

mon·key·shine \'məŋ-kē-ˌshīn\ *n* : a mischievous trick : PRANK — usually used in pl.

monkey wrench *n* : a wrench with one fixed and one adjustable jaw

monks·hood \'məŋ(k)s-ˌhud\ *n* : any of a genus of poisonous plants related to the buttercups; *esp* : a tall Old World plant that is grown for its white or purplish flowers or as a source of drugs

mono- — see MON-

mono·chro·mat·ic \ˌmän-ə-krō-'mat-ik\ *adj* **1** : having or consisting of one color **2** : consisting of radiation (as light) of a single wavelength

mono·chrome \'män-ə-ˌkrōm\ *n* : a painting, drawing, or photograph in a single color — **monochrome** *adj*

mon·o·cle \'män-i-kəl\ *n* : an eyeglass for one eye — **mon·o·cled** \-kəld\ *adj*

mono·cot \'män-ə-ˌkät\ *n* : MONOCOTYLEDON — **monocot** *adj*

mono·cot·y·le·don \ˌmän-ə-ˌkät-ᵊl-'ēd-ᵊn\ *n* : any of a group of seed plants (as the palms and grasses) having an embryo with a single cotyledon and usually leaves with parallel veins and flower parts in groups of three — **mono·cot·y·le·don·ous** \-ᵊl-'ēd-ᵊn-əs\ *adj*

monocle

mono·cyte \'män-ə-ˌsīt\ *n* : a large white blood cell that takes in and uses up foreign bodies and bits of material

mon·oe·cious \mə-'nē-shəs, (')mä-\ *adj* : having on the same plant flowers with stamens only and flowers with pistils only

mo·nog·a·my \mə-'näg-ə-mē\ *n* : marriage with only one person at a time — **mo·nog·a·mous** \-məs\ *adj*

mono·gram \'män-ə-ˌgram\ *n* : an identifying or decorative symbol usually made up of a person's initials — **mono·grammed** \-ˌgramd\ *adj*

mono·lith \'män-ᵊl-ˌith\ *n* **1** : a single great stone often in the form of a monument or column **2** : something large and powerful (as a political organization) that is thought to function as a unified whole — **mono·lith·ic** \ˌmän-ᵊl-'ith-ik\ *adj*

mono·logue *or* **mono·log** \'män-ᵊl-ˌóg, -ˌäg\ *n* **1** : a short dramatic work performed by one actor **2** : a long uninterrupted speech delivered by one person in the presence of others — **mono·logu·ist** \-ᵊl-ˌóg-əst, -ˌäg-\ *or* **mo·no·lo·gist** \mə-'näl-ə-jəst; 'män-ᵊl-ˌóg-əst, -ˌäg-\ *n*

mono·pho·nic \ˌmän-ə-'fän-ik\ *adj* : of or relating to sound recording or reproduction involving a single transmission path

mono·plane \'män-ə-ˌplān\ *n* : an airplane with only one set of wings

mo·nop·o·list \mə-'näp-ə-ləst\ *n* : one who monopolizes — **mo·nop·o·lis·tic** \-ˌnäp-ə-'lis-tik\ *adj*

mo·nop·o·lize \mə-'näp-ə-ˌlīz\ *vb* **-lized; -liz·ing** : to acquire or have complete control over ⟨insisted always on *monopolizing* the conversation⟩ — **mo·nop·o·li·za·tion** \-ˌnäp-ə-lə-'zā-shən\ *n* — **mo·nop·o·liz·er** \-'näp-ə-ˌlī-zər\ *n*

mo·nop·o·ly \mə-'näp-(ə-)lē\ *n, pl* **-lies** **1 a** : complete control over the entire supply of goods or a service in a certain market **b** : complete possession **2** : a commercial product or service controlled by one person or company **3** : a company that has a monopoly

mono·rail \'män-ə-ˌrāl\ *n* : a single rail serving as a track for cars that balance on or hang from it; *also* : a car using such a track

mono·sac·cha·ride \ˌmän-ə-'sak-ə-ˌrīd\ *n* : a sugar that cannot be split into simpler sugars by reaction with water — called also *simple sugar*

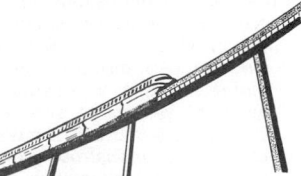

monorail

\ə\ **abut**	\au\ **out**	\i\ **tip**	\ó\ **saw**	\u\ **foot**
\ər\ **further**	\ch\ **chin**	\ī\ **life**	\ói\ **coin**	\y\ **yet**
\a\ **mat**	\e\ **pet**	\j\ **job**	\th\ **thin**	\yü\ **few**
\ā\ **take**	\ē\ **easy**	\ŋ\ **sing**	\t̲h̲\ **this**	\yu̇\ **cure**
\ä\ **cot, cart**	\g\ **go**	\ō\ **bone**	\ü\ **food**	\zh\ **vision**

mono·so·di·um glu·ta·mate \,män-ə-,sŏd-ē-əm-'glüt-ə-,māt\ *n* : a salt used for seasoning foods

mono·syl·la·ble \'män-ə-,sil-ə-bəl, ,män-ə-'sil-\ *n* : a word of one syllable — **mono·syl·lab·ic** \,män-ə-sə-'lab-ik\ *adj*

mono·the·ism \'män-ə-(,)thē-,iz-əm\ *n* : the belief that there is only one God — **mono·the·ist** \-,thē-əst\ *n* — **mono·the·is·tic** \,män-ə-thē-'is-tik\ *adj*

mono·tone \'män-ə-,tōn\ *n* **1** : a series of syllables, words, or sentences on one unchanging key or pitch ⟨speak in a *monotone*⟩ **2** : a single unchanging musical tone **3 a** : sameness of tone or style ⟨a poem written in *monotone*⟩ **b** : sameness of color ⟨engravings in *monotone*⟩

mo·not·o·nous \mə-'nät-°n-əs, -'nät-nəs\ *adj* **1** : uttered or sounded in one unchanging tone **2** : boring from being always the same ⟨a *monotonous* task⟩ — **mo·not·o·nous·ly** *adv* — **mo·not·o·nous·ness** *n*

mo·not·o·ny \mə-'nät-°n-ē, -'nät-nē\ *n, pl* **-nies** **1** : sameness of tone or sound **2** : lack of variety; *esp* : a lack of change that causes boredom

mono·treme \'män-ə-,trēm\ *n* : any of an order of primitive egg-laying mammals that include the platypuses and echidnas

mono·un·sat·u·rat·ed \,män-ō-,ən-'sach-ə-,rāt-ed\ *adj* : containing one double or triple bond per molecule — used especially of an oil or fatty acid

mon·ox·ide \mə-'näk-,sīd\ *n* : an oxide containing only one oxygen atom in the molecule

mon·sei·gneur \,mōn-,sān-'yər\ *n, pl* **mes·sei·gneurs** \,mā-,sān-'yər(z)\ : a high-ranking Frenchman (as a prince or archbishop) — used as a title before a title of office or rank

mon·sieur \məsh-(')yə(r), məs-, mə-'si(ə)r\ *n, pl* **mes·sieurs** \məsh-(')yə(r)(z), məs-, mäs-; mə-'si(ə)r(z)\ — used as a title equal to *Mister* for a Frenchman

mon·si·gnor \män-'sē-nyər, mən-\ *n, pl* **monsignors** *or* **mon·si·gno·ri** \,män-'sēn-'yōr-ē, -'yór-\ — used as a title for Roman Catholic priests

mon·soon \män-'sün\ *n* **1** : a wind in the Indian ocean and southern Asia that blows from the southwest from April to October and from the northeast from October to April **2** : the rainy season that accompanies the southwest monsoon

¹mon·ster \'män(t)-stər\ *n* **1** : an animal or plant of abnormal form or structure **2** : a strange or horrible creature **3** : something unusually large **4** : an extremely wicked or cruel person

²monster *adj* : very large : ENORMOUS

mon·strance \'män(t)-strən(t)s\ *n* : a vessel in which the consecrated Host is exposed

mon·stros·i·ty \män-'sträs-ət-ē\ *n, pl* **-ties** **1** : the condition of being monstrous **2** : MONSTER 1, 2, 3

mon·strous \'män(t)-strəs\ *adj* **1** : unusually large : GIGANTIC **2** : very ugly or vicious : HORRIBLE **3** : shockingly wrong or ridiculous **4** : very different from the usual form : ABNORMAL — **mon·strous·ly** *adv*

> **syn** MONSTROUS, TREMENDOUS, STUPENDOUS, COLOSSAL mean of very great size. MONSTROUS suggests that something is unusually big when compared to others of its kind ⟨a *monstrous* cow⟩ TREMENDOUS suggests something so big that it causes wonder or fear ⟨the *tremendous* size of the blue whale⟩ STUPENDOUS suggests something that is amazing simply because of its size ⟨a *stupendous* wedding cake⟩ COLOSSAL suggests a size that is almost too great to imagine ⟨the *colossal* size of the largest planets⟩

mon·tage \män-'täzh, mōn-\ *n* **1** : an artistic composition made up of several different kinds of items (as strips of newspaper, pictures, bits of wood) arranged together **2** : a rapid succession of distinct scenes or images in a motion picture to illustrate associated ideas

month \'mən(t)th\ *n, pl* **months** \'mən(t)s, 'mən(t)ths\ : one of the 12 parts into which the year is divided

¹month·ly \'mən(t)th-lē\ *adj* **1** : occurring, done, produced, or published every month **2** : due or calculated by the month ⟨*monthly* salary⟩ **3** : lasting a month — **monthly** *adv*

²monthly *n, pl* **monthlies** **1** : a monthly magazine **2** *pl* : a menstrual period

mon·u·ment \'män-yə-mənt\ *n* **1** : something that serves as a memorial; *esp* : a building, pillar, stone, or statue honoring a person or event **2** : a work, saying, or deed that lasts or that is worth preserving ⟨the book is a *monument* of scholarship⟩ **3** : a boundary marker (as a stone) **4** : a place of historic interest or natural beauty set aside and maintained by the government as public property

mon·u·men·tal \,män-yə-'ment-°l\ *adj* **1** : of or relating to a monument **2** : serving as or resembling a monument : MASSIVE; *also* : highly significant : OUTSTANDING **3** : very great ⟨*monumental* stupidity⟩ — **mon·u·men·tal·ly** \-°l-ē\ *adv*

¹moo \'mü\ *vb* : to make the low sound of a cow : LOW

²moo *n* : the sound a cow makes when it moos

mooch \'müch\ *vb* **1** : to wander about **2** : BEG 1, SPONGE — **mooch·er** *n*

¹mood \'müd\ *n* **1** : a conscious and emotional state of mind or feeling; *also* : the feeling expressed in a work of art or literature **2** : a dominant attitude or spirit ⟨the *mood* of the country was grim⟩ [Old English *mōd* "a state of mind"]

²mood *n* : a set of forms of a verb that show whether the action or state expressed is to be thought of as a fact, a command, or a wish or possibility [an altered form of *mode*]

moody \'müd-ē\ *adj* **mood·i·er; -est** **1** : frequently influenced by moods; *esp* : affected by changeable and gloomy moods or bad temper **2** : expressing a mood ⟨a *moody* face⟩ — **mood·i·ly** \'müd-°l-ē\ *adv* — **mood·i·ness** \'müd-ē-nəs\ *n*

¹moon \'mün\ *n* **1 a** : the earth's natural satellite that shines by reflecting light from the sun and revolves about the earth in about 29½ days **b** : SATELLITE 2a **2** : the average period of revolution of the moon about the earth equal to about 29½ days **3** : ¹MOONLIGHT — **moon·less** \-ləs\ *adj*

²moon *vb* : to spend time daydreaming

moon·beam \'mün-,bēm\ *n* : a ray of light from the moon

¹moon·light \-,līt\ *n* : the light of the moon

²moonlight *vb* : to work at a second job in addition to a regular one — **moon·light·er** *n*

moon·lit \'mün-,lit\ *adj* : lighted by the moon

moon·scape \'mün-,skāp\ *n* : the surface of the moon as seen or as pictured

moon·shine \'mün-,shīn\ *n* **1** : ¹MOONLIGHT **2** : meaningless talk : NONSENSE **3** : alcoholic liquor; *esp* : illegally produced whiskey made from corn — **moon·shin·er** \-,shī-nər\ *n*

moon·stone \-,stōn\ *n* : a partly transparent shiny stone used as a gem

moon·struck \-,strək\ *adj* **1** : mentally unbalanced **2** : romantically sentimental **3** : lost in daydreams or fantasy

moony \'mü-nē\ *adj* : MOONSTRUCK 2, 3, DREAMY

¹moor \'mu̇(ə)r\ *n* : a broad area of open land that is usually too wet or too poor for farming [Old English *mōr* "an area of open and wet wasteland"]

²moor *vb* : to fasten in place with cables, lines, or anchors ⟨*moor* a boat⟩ [Middle English *moren* "to fasten (a boat) in place"] — **moor·age** \-ij\ *n*

Moor \'mu̇(ə)r\ *n* : one of a North African people that conquered Spain in the 8th century and ruled until 1492 [Middle English *More* "Moor", from early French *More* (same meaning), from Latin *Maurus* "a person from Mauretania (a country in Africa)"] — **Moor·ish** \-ish\ *adj*

moor·hen \'mu̇(ə)r-ˌhen\ *n* : a common gallinule found in the New World, Eurasia, and Africa

moor·ing \'mu̇(ə)r-iŋ\ *n* **1** : a place or object to which a boat or aircraft can be fastened **2** : a device or line by which a boat or aircraft is moored

moor·land \'mu̇(ə)r-lənd, -ˌland\ *n* : land consisting of moors

moose \'müs\ *n, pl* **moose**
1 : a large cud-chewing mammal with broad flat-tened antlers and humped shoulders that is related to the deer and lives in for-ests of Canada and the northern U.S. **2** : ELK 1

moose 1

¹**moot** \'müt\ *vb* **1** : to bring up for discussion **2** : ²DEBATE 1

²**moot** *adj* : open to question or discussion : DEBATABLE ⟨a *moot* question⟩

¹**mop** \'mäp\ *n* **1** : a tool for cleaning made of a bundle of cloth or yarn or a sponge fastened to a handle **2** : some-thing resembling a mop ⟨a tangled *mop* of hair⟩

²**mop** *vb* **mopped; mop·ping** : to wipe or clean with or as if with a mop ⟨*mop* the floor⟩ ⟨*mopped* my brow with a hand-kerchief⟩

¹**mope** \'mōp\ *vb* **moped; mop·ing** **1** : to be in a dull and gloomy state **2** : to move slowly and aimlessly : DAWDLE — **mop·er** *n*

²**mope** *n* **1** : a person who lacks energy or enthusiasm **2** *pl* : low spirits : BLUES ⟨a fit of the *mopes*⟩

mo·ped \'mō-ˌped\ *n* : a lightweight low-powered motorbike that can be pedaled

mop·pet \'mäp-ət\ *n* : a young child

mo·raine \mə-'rān\ *n* : a pile of earth and stones carried and deposited by a glacier

¹**mor·al** \'mȯr-əl, 'mär-\ *adj* **1 a** : of or relating to the judg-ment of right and wrong in human behavior : ETHICAL **b** : expressing or teaching an idea of right behavior ⟨a *moral* poem⟩ **c** : agreeing with a standard of right behavior : GOOD ⟨*moral* conduct⟩ **d** : able to choose between right and wrong **2** : likely but not proved : VIRTUAL ⟨a *moral* certainty⟩ — **mor·al·ly** \-ə-lē\ *adv*

²**moral** *n* **1** : the lesson to be learned from a story or an experience **2** *pl* : moral conduct ⟨a high standard of *mor-als*⟩ **3** *pl* : moral teachings or rules

mo·rale \mə-'ral\ *n* : the mental and emotional condition (as of enthusiasm, spirit, or loyalty) of an individual or a group with regard to a task or goal to be accomplished

mor·al·ist \'mȯr-ə-ləst, 'mär-\ *n* **1** : a person who leads a moral life **2** : a person who teaches, studies, or points out morals **3** : a person who is concerned with regulating the morals of others

mor·al·is·tic \ˌmȯr-ə-'lis-tik, ˌmär-\ *adj* **1** : teaching or pointing out morals ⟨a *moralistic* story⟩ **2** : having or ex-pressing a conservative moral attitude ⟨a *moralistic* atti-tude toward the problems of youth⟩

mo·ral·i·ty \mə-'ral-ət-ē\ *n, pl* **-ties** **1** : moral quality : VIR-TUE ⟨judge the *morality* of an action⟩ **2** : a system of moral rules

morality play *n* : a type of play popular especially in the 15th and 16th centuries in which the characters stand for moral qualities (as virtue or vice) or conditions (as death)

mor·al·ize \'mȯr-ə-ˌlīz, 'mär-\ *vb* **-ized; -iz·ing** **1** : to ex-plain in a moral sense : draw a moral from **2** : to make moral or morally better **3** : to make moral comments — **mor·al·iza·tion** \ˌmȯr-ə-lə-'zā-shən, ˌmär-\ *n* — **mor-al·iz·er** \'mȯr-ə-ˌlī-zər, 'mär-\ *n*

mo·rass \mə-'ras\ *n* : MARSH, SWAMP

mor·a·to·ri·um \ˌmȯr-ə-'tōr-ē-əm, ˌmär-, -'tȯr-\ *n, pl* **-ri-ums** *or* **-ria** \-ē-ə\ **1** : a legally approved period of delay in the payment of a debt or the performance of a duty **2** : ²BAN 2, SUSPENSION ⟨a *moratorium* on atomic testing⟩

mo·ray \mə-'rā, 'mȯr-ā\ *n* : any of numerous often brightly colored eels that have sharp teeth capable of biting and live in warm seas

mor·bid \'mȯr-bəd\ *adj* **1** : not healthful : DISEASED ⟨*mor-bid* condition⟩ **2** : characterized by gloomy or sick ideas or feelings ⟨takes a *morbid* interest in funerals⟩ — **mor-bid·ly** *adv*

mor·dant \'mȯrd-ᵊnt\ *adj* : SARCASTIC, BITING ⟨*mordant* crit-icism⟩

¹**more** \'mō(ə)r, 'mȯ(ə)r\ *adj* **1** : greater in amount, num-ber, or size ⟨felt *more* pain⟩ **2** : ¹EXTRA, ADDITIONAL ⟨bought *more* apples⟩

²**more** *adv* **1** : in addition ⟨wait one day *more*⟩ **2** : to a greater or higher extent — often used with an adjective or adverb to form the comparative ⟨*more* active⟩ ⟨*more* ac-tively⟩

³**more** *n* **1 a** : a greater amount or number ⟨got *more* than we expected⟩ **b** : additional persons or things ⟨the *more* the merrier⟩ **2** : an additional amount ⟨too full to eat *more*⟩

mo·rel \mə-'rel, mȯ-\ *n* : any of several large edible fungi with pits on the outside of the fruiting part at the top

more or less *adv* **1** : to a varying or uncertain degree : SOMEWHAT ⟨they were *more or less* willing to help⟩ **2** : with small variations : APPROXIMATELY ⟨contains 16 acres *more or less*⟩

more·over \mōr-'ō-vər, mȯr-\ *adv* : in addition to what has been said : BESIDES

mo·res \'mō(ə)r-ˌāz, 'mȯ(ə)r- *also* -ēz\ *n pl* **1** : the un-changing customs of a particular group that are accepted by all group members as moral and necessary for the group's survival **2** : usual behavior : HABITS, MANNERS

Mor·gan \'mȯr-gən\ *n* : any of an American breed of light strong horses

mor·ga·nat·ic marriage \ˌmȯr-gə-ˌnat-ik-\ *n* : a le-gal and recognized mar-riage between a member of a royal or noble family and a person of lower rank who does not take on the title of the higher ranked person and whose chil-dren do not acquire the ti-tle or inheritance of the parent of higher rank

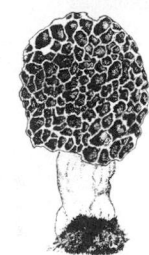

morel

morgue \'mȯ(ə)rg\ *n* **1** : a place where the bodies of the dead are kept temporarily until they are identified or re-leased for burial **2** : a department of a newspaper where reference material is filed

mor·i·bund \'mȯr-ə-(ˌ)bənd, 'mär-\ *adj* : nearly dead

Mor·mon \'mȯr-mən\ *adj* : of or relating to the Church of Jesus Christ of Latter-day Saints — **Mormon** *n* — **Mor-mon·ism** \'mȯr-mə-ˌniz-əm\ *n*

morn \'mȯ(ə)rn\ *n* : MORNING

morn·ing \'mȯr-niŋ\ *n* **1 a** : ²DAWN 1 **b** : the time from sunrise to noon **c** : the time from midnight to noon **2** : the first or early part : BEGINNING ⟨the *morning* of life⟩

morning glory *n* : any of various usually twining plants with showy trumpet-shaped flowers that usually close by the middle of the day; *also* : any of various related plants in-cluding herbs, vines, shrubs, or trees that usually have fun-nel-shaped flowers

\ə\ abut	\au̇\ out	\i\ tip	\ȯ\ saw	\u̇\ foot
\ər\ further	\ch\ chin	\ī\ life	\ȯi\ coin	\y\ yet
\a\ mat	\e\ pet	\j\ job	\th\ thin	\yü\ few
\ā\ take	\ē\ easy	\ŋ\ sing	\th\ this	\yu̇\ cure
\ä\ cot, cart	\g\ go	\ō\ bone	\ü\ food	\zh\ vision

morning sickness *n* : nausea on getting up in the morning that is usually associated with early pregnancy

morning star *n* : a bright planet (as Venus) seen in the eastern sky before or at sunrise

mo·roc·co \mə-ˈräk-ō\ *n* : a fine leather made of goat skins tanned with sumac

mo·ron \ˈmō(ə)r-ˌän, ˈmȯ(ə)r-\ *n* **1** : a feebleminded person who is able to develop to a mental age of between 8 and 12 years and is capable of doing routine work under supervision **2** : a very stupid person — **mo·ron·ic** \mə-ˈrän-ik, mȯ-\ *adj*

mo·rose \mə-ˈrōs, mȯ-\ *adj* : SULLEN 1a, GLOOMY — **mo·rose·ly** *adv* — **mo·rose·ness** *n*

mor·pheme \ˈmȯr-ˌfēm\ *n* : a word or a part of a word (as *re-* or *-call* in *recall*) that contains no smaller unit of meaning — **mor·phe·mic** \mȯr-ˈfē-mik\ *adj*

mor·phine \ˈmȯr-ˌfēn\ *n* : a bitter white habit-forming narcotic made from opium and used especially to deaden pain [derived from *Morpheus* "Greek god of dreams"]

mor·phol·o·gy \mȯr-ˈfäl-ə-jē\ *n* **1 a** : a branch of biology that deals with the form and structure of animals and plants **b** : the form and structure of a plant or animal or any of its parts **2** : the part of grammar dealing with word formation **3** : [1]STRUCTURE 3, FORM ⟨the *morphology* of rocks⟩ — **mor·pho·log·i·cal** \ˌmȯr-fə-ˈläj-i-kəl\ *adj*

mor·ris \ˈmȯr-əs, ˈmär-\ *n* : a vigorous English dance traditionally performed by men wearing costumes and bells [Middle English *moreys* "Moorish"]

mor·ris chair \ˌmȯr-əs-, -ˌmär-\ *n* : an easy chair with adjustable back and removable cushions

mor·row \ˈmär-ō, ˈmȯr-\ *n* **1** *archaic* : MORNING **2** : the next day

Morse code \ˈmȯrs-\ *n* : either of two codes consisting of dots and dashes or long and short sounds used for sending messages

INTERNATIONAL MORSE CODE

A •—	N —•	Á •——•—	8 ———••
B —•••	O ———	Ä •—•—	9 ————•
C —•—•	P •——•	É ••—••	0 —————
D —••	Q ——•—	Ñ ——•——	, (comma) ——••——
E •	R •—•	Ö ———•	. •—•—•—
F ••—•	S •••	Ü ••——	? ••——••
G ——•	T —	1 •————	; —•—•—•
H ••••	U ••—	2 ••———	: ———•••
I ••	V •••—	3 •••——	' (apostrophe) •————•
J •———	W •——	4 ••••—	- (hyphen) —••••—
K —•—	X —••—	5 •••••	/ —••—•
L •—••	Y —•——	6 —••••	parenthesis —•——•—
M ——	Z ——••	7 ——•••	underline ••——•—

mor·sel \ˈmȯr-səl\ *n* **1** : a small piece of food : BITE **2** : a small quantity or piece [Middle English *morsel* "a small piece of food", from early French *morsel* (same meaning), from *mors* "a bite", derived from Latin *morsus*, past participle of *mordēre* "to bite" — related to REMORSE; see *Word History* at REMORSE]

[1]mor·tal \ˈmȯrt-ᵊl\ *adj* **1** : capable of causing death ⟨a *mortal* wound⟩ **2** : certain to die ⟨animals are *mortal*⟩ **3** : extremely unfriendly ⟨a *mortal* enemy⟩ **4 a** : considered such a great offense as to deserve eternal punishment ⟨a *mortal* sin⟩ **b** : very great or severe ⟨in *mortal* fear⟩ **5** : [1]HUMAN 1 ⟨*mortal* limitations⟩ **6** : of, relating to, or connected with death ⟨*mortal* agony⟩ **syn** see DEADLY — **mor·tal·ly** \-ᵊl-ē\ *adv*

[2]mortal *n* : a human being

mor·tal·i·ty \mȯr-ˈtal-ət-ē\ *n, pl* **-ties** **1** : the quality or state of being mortal **2** : the death of large numbers (as of animals or people) **3 a** : the number of deaths in a given time or place **b** : the ratio of deaths occurring in a certain time in a given population to the number of individuals in the population

[1]mor·tar \ˈmȯrt-ər\ *n* **1** : a strong deep bowl in which substances are pounded or crushed with a pestle **2** : a short muzzle-loading cannon used to fire shells at a low speed and at high angles

[2]mortar *n* : a building material made of lime and cement mixed with sand and water that is spread between bricks or stones so as to hold them together when it hardens — **mortar** *vb*

mor·tar·board \ˈmȯrt-ər-ˌbō(ə)rd, -ˌbȯ(ə)rd\ *n* **1** : a board used to hold mortar while it is being applied **2** : an academic cap with a broad flat square top and tassel that is worn at graduation and other ceremonies

mortarboard 2

[1]mort·gage \ˈmȯr-gij\ *n* **1** : a transfer of rights to a piece of property (as a house) usually in return for a loan and that is canceled when the loan is paid **2** : the document recording such a transfer

[2]mortgage *vb* **mort·gaged; mort·gag·ing** **1** : to transfer rights to a piece of property by a mortgage **2** : to place under an obligation : pledge in advance

mort·gag·ee \ˌmȯr-gi-ˈjē\ *n* : a person to whom property is mortgaged

mort·gag·or \ˌmȯr-gi-ˈjȯ(ə)r\ *also* **mort·gag·er** \ˈmȯr-gi-jər\ *n* : a person who mortgages his or her property

mor·ti·cian \mȯr-ˈtish-ən\ *n* : UNDERTAKER

mor·ti·fy \ˈmȯrt-ə-ˌfī\ *vb* **-fied; -fy·ing** **1** : to attempt to reduce or control bodily needs and desires through punishment and self-denial **2** : to embarrass greatly : HUMILIATE — **mor·ti·fi·ca·tion** \ˌmȯrt-ə-fə-ˈkā-shən\ *n*

[1]mor·tise \ˈmȯrt-əs\ *n* : a hole or groove cut in a piece of wood or other material into which another piece fits so as to form a joint

[2]mortise *vb* **mor·tised; mor·tis·ing** **1** : to join or fasten securely especially by a tenon and mortise **2** : to cut a mortise in

[1]mor·tu·ary \ˈmȯr-chə-ˌwer-ē\ *n, pl* **-ar·ies** : a place in which the bodies of the dead are kept until burial

[2]mortuary *adj* : of or relating to death or burial

mo·sa·ic \mō-ˈzā-ik\ *n* **1** : a decoration on a surface made by setting small pieces of glass or stone of different colors into another material so as to make pictures or patterns **2** : the process of making mosaics **3** : something resembling a mosaic; *esp* : a virus disease of plants characterized by mottling of the foliage — **mosaic** *adj*

mosquito

Moslem *variant of* MUSLIM

mosque \ˈmäsk\ *n* : a Muslim place of worship

mos·qui·to \mə-ˈskēt-ō\ *n, pl* **-toes** *also* **-tos** : any of numerous two-winged flies of which the females have a needlelike mouth region adapted to puncture the skin and suck the blood of animals [from Spanish *mosquito* "mosquito", literally "little fly", from *mosca* "fly"] — **mos·qui·to·ey** \-ˈskēt-ə-wē\ *adj*

mosquito net *n* : a net for keeping out mosquitoes

moss \ˈmȯs\ *n* **1** : any of a class of plants that have no flowers and produce small leafy stems forming sex organs at their tips and that grow in patches like cushions clinging to rocks, bark, or damp ground **2** : any of various plants (as lichens) resembling mosses — compare REINDEER MOSS — **moss·like** \-,līk\ adj — **mossy** \'mȯ-sē\ adj

mossy zinc n : a form of zinc made by pouring melted zinc into water

¹most \'mōst\ adj **1** : the majority of ⟨most people believe this⟩ **2** : greatest in amount or extent ⟨the most ability⟩

²most adv **1** : to the greatest or highest level or extent — often used with an adjective or adverb to form the superlative ⟨most active⟩ ⟨most actively⟩ **2** : to a very great extent ⟨a most careful driver⟩

³most n : the greatest amount, number, or part ⟨the most that can be accomplished⟩

⁴most adv : ALMOST ⟨the cost of most everything is higher⟩

-most \,mōst\ adj suffix : most ⟨innermost⟩ [Middle English -most "most"]

most·ly \'mōst-lē\ adv : for the greatest part : MAINLY

mote \'mōt\ n : a small particle : SPECK

mo·tel \mō-'tel\ n : a building or group of buildings which provide lodgings and in which the rooms are usually reached directly from an outdoor parking lot

mo·tet \mō-'tet\ n : a form of church music to be sung by several voices usually without accompanying instruments and with several melodies woven together

moth \'mȯth\ n, pl **moths** \'mȯthz, 'mȯths\ : any of a group of insects that are lepidoptera, usually fly at night, and have antennae that are often feathery, duller coloring and a stouter body in relation to the size of the wings than the related butterflies, and larvae that are usually plant-eating caterpillars — compare CLOTHES MOTH

moth·ball \'mȯth-,bȯl\ n **1** : a ball (as of naphthalene) used to keep moths out of clothing **2** pl : protective storage ⟨a fleet put in mothballs after the war⟩

moth–eat·en \'mȯ-,thēt-ᵊn\ adj **1** : eaten into by moths **2** : so old as to be no longer acceptable or usable

¹moth·er \'məth-ər\ n **1 a** : a female parent **b** : a woman in authority; esp : a nun in charge of a convent **2** : an elderly woman **3** : ¹CAUSE 1, ORIGIN ⟨necessity is the mother of invention⟩ — **moth·er·hood** \-,hu̇d\ n — **moth·er·less** \-ləs\ adj

²mother adj **1 a** : of or relating to a mother ⟨mother love⟩ **b** : being in the relation of a mother to others ⟨a mother country⟩ **2** : gotten from or as if from one's mother

³mother vb **moth·ered; moth·er·ing** \'məth-(ə-)riŋ\ : to be or act as mother to

moth·er·board \'məth-ər-,bō(ə)rd, -,bȯ(ə)rd\ n : the main circuit board especially of a microcomputer

Mother Car·ey's chicken \,məth-ər-,kar-ēz, -,ker-\ n : any of several small petrels

Mother Hub·bard \,məth-ər-'həb-ərd\ n : a loose usually shapeless dress

moth·er–in–law \'məth-(ə-)rən-,lȯ, 'məth-ərn-,lȯ\ n, pl **moth·ers–in–law** \'məth-ər-zən-\ : the mother of one's husband or wife

moth·er·land \'məth-ər-,land\ n : FATHERLAND

moth·er·ly \'məth-ər-lē\ adj **1** : of, relating to, or characteristic of a mother ⟨motherly affection⟩ **2** : resembling a mother — **moth·er·li·ness** n

moth·er–of–pearl \,məth-ə-rə(v)-'pər(-ə)l\ n : the hard pearly material that lines the shell of some mollusks (as mussels) and is often used for ornamental objects and buttons

mother of vinegar : a slimy mass of yeast cells and bacteria that forms on the surface of liquids in a process of alcoholic fermentation and is added to wine or cider to produce vinegar — called also **mother**

Mother's Day n : the second Sunday in May set aside for the honoring of mothers

mother tongue n **1** : one's native language **2** : a language from which another language develops

mo·tif \mō-'tēf\ n **1** : an important and usually repeating idea or theme in a work of art **2** : a feature in a decoration or design ⟨a flower motif in wallpaper⟩

mo·tile \'mōt-ᵊl, 'mō-,tīl\ adj : moving or able to move — **mo·til·i·ty** \mō-'til-ət-ē\ n

¹mo·tion \'mō-shən\ n **1** : a formal plan or suggestion for action offered according to the rules of a meeting ⟨a motion to adjourn⟩ **2** : an act or process of changing place or position : MOVEMENT — **mo·tion·less** \-ləs\ adj — **mo·tion·less·ly** adv — **mo·tion·less·ness** n

²motion vb **mo·tioned; mo·tion·ing** \'mō-sh(ə-)niŋ\ : to direct or signal by a movement or sign ⟨motioned me to come forward⟩

motion picture n **1** : a series of pictures projected on a screen rapidly one after another so as to give the appearance of a continuous picture in which the objects move **2** : MOVIE 2

motion sickness n : sickness caused by motion (as in travel by air, car, or ship) and characterized by nausea

mo·ti·vate \'mōt-ə-,vāt\ vb **-vat·ed; -vat·ing** : to provide with a reason for doing something : INDUCE

mo·ti·va·tion \,mōt-ə-'vā-shən\ n **1 a** : the act or process of motivating **b** : the condition of being motivated **2** : a motivating force or influence : INCENTIVE

¹mo·tive \'mōt-iv, sense 2 is also mō-'tēv\ n **1** : something (as a need or desire) that leads or influences a person to do something ⟨their motive in running away was to avoid trouble⟩ **2** : MOTIF syn see CAUSE

²mo·tive \'mōt-iv\ adj : of, relating to, or causing motion ⟨motive power⟩

¹mot·ley \'mät-lē\ adj **1** : having various colors **2** : composed of various often unlike kinds or parts ⟨a motley collection of junk⟩

²motley n **1 a** : a garment of mixed colors worn by a court jester **b** : ¹FOOL 2 **2** : a mixture of different elements

mo·to·neu·ron \,mōt-ə-'n(y)ü-,rän, -'n(y)u̇(ə)r-,än\ n : a neuron that passes from the central nervous system or a ganglion toward or to a muscle and carries a nerve impulse that causes movement — called also **motor neuron**

¹mo·tor \'mōt-ər\ n **1** : a machine that produces motion or power for doing work ⟨a gasoline motor⟩ ⟨electric motors⟩ **2** : MOTOR VEHICLE; esp : ²AUTOMOBILE — **mo·tored** \'mōt-ərd\ adj — **mo·tor·less** \-ləs\ adj

²motor adj **1** : causing or giving motion ⟨motor power⟩ **2 a** : of, relating to, or being a nerve, neuron, or nerve fiber that carries a nerve impulse to a muscle causing movement ⟨motor nerves⟩ **b** : concerned with or involving muscular movement ⟨motor areas of the brain⟩ ⟨a motor reaction⟩ **3 a** : equipped with or driven by a motor **b** : of, relating to, or designed for use in an automobile ⟨a motor accident⟩ ⟨a motor mechanic⟩

³motor vb : to travel or transport by automobile : DRIVE

mo·tor·bike \'mōt-ər-,bīk\ n : a light motorcycle

mo·tor·boat \-,bōt\ n : a boat driven by a motor

mo·tor·cade \'mōt-ər-,kād\ n : a parade of motor vehicles

mo·tor·car \'mōt-ər-,kär\ n : ²AUTOMOBILE

motor court n : MOTEL

mo·tor·cy·cle \'mōt-ər-,sī-kəl\ n : a motorized vehicle for one or two passengers that has two wheels — **motorcycle** vb — **mo·tor·cy·clist** \-,sī-k(ə-)ləst\ n

motor home n : a large motor vehicle equipped as a complete traveling home

mo·tor·ist \'mōt-ə-rəst\ n : a person who travels by automobile

mo·tor·ize \'mōt-ə-,rīz\ vb **-ized; -iz·ing** **1** : to equip with a motor **2** : to equip with motor-driven vehicles for transportation ⟨motorized troops⟩

mo·tor·man \'mōt-ər-mən\ n : an operator of a motor-

\ə\ **abut**	\au̇\ **out**	\i\ **tip**	\ȯ\ **saw**	\u̇\ **foot**
\ər\ **further**	\ch\ **chin**	\ī\ **life**	\ȯi\ **coin**	\y\ **yet**
\a\ **mat**	\e\ **pet**	\j\ **job**	\th\ **thin**	\yü\ **few**
\ā\ **take**	\ē\ **easy**	\ŋ\ **sing**	\th\ **this**	\yu̇\ **cure**
\ä\ **cot, cart**	\g\ **go**	\ō\ **bone**	\ü\ **food**	\zh\ **vision**

driven vehicle (as a streetcar or a subway train)

motor scooter *n* : a motorized vehicle with two or three wheels like a child's scooter but having a seat

mo·tor·truck \'mōt-ər-ˌtrək\ *n* : a self-propelled truck for transporting freight

motor vehicle *n* : a motorized vehicle (as an automobile or motorcycle) not operated on rails

¹**mot·tle** \'mät-ᵊl\ *n* **1** : a colored spot **2** : a pattern of colored spots or blotches — **mot·tled** \-ᵊld\ *adj*

²**mottle** *vb* **mot·tled; mot·tling** \'mät-liŋ, -ᵊl-iŋ\ : to mark with spots or blotches of different color or shades of color as if stained

mot·to \'mät-ō\ *n, pl* **mottoes** *also* **mottos** **1** : a sentence, phrase, or word inscribed on something (as a coin or public building) to suggest its use or nature **2** : a short expression of a guiding rule of conduct

mould *variant of* MOLD

moult *variant of* MOLT

¹**mound** \'maůnd\ *n* **1** : a small hill or heap of dirt or stones (as one made to mark a grave) **2** : the slightly raised ground on which a baseball pitcher stands

²**mound** *vb* : to form into a mound

¹**mount** \'maůnt\ *n* : a high hill : MOUNTAIN — used especially before an identifying name ⟨*Mount* Everest⟩ [from Old English *munt* and early French *mont,* both meaning "hill, mount" and both from Latin *mont-, mons* (same meaning)]

²**mount** *vb* **1 a** : ¹RISE 5a, ASCEND **b** : to go up : CLIMB ⟨*mount* a ladder⟩ **2** : to get up onto something ⟨*mount* a platform⟩ **3** : to furnish with riding animals or vehicles ⟨*mounted* infantry⟩ **4** : to increase rapidly in amount : ACCUMULATE ⟨*mounting* debts⟩ **5 a** : to prepare for use or display especially by fastening in position on a support ⟨*mount* a picture on cardboard⟩ ⟨*mount* an engine⟩ **b** : to prepare (a specimen) for examination and display **6** : to furnish with scenery and costumes : STAGE **7** : to place in position for the purpose of defense or observation ⟨*mounted* some guards⟩ [Middle English *mounten* "to increase, rise", from early French *monter* (same meaning), derived from Latin *mont-, mons* "hill, mount"]

³**mount** *n* **1** : FRAME, SUPPORT: as **a** : a jewelry setting **b** : an object mounted on a slide for examination under a microscope **2** : SADDLE HORSE

moun·tain \'maůnt-ᵊn\ *n* **1** : an elevation higher than a hill **2** : a great mass or huge number ⟨a *mountain* of mail⟩

mountain ash *n* : any of various trees related to the roses and having leaves divided into numerous leaflets and red or orange fruits

moun·tain·eer \ˌmaůnt-ᵊn-'i(ə)r\ *n* **1** : a person who lives in the mountains **2** : a mountain climber — **mountaineer** *vb*

mountain goat *n* : an antelope of the mountains of western North America that has a thick white hairy coat and slightly curved black horns and closely resembles a goat

mountain laurel *n* : a North American evergreen shrub that is related to the rhododendrons and has glossy leaves and pink or white cup-shaped flowers

mountain goat

mountain lion *n* : COUGAR

moun·tain·ous \'maůnt-ᵊn-əs, -nəs\ *adj* **1** : having many mountains **2** : resembling a mountain : HUGE

mountain range *n* : a series of mountains or mountain ridges closely related in direction and position

mountain sheep *n* : any of various wild sheep (as a bighorn) that live in high mountains

moun·tain·side \'maůnt-ᵊn-ˌsīd\ *n* : the side of a mountain

mountain time *n, often cap M* : the time of the seventh time zone west of Greenwich that includes the Rocky mountain states of the U.S.

moun·tain·top \'maůnt-ᵊn-ˌtäp\ *n* : the peak of a mountain

moun·te·bank \'maůnt-i-ˌbaŋk\ *n* **1** : a person who peddles fake medicines (as at fairs and carnivals) by trickery **2** : a boastful dishonest pretender : CHARLATAN

Mount·ie \'maůnt-ē\ *n* : a member of the Royal Canadian Mounted Police

mount·ing \'maůnt-iŋ\ *n* **1** : the act of a person who mounts **2** : something that serves as a mount : SUPPORT ⟨a *mounting* for an engine⟩ ⟨a *mounting* for a diamond⟩

mourn \'mō(ə)rn, 'mȯ(ə)rn\ *vb* **1** : to feel or show grief or sorrow especially over someone's death **2** : to display the customary signs of grief for a death especially by wearing mourning — **mourn·er** *n*

mourn·ful \'mō(ə)rn-fəl, 'mȯ(ə)rn-\ *adj* **1** : expressing or full of sorrow : SORROWFUL ⟨a *mournful* face⟩ **2** : causing sorrow ⟨a *mournful* story⟩ — **mourn·ful·ly** \-fə-lē\ *adv* — **mourn·ful·ness** *n*

mourn·ing \'mōr-niŋ, 'mȯr-\ *n* **1** : the act of sorrowing **2** : an outward sign (as black clothes or a black arm band) of grief for a person's death ⟨to wear *mourning*⟩ **3** : a period of time during which signs of grief are shown

mourning cloak *n* : a blackish brown butterfly of Europe, Asia, and North America having a broad yellow border on the wings

mourning dove *n* : a wild dove of the U.S. with a mournful call

¹**mouse** \'maůs\ *n, pl* **mice** \'mīs\ **1** : any of numerous small rodents with pointed snout, rather small ears, and a slender hairless tail **2** : a person without spirit or courage — **mouse·like** \-ˌlīk\ *adj*

mouse 1

²**mouse** \'maůz\ *vb* **moused; mous·ing** **1** : to hunt mice **2** : to search or move slyly and carefully (as a cat hunting mice) **3** : to move about softly like a mouse

mous·er \'maů-zər\ *n* : a cat good at catching mice

mous·sa·ka \ˌmü-sə-'kä\ *n* : a Middle Eastern dish of ground meat (as lamb or beef) and sliced eggplant often topped with a seasoned sauce [from modern Greek *mousakas* "moussaka"]

¹**mousse** \'müs\ *n* **1** : a light whipped or molded food; *esp* : a frozen dessert of sweetened and flavored whipped cream or egg whites and gelatin **2** : a foamy preparation used in styling hair

²**mousse** *vb* **moussed; mouss·ing** : to style (hair) with mousse

moustache *variant of* MUSTACHE

mousy *or* **mous·ey** \'maů-sē, -zē\ *adj* **mous·i·er; -est** : of, relating to, or resembling a mouse: as **a** : ²QUIET 1a, STEALTHY **b** : ¹SHY 1a, TIMID **c** : dull in color : DRAB

¹**mouth** \'maůth\ *n, pl* **mouths** \'maůthz *also* 'maůths\ **1 a** : the opening through which food passes into the body of an animal **b** : the cavity that encloses the tongue, gums, and teeth in the usual vertebrate **2** : GRIMACE ⟨make a *mouth*⟩ **3** : an opening that is like a mouth ⟨the *mouth* of a cave⟩ ⟨the *mouth* of a container⟩ **4** : the place where a stream enters a larger body of water

²**mouth** \'maůth\ *vb* **1 a** : to speak or utter especially proudly or loudly : DECLAIM **b** : to repeat without belief or understanding ⟨*mouth* empty phrases⟩ **2 a** : to form with the lips without speaking ⟨the librarian *mouthed* "quiet"⟩ **b** : ¹MUMBLE 1 **3** : to take into the mouth — **mouth·er** *n*

mouthed \'maůthd, 'maůtht\ *adj* : having such a mouth ⟨a large-*mouthed* jar⟩

mouth·ful \'maůth-ˌfůl\ *n* **1 a** : as much as a mouth will hold **b** : the amount put into the mouth at one time **2**

: a small quantity **3 a** : a word or phrase that is very long or difficult to say **b** : a comment or remark that is rich in meaning ⟨you said a *mouthful*⟩

mouth organ *n* : HARMONICA

mouth·part \'maúth-ˌpärt\ *n* : a bodily structure that is near the mouth (as of an insect) especially when used to gather or eat food

mouth·piece \-ˌpēs\ *n* **1** : the part put to, between, or near the lips ⟨the *mouthpiece* of a trumpet⟩ ⟨the *mouthpiece* of a telephone⟩ **2** : someone who expresses another person's ideas : SPOKESPERSON

mouth–to–mouth \ˌmaúth-tə-ˌmaúth\ *adj* : of, relating to, or being a method of artificial respiration in which the rescuer's mouth is placed tightly over the victim's mouth in order to force air into the lungs by blowing hard enough every few seconds to inflate them

mouth·wash \'maúth-ˌwȯsh, -ˌwäsh\ *n* : a liquid that usually kills germs and is used to clean the mouth and teeth and freshen the breath

mou·ton \'mü-ˌtän\ *n* : sheepskin that has been sheared, treated, and dyed to look like the pelt of a beaver or seal

¹mov·able *or* **move·able** \'mü-və-bəl\ *adj* **1** : capable of being moved : not fixed **2** : changing date from year to year ⟨Thanksgiving is a *movable* holiday⟩ — **mov·ably** \-blē\ *adv*

²movable *or* **moveable** *n* : a piece of property (as an article of furniture) that can be moved

¹move \'müv\ *vb* **moved; mov·ing** **1** : to change the place or position of : SHIFT ⟨*move* the chair closer⟩ **2** : to go from one place to another ⟨*move* into the shade⟩ **3** : to set in motion ⟨*moved* their feet⟩ **4 a** : to cause a person to act or decide : PERSUADE ⟨the report *moved* me to change my mind⟩ **b** : to take action : ACT **5** : to affect the feelings of ⟨the sad story *moved* me to tears⟩ **6** : to suggest according to the rules of a meeting ⟨*move* to adjourn⟩ **7** : to change hands or cause to change hands through sale or rental ⟨the store's stock must be *moved*⟩ **8 a** : to change residence **b** : to change place or position : STIR **9** : to cause to function : OPERATE ⟨*move* the handle to increase pressure⟩ **10** : to proceed in a certain direction ⟨we're *moving* up in the world⟩ **11** : to carry on one's life in a particular environment ⟨*moves* in high circles⟩ **12** : to go away : DEPART ⟨told them to *move* on⟩ **13** : to transfer a piece in a game (as chess) from one place to another **14** : to empty or cause to empty ⟨*move* the bowels⟩

²move *n* **1 a** : the act of moving a piece in a game **b** : the turn of a player to move **2 a** : a step taken to achieve a goal : MANEUVER **b** : the action of moving : MOVEMENT **c** : a change of residence or location — **on the move** **1** : moving from place to place **2** : moving ahead or making progress

move·less \'müv-ləs\ *adj* : not moving : FIXED, MOTIONLESS

move·ment \'müv-mənt\ *n* **1 a** : the act or process of moving **b** : an instance or manner of moving ⟨observe the *movement* of a star⟩ **2** : a tendency or trend ⟨detected a *movement* toward fairer pricing⟩ **3 a** : a program or series of acts working toward a desired end ⟨a *movement* for political reform⟩ **b** : the group taking part in such a series of acts ⟨join the *movement*⟩ **4** : a mechanical arrangement (as of wheels) for causing a particular motion (as in a clock or watch) **5** : a section of a longer piece of music **6** : an emptying of the bowels; *also* : the material emptied

mov·er \'mü-vər\ *n* : one that moves or sets something in motion; *esp* : a person or company that moves the belongings of others from one home or place of business to another

mov·ie \'mü-vē\ *n* **1** : MOTION PICTURE 1 **2 a** : a story represented in motion pictures **b** : a showing of a motion picture — often used in pl. with *the* **3** *pl* : the motion picture industry

mov·ie·go·er \-ˌgō(-ə)r\ *n* : a person who frequently attends the movies

mov·ing \'mü-viŋ\ *adj* **1** : changing place or position ⟨a *moving* target⟩ **2** : causing motion or action **3** : having the power to affect the feelings or sympathies ⟨a *moving* story of a faithful dog⟩ **4 a** : of or relating to a change of residence ⟨*moving* expenses⟩ **b** : used for moving belongings from one place to another ⟨a *moving* van⟩ — **mov·ing·ly** *adv*

moving picture *n* : MOTION PICTURE

¹mow \'maú\ *n* **1** : a stack of hay or straw **2** : the part of a barn where hay or straw is stored [Old English *mūga* "heap, stack"]

²mow \'mō\ *vb* **mowed; mowed** *or* **mown** \'mōn\; **mow·ing** **1** : to cut down with a scythe or machine ⟨*mow* hay⟩ **2** : to cut the standing leafy plant cover from ⟨*mow* a lawn⟩ **3** : to kill or destroy in great numbers **4** : to overcome completely : ROUT ⟨*mow* down the other team⟩ [Old English *māwan* "to mow (as hay)"] — **mow·er** \'mō(-ə)r\ *n*

moz·za·rel·la \ˌmät-sə-'rel-ə\ *n* : a moist white rubbery mild-flavored cheese that is much used in Italian cooking

Mr. \ˌmis-tər\ *n, pl* **Messrs.** \ˌmes-ərz\ **1** — used as a title before a man's last name or title of office ⟨*Mr.* President⟩ **2** — used to form a title for a man who represents the thing indicated ⟨*Mr.* Baseball⟩ [Middle English *Mr.*, an abbreviation of *master*]

Mrs. \ˌmis-əz, -əs, *especially Southern* ˌmiz-əz, -əs, *or* (ˌ)miz\ *n, pl* **Mes·dames** \mā-'däm, -'dam\ — used as a title before a married woman's last name [an abbreviation of *mistress*]

Ms. \(ˌ)miz\ *n* — used instead of *Miss* or *Mrs.* (as when it is unknown or unimportant whether the woman addressed is married or single) [probably a combination of *Miss* and *Mrs.*]

mu \'myü, 'mü\ *n* : the twelfth letter of the Greek alphabet — M or μ

¹much \'məch\ *adj* **more** \'mō(ə)r, 'mȯ(ə)r\; **most** \'mōst\ : great in quantity, amount, or extent ⟨has *much* money⟩ ⟨takes too *much* time⟩

²much *adv* **more; most** **1** : to a great or high level or extent ⟨*much* happier⟩ **2** : just about : NEARLY ⟨looks *much* as it did years ago⟩

³much *n* **1** : a great quantity, amount, extent, or part ⟨*much* that was said is false⟩ **2** : something important or impressive ⟨not *much* to look at⟩

mu·ci·lage \'myü-s(ə-)lij\ *n* **1** : a jellylike substance obtained especially from seaweeds that is similar to plant gums **2** : a water solution of a gum or similar substance used especially as an adhesive

muck \'mək\ *n* **1** : soft moist barnyard manure **2** : DIRT 1, FILTH **3 a** : dark rich soil **b** : MUD, MIRE — **mucky** \'mək-ē\ *adj*

muck·rak·er \'mək-ˌrā-kər\ *n* : one of a group of writers noted for seeking out and exposing abuses and misconduct in American business, government, and society at the beginning of the 20th century — **muck·rake** \-ˌrāk\ *vb*

mu·cous \'myü-kəs\ *adj* **1** : of, relating to, or resembling mucus ⟨*mucous* discharges⟩ **2** : producing or containing mucus ⟨a *mucous* gland⟩

mucous membrane *n* : a membrane rich in mucous glands; *esp* : one lining body passages and cavities which connect directly or indirectly with the outside

mu·cus \'myü-kəs\ *n* : a slippery sticky substance produced especially by mucous membranes (as of the nose and throat) which it moistens and protects

mud \'məd\ *n* : soft wet earth

\ə\ **abut**	\aú\ **out**	\i\ **tip**	\ȯ\ **saw**	\ú\ **foot**
\ər\ **further**	\ch\ **chin**	\ī\ **life**	\ȯi\ **coin**	\y\ **yet**
\a\ **mat**	\e\ **pet**	\j\ **job**	\th\ **thin**	\yü\ **few**
\ā\ **take**	\ē\ **easy**	\ŋ\ **sing**	\th\ **this**	\yú\ **cure**
\ä\ **cot, cart**	\g\ **go**	\ō\ **bone**	\ü\ **food**	\zh\ **vision**

mud dauber *n* : any of various wasps that construct mud cells in which the female places an egg with paralyzed insects or spiders as food for the larva

¹mud·dle \'məd-ªl\ *vb* **mud·dled; mud·dling** \'məd-liŋ, -ªl-iŋ\ **1** : to be or cause to be confused or bewildered : STUPEFY ⟨*muddled* by too much advice⟩ **2** : to mix up in a confused way ⟨*muddle* the household accounts⟩ **3** : to think or act in a confused way : BUNGLE ⟨*muddle* through a task⟩ — **mud·dler** \-lər, -ªl-ər\ *n*

²muddle *n* **1** : a state of confusion or bewilderment **2** : a confused mess : JUMBLE

¹mud·dy \'məd-ē\ *adj* **mud·di·er; -est 1** : filled or covered with mud ⟨a *muddy* pond⟩ ⟨*muddy* shoes⟩ **2** : resembling mud ⟨a *muddy* color⟩ ⟨*muddy* coffee⟩ **3** : not clear or bright : DULL, CLOUDY ⟨a *muddy* complexion⟩ **4** : unclear in meaning : MUDDLED ⟨*muddy* thinking⟩ — **mud·di·ness** *n*

²muddy *vb* **mud·died; mud·dy·ing 1** : to soil or stain with or as if with mud **2** : to make cloudy or dull **3** : to become or cause to become confused

mud puppy *n* : any of several large American salamanders; *esp* : one that has gills on the outside and is gray to rusty brown usually with bluish black spots

mud turtle *n* : any of various turtles that live on the bottom of bodies of fresh water

mu·ez·zin \m(y)ü-'ez-ªn\ *n* : a crier who summons Muslims to prayer

¹muff \'məf\ *n* : a soft thick tube-like covering with open ends in which both hands may be inserted for protection from cold [from Dutch *mof* "a cover for the hands", from early French *moufle* "mitten"]

²muff *n* : a clumsy or bungled performance; *esp* : a failure to hold a ball in attempting a catch [origin unknown] — **muff** *vb*

muf·fin \'məf-ən\ *n* : a bread made of batter containing egg that is baked in a small cup-shaped container

¹muff

muf·fle \'məf-əl\ *vb* **muf·fled; muf·fling** \'məf-(ə-)liŋ\ **1** : to wrap up so as to conceal or protect **2** : to deaden the sound of ⟨*muffle* a cry⟩

muf·fler \'məf-lər\ *n* **1** : a scarf worn to protect the neck **2** : something that deadens noises; *esp* : a device attached to the exhaust system of an automobile

muf·ti \'məf-tē\ *n* : civilian clothes ⟨an off-duty soldier in *mufti*⟩

¹mug \'məg\ *n* **1** : a usually large drinking cup with a handle **2** : the face or mouth of a person **3** : ¹PUNK, THUG

²mug *vb* **mugged; mug·ging 1** : to make faces especially to attract attention : GRIMACE **2** : ²PHOTOGRAPH; *esp* : to take a police photograph of

³mug *vb* **mugged; mug·ging** : to assault especially with the intention of robbing — **mug·ger** *n*

mug·gy \'məg-ē\ *adj* **mug·gi·er; -est** : being warm and humid ⟨a *muggy* day in August⟩ — **mug·gi·ness** *n*

Mu·ham·mad·an *or* **Mo·ham·med·an** \'mō-'ham-əd-ən *also* mü-\ *n* : MUSLIM — **Muhammadan** *adj* — **Mu·ham·mad·an·ism** \-,iz-əm\ *n*

muk·luk \'mək-,lək\ *n* **1** : an Eskimo boot of sealskin or reindeer skin **2** : a boot with a soft leather sole worn over several pairs of socks

mu·lat·to \m(y)ü-'lat-ō\ *n, pl* **-toes** *or* **-tos 1** : a person with one black and one white parent **2** : a person of mixed white and black descent

mul·ber·ry \'məl-,ber-ē\ *n* **1** : any of a genus of trees that have edible usually purple fruits resembling berries and leaves on which silkworms can be fed; *also* : the fruit of a mulberry **2** : a dark purple or purplish black

¹mulch \'məlch\ *n* : a covering (as of straw or sawdust) spread over the ground to protect the roots of plants from heat, cold, or evaporation, prevent soil loss, control weeds, enrich the soil, or keep fruit (as strawberries) clean

²mulch *vb* : to cover with mulch

¹mulct \'məlkt\ *n* : ¹FINE

²mulct *vb* **1** : to punish by a fine **2 a** : to defraud especially of money **b** : to obtain by dishonest means

¹mule \'myü(ə)l\ *n* **1** : the hybrid offspring of a horse and a donkey; *esp* : the offspring of a male donkey and a mare **2** : a very stubborn person **3** : a machine that draws and twists fiber into yarn or thread and winds it onto spindles [Middle English *mule* "the offspring of a donkey and a horse", from early French *mul* (same meaning), from Latin *multus* (same meaning)]

²mule *n* : a slipper that is open at the heel [from early French *mule* "slipper", from *mulleus* "a shoe worn by public officials"]

mule deer *n* : a long-eared deer of western North America that is larger and more heavily built than the common white-tailed deer

mule skinner *n* : a driver of mules

mu·le·teer \,myü-lə-'ti(ə)r\ *n* : a driver of mules

mul·ish \'myü-lish\ *adj* : STUBBORN 1a, INFLEXIBLE — **mul·ish·ly** *adv* — **mul·ish·ness** *n*

¹mull \'məl\ *vb* : to think about slowly and carefully : PONDER ⟨*mull* over an idea⟩ [Middle English *mullen* "to grind up or mix thoroughly", from *mul, mol* "dust"]

²mull *vb* : to sweeten, spice, and heat ⟨*mulled* wine⟩ [origin unknown]

mul·lein *also* **mul·len** \'məl-ən\ *n* : a tall herb related to the snapdragons and having coarse woolly leaves and spikes of usually yellow flowers

mul·let \'məl-ət\ *n, pl* **mullet** *or* **mullets 1** : any of a family of mostly gray food fishes **2** : any of a family of medium-sized usually red or golden fishes with two stringy feelers on the chin

mul·lion \'məl-yən\ *n* : a slender upright bar which separates the panes of a window or panels of a door — **mullion** *vb*

multi- *combining form* **1 a** : many : much ⟨*multi*colored⟩ **b** : more than two ⟨*multi*national⟩ ⟨*multi*racial⟩ **2** : many times over ⟨*multi*millionaire⟩ [derived from Latin *multus* "much, many"]

mul·ti·cel·lu·lar \,məl-ti-'sel-yə-lər, -,tī-\ *adj* : having or consisting of many cells — **mul·ti·cel·lu·lar·i·ty** \-,sel-yə-'lar-ət-ē\ *n*

mul·ti·col·ored \,məl-ti-'kəl-ərd\ *adj* : having, made up of, or including many colors

mul·ti·cul·tur·al \,məl-ti-'kəlch-rəl, -,tī-, -ə-rəl\ *adj* : of, relating to, reflecting, or adapted to diverse cultures ⟨a *multicultural* society⟩ — **mul·ti·cul·tur·al·ism** \-rə-,liz-əm\ *n*

mul·ti·di·men·sion·al \,məl-ti-də-'mench-nəl, -'mench-ən-ªl\ *adj* : made up of or involving two or more dimensions

mul·ti·far·i·ous \,məl-tə-'far-ē-əs, -'fer-\ *adj* : of many and various kinds ⟨the *multifarious* sounds of the city⟩

mul·ti·form \'məl-ti-,fȯrm\ *adj* : having many forms, shapes, or appearances

mul·ti·lat·er·al \,məl-ti-'lat-ə-rəl, -,tī-, -'la-trəl\ *adj* **1** : having many sides **2** : involving or taken part in by more than two nations or groups ⟨a *multilateral* treaty⟩ — **mul·ti·lat·er·al·ly** \-ē\ *adv*

mul·ti·lay·ered \,məl-ti-'lā-ərd, -'le(-ə)rd\ *or* **mul·ti·lay·er** \-'lā-ər, -'le(-ə)r\ *adj* : made up of or involving two or more layers or levels

mul·ti·me·dia \,məl-ti-'mēd-ē-ə\ *adj* : using or composed of more than one form of communication or expression ⟨a *multimedia* exhibit of photographs, films, and music⟩

mul·ti·mil·lion·aire \,məl-ti-,mil-yə-'na(ə)r, -,tī-, -'ne(ə)r, -'mil-yə-,na(ə)r, -,ne(ə)r\ *n* : a person whose wealth is estimated at several millions (as of dollars)

¹mul·ti·na·tion·al \,məl-ti-'nash-nəl, -ən-°l\ *adj* **1** : of, relating to, or involving more than two nations **2** : having divisions in more than two countries

²multinational *n* : a multinational corporation

¹mul·ti·ple \'məl-tə-pəl\ *adj* **1** : containing, involving, or consisting of more than one ⟨*multiple* copies⟩ **2** : ¹MANY 1 ⟨a person of *multiple* achievements⟩

²multiple *n* : the product of a quantity by an integer ⟨35 is a *multiple* of 7⟩

mul·ti·ple–choice \,məl-tə-pəl-'chȯis\ *adj* **1** : having several answers from which one is to be chosen **2** : made up of multiple-choice questions ⟨a *multiple-choice* test⟩

multiple fruit *n* : a fruit (as a mulberry) formed from a cluster of flowers

multiple sclerosis *n* : a disease marked by patches of hardened tissue in the brain or spinal cord resulting in partial or complete paralysis and muscular twitching

¹mul·ti·plex \'məl-tə-,pleks\ *adj* **1** : MULTIPLE **2** : being or relating to a system of transmitting several messages simultaneously on the same circuit or channel

²multiplex *n* : a complex that houses several movie theaters

mul·ti·pli·cand \,məl-tə-pli-'kand\ *n* : the number that is to be multiplied by another

mul·ti·pli·ca·tion \,məl-tə-plə-'kā-shən\ *n* **1** : the act or process of multiplying **2** : a mathematical operation that for the set of integers is equivalent to adding a column containing only one number repeated the number of times specified by the other and that is extended to other sets of numbers (as rational numbers or real numbers) by rules that are true for the integers

multiplication sign *n* : a symbol used to indicate multiplication: **a** : TIMES SIGN **b** : DOT 2c

mul·ti·pli·ca·tive \,məl-tə-'plik-ət-iv, 'məl-tə-plə-,kāt-\ *adj* : of, relating to, or associated with a mathematical operation of multiplication ⟨the *multiplicative* property of 0 requires that $a \cdot 0 = 0$ and $0 \cdot a = 0$⟩

multiplicative identity *n* : an element of a set that when multiplied by any element of the set leaves the element unchanged ⟨the integer 1 is a *multiplicative identity* in the set of real numbers⟩

multiplicative inverse *n* : an element (as a reciprocal) of a mathematical set that when multiplied by a given element gives the identity element ⟨in the set of all rational numbers the *multiplicative inverse* of 2 is ½ since $2 \times ½ = 1$⟩

mul·ti·plic·i·ty \,məl-tə-'plis-ət-ē\ *n, pl* **-ties** **1** : the quality or state of being multiple or various **2** : a great number

mul·ti·pli·er \'məl-tə-,plī(-ə)r\ *n* **1** : one that multiplies **2** : a number by which another number is multiplied

mul·ti·ply \'məl-tə-,plī\ *vb* **-plied; -ply·ing** **1 a** : to increase in number : make or become more numerous **b** : to produce offspring : BREED ⟨rabbits *multiply* rapidly⟩ **2 a** : to use in finding a product by multiplication ⟨*multiply* 7 and 8⟩ ⟨*multiply* 7 by 8⟩ **b** : to perform multiplication ⟨first divide and then *multiply*⟩

mul·ti·pur·pose \,məl-ti-'pər-pəs, -,tī-\ *adj* : having more than one use ⟨*multipurpose* furniture⟩

mul·ti·ra·cial \,məl-ti-'rā-shəl, -,tī-\ *adj* : composed of, relating to, or representing various races

mul·ti·stage \'məl-tl-,stāj\ *adj* : operating in or involving two or more stages ⟨a *multistage* rocket⟩

mul·ti·tude \'məl-tə-,t(y)üd\ *n* : a great number of things or people

syn MULTITUDE, CROWD, THRONG, MOB mean a large number of individuals. MULTITUDE usually suggests a truly great number ⟨*multitudes* made homeless by war⟩ ⟨a *multitude* of stars⟩ CROWD suggests a disorganized group that is closely packed together ⟨a *crowd* of onlookers at the scene of the accident⟩ THRONG suggests many people gathered together and wandering about ⟨*throngs* of people were at the fair⟩ MOB suggests disorderly behavior and disturbance and the possibility of violence ⟨police faced an angry *mob* of demonstrators⟩

mul·ti·tu·di·nous \,məl-tə-'t(y)üd-nəs, -°n-əs\ *adj* : consisting of a multitude ⟨*multitudinous* questions⟩

mul·ti·vi·ta·min \,məl-ti-'vīt-ə-mən\ *adj* : containing several vitamins and especially all known to be necessary to health ⟨a *multivitamin* formula⟩

¹mum \'məm\ *adj* : SILENT 1 ⟨keep *mum*⟩

²mum *n* : CHRYSANTHEMUM

³mum *chiefly British variant of* MOM

¹mum·ble \'məm-bəl\ *vb* **mum·bled; mum·bling** \-b(ə-)liŋ\ **1** : to speak softly and unclearly **2** : to eat with or as if with toothless gums ⟨a baby *mumbling* its food⟩ — **mum·bler** \-b(ə-)lər\ *n* — **mum·bling·ly** \-bliŋ-lē\ *adv*

²mumble *n* : speech that is not clear enough to be understood

mum·bo jum·bo \,məm-bō-'jəm-bō\ *n* **1** : a complicated ceremony **2** : confusing or meaningless talk

mum·mer \'məm-ər\ *n* **1** : a person who celebrates a holiday (as Christmas) by making merry in disguise **2** : ACTOR

mum·mery \'məm-ə-rē\ *n, pl* **-mer·ies** **1** : a performance by mummers **2** : a ridiculous ceremony

mum·mi·fy \'məm-i-,fī\ *vb* **-fied; -fy·ing** **1** : to embalm and dry as or like a mummy **2** : to dry up like the skin of a mummy : SHRIVEL — **mum·mi·fi·ca·tion** \,məm-i-fə-'kā-shən\ *n*

mum·my \'məm-ē\ *n, pl* **mummies** **1** : a body prepared for burial in the manner of the ancient Egyptians **2** : an unusually well-preserved body

mumps \'məm(p)s\ *n sing or pl* : a contagious disease caused by a virus and marked by fever and by swelling especially of salivary glands

mumu *variant of* MUUMUU

munch \'mənch\ *vb* : to chew with a crunching sound : eat with enjoyment — **munch·er** *n*

mun·dane \,mən-'dān, 'mən-,dān\ *adj* **1** : of or relating to the world : WORLDLY **2** : having to do with the practical details of everyday life — **mun·dane·ly** *adv*

mu·nic·i·pal \myu̇-'nis-(ə-)pəl\ *adj* : of or relating to a municipality ⟨*municipal* government⟩

mu·nic·i·pal·i·ty \myu̇-,nis-ə-'pal-ət-ē\ *n, pl* **-ties** : a self-governing city or town

mu·nif·i·cent \myu̇-'nif-ə-sənt\ *adj* **1** : very generous in giving ⟨a *munificent* host⟩ **2** : given generously or in plenty ⟨a *munificent* gift⟩ — **mu·nif·i·cent·ly** *adv*

mu·ni·tions \myu̇-'nish-ənz\ *n pl* : military supplies and equipment; *esp* : AMMUNITION

¹mu·ral \'myu̇r-əl\ *adj* **1** : of or relating to a wall **2** : applied to and made part of a wall surface ⟨a *mural* painting⟩

²mural *n* : a mural work of art

¹mur·der \'mərd-ər\ *n* **1** : the intentional and unlawful killing of a person **2** : something that is difficult or dangerous ⟨that test was *murder*⟩ ⟨traffic was *murder* this morning⟩

²murder *vb* **mur·dered; mur·der·ing** \'mərd-(ə-)riŋ\ **1** : to commit murder **2** : to spoil by performing or using poorly ⟨*murder* a song⟩ ⟨*murder* the English language⟩ **syn** see KILL — **mur·der·er** \-ər-ər\ *n*

mur·der·ous \'mərd-(ə-)rəs\ *adj* **1** : intending or capable of causing murder or bloodshed : DEADLY ⟨*murderous* ma-

\ə\ abut		\au̇\ out		\i\ tip		\ȯ\ saw	\u̇\ foot
\ər\ further		\ch\ chin		\ī\ life		\ȯi\ coin	\y\ yet
\a\ mat		\e\ pet		\j\ job		\th\ thin	\yü\ few
\ā\ take		\ē\ easy		\ŋ\ sing		\th\ this	\yu̇\ cure
\ä\ cot, cart		\g\ go		\ō\ bone		\ü\ food	\zh\ vision

chine-gun fire) **2** : very difficult to bear or withstand (a *murderous* glance) (*murderous* heat) — **mur·der·ous·ly** *adv*

murk \ˈmərk\ *n* : deep darkness or gloom; *also* : ¹FOG 1a

murky \ˈmər-kē\ *adj* **murk·i·er; -est 1** : very dark or gloomy **2** : FOGGY 1, MISTY **3** : difficult to understand (a *murky* reply designed to confuse) — **murk·i·ness** *n*

¹**mur·mur** \ˈmər-mər\ *n* **1** : a muttered complaint : GRUMBLE **2** : a low, faint, and continuous sound (the *murmur* of bees) **3** : an irregular heart sound indicating an abnormality in the heart's function or structure — called also *heart murmur*

²**murmur** *vb* **1** : to make a murmur (the breeze *murmured* in the pines) **2** : to say in a voice too low to be heard clearly — **mur·mur·er** *n*

mur·mur·ous \ˈmərm-(ə-)rəs\ *adj* : filled with or characterized by murmurs

mur·rain \ˈmər-ən, ˈmə-rən\ *n* : a disease that spreads among domestic animals or plants

murre \ˈmər\ *n* : any of several auks of northern seas that have narrow bills

mus·ca·tel \ˌməs-kə-ˈtel\ *n* : a sweet wine that is golden to dark amber in color

¹**mus·cle** \ˈməs-əl\ *n* **1 a** : a body tissue consisting of long cells that can contract and produce motion **b** : an organ that is a mass of muscle tissue attached at either end (as to bones) and that by contracting moves or checks the movement of a body part **2 a** : muscular strength : BRAWN **b** : ¹POWER 2 (lacks the *muscle* to make good on campaign promises)

Word History Few people today are likely to think of their muscles as resembling mice. The ancient Romans, however, saw a likeness, especially in the major muscles of the arms and legs. For that reason the Latin word *musculus,* which originally meant "little mouse", came to be used to mean "muscle". Latin *musculus* became *muscle* in early French, from which it came into English. [from early French *muscle* "muscle", from Latin *musculus* "muscle, little mouse", from *mus* "mouse"]

²**muscle** *vb* **mus·cled; mus·cling** \ˈməs-(ə-)liŋ\ **1** : to force from a position (was *muscled* out of office by political opponents) **2** : to force one's way (*muscled* through the crowd)

mus·cle–bound \ˈməs-əl-ˌbau̇nd\ *adj* : having abnormally large muscles that do not move and stretch easily

muscle tone *n* : the state of being partly contracted that is characteristic of normal muscle

muscle spindle *n* : a structure at the ending of a group of nerve fibers in a muscle that is sensitive to stretching of the muscle, consists of small striated muscle fibers richly supplied with nerve fibers, and is enclosed in a sheath of connective tissue — called also *stretch receptor*

Mus·co·vite \ˈməs-kə-ˌvīt\ *n* : a person born or living in Moscow — **Muscovite** *adj*

mus·cu·lar \ˈməs-kyə-lər\ *adj* **1 a** : of, relating to, or being muscle **b** : performed by the muscles **2** : having well-developed muscles : STRONG

muscular dys·tro·phy \-ˈdis-trə-fē\ *n* : an inherited disease characterized by increasing weakness of muscles

mus·cu·la·ture \ˈməs-kyə-lə-ˌchu̇(ə)r\ *n* : the muscles of the body or of one of its parts

¹**muse** \ˈmyüz\ *vb* **mused; mus·ing** : PONDER, MEDITATE [Middle English *musen* "to ponder", from early French *muser* "to gape, muse", from *muse* "mouth of an animal"]

²**muse** *n* **1** *cap* : any of the nine sister goddesses of song and poetry and the arts and sciences in Greek mythology **2** : a source of inspiration [Middle English *Muse* "one of the nine goddesses of the arts", from early French *Muse* (same meaning), from Latin *Musa* (same meaning), from Greek *Mousa* "Muse"]

mu·se·um \myu̇-ˈzē-əm\ *n* : a building or part of a building in which objects of interest in one or more of the arts or sciences are displayed

Word History The ancient Greeks worshiped nine sister goddesses, each of whom was called a *Mousa.* In English we now refer to them as the Muses. The Greeks believed that each Muse was the goddess of a particular art or science. A place that was dedicated to these goddesses — and to the arts and sciences for which they stood — was called a *Mouseion.* The Greek *Mouseion* became *Museum* in Latin, from which it was borrowed into English about 300 years ago. [from Latin *Museum* "a place devoted to the Muses, a place for the study of special arts and sciences", from Greek *Mouseion* (same meaning), from *Mouseios* "of the Muses", from *Mousa* "Muse, goddess of an art or science" — related to MUSIC]

¹**mush** \ˈməsh\ *n* **1** : cornmeal boiled in water **2** : something soft and spongy or shapeless **3** : sickeningly sweet sentimentality [probably an altered form of *mash*] — **mush·i·ly** \-ə-lē\ *adv* — **mushy** \-ē\ *adj*

²**mush** *vb* : to travel over snow with a sled drawn by dogs — often used as a command to a dog team [probably from *moncher,* a word in the French of Canada and the northern United States meaning "to go fast"] — **mush·er** *n*

³**mush** *n* : a trip across snow with a dog team

¹**mush·room** \ˈməsh-ˌrüm, -ˌru̇m\ *n* **1** : a fleshy part of a fungus that bears spores, grows above ground, and suggests an umbrella in shape; *esp* : one that is edible **2** : FUNGUS 1

²**mushroom** *vb* : to appear or develop suddenly or increase rapidly (the population *mushroomed*)

mu·sic \ˈmyü-zik\ *n* **1 a** : the art of producing pleasing or expressive combinations of tones especially with melody, rhythm, and usually harmony **b** : compositions made according to the rules of music **c** : a musical composition set down on paper (bring your *music*) **2 a** : sounds that have rhythm, harmony, and melody **b** : an agreeable sound (the *music* of a brook) [Middle English *musik* "music", from early French *musique* (same meaning), from Latin *musica* (same meaning), from Greek *mousikē* "any art under the control or guidance of the Muses", derived from *Mousa* "Muse" — related to MUSEUM; see *Word History* at MUSEUM]

¹**mu·si·cal** \ˈmyü-zi-kəl\ *adj* **1 a** : of or relating to music or the writing or performance of music (*musical* instruments) **b** : having the pleasing harmonious qualities of music (a *musical* voice) **2** : fond of or gifted in music (a *musical* family) **3** : set to or accompanied by music — **mu·si·cal·ly** \-k(ə-)lē\ *adv*

²**musical** *n* : a film or play that tells a story and that includes both musical numbers and dialogue

musical comedy *n* : ²MUSICAL

mu·si·cale \ˌmyü-zi-ˈkal\ *n* : a usually private social gathering to hear music

mu·si·cal·i·ty \ˌmyü-zi-ˈkal-ət-ē\ *n* : the quality of being musical or melodious

music box *n* : a box containing a mechanical device that uses gears like those of a clock to play a tune

mu·si·cian \myu̇-ˈzish-ən\ *n* : a person who writes, sings, or plays music and especially as a profession — **mu·si·cian·ship** \-ˌship\ *n*

musk \ˈməsk\ *n* : a strong-smelling substance obtained usually from the male musk deer and used in perfume; *also* : an odor of or resembling that of musk — **musky** \ˈməs-kē\ *adj*

mushroom 1

musk deer *n* : a small hornless deer about one meter long and 50 centimeters tall that lives in the high regions of central Asia

mus·keg \'məs-ˌkeg\ *n* : ¹BOG; *esp* : a bog of northern North America that is composed of many layers of half-decayed plants and especially sphagnum

mus·kel·lunge \'məs-kə-ˌlənj\ *n, pl* **muskellunge** : a large North American pike that may weigh 27 to 36 kilograms and is a valuable sport fish

mus·ket \'məs-kət\ *n* : a muzzle-loading firearm that was once used by soldiers

mus·ke·teer \ˌməs-kə-'ti(ə)r\ *n* : a soldier armed with a musket

mus·kie *or* **mus·ky** \'məs-kē\ *n, pl* **muskies** : MUSKELLUNGE

musk·mel·on \'məsk-ˌmel-ən\ *n* : a small round to oval melon that is related to the cucumber and has usually sweet edible green or orange flesh — compare CANTALOUPE

musk–ox \'məs-ˌkäks\ *n* : a large shaggy-coated wild ox native to Greenland and the barren lands of northern North America

musk·rat \'məs-ˌkrat\ *n, pl* **muskrat** *or* **muskrats** : a North American rodent that lives in or near the water, has a long scaly tail and webbed hind feet, and is valued for its glossy usually dark brown fur; *also* : its fur or pelt

musk-ox

musk turtle *n* : any of several small American freshwater turtles with a strong musky odor

Mus·lim \'məz-ləm, 'mus-, 'muz-\ *or* **Mos·lem** \'mäz- *also* 'mäs-\ *n* : a follower of Islam [from Arabic *muslim,* literally "one who surrenders (to God)"] — **Muslim** *or* **Moslem** *adj*

mus·lin \'məz-lən\ *n* : a cotton fabric of plain weave [from French *mousseline* "muslin", derived from Arabic *mawṣilīy* "of Mosul (a city in Iraq)"]

¹**muss** \'məs\ *n* : a state of disorder : MESS — **mussy** \-ē\ *adj*

²**muss** *vb* : to make untidy : RUMPLE ⟨*mussed* my hair⟩

mus·sel \'məs-əl\ *n* **1** : an edible saltwater mollusk with a long dark hinged double shell **2** : any of numerous freshwater mollusks of the central U.S. whose hinged double shells are lined with mother-of-pearl

¹**must** \məs(t), 'məst\ *helping verb, present & past all persons* **must** **1** : is commanded, requested, or urged to ⟨the train *must* stop⟩ ⟨you *must* read that book⟩ **2** : is forced, required, or obliged to ⟨leaves *must* fall⟩ ⟨one *must* eat to live⟩ ⟨we *must* be quiet⟩ **3** : is determined to ⟨if you *must* go⟩ **4** : is very likely to ⟨it *must* be time⟩ ⟨*must* have lost it⟩ **5** : is certain to ⟨the bus *must* be coming⟩

²**must** \'məst\ *n* : something required or absolutely necessary ⟨new shoes are a *must*⟩

mus·tache *or* **mous·tache** \'məs-ˌtash, (ˌ)məs-'tash\ *n* **1** : the hair growing on the human upper lip **2** : hair or bristles about the mouth of an animal

mus·ta·chio \(ˌ)məs-'tash-(ē-)ō, -'täsh-\ *n, pl* **-chios** : MUSTACHE; *esp* : a large mustache [from Spanish *mostacho* and Italian *mustaccio,* both meaning "'mustache'"] — **mus·ta·chioed** \-(ē-)ōd\ *adj*

mus·tang \'məs-ˌtaŋ\ *n* **1** : the small hardy half-wild horse of the western plains of North America directly descended from horses brought in by the Spaniards **2** : BRONCO 1

　　Word History Many American cowboy practices can be traced back to those of the Spanish. One such practice is a yearly roundup of unbranded or stray cattle. Centuries ago in Spain, cattle without owners were rounded up each year and sold. The Spanish word for this roundup was *mesta,* which came from a Latin phrase that meant "mixed animals". From *mesta,* the Spanish created the word *mestengo,* meaning "a wild or stray animal". In the form of Spanish spoken in Mexico, *mestengo* came to be used for wild or stray horses. As these horses became more and more common in the western plains of the United States, English borrowed the Mexican Spanish word *mestengo* as *mustang.* [from American Spanish *mestengo* "a wild or stray horse", from Spanish *mestengo* "a stray animal", derived from *mesta* "an annual roundup of stray cattle", from Latin *(animalia) mixta* "mixed animals"]

mus·tard \'məs-tərd\ *n* **1** : a yellow sharp-tasting powder of the seeds of a common mustard used in food seasonings or in medicine **2** : any of several yellow-flowered herbs related to the turnips and cabbages

mustard gas *n* : a poisonous gas used in war which has violent irritating and especially blistering effects

mustard plaster *n* : a dressing made of a paste containing powdered mustard that is applied to the skin (as of the back or chest) to cause redness and irritation in the surface layers of the skin and reduce inflammation deeper down

¹**mus·ter** \'məs-tər\ *vb* **mus·tered; mus·ter·ing** \-t(ə-)riŋ\ **1** : to assemble (as troops) for roll call or inspection **2** : to collect and display ⟨all the strength I could *muster*⟩

²**muster** *n* **1 a** : an act of assembling; *esp* : a formal military inspection or drill **b** : an assembled group : COLLECTION **2** : critical examination ⟨work that would never pass *muster*⟩

muster out *vb* : to discharge from service

mustn't \'məs-ᵊnt\ : must not

musty \'məs-tē\ *adj* **must·i·er; -est** **1 a** : affected by dampness or mildew : MOLDY **b** : tasting or smelling of dampness and decay **2** : smelling of musk **3 a** : ¹STALE 2, TRITE **b** : OUTMODED, ANTIQUATED — **must·i·ness** *n*

mu·ta·ble \'myüt-ə-bəl\ *adj* **1** : likely to change often : INCONSTANT **2 a** : capable of change **b** : able or likely to mutate — **mu·ta·bil·i·ty** \ˌmyüt-ə-'bil-ət-ē\ *n*

¹**mu·tant** \'myüt-ᵊnt\ *adj* : of, relating to, or produced by mutation

²**mutant** *n* : a mutant individual

mu·tate \'myü-ˌtāt\ *vb* **mu·tat·ed; mu·tat·ing** : to undergo or cause to undergo mutation

mu·ta·tion \myü-'tā-shən\ *n* **1** : a basic and important change **2 a** : an inherited change in genetic material involving either a physical change (as breaking and inverting a part) in a chromosome or a change in the chemical structure of a gene; *also* : the process of producing a mutation **b** : an individual, strain, or trait resulting from mutation

¹**mute** \'myüt\ *adj* **mut·er; mut·est** **1** : unable to speak often because of a problem (as from never having learned speech) that can be corrected **2** : felt but not expressed ⟨*mute* sympathy⟩ **3** : not pronounced : SILENT ⟨the *mute* "b" in "thumb"⟩ — **mute·ly** *adv* — **mute·ness** *n*

²**mute** *n* **1** : a person who cannot or does not speak **2** : a device on a musical instrument that deadens, softens, or muffles its tone **3** : ²STOP 9

³**mute** *vb* **mut·ed; mut·ing** **1** : to muffle or reduce the sound

mute 2

\ə\ **abut**		\aú\ **out**	\i\ **tip**	\ȯ\ **saw**	\ú\ **foot**
\ər\ **further**		\ch\ **chin**	\ī\ **life**	\ȯi\ **coin**	\y\ **yet**
\a\ **mat**		\e\ **pet**	\j\ **job**	\th\ **thin**	\yü\ **few**
\ā\ **take**		\ē\ **easy**	\ŋ\ **sing**	\th\ **this**	\yú\ **cure**
\ä\ **cot, cart**		\g\ **go**	\ō\ **bone**	\ü\ **food**	\zh\ **vision**

of **2** : to tone down ⟨*muted* his criticism⟩

mu·ti·late \'myüt-ᵊl-,āt\ *vb* **-lat·ed; -lat·ing** **1** : to cut off or destroy a necessary part (as a limb) : MAIM **2** : to make imperfect by cutting or altering severely : RUIN ⟨*mutilate* a play⟩ — **mu·ti·la·tion** \,myüt-ᵊl-'ā-shən\ *n* — **mu·ti·la·tor** \'myüt-ᵊl-,āt-ər\ *n*

mu·ti·neer \,myüt-ᵊn-'i(ə)r\ *n* : a person who is guilty of mutiny

mu·ti·nous \'myüt-ᵊn-əs, 'myüt-nəs\ *adj* **1** : inclined to or in a state of mutiny : REBELLIOUS ⟨a *mutinous* crew⟩ **2** : relating to or being mutiny ⟨*mutinous* acts⟩ — **mu·ti·nous·ly** *adv*

mu·ti·ny \'myüt-ᵊn-ē, 'myüt-nē\ *n, pl* **-nies** : refusal to obey authority; *esp* : a military outbreak against the officer in charge   **syn** see REBELLION — **mutiny** *vb*

mutt \'mət\ *n* : a mongrel dog : CUR

mut·ter \'mət-ər\ *vb* **1** : ¹MUMBLE 1 **2** : to murmur complainingly or angrily : GRUMBLE — **mutter** *n* — **mut·ter·er** \-ər-ər\ *n*

mut·ton \'mət-ᵊn\ *n* : the flesh of a mature sheep [from French *mouton* "sheep"]

mut·ton·chops \'mət-ᵊn-,chäps\ *n pl* : whiskers framing a man's face that are narrow at the temple and broad and round by the lower jaws

mu·tu·al \'myüch-(ə-)wəl, 'myü-chəl\ *adj* **1 a** : given and received in equal amount ⟨*mutual* favors⟩ **b** : having the same relation one to the other ⟨*mutual* enemies⟩ **2** : owned, shared, or enjoyed by two or more at the same time : JOINT ⟨our *mutual* friend⟩ ⟨*mutual* defense⟩ **3** : organized so that the customers share directly in the company's profits and losses ⟨a *mutual* savings bank⟩ ⟨a *mutual* insurance company⟩ — **mu·tu·al·ly** \-ē\ *adv*

mu·tu·al·ism \'myüch-(ə-)wə-,liz-əm, 'myü-chə-,liz-\ *n* : association between different kinds of organisms that benefits both

muu·muu *or* **mu·mu** \'mü-,mü\ *n* : a usually long, loose-fitting, and brightly-colored dress originally worn in Hawaii

¹muz·zle \'məz-əl\ *n* **1** : the nose and jaws of an animal : SNOUT **2** : a covering for the mouth and jaws of an animal used to keep it from eating or biting **3** : the open end of a weapon from which the missile is fired

²muzzle *vb* **muz·zled; muz·zling** \'məz-(ə-)liŋ\ **1** : to put a muzzle on **2** : to prevent free or normal expression by : GAG ⟨the dictator *muzzled* the press⟩

muz·zle–load·er \,məz-əl-'(l)ōd-ər\ *n* : a gun that is loaded through the muzzle — **muz·zle–load·ing** \-'(l)ōd-iŋ\ *adj*

my \(')mī, mə\ *adj* : of or relating to me or myself ⟨*my* head⟩ ⟨kept *my* promise⟩ ⟨*my* injuries⟩

my·ce·li·um \mī-'sē-lē-əm\ *n, pl* **-lia** \-lē-ə\ *also* **-li·ums** : the part of the body of a fungus that does not reproduce and usually consists of a mass of hyphae that are often growing in something else (as soil, organic matter, or the tissues of a plant or animal host) — **my·ce·li·al** \-lē-əl\ *adj*

-my·cin \'mīs-ᵊn\ *combining form* : a substance made from a fungus-like bacterium [strepto*mycin*]

my·col·o·gist \mī-'käl-ə-jəst\ *n* : a person who is a specialist or expert in mycology

my·col·o·gy \mī-'käl-ə-jē\ *n* **1** : a branch of botany dealing with fungi **2** : fungal life

my·elin \'mī-ə-lən\ *n* : a soft white somewhat fatty material that forms a thick covering surrounding certain nerve fibers

my·elin·at·ed \'mī-ə-lə-,nāt-əd\ *adj* : having a myelin covering ⟨*myelinated* nerve fibers⟩

myelin sheath *n* : a layer of myelin surrounding some nerve fibers

my·nah *or* **my·na** \'mī-nə\ *n* : any of various Asian starlings; *esp* : one that is mostly black and is often tamed and trained to imitate the sounds of words

myn·heer \mə-'ne(ə)r\ *n* : a male Netherlander — used as a title equal to *Mr.*

myo·fi·bril \,mī-ō-'fīb-rəl, -'fib-\ *n* : any of the long thin con-

tracting protein elements of a muscle cell that are composed of actin and myosin

my·o·pia \mī-'ō-pē-ə\ *n* : the condition of being nearsighted or shortsighted — **my·o·pic** \-'ō-pik, -'äp-ik\ *adj*

my·o·sin \'mī-ə-sən\ *n* : a protein of muscle that with actin is active in muscular contraction

¹myr·i·ad \'mir-ē-əd\ *n* **1** : ten thousand **2** : a large but not specified or counted number ⟨the *myriads* of stars⟩

²myriad *adj* : extremely numerous ⟨the *myriad* grains of sand on a beach⟩

myr·ia·pod *also* **myr·io·pod** \'mir-ē-ə-,päd\ *n* : any of a group of arthropods including the millipedes and centipedes — **myriapod** *also* **myriopod** *adj*

myrrh \'mər\ *n* : a brown slightly bitter gum obtained from African and Arabian trees and used especially in perfumes or formerly in incense

myr·tle \'mərt-ᵊl\ *n* **1** : a common evergreen shrub of southern Europe with shining leaves, fragrant white or rosy flowers, and black berries **2 a** : any of the family of chiefly tropical shrubs or trees (as eucalyptus or guava) to which the common myrtle belongs **b** : ¹PERIWINKLE

myrtle 1

my·self \mī-'self, mə-\ *pron* **1** : the one that is I — used for emphasis or to show that the subject and object of the verb are the same ⟨I'll go *myself*⟩ ⟨I'm going to get *myself* a new job⟩ **2** : my normal or healthy self ⟨didn't feel *myself* yesterday⟩

mys·te·ri·ous \mis-'tir-ē-əs\ *adj* : containing, suggesting, or presenting a mystery : difficult or impossible to understand ⟨the *mysterious* ways of nature⟩ — **mys·te·ri·ous·ly** *adv*

mys·tery \'mis-t(ə-)rē\ *n, pl* **-ter·ies** **1 a** : a religious truth that cannot be fully understood **b** : any of the 15 events (as the Nativity, the Crucifixion, or the Assumption) which serve as subjects for meditation by Roman Catholics as they say the rosary **2 a** : something that has not been or cannot be explained ⟨where they went is a *mystery*⟩ **b** : a deep secret ⟨kept their plans a *mystery*⟩ **3** : a work of fiction dealing with the solution of a mysterious crime

  syn MYSTERY, ENIGMA, PUZZLE mean something which is hard to understand or explain. MYSTERY applies to what cannot be fully understood by human reason or easily explained ⟨the *mystery* surrounding the building of those ancient temples⟩ ENIGMA applies to words or actions very difficult to interpret correctly ⟨what she meant by her last remark is an *enigma*⟩ PUZZLE applies to a tricky problem that challenges one to provide a solution ⟨it's a *puzzle* who took the chairs from the room and why⟩

mystery play *n* : a play in the Middle Ages based on stories from the Bible (as the creation of the world or the life and death of Jesus Christ

¹mys·tic \'mis-tik\ *adj* **1** : MYSTICAL 1 **2** : of or relating to magic : OCCULT **3** : MYSTERIOUS, AWESOME

²mystic *n* : a person who seeks direct knowledge of God through meditation and prayer

mys·ti·cal \'mis-ti-kəl\ *adj* **1** : having a spiritual meaning or reality that is not immediately apparent to the senses or the mind **2** : of, relating to, or resulting from communication directly with God — **mys·ti·cal·ly** \-k(ə-)lē\ *adv*

mys·ti·cism \'mis-tə-,siz-əm\ *n* **1** : the experience of mystical union or direct communication with God **2** : the belief that direct knowledge of God or of spiritual truth can be achieved through deep meditation

mys·ti·fy \'mis-tə-,fī\ *vb* **-fied; -fy·ing** : to confuse thoroughly the understanding of **syn** see PUZZLE — **mys·ti·fi·ca·tion** \,mis-tə-fə-'kā-shən\ *n*

mys·tique \mis-'tēk\ *n* : a set of beliefs and attitudes developing around an object or associated with a group or activity ⟨the *mystique* of mountain climbing⟩

myth \'mith\ *n*　**1** : a legend often describing the adventures of superhuman beings that is usually part of a people's religion and that attempts to describe the origin of their customs or beliefs or to explain mysterious events (as the changing of the seasons)　**2** : a person or thing that exists only in the imagination ⟨the dragon is a *myth*⟩　**3** : a popular belief that is false or unsupported

myth·i·cal \'mith-i-kəl\ *also* **myth·ic** \'mith-ik\ *adj*　**1** : based on, described in, or being a myth ⟨Hercules is a *mythical* hero⟩　**2** : existing only in the imagination : IMAGINARY ⟨the gremlin is a *mythical* creature⟩ — **myth·i·cal·ly** \-i-k(ə-)lē\ *adv*

my·thol·o·gy \mith-'äl-ə-jē\ *n, pl* **-gies**　**1** : a collection of myths; *esp* : the myths dealing with the gods and heroes of a particular people ⟨Greek *mythology*⟩　**2** : a branch of knowledge that deals with myth — **myth·o·log·i·cal** \,mith-ə-'läj-i-kəl\ *adj*

myxo·my·cete \,mik-sō-'mī-,sēt, -(,)mī-'sēt\ *n* : SLIME MOLD

N

n \'en\ *n, often cap*　**1** : the 14th letter of the English alphabet　**2** : an unspecified quantity ⟨*n* samples of vaccine⟩

-n — see [1]-EN

nab \'nab\ *vb* **nabbed; nab·bing**　**1** : to seize and take into custody : ARREST　**2** : to seize suddenly; *esp* : [1]STEAL 2a

na·bob \'nā-,bäb\ *n*　**1** : a governor of a province of the Mogul empire in India　**2** : a person of great wealth or importance

na·celle \nə-'sel\ *n* : an enclosed shelter on an aircraft for an engine or sometimes for the crew

na·cre \'nā-kər\ *n* : MOTHER-OF-PEARL

na·dir \'nā-,di(ə)r, 'nād-ər\ *n*　**1** : the point of the celestial sphere that is directly opposite the zenith and directly under the observer　**2** : the lowest point ⟨our hopes reached their *nadir*⟩

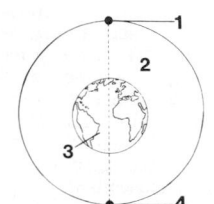

nadir 1: *1* zenith, *2* celestial sphere, *3* earth, *4* nadir

¹nag \'nag\ *n* : [1]HORSE 1a; *esp* : an old or broken-down horse [Middle English *nagge* "horse"]

²nag *vb* **nagged; nag·ging**　**1** : to find fault constantly : COMPLAIN　**2** : to be a continuing cause of annoyance or pain ⟨a *nagging* toothache⟩ [probably of Scandinavian origin] — **nag·ger** *n*

Na·hum \'nā-(h)əm\ *n* — see BIBLE table

na·iad \'nā-əd, 'nī-, -,ad\ *n, pl* **na·iads** *or* **na·ia·des** \-ə-,dēz\　**1** : one of the nymphs living in lakes, rivers, springs, and fountains　**2** : the water-dwelling larva of some insects (as a mayfly, dragonfly, damselfly, or stone fly)

¹nail \'nā(ə)l\ *n*　**1** : a horny covering or claw at the end of the fingers and toes of human beings, apes, and many other mammals　**2** : a slender usually pointed fastener with a head designed to be pounded in

²nail *vb*　**1** : to fasten with or as if with a nail　**2** : [1]CATCH 1, TRAP ⟨*nail* a thief⟩ — **nail·er** *n*

nail·brush \'nāl-,brəsh\ *n* : a small brush for cleaning the hands and fingernails

nail file *n* : a small flat file (as of metal or cardboard) that is used for shaping fingernails

na·ive *or* **na·ïve** \nä-'ēv\ *adj* **na·iv·er; na·iv·est**　**1** : marked by honest simplicity : ARTLESS　**2** : showing lack of informed judgment : CREDULOUS [from French *naïve* "having a natural simplicity and honesty", from early French *naïf* "being part of the nature of a person from birth, native, inborn", from Latin *nativus* "native", from *natus*, past participle of *nasci* "to be born" — related to NATIVE] — **na·ive·ly** *adv*

na·ïve·té *also* **na·ive·té** \(,)nä-,ēv(-ə)-'tā, nä-'ēv(-ə)-tā\ *n*

1 : the quality or state of being naive　**2** : a naive remark or action

na·ked \'nā-kəd, *especially Southern* 'nek-əd\ *adj*　**1** : having no clothes on　**2 a** : lacking a usual or natural covering (as of leaves, plants, or feathers) ⟨*naked* hills⟩　**b** : not enclosed in a case or covering ⟨a *naked* sword⟩　**c** : lacking protective covering parts (as membranes, scales, or shells) ⟨a *naked* seed⟩ ⟨slugs and other *naked* mollusks⟩　**3** : [2]PLAIN 2, UNADORNED ⟨the *naked* truth⟩　**4** : not aided by artificial means ⟨seen by the *naked* eye⟩ — **na·ked·ly** *adv* — **na·ked·ness** *n*

¹name \'nām\ *n*　**1** : a word or combination of words by which a person or thing is regularly known　**2** : a descriptive often insulting word or phrase ⟨called him *names*⟩　**3** : REPUTATION 2 ⟨made a *name* for herself⟩　**4** : appearance as opposed to fact ⟨a friend in *name* only⟩

²name *vb* **named; nam·ing**　**1** : to give a name to : CALL　**2 a** : to mention or identify by name　**b** : to accuse by name　**3** : to nominate for office : APPOINT ⟨*named* a career diplomat Secretary of State⟩　**4** : to decide upon : CHOOSE ⟨*name* the date for a wedding⟩　**5** : to speak about : MENTION ⟨*name* a price⟩ — **nam·er** *n*

³name *adj*　**1** : bearing a name ⟨*name* tag⟩　**2** : having an established reputation ⟨*name* performers⟩ ⟨*name* brands⟩

name·less \'nām-ləs\ *adj*　**1** : having no name　**2** : not marked with a name ⟨a *nameless* grave⟩　**3** : [1]UNKNOWN, ANONYMOUS ⟨a *nameless* hero⟩ ⟨a *nameless* author⟩　**4 a** : impossible to describe ⟨*nameless* fears⟩　**b** : too disgusting or disturbing to be described ⟨*nameless* acts of cruelty⟩

name·ly \'nām-lē\ *adv* : that is to say ⟨the cat family, *namely*, lions, tigers, and related animals⟩

name·sake \'nām-,sāk\ *n* : one that has the same name as another; *esp* : one named after another

nan·keen \(')nan-'kēn\ *n* : a durable brownish yellow cotton fabric originally from China

nan·ny goat \'nan-ē-\ *n* : a female goat

nano·sec·ond \'nan-ə-,sek-ənd, -ənt\ *n* : one billionth of a second

¹nap \'nap\ *vb* **napped; nap·ping**　**1** : to sleep briefly especially during the day　**2** : to be off guard ⟨was caught *napping*⟩ [Old English *hnappian* "to doze"]

²nap *n* : a short sleep especially during the day ⟨takes a *nap* every day after lunch⟩

³nap *n* : a hairy or soft feathery surface on a woven fabric or leather [Middle English *noppe* "soft surface on a fabric"; of Dutch origin] — **nap·py** \'nap-ē\ *adj*

\ə\ **abut**	\aú\ **out**	\i\ **tip**	\ȯ\ **saw**	\ú\ **foot**
\ər\ **further**	\ch\ **chin**	\ī\ **life**	\ȯi\ **coin**	\y\ **yet**
\a\ **mat**	\e\ **pet**	\j\ **job**	\th\ **thin**	\yü\ **few**
\ā\ **take**	\ē\ **easy**	\ŋ\ **sing**	\t̲h̲\ **this**	\yü\ **cure**
\ä\ **cot, cart**	\g\ **go**	\ō\ **bone**	\ü\ **food**	\zh\ **vision**

⁴nap *vb* **napped; nap·ping** : to raise a nap on fabric or leather

na·palm \'nā-,päm, -,pälm\ *n* **1** : a mixture of aluminum soaps used to make gasoline jellylike (as for bombs) **2** : fuel made jellylike with napalm

nape \'nāp, 'nap\ *n* : the back of the neck

naph·tha \'naf-thə, 'nap-\ *n* : any of various often flammable liquids prepared from coal or petroleum and used especially to dissolve substances

naph·tha·lene \'naf-thə-,lēn, 'nap-\ *n* : a hydrocarbon in the form of crystals usually obtained from coal tar and used in chemical manufacture and as a moth repellent

Na·pier's bones \'nā-pē-ərz-\ *n* : a set of 11 rods invented by the Scottish mathematician Napier and used to multiply and divide large numbers

nap·kin \'nap-kən\ *n* **1** : a small square of cloth or paper used during a meal to wipe the lips or fingers and protect the clothes **2** : a small cloth or towel [Middle English *nappekin* "napkin", from *nappe* "tablecloth", derived from Latin *mappe* "napkin" — related to APRON, MAP]

na·po·leon \nə-'pōl-yən, -'pō-lē-ən\ *n* **1** : a French 20-franc gold coin **2** : an oblong pastry with a filling of cream, custard, or jelly between layers of crust [from French *napoléon* "coin worth 20 francs", named for *Napoléon I*]

narc *or* **nark** \'närk\ *n, slang* : a person (as a government agent) who investigates narcotics violations

nar·cis·sus \när-'sis-əs\ *n, pl* **-cissus** *or* **-cis·sus·es** \-'sis-ə-səz\ *or* **-cis·si** \-'sis-,ī, -ē\ : DAFFODIL; *esp* : one whose flowers have a short tube and grow separately on the stalk — compare JONQUIL

nar·co·sis \när-'kō-səs\ *n, pl* **-co·ses** \-'kō-,sēz\ : a dazed, unconscious, or inactive condition produced by chemicals (as narcotics)

¹nar·cot·ic \när-'kät-ik\ *n* **1** : a drug (as opium) that in small doses dulls the senses, relieves pain, and causes sleep but in large doses is a dangerous poison **2** : something that soothes, relieves, or lulls

²narcotic *adj* **1** : acting as or being the source of a narcotic ⟨*narcotic* drugs⟩ ⟨the opium poppy is a *narcotic* plant⟩ **2** : of or relating to narcotics or their use or control ⟨*narcotic* laws⟩

na·ris \'nar-əs, 'ner-\ *n, pl* **na·res** \'nā(ə)r-(,)ēz, 'ne(ə)r-\ : any of the openings of the nose or nasal cavity of a vertebrate

nar·rate \'na(ə)r-,āt, na-'rāt\ *vb* **nar·rat·ed; nar·rat·ing** : RELATE 1, TELL ⟨*narrate* a story⟩ — **nar·ra·tor** \'na(ə)r-,āt-ər, na-'rāt-, nə-; 'nar-ət-\ *n*

nar·ra·tion \na-'rā-shen, nə-\ *n* **1** : the act or process or an instance of telling a story **2** : ¹STORY 1a, NARRATIVE — **nar·ra·tion·al** \-shnəl, -shən-ᵊl\ *adj*

nar·ra·tive \'nar-ət-iv\ *n* **1** : something (as a story) that is told or written **2** : the art or practice of telling stories — **narrative** *adj*

   syn NARRATIVE, ACCOUNT, RECITAL mean a statement of facts or events. NARRATIVE suggests a series of connected events told like a story ⟨a *narrative* of the early pioneers⟩ ACCOUNT suggests a simple repeating of the facts or events ⟨give the police an *account* of what happened⟩ RECITAL may suggest either an account with many details or a list of memorized facts ⟨the speaker gave a *recital* of the scientist's many achievements⟩

¹nar·row \'nar-ō\ *adj* **1** : of slender or of less than usual width **2** : limited in size or space or opportunity for action ⟨the poor economy offered a *narrow* choice of jobs⟩ **3** : not broad or open in views or opinions ⟨*narrow* in their thinking⟩ **4** : barely enough for the purpose : CLOSE ⟨a *narrow* escape⟩ ⟨won by a *narrow* margin⟩ — **nar·row·ly** *adv* — **nar·row·ness** *n*

²narrow *n* : a narrow part or passage; *esp* : a strait connecting two bodies of water — usually used in pl.

³narrow *vb* : to lessen in width or extent : CONTRACT

nar·row–mind·ed \,nar-ō-'mīn-dəd\ *adj* : INTOLERANT 2, BIGOTED — **nar·row–mind·ed·ness** *n*

nar·whal \'när-, wäl, -,hwäl, -wəl\ *n* : an arctic sea mammal that is about six meters long, is related to the dolphin, and in the male has a long twisted ivory tusk

narwhal

¹na·sal \'nā-zəl\ *n* : a nasal consonant or vowel

²nasal *adj* **1** : of or relating to the nose **2 a** : uttered with the mouth passage closed and the nose passage open ⟨the *nasal* consonants \m\, \n\, and \ŋ\⟩ **b** : uttered with the nose and mouth passages open ⟨the *nasal* vowels in French⟩ **c** : marked by resonance produced through the nose ⟨speaking in a *nasal* tone⟩ — **na·sal·i·ty** \nā-'zal-ət-ē\ *n* — **na·sal·ly** \'nāz-(ə-)lē\ *adv*

nasal cavity *n* : an incompletely divided chamber that lies between the floor of the skull and the roof of the mouth and functions in the warming and filtering of inhaled air and in the sensing of odors

nas·tur·tium \nə-'stər-shəm, na-\ *n* : any of a genus of herbs with juicy stems, showy flowers, and sharp-tasting seeds

nas·ty \'nas-tē\ *adj* **nas·ti·er; -est** **1** : very dirty or foul : FILTHY **2** : morally disgusting or degrading **3** : DISAGREEABLE 1, UNPLEASANT ⟨*nasty* weather⟩ **4** : SPITEFUL, ILL-NATURED ⟨a *nasty* temper⟩ **5** : deserving scorn : CONTEMPTIBLE ⟨a *nasty* trick⟩ **6** : HARMFUL, DANGEROUS ⟨a *nasty* fall on the ice⟩ — **nas·ti·ly** \-tə-lē\ *adv* — **nas·ti·ness** \-tē-nəs\ *n*

na·tal \'nāt-ᵊl\ *adj* : of or relating to birth

na·tion \'nā-shən\ *n* **1** : NATIONALITY 3 **2** : a community of people composed of one or more nationalities usually with its own territory and government **3** : the territory of a nation

¹na·tion·al \'nash-nəl, -ən-ᵊl\ *adj* : of or relating to a nation ⟨the *national* government⟩ — **na·tion·al·ly** \-ē\ *adv*

²national *n* **1** : a citizen or subject of a nation **2** : an organization (as a labor union) having local units throughout a nation

national bank *n* : a commercial bank organized under laws passed by Congress and chartered by the national government

National Guard *n* **1** : a militia force recruited by each state, equipped by the federal government, and subject to the call of either **2** : a military force serving as a national police and defense force

na·tion·al·ism \'nash-nəl-,iz-əm, -ən-ᵊl-\ *n* : loyalty and devotion to a nation especially as expressed in a glorifying of one nation above all others and a stressing of the promotion of its culture and interests

na·tion·al·ist \'nash-nəl-əst, -ən-ᵊl-əst\ *n* **1** : a supporter of nationalism **2** *cap* : a member of a group promoting national independence — **nationalist** *adj, often cap* — **na·tion·al·is·tic** \,nash-nəl-'is-tik, -ən-ᵊl-\ *adj*

na·tion·al·i·ty \,nash-(ə-)'nal-ət-ē\ *n, pl* **-ties** **1** : the fact or state of belonging to a nation ⟨a person of French *nationality*⟩ **2** : political independence as a nation **3** : a people having a common beginning, tradition, or language

na·tion·al·ize \'nash-nəl-,īz, -ən-ᵊl-\ *vb* **-ized; -iz·ing** **1** : to make national **2** : to remove from private ownership and place under government control ⟨*nationalize* railroads⟩ — **na·tion·al·iza·tion** \-ə-'zā-shən\ *n*

na·tion·wide \,nā-shən-'wīd\ *adj* : extending throughout a nation

¹na·tive \'nāt-iv\ *adj* **1** : INBORN 1, NATURAL ⟨*native* ability⟩ **2** : born in a particular place or country ⟨*native* Hawaiians⟩

3 : belonging to one because of the place or circumstances of one's birth ⟨my *native* language⟩ **4 a** : grown, produced, or having its beginning in a particular region ⟨*native* art⟩ **b** : living or growing naturally in a particular region ⟨*native* plants⟩ **5** : found in nature especially in a pure form : not artificially prepared ⟨*native* salt⟩ [Middle English *natif* "native", from early French *natif* (same meaning), from Latin *nativus* (same meaning), from *natus*, past participle of *nasci* "to be born" — related to INNATE, NAIVE, NATURE] — **na·tive·ly** *adv*

²**native** *n* **1** : one born or raised in a particular place ⟨a *native* of Milwaukee⟩ **2** : one of a people living in a place before the arrival of foreigners **3** : something native to or produced in a locality

Native American *n* : AMERICAN INDIAN — **Native American** *adj*

na·tiv·i·ty \nə-'tiv-ət-ē, nā-\ *n, pl* **-ties** **1** *cap* : the birth of Jesus **2** *cap* : CHRISTMAS 1 **3** : the time, place, or manner of being born : BIRTH

nat·ty \'nat-ē\ *adj* **nat·ti·er; -est** : trimly neat and tidy : SMART — **nat·ti·ly** \'nat-ᵊl-ē\ *adv* — **nat·ti·ness** \'nat-ē-nəs\ *n*

¹**nat·u·ral** \'nach-(ə-)rəl\ *adj* **1** : born in or with one : INNATE ⟨*natural* ability⟩ **2** : being such by nature : BORN ⟨a *natural* musician⟩ **3** : born of unmarried parents : ILLEGITIMATE **4 a** : growing without human care ⟨*natural* forests⟩ **b** : existing in or produced by nature ⟨*natural* scenery⟩ **c** : relating to or being natural food **5** : ¹HUMAN 1 ⟨it is not *natural* to hate your children⟩ **6** : of, relating to, or following the usual events and happenings of nature or the physical world : not miraculous ⟨*natural* causes⟩ **7** : not made or changed by humans ⟨*natural* silk⟩ ⟨a person's *natural* complexion⟩ **8** : being simple and sincere ⟨*natural* manners⟩ **9** : LIFELIKE ⟨the people in the picture look *natural*⟩ **10 a** : having neither sharps nor flats in the key signature **b** : having a sharp or a flat changed in pitch by a natural sign — **nat·u·ral·ness** *n*

²**natural** *n* **1 a** : a character ♮ placed on a line or space of the musical staff to change a sharp or flat in the key signature back to the natural tone value **b** : a note or tone changed by the natural sign **2** : one naturally able to do or to learn easily how to do something ⟨a *natural* at golf⟩ **3** : ²AFRO

natural childbirth *n* : a system of managing childbirth in which the mother receives training in order to remain conscious and to help in the process of birth without the use of drugs (as anesthetics)

natural food *n* : food that has been processed as little as possible and contains no added artificial substances to keep it fresh or give it flavor

natural gas *n* : gas that comes from the earth's crust through natural openings or bored wells; *esp* : a flammable mixture of hydrocarbons and especially methane used chiefly as a fuel and raw material

natural history *n* : the study of natural objects and especially plants and animals as they live in nature from an amateur or popular point of view

nat·u·ral·ist \'nach-(ə-)rə-ləst\ *n* : a student of natural history; *esp* : a field biologist — **naturalist** *adj*

nat·u·ral·iza·tion \,nach-(ə-)rə-lə-'zā-shən\ *n* : the act or process of naturalizing : the state of being naturalized

nat·u·ral·ize \'nach-(ə-)rə-,līz\ *vb* **-ized; -iz·ing** **1** : to introduce into common use ⟨*naturalize* a foreign word⟩ **2** : to become or cause to become established as if native ⟨*naturalized* weeds⟩ **3** : to give the rights and privileges of citizenship to ⟨*naturalize* a foreign-born person⟩

nat·u·ral·ly \'nach-(ə-)rə-lē, 'nach-ər-lē\ *adv* **1** : by natural character or ability ⟨*naturally* timid⟩ **2** : according to the usual course of things ⟨we *naturally* dislike being hurt⟩ **3 a** : without artificial aid ⟨hair that curls *naturally*⟩ **b** : in a simple and sincere manner ⟨speak *naturally*⟩ **4** : in a lifelike manner ⟨paints flowers *naturally*⟩

natural number *n* : the number 1 or any number (as 3, 12, or 432) obtained by adding 1 to it one or more times — called also *counting number*

natural resource *n* : something (as a mineral, waterpower source, forest, or kind of animal) that is found in nature and is valuable to humans

natural science *n* : any of the sciences (as physics, chemistry, or biology) that deal with matter, energy, and their relationships and transformations or with measurable natural events

natural selection *n* : a natural process in which individuals or groups best adapted to the conditions under which they live survive and poorly adapted forms are eliminated

na·ture \'nā-chər\ *n* **1** : the basic quality, character, or way in which a thing or person exists or has been formed ⟨the *nature* of steel⟩ **2** : ¹KIND 1a, SORT ⟨and things of that *nature*⟩ **3** : DISPOSITION 3a, TEMPERAMENT ⟨behavior contrary to one's *nature*⟩ **4** *often cap* : a power or set of forces thought of as controlling the universe ⟨Mother *Nature*⟩ **5** : natural feeling especially as shown in one's attitude toward others ⟨your good *nature* is well-known⟩ **6** : humanity's original or natural condition : primitive life ⟨return to *nature*⟩ **7** : the physical universe ⟨the study of *nature*⟩ **8** : the working of a living body ⟨leave a cure to *nature*⟩ ⟨sex is a part of *nature*⟩ **9** : natural scenery ⟨the beauties of *nature*⟩ [Middle English *nature* "normal or essential quality of something, nature", from early French *nature* (same meaning), from Latin *natura* (same meaning), from *natus*, past participle of *nasci* "to be born" — related to INNATE, NATIVE]

naught *or* **nought** \'not, 'nät\ *n* **1 a** : ³NOTHING 1a **b** : the quality or state of being nothing **2** : ¹ZERO 1 — see NUMBER table

naugh·ty \'not-ē, 'nät-\ *adj* **naugh·ti·er; -est** : behaving badly or improperly — **naugh·ti·ly** \'not-ᵊl-ē, 'nät-\ *adv* — **naugh·ti·ness** \'not-ē-nəs, 'nät-\ *n*

nau·sea \'no-zē-ə, -sē-ə; 'no-zhə, -shə\ *n* **1** : a disturbed condition of the stomach in which one feels like vomiting **2** : extreme disgust

Word History The ancient Greeks were a seagoing people, so seasickness was not rare for them. Their word for seasickness, *nausia* or *nautia*, came from their word for ship, *naus*. But *nautia* or *nausia* also meant the worst symptom of seasickness, the stomach upset and urge to vomit. *Nausea*, as we call this feeling in English, can be caused by something other than the motion of a ship. The ancient Greeks and the ancient Romans, who spoke Latin, needed only one word for both seasickness and the upset in the stomach. The Romans borrowed the Greek word, spelling it *nausea* in Latin. English took the word directly from Latin. [from Latin *nausea* "seasickness, the stomach upset that causes an urge to vomit", from Greek *nausia*, *nautia* (same meaning), literally "ship sickness", from *naus* "ship" — related to ASTRONAUT, NAUTICAL, NOISE; see *Word History* at NOISE]

nau·se·ate \'no-zē-,āt, -sē-, -zhē-, -shē-\ *vb* **-at·ed; -at·ing** : to affect or become affected with nausea

nau·se·at·ing \'no-zē-,āt-iŋ, -sē-, -zhē-, -shē-\ *adj* : causing nausea and especially disgust — **nau·se·at·ing·ly** *adv*

nau·seous \'no-shəs, 'no-zē-əs\ *adj* : affected with or causing nausea ⟨feel *nauseous*⟩ ⟨a *nauseous* odor⟩ — **nau·seous·ly** *adv*

nau·ti·cal \'not-i-kəl, 'nät-\ *adj* : of or relating to sailors, navigation, or ships [from Latin *nauticus* "nautical", from Greek *nautikos* (same meaning), from *nautēs* "sailor",

\ə\ abut	\au̇\ out	\i\ tip	\ȯ\ saw	\u̇\ foot
\ər\ further	\ch\ chin	\ī\ life	\ȯi\ coin	\y\ yet
\a\ mat	\e\ pet	\j\ job	\th\ thin	\yü\ few
\ā\ take	\ē\ easy	\ŋ\ sing	\th\ this	\yu̇\ cure
\ä\ cot, cart	\g\ go	\ō\ bone	\ü\ food	\zh\ vision

from *naus* "ship" — related to ASTRONAUT, NAUSEA; see *Word History* at NAUSEA] — **nau·ti·cal·ly** \-k(ə-)lē\ *adv*

nautical mile *n* : any of various units of distance used for sea and air navigation; *esp* : a unit of distance equal to 6076.115 feet (1852 meters)

nau·ti·lus \'nȯt-ᵊl-əs, 'nät-\ *n, pl* **-lus·es** *or* **-li** \-ᵊl-ī, -,ē\ **1** : any of a genus of mollusks of the South Pacific and Indian oceans that are cephalopods and have a spiral chambered shell that is pearly on the inside — called also *chambered nautilus* **2** : PAPER NAUTILUS

nautilus 1

Na·va·jo *also* **Na·va·ho** \'nav-ə-,hō, 'näv-\ *n* : a member of an American Indian people of northern New Mexico and Arizona

na·val \'nā-vəl\ *adj* : of or relating to a navy or warships

naval stores *n pl* : products (as pitch, turpentine, or rosin) obtained from coniferous trees (as pines)

¹nave \'nāv\ *n* : the hub of a wheel

²nave *n* : the long central main part of a church

na·vel \'nā-vəl\ *n* : a hollowed out place on the outside wall of the middle of the abdomen marking the point of attachment of the umbilical cord

navel orange *n* : an orange that is usually without seeds and contains a small or partial second fruit at one end resembling a navel

nav·i·ga·ble \'nav-i-gə-bəl\ *adj* **1** : deep and wide enough to permit passage to ships ⟨*navigable* rivers⟩ **2** : capable of being steered ⟨a *navigable* balloon⟩ — **nav·i·ga·bil·i·ty** \,nav-i-gə-'bil-ət-ē\ *n*

nav·i·gate \'nav-ə-,gāt\ *vb* **-gat·ed; -gat·ing** **1 a** : to travel by water **b** : to sail over, on, or through **2 a** : to direct one's course in a ship or aircraft **b** : to control the course of : STEER

nav·i·ga·tion \,nav-ə-'gā-shən\ *n* **1** : the act or practice of navigating **2** : the science of getting ships, aircraft, or spacecraft from place to place; *esp* : the method of figuring out position, course, and distance traveled — **nav·i·ga·tion·al** \-shnəl, -shən-ᵊl\ *adj*

nav·i·ga·tor \'nav-ə-,gāt-ər\ *n* : one that navigates or is qualified to navigate

nav·vy \'nav-ē\ *n, pl* **navvies** *chiefly British* : an unskilled laborer

na·vy \'nā-vē\ *n, pl* **navies** **1** : a fleet of ships **2** : a nation's warships **3** *often cap* : a nation's complete equipment and organization for sea warfare **4** : a dark purplish blue

navy bean *n* : a kidney bean grown especially for its small white seeds that are valuable as food

navy yard *n* : a naval shore station where ships are built or repaired

na·wab \nə-'wäb\ *n* : a Muslim prince of India

¹nay \'nā\ *adv* **1** : ¹NO 3 **2** : not merely this but also : not only so but ⟨the letter made him happy, *nay*, ecstatic⟩

²nay *n* **1** : DENIAL 1, REFUSAL **2 a** : a negative reply or vote **b** : one who votes no

Naz·a·rene \,naz-ə-'rēn\ *n* **1** : a person born or living in Nazareth **2** : JESUS — **Nazarene** *adj*

Na·zi \'nät-sē, 'nat-\ *n* : a member of a German fascist party controlling Germany from 1933 to 1945 — **Nazi** *adj* — **Na·zism** \'nät-,siz-əm, 'nat-\

NC–17 \'en-'sē-,sev-ən-'tēn\ *trademark* — used to certify that a motion picture is of such a nature that no one under the age of 17 can be admitted

¹Ne·an·der·thal \nē-'an-dər-,thȯl, -,tȯl; nā-'än-dər-,täl\ *adj* **1** : being, relating to, or resembling Neanderthal man **2** : suggesting a caveman in appearance or behavior

²Neanderthal *or* **Ne·an·der·thal·er** \-ər\ *n* **1** : a member of the Neanderthal race **2** : a person who resembles a caveman in appearance or behavior

Neanderthal man *n* : a prehistoric human being that is between modern human beings and the pithecanthropines in some characteristics

Ne·a·pol·i·tan ice cream \,nē-ə-'päl-ət-ᵊn-\ *n* : a brick of ice cream with layers of different flavors (as vanilla, chocolate, and strawberry)

neap tide \'nēp-\ *n* : a tide of least range occurring at the first and third quarters of the moon

¹near \'ni(ə)r\ *adv* **1** : at, within, or to a short distance or time **2** : in a condition or state resembling or close to : ALMOST ⟨*near* dead⟩ **3** : in a very close manner ⟨*near* related⟩ [Old English *nēar* "nearer", comparative form of *nēah* "near, close" — related to NEIGHBOR, NIGH; see *Word History* at NEIGHBOR]

²near \(')ni(ə)r\ *prep* : close to ⟨standing *near* the door⟩

³near \'ni(ə)r\ *adj* **1** : closely related or associated **2 a** : not far away **b** : barely avoided ⟨a *near* disaster⟩ **c** : almost not happening ⟨a *near* miss⟩ **3** : being the closer of two ⟨the *near* side of a hill⟩ **4** : ²DIRECT 1, SHORT ⟨the *nearest* route⟩ **5** : closely resembling a model or a genuine example ⟨*near* silk⟩ — **near·ly** *adv* — **near·ness** *n*

⁴near \'ni(ə)r\ *vb* : to come near : APPROACH

near·by \ni(ə)r-'bī, 'ni(ə)r-,bī\ *adv or adj* : close at hand

near·sight·ed \'ni(ə)r-'sīt-əd\ *adj* : able to see near things more clearly than distant ones : MYOPIC — **near·sight·ed·ness** *n*

neat \'nēt\ *adj* **1** : being orderly and clean : TIDY **2** : not mixed or diluted : STRAIGHT ⟨*neat* brandy⟩ **3** : marked by tasteful simplicity **4** : SKILLFUL 2, ADROIT **5** : ³FINE 4, SPLENDID — **neat·ly** *adv* — **neat·ness** *n*

Word History Today a popular use of the word *neat* is to mean "fine, splendid". It is a use that does not appear to have much in common with earlier meanings of the word such as "tidy" or "undiluted". But in its newest sense of "splendid", something that is "neat" might be thought of as a brilliant or shining example of the best of its kind. And this idea is very close to the origin of the word. *Neat* first began to be used in English about 400 years ago. It was borrowed from the early French word *net*, which in turn was taken from Latin *nitidus*, meaning "bright, shining". At first *neat* was used in English with the same meaning, as in "a neat new metal pin". This original sense in time fell out of use. But the idea of something bright and clean and sparkling and new gave us other meanings. One of these is the sense of "tidy", as in "a neat room or desk". Perhaps the idea of something clean also gave rise to the sense of *neat* meaning "not mixed or diluted" with anything. The idea of "tidy" certainly must have been the basis of the sense of "marked by tasteful simplicity". And since all of these senses suggest something that is viewed as ideal, it is easy to understand that they should lead to the newest sense of *neat,* meaning "splendid". When first used in English, *splendid* also meant "shining", coming from a Latin verb meaning "to shine". [from earlier *neat* "bright, shining", from early French *net* (same meaning), from Latin *nitidus* (same meaning), from *nitēre* "to shine" — related to ³NET]

syn NEAT, TIDY, TRIM mean showing care and concern for order. NEAT stresses that something is clean in addition to being orderly ⟨your clothes should always be *neat*⟩ TIDY suggests that something is continually kept orderly and neat ⟨I work hard to keep my room *tidy*⟩ TRIM stresses that something is orderly and compact ⟨*trim* comfortable houses⟩

neb·u·la \'neb-yə-lə\ *n, pl* **-las** *or* **-lae** \-,lē, -,lī\ **1** : any of many huge clouds of gas or dust in deep space **2** : GALAXY 2 — **neb·u·lar** \-lər\ *adj*

neb·u·lous \'neb-yə-ləs\ *adj* **1** : of, relating to, or resembling a nebula   **2** : not clear or sharp : VAGUE — **neb·u·lous·ly** *adv* — **neb·u·lous·ness** *n*

¹nec·es·sary \'nes-ə-ˌser-ē\ *adj*   **1** : going to happen with no way of preventing it : INEVITABLE   **2** : being the only logically possible result of an argument or situation   **3** : being compulsory or required ⟨it is *necessary* that you do your homework⟩   **4** : impossible to do without : INDISPENSABLE ⟨food is *necessary* for life⟩ [Middle English *necessarie* "necessary, required", derived from Latin *necesse* "necessary, unavoidable", from *ne-* "not" and *cedere* "to go, go away" — related to CONCEDE, SUCCEED] — **nec·es·sar·i·ly** \ˌnes-ə-'ser-ə-lē\ *adv*

²necessary *n, pl* **-sar·ies** : something necessary : REQUIREMENT ⟨the *necessaries* of life⟩

ne·ces·si·tate \ni-'ses-ə-ˌtāt\ *vb* **-tat·ed; -tat·ing** : to make necessary ⟨sick enough to *necessitate* staying home⟩ — **ne·ces·si·ta·tion** \-ˌses-ə-'tā-shən\ *n*

ne·ces·si·ty \ni-'ses-ət-ē, -'ses-tē\ *n, pl* **-ties**   **1** : very great need of help or relief ⟨call in case of *necessity*⟩   **2** : something badly needed   **3** : the quality or state of being in need : POVERTY   **4** : conditions that cannot be changed ⟨forced by *necessity*⟩

neck \'nek\ *n*   **1** : the part of the body connecting the head and the main part of the body   **2** : the part of a garment covering or nearest to the neck   **3 a** : something like a neck in shape or position ⟨the *neck* of a bottle⟩ ⟨a *neck* of land⟩   **b** : the part of a tooth between the crown and the root — **necked** \'nekt\ *adj* — **neck and neck** : so nearly equal (as in a race) that one cannot be said to be ahead of the other

neck·er·chief \'nek-ər-chəf, -(ˌ)chif, -ˌchēf\ *n, pl* **-chiefs** *also* **-chieves** \-chəfs, -(ˌ)chifs, -ˌchēvz, -ˌchēfs\ : a square of cloth worn folded about the neck like a scarf

neck·lace \'nek-ləs\ *n* : an ornament (as a string of beads) worn around the neck

neck·line \-ˌlīn\ *n* : the outline of the neck opening of a garment

neck·piece \-ˌpēs\ *n* : an article of apparel (as a fur scarf) worn about the neck

neckerchief

neck·tie \-ˌtī\ *n* : a narrow length of cloth worn about the neck and tied in front

neck·wear \-ˌwa(ə)r, -ˌwe(ə)r\ *n* : articles (as scarves or neckties) for wear around the neck

nec·ro·man·cy \'nek-rə-ˌman(t)-sē\ *n*   **1** : the art or practice of calling up the spirits of the dead for magical purposes   **2** : MAGIC 1 — **nec·ro·man·cer** \-sər\ *n*

nec·tar \'nek-tər\ *n*   **1** : the drink of the Greek and Roman gods   **2** : a sweet liquid given off by plants and used by bees in making honey

nec·tar·ine \ˌnek-tə-'rēn\ *n* : a smooth-skinned peach; *also* : a tree producing this fruit

nec·tary \'nek-t(ə-)rē\ *n, pl* **-tar·ies** : a plant gland that secretes nectar

née *or* **nee** \'nā\ *adj* : BORN 1a — used to identify a woman by her maiden family name ⟨Mrs. Jane Doe, *née* Roe⟩

¹need \'nēd\ *n*   **1** : necessary duty : OBLIGATION   **2 a** : a lack of something necessary, desirable, or useful   **b** : a mental or physical requirement for keeping a living thing in normal condition   **3** : a situation requiring supply or relief   **4** : something necessary or desired ⟨our daily *needs*⟩   **5** : POVERTY 1, WANT

²need *vb*   **1** : to be in want   **2** : to be in need of : REQUIRE ⟨they *need* advice⟩   **3** : to be required or obliged ⟨we *need* to look at the facts⟩ ⟨you *need* not answer⟩   **4** : to be necessary ⟨something *needs* to be done⟩

need·ful \'nēd-fəl\ *adj* : necessary for a purpose — **need·ful·ly** \-fə-lē\ *adv* — **need·ful·ness** *n*

¹nee·dle \'nēd-ᵊl\ *n*   **1 a** : a slender usually steel instrument having an eye for thread and used for sewing   **b** : a device for carrying thread and making stitches (as in sewing up a wound)   **c** : a slender hollow instrument by which material is put into or taken from the body through the skin   **2** : a slender pointer on a dial   **3 a** : a slender pointed object (as a pointed crystal or an obelisk)   **b** : a leaf (as of a pine) shaped like a needle   **4** : a slender piece of jewel or steel with a rounded tip used in a phonograph to transmit vibrations from the record — **nee·dle·like** \'nēd-ᵊl-ˌ(l)īk\ *adj*

²needle *vb* **nee·dled; nee·dling** \'nēd-liŋ, -ᵊl-iŋ\   **1** : ¹TEASE 2a, TAUNT   **2** : to cause to take action by repeated stinging remarks — **nee·dler** \'nēd-lər, -ᵊl-ər\ *n* — **nee·dling** *n*

nee·dle·leaf \'nēd-ᵊl-ˌlēf\ *adj* : populated with trees having leaves that are needles (*needleleaf* evergreen forests); *also* : having leaves that are needles (*needleleaf* trees)

nee·dle·point \'nēd-ᵊl-ˌpȯint\ *n* : embroidery done on canvas or plastic usually in simple even stitches across counted threads

need·less \'nēd-ləs\ *adj* : UNNECESSARY — **need·less·ly** *adv*

nee·dle·work \'nēd-ᵊl-ˌwərk\ *n* : work done with a needle; *esp* : EMBROIDERY

needn't \'nēd-ᵊnt\ : need not

needs \'nēdz\ *adv* : because of necessity : NECESSARILY ⟨must *needs* be recognized⟩

needy \'nēd-ē\ *adj* **need·i·er; -est** : being in want : very poor — **need·i·ness** *n*

ne'er \(')ne(ə)r, (')na(ə)r\ *adv* : NEVER

ne'er–do–well \'ne(ə)r-dù-ˌwel, 'na(ə)r-\ *n* : an idle worthless person

ne·far·i·ous \ni-'far-ē-əs, -'fer-\ *adj* : very wicked : EVIL — **ne·far·i·ous·ly** *adv* — **ne·far·i·ous·ness** *n*

ne·gate \ni-'gāt\ *vb* **ne·gat·ed; ne·gat·ing**   **1** : to deny the existence or truth of   **2** : to cause to be ineffective or invalid

ne·ga·tion \ni-'gā-shən\ *n*   **1 a** : the action of negating : DENIAL   **b** : a negative statement   **2** : something that is the opposite of something positive ⟨death is the *negation* of life⟩

¹neg·a·tive \'neg-ət-iv\ *adj*   **1** : marked by denial, prohibition, or refusal ⟨a *negative* reply⟩   **2** : not positive or helpful ⟨a *negative* attitude⟩ ⟨*negative* criticism⟩   **3 a** : less than zero and opposite in sign to a positive number that when added to the number gives zero   **b** : extending or measured in a direction opposite to one chosen as positive ⟨a *negative* angle⟩   **4 a** : of, being, or relating to electricity of a kind of which the electron is the elementary unit ⟨a *negative* charge⟩   **b** : having more electrons than protons ⟨a *negative* particle⟩   **c** : being the part toward which the electric current flows from the outside circuit ⟨the *negative* pole of a battery⟩   **5 a** : not indicating the presence of a particular germ or condition ⟨a *negative* TB test⟩   **b** : directed or moving away from a source of stimulation ⟨a *negative* tropism⟩   **6** : having the light and dark parts approximately opposite to those of the thing or person photographed — **neg·a·tive·ly** *adv* — **neg·a·tive·ness** *n* — **neg·a·tiv·i·ty** \ˌneg-ə-'tiv-ət-ē\ *n*

²negative *n*   **1** : a reply that indicates denial or contradiction : REFUSAL   **2** : something that is the opposite or negation of something else   **3** : an expression (as the word *no*) of negation or denial   **4** : a negative number   **5** : the side that argues or votes against something in a debate   **6** : a negative photographic image on transparent material used

\ə\ abut	\aù\ out	\i\ tip	\ȯ\ saw	\ù\ foot
\ər\ further	\ch\ chin	\ī\ life	\ȯi\ coin	\y\ yet
\a\ mat	\e\ pet	\j\ job	\th\ thin	\yü\ few
\ā\ take	\ē\ easy	\ŋ\ sing	\th\ this	\yù\ cure
\ä\ cot, cart	\g\ go	\ō\ bone	\ü\ food	\zh\ vision

for printing positive pictures; *also* : the material that carries such an image

³negative *vb* **-tived; -tiv·ing** **1** : to refuse to accept or approve **2** : to vote against **3** : DENY 1, CONTRADICT

¹ne·glect \ni-'glekt\ *vb* **1** : to give little attention or respect to **2** : to leave undone or not attended to especially through carelessness — **ne·glect·er** *n*

syn NEGLECT, DISREGARD, IGNORE mean to pass over something without giving it any or enough attention. NEGLECT suggests that one has not given enough attention to something that deserves or requires attention, but the lack of attention may not be deliberate ⟨you have been *neglecting* your homework⟩ DISREGARD suggests deliberately overlooking something usually because one feels that it is not worth noticing ⟨*disregarded* the "No Exit" sign and left through that door⟩ IGNORE suggests deliberately overlooking something easily seen ⟨my grandmother politely *ignored* the messy room⟩

²neglect *n* **1** : an act or instance of neglecting something **2** : the condition of being neglected

ne·glect·ful \ni-'glekt(t)-fəl\ *adj* : given to neglecting : CARELESS — **ne·glect·ful·ly** \-fə-lē\ *adv*

neg·li·gee *also* **neg·li·gé** \,neg-lə-'zhā\ *n* **1** : a woman's long flowing dressing gown **2** : informal clothes [derived from French *négligé,* past participle of *négliger* "to neglect"]

neg·li·gence \'neg-li-jən(t)s\ *n* **1** : the quality or state of being negligent; *esp* : failure to take the care that a reasonably cautious person usually takes **2** : an act or instance of negligence

neg·li·gent \'neg-li-jənt\ *adj* **1** : marked by or likely to show neglect **2** : failing to take proper or normal care — **neg·li·gent·ly** *adv*

neg·li·gi·ble \'neg-li-jə-bəl\ *adj* : so small or unimportant as to deserve little or no attention — **neg·li·gi·bly** \-blē\ *adv*

ne·go·tia·ble \ni-'gō-sh(ē-)ə-bəl\ *adj* : capable of being negotiated; *esp* : capable of being passed from one person to another without being signed in return for something of equal value ⟨*negotiable* bonds⟩ — **ne·go·tia·bil·i·ty** \-,gō-sh(ē-)ə-'bil-ət-ē\ *n*

ne·go·ti·ate \ni-'gō-shē-,āt\ *vb* **-at·ed; -at·ing** **1 a** : to discuss with another so as to arrive at an agreement **b** : to arrange for or bring about by such conference ⟨*negotiate* a treaty⟩ **2** : to transfer to another in return for something of equal value ⟨*negotiate* a check⟩ **3** : to get through, around, or over successfully ⟨*negotiate* a turn⟩ — **ne·go·ti·a·tion** \-,gō-shē-'ā-shən, -sē-\ *n* — **ne·go·ti·a·tor** \-'gō-shē-,āt-ər\ *n*

Ne·gri·to \nə-'grēt-ō\ *n, pl* **-tos** *or* **-toes** : a member of any of a group of Negroid peoples that are of small size and live in Oceania and southeastern Asia

ne·gri·tude \'neg-rə-,t(y)üd, 'nē-grə-\ *n* : awareness of and pride in the cultural values that make up the African heritage

Ne·gro \'nē-grō\ *n, pl* **Negroes** **1** : a member of the black race of humanity distinguished from members of other races by physical features without regard to language or culture; *esp* : a member of a people belonging to the African branch of the black race **2** : a person of Negro ancestry [from Spanish *Negro* or Portuguese *Negro* "a person of a black race", derived from Latin *nigr-, niger* "black"] — **Negro** *adj*

Ne·groid \'nē-,groid\ *adj* : of, resembling, or related to the Negro race ⟨a *Negroid* people of Oceania⟩ — **Negroid** *n*

Ne·he·mi·ah \,nē-(h)ə-'mī-ə\ *n* — see BIBLE table

neigh \'nā\ *vb* : to make the loud drawn-out cry of a horse — **neigh** *n*

¹neigh·bor \'nā-bər\ *n* **1** : a person who lives near another **2** : a person or thing located near another ⟨Canada is a *neighbor* of the U.S.⟩ **3** : a fellow human being

Word History The words *near* and *nigh* are both re-

lated to — and have the same meaning as — the Old English word *nēah.* Another word which can be traced, at least in part, to *nēah* is *neighbor.* The combination of *nēah,* meaning "near", and *gebūr,* meaning "dweller", produced the Old English word *nēahgebūr.* This word was used for "a person living near another". The spelling of *nēahgebūr* has changed over the centuries to give us *neighbor,* but the word's basic meaning has remained the same. [Old English *nēahgebūr* "neighbor", from *nēah* "near" + *gebūr* "dweller" — related to NEAR, NIGH]

²neighbor *vb* **neigh·bored; neigh·bor·ing** \-b(ə-)riŋ\ : to be next to or near to ⟨*neighboring* towns⟩

neigh·bor·hood \'nā-bər-,hud\ *n* **1** : the quality or state of being neighbors **2 a** : a place or region near : VICINITY **b** : a number or amount near ⟨cost in the *neighborhood* of $10⟩ **3 a** : the people living near one another **b** : a section lived in by people who consider themselves neighbors

neigh·bor·ly \'nā-bər-lē\ *adj* : of, relating to, or characteristic of neighbors : FRIENDLY — **neigh·bor·li·ness** *n*

¹nei·ther \'nē-thər *also* 'nī-\ *pron* : not the one and not the other ⟨*neither* of the two⟩

²neither *conj* **1** : both not : equally not ⟨*neither* black nor white⟩ **2** : also not ⟨*neither* did I⟩

³neither *adj* : not either ⟨*neither* hand⟩

nek·ton \'nek-tən, -,tän\ *n* : strong-swimming water-dwelling animals (as whales and squid) that are largely independent of the action of waves and currents

nem·a·tode \'nem-ə-,tōd\ *n* : any of a major group of long cylinder-shaped worms that are parasites in animals or plants or live in soil or water

nem·e·sis \'nem-ə-səs\ *n, pl* **-e·ses** \-ə-,sēz\ **1** : one that punishes or avenges **2** : an act or instance of just punishment

neo- *combining form* : new : recent [derived from Greek *neos* "new"]

neo·clas·sic \,nē-ō-'klas-ik\ *adj* : of or relating to a renewal or a renewal with some changes of the classical style especially in literature, art, or music — **neo·clas·si·cal** \-'klas-i-kəl\ *adj* — **neo·clas·si·cism** \-'klas-ə-,siz-əm\ *n*

neo·dym·i·um \,nē-ō-'dim-ē-əm\ *n* : a yellow metallic chemical element — see ELEMENT table

Neo·lith·ic \,nē-ə-'lith-ik\ *adj* : of, relating to, or being the latest period of the Stone Age which is marked by the use of polished stone tools

ne·ol·o·gism \nē-'äl-ə-,jiz-əm\ *n* : a new word or expression — **ne·ol·o·gis·tic** \-,äl-ə-'jis-tik\ *adj*

ne·on \'nē-,än\ *n* **1** : a colorless odorless gaseous element found in very small amounts in air and used in electric lamps — see ELEMENT table **2 a** : a lamp in which the gas contains a large amount of neon that gives a reddish glow when a current is passed through it **b** : a sign composed of such lamps — **neon** *adj*

neo·phyte \'nē-ə-,fīt\ *n* **1** : a person who has recently joined a religious group **2** : BEGINNER, NOVICE

neo·plasm \'nē-ə-,plaz-əm\ *n* : a new growth of tissue that serves no useful purpose in the body : TUMOR

ne·pen·the \nə-'pen(t)-thē\ *n* : a potion used by the ancient peoples to dull pain and sorrow

neph·ew \'nef-yü\ *n* : a son of one's brother, sister, brother-in-law, or sister-in-law

ne·phri·tis \ni-'frīt-əs\ *n, pl* **ne·phrit·i·des** \-'frit-ə-,dēz\ : inflammation of the kidneys

neph·ron \'nef-,rän\ *n* : a single unit that functions in giving off bodily waste especially in a vertebrate kidney

nep·o·tism \'nep-ə-,tiz-əm\ *n* : favoritism shown to a relative (as in the distribution of political offices)

Nep·tune \'nep-,t(y)ün\ *n* : the planet eighth in order from the sun — see PLANET table — **Nep·tu·ni·an** \nep-'t(y)ü-nē-ən\ *adj*

nep·tu·ni·um \nep-'t(y)ü-nē-əm\ *n* : a radioactive metallic element similar to uranium and obtained in nuclear reactors in the production of plutonium — see ELEMENT table

nerd \'nərd\ *n* **1** : an unstylish, unattractive, or socially awkward person **2** : a person slavishly devoted to intellectual or academic pursuits — **nerdy** \'nər-dē\ *adj*

Ne·re·id \'nir-ē-əd\ *n* : any of the sea nymphs held in Greek mythology to be the daughters of the sea-god Nereus

¹nerve \'nərv\ *n* **1** : TENDON ⟨strain every *nerve*⟩ **2** : one of the stringy bands of nervous tissue connecting the nervous system with other organs and carrying nerve impulses **3 a** : power of endurance or control **b** : fearless boldness **c** : behavior marked by a rude or disrespectful boldness **4 a** : a sore or sensitive point **b** *pl* : a condition of being very nervous : JITTERS, HYSTERIA **5** : a vein in a leaf or in the wing of an insect **6** : the sensitive soft inner part of a tooth — **nerved** \'nərvd\ *adj*

²nerve *vb* **nerved; nerv·ing** : to give strength or courage to

nerve cell *n* : NEURON; *also* : CELL BODY

nerve center *n* : ¹CENTER 2b

nerve cord *n* **1** : a pair of closely united nerves that run along the inside of the body on the lower side of many long-bodied invertebrates (as earthworms and insects) **2** : a tube-shaped cord of nervous tissue in the back or upper side of a chordate above the notochord that makes up or develops into the central nervous system

nerve ending *n* : a structure forming an end of a nerve axon that is distant from the cell body

nerve fiber *n* : any of the long thin parts that lead to or away from the cell body of a neuron and include axons and dendrites

nerve gas *n* : a war gas damaging especially to the nervous and respiratory systems

nerve impulse *n* : a change that moves along a nerve fiber after it is stimulated and that carries a record of sensation or an instruction to act — called also *nervous impulse*

nerve·less \'nərv-ləs\ *adj* **1** : lacking strength or courage : FEEBLE **2** : showing or having control : not nervous — **nerve·less·ly** *adv*

nerve net *n* : a network of nerve cells that seem to be continuous one with another and carry impulses in all directions; *also* : a nervous system (as in a jellyfish) consisting of such a network

ner·vous \'nər-vəs\ *adj* **1 a** : of, relating to, or composed of neurons **b** : of or relating to the nerves **c** : having its source in or affected by the nerves ⟨*nervous* energy⟩ **2 a** : easily excited or irritated **b** : TIMID, FEARFUL ⟨a *nervous* smile⟩ **3 a** : causing uncomfortable feelings ⟨a *nervous* situation⟩ **b** : not steady : UNSTABLE — **ner·vous·ly** *adv* — **ner·vous·ness** *n*

nervous breakdown *n* : an attack of mental or emotional disorder that is severe enough to require hospitalization

nervous system *n* : the bodily system that receives stimuli, decides on their importance, and sends nerve impulses to the organs of action and that in vertebrates is made up of brain and spinal cord, nerves, ganglia, and parts of the receptor organs

nervy \'nər-vē\ *adj* **nerv·i·er; -est** **1 a** : showing calm courage : FEARLESS **b** : rudely bold : IMPUDENT ⟨a *nervy* salesperson⟩ **2** : EXCITABLE 1, NERVOUS — **nerv·i·ness** *n*

-ness \nəs\ *n suffix* : state : condition : quality ⟨good*ness*⟩ [Old English *-nes* (suffix) "state, condition, quality"]

¹nest \'nest\ *n* **1 a** : a bed or shelter prepared by a bird for its eggs and young **b** : a place where eggs (as of insects, fishes, or turtles) are laid and hatched **2 a** : a place of rest, shelter, or lodging **b** : DEN 2, HANGOUT **3** : the occupants of a nest ⟨a *nest* of baby birds⟩ **4** : a group of objects made to fit one within another ⟨a *nest* of measuring cups⟩

²nest *vb* **1** : to build or live in a nest ⟨robins *nested* in the

underbrush⟩ **2** : to fit compactly together or within one another

nest egg *n* : a fund of money set aside as a reserve

nest·er \'nes-tər\ *n* **1** : one that nests **2** *West* : a person who settles on open range in order to farm

nes·tle \'nes-əl\ *vb* **nes·tled; nes·tling** \-(ə-)liŋ\ **1** : to lie close and snug : CUDDLE **2** : to settle as if in a nest — **nes·tler** \-(ə-)lər\ *n*

nest·ling \'nest-liŋ\ *n* **1** : a young bird not yet able to leave the nest **2** : a young child

¹net \'net\ *n* **1** : a fabric made of threads, cords, ropes, or wires that weave in and out with much open space **2** : something made of net: as **a** : a device for catching fish, birds, or insects **b** : a fabric barricade which divides a court in half (as in tennis or badminton) **3** : something that traps like a net **4** : a network of lines, fibers, or figures [Old English *nett* "net fabric"] — **net·like** \-‚līk\ *adj* — **net·ted** \'net-əd\ *adj*

²net *vb* **net·ted; net·ting** **1** : to cover with or as if with a net **2** : to catch in or as if in a net ⟨*net* fish⟩ **3** : to hit the ball into the net in a racket game — **net·ter** *n*

³net *adj* : free from all charges or deductions ⟨*net* profit⟩ ⟨*net* weight⟩ [from earlier *net* "neat", from Middle English *net* "clean, bright", derived from Latin *nitidus* "bright, lustrous" — related to NEAT; see *Word History* at NEAT]

⁴net *vb* **net·ted; net·ting** : to gain or produce as profit ⟨*net·ted* five dollars on the sale⟩

⁵net *n* : a net amount, profit, weight, or price

neth·er \'ne_th_-ər\ *adj* : ³LOWER 1

neth·er·most \'ne_th_-ər-‚mōst\ *adj* : being the farthest down

neth·er·world \'ne_th_-ər-‚wərld\ *n* : the world of the dead

net·ting \'net-iŋ\ *n* **1** : NETWORK 1 **2** : the act or process of making a net

¹net·tle \'net-ᵊl\ *n* : any of several tall coarse herbs with stinging hairs

²nettle *vb* **net·tled; net·tling** \'net-liŋ, -ᵊl-iŋ\ **1** : to sting with nettles **2** : ANNOY, VEX

net–veined \'net-'vānd\ *adj* : having veins that branch and come together again to form a network ⟨dicotyledons such as asters, oaks, or a cabbage plant have *net-veined* leaves⟩ — compare PARALLEL-VEINED

nettle

net·work \'net-‚wərk\ *n* **1** : a fabric or structure of cords or wires that cross with even spacings **2** : a system of lines or channels resembling a network **3** : a group or system of related or connected parts; *esp* : a group of connected radio or television stations

neu·ral \'n(y)ùr-əl\ *adj* : of, relating to, or involving a nerve or the nervous system

neu·ral·gia \n(y)ù-'ral-jə\ *n* : pain that follows the course of a nerve; *also* : a condition marked by such pain

neu·ro·hor·mone \‚n(y)ùr-ō-'hòr-‚mōn\ *n* : a hormone produced by or acting on nervous tissue

neu·ro·hu·mor \‚n(y)ùr-ō-'hyü-mər, -'yü-\ *n* : NEUROHORMONE; *esp* : a substance that carries a nerve impulse from one neuron to another

neu·rol·o·gist \n(y)ù-'räl-ə-jəst\ *n* : a specialist in neurology; *esp* : a physician who specializes in identifying and treating diseases of the nervous system

\ə\ abut		\aú\ out	\i\ tip	\ò\ saw	\ú\ foot
\ər\ further		\ch\ chin	\ī\ life	\òi\ coin	\y\ yet
\a\ mat		\e\ pet	\j\ job	\th\ thin	\yü\ few
\ā\ take		\ē\ easy	\ŋ\ sing	_th_\ this	\yù\ cure
\ä\ cot, cart		\g\ go	\ō\ bone	\ü\ food	\zh\ vision

neu·rol·o·gy \n(y)ù-'räl-ə-jē\ *n* : the scientific study of the nervous system — **neu·ro·log·i·cal** \,n(y)ùr-ə-'läj-i-kəl\ *or* **neu·ro·log·ic** \-'läj-ik\ *adj*

neu·ron \'n(y)ü-,rän, 'n(y)ù(ə)r-,än\ *also* **neu·rone** \-,rōn, -,ōn\ *n* : a grayish or reddish cell that is the basic working unit of the nervous system and has an axon and dendrites that carry nerve impulses

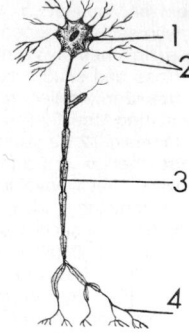

neu·ro·sis \n(y)ù-'rō-səs\ *n, pl* **-ro·ses** \-'rō-,sēz\ : any of various mental and emotional disorders that affect only part of a person's personality, are less serious than a psychosis, and involve reactions (as abnormal fears, imaginary physical ailments, or the development of separated parts to the personality) to anxiety that are harmful to oneself

neuron: *1* cell body, *2* dendrite, *3* axon, *4* nerve ending

neu·ros·po·ra \n(y)ù-'räs-pə-rə\ *n* : any of a genus of fungi that often have pink spores, are important in genetic research, and are severe pests in bakeries

neu·ro·sur·geon \,n(y)ùr-ō-'sər-jən\ *n* : a surgeon who specializes in the surgery of nervous structures (as nerves, the brain, or the spinal cord)

¹neu·rot·ic \n(y)ù-'rät-ik\ *adj* : of, relating to, being, or affected with neurosis — **neu·rot·i·cal·ly** \-i-k(ə-)lē\ *adv*

²neurotic *n* **1** : a person affected with a neurosis **2** : an emotionally unstable person

¹neu·ter \'n(y)üt-ər\ *adj* **1** : relating to or being the class of words that ordinarily includes most of those referring to things that are neither male nor female ⟨a *neuter* noun⟩ ⟨the *neuter* gender⟩ **2** : lacking sex organs; *also* : having imperfectly developed sex organs

²neuter *n* **1 a** : a word or form of the neuter gender **b** : the neuter gender **2** : WORKER 2

³neuter *vb* : CASTRATE, ALTER 2

¹neu·tral \'n(y)ü-trəl\ *n* **1** : one that is neutral **2** : a neutral color **3** : a state in which transmission gears (as of a motor vehicle) are not in contact so that power from the engine is not passed to the drive shaft

²neutral *adj* **1 a** : not favoring either side in a quarrel, contest, or war **b** : of or relating to a neutral country **2** : neither one thing nor the other **3** : having no color that stands out : somewhat gray **4** : neither acid nor basic **5** : not electrically charged — **neu·tral·ly** \-trə-lē\ *adv*

neu·tral·ism \'n(y)ü-trə-,liz-əm\ *n* : a policy of neutrality in international affairs

neu·tral·ist \'n(y)ü-trə-ləst\ *n* **1** : one that favors or practices neutrality **2** : one that favors keeping or making a state or region neutral

neu·tral·i·ty \n(y)ü-'tral-ət-ē\ *n* : the quality or state of being neutral especially in time of war

neu·tral·ize \'n(y)ü-trə-,līz\ *vb* **-ized; -iz·ing** **1** : to make chemically neutral ⟨*neutralize* an acid with a base⟩ **2** : to make ineffective : NULLIFY ⟨*neutralize* an opponent's move⟩ **3** : to make electrically neutral by combining equal positive and negative quantities **4** : to make politically neutral ⟨*neutralize* a country⟩ — **neu·tral·iza·tion** \,n(y)ü-trə-lə-'zā-shən\ *n* — **neu·tral·iz·er** \'n(y)ü-trə-,līz-ər\ *n*

neu·tri·no \n(y)ü-'trē-nō\ *n, pl* **-nos** : an uncharged elementary particle believed to have no mass

neu·tron \'n(y)ü-,trän\ *n* : an uncharged atomic particle that has a mass nearly equal to that of the proton and is present in all known atomic nuclei except the hydrogen nucleus

neutron star *n* : an object in space that is believed to be very small and very dense, to consist mostly of closely packed neutrons, and to be produced by the collapse of a star with a mass greater than 1.4 times the mass of the sun

neu·tro·phil \'n(y)ü-trə-,fil\ *n* : a cell with fine grains in it that is the white blood cell doing most of the work in collecting and taking in stray and foreign matter

nev·er \'nev-ər\ *adv* **1** : not ever : at no time ⟨*never* saw it before⟩ ⟨*never* had a sick day in my life⟩ **2** : not to any extent or in any way ⟨*never* fear⟩

nev·er·more \,nev-ər-'mō(ə)r, -'mó(ə)r\ *adv* : never again

nev·er·the·less \,nev-ər-thə-'les\ *adv* : in spite of that : HOWEVER

¹new \'n(y)ü\ *adj* **1** : not old : RECENT, MODERN **2** : not the same as the former : taking the place of one that came before ⟨a *new* teacher⟩ **3** : recently discovered or learned about ⟨*new* lands⟩ ⟨*new* plants and animals⟩ **4** : not known or experienced before ⟨*new* feelings⟩ **5** : not accustomed ⟨*new* to this work⟩ **6** : beginning as a repeating of some previous act or thing ⟨the *new* year⟩ **7** : refreshed in spirits or vigor ⟨felt like a *new* person after my vacation⟩ **8** : being in a position or place for the first time ⟨a *new* member⟩ — **new·ness** *n*

syn NEW, NOVEL, ORIGINAL, FRESH mean having recently come into existence or use. NEW may apply to what is freshly made and unused ⟨*new* bricks⟩ or has not been known before ⟨*new* design⟩ or not experienced before ⟨starts a *new* job⟩ NOVEL applies to what is not only new but strange or untried ⟨a *novel* way of solving the problem⟩ ORIGINAL applies to what is the first of its kind to exist ⟨a person without one *original* idea⟩ FRESH applies to what has not lost its original qualities of newness such as liveliness, energy, or brightness ⟨*fresh* towels⟩ ⟨a *fresh* start in life⟩

²new *adv* : just recently ⟨*new*-mown hay⟩

¹new·born \'n(y)ü-'bò(ə)rn\ *adj* **1** : recently born **2** : born anew

²newborn *n, pl* **newborn** *or* **newborns** : a newborn individual

new·com·er \'n(y)ü-,kəm-ər\ *n* **1** : one recently arrived **2** : BEGINNER

new·el \'n(y)ü-əl\ *n* **1** : an upright post about which the steps of a circular staircase wind **2** : a post at the foot of a straight stairway or one at a landing

new·fan·gled \'n(y)ü-'faŋ-gəld\ *adj* : of the newest style : NOVEL ⟨*newfangled* ideas⟩ ⟨a *newfangled* contraption⟩

new–fash·ioned \'n(y)ü-'fash-ənd\ *adj* : UP-TO-DATE 2, MODERN

New·found·land \'n(y)ü-fən-(d)lənd, -,(d)land; n(y)ü-'faùn-(d)lənd\ *n* : any of a breed of very large usually black dogs developed in Newfoundland

Newfoundland

new·ly \'n(y)ü-lē\ *adv* **1** : not long ago : RECENTLY ⟨a *newly* married couple⟩ **2** : in a new or different way : ANEW ⟨a *newly* furnished house⟩

new·ly·wed \'n(y)ü-lē-,wed\ *n* : a person recently married

new moon *n* : the moon's phase when its dark side is toward the earth; *also* : the thin curved outline of the moon seen shortly after sunset for a few days after the actual occurrence of the new moon phase

news \'n(y)üz\ *n* **1** : a report of recent events or of something unknown ⟨brought us the office *news*⟩ **2** : material reported in a newspaper or news periodical or on a newscast **3** : an event that is interesting enough to be reported

news agency *n* : an organization that supplies news to subscribing newspapers, magazines, and newscasters

news·boy \'n(y)üz-,bòi\ *n* : a person who delivers or sells newspapers

news·cast \-,kast\ *n* : a radio or television broadcast of news — **news·cast·er** \-,kas-tər\ *n*

news·let·ter \-,let-ər\ *n* : a bulletin or small newspaper of interest chiefly to a special group

news·man \-mən, -,man\ *n* : one who gathers or reports the news : REPORTER, CORRESPONDENT

news·pa·per \'n(y)üz-,pā-pər, 'n(y)üs-\ *n* : a paper that is printed and distributed usually daily or weekly and contains news, articles of opinion, features, and advertising

news·pa·per·man \-,man\ *n* : one who owns or is employed by a newspaper; *esp* : one who writes or edits copy for a newspaper

news·print \'n(y)üz-,print\ *n* : paper made chiefly from wood pulp and used mostly for newspapers

news·reel \-,rēl\ *n* : a short motion picture dealing with current events

news·stand \-,stand\ *n* : a place where newspapers and magazines are sold

news·wor·thy \-,wər-the\ *adj* : sufficiently interesting to the average person to deserve reporting

newsy \'n(y)ü-zē\ *adj* **news·i·er; -est** : filled with news; *esp* : CHATTY 2 ⟨a *newsy* letter⟩

newt \'n(y)üt\ *n* : any of various small salamanders that live mostly in water

New Testament *n* : the second of the two chief divisions of the Bible — see BIBLE table

newt

new·ton \'n(y)üt-°n\ *n* : the unit of force in the metric system that is of such size that under its influence a body whose mass is one kilogram would experience an acceleration of one meter per second per second

New Year *n* **1** : NEW YEAR'S DAY; *also* : the first days of the year **2** : ROSH HASHANAH

New Year's Day *n* : January 1 observed as a legal holiday in many countries

¹next \'nekst\ *adj* : coming immediately before or following ⟨the *next* page⟩ ⟨the house *next* to ours⟩

²next \(')nekst\ *prep* : ¹NEXT TO

³next \'nekst\ *adv* **1** : in the nearest time, place, or order following ⟨open this package *next*⟩ **2** : at the first time to come after this ⟨when *next* we meet⟩

next–door *adj* : located or living in the next building, house, apartment, or room ⟨*next-door* neighbors⟩

next door *adv* : in or to the next building, house, apartment, or room

¹next to *prep* : immediately following : being close to ⟨*next to* the head of her class⟩

²next to *adv* : very nearly : ALMOST

Nez Percé \'nez-'pərs, 'nes-'pe(ə)rs, *French* nā-per-sā\ *n* : a member of an American Indian people of central Idaho and neighboring parts of Washington and Oregon [French, literally "pierced nose"]

ni·a·cin \'nī-ə-sən\ *n* : an acid of the vitamin B complex that is found widely in plants and animals and is used especially against pellagra — called also *nicotinic acid*

ni·a·cin·amide \,nī-ə-'sin-ə-,mīd\ *n* : a compound of the vitamin B complex that is used like niacin

nib \'nib\ *n* **1** : ¹BILL 1, BEAK **2** : the point of a pen **3** : a part that is pointed or sticks out

nib·ble \'nib-əl\ *vb* **nib·bled; nib·bling** \-(ə-)liŋ\ : to bite or chew gently or bit by bit — **nibble** *n* — **nib·bler** \-(ə-)lər\ *n*

nice \'nīs\ *adj* **1** : finicky in tastes or habits **2 a** : not obvious : SUBTLE ⟨a *nice* distinction⟩ **b** : having the ability to notice small differences ⟨a *nice* ear for music⟩ **3** : PLEASING, AGREEABLE ⟨a *nice* time⟩ ⟨a *nice* person⟩ **4** : well behaved : RESPECTABLE ⟨wasn't a *nice* thing to do⟩

— **nice·ly** *adv* — **nice·ness** *n*

Word History Five hundred years ago, when *nice* was first used in English, it meant "foolish or stupid". This is not as surprising as it may seem, since it came through early French from the Latin *nescius,* meaning "ignorant". By the 16th century, the sense of being "very particular" or "finicky" had developed. In the 19th century, *nice* came to mean "pleasant or agreeable" and then "respectable", a sense quite unlike its original meaning. [Middle English *nice* "foolish, stupid", from early French *nice* (same meaning), from Latin *nescius* "ignorant", from *nescire* "not to know", from *ne-* "not" and *scire* "to know" — related to SCIENCE]

nice·ty \'nī-sət-ē, -stē\ *n, pl* **-ties** **1** : a dainty, delicate, or elegant thing ⟨enjoy the *niceties* of life⟩ **2** : a small point or detail ⟨*niceties* of table manners⟩ **3** : careful attention to details ⟨*nicety* is needed in making watches⟩ **4** : the point at which a thing is at its best ⟨roasted to a *nicety*⟩

niche \'nich\ *n* **1** : a hollowed-out place in a wall especially for a statue **2** : a place, use, or work for which a person is best fitted **3 a** : a habitat that contains the things necessary for a particular plant or animal to live **b** : the part that a particular living thing plays in an ecological community

¹nick \'nik\ *n* **1** : a small groove : NOTCH **2** : ¹CHIP 4 ⟨a *nick* in a cup⟩ **3** : the last moment at which the result of an event can be changed ⟨the rescue team arrived in the *nick* of time⟩

²nick *vb* **1** : to make a nick in **2** : to touch lightly : GRAZE ⟨*nicked* by a bullet⟩

¹nick·el \'nik-əl\ *n* **1** : a silver-white hard metallic element that can be hammered and shaped and is capable of a high polish, resistant to wearing away, and used chiefly in alloys — see ELEMENT table **2 a** *also* **nick·le** : the U.S. five-cent piece made of nickel and copper **b** : five cents

Word History When copper miners in the German state of Saxony first dug out chunks of what is now known to be nickel ore, they thought it was copper. But even though it was reddish-brown like copper, the ore broke easily and did not seem to have any use. Because they were at first fooled, the Germans called this ore *kupfernickel,* meaning literally "copper demon" or "copper goblin". *Kupfer* is the German word for "copper" and *nickel* in German means "demon" or "goblin". Even though the metal turned out to be quite valuable, it kept its old name. For a while the term was *copper nickel* in English, and then simply *nickel,* for both the metal and the American five-cent coin made out of a combination of nickel and copper. [derived from German *kupfernickel* "a compound of nickel and arsenic", literally "copper demon", from *kupfer* "copper" and *nickel* "demon"]

²nick·el *vb* **-eled** *or* **-elled; -el·ing** *or* **-el·ling** \'nik-(ə-)liŋ\ : to plate with nickel

nick·el·ode·on \,nik-ə-'lōd-ē-ən\ *n* **1** : an early movie theater charging five cents for admission **2** : JUKEBOX

nick·er \'nik-ər\ *vb* **nick·ered; nick·er·ing** \-(ə-)riŋ\ : NEIGH, WHINNY — **nicker** *n*

¹nick·name \'nik-,nām\ *n* **1** : an often descriptive name (as "Shorty" or "Tex") given in addition to the one belonging to an individual **2** : a form of a proper name (as "Billy" for "William") used by family or friends

Word History The Middle English word *eke* meant "something added on". An *ekename* was therefore an added name given to a person or place. Many people who heard the phrase "an ekename", however, thought they were hearing "a nekename". Because of that con-

\ə\ **abut**	\au̇\ **out**	\i\ **tip**	\ȯ\ **saw**	\u̇\ **foot**
\ər\ **further**	\ch\ **chin**	\ī\ **life**	\ȯi\ **coin**	\y\ **yet**
\a\ **mat**	\e\ **pet**	\j\ **job**	\th\ **thin**	\yü\ **few**
\ā\ **take**	\ē\ **easy**	\ŋ\ **sing**	\th\ **this**	\yu̇\ **cure**
\ä\ **cot, cart**	\g\ **go**	\ō\ **bone**	\ü\ **food**	\zh\ **vision**

fusion over the course of many years, the word *ekename* became *nekename*. Later changes in spelling have given us the modern word *nickname*. [Middle English *nekename* "an additional name", from the phrase *an ekename* (misunderstood as being *a nekename*), from *eke* "something added on" and *name* "name"]

²nickname *vb* : to give a nickname to

nic·o·tine \'nik-ə-ˌtēn\ *n* : a poisonous substance found in tobacco and used especially as an insecticide

nic·o·tin·ic acid \ˌnik-ə-'tē-nik-, -'tin-ik-\ *n* : NIACIN

nic·ti·tat·ing membrane \ˌnik-tə-ˌtāt-iŋ-\ *n* : a thin membrane found in many animals at the inner angle or beneath the lower lid of the eye and capable of extending across the eyeball

niece \'nēs\ *n* : a daughter of one's brother, sister, brotherin-law, or sister-in-law

nif·ty \'nif-tē\ *adj* **nif·ti·er; -est** : very good : very attractive — **nifty** *n*

nig·gard \'nig-ərd\ *n* : a mean stingy person : MISER — **niggard** *adj*

nig·gard·ly \'nig-ərd-lē\ *adj* **1** : STINGY 1, MISERLY **2** : characteristic of a niggard : SCANTY — **niggardly** *adv*

¹nigh \'nī\ *adv* **1** : near in place, time, or relationship **2** : ALMOST, NEARLY [Old English *nēah* "near, nigh" — related to NEAR, NEIGHBOR; see *Word History* at NEIGHBOR]

²nigh *adj* : not far : CLOSE, NEAR

night \'nīt\ *n* **1** : the time between dusk and dawn when there is no sunlight **2** : NIGHTFALL **3** : the darkness of night — **night** *adj*

night blindness *n* : subnormal vision in faint light (as at night) — **night–blind** *adj*

night–bloom·ing ce·re·us \ˌnīt-ˌblüm-in-'sir-ē-əs\ *n* : any of several cacti that bloom at night; *esp* : a slender spreading or climbing cactus often grown for its large showy fragrant white flowers

night·cap \'nīt-ˌkap\ *n* **1** : a cap worn with nightclothes **2** : a drink taken at bedtime **3** : the final race or contest of a day's sports activities

night·clothes \-ˌklō(th)z\ *n pl* : garments worn in bed

night·club \-ˌkləb\ *n* : a place of entertainment open in the evening and usually serving food and liquor, having a floor show, and providing music for dancing

night crawler *n* : EARTHWORM; *esp* : a large earthworm found on the soil surface at night

night·dress \'nīt-ˌdres\ *n* : NIGHTGOWN

night·fall \-ˌfȯl\ *n* : the coming of night : DUSK

night·gown \-ˌgaun\ *n* : a long loose garment worn in bed

night·hawk \-ˌhȯk\ *n* **1** : any of several insect-eating birds that resemble the related whippoorwill **2** : NIGHT OWL

night·in·gale \'nīt-ᵊn-ˌgāl\ *n* : any of several Old World thrushes noted for the sweet song of the male

night·ly \'nīt-lē\ *adj* **1** : of or relating to the night or every night **2** : happening, done, or produced by night or every night — **nightly** *adv*

night·mare \'nīt-ˌma(ə)r, -ˌme(ə)r\ *n* **1** : a frightening dream **2** : a frightening or horrible experience — **night·mar·ish** \-ish\ *adj*

nightingale

> **Word History** In the Middle Ages many people believed in a type of evil spirit that was said to haunt people while they slept. Such a demon was known in Old English as a *mare*. Because it was believed to come in the night, it later became known in Middle English as a *nightmare*. It was not until the 16th century that the word *nightmare* came to mean "a frightening dream". This meaning probably came from the belief that such dreams were caused by evil spirits. [Middle English *nightmare* "evil spirit thought to haunt people during sleep", from *night* "night" and *mare* "spirit", from Old English *mare* "evil spirit haunting people in sleep"]

night owl *n* : a person who usually stays up late at night

night·shade \'nīt-ˌshād\ *n* : any of a family of herbs, shrubs, and trees having clusters of usually white, yellow, or purple flowers, and fruits that are berries and including many poisonous forms (as belladonna) and important food plants (as the potato, tomato, and eggplant)

night·shirt \-ˌshərt\ *n* : a nightgown resembling a shirt

night·stick \-ˌstik\ *n* : a police officer's club

night·time \'nīt-ˌtīm\ *n* : the time from dusk to dawn — **nighttime** *adj*

nil \'nil\ *n* : nothing at all : ZERO — **nil** *adj*

Ni·lot·ic \nī-'lät-ik\ *adj* : of or relating to the Nile or the peoples of the Nile basin

nim·ble \'nim-bəl\ *adj* **nim·bler** \-b(ə-)lər\; **nim·blest** \-b(ə-)ləst\ **1** : quick and light in motion : AGILE ⟨a *nimble* dancer⟩ **2** : quick in understanding and learning : CLEVER ⟨a *nimble* mind⟩ — **nim·ble·ness** \-bəl-nəs\ *n* — **nim·bly** \-blē\ *adv*

nim·bo·stra·tus \ˌnim-bō-'strāt-əs, -'strat-\ *n* : a low dark gray rainy cloud layer

nim·bus \'nim-bəs\ *n, pl* **nim·bi** \-ˌbī, -ˌbē\ *or* **nim·bus·es** **1** : a shining cloud about a god or goddess when on earth **2** : an indication (as a circle) of radiant light about the head of a drawn or sculptured god or saint **3** : a rain cloud that is evenly gray and extends over the entire sky

nimbus 2

nin·com·poop \'nin-kəm-ˌpüp, 'niŋ-\ *n* : ¹FOOL 1, SIMPLETON

nine \'nīn\ *n* **1** — see NUMBER table **2** : the ninth in a set or series **3** : a baseball team — **nine** *adj or pron*

nine·pin \-ˌpin\ *n* **1** *pl* : a bowling game resembling tenpins played without the headpin **2** : a pin used in ninepins

nine·teen \(')nīn(t)-'tēn\ *n* — see NUMBER table — **nineteen** *adj or pron* — **nine·teenth** \-'tēn(t)th\ *adj or n*

nine·ty \'nīnt-ē\ *n, pl* **nineties** **1** — see NUMBER table **2** *pl* : the numbers 90 to 99 and specifically the years 90 to 99 in a lifetime or century — **nine·ti·eth** \-ē-əth\ *adj or n* — **ninety** *adj or pron*

nin·ja \'nin-jə, -(ˌ)jä\ *n, pl* **ninja** *also* **ninjas** : a person trained in ancient Japanese arts of combat and self-defense and employed especially for espionage and assassinations

nin·ny \'nin-ē\ *n, pl* **ninnies** : ¹FOOL 1, SIMPLETON

ninth \'nīn(t)th\ *n, pl* **ninths** — see NUMBER table — **ninth** *adj or adv*

ni·o·bi·um \nī-'ō-bē-əm\ *n* : a shiny gray metallic element used in alloys — see ELEMENT table

¹nip \'nip\ *vb* **nipped; nip·ping** **1** : to catch hold of and squeeze tightly between two surfaces, edges, or points ⟨the dog *nipped* my ankle⟩ **2** : to cut off by pinching or clipping **3** : to destroy the growth or progress of ⟨*nipped* in the bud⟩ **4** : to make numb with cold : CHILL **5** : to seize suddenly and forcibly : SNATCH, STEAL **6** : to move quickly or nimbly [Middle English *nippen* "to nip"]

²nip *n* **1** : something (as a sharp stinging cold or a biting flavor) that nips ⟨cheese with a *nip*⟩ **2** : the act of nipping : PINCH, BITE **3** : a small portion : BIT

³nip *n* : a small quantity of liquor ⟨takes a *nip* now and then⟩ [probably a shortened form of *nipperkin* "a liquor container"; of unknown origin]

nip and tuck \ˌnip-ən-'tək\ *adj or adv* : so close that the advantage shifts rapidly from one contestant to another

nip·per \'nip-ər\ *n* **1** : a device (as pincers) for nipping — usually used in pl. **2** : a small boy

nip·ple \\'nip-əl\\ *n* **1** : the part of the female breast from which a baby or young mammal sucks milk **2** : something resembling a nipple; *esp* : the rubber mouthpiece of a baby's nursing bottle

Nip·pon·ese \\,nip-ə-'nēz, -'nēs\\ *adj* : of or relating to Japan or Japanese : JAPANESE — **Nipponese** *n*

nip·py \\'nip-ē\\ *adj* **nip·pi·er; -est** **1** : quick in movement : NIMBLE, BRISK **2** : having a biting flavor **3** : CHILLY ⟨a *nippy* day⟩

ni·sei \\(')nē-'sā, 'nē-,sā\\ *n, pl* **nisei** *also* **niseis** : a son or daughter of immigrant Japanese parents who is born and educated in America [Japanese, literally "second generation"]

nit \\'nit\\ *n* : the egg of a louse or similar insect; *also* : the insect itself when young

ni·ter \\'nīt-ər\\ *n* **1** : POTASSIUM NITRATE **2** : SODIUM NITRATE

nit·pick \\'nit-,pik\\ *vb* : to criticize for tiny faults that are usually of little importance — **nit·pick·er** *n*

ni·trate \\'nī-,trāt, -trət\\ *n* **1** : a chemical compound formed by the reaction of nitric acid with another substance **2** : nitrate of sodium or potassium used as a fertilizer

nitric acid \\'nī-trik-\\ *n* : a strong liquid nitrogen-containing acid used in making fertilizers, explosives, and dyes

ni·tri·fi·ca·tion \\,nī-trə-fə-'kā-shən\\ *n* : the process of combining, mixing, or filling with nitrogen or one of its compounds; *esp* : the oxidation (as by bacteria) of ammonium salts to nitrites and then to nitrates

ni·tri·fi·er \\'nī-trə-,fī-(-ə)r\\ *n* : any of various soil bacteria capable of nitrification

ni·tri·fy·ing \\'nī-trə-,fī-iŋ\\ *adj* : active in nitrification ⟨*nitrifying* bacteria⟩

ni·trite \\'nī-,trīt\\ *n* : a salt of a certain unstable nitrogen-containing acid that is known only in solution or in the form of its salts

ni·tro·gen \\'nī-trə-jən\\ *n* : a colorless tasteless odorless gaseous element that makes up 78 percent of the atmosphere and forms a part of all living tissues — see ELEMENT table — **ni·trog·e·nous** \\nī-'träj-ə-nəs\\ *adj*

nitrogen cycle *n* : a continuous series of natural processes by which nitrogen passes from air to soil to living things and back to the air by means of nitrogen fixation, nitrification, decay, and denitrification

nitrogen dioxide *n* : a brownish to yellowish poisonous gas that is used especially in making nitric acid and is an air pollutant formed from automobile exhausts

nitrogen fixation *n* : the changing of free nitrogen in the air into combined forms especially by bacteria in the soil and in roots

nitrogen–fixer *n* : any of various living things (as bacteria) in the soil that are capable of nitrogen fixation

nitrogen–fixing *adj* : capable of nitrogen fixation

nitrogen oxide *n* : any of several oxides of nitrogen (as nitrous oxide) that may be formed by the reaction of nitrogen with oxygen, by the reaction of nitric acid with another substance, or by the breaking down of compounds containing nitrogen

ni·tro·glyc·er·in *or* **ni·tro·glyc·er·ine** \\,nī-trə-'glis-(ə-)rən\\ *n* : a heavy oily explosive poisonous liquid used chiefly in making dynamites and in medicine to relax blood vessels

nitrous oxide *n* : a colorless gas that when inhaled causes loss of the ability to feel pain and sometimes produces laughter and is used especially in dentistry — called also *laughing gas*

nit·ty–grit·ty \\'nit-ē-,grit-ē, ,nit-ē-'grit-ē\\ *n* : what is essential and basic ⟨getting down to the *nitty-gritty* of the problem⟩

nit·wit \\'nit-,wit\\ *n* : a stupid or silly person

¹no \\(')nō\\ *adv* **1** — used to express the negative of an alternative ⟨shall we go to the game or *no*⟩ **2** : in no respect or degree — used in comparisons ⟨it is *no* better

than I expected it to be⟩ **3** : not so — used to express disagreement or refusal ⟨*no*, I'm not hungry⟩ **4** — used with a following adjective to imply a meaning expressed by the opposite positive statement ⟨*no* uncertain terms⟩ **5** — used to emphasize a following negative or to introduce a statement that is clearer or has more emphasis ⟨has the right, *no*, the duty, to continue⟩ **6** — used to express surprise, doubt, or disbelief ⟨*no* — you don't say⟩

²no *adj* **1 a** : not any ⟨has *no* money⟩ **b** : hardly any : very little ⟨finished in *no* time⟩ **2** : not a ⟨I'm *no* expert⟩

³no \\'nō\\ *n, pl* **noes** *or* **nos** \\'nōz\\ **1** : an act or instance of refusing or denying by the use of the word *no* : DENIAL **2 a** : a negative vote or decision **b** *pl* : persons voting in the negative

no·bel·i·um \\nō-'bel-ē-əm\\ *n* : a radioactive element produced artificially — see ELEMENT table

No·bel prize \\(,)nō-,bel-\\ *n* : an annual prize (as in literature, medicine, peace) established by the will of Alfred Nobel for the encouragement of people who work for the interests of humanity

no·bil·i·ty \\nō-'bil-ət-ē\\ *n, pl* **-ties** **1** : the quality or state of being noble ⟨*nobility* of character⟩ **2** : the body of persons forming the noble class in a country or state ⟨a member of the *nobility*⟩

¹no·ble \\'nō-bəl\\ *adj* **no·bler** \\-b(ə-)lər\\; **no·blest** \\-b(ə-)ləst\\ **1** : FAMOUS, NOTABLE ⟨*noble* deed⟩ **2** : of high birth or rank : ARISTOCRATIC **3** : possessing very high qualities : EXCELLENT **4** : grand especially in appearance : IMPOSING ⟨a *noble* cathedral⟩ **5** : having or characterized by superiority of mind or character : MAGNANIMOUS ⟨a *noble* nature⟩ **6** : chemically inactive especially toward oxygen ⟨*noble* metal⟩ — **no·ble·ness** \\-bəl-nəs\\ *n* — **no·bly** \\-blē\\ *adv*

²noble *n* : a person of noble rank or birth

no·ble·man \\'nō-bəl-mən\\ *n* : a man of noble rank

no·ble·wom·an \\-,wùm-ən\\ *n* : a woman of noble rank

¹no·body \\'nō-bəd-ē, -,bäd-ē\\ *pron* : no person : not anybody ⟨*nobody* lives in that house⟩

²nobody *n, pl* **no·bod·ies** : a person of no importance

noc·tur·nal \\näk-'tərn-ᵊl\\ *adj* **1** : of, relating to, or occurring in the night ⟨a *nocturnal* journey⟩ **2** : active at night ⟨*nocturnal* insects⟩ [from early French *nocturnal, nocturnel* or Latin *nocturnalis*, both meaning "nocturnal", derived from earlier Latin *noct-, nox* "night" — related to EQUINOX] — **noc·tur·nal·ly** \\-ᵊl-ē\\ *adv*

noc·turne \\'näk-,tərn\\ *n* : a work of art dealing with evening or night; *esp* : a dreamy composition for the piano

¹nod \\'näd\\ *vb* **nod·ded; nod·ding** **1** : to bend the head downward or forward (as in bowing or going to sleep or as a way of answering "yes") **2** : to move up and down ⟨the tulips *nodded* in the breeze⟩ **3** : to show by a nod of the head ⟨*nod* agreement⟩ **4** : to let one's attention roam for a moment and make an error — **nod·der** *n*

²nod *n* : the action of nodding

nod·ding \\'näd-iŋ\\ *adj* : bending downward or forward ⟨a plant with *nodding* flowers⟩

nod·dle \\'näd-ᵊl\\ *n* : ¹HEAD 1

nod·dy \\'näd-ē\\ *n, pl* **nod·dies** : any of several stout-bodied terns of warm seas

node \\'nōd\\ *n* **1 a** : a

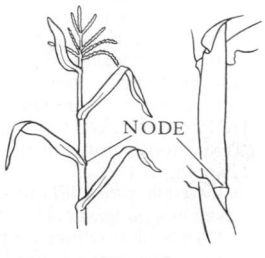

NODE

node 2

\\ə\\ abut	\\au̇\\ out	\\i\\ tip	\\ȯ\\ saw	\\u̇\\ foot
\\ər\\ further	\\ch\\ chin	\\ī\\ life	\\ȯi\\ coin	\\y\\ yet
\\a\\ mat	\\e\\ pet	\\j\\ job	\\th\\ thin	\\yü\\ few
\\ā\\ take	\\ē\\ easy	\\ŋ\\ sing	\\th\\ this	\\yu̇\\ cure
\\ä\\ cot, cart	\\g\\ go	\\ō\\ bone	\\ü\\ food	\\zh\\ vision

thickened or swollen enlargement (as of a joint with rheumatism)   **b** : a body part resembling a knot   **2** : a point on a stem at which a leaf is inserted — **nod·al** \'nōd-ᵊl\ *adj*

nod·ule \'näj-(,)ü(ə)l\ *n*   **1** : a small rounded mass ⟨manganese *nodules* on the ocean floor⟩   **2** : a swelling on the root of a plant of the legume family that contains nitrogen-fixing bacteria — **nod·u·lar** \'näj-ə-lər\ *adj*

no·el \nō-'el\ *n*   **1** : a Christmas carol   **2** *cap* : the Christmas season [from French *noël* "Christmas, a carol", from Latin *natalis* "birthday"]

nog·gin \'näg-ən\ *n*   **1** : a small mug   **2** : a small quantity of drink usually equal to a gill   **3** : a person's head

no–good \,nō-'gud\ *adj* : having no worth, use, or chance of success — **no–good** \'nō-,gud\ *n*

no–hit·ter \(')nō-'hit-ər\ *n* : a baseball game in which a pitcher allows the opposition no base hits

¹noise \'nȯiz\ *n*   **1** : a loud, confused, or senseless shouting or outcry   **2 a** : ³SOUND 1b; *esp* : a loud, harsh, or unharmonious sound   **b** : an unwanted signal in an electronic communication system

> **Word History** Although loud noise may make us sick, we probably do not think of the words *noise* and *nausea* as having much in common. But the word *noise* came into English from early French, in which it meant "quarrel, loud noise". French had it from the Latin word *nausea* meaning "seasickness, nausea". Perhaps the original connection was with the unpleasant sounds or complaints made by seasick passengers or sailors. *Nausea*, after all, came from the Greek word for sailor, *nautēs*. [Middle English *noise* "noise", from early French *noise* "quarrel, loud noise", from Latin *nausea* "seasickness, nausea", derived from Greek *nautēs* "sailor" — related to NAUSEA; see *Word History* at NAUSEA]

²noise *vb* **noised; nois·ing** : to spread by rumor or report ⟨*noised* it about that we would be allowed to leave early⟩

noise·less \'nȯiz-ləs\ *adj* : making or causing no noise ⟨kittens on *noiseless* feet⟩ — **noise·less·ly** *adv*

noise·mak·er \'nȯiz-,mā-kər\ *n* : one that makes noise; *esp* : a device used to make noise at parties

noise pollution *n* : environmental pollution consisting of annoying or harmful noise — called also *sound pollution*

noi·some \'nȯi-səm\ *adj*   **1** : not wholesome ⟨a *noisome* slum⟩   **2** : disagreeable especially to the sense of smell : DISGUSTING ⟨*noisome* odors⟩

noisy \'nȯi-zē\ *adj* **nois·i·er; -est**   **1** : making noise   **2** : full of or characterized by noise ⟨a *noisy* street⟩ — **nois·i·ly** \-zə-lē\ *adv* — **nois·i·ness** \-zē-nəs\ *n*

no·mad \'nō-,mad\ *n*   **1** : a member of a people that has no fixed home but wanders from place to place   **2** : an individual who roams about without a goal or purpose — **nomad** *or* **no·mad·ic** \nō-'mad-ik\ *adj* — **no·mad·ism** \'nō-,mad-,iz-əm\ *n*

no–man's–land \'nō-,manz-,land\ *n* : an unoccupied area between opposing armies

nom de plume \,näm-di-'plüm\ *n, pl* **noms de plume** \,näm(z)-di-\ : PEN NAME [a phrase believed to have been made up in English as a French translation of *pen name*; from French *nom* "name" and *de* "of" and *plume* "(the) pen"]

no·men·cla·ture \'nō-mən-,klā-chər\ *n* : a system of terms used in a particular science, field of knowledge, or art; *esp* : the scientific names for plants and animals used in biology — compare BINOMIAL NOMENCLATURE [from Latin *nomenclatura* "a calling by name, list of names", derived from *nomen* "name" and *calatus,* past participle of *calare* "to call"]

nom·i·nal \'näm-ən-ᵊl, 'näm-nəl\ *adj*   **1** : being such in name or form only ⟨the *nominal* head of the party⟩   **2** : very small : TRIFLING ⟨a *nominal* price⟩ — **nom·i·nal·ly** \-ē\ *adv*

nom·i·nate \'näm-ə-,nāt\ *vb* **-nat·ed; -nat·ing** : to choose as a candidate for election, appointment, or honor; *esp* : to propose for office ⟨*nominated* a senator for president⟩ — **nom·i·na·tor** \-,nāt-ər\ *n*

nom·i·na·tion \,näm-ə-'nā-shən\ *n*   **1** : the act, process, or an instance of nominating   **2** : the state of being nominated

nom·i·na·tive \'näm-(ə-)nət-iv\ *adj* : being or belonging to the case of a noun or pronoun that is usually the subject of a verb — **nominative** *n*

nom·i·nee \,näm-ə-'nē\ *n* : a person nominated for an office, duty, or position

no·mo·gram \'näm-ə-,gram, 'nō-mə-\ *n* : a set of several lines marked off to scale and arranged in such a way that by using a straightedge to connect known values on two lines an unknown value can be read at the point of intersection with another line

no·mo·graph \'näm-ə-,graf, 'nō-mə-\ *n* : NOMOGRAM

non- \(')nän, ,nän\ *prefix* : not : reverse of : absence of ⟨*non*resident⟩ ⟨*non*fiction⟩ [derived from Latin *non* "not"]

nonabsorbent	nonconflicting	nonessential
nonabstainer	nonconforming	nonexclusive
nonacademic	nonconscious	nonexempt
nonacid	nonconstitutional	nonexistence
nonaction	nonconstructive	nonexistent
nonactive	noncontemporary	nonexplosive
nonadhesive	noncontinuous	nonfarm
nonadjacent	noncontradictory	nonfatal
nonadjustable	noncontributing	nonfattening
nonaggression	noncontrolled	nonfederal
nonagreement	noncontrolling	nonfederated
nonagricultural	noncontroversial	nonferrous
nonalcoholic	nonconventional	nonfigurative
nonathlete	nonconvertible	nonfinancial
nonathletic	noncorporate	nonfissionable
nonattendance	noncorrosive	nonflagellated
nonautomatic	noncreative	nonflammable
nonbeliever	noncriminal	nonflying
nonbelligerent	noncritical	nonfood
nonbinding	noncrystalline	nonfreezing
nonbiodegradable	nondeductible	nonfulfillment
nonbiting	nondegenerate	nonfunctional
nonbreakable	nondelivery	nonfunctioning
nonbusiness	nondemocratic	nongaseous
noncaking	nondenominational	nongovernmental
noncellular	nonderivative	nonhandicapped
nonchargeable	nondestructive	nonhardy
nonchlorine	nondevelopment	nonhereditary
non–Christian	nondigestible	nonhistorical
noncitizen	nondirectional	nonhuman
nonclassical	nondisabled	nonimmigrant
nonclerical	nondisclosure	non–Indo–European
nonclinical	nondiscrimination	nonindustrial
nonclotting	nondisjoint	noninfectious
noncoated	nondistinctive	noninflammable
noncoercive	nondistribution	noninstitutional
noncollectable	nondivided	noninstructional
noncollegiate	nondocumentary	nonintegrated
noncombat	nondollar	nonintellectual
noncombustible	nondomesticated	noninterference
noncommercial	nondramatic	nonintersecting
noncommunicable	nondurable	nonintoxicating
noncompetent	noneconomic	noninvolvement
noncompeting	noneducational	nonionized
noncompetitive	noneffervescent	nonirritating
noncomplementary	nonelastic	non–Jewish
noncompliance	nonelective	nonleaded
noncompressible	nonelectric	nonlegal
nonconclusive	nonelectrical	nonlethal
nonconducting	noneligible	nonlexical
nonconfidence	nonempirical	nonliquid

nonliterary
nonliterate
nonliturgical
nonliving
nonlocal
nonlogical
nonluminous
nonmagnetic
nonmalleable
nonmaterial
nonmeat
nonmechanical
nonmedicinal
nonmember
nonmembership
nonmetric
nonmetrical
nonmigratory
nonmilitary
nonmolecular
nonmoral
nonmotile
nonmoving
nonmusical
nonnational
nonnative
nonnatural
nonnecessity
nonnegotiable
nonnumerical
nonnutritious
nonobligatory
nonobservance
nonoccurrence
nonoily
nonoperating
nonorganic
nonorthodox
nonparallel
nonparalytic
nonparasitic
nonparticipant
nonparty
nonpathogenic
nonpayment
nonpecuniary
nonperformance
nonperishable
nonpersistent
nonpersonal
nonphysical
nonpoisonous
nonpolar
nonpolitical
nonpolluting

nonporous
nonpossession
nonpractical
nonpregnant
nonprint
nonprinting
nonproducer
nonprofessional
nonprogressive
nonprotein
nonproven
nonpublic
nonracial
nonradical
nonradioactive
nonrated
nonrational
nonreactive
nonreader
nonrealistic
nonreciprocal
nonrecoverable
nonrecurrent
nonreducing
nonregistered
nonregulation
nonreligious
nonrepresentative
nonresidential
nonrestraint
nonrestricted
nonretractile
nonreturnable
nonreusable
nonrevenue
nonreversible
nonrhetorical
nonrotating
nonsalable
nonscientific
nonscientist
nonseasonal
nonsecret
nonsegregated
nonsegregation
nonselective
nonsensitive
nonsensuous
nonsexist
nonsexual
nonshrinkable
nonsinkable
nonsmoker
nonsocial

nonsolar
nonsolid
nonspatial
nonspeaking
nonspecialist
nonspecialized
nonspecific
nonspeculative
nonstaining
nonstationary
nonstatistical
nonstellar
nonstrategic
nonstriated
nonstriker
nonstructural
nonsubscriber
nonsuccess
nonsugar
nonsurgical
nonswimmer
nonsymbolic
nonsymmetrical
nontaxable
nontechnical
nontemporal
nonterritorial
nontheatrical
nonthermal
nonthreatening
nontoxic
nontraditional
nontransferable
nontransparent
nontropical
nontypical
nonuniform
nonuniversal
nonurgent
nonuser
nonvalid
nonvascular
nonvenomous
nonvibratory
nonviewer
nonviolation
nonviscous
nonvisual
nonvocal
nonvocational
nonvoting
nonwoody
nonworker
nonzero

no·na·gon \\'nō-nə-ˌgän\\ *n*
: a polygon of nine angles
and nine sides

nonce \\'nän(t)s\\ *n* : the one,
particular, or present occasion, purpose, or use ⟨for
the *nonce*⟩

non·cha·lance \\ˌnän-shə-
ˈlän(t)s, 'nän-shə-ˌlän(t)s\\ *n*
: the quality or state of being
nonchalant

non·cha·lant \\ˌnän-shə-
ˈlänt, 'nän-shə-ˌlänt\\ *adj*
: having a confident and
easy manner ⟨face a crowd
with *nonchalant* ease⟩ [from French *nonchalant* "not ex-

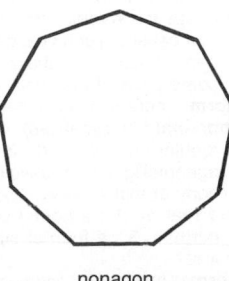

nonagon

cited", derived from early French *nonchaloir* "to disregard,
be unconcerned", from *non-* "not" and *chaloir* "to care, to
be hot", from Latin *calēre* "to be hot" — related to CALD-
RON, CALORIE] — **non·cha·lant·ly** *adv*

non·com \\'nän-ˌkäm\\ *n* : NONCOMMISSIONED OFFICER

non·com·ba·tant \\ˌnän-kəm-ˈbat-ᵊnt, (')nän-ˈkäm-bət-ənt\\
n **1** : a member (as a chaplain) of the armed forces
whose duties do not include fighting **2** : CIVILIAN — **non-
combatant** *adj*

non·com·mis·sioned officer \\ˌnän-kə-ˌmish-ənd-\\ *n* : an
officer in the Army, Air Force, or Marine Corps appointed
from among the enlisted persons

non·com·mit·tal \\ˌnän-kə-ˈmit-ᵊl\\ *adj* : not telling or showing what a person thinks or has decided ⟨a *noncommittal*
answer⟩ — **non·com·mit·tal·ly** \\-ᵊl-ē\\ *adv*

non·con·duc·tor \\ˌnän-kən-ˈdək-tər\\ *n* : a substance that
conducts heat, electricity, or sound at a very low rate

non·con·form·ist \\ˌnän-kən-ˈfor-məst\\ *n* **1** *often cap* : a
person who does not conform to an established church **2**
: a person who does not conform to generally accepted
standards or customs — **nonconformist** *adj, often cap*

non·con·for·mi·ty \\ˌnän-kən-ˈfor-mət-ē\\ *n* : failure or refusal to conform

non·dairy \\'nän-ˈde(ə)r-ē\\ *adj* : containing no milk or milk
products ⟨*nondairy* whipped topping⟩

non·de·script \\ˌnän-di-ˈskript\\ *adj* : belonging or appearing
to belong to no particular class or kind : not easily described — **nondescript** *n*

non·di·vid·ing \\ˌnän-də-ˈvīd-iŋ\\ *adj* : not undergoing cell
division

¹none \\'nən\\ *pron* **1** : not any ⟨*none* of them went⟩ ⟨*none*
of it is needed⟩ **2** : not one ⟨*none* of the family⟩ **3** : not
any such thing or person ⟨half a loaf is better than *none*⟩

²none *adv* **1** : by no means : not at all ⟨*none* too soon to
begin⟩ **2** : in no way : to no extent ⟨*none* the worse for
wear⟩

non·elec·tro·lyte \\ˌnän-ə-ˈlek-trə-ˌlīt\\ *n* : a substance that
does not readily form ions when dissolved or melted and
that is a poor conductor of electricity

non·en·ti·ty \\nä-ˈnen(t)-ət-ē\\ *n, pl* **-ti·ties** **1** : something
that does not exist or exists only in the imagination **2** : a
person of no importance

non·es·sen·tial \\ˌnän-i-ˈsen-chəl\\ *adj* : not necessary or
essential — **nonessential** *n*

none·the·less \\ˌnən-thə-ˈles\\ *adv* : NEVERTHELESS

non·fat \\'nän-ˈfat\\ *adj* : having no fat solids : having fat
solids removed ⟨*nonfat* milk⟩

non·fic·tion \\'nän-ˈfik-shən\\ *n* : literature that is not fictional — **non·fic·tion·al** \\(')nän-ˈfik-shnəl, -shən-ᵊl\\ *adj*

non·flow·er·ing \\(')nän-ˈflaú-(ə-)riŋ\\ *adj* : producing no
flowers; *esp* : having no flowering stage in the life cycle

non·green \\'nän-ˈgrēn\\ *adj* : having no chlorophyll ⟨*non-
green* plants⟩

no·nil·lion \\nō-ˈnil-yən\\ *n* — see NUMBER table

non·in·ter·ven·tion \\ˌnän-ˌint-ər-ˈven-chən\\ *n* **1** : the
state or habit of not intervening **2** : refusal or failure to
intervene

non·met·al \\(')nän-ˈmet-ᵊl\\ *n* : an element (as carbon or
nitrogen) that lacks the characteristics of a metal

non·me·tal·lic \\ˌnän-mə-ˈtal-ik\\ *adj* **1** : not metallic **2**
: of, relating to, or being a nonmetal

non·neg·a·tive \\(')nän-ˈneg-ət-iv\\ *adj* : not negative; *esp*
: being either positive or zero ⟨a *nonnegative* integer⟩

non·nu·cle·ar \\(')nän-ˈn(y)ü-klē-ər\\ *adj* : not operated by
or involving atomic energy ⟨electricity from a *nonnuclear*
power plant⟩

\ə\ abut	\aú\ out	\i\ tip	\ó\ saw	\ú\ foot
\ər\ further	\ch\ chin	\ī\ life	\ói\ coin	\y\ yet
\a\ mat	\e\ pet	\j\ job	\th\ thin	\yü\ few
\ā\ take	\ē\ easy	\ŋ\ sing	\th\ this	\yú\ cure
\ä\ cot, cart	\g\ go	\ō\ bone	\ü\ food	\zh\ vision

no–no \'nō-ˌnō\ *n, pl* **no–no's** *or* **no–nos** : something that is unacceptable or forbidden

non·ob·jec·tive \ˌnän-əb-'jek-tiv\ *adj* : intended to represent no natural or actual object or likeness ⟨*nonobjective* art⟩

no–nonsense *adj* : putting up with or including no nonsense : SERIOUS

¹**non·pa·reil** \ˌnän-pə-'rel\ *adj* : having no equal : PEERLESS

²**nonpareil** *n* **1** : an individual of unequaled excellence : PARAGON **2** : PAINTED BUNTING

non·par·ti·san \(')nän-'pärt-ə-zən, -sən\ *adj* : not partisan; *esp* : free from party ties, bias, or designation ⟨a *nonpartisan* ballot⟩ ⟨a *nonpartisan* committee⟩

non·pay·ment \(')nän-'pā-mənt\ *n* : failure to pay

non·plus \(')nän-'pləs\ *vb* **non·plussed;** **non·plus·sing** *also* **non·plus·ing** : to cause to be at a loss as to what to say, think, or do : PERPLEX

non·pre·scrip·tion \ˌnän-pri-'skrip-shən\ *adj* : capable of being bought without a doctor's prescription ⟨*nonprescription* pain reliever⟩

non·pro·duc·tive \ˌnän-prə-'dək-tiv\ *adj* **1** : failing to produce : UNPRODUCTIVE ⟨a *nonproductive* oil well⟩ **2** : not directly productive ⟨*nonproductive* labor⟩

non·prof·it \'nän-'präf-ət\ *adj* : not existing or carried on for the purpose of making a profit ⟨a *nonprofit* organization⟩

non·ran·dom \(')nän-'ran-dəm\ *adj* : not governed strictly by chance : following a pattern or plan

non·re·new·able \ˌnän-ri-'n(y)ü-ə-bəl\ *adj* : not renewable; *esp* : not restored or replaced by natural processes ⟨*nonrenewable* resources⟩

non·res·i·dent \(')nän-'rez-əd-ənt, -'rez-dənt, -'rez-əˌdent\ *adj* : not living in a particular place — **nonresident** *n*

non·re·sis·tance \ˌnän-ri-'zis-tən(t)s\ *n* : the policy or practice of yielding to authority even when unjust or cruel — **non·re·sis·tant** \-tənt\ *adj*

non·re·stric·tive \ˌnän-ri-'strik-tiv\ *adj* **1** : not serving or tending to restrict **2** : not limiting the reference of the word or phrase modified ⟨a *nonrestrictive* clause⟩

non·sched·uled \(')nän-'skej-(ˌ)ü(ə)ld, -'skej-əld\ *adj* : licensed to carry passengers or freight by air without a regular schedule ⟨a *nonscheduled* airline⟩

non·sec·tar·i·an \ˌnän-(ˌ)sek-'ter-ē-ən\ *adj* : not having a sectarian character : not restricted to a particular religious group

non·sense \'nän-ˌsen(t)s, 'nän(t)-sən(t)s\ *n* **1** : foolish or meaningless words or actions **2** : things of no importance or value — **non·sen·si·cal** \(')nän-'sen(t)-si-kəl\ *adj* — **non·sen·si·cal·ly** \-k(ə-)lē\ *adv* — **non·sen·si·cal·ness** \-kəl-nəs\ *n*

non·skid \(')nän-'skid\ *adj* : designed to prevent skidding

non·stan·dard \(')nän-'stan-dərd\ *adj* **1** : not standard **2** : not agreeing in pronunciation, grammatical construction, idiom, or choice of word with the usage generally characteristic of educated native speakers of the language

non·stick \'nän-'stik\ *adj* : allowing easy removal of cooked food particles ⟨a *nonstick* coating in a pan⟩

non·stop \'nän-'stäp\ *adj* : done, made, or held without a stop ⟨a *nonstop* flight to Chicago⟩ — **nonstop** *adv*

non·sup·port \ˌnän(t)-sə-'pō(ə)rt, -'pȯ(ə)rt\ *n* : failure to support; *esp* : failure to provide legally required financial support

non·tast·er \(')nän-'tā-stər\ *n* : a person unable to taste the chemical phenylthiocarbamide

non·union \(')nän-'yün-yən\ *adj* **1** : not belonging to a trade union ⟨*nonunion* carpenters⟩ **2** : not recognizing or favoring trade unions or their members ⟨*nonunion* employers⟩

non·ver·bal \(')nän-'vər-bəl\ *adj* **1** : being other than verbal ⟨*nonverbal* symbols⟩ **2** : involving little use of language ⟨*nonverbal* tests⟩ — **non·ver·bal·ly** \-bə-lē\ *adv*

non·vi·o·lence \(')nän-'vī-ə-lən(t)s\ *n* **1** : the avoidance of the use of violence as a matter of principle; *also* : the principle of not using violence to achieve one's goals **2** : nonviolent demonstrations for the purpose of achieving political goals

non·vi·o·lent \(')nän-'vī-ə-lənt\ *adj* **1** : not using violence : PEACEFUL **2** : of, relating to, or marked by nonviolence

non–West·ern \(')nän-'wes-tərn\ *adj* **1** : not being part of the western tradition ⟨*non-Western* countries⟩ **2** : of or relating to non-Western societies ⟨*non-Western* values⟩

non·white \(')nän-'hwīt, -'wīt\ *n* : a person whose features and especially whose skin color are different from those of white people of northwestern Europe — **nonwhite** *adj*

non·woody \(')nän-'wud-ē\ *adj* : not woody ⟨*nonwoody* plants⟩

non·woven \(')nän-'wō-vən\ *adj* **1** : made of fibers held together by interlocking or bonding (as by chemical means) ⟨*nonwoven* fabric⟩ **2** : made of nonwoven fabric ⟨a *nonwoven* dress⟩ — **nonwoven** *n*

noo·dle \'nüd-ᵊl\ *n* : a food like macaroni made with egg and shaped into flat strips ⟨a casserole of tuna and *noodles*⟩

nook \'nuk\ *n* **1** : an interior angle or corner formed usually by two walls ⟨a chimney *nook*⟩ **2** : a sheltered or hidden place ⟨a shady *nook*⟩

noon \'nün\ *n* : the middle of the day : 12 o'clock in the daytime — **noon** *adj*

> **Word History** *Noon* has not always meant "12 o'clock in the daytime". In the ancient Roman way of keeping track of time, the hours of the day were counted from sunrise to sunset. The ninth hour of the their day (about three p.m. nowadays) was called *nona,* Latin for "ninth". In the early period of English, the word was borrowed as *nōn,* also referring to the ninth hour after sunrise. By the 14th century, however, the word came to be used for midday, 12 o'clock, as we use it today. [Old English *nōn* "ninth hour from sunrise", derived from Latin *nona,* a feminine form of *nonus* "ninth", from *novem* "nine"]

noon·day \-ˌdā\ *n* : NOON

no one *pron* : NOBODY ⟨*no one* was home⟩

noon·tide \'nün-ˌtīd\ *n* : NOON

noon·time \-ˌtīm\ *n* : NOON

noose \'nüs\ *n* : a loop that passes through a knot at the end of a line so that it gets smaller when the other end of the line is pulled

nor \nər, (')nȯ(ə)r\ *conj* : and not ⟨not for you *nor* for me⟩ — used especially between two words or phrases preceded by *neither* ⟨neither here *nor* there⟩

noose

nor·adren·a·line \ˌnȯr-ə-'dren-ᵊl-ən\ *n* : NOREPINEPHRINE

nor·epi·neph·rine \ˌnȯ(ə)r-ˌep-ə-'nef-rən\ *n* : a hormone that causes blood vessels to contract and helps to transmit nerve impulses in the sympathetic nervous system and in some parts of the central nervous system

norm \'nȯ(ə)rm\ *n* : ¹AVERAGE 2, STANDARD

¹**nor·mal** \'nȯr-məl\ *adj* **1** : ¹PERPENDICULAR 2 **2** : of the regular or usual kind **3 a** : relating to or marked by average intelligence or development **b** : free from sickness of body or mind : SANE, SOUND — **nor·mal·ly** \-mə-lē\ *adv*

²**normal** *n* **1** : a normal line **2** : a person or thing that is normal **3** : a form or state regarded as the usual : AVERAGE

normal curve *n* : a symmetrical bell-shaped curve that often gives a close approximation to the graph of scores or measurements consisting of many bunched values near the average in the middle and a few large and a few small values arranged toward the opposite ends

nor·mal·cy \'nȯr-məl-sē\ *n* : NORMALITY

nor·mal·i·ty \nȯr-'mal-ət-ē\ *n* : the quality or state of being normal

nor·mal·ize \'nȯr-mə-ˌlīz\ *vb* **-ized; -iz·ing** : to make normal or average — **nor·mal·iza·tion** \ˌnȯr-mə-lə-'zā-shən\ *n*

Nor·man \'nȯr-mən\ *n* **1** : one of the Scandinavians who conquered Normandy in the 10th century **2** : one of the people of mixed Norman and French blood who conquered England in 1066 **3** : a person born or living in Normandy — **Nor·man** *adj*

Norse \'nȯ(ə)rs\ *n* **1** *pl* **Norse a** : the Scandinavian people **b** : the Norwegian people **2 a** : NORWEGIAN 2 **b** : any of the Scandinavian languages — **Norse** *adj*

Norse·man \'nȯr-smən\ *n* : any of the ancient Scandinavians

¹north \'nȯ(ə)rth\ *adv* : to or toward the north

²north *adj* **1** : placed or lying toward or at the north ⟨the *north* entrance⟩ **2** : coming from the north ⟨a *north* wind⟩

³north *n* **1 a** : the direction to the left of one facing east **b** : the compass point opposite to south **2** *cap* : regions or countries north of a point that is mentioned or understood

north·bound \'nȯrth-ˌbau̇nd\ *adj* : headed north

¹north·east \nȯr-'thēst, *nautical* nȯ-'rēst\ *adv* : to or toward the northeast

²northeast *n* **1** : the direction between north and east **2** *cap* : regions or countries northeast of a point that is mentioned or understood

³northeast *adj* **1** : placed or lying toward or at the northeast ⟨the *northeast* corner⟩ **2** : coming from the northeast ⟨a *northeast* wind⟩

north·east·er \nȯr-'thē-stər, nȯ-'rē-\ *n* **1** : a strong northeast wind **2** : a storm with northeast winds

north·east·er·ly \nȯr-'thē-stər-lē\ *adv or adj* **1** : from the northeast **2** : toward the northeast

north·east·ern \nȯr-'thē-stərn\ *adj* **1** *often cap* : of, relating to, or characteristic of the Northeast **2** : lying toward or coming from the northeast

North·east·ern·er \nȯr-'thē-stə(r)-nər\ *n* : a person born or living in a northeastern region (as of the U.S.)

north·east·ward \nȯr-'thēs-twərd\ *adv or adj* : toward the northeast — **north·east·wards** \-twərdz\ *adv*

north·er \'nȯr-thər\ *n* **1** : a strong north wind **2** : a storm with north winds

¹north·er·ly \'nȯr-thər-lē\ *adj or adv* **1** : placed or lying toward the north ⟨the *northerly* border⟩ **2** : coming from the north ⟨a *northerly* wind⟩

²northerly *n, pl* **-lies** : a wind from the north

north·ern \'nȯr-thə(r)n\ *adj* **1** *cap* : of, relating to, or characteristic of the North **2** : lying toward or coming from the north ⟨a *northern* storm⟩ — **north·ern·most** \-ˌmōst\ *adj*

North·ern·er \'nȯr-thə(r)-nər\ *n* : a person born or living in the North (as of the U.S.)

northern hemisphere *n, often cap N & H* : the half of the earth that lies north of the equator

northern lights *n pl* : AURORA BOREALIS

north·land \'nȯrth-ˌland, -lənd\ *n, often cap* : land in the north : the north of a country or region

North·man \-mən\ *n* : NORSEMAN

north pole *n* **1 a** *often cap N & P* : the northernmost point of the earth : the northern end of the earth's axis **b** : the point in the sky directly overhead at the north pole **2** : the pole of a magnet that points toward the north

north–seeking pole *n* : NORTH POLE 2

North Star *n* : the star toward which the northern end of the earth's axis very nearly points — called also *polestar*

north·ward \'nȯrth-wərd\ *adv or adj* : toward the north — **north·wards** \-wərdz\ *adv*

¹north·west \nȯrth-'west, *nautical* nȯr-'west\ *adv* : to or toward the northwest

²northwest *n* **1** : the direction between north and west **2** *cap* : the regions or countries northwest of a point that is mentioned or understood

³northwest *adj* **1** : coming from the northwest ⟨a *northwest* wind⟩ **2** : placed or lying toward or at the northwest ⟨the *northwest* corner⟩

north·west·er \nȯr(th)-'wes-tər\ *n* : a strong northwest wind

north·west·er·ly \nȯrth-'wes-tər-lē\ *adv or adj* **1** : from the northwest **2** : toward the northwest

north·west·ern \nȯrth-'wes-tərn\ *adj* **1** *often cap* : of, relating to, or characteristic of the Northwest **2** : lying toward or coming from the northwest

North·west·ern·er \nȯrth-'wes-tə(r)-nər\ *n* : a person born or living in a northwestern region (as of the U.S.)

north·west·ward \nȯrth-'wes-twərd\ *adv or adj* : toward the northwest — **north·west·wards** \-twərdz\ *adv*

Nor·way maple \ˌnȯ(ə)r-ˌwā-\ *n* : a European maple with dark green or often reddish or red veined leaves that is often planted for shade in the U.S.

Nor·we·gian \nȯr-'wē-jən\ *n* **1** : a person born or living in Norway **2** : the Germanic language of the Norwegian people — **Norwegian** *adj*

nos *pl of* NO

¹nose \'nōz\ *n* **1 a** : the part of the face or head that contains the nostrils and covers the front or outer part of the nasal cavity; *also* : this part together with the nasal cavity **b** : the front part of the head above or sticking out beyond the jaws ⟨the length of a whale from the tip of the *nose* to the middle of the tail⟩ **2** : the sense of smell **3** : the organ of smell of a vertebrate **4** : something (as a point, edge, or projection) like a nose ⟨the *nose* of a plane⟩ **5** : an ability to discover ⟨a *nose* for news⟩ — **nosed** \'nōzd\ *adj*

²nose *vb* **nosed; nos·ing** **1** : to detect by or as if by smell : SCENT **2** : to push or move with the nose **3** : to touch or rub with the nose : NUZZLE **4** : to search especially into other peoples' business : PRY **5** : to move ahead slowly or cautiously ⟨the boat *nosed* around the bend⟩

nose·bleed \'nōz-ˌblēd\ *n* : a bleeding from the nose

nose cone *n* : a protective cone forming the forward end of a rocket or missile

nose·dive \'nōz-ˌdīv\ *n* **1** : a downward nose-first plunge (as of an airplane) **2** : a sudden extreme drop (as in prices)

nose–dive *vb* **nose–dived; nose–div·ing** : to plunge suddenly or sharply

nose·gay \-ˌgā\ *n* : a small bunch of flowers : POSY

nose out *vb* : to defeat by a narrow margin ⟨the home team barely *nosed out* the visitors⟩

nose·piece \-ˌpēs\ *n* : the end piece of a microscope body to which a lens or set of lenses is attached

nose cone

nose·wheel \-ˌhwēl, -ˌwēl\ *n* : a landing-gear wheel under the nose of an aircraft

nos·tal·gia \nä-'stal-jə, nə-\ *n* : a longing for something past — **nos·tal·gic** \-jik\ *adj* — **nos·tal·gi·cal·ly** \-ji-k(ə-)lē\ *adv*

nos·tril \'näs-trəl\ *n* : either of the outer openings of the nose through which one breathes; *also* : either fleshy wall forming a side of the nose [Old English *nosthyrl* "nostril",

\ə\ abut	\au̇\ out	\i\ tip	\ȯ\ saw	\u̇\ foot
\ər\ further	\ch\ chin	\ī\ life	\ȯi\ coin	\y\ yet
\a\ mat	\e\ pet	\j\ job	\th\ thin	\yü\ few
\ā\ take	\ē\ easy	\ŋ\ sing	\th\ this	\yu̇\ cure
\ä\ cot, cart	\g\ go	\ō\ bone	\ü\ food	\zh\ vision

literally "nose hole", from *nosu* "nose" and *thyrel* "hole" — related to THRILL; see *Word History* at THRILL]

nosy *or* **nos·ey** \'nō-zē\ *adj* **nos·i·er; -est** : tending to pry into someone else's business — **nos·i·ly** \-zə-lē\ *adv* — **nos·i·ness** \-zē-nəs\ *n*

not \(')nät\ *adv* **1** — used to make a word or group of words negative ⟨the books are *not* here⟩ **2** — used to stand for the negative of a group of words that comes before ⟨is sometimes hard to see and sometimes *not*⟩

¹no·ta·ble \'nōt-ə-bəl\ *adj* **1** : deserving special notice : REMARKABLE ⟨a *notable* sight⟩ **2** : DISTINGUISHED, PROMINENT ⟨a *notable* writer⟩ — **no·ta·bly** \-blē\ *adv*

²notable *n* : a famous person

no·ta·rize \'nōt-ə-,rīz\ *vb* **-rized; -riz·ing** : to sign as a notary public to show that a document is authentic — **no·ta·ri·za·tion** \,nōt-ə-rə-'zā-shən\ *n*

no·ta·ry public \,nōt-ə-rē-\ *n, pl* **notaries public** *or* **notary publics** : a public officer who witnesses the making of a document (as a deed) and signs it to show that it is authentic — called also *notary*

no·ta·tion \nō-'tā-shən\ *n* **1** : ²NOTE 3a ⟨make *notations* on a paper⟩ **2** : the act of noting **3** : a system of marks, signs, figures, or characters used to give specified information ⟨musical *notation*⟩ ⟨scientific *notation*⟩ — **no·ta·tion·al** \-shən-ᵊl\ *adj*

¹notch \'näch\ *n* **1** : a cut in the shape of a V in an edge or surface **2** : a narrow pass between mountains : GAP **3** : DEGREE 1, STEP ⟨turn the radio up a *notch*⟩

²notch *vb* **1** : to cut or make a notch in **2 a** : to mark or record by a notch **b** : ACHIEVE 2, SCORE

notched \'nächt\ *adj* : having a notch or notches

¹note \'nōt\ *vb* **not·ed; not·ing** **1 a** : to notice or observe with care **b** : to record or preserve in writing **2** : to make special mention of : NOTICE — **not·er** *n*

²note *n* **1 a** : a musical sound : TONE **b** : an animal's cry, call, or sound ⟨a bird's *note*⟩ **c** : a symbol in music that by its shape and position on the staff shows the pitch of a tone and the length of time it is to be held **2** : a quality that shows a feeling ⟨a *note* of sadness in your voice⟩ **3 a** : something written down often to aid the memory ⟨I'll make a *note* of the appointment⟩ **b** : a brief and informal record **c** : a written or printed comment that helps explain part of the book ⟨*notes* in the back of the book⟩ **4 a** : a written promise to pay **b** : a piece of paper money **5 a** : a short informal letter **b** : a formal diplomatic or official communication **6 a** : REPUTATION 1, DISTINCTION ⟨a scientist of *note*⟩ **b** : careful notice ⟨take *note* of the exact time⟩

	whole
	half
	quarter
	eighth
	sixteenth
	thirty-second
	sixty-fourth

note 1c

note·book \'nōt-,buk\ *n* : a book for notes

not·ed \'nōt-əd\ *adj* : well-known and highly regarded : FAMOUS — **not·ed·ly** *adv*

note·pad \'nōt-,pad\ *n* : ²PAD 4

note·wor·thy \-,wər-thē\ *adj* : worthy of note : REMARKABLE — **note·wor·thi·ness** *n*

¹noth·ing \'nəth-iŋ\ *pron* **1** : not anything ⟨there's *nothing* in the box⟩ **2** : one of no interest, value, or importance ⟨your opinion means *nothing* to me⟩ — **nothing doing** : by no means : definitely no

²nothing *adv* : not at all : in no way

³nothing *n* **1 a** : something that does not exist **b** : absence of quantity : ZERO **2** : something of little or no worth or importance — **noth·ing·ness** *n*

¹no·tice \'nōt-əs\ *n* **1** : warning or indication of something

: ANNOUNCEMENT ⟨her footsteps gave *notice* of her coming⟩ **2** : notification of the ending of an agreement at a specified time ⟨gave my employer *notice*⟩ **3** : ATTENTION 1, HEED ⟨take no *notice* of them⟩ **4** : a written or printed announcement **5** : a brief published criticism (as of a book)

²notice *vb* **no·ticed; no·tic·ing** **1** : to make mention of : remark on **2** : to take notice of : OBSERVE, MARK ⟨*notice* details⟩

no·tice·able \'nōt-ə-sə-bəl\ *adj* **1** : worthy of notice ⟨*noticeable* for its fine coloring⟩ **2** : capable of being or likely to be noticed ⟨a *noticeable* improvement⟩ — **no·tice·ably** \-blē\ *adv*

syn NOTICEABLE, PROMINENT, OUTSTANDING, CONSPICUOUS mean attracting notice or attention. NOTICEABLE suggests that something is likely to be seen ⟨an essay with many *noticeable* mistakes⟩ PROMINENT suggests that something calls attention to itself by standing out from its surroundings ⟨a *prominent* bruise on the forehead⟩ OUTSTANDING applies to something that rises above and is better than others of the same kind ⟨an *outstanding* baseball player⟩ CONSPICUOUS applies to something that is easily observed and certain to attract attention ⟨his loud voice made him *conspicuous* at the party⟩

no·ti·fi·ca·tion \,nōt-ə-fə-'kā-shən\ *n* **1** : the act or an instance of notifying **2** : written or printed matter that gives notice

no·ti·fy \'nōt-ə-,fī\ *vb* **-fied; -fy·ing** : to give notice to : INFORM ⟨*notify* the police⟩ — **no·ti·fi·er** \-,fī(-ə)r\ *n*

no·tion \'nō-shən\ *n* **1 a** : IDEA 2, CONCEPTION ⟨have a *notion* of a poem's meaning⟩ **b** : a belief held : OPINION **c** : a sudden wish or desire : WHIM ⟨just had a *notion* to go home⟩ **2** *pl* : small useful articles (as pins, needles, or thread)

no·to·chord \'nōt-ə-,kô(ə)rd\ *n* : a flexible rod of cells that in the lowest chordates (as lancelets and the lampreys) and in the embryos of the higher vertebrates forms a support for the body

no·to·ri·ety \,nōt-ə-'rī-ət-ē\ *n, pl* **-eties** : the quality or state of being notorious

no·to·ri·ous \nō-'tōr-ē-əs, nə-, -'tôr-\ *adj* : generally known and talked of; *esp* : widely and unfavorably known syn see FAMOUS — **no·to·ri·ous·ly** *adv*

¹not·with·stand·ing \,nät-with-'stan-diŋ, -with-\ *prep* : ²DESPITE ⟨we went ahead with our plan *notwithstanding* their objections⟩

²notwithstanding *adv* : NEVERTHELESS, HOWEVER

nou·gat \'nü-gət\ *n* : a candy of nuts or fruit pieces in a sugar paste

nought *variant of* NAUGHT

noun \'naun\ *n* : a word that is the name of something (as a person, animal, place, thing, quality, idea, or action) and that is typically used in a sentence as subject or object of a verb or as object of a preposition

nour·ish \'nər-ish, 'nə-rish\ *vb* **1** : to promote the growth or development of **2 a** : to provide with food : FEED ⟨plants *nourished* by rain and soil⟩ **b** : to provide for : SUPPORT, MAINTAIN ⟨a friendship *nourished* by trust⟩

nour·ish·ing *adj* : giving nourishment : NUTRITIOUS

nour·ish·ment \'nər-ish-mənt, 'nə-rish-\ *n* **1** : something that nourishes : FOOD, NUTRIMENT **2** : the act of nourishing : the state of being nourished

no·va \'nō-və\ *n, pl* **novas** *or* **no·vae** \-vē, -,vī\ : a star that suddenly increases greatly in brightness and then within a few months or years grows dim again

¹nov·el \'näv-əl\ *adj* **1** : new and different from what has been known before **2** : original or striking in design or appearance ⟨a *novel* way to make money⟩ syn see NEW

²novel *n* : a long prose narrative that usually portrays imaginary characters and events

nov·el·ette \,näv-ə-'let\ *n* : a brief novel

nov·el·ist \'näv-(ə-)ləst\ *n* : a writer of novels

no·vel·la \nō-'vel-ə\ *n* : NOVELETTE

nov·el·ty \'näv-əl-tē\ *n, pl* **-ties** **1** : something new or unusual **2** : the quality or state of being novel : NEWNESS **3** : a small article intended mainly as an unusual ornament or toy — usually used in pl.

No·vem·ber \nō-'vem-bər\ *n* : the 11th month of the year

Word History The first calendar used in ancient Rome began the year with the month of March. The ninth month of the year was called *November,* from the Latin word *novem,* meaning "nine". When the name was first borrowed into Middle English from early French, it was spelled *Novembre.* But in time the original Latin spelling became the one used in English. [Middle English *Novembre* "November (the 11th month)", from early French *Novembre* (same meaning), from Latin *November* "November (ninth month)", from *novem* "nine"]

no·ve·na \nō-'vē-nə\ *n, pl* **-nas** *or* **-nae** \-nē\ : a Roman Catholic devotion in which prayers are said for the same intention on nine days in a row

nov·ice \'näv-əs\ *n* **1** : a new member of a religious order who is preparing to take the vows of religion **2** : a person who has no previous experience with something

no·vi·tiate \nō-'vish-ət\ *n* **1** : the period or state of being a novice **2** : NOVICE 1 **3** : a place where novices are trained

¹now \(')naù\ *adv* **1 a** : at the present time ⟨they are busy *now*⟩ **b** : in the time immediately before the present ⟨thought of them just *now*⟩ **c** : in the time immediately to follow ⟨come in *now*⟩ **2** — used with the sense of present time weakened or lost (as to express command or introduce an important point) ⟨*now* hear this⟩ **3** : SOMETIMES ⟨*now* one and *now* another⟩ **4** : under the present circumstances ⟨*now* the trouble began⟩ — **now and then** : from time to time : OCCASIONALLY

²now *conj* : in view of the fact that : SINCE — often followed by *that* ⟨*now* that we are here⟩

³now \'naù\ *n* : the present time ⟨been ill up to *now*⟩

⁴now \'naù\ *adj* : of or relating to the present time : EXISTING ⟨the *now* president⟩

now·a·days \'naù-(ə-),dāz\ *adv* : at the present time

no·way \'nō-,wā\ *or* **no·ways** \-,wāz\ : NOWISE 2 *usually* **no way** \-'wā\ : certainly not

¹no·where \'nō-,hwe(ə)r, -,we(ə)r, -,hwa(ə)r, -,wa(ə)r, -hwər, -wər\ *adv* **1** : not in or at any place **2** : to no place

²nowhere *n* : a place that does not exist ⟨sounds seeming to come from *nowhere*⟩

nowhere near *adv* : not nearly

no·wise \'nō-,wīz\ *adv* : not at all

nox·ious \'näk-shəs\ *adj* : harmful especially to health : UNWHOLESOME ⟨*noxious* fumes⟩

noz·zle \'näz-əl\ *n* : a short tube that narrows in the middle or toward one end and is often used on a hose or pipe to direct or speed up a flow of fluid

-n't \(ə)nt, ənt\ *vb combining form* : not ⟨*isn't*⟩

nth \'en(t)th\ *adj* **1** : numbered with an unspecified or indefinitely large ordinal number ⟨for the *nth* time⟩ **2** : UTMOST 2, EXTREME ⟨to the *nth* degree⟩

nu \'n(y)ü\ *n* : the 13th letter of the Greek alphabet — N or *ν*

nu·ance \'n(y)ü-,än(t)s, n(y)ü-'än(t)s\ *n* : a slight shade or degree of difference (as in color, tone, or meaning)

nub \'nəb\ *n* **1** : KNOB 1a, LUMP **2** : the main point of a matter ⟨the *nub* of the story⟩

nub·bin \'nəb-ən\ *n* **1** : a small or imperfect ear of Indian corn; *also* : any small shriveled or undeveloped fruit **2** : a small part or bit

nub·ble \'nəb-əl\ *n* : a small knob or lump — **nub·bly** \-(ə-)lē\ *adj*

nub·by \'nəb-ē\ *adj* **nub·bi·er; -est** : having small knobs or lumps ⟨a *nubby* knit fabric⟩

nu·cle·ar \'n(y)ü-klē-ər\ *adj* **1** : of, relating to, or being a nucleus (as of a cell) **2** : of, relating to, or using the atomic nucleus, atomic energy, the atom bomb, or atomic power

nuclear energy *n* : ATOMIC ENERGY

nuclear family *n* : a family group that consists only of father, mother, and children

nuclear membrane *n* : the boundary of a cell nucleus

nuclear reactor *n* : REACTOR 2

nu·cle·ic acid \n(y)ü-,klā-ik-, -,klē-\ *n* : any of various acids (as DNA or RNA) composed of a chain of nucleotides and found especially in cell nuclei

nu·cle·o·lus \n(y)ü-'klē-ə-ləs\ *n, pl* **-li** \-,lī\ : a sphere-shaped body in the cell nucleus that becomes enlarged during the manufacture of proteins, is associated with a particular part of a chromosome, and is rich in RNA

nu·cleo·plasm \'n(y)ü-klē-ə-,plaz-əm\ *n* : the protoplasm of a nucleus

nu·cle·o·tide \'n(y)ü-klē-ə-,tīd\ *n* : any of the basic units of structure of DNA or RNA that consist of a base (as adenine, cytosine, guanine, or thymine) joined to a sugar with five carbon atoms in a molecule and to a phosphate group

nu·cle·us \'n(y)ü-klē-əs\ *n, pl* **-clei** \-klē-,ī\ *also* **-cle·us·es** : a central point, group, or mass of something: as **a** : the small, brighter, and denser part of a galaxy or of the head of a comet **b** : a cell part that is characteristic of all living things with the exception of viruses, bacteria, and blue-green algae, that is necessary for heredity and for making proteins, that contains the nucleoli and the chromosomes with their genes, and that is enclosed in a nuclear membrane **c** : a mass of gray matter or group of nerve cells in the central nervous system **d** : the central part of an atom that includes nearly all of the atomic mass and consists of protons and neutrons except in hydrogen in which it consists of one proton only [from modern Latin *nucleus* "the central part of something", from Latin *nucleus* "kernel", derived from *nux* "nut"]

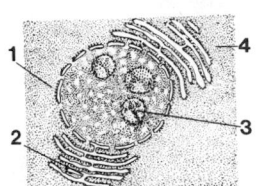

nucleus b: *1* nuclear membrane, *2* endoplasmic reticulum, *3* nucleolus, *4* cytoplasm

nu·clide \'n(y)ü-,klīd\ *n* : a kind of atom marked by the number of protons and neutrons and by the amount of energy contained in its nucleus

¹nude \'n(y)üd\ *adj* **nud·er; nud·est** : having no clothes on — **nude·ness** *n*

²nude *n* **1** : a nude human figure especially as shown in art **2** : the condition of being nude ⟨in the *nude*⟩

nudge \'nəj\ *vb* **nudged; nudg·ing** : to touch or push gently; *esp* : to attract the attention of by a push of the elbow — **nudge** *n*

nud·ism \'n(y)üd-,iz-əm\ *n* : the practice of going nude especially in sexually mixed groups and at specially secluded places — **nud·ist** \'n(y)üd-əst\ *n or adj*

nu·di·ty \'n(y)üd-ət-ē\ *n* : the quality or state of being nude

nug·get \'nəg-ət\ *n* : a solid lump especially of precious metal

nui·sance \'n(y)üs-ⁿt(s)\ *n* : an annoying or troublesome person, thing, or way of doing something

null \'nəl\ *adj* **1** : having no legal or binding force : INVALID **2** : having no value : INSIGNIFICANT **3** : having no members ⟨the *null* set⟩

\ə\ abut	\aù\ out	\i\ tip	\ò\ saw	\ù\ foot
\ər\ further	\ch\ chin	\ī\ life	\òi\ coin	\y\ yet
\a\ mat	\e\ pet	\j\ job	\th\ thin	\yü\ few
\ā\ take	\ē\ easy	\ŋ\ sing	\t̲h̲\ this	\yù\ cure
\ä\ cot, cart	\g\ go	\ō\ bone	\ü\ food	\zh\ vision

TABLE OF NUMBERS

CARDINAL NUMBERS[1]			ORDINAL NUMBERS[4]	
NAME[2]	SYMBOL		NAME[5]	SYMBOL[6]
	Arabic	*Roman*[3]		
zero *or* naught *or* cipher	0		first	1st
one	1	I	second	2d *or* 2nd
two	2	II	third	3d *or* 3rd
three	3	III	fourth	4th
four	4	IV	fifth	5th
five	5	V	sixth	6th
six	6	VI	seventh	7th
seven	7	VII	eighth	8th
eight	8	VIII	ninth	9th
nine	9	IX	tenth	10th
ten	10	X	eleventh	11th
eleven	11	XI	twelfth	12th
twelve	12	XII	thirteenth	13th
thirteen	13	XIII	fourteenth	14th
fourteen	14	XIV	fifteenth	15th
fifteen	15	XV	sixteenth	16th
sixteen	16	XVI	seventeenth	17th
seventeen	17	XVII	eighteenth	18th
eighteen	18	XVIII	nineteenth	19th
nineteen	19	XIX	twentieth	20th
twenty	20	XX	twenty-first	21st
twenty-one	21	XXI	twenty-second	22d *or* 22nd
twenty-two	22	XXII	twenty-third	23d *or* 23rd
twenty-three	23	XXIII	twenty-fourth	24th
twenty-four	24	XXIV	twenty-fifth	25th
twenty-five	25	XXV	twenty-sixth	26th
twenty-six	26	XXVI	twenty-seventh	27th
twenty-seven	27	XXVII	twenty-eighth	28th
twenty-eight	28	XXVIII	twenty-ninth	29th
twenty-nine	29	XXIX	thirtieth	30th
thirty	30	XXX	thirty-first *etc*	31st
thirty-one *etc*	31	XXXI	fortieth	40th
forty	40	XL	fiftieth	50th
fifty	50	L	sixtieth	60th
sixty	60	LX	seventieth	70th
seventy	70	LXX	eightieth	80th
eighty	80	LXXX	ninetieth	90th
ninety	90	XC	hundredth *or* one hundredth	100th
one hundred	100	C	hundred and first *or*	101st
one hundred one *or*	101	CI	one hundred and first *etc*	
one hundred and one *etc*			two hundredth	200th
two hundred	200	CC	three hundredth	300th
three hundred	300	CCC	four hundredth	400th
four hundred	400	CD	five hundredth	500th
five hundred	500	D	six hundredth	600th
six hundred	600	DC	seven hundredth	700th
seven hundred	700	DCC	eight hundredth	800th
eight hundred	800	DCCC	nine hundredth	900th
nine hundred	900	CM	thousandth *or* one thousandth	1,000th
one thousand *or* ten	1,000	M	two thousandth *etc*	2,000th
hundred *etc*			five thousandth	5,000th
two thousand *etc*	2,000	MM	ten thousandth	10,000th
five thousand	5,000	$\overline{\text{V}}$	hundred thousandth *or*	100,000th
ten thousand	10,000	$\overline{\text{X}}$	one hundred thousandth	
one hundred thousand	100,000	$\overline{\text{C}}$	millionth *or* one millionth	1,000,000th
one million	1,000,000	$\overline{\text{M}}$		

(continued on next page)

[1]The cardinal numbers are used in simple counting or in answer to "how many?" The words for these numbers may be used as nouns (I counted to *twelve*), as pronouns (*twelve* were found), or as adjectives (*twelve* cows).
[2]In formal writing the numbers one to one hundred and in less formal writing the numbers one to nine are commonly written out, while larger numbers are given in numerals. A number occurring at the beginning of a sentence is usually written out. Except in very formal writing numerals are used for dates. Arabic numerals from 1,000 to 9,999 are often written without commas (1000; 9999). Year numbers are always written without commas (1783).
[3]The Roman numerals are written either in capitals or in lowercase letters.
[4]The ordinal numbers are used to show the order in which such items as names, objects, and periods of time are considered (the *twelfth* month; the *fourth* row of seats; the *18th* century).
[5]Each of the names of the ordinal numbers except *first* and *second* is used for one of the equal parts into which a whole may be divided (a *fourth*; a *sixth*; a *tenth*) and also as the denominator in fractions (*one fourth*; *three fifths*). Fractions used as nouns are usually written as two words, but fractions used as adjectives are usually hyphenated (a *two-thirds* majority). When a two-word ordinal number is used as a noun to name a denominator, a hyphen is usually used to make sure that there is only one meaning (*six hundred ten-thousandths* means only 600/10,000 and not 610/1000). When fractions are written in numerals, the cardinal symbols are used (¼, ⅗, ⅙).
[6]The Arabic symbols for the cardinal numbers may be read as ordinals (January 1 = January first; 2 Samuel = Second Samuel). The Roman numerals are sometimes read as ordinals (Henry IV = Henry the Fourth); sometimes they are written with the ordinal suffixes (XIXth Dynasty).

DENOMINATIONS ABOVE ONE MILLION

NAME	American system[1] VALUE IN POWERS OF TEN	NUMBER OF ZEROS[2]	NUMBER OF GROUPS OF THREE 0's AFTER 1,000	NAME	British system[1] VALUE IN POWERS OF TEN	NUMBER OF ZEROS[2]	POWERS OF 1,000,000
billion	10^9	9	2	milliard	10^9	9	—
trillion	10^{12}	12	3	billion	10^{12}	12	2
quadrillion	10^{15}	15	4	trillion	10^{18}	18	3
quintillion	10^{18}	18	5	quadrillion	10^{24}	24	4
sextillion	10^{21}	21	6	quintillion	10^{30}	30	5
septillion	10^{24}	24	7	sextillion	10^{36}	36	6
octillion	10^{27}	27	8	septillion	10^{42}	42	7
nonillion	10^{30}	30	9	octillion	10^{48}	48	8
decillion	10^{33}	33	10	nonillion	10^{54}	54	9
				decillion	10^{60}	60	10

[1]The American system for numbers above one million was based on the French number system, but the French later changed their system to follow the British. In the American system the number for each different name is 1,000 times greater than the one before (one billion = 1,000 million; one trillion = 1,000 billion). In the British system 1,000 million (the American *billion*) is called a *milliard,* and 1,000 milliard (the American *trillion*) is called a *billion.* After that, the number for each different name in the British system is 1,000,000 times greater than the one before (one trillion = 1,000,000 billion; one quadrillion = 1,000,000 trillion).
[2]For ease in reading large numerals the thousands, millions, etc., are usually separated by commas (21,530; 1,155,465) or sometimes by spaces (1 155 465).

null and void *adj* : having no force, binding power, or validity
nul·li·fi·ca·tion \ˌnəl-ə-fə-'kā-shən\ *n*　**1** : the act of nullifying : the state of being nullified　**2** : the action of a state blocking or attempting to prevent the enforcement within its territory of a federal law of the U.S. — **nul·li·fi·ca·tion·ist** \-sh(ə-)nəst\ *n*
nul·li·fy \'nəl-ə-ˌfī\ *vb* **-fied; -fy·ing** : to make null or valueless; *esp* : ANNUL
¹numb \'nəm\ *adj*　**1** : lacking in sensation especially from cold　**2** : lacking in emotion : INDIFFERENT — **numb·ly** *adv* — **numb·ness** *n*
²numb *vb* : to make or become numb
¹num·ber \'nəm-bər\ *n*　**1 a** : the total of persons, things, or units taken together : AMOUNT ⟨the *number* of people in the room⟩　**b** : the possibility of being counted ⟨mosquitoes in swarms beyond *number*⟩　**c** : a total that is not specified : MANY ⟨a *number* of accidents occur on wet roads⟩　**2 a** : a unit (as an integer or irrational number) belonging to a mathematical system and subject to its laws　**b** *pl* : ARITHMETIC　**3** : a quality of a word form that shows whether the word is singular or plural ⟨a verb agrees in *number* with its subject⟩　**4 a** : a word or symbol used to represent a mathematical number; *esp* : NUMERAL 1　**b** : a certain numeral for telling one person or thing from another or from others ⟨a phone *number*⟩　**5** : one in a series ⟨the June *number* of a magazine⟩　**6** : a musical, theatrical, or literary selection — **by the numbers**　**1** : all together in time to a specific count or cadence　**2** : in a manner lacking freshness and individuality
²number *vb* **num·bered; num·ber·ing** \-b(ə-)riŋ\　**1** : ¹COUNT 1a, ENUMERATE　**2** : to claim as part of a total : INCLUDE ⟨was *numbered* among the guests⟩　**3** : to restrict to a definite number ⟨vacation days are *numbered* now⟩　**4** : to assign a number to ⟨*number* the pages of a scrapbook⟩　**5** : to add up to or have a total of ⟨our group *numbered* ten in all⟩ — **num·ber·er** \-bər-ər\ *n*
number crunch·er \-'krən-chər\ *n*　**1** : a computer that performs fast numerical calculations especially on large amounts of data　**2** : a person concerned with complex numerical data — **number crunching** *n*
num·ber·less \'nəm-bər-ləs\ *adj* : too many to count : INNUMERABLE ⟨the *numberless* stars in the sky⟩
number line *n* : a line without ends whose points are matched to the real numbers by their distance from a given point labeled zero
Num·bers \'nəm-bərz\ *n* — see BIBLE table
nu·mer·al \'n(y)üm-(ə-)rəl\ *n*　**1** : a symbol or group of symbols representing a number　**2** *pl* : numbers that designate by year a school or college class and that are awarded for distinction (as in sports)
nu·mer·ate \'n(y)ü-mə-ˌrāt\ *vb* **-at·ed; -at·ing** : ENUMERATE
nu·mer·a·tion \ˌn(y)ü-mə-'rā-shən\ *n*　**1** : the act or process or a system or instance of counting or naming one by one ⟨decimal *numeration*⟩　**2** : the act of reading in words numbers expressed by numerals
nu·mer·a·tor \'n(y)ü-mə-ˌrāt-ər\ *n*　**1** : the part of a fraction written above the line that signifies the number of parts of the denominator taken ⟨3 is the *numerator* of the fraction ⅜⟩　**2** : one that counts something
nu·mer·ic \n(y)ü-'mer-ik\ *adj* : NUMERICAL; *esp* : indicating a number or a system of numbers ⟨*numeric* code⟩
nu·mer·i·cal \n(y)ü-'mer-i-kəl\ *adj*　**1** : of or relating to numbers　**2** : shown in or involving numbers or a number system ⟨*numerical* standing in a class⟩ — **nu·mer·i·cal·ly** \-k(ə-)lē\ *adv*
nu·mer·ous \'n(y)üm-(ə-)rəs\ *adj* : consisting of great numbers ⟨*numerous* friends⟩ — **nu·mer·ous·ly** *adv*
nu·mis·mat·ics \ˌn(y)ü-məz-'mat-iks, -məs\ *n* : the study or collection of coins, paper money, and sometimes related objects (as medals) — **nu·mis·mat·ic** \-ik\ *adj* — **nu·mis·ma·tist** \n(y)ü-'miz-mət-əst\ *n*
num·skull *or* **numb·skull** \'nəm-ˌskəl\ *n* : a stupid person
nun \'nən\ *n* : a woman belonging to a religious order; *esp* : one living under solemn vows of poverty, chastity, and obedience
nun·cio \'nən(t)-sē-ˌō, 'nün(t)-\ *n, pl* **-ci·os** : a papal representative to a civil government
nun·nery \'nən-(ə-)rē\ *n, pl* **-ner·ies** : a convent of nuns
¹nup·tial \'nəp-shəl, -chəl\ *adj*　**1** : of or relating to marriage or a wedding　**2** : characteristic of the breeding season
²nuptial *n* : MARRIAGE 2, WEDDING — usually used in pl.
¹nurse \'nərs\ *n*　**1** : a woman who has the care of a young child　**2** : a person skilled or trained in caring for the sick especially under the supervision of a physician　**3** : a worker of a social insect that cares for the young
²nurse *vb* **nursed; nurs·ing**　**1** : to feed at the breast : SUCKLE　**2** : ¹REAR 3b, EDUCATE　**3** : to manage with care or economy ⟨*nursed* the business through hard times⟩　**4** : to care for and wait on (as a young child or sick person) ⟨*nursed* me back to health⟩　**5** : to hold in one's memory

\ə\ abut		\aú\ out	\i\ tip		\ó\ saw		\ú\ foot
\ər\ further		\ch\ chin	\ī\ life		\ói\ coin		\y\ yet
\a\ mat		\e\ pet	\j\ job		\th\ thin		\yü\ few
\ā\ take		\ē\ easy	\ŋ\ sing		\th\ this		\yú\ cure
\ä\ cot, cart		\g\ go	\ō\ bone		\ü\ food		\zh\ vision

⟨*nurse* a grudge⟩ **6** : to treat with special care ⟨*nursed* the car over the rough road⟩ — **nurs·er** *n*

nurse·maid \'nər-ˌsmād\ *n* : a girl or woman employed to look after children

nurs·ery \'nərs-(ə-)rē\ *n, pl* **-er·ies 1 a** : a child's bedroom **b** : a place where children are temporarily cared for in their parents' absence **2** : a place where plants (as trees or shrubs) are grown for transplanting, for use as stocks in grafting, or for sale

nurs·ery·man \-mən\ *n* : a person who keeps or works in a plant nursery

nursery rhyme *n* : a short rhyme for children that often tells a story

nursery school *n* : a school for children usually under five years of age

nurse's aid *n* : a worker who assists trained nurses in a hospital by performing unspecialized services (as giving baths)

nurse shark *n* : a shark of the warmer parts of the Atlantic ocean

nursing bottle *n* : a bottle with a rubber nipple used for feeding a baby

nursing home *n* : a privately operated establishment where nursing care is provided for persons (as the aged) who are unable to care for themselves

nurs·ling \'nər-sliŋ\ *n* **1** : one that is tended with special care **2** : a nursing child

nur·tur·ance \'nər-chə-rən(t)s\ *n* : affectionate care and attention — **nur·tur·ant** \-rənt\ *adj*

¹nur·ture \'nər-chər\ *n* **1** : TRAINING 1, UPBRINGING **2** : something that nourishes : FOOD

²nurture *vb* **nur·tured; nur·tur·ing** \'nərch-(ə-)riŋ\ **1** : to supply with nourishment **2** : EDUCATE 2 **3** : to further the development of : FOSTER

nut \'nət\ *n* **1 a** : a hard-shelled dry fruit (as a peanut in the shell) or seed (as a Brazil nut) with an inner kernel; *also* : this kernel **b** : a dry one-seeded fruit (as an acorn, hazelnut, or chestnut) that has a woody outer layer and does not break open when it is ripe **2** : a block of metal with a hole in it that is fastened to a bolt or screw by means of a screw thread within the hole **3** : the ridge on the upper end of the fingerboard of a stringed instrument over which the strings pass **4 a** : a foolish, odd, or crazy person **b** : ENTHUSIAST ⟨a movie *nut*⟩ [Old English *hnutu* "nut"]

nut·crack·er \'nət-ˌkrak-ər\ *n* : a device for cracking the shells of nuts

nut·hatch \'nət-ˌhach\ *n* : any of a group of small birds that climb trees and eat insects and are noted for their habit of going down tree trunks head-first

nut·let \'nət-lət\ *n* : a small nut

nut·meg \'nət-ˌmeg\ *n* : a spice that consists of the ground seeds of a small tropical evergreen tree grown in the East and West Indies and Brazil

nu·tria \'n(y)ü-trē-ə\ *n* : a South American water-dwelling rodent with webbed feet and mammary glands on its back that has been introduced into the U.S. on the Gulf coast and in the Pacific Northwest — called also *coypu*

nuthatch

¹nu·tri·ent \'n(y)ü-trē-ənt\ *adj* : furnishing nourishment

²nutrient *n* : a nutrient substance or ingredient

nu·tri·ment \'n(y)ü-trə-mənt\ *n* : something that nourishes

nu·tri·tion \n(y)ü-'trish-ən\ *n* : the act or process of nourishing or being nourished; *esp* : the processes by which an animal or plant takes in and makes use of food substances

nu·tri·tion·al \n(y)ü-'trish-nəl, -ən-ᵊl\ *adj* : of or relating to nutrition — **nu·tri·tion·al·ly** \-ē\ *adv*

nu·tri·tious \n(y)ü-'trish-əs\ *adj* : providing nutrients

nu·tri·tive \'n(y)ü-trət-iv\ *adj* **1** : of or relating to nutrition **2** : NUTRITIOUS

nuts \'nəts\ *adj* **1** : ENTHUSIASTIC, KEEN ⟨was *nuts* about baseball⟩ **2** : CRAZY 1, DEMENTED

nut·shell \'nət-ˌshel\ *n* : the shell of a nut — **in a nutshell** : in a very brief statement

nut·ty \'nət-ē\ *adj* **nut·ti·er; -est 1** : containing or suggesting nuts (as in flavor) **2** : not showing good sense; *also* : mentally unbalanced — **nut·ti·ness** *n*

nuz·zle \'nəz-əl\ *vb* **nuz·zled; nuz·zling** \-(ə-)liŋ\ **1** : to push or rub with the nose **2** : to lie close : NESTLE

ny·lon \'nī-ˌlän\ *n* **1** : any of numerous strong tough elastic synthetic materials used especially in textiles and plastics **2** *pl* : stockings made of nylon [coined from meaningless word elements] — **nylon** *adj*

nymph \'nim(p)f\ *n* **1** : one of many goddesses in old legends represented as beautiful young girls living in mountains, forests, meadows, and waters **2** : any of various immature insects; *esp* : an immature insect that differs from the adult chiefly in the size and proportions of the body

O

o \'ō\ *n, often cap* **1** : the 15th letter of the English alphabet **2** : ¹ZERO 1

o' *also* **o** \ə\ *prep* : OF ⟨one *o'*clock⟩

O *variant of* ¹OH

oaf \'ōf\ *n* : a stupid or awkward person — **oaf·ish** \'ō-fish\ *adj* — **oaf·ish·ness** *n*

Word History When most people in England believed in elves, it was supposed that the elves would secretly exchange their own babies for those of human parents. An infant might be very ugly or deformed in some way. Then it was said that the elves had traded this baby of theirs, called an *oaf,* for the beautiful and healthy child the human parents had actually given birth to. Over the years, this connection with elves was forgotten. Any person who was considered stupid, slow, awkward, or disagreeable was called an *oaf.* [from obsolete English *oaf* "a baby left in place of another by elves"; of Scandina-

vian origin]

oak \'ōk\ *n, pl* **oaks** *or* **oak 1** : any of various hardwood timber trees or shrubs closely related to the beech and having a rounded one-seeded thin-shelled nut **2** : the tough hard wood of the oak much used for furniture and flooring — **oak·en** \'ō-kən\ *adj*

oa·kum \'ō-kəm\ *n* : hemp or jute fiber soaked with tar or something like tar and used in caulking seams (as of wooden ships) and packing joints (as of pipes)

¹oar \'ō(ə)r, 'ȯ(ə)r\ *n* **1** : a long pole with a broad blade at one end used for rowing or steering a boat **2** : OARSMAN — **oared** \'ō(ə)rd, 'ȯ(ə)rd\ *adj*

²oar *vb* : ¹ROW 1

oar·lock \'ō(ə)r-ˌläk, 'ȯ(ə)r-\ *n* : a usually U-shaped device for holding an oar in place

oars·man \'ō(ə)rz-mən, 'ȯ(ə)rz-\ *n* : a person who rows especially in a racing crew

oa·sis \ō-'ā-səs\ *n, pl* **oa·ses** \-'ā-ˌsēz\ **1** : a fertile or green spot in a desert **2** : something or some place that provides refreshing relief

oat \'ōt\ *n* : a grain that is widely grown for its long loose clusters of seeds which are used for human food and for livestock feed — **oat·en** \'ōt-ᵊn\ *adj*

oath \'ōth\ *n, pl* **oaths** \'ōthz, 'ōths\ **1** : a solemn appeal to God or to some deeply respected person or thing to witness to the truth of one's word or the sacredness of a promise ⟨under *oath* to tell the truth⟩ **2** : a careless or improper use of a sacred name

oat·meal \'ōt-ˌmēl, ōt-'mē(ə)l\ *n* **1** : oats husked and ground into meal or flattened into flakes **2** : a hot cereal made from oatmeal

Oba·di·ah \ˌō-bə-'dī-ə\ *n* — see BIBLE table

¹ob·bli·ga·to \ˌäb-lə-'gät-ō\ *adj* : not to be left out — used as a direction in music

²obbligato *n, pl* **-tos** *also* **-ti** \-ē\ : an important melody part usually played by a single instrument to accompany another instrument or a singer ⟨a violin *obbligato*⟩

ob·du·ra·cy \'äb-d(y)ə-rə-sē, äb-'d(y)ùr-ə-\ *n, pl* **-cies** : the quality or state or an instance of being obdurate

ob·du·rate \'äb-d(y)ə-rət, äb-'d(y)ùr-ət\ *adj* **1** : hardened in feelings **2** : UNYIELDING 2, STUBBORN — **ob·du·rate·ly** *adv*

obe·di·ence \ō-'bēd-ē-ən(t)s, ə-\ *n* **1** : an act or instance of obeying **2** : the quality or state of being obedient

obe·di·ent \ō-'bēd-ē-ənt, ə-\ *adj* : willing to obey — **obe·di·ent·ly** *adv*

obei·sance \ō-'bēs-ᵊn(t)s, -'bās-\ *n* : a movement of the body (as a bow) made as a sign of respect

obe·lia \ō-'bēl-yə\ *n* : any of a genus of small marine hydroids that form colonies branched like trees

obe·lisk \'äb-ə-ˌlisk\ *n* : a four-sided pillar that becomes narrower toward the top and ends in a pyramid

obese \ō-'bēs\ *adj* : very fat — **obe·si·ty** \ō-'bē-sət-ē\ *n*

obey \ō-'bā, ə-\ *vb* **obeyed; obeying** **1** : to follow the commands or guidance of **2** : to act in agreement with : CARRY OUT ⟨*obey* an order⟩ ⟨*obey* the rules⟩

obi \'ō-bē\ *n* : a broad sash worn with a Japanese kimono

obit·u·ary \ə-'bich-ə-ˌwer-ē\ *n, pl* **-ar·ies** : a notice of a person's death (as in a newspaper) — **obituary** *adj*

¹ob·ject \'äb-jikt\ *n* **1 a** : something that may be seen or felt ⟨tables and chairs are *objects*⟩ **b** : something that arouses feelings in an observer ⟨the *object* of their envy⟩ **2** : something that is the target of thought or feeling ⟨an *object* of study⟩ ⟨the *object* of my affections⟩ **3** : the goal or purpose of some activity ⟨the *object* is to raise money⟩ **4** : a noun or term behaving like a noun that receives the action of a verb or completes the meaning of a preposition — **ob·ject·less** \'äb-jik-tləs\ *adj*

²ob·ject \əb-'jekt\ *vb* **1** : to offer or mention as an objection ⟨*objected* that the price was too high⟩ **2** : to oppose something firmly usually with words ⟨*objected* to the plan⟩ — **ob·jec·tor** \-'jek-tər\ *n*

oat

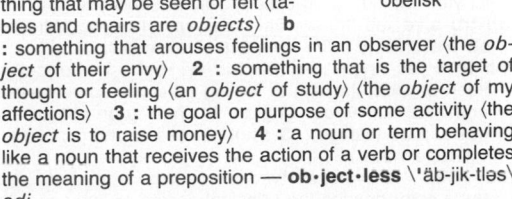

obelisk

object ball \'äb-jik(t)-\ *n* : the ball struck by the cue ball in pool or billiards

ob·jec·tion \əb-'jek-shən\ *n* **1** : an act of objecting **2** : a reason for or a feeling of disapproval

ob·jec·tion·able \əb-'jek-sh(ə-)nə-bəl\ *adj* : arousing objection : OFFENSIVE ⟨uses *objectionable* language⟩ — **ob·jec·tion·ably** \-blē\ *adv*

¹ob·jec·tive \əb-'jek-tiv\ *adj* **1** : being outside of the mind and independent of it ⟨*objective* reality⟩ **2** : being or belonging to the case of a noun or pronoun that is an object of a transitive verb or a preposition **3** : dealing with facts without letting one's feelings interfere with them ⟨an *objective* judgment⟩ — **ob·jec·tive·ly** *adv* — **ob·jec·tiv·i·ty** \(ˌ)äb-ˌjek-'tiv-ət-ē, əb-\ *n*

²objective *n* **1** : a lens or system of lenses (as in a microscope) that forms an image of an object **2** : a goal or end of action **syn** see INTENTION

objective lens *n* : ²OBJECTIVE 1

object lesson \'äb-jikt-\ *n* : a real example of how some general idea or role works

ob·jet d'art \ˌōb-ˌzhā-'där\ *n, pl* **ob·jets d'art** \ˌōb-ˌzhā-'där\ : an article of artistic value

ob·li·gate \'äb-lə-ˌgāt\ *vb* **-gat·ed; -gat·ing** **1** : to make (someone) do something by law or because it is right **2** : OBLIGE 2

ob·li·ga·tion \ˌäb-lə-'gā-shən\ *n* **1** : an act of making oneself responsible for doing something **2 a** : something (as a promise or contract) that requires one to do something **b** : something one must do : DUTY **3** : a feeling of being indebted for an act of kindness

oblig·a·to·ry \ə-'blig-ə-ˌtōr-ē, -ˌtòr- *also* ˌäb-li-gə-\ *adj* : not to be left out, forgotten, or ignored : being required

oblige \ə-'blīj\ *vb* **obliged; oblig·ing** **1** : ²FORCE 1, COMPEL ⟨the soldiers were *obliged* to retreat⟩ **2 a** : to earn the gratitude of ⟨you will *oblige* me by coming early⟩ **b** : to do a favor for or do something as a favor ⟨glad to *oblige*⟩ — **oblig·er** *n*

oblig·ing \ə-'blī-jiŋ\ *adj* : willing to do favors — **oblig·ing·ly** *adv*

oblique \ō-'blēk, ə-, -'blīk; *military usually* ī\ *adj* **1** : having a slanting direction or position : neither perpendicular nor parallel **2** *of a solid* : having the axis not perpendicular to the base ⟨*oblique* circular cylinder⟩ — **oblique·ly** *adv* — **oblique·ness** *n*

oblique angle *n* : an acute or obtuse angle

oblit·er·ate \ə-'blit-ə-ˌrāt, ō-\ *vb* **-at·ed; -at·ing** : to remove or destroy completely : WIPE OUT — **oblit·er·a·tion** \-ˌblit-ə-'rā-shən\ *n*

obliv·i·on \ə-'bliv-ē-ən, ō-, ä-\ *n* **1** : the state of forgetting or having forgotten or of being unaware or unconscious **2** : the state of being forgotten

obliv·i·ous \ə-'bliv-ē-əs, ō-, ä-\ *adj* : not being conscious or aware ⟨*oblivious* to the danger⟩ ⟨*oblivious* of the crowd⟩ — **obliv·i·ous·ly** *adv* — **obliv·i·ous·ness** *n*

¹ob·long \'äb-ˌlòŋ\ *adj* : longer in one direction than in the other with opposite sides parallel ⟨an *oblong* shoe box⟩

²oblong *n* : an oblong figure or object

ob·nox·ious \äb-'näk-shəs, əb-\ *adj* : very disagreeable : HATEFUL — **ob·nox·ious·ly** *adv* — **ob·nox·ious·ness** *n*

oboe \'ō-bō\ *n* : a musical instrument in the form of a slender tube that has holes and keys and that is played by blowing into a reed mouthpiece — **obo·ist** \'ō-ˌbō-əst\ *n*
Word History The musical instrument we now call an *oboe* was developed in France in the 17th century. The French called it a *hautbois*, a word pronounced some-

\ə\ abut	\aù\ out	\i\ tip	\ò\ saw	\ù\ foot
\ər\ further	\ch\ chin	\ī\ life	\òi\ coin	\y\ yet
\a\ mat	\e\ pet	\j\ job	\th\ thin	\yü\ few
\ā\ take	\ē\ easy	\ŋ\ sing	\th\ this	\yù\ cure
\ä\ cot, cart	\g\ go	\ō\ bone	\ü\ food	\zh\ vision

thing like English *o boy* and made up of *haut,* meaning "high", and *bois,* meaning "wood". The *hautbois* was the highest pitched member of a group of woodwind instruments played with a reed. For a time the English simply used the French word for the instrument. Sometimes they spelled it *hautbois,* sometimes *hautboy,* and sometimes they changed the spelling to *oboy* or *hoboy.* Meanwhile, the Italians took the French word as *oboe,* a spelling closer to the way they pronounced it. In the 18th century it became fashionable in England to prefer Italian musical terms. The English then started using the form *oboe* instead of *hautbois,* and so *oboe* is the form we use today. [from Italian *oboe* "oboe", from French *hautbois* (same meaning), from *haut* "high" and *bois* "wood"]

oboe

ob·scene \äb-'sēn, əb-\ *adj* **1** : REPULSIVE, DISGUSTING **2** : very shocking to one's sense of what is moral or decent — **ob·scene·ly** *adv*

ob·scen·i·ty \äb-'sen-ət-ē, əb-\ *n, pl* **-ties** **1** : the quality or state of being obscene **2** : something that is obscene

¹ob·scure \äb-'skyü(ə)r, əb-\ *adj* **1 a** : not having enough light : DARK, GLOOMY **b** : not clearly seen : FAINT **2** : not easily understood or not clearly expressed **3 a** : SECLUDED 1, REMOTE **b** : not widely known — **ob·scure·ly** *adv*

²obscure *vb* **ob·scured; ob·scur·ing** : to make obscure

ob·scu·ri·ty \äb-'skyur-ət-ē, əb-\ *n, pl* **-ties** **1** : the quality or state of being obscure **2** : something that is obscure

ob·se·qui·ous \əb-'sē-kwē-əs, äb-\ *adj* : ready or prompt to help or obey like a servant or slave at the wish or command of another person

ob·serv·able \əb-'zər-və-bəl\ *adj* : able to be observed : NOTICEABLE — **ob·serv·ably** \-blē\ *adv*

ob·ser·vance \əb-'zər-vən(t)s\ *n* **1** : an established practice or ceremony ⟨religious *observances*⟩ **2** : an act of following a custom, rule, or law **3** : an act or instance of watching

ob·ser·vant \əb-'zər-vənt\ *adj* **1** : paying careful attention : WATCHFUL **2** : quick to observe : KEEN **3** : careful in observing : MINDFUL — **ob·ser·vant·ly** *adv*

ob·ser·va·tion \,äb-sər-'vā-shən, -zər-\ *n* **1** : an act or the power of seeing or fixing the mind upon something **2** : the gathering of information (as for scientific studies) by noting facts or occurrences ⟨weather *observations*⟩ **3** : an opinion formed or expressed after observing **4** : the fact of being observed **syn** see REMARK — **ob·ser·va·tion·al** \-shnəl, -shən-ᵊl\ *adj*

ob·ser·va·to·ry \əb-'zər-və-,tōr-ē, -,tȯr-\ *n, pl* **-ries** **1** : a place or institution equipped with instruments for observation of natural objects and events (as in astronomy) **2** : a place providing a wide view

ob·serve \əb-'zərv\ *vb* **ob·served; ob·serv·ing** **1** : to act in agreement with : OBEY ⟨*observe* the law⟩ **2** : to celebrate or honor (as a holiday) with special events or customs **3 a** : to watch carefully ⟨*observed* how the food was prepared⟩ **b** : to make a scientific observation of ⟨*observe* an eclipse⟩ **4** : to come to understand or know especially by thinking about facts that have been noted ⟨I have *observed* that it happens more often on Tuesdays⟩ **5** : to say as a remark ⟨*observed* that it was a fine day and we agreed⟩ **syn** see KEEP — **ob·serv·er** *n*

ob·sess \əb-'ses, äb-\ *vb* : to occupy the mind of completely or abnormally ⟨*obsessed* with this new scheme⟩

ob·ses·sion \äb-'sesh-ən, əb-\ *n* : a disturbing concern with an idea or feeling that cannot be put out of mind even when it is seen to be unreasonable; *also* : such a thought or feeling

ob·ses·sive \äb-'ses-iv, əb-\ *adj* : of, relating to, having, or being an obsession — **ob·ses·sive·ly** *adv*

ob·sid·i·an \əb-'sid-ē-ən\ *n* : a dark natural glass formed by the cooling of lava

ob·so·les·cence \,äb-sə-'les-ᵊn(t)s\ *n* : the process of becoming obsolete or the state of being nearly obsolete

ob·so·les·cent \,äb-sə-'les-ᵊnt\ *adj* : going out of use : becoming obsolete

ob·so·lete \,äb-sə-'lēt, 'äb-sə-,lēt\ *adj* **1** : no longer in use ⟨an *obsolete* word⟩ **2** : of a kind or style no longer current : OUTMODED ⟨*obsolete* machinery⟩ — **ob·so·lete·ly** *adv* — **ob·so·lete·ness** *n*

ob·sta·cle \'äb-sti-kəl\ *n* : something that stands in the way or opposes : HINDRANCE

ob·stet·ric \əb-'ste-trik, äb-\ *or* **ob·stet·ri·cal** \-tri-kəl\ *adj* : of or relating to childbirth or obstetrics

ob·ste·tri·cian \,äb-stə-'trish-ən\ *n* : a physician specializing in obstetrics

ob·stet·rics \əb-'ste-triks, äb-\ *n* : a branch of medical science that deals with childbirth and with the care of women before, during, and after this

ob·sti·na·cy \'äb-stə-nə-sē\ *n* : the quality or state of being obstinate

ob·sti·nate \'äb-stə-nət\ *adj* **1** : sticking to an opinion, purpose, or course in spite of reason, arguments, or persuasion **2** : not easily overcome or removed ⟨an *obstinate* fever⟩ — **ob·sti·nate·ly** *adv*

syn OBSTINATE, DOGGED, STUBBORN mean unwilling to change course or give up one's intention. OBSTINATE suggests that one sticks to a course of action to the point of being unreasonable ⟨an *obstinate* player who would not pass the ball⟩ DOGGED suggests that one goes after something and never tires or quits ⟨a *dogged* reporter determined to get the real story⟩ STUBBORN suggests that one has a fixed mind and opposes all attempts to change it ⟨too *stubborn* to admit the mistake⟩

ob·strep·er·ous \əb-'strep-(ə-)rəs, äb-\ *adj* : noisy and hard to control — **ob·strep·er·ous·ly** *adv* — **ob·strep·er·ous·ness** *n*

ob·struct \əb-'strəkt, äb-\ *vb* **1** : to stop up by an obstacle **2** : to be or get in the way of : HINDER

ob·struc·tion \əb-'strək-shən, äb-\ *n* **1** : an act of obstructing : the state of being obstructed **2** : something that gets in the way : OBSTACLE

ob·struc·tion·ism \əb-'strək-shə-,niz-əm, äb-\ *n* : deliberate interference with business especially in a legislative body — **ob·struc·tion·ist** \-sh(ə-)nəst\ *n or adj*

ob·struc·tive \əb-'strək-tiv, äb-\ *adj* : tending or serving to obstruct

ob·tain \əb-'tān, äb-\ *vb* **1** : to gain or acquire usually by planning or effort **2** : PREVAIL 3b ⟨perfect courtesy *obtained*⟩ **syn** see GET — **ob·tain·able** \-'tā-nə-bəl\ *adj*

ob·trude \əb-'trüd, äb-\ *vb* **ob·trud·ed; ob·trud·ing** **1** : to stick out ⟨the tortoise *obtruded* its head⟩ **2** : to put forward without being asked ⟨*obtrude* one's views⟩

ob·tru·sive \əb-'trü-siv, äb-, -ziv\ *adj* : likely to obtrude — **ob·tru·sive·ly** *adv* — **ob·tru·sive·ness** *n*

ob·tuse \äb-'t(y)üs\ *adj* **ob·tus·er; -est** **1** : not quick or keen of understanding or feeling **2 a** : being between 90° and 180° ⟨an *obtuse* angle⟩ **b** : having an obtuse angle ⟨an *obtuse* triangle⟩ **3** : not pointed or sharp : BLUNT — **ob·tuse·ness** *n*

ob·verse \'äb-,vərs, äb-'vərs\ *n* **1** : the side of something (as a coin) bearing the principal design or lettering **2** : a front or principal surface **3** : COUNTERPART 3

ob·vi·ate \'äb-vē-,āt\ *vb* **-at·ed; -at·ing** : to anticipate and take care of beforehand ⟨*obviate* an objection⟩

ob·vi·ous \'äb-vē-əs\ *adj* : easily found, seen, or understood : PLAIN ⟨an *obvious* mistake⟩ — **ob·vi·ous·ness** *n*

ob·vious·ly \'äb-vē-əs-lē\ *adv* **1** : in an obvious manner : PLAINLY, CLEARLY ⟨*obviously* enjoys her work⟩ ⟨dealing with an *obviously* difficult subject⟩ **2** : it is obvious ⟨*obviously*, this is only a beginning⟩

oc·a·ri·na \,äk-ə-'rē-nə\ *n* : a simple musical instrument having an oval body with finger holes and a projecting mouthpiece and giving soft flutelike tones

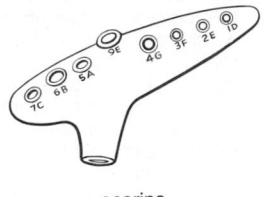

ocarina

¹oc·ca·sion \ə-'kā-zhən\ *n* **1** : a favorable opportunity : a good chance ⟨sorry not to have had *occasion* to meet them⟩ **2** : a situation that provides a reason ⟨an *occasion* for rejoicing⟩ **3** : something that brings about an event ⟨the remark was the *occasion* of a bitter quarrel⟩ **4** : a time at which something happens ⟨on the *occasion* of the wedding⟩ **5** : a need that arises ⟨have *occasion* to travel⟩ **6** : a special event or ceremony : CELEBRATION ⟨a big *occasion*⟩

²occasion *vb* **-sioned; -sion·ing** \-'kāzh-(ə-)niŋ\ : to give occasion to : CAUSE

oc·ca·sion·al \ə-'kāzh-nəl, -ən-ᵊl\ *adj* **1** : relating to or created for a special occasion ⟨*occasional* verse⟩ **2** : happening, appearing, or met with now and then ⟨an *occasional* visitor⟩ — **oc·ca·sion·al·ly** \-ē\ *adv*

Oc·ci·dent \'äk-səd-ənt, -sə-,dent\ *n* : ³WEST 2 [Middle English *occident* "the West", from early French *occident* (same meaning), from Latin *occident-, occidens* "the West, the part of the world lying in the direction in which the sun sets, the part of the world opposite the Orient", derived from *occidere* "to fall, set behind the horizon", from *oc-, ob-* "toward, over" and *cadere* "to fall"]

oc·ci·den·tal \,äk-sə-'dent-ᵊl\ *adj, often cap* **1** : of, relating to, or located in the Occident : WESTERN **2** : of or relating to Occidentals

Occidental *n* : a person of European ancestry

¹oc·cip·i·tal \äk-'sip-ət-ᵊl\ *adj* : of or relating to the back part of the head or skull or to the occipital bone

²occipital *n* : OCCIPITAL BONE

occipital bone *n* : a compound bone that forms the back part of the skull

oc·clud·ed front \ə-'klüd-əd-, ä-\ *n* : the front formed by a cold front overtaking a warm front and lifting the warm air over the cold air

oc·clu·sion \ə-'klü-zhən\ *n* : the coming together of the opposing surfaces of the teeth of the two jaws

¹oc·cult \ə-'kəlt, ä-\ *vb* : to shut off from view : COVER, ECLIPSE

²oc·cult \ə-'kəlt, ä-; 'äk-əlt\ *adj* **1** : beyond understanding : MYSTERIOUS **2** : of or relating to supernatural forces

³occult \ə-'kəlt, ä-; 'äk-əlt\ *n* : matters thought to involve the influence of supernatural forces

oc·cult·ism \ə-'kəl-,tiz-əm, ä-; 'äk-,əl-,tiz-əm\ *n* : a belief in the action or influence of supernatural powers — **oc·cult·ist** \-təst\ *n*

oc·cu·pan·cy \'äk-yə-pən-sē\ *n, pl* **-cies** **1** : the act of occupying or taking possession **2** : the state of being occupied

oc·cu·pant \'äk-yə-pənt\ *n* : a person who occupies something; *esp* : ²RESIDENT 1

oc·cu·pa·tion \,äk-yə-'pā-shən\ *n* **1** : one's business or profession **2** : the taking possession and control of an area ⟨*occupation* of a conquered country⟩

oc·cu·pa·tion·al \,äk-yə-'pā-shnəl, -shən-ᵊl\ *adj* : of or relating to one's occupation — **oc·cu·pa·tion·al·ly** \-ē\ *adv*

oc·cu·py \'äk-yə-,pī\ *vb* **-pied; -py·ing** **1 a** : to take up the attention or energies of ⟨reading *occupied* me most of the summer⟩ **b** : to fill up (space or time) ⟨sports *occupied* most of their spare time⟩ ⟨a liter of water *occupies* 1000 cubic centimeters of space⟩ **2 a** : to take or hold possession of ⟨enemy troops *occupied* the town⟩ **b** : to live in as owner or tenant ⟨*occupy* an apartment⟩ — **oc·cu·pi·er** \-,pī(-ə)r\ *n*

oc·cur \ə-'kər\ *vb* **oc·curred; oc·cur·ring** \-'kər-iŋ\ **1** : to be found or met with : APPEAR ⟨plants that *occur* in meadows⟩ **2** : to present itself : come by or as if by chance ⟨an accident *occurred* on the way to school⟩ ⟨success isn't just *occur*, it is earned⟩ **3** : to come into the mind ⟨it just *occurred* to me⟩ [from Latin *occurrere* "to exist, happen, meet with", literally "to run up against", from *oc-, ob-* "toward, against" and *currere* "to run" — related to CURRENT, INCUR]

oc·cur·rence \ə-'kər-ən(t)s, -'kə-rən(t)s\ *n* **1** : something that occurs **2** : the action or process of occurring **3** : the presence of a natural form or material in a particular place ⟨the *occurrence* of oil in Oklahoma⟩

ocean \'ō-shən\ *n* **1** : the whole body of salt water that covers nearly three fourths of the surface of the earth **2** : one of the large bodies of water into which the ocean is divided — **oce·an·ic** \,ō-shē-'an-ik\ *adj*

ocean·go·ing \-,gō-iŋ\ *adj* : made to travel on the ocean ⟨*oceangoing* ships⟩

ocean·og·ra·pher \,ō-shə-'näg-rə-fər\ *n* : a person who specializes in oceanography

ocean·og·ra·phy \,ō-shə-'näg-rə-fē\ *n* : a science that deals with the ocean — **ocean·o·graph·ic** \-nə-'graf-ik\ *adj* — **ocean·o·graph·i·cal·ly** \-i-k(ə-)lē\ *adv*

oce·lot \'äs-ə-,lät, 'ō-sə-\ *n* : a medium-sized American wildcat that is found from Texas to Patagonia and has a tawny yellow or grayish coat marked with black

ocher *or* **ochre** \'ō-kər\ *n* **1** : an earthy usually red or yellow and often impure iron ore used as coloring matter **2** : the color of yellow ocher

o'·clock \ə-'kläk\ *adv* **1** : according to the clock ⟨the time is three *o'clock*⟩ **2** — used for indicating position or direction as if on a clock dial ⟨an airplane approaching at eleven *o'clock*⟩

octa- *or* **octo-** *also* **oct-** *combining form* : eight [derived from Greek *oktō* and Latin *octo*, both meaning "eight"]

oc·ta·gon \'äk-tə-,gän\ *n* : a plane figure with eight angles and eight sides — **oc·tag·o·nal** \äk-'tag-ən-ᵊl\ *adj*

oc·ta·he·dron \,äk-tə-'hē-drən\ *n, pl* **-drons** *or* **-dra** \-drə\ : a solid bounded by eight plane faces

oc·tal \'äk-tᵊl\ *adj* : of, relating to, or being a number system with a base of eight

oc·tane \'äk-,tān\ *n* **1** : any of several liquid chemical compounds containing 8 carbon atoms and 18 hydrogen atoms **2** : a number that is used to measure the antiknock characteristics of gasoline and that increases as the chance of knocking decreases

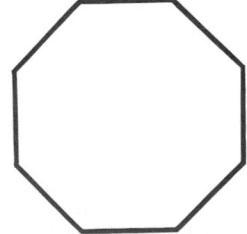

octagon

oc·tave \'äk-tiv, -təv, -,tāv\ *n* **1** : a group of eight lines of poetry (as the first eight lines of a sonnet) **2 a** : the difference in pitch between the first and eighth tone on the scale **b** : a tone or note that is eight steps above or below

\ə\ abut	\au̇\ out	\i\ tip	\ȯ\ saw	\u̇\ foot
\ər\ further	\ch\ chin	\ī\ life	\ȯi\ coin	\y\ yet
\a\ mat	\e\ pet	\j\ job	\th\ thin	\yü\ few
\ā\ take	\ē\ easy	\ŋ\ sing	\th\ this	\yu̇\ cure
\ä\ cot, cart	\g\ go	\ō\ bone	\ü\ food	\zh\ vision

another note or tone
3 : a group of eight

oc·ta·vo \äk-'tā-vō, -'täv-ō\ *n, pl* **-vos** : a book made up of sheets of paper that have been folded to produce eight leaves

octave 2a

oc·tet \äk-'tet\ *n* **1 a** : a piece of music written for eight voices or eight instruments **b** : the performers of an octet **2** : a group or set of eight

oc·til·lion \äk-'til-yən\ *n* — see NUMBER table

Oc·to·ber \äk-'tō-bər\ *n* : the tenth month of the year

Word History According to its origin, the name *October,* which we know as the tenth month of the year, really means "eighth month". In the first calendar used in ancient Rome, the year had only ten months, starting in March and ending in December. The extra period between December and March was not considered part of the series of months. Later, when two extra months were added to the calendar, October became the tenth month but kept its old name. The Latin name came into Old English as *october* and into early French as *octobre.* It was spelled both ways in Middle English. But in time the influence of Latin fixed the spelling as *october.* [Middle English *october, octobre* "the tenth month", from Old English *october* and early French *octobre* (both, same meaning), both from Latin *october* "the eighth month", from *octo* "eight"]

oc·to·ge·nar·i·an \,äk-tə-jə-'ner-ē-ən\ *n* : a person who is 80 or more but less than 90 years old

oc·to·pus \'äk-tə-pəs\ *n, pl* **-pus·es** *or* **-pi** \-,pī\ **1** : any of various sea mollusks that are cephalopods having eight muscular arms with two rows of suckers which hold objects (as its prey) **2** : something suggestive of an octopus; *esp* : a powerful grasping organization with many branches [from scientific Latin *Octopod-, Octopus* "octopus", from Greek *oktōpous,* literally "eight-footed", from *oktō* "eight" and *pous* "foot"]

¹oc·u·lar \'äk-yə-lər\ *adj* : of or relating to the eye or the eyesight

²ocular *n* : EYEPIECE

oc·u·list \'äk-yə-ləst\ *n* **1** : OPHTHALMOLOGIST **2** : OPTOMETRIST

¹OD \(')ō-'dē\ *n* : an overdose of a drug and especially a narcotic

²OD *vb* **OD'd** *or* **ODed** \(')ō-'dēd\; **OD'ing** \(')ō-'dē-iŋ\ : to become ill or die from an OD

odd \'äd\ *adj* **1** : being only one of a pair or set ⟨an *odd* shoe⟩ **2 a** : not divisible by two without leaving a remainder ⟨1, 3, 5, and 7 are *odd* numbers⟩ **b** : numbered with an odd number ⟨an *odd* year⟩ **3** : somewhat more than the number mentioned ⟨50 *odd* years ago⟩ **4** : additional to or apart from what is usual, expected, or planned on ⟨*odd* jobs⟩ **5** : not usual or traditional : STRANGE ⟨what an *odd* thing to do⟩ — **odd·ly** *adv* — **odd·ness** *n*

Word History In the early Norse language, the word *oddi* was first used to mean "a point of land". Then, because one corner of a triangle looks something like a point of land sticking out into the sea, *oddi* came to mean "triangle". A triangle that has one long point, like a point of land, may be thought of as having two paired angles and one angle left over. In time, the Norse came to call something that was not matched or paired up "oddi". This was used for an odd number, one left over after all other numbers were paired up. It was also used for an odd man, one who in a voting situation could break a tie with his vote. When the word was taken into English in the 14th century, it had the meaning of an odd number like 3, 5, or 7 that cannot be divided evenly by 2. Later it came to mean something that stood out from

others as being different or strange. [Middle English *odde* "odd", from an early Norse word *oddi* (noun) "a point of land, triangle, odd number"]

odd·ball \-,bȯl\ *n* : a person who behaves strangely

odd·i·ty \'äd-ət-ē\ *n, pl* **-ties 1** : something odd **2** : the quality or state of being odd

odd·ment \'äd-mənt\ *n* : something left over : REMNANT

odds \'ädz\ *n pl* **1** : a difference by which one thing is favored over another ⟨the *odds* are in favor of our side⟩ **2 a** : the probability that one thing is so or will happen instead of another **b** : the ratio of the probability of one event to that of an event that can happen instead ⟨the *odds* of success to failure in throwing a six with two dice are 1 to 5⟩ **3** : a state of disagreement

odds and ends *n pl* : miscelleanous articles, leftovers, or things to do

ode \'ōd\ *n* : a lyric poem that expresses a noble feeling with dignity

-ode \,ōd\ *n combining form* **1** : way : path ⟨electr*ode*⟩ **2** : electrode ⟨di*ode*⟩ [derived from Greek *hodos* "way, path"]

odi·ous \'ōd-ē-əs\ *adj* : causing hatred or strong dislike : worthy of hatred — **odi·ous·ly** *adv*

odi·um \'ōd-ē-əm\ *n* **1** : the state of being generally hated **2** : the disgrace or shame attached to something considered hateful

odom·e·ter \ō-'däm-ət-ər\ *n* : an instrument for measuring distance traveled (as by a vehicle)

odor \'ōd-ər\ *n* **1** : a quality of something that one becomes aware of through the sense of smell : SCENT **2** : a smell whether pleasant or unpleasant — **odor·less** \-ləs\ *adj*

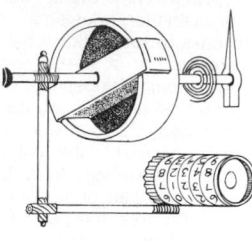

odometer

odor·if·er·ous \,ōd-ə-'rif-(ə-)rəs\ *adj* : ODOROUS

odor·ous \'ōd-ə-rəs\ *adj* : having or giving off an odor

od·ys·sey \'äd-ə-sē\ *n, pl* **-seys** : a long wandering or series of travels [named for the *Odyssey,* a long poem from ancient Greece telling the story of the 10-year wanderings of Odysseus, a Greek hero and king]

o'er \'ō(ə)r, 'ȯ(ə)r\ *adv or prep* : OVER

of \əv, 'əv, 'äv\ *prep* **1** — used to indicate a point from which something is located ⟨north *of* the lake⟩ **2 a** — used to indicate origin ⟨*of* noble birth⟩ **b** — used to indicate cause or reason ⟨afraid *of* the dark⟩ ⟨died *of* flu⟩ **c** : by as author or doer ⟨the plays *of* Shakespeare⟩ **d** : on the part of ⟨very kind *of* you⟩ **3 a** : made from ⟨a ring *of* gold⟩ **b** — used to indicate contents ⟨a cup *of* water⟩ **c** — used to indicate the number or amount in or making up something ⟨a class *of* 20 students⟩ ⟨interest *of* 5¼%⟩ **4 a** — used to indicate the whole that includes an amount or part mentioned first ⟨most *of* the team⟩ **b** — used to indicate the whole or quantity from which part is removed or used ⟨gave freely *of* their time⟩ **5 a** : relating to : ABOUT ⟨stories *of* her adventures⟩ **b** : in respect to ⟨slow *of* speech⟩ ⟨great *of* heart⟩ **6 a** — used to indicate belonging or possession ⟨queen *of* France⟩ ⟨courage *of* the pioneers⟩ **b** — used to indicate relationship between a result and something upon which an operation or procedure is performed to produce it ⟨the product *of* two numbers⟩ ⟨the solution *of* an equation⟩ **7** — used to indicate something that is removed ⟨cured *of* her disease⟩ ⟨relieved *of* his command⟩ ⟨rid the barn *of* rats⟩ **8** — used to indicate that an example belongs to a certain class ⟨the city *of* Rome⟩ **9** — used to indicate what a noun, verb, or adjective applies to ⟨love *of* nature⟩ ⟨cheated *of* a dollar⟩ ⟨fond *of* oranges⟩ **10** : having as a quality or possession ⟨a thing *of* no importance⟩ **11** : ²BEFORE 3 ⟨ten minutes *of* eight⟩

¹off \'óf\ *adv* **1 a** : from a place or position ⟨march *off*⟩ ⟨stood 10 paces *off*⟩ ⟨drove the dogs *off*⟩ **b** : from a course : ASIDE ⟨turned *off* onto a side street⟩ **c** : into an unconscious state ⟨dozed *off*⟩ **2** : so as not to be supported, or covering or enclosing, or attached ⟨rolled to the edge of the table and *off*⟩ ⟨the handle came *off*⟩ **3** : so as to be divided ⟨surface marked *off* into squares⟩ **4** : so as to be stopped or finished ⟨shut *off* an engine⟩ ⟨a coat of paint to finish it *off*⟩ **5** : away from work ⟨took the day *off*⟩

²off \(')óf\ *prep* **1** : away from the surface or top of ⟨take it *off* the table⟩ **2** : at the expense of ⟨still living *off* my parents⟩ **3 a** : released or freed from ⟨*off* duty⟩ **b** : below the usual level of ⟨*off* her game⟩ ⟨a dollar *off* the price⟩ **4** : away from ⟨just *off* the highway⟩

³off \(')óf\ *adj* **1 a** : more distant ⟨the *off* side of the building⟩ **b** : not left : RIGHT ⟨the *off* horse⟩ **2** : started on the way ⟨*off* on a trip⟩ ⟨they're *off* and running⟩ **3 a** : not taking place ⟨the game is *off*⟩ **b** : not operating ⟨the radio is *off*⟩ **4** : not correct : WRONG ⟨these numbers are *off*⟩ ⟨your guess is way *off*⟩ **5 a** : not very good : POOR ⟨an *off* grade of oil⟩ **b** : below or down from the normal ⟨stocks were *off*⟩ ⟨offered at 15% *off*⟩ **c** : not entirely sane **6** : small in degree : SLIGHT ⟨an *off* chance⟩ **7** : provided for or taken care of ⟨we were better *off* before⟩

of·fal \'ò-fəl, 'äf-əl\ *n* : the waste or by-product of a process; *esp* : the inside organs of and parts trimmed from an animal killed and prepared for food ⟨fish *offal*⟩

¹off·beat \'óf-,bēt\ *n* : a musical beat that is not accented

²offbeat *adj* : not ordinary : UNUSUAL

offence *chiefly British variant of* OFFENSE

of·fend \ə-'fend\ *vb* **1** : to do wrong : SIN **2** : to cause to be angry or annoyed : DISPLEASE — **of·fend·er** *n*

of·fense \ə-'fen(t)s, *especially for sense 2* 'äf-,en(t)s, 'óf-\ *n* **1** : something that offends **2 a** : an act of attacking : ASSAULT **b** : the side that is attacking **c** : the side that is attempting to score in a game or contest **3 a** : the act of offending **b** : the state of being offended **4 a** : a violation of a social or moral code **b** : a breaking of the law
syn OFFENSE, SIN, VICE, CRIME mean a violation of law. OFFENSE applies to the breaking of any law, rule, or code ⟨students will be expelled for major *offenses*⟩ SIN applies especially to a breaking of moral law ⟨the *sin* of greed⟩ VICE applies to a habit that degrades or ruins ⟨one of their worst *vices* was gambling⟩ CRIME applies to a serious offense punishable by the law of the state ⟨robbery is a *crime*⟩

¹of·fen·sive \ə-'fen(t)-siv\ *adj* **1 a** : relating to or made or suited for attack ⟨*offensive* weapons⟩ **b** : of or relating to the attempt to score in a game or contest ⟨the *offensive* team⟩ **2** : causing displeasure or resentment ⟨an *offensive* smell⟩ ⟨an *offensive* remark⟩ — **of·fen·sive·ly** *adv* — **of·fen·sive·ness** *n*

²offensive *n* **1** : the state or attitude of one who is making an attack ⟨on the *offensive*⟩ **2** : ²ATTACK 1 ⟨launch an *offensive*⟩

¹of·fer \'óf-ər, 'äf-\ *vb* **of·fered; of·fer·ing** \-(ə-)riŋ\ **1** : to present as an act of worship : SACRIFICE **2** : to present (something) to be accepted or rejected ⟨was *offered* the job⟩ ⟨*offer* $10 for the lamp⟩ ⟨*offer* fruit for sale⟩ **3 a** : to present for consideration : SUGGEST ⟨*offer* a suggestion⟩ **b** : to declare one's willingness ⟨*offered* to help⟩ **4** : to try to make or do : PUT UP ⟨*offered* stubborn resistance⟩ **5** : to make available ⟨the hut *offered* protection from the wind and rain⟩ [Old English *offrian* "to present as an act of worship", derived from Latin *offerre* "to present, offer", from *of-, ob-* "to, toward" and *ferre* "to bear, carry, yield" — related to ¹DEFER, REFER]

²offer *n* **1** : an act of offering ⟨an *offer* to help⟩ **2** : a price suggested by one prepared to buy : BID

of·fer·ing \'óf-(ə-)riŋ, 'äf-\ *n* **1** : the act of one who offers **2 a** : something offered **b** : a sacrifice offered as a part of worship **3** : a contribution to the support of a church

of·fer·to·ry \'óf-ə(r)-,tōr-ē, 'äf-, -,tór-\ *n, pl* **-ries** **1** *often cap* **a** : the offering of the sacramental bread and wine to God before they are consecrated **b** : a verse from a psalm said or sung at the beginning of the offertory **2 a** : the presentation of the offerings of the congregation in church **b** : the music played or sung during an offertory

off·hand \'óf-'hand\ *adv* : without previous thought or preparation ⟨can't say *offhand* how many there are⟩

off·hand·ed \'óf-'han-dəd\ *adj* : OFFHAND ⟨*offhanded* remarks⟩ — **off·hand·ed·ly** *adv*

of·fice \'äf-əs, 'óf-\ *n* **1** : a special duty or post and especially one of authority in government ⟨hold public *office*⟩ **2** : a prescribed form or service of worship : RITE **3** : something done for another : SERVICE **4** : a place where a business is carried on ⟨ticket *office*⟩ ⟨a dentist's *office*⟩ **5** : a large government department ⟨Patent *Office*⟩

of·fice·hold·er \-,hōl-dər\ *n* : a person holding a public office

of·fi·cer \'äf-ə-sər, 'óf-\ *n* **1** : a person given the responsibility of enforcing the law ⟨a police *officer*⟩ **2** : a person who holds an office ⟨an *officer* of the company⟩ **3** : a person who holds a commission in the armed forces

¹of·fi·cial \ə-'fish-əl\ *n* **1** : a person who holds an office ⟨public *officials*⟩ **2** : a person who enforces the rules in a game or sport ⟨the *officials* of a football game⟩

²official *adj* **1** : of or relating to an office ⟨*official* duties⟩ **2** : having authority to perform a duty ⟨the *official* government of the 13 colonies⟩ **3** : prescribed or permitted by authority ⟨the *official* language⟩ ⟨an *official* American League baseball⟩ **4** : proper for a person in office ⟨an *official* greeting⟩ — **of·fi·cial·ly** \-'fish-(ə-)lē\ *adv*

of·fi·cial·dom \ə-'fish-əl-dəm\ *n* : officials as a class

of·fi·ci·ate \ə-'fish-ē-,āt\ *vb* **-at·ed; -at·ing** **1** : to perform a ceremony ⟨*officiate* at a wedding⟩ **2** : to act as an officer ⟨*officiated* at the annual meeting⟩

of·fi·cious \ə-'fish-əs\ *adj* : volunteering one's services where they are not asked for or needed — **of·fi·cious·ly** *adv* — **of·fi·cious·ness** *n*

off·ing \'óf-iŋ, 'äf-\ *n* : the near distance or near future ⟨sees trouble in the *offing*⟩

off–key \'óf-'kē\ *adj or adv* : above or below the proper tone of a melody ⟨singing *off-key*⟩

off–limits \'ò-'flim-əts\ *adj* : not to be entered or used by a certain group of people

off–line \'ò-'flīn\ *adj* : not connected to or controlled by a computer ⟨an *off-line* printer⟩

off of *prep* : ²OFF

off–road \'óf-'rōd\ *adj* : of, relating to, done with, or being a vehicle designed especially to operate away from public roads

off–season \'óf-,sēz-ᵊn\ *n* : a time when some activity is suspended or reduced

¹off·set \'óf-,set\ *n* **1** : a short shoot arising from the base of a plant and growing flat on the ground **2** : something that serves to make up for something else

²off·set \'óf-,set *also* óf-'set\ *vb* **-set; -set·ting** : to make up for ⟨gains in one state *offset* losses in another⟩

off·shoot \'óf-,shüt\ *n* **1** : something that branches out from something else **2** : a branch of a main stem of a plant

offset 1

¹off·shore \'òf-'shō(ə)r, -'shȯ(ə)r\ *adv* : from the shore : at a distance from the shore

²off·shore \'òf-,shō(ə)r, -,shȯ(ə)r\ *adj* **1** : coming or moving away from the shore ⟨an *offshore* breeze⟩ **2** : located off the shore ⟨*offshore* islands⟩ ⟨an *offshore* oil rig⟩

off·side \'òf-'sīd\ *adv or adj* : illegally in advance of the ball or puck

off·spring \'òf-,spriŋ\ *n, pl* **offspring** *also* **offsprings** : the young of a person, animal, or plant

off·stage \'òf-'stāj, -,stāj\ *adv or adj* : off or away from the stage

off–white \'òf-'hwīt, -'wīt\ *n* : a yellowish or grayish white

oft \'òft\ *adv* : OFTEN ⟨an *oft* neglected factor⟩

of·ten \'ò-fən, 'òf-tən\ *adv* : many times : FREQUENTLY

of·ten·times \-,tīmz\ *or* **oft·times** \'òf(t)-,tīmz\ *adv* : OFTEN

ogle \'ōg-əl *also* 'äg-\ *vb* **ogled**; **ogling** \-(ə)liŋ\ : to look at in a flirting way or with unusual attention or desire — **ogle** *n* — **ogler** \-(ə)lər\ *n*

ogre \'ō-gər\ *n* **1** : an ugly giant of fairy tales and folklore that eats people **2** : a dreaded person or object — **ogre·ish** \'ō-g(ə)rish\ *adj*

¹oh *or* **O** \(')ō\ *interj* **1** — used to express an emotion (as astonishment or desire) or in response to a physical sensation (as pain) **2** — used in direct address ⟨*Oh* sir, you forgot your change⟩

²oh \'ō\ *n* : ¹ZERO 1

ohm \'ōm\ *n* : a unit of electric resistance equal to the resistance of a circuit in which a potential difference of one volt produces a current of one ampere — **ohm·ic** \'ō-mik\ *adj*

ohm·me·ter \'ō(m)-,mēt-ər\ *n* : an instrument for indicating resistance in ohms directly

Ohm's law \'ōmz-\ *n* : a law in electricity that states that the current in a circuit is equal to the potential difference divided by the resistance of the circuit

¹-oid \,òid\ *n suffix* : something resembling a (specified) object or having a (specified) quality ⟨planet*oid*⟩

²-oid *adj suffix* : resembling : having the form or appearance of [derived from Greek *-oeidēs* "resembling, having a specified form"]

¹oil \'òi(ə)l\ *n* **1 a** : any of numerous greasy flammable usually liquid substances from plant, animal, or mineral sources that do not dissolve in water and are used especially as lubricants, fuels, and food **b** : PETROLEUM **2** : something (as a cosmetic) like oil or containing an oil ⟨bath *oil*⟩ ⟨suntan *oil*⟩ **3 a** : artist's paints made of pigments and oil **b** : a painting done in oils

²oil *vb* : to put oil in or on

oil·cloth \'òi(ə)l-,klòth\ *n* : cloth treated with oil or paint so as to be waterproof and used for table and shelf coverings

oil·er \'òi-lər\ *n* **1** : a person (as a worker) who oils something **2** : a device for applying oil

oil field *n* : a region rich in oil deposits

oil gland *n* : a gland (as of the skin) that gives off an oily substance

oil of wintergreen : a chemical compound made from salicylic acid and used in liniments and as a flavoring

oil paint *n* : paint made with a drying oil

oil painting *n* : a painting done with oil paints

oil palm *n* : a palm that is cultivated for its clusters of fruits from which a vegetable oil is obtained

oil·seed \'òi(ə)l-,sēd\ *n* : a seed or crop grown mainly for the oil obtained from it

oil shale *n* : a rock (as shale) from which oil can be recovered

oil·skin \'òi(ə)l-,skin\ *n* **1** : a waterproof cloth **2** : an oilskin raincoat **3** *pl* : an oilskin coat and trousers

oil slick *n* : a film of oil floating on water

oily \'òi-lē\ *adj* **oil·i·er**; **-est** **1** : of, relating to, or consisting of oil **2** : covered or soaked with oil — **oil·i·ness** *n*

oint·ment \'òint-mənt\ *n* : a semisolid greasy medicine for use on the skin

Ojib·wa *or* **Ojib·way** \ō-'jib-wä\ *n* : a member of an American Indian people originally of Michigan

¹OK *or* **okay** \ō-'kā\ *adv or adj* : all right

> **Word History** In the late 1830s Boston newspapers were filled with abbreviations. Abbreviation was apparently the fashion at that time. Any phrase might be shortened. The fad even went so far as to produce abbreviations for intentional misspellings. Such popular expressions as *N.G.* (no go) and *A.R.* (all right) gave way to *K.G.* (know go) and *O.W.* (oll wright). The abbreviation *O.K.* stood for *oll korrect*, a deliberate misspelling of *all correct*. Several of these abbreviated misspellings became popular for a time, but *O.K.* was the only one to gain a lasting place in the language. [an abbreviation of *oll korrect*, an altered form of *all correct*]

²OK *or* **okay** *vb* **OK'd** *or* **okayed**; **OK'·ing** *or* **okay·ing** : APPROVE 2

³OK *or* **okay** *n* : APPROVAL

oka·pi \ō-'käp-ē\ *n* : an African mammal closely related to the giraffe but lacking the long neck

okra \'ō-krə\ *n* : a tall plant related to the hollyhocks and grown for its edible green pods which are used especially in soups and stews; *also* : these pods

okapi

¹old \'ōld\ *adj* **1 a** : dating from the distant past ⟨an *old* custom⟩ **b** : having lasted or been such for a long time ⟨an *old* friend⟩ **2** *cap* : belonging to an early period in development ⟨*Old* Irish⟩ **3** : having existed for a specified length of time ⟨a girl three years *old*⟩ **4** : having lived a long time ⟨*old* people⟩ **5** : FORMER 1 ⟨my *old* teachers⟩ **6** : showing the effects of time or use ⟨wore an *old* coat⟩ **7** : long familiar ⟨it's still the same *old* story⟩

> **syn** OLD, ANCIENT, ANTIQUE, ARCHAIC mean having come into being or use in the distant past. OLD may apply to a period of time that is truly long or only longer than average ⟨*old* houses that were built two hundred years ago⟩ ⟨an *old* sweater of mine⟩ ANCIENT applies to things that happened or existed in the very distant past ⟨an *ancient* custom⟩ or to things that still survive from early times ⟨the *ancient* pyramids of Egypt⟩ ANTIQUE applies to things that have been handed down from times gone by ⟨collected *antique* furniture⟩ ARCHAIC suggests something that has the characteristics of a much earlier time ⟨the play used *archaic* language so as to give the audience a feeling for those days⟩

²old *n* : old or earlier time ⟨in days of *old*⟩

old country *n* : the country that a person has emigrated from

old·en \'ōl-dən\ *adj* : of or relating to earlier days

Old English *n* : the language of the English people before about 1100

old·fan·gled \'ōl(d)-'faŋ-gəld\ *adj* : OLD-FASHIONED

old–fash·ioned \'ōl(d)-'fash-ənd\ *adj* **1** : of, relating to, or like that of an earlier time ⟨*old-fashioned* clothes⟩ **2** : holding fast to old ways : CONSERVATIVE

Old French *n* : the French language from the 9th to the 16th century

Old Glory *n* : the flag of the U.S.

old hand *n* : VETERAN 1

old·ish \'ōl-dish\ *adj* : somewhat old or elderly

old maid *n* **1** : an elderly unmarried woman **2** : a very neat fussy person **3** : a card game in which cards are matched in pairs and the player holding the extra queen at the end loses — **old–maid·ish** \'ōl(d)-'mād-ish\ *adj*

old man *n* **1** : one's husband or father **2** *cap O & M* : a person (as one's boss or commanding officer) who is in charge

Old Norse *n* : the Germanic language of the Scandinavian peoples before about 1350

old·ster \'ōl(d)-stər\ *n* : an old or elderly person

Old Style *n* : the way the calendar was calculated before the adoption of the Gregorian calendar

Old Testament *n* : the first of the two chief divisions of the Bible — see BIBLE table

old–time \,ōl(d)-,tīm\ *adj* : of, relating to, or typical of an earlier period

old–tim·er \ōl(d)-'tī-mər\ *n* **1 a** : VETERAN 1 **b** : OLDSTER **2** : something old-fashioned

old wives' tale *n* : a belief that is not based on fact : SUPER-STITION

old–world \'ōl-'(d)wər(-ə)ld\ *adj* **1** : of or relating to the Old World **2** : having old-fashioned charm

ole·an·der \'ō-lē-,an-dər\ *n* : a poisonous evergreen shrub with showy fragrant white, red, or pink flowers

ole·fin \'ō-lə-fən\ *n* : a chemical compound made up of carbon and hydrogen atoms that contains at least one double bond; *esp* : any of various long-chain synthetic polymers (as of ethylene) used especially as textile fibers

oleo \'ō-lē-,ō\ *n*, *pl* **ole·os** : MARGARINE

oleo·mar·ga·rine \,ō-lē-ō-'märj-(ə-)rən, -'märj-ə-,rēn\ *n* : MARGARINE

O level *n* : the earlier of two British examinations in a secondary school subject

ol·fac·to·ry \äl-'fak-t(ə-)rē, ōl-\ *adj* : of, relating to, or concerned with the sense of smell

olfactory lobe *n* : a lobe of the brain that lies on the underside of each cerebral hemisphere pointing forward and that is continuous in front with the olfactory nerve

olfactory nerve *n* : either of a pair of sensory nerves that are the first cranial nerves, arise in the nose, and carry odor stimuli to the brain

oli·gar·chy \'äl-ə-,gär-kē, 'ō-lə-\ *n*, *pl* **-chies** **1** : government by the few **2** : a government in which a small group exercises control; *also* : a group exercising such control

Oli·go·cene \'äl-i-gō-,sēn, 'ō-li-; ə-'lig-ə-\ *adj* : of, relating to, or being an epoch of the Tertiary period of geological history or the corresponding system of rocks — see GEO-LOGIC TIME table — **Oligocene** *n*

ol·ive \'äl-iv, -əv\ *n* **1** : an Old World evergreen tree grown for its fruit **2** : the edible fruit of the olive tree that is the source of an oil **3** : a yellowish green — **olive** *adj*

olive branch *n* **1** : a branch of the olive tree especially when used as a symbol of peace **2** : something meant to show intentions of peace or goodwill

ol·iv·ine \'äl-ə-,vēn\ *n* : a usually greenish mineral that is a silicate of magnesium and iron

olym·pi·ad \ə-'lim-pē-,ad, ō-\ *n*, *often cap* : one of the four-year periods between Olympic Games

¹Olym·pi·an \ə-'lim-pē-ən, ō-\ *adj* **1** : of or relating to the ancient Greek region of Olympia **2** : OLYMPIC

²Olympian *n* : an athlete who competes in the Olympic Games

³Olympian *adj* **1** : of or relating to Olympus **2** : relating to or proper for one of the Greek gods of Olympus : LOFTY

⁴Olympian *n* : one of the Greek gods living on Olympus

Olym·pic \ə-'lim-pik, ō-\ *adj* : of or relating to the Olympic Games ⟨the U.S. *Olympic* team⟩

olive 1 and 2

Olympic Games *n pl* : a series of international athletic contests held in a different country once every four years

Olym·pics \ə-'lim-piks, ō-\ *n pl* : OLYMPIC GAMES

om·buds·man \'äm-,bùdz-mən, 'ōm-, -bədz-, -,man; äm-'bùdz-, ōm-\ *n*, *pl* **om·buds·men** \-,mən\ : a government official who investigates complaints made by people about unfair acts of public officials

ome·ga \ō-'meg-ə, -'mē-gə, -'mä-gə\ *n* : the 24th and last letter of the Greek alphabet — Ω or ω [from Greek *ō mega*, literally "big o"]

om·elet *also* **om·elette** \'äm-(ə-)lət\ *n* : beaten eggs cooked without stirring and served folded in half

> **Word History** Because of various spelling changes, the word *omelet* does not look much like its Latin source *lamina*. From *lamina*, meaning "a thin plate", the Romans formed *lamella*, meaning "a small thin metal plate". This word was borrowed into early French as *la lemelle*, literally meaning "the blade of a sword or knife". During its history in French, the word changed in spelling to *l'alemelle* and *alumelle* and then to *alumette*. *Alumette* took on the added meaning of "beaten eggs fried until set without stirring", probably because of the thin flat shape. *Alumette* became *amelette* and finally *omelette* in modern French. In the 17th century the word was taken into English both as *omelette* and in the shorter form *omelet*. [from French *omelette* "omelet", derived from early French *amelette*, *alumette*, altered forms of *alumelle* "omelet", literally "knife blade, sword blade", derived from *la lemelle* (same meaning), derived from Latin *lamella* "a small thin metal plate", from *lamina* "a thin plate"]

omen \'ō-mən\ *n* : a happening believed to be a sign or warning of some future event

omi·cron \'äm-ə-,krän, 'ōm-\ *n* : the 15th letter of the Greek alphabet — O or o [from Greek *o mikron*, literally "small o"]

om·i·nous \'äm-ə-nəs\ *adj* : being or showing a sign of evil or misfortune to come ⟨*ominous* clouds⟩ — **om·i·nous·ly** *adv*

omis·sion \ō-'mish-ən, ə-\ *n* **1** : something omitted **2** : the act of omitting : the state of being omitted

omit \ō-'mit, ə-\ *vb* **omit·ted; omit·ting** **1** : to leave out ⟨*omitted* your name from the list⟩ **2** : to fail to do : leave undone : NEGLECT ⟨*omitted* to mention that it was my fault⟩

¹om·ni·bus \'äm-ni-(,)bəs\ *n* : BUS

²omnibus *adj* : of, relating to, or providing for many things at once ⟨an *omnibus* legislative bill⟩

om·nip·o·tence \äm-'nip-ət-ən(t)s\ *n* : the quality or state of being omnipotent

om·nip·o·tent \äm-'nip-ət-ənt\ *adj* : having power or authority without limit : ALMIGHTY — **om·nip·o·tent·ly** *adv*

om·ni·pres·ent \,äm-ni-'prez-°nt\ *adj* : present in all places at all times

om·ni·science \äm-'nish-ən(t)s\ *n* : the quality or state of being omniscient

om·ni·scient \äm-'nish-ənt\ *adj* : knowing everything [from modern Latin *omniscient-, omnisciens* "knowing all things, all-knowing", derived from *omni-* (from *omnis* "all") and *scient-, sciens* "knowing", from *scire* "to know" — related to SCIENCE] — **om·ni·scient·ly** *adv*

om·ni·vore \'äm-ni-,vō(ə)r, -,vò(ə)r\ *n* : one that is omnivorous

om·niv·o·rous \äm-'niv-(ə-)rəs\ *adj* : feeding on both animal and vegetable substances

¹on \(')ón, (')än\ *prep* **1 a** : in contact with and supported

\ə\ abut	\aù\ out	\i\ tip	\ò\ saw	\ù\ foot
\ər\ further	\ch\ chin	\ī\ life	\òi\ coin	\y\ yet
\a\ mat	\e\ pet	\j\ job	\th\ thin	\yü\ few
\ā\ take	\ē\ easy	\ŋ\ sing	\th\ this	\yù\ cure
\ä\ cot, cart	\g\ go	\ō\ bone	\ü\ food	\zh\ vision

by 〈the book *on* the table〉 **b** : in a position in contact with or near 〈a fly *on* the wall〉 〈a town *on* the river〉 **c** : in the direction of 〈*on* the right〉 **2 a** — used to indicate means of being attached or supported 〈*on* a string〉 〈stood *on* one foot〉 〈hang your coat *on* the peg〉 〈you can rely *on* me〉 〈lives *on* insects〉 **b** — used to indicate means of being carried 〈rode *on* a horse〉 〈went *on* the bus〉 〈have only five dollars *on* me〉 **3** — used to indicate a time 〈arrived *on* Monday〉 〈news *on* the hour〉 **4 a** — used to indicate the way something is done 〈told her *on* the sly〉 **b** — used to indicate what something is done with or done by 〈cut *on* broken glass〉 〈talk *on* the phone〉 〈type *on* a keyboard〉 〈displayed *on* a TV screen〉 **5 a** : in connection, association, or activity with or with regard to 〈*on* a committee〉 〈*on* tour〉 **b** : in a state or process of 〈*on* fire〉 〈*on* the increase〉 **6 a** — used to indicate a reason or basis 〈*on* one condition〉 〈interest of 10 cents *on* the dollar〉 **b** — used to indicate who or what is responsible 〈this treat is *on* me〉 〈blamed it *on* the weather〉 **7** — used to indicate someone or something an action or feeling is directed toward 〈was creeping up *on* us〉 〈have pity *on* me〉 〈the joke's *on* you〉 **8** : CONCERNING, ABOUT 〈a book *on* cats〉 〈agree *on* price〉 **9** : following in series 〈loss *on* loss〉

²on \'ȯn, 'än\ *adv* **1** : in or into contact with a surface 〈put the kettle *on*〉 〈has new shoes *on*〉 **2** : forward in space, time, or action 〈went *on* home〉 〈*on* came the storm〉 〈getting *on* in years〉 **3** : from one to another 〈pass the word *on*〉 〈and so *on*〉 **4** : into operation or a position allowing operation 〈turn the light *on*〉

³on \'ȯn, 'än\ *adj* **1** : doing an activity (as a role in a play) 〈you're *on* next〉 **2 a** : being in operation 〈the radio is *on*〉 **b** : set so as to permit operation 〈the switch is *on*〉 **c** : taking place 〈the game is *on*〉 **3** : having been planned 〈has nothing *on* for tonight〉

¹once \'wən(t)s\ *adv* **1** : one time only 〈will repeat the question *once*〉 **2** : at any one time : EVER 〈*once* you hesitate, it's too late〉 **3** : at some time in the past : FORMERLY 〈it was *once* done that way〉 **4** : by one degree of relationship 〈cousin *once* removed〉

²once *n* : one single time 〈just this *once*〉 — **at once 1** : at the same time : SIMULTANEOUSLY 〈two people talking at *once*〉 **2** : IMMEDIATELY 2 〈leave at *once*〉

³once *conj* : AS SOON AS 〈*once* that is done, all will be well〉

once–over \'wən(t)-,sō-vər\ *n* : a quick glance or examination

on·cho·cer·ci·a·sis \,äŋ-kō-sər-'kī-ə-səs\ *n, pl* **-a·ses** \-,sēz\ : RIVER BLINDNESS

on·co·gene \'äŋ-kō-,jēn\ *n* : a gene having the potential to cause a normal cell to become cancerous

on·com·ing \'ȯn-,kəm-iŋ, 'än-\ *adj* : coming nearer 〈*oncoming* traffic〉

¹one \'wən, ,wən\ *adj* **1** : being a single unit or thing — see NUMBER table **2** : being a certain unit or thing 〈early *one* morning〉 **3 a** : being the same in kind or quality 〈members of *one* class〉 **b** : not divided **4** : not definitely fixed or placed 〈will see you again *one* day〉

²one *pron* **1** : a single member or individual 〈saw *one* of your friends〉 **2** : any person 〈*one* never knows〉

³one *n* **1** : the number indicating a single unit **2** : the first in a set or series **3** : a single person or thing

one another *pron* : EACH OTHER

one–dimensional *adj* : STEREOTYPED

one–horse *adj* : small and unimportant 〈a *one-horse* town〉

one·ness \'wən-nəs\ *n* : the quality, state, or fact of being one 〈our *oneness* with the rest of humanity〉

oner·ous \'än-ə-rəs, 'ō-nə-\ *adj* : being difficult and unpleasant to do or to deal with 〈an *onerous* task〉

ones digit *n* : UNITS DIGIT

one·self \(,)wən-'self\ *pron* **1** : one's own self 〈one can feel proud of *oneself*〉 **2** : one's normal or healthy self

one–sid·ed \'wən-'sīd-əd\ *adj* **1 a** : having or happening on one side only **b** : having one side more developed **2**

: favoring one side : PARTIAL 〈a *one-sided* view of the case〉 — **one–sid·ed·ly** *adv* — **one–sid·ed·ness** *n*

ones place *n* : UNITS PLACE

one·time \'wən-,tīm\ *adj* : FORMER 1 〈a *onetime* boxing champion〉

one–to–one \,wən-tə-'wən\ *adj* : pairing each element of a set with one and only one element of another set 〈a *one-to-one* correspondence between the real numbers and the points on a straight line〉

one–way *adj* : moving or allowing movement in one direction only

on·go·ing \'ȯn-,gō-iŋ, 'än-\ *adj* : being in progress or movement

on·ion \'ən-yən\ *n* : a widely grown Asian herb related to the lilies and having edible bulbs that have a sharp odor and taste and are used as a vegetable and to season foods; *also* : its bulb

on·ion·skin \-,skin\ *n* : a thin strong nearly transparent paper of very light weight

on–line \'ȯn-'līn, 'än-\ *adj* : being controlled directly by or connected to a computer 〈an *on-line* terminal for graphics display〉

on·look·er \'ȯn-,lúk-ər, 'än-\ *n* : SPECTATOR

¹on·ly \'ōn-lē\ *adj* **1** : the best without doubt 〈it's the *only* thing for me〉 **2** : alone in or of a class or kind : SOLE 〈the *only* survivor of the crash〉

²only *adv* **1 a** : as a single fact or instance and nothing more or different 〈worked *only* in the mornings〉 **b** : no one or nothing other than 〈*only* you know〉 **2** : at the very least 〈it was *only* too true〉 **3 a** : in the end 〈it will *only* make you sick〉 **b** : with the result, even so 〈found my pen, *only* to lose it again a week later〉 **4 a** : as recently as 〈*only* last week〉 **b** : in the immediate past 〈*only* just talked to her〉

³only *conj* : except that 〈I'd play, *only* I'm too tired〉

on·o·mas·tics \,än-ə-'mas-tiks\ *n sing or pl* : the study of the proper names of people and places

on·o·mato·poe·ia \,än-ə-,mat-ə-'pē-(y)ə\ *n* **1** : formation of words in imitation of natural sounds **2** : the use of words whose sound suggests the sense — **on·o·mato·poe·ic** \-'pē-ik\ *or* **on·o·mato·po·et·ic** \-pō-'et-ik\ *adj*

on·rush \'ȯn-,rəsh, 'än-\ *n* : a rushing forward or onward — **on·rush·ing** \-iŋ\ *adj*

on·set \'ȯn-,set, 'än-\ *n* **1** : ²ATTACK 1 **2** : BEGINNING 1

on·shore \'ȯn-,shō(ə)r, 'än-, -,shò(ə)r\ *adj* : moving toward the shore 〈*onshore* winds〉 — **on·shore** \'ȯn-'shō(ə)r, 'än-, -'shò(ə)r\ *adv*

on·slaught \'än-,slȯt, 'ȯn-\ *n* : a violent attack

on–the–job *adj* : received or learned while working at a job 〈*on-the-job* training〉

on·to \,ȯn-tə, 'än-; 'ȯn-tü, 'än-\ *prep* **1** : to a position on or against 〈leaped *onto* the horse〉 〈climbed *onto* the roof〉 **2** : in a state of knowing about or becoming aware of 〈I'm *onto* their little game〉

¹on·ward \'ȯn-wərd, 'än-\ *also* **on·wards** \-wərdz\ *adv* : toward or at a point lying ahead in space or time : FORWARD 〈kept moving *onward*〉

²onward *adj* : directed or moving onward 〈the *onward* march of time〉

on·yx \'än-iks\ *n* : chalcedony with straight parallel alternating bands of color or dyed jet black

oo·dles \'üd-ᵊlz\ *n pl* : a great quantity

oo·gen·e·sis \,ō-ə-'jen-ə-səs\ *n* : the process of female gamete formation including meiosis and formation of eggs

oo·lite \'ō-ə-,līt\ *n* : a rock consisting of small round grains

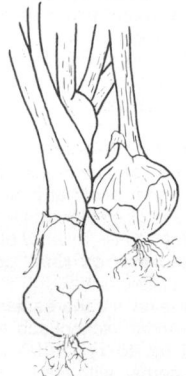

onion

usually of calcium carbonate firmly joined together

oo·long \'ü-,lȯn\ *n* : tea that has undergone partial fermentation before being dried

oops \'(w)ů(ə)ps\ *interj* — used to express mild apology, surprise, or distress (as at spilling something or saying the wrong thing)

oo·tid \'ō-ə-,tid\ *n* : an egg cell after meiosis but before it is a fully mature egg

¹ooze \'üz\ *n* : soft mud or slime (as on the bottom of a lake)

²ooze *n* : something that oozes

³ooze *vb* **oozed; ooz·ing** **1** : to flow or leak slowly ⟨sap *oozed* from the tree⟩ **2** : EMIT 1a ⟨a manner that *oozed* confidence⟩

oozy \'ü-zē\ *adj* **ooz·i·er; -est** : consisting of or resembling ooze

opac·i·ty \ō-'pas-ət-ē\ *n, pl* **-ties** : the quality or state of being opaque

opal \'ō-pəl\ *n* : a mineral with soft changeable colors that is used as a gem

opaque \ō-'pāk\ *adj* **1** : not letting light through : not transparent **2** : hard to understand **3** : not reflecting light — **opaque·ly** *adv* — **opaque·ness** *n*

ope \'ōp\ *vb* **oped; op·ing** *archaic* : ²OPEN

¹open \'ō-pən, 'ōp-°m\ *adj* **1** : allowing passage : not shut or blocked ⟨an *open* door⟩ ⟨*open* books⟩ ⟨*open* pores⟩ **2 a** : not enclosed or covered ⟨an *open* boat⟩ ⟨an *open* fire⟩ ⟨*open* wounds⟩ **b** : LIABLE 2 ⟨*open* to challenge⟩ **c** : not completely enclosed by lines ⟨an *open* geometric figure⟩ **3** : not secret : PUBLIC ⟨*open* dislike⟩ **4 a** : free to be used, entered, or taken part in by all ⟨an *open* meeting⟩ ⟨an *open* golf tournament⟩ **b** : easy to enter, get through, or see ⟨*open* country⟩ **5** : not drawn together : spread out ⟨an *open* flower⟩ ⟨an *open* umbrella⟩ **6 a** : not decided or settled ⟨an *open* question⟩ **b** : waiting to be filled ⟨the job is still *open*⟩ **c** : available for purchase all or most of the time ⟨these items are in *open* stock⟩ **7** : ready to consider appeals or ideas ⟨an *open* mind⟩ ⟨*open* to suggestion⟩ **8** : not allowing the flow of electricity : being an incomplete electrical circuit ⟨an *open* switch⟩ — **open·ly** \'ō-pən-lē\ *adv* — **open·ness** \'ō-pən-nəs\ *n*

²open \'ō-pən, 'ōp-°m\ *vb* **opened** \'ō-pənd, 'ōp-°md\; **open·ing** \'ōp-(ə-)niṅ\ **1 a** : to change or move from a shut condition ⟨*open* a book⟩ ⟨the door *opened*⟩ **b** : to clear by or as if by removing something in the way ⟨*open* a road blocked with snow⟩ ⟨the clouds *opened*⟩ **c** : to make an opening in ⟨*open* a boil⟩ **2 a** : to make or become ready for use ⟨*open* a new store⟩ **b** : to make available for a certain purpose ⟨*open* land for settlement⟩ ⟨*opened* Japan to foreign trade⟩ ⟨the office *opens* at eight⟩ **3** : to have an opening ⟨the rooms *open* onto a hall⟩ **4** : BEGIN 1, START ⟨*opened* fire⟩ ⟨*open* talks⟩

³open *n* **1** : open space; *esp* : ²OUTDOORS ⟨go out in the *open*⟩ **2** : a contest or tournament that is open **3** : a state or position that is public or is not concealed

open air *n* : ²OUTDOORS 1 — **open–air** *adj*

open–and–shut \,ōp-(ə-)nən-'shət\ *adj* : perfectly plain : easily decided : OBVIOUS ⟨an *open-and-shut* case⟩

open dating *n* : the placing of dates on goods (as dairy products) so that the consumer can tell how old they are

open door *n* : a policy of giving equal opportunity for trade to all nations — **open–door** *adj*

open·er \'ōp-(ə-)nər\ *n* : something used for opening ⟨a bottle *opener*⟩ ⟨a conversation *opener*⟩ — **for openers** : to begin with

open–eyed \,ō-pə-'nīd\ *adj* **1** : having the eyes open **2** : watching carefully : ALERT

open·hand·ed \,ō-pən-'han-dəd\ *adj* : GENEROUS 1, LIBERAL — **open·hand·ed·ly** *adv* — **open·hand·ed·ness** *n*

open–heart *adj* : of, relating to, or done on a heart temporarily laid open for inspection and treatment ⟨*open-heart* surgery⟩

open·heart·ed \,ō-pən-'härt-əd\ *adj* **1** : FRANK **2** : GENEROUS 1 — **open·heart·ed·ly** *adv* — **open·heart·ed·ness** *n*

open–hearth *adj* : being or relating to a process of making steel from pig iron in a furnace that reflects heat from the roof onto the material

open house *n* : usually informal hospitality or entertainment for all comers

open·ing \'ōp-(ə-)niṅ\ *n* **1** : an act or instance of making or becoming open ⟨the *opening* of a new store⟩ ⟨welcome to our grand *opening*⟩ **2** : an open place ⟨an *opening* in the woods⟩ **3** : BEGINNING 2 **4 a** : ¹OCCASION 1 **b** : a job opportunity ⟨*openings* for welders and machinists⟩

open letter *n* : a letter (as one addressed to an official) for the public to see and printed in a newspaper or magazine

open–mind·ed \,ō-pən-'mīn-dəd\ *adj* : open to arguments or ideas : not prejudiced — **open–mind·ed·ly** *adv* — **open–mind·ed·ness** *n*

open·mouthed \,ō-pən-'maůthd, -'maůtht\ *adj* **1** : having the mouth wide open **2** : struck with amazement or wonder

open–pit *adj* : having the surface exposed to the air or worked from the exposed surface ⟨an *open-pit* mine⟩

open secret *n* : something supposed to be a secret but in fact generally known

open sentence *n* : a statement (as in mathematics) that contains at least one blank or unknown and that becomes true or false when the blank is filled or a quantity is substituted for the unknown ("$n + 5 = 3$" and "It is divisible by 6" are *open sentences*⟩

open sesame *n* : something that always works to bring about a desired result ⟨believed education was the *open sesame* to the good life⟩ [from *open sesame,* the magical command used by Ali Baba to open the door of the robbers' den in the story *Ali Baba and the Forty Thieves*]

open up *vb* : to begin firing (as with a weapon or with questions)

open·work \'ō-pən-,wərk\ *n* : something made or work done so as to show openings through the fabric or material — **open–worked** \-,wərkt\ *adj*

¹opera *pl of* OPUS

²op·era \'äp-(ə-)rə\ *n* : a play in which usually the entire text is sung with orchestral accompaniment — **op·er·at·ic** \,äp-ə-'rat-ik\ *adj*

op·er·a·ble \'äp-(ə-)rə-bəl\ *adj* **1** : fit, possible, or desirable to use **2** : likely to have a favorable result upon surgical treatment ⟨an *operable* cancer⟩

opera glasses *n pl* : small binoculars or field glasses of low power for use in a theater

¹op·er·ant \'äp-ə-rənt\ *adj* : of, relating to, or being an operant or operant conditioning

²operant *n* : behavior (as bar pressing by a rat to obtain food) that operates on the environment to produce effects that are needed, pleasant, or desired

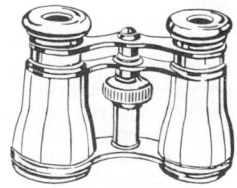

opera glasses

operant conditioning *n* : conditioning in which the desired behavior or increasingly closer approximations to it are followed by a stimulus that is needed, pleasant, or desired

op·er·ate \'äp-(ə-),rāt\ *vb* **-at·ed; -at·ing** **1** : to work or cause to work in a proper way ⟨how to *operate* the new microwave oven⟩ **2** : to take effect ⟨a drug that *operates*

\ə\ abut	\aů\ out	\i\ tip	\ȯ\ saw	\ů\ foot
\ər\ further	\ch\ chin	\ī\ life	\ȯi\ coin	\y\ yet
\a\ mat	\e\ pet	\j\ job	\th\ thin	\yü\ few
\ā\ take	\ē\ easy	\ṅ\ sing	\th\ this	\yů\ cure
\ä\ cot, cart	\g\ go	\ō\ bone	\ü\ food	\zh\ vision

quickly⟩ **3** : MANAGE 1 ⟨*operate* a business⟩ **4 a** : to perform an operation or a series of operations **b** : to perform surgery ⟨*operate* on a tumor⟩ [from Latin *operatus*, past participle of *operari* "to work" — related to MANEUVER; see *Word History* at MANEUVER]

operating system *n* : a program or set of programs that controls the operation of a computer and directs the processing of the user's programs (as by assigning space for storage in memory and controlling input and output functions)

op·er·a·tion \ˌäp-ə-ˈrā-shən\ *n* **1** : the act, process, method, or result of operating ⟨does the whole *operation* without stopping⟩ ⟨the *operation* of a drug⟩ **2** : the quality or state of being able to work or function ⟨put a factory into *operation*⟩ **3** : a surgical procedure **4** : a mathematical or logical process (as addition or multiplication) for getting one mathematical expression from others according to a rule **5** : the process of putting military or naval forces into action ⟨naval *operations*⟩

op·er·a·tion·al \ˌäp-ə-ˈrā-shnəl, -shən-ᵊl\ *adj* **1** : of or relating to operation or an operation **2** : ready for operation

¹op·er·a·tive \ˈäp-(ə-)rət-iv, ˈäp-ə-ˌrāt-\ *adj* **1** : producing a normal or desired effect **2** : being in operation

²operative *n* **1** : OPERATOR 1 **2 a** : a secret agent : SPY **b** : ²DETECTIVE

op·er·a·tor \ˈäp-(ə-)ˌrāt-ər\ *n* **1** : a person who operates something ⟨a computer *operator*⟩ ⟨the *operator* of an automobile⟩ **2** : a person in charge of a telephone switchboard

op·er·et·ta \ˌäp-ə-ˈret-ə\ *n* : a light play set to music with speaking, singing, and dancing scenes

oph·thal·mol·o·gist \ˌäf-thə(l)-ˈmäl-ə-jəst, ˌäp-, -, thal-\ *n* : a physician specializing in ophthalmology — compare OPTICIAN 2, OPTOMETRIST

oph·thal·mol·o·gy \ˌäf-thə(l)-ˈmäl-ə-jē, ˌäp-, -, thal-\ *n* : a branch of medical science dealing with the structure, functions, and diseases of the eye

oph·thal·mo·scope \äf-ˈthal-mə-ˌskōp, äp-\ *n* : an optical instrument for viewing the inside of the eye

¹opi·ate \ˈō-pē-ət, -ˌāt\ *adj* **1** : of, relating to, or being opium or an opiate **2 a** : causing sleep **b** : causing dullness or idleness

²opiate *n* **1** : a preparation of opium or a substance (as morphine or heroin) made or obtained from it; *also* : ¹NARCOTIC 1 **2** : something restful or soothing ⟨the *opiate* of sleep⟩

opine \ō-ˈpīn\ *vb* **opined; opin·ing** : to have or express an opinion

opin·ion \ə-ˈpin-yən\ *n* **1** : a belief based on experience and on seeing certain facts but falling short of positive knowledge **2** : a judgment about a person or thing ⟨a high *opinion* of themselves⟩ **3** : a statement by an expert after careful study ⟨you better get an *opinion* from a lawyer⟩

syn OPINION, BELIEF, CONVICTION mean something that one thinks is true. OPINION suggests a judgment that may not be shared by all ⟨heard more than one *opinion* on that issue⟩ BELIEF suggests a view that one has come to accept fully in one's own mind ⟨a basic *belief* in a supreme being⟩ CONVICTION suggests a firm unchangeable belief ⟨a *conviction* that all life is valuable⟩

opin·ion·at·ed \ə-ˈpin-yə-ˌnāt-əd\ *adj* : holding to one's own opinions and ideas too strongly

opi·um \ˈō-pē-əm\ *n* **1** : a bitter brownish narcotic drug that causes addiction and is the dried juice of the opium poppy **2** : something having an effect like that of opium

opium poppy *n* : an annual Eurasian poppy grown for opium, for its edible oily seeds, and for its showy flowers

opos·sum \(ə-)ˈpäs-əm\ *n, pl* **-sums** *also* **-sum** : a common marsupial mammal of the eastern U.S. that usually is active at night and dwells in trees [from *âpüsûm*, an American Indian word meaning literally "white animal"]

op·po·nent \ə-ˈpō-nənt\ *n* : a person or thing that opposes another

op·por·tune \ˌäp-ər-ˈt(y)ün\ *adj* : SUITABLE 1, TIMELY ⟨an *opportune* moment to act⟩ — **op·por·tune·ly** *adv*

opossum

Word History The Latin adjective *opportunus* was used to mean "fit, suitable, or convenient". It was formed from the prefix *op-, ob-,* meaning "at or toward" and *portus,* meaning "port or harbor". The Romans considered something "at the port" to be suitable and ready for use. The French took the word as *opportun* with the same basic meaning, and the word came into English as *opportune* in the 15th century. Nowadays it is often applied to a suitable or favorable time for something or to something that occurs or is done at just the right time. [Middle English *opportune* "opportune, suitable, fit", from early French *opportun* (same meaning), from Latin *opportunus* "fit, suitable, convenient", from *op-, ob-* "toward, at" and *portus* "port, harbor"]

op·por·tun·ism \ˌäp-ər-ˈt(y)ü-ˌniz-əm\ *n* : the practice of taking advantage of opportunities or circumstances regardless of what one should do or what might happen — **op·por·tun·ist** \-ˈt(y)ü-nəst\ *n or adj* — **op·por·tu·nis·tic** \-ˌt(y)ü-ˈnis-tik\ *adj*

op·por·tu·ni·ty \ˌäp-ər-ˈt(y)ü-nət-ē\ *n, pl* **-ties** **1** : a favorable combination of circumstances, time, and place **2** : a chance to better oneself

op·pos·able \ə-ˈpō-zə-bəl\ *adj* : capable of being placed against one or more of the remaining digits of a hand or foot ⟨the *opposable* human thumb⟩

op·pose \ə-ˈpōz\ *vb* **op·posed; op·pos·ing** **1** : to be or place opposite or against something **2** : to offer resistance to : stand against : RESIST

¹op·po·site \ˈäp-ə-zət, ˈäp-sət\ *adj* **1 a** : being at the other end, side, or corner ⟨lived on *opposite* sides of the street⟩ ⟨the *opposite* sides of a rectangle⟩ **b** : being one of two angles of a four-sided figure (as a square or parallelogram) that are not next to each other **2 a** : being in a position to oppose or cancel out ⟨*opposite* sides of the question⟩ **b** : as different as possible : CONTRARY ⟨reached *opposite* conclusions⟩ ⟨went off in *opposite* directions⟩ **3** : being the other of a matching or contrasting pair ⟨the *opposite* sex⟩ — **op·po·site·ly** *adv* — **op·po·site·ness** *n*

²opposite *n* **1** : someone or something that is opposite **2** : ANTONYM **3** : ADDITIVE INVERSE; *esp* : the additive inverse of a real number ⟨+3 and −3 are *opposites*⟩

³opposite *adv* : on the opposite side

⁴opposite *prep* : across from and usually facing or on the same level with ⟨the house *opposite* ours⟩

opposite angle *n* : VERTICAL ANGLE

op·po·si·tion \ˌäp-ə-ˈzish-ən\ *n* **1** : the state of being opposite **2** : the action of resisting ⟨offer *opposition* to a plan⟩ ⟨the *opposition* of two forces⟩ **3 a** : a group of persons (as a team or an enemy force) that oppose someone or something **b** *often cap* : a political party opposing the party in power

op·press \ə-ˈpres\ *vb* **1** : to cause to feel burdened in spirit ⟨*oppressed* by grief⟩ **2** : to control or rule in a harsh or cruel way ⟨a country *oppressed* by a dictator⟩ — **op·pres·sor** \-ˈpres-ər\ *n*

op·pres·sion \ə-ˈpresh-ən\ *n* **1** : cruel or unjust use of authority or power **2** : a feeling of low spirits

op·pres·sive \ə-ˈpres-iv\ *adj* **1** : cruel or harsh without just cause ⟨*oppressive* taxes⟩ **2** : causing a feeling of oppression ⟨*oppressive* heat⟩ — **op·pres·sive·ly** *adv* — **op·pres·sive·ness** *n*

op·pro·bri·ous \ə-'prō-brē-əs\ *adj* : expressing very strong disapproval ⟨the *opprobrious* term "murderer"⟩

op·pro·bri·um \ə-'prō-brē-əm\ *n* : very strong disapproval

opt \'äpt\ *vb* : to make a choice

op·tic \'äp-tik\ *adj* : of or relating to vision or the eye [Middle English *optic* "relating to the eye", from early French *optique* (same meaning), from Latin *opticus* (same meaning), from Greek *optikos* (same meaning), from *opsesthai* "to be going to see" — related to AUTOPSY]

op·ti·cal \'äp-ti-kəl\ *adj* **1** : relating to optics **2** : OPTIC **3 a** : of, relating to, or using light ⟨an *optical* telescope⟩ **b** : involving the use of devices that sense light to acquire information for a computer ⟨an *optical* scanner⟩ — **op·ti·cal·ly** \-k(ə-)lē\ *adv*

optical illusion *n* : ILLUSION 1

op·ti·cian \äp-'tish-ən\ *n* **1** : a maker of or dealer in optical items and instruments **2** : a person who grinds eyeglass lenses to prescription and sells glasses — compare OPHTHALMOLOGIST, OPTOMETRIST

optic lobe *n* : either of a pair of lobes in the midbrain that are concerned with vision

optic nerve *n* : either of a pair of sensory nerves that are the second pair of cranial nerves and carry visual information from the retina of the eye to the brain

op·tics \'äp-tiks\ *n* : a science that deals with the nature and properties of light and the effects that it undergoes and produces

op·ti·mal \'äp-tə-məl\ *adj* : ²OPTIMUM — **op·ti·mal·ly** \-mə-lē\ *adv*

op·ti·mism \'äp-tə-,miz-əm\ *n* : a habit of expecting everything to turn out for the best

op·ti·mist \'äp-tə-məst\ *n* : an optimistic person

op·ti·mis·tic \,äp-tə-'mis-tik\ *adj* : showing optimism : expecting everything to come out all right : HOPEFUL — **op·ti·mis·ti·cal·ly** \-ti-k(ə-)lē\ *adv*

¹op·ti·mum \'äp-tə-məm\ *n, pl* **-ma** \-mə\ *also* **-mums** : the best or most favorable amount or degree

²optimum *adj* : most desirable or satisfactory ⟨under *optimum* conditions⟩

op·tion \'äp-shən\ *n* **1** : the power or right to choose **2** : a right to buy or sell something at a specified price during a specified period ⟨took an *option* on the house⟩ **3** : something offered for choice ⟨a tape deck was one of the *options* you could get on the car⟩

op·tion·al \'äp-shnəl, -shən-ᵊl\ *adj* : left to one's choice : not required ⟨*optional* equipment on a new car⟩ — **op·tion·al·ly** \-ē\ *adv*

op·tom·e·trist \äp-'täm-ə-trəst\ *n* : a specialist licensed in optometry — compare OPHTHALMOLOGIST, OPTICIAN 2

op·tom·e·try \äp-'täm-ə-trē\ *n* : the profession of examining the eyesight and prescribing glasses or exercise to improve it but not drugs or surgery — **op·to·met·ric** \,äp-tə-'me-trik\ *adj*

op·u·lence \'äp-yə-lən(t)s\ *n* : great wealth

op·u·lent \'äp-yə-lənt\ *adj* : having or showing much wealth — **op·u·lent·ly** *adv*

opus \'ō-pəs\ *n, pl* **opera** \'ō-pə-rə, 'äp-ə-\ *also* **opus·es** \'ō-pə-səz\ : ¹WORK 7; *esp* : a musical composition or set of compositions

or \ər, (,)ȯ(ə)r\ *conj* — used to indicate an alternative ⟨coffee *or* tea⟩ ⟨sink *or* swim⟩

¹-or \ər, ,ȯ(ə)r, 'ȯ(ə)r\ *n suffix* : one that does a specified thing ⟨elevat*or*⟩ [derived from Latin *-or* or *-ator*, both meaning "one that does something"]

²-or \ər\ *n suffix* : condition : activity ⟨demean*or*⟩ [derived from Latin *-or* "condition, activity"]

or·a·cle \'ȯr-ə-kəl, 'är-\ *n* **1** : a person (as a priestess of ancient Greece) through whom a god is believed to speak **2** : the place where a god speaks through an oracle **3** : an answer given by an oracle [Middle English *oracle* "a

person through whom a god speaks", from early French *oracle* (same meaning), from Latin *oraculum* (same meaning), from *orare* "to speak, pray" — related to ADORE, ORATION]

orac·u·lar \ȯ-'rak-yə-lər, ə-\ *adj* **1** : of, relating to, or being an oracle **2** : resembling an oracle — **orac·u·lar·ly** *adv*

oral \'ȯr-əl, 'ȯr-, 'är-\ *adj* **1** : uttered by the mouth : SPOKEN **2** : of, relating to, given by, or near the mouth ⟨*oral* hygiene⟩ — **oral·ly** \-ə-lē\ *adv*

syn ORAL, VERBAL mean expressed or communicated in words. ORAL applies only to the spoken word and not to what is written ⟨made an *oral* report before the class⟩ VERBAL applies to either speech or writing and may stress the use of words as opposed to other forms of expression or communication ⟨a test of your *verbal* and mathematical skills⟩

¹or·ange \'är-inj, 'ȯr-, -ənj\ *n* **1 a** : a round usually sweet juicy fruit with a reddish yellow rind **b** : any of various rather small evergreen citrus trees having shining leaves, fragrant white flowers, and fruits which are oranges **2** : a color between red and yellow

²orange *adj* **1** : of or relating to the orange **2** : of the color orange

or·ange·ade \,är-in-'jād, 'ȯr-, -ən-\ *n* : a drink made of orange juice, sugar, and water

orange hawkweed *n* : a European plant that is related to the daisies, has bright orange-red flower heads, and is a troublesome weed in northeastern North America

or·ange·wood \'är-inj-,wu̇d, 'ȯr-, -ənj-\ *n* : the wood of an orange tree

orang·utan \ə-'raŋ-ə-,taŋ, -,tan\ *n* : a large anthropoid ape of Borneo and Sumatra that is about two thirds as large as a gorilla, eats plants, lives in trees, and has very long arms, long thin reddish brown hair, and a hairless face, feet, and hands

orangutan

Word History The orangutan is a large, long-haired ape found on the islands of Borneo and Sumata, part of Indonesia in southeast Asia. Malay is the language of the original people of this area. The name of the animal in Malay is *orang hutan,* literally meaning "person of the forest". The Malay name is a good one for this ape that combines a somewhat human appearance with a habit of living in trees. The animal has been known in Europe since the 17th century. Its Malay name has been borrowed by most European languages in a form similar to the English *orangutan.* [from the native name in Malay (the language of the original people of the Malay peninsula) *orang hutan,* literally "person of the forest"]

orate \ȯ-'rāt\ *vb* **orat·ed; orat·ing** : to speak as if giving an oration

ora·tion \ə-'rā-shən, ȯ-\ *n* : an important speech given on some special occasion [from Latin *oration-, oratio* "speech", from *oratus,* past participle of *orare* "to speak, pray" — related to ADORE, ORACLE]

or·a·tor \'ȯr-ət-ər, 'är-\ *n* : a public speaker noted for skill and power in speaking

or·a·tor·i·cal \,ȯr-ə-'tȯr-i-kəl, ,är-ə-'tär-\ *adj* : of, relating

\ə\ **abut**		\au̇\ **out**	\i\ **tip**	\ȯ\ **saw**	\u̇\ **foot**
\ər\ **further**		\ch\ **chin**	\ī\ **life**	\ȯi\ **coin**	\y\ **yet**
\a\ **mat**		\e\ **pet**	\j\ **job**	\th\ **thin**	\yü\ **few**
\ā\ **take**		\ē\ **easy**	\ŋ\ **sing**	\th\ **this**	\yu̇\ **cure**
\ä\ **cot, cart**		\g\ **go**	\ō\ **bone**	\ü\ **food**	\zh\ **vision**

to, or characteristic of an orator or oratory — **or·a·tor·i·cal·ly** \-k(ə-)lē\ adv

or·a·to·rio \ˌȯr-ə-'tȯr-ē-ˌō, ˌär-, -'tȯr-\ n, pl **-ri·os** : a vocal and orchestral work usually dramatizing a biblical subject without action or scenery

¹or·a·to·ry \'ȯr-ə-ˌtȯr-ē, 'är-, -ˌtȯr-\ n, pl **-ries** : a place for prayer; esp : a private chapel

²oratory n **1** : the art of an orator **2** : oratorical language or speeches

orb \'ȯ(ə)rb\ n **1** : something (as a planet) in the shape of a ball **2** : ¹EYE 1

¹or·bit \'ȯr-bət\ n : one of the bone-lined cavities for the eyes in the vertebrate skull — called also eye socket [Middle English orbit "eye socket", from Latin orbita (same meaning), from earlier orbita "path, rut, track"]

²orbit n : the path taken by one body circling around another body ⟨the orbit of the earth around the sun⟩; also : one complete circle that makes up such a path [from Latin orbita "path, rut, track"] — **or·bit·al** \-ᵊl\ adj

³orbit vb **1** : to move in an orbit around : CIRCLE ⟨the moon orbits the earth⟩ **2** : to send up so as to move in an orbit ⟨orbit a satellite⟩ — **or·bit·er** n

or·chard \'ȯr-chərd\ n **1** : a place where fruit or nut trees are grown **2** : the trees in an orchard

or·ches·tra \'ȯr-kə-strə, -ˌkes-trə\ n **1** : a group of musicians who perform instrumental music using mostly stringed instruments **2** : the front part of the main floor of a theater

Word History In front of the ancient Greek stage was a semicircular space where a chorus danced, sang, and commented on the action of the play. The Greek word orchēstra referred to this space. It came from the verb orcheisthai, meaning "to dance". The word was borrowed into Latin, but the Roman orchestra was reserved for the seats of prominent persons, such as senators, instead of for a chorus. When English borrowed the word, it indicated the space occupied by a group of musicians, usually right in front of the stage. It also was used to refer to the group of musicians itself. Later, orchestra came to mean the forward part or all of the main floor of a theater. [from Latin orchestra "the place in front of the stage where prominent persons sit", from Greek orchēstra "a semicircular area in front of the stage of a theater where the chorus dances", from orcheisthai "to dance"]

or·ches·tral \ȯr-'kes-trəl\ adj : of, relating to, or written for an orchestra

or·ches·trate \'ȯr-kə-ˌstrāt\ vb **-trat·ed; -trat·ing** **1** : to write or arrange music for an orchestra **2** : to arrange or combine so as to get the best effect — **or·ches·tra·tion** \ˌȯr-kə-'strā-shən\ n

or·chid \'ȯr-kəd\ n **1** : any plant or flower of a large family of plants that have usually showy flowers with three petals of which the middle petal is enlarged and differs from the others in shape and color **2** : a light purple

or·chis \'ȯr-kəs\ n : ORCHID 1; esp : any of a genus of woodland plants having fleshy roots and a spur on the middle petal

or·dain \ȯr-'dān\ vb **1** : to make a person a Christian minister or priest by a special ceremony **2 a** : ²DECREE ⟨it was ordained by law⟩ **b** : DESTINE 1 ⟨we seem ordained to fail⟩

or·deal \ȯr-'dē(-ə)l\ n **1** : a method of deciding guilt or innocence by making the accused person take dangerous or painful tests ⟨ordeal by fire⟩ **2** : a severe test or experience

¹or·der \'ȯrd-ər\ vb **or·dered; or·der·ing** \'ȯrd-(ə-)riŋ\ **1** : to put in order : ARRANGE, REGULATE **2 a** : to give an order to or for ⟨ordered them to clean their rooms⟩ ⟨order groceries⟩ **b** : to command to go or come to a certain place ⟨order troops to the front⟩ — **or·der·er** \'ȯrd-ər-ər\ n

²order n **1 a** : a group of people united in some way (as by living under the same religious rules or by loyalty to common interests and duties) ⟨an order of monks⟩ ⟨an order of knighthood⟩ **b** : the badge or emblem of such an order **c** : a military medal or award **2** pl : the Christian ministry ⟨in orders⟩ **3 a** : a rank or class in society ⟨the lower orders⟩ **b** : ¹CLASS 3a, KIND **c** : a category of biological classification ranking above the family and below the class **4 a** : the way objects in space or events in time are arranged or follow one another ⟨the order of the seasons⟩ ⟨in alphabetical order⟩ **b** : the property or state of being mathematically ordered **c** : the established way or arrangement ⟨the old order⟩ ⟨the order of worship⟩ **d** : regular or harmonious arrangement or a condition having such an arrangement ⟨kept my room in order⟩ **5 a** : the state of things when law or authority is obeyed ⟨restored order after the riot⟩ **b** : a certain rule or direction : COMMAND **6 a** : a style of building **b** : a type of architectural column with its related parts **7** : good working condition ⟨out of order⟩ **8 a** : a direction to pay or not to pay money, to buy or sell, or to supply goods or services **b** : goods or items bought or sold ⟨an order of ham and eggs⟩ — **in order to** or **in order that** : for the purpose of — **on the order of** : similar to : LIKE ⟨cloth on the order of tweed⟩ — **to order** : according to the instructions of an order ⟨a suit made to order⟩

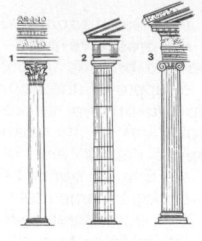

order 6b: 1 Corinthian, 2 Doric, 3 Ionic

or·dered \'ȯrd-ərd\ adj **1** : carefully regulated or managed **2** : having the property that for any two different elements a and b either a is greater than b or a is less than b ⟨the set of real numbers is ordered⟩

ordered pair n : a set with two elements in which one element is identified as the first and the other as the second

¹or·der·ly \'ȯrd-ər-lē\ adj **1 a** : being in order; esp : ¹TIDY 1, NEAT **b** : METHODICAL 2 ⟨an orderly thinker⟩ **2** : regulated by law or system ⟨an orderly universe⟩ **3** : well behaved ⟨an orderly crowd⟩ — **or·der·li·ness** n — **orderly** adv

²orderly n, pl **-lies** **1** : a soldier who carries messages and performs services for an officer **2** : a person who waits on others, cleans, and does general work in a hospital

or·di·nal \'ȯrd-nəl, -ᵊn-əl\ n : ORDINAL NUMBER

ordinal number n : a number indicating the place (as first, fifth, 22d) of an item in an ordered sequence — see NUMBER table

or·di·nance \'ȯrd-nən(t)s, -ᵊn-ən(t)s\ n : a law or regulation especially of a city or town

¹or·di·nary \'ȯrd-ᵊn-ˌer-ē\ n, pl **-nar·ies** **1** : regular or usual condition or course of things ⟨nothing out of the ordinary⟩ **2** chiefly British : a tavern or eating house serving regular meals

²ordinary adj **1** : to be expected : NORMAL, USUAL ⟨ordinary problems⟩ **2** : neither good nor bad : AVERAGE ⟨an ordinary person⟩ — **or·di·nari·ly** \ˌȯrd-ᵊn-'er-ə-lē\ adv — **or·di·nari·ness** \'ȯrd-ᵊn-ˌer-ē-nəs\ n

ordinary life insurance n : life insurance for which payments are made to the insurance company as long as the insured person lives

or·di·nate \'ȯrd-nət, -ᵊn-ət, -ᵊn-ˌāt\ n : the second number of an ordered pair of numbers locating a point in a plane coordinate system that is the distance of the point from the x-axis found by measuring along a line parallel to the y-axis — compare ABSCISSA

or·di·na·tion \ˌȯrd-ᵊn-'ā-shən\ n : the act of ordaining : the state of being ordained

ord·nance \'ȯrd-nən(t)s\ n **1** : military supplies; also : the branch of the army that obtains and gives out military supplies **2** : ARTILLERY 1

Or·do·vi·cian \ˌȯrd-ə-'vish-ən\ *adj* : of, relating to, or being a period of the Paleozoic era of geological history or the corresponding system of rocks — see GEOLOGIC TIME table — **Ordovician** *n*

ore \'ō(ə)r, 'ȯ(ə)r\ *n* : a mineral mined to obtain a substance that it contains ⟨iron *ore*⟩

ore·ad \'ōr-ē-ˌad, 'ȯr-, -ē-əd\ *n* : a nymph of mountains and hills

oreg·a·no \ə-'reg-ə-ˌnō\ *n, pl* **-nos** : a bushy mint used as a seasoning and a source of a fragrant oil

or·gan \'ȯr-gən\ *n* **1 a** : a keyboard musical instrument that has pipes played by compressed air **b** : an electronic musical instrument by which sounds like those of an organ are made **2** : a part of a person, plant, or animal that consists of cells and tissues and is specialized to do a particular task — compare SYSTEM 1c, TISSUE 3 **3** : a way of getting something done ⟨courts are *organs* of government⟩ **4** : a publication (as a newspaper or magazine) of a special group

or·gan·dy *also* **or·gan·die** \'ȯr-gən-dē\ *n, pl* **-dies** : a fine transparent cotton fabric with a stiff finish and a plain weave

or·gan·elle \ˌȯr-gə-'nel\ *n* : a structure in a single-celled living thing that has a special task as an organ does in a many-celled living thing

or·gan–grind·er \'ȯr-gən-ˌgrīn-dər\ *n* : a traveling street musician who plays a hand organ

or·gan·ic \ȯr-'gan-ik\ *adj* **1 a** : of, relating to, or arising in a bodily organ **b** : affecting the structure of the living thing ⟨an *organic* disease⟩ **2 a** : of, relating to, or obtained from living things ⟨*organic* matter⟩ **b** : of, relating to, or containing carbon compounds **c** : of, relating to, or dealt with by a branch of chemistry concerned with the carbon compounds of living things and most other carbon compounds **d** : relating to, producing, dealing in, or involving foods produced with the use of feed or fertilizer obtained from plants or animals and without the use of laboratory-made fertilizers, growth substances, antibiotics, or pesticides ⟨*organic* gardeners⟩ ⟨*organic* food stores⟩ **3 a** : forming an important part of a whole : FUNDAMENTAL **b** : having the parts related together ⟨an *organic* whole⟩ — **or·gan·i·cal·ly** \-i-k(ə-)lē\ *adv*

or·gan·ism \'ȯr-gə-ˌniz-əm\ *n* **1** : something having many related parts that function together as a whole **2** : an individual living thing that carries on the activities of life by means of organs which have separate functions but are dependent on each other : a living person, plant, or animal — **or·gan·is·mic** \ˌȯr-gə-'niz-mik\ *adj*

or·gan·ist \'ȯr-gə-nəst\ *n* : one who plays an organ

¹or·ga·ni·za·tion \ˌȯrg-(ə-)nə-'zā-shən\ *n* **1** : the act or process of organizing **2** : the condition or manner of being organized ⟨a high degree of *organization*⟩ **3** : a group of persons organized for some purpose ⟨a business *organization*⟩ — **or·ga·ni·za·tion·al** \-shnəl, -shən-ᵊl\ *adj*

²organization *adj* : behaving and thinking in a way that an organization would approve of

or·ga·nize \'ȯr-gə-ˌnīz\ *vb* **-nized; -niz·ing** **1** : to make separate parts into one united whole : form or form into an organization **2** : to put into order : SYSTEMATIZE ⟨*organize* your work⟩ — **or·ga·niz·er** *n*

or·ga·nized *adj* : having an organization

organ of Cor·ti \-'kȯrt-ē\ *n* : a complicated structure in the cochlea that is the chief part of the ear which receives sound and changes it into signals carrying information to the brain

or·gasm \'ȯr-ˌgaz-əm\ *n* : the climax of sexual excitement

or·gy \'ȯr-jē\ *n, pl* **orgies** **1** : secret ceremonies in honor of an ancient Greek or Roman god usually celebrated by wild singing and dancing **2** : something (as a party) that resembles an orgy in lack of control

ori·el \'ōr-ē-əl, 'ȯr-\ *n* : a large window that sticks out from and is supported against a wall

ori·ent \'ōr-ē-ˌent, 'ȯr-\ *vb* **1 a** : to cause to face toward the east **b** : to set or arrange in a definite position especially in relation to the points of the compass **2** : to acquaint with a situation or environment ⟨*orient* new students⟩ **3** : to direct towards the interests or subject of : RELATE ⟨movies that are *oriented* toward teenagers⟩ — **ori·en·ta·tion** \ˌōr-ē-ən-'tā-shən, ˌȯr-, -ē-ˌen-\ *n*

Ori·ent \'ōr-ē-ənt, 'ȯr-, -ē-ˌent\ *n* : ³EAST 2; *esp* : the countries of eastern Asia

oriel

Word History The Romans had no magnetic compasses, so they depended on the position of the rising sun to determine directions in the daytime. The direction from which the sun rose (which we know as east) was called *oriens*. This word was formed from the verb *oriri*, meaning "to rise, come forth". The word *oriens* also came to be used for the part of the world in the direction from which the sun rose, that is, the area we call the East. The English word *Orient*, taken from the Latin *oriens*, was used for the same general area to the east of Europe, and especially eastern Asia. When the verb *orient* was first used in English, it meant "to set or face toward the east". To orient a church means to build it so that the aisles lead up to the main alter at the eastern end of the building. Other senses of the verb developed later. [Middle English *orient* "east", from early French *orient* (same meaning), from Latin *orient-, oriens* "the direction in which the sun rises", from *oriri* "to rise" — related to ORIGIN]

ori·en·tal \ˌōr-ē-'ent-ᵊl, ˌȯr-\ *adj, often cap* : of or relating to the Orient — **ori·en·tal·ly** \-ᵊl-ē\ *adv*

Oriental *n* : a member of any of the native peoples of the Orient

Oriental poppy *n* : an Asian perennial poppy widely grown for its very large showy flowers

ori·en·tate \'ōr-ē-ən-ˌtāt, 'ȯr-, -ˌen-\ *vb* **-tat·ed; -tat·ing** : ORIENT

-ories *pl of* -ORY

or·i·fice \'ȯr-ə-fəs, 'är-\ *n* : an opening (as a mouth or hole) through which something may pass

ori·ga·mi \ˌȯr-ə-'gäm-ē\ *n* : the Japanese art of folding paper

or·i·gin \'ȯr-ə-jən, 'är-\ *n* **1** : ANCESTRY 1, PARENTAGE ⟨of French *origin*⟩ **2 a** : a rising, beginning, or coming from a source **b** : basic source or cause **3** : the intersection of the x-axis and y-axis on a graph [Middle English *origine* "ancestry", probably from early French *origine* (same meaning), from Latin *origin-, origo* "source, point at which something begins or arises", from *orire* "to rise" — related to ABORIGINE, ORIENT; see *Word History* at ORIENT]

¹orig·i·nal \ə-'rij-ən-ᵊl, -nəl\ *n* : something from which a copy or translation is made

²original *adj* **1** : relating to or being the origin or beginning : FIRST, EARLIEST ⟨the *original* part of an old house⟩ ⟨*original* owners⟩ **2** : not copied or imitated from something else ⟨*original* paintings⟩ ⟨an *original* idea⟩ **3** : being an

\ə\ abut	\au̇\ out	\i\ tip	\ȯ\ saw	\u̇\ foot
\ər\ further	\ch\ chin	\ī\ life	\ȯi\ coin	\y\ yet
\a\ mat	\e\ pet	\j\ job	\th\ thin	\yü\ few
\ā\ take	\ē\ easy	\ŋ\ sing	\th\ this	\yu̇\ cure
\ä\ cot, cart	\g\ go	\ō\ bone	\ü\ food	\zh\ vision

original **4** : able to think up new things : INVENTIVE **syn** see NEW

orig·i·nal·i·ty \ə-ˌrij-ə-'nal-ət-ē\ *n* **1** : the quality or state of being original : FRESHNESS ⟨the *originality* of an idea⟩ **2** : the power or ability to think, to act, or to do something in new ways : CREATIVITY ⟨an artist of great *originality*⟩

orig·i·nal·ly \ə-'rij-ən-ᵊl-ē, -nəl-ē\ *adv* **1** : in the beginning : in the first place ⟨it *originally* belonged to me⟩ **2** : in an original manner

original sin *n* : the state of sin that according to Christian teaching all people are born in as a result of Adam's sin in Eden

orig·i·nate \ə-'rij-ə-ˌnāt\ *vb* **-nat·ed; -nat·ing** **1** : to bring into existence : cause to be : INITIATE, INVENT **2** : to come into existence : ARISE — **orig·i·na·tion** \-ˌrij-ə-'nā-shən\ *n* — **orig·i·na·tor** \-'rij-ə-ˌnāt-ər\ *n*

ori·ole \'ōr-ē-ˌōl, 'ȯr-, -ē-əl\ *n* **1** : any of a family of usually brightly colored Old World birds related to the crows **2** : any of a family of New World birds of which the males are usually black and yellow or orange and the females chiefly greenish or yellowish

Ori·on \ə-'rī-ən, ȯ-\ *n* : a group of stars on the equator east of Taurus represented on charts by the figure of a hunter with belt and sword

or·i·son \'ȯr-ə-sən, 'är-, -zən\ *n* : PRAYER 1, 2a

Or·lon \'ȯ(ə)r-ˌlän\ *trademark* — used for an acrylic fiber

¹or·na·ment \'ȯr-nə-mənt\ *n* **1** : something that adds beauty : DECORATION **2** : addition of something that beautifies ⟨a satin bow applied for *ornament*⟩

²or·na·ment \'ȯr-nə-ˌment\ *vb* : ADORN, DECORATE — **or·na·men·ta·tion** \ˌȯr-nə-mən-'tā-shən, -ˌmen-\ *n*

¹or·na·men·tal \ˌȯr-nə-'ment-ᵊl\ *adj* : of, relating to, or serving as ornament — **or·na·men·tal·ly** \-ᵊl-ē\ *adv*

²ornamental *n* : a decorative object; *esp* : a plant cultivated for its beauty rather than for use

or·nate \ȯr-'nāt\ *adj* : decorated in a fancy way — **or·nate·ly** *adv* — **or·nate·ness** *n*

or·nery \'ȯrn-(ə-)rē, 'än-\ *adj* **or·neri·er; -est** : having an irritable disposition — **or·neri·ness** *n*

or·ni·thol·o·gist \ˌȯr-nə-'thäl-ə-jəst\ *n* : a person who specializes in ornithology

or·ni·thol·o·gy \ˌȯr-nə-'thäl-ə-jē\ *n* : a branch of zoology dealing with birds

¹or·phan \'ȯr-fən\ *n* : a child whose parents are dead — **orphan** *adj*

²orphan *vb* **or·phaned; or·phan·ing** \'ȯrf-(ə-)niŋ\ : to cause to become an orphan ⟨a child *orphaned* by a plane wreck⟩

or·phan·age \'ȯrf-(ə-)nij\ *n* : an institution for the care of orphans

or·tho·clase \'ȯr-thə-ˌklās, -ˌklāz\ *n* : a mineral consisting of common potassium feldspar often with sodium in place of some of the potassium

orth·odon·tics \ˌȯr-thə-'dänt-iks\ *n* : a branch of dentistry dealing with faults in the arrangement and placing of teeth and with their correction — **orth·odon·tic** \-'dänt-ik\ *adj*

orth·odon·tist \ˌȯr-thə-'dänt-əst\ *n* : a dentist who specializes in orthodontics

or·tho·dox \'ȯr-thə-ˌdäks\ *adj* **1** : holding established beliefs especially in religion ⟨an *orthodox* Christian⟩ **2** : approved as measuring up to some standard : USUAL, CONVENTIONAL ⟨take an *orthodox* approach to a problem⟩ **3 a** : EASTERN ORTHODOX **b** : of, relating to, or following Orthodox Judaism

Word History When someone has the same opinions and beliefs as those held by most other people, these opinions are usually considered the "right" opinions to have. In English such opinions might be called "orthodox". The English word *orthodox* comes originally from the Greek words *orthos,* meaning "right, true" and *doxa,* meaning "opinion". These two words were combined to form the Greek verb *orthodoxein,* meaning "to

have the right opinion". From *orthodoxein* came the Greek adjective *orthodoxos,* which was borrowed into Latin as *orthodoxus.* The English adjective *orthodox* comes from this Latin adjective. [from early French *orthodoxe* or Latin *orthodoxus,* both meaning "orthodox", from Greek *orthodoxos* (same meaning), from *orthodoxein* "to have the right or true opinion", derived from *orthos* "right, true" and *doxa* "opinion"]

Orthodox Judaism *n* : Judaism that considers the Torah sacred and that strictly follows Jewish laws and traditions in everyday life

or·tho·doxy \'ȯr-thə-ˌdäk-sē\ *n, pl* **-dox·ies** **1** : the quality or state of being orthodox **2** : an orthodox belief or practice

or·thog·ra·phy \ȯr-'thäg-rə-fē\ *n, pl* **-phies** **1** : correct spelling **2** : a way or style of spelling — **or·tho·graph·ic** \ˌȯr-thə-'graf-ik\ *also* **or·tho·graph·i·cal** \-i-kəl\ *adj* — **or·tho·graph·i·cal·ly** \-i-k(ə-)lē\ *adv*

or·tho·pe·dic \ˌȯr-thə-'pēd-ik\ *adj* **1** : of or relating to orthopedics **2** : marked by deformities or crippling

or·tho·pe·dics \ˌȯr-thə-'pēd-iks\ *n sing or pl* : the correction or prevention of deformities of the skeleton

or·tho·pe·dist \ˌȯr-thə-'pēd-əst\ *n* : a physician who specializes in orthopedics

¹-o·ry \ˌ-ōr-ē, ˌȯr-ē, (ˌ)ȯr-ē\ *n suffix, pl* **-ories** : place of or for ⟨observat*ory*⟩ [derived from Latin *-orius* (adjective suffix)]

²-ory *adj suffix* : of, relating to, serving for, or characterized by ⟨regulat*ory*⟩

oryx \'ōr-iks, 'ȯr-, 'är-\ *n, pl* **oryx·es** *or* **oryx** : any of several African antelopes having long horns that are straight or that curve backward

oryx

Osage \ō-'sāj, 'ō-ˌsāj\ *n* : a member of an American Indian people originally of Missouri

os·cil·late \'äs-ə-ˌlāt\ *vb* **-lat·ed; -lat·ing** **1 a** : to swing backward and forward like a pendulum **b** : to move or travel back and forth between two points **2** : to have trouble deciding between opposing beliefs, feelings, or ideas — **os·cil·la·to·ry** \'äs-ə-lə-ˌtōr-ē, -ˌtȯr-\ *adj*

os·cil·la·tion \ˌäs-ə-'lā-shən\ *n* **1** : the action or state of oscillating : VIBRATION **2** : VARIATION 1, FLUCTUATION **3** : a single swing (as of an oscillating body) from one extreme limit to the other

os·cil·la·tor \'äs-ə-ˌlāt-ər\ *n* **1** : one that oscillates **2** : a device for producing alternating current; *esp* : a radio-frequency or audio-frequency generator

os·cil·lo·scope \ä-'sil-ə-ˌskōp, ə-\ *n* : an instrument in which the variations in a continually changing electrical quantity appear temporarily as a visible wave form on the screen of a cathode-ray tube

Osee \'ō-ˌzē, ō-'zā-ə\ *n* — see BIBLE table

osier \'ō-zhər\ *n* **1** : any of various willows with easily bent twigs used for making furniture and baskets **2** : a willow rod used for making baskets **3** : any of several American dogwoods

os·mi·um \'äz-mē-əm\ *n* : a hard brittle blue-gray or blue⸗black metallic element with a high melting point that is the heaviest metal known — see ELEMENT table

os·mo·sis \äz-'mō-səs, äs-\ *n* **1** : the passage of material (as a solvent) through a membrane (as of a plant or animal cell) that will not allow all kinds of molecules to pass **2** : a taking in (as of knowledge) as if by the process of osmosis — **os·mot·ic** \-'mät-ik\ *adj*

os·prey \'äs-prē, -ˌprā\ *n, pl* **ospreys** : a large hawk that is dark brown above and mostly white below and that feeds chiefly on fish — called also *fish hawk*

os·si·fi·ca·tion \ˌäs-ə-fə-'kā-shən\ *n* : the natural process of bone formation

os·si·fy \'äs-ə-ˌfī\ *vb* **-fied; -fy·ing**   **1** : to become or change into bone or bony tissue   **2** : to become or make hardened or set in one's ways

os·ten·si·ble \ä-'sten(t)-sə-bəl, ə-\ *adj* : shown outwardly : APPARENT

os·ten·si·bly \ä-'sten(t)-sə-blē, ə-\ *adv* : to all outward appearances : SEEMINGLY ⟨everything they said was *ostensibly* true⟩

os·ten·ta·tion \ˌäs-tən-'tā-shən\ *n* : unnecessary show to attract attention, admiration, or envy

os·ten·ta·tious \ˌäs-tən-'tā-shəs\ *adj* : fond of or showing ostentation — **os·ten·ta·tious·ly** *adv* — **os·ten·ta·tious·ness** *n*

os·teo·ar·thri·tis \ˌäs-tē-ō-är-'thrīt-əs\ *n* : arthritis marked by the breakdown of cartilage and bone of joints

os·teo·path \'äs-tē-ə-ˌpath\ *n* : a person who practices osteopathy

os·te·op·a·thy \ˌäs-tē-'äp-ə-thē\ *n* : a system of treating diseases that uses procedures involving especially the manipulation of bones but does not exclude other treatment (as the use of medicine and surgery) — **os·teo·path·ic** \ˌäs-tē-ə-'path-ik\ *adj*

ostler *variant of* HOSTLER

os·tra·cism \'äs-trə-ˌsiz-əm\ *n*   **1** : a method of temporary banishment by popular vote without trial practiced in ancient Greece   **2** : a general refusal to include someone as part of a social group

os·tra·cize \'äs-trə-ˌsīz\ *vb* **-cized; -ciz·ing** : to force to leave or refuse to include by ostracism

> **Word History** The ancient Greek word *ostrakon* had several meanings, including "a shell" and "a fragment of pottery". Such pottery fragments were used in ancient Athens as ballots in a particular kind of popular vote. Once a year the citizens would gather in the marketplace to decide who, if anyone, should be forced to go away temporarily for the good of the city. Each voter wrote a name on an *ostrakon.* If enough votes were cast against one person, then that person was sent away from the city, or *ostracized.* [from Greek *ostrakizein* "to banish by voting with pottery fragments," from *ostrakon* "shell, pottery fragment"]

os·trich \'äs-trich, 'òs-\ *n*   **1** : a very large bird of Africa and Arabia that often weighs as much as 135 kilograms, runs very swiftly but cannot fly, and has large valuable wing and tail feathers   **2** : one who tries to avoid danger by refusing to face it

¹oth·er \'əth-ər\ *adj*   **1** : not being the one or ones first mentioned or included ⟨broke my *other* arm⟩   **2** : having one come before that is not included or counted : SECOND ⟨every *other* day⟩   **3** : not the same : DIFFERENT ⟨any *other* color would be better⟩   **4** : ADDITIONAL ⟨some *other* guests are coming⟩   **5** : recently past ⟨the *other* evening⟩

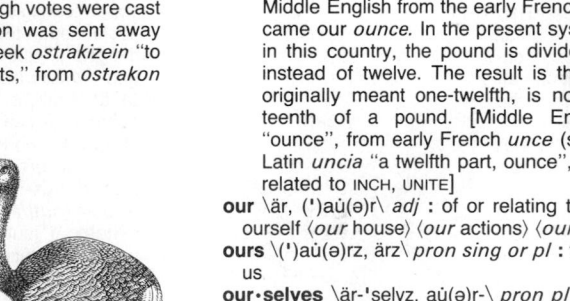

ostrich 1

²other *n*   **1** : a remaining one ⟨lift one foot and then the *other*⟩   **2** : a different or additional one ⟨the *others* came later⟩

³other *pron* : a different or additional one ⟨something or *other*⟩

⁴other *adv* : OTHERWISE 1 ⟨could not get there *other* than by helicopter⟩

oth·er·wise \'ə-thər-ˌwīz\ *adv*   **1** : in a different way : DIFFERENTLY ⟨could not do *otherwise*⟩   **2** : in other circum-

stances ⟨*otherwise* we might have won⟩   **3** : in other respects ⟨the *otherwise* busy street⟩

oth·er·world \'əth-ər-ˌwərld\ *n* : a world beyond death

oto·lar·yn·gol·o·gy \ˌōt-ō-ˌlar-ən-'gäl-ə-jē\ *n* : a medical specialty concerned with the ear, nose, and throat

ot·ter \'ät-ər\ *n, pl* **otter** *or* **otters**   **1** : any of several water-dwelling fish-eating mammals that are related to the weasels and minks and have webbed feet with claws and dark brown fur   **2** : the fur or pelt of an otter

ot·to·man \'ät-ə-mən\ *n, pl* **-mans**   **1** *cap* : TURK   **2** : an upholstered footstool — **Ottoman** *adj*

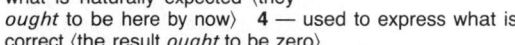
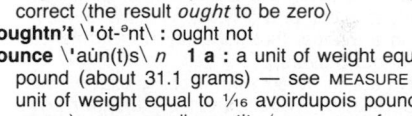

otter 1

ouch \'aùch\ *interj* — used to express sudden pain

ought \'òt\ *helping verb*   **1** — used to express duty ⟨we *ought* to pay our debts⟩   **2** — used to express what it would be wise to do ⟨you *ought* to take care of yourself⟩   **3** — used to express what is naturally expected ⟨they *ought* to be here by now⟩   **4** — used to express what is correct ⟨the result *ought* to be zero⟩

oughtn't \'òt-ᵊnt\ : ought not

ounce \'aùn(t)s\ *n*   **1 a** : a unit of weight equal to 1/12 troy pound (about 31.1 grams) — see MEASURE table   **b** : a unit of weight equal to 1/16 avoirdupois pound (about 28.3 grams)   **c** : a small quantity ⟨an *ounce* of common sense⟩   **2** : FLUIDOUNCE

> **Word History** The Latin word *uncia* was used to mean "a twelfth part of something". In reference to length, it meant one-twelfth of a *pes* "foot". In reference to weight, it meant one-twelfth of a *libra* "pound". *Uncia,* as a unit of length, came into Old English as *ince* or *ynce,* which became our *inch. Uncia,* as a unit of weight, came into Middle English from the early French word *unce* and became our *ounce.* In the present system of weights used in this country, the pound is divided into sixteen parts instead of twelve. The result is that the ounce, which originally meant one-twelfth, is now equal to one-sixteenth of a pound. [Middle English *unce, ounce* "ounce", from early French *unce* (same meaning), from Latin *uncia* "a twelfth part, ounce", from *unus* "one" — related to INCH, UNITE]

our \är, (')aù(ə)r\ *adj* : of or relating to us or ourselves or ourself ⟨*our* house⟩ ⟨*our* actions⟩ ⟨*our* being chosen⟩

ours \(')aù(ə)rz, ärz\ *pron sing or pl* : that which belongs to us

our·selves \är-'selvz, aù(ə)r-\ *pron pl*   **1** : our own selves — used for emphasis or to show that the subject and object of the verb are the same ⟨we amused *ourselves*⟩ ⟨we did it *ourselves*⟩   **2** : our normal or healthy selves ⟨just not *ourselves* today⟩

-ous \əs\ *adj suffix*   **1** : full of : having plenty of ⟨clamor*ous*⟩   **2** : having : possessing the qualities of ⟨poison*ous*⟩ [derived from Latin *-osus* (adjective suffix)]

oust \'aùst\ *vb* : to force or drive out (as from office or from possession of something)

oust·er \'aùs-tər\ *n* : the act or an instance of ousting or being ousted

¹out \'aùt\ *adv*   **1 a** : in a direction away from the inside, center, or surface ⟨look *out* of a window⟩   **b** : ¹OUTDOORS

\ə\ abut	\aù\ **out**	\i\ tip	\ò\ **saw**	\ù\ **foot**
\ər\ **further**	\ch\ **chin**	\ī\ **life**	\òi\ **coin**	\y\ **yet**
\a\ **mat**	\e\ **pet**	\j\ **job**	\th\ **thin**	\yü\ **few**
\ā\ **take**	\ē\ **easy**	\ŋ\ **sing**	\th\ **this**	\yù\ **cure**
\ä\ **cot, cart**	\g\ **go**	\ō\ **bone**	\ü\ **food**	\zh\ **vision**

⟨it's raining *out*⟩ **c** : from among others ⟨picked *out* a hat⟩ **2** : away from home, business, or usual or proper place ⟨*out* to lunch⟩ ⟨left a word *out*⟩ **3** : into a state of loss or defeat ⟨was voted *out* of office⟩ **4** : beyond control or possession ⟨let a secret *out*⟩ ⟨lent *out* money⟩ **5 a** : so as to be exhausted, completed, or discontinued ⟨the food ran *out*⟩ ⟨the light burned *out*⟩ **b** : at an end ⟨before the week is *out*⟩ **6 a** : in or into the open ⟨the sun came *out*⟩ **b** : ALOUD ⟨cried *out*⟩ **7** : in the fullest way — used to stress the sense of the verb ⟨all decked *out*⟩ ⟨sketch *out* plans⟩ **8** : so as to put out or be put out in baseball ⟨the catcher threw the runner *out*⟩ ⟨grounded *out* to shortstop⟩

²out *vb* : to become known ⟨the truth will *out*⟩

³out \(ˌ)aut\ *prep* **1** : out through ⟨ran *out* the door⟩ **2** : outward along or on ⟨drive *out* the old road⟩

⁴out \ˈaut\ *adj* **1** : located outside or at a distance ⟨the *out* islands⟩ **2** : not being in power ⟨the *out* party⟩ **3** : not allowed to continue batting, to occupy a base, or to score in baseball ⟨the runner was *out*⟩ **4** : directed outward or directing something outward ⟨a letter in the *out* basket⟩ **5** : ¹ABSENT 1, MISSING ⟨a basket with its bottom *out*⟩ **6** : no longer in fashion **7** : not to be considered ⟨that choice was *out* as far as we were concerned⟩

⁵out \ˈaut\ *n* **1** : one who is out of power **2 a** : the putting out of a batter or base runner in baseball **b** : a player who has been put out **3** : a way of escaping from an embarrassing situation or a difficulty

out- *prefix* : in a manner that goes beyond ⟨*out*maneuver⟩ [derived from *out* (adverb)]

out–and–out \ˌaut-ᵊn-ˈ(d)aut\ *adj* : being exactly what is stated : COMPLETE, THOROUGHGOING ⟨an *out-and-out* crook⟩

out·bid \(ˈ)aut-ˈbid\ *vb* **-bid; -bid·ding** : to make a higher bid than

¹out·board \ˈaut-ˌbō(ə)rd, -ˌbò(ə)rd\ *adj* **1** : located outboard **2** : having or using an outboard motor

²outboard *adv* **1** : outside a ship's hull : away from the long axis of a ship **2** : in a position closer to the wing tips of an airplane

³outboard *n* : OUTBOARD MOTOR

outboard motor *n* : a small internal-combustion engine with propeller attached for mounting at the stern of a small boat

out·bound \ˈaut-ˌbaund\ *adj* : outward bound ⟨*outbound* traffic⟩

out·brave \(ˈ)aut-ˈbrāv\ *vb* **1** : to face or resist boldly **2** : to have more courage than

out·break \ˈaut-ˌbrāk\ *n* **1** : a sudden or violent development of activity, use, or acceptance ⟨the *outbreak* of war⟩ **2** : something (as an epidemic or revolution) that breaks out

outboard motor

out·breed·ing \-ˌbrēd-iŋ\ *n* : the interbreeding of individuals that are unrelated or only distantly related

out·build·ing \-ˌbil-diŋ\ *n* : a building separate from and smaller than the main one

out·burst \-ˌbərst\ *n* **1** : a sudden violent expression of strong feeling ⟨an *outburst* of anger⟩ **2** : a sudden increase in activity or growth

out·cast \-ˌkast\ *n* : a person who is cast out by society : PARIAH — **outcast** *adj*

out·caste \-ˌkast\ *n* **1** : a Hindu who has been forced out of a caste for violation of its rules **2** : one who has no caste

out·class \(ˈ)aut-ˈklas\ *vb* : to do or be so much better than as to appear of a higher class

out·come \ˈaut-ˌkəm\ *n* : ²RESULT 1

¹out·crop \ˈaut-ˌkräp\ *n* **1** : a coming out of bedrock to the surface of the ground **2** : the part of a rock formation that appears at the surface of the ground

²out·crop \ˈaut-ˌkräp, (ˈ)aut-ˈkräp\ *vb* : to come to the surface : APPEAR ⟨granite *outcropping* through softer rocks⟩

out·crop·ping \ˈaut-ˌkrä-piŋ\ *n* : ¹OUTCROP

¹out·cross \ˈaut-ˌkròs\ *n* **1** : a cross made by outcrossing two individuals or strains **2** : the offspring resulting from an outcross

²outcross *vb* : to cross with an unrelated individual or strain or one that is only distantly related

out·cry \ˈaut-ˌkrī\ *n* **1** : a loud cry : CLAMOR **2** : a strong protest

out·dat·ed \(ˈ)aut-ˈdāt-əd\ *adj* : not up-to-date

out·dis·tance \-ˈdis-tən(t)s\ *vb* : to go far ahead of (as in a race) : OUTSTRIP

out·do \-ˈdü\ *vb* **-did** \-ˈdid\; **-done** \-ˈdən\; **-do·ing** \-ˈdü-iŋ\ : to go beyond in achievement or performance **syn** see EXCEED

out·door \ˌaut-ˈdō(ə)r, -ˈdò(ə)r\ *also* **out·doors** \-ˈdō(ə)rz, -ˈdò(ə)rz\ *adj* **1** : of or relating to the outdoors ⟨an *outdoor* setting⟩ **2** : done outdoors ⟨*outdoor* games⟩ **3** : having no roof and walls ⟨an *outdoor* theater⟩

¹out·doors \(ˈ)aut-ˈdō(ə)rz, -ˈdò(ə)rz\ *adv* : outside a building : in or into the open air

²outdoors *n* **1** : a place away from or outside a building **2** : the world away from human dwellings

out·er \ˈaut-ər\ *adj* **1** : located on the outside or farther out ⟨the *outer* wall⟩ **2** : being away from a center ⟨the *outer* planets of the solar system⟩

outer ear *n* : the outer visible part of the ear that collects and directs sound waves toward the eardrum by way of a canal through the temporal bone

out·er·most \ˈaut-ər-ˌmōst\ *adj* : farthest out

outer space *n* : ¹SPACE 4; *esp* : the region beyond the solar system

out·er·wear \ˈaut-ər-ˌwa(ə)r, -ˌwe(ə)r\ *n* : clothing for outdoor wear

out·field \ˈaut-ˌfēld\ *n* **1** : the part of a baseball field beyond the infield and between the foul lines **2** : the players positioned in the outfield — **out·field·er** \-ˌfēl-dər\ *n*

out·fight \(ˈ)aut-ˈfīt\ *vb* **-fought** \-ˈfòt\; **-fight·ing** : to fight better than : DEFEAT

¹out·fit \ˈaut-ˌfit\ *n* **1** : the equipment or clothing for some purpose ⟨a camping *outfit*⟩ ⟨a sports *outfit*⟩ **2** : a group of persons working together or associated in the same activity ⟨soldiers belonging to the same *outfit*⟩

²outfit *vb* **out·fit·ted; out·fit·ting** : to furnish with an outfit : EQUIP ⟨*outfit* an expedition⟩ — **out·fit·ter** *n*

out·flank \(ˈ)aut-ˈflaŋk\ *vb* : to get around the side of (a military formation) ⟨*outflank* the enemy⟩

out·flow \ˈaut-ˌflō\ *n* **1** : a flowing out ⟨an *outflow* of fans from the stadium⟩ **2** : something that flows out

out·fox \(ˈ)aut-ˈfäks\ *vb* : OUTWIT

out·go \ˈaut-ˌgō\ *n, pl* **outgoes** : money spent : OUTLAY

out·go·ing \ˈaut-ˌgō-iŋ\ *adj* **1 a** : going out : DEPARTING ⟨*outgoing* tide⟩ **b** : retiring from a position ⟨the *outgoing* governor⟩ **2** : being at ease and friendly when dealing with others ⟨an *outgoing* person⟩

out·grow \(ˈ)aut-ˈgrō\ *vb* **-grew** \-ˈgrü\; **-grown** \-ˈgrōn\; **-grow·ing** **1** : to grow faster than **2** : to grow too large or too mature for ⟨*outgrew* their clothes⟩ ⟨*outgrow* old friends⟩

out·growth \ˈaut-ˌgrōth\ *n* **1** : something that grows out of or develops from something else **2** : OFFSHOOT 1, BY-PRODUCT

out·guess \(ˈ)aut-ˈges\ *vb* : to correctly foresee the plans, actions, or activities of

out·house \ˈaut-ˌhaus\ *n* : OUTBUILDING; *esp* : ²PRIVY 1

out·ing \ˈaut-iŋ\ *n* : a brief usually outdoor pleasure trip often with a picnic

out·land·er \ˈaut-ˌlan-dər\ *n* : a person from another country or region

out·land·ish \('\)aut-'lan-dish\ *adj* : of foreign or strange appearance or manner : BIZARRE — **out·land·ish·ly** *adv* — **out·land·ish·ness** *n*

out·last \'aut-'last\ *vb* : to last longer than : SURVIVE

¹**out·law** \'aut-,lò\ *n* **1** : a person who is not given the protection of the law **2** : a lawless person or one who is running away from the law **3** : an animal (as a horse) that is wild and hard to control — **outlaw** *adj*

²**outlaw** *vb* **1** : to deprive of the protection of law **2** : to make illegal ⟨dueling was *outlawed*⟩ — **out·law·ry** \'aut-,lò\)r-ē\ *n*

out·lay \'aut-,lā\ *n* **1** : the act of spending **2** : an amount spent : PAYMENT

out·let \'aut-,let, -lət\ *n* **1** : a place or opening through which something is let out : EXIT, VENT **2** : a means of release or satisfaction ⟨an *outlet* for her grief⟩ **3** : a market for a product or an agency through which a product is marketed **4** : an electrical device (as in a wall) into which an appliance may be plugged

¹**out·line** \'aut-,līn\ *n* **1** : a line that traces or forms the outer limits of an object or figure and shows its shape **2 a** : a drawing or picture giving only the outlines of something **b** : this method of drawing **3 a** : a brief summary often in numbered divisions **b** : a brief treatment of a subject

²**outline** *vb* **1** : to draw or trace the outline of **2** : to indicate the main features or parts of ⟨*outlined* our responsibilities⟩

out·live \('\)aut-'liv\ *vb* : to live longer than : OUTLAST

out·look \'aut-,lùk\ *n* **1 a** : a place offering a view **b** : a view from a particular place **2** : POINT OF VIEW **3** : conditions that seem to lie ahead ⟨the *outlook* for business⟩

out loud *adv* : loudly enough to be heard : ALOUD

out·ly·ing \'aut-,lī-iŋ\ *adj* : being far from a center or main body ⟨an *outlying* suburb⟩

out·ma·neu·ver \,aut-mə-'n(y)ü-vər\ *vb* : to be more skillful or successful than in maneuvering

out·mod·ed \('\)aut-'mōd-əd\ *adj* : no longer acceptable, usable, or fashionable ⟨*outmoded* beliefs⟩

out·most \'aut-,mōst\ *adj* : OUTERMOST

out·num·ber \('\)aut-'nəm-bər\ *vb* : to be more than in number ⟨girls *outnumber* boys in the class⟩

out of *prep* **1 a** : from within to the outside of ⟨walked *out of* the room⟩ **b** — used to indicate a change in quality, state, or form ⟨woke *out of* a deep sleep⟩ **c** : beyond the range or limits of ⟨moved *out of* sight⟩ **2** — used to indicate source, material, or cause ⟨built *out of* old lumber⟩ ⟨came *out of* curiosity⟩ **3** — used to indicate the state or condition of being without something especially that was there before ⟨the store is *out of* bread⟩ ⟨cheated us *out of* our savings⟩ **4** : from among ⟨one *out of* four survived⟩

out–of–bounds \,aut-ə(v)-'baun(d)z\ *adv or adj* : outside the limits of the playing area ⟨the pass went *out-of-bounds*⟩

out–of–date \-'dāt\ *adj* : OUTMODED, OBSOLETE

out–of–door \-'dō(ə)r, -'dò(ə)r\ *or* **out–of–doors** \-'dō(ə)rz, -'dò(ə)rz\ *adj* : OUTDOOR 1, 2

out–of–doors *n* : ²OUTDOORS

out–of–the–way \,aut-ə(v)-thə-'wā\ *adj* **1** : being off the usual paths ⟨an *out-of-the-way* village⟩ **2** : not commonly found or met : UNUSUAL ⟨the store specializes in *out-of-the-way* books⟩

out·pace \('\)aut-'pās\ *vb* : OUTRUN

out·pa·tient \'aut-,pā-shənt\ *n* : a patient who visits a hospital for diagnosis or treatment without staying overnight — compare INPATIENT

out·play \('\)aut-'plā\ *vb* : to play better than

out·post \'aut-,pōst\ *n* **1** : a guard stationed at a distance from a military force or camp **2** : the position occupied by an outpost **3** : a settlement on a frontier or in a faraway place

out·pour·ing \-,pōr-iŋ, -,pòr-\ *n* **1** : the act of pouring out **2 a** : something that pours out or is poured out **b** : OUTBURST 1

¹**out·put** \'aut-,pùt\ *n* **1** : something produced: as **a** : agricultural or industrial production ⟨steel *output*⟩ **b** : mental or artistic production ⟨writing *output*⟩ **c** : the amount produced by a person in a given time **d** : power or energy delivered or produced by a machine or system ⟨light *output* of the sun⟩ **e** : the information generated by a computer **2** : a point at which something (as power, an electronic signal, or data) comes out

²**output** *vb* **out·put·ted** *or* **output; out·put·ting** : to produce as output

¹**out·rage** \'aut-,rāj\ *n* **1** : a violent or brutal act **2** : an act that hurts someone or shows disrespect for a person's feelings **3** : the angry feelings caused by injury or insult [Old English *outrage* "excessive, disorderly, or violent action or behavior", from early French *outrage* (same meaning), from *outre* "beyond" (from Latin *ultra* "beyond") and *-age* "action"]

²**outrage** *vb* **out·raged; out·rag·ing** **1** : to cause to suffer violent injury or abuse **2** : to cause to feel anger or resentment

out·ra·geous \aut-'rā-jəs\ *adj* : extremely annoying, insulting, or shameful : SHOCKING — **out·ra·geous·ly** *adv* — **out·ra·geous·ness** *n*

out·rank \('\)aut-'raŋk\ *vb* : to rank higher or be more important than

ou·tré \ü-'trā\ *adj* : very strange or unusual : BIZARRE [French]

out·rid·er \'aut-,rīd-ər\ *n* : a mounted escort

out·rig·ger \'aut-,rig-ər\ *n* **1** : a frame that extends from the side of a canoe or boat to prevent upsetting **2** : a craft equipped with an outrigger

outrigger 2

¹**out·right** \('\)aut-'rīt\ *adv* **1 a** : in entirety : COMPLETELY ⟨sold *outright*⟩ **b** : without holding back ⟨laughed *outright*⟩ **2** : on the spot : INSTANTANEOUSLY ⟨killed *outright*⟩

²**out·right** \'aut-,rīt\ *adj* **1** : being exactly what is stated ⟨an *outright* lie⟩ **2** : given without restriction ⟨an *outright* gift⟩

out·run \('\)aut-'rən\ *vb* **-ran** \-'ran\; **-run; -run·ning** **1** : to run or go faster than **2** : EXCEED 1 ⟨our needs *outran* our funds⟩

out·sell \-'sel\ *vb* **-sold** \-'sōld\; **-sell·ing** **1** : to be sold more than ⟨corn *outsold* beets⟩ **2** : to sell more than ⟨we *outsell* our competitors⟩

out·set \'aut-,set\ *n* : BEGINNING 1, START

out·shine \('\)aut-'shīn\ *vb* **-shone** \-'shōn\; **-shin·ing** **1** : to shine brighter than **2** : EXCEL, SURPASS

¹**out·side** \('\)aut-'sīd, 'aut-,sīd\ *n* **1** : a place or region beyond an enclosure or boundary **2** : an outer side or surface **3** : the extreme limit of a guess : MOST ⟨the crowd numbered 10,000 at the *outside*⟩

²**outside** *adj* **1** : of, relating to, or being on the outside ⟨the *outside* edge⟩ **2** : connected with or leading to the outside ⟨an *outside* door⟩ **3** : coming from outside ⟨*outside* influences⟩ **4** : barely possible : REMOTE ⟨an *outside* chance⟩

³**outside** *adv* : on or to the outside ⟨waited *outside* in the

hall); *esp* : ¹OUTDOORS ⟨took the dog *outside*⟩

⁴**outside** *prep* **1** : on or to the outside of ⟨*outside* the house⟩ **2** : beyond the limits of ⟨*outside* the law⟩ **3** : ²EXCEPT 2, BESIDES ⟨nobody *outside* a few close friends⟩

outside of *prep* : ⁴OUTSIDE 2, 3

out·sid·er \(')aut-'sīd-ər\ *n* : a person who does not belong to a particular group

¹**out·size** \'aut-,sīz\ *n* : a size different and especially larger than the standard

²**outsize** *also* **out·sized** \-,sīzd\ *adj* : unusually large or heavy

out·skirts \'aut-,skərts\ *n pl* : the parts far from the center of a place or town

out·smart \(')aut-'smärt\ *vb* : OUTWIT

out·spo·ken \aut-'spō-kən\ *adj* : direct and open in speech or expression : FRANK — **out·spo·ken·ness** \-kən-nəs\ *n*

out·spread \-'spred\ *vb* **-spread; -spread·ing** : to spread out : EXTEND — **out·spread** \'aut-,spred\ *adj*

out·stand·ing \-'stan-diŋ\ *adj* **1** : sticking out : PROJECTING **2 a** : not yet paid : UNPAID ⟨*outstanding* bills⟩ **b** : continuing in being : UNRESOLVED ⟨problems *outstanding*⟩ **3** : attracting notice especially because of excellence ⟨an *outstanding* scholar⟩ **syn** *see* NOTICEABLE — **out·stand·ing·ly** \-diŋ-lē\ *adv*

out·stay \(')aut-'stā\ *vb* **1** : to stay beyond or longer than ⟨*outstayed* their welcome⟩ **2** : to be able to hold out longer than

out·stretch \aut-'strech\ *vb* : to stretch out : EXTEND

out·strip \-'strip\ *vb* **1** : to go faster or farther than ⟨*outstripped* the other runners⟩ **2 a** : EXCEL ⟨*outstripped* all rivals⟩ **b** : EXCEED 1 ⟨demand *outstrips* supply⟩

¹**out·ward** \'aut-wərd\ *adj* **1** : moving or directed toward the outside or away from a center ⟨the *outward* journey⟩ **2** : showing on the outside : EXTERNAL ⟨*outward* signs of fear⟩

²**outward** *or* **out·wards** \-wərdz\ *adv* : toward the outside ⟨the city stretches *outward* for miles⟩ ⟨fold it *outward*⟩

out·ward·ly \'aut-wərd-lē\ *adv* : on the outside : in outward appearance ⟨*outwardly* calm⟩

out·wear \(')aut-'wa(ə)r, -'we(ə)r\ *vb* **-wore** \-'wō(ə)r, -'wȯ(ə)r\; **-worn** \-'wō(ə)rn, -'wȯ(ə)rn\; **-wear·ing** : to wear or last longer than ⟨a fabric that *outwears* others⟩

out·weigh \-'wā\ *vb* : to be greater than in weight, value, or importance ⟨the benefits *outweigh* the disadvantages⟩

out·wit \aut-'wit\ *vb* **-wit·ted; -wit·ting** : to get the better of by cleverness **syn** *see* FRUSTRATE

¹**out·work** \(')aut-'wərk\ *vb* : to outdo in working

²**out·work** \'aut-,wərk\ *n* : a small protected position constructed outside a main defense (as a castle)

out·worn \aut-'wō(ə)rn, -'wȯ(ə)rn\ *adj* : WORN-OUT 1, OUT-OF-DATE ⟨an *outworn* system⟩

ou·zel \'ü-zəl\ *n* : DIPPER 1

ova *pl of* OVUM

¹**oval** \'ō-vəl\ *n* : an oval figure or object

²**oval** *adj* : having the shape or outline of an egg [from Latin *ovalis* (adjective) "having the shape of an egg", derived from earlier *ovum* "egg"]

oval window *n* : an oval opening between the middle ear and inner ear having the base of the stapes attached to its membrane

ovar·i·an \ō-'var-ē-ən, -'ver-\ *adj* : of, relating to, or produced by an ovary ⟨*ovarian* hormones⟩

ova·ry \'ōv-(ə-)rē\ *n, pl* **-ries** **1** : a usually paired organ in the body of female animals that produces eggs and in vertebrates female sex hormones **2** : the enlarged rounded lower part of the pistil of a flower in which seeds are formed

ovate \'ō-,vāt\ *adj* : shaped like an egg in outline with the base wider than the end ⟨*ovate* leaves⟩

ova·tion \ō-'vā-shən\ *n* : a public expression of praise : enthusiastic applause

ov·en \'əv-ən\ *n* : a chamber (as in a stove) used for bak-ing, heating, or drying

ov·en·bird \-,bərd\ *n* : an olive-green American warbler that builds a dome-shaped nest on the ground

ovenbird

¹**over** \'ō-vər\ *adv* **1 a** : across a barrier or space ⟨fly *over* to London⟩ **b** : in a direction down or forward and down ⟨fell *over*⟩ **c** : across the brim ⟨soup boiled *over*⟩ **d** : so as to bring the underside up ⟨turned his cards *over*⟩ **e** : from one person or side to another ⟨hand it *over*⟩ ⟨won them *over*⟩ **f** : to one's home ⟨ask them *over*⟩ **g** : at a distance from a certain point ⟨two streets *over*⟩ **2** : ¹ACROSS 3 ⟨got their point *over*⟩ **3 a** : beyond a limit ⟨show ran a minute *over*⟩ **b** : more than needed : too many or too much ⟨has two cards left *over*⟩ ⟨*over* fond of food⟩ **4** : so as to cover the whole surface ⟨windows boarded *over*⟩ **5 a** : ²THROUGH 2a ⟨read it *over*⟩ **b** : once more : AGAIN ⟨do it *over*⟩

²**over** \,ō-vər, 'ō-\ *prep* **1** : higher than : ABOVE ⟨towered *over* my mother⟩ **2 a** : above in authority, power, or worth ⟨respected those *over* us⟩ **b** : in front of : AHEAD OF, BEYOND ⟨a big lead *over* the others⟩ **3** : more than ⟨cost *over* $5⟩ **4 a** : down upon especially so as to cover ⟨laid a blanket *over* the child⟩ **b** : all through or throughout ⟨all *over* town⟩ ⟨went *over* her notes⟩ **c** : on or along the surface of ⟨*over* the road⟩ **5 a** : ²ACROSS 1 ⟨jump *over* a stream⟩ **b** : to or on the other side of ⟨climb *over* the fence⟩ **c** : down from : OFF ⟨fell *over* the edge⟩ **6** : DURING ⟨*over* the past 25 years⟩ **7** — used to indicate an object of concern ⟨trouble *over* money⟩ **8** : by means of ⟨heard the news *over* TV⟩

³**over** \'ō-vər, ,ō-\ *adj* **1** : having or being more than is needed ⟨the cash was $3 *over* in our books⟩ **2** : brought or having come to an end : DONE ⟨the day is *over*⟩

over- *prefix* **1** : so as to be greater, better, or stronger than **2** : so as to be too much too great [from *over* (adverb or adjective)]

overabundant	overextend	overproduction
overambitious	overfamiliar	overprotect
overanxious	overfeed	overprotective
overbake	overfull	overproud
overbold	overgenerous	overrefined
overburden	overgraze	oversensitive
overcareful	overhasty	oversensitiveness
overcautious	overheat	oversimplification
overconfidence	overindulge	oversimplify
overconfident	overindulgence	oversize
overconscientious	overindulgent	oversized
overcooked	overlarge	overspecialization
overcritical	overlearn	overspecialize
overcrowd	overliberal	overstrict
overdecorated	overlong	oversubtle
overdependent	overmodest	oversuspicious
overeager	overnice	overtax
overeat	overpay	overtip
overemphasis	overpolite	overtired
overemphasize	overpopulate	overtrain
overenthusiastic	overpopulation	overvalue
overexcite	overpraise	overwithhold
overexert	overprice	overzealous
overexertion	overproduce	

over·abun·dance \,ō-vər-ə-'bən-dən(t)s\ *n* : a supply that is too great : EXCESS

over·act \,ō-və-'rakt\ *vb* : to exaggerate in acting

over·ac·tive \ˌō-və-'rak-tiv\ *adj* : very active and especially abnormally so ⟨an *overactive* thyroid⟩ — **over·ac·tiv·i·ty** \-ˌrak-'tiv-ət-ē\ *n*

¹**over·age** \ˌō-və-'rāj\ *adj* : older than is normal for one's position ⟨*overage* students⟩

²**over·age** \'ōv-(ə-)rij\ *n* : ¹EXCESS 1, SURPLUS

¹**over·all** \ˌō-və-'rȯl\ *adv* : as a whole : GENERALLY ⟨we find your work satisfactory, *overall*⟩

²**overall** \ˌō-və-'rȯl, 'ō-və-ˌrȯl\ *adj* 1 : including everything ⟨*overall* expenses⟩ 2 : viewed as a whole : GENERAL

over·alls \'ō-və-ˌrȯlz\ *n pl* : loose trousers made of strong material usually with a bib and shoulder straps

over and above *prep* : ¹BESIDES

over and over *adv* : many times : OFTEN

over·arm \'ō-və-ˌrärm\ *adj* 1 : ¹OVERHAND 2 : made with the arm lifted out of the water and stretched forward ⟨an *overarm* swimming stroke⟩

over·awe \ˌō-və-'rȯ\ *vb* : to make quiet or peaceful with fear, respect, or wonder

over·bal·ance \ˌō-vər-'bal-ən(t)s\ *vb* 1 : to have greater weight or importance than ⟨your good qualities *overbalanced* your shortcomings⟩ 2 : to lose or cause to lose balance ⟨a boat *overbalanced* by shifting cargo⟩

over·bear \ˌō-vər-'ba(ə)r, -'be(ə)r\ *vb* **-bore** \-'bō(ə)r, -'bȯ(ə)r\; **-borne** \-'bō(ə)rn, -'bȯ(ə)rn\ *also* **-born** \-'bȯ(ə)rn\; **-bear·ing** : OVERCOME

over·bear·ing \-'ba(ə)r-iŋ, -'be(ə)r-\ *adj* : ARROGANT, DOMINEERING — **over·bear·ing·ly** *adv*

over·bid \ˌō-vər-'bid\ *vb* **-bid; -bid·ding** : to bid too high — **over·bid** \'ō-vər-ˌbid\ *n*

over·board \'ō-vər-ˌbō(ə)rd, -ˌbȯ(ə)rd\ *adv* 1 : over the side of a ship into the water 2 : to extremes of enthusiasm ⟨go *overboard* for a new fad⟩

over·buy \ˌō-vər-'bī\ *vb* **-bought** \-'bȯt\; **-buy·ing** : to buy more than is needed or can be afforded

¹**over·cast** \'ō-vər-ˌkast; -'cast; -cast·ing 1 \ˌō-vər-'kast, 'ō-vər-ˌkast\ : DARKEN 1, OVERSHADOW 2 \'ō-vər-ˌkast\ : to sew with stitches that prevent the material at the edge of a seam from coming apart

²**over·cast** \ˌō-vər-'kast, ˌō-vər-'kast\ *adj* : clouded over : GLOOMY ⟨an *overcast* night⟩

over·charge \ˌō-vər-'chärj\ *vb* 1 : to charge too much 2 : to fill or load too full ⟨a cannon *overcharged* with powder⟩ — **over·charge** \'ō-vər-ˌchärj\ *n*

over·cloud \-'klaúd\ *vb* : to overspread with clouds : DARKEN

over·coat \'ō-vər-ˌkōt\ *n* : a warm coat worn over indoor clothing

over·come \ˌō-vər-'kəm\ *vb* **-came** \-'kām\; **-come; -com·ing** 1 : to gain an advantage or victory over ⟨*overcome* an enemy⟩ 2 : to make helpless or exhausted ⟨was *overcome* by gas⟩ **syn** see CONQUER

over·do \-'dü\ *vb* **-did** \-'did\; **-done** \-'dən\; **-do·ing** \-'dü-iŋ\ 1 : to do too much ⟨*overdoes* it getting ready for a party⟩ 2 : EXAGGERATE ⟨*overdo* praise⟩ 3 : to cook too long ⟨meat that is *overdone*⟩

¹**over·dose** \'ō-vər-ˌdōs\ *n* : too great a dose — **over·dos·age** \ˌō-vər-'dō-sij\ *n*

²**over·dose** \ˌō-vər-'dōs\ *vb* : to give an overdose or too many doses to

over·draft \'ō-vər-ˌdraft\ *n* : an overdrawing of a bank account or the amount overdrawn

over·draw \ˌō-vər-'drȯ\ *vb* **-drew** \-'drü\; **-drawn** \-'drȯn\; **-draw·ing** 1 : to draw checks on (a bank account) for more than the balance in it 2 : EXAGGERATE, OVERSTATE ⟨*overdrew* the dangers in the task⟩

¹**over·dress** \ˌō-vər-'dres\ *vb* : to dress too richly for an occasion

²**over·dress** \'ō-vər-ˌdres\ *n* : a dress worn over another

over·drive \'ō-vər-ˌdrīv\ *n* : a transmission gear in an automobile that allows the drive shaft to operate at a speed greater than that of the engine crankshaft

over·due \ˌō-vər-'d(y)ü\ *adj* 1 a : unpaid when due ⟨*overdue* bills⟩ b : not appearing or presented on time ⟨an *overdue* train⟩ ⟨an *overdue* book⟩ 2 : more than ready ⟨a country *overdue* for governmental reform⟩

over·es·ti·mate \ˌō-və-'res-tə-ˌmāt\ *vb* : to estimate too highly — **over·es·ti·mate** \-mət\ *n* — **over·es·ti·ma·tion** \-ˌres-tə-'mā-shən\ *n*

over·ex·pose \ˌō-və-rik-'spōz\ *vb* : to expose (as photographic material) for a longer time than is needed or desirable — **over·ex·po·sure** \-'spō-zhər\ *n*

over·fill \ˌō-vər-'fil\ *vb* : to fill to overflowing

over·fish \-'fish\ *vb* : to fish too much for (a kind of fish) or in (a certain area)

over·flight \'ō-vər-ˌflīt\ *n* : a flight over an area

¹**over·flow** \ˌō-vər-'flō\ *vb* 1 : to cover with or as if with water : INUNDATE 2 : to flow over the brim or top of ⟨the river *overflowed* its banks⟩ 3 : to flow over bounds ⟨the creek *overflows* every spring⟩ 4 : to fill a space up and spread beyond its limits ⟨the paragraph *overflowed* the page⟩

²**over·flow** \'ō-vər-ˌflō\ *n* 1 : a flowing over : FLOOD 2 : something that flows over : SURPLUS 3 : an outlet or container for liquid that overflows

over·fly \ˌō-vər-'flī\ *vb* **-flew** \-'flü\; **-flown** \-'flōn\; **-fly·ing** : to fly over; *esp* : to pass over in an airplane or spacecraft

over·gar·ment \'ō-vər-ˌgär-mənt\ *n* : an outer garment

over·grow \ˌō-vər-'grō\ *vb* **-grew** \-'grü\; **-grown** \-'grōn\; **-grow·ing** 1 : to grow over so as to cover 2 : OUTGROW 3 : to grow too big ⟨an *overgrown* puppy⟩ — **over·growth** \'ō-vər-ˌgrōth\ *n*

¹**over·hand** \'ō-vər-ˌhand\ *adj* : made with the hand brought forward and down from above shoulder level ⟨an *overhand* pitch⟩ ⟨an *overhand* tennis stroke⟩ — **overhand** *adv* — **over·hand·ed** \ˌō-vər-'han-dəd\ *adv*

²**overhand** *n* : an overhand stroke (as in tennis)

overhand knot \ˌō-vər-ˌhan(d)-\ *n* : a small knot often used to prevent the end of a cord from pulling apart

¹**over·hang** \'ō-vər-ˌhaŋ, ˌō-vər-'haŋ\ *vb* **-hung** \-ˌhəŋ, -'həŋ\; **-hang·ing** 1 : to stick out or hang over 2 : THREATEN 3

²**over·hang** \'ō-vər-ˌhaŋ\ *n* : a part that overhangs ⟨the *overhang* of a roof⟩

over·haul \ˌō-vər-'hȯl\ *vb* 1 : to make a thorough examination of and make necessary repairs and adjustments on ⟨*overhaul* an engine⟩ 2 : OVERTAKE 1a — **over·haul** \'ō-vər-ˌhȯl\ *n*

overhang

¹**over·head** \ˌō-vər-'hed\ *adv* : above one's head : ALOFT ⟨geese flying *overhead*⟩

²**over·head** \'ō-vər-ˌhed\ *adj* 1 : operating or lying above ⟨an *overhead* door⟩ 2 : of or relating to business expense

³**over·head** \'ō-vər-ˌhed\ *n* 1 : general business expenses (as rent, heat, or lighting) 2 : a stroke in a racket game made above head height : SMASH

over·hear \ˌō-vər-'hi(ə)r\ *vb* **-heard** \-'hərd\; **-hear·ing** \-'hi(ə)r-iŋ\ : to hear without the speaker's knowledge or intention

over·joy \ˌō-vər-'jȯi\ *vb* : to fill with great joy

over·kill \-'kil\ *n* 1 : a much greater capacity for destruc-

\ə\ abut	\aú\ out	\i\ tip	\ȯ\ saw	\ú\ foot
\ər\ further	\ch\ chin	\ī\ life	\ȯi\ coin	\y\ yet
\a\ mat	\e\ pet	\j\ job	\th\ thin	\yü\ few
\ā\ take	\ē\ easy	\ŋ\ sing	\t͟h\ this	\yú\ cure
\ä\ cot, cart	\g\ go	\ō\ bone	\ü\ food	\zh\ vision

tion than is needed for a particular target **2** : an excess beyond what is needed or suitable ⟨advertising *overkill*⟩

over·land \'ō-vər-ˌland, -lənd\ *adv or adj* : by, on, or across land

over·lap \ˌō-vər-'lap\ *vb* **1** : to lay or lie over (something) so as to partly cover **2** : to have something in common ⟨political and social interests that often *overlap*⟩ — **over·lap** \'ō-vər-ˌlap\ *n*

¹over·lay \ˌō-vər-'lā\ *vb* **-laid** \-'lād\; **-lay·ing 1** : to lay or spread over or across **2** : OVERLIE

²over·lay \'ō-vər-ˌlā\ *n* : something (as a veneer on wood) that is overlaid

over·leap \ˌō-vər-'lēp\ *vb* **-leaped** *or* **-leapt** \-'lept *also* -'lēpt\; **-leap·ing** \-'lē-piŋ\ **1** : to leap over or across ⟨*overleap* a ditch⟩ **2** : to defeat (oneself) by going too far

over·lie \-'lī\ *vb* **-lay** \-'lā\; **-lain** \-'lān\; **-ly·ing** \-'lī-iŋ\ : to lie over or upon

¹over·load \ˌō-vər-'lōd\ *vb* : to load too much

²over·load \'ō-vər-ˌlōd\ *n* : a load or amount that is too great

over·look \ˌō-vər-'lùk\ *vb* **1** : to look over : INSPECT **2 a** : to look down upon from above **b** : to provide a view of from above ⟨the mountain *overlooks* a lake⟩ **3 a** : to fail to see : MISS **b** : to pay no attention to : IGNORE ⟨*overlook* a beginner's mistakes⟩

over·lord \'ō-vər-ˌlò(ə)rd\ *n* **1** : a lord who rules over other lords **2** : an absolute or supreme ruler

over·ly \'ō-vər-lē\ *adv* : TOO 2, EXCESSIVELY

over·mas·ter \ˌō-vər-'mas-tər\ *vb* : OVERPOWER, SUBDUE

over·match \-'mach\ *vb* **1** : to be more than a match for : DEFEAT **2** : to match with a stronger opponent ⟨a boxer who was badly *overmatched*⟩

¹over·much \ˌō-vər-'məch\ *adj or adv* : too much

²over·much \'ō-vər-ˌməch, ˌō-vər-'məch\ *n* : too great an amount

¹over·night \ˌō-vər-'nīt\ *adv* **1** : on or during the evening or night ⟨stayed away *overnight*⟩ **2** : very quickly or suddenly ⟨became famous *overnight*⟩

²overnight *adj* **1** : of, lasting, or staying the night ⟨*overnight* trip⟩ ⟨*overnight* guests⟩ **2** : for use on short trips

¹over·pass \ˌō-vər-'pas\ *vb* **1** : to pass across, over, or beyond **2** : SURPASS **3** : ¹DISREGARD, IGNORE

²over·pass \'ō-vər-ˌpas\ *n* **1** : a crossing (as of two highways or of a highway and railroad) at different levels usually by means of a bridge **2** : the upper level of an overpass

overpass 1

over·play \ˌō-vər-'plā\ *vb* **1** : EXAGGERATE, OVEREMPHASIZE ⟨newspapers *overplayed* the story⟩ **2** : to rely too much on the strength of ⟨*overplayed* my hand and lost everything⟩

over·pop·u·la·tion \-ˌpäp-yə-'lā-shən\ *n* : the condition of having too many people living in a certain area — **over·pop·u·lat·ed** \-'päp-yə-ˌlāt-əd\ *adj*

over·pow·er \ˌō-vər-'paù-(ə)r\ *vb* **1** : to overcome by greater force : DEFEAT **2** : OVERWHELM 2 ⟨*overpowered* by hunger⟩ — **over·pow·er·ing·ly** \-'paùr-iŋ-lē\ *adv*

over·price \ˌō-vər-'prīs\ *vb* : to price too high

over·print \-'print\ *vb* : to print over with something additional — **over·print** \'ō-vər-ˌprint\ *n*

over·pro·duc·tion \-prə-'dək-shən\ *n* : too much production especially to the point that supply is greater than demand

over·rate \ˌō-və(r)-'rāt\ *vb* : to rate too highly ⟨a book that was *overrated*⟩

over·reach \-'rēch\ *vb* **1** : to reach above or beyond : OVERTOP **2** : to defeat (oneself) by trying to do or gain

too much **3** : OUTWIT, TRICK **4** : to reach or go too far — **over·reach·er** *n*

over·ride \-'rīd\ *vb* **-rode** \-'rōd\; **-rid·den** \-'rid-ᵊn\; **-rid·ing** \-'rīd-iŋ\ **1 a** : to ride over or across **b** : TRAMPLE 1 **2** : to ride a horse too much or too hard **3 a** : to take power away from : DOMINATE **b** : ANNUL 2 ⟨the congress *overrode* the president's veto⟩

over·ripe \-'rīp\ *adj* : passed beyond ripeness toward decay

over·rule \-'rül\ *vb* **1** : to decide against ⟨the judge *overruled* the objection⟩ **2** : to reverse or set aside (a decision or ruling made by a lesser authority)

¹over·run \ˌō-və(r)-'rən\ *vb* **-ran** \-'ran\; **-run; -run·ning 1 a** : to invade and occupy ⟨the island was *overrun* by the enemy⟩ **b** : INFEST 1 ⟨rats *overran* the ship⟩ **2** : to run or go beyond or past ⟨*overran* third base⟩ ⟨the program *overran* the time allowed⟩ **3** : to spread or grow over ⟨a garden *overrun* with weeds⟩

²over·run \'ō-və(r)-ˌrən\ *n* **1** : an act or instance of overrunning **2** : the amount by which something overruns

over·sea \ˌō-vər-'sē, 'ō-vər-ˌsē\ *adj or adv* : OVERSEAS

over·seas \-'sēz, -ˌsēz\ *adv or adj* : beyond or across the sea

over·see \ˌō-vər-'sē\ *vb* **-saw** \-'sò\; **-seen** \-'sēn\; **-see·ing 1** : to look down upon : SURVEY **2 a** : to look over : EXAMINE **b** : SUPERINTEND, SUPERVISE

over·seer \'ō-və(r)-ˌsi(ə)r, -ˌsē-ər; ˌō-və(r)-'si(ə)r, -'sē-ər\ *n* : one that oversees : SUPERINTENDENT

over·sell \ˌō-vər-'sel\ *vb* **-sold** \-'sōld\; **-sell·ing** : to sell too much to or of

over·shad·ow \-'shad-ō\ *vb* **1** : to cast a shadow over : DARKEN **2** : to become more important than : OUTWEIGH ⟨the win *overshadowed* the player's injury⟩

over·shoe \'ō-vər-ˌshü\ *n* : a shoe (as of rubber) worn over another for protection; *esp* : GALOSH

over·shoot \ˌō-vər-'shüt\ *vb* **-shot** \-'shät\; **-shoot·ing 1** : to miss by going beyond ⟨the plane *overshot* the runway⟩ **2** : to shoot over or beyond ⟨*overshot* the target⟩

over·shot \'ō-vər-ˌshät\ *adj* : moved by water shooting over from above ⟨an *overshot* waterwheel⟩

over·sight \-ˌsīt\ *n* **1** : the act or duty of overseeing : SUPERVISION ⟨have the *oversight* of a job⟩ **2** : an error or a leaving something out through carelessness or haste

over·sim·pli·fy \ˌō-vər-'sim-plə-ˌfī\ *vb* : to simplify something so much that the result is confusing, misleading, or wrong

over·skirt \-ˌskərt\ *n* : a skirt worn over another skirt

over·sleep \ˌō-vər-'slēp\ *vb* **-slept** \-'slept\; **-sleep·ing** : to sleep beyond the usual time or beyond the time set for getting up

over·spread \-'spred\ *vb* **-spread; -spread·ing** : to spread over or above ⟨branches *overspreading* a garden path⟩

over·state \-'stāt\ *vb* : to state in too strong terms : EXAGGERATE — **over·state·ment** \-mənt\ *n*

over·stay \-'stā\ *vb* : to stay beyond the time or the limits of ⟨*overstayed* their welcome⟩

over·step \-'step\ *vb* : to step over or beyond : EXCEED ⟨*overstepped* their authority⟩

over·stock \-'stäk\ *vb* : to stock more than there is need or room for ⟨stores *overstocked* with toys⟩ — **over·stock** \'ō-vər-ˌstäk\ *n*

over·stuffed \ˌō-vər-'stəft\ *adj* **1** : stuffed too full **2** : covered completely and deeply with upholstery ⟨an *overstuffed* chair⟩

over·sub·scribe \-səb-'skrīb\ *vb* : to subscribe for more of than is available ⟨*oversubscribe* a stock issue⟩

over·sup·ply \-sə-'plī\ *n* : a supply that is too large : SURPLUS

overt \ō-'vərt, 'ō-(ˌ)vərt\ *adj* : open to view : not secret — **overt·ly** *adv*

over·take \ˌō-vər-'tāk\ *vb* **-took** \-'tùk\; **-tak·en** \-'tā-kən\; **-tak·ing 1 a** : to catch up with **b** : to catch up with and pass by **2** : to come upon suddenly ⟨a blizzard *overtook* the hunting party⟩

over·throw \-'thrō\ *vb* **-threw** \-'thrü\; **-thrown** \-'thrōn\; **-throw·ing** **1** : OVERTURN 1, UPSET ⟨lawn chairs *overthrown* by the gale⟩ **2** : ¹DEFEAT, DESTROY ⟨a government *overthrown* by rebels⟩ **3** : to throw something (as a ball) over or past ⟨*overthrew* second base⟩ **syn** see CONQUER — **over·throw** \'ō-vər-,thrō\ *n*

over·time \'ō-vər-,tīm\ *n* **1** : time beyond a set limit; *esp* : working time beyond a standard day or week **2** : the wage paid for overtime — **overtime** *adv or adj*

over·tone \-,tōn\ *n* **1** : any of a series of higher tones related to and produced along with a base tone that make up the whole sound of a musical tone **2** : an accompanying result, quality, or meaning : SUGGESTION ⟨the words carried an *overtone* of menace⟩

over·top \,ō-vər-'täp\ *vb* **1** : to rise above the top of : go beyond in height **2** : SURPASS

over·ture \'ō-və(r)-,chů(ə)r, -chər\ *n* **1** : an opening offer : PROPOSAL ⟨the enemy made *overtures* for peace⟩ **2 a** : a musical composition played by the orchestra as the introduction to an opera or musical play **b** : a piece of music in the style of an overture for concert performance

over·turn \,ō-vər-'tərn\ *vb* **1** : to turn over or upside down **2** : INVALIDATE, DESTROY — **over·turn** \'ō-vər-,tərn\ *n*

¹over·use \-'yüz\ *vb* : to use too much ⟨an *overused* phrase⟩

²over·use \-'yüs\ *n* : too much use

over·view \'ō-vər-,vyü\ *n* : a view that includes everything

over·ween·ing \,ō-vər-'wē-niŋ\ *adj* **1** : ARROGANT, CONCEITED **2** : IMMODERATE, EXAGGERATED ⟨*overweening* pride⟩ — **over·ween·ing·ly** *adv*

over·weigh \,ō-vər-'wā\ *vb* : to weigh more than : OVERBALANCE

¹over·weight \'ō-vər-,wāt, *sense 2 is usually* ,ō-vər-'wāt\ *n* **1** : weight above what is required or allowed **2** : bodily weight greater than normal for one's age, height, and build

²over·weight \,ō-vər-'wāt\ *adj* : more than the expected, normal, or proper weight; *esp* : having greater than normal bodily weight for one's age, height, and build

over·whelm \,ō-vər-'hwelm, -'welm\ *vb* **1** : to cover over completely : SUBMERGE ⟨a boat *overwhelmed* by a wave⟩ **2** : to overcome completely : CRUSH ⟨*overwhelmed* by grief⟩

over·whelm·ing \,ō-vər-'hwel-miŋ, -wel-\ *adj* : GREAT 4, EXTREME — **over·whelm·ing·ly** *adv*

over·wind \,ō-vər-'wīnd\ *vb* **-wound** \-'waůnd\; **-wind·ing** : to wind too much

over·win·ter \-'wint-ər\ *vb* : to spend or survive the winter

over·work \-'wərk\ *vb* **1** : to work or cause to work too hard or long ⟨*overworked* the crew⟩ **2** : to use too much ⟨*overworked* phrases⟩ — **overwork** *n*

over·write \,ō-və(r)-'rīt\ *vb* **-wrote** \-'rōt\; **-writ·ten** \-'ritᵉn\; **-writ·ing** \-'rīt-iŋ\ : to write over the surface of : write on top of

over·wrought \,ō-və(r)-'rȯt\ *adj* **1** : extremely excited : AGITATED ⟨*overwrought* feelings⟩ **2** : decorated too much : OVERDONE

ovi·duct \'ō-və-,dəkt\ *n* : a tube for the passage of eggs from the ovary of an animal [from scientific Latin *oviductus* "oviduct", from Latin *ovi-* "egg" (from *ovum* "egg") and Latin *ductus* "tube, duct"]

ovip·a·rous \ō-'vip-(ə-)rəs\ *adj* : producing eggs that develop and hatch outside the body of the female

ovi·pos·i·tor \'ō-və-,päz-ət-ər\ *n* : a specialized organ (as of an insect) for depositing eggs

ovoid \'ō-,vȯid\ *adj* : OVATE

ovu·late \'äv-yə-,lāt, 'ōv-\ *vb* **-lat·ed; -lat·ing** : to produce eggs or release them from an ovary — **ovu·la·tion** \,äv-yə-'lā-shən, ,ōv-\ *n*

ovule \'ō-vyü(-,)l, 'ōv-\ *n* **1** : an outgrowth of the ovary of a seed plant that after fertilization develops into a seed **2** : a small egg; *esp* : one in an early stage of growth

ovum \'ō-vəm\ *n, pl* **ova** \-və\ : ²EGG 1c

ow \'aů, 'ü\ *interj* — used especially to express sudden pain

owe \'ō\ *vb* **owed; ow·ing** **1 a** : to be obligated to pay or repay ⟨*owes* me \$5⟩ **b** : to be indebted to ⟨*owes* the grocer for supplies⟩ **c** : to be in debt ⟨*owes* for her house⟩ **2** : to have or possess as something obtained from or given to ⟨*owes* much to good luck⟩

ow·ing \'ō-iŋ\ *adj* : due to be paid : OWED ⟨have bills *owing*⟩ ⟨claim no more than is *owing*⟩

owing to *prep* : BECAUSE OF ⟨absent *owing to* illness⟩

owl \'aů(ə)l\ *n* : any of an order of birds of prey that are active mainly at night and that have a broad head, very large eyes, and a powerful hooked beak and claws

owl·et \'aů-lət\ *n* : a young or small owl

owl·ish \'aů-lish\ *adj* : resembling or suggesting an owl — **owl·ish·ly** *adv*

¹own \'ōn\ *adj* : belonging to oneself or itself ⟨my *own* room⟩

²own *vb* **1** : to have or hold as property : POSSESS **2** : to admit that something is true : CONFESS ⟨*owned* to being scared⟩ ⟨if you break a window, *own* up⟩ **syn** see ACKNOWLEDGE — **own·er** \'ō-nər\ *n* — **own·er·ship** \-,ship\ *n*

³own *pron sing or pl* : one or ones belonging to oneself — used after a possessive ⟨dog of his *own*⟩ — **on one's own** : without outside help or control ⟨we're *on our own* now⟩ ⟨did the whole thing *on her own*⟩

ox \'äks\ *n, pl* **ox·en** \'äk-sən\ *also* **ox** **1** : an individual of the common large domestic cattle which is kept for milk, draft, and meat and of which the female is a cow and the male a bull; *esp* : an adult castrated male **2** : any of the larger hollow-horned cud-chewing mammals (as the domestic ox, buffaloes, and the yak) that have hoofs with an even number of toes and do not include the related but smaller forms (as sheep and goats)

ox·blood \'äks-,bləd\ *n* : a medium reddish brown

ox·bow \-,bō\ *n* **1** : a U-shaped collar worn by a draft ox **2** : something (as a bend in a river) resembling an oxbow — **oxbow** *adj*

oxbow 1

ox·cart \-,kärt\ *n* : a cart drawn by oxen

ox·eye \'äk-,sī\ *n* : any of several plants related to the asters and having heads with both disk and ray flowers

oxeye daisy *n* : DAISY 1b

ox·ford \'äks-fərd\ *n* : a low shoe laced over the middle of the foot

oxford cloth *n* : a soft strong cotton or synthetic fabric that has a weave like or like that of a basket

ox·i·da·tion \,äk-sə-'dā-shən\ *n* **1** : the process of oxidizing **2** : the state or result of being oxidized — **ox·i·da·tive** \'äk-sə-,dāt-iv\ *adj*

oxidation number *n* : a positive or negative number that represents the effective charge of an atom or element and indicates the extent of or possibility for oxidation of the atom or element ⟨the usual *oxidation number* of sodium is +1 and of oxygen −2⟩

ox·ide \'äk-,sīd\ *n* : a compound of oxygen with another element or chemical group

ox·i·dize \'äk-sə-,dīz\ *vb* **-dized; -diz·ing** **1** : to combine

\ə\ abut	\aů\ out	\i\ tip	\ȯ\ saw	\ů\ foot	
\ər\ further	\ch\ chin	\ī\ life	\ȯi\ coin	\y\ yet	
\a\ mat	\e\ pet	\j\ job	\th\ thin	\yü\ few	
\ā\ take	\ē\ easy	\ŋ\ sing	\th\ this	\yů\ cure	
\ä\ cot, cart	\g\ go	\ō\ bone	\ü\ food	\zh\ vision	

with oxygen **2** : to remove hydrogen from especially by the action of oxygen **3** : to remove one or more electrons from (an atom, ion, or molecule) **4** : to become oxidized — **ox·i·diz·er** *n*

oxy·acet·y·lene \ˌäk-sē-ə-'set-ᵊl-ən, -ᵊl-ˌēn\ *adj* : of, relating to, or using a mixture of oxygen and acetylene ⟨*oxyacetylene* torch⟩

ox·y·gen \'äk-si-jən\ *n* : an element that is found free as a colorless tasteless odorless gas, forms about 21 percent of the atmosphere, is capable of combining with almost all elements, and is necessary for life — see ELEMENT table

> **Word History** Oxygen was discovered by two scientists working independently, Joseph Priestley of England and Carl Scheele of Sweden. However, it was the French chemist Antoine Lavoisier who later gave the gas its name. He said the most common characteristic of this element was its ability to combine with other substances to form acids. For this reason Lavoisier named it *oxygène,* literally meaning "acid producer". The origin of his word was two Greek elements, *oxys,* meaning "sharp, sour", and *-genēs,* meaning "born, generated". [from French *oxygène* "oxygen", literally "acid producer", from *oxy-* "sharp, acid" (from Greek *oxys* "sharp, sour") and *-gène* "one that produces or generates (from Greek *-genēs* "born, generated")]

ox·y·gen·ate \'äk-si-jə-ˌnāt, äk-'sij-ə-\ *vb* **-at·ed; -at·ing** : to combine or supply with oxygen — **ox·y·gen·ation** \ˌäk-si-jə-'nā-shən, äk-ˌsij-ə-\ *n*

oxygen debt *n* : a lack of oxygen that develops in the body during periods of intense activity and must be made good when the body returns to rest

oxygen mask *n* : a device worn over the nose and mouth through which oxygen is supplied from a storage tank

oxygen tent *n* : a flexible enclosure which can be placed over and around a person in bed and within which a flow of oxygen can be maintained

oxy·he·mo·glo·bin \ˌäk-si-'hē-mə-ˌglō-bən\ *n* : a compound of hemoglobin with oxygen that is the chief means of transportation of oxygen from the air (as in the lungs) by way of the blood to the tissues

oyez \ō-'yā, -'yes\ *imperative verb* — used as a call to gain attention before a public announcement

oys·ter \'ȯi-stər\ *n* : any of various marine mollusks that include important edible shellfish and have a rough uneven shell made up of two hinged parts and closed by a single muscle

oyster bed *n* : a place where oysters grow or are cultivated

ozone \'ō-ˌzōn\ *n* **1** : a form of oxygen that is a bluish irritating sharp-smelling gas containing three atoms per molecule, is generated commercially by a silent electric discharge in ordinary oxygen or air, and is used especially in disinfecting, deodorizing, and bleaching **2** : pure and refreshing air

ozone hole *n* : an area of the ozone layer (as near the south pole) that is seasonally depleted of ozone

ozone layer *n* : a layer of the earth's atmosphere at heights of about 32 to 48 kilometers that is normally characterized by high ozone content which blocks most of the sun's ultraviolet radiation from entry into the lower atmosphere

P

p \'pē\ *n, often cap* : the 16th letter of the English alphabet

pa \'pä, 'pȯ\ *n* : ¹FATHER 1a

¹pace \'pās\ *n* **1 a** : rate of moving especially on foot **b** : rate of progress ⟨the *pace* of the story was slow⟩ **2 a** : a manner of going on foot : GAIT **b** : a fast gait of a horse in which legs on the same side move together **3** : a single step or a measure based on the length of a human step

²pace *vb* **paced; pac·ing** **1** : to walk with slow steady steps **2** : to go or cover at a pace ⟨*pace* the floor⟩ **3** : to measure by paces **4** : to set or regulate the pace of — **pac·er** *n*

pace·mak·er \'pā-ˌsmā-kər\ *n* **1** : a bodily part (as of the heart) that serves to establish and maintain a bodily activity **2** : an electrical device for steadying or establishing the heartbeat

pachy·derm \'pak-i-ˌdərm\ *n* : any of various thick-skinned hoofed mammals (as an elephant or a rhinoceros)

pa·cif·ic \pə-'sif-ik\ *adj* **1** : tending to lessen or avoid fights or disagreements **2** : having a peaceful nature — **pa·cif·i·cal·ly** \-i-k(ə-)lē\ *adv*

Pacific time *n* : the time of the 8th time zone west of Greenwich that includes the Pacific coastal region of the U.S. — see TIME ZONE illustration

pac·i·fi·er \'pas-ə-ˌfī-(ə)r\ *n* **1** : one that pacifies **2** : a usually nipple-shaped device for babies to suck or bite on

pac·i·fism \'pas-ə-ˌfiz-əm\ *n* : opposition to war or violence as a means of settling disputes — **pac·i·fist** \-fəst\ *n*

pac·i·fy \'pas-ə-ˌfī\ *vb* **-fied; -fy·ing** **1** : to make peaceful or quiet ⟨*pacify* a crying child⟩ **2** : to restore to a peaceful state : SETTLE, SUBDUE [Middle English *pacifien* "to soothe the anger or disturbance of, make peaceful", from Latin *pacificare* (same meaning), from *pac-, pax* "peace" — related to APPEASE, PEACE] — **pac·i·fi·ca·tion** \ˌpas-ə-fə-'kā-shən\ *n*

syn PACIFY, MOLLIFY, APPEASE, PLACATE mean to calm the feelings of. PACIFY suggests the quieting of persons who are upset or angry ⟨*pacify* a crying baby with a toy⟩ MOLLIFY suggests a comforting of hurt feelings ⟨an apology would probably *mollify* your friend⟩ APPEASE suggests dealing with another's anger or threats by giving in to demands ⟨some were willing to *appease* the dictator in order to keep peace⟩ PLACATE suggests changing anger or bitterness to goodwill ⟨the builders *placated* the people of the neighborhood by including a playground in their plans⟩

¹pack \'pak\ *n* **1 a** : a bundle arranged for carrying especially on the back of a person or animal **b** : a group of items packaged as a unit ⟨a *pack* of cards⟩ **c** : PACKET 2, CONTAINER **d** : a stack of magnetic disks in a container for use as a storage device **2** : the contents of a pack **3 a** : a group of similar persons or animals ⟨a *pack* of thieves⟩ ⟨a wolf *pack*⟩ **b** : an organized troop ⟨a *pack* of Cub Scouts⟩ **4** : a tight mass or group; *esp* : a mass of ice chunks floating on the sea **5** : absorbent material (as gauze pads) used to press upon a bodily part, to plug body cavities in order to stop bleeding, or to apply medicine [Middle English *pack* "a bundle for carrying on the back"; of Germanic origin]

²pack *vb* **1 a** : to place articles in (as for transportation or storage) ⟨*pack* a suitcase⟩ **b** : to cover or fill so as to prevent passage (as of air or water) ⟨*pack* the joint of a pipe⟩ **c** : to place closely and securely in a container or bundle ⟨*pack* goods⟩ **2 a** : to crowd in ⟨people *packed* the hall⟩ **b** : to form into a pack ⟨ice is *packing* in the gorge⟩ **3** : to send or go away without delay ⟨*pack* a child off to school⟩ **4** : to transport in packs **5** : ¹CARRY 6 ⟨*pack* a gun⟩ **6** : to prepare (foods) for sale

syn PACK, CRAM, STUFF mean to fill something to its limit or beyond. PACK may suggest filling something up in a way that is tight but orderly ⟨*pack* a trunk⟩ or it may suggest filling something too much ⟨people were *packed* into the room like sardines⟩ CRAM usually suggests that something has been filled in a forceful, careless, or disorderly way ⟨*crammed* everything into one small box⟩ STUFF suggests filling something with as much as it will hold and often to the point that it bulges ⟨I *stuffed* my pockets with apples⟩

³**pack** *vb* : to choose or bring together dishonestly so as to be assured of a favorable vote ⟨*pack* a jury⟩ [probably from obsolete *pack* "a secret agreement", from *pact* "agreement, treaty"]

¹**pack·age** \'pak-ij\ *n* **1** : a small or medium-sized pack : PARCEL **2** : a covering wrapper or container **3** : PACKAGE DEAL **4** : a collection of related items to be considered together

²**package** *vb* **pack·aged; pack·ag·ing** : to make into or enclose in a package — **pack·ag·er** *n*

package deal *n* : an offer containing several items all or none of which must be accepted

package store *n* : a store that sells alcoholic beverages only in containers that may not be opened in the store

pack animal *n* : an animal (as a horse or donkey) used for carrying packs

packed \'pakt\ *adj* : that is crowded or stuffed — often used in combination ⟨an action-*packed* story⟩

pack·er \'pak-ər\ *n* : one that packs; *esp* : a dealer who prepares and packs foods for the market

pack·et \'pak-ət\ *n* **1** : a passenger boat carrying mail and cargo on a regular schedule **2** : a small bundle or parcel

pack ice *n* : sea ice formed into a mass by the crushing together of chunks and sheets of ice

pack·ing·house \'pak-iŋ-,haus\ *n* : an establishment for preparing foods and especially meat

pack rat *n* : WOOD RAT; *esp* : a large bushy-tailed rodent of the Rocky mountain area that stores food and loose objects

pack rat

pack·sad·dle \'pak-,sad-ᵊl\ *n* : a saddle that supports the load on the back of a pack animal

pack·thread \-,thred\ *n* : strong thread or twine used especially for sewing or tying packs or parcels

pact \'pakt\ *n* : AGREEMENT 2; *esp* : a treaty between countries [Middle English *pact* "agreement", from early French *pact* (same meaning), from Latin *pactum* (same meaning), derived from *pacisci* "to agree, contract"]

¹**pad** \'pad\ *vb* **pad·ded; pad·ding** **1** : to go on foot **2** : to move along with a muffled step [probably from early Dutch *paden* "to follow a path"]

²**pad** *n* **1 a** : something soft used for protection or comfort : CUSHION **b** : a piece of material that holds ink for inking a rubber stamp **2 a** : the hairy foot of some mammals (as a fox or hare) **b** : the soft thickening of the underside of the toes of some mammals **3** : a floating leaf of a water plant **4** : a number of sheets of writing paper glued together at one edge **5** : LAUNCH PAD **6 a** : living quarters : HOME **b** : ¹BED 1a [origin unknown]

³**pad** *vb* **pad·ded; pad·ding** **1** : to furnish with a pad or padding **2** : to expand with unnecessary or unimportant material ⟨*pad* a speech⟩

⁴**pad** *n* : a soft muffled or slapping sound

pad·ding \'pad-iŋ\ *n* : material used to pad something

¹**pad·dle** \'pad-ᵊl\ *vb* **pad·dled; pad·dling** \'pad-liŋ, -ᵊl-iŋ\ : to move the hands or feet about in shallow water [origin unknown]

²**paddle** *n* **1** : an instrument with a flat blade to move and steer a small boat (as a canoe) **2 a** : an instrument used for stirring, mixing, or beating **b** : a short bat with a broad flat blade used to hit the ball in various games (as table tennis) **c** : a small hand-held device with a dial used to control movement of an object along a line on a computer display screen **3** : one of the broad boards at the outer rim of a paddle wheel or waterwheel [Middle English *padell* "a device for cleaning a plow"]

³**paddle** *vb* **pad·dled; pad·dling** \'pad-liŋ, -ᵊl-iŋ\ **1** : to move or drive forward with or as if with a paddle **2** : to stir or mix with a paddle **3** : to beat with or as if with a paddle

paddle wheel *n* : a wheel with boards around its outer edge used to move a vessel

pad·dock \'pad-ək, -ik\ *n* **1** : an enclosed area where animals are put to eat grass or to exercise **2** : an enclosed area where racehorses are saddled and paraded

pad·dy \'pad-ē\ *n, pl* **paddies** : wet land in which rice is grown

pad·dy wagon \'pad-ē-\ *n* : PATROL WAGON

pad·lock \'pad-,läk\ *n* : a removable lock with a curved piece that snaps into a catch — **padlock** *vb*

pa·dre \'päd-rā, -rē\ *n* **1** : PRIEST **2** : a military chaplain [from Spanish or Italian or Portuguese *padre* "priest", all from Latin *pater* "bishop", from earlier *pater* "father" — related to PATERNAL, PATRON, PATTERN]

pae·an \'pē-ən\ *n* : a song of joy, praise, or triumph

pa·gan \'pā-gən\ *n* **1** : HEATHEN 1 **2** : a person who is not religious — **pagan** *adj* — **pa·gan·ism** \-gə-,niz-əm\ *n*

Word History In ancient Rome a person living in a rural area or village was called *paganus*, a word derived from the Latin noun *pagus*, meaning "village, district". In time *paganus* came to refer to a civilian as opposed to a soldier. When Christianity became generally accepted in the towns and cities of the empire, *paganus* was used to refer to a villager who continued to worship the old gods. Christians used the term for anyone not of their faith or of the Jewish faith. The word in Old English for such a person was what is now *heathen*. In the 14th century, English borrowed the Latin *paganus* as *pagan*, and used it with the same meaning. In time both *heathen* and *pagan* also took on the meaning of "a person having no religion". [Middle English *pagan* "heathen", from Latin *paganus* (same meaning), from earlier *paganus* "person who lives in a rural area", from *pagus* "village, district"]

¹**page** \'pāj\ *n* **1** : a youth in the Middle Ages being trained for knighthood and in the service of a knight **2** : a youth serving a person of rank **3** : a person employed especially to deliver messages or perform personal services (as in a hotel) [Middle English *page* "a youth trained to serve a knight", from early French *page* (same meaning), from Italian *paggio* (same meaning), perhaps derived from Greek *pais* "child, boy"]

²**page** *vb* **paged; pag·ing** **1** : to serve as a page **2** : to send for by calling out the name of

³**page** *n* **1 a** : one side of a printed or written leaf **b** : the entire leaf **c** : the material printed or written on a page **2 a** : a written record **b** : an event worth recording **3** : a large section of computer memory [from early French *page* "a leaf in a book", from Latin *pagina* (same meaning)]

⁴**page** *vb* **paged; pag·ing** **1** : to number or mark the pages of **2** : to turn the pages (as of a book or magazine) especially in a quick steady manner

\ə\ abut	\au\ out	\i\ tip	\o\ saw	\u̇\ foot
\ər\ further	\ch\ chin	\ī\ life	\oi\ coin	\y\ yet
\a\ mat	\e\ pet	\j\ job	\th\ thin	\yü\ few
\ā\ take	\ē\ easy	\ŋ\ sing	\t͟h\ this	\yu̇\ cure
\ä\ cot, cart	\g\ go	\ō\ bone	\ü\ food	\zh\ vision

pag·eant \'paj-ənt\ *n*   **1** : an impressive exhibition or spectacle   **2** : an entertainment consisting of scenes based on history or legend

pag·eant·ry \'paj-ən-trē\ *n, pl* **-tries**   **1** : pageants and the presentation of pageants   **2** : splendid display

pag·er \'pā-jər\ *n* : one that pages; *esp* : BEEPER

pa·go·da \pə-'gōd-ə\ *n* : a Far Eastern tower of several stories erected as a temple or memorial

¹paid \'pād\ *past and past participle of* PAY

²paid *adj* : being or having been paid or paid for ⟨a *paid* political announcement⟩

pail \'pā(ə)l\ *n*   **1** : a round container that is open at the top and has a handle : BUCKET   **2** : the quantity held by a pail ⟨fetch a pail of water⟩

pail·ful \'pā(ə)l-ˌfu̇l\ *n* : PAIL 2

¹pain \'pān\ *n*   **1** : PUNISHMENT 2 ⟨under *pain* of death⟩   **2 a** : physical suffering associated with disease, injury, or other bodily disorder ⟨a *pain* in the back⟩

pagoda

b : a basic bodily sensation that is caused by something harmful, is accompanied by physical discomfort (as pricking, throbbing, or aching), and usually makes one try to escape its source   **3** : mental distress : GRIEF   **4** *pl* : the suffering experienced during childbirth   **5** *pl* : great care or effort ⟨took *pains* with their work⟩ — **pain·less** \-ləs\ *adj* — **pain·less·ly** *adv*

²pain *vb*   **1** : to cause pain in or to : HURT   **2** : to give or feel pain

pain·ful \'pān-fəl\ *adj* : feeling or giving pain — **pain·ful·ly** \-f(ə-)lē\ *adv* — **pain·ful·ness** \-fəl-nəs\ *n*

pain·kill·er \'pān-ˌkil-ər\ *n* : something (as a drug) that relieves pain — **pain·kill·ing** \-iŋ\ *adj*

pains·tak·ing \'pān-ˌstā-kiŋ\ *adj* : taking or showing great care and effort ⟨a *painstaking* search⟩ — **pains·tak·ing·ly** \-kiŋ-lē\ *adv*

¹paint \'pānt\ *vb*   **1** : to apply paint or a covering or coloring substance to ⟨*paint* a wall⟩   **2 a** : to make a picture or design by using paints ⟨*paint* a portrait⟩   **b** : to describe clearly ⟨*paint* a scene in words⟩   **3** : to practice the art of painting

²paint *n*   **1** : MAKEUP 2   **2** : a mixture of coloring matter and a suitable liquid to form a thin coating when spread on a surface

paint·brush \'pānt-ˌbrəsh\ *n*   **1** : a brush for applying paint   **2** : INDIAN PAINTBRUSH 1

painted bunting *n* : a brightly colored finch of the southern U.S.

painted lady *n* : a butterfly with brown, orange, red, and white wings that migrates long distances

painted turtle *n* : any of several common freshwater turtles that are found chiefly in the eastern U.S. and have a greenish black upper shell with yellow bands and red markings and a yellow lower shell

¹paint·er \'pānt-ər\ *n* : one that paints; *esp* : an artist who paints [from *paint* (verb) and *-er* (noun suffix)]

²pain·ter *n* : a line used for attaching or towing a boat [Middle English *paynter* "a line used for securing a boat", probably from early French *pendoir, pentoir* "clothesline"]

³pain·ter *n* : COUGAR [an altered form of *panther*]

paint·ing *n*   **1** : a painted work of art   **2** : the art or occupation of painting

¹pair \'pa(ə)r, 'pe(ə)r\ *n, pl* **pairs** *also* **pair**   **1** : two things that match or are meant to be used together ⟨a *pair* of hands⟩ ⟨a *pair* of gloves⟩   **2** : a thing having two connected matching parts ⟨a *pair* of scissors⟩   **3** : a set of two like or associated things [Middle English *paire* "two things

that match or go together", from early French *paire* (same meaning), from Latin *paria* "equal things", derived from *par* "equal" — related to COMPARE, PAR, PEER, UMPIRE; see *Word History* at UMPIRE]

²pair *vb*   **1** : to make a pair of or arrange in pairs ⟨*paired* off the animals⟩   **2** : to form a pair or pairs ⟨*paired* off for the next dance⟩

pais·ley \'pāz-lē\ *adj, often cap* : made with colorful curved figures ⟨a *paisley* shawl⟩ — **pais·ley** *n*

Pai·ute \'pī-ˌ(y)üt\ *n* : a member of an American Indian people originally of Utah, Arizona, Nevada, and California

pa·ja·mas \pə-'jäm-əz, -'jam-\ *n pl* : a loose lightweight usually two-piece garment worn for sleeping or lounging [from *pājama,* a word in Hindi, the principal language in India, meaning "loose lightweight trousers", from Persian *pā* "leg" and Persian *jāma* "garment"]

¹pal \'pal\ *n* : a close friend

²pal *vb* **palled; pal·ling** : to be or become pals

pal·ace \'pal-əs\ *n*   **1** : the official residence of a ruler   **2** : a large splendid house   **3** : a large public building (as for a legislature, court, or governor) [Middle English *palais* "palace", from early French *palais* (same meaning), from Latin *palatium* (same meaning), from *Palatium,* name of one of the Seven Hills of Rome on which the Caesars had their residences]

pal·a·din \'pal-əd-ən\ *n* : a person who fights for a cause as a knight fought for a king in the Middle Ages

pa·lan·quin \ˌpal-ən-'kēn, -'k(w)in, pə-'laŋ-kwən\ *n* : a boxlike structure in which a person is carried on the shoulders of servants using poles

pal·at·able \'pal-ət-ə-bəl\ *adj*   **1** : agreeable to the taste   **2** : AGREEABLE 1, ACCEPTABLE — **pal·at·abil·i·ty** \ˌpal-ət-ə-'bil-ət-ē\ *n* — **pal·at·ably** \'pal-ət-ə-blē\ *adv*

pal·ate \'pal-ət\ *n*   **1** : the roof of the mouth that separates the mouth from the nasal cavity and is made up of a bony front part and a soft flexible back part   **2** : the sense of taste

pa·la·tial \pə-'lā-shəl\ *adj* : of, resembling, or fit for a palace — **pa·la·tial·ly** \-shə-lē\ *adv*

¹pa·la·ver \pə-'lav-ər, -'läv-\ *n*   **1** : a long discussion usually between persons of different levels of culture   **2** : ²TALK 1; *esp* : idle or flattering talk

²palaver *vb* **pa·la·vered; pa·la·ver·ing** \-(ə-)riŋ\ : to talk especially at length or idly

¹pale \'pā(ə)l\ *adj* **pal·er; pal·est**   **1 a** : light in color or shade : not vivid ⟨a *pale* pink⟩   **b** : not having the warm skin color of a person in good health : WAN ⟨became *pale*⟩   **2** : not bright or brilliant : DIM [Middle English *pale* "lacking in color", from early French *pale* (same meaning), from Latin *pallidus* (same meaning), from *pallēre* "to be pale"] — **pale·ly** *adv* — **pale·ness** *n*

²pale *vb* **paled; pal·ing** : to make or become pale

³pale *n*   **1** : a stake or picket of a fence   **2** : an enclosed place   **3** : territory within clearly marked bounds or under a particular authority [Middle English *pale* "paling, picket", from early French *pal* "stake", from Latin *palus* (same meaning) — related to TRAVEL; see *Word History* at TRAVEL]

pale·face \'pā(ə)l-ˌfās\ *n* : a white person : CAUCASIAN

Pa·leo·cene \'pā-lē-ə-ˌsēn\ *adj* : of, relating to, or being the earliest epoch of the Tertiary period of geological history or the corresponding system of rocks — see GEOLOGIC TIME table — **Paleocene** *n*

Pa·leo·lith·ic \ˌpā-lē-ə-'lith-ik\ *adj* : of, relating to, or being the second period of the Stone Age marked by rough or crudely chipped stone implements

pa·le·on·tol·o·gist \ˌpā-lē-ˌän-'täl-ə-jəst\ *n* : a specialist in paleontology

pa·le·on·tol·o·gy \ˌpā-lē-ˌän-'täl-ə-jē\ *n* : a science dealing with the life of past geological periods as known especially from fossil remains — **pa·le·on·to·log·i·cal** \-ˌänt-ᵊl-'äj-i-kəl\ *or* **pa·le·on·to·log·ic** \-ik\ *adj*

Pa·leo·zo·ic \,pā-lē-ə-'zō-ik\ *adj* : of, relating to, or being an era of geological history ending about 245,000,000 years ago in which vertebrates and land plants first appeared; *also* : relating to the corresponding system of rocks — see GEOLOGIC TIME table — **Paleozoic** *n*

pal·ette \'pal-ət\ *n* **1** : a thin usually oval board or tablet with a hole for the thumb at one end used by a painter to lay and mix pigments on **2** : the colors put on the palette

pal·frey \'pòl-frē\ *n, pl* **pal·freys** *archaic* : a saddle horse that is not a war horse

pal·in·drome \'pal-ən-,drōm\ *n* : a word, phrase, or sentence (as "Step on no pets") or a number (as 1881) that reads the same backward or forward

palette 1

pal·ing \'pā-liŋ\ *n* **1** : ³PALE 1, PICKET **2** : pales or a fence of pales

¹pal·i·sade \,pal-ə-'sād\ *n* **1 a** : a stout high fence of stakes especially for defense **b** : a long strong pointed stake set close with others as a defense **2** : a line of steep cliffs

²palisade *vb* **-sad·ed; -sad·ing** : to surround or protect with palisades

palisade cell *n* : a cell of the palisade layer

palisade layer *n* : a layer of cylinder-shaped cells that are rich in chloroplasts, have small spaces between the cells, and are usually found just beneath the upper epidermis of leaves

¹pall \'pòl\ *n* **1** : a heavy cloth covering for a coffin, hearse, or tomb **2** : a chalice cover made of a square piece of stiffened linen **3** : something that covers, darkens, or produces a gloomy effect

²pall *vb* : to become dull or uninteresting : lose the ability to give pleasure ⟨the excitement of the party quickly began to *pall*⟩

pal·la·di·um \pə-'lād-ē-əm\ *n* : a silver-white metallic element that is used especially in alloys — see ELEMENT table

pall·bear·er \'pòl-,bar-ər, -,ber-\ *n* : a person who helps to carry the coffin at a funeral

palled *past and past participle of* PAL

pal·let \'pal-ət\ *n* **1** : a straw-filled mattress **2** : a small, hard, or temporary bed

pal·li·ate \'pal-ē-,āt\ *vb* **-at·ed; -at·ing** **1** : to make less harmful or harsh **2** : to find excuses for : EXCUSE

¹pal·li·a·tive \'pal-ē-,āt-iv, 'pal-yət-\ *adj* : serving to palliate

²palliative *n* : something that palliates

pal·lid \'pal-əd\ *adj* : lacking healthy color : PALE — **pal·lid·ly** *adv*

palling *present participle of* PAL

pal·lor \'pal-ər\ *n* : paleness especially of the face

¹palm \'päm, 'pälm\ *n* **1** : any of a family of mostly tropical or subtropical woody trees, shrubs, or vines usually with a simple but often tall stem topped by a crown of huge feathery or fan-shaped leaves **2 a** : a palm leaf especially when carried as a symbol of victory or rejoicing **b** : an emblem of success or triumph [Old English *palm* "palm tree", from Latin *palma* "palm of the hand"; so called because the leaves resemble an outstretched hand] — **palm·like** \-,līk\ *adj*

²palm *n* **1** : the under part of the hand between the fingers and the wrist **2** : a measure of length based on the width or length of the palm [Middle English *paume* "palm of the hand", from early French *paume* (same meaning), from Latin *palma* "palm of the hand"]

³palm *vb* : to conceal in or pick up secretly with the hand

pal·mate \'pal-,māt, 'pälm-,āt, 'pam-\ *adj* : resembling a hand with the fingers spread ⟨*palmate* leaves⟩

palm·er \'päm-ər, 'pāl-mər\ *n* : a person wearing two crossed palm leaves as a sign of having gone on a pilgrimage to the Holy Land

pal·met·to \pal-'met-ō\ *n, pl* **-tos** or **-toes** : any of several usually low-growing palms with fan-shaped leaves

palm·ist·ry \'päm-ə-strē, 'pāl-mə-\ *n* : the art or practice of reading a person's character or future from markings on the palm of the hand — **palm·ist** \'päm-əst, 'pāl-məst\ *n*

palm off *vb* : to get rid of or pass on (as something fake, useless, or of poor quality) in a dishonest way ⟨*palmed off* fake antiques on unsuspecting customers⟩

Palm Sunday *n* : the Sunday before Easter celebrated in memory of Jesus' entry into Jerusalem

palmy \'päm-ē, 'pāl-mē\ *adj* **palm·i·er; -est** **1** : having palms ⟨a *palmy* beach⟩ **2** : marked by success : PROSPEROUS

pal·o·mi·no \,pal-ə-'mē-nō\ *n, pl* **-nos** : a horse with a light golden coat and cream or white mane and tail

pal·pa·ble \'pal-pə-bəl\ *adj* **1** : capable of being touched or felt : TANGIBLE **2** : easily sensed : NOTICEABLE **3** : easily understood or recognized : OBVIOUS ⟨a *palpable* error⟩ — **pal·pa·bil·i·ty** \,pal-pə-'bil-ət-ē\ *n* — **pal·pa·bly** \'pal-pə-blē\ *adv*

pal·pi·tate \'pal-pə-,tāt\ *vb* **-tat·ed; -tat·ing** : to beat rapidly and strongly : THROB, QUIVER

pal·pi·ta·tion \,pal-pə-'tā-shən\ *n* : an act or instance of palpitating; *esp* : an abnormally rapid beating of the heart

pal·pus \'pal-pəs\ *n, pl* **pal·pi** \-,pī, -,pē\ : a part that sticks out from a mouthpart of an arthropod and is used in sensing by touch or in feeding

pal·sied \'pòl-zēd\ *adj* : affected with or as if with palsy

pal·sy \'pòl-zē\ *n* **1** : PARALYSIS **2** : a condition marked by uncontrollable trembling or shaking of the body or a part (as the head or hands)

pal·ter \'pòl-tər\ *vb* **pal·tered; pal·ter·ing** \-t(ə-)riŋ\ **1** : to act or speak insincerely **2** : HAGGLE, BARGAIN — **pal·ter·er** \-tər-ər\ *n*

pal·try \'pòl-trē\ *adj* **pal·tri·er; -est** **1** : PETTY 3, MEAN ⟨a *paltry* trick⟩ **2** : TRIVIAL 2, WORTHLESS ⟨a *paltry* sum⟩ — **pal·tri·ness** *n*

pam·pas \'pam-pəz, -pəs\ *n pl* : wide generally grass-covered plains of South America

pam·per \'pam-pər\ *vb* **pam·pered; pam·per·ing** \-p(ə-)riŋ\ : to treat with too much care and attention

pam·phlet \'pam(p)-flət\ *n* : a short printed publication with no cover or with a paper cover

pam·phle·teer \,pam(p)-flə-'ti(ə)r\ *n* : a writer of pamphlets usually attacking something or urging a cause — **pamphleteer** *vb*

¹pan \'pan\ *n* **1 a** : a usually broad, shallow, and open container for cooking **b** : something resembling a pan **2** : a basin or depression in the earth ⟨a salt *pan*⟩ [Old English *panne* "pan for cooking", from Latin *patina* (same meaning)]

²pan *vb* **panned; pan·ning** **1** : to wash earthy material in a pan to concentrate bits of metal ⟨*pan* for gold⟩ **2** : to yield precious metal in panning **3** : to criticize severely

³pan *vb* **panned; pan·ning** : to move a motion-picture or television camera so as to keep a moving object in view or to scan a scene [derived from *panorama*]

pan·a·cea \,pan-ə-'sē-ə\ *n* : a remedy for all ills or difficulties : CURE-ALL

pan·a·ma \'pan-ə-,mä, -,mò\ *n, often cap* : a lightweight hat made of narrow strips from the young leaves of a trop-

\ə\ abut		\aù\ out	\i\ tip	\ò\ saw	\ù\ foot
\ər\ further		\ch\ chin	\ī\ life	\òi\ coin	\y\ yet
\a\ mat		\e\ pet	\j\ job	\th\ thin	\yü\ few
\ā\ take		\ē\ easy	\ŋ\ sing	\th\ this	\yü\ cure
\ä\ cot, cart		\g\ go	\ō\ bone	\ü\ food	\zh\ vision

ical American tree

Pan–Amer·i·can \ˌpan-ə-ˈmer-ə-kən\ *adj* : of, relating to, or involving the independent republics of North and South America

pan·broil \ˈpan-ˌbroi(ə)l\ *vb* : to cook uncovered on a hot metal surface (as a frying pan) with little or no fat

pan·cake \ˈpan-ˌkāk\ *n* : a flat cake made of thin batter and cooked on both sides on a griddle or in a frying pan

pan·chro·mat·ic \ˌpan-krō-ˈmat-ik\ *adj* : sensitive to light of all colors in the visible spectrum ⟨*panchromatic* film⟩

pan·cre·as \ˈpaŋ-krē-əs, ˈpan-\ *n* : a large compound gland of vertebrates that lies near the stomach and produces digestive enzymes and insulin — **pan·cre·at·ic** \ˌpaŋ-krē-ˈat-ik, ˌpan-\ *adj*

pancreatic duct *n* : a duct leading from the pancreas and opening into the duodenum

pancreatic juice *n* : a clear digestive fluid containing enzymes produced by the pancreas that is poured into the duodenum

pan·da \ˈpan-də\ *n* **1** : a reddish animal that is smaller than the related panda **2** : a large black-and-white mammal of Tibet that looks like a bear but is related to the raccoon

¹pan·dem·ic \pan-ˈdem-ik\ *adj* : occurring over a wide area and affecting many individuals ⟨*pandemic* malaria⟩

²pandemic *n* : a pandemic outbreak of a disease

panda: *left* 1, *right* 2

pan·de·mo·ni·um \ˌpan-də-ˈmō-nē-əm\ *n* : a wild uproar : TUMULT [from *Pandemonium*, name of the place of demons in *Paradise Lost* by John Milton, derived from Greek *pan-* "all, every, completely" and Greek *daimon* "devil, demon"]

pan·der \ˈpan-dər\ *or* **pan·der·er** \-dər-ər\ *n* : one who takes advantage of or profits from the weaknesses and mean desires of others — **pander** *vb*

pane \ˈpān\ *n* **1** : a piece, section, or side of something (as a sheet of glass in a window) **2** : one of the sections (as of 50 or 100 stamps) into which a sheet of postage stamps is divided

pan·e·gy·ric \ˌpan-ə-ˈjir-ik, -ˈjī-rik\ *n* : formal or elaborate praise

¹pan·el \ˈpan-ᵊl\ *n* **1 a** : a list or a group of persons selected as jurors **b** : a group of persons who discuss a topic before an audience **c** : a group of entertainers or guests who are players in a quiz or guessing game on a radio or television program **2** : a separate or different part of a surface: as **a** : a usually rectangular and sunken or raised section of a door, wall, or ceiling **b** : a flat usually rectangular piece of construction material (as plywood) made to form part of a surface **c** : a lengthwise section of cloth (as in a skirt or dress) **3 a** : a thin flat piece of wood on which a picture is painted **b** : a painting on such a surface **4** : a usually vertical mount for controls or dials (as of instruments of measurement)

²panel *vb* **-eled** *or* **-elled; -el·ing** *or* **-el·ling** : to furnish or decorate with panels

pan·el·ing \ˈpan-ᵊl-iŋ\ *n* : panels joined in a continuous surface

pan·el·ist \ˈpan-ᵊl-əst\ *n* : a member of a panel

pan·fish \ˈpan-ˌfish\ *n* : a small food fish (as a sunfish) usually caught with a hook and line but not sold on the market

pan·fry \ˈpan-ˌfrī, pan-ˈfrī\ *vb* **pan·fried; pan·fry·ing** : to cook in a frying pan with a small amount of fat

pang \ˈpaŋ\ *n* : a sudden sharp attack of pain or distress ⟨hunger *pangs*⟩

pan·go·lin \ˈpaŋ-gə-lən, ˈpan-\ *n* : any of several Asian and African mammals having the body covered with large overlapping horny scales

pangolin

¹pan·han·dle \ˈpan-ˌhan-dᵊl\ *n* : a narrow strip of territory that extends from a larger territory (as a state) ⟨the Texas *Panhandle*⟩

²panhandle *vb* **-dled; -dling** \-ˌhan-(d)liŋ, -dᵊl-iŋ\ : to beg for money on the street — **pan·han·dler** \-(d)lər, -dᵊl-ər\ *n*

¹pan·ic \ˈpan-ik\ *n* **1** : a sudden overpowering fright especially without reasonable cause **2** : a sudden widespread fright concerning financial affairs causing hurried selling and a sharp fall in prices — **panic** *adj* — **pan·icky** \ˈpan-i-kē\ *adj*

Word History The ancient Greeks worshiped a god of pastures, flocks, and shepherds whom they named *Pan*. Pan was believed to be able to cause great fear at times. The people of Athens believed that it was Pan who had caused the Persians to flee in terror from the battle of Marathon. The Greek adjective *panikos*, literally meaning "of Pan", was used to describe the kind of sudden fear that Pan was thought to cause. The English word *panic* comes from the Greek *panikos*. [probably from earlier *panic* (adjective), from French *panique* (adjective) "wild, panicky", from Greek *panikos* "relating to the fear caused by Pan", from *Pan,* name of a god of woods and shepherds]

²panic *vb* **pan·icked** \-ikt\; **pan·ick·ing** : to affect or be affected with panic

pan·i·cle \ˈpan-i-kəl\ *n* : a branched flower cluster (as of a lilac or some grasses) in which each branch from the main stem has one or more flowers

pan·ic-strick·en \ˈpan-ik-ˌstrik-ən\ *adj* : overcome with panic

panned *past and past participle of* PAN

pan·nier \ˈpan-yər, ˈpan-ē-ər\ *n* : a large basket; *esp* : one carried on the back of an animal or the shoulder of a person

panning *present participle of* PAN

pan·o·ply \ˈpan-ə-plē\ *n, pl* **-plies** **1** : a full suit of armor **2** : a protective covering **3** : a magnificent arrangement or display — **pan·o·plied** \-plēd\ *adj*

pan·ora·ma \ˌpan-ə-ˈram-ə, -ˈräm-\ *n* **1** : a picture shown a part at a time by being unrolled before the spectator **2** : a full and clear view in every direction **3** : a complete presentation of a subject — **pan·oram·ic** \-ˈram-ik\ *adj*

pan out *vb* : TURN OUT 5; *esp* : to give a good result : SUCCEED

pan·pipe \ˈpan-ˌpīp\ *n* : a musical instrument made up of several short pipes of different lengths fixed together and played by blowing air across the top — usually used in pl.

pan·sy \ˈpan-zē\ *n, pl* **pansies** : a garden plant that is related to the violets and has large velvety flowers with five petals usually in shades of yellow, purple, or brownish red; *also* : its flower

panpipe

pant \ˈpant\ *vb* **1 a** : to breathe hard or quickly : GASP **b** : to make a puffing sound **c** : to move forward with panting ⟨the car *panted* up the hill⟩ **2** : to wish for eagerly : YEARN **3** : to utter with panting ⟨ran up and *panted* out the message⟩ — **pant** *n*

pan·ta·loons \,pant-ªl-'ünz\ *n pl* : close-fitting trousers usually with straps passing under the insteps

pan·ther \'pan(t)-thər\ *n, pl* **panthers** *also* **panther** **1** : LEOPARD; *esp* : one of the black form **2** : COUGAR **3** : JAGUAR

pant·ie *or* **panty** \'pant-ē\ *n, pl* **pant·ies** : a woman's or child's undergarment covering the lower trunk — usually used in pl.

pan·to·graph \'pant-ə-,graf\ *n* : an instrument for copying a figure (as a map or plan) by hand using a previously chosen scale

pan·to·mime \'pant-ə-,mīm\ *n* **1** : PANTOMIMIST **2** : a performance in which a story is told by expressive movements of the body or face **3** : expression of information by movements of the body or face — **pantomime** *vb*

pan·to·mim·ist \'pant-ə-,mim-əst, -,mīm-\ *n* : an actor or dancer in pantomimes

pan·to·the·nate \,pant-ə-'then-,āt, pan-'täth-ə-,nāt\ *n* : a compound formed by the reaction of pantothenic acid with another substance

pan·to·then·ic acid \,pant-ə-,then-ik-\ *n* : an oily acid of the vitamin B complex found in all living tissues and necessary for growth

pan·try \'pan-trē\ *n, pl* **pantries** : a small room in which food and dishes are kept [Middle English *panetrie* "pantry", derived from early French *panetier* "servant in charge of food or bread", from *pan* "bread", from Latin *panis* "bread, food" — related to COMPANION]

pants \'pan(t)s\ *n pl* **1** : an outer garment extending from the waist to the ankle and covering each leg separately : TROUSERS **2** : UNDERPANTS; *esp* : PANTIE

Word History A form of comic entertainment that had its start in Italy became popular throughout Europe several hundred years ago. A small group of actors would put on a play with a standard set of humorous characters. One of the standard characters was a bad-tempered old man called *Pantalone* or *Pantaloon*. Pantaloon always wore a tight-fitting combination of trousers and stockings. Because he did, such clothing became known as *pantaloons*. The word *pantaloons*, which was later used for various types of trousers, is still sometimes heard today. The usual term now, however, is *pants*, which is a short way of saying *pantaloons*. [a shortened form of *pantaloons* "trousers", from *Pantaloon, Pantalone*, name of a clown in stage entertainment]

pant·suit \'pant-,süt\ *n* : a woman's outfit consisting usually of a long jacket and pants made of the same material

panty hose *n pl* : a one-piece undergarment for women consisting of hosiery combined with panties

pap \'pap\ *n* : soft or bland food for infants or invalids

pa·pa \'päp-ə\ *n* : ¹FATHER 1a

pa·pa·cy \'pā-pə-sē\ *n, pl* **-cies** **1** : the office of pope **2** : the term of a pope's reign **3** *cap* : the government of the Roman Catholic Church of which the pope is the head

pa·pa·in \pə-'pā-ən, -'pī-ən\ *n* : an enzyme in papaya juice used especially to make meat tender and in medicine

pa·pal \'pā-pəl\ *adj* : of or relating to the pope or the papacy — **pa·pal·ly** \-pə-lē\ *adv*

pa·paw *or* **paw·paw** *n* **1** \pə-'pȯ\ : PAPAYA **2** \'päp-(,)ȯ, 'pȯp-\ : a North American tree having purple flowers and a yellow edible fruit; *also* : its fruit

pa·pa·ya \pə-'pī-ə\ *n* : an oblong edible fruit with black seeds that grows on a tropical American tree with large leaves; *also* : the tree

¹pa·per \'pā-pər\ *n* **1 a** : a thin sheet made usually from rags, wood, straw, or bark and used to write or print on, to wrap things in, or to cover walls **b** : a sheet or piece of paper **2 a** : a piece of paper having something written or printed on it **b** : a written composition **3** : NEWSPAPER **4** : WALLPAPER [Middle English *papir* "paper", from early

French *papier* (same meaning), from Latin *papyrus* "paper, papyrus" — related to PAPYRUS]

²paper *or* **pa·pered; pa·per·ing** \'pā-p(ə-)riŋ\ : to cover or line with paper and especially wallpaper ⟨*paper* a room⟩ — **pa·per·er** \-pər-ər\

³paper *adj* **1 a** : of, relating to, or made of paper or paperboard ⟨*paper* carton⟩ ⟨*paper* mills⟩ **b** : PAPERY ⟨nuts with *paper* shells⟩ **2** : NOMINAL 1

pa·per·back \'pā-pər-,bak\ *n* : a book with a flexible paper binding — **paperback** *adj*

paper birch *n* : an American birch with white bark that peels off the tree easily

pa·per·board \-,bō(ə)rd, -,bȯ(ə)rd\ *n* : a material made from cellulose fiber (as wood pulp) like paper but usually thicker

paper clip *n* : a length of wire bent into flat loops that is used to hold papers together

pa·per·hang·er \'pā-pər-,haŋ-ər\ *n* : a person who applies wallpaper to walls especially as an occupation — **pa·per·hang·ing** \-,haŋ-iŋ\ *n*

paper money *n* : money consisting of government notes and bank notes

paper mulberry *n* : an Asian tree of the mulberry family widely grown as a shade tree

paper nautilus *n* : a mollusk with eight arms which is related to the octopuses and of which the female has a thin fragile shell — called also *argonaut*

pa·per·weight \'pā-pər-,wāt\ *n* : an object used to hold down loose papers by its weight

pa·per·work \-,wərk\ *n* : routine office or record-keeping work

pa·pery \'pā-p(ə-)rē\ *adj* : resembling paper in thinness or firmness — **pa·per·i·ness** *n*

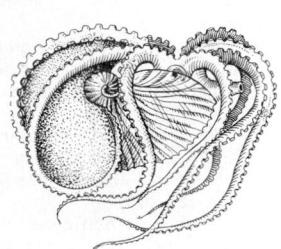
paper nautilus

pa·pier–mâ·ché \,pā-pər-mə-'shā, ,pap-,yā-mə-; -(,)ma-\ *n* : a light strong molding material made of paper pulp mixed with glue and other substances [French, literally "chewed paper"] — **papier–mâché** *adj*

pa·pil·la \pə-'pil-ə\ *n, pl* **-pil·lae** \-'pil-ē, -,ī\ : a small bodily structure (as one of the nubs on the surface of the tongue) that resembles a tiny nipple in form

pa·poose \pa-'püs, pə-\ *n* : a North American Indian infant

pa·pri·ka \pə-prē-kə, pa-\ *n* : a mild red spice consisting of the dried finely ground fruit of various cultivated sweet peppers

Pap smear \'pap-\ *n* : a test for the early detection of cancer especially of the uterus and cervix using cells that are shed or scraped off and stained in a special way — called also *Pap test*

pa·py·rus \pə-'pī-rəs\ *n, pl* **pa·py·rus·es** *or* **pa·py·ri** \-'pī(ə)r-ē, -,ī\ **1** : a tall sedge of the Nile valley **2** : the soft central part of papyrus stems especially when cut in strips and pressed into a writing material **3** : a writing on or written scroll of papyrus [Middle English *papyrus* "papyrus", from Latin *papyrus* "papyrus, paper", from Greek *papyros* "papyrus" — related to PAPER]

par \'pär\ *n* **1 a** : the fixed value of the unit of money of one country expressed in terms of the unit of money of another country **b** : the face value or issuing price of a stock or bond **2** : common level : EQUALITY **3** : an accepted standard (as of health) ⟨not feeling up to *par*⟩ **4**

\ə\ abut	\au̇\ **out**	\i\ **tip**	\ȯ\ **saw**	\u̇\ **foot**
\ər\ **further**	\ch\ **chin**	\ī\ **life**	\ȯi\ **coin**	\y\ **yet**
\a\ **mat**	\e\ **pet**	\j\ **job**	\th\ **thin**	\yü\ **few**
\ā\ **take**	\ē\ **easy**	\ŋ\ **sing**	\t̲h̲\ **this**	\yu̇\ **cure**
\ä\ **cot, cart**	\g\ **go**	\ō\ **bone**	\ü\ **food**	\zh\ **vision**

: the standard score for a golf hole or course [from Latin *par* (noun) "one that is equal", from *par* (adjective) "equal" — related to COMPARE, PAIR, PEER, UMPIRE; see *Word History* at UMPIRE] — **par** *adj*

par·a·ble \'par-ə-bəl\ *n* : a short simple story illustrating a moral or spiritual truth

pa·rab·o·la \pə-'rab-ə-lə\ *n* **1** : a curve formed by the intersection of a cone with a plane parallel to a straight line in its surface : a plane curve formed by a point moving so that its distance from a fixed point is equal to its distance from a fixed line **2** : something that is bowl-shaped — **par·a·bol·ic** \,par-ə-'bäl-ik\ *adj*

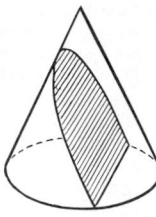

parabola 1

¹**para·chute** \'par-ə-,shüt\ *n* **1** : a folding umbrella-shaped device of light fabric used especially for making a safe jump from an aircraft **2** : something (as the bunch of hairs on a dandelion seed) that is like a parachute in form, use, or operation

²**parachute** *vb* **-chut·ed; -chut·ing** : to transport or come down by means of a parachute — **para·chut·ist** \-,shüt-əst\ *n*

¹**pa·rade** \pə-'rād\ *n* **1** : great show or display **2** : a formation of a body of troops before a superior officer **3** : a public procession **4** : a crowd of strolling people ⟨the Easter *parade*⟩

²**parade** *vb* **pa·rad·ed; pa·rad·ing** **1 a** : to cause to march **b** : to march in a parade **2** : ²PROMENADE **3** : SHOW OFF 1 ⟨*parade* one's knowledge⟩ **syn** see SHOW — **pa·rad·er** *n*

para·di·chlo·ro·ben·zene \,par-ə-,dī-,klōr-ə-'ben-,zēn, -,klȯr-, -,ben-'zēn\ *n* : a white compound that contains chlorine and benzene and is used chiefly in moth balls

par·a·digm \'par-ə-,dīm, -,dim\ *n* **1** : an example showing how something is to be done : MODEL **2** : an example of a conjugation or declension showing a word in all its inflectional forms — **par·a·dig·mat·ic** \,par-ə-dig-'mat-ik\ *adj*

par·a·dise \'par-ə-,dīs, -,dīz\ *n* **1** : EDEN 1 **2** : HEAVEN 2 **3** : a place or state of great happiness [Middle English *paradis* "the Garden of Eden", from early French *paradis* (same meaning), from Latin *paradisus* (same meaning), from Greek *paradeisos* "Garden of Eden", literally "enclosed park"]

par·a·dox \'par-ə-,däks\ *n* **1 a** : a statement that seems to go against common sense but may still be true **b** : a false statement that at first seems true **2** : a person or thing having qualities that seem to be opposites — **par·a·dox·i·cal** \,par-ə-'däk-si-kəl\ *adj* — **par·a·dox·i·cal·ly** \-k(ə-)lē\ *adv*

par·af·fin \'par-ə-fən\ *n* : a flammable waxy substance obtained from wood, coal, or petroleum and used chiefly in coating and sealing, in candles, and in drugs and cosmetics

par·a·gon \'par-ə-,gän, -gən\ *n* : a model of excellence or perfection

¹**para·graph** \'par-ə-,graf\ *n* **1** : a part of a writing or speech that develops in an organized manner one point of a subject or gives the words of one speaker **2** : a short written article (as in a newspaper) complete in one section

²**paragraph** *vb* : to divide into or write paragraphs

par·a·keet *also* **par·ra·keet** \'par-ə-,kēt\ *n* : any of numerous usually small slender parrots with a long tail

Par·a·li·pom·e·non \,par-ə-lə-'päm-ə-,nän, -lī-\ *n* — see BIBLE table

par·al·lax \'par-ə-,laks\ *n* : the apparent shift in position of an object as seen from two different points not on a straight line with the object

¹**par·al·lel** \'par-ə-,lel\ *adj* **1** : lying or moving in the same direction but always the same distance apart ⟨train tracks are *parallel*⟩ **2 a** : being or relating to an electrical circuit having a number of conductors in parallel **b** : being or relating to a connection in a computer system in which the bits of a byte are transmitted over separate wires at the same time **3** : ³LIKE, SIMILAR ⟨*parallel* situations⟩

²**parallel** *n* **1** : a parallel line, curve, or surface **2 a** : one of the imaginary circles on the surface of the earth parallel to the equator that mark latitude **b** : a corresponding line on a globe or map **3 a** : COUNTERPART 1, EQUAL ⟨a victory without *parallel*⟩ **b** : SIMILARITY 1, LIKENESS **c** : a tracing of similarity ⟨draw a *parallel* between two periods of history⟩ **4** : an arrangement of electrical devices in a circuit in which the same potential difference is applied to two or more resistances with each resistance on a parallel branch

³**parallel** *vb* **1** : to be like or equal to **2** : to lie, run, or move in a direction parallel to ⟨the highway *parallels* the river⟩

⁴**parallel** *adv* : in a parallel manner — often used with *with* or *to*

parallel bars *n pl* : a pair of horizontal bars that are used for swinging and balancing exercises in gymnastics

par·al·lel·ism \'par-ə-,lel-,iz-əm\ *n* : the quality or state of being parallel; *esp* : similarity of construction of word groups especially for effect or rhythm

par·al·lel·o·gram \,par-ə-'lel-ə-,gram\ *n* : a four-sided figure whose opposite sides are parallel and equal

par·al·lel–veined \,par-ə-,lel-'vānd\ *adj* : having straight or curved veins that do not branch and come together again ⟨monocotyledons such as grasses and lilies have *parallel-veined* leaves⟩ — compare NET-VEINED

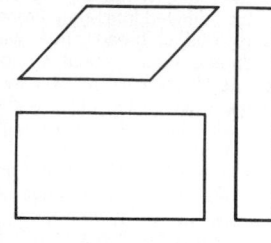

parallelogram

pa·ral·y·sis \pə-'ral-ə-səs\ *n, pl* **-y·ses** \-ə-,sēz\ : complete or partial loss of function especially when involving motion or sensation in a part of the body

¹**par·a·lyt·ic** \,par-ə-'lit-ik\ *adj* **1** : affected with or marked by paralysis **2** : of, relating to, or resembling paralysis

²**paralytic** *n* : one affected with paralysis

par·a·lyze \'par-ə-,līz\ *vb* **-lyzed; -lyz·ing** **1** : to affect with paralysis **2** : to make powerless or unable to act, function, or move

par·a·me·cium \,par-ə-'mē-sh(ē-)əm, -sē-əm\ *n, pl* **-cia** \-sh(ē-)ə, -sē-ə\ *also* **-ciums** : any of a genus of one-celled somewhat slipper-shaped protozoans that move by cilia

para·med·ic \,par-ə-'med-ik\ *n* : a person who works in a health field by helping a physician (as by taking X rays or giving injections) [from *para-* "alongside of, associated with in a secondary or assisting role" and *medic* "a person trained in or studying medical work"; *para-* derived from Greek *para* "beside, alongside of" and *medic* from Latin *medicus* "physician"]

para·med·i·cal \,par-ə-'med-i-kəl\ *adj* : concerned with helping with the work of highly trained medical professionals

pa·ram·e·ter \pə-'ram-ət-ər\ *n* **1** : an independent variable used to express the coordinates of points represented by a mathematical function **2** : any of a set of properties whose values determine the characteristics or behavior of something — **para·met·ric** \,par-ə-'me-trik\ *adj*

paramecium

par·a·mount \'par-ə-ˌmaúnt\ *adj* : superior to all others : SUPREME ⟨of *paramount* importance⟩

para·noia \ˌpar-ə-'nói-ə\ *n* **1** : a serious mental disorder marked by feelings of persecution or of twisted and incorrect ideas of one's own importance usually without hallucinations **2** : a tendency toward being overly suspicious and distrustful

¹para·noid \'par-ə-ˌnóid\ *adj* **1** : resembling paranoia **2** : marked by suspiciousness, feelings of persecution, or an exaggerated sense of one's own importance

²paranoid *n* : one who is paranoid

par·a·pet \'par-ə-pət, -ˌpet\ *n* **1** : a wall of earth or stone to protect soldiers **2** : a low wall or railing at the edge of a platform, roof, or bridge

par·a·pher·na·lia \ˌpar-ə-fə(r)-'nāl-yə\ *n sing or pl* **1** : personal belongings **2** : FURNISHINGS, APPARATUS

¹para·phrase \'par-ə-ˌfrāz\ *n* : a way of stating something again by giving the meaning in different words

²paraphrase *vb* **-phrased; -phras·ing** : to give the meaning in different words — **para·phras·er** *n*

para·pro·fes·sion·al \ˌpar-ə-prə-'fesh-nəl, -ən-ᵊl\ *n* : a person trained to assist a professional person (as a teacher or doctor) — **paraprofessional** *adj*

par·a·site \'par-ə-ˌsīt\ *n* **1** : a person who lives at the expense of another **2** : a living thing which lives in or on another living thing in parasitism **3** : a person dependent on something else for life or support without making proper return

par·a·sit·ic \ˌpar-ə-'sit-ik\ *adj* : of or relating to parasites or their way of life : being a parasite — **par·a·sit·i·cal·ly** \-i-k(ə-)lē\ *adv*

par·a·sit·ism \'par-ə-sə-ˌtiz-əm, -ˌsīt-ˌiz-\ *n* : a close association between living things of two or more kinds of which one is a parasite and obtains benefits from the other which is a host and is usually harmed in some way

par·a·sit·ize \'par-ə-sə-ˌtīz, -ˌsīt-ˌīz\ *vb* **-ized; -iz·ing** : to infest or live on or with as a parasite

para·sol \'par-ə-ˌsól\ *n* : a light umbrella for protection against the sun

para·sym·pa·thet·ic \ˌpar-ə-ˌsim-pə-'thet-ik\ *adj* : of, relating to, being, or acting on the parasympathetic nervous system

parasympathetic nervous system *n* : the part of the autonomic nervous system that is concerned with controlling the body during normal routine situations, that narrows the pupil of the eye, has primary control over the secretion of the digestive and salivary glands, and decreases the activity of the heart, and that acts on bodily organs by releasing acetylcholine at the ends of nerve fibers supplying them — compare SYMPATHETIC NERVOUS SYSTEM

par·a·thor·mone \ˌpar-ə-'thór-ˌmōn\ *n* : the parathyroid hormone

para·thy·roid \ˌpar-ə-'thī-ˌroid\ *adj* : of, relating to, or produced by the parathyroid glands

parathyroid gland *n* : any of usually four small endocrine glands next to or located in the thyroid gland that produce a hormone concerned with calcium metabolism

para·troops \'par-ə-ˌtrüps\ *n pl* : troops trained and equipped to parachute from an airplane — **para·troop** \-ˌtrüp\ *adj* — **para·troop·er** \-ˌtrü-pər\ *n*

¹para·ty·phoid \ˌpar-ə-'tī-ˌfóid, -(ˌ)tī-'fóid\ *adj* **1** : resembling typhoid fever **2** : of or relating to paratyphoid or the bacteria that cause it

²paratyphoid *n* : a disease caused by bacteria, resembling typhoid fever, and occurring as a food poisoning

par·boil \'pär-ˌbóil\ *vb* : to boil briefly usually before cooking in another manner

¹par·cel \'pär-səl\ *n* **1** : ¹PORTION 3, PART **2** : a plot of land **3** : ¹GROUP 1, LOT **4** : ¹BUNDLE 1, PACKAGE

²parcel *vb* **par·celed** *or* **par·celled; par·cel·ing** *or* **par·cel·ling** \'pär-s(ə-)liŋ\ **1** : to divide into parts : DISTRIBUTE **2** : to wrap up into a parcel

parcel post *n* **1** : a mail service handling parcels **2** : packages handled by parcel post

parch \'pärch\ *vb* **1** : to toast by dry heat **2** : to wilt with heat

parch·ment \'pärch-mənt\ *n* **1** : the skin of a sheep or goat prepared as a writing material **2** : a paper like parchment **3** : something written on parchment

¹par·don \'pärd-ᵊn\ *n* : the excusing of an offense without a penalty — **par·don·able** \'pärd-nə-bəl, -ᵊn-ə-bəl\ *adj* — **par·don·ably** \-blē\ *adv*

²pardon *vb* **par·doned; par·don·ing** \'pärd-niŋ, -ᵊn-iŋ\ **1** : to free from penalty **2** : to allow an offense to pass without punishment

pare \'pa(ə)r, 'pe(ə)r\ *vb* **pared; par·ing** **1** : to cut or shave off the outside or the ends of ⟨*pare* an apple⟩ **2** : to reduce as if by paring ⟨*pare* expenses⟩

par·e·gor·ic \ˌpar-ə-'gór-ik, -'gór-, -'gär-\ *n* : a liquid mixture of opium and camphor in alcohol used especially to relieve pain

pa·ren·chy·ma \pə-'ren-kə-mə\ *n* **1** : a tissue of higher plants consisting of thin-walled living cells that remain capable of cell division even when mature, are the location where photosynthesis takes place and materials and food are stored, and make up much of the substance of leaves and roots and the pulp of fruits as well as parts of stems and supporting structures **2** : the tissue of an animal organ (as a gland) that performs the work of the organ as compared to tissue which only gives support or serves as a framework

par·ent \'par-ənt, 'per-\ *n* **1 a** : one that is a father or mother **b** : an animal or plant that produces offspring **2** : the original source of something — **parent** *adj* — **par·ent·hood** \-ˌhúd\ *n*

par·ent·age \'par-ənt-ij, 'per-\ *n* : descent from parents or ancestors : LINEAGE

pa·ren·tal \pə-'rent-ᵊl\ *adj* : of, typical of, or being parents

pa·ren·the·sis \pə-'ren(t)-thə-səs\ *n, pl* **-the·ses** \-thə-ˌsēz\ **1** : a word, phrase, or sentence inserted in a passage to explain or comment on it **2** : one of a pair of marks ( ) used to enclose a parenthesis or to group units in a mathematical expression — **par·en·thet·ic** \ˌpar-ən-'thet-ik\ *or* **par·en·thet·i·cal** \-'thet-i-kəl\ *adj* — **par·en·thet·i·cal·ly** \-i-k(ə-)lē\ *adv*

par·ent·ing \'par-ənt-iŋ, 'per-\ *n* : the raising of a child by its parents

par ex·cel·lence \ˌpär-,ek-sə-'läns\ *adv or adj* : in the highest degree : above all others

par·fait \pär-'fā\ *n* **1** : a flavored custard containing whipped cream and syrup frozen without stirring **2** : a dessert made of layers of fruit, syrup, ice cream, and whipped cream

pa·ri·ah \pə-'rī-ə\ *n* : a person despised or rejected by society : OUTCAST

pa·ri·etal \pə-'rī-ət-ᵊl\ *adj* : of, relating to, or forming the upper back wall of the head

par·ing \'pa(ə)r-iŋ, 'pe(ə)r-\ *n* **1** : the act of cutting away an edge or surface **2** : something pared off

Par·is green \ˌpar-əs-\ *n* : a poisonous bright green powder containing copper and arsenic that is used as an insecticide

par·ish \'par-ish\ *n* **1 a** : a section of a church district in the care of a priest or minister **b** : the persons who live in such a section and attend the parish church **2** : the members of a church **3** : a division of the state of Louisiana that is similar to a county in other states

pa·rish·io·ner \pə-'rish-(ə-)nər\ *n* : a member or resident

\ə\ abut	\aú\ out	\i\ tip	\ó\ saw	\ú\ foot
\ər\ further	\ch\ chin	\ī\ life	\ói\ coin	\y\ yet
\a\ mat	\e\ pet	\j\ job	\th\ thin	\yü\ few
\ā\ take	\ē\ easy	\ŋ\ sing	\th\ this	\yú\ cure
\ä\ cot, cart	\g\ go	\ō\ bone	\ü\ food	\zh\ vision

of a parish

par·i·ty \'par-ət-ē\ *n, pl* **-ties** **1** : the quality or state of being equal or equivalent : EQUALITY **2** : the state of being odd or even used as the foundation of a method of detecting errors in binary-coded data

¹**park** \'pärk\ *n* **1** : an area around a country house used for recreation (as hunting or riding) **2 a** : a piece of ground in or near a city or town kept as a place of beauty or recreation **b** : an area maintained in its natural state as a public property **3** : PARKING LOT **4** : an enclosed field for ball games

²**park** *vb* **1** : to leave a vehicle standing temporarily (as in a parking lot or garage) **2** : to set and leave temporarily ⟨*park* yourself in that chair⟩

par·ka \'pär-kə\ *n* : a very warm jacket with a hood

parking lot *n* : an outdoor area for parking motor vehicles

Par·kin·son's disease \'pär-kən-sənz-\ *n* : a nervous disease of later life that tends to get steadily worse and is marked by trembling and weakness of resting muscles and by a characteristic way of walking

park·way \'pär-ˌkwā\ *n* : a broad landscaped highway

par·lance \'pär-lən(t)s\ *n* : manner of speech

par·lay \'pär-ˌlā, -lē\ *vb* : to increase or change into something of much greater value ⟨*parlayed* a handicap into an asset⟩ [from *parlay* "to make a series of bets so that winnings from earlier bets are all wagered on later contests", from French *paroli* (noun) "a parlayed bet", derived from an Italian dialect word *paroli*, plural of *parolo* "a parlayed bet", from *para* "equal"]

par·ley \'pär-lē\ *vb* **par·leyed; par·ley·ing** : CONFER 2; *esp* : to discuss terms with an enemy [from early French *parler* "to speak" — related to PARLIAMENT, PARLOR; see *Word History* at PARLOR] — **parley** *n*

par·lia·ment \'pär-lə-mənt *also* 'pärl-yə-\ *n* : the supreme legislative body of various political units ⟨the British *parliament*⟩ [Middle English *parliament* "a council for discussing government business", from early French *parlement* (same meaning), from *parler* "to speak" — related to PARLEY, PARLOR; see *Word History* at PARLOR]

par·lia·men·tar·i·an \ˌpär-lə-ˌmen-'ter-ē-ən, -mən- *also* ˌpärl-yə-\ *n* : an expert in parliamentary procedure

par·lia·men·ta·ry \ˌpär-lə-'ment-ə-rē, -'men-trē *also* ˌpärl-yə-\ *adj* **1** : of, relating to, or enacted by a parliament **2** : of or relating to government by a cabinet whose members belong to and are responsible to the legislature **3** : of or according to the rules governing the way in which official meetings (as of a parliament or congress) are conducted ⟨*parliamentary* procedure⟩

par·lor \'pär-lər\ *n* **1** : a room in a home, hotel, or club used for conversation or the reception of guests **2** : any of various business places ⟨funeral *parlor*⟩ ⟨beauty *parlor*⟩

Word History In some monasteries during the Middle Ages, monks were not allowed to speak except when they were in a special room. Such a room was known in early French as a *parlour*. The word *parlour* comes from the French verb *parler*, which means "to speak". In the 13th century, *parlour* was borrowed into English as *parlor*. Before long it had acquired the meaning that it has today. Other English words that can be traced to the verb *parler* include *parley* and *parliament*. [Middle English *parlour* "a room for receiving and talking with guests", from early French *parlour* (same meaning), from *parler* "to speak" — related to PARLEY, PARLIAMENT]

par·lous \'pär-ləs\ *adj* : DANGEROUS 1, RISKY — **par·lous·ly** *adv*

Par·me·san \'pär-mə-ˌzän, -ˌzhän, -zən, -ˌzan\ *n* : a very hard dry sharply flavored cheese that is sold grated or in wedges

pa·ro·chi·al \pə-'rō-kē-əl\ *adj* **1** : of or relating to a parish **2** : restricted or limited in range : NARROW, PROVINCIAL ⟨a *parochial* point of view⟩ — **pa·ro·chi·al·ism** \-kē-ə-ˌliz-

əm\ *n* — **pa·ro·chi·al·ly** \-kē-ə-lē\ *adv*

parochial school *n* : a school maintained by a religious body

par·o·dy \'par-əd-ē\ *n, pl* **-dies** **1** : a written or musical work in which the style of an author or work is imitated for comic effect **2** : a poor imitation — **par·o·dist** \-əd-əst\ *n* — **parody** *vb*

¹**pa·role** \pə-'rōl\ *n* : an early release of a prisoner who meets specified requirements

²**parole** *vb* **pa·roled; pa·rol·ing** : to release on parole — **pa·rol·ee** \pə-ˌrō-'lē\ *n*

pa·rot·id \pə-'rät-əd\ *adj* : of or relating to the parotid gland

parotid gland *n* : either of a pair of large salivary glands located below and in front of the ear

par·ox·ysm \'par-ək-ˌsiz-əm\ *n* **1** : a fit, attack, or sudden increase of violence of a disease that occurs, quiets down, and occurs again and again ⟨a *paroxysm* of coughing⟩ **2** : a sudden violent emotion or action ⟨*paroxysms* of rage⟩

par·quet \'pär-ˌkā, pär-'kā\ *n* : a flooring of parquetry

par·que·try \'pär-kə-trē\ *n, pl* **-tries** : a patterned wood inlay used especiallly for floors

parrakeet *variant of* PARAKEET

¹**par·rot** \'par-ət\ *n* **1** : a bright-colored tropical bird of a family marked by a strong hooked bill, by toes arranged in pairs with two in front and two behind, and often by the ability to mimic speech **2** : a person who repeats the words of others without understanding what they mean

²**parrot** *vb* : to repeat words like a parrot

parquetry

parrot fever *n* : PSITTACOSIS

parrot fish *n* : any of numerous sea fishes that are related to the perches and have the teeth united into a cutting plate resembling a beak

par·ry \'par-ē\ *vb* **par·ried; par·ry·ing** **1** : to turn aside skillfully : DEFLECT ⟨*parry* a blow⟩ **2** : EVADE 1 ⟨*parry* an embarrassing question⟩ — **parry** *n*

parse \'pärs, 'pärz\ *vb* **parsed; pars·ing** **1** : to analyze a sentence by naming its parts and their relations to each other **2** : to give the part of speech of a word and explain its relation to other words in a sentence

Par·si *also* **Par·see** \'pär-ˌsē\ *n* : a Zoroastrian descended from Persian refugees settled principally at Bombay

par·si·mo·ny \'pär-sə-ˌmō-nē\ *n* : the quality of being overly sparing with money : MISERLINESS — **par·si·mo·ni·ous** \ˌpär-sə-'mō-nē-əs\ *adj* — **par·si·mo·ni·ous·ly** *adv* — **par·si·mo·ni·ous·ness** *n*

pars·ley \'pär-slē\ *n, pl* **parsleys** : a southern European herb related to the carrot and widely grown for its finely divided leaves which are used to season or decorate foods

pars·nip \'pär-snəp\ *n* : a European herb related to the carrot and grown for its long white root used as a vegetable; *also* : this root

par·son \'pärs-ᵊn\ *n* **1** : a minister in charge of a parish **2** : a member of the clergy; *esp* : a Protestant pastor [Middle English *persone* "parson", from early French *persone* (same meaning), from Latin *persona*, literally "person"; so called because the parson was the legal "person" representing the church]

par·son·age \'pär-snij, 'pärs-ᵊn-ij\ *n* : the house provided by a church for

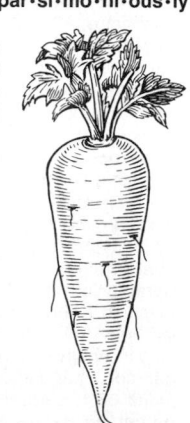

parsnip

its pastor

¹part \'pärt\ *n* **1 a** : one of the pieces into which something can be divided   **b** : one of the equal units of which something is composed ⟨a fifth *part* for each⟩   **c** : a portion of a plant or animal body : MEMBER, ORGAN ⟨wash the injured *part*⟩   **d** : a particular melody or line of music for one voice or instrument or a certain group of voices or instruments in harmony with others   **e** : a piece of a machine or equipment   **2** : a person's share, duty, or function ⟨did my *part*⟩   **3** : one of the sides in a conflict ⟨take another's *part* in a quarrel⟩   **4** : a general area : REGION — usually used in pl. ⟨you're not from around these *parts*⟩   **5** : a role in a play   **6** : the line where the hair is divided in combing — **in part** : PARTLY — **on the part of** : relating to the one specified

    syn PART, PORTION, SECTION, FRAGMENT mean something less than the whole. PART is a general word and can be used when it is not necessary to be exact ⟨they ran only *part* of the way⟩ PORTION suggests a part that is assigned or given as one's share ⟨divided the food into six *portions*⟩ SECTION applies to a part that is fairly small or is clearly seen as a unit ⟨the sports *section* of the newspaper⟩ FRAGMENT applies to a part made by or as if by breaking something ⟨while digging they found *fragments* of old pottery⟩ ⟨some ancient literature is now known only in *fragments*⟩

²part *vb* **1** : to separate from or leave someone : go away : DEPART   **2** : to become separated, detached, or broken ⟨the ice *parted*⟩   **3** : to give up possession or control ⟨wouldn't *part* with their old car⟩   **4 a** : to divide into parts   **b** : to separate by combing on each side of a line   **syn** see SEPARATE

³part *adv* : PARTLY ⟨was only *part* right⟩

par·take \pär-'tāk, pər-\ *vb* **par·took** \-'tůk\; **par·tak·en** \-'tā-kən\; **par·tak·ing** **1 a** : to take a share or part ⟨*partake* of a meal⟩   **b** : to take part in something ⟨all may *partake* in the ceremony⟩   **2** : to have some of the qualities of something ⟨the story *partook* of the nature of drama⟩ — **par·tak·er** *n*

    syn PARTAKE, PARTICIPATE, SHARE mean to take part together. PARTAKE applies especially to the common enjoyment of food and drink ⟨shall we *partake* of the feast prepared for us?⟩ PARTICIPATE suggests a business or activity in which persons work or act as a group ⟨the whole class *participated* in singing the songs⟩ SHARE can apply either to situations in which one person allows another the use or enjoyment of some possession ⟨she was nice enough to *share* her lunch with me⟩ or to situations involving the use of something by two or more people ⟨everyone in the group had to *share* one computer⟩

par·tial \'pär-shəl\ *adj* **1** : inclined to favor one side over another : BIASED   **2** : fond of someone or something ⟨*partial* to pizza⟩   **3** : relating to or being a part rather than the whole : not total or complete ⟨a *partial* eclipse⟩ ⟨a *partial* rhyme⟩ — **par·tial·ly** \'pärsh-(ə-)lē\ *adv*

par·tial·i·ty \,pär-shē-'al-ət-ē, pär-'shal-\ *n, pl* **-ties** **1** : the quality or state of being partial   **2** : a special taste or liking

partial product *n* : one of the products obtained by multiplying one after another the multiplicand by each digit of the multiplier

par·tic·i·pant \pər-'tis-ə-pənt, pär-\ *n* : one that participates

par·tic·i·pate \pər-'tis-ə-,pāt, pär-\ *vb* **-pat·ed; -pat·ing** : to take part or have a share in something in common with others ⟨*participate* in sports⟩   **syn** see PARTAKE — **par·tic·i·pa·tion** \-,tis-ə-'pā-shən\ *n* — **par·tic·i·pa·tor** \-'tis-ə-,pāt-ər\ *n*

par·ti·cip·i·al \,pärt-ə-'sip-ē-əl\ *adj* : of, relating to, or formed with a participle ⟨*participial* phrase⟩ — **par·ti·cip·i·al·ly** \-ē-ə-lē\ *adv*

par·ti·ci·ple \'pärt-ə-,sip-əl\ *n* : a word that functions like an adjective and also shows such features of a verb as tense and voice and the ability to take an object

par·ti·cle \'pärt-i-kəl\ *n* **1** : one of the very small parts of matter (as a molecule, atom, or electron)   **2** : a very small quantity or piece   **3** : the smallest possible portion

par·ti·cle·board \-,bō(ə)rd, -,bȯ(ə)rd\ *n* : a board made of very small pieces of wood stuck together

¹par·tic·u·lar \pə(r)-'tik-(y)ə-lər, -'tik-lər\ *adj* **1** : of or relating to the separate parts of a whole ⟨each *particular* item on the list⟩   **2** : of or relating to a single person or thing ⟨my *particular* skills⟩   **3** : very unusual : SPECIAL ⟨a storm of *particular* violence⟩   **4** : hard to please : FASTIDIOUS ⟨*particular* about their clothes⟩

²particular *n* : an individual fact, detail, or item — **in particular** : PARTICULARLY 2

par·tic·u·lar·i·ty \pə(r)-,tik-yə-'lar-ət-ē\ *n, pl* **-ties** **1** : a very small detail   **2** : careful attention to detail : EXACTNESS, CARE

par·tic·u·lar·ize \pə(r)-'tik-(yə-)lə-,rīz\ *vb* **-ized; -iz·ing** : to state in detail : SPECIFY — **par·tic·u·lar·iza·tion** \-,tik-(yə-)lə-rə-'zā-shən\ *n*

par·tic·u·lar·ly \pə(r)-'tik-yə-(lər)lē, -yə-lə-lē; pə(r)-'tik-(ə-)lē\ *adv* **1** : in a particular manner   **2** : to an unusual degree : ESPECIALLY

par·tic·u·late \pər-'tik-yə-lət, pär-, -,lāt\ *n* : a substance made up of very small separate particles

¹part·ing \'pärt-iŋ\ *n* **1** : SEPARATION 1, DIVISION   **2** : a place where a division or separation occurs ⟨a *parting* of the ways⟩   **3** : LEAVE-TAKING ⟨shake hands at *parting*⟩

²parting *adj* **1** : being in the process of departing   **2** : serving to divide : SEPARATING   **3** : given, taken, or performed at parting ⟨a *parting* kiss⟩

par·ti·san \'pärt-ə-zən\ *n* **1** : a person who is strongly devoted to a particular cause or group   **2** : GUERRILLA — **partisan** *adj* — **par·ti·san·ship** \-,ship\ *n*

par·ti·tion \pər-'tish-ən, pär-\ *n* **1** : DIVISION 1a, SEPARATION   **2** : an interior dividing wall   **3** : ¹PART 1a, SECTION — **partition** *vb* — **par·ti·tion·er** \-'tish-(ə-)nər\ *n*

part·ly \'pärt-lē\ *adv* : in some measure or degree : not completely ⟨a statement that is only *partly* true⟩

part·ner \'pärt-nər\ *n* **1** : one associated in action with another : COLLEAGUE   **2** : either of a couple who dance together   **3** : one of two or more persons who play together in a game against an opposing side   **4** : SPOUSE   **5** : a member of a partnership

part·ner·ship \'pärt-nər-,ship\ *n* **1** : the state of being a partner   **2** : a business organization owned by two or more persons who agree to share the profits and losses

part of speech : a class of words (as adjectives, adverbs, conjunctions, interjections, nouns, prepositions, pronouns, or verbs) identified according to the kinds of ideas they express and the way they work in a sentence

partook *past of* PARTAKE

par·tridge \'pär-trij\ *n, pl* **par·tridge** *or* **par·tridg·es** : any of several plump Old World game birds related to the common chicken; *also* : any of various American birds (as a bobwhite or ruffed grouse) that are related to and resemble partridges of the Old World

partridge

par·tridge·ber·ry \-,ber-ē\ *n* : an American evergreen

plant that grows along the ground and produces rather tasteless scarlet berries

part–song \'pärt-,sȯŋ\ *n* : a song consisting of two or more voice parts

part–time \'pärt-'tīm\ *adj or adv* : involving or working less than a full or regular schedule

par·tu·ri·tion \,pärt-ə-'rish-ən, ,pär-chə-\ *n* : CHILDBIRTH

part·way \'pärt-'wā\ *adv* : to a part of a distance ⟨followed us *partway* home⟩

par·ty \'pärt-ē\ *n, pl* **parties** **1** : one side in a dispute or contest ⟨the *parties* to a lawsuit⟩ **2** : a group of persons organized to influence or direct the policies of a government or to overthrow an established government **3** : a person or group that takes part with others in an action or affair ⟨a *party* to a contract⟩ **4** : PERSON 1 **5** : a small group involved in a task ⟨a scouting *party*⟩ **6 a** : a social gathering **b** : entertainment for such a gathering — **party** *adj*

party poop·er \-'pü-pər\ *n* : one who spoils the pleasure of others especially at a party : KILLJOY

pas·cal \pas-'kal\ *n* **1** : a unit of pressure in the metric system equal to one newton per square meter **2** *usu cap P or all cap* : a computer programming language in which a problem is solved by a step-by-step process and each step is done by a separate part of a program [named for Blaise *Pascal* 1623–1662 French mathematician]

Pas·cal's triangle \pas-'kalz-\ *n* : a set of numbers which are arranged in rows in the shape of a triangle with the first row containing only 1, the second row 1 1, the third 1 3 3 1, and in general the *n*th row containing the coefficients in the expansion of $(a + b)^n$

pas·chal \'pas-kəl\ *adj* : of or relating to Passover or Easter [from earlier *Pasch* "Passover, Easter", derived from Greek *pascha* "Passover", from Hebrew *pesaḥ* "Passover"]

pa·sha \'päsh-ə, 'pash-ə, pə-'shä\ *n* : a Middle Eastern official of high rank

¹pass \'pas\ *vb* **1** : ¹MOVE 2, PROCEED **2 a** : to go away ⟨the pain will soon *pass*⟩ **b** : ¹DIE 1 — often used with *on* **3** : to go by or beyond or move past **4** : to go to allow to go across, over, or through ⟨let no one *pass*⟩ **5** : to change or transfer ownership or possession ⟨recipes *passed* down through the family⟩ **6** : HAPPEN 2, OCCUR **7 a** : to gain the approval of a legislative body ⟨the bill *passed* both houses⟩ **b** : to approve officially ⟨*pass* a new law⟩ **8** : to go or allow to go through an examination or course of study successfully ⟨*passed* my French course⟩ **9** : to cause to be considered ⟨*passed* for an expert⟩ **10** : to transfer or become transferred from one person to another ⟨*pass* the butter⟩ ⟨*pass* a football⟩ **11** : to decide not to bid, bet, or draw in a card game **12** : to cause or permit to elapse : SPEND ⟨*pass* time⟩ **13** : to state judicially ⟨*pass* sentence⟩ — **pass·er** *n*

²pass *n* **1** : PASSAGE 2a, WAY **2** : a gap in a mountain range

³pass *n* **1** : the act or an instance of passing : PASSAGE **2** : ACCOMPLISHMENT 1, REALIZATION — used in the phrases *come to pass* and *bring to pass* **3** : SITUATION 3, CONDITION ⟨have come to a strange *pass*⟩ **4** : a written permission to enter or leave or to move about freely ⟨a soldier's three-day *pass*⟩ **5** : a moving of the hands over or along something **6** : a transfer of a ball or puck from one player to another; *esp* : FORWARD PASS **7** : BASE ON BALLS **8** : an act of passing in a card game **9** : EFFORT 2, TRY ⟨make a *pass* at it⟩

pass·able \'pas-ə-bəl\ *adj* **1** : capable of being passed, crossed, or traveled on ⟨*passable* roads⟩ **2** : barely good enough : TOLERABLE ⟨a *passable* imitation⟩ — **pass·ably** \-blē\ *adv*

pas·sage \'pas-ij\ *n* **1** : the action or process of passing from one place or condition to another **2 a** : a road, path, channel, or course by which something can pass **b**

: CORRIDOR 1 **3 a** : ¹VOYAGE, JOURNEY **b** : a right to travel as a passenger ⟨book *passage* on an airplane⟩ **4** : the passing of a law **5** : a usually brief portion of a written work or speech or of a musical composition

pas·sage·way \-,wā\ *n* : a road or way by which a person or thing may pass

pass away *vb* : ¹DIE 1

pass·book \'pas-,bùk\ *n* : BANKBOOK

pas·sé \pa-'sā\ *adj* : OUTMODED, OUT-OF-DATE [French, literally "past, gone by"]

pas·sel \'pas-əl\ *n* : a large number : GROUP

pas·sen·ger \'pas-ᵊn-jər\ *n* : a person riding in or on a vehicle

passenger pigeon *n* : an extinct but formerly very common North American pigeon that migrated long distances

pass·er·by \,pas-ər-'bī\ *n, pl* **pass·ers·by** \,pas-ərz-\ : one who passes by

¹pass·ing \'pas-iŋ\ *n* **1** : the act of one that passes or causes to pass **2** : DEATH 1 — **in passing** : BY THE WAY, INCIDENTALLY

²passing *adj* **1** : going by or past ⟨the *passing* crowd⟩ **2** : lasting only for a short time; *esp* : showing haste or lack of attention : HASTY, SUPERFICIAL ⟨a *passing* glance⟩ **3** : used for the act or process of passing ⟨the *passing* lane⟩ **4** : given on satisfactory completion of an examination or course of study ⟨a *passing* grade⟩

pas·sion \'pash-ən\ *n* **1** *often cap* : the sufferings of Jesus between the night of the Last Supper and his death **2 a** *pl* : the emotions in general **b** : strong feeling or emotion **3 a** : great affection : LOVE **b** : a strong liking **c** : an object of desire or deep interest

pas·sion·ate \'pash-(ə-)nət\ *adj* **1** : excited or easily excited to strong feeling **2** : showing or expressing strong feeling **3** : strongly affected with sexual desire — **pas·sion·ate·ly** *adv*

passion play *n, often cap 1st P* : a play representing scenes connected with Jesus' suffering and crucifixion

Passion Sunday *n* : the 5th Sunday in Lent

Pas·sion·tide \'pash-ən-,tīd\ *n* : the last two weeks of Lent

Passion Week *n* **1** : HOLY WEEK **2** : the 2d week before Easter

¹pas·sive \'pas-iv\ *adj* **1 a** : not active but acted upon ⟨*passive* spectators⟩ **b** : indicating that the person or thing represented by the subject is acted on by the verb ("was hit" in "he was hit by the ball" is *passive*) **2 a** : not operating **b** : of, relating to, or making use of the sun's heat usually without the aid of mechanical devices **3** : offering no resistance — **pas·sive·ly** *adv* — **pas·sive·ness** *n* — **pas·siv·i·ty** \pa-'siv-ət-ē\ *n*

²passive *n* **1** : a passive verb form **2** : the passive voice

passive immunity *n* : temporary immunity acquired by transfer (as by injection) of antibodies especially from an individual with active immunity

pass·key \'pas-,kē\ *n* **1** : a key for opening two or more locks **2** : SKELETON KEY

pass off *vb* : to give a false identity to : describe untruthfully

pass out *vb* : to lose consciousness

Pass·over \'pas-,ō-vər\ *n* : a Jewish holiday celebrated in March or April in honor of the freeing of the Hebrews from slavery in Egypt [so called because in Exodus 12:23–27 the Lord passes over the homes of the Israelites in killing the firstborn in Egypt]

pass over \(')pas-'ō-vər\ *vb* **1** : to ignore in passing **2** : to pay no attention to

pass·port \'pas-,pō(ə)rt, -,pȯ(ə)rt\ *n* **1** : a government-issued document that serves to identify a citizen and allows him or her to travel to foreign countries **2** : something that allows a person to reach a desired goal ⟨education can be a *passport* to a successful future⟩

pass·word \-,wərd\ *n* : a word or phrase that must be spoken by a person in order to pass a guard

¹past \'past\ *adj* **1 a** : AGO ⟨10 years *past*⟩ **b** : just gone by ⟨for the *past* few months⟩ **2** : having existed or taken place in a period before the present ⟨*past* customs⟩ **3** : of, relating to, or being a verb tense that in English is usually formed by internal vowel change (as in *sang*) or by the addition of a suffix (as in *laughed*) and that expresses time gone by **4** : no longer serving ⟨a *past* president⟩

²past *prep* **1** : ²BEYOND 1 ⟨*past* 50 years old⟩ ⟨half *past* ten⟩ **2** : in a course by and then beyond ⟨the road goes *past* the house⟩

³past *n* **1** : a former time or event **2 a** : PAST TENSE **b** : a verb form in the past tense **3** : a past life or history; *esp* : a past life that is secret or questionable

⁴past *adv* : so as to pass by ⟨a deer ran *past*⟩

pas·ta \'päs-tə\ *n* **1** : a dough of flour, eggs, and water made in different shapes and dried (as spaghetti or macaroni) or used fresh (as ravioli) **2** : a dish of cooked pasta

¹paste \'pāst\ *n* **1 a** : a dough rich in fat used for pastry **b** : a candy made by evaporating fruit with sugar or by flavoring a gelatin, starch, or gum arabic preparation **c** : a smooth food product made by evaporation or grinding ⟨almond *paste*⟩ **2** : a preparation of flour or starch and water used for sticking things together **3** : a soft plastic substance or mixture **4** : a very brilliant glass used for artificial gems [Middle English *paste* "pastry dough", from early French *paste* (same meaning), from Latin *pasta* "paste, dough"]

²paste *vb* **past·ed; past·ing** **1** : to stick on or together by paste **2** : to cover with something pasted on

³paste *vb* **past·ed; past·ing** : to hit hard [an altered form of earlier *baste* "to hit, beat"]

paste·board \'pās(t)-,bō(ə)rd, -,bȯ(ə)rd\ *n* : a stiff material made of sheets of paper pasted together; *also* : PAPERBOARD

¹pas·tel \pas-'tel\ *n* **1 a** : a paste made of ground color and used for making crayons **b** : a crayon of such paste **2** : a drawing in pastel **3** : any of various pale or light colors

²pastel *adj* **1** : of, relating to, or made with pastels **2** : pale and light in color

pas·tern \'pas-'tərn\ *n* : the part of the foot of a horse between the fetlock and the joint at the hoof; *also* : the corresponding part of some other four-footed animals

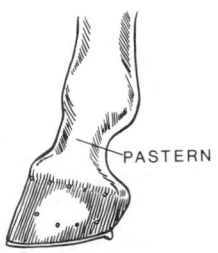

→PASTERN

pastern

pas·teur·iza·tion \,pas-chə-rə-'zā-shən, ,pas-tə-\ *n* : the process of heating a fluid (as milk) to a temperature high enough and keeping it at that temperature long enough to kill many objectionable germs and then cooling it rapidly without causing a major change in its chemical composition

pas·teur·ize \'pas-chə-,rīz, 'pas-tə-\ *vb* **-ized; -iz·ing** : to expose to pasteurization [named for Louis *Pasteur* 1822–1895 French chemist] — **pas·teur·iz·er** *n*

pas·time \'pas-,tīm\ *n* : something that helps to make time pass agreeably

past master *n* : one who is experienced : EXPERT

pas·tor \'pas-tər\ *n* : a minister or priest in charge of a church or parish — **pas·tor·ship** \-,ship\ *n*

¹pas·to·ral \'pas-t(ə-)rəl\ *adj* **1 a** : of or relating to shepherds or rural life **b** : devoted to or based on livestock raising **2** : of or relating to the pastor of a church

²pas·to·ral \'pas-t(ə-)rəl, *sense 3 is often* ,pas-tə-'räl, -'ral\ *n* **1** : a literary work dealing with shepherds or rural life **2** : a rural picture or scene **3** : PASTORALE

pas·to·rale \,pas-tə-'räl, -'ral\ *n* : a piece of music for instruments or voices that suggests rural scenes

pas·tor·ate \'pas-t(ə-)rət\ *n* **1** : the office, duties, or term

of service of a pastor **2** : a body of pastors

past participle *n* : a participle that expresses completed action and that is one of the principal parts of the verb ("raised" in "Many hands were raised" and "thrown" in "The ball has been thrown" are *past participles*)

past perfect tense *n* : a verb tense formed in English with *had* and expressing an action or state completed at or before a past time spoken of

pas·tra·mi \pə-'sträm-ē\ *n* : a highly seasoned smoked beef

pas·try \'pā-strē\ *n, pl* **pastries** **1** : sweet baked goods (as cakes, or tarts) made of dough or having a crust made of enriched dough **2** : a piece of pastry

past tense *n* : a verb tense expressing action or state in the past

pas·tur·age \'pas-chə-rij\ *n* : ¹PASTURE

¹pas·ture \'pas-chər\ *n* **1** : plants (as grass) for feeding especially grazing animals **2** : land or a plot of land used for grazing

²pasture *vb* **pas·tured; pas·tur·ing** **1** : ¹GRAZE 1 **2** : to feed (as cattle) on pasture

pas·ture·land \'pas-chər-,land\ *n* : ¹PASTURE 2

¹pas·ty \'pas-tē\ *n, pl* **pas·ties** : ¹PIE 1; *esp* : a meat pie

²pasty \'pā-stē\ *adj* **past·i·er; -est** : resembling paste; *esp* : pale and unhealthy in appearance — **past·i·ness** *n*

PA system \pē-'ā-\ *n* : PUBLIC-ADDRESS SYSTEM

¹pat \'pat\ *n* **1** : a light blow especially with the hand or a flat instrument **2** : a light tapping sound **3** : something (as butter) shaped into a small flat portion

²pat *vb* **pat·ted; pat·ting** **1** : to strike lightly with the hand or a flat instrument : strike or beat gently **2** : to flatten, smooth, or shape with pats **3** : to tap or stroke gently with the hand to soothe or to show affection or approval

³pat *adj* **pat·ter; pat·test** **1** : exactly suited : APT, TIMELY ⟨a *pat* answer⟩ **2** : learned exactly ⟨have a lesson down *pat*⟩ **3** : ¹FIRM 2b, UNYIELDING ⟨stand *pat*⟩

¹patch \'pach\ *n* **1** : a piece of material used to mend or cover a hole, a torn place, or a weak spot **2** : a shield (as of cloth) worn over an injured eye **3** : a small piece : SCRAP **4 a** : a small area or plot different from its surroundings ⟨a *patch* of oats⟩ ⟨a *patch* of blistered skin⟩ **b** : a spot of color : BLOTCH **5** : a piece of cloth worn (as on the shoulder of a uniform) as an ornament or insignia

²patch *vb* **1** : to mend, cover, or fill up a hole or weak spot in **2** : to provide with a patch **3 a** : to make out of patches **b** : to mend or put together especially hastily or clumsily **c** : ²SETTLE 6, ADJUST — usually used with *up* ⟨*patched* up their differences⟩ **syn** see MEND

patch pocket *n* : a pocket that is sewn on the outside of a garment

patch test *n* : a test for finding out if a person is sensitive to an allergy-producing substance that is made by putting small pads soaked with the substance in question on the unbroken skin

patch·work \'pach-,wərk\ *n* **1** : something made up of various parts **2** : pieces of cloth of various colors and shapes sewn together usually in a pattern — **patchwork** *adj*

patchy \'pach-ē\ *adj* **patch·i·er; -est** : consist-

patchwork 2

\ə\ abut	\au̇\ out	\i\ tip	\ȯ\ saw	\u̇\ foot
\ər\ further	\ch\ chin	\ī\ life	\ȯi\ coin	\y\ yet
\a\ mat	\e\ pet	\j\ job	\th\ thin	\yü\ few
\ā\ take	\ē\ easy	\ŋ\ sing	\th\ this	\yu̇\ cure
\ä\ cot, cart	\g\ go	\ō\ bone	\ü\ food	\zh\ vision

ing of or marked by patches : resembling patchwork

pate \'pāt\ *n* : ¹HEAD 1; *esp* : the top of the head — **pat·ed** \'pāt-əd\ *adj*

pa·tel·la \pə-'tel-ə\ *n, pl* **-tel·lae** \-'tel-ē, -,ī\ *or* **-tellas** : KNEECAP

pat·en \'pat-ᵊn\ *n* **1** : a plate of precious metal for the eucharistic bread **2** : a metal plate **3** : a thin disk (as of metal)

¹**pat·ent** *sense 1 is* 'pat-ᵊnt, *sense 2 is* 'pāt-, 'pat-\ *adj* **1 a** : protected by a patent **b** : of, relating to, or concerned with patents ⟨a *patent* lawyer⟩ **c** : ²PROPRIETARY 2 ⟨a *patent* can opener⟩ **2** : ²PLAIN 4a, OBVIOUS ⟨a *patent* lie⟩ — **pat·ent·ly** *adv*

²**pat·ent** \'pat-ᵊnt\ *n* **1** : an official document granting a right or privilege; *esp* : a writing granting to an inventor for a term of years the only right to make, use, or sell his or her invention **2** : the right granted by a patent

³**pat·ent** \'pat-ᵊnt\ *vb* : to protect by patent — **pat·ent·able** \'pat-ᵊn-tə-bəl\ *adj*

pat·en·tee \,pat-ᵊn-'tē\ *n* : one to whom a patent is granted

pat·ent leather \,pat-ᵊn(t)-\ *n* : a leather with a hard smooth glossy surface

patent medicine *n* : a medicine available for sale to the public without a doctor's prescription and having a label giving the name of the medicine, the manufacturer's name, and directions for use

pa·ter·nal \pə-'tərn-ᵊl\ *adj* **1** : FATHERLY ⟨*paternal* advice⟩ **2** : received or inherited from one's father **3** : related through the father ⟨a *paternal* grandfather⟩ [from Latin *paternalis* "fatherly", from earlier *paternus* (same meaning), from *pater* "father" — related to PADRE, PATRON, PATTERN] — **pa·ter·nal·ly** \-ᵊl-ē\ *adv*

pa·ter·ni·ty \pə-'tər-nət-ē\ *n* **1** : the state of being a father **2** : origin from a father

path \'path, 'päth\ *n, pl* **paths** \'pathz, 'paths, 'päthz, 'päths\ **1 a** : a track made by foot travel **b** : a track constructed for a particular use (as horseback riding) **2 a** : the way along which something moves : COURSE **b** : a way of life, conduct, or thought — **path·less** \-ləs\ *adj*

pa·thet·ic \pə-'thet-ik\ *adj* : causing one to feel tenderness, pity, or sorrow — **pa·thet·i·cal·ly** \-i-k(ə-)lē\ *adv*

path·find·er \'path-,fīn-dər, 'päth-\ *n* : one that discovers a way and especially a new route for travelers in unexplored regions

patho·gen \'path-ə-jən\ *n* : a germ (as a bacterium or virus) that causes disease

patho·gen·ic \,path-ə-'jen-ik\ *adj* : causing or capable of causing disease

patho·log·i·cal \,path-ə-'läj-i-kəl\ *also* **patho·log·ic** \-ik\ *adj* **1** : of or relating to pathology **2** : changed or caused by disease — **patho·log·i·cal·ly** \-i-k(ə-)lē\ *adv*

pa·thol·o·gist \pə-'thäl-ə-jəst, pa-\ *n* : a specialist in pathology

pa·thol·o·gy \pə-'thäl-ə-jē\ *n, pl* **-gies** **1** : the study of diseases and especially of the changes in the body produced by them **2** : something abnormal; *esp* : the disorders in structure and function that occur in a particular disease

pa·thos \'pā-,thäs, -,thȯs\ *n* : an element in life or in artistic representation of it that moves one to pity

path·way \'path-,wā, 'päth-\ *n* : PATH

pa·tience \'pā-shən(t)s\ *n* : the quality or state of being patient

¹**pa·tient** \'pā-shənt\ *adj* **1** : putting up with pains or hardships calmly or without complaint **2** : showing calm self-control **3** : not hasty or reckless **4** : STEADFAST 2, PERSEVERING ⟨years of *patient* labor⟩ — **pa·tient·ly** *adv*

²**patient** *n* : an individual awaiting or under medical care and treatment

pa·tio \'pat-ē-,ō *also* 'pät-\ *n, pl* **pa·ti·os** **1** : COURTYARD; *esp* : an inner court open to the sky **2** : an often paved recreation area next to a dwelling

pa·tois \'pa-,twä, 'pä-\ *n, pl* **patois** \-,twäz\ : DIALECT

pa·tri·arch \'pā-trē-,ärk\ *n* **1 a** : one of the Old Testament fathers of the human race or of the Hebrew people **b** : the father and ruler of a family or tribe **c** : an old man deserving respect **2** : any of various bishops of highest rank and dignity — **pa·tri·ar·chal** \,pā-trē-'är-kəl\ *adj*

pa·tri·ar·chy \'pā-trē-,är-kē\ *n, pl* **-chies** **1** : social organization in which the father is head of the family and ancestry and inheritance are traced in the male line **2** : a society organized according to the principles of patriarchy

pa·tri·cian \pə-'trish-ən\ *n* **1** : a member of one of the original citizen families of ancient Rome **2** : a person of high birth or position : ARISTOCRAT — **patrician** *adj*

pat·ri·mo·ny \'pa-trə-,mō-nē\ *n, pl* **-nies** **1** : an estate inherited from one's father or ancestors **2** : something passed down from one's father or ancestors : HERITAGE — **pat·ri·mo·ni·al** \,pa-trə-'mō-nē-əl\ *adj*

pa·tri·ot \'pā-trē-ət, -trē-,ät\ *n* : a person who loves his or her country and supports its authority and interests

pa·tri·ot·ic \,pā-trē-'ät-ik\ *adj* **1** : having or showing patriotism **2** : suitable or proper for a patriot — **pa·tri·ot·i·cal·ly** \-i-k(ə-)lē\ *adv*

pa·tri·o·tism \'pā-trē-ə-,tiz-əm\ *n* : love of one's own country

¹**pa·trol** \pə-'trōl\ *n* **1 a** : the action of going the rounds of an area for observation or guard **b** : the person or group doing the patrolling **2** : a part of a Boy Scout or Girl Scout troop

²**patrol** *vb* **pa·trolled; pa·trol·ling** : to carry out a patrol or a patrol of — **pa·trol·ler** *n*

pa·trol·man \pə-'trōl-mən\ *n* : a police officer who has a regular beat

patrol wagon *n* : an enclosed police truck used to carry prisoners

pa·tron \'pā-trən\ *n* **1** : a person chosen as a special guardian or supporter ⟨a *patron* of poets⟩ **2** : one who gives generous support or approval ⟨a *patron* of the arts⟩ **3** : a person who buys the goods or uses the services offered (as by a business) [Middle English *patroun* "a special guardian or protector", from early French *patrun*, *patron* (same meaning), from Latin *patronus* "patron, patron saint", from earlier *patronus* "defender", from *patr-*, *pater* "father" — related to PADRE, PATERNAL, PATTERN]

pa·tron·age \'pa-trə-nij, 'pā-\ *n* **1** : the support or influence of a patron **2** : business or activity provided by patrons **3** : the power to give out government jobs, contracts, or favors

pa·tron·ess \'pā-trə-nəs\ *n* : a woman who is a patron: as **a** : a woman chosen as a special guardian or supporter **b** : a woman who gives generous support or approval

pa·tron·ize \'pā-trə-,nīz, 'pa-\ *vb* **-ized; -iz·ing** **1** : to act as a patron to or of : give aid or support to ⟨*patronize* the arts⟩ **2** : to act as if one were better than **3** : to be a patron of ⟨*patronize* a store⟩ ⟨*patronize* the library⟩ — **pa·tron·iz·ing·ly** \-,nī-ziŋ-lē\ *adv*

patron saint *n* : a saint to whom a person, society, church, or place is dedicated

pa·troon \pə-'trün\ *n* : a landowner of a large estate in New York or New Jersey granted by the Dutch

patted *past and past participle of* ²PAT

¹**pat·ter** \'pat-ər\ *vb* : to talk quickly and smoothly or mechanically [Middle English *patren* "to patter, chant prayers mechanically", from *paternoster* "Lord's Prayer, Our Father", derived from Latin *pater noster* "our father" (first words of the prayer)]

²**patter** *n* **1** : JARGON 2, CANT **2** : fast talk used especially to attract attention or to entertain

³**patter** *vb* **1** : to strike or pat rapidly and repeatedly ⟨rain *pattering* on a roof⟩ **2** : to run with quick light-sounding steps [from *pat* "to tap or strike"]

⁴**patter** *n* : a series of quick light sounds ⟨the *patter* of little feet⟩

¹pat·tern \\'pat-ərn\\ *n*　**1** : something worth imitating or us- ing as a guide　**2** : a model or guide for making something ⟨a dress *pattern*⟩　**3** : an artistic form, figure, or design ⟨chintz with a small *pattern*⟩　**4** : a set of characteristics that are displayed repeatedly ⟨behavior *patterns*⟩ [Middle English *patron* "pattern", from early French *patron* (same meaning), from Latin *patronus* "patron, patron saint", from earlier *patronus* "defender, protector", from *patr-*, *pater* "father" — related to PADRE, PATERNAL, PATRON] — **pat- terned** \\-ərnd\\ *adj*

　　syn PATTERN, EXAMPLE, MODEL, IDEAL mean someone or something that one should follow or imitate. PATTERN suggests a carefully worked out design that should be followed closely ⟨other countries have used our laws as a *pattern*⟩ EXAMPLE applies to something that should be followed or sometimes to something certainly not to be followed ⟨set a good *example* for others⟩ ⟨they were punished for bad behavior and let that be an *example* for you⟩ MODEL suggests that the person or thing imi- tated is very worthy of imitation ⟨a leader who can be a *model* for all children⟩ IDEAL suggests something real or imagined that is thought to be the best of its kind that can exist ⟨the *ideal* of beauty⟩

²pattern *vb* : to make or design by following a pattern
patting *present participle of* ²PAT
pat·ty *also* **pat·tie** \\'pat-ē\\ *n, pl* **patties**　**1** : a little pie　**2** : a small flat cake of chopped food　**b** : a small flat candy
pau·ci·ty \\'pò-sət-ē\\ *n* : smallness of number or quantity : SCARCITY
paunch \\'pònch, 'pänch\\ *n*　**1** : the belly together with its contents　**2** : POTBELLY 1
paunchy \\'pòn-chē, 'pän-\\ *adj* **paunch·i·er; -est** : having a potbelly — **paunch·i·ness** *n*
pau·per \\'pò-pər\\ *n* : a very poor person; *esp* : one sup- ported by charity — **pau·per·ism** \\-pə-,riz-əm\\ *n* — **pau- per·ize** \\-,rīz\\ *vb*
¹pause \\'pòz\\ *n*　**1** : a temporary stop or rest　**2** : the sign ⌒ or ⌣ placed over or under a musical note, chord, or rest to show that it is to be held longer than usual　**3** : a reason for pausing ⟨a thought that should give *pause*⟩ [Middle English *pause* "a temporary stop, pause", from Latin *pausa* "a pause" — related to ¹REPOSE]
²pause *vb* **paused; paus·ing**　**1** : to stop temporarily　**2** : to linger for a time ⟨*pause* on a high note⟩
pave \\'pāv\\ *vb* **paved; pav·ing** : to lay or cover with mate- rial (as stone or concrete) that forms a firm level surface for travel — **pave the way** : to prepare a smooth easy way
pave·ment \\'pāv-mənt\\ *n*　**1** : a paved surface (as of a street)　**2** : the material with which something is paved
pa·vil·ion \\pə-'vil-yən\\ *n* **1** : a usually large tent with a peaked or rounded top　**2** : a lightly con- structed building serving as a shelter in a park, gar- den, or athletic field　**3** : a part of a building that ex- tends from the main part　**4** : a building partly or completely detached from the main building or group of buildings

pavilion 2

Word History The Latin word *papilio* meant "butterfly". From *papilio* came the early French word *paveillon*, which also meant "butterfly". But *paveillon* also came to be used to mean "a tent". Probably this happened because the top of a colorful tent looked like the spread wings of a butterfly. This early French word was borrowed into English as *pavilon*, now spelled *pa- vilion*. Over the years *pavilion* has acquired additional meanings in English, all having to do with a building of

some kind. But a tent that is large and richly decorated — as colorful as a butterfly — is still sometimes called a *pavilion*. [Middle English *pavilon* "a large decorated tent", from early French *paveillon* "tent, butterfly", from Latin *papilion-*, *papilio* "butterfly"]

pav·ing \\'pā-viŋ\\ *n* : PAVEMENT
¹paw \\'pò\\ *n* : the foot of a four-footed animal (as a lion or dog) having claws; *also* : the foot of an animal
²paw *vb*　**1** : to touch or handle clumsily or rudely　**2** : to touch or strike with a paw　**3** : to scrape or beat with or as if with a hoof　**4** : to grab at wildly
pawl \\'pòl\\ *n* : a tongue or sliding bolt on a machine part that is made to fall into notches on another part (as a ratchet wheel) so as to permit motion in only one direction
¹pawn \\'pòn, 'pän\\ *n*　**1** : the piece of least value in the game of chess　**2** : one that can be used to further the purposes of another [Middle English *pawn* "chess piece representing an ordinary soldier", from early French *poon* (same meaning), from Latin *pedon-*, *pedo* "foot soldier", derived from earlier *ped-*, *pes* "foot" — related to PEDES- TRIAN]
²pawn *n*　**1** : something given as a guarantee of repayment of a loan　**2** : the state of being pledged ⟨the watch was in *pawn*⟩ [Middle English *paun* "something given as a guarantee of repayment of a loan"]
³pawn *vb* : to leave as a guarantee of repayment of a loan ⟨*pawn* a watch⟩ — **pawn·er** *n*
pawn·bro·ker \\'pòn-,brō-kər, 'pän-\\ *n* : a person who makes a business of lending money and keeping personal property as a guarantee — **pawn·bro·king** \\-kiŋ\\ *n*
Paw·nee \\pò-'nē, pä-\\ *n* : a member of an American Indian people originally of Nebraska and Kansas
pawn·shop \\'pòn-,shäp, 'pän-\\ *n* : a pawnbroker's shop
pawpaw *variant of* PAPAW
¹pay \\'pā\\ *vb* **paid** \\'pād\\ *also in sense 6* **payed; paid; pay·ing**　**1** : to give (as money) in return for services re- ceived or for something bought ⟨*pay* the taxi driver⟩ ⟨*pay* for a ticket⟩　**2** : to give what is owed ⟨*pay* a tax⟩　**3** : to get even with ⟨*pay* someone back for an insult⟩　**4** : to give or offer freely ⟨*pay* a compliment⟩ ⟨*pay* attention⟩　**5 a** : to return value or profit to ⟨it *pays* to drive carefully⟩　**b** : to give as a return ⟨a bank account *paying* eight percent⟩　**6** : to make slack and allow to run out ⟨*pay* out a rope⟩ — **pay·er** \\'pā-ər\\ *also* **pay·or** \\'pā-ər, pā-'ò(ə)r\\ *n*
²pay *n*　**1 a** : the act of paying　**b** : the state of being paid or employed for money　**2** : something paid; *esp* : ²WAGE, SALARY
³pay *adj*　**1** : containing or leading to something valuable　**2** : having a coin slot for receiving money for use ⟨a *pay* phone⟩
pay·able \\'pā-ə-bəl\\ *adj* : that may, can, or must be paid ⟨accounts *payable*⟩
pay·check \\'pā-,chek\\ *n* : a check in payment of wages or salary
pay·day \\'pā-,dā\\ *n* : a regular day on which wages are paid
pay dirt *n*　**1** : earth or ore that produces a profit for a miner　**2** : a useful or profitable discovery or object
pay·ee \\pā-'ē\\ *n* : one to whom money is paid or is to be paid
pay·load \\'pā-,lōd\\ *n* : something (as cargo, passengers, instruments, or explosives) carried by a vehicle in addition to what is necessary for its operation
pay·mas·ter \\-,mas-tər\\ *n* : an officer or agent of an em- ployer whose duty it is to pay salaries or wages
pay·ment \\'pā-mənt\\ *n*　**1** : the act of paying　**2** : money

\\ə\\ abut	\\aú\\ **out**	\\ι\\ t**lp**	\\ò\\ **saw**	\\ú\\ **foot**
\\ər\\ **further**	\\ch\\ **chin**	\\ī\\ **life**	\\òi\\ **coin**	\\y\\ **yet**
\\a\\ **mat**	\\e\\ **pet**	\\j\\ **job**	\\th\\ **thin**	\\yü\\ **few**
\\ā\\ **take**	\\ē\\ **easy**	\\ŋ\\ **sing**	\\th\\ **this**	\\yú\\ **cure**
\\ä\\ **cot, cart**	\\g\\ **go**	\\ō\\ **bone**	\\ü\\ **food**	\\zh\\ **vision**

given to pay a debt **3** : ²PAY 2

pay·off \'pā-ˌȯf\ *n* **1** : ¹PROFIT 2 **2** : the last and most interesting part of an incident ⟨the *payoff* of a story⟩

pay off \(')pā-'ȯf\ *vb* **1** : to pay in full ⟨*pay off* a mortgage⟩ **2** : to produce a profit ⟨investments that *pay off*⟩

pay·roll \'pā-ˌrōl\ *n* **1** : a list of persons entitled to receive pay with the amounts due to each **2** : the amount of money necessary to pay those on a payroll

pay up *vb* : to pay in full

pea \'pē\ *n, pl* **peas** *also* **pease** \'pēz\ **1 a** : a plant of the legume family that is widely grown for its pods of protein-rich edible rounded seeds **b** : the seed of a pea **2** : a plant (as the sweet pea) related to the pea

peace \'pēs\ *n* **1** : a state of quiet; *esp* : freedom from public disturbance or war **2** : freedom from upsetting thoughts or feelings **3** : harmony in personal relations **4 a** : a state or period of peace between governments **b** : an agreement to end a war [Middle English *pees* "peace", from early French *pais* (same meaning), from Latin *pac-, pax* "peace" — related to APPEASE, PACIFY]

peace·able \'pē-sə-bəl\ *adj* **1** : PEACEFUL 1 **2** : PEACEFUL 3 — **peace·ably** \-blē\ *adv*

peace·ful \'pēs-fəl\ *adj* **1** : enjoying peace and quiet ⟨a *peaceful* people⟩ **2** : ²QUIET 1c, TRANQUIL ⟨a *peaceful* countryside⟩; *esp* : not at war **3** : not involving violence or force ⟨settled the conflict by *peaceful* means⟩ **syn** see CALM — **peace·ful·ly** \-fə-lē\ *adv* — **peace·ful·ness** *n*

peace·keep·ing \'pē-ˌskē-piŋ\ *n* : the enforcing of a truce between countries or groups by an international military force

peace·mak·er \'pē-ˌsmā-kər\ *n* : a person who settles an argument or stops a fight — **peace·mak·ing** \-kiŋ\ *n or adj*

peace·time \'pē-ˌstīm\ *n* : a time when a nation is not at war

peach \'pēch\ *n* **1** : a sweet juicy fruit with white or yellow flesh, a thin downy skin, and a single rough hard stone that is produced by a low spreading Chinese tree related to the plums and cherries and grown in most temperate areas; *also* : this tree **2** : a moderate yellowish pink

pea·cock \'pē-ˌkäk\ *n* : the male of a very large Asian pheasant having a very long brightly colored tail that can be spread or raised, a small crest, and in most forms brilliant blue or green feathers on the neck and shoulders

pea jacket \'pē-\ *n* : a heavy woolen double-breasted jacket originally worn by sailors

peacock

¹peak \'pēk\ *n* **1** : a part of a piece of clothing that is pointed or sticks out; *esp* : the front part of a cap or hat **2 a** : the top of a hill or mountain **b** : a mountain all by itself **3** : the highest point of development ⟨the *peak* of perfection⟩ — **peak** *adj*

²peak *vb* : to reach or cause to come to a peak, point, or maximum

¹peaked \'pēkt *also* 'pē-kəd\ *adj* : having a peak : POINTED ⟨a *peaked* roof⟩

²peak·ed \'pē-kəd\ *adj* : looking pale and sick

peal \'pē(ə)l\ *n* **1** : the loud ringing of bells **2** : a loud sound or series of sounds ⟨a *peal* of laughter⟩ ⟨a *peal* of thunder⟩ — **peal** *vb*

pea·nut \'pē-(ˌ)nət\ *n* **1** : a plant of the legume family that has yellow flowers and is grown for its underground pods of oily nutlike edible seeds which yield peanut oil or are crushed to make peanut butter; *also* : this pod or one of the oily edible seeds it contains **2** *pl* : a very small amount

peanut butter *n* : a paste made chiefly of ground roasted peanuts

peanut oil *n* : a colorless to yellow fatty oil that is obtained from peanuts

pear \'pa(ə)r, 'pe(ə)r\ *n* : a fleshy fruit that grows on a tree related to the apple and is commonly larger at the end opposite the stem; *also* : this tree

¹pearl \'pər(-ə)l\ *n* **1 a** : a dense smooth shiny body that is considered a gem and is formed in layers as an abnormal growth in the body of some mollusks usually around something irritating (as a grain of sand) which has gotten into the shell **b** : MOTHER-OF-PEARL **2** : something like a pearl (as in shape, color, or value) **3** : a light bluish gray

²pearl *adj* **1** : of, relating to, or resembling pearl **2** : made of pearls

pearly \'pər-lē\ *adj* **pearl·i·er; -est** : resembling pearls or mother-of-pearl

peas·ant \'pez-ᵊnt\ *n* **1** : a European small farmer or farm laborer **2** : a member of a similar agricultural class elsewhere

peas·ant·ry \-ᵊn-trē\ *n* : peasants as a group

pease *pl of* PEA

peat \'pēt\ *n* : a dark brown or blackish material that is the remains of plants partly decayed in water and is dug up and dried for use as fuel

peat moss *n* : SPHAGNUM

¹peb·ble \'peb-əl\ *n* **1** : a small rounded stone **2** : an uneven, wrinkled, or grainy surface — **peb·ble·like** \-əl-ˌ(l)īk\ *adj* — **peb·bly** \-(ə-)lē\ *adj*

²pebble *vb* **peb·bled; peb·bling** \'peb-(ə-)liŋ\ : to produce an uneven, wrinkled, or grainy surface on

pe·can \pi-'kän, -'kan\ *n* : an oblong edible nut that usually has a thin shell and is the fruit of a tall tree of the central and southern U.S.; *also* : this tree which is one of the hickories

pec·ca·dil·lo \ˌpek-ə-'dil-ō\ *n, pl* **-loes** *or* **-los** : a slight offense or fault

pec·ca·ry \'pek-ə-rē\ *n, pl* **-ries** : either of two American chiefly tropical mammals that gather in herds, are active at night, and look like but are much smaller than the related pigs

peccary

¹peck \'pek\ *n* **1** — see MEASURE table **2** : a large quantity ⟨a *peck* of trouble⟩ [Middle English *pek* "unit of measure", from early French *pek* (same meaning)]

²peck *vb* **1 a** : to strike with the bill : thrust the beak into **b** : to make by pecking ⟨*peck* holes⟩ **2** : to strike with a sharp instrument (as a pick) **3** : to pick up with the bill ⟨a chicken *pecking* corn⟩ **4** : to bite daintily : NIBBLE ⟨*peck* at one's food⟩ [Middle English *pecken* "to strike or pierce repeatedly", an altered form of *piken* "pierce, pick" — related to ¹PICK]

³peck *n* **1** : a mark or hole made by pecking **2** : a quick sharp stroke

pecking order *also* **peck order** *n* : a basic pattern of social organization within a flock of poultry in which each bird pecks another lower in the scale without being pecked in return and allows pecking by one of higher rank

pec·tin \'pek-tən\ *n* : any of various substances in plant tissues that dissolve in water and produce a gel which is the basis of fruit jellies; *also* : a commercial product rich in pectins

pec·to·ral \'pek-t(ə-)rəl\ *adj* : of, relating to, or situated in, near, or on the chest

pectoral fin *n* : either of a pair of fins in a fish that correspond to the front limbs of a four-footed animal — compare

PELVIC FIN

pectoral muscle *n* : any of the muscles which connect the front walls of the chest with the bones of the upper arm and shoulder and of which there are two on each side in the human body

pe·cu·liar \pi-'kyül-yər\ *adj* **1** : one's own : of or limited to some one person, thing, or place ⟨a custom *peculiar* to England⟩ **2** : different from the usual or normal ⟨*peculiar* behavior⟩ — **pe·cu·liar·ly** *adv*

pe·cu·liar·i·ty \pi-,kyül-'yar-ət-ē, -,kyü-lē-'ar-\ *n, pl* **-ties** **1** : the quality or state of being peculiar **2** : something different or individual **3** : something odd or abnormal

pe·cu·ni·ary \pi-'kyü-nē-,er-ē\ *adj* : of, relating to, or consisting of money

ped·a·gog·ics \,ped-ə-'gäj-iks\ *n* : PEDAGOGY

ped·a·gogue \'ped-ə-,gäg\ *n* : TEACHER, SCHOOLMASTER

Word History In ancient Greece a rich family had many servants. One of the servants was in charge of caring for the children. This servant's duties included escorting the children to and from school. As a name for this servant, the Greek prefix *paid-*, meaning "child", and the noun *agōgos*, meaning "leader", were combined to form *paidagōgos.* This word might be translated literally as "child-leader". The English word *pedagogue* can be traced to the Greek *paidagōgos.* It is now a name for a person who leads children by teaching them, rather than just by escorting them. [Middle English *pedagoge* "teacher", from early French *pedagoge* (same meaning), from Latin *paedagogus* (same meaning), from Greek *paidagōgos* "a servant who escorted children to school", from *paid-* "child" and *agōgos* "leader"]

ped·a·go·gy \'ped-ə-,gōj-ē *also* -,gäj-,ē\ *n* : the art, science, or profession of teaching : EDUCATION — **ped·a·gog·i·cal** \-i-kəl\ *adj* — **ped·a·gog·i·cal·ly** \-i-k(ə-)lē\ *adv*

¹ped·al \'ped-ªl\ *n* : a lever (as on a piano, bicycle, or sewing machine) worked by the foot [from early French *pedale* "a foot lever on an organ", from Italian *pedale* (same meaning), from Latin *pedalis* "of the foot", from *ped-, pes* "foot" — related to PEDESTRIAN]

²pedal *vb* **ped·aled** *also* **ped·alled; ped·al·ing** *also* **ped·al·ling** \'ped-ªl-iŋ, -liŋ\ **1** : to use or work the pedals of something **2** : to ride a bicycle

pedal pushers *n pl* : women's and girls' calf-length trousers

ped·ant \'ped-ªnt\ *n* **1** : a person who shows off his or her learning **2** : a dull and overly exact teacher — **pe·dan·tic** \pi-'dant-ik\ *adj* — **pe·dan·ti·cal·ly** \-i-k(ə-)lē\ *adv*

ped·ant·ry \'ped-ªn-trē\ *n, pl* **-ries** : dull and overly exact presentation of knowledge or learning

ped·dle \'ped-ªl\ *vb* **ped·dled; ped·dling** \-liŋ, -ªl-iŋ\ **1** : to travel about especially from house to house with goods for sale **2** : to sell from place to place usually in small quantities — **ped·dler** *also* **ped·lar** \'ped-lər\ *n*

ped·es·tal \'ped-əs-tªl\ *n* **1** : the support or foot of a column **2** : the base of something upright (as a vase, lamp, or statue) **3** : a position of high regard

¹pe·des·tri·an \pə-'des-trē-ən\ *adj* **1** : not interesting : ORDINARY **2 a** : going on foot **b** : of, relating to, or designed for walking ⟨*pedestrian* traffic⟩ ⟨a *pedestrian* mall⟩ [from Latin *pedestri-, pedestris* "going on foot", from *pedes* "one who goes on foot", from *ped-, pes* "foot" — related to CENTIPEDE, IMPEDE, ¹PAWN, PEDAL] — **pe·des·tri·an·ism** \-trē-ə-,niz-əm\ *n*

²pedestrian *n* : a person who is walking

pe·di·a·tri·cian \,pēd-ē-ə-'trish-ən\ *n* : a doctor who specializes in the care, development, and diseases of babies and children

pe·di·at·rics \,pēd-ē-'a-triks\ *n sing or pl* : a branch of medicine concerned with the development, care, and diseases of babies and children — **pe·di·at·ric** \-trik\ *adj*

pe·dic·u·lo·sis \pi-,dik-yə-'lō-səs\ *n* : the condition of having lice (as in the hair or on the body)

ped·i·cure \'ped-i-,kyù(ə)r\ *n* : care of the feet, toes, and nails; *also* : a single treatment of these parts

ped·i·gree \'ped-ə-,grē\ *n* **1** : a table or list showing the line of ancestors of a person or animal **2** : an ancestral line : LINEAGE **3** : purity of breed recorded by a pedigree — **ped·i·greed** \-,grēd\ *adj*

ped·i·ment \'ped-ə-mənt\ *n* : a triangular space forming the gable of a roof in classic architecture

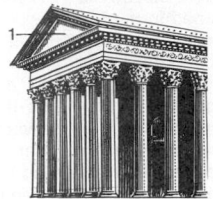

pe·dom·e·ter \pi-'däm-ət-ər\ *n* : an instrument that measures the distance one covers in walking

pe·dun·cle \'pē-,dən-kəl, pi-'dəŋ-\ *n* : a narrow part by which some larger part or the body of a living thing is attached; *esp* : a stalk that supports a flower cluster

1 pediment

peek \'pēk\ *vb* **1** : to look cautiously or briefly **2** : to look through a crack or hole or from a hiding place — **peek** *n*

¹peel \'pē(ə)l\ *vb* **1** : to strip off the skin or bark of ⟨*peel* an apple⟩ **2** : to strip or tear off ⟨*peeled* off their coats⟩ **3 a** : to come off in strips or patches ⟨the paint is *peeling*⟩ **b** : to lose the skin or bark ⟨your face is *peeling*⟩ — **peel·er** *n*

²peel *n* : an outer covering and especially the skin of a fruit

peel·ing \'pē-liŋ\ *n* : a peeled-off piece or strip (as of skin or rind)

¹peep \'pēp\ *vb* **1** : to make a feeble shrill sound as of a bird newly hatched **2** : to speak with a small weak voice [Middle English *pepen* "to peep, make the sound of a young bird"; the word began as an imitation of the sound made by a young bird]

²peep *n* : a feeble shrill sound

³peep *vb* **1** : PEEK 2, PEER **2** : to show slightly ⟨crocuses *peeping* through the snow⟩ [Middle English *pepen* "to peek", an altered form of earlier *piken* "to peek"]

⁴peep *n* **1** : the first appearance ⟨the *peep* of dawn⟩ **2** : a brief or sly look

¹peep·er \'pē-pər\ *n* : one that peeps; *esp* : any of various small frogs that peep in spring

²peeper *n* **1** : one that peeps; *esp* : PEEPING TOM **2** : ¹EYE 1

peep·hole \'pēp-,hōl\ *n* : a hole or crack to peep through

peep·ing Tom \,pē-piŋ-'täm\ *n* : a person who spies into the windows of private dwellings

Word History According to an ancient English legend, the lord of the town of Coventry had burdened the citizens with heavy taxes. His wife, Lady Godiva, was constantly urging the lord to lower the taxes. Finally he promised to do away with the taxes, but only if Lady Godiva would ride naked on a horse through the town. Wanting to help the townspeople, Godiva agreed and made the ride, covered only by her very long hair. For their part, the people decided to stay in their homes and not look at her nakedness. However, a tailor named Tom could not resist the temptation to peep at her. For this, it is said, he was struck blind. He is remembered as "Peeping Tom", and his name is used for a person who sneakily peeps at the private activities of others.

peep show *n* : an entertainment consisting of objects or pictures viewed through a small hole usually fitted with a lens

¹peer \'pi(ə)r\ *n* **1** : a person of the same rank or class as another **2 a** : a member of one of the five ranks of the

\ə\ abut	\aù\ out	\i\ tip	\ò\ saw	\ù\ foot
\ər\ further	\ch\ chin	\ī\ life	\òi\ coin	\y\ yet
\a\ mat	\e\ pet	\j\ job	\th\ thin	\yü\ few
\ā\ take	\ē\ easy	\ŋ\ sing	\th\ this	\yù\ cure
\ä\ cot, cart	\g\ go	\ō\ bone	\ü\ food	\zh\ vision

British nobility **b** : ²NOBLE [Middle English *peer* "one on equal standing with another", derived from early French *per* (adjective) "equal", from Latin *par* "equal" — related to COMPARE, PAIR, PAR, UMPIRE; see *Word History* at UMPIRE]

²**peer** *vb* **1** : to look closely or curiously ⟨*peered* into the dark closet⟩ **2** : ³PEEP 2 [perhaps an altered and shortened form of *appear*]

peer·age \'pi(ə)r-ij\ *n* **1** : NOBILITY 2 **2** : a list or register of peers

peer·less \'pi(ə)r-ləs\ *adj* : having no equal ⟨*peerless* beauty⟩ — **peer·less·ly** *adv* — **peer·less·ness** *n*

¹**peeve** \'pēv\ *vb* **peeved; peev·ing** : to make irritable or resentful : ANNOY, IRRITATE

²**peeve** *n* **1** : a feeling or mood of resentment **2** : something one finds annoying ⟨a pet *peeve*⟩

pee·vish \'pē-vish\ *adj* **1** : IRRITABLE **2** : STUBBORN 1a — **pee·vish·ly** *adv* — **pee·vish·ness** *n*

pee·wee \'pē-wē\ *n* **1** : PEWEE **2** : a tiny person or thing

pee·wit *or* **pe·wit** \'pē-ˌwit, 'pyü-ət\ *n* : any of several birds (as a small gull or a pewee)

¹**peg** \'peg\ *n* **1 a** : a small usually cylindrical pointed piece (as of wood) used to pin down or fasten things or to fit into or close holes ⟨a tent *peg*⟩ **b** : a tapered wooden piece in a musical instrument (as a violin) that is turned to tighten or loosen a string to adjust pitch **2** : a piece that sticks out and is used as a support or boundary marker **3** : ¹STEP 5, DEGREE ⟨take someone down a *peg*⟩ **4** : ²THROW 1 ⟨a quick *peg* to first base⟩

²**peg** *vb* **pegged; peg·ging** **1 a** : to fasten or mark with pegs **b** : to fix or hold (as prices) at a level or rate of increase **2** : to place in a class or group **3** : ¹THROW 1a **4** : to work steadily and diligently

Peg·a·sus \'peg-ə-səs\ *n* : a group of stars that is located just north of Aquarius and Pisces and that is recognized by four bright stars in the form of a large square

Peg–Board \'peg-ˌbō(ə)rd, -ˌbȯ(ə)rd\ *trademark* — used for material (as fiberboard) with evenly spaced holes into which hooks may be inserted for the storage or display of articles

peg·ma·tite \'peg-mə-ˌtīt\ *n* : a grainy variety of granite that occurs in layers in rock

Pe·king·ese *or* **Pe·kin·ese** \ˌpē-kən-'ēz, -kiŋ-, -'ēs\ *n, pl* **Pekingese** *or* **Pekinese** **1 a** : the Chinese dialect of Peking **b** : a person born or living in Peking **2** : any of a Chinese breed of small short-legged dogs with a broad flat face and a long soft coat

Pekingese 2

Pe·king man \ˌpē-ˌkiŋ-\ *n* : an extinct Pleistocene human being known from skeletal and cultural remains in cave deposits found in northeastern China and now classified with the pithecanthropines

pe·koe \'pē-kō\ *n* : a black tea made from small-sized tea leaves especially in India and Ceylon

pel·age \'pel-ij\ *n* : the hairy covering of an animal

pe·lag·ic \pə-'laj-ik\ *adj* : of, relating to, or living or occurring in the open sea : OCEANIC

pelf \'pelf\ *n* : MONEY 1a, RICHES

pel·i·can \'pel-i-kən\ *n* : any of a genus of large web-footed birds with a very large bill having a pouch on the lower part used to scoop in fish for food

pel·la·gra \pə-'lag-rə, -'lāg-, -'läg-\ *n* : a disease caused by a diet with too little niacin and protein and marked by a skin rash, disease of the digestive system, and certain nervous and mental symptoms

pel·let \'pel-ət\ *n* **1** : a little ball (as of food or medicine) **2 a** : BULLET **b** : a piece of small shot

pel·li·cle \'pel-i-kəl\ *n* : a thin skin or membrane (as of a cell)

pell–mell \'pel-'mel\ *adv* **1** : in confusion or disorder **2** : in great haste — **pell–mell** *adj*

pel·lu·cid \pə-'lü-səd\ *adj* : extremely clear or transparent

¹**pelt** \'pelt\ *n* : a usually unfinished skin with its hair, wool, or fur [Middle English *pelt* "skin and attached fur of an animal"]

²**pelt** *vb* **1** : to strike with a series of blows, missiles, or words **2** : HURL 1, THROW **3** : to beat against again and again **4** : to move quickly [Middle English *pelten* "to hit with a series of blows, pelt"]

pel·vic \'pel-vik\ *adj* : of, relating to, or located in or near the pelvis ⟨*pelvic* bones⟩

pelvic fin *n* : either of a pair of fins on a fish that correspond to the hind limbs of a four-footed animal — compare PECTORAL FIN

pelvic girdle *n* : an arch of bone or cartilage that supports the hind limbs of a vertebrate — called also *hip girdle*

pel·vis \'pel-vəs\ *n, pl* **pel·vis·es** *or* **pel·ves** \'pel-ˌvēz\ : a basin-shaped structure in the skeleton of many vertebrates formed by the pelvic girdle and the nearby bones of the spine; *also* : its cavity

Pem·broke Welsh corgi \'pem-ˌbrōk-, -ˌbrük-\ *n* : any of a breed of Welsh corgis with pointed ears, straight forelegs, and a short tail — called also *Pembroke*

Pembroke Welsh corgi

pem·mi·can \'pem-i-kən\ *n* : dried lean meat pounded fine and mixed with melted fat

¹**pen** \'pen\ *n* **1** : a small enclosure for animals **2** : a small place of confinement or storage [Old English *penn* "an enclosure for animals"]

²**pen** *vb* **penned; pen·ning** : to shut in a pen

³**pen** *n* : an instrument for writing or drawing with ink

Word History The words *pen* and *pencil* look very much alike, and the writing instruments themselves have much in common. But these two words are not at all related. *Pen* can be traced back to the Latin word *penna* or *pinna*, meaning "feather". The early pens were made of long feathers trimmed to a point to hold ink. In time, pens came to be made with metal points and later with rolling balls instead of points. For this reason we no longer associate the word *pen* with feathers. *Pencil* can be traced to the Latin word *penicillus*, which meant "little tail" or "brush". (It also gave us our word *penicillin*.) The first pencils were artists' brushes that had fine hairs drawn to a point, like the tail of a tiny animal. From these first pencils, used for painting fine lines, the word came to be used for other instruments used to draw marks. Some pencils were sticks of charcoal. Others were sticks of slate or lead. Still others were sticks of colored material like crayons. In time, we began using our modern wood and graphite pencils, which are not at all like the original "little tails". [Middle English *penne* "a writing instrument made from a bird's feather", from early French *penne* "a bird's feather, pen", from Latin *penna, pinna* "feather"]

⁴**pen** *vb* **penned; pen·ning** : to write especially with a pen

⁵**pen** *n, slang* : PENITENTIARY [a shortened form of *penitentiary*]

pe·nal \'pēn-ᵊl\ *adj* : of or relating to punishment ⟨*penal* laws⟩ ⟨a *penal* colony⟩

pe·nal·ize \'pēn-ᵊl-ˌīz, 'pen-\ *vb* **-ized; -iz·ing** **1** : to give a penalty to **2** : to place at a disadvantage

pen·al·ty \'pen-ᵊl-tē\ *n, pl* **-ties** **1** : punishment for a crime or offense **2** : something forfeited when one fails to do what one has agreed to do **3** : disadvantage, loss, or hardship due to some action or condition **4** : a punishment or handicap given for breaking a rule in a sport or game

pen·ance \'pen-ən(t)s\ *n* **1** : an act showing sorrow or regret for sin **2** : a sacrament consisting of regret for sin, confession to a priest, an act showing sorrow or regret ordered by the confessor, and forgiveness

pence *pl of* PENNY

pen·chant \'pen-chənt\ *n* : a strong liking

¹**pen·cil** \'pen(t)-səl\ *n* **1** : an instrument for writing, drawing, or marking consisting of or containing a slender cylinder or strip of a solid marking substance **2** : something like a pencil in form or use ⟨an eyebrow *pencil*⟩ [Middle English *pensel* "an artist's brush, pencil", from early French *pincel* (same meaning), derived from Latin *penicillus*, literally "little tail" — related to PENICILLIN; see *Word History* at ³PEN]

²**pencil** *vb* **-ciled** *or* **-cilled; -cil·ing** *or* **-cil·ling** \'pen(t)-s(ə-)liŋ\ : to mark, draw, or write with or as if with a pencil

pen·dant *also* **pen·dent** \'pen-dənt\ *n* : something that hangs down especially as an ornament

pen·dent *or* **pen·dant** \'pen-dənt\ *adj* **1** : sticking out or hanging over **2** : supported from above **3** : ²PENDING 1

¹**pend·ing** \'pen-diŋ\ *prep* : while waiting for ⟨held in jail *pending* a trial⟩

²**pending** *adj* **1** : not yet decided or acted on ⟨bills *pending* in Congress⟩ **2** : being about to take place ⟨signs of a *pending* victory⟩

pen·du·lous \'pen-jə-ləs\ *adj* **1** : hanging so as to swing freely **2** : hanging downward — **pen·du·lous·ly** *adv*

pen·du·lum \'pen-jə-ləm\ *n* : a body hung from a fixed point so as to swing freely back and forth under the action of gravity [from scientific Latin *pendulum* "something suspended so as to swing freely", from Latin *pendulus* "suspended", from *pendēre* "to hang" — related to DEPEND, PERPENDICULAR]

pe·ne·plain *also* **pe·ne·plane** \'pēn-i-ˌplān, 'pen-\ *n* : a large almost flat land surface shaped by erosion

pen·e·tra·ble \'pen-ə-trə-bəl\ *adj* : capable of being penetrated — **pen·e·tra·bil·i·ty** \ˌpen-ə-trə-'bil-ət-ē\ *n*

pen·e·trate \'pen-ə-ˌtrāt\ *vb* **-trat·ed; -trat·ing** **1 a** : to pass into or through **b** : to enter by piercing **2** : to come to understand **3** : to move deeply

pen·e·trat·ing *adj* **1** : having the power of entering or piercing ⟨*penetrating* cold⟩ **2** : ACUTE 3, DISCERNING ⟨a *penetrating* mind⟩ — **pen·e·trat·ing·ly** \-ˌtrāt-iŋ-lē\ *adv*

pen·e·tra·tion \ˌpen-ə-'trā-shən\ *n* **1** : the act or process of penetrating **2 a** : the depth to which something penetrates **b** : keen understanding

pen·guin \'pen-gwən, 'peŋ-\ *n* : any of various short-legged seabirds of the southern hemisphere that cannot fly and have the wings reduced to flippers and used in swimming

pen·i·cil·lin \ˌpen-ə-'sil-ən\ *n* : any of several antibiotics or a mixture of these produced by penicillia or in the laboratory and used especially against round disease-producing bacteria [from scientific Latin *Penicillium* "a genus of fungi", from Latin *penicillus*, literally "little tail" — related to PENCIL]

pen·i·cil·li·um \ˌpen-ə-'sil-ē-əm\ *n, pl* **-lia** \-ē-ə\ : any of a genus of fungi of which most are blue molds found chiefly on moist nonliving organic matter

pen·in·su·la \pə-'nin(t)-s(ə-)lə, -'nin-chə-lə\ *n* : a piece of land nearly surrounded by water or sticking out into the water [from Latin *paeninsula* "peninsula", from *paene-* "almost" and *insula* "island" — related to INSULATE, ISLE, ISOLATE] — **pen·in·su·lar** \-s(ə-)lər, -chə-lər\ *adj*

pe·nis \'pē-nəs\ *n, pl* **pe·nes** \'pē-ˌnēz\ *or* **pe·nis·es** : a male organ of copulation that in mammals including humans usually also contains the channel by which urine leaves the body — **pe·nile** \-ˌnīl\ *adj*

penguin

pen·i·tence \'pen-ə-tən(t)s\ *n* : sorrow for one's sins or faults : REPENTANCE — **pen·i·tent** \-tənt\ *adj* — **pen·i·tent·ly** *adv*

penitent *n* : a person who repents or is doing penance

pen·i·ten·tial \ˌpen-ə-'ten-chəl\ *adj* : of or relating to penitence or penance — **pen·i·ten·tial·ly** \-'tench-(ə-)lē\ *adv*

pen·i·ten·tia·ry \ˌpen-ə-'tench-(ə-)rē\ *n, pl* **-ries** : a usually state or federal prison in which criminals are kept

pen·knife \'pen-ˌnīf\ *n* : a small pocketknife usually with only one blade [so called from the fact that it was originally used for sharpening the points of quill (feather) pens]

pen·light \-ˌlīt\ *n* : a small flashlight resembling a fountain pen in size or shape

pen·man \-mən\ *n* : AUTHOR 1

pen·man·ship \-mən-ˌship\ *n* **1** : the art or practice of writing with the pen **2** : quality or style of handwriting

pen name *n* : a false name used by an author

pen·nant \'pen-ənt\ *n* **1** : a flag with a usually tapering or forked tail that is used especially for signaling **2** : a flag that serves as the emblem of championship

pen·ni·less \'pen-i-ləs, 'pen-ᵊl-əs\ *adj* : having no money : very poor

pen·non \'pen-ən\ *n* **1** : a long triangular or forked streamer attached to the head of a lance as a flag **2** : ²FLAG 1, PENNANT

Penn·syl·va·nia Dutch \ˌpen(t)-səl-ˌvā-nyə-, -nē-ə-\ *n* **1** : a people living mostly in eastern Pennsylvania whose culture goes back to the German migrations of the 18th century **2** : the German dialect of the Pennsylvania Dutch — **Pennsylvania Dutchman** *n*

Penn·syl·va·nian \ˌpen(t)-səl-'vā-nyən, -nē-ən\ *adj* **1** : of or relating to Pennsylvania or its people **2** : of, relating to, or being the later part of the Carboniferous period in the Paleozoic era of geological history in North America marked by the first appearance of reptiles; *also* : relating to the corresponding system of rocks — see GEOLOGIC TIME table — **Pennsylvanian** *n*

pen·ny \'pen-ē\ *n, pl* **pen·nies** \-ēz\ *or* **pence** \'pen(t)s\ **1 a** : a British unit of money formerly equal to ¹⁄₂₄₀ pound but now equal to ¹⁄₁₀₀ pound **b** : a coin representing this unit **2** *pl* **pennies** : CENT **3** : a sum of money ⟨earn an

\ə\ **abut**	\au̇\ **out**	\i\ **tip**	\ȯ\ **saw**	\u̇\ **foot**
\ər\ **further**	\ch\ **chin**	\ī\ **life**	\ȯi\ **coin**	\y\ **yet**
\a\ **mat**	\e\ **pet**	\j\ **job**	\th\ **thin**	\yü\ **few**
\ā\ **take**	\ē\ **easy**	\ŋ\ **sing**	\th\ **this**	\yu̇\ **cure**
\ä\ **cot, cart**	\g\ **go**	\ō\ **bone**	\ü\ **food**	\zh\ **vision**

honest *penny*⟩

penny arcade *n* : an amusement center where each device for entertainment may be operated for a small sum

pen·ny·weight \'pen-ē-,wāt\ *n* — see MEASURE table

pen·ny–wise \-,wīz\ *adj* : wise only in small or unimportant matters

pen pal *n* : a friend made and kept through letter-writing

¹**pen·sion** \'pen-chən\ *n* : a sum paid regularly to a person especially following retirement or to surviving dependents

²**pension** *vb* **pen·sioned; pen·sion·ing** \'pench-(ə-)niŋ\ : to pay a pension to

pen·sion·er \'pench-(ə-)nər\ *n* : a person who receives or lives on a pension

pen·sive \'pen(t)-siv\ *adj* **1** : dreamily thoughtful **2** : suggestive of sad thoughtfulness — **pen·sive·ly** *adv* — **pen·sive·ness** *n*

pen·stock \'pen-,stäk\ *n* **1** : a gate or valve for regulating a flow (as of water) **2** : a pipe for carrying water

pent \'pent\ *adj* : shut up : CONFINED ⟨*pent*-up feelings⟩

pen·ta·gon \'pent-ə-,gän\ *n* : a figure of five angles and five sides

pen·tag·o·nal \pen-'tag-ən-ᵊl\ *adj* **1** : having five sides and five angles **2** : having a pentagon as a cross section or as a base ⟨a *pentagonal* pyramid⟩

pen·tam·e·ter \pen-'tam-ət-ər\ *n* : a line consisting of five metrical feet

pen·tath·lon \pen-'tath-lən, -,län\ *n* : an athletic contest made up of five different track-and-field events

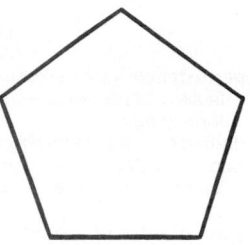

pentagon

Pen·te·cost \'pent-i-,kóst, -,käst\ *n* **1** : SHABUOTH **2** : the seventh Sunday after Easter observed as a Christian church festival in memory of the appearance of the Holy Spirit to the apostles — **Pen·te·cos·tal** \,pent-i-'käs-tᵊl, -'kós-\ *adj or n*

pent·house \'pent-,haús\ *n* **1** : a sloping roof or a shed attached to a wall or building **2** : a structure (as an apartment) built on the roof of a building

pen·tose \'pen-,tōs\ *n* : any of various sugars containing five carbon atoms in a molecule

pe·nult \'pē-,nəlt, pi-'nəlt\ *n* : the next to the last syllable of a word

pen·ul·ti·mate \pi-'nəl-tə-mət\ *adj* : next to the last — **pen·ultimate** *n*

pen·um·bra \pə-'nəm-brə\ *n, pl* **-brae** \-brē, -,brī\ *or* **-bras** : the partial shadow surrounding a perfect shadow (as in an eclipse) — **pen·um·bral** \-brəl\ *adj*

pe·nu·ri·ous \pə-'n(y)úr-ē-əs\ *adj* **1** : marked by or suffering from penury **2** : extremely stingy : MISERLY — **pe·nu·ri·ous·ly** *adv* — **pe·nu·ri·ous·ness** *n*

pen·u·ry \'pen-yə-rē\ *n* : extreme poverty

pe·on \'pē-,än, -ən\ *n* **1** : a member of the landless laboring class in Spanish America **2** : a person who does hard or dull work — **pe·on·age** \'pē-ə-nij\ *n*

pe·o·ny \'pē-ə-nē\ *n, pl* **-nies** : any of a genus of plants that are related to the buttercups, live for years, and are widely grown for their large usually double red, pink, or white flowers

¹**peo·ple** \'pē-pəl\ *n, pl* **people** **1** *pl* : human beings : PERSONS — often used in compounds instead of *persons* ⟨sales*people*⟩ **2** *pl* : the members of a family : KINDRED **3** *pl* : the mass of a community as distinguished from a special class **4** *pl* **peoples** : a body of persons united by a common culture, tradition, or sense of kinship, and usually language **5** : the body of voters of a state

²**people** *vb* **peo·pled; peo·pling** \'pē-p(ə-)liŋ\ **1** : to supply or fill with people **2** : INHABIT

¹**pep** \'pep\ *n* : brisk energy : LIVELINESS — **pep·pi·ness** \-ē-nəs\ *n* — **pep·py** \-ē\ *adj*

²**pep** *vb* **pepped; pep·ping** : to put pep into : STIMULATE ⟨let's try to *pep* things up⟩

¹**pep·per** \'pep-ər\ *n* **1** : either of two sharp-tasting products from the fruit of an East Indian plant used as a seasoning or in medicine: **a** : BLACK PEPPER **b** : WHITE PEPPER **2** : a woody vine with rounded leaves and flowers arranged in a spike that is widely cultivated in the tropics for its red berries from which pepper is prepared **3** : any of several products similar to pepper that are obtained from close relatives of the pepper **4** : any of a genus of tropical herbs and shrubs related to the potato and widely cultivated for their many-seeded fruits that usually have fleshy walls; *esp* : one of the New World whose fruits are hot peppers or sweet peppers — **pepper** *adj*

pepper 2

²**pepper** *vb* **pep·pered; pep·per·ing** \'pep-(ə-)riŋ\ **1** : to sprinkle or season with or as if with pepper **2** : to hit with a shower of blows or objects

pep·per·corn \'pep-ər-,kó(ə)rn\ *n* : a dried berry of the East Indian pepper

peppered moth *n* : a European moth that normally has white wings with small black specks but often has black wings in areas with heavy air pollution

pep·per·mint \'pep-ər-,mint, -mənt\ *n* **1** : a mint with stalks of small usually pink flowers that is the source of an oil which is sharp in flavor and is used especially to flavor candies **2** : candy flavored with peppermint

pep·per·o·ni \,pep-ə-'rō-nē\ *n* : a highly seasoned beef and pork sausage

pep·pery \'pep-(ə-)rē\ *adj* **1** : of, relating to, or having the qualities of pepper : HOT **2** : having a hot temper **3** : FIERY 3a

pep·sin \'pep-sən\ *n* **1** : an enzyme given off by glands in the wall of the stomach that begins the digestion of most proteins **2** : a preparation of pepsin obtained especially from the stomach of the hog and used in medicine

pep·tic \'pep-tik\ *adj* **1** : relating to or promoting digestion **2** : resulting from the action of digestive juices ⟨a *peptic* ulcer⟩

pep·ti·dase \'pep-tə-,dās, -,dāz\ *n* : an enzyme that breaks down simple pieces of proteins

pep·tone \'pep-,tōn\ *n* : any of various products that result from the partial breakdown of proteins and that dissolve in water

per \(')pər\ *prep* **1** : by means of **2** : to or for each ⟨$10 *per* day⟩ **3** : as indicated by : ACCORDING TO ⟨*per* list price⟩

¹**per·ad·ven·ture** \'pər-əd-,ven-chər, 'per-; ,pər-əd-'ven-, ,per-\ *adv, archaic* : PERHAPS, POSSIBLY

²**peradventure** *n* : a possibility of error or uncertainty

per·am·bu·late \pə-'ram-byə-,lāt\ *vb* **-lat·ed; -lat·ing** **1** : to walk over or through **2** : STROLL, RAMBLE — **per·am·bu·la·tion** \-,ram-byə-'lā-shən\ *n*

per·am·bu·la·tor \pə-'ram-byə-,lāt-ər\ *n* **1** : one that perambulates **2** *chiefly British* : a baby carriage

per an·num \(,)pər-'an-əm\ *adv* : in or for each year : ANNUALLY

per·cale \(,)pər-'kā(ə)l, 'pər-,kā(ə)l, (,)pər-'kal\ *n* : a fine closely woven cotton cloth used especially to make sheets and pillowcases

per cap·i·ta \(,)pər-'kap-ət-ə\ *adv or adj* : by or for each person ⟨*per capita* income⟩

per·ceive \pər-'sēv\ *vb* **perceived; per·ceiv·ing** **1** : UN-

DERSTAND 1a, COMPREHEND   **2** : to become aware of through the senses and especially through sight — **per·ceiv·er** *n*

¹per·cent \pər-'sent\ *adv* : in the hundred : of each hundred

²percent *adj* : measured or counted on the basis of a whole divided into one hundred parts

³percent *n, pl* **percent** *or* **percents**   **1** : one part in a hundred : HUNDREDTH   **2** : PERCENTAGE 1

per·cent·age \pər-'sent-ij\ *n*   **1 a** : a part of a whole expressed in hundredths   **b** : the result obtained by multiplying a number by a percent   **2 a** : PROBABILITY 3a ⟨play the *percentages*⟩   **b** : favorable odds

per·cep·ti·ble \pər-'sep-tə-bəl\ *adj* : capable of being noticed or observed ⟨a *perceptible* change⟩ — **per·cep·ti·bly** \-blē\ *adv*

per·cep·tion \pər-'sep-shən\ *n*   **1** : a result of perceiving : OBSERVATION   **2** : the act, process, or power of perceiving; *esp* : awareness of the elements of environment through sensation ⟨color *perception*⟩   **3** : capacity for understanding

per·cep·tive \pər-'sep-tiv\ *adj* : capable of or showing a keen ability to observe and understand

¹perch \'pərch\ *n*   **1** : a roost for a bird   **2** : a raised seat or position [Middle English *perche* "a peg on which something is hung", from early French *perche* (same meaning), from Latin *pertica* "pole"]

²perch *vb*   **1** : to place on a perch   **2** : to land, settle, or rest on or as if on a perch

³perch *n, pl* **perch** *or* **perch·es**   **1** : a common North American fish with spiny fins that is yellowish with dark green bands and is an excellent food and sport fish — called also *yellow perch*   **2** : any of various fishes related to or resembling the perch [Middle English *perche* "a kind of fish", from early French *perche* (same meaning), from Latin *perca* (same meaning), from Greek *perkē* "perch (fish)"]

per·chance \pər-'chan(t)s\ *adv* : PERHAPS, POSSIBLY

per·chlo·rate \(')pər-'klō(ə)r-,āt, -'klō(ə)r-\ *n* : a chemical compound formed by the reaction of perchloric acid with another substance

per·chlo·ric acid \(,)pər-,klōr-ik-, -,klȯr-\ *n* : a fuming strong acid that is a powerful oxidizing agent when heated

per·co·late \'pər-kə-,lāt\ *vb* **-lat·ed; -lat·ing**   **1** : to trickle or cause to trickle through something porous : FILTER, SEEP ⟨water *percolating* through sand⟩   **2** : to prepare coffee in a percolator   **3** : to be or become spread through : PENETRATE

per·co·la·tion \,pər-kə-'lā-shən\ *n* : the act or process of percolating

per·co·la·tor \'pər-kə-,lāt-ər\ *n* : a coffeepot in which boiling water rising through a tube is repeatedly turned downward through a basket with holes that contains ground coffee beans to make coffee

per·cus·sion \pər-'kəsh-ən\ *n*   **1** : the act of tapping sharply; *esp* : the striking of a percussion cap so as to set off the charge in a firearm   **2** : the striking of sound sharply on the ear

percussion cap *n* : ¹CAP 4

percussion instrument *n* : a musical instrument (as a drum, cymbal, or maraca) sounded by striking or shaking — compare BRASS INSTRUMENT, STRINGED INSTRUMENT, WOODWIND

per·cus·sion·ist \pər-'kəsh-(ə-)nəst\ *n* : a person who plays percussion instruments

per di·em \(,)pər-dē-əm, -'dī-\ *adv* : by the day : for each day — **per diem** *adj*

per·di·tion \pər-'dish-ən\ *n*   **1** : eternal damnation   **2** : HELL 2

per·e·gri·nate \'per-ə-grə-,nāt\ *vb* **-nat·ed; -nat·ing** : to travel especially on foot — **per·e·gri·na·tion** \,per-ə-grə-'nā-shən\ *n*

per·e·grine falcon \'per-ə-grən-, -,grēn-\ *n* : a dark swift widely distributed falcon that can be tamed and trained to hunt game

pe·remp·to·ry \pə-'rem(p)-t(ə-)rē\ *adj*   **1** : not to be refused ⟨a *peremptory* summons from the boss⟩   **2** : expressing command ⟨called for silence with a *peremptory* gesture⟩   **3** : showing the attitude of one accustomed to command : ARROGANT ⟨the *peremptory* tone caused resentment⟩ — **pe·remp·to·ri·ly** \-t(ə-)rə-lē\ *adv* — **pe·remp·to·ri·ness** \-t(ə-)rē-nəs\ *n*

peregrine falcon

¹pe·ren·ni·al \pə-'ren-ē-əl\ *adj*   **1** : present at all seasons of the year ⟨*perennial* springs⟩   **2** : living for several years usually with new leafy growth produced from the base each year ⟨*perennial* asters⟩   **3 a** : PERSISTENT 1, CONSTANT   **b** : RECURRENT 2 ⟨flooding is a *perennial* problem⟩ — **pe·ren·ni·al·ly** \-ē-ə-lē\ *adv*

²perennial *n* : a perennial plant

¹per·fect \'pər-fikt\ *adj*   **1 a** : being entirely without fault or defect : FLAWLESS   **b** : meeting all requirements : ACCURATE, EXACT ⟨a *perfect* circle⟩ ⟨a *perfect* copy⟩   **c** : PURE 3, TOTAL ⟨*perfect* stillness⟩   **d** : ¹COMPLETE 1, WHOLE   **2** : of an extreme kind ⟨a *perfect* fool⟩   **3** : of, relating to, or being a verb form in the perfect tense   **4** : having both stamens and pistil ⟨a *perfect* flower⟩ [Middle English *perfit* "complete, thoroughly or accurately done", from early French *parfit* (same meaning), from Latin *perfectus* "complete, perfect", derived from *perficere* "to carry out, complete", from *per-* "completely" and *-ficere*, from *facere* "to make, do" — related to ARTIFICIAL, FASHION, SATISFY] — **per·fect·ness** \-fik(t)-nəs\ *n*

²per·fect \pər-'fekt *also* 'pər-fikt\ *vb*   **1** : to make perfect   **2** : to bring to final form — **per·fect·er** *n*

³per·fect \'pər-fikt\ *n*   **1** : PERFECT TENSE   **2** : a verb form in the perfect tense

per·fect·ible \pər-'fek-tə-bəl *also* 'pər-fik-\ *adj* : capable of improvement or perfection — **per·fect·ibil·i·ty** \pər-,fek-tə-'bil-ət-ē ,pər-fik-\ *n*

per·fec·tion \pər-'fek-shən\ *n*   **1** : the quality or state of being perfect   **2** : a perfect quality or thing   **3** : a degree of accuracy or excellence that cannot be bettered ⟨cooked to *perfection*⟩   **4** : the act or process of perfecting

per·fec·tion·ist \pər-'fek-sh(ə-)nəst\ *n* : a person who is not content with anything less than perfection — **perfectionist** *adj*

per·fect·ly \'pər-fik-(t)lē\ *adv*   **1** : in a perfect manner ⟨understand *perfectly*⟩   **2** : QUITE 1, ALTOGETHER ⟨I was *perfectly* willing⟩

perfect number *n* : an integer that is equal to the sum of all its divisors except itself ⟨28 is a *perfect number* because it is the sum of $1 + 2 + 4 + 7 + 14$⟩

perfect square *n* : an integer whose square root is an integer ⟨9 is a *perfect square*⟩

perfect tense *n* : a verb tense that expresses an action or state completed at the time of speaking or at a time spoken of

per·fid·i·ous \(,)pər-'fid-ē-əs\ *adj* : of, relating to, or characterized by perfidy : TREACHEROUS — **per·fid·i·ous·ly** *adv* — **per·fid·i·ous·ness** *n*

per·fi·dy \'pər-fəd-ē\ *n, pl* **-dies** : the quality or state of being faithless or disloyal : TREACHERY

per·fo·rate \'pər-fə-,rāt\ *vb* **-rat·ed; -rat·ing** : to make a hole or series of holes through; *esp* : to make a line of

\ə\ abut	\au̇\ out	\i\ tip	\ȯ\ saw	\u̇\ foot
\ər\ further	\ch\ chin	\ī\ life	\ȯi\ coin	\y\ yet
\a\ mat	\e\ pet	\j\ job	\th\ thin	\yü\ few
\ā\ take	\ē\ easy	\ŋ\ sing	\th\ this	\yu̇\ cure
\ä\ cot, cart	\g\ go	\ō\ bone	\ü\ food	\zh\ vision

holes to make tearing easy and neat ⟨sheets of stamps are *perforated*⟩ — **per·fo·rate** \'pər-f(ə-)rət, -fə-ˌrāt\ *adj* — **per·fo·ra·tor** \-fə-ˌrāt-ər\ *n*

per·fo·ra·tion \ˌpər-fə-'rā-shən\ *n* **1** : the act or process of perforating **2** : a hole, pattern, or series of holes made by perforating

per·force \pər-'fō(ə)rs, -'fo(ə)rs\ *adv* : by force of circumstances or of necessity

per·form \pə(r)-'fo(ə)rm\ *vb* **1 a** : CARRY OUT, DO **b** : ²ACT 4, FUNCTION **2** : to do something requiring special skill **3 a** : to do according to rules or in an established way ⟨*perform* a wedding⟩ **b** : to give a performance of ⟨*perform* a play⟩ — **per·form·able** \-'for-mə-bəl\ *adj* — **per·form·er** \-'for-mər\ *n*

per·for·mance \pə(r)-'for-mən(t)s\ *n* **1 a** : the doing of an action **b** : something accomplished : DEED, FEAT **2 a** : the action of representing a character in a play **b** : a public presentation **3** : the manner in which something performs ⟨an engine's *performance*⟩

¹per·fume \'pər-ˌfyüm, (ˌ)pər-'fyüm\ *n* **1** : the scent of something usually sweet-smelling **2** : a substance that gives off a pleasant odor; *esp* : a liquid containing fragrant oils (as from flowers) mixed with alcohol and applied to the body to give it a pleasant odor

²per·fume \(ˌ)pər-'fyüm, 'pər-ˌfyüm\ *vb* **-fumed; -fum·ing** : to fill with a pleasing odor (as of flowers)

per·fum·ery \pə(r)-'fyüm-(ə-)rē\ *n, pl* **-er·ies** **1** : the art or process of making perfume **2** : a place where perfumes are made

per·func·to·ry \pər-'fəŋ(k)-t(ə)rē\ *adj* **1** : done mechanically or carelessly ⟨a *perfunctory* inspection⟩ **2** : lacking in interest or enthusiasm : INDIFFERENT — **per·func·to·ri·ly** \-t(ə-)rə-lē\ *adv* — **per·func·to·ri·ness** \-t(ə-)rē-nəs\ *n*

per·haps \pər-'(h)aps, 'praps\ *adv* : possibly but not certainly [from *per* (preposition) "by, according to" and *haps*, plural of *hap* "chance, chance occurrence" — related to HAPPEN, HAPPY, MISHAP]

peri·car·di·um \ˌper-ə-'kärd-ē-əm\ *n, pl* **-car·dia** \-ē-ə\ : the cone-shaped structure of membrane that encloses the vertebrate heart and the nearby parts of the large arteries and veins leading to or away from it — **peri·car·di·al** \-ē-əl\ *adj*

peri·gee \'per-ə-jē\ *n* : the point nearest a planet or a satellite (as the moon) reached by an object orbiting it — compare APOGEE

peri·he·lion \ˌper-ə-'hēl-yən\ *n* : the point in the path of a heavenly body (as a planet) that is nearest to the sun

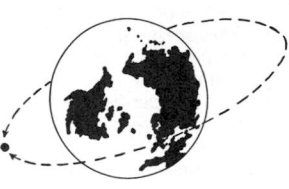

perigee

per·il \'per-əl\ *n* **1** : the state of being in danger of injury, loss, or destruction **2** : something that presents immediate danger ⟨*perils* of the highway⟩ **syn** see DANGER

per·il·ous \'per-ə-ləs\ *adj* : full of or involving peril — **per·il·ous·ly** *adv* — **per·il·ous·ness** *n*

pe·rim·e·ter \pə-'rim-ət-ər\ *n* : the boundary of a closed plane figure or area; *also* : the length of such a boundary

pe·ri·od \'pir-ē-əd\ *n* **1** : the completion of a cycle, a series of events, or an action **2** : a point . used to mark the end (as of a declarative sentence or an abbreviation) **3 a** : a portion of time marked by some repeating event **b** : the length of time required for a motion or event to complete a cycle and begin to repeat itself ⟨the *period* of a pendulum⟩ **c** : a single occurrence of menstruation **4 a** : ¹STAGE 4e **b** : a division of geologic time longer than an epoch and included in an era **c** : a stage or portion of time in the history of something ⟨the colonial *period*⟩ **5 a**

: one of the divisions of the school day **b** : one of the divisions of the playing time of a game **6** : a series of elements of increasing atomic number as listed in horizontal rows in the periodic table

syn PERIOD, ERA, AGE mean a portion of time. PERIOD can be used of any portion of time, no matter how long or short ⟨talked for a *period* of five minutes⟩ ⟨was a farmer for a *period* of twenty years⟩ ERA suggests a period of history noted for new or remarkable events ⟨an *era* of space exploration⟩ AGE suggests a long period of time that is associated with an important person ⟨the *age* of Thomas Jefferson⟩ or an outstanding thing ⟨the atomic *age*⟩

pe·ri·od·ic \ˌpir-ē-'äd-ik\ *adj* **1** : occurring at regular intervals **2** : consisting of or containing a series of repeated stages ⟨*periodic* vibrations⟩

¹pe·ri·od·i·cal \ˌpir-ē-'äd-i-kəl\ *adj* **1** : PERIODIC 1 **2** : published at regular intervals — **pe·ri·od·i·cal·ly** \-k(ə-)lē\ *adv*

²periodical *n* : a periodical publication

periodic table *n* : an arrangement of chemical elements in order of atomic number that groups elements with common characteristics in the same area of the table

peri·os·te·um \ˌper-ē-'äs-tē-əm\ *n, pl* **-tea** \-tē-ə\ : the membrane of connective tissue that covers all bones except at the surfaces in a joint

peri·pa·tet·ic \ˌper-ə-pə-'tet-ik\ *adj* : going about from place to place : ITINERANT

¹pe·riph·er·al \pə-'rif-(ə-)rəl\ *adj* **1** : of, relating to, located in, or forming a periphery **2** : ¹AUXILIARY, SUPPLEMENTARY ⟨*peripheral* equipment⟩ — **pe·riph·er·al·ly** \-ē\ *adv*

²peripheral *n* : a device connected to a computer to provide communication (as input and output) or extra storage capacity

peripheral nervous system *n* : the part of the nervous system that is outside the central nervous system and is made up of the autonomic nervous system, the spinal nerves, and the cranial nerves except the optic nerve

pe·riph·ery \pə-'rif-(ə-)rē\ *n, pl* **-er·ies** **1** : the boundary or surface of a body or figure **2** : the outer or outermost part

peri·scope \'per-ə-ˌskōp\ *n* : an instrument containing lenses and mirrors by which an observer (as on a submerged submarine) can get a view that would otherwise be blocked — **peri·scop·ic** \ˌper-ə-'skäp-ik\ *adj*

per·ish \'per-ish\ *vb* : to pass away completely : become destroyed

per·ish·able \'per-ish-ə-bəl\ *adj* : likely to spoil or decay ⟨*perishable* fruit⟩ — **perishable** *n*

peri·stal·sis \ˌper-ə-'stòl-səs, -'stäl-, -'stal-\ *n, pl* **-stal·ses** \-ˌsēz\ : the contracting and expanding movements by which food is forced through the digestive tube — **peri·stal·tic** \-tik\ *adj*

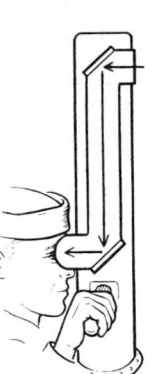

periscope

peri·to·ne·um \ˌper-ət-ᵊn-'ē-əm\ *n, pl* **-ne·ums** *or* **-nea** \-ᵊn-ē-ə\ : the smooth transparent membrane that lines the cavity of the abdomen and encloses the abdominal and pelvic organs

peri·to·ni·tis \ˌper-ət-ᵊn-'īt-əs\ *n* : inflammation of the peritoneum

peri·wig \'per-i-ˌwig\ *n* : WIG

¹per·i·win·kle \'per-i-ˌwiŋ-kəl\ *n* : an evergreen herb that spreads along the ground and has shiny leaves and blue or white flowers [Old English *perwince* "periwinkle vine", from Latin *pervinca* (same meaning)]

²periwinkle *n* **1** : any of numerous small edible marine

per·jure \'pər-jər\ *vb* **per·jured; per·jur·ing** \'pərj-(ə-)riŋ\ : to make (oneself) guilty of perjury — **per·jur·er** \'pər-jər-ər\ *n*

per·ju·ry \'pərj-(ə-)rē\ *n, pl* **-ries** : an act of swearing to what one knows is untrue

perk \'pərk\ *vb* **1** : to lift quickly or alertly ⟨the dog *perked* up its ears⟩ **2** : to make fresher in appearance ⟨new paint *perked* up the room⟩ **3** : to become more lively or cheerful — usually used with *up* ⟨we *perked* up at the good news⟩

perky \'pər-kē\ *adj* **perk·i·er; -est** : being lively and cheerful — **perk·i·ness** *n*

per·ma·frost \'pər-mə-,fròst\ *n* : a permanently frozen layer at variable depth below the surface in frigid regions of a planet (as earth)

¹per·ma·nent \'pərm(-ə)-nənt\ *adj* : lasting or intended to last for a very long time : not temporary or changing **syn** see LASTING — **per·ma·nence** \-nən(t)s\ *n* — **per·ma·nen·cy** \-nən-sē\ *n* — **per·ma·nent·ly** *adv* — **per·ma·nent·ness** *n*

²permanent *n* : a long-lasting hair wave produced by mechanical and chemical means

permanent magnet *n* : a magnet that retains its magnetism after removal of the magnetizing force

permanent press *n* : the process of treating a fabric chemically to resist wrinkling — **permanent–press** *adj*

permanent tooth *n* : one of the second set of teeth of a mammal that follow the milk teeth, usually last into old age, and in human beings are 32 in number

per·me·abil·i·ty \,pər-mē-ə-'bil-ət-ē\ *n* : the quality or state of being permeable

per·me·able \'pər-mē-ə-bəl\ *adj* : having pores or openings that permit liquids or gases to pass through ⟨a *permeable* membrane⟩ ⟨*permeable* limestone⟩

per·me·ate \'pər-mē-,āt\ *vb* **-at·ed; -at·ing** **1** : to spread throughout ⟨a room *permeated* with the scent of flowers⟩ **2** : to pass through something which has pores or small openings or is of loose texture : seep through ⟨water *permeates* sand⟩ — **per·me·ation** \,pər-mē-'ā-shən\ *n*

Perm·ian \'pər-mē-ən\ *adj* : of, relating to, or being the latest period of the Paleozoic era of geological history or the corresponding system of rocks — see GEOLOGIC TIME table — **Permian** *n*

per·mis·si·ble \pər-'mis-ə-bəl\ *adj* : that may be permitted : ALLOWABLE — **per·mis·si·bil·i·ty** \-,mis-ə-'bil-ət-ē\ *n* — **per·mis·si·ble·ness** \-'mis-ə-bəl-nəs\ *n* — **per·mis·si·bly** \-blē\ *adv*

per·mis·sion \pər-'mish-ən\ *n* **1** : the act of permitting **2** : the consent of a person in authority ⟨has *permission* to leave⟩

per·mis·sive \pər-'mis-iv\ *adj* **1** : granting or tending to grant permission : ALLOWING **2** : not forbidden : ALLOWABLE — **per·mis·sive·ly** *adv* — **per·mis·sive·ness** *n*

¹per·mit \pər-'mit\ *vb* **per·mit·ted; per·mit·ting** **1** : to consent to : give permission : ALLOW **2** : to make possible : give an opportunity ⟨if time *permits*⟩ — **per·mit·ter** *n*

²per·mit \'pər-,mit, pər-'mit\ *n* : a written statement of permission given by one having authority : LICENSE

per·mu·ta·tion \,pər-myü-'tā-shən\ *n* : an ordered arrangement of a set of objects

per·ni·cious \pər-'nish-əs\ *adj* : very destructive or harmful ⟨a *pernicious* disease⟩ — **per·ni·cious·ly** *adv*

pernicious anemia *n* : a severe anemia in which the red blood cells decrease in number and increase in size and which is caused by a reduced ability to absorb vitamin B_{12}

per·ora·tion \'per-ər-,ā-shən, 'pər-\ *n* : the last part of a speech

per·ox·ide \pə-'räk-,sīd\ *n* : an oxide containing a high proportion of oxygen; *esp* : HYDROGEN PEROXIDE

¹per·pen·dic·u·lar \,pər-pən-'dik-yə-lər\ *adj* **1** : exactly vertical or upright **2** : forming a right angle with each other or with a given line or plane [Middle English *perpendiculer* "exactly upright", from early French *perpendiculer* (same meaning), from Latin *perpendicularis* (same meaning), derived from *per-* "thoroughly" and *pendēre* "to hang" — related to DEPEND, PENDULUM] — **per·pen·dic·u·lar·ly** *adv*

²perpendicular *n* : a perpendicular line

per·pe·trate \'pər-pə-,trāt\ *vb* **-trat·ed; -trat·ing** : to be guilty of doing : COMMIT — **per·pe·tra·tion** \,pər-pə-'trā-shən\ *n* — **per·pe·tra·tor** \'pər-pə-,trāt-ər\ *n*

horizontal | perpendicular

perpendicular

per·pet·u·al \pər-'pech-(ə-)wəl, -'pech-əl\ *adj* **1** : continuing forever : EVERLASTING **2** : occurring continually : CONSTANT — **per·pet·u·al·ly** \-ē\ *adv*

per·pet·u·ate \pər-'pech-ə-,wāt\ *vb* **-at·ed; -at·ing** : to make perpetual or cause to last indefinitely — **per·pet·u·a·tion** \-,pech-ə-'wā-shən\ *n* — **per·pet·u·a·tor** \-'pech-ə-,wāt-ər\ *n*

per·pe·tu·ity \,pər-pə-'t(y)ü-ət-ē\ *n, pl* **-ities** **1** : perpetual existence **2** : endless time : ETERNITY

per·plex \pər-'pleks\ *vb* **1** : to block the understanding of; *esp* : CONFUSE 1a, BEWILDER **2** : to make difficult to understand : COMPLICATE **syn** see PUZZLE — **per·plexed** \-'plekst\ *adj* — **per·plexed·ly** \-'plek-səd-lē, -'pleks-tlē\ *adv*

per·plex·i·ty \pər-'plek-sət-ē\ *n, pl* **-ties** **1** : the state of being perplexed : BEWILDERMENT **2** : something that perplexes

per·qui·site \'pər-kwə-zət\ *n* **1** : a privilege or profit made in addition to regular pay **2** : ¹⁰TIP

per·se·cute \'pər-si-,kyüt\ *vb* **-cut·ed; -cut·ing** **1** : to treat continually in a way meant to be cruel or harmful; *esp* : to cause to suffer because of belief **2** : ANNOY, PESTER — **per·se·cu·tor** \-,kyüt-ər\ *n* — **per·se·cu·to·ry** \-kyü-,tōr-ē, -,tòr-\ *adj*

per·se·cu·tion \,pər-si-'kyü-shən\ *n* **1** : the act or practice of persecuting **2** : the condition of being persecuted

Per·seus \'pər-,süs, -sē-əs\ *n* : a northern group of stars between Taurus and Cassiopeia

per·se·ver·ance \,pər-sə-'vir-ən(t)s\ *n* : the action, state, or an instance of persevering

per·se·vere \,pər-sə-'vi(ə)r\ *vb* **-vered; -ver·ing** : to keep at something in spite of difficulties, opposition, or discouragement

per·se·ver·ing \,pər-sə-'vi(ə)r-iŋ\ *adj* : showing perseverance — **per·se·ver·ing·ly** *adv*

Per·sian \'pər-zhən\ *n* **1** : a native or inhabitant of ancient Persia or modern Iran **2** : the language of the Persians — **Persian** *adj*

Persian cat *n* : any of a breed of domestic cats with a round head, stocky body, and long silky fur

Persian cat

\ə\ **abut**	\aủ\ **out**	\i\ **tip**	\ò\ **saw**	\ủ\ **foot**
\ər\ **further**	\ch\ **chin**	\ī\ **life**	\òi\ **coin**	\y\ **yet**
\a\ **mat**	\e\ **pet**	\j\ **job**	\th\ **thin**	\yü\ **few**
\ā\ **take**	\ē\ **easy**	\ŋ\ **sing**	\th\ **this**	\yủ\ **cure**
\ä\ **cot, cart**	\g\ **go**	\ō\ **bone**	\ü\ **food**	\zh\ **vision**

Persian lamb *n* : a pelt that is obtained from a karakul lamb and has very silky tightly curled fur

per·si·flage \'pər-si-ˌfläzh, 'per-\ *n* : silly or lightly joking talk

per·sim·mon \pər-'sim-ən\ *n* **1** : any of a genus of trees with hard fine wood, oblong leaves, and small bell-shaped white flowers **2** : the usually orange fruit of a persimmon that resembles a plum and is edible when fully ripe

per·sist \pər-'sist, -'zist\ *vb* **1** : to continue to do something in spite of opposition, warnings, or pleas : PERSEVERE **2** : to last on and on : continue to exist — **per·sist·er** *n*

per·sis·tence \pər-'sis-tən(t)s, -'zis-\ *n* **1** : the act or fact of persisting **2** : the quality of being persistent

per·sis·tent \pər-'sis-tənt, -'zis-\ *adj* **1** : continuing, existing, or acting for a long or longer than usual time ⟨a *persistent* cold⟩ ⟨*persistent* gills⟩ **2** : stubbornly determined — **per·sis·tent·ly** *adv*

per·son \'pərs-ᵊn\ *n* **1** : a human being : INDIVIDUAL — used in combination especially by those who prefer to avoid *man* in compounds that apply to both sexes ⟨chairperson⟩ **2** : a character or part in or as if in a play **3** : the body of a human being **4** : reference to the speaker, to one spoken to, or to one spoken of as indicated especially by means of certain pronouns [Middle English *person* "human being", from early French *persone* (same meaning), from Latin *persona* "person, character in a play", originally "an actor's mask"] — **in person** : as one who is or was actually present ⟨the president appeared *in person*⟩ ⟨spoke to her *in person*⟩

per·son·able \'pərs-nə-bəl, -ᵊn-ə-bəl\ *adj* : pleasing in appearance or manner — **per·son·able·ness** *n*

per·son·age \'pərs-nij, -ᵊn-ij\ *n* **1** : an important or famous person **2** : a character in a book or play

¹per·son·al \'pərs-nəl, -ᵊn-əl\ *adj* **1** : of, relating to, or belonging to a person : PRIVATE ⟨*personal* property⟩ **2 a** : done in person **b** : proceeding from or directed to a single person **c** : carried on between individuals directly **3** : relating to the person or body ⟨your *personal* appearance⟩ **4** : closely related to an individual : INTIMATE **5** : indicating grammatical person

²personal *n* : a short paragraph or ad in a newspaper relating to personal matters

personal computer *n* : MICROCOMPUTER

per·son·al·i·ty \ˌpərs-ᵊn-'al-ət-ē, ˌpər-'snal-\ *n, pl* **-ties** **1** : the state of being a person **2** : the whole collection of individual emotions and behavior that make one person different from others : INDIVIDUALITY **3** : an insulting mention of a person ⟨use *personalities* in an argument⟩ **4** : pleasing qualities of character ⟨has lots of *personality*⟩ **5** : a person who is well-known ⟨a television *personality*⟩

per·son·al·ize \'pərs-nə-ˌlīz, -ᵊn-ə-\ *vb* **-ized; -iz·ing** **1** : PERSONIFY 1 **2** : to make personal; *esp* : to mark as belonging to a particular person ⟨*personalized* stationery⟩

per·son·al·ly \'pərs-nə-lē, -ᵊn-ə-\ *adv* **1** : in person ⟨attend to the matter *personally*⟩ **2** : as a person : in personality ⟨*personally* attractive⟩ **3** : for oneself : as far as oneself is concerned ⟨*personally*, I am against it⟩

personal pronoun *n* : a pronoun (as *I, you,* or *they*) used as a substitute for a noun that names a definite person or thing

per·son·al·ty \'pərs-nəl-tē, -ᵊn-əl-\ *n, pl* **-ties** : personal property as distinguished from real estate

per·son·i·fi·ca·tion \pər-ˌsän-ə-fə-'kā-shən\ *n* **1** : the representation of a thing or idea as a person or by the human form **2** : an imaginary being thought of as representing a thing or an idea ⟨Uncle Sam is the *personification* of the U.S.⟩ **3** : a perfect example : EMBODIMENT ⟨you are the very *personification* of generosity⟩

per·son·i·fy \pər-'sän-ə-ˌfī\ *vb* **-fied; -fy·ing** **1** : to think of or represent as a person ⟨*personify* the forces of nature⟩ **2** : to be the perfect example of ⟨she *personified* kindness⟩

per·son·nel \ˌpərs-ᵊn-'el\ *n* : a group of persons employed (as in a public service, a factory, or an office)

¹per·spec·tive \pər-'spek-tiv\ *n* **1** : the art or technique of painting or drawing a scene so that objects in it seem to have depth and distance **2 a** : the relationship in which a subject or its parts are viewed mentally ⟨places the issues in *perspective*⟩ **b** : POINT OF VIEW ⟨from a conservative *perspective*⟩ **3** : the power to understand things in their true relationship to each other ⟨try to keep your *perspective* and not get flustered⟩ **4** : the appearance to the eye of objects in space with respect to their distance and positions in relation to each other

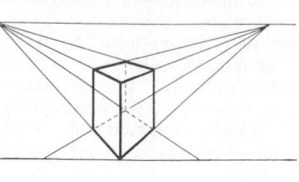
perspective 1

²perspective *adj* : of, relating to, or seen in perspective

per·spi·ca·cious \ˌpər-spə-'kā-shəs\ *adj* : having or showing keen understanding — **per·spi·ca·cious·ly** *adv* — **per·spi·cac·i·ty** \-'kas-ət-ē\ *n*

per·spic·u·ous \pər-'spik-yə-wəs\ *adj* **1** : plain to the understanding : CLEAR **2** : expressing oneself clearly — **per·spi·cu·ity** \ˌpər-spə-'kyü-ət-ē\ *n* — **per·spic·u·ous·ly** \pər-'spik-yə-wə-slē\ *adv* — **per·spic·u·ous·ness** *n*

per·spi·ra·tion \ˌpər-spə-'rā-shən\ *n* **1** : the act or process of perspiring **2** : a salty fluid given off by the sweat glands : SWEAT

per·spire \pər-'spī(ə)r\ *vb* **per·spired; per·spir·ing** : to give off perspiration : SWEAT

per·suade \pər-'swād\ *vb* **per·suad·ed; per·suad·ing** : to win over to a belief or to a course of action by argument or earnest request — **per·suad·able** \-'swäd-ə-bəl\ *adj* — **per·suad·er** *n*

per·sua·si·ble \pər-'swā-zə-bəl, -'swā-sə-\ *adj* : capable of being persuaded

per·sua·sion \pər-'swā-zhən\ *n* **1** : the act of persuading **2** : the power or ability to persuade **3** : the state of being persuaded **4 a** : BELIEF 2; *esp* : a system of religious beliefs **b** : a group having the same religious beliefs

per·sua·sive \pər-'swā-siv, -ziv\ *adj* : tending to persuade ⟨a *persuasive* argument⟩ — **per·sua·sive·ly** *adv* — **per·sua·sive·ness** *n*

pert \'pərt\ *adj* **1** : IMPUDENT **2** : being trim and chic **3** : VIVACIOUS, LIVELY — **pert·ly** *adv* — **pert·ness** *n*

per·tain \pər-'tān\ *vb* **1** : to belong to a person or thing as a part, quality, or function ⟨duties that *pertain* to an office⟩ **2** : to have reference ⟨books *pertaining* to birds⟩

per·ti·na·cious \ˌpərt-ᵊn-'ā-shəs\ *adj* **1** : holding strongly to an opinion, purpose, or course of action **2** : stubbornly persistent — **per·ti·na·cious·ly** *adv* — **per·ti·na·cious·ness** *n* — **per·ti·nac·i·ty** \-'as-ət-ē\ *n*

per·ti·nence \'pərt-ᵊn-ən(t)s, 'pərt-nən(t)s\ *n* : the quality or state of being pertinent : RELEVANCE

per·ti·nen·cy \'pərt-ᵊn-ən-sē, 'pərt-nən-sē\ *n* : PERTINENCE

per·ti·nent \'pərt-ᵊn-ənt, 'pərt-nənt\ *adj* : having to do with the matter being thought about or discussed : RELEVANT ⟨a *pertinent* question⟩ — **per·ti·nent·ly** *adv*

per·turb \pər-'tərb\ *vb* : to disturb greatly especially in mind — **per·turb·able** \-'tər-bə-bəl\ *adj*

per·tur·ba·tion \ˌpərt-ər-'bā-shən, ˌpər-ˌtər-\ *n* **1 a** : the action of perturbing **b** : the state of being perturbed **2** : a cause of worry or disturbance — **per·tur·ba·tion·al** \-shnəl, -shən-ᵊl\ *adj*

per·tus·sis \pər-'təs-əs\ *n* : WHOOPING COUGH

pe·ruke \pə-'rük\ *n* : a kind of wig popular in the 17th and 18th centuries

pe·rus·al \pə-'rü-zəl\ *n* : the action of perusing

pe·ruse \pə-'rüz\ *vb* **pe·rused; pe·rus·ing** : [1]READ 1a; *esp* : to read carefully or thoroughly — **pe·rus·er** *n*

per·vade \pər-'vād\ *vb* **per·vad·ed; per·vad·ing** : to spread through all parts of : PERMEATE

per·va·sive \pər-'vā-siv, -ziv\ *adj* : spread throughout so thoroughly as to be seen or felt everywhere ⟨the *pervasive* influence of television⟩ ⟨the *pervasive* dampness of the mines⟩ — **per·va·sive·ly** *adv* — **per·va·sive·ness** *n*

per·verse \(,)pər-'vərs, 'pər-,vərs\ *adj* **1** : morally bad : CORRUPT **2** : stubborn in being wrong **3** : IRRITABLE, CRANKY — **per·verse·ly** *adv* — **per·verse·ness** *n*

per·ver·sion \pər-'vər-zhən\ *n* **1 a** : the action of perverting **b** : the state of being perverted **2** : abnormal sexual behavior

per·ver·si·ty \pər-'vər-sət-ē, -stē\ *n, pl* **-ties** : the quality, state, or an instance of being perverse

[1]per·vert \pər-'vərt\ *vb* **1** : to cause to turn away from what is good or true or right : CORRUPT **2** : to put to a wrong use **3** : to give a wrong meaning to : MISINTERPRET

[2]per·vert \'pər-,vərt\ *n* : one that is perverted; *esp* : one given to some form of sexual perversion

Pe·sach \'pā-,säk\ *n* : PASSOVER

pe·se·ta \pə-'sāt-ə\ *n* **1** : the basic unit of money of Spain **2** : a coin or bill representing one peseta

pes·ky \'pes-kē\ *adj* **pes·ki·er; -est** : TROUBLESOME 2 — **pes·ki·ly** \-kə-lē\ *adv* — **pes·ki·ness** \-kē-nəs\ *n*

pe·so \'pā-sō\ *n, pl* **pesos** **1** : an old silver coin of Spain or Spanish America **2 a** : the basic unit of money of Bolivia, Chile, Colombia, Cuba, Dominican Republic, Mexico, Philippines, and Uruguay **b** : a coin or bill representing one peso

pes·si·mism \'pes-ə-,miz-əm\ *n* **1** : a tending to expect the worst possible outcome **2** : a belief that evil is more common than good in life — **pes·si·mist** \-məst\ *n*

pes·si·mis·tic \,pes-ə-'mis-tik\ *adj* : of, relating to, or marked by pessimism : GLOOMY — **pes·si·mis·ti·cal·ly** \-ti-k(ə-)lē\ *adv*

pest \'pest\ *n* **1** : an epidemic disease which causes a large number of deaths; *esp* : [1]PLAGUE 2 **2** : something resembling a pest in destructiveness; *esp* : a plant or animal harmful to human beings **3** : one that pesters or annoys : NUISANCE — **pesty** \'pes-tē\ *adj*

pes·ter \'pes-tər\ *vb* **pes·tered; pes·ter·ing** \-t(ə-)riŋ\ : ANNOY, BOTHER

pest·hole \'pest-,hōl\ *n* : a place in which diseases are common

pes·ti·cide \'pes-tə-,sīd\ *n* : a substance used to destroy pests — **pes·ti·cid·al** \,pes-tə-'sīd-ᵊl\ *adj*

pes·tif·er·ous \pes-'tif-(ə-)rəs\ *adj* **1** : dangerous to society : PERNICIOUS **2** : TROUBLESOME 2

pes·ti·lence \'pes-tə-lən(t)s\ *n* : a contagious or infectious epidemic disease that spreads quickly and is often fatal; *esp* : BUBONIC PLAGUE

pes·ti·lent \'pes-tə-lənt\ *adj* **1** : dangerous or destructive to life : DEADLY ⟨a *pestilent* drug⟩ **2** : harmful or dangerous to society : PERNICIOUS **3** : causing displeasure or annoyance **4** : INFECTIOUS 1, CONTAGIOUS

pes·ti·len·tial \,pes-tə-'len-chəl\ *adj* : causing or likely to cause pestilence

pes·tle \'pes-əl, 'pes-tᵊl\ *n* : a usually club-shaped tool for pounding or grinding substances in a mortar

[1]pet \'pet\ *n* **1** : a tame animal kept for pleasure rather than for use **2** : someone given special treatment or consideration ⟨teacher's *pet*⟩

[2]pet *adj* **1** : kept or treated as a pet **2** : showing fondness ⟨a *pet* name⟩ **3** : [2]FAVORITE ⟨my *pet* project⟩

pestle with mortar

[3]pet *vb* **pet·ted; pet·ting** **1** : FONDLE, CARESS **2** : to treat as a pet : PAMPER **3** : to engage in embracing, caressing, and kissing

[4]pet *n* : a spell of sulkiness or anger

pet·al \'pet-ᵊl\ *n* : one of the often brightly colored modified leaves that make up the corolla of a flower — **pet·aled** *or* **pet·alled** \-ᵊld\ *adj* — **pet·al·like** \-ᵊl-,(l)īk\ *adj*

pe·ter \'pēt-ər\ *vb* : to become exhausted — usually used with *out*

Pe·ter \'pēt-ər\ *n* — see BIBLE table

pet·i·ole \'pet-ē-,ōl\ *n* : the stem of a leaf

pe·tite \pə-'tēt\ *adj* : having a small trim figure

pe·tit four \,pet-ē-'fō(ə)r, -'fō(ə)r\ *n, pl* **petits fours** *or* **petit fours** \-ē-'fō(ə)rz, -'fō(ə)rz\ : a small frosted cake

[1]pe·ti·tion \pə-'tish-ən\ *n* **1** : an earnest request : ENTREATY **2** : a formal written request made to a superior or authority

[2]petition *vb* **pe·ti·tioned; pe·ti·tion·ing** \-'tish-(ə-)niŋ\ : to make a request to or for; *esp* : to make a formal written request — **pe·ti·tion·er** \-(ə-)nər\ *n*

pet·it jury \'pet-ē-\ *n* : a jury of 12 persons for a trial in court

petr- *or* **petri-** *or* **petro-** *combining form* : stone : rock [derived from Greek *petros* "stone" and *petra* "rock"]

pe·trel \'pe-trəl, 'pē-\ *n* : any of various seabirds with long wings that fly far from land

Pe·tri dish \,pē-trē-\ *n* : a small shallow dish of thin glass with a loose cover used especially for cultures of bacteria

pet·ri·fac·tion \,pe-trə-'fak-shən\ *n* **1** : the process of petrifying or state of being petrified **2** : something that is petrified

pet·ri·fi·ca·tion \,pe-trə-fə-'kā-shən\ *n* : PETRIFACTION

pet·ri·fy \'pe-trə-,fī\ *vb* **-fied; -fy·ing** **1** : to convert into stone or a stony substance **2** : to make lifeless or inactive : DEADEN **3** : to paralyze with fear, amazement, or awe : STUN

pet·ro·chem·i·cal \,pe-trō-'kem-i-kəl\ *n* : a chemical obtained from petroleum or natural gas

pet·rol \'pe-trəl, -,träl\ *n, British* : GASOLINE

pe·tro·leum \pə-'trō-lē-əm, -'trōl-yəm\ *n* : an oily flammable liquid that may vary from almost colorless to black, is obtained from wells drilled in the ground, and is the source of gasoline, kerosene, fuel oils, and other products

petroleum jelly *n* : a tasteless, odorless, and oily or greasy substance from petroleum that is used especially in ointments and dressings

[1]pet·ti·coat \'pet-ē-,kōt\ *n* : a skirt or slip worn under a dress or outer skirt

[2]petticoat *adj* : of, relating to, or controlled by women : FEMALE ⟨*petticoat* government⟩

pet·ti·fog \'pet-ē-,fóg, -,fäg\ *vb* **-fogged; -fog·ging** **1** : to engage in legal trickery **2** : to argue about unimportant details : BICKER — **pet·ti·fog·ger** *n* — **pet·ti·fog·gery** \-,fóg-(ə-)rē, -,fäg-\ *n*

petting zoo *n* : a collection of farm animals or gentle exotic animals for children to pet and feed

pet·tish \'pet-ish\ *adj* : IRRITABLE, PEEVISH — **pet·tish·ly** *adv* — **pet·tish·ness** *n*

pet·ty \'pet-ē\ *adj* **pet·ti·er; -est** **1** : lesser in rank or importance : MINOR ⟨a *petty* prince⟩ **2** : having little or no importance or meaning ⟨*petty* details⟩ **3** : having or displaying a mean narrow-minded attitude : SMALL-MINDED [Middle English *pety* "small, minor", an altered form of *petit* (same meaning), from early French *petit* "small"] — **pet·ti·ly** \'pet-ᵊl-ē\ *adv* — **pet·ti·ness** \'pet-ē-nəs\ *n*

petty cash *n* : a small amount of money kept on hand in an

\ə\ abut	\au̇\ out	\i\ tip	\ȯ\ saw	\u̇\ foot
\ər\ further	\ch\ chin	\ī\ life	\ȯi\ coin	\y\ yet
\a\ mat	\e\ pet	\j\ job	\th\ thin	\yü\ few
\ā\ take	\ē\ easy	\ŋ\ sing	\th\ this	\yu̇\ cure
\ä\ cot, cart	\g\ go	\ō\ bone	\ü\ food	\zh\ vision

office to pay for minor items

petty officer *n* : an officer in the Navy or Coast Guard appointed from among enlisted personnel

petty officer first class *n* : a naval petty officer with a rank just below that of chief petty officer

petty officer second class *n* : a naval petty officer with a rank just below that of petty officer first class

petty officer third class *n* : a naval petty officer with a rank just below that of petty officer second class

pet·u·lance \'pech-ə-lən(t)s\ *n* : the quality or state of being petulant

pet·u·lant \'pech-ə-lənt\ *adj* : marked by displays of rudeness or ill temper — **pet·u·lant·ly** *adv*

pe·tu·nia \pi-'t(y)ün-yə\ *n* : any of a genus of tropical American herbs related to the potato and widely grown for their showy funnel-shaped flowers

pew \'pyü\ *n* : one of the benches with backs and sometimes doors set in rows in a church

pe·wee \'pē-wē\ *n* : any of various small grayish or greenish brown birds that eat flying insects

petunia

pe·wit *variant of* PEEWIT

pew·ter \'pyüt-ər\ *n* 1 : any of various metallic substances made mostly of tin; *esp* : a dull metallic substance containing lead formerly used for utensils 2 : utensils made of pewter — **pewter** *adj*

pey·o·te \pā-'ōt-ē\ *n* : MESCAL 1; *also* : a drug obtained from the mescal cactus

pfen·nig \'fen-ig, -ik\ *n, pl* **pfennig** *also* **pfennigs** *or* **pfen·ni·ge** \'fen-i-gə\ 1 : a unit of money equal to 1/100 deutsche mark 2 : a coin representing one pfennig

PG \'pē-'jē\ *trademark* — used to certify that a motion picture is of such a nature that persons of all ages may be admitted but parental guidance is suggested

PG–13 \,pē-,jē-,thər(t)-'tēn\ *trademark* — used to certify that a motion picture is of such a nature that persons of all ages may be admitted but parental guidance is suggested especially for children under 13 years of age

pH \(')pē-'āch\ *n* : a number used in expressing acidity or alkalinity on a scale whose values run from 0 to 14 with 7 representing neutrality, numbers less than 7 increasing acidity, and numbers greater than 7 increasing alkalinity; *also* : the condition represented by such a number

phage \'fāj *also* 'fāzh\ *n* : BACTERIOPHAGE

pha·lanx \'fā-,laŋ(k)s\ *n, pl* **pha·lanx·es** *or* **pha·lan·ges** \fə-'lan-(,)jēz, fā-\ 1 : a body of heavily armed infantry of ancient Greece 2 *pl* **phalanges** : one of the bones of a finger or toe of a vertebrate

phal·a·rope \'fal-ə-,rōp\ *n* : any of various small shorebirds that resemble sandpipers but have thicker toes and are good swimmers

phal·lus \'fal-əs\ *n, pl* **phal·li** \'fal-,ī, -,ē\ *or* **phal·lus·es** 1 : a symbol or likeness of the male sex organ 2 : PENIS — **phal·lic** \'fal-ik\ *adj*

Phan·er·o·zo·ic \,fan-ə-rə-'zō-ik\ *adj* : of, relating to, or being an eon of geological history that is made up of the Paleozoic, Mesozoic, and Cenozoic eras or the corresponding system of rocks — see GEOLOGIC TIME table — **Phanerozoic** *n*

phan·tasm \'fan-,taz-əm\ *n* 1 : a misleading image or appearance (as a mirage) : ILLUSION 2 : GHOST, SPECTER 3 : a product of the imagination : FANTASY — **phan·tas·mal** \fan-'taz-məl\ *adj*

phantasy *variant of* FANTASY

¹phan·tom \'fant-əm\ *n* : something (as a ghost) that seems to be there but is not real : APPARITION

²phantom *adj* 1 : suggesting or being a phantom 2 : existing in name only : not real : FICTITIOUS ⟨*phantom* voters⟩

pha·raoh \'fe(ə)r-ō, 'fa(ə)r-; 'fā-rō\ *n, often cap* : a ruler of ancient Egypt [Old English *pharao* "pharaoh", from Latin *pharaon-, pharao* (same meaning), from Greek *pharaō* (same meaning), from Hebrew *par'ōh* "pharaoh"; of Egyptian origin]

¹phar·ma·ceu·ti·cal \,fär-mə-'süt-i-kəl\ *adj* : of or relating to pharmacy or pharmacists — **phar·ma·ceu·ti·cal·ly** \-i-k(ə-)lē\ *adv*

²pharmaceutical *n* : a drug or preparation used in medicine

phar·ma·cist \'fär-mə-səst\ *n* : one trained in pharmacy

phar·ma·col·o·gist \,fär-mə-'käl-ə-jəst\ *n* : a person who specializes in pharmacology

phar·ma·col·o·gy \,fär-mə-'käl-ə-jē\ *n* 1 : the study of drugs, their composition, effects, and use in medicine 2 : the properties and reactions of drugs especially with relation to their medical value — **phar·ma·co·log·i·cal** \-kə-'läj-i-kəl\ *also* **phar·ma·co·log·ic** \-'läj-ik\ *adj* — **phar·ma·co·log·i·cal·ly** \-i-k(ə-)lē\ *adv*

phar·ma·co·poe·ia *also* **phar·ma·co·pe·ia** \,fär-mə-kə-'pē-(y)ə\ *n* 1 : a book describing drugs, chemicals, and preparations used in medicine 2 : a collection or stock of drugs

phar·ma·cy \'fär-mə-sē\ *n, pl* **-cies** 1 : the art, practice, or profession of preparing drugs according to a doctor's prescription 2 a : a place where medicines are made or distributed b : DRUGSTORE

pha·ryn·geal \,far-ən-'jē-əl, fə-'rin-j(ē-)əl\ *adj* : relating to, located in, or produced in the region of the pharynx

phar·ynx \'far-iŋ(k)s\ *n, pl* **pha·ryn·ges** \fə-'rin-(,)jēz\ *also* **phar·ynx·es** : the space in a vertebrate just behind the cavity of the mouth into which the nostrils, Eustachian tubes, esophagus, and trachea open

¹phase \'fāz\ *n* 1 : a particular appearance or state in a repeating series of changes ⟨*phases* of the moon⟩ 2 : a step or part in a series of events or actions : STAGE 3 : a particular part or feature (as of an activity, situation, or a subject being considered) : ASPECT 4 : a physically different portion or kind of matter present in a mixed system ⟨the three *phases* ice, water, and steam⟩

²phase *vb* **phased; phas·ing** 1 : to do in steps according to a plan ⟨successfully *phased* orphaned animals back to the wild⟩ 2 : to introduce in stages — often used with *in* ⟨*phase* in new models⟩

phase out *vb* : to discontinue doing, producing, or using ⟨*phasing out* old machinery⟩

pheas·ant \'fez-ᵊnt\ *n, pl* **pheasant** *or* **pheasants** : any of numerous large long-tailed brightly colored birds that are related to the domestic chicken and many of which are raised as ornamental or game birds

phe·no·bar·bi·tal \,fē-nō-'bär-bə-,tól\ *n* : a drug that is a barbiturate used to calm one down and cause sleep

phe·nol \'fē-,nōl, -,nól; fi-'nōl, -'nól\ *n* : a white poisonous acidic compound present in tars from coal and wood that when dissolved to make a weak liquid mixture is used as a disinfectant — called also *carbolic acid* — **phe·no·lic** \fi-'nō-lik, -'näl-ik\ *adj*

phe·nol·phtha·lein \,fēn-ᵊl-'thal-ē-ən, -'thal-,ēn, -'thāl-\ *n* : a white or yellowish white compound used as a laxative and as an acid-base indicator because its solution is brilliant red in alkalies and clear in acids

phe·nom·e·nal \fi-'näm-ən-ᵊl\ *adj* 1 : of, relating to, or being a phenomenon 2 : very remarkable : EXTRAORDINARY ⟨a *phenomenal* memory⟩ — **phe·nom·e·nal·ly** \-ᵊl-ē\ *adv*

phe·nom·e·non \fi-'näm-ə-,nän, -nən\ *n, pl* **-na** \-nə, -,nä\ *or* **-nons** 1 *pl* **phenomena** : an observable fact or event 2 : a fact, feature, or event of scientific interest 3 a : a rare or important fact or event b *pl* **phenomenons** : an exceptional, unusual, or abnormal person or thing

phe·no·type \'fē-nə-,tīp\ *n* : the visible characteristics of a plant or animal that result from the combined effects of the genes and the environment — **phe·no·typ·ic** \,fē-nə-'tip-ik\ *adj*

phe·nyl·ke·ton·uria \,fen-ᵊl-,kēt-ᵊn-'(y)ûr-ē-ə, ,fēn-\ *n* : an inherited disease of human beings that is marked by the inability to oxidize a certain chemical in the body and may cause severe brain damage if not treated properly

phen·yl·thio·car·ba·mide \,fen-ᵊl-,thī-ō-'kär-bə-,mīd\ *n* : a compound that is extremely bitter or tasteless depending on the presence or absence of a single dominant gene in the taster — called also *PTC*

pher·o·mone \'fer-ə-,mōn\ *n* : a chemical substance that is produced by an animal (as an insect) and serves as a signal to other individuals of the same species to engage in some kind of behavior (as mating)

phi \'fī\ *n* : the 21st letter of the Greek alphabet — Φ or φ

phi·al \'fī(-ə)l\ *n* : VIAL

phi·lan·der \fə-'lan-dər\ *vb* **phi·lan·dered; phi·lan·der·ing** \-d(ə-)riŋ\ **1** : to make love without serious intention : FLIRT **2** : to have many love affairs — **phi·lan·der·er** \-dər-ər\ *n*

phil·an·throp·ic \,fil-ən-'thräp-ik\ *adj* : of, relating to, or devoted to philanthropy : CHARITABLE, BENEVOLENT — **phil·an·throp·i·cal** \-'thräp-i-kəl\ *adj*

phi·lan·thro·py \fə-'lan(t)-thrə-pē\ *n, pl* **-pies** **1** : a spirit of goodwill toward all people especially when expressed in active and generous efforts to help others **2** : a charitable act or gift **3** : an organization which distributes or is supported by charitable contributions — **phi·lan·thro·pist** \-pəst\ *n*

phi·lat·e·list \fə-'lat-ᵊl-əst\ *n* : someone who collects or studies postage stamps

phi·lat·e·ly \fə-'lat-ᵊl-ē\ *n* : the collection and study of postage stamps — **phil·a·tel·ic** \,fil-ə-'tel-ik\ *adj*

¹-phile \,fīl\ *n combining form* : one that loves or is strongly attracted to ⟨audio*phile*⟩ [derived from Greek *-philos* "loving"]

²-phile *adj combining form* : being strongly attracted to

Phi·le·mon \fə-'lē-mən, fī-\ *n* — see BIBLE table

Phil·har·mon·ic \,fil-ər-'män-ik, ,fil-(,)(h)är-\ *n* : SYMPHONY ORCHESTRA

Phi·lip·pi·ans \fə-'lip-ē-ənz\ *n* — see BIBLE table

Phi·lis·tine \'fil-ə-,stēn; fə-'lis-tən, -,tēn\ *n* **1** : a member of an ancient race that lived in the coastal regions of Palestine **2** *often not cap* **a** : an individual who dislikes or is indifferent to art and cultural activities and whose only interest is in making money **b** : a person who lacks taste or knowledge — **philistine** *adj, often cap* — **phi·lis·tin·ism** \-,stē-,niz-əm; -tə-,niz-, -,tē-, -stə-\ *n, often cap*

philo·den·dron \,fil-ə-'den-drən\ *n, pl* **-drons** *or* **-dra** \-drə\ : any of several plants that can stand shade and are often grown for their showy leaves

phi·lol·o·gy \fə-'läl-ə-jē\ *n* : the study of language and especially of historical development in languages — **phil·o·log·i·cal** \,fil-ə-'läj-i-kəl\ *adj* — **phi·lol·o·gist** \fə-'läl-ə-jəst\ *n*

philo·pro·gen·i·tive·ness \,fil-ə-prō-'jen-ət-iv-nəs\ *n* : love of one's children

phi·los·o·pher \fə-'läs-(ə-)fər\ *n* **1** : a student of philosophy **2** : a person who is calm and patient when faced with trouble

philosophers' stone *n* : an imaginary stone, substance, or mixture believed by alchemists to have the power to change other metals into gold

philo·soph·i·cal \,fil-ə-'säf-i-kəl\ *or* **philo·soph·ic** \-ik\ *adj* **1** : of, relating to, or based on philosophy **2** : calm and patient when faced with trouble — **philo·soph·i·cal·ly** \-i-k(ə-)lē\ *adv*

phi·los·o·phize \fə-'läs-ə-,fīz\ *vb* **-phized; -phiz·ing** **1** : to think like a philosopher **2** : to talk about life as if one were a philosopher — **phi·los·o·phiz·er** \-,fīz-ər\ *n*

phi·los·o·phy \fə-'läs-(ə-)fē\ *n, pl* **-phies** **1** : the study of

the basic ideas about knowledge, truth, right and wrong, God, and the nature and meaning of life **2** : the philosophical teachings or principles of a person or group ⟨Greek *philosophy*⟩ **3** : the general principles of a field of study or activity ⟨*philosophy* of history⟩ ⟨*philosophy* of cooking⟩ **4** : someone's basic beliefs about the way people should live

phlegm \'flem\ *n* **1** : thick mucus produced in abnormal quantity in the respiratory passages **2 a** : cold indifference **b** : cool bravery — **phlegmy** \'flem-ē\ *adj*

phleg·mat·ic \fleg-'mat-ik\ *adj* : not easily excited : slow to respond [from earlier *phlegm* "one of the four body fluids once believed to affect a person's health", from Middle English *fleume* (same meaning), from early French *fleume* (same meaning), from Latin *phlegma* (same meaning), from Greek *phlegma* "flame, phlegm" — see *Word History* at HUMOR] — **phleg·mat·i·cal·ly** \-i-k(ə-)lē\ *adv*

phlo·em \'flō-,em\ *n* : a tissue of higher plants that contains tubes serving to carry dissolved food material and that lies mostly outside the cambium — compare XYLEM

phlo·gis·ton \flō-'jis-tən\ *n* : the substance thought by early chemists to be given off as smoke and flame when something is burned

phlox \'fläks\ *n, pl* **phlox** *or* **phlox·es** : any of a genus of American herbs widely grown for their showy clusters of usually white, pink, or purplish flowers

-phobe \,fōb\ *n combining form* : one fearing or disliking [derived from Greek *-phobos* "fearing"] — **-pho·bic** \'fō-bik\ *adj combining form*

pho·bia \'fō-bē-ə\ *n* : an unreasonable, abnormal, and lasting fear of something

phlox

phoe·be \'fē-bē\ *n* : any of several American flycatchers; *esp* : one of the eastern U.S. that has a slight crest and is plain grayish brown above and yellowish white below

Phoe·ni·cian \fi-'nish-ən, -'nē-shən\ *n* **1** : a person born or living in ancient Phoenicia **2** : the Semitic language of ancient Phoenicia — **Phoenician** *adj*

phoe·nix \'fē-niks\ *n* : a legendary bird which was thought to live for 500 years, burn itself to death, and then rise newborn from the ashes

phon- *or* **phono-** *combining form* : sound : voice : speech ⟨*phon*ic⟩ ⟨*phono*graph⟩ [derived from Greek *phōnē* "voice, sound"]

pho·na·tion \fō-'nā-shən\ *n* : the act or process of producing speech sounds ⟨organs of *phonation*⟩ — **pho·nate** \'fō-,nāt\ *vb*

¹phone \'fōn\ *n* **1** : HEADPHONE **2** : ¹TELEPHONE

²phone *vb* **phoned; phon·ing** : ²TELEPHONE

-phone \,fōn\ *n combining form* : sound ⟨homo*phone*⟩ — often in names of musical instruments and sound-sending devices ⟨radio*phone*⟩ ⟨xylo*phone*⟩ [derived from Greek *phōnē* "voice, sound"]

pho·neme \'fō-,nēm\ *n* : one of the smallest units of speech that distinguishes one utterance from another (\n\ and \t\ in "pin" and "pit" are different *phonemes*)

pho·ne·mic \fə-'nē-mik\ *adj* **1** : of, relating to, or having the characteristics of a phoneme **2** : being different phonemes (in English \n\ and \ŋ\ are *phonemic*) — **pho·ne·mi·cal·ly** \-mi-k(ə-)lē\ *adv*

\ə\ abut	\au̇\ out	\i\ tip	\o̅\ saw	\u̇\ foot
\ər\ further	\ch\ chin	\ī\ life	\oi\ coin	\y\ yet
\a\ mat	\e\ pet	\j\ job	\th\ thin	\yü\ few
\ā\ take	\ē\ easy	\ŋ\ sing	\th\ this	\yu̇\ cure
\ä\ cot, cart	\g\ go	\ō\ bone	\ü\ food	\zh\ vision

pho·net·ic \fə-'net-ik\ adj **1 a** : of or relating to spoken language or speech sounds **b** : of or relating to phonetics **2** : representing speech sounds [from modern Latin *phoneticus* "relating to speech sounds", from Greek *phōnētikos* (same meaning), derived from *phōnē* "voice, sound" — related to EUPHONY, SYMPHONY] — **pho·net·i·cal·ly** \-i-k(ə-)lē\ adv

pho·net·ics \fə-'net-iks\ n : the study and classification of speech sounds — **pho·ne·ti·cian** \,fō-nə-'tish-ən\ n

pho·nic \'fän-ik also 'fō-nik\ adj **1** : of, relating to, or producing sound **2** : of or relating to speech sounds or to phonics — **pho·ni·cal·ly** \-(ə-)lē\ adv

phon·ics \'fän-iks\ n : a method of teaching beginners to read and pronounce words by learning the characteristic sounds of letters, letter groups, and especially syllables

pho·no·graph \'fō-nə-,graf\ n : an instrument that reproduces sound recorded on a grooved disk — **pho·no·graph·ic** \,fō-nə-'graf-ik\ adj — **pho·no·graph·i·cal·ly** \-i-k(ə-)lē\ adv

¹pho·ny or **pho·ney** \'fō-nē\ adj **pho·ni·er; -est** : not genuine or real: as **a** (1) : intended to deceive or mislead (2) : ²COUNTERFEIT 1 ⟨a *phony* $10 bill⟩ **b** : causing suspicion : probably dishonest ⟨sounds like a *phony* excuse to me⟩ **c** : FICTITIOUS, FALSE ⟨gave a *phony* name to the police⟩ — **pho·ni·ness** n

²phony or **phoney** n, pl **phonies** or **phoneys** : a phony person or thing

phoo·ey \'fü-ē\ interj — used to express disapproval or disgust

phos·phate \'fäs-,fāt\ n **1** : a salt of a phosphoric acid **2** : a drink made of carbonated water and fruit syrup with a little phosphoric acid added for tang

phos·phor \'fäs-fər, -,fó(ə)r\ n : a phosphorescent substance

phos·pho·res·cence \,fäs-fə-'res-ᵊn(t)s\ n **1** : a light given off at low temperatures that is caused by the absorption of radiations (as X rays or ultraviolet light) and continuing for a noticeable time after these radiations have stopped **2** : an enduring light given off with very little heat

phos·pho·res·cent \,fäs-fə-'res-ᵊnt\ adj : exhibiting phosphorescence

phos·phor·ic acid \fäs-,fór-ik-, -,fär-\ n : any of several oxygen-containing acids of phosphorus

phos·pho·rite \'fäs-fə-,rīt\ n : a rock that consists largely of calcium phosphate usually together with other minerals (as calcium carbonate), is used in making fertilizers, and is a source of phosphorus compounds

phos·pho·rus \'fäs-f(ə-)rəs\ n **1** : a phosphorescent substance; esp : one that glows in the dark **2** : a nonmetallic element that has characteristics similar to nitrogen and occurs widely especially as phosphates — see ELEMENT table — **phos·phor·ic** \fäs-'fór-ik, -'fär-\ adj — **phos·pho·rous** \'fäs-f(ə-)rəs; fäs-'fōr-əs, -'fór-\ adj

phot- or **photo-** combining form **1** : light ⟨*phot*on⟩ ⟨*pho*tography⟩ **2** : photograph : photographic ⟨*photo*copy⟩ **3** : photoelectric ⟨*photo*cell⟩ [derived from Greek *phot-, phos* "light"]

¹pho·to \'fōt-ō\ n, pl **photos** : ¹PHOTOGRAPH

²photo vb : ²PHOTOGRAPH

³photo adj : PHOTOGRAPHIC 1

pho·to·cell \'fōt-ə-,sel\ n : PHOTOELECTRIC CELL

pho·to·copy \'fōt-ə-,käp-ē\ n : a photographic copy (as of a printed page) — **photocopy** vb

pho·to·elec·tric \,fōt-ō-i-'lek-trik\ adj : involving, relating to, or using any of various electrical effects due to the action of radiation (as light) on matter

photoelectric cell n : a cell in which variations of light are converted into corresponding variations in an electric current

photoelectric effect n : the giving off of free electrons from a metal surface when light strikes it

photo finish n **1** : a finish of a race in which contestants

are so close that a photograph of them crossing the finish line has to be examined to decide the winner **2** : a close contest (as in an election)

pho·to·gen·ic \,fōt-ə-'jen-ik, -'jēn-\ adj : suitable for being photographed : likely to photograph well ⟨a *photogenic* child⟩ — **pho·to·ge·ni·cal·ly** \-i-k(ə-)lē\ adv

¹pho·to·graph \'fōt-ə-,graf\ : a picture obtained by photography

²photograph vb **1** : to take a photograph of **2** : to take photographs **3** : to be photographed — **pho·tog·ra·pher** \fə-'täg-rə-fər\ n

pho·to·graph·ic \,fōt-ə-'graf-ik\ adj **1** : relating to, obtained by, or used in photography ⟨*photographic* supplies⟩ **2** : capable of remembering details exactly ⟨a *photographic* mind⟩ — **pho·to·graph·i·cal·ly** \-i-k(ə-)lē\ adv

pho·tog·ra·phy \fə-'täg-rə-fē\ n : the art or process of making pictures by means of a camera that directs the image of an object onto a film made sensitive to light

pho·to·mi·cro·graph \,fōt-ə-'mī-krə-,graf\ n : a photograph of a magnified image of a small object

pho·ton \'fō-,tän\ n : a tiny particle or bundle of radiant energy

pho·to·play \'fōt-ō-,plā\ n : MOVIE 2a

pho·to·sphere \'fōt-ə-,sfi(ə)r\ n : the shining surface of the sun or a star — **pho·to·spher·ic** \,fōt-ə-'sfi(ə)r-ik, -'sfer-\ adj

pho·to·syn·the·sis \,fōt-ə-'sin(t)-thə-səs\ n : the process by which plants that contain chlorophyll make carbohydrates from water and from carbon dioxide in the air in the presence of light — **pho·to·syn·thet·ic** \-sin-'thet-ik\ adj

pho·to·tax·is \,fōt-ō-'tak-səs\ n : a movement of a living thing that is made in response to light

pho·tot·ro·pism \fō-'tä-trə-,piz-əm\ n : a movement or growing in a particular direction that is made by a living thing in response to light — **pho·to·tro·pic** \,fōt-ə-'träp-ik\ adj

¹phrase \'frāz\ n **1** : a characteristic style or manner of speech or expression : DICTION **2** : a brief expression; esp : one commonly used **3** : a small unit of a musical passage usually several measures long **4** : a group of two or more words that express a single idea but do not form a complete sentence ⟨"out the door" in "they ran out the door" is a *phrase*⟩ — **phras·al** \'frā-zəl\ adj — **phras·al·ly** \-zə-lē\ adv

²phrase vb **phrased; phras·ing** **1** : to express in words ⟨*phrased* his thoughts well⟩ **2** : to divide into musical phrases

phrase·ol·o·gy \,frā-zē-'äl-ə-jē, frä-'zäl-\ n **1** : manner of speaking and writing : STYLE **2** : choice of words

phras·ing \'frā-ziŋ\ n **1** : PHRASEOLOGY 1 **2** : the act, method, or result of grouping notes into musical phrases

phy·lac·tery \fə-'lak-t(ə-)rē\ n, pl **-ter·ies** **1** : either of two small square leather boxes containing scripture passages on slips of paper that are traditionally worn on the left arm and the head by Jewish men during morning prayers **2** : AMULET

phy·log·e·ny \fī-'läj-ə-nē\ n, pl **-nies** : the development of a group of related living things by evolution over a long period of time in contrast to the development of a particular individual from its first immature stage to an adult

phylactery 1

phy·lum \'fī-ləm\ n, pl **phy·la** \-lə\ : a group of animals or in some classifications plants sharing one or more major characteristics that set them apart from all other animals or plants and forming one of the important groups into which the animal or plant kingdom is divided

phys·ic \'fiz-ik\ *n* : a remedy for disease; *esp* : a strong laxative

phys·i·cal \'fiz-i-kəl\ *adj* **1 a** : having material existence **b** : of or relating to material things **2 a** : of or relating to natural science **b** : of or relating to physics **3** : of or relating to the body : BODILY — **phys·i·cal·ly** \-k(ə-)lē\ *adv*

physical education *n* : instruction in the care and development of the body

physical science *n* : any of the natural sciences (as physics, geology, and astronomy) that deal primarily with nonliving materials

physical therapist *n* : a person who is a specialist in physical therapy

physical therapy *n* : the treatment of disease especially by massage, exercise, water, or heat

phy·si·cian \fə-'zish-ən\ *n* : a specialist in healing human diseases : a doctor of medicine

phys·i·cist \'fiz-(ə-)səst\ *n* : a specialist in physics

phys·ics \'fiz-iks\ *n* **1** : a science that deals with matter and energy and their actions upon each other in the fields of mechanics, heat, light, electricity, sound, and the atomic nucleus **2** : physical composition, characteristics, or processes ⟨the *physics* of sound⟩

phys·i·og·no·my \,fiz-ē-'ä(g)-nə-mē\ *n, pl* **-mies** : facial features or expression thought to reveal qualities of mind or character

phys·i·og·ra·phy \,fiz-ē-'äg-rə-fē\ *n* : a branch of geography that deals with the exterior features and changes of the earth — **phys·i·og·ra·pher** \-fər\ *n* — **phys·io·graph·ic** \,fiz-ē-ō-'graf-ik\ *adj*

phys·i·o·log·i·cal \,fiz-ē-ə-'läj-i-kəl\ *or* **phys·i·o·log·ic** \-'läj-ik\ *adj* **1** : of or relating to physiology **2** : characteristic of healthy or normal functioning of the body — **phys·i·o·log·i·cal·ly** \-i-k(ə-)lē\ *adv*

phys·i·ol·o·gist \,fiz-ē-'äl-ə-jəst\ *n* : a specialist in physiology

phys·i·ol·o·gy \,fiz-ē-'äl-ə-jē\ *n* **1** : a branch of biology dealing with the processes and activities by which life is carried on and which are special features of the functioning of living things, tissues, and cells **2** : the life processes and activities of a living thing or any of its parts or of a particular bodily process

phys·io·ther·a·py \,fiz-ē-ō-'ther-ə-pē\ *n* : PHYSICAL THERAPY

phy·sique \fə-'zēk\ *n* : the build of a person's body

-phyte \,fīt\ *n combining form* : plant having a (specified) characteristic or habitat ⟨sporo*phyte*⟩ [derived from Greek *phyton* "plant"]

pi \'pī\ *n, pl* **pis** \'pīz\ **1** : the 16th letter of the Greek alphabet — Π or π **2 a** : the symbol π representing the ratio of the circumference of a circle to its diameter **b** : the ratio itself having a value of approximately 3.1416

pi·a·nis·si·mo \,pē-ə-'nis-ə-,mō\ *adv or adj* : very softly — used as a direction in music

¹pi·a·no \pē-'än-ō\ *adv or adj* : in a soft or quiet manner — used as a direction in music

²pi·ano \pē-'an-ō\ *n, pl* **pianos** : a musical instrument consisting of a large frame holding steel wire strings that sound when struck by felt-covered hammers which are operated from a keyboard [from Italian *piano* "a keyboard musical instrument", a shortened form of *pianoforte,* from *piano* "soft" and *forte* "loud"; so called because, unlike earlier keyboard instruments, it could be played with varying degrees of loudness] — **pi·a·nist** \pē-'an-əst, 'pē-ə-nəst\ *n*

pi·ano·forte \pē-'an-ə-,fō(ə)rt, -,fô(ə)rt, -,fort-ē\ *n* : ²PIANO

pi·az·za \pē-'az-ə, *sense 1 is usually* -'at-sə, -'ät-\ *n, pl* **piazzas** *or* **pi·az·ze** \-'at-sä, -'ät-\ **1** : an open square especially in an Italian town : PLAZA **2 a** : a long hall with an arched roof **b** *dialect* : VERANDA, PORCH

pi·broch \'pē-,bräk, -,bräĸ\ *n* : a set of variations for the Scottish bagpipe

pi·ca \'pī-kə\ *n* : a typewriter type providing 10 characters to the inch

pic·a·dor \'pik-ə-,dó(ə)r\ *n, pl* **picadors** \-,dó(ə)rz\ *or* **pic·a·do·res** \,pik-ə-'dōr-ēz, -'dór-\ : a rider on horseback in a bullfight who jabs the bull with a lance

pic·a·resque \,pik-ə-'resk, ,pē-kə-\ *adj* : of, relating to, or being a type of fiction which presents the adventures of a usually rascally character ⟨a *picaresque* novel⟩

pic·a·yune \,pik-ē-'(y)ün\ *adj* : of little value : PALTRY; *also* : PETTY 3

pic·ca·lil·li \,pik-ə-'lil-ē\ *n* : a spicy relish of chopped vegetables

pic·co·lo \'pik-ə-,lō\ *n, pl* **-los** : a small shrill flute [from Italian *piccolo* "piccolo", a shortened form of *piccolo flauto* "little flute"] — **pic·co·lo·ist** \-əst\ *n*

¹pick \'pik\ *vb* **1** : to strike, pierce, or break up with a pointed tool **2 a** : to remove matter from bit by bit by or as if by plucking ⟨*picked* the bone clean⟩ **b** : to gather by plucking ⟨*pick* berries⟩ **c** : to play by plucking ⟨*pick* a guitar⟩ **3 a** : ²SELECT, CHOOSE ⟨*pick* out a dress⟩ **b** : to make (one's way) slowly and carefully **4** : to steal or pilfer from ⟨*pick* pockets⟩ **5** : to start (a fight) with someone else deliberately **6** : to dig at or into : PROBE **7** : to eat sparingly or in a finicky manner **8** : to unlock without a key ⟨*pick* a lock⟩ [Middle English *piken* "to pierce, pick", probably from Old English *pīcian* (same meaning) and from early French *piquer* "to prick" — related to ³PIKE] — **pick·er** *n* — **pick on** : to select especially for unwanted attention (as by bullying or teasing)

²pick *n* **1** : a blow or stroke with a pointed instrument **2 a** : the act or opportunity of choosing : CHOICE ⟨take your *pick*⟩ **b** : the best or choicest one or portion ⟨took only the *pick* of the crop⟩

³pick *n* **1** : a heavy tool with a wooden handle and a blade pointed at one or both ends used especially to loosen or break up soil or rock **2** : a slender pointed instrument ⟨ice *pick*⟩ **3** : a small thin piece of metal or plastic used to pluck a stringed instrument **4** : a comb with long widely spaced teeth used in grooming hair [Middle English *pik* "a pick for digging"]

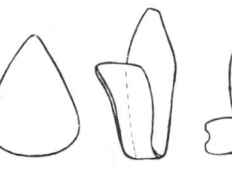

³pick 3

pickaback *variant of* PIGGYBACK

pick·a·nin·ny *or* **pic·a·nin·ny** \'pik-ə-,nin-ē, ,pik-ə-'nin-ē\ *n, pl* **-nies** : a Negro child — often taken to be offensive

pick·ax \'pik-,aks\ *n* : ³PICK 1

picked \'pikt\ *adj* : selected as being the best available ⟨a *picked* crew⟩

pick·er·el \'pik-(ə-)rəl\ *n, pl* **pickerel** *or* **pickerels** **1** : any of several fairly small pike **2** : WALLEYE

pick·er·el·weed \-,wēd\ *n* : an American plant that grows in shallow water and has thick arrow-shaped leaves and blue flowers

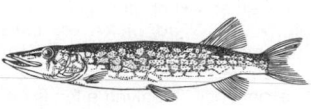

pickerel 1

¹pick·et \'pik-ət\ *n* **1** : a pointed stake or post (as for a fence) **2** : a soldier or a group of soldiers assigned to stand guard **3** : a person (as a striking worker or a demonstrator) on a picket line

²**picket** *vb* **1** : to enclose, fence, or strengthen with pickets **2** : to guard with or station as a picket **3** : ²TETHER ⟨*picket* a horse⟩ **4 a** : to station pickets or act as a picket at ⟨*picket* a factory⟩ **b** : to serve as a picket — **pick·et·er** *n*

picket line *n* **1** : a position held by a line of military pickets **2** : a line of individuals (as striking workers or protestors) who are demonstrating against a business, organization, or institution

¹**pick·le** \'pik-əl\ *n* **1** : a liquid used for preserving or cleaning; *esp* : a saltwater or vinegar solution in which foods are preserved : BRINE **2** : an unpleasant or difficult situation : PLIGHT **3** : an article of food (as a cucumber) preserved in a saltwater or vinegar solution

²**pickle** *vb* **pick·led; pick·ling** \'pik-(ə-)liŋ\ : to treat, preserve, or clean in or with a pickle

pick·led *adj* : preserved with pickle

pick–me–up \'pik-mē-,əp\ *n* : something that stimulates or refreshes

pick off *vb* **1** : to shoot or bring down one by one or with a single shot **2** : to put out (a base runner who is off base) with a quick throw

pick out *vb* **1** : to see or detect with some difficulty ⟨*picked out* the trail in the snow⟩ **2** : to play the notes of by ear or one by one ⟨*pick out* a tune⟩

pick over *vb* : to examine in order to select the best or remove the unwanted

pick·pock·et \'pik-,päk-ət\ *n* : a thief who steals from pockets and purses

pick·up \'pik-,əp\ *n* **1 a** : an increase in activity ⟨a *pickup* in business⟩ **b** : ACCELERATION 1 **2** : one (as a hitchhiker or chance acquaintance) that is picked up **3 a** : the changing of mechanical movements into electrical energy in the reproduction of sound **b** : a device (as on a phonograph) for making such a change **4 a** : the receiving of sound or an image into a radio or television transmitting device **b** : a device (as a microphone or a television camera) for converting sound or an image into electrical signals **5** : a light truck with an open body and low sides — called also *pickup truck*

pick up \(')pik-'əp\ *vb* **1 a** : to take hold of and lift ⟨*picked* the book *up*⟩ **b** : to gather together : COLLECT ⟨*picked up* every piece⟩ **c** : to clean up : TIDY ⟨*pick up* your room⟩ **2** : to take (passengers or freight) into a vehicle **3 a** : to acquire without great effort or by chance ⟨*pick up* a habit⟩ ⟨*picked up* a nasty cold⟩ **b** : to gain by study or experience ⟨*picked up* a new language while traveling⟩ **c** : to obtain especially by buying or as a bargain ⟨*picked up* the shirts on sale⟩ **d** : to form a brief or chance acquaintance with a stranger **e** : to take into custody ⟨was *picked up* by the police⟩ **4** : to find and follow ⟨*picked up* the outlaw's trail⟩ **5** : to bring within range of sight or hearing ⟨a radio that *picks up* foreign broadcasts⟩ **6** : to gather or regain speed or strength

picky \'pik-ē\ *adj* **pick·i·er; -est** : FUSSY 2b, FINICKY

¹**pic·nic** \'pik-(,)nik\ *n* **1** : a meal eaten outdoors often during a trip away from home **2 a** : a pleasant or carefree experience ⟨breaking a leg is no *picnic*⟩ **b** : an easy task **3** : a shoulder of pork that is often smoked and boned — **pic·nic·ky** *adj*

²**picnic** *vb* **pic·nicked; pic·nick·ing** : to go on a picnic : eat as if on a picnic — **pic·nick·er** *n*

pi·co- \'pē-kō, -kə\ *combining form* : one trillionth part of [derived from Italian *piccolo* "small"]

pi·cot \'pē-kō, pē-'kō\ *n* : one of a series of small loops forming an ornamental edging on ribbon or lace

pic·to·gram \'pik-tə-,gram\ *n* : PICTOGRAPH

pic·to·graph \'pik-tə-,graf\ *n* **1** : an ancient or prehistoric drawing or painting on a rock wall **2** : one of the symbols

of a system of picture writing **3** : a diagram representing statistical information by pictures which can be varied in color, size, or number to indicate change — **pic·to·graph·ic** \,pik-tə-'graf-ik\ *adj*

pictograph 1

pic·to·ri·al \pik-'tōr-ē-əl, -'tòr-\ *adj* **1** : of or relating to painting or drawing ⟨*pictorial* art⟩ **2** : consisting of or illustrated by pictures ⟨*pictorial* magazines⟩ **3** : suggesting or communicating vivid mental images ⟨*pictorial* poetry⟩ — **pic·to·ri·al·ly** \-ē-ə-lē\ *adv*

¹**pic·ture** \'pik-chər\ *n* **1** : a design or image made on a surface (as by painting, drawing, or photography) **2 a** : a clear description in words ⟨the book gives us a *picture* of another way of life⟩ **b** : a mental image : IDEA ⟨do you get the *picture*?⟩ **3** : a particular combination of circumstances : SITUATION ⟨an improvement of the economic *picture*⟩ **4 a** : an exact likeness : COPY **b** : a perfect symbol of something : EMBODIMENT ⟨the *picture* of health⟩ **5 a** : an image on a screen **b** : MOTION PICTURE — **picture** *adj*

²**picture** *vb* **pic·tured; pic·tur·ing** \'pik-chə-riŋ, 'pik-shriŋ\ **1** : to draw or paint a picture of : DEPICT **2** : to describe vividly **3** : to form a mental image of : IMAGINE

picture book *n* : a book that consists entirely or chiefly of pictures

picture graph *n* : PICTOGRAPH 3

pic·tur·esque \,pik-chə-'resk\ *adj* **1 a** : resembling or suitable for a painted picture **b** : CHARMING, QUAINT ⟨*picturesque* customs⟩ **2** : calling forth a striking mental picture **syn** see GRAPHIC — **pic·tur·esque·ly** *adv* — **pic·tur·esque·ness** *n*

picture tube *n* : a cathode-ray tube on which the picture in a television set appears

picture window *n* : a large window designed to frame a view

picture writing *n* : pictures that stand for actions or facts

pid·dling \'pid-lən, -liŋ, -ᵊl-ən, -ᵊl-iŋ\ *adj* : lacking size or importance : TRIVIAL

pid·gin \'pij-ən\ *n* : a simplified speech used for communication by people who speak different languages

pie \'pī\ *n* **1** : a dish consisting of a pastry crust and a filling (as of fruit or meat) **2** : a layer cake with a thick filling (as of jam or custard)

¹**pie·bald** \'pī-,bòld\ *adj* : spotted or blotched with two different colors and especially with black and white ⟨a *piebald* horse⟩

²**piebald** *n* : a piebald animal

¹**piece** \'pēs\ *n* **1** : a part cut, torn, or broken from a thing : FRAGMENT ⟨a *piece* of string⟩ **2** : one of a class, group, or set of things ⟨a *piece* of mail⟩ ⟨a three-*piece* suite of furniture⟩ ⟨a chess *piece*⟩ **3** : a short distance ⟨down the road a *piece*⟩ **4** : a portion marked off ⟨a *piece* of land⟩ **5** : a single item or example ⟨a *piece* of news⟩ **6** : a standard quantity or size in which an article is made or sold ⟨buy lumber by the *piece*⟩ **7** : something made, composed, or written ⟨a *piece* written for the piano⟩ **8** : ¹COIN 1 ⟨a 50-cent *piece*⟩ **9** : FIREARM — **of a piece** : of the same kind or character throughout : CONSISTENT — **piece of one's mind** : a severe scolding — **to pieces** **1** : very well : THOROUGHLY ⟨knew the countryside all *to pieces*⟩ **2** : out of control : CRAZY ⟨went *to pieces* after the accident⟩

²**piece** *vb* **pieced; piec·ing** **1** : to repair, form, or complete by adding pieces ⟨helped to *piece* a quilt⟩ ⟨*pieced* a jigsaw puzzle⟩ **2** : to join into a whole ⟨*pieced* their stories together⟩ — **piec·er** *n*

piece by piece *adv* : a little at a time : BIT BY BIT

pièce de ré·sis·tance \pē-,es-də-rə-,zē-'stän(t)s\ *n, pl*

pièces de ré·sis·tance \same\ **1** : the main dish of a meal **2** : an outstanding item or event : SHOWPIECE [French, literally "piece of resistance"]

¹piece·meal \'pē-,smēl\ adv **1** : one piece at a time : GRADUALLY **2** : in or into pieces : APART

²piecemeal adj : done, made, or accomplished piece by piece or in an incomplete way ⟨piecemeal reforms⟩

piece of cake : something easy to do ⟨the quiz was a piece of cake⟩

piece of eight : an old Spanish peso of eight reals

piece·work \'pē-,swərk\ n : work paid for at a rate based on the number of articles produced rather than the time spent working — **piece·work·er** \-,swər-kər\ n

pie chart n : a circular chart that shows quantities or frequencies by parts of a circle shaped like pieces of pie — called also circle graph, pie graph

pied \'pīd\ adj : having blotches of two or more colors

pied·mont \'pēd-,mänt\ adj : lying or formed at the base of mountains — **piedmont** n

pie chart

pie plant n : garden rhubarb

pier \'pi(ə)r\ n **1** : a support for a bridge **2** : a structure built out into the water for use as a landing place or walk or to protect or form a harbor **3** : an upright supporting part (as a pillar or buttress) of a building or structure

pierce \'pi(ə)rs\ vb **pierced; pierc·ing** **1 a** : to run into or through as a pointed weapon does : STAB **b** : to enter or thrust into sharply or painfully **2** : to make a hole in or through ⟨have one's ears pierced⟩ **3** : to force or make a way into or through ⟨pierce the enemy's line⟩ **4** : to penetrate with the eye or mind : see through **5** : to stir the emotions of : MOVE — **pierc·ing·ly** \'pir-siŋ-lē\ adv

pierc·ing adj : having the ability to enter, pierce, or penetrate: as **a** : loud and shrill ⟨piercing screams⟩ **b** : PERCEPTIVE, KEEN ⟨a piercing glance⟩ **c** : very cold ⟨a piercing wind⟩

pier glass n : a tall narrow mirror

pi·ety \'pī-ət-ē\ n, pl **pi·eties** **1** : the state or fact of being pious : devotion to one's god **2** : a pious act

pif·fle \'pif-əl\ n : NONSENSE 1

pig \'pig\ n **1 a** : a young swine **b** : a wild or domestic swine **2 a** : PORK **b** : PIGSKIN 1 **3** : a metal cast (as of iron) poured directly from the smelting furnace into a mold

pi·geon \'pij-ən\ n **1** : any of numerous birds with a stout body, usually short legs, and smooth feathers **2** : someone who is easily fooled or cheated

¹pi·geon·hole \-,hōl\ n : a small open compartment (as in a desk) for keeping letters or papers

²pigeonhole vb : to place in or as if in the pigeonhole of a desk

pi·geon–toed \,pij-ən-'tōd\ adj : having the toes turned in

pig·gish \'pig-ish\ adj : resembling or suggesting a pig (as in greed or dirtiness) — **pig·gish·ly** adv

pig·gy·back \'pig-ē-,bak\ or **pick·a·back** \'pig-ē-,bak, 'pik-ə-\ adv or adj **1** : on the back or shoulders **2** : on a railroad flatcar

piggy bank n : a bank for coins often shaped like a pig

pig·head·ed \'pig-'hed-əd\ adj : STUBBORN 1a, OBSTINATE

pig iron n : crude iron that is the direct product of the blast furnace and when refined yields steel, wrought iron, or ingot iron

pig latin n, often cap L : a play language usually formed by placing the first consonants and "-ay" at the end of each word (as "utshay the oorday" for "shut the door")

pig·let \'pig-lət\ n : a baby pig

pig·ment \'pig-mənt\ n **1** : a substance that gives color to other materials; esp : a powder mixed with a liquid to give color **2** : a natural coloring matter in animals and plants — **pig·ment·ed** \-mənt-əd, -,ment-\ adj

pig·men·ta·tion \,pig-mən-'tā-shən, -,men-\ n : a coloring with pigment; esp : an amount of bodily pigment that is greater than normal

pigmy variant of PYGMY

pig out vb **pigged out; pig·ging out** slang : to eat greedily

pig·pen \'pig-,pen\ n **1** : a pen for pigs **2** : a dirty or messy place

pig·skin \-,skin\ n **1** : the skin of a swine or leather made of it **2** : FOOTBALL 2

pig·sty \'pig-,stī\ n : PIGPEN

pig·tail \-,tāl\ n : a tight braid of hair — **pig·tailed** \-,tāld\ adj

pig·weed \-,wēd\ n : any of various weedy plants especially of the two families to which the goosefoots and amaranths belong

pi·ka \'pē-kə\ n : any of various small short-eared mammals of rocky uplands of Asia and western North America that are related to the rabbits

¹pike \'pīk\ n **1** : PIKESTAFF 1 **2** : a sharp point or spike (as the tip of a spear) [Old English pic "pick used for digging"] — **piked** \'pīkt\ adj

²pike n, pl **pike** or **pikes** **1** : a large freshwater fish with a long body and long snout that is valued for food and sport and is widely distributed in cool northern waters **2** : any of various fishes related to or like the pike [Middle English pike "a fish", from pic "a pick used for digging"]

pika

³pike n : a long wooden pole with a steel point once used as a weapon [from early French pique "a long weapon of war", from piquer "to prick", probably derived from a Latin word piccus "woodpecker" — related to ¹PICK]

⁴pike n : TURNPIKE [a shortened form of turnpike]

pik·er \'pī-kər\ n **1** : one who does things on a small scale; esp : one who gambles with a small amount of money **2** : CHEAPSKATE, CHISELER

pike·staff \'pīk-,staf\ n **1** : a sharply pointed walking stick **2** : the shaft of a soldier's pike

pi·laf or **pi·laff** \pi-'läf, 'pē-,läf\ or **pi·lau** \pi-'lō, -'lō, 'pē-; Southern often 'pər-lü, -lō\ n : a dish made of seasoned rice and often meat

pi·las·ter \'pī-,las-tər\ n : an upright rectangular column that ornaments or helps to support a wall from which it sticks out slightly

¹pile \'pī(ə)l\ n : a long slender post usually of timber, steel, or concrete driven into the ground to support a load [Old English pil "dart, stake", from Latin pilum "spear, javelin"]

²pile vb **piled; pil·ing** : to equip or support with piles

³pile n **1 a** : a quantity of things heaped together **b** : a heap of wood for burning a corpse or a sacrifice **2** : a great amount **3** : REACTOR 2 [Middle English pile "heap, stack", from early French pile (same meaning), from Latin pila "pillar"]

⁴pile vb **piled; pil·ing** **1** : to lay or place something in a pile : STACK **2** : to heap in abundance : LOAD **3** : to move or push forward hastily or in a disorganized way : CROWD

\ə\ abut	\aú\ out	\i\ tip	\ò\ saw	\ú\ foot
\ər\ further	\ch\ chin	\ī\ life	\òi\ coin	\y\ yet
\a\ mat	\e\ pet	\j\ job	\th\ thin	\yü\ few
\ā\ take	\ē\ easy	\ŋ\ sing	\th\ this	\yú\ cure
\ä\ cot, cart	\g\ go	\ō\ bone	\ü\ food	\zh\ vision

⟨*piled* into the car⟩

⁵pile *n* **1** : a coat or surface of usually short close fine furry hairs **2** : raised loops on the surface of a fabric which may be cut or uncut and which produce a velvety or fuzzy texture [Middle English *pile* "fuzzy surface of a fabric", from Latin *pilus* "hair" — related to CATERPILLAR; see *Word History* at CATERPILLAR] — **piled** *adj*

⁶pile *n* **1** : HEMORRHOID 1 **2** *pl* : HEMORRHOID 2 [Middle English *pile* "hemorrhoid", from Latin *pila* "ball"]

pil·e·at·ed woodpecker \,pī-lē-,āt-əd-, ,pil-ē-\ *n* : a North American woodpecker that is black with a red crest and white on the wings and sides of the neck

pile driver *n* : a machine for hammering piles into place

pil·fer \'pil-fər\ *vb* **pil·fered; pil·fer·ing** \-f(ə-)riŋ\ : to steal articles of small value or in small amounts — **pil·fer·age** \-f(ə-)rij\ *n* — **pil·fer·er** \-fər-ər\ *n*

pil·grim \'pil-grəm\ *n* **1** : one who journeys in foreign lands : TRAVELER **2** : a person who travels to a shrine or holy place to worship **3** *cap* : one of the English colonists who founded the first permanent settlement in New England at Plymouth in 1620

pil·grim·age \'pil-grə-mij\ *n* : a journey of a pilgrim — **pil·grimage** *vb*

pil·ing \'pī-liŋ\ *n* : a structure of piles especially one built in or near water; *also* : a number of piles (as of concrete)

¹pill \'pil\ *n* **1 a** : medicine in a small rounded mass to be swallowed whole **b** : *often cap* : an oral contraceptive — usually used with *the* **2** : something resembling a pill in shape or size **3** : something unpleasant that must be accepted or endured

²pill *vb, of a garment* : to develop small balls of fiber on the surface because of wear

¹pil·lage \'pil-ij\ *n* : the act of robbing by force especially in war

²pillage *vb* **pil·laged; pil·lag·ing** : to strip of goods and possessions with ruthless violence : PLUNDER, LOOT — **pil·lag·er** *n*

¹pil·lar \'pil-ər\ *n* **1** : a firm upright support (as for a roof) **2** : a column or shaft standing alone (as for a monument) **3** : something like a pillar : a main support ⟨a *pillar* of society⟩

²pillar *vb* : to provide or support with or as if with pillars ⟨a long *pillared* hall⟩

pill·box \'pil-,bäks\ *n* **1** : a small usually shallow box for pills **2** : a small low fortification for machine guns and antitank weapons **3** : a small round hat without a brim

pill bug *n* : WOOD LOUSE

pil·lion \'pil-yən\ *n* **1** : a cushion or pad placed behind a saddle for an extra rider **2** : a saddle for a passenger on a motorcycle or bicycle

pil·lo·ry \'pil-(ə-)rē\ *n, pl* **-ries** **1** : a device formerly used for the public punishment of wrongdoers that consists of a wooden frame with holes in which the head and hands can be locked **2** : exposure to public scorn or ridicule — **pillory** *vb*

¹pil·low \'pil-ō\ *n* : a bag filled with soft or springy material used as a cushion usually for the head of a person lying down

²pillow *vb* **1** : to place on or as if on a pillow **2** : to serve as a pillow for

pil·low·case \'pil-ō-,kās\ *n* : a removable covering for a pillow

pillory 1

¹pi·lot \'pī-lət\ *n* **1 a** : a person who steers a ship **b** : a person qualified to guide a ship into and out of a port or in specified waters **2** : someone who provides guidance and direction : LEADER **3** : one who flies or is qualified to fly an aircraft or spacecraft **4** : PILOT LIGHT — **pi·lot·less** \-ləs\ *adj*

²pilot *vb* : to act as pilot of : GUIDE

³pilot *adj* : serving as a guiding or tracing device, as an activating or auxiliary unit, or to test a new invention or idea ⟨a *pilot* study⟩

pilot balloon *n* : a small unmanned balloon sent up to show the direction and speed of the wind

pilot fish *n* : a fish with spiny fins, a narrow body, and a widely forked tail that often accompanies a shark

pi·lot·house \'pī-lət-,haus\ *n* : an enclosed place for the helmsman of a ship that contains the steering and navigating equipment

pilot light *n* : a small permanent flame used to ignite gas at a burner

pi·men·to \pə-'ment-ō\ *n, pl* **-tos** *or* **-to** : PIMIENTO

pi·mien·to \pə-'ment-ō, pəm-'yent-\ *n, pl* **-tos** : any of various sweet peppers that have thick flesh and a mild flavor

pim·ple \'pim-pəl\ *n* : a small swelling of the skin often containing pus : PUSTULE — **pim·pled** \-pəld\ *adj* — **pim·ply** \-p(ə-)lē\ *adj*

¹pin \'pin\ *n* **1 a** : a piece of wood, metal, or plastic used especially for fastening articles together or for hanging one article from another **b** : something that resembles a pin especially in long slender form ⟨a *pin* that makes an electrical connection⟩ **c** : one of the pieces that make up the target in various games (as bowling) **d** : the staff of the flag marking a hole on a golf course **e** : a peg for regulating the tension of the strings of a musical instrument **2 a** : a small pointed piece of wire with a head used especially for fastening cloth or paper **b** : something of small value : TRIFLE ⟨doesn't care a *pin* what they think⟩ **c** : an ornament or emblem fastened to clothing with a pin **d** : a device (as a hairpin or safety pin) for fastening **3** : ¹LEG 1

²pin *vb* **pinned; pin·ning** **1 a** : to fasten, join, or secure with or as if with a pin **b** : to prevent or be prevented from moving ⟨*pinned* under the wreckage⟩ **2** : to assign the blame or responsibility for

pin·afore \'pin-ə-,fō(ə)r, -,fo(ə)r\ *n* : a low-necked sleeveless garment worn especially by children

pi·ña·ta \pēn-'yät-ə\ *n* : a decorated container filled with candies, fruits, and gifts which is hung from the ceiling to be broken open with bats by blindfolded persons during festivities [Spanish, literally "pot"]

pin·ball machine \'pin-,bȯl-\ *n* : a game in which a ball shot by a plunger scores points as it rolls around a slanting surface among pins and targets

piñata

pince–nez \pan(t)-'snā\ *n, pl* **pince–nez** \-'snā(z)\ : eyeglasses clipped to the nose by a spring

pin·cer \'pin-chər, 'pin(t)-sər\ *n* **1** *pl* : an instrument having two handles and two jaws that is used to grip things **2** : a claw (as of a lobster) resembling a pair of pincers : CHELA — **pin·cer·like** \-,līk\ *adj*

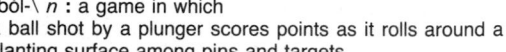

pince-nez

¹pinch \'pinch\ *vb* **1 a** : to squeeze between the finger and thumb or between the jaws of an instrument **b** : to squeeze painfully **c** : to nip off (a bud) to control flowering or prune the tip of (a young shoot) to cause branching **2** : to cause to appear thin or shrunken ⟨a face *pinched* with cold⟩ **3 a** : to be thrifty or stingy **b** : to confine or limit narrowly **4 a** : ¹STEAL 2a **b** : ¹ARREST 2 **5 a** : ³NARROW, TAPER **b** : to sharply reduce the length or quantity of

²**pinch** *n* **1 a** : a critical time or point : EMERGENCY ⟨help out in a *pinch*⟩ **b** : painful pressure or stress ⟨the *pinch* of hunger⟩ **2 a** : an act of pinching **b** : as much as may be taken between the finger and thumb ⟨a *pinch* of salt⟩ **c** : a small amount **3** *slang* **a** : THEFT **b** : a police raid; *also* : ²ARREST 2

pinch·er \'pin-chər\ *n* **1** : one that pinches **2** *pl* : PINCER 1

pinch hitter *n* **1** : a baseball player sent in to bat for another especially when a hit is needed **2** : a person called upon to do another's work in an emergency — **pinch–hit** \(')pinch-'hit\ *vb*

pin·cush·ion \'pin-,kush-ən\ *n* : a small cushion in which pins may be stuck

¹**pine** \'pīn\ *vb* **pined; pin·ing** **1** : to lose energy, health, or weight through grief, worry, or distress ⟨*pine* away⟩ **2** : to long for very much **syn** see YEARN

²**pine** *n* **1** : any of a genus of evergreen trees that have narrow needles for leaves, cones, and wood ranging from very soft to hard and that include valuable timber trees as well as many ornamentals **2** : the white or yellow wood of a pine — **piny** *or* **pin·ey** \'pī-nē\ *adj*

pi·ne·al gland \'pī-nē-əl, pī-'nē-\ *n* : a small usually cone-shaped part of the brain of most vertebrates that has an eyelike structure in reptiles and functions in time measurement in birds — called also *pineal body*

pine·ap·ple \'pī-,nap-əl\ *n* : a tropical plant with stiff spiny sword-shaped leaves and a short flowering stalk that develops into a fleshy edible fruit; *also* : this fruit [Middle English *pinappel* "the cone of a pine"; so called because the fruit looks like the cone from a pine tree]

pine·cone \'pīn-,kōn\ *n* : the cone of a pine tree

pine tar *n* : tar obtained from pinewood and used especially in roofing and soaps and in the treatment of skin diseases

pine·wood \'pīn-,wud\ *n* **1** : a wood or growth of pines **2** : ²PINE 2

pin·feath·er \'pin-,feth-ər\ *n* : an incompletely developed feather just breaking through the skin

ping \'pin\ *n* **1** : a sharp sound like that of a bullet striking **2** : ²KNOCK 3b — **ping** *vb*

Ping–Pong \'pin-,pän, -,pon\ *trademark* — used for table tennis

pin·head \'pin-,hed\ *n* **1** : the head of a pin **2** : a very stupid person

pin·hole \-,hōl\ *n* : a very small hole made by or as if by a pin

¹**pin·ion** \'pin-yən\ *n* **1** : the end part of a bird's wing; *also* : ¹WING 1 **2** : ¹FEATHER 1

²**pinion** *vb* **1** : to prevent a bird from flying especially by cutting off the pinion of one wing **2** : to restrain especially by binding the arms

³**pinion** *n* **1** : a gear with a small number of teeth designed to fit together with a larger wheel or rack **2** : the smallest of a set of gear wheels

¹**pink** \'pink\ *n* **1** : any of a genus of herbs that have narrow leaves and stems with thick joints and are often grown for their showy flowers produced singly or in clusters **2** : the highest degree ⟨athletes in the *pink* of condition⟩ [origin unknown]

²**pink** *n* : a pale red — **pink** *adj* — **pink·ish** \'pin-kish\ *adj* — **pink·ness** *n*

³**pink** *vb* : to cut cloth, leather, or paper in an ornamental pattern or with a saw-toothed edge [from earlier *pink* "stab, pierce", from Middle English *pinken* "to thrust"]

pink·eye \'pin-,kī\ *n* : a painful and infectious disease in which the inner surface of the eyelid and part of the eyeball

become pinkish and sore

pin·kie *or* **pin·ky** \'pin-kē\ *n* : LITTLE FINGER [probably from Dutch *pinkje* "little finger"]

pinking shears *n pl* : dressmaking shears that make a zigzag cut

pin money *n* : money for small expenses

pin·na \'pin-ə\ *n, pl* **pin·nae** \'pin-ē, -,ī\ *or* **pin·nas** **1** : a feather, wing, or fin or a part like one **2** : the part of the ear that is outside the head and is made of cartilage

pin·nace \'pin-əs\ *n* **1** : a light sailing ship **2** : a ship's boat

pin·na·cle \'pin-i-kəl\ *n* **1** : a slender tower generally coming to a point at the top **2** : a high pointed peak **3** : the highest point of achievement or development

pin·nate \'pin-,āt\ *adj* : resembling a feather especially in having similar parts arranged on opposite sides of a long thin central part like a stem ⟨a *pinnate* leaf⟩ — **pin·nate·ly** *adv*

pinned *past and past participle of* PIN

pinning *present participle of* PIN

pi·noch·le \'pē-,nək-əl\ *n* : a card game played with two cards of each suit with 9 the lowest card

pi·ñon \'pin-,yōn, -,yän, -yən; pin-'yōn\ *n, pl* **piñons** *or* **pi·ño·nes** \pin-'yō-nēz\ : any of various low-growing pines of western North America with edible seeds; *also* : the edible seed of a piñon

¹**pin·point** \'pin-,point\ *n* **1** : the point of a pin **2** : an extremely small or sharp point ⟨a *pinpoint* of light in the darkness⟩

²**pinpoint** *vb* : to locate or identify exactly ⟨*pinpoint* your career interests⟩

³**pinpoint** *adj* **1** : extremely fine or exact ⟨*pinpoint* accuracy⟩ **2** : located, fixed, or directed with great exactness

pin·prick \'pin-,prik\ *n* : a small puncture made by or as if by a pin; *also* : a small but unpleasant sensation ⟨the steady *pinprick* of a guilty conscience⟩

pins and needles *n pl* : a pricking tingling feeling in an arm or leg that is recovering from numbness — **on pins and needles** : in a nervous or jumpy state of expectation

pin·stripe \'pin-,strīp\ *n* : a very fine stripe on a fabric; *also* : a fabric that has such stripes — **pin–striped** \-,strīpt\ *adj*

pint \'pīnt\ *n* **1** — see MEASURE table **2** : a pint container

pin·tail \'pin-,tāl\ *n, pl* **pintail** *or* **pintails** : a bird (as a duck or grouse) with long central tail feathers

¹**pin·to** \'pin-tō\ *n, pl* **pintos** *also* **pintoes** : a spotted horse or pony

²**pinto** *adj* : PIED, MOTTLED

pinto bean *n* : a spotted seed produced by a kind of kidney bean and used for food; *also* : a plant producing pinto beans that is often used to feed livestock

pint–size \'pīnt–,sīz\ *or* **pint–sized** \-,sīzd\ *adj* : TINY, SMALL

pinto

pin tuck *n* : a very narrow tuck

pin·wale \'pin-,wāl\ *adj* : made with narrow wales ⟨*pinwale* corduroy⟩

pin·wheel \-,hwēl\ *n* **1** : a fireworks device in the form of a spinning wheel of colored fire **2** : a toy made of a stick with fanlike blades that spin in the wind attached at one end

pin·worm \-,wərm\ *n* : any of numerous small roundworms

\ə\ abut	\au̇\ out	\i\ tip	\o̊\ saw	\u̇\ foot
\ər\ further	\ch\ chin	\ī\ life	\o̊i\ coin	\y\ yet
\a\ mat	\e\ pet	\j\ job	\th\ thin	\yü\ few
\ā\ take	\ē\ easy	\ŋ\ sing	\th\ this	\yu̇\ cure
\ä\ cot, cart	\g\ go	\ō\ bone	\ü\ food	\zh\ vision

that infest the intestines and usually the cecum of various vertebrates; *esp* : one that infests human beings

pin·yin \'pin-'yin\ *n, often cap* : a system for writing Chinese words by using Roman letters to represent the sounds [from a Chinese word meaning "to write according to sound or pronunciation"]

¹**pi·o·neer** \,pī-ə-'ni(ə)r\ *n* **1** : a person or group that explores new areas of thought or activity ⟨*pioneers* of American medicine⟩ **2** : one of the first to settle in an area : COLONIST — **pioneer** *adj*

²**pioneer** *vb* **1** : to act as a pioneer **2** : to open or prepare for others to follow; *esp* : ²SETTLE 2a **3** : to begin or take part in the development of something new

pi·ous \'pī-əs\ *adj* **1** : having or showing love for God : DEVOUT **2** : displaying great loyalty to a person or thing (as a family, custom, or philosophy) **3** : marked by a false show of goodness ⟨a *pious* fraud⟩ — **pi·ous·ly** *adv* — **pi·ous·ness** *n*

¹**pip** \'pip\ *vb* **pipped; pip·ping** **1** : to break through the shell of the egg in hatching **2** : to be broken by a pipping bird ⟨eggs starting to *pip*⟩ [a word that imitates the sound made by a bird in breaking through the shell]

²**pip** *n* **1** : a dot or spot (as on dice or playing cards) that indicates numerical value **2** : BLIP [origin unknown]

³**pip** *n* **1** : a small fruit seed ⟨apple *pips*⟩ **2** : something very good of its kind [a shortened form of *pippin* "a kind of apple"]

¹**pipe** \'pīp\ *n* **1 a** : a musical instrument consisting of a tube of reed, wood, or metal that is played by blowing **b** : one of the tubes of a pipe organ **c** : BAGPIPE — usually used in pl. **d** : the whistle, call, or note especially of a bird or an insect **2** : a long tube or hollow body for carrying a substance (as water, steam, or gas) **3 a** : a tube with a small bowl at one end used for smoking tobacco **b** : a toy pipe for blowing bubbles **4** : a large barrel used especially to hold oil or wine

²**pipe** *vb* **piped; pip·ing** **1 a** : to play on a pipe **b** : to receive on board or signal the departure of by the sounding of a boatswain's pipe **2** : to speak, call, or play with a high shrill tone **3** : to furnish or trim with piping **4** : to carry by or as if by pipes ⟨*pipe* water⟩ — **pip·er** *n*

pipe cleaner *n* : a piece of flexible wire in which tufted fabric is twisted and which is used to clean the stem of a tobacco pipe

pipe dream *n* : an unreal and fantastic idea, wish, or story

pipe·fish \'pīp-,fish\ *n* : any of various long slender fishes that are related to the sea horses and have a tube-shaped snout and a body covered with bony plates

pipe fitter *n* : a person who installs and repairs piping

pipe·line \'pī-,plīn\ *n* **1** : a line of pipe with pumps, valves, and control devices for carrying liquids, gases, or finely divided solids **2** : a direct channel for information or supplies

pipe organ *n* : ORGAN 1a

pi·pette *or* **pi·pet** \pī-'pet\ *n* : a device for measuring and transferring small volumes of liquid that typically consists of a narrow glass tube into which the liquid is drawn by suction and kept by blocking the upper end — **pipette** *vb*

pip·ing \'pī-piŋ\ *n* **1 a** : the music of a pipe **b** : a shrill sound or call ⟨the *piping* of frogs⟩ **2** : a quantity or system of pipes **3** : a narrow fold of fabric used to decorate seams or edges

pip·ing hot *adj* : very hot

pi·quan·cy \'pē-kən-sē\ *n* : the quality or state of being piquant

pi·quant \'pē-kənt, -,känt\ *adj* **1** : agreeably stimulating to the taste; *esp* : SPICY 1 **2** : pleasingly exciting ⟨a *piquant* bit of gossip⟩ — **pi·quant·ly** *adv*

¹**pique** \'pēk\ *n* **1** : offense taken by one treated with disrespect or looked down upon **2** : a sudden feeling of resentment

²**pique** *vb* **piqued; piqu·ing** **1** : to arouse anger or resent-

ment in : IRRITATE; *esp* : to offend by treating with disrespect **2** : EXCITE 1, AROUSE ⟨the package *piqued* my curiosity⟩

pi·qué *or* **pi·que** \pi-'kā, 'pē-,kā\ *n* : a ribbed fabric of cotton, rayon, or silk

pi·ra·cy \'pī-rə-sē\ *n, pl* **-cies** **1** : robbery on the high seas **2** : the use of another's production or invention without permission

pi·ra·nha \pə-'rän-yə, -'rän-(y)ə\ *n* : a small flesh-eating South American freshwater fish that often attacks human beings and animals in the water

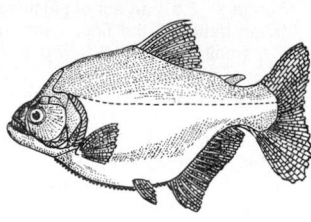
piranha

¹**pi·rate** \'pī-rət\ *n* : a person who commits piracy — **pi·rat·i·cal** \pə-'rat-i-kəl, pī-\ *adj* — **pi·rat·i·cal·ly** \-i-k(ə-)lē\ *adv*

²**pirate** *vb* **pi·rat·ed; pi·rat·ing** : to take by piracy ⟨*pirate* an invention⟩

pi·rogue \'pē-,rōg\ *n* **1** : DUGOUT 1 **2** : a boat like a canoe

pir·ou·ette \,pir-ə-'wet\ *n* : a rapid whirling of the body; *esp* : a full turn on the toe or ball of one foot in ballet — **pirouette** *vb*

pis *pl of* PI

Pi·sces \'pī-,sēz, 'pis-,ēz\ *n* **1** : a group of stars between Aquarius and Aries usually pictured as a pair of fish **2 a** : the 12th sign of the zodiac — see ZODIAC table **b** : a person whose sign of the zodiac is Pisces

pis·ta·chio \pə-'stash-(ē-,)ō, -'stäsh-\ *n, pl* **-chios** : a small tree that is related to the sumacs and has a fruit containing a greenish edible seed; *also* : its seed

pis·til \'pis-tᵊl\ *n* : the seed-producing part of a flower consisting usually of stigma, style, and ovary [from scientific Latin *pistillum* "pistil", from Latin *pistillum* "pestle for grinding material in a mortar"]

pis·til·late \'pis-tə-,lāt\ *adj* : having pistils; *esp* : having pistils but no stamens

pis·tol \'pis-tᵊl\ *n* : a short firearm made to be aimed and fired with one hand [from early French *pistole* "pistol", from German *pistole* (same meaning), derived from Czech *pištal*, literally "pipe"]

pis·ton \'pis-tən\ *n* : a sliding piece moved by or moving against the pressure of a fluid (as steam or hot gases) that usually consists of a short cylinder moving within a larger cylinder

¹**pit** \'pit\ *n* **1** : a hole, shaft, or cavity in the ground ⟨gravel *pit*⟩ **2** : an area set off from and often sunken below neighboring areas: as **a** : an enclosure where animals (as cocks) are set to fight **b** : the space occupied by an orchestra in a theater **3 a** : a hollowed or indented area especially in the surface of the body ⟨the *pit* of the stomach⟩ **b** : an indented scar (as from a boil) **4** : any of the areas alongside an auto racetrack used for servicing cars during a race — often used in pl. with *the* [Old English *pytt* "pit, hole in the ground"]

²**pit** *vb* **pit·ted; pit·ting** **1 a** : to put into or store in a pit **b** : to make pits in; *esp* : to scar with pits **2** : to set against another in a fight or contest ⟨*pitted* the courageous fighter against the champion⟩ **3** : to become marked with pits

³**pit** *n* : the stone of a fruit (as the cherry or peach) that is a drupe [from Dutch *pit* "the seed-containing stone of a fruit"]

⁴**pit** *vb* **pit·ted; pit·ting** : to remove the pit from ⟨*pitted* dates⟩

pi·ta \'pēt-ə\ *n* : a thin flat bread

pit–a–pat \,pit-i-'pat\ *n* : PITTER-PATTER — **pit–a–pat** *adv or adj* — **pit–a–pat** *vb*

¹pitch \'pich\ *n* **1** : a dark sticky substance left over from distilling tar and used in making roofing paper, in waterproofing seams, and in paving **2** : resin from various cone-bearing trees [Old English *pic* "a tar-like substance", from Latin *pic-, pix* (same meaning)]

²pitch *vb* : to cover, smear, or treat with pitch

³pitch *vb* **1** : to erect and fix firmly in place ⟨*pitch* a tent⟩ **2** : to throw usually toward a certain point ⟨*pitch* hay into a wagon⟩ **3 a** : to fix or set at a particular pitch or level ⟨*pitch* a tune too high⟩ **b** : to cause to be set at a certain angle : SLOPE **4 a** : to fall or plunge forward ⟨*pitch* from a cliff⟩ **b** : to move in such a way that one end falls while the other end rises ⟨a ship *pitching* in a rough sea⟩ **c** : ²BUCK 1a ⟨a *pitching* horse⟩ **5 a** : to throw a ball to a batter **b** : to play ball as a pitcher [Middle English *pichen* "to erect in place"]

⁴pitch *n* **1** : the action or a manner of pitching; *esp* : an up-and-down movement **2** : slope or degree of slope **3** : the forward distance advanced by a propeller as it makes one revolution **4** : the amount or level of something (as a feeling) ⟨excitement reached a high *pitch*⟩ **5 a** : highness or lowness of sound **b** : a standard frequency for tuning instruments ⟨the oboe sounded the *pitch*⟩ **6** : a high-pressure sales talk **7** : the delivery of a baseball by a pitcher to a batter — **pitched** \'picht\ *adj*

pitch–black \'pich-'blak\ *adj* : extremely dark or black

pitch·blende \'pich-,blend\ *n* : a brown to black mineral that is a source of uranium and radium

pitch–dark \'pich-'därk\ *adj* : extremely dark

pitched battle \'pich(t)-\ *n* : a fiercely fought battle in which the opposing forces are locked in close combat

¹pitch·er \'pich-ər\ *n* : a container for holding and pouring liquids that usually has a lip or spout and a handle [Middle English *picher* "container for pouring liquids", from early French *pichier* (same meaning), from Latin *bicarius* "drinking vessel, goblet"]

²pitcher *n* : one that pitches; *esp* : a baseball player who pitches [from *pitch* "to erect in place, throw a ball" and *-er*, noun suffix]

pitcher plant *n* : any of various plants with modified leaves which have a hollow leaf stem and base of the blade forming a long container for catching and digesting small arthropods (as insects)

pitch·fork \'pich-,fȯ(ə)rk\ *n* : a fork with a long handle used especially in pitching hay

pitch in *vb* **1** : to begin to work **2** : to contribute to a common task ⟨all the students *pitched in* to make the dance a success⟩

pitch·out \'pich-,aut\ *n* **1** : a pitch in baseball deliberately out of reach of the batter to let the catcher check or put out a base runner **2** : a lateral pass in football between two backs behind the line of scrimmage

¹pitcher

pitch pipe *n* : a small pipe blown to establish the pitch in singing or in tuning an instrument

pitchy \'pich-ē\ *adj* **1 a** : full of pitch : TARRY **b** : of, relating to, or having the qualities of pitch **2** : PITCH-BLACK

pit·e·ous \'pit-ē-əs\ *adj* : of a kind to move to pity ⟨*piteous* cries for help⟩ — **pit·e·ous·ly** *adv*

pit·fall \'pit-,fȯl\ *n* **1** : ¹TRAP 1, SNARE; *esp* : a covered or camouflaged pit used to capture animals or people **2** : a danger or difficulty that is hidden or is not easily recognized

pith \'pith\ *n* **1 a** : the loose spongy tissue that forms the center of the stem in some plants and probably functions chiefly in storage **b** : the spongy inside of a bone or feather **2** : the essential part : CORE ⟨the *pith* of the problem⟩

pith·ec·an·thro·pine \,pith-i-'kan(t)-thrə-,pīn\ *n* : any of a group of extinct human beings (as Java man and Peking man) that lived in the Pleistocene geologic epoch, had a smaller brain and larger canine and incisor teeth than human beings alive today, and were formerly classified as separate species but are now grouped in a single species

pith·ec·an·thro·pus \,pith-i-'kan(t)-thrə-pəs, -,kan-'thrō-\ *n, pl* **-pi** \-,pī, -,pē\ : PITHECANTHROPINE

pithy \'pith-ē\ *adj* **pith·i·er; -est** **1** : consisting of or filled with pith **2** : being short and to the point ⟨a *pithy* saying⟩ — **pith·i·ly** \'pith-ə-lē\ *adv* — **pith·i·ness** \'pith-ē-nəs\ *n*

piti·able \'pit-ē-ə-bəl\ *adj* : PITIFUL — **piti·ably** \-blē\ *adv*

piti·ful \'pit-i-fəl\ *adj* **1** : deserving or arousing pity or sympathy ⟨a *pitiful* mongrel⟩ **2** : deserving pitying scorn (as by not being adequate) ⟨a *pitiful* excuse⟩ — **piti·ful·ly** \-f(ə-)lē\ *adv*

piti·less \'pit-i-ləs, 'pit-ᵊl-əs\ *adj* : having no pity : MERCILESS — **piti·less·ly** *adv*

pi·ton \'pē-,tän\ *n* : a spike or peg that is driven into a rock for support (as for a mountain climber)

pit·tance \'pit-ᵊn(t)s\ *n* : a small portion, amount, or allowance especially of money

pitted *past and past participle of* PIT

pit·ter–pat·ter \'pit-ər-,pat-ər, 'pit-ē-,pat-\ *n* : a rapid series of light sounds or beats — **pit·ter–pat·ter** \,pit-ər-'pat-, ,pit-ē-'pat-\ *adv or adj* — **pitter–patter** \like *adv*\ *vb*

pitting *present participle of* PIT

¹pi·tu·itary \pə-'t(y)ü-ə-,ter-ē\ *adj* : of, relating to, or being the pituitary gland

²pituitary *n, pl* **-itar·ies** : PITUITARY GLAND

pituitary gland *n* : a small oval endocrine organ located at the base of the brain that produces various hormones that regulate especially growth and reproduction — called also *pituitary body*

pit viper *n* : any of a family of mostly New World poisonous snakes that have a small pit on each side of the head and hollow fangs with holes in them

¹pity \'pit-ē\ *n, pl* **pit·ies** **1** : sympathetic sorrow for one suffering, distressed, or unhappy : COMPASSION **2** : something to be regretted ⟨it's a *pity* you can't go⟩

²pity *vb* **pit·ied; pity·ing** : to feel pity for

¹piv·ot \'piv-ət\ *n* **1** : a shaft or pin on which something turns **2** : something on which something else turns or depends : a central member, part, or point

²pivot *vb* **1** : to turn on or as if on a pivot ⟨the guns are mounted in such a way as to *pivot* easily⟩ ⟨the future *pivots* on what is done today⟩ **2** : to provide with, mount on, or attach by a pivot

piv·ot·al \'piv-ət-ᵊl\ *adj* **1** : of, relating to, or functioning as a pivot **2** : extremely important : CRUCIAL — **piv·ot·al·ly** \-ᵊl-ē\ *adv*

pix·el \'pik-səl, -,sel\ *n* : any of the small elements that together make up an image (as on a television screen) [from *pix,* an altered form of *pictures,* and *el*ement]

pix·ie *or* **pixy** \'pik-sē\ *n, pl* **pix·ies** : a mischievous elf or fairy — **pix·ie·ish** \-sē-ish\ *adj*

piz·za \'pēt-sə\ *n* : an open pie made typically of thinly rolled bread dough spread with a spiced mixture (as of tomatoes, cheese, and ground meat) and baked — called also *pizza pie* [from Italian *pizza* "pizza", probably derived from Latin *pinsa* "a board for kneading dough"]

piz·ze·ria \,pēt-sə-'rē-ə\ *n* : an establishment where pizzas are made or sold

\ə\ abut	\au̇\ out	\i\ tip	\ȯ\ saw	\u̇\ foot	
\ər\ further	\ch\ chin	\ī\ life	\ȯi\ coin	\y\ yet	
\a\ mat	\e\ pet	\j\ job	\th\ thin	\yü\ few	
\ā\ take	\ē\ easy	\ŋ\ sing	\th\ this	\yu̇\ cure	
\ä\ cot, cart	\g\ go	\ō\ bone	\ü\ food	\zh\ vision	

piz·zi·ca·to \,pit-si-'kät-ō\ *adv or adj* : by means of plucking by the fingers instead of bowing — used as a direction in music

pj's \(')pē-'jäz\ *n pl* : PAJAMAS

¹plac·ard \'plak-ərd, -,ärd\ *n* : a notice posted in a public place : POSTER

²plac·ard \'plak-,ärd, -ərd\ *vb* **1** : to post in a public place **2** : to announce by or as if by posting

pla·cate \'plāk-,āt, 'plak-\ *vb* **pla·cat·ed; pla·cat·ing** : to calm the anger or bitterness of **syn** see PACIFY

¹place \'plās\ *n* **1** : an available space : ROOM ⟨make a *place* for the newcomer⟩ **2 a** : a region not made clear in description ⟨all over the *place*⟩ **b** : a building or spot set apart for a special purpose ⟨a *place* of worship⟩ **3 a** : a certain region or center of population ⟨a *place* on the map⟩ **b** : ¹HOUSE 1, DWELLING ⟨nice *place* you have here⟩ ⟨our summer *place*⟩ **4** : a certain part of a surface or body : SPOT ⟨a sore *place* on my shoulder⟩ ⟨lost my *place* in the book⟩ **5** : relative position in a scale or series ⟨kept them in their *place*⟩ ⟨in the first *place*, you're wrong⟩ ⟨finished in last *place*⟩ **6 a** : a proper position ⟨the *place* of education in society⟩ **b** : a suitable moment or point ⟨this is not the *place* to discuss that problem⟩ **7 a** : an available seat or accommodation ⟨needs a *place* to stay⟩ **b** : usual space or use ⟨paper towels take the *place* of linen⟩ **8** : the position of a figure in a numeral ⟨12 is a two *place* number⟩ ⟨in 316 the figure 1 holds the *place* for the tens digit⟩ **9** : JOB 3, POSITION **10** : a public square **11** : a short street **12** : second position at the finish ⟨as of a horse race⟩

²place *vb* **placed; plac·ing** **1** : to put or arrange in a certain place or position **2 a** : to appoint to a position ⟨was *placed* in command⟩ **b** : to find a job or home for ⟨*place* a child for adoption⟩ **3 a** : to assign to a position in a series or category : RANK **b** : ¹ESTIMATE 1 ⟨*placed* the value of the ring too high⟩ **c** : to identify by association ⟨couldn't quite *place* her face⟩ **4** : to give an order for ⟨*place* a bet⟩ **5** : to come in second ⟨as in a horse race⟩

place·hold·er \'plās-,hōl-dər\ *n* : a symbol used in mathematics in the place of a numeral not yet known

place·kick \'plā-,skik\ *n* : a kick in football made with the ball held in place on the ground — **place·kick** *vb*

place mat *n* : a small table mat on which a place setting is laid

place·ment \'plā-smənt\ *n* **1** : an act or instance of placing; *esp* : the assignment of a person to a suitable place ⟨as a class in school or a job⟩ **2** : PLACEKICK

pla·cen·ta \plə-'sent-ə\ *n, pl* **-centas** or **-cen·tae** \-'sent-ē\ : the organ in most mammals by which the fetus is joined to the uterus of the mother and is nourished — **pla·cen·tal** \-'sent-ᵊl\ *adj*

plac·er \'plas-ər\ *n* : a deposit of sand or gravel containing particles of valuable mineral ⟨as gold⟩ — **placer miner** *n* — **placer mining** *n*

place setting *n* : a set of dishes and silverware for one person

place value *n* : the value of the location of a digit in a number ⟨in 425 the location of the digit 2 has a *place value* of ten while the digit itself indicates that there are two tens⟩

plac·id \'plas-əd\ *adj* : peacefully free of interruption or disturbance : PEACEFUL, CALM ⟨a *placid* disposition⟩ — **pla·cid·i·ty** \pla-'sid-ət-ē, plə-\ *n* — **plac·id·ly** \'plas-əd-lē\ *adv*

plack·et \'plak-ət\ *n* : a slit in a garment ⟨as a skirt⟩ which closes after the garment has been put on

pla·gia·rism \'plā-jə-,riz-əm\ *n* **1** : an act of plagiarizing **2** : something plagiarized — **pla·gia·rist** \-rəst\ *n* — **pla·gia·ris·tic** \,plā-jə-'ris-tik\ *adj*

pla·gia·rize \'plā-jə-,rīz\ *vb* **-rized; -riz·ing** : to steal and pass off ⟨as the ideas or words of another⟩ as one's own ⟨*plagiarized* a classmate's homework⟩ — **pla·gia·riz·er** *n*

¹plague \'plāg\ *n* **1 a** : a disastrous evil **b** : a large number of destructive pests ⟨a *plague* of locusts⟩ **2** : an epidemic disease causing a high rate of death : PESTILENCE; *esp* : a serious disease that is caused by a bacterium, occurs or has occurred in several forms including bubonic plague, and is usually passed to human beings from rodents and especially rats by the bite of an infected flea or is passed directly from person to person **3** : a cause or occasion of annoyance : NUISANCE

²plague *vb* **plagued; plagu·ing** **1** : to strike or afflict with or as if with disease or evil **2** : to cause worry or distress to ⟨*plagued* by a sense of guilt⟩

plaid \'plad\ *n* **1** : a rectangular length of tartan worn over the shoulder as part of the Scottish national costume **2** : TARTAN 2 **3 a** : TARTAN 1 **b** : a pattern of unevenly spaced repeated stripes crossing at right angles — **plaid** *adj*

¹plain \'plān\ *n* : a broad area of level or rolling treeless country [Middle English *plain* "a stretch of nearly level treeless country", from early French *plain* (same meaning), derived from Latin *planus* "flat" — related to ¹PLANE]

²plain *adj* **1** : having no pattern or decoration ⟨a *plain* cloth⟩ ⟨her dress was *plain*⟩ **2** : free of added or extra matter : PURE ⟨a glass of *plain* water⟩ **3** : open and clear to the sight ⟨in *plain* view⟩ **4 a** : clear to the mind ⟨your meaning was *plain*⟩ **b** : FRANK, BLUNT ⟨*plain* speaking⟩ **5 a** : of common or average accomplishments or position : ORDINARY ⟨*plain* people⟩ **b** : not complicated or hard to do ⟨*plain* sewing⟩ **6** : not handsome or beautiful — **plain·ly** *adv* — **plain·ness** \'plān-nəs\ *n*

³plain *adv* : in a plain or simple manner

⁴plain *adv* : to a complete degree : TOTALLY ⟨were *plain* overcome by all the problems⟩ [partly from Middle English *plein* (adjective) "entire, complete" (derived from Latin *plenus* "full") and partly from *plain* (adverb) "in a plain manner" (derived from Latin *planus* "flat, level")]

plain·clothes·man \'plān-'klō(th)z-mən, -,man\ *n* : a police officer who does not wear a uniform on duty : DETECTIVE

Plains \'plānz\ *adj* : of or relating to North American Indians of the Great Plains or to their culture

plains·man \'plānz-mən\ *n* : a person who lives on the plains

plain·song \'plān-,sȯn\ *n* : a liturgical chant sung in various Christian ceremonies

plain·spo·ken \-'spō-kən\ *adj* : speaking or spoken frankly

plaint \'plānt\ *n* **1** : a crying out : WAIL **2** : ¹PROTEST, COMPLAINT

plain·tiff \'plānt-əf\ *n* : the complaining party in a lawsuit

plain·tive \'plānt-iv\ *adj* : showing or expressing sorrow : MOURNFUL, SAD ⟨a *plaintive* sigh⟩ — **plain·tive·ly** *adv* — **plain·tive·ness** *n*

plain weave *n* : a weave in which the threads cross by lacing together alternately — **plain–woven** *adj*

¹plait \'plāt, 'plat\ *vb* **1** : PLEAT 1 **2 a** : ¹BRAID 1 **b** : to make by braiding ⟨*plaiting* a basket⟩ — **plait·er** *n*

²plait *n* **1** : a flat fold : PLEAT **2** : a flat braid ⟨as of hair⟩

¹plan \'plan\ *n* **1** : a drawing or diagram showing the parts or outline of something **2** : a method or scheme of acting, doing, or arranging ⟨a civil defense *plan*⟩ ⟨vacation *plans*⟩ **3** : GOAL 2, AIM ⟨our *plan* was to stop them at the bridge⟩ — **plan·less** \-ləs\ *adj*

syn PLAN, PLOT, SCHEME mean a method of making or doing something or achieving a goal. PLAN suggests that some thinking was done beforehand and often that the thinking resulted in something written down or pictured ⟨a *plan* for a new school⟩ PLOT suggests a complicated carefully shaped plan of several parts. PLOT can be used of the plan of a story ⟨a novel with a good *plot*⟩ or it can be used of a secret and usually evil plan ⟨a *plot* to take over the government⟩ SCHEME suggests a sly plan often for evil reasons ⟨a *scheme* to cheat simple people⟩

²plan *vb* **planned; plan·ning** **1** : to form a plan of or for; *esp* : to arrange the parts or details of ahead of time ⟨*plan* a church⟩ ⟨*plan* a party⟩ **2** : to have in mind : INTEND **3**

: to make plans — **plan·ner** *n*

pla·nar·ia \plə-'nar-ē-ə, -'ner-\ *n* : PLANARIAN; *esp* : any of a common freshwater genus

pla·nar·i·an \plə-'nar-ē-ən, -'ner-\ *n* : any of a family or order of small soft-bodied mostly water-dwelling flatworms having cilia

¹plane \'plān\ *vb* **planed; plan·ing 1** : to make smooth or level especially with a plane **2** : to remove by planing — often used with *away* or *off* [Middle English *planen* "to make smooth or level", from early French *planer* (same meaning), derived from Latin *planus* "level" — related to ¹PLAIN] — **plan·er** *n*

²plane *n* : a tool for smoothing or shaping wood

³plane *n* **1 a** : a surface which contains at least three points not all lying on one straight line and any two points of which can be joined by a straight line lying wholly within the surface **b** : a flat or level surface **2** : a level of existence or development ⟨on the intellectual *plane*⟩ **3 a** : one of the main supporting surfaces of an airplane **b** : AIRPLANE

⁴plane *adj* **1** : having no elevations or depressions : FLAT **2 a** : of, relating to, or dealing with planes ⟨*plane* geometry⟩ **b** : lying within a plane ⟨a closed *plane* curve⟩ [from Latin *planus* "level"]

⁵plane *vb* **planed; plan·ing 1** : to fly while keeping the wings still **2** : to travel by airplane [from French *planer* "to fly while keeping the wings motionless", from *plan* "plane"; so called from the fact that the wings of a soaring bird form a level surface]

plan·et \'plan-ət\ *n* : a heavenly body other than a comet, asteroid, or satellite that travels in orbit around the sun; *also* : such a body orbiting another star

Word History Most of the stars seem to have fixed positions when they are compared to other stars. There are some heavenly bodies, however, that clearly change their positions in relation to the stars and to each other. They seem to wander about among the fixed stars. The ancient Greek name for such a heavenly body was *planēs*, which means "wanderer". The English word *planet* comes from the Greek *planēs*. Unlike the ancient Greeks, we now know that the planets "wander" across the sky because they, like the planet Earth, are revolving around the sun. [Middle English *planete* "planet", from early French *planet* (same meaning), from Latin *planeta* (same meaning), from Greek *planēt-, planēs* "planet", literally "wanderer"]

planarian

PLANETS

SYMBOL	NAME	MEAN DISTANCE FROM THE SUN		PERIOD OF REVOLUTION IN DAYS OR YEARS	EQUA-TORIAL DIAMETER IN KILOMETERS
		astronomical units	million kilometers		
☿	Mercury	0.387	57.9	87.97 d.	4,878
♀	Venus	0.723	108.2	224.70 d.	12,104
⊕	Earth	1.000	149.6	365.26 d.	12,756
♂	Mars	1.524	228.0	686.98 d.	6,787
♃	Jupiter	5.203	778.4	11.86 y.	142,800
♄	Saturn	9.569	1431.5	29.46 y.	120,000
♁	Uranus	19.309	2888.6	84.01 y.	50,800
Ψ	Neptune	30.284	4530.5	164.79 y.	48,600
♇	Pluto	39.781	5951.2	247.69 y.	3,000

plan·e·tar·i·um \,plan-ə-'ter-ē-əm\ *n, pl* **-i·ums** *or* **-ia** \-ē-ə\ **1** : a device that projects images of heavenly bodies on a ceiling shaped like a dome **2** : a building or room housing a planetarium

plan·e·tary \'plan-ə-,ter-ē\ *adj* **1 a** : of or relating to a planet **b** : having a motion like that of a planet ⟨*planetary* electrons of the atomic nucleus⟩ **2** : WORLDWIDE, GLOBAL ⟨a matter of *planetary* concern⟩

plan·e·tes·i·mal \,plan-ə-'tes-ə-məl, -tez-\ *n* : one of numerous small solid heavenly bodies which may have existed at an early stage of the development of the solar system and from which the planets may have been formed

plan·e·toid \'plan-ə-,tȯid\ *n* **1** : a body resembling a planet **2** : ASTEROID

¹plank \'plaŋk\ *n* **1** : a wide heavy thick board **2** : an item in the list of beliefs and goals of a political party

²plank *vb* **1** : to cover or floor with planks **2** : to set down forcefully ⟨*planked* the book on the table⟩ **3** : to cook and serve on a board ⟨*planked* steak⟩

plank·ton \'plaŋ(k)-tən, -,tän\ *n* : the floating or weakly swimming animal and plant life of a body of water — **plank·ton·ic** \plaŋ(k)-'tän-ik\ *adj*

pla·no·con·cave \,plā-nō-kän-'kāv, -'kän-,kāv\ *adj* : flat on one side and concave on the other

pla·no·con·vex \,plā-nō-kän-'veks, -'kän-,veks, -kən-'veks\ *adj* : flat on one side and convex on the other

¹plant \'plant\ *vb* **1 a** : to put or set in the ground to grow ⟨*plant* seeds⟩ **b** : to set permanently in the consciousness of : IMPLANT ⟨*plant* good habits⟩ **2 a** : to cause to become established ⟨*plant* colonies⟩ **b** : to stock or provide with something usually to grow or increase ⟨*plant* fields to corn⟩ ⟨*plant* a stream with trout⟩ **3 a** : to place or fix in the ground ⟨*planted* stakes to hold the vines⟩ **b** : to place firmly or forcibly ⟨*planted* a blow on his nose⟩ ⟨*planted* themselves right in our way⟩ **4** : to place or introduce so as to mislead ⟨*plant* a spy in an office⟩ ⟨*plant* a rumor⟩

²plant *n* **1** : any of a kingdom of living things usually lacking the ability to move from place to place under their own power, having no obvious nervous or sensory organs, possessing cellulose cell walls, and often having a body that is able to keep growing without taking on a fixed size and shape **2 a** : the land, buildings, and equipment of an organization ⟨the college *plant*⟩ **b** : a building or workshop for the manufacture of a product : FACTORY **3** : something or someone planted ⟨left muddy footprints as a *plant* to confuse the police⟩ — **plant·like** \-,līk\ *adj*

¹plan·tain \'plant-ᵊn\ *n* : any of several common weeds having a short stem or none at all, leaves with parallel veins, and a long stalk of tiny greenish flowers

²plantain *n* : the large greenish starchy fruit of a kind of banana plant that is eaten cooked and is an important food in the tropics; *also* : this plant

plan·ta·tion \plan-'tā-shən\ *n* **1** : a group of plants and especially trees planted and cared for **2** : a settlement in a new country or region : COLONY **3** : a planted area; *esp* : an agricultural estate worked by laborers

plant·er \'plant-ər\ *n* **1** : one that plants or cultivates ⟨a mechanical corn *planter*⟩; *esp* : a person who owns or operates a plantation **2** : a container in which ornamental plants are grown

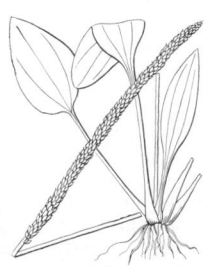

¹plantain

plant food *n* **1** : FOOD 2b **2** : FERTILIZER

plant hormone *n* : an organic substance other than food that in small amounts changes one of the life processes of a plant; *esp* : one made by the plant itself and acting somewhere other than at the site where it is produced

plant kingdom *n* : the one of the three or sometimes four basic groups of natural objects that includes all living and extinct plants — compare ANIMAL KINGDOM, MINERAL KINGDOM, PROTIST

plant louse *n* : APHID; *also* : any of various small insects that are like aphids

plaque \'plak\ *n* **1** : an ornamental pin; *esp* : an honorary badge **2** : a flat thin piece (as of metal) used for decoration or inscribed as a memorial or marker **3** : a thin film containing bacteria, mucus, and bits of food that forms on teeth

plash \'plash\ *n* : ²SPLASH — **plash** *vb*

plas·ma \'plaz-mə\ *n* **1** : the watery part of blood, lymph, or milk **2** : a collection of charged particles (as in the atmospheres of stars) that shows some characteristics of a gas but that differs from a gas in being a good conductor of electricity and in being affected by a magnetic field

plas·mo·di·um \plaz-'mōd-ē-əm\ *n, pl* **-dia** \-ē-ə\ : a parasite that causes malaria

¹plas·ter \'plas-tər\ *n* **1** : a medicated or protective dressing consisting of a film (as of cloth or plastic) spread with a substance that clings to the skin ⟨adhesive *plaster*⟩ **2** : a paste (as of lime, water, and sand) that hardens on drying and is used for coating walls and ceilings — **plas·tery** \-t(ə-)rē\ *adj*

²plaster *vb* **plas·tered; plas·ter·ing** \-t(ə-)riŋ\ **1** : to apply a plaster to **2** : to cover over as if with a coat of plaster **3** : to smooth down with a sticky or shiny substance ⟨*plastered* my hair down⟩ **4** : to fasten or apply tightly to another surface ⟨wet clothes *plastered* to his body⟩ **5** : to affix to or place on especially in large numbers ⟨*plaster* posters to a wall⟩ **6** : to apply plaster — **plas·ter·er** \-tər-ər\

plas·ter·board \'plas-tər-,bō(ə)rd, -,bȯ(ə)rd\ *n* : a board used in sheets and consisting of fiberboard, paper, or felt over a plaster core

plaster cast *n* : a rigid dressing of gauze filled with plaster of paris

plaster of par·is \-'par-əs\ *often cap 2d P* : a white powder made from gypsum that mixes with water to form a paste that hardens quickly and is used chiefly for casts and molds

¹plas·tic \'plas-tik\ *adj* **1** : capable of being molded or modeled ⟨*plastic* clay⟩ **2** : marked by or using modeling ⟨sculpture is a *plastic* art⟩ **3** : made or consisting of a plastic ⟨*plastic* dishes⟩ — **plas·ti·cal·ly** \-ti-k(ə-)lē\ *adv*

²plastic *n* : a plastic substance; *esp* : any of numerous synthetic or processed materials that can be formed into objects, films, or fibers

plas·tic·i·ty \pla-'stis-ət-ē\ *n* : the quality or state of being plastic; *esp* : capacity for being molded or changed in form or shape

plastic surgeon *n* : a surgeon skilled in plastic surgery

plastic surgery *n* : surgery concerned with the repair of lost, injured, or deformed parts of the body

plas·tid \'plas-təd\ *n* : any of various small bodies of protoplasm in cells of many plants and some protozoans that often serve as centers for special activities of metabolism

plat \'plat\ **1** : a small plot of ground **2** : a plan or map of an area with lots marked out

¹plate \'plāt\ *n* **1 a** : a flat thin piece of material **b** : metal in sheets ⟨steel *plate*⟩ **c** : a thin layer of one metal deposited on another **2 a** : one of the broad metal pieces used in armor **b** : armor made of plates **3** : a usually flat bony or horny bodily part forming part of a covering of an animal (as some fishes or reptiles) **4** : HOME PLATE **5** : any of the huge movable segments into which the earth's crust is divided and which are held to float on and travel over the mantle **6 a** : precious metal; *esp* : silver bullion **b** : vessels (as bowls or cups) used in the home and made of or plated with precious metal (as silver) **7 a** : a shallow usually circular dish from which food is eaten or served **b** : a main food course served on a plate ⟨a *plate* of spaghetti⟩ **c** : food and service for one person ⟨a dinner at $10 a *plate*⟩ **d** : a dish or pouch used in taking a collection (as in a church) **8 a** : a prepared surface from which printing is done **b** : a sheet of glass coated with a chemical sensitive to light for use in a camera **9** : LICENSE PLATE **10** : the part of a denture that holds the false teeth and fits to the mouth **11** : a full-page illustration ⟨color *plates*⟩ — **plate·like** \-,līk\ *adj*

²plate *vb* **plat·ed; plat·ing** : to cover or equip with plate ⟨*plate* the teapot with silver⟩

pla·teau \pla-'tō, 'pla-,tō\ *n, pl* **plateaus** *or* **pla·teaux** \-'tōz, -,tōz\ **1** : a broad flat area of high land **2** : a stable level, period, or condition [from French *plateau* "flat land raised above the surrounding land", from early French *plateau* "platter, plate"]

plate·ful \'plāt-,fu̇l\ *n, pl* **platefuls** \-,fu̇lz\ *also* **plates·ful** \'plāts-,fu̇l\ : a quantity to fill a plate

plate glass *n* : fine glass in large sheets that has been ground and polished

plate·let \'plāt-lət\ *n* : BLOOD PLATELET

plat·form \'plat-,fȯrm\ *n* **1** : a declaration of the beliefs and goals of a political party or candidate **2 a** : a level usually raised surface ⟨a railroad station *platform*⟩ **b** : a raised floor or stage for performers or speakers **3** : a thick sole for a shoe or a shoe with such a sole

plat·ing \'plāt-iŋ\ *n* **1** : the act or process of covering especially with metal plate **2** : a coating of metal plates or plate ⟨armor *plating*⟩ ⟨the *plating* wore off the spoons⟩

plat·i·num \'plat-nəm, -ᵊn-əm\ *n* : a heavy precious grayish white metallic element that is difficult to melt and is used especially in chemical ware and equipment and in jewelry — see ELEMENT table

plat·i·tude \'plat-ə-,t(y)üd\ *n* **1** : the quality or state of being dull or not stimulating **2** : an obvious, stale, or shallow remark

pla·toon \plə-'tün, pla-\ *n* **1** : a part of a military company consisting of two or more squads **2** : a group of football players sent into or withdrawn from the game as a body

platoon sergeant *n* : a noncommissioned officer in the army with a rank just below that of first sergeant

plat·ter \'plat-ər\ *n* **1** : a large plate used especially for serving meat **2** : a phonograph record

platy \'plat-ē\ *n, pl* **platy** *or* **plat·ys** *or* **plat·ies** : either of two small fish that are often kept in tropical aquariums and are noted for their varied and brilliant colors

platy·pus \'plat-i-pəs, -,pu̇s\ *n, pl* **platy·pus·es** *also* **platy·pi** \-,pī, -,pē\ : a small water-dwelling egg-laying mammal of southern and eastern Australia and Tasmania with a fleshy bill resembling that of a duck, webbed feet, and a broad flattened tail

platypus

plau·dit \'plȯd-ət\ *n* **1** : APPLAUSE **2** : enthusiastic approval — usually used in pl. ⟨received the *plaudits* of the critics⟩ [from Latin *plaudite*, a form of *plaudere* "to clap" — related to APPLAUD, EXPLODE, PLAUSIBLE; see *Word History* at EXPLODE, PLAUSIBLE]

plau·si·ble \'plȯ-zə-bəl\ *adj* **1** : seemingly fair, reasonable, or valuable but often not so ⟨a *plausible* excuse⟩ **2** : appearing worthy of belief ⟨the argument was both *plausible* and powerful⟩ — **plau·si·bil·i·ty** \,plȯ-zə-'bil-ət-ē\

n — **plau·si·bly** \ˈplȯ-zə-blē\ *adv*

Word History A plausible explanation is one that sounds as if it could be true. Such an explanation is not usually greeted with applause, but the origin of *plausible* suggests that it might be. *Plausible* comes from the Latin word *plausibilis,* meaning "worthy of applause". The first use of *plausible* in English was to describe a person or thing that deserved special praise. That use is now obsolete. To call something *plausible* now is to praise it only slightly, if at all. [from Latin *plausibilis* "deserving applause, pleasing", from *plausus,* past participle of *plaudere* "to clap" — related to APPLAUD, EXPLODE, PLAUDIT; see *Word History* at EXPLODE]

¹**play** \ˈplā\ *n* **1 a :** a brisk handling or using ⟨the *play* of a sword⟩ **b :** the conduct, course, or action of a game ⟨rain held up *play*⟩ **c :** a particular act or maneuver in a game ⟨a great *play* by the shortstop⟩ **d :** one's turn in a game ⟨it's your *play*⟩ **2 a :** exercise or activity for amusement ⟨children at *play*⟩ **b :** absence of any bad intention ⟨said it in *play*⟩ **c :** the act or an instance of playing on words : PUN **d :** the act of playing a game and risking something on an uncertain event : GAMBLING, GAMING **3 a :** a way or manner of acting or proceeding : ACTION, CONDUCT ⟨fair *play*⟩ **b :** OPERATION 1, ACTIVITY **c :** brisk or light movement ⟨the light *play* of a breeze⟩ **d :** freedom of motion ⟨too much *play* in the steering wheel⟩ **e :** opportunity for action ⟨the new job gave *play* to my talents⟩ **4 a :** the stage representation of an action or story **b :** a dramatic composition : DRAMA — **in play :** in condition or position to be legitimately played ⟨the ball was *in play*⟩ — **out of play :** not in play

²**play** *vb* **1 a :** to engage in sport or recreation and especially in activity for amusement ⟨children *playing*⟩ **b :** to treat or behave lightly or without respect that is due ⟨*play* with a new idea⟩ **c :** to make use of double meaning or the similarity of sound of two words for humorous effect : PUN **d :** to handle something in an absentminded way : TOY ⟨*played* with the pencil⟩ **2 a :** to take advantage ⟨*played* upon the people's fears⟩ **b :** to move swiftly or lightly ⟨shadows *playing* on the wall⟩ **c :** to move freely **d :** to let go in a stream ⟨hoses *playing* on the fire⟩ **3 a :** to sound in performance ⟨listen to an organ *playing*⟩ **b :** to be performed ⟨a new show *playing* for one week⟩ ⟨the music began to *play*⟩ **c :** to be staged or presented ⟨what's *playing* at the movies⟩ **4 :** to behave in a particular way ⟨*play* safe⟩ **5 a :** to take part in ⟨*play* cards⟩ ⟨*play* ball⟩ **b :** to pretend to take part in the activities of ⟨children *playing* house⟩ **c :** to do for amusement or from mischief ⟨*play* a trick on someone⟩ **d :** to give a particular degree of importance to — usually used with *up* or *down* ⟨*played* up their good grades⟩ ⟨*played* down the loss of the game⟩ **6 a :** to perform on or as if on the stage ⟨*play* a part⟩ **b :** to act the part of ⟨*play* the fool⟩ **7 a :** to contend against in a game ⟨*playing* the Dodgers today⟩ **b :** to put or keep in action ⟨*play* a card in a game⟩ ⟨*play* a fish on a line⟩ **8 :** to cause something to produce music or sound ⟨*play* the piano⟩ ⟨*play* a record⟩ — **play·able** \ˈplā-ə-bəl\ *adj* — **play ball :** COOPERATE — **play hooky** \-ˈhu̇k-ē\ **:** to stay out of school without permission

play·act·ing \ˈplā-ˌak-tiŋ\ *n* **1 :** performance in theatrical productions **2 :** behavior that is not sincere or natural

play·back \ˈplā-ˌbak\ *n* **:** the action of reproducing recorded sound or pictures often immediately after recording

play back \(ˈ)plā-ˈbak\ *vb* **:** to perform a playback of (a disc or tape)

play·bill \ˈplā-ˌbil\ *n* **:** a poster advertising a play

play·boy \-ˌbȯi\ *n* **:** a man whose chief interest is the pursuit of pleasure

play·er \ˈplā-ər\ *n* **1 a :** a person who plays a game **b :** MUSICIAN **c :** ACTOR **2 :** a mechanical device for automatically playing a musical instrument (as a piano)

player piano *n* **:** a piano containing a mechanical player

play·fel·low \ˈplā-ˌfel-ō\ *n* **:** PLAYMATE

play·ful \ˈplā-fəl\ *adj* **1 :** full of play : fond of playing ⟨a *playful* kitten⟩ **2 :** HUMOROUS ⟨a *playful* tone of voice⟩ — **play·ful·ly** \-fə-lē\ *adv* — **play·ful·ness** *n*

play·ground \ˈplā-ˌgrau̇nd\ *n* **:** a piece of land used for games and recreation especially by children

play·house \-ˌhau̇s\ *n* **1 :** THEATER 1 **2 :** a small house for children to play in

playing card *n* **:** any of a set of cards marked to show rank and suit (as spades, hearts, diamonds, or clubs) and used in playing games

playing field *n* **:** a field for various games; *esp* **:** the part of a field marked off for play

play·let \ˈplā-lət\ *n* **:** a short play

play·mate \ˈplā-ˌmāt\ *n* **:** a companion in play

play–off \ˈplā-ˌȯf\ *n* **1 :** a final contest or series of contests to break a tie **2 :** a series of contests played after the end of the regular season to determine a championship

play off \(ˈ)plā-ˈȯf\ *vb* **:** to break a tie by a play-off

play out *vb* **1 :** to perform to the end **2 a :** to use up or finish **b :** to become exhausted : TIRE **3 :** UNREEL, UNFOLD

play·pen \ˈplā-ˌpen\ *n* **:** a portable enclosure in which a baby or young child is placed to play

play·thing \-ˌthiŋ\ *n* **:** ¹TOY 2

play·wright \ˈplā-ˌrīt\ *n* **:** a person who writes plays

pla·za \ˈplaz-ə, ˈpläz-\ *n* **:** a public square in a city or town

plea \ˈplē\ *n* **1 :** a defendant's answer to a lawsuit or to a criminal charge ⟨a *plea* of guilty⟩ **2 :** something offered as an excuse ⟨left early with the *plea* of a headache⟩ **3 :** an earnest appeal ⟨a *plea* for mercy⟩

plead \ˈplēd\ *vb* **plead·ed** \ˈplēd-əd\ *or* **pled** \ˈpled\; **plead·ing 1 :** to argue a case in a court of law **2 :** to answer to a claim or charge in a court of law ⟨*plead* not guilty⟩ **3 a :** to argue for or against a claim ⟨*plead* a case before a jury⟩ **b :** to appeal earnestly : BEG **4 :** to offer as a defense, apology, or excuse ⟨*plead* sickness⟩ — **plead·er** *n*

pleas·ant \ˈplez-ᵊnt\ *adj* **1 :** giving pleasure : AGREEABLE ⟨a *pleasant* day⟩ **2 :** having or marked by pleasing manners, behavior, or appearance ⟨the new teacher is very *pleasant*⟩ — **pleas·ant·ly** *adv* — **pleas·ant·ness** *n*

pleas·ant·ry \ˈplez-ᵊn-trē\ *n, pl* **-ries 1 :** agreeable playfulness in conversation **2 a :** a humorous act or speech **b :** a light or casual polite remark

¹**please** \ˈplēz\ *vb* **pleased; pleas·ing 1 :** to give pleasure or satisfaction ⟨the new show will really *please* you⟩ **2 :** to feel the desire : LIKE ⟨do what you *please*⟩

²**please** *adv* — used to express politeness in a request ⟨*please* come in⟩

pleas·ing \ˈplē-ziŋ\ *adj* **:** giving pleasure : AGREEABLE — **pleas·ing·ly** *adv*

plea·sur·able \ˈplezh-(ə-)rə-bəl, ˈplāzh-\ *adj* **:** PLEASANT 1 — **plea·sur·ably** \-blē\ *adv*

plea·sure \ˈplezh-ər, ˈplāzh-\ *n* **1 :** a particular desire or purpose : INCLINATION ⟨what's your *pleasure*⟩ **2 :** the feeling that comes when one's wishes are met **3 :** a source of delight or joy

syn PLEASURE, JOY, ENJOYMENT mean the agreeable feeling that accompanies getting something good or much wanted. PLEASURE suggests an inner satisfaction rather than an open display of feeling ⟨the *pleasure* felt after helping others⟩ JOY suggests a very strong feeling that is shown openly ⟨you could see the winner's *joy*⟩ ENJOYMENT suggests a conscious reaction to something intended to make one happy ⟨the songs added to our

\ə\ abut	\au̇\ out	\i\ tip	\ȯ\ saw	\u̇\ foot
\ər\ further	\ch\ chin	\ī\ life	\ȯi\ coin	\y\ yet
\a\ mat	\e\ pet	\j\ job	\th\ thin	\yü\ few
\ā\ take	\ē\ easy	\ŋ\ sing	\th̲\ this	\yu̇\ cure
\ä\ cot, cart	\g\ go	\ō\ bone	\ü\ food	\zh\ vision

enjoyment of the movie⟩

¹pleat \'plēt\ vb **1** : to fold or arrange in pleats ⟨pleat a skirt⟩ **2** : ¹BRAID 1 — **pleat·ed** adj — **pleat·er** n

²pleat n : a fold (as in cloth) made by doubling material over on itself

ple·be·ian \pli-'bē-(y)ən\ n **1** : a member of the common people in ancient Rome **2** : one of the common people — **plebeian** adj

pleb·i·scite \'pleb-ə-,sīt, -sət\ n : a vote by which the people of an entire country or district express an opinion for or against a proposal especially on a choice of government or ruler

plec·trum \'plek-trəm\ n, pl **plec·tra** \-trə\ or **plectrums** : ³PICK 3

¹pledge \'plej\ n **1** : the handing over of something to another to assure that the giver will keep his or her promise; also : the thing handed over **2** : the state of being held as a security ⟨given in pledge⟩ **3** : something that is a token or sign of something else ⟨the ring is a pledge of love⟩ **4** : ²TOAST 3 **5** : a promise or agreement that must be kept

²pledge vb **pledged**; **pledg·ing** **1** : to give as a pledge **2** : ³TOAST **3** : to obligate by a pledge ⟨pledged myself to give $50⟩ **4** : to promise by a pledge ⟨pledge money to charity⟩

Ple·ia·des \'plē-ə-,dēz\ n pl : a loose cluster of stars in Taurus that is easily seen by a person with average sight

Pleis·to·cene \'plī-stə-,sēn\ adj : of, relating to, or being the earlier epoch of the Quaternary period of geological history or the corresponding system of rocks — see GEOLOGIC TIME table — **Pleistocene** n

ple·na·ry \'plē-nə-rē, 'plen-ə-\ adj **1** : complete in all ways : FULL ⟨plenary powers⟩ **2** : including all who have a right to attend ⟨a plenary session of an assembly⟩

pleni·po·ten·tia·ry \,plen-ə-pə-'tench-(ə-)rē, -'ten-chē-,er-ē\ n, pl **-ries** : a person and especially a diplomatic agent having full power to carry on business — **plenipotentiary** adj

plen·i·tude \'plen-ə-,t(y)üd\ n : the quality or state of being full or plentiful : ABUNDANCE

plen·te·ous \'plent-ē-əs\ adj : PLENTIFUL 2 — **plen·te·ous·ly** adv

plen·ti·ful \'plent-i-fəl\ adj **1** : giving or containing plenty ⟨a plentiful land⟩ **2** : present in large numbers or amount ⟨plentiful rain⟩ — **plen·ti·ful·ly** \-fə-lē\ adv

syn PLENTIFUL, AMPLE, ABUNDANT, COPIOUS mean more than enough yet not too much. PLENTIFUL suggests a great or rich supply ⟨vegetables are cheap when plentiful⟩ AMPLE suggests an amount more than enough to meet a particular need ⟨an income ample for the way that I live⟩ ABUNDANT suggests a supply far greater than needed ⟨an unexpectedly abundant corn harvest⟩ COPIOUS suggests more often a large quantity or number than a rich supply ⟨took copious notes during the lecture⟩

plen·ti·tude \'plen(t)-ə-,t(y)üd\ n : PLENITUDE

¹plen·ty \'plent-ē\ n **1 a** : a full supply ⟨had plenty of time to finish⟩ **b** : a large number or amount ⟨is in plenty of trouble⟩ **2** : the state of being plentiful ⟨times of plenty⟩

²plenty adv : QUITE 2 ⟨the game was plenty exciting⟩

ple·sio·saur \'plē-sē-ə-,sȯr, 'plē-zē- 'plē-zē-\ n : any of a group of Mesozoic marine reptiles with flattened bodies and limbs changed into paddles

pleu·ra \'plur-ə\ n, pl **pleu·rae** \'plu̇(ə)r-,ē, -,ī\ or **pleuras** : the delicate membrane lining each half of the chest of mammals and folded back over the surface of the lung of the same side — **pleu·ral** \'plu̇r-əl\ adj

pleu·ri·sy \'plur-ə-sē\ n : inflammation of the pleura usually with fever, painful breathing, and coughing

plex·us \'plek-səs\ n, pl **plex·us·es** : a network especially of blood vessels or nerves

pli·able \'plī-ə-bəl\ adj **1** : possible to bend without break-

ing **2** : easily influenced — **pli·abil·i·ty** \,plī-ə-'bil-ət-ē\ n

pli·ant \'plī-ənt\ adj **1** : PLIABLE 1 ⟨pliant willow twigs⟩ **2** : PLIABLE 2 **3** : adjusting to changing conditions : ADAPTABLE — **pli·ant·ly** adv

plied past and past participle of PLY

pli·ers \'plī-(ə)rz\ n pl : a small pincers for holding small objects or for bending and cutting wire

plies pl of PLY

¹plight \'plīt\ vb : to put or give in pledge — **plight·er** n

²plight n : a usually bad condition or state : PREDICAMENT ⟨in a sorry plight⟩

plinth \'plin(t)th\ n **1** : the lowest part of the base of an architectural column **2** : a block used as a base (as for a vase)

Plio·cene \'plī-ə-,sēn\ adj : of, relating to, or being the latest epoch of the Tertiary period of geological history or the corresponding system of rocks — see GEOLOGIC TIME table — **Pliocene** n

plod \'pläd\ vb **plod·ded**; **plod·ding** **1** : to walk heavily or slowly : TRUDGE **2** : to work or study with effort — **plod** n — **plod·der** n — **plod·ding·ly** \-iŋ-lē\ adv

plop \'pläp\ vb **plopped**; **plop·ping** **1** : to make or move with a sound like that of something dropping into water **2** : to set, drop, or throw heavily ⟨plopped myself in a chair⟩ — **plop** n

¹plot \'plät\ n **1** : a small area of ground : LOT ⟨a cemetery plot⟩ **2** : a plan of a floor of a building **3** : the main story of a literary work **4** : a secret plan; esp : an evil or unlawful scheme **5** : ¹DIAGRAM, CHART

²plot vb **plot·ted**; **plot·ting** **1 a** : to make a plot, map, or plan of **b** : to mark, note, or locate on a map or chart ⟨plot a ship's position⟩ **2** : to plan especially secretly : SCHEME **3 a** : to locate (a point) by means of coordinates **b** : to locate (a curve) by plotted points **syn** see PLAN — **plot·ter** n

plo·ver \'pləv-ər, 'plō-vər\ n, pl **plover** or **plovers** : any of numerous shorebirds differing from the related sandpipers in having shorter and stouter bills

plover

¹plow or **plough** \'plau̇\ n **1** : a farm machine used to cut, lift, and turn over soil **2** : a device (as a snowplow) used to spread or clear away matter on the ground

²plow or **plough** vb **1** : to open, break up, or work with a plow ⟨plow a furrow⟩ ⟨plow a road out with a snowplow⟩ **2** : to move through or cut as a plow does ⟨a ship plowing the waves⟩ **3** : to go steadily and with great effort : PLOD ⟨plow through a report⟩

plow·boy \'plau̇-,bȯi\ n **1** : a boy who guides a plow or leads the horse drawing it **2** : a country youth

plow·man \-mən\ n **1** : one that plows **2** : a farm laborer

plow·share \-,she(ə)r, -,sha(ə)r\ n : the part of a plow that cuts the earth

ploy \'plȯi\ n : a trick designed to embarrass or upset an opponent

¹pluck \'plək\ vb **1 a** : to pull or pick off or out ⟨pluck a flower⟩ **b** : to remove something (as feathers) from by or as if by plucking ⟨pluck a chicken⟩ **2** : to move or separate forcibly : SNATCH ⟨plucked the child from danger⟩ **3** : to play by pulling the strings ⟨pluck a guitar⟩ — **pluck·er** n

²pluck n **1** : a sharp pull : TUG **2** : COURAGE, SPIRIT

plucky \'plək-ē\ adj **pluck·i·er**; **-est** : COURAGEOUS, BRAVE

¹plug \'pləg\ n **1** : a piece used to close or fill a hole **2** : a flat cake of tightly pressed tobacco leaves **3** : something of lesser quality; *esp* : a worn-out horse **4** : SPARK PLUG 1 **5** : a lure with several hooks used in casting for fish **6** : a device usually on a cord used to make an electrical connection by putting it into another part (as a socket) **7** : a piece of favorable publicity

²**plug** *vb* **plugged; plug·ging 1** : to stop, make tight, or secure by or as if with a plug ⟨*plug* the leak with tar⟩ **2** : to hit with a bullet : SHOOT **3** : to advertise or publicize over and over **4** : to become plugged — usually used with *up* ⟨the drain was *plugged* up⟩ **5** : to keep steadily at work or in action ⟨*plugged* away at my homework⟩ — **plug·ger** *n* — **plug into** : to connect or become connected to by or as if by means of a plug ⟨the generator *plugs into* the power grid⟩

plug in *vb* : to establish an electric circuit by inserting a plug

plum \ˈpləm\ *n* **1 a** : any of numerous trees and shrubs related to the peach and cherries and having globe-shaped to oval fruits with an oblong stone **b** : the edible smooth‍-skinned fruit of a plum **2** : a raisin when used in desserts (as puddings or cake) **3** : something very desirable **4** : a dark reddish purple — **plum·like** \-ˌlīk\ *adj*

plum·age \ˈplü-mij\ *n* : the entire clothing of feathers of a bird

¹**plumb** \ˈpləm\ *n* : a weight attached to a line especially to show a vertical direction or distance — **out of plumb** or **off plumb** : not vertical or true

²**plumb** *adv* **1** : straight down or up : VERTICALLY **2** *chiefly dialect* : to a complete degree : ABSOLUTELY **3** : in a direct manner : EXACTLY

³**plumb** *vb* **1** : to measure, adjust, or test with a plumb ⟨*plumb* a wall⟩ ⟨*plumb* the depth of the well⟩ **2** : to see into and come to understand ⟨*plumbed* their motives⟩

⁴**plumb** *adj* : exactly vertical or true ⟨the wall is *plumb*⟩

plumb bob *n* : the metal bob of a plumb line

plumb·er \ˈpləm-ər\ *n* : a person who puts in or repairs plumbing

plumber's helper *n* : PLUNGER b

plumb·ing \ˈpləm-iŋ\ *n* **1** : a plumber's work **2** : a system of pipes for supplying and carrying off water in a building

plumb line *n* : a line that has a weight (as a plumb bob) at one end and is used to find out whether something is vertical or to measure depth

¹**plume** \ˈplüm\ *n* **1** : a feather of a bird; *esp* : one that is large and showy **2 a** : a feather or tuft of feathers worn as an ornament (as on a hat) **b** : a deserved prize or reward **3** : something that resembles a feather (as in shape or lightness) ⟨a *plume* of smoke⟩ — **plumy** \ˈplü-mē\ *adj*

²**plume** *vb* **plumed; plum·ing 1** : to provide or adorn with feathers **2** : to act with too much pride in oneself ⟨*plumed* himself on his swimming skill⟩ **3** : to arrange the feathers of : PREEN ⟨a bird *pluming* itself⟩

¹**plum·met** \ˈpləm-ət\ *n* **1** : ¹PLUMB **2** : PLUMB LINE

²**plummet** *vb* : to fall straight down : PLUNGE

¹**plump** \ˈpləmp\ *vb* **1** : to drop, sink, or come in contact suddenly or heavily ⟨*plumped* down in the chair⟩ **2** : to support someone or something strongly — used with *for* ⟨*plump* for a candidate⟩ [Middle English *plumpen* "to drop or sink heavily"]

²**plump** *n* : a sudden plunge or blow

³**plump** *adv* **1** : with a sudden or heavy drop **2** : ¹DIRECTLY 1 ⟨ran *plump* into the wall⟩

⁴**plump** *vb* : to make or become plump ⟨*plump* up a pillow⟩ [Middle English *plump* (adjective) "dull, blunt"]

⁵**plump** *adj* : having a full rounded form : CHUBBY — **plump·ness** *n*

plum pudding *n* : a rich boiled or steamed pudding containing fruits (as raisins) and spices

plu·mule \ˈplü-myü(ə)l\ *n* : the shoot or bud of a plant embryo that is located between the cotyledons and grows into the stem and leaves

plun·der \ˈplən-dər\ *vb* **plun·dered; plun·der·ing**

\-d(ə-)riŋ\ : to rob especially openly and by force (as in a raid) — **plunder** *n* — **plun·der·er** \-dər-ər\ *n*

¹**plunge** \ˈplənj\ *vb* **plunged; plung·ing 1** : to push or drive with force ⟨*plunged* my arm into the pipe⟩ **2** : to leap or dive into water **3 a** : to rush with reckless haste ⟨*plunged* into debt⟩ **b** : to bring into an unpleasant state ⟨*plunged* the family into gloom⟩ **4** : to dip or move suddenly downward or forward and downward ⟨the road *plunges* along the slope⟩

²**plunge** *n* : a sudden dive, leap, or rush

plung·er \ˈplən-jər\ *n* : one that plunges: as **a** : a device (as a piston in a pump) that acts with a plunging motion **b** : a rubber suction cup on a handle used to free plumbing traps and waste outlets of something blocking them

plunk \ˈpləŋk\ *vb* **1** : to make or cause to make a hollow, metallic, or harsh sound ⟨*plunk* the strings of a banjo⟩ **2** : to drop or set down suddenly ⟨*plunk* a suitcase on the bench⟩ — **plunk** *n*

¹**plu·ral** \ˈplur-əl\ *adj* : of, relating to, or being a word form used to indicate more than one ⟨*plural* nouns⟩ — **plu·ral·ly** \-ə-lē\ *adv*

²**plural** *n* : a form of a word used to show that more than one person or thing is meant

plu·ral·i·ty \plu̇-ˈral-ət-ē\ *n, pl* **-ties 1** : the state of being plural or numerous **2 a** : the greater number or part ⟨a *plurality* of the nations want peace⟩ **b** : the number of votes by which one candidate wins over another **c** : a number of votes cast for a candidate in a contest of more than two candidates that is greater than the number cast for any other candidate but is not more than half the total votes cast

plu·ral·ize \ˈplur-ə-ˌlīz\ *vb* **-ized; -iz·ing** : to make plural or express in the plural form — **plu·ral·iza·tion** \ˌplur-ə-lə-ˈzā-shən\ *n*

¹**plus** \ˈpləs\ *adj* **1** : mathematically positive ⟨a *plus* and minus 4⟩ **2** : having, receiving, or being in addition to what is expected ⟨now she is *plus* a kitten⟩ **3** : falling high in a certain range ⟨a grade of C *plus*⟩ **4** : electrically positive

²**plus** *n, pl* **plus·es** \ˈpləs-əz\ *also* **plus·ses 1** : an added quantity **2** : something that is an advantage ⟨that the machine operated quietly was a *plus*⟩

³**plus** *prep* : increased by : with the addition of ⟨4 *plus* 5 is 9⟩

¹**plush** \ˈpləsh\ *n* : a fabric like a very thick soft velvet

²**plush** *adj* **1** : made of or like plush **2** : very luxurious ⟨a *plush* home⟩

plus sign *n* : a sign + used especially in mathematics to indicate addition (as in 8 + 6 = 14) or a positive quantity (as in +10°)

Plu·to \ˈplüt-ō\ *n* : the planet farthest from the sun — see PLANET table

plu·toc·ra·cy \plü-ˈtäk-rə-sē\ *n, pl* **-cies 1** : government by the wealthy **2** : a controlling class of the wealthy — **plu·to·crat** \ˈplüt-ə-ˌkrat\ *n* — **plu·to·crat·ic** \ˌplüt-ə-ˈkrat-ik\ *adj*

plu·to·ni·an \plü-ˈtō-nē-ən\ *adj, often cap* : of, relating to, or like Pluto or the lower world : INFERNAL

plu·to·ni·um \plü-ˈtō-nē-əm\ *n* : a radioactive metallic ele-

plunger b

\ə\ **abut**	\au̇\ **out**	\i\ **tip**	\ȯ\ **saw**	\u̇\ **foot**
\ər\ **further**	\ch\ **chin**	\ī\ **life**	\ȯi\ **coin**	\y\ **yet**
\a\ **mat**	\e\ **pet**	\j\ **job**	\th\ **thin**	\yü\ **few**
\ā\ **take**	\ē\ **easy**	\ŋ\ **sing**	\th\ **this**	\yu̇\ **cure**
\ä\ **cot, cart**	\g\ **go**	\ō\ **bone**	\ü\ **food**	\zh\ **vision**

ment that is chemically similar to uranium, that is formed by decay of neptunium and found in minute quantities in pitchblende, that decays slowly to form uranium, and that will produce atomic energy by fission — see ELEMENT table

¹ply \'plī\ vb **plied; ply·ing** **1 a** : to use steadily or forcefully ⟨ply an ax⟩ **b** : to work at ⟨ply one's trade⟩ **2** : to keep furnishing or supplying something to ⟨ply a guest with food⟩ **3** : to go or travel regularly [Middle English plier, a shortened form of applier "to apply"]

²ply n, pl **plies** : one of the folds, layers, or strands of which something (as yarn or plywood) is made up [Middle English plien "to fold", from early French plier (same meaning), from Latin plicare (same meaning)]

Plym·outh Rock \,plim-əth-\ n : any of an American breed of medium-sized domestic chickens having a single comb

ply·wood \'plī-,wud\ n : a strong board made by gluing thin sheets of wood together under heat and pressure

pneu·mat·ic \n(y)u-'mat-ik\ adj **1** : of, relating to, or using air, wind, or other gas **2** : moved or worked by air pressure ⟨a pneumatic drill⟩ **3** : made to hold or be inflated with compressed air ⟨pneumatic tires⟩ [from Latin pneumaticus "relating to or using air", from Greek pneumatikos (same meaning), from pneumat-, pneuma "air, breath"] — **pneu·mat·i·cal·ly** \-i-k(ə-)lē\ adv

pneu·mo·coc·cus \,n(y)u-mə-'käk-əs\ n, pl **-coc·ci** \-'käk-(s)ī, -'käk-(,)(s)ē\ : a bacterium that causes pneumonia — **pneu·mo·coc·cal** \-'käk-əl\ adj

pneu·mo·nia \n(y)u-'mō-nyə\ n : a disease of the lungs marked by inflammation and congestion and caused by infection or irritants

¹poach \'pōch\ vb : to cook in simmering liquid ⟨poached eggs⟩ [Middle English pochen "to boil an egg without its shell so that the white covers the yolk like a bag", from early French pocher (same meaning), from earlier pochier, literally "to put into a bag", from poche "bag, pocket"]

²poach vb : to hunt or fish unlawfully usually on private property [from early French pocher "to trespass on, thrust one's fingers into, poke"] — **poach·er** n

pock \'päk\ n : a small swelling on the skin like a pimple (as in chicken pox or smallpox); also : the scar it leaves

¹pock·et \'päk-ət\ n **1 a** : a small bag carried by a person : PURSE **b** : a small bag open at the top or side inserted in a garment ⟨coat pocket⟩ **2** : supply of money : MEANS **3** : CONTAINER; esp : a bag at the corner or side of a billiard table **4** : something like a pocket ⟨a pocket of ore in a mine⟩ **5** : AIR POCKET

²pocket vb **1 a** : to put or enclose in a pocket ⟨pocketed the change⟩ **b** : to take for one's own use especially dishonestly ⟨pocket the profits⟩ **2** : to set aside : SUPPRESS ⟨pocketed my anger⟩ **3** : to supply with pockets

³pocket adj **1 a** : small enough to fit in the pocket ⟨a pocket dictionary⟩ **b** : smaller than the usual size ⟨a pocket park⟩ **2** : carried in or paid from one's pocket ⟨pocket expenses⟩

pock·et·book \'päk-ət-,buk\ n **1** often **pocket book** : a small especially paperback book **2** : a container for money and personal papers : WALLET **3 a** : ¹PURSE 1 **b** : HANDBAG 2 **4** : financial resources : INCOME ⟨a price suited to your pocketbook⟩

pock·et·ful \'päk-ət-,ful\ n, pl **pocketfuls** \-,fulz\ or **pock·ets·ful** \-əts-,ful\ : as much or as many as the pocket will contain

pocket gopher n : any of various compact burrowing North American rodents with fur-lined cheek pouches

pock·et·knife \'päk-ət-,nīf\ n : a knife that has one or more blades that fold into the handle and that can be carried in the pocket

pocket money n : money for small personal expenses

pock·et–size \'päk-ət-,sīz\ also **pock·et–sized** \-,sīzd\ adj : of a size convenient for carrying in the pocket ⟨a pocket-size calculator⟩

pocket veto n : a veto of a legislative bill by an executive

(as the president) accomplished through holding the bill unsigned until after the session of the legislature is over

¹pock·mark \'päk-,märk\ n : the scar left by a pock especially of smallpox; also : an imperfection suggesting a pockmark

²pockmark vb : to cover with or as if with pockmarks

¹pod \'päd\ n **1** : a fruit that is dry when ripe and then splits open to free its seeds; esp : LEGUME 2 **2** : any of various natural protective coverings (as a cocoon) or cases (as for grasshopper eggs) **3** : a streamlined compartment under the wings or body of an airplane used as a container (as for fuel or a jet engine)

²pod n : a number of animals (as seals) assembled together

po·di·a·trist \pə-'dī-ə-trəst\ n : a specialist in podiatry — called also chiropodist

po·di·a·try \pə-'dī-ə-trē\ n : professional care and treatment of the human foot in health and disease — called also chiropody

po·di·um \'pōd-ē-əm\ n, pl **podiums** or **po·dia** \-ē-ə\ : a raised platform especially for an orchestral conductor

po·em \'pō-əm, -im, 'pōm, also 'pō-,em\ n : a composition in verse

po·esy \'pō-ə-zē, -sē\ n, pl **po·esies** : poetic form or composition : POETRY

po·et \'pō-ət, -it\ n : a person who writes poetry

po·et·ess \'pō-ət-əs, -it-\ n : a girl or woman who writes poetry

po·et·ic \pō-'et-ik\ adj **1** : of, relating to, or characteristic of poets or poetry ⟨poetic words⟩ **2** : written in verse — **po·et·i·cal** \-i-kəl\ adj — **po·et·i·cal·ly** \-k(ə-)lē\ adv

poet laureate n, pl **poets laureate** or **poet laureates** **1** : a poet appointed by an English ruler as a member of the royal household and formerly expected to write poems for court and national occasions **2** : a poet regarded by a country or region as its most outstanding

po·et·ry \'pō-ə-trē, -i-trē\ n **1 a** : writing usually with a rhythm that repeats : VERSE **b** : the productions of a poet : POEMS **2** : writing chosen and arranged to create a certain emotional response through meaning, sound, and rhythm

poi \'poi\ n, pl **poi** or **pois** : a Hawaiian food made of cooked taro root pounded to a paste and often fermented

poi·gnan·cy \'poi-nyən-sē\ n : the quality or state of being poignant

poi·gnant \'poi-nyənt\ adj **1** : painfully affecting the feelings : SHARP, PIERCING ⟨poignant grief⟩ **2** : deeply affecting : TOUCHING — **poi·gnant·ly** adv

poin·set·tia \poin-'set-ē-ə, -'set-ə\ n : a showy Mexican and South American plant with large scarlet bracts that grow like petals about its small yellow flowers

¹point \'point\ n **1 a** : an individual detail : ITEM ⟨two points that were important to remember⟩ **b** : a distinguishing detail : CHARACTERISTIC ⟨politeness was a strong point⟩ **c** : the chief part or meaning

poinsettia

⟨the point of the joke⟩ **2** : a goal to be achieved : PURPOSE ⟨there's no point in continuing⟩ **3 a** : a geometric element that has position but no dimensions and is pictured as a small dot **b** : a usually small or precise place : LOCALITY ⟨a starting point⟩ **c** : an exact moment ⟨at this point they were ready⟩ **d** : a step, stage, or degree in development or rank ⟨the melting point of ice⟩ ⟨up to a point it was a good performance⟩ **4 a** : the usually sharp or tapering end of something (as a sword or pencil) : TIP **b** : either of two metal pieces in a distributor through which the circuit is made or broken **5** : a piece of land that sticks out **6 a** : a very small mark : DOT **b** : PUNCTUATION MARK; *esp* : PERIOD 2 **c** : DECIMAL POINT **7 a** : one of the 32 marks indicating direction on a compass used by seamen **b** : the difference of 11¼ degrees between two such adjacent points **8** : a unit used in giving a value or score ⟨scored fifteen *points*⟩ **9** : the action of pointing — **in point** : having something to do with the matter at hand : PERTINENT ⟨a case *in point*⟩ — **in point of** : in the matter of ⟨*in point of* fact⟩ — **to the point** : PERTINENT ⟨a remark that was quite *to the point*⟩

²**point** *vb* **1 a** : to furnish with a point ⟨*point* a pencil with a knife⟩ **b** : to give force to ⟨*point* up a remark with actual examples⟩ **2 a** : PUNCTUATE 1 **b** : to separate a decimal fraction from an integer by a decimal point ⟨*point* off three decimal places⟩ **3 a** : to show the position or direction of especially by extending a finger ⟨*point* out a house⟩ **b** : to direct someone's attention to ⟨*point* out a mistake⟩ **c** : to indicate game by freezing into a fixed position with head and gaze directed toward the object hunted ⟨a dog that *points* well⟩ **4** : to turn, face, or cause to be turned in a particular direction : AIM ⟨*point* a gun⟩ **5** : to indicate the fact or probability of something ⟨everything *points* to a bright future⟩

point–blank \ˈpȯint-ˈblaŋk\ *adj* **1** : aimed at a target from a very short distance away ⟨fired from *point-blank* range⟩ **2** : ¹BLUNT 3, DIRECT ⟨a *point-blank* refusal⟩ — **point–blank** *adv*

point·ed \ˈpȯint-əd\ *adj* **1** : having a point **2 a** : being to the point : PERTINENT **b** : aimed at a particular person or group ⟨*pointed* remarks⟩ — **point·ed·ly** *adv* — **point·ed·ness** *n*

point·er \ˈpȯint-ər\ *n* **1** : one that points; *esp* : a rod used to direct attention **2** : a large dog with long ears and short hair that is usually white with colored spots, hunts by scent, and points game **3** : a useful hint : TIP ⟨*pointers* on how to study⟩

point·less \ˈpȯint-ləs\ *adj* **1** : having no point **2** : lacking meaning : SENSELESS ⟨a *pointless* remark⟩ **3** : INEFFECTIVE ⟨*pointless* attempts to be funny⟩ — **point·less·ly** *adv* — **point·less·ness** *n*

point of view : a way of looking at or thinking about something : STANDPOINT

¹**poise** \ˈpȯiz\ *vb* **poised; pois·ing** **1 a** : ²BALANCE 5; *esp* : to hold or make firm or steady by balancing **b** : to hold without motion in a steady position : HOVER ⟨a bird *poised* in the air⟩ **2** : to put into readiness : BRACE ⟨*poised* for action⟩

²**poise** *n* **1** : ¹BALANCE 4, EQUILIBRIUM **2 a** : a dignified self-confident manner ⟨a speaker of great *poise*⟩ **b** : a way of carrying oneself : BEARING

¹**poi·son** \ˈpȯiz-ən\ *n* **1** : a substance that by its chemical action can kill or injure a living thing **2** : something destructive or harmful [Middle English *poison* "poison, a poisonous drink", from early French *poison* "drink, poisonous drink", from Latin *potion-, potio* "a drink, potion" — related to POTION]

²**poison** *vb* **poi·soned; poi·son·ing** \ˈpȯiz-niŋ, -ᵊn-iŋ\ **1 a** : to injure or kill with poison **b** : to put poison in or on ⟨*poisoned* the air with its fumes⟩ **2** : to exert a harmful influence on : CORRUPT ⟨*poisoned* their minds⟩ — **poi·son·er** \ˈpȯiz-nər, -ᵊn-ər\ *n*

³**poison** *adj* : POISONOUS ⟨a *poison* plant⟩

poison gas *n* : a poisonous gas or a liquid or a solid giving off poisonous vapors designed (as in chemical warfare) to kill or injure

poison ivy *n* **1** : a usually climbing plant that is related to the sumacs, has leaves usually with three leaflets, greenish flowers and berries, and leaves and stems that when bruised and touched may cause an itching rash on the skin **2** : a skin rash caused by poison ivy

poison oak *n* : any of several shrubby poison ivies

poi·son·ous \ˈpȯiz-nəs, -ᵊn-əs\ *adj* : containing poison : having or causing an effect of poison — **poi·son·ous·ly** *adv*

poison sumac *n* : a swamp shrub related to poison ivy, having smooth leaves with 7 to 13 leaflets, and producing an irritating oil that causes a severe rash on the skin of many people

¹**poke** \ˈpōk\ *n, chiefly Southern & Midland* : ¹BAG 1a, SACK [Middle English *poke* "bag, sack", from an early French dialect word *poke* (same meaning)]

²**poke** *vb* **poked; pok·ing** **1 a** : JAB, PROD ⟨*poke* a stick at a snake⟩ ⟨*poked* me in the ribs⟩ **b** : ¹THRUST 3, STAB **c** : to produce by piercing, stabbing, or jabbing ⟨*poke* a hole⟩ **2** : to stick out or cause to stick out ⟨*poked* her head out the window⟩ **3** : to be nosy especially about things that do not concern one **4** : to search over or through usually without purpose : RUMMAGE ⟨*poking* around in the attic⟩ **5** : to move slowly or lazily ⟨they were just *poking* along home⟩ [Middle English *poken* "to jab, prod"] — **poke fun at** : DERIDE, MOCK

³**poke** *n* : a quick thrust : JAB

poke bonnet *n* : a woman's bonnet with a brim that sticks out

¹**pok·er** \ˈpō-kər\ *n* : one that pokes; *esp* : a metal rod for stirring a fire

²**po·ker** \ˈpō-kər\ *n* : a card game in which a player bets on the value of his or her hand

poke·weed \ˈpō-ˌkwēd\ *n* : an American herb with spikes of white flowers, dark purple juicy berries, a poisonous root, and young shoots sometimes used as greens

poky *or* **pok·ey** \ˈpō-kē\ *adj* **pok·i·er; -est** **1** : being small and cramped ⟨a *poky* room⟩ **2** : so slow as to be annoying — **pok·i·ness** *n*

po·lar \ˈpō-lər\ *adj* **1 a** : of or relating to a geographical pole or the region around it **b** : coming from or having the characteristics of a polar region ⟨*polar* cold⟩ **2** : of or relating to one or more poles (as of a magnet) **3** : diametrically opposite **4** : showing polarity ⟨water molecules are *polar*⟩

polar bear *n* : a large creamy-white bear that lives in arctic regions

polar body *n* : a cell that separates from the immature ovum during meiosis and that contains a nucleus produced in the first or second division of meiosis but very little cytoplasm

polar bear

Po·lar·is \pə-ˈlar-əs, -ˈlär-\ *n* : NORTH STAR

po·lari·scope \pō-ˈlar-ə-ˌskōp\ *n* : an instrument for studying the characteristics of substances in polarized light

po·lar·i·ty \pō-ˈlar-ət-ē, pə-\ *n, pl* **-ties** **1** : the condition of having poles and especially magnetic or electrical poles **2** : attraction toward a particular object or in a specific direction

po·lar·ize \ˈpō-lə-ˌrīz\ *vb* **-ized; -iz·ing** **1** : to cause to vibrate (as light waves) in a definite pattern **2** : to give physical polarity to **3** : to break up into opposing groups **4** : to become polarized — **po·lar·iza·tion** *n*

Po·lar·oid \ˈpō-lə-ˌrȯid\ *trademark* — used especially for a material that polarizes light and is used chiefly in eyeglasses and in various optical devices

\ə\ abut	\au̇\ out	\i\ tip	\ȯ\ saw	\u̇\ foot
\ər\ further	\ch\ chin	\ī\ life	\ȯi\ coin	\y\ yet
\a\ mat	\e\ pet	\j\ job	\th\ thin	\yü\ few
\ā\ take	\ē\ easy	\ŋ\ sing	\th\ this	\yu̇\ cure
\ä\ cot, cart	\g\ go	\ō\ bone	\ü\ food	\zh\ vision

¹pole \'pōl\ *n* **1** : a long slender piece of material (as wood or metal) ⟨telephone *poles*⟩ **2** : ROD 2 [Old English *pāl* "stake, pole"]

²pole *vb* **poled; pol·ing** : to push or move with a pole ⟨*pole* a boat⟩ — **pol·er** *n*

³pole *n* **1** : either end of an axis of a globe and especially of the earth's axis **2 a** : one of the two terminals of an electric cell or battery **b** : one of two or more regions in a magnetized body at which the magnetism seems to be concentrated **3** : either of two specialized areas at opposite ends of an axis in an organism or cell ⟨chromosomes moving toward the *poles* of a dividing cell⟩ [Middle English *pool* "axis of the earth", from Latin *polus* (same meaning), from Greek *polos* "pivot, axis"]

Pole \'pōl\ *n* : a person born or living in Poland

pole bean *n* : a cultivated bean with long coiling stems that is usually trained to grow upright on supports

pole·cat \'pōl-ˌkat\ *n, pl* **polecats** *or* **polecat** **1** : a European flesh-eating mammal related to the weasel **2** : ¹SKUNK 1

polecat 1

Word History A polecat is not a cat at all, and its name has nothing to do with poles. The European polecat looks like a large weasel with a bandit's mask of darker fur around its eyes. The polecat has long been known as a killer of poultry, and its name reflects its reputation. *Polecat* was spelled *polcat* in Middle English. This word was probably formed from *pol* or *poul*, the early French word for "cock", and the Middle English word *cat.* During the Middle English period people often gave the name *cat* to small animals, like the polecat, that looked something like the ordinary house cat. [Middle English *polcat* "polecat", probably from early French *pol, poul* "cock" and Middle English *cat* "cat, a small animal"]

po·lem·ic \pə-'lem-ik\ *n* : an aggressive attack on the opinions or beliefs of another — **polemic** *or* **po·lem·i·cal** \-'lem-i-kəl\ *adj* — **po·lem·i·cal·ly** \-i-k(ə-)lē\ *adv*

pole·star \'pōl-ˌstär\ *n* : NORTH STAR

pole vault *n* : a track-and-field event in which contestants use a pole to jump for height over a crossbar — **pole–vault** *vb* — **pole–vault·er** *n*

¹po·lice \pə-'lēs\ *vb* **po·liced; po·lic·ing** **1** : to control, regulate, or keep in order by use of police ⟨*police* a city⟩ **2** : to make clean and put in order ⟨*police* the area⟩

²police *n, pl* **police** **1** : the department of government that keeps order and enforces law, investigates crimes, and makes arrests **2** *pl* : members of a police force **3** : a private or military force like a police force ⟨campus *police*⟩

police dog *n* **1** : a dog trained to help police (as in drug detection) **2** : GERMAN SHEPHERD

police force *n* : a body of officers trained and entrusted by a government to keep public peace, enforce laws, and prevent and detect crime

po·lice·man \pə-'lē-smən\ *n* : POLICE OFFICER

police officer *n* : a member of a police force

police state *n* : a state in which the activities of the people are under the power of the government often acting through a secret police force

po·lice·wom·an \pə-'lē-ˌswùm-ən\ *n* : a woman who is a police officer

¹pol·i·cy \'päl-ə-sē\ *n, pl* **-cies** : a course of action chosen in order to guide people in making decisions ⟨a country's foreign *policy*⟩

²policy *n, pl* **-cies** : a document that contains the agreement made by an insurance company with a person whose life or property is insured

pol·i·cy·hold·er \'päl-ə-sē-ˌhōl-dər\ *n* : the owner of an insurance policy

pol·i·cy–mak·ing \-ˌmā-kiŋ\ *n* : the development of governmental policy by high-ranking officials

po·lio \'pō-lē-ˌō\ *n* : POLIOMYELITIS

po·lio·my·eli·tis \ˌpō-lē-ˌō-ˌmī-ə-'līt-əs\ *n* : an infectious virus disease marked by inflammation of nerve cells in the spinal cord accompanied by fever and often paralysis and wasting of muscles — called also *infantile paralysis*

¹pol·ish \'päl-ish\ *vb* **1** : to make smooth and glossy usually by rubbing **2** : to smooth or improve in manners, condition, or style — **pol·ish·er** *n*

²polish *n* **1 a** : a smooth glossy surface : LUSTER **b** : good manners : REFINEMENT **2** : the action or process of polishing **3** : a substance prepared for use in polishing ⟨shoe *polish*⟩ ⟨nail *polish*⟩

¹Pol·ish \'pō-lish\ *adj* : of, relating to, or characteristic of Poland, the Poles, or Polish

²Polish *n* : the Slavic language of the Poles

polish off *vb* : to finish off or dispose of rapidly or completely ⟨*polished off* the whole meal⟩

po·lite \pə-'līt\ *adj* **po·lit·er; -est** **1** : showing good taste or training : REFINED ⟨*polite* society⟩ ⟨*polite* forms of address⟩ **2** : showing consideration and courtesy : COURTEOUS — **po·lite·ly** *adv* — **po·lite·ness** *n*

pol·i·tic \'päl-ə-ˌtik\ *adj* : wise especially in dealing with others or in carrying out a policy

po·lit·i·cal \pə-'lit-i-kəl\ *adj* **1** : of or relating to a government or the conduct of government **2** : of or relating to politics **3** : organized in governmental terms ⟨*political* units⟩ **4** : involving, concerned with, or accused of acts against a government or political system ⟨*political* prisoners⟩ — **po·lit·i·cal·ly** \-k(ə-)lē\ *adv*

political science *n* : the study of government and politics — **political scientist** *n*

pol·i·ti·cian \ˌpäl-ə-'tish-ən\ *n* : a person who takes an active part in party politics or in government business

pol·i·tics \'päl-ə-ˌtiks\ *n sing or pl* **1 a** : POLITICAL SCIENCE **b** : the art of guiding or influencing governmental policy **c** : the art of winning and holding control over a government **2** : political affairs or business; *esp* : competition between groups or individuals for power and leadership **3** : political opinions

pol·ka \'pōl-kə\ *n* : a lively dance that originated in Bohemia — **polka** *vb*

pol·ka dot \'pō-kə-\ *n* : a dot in a textile pattern of evenly spaced dots

¹poll \'pōl\ *n* **1 a** : ¹HEAD 1 **b** : the top or back of the head **2 a** : the casting or recording of votes **b** : the place where votes are cast or recorded — usually used in pl. ⟨at the *polls*⟩ **3** : a questioning of persons to obtain information or opinions

²poll *vb* **1 a** : to take and record the votes of **b** : to request each member of to declare his or her vote individually ⟨*poll* a jury⟩ **2** : to receive votes in an election (the candidate *polled* 10,000 votes⟩ **3** : to question (people) or cover (an area) in a poll **4** : to cast one's vote at a poll — **poll·er** \'pō-lər\ *n*

pol·lack *or* **pol·lock** \'päl-ək\ *n, pl* **pollack** *or* **pollock** **1** : an important food fish of the north Atlantic that resembles the related cods but is darker **2** : an important food fish of the north Pacific that is related to and resembles the pollack of the north Atlantic

polled \'pōld\ *adj* : having no horns ⟨*polled* cattle⟩

pol·len \'päl-ən\ *n* : a mass of tiny particles in the anthers of a flower that fertilize the seeds and usually appear as fine yellow dust

pollen basket *n* : a flat or hollow area bordered with stiff hairs on the hind leg of a bee in which it carries pollen to the hive or nest

pollen grain *n* : one of the microscopic grains of which pollen is made up

pollen sac *n* : one of the pouches of a seed plant anther in which pollen is formed

pol·len tube *n* : a tube that is formed by a pollen grain as it grows down the style and that carries the sperm nuclei to the embryo sac of a flower

pol·li·nate \'päl-ə-ˌnāt\ *vb* **-nat·ed; -nat·ing** : to place pollen on the stigma of

pol·li·na·tion \ˌpäl-ə-'nā-shən\ *n* : the act or process of pollinating

pol·li·na·tor \'päl-ə-ˌnāt-ər\ *n* : something (as an insect) that pollinates flowers

poll·ster \'pōl-stər\ *n* : one that conducts a poll or collects data obtained by a poll

poll tax *n* : a tax of a fixed amount per person that must be paid in order to vote

pol·lut·ant \pə-'lüt-ᵊnt\ *n* : something that pollutes

pol·lute \pə-'lüt\ *vb* **pol·lut·ed; pol·lut·ing** : to make impure; *esp* : to spoil (as a natural resource) with waste made by humans ⟨industrial wastes *polluted* the river⟩

pol·lu·tion \pə-'lü-shən\ *n* : the action of polluting : the state of being polluted ⟨air *pollution*⟩ — compare NOISE POLLUTION, THERMAL POLLUTION

Pol·lux \'päl-əks\ *n* : a bright star in Gemini [derived from Latin *Pollux* "Pollux, one of the twin heroes of Greek mythology", from Greek *Polydeukēs* "Pollux" — see *Word History* at GEMINI]

pol·ly·wog *or* **pol·li·wog** \'päl-ē-ˌwäg, -ˌwȯg\ *n* : TADPOLE

po·lo \'pō-lō\ *n* : a game played by teams of players on horseback using long-handled mallets to drive a wooden ball — **po·lo·ist** \'pō-lō-əst\ *n*

po·lo·naise \ˌpäl-ə-'nāz, ˌpō-lə-\ *n* : a dignified 19th century Polish dance [from French *polonaise* "a fancy woman's dress or gown", literally "a Polish gown", from *polonaise* (adjective), feminine form of *polonais* "Polish"]

po·lo·ni·um \pə-'lō-nē-əm\ *n* : a radioactive metallic element that is chemically similar to tellurium and bismuth, is found in pitchblende, and decays to form lead — see ELEMENT table

polo shirt *n* : a close-fitting pullover shirt of knitted fabric

pol·ter·geist \'pōl-tər-ˌgīst\ *n* : a mischievous ghost thought to be the cause of mysterious noises (as rappings)

pol·troon \päl-'trün\ *n* : COWARD

poly- *combining form* : many : several [Middle English *poly-* "many", from Latin *poly-* (same meaning), derived from Greek *polys* "many, several, much"]

poly·an·thus \ˌpäl-ē-'an(t)-thəs\ *n* **1** : any of various hybrid primroses **2** : a narcissus having small white or yellow flowers

poly·chro·mat·ic \ˌpäl-i-krō-'mat-ik\ *adj* : showing a variety or change of colors : MULTICOLORED

poly·chrome \'päl-i-ˌkrōm\ *adj* : relating to, made with, or decorated in several colors ⟨*polychrome* pottery⟩

poly·dac·ty·ly \ˌpäl-i-'dak-tə-lē\ *n* : the condition of having extra fingers or toes

poly·es·ter \'päl-ē-ˌes-tər\ *n* : any of a group of polymers that consist basically of repeated units of an ester and are used chiefly in making fibers or plastics

poly·eth·yl·ene \ˌpäl-ē-'eth-ə-ˌlēn\ *n* : a lightweight plastic resistant to chemicals and moisture and used chiefly in packaging

po·lyg·a·mous \pə-'lig-ə-məs\ *adj* **1** : of or relating to marriage in which a spouse has more than one mate at one time **2** : having more than one mate at one time — **po·lyg·a·mist** \-məst\ *n* — **po·lyg·a·my** \-mē\ *n*

poly·glot \'päl-i-ˌglät\ *adj* **1** : speaking or writing several languages **2** : containing or composed of several languages — **polyglot** *n*

poly·gon \'päl-i-ˌgän\ *n* : a closed plane figure bounded by straight lines — **po·lyg·o·nal** \pə-'lig-ən-ᵊl\ *adj*

poly·graph \'päl-i-ˌgraf\ *n* : an instrument for recording changes in several bodily functions (as blood pressure and rate of breathing) at the same time; *also* : LIE DETECTOR

poly·he·dron \ˌpäl-i-'hē-drən\ *n, pl* **-drons** *or* **-dra** \-drə\

: a solid that is formed by plane faces each of which has a boundary that is a polygon — **poly·he·dral** \-drəl\ *adj*

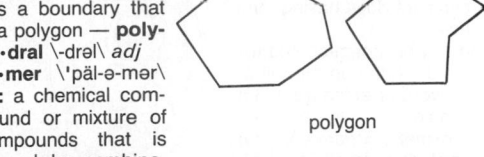

polygon

poly·mer \'päl-ə-mər\ *n* : a chemical compound or mixture of compounds that is formed by combination of smaller molecules and consists basically of repeating structural units — **poly·mer·ic** \ˌpäl-ə-'mer-ik\ *adj*

po·ly·mer·iza·tion \pə-ˌlim-ə-rə-'zā-shən, ˌpäl-ə-mə-rə-\ *n* : a chemical reaction in which two or more small molecules combine to form larger molecules — **po·ly·mer·ize** \pə-'lim-ə-ˌrīz, 'päl-ə-mə-\ *vb*

Poly·ne·sian \ˌpäl-ə-'nē-zhən, -shən\ *n* **1** : a member of any of the native peoples of Polynesia **2** : a group of languages spoken in Polynesia — **Polynesian** *adj*

¹poly·no·mi·al \ˌpäl-i-'nō-mē-əl\ *n* : an algebraic expression having two or more terms ⟨the *polynomial* $a^2 + 2ab - b^2$⟩

²polynomial *adj* : relating to, composed of, or expressed as one or more polynomials ⟨7023 written as $7(10^3) + 0(10^2) + 2(10^1) + 3(10^0)$ is in *polynomial* form⟩

pol·yp \'päl-əp\ *n* : an invertebrate animal (as a sea anemone or a coral) that is a coelenterate having a hollow cylinder-shaped body closed and attached at one end and opening at the other by a central mouth surrounded by tentacles armed with minute stinging organs

po·lyph·o·ny \pə-'lif-ə-nē\ *n* : music consisting of two or more independent but harmonious melodies — **poly·phon·ic** \ˌpäl-i-'fän-ik\ *adj*

poly·sac·cha·ride \ˌpäl-i-'sak-ə-ˌrīd\ *n* : a carbohydrate that can be broken down into two or more molecules of simple sugars

poly·sty·rene \ˌpäl-i-'stī(ə)r-ˌēn\ *n* : a stiff transparent plastic used chiefly in molded products, foams, and sheet materials

poly·syl·lab·ic \ˌpäl-i-sə-'lab-ik\ *adj* : having many syllables; *esp* : having more than three syllables — **poly·syl·lab·i·cal·ly** \-'lab-i-k(ə-)lē\ *adv* — **poly·syl·la·ble** \'päl-i-ˌsil-ə-bəl, ˌpäl-i-'sil-\ *n*

poly·tech·nic \ˌpäl-i-'tek-nik\ *adj* : relating to or devoted to instruction in many technical arts or applied sciences ⟨a *polytechnic* school⟩

poly·the·ism \'päl-i-(ˌ)thē-ˌiz-əm\ *n* : belief in or worship of more than one god — **poly·the·ist** \-ˌthē-əst\ *adj or n* — **poly·the·is·tic** \ˌpäl-i-thē-'is-tik\ *adj*

poly·un·sat·u·rat·ed \ˌpäl-ē-ˌən-'sach-ə-ˌrāt-əd\ *adj, of an oil or fatty acid* : having many double or triple bonds in a molecule

pome \'pōm\ *n* : a fleshy fruit (as an apple) consisting of a central core that has usually five seeds and is surrounded by a thick fleshy outer layer

pome·gran·ate \'päm-(ə-),gran-ət, 'pəm-,gran-\ *n* : a reddish fruit about the size of an orange that has a thick skin and many seeds in a pulp of acid flavor; *also* : a tropical Old World tree that produces pomegranates [Middle English *poumgarnet, pomegranard* "pomegranate", from early French *pomme grenate* "pomegranate", literally "seedy apple"; *pomme* from earlier *pome* "apple" and *grenate* derived from Latin *granum* "grain, seed" — related to GARNET, GRAIN, GRENADE; see *Word History* at GARNET]

\ə\ **abut**	\au̇\ **out**	\i\ **tip**	\o̅\ **saw**	\u̇\ **foot**
\ər\ **further**	\ch\ **chin**	\ī\ **life**	\o̅i\ **coin**	\y\ **yet**
\a\ **mat**	\e\ **pet**	\j\ **job**	\th\ **thin**	\yü\ **few**
\ā\ **take**	\ē\ **easy**	\ŋ\ **sing**	\th\ **this**	\yu̇\ **cure**
\ä\ **cot, cart**	\g\ **go**	\ō\ **bone**	\ü\ **food**	\zh\ **vision**

Pom·er·a·nian \,päm-ə-'rā-nē-ən, -nyən\ *n* : any of a breed of very small compact dogs having long hair

¹**pom·mel** \'pəm-əl, 'päm-\ *n* : the knob on the hilt of a sword or at the front of a saddle

²**pom·mel** \'pəm-əl\ *vb* **-meled** *or* **-melled; -mel·ing** *or* **-mel·ling** \-(ə-)liŋ\ : ²POUND 2a, PUMMEL

pomp \'pämp\ *n* **1** : a show of magnificence : SPLENDOR ⟨the *pomp* of a royal ceremony⟩ **2** : showy display

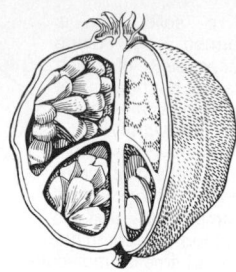
pomegranate

pom·pa·dour \'päm-pə-,dō(ə)r, -,dȯ(ə)r\ *n* : a hairdo in which the hair is combed high over the forehead; *also* : hair dressed in this style

pom·pa·no \'päm-pə-,nō, 'pəm-\ *n, pl* **-nos** : a food fish that occurs along the coasts of the south Atlantic and the Gulf of Mexico having a narrow body and forked tail; *also* : any of several related fishes

pom–pom \'päm-,päm\ *n* : a fluffy ball used as trimming on clothing

pomp·ous \'päm-pəs\ *adj* **1** : making a show of importance or dignity ⟨a *pompous* manner⟩ **2** : having an overly high opinion of one's importance ⟨a *pompous* politician⟩ — **pomp·ous·ly** *adv* — **pomp·ous·ness** *n*

pon·cho \'pän-chō\ *n, pl* **ponchos** **1** : a cloak like a blanket with a slit in the middle for the head **2** : a waterproof garment like a poncho

pond \'pänd\ *n* : a body of water usually smaller than a lake

pon·der \'pän-dər\ *vb* **pon·dered; pon·der·ing** \-d(ə-)riŋ\ : to consider carefully — **pon·der·er** \-dər-ər\ *n*

pon·der·o·sa pine \,pän-də-,rō-sə-, -zə-\ *n* : a tall timber pine of western North America with long needles in groups of 2 to 5; *also* : its strong reddish straight-grained wood

pon·der·ous \'pän-d(ə-)rəs\ *adj* **1** : very heavy **2** : unpleasantly dull ⟨fell asleep during the *ponderous* speech⟩ — **pon·der·ous·ly** *adv* — **pon·der·ous·ness** *n*

pond lily *n* : WATER LILY

pond scum *n* **1** : SPIROGYRA; *also* : any of various related algae **2** : a mass of tangled threads of algae in still water

pond·weed \'pän-,dwēd\ *n* : any of several water plants with leaves that float or are under the water and spikes of greenish flowers

pone \'pōn\ *n, Southern & Midland* : CORN PONE

pon·gee \(')pän-'jē, 'pän-,jē\ *n* **1** : a thin soft silk fabric of Chinese origin **2** : an imitation of pongee in cotton or synthetic fiber

pon·iard \'pän-yərd\ *n* : a slender dagger

pon·tiff \'pänt-əf\ *n* : BISHOP 1; *esp* : POPE — **pon·tif·i·cal** \pän-'tif-i-kəl\ *adj*

¹**pon·tif·i·cate** \pän-'tif-i-kət, -'tif-ə-,kāt\ *n* : the office or term of office of a pontiff

²**pon·tif·i·cate** \pän-'tif-ə-,kāt\ *vb* **-cat·ed; -cat·ing** : to speak pompously

pon·toon \pän-'tün\ *n* **1** : a flat-bottomed boat **2** : a float used in building a floating bridge **3** : a float of an airplane [from French *ponton* "a floating bridge, punt", from Latin *ponton-, ponto* (same meaning), from *pont-, pons*

poncho 1

"bridge" — related to ¹PUNT]

po·ny \'pō-nē\ *n, pl* **ponies** **1** : a horse of any of several breeds of very small compact animals **2** : a word-for-word translation of a foreign language text

Pony Express *n* : a rapid postal system across the western U.S. in 1860–61 that operated by changing horses and riders along the way

po·ny·tail \'pō-nē-,tāl\ *n* : hair arranged to resemble the tail of a pony

pooch \'pu̇ch\ *n* : ¹DOG 1a

poo·dle \'püd-ºl\ *n* : any of a breed of active intelligent dogs with heavy coats of solid color that occur in three sizes

Word History Poodles are often seen with their coats clipped or cut in different patterns. Both their haircuts and their name go back to a time when poodles were kept not as house pets but as retrievers. Poodles were especially good at retrieving game in the water. The dogs were good swimmers, and they had heavy coats that kept them warm even in icy water. Hunters came up with the idea of cutting their dogs' hair shorter in a pattern that would make swimming easier. Cutting poodles' hair in a pattern soon became a tradition. The German name for this skillful swimmer was *pudelhund*. This word combined *pudeln*, meaning "to splash", and *hund*, meaning "dog". It was then shortened to *pudel*, which English borrowed as *poodle*. [from German *pudel*, a shortened form of *pudelhund* "poodle", from *pudeln* "to splash" and *hund* "dog"]

pooh \'pü, 'pu̇\ *interj* — used to express disapproval

pooh–pooh \'pü-,pü, pü-'pü\ *also* **pooh** \'pü\ *vb* **1** : to express scorn or impatience **2** : to treat with scorn : DERIDE ⟨*pooh-pooh* the idea of ghosts⟩

¹**pool** \'pül\ *n* **1** : a small deep body of water **2** : a small body of standing liquid : PUDDLE [Old English *pōl* "a small body of water"]

²**pool** *n* **1** : the money bet by a number of persons on an event or in a game **2** : a game played on a billiard table having six pockets with usually 15 object balls **3** : a common fund for making investments **4 a** : a readily available supply ⟨a *pool* of talent⟩ ⟨a typing *pool*⟩ **b** : a group sharing in some activity ⟨a car *pool*⟩ [from French *poule* "the amount of money bet in a card game", literally "hen", derived from early French *poul* "a male chicken, cock" — related to PULLET]

³**pool** *vb* : to contribute to a common fund or effort ⟨*pooled* their resources⟩

poop \'püp\ *n* : an enclosed raised structure at the stern of a ship

¹**poor** \'pu̇(ə)r, 'pō(ə)r\ *adj* **1** : lacking riches or possessions **2** : less than enough ⟨a *poor* crop⟩ **3** : not good in quality or character of work **4** : FEEBLE 1 ⟨*poor* health⟩ **5** : lacking fertility ⟨*poor* land⟩ **6** : not satisfactory ⟨the patient had a *poor* day⟩ **7** : lacking in signs of wealth or good taste ⟨*poor* furnishings⟩ **8** : not efficient or capable ⟨a *poor* carpenter⟩ **9** : worthy of pity or sympathy ⟨the *poor* kitten hurt its paw⟩ — **poor·ly** *adv* — **poor·ness** *n*

²**poor** *n pl* : poor people ⟨charity for the *poor*⟩

poor boy *n, chiefly Southern* : ²SUBMARINE 2

poor farm *n* : a farm kept by the government and worked by poor people

poor·house \'pu̇(ə-)r-,hȧus, 'pō(ə)r-\ *n* : a place maintained at public expense to house needy or dependent persons

poor·ly \'pu̇(ə)r-lē, 'pō(ə)r-\ *adj* : somewhat ill : INDISPOSED

¹**pop** \'päp\ *vb* **popped; pop·ping** **1** : to burst or cause to burst with a pop ⟨the balloon *popped*⟩ ⟨we *popped* corn⟩ **2** : to go, come, push, or enter quickly or suddenly ⟨*pop* into bed⟩ ⟨*popped* a grape into my mouth⟩ **3** : to shoot with a gun **4** : to bulge from the sockets ⟨eyes *popping* with surprise⟩ **5** : to hit a pop fly [Middle English *poppen* "to hit, burst open"; a word created to imitate the sound made when something bursts open]

²pop *n* **1** : a sharp explosive sound **2** : a shot from a gun **3** : a flavored carbonated beverage

³pop *adv* : like or with a pop : SUDDENLY

⁴pop *n* : FATHER 1a [a shortened form of *poppa,* an altered form of *papa*]

⁵pop *adj* **1 a** : POPULAR 2 ⟨*pop* music⟩ **b** : of or relating to pop music ⟨a *pop* singer⟩ **2** : of, relating to, or being the behavior and interests of average people and especially young people [a shortened form of *popular*]

⁶pop *n* : a popular song ⟨the top *pops*⟩

pop·corn \'päp-ˌkò(ə)rn\ *n* : an Indian corn with kernels that burst open to form a white starchy mass when heated

pope \'pōp\ *n, often cap* : the head of the Roman Catholic Church

pop·eyed \'päp-ˌīd\ *adj* : having eyes that bulge

pop fly *n* : a short high fly in baseball

pop·gun \'päp-ˌgən\ *n* : a toy gun for shooting pellets or corks by compressed air

pop·in·jay \'päp-ən-ˌjā\ *n* : a proud talkative thoughtless person

pop·lar \'päp-lər\ *n* **1** : any of a genus of slender quick‑growing trees (as an aspen or cottonwood) that have catkins for flowers and are related to the willows **2** : the wood of a poplar

pop·lin \'päp-lən\ *n* : a strong ribbed fabric in plain weave

pop·over \'päp-ˌō-vər\ *n* : a quick bread shaped like a hollow muffin and made from eggs, milk, and flour

pop·per \'päp-ər\ *n* : one that pops; *esp* : a utensil for popping corn

pop·py \'päp-ē\ *n, pl* **poppies** : any of a genus of herbs or shrubs that have milky juice, showy flowers, and a fruit that is a capsule and include one that is the source of opium and several that are grown as ornamental plants

Pop·si·cle \'päp-ˌsik-əl\ *trademark* — used for flavored and colored water frozen in a rectangular shape on two flat handles

pop·u·lace \'päp-yə-ləs\ *n* **1** : the common people : MASSES **2** : POPULATION 1

pop·u·lar \'päp-yə-lər\ *adj* **1** : of, relating to, or coming from the whole body of people ⟨*popular* government⟩ ⟨*popular* opinion⟩ **2** : suitable for the average person (as in low price or ease of understanding) ⟨*popular* prices⟩ ⟨*popular* science⟩ **3** : generally current : PREVALENT ⟨*popular* opinion⟩ **4** : commonly liked or approved ⟨a *popular* teacher⟩ [from Latin *popularis* "of the people", from *populus* "the people" — related to PUBLIC] — **pop·u·lar·i·ty** \ˌpäp-yə-'lar-ət-ē\ *n* — **pop·u·lar·ly** *adv*

pop·u·lar·ize \'päp-yə-lə-ˌrīz\ *vb* **-ized; -iz·ing** : to make popular — **pop·u·lar·iza·tion** \ˌpäp-yə-lə-rə-'zā-shən\ *n* — **pop·u·lar·iz·er** \'päp-yə-lə-ˌrī-zər\ *n*

pop·u·late \'päp-yə-ˌlāt\ *vb* **-lat·ed; -lat·ing** **1** : to have a place in : OCCUPY, INHABIT **2** : to provide with inhabitants : PEOPLE

pop·u·la·tion \ˌpäp-yə-'lā-shən\ *n* **1** : the whole number of people living in a country or region **2** : the act or process of populating **3** : a group of one or more species of organisms living in a particular area or habitat

pop·u·lous \'päp-yə-ləs\ *adj* : having a large population

por·ce·lain \'pōr-s(ə)lən, 'pòr-\ *n* : a hard white ceramic ware used especially for dishes and chemical utensils

porch \'pōrch, 'pòrch\ *n* **1** : a covered entrance to a building usually with a separate roof **2** : VERANDA

por·cu·pine \'pòr-kyə-ˌpīn\ *n* : any of various rather large ro-

porcupine

dents with stiff sharp quills among the hairs on the body [Middle English *porkepin* "porcupine", from early French *porc espin,* literally "thorny pig", derived from Latin *porcus* "pig" and *spina* "thorn, spiral, column" — related to PORK, PORPOISE, SPINE; see *Word History* at PORPOISE]

porcupine fish *n* : any of various fish that are not usually fit to eat, are widespread in tropical seas, and have the body covered with spines and the teeth of each jaw united into a cutting plate

¹pore \'pō(ə)r, 'pò(ə)r\ *vb* **pored; por·ing** : to read with great attention : STUDY ⟨*pore* over a book⟩

²pore *n* : a tiny opening or space (as in the skin or the soil) — **pored** \'pō(ə)rd, 'pò(ə)rd\ *adj*

por·gy \'pòr-gē\ *n, pl* **porgies** *also* **porgy** : a blue-spotted crimson food fish of the coasts of Europe and America; *also* : any of various other fishes

pork \'pō(ə)rk, 'pò(ə)rk\ *n* : the flesh of a pig used for food [Middle English *pork* "meat from a pig", from early French *porc* "pig", from Latin *porcus* "pig" — related to PORCUPINE, PORPOISE; see *Word History* at PORPOISE]

pork·er \'pōr-kər, 'pòr-\ *n* : HOG 1a; *esp* : a young pig suitable for use as fresh pork

por·nog·ra·phy \pòr-'näg-rə-fē\ *n* : pictures or writings describing sexual behavior and intended to cause sexual excitement — **por·no·graph·ic** \ˌpòr-nə-'graf-ik\ *adj*

po·ros·i·ty \pə-'räs-ət-ē, pōr-'äs-, pò-'räs-\ *n, pl* **-ties** : the quality or state of being porous

po·rous \'pōr-əs, 'pòr-\ *adj* **1** : full of pores **2** : capable of absorbing liquids

por·phy·ry \'pòr-f(ə-)rē\ *n, pl* **-ries** : a rock consisting of feldspar crystals set firmly in a compact dark red or purple base of glassy or fine-grained texture — **por·phy·rit·ic** \ˌpòr-fə-'rit-ik\ *adj*

por·poise \'pòr-pəs\ *n* **1** : any of several small toothed whales with blunt rounded snouts that live and travel in groups **2** : DOLPHIN 1a

porpoise 1

Word History The small whale we call a porpoise is a swift and graceful swimmer. However, both its name and *pork,* the English word for the meat of hogs, can be traced back to Latin *porcus,* meaning "pig". The porpoise's rounded face must have reminded the ancient Romans of a pig's snout. They named the animal *porcus marinus,* meaning "pig of the sea". In the Middle Ages this became *porcopiscus,* from Latin *porcus* "pig" and *piscis* "fish". In early French the word was borrowed as *porpois.* It is from the French that we derived our English word *porpoise.* [Middle English *porpoys* "porpoise", from early French *porpois* (same meaning), from Latin *porcopiscis,* literally "pig fish", from *porcus* "pig" and *piscis* "fish"; originally in Latin called *porcus marinus,* literally "pig of the sea" — related to PORCUPINE, PORK]

por·ridge \'pòr-ij, 'pär-\ *n* : a soft food made by boiling meal or a vegetable in milk or water until it thickens ⟨oatmeal *porridge*⟩

por·rin·ger \'pòr-ən-jər, 'pär-\ *n* : a low metal bowl or cup with a handle

¹port \'pōrt, 'pòrt\ *n* **1** : a place where ships may take shelter from storms **2** : a harbor where ships load or unload cargo **3** : AIRPORT [Middle English *port* "a place for ships

\ə\ abut	\aů\ out	\i\ tip	\ò\ saw	\ů\ foot
\ər\ further	\ch\ chin	\ī\ life	\òi\ coin	\y\ yet
\a\ mat	\e\ pet	\j\ job	\th\ thin	\yů\ few
\ā\ take	\ē\ easy	\ŋ\ sing	\th\ this	\yü\ cure
\ä\ cot, cart	\g\ go	\ō\ bone	\ü\ food	\zh\ vision

to be secured", from Old English *port* and early French *port* (both, same meaning), from Latin *portus* (same meaning)]

²**port** *n* **1 a** : an opening (as in machinery) for gas, steam, or water to go in or out **b** : a place of entry into a system **2** : PORTHOLE 1 [Middle English *porte* "gate, an opening in the side of a ship for light or moving cargo in or out", from early French *porte* "door, gate", from Latin *porta* "passage, gate" — related to PORTAL]

³**port** *vb* : to turn to the left

⁴**port** *n* : the left side of a ship or aircraft looking forward [probably from ¹*port* "a place for ships to be secured" or ²*port* "an opening in the side of a ship"; so called from the fact that very early sailing vessels would keep the left side toward the port because the steering mechanism was always on the right side — see *Word History* at STARBOARD] — **port** *adj*

⁵**port** *n* : a rich sweet wine [named for *Oporto,* a city in Portugal from which the wine was exported]

por·ta·ble \'pȯrt-ə-bəl, 'pȯrt-\ *adj* : possible to carry or move about [Middle English *portable* "capable of being carried or moved about", from early French *portable* (same meaning), from Latin *portabilis* (same meaning), from earlier *portare* "to carry" — related to PORTFOLIO, TRANSPORT]

¹**por·tage** \'pȯrt-ij, 'pȯrt-; pȯr-'täzh\ *n* **1** : the carrying of boats or goods overland from one body of water to another **2** : a route for such carrying

²**portage** *vb* **por·taged; por·tag·ing** : to go or carry over a portage

por·tal \'pȯrt-ᵊl, 'pȯrt-\ *n* : a large or magnificent door or gate [Middle English *portal* "door, the structure around a door", from early French *portal* (same meaning), derived from Latin *portalis* (adjective) "of a gate", from *porta* "gate, passage" — related to ²PORT]

portal vein *n* : a vein that collects blood from one part of the body and distributes it to another through capillaries; *esp* : one that carries blood from the digestive organs and spleen to the liver

port·cul·lis \pȯrt-'kəl-əs, pȯrt-\ *n* : a heavy iron gate that can be lowered to prevent entrance (as to a castle)

por·tend \pȯr-'tend, pȯr-\ *vb* : to give a sign or warning of beforehand ⟨the distant thunder *portended* a storm⟩

por·tent \'pȯ(ə)r-,tent, 'pō(ə)r-\ *n* : a sign or warning usually of evil : OMEN

portcullis

por·ten·tous \pȯr-'tent-əs, pōr-\ *adj* **1** : being a portent : THREATENING **2** : causing wonder — **por·ten·tous·ly** *adv* — **por·ten·tous·ness** *n*

¹**por·ter** \'pȯrt-ər, 'pȯrt-\ *n, chiefly British* : DOORKEEPER

²**porter** *n* **1** : a person who carries baggage (as at a hotel) **2** : a railroad employee who waits on passengers **3** : a dark heavy ale

port·er·house \'pȯrt-ər-,hȧus, 'pȯrt-\ *n* : a beefsteak with a large piece of tenderloin on a T-shaped bone

port·fo·lio \pȯrt-'fō-lē-,ō, pȯrt-\ *n, pl* **-lios** **1** : a case for carrying papers or drawings **2** : the office and functions of a minister of state or member of a cabinet **3** : the stocks and bonds held by an investor or investment firm [an altered form of earlier *porto folio* "portfolio", from Italian *portafoglio* (same meaning), from *portare* "to carry" and *foglio* "leaf, sheet"; *portare* from Latin *portare* "to carry" and *foglio* from Latin *folium* "leaf" — related to FOLIAGE, PORTABLE]

port·hole \'pȯrt-,hōl, 'pȯrt-\ *n* **1** : an opening in the side

of a ship or aircraft **2** : an opening (as in a wall) to shoot through

por·ti·co \'pȯrt-i-,kō, 'pȯrt-\ *n, pl* **-coes** *or* **-cos** : a row of columns supporting a roof around or at the entrance of a building

¹**por·tion** \'pōr-shən, 'pȯr-\ *n* **1 a** : one's share of a whole ⟨a *portion* of food⟩ **b** : DOWRY **2** : one's lot or fate **3** : a part of a whole **syn** see PART

²**portion** *vb* **por·tioned; por·tion·ing** \-sh(ə-)niŋ\ : APPORTION

port·land cement \,pȯrt-lən(d)-, ,pȯrt-\ *n* : a cement made by burning and grinding a mixture usually of clay and limestone

port·ly \'pȯrt-lē, 'pȯrt-\ *adj* **port·li·er; -est** : heavy of body : STOUT — **port·li·ness** *n*

port·man·teau \pȯrt-'man-tō, pȯrt-\ *n, pl* **-teaus** *or* **-teaux** \-tōz\ : TRAVELING BAG

por·trait \'pōr-trət, 'pȯr-, -,trāt\ *n* **1** : a picture of a person usually showing the face **2** : a portrayal in words

por·tray \pōr-'trā, pȯr-\ *vb* **1** : to make a portrait of **2 a** : to describe in words **b** : to play the role of — **por·tray·er** *n*

por·tray·al \pōr-'trā(-ə)l, pȯr-\ *n* **1** : the act or process of portraying : REPRESENTATION **2** : PORTRAIT 1

Por·tu·guese \'pōr-chə-,gēz, 'pȯr-, -,gēs; ,pōr-chə-'gēz, ,pȯr-, -'gēs\ *n, pl* **Portuguese** **1** : a person born or living in Portugal **2** : the language of Portugal and Brazil — **Portuguese** *adj*

Portuguese man–of–war *n, pl* **Portuguese men–of–war** : any of several large colonial invertebrate animals that belong to the coelenterates and float on the surface of the sea by means of a large gas-filled structure like a bag

¹**pose** \'pōz\ *vb* **posed; pos·ing** **1 a** : to hold or cause to hold a special position of the body ⟨*posed* for fashion photographers⟩ **b** : to pretend to be what one is not ⟨*pose* as a soldier⟩ **2** : PROPOSE 1 ⟨*posed* a question⟩

²**pose** *n* **1** : a position of the body held for a special purpose **2** : a pretended attitude ⟨my cheerfulness was a *pose*⟩

¹**pos·er** \'pō-zər\ *n* : a puzzling or baffling question

²**poser** *n* : a person who poses

Portuguese man-of-war

po·seur \pō-'zər\ *n* : a person who pretends to be what he or she is not

posh \'päsh\ *adj* : ELEGANT 1, FASHIONABLE

posies *pl of* POSY

¹**po·si·tion** \pə-'zish-ən\ *n* **1 a** : the manner in which something is placed or arranged **b** : a certain arrangement of the body ⟨exercise while in a sitting *position*⟩ **2** : a stand taken on a question **3** : the point or area occupied by something **4 a** : one's rank in an organization or in society **b** : JOB 3 [Middle English *posycion* "position", from early French *position* (same meaning), from Latin *positio* "position", derived from *ponere* "to put, place" — related to ¹COMPOUND] — **po·si·tion·al** \-'zish-(ə-)nəl\ *adj*

²**position** *vb* **po·si·tioned; po·si·tion·ing** \-'zish-(ə-)niŋ\ : to put in proper position

¹**pos·i·tive** \'päz-ət-iv, 'päz-tiv\ *adj* **1 a** : clearly or definitely stated ⟨*positive* orders⟩ **b** : filled with confidence : CERTAIN ⟨were *positive* we would win⟩ **2** : of, relating to, or having the form of an adjective or adverb that shows no degree of comparison **3 a** : having or showing real existence or activity ⟨*positive* change in temperature⟩ **b**

: having the light and dark areas the same as in the original subject ⟨a *positive* photographic image⟩ **c** : being numerically greater than zero ⟨+2 is a *positive* integer⟩ **d** : reckoned or proceeding in a direction taken as that of increase or progress **e** : directed or moving toward the source of a stimulus ⟨a *positive* tropism⟩ **4 a** : of, being, or relating to electricity of a kind that is produced in a glass rod rubbed with silk ⟨a *positive* charge⟩ **b** : charged with positive electricity : having a deficiency of electrons ⟨a *positive* particle⟩ **c** : being the part from which the current flows to the external circuit ⟨the *positive* pole of a storage battery⟩ **d** : electron-collecting — used of an electrode in an electron tube **5 a** : showing acceptance or approval ⟨a *positive* answer to the question⟩ **b** : showing the presence of what is sought or suspected to be present ⟨the test for tuberculosis was *positive*⟩ — **pos·i·tive·ly** \'päz-ət-iv-lē, 'päz-tiv-lē, ,päz-ə-'tiv-lē\ *adv* — **pos·i·tive·ness** *n*

²**positive** *n* : something positive: as **a** : the positive degree or a positive form in a language **b** : a positive photograph or a print from a negative

pos·i·tron \'päz-ə-,trän\ *n* : a positively charged particle having the same mass and size of charge as the electron

pos·se \'päs-ē\ *n* **1** : a group of people called upon by a sheriff for help (as in pursuit of a criminal) **2** : a number of people organized to make a search (as for a lost child)

pos·sess \pə-'zes\ *vb* **1 a** : to have and hold as property : OWN **b** : to have as a characteristic, knowledge, or skill ⟨*possesses* a keen wit⟩ **2** : to enter into and control firmly : DOMINATE ⟨*possessed* by a demon⟩ ⟨whatever *possessed* you to do such a stupid thing⟩ — **pos·sess·or** \-'zes-ər\ *n*

pos·ses·sion \pə-'zesh-ən\ *n* **1 a** : the act of possessing or holding as one's own : OWNERSHIP **b** : control of property without regard to ownership **2 a** : something held as one's own **b** : an area under the control of but not actually part of a nation ⟨island *possessions* of the U.S.⟩ **3** : control by an idea or influence from outside oneself

¹**pos·ses·sive** \pə-'zes-iv\ *adj* **1** : of, relating to, or being a grammatical case that shows ownership or a similar relation **2** : showing the desire to possess or control ⟨a *possessive* attitude⟩ — **pos·ses·sive·ly** *adv* — **pos·ses·sive·ness** *n*

²**possessive** *n* **1** : the possessive case **2** : a noun or pronoun in the possessive case

pos·si·bil·i·ty \,päs-ə-'bil-ət-ē\ *n, pl* **-ties** **1** : the state or fact of being possible **2** : something possible

pos·si·ble \'päs-ə-bəl\ *adj* **1** : being something that can be done or brought about ⟨a task *possible* only to skilled workers⟩ **2** : being something that may or may not occur ⟨plan against *possible* dangers⟩ **3** : able or fitted to be or to become ⟨a *possible* site for a camp⟩

pos·si·bly \'päs-ə-blē\ *adv* **1** : by possible means : by any possibility ⟨that cannot *possibly* be true⟩ **2** : PERHAPS ⟨may *possibly* recover⟩

pos·sum \'päs-əm\ *n* : OPOSSUM

¹**post** \'pōst\ *n* **1** : a piece of timber or metal fixed upright especially as a support : PILLAR **2** : a pole or stake set up as a marker ⟨the starting *post*⟩ **3** : a metallic fixture attached to an electrical device (as a battery) for making connections [Old English *post* "an upright timber for support, pillar", from Latin *postis* (same meaning)]

²**post** *vb* **1 a** : to fix notices to or on a suitable place (as a bulletin board) **b** : to publish or announce by or as if by a notice ⟨*posted* the students' grades⟩ **2** : to forbid persons from entering or using by putting up warning notices ⟨*post* a trout stream⟩ **3** : ²SCORE 1a ⟨*posted* a 72 for the round⟩

³**post** *n* **1** *chiefly British* : POSTAL SERVICE **2** *chiefly British* : the mail handled by the post **3** *chiefly British* : a single shipment of mail [from early French *poste* "a relay station, one who carries messages", from early Italian

posta "relay station", derived from *porre* (verb) "to place", from Latin *ponere* "to place" — related to ⁵POST]

⁴**post** *vb* **1** : to ride or travel with haste : HURRY **2** : ²MAIL **3** : to transfer a bookkeeping item from a book of original entry to an account book **4** : to make familiar with a subject : INFORM

⁵**post** *n* **1 a** : the place at which a soldier or guard is stationed **b** : a station or task to which a person is assigned **c** : a place to which troops are assigned : CAMP **2** : an office or position to which a person is appointed **3** : TRADING POST [from early French *poste* "place where soldiers are stationed", from early Italian *posto* (same meaning), derived from *porre* (verb) "to place", from Latin *ponere* "to place" — related to ³POST]

⁶**post** *vb* **1** : to station in a given place ⟨*post* a guard⟩ **2** : to give as a guarantee of payment ⟨*post* a bond⟩

post- *prefix* **1 a** : after : later ⟨*post*date⟩ **b** : behind **2** : following : later than ⟨*post*script⟩ [derived from Latin *post* "after, later"]

post·age \'pō-stij\ *n* : the charge fixed by law for carrying an article by mail

postage stamp *n* : a government stamp used on mail to show that postage has been paid

post·al \'pōs-t°l\ *adj* : of or relating to the mails or to the post office

postal card *n* **1** : a blank card with a postage stamp printed on it **2** : POSTCARD 1

postal service *n* : a government department in charge of handling the mail

post·card \'pōs(t)-,kärd\ *n* **1** : a card on which a message may be sent by mail without an envelope **2** : POSTAL CARD 1

post·date \(')pōs(t)-'dāt\ *vb* **1** : to assign a date to that is later than the actual or current date ⟨*postdate* a check⟩ **2** : to follow in time

post·er \'pō-stər\ *n* : a notice or advertisement for posting in a public place or for decorative or pictorial display

¹**pos·te·ri·or** \pō-'stir-ē-ər, pä-\ *adj* **1** : later in time : SUBSEQUENT **2** : located behind or toward the back — **pos·te·ri·or·ly** *adv*

²**pos·te·ri·or** \pä-'stir-ē-ər, pō-\ *n* : the hind end of the body; *esp* : BUTTOCK 2

pos·ter·i·ty \pä-'ster-ət-ē\ *n* **1** : the line of individuals descended from one ancestor **2** : all future generations

pos·tern \'pōs-tərn, 'päs-\ *n* **1** : a back door or gate **2** : a private or side entrance or way — **postern** *adj*

post exchange *n* : a store at a military post that sells to people in or associated with the armed forces

¹**post·grad·u·ate** \(')pōst-'graj-(ə-)wət, -ə-,wāt\ *adj* : ²GRADUATE 2

²**postgraduate** *n* : a student continuing his or her education after graduation

post·haste \'pōst-'hāst\ *adv* : with great speed ⟨sent *posthaste* for the doctor⟩

post·hole \'pōst-,hōl\ *n* : a hole sunk in the ground to hold a fence post

post·hu·mous \'päs-chə-məs\ *adj* **1** : born after the death of the father ⟨a *posthumous* son⟩ **2** : published after the death of the author **3** : following or occurring after one's death ⟨*posthumous* fame⟩ ⟨a *posthumous* award⟩ — **post·hu·mous·ly** *adv*

pos·til·ion *or* **pos·til·lion** \pō-'stil-yən, pə-\ *n* : a person who rides as a guide on the left-hand horse of a pair drawing a coach

post·lude \'pōst-,lüd\ *n* : a closing piece of music; *esp* : an organ piece at the end of a church service

\ə\ abut	\aú\ out	\i\ tIp	\ò\ saw	\ú\ foot	
\ər\ further	\ch\ chin	\ī\ life	\òi\ coin	\y\ yet	
\a\ mat	\e\ pet	\j\ job	\th\ thin	\yü\ few	
\ā\ take	\ē\ easy	\ŋ\ sing	\th\ this	\yú\ cure	
\ä\ cot, cart	\g\ go	\ō\ bone	\ü\ food	\zh\ vision	

post·man \'pōs(t)-mən, -,man\ *n* : LETTER CARRIER

post·mark \-,märk\ *n* : a mark canceling the postage stamp on a piece of mail and giving the date and place of sending — **postmark** *vb*

post·mas·ter \-,mas-tər\ *n* : a person in charge of a post office

postmaster general *n, pl* **postmasters general** : an official in charge of a national post office department or postal service

post me·ri·di·em \'pōs(t)-mə-'rid-ē-əm, -ē-,em\ *adj* : being after noon — abbr. *p.m.*

post·mis·tress \'pōs(t)-,mis-trəs\ *n* : a woman in charge of a post office

¹post·mor·tem \(')pōs(t)-'mȯrt-əm\ *adj* : occurring after death

²postmortem *n* : POSTMORTEM EXAMINATION

postmortem examination *n* : an examination of a dead body especially to find out the cause of death

post·na·tal \(')pōs(t)-'nāt-°l\ *adj* : following birth; *also* : of or relating to a newborn child ⟨*postnatal* care⟩

post office *n* **1** : POSTAL SERVICE **2** : a local branch of the postal service handling the mail for a particular place

post·paid \'pōs(t)-'pād\ *adv* : with postage paid by the sender

post·pone \pōs(t)-'pōn\ *vb* **post·poned; post·pon·ing** : to hold back the doing of until a later time — **post·pone·ment** \-mənt\ *n*

post road *n* : a road over which mail is carried

post·script \'pō(s)-,skript\ *n* : a note or series of notes added at the end of a letter, article, or book

¹pos·tu·late \'päs-chə-,lāt\ *vb* **-lat·ed; -lat·ing** : to claim as true : assume as a postulate ⟨*postulates* that all people are created equal⟩

²pos·tu·late \'päs-chə-lət, -,lāt\ *n* : a statement or claim assumed to be true especially as the basis of a process of reasoning

¹pos·ture \'päs-chər\ *n* **1** : the position of one part of the body with relation to other parts : the general way of holding the body **2** : a particular condition or state ⟨a country's defense *posture*⟩ — **pos·tur·al** \-chə-rəl\ *adj*

²posture *vb* **pos·tured; pos·tur·ing** : to take a particular posture : POSE

post·war \'pōst-'wȯ(ə)r\ *adj* : of, relating to, or being a period after a war ⟨*postwar* Europe⟩

po·sy \'pō-zē\ *n, pl* **posies 1** : a bunch of flowers : BOUQUET **2** : ¹FLOWER 1c

¹pot \'pät\ *n* **1 a** : a deep rounded container for household purposes ⟨cooking *pot*⟩ **b** : the quantity held by a pot ⟨a *pot* of tea⟩ **2** : an enclosed trap for catching fish or lobsters **3 a** : a large quantity or sum **b** : the total of the bets at stake at one time **4** : ¹RUIN 1 ⟨business went to *pot*⟩ **5** : MARIJUANA

²pot *vb* **pot·ted; pot·ting 1** : to preserve in a sealed pot, jar, or can **2** : to plant or grow in a pot

po·ta·ble \'pōt-ə-bəl\ *adj* : suitable for drinking — **po·ta·bil·i·ty** \,pōt-ə-'bil-ət-ē\ *n*

pot·ash \'pät-,ash\ *n* : potassium or a potassium compound

po·tas·si·um \pə-'tas-ē-əm\ *n* : a silver-white soft light metallic element that has a low melting point and occurs abundantly in nature especially combined in minerals — see ELEMENT table

potassium chlorate \-'klō(ə)r-,āt, -'klȯ(ə)r-\ *n* : a salt used to supply oxygen for matches, fireworks, and explosives

potassium chloride *n* : a salt used as a fertilizer

potassium cyanide *n* : a very poisonous salt used especially to obtain gold and silver from ore

potassium dichromate \-(')dī-'krō-,māt, -'dī-krō-\ *n* : a salt that dissolves in water, forms large orange-red crystals, and is used especially in dyeing and photography

potassium hydroxide *n* : a white solid that dissolves in water to form a very alkaline liquid and is used in making soap

potassium nitrate *n* : a salt used in making gunpowder, in preserving meat, and in medicine

potassium permanganate \-(,)pər-'maŋ-gə-,nāt\ *n* : a dark purple salt used especially as a disinfectant

potassium sulfate *n* : a white salt used especially as a fertilizer

po·ta·to \pə-'tāt-ō, pət-'āt-\ *n, pl* **-toes 1** : SWEET POTATO 1 **2 a** : an erect American herb widely cultivated for its thick starchy edible underground tubers **b** : one of these edible tubers — called also *Irish potato, white potato*

potato beetle *n* : COLORADO POTATO BEETLE

potato bug *n* : COLORADO POTATO BEETLE

potato chip *n* : a thin slice of potato fried in deep fat

pot·bel·ly \'pät-,bel-ē\ *n* **1** : an enlarged abdomen or one that bulges outward **2** : a stove with a bulging body — **pot·bel·lied** \-'bel-ēd\ *adj*

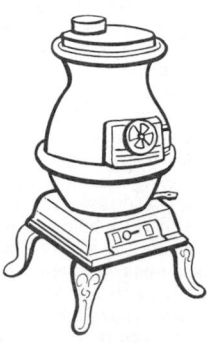

potbelly 2

po·ten·cy \'pōt-°n-sē\ *n, pl* **-cies** : the quality or state of being potent ⟨vitamins of high *potency*⟩; *esp* : power to bring about a certain result

po·tent \'pōt-°nt\ *adj* **1** : having or wielding force, authority, or influence : POWERFUL ⟨*potent* arguments for a strong defense⟩ **2 a** : very effective ⟨*potent* medicine⟩ **b** : rich in a particular quality : STRONG ⟨*potent* tea⟩ — **po·tent·ly** *adv*

po·ten·tate \'pōt-°n-,tāt\ *n* : a person who has controlling power : SOVEREIGN

¹po·ten·tial \pə-'ten-chəl\ *adj* : capable of becoming real : POSSIBLE ⟨aware of the *potential* dangers in a scheme⟩ — **po·ten·tial·ly** \-'tench-(ə-)lē\ *adv*

²potential *n* **1 a** : something that can develop or become actual : POSSIBILITY **b** : POTENTIALITY 1 **2 a** : the work required to move a unit positive charge from a reference point (as at infinity) to a point in question **b** : POTENTIAL DIFFERENCE

potential difference *n* : the difference in potential between two points that represents the work involved or the energy released in the transfer of a unit quantity of electricity from one point to the other

potential energy *n* : the amount of energy a thing (as a weight raised to a height or a coiled spring) has because of its position or because of the arrangement of its parts

po·ten·ti·al·i·ty \pə-,ten-chē-'al-ət-ē\ *n, pl* **-ties 1** : the ability to develop or to come into existence **2** : ²POTENTIAL 1a

pot·ful \'pät-,fŭl\ *n* : the quantity held by a pot

pot·head \'pät-,hed\ *n* : a person who smokes marijuana

poth·er \'päth-ər\ *n* : ¹FUSS 1

pot·herb \'pät-,(h)ərb\ *n* : an herb whose leaves or stems are boiled for use as greens; *also* : one (as mint) used to season food

pot holder *n* : a small cloth pad used for handling hot cooking utensils

pot·hole \'pät-,hōl\ *n* : a deep round hole (as in a road)

pot·hook \-,hŭk\ *n* : an S-shaped hook for hanging pots over an open fire

po·tion \'pō-shən\ *n* : a drink especially of a medicine or of a poison [Middle English *pocioun* "a mixture of liquids", from early French *potion* (same meaning), from Latin *potion-, potio* "a drink, potion", derived from *potare* "to drink" — related to POISON]

pot·luck \'pät-'lək\ *n* : a regular meal for which no special preparations have been made

pot·pie \-'pī\ *n* : pastry-covered meat and vegetables cooked in a deep dish

pot·pour·ri \ˌpō-pù-'rē\ *n* **1** : a jar of flower petals and spices used for scent **2** : a miscellaneous collection : MEDLEY

pot roast *n* : a piece of meat (as beef) cooked by braising usually on top of the stove

pot·shot \'pät-ˌshät\ *n* : a shot taken in a casual manner or at an easy target

pot·tage \'pät-ij\ *n* : a thick soup of vegetables or vegetables and meat

potted *past and past participle of* POT

¹pot·ter \'pät-ər\ *n* : one that makes pottery

²potter *vb* : ³PUTTER — **pot·ter·er** *n*

potter's field *n* : a public burial place for the poor, unknown persons, and criminals

potter's wheel *n* : a horizontal disk revolving on a spindle and carrying the clay being shaped by a potter

pot·tery \'pät-ə-rē\ *n, pl* **-ter·ies** **1** : a place where clay articles (as pots and vases) are made **2** : the art of the potter : CERAMICS **3** : articles made from clay that is shaped while moist and hardened by heat

potting *present participle of* POT

potter's wheel

¹pouch \'paùch\ *n* **1** : a small bag that can be closed (as with a string) ⟨tobacco *pouch*⟩ **2** : a structure in the form of a bag; *esp* : one for carrying the young on the abdomen of a female marsupial (as a kangaroo or opossum) — **pouched** \'paùcht\ *adj*

²pouch *vb* : to put or form into or as if into a pouch

poul·tice \'pōl-təs\ *n* : a soft usually heated mass that often contains medicine, is spread on cloth, and is applied especially to sores

poul·try \'pōl-trē\ *n* : domesticated birds kept for eggs or meat [Middle English *pultrie* "fowl raised for food", derived from early French *pouleterie* (same meaning), from *pouletier* "one who raises poultry", from *poulet* "a young chicken or fowl", derived from *poul* "a male chicken" — related to PULLET]

poul·try·man \-mən\ *n* : one who raises or deals in poultry

pounce \'paùn(t)s\ *vb* **pounced; pounc·ing** **1** : to swoop down on and seize something ⟨a cat waiting to *pounce*⟩ **2** : to make a sudden assault or approach ⟨a clerk *pounced* on me immediately⟩ — **pounce** *n*

¹pound \'paùnd\ *n, pl* **pounds** *also* **pound** **1** : any of various units of mass and weight; *esp* : a unit in general use among English-speaking peoples equal to 16 ounces (about 0.454 kilograms) — see MEASURE table **2 a** : the basic unit of money of the United Kingdom — called also *pound sterling* **b** : the basic unit of money of Cyprus, Egypt, Ireland, Lebanon, Malta, Sudan, and Syria **c** : a coin or bill representing one pound [Old English *pund* "pound weight", from Latin *pondo* (same meaning)]

²pound *vb* **1** : to crush to powder or pulp by beating **2 a** : to strike heavily or again and again ⟨*pound* the piano⟩ **b** : to produce by pounding ⟨*pound* out a tune on the piano⟩ **c** : ¹DRIVE 1b ⟨*pound* a nail⟩ **3** : to move heavily ⟨the horses *pounded* along the lane⟩ [Old English *pūnian* "to beat into a powder"] — **pound·er** *n*

³pound *n* : an act or sound of pounding

⁴pound *n* **1** : a public enclosure for stray animals ⟨the dog *pound*⟩ **2** : an enclosure within which fish or shellfish are caught or stored [Old English *pund-* "an enclosure for animals"]

pound cake *n* : a cake made with a large amount of butter and eggs

pour \'pō(ə)r, 'pȯ(ə)r\ *vb* **1** : to flow or to cause to flow in a stream ⟨*pour* the tea⟩ ⟨tears *pouring* down their cheeks⟩ **2** : to let loose something without restraint ⟨*poured* out my troubles to anyone who would listen⟩ **3** : to rain very hard

— **pour·er** *n*

¹pout \'paùt\ *vb* **1** : to show displeasure by pushing out the lips **2** : ¹SULK

²pout *n* **1** : an act of pouting **2** *pl* : a state of bad humor

pov·er·ty \'päv-ərt-ē\ *n* **1** : the state of being poor : lack of money or possessions : WANT **2** : a small supply : DEARTH ⟨a *poverty* of information about the new disease⟩ **3** : lack of fertility ⟨*poverty* of the soil⟩

pov·er·ty–strick·en \-ˌstrik-ən\ *adj* : very poor : DESTITUTE

¹pow·der \'paùd-ər\ *n* **1 a** : dry material made up of fine particles **b** : something (as a food, medicine, or cosmetic) made in or changed to the form of a powder **2** : a solid explosive used in shooting or blasting

²powder *vb* **1** : to sprinkle or cover with or as if with powder **2** : to crush to or become powder — **pow·der·er** \-ər-ər\ *n*

powder blue *n* : a pale blue

powder horn *n* : a flask for carrying gunpowder; *esp* : one made of the horn of an ox or cow

pow·dery \'paùd-ə-rē\ *adj* **1 a** : resembling or consisting of powder **b** : easily made into a powder : CRUMBLY **2** : covered with or as if with powder : DUSTY

powdery mildew *n* : a fungus that is a parasite and produces a large number of powdery spores on the host; *also* : a plant disease caused by such a fungus

¹pow·er \'paù(-ə)r\ *n* **1 a** : possession of control, authority, or influence over others ⟨a politician hungry for *power*⟩ **b** : one having such power; *esp* : an independent state ⟨China is a major *power* in Asia⟩ **2** : ability to act or do something ⟨lose the *power* of speech⟩ **3 a** : physical might **b** : mental strength **4** : the number of times as indicated by an exponent a number occurs as a factor in a product; *also* : the product obtained by raising a number to a power ⟨10^3, or 10·10·10, is the 3d *power* of 10⟩ **5 a** : force or energy that is or can be applied to work ⟨electric *power*⟩ **b** : the time rate at which work is done or energy given off or transferred **6** : MAGNIFICATION 2b

syn POWER, ENERGY, STRENGTH mean the ability to put out effort or force. POWER applies to the ability to act, whether only possible or actually used ⟨the king had the *power* to coin money⟩ ENERGY applies to stored-up power that can be used to do work ⟨the sun could be a great source of new *energy* for us⟩ STRENGTH applies to that quality which gives a person or thing the ability to put out force or to oppose another's force or attack ⟨test the *strength* of this rope⟩

²power *adj* : relating to, supplying, or using power ⟨a *power* drill⟩ ⟨*power* failure⟩

³power *vb* : to supply with power

pow·er·boat \'paù(-ə)r-ˌbōt\ *n* : MOTORBOAT

power dive *n* : a dive of an airplane accelerated by the power of the engine — **power–dive** *vb*

pow·er·ful \'paù(-ə)r-fəl\ *adj* : full of or having power or influence : STRONG, EFFECTIVE — **pow·er·ful·ly** \-f(ə-)lē\ *adv*

pow·er·house \'paù(-ə)r-ˌhaùs\ *n* **1** : POWER PLANT **2** : a person or thing having unusual strength or energy

pow·er·less \'paù(-ə)r-ləs\ *adj* **1** : lacking power, force, or energy **2** : lacking authority to act — **pow·er·less·ly** *adv* — **pow·er·less·ness** *n*

power plant *n* : a building in which electric power is generated

power station *n* : POWER PLANT

pow·wow \'paù-ˌwaù\ *n* **1** : an American Indian ceremony or conference **2** : a meeting for discussion — **powwow** *vb*

\ə\ abut	\aù\ **out**	\i\ tip	\ȯ\ saw	\ù\ foot	
\ər\ further	\ch\ **chin**	\ī\ life	\ȯi\ coin	\y\ yet	
\a\ mat	\e\ pet	\j\ job	\th\ thin	\yü\ few	
\ā\ take	\ē\ **easy**	\ŋ\ sing	\th\ this	\yù\ cure	
\ä\ cot, cart	\g\ go	\ō\ bone	\ü\ food	\zh\ vision	

pox \'päks\ *n* : a disease (as smallpox, chicken pox, or syphilis) that causes a rash on the skin

prac·ti·ca·ble \'prak-ti-kə-bəl\ *adj* 1 : capable of being done, put into practice, or accomplished : FEASIBLE ⟨an interesting but not *practicable* idea⟩ 2 : USABLE ⟨a *practicable* weapon⟩ — **prac·ti·ca·bil·i·ty** \,prak-ti-kə-'bil-ət-ē\ *n*

prac·ti·cal \'prak-ti-kəl\ *adj* 1 : of or relating to action and practice rather than ideas or thought ⟨for *practical* purposes⟩ 2 : being such in practice or effect : VIRTUAL ⟨a *practical* failure⟩ 3 : capable of being put to use or account : USEFUL ⟨a *practical* knowledge of farming⟩ 4 : good at putting ideas or plans into action ⟨a *practical* mind⟩ — **prac·ti·cal·i·ty** \,prak-ti-'kal-ət-ē\ *n*

practical joke *n* : a joke involving something that is done rather than said; *esp* : a trick played on a person — **practical joker** *n*

prac·ti·cal·ly \'prak-ti-k(ə-)lē\ *adv* 1 : in a practical manner ⟨talked *practically* about the problem⟩ 2 : ALMOST, NEARLY ⟨*practically* everyone went to the game⟩

practical nurse *n* : a nurse who cares for the sick professionally without having the training or experience required of a registered nurse; *esp* : LICENSED PRACTICAL NURSE

¹prac·tice *or* **prac·tise** \'prak-təs\ *vb* **prac·ticed** *or* **prac·tised; prac·tic·ing** *or* **prac·tis·ing** 1 : to perform or work at over and over so as to become skilled ⟨*practice* juggling⟩ 2 : CARRY OUT, APPLY ⟨*practice* what you preach⟩ 3 : to do or perform often or usually ⟨*practice* politeness⟩ 4 : to engage in or work at as a profession ⟨*practice* medicine⟩ — **prac·tic·er** *n*

²practice *also* **practise** *n* 1 a : actual performance or application b : a repeated or usual action ⟨it was our *practice* to rise early⟩ c : the usual way of doing something ⟨local *practice*⟩ 2 a : action done over and over in order to acquire skill ⟨*practice* makes perfect⟩ b : the condition of being skilled through practice ⟨get in *practice*⟩ 3 a : continuous work in a profession ⟨the *practice* of law⟩ b : a professional business ⟨the doctor has expanded her *practice*⟩ **syn** see HABIT

prac·ticed *or* **prac·tised** \'prak-təst\ *adj* 1 : EXPERIENCED, SKILLED 2 : learned by practice

prac·ti·tio·ner \prak-'tish-(ə-)nər\ *n* : a person who practices a profession and especially law or medicine

prae·tor \'prēt-ər\ *n* : an ancient Roman official ranking below a consul and acting as a judge

¹prae·to·ri·an \prē-'tōr-ē-ən, -'tòr-\ *adj* 1 : of or relating to a Roman praetor 2 *often cap* : of, relating to, or being the bodyguard of a Roman emperor ⟨the *praetorian* guard⟩

²praetorian *n, often cap* : a member of the praetorian guard

prag·mat·ic \prag-'mat-ik\ *also* **prag·mat·i·cal** \-i-kəl\ *adj* : concerned with practical rather than intellectual or artistic matters — **prag·mat·i·cal·ly** \-i-k(ə-)lē\ *adv*

prag·ma·tism \'prag-mə-,tiz-əm\ *n* 1 : a practical approach to problems and affairs 2 : a doctrine that truth is to be tested by the practical effects of belief — **prag·ma·tist** \-mət-əst\ *adj or n*

prai·rie \'pre(ə)r-ē\ *n* : a large area of level or rolling grassland

prairie chicken *n* : a grouse of the Mississippi valley with a patch of bare skin on the neck

prairie dog *n* : a buff or grayish American burrowing rodent related to the marmots and living in colonies

prairie schooner *n* : a long covered wagon used by pioneers to cross the prairies

praise \'prāz\ *vb* **praised;**

prairie chicken

prais·ing 1 : to express approval of : COMMEND 2 : to glorify (God or a saint) especially in song [Middle English *praisen* "to praise", from early French *preisier* "to praise, prize", from Latin *pretiare* "to prize", from earlier *pretium* (noun) "price, money" — related to PRICE] — **praise** *n*

praise·wor·thy \-,wər-thē\ *adj* : worthy of praise

pra·line \'prä-,lēn, 'prā-\ *n* : a candy of nuts in boiled brown sugar or maple sugar

prance \'pran(t)s\ *vb* **pranced; pranc·ing** 1 : to rise up or move about on the hind legs 2 : to ride on a prancing horse 3 : to walk or move about in a lively and proud manner : STRUT — **prance** *n* — **pranc·er** \'pran(t)-sər\ *n*

prank \'praŋk\ *n* : a playful or mischievous act : TRICK — **prank·ish** \'praŋ-kish\ *adj* — **prank·ish·ness** *n*

prank·ster \'praŋ(k)-stər\ *n* : a player of pranks

pra·seo·dym·i·um \,prā-zē-ō-'dim-ē-əm\ *n* : a yellowish white metallic element used chiefly in the form of its salts in coloring glass greenish yellow — see ELEMENT table

prate \'prāt\ *vb* **prat·ed; prat·ing** : to talk at great length but with little meaning : CHATTER — **prate** *n*

prat·fall \'prat-,fȯl\ *n* : a fall on the backside

prat·tle \'prat-ᵊl\ *vb* **prat·tled; prat·tling** \-liŋ, -ᵊl-iŋ\ 1 : PRATE 2 : ¹BABBLE 1a — **prattle** *n* — **prat·tler** \-lər, -ᵊl-ər\ *n*

prawn \'prȯn, 'prän\ *n* : any of numerous widespread edible crustaceans that resemble shrimps; *also* : ¹SHRIMP 1

pray \'prā\ *vb* 1 : to ask earnestly : BEG ⟨I *pray* you, tell me where they went⟩ 2 : to address God with adoration, confession, pleading, or thanksgiving

prayer \'pra(ə)r, 'pre(ə)r\ *n* 1 : the act or practice of praying to God ⟨a moment of silent *prayer*⟩ 2 a : a set of words addressed to God ⟨a *prayer* of thanksgiving⟩ b : an earnest request or wish : PLEA 3 : a religious practice consisting chiefly of prayers ⟨had regular family *prayers*⟩

prayer·ful \'pra(ə)r-fəl, 'pre(ə)r-\ *adj* 1 : given to or marked by prayer : DEVOUT 2 : ²EARNEST 1 — **prayer·ful·ly** \-fə-lē\ *adv*

praying mantis *n* : MANTIS

pre- *prefix* 1 a : earlier than : before ⟨*pre*historic⟩ b : in preparation for : required for ⟨*pre*medical⟩ 2 : in advance : beforehand ⟨*pre*pay⟩ 3 : in front of : front ⟨*pre*molar⟩ [Middle English *pre-* "before", from early French *pre-* and Latin *prae-* (both, same meaning), from Latin *prae* "ahead, before"]

preach \'prēch\ *vb* 1 a : to deliver a sermon : utter publicly b : to set forth in a sermon ⟨*preach* the gospel⟩ 2 : to urge publicly : ADVOCATE ⟨*preach* brotherhood⟩

preach·er \'prē-chər\ *n* : one that preaches; *esp* : ¹MINISTER 1b

pre·am·ble \'prē-,am-bəl, prē-'am-\ *n* 1 : an introduction (as to a law) that often gives the reasons for the parts that follow 2 : a fact or condition that comes before the main event

pre·ar·range \,prē-ə-'rānj\ *vb* : to arrange beforehand — **pre·ar·range·ment** \-mənt\ *n*

Pre·cam·bri·an \(')prē-'kam-brē-ən\ *adj* : of, relating to, or being the very long stage of geological history extending from the time when the earth's crust was formed to about 570,000,000 years ago and including the Archean and Proterozoic eons; *also* : relating to the rocks formed during this time — see GEOLOGIC TIME table — **Precambrian** *n*

pre·car·i·ous \pri-'kar-ē-əs, -'ker-\ *adj* 1 : depending on unknown conditions or chance events 2 : dangerously lacking in security or steadiness ⟨*precarious* health⟩ — **pre·car·i·ous·ly** *adv* — **pre·car·i·ous·ness** *n*

pre·cau·tion \pri-'kȯ-shən\ *n* 1 : care taken in advance : FORESIGHT 2 : a measure taken beforehand to prevent harm or to bring about a good result ⟨take *precautions* against fire⟩ — **pre·cau·tion·ary** \-shə-,ner-ē\ *adj*

pre·cede \pri-'sēd\ *vb* **pre·ced·ed; pre·ced·ing** : to be, go, or come before (as in rank, position, or time)

pre·ce·dence \'pres-əd-ən(t)s, pri-'sēd-ᵊn(t)s\ *n* 1 : the act or fact of preceding   **2** : consideration based on order of importance : PRIORITY

¹pre·ce·dent \pri-'sēd-ᵊnt, 'pres-əd-ənt\ *adj* : going before in time, order, arrangement, or importance

²prec·e·dent \'pres-əd-ənt\ *n*   **1** : an earlier occurrence of something similar   **2** : something that may serve as an example or rule to be followed in the future

pre·ced·ing \pri-'sēd-in\ *adj* : going before : PREVIOUS

pre·cept \'prē-,sept\ *n* : a command or principle intended as a general rule of action

pre·cep·tor \pri-'sep-tər, 'prē-,sep-\ *n*   **1** : TEACHER, TUTOR   **2** : the principal of a school

pre·ces·sion \prē-'sesh-ən\ *n* : a comparatively slow circling of the rotation axis of a spinning body about another line intersecting it — **pre·cess** \prē-'ses, 'prē-,ses\ *vb*

pre·cinct \'prē-,sin(k)t\ *n*   **1** : an administrative district especially of a town or city ⟨a police *precinct*⟩ ⟨an electoral *precinct*⟩   **2** : a surrounding or enclosed area ⟨within the *precincts* of the college⟩

pre·cious \'presh-əs\ *adj*   **1** : of great value or high price ⟨diamonds and other *precious* stones⟩   **2** : greatly loved : DEAR ⟨*precious* memories⟩ [Middle English *precious* "of great value", from early French *precios* (same meaning), from Latin *pretiosus* (same meaning), from *pretium* "price, money" — related to PRICE] — **pre·cious·ly** *adv* — **pre·cious·ness** *n*

prec·i·pice \'pres-(ə-)pəs\ *n* : a very steep and high face of a rock or mountain

¹pre·cip·i·tate \pri-'sip-ə-,tāt\ *vb* **-tat·ed; -tat·ing**   **1 a** : to throw violently : HURL   **b** : to fall headlong   **2** : to bring about suddenly ⟨an event that *precipitated* war⟩   **3 a** : to separate or cause to separate from solution or suspension   **b** : to change from a vapor to a liquid or solid and fall as rain or snow — **pre·cip·i·ta·tor** \-,tāt-ər\ *n*

²pre·cip·i·tate \pri-'sip-ət-ət, -ə-,tāt\ *n* : a usually solid substance separated from a solution or suspension by chemical or physical change

³pre·cip·i·tate \pri-'sip-ət-ət\ *adj* : HASTY 2 ⟨a *precipitate* attack⟩ — **pre·cip·i·tate·ly** *adv*

pre·cip·i·ta·tion \pri-,sip-ə-'tā-shən\ *n*   **1** : unwise haste   **2** : the process of precipitating or forming a precipitate   **3** : water or the amount of water that falls to the earth as hail, mist, rain, sleet, or snow

pre·cip·i·tous \pri-'sip-ət-əs\ *adj*   **1** : showing unwise and unnecessary haste ⟨a *precipitous* act⟩   **2** : falling very quickly : very rapid ⟨*precipitous* flow of floodwaters⟩   **3** : steep like a precipice — **pre·cip·i·tous·ly** *adv* — **pre·cip·i·tous·ness** *n*

pré·cis \prā-'sē, 'prā-sē\ *n, pl* **pré·cis** \-'sēz, -sēz\ : a brief summary of the essential points of something

pre·cise \pri-'sīs\ *adj*   **1** : exactly or sharply explained or stated   **2** : very exact ⟨*precise* scales⟩ ⟨their *precise* time of arrival⟩   **3** : agreeing exactly with a rule or standard ⟨*precise* daily habits⟩   **syn** see CORRECT — **pre·cise·ly** *adv* — **pre·cise·ness** *n*

¹pre·ci·sion \pri-'sizh-ən\ *n* : the quality or state of being precise : EXACTNESS, ACCURACY

²precision *adj*   **1** : designed for very accurate measurement or operation ⟨a *precision* gauge⟩   **2** : marked by precision ⟨*precision* drilling⟩

pre·clude \pri-'klüd\ *vb* **pre·clud·ed; pre·clud·ing** : to make impossible beforehand : PREVENT ⟨the injury *precluded* the possibility of a career in sports⟩

pre·co·cious \pri-'kō-shəs\ *adj* : showing the qualities or abilities of an adult at an unusually early age ⟨a *precocious* child⟩ — **pre·co·cious·ly** *adv* — **pre·co·cious·ness** *n* — **pre·coc·i·ty** \pri-'käs-ət-ē\ *n*

Word History The process of growing from a child to an adult is sometimes thought of as being like the slow ripening of fruit. That was the image which gave us the word *precocious*. Like many English words, *precocious* comes from Latin. The Latin prefix *prae-*, meaning

"ahead of, before", and the verb *coquere,* meaning "to ripen, cook", were combined to form the adjective *praecoc-, praecox,* which meant "ripening early or before its time". The Latin word was first used to describe certain plants and fruits. In time it also came to be used to describe a child who is unusually mature at an early age. [from Latin *praecoc-, praecox* "ripening early, ripening before its time", from *prae-* "ahead of, before" and *coquere* "to ripen, cook"]

pre·con·ceive \,prē-kən-'sēv\ *vb* : to form (an opinion or idea) beforehand ⟨*preconceived* notions about foreign lands⟩ — **pre·con·cep·tion** \-'sep-shən\ *n*

pre·con·cert·ed \,prē-kən-'sərt-əd\ *adj* : arranged or agreed upon in advance ⟨at a *preconcerted* signal we all stood⟩

pre·cook \(')prē-'kůk\ *vb* : to cook partially or entirely before final cooking or reheating

pre·cur·sor \pri-'kər-sər, 'prē-,kər-\ *n* : PREDECESSOR

pre·da·cious *or* **pre·da·ceous** \pri-'dā-shəs\ *adj* : PREDATORY 2

pre·date \(')prē-'dāt\ *vb* : ANTEDATE 1

pre·da·tion \pri-'dā-shən\ *n* : a way of life in which food is got mostly by killing and eating animals

pred·a·tor \'pred-ət-ər, -ə-,tȯ(ə)r\ *n* : an animal that lives by killing and eating other animals

pred·a·to·ry \'pred-ə-,tōr-ē, -,tȯr-\ *adj*   **1** : of, relating to, or marked by robbing or using others for personal gain ⟨*predatory* raids⟩   **2** : living by predation ⟨*predatory* animals⟩

pre·de·ces·sor \'pred-ə-,ses-ər, 'prēd-\ *n* : one that precedes; *esp* : a person who has held a position or office before another [Middle English *predecessour* "predecessor", from early French *predecesseur* (same meaning), from Latin *praedecessor* "one that goes before", from *prae-* "before, pre-", and *decessor* "retiring governor", derived from *decedere* "to depart", from *de-* "from" and *cedere* "to go, go away" — related to ANCESTOR, CONCEDE]

pre·des·ti·na·tion \(,)prē-,des-tə-'nā-shən\ *n*   **1 a** : the act of predestining   **b** : the state of being predestined   **2** : the doctrine that God has predestined some persons to eternal happiness and others to eternal punishment

pre·des·tine \(')prē-'des-tən\ *vb* : to decide beforehand especially by divine command

pre·de·ter·mine \,prēd-i-'tər-mən\ *vb*   **1** : PREDESTINE   **2** : to decide or settle beforehand ⟨meet at a *predetermined* place⟩ — **pre·de·ter·mi·na·tion** \-,tər-mə-'nā-shən\ *n*

pre·dic·a·ment \pri-'dik-ə-mənt\ *n* : a difficult, puzzling, or trying situation : FIX

¹pred·i·cate \'pred-i-kət\ *n* : the part of a sentence or clause that expresses what is said about the subject ⟨"threw the ball" in "the child threw the ball" is the *predicate*⟩ — **pred·i·ca·tive** \'pred-i-kət-iv, 'pred-ə-,kāt-\ *adj*

²pred·i·cate \'pred-ə-,kāt\ *vb* **-cat·ed; -cat·ing** : ²BASE 2 ⟨your theory is *predicated* on the belief that ghosts exist⟩ — **pred·i·ca·tion** \,pred-ə-'kā-shən\ *n*

³pred·i·cate \'pred-i-kət\ *adj* : belonging to the predicate; *esp* : completing the meaning of a linking verb ⟨*hot* in "the sun is hot" is a *predicate* adjective⟩ — compare ATTRIBUTIVE

pre·dict \pri-'dikt\ *vb* : to declare in advance : foretell on the basis of observation, experience, or reasoning [from Latin *praedictus,* past participle of *praedicere* "to predict, tell ahead of time", from *prae-* "pre-, earlier than, before" and *dicere* "to say" — related to DICTATE] **syn** see FORETELL — **pre·dict·able** \-'dik-tə-bəl\ *adj* — **pre·dict·ably** \-blē\ *adv*

\ə\ abut	\aů\ out	\i\ tip	\ȯ\ saw	\ů\ foot
\ər\ further	\ch\ chin	\ī\ life	\ȯi\ coin	\y\ yet
\a\ mat	\e\ pet	\j\ job	\th\ thin	\yü\ few
\ā\ take	\ē\ easy	\ŋ\ sing	\t̲h̲\ this	\yů\ cure
\ä\ cot, cart	\g\ go	\ō\ bone	\ü\ food	\zh\ vision

pre·dic·tion \pri-'dik-shən\ *n* **1** : an act of predicting **2** : something predicted : FORECAST ⟨a *prediction* that there would be an earthquake⟩ — **pre·dic·tive** \-'dik-tiv\ *adj*

pre·di·lec·tion \‚pred-ºl-'ek-shən, ‚prēd-\ *n* : a natural liking for something ⟨a *predilection* for adventure stories⟩

pre·dis·pose \‚prēd-is-'pōz\ *vb* : to dispose in advance : INCLINE — **pre·dis·po·si·tion** \‚prē-‚dis-pə-'zish-ən\ *n*

pre·dom·i·nance \pri-'däm-ə-nən(t)s\ *n* : the quality or state of being predominant

pre·dom·i·nant \pri-'däm-ə-nənt\ *adj* : greater in importance, strength, influence, or authority : PREVAILING ⟨the *predominant* color in a painting⟩ — **pre·dom·i·nant·ly** *adv*

pre·dom·i·nate \pri-'däm-ə-‚nāt\ *vb* **1** : to be predominant : PREVAIL **2** : to go beyond others in number or quantity ⟨cottages *predominated*⟩ — **pre·dom·i·na·tion** \-‚däm-ə-'nā-shən\ *n*

pre·em·i·nence \prē-'em-ə-nən(t)s\ *n* : the quality or state of being preeminent

pre·em·i·nent \prē-'em-ə-nənt\ *adj* : having supreme rank, dignity, or importance : OUTSTANDING — **pre·em·i·nent·ly** *adv*

pre·empt \prē-'em(p)t\ *vb* **1 a** : to settle upon (as public land) with the right to purchase before others **b** : to take by such a right **2** : to take before someone else can : APPROPRIATE ⟨*preempt* a seat at the stadium⟩ **3** : to take the place of ⟨the president's speech *preempted* the regular program⟩ — **pre·emp·tion** \-'em(p)-shən\ *n* — **pre·emp·tive** \-'em(p)-tiv\ *adj* — **pre·emp·tor** \-tər\ *n*

preen \'prēn\ *vb* **1** : to trim or dress with the bill ⟨a bird *preening* its feathers⟩ **2** : to make one's appearance neat and tidy ⟨*preened* in front of the mirror⟩

pre·ex·ist \‚prē-ig-'zist\ *vb* : to exist before something else

pre·ex·is·tence \‚prē-ig-'zis-tən(t)s\ *n* : existence in a former state or before something else; *esp* : existence of the soul before its union with the body — **pre·ex·is·tent** \-tənt\ *adj*

pre·fab \('*)prē-'fab, 'prē-‚fab\ *n* : a prefabricated structure

pre·fab·ri·cate \(')prē-'fab-ri-‚kāt\ *vb* : to manufacture the parts of something beforehand so that it can be built by putting the parts together — **pre·fab·ri·ca·tion** \‚prē-‚fab-ri-'kā-shən\ *n*

¹pref·ace \'pref-əs\ *n* : a section that introduces a book or a speech

²preface *vb* **pref·aced; pref·ac·ing** : to introduce by or begin with a preface ⟨*prefaced* the talk with a funny story⟩

pre·fect \'prē-‚fekt\ *n* **1** : a high official or judge (as of ancient Rome or France) **2** : a student assistant in some schools

pre·fec·ture \'prē-‚fek-chər\ *n* **1** : the office or term of office of a prefect **2** : the district governed by a prefect — **pre·fec·tur·al** \'prē-'fek-chə-rəl\ *adj*

pre·fer \pri-'fər\ *vb* **pre·ferred; pre·fer·ring** **1** : to choose or like better than another ⟨*prefer* dark clothes⟩ **2** : to present for action or consideration ⟨*prefer* charges against a thief⟩

pref·er·a·ble \'pref-(ə-)rə-bəl, 'pref-ər-bəl\ *adj* : worthy to be preferred : more desirable — **pref·er·a·bil·i·ty** \‚pref-(ə-)rə-'bil-ət-ē\ *n* — **pref·er·a·bly** \'pref-(ə-)rə-blē, 'pref-ər-\ *adv*

pref·er·ence \'pref-ərn(t)s, 'pref-(ə-)rən(t)s\ *n* **1 a** : the act of preferring **b** : the state of being preferred **2** : the power or opportunity of choosing ⟨gave him his *preference*⟩ **3** : one that is preferred : FAVORITE ⟨my *preference* is soul music⟩ **4** : the act of giving advantages to some over others ⟨show *preference* in giving out jobs⟩

pref·er·en·tial \‚pref-ə-'ren-chəl\ *adj* **1** : of or relating to preference **2** : showing preference ⟨*preferential* treatment⟩ **3** : creating or using preference in trading **4** : permitting the showing of order of preference (as of candidates in an election) ⟨a *preferential* ballot⟩ — **pref·er·en·tial·ly** \-'rench-(ə-)lē\ *adv*

pre·fer·ment \pri-'fər-mənt\ *n* **1** : advancement or promotion in dignity, office, or rank **2** : a position or office of honor or importance

pre·fig·ure \(')prē-'fig-yər, *especially British* -'fig-ər\ *vb* **1** : to show, suggest, or announce by an earlier type, image, or likeness ⟨the first crocus *prefigures* the arrival of spring⟩ **2** : to picture or imagine beforehand ⟨*prefigure* the outcome of the game⟩ — **pre·fig·u·ra·tion** \(‚)prē-‚fig-(y)ə-'rā-shən\ *n* — **pre·fig·ure·ment** \(')prē-'fig-yər-mənt, *especially British* -'fig-ər-\ *n*

¹pre·fix \'prē-‚fiks, prē-'fiks\ *vb* : to place in front; *esp* : to add as a prefix ⟨*prefix* a syllable to a word⟩

²pre·fix \'prē-‚fiks\ *n* : a letter or group of letters that comes at the beginning of a word and has a meaning of its own

preg·nan·cy \'preg-nən(t)-sē\ *n, pl* **-cies** : the condition of being pregnant : GESTATION

preg·nant \'preg-nənt\ *adj* **1** : containing unborn young within the body **2** : full of meaning ⟨a *pregnant* pause⟩ — **preg·nant·ly** *adv*

pre·heat \(')prē-'hēt\ *vb* : to heat beforehand ⟨*preheat* the oven to 400 degrees⟩

pre·hen·sile \prē-'hen(t)-səl\ *adj* : capable of grasping especially by wrapping around ⟨a *prehensile* tail⟩

pre–His·pan·ic \‚prē-(h)i-'span-ik\ *adj* : of, relating to, or being the time prior to Spanish conquests in the western hemisphere

pre·his·tor·ic \‚prē-(h)is-'tȯr-ik, -'tär-\ *adj* : of, relating to, or existing in times before written history ⟨*prehistoric* animals⟩ — **pre·his·tor·i·cal·ly** \-i-k(ə-)lē\ *adv*

pre·his·to·ry \(')prē-'his-t(ə-)rē\ *n* : the study of prehistoric man — **pre·his·to·ri·an** \‚prē-(h)is-'tȯr-ē-ən, -'tȯr-\ *n*

pre·judge \(')prē-'jəj\ *vb* : to judge before receiving all or enough of the facts — **pre·judg·ment** \-'jəj-mənt\ *n*

¹prej·u·dice \'prej-əd-əs\ *n* **1** : injury or damage to a case at law or to one's rights **2 a** : a favoring or dislike of something without good reason **b** : unfriendly feelings directed against an individual, a group, or a race [Middle English *prejudice* "injury from a judgment, an opinion formed before knowing the facts", from early French *prejudice* (same meaning), from Latin *praejudicium* "previous judgment", from *prae-* "pre-, before" and *judicium* "judgment", from *judic-, judex* "judge", from *jus* "right, law" and *dicere* "to say" — related to JUDGE, JUST]

²prejudice *vb* **-diced; -dic·ing** **1** : to cause damage to (as a case at law) ⟨newspaper stories *prejudiced* the murder case⟩ **2** : to cause to have prejudice : BIAS ⟨the incident *prejudiced* them against that company⟩

prej·u·di·cial \‚prej-ə-'dish-əl\ *adj* : tending to cause damage : DETRIMENTAL

prel·ate \'prel-ət\ *n* : a high-ranking member of the clergy (as a bishop)

¹pre·lim·i·nary \pri-'lim-ə-‚ner-ē\ *n, pl* **-nar·ies** : something preliminary

²preliminary *adj* : coming before the main part or item : INTRODUCTORY — **pre·lim·i·nar·i·ly** \-‚lim-ə-'ner-ə-lē\ *adv*

pre·lit·er·ate \(')prē-'lit-ə-rət, -'li-trət\ *adj* : existing before or lacking the use of writing ⟨*preliterate* societies⟩

¹pre·lude \'prel-‚(y)üd, 'prā-‚l(y)üd\ *n* **1** : something that comes before and prepares for the main or more important parts ⟨the wind was a *prelude* to the storm⟩ **2 a** : a short musical introduction (as to an opera) **b** : a musical piece (as an organ solo) played at the beginning of a church service

²prelude *vb* **pre·lud·ed; pre·lud·ing** : to give, play, or serve as a prelude

pre·ma·ture \‚prē-mə-'t(y)ù(ə)r, -'chù(ə)r\ *adj* : happening, coming, existing, or done before the proper or usual time; *esp* : born after a period of pregnancy of less than 37 weeks ⟨*premature* babies⟩ — **pre·ma·ture·ly** *adv* — **pre·ma·tu·ri·ty** \-'t(y)ùr-ət-ē, -'chùr-\ *n*

pre·med·i·cal \(')prē-'med-i-kəl\ *adj* : coming before and preparing for the study of medicine

pre·med·i·tate \pri-'med-ə-,tāt, 'prē-\ *vb* : to think about and plan beforehand ⟨*premeditated* murder⟩ — **pre·med·i·ta·tion** \pri-,med-ə-'tā-shən, ,prē-\ *n*

pre·men·stru·al \(')prē-'men(t)-strə-wəl\ *adj* : of, relating to, occurring in, or being the time period just preceding menstruation ⟨*premenstrual* tension⟩

premenstrual syndrome *n* : a varying group of symptoms experienced by some women prior to menstruation that may include insomnia, fatigue, anxiety, depression, headache, and abdominal pain

¹**pre·mier** \pri-'m(y)i(ə)r; 'prē-mē-ər, 'prem-ē-\ *adj* **1** : first in position, rank, or importance : PRINCIPAL **2** : first in time : EARLIEST

²**premier** *n* : the chief minister of government : PRIME MINISTER — **pre·mier·ship** \-,ship\ *n*

¹**pre·miere** \pri-'mye(ə)r, -'mi(ə)r\ *n* : a first performance or showing ⟨*premiere* of a play⟩

²**premiere** *adj* : PREMIER

¹**prem·ise** \'prem-əs\ *n* **1** : a statement taken to be true and used as a basis for argument or reasoning **2** *pl* **a** : a piece of land with the buildings on it **b** : a building or part of a building usually with its grounds

²**premise** \'prem-əs, pri-'mīz\ *vb* **pre·mised; pre·mis·ing** : to base on certain assumptions ⟨a brief *premised* on stereotypes⟩

¹**pre·mi·um** \'prē-mē-əm\ *n* **1 a** : a reward for an act **b** : a sum over and above a regular or stated price **c** : something given free or at a lower price with the purchase of a product or service **2** : the amount paid for a contract of insurance **3** : a high or extra value ⟨put a *premium* on accuracy⟩ [Middle English *primier* "first in rank, chief", from early French *premier* "first, chief", from Latin *primarius* "primary, principal", from *primus* "first" — related to PRIME]

²**premium** *adj* : of high quality, value, or price

¹**pre·mo·lar** \(')prē-'mō-lər\ *adj* : located in front of the molar teeth; *also* : being or relating to the premolars

²**premolar** *n* : any of the double-pointed grinding teeth which are located between the canines and the true molars and of which there are two on each side of each jaw — called also *bicuspid*

pre·mo·ni·tion \,prē-mə-'nish-ən, ,prem-ə-\ *n* : a feeling that something is going to happen ⟨a *premonition* of disaster⟩ — **pre·mon·i·to·ry** \pri-'män-ə-,tōr-ē, -,tòr-\ *adj*

pre·na·tal \(')prē-'nāt-ᵊl\ *adj* : occurring or existing before birth ⟨*prenatal* care⟩ ⟨*prenatal* development⟩

pre·oc·cu·pied \(')prē-'äk-yə-,pīd\ *adj* **1** : lost in thought : ENGROSSED **2** : already occupied

pre·oc·cu·py \(')prē-'äk-yə-,pī\ *vb* **1** : to hold the attention of beforehand **2** : to take possession of before another — **pre·oc·cu·pa·tion** \(,)prē-,äk-yə-'pā-shən\ *n*

pre·or·dain \,prē-òr-'dān\ *vb* : FOREORDAIN — **pre·or·di·na·tion** \(,)prē-,òrd-ᵊn-'ā-shən\ *n*

pre·pack·age \(')prē-'pak-ij\ *vb* : to package (as food) before offering for sale

prep·a·ra·tion \,prep-ə-'rā-shən\ *n* **1** : the action or process of making ready in advance **2** : a state of being prepared : READINESS **3** : an act or measure that prepares ⟨busy with *preparations* for the picnic⟩ **4** : something prepared ⟨a medicinal *preparation*⟩

pre·pa·ra·to·ry \pri-'par-ə-,tōr-ē, -,tòr-\ *adj* : preparing or serving to prepare for something : INTRODUCTORY

preparatory school *n* **1** : a usually private school preparing students primarily for college **2** *British* : a private elementary school preparing students primarily for public schools

pre·pare \pri-'pa(ə)r, -'pe(ə)r\ *vb* **pre·pared; pre·par·ing** **1** : to make ready beforehand ⟨*prepared* us for the news⟩ ⟨*prepare* for a test⟩ **2** : to put together the elements of : COMPOUND ⟨*prepare* a prescription⟩ — **pre·par·er** *n*

pre·pared \pri-'pa(ə)rd, -'pe(ə)rd\ *adj* : treated with a special process : given a special treatment

pre·pared·ness \pri-'par-əd-nəs, -'per- *also* -'pa(ə)rd-nəs *or* -'pe(ə)rd-\ *n* : the quality or state of being prepared; *esp* : a state of readiness for war

pre·pay \(')prē-'pā\ *vb* **pre·paid** \-'pād\; **pre·pay·ing** : to pay or pay for in advance — **pre·pay·ment** \-'pā-mənt\ *n*

pre·pon·der·ance \pri-'pän-d(ə-)rən(t)s\ *n* : a greater quantity, number, weight, or importance ⟨the *preponderance* of evidence suggests that the accused is guilty⟩

pre·pon·der·ant \pri-'pän-d(ə-)rənt\ *adj* **1** : having greater weight, force, or influence : PREDOMINANT **2** : having greater frequency — **pre·pon·der·ant·ly** *adv*

prep·o·si·tion \,prep-ə-'zish-ən\ *n* : a word or group of words that combines with a noun or pronoun to form a phrase that usually acts as an adverb, adjective, or noun ⟨"with" in "the house with the red door" is a *preposition*⟩ — **prep·o·si·tion·al** \-'zish-nəl, -ən-ᵊl\ *adj*

pre·pos·sess \,prē-pə-'zes\ *vb* **1** : PREOCCUPY 1 **2** : to influence beforehand especially so as to win approval

pre·pos·sess·ing *adj* : creating a good impression : ATTRACTIVE ⟨a *prepossessing* appearance⟩

pre·pos·ses·sion \,prē-pə-'zesh-ən\ *n* **1** : an attitude, belief, or impression formed beforehand : PREJUDICE **2** : great concern with just one idea or object

pre·pos·ter·ous \pri-'päs-t(ə-)rəs\ *adj* : making little or no sense : ABSURD — **pre·pos·ter·ous·ly** *adv* — **pre·pos·ter·ous·ness** *n*

Word History The familiar expression "putting the cart before the horse" comes very close to the literal sense of the word *preposterous*. The Romans formed their Latin adjective *praeposterus* from *prae-*, meaning "before", and *posterus*, meaning "following". They at first used it to mean "having that first which ought to be last", like having a cart ahead of the horse that is pulling it. *Praeposterus* was used to describe something that was out of the normal or logical order or position. From this developed the more general sense of "ridiculous, absurd". These meanings were borrowed into English in the 16th century. Although *preposterous* is seldom used in its literal sense nowadays, we still use it to describe something that seems so unreasonable as to be ridiculous. [from Latin *praeposterus*, literally "having the rear part in front", from *prae-* "in front, before" and *posterus* "coming behind, following"]

pre·puce \'prē-,pyüs\ *n* : FORESKIN

pre·re·cord \,prē-ri-'kò(ə)rd\ *vb* : to record (as a radio or television program) in advance of presentation or use

pre·req·ui·site \(')prē-'rek-wə-zət\ *n* : something required beforehand or necessary as preparation for something else ⟨the course is a *prerequisite* for advanced study⟩ — **prerequisite** *adj*

pre·rog·a·tive \pri-'räg-ət-iv\ *n* : a special right or privilege given because of one's rank or position

¹**pres·age** \'pres-ij\ *n* **1** : OMEN **2** : a warning or suggestion of future events

²**pre·sage** \'pres-ij, pri-'sāj\ *vb* **pre·saged; pre·sag·ing** **1** : to give a sign or warning of : PORTEND **2** : FORETELL, PREDICT

pres·by·ter \'prez-bət-ər, 'pres-\ *n* : a member of the governing body of an early Christian church

Pres·by·te·ri·an \,prez-bə-'tir-ē-ən, ,pres-\ *adj* **1** *often not cap* : having a system of representative governing councils of ministers and elders **2** : of, relating to, or being a Protestant Christian church that is presbyterian in government — **Presbyterian** *n* — **Pres·by·te·ri·an·ism** \-ē-ə-,niz-əm\ *n*

pre·school \'prē-'skül\ *adj* : of, relating to, or being the pe-

\ə\ abut		\au̇\ out		\i\ tip		\ȯ\ saw		\u̇\ foot
\ər\ further		\ch\ chin		\ī\ life		\ȯi\ coin		\y\ yet
\a\ mat		\e\ pet		\j\ job		\th\ thin		\yü\ few
\ā\ take		\ē\ easy		\ŋ\ sing		\th\ this		\yu̇\ cure
\ä\ cot, cart		\g\ go		\ō\ bone		\ü\ food		\zh\ vision

riod in a child's life to the age of five or six that ordinarily precedes attendance at school

pre·school·er \'prē-'skü-lər\ *n* : a child of preschool age

pre·science \'prēsh(-ē)-ən(t)s, 'presh-\ *n* : FORESIGHT 1

pre·scient \'prēsh(-ē)-ənt, 'presh-\ *adj* : having foresight — **pre·scient·ly** *adv*

pre·scribe \pri-'skrīb\ *vb* **pre·scribed; pre·scrib·ing 1** : to lay down as a rule of action ⟨the route that was *prescribed*⟩ **2** : to order or direct the use of something as a remedy — **pre·scrib·er** *n*

pre·scrip·tion \pri-'skrip-shən\ *n* **1** : the action of prescribing rules or directions **2 a** : a written direction or order for the preparation and use of a medicine **b** : a medicine that is prescribed — **pre·scrip·tive** \-'skrip-tiv\ *adj*

pres·ence \'prez-ᵊn(t)s\ *n* **1** : the fact or state of being present ⟨no one noticed the stranger's *presence*⟩ **2** : position close to a person ⟨in the *presence* of a guest⟩ **3** : a person's appearance ⟨a stately *presence*⟩ **4** : something felt or believed to be present ⟨a ghostly *presence* in the room⟩

presence of mind : ability to think clearly and act quickly in an emergency

¹pres·ent \'prez-ᵊnt\ *n* : something presented

²pre·sent \pri-'zent\ *vb* **1 a** : to introduce one person to another **b** : to bring before the public ⟨*present* a play⟩ **2** : to make a gift to ⟨*presented* me with a watch⟩ **3** : to give or hand over with ceremony ⟨*present* a medal⟩ **4** : to make an accusation against someone ⟨*present* a charge⟩ **5** : to offer to view : DISPLAY, SHOW ⟨*presents* a fine appearance⟩ **syn** see GIVE — **pre·sent·er** *n*

³pres·ent \'prez-ᵊnt\ *adj* **1** : being or going on now : not past or future ⟨the *present* situation⟩ **2** : being before or near a person or in sight : being at a certain place and not elsewhere ⟨all the pupils were *present*⟩ ⟨was *present* at the ceremony⟩ **3** : of, relating to, or being a verb tense that expresses present time or the time of speaking

⁴pres·ent \'prez-ᵊnt\ *n* **1 a** : PRESENT TENSE **b** : a verb form in the present tense **2** : the present time

pre·sent·able \pri-'zent-ə-bəl\ *adj* : having a satisfactory or pleasing appearance — **pre·sent·ably** \-blē\ *adv*

pre·sen·ta·tion \ˌprē-ˌzen-'tā-shən, ˌprez-ᵊn-, ˌprēz-ᵊn-\ *n* **1** : the act of presenting **2 a** : something (as a gift or an award) presented **b** : something set forth for attention (as a play or a sales demonstration) **3** : the position in which the fetus lies in the uterus in labor with respect to the opening through which it passes in birth — compare BREECH PRESENTATION — **pre·sen·ta·tion·al** \-shnəl, -shən-ᵊl\ *adj*

pres·ent–day \'prez-ᵊnt-'dā\ *adj* : being or happening now

pre·sen·ti·ment \pri-'zent-ə-mənt\ *n* : a feeling that something will or is about to happen

pres·ent·ly \'prez-ᵊnt-lē\ *adv* **1** *archaic* : at once **2** : before long : after a while ⟨*presently* they arrived⟩ **3** : at the present time : NOW ⟨*presently* such materials are hard to find⟩

pre·sent·ment \pri-'zent-mənt\ *n* : the act of presenting to an authority a statement of the matter to be dealt with ⟨a *presentment* returned by a grand jury⟩

pres·ent participle \'prez-ᵊnt-\ *n* : a participle that expresses present action, that in English is formed with the suffix *-ing*, and that indicates action going on

present perfect tense *n* : a tense formed in English with *have* and expressing action or state completed at the time of speaking

present tense *n* : a tense that expresses action or state in the present time and is used of what is true at the time of speaking or is always true

pres·er·va·tion \ˌprez-ər-'vā-shən\ *n* : a keeping from injury, loss, or decay

¹pre·ser·va·tive \pri-'zər-vət-iv\ *adj* : having the power of preserving

²preservative *n* : something that preserves or has the power

of preserving; *esp* : a substance added to food to prevent spoiling or discoloring

¹pre·serve \pri-'zərv\ *vb* **pre·served; pre·serv·ing 1** : to keep or save from injury, loss, or ruin : PROTECT ⟨*preserve* the republic⟩ **2** : MAINTAIN 1, CONTINUE ⟨*preserve* silence⟩ **3** : to prepare (as vegetables, fruits, or meats) to be kept for future use — **pre·serv·er** *n*

²preserve *n* **1** : fruit cooked in sugar or made into jams or jellies ⟨strawberry *preserves*⟩ **2** : an area where natural resources (as fish, game, or trees) are protected

pre·set \(')prē-'set\ *vb* **preset; pre·set·ting** : to set ahead of time ⟨*preset* the oven to 350 degrees⟩

pre·shrink \(')prē-'shrink\ *vb* **pre·shrank** \-'shrank\; **pre·shrunk** \-'shrənk\ : to shrink (as a fabric) before making into a garment so that the garment will not shrink much when washed

pre·side \pri-'zīd\ *vb* **pre·sid·ed; pre·sid·ing 1** : to be in the place of authority : act as president, chairperson, or moderator ⟨*preside* over a meeting⟩ **2** : to be in charge

pres·i·den·cy \'prez-əd-ən-sē, 'prez-dən-; 'prez-ə-ˌden(t)-sē\ *n, pl* **-cies 1** : the office of president **2** : the term during which a president holds office

pres·i·dent \'prez-əd-ənt, 'prez-dənt, 'prez-ə-ˌdent\ *n* **1** : a person who presides over a meeting **2** : the chief officer of an organization ⟨a bank *president*⟩ ⟨college *president*⟩ ⟨*president* of our club⟩ **3** : the chief executive officer or the chief of state in a republic — **pres·i·den·tial** \ˌprez(-ə)-'den-chəl\ *adj*

Presidents' Day *n* : WASHINGTON'S BIRTHDAY 2

¹pre·soak \(')prē-'sōk\ *vb* : to soak before washing

²pre·soak \'prē-ˌsōk\ *n* **1** : an instance of presoaking **2** : a product used for presoaking clothes

¹press \'pres\ *n* **1** : ²CROWD 1, THRONG **2** : a machine or device that uses pressure to shape, flatten, squeeze, or stamp ⟨a cookie *press*⟩ ⟨a cider *press*⟩ **3** : ¹CLOSET 2 **4 a** : an act of pressing : PRESSURE **b** : an aggressive defense in basketball **5** : the smoothed and creased condition of a freshly pressed garment **6 a** : PRINTING PRESS **b** : a printing or publishing business **7 a** : the gathering and publishing or broadcasting of news **b** : the newspapers and magazines of a country **c** : news reporters and broadcasters

press 2

²press *vb* **1** : to bear down upon : push steadily against **2** : to squeeze so as to force out the juice or contents of ⟨*press* apples to make cider⟩ **3** : to flatten out or smooth by bearing down upon (as with an iron) ⟨*press* clothes⟩ **4 a** : to put pressure on : FORCE, COMPEL ⟨*pressed* by business to return⟩ **b** : to ask or urge strongly ⟨*pressed* us to go with them⟩ **5 a** : to insist on ⟨didn't *press* the issue⟩ **b** : to make a demand ⟨*pressing* for higher wages⟩ **6 a** : to crowd closely ⟨reporters *pressed* around the celebrity⟩ **b** : to force or push one's way ⟨*pressed* deeper into the jungle⟩ — **press·er** *n*

³press *vb* : to force into emergency service

press agent *n* : a person employed to establish and keep up good public relations by publicity

press conference *n* : an interview given by a public figure to the press

presser foot *n* : a piece on a sewing machine that holds the fabric down while stitching

press·ing \'pres-in\ *adj* : needing one's immediate attention — **press·ing·ly** \-in-lē\ *adv*

press secretary *n* : a person in charge of relations with the press for a public figure

¹pres·sure \'presh-ər\ *n* **1** : a force or influence that cannot be avoided ⟨social *pressure*⟩ **2** : the application of force to something by something else in direct contact with it ⟨keep steady *pressure* on the gas pedal⟩ **3 a** : the action of a force against an opposing force **b** : the force applied over a surface divided by its area **4** : the stress or burden of matters demanding attention ⟨works well under *pressure*⟩

²pressure *vb* **pres·sured; pres·sur·ing** \'presh-(ə-)riŋ\ **1** : to apply pressure to **2** : PRESSURIZE

pressure cooker *n* : a utensil for cooking or preserving foods by means of steam under pressure — **pressure–cook** \,presh-ər-'kúk\ *vb*

pressure point *n* : a point where a blood vessel runs near a bone and can be compressed (as to stop bleeding) by pressure against the bone

pres·sur·ize \'presh-ə-,rīz\ *vb* **-ized; -iz·ing 1** : to maintain near-normal atmospheric pressure in ⟨*pressurize* an airplane cabin⟩ **2** : to apply pressure to — **pres·sur·iza·tion** \,presh-(ə-)rə-'zā-shən\ *n*

pres·ti·dig·i·ta·tion \,pres-tə-,dij-ə-'tā-shən\ *n* : SLEIGHT OF HAND **1** — **pres·ti·dig·i·ta·tor** \-'dij-ə-,tāt-ər\ *n*

pres·tige \pre-'stēzh, -'stēj\ *n* : importance in the eyes of other people — **pres·ti·gious** \-'stij-əs\ *adj* — **pres·ti·gious·ly** *adv* — **pres·ti·gious·ness** *n*

pres·to \'pres-tō\ *adv or adj* **1** : suddenly as if by magic ⟨a wave of the hand and, *presto*, it's gone⟩ **2** : at a rapid tempo — used as a direction in music

pre·sum·ably \pri-'zü-mə-blē\ *adv* : one would presume : it seems likely : PROBABLY ⟨*presumably* he'll come later⟩

pre·sume \pri-'züm\ *vb* **pre·sumed; pre·sum·ing 1** : to undertake without permission or good reason : DARE ⟨*presume* to question the authority of a superior⟩ **2** : to expect or assume with confidence : feel sure ⟨I *presume* you'll fly if you do go⟩ **3** : to suppose to be true without proof ⟨*presume* a person innocent until proved guilty⟩ — **pre·sum·able** \-'zü-mə-bəl\ *adj*

pre·sump·tion \pri-'zəm(p)-shən\ *n* **1** : presumptuous attitude or behavior **2 a** : strong reason for believing something to be so in spite of lack of proof **b** : something believed but not proved

pre·sump·tu·ous \pri-'zəm(p)-ch(ə-w)əs\ *adj* : going beyond what is proper — **pre·sump·tu·ous·ly** *adv* — **pre·sump·tu·ous·ness** *n*

pre·sup·pose \,prē-sə-'pōz\ *vb* : to take something to be true : suppose ahead of time ⟨the book *presupposes* its readers will know something about the subject⟩ — **pre·sup·po·si·tion** \(,)prē-,səp-ə-'zish-ən\ *n*

pre·sweet·ened \'prē-'swēt-ºnd\ *adj* : sweetened by the manufacturer ⟨*presweetened* cereal⟩

¹pre·teen \'prē-'tēn\ *n* : a boy or girl not yet 13 years old

²preteen *adj* **1** : relating to or produced for children especially in the 9 to 12 year-old age group ⟨*preteen* fashions⟩ **2** : being younger than 13

¹pre·tend \pri-'tend\ *vb* **1** : to give the appearance of being, having, or doing ⟨I don't *pretend* to be a doctor, but you should do something about that cough⟩ **2** : to make believe : act a part or role ⟨*pretend* to be a bear⟩ ⟨*pretend* I'm your boss. What would you say?⟩

²pretend *adj* : IMAGINARY, MAKE-BELIEVE

pre·tend·er \pri-'ten-dər\ *n* **1** : a person who pretends **2** : a person who claims a throne without right

pre·tense *or* **pre·tence** \'prē-'ten(t)s, pri-'ten(t)s\ *n* **1** : a claim usually not supported by facts **2** : the quality or state of being pretentious ⟨free from *pretense*⟩ **3** : an effort to reach a certain condition or quality ⟨let's have some *pretense* of order around here⟩ ⟨the book makes no *pretense* at completeness⟩ **4** : a pretended purpose ⟨was there under false *pretenses*⟩ **5** : a false show : SIMULATION ⟨making a *pretense* of reaching for the dinner check⟩

pre·ten·sion \pri-'ten-chən\ *n* **1** : PRETENSE 1 **2** : something one hopes to reach : ASPIRATION, AMBITION ⟨has serious *pretensions* as a writer⟩ **3** : PRETENSE 2

pre·ten·tious \pri-'ten-chəs\ *adj* : appearing or trying to ap-

pear more important or more valuable than is the case — **pre·ten·tious·ly** *adv* — **pre·ten·tious·ness** *n*

pret·er·it *or* **pret·er·ite** \'pret-ə-rət\ *n* : PAST TENSE

pre·ter·nat·u·ral \,prēt-ər-'nach(-ə)-rəl\ *adj* : beyond what is natural : unable to be explained by ordinary means — **pre·ter·nat·u·ral·ly** \-'nach(-ə)-rə-lē, -'nach-ər-lē\ *adv*

pre·test \(')prē-'test\ *n* : a test to find out if students are prepared for further studies

pre·text \'prē-,tekst\ *n* : a reason put forward in order to hide the real reason

pre·treat \(')prē-'trēt\ *vb* : to treat (as soiled clothes) before laundering — **pre·treat·ment** \-mənt\ *n*

¹pret·ty \'prit-ē, 'púrt-\ *adj* **pret·ti·er; -est** : delicately or gracefully attractive to the eye or ear ⟨a *pretty* face⟩ ⟨*pretty* tunes⟩ **syn** see BEAUTIFUL — **pret·ti·ly** \'prit-ºl-ē, 'púrt-\ *adv* — **pret·ti·ness** \'prit-ē-nəs, \'púrt-\ *n*

²pret·ty \'prit-ē, pərt-ē\ *adv* : in some degree : FAIRLY, MODERATELY ⟨*pretty* big⟩ ⟨was *pretty* much ignored⟩

³pretty *\ike* ¹\ *n, pl* **pretties** : a pretty person or thing

pret·zel \'pret-səl\ *n* : a brown cracker that is salted and usually hard and shaped like a loose knot

> **Word History** Pretzels were probably first made in the United States during the 19th century by immigrants from Germany. The English word *pretzel* comes from the German *brezel*. The familiar knot-shaped pretzel has been known in Germanic countries for centuries. Its German name comes from the Latin *brachiatus*, which means "having branches like arms". The pretzel seems to have got its name because its knot shape looks something like a pair of folded arms. [from German *brezel* "pretzel", derived from Latin *brachiatus* (adjective) "having branches like arms", from *brachium*, *brachium* "arm" — related to ²BRACE]

pre·vail \pri-'vā(ə)l\ *vb* **1** : to win against opposition : be successful ⟨our team *prevailed*⟩ ⟨will truth *prevail* over error⟩ ⟨believed injustice should not *prevail*⟩ **2** : to urge successfully ⟨*prevailed* upon me to play a few tunes⟩ **3 a** : to be frequent ⟨the storms that *prevail* there in winter⟩ **b** : to be or continue to be in use or fashion ⟨lower rates *prevail* in the evening⟩ ⟨customs that still *prevail* in Europe⟩

pre·vail·ing \pri-'vā-liŋ\ *adj* **1** : having greater force or influence **2 a** : most frequent ⟨*prevailing* winds⟩ **b** : generally current : COMMON — **pre·vail·ing·ly** *adv*

prev·a·lence \'prev-(ə)-lən(t)s\ *n* : the state of being prevalent

prev·a·lent \'prev-(ə)-lənt\ *adj* : accepted, practiced, or happening often or over a wide area — **prev·a·lent·ly** *adv*

pre·var·i·cate \pri-'var-ə-,kāt\ *vb* **-cat·ed; -cat·ing** : ³LIE 1 — **pre·var·i·ca·tion** \-,var-ə-'kā-shən\ *n* — **pre·var·i·ca·tor** \-'var-ə-,kāt-ər\ *n*

pre·vent \pri-'vent\ *vb* **1** : to keep from happening ⟨*prevent* accidents⟩ **2** : to hold or keep back : HINDER, STOP ⟨bad weather *prevented* us from leaving⟩ — **pre·vent·able** *also* **pre·vent·ible** \-ə-bəl\ *adj*

pre·ven·ta·tive \pri-'vent-ət-iv\ *adj or n* : PREVENTIVE

pre·ven·tion \pri-'ven-chən\ *n* : the act or practice of preventing something ⟨the *prevention* of fires⟩

¹pre·ven·tive \pri-'vent-iv\ *n* : something that prevents; *esp* : something used to prevent disease

²preventive *adj* : concerned with or used for prevention ⟨*preventive* measures⟩ ⟨*preventive* medicine⟩

¹pre·view \'prē-,vyü\ *vb* : to view or show in advance

²preview *n* **1** : a showing of something (as a movie) before regular showings **2** *also* **pre·vue** \-,vyü\ : a showing of

\ə\ abut		\aú\ out		\i\ tip		\ó\ saw	\ú\ foot
\ər\ further		\ch\ chin		\ī\ life		\ói\ coin	\y\ yet
\a\ mat		\e\ pet		\j\ job		\th\ thin	\yü\ few
\ā\ take		\ē\ easy		\ŋ\ sing		\ṯh\ this	\yú\ cure
\ä\ cot, cart		\g\ go		\ō\ bone		\ü\ food	\zh\ vision

bits from a movie that is to be shown in the near future

pre·vi·ous \'prē-vē-əs\ *adj* : going before in time or order : PRECEDING, PRIOR — **pre·vi·ous·ly** *adv*

previous to *prep* : PRIOR TO, BEFORE

pre·war \'prē-'wȯ(ə)r\ *adj* : occurring or existing before a war

pre·wash \(')prē-'wȯsh, -'wäsh\ *vb* : to wash beforehand

pre·writ·ing \'prē-,rīt-iŋ\ *n* : planning and getting ideas in order before writing

¹prey \'prā\ *n* **1** : an animal hunted or killed by another animal for food **2** : a person who is helpless or unable to escape attack : VICTIM **3** : the act or habit of seizing and pouncing upon

²prey *vb* **preyed; prey·ing** **1 a** : to seize and eat something as prey **b** : to do violent or dishonest acts ⟨robbers who *preyed* on travelers⟩ **2** : to have a harmful effect ⟨fears that *prey* on the mind⟩

¹price \'prīs\ *n* **1** : the quantity of one thing and especially money that is exchanged or demanded in exchange for another **2** : ²REWARD 1 ⟨a *price* on an outlaw's head⟩ **3** : the cost at which something is gotten or done ⟨victory at any *price*⟩ [Middle English *pris* "prize, price", from early French *pris* (same meaning), from Latin *pretium* "price, money" — related to APPRECIATE, PRAISE, PRECIOUS, ¹PRIZE]

> **syn** PRICE, CHARGE, FEE mean payment in exchange for something. PRICE usually refers to the payment asked for goods ⟨the *price* of a pair of shoes⟩ CHARGE usually refers to the payment asked for services ⟨the *charge* for dry-cleaning a pair of pants⟩ FEE refers to a charge fixed (as by law or a business) for a service or permit ⟨the *fee* for a driver's license⟩

²price *vb* **priced; pric·ing** **1** : to set a price on **2** : to ask the price of — **pric·er** *n*

price·less \'prī-sləs\ *adj* **1** : too valuable to have a price : not to be bought at any price **2** : very funny or strange ⟨a *priceless* remark⟩

¹prick \'prik\ *n* **1** : a mark or small wound made by a pointed instrument **2** : something sharp or pointed **3** : an instance of pricking **4** : the sensation of being pricked

²prick *vb* **1** : to pierce slightly with a sharp point **2** : to have or cause a feeling of or as if of being pricked **3** : to point forward or upward ⟨the dog's ears *pricked* up at the sound⟩ — **prick up one's ears** : to listen with close attention

prick·er \'prik-ər\ *n* **1** : one that pricks **2** : ¹PRICKLE 1

¹prick·le \'prik-əl\ *n* **1** : a small sharp point or a sharp pointed part (as a thorn on a plant) that sticks out **2** : a slight stinging or tingling sensation

²prickle *vb* **prick·led; prick·ling** \'prik-(ə-)liŋ\ : ²PRICK 2

prick·ly \'prik-lē, -ə-lē\ *adj* **prick·li·er; -est** **1** : full of or covered with prickles ⟨*prickly* plants⟩ **2** : being or having a pricking ⟨a *prickly* sensation⟩ ⟨a *prickly* thumb⟩ — **prick·li·ness** *n*

prickly heat *n* : a rash around the openings of the sweat glands with pimples, itching, and tingling that is caused by inflammation

prickly pear *n* **1** : any of numerous flat-jointed often prickly cacti **2** : the pear-shaped sweet edible pulpy fruit of a prickly pear

¹pride \'prīd\ *n* **1** : too high an opinion of one's own ability or worth : a feeling of being better than others **2** : a reasonable and justifiable sense of one's own worth : SELF-RESPECT **3** : a sense of pleasure that comes from some act or possession **4**

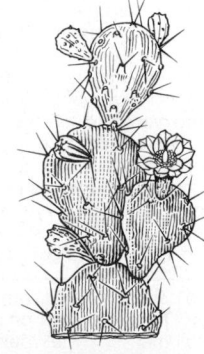

prickly pear 1

: something of which one is proud ⟨our *pride* and joy⟩ **5** : a group of lions

²pride *vb* **prid·ed; prid·ing** : to think highly of (oneself)

pride·ful \'prīd-fəl\ *adj* : full of pride — **pride·ful·ly** *adv* \-fə-lē\ — **pride·ful·ness** *n*

pried *past and past participle of* PRY

priest \'prēst\ *n* : a person who has the authority to lead or perform religious ceremonies [Old English *prēost* "priest", from Latin *presbyter* "priest, church leader", from Greek *presbyteros,* comparative form of *presbys* "old man"]

priest·ess \'prē-stəs\ *n* : a woman who is a priest

priest·hood \'prēst-,hu̇d, 'prē-,stu̇d\ *n* **1** : the office or dignity of a priest **2** : the whole group of priests

priest·ly \'prēst-lē\ *adj* **priest·li·er; -est** **1** : of or relating to a priest or the priesthood **2** : characteristic of or suitable for a priest — **priest·li·ness** *n*

prig \'prig\ *n* : a person who annoys others by being too precise about speech and manners — **prig·gish** \'prig-ish\ *adj* — **prig·gish·ly** *adv* — **prig·gish·ness** *n*

prim \'prim\ *adj* **prim·mer; prim·mest** : very fussy about one's appearance and behavior — **prim·ly** *adv* — **prim·ness** *n*

pri·ma·cy \'prī-mə-sē\ *n, pl* **-cies** **1** : the state of being first (as in time, place, or rank) **2** : the office or dignity of a bishop of the highest rank

pri·ma don·na \,prim-ə-'dän-ə, ,prē-mə-\ *n, pl* **prima don·nas** **1** : a principal female singer (in an opera or concert organization **2** : a person who is easily hurt or upset or is stuck-up [Italian, literally "first lady"; *prima* from Latin *prima,* a feminine form of *primus* "first", *donna* from Latin *domina* "lady, mistress", a feminine form of *dominus* "master" — related to DAME, PRIME]

pri·mal \'prī-məl\ *adj* **1** : of or relating to the first period or state : PRIMITIVE **2** : first in importance : BASIC

pri·mar·i·ly \prī-'mer-ə-lē\ *adv* **1** : for the most part : CHIEFLY **2** : in the first place : ORIGINALLY

¹pri·ma·ry \'prī-,mer-ē, 'prim-(ə-)rē\ *adj* **1** : first in time or development : INITIAL, PRIMITIVE ⟨the *primary* stage of a civilization⟩ **2 a** : of first rank, importance, or value ⟨our *primary* duties⟩ **b** : ¹BASIC 1, FUNDAMENTAL ⟨the family is the *primary* unit of human association⟩ **c** : of, relating to, or being one of the principal quills of a bird's wing located on the outer joint **d** : of, relating to, or being the strongest of three levels of stress in pronunciation **3 a** : not made or coming from something else : FIRSTHAND ⟨a *primary* source of information⟩ **b** : of, relating to, or being the current or circuit that is connected to the source of electricity in an induction coil or transformer

²primary *n, pl* **-ma·ries** **1** : a primary quill or feather **2** : PRIMARY COLOR **3** : an election in which members of a political party nominate candidates for office **4** : the coil that is connected to the source of electricity in an induction coil or transformer — called also *primary coil*

primary color *n* : any of a set of colors from which all other colors may be made with the colors for light being red, green, and blue and for pigments or paint being red, yellow, and blue

pri·mate \'prī-,māt *or especially for 1* -mət\ *n* **1** : a bishop or archbishop of the highest rank in a district, nation, or church **2** : any of an order of mammals including human beings, apes, monkeys, and related forms (as lemurs and tarsiers)

¹prime \'prīm\ *n* **1** : the first part : the earliest stage **2** : the period in life when a person is best in health, looks, or strength **3** : the best individual or part **4** : PRIME NUMBER **5** : the symbol ′ [Old English *prīm* "a religious duty for the first hour of the day", from Latin *prima (hora)* "first (hour)", from *primus* "first" — related to PREMIER, PRIMA DONNA, PRIMEVAL, PRINCE]

²prime *adj* **1** : first in time : ORIGINAL **2 a** : of, relating to, or being a prime number **b** : expressed as a product of prime factors ⟨the *prime* factorization of 12 is 2 · 2 · 3⟩ **3**

a : first in rank or importance ⟨our *prime* responsibility⟩ **b** : being highest in quality or value ⟨*prime* farmland⟩ **c** : of the highest grade of meat ⟨*prime* beef⟩

³**prime** *vb* **primed; prim·ing** **1** : to get ready for firing by putting in priming ⟨*prime* a rifle⟩ **2** : to put a first color or coating on (an unpainted surface) **3** : to put into working order by filling ⟨*prime* a pump⟩ **4** : to tell what to say beforehand ⟨they had you all *primed* to tell me that⟩

prime meridian *n* : the meridian of 0° longitude from which other longitudes are calculated

prime minister *n* : the chief officer of the government in some countries

prime number *n* : an integer other than 0 or +1 that is not divisible without a remainder by any other integers except ±1 and ± itself

¹**prim·er** \'prim-ər, *especially British* 'prī-mər\ *n* **1** : a small book for teaching children to read **2** : a book of first instructions in a subject

²**prim·er** \'prī-mər\ *n* **1** : a device (as a cap or tube) containing a small explosive charge that is used for setting off a larger explosive charge (as in a cartridge) **2** : material used in priming a surface

prime time *n* : the time in the evening when television has its largest number of viewers

pri·me·val \prī-'mē-vəl\ *adj* : belonging to the earliest time : PRIMITIVE [from Latin *primaevus* "relating to the very earliest ages", from *primus* "first" and *aevum* "age" — related to PRIME] — **pri·me·val·ly** \-və-lē\ *adv*

prim·ing \'prī-miŋ\ *n* **1** : the explosive used in priming a charge **2** : ²PRIMER 2

¹**prim·i·tive** \'prim-ət-iv\ *adj* **1 a** : of or relating to the earliest age or period ⟨*primitive* forests⟩ ⟨the *primitive* church⟩ **b** : closely resembling an ancient ancestor ⟨a *primitive* fish⟩ **2** : of or relating to an early stage of development ⟨*primitive* tools⟩ **3** : being or made by a self-taught artist — **prim·i·tive·ly** *adv* — **prim·i·tive·ness** *n*

²**primitive** *n* **1** : something primitive : something basic or original **2** : a member of a primitive people

pri·mor·di·al \prī-'mord-ē-əl\ *adj* : first created or developed : PRIMEVAL — **pri·mor·di·al·ly** \-ē-ə-lē\ *adv*

primp \'primp\ *vb* : to dress or arrange in a careful or fussy manner

prim·rose \'prim-ˌrōz\ *n* : any of a genus of herbs with large leaves arranged at the base of the stem and showy variously colored flowers in clusters on leafless stalks — compare EVENING PRIMROSE

prince \'prin(t)s\ *n* **1** : MONARCH 1 **2** : a son or grandson of a monarch : a male member of a royal family **3** : a nobleman of very high rank **4** : a person of high standing in his class or profession [Middle English *prince* "ruler, king", from early French *prince* (same meaning), from Latin *princip-, princeps* "first person, chief", literally "one who takes the first part", from *primus* "first" and *capere* "to take" — related to PRIME]

primrose

Prince Al·bert \prin-'sal-bərt\ *n* : a long double-breasted coat

prince consort *n, pl* **princes consort** : the husband of a reigning queen

prince·ly \'prin(t)-slē\ *adj* **prince·li·er; -est** **1** : of or relating to a prince **2** : suitable for a prince ⟨a *princely* sum⟩

prin·cess \'prin(t)-səs, 'prin-ˌses, prin-'ses\ *n* **1** : a daughter or granddaughter of a monarch : a female member of a royal family **2** : the wife of a prince

¹**prin·ci·pal** \'prin(t)-s(ə-)pəl, -sə-bəl\ *adj* : most important

: CHIEF ⟨the *principal* ingredient of the stew⟩ — **prin·ci·pal·ly** \-ē, prin(t)-splē\ *adv*

²**principal** *n* **1 a** : a leading or most important person **b** : the head of a school **2** : a sum of money that is placed to earn interest, is owed as a debt, or is used as a fund

prin·ci·pal·i·ty \ˌprin(t)-sə-'pal-ət-ē\ *n, pl* **-ties** : a small territory that is ruled by a prince

principal parts *n pl* : the infinitive, the past tense, and the past and present participles of an English verb

prin·ci·ple \'prin(t)-s(ə-)pəl, -sə-bəl\ *n* **1** : a general or basic truth on which other truths or theories can be based ⟨scientific *principles*⟩ **2** : a rule of conduct ⟨a person of high *principles*⟩ **3** : a law or fact of nature which makes possible the working of a machine or device ⟨the *principle* of magnetism⟩ ⟨the *principle* of the lever⟩

prin·ci·pled \'prin(t)-s(ə-)pəld, -sə-bəld\ *adj* : based on or marked by principle ⟨high-*principled*⟩

prink \'priŋk\ *vb* : PRIMP

¹**print** \'print\ *n* **1 a** : a mark made by pressure **b** : something that has been stamped with an impression or formed in a mold ⟨a *print* of butter⟩ **2 a** : printed state or form ⟨put a manuscript into *print*⟩ **b** : printed matter **c** : printed letters **3** : a picture, copy, or design made by printing (as from an engraving or a photographic negative) **4 a** : cloth with a printed pattern **b** : an article of such cloth

²**print** *vb* **1** : to put or stamp something in or on **2 a** : to make a copy of by pressing paper against an inked surface (as type or an engraving) **b** : to stamp with a design by pressure ⟨*print* wallpaper⟩ **c** : to publish in printed form ⟨*print* a newspaper⟩ **d** : to write or cause to be written on a surface (as a computer display screen) for viewing ⟨the computer will *print* the message at the top of the screen⟩ **3** : to write in separate letters like those made by a typewriter **4** : to make a picture from a photographic negative

print·able \'print-ə-bəl\ *adj* : considered suitable to be published

print·er \'print-ər\ *n* **1** : a person whose business is printing **2** : a device used for printing or for making printouts

printer's devil *n* : an apprentice in a printing office

print·ing \'print-iŋ\ *n* **1** : the process of putting something in printed form **2** : the art or business of a printer

printing press *n* : a machine that produces printed copies

print·mak·er \'print-ˌmā-kər\ *n* : an artist who makes prints

print·out \'print-ˌaut\ *n* : a printed record produced by a computer

print out \(')print-'aut\ *vb* : to produce a printed record of

¹**pri·or** \'prī(-ə)r\ *n* : a monk who is head of a priory

²**prior** *adj* **1** : earlier in time or order : PREVIOUS ⟨better than in *prior* years⟩ ⟨without *prior* warning⟩ **2** : being more important than something else : having priority ⟨has a *prior* claim to our attention⟩

pri·or·ess \'prī-ə-rəs\ *n* : a nun who is head of a priory

pri·or·i·ty \prī-'òr-ət-ē, -'är-\ *n, pl* **-ties** **1** : the quality or state of coming before another in time or importance **2** : a condition of being given attention before others ⟨this project has top *priority*⟩ ⟨list your needs in order of *priority*⟩

printing press

\ə\ abut	\au\ out	\i\ tip	\ò\ saw	\u\ foot
\ər\ further	\ch\ chin	\ī\ life	\òi\ coin	\y\ yet
\a\ mat	\e\ pet	\j\ job	\th\ thin	\yü\ few
\ā\ take	\ē\ easy	\ŋ\ sing	\th\ this	\yu\ cure
\ä\ cot, cart	\g\ go	\ō\ bone	\ü\ food	\zh\ vision

prior to *prep* : in advance of : BEFORE

pri·o·ry \'prī-(ə-)rē\ *n, pl* **-ries** : a religious house under a prior or prioress

prise \'prīz\ *vb* **prised; pris·ing** *chiefly British* : ⁵PRIZE, PRY

prism \'priz-əm\ *n* **1** : a solid having two opposite ends that are parallel polygons of exactly the same size and shape and faces that are parallelograms **2** : a transparent object that usually has three sides and bends light so that it breaks up into rainbow colors

pris·on \'priz-°n\ *n* **1** : a state of confinement or captivity **2** : a place where criminals or prisoners are locked up

prison camp *n* : a camp where prisoners are held

pris·on·er \'priz-nər, -°n-ər\ *n* : a person who has been captured or locked up

prisoner of war : a member of the armed forces of a nation who has been captured by the enemy

pris·tine \'pris-,tēn\ *adj* : being fresh and clean

prith·ee \'prith-ē, 'prith-\ *interj, archaic* — used to express a wish or request

pri·va·cy \'prī-və-sē\ *n, pl* **-cies** **1 a** : the quality or state of being out of the sight and hearing of other people : SE-CLUSION ⟨the *privacy* of the home⟩ **b** : freedom from being intruded upon ⟨one's right to *privacy*⟩ **2** : SECRECY **2** ⟨talk in *privacy*⟩

¹**pri·vate** \'prī-vət\ *adj* **1** : having to do with or for the use of a single person or group : not public ⟨*private* property⟩ ⟨a *private* beach⟩ **2 a** : not holding any public office ⟨a *private* citizen⟩ **b** : not relating to one's official position : PERSONAL ⟨*private* letters⟩ ⟨your own *private* opinion⟩ **3** : not known or meant to be known publicly ⟨*private* meet-ings⟩ ⟨keep personal information *private*⟩ **4** : not under public control ⟨a *private* school⟩ — **pri·vate·ly** *adv* — **pri·vate·ness** *n*

²**private** *n* : a person of low or lowest rank in an organized group (as a police or fire department); *esp* : an enlisted person of the lowest ranks in the army or marines — **in private** : where no one else can hear ⟨would like to speak to you *in private*⟩

¹**pri·va·teer** \,prī-və-'ti(ə)r\ *n* **1** : an armed private ship permitted by its government to make war on ships of an enemy country **2** : a sailor on a privateer

²**privateer** *vb* : to cruise in or as a privateer

private first class *n* : an enlisted person with a rank just below corporal in the army or just below lance corporal in the marines

pri·va·tion \prī-'vā-shən\ *n* : the state of being deprived

priv·et \'priv-ət\ *n* : a shrub that is related to the lilac, has small white flowers, and is widely used for hedges

¹**priv·i·lege** \'priv-(ə-)lij\ *n* : a right or liberty granted as a favor or benefit es-pecially to some and not others

²**privilege** *vb* **-leged; -leg·ing** : to grant a privilege to

priv·i·leged \'priv-(ə-)lijd\ *adj* : having more things and a better chance in life than most people ⟨*privileged* classes of society⟩

priv·i·ly \'priv-ə-lē\ *adv* : in private : SECRETLY

¹**privy** \'priv-ē\ *adj* **1** : ¹PRIVATE 1, 2b, 3 **2** : sharing in a secret ⟨*privy* to the conspiracy⟩

²**privy** *n, pl* **priv·ies** **1** : a small building without plumbing used as a toilet **2** : TOILET 2b

¹**prize** \'prīz\ *n* **1** : something won or to be won in a contest **2** : something unusually valuable or eagerly sought [Middle English *pris* "prize, price, value", from early French *pris* (same meaning), from Latin *pretium* "price, money" — re-

privet

lated to PRICE]

²**prize** *adj* **1 a** : awarded a prize ⟨a *prize* essay⟩ **b** : awarded as a prize ⟨*prize* money⟩ **2** : outstanding of its kind ⟨a *prize* fool⟩ ⟨a *prize* student⟩

³**prize** *vb* **prized; priz·ing** **1** : to estimate the value of **2** : to value highly : TREASURE [Middle English *prisen* "to value, treasure", from early French *prisier* (same mean-ing), from Latin *pretiare* (same meaning), from earlier *pre-tium* (noun) "price, value"]

⁴**prize** *n* : something taken (as in war) especially at sea [Mid-dle English *prise* "something taken by force or threat", from early French *prise* "the act of taking", from *prendre* "to take", from Latin *prehendere* "to take"]

⁵**prize** *vb* **prized; priz·ing** : to force or move with or as if with a lever : PRY

prize·fight \'prīz-,fīt\ *n* : a contest between professional boxers for pay — **prize·fight·er** \-ər\ *n* — **prize·fight·ing** \-iŋ\ *n*

prize·win·ner \-,win-ər\ *n* : a winner of a prize — **prize·win·ning** \-,win-iŋ\ *adj*

¹**pro** \'prō\ *n, pl* **pros** \'prōz\ : an argument or evidence in favor of something ⟨discuss the *pros* and cons⟩ [Middle English *pro* "an argument in favor of something", from Latin *pro* (preposition) "in favor of, for"]

²**pro** *adv* : in favor of something

³**pro** *n or adj* : PROFESSIONAL [a shortened form of *profes-sional*]

¹**pro-** *prefix* : located in front of or at the front of ⟨*pro*thorax⟩ [derived from Greek *pro* "before, forward"]

²**pro-** *prefix* **1** : taking the place of : substituting for **2** : favoring : supporting ⟨*pro*-American⟩ [derived from Latin *pro* "in front of, for"]

prob·a·bil·i·ty \,präb-ə-'bil-ət-ē\ *n, pl* **-ties** **1** : the quality or state of being probable **2** : something probable **3 a** : a measure of how often a particular event will happen if something (as tossing a coin) is done repeatedly which re-sults in any of a number of possible events ⟨the *probabil-ity* of a coin coming up heads is ½⟩ **b** : a branch of math-ematics concerned with the study of probabilities

prob·a·ble \'präb-ə-bəl\ *adj* : reasonably sure but not cer-tain of happening or being true : LIKELY

prob·a·bly \'präb-(ə-)blē, 'präb-lē\ *adv* : without much doubt : very likely

¹**pro·bate** \'prō-,bāt\ *n* **1** : proof before a probate court that the will of a deceased person is genuine **2** : judicial determination of the legal force of a will

²**probate** *vb* **pro·bat·ed; pro·bat·ing** : to establish by pro-bate as genuine and as having legal force

probate court *n* : a court that probates wills and administers estates of deceased persons

pro·ba·tion \prō-'bā-shən\ *n* **1** : a period of trial for finding out or testing a person's fitness (as for a job) **2** : the suspending of a convicted offender's sentence during good behavior under the supervision of a probation officer — **pro·ba·tion·al** \-shnəl, -shən-°l\ *adj* — **pro·ba·tion·ary** \-shə-,ner-ē\ *adj*

pro·ba·tion·er \prō-'bā-sh(ə-)nər\ *n* : a person who is on probation

probation officer *n* : an officer appointed to supervise con-victed offenders on probation

¹**probe** \'prōb\ *n* **1** : a slender instrument especially for ex-amining a cavity (as a deep wound) **2** : a device used to penetrate or send back information especially from outer space **3** : a careful investigation **4** : an attempt to ex-plore or learn about some unknown place ⟨a space *probe*⟩

²**probe** *vb* **probed; prob·ing** **1** : to examine with or as if with a probe **2** : to investigate thoroughly — **prob·er** *n*

pro·bi·ty \'prō-bət-ē\ *n* : HONESTY, UPRIGHTNESS

¹**prob·lem** \'präb-ləm\ *n* **1** : something to be worked out or solved ⟨a *problem* in arithmetic⟩ **2 a** : something that is hard to understand, deal with, or correct ⟨social *prob-lems*⟩ ⟨have a *problem* with the car⟩ **b** : something that

causes one trouble or irritation ⟨of course the mosquitoes are a *problem*⟩

²**problem** *adj* **1** : dealing with a problem of human conduct or social justice ⟨a *problem* play⟩ **2** : difficult to deal with ⟨a *problem* child⟩

prob·lem·at·ic \,präb-lə-'mat-ik\ *or* **prob·lem·at·i·cal** \-'mat-i-kəl\ *adj* **1** : difficult to solve or decide : PUZZLING ⟨a *problematic* situation⟩ **2** : not settled : UNCERTAIN ⟨their future is still *problematic*⟩

pro·bos·cis \prə-'bäs-əs, -kəs\ *n, pl* **-bos·cis·es** *also* **-bos·ci·des** \-'bäs-ə-,dēz\ **1** : the trunk of an elephant; *esp* : ¹TRUNK 3 **2** : a long tube-shaped bodily part in the mouth region of an invertebrate (as the sucking organ of a butterfly)

proboscis 2

pro·caine \'prō-,kān\ *n* : a drug resembling cocaine that is used as a local anesthetic in dentistry and medicine

pro·ce·dure \prə-'sē-jər\ *n* **1** : a manner or method in which a business or action is carried on **2 a** : an action or series of actions **b** : a series of instructions for a computer that has a name by which it can be called into action — **pro·ce·dur·al** \-'sēj-(ə-)rəl\ *adj*

pro·ceed \prō-'sēd, prə-\ *vb* **1** : to come from a source **2 a** : to continue after a pause or interruption **b** : to go or act by an orderly method **3 a** : to carry on an action, process, or movement **b** : to be in the process of being done **4** : to go forward or onward : ADVANCE

pro·ceed·ing *n* **1** : PROCEDURE 2a **2** *pl* : things that happen **3** : a legal action

pro·ceeds \'prō-,sēdz\ *n pl* : the money or profit that comes from a business deal

¹**pro·cess** \'präs-,es, 'prōs-, -əs\ *n, pl* **pro·cess·es** \-,es-əz, -ə-səz, -ə-,sēz\ **1 a** : ²ADVANCE 1 ⟨the *process* of time⟩ **b** : something going on **2 a** : a natural continuing action or series of actions or changes ⟨the *process* of growth⟩ ⟨life *processes*⟩ ⟨mental *processes*⟩ **b** : a series of actions or operations leading to a result ⟨a manufacturing *process*⟩ **3** : the carrying on of a legal action ⟨due *process* of law⟩ **4** : a bodily part that sticks out or is conspicuous : OUTGROWTH ⟨a bony *process*⟩

²**process** *vb* **1** : to change or prepare by special treatment ⟨*process* foods⟩ **2 a** : to take care of according to a routine ⟨*process* people looking for a job⟩ ⟨*process* insurance claims⟩ **b** : to take in and organize for use in a variety of ways ⟨computers *process* data⟩ ⟨*process* information⟩

process cheese *n* : cheese made by blending different cheeses

pro·ces·sion \prə-'sesh-ən\ *n* **1** : continuous forward movement : PROGRESSION **2** : a group of individuals moving along in an orderly often ceremonial way ⟨a funeral *procession*⟩

¹**pro·ces·sion·al** \prə-'sesh-nəl, -ən-ᵊl\ *n* : a hymn sung during a church procession

²**processional** *adj* : of, relating to, or moving in a procession

pro·ces·sor \'präs-,es-ər, 'prōs-\ *n* **1** : a person or machine that processes **2** : the part of a computer that operates on data

pro·claim \prō-'klām\ *vb* : to announce publicly : DECLARE ⟨*proclaim* a holiday⟩ — **pro·claim·er** *n*

proc·la·ma·tion \,präk-lə-'mā-shən\ *n* **1** : the act of proclaiming **2** : something proclaimed

pro·cliv·i·ty \prō-'kliv-ət-ē\ *n, pl* **-ties** : a natural tendency of the mind or personality ⟨showed artistic *proclivities* at an early age⟩; *esp* : such a tendency toward something bad ⟨a *proclivity* for violence⟩

pro·con·sul \(')prō-'kän(t)-səl\ *n* : a powerful administrator

(as of a colony)

pro·cras·ti·nate \p(r)ə-'kras-tə-,nāt, prō-\ *vb* **-nat·ed; -nat·ing** : to keep putting off something supposed to be done — **pro·cras·ti·na·tion** \-,kras-tə-'nā-shən\ *n* — **pro·cras·ti·na·tor** \-'kras-tə-,nāt-ər\ *n*

proc·tor \'präk-tər\ *n* : a person who supervises students during an examination — **proctor** *vb*

proc·u·ra·tor \'präk-yə-,rāt-ər\ *n* : a person who handles the business affairs of another : AGENT

pro·cure \prə-'kyü(ə)r\ *vb* **pro·cured; pro·cur·ing** **1** : to get possession of **2** : BRING ABOUT, ACHIEVE   **syn** see GET — **pro·cur·able** \-'kyür-ə-bəl\ *adj* — **pro·cure·ment** \-'kyü(ə)r-mənt\ *n*

¹**prod** \'präd\ *vb* **prod·ded; prod·ding** **1** : to poke with something **2** : to stir a person or animal to action — **prod·der** *n*

²**prod** *n* **1** : something used for prodding **2** : an act of prodding : a sharp urging or reminder

¹**prod·i·gal** \'präd-i-gəl\ *adj* : carelessly wasteful ⟨a *prodigal* spender⟩ — **prod·i·gal·i·ty** \,präd-ə-'gal-ət-ē\ *n* — **prod·i·gal·ly** \'präd-i-g(ə-)lē\ *adv*

²**prodigal** *n* : somebody who wastes money carelessly

pro·di·gious \prə-'dij-əs\ *adj* **1** : exciting amazement or wonder ⟨performs *prodigious* feats⟩ **2** : very big : HUGE ⟨a *prodigious* amount of food⟩ — **pro·di·gious·ly** *adv*

prod·i·gy \'präd-ə-jē\ *n, pl* **-gies** **1** : an amazing event or action : WONDER **2** : an unusually talented child

¹**pro·duce** \prə-'d(y)üs\ *vb* **pro·duced; pro·duc·ing** **1** : to bring to view : EXHIBIT ⟨*produce* evidence⟩ ⟨*produced* a permit when asked⟩ **2** : to give birth or rise to ⟨a tree *producing* good fruit⟩ ⟨the offspring an insect can *produce*⟩ **3** : to prepare to present to the public ⟨*produce* a play⟩ **4** : to cause to be or happen : BRING ABOUT ⟨the insect bite *produced* a rash⟩ ⟨this will *produce* results⟩ **5 a** : to bring something out by work ⟨the crops the peasants *produced*⟩ ⟨*produced* articles and illustrations⟩ **b** : ²MANUFACTURE 2 ⟨a factory *producing* steel⟩ — **pro·duc·ible** \-'d(y)ü-sə-bəl\ *adj*

²**pro·duce** \'präd-(,)üs, 'prōd- *also* -(,)yüs\ *n* **1** : something produced **2** : fresh fruits and vegetables

pro·duc·er \prə-'d(y)ü-sər\ *n* **1** : one that produces; *esp* : a person who grows agricultural products or manufactures articles **2** : a person who supervises or finances a play, a movie, or a radio or television program **3** : a living thing (as a green plant) that makes its food from simple inorganic substances

prod·uct \'präd-(,)əkt\ *n* **1** : the number or expression resulting from the multiplication of two or more numbers or expressions ⟨15 is the *product* of 3 and 5⟩ **2** : something produced

pro·duc·tion \prə-'dək-shən\ *n* **1** : something produced **2** : the act or process of producing **3** : the amount produced : total output ⟨annual *production* of coal⟩

pro·duc·tive \prə-'dək-tiv\ *adj* **1** : having the power to produce plentifully ⟨*productive* soil⟩ ⟨*productive* fishing waters⟩ **2** : producing something ⟨your efforts have been *productive* of much good⟩ **3** : giving results ⟨a *productive* meeting⟩ — **pro·duc·tive·ly** *adv* — **pro·duc·tive·ness** *n*

pro·duc·tiv·i·ty \(,)prō-,dək-'tiv-ət-ē, ,präd-(,)ək-, prə-,dək-\ *n* **1** : the quality or state of being productive **2** : rate of production especially of food through use of the sun's energy by living things that are producers

prof \'präf\ *n* : PROFESSOR

¹**pro·fane** \prō-'fān, prə-\ *vb* **pro·faned; pro·fan·ing** **1** : to treat with great disrespect **2** : to put to a wrong or

\ə\ abut	\aü\ out	\i\ tip	\ȯ\ saw	\u̇\ foot
\ər\ further	\ch\ chin	\ī\ life	\ȯi\ coin	\y\ yet
\a\ mat	\e\ pet	\j\ job	\th\ thin	\yü\ few
\ā\ take	\ē\ easy	\ŋ\ sing	\th\ this	\yu̇\ cure
\ä\ cot, cart	\g\ go	\ō\ bone	\ü\ food	\zh\ vision

vulgar use : DEBASE — **pro·fa·na·tion** \‚präf-ə-'nā-shən, ‚prō-fə-\ *n*

²profane *adj* **1** : not concerned with religion or religious purposes : SECULAR, WORLDLY **2** : showing no respect for God or holy things ⟨*profane* language⟩ — **pro·fane·ly** *adv*

pro·fan·i·ty \prō-'fan-ət-ē, prə-\ *n, pl* **-ties** **1** : the quality or state of being profane **2** : profane language

pro·fess \prə-'fes\ *vb* **1** : to declare openly or freely ⟨*profess* confidence in a friend⟩ **2** : ¹PRETEND 1, CLAIM ⟨*professed* to be our friends⟩

pro·fessed \prə-'fest\ *adj* **1** : openly declared ⟨failed in its *professed* task⟩ **2** : claiming to be qualified ⟨a *professed* expert⟩

pro·fess·ed·ly \prə-'fes-əd-lē, -'fest-lē\ *adv* **1** : by one's own declaration ⟨a *professedly* serious novelist⟩ **2** : supposedly but not really ⟨was *professedly* open to all, but actually was not⟩

pro·fes·sion \prə-'fesh-ən\ *n* **1** : the act of taking the vows of a religious community **2** : a public declaring or claiming (as of a belief, faith, or opinion) **3 a** : an occupation (as medicine, law, or teaching) that is not mechanical or agricultural and that requires special education **b** : a principal occupation or employment **c** : the people working in a profession

¹pro·fes·sion·al \prə-'fesh-nəl, -ən-ᵊl\ *adj* **1 a** : of, relating to, or resembling that of a profession **b** : working in a profession ⟨a *professional* dry cleaner⟩ ⟨a *professional* soldier⟩ **2 a** : taking part for money in an activity (as sport) that others do for pleasure ⟨*professional* golfers⟩ **b** : engaged in by professionals ⟨*professional* football⟩ — **pro·fes·sion·al·ly** \-ē\ *adv*

²professional *n* : a person who engages in an activity professionally

pro·fes·sion·al·ize \prə-'fesh-nəl-‚īz, -ən-ᵊl-\ *vb* **-ized; -iz·ing** : to give a professional nature to

pro·fes·sor \prə-'fes-ər\ *n* : a teacher especially of the highest rank at a college or university — **pro·fes·so·ri·al** \‚prō-fə-'sōr-ē-əl, ‚präf-ə-, -'sòr-\ *adj* — **pro·fes·so·ri·al·ly** \-ē-ə-lē\ *adv*

pro·fes·sor·ship \prə-'fes-ər-‚ship\ *n* : the office, duties or position of a professor

prof·fer \'präf-ər\ *vb* **prof·fered; prof·fer·ing** \'präf-(ə-)riŋ\ : ¹OFFER 2 — **proffer** *n*

pro·fi·cien·cy \prə-'fish-ən-sē\ *n, pl* **-cies** : the quality or state of being proficient

pro·fi·cient \prə-'fish-ənt\ *adj* : very good at doing something especially through practice **syn** see SKILLFUL — **pro·fi·cient·ly** *adv*

pro·file \'prō-‚fīl\ *n* **1** : a head or face seen or drawn from the side **2** : something seen in outline **3** : a vertical section of soil that shows the various layers — called also *soil profile* **4** : a set of data often in the form of a graph that shows the important characteristics of something **5** : level of activity that attracts attention ⟨tried to keep a low *profile*⟩

profile 1

¹prof·it \'präf-ət\ *n* **1** : the gain or benefit from something **2** : the gain after all the expenses are subtracted from the amount received — **prof·it·less** \-ləs\ *adj*

²profit *vb* **1** : to get some good out of something : GAIN ⟨*profit* by experience⟩ **2** : to be of use to (someone) : BENEFIT ⟨an agreement that *profited* us all⟩

prof·it·able \'präf-ət-ə-bəl, 'präf-tə-bəl\ *adj* : producing profit — **prof·it·ably** \-blē\ *adv*

prof·i·teer \‚präf-ə-'ti(ə)r\ *n* : a person who makes an unfair profit especially on essential goods during an emer-

gency — **profiteer** *vb*

prof·li·ga·cy \'präf-li-gə-sē\ *n* : the quality or state of being profligate

prof·li·gate \'präf-li-gət\ *adj* **1** : wicked in character or morals : DISSIPATED **2** : very wasteful — **profligate** *n*

pro·found \prə-'faünd\ *adj* **1** : having or showing great knowledge or understanding ⟨a *profound* thinker⟩ **2** : very deeply felt ⟨*profound* sorrow⟩ **3** : ABSOLUTE 1a, COMPLETE ⟨a *profound* silence⟩ — **pro·found·ly** \-'faün-(d)lē\ *adv* — **pro·found·ness** \-'faün(d)-nəs\ *n*

pro·fun·di·ty \prə-'fən-dət-ē\ *n, pl* **-ties** **1** : great knowledge or understanding **2** : something profound

pro·fuse \prə-'fyüs\ *adj* **1** : pouring forth in great amounts ⟨*profuse* apologies⟩ ⟨*profuse* in their thanks⟩ **2** : very plentiful ⟨a *profuse* harvest⟩ ⟨a *profuse* variety of minerals⟩ — **pro·fuse·ly** *adv*

pro·fu·sion \prə-'fyü-zhən\ *n* : a plentiful supply : great quantity ⟨lilacs blooming in *profusion*⟩

prog·e·ny \'präj-(ə-)nē\ *n, pl* **-nies** : human descendants or animal offspring

pro·ges·ter·one \prō-'jes-tə-‚rōn\ *n* : a hormone that is produced by the corpus luteum and causes the uterus to change so that it provides a suitable environment for a fertilized egg

prog·no·sis \präg-'nō-səs\ *n, pl* **-no·ses** \-'nō-‚sēz\ **1** : the prospect of recovery of an individual who has a disease based on the usual course of the disease and the characteristics of the individual who is sick **2** : ²FORECAST

prog·nos·ti·cate \präg-'näs-tə-‚kāt\ *vb* **-cat·ed; -cat·ing** : PREDICT, PROPHESY — **prog·nos·ti·ca·tor** \-‚kāt-ər\ *n*

prog·nos·ti·ca·tion \(‚)präg-‚näs-tə-'kā-shən\ *n* : ²FORECAST

¹pro·gram \'prō-‚gram, -grəm\ *n* **1** : a brief statement or written outline (as of a concert or play) **2** : a performance that is broadcast ⟨a television *program*⟩ **3** : a plan of action ⟨a *program* of regular dental checkups⟩ ⟨a political *program*⟩ **4** : a set of step-by-step instructions that tell a computer to do something with data

²program *vb* **pro·grammed** *or* **pro·gramed** \-‚gramd, -grəmd\; **pro·gram·ming** *or* **pro·gram·ing** : to provide with a program ⟨*program* a computer⟩ — **pro·gram·ma·ble** \'prō-‚gram-ə-bəl\ *adj*

pro·gramme *chiefly British variant of* PROGRAM

pro·gram·mer *or* **pro·gram·er** \'prō-‚gram-ər, -grə-mər\ *n* : a person who writes computer programs

pro·gram·ming *or* **pro·gram·ing** \'prō-‚gram-iŋ, -grə-miŋ\ *n* : the design and production of computer programs

program music *n* : music that is inspired by or that describes a story or a sequence of images

¹prog·ress \'präg-rəs, -‚res, *chiefly British* 'prō-‚gres\ *n* **1** : a moving toward a goal ⟨the *progress* of a ship⟩ **2** : gradual improvement or advancement ⟨the *progress* of science⟩

²pro·gress \prə-'gres\ *vb* **1** : to move forward : ADVANCE, PROCEED **2** : to move toward a higher, better, or more advanced stage

pro·gres·sion \prə-'gresh-ən\ *n* **1** : the action of progressing or moving forward **2** : a continuous and connected series (as of acts, events, or steps) **3** : a changing from one chord to another by means of several notes or chords coming one after the other

¹pro·gres·sive \prə-'gres-iv\ *adj* **1 a** : of, relating to, or showing progress or progression **b** : making use of or interested in new ideas ⟨a *progressive* city⟩ **c** : allowing more freedom to the pupils than an ordinary school ⟨a *progressive* school⟩ **2 a** : moving forward or onward : ADVANCING ⟨the *progressive* movements of the hands of a clock⟩ **b** : spreading and becoming worse ⟨a *progressive* disease⟩ **c** : increasing in rate as the base amount increases ⟨a *progressive* tax⟩ **3** : of or relating to political progressives **4** : of, relating to, or being a verb form that expresses action or state in progress at the time of speaking or a time spoken of — **pro·gres·sive·ly** *adv* — **pro·gres·sive·ness** *n*

²progressive *n* : a person believing in gradual political change and social improvement by government action

pro·hib·it \prō-'hib-ət\ *vb* **1** : to forbid by authority ⟨*prohibit* parking⟩ **2** : to make impossible ⟨the high walls *prohibit* escape⟩

pro·hi·bi·tion \,prō-ə-'bish-ən\ *n* **1** : the act of prohibiting **2** : an order forbidding something **3** : the forbidding by law of the sale and manufacture of alcoholic beverages

pro·hi·bi·tion·ist \'pro-ə-'bish-(ə-)nəst\ *n* : a person who is in favor of prohibiting the manufacture and sale of alcoholic beverages

pro·hib·i·tive \prō-'hib-ət-iv\ *adj* : likely to discourage use or purchase ⟨*prohibitive* prices⟩ — **pro·hib·i·tive·ly** *adv*

¹proj·ect \'präj-,ekt, -ikt\ *n* **1** : a plan or scheme to do something **2** : a task or problem in school ⟨my science *project*⟩ **3** : a group of houses or apartment buildings built according to a single plan

²pro·ject \prə-'jekt\ *vb* **1 a** : to work out in the mind **b** : to plan, figure, or estimate for the future ⟨*project* next year's costs⟩ **2** : to throw forward **3** : STICK OUT 1a **4** : to cause to fall upon a surface ⟨*project* motion pictures on a screen⟩

pro·jec·tile \prə-'jek-t°l\ *n* : something (as a bullet or rocket) thrown or driven forward especially from or for use as a weapon

pro·jec·tion \prə-'jek-shən\ *n* **1** : a method of showing a curved surface (as the earth) on a flat one (as a map) **2** : the act of throwing or shooting forward **3** : something that sticks out **4** : the act or process of projecting something on a surface (as by motion

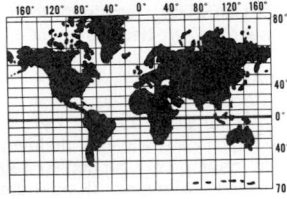

projection 1

pictures or slides) **5** : an estimate of what might happen in the future based on what is happening now

pro·jec·tion·ist \prə-'jek-sh(ə-)nəst\ *n* : a person who operates a motion-picture projector or television equipment

pro·jec·tor \prə-'jek-tər\ *n* : a machine for projecting an image or pictures upon a surface ⟨a motion-picture *projector*⟩ ⟨a slide *projector*⟩

pro·leg \'prō-,leg\ *n* : a fleshy leg on the abdomen of some insect larvae

pro·le·tar·i·an \,prō-lə-'ter-ē-ən\ *n* : a member of the proletariat — **proletarian** *adj*

pro·le·tar·i·at \,prō-lə-'ter-ē-ət, -'tar-, -ē-,at\ *n* **1** : the lowest social or economic class of a community **2** : industrial workers who sell their labor to live

pro·lif·er·ate \prə-'lif-ə-,rāt\ *vb* **-at·ed; -at·ing** : to grow or increase rapidly — **pro·lif·er·a·tion** \-,lif-ə-'rā-shən\ *n*

pro·lif·ic \prə-'lif-ik\ *adj* **1** : producing young or fruit in large numbers ⟨a *prolific* orchard⟩ **2** : highly inventive : PRODUCTIVE ⟨a *prolific* mind⟩ **syn** see FERTILE — **pro·lif·i·cal·ly** \-'lif-i-k(ə-)lē\ *adv*

pro·lix \prō-'liks, 'prō-(,)liks\ *adj* : too long-winded or wordy — **pro·lix·i·ty** \prō-'lik-sət-ē\ *n*

pro·logue \'prō-,lóg\ *n* **1** : an introduction to a book or play **2** : an act or event that comes before or introduces something

pro·long \prə-'lón\ *vb* : to make longer than usual

pro·lon·ga·tion \(,)prō-,lón-'gā-shən\ *n* **1** : a making longer **2** : something that prolongs or is prolonged

prom \'präm\ *n* : a usually formal dance given by a high school or college class [a shortened form of *promenade* "a march by couples at the beginning of a formal ball"]

¹prom·e·nade \,präm-ə-'nād, -'näd\ *n* **1** : a walk or ride for pleasure or to be seen **2** : a place for strolling

²promenade *vb* **-nad·ed; -nad·ing** : to take or go on a walk

pro·me·thi·um \prə-'mē-thē-əm\ *n* : a radioactive metallic element obtained from the splitting of uranium atoms — see ELEMENT table

prom·i·nence \'präm-(ə-)nən(t)s\ *n* **1** : the quality, state, or fact of being prominent : DISTINCTION ⟨a person of *prominence*⟩ **2** : something (as a mountain) that is prominent **3** : a mass of gas resembling a cloud that arises from the chromosphere of the sun

prom·i·nent \'präm-(ə-)nənt\ *adj* **1** : sticking out beyond a surface or line **2** : easily noticeable **3** : DISTINGUISHED, EMINENT **syn** see NOTICEABLE — **prom·i·nent·ly** *adv*

prom·is·cu·ity \,präm-əs-'kyü-ət-ē\ *n, pl* **-ities** : the quality or state of being promiscuous

pro·mis·cu·ous \prə-'mis-kyə-wəs\ *adj* **1** : composed of all sorts of persons and things : MISCELLANEOUS **2 a** : INDISCRIMINATE **b** : having sexual intercourse with a number of persons — **pro·mis·cu·ous·ly** *adv*

¹prom·ise \'präm-əs\ *n* **1** : a statement by a person that he or she will or will not do something ⟨a *promise* to pay within a month⟩ **2** : something promised **3** : a cause or ground for hope ⟨give *promise* of success⟩ ⟨shows *promise*⟩ [Middle English *promisse, promis* "promise", derived from Latin *promissus,* past participle of *promittere* "to send forth, promise", from *pro-* "forward, forth" and *mittere* "to send, throw" — related to MESSAGE]

²promise *vb* **prom·ised; prom·is·ing** **1** : to give a promise about one's own actions ⟨I *promise* to clean my room this afternoon⟩ **2** : to give reason to expect ⟨dark clouds *promising* rain⟩ — **prom·i·sor** \,präm-ə-'só(ə)r\ *also* **prom·is·er** \'präm-ə-sər\ *n*

promised land *n* : a better place or state that one hopes to reach [so called from the biblical promise God made in Genesis 17:8 and Exodus 3:8 to give the land of Canaan to Abraham and his descendants]

prom·is·ing \'präm-ə-siŋ\ *adj* : likely to turn out well ⟨a *promising* pupil⟩ — **prom·is·ing·ly** \-siŋ-lē\ *adv*

prom·is·so·ry \'präm-ə-,sōr-ē, -,sòr-\ *adj* : containing a promise to pay ⟨a *promissory* note⟩

prom·on·to·ry \'präm-ən-,tōr-ē, -,tòr-\ *n, pl* **-ries** : a high point of land sticking out into the sea

pro·mote \prə-'mōt\ *vb* **pro·mot·ed; pro·mot·ing** **1** : to move up in position or rank ⟨was *promoted* to the next grade⟩ **2** : to help (something) grow or develop ⟨good soil *promotes* plant growth⟩ **3** : to help increase the sales of ⟨a sports star *promoting* a new product⟩

pro·mot·er \prə-'mōt-ər\ *n* : a person who promotes; *esp* : one who finances a sporting event ⟨a *promoter* of prizefights⟩

pro·mo·tion \prə-'mō-shən\ *n* **1** : a moving up in position or rank **2** : the promoting of something — **pro·mo·tion·al** \-shnəl, -shən-°l\ *adj*

¹prompt \'präm(p)t\ *vb* **1** : to lead to do something ⟨curiosity *prompted* her to ask the question⟩ **2** : to remind of something forgotten or poorly learned ⟨*prompt* an actor⟩ **3** : to be the cause of : INSPIRE ⟨pride *prompted* the act⟩

²prompt *adj* **1 a** : being ready and quick to act ⟨*prompt* to answer⟩ **b** : being on time : PUNCTUAL ⟨*prompt* in arriving⟩ **2** : done at once : given without delay ⟨*prompt* assistance⟩ **syn** see QUICK — **prompt·ly** *adv* — **prompt·ness** *n*

³prompt *n* : something that prompts

prompt·er \'präm(p)-tər\ *n* : a person who reminds another of the words to be spoken next (as in a play)

promp·ti·tude \'präm(p)-tə-,t(y)üd\ *n* : the quality or habit of being prompt : PROMPTNESS

\ə\ **abut**		\aů\ **out**	\i\ **tip**	\ó\ **saw**	\ů\ **foot**
\ər\ **further**		\ch\ **chin**	\ī\ **life**	\ói\ **coin**	\y\ **yet**
\a\ **mat**		\e\ **pet**	\j\ **job**	\th\ **thin**	\yü\ **few**
\ā\ **take**		\ē\ **easy**	\ŋ\ **sing**	\th\ **this**	\yů\ **cure**
\ä\ **cot, cart**		\g\ **go**	\ō\ **bone**	\ü\ **food**	\zh\ **vision**

pro·mul·gate \'präm-əl-ˌgāt; prō-'məl-\ *vb* **-gat·ed; -gat·ing** : to make known or make public ⟨*promulgate* a new law⟩ — **pro·mul·ga·tion** \ˌpräm-əl-'gā-shən, ˌprō-(ˌ)məl-\ *n*

prone \'prōn\ *adj* **1** : likely to be or act a certain way ⟨was *prone* to laziness⟩ ⟨devices *prone* to fail⟩ ⟨accident-*prone*⟩ **2** : having the front surface downward ⟨lying *prone* on the floor⟩ — **prone·ness** \'prōn-nəs\ *n*

prong \'prȯṅ, 'präṅ\ *n* **1** : ¹FORK 1 **2** : one of the sharp points of a fork : TINE **3** : a slender pointed part that sticks out (as on an antler) **4** : something shaped like a fork — **pronged** \'prȯṅd, 'präṅd\ *adj*

prong·horn \'prȯṅ-ˌhȯ(ə)rn, 'präṅ-\ *n, pl* **pronghorn** *also* **pronghorns** : a cud-chewing mammal of treeless parts of western North America resembling an antelope — called also *pronghorn antelope*

pronghorn

pro·nom·i·nal \prō-'näm-ən-ᵊl\ *adj* : of, relating to, or being a pronoun

pro·noun \'prō-ˌnaún\ *n* : a word that is used as a substitute for a noun

pro·nounce \prə-'naún(t)s\ *vb* **pro·nounced; pro·nounc·ing 1** : to state in an official or solemn way ⟨I *pronounced* a blessing on it⟩ ⟨the judge *pronounced* sentence⟩ **2** : to give as an opinion ⟨*pronounced* the party a success⟩ **3 a** : to use the voice to make the sounds of ⟨practice *pronouncing* foreign words⟩ **b** : to say or speak correctly ⟨I can't *pronounce* your name⟩ — **pro·nounc·er** *n*

pro·nounced \prə-'naún(t)st\ *adj* : very noticeable ⟨walk with a *pronounced* limp⟩ — **pro·nounc·ed·ly** \-'naún(t)-səd-lē\ *adv*

pro·nounce·ment \prə-'naún(t)-smənt\ *n* : an official or solemn statement or announcement

pron·to \'prän-ˌtō\ *adv* : without delay : right away

pro·nun·ci·a·tion \prə-ˌnən(t)-sē-'ā-shən\ *n* : the act or way of pronouncing a word or words

¹proof \'prüf\ *n* **1 a** : evidence of truth or correctness ⟨gave *proof* of her statement⟩ **b** : an act or process of showing or finding out that something is true especially by reasoning or by experiment ⟨a *proof* that the theorem is true⟩ ⟨put a theory to the *proof*⟩ **2 a** : a copy (as of something set in type) taken for study and correction **b** : a test print made from a photographic negative

²proof *adj* : designed or made to prevent or keep out something that could be harmful ⟨*proof* against tampering⟩ — usually used in compounds ⟨water*proof*⟩

³proof *vb* : to test the activeness of (yeast)

proof·read \'prü-ˌfrēd\ *vb* **-read** \-ˌfred\; **-read·ing** : to read over and fix mistakes in — **proof·read·er** *n*

¹prop \'präp\ *n* : something that props or supports

²prop *vb* **propped; prop·ping 1 a** : to hold up or keep from falling or slipping by placing a support under or against ⟨*prop* up a broken chair⟩ **b** : to support by placing against something ⟨*propped* the rake against a tree⟩ **2** : to give help, encouragement, or support to ⟨*propped* up by his faith in times of crisis⟩

³prop *n* : PROPERTY 4

⁴prop *n* : PROPELLER

pro·pa·gan·da \ˌpräp-ə-'gan-də, ˌprō-pə-\ *n* : an organized spreading of certain ideas; *also* : the ideas spread in this way — **pro·pa·gan·dist** \-dəst\ *n or adj* — **pro·pa·gan·dis·tic** \-ˌgan-'dis-tik\ *adj*

pro·pa·gan·dize \ˌpräp-ə-'gan-ˌdīz, ˌprō-pə-\ *vb* **-dized; -diz·ing 1** : to spread propaganda **2** : to try to influence by propaganda

prop·a·gate \'präp-ə-ˌgāt\ *vb* **-gat·ed; -gat·ing 1** : to

have or cause to have offspring ⟨ways to *propagate* plants without seeds⟩ ⟨*propagate* an apple by grafting⟩ **2** : to cause (as an idea or belief) to spread out and affect a greater number or wider area ⟨*propagate* a faith⟩

prop·a·ga·tion \ˌpräp-ə-'gā-shən\ *n* : the act or process of propagating: as **a** : multiplication (as of a kind of living thing) in number of individuals **b** : the spreading of something (as a belief) abroad or into new regions ⟨*propagation* of a faith⟩

pro·pane \'prō-ˌpān\ *n* : a heavy flammable gas found in crude petroleum and natural gas and used especially as fuel and in the chemical industry

pro·pel \prə-'pel\ *vb* **pro·pelled; pro·pel·ling** : to push or drive usually forward or onward ⟨a bicycle is *propelled* by pedals⟩

pro·pel·lant *also* **pro·pel·lent** \prə-'pel-ənt\ *n* : something that propels: as **a** : fuel plus a chemical to supply oxygen used by a rocket engine **b** : a gas under pressure in a can for expelling the contents when the pressure is released

pro·pel·ler \prə-'pel-ər\ *n* : a device consisting of a hub fitted with blades that is made to turn rapidly by an engine and is used especially for propelling airplanes and ships

propeller

pro·pen·si·ty \prə-'pen(t)-sət-ē\ *n, pl* **-ties** : a natural talent or liking : BENT

prop·er \'präp-ər\ *adj* **1** : appointed for the liturgy of a particular day **2** : belonging naturally to something : SPECIAL ⟨diseases *proper* to the tropics⟩ **3** : considered without surrounding places, things, or events ⟨lived outside the city *proper*⟩ **4 a** : strictly accurate : CORRECT **b** : obeying social rules : GENTEEL **5** : suitable because of an essential nature or condition **syn** see FIT

proper adjective *n* : an adjective formed from a proper noun ⟨"Italian" in "Italian paintings" is a *proper adjective*⟩

proper fraction *n* : a fraction in which the numerator is less than the denominator

prop·er·ly \'präp-ər-lē\ *adv* **1** : in a fit or suitable way ⟨behave *properly* in church⟩ **2** : according to fact : CORRECTLY ⟨*properly* labeled goods⟩ ⟨*properly* speaking, whales are not fish⟩

proper name *n* : PROPER NOUN

proper noun *n* : a noun that names a particular person, place, or thing

prop·er·tied \'präp-ərt-ēd\ *adj* : owning property

prop·er·ty \'präp-ərt-ē\ *n, pl* **-ties 1** : a special quality of something ⟨the commutative *property* for addition⟩ ⟨sweetness is a *property* of sugar⟩ **2** : something (as land, goods, or money) that is owned ⟨that lamp is my aunt's *property*⟩; *esp* : a piece of real estate ⟨a business *property*⟩ **3** : something other than scenery or costumes that is used in a play or movie — **prop·er·ty·less** \-ē-ləs\ *adj*

pro·phase \'prō-ˌfāz\ *n* : the first stage of mitosis or meiosis in which chromosomes become visible as threads

proph·e·cy \'präf-ə-sē\ *n, pl* **-cies 1** : the sayings of a prophet **2** : the foretelling of the future ⟨the gift of *prophecy*⟩ **3** : something foretold : PREDICTION

proph·e·sy \'präf-ə-ˌsī\ *vb* **-sied; -sy·ing 1** : to speak or write like a prophet **2** : FORETELL, PREDICT — **proph·e·si·er** \-ˌsī(-ə)r\ *n*

proph·et \'präf-ət\ *n* **1** : one who declares publicly a message that one believes has come from God or a god **2** : one who foretells future events

proph·et·ess \'präf-ət-əs\ *n* : a woman who is a prophet

pro·phet·ic \prə-'fet-ik\ *or* **pro·phet·i·cal** \-'fet-i-kəl\ *adj* : of or relating to a prophet or prophecy — **pro·phet·i·**

cal·ly \-i-k(ə-)lē\ *adv*

Proph·ets \'präf-əts\ *n pl* : the second part of the Jewish scriptures — compare HAGIOGRAPHA, LAW 2

pro·pi·ti·ate \prō-'pish-ē-,āt\ *vb* **-at·ed; -at·ing** : to gain or regain the favor or goodwill of — **pro·pi·ti·a·tion** \-,pish-ē-'ā-shən\ *n* — **pro·pi·tia·to·ry** \-'pish-(ē-)ə-,tōr-ē, -,tȯr-\ *adj*

pro·pi·tious \prə-'pish-əs\ *adj* **1** : PROMISING, ADVANTAGEOUS **2** : likely to produce good results

pro·po·nent \prə-'pō-nənt, 'prō-,pō-nənt\ *n* : one who argues in favor of something

¹pro·por·tion \p(r)ə-'pōr-shən, -'pȯr-\ *n* **1** : the size, number, or amount of one thing or group as compared to the size, number, or amount of another ⟨the *proportion* of boys to girls in our class is three to one⟩ **2** : a balanced or pleasing arrangement ⟨out of *proportion*⟩ **3** : a statement of the equality of two ratios (as ½ = ¹⁰⁄₂₀) — compare ²EXTREME 2, ⁴MEAN 2b **4** : a fair or just share ⟨did our *proportion* of the work⟩ **5** : DIMENSION 1b ⟨a crisis of large *proportions*⟩ ⟨the *proportions* of a room⟩ — **in proportion** : PROPORTIONAL 1

²proportion *vb* **-tioned; -tion·ing** \-sh(ə-)niŋ\ **1** : to adjust something to fit with something else **2** : to make the parts of fit well with each other

pro·por·tion·al \p(r)ə-'pōr-shnəl, -'pȯr-, -shən-ᵊl\ *adj* **1 a** : being equivalent in size, amount, or strength **b** : having the same or a constant ratio **2** : set with reference to proportions — **pro·por·tion·al·i·ty** \-,pōr-shə-'nal-ət-ē, -,pȯr-\ *n* — **pro·por·tion·al·ly** \-'pōr-shnə-lē, -'pȯr-, -shən-ᵊl-ē\ *adv*

pro·por·tion·ate \p(r)ə-'pōr-sh(ə-)nət, -'pȯr-\ *adj* : PROPORTIONAL 1 — **pro·por·tion·ate·ly** *adv*

pro·pos·al \prə-'pō-zəl\ *n* **1** : a stating or putting forward something for consideration **2 a** : something proposed : SUGGESTION **b** : an offer of marriage

pro·pose \prə-'pōz\ *vb* **pro·posed; pro·pos·ing** **1** : to make a suggestion to be thought over and talked about : SUGGEST ⟨*propose* a new theory⟩ **2** : to make plans : INTEND ⟨*propose* to buy a new house⟩ **3** : to suggest for filling a place or office ⟨*propose* someone for membership⟩ **4** : to make an offer of marriage — **pro·pos·er** *n*

prop·o·si·tion \,präp-ə-'zish-ən\ *n* **1** : something offered to be thought about or accepted : PROPOSAL ⟨a business *proposition*⟩ **2** : a statement to be proved or explained **3** : something with which one is involved or with which one must deal ⟨the mine will never be a paying *proposition*⟩ ⟨fixing that roof will be a tough *proposition*⟩

pro·pound \prə-'paund\ *vb* : PROPOSE 1 — **pro·pound·er** *n*

¹pro·pri·etary \p(r)ə-'prī-ə-,ter-ē\ *n, pl* **-etar·ies** : PROPRIETOR 1

²proprietary *adj* **1 a** : of or relating to a proprietor ⟨*proprietary* rights⟩ **b** : resembling that of a proprietor ⟨a *proprietary* pride in their hometown⟩ **2** : made and sold by one having the exclusive right to manufacture and sell ⟨a *proprietary* drug⟩ **3** : privately owned and managed ⟨a *proprietary* nursing home⟩

proprietary colony *n* : a colony (as one of the original 13 American colonies) granted to a proprietor with full powers of government

pro·pri·etor \p(r)ə-'prī-ət-ər\ *n* **1** : a person to whom ownership of a colony is granted **2** : a person who is owner ⟨the *proprietor* of the store⟩ — **pro·pri·etor·ship** \-,ship\ *n*

pro·pri·ety \p(r)ə-'prī-ət-ē\ *n, pl* **-eties** **1** : the quality or state of being proper **2** : correctness in manners or behavior : POLITENESS **3** *pl* : the rules and customs of behavior followed by polite people

prop root *n* : a root that braces or supports a plant

pro·pul·sion \prə-'pəl-shən\ *n* **1** : the action or process of propelling **2** : something that propels — **pro·pul·sive** \-'pəl-siv\ *adj*

pro ra·ta \(')prō-'rät-ə, -'rät-ə\ *adv* : in proportion to the share of each : PROPORTIONATELY — **pro rata** *adj*

pro·rate \(')prō-'rāt\ *vb* **pro·rat·ed; pro·rat·ing** : to divide or spread proportionately — **pro·ra·tion** \prō-'rā-shən\ *n*

pros *pl of* ¹PRO

pro·sa·ic \prō-'zā-ik\ *adj* : being dull, ordinary, or uninteresting — **pro·sa·i·cal·ly** \-'zā-ə-k(ə-)lē\ *adv*

pro·sce·ni·um \prō-'sē-nē-əm\ *n* **1** : the part of a stage in front of the curtain **2** : the wall containing the arch that frames the stage

pro·scribe \prō-'skrīb\ *vb* **pro·scribed; pro·scrib·ing** **1** : ²OUTLAW 1 **2** : PROHIBIT 1

proscenium 1 and 2

pro·scrip·tion \prō-'skrip-shən\ *n* **1** : the act of proscribing : the state of being proscribed **2** : PROHIBITION 2

prose \'prōz\ *n* **1** : the ordinary language that people use when they speak or write **2** : writing that does not have the repeating rhythm used in poetry — **prose** *adj*

pros·e·cute \'präs-i-,kyüt\ *vb* **-cut·ed; -cut·ing** **1** : to follow up to the end : keep at ⟨*prosecute* a war⟩ **2** : to carry on a legal action against an accused person to prove his or her guilt — **pros·e·cut·able** \-,kyüt-ə-bəl\ *adj*

prosecuting attorney *n* : DISTRICT ATTORNEY

pros·e·cu·tion \,präs-i-'kyü-shən\ *n* **1** : the act or process of prosecuting especially a criminal case in court **2** : the one bringing charges of crime against a person being tried; *esp* : the state's lawyers in a criminal case

pros·e·cu·tor \'präs-i-,kyüt-ər\ *n* : a person (as a district attorney) who prosecutes especially a criminal case as lawyer for the state

pros·e·lyte \'präs-ə-,līt\ *n* : a new convert especially to a religion

pros·e·ly·tize \'präs-(ə-)lə-,tīz\ *vb* **-tized; -tiz·ing** **1** : to talk someone into changing religious faith **2** : to try to get new people to join one's cause or group

pro·sim·i·an \(')prō-'sim-ē-ən\ *n* : a mammal (as a lemur) that is one of the lower primates — **prosimian** *adj*

pros·o·dy \'präs-əd-ē\ *n, pl* **-dies** : the study of the structure of poetry

¹pros·pect \'präs-,pekt\ *n* **1** : a wide view **2** : an imagining of something to come : ANTICIPATION ⟨the *prospect* of a good time⟩ **3** : something that is waited for or expected : POSSIBILITY ⟨what is the *prospect* of our seeing you again soon?⟩ **4 a** : a possible buyer or customer **b** : a likely candidate ⟨a presidential *prospect*⟩

²prospect *vb* : to explore especially for mineral deposits

pro·spec·tive \prə-'spek-tiv *also* 'prä-,spek-, prō-'spek-, prä-'spek-\ *adj* **1** : likely to come about ⟨*prospective* benefits⟩ **2** : likely to become ⟨a *prospective* buyer⟩

pros·pec·tor \'präs-,pek-tər\ *n* : a person who explores a region in search of valuable minerals (as metals or oil)

pro·spec·tus \prə-'spek-təs, prä-\ *n, pl* **-tus·es** : a printed statement that describes something (as a new business) and is sent out to people who may want to take part (as by investing)

pros·per \'präs-pər\ *vb* **pros·pered; pros·per·ing** \-p(ə-)riŋ\ **1** : to succeed or make money in something one is doing **2** : THRIVE 1, FLOURISH **3** : to cause to become prosperous

pros·per·i·ty \prä-'sper-ət-ē\ *n* : the state of being pros-

\ə\ **abut**	\au̇\ **out**	\i\ **tip**	\ȯ\ **saw**	\u̇\ **foot**	
\ər\ **further**	\ch\ **chin**	\ī\ **life**	\ȯi\ **coin**	\y\ **yet**	
\a\ **mat**	\e\ **pet**	\j\ **job**	\th\ **thin**	\yü\ **few**	
\ā\ **take**	\ē\ **easy**	\ŋ\ **sing**	\th\ **this**	\yu̇\ **cure**	
\ä\ **cot, cart**	\g\ **go**	\ō\ **bone**	\ü\ **food**	\zh\ **vision**	

perous or successful

pros·per·ous \'präs-p(ə-)rəs\ *adj* **1** : having or showing success or financial good fortune **2** : strong and healthy in growth — **pros·per·ous·ly** *adv*

pros·tate \'präs-ˌtāt\ *also* **pros·tat·ic** \prä-'stat-ik\ *adj* : of, relating to, or being the prostate gland

prostate gland *n* : a body around the base of the male urethra in mammals that is part muscle and part gland and produces a secretion that is a major part of the fluid given off usually during an orgasm

pros·the·sis \präs-'thē-səs, 'präs-thə-\ *n, pl* **-the·ses** \-ˌsēz\ : an artificial device that replaces a missing part of the body

¹pros·ti·tute \'präs-tə-ˌt(y)üt\ *vb* **-tut·ed; -tut·ing** : to put (as one's talents) to unworthy uses : DEBASE

²prostitute *n* : a person who engages in sexual activities for money

pros·ti·tu·tion \ˌpräs-tə-'t(y)ü-shən\ *n* **1** : the acts or practices of a prostitute **2** : the state of being prostituted

¹pros·trate \'präs-ˌtrāt\ *adj* **1** : stretched out with the face on the ground **2** : lacking strength or energy

²prostrate *vb* **pros·trat·ed; pros·trat·ing** **1** : to throw or put into a prostrate position **2** : to bring to a weak or powerless condition ⟨*prostrated* with grief⟩

pros·tra·tion \prä-'strā-shən\ *n* **1 a** : the act of assuming a prostrate position **b** : the state of being prostrate **2** : complete physical or mental exhaustion : COLLAPSE

prosy \'prō-zē\ *adj* **pros·i·er; -est** : PROSAIC

prot·ac·tin·i·um \ˌprōt-ˌak-'tin-ē-əm\ *n* : a shiny metallic radioactive element of short life — see ELEMENT table

pro·tag·o·nist \prō-'tag-ə-nəst\ *n* : the chief character in a play, novel, or story

pro·te·an \'prōt-ē-ən\ *adj* : easily taking different shapes or roles [from *Proteus,* a god of the sea in Greek mythology who could change his form at will]

pro·tect \prə-'tekt\ *vb* : to cover or shield from something that would destroy or injure : GUARD

pro·tec·tion \prə-'tek-shən\ *n* **1 a** : the act of protecting ⟨under our *protection*⟩ **b** : the state of being protected ⟨the open boat offered no *protection* from the weather⟩ **2** : a person or thing that protects

pro·tec·tive \prə-'tek-tiv\ *adj* : giving or meant to give protection — **pro·tec·tive·ly** *adv* — **pro·tec·tive·ness** *n*

protective coloration *n* : coloration by which a living thing appears less visible or less attractive to predators

pro·tec·tor \prə-'tek-tər\ *n* **1** : a person or thing that protects or is intended to protect **2** : a person who takes charge of a kingdom while the king or queen is too young to rule : REGENT

pro·tec·tor·ate \prə-'tek-t(ə-)rət\ *n* **1 a** : government by a protector **b** : the office or period of rule of a protector **2** : a small country ruled by a larger one

pro·té·gé \'prōt-ə-ˌzhā\ *n* : a person under the care and protection of another [French, derived from *protéger* "to protect"]

pro·tein \'prō-ˌtēn, 'prōt-ē-ən\ *n* : any of numerous nitrogen-containing substances that consist of chains of amino acids, are important parts of all living cells, are a necessary part of the human diet, and are supplied especially by such foods as meat, milk, and eggs — **pro·tein·aceous** \ˌprō-ˌ°n-'ā-shəs, ˌprō-ˌtēn-, ˌprōt-ē-ən-\ *adj*

pro tem·po·re \prō-'tem-pə-rē\ *adv* : for the present ⟨president *pro tempore*⟩

Pro·tero·zo·ic \ˌprät-ə-rə-'zō-ik, ˌprōt-\ *adj* : of, relating to, or being an eon of geological history that includes the span of time between the Archean and the Phanerozoic, perhaps exceeds in length all of following geological time, and is marked by rocks which contain a few fossils indicating the existence of worms related to the earthworms and of primitive plants; *also* : relating to the corresponding system of rocks — see GEOLOGIC TIME table — **Proterozoic** *n*

¹pro·test \'prō-ˌtest\ *n* : a complaint, objection, or display of unwillingness or disapproval

²pro·test \prə-'test, 'prō-ˌtest, prō-'test\ *vb* **1** : to declare positively : ASSERT ⟨*protested* their innocence⟩ **2 a** : to make a protest against ⟨*protested* the higher tax rate⟩ **b** : to object strongly ⟨*protest* against a ruling⟩ — **pro·test·er** *or* **pro·tes·tor** \-'tes-tər, -ˌtes-\ *n*

prot·es·tant \'prät-əs-tənt, *sense 2 is also* prə-'tes-\ *n* **1** *cap* : a member of one of the Christian churches that separated from the Roman Catholic church in the 16th century or of a church founded by members of these churches **2** : one who protests — **protestant** *adj, often cap* — **Prot·es·tant·ism** \'prät-əs-tənt-ˌiz-əm\ *n*

pro·tes·ta·tion \ˌprät-əs-'tā-shən, ˌprō-ˌtes-\ *n* **1** : the act of protesting **2** : a positive declaration

pro·tho·rax \(')prō-'thō(ə)r-ˌaks, -'thó(ə)r-\ *n* : the first segment of the thorax of an insect

pro·tist \'prōt-əst\ *n* : any of a group or in some classifications a kingdom of one-celled or noncellular organisms including bacteria, protozoans, various algae and fungi, and sometimes viruses — compare ANIMAL KINGDOM, MINERAL KINGDOM, PLANT KINGDOM

pro·to·coc·cus \ˌprōt-ə-'käk-əs\ *n* : any of a genus of globe-shaped green algae most of which live on land

pro·to·col \'prōt-ə-ˌkȯl\ *n* **1** : an original copy or record of a document **2** : a code of diplomatic or military rules of behavior

pro·ton \'prō-ˌtän\ *n* : an atomic particle that occurs in the nucleus of every atom and carries a positive charge equal in size to the negative charge of an electron — **pro·ton·ic** \prō-'tän-ik\ *adj*

pro·to·plan·et \'prōt-ō-ˌplan-ət\ *n* : a whirling mass of gas that rotates around a sun and is believed to become a planet

pro·to·plasm \'prōt-ə-ˌplaz-əm\ *n* : a mixture of protein, various organic and inorganic substances, and water that makes up the living nucleus, cytoplasm, plastids, and mitochondria of the cell and is considered the physical basis of life — **pro·to·plas·mic** \ˌprōt-ə-'plaz-mik\ *adj*

pro·to·type \'prōt-ə-ˌtīp\ *n* : an original model on which something is patterned

pro·to·zoa \ˌprōt-ə-'zō-ə\ *n pl* : tiny animals that are protozoans

pro·to·zo·an \ˌprōt-ə-'zō-ən\ *n* : any of a phylum or group of tiny animals that are not divided into cells and have varied structure and physiology and often complicated life cycles — **protozoan** *adj*

pro·to·zo·ol·o·gist \ˌprōt-ə-zō-'äl-ə-jəst, -zə-'wäl-\ *n* : a specialist in protozoology

pro·to·zo·ol·o·gy \ˌprōt-ə-zō-'äl-ə-jē, -zə-'wäl-\ *n* : a branch of zoology dealing with protozoans

pro·tract \prō-'trakt\ *vb* : PROLONG

pro·trac·tor \prō-'trak-tər\ *n* : an instrument for drawing and measuring angles

pro·trude \prō-'trüd\ *vb* **pro·trud·ed; pro·trud·ing** : to stick out or cause to stick out

protractor

pro·tru·sion \prō-'trü-zhən\ *n* **1** : the act of protruding : the state of being protruded **2** : something that protrudes

pro·tu·ber·ance \prō-'t(y)ü-b(ə-)rən(t)s\ *n* **1** : the quality or state of bulging beyond a surrounding surface **2** : ¹BULGE

pro·tu·ber·ant \prō-'t(y)ü-b(ə-)rənt\ *adj* : bulging beyond the surrounding surface

proud \'praud\ *adj* **1 a** : having or displaying excessive self-esteem ⟨a *proud* manner⟩ **b** : much pleased ⟨*proud* parents of a hero⟩ **c** : having proper self-respect ⟨too *proud* to beg⟩ **2** : MAGNIFICENT 1, GLORIOUS ⟨a *proud* record⟩ **3** : VIGOROUS 1, SPIRITED ⟨a *proud* horse⟩ — **proud·ly** *adv*

prove \'prüv\ *vb* **proved; proved** *or* **prov·en** \'prü-vən\; **prov·ing** **1** : to test by an experiment or a standard **2 a** : to show the truth of by evidence **b** : to check the correctness of (as an arithmetic problem) **3** : to show the genuineness of ⟨*prove* a will⟩ **4** : to turn out especially after trial or test ⟨the new automobile engine *proved* to be impractical⟩ — **prov·able** \'prü-və-bəl\ *adj*

Pro·ven·çal \,präv-ən-'säl, ,prōv-\ *n* **1** : a person born or living in Provence **2** : a Romance language spoken in southeastern France — **Provençal** *adj*

prov·en·der \'präv-ən-dər\ *n* **1** : dry food for domestic animals : FEED **2** : FOOD 1

prov·erb \'präv-,ərb\ *n* : a brief popular saying expressing a wise thought

pro·ver·bi·al \prə-'vər-bē-əl\ *adj* **1** : of, relating to, or resembling a proverb ⟨*proverbial* wisdom⟩ **2** : commonly spoken of ⟨the *proverbial* beginner's luck⟩ — **pro·ver·bi·al·ly** \-bē-ə-lē\ *adv*

Prov·erbs \'präv-,ərbz\ *n* — see BIBLE table

pro·vide \prə-'vīd\ *vb* **pro·vid·ed; pro·vid·ing** **1** : to take care of beforehand ⟨*provide* against a possible scarcity⟩ **2** : to state as a condition : STIPULATE ⟨the contract *provided* for 10 paid holidays⟩ **3** : to supply what is needed for support ⟨*provides* for a large family⟩ **4** : ¹SUPPLY 2b, YIELD ⟨cows *provide* milk⟩ [Middle English *providen* "to provide", from Latin *providēre*, literally "to see ahead", from *pro-* "ahead, forward" and *vidēre* "to see" — related to VISION] — **pro·vid·er** *n*

pro·vid·ed \prə-'vīd-əd\ *conj* : IF 1

prov·i·dence \'präv-əd-ən(t)s, -ə-,den(t)s\ *n* **1 a** *often cap* : divine guidance or care **b** *cap* : God as the guide and protector of all human beings **2** : the quality or state of being provident : PRUDENCE

prov·i·dent \'präv-əd-ənt, -ə-,dent\ *adj* **1** : providing for future needs **2** : FRUGAL — **prov·i·dent·ly** *adv*

prov·i·den·tial \,präv-ə-'den-chəl\ *adj* **1** : of, relating to, or determined by Providence ⟨a *providential* plan⟩ **2** : FORTUNATE 1, TIMELY ⟨a *providential* escape⟩ — **prov·i·den·tial·ly** \-'dench-(ə-)lē\ *adv*

prov·ince \'präv-ən(t)s\ *n* **1 a** : a country or region brought under the control of the ancient Roman government **b** : a usually large division of a country having its own government ⟨Canadian *provinces*⟩ **c** *pl* : all of a country except the capital or chief city **2** : the jurisdiction of an archbishop or metropolitan or of a religious province **3** : proper or appropriate business or area of skill, knowledge, or interest ⟨a legal question outside the physician's *province*⟩

¹**pro·vin·cial** \prə-'vin-chəl\ *n* **1** : a person living in or coming from a province **2** : a provincial person

²**provincial** *adj* **1** : of, relating to, or coming from a province **2 a** : limited in outlook : NARROW **b** : lacking the ways and manners of city people **3** : of or relating to a style (as in furniture) marked by simple design and plain decoration — **pro·vin·ci·al·i·ty** \-,vin-chē-'al-ət-ē\ *n* — **pro·vin·cial·ly** \-'vinch-(ə-)lē\ *adv*

pro·vin·cial·ism \prə-'vin-chə-,liz-əm\ *n* **1** : a local word, phrase, or idiom **2** : the quality or state of being provincial

proving ground *n* : a place for scientific testing

¹**pro·vi·sion** \prə-'vizh-ən\ *n* **1 a** : the act or process of providing ⟨*provision* of transportation for the trip⟩ **b** : something done beforehand : PREPARATION ⟨make *provision* for emergencies⟩ **2** : a stock of materials or supplies; *esp* : a stock of food — usually used in pl. **3** : ¹CONDITION 1 ⟨a constitutional *provision*⟩

²**provision** *vb* **pro·vi·sioned; pro·vi·sion·ing** \-'vizh-(ə-)niŋ\ : to supply with provisions

pro·vi·sion·al \prə-'vizh-nəl, -ən-ᵊl\ *adj* : serving for the time being ⟨a *provisional* government⟩ ⟨*provisional* arrangements⟩ — **pro·vi·sion·al·ly** \-ē\ *adv*

pro·vi·so \prə-'vī-zō\ *n, pl* **-sos** *or* **-soes** **1** : a sentence or clause in a legal document in which a condition is stated **2** : a limiting statement ⟨released them with the *proviso* that they behave⟩

prov·o·ca·tion \,präv-ə-'kā-shən\ *n* **1** : the act of provoking **2** : something that provokes

pro·voc·a·tive \prə-'väk-ət-iv\ *adj* : serving or tending to provoke ⟨*provocative* comments⟩ — **pro·voc·a·tive·ly** *adv* — **pro·voc·a·tive·ness** *n*

pro·voke \prə-'vōk\ *vb* **pro·voked; pro·vok·ing** **1** : to arouse to action or feeling; *esp* : to excite to anger **2** : to stir up : BRING ABOUT ⟨*provoke* an argument⟩ [Middle English *provoken* "to arouse to strong feeling or action", from early French *provoquer* (same meaning), from Latin *provocare* "to call forth, stir up", from *pro-* "forth, forward" and *vocare* "to call" — related to ADVOCATE, REVOKE, VOCATION]

syn PROVOKE, EXCITE, STIMULATE mean to arouse into doing or feeling something. PROVOKE stresses the feeling or action called forth ⟨my stories usually *provoke* laughter⟩ EXCITE suggests the stirring up of great feeling ⟨news of the victory *excited* joy and relief⟩ STIMULATE suggests a rousing out of laziness, slumber, or unconcern ⟨a speech that *stimulated* the crowd to shout slogans⟩

pro·vok·ing \prə-'vō-kiŋ\ *adj* : causing mild anger : ANNOYING ⟨a *provoking* delay⟩ — **pro·vok·ing·ly** \-kiŋ-lē\ *adv*

pro·vost \'prō-,vōst, 'präv-əst, *before* "marshal" *often* ,prō-vō-\ *n* : a high managing officer (as in a university)

provost marshal *n* : a military police chief

prow \'prau̇\ *n* : the bow of a ship

prow·ess \'prau̇-əs\ *n* **1** : great bravery especially in battle **2** : very great ability

prowl \'prau̇(ə)l\ *vb* **1** : to move about or wander like a wild beast seeking prey **2** : to roam over like a wild beast ⟨*prowl* the streets⟩ — **prowl** *n* — **prowl·er** *n*

prowl car *n* : SQUAD CAR

prox·im·i·ty \präk-'sim-ət-ē\ *n* : the state or condition of being near : NEARNESS

proxy \'präk-sē\ *n, pl* **prox·ies** **1** : authority held by one person to act for another (as in voting) **2 a** : a person holding authority to act for another **b** : a written paper giving a person such authority — **proxy** *adj*

prude \'prüd\ *n* : a person who cares so much about proper speech and conduct as to be annoying to others — **prud·ish** \'prüd-ish\ *adj* — **prud·ish·ly** *adv* — **prud·ish·ness** *n*

pru·dence \'prüd-ᵊn(t)s\ *n* **1** : the ability to govern and discipline oneself by the use of reason **2** : skill and good judgment in the management of affairs

pru·dent \'prüd-ᵊnt\ *adj* **1** : clever and careful in action and judgment **2** : DISCREET **3** : FRUGAL — **pru·dent·ly** *adv*

pru·den·tial \prü-'den-chəl\ *adj* **1** : of, relating to, or resulting from prudence **2** : using prudence

prud·ery \'prüd-(ə-)rē\ *n, pl* **-er·ies** **1** : the quality or state of being prudish **2** : a prudish remark or act

¹**prune** \'prün\ *n* : a dried plum

²**prune** *vb* **pruned; prun·ing** **1** : to cut off the parts of a woody plant that are dead or not wanted ⟨*prune* the hedge⟩ **2 a** : to reduce by getting rid of matter that is not necessary or wanted ⟨*prune* an essay⟩ ⟨*prune* a budget⟩ **b** : to remove as unnecessary — **prun·er** *n*

\ə\ abut	\au̇\ out	\i\ tip	\ȯ\ saw	\u̇\ foot
\ər\ further	\ch\ chin	\ī\ life	\ȯi\ coin	\y\ yet
\a\ mat	\e\ pet	\j\ job	\th\ thin	\yü\ few
\ā\ take	\ē\ easy	\ŋ\ sing	\th\ this	\yu̇\ cure
\ä\ cot, cart	\g\ go	\ō\ bone	\ü\ food	\zh\ vision

pru·ri·ent \'prür-ē-ənt\ *adj* : having or revealing indecent desires or thoughts — **pru·ri·ent·ly** *adv*

¹pry \'prī\ *vb* **pried; pry·ing** : to look closely : PEER; *esp* : to search curiously into other people's affairs [Middle English *prien* "to look at closely"]

²pry *vb* **pried; pry·ing** **1** : to raise, move, or pull apart with or as if with a lever ⟨*pry* off a tight lid⟩ **2** : to force out, detach, or open with difficulty ⟨could not *pry* a secret out of her⟩ [an altered form of *prize* "to move with or as if with a lever"]

³pry *n* : a tool for prying

pry·ing *adj* : given to asking about other people's affairs especially in an annoying or meddlesome way — **syn** see CURIOUS — **pry·ing·ly** \-iŋ-lē\ *adv*

psalm \'säm, 'sälm\ *n* **1** : a sacred song or poem **2** *cap* : one of the hymns that make up the Old Testament Book of Psalms

> **Word History** The Greek word *psallein* originally meant "to pull" or "to pluck". It then came to be used with the meaning "to play a stringed musical instrument". From this verb came the noun *psalmos,* which literally meant "the twanging of a harp". Since harp music often accompanied singing, *psalmos* took on the meaning of "a song sung to harp music" and later simply "a song or poem". It was borrowed into Latin as *psalmus* and came into English as *psalm.* [Old English *psealm* "psalm", from Latin *psalmus* (same meaning), from Greek *psalmos* "psalm", literally "twanging of a harp", from *psallein* "to pluck, play a stringed musical instrument"]

psalm·ist \'säm-əst, 'säl-məst\ *n* : a writer or composer of psalms

psalm·o·dy \'säm-əd-ē, 'säl-məd-\ *n, pl* **-dies** **1** : the art or practice of singing psalms in worship **2** : a collection of psalms

Psalms \'sämz, 'sälmz\ *n* — see BIBLE table

Psal·ter \'sól-tər\ *n* **1** : the Book of Psalms **2** : a collection of Psalms

psal·tery *also* **psal·try** \'sól-t(ə-)rē\ *n pl* **-ter·ies** *also* **-tries** : an ancient stringed musical instrument resembling the zither

p's and q's \ˌpēz-°n-'kyüz\ *n* : something (as manners) that one should be careful about ⟨always minded my *p's and q's* around my aunts and uncles⟩

pseudo- *combining form* : not genuine : fake [derived from Greek *pseudēs* "false"]

pseu·do \'süd-ō\ *adj* : not genuine : FAKE

pseud·onym \'süd-°n-ˌim\ *n* : a fictitious name; *esp* : PEN NAME

pseu·do·pod \'süd-ə-ˌpäd\ *n* : PSEUDOPODIUM

pseu·do·po·di·um \ˌsüd-ə-'pōd-ē-əm\ *n, pl* **-po·dia** \-ē-ə\ : an outward extension of part of a cell that is produced by the pressure of moving cytoplasm (as in an amoeba) and that helps to move the cell and to take in its food

pshaw \'shó\ *interj* — used to express irritation, contempt, or disbelief

psi \'sī\ *n* : the 23d letter of the Greek alphabet — Ψ or ψ

psi·lo·cy·bin \ˌsī-lə-'sī-bən\ *n* : a chemical that is obtained from a fungus and causes hallucinations

psit·ta·co·sis \ˌsit-ə-'kō-səs\ *n* : an infectious disease of birds caused by a rickettsia, marked by diarrhea and loss of weight and strength, and capable of being passed on to human beings — called also *parrot fever*

psych *also* **psyche** \'sīk\ *vb* **psyched; psych·ing** **1** : to make oneself psychologically ready — usually used with *up* ⟨*psyched* themselves up for the race⟩ **2** : to make uneasy — often used with *out*

psy·che \'sī-kē\ *n* **1** : ¹SOUL 2, SELF **2** : ¹MIND 2

¹psy·che·del·ic \ˌsī-kə-'del-ik\ *adj* **1** : of, relating to, or being a drug that has a serious effect on thinking or the way the mind works only temporarily **2 a** : imitating the effects of psychedelic drugs **b** : glowing brightly

²psychedelic *n* : a psychedelic drug

psy·chi·a·trist \sə-'kī-ə-trəst, sī-\ *n* : a specialist in psychiatry

psy·chi·a·try \sə-'kī-ə-trē, sī-\ *n* : a branch of medicine that deals with the mind, emotions, and behavior — **psy·chi·at·ric** \ˌsī-kē-'a-trik\ *adj*

¹psy·chic \'sī-kik\ *also* **psy·chi·cal** \-ki-kəl\ *adj* **1** : of or relating to the psyche **2** : not physical; *esp* : not to be explained by knowledge of natural laws **3** : sensitive to influences or forces believed to come from beyond the natural world — **psy·chi·cal·ly** \-ki-k(ə-)lē\ *adv*

²psychic *n* : a psychic person (as a medium)

psycho- *combining form* : mind : mental processes and activities ⟨*psycho*therapy⟩ [derived from Greek *psychē* "soul, mind, principle of life"]

psy·cho·anal·y·sis \ˌsī-kō-ə-'nal-ə-səs, -ˌsēz\ *n, pl* **-y·ses** \-ˌsēz\ : a method of explaining and treating mental and emotional disorders by having the patient talk freely about himself or herself and especially about dreams, problems, and early childhood memories and experiences

psy·cho·an·a·lyst \ˌsī-kō-'an-°l-əst\ *n* : a medical specialist who uses psychoanalysis to treat patients with mental or emotional disorders

psy·cho·an·a·lyt·ic \ˌsī-kō-ˌan-°l-'it-ik\ *also* **psy·cho·an·a·lyt·i·cal** \-i-kəl\ *adj* : of, relating to, or using psychoanalysis or its principles and techniques

psy·cho·an·a·lyze \ˌsi-kō-'an-°l-ˌīz\ *vb* : to treat by means of psychoanalysis

psy·cho·log·i·cal \ˌsī-kə-'läj-i-kəl\ *also* **psy·cho·log·ic** \-'läj-ik\ *adj* **1 a** : of or relating to psychology **b** : MENTAL 1 **2** : meant to influence the will or mind — **psy·cho·log·i·cal·ly** \-i-k(ə-)lē\ *adv*

psy·chol·o·gist \sī-'käl-ə-jəst\ *n* : a specialist in psychology

psy·chol·o·gy \sī-'käl-ə-jē\ *n, pl* **-gies** **1** : the science or study of mind and behavior **2** : the particular ways in which an individual or group thinks or behaves [from scientific Latin *psychologia* "the study of the mind and behavior", derived from Greek *psychē* "soul, mind" and Greek *-logia* "science, study"]

psy·cho·path \'sī-kə-ˌpath\ *n* : a mentally ill or unstable person; *esp* : one who has a poorly balanced personality and does not feel guilty about not living up to normal social and moral responsibilities

psy·cho·sis \sī-'kō-səs\ *n, pl* **-cho·ses** \-'kō-ˌsēz\ : a serious mental illness marked by loss of or greatly lessened ability to test whether what one is thinking and feeling about the real world is really true

psy·cho·ther·a·pist \ˌsī-kō-'ther-ə-pəst\ *n* : a person (as a doctor or psychologist) who treats patients by psychotherapy

psy·cho·ther·a·py \ˌsī-kō-'ther-ə-pē\ *n* : treatment of mental or emotional disorder or of related bodily illnesses by psychological means

¹psy·chot·ic \sī-'kät-ik\ *adj* : of, relating to, or marked by psychosis

²psychotic *n* : a psychotic person

psy·chrom·e·ter \sī-'kräm-ət-ər\ *n* : an instrument for measuring the water vapor in the atmosphere by means of the difference in the readings of two thermometers when one of them is kept wet so that it is cooled by evaporation

ptar·mi·gan \'tär-mi-gən\ *n, pl* **ptarmigans** *or* **ptarmigan** : any of various grouses of northern regions with completely feathered feet

PT boat \(')pē-'tē-\ *n* : a high-speed motorboat usually equipped with tor-

ptarmigan: *top* summer, *bottom* winter

pedoes, machine guns, and depth charges

PTC \ˌpē-ˌtē-ˈsē\ *n* : PHENYLTHIOCARBAMIDE

pte·ri·do·phyte \tə-ˈrid-ə-ˌfīt\ *n* : any of a group of vascular plants that have roots, stems, and leaves, lack flowers or seeds, and include the ferns and related forms

ptero·dac·tyl \ˌter-ə-ˈdak-tᵊl\ *n* : an extinct flying reptile having a featherless membrane extending from the body along the arms and forming the supporting surface of the wings [from scientific Latin *Pterodactylus* "scientific name for the pterodactyl", from Greek *pteron* "wing" and Greek *daktylos* "finger"]

ptero·saur \ˈter-ə-ˌsȯ(ə)r\ *n* : PTERODACTYL

pto·maine \ˈtō-ˌmān, tō-ˈmān\ *n* : any of various organic compounds formed by the action of decay-producing bacteria on nitrogen-containing matter and including some which are poisonous

ptomaine poisoning *n* : food poisoning caused usually by bacteria or their products

pty·a·lin \ˈtī-ə-lən\ *n* : an enzyme found in the saliva of many animals that helps change starch into sugar

pub \ˈpəb\ *n, chiefly British* : PUBLIC HOUSE 2

pu·ber·ty \ˈpyü-bərt-ē\ *n* **1** : the condition of being or the period of becoming first capable of reproducing sexually that is marked by maturing of the sex organs, development of secondary sex characteristics, and in the human female by the occurring of the first menstruation **2** : the age at which puberty occurs often defined legally as 14 in boys and 12 in girls

pu·bic \ˈpyü-bik\ *adj* : of, relating to, or located near the pubis

pu·bis \ˈpyü-bəs\ *n, pl* **pu·bes** \-ˌbēz\ : the front and lower of the three principal bones composing each hipbone

¹pub·lic \ˈpəb-lik\ *adj* **1 a** : of, relating to, belonging to, or affecting all the people ⟨*public* law⟩ **b** : provided by the government ⟨*public* education⟩ **c** : relating to or engaged in the service of the community or nation ⟨*public* life⟩ **2** : of or relating to community interests as opposed to private affairs ⟨a radio program in the *public* interest⟩ **3** : devoted to the general welfare ⟨needed leaders with *public* spirit⟩ **4** : open to or shared by all ⟨a *public* meeting⟩ ⟨the *public* library⟩ **5 a** : generally known ⟨the story became *public*⟩ **b** : WELL-KNOWN ⟨a *public* figure⟩ [Middle English *publique* "relating to the people as a whole, public", from early French *public, publique* (same meaning), from Latin *publicus* "belonging to the people as a whole" from an earlier variant form *poplicus* (same meaning), from *populus* "the people" — related to POPULAR, REPUBLIC] — **pub·lic·ly** *adv*

²public *n* **1** : a place open or visible to people ⟨seen in *public*⟩ **2** : the people as a whole ⟨a lecture open to the *public*⟩ **3** : a particular group of people ⟨a writer's *public*⟩

public–address system *n* : a set of equipment including microphone and loudspeakers used for broadcasting to a large audience in an auditorium or out of doors

pub·li·can \ˈpəb-li-kən\ *n* : a tax collector for the ancient Romans

pub·li·ca·tion \ˌpəb-lə-ˈkā-shən\ *n* **1** : the act or process of publishing **2** : a published work

public house *n* **1** : INN, HOTEL **2** *chiefly British* : a licensed saloon or bar

pub·li·cist \ˈpəb-lə-səst\ *n* **1 a** : an expert in international law **b** : an expert on public affairs **2** : PRESS AGENT

pub·lic·i·ty \(ˌ)pə-ˈblis-ət-ē\ *n* **1** : the condition of being public or publicly known **2** : an act or device designed to attract public interest; *esp* : information with a news value designed to further the interests of a place, person, or cause **3 a** : an action that gains public attention **b** : the attention so gained

pub·li·cize \ˈpəb-lə-ˌsīz\ *vb* **-cized; -ciz·ing** : to give publicity to

public relations *n* **1** : the business of creating public goodwill for a person, firm, or institution **2** : the degree of un-

derstanding and goodwill achieved

public school *n* **1** : a British private school that gives a liberal education and prepares students for the universities **2** : an elementary or secondary school supported by taxes and operated by a local government

public servant *n* : a governmental official or employee

public service *n* **1** : the business of supplying a commodity (as electricity or gas) or service (as transportation) to any or all members of a community **2** : governmental employment; *esp* : CIVIL SERVICE

public television *n* : a television broadcasting service whose programs do not include commercial messages

public utility *n* : a business organization performing a public service and subject to special governmental regulation

public works *n pl* : works (as schools, highways, or docks) constructed with public funds for public use

pub·lish \ˈpəb-lish\ *vb* **1** : to make generally known : make public announcement of **2 a** : to produce or release for publication; *esp* : ²PRINT 2c **b** : to print the work of ⟨*publish* a poet⟩ — **pub·lish·able** \-ə-bəl\ *adj*

pub·lish·er \ˈpəb-lish-ər\ *n* : one that publishes; *esp* : one that sends out and offers for sale printed matter (as books, magazines, or newspapers)

¹puck \ˈpək\ *n* : a fairy or spirit who plays tricks on human beings [Old English *pūca* "a fairy who plays tricks"]

²puck *n* : a rubber disk used in ice hockey [from a dialect word *puck* "to hit, poke", derived from *poke* "jab, prod"]

¹puck·er \ˈpək-ər\ *vb* **puck·ered; puck·er·ing** \-(ə-)riŋ\ : to contract into folds or wrinkles ⟨*pucker* one's lips⟩

²pucker *n* : a fold or wrinkle caused by puckering — **puck·ery** \ˈpək-(ə-)rē\ *adj*

pud·ding \ˈpu̇d-iŋ\ *n* **1** : a boiled or baked soft food usually with a cereal base ⟨corn *pudding*⟩ **2** : a soft, spongy, or thick creamy dessert ⟨bread *pudding*⟩

pudding stone *n* : ³CONGLOMERATE 1

¹pud·dle \ˈpəd-ᵊl\ *n* : a very small pool (as of dirty or muddy water)

²puddle *vb* **pud·dled; pud·dling** \ˈpəd-liŋ, -ᵊl-iŋ\ **1** : to make muddy **2** : to cover with puddles — **pud·dler** \-lər, -ᵊl-ər\ *n*

pudgy \ˈpəj-ē\ *adj* **pudg·i·er; -est** : short and plump — **pudg·i·ness** *n*

pueb·lo \pü-ˈeb-lō, ˈpweb-, pyü-ˈeb-\ *n, pl* **pueblos** **1** : an Indian village of Arizona or New Mexico consisting of flat-roofed stone or adobe houses joined in groups sometimes several stories high **2** *cap* : a member of any of several American Indian peoples of Arizona and New Mexico [from Spanish *pueblo* "village", literally "people", from Latin *populus* "people"]

pu·er·ile \ˈpyü(-ə)r-əl, -ˌīl\ *adj* : showing a lack of maturity, seriousness, or good judgment ⟨*puerile* remarks⟩ — **pu·er·il·i·ty** \ˌpyü(-ə)r-ˈil-ət-ē\ *n*

¹puff \ˈpəf\ *vb* **1 a** : to blow in short gusts **b** : to breathe hard ⟨*puffed* as we climbed the hill⟩ **c** : to blow by or as if by puffs ⟨the locomotive *puffed* smoke⟩ **2** : to swell or become swollen with or as if with air ⟨the sprained ankle *puffed* up⟩ ⟨*puffed* up with pride⟩

²puff *n* **1 a** : an act or instance of puffing : WHIFF, GUST **b** : a cloud (as of smoke or steam) given off in a puff **2** : a light pastry that rises high in baking **3 a** : a slight swelling **b** : a small fluffy pad for applying cosmetic powder **c** : a quilted bed covering — **puff·i·ness** \ˈpəf-ē-nəs\ *n* — **puffy** \ˈpəf-ē\ *adj*

puff adder *n* : HOGNOSE SNAKE

puff·ball \ˈpəf-ˌbȯl\ *n* : any of various mostly edible globe-shaped fungi that release ripe spores in a cloud resem-

\ə\ abut	\au̇\ out	\i\ tip	\ȯ\ saw	\u̇\ foot
\ər\ further	\ch\ chin	\ī\ life	\ȯi\ coin	\y\ yet
\a\ mat	\e\ pet	\j\ job	\th\ thin	\yü\ few
\ā\ take	\ē\ easy	\ŋ\ sing	\th\ this	\yu̇\ cure
\ä\ cot, cart	\g\ go	\ō\ bone	\ü\ food	\zh\ vision

bling smoke when they are disturbed

puff·er \'pəf-ər\ *n* **1** : one that puffs **2** : any of various fishes which can inflate their bodies with air and many of which are very poisonous

puf·fin \'pəf-ən\ *n* : any of several seabirds that are related to the auks and have a short thick neck and a deep grooved bill marked with different colors

pug \'pəg\ *n* : any of a breed of small sturdy compact dogs having a short coat, tightly curled tail, and broad wrinkled face

pug

pu·gi·list \'pyü-jə-ləst\ *n* : [1]BOXER — **pu·gi·lis·tic** \,pyü-jə-'lis-tik\ *adj*

pug·na·cious \,pəg-'nā-shəs\ *adj* : showing a readiness to fight **syn** see BELLIGERENT — **pug·na·cious·ly** *adv* — **pug·nac·i·ty** \-'nas-ət-ē\ *n*

pug nose *n* : a usually short nose turning up at the end — **pug–nosed** \'pəg-'nōzd\ *adj*

puis·sance \'pwis-³n(t)s, 'pyü-ə-sən(t)s\ *n* : STRENGTH 1, POWER — **puis·sant** \-³nt, -sənt\ *adj*

pule \'pyü(ə)l\ *vb* **puled; pul·ing** : [1]WHINE, WHIMPER

[1]pull \'pul\ *vb* **1** : to separate forcibly from a natural or firm attachment ⟨*pull* a tooth⟩ ⟨*pull* up carrots⟩ **2 a** : to use force on so as to cause or tend to cause motion toward the force ⟨*pull* a wagon⟩ ⟨*pull* at a rope⟩ **b** : to stretch repeatedly ⟨*pull* taffy⟩ **c** : to strain by stretching ⟨*pull* a tendon⟩ **d** : [1]MOVE 1 ⟨the car *pulled* out of the driveway⟩ **3** : to draw apart : TEAR **4** : [1]REMOVE 2 ⟨*pulled* the pitcher in the third inning⟩ **5** : to bring into the open ⟨*pulled* a knife⟩ **6** : to carry out with skill or daring : COMMIT ⟨*pull* a robbery⟩ **7** : ATTRACT 2 ⟨*pull* customers⟩ — **pull·er** *n* — **pull oneself together** : to regain one's calmness — **pull one's leg** : to deceive someone playfully — **pull together** : to work in harmony : COOPERATE

[2]pull *n* **1 a** : the act or an instance of pulling **b** : the effort put forth in pulling ⟨a long *pull* uphill⟩ **2** : special influence ⟨got his job through *pull*⟩ **3** : a device for pulling ⟨a drawer *pull*⟩ **4** : a force that attracts or influences ⟨the *pull* of gravity⟩

pul·let \'pul-ət\ *n* : a young hen; *esp* : a hen of the domestic chicken that is less than a year old [Middle English *polet* "a very young chicken or fowl", from early French *poulet* (same meaning), derived from earlier *poul* "a male chicken, cock" — related to [2]POOL, POULTRY]

pul·ley \'pul-ē\ *n, pl* **pulleys** : a small wheel with a grooved rim used with a rope or chain to change the direction of a pulling force and in combination to increase the force applied for lifting

Pull·man \'pul-mən\ *n* : a railroad passenger car with comfortable furnishings especially for night travel

[1]pull·over \,pul-,ō-vər\ *adj* : put on by being pulled over the head ⟨*pullover* sweater⟩

[2]pull·over \'pul-,ō-vər\ *n* : a pullover garment

pull through *vb* : to help through or to survive a dangerous or difficult period or situation ⟨had pneumonia but she *pulled through*⟩

pul·mo·nary \'pul-mə-,ner-ē, 'pəl-\ *adj* **1** : of or relating to the lungs **2** : carried on by the lungs

pulmonary artery *n* : an artery that carries blood containing carbon dioxide from the right side of the heart to the lungs

pulley

pulmonary circulation *n* : the passage of blood from the right side of the heart through arteries to the lungs where it picks up oxygen and is returned to the left side of the heart by veins

pulmonary vein *n* : a vein that returns oxygen-rich blood from the lungs to the left side of the heart

[1]pulp \'pəlp\ *n* **1 a** : the soft juicy or fleshy part of a fruit or vegetable ⟨the *pulp* of an apple⟩ **b** : a mass of vegetable matter from which the moisture has been squeezed ⟨*pulp* left from making orange juice⟩ **2** : the soft sensitive tissue that fills the central cavity of a tooth **3** : a material prepared chiefly from wood but also from other materials (as rags) and used in making paper products **4** : pulpy state ⟨beaten to a *pulp*⟩ **5** : a magazine or book on rough-surfaced paper and often dealing with sensational material

[2]pulp *vb* : to make into a pulp — **pulp·er** *n*

pul·pit \'pul-,pit *also* 'pəl-, -pət\ *n* **1** : a raised platform or high desk used in preaching or leading a worship service **2** : the preaching profession **3** : a job as a preacher

pulp·wood \'pəlp-,wud\ *n* : wood (as of aspen, hemlock, pine, or spruce) used in making pulp for paper

pulpy \'pəl-pē\ *adj* **pulp·i·er; -est** : resembling or consisting of pulp — **pulp·i·ness** *n*

pul·sate \'pəl-,sāt\ *vb* **pul·sat·ed; pul·sat·ing** : to expand and contract in a rhythmic manner ⟨my heart *pulsated* visibly⟩

pul·sa·tion \,pəl-'sā-shən\ *n* : expanding and contracting movement or action (as of an artery); *also* : a single throb of such movement

[1]pulse \'pəls\ *n* : the edible seeds of several crops (as peas, beans, or lentils) of the legume family; *also* : a plant yielding pulse

[2]pulse *n* **1** : a regular throbbing caused in the arteries by the contractions of the heart **2 a** : rhythmical beating or throbbing **b** : PULSATION, BEAT, THROB **3 a** : a brief variation of a quantity (as electrical current) whose value is normally constant **b** : an electromagnetic wave or a sound wave lasting only a short length of time

[3]pulse *vb* **pulsed; puls·ing** : to display a pulse or pulsation ⟨the veins in your forehead *pulsed*⟩

pul·ver·ize \'pəl-və-,rīz\ *vb* **-ized; -iz·ing** **1** : to beat or grind into a powder or dust **2** : to destroy as if by pulverizing

pu·ma \'p(y)ü-mə\ *n, pl* **pumas** *also* **puma** : COUGAR

pum·ice \'pəm-əs\ *n* : a very light glass that is formed by the rapid cooling of lava from volcanoes, is full of small holes, and is used especially in powder form for smoothing and polishing

pum·mel \'pəm-əl\ *vb* **-meled** *or* **-melled; -mel·ing** *or* **-mel·ling** \-(ə-)liŋ\ : [2]POUND 2a, BEAT, THUMP

[1]pump \'pəmp\ *n* : a device that raises, transfers, or compresses fluids especially by suction or pressure or both

[2]pump *vb* **1** : to raise, transfer, or compress by means of a pump ⟨*pump* up water⟩ **2** : to free (as from water or air) by the use of a pump ⟨*pump* a boat dry⟩ **3** : to fill by using a pump ⟨*pump* up a tire⟩ **4** : to draw, force, or drive onward in the manner of a pump ⟨the heart *pumps* blood into the arteries⟩ **5** : to move up and down like a pump handle ⟨*pump* the hand of a friend⟩ **6 a** : to question again and again to find out something **b** : to draw out by such questioning — **pump·er** *n*

[3]pump *n* : a low shoe gripping the foot chiefly at the toe and heel

pum·per·nick·el \'pəm-pər-,nik-əl\ *n* : a dark coarse somewhat sour rye bread

pump·kin \'pəŋ-kən, 'pəm(p)-kən\ *n* **1** : the usually round orange fruit of a vine related to the squashes and cucumber and widely used as food; *also* : a fruit (as a crookneck squash) of a closely related vine **2** : a usually hairy prickly vine that produces pumpkins

pump·kin·seed \-,sēd\ *n* **1** : a small brilliantly colored

North American freshwater sunfish   **2** : BLUEGILL

pun \'pən\ *n* : the humorous use of a word in such a way as to suggest different meanings or of words having the same sound but different meanings — **pun** *vb*

¹punch \'pənch\ *vb*   **1 a** : ¹PROD 1, POKE   **b** : ¹DRIVE 1a, HERD ⟨*punch* cattle⟩   **2 a** : to strike with the fist   **b** : to press, strike, or cause to work by or as if by punching ⟨*punch* a typewriter⟩   **3** : to pierce or stamp with a punch   **4** : to enter (as data) by punching keys [Middle English *punchen* "to prod, herd", from early French *poinçonner* "to prick, stamp", from *poinçon* "a pointed tool for making holes"] — **punch·er** *n*

²punch *n*   **1 a** : a quick blow with or as if with the fist   **2** : effective force ⟨the team was well trained but lacked *punch*⟩

³punch *n*   **1 a** : a tool for piercing, cutting, or stamping or for driving a nail   **b** : a device or machine for cutting holes or notches (as in paper or cardboard)   **2** : a hole or notch made by a punch

⁴punch *n* : a drink made of various and usually many ingredients and often flavored with wine or liquor [perhaps from a word in Hindi (the official language of India) *pāc* "five"; so called from the fact that it originally had five ingredients]

punch card *n* : a card with holes punched in particular positions to represent data — called also *punched card*

pun·cheon \'pən-chən\ *n* : a large barrel of varying size

punc·til·io \,pəŋ(k)-'til-ē-,ō\ *n, pl* **-i·os** : **1** : a small but important detail of conduct in a ceremony or in following a set of rules   **2** : careful following of set ways of doing things (as in social conduct)

punc·til·i·ous \,pəŋ(k)-'til-ē-əs\ *adj* : following exactly the details of proper ways of behaving — **punc·til·i·ous·ly** *adv* — **punc·til·i·ous·ness** *n*

punc·tu·al \'pəŋ(k)-chə(-wə)l\ *adj* : acting or usually acting at an appointed time or at a regularly scheduled time ⟨the trains were *punctual*⟩ — **punc·tu·al·i·ty** \,pəŋ(k)-chə-'wal-ət-ē\ *n* — **punc·tu·al·ly** \'pəŋ(k)-chə(-wə)-lē\ *adv*

punc·tu·ate \'pəŋ(k)-chə-,wāt\ *vb* **-at·ed; -at·ing**   **1** : to mark or divide with punctuation marks   **2** : to interrupt at intervals ⟨a speech *punctuated* by a harsh cough⟩

punc·tu·a·tion \,pəŋ(k)-chə-'wā-shən\ *n* : the act, practice, or system of inserting punctuation marks in written matter to make the meaning clear and separate parts (as clauses or sentences)

punctuation mark *n* : any of various marks or signs used in punctuation

PUNCTUATION MARKS

,	comma
;	semicolon
:	colon
.	period
— *or* –	dash
-	hyphen
⸗	double hyphen
?	question mark *or* interrogation point
¿ ?	question marks, Spanish
!	exclamation point
¡ !	exclamation points, Spanish
'	apostrophe
/	slash
( )	parentheses
[ ]	brackets *or* square brackets
⟨ ⟩	brackets *or* angle brackets
{ }	braces
" "	quotation marks
' '	quotation marks, single
« » *or* „ "	quotation marks, European
. . . *or*	ellipsis

¹punc·ture \'pəŋ(k)-chər\ *n*   **1** : the act of puncturing   **2**

: a hole or wound made by puncturing ⟨a slight *puncture* of the skin⟩ ⟨a tire *puncture*⟩

²puncture *vb* **punc·tured; punc·tur·ing** \'pəŋ(k)-chə-riŋ, 'pəŋ(k)-shriŋ\   **1** : to make a hole with a point ⟨a nail *punctured* the tire⟩   **2** : to suffer a puncture of ⟨*punctured* the tire on a nail⟩   **3** : to become punctured ⟨worn tires *puncture* easily⟩   **4** : to make useless or ridiculous as if by a puncture ⟨*puncture* an argument⟩

pun·gen·cy \'pən-jən-sē\ *n* : the quality or state of being pungent

pun·gent \'pən-jənt\ *adj*   **1** : sharply exciting to the mind ⟨*pungent* criticism⟩ ⟨*pungent* wit⟩   **2** : causing a sharp or irritating sensation; *esp* : sharp or harsh to the sense of taste or smell — **pun·gent·ly** *adv*

pun·ish \'pən-ish\ *vb*   **1** : to cause to experience pain or suffering for having done wrong ⟨*punish* criminals with imprisonment⟩   **2** : to inflict punishment for ⟨*punish* misbehavior⟩   **3** : to deal with or handle severely or roughly ⟨badly *punished* by an opponent⟩ — **pun·ish·able** \-ə-bəl\ *adj* — **pun·ish·er** *n*

syn PUNISH, DISCIPLINE mean to put a penalty on someone for doing wrong. PUNISH stresses giving some kind of pain or suffering to the wrongdoer rather than trying to reform the person ⟨*punished* the burglars by sending them to prison⟩ DISCIPLINE suggests penalizing the wrongdoer but stresses the effort to bring the person under control ⟨parents must *discipline* their children⟩

pun·ish·ment \'pən-ish-mənt\ *n*   **1 a** : the act of punishing   **b** : the state or fact of being punished ⟨persons undergoing *punishment*⟩   **2** : the penalty for a fault or crime ⟨the *punishment* for robbery⟩   **3** : severe, rough, or disastrous treatment

pu·ni·tive \'pyü-nət-iv\ *adj*   **1** : of or relating to punishment or penalties ⟨*punitive* law⟩   **2** : intended to inflict punishment ⟨a *punitive* expedition against outlaws⟩ — **pu·ni·tive·ly** *adv*

¹punk \'pəŋk\ *n* : a brutal ruffian : THUG [origin unknown]

²punk *adj* : very poor in quality : BAD, MISERABLE

³punk *n*   **1** : wood so decayed as to be dry, crumbly, and useful for starting a fire   **2** : a dry spongy substance prepared from plants and used to light fuses especially of fireworks [perhaps an altered form of *spunk* "delicate piece of wood suitable for starting a fire"]

¹punt \'pənt\ *n* : a long narrow flat-bottomed boat with square ends usually pushed along with a pole [probably from Old English *punt* "a flat-bottomed boat pushed along with a pole", from Latin *ponton-, ponto* "punt, floating bridge, pontoon" — related to PONTOON]

¹punt

²punt *vb* : to propel (as a punt) with a pole

³punt *vb* : to kick a football before it touches the ground when dropped from the hands [origin unknown] — **punt·er** *n*

⁴punt *n* : the act or an instance of punting a ball

pu·ny \'pyü-nē\ *adj* **pu·ni·er; -est** : slight or lesser in power, size, or importance : WEAK [from early French *puisné* "younger", literally "born afterward", from *puis* "afterward" and *né* "born"] — **pu·ni·ness** *n*

pup \'pəp\ *n* : PUPPY; *also* : one of the young of various

\ə\ abut		\aú\ out		\i\ tip		\ó\ saw		\ú\ foot
\ər\ further		\ch\ chin		\ī\ life		\ói\ coin		\y\ yet
\a\ mat		\e\ pet		\j\ job		\th\ thin		\yü\ few
\ā\ take		\ē\ easy		\ŋ\ sing		\th\ this		\yú\ cure
\ä\ cot, cart		\g\ go		\ō\ bone		\ü\ food		\zh\ vision

animals (as a seal or rat)

pu·pa \'pyü-pə\ *n, pl* **pu·pae** \-pē, -,pī\ *or* **pupas** : a form of an insect (as a bee, moth, or beetle) having complete metamorphosis that occurs between the larva and the adult, is usually enclosed in a cocoon or case, and goes through changes inside by which structures of the larva are replaced by those of the adult — **pu·pal** \'pyü-pəl\ *adj*

pu·pate \'pyü-,pāt\ *vb* **pu·pat·ed; pu·pat·ing** : to become a pupa : pass through the stage of the pupa — **pu·pa·tion** \pyü-'pā-shən\ *n*

¹pu·pil \'pyü-pəl\ *n* **1** : a child or young person in school or in the care of a tutor or teacher **2** : one who has been taught or influenced by a person of fame : DISCIPLE [Middle English *pupille* "a child under the care of a guardian", from early French *pupille* (same meaning), from Latin *pupillus* "a boy under the care of a guardian" and *pupilla* "a girl under the care of a guardian, pupil of the eye"; *pupillus* derived from *pupus* "boy"; *pupilla* derived from *pupa* "girl, doll" — related to ²PUPIL]

²pupil *n* : the usually round opening in the iris that contracts and expands in order to regulate the amount of light entering the eye

> **Word History** If you look into another person's eye, you can see a small reflection of yourself. That small image made the ancient Romans think of a doll. Thus, they called the part of the eye in which it appears the *pupilla*. This word literally meant "little doll". The English word for that part of the eye, *pupil*, can be traced to the Latin *pupilla*. *Pupilla* also had another meaning. A little girl who was an orphan and was in the care of a guardian was called a *pupilla*. A little boy in the same situation was called a *pupillus*. From these two Latin words we get the other English *pupil*, meaning "a young student in the care of a tutor or in school". [derived from Latin *pupilla* "pupil of the eye, girl under the care of a guardian", literally "little doll", derived from *pupa* "doll, girl"; so called because the tiny image of oneself seen in another's eye is like a tiny doll]

pup·pet \'pəp-ət\ *n* **1** : a doll moved by hand or by strings or wires **2** : DOLL 1 **3** : a person or a government whose acts are controlled by an outside force or influence

pup·pe·teer \,pəp-ə-'ti(ə)r\ *n* : one who works puppets

pup·py \'pəp-ē\ *n, pl* **puppies** : a young domestic dog; *esp* : one less than a year old

pur·blind \'pər-,blīnd\ *adj* **1** : partly blind **2** : lacking in understanding

¹pur·chase \'pər-chəs\ *vb* **pur·chased; pur·chas·ing** : to get by paying money for : BUY ⟨*purchase* a house⟩ — **pur·chas·able** \-chə-sə-bəl\ *adj* — **pur·chas·er** *n*

²purchase *n* **1** : an act or instance of purchasing **2** : something purchased **3** : a secure hold, grasp, or place to stand ⟨could not get a *purchase* on the ledge⟩

pure \'pyü(ə)r\ *adj* **1** : not mixed with anything else : free from everything that might make dirty, change, or lower the quality ⟨*pure* water⟩ **2** : free from sin or guilt; *esp* : CHASTE 1a **3** : nothing other than ⟨*pure* nonsense⟩ **4** : not applied to everyday problems : THEORETICAL ⟨*pure* science⟩ ⟨*pure* mathematics⟩ **5 a** : of unmixed ancestry **b** : producing offspring which do not vary from the type of the parents or among themselves with respect to one or more characters

pure·bred \-'bred\ *adj* : bred from members of a recognized breed, strain, or kind without cross-breeding over many generations — **pure·bred** \-,bred\ *n*

¹pu·ree \pyü-'rā, -'rē\ *n* **1** : a paste or thick liquid usually made by rubbing cooked food through a sieve **2** : a thick soup having pureed vegetables as a base

²puree *vb* **pu·reed; pu·ree·ing** : to boil soft and then rub through a sieve

pure line *n* : a strain of living things (as corn plants) that shows little variation from individual to individual and is usually formed by repeated inbreeding

pure·ly \'pyü(ə)r-lē\ *adv* **1** : to the full or entire extent **2** : without the addition of anything harmful or different **3** : for no other reason than : ONLY ⟨done *purely* for fun⟩ **4** : in an innocent manner

pur·ga·tive \'pər-gət-iv\ *adj* : tending to act as a strong laxative

²purgative *n* : a strong laxative

pur·ga·to·ry \'pər-gə-,tōr-ē, -,tôr-\ *n, pl* **-ries** : a state after death in which according to Roman Catholic belief the souls of those who die in God's grace are purified of their sins by suffering

¹purge \'pərj\ *vb* **purged; purg·ing** **1** : to make clean **2** : to have or cause strong and usually repeated emptying of the bowels

²purge *n* **1** : an act or instance of purging **2** : something that purges

pu·ri·fy \'pyür-ə-,fī\ *vb* **-fied; -fy·ing** : to make or become pure — **pu·ri·fi·ca·tion** \,pyür-ə-fə-'kā-shən\ *n* — **pu·ri·fi·er** \'pyür-ə-,fī(-ə)r\ *n*

Pu·rim \'pùr-(,)im, pùr-'im\ *n* : a Jewish holiday observed in February or March that celebrates the rescue of the Jews from a plot to massacre them [from Hebrew *pūrīm* (plural), literally "lots cast in determining something by chance"; so called because Haman in the biblical story in Esther 9:24–26 cast lots to decide a day on which he planned to destroy the Jews]

pu·rine \'pyù(ə)r-,ēn\ *n* : any of a group of bases including several (as cytosine or thymine) that are important parts of DNA and RNA — compare PYRIMIDINE

pur·ism \'pyù(ə)r-,iz-əm\ *n* : a strict following of what is considered absolutely correct especially in the use of words — **pur·ist** \-əst\ *n*

pu·ri·tan \'pyùr-ət-°n\ *n* **1** *cap* : a member of a 16th and 17th century Protestant group in England and New England opposing many customs of the Church of England **2** : one who practices or preaches a stricter moral code than is generally followed — **puritan** *adj, often cap* — **pu·ri·tan·i·cal** \,pyùr-ə-'tan-i-kəl\ *adj* — **pu·ri·tan·ism** \'pyùr-ət-°n-,iz-əm\ *n, often cap*

pu·ri·ty \'pyùr-ət-ē\ *n* **1** : the quality or state of being pure : freedom from impurities **2** : freedom from guilt or sin

¹purl \'pər(-ə)l\ *vb* : to invert the stitches in knitting [from obsolete *pirl* "to twist"]

²purl *n* **1** : a swirling stream **2** : a gentle murmur [probably of Scandinavian origin]

³purl *vb* **1** : ²EDDY, SWIRL **2** : to make a murmuring sound

pur·lieu \'pərl-,yü\ *n* **1** : an outlying or neighboring district **2** *pl* : SURROUNDINGS

pur·loin \(,)pər-'lóin, 'pər-,lóin\ *vb* : ¹STEAL 2a — **pur·loin·er** *n*

¹pur·ple \'pər-pəl\ *adj* **pur·pler** \-p(ə-)lər\; **pur·plest** \-p(ə-)ləst\ : of the color purple

²purple *n* : a color midway between red and blue

³purple *vb* **pur·pled; pur·pling** \'pər-p(ə-)liŋ\ : to turn purple

pur·plish \'pər-p(ə-)lish\ *adj* : somewhat purple

¹pur·port \'pər-,pō(ə)rt, -,pò(ə)rt\ *n* **1** : meaning stated, suggested, or hinted **2** : the main point of a talk or subject

²pur·port \(,)pər-'pō(ə)rt, -'pò(ə)rt\ *vb* : to give the impression of being ⟨*purports* to be a physician⟩

pur·pose \'pər-pəs\ *n* **1** : something set up as an end to be attained **2** : an object or result achieved ⟨worked to little *purpose*⟩ **syn** see INTENTION — **pur·pose·ful** \-fəl\ *adj* — **pur·pose·ful·ly** \-fə-lē\ *adv* — **pur·pose·ful·ness** \-fəl-nəs\ *n* — **pur·pose·less** \-pəs-ləs\ *adj* — **on purpose** : by intention

pur·pose·ly \'pər-pəs-lē\ *adv* : with a clear or known purpose

purr \'pər\ *n* : a low murmuring sound of a contented cat — **purr** *vb*

¹purse \'pərs\ *n* **1** : a small container (as a wallet) for money; *esp* : a woman's pocketbook **2** : a source of supply or support **3** : a sum of money offered as a prize or present [Old English *purs* "a small bag for money, purse", from Latin *bursa* "purse", from earlier *bursa* "a small leather bag" — related to DISBURSE, REIMBURSE]

²purse *vb* **pursed; purs·ing 1** : to put into a purse **2** : ¹PUCKER ⟨*pursed* lips⟩

purs·er \'pər-sər\ *n* : an official on a ship who keeps accounts and attends to passengers

pur·su·ance \pər-'sü-ən(t)s\ *n* : the act of pursuing or carrying out ⟨in *pursuance* of their plans⟩

pur·su·ant to \pər-'sü-ənt-\ *prep* : in carrying out : ACCORDING TO

pur·sue \pər-'sü\ *vb* **pur·sued; pur·su·ing 1** : to follow in order to catch up with and seize **2** : to try to obtain or accomplish : SEEK ⟨*pursue* pleasure⟩ **3** : to proceed along ⟨*pursue* a northerly course⟩ **4** : to engage in : PRACTICE ⟨*pursue* a hobby⟩ **5** : HARASS 1, HAUNT ⟨*pursued* by fear⟩ [Middle English *pursuen* "persecute", derived from early French *poursivre, pousuir* (same meaning), derived from Latin *prosequi* "to follow after, pursue", from *pro-* "forward" and *sequi* "to follow" — related to SEQUEL] **syn** *see* CHASE — **pur·su·er** *n*

pur·suit \pər-'süt\ *n* **1** : the act of pursuing **2** : an activity done especially for pleasure

pur·vey \(,)pər-'vā, 'pər-,vā\ *vb* **pur·veyed; pur·vey·ing** : to supply usually as a business — **pur·vey·ance** \-ən(t)s\ *n* — **pur·vey·or** \-ər\ *n*

pus \'pəs\ *n* : thick cloudy usually yellowish white fluid matter formed at a place of inflammation and infection (as an abscess) and containing white blood cells, tissue debris, and germs

¹push \'push\ *vb* **1** : to press against with force in order to drive **2** : to force forward, downward, or outward **3** : to go or make go ahead ⟨*push* the job to completion⟩ **4** : to press hard against so as to involve in difficulty ⟨was *pushed* for time⟩

²push *n* **1** : a strong advance against obstacles **2** : a sudden thrust : SHOVE **3** : a steady applying of force in a direction away from the body from which it comes

push–button *adj* : using or dependent on complicated automatic machines ⟨*push-button* warfare⟩ ⟨a *push-button* civilization⟩

push button *n* : a small button or knob that when pushed operates something especially by closing an electric circuit

push·cart \'push-,kärt\ *n* : a cart pushed by hand

push·er \'push-ər\ *n* **1** : one that pushes **2** : a peddler of illegal drugs

push·over \'push-,ō-vər\ *n* **1** : an opponent easy to defeat or incapable of resistance **2** : someone unable to resist an attraction or appeal **3** : something easily done : SNAP

push–up \'push-,əp\ *n* : an exercise performed while lying facedown by raising and lowering the body with the straightening and bending of the arms

pu·sil·lan·i·mous \,pyü-sə-'lan-ə-məs\ *adj* : COWARDLY

¹puss \'pus\ *n* **1** : CAT 1a **2** : GIRL 1 [origin unknown]

²puss *n, slang* : ¹FACE 1 [from Irish Gaelic (the original language of Ireland) *pus* "mouth"]

pussy \'pus-ē\ *n, pl* **puss·ies 1** : ¹PUSS 1 **2** : a catkin of the pussy willow

pussy·foot \-,fut\ *vb* **1** : to walk or move in a careful or sneaky manner **2** : to avoid taking a firm stand (as in a dispute)

pussy willow *n* : a willow having large silky catkins

pus·tule \'pəs-chü(ə)l\ *n* **1** : a small elevation of the skin having an inflamed base and containing pus **2** : a small elevation resembling a pimple or blister

¹put \'put\ *vb* **put; put·ting 1 a** : to place in or move into a position or relationship ⟨*put*

pussy willow

the book down⟩ **b** : to throw with an overhand pushing motion ⟨*put* the shot⟩ **c** : to bring into a state ⟨*put* it to use⟩ ⟨*put* the matter right⟩ **2 a** : to cause to undergo something ⟨was *put* to death⟩ **b** : IMPOSE 1a ⟨*put* a special tax on luxuries⟩ **3** : to set before one for judgment or decision (as by a formal vote) ⟨*put* the motion⟩ **4** : ⁴EXPRESS 1a ⟨*put* your feelings into words⟩ **5 a** : to devote or urge to an activity or end ⟨*put* your mind to the problem⟩ ⟨*put* them to work⟩ **b** : ²INVEST 1 ⟨*put* our money in the company⟩ **6 a** : ¹ESTIMATE 1 ⟨*put* the time at about eleven⟩ **b** : ATTACH 5 ⟨*puts* a high value on friendship⟩ **7** : ¹GO 1, PROCEED ⟨the ship *put* to sea⟩ — **put forth 1** : DISCLOSE, ISSUE **2** : to bring into action **3** : to produce or send out by growth ⟨*put forth* leaves⟩ — **put forward** : PROPOSE 1 ⟨*put forward* a theory⟩ — **put in mind** : REMIND — **put together 1** : to create as a whole : CONSTRUCT **2** : ADD 1b, COMBINE — **put to it** : to give difficulty to ⟨was *put to it* to keep up⟩

²put *n* : a throw made with an overhand pushing motion

³put *adj* : FIXED 1a, SET ⟨stay *put* until I come back⟩

put about *vb* : to change course or direction ⟨after sailing north, they *put about* and headed east⟩

put across *vb* : to gain or communicate successfully ⟨*put across* a plan⟩

put by *vb* : to lay aside : SAVE ⟨have money *put by* for an emergency⟩

put down *vb* **1** : to bring to an end by force ⟨*put down* a riot⟩ **2** : to write down (as in a list) **3** : BELITTLE, CRITICIZE — **put–down** \'put-,daun\ *n*

put in *vb* **1** : to make or make as a request, offer, or declaration ⟨*put in* a plea of guilty⟩ ⟨*put in* for a job at the store⟩ **2** : to spend at some activity or place ⟨*put in* six hours at the office⟩ **3** : ¹PLANT 1a ⟨*put in* a crop⟩ **4** : to enter a harbor or port ⟨the freighter *put in* for overnight⟩

put off *vb* **1** : to cause negative feelings in ⟨your sloppy appearance *put* them *off*⟩ **2** : POSTPONE, DEFER ⟨*put off* my visit to the dentist⟩ **3** : to rid oneself of ⟨*put off* your coat⟩

put–on \'put-,ȯn, -,än\ *n* **1** : a false appearance or presentation ⟨my bravery was all a *put-on*⟩ **2** : a joke in which someone is fooled

put on \(')put-'ȯn, -'än\ *vb* **1 a** : to dress oneself in **b** : to make part of one's appearance or behavior **c** : ¹PRETEND 1 ⟨*put on* a show of anger⟩ **2** : EXAGGERATE, OVERSTATE ⟨they're *putting* it *on* when they make such claims⟩ **3** : PERFORM 3b, PRODUCE ⟨*put on* an entertaining act⟩ **4** : ²KID 1, FOOL ⟨you're *putting* me *on*⟩ — **put–on** *adj*

put·out \'put-,aut\ *n* : the act of causing a base runner or batter to be out in baseball

put out \,put-'aut, 'put-\ *vb* **1** : EXTINGUISH 1 ⟨*put* the fire *out*⟩ **2** : EXERT 1, USE ⟨*put out* all my strength to move the piano⟩ **3** : ¹PRODUCE 4 : IRRITATE 1, PROVOKE ⟨my father was *put out* by my failure⟩ **5** : to cause to be out (as in baseball) **6** : to set out from shore ⟨Columbus *put out* for the New World⟩

put over *vb* : PUT ACROSS ⟨*put over* a song⟩

pu·tre·fac·tion \,pyü-trə-'fak-shən\ *n* **1** : the rotting of organic matter **2** : the state of being putrefied : CORRUPTION

pu·tre·fy \'pyü-trə-,fī\ *vb* **-fied; -fy·ing** : to make or become putrid

pu·trid \'pyü-trəd\ *adj* **1 a** : being in a state of putrefaction : ROTTEN ⟨*putrid* meat⟩ **b** : characteristic of putrefaction : FOUL ⟨a *putrid* odor⟩ **2** : morally objectionable

putt \'pət\ *n* : a golf stroke made to cause the ball to roll into or near the hole — **putt** *vb*

\ə\ abut	\au̇\ out	\i\ tip	\ȯ\ saw	\u̇\ foot
\ər\ further	\ch\ chin	\ī\ life	\ȯi\ coin	\y\ yet
\a\ mat	\e\ pet	\j\ job	\th\ thin	\yü\ few
\ā\ take	\ē\ easy	\ŋ\ sing	\th\ this	\yu̇\ cure
\ä\ cot, cart	\g\ go	\ō\ bone	\ü\ food	\zh\ vision

¹**put·ter** \'pût-ər\ *n* : one that puts [from *put* and *-er* (noun suffix)]

²**putt·er** \'pət-ər\ *n* **1** : a golf club used in putting **2** : a person who putts [from *putt* and *-er* (noun suffix)]

³**put·ter** \'pət-ər\ *vb* **1** : to move or act without obvious purpose **2** : to work by chance or without skill [an altered form of earlier *potter* "to move about idly without aim or purpose"] — **put·ter·er** \-ər-ər\ *n*

put through *vb* : to carry to a conclusion ⟨*put through* a number of reforms⟩

putting *present participle of* PUT

¹**put·ty** \'pət-ē\ *n, pl* **putties** : a soft cement (as for holding glass in a window frame)

²**putty** *vb* **put·tied; put·ty·ing** : to cement or seal up with putty

put up *vb* **1 a** : to prepare for later use ⟨*put up* a lunch⟩; *esp* : ³CAN 1 ⟨*put up* peaches⟩ **b** : to put away out of use ⟨*put up* your sword⟩ **2 a** : to nominate for election **b** : to offer for public sale ⟨*put* their possessions *up* for auction⟩ **3** : to give or obtain food and shelter : LODGE ⟨*put* us *up* overnight⟩ **4** : ¹BUILD 1, ERECT **5** : CARRY ON 3 ⟨*put up* a struggle⟩ **6** : to make available ⟨*put up* a prize for the best essay⟩ — **put up to** : to urge or cause to do ⟨*put* them *up to* doing the stunts⟩ — **put up with** : TOLERATE 1

¹**puz·zle** \'pəz-əl\ *vb* **puz·zled; puz·zling** \-(ə-)liŋ\ **1** : to confuse the understanding of **2** : to solve with difficulty or cleverness — **puz·zler** \-(ə-)lər\ *n*

> **syn** PUZZLE, PERPLEX, MYSTIFY mean to baffle (someone) by preventing the understanding of something. PUZZLE suggests that a particular part of something is hard to understand or explain ⟨it is the cause of the disease that *puzzles* doctors⟩ PERPLEX adds a suggestion of worry or distress ⟨*perplexed* by the sudden departure of their friend⟩ MYSTIFY stresses the completeness of one's failure to understand ⟨modern art *mystifies* me entirely⟩

²**puzzle** *n* **1** : PUZZLEMENT 1 **2** : something that puzzles **b** : a question, problem, or device designed for testing skill or cleverness **syn** see MYSTERY

puz·zle·ment \'pəz-əl-mənt\ *n* **1** : the state of being puzzled **2** : ²PUZZLE 2a

pyg·my \'pig-mē\ *n, pl* **pygmies** **1** *cap* : one of a small people of equatorial Africa ranging under five feet in height **2** : a person or thing very small for its kind : DWARF — **pygmy** *adj*

> **Word History** In ancient Greek the word *pygmē* was used to mean "a measure of length from the elbow to the knuckles". It also came to refer to the fist. From this word Greek writers formed the word *pygmios* for "a tiny person no longer than the forearm". They were assumed to be writing about imaginary figures, not real people. Later, this Greek word was taken into Latin as *pygmaeus*, meaning "dwarf". From Latin *pygmaeus* English formed the word *pygmy*. In the 19th century this word was applied to a member of a race of small people found living in Africa. [Middle English *pigmei* "pygmy, dwarf", from Latin *pygmaeus* (noun and adjective) "pygmy, dwarfish", from Greek *pygmios* (same meaning), literally "one no longer than the forearm", from *pygmē* "fist, measure of length from the elbow to the knuckles"]

py·ja·mas \pə-'jä-məz\ *chiefly British variant of* PAJAMAS

py·lon \'pī-ˌlän, -lən\ *n* **1** : a tower for supporting a long span of wire; *also* : any of various structures like a tower **2** : a post or tower marking a prescribed course of flight for an airplane

py·lo·rus \pī-'lōr-əs, -'lȯr-\ *n, pl* **-lo·ri** \-'lō(ə)r-ˌī, -, -ē\ : the opening in a vertebrate animal from the stomach into the intestine — **py·lo·ric** \pī-'lōr-ik, pə-, -'lȯr-\ *adj*

py·or·rhea \ˌpī-ə-'rē-ə\ *n* : an inflammation with pus of the sockets of the teeth leading usually to loosening of the teeth

¹**pyr·a·mid** \'pir-ə-ˌmid\ *n* **1** : a massive structure built es-

pecially in ancient Egypt that usually has a square base and four triangular sides meeting at a point **2** : something that resembles a pyramid in shape or organization ⟨the social *pyramid*⟩ **3** : a solid having a polygon for its base and three or more triangles for its sides that meet at a point to form the top — **py·ra·mi·dal** \pə-'ram-əd-ᵊl, ˌpir-ə-'mid-\ *adj*

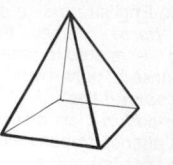
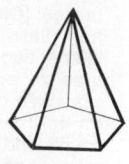

pyramid 3

²**pyramid** *vb* : to build up in the form of a pyramid

pyre \'pī(ə)r\ *n* : a heap of wood for burning a dead body; *also* : a pile of material to be burned

py·re·thrum \pī-'rē-thrəm, -'reth-rəm\ *n* **1** : any of several chrysanthemums that have finely divided leaves and include ornamental plants as well as important sources of insecticides **2** : an insecticide consisting of the dried heads of some Old World pyrethrums

Py·rex \'pī(ə)r-ˌeks\ *trademark* — used for glass and glassware that is resistant to heat, chemicals, and electricity

pyr·i·dox·ine \ˌpir-ə-'däk-ˌsēn, -sən\ *n* : an alcohol of the vitamin B_6 group found especially in cereals

py·rim·i·dine \pī-'rim-ə-ˌdēn, pə-\ *n* : any of a group of bases including several (as cytosine and thymine) that are important parts of DNA or RNA — compare PURINE

py·rite \'pī-ˌrīt\ *n* : a common mineral that consists of iron combined with sulfur, has a pale brass-yellow color and metallic luster, and is used especially in making sulfuric acid

pyro- *combining form* : fire : heat [derived from Greek *pyr-* "fire"]

py·ro·lu·site \ˌpī-rō-'lü-ˌsīt\ *n* : a mineral consisting of manganese dioxide that is of an iron-black or dark steel-gray color and metallic luster, is usually soft, and is the most important ore of manganese

py·rox·ene \pī-'räk-ˌsēn\ *n* : any of various silicate minerals that usually contain aluminum, calcium, sodium, magnesium, or iron

py·ru·vic acid \pī-ˌrü-vik-\ *n* : an acid that can be formed from either glucose or glycogen and is an important chemical in the production of energy from food in animals

Py·thag·o·re·an numbers \pə-ˌthag-ə-ˌrē-ən-, (ˌ)pī-\ *n pl* : any set of three positive integers (as 3, 4, 5) that satisfy the equation $x^2 + y^2 = z^2$

Pythagorean theorem *n* : a theorem in geometry: the square of the length of the hypotenuse of a right triangle equals the sum of the squares of the lengths of the other two sides

py·thon \'pī-ˌthän, -thən\ *n* : a large snake (as a boa) that squeezes and suffocates its prey; *esp* : any of an Old World genus including the largest snakes living at the present time

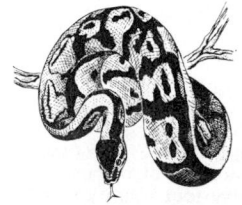

python

> **Word History** *Python*, in Greek legend, was the name of a monstrous serpent that lived in the caves of Mt. Parnassus near the town of Delphi. This serpent attacked the mother of the god Apollo. Zeus, fortunately, came to her aid and removed her to a place of safety. Later, Apollo sought revenge for the attack. With bow and arrow he hunted the dreaded Python. After struggling with and finally slaying the serpent, Apollo buried it in the

temple at Delphi. To celebrate this victory a festival of games was held, including athletic and musical contests and a dramatic performance of Apollo's slaying of Python. These games continued to be held every four years until the 4th century A. D. They were called the Pythian games and ranked second to the Olympic games in popularity. Its was not until the 19th century that the word *python* was used for a large snake that crushes its prey. [named for *Python,* a monstrous serpent in Greek Legend]

Q

q \'kyü\ *n, often cap* : the 17th letter of the English alphabet

¹quack \'kwak\ *n* : the cry of a duck; *also* : a sound resembling this cry [a word created to imitate the sound made by a duck]

²quack *vb* : to make a quack

³quack *n* : a person who makes false claims to special knowledge or ability; *esp* : one who pretends to have medical skill [a shortened form of earlier *quacksalver* "a person who pretends to have medical skill"; of Dutch origin]

⁴quack *adj* : of, relating to, or resembling that of a quack ⟨*quack* medicines⟩

quack·ery \'kwak-(ə-)rē\ *n* : the practices or claims of a quack

quack grass *n* : a European grass that is found throughout North America as a weed and that spreads by creeping underground stems

quad \'kwäd\ *n* : QUADRUPLET

quad·ran·gle \'kwäd-,raŋ-gəl\ *n* **1** : ²QUADRILATERAL **2 a** : a four-sided enclosure especially when surrounded by buildings **b** : the buildings enclosing a quadrangle — **qua·dran·gu·lar** \kwä-'draŋ-gyə-lər\ *adj*

quad·rant \'kwäd-rənt\ *n* **1** : an arc of 90° : one quarter of a circle **2** : any of the four quarters into which something is divided by two real or imaginary lines that intersect each other at right angles

quad·ra·phon·ic \,kwäd-rə-'fän-ik\ *adj* : of or relating to the transmission, recording, or reproduction of sound using four transmission channels

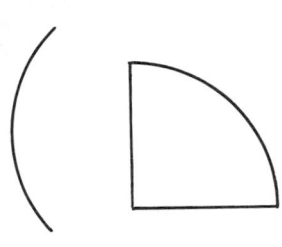

quadrant 1

¹qua·drat·ic \kwä-'drat-ik\ *adj* : having or being a term in which the variable (as *x*) is squared but containing no term in which the variable is raised to a higher power than a square ⟨a *quadratic* expression⟩ ⟨a *quadratic* function⟩

²quadratic *n* : a quadratic polynomial or equation

quadratic equation *n* : an equation containing one quadratic term in the unknown but containing no term in which the unknown is raised to a power higher than two ⟨$x^2 + 4x + 4 = 0$ is a *quadratic equation*⟩

quadratic formula *n* : a formula that gives the solutions of the general quadratic equation $ax^2 + bx + c = 0$ and that is usually written in the form

$$x = \frac{-b \pm \sqrt{b^2 - 4ac}}{2a}$$

quadri- *or* **quadr-** *or* **quadru-** *combining form* : four [derived from Latin *quattuor* "four"]

¹quad·ri·lat·er·al \,kwäd-rə-'lat-ə-rəl, -'la-trəl\ *adj* : having four sides

²quadrilateral *n* : a plane figure of four sides and four angles

qua·drille \kwä-'dril, k(w)ə-\ *n* : a square dance for four couples or music for this dance

qua·dril·lion \kwä-'dril-yən\ *n* — see NUMBER table

quad·ri·ple·gic \,kwäd-rə-'plē-jik\ *n* : a person who is paralyzed in both arms and both legs

quad·ru·ped \'kwäd-rə-,ped\ *n* : an animal having four feet

¹qua·dru·ple \kwä-'drüp-əl, -'drəp-; 'kwäd-rəp-\ *vb* **qua·dru·pled; qua·dru·pling** \-(ə-)liŋ\ : to make or become four times as great or as many

²quadruple *adj* **1** : having four units or members **2** : being four times as great or as many **3** : marked by four beats per measure ⟨*quadruple* time⟩ — **quadruple** *n*

qua·dru·plet \kwä-'drü-plət, -'drəp-lət; 'kwäd-rə-plət\ *n* **1** : one of four offspring born at one birth **2** : a combination of four of a kind

qua·dru·pli·cate \kwä-'drü-pli-kət\ *n* **1** : four copies all alike — used with *in* ⟨papers typed in *quadruplicate*⟩ **2** : one of four things exactly alike; *esp* : one of four identical copies

quaff \'kwäf, 'kwaf\ *vb* : to drink freely — **quaff** *n*

quag·mire \'kwag-,mī(ə)r, 'kwäg-\ *n* **1** : soft muddy ground that gives under the foot **2** : a difficult situation from which it is hard to escape

¹quail \'kwā(ə)l\ *n, pl* **quail** *or* **quails** : any of various mostly small plump game birds (as the bobwhite) that are related to the common domestic chicken [Middle English *quaille* "quail (bird)", from early French *quaille* (same meaning), from Latin *quaccula* (same meaning)]

²quail *vb* : to lose courage : shrink in fear [Middle English *quailen* "to curdle", from early French *quailler* (same meaning), from Latin *coagulare* "to curdle" — related to COAGULATE]

quail

quaint \'kwānt\ *adj* : unusual or different in quality or appearance; *esp* : pleasingly old-fashioned or unfamiliar ⟨a *quaint* fishing village⟩ — **quaint·ly** *adv* — **quaint·ness** *n*

¹quake \'kwāk\ *vb* **quaked; quak·ing** **1** : to shake or vibrate usually from shock or lack of stability **2** : to tremble or shudder usually from cold or fear

²quake *n* : a shaking or trembling; *esp* : EARTHQUAKE

quak·er \'kwā-kər\ *n* **1** : one that quakes **2** *cap* : FRIEND 4 — **Quak·er·ism** \-kə-,riz-əm\ *n*

qual·i·fi·ca·tion \,kwäl-ə-fə-'kā-shən\ *n* **1** : the act or an instance of qualifying **2** : the state of being qualified **3 a** : a special skill, knowledge, or ability that fits a person for a particular work or position **b** : a condition that must be met (as to gain a privilege)

qual·i·fied \'kwäl-ə-,fīd\ *adj* **1** : having the necessary qualifications : FITTED **2** : limited in some way ⟨a *qualified* yes to the question⟩

\ə\ abut	\au̇\ out	\i\ tip	\o̊\ saw	\u̇\ foot
\ər\ further	\ch\ chin	\ī\ life	\oi\ coin	\y\ yet
\a\ mat	\e\ pet	\j\ job	\th\ thin	\yü\ few
\ā\ take	\ē\ easy	\ŋ\ sing	\th\ this	\yu̇\ cure
\ä\ cot, cart	\g\ go	\ō\ bone	\ü\ food	\zh\ vision

qual·i·fi·er \'kwäl-ə-ˌfī(-ə)r\ *n* **1** : a person or thing that meets requirements **2** : a word or word group that limits the meaning of another word or word group : MODIFIER

qual·i·fy \'kwäl-ə-ˌfī\ *vb* **-fied; -fy·ing 1 a** : to make less general or more limited : MODIFY ⟨*qualify* a statement⟩ **b** : to make less harsh or strict : MODERATE ⟨*qualify* a punishment⟩ **c** : to limit the meaning of (as a noun) **2** : to describe in a particular way ⟨would you *qualify* her as smart⟩ **3 a** : to fit or be fit (as by training, skill, or ability) for a special purpose ⟨*qualify* for a race⟩ **b** : ²LICENSE ⟨*qualified* to practice law⟩

qual·i·ta·tive \'kwäl-ə-ˌtāt-iv\ *adj* : of, relating to, or involving quality or kind — **qual·i·ta·tive·ly** *adv*

qual·i·ty \'kwäl-ət-ē\ *n, pl* **-ties 1 a** : basic and individual nature ⟨a person with a kindly *quality*⟩ **b** : a basic characteristic ⟨hardness is a *quality* of steel⟩ **2** : grade of excellence ⟨food of high *quality*⟩ **3** : high social rank ⟨marry a person of *quality*⟩ **4** : something that sets a person or thing apart **5** : TIMBRE

qualm \'kwäm, 'kwälm *also* 'kwȯm\ *n* **1** : a sudden attack of illness, faintness, or nausea **2** : a sudden fear **3** : a feeling of doubt or indecision in matters of right and wrong ⟨had *qualms* about coming home late⟩ — **qualmy** \-ē\ *adj*
syn QUALM, SCRUPLE, COMPUNCTION mean an uneasy feeling about what one is doing or going to do. QUALM suggests an uneasy fear that one is not following one's conscience or better judgment ⟨started having *qualms* about going along with the crowd⟩ SCRUPLE suggests doubt about the rightness of an act based upon one's moral code ⟨citizens with *scruples* won't cheat on their taxes⟩ COMPUNCTION suggests an inner feeling that one is doing wrong to another person ⟨don't you have any *compunctions* about spreading gossip?⟩

qualm·ish \'kwäm-ish, 'kwälm- *also* 'kwȯm-ish\ *adj* **1** : feeling qualms : NAUSEATED **2** : of, relating to, or producing qualms — **qualm·ish·ness** *n*

quan·da·ry \'kwän-d(ə-)rē\ *n, pl* **-ries** : a state of confusion or doubt ⟨in a *quandary* about which to choose⟩

quan·ti·ta·tive \'kwän(t)-ə-ˌtāt-iv\ *adj* : of, relating to, or involving the measurement of quantity — **quan·ti·ta·tive·ly** *adv* — **quan·ti·ta·tive·ness** *n*

quan·ti·ty \'kwän(t)-ət-ē\ *n, pl* **-ties 1 a** : an amount or number that is not fixed **b** : a great amount or number ⟨buys food in *quantity*⟩ **2 a** : the character of something that makes it possible to measure or number it **b** : the subject of a mathematical operation [Middle English *quantite* "amount", from early French *quantité* (same meaning), derived from Latin *quantus* "how much?, how large?"]

quan·tum \'kwänt-əm\ *n, pl* **quan·ta** \'kwänt-ə\ : the smallest amount of many forms of energy (as light)

quantum theory *n* : a theory in physics based on the idea that radiant energy (as light) is composed of small separate packets of energy

¹quar·an·tine \'kwȯr-ən-ˌtēn, 'kwär-\ *n* **1** : a period during which a ship arriving in port and suspected of carrying contagious disease is forbidden contact with the shore **2** : a limiting or forbidding of movements of persons or goods that is designed to prevent the spread of disease or pests **3** : the period during which a person with a contagious disease is under quarantine **4** : a place where persons are kept in quarantine
> **Word History** As bad as contagious diseases are today, they were much more frightening in the Middle Ages. No effective treatment or cure was known then. When it was found out that ships could carry diseases from port to port, authorities acted to protect their citizens. Any ship suspected of carrying a disease was forced to remain offshore for a time. Usually about forty days had to pass before it was allowed to dock. Then if no signs of disease were found on the ship, it was allowed to unload its passengers and cargo. The Italians called this restric-

tion period *quarantina*. They based the word on a French word *quarantaine*, meaning "a period of forty days". This French word was derived from the Latin *quadraginta*, meaning "forty". It was the Italian word that was taken into English as *quarantine* in the 17th century. [from Italian *quarantina, quaranténa* "quarantine, period of forty days", probably from early French *quarantaine* "period of forty days", from earlier *quarante* "forty", from Latin *quadraginta* "forty", from *quadra-* "four"]

²quarantine *vb* **-tined; -tin·ing** : to put or hold in quarantine : ISOLATE

¹quar·rel \'kwȯr-(ə)l, 'kwär-(ə)l\ *n* **1** : a cause of dispute or complaint **2** : an angry difference of opinion : DISPUTE

²quarrel *vb* **-reled** *or* **-relled; -rel·ing** *or* **-rel·ling 1** : to find fault ⟨I *quarrel* with your version of what happened⟩ **2** : to argue forcefully or loudly : SQUABBLE — **quar·rel·er** *or* **quar·rel·ler** *n*

quar·rel·some \'kwȯr-(ə)l-səm, 'kwär-(ə)l-\ *adj* : usually ready to quarrel **syn** see BELLIGERENT

¹quar·ry \'kwȯr-ē, 'kwär-\ *n, pl* **quarries 1** : an animal or bird hunted as game or prey **2** : something sought or chased after
> **Word History** The quarry a hunter chases is not related to the quarry that supplies building stones. The word for a hunter's quarry can be traced back to a ceremony that was once part of every successful hunt. The hounds used for chasing the game were rewarded after the kill by being allowed to eat part of the dead animal. The French word for this hounds' share was *cuiree*, which was borrowed into Middle English as *querre*. The word later came to be used for the live game animal itself. Now a quarry is anything that is pursued. [Middle English *querre* "the part of a game animal given to the hounds", from early French *cuiree* (same meaning), probably derived from earlier *coree* "the internal organs of an animal", derived from Latin *cor* "heart"]

²quarry *n, pl* **quarries** : an open pit usually for obtaining building stone, slate, or limestone [Middle English *quarey*, an altered form of *quarrere* "a place for digging stones for use in building", from early French *quarriere* (same meaning), probably from earlier *quarre* "squared stones", from Latin *quadrum* "a square"]

³quarry *vb* **quar·ried; quar·ry·ing 1** : to dig or take from or as if from a quarry **2** : to make a quarry in — **quar·ri·er** *n*

quart \'kwȯ(ə)rt\ *n* **1** — see MEASURE table **2** : a container or measure having a capacity of one quart

¹quar·ter \'kwȯ(r)t-ər\ *n* **1** : one of four equal parts **2** : a unit (as of weight or length) that equals one fourth of some larger unit **3 a** : any of four 3-month divisions of a year **b** : a school term of about 12 weeks **c** : a coin worth a fourth of a dollar **d** : the sum of 25 cents **e** : one fourth part of a slaughtered animal including a leg ⟨*quarter* of beef⟩ **f** : a fourth part of the moon's period ⟨a moon in its first *quarter*⟩ **g** : one of the four equal parts into which the playing time of some games is divided **4** : someone or something (as a place, direction, or group) not named ⟨complaints came from all *quarters*⟩ **5 a** : a particular division or district of a city **b** : an assigned station especially of a member of a crew ⟨call to *quarters*⟩ **c** *pl* : the place where one lives : LODGING **6** : MERCY 1a ⟨show no *quarter* to the enemy⟩ [Middle English *quarter* "a fourth part", from early French *quartier* (same meaning), derived from Latin *quartus* "a fourth"] — **at close quarters** : at close range or in immediate contact

²quarter *vb* **1 a** : to divide into four equal parts **b** : to separate into parts ⟨peel and *quarter* an orange⟩ **2** : to provide with lodging or shelter

³quarter *adj* : consisting of or equal to a quarter

quar·ter·back \'kwȯ(r)t-ər-ˌbak\ *n* : an offensive football back who calls the signals and directs the offensive play

of the team — **quarterback** *vb*

quar·ter·deck \-,dek\ *n* : the part of the upper deck that is located toward the rear of a ship

quarter horse *n* : a stocky muscular horse capable of high speed for short distances

quarter horse

Word History *Quarter horse* might seem like a strange name for an animal that is not only full-sized but quite sturdy and muscular. However, the breed gets its name not because it is a fraction of a horse but because it can run very fast for short distances. Unlike the slender, long-legged Thoroughbred horse, the compact quarter horse is built for quick bursts of speed. For about a quarter-mile the quarter horse probably can run faster than any other breed of horse. After that distance the quarter horse begins to slow down and can be beaten in a race with other horses.

quarter hour *n* **1** : any of the quarter points of an hour **2** : 15 minutes

quar·ter·ing \'kwȯ(r)t-ə-riŋ\ *adj* : coming from a direction behind and to the side (as of a ship) ⟨a *quartering* wind⟩

¹quar·ter·ly \'kwȯ(r)t-ər-lē\ *adv* : four times a year ⟨interest compounded *quarterly*⟩

²quarterly *adj* : coming or happening every three months ⟨*quarterly* premium⟩ ⟨*quarterly* meeting⟩

³quarterly *n, pl* **-lies** : a magazine published four times a year

quar·ter·mas·ter \'kwȯ(r)t-ər-,mas-tər\ *n* : an army officer who provides clothing and supplies for troops

quarter note *n* : a musical note equal in time to ¼ of a whole note

quar·ter·staff \'kwȯ(r)t-ər-,staf\ *n, pl* **-staves** \-,stavz, -,stävz\ : a long strong staff used long ago as a weapon

quar·tet *also* **quar·tette** \kwȯr-'tet\ *n* **1 a** : a musical composition for four instruments or voices **b** : the performers of a quartet **2** : a group or set of four

quar·to \'kwȯrt-ō\ *n, pl* **quartos** : a book made up of sheets of paper that have been folded to produce four leaves

quartz \'kwȯ(ə)rts\ *n* : a common mineral consisting of silicon dioxide that is often found in the form of colorless transparent crystals but is sometimes (as in amethysts, agates, and jaspers) brightly colored

quartz·ite \'kwȯrt-,sīt\ *n* : a compact grainy rock composed of quartz and made from sandstone by the earth's heat and pressure

qua·sar \'kwā-,zär *also* -,sär\ *n* : any of the very distant starlike heavenly objects that give off very strong blue and ultraviolet light and powerful radio waves

¹quash \'kwäsh, 'kwȯsh\ *vb* : to cancel by court action ⟨*quash* a criminal charge⟩

²quash *vb* : to put down completely : QUELL ⟨*quash* a rebellion⟩

qua·si- \'kwā-,zī, -,sī; 'kwäz-ē, 'kwäs-\ *combining form* : in some sense or degree ⟨*quasi*-historical⟩ ⟨*quasi*-officially⟩ [from Latin *quasi* "as if"]

Qua·ter·na·ry \'kwät-ə(r)-,ner-ē, kwə-'tər-nə-rē\ *adj* : of, relating to, or being the period of geological history from the end of the Tertiary period to the present time or the corresponding system of rocks — see GEOLOGIC TIME table — **Quaternary** *n*

qua·train \'kwä-,trān\ *n* : a unit or group of four lines of verse

¹qua·ver \'kwā-vər\ *vb* **qua·vered; qua·ver·ing** \'kwāv-(ə-)riŋ\ **1** : ¹TREMBLE 1 **2** : to utter sound in trembling unsteady tones ⟨a voice that *quavered*⟩ **3** : to say or sing

with a quavering voice — **qua·ver·ing·ly** \'kwāv-(ə-)riŋ-lē\ *adv* — **qua·very** \'kwāv-(ə-)rē\ *adj*

²quaver *n* **1** : EIGHTH NOTE **2** : a trembling sound

quay \'kē, 'k(w)ā\ *n* : a structure built along the bank of a waterway for use as a landing place

quea·sy *also* **quea·zy** \'kwē-zē\ *adj* **quea·si·er; -est 1** : somewhat nauseated ⟨the boat ride made me *queasy*⟩ **2** : full of doubt ⟨*queasy* about taking the test⟩ — **quea·si·ly** \-zə-lē\ *adv* — **quea·si·ness** \-zē-nəs\ *n*

Que·chua \'kech-(ə-)wə, kə-'chü-ə\ *n, pl* **Quechua** *or* **Que·chuas 1** : a member of an American Indian people of central Peru **2** : the language of the Quechua people widely spoken by other American Indian peoples of southern and western South America

¹queen \'kwēn\ *n* **1** : the wife or widow of a king **2** : a woman who rules a kingdom in her own right **3 a** : a woman of supreme rank, power, or attractiveness ⟨a society *queen*⟩ **b** : something thought of as female and being at the top in a particular field ⟨*queen* of the ocean liners⟩ **4** : the most powerful piece in the game of chess **5** : a playing card bearing the figure of a queen **6** : the fertile fully developed female of social bees, ants, and termites whose purpose is to lay eggs [Old English *cwēn* "woman, wife, queen"]

²queen *vb* **1** : to act like a queen; *esp* : put on airs ⟨she *queened* it over her friends⟩ **2** : to become or promote to a queen in chess

Queen Anne's lace \-'anz-\ *n* : WILD CARROT

queen·ly \'kwēn-lē\ *adj* : resembling a queen

queen mother *n* : the widowed mother of the king or queen who is currently reigning

¹queer \'kwi(ə)r\ *adj* **1** : oddly unlike the usual or normal ⟨a *queer* smell⟩ **2** : not quite well : QUEASY ⟨feeling a little *queer* today⟩ — **queer·ish** \-ish\ *adj* — **queer·ly** *adv* — **queer·ness** *n*

²queer *vb* : to spoil the effect or success of : DISRUPT ⟨a stupid mistake *queered* our plans⟩

quell \'kwel\ *vb* **1** : to put down by force ⟨*quell* a riot⟩ **2** : ³QUIET ⟨*quell* fears⟩ — **quell·er** *n*

quench \'kwench\ *vb* **1** : EXTINGUISH 1 ⟨*quench* a fire⟩ **2** : to bring to an end **3** : SATISFY 2b ⟨a drink that will *quench* your thirst⟩ — **quench·able** \'kwen-chə-bəl\ *adj* — **quench·er** *n*

quer·u·lous \'kwer-(y)ə-ləs\ *adj* **1** : always eager to complain **2** : showing a complaining attitude ⟨a *querulous* voice⟩ — **quer·u·lous·ly** *adv* — **quer·u·lous·ness** *n*

¹que·ry \'kwi(ə)r-ē, 'kwe(ə)r-\ *n, pl* **queries** : ¹QUESTION 1a

²query *vb* **que·ried; que·ry·ing 1** : to ask questions about especially in order to clear up doubts **2** : to put as a question ⟨*queried* the matter to their teacher⟩ **3** : to ask questions of ⟨*queried* the professor⟩

¹quest \'kwest\ *n* **1** : an act or instance of seeking **2 a** : ²SEARCH ⟨in *quest* of game⟩ **b** : an adventurous journey by a knight in quest of olden days

²quest *vb* **1** : to go on a quest : SEEK **2** : to search for : PURSUE **3** : to ask for : DEMAND

¹ques·tion \'kwes-chən, 'kwesh-\ *n* **1 a** : something asked ⟨try to make your *questions* brief⟩ **b** : a topic to be talked or argued about ⟨arms control and other *questions* of the day⟩ **c** : a suggestion to be voted on ⟨put the *question* to the members⟩ **2 a** : an act or instance of asking : INQUIRY **b** : OBJECTION 1 ⟨obey without *question*⟩ **c** : POSSIBILITY 1 ⟨no *question* of escape⟩

²question *vb* **1** : to ask questions of or about **2** : to doubt the correctness of ⟨*question* the decision of the judges⟩ **3** : to look at or consider carefully : EXAMINE — **ques·tion-**

\ə\ **abut**	\au̇\ **out**	\i\ **tip**	\ȯ\ **saw**	\u̇\ **foot**
\ər\ **further**	\ch\ **chin**	\ī\ **life**	\ȯi\ **coin**	\y\ **yet**
\a\ **mat**	\e\ **pet**	\j\ **job**	\th\ **thin**	\yü\ **few**
\ā\ **take**	\ē\ **easy**	\ŋ\ **sing**	\th\ **this**	\yu̇\ **cure**
\ä\ **cot, cart**	\g\ **go**	\ō\ **bone**	\ü\ **food**	\zh\ **vision**

er *n* — **ques·tion·ing·ly** \-chə-niŋ-lē\ *adv*
ques·tion·able \'kwes-chə-nə-bəl, 'kwesh-\ *adj* **1** : open to doubt, question, or challenge : not certain or exact ⟨milk of *questionable* purity⟩ ⟨a *questionable* decision⟩ **2** : believed to be bad, false, or unsound : DUBIOUS ⟨*questionable* motives⟩ — **ques·tion·ably** \-blē\ *adv*
question mark *n* : a punctuation mark ? used chiefly at the end of a sentence to indicate a direct question
ques·tion·naire \,kwes-chə-'na(ə)r, -'ne(ə)r\ *n* : a set of questions to be asked of a number of persons usually in order to gather information (as on opinions)
quet·zal \ket-'säl, -'sal\ *n, pl* **quetzals** *or* **quet·za·les** \-'säl-ās\ : a Central American bird with a narrow crest on the head and brightly colored feathers and in the male with tail feathers often over two feet in length
¹**queue** \'kyü\ *n* **1** : a pigtail usually worn hanging at the back of the head **2** : a waiting line ⟨a *queue* at a ticket window⟩ **3** : a sequence of messages or jobs held in auxiliary storage in a computer awaiting transmission or processing
Word History The Latin word *cauda* or *coda,* meaning "tail", passed into French and in time ended up being spelled *queue.* English borrowed this word, giving it the meaning "a long braid of hair", one that hangs from a person's head like a tail. This sense is still in use, but we more commonly refer to such a braid as *pigtail* today. In the 19th century, *queue* came to be used for something else that looked like a tail — a number of people waiting in line. [from French *queue,* literally "tail", from Latin *coda, cauda* "tail" — related to CODA, COWARD, ³CUE; see *Word History* at COWARD]
²**queue** *vb* **queued; queu·ing** *or* **queue·ing** **1** : to arrange or form in a queue **2** : to line up or wait in a queue ⟨the crowd *queued* up for tickets⟩ — **queu·er** *n*
¹**quib·ble** \'kwib-əl\ *vb* **quib·bled; quib·bling** \-(ə-)liŋ\ **1** : to talk about unimportant things rather than the real point ⟨stop *quibbling* about words and tell what happened⟩ **2** : to find fault or argue over unimportant points ⟨people ignored the main point of the speech and *quibbled* about its length⟩ — **quib·bler** \-(ə-)lər\ *n*
²**quibble** *n* **1** : a statement that deals with a minor matter and not the real point under discussion **2** : a minor objection or criticism
¹**quick** \'kwik\ *adj* **1** *archaic* : not dead : LIVING, ALIVE **2 a** : fast in understanding, thinking, or learning : mentally keen **b** : reacting with speed and alertness **c** : aroused immediately and easily ⟨*quick* temper⟩ **d** : fast in development or occurrence ⟨gave a *quick* look⟩ **e** : marked by speed, readiness, or promptness of action or movement — **quick** *adv* — **quick·ly** *adv* — **quick·ness** *n*
syn QUICK, PROMPT, READY, APT mean able to respond right away. QUICK stresses that the response is immediate and often suggests that the ability is part of one's nature ⟨she always had a *quick* mind⟩ PROMPT suggests that the ability to respond quickly is the product of training and discipline ⟨the store gives *prompt* service⟩ READY suggests ease or smoothness in response ⟨he always had a *ready* answer to any question⟩ APT stresses the person's intelligence or talent that allows the giving of a quick response ⟨an *apt* student who learned computer programming in no time⟩
²**quick** *n* **1** : living persons ⟨the *quick* and the dead⟩ **2** : a very tender area of flesh (as under a fingernail) **3** : one's innermost feelings ⟨hurt to the *quick* by the remark⟩ **4** : the very center of something : HEART ⟨the *quick* of the matter⟩

quetzal

quick bread *n* : a bread made with baking powder or baking soda that does not have to be allowed to rise before baking
quick·en \'kwik-ən\ *vb* **quick·ened; quick·en·ing** \-(ə-)niŋ\ **1 a** : to make or become alive : REVIVE ⟨warm spring days that *quickened* the earth⟩ **b** : AROUSE 2, STIMULATE ⟨curiosity *quickened* her interest⟩ **2** : to make or become quicker : HASTEN ⟨*quickened* her steps⟩ **3 a** : to begin growth and development ⟨seeds *quickening* in the soil⟩ **b** : to reach the stage of fetal growth at which motion is begun
quick–freeze \'kwik-'frēz\ *vb* **-froze** \-'frōz\; **-fro·zen** \-'frōz-ᵊn\; **-freez·ing** : to freeze food so rapidly that the natural juices and flavor are not lost
quick·ie \'kwik-ē\ *n* : something done or made in a hurry
quick·sand \'kwik-,sand\ *n* : a deep mass of loose sand mixed with water into which heavy objects sink
quick·sil·ver \-,sil-vər\ *n* : MERCURY 1a
Word History The metal mercury resembles silver in color. Unlike silver and most other metals, though, mercury is liquid at ordinary temperatures. For that reason it is able to flow and to move almost as if it were alive. The Old English word for mercury was *cwicseolfor,* a combination of *cwic,* meaning "alive" or "moving", and *seolfor,* meaning "silver". The Modern English *quicksilver* comes from the Old English *cwicseolfor.* [Old English *cwicseolfor,* from *cwic* "alive" and *seolfor* "silver"]
quick–tem·pered \'kwik-'tem-pərd\ *adj* : easily angered : IRASCIBLE
quick–wit·ted \'kwik-'wit-əd\ *adj* : quick in thinking and understanding : mentally alert **syn** see INTELLIGENT — **quick–wit·ted·ness** *n*
quid \'kwid\ *n* : a lump of something chewable
qui·es·cent \kwī-'es-ᵊnt, kwē-\ *adj* : marked by a lack of action or movement — **qui·es·cence** \-ᵊn(t)s\ *n* — **qui·es·cent·ly** *adv*
¹**qui·et** \'kwī-ət\ *n* : the quality or state of being quiet — **on the quiet** : in a secretive manner
²**quiet** *adj* **1 a** : marked by little or no motion, activity, or noise : CALM **b** : GENTLE 2b, EASYGOING ⟨a *quiet* disposition⟩ **c** : not disturbed : PEACEFUL ⟨enjoyed a *quiet* dinner for two⟩ **2** : not colorful or showy : CONSERVATIVE ⟨*quiet* clothes⟩ **3** : hidden from public view ⟨a *quiet* corner⟩ — **quiet** *adv* — **qui·et·ly** *adv* — **qui·et·ness** *n*
³**quiet** *vb* : to make or become quiet — **qui·et·er** *n*
qui·etude \'kwī-ə-,t(y)üd\ *n* : the state of being quiet : TRANQUILLITY
qui·etus \kwī-'ēt-əs\ *n* **1** : a final freeing from something (as a debt, an office or duty, or life) **2** : something that quiets or brings under control ⟨put the *quietus* on a scandal⟩
quill \'kwil\ *n* **1 a** : the hollow tubelike part of a feather **b** : one of the large stiff feathers of the wing or tail **2** : one of the hollow sharp spines of a porcupine or hedgehog **3** : a pen made from a feather
¹**quilt** \'kwilt\ *n* : a bed cover made of two layers of cloth with a filling of wool, cotton, or down held together by patterned stitching
²**quilt** *vb* : to construct (as by padding, covering with patterns, or sewing layers together) like a quilt — **quilt·er** *n*
quilt·ing *n* **1** : material that is quilted or used for making quilts **2** : the process of quilting
quince \'kwin(t)s\ *n* : the fruit of an Asian tree that resembles a yellow apple with hard flesh and is used especially for marmalade,

quince

jelly, and preserves; *also*: this tree

qui·nine \'kwī-,nīn *also* 'kwin-,īn\ *n* : a bitter white drug obtained from cinchona bark and used especially to treat malaria; *also* : a salt of quinine

qui·noa \ki-'nō-ə\ *n* : a pigweed of the high Andes with seeds that are ground and widely used as food in Peru

Quin·qua·ge·si·ma \,kwiŋ-kə-'jes-ə-mə, -'jä-zə-\ *n* : the Sunday before Lent

quint \'kwint\ *n* : QUINTUPLET

quin·tal \'kwint-ᵊl\ *n* : HUNDREDWEIGHT

quin·tes·sence \kwin-'tes-ᵊn(t)s\ *n* **1** : the purest form of something **2** : the most perfect type or example [Middle English *quintessence* "the purest or most perfect form or example of something", from early French *quinte essence* (same meaning), from Latin *quinta essentia*, literally "fifth essence", from earlier *quinta*, feminine form of *quintus* "fifth", and earlier *essentia* "essence"] — **quin·tes·sen·tial** \,kwint-ə-'sen-chəl\ *adj*

quin·tet \kwin-'tet\ *n* **1 a** : a musical composition for five instruments or voices **b** : the performers of a quintet **2** : a group or set of five

quin·til·lion \kwin-'til-yən\ *n* — see NUMBER table

¹quin·tu·ple \kwin-'t(y)üp-əl, -'təp-; 'kwint-əp-\ *adj* **1** : having five units or members **2** : being five times as great or as many — **quintuple** *n*

²quintuple *vb* **quin·tu·pled; quin·tu·pling** \-(ə-)liŋ\ : to make or become five times as great or as many

quin·tu·plet \kwin-'təp-lət, -'t(y)üp-; 'kwint-əp-\ *n* **1** : a group of five **2** : one of five offspring born at one birth

¹quip \'kwip\ *n* **1** : a clever remark **2** : a witty or funny saying

²quip *vb* **quipped; quip·ping** : to make quips

quirk \'kwərk\ *n* **1** : a sudden turn, twist, or curve **2** : an odd personal habit : IDIOSYNCRASY — **quirky** \'kwər-kē\ *adj*

quirt \'kwərt\ *n* : a riding whip with a short handle and a rawhide tip

quis·ling \'kwiz-liŋ\ *n* : one who helps the invaders of one's own country [named for Vidkun *Quisling* 1887–1945 a Norwegian politician who helped the German invaders in World War II]

¹quit \'kwit\ *adj* : released from duty, responsibility, or penalty : FREE ⟨*quit* of debt⟩

²quit *vb* **quit** *also* **quit·ted; quit·ting** **1** : to make full payment to or for : REPAY ⟨*quit* a debt⟩ **2** : ²CONDUCT 4 ⟨the children *quit* themselves well in the woods⟩ **3 a** : to depart from : LEAVE ⟨*quit* the scene of the accident⟩ **b** : to bring to an end : ABANDON **c** : to give up (as an action or activity) for good ⟨*quit* bragging⟩ ⟨*quit* a job⟩ **4** : to admit defeat : SURRENDER

quite \'kwīt\ *adv* **1** : beyond question or doubt : COMPLETELY ⟨*quite* alone⟩ ⟨*quite* sure⟩ **2** : MORE OR LESS 1, RATHER ⟨we live *quite* near the school⟩

quits \'kwits\ *adj* : even or equal with another (as by repaying a debt, returning a favor, or paying back an enemy)

quit·tance \'kwit-ᵊn(t)s\ *n* **1 a** : a freeing from a debt or responsibility **b** : a document certifying quittance **2** : something given in return : RECOMPENSE

quit·ter \'kwit-ər\ *n* : a person who gives up too easily

¹quiv·er \'kwiv-ər\ *n* **1** : a case for carrying arrows **2** : the arrows in a quiver [Middle English *quiver* "a case for carrying arrows", from early French *quivre* (same meaning); of Germanic origin]

¹quiver 1

²quiver *vb* **quiv·ered; quiv·er·ing** \'kwiv-(ə-)riŋ\ : to move with a slight shaking motion [Middle English *quiveren* "to quiver", probably from *quiver* "agile, quick"]

³quiver *n* : the act or action of quivering : TREMOR

quix·ot·ic \kwik-'sät-ik\ *adj* : impractical especially in the foolish pursuit of ideals [from Don *Quixote*, hero of the novel *Don Quixote de la Mancha* by Cervantes] — **quix·ot·i·cal·ly** \-'sät-i-k(ə-)lē\ *adv*

¹quiz \'kwiz\ *n, pl* **quiz·zes** **1** : a person who mocks **2** : the act or action of quizzing; *esp* : a short oral or written test

²quiz *vb* **quizzed; quiz·zing** **1** : to make fun of : MOCK **2** : to ask many questions — **quiz·zer** *n*

quiz·zi·cal \'kwiz-i-kəl\ *adj* **1** : teasing in a good-natured way **2 a** : showing doubt in a good-natured way **b** : showing puzzlement or curiosity — **quiz·zi·cal·ly** \-k(ə-)lē\ *adv*

quoit \'kwāt, 'k(w)óit\ *n* **1** : a ring of iron or circle of rope to be thrown over a peg in a game **2** *pl* : a game played with quoits

quo·rum \'kwōr-əm, 'kwór-\ *n* : the number of members of an organization required to be present in order for business to be carried on

quo·ta \'kwōt-ə\ *n* **1** : a share or part assigned to each member of a group **2** : the number or amount making up a quota

quot·able \'kwōt-ə-bəl\ *adj* : fit for or worth quoting

quo·ta·tion \kwō-'tā-shən\ *n* **1** : the act or process of quoting **2** : the prices currently bid or offered for stocks, bonds, or goods **3** : something that is quoted

quotation mark *n* : one of a pair of punctuation marks " " or ' ' used chiefly to indicate the beginning and the end of a direct quotation

¹quote \'kwōt\ *vb* **quot·ed; quot·ing** **1** : to repeat (someone else's words) exactly ⟨*quote* Shakespeare⟩ **2** : to give as an example **3** : to set off written material by quotation marks

²quote *n* **1** : QUOTATION 3 **2** : QUOTATION MARK

quoth \(')kwōth\ *vb past, archaic* : SAID — used chiefly in the first and third persons and placed before the subject

quo·tient \'kwō-shənt\ *n* : the number obtained from the division of one number by another [Middle English *quocient*, an altered form of Latin *quotiens* "how many times?"]

\ə\ **abut**	\aú\ **out**	\i\ **tip**	\ó\ **saw**	\ú\ **foot**
\ər\ **further**	\ch\ **chin**	\ī\ **life**	\ói\ **coin**	\y\ **yet**
\a\ **mat**	\e\ **pet**	\j\ **job**	\th\ **thin**	\yü\ **few**
\ā\ **take**	\ē\ **easy**	\ŋ\ **sing**	\t̲h̲\ **this**	\yú\ **cure**
\ä\ **cot, cart**	\g\ **go**	\ō\ **bone**	\ü\ **food**	\zh\ **vision**

R

r \'är\ *n, often cap* : the 18th letter of the English alphabet

R *trademark* — used to certify that a motion picture is of such a nature that admission is restricted to persons over a specified age (as 17) unless accompanied by a parent or guardian

rab·bi \'rab-,ī\ *n* **1** : ¹MASTER 1a, TEACHER — used as a term of address for Jewish religious leaders **2** : a professionally trained leader of a Jewish congregation [Old English *rabbi* "term of address used by Jews", from Latin *rabbi* (same meaning), from Greek *rhabbi* (same meaning), from Hebrew *rabbī* "my master", from *rabh* "master" and the suffix *-ī* "my"] — **rab·bin·ic** \rə-'bin-ik, ra-\ *or* **rab·bin·i·cal** \-i-kəl\ *adj*

rab·bin·ate \'rab-ə-nət, -,nāt\ *n* **1** : the office of a rabbi **2** : a group of rabbis

rab·bit \'rab-ət\ *n, pl* **rab·bits** *also* **rabbit** : a burrowing mammal that is smaller than the related hare and is born blind and naked; *also* : its pelt

rabbit

rabbit punch *n* : a short chopping blow to the back of the neck that is illegal in boxing

rab·ble \'rab-əl\ *n* **1** : a crowd that is noisy and hard to control : MOB **2** : a group of people looked down upon as ignorant and hard to control

rab·ble–rous·er \'rab-əl-,rau̇-zər\ *n* : a person who stirs up the people especially to hatred or violence

ra·bid \'rab-əd *also* 'rā-bəd\ *adj* **1** : extremely violent : FURIOUS **2** : going to extreme lengths (as in interest or opinion) **3** : affected with rabies — **ra·bid·ly** *adv*

ra·bies \'rā-bēz\ *n* : a deadly disease of the nervous system of warm-blooded animals that is usually passed on by the bite of an animal already infected with it — called also *hydrophobia*

rac·coon *also* **ra·coon** \ra-'kün\ *n, pl* **raccoon** *or* **raccoons** : a small North American mammal that is chiefly gray, has a bushy ringed tail, lives chiefly in trees, and eats a varied diet including small animals, fruits, and nuts; *also* : its pelt [from *ärähkun,* a word meaning "raccoon" in an American Indian language from the area that is now Virginia]

raccoon

¹race \'rās\ *n* **1** : a strong or rapid current of water or its channel **2 a** : a contest of speed **b** : a contest involving progress toward a goal (the *race* for governor) [Middle English *ras* "the act of running, a rapid current of water", of Norse origin]

²race *vb* **raced; rac·ing** **1** : to take part in a race **2** : to go, move, or drive at top speed **3** : to take part in a race against **4** : to cause the engine of a motor vehicle to go fast especially when in neutral

³race *n* **1 a** : a group of people of common ancestry or stock (the English *race*) (scion of a noble *race*) **b** : a class or kind of people unified by common interests, habits, or characteristics (a new *race* of scientists) **2 a** : a variety or breed of animals or plants **b** : a division of mankind possessing traits that are transmissible by descent and sufficient to character-ize it as a distinct human type **3** : a major group of living things (the human *race*) (the *race* of birds) [from early French *race* "generation", from early Italian *razza* (same meaning)]

race·course \'rā-,skō(ə)rs, -,skȯ(ə)rs\ *n* : a place for racing

race·horse \'rās-,hȯ(ə)rs\ *n* : a horse bred or kept for racing

rac·er \'rā-sər\ *n* **1** : one that races or is used for racing **2** : any of various long swift slender American snakes; *esp* : a common blacksnake

race runner *n* : a North American lizard that has a long tail and moves quickly

race·track \'rās-,strak\ *n* : a usually oval course on which races are run

race·way \'rā-,swā\ *n* **1** : a channel for a current of water **2** : RACETRACK; *esp* : one for harness racing

ra·cial \'rā-shəl\ *adj* : of, relating to, or based on race — **ra·cial·ly** \-shə-lē\ *adv*

ra·cial·ism \'rā-shə-,liz-əm\ *n* : RACISM — **ra·cial·ist** \-ləst\ *n or adj* — **ra·cial·is·tic** \rā-shə-'lis-tik\ *adj*

rac·ism \'rā-,siz-əm\ *n* **1** : belief that certain races of people are by birth and nature superior to others **2** : discrimination or hatred based on race — **rac·ist** \'rā-səst\ *n or adj*

¹rack \'rak\ *n* **1** : a framework for holding fodder for livestock **2** : an instrument of torture on which a body is stretched **3** : a framework or stand on or in which articles are placed (hat *rack*) (bicycle *rack*) **4** : a bar with teeth on one side for fitting together with those of a pinion

²rack *vb* **1** : to cause to suffer torture, pain, or sorrow (*racked* by a cough) **2** : to stretch or strain violently **3** : to place (as pool balls) in a rack

³rack *n* : a showy gait of a horse that is faster than a walk but slower than a trot

¹rack·et *also* **rac·quet** \'rak-ət\ *n* **1** : a light implement consisting of a handle attached to an open frame with a network of strings stretched across it that is used to hit the object in play (as a ball) in various games (as tennis, badminton, or racquetball) **2** : ²PADDLE 2b [from early French *raquette* "racket", from Arabic *rāḥah* "palm of the hand"]

²racket *n* **1** : a loud confused noise **2 a** : a dishonest scheme for obtaining money (as by cheating or threats) **b** : an easy way to make money or earn a living (is that all you do? What a *racket*) [origin unknown]

³racket *vb* : to make a racket

rack·e·teer \,rak-ə-'ti(ə)r\ *n* : one who gets money or advantages by using force or threats — **racketeer** *vb*

rack up *vb* : ²SCORE 4a (*racked* 30 points *up* in the first half)

racoon *variant of* RACCOON

rac·quet·ball \'rak-ət-,bȯl\ *n* : a game for two or four played on a four-walled court with short-handled rackets and a rubber ball

¹racy \'rā-sē\ *adj* **rac·i·er; -est** **1** : full of energy or keen enjoyment **2** : slightly indecent or improper — **rac·i·ly** \-sə-lē\ *adv* — **rac·i·ness** \-sē-nəs\ *n*

²racy *adj* : being long-bodied and lean

ra·dar \'rā-,där\ *n* : a device that sends out radio waves for detecting and locating an object by the reflection of the radio waves and that may use this reflection to find out the position and speed of the object [from *radio detecting and ranging*]

¹ra·di·al \'rād-ē-əl\ *adj* **1** : arranged or having parts arranged like rays around a common center (the *radial* form of a starfish) **2** : relating to, placed like, or moving along a bodily radius (as the bone of the forearm) — **ra·di·al·ly** \-ē-ə-lē\ *adv*

²radial *n* **1** : a radial part **2** : RADIAL TIRE

radial symmetry *n* : plant and animal symmetry in which similar parts are arranged in a balanced way around the center of the body — compare BILATERAL SYMMETRY

radial tire *n* : a tire in which the ply cords are at right angles to the centerline of the tread

ra·di·ance \'rād-ē-ən(t)s\ *n* : the quality or state of being radiant

ra·di·ant \'rād-ē-ənt\ *adj* **1 a** : giving out or reflecting light ⟨a *radiant* jewel⟩ **b** : vividly bright and gleaming **2** : glowing with love, confidence, or happiness ⟨a *radiant* smile⟩ **3** : transmitted by radiation ⟨*radiant* heat⟩ [Middle English *radiant* "reflecting light beams", from Latin *radiant-, radians,* present participle of *radiare* "to emit beams of light", from *radius* "ray, beam, spoke" — related to RADIO, RADIUS, [2]RAY] **syn** see BRIGHT — **ra·di·ant·ly** *adv*

radiant energy *n* : energy (as heat waves, light waves, radio waves, X rays) transmitted in the form of electromagnetic waves

ra·di·ate \'rād-ē-ˌāt\ *vb* **-at·ed; -at·ing** **1** : to proceed in a direct line from or toward a center **2 a** : to send out rays : SHINE **b** : to come forth in the form or as if in the form of rays **3** : to spread around from or as if from a center

ra·di·a·tion \ˌrād-ē-'ā-shən\ *n* **1** : something that is radiated; *esp* : energy radiated in the form of waves or particles **2** : the action or process of radiating; *esp* : the process of giving off radiant energy in the form of waves or particles — **ra·di·a·tion·al** \-shnəl, -shən-ᵊl\ *adj*

ra·di·a·tor \'rād-ē-ˌāt-ər\ *n* : one that radiates; *esp* : any of various devices (as a set of pipes or tubes) for transferring heat from a fluid within to an area or object outside

[1]rad·i·cal \'rad-i-kəl\ *adj* **1** : of, relating to, or proceeding from a root **2 a** : departing sharply from the usual or ordinary : EXTREME **b** : of or relating to radicals in politics — **rad·i·cal·ly** \-k(ə-)lē\ *adv* — **rad·i·cal·ness** *n*

Word History Our word *radical* was formed from the Latin adjective *radicalis,* which simply meant "of or relating to a root". The Latin word *radix* meant "root". This meaning was kept when the word *radicalis* came into English as *radical,* but new senses developed too. Since a root is at the bottom of something, *radical* came to describe what is at the base or beginning, in other words, what is "basic, fundamental". Later, *radical* was used to describe something that was extremely different from the usual. Then, as a noun *radical* came to be applied to a person who wants to make extreme or "radical" changes in the government or in society. In mathematics, a *radical* sign indicates a root of a number. The words *radish* and *eradicate* also come from the Latin *radix.* [Middle English *radical* "relating to a root", from Latin *radicalis* (same meaning), from earlier *radic-, radix* "root" — related to ERADICATE, RADISH]

[2]radical *n* **1** : [1]ROOT 5 **2** : a person who favors rapid and sweeping changes especially in laws and methods of government **3** : a group of atoms bonded together that is considered as a unit in various kinds of reactions **4 a** : the indicated root of a mathematical expression **b** : RADICAL SIGN

rad·i·cal·ism \'rad-i-kə-ˌliz-əm\ *n* : the quality or state of being radical

rad·i·cal·ize \'rad-i-kə-ˌlīz\ *vb* **-ized; -iz·ing** : to make radical

radical sign *n* : the sign √ placed before an expression in mathematics to indicate that its root is to be found

rad·i·cand \ˌrad-ə-'kand\ *n* : the expression under a radical sign

radial symmetry

radii *pl of* RADIUS

[1]ra·dio \'rād-ē-ˌō\ *n, pl* **ra·di·os** **1 a** : the sending or receiving of signals using electromagnetic waves without a connecting wire ⟨*radio* includes television and radar⟩ **b** : the use of these waves to carry sound energy that has been changed into electrical energy **2** : a radio receiving set ⟨a transistor *radio*⟩ **3** : the radio broadcasting industry [a shortened form of *radiotelegraphy,* literally "telegraphy by rays"; *radio-* from French *radio-* "radial, radiating", from Latin *radius* "ray, beam, spoke" — related to RADIANT, RADIUS, [2]RAY]

[2]radio *adj* **1** : of, relating to, or operated by radiant energy and especially by radio frequencies **2** : of, relating to, or used in radio or a radio

[3]radio *vb* : to communicate or send a message to by radio

radio- *combining form* **1** : radiant energy : radiation ⟨*radio*active⟩ **2** : radioactive ⟨*radio*carbon⟩ [derived from Latin *radius* "ray, beam, spoke"]

ra·dio·ac·tive \ˌrād-ē-ō-'ak-tiv\ *adj* : of, caused by, or exhibiting radioactivity — **ra·dio·ac·tive·ly** *adv*

ra·dio·ac·tiv·i·ty \-ˌak-'tiv-ət-ē\ *n* : the giving off of rays of energy or particles by the breaking apart of atoms of certain elements (as uranium)

radio astronomy *n* : astronomy dealing with electromagnetic waves of radio frequency received from outside the earth's atmosphere — **radio astronomer** *n*

ra·dio·car·bon \ˌrād-ē-ō-'kär-bən\ *n* : radioactive carbon; *esp* : CARBON 14

radio frequency *n* : any of the electromagnetic wave frequencies between audio frequencies and infrared frequencies and used especially in radio and television transmission

ra·dio·gram \'rād-ē-ō-ˌgram\ *n* : a message transmitted by radio

ra·dio·iso·tope \ˌrād-ē-ō-'ī-sə-ˌtōp\ *n* : a radioactive isotope

ra·di·o·lar·i·an \ˌrād-ē-ō-'lar-ē-ən, -'ler-\ *n* : any of an order of marine protozoans that have small spines radiating from the shell and have a skeleton containing silica

ra·dio·man \'rād-ē-ō-ˌman\ *n* : a radio operator (as on a ship)

ra·di·om·e·ter \ˌrād-ē-'äm-ət-ər\ *n* : an instrument for measuring the strength of radiant energy — **ra·dio·met·ric** \ˌrād-ē-ō-'me-trik\ *adj* — **ra·di·om·e·try** \-'äm-ə-trē\ *n*

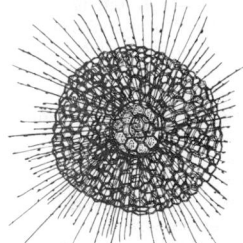

radiolarian

ra·dio·phone \'rād-ē-ə-ˌfōn\ *n* : RADIOTELEPHONE

ra·dio·sonde \'rād-ē-ō-ˌsänd\ *n* : a miniature radio transmitter that is carried aloft (as by a balloon) with instruments for broadcasting the humidity, temperature, and pressure

ra·dio·tele·phone \ˌrād-ē-ō-'tel-ə-ˌfōn\ *n* : a telephone that uses radio waves wholly or partly instead of connecting wires — **ra·dio·te·le·pho·ny** \-tə-'lef-ə-nē, -'tel-ə-ˌfō-nē\ *n*

radio telescope *n* : a radio receiver-antenna combination used for observation in radio astronomy

ra·dio·ul·na \ˌrād-ē-ō-'əl-nə\ *n* : a bone of some lower vertebrates (as the toad) equivalent to the radius and ulna of higher forms that have become united to form a single bone

\ə\ abut		\aú\ **out**	\i\ **tip**	\ȯ\ **saw**	\ù\ **foot**
\ər\ **further**		\ch\ **chin**	\ī\ **life**	\ȯi\ **coin**	\y\ **yet**
\a\ **mat**		\e\ **pet**	\j\ **job**	\th\ **thin**	\yü\ **few**
\ā\ **take**		\ē\ **easy**	\ŋ\ **sing**	\th\ **this**	\yù\ **cure**
\ä\ **cot, cart**		\g\ **go**	\ō\ **bone**	\ü\ **food**	\zh\ **vision**

radio wave *n* : an electromagnetic wave with radio frequency

rad·ish \'rad-ish, 'red-\ *n* : the fleshy edible root of a plant related to the mustards; *also* : a plant that produces radishes [Old English *rædic* "radish", from Latin *radic-, radix* "root" — related to ERADICATE, RADICAL; see *Word History* at RADICAL]

ra·di·um \'rād-ē-əm\ *n* : a strongly radioactive shining white metallic element that is chemically similar to barium, occurs in combination in very small quantities in minerals (as pitchblende), and is used in the treatment of cancer — see ELEMENT table

ra·di·us \'rād-ē-əs\ *n, pl* **-dii** \-ē-,ī\ *also* **-di·us·es** **1** : the bone on the thumb side of the human forearm; *also* : a corresponding bone of vertebrates above fishes **2** : a line extending from the center of a circle or sphere to the circumference or surface **3 a** : the length of a radius **b** : a circular area defined by a given radius ⟨deer may wander within a *radius* of several kilometers⟩ **4** : a radial part or plane [from Latin *radius* "ray, beam, spoke" — related to RADIANT, RADIO, ²RAY]

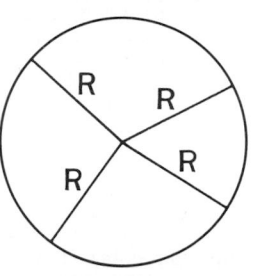

R radius 2

ra·don \'rā-,dän\ *n* : a heavy radioactive gaseous element formed by the breaking apart of radium atoms — see ELEMENT table

raf·fia \'raf-ē-ə\ *n* : fiber from a palm of Madagascar used to braid or weave various articles (as baskets or hats)

raff·ish \'raf-ish\ *adj* **1** : vulgarly crude or flashy ⟨*raffish* language⟩ **2** : careless about moral behavior : DISREPUTABLE — **raff·ish·ly** *adv* — **raff·ish·ness** *n*

¹raf·fle \'raf-əl\ *vb* **raf·fled; raf·fling** \'raf-(ə-)liŋ\ : to dispose of by a raffle ⟨*raffle* off a turkey⟩

²raffle *n* : the sale of chances for a prize whose winner is the one whose ticket is picked at a drawing

¹raft \'raft\ *n* : a flat structure (as a group of logs fastened together) for support or transportation on water [Middle English *rafte* "rafter, raft"; of Norse origin]

²raft *vb* : to transport or move on or by means of a raft

³raft *n* : a large amount or number [probably an altered form of earlier *raff* "jumble"]

raf·ter \'raf-tər\ *n* : one of the usually sloping timbers that support a roof — **raf·tered** \-tərd\ *adj*

¹rag \'rag\ *n* **1** : a waste or worn piece of cloth **2** *pl* : shabby or very worn clothing ⟨dressed in *rags*⟩

²rag *n* : a composition in ragtime

rag·a·muf·fin \'rag-ə-,məf-ən\ *n* : a poorly clothed often dirty child

rag·bag \'rag-,bag\ *n* : a bag for scraps of cloth

rag doll *n* : a cloth doll that is stuffed and usually painted

¹rage \'rāj\ *n* **1 a** : very strong and uncontrolled anger **b** : a fit of violent anger **2** : violent action (as of wind or sea) **3** : FAD ⟨the current *rage*⟩ **syn** see ANGER

²rage *vb* **raged; rag·ing** **1** : to be in a rage **2** : to continue out of control ⟨the fire *raged* for hours⟩

rag·ged \'rag-əd\ *adj* **1** : having a rough or uneven edge or outline ⟨*ragged* cliffs⟩ **2 a** : torn or worn to or as if to tatters ⟨a *ragged* dress⟩ **b** : wearing tattered clothes **3** : done in an uneven way ⟨a *ragged* performance⟩ — **rag·ged·ly** *adv* — **rag·ged·ness** *n*

rag·gedy \'rag-əd-ē\ *adj* : RAGGED 2

rag·lan sleeve \'rag-lən-\ *n* : a sleeve sewn in by seams slanted from the underarm to the neck

rag·man \'rag-,man\ *n* : a collector of or dealer in rags

ra·gout \ra-'gü\ *n* : a highly seasoned stew of meat and vegetables

rag·pick·er \'rag-,pik-ər\ *n* : a person who collects rags and waste for a living

rag·tag \'rag-,tag\ *adj* : RAGGED 2b

rag·time \'rag-,tīm\ *n* : music played with a strong march-style rhythm and a lively melody with accented notes falling on beats that are not usually accented

rag·weed \'rag-,wēd\ *n* : any of various chiefly North American weedy herbs related to the daisies and producing pollen irritating to the eyes and noses of some persons

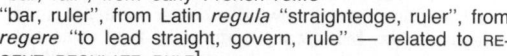

ragweed

rah \'rä, 'rò\ *interj* : HURRAH — used to cheer a team on

¹raid \'rād\ *n* : a sudden attack or invasion

²raid *vb* : to make a raid on — **raid·er** *n*

¹rail \'rā(ə)l\ *n* **1 a** : a bar extending from one support to another and serving as a guard or barrier **b** : RAILING 1 **2 a** : a bar of steel forming a track for wheeled vehicles **b** : RAILROAD [Middle English *raile* "bar, rail", from early French *reille* "bar, rail", from Latin *regula* "straightedge, ruler", from *regere* "to lead straight, govern, rule" — related to REGENT, REGULATE, RULE]

²rail *vb* : to provide with a railing

³rail *n, pl* **rails** *or* **rail** : any of a family of small wading birds related to the cranes and often hunted as game birds [Middle English *raile* "rail (the bird)", from early French *raale* (same meaning)]

⁴rail *vb* : to scold or complain in harsh or bitter language [Middle English *railen* "to scold, be abusive to", from early French *railler* "to mock", probably derived from Latin *regulare* "to bray like a horse"] — **rail·er** *n*

rail·ing \'rā-liŋ\ *n* **1** : a barrier (as a fence) consisting of rails and their supports **2** : material for rails

rail·lery \'rā-lə-rē\ *n, pl* **-ler·ies** : an act or an instance of making fun of somebody in a good-natured way

¹rail·road \'rā(ə)l-,rōd\ *n* **1** : a permanent road that has parallel steel rails which make a track for cars **2** : a railroad together with the lands, buildings, locomotives, cars, and other equipment that belong to it

²railroad *vb* **1 a** : to send by railroad **b** : to work on a railroad **2 a** : to push (as a bill) through a legislature in a rush **b** : to convict and send to prison without very much evidence or by means of false charges — **rail·road·er** *n*

rail·road·ing *n* : the building or running of a railroad

rail·way \'rā(ə)l-,wā\ *n* : ¹RAILROAD

rai·ment \'rā-mənt\ *n* : CLOTHING 1

¹rain \'rān\ *n* **1 a** : water falling in drops from clouds **b** : the falling of such water **2 a** : RAINSTORM **b** *pl* : the rainy season **3** : rainy weather ⟨a week of *rain*⟩ **4** : a heavy fall of objects ⟨a *rain* of ashes⟩ — **rain·less** \-ləs\ *adj*

²rain *vb* **1** : to fall as water in drops from the clouds **2** : to send down rain **3** : to fall like rain ⟨ashes *rained* from the volcano⟩ **4** : to give in large amounts ⟨*rained* blows on each other⟩ — **rain cats and dogs** : to rain very hard

rain·bow \'rān-,bō\ *n* : an arc or circle of colors that appears in the sky opposite the sun and is caused by the sun shining through raindrops, spray, or mist

rainbow trout *n* : a large trout native to western North America that usually has red or pink stripes with black dots on its sides

³rail

rain·coat \'rān-ˌkōt\ *n* : a coat of waterproof or water-resistant material

rain·drop \-ˌdräp\ *n* : a drop of rain

rain·fall \-ˌfȯl\ *n* **1** : a fall of rain **2** : amount of precipitation ⟨an annual *rainfall* of 50 centimeters⟩

rain forest *n* **1** : an often tropical woodland with a high annual rainfall and very tall trees — called also *tropical rain forest* **2** : TEMPERATE RAIN FOREST

rain gauge *n* : an instrument for measuring rainfall

rain·mak·ing \'rān-ˌmā-kiŋ\ *n* : the action or process of attempting to produce rain by artificial means — **rain·mak·er** \-kər\ *n*

rain·proof \-ˈprüf\ *adj* : keeping rain out

rain·storm \-ˌstȯ(ə)rm\ *n* : a storm of or with rain

rain·wa·ter \-ˌwȯt-ər, -ˌwät-\ *n* : water falling or fallen as rain

rain·wear \-ˌwa(ə)r, -ˌwe(ə)r\ *n* : waterproof or water-resistant clothing

rainy \'rā-nē\ *adj* **rain·i·er; -est** : having much rain

rainy day *n* : a period of need ⟨set a little money aside for a *rainy day*⟩

¹raise \'rāz\ *vb* **raised; rais·ing** **1** : to cause to rise ⟨*raise* a window⟩ ⟨*raise* dust⟩ **2 a** : to give life to : AROUSE ⟨enough noise to *raise* the dead⟩ **b** : to stir up : INCITE ⟨*raise* a rebellion⟩ **3 a** : to set upright by lifting or building ⟨*raise* a monument⟩ **b** : to place higher especially in rank : PROMOTE ⟨was *raised* to captain⟩ **4** : ²COLLECT 1b ⟨*raise* funds⟩ **5 a** : to look after the growth and development of : GROW ⟨*raise* hogs for market⟩ ⟨*raise* olives⟩ **b** : to bring up a child : REAR ⟨was *raised* in the city⟩ **6** : BRING ABOUT ⟨*raised* a laugh⟩ **7** : to bring to notice ⟨*raise* an issue⟩ **8 a** : to increase the strength of ⟨don't *raise* your voice⟩ **b** : to increase the amount of ⟨*raise* the rent⟩ **c** : to increase a bid or bet **9** : to make light and airy ⟨*raise* dough⟩ **10** : to multiply a quantity by itself a specified number of times **11** : to bring into sight on the horizon by approaching ⟨*raised* land at last⟩ **12** : to cause to form on the skin ⟨*raise* a blister⟩ — **rais·er** *n*

> **syn** RAISE, LIFT, HEAVE, HOIST mean to move from a lower to a higher place or position. RAISE often suggests a suitable or intended higher position to which something is brought ⟨*raise* the flag to the top of the pole⟩ LIFT suggests a bringing up especially from the ground and may also suggest the need for exertion in order to pick up something heavy ⟨*lift* those boxes onto the table⟩ HEAVE suggests lifting with great effort or strain ⟨*heave* those bales of hay onto the truck⟩ HOIST often suggests the use of pulleys to increase the force applied in raising something very heavy ⟨*hoist* the crates onto the ship⟩

— **raise Cain** : to cause trouble

²raise *n* **1** : an increase in the amount of a bet or bid **2** : an increase in pay

raised *adj* **1** : done in relief ⟨*raised* needlework⟩ **2** : having a nap ⟨*raised* fabric⟩

rai·sin \'rāz-ⁿn\ *n* : a grape usually of a special type dried for food

ra·ja *or* **ra·jah** \'räj-ə, 'räzh-\ *n* : an Indian prince [from a word in Hindi (the official language of India) *rājā* "prince, chief"]

¹rake \'rāk\ *n* **1** : a garden tool with a long handle and a bar with teeth or prongs at the end **2** : a machine for gathering hay [Old English *racu* "a tool for gathering up grass or straw"]

²rake *vb* **raked; rak·ing** **1** : to gather, loosen, or smooth with or as if with a rake ⟨*rake* leaves⟩ ⟨*raking* in money⟩ **2** : to search through : RANSACK ⟨*rake* the records for evidence⟩ **3** : to sweep the length of with or as if with gunfire — **rak·er** *n*

³rake *n* : LIBERTINE [a shortened form of earlier *rakehell* (same meaning), probably from earlier *rackle* "rash, impetuous"]

¹rak·ish \'rā-kish\ *adj* : of or resembling that of a rake

: DISSOLUTE [from *rake* "libertine"] — **rak·ish·ly** *adv* — **rak·ish·ness** *n*

²rakish *adj* **1** : having a neat or streamlined look that suggests speed ⟨a *rakish* ship⟩ ⟨a *rakish* sports car⟩ **2** : JAUNTY, DASHING ⟨hat perched at a *rakish* angle⟩ [from earlier *rake* "the amount of slope or lean of a ship's mast or the amount of overhang of a ship's bow"] — **rak·ish·ly** *adv* — **rak·ish·ness** *n*

rale \'ral, 'räl\ *n* : an abnormal sound that accompanies the sounds of normal breathing (as in bronchitis)

¹ral·ly \'ral-ē\ *vb* **ral·lied; ral·ly·ing** **1 a** : to bring or come together for a common purpose ⟨*rallied* to the cause⟩ **b** : to bring back to order ⟨*rallied* the retreating troops⟩ **2** : to rouse from low spirits or weakness ⟨the patient *rallied*⟩ **3** : to make a comeback ⟨the team *rallied* in the fourth quarter⟩ ⟨stock prices *rallied* at the close of trading⟩ [from French *rallier* "to call or come together for a common purpose", from early French *ralier* (same meaning), from *re-* "again, back" and *alier* "to unite"]

²rally *n*, *pl* **rallies** **1** : the action of rallying **2** : a big meeting intended to arouse enthusiasm **3** : a series of shots hit back and forth between players (as in tennis) before a point is won

³rally *vb* **ral·lied; ral·ly·ing** : to tease in a good-natured way [from French *railler* "to mock, tease", from early French *railler* (same meaning) — related to ⁴RAIL]

¹ram \'ram\ *n* **1** : a male sheep **2** : BATTERING RAM

²ram *vb* **rammed; ram·ming** **1** : to strike or strike against with violence : CRASH **2** : to force in, down, or through by or as if by driving or pressing — **ram·mer** *n*

RAM \'ram\ *n* : RANDOM-ACCESS MEMORY

¹ram·ble \'ram-bəl\ *vb* **ram·bled; ram·bling** \-b(ə-)liŋ\ **1** : to move from place to place for no special reason **2** : to talk or write without a clear purpose or point **3** : to grow or extend irregularly **syn** see WANDER

²ramble *n* : a long stroll with no particular destination

ram·bler \'ram-blər\ *n* **1** : a person who rambles **2** : a climbing rose with rather small often double flowers in large clusters

ram·bunc·tious \ram-ˈbəŋ(k)-shəs\ *adj* : not under control : UNRULY, EXUBERANT — **ram·bunc·tious·ly** *adv* — **ram·bunc·tious·ness** *n*

rambler 2

ram·i·fi·ca·tion \ˌram-ə-fə-ˈkā-shən\ *n* **1** : the act or process of branching **2** : something that comes from another like a branch ⟨the *ramifications* of a problem⟩

ram·i·fy \'ram-ə-ˌfī\ *vb* **-fied; -fy·ing** : to spread out or split up into branches or divisions

ram·jet engine \ˌram-ˌjet-\ *n* : a jet engine that depends on the speed of flight for the compression of the air it takes in rather than using a mechanical compressor

ramp \'ramp\ *n* : a sloping passage or roadway connecting different levels

¹ram·page \'ram-ˌpāj, (ˈ)ram-ˈpāj\ *vb* **ram·paged; ram·pag·ing** : to rush wildly about

²ram·page \'ram-ˌpāj\ *n* : a course of violent or reckless action or behavior — **ram·pa·geous** \ram-ˈpā-jəs\ *adj*

ram·pant \'ram-pənt *also* -ˌpant\ *adj* **1** : standing on the hind legs like a horse rearing **2** : not checked in growth

\ə\ abut		\aú\ out		\i\ tip		\ȯ\ saw		\ú\ foot
\ər\ further		\ch\ chin		\ī\ life		\ȯi\ coin		\y\ yet
\a\ mat		\e\ pet		\j\ job		\th\ thin		\yü\ few
\ā\ take		\ē\ easy		\ŋ\ sing		\th\ this		\yú\ cure
\ä\ cot, cart		\g\ go		\ō\ bone		\ü\ food		\zh\ vision

or spread ⟨rumor ran *rampant*⟩ — **ram·pant·ly** *adv*

ram·part \'ram-,pärt, -pərt\ *n* : a broad bank or wall raised as a protective barrier; *also* : any barrier that provides protection

¹ram·rod \'ram-,räd\ *n* : a rod for ramming the charge down the barrel in a muzzle-loading firearm

²ramrod *adj* : not flexible : very strict

ram·shack·le \'ram-,shak-əl\ *adj* : looking ready to fall down ⟨a *ramshackle* old barn⟩

ran *past of* RUN

¹ranch \'ranch\ *n* **1** : a place for the raising of livestock (as cattle, horses, or sheep) on range **2** : a farm devoted to a special crop or kind of animal ⟨a fruit *ranch*⟩ ⟨a mink *ranch*⟩ **3** : RANCH HOUSE 2

²ranch *vb* : to live or work on a ranch

ranch·er \'ran-chər\ *n* : a person who owns or works on a ranch

ran·che·ro \ran-'che(ə)r-ō, rän-\ *n, pl* **-ros** : RANCHER

ranch house *n* **1** : the main house on a ranch **2** : a one-story house usually with a low-pitched roof

ranch·man \'ranch-mən\ *n* : RANCHER

ran·cid \'ran(t)-səd\ *adj* : having a strong disagreeable smell or taste of stale oil or fat ⟨*rancid* butter⟩ — **ran·cid·i·ty** \ran-'sid-ət-ē\ *n*

ran·cor \'ran-kər\ *n* : deep hatred — **ran·cor·ous** \-k(ə-)rəs\ *adj* — **ran·cor·ous·ly** *adv*

R and D *n* : research and development

¹ran·dom \'ran-dəm\ *n* : something that is random — **at random** : without definite aim, direction, rule, or method

²random *adj* **1** : showing no clear plan, purpose, or pattern ⟨a *random* arrangement⟩ **2** : having a definite and especially an equal probability of occurring ⟨*random* number⟩ — **ran·dom·ly** *adv* — **ran·dom·ness** *n*

ran·dom–ac·cess \,ran-dəm-'ak-,ses\ *adj* : permitting access to stored data in any order the user desires

random–access memory *n* : a computer memory that provides the main internal storage available to the user for programs and data — compare READ-ONLY MEMORY

ran·dom·ize \'ran-də-,mīz\ *vb* **-ized; -iz·ing** : to make random ⟨shuffling *randomizes* playing cards⟩

rang *past of* RING

¹range \'rānj\ *n* **1** : a series of things in a line ⟨a *range* of mountains⟩ **2** : a cooking stove **3 a** : open land over which livestock may roam and feed **b** : the place where a certain kind of animal or plant naturally lives **4** : the act of ranging about **5 a** : the maximum distance a weapon can shoot, a missile can travel, or a vehicle can go without refueling ⟨the *range* of an airplane⟩ **b** : the distance between a weapon and its target **c** : a place where shooting is practiced ⟨a rifle *range*⟩ **6** : the distance or amount included or gone over : SCOPE ⟨the *range* of one's knowledge⟩ **7 a** : a variation or variety between limits ⟨out of our price *range*⟩ ⟨a wide *range* of colors⟩ **b** : the difference between the least and greatest of a set of values

²range *vb* **ranged; rang·ing** **1 a** : to set in a row or in proper order **b** : to set in place among others of the same kind **2** : to rove over or through : roam freely **3** : to vary within limits ⟨the temperature *ranged* from 50° to 90°⟩ **4** : to find the range of an object by instrument (as radar)

range finder *n* : a device used to find out the distance of an object (as a target)

rang·er \'rān-jər\ *n* **1** : FOREST RANGER **2 a** : a member of a body of troops who range over a region **b** : a soldier in an army unit with special training (as parachute jumping and scuba diving) for making surprise attacks and raids

rangy \'rān-jē\ *adj* **rang·i·er; -est** **1** : having long limbs and a long body ⟨*rangy* cattle⟩ **2** : tall and slender in body build — **rang·i·ness** *n*

ra·ni *or* **ra·nee** \rä-'nē, 'rän-,ē\ *n* : an Indian queen : a raja's wife

¹rank \'rank\ *adj* **1** : strong and active in growth ⟨*rank* weeds⟩ **2** : unpleasant to smell ⟨a faint *rank* smell of a

mountain lion⟩ ⟨the uncollected garbage was *rank*⟩ **3 a** : very noticeable ⟨*rank* dishonesty⟩ **b** : ¹EXTREME 1 ⟨a *rank* beginner⟩ — **rank·ly** *adv* — **rank·ness** *n*

²rank \'rank\ *n* **1** : ³ROW 1, SERIES ⟨*ranks* of houses⟩ **2 a** : a line of soldiers standing side by side **b** : the body of enlisted persons in an army ⟨rose from the *ranks*⟩ **3** : a group of individuals classed together — usually used in pl. ⟨in the *ranks* of the unemployed⟩ **4** : position within a group ⟨a poet of high *rank*⟩ **5** : official grade or position ⟨the *rank* of general⟩ **6** : high social position ⟨a person of *rank*⟩

³rank *vb* **1** : to arrange in lines or in a formation **2** : to arrange in a classification **3** : to take or have a certain position in a group ⟨*ranks* third in the class⟩

rank and file *n* **1** : the enlisted persons of one of the armed forces **2** : the ordinary members that make up the body of a group when considered apart from the leaders

ran·kle \'ran-kəl\ *vb* **ran·kled; ran·kling** \-k(ə-)lin\ : to cause anger, irritation, or deep bitterness

Word History The Greek word *drakōn*, meaning "serpent, dragon", was borrowed into Latin as *draco*. Later, the noun *dracunculus*, meaning "little serpent", was formed from *draco*. The French borrowed this noun as *draoncle* or *raoncle* but used it for something different: "a festering sore or ulcer". It seems that the form of such a sore looked something like the form of a small serpent. From the noun the French formed the verb *rancler*, "to fester". In the 14th century, the verb was taken in English as *rankle*, with the same meaning. Our word *dragon* also comes from the Greek *drakōn* by way of the Latin *draco*. [Middle English *ranclen* "to fester", from early French *rancler* (same meaning), derived from earlier *draoncle, raoncle* "a festering sore", from Latin *dracunculus* "little serpent, little dragon", from earlier *draco* "serpent, dragon", from Greek *drākon* "serpent, dragon" — related to DRAGON]

ran·sack \'ran-,sak, (')ran-'sak\ *vb* **1** : to search thoroughly **2** : to search through in order to rob — **ran·sack·er** *n*

¹ran·som \'ran(t)-səm\ *n* **1** : something paid or demanded for the freedom of a captured person **2** : the act of ransoming

²ransom *vb* : to free from captivity or punishment by paying a price — **ran·som·er** *n*

¹rant \'rant\ *vb* : to talk loudly and wildly ⟨*rant* and rave in anger⟩ — **rant·er** *n*

²rant *n* : loud and wild speech

¹rap \'rap\ *n* **1** : a sharp blow or knock **2 a** : the blame for an action ⟨took the *rap*⟩ **b** : a criminal charge ⟨a murder *rap*⟩ [Middle English *rappe* "a hard blow"]

²rap *vb* **rapped; rap·ping** **1** : to give a quick sharp blow : KNOCK ⟨*rap* on the door⟩ **2** : to utter suddenly with force

³rap *n* : the least bit ⟨doesn't care a *rap*⟩

⁴rap *vb* **rapped; rap·ping** **1** : to talk freely and frankly **2** : to perform rap music

⁵rap *n* **1** : an informal talk : CHAT, CONVERSATION; *also* : a line of talk : PATTER **2 a** : a rhythmic chanting often in unison of usually rhymed couplets to a musical accompaniment **b** : a piece so performed

ra·pa·cious \rə-'pā-shəs\ *adj* **1** : very greedy **2** : PREDATORY 2 — **ra·pa·cious·ly** *adv* — **ra·pa·cious·ness** *n*

ra·pac·i·ty \rə-'pas-ət-ē\ *n* : the quality of being rapacious

¹rape \'rāp\ *n* : an herb related to the mustards that is grown for animals to graze on and for its seeds which are used as birdseed and as a source of oil [Middle English *rape* "the herb rape", from Latin *rapa, rapum* "turnip, rape"]

²rape *vb* **raped; rap·ing** **1** *archaic* : to take away by force **2** : to have sexual intercourse with by force [Middle English *rapen* "to take away by force", from Latin *rapere* "to seize"] — **rap·er** *n* — **rap·ist** \'rā-pəst\ *n*

³rape *n* : an act of raping

¹rap·id \'rap-əd\ *adj* : very fast **syn** see FAST — **ra·pid·i·ty** \rə-'pid-ət-ē, ra-\ *n* — **rap·id·ly** *adv* — **rap·id·ness** *n*

²rapid *n* : a part of a river where the current flows fast usually over rocks — usually used in pl.

rapid eye movement *n* : rapid movement of the eyes which occurs during the dreaming period of sleep

rap·id–fire \,rap-əd-'fī(ə)r\ *adj* **1** : able to fire shots rapidly ⟨a *rapid-fire* weapon⟩ **2** : marked by a rapid rate or pace ⟨spoke *rapid-fire* Spanish⟩

rapid transit *n* : fast public passenger transportation (as by subway) in cities

ra·pi·er \'rā-pē-ər\ *n* : a straight sword with a narrow blade having both edges sharp

rap·ine \'rap-ən, -,īn\ *n* : the seizing and carrying away of something by force

rap·pel \ra-'pel, ra-\ *vb* : to descend (as from a cliff) by sliding down a rope

rap·port \ra-'pō(ə)r, -'pó(ə)r\ *n* : a friendly relationship

rap·proche·ment \,rap-,rōsh-'män\ *n* : the establishment of or a state of friendly relations

rap·scal·lion \rap-'skal-yən\ *n* : RASCAL

rapier

rapt \'rapt\ *adj* : showing complete delight or interest ⟨listened with *rapt* attention⟩ — **rapt·ly** \'rap-(t)lē\ *adv* — **rapt·ness** \'rap(t)-nəs\ *n*

rap·ture \'rap-chər\ *n* : a strong feeling of joy, delight, or love — **rap·tur·ous** \-chə-rəs, -shrəs\ *adj* — **rap·tur·ous·ly** *adv* — **rap·tur·ous·ness** *n*

¹rare \'ra(ə)r, 're(ə)r\ *adj* **rar·er; rar·est** **1** : not thick or dense : THIN ⟨the atmosphere is *rare* at high altitudes⟩ **2** : very fine : EXCELLENT, SPLENDID ⟨a *rare* June day⟩ **3** : very uncommon ⟨rain is *rare* in the desert⟩ ⟨a collection of *rare* books⟩ [Middle English *rare* "thin", from Latin *rarus* "rare"] — **rare·ness** *n*

  syn RARE, SCARCE mean being in short supply. RARE usually applies to an object or quality of which only a few examples are to be found and which is thus greatly prized and cherished ⟨a *rare* gem⟩ SCARCE applies to something that for the present is in too short supply to meet the demand for it ⟨food was *scarce* that winter⟩

²rare *adj* **rar·er; rar·est** : cooked so that the inside is still red ⟨*rare* roast beef⟩ [Old English *hrēre* "boiled lightly"]

rare·bit \'ra(ə)r-bət, 're(ə)r-\ *n* : WELSH RABBIT

rar·efac·tion \,rar-ə-'fak-shən, ,rer-\ *n* **1** : the action or process of rarefying **2** : the state of being rarefied **3** : a state or region of minimum pressure in a substance (as air) being traveled through by a wave formed by compression (as sound)

rar·efy *also* **rar·i·fy** \'rar-ə-,fī, 'rer-\ *vb* **-efied; -efy·ing** : to make or become rare, thin, or less dense

rare·ly \'ra(ə)r-lē, 're(ə)r-\ *adv* : not often : SELDOM

rar·ing \'ra(ə)r-ən, 're(ə)r-, -iŋ\ *adj* : full of enthusiasm or eagerness ⟨*raring* to go⟩

rar·i·ty \'rar-ət-ē, 'rer-\ *n, pl* **-ties** **1** : the quality, state, or fact of being rare **2** : someone or something rare

ras·cal \'ras-kəl\ *n* **1** : a mean or dishonest person **2** : a mischievous person

ras·cal·i·ty \ra-'skal-ət-ē\ *n, pl* **-ties** : the actions or character of a rascal

ras·cal·ly \'ras-kə-lē\ *adj* : of or resembling that of a rascal ⟨a *rascally* trick⟩ — **rascally** *adv*

¹rash \'rash\ *adj* : marked by or coming from being too hasty in speech or action or in making decisions — **rash·ly** *adv* — **rash·ness** *n*

²rash *n* : a breaking out of the skin with red spots (as in measles)

¹rasp \'rasp\ *vb* **1** : to rub with or as if with a rough file ⟨*rasp* off a rough edge⟩ **2** : IRRITATE 1 **3** : to speak or say in an irritated tone **4** : to make a harsh grating sound

²rasp *n* **1** : a coarse file with cutting points instead of lines **2** : a rasping sound or sensation

rasp·ber·ry \'raz-,ber-ē, -b(ə-)rē\ *n* **1 a** : any of various black or red edible berries that are rounder and smaller than the related blackberries **b** : a usually prickly plant that produces raspberries **2** : a sound of scorn made by sticking out the tongue and blowing hard so as to make it vibrate

raspy \'ras-pē\ *adj* : making a harsh grating sound ⟨a *raspy* voice⟩

¹rat \'rat\ *n* **1** : any of numerous rodents with brown, black, white, or grayish fur and a naked tail that look like but are larger than the related mice **2** : a person who betrays friends

²rat *vb* **rat·ted; rat·ting** **1** : to betray one's friends **2** : to catch or hunt rats

rat·able *or* **rate·able** \'rāt-ə-bəl\ *adj* : able to be rated or estimated

ratch·et \'rach-ət\ *n* **1** : a mechanical device that consists of a bar or wheel having slanted teeth into which a pawl drops so as to allow motion in one direction only **2** : PAWL

ratchet wheel *n* : a toothed wheel held in position or turned by a pawl

¹rate \'rāt\ *vb* **rat·ed; rat·ing** : to scold violently : BERATE [Middle English *raten* "to scold violently"]

²rate *n* **1 a** : a constant ratio between two things ⟨a *rate* of exchange⟩ **b** : a price or charge set according to a scale or standard ⟨hotel *rates*⟩ ⟨tax *rate*⟩ **3** : a quantity, amount, or degree of something measured in units of something else ⟨the unemployment *rate*⟩ **4** : a level of quality : CLASS [Middle English *rate* "an estimated or determined value", from early French *rate* (same meaning), derived from Latin *rata*, literally "fixed, determined", from *(pro) rata (parte)* "according to the fixed proportion"] — **at any rate** : without regard to or in spite of other considerations

ratchet wheel: *1* wheel, *2* reciprocating lever, *3* pawl for communicating motion, *4* pawl for preventing backward motion

³rate *vb* **rat·ed; rat·ing** **1** : CONSIDER 3, REGARD ⟨*rated* a good pianist⟩ **2** : to set an estimate on : EVALUATE **3** : to have a rating : be classed ⟨*rates* high in math⟩ **4** : to have a right to : DESERVE ⟨*rate* a promotion⟩

rath·er \'rath-ər, 'räth-, 'rəth-\ *adv* **1** : more willingly ⟨would *rather* stay home⟩ **2** : more exactly : more properly ⟨my father, or, *rather*, my stepfather⟩ **3** : INSTEAD ⟨was no better but *rather* grew worse⟩ **4** : ²SOMEWHAT ⟨*rather* cold today⟩

rat·i·fi·ca·tion \,rat-ə-fə-'kā-shən\ *n* : the action of ratifying

rat·i·fy \'rat-ə-,fī\ *vb* **-fied; -fy·ing** : to give legal or official approval to ⟨*ratify* a treaty⟩

rat·ing \'rāt-iŋ\ *n* : a position within a grading system ⟨credit *rating*⟩

ra·tio \'rā-shō, -shē-,ō\ *n, pl* **ra·tios** **1** : the quotient of two numbers or mathematical expressions ⟨the *ratio* of 6 to 3 may be expressed as 6:3, ⅔, and 2⟩ **2** : the relationship in quantity, amount, or size between two or more things ⟨women outnumbered men in the *ratio* of three to one⟩

\ə\ abut	\au̇\ out	\i\ tip	\ȯ\ saw	\u̇\ foot
\ər\ further	\ch\ chin	\ī\ life	\ȯi\ coin	\y\ yet
\a\ mat	\e\ pet	\j\ job	\th\ thin	\yü\ few
\ā\ take	\ē\ easy	\ŋ\ sing	\th\ this	\yu̇\ cure
\ä\ cot, cart	\g\ go	\ō\ bone	\ü\ food	\zh\ vision

¹ra·tion \'rash-ən, 'rā-shən\ *n* **1 a** : a food allowance for one day **b** *pl* : ¹PROVISION 2 **2** : the amount one is allowed by authority

²ration *vb* **ra·tioned; ra·tion·ing** \'rash-(ə-)niŋ, 'rāsh-\ **1** : to control the amount one can use ⟨during the war the government *rationed* gasoline⟩ **2** : to use sparingly ⟨you'll have to *ration* your food if you expect to stick to your diet⟩

¹ra·tio·nal \'rash-nəl, -ən-ᵊl\ *adj* **1 a** : having the ability to reason ⟨*rational* beings⟩ **b** : relating to, based on, or showing reason ⟨*rational* behavior⟩ **2** : relating to or involving rational numbers ⟨a *rational* fraction⟩ — **ra·tio·nal·ly** \-ē\ *adv*

²rational *n* : something rational; *esp* : RATIONAL NUMBER

ra·tio·nale \,rash-ə-'nal\ *n* : a basic reason or explanation for something

ra·tio·nal·i·ty \,rash-ə-'nal-ət-ē\ *n* : the quality or state of being rational

ra·tio·nal·ize \'rash-nə-,līz, -ən-ᵊl-,īz\ *vb* **-ized; -iz·ing** **1** : to remove radicals from ⟨*rationalize* a denominator⟩ **2** : to find believable but untrue reasons for (one's conduct) — **ra·tio·nal·iza·tion** \,rash-nə-lə-'zā-shən, -ən-ᵊl-ə-\ *n*

rational number *n* : a number that can be expressed as an integer or the quotient of two integers

rat·line \'rat-lən\ *n* : any of the small cross ropes attached to the shrouds of a ship so as to form the steps of a rope ladder

rat snake *n* : any of various large snakes that eat rodents and birds and that kill their prey by squeezing and suffocating it

rat·tan \ra-'tan, rə-\ *n* **1** : a climbing palm with very long tough stems **2** : a part of a rattan stem used especially for wickerwork

ratted *past and past participle of* RAT

rat·ter \'rat-ər\ *n* : a rat-catching dog or cat

ratting *present participle of* RAT

ratline

¹rat·tle \'rat-ᵊl\ *vb* **rat·tled; rat·tling** \'rat-liŋ, -ᵊl-iŋ\ **1** : to make or cause to make a rattle ⟨windows *rattling* in the wind⟩ **2** : CHATTER 2 ⟨*rattled* on and on about the party⟩ **3** : to move with a rattle ⟨the old truck *rattled* down the street⟩ **4** : to say or do in a brisk lively way ⟨*rattled* off the answers⟩ **5** : to disturb the calmness of : UPSET ⟨*rattled* the speaker⟩

²rattle *n* **1** : a series of short sharp sounds : CLATTER **2** : a device (as a toy) for making a rattling sound **3** : a rattling organ at the end of a rattlesnake's tail made up of horny joints **4** : a noise in the throat caused by air passing through mucus especially at the approach of death

rat·tler \'rat-lər, -ᵊl-ər\ *n* : RATTLESNAKE

rat·tle·snake \'rat-ᵊl-,snāk\ *n* : any of various poisonous American snakes with a rattle at the end of the tail

rat·tle·trap \-,trap\ *n* : something (as an old car) that is rickety and makes rattling noises

¹rat·tling \'rat-liŋ\ *adj* : very brisk : LIVELY ⟨going at a *rattling* pace⟩

²rattling *adv* : ²VERY 1 ⟨a *rattling* good tale⟩

rat·tly \'rat-lē, -ᵊl-ē\ *adj* : likely to rattle : making a rattle ⟨a *rattly* old car⟩

rat·ty \'rat-ē\ *adj* **rat·ti·er; -est** **1 a** : full of rats ⟨*ratty* dockside warehouses⟩ **b** : of or relating to rats **2**

rattlesnake

: SHABBY 2a ⟨a *ratty* old sweater⟩

rau·cous \'rò-kəs\ *adj* **1** : being harsh and unpleasant ⟨a *raucous* voice⟩ **2** : behaving in a rough and noisy way ⟨a *raucous* crowd⟩ — **rau·cous·ly** *adv* — **rau·cous·ness** *n*

¹rav·age \'rav-ij\ *n* : violently destructive action or effect

²ravage *vb* **rav·aged; rav·ag·ing** : to attack or act upon with great violence ⟨a forest *ravaged* by fire⟩ — **rav·ag·er** *n*

¹rave \'rāv\ *vb* **raved; rav·ing** **1** : to talk wildly as if crazy **2** : to talk with great enthusiasm ⟨*raved* about the new play⟩ — **rav·er** *n*

²rave *n* : a statement of enthusiastic praise

¹rav·el \'rav-əl\ *vb* **-eled** *or* **-elled; -el·ing** *or* **-el·ling** \-(ə-)liŋ\ : UNRAVEL 1 — **rav·el·er** *or* **rav·el·ler** \-(ə-)lər\ *n*

²ravel *n* : something that is raveled

rav·el·ing *or* **rav·el·ling** \'rav-(ə-)liŋ, -lən\ *n* : something raveled or frayed; *esp* : a thread raveled out of a fabric

¹ra·ven \'rā-vən\ *n* : a bird of northern Europe, Asia, and America that has glossy black feathers and is larger than the related crow

²raven *adj* : shiny and black like a raven's feathers

rav·en·ous \'rav-(ə-)nəs\ *adj* : very eager for food or satisfaction — **rav·en·ous·ly** *adv* — **rav·en·ous·ness** *n*

raven

ra·vine \rə-'vēn\ *n* : a small narrow valley with steep sides that is larger than a gully and smaller than a canyon

rav·i·o·li \,rav-ē-'ō-lē, ,räv-\ *n, pl* **ravioli** *or* **raviolis** \-lēz\ : little pockets of pasta with a filling (as of meat or cheese); *also* : a dish of cooked ravioli served with tomato sauce [Italian, from a plural of a dialect word *raviolo*, literally "little turnip"]

rav·ish \'rav-ish\ *vb* **1** : to seize and take away by violence **2** : to overcome with a feeling and especially a feeling of joy or delight — **rav·ish·er** *n*

rav·ish·ing \'rav-ish-iŋ\ *adj* : very attractive or pleasing — **rav·ish·ing·ly** \-iŋ-lē\ *adv*

¹raw \'rò\ *adj* **raw·er** \'rò-(ə)r\; **raw·est** \'rò-əst\ **1** : not cooked ⟨a *raw* carrot⟩ **2 a** : being in or nearly in the natural state : not processed or purified ⟨*raw* milk⟩ ⟨*raw* sewage⟩ **b** : not in a finished, organized, or polished form ⟨the *raw* edge of a seam⟩ ⟨*raw* data⟩ **3 a** : having the surface scraped or roughened ⟨*raw* red hands⟩ **b** : very sore or irritated ⟨a *raw* throat⟩ **4** : not trained or experienced ⟨a *raw* recruit⟩ **5** : unpleasantly damp or cold ⟨a *raw* wind⟩ — **raw·ly** *adv* — **raw·ness** *n*

²raw *n* : a raw place or state

raw·boned \'rò-'bōnd\ *adj* : extremely thin : GAUNT

raw deal *n* : an instance of unfair treatment

¹raw·hide \'rò-,hīd\ *n* **1** : a whip of untanned hide **2** : untanned cattle skin

²rawhide *vb* **-hid·ed; -hid·ing** : to whip or drive with or as if with a rawhide

raw material *n* : something from which a useful or desirable product can be manufactured ⟨wheat and rye are the *raw materials* for a flour mill⟩ ⟨collect *raw material* for writing a story⟩

¹ray \'rā\ *n* : any of numerous flat broad fishes related to the sharks that live on the sea bottom and have their eyes on the upper surface of their bodies and a long narrow tail [Middle English *raye* "the ray (fish)", from early French *raie* (same meaning), from Latin *raia* (same meaning)]

²ray *n* **1 a** : one of the lines of light that appear to be given off by a bright object **b** : a thin beam of radiant energy (as light) **c** : a stream of particles (as electrons) traveling in the same line   **2 a** : any of a group of lines coming from a common center   **b** : HALF LINE   **3** : a plant or animal structure (as an arm of a starfish) that resembles a ray   **4** : a tiny bit ⟨a *ray* of hope⟩ [Middle English *ray* "a beam of light", from early French *rai* (same meaning), from Latin *radius* "ray, beam, spoke" — related to RADIANT, RADIO, RADIUS]

rayed \'rād\ *adj* : having rays

ray flower *n* : one of the flowers with long flat petals that grow on the outer edge of the head of a composite plant (as a daisy)

ray·on \'rā-,än\ *n* : a yarn, thread, or fabric made from fibers produced chemically from cellulose

raze \'rāz\ *vb* **razed**; **raz·ing** : to destroy completely by knocking down or breaking to pieces : DEMOLISH ⟨*razed* the building⟩

ra·zor \'rā-zər\ *n* : a sharp cutting instrument used to shave off hair

ra·zor·back \-,bak\ *n* : a thin-bodied long-legged half-wild mongrel hog chiefly of the southeastern U.S.

razz \'raz\ *vb* : ¹TEASE 2a

re \'rā\ *n* : the second note of the musical scale

re- \(')rē *before* '-*stressed syllable,* (,)rē *before* ,-*stressed syllable,* ,rē *before unstressed syllable*\ *prefix* **1** : again ⟨*refill*⟩   **2** : back : backward ⟨*recall*⟩ [derived from Latin *re-, red-* "again, back, against"]

reaccommodate	rebutton	redelivery
reacquire	rebuy	redeposit
reactivate	recarbonize	redevelop
reactivation	rechannel	redeveloper
readapt	recharge	redevelopment
readdress	recharter	redigest
readjust	recheck	redigestion
readmission	reclean	redip
readmit	recolor	rediscover
readopt	recomb	rediscovery
reaffirm	recombine	redispose
realign	recommission	redissolve
reanalysis	recompile	redistill
reanalyze	recompress	redistribute
reanimate	recompression	redistribution
reanimation	recompute	redivide
reappear	reconceive	redivision
reappearance	reconcentrate	redraft
reapplication	reconception	redraw
reapply	recondensation	redry
reappoint	recondense	reeligible
reappointment	reconduct	reembodiment
reapportionment	reconnect	reembody
reappraisal	reconquer	reemerge
reappraise	reconquest	reemission
reapprove	reconsecrate	reemit
reargue	reconsecration	reemphasis
rearrest	reconsult	reemphasize
reassail	reconsultation	reenergize
reassemble	recontact	reenlist
reassembly	recontaminate	reenlistment
reassess	recontamination	reenroll
reassign	recontract	reequip
reattach	reconvene	reestablish
reattack	recook	reestablishment
reawake	recopy	reevaluate
reawaken	recouple	reexamination
rebalance	recross	reexamine
rebaptism	recut	reexchange
rebaptize	redate	reexplore
rebid	redeal	reface
reboil	rededicate	refasten
rebroadcast	rededication	refigure
reburial	redefine	refilm
rebury	redeliver	refilter

refinance	remarry	restaff
refind	remelt	restage
refix	remix	restart
refloat	remold	restock
refly	renumber	restraighten
refreeze	reoccupy	restrengthen
refurnish	reordination	restrike
regather	reorient	restring
regild	reorientate	restructure
regive	repack	restudy
reglue	repaint	restyle
regrade	repeople	resubmit
regrind	rephotograph	resummon
regrowth	replay	resupply
rehandle	repopulate	resurface
rehear	reprice	resurvey
reheat	reprocess	resynthesis
reimpose	repurchase	resynthesize
reimposition	reread	retag
reincorporate	rerecord	retaste
reinsert	reroll	retell
reintroduce	resaw	rethink
reintroduction	resay	retrack
reinvade	reschedule	retrain
reinvasion	rescore	retransmission
reinvent	reseal	retransmit
reinvention	reseat	reverify
reissue	resell	revisit
rekindle	reset	rewash
relaunch	resettle	reweave
relearn	resew	rewed
reletter	reshow	reweigh
relight	resow	reweld
reload	respell	rewind
remanufacture		

're \(ə)r\ *vb* : ¹ARE ⟨sorry, we*'re* sold out⟩

¹reach \'rēch\ *vb* **1** : to stretch out : EXTEND ⟨*reached* out her arm⟩   **2 a** : to touch or move to touch or take by sticking out a part of the body (as the hand) or something held in the hand ⟨couldn't *reach* the apple, even standing on tiptoes⟩ ⟨*reached* for the catsup⟩   **b** : to extend or stretch to ⟨their land *reaches* the river⟩   **c** : to get up to or as far as : come to ⟨your letter *reached* me yesterday⟩ ⟨tried to *reach* an agreement⟩   **d** : to communicate with ⟨tried to *reach* you by phone⟩   **3** : ²HAND 2, PASS ⟨please *reach* me the salt⟩ — **reach·able** \'rē-chə-bəl\ *adj* — **reach·er** *n*

²reach *n* **1** : an unbroken stretch (as of a river)   **2 a** : the action or an act of reaching   **b** : the distance one can reach ⟨kept it in easy *reach*⟩   **c** : ability to stretch so as to touch something ⟨you have a long *reach*⟩   **d** : the ability to reach something as if by using the hands ⟨a new car is beyond our *reach* right now⟩

re·act \rē-'akt\ *vb* **1** : to act or behave in response (as to stimulation or an influence) ⟨the colonists *reacted* to the tax by boycotting tea⟩   **2** : to oppose a force or influence — usually used with *against* ⟨*reacted* against their unfair treatment⟩   **3** : to go through or cause to go through a chemical reaction

re·ac·tant \rē-'ak-tənt\ *n* : a substance that enters into and is changed by a chemical reaction

re·ac·tion \rē-'ak-shən\ *n* **1 a** : an instance of reacting ⟨our *reaction* to the news⟩   **b** : an action or attitude opposing current political or social forces or ideas   **2** : a response (as of body or mind) to a stimulus; *esp* : the response of the body to a foreign substance (as a drug)   **3**

\ə\ abut	\au̇\ out	\i\ tip	\ȯ\ saw	\u̇\ foot
\ər\ further	\ch\ chin	\ī\ life	\ȯi\ coin	\y\ yet
\a\ mat	\e\ pet	\j\ job	\th\ thin	\yü\ few
\ā\ take	\ē\ easy	\ŋ\ sing	\t̲h̲\ this	\yu̇\ cure
\ä\ cot, cart	\g\ go	\ō\ bone	\ü\ food	\zh\ vision

: the force that opposes the action of a force applied to one body by another body   **4 a** : chemical transformation or change : the action between atoms or molecules to form one or more new substances   **b** : a process involving change in atomic nuclei

¹re·ac·tion·ary \rē-'ak-shə-,ner-ē\ *adj* : of, relating to, or favoring old-fashioned political or social ideas

²reactionary *n, pl* **-ar·ies** : a reactionary person

re·ac·tive \rē-'ak-tiv\ *adj*   **1** : of or relating to reaction   **2** : reacting or tending to react — **re·ac·tive·ly** *adv* — **re·ac·tive·ness** *n* — **re·ac·tiv·i·ty** \(,)rē-,ak-'tiv-ət-ē\ *n*

re·ac·tor \rē-'ak-tər\ *n*   **1** : one that reacts   **2** : a device for the controlled release of atomic energy (as for producing heat)

¹read \'rēd\ *vb* **read** \'red\; **read·ing** \'rēd-iŋ\   **1 a** : to go over and take in and understand the meaning of letters or symbols (learn to *read*) (*read* braille) (can you *read* decimals) (I can't *read* your writing)   **b** : to study the movements of (a speaker's lips) and so understand what is being said   **c** : to speak aloud written or printed words (*read* us a story)   **d** : to go over and take in the contents of (*reading* a book)   **e** : to understand the written form of (*reads* Spanish)   **f** : to be able to be read   **2** : to learn from what one has seen in writing or printing (*read* about the fire)   **3 a** : to discover or figure out the meaning of (*read* palms)   **b** : to watch carefully in order to tell what will happen (*reading* the rapids while canoeing)   **4** : to show by numbers or letters (the thermometer *reads* zero)   **5 a** : to acquire data or information (a scanner *reads* the bar code)   **b** : to send to or get from storage (*read* your program back in) — **read between the lines** : to understand more than is directly stated

²read \'red\ *adj* : taught or informed by reading (a well-*read* person)

read·able \'rēd-ə-bəl\ *adj* : able to be read easily — **read·abil·i·ty** \,rēd-ə-'bil-ət-ē\ *n* — **read·able·ness** \'rēd-ə-bəl-nəs\ *n* — **read·ably** \-blē\ *adv*

read·er \'rēd-ər\ *n*   **1** : a person who reads   **2 a** : a device that makes a readable image (a microfilm *reader*)   **b** : a machine for acquiring data (as for a computer) (a card *reader*)   **3** : a book for learning or practicing reading

read·er·ship \'rēd-ər-,ship\ *n* : a group of readers

read·ing \'rēd-iŋ\ *n*   **1** : something to be read or for reading   **2** : a particular version   **3** : the number or fact shown on an instrument (the thermometer *reading* was 20 degrees)   **4** : an individual explanation of something

read–on·ly memory \'rēd-'ōn-lē-\ *n* : a usually small computer memory that contains special-purpose information (as a program) which cannot be altered — compare RANDOM-ACCESS MEMORY

read·out \'rēd-,aút\ *n*   **1** : the process of removing information from an automatic device (as a computer) and displaying it in an understandable form   **2** : the information removed from an automatic device and displayed or recorded (as by a printing device or magnetic tape)   **3** : an electronic device that presents information in visual form

¹ready \'red-ē\ *adj* **readi·er**; **-est**   **1** : prepared for use or action (dinner is *ready*)   **2** : likely to do something (*ready* to cry)   **3** : WILLING 1 (*ready* to give aid)   **4** : showing ease and promptness (a *ready* answer)   **5** : available right away : HANDY (*ready* money)   **syn** see QUICK — **readi·ly** \'red-ᵊl-ē\ *adv* — **readi·ness** \'red-ē-nəs\ *n*

²ready *vb* **read·ied**; **ready·ing** : to make ready : PREPARE

¹ready–made \,red-ē-'mād\ *adj* : made beforehand in large numbers (*ready-made* clothes)

²ready–made *n* : something that is ready-made

ready room *n* : a room in which a pilot or an astronaut waits before a mission

ready–to–wear \,red-ēt-ə-'wa(ə)r, -'we(ə)r\ *adj* : ¹READY-MADE

¹re·al \'rē(-ə)l, 'ri(-ə)l\ *adj*   **1** : of, relating to, or made up of land and buildings (*real* property)   **2 a** : not artificial or

fake : GENUINE (*real* leather)   **b** : not imaginary : ACTUAL (*real* life)   **c** : belonging to or containing elements that belong to the set of real numbers (an equation with two *real* solutions)   **3** : ABSOLUTE 1a, COMPLETE (there's a *real* surprise at the end) [Middle English *real* "real, relating to things", from early French *real* (same meaning), derived from Latin *res* "thing, matter" — related to REBUS, REPUBLIC] — **re·al·ness** *n*

syn REAL, ACTUAL, TRUE mean agreeing with known facts. REAL may suggest that a thing is what it appears to be (this is a *real* diamond) ACTUAL stresses that someone or something does or did occur or exist (was Robin Hood an *actual* person?) TRUE may apply to something that is real or actual (a *true* story) or to something that agrees with a standard (seaweeds are not *true* plants)

²real *adv* : ²VERY 1 (we had a *real* good time)

³re·al \rā-'äl\ *n, pl* **re·als** *or* **re·ales** \-'äl-ās\ : an old silver coin of Spain

real estate *n* : property consisting of buildings and land

real image *n* : an image of an object formed by rays of light coming to a focus (as after passing through a lens)

re·al·ism \'rē-ə-,liz-əm, 'ri-ə-\ *n*   **1** : willingness to face facts and to give in to what is necessary   **2** : the showing of things as they really are in art, literature, and theater — **re·al·ist** \-ləst\ *n*

re·al·is·tic \,rē-ə-'lis-tik, ,ri-ə-\ *adj*   **1** : true to life or nature (a *realistic* painting)   **2** : ready to see things as they really are and deal with them sensibly (a *realistic* approach) — **re·al·is·ti·cal·ly** \-ti-k(ə-)lē\ *adv*

re·al·i·ty \rē-'al-ət-ē\ *n, pl* **-ties**   **1** : the quality or state of being real   **2** : someone or something real or actual (our dream became a *reality*) — **in reality** : in actual fact

re·al·ize \'rē-ə-,līz, 'ri-ə-\ *vb* **-ized**; **-iz·ing**   **1** : to bring into being : ACCOMPLISH (*realize* a lifelong ambition)   **2** : to get by sale or effort : GAIN (*realize* a profit)   **3** : to be aware of (*realized* their danger) — **re·al·iz·able** \-,lī-zə-bəl\ *adj* — **re·al·iza·tion** \,rē-ə-lə-'zā-shən, ,ri-ə-\ *n*

real–life *adj* : happening in reality : being like real life (*real-life* problems) (a *real-life* drama)

re·al·ly \'rē-(ə-)lē, 'ri-(ə)l-ē\ *adv*   **1** : in actual fact : ACTUALLY (didn't *really* mean it)   **2** : without question : TRULY (a *really* beautiful day)   **3** : to be honest : FRANKLY (*really*, you're being ridiculous)

realm \'relm\ *n*   **1** : KINGDOM 1   **2** : field of influence or activity (the *realm* of art)

real number *n* : a number (as −2, 3, ⅞, .25, 12, π) that is rational or irrational

Re·al·tor \'rē(-ə)l-tər, -,tȯ(ə)r\ *collective mark* — used for a real estate agent who is a member of the National Association of Realtors

re·al·ty \'rē(-ə)l-tē\ *n, pl* **-ties** : REAL ESTATE

¹ream \'rēm\ *n*   **1** : a quantity of paper that may equal 480, 500, or 516 sheets   **2** : a great amount — usually used in pl. (*reams* of notes) [Middle English *reme* "a quantity of paper", from early French *raime* (same meaning), from Arabic *rizmah*, literally "bundle"]

²ream *vb* : to shape, make larger, or clean or clear with a reamer [probably from an Old English dialect word *rēman* "to open up"]

ream·er \'rē-mər\ *n* : a tool with cutting edges for enlarging or shaping a hole

reap \'rēp\ *vb*   **1 a** : to cut (as grain) or clear (as a field) with a sickle, scythe, or machine   **b** : ²HARVEST 1 (*reap* a crop)   **2** : to get as a result (*reap* the benefit of hard work)

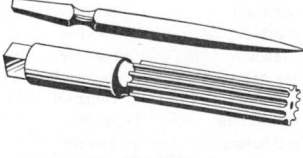

reamer

reap·er \'rē-pər\ *n*   **1** : a worker who reaps crops   **2** : a machine for reaping grain

¹rear \'ri(ə)r\ *vb* **1** : to put up by building : CONSTRUCT **2** : to raise or set on end **3 a** : to take care of the breeding and raising of ⟨*rear* cattle⟩ **b** : BRING UP 1 ⟨*rear* children⟩ **4** : to rise high **5** : to rise up on the hind legs ⟨the horse *reared* in fright⟩

²rear *n* **1** : the part (as of an army) or area farthest from the enemy **2** : BUTTOCK 2 **3** : the space or position at the back

³rear *adj* : being at the back

rear admiral *n* : a naval commissioned officer with a rank just below that of vice admiral

rear guard *n* : soldiers who protect the rear of an army

re·arm \(')rē-'ärm\ *vb* : to arm again with new or better weapons — **re·ar·ma·ment** \-'är-mə-mənt\ *n*

rear·most \'ri(ə)r-ˌmōst\ *adj* : farthest in the rear : LAST

re·ar·range \ˌrē-ə-'rānj\ *vb* : to arrange again usually in a different way ⟨*rearranged* the furniture⟩

rear·view mirror \ˌri(ə)r-ˌvyü-\ *n* : a mirror (as in a car) that gives a view to the rear

¹rear·ward \'ri(ə)r-wərd\ *adj* **1** : located at, near, or toward the rear **2** : directed toward the rear : BACKWARD — **rear·ward·ly** *adv*

²rearward *also* **rear·wards** \-wərdz\ *adv* : at, near, or toward the rear : BACKWARD

¹rea·son \'rēz-ⁿn\ *n* **1 a** : a statement given to explain a belief or act ⟨gave a *reason* for my absence⟩ **b** : a good basis ⟨*reasons* for thinking life may exist on other planets⟩ **c** : the thing that makes some fact understandable : CAUSE ⟨wanted to know the *reason* for earthquakes⟩ **2 a** : the power to think : INTELLIGENCE **b** : a sound mind **syn** see CAUSE — **within reason** : within reasonable limits — **with reason** : with good cause

²reason *vb* **rea·soned; rea·son·ing** \'rēz-niŋ, -ⁿn-iŋ\ **1** : to talk with another in order to cause a change of mind ⟨*reason* with someone⟩ **2 a** : to use the power of reason **b** : to state or conclude by use of reason ⟨*reasoned* that both statements couldn't be true⟩

rea·son·able \'rēz-nə-bəl, -ⁿn-ə-bəl\ *adj* **1 a** : not beyond what is usual or expected : MODERATE ⟨a *reasonable* request⟩ ⟨a *reasonable* chance of success⟩ **b** : not expensive **2** : able to reason : RATIONAL — **rea·son·abil·i·ty** \ˌrēz-nə-'bil-ət-ē, -ⁿn-ə-\ *n* — **rea·son·able·ness** \'rēz-nə-bəl-nəs, -ⁿn-ə-\ *n* — **rea·son·ably** \-blē\ *adv*

rea·son·ing *n* **1** : the use of reason **2** : the reasons used in and the proofs that result from thought : ARGUMENT

re·as·sur·ance \ˌrē-ə-'shùr-ən(t)s\ *n* : the action of reassuring : the state of being reassured

re·as·sure \ˌrē-ə-'shù(ə)r\ *vb* **1** : to assure again **2** : to give fresh confidence to : free from fear

re·ata \rē-'at-ə, -'ät-\ *n* : LARIAT

¹re·bate \'rē-ˌbāt, ri-'bāt\ *vb* **re·bat·ed; re·bat·ing** : to make a rebate of : give as a rebate

²re·bate \'rē-ˌbāt\ *n* : a return of part of a payment or an amount owed

¹reb·el \'reb-əl\ *adj* **1** : being or fighting against one's government or ruler **2** : not obeying

²rebel *n* : a person who refuses to give in to authority

³re·bel \ri-'bel\ *vb* **re·belled; re·bel·ling** **1 a** : to be against or fight against authority and especially the authority of one's government **2** : to feel or show anger or strong dislike

re·bel·lion \ri-'bel-yən\ *n* **1** : open opposition to authority **2** : open fighting against authority (as one's government)
syn REBELLION, REVOLUTION, UPRISING, MUTINY mean an armed outbreak against authority. REBELLION suggests an outbreak that is serious and widespread but does not succeed ⟨the *rebellion* lasted a year before the government put it down⟩ REVOLUTION applies to a successful rebellion that ends in a major change (as of government) ⟨the American *revolution* brought about the creation of a new country⟩ UPRISING suggests a rebellion that quickly fails ⟨*uprisings* on the frontier⟩ MUTINY applies to

an outbreak against authority at sea ⟨the sailors planned a *mutiny*⟩

re·bel·lious \ri-'bel-yəs\ *adj* **1** : taking part in rebellion **2** : tending to fight against or disobey authority — **re·bel·lious·ly** *adv* — **re·bel·lious·ness** *n*

re·birth \(')rē-'bərth\ *n* **1** : a new or second birth **2** : a return to importance

re·born \(')rē-'bò(ə)rn\ *adj* : born again

¹re·bound \ri-'baùnd\ *vb* **1** : to spring back on hitting something **2** : to recover from a loss or disappointment **3** : to gain possession of a rebound in basketball

²re·bound \'rē-ˌbaùnd, ri-'baùnd\ *n* **1** : the action of rebounding : a springing back **2 a** : a basketball or hockey puck that rebounds **b** : the act of gaining possession of a basketball rebound ⟨led the league in *rebounds*⟩ **3** : an immediate reaction especially to a loss or disappointment

re·bo·zo \ri-'bō-zō, -sō\ *n, pl* **-zos** : a long scarf worn chiefly by Mexican women

re·branch \(')rē-'branch\ *vb* : to branch again ⟨the arteries branched and *rebranched*⟩

¹re·buff \ri-'bəf\ *vb* : to refuse or check sharply ⟨the suggestion was *rebuffed*⟩

²rebuff *n* : a refusal to meet an advance or offer

re·build \(')rē-'bild\ *vb* **-built** \-'bilt\; **-build·ing** **1** : to make important repairs to or changes in ⟨*rebuild* an old house⟩ **2** : to build again ⟨planned to *rebuild* after the fire⟩

¹re·buke \ri-'byük\ *vb* **re·buked; re·buk·ing** : to criticize sharply

syn REBUKE, REPRIMAND, ADMONISH, CHIDE mean to express criticism of. REBUKE suggests a severe or stern criticism ⟨*rebuked* the students for bad conduct at the game⟩ REPRIMAND suggests a formal and often public or official rebuke ⟨the general was *reprimanded* by the President for an unwise speech⟩ ADMONISH suggests an earnest or friendly warning or piece of advice ⟨we were *admonished* for talking too loud⟩ CHIDE suggests a mild scolding that expresses displeasure or disappointment ⟨my parents *chided* me for my table manners⟩

²rebuke *n* : an expression of strong disapproval

re·bus \'rē-bəs\ *n* : a riddle or puzzle made up of letters, pictures, and symbols whose names sound like the syllables and words of a phrase or sentence [from Latin *rebus* "by things", from *res* "thing, matter" — related to REAL, RE-PUBLIC]

rebus

re·but \ri-'bət\ *vb* **re·but·ted; re·but·ting** **1** : to oppose by argument **2** : to prove to be wrong especially by argument or by proof that the opposite is true

re·but·tal \ri-'bət-ⁿl\ *n* : the act of rebutting; *also* : argument or proof that rebuts

re·cal·ci·trance \ri-'kal-sə-trən(t)s\ *n* : the state of being recalcitrant

re·cal·ci·trant \ri-'kal-sə-trənt\ *adj* : stubbornly refusing to give in to authority

¹re·call \ri-'kòl\ *vb* **1 a** : to call back ⟨soldiers *recalled* to active duty⟩ ⟨*recalled* cars with brake problems⟩ **b** : to bring back to mind : REMEMBER ⟨as I *recall*⟩ **2** : CANCEL 2a, REVOKE ⟨*recalled* the order⟩ — **re·call·able** \-'kò-lə-bəl\ *adj*

\ə\ abut		\aù\ **out**	\i\ **tip**	\ò\ **saw**	\ù\ **foot**
\ər\ **further**		\ch\ **chin**	\ī\ **life**	\òi\ **coin**	\y\ **yet**
\a\ **mat**		\e\ **pet**	\j\ **job**	\th\ **thin**	\yü\ **few**
\ā\ **take**		\ē\ **easy**	\ŋ\ **sing**	\th\ **this**	\yù\ **cure**
\ä\ **cot, cart**		\g\ **go**	\ō\ **bone**	\ü\ **food**	\zh\ **vision**

²**re·call** \ri-'kȯl, 'rē-ˌkȯl\ *n* **1** : a command to return **2** : a way in which a public official may be removed from office by vote of the people **3** : remembrance of what has been learned or experienced **4** : the act of canceling (as an order) **5** : a call by a manufacturer for the return of a product that may be defective or contaminated

re·cant \ri-'kant\ *vb* : to take back publicly an opinion or belief — **re·can·ta·tion** \ˌrē-ˌkan-'tā-shən\ *n*

¹**re·cap** \'rē-ˌkap, ri-'kap\ *vb* **re·capped; re·cap·ping** : RECAPITULATE ⟨now, to *recap* the news⟩

²**re·cap** \'rē-ˌkap\ *n* : a brief summary : RECAPITULATION

³**re·cap** \(')rē-'kap\ *vb* **re·capped; re·cap·ping** : ¹RETREAD

⁴**re·cap** \'rē-ˌkap\ *n* : ²RETREAD 2

re·ca·pit·u·late \ˌrē-kə-'pich-ə-ˌlāt\ *vb* **-lat·ed; -lat·ing** : to give a brief summary : SUMMARIZE — **re·ca·pit·u·la·tion** \-ˌpich-ə-'lā-shən\ *n*

re·cap·ture \(')rē-'kap-chər\ *vb* **1** : to capture again ⟨*recaptured* the escaped prisoner⟩ **2** : to experience again ⟨trying to *recapture* those happy times⟩

re·cast \(')rē-'kast\ *vb* **-cast; -cast·ing** **1** : to cast again ⟨*recast* a cannon⟩ ⟨*recast* a play⟩ **2** : to change around : REVISE, REMODEL ⟨*recast* a sentence to make it clearer⟩

re·cede \ri-'sēd\ *vb* **re·ced·ed; re·ced·ing** **1 a** : to move back or away ⟨the flood waters *receded*⟩ **b** : to slant backward **2** : to grow smaller

¹**re·ceipt** \ri-'sēt\ *n* **1** : RECIPE 2 **2** : the act or process of receiving **3** : something received — usually used in pl. **4** : a written statement saying that money or goods have been received

²**receipt** *vb* **1** : to give a receipt for **2** : to mark as paid ⟨*receipt* a bill⟩

re·ceiv·able \ri-'sē-və-bəl\ *adj* **1** : capable of being received **2** : not yet paid : DUE ⟨accounts *receivable*⟩

re·ceiv·ables \ri-'sē-və-bəlz\ *n pl* : amounts of money receivable

re·ceive \ri-'sēv\ *vb* **re·ceived; re·ceiv·ing** **1** : to take or get something that is given, paid, or sent ⟨*receive* the money⟩ ⟨*receive* a letter⟩ **2** : to welcome on arrival : GREET ⟨*receive* friends⟩ **3** : to hold a reception ⟨*receive* from four to six o'clock⟩ **4** : ²EXPERIENCE ⟨*receive* a shock⟩ **5** : to change incoming radio waves into sounds or pictures [Middle English *receiven* "to gain possession of", from early French *receivre* (same meaning), from Latin *recipere* "receive, take back", from *re-* "back, again" and *capere* "to take" — related to ACCEPT, CAPTURE]

re·ceiv·er \ri-'sē-vər\ *n* : one that receives: as **a** : a person appointed to take control of property that is involved in a lawsuit or of a business that is bankrupt or is being reorganized **b** : equipment for receiving radio or television broadcasts **c** : a device for changing electricity or radio waves into light or sound **d** : an offensive football player who may catch a forward pass

re·ceiv·er·ship \ri-'sē-vər-ˌship\ *n* **1** : the office or role of a receiver **2** : the state of being in the control of a receiver

re·cen·cy \'rēs-ⁿn-sē\ *n* : the state of being recent

re·cent \'rēs-ⁿnt\ *adj* **1 a** : of or relating to a time not long past ⟨*recent* history⟩ **b** : having lately appeared or come into existence : NEW, FRESH ⟨*recent* events⟩ **2** *cap* : HOLOCENE — **re·cent·ly** *adv* — **re·cent·ness** *n*

re·cep·ta·cle \ri-'sep-ti-kəl\ *n* **1** : something used to receive and contain smaller objects : CONTAINER **2** : the enlarged end of a flower stalk upon which the parts of the flower grow

re·cep·tion \ri-'sep-shən\ *n* **1** : the act or process of receiving, welcoming, or accepting ⟨a warm *reception*⟩ **2** : the receiving of a radio or television broadcast **3** : a social gathering ⟨a wedding *reception*⟩

re·cep·tion·ist \ri-'sep-sh(ə-)nəst\ *n* : an office employee who greets callers, answers questions, and arranges appointments

re·cep·tive \ri-'sep-tiv\ *adj* **1** : able or willing to receive

especially ideas **2** : able to receive and pass on stimuli : SENSORY — **re·cep·tive·ly** *adv* — **re·cep·tive·ness** *n* — **re·cep·tiv·i·ty** \ˌrē-ˌsep-'tiv-ət-ē, ri-\ *n*

re·cep·tor \ri-'sep-tər\ *n* : a cell or group of cells that receives stimuli : SENSE ORGAN

¹**re·cess** \'rē-ˌses, ri-'ses\ *n* **1** : a hidden or secret place **2 a** : a space or little hollow set back (as from the main line of a coast or mountain range) **b** : ALCOVE 1 **3** : a brief period for relaxation between periods of work

²**recess** *vb* **1** : to put into a recess ⟨*recessed* lighting⟩ **2** : to make a recess in **3** : to interrupt for or take a recess

re·ces·sion \ri-'sesh-ən\ *n* **1** : the act or fact of receding or withdrawing **2** : a group of individuals departing in an orderly often ceremonial way **3** : a downward turn in business activity; *also* : the period of such a downward turn

re·ces·sion·al \ri-'sesh-nəl, -ən-ᵊl\ *n* : a hymn or musical piece at the conclusion of a service or program; *also* : RECESSION 2

¹**re·ces·sive** \ri-'ses-iv\ *adj* **1** : tending to go back **2** : producing or being a bodily characteristic that is masked or not expressed when a contrasting dominant gene or trait is present ⟨*recessive* genes⟩ — **re·ces·sive·ly** *adv* — **re·ces·sive·ness** *n*

²**recessive** *n* **1** : a recessive characteristic or gene **2** : an individual that has one or more recessive characteristics

rec·i·pe \'res-ə-(ˌ)pē\ *n* **1** : PRESCRIPTION 2a **2** : a set of instructions for making something (as a food dish) from various things ⟨a *recipe* for beef stew⟩ **3** : method of proceeding ⟨a *recipe* for success⟩

re·cip·i·ent \ri-'sip-ē-ənt\ *n* : one that receives ⟨the *recipient* of many honors⟩ — **recipient** *adj*

¹**re·cip·ro·cal** \ri-'sip-rə-kəl\ *adj* **1** : done, given, or felt equally by both sides ⟨*reciprocal* affection⟩ **2** : related to each other in such a way that one completes the other or is the equal of the other — **re·cip·ro·cal·ly** \-k(ə-)lē\ *adv*

²**reciprocal** *n* **1** : something in a reciprocal relationship to another **2** : one of a pair of numbers (as 9, ⅑ or ⅔, 3⁄2) whose product is one

re·cip·ro·cate \ri-'sip-rə-ˌkāt\ *vb* **-cat·ed; -cat·ing** **1** : to give and take mutually : EXCHANGE **2** : to make a return for something ⟨*reciprocate* a favor⟩ — **re·cip·ro·ca·tion** \ri-ˌsip-rə-'kā-shən\ *n*

rec·i·proc·i·ty \ˌres-ə-'präs-ət-ē\ *n, pl* **-ties** **1** : shared dependence, cooperation, or exchange between persons, groups, or states **2** : an exchange of commercial benefits between countries

re·cit·al \ri-'sīt-ᵊl\ *n* **1** : a reciting of something; *esp* : a story told in detail **2** : a program of music usually given by a single performer ⟨a piano *recital*⟩ **3** : a public performance by music or dance pupils **syn** see NARRATIVE — **re·cit·al·ist** \-ᵊl-əst\ *n*

rec·i·ta·tion \ˌres-ə-'tā-shən\ *n* **1** : a complete telling or listing of something **2** : the act or an instance of reading or repeating aloud especially before an audience **3** : a student's oral reply to questions

rec·i·ta·tive \ˌres-ə-(ə)tə-'tēv\ *n* : a style of singing without a fixed rhythm that imitates speech and is used sometimes in operas and oratorios; *also* : a passage in this style — **recitative** *adj*

re·cite \ri-'sīt\ *vb* **re·cit·ed; re·cit·ing** **1** : to repeat from memory or read aloud before an audience ⟨*recite* a poem⟩ **2** : to tell all the details of **3** : to answer questions about a lesson — **re·cit·er** *n*

reck·less \'rek-ləs\ *adj* : showing lack of caution : IRRESPONSIBLE, WILD — **reck·less·ly** *adv* — **reck·less·ness** *n*

reck·on \'rek-ən\ *vb* **reck·oned; reck·on·ing** \-(ə-)niŋ\ **1 a** : COUNT 1a, COMPUTE ⟨*reckon* the days till the wedding⟩ **b** : to estimate by calculating ⟨*reckon* the height of a building⟩ **2** : CONSIDER 3, REGARD ⟨was *reckoned* among the leaders⟩ **3** *chiefly dialect* : THINK 2, SUPPOSE **4** : to look forward to as certain : DEPEND ⟨*reckon* on support⟩ —

reck·on·er \-(ə-)nər\ *n*

reck·on·ing *n* **1** : the act or an instance of calculating **2** : a settling of accounts ⟨day of *reckoning*⟩

re·claim \ri-'klām\ *vb* **1** : to make someone better in behavior or character : REFORM ⟨*reclaim* criminals⟩ **2** : to change to a desirable condition or state ⟨*reclaim* swampland for agriculture⟩ **3** : to obtain from a waste product or by-product : RECOVER ⟨*reclaimed* wool⟩ — **re·claim·able** \-'klā-mə-bəl\ *adj*

rec·la·ma·tion \,rek-lə-'mā-shən\ *n* : the act or process of reclaiming : the state of being reclaimed

re·cline \ri-'klīn\ *vb* **re·clined; re·clin·ing 1** : to lean or cause to lean backwards **2** : ¹REPOSE 2, LIE ⟨*reclining* on the sofa⟩

re·cluse \'rek-,lüs, ri-'klüs\ *n* : a person who lives away from others — **re·clu·sive** \ri-'klü-siv, -ziv\ *adj*

rec·og·ni·tion \,rek-ig-'nish-ən, ,rek-əg-\ *n* **1** : the act of recognizing **2** : acknowledgment of something done or given ⟨got a medal in *recognition* of bravery⟩ **3** : formal acknowledgment of the political existence of a government or nation **4** : special attention or notice

re·cog·ni·zance \ri-'käg-nə-zən(t)s, -'kän-ə-\ *n* : a recorded legal promise to do something (as to appear in court)

rec·og·nize \'rek-ig-,nīz, 'rek-əg-\ *vb* **-nized; -niz·ing 1** : to be willing to admit : ACKNOWLEDGE ⟨*recognized* my own faults⟩ **2** : to admit as qualified to be heard at a meeting ⟨*recognizes* the delegate from Arkansas⟩ **3** : to grant diplomatic recognition to ⟨*recognized* the new government⟩ **4** : to take approving notice of ⟨*recognize* an act of bravery with a medal⟩ **5** : to show one is acquainted with ⟨*recognize* someone with a nod⟩ **6** : to know and remember upon seeing ⟨I didn't *recognize* you in that new hairdo⟩ [derived from early French *reconoistre* "to recognize", from Latin *recognoscere* "to know again", from *re-* "again" and *cognoscere* "to know" — related to CONNOISSEUR, INCOGNITO] — **rec·og·niz·abil·i·ty** \,rek-ig-,nī-zə-'bil-ət-ē, ,rek-əg-\ *n* — **rec·og·niz·able** \'rek-əg-,nī-ze-bəl, 'rek-ig-\ *adj* — **rec·og·niz·ably** \-,nī-zə-blē\ *adv*

¹re·coil \ri-'koi(ə)l\ *vb* **1 a** : to fall back under pressure : RETREAT **b** : to shrink back ⟨*recoil* in horror⟩ **2** : to spring back to or as if to a starting point ⟨the compressed spring *recoiled* upon release⟩ ⟨the big gun *recoiled* upon firing⟩

²re·coil \'rē-,koil, ri-'koi(ə)l\ *n* **1** : the act or action of recoiling **2** : the distance through which something (as a spring) recoils

rec·ol·lect \,rek-ə-'lekt\ *vb* **1** : to recall to mind : REMEMBER **2** : to remind oneself of something temporarily forgotten

re-col·lect \,rē-kə-'lekt\ *vb* : to collect again; *esp* : ¹RALLY 2, RECOVER

rec·ol·lec·tion \,rek-ə-'lek-shən\ *n* **1** : the action or power of recalling to mind **2** : something recalled to the mind **syn** *see* MEMORY

re·com·bi·na·tion \,rē-,käm-bə-'nā-shən\ *n* : the formation of new combinations of genes

rec·om·mend \,rek-ə-'mend\ *vb* **1** : to make a statement in praise of ⟨*recommend* a person for a promotion⟩ **2** : to cause to receive favorable attention ⟨children *recommended* by their good manners⟩ **3** : to put forward or suggest as one's advice, as one's choice, or as having one's support — **rec·om·mend·able** \-'men-də-bəl\ *adj* — **rec·om·mend·er** *n*

rec·om·men·da·tion \,rek-ə-mən-'dā-shən, -,men-\ *n* **1** : the act of recommending **2** : a thing or course of action recommended **3** : something that recommends ⟨a written *recommendation*⟩

re·com·mit \,rē-kə-'mit\ *vb* **1** : to refer (as a bill) again to a committee **2** : to commit again — **re·com·mit·ment** \-mənt\ *n* — **re·com·mit·tal** \-'mit-ᵊl\ *n*

rec·om·pense \'rek-əm-,pen(t)s\ *vb* **-pensed; -pens·ing** : to pay for or pay back — **recompense** *n*

rec·on·cile \'rek-ən-,sīl\ *vb* **-ciled; -cil·ing 1** : to make friendly again ⟨*reconcile* friends who have quarreled⟩ **2** : to settle by agreement : ADJUST ⟨*reconcile* differences⟩ **3** : to make agree ⟨a story that cannot be *reconciled* with the facts⟩ **4** : to cause to give in or to accept : make content ⟨*reconciled* myself to the loss⟩ — **rec·on·cil·able** \,rek-ən-'sī-lə-bəl, 'rek-ən-,sīl-\ *adj* — **rec·on·cile·ment** \'rek-ən-,sīl-mənt\ *n* — **rec·on·cil·er** *n* — **rec·on·cil·i·a·tion** \,rek-ən-,sil-ē-'ā-shən\ *n*

re·con·dite \'rek-ən-,dīt, ri-'kän-\ *adj* **1** : hidden from sight **2** : difficult to understand : DEEP ⟨a *recondite* subject⟩

re·con·di·tion \,rē-kən-'dish-ən\ *vb* : to return to good condition ⟨*reconditioned* a used car⟩

re·con·firm \,rē-kən-'fərm\ *vb* **1** : to confirm again **2** : to establish more strongly — **re·con·fir·ma·tion** \(,)rē-,kän-fər-'mā-shən\ *n*

re·con·nais·sance \ri-'kän-ə-zən(t)s\ *n* : a survey (as of enemy territory) to gain information

re·con·noi·ter *or* **re·con·noi·tre** \,rē-kə-'nòit-ər *also* ,rek-ə-\ *vb* : to make a reconnaissance (as in preparation for military action)

re·con·sid·er \,rē-kən-'sid-ər\ *vb* : to consider again especially with the possibility of change or reversal — **re·con·sid·er·a·tion** \-,sid-ə-'rā-shən\ *n*

re·con·sti·tute \(')rē-'kän(t)-stə-,t(y)üt\ *vb* : to return to a former condition by adding water

re·con·struct \,rē-kən-'strəkt\ *vb* : to construct again : REBUILD, REMODEL

re·con·struc·tion \,rē-kən-'strək-shən\ *n* **1 a** : the action of reconstructing : the state of being reconstructed **b** *often cap* : the reorganization and reestablishment of the Confederate states in the Union after the American Civil War **2** : something reconstructed

re·con·ver·sion \,rē-kən-'vər-zhən\ *n* : conversion back to a previous state

re·con·vert \,rē-kən-'vərt\ *vb* : to convert back

¹re·cord \ri-'kò(ə)rd\ *vb* **1 a** : to set down in writing **b** : to deposit an authentic official copy of ⟨*record* a deed⟩ **c** : to register permanently ⟨events *recorded* in history⟩ **d** : INDICATE 1a, READ ⟨the thermometer *recorded* 40°⟩ **2** : to give evidence of **3** : to change sound or visual images into a form (as on magnetic tape) that can be listened to or watched at a later time

²rec·ord \'rek-ərd *also* -,òrd\ *n* **1** : the state or fact of being recorded ⟨on *record*⟩ **2 a** : something that recalls or tells about past events **b** : an official writing that records what has been said or done by a group, organization, or official **c** : an authentic official copy of a document **3 a** : the known or recorded facts about something or someone ⟨my school *record*⟩ **b** : a recorded top performance or achievement ⟨broke the high jump *record*⟩ **4** : something on which sound or visual images have been recorded

³rec·ord \'rek-ərd\ *adj* : setting a record : outstanding among other like things ⟨a *record* crop⟩ ⟨*record* prices⟩

recorder 2

re·cord·er \ri-'kòrd-ər\ *n* **1** : a person or device

that records **2** : a musical instrument consisting of a usually wooden tube with finger holes and a whistle mouthpiece

re·cord·ing \ri-'kȯrd-iŋ\ *n* : ²RECORD 4

rec·ord player \'rek-ərd-\ *n* : an electronic instrument for playing phonograph records

¹re·count \ri-'kaůnt\ *vb* : to tell about in detail : NARRATE ⟨*recount* an adventure⟩ [Middle English *recounten* "to tell about", from early French *reconter* (same meaning), from *re-* "again" and *conter* "relate, count"]

²re·count \(')rē-'kaůnt\ *vb* : to count again [from English *re-* (prefix) and *count*]

³re·count \'rē-,kaůnt, (')rē-'kaůnt\ *n* : a second or fresh count (as of election votes)

re·coup \ri-'küp\ *vb* **1** : to make up for : RECOVER ⟨*recoup* a loss⟩ **2** : REIMBURSE, COMPENSATE ⟨*recoup* a person for losses⟩ — **re·coup·ment** \-'küp-mənt\ *n*

re·course \'rē-,kō(ə)rs, -,kȯ(ə)rs; ri-'kō(ə)rs, -'kȯ(ə)rs\ *n* **1** : a turning for assistance or protection ⟨have *recourse* to the law⟩ **2** : a source of help or strength : RESORT

re·cov·er \ri-'kəv-ər\ *vb* **re·cov·ered; re·cov·er·ing** \-'kəv-(ə-)riŋ\ **1** : REGAIN 1 ⟨*recover* a lost wallet⟩ ⟨*recovered* my breath⟩ **2** : to regain or bring back to normal health, self-confidence, or position ⟨stumbled, then *recovered* myself⟩ ⟨*recovered* from the flu⟩ **3** : to make up for ⟨*recover* lost time⟩ **4** : to obtain something useful by separating it from a source (as ore or waste) : RECLAIM ⟨*recover* gold from gravel⟩ — **re·cov·er·able** \-'kəv-(ə-)rə-bəl\ *adj*

re–cov·er \(')rē-'kəv-ər\ *vb* : to cover again

re·cov·ery \ri-'kəv-(ə-)rē\ *n, pl* **-er·ies** : the act or process or an instance of recovering

recovery room *n* : a hospital room where patients are temporarily placed for special care and observation after an operation

¹rec·re·ant \'rek-rē-ənt\ *adj* **1** : crying for mercy : COWARDLY **2** : unfaithful to duty or allegiance

²recreant *n* **1** : COWARD **2** : one that is unfaithful : BETRAYER, DESERTER

rec·re·ate \'rek-rē-,āt\ *vb* **-at·ed; -at·ing** **1** : to give new life or freshness to **2** : to take recreation — **rec·re·ative** \-,āt-iv\ *adj*

re–cre·ate \,rē-krē-'āt\ *vb* : to create again especially in the imagination — **re–cre·ation** \-'ā-shən\ *n* — **re–cre·ative** \-'āt-iv\ *adj*

rec·re·ation \,rek-rē-'ā-shən\ *n* **1** : refreshment of mind or body after work or worry : DIVERSION **2** : a way of refreshing mind or body ⟨hiking and gardening are our favorite *recreations*⟩ — **rec·re·ation·al** \-shnəl, -shən-ᵊl\ *adj*

re·crim·i·nate \ri-'krim-ə-,nāt\ *vb* **-nat·ed; -nat·ing** **1** : to make a return charge against an accuser **2** : to respond bitterly — **re·crim·i·na·tion** \-,krim-ə-'nā-shən\ *n*

re·cru·des·cence \,rē-krü-'des-ᵊn(t)s\ *n* : a renewal or breaking out again especially of something unhealthful or dangerous

¹re·cruit \ri-'krüt\ *vb* **1 a** : to increase the number of by enlisting new members **b** : to get the services of : ENGAGE ⟨*recruited* new teachers⟩ **2** : REPLENISH ⟨*recruited* their finances⟩ **3** : to return or increase the health, energy, or strength of — **re·cruit·er** *n* — **re·cruit·ment** \-'krüt-mənt\ *n*

²recruit *n* : a newcomer to a field or activity; *esp* : a newly enlisted or drafted member of the armed forces

> **Word History** The French formed the noun *recrute,* meaning "fresh growth", from their verb *recroistre* "to grow up again". This verb was taken from the Latin verb *recrescere,* which had the same meaning. Later, someone saw a likeness between "a fresh growth of plants" and "a fresh supply of soldiers". Thus they began using the word *recrute* for the new soldiers. In the 17th century this sense of *recrute* came to the attention of the English. They borrowed the word as *recruit* and began

using it as a verb and noun. In time it acquired broader senses not related to the military. [from French *recrute, recrue* (noun) "new growth, a batch of new soldiers", derived from early French *recroistre* "to grow up again", from Latin *recrescere* (same meaning), from *re-* "again" and *crescere* "to grow"]

re·crys·tal·lize \(')rē-'kris-tə-,līz\ *vb* : to form or cause to form crystals after being dissolved or melted — **re·crys·tal·li·za·tion** \(,)rē-,kris-tə-lə-'zā-shən\ *n*

rect·an·gle \'rek-,taŋ-gəl\ *n* : a four-sided figure with four right angles and with the two pairs of opposite sides equal and parallel [from Latin *rectangulus* "having a right angle", from earlier Latin *rectus* "right" and *angulus* "angle"]

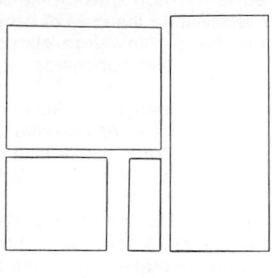

rectangle

rect·an·gu·lar \rek-'taŋ-gyə-lər\ *adj* **1** : of, relating to, or having the shape of a rectangle ⟨a *rectangular* drawing⟩ **2** : having edges, faces, or surfaces that meet at right angles : having faces or surfaces shaped like rectangles ⟨*rectangular* solid⟩ ⟨*rectangular* prism⟩

rec·ti·fy \'rek-tə-,fī\ *vb* **-fied; -fy·ing** : to set or make right **syn** see CORRECT — **rec·ti·fi·able** \-,fī-ə-bəl\ *adj* — **rec·ti·fi·ca·tion** \,rek-tə-fə-'kā-shən\ *n*

rec·ti·tude \'rek-tə-,t(y)üd\ *n* **1** : the quality or state of being straight **2** : moral honesty : RIGHTEOUSNESS

rec·tor \'rek-tər\ *n* **1** : a member of the clergy who has charge of a church or parish **2** : the priest in charge of certain Roman Catholic religious houses **3** : the head of a university or school

rec·to·ry \'rek-t(ə-)rē\ *n, pl* **-ries** : a residence of a rector or a parish priest

rec·tum \'rek-təm\ *n, pl* **rectums** or **rec·ta** \-tə\ : the end of the large intestine that links the colon to the anus — **rec·tal** \-tᵊl\ *adj*

rec·tus \'rek-təs\ *n, pl* **rec·ti** \-,tī, -,tē\ : any of several straight muscles (as of the abdomen)

re·cum·bent \ri-'kəm-bənt\ *adj* **1** : being in a state of rest **2** : lying down

re·cu·per·ate \ri-'k(y)ü-pə-,rāt\ *vb* **-at·ed; -at·ing** : RECOVER 2; *esp* : to regain health or strength — **re·cu·per·a·tion** \-,k(y)ü-pə-'rā-shən\ *n*

re·cur \ri-'kər\ *vb* **re·curred; re·cur·ring** **1** : to go or come back in thought or discussion **2** : to come again into the mind **3** : to occur or appear again — **re·cur·rence** \-'kər-ən(t)s, -'kə-rən(t)s\ *n*

re·cur·rent \ri-'kər-ənt, -'kə-rənt\ *adj* **1** : running or turning back in direction ⟨a *recurrent* vein⟩ **2** : returning from time to time ⟨a *recurrent* fever⟩ — **re·cur·rent·ly** *adv*

re·cy·cle \(')rē-'sī-kəl\ *vb* **1** : to process (as liquid body waste, glass, or cans) in order to regain materials for human use **2** : RECOVER 4

¹red \'red\ *adj* **red·der; red·dest** **1** : of the color red **2 a** : flushed especially with anger or embarrassment **b** : BLOODSHOT ⟨eyes *red* from weeping⟩ **3 a** : openly supporting sweeping social or political change especially by force **b** : encouraging, aiding, or furthering Communism : COMMUNIST **c** : of or relating to the U.S.S.R. or a Communist country — **red·ly** *adv* — **red·ness** *n*

²red *n* **1** : a color like that of blood or a ruby **2** : one that is of a red color **3** : a dye that colors red **4 a** : a person who seeks the overthrow of a social or political order : REVOLUTIONARY **b** *often cap* : a member or follower of a Communist party : COMMUNIST **5** : the condition of showing a loss ⟨in the *red*⟩

red alga *n* : any of several reddish algae that often grow in

the ocean

red·bird \'red-ˌbərd\ *n* : any of several birds (as a cardinal) with mostly red feathers

red blood cell *n* : a reddish cell of the blood that contains hemoglobin and carries oxygen from the lungs to the tissues — called also *red blood corpuscle, red cell, red corpuscle*

red–blood·ed \'red-'bləd-əd\ *adj* : ENERGETIC, VIGOROUS

red·breast \-ˌbrest\ *n* : a bird (as a robin) with a reddish breast

red·cap \-ˌkap\ *n* : ²PORTER 1

red–car·pet \-'kär-pət\ *adj* : marked by ceremonial courtesy ⟨*red-carpet* treatment⟩

red cedar *n* **1** : any of several American evergreens related to the junipers that have fragrant red wood **2** : the wood of a red cedar

red cell *n* : RED BLOOD CELL

red clover *n* : a Eurasian clover with globe-shaped reddish purple flowers that is grown for animals to graze on

red·coat \'red-ˌkōt\ *n* : a British soldier especially during the Revolutionary War

red corpuscle *n* : RED BLOOD CELL

red cross *n* : a red-colored cross on a white background used as a badge for hospitals and for members of a worldwide organization that helps the suffering especially in areas of war or disaster

red deer *n* : the common deer of Europe and Asia related to but smaller than the elk

red·den \'red-ᵊn\ *vb* **red·dened; red·den·ing** \'red-niŋ, -ᵊn-iŋ\ : to make or become red; *esp* : ¹BLUSH 1

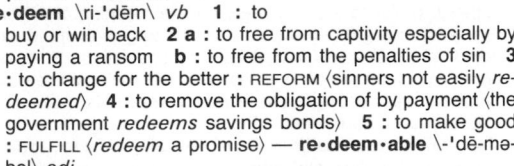
red deer

red·dish \'red-ish\ *adj* : somewhat red — **red·dish·ness** *n*

re·dec·o·rate \(')rē-'dek-ə-ˌrāt\ *vb* : to freshen or change a decorative scheme — **re·dec·o·ra·tion** \(ˌ)rē-ˌdek-ə-'rā-shən\ *n*

re·deem \ri-'dēm\ *vb* **1** : to buy or win back **2 a** : to free from captivity especially by paying a ransom **b** : to free from the penalties of sin **3** : to change for the better : REFORM ⟨sinners not easily *redeemed*⟩ **4** : to remove the obligation of by payment ⟨the government *redeems* savings bonds⟩ **5** : to make good : FULFILL ⟨*redeem* a promise⟩ — **re·deem·able** \-'dē-mə-bəl\ *adj*

re·deem·er \ri-'dē-mər\ *n* : a person who redeems; *esp, cap* : Jesus

re·demp·tion \ri-'dem(p)-shən\ *n* : the act or process or an instance of redeeming — **re·demp·tive** \-'dem(p)-tiv\ *adj*

re·de·sign \ˌrēd-i-'zīn\ *vb* : to change what something looks like, is used for, or contains — **redesign** *n*

red fox *n* : a fox with orange-red to reddish brown fur

red giant *n* : a star that has a low surface temperature and a diameter that is much larger than that of the sun

red fox

red–hand·ed \'red-'han-dəd\ *adv or adj* : in the act of doing something wrong

red·head \-ˌhed\ *n* : a person having red hair

red·head·ed \-'hed-əd\ *adj* : having red hair or a red head

redheaded woodpecker *n* : a large North American woodpecker that has a red head, a black back, and white patches on the wings

red herring *n* : something intended to distract attention from the real problem

red–hot \'red-'hät\ *adj* **1** : glowing red with heat **2** : marked by much feeling, enthusiasm, or energy ⟨a *red= hot* political campaign⟩ **3** : of or relating to the immediate present : including the very latest information ⟨*red-hot* news⟩

re·di·rect \ˌrēd-ə-'rekt, ˌrē-(ˌ)dī-\ *vb* : to change the course or direction of — **re·di·rec·tion** \-'rek-shən\ *n*

re·dis·trict \(')rē-'dis-(ˌ)trikt\ *vb* : to divide into new districts; *esp* : to reorganize the legislative districts of

red lead *n* : an orange-red to brick-red oxide of lead used in storage-battery plates, in glass, and in paint

red–let·ter \ˌred-'let-ər\ *adj* : worth remembering especially in a happy or joyful way ⟨a *red-letter* day⟩ [from the practice of marking holy days in red letters in church calendars]

red maple *n* : an American maple with reddish twigs and rather soft wood that grows mainly in moist soils

red marrow *n* : reddish bone marrow that produces red blood cells

re·do \(')rē-'dü\ *vb* **-did** \-'did\; **-done** \-'dən\; **-do·ing** \-'dü-iŋ\ : to do over or again; *esp* : REDECORATE

red oak *n* **1** : any of numerous North American oaks with acorns that take two years to mature and leaves with bristles on the edge **2** : the wood of a red oak

red·o·lence \'red-ᵊl-ən(t)s\ *n* **1** : the quality or state of being redolent **2** : ¹SCENT 1b, AROMA

red·o·lent \'red-ᵊl-ənt\ *adj* **1** : AROMATIC **2** : full of a fragrance or odor : SCENTED ⟨a room *redolent* of cooked cabbage⟩

re·dou·ble \(')rē-'dəb-əl\ *vb* : to make or become doubled (as in size or amount) ⟨*redoubled* their efforts⟩

re·doubt·able \ri-'daut-ə-bəl\ *adj* : causing fear or dread : FORMIDABLE ⟨a *redoubtable* warrior⟩ — **re·doubt·ably** \-blē\ *adv*

re·dound \ri-'daund\ *vb* : to have a result for good or bad

red pepper *n* : CAYENNE PEPPER

¹re·dress \ri-'dres\ *vb* : to set (as a wrong) right : REMEDY, RELIEVE — **re·dress·er** *n*

²re·dress \ri-'dres, 'rē-ˌdres\ *n* **1 a** : relief from distress **b** : the way or possibility of seeking a remedy **2** : something that makes up for wrong or loss **3** : an act or instance of redressing

red·shift \'red-'shift\ *n* : displacement of a spectrum especially of a heavenly body toward longer wavelengths

red snapper *n* : any of several reddish sea fishes including some used for food or sport

red spider *n* : any small web-spinning mite that attacks crop plants and fruit trees

red spruce *n* : a cone-bearing tree of eastern North America that is an important source of lumber and pulpwood

red·start \'red-ˌstärt\ *n* : an American fly-catching warbler

red–tailed hawk \ˌred-ˌtāld-\ *n* : an American hawk that eats small mammals and birds and that has a rather short usually reddish tail — called also *redtail*

red tape *n* : rules and regulations that waste people's time

red tide *n* : seawater discolored and made poisonous by the presence of large numbers of microscopic living things and especially by dinoflagellates

re·duce \ri-'d(y)üs\ *vb* **re·duced; re·duc·ing** **1** : to make smaller in size, amount, or number ⟨*reduce* the number of accidents⟩; *esp* : to lose weight by dieting **2** : to bring to a specified state or condition **3 a** : to lower in grade or rank : DEMOTE **b** : to be driven by poverty or need ⟨was *reduced* to begging⟩ **c** : to lessen the strength of **4** : to change an arithmetic expression to a simpler form without

\ə\ abut	\au̇\ out	\i\ tip	\ȯ\ saw	\u̇\ foot
\ər\ further	\ch\ chin	\ī\ life	\ȯi\ coin	\y\ yet
\a\ mat	\e\ pet	\j\ job	\th\ thin	\yü\ few
\ā\ take	\ē\ easy	\ŋ\ sing	\t̲h̲\ this	\yu̇\ cure
\ä\ cot, cart	\g\ go	\ō\ bone	\ü\ food	\zh\ vision

changing the value ⟨*reduce* a fraction to lowest terms⟩ **5** : to break down (as by crushing or grinding) ⟨*reduce* stone to powder⟩ **6 a :** DEOXIDIZE **b :** to combine with or subject to the action of hydrogen **c :** to add one or more electrons to (an atom or ion or molecule) — **re·duc·er** *n* — **re·duc·ibil·i·ty** \-,d(y)ü-sə-'bil-ət-ē\ *n* — **re·duc·ible** \-'d(y)ü-sə-bəl\ *adj*

re·duc·tion \ri-'dək-shən\ *n* **1 :** the act or process of reducing : the state of being reduced **2 a :** something made by reducing **b :** the amount by which something is reduced in price **3 :** MEIOSIS; *esp* : halving of the chromosome number in the reduction division — **re·duc·tive** \-'dək-tiv\ *adj*

reduction division *n* : the first cell division in the formation of sex cells in which the number of chromosomes in each cell is halved; *also* : MEIOSIS

re·dun·dan·cy \ri-'dən-dən-sē\ *n, pl* **-cies** **1 :** the quality or state of being redundant **2 a :** the use of unnecessary words **b :** an act or instance of needless repetition

re·dun·dant \ri-'dən-dənt\ *adj* **1 :** more than what is necessary or normal **2 :** using or having more words than necessary : REPETITIOUS — **re·dun·dant·ly** *adv*

re·du·pli·cate \ri-'d(y)ü-pli-,kāt, 'rē-\ *vb* : to make or perform again : COPY — **re·du·pli·cate** \-kət\ *adj*

re·du·pli·ca·tion \ri-,d(y)ü-pli-'kā-shən, ,rē-\ *n* : an act or instance of doubling or repeating : DUPLICATION — **re·du·pli·ca·tive** \ri-'d(y)ü-pli-,kāt-iv, 'rē-\ *adj*

red–winged blackbird \,red-,wind-\ *n* : an American blackbird of which the adult male is black with a patch of bright red on the wing — called also *redwing blackbird*

red·wood \'red-,wüd\ *n* : a tall cone-producing evergreen tree of the western coast of North America; *also* : its light long-lasting brownish red wood

re·echo \(')rē-'ek-ō\ *vb* : to echo back : REVERBERATE

reed \'rēd\ *n* **1 a** : any of various tall slender grasses (as bamboo) of wet areas that have stems with large joints **b** : a stem of such a grass **c** : a growth or mass of reeds **2** : a musical instrument made of the hollow joint of a plant **3** : a thin flexible strip (as of cane, wood, metal, or plastic) fastened at one end to the mouthpiece of a musical instrument (as a clarinet) or over an air opening (as in an accordion) and set in vibration by an air current (as the breath)

reed 3

re·ed·u·cate \(')rē-'ej-ə-,kāt\ *vb* : to train again; *esp* : to cause to develop new attitudes or habits through education — **re·ed·u·ca·tion** \(,)rē-,ej-ə-'kā-shən\ *n*

reedy \'rēd-ē\ *adj* **reed·i·er; -est** **1 :** full of or covered with reeds ⟨a *reedy* marsh⟩ **2 :** made of or resembling reeds; *esp* : long and slender like a reed ⟨*reedy* arms⟩

¹reef \'rēf\ *n* **1 :** a part of a sail taken in or let out in regulating size **2 :** the reduction in sail area made by reefing [Middle English *riff* "reef of a sail"; of Norse origin]

²reef *vb* : to reduce the area of (a sail) by rolling or folding a portion

³reef *n* : a chain of rocks or ridge of sand at or near the surface of water [from Dutch *rif* "reef of rocks or sand"; of Scandinavian origin]

¹reef·er \'rē-fər\ *n* **1 :** one that reefs **2 :** a close-fitting jacket of thick cloth

²reefer *n* : a marijuana cigarette

¹reek \'rēk\ *n* **1 :** VAPOR 1, FOG **2 :** a strong or disagreeable fume or odor

²reek *vb* **1 :** to give off smoke or vapor **2 a :** to have a strong or unpleasant smell **b :** to give a strong impression

of something unpleasant ⟨she *reeks* of wealth⟩ — **reeky** \'rē-kē\ *adj*

¹reel \'rē(ə)l\ *n* **1 a :** a device that can be turned round and round and on which something flexible is wound **b :** a device which is set on the handle of a fishing pole and used for winding up or letting out the line **c :** a narrow spool with a rim used to guide photographic film or magnetic tape **2 :** a quantity of something wound on a reel **3 :** a frame for drying clothes

²reel *vb* **1 :** to wind on or as if on a reel **2 :** to pull (as a fish) by reeling a line **3 :** to wind or turn a reel — **reel·able** \'rē-lə-bəl\ *adj* — **reel·er** *n*

³reel *vb* **1 a :** to whirl around ⟨*reeling* in a dance⟩ **b :** to be in a whirl ⟨heads *reeling* with excitement⟩ **2 :** to fall back (as from a blow) : RECOIL **3 :** to stagger or sway dizzily

⁴reel *n* : a reeling motion

⁵reel *n* : a lively dance originally of the Scottish Highlands; *also* : the music for this dance

re·elect \,rē-ə-'lekt\ *vb* : to elect for another term in office — **re·elec·tion** \-'lek-shən\ *n*

reel off *vb* : to tell or recite rapidly and easily ⟨*reeled off* the right answers⟩

re·en·act \,rē-ə-'nakt\ *vb* **1 :** to enact again **2 :** to perform again — **re·en·act·ment** \-'nak(t)-mənt\ *n*

re·en·ter \(')rē-'ent-ər\ *vb* : to enter again

re·en·trance \(')rē-'en-trən(t)s\ *n* : REENTRY

re·en·try \(')rē-'en-trē\ *n* **1 :** a second or new entry **2** : the action of reentering the earth's atmosphere after travel in space

reeve \'rēv\ *n* : an English manor officer of the Middle Ages

ref \'ref\ *n* : ¹REFEREE 2

re·fash·ion \(')rē-'fash-ən\ *vb* : to make again : MAKE OVER, ALTER

re·fec·to·ry \ri-'fek-t(ə-)rē\ *n, pl* **-ries** : a dining hall

refectory table *n* : a long narrow table with heavy legs

re·fer \ri-'fər\ *vb* **re·ferred; re·fer·ring** **1 :** to explain in terms of a general cause ⟨*referred* the defeat to poor training⟩ **2 :** to go, send, or guide to some person or place for treatment, help, advice, or information ⟨*refer* them to a dictionary⟩ ⟨*refer* to the dictionary for the meaning of a word⟩ **3 :** to have relationship : RELATE **4 :** to give or hand over to someone else ⟨*refer* a patient to a specialist⟩ **5 :** to call attention : make reference ⟨no one *referred* to yesterday's quarrel⟩ [Middle English *referren, referen* "to think of or place in a certain relationship, make a connection with in the mind", from Latin *referre,* literally "to carry back", from *re-* "back, again" and *ferre* "to bear, carry, yield" — related to ¹DEFER, OFFER] — **re·fer·able** \'ref-(ə-)rə-bəl, ri-'fər-ə-\ *adj* — **re·fer·rer** \ri-'fər-ər\ *n*

¹ref·er·ee \,ref-ə-'rē\ *n* **1 :** a person to whom something that is to be investigated or decided is referred **2 :** a sports official usually having final authority in conducting a game

²referee *vb* **-eed; -ee·ing** : to conduct as a referee

¹ref·er·ence \'ref-ərn(t)s, 'ref-(ə-)rən(t)s\ *n* **1 :** the act of referring **2 :** a relation to or concern with something : RESPECT ⟨with *reference* to what was said⟩ **3 a :** a remark referring to something : ALLUSION ⟨made *reference* to our agreement⟩ **b :** a sign or indication referring a reader to another book or portion of a written work **c :** use as sources of information ⟨volumes for ready *reference*⟩ **4 a** : a person to whom questions as to another person's honesty or ability can be addressed **b :** a statement of the qualifications of a person seeking employment or appointment given by someone familiar with them **c :** a book, document, or portion of a written work to which a reader is referred

²reference *adj* : used or usable for reference ⟨a *reference* point⟩

reference mark *n* : a conventional mark (as *, †, or ‡) placed in written or printed text to call the reader's attention especially to a footnote

ref·er·en·dum \,ref-ə-'ren-dəm\ *n, pl* **-da** \-də\ *or* **-dums** : the idea or practice of letting voters approve or disapprove laws or suggested laws; *also* : such a vote

ref·er·ent \'ref-(ə-)rənt\ *n* : something that refers or is referred to; *esp* : the thing a word represents — **referent** *adj*

re·fer·ral \ri-'fər-əl\ *n* : the act or an instance of referring

¹re·fill \(')rē-'fil\ *vb* : to fill or become filled again — **re·fill·able** \-'fil-ə-bəl\ *adj*

²re·fill \'rē-,fil\ *n* : a new or fresh supply of something ⟨a *refill* for a ball-point pen⟩

re·fine \ri-'fīn\ *vb* **re·fined; re·fin·ing** **1** : to come or bring to a pure state ⟨*refine* sugar⟩ **2** : to make or become improved **3** : to free from what is vulgar **4** : to improve by introducing something that makes a small difference ⟨*refined* upon the older methods⟩ — **re·fin·er** *n*

re·fined \ri-'fīnd\ *adj* **1** : WELL-BRED, CULTURED ⟨very *refined* manners⟩ **2** : freed from impurities : PURE ⟨*refined* sugar⟩ **3** : carried to a fine point : SUBTLE ⟨*refined* measurements⟩

re·fine·ment \ri-'fīn-mənt\ *n* **1** : the action or process of refining **2** : the state of being refined ⟨CULTIVATION **3 a** : something that has been refined ⟨*refinements* in dress and behavior⟩ **b** : something intended to improve or refine

re·fin·ery \ri-'fīn-(ə-)rē\ *n, pl* **-er·ies** : a building and equipment for refining metals, oil, or sugar

re·fin·ish \(')rē-'fin-ish\ *vb* : to give (as furniture) a new surface — **re·fin·ish·er** *n*

re·fit \(')rē-'fit\ *vb* : to get ready for use again ⟨*refit* a ship for service⟩ — **re·fit** \'rē-,fit, (')rē-'fit\ *n*

re·flect \ri-'flekt\ *vb* **1** : to bend or throw back waves of light, sound, or heat ⟨a polished surface *reflects* light⟩ **2** : to give back an image or likeness of as if by a mirror **3** : to bring as a result **4** : to cast disapproval or blame ⟨our bad conduct *reflects* upon our training⟩ **5** : to think seriously and carefully : MEDITATE

reflecting telescope *n* : a telescope in which the principal light-gathering element is a mirror

re·flec·tion \ri-'flek-shən\ *n* **1** : an instance of reflecting; *esp* : the return of light or sound waves from a surface **2** : the production of an image by or as if by a mirror **3** : an image produced by or as if by a mirror **4** : something that brings blame or disgrace ⟨a *reflection* on my honesty⟩ **5** : an opinion formed or a remark made after careful thought **6** : careful thought ⟨much *reflection* on the problem⟩ — **re·flec·tion·al** \-shnəl, -shən-ᵊl\ *adj*

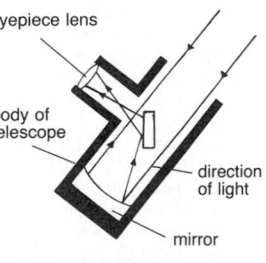

eyepiece lens

body of telescope

direction of light

mirror

reflecting telescope

re·flec·tive \ri-'flek-tiv\ *adj* **1** : capable of reflecting light, images, or sound waves **2** : marked by reflection : THOUGHTFUL **3** : of, relating to, or caused by reflection — **re·flec·tive·ly** *adv* — **re·flec·tive·ness** *n* — **re·flec·tiv·i·ty** \,rē-,flek-'tiv-ət-ē, ri-\ *n*

re·flec·tor \ri-'flek-tər\ *n* : one that reflects; *esp* : a polished surface for reflecting light or heat

¹re·flex \'rē-,fleks\ *n* **1** : an automatic response to a stimulus in which a nerve message passes from a sense organ to the spinal cord and then to a point of action (as a muscle or gland) without going to the brain ⟨the knee-jerk *reflex*⟩ — compare HABIT **3** **2** *pl* : the power of acting or responding with enough speed ⟨an athlete with great *reflexes*⟩

²reflex *adj* **1** : produced in reaction, resistance, or return **2** : of, relating to, or produced by a reflex of the nervous system ⟨*reflex* action⟩ — **re·flex·ly** *adv*

reflex arc *n* : the complete nervous path involved in a reflex

re·flex·ion \ri-'flek-shən\ *chiefly British variant of* REFLECTION

¹re·flex·ive \ri-'flek-siv\ *adj* **1** : turned back upon itself **2** : of, relating to, or being an action directed back upon the doer or the grammatical subject **3** : of, relating to, or being a relation which exists between a thing and itself ⟨the relation of equality or "is equal to" is *reflexive* but the relation "is the parent of" is not⟩ — **re·flex·ive·ly** *adv*

²reflexive *n* : a pronoun that refers to the grammatical subject and is the object of the verb ⟨in the sentence "We forced ourselves to finish the assignment", the word "ourselves" is a *reflexive*⟩

re·flux \'rē-,fleks\ *n* : a flowing back : EBB

re·for·es·ta·tion \(,)rē-,fôr-ə-'stā-shən, -,fär-\ *n* : the action of renewing a forest by planting seeds or young trees — **re·for·est** \(')rē-'fôr-əst, -'fär-\ *vb*

¹re·form \ri-'fô(ə)rm\ *vb* **1** : to make better by removal of faults ⟨*reform* a prisoner⟩ **2** : to correct or improve one's own behavior or habits — **re·form·able** \-'fôr-mə-bəl\ *adj*

²reform *n* **1** : improvement in what is bad **2** : a removal or correction of an abuse, a wrong, or errors

re–form \(')rē-'fô(ə)rm\ *vb* : to form again ⟨the ice *re-formed* on the lake⟩

ref·or·ma·tion \,ref-ər-'mā-shən\ *n* **1** : the act of reforming : the state of being reformed **2** *cap* : a 16th century series of religious actions which led to establishment of the Protestant churches — **ref·or·ma·tion·al** \-shnəl, -shən-ᵊl\ *adj*

re·for·ma·tive \ri-'fôr-mət-iv\ *adj* : tending or likely to reform

¹re·for·ma·to·ry \ri-'fôr-mə-,tōr-ē, -,tôr-\ *adj* : REFORMATIVE

²reformatory *n, pl* **-ries** : an institution for reforming usually young or female criminals or those in jail for the first time

re·form·er \ri-'fôr-mər\ *n* : one that works for reform

Reform Judaism *n* : a 19th and 20th century development of Judaism marked by the nonobservance of much legal tradition no longer considered appropriate, by simplified traditional ceremonies, and by stress on the religious rather than the national quality of Judaism

reform school *n* : a reformatory for boys or girls

re·fract \ri-'frakt\ *vb* : to cause to go through refraction

refracting telescope *n* : a telescope in which the principal light-gathering element is a lens

re·frac·tion \ri-'frak-shən\ *n* : the bending of a ray when it passes at an angle from one medium into another in which its speed is different (as when light passes from air into water) — **re·frac·tive** \-'frak-tiv\ *adj*

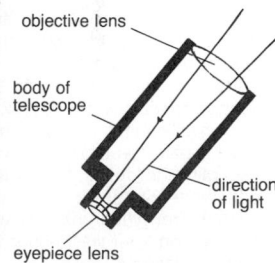

objective lens

body of telescope

direction of light

eyepiece lens

refracting telescope

re·frac·to·ry \ri-'frak-t(ə-)rē\ *adj* **1** : resisting control or authority : STUBBORN ⟨a *refractory* child⟩ **2** : resistant to treatment : UNRESPONSIVE **3** : capable of enduring high temperatures — **re·frac·to·ri·ness** \-t(ə-)rē-nəs\ *n*

¹re·frain \ri-'frān\ *vb* : to hold oneself back ⟨*refrain* from laughing⟩

²refrain *n* : a regularly repeated phrase or verse of a poem or song : CHORUS

\ə\ abut	\au̇\ out	\i\ tip	\ȯ\ saw	\u̇\ foot
\ər\ further	\ch\ chin	\ī\ life	\ȯi\ coin	\y\ yet
\a\ mat	\e\ pet	\j\ job	\th\ thin	\yü\ few
\ā\ take	\ē\ easy	\ŋ\ sing	\th\ this	\yu̇\ cure
\ä\ cot, cart	\g\ go	\ō\ bone	\ü\ food	\zh\ vision

re·fresh \ri-'fresh\ *vb* **1** : to make fresh or fresher : REVIVE ⟨sleep *refreshes* the body⟩ ⟨*refreshed* my memory by looking at my notes⟩ **2** : to restore or maintain by renewing supply

re·fresh·en \ri-'fresh-ən\ *vb* : REFRESH

re·fresh·er \ri-'fresh-ər\ *n* **1** : something that refreshes **2** : review or instruction designed especially to keep one familiar with professional progress

re·fresh·ing \ri-'fresh-iŋ\ *adj* : serving to refresh; *esp* : pleasing because of freshness or newness

re·fresh·ment \ri-'fresh-mənt\ *n* **1** : the act of refreshing : the state of being refreshed **2 a** : something that refreshes **b** *pl* : a light meal ⟨*refreshments* will be served after the meeting⟩

re·fried beans \(,)rē-'frīd-\ *n pl* : beans cooked with seasonings, fried, then mashed and fried again

re·frig·er·ant \ri-'frij-(ə-)rənt\ *n* : a substance (as ice, ammonia, or carbon dioxide) used in refrigeration

re·frig·er·ate \ri-'frij-ə-,rāt\ *vb* **-at·ed; -at·ing** : to make or keep cold or cool; *esp* : to freeze or chill food to preserve it — **re·frig·er·a·tion** \-,frij-ə-'rā-shən\ *n*

re·frig·er·a·tor \ri-'frij-ə-,rāt-ər\ *n* : a device or room for keeping articles (as food) cool

re·fu·el \(')rē-'fyü-əl\ *vb* : to provide with or take on more fuel

ref·uge \'ref-,yüj\ *n* **1** : shelter or protection from danger or distress **2** : a place that provides shelter or protection ⟨wildlife *refuges*⟩

ref·u·gee \,ref-yù-'jē, 'ref-yù-,jē\ *n* : a person who flees for safety especially to a foreign country [from French *réfugié*, past participle of *réfugier* "to put in a place of safety", from Latin *refugium* "a refuge", from *refugere* "to run away from, escape", from *re-* "again, against" and *fugere* "to run away, flee" — related to CENTRIFUGAL, FUGITIVE]

re·ful·gence \ri-'fùl-jən(t)s, -'fəl-\ *n* : a radiant or shining quality or state : BRILLIANCE — **re·ful·gent** \-jənt\ *adj*

¹re·fund \ri-'fənd, 'rē-,fənd\ *vb* : to return money in repayment — **re·fund·able** \-ə-bəl\ *adj*

²re·fund \'rē-,fənd\ *n* **1** : the act of refunding **2** : an amount of money refunded

³re·fund \(')rē-'fənd\ *vb* : to fund a debt again

re·fur·bish \ri-'fər-bish\ *vb* : to brighten or freshen up : RENOVATE ⟨*refurbish* an old house⟩ — **re·fur·bish·ment** \-mənt\ *n*

re·fus·al \ri-'fyü-zəl\ *n* **1** : the act of refusing or denying **2** : the opportunity or right of refusing or taking (as a purchase) before others

¹re·fuse \ri-'fyüz\ *vb* **1** : to say one will not accept : REJECT ⟨*refused* the money⟩ **2 a** : to show or express positive unwillingness ⟨*refused* to act⟩ **b** : to say one will not grant : DENY ⟨was *refused* entrance⟩ **3** : to withhold the accepting, following, or permitting of something **syn** see DECLINE — **re·fus·er** *n*

²ref·use \'ref-,yüs, -,yüz\ *n* : worthless things : TRASH

ref·u·ta·tion \,ref-yù-'tā-shən\ *n* : the act or process of refuting : DISPROOF

re·fute \ri-'fyüt\ *vb* **re·fut·ed; re·fut·ing** : to prove wrong by argument or evidence : show to be false ⟨*refute* the testimony of a witness⟩ — **re·fut·able** \-'fyüt-ə-bəl\ *adj* — **re·fut·er** *n*

re·gain \ri-'gān\ *vb* **1** : to gain or get again ⟨*regained* my health⟩ **2** : to get back to : reach again ⟨*regain* the shore⟩

re·gal \'rē-gəl\ *adj* **1** : of, relating to, or suitable for a king **2** : of remarkable excellence or magnificence : SPLENDID — **re·gal·ly** \'rē-gə-lē\ *adv*

re·gale \ri-'gā(ə)l\ *vb* **re·galed; re·gal·ing** **1** : to entertain richly **2** : to give pleasure or amusement to **3** : to feast oneself : FEED

re·ga·lia \ri-'gāl-yə\ *n sing or pl* **1** : the emblems and symbols (as the crown) of royalty **2** : the emblem of an office or association **3** : special dress : FINERY

¹re·gard \ri-'gärd\ *n* **1 a** : CONSIDERATION 2, CONCERN ⟨little

regard for others' feelings⟩ **b** : the act or an instance of looking : GAZE **2 a** : the worth or estimation in which something is held **b** : a feeling of respect and affection : ESTEEM ⟨a high *regard* for my teacher⟩ **c** *pl* : friendly greetings ⟨give them my *regards*⟩ **3** : ¹REFERENCE 2, RESPECT ⟨this is in *regard* to your unpaid balance⟩ **4** : a point to be taken into consideration ⟨nothing to worry about in that *regard*⟩

²regard *vb* **1** : to pay attention to : take into consideration **2 a** : to show respect or consideration for **b** : to have a high opinion of **3** : to look at **4** *archaic* : to relate to **5** : to think of : look upon ⟨*regarded* you as a friend⟩ — **as regards** : with respect to : REGARDING

re·gard·ful \ri-'gärd-fəl\ *adj* **1** : HEEDFUL, OBSERVANT **2** : full or expressive of regard or respect : RESPECTFUL

re·gard·ing *prep* : CONCERNING

¹re·gard·less \ri-'gärd-ləs\ *adj* : having or taking no regard : HEEDLESS, CARELESS ⟨*regardless* of what might happen⟩

²regardless *adv* : in spite of everything

re·gat·ta \ri-'gät-ə, -'gat-\ *n* : a boat race or a series of boat races

re·gen·cy \'rē-jən-sē\ *n, pl* **-cies** **1** : the office, authority, or government of a regent or body of regents **2** : the period of rule of a regent or body of regents

¹re·gen·er·ate \ri-'jen-(ə-)rət\ *adj* : spiritually reborn or renewed

²re·gen·er·ate \ri-'jen-ə-,rāt\ *vb* **1** : to cause to be reborn spiritually **2** : to reform completely in ways of thinking and behaving **3** : to generate or produce again; *esp* : to renew (a lost or damaged body part) by a new growth of tissue **4** : to give new life to : REVIVE ⟨land *regenerated* by rotation of crops⟩

re·gen·er·a·tion \ri-,jen-ə-'rā-shən, ,rē-\ *n* : an act or the process of regenerating : the state of being regenerated

re·gen·er·a·tive \ri-'jen-ə-,rāt-iv\ *adj* **1** : of, relating to, or marked by regeneration **2** : tending to regenerate

re·gent \'rē-jənt\ *n* **1** : one who governs a kingdom when a monarch is not able to **2** : a member of a governing group (as of a state university) [Middle English *regent* "one who governs", from

regeneration

early French *regent* or Latin *regent-, regens* (both, same meaning), from earlier Latin *regens*, a form of the verb *regere* "to lead straight, govern, rule" — related to ¹RAIL, REGULATE, RULE] — **regent** *adj*

reg·gae \'reg-(,)ā, 'räg-\ *n* : popular music of Jamaican origin that combines native styles with elements of U.S. black popular music and is performed at moderate tempos with the accent on the offbeat

reg·i·cide \'rej-ə-,sīd\ *n* **1** : one who kills or helps to kill a king **2** : the killing of a king — **reg·i·cid·al** \,rej-ə-'sīd-əl\ *adj*

re·gime *also* **ré·gime** \rā-'zhēm, ri-\ *n* **1 a** : REGIMEN 1 **b** : a regular pattern of doing something **2 a** : a method of rule or management **b** : a form of government or administration; *esp* : a governmental or social system **c** : a period of rule of a regime

reg·i·men \'rej-ə-mən, -,men\ *n* **1** : a regular course of treatment **2** : a form of government : RULE

¹reg·i·ment \'rej-(ə-)mənt\ *n* : a military unit consisting usually of a number of battalions — **reg·i·men·tal** \,rej-ə-'ment-əl\ *adj*

²reg·i·ment \'rej-ə-,ment\ *vb* **1** : to organize for the sake of regulation or control **2** : to make orderly or the same as others — **reg·i·men·ta·tion** \,rej-ə-mən-'tā-shən, -,men-\ *n*

reg·i·men·tals \ˌrej-ə-'ment-ᵊlz\ *n pl* **1** : a regimental uniform **2** : military dress

re·gion \'rē-jən\ *n* **1** : an area, division, or district of administration **2 a** : a part, portion, or area having no fixed boundaries ⟨darker *regions* of the night sky⟩ **b** : a broad geographical area **3** : VICINITY 2 ⟨a pain in the *region* of the heart⟩ **4** : a set of points any two of which can be connected by a line lying wholly within the set together with none, some, or all of the points on its boundary ⟨a rectangular *region*⟩

re·gion·al \'rēj-nəl, -ən-ᵊl\ *adj* **1** : of, relating to, or characteristic of a region **2** : affecting a particular region : LOCALIZED ⟨*regional* pain⟩ — **re·gion·al·ly** \-ē\ *adv*

re·gion·al·ism \'rēj-nəl-ˌiz-əm, -ən-ᵊl-\ *n* **1** : the quality of being conscious of and loyal to a particular region **2** : the practice of using a particular region as the setting in art or literature **3** : an individual quality (as of speech) of a geographic area — **re·gion·al·ist** \-əst\ *n or adj* — **re·gion·al·is·tic** \ˌrēj-nᵊl 'io tik, -ən-ᵊl-\ *adj*

¹reg·is·ter \'rej-ə-stər\ *n* **1 a** : a written record or list of items **b** : a book for such a record ⟨a *register* of deeds⟩ **2** : a part of the range of a human voice or a musical instrument made up of tones similarly produced or of the same quality **3** : a device (as in a floor or wall) that regulates the flow of heated air from a furnace **4 a** : an automatic device registering a number or a quantity **b** : a number or quantity registered by such a device **5** : a device (as in a computer) for storing small amounts of data

²register *vb* **reg·is·tered; reg·is·ter·ing** \-st(ə-)riŋ\ **1 a** : to record exactly and legally in a register ⟨*register* a will⟩ **b** : to enroll especially as a voter or student **c** : to record automatically : INDICATE ⟨the thermometer *registered* zero⟩ **2** : to get special protection for (a piece of mail) by prepayment of a fee **3** : to show by expression and bodily movements alone ⟨your face *registered* surprise⟩ **4** : to write one's name in a register ⟨*register* at a hotel⟩ ⟨*register* for the draft⟩ **5** : to make an impression ⟨your name didn't *register* with me⟩

³register *n* : REGISTRAR

registered nurse *n* : a graduate trained nurse who has been licensed to practice by a state authority

reg·is·trant \'rej-ə-strənt\ *n* : one that registers or is registered

reg·is·trar \'rej-ə-ˌsträr\ *n* : an official who records or keeps records

reg·is·tra·tion \ˌrej-ə-'strā-shən\ *n* **1** : an act or the fact of registering **2** : something recorded in a register **3** : the number of individuals registered : ENROLLMENT **4** : a document certifying an act of registering ⟨automobile *registration*⟩

reg·is·try \'rej-ə-strē\ *n, pl* **-tries** **1** : REGISTRATION 3 **2** : a place of registration **3 a** : a book in which things are recorded exactly and legally **b** : something recorded in a registry

re·gress \ri-'gres\ *vb* : to go or cause to go back especially to a previous level or condition

re·gres·sion \ri-'gresh-ən\ *n* : an act or the fact of regressing : RETROGRESSION

re·gres·sive \ri-'gres-iv\ *adj* **1** : of, relating to, or tending toward regression **2** : gradually decreasing ⟨a *regressive* tax⟩

¹re·gret \ri-'gret\ *vb* **re·gret·ted; re·gret·ting** **1 a** : to mourn the loss or death of **b** : to miss very much **2** : to be keenly sorry for **3** : to experience regret

²regret *n* **1** : sorrow aroused by events beyond one's control **2 a** : an expression of sorrow or disappointment **b** *pl* : a note politely turning down an invitation — **re·gret·ful** \-'gret-fəl\ *adj*

re·gret·ful·ly \ri-'gret-fə-lē\ *adv* **1** : in a way that is full of regret ⟨I must *regretfully* decline your invitation⟩ **2** : I regret : we regret ⟨*regretfully*, we can't go⟩

re·gret·ta·ble \ri-'gret-ə-bəl\ *adj* : deserving regret

re·gret·ta·bly \ri-'gret-ə-blē\ *adv* **1** : to an extent deserving regret ⟨a *regrettably* big decline in wages⟩ **2** : it is regrettable : UNFORTUNATELY ⟨*regrettably*, I could not agree⟩

re·group \(')rē-'grüp\ *vb* : to form into a new group ⟨in order to subtract 129 from 531 *regroup* 531 into 5 hundreds, 2 tens, and 11 ones⟩

re·grow \(')rē-'grō\ *vb* **-grew** \-'grü\; **-grown** \-'grōn\; **-grow·ing** : to grow (as a missing part) again

¹reg·u·lar \'reg-yə-lər\ *adj* **1** : belonging to a religious community and living by its rules **2 a** : formed, built, arranged, or ordered according to an established rule, law, or type **b** : having all sides or faces equal and all angles equal ⟨a *regular* polygon⟩ **c** : even or balanced in form or structure; *esp* : having radial symmetry ⟨*regular* flowers⟩ **3 a** : being in the habit of following a method : ORDERLY, METHODICAL **b** : returning or acting at fixed times **4 a** : following established or prescribed uses or rules **b** : being such without any doubt : COMPLETE, UNMITIGATED ⟨a *regular* scoundrel⟩ **c** : following the normal or usual manner of changing tense ⟨*regular* verbs⟩ **5** : of, relating to, or being a permanent army of a country — **reg·u·lar·ly** \'reg-yə-lər-lē\ *adv*

²regular *n* **1** : a member of the clergy who belongs to a religious community **2** : a soldier in a regular army **3** : a player on an athletic team who usually starts every game

reg·u·lar·i·ty \ˌreg-yə-'lar-ət-ē\ *n, pl* **-ties** **1** : the quality or state of being regular **2** : something that is regular

reg·u·lar·ize \'reg-yə-lə-ˌrīz\ *vb* **-ized; -iz·ing** : to make regular

reg·u·late \'reg-yə-ˌlāt\ *vb* **-lat·ed; -lat·ing** **1 a** : to govern or direct according to rule **b** : to bring under the control of authority ⟨*regulate* prices⟩ **2** : to bring order or method to ⟨*regulate* one's habits⟩ **3** : to fix or adjust the time, amount, degree, or rate of ⟨*regulate* the pressure of a tire⟩ ⟨the brain *regulates* the heartbeat⟩ [from Latin *regulatus*, past participle of *regulare* "to regulate, direct", from *regula* "a rule, straightedge" — related to ¹RAIL, REGENT, RULE] — **reg·u·la·tor** \-ˌlāt-ər\ *n* — **reg·u·la·to·ry** \-lə-ˌtōr-ē, -ˌtȯr-\ *adj*

¹reg·u·la·tion \ˌreg-yə-'lā-shən\ *n* **1** : the act of regulating : the state of being regulated **2 a** : a rule or order telling how something is to be done ⟨safety *regulations* in a factory⟩ **b** : a rule or order having the force of law

²regulation *adj* : being in agreement with regulations ⟨*regulation* baseball⟩

re·gur·gi·tate \(')rē-'gər-jə-ˌtāt\ *vb* **-tat·ed; -tat·ing** : to throw or be thrown back or out again ⟨*regurgitate* undigested food⟩ — **re·gur·gi·ta·tion** \(ˌ)rē-ˌgər-jə-'tā-shən\ *n*

re·ha·bil·i·tate \ˌrē-(h)ə-'bil-ə-ˌtāt\ *vb* **-tat·ed; -tat·ing** **1** : to restore to a former status or reputation **2 a** : to restore to a state of efficiency, good management, or repair ⟨*rehabilitate* slum areas⟩ **b** : to restore to a condition of health or useful and constructive activity ⟨*rehabilitate* criminals⟩ — **re·ha·bil·i·ta·tion** \-ˌbil-ə-'tā-shən\ *n*

re·hash \(')rē-'hash\ *vb* : to present or use (as an argument) again in another form without much change or improvement — **re·hash** \'rē-ˌhash\ *n*

re·hears·al \ri-'hər-səl\ *n* **1** : a private performance or practice session in preparation for a public appearance **2** : a practice exercise : TRIAL

re·hearse \ri-'hərs\ *vb* **re·hearsed; re·hears·ing** **1 a** : to say again : REPEAT **b** : to recount in order : ENUMERATE ⟨they *rehearsed* their complaints in a letter⟩ **2 a** : to prac-

\ə\ abut	\au̇\ out	\i\ tip	\ȯ\ saw	\u̇\ foot
\ər\ further	\ch\ chin	\ī\ life	\ȯi\ coin	\y\ yet
\a\ mat	\e\ pet	\j\ job	\th\ thin	\yü\ few
\ā\ take	\ē\ easy	\ŋ\ sing	\th\ this	\yu̇\ cure
\ä\ cot, cart	\g\ go	\ō\ bone	\ü\ food	\zh\ vision

tice (a play or scene) for public performance   **b** : to train or instruct (as actors) by rehearsal   **3** : to engage in a rehearsal — **re·hears·er** *n*

Word History In the Middle Ages, French farmers used a tool they called a *herce*. This was a triangular wooden frame with sturdy pegs or teeth on one side. It was pulled over plowed farmland to break up the soil in order to make it smooth for planting. The early French verb used to describe this action was *hercier*, which meant "to harrow". In most cases the process had to be repeated over and over, so the word *rehercier* was formed, meaning "to harrow again" or "reharrow". In time, *rehercier* came to be used with more general meanings like "to go over something again (and again)", as in repeating a school lesson or a story. The word came into Middle English as *rehersen,* meaning "to say again, repeat". Through the years the English word, now spelled *rehearse,* has picked up new meanings. Perhaps the most familiar one now is "to go through (a scene or play) over and over for practice until it is ready for performance". [Middle English *rehersen* "to say again, repeat", from early French *rehercier* "to go over again and again", literally "to harrow again", from *re-* "again" and *hercier* "to harrow", from *herce* "a harrow"]

re·hy·drate \(')rē-'hī-,drāt\ *vb* : to restore fluid to (something dehydrated) — **re·hy·dra·tion** \,rē-,hī-'drā-shən\ *n*

reichs·mark \'rīk-,smärk\ *n, pl* **reichsmarks** *also* **reichsmark** : the German unit of money from 1925 to 1948

¹reign \'rān\ *n*   **1** : the authority or rule of a monarch   **2** : the time during which a monarch reigns

²reign *vb*   **1** : to govern as a monarch   **2** : to exercise authority in the manner of a monarch   **3** : to be usual or widespread ⟨silence *reigned*⟩

reign of terror : a period marked by violence that is often carried out by those in power and produces terror among the people involved

re·im·burse \,rē-əm-'bərs\ *vb* **-bursed; -burs·ing** : to pay back : REPAY ⟨*reimburse* travel expenses⟩ [from *re-* "again, back" and obsolete *imburse* "pay, put in the pocket", from Latin *imbursare* (same meaning), from earlier *in-* "in" and *bursa* "purse, small leather bag" — related to DISBURSE, PURSE] — **re·im·burs·able** \-'bər-sə-bəl\ *adj* — **re·im·burse·ment** \-'bər-smənt\ *n*

¹rein \'rān\ *n*   **1** : a line or strap fastened to a bit on each side for controlling an animal (as a horse) — usually used in pl.   **2 a** : an influence that slows, limits, or holds back ⟨kept the child under a tight *rein*⟩   **b** : controlling or guiding power — usually used in pl. ⟨seized the *reins* of government⟩   **3** : complete freedom : SCOPE ⟨gave full *rein* to her imagination⟩

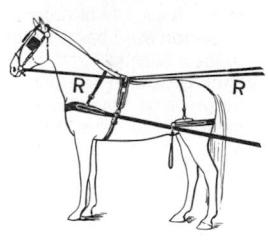

R rein 1

²rein *vb* : to check, control, or stop by or as if by reins ⟨*reined* in the horse⟩ ⟨couldn't *rein* his impatience⟩

re·in·car·nate \,rē-ən-'kär-,nāt\ *vb* **-nat·ed; -nat·ing** : to give a new or different body or form to

re·in·car·na·tion \(,)rē-,in-,kär-'nā-shən\ *n*   **1** : the action of reincarnating : the state of being reincarnated   **2** : rebirth in new bodies or forms of life; *esp* : a rebirth of a soul in a new human body

rein·deer \'rān-,di(ə)r\ *n, pl* **reindeer** *also* **rein·deers** : any of several large deer of northern regions that have antlers in both sexes and are now classified with the caribou in a single species

reindeer moss *n* : a gray lichen of northern regions that has many branches and is an important food for reindeer

re·in·fec·tion \,rē-ən-'fek-shən\ *n* : infection following recovery from or in addition to another infection of the same kind — **re·in·fect** \,re-ən-'fekt\ *vb*

re·in·force \,rē-ən-'fō(ə)rs, -'fȯ(ə)rs\ *vb*   **1** : to strengthen or increase by fresh additions ⟨were *reinforcing* their pitching staff⟩   **2** : to strengthen by additional assistance, material, or support ⟨*reinforce* the elbows of a jacket⟩ ⟨*reinforce* the argument with facts⟩

reindeer

re·in·force·ment \,rē-ən-'fȯr-smənt, -'fȯr-\ *n*   **1** : the action of reinforcing : the state of being reinforced   **2** : something that reinforces

re·in·forc·er \,rē-ən-'fȯr-sər, -'fȯr-\ *n*   **1** : one that reinforces   **2** : a stimulus (as a reward or the removal of something unpleasant) given after an action or reply that helps to make the individual act or reply in the same way when the conditions are repeated

re·in·state \,rē-ən-'stāt\ *vb* **-stat·ed; -stat·ing** : to place again in a former position or condition ⟨*reinstate* an official⟩ — **re·in·state·ment** \-mənt\ *n*

re·in·ter·pret \,rē-ən-'tər-prət\ *vb* : to interpret again; *esp* : to give a new or different interpretation to — **re·in·ter·pre·ta·tion** \-,tər-prə-'tā-shən\ *n*

re·in·vest \,rē-ən-'vest\ *vb* : to invest again or anew — **re·in·vest·ment** \-'ves(t)-mənt\ *n*

re·it·er·ate \rē-'it-ə-,rāt\ *vb* **-at·ed; -at·ing** : to say or do over again or repeatedly — **re·it·er·a·tion** \(,)rē-,it-ə-'rā-shən\ *n* — **re·it·er·a·tive** \rē-'it-ə-,rāt-iv, -rət-\ *adj* — **re·it·er·a·tive·ly** *adv* — **re·it·er·a·tive·ness** *n*

¹re·ject \ri-'jekt\ *vb*   **1** : to refuse to admit, believe, or receive   **2** : to throw away as useless or unsatisfactory   **3** : to refuse to grant or consider   **4** : to cause the rejection of by the immune system ⟨the body of the patient started to *reject* the transplanted heart⟩   **syn** see DECLINE

²re·ject \'rē-,jekt\ *n* : a rejected person or thing

re·jec·tion \ri-'jek-shən\ *n*   **1** : the action of rejecting : the state of being rejected   **2** : something rejected   **3** : the process by which the immune system causes foreign tissue or an organ (as a transplant) to separate from and stop functioning with the organs and tissues of the animal or human being that has received it

re·joice \ri-'jȯis\ *vb* **re·joiced; re·joic·ing**   **1** : to give joy to : GLADDEN ⟨news that *rejoices* the heart⟩   **2** : to feel joy or great delight ⟨*rejoice* over a friend's good luck⟩ — **re·joic·er** *n* — **re·joic·ing·ly** \-'jȯi-siŋ-lē\ *adv*

re·joic·ing \ri-'jȯi-siŋ\ *n*   **1** : the action of one that rejoices   **2** : a time or an expression of joy

re·join *vb*   **1** \(')rē-'jȯin\ : to join again : return to ⟨*rejoined* my family after a week in camp⟩   **2** \ri-\ : to say in reply

re·join·der \ri-'jȯin-dər\ *n* : ²REPLY; *esp* : an answer to a reply

re·ju·ve·nate \ri-'jü-və-,nāt\ *vb* **-nat·ed; -nat·ing** : to make young or youthful again : give new vigor to — **re·ju·ve·na·tion** \-,jü-və-'nā-shən\ *n* — **re·ju·ve·na·tor** \-'jü-və-,nāt-ər\ *n*

relaid *past and past participle of* RELAY

¹re·lapse \ri-'laps, 'rē-,laps\ *n* : a relapsing; *esp* : a fresh period of an illness after an improvement

²re·lapse \ri-'laps\ *vb* **re·lapsed; re·laps·ing** : to slip or fall back into a former worse state — **re·laps·er** *n*

re·late \ri-'lāt\ *vb* **re·lat·ed; re·lat·ing**   **1** : to give an account of : TELL ⟨*relate* a story⟩   **2** : to show or establish a relationship between ⟨*relate* cause and effect⟩   **3** : to have relationship or connection : REFER ⟨the readings *relate* to the class discussions⟩   **4** : to have or establish a social relationship ⟨the way a child *relates* to a teacher⟩ **5** : to respond especially in a favorable way ⟨can't *relate* to that kind of music⟩ — **re·lat·able** \-'lāt-ə-bəl\ *adj*

re·lat·ed *adj* **1** : connected through a relation that is known or can be discovered ⟨painting and the *related* arts⟩ **2** : connected by common ancestry or by marriage

re·la·tion \ri-'lā-shən\ *n* **1** : the act of telling or describing **2** : CONNECTION 2, RELATIONSHIP ⟨the *relation* of employer to employee⟩ **3** : a related person : RELATIVE **4** : ¹REF-ERENCE 2, RESPECT ⟨in *relation* to this matter⟩ **5 a** : the state of sharing an interest (as in social or business matters) **b** *pl* : business or public affairs ⟨good trade *relations*⟩ ⟨foreign *relations*⟩ **c** *pl* : dealings between persons or groups ⟨improved his *relations* with his family⟩ — **re·la·tion·al** \-shnəl, -shən-ᵊl\ *adj*

re·la·tion·ship \ri-'lā-shən-,ship\ *n* **1** : the state of being related ⟨study language *relationships*⟩ **2 a** : KINSHIP ⟨claimed *relationship* with the mayor⟩ **b** : a specific instance or type of this ⟨family *relationships*⟩

¹**rel·a·tive** \'rel-ət-ɪv\ *n* **1** : a word referring grammatically to one that comes before it **2** : a person connected with another by blood or marriage

²**relative** *adj* **1 a** : introducing a subordinate clause that qualifies an expressed or implied antecedent ⟨*relative* pronoun⟩ **b** : introduced by a word having such an antecedent ⟨*relative* clause⟩ **2** : RELEVANT, PERTINENT ⟨questions *relative* to the topic⟩ **3** : existing in comparison to something else ⟨the *relative* value of two houses⟩ **4** : having the same key signature — used of major and minor keys and scales — **rel·a·tive·ness** *n*

relative humidity *n* : the amount of water vapor actually present in the air compared to the greatest amount possible at the same temperature

rel·a·tive·ly \'rel-ət-iv-lē\ *adv* : ²SOMEWHAT

relative to *prep* : in relation to ⟨the angle of the pole *relative to* the ground⟩

rel·a·tiv·ism \'rel-ət-iv-,iz-əm\ *n* : RELATIVITY — **rel·a·tiv·ist** \-iv-əst\ *n*

rel·a·tiv·is·tic \,rel-ət-iv-'is-tik\ *adj* : of, relating to, or characterized by relativity — **rel·a·tiv·is·ti·cal·ly** \-ti-k(ə-)lē\ *adv*

rel·a·tiv·i·ty \,rel-ə-'tiv-ət-ē\ *n, pl* **-ties** **1** : the quality or state of being relative; *esp* : dependence on something else **2 a** : a theory in physics that considers mass and energy to be equal and that states that a moving object will experience changes in mass, size, and time which are related to its speed and are not noticeable except at speeds approaching that of light **b** : an extension of the theory to include gravity and its related acceleration effects

re·lat·er *or* **re·la·tor** \ri-'lāt-ər\ *n* : one that relates : NAR-RATOR

re·lax \ri-'laks\ *vb* **1** : to make or become loose or less tense ⟨*relaxed* my attention⟩ **2** : to make or become less severe or strict ⟨*relax* discipline⟩ **3** : to get rid of nervous tension or anxiety ⟨couldn't *relax* in crowds⟩ **4** : to rest or enjoy oneself away from one's usual duties ⟨*relaxed* at the beach⟩ — **re·lax·er** *n*

¹**re·lax·ant** \ri-'lak-sənt\ *adj* : producing relaxation

²**relaxant** *n* : a relaxing agent; *esp* : a drug that causes muscular relaxation

re·lax·ation \,rē-,lak-'sā-shən, ri-\ *n* **1** : the act of relaxing : the state of being relaxed **2** : a relaxing activity or pastime ⟨play the guitar as a *relaxation*⟩ **3** : the lengthening that characterizes inactive muscle

re·laxed \ri-'lakst\ *adj* **1** : lacking in precision or strictness ⟨*relaxed* rules for doing something⟩ **2** : set or being at ease ⟨found her in a *relaxed* moment⟩ **3** : easy of manner : INFORMAL ⟨a *relaxed* style of comedy⟩ — **re·laxed·ly** \-'lak-səd-lē, -'laks-tlē\ *adv* — **re·laxed·ness** \-'lak-səd-nəs, -'laks(t)-nəs\ *n*

¹**re·lay** \'rē-,lā\ *n* **1** : a fresh supply (as of horses or people) arranged to relieve others **2 a** : a race between

teams in which each team member covers an assigned part of the course **b** : one of the divisions of a relay **3** : an electromagnetic device in which the opening or closing of one circuit operates another device (as a switch in another circuit) **4** : the act of passing along (as a message or a ball) by stages; *also* : one of such stages ⟨the shortstop's *relay* from center field was too late to catch the runner⟩

²**re·lay** \'rē-,lā, ri-'lā\ *vb* **re·layed; re·lay·ing** **1 a** : to place or arrange in relays **b** : to provide with relays **2** : to pass along by stages ⟨news was *relayed* by satellites⟩

³**re·lay** \(')rē-'lā\ *vb* **-laid** \-'lād\; **-lay·ing** : to lay again

¹**re·lease** \ri-'lēs\ *vb* **re·leased; re·leas·ing** **1** : to set free (as from confinement) ⟨*release* a prisoner⟩ ⟨*release* a bird from a cage⟩ **2** : to relieve from something that holds or burdens ⟨*released* from our promise⟩ **3** : to give up in favor of another : RELINQUISH ⟨*release* a claim to property⟩ **4** : to give permission for publication, performance, exhibition, or sale of (as a movie or news story) — **re·leas·able** \-'lē-sə-bəl\ *adj*

²**release** *n* **1** : relief or rescue from sorrow, suffering, or trouble **2 a** : a discharge from an obligation (as a debt) **b** : a giving up of a right or claim **3** : the act or an instance of setting free or letting go **4** : a document that contains a release **5** : the state of being freed **6 a** : a device adapted to hold or release a mechanism as required **7 a** : the act of permitting performance or publication **b** : the matter released; *esp* : a statement prepared for the press

re·leas·er \ri-'lē-sər\ *n* : one that releases; *esp* : a stimulus that serves to start complicated behavior

rel·e·gate \'rel-ə-,gāt\ *vb* **-gat·ed; -gat·ing** **1** : to remove or dismiss to a less important place ⟨*relegate* some old books to the attic⟩ **2** : to refer or hand over for decision or carrying out ⟨*relegate* that matter to a special committee⟩ — **rel·e·ga·tion** \,rel-ə-'gā-shən\ *n*

re·lent \ri-'lent\ *vb* **1** : to become less severe, harsh, or strict **2** : SLACKEN 1

re·lent·less \ri-'lent-ləs\ *adj* : not lessening in harshness or sternness — **re·lent·less·ly** *adv* — **re·lent·less·ness** *n*

rel·e·vance \'rel-ə-vən(t)s\ *n* : relation to the matter at hand : PERTINENCE

rel·e·van·cy \'rel-ə-vən-sē\ *n, pl* **-cies** : RELEVANCE

rel·e·vant \'rel-ə-vənt\ *adj* : having something to do with the matter being considered : PERTINENT ⟨a *relevant* question⟩ — **rel·e·vant·ly** *adv*

re·li·abil·i·ty \ri-,lī-ə-'bil-ət-ē\ *n, pl* **-ties** : the quality or state of being reliable

re·li·able \ri-'lī-ə-bəl\ *adj* : fit to be trusted : DEPENDABLE — **re·li·able·ness** *n* — **re·li·ably** \-blē\ *adv*

re·li·ance \ri-'lī-ən(t)s\ *n* **1** : the act of relying **2** : the condition or attitude of one who relies : DEPENDENCE **3** : something or someone relied on

re·li·ant \ri-'lī-ənt\ *adj* : having reliance on something or someone : TRUSTING ⟨*reliant* on the family for news⟩ — **re·li·ant·ly** *adv*

rel·ic \'rel-ik\ *n* **1** : an object treated with great respect because of its connection with a saint or martyr **2** : something left behind after decay or disappearance ⟨*relics* of ancient cities⟩

rel·ict \'rel-ikt\ *n* : WIDOW

relied *past and past participle of* RELY

re·lief \ri-'lēf\ *n* **1 a** : removal or lightening of something painful, troubling, burdensome, or dangerous **b** : WEL-FARE 3 **c** : military assistance to a post or force in extreme danger **d** : a means of breaking boredom : DIVER-

\ə\ abut		\au̇\ out	\i\ tip	\ȯ\ saw	\u̇\ foot
\ər\ further		\ch\ chin	\ī\ life	\ȯi\ coin	\y\ yet
\a\ mat		\e\ pet	\j\ job	\th\ thin	\yü\ few
\ā\ take		\ē\ easy	\ŋ\ sing	\th\ this	\yu̇\ cure
\ä\ cot, cart		\g\ go	\ō\ bone	\ü\ food	\zh\ vision

SION ⟨a quick swim was a welcome *relief* from the job⟩ **2** : release from duty **3** : one that takes the place of another on duty **4** : the legal correction of a wrong **5 a** : elevation of figures or designs from the background (as in sculpture) **b** : a work of art with such raised figures **c** : projecting detail or figures in sculpture **6** : sharpness of outline ⟨a roof in bold *relief* against the sky⟩ **7** : the elevations of a land surface ⟨a map showing *relief*⟩

relief map *n* : a map or model in which unevenness of surface is shown in relief

relief pitcher *n* : a baseball pitcher who takes over for another during a game

relief 5b

re·lieve \ri-'lēv\ *vb* **re·lieved; re·liev·ing** **1** : to free partly or wholly from a burden or from distress ⟨*relieve* parents of worry⟩ **2** : to bring about the removal or reduction of ⟨efforts to *relieve* world hunger⟩ **3** : to release from a post or duty ⟨*relieve* a sentry⟩ **4** : to break the sameness of ⟨a black dress *relieved* by a white collar⟩ **5** : to put or stand out in relief : set off by contrast (as in sculpture or painting) — **re·liev·er** *n*

re·li·gion \ri-'lij-ən\ *n* **1 a** : the service and worship of God or the supernatural **b** : belief in or devotion to religious faith or observance **c** : the state of a person in the religious life ⟨a nun in her 20th year of *religion*⟩ **2** : a set or system of religious attitudes, beliefs, and ways of doing things **3** : a cause, principle, or system of beliefs held with faith and strong feeling

¹re·li·gious \ri-'lij-əs\ *adj* **1** : devoted to God or to the powers or forces believed to govern life ⟨a very *religious* person⟩ **2** : of or relating to religion ⟨*religious* beliefs⟩ **3** : very devoted and faithful ⟨performed his duties with *religious* regularity⟩ — **re·li·gious·ly** *adv* — **re·li·gious·ness** *n*

²religious *n, pl* **religious** : a member of a religious order

re·line \(')rē-'līn\ *vb* : to put new lines on or a new lining in ⟨*reline* a coat⟩

re·lin·quish \ri-'liŋ-kwish\ *vb* **1** : to withdraw or retreat from : leave behind ⟨*relinquished* their homes and sailed to the New World⟩ **2** : to give over to the control or possession of another ⟨*relinquish* a title⟩ **3** : to let go of : RELEASE ⟨*relinquish* your grip on the bar⟩ ⟨few leaders willingly *relinquish* power⟩ — **re·lin·quish·ment** \-mənt\ *n*

rel·i·quary \'rel-ə-,kwer-ē\ *n, pl* **-quar·ies** : a small box or shrine in which sacred relics are kept

¹rel·ish \'rel-ish\ *n* **1** : a pleasing appetizing taste **2** : a small bit added for flavor : DASH **3 a** : enjoyment or delight in something ⟨eat with great *relish*⟩ **b** : a strong liking ⟨has little *relish* for work⟩ **4** : a highly seasoned food (as of pickles or mustard) eaten with other food to add flavor

²relish *vb* **1** : to add relish to **2** : to be pleased by : ENJOY **3** : to eat or drink with pleasure — **rel·ish·able** \-ə-bəl\ *adj*

re·live \(')rē-'liv\ *vb* : to live over again; *esp* : to experience again in imagination

re·lo·cate \(')rē-'lō-,kāt, ,rē-lō-'kāt\ *vb* **1** : to locate again **2** : to move to a new location ⟨*relocate* a factory⟩ — **re·lo·ca·tion** \,rē-lō-'kā-shən\ *n*

re·luc·tance \ri-'lək-tən(t)s\ *n* : the quality or state of being reluctant

re·luc·tant \ri-'lək-tənt\ *adj* : showing doubt or unwillingness ⟨*reluctant* to answer⟩ — **re·luc·tant·ly** *adv*

re·ly \ri-'lī\ *vb* **re·lied; re·ly·ing** **1** : to have confidence based on experience ⟨someone you can *rely* on⟩ **2** : to

be dependent ⟨the system on which we *rely* for water⟩

REM \'rem\ *n* : RAPID EYE MOVEMENT

¹re·main \ri-'mān\ *vb* **1 a** : to be a part not destroyed, taken, or used up ⟨little *remained* after the fire⟩ **b** : to be something yet to be shown, done, or treated ⟨that *remains* to be seen⟩ **2** : to stay in the same place or with the same person or group; *esp* : to stay behind **3** : to continue unchanged ⟨the weather *remained* cold⟩

²remain *n* **1** : whatever is left over or behind — usually used in pl. ⟨the *remains* of a meal⟩ **2** *pl* : a dead body

re·main·der \ri-'mān-dər\ *n* **1** : a remaining group or part **2** : the number left after a subtraction **3** : the number that is left over from the dividend after division and is less than the divisor

¹re·make \(')rē-'māk\ *vb* **-made** \-'mād\; **-mak·ing** : to make anew or in a different form

²re·make \'rē-,māk\ *n* : one that has been remade; *esp* : a new version of a motion picture

¹re·mand \ri-'mand\ *vb* **1** : to send back a case to another court for further action **2** : to return to custody to be held longer or to await trial

²remand *n* : the act of remanding : the state of being remanded ⟨sent back on *remand*⟩

¹re·mark \ri-'märk\ *n* **1** : the act of remarking : NOTICE **2** : mention of that which deserves attention or notice **3** : a briefly expressed opinion

syn REMARK, OBSERVATION, COMMENT mean something said or written that gives an opinion. REMARK suggests a quick thought or offhand judgment ⟨made a brief *remark* about the weather⟩ OBSERVATION suggests a careful opinion expressed after looking closely at something ⟨she published her *observations* on whales after ten years of study⟩ COMMENT suggests a remark that is meant to explain or criticize ⟨after the play was over, he made his *comments* on it⟩

²remark *vb* **1** : to take note of ⟨*remarked* his strange manner⟩ **2** : to express as a comment ⟨"Nice day," she *remarked*⟩ **3** : to make a comment ⟨*remarked* on how well the team was doing⟩

re·mark·able \ri-'mär-kə-bəl\ *adj* : worthy of being or likely to be noticed especially as being uncommon or extraordinary — **re·mark·able·ness** *n* — **re·mark·ably** \-blē\ *adv*

re·mar·riage \(')rē-'mar-ij\ *n* : a second or later marriage

re·match \(')rē-'mach, 'rē-,mach\ *n* : a second meeting between the same contestants

re·me·di·a·ble \ri-'mēd-ē-ə-bəl\ *adj* : capable of being made better

re·me·di·al \ri-'mēd-ē-əl\ *adj* : intended to make something better ⟨*remedial* measures⟩ ⟨*remedial* classes⟩

¹rem·e·dy \'rem-əd-ē\ *n, pl* **-dies** **1** : a medicine or treatment that cures or relieves **2** : something that corrects an evil, rights a wrong, or makes up for a loss

²remedy *vb* **-died; -dy·ing** : to provide or serve as a remedy for : RELIEVE

re·mem·ber \ri-'mem-bər\ *vb* **-bered; -ber·ing** \-b(ə-)riŋ\ **1** : to bring to mind or think of again ⟨*remembers* the old days⟩ **2 a** : to keep in mind for attention ⟨*remember* friends at Christmas⟩ **b** : ¹REWARD 1 ⟨was *remembered* in the will⟩ **3** : to keep in the memory ⟨*remember* the facts for the test⟩ **4** : to pass along greetings from ⟨*remember* us to your family⟩ — **re·mem·ber·able** \-b(ə-)rə-bəl\ *adj* — **re·mem·ber·er** \-bər-ər\ *n*

re·mem·brance \ri-'mem-brən(t)s\ *n* **1** : the act of remembering **2** : something remembered **3** : something (as a souvenir) that serves to keep in or bring to mind : REMINDER **b** : something (as a greeting or gift) recalling or expressing friendship **syn** see MEMORY

re·mind \ri-'mīnd\ *vb* : to put in mind of something : cause to remember ⟨*remind* a child that it is bedtime⟩ — **re·mind·er** *n*

rem·i·nisce \,rem-ə-'nis\ *vb* **-nisced; -nisc·ing** : to talk or think about things that happened in the past

rem·i·nis·cence \,rem-ə-'nis-°n(t)s\ *n* **1** : a recalling or telling of a past experience ⟨spent a pleasant hour in *reminiscence*⟩ **2** : an account of a memorable experience — often used in pl. **syn** see MEMORY

rem·i·nis·cent \,rem-ə-'nis-°nt\ *adj* **1** : of, relating to, or engaging in reminiscence **2** : reminding one of someone or something else

re·miss \ri-'mis\ *adj* **1** : careless in the performance of work or duty ⟨*remiss* in paying one's bills⟩ **2** : showing neglect or lack of attention ⟨service at the restaurant was *remiss*⟩ — **re·miss·ly** *adv* — **re·miss·ness** *n*

re·mis·si·ble \ri-'mis-ə-bəl\ *adj* : that may be forgiven ⟨*remissible* sins⟩ — **re·mis·si·bly** \-blē\ *adv*

re·mis·sion \ri-'mish-ən\ *n* : the act or process of remitting

re·mit \ri-'mit\ *vb* **re·mit·ted; re·mit·ting** **1 a** : to lay aside a mood or disposition partly or wholly **b** : to stop something one is doing **c** : to let (as attention) slacken : RELAX **2 a** : to release from the guilt or penalty of : PARDON ⟨*remit* sins⟩ **b** : to keep from inflicting ⟨*remit* a penalty⟩ **3** : to give over for consideration, judgment, decision, or action ⟨*remit* the proposal to a special committee⟩ **4** : to send money especially in payment **5** : to lessen in intensity or severity often temporarily : MODERATE ⟨the fever had *remitted*⟩ — **remit** *n* — **re·mit·ment** \-'mit-mənt\ *n* — **re·mit·ta·ble** \-'mit-ə-bəl\ *adj* — **re·mit·ter** *n*

re·mit·tal \ri-'mit-°l\ *n* : REMISSION

re·mit·tance \ri-'mit-°n(t)s\ *n* **1** : money sent especially in payment **2** : a sending of money (as to a distant place)

rem·nant \'rem-nənt\ *n* **1** : something that remains or is left over ⟨a *remnant* of cloth⟩ **2** : a surviving usually small part ⟨*remnants* of a great civilization⟩

re·mod·el \(')rē-'mäd-°l\ *vb* : to change the structure of

re·mon·strance \ri-'män(t)-strən(t)s\ *n* : an act or instance of protest

re·mon·strant \ri-'män(t)-strənt\ *adj* : strongly objecting or opposing — **re·mon·strant·ly** *adv*

re·mon·strate \ri-'män-,strāt\ *vb* **-strat·ed; -strat·ing** : to present and urge reasons in opposition ⟨*remonstrate* with a student for being late⟩

rem·o·ra \'rem-ə-rə\ *n* : a fish that has a suction disk on the top of its head by means of which it clings to other fishes and to ships

re·morse \ri-'mó(ə)rs\ *n* : a deep regret coming from a sense of guilt for past wrongs : SELF-REPROACH

remora

Word History The Latin verb *remordēre* literally meant "to bite again". The Romans, however, usually used it with the meaning "to torment", because being tormented was like getting bitten again and again. The past participle of this verb is *remorsus,* which in early French was used to form the noun *remors.* This noun was used to refer to the deep regret one feels after doing something sinful, wrong, or hurtful. Such regret was felt to be a kind of torment. In the 15th century, this French word was taken into English as *remorse* with the same meaning. [Middle English *remorse* "a deep regret coming from a sense of guilt", from early French *remors* (same meaning), derived from Latin *remorsus,* past participle of *remordēre* "to bite again", from *mordēre* "to bite" — related to MORSEL]

re·morse·ful \ri-'mórs-fəl\ *adj* : moved or marked by remorse — **re·morse·ful·ly** \-fə-lē\ *adv* — **re·morse·ful·ness** *n*

re·morse·less \ri-'mór-sləs\ *adj* : having no remorse : MERCILESS ⟨*remorseless* cruelty⟩ — **re·morse·less·ly** *adv* — **re·morse·less·ness** *n*

re·mote \ri-'mōt\ *adj* **re·mot·er; -est** **1** : far removed in place, time, or relation ⟨*remote* countries⟩ ⟨*remote* ages⟩ ⟨*remote* cousins⟩ **2** : SECLUDED 1 ⟨a *remote* valley⟩ **3** : acting, acted on, or controlled indirectly or from a distance ⟨*remote* computer operation⟩ **4** : small in degree : SLIGHT ⟨a *remote* possibility⟩ **5** : distant in manner : ALOOF — **re·mote·ly** *adv* — **re·mote·ness** *n*

[1]re·mount \(')rē-'maunt\ *vb* **1** : to mount something again ⟨*remount* the picture on the other wall⟩ **2** : to mount again ⟨*remount* at once and ride back⟩

[2]re·mount \'rē-,maunt, (')rē-'maunt\ *n* : a fresh horse to take the place of one no longer available

re·mov·able \ri-'mü-və-bəl\ *adj* : possible to remove — **re·mov·abil·i·ty** \-,mü-və-'bil-ət-ē\ *n* — **re·mov·able·ness** \-'mü-və-bəl-nəs\ *n* — **re·mov·ably** \-blē\ *adv*

re·mov·al \ri-'mü-vəl\ *n* : the act of removing : the fact of being removed

[1]re·move \ri-'müv\ *vb* **re·moved; re·mov·ing** **1** : to change or cause to change to another location, position, station, or residence ⟨*remove* soldiers to the front⟩ ⟨*remove* from the city to the country⟩ **2** : to move by lifting, pushing aside, or taking away or off ⟨please *remove* your hat⟩ **3** : to dismiss from office ⟨the treasurer was *removed* after a year⟩ **4** : to get rid of ⟨*remove* the causes of poverty⟩ **5** : to go away **6** : to be capable of being removed ⟨a bottle cap that *removes* easily⟩

[2]remove *n* **1** : REMOVAL; *esp* : [2]MOVE 2c **2 a** : a distance separating one thing from another **b** : a degree or stage of separation ⟨at one *remove*⟩

re·moved \ri-'müvd\ *adj* **1** : being a generation older or younger ⟨the children of your first cousin are your first cousins once *removed*⟩ **2** : far away or separate ⟨a town far *removed* from cities⟩

re·mov·er \ri-'müv-ər\ *n* : something (as a chemical) used in removing a substance ⟨paint *remover*⟩

re·mu·ner·ate \ri-'myü-nə-,rāt\ *vb* **-at·ed; -at·ing** : to pay an equivalent to for a service, loss, or expense : RECOMPENSE — **re·mu·ner·a·tor** \-,rāt-ər\ *n*

re·mu·ner·a·tion \ri-,myü-nə-'rā-shən\ *n* **1** : something that pays back an equivalent **2** : an act or fact of paying back an equivalent

re·mu·ner·a·tive \ri-'myü-nə-rət-iv, -,rāt-\ *adj* **1** : serving to remunerate **2** : PROFITABLE ⟨made a highly *remunerative* investment⟩ — **re·mu·ner·a·tive·ly** *adv* — **re·mu·ner·a·tive·ness** *n*

Re·nais·sance \,ren-ə-'sän(t)s, -'zän(t)s\ *n* **1** : the period of European history between the 14th and 17th centuries marked by a fresh interest in ancient art and literature and by the beginnings of modern science **2** *often not cap* : a movement or period of great activity (as in literature, science, and the arts)

re·nal \'rēn-°l\ *adj* : relating to, involving, or located in the region of the kidneys

re·name \(')rē-'nām\ *vb* : to give a new name to

re·na·scence \ri-'nas-°n(t)s, -'nās-\ *n, often cap* : RENAISSANCE 2 — **re·na·scent** \-°nt\ *adj*

rend \'rend\ *vb* **rent** \'rent\ *also* **rend·ed; rend·ing** **1** : to remove from place by force : WREST **2** : to split or tear apart or in pieces by force **3** : to tear (the hair or clothing) as a sign of anger, grief, or despair **4** : to affect as if splitting or tearing ⟨silence *rent* by a scream⟩

ren·der \'ren-dər\ *vb* **ren·dered; ren·der·ing** \-d(ə-)riŋ\ **1** : to obtain by heating ⟨*render* lard from fat⟩ **2 a** : to furnish or give to another : DELIVER ⟨*render* a report⟩ ⟨*render* aid⟩ **b** : [1]SURRENDER 1, GIVE UP ⟨*rendered* their lives to save others⟩ **3** : to give in return ⟨*render* thanks⟩ **4 a**

\ə\ abut		\au\ out	\i\ tip	\ȯ\ saw	\u̇\ foot
\ər\ further	\ch\ chin	\ī\ life	\ȯi\ coin	\y\ yet
\a\ mat	\e\ pet	\j\ job	\th\ thin	\yü\ few
\ā\ take	\ē\ easy	\ŋ\ sing	\th\ this	\yu̇\ cure
\ä\ cot, cart	\g\ go	\ō\ bone	\ü\ food	\zh\ vision

: to cause to be or become ⟨*render* a person helpless⟩ **b** : PERFORM 3a ⟨*render* a salute⟩ **c** : PERFORM 3b ⟨*render* a song⟩ **d** : TRANSLATE 3a, b ⟨*render* Latin into English⟩ — **ren·der·able** \-d(ə-)rə-bəl\ *adj* — **ren·der·er** \-dər-ər\ *n*

¹**ren·dez·vous** \'rän-di-,vü, -dā-\ *n, pl* **ren·dez·vous** \-,vüz\ **1 a** : a place agreed on for assembling or meeting **b** : a place that many people visit **2** : a planned meeting [from early French *rendezvous* "a place to meet", from the phrase *rendez vous* "present yourself"]

²**rendezvous** *vb* **-voused** \-,vüd\; **-vous·ing** \-,vü-iŋ\; **-vouses** \-,vüz\ : to come or bring together at a rendezvous

ren·di·tion \ren-'dish-ən\ *n* : an act or result of rendering ⟨sang their *rendition* of the old song⟩

¹**ren·e·gade** \'ren-i-,gād\ *n* : a person who deserts a faith, cause, or party

²**renegade** *adj* : having deserted a faith, cause, or party

re·nege \ri-'nig, -'neg, -'nēg, -'nāg\ *vb* **re·neged; re·neg·ing** **1** : to violate a rule in a card game by failing to follow suit when able **2** : to go back on a promise or agreement ⟨*reneged* on paying the debt⟩ — **re·neg·er** *n*

re·new \ri-'n(y)ü\ *vb* **1** : to make or become new, fresh, or strong again ⟨strength *renewed* by a night's rest⟩ **2** : to restore to existence ⟨*renew* the splendor of a palace⟩ **3** : to do or make again ⟨*renew* a complaint⟩ **4** : to begin again : RESUME ⟨*renewed* efforts to make peace⟩ **5** : to put in a fresh supply of : REPLACE ⟨*renew* the water in a tank⟩ **6** : to grant or obtain an extension of : continue in force for a fresh period ⟨*renew* a lease⟩ ⟨*renew* a subscription⟩ — **re·new·er** *n*

re·new·able \ri-'n(y)ü-ə-bəl\ *adj* **1** : capable of being renewed **2** : capable of being replaced by natural ecological cycles or sound management procedures ⟨*renewable* resources like water, wildlife, forests, and grasslands⟩

re·new·al \ri-'n(y)ü-əl\ *n* **1** : the act of renewing : the state of being renewed **2** : something renewed

ren·net \'ren-ət\ *n* **1 a** : the contents of the stomach of a young animal and especially a calf **b** : a part of the lining of the stomach that is used to curdle milk **2** : something used to curdle milk; *esp* : RENNIN

ren·nin \'ren-ən\ *n* : a stomach enzyme that curdles milk

re·nom·i·nate \(')rē-'näm-ə-,nāt\ *vb* : to nominate again especially for a term right after one just served — **re·nom·i·na·tion** \(,)rē-,näm-ə-'nā-shən\ *n*

re·nounce \ri-'naun(t)s\ *vb* **re·nounced; re·nounc·ing** **1** : to give up, abandon, or resign usually by public declaration ⟨*renounced* the throne⟩ **2** : to refuse further to follow, obey, or recognize : REPUDIATE ⟨*renounced* the authority of her political party⟩ — **re·nounce·ment** \-'naun(t)-smənt\ *n* — **re·nounc·er** *n*

ren·o·vate \'ren-ə-,vāt\ *vb* **-vat·ed; -vat·ing** : to make like new again : put in good condition — **ren·o·va·tion** \,ren-ə-'vā-shən\ *n* — **ren·o·va·tor** \'ren-ə-,vāt-ər\ *n*

re·nown \ri-'naun\ *n* : a state of being widely known and highly honored : FAME

re·nowned \ri-'naund\ *adj* : having renown : CELEBRATED **syn** see FAMOUS

¹**rent** \'rent\ *n* : money paid for the use of property : a periodic payment made by a tenant to the owner for the use of the owner's property [Middle English *rente* "income from property", from early French *rente* (same meaning), derived from Latin *rendere* "to yield"] — **for rent** : available for use or service at a price

²**rent** *vb* **1** : to take and hold property under an agreement to pay rent **2** : to give the possession and use of in return for rent ⟨*rented* a cottage to friends⟩ **3** : to be for rent ⟨the room *rents* for $40 a week⟩ — **rent·able** \-ə-bəl\ *adj* — **rent·er** *n*

³**rent** *past and past participle of* REND

⁴**rent** *n* **1** : an opening (as in cloth) made by or as if by tearing **2** : an act or instance of tearing [from a dialect word *rent* "to tear", from Middle English *renten*, an altered form of *renden* "to tear, rend"]

¹**rent·al** \'rent-ªl\ *n* **1** : an amount paid or collected as rent **2** : an act of renting

²**rental** *adj* **1** : of, relating to, or available for rent ⟨a *rental* car⟩ **2** : dealing in rental property ⟨a *rental* agency⟩

re·nun·ci·a·tion \ri-,nən(t)-sē-'ā-shən\ *n* : the act or practice of renouncing

re·open \(')rē-'ō-pən, -'ōp-ªn\ *vb* **1** : to open again **2** : to take up again : RESUME ⟨*reopen* the discussion⟩

¹**re·or·der** \(')rē-'ord-ər\ *vb* **1** : to arrange in a different way **2** : to place a reorder

²**reorder** *n* : an order like a previous order from the same supplier

re·or·ga·ni·za·tion \(,)rē-,org-(ə-)nə-'zā-shən\ *n* : the act of reorganizing : the state of being reorganized; *esp* : the changing of the financial structure of a business

re·or·ga·nize \(')rē-'or-gə-,nīz\ *vb* : to organize again or anew; *esp* : to bring about a reorganization (as of a business) — **re·or·ga·niz·er** *n*

re·pack·age \(')rē-'pak-ij\ *vb* : to package again or anew; *esp* : to put into a more attractive form

¹**re·pair** \ri-'pa(ə)r, -'pe(ə)r\ *vb* : to make one's way : GO ⟨*repair* to an inner office⟩

²**repair** *vb* **1** : to put back in good condition ⟨*repair* a broken toy⟩ **2** : to make up for : REMEDY ⟨*repair* an injustice⟩ **syn** see MEND — **re·pair·able** \-'par-ə-bəl, -'per-\ *adj* — **re·pair·er** \-ər\ *n*

³**repair** *n* **1 a** : the act or process of repairing ⟨make *repairs*⟩ **b** : the result of repairing ⟨a tire with three *repairs*⟩ **2 a** : condition with respect to soundness or need of fixing ⟨the car is in poor *repair*⟩ **b** : good condition ⟨a house in *repair*⟩

re·pair·man \ri-'pa(ə)r-,man, -'pe(ə)r-, -mən\ *n* : a person whose occupation is making repairs ⟨TV *repairman*⟩

rep·a·ra·ble \'rep-(ə-)rə-bəl\ *adj* : capable of being repaired

rep·a·ra·tion \,rep-ə-'rā-shən\ *n* **1** : a repairing or keeping in repair ⟨a building in need of constant *reparation*⟩ **2** : the act of making up for a wrong **3** : money or materials paid or to be paid by a country losing a war to the winner to make up for damages done in the war — usually used in pl.

re·par·a·tive \ri-'par-ət-iv\ *adj* : of, relating to, or serving to repair

rep·ar·tee \,rep-ər-'tē, -,är-, -'tā\ *n* **1** : a clever witty reply **2** : skill in making clever replies

re·past \ri-'past\ *n* : ¹MEAL 1, FEAST

¹**re·pa·tri·ate** \(')rē-'pā-trē-,āt, -'pa-\ *vb* **-at·ed; -at·ing** : to return to the country of origin, allegiance, or citizenship ⟨*repatriate* prisoners of war⟩ — **re·pa·tri·a·tion** \(,)rē-,pā-trē-'ā-shən, -,pa-\ *n*

²**re·pa·tri·ate** \(')rē-'pā-trē-ət, -tre-,āt\ *n* : one that is repatriated

re·pay \(')rē-'pā\ *vb* **-paid** \-'pād\; **-pay·ing** **1** : to pay back ⟨*repay* a loan⟩ **2** : to make a return payment to ⟨*repay* a creditor⟩ — **re·pay·able** \-'pā-ə-bəl\ *adj* — **re·pay·ment** \-'pā-mənt\ *n*

re·peal \ri-'pē(ə)l\ *vb* : to do away with especially by legislative action ⟨*repeal* a law⟩ — **repeal** *n* — **re·peal·able** \-'pē-lə-bəl\ *adj* — **re·peal·er** *n*

¹**re·peat** \ri-'pēt\ *vb* **1 a** : to say or state again ⟨*repeated* the question⟩ **b** : to say from memory : RECITE ⟨*repeat* a poem⟩ **c** : to say after another ⟨*repeat* the following words after me⟩ **d** : to tell to others ⟨*repeat* gossip⟩ **2** : to make, do, or perform again ⟨*repeat* a mistake⟩ — **re·peat·able** \-ə-bəl\ *adj* — **repeat oneself** : to say or do the same thing more than once

²**re·peat** \ri-'pēt, 'rē-,pēt\ *n* **1** : the act of repeating **2** : something repeated

re·peat·ed \ri-'pēt-əd\ *adj* : done or happening again and again : FREQUENT — **re·peat·ed·ly** *adv*

re·peat·er \ri-ˈpēt-ər\ *n* **1** : a firearm that fires several times without reloading **2** : a person who violates the laws again and again **3** : a student who is taking a class or course again

repeating decimal *n* : a decimal in which after a certain point a particular digit or sequence of digits repeats itself indefinitely — compare TERMINATING DECIMAL

re·pel \ri-ˈpel\ *vb* **re·pelled; re·pel·ling** **1 a** : to drive back ⟨*repel* the enemy⟩ **b** : to fight against : RESIST **2** : to refuse to accept : REJECT ⟨*repel* a suggestion⟩ **3 a** : to be incapable of sticking to, mixing with, taking up, or holding ⟨a fabric that *repels* water⟩ **b** : to force away or apart or tend to do so by mutual action at a distance ⟨two like electrical charges *repel* each other⟩ **4** : DISGUST ⟨a sight that *repelled* everyone⟩ — **re·pel·ler** *n*

re·pel·len·cy \ri-ˈpel-ən-sē\ *n* : the quality of repelling : the ability to repel

¹re·pel·lent *also* **re·pel·lant** \ri-ˈpel-ənt\ *adj* **1** : serving or tending to drive away — often used in combination ⟨a water-*repellent* jacket⟩ **2** : causing disgust — **re·pel·lent·ly** *adv*

²repellent *also* **repellant** *n* : something that repels; *esp* : a substance used to keep off pests (as insects)

re·pent \ri-ˈpent\ *vb* **1** : to feel sorrow for one's sin and make up one's mind to do what is right **2** : to feel sorry for or dissatisfied with something one has done : REGRET — **re·pent·er** *n*

re·pen·tance \ri-ˈpent-ᵊn(t)s\ *n* : the action or process of repenting especially for one's sins

re·pen·tant \ri-ˈpent-ᵊnt\ *adj* : feeling or showing repentance — **re·pen·tant·ly** *adv*

re·per·cus·sion \ˌrē-pər-ˈkəsh-ən, ˌrep-ər-\ *n* **1** : a return action or effect **2** : a widespread, indirect, or unexpected effect of something said or done ⟨the new policy had *repercussions* for everyone⟩

re·per·cus·sive \ˌrē-pər-ˈkəs-iv, ˌrep-ər-\ *adj* : of, marked by, or creating repercussion

rep·er·toire \ˈrep-ə(r)-ˌtwär\ *n* **1** : a list or supply of dramas, operas, pieces, or parts that a company or person is prepared to perform **2** : a supply of skills or devices possessed by a person ⟨passing is part of the *repertoire* of a quarterback⟩

rep·er·to·ry \ˈrep-ə(r)-ˌtōr-ē, -ˌtȯr-\ *n, pl* **-ries** **1** : a stock or store of something : COLLECTION **2 a** : REPERTOIRE **b** : a theater in which a company performs different plays or pieces in the course of a season

rep·e·ti·tion \ˌrep-ə-ˈtish-ən\ *n* **1** : the act or an instance of repeating **2** : the fact of being repeated **3** : something repeated

rep·e·ti·tious \ˌrep-ə-ˈtish-əs\ *adj* : marked by repetition; *esp* : tiresomely repeating — **rep·e·ti·tious·ly** *adv* — **rep·e·ti·tious·ness** *n*

re·pet·i·tive \ri-ˈpet-ət-iv\ *adj* : REPETITIOUS — **re·pet·i·tive·ly** *adv* — **re·pet·i·tive·ness** *n*

re·phrase \(ˈ)rē-ˈfrāz\ *vb* : to phrase over again in a different form

re·pine \ri-ˈpīn\ *vb* **1** : to feel or express sadness or discontent : COMPLAIN **2** : to long restlessly for something — **re·pin·er** *n*

re·place \ri-ˈplās\ *vb* **1** : to put back in a proper or former place ⟨*replace* a card in a file⟩ **2** : to take the place of ⟨paper money has *replaced* gold coins⟩ **3** : to put something new in the place of ⟨*replace* a broken dish⟩ — **re·place·able** \-ˈplā-sə-bəl\ *adj*

re·place·ment \ri-ˈplā-smənt\ *n* **1** : the act of replacing : the state of being replaced **2** : one that replaces another : SUBSTITUTE

replacement set *n* : a set of elements any one of which may be used to replace a given variable or placeholder in a mathematical sentence or expression (as an equation)

re·plant \(ˈ)rē-ˈplant\ *vb* **1** : to plant again or anew ⟨*replanted* the tree farther from the house⟩ **2** : to provide with new plants ⟨*replanted* the park⟩

re·plen·ish \ri-ˈplen-ish\ *vb* : to make full or complete once more ⟨*replenish* a supply of fuel⟩ — **re·plen·ish·er** *n* — **re·plen·ish·ment** \-mənt\ *n*

re·plete \ri-ˈplēt\ *adj* **1** : fully or well provided or filled ⟨a book *replete* with illustrations⟩ **2** : well fed — **re·plete·ness** *n*

re·ple·tion \ri-ˈplē-shən\ *n* **1** : the act of eating too much : the state of being fed too much ⟨made sick by *repletion*⟩ **2** : fulfillment of a need or desire : SATISFACTION

rep·li·ca \ˈrep-li-kə\ *n* **1** : a close reproduction especially by the maker of the original **2** : ¹COPY 1, DUPLICATE

¹rep·li·cate \ˈrep-lə-ˌkāt\ *vb* **-cat·ed; -cat·ing** **1** : ²DUPLICATE 1, REPEAT **2** : to produce one or more exact copies of itself ⟨DNA *replicates* in the cell nucleus⟩

²rep·li·cate \ˈrep-li-kət\ *n* : one of several identical experiments, processes, or samples

rep·li·ca·tion \ˌrep-lə-ˈkā-shən\ *n* : very exact copying or duplication; *also* : an act or process of this

¹re·ply \ri-ˈplī\ *vb* **re·plied; re·ply·ing** **1** : to respond in words or writing ⟨*reply* to a letter⟩ **2** : to do something in response; *esp* : to return gunfire or an attack **3** : to give as an answer ⟨*replied* not a word⟩ — **re·pli·er** \-ˈplī-(ə)r\ *n*

²reply *n, pl* **replies** : something said, written, or done in answer or response

¹re·port \ri-ˈpō(ə)rt, -ˈpȯ(ə)rt\ *n* **1 a** : common talk : RUMOR **b** : REPUTATION 1 ⟨people of evil *report*⟩ **2** : a usually detailed account or statement ⟨a news *report*⟩ ⟨wrote a *report* of the meeting⟩ **3** : an explosive noise ⟨the *report* of a gun⟩

²report *vb* **1** : to make a statement about or description of : RELATE **2** : to describe and discuss in a newspaper article or broadcast ⟨*report* a baseball game⟩ **3 a** : to return or present (a matter officially given over to a committee) with conclusions and suggestions **b** : to make known to the proper authorities ⟨*report* a fire⟩ **c** : to make a charge of misconduct against ⟨*report* a student for lateness⟩ **4** : to present oneself ⟨*report* for duty⟩ — **re·port·able** \-ˈpōrt-ə-bəl, -ˈpȯrt-\ *adj*

report card *n* : a report containing a student's grades that is regularly sent by a school to the student's parents or guardian

re·port·ed·ly \ri-ˈpōrt-əd-lē, -ˈpȯrt-\ *adv* : according to report

re·port·er \ri-ˈpōrt-ər, -ˈpȯrt-\ *n* : a person who reports; *esp* : one employed by a newspaper, magazine, or radio or television station to gather, write, or report news

re·por·to·ri·al \ˌrep-ə(r)-ˈtōr-ē-əl, ˌrēp-, -ˈtȯr-\ *adj* : of, relating to, or characteristic of a reporter or report — **re·por·to·ri·al·ly** \-ē-ə-lē\ *adv*

¹re·pose \ri-ˈpōz\ *vb* **re·posed; re·pos·ing** **1** : to lay at rest ⟨*reposed* her head on a cushion⟩ **2** : to lie at rest ⟨*reposing* on the couch⟩ [Middle English *reposen* "to lay at rest", from early French *reposer* (same meaning), derived from Latin *repausare* (same meaning), from earlier *re-* "back, again" and *pausare* "to stop", from Latin *pausa* "a pause" — related to PAUSE]

²repose *n* **1** : a state of resting after effort or strain; *esp* : rest in sleep **2** : freedom from disturbance or excitement : CALM **3** : absence or stopping of activity or movement ⟨a face in *repose*⟩

³re·pose *vb* **re·posed; re·pos·ing** **1** : to place (as trust or confidence) in someone or something **2** : to place for control, management, or use [Middle English *reposen* "to replace", from Latin *reponere* "replace"]

\ə\ abut	\au̇\ **out**	\i\ **tip**	\ȯ\ **saw**	\u̇\ **foot**
\ər\ **further**	\ch\ **chin**	\ī\ **life**	\ȯi\ **coin**	\y\ **yet**
\a\ **mat**	\e\ **pet**	\j\ **job**	\th\ **thin**	\yü\ **few**
\ā\ **take**	\ē\ **easy**	\ŋ\ **sing**	\t̲h̲\ **this**	\yu̇\ **cure**
\ä\ **cot, cart**	\g\ **go**	\ō\ **bone**	\ü\ **food**	\zh\ **vision**

re·pose·ful \ri-'pōz-fəl\ *adj* : likely to bring on relaxation — **re·pose·ful·ly** \-fə-lē\ *adv* — **re·pose·ful·ness** *n*

re·po·si·tion \,rē-pə-'zish-ən\ *vb* : to change the position of

re·pos·i·to·ry \ri-'päz-ə-,tōr-ē, -,tȯr-\ *n, pl* **-ries** : a place or container where something is deposited or stored

re·pos·sess \,rē-pə-'zes\ *vb* : to regain or retake possession of — **re·pos·ses·sion** \-'zesh-ən\ *n*

rep·re·hend \,rep-ri-'hend\ *vb* : to find fault with usually with sternness

rep·re·hen·si·ble \,rep-ri-'hen(t)-sə-bəl\ *adj* : worthy of or deserving blame or condemnation ⟨*reprehensible* acts⟩ — **rep·re·hen·si·ble·ness** *n* — **rep·re·hen·si·bly** \-blē\ *adv*

rep·re·hen·sion \,rep-ri-'hen-chən\ *n* : the act of reprehending : CONDEMNATION

rep·re·sent \,rep-ri-'zent\ *vb* **1** : to serve as a sign or symbol of ⟨the flag *represents* our country⟩ **2** : to present a picture, image, or likeness of : PORTRAY ⟨this picture *represents* a scene at Queen Elizabeth's court⟩ **3 a** : to take the place of in some respect **b** : to act for or in the place of (as in a legislative body) **4** : to describe as having a certain character or quality ⟨*represented* himself as being poor⟩ **5** : to serve as an example or instance of — **rep·re·sent·able** \-ə-bəl\ *adj* — **rep·re·sent·er** *n*

rep·re·sen·ta·tion \,rep-ri-,zen-'tā-shən\ *n* **1** : one (as a picture or symbol) that represents something else **2** : the act or action of representing : the state of being represented (as in a legislative body)

rep·re·sen·ta·tion·al \,rep-ri-,zen-'tā-shnəl, -shən-ᵊl\ *adj* : of, based on, or having the nature of representation ⟨*representational* art⟩

¹rep·re·sen·ta·tive \,rep-ri-'zent-ət-iv\ *adj* **1** : serving to represent ⟨a painting *representative* of a battle⟩ **2** : standing or acting for another especially through delegated authority **3** : of, based upon, or being a government in which the people are represented by persons chosen from among them usually by election **4** : serving as a typical example of the thing mentioned ⟨a *representative* athlete⟩ — **rep·re·sen·ta·tive·ly** *adv* — **rep·re·sen·ta·tive·ness** *n*

²representative *n* **1** : a typical example of a group, class, or quality **2** : one that represents another or others : DELEGATE, AGENT; *esp* : a member of the house of representatives of the U.S. Congress or a state legislature

re·press \ri-'pres\ *vb* **1 a** : to check by or as if by pressure ⟨injustice was *repressed*⟩ **b** : to put down by force : SUBDUE **2 a** : to hold in by self-control ⟨*repressed* a laugh⟩ **b** : to prevent the natural or normal expression, activity, or development of ⟨*repress* one's anger⟩ **3** : to shut out of consciousness ⟨*repressed* painful past experiences⟩ — **re·pres·sive** \-'pres-iv\ *adj*

re·pressed \ri-'prest\ *adj* **1** : subjected to or marked by repression ⟨a *repressed* child⟩ **2** : characterized by a keeping in check

re·pres·sion \ri-'presh-ən\ *n* **1** : the act of repressing : the state of being repressed **2** : a process of the mind by which painful or disturbing thoughts or desires are kept from conscious awareness

re·pres·sor \ri-'pres-ər\ *n* : one that represses; *esp* : a protein that keeps a special region of a chromosome from acting to start the manufacture of messenger RNA

¹re·prieve \ri-'prēv\ *vb* **re·prieved; re·priev·ing** **1** : to delay the punishment of (as a condemned prisoner) **2** : to give relief or deliverance to for a time

²reprieve *n* **1 a** : the act of reprieving : the state of being reprieved **b** : a postponing of a prison or death sentence **2** : a temporary escape (as from pain or trouble)

¹rep·ri·mand \'rep-rə-,mand\ *n* : a severe or formal criticism

²reprimand *vb* : to criticize (a person) severely especially from a position of authority **syn** see REBUKE

¹re·print \(')rē-'print\ *vb* : to print again — **re·print·er** *n*

²re·print \'rē-,print\ *n* **1** : a new or additional printing without change in the text **2** : a separately printed piece of writing

re·pri·sal \ri-'prī-zəl\ *n* **1** : the use of force short of war by one nation against another in return for damage or loss suffered ⟨economic *reprisals*⟩ **2** : an act of getting back at especially in war

¹re·proach \ri-'prōch\ *n* **1 a** : something that deserves blame or disgrace ⟨their dirty yard is a *reproach* to the whole street⟩ **b** : loss of reputation : DISGRACE **2** : the act or action of disapproving ⟨was beyond *reproach*⟩ **3** : an expression of disapproval — **re·proach·ful** \-fəl\ *adj* — **re·proach·ful·ly** \-fə-lē\ *adv* — **re·proach·ful·ness** *n*

²reproach *vb* : to find fault with : BLAME ⟨*reproached* him for his cowardice⟩ — **re·proach·able** \-'prō-chə-bəl\ *adj* — **re·proach·er** *n* — **re·proach·ing·ly** \-'prō-chiŋ-lē\ *adv*

¹rep·ro·bate \'rep-rə-,bāt\ *vb* **-bat·ed; -bat·ing** : to condemn strongly as unworthy or evil — **rep·ro·ba·tion** \,rep-rə-'bā-shən\ *n*

²reprobate *adj* **1** : doomed to hell : CONDEMNED **2** : being without any morals : CORRUPT

³reprobate *n* : a wicked person

re·pro·duce \,rē-prə-'d(y)üs\ *vb* **1 a** : to produce new individuals of the same kind **b** : to cause to exist again ⟨*reproduce* water from steam⟩ **c** : to imitate closely ⟨sound effects can *reproduce* the sound of thunder⟩ **d** : to present again **e** : to make an image or copy of ⟨*reproduce* a face on canvas⟩ **f** : to translate a recording into sound **2** : to go through reproduction ⟨her voice *reproduces* well⟩ **3** : to produce offspring — **re·pro·duc·er** *n*

re·pro·duc·tion \,rē-prə-'dək-shən\ *n* **1** : the act or process of reproducing; *esp* : the process by which plants and animals produce offspring **2** : something reproduced : COPY

re·pro·duc·tive \,rē-prə-'dək-tiv\ *adj* : of, relating to, capable of, or concerned with reproduction

re·proof \ri-'prüf\ *n* : criticism for a fault : REBUKE

re·prove \ri-'prüv\ *vb* **re·proved; re·prov·ing** **1** : to scold or correct usually in a gentle way ⟨*reprove* a tardy student⟩ **2** : to express disapproval of ⟨*reprove* a fault⟩

¹rep·tile \'rep-tᵊl, -,tīl\ *n* : any of a group of cold-blooded air-breathing vertebrates (as snakes, lizards, turtles, and alligators) that usually lay eggs and have skin covered with scales or bony plates

²reptile *adj* : characteristic of a reptile : REPTILIAN

rep·til·i·an \rep-'til-ē-ən\ *adj* : of, relating to, or resembling reptiles

re·pub·lic \ri-'pəb-lik\ *n* **1** : a government having a chief of state who is not a monarch and who is usually a president **2** : a government in which supreme power belongs to the citizens through their right to vote **3** : a political unit having a republican form of government **4** : a political and territorial unit of the U.S.S.R., Czechoslovakia, or Yugoslavia [from French *république* "republic", derived from Latin *respublica* "republic, public matters, commonweal", literally "public things", from *res* "thing, matter" and *publica*, a feminine form of *publicus* "relating to the people as a whole, public" — related to PUBLIC, REAL, REBUS]

¹re·pub·li·can \ri-'pəb-li-kən\ *adj* **1 a** : of, relating to, or resembling a republic **b** : favoring or supporting a republic **2** *cap* **a** : DEMOCRATIC-REPUBLICAN **b** : of, relating to, or being one of the two major political parties in the U.S.

²republican *n* **1** : one that favors or supports a republican form of government **2** *cap* **a** : a member of a political party favoring republicanism **b** : a member of the Republican party of the U.S.

re·pub·li·can·ism \ri-'pəb-li-kə-,niz-əm\ *n* **1** : support or desire for a republican form of government **2** : the principles or ideas of republican government **3** *cap* : the principles, policy, or practices of the Republican party of the U.S.

re·pu·di·ate \ri-'pyüd-ē-,āt\ vb **-at·ed; -at·ing** **1** : to refuse to have anything to do with **2** : to refuse to accept or pay ⟨repudiate a debt⟩ — **re·pu·di·a·tion** \-,pyüd-ē-'ā-shən\ n — **re·pu·di·a·tor** \-'pyüd-ē-,āt-ər\ n

re·pug·nance \ri-'pəg-nən(t)s\ n : a strong feeling of dislike

re·pug·nant \ri-'pəg-nənt\ adj **1** : INCOMPATIBLE 1 **2** : causing a feeling of dislike or disgust : REPULSIVE — **re·pug·nant·ly** adv

¹**re·pulse** \ri-'pəls\ vb **re·pulsed; re·puls·ing** **1** : to drive or beat back : REPEL ⟨repulse an attack⟩ **2** : to cause dislike or disgust in

²**repulse** n **1** : a cold unfriendly rejection **2** : the action of driving back an attacker

re·pul·sion \ri-'pəl-shən\ n **1** : the action of repulsing : the state of being repulsed **2** : the force with which bodies, particles, or like forces repel one another **3** : a feeling of great dislike : REPUGNANCE

re·pul·sive \ri-'pəl-siv\ adj : causing disgust — **re·pul·sive·ly** adv — **re·pul·sive·ness** n

rep·u·ta·ble \'rep-yət-ə-bəl\ adj : having a good reputation : RESPECTED — **rep·u·ta·bil·i·ty** \,rep-yət-ə-'bil-ət-ē\ n — **rep·u·ta·bly** \'rep-yət-ə-blē\ adv

rep·u·ta·tion \,rep-yə-'tā-shən\ n **1** : overall quality or character as seen or judged by people in general ⟨a car with a good reputation⟩ **2** : notice by other people of some quality or ability ⟨has the reputation of being a good tennis player⟩

¹**re·pute** \ri-'pyüt\ vb **re·put·ed; re·put·ing** : to have the opinion that : CONSIDER, SUPPOSE ⟨reputed to be a millionaire⟩

²**repute** n **1** : REPUTATION 1 **2** : good reputation ⟨a scientist of repute⟩

re·put·ed \ri-'pyüt-əd\ adj **1** : having a good reputation ⟨a highly reputed lawyer⟩ **2** : believed by most people to be such ⟨the movie was a reputed success⟩ — **re·put·ed·ly** adv

¹**re·quest** \ri-'kwest\ n **1** : an asking for something **2** : something asked for ⟨granted me three requests⟩ **3** : the condition of being requested ⟨tickets are available upon request⟩

²**request** vb **1** : to make a request to or of **2** : to ask for — **re·quest·er** n

re·qui·em \'rek-wē-əm also 'rāk- or 'rēk-\ n **1** : a Mass for a dead person **2** : a musical service or hymn in honor of the dead [Middle English requiem "a mass for the dead", from Latin requiem "rest", the first word of the phrase Requiem aeternum dona eis "Eternal rest grant to them", said or sung at the begining of the Mass]

requiem shark n : any of several large sharks usually found in warm seas that sometimes attack human beings

re·quire \ri-'kwī(ə)r\ vb **re·quired; re·quir·ing** **1** : to have a need for ⟨a game that requires skill⟩ **2** : ¹ORDER 2a ⟨the law requires that everyone pay the tax⟩

re·quire·ment \ri-'kwī(ə)r-mənt\ n : something that is required or necessary ⟨requirements for graduation⟩

req·ui·site \'rek-wə-zət\ adj : needed for reaching a goal or achieving a purpose — **requisite** n — **req·ui·site·ness** n

¹**req·ui·si·tion** \,rek-wə-'zish-ən\ n **1** : the act of requiring or demanding **2** : a demand or request made by proper authority ⟨a requisition for supplies⟩

²**requisition** vb **-si·tioned; -si·tion·ing** \-'zish-niŋ, -ᵊn-iŋ\ : to make a requisition for

re·quit·al \ri-'kwīt-ᵊl\ n **1** : something given in payment or in return **2** : the act or action of requiting : the state of being requited

re·quite \ri-'kwīt\ vb **re·quit·ed; re·quit·ing** **1** : to make return for (as a favor or an injury) **2** : to make suitable return to — **re·quit·er** n

re·ra·di·ate \(')rē-'rād-ē-,āt\ vb : to radiate anew ⟨the

ground reradiates the heat obtained from the sun⟩ — **re·ra·di·a·tion** \(,)rē-,rād-ē-'ā-shən\ n

¹**re·run** \(')rē-'rən\ vb : to run again or anew

²**re·run** \'rē-,rən, (')rē-'rən\ n **1** : the act or action or an instance of rerunning **2** : a television program or movie that is rerun

re·sale \'rē-,sāl, (')rē-'sā(ə)l\ n : the act or an instance of selling again

re·scind \ri-'sind\ vb **1** : CANCEL 2a ⟨rescind a contract⟩ **2** : to do away with by legislative action ⟨rescind a law⟩ — **re·scind·er** n

re·scis·sion \ri-'sizh-ən\ n : an act of rescinding

res·cue \'res-kyü\ vb **res·cued; res·cu·ing** : to free from danger or evil : SAVE — **res·cue** n — **res·cu·er** n

re·search \ri-'sərch, 'rē-,sərch\ n **1** : careful study and investigation for the purpose of discovering and explaining new knowledge **2** : the collecting of information about a subject — **research** vb — **re·search·er** n

re·seed \(')rē-'sēd\ vb : to sow seed on again

re·sem·blance \ri-'zem-blən(t)s\ n **1 a** : the quality or state of resembling : SIMILARITY **b** : a point of likeness **2** : REPRESENTATION 1

re·sem·ble \ri-'zem-bəl\ vb **-bled; -bling** \-b(ə-)liŋ\ : to be like or similar to

re·sent \ri-'zent\ vb : to feel or state annoyance or anger at

re·sent·ful \ri-'zent-fəl\ adj **1** : full of resentment ⟨a resentful child⟩ **2** : caused or marked by resentment ⟨a resentful reply to a letter⟩ — **re·sent·ful·ly** \-fə-lē\ adv — **re·sent·ful·ness** n

re·sent·ment \ri-'zent-mənt\ n : a feeling of angry displeasure at something regarded as a wrong, insult, or injury

res·er·va·tion \,rez-ər-'vā-shən\ n **1** : the act of reserving **2** : an arrangement to have something (as a motel room or a seat on a plane) held for one's use **3** : something reserved for a special use; esp : an area of public lands so reserved ⟨an Indian reservation⟩ **4** : a limiting condition : EXCEPTION ⟨agree without reservations⟩

¹**re·serve** \ri-'zərv\ vb **re·served; re·serv·ing** **1** : to keep in store for future or special use ⟨reserve that shirt for special occasions⟩ **2** : to hold over to a future time or place : DEFER ⟨reserve judgment on that matter⟩ **3** : to arrange to have set aside and held for one's use ⟨reserve a hotel room⟩

²**reserve** n **1** : something stored or available for future use : STOCK ⟨oil reserves⟩ **2 a** : military forces held back or available for later use — usually used in pl. **b** : the military forces of a country not part of the regular services **3** : an area of land set apart ⟨wild game reserve⟩ **4** : restraint, closeness, or caution in one's words and behavior **5** : ¹SUBSTITUTE ⟨the reserves of the football team⟩ — **in reserve** : set aside for future or special use

re·served \ri-'zərvd\ adj **1** : cautious in words and actions ⟨a reserved young woman⟩ **2** : kept or set apart or aside for future or special use ⟨a reserved parking space⟩ **syn** see SILENT — **re·serv·ed·ly** \-'zər-vəd-lē\ adv — **re·served·ness** \-'zər-vəd-nəs\ n

re·serv·ist \ri-'zər-vəst\ n : a member of a military reserve

res·er·voir \'rez-ə(r)v-,wär, -ə(r)v-,(w)ȯr\ n **1** : a place where something is kept in store; esp : an artificial or natural lake where water is col-

reservoir 1

\ə\ abut		\aů\ out	\i\ tip	\ȯ\ saw	\ů\ foot
\ər\ further	\ch\ chin		\ī\ life	\ȯi\ coin	\y\ yet
\a\ mat		\e\ pet	\j\ job	\th\ thin	\yü\ few
\ā\ take		\ē\ easy	\ŋ\ sing	\th\ this	\yů\ cure
\ä\ cot, cart		\g\ go	\ō\ bone	\ü\ food	\zh\ vision

lected as a water supply   **2** : an extra supply : RESERVE [from French *réservoir* "place where something is kept in reserve", from *reserver* "to reserve, keep for future use"]

re·shape \(')rē-'shāp\ *vb* : to give a new form to

re·shuf·fle \(')rē-'shəf-əl\ *vb*   **1** : to shuffle again   **2** : to reorganize usually by switching around existing parts ⟨the President *reshuffled* the cabinet⟩ — **reshuffle** *n*

re·side \ri-'zīd\ *vb* **re·sid·ed; re·sid·ing**   **1** : to live permanently or continuously ⟨*reside* in St. Louis⟩   **2** : to live ⟨the power of veto *resides* in the president⟩ — **re·sid·er** *n*

res·i·dence \'rez-əd-ən(t)s, -ə-,den(t)s\ *n*   **1** : the act or state of living or working continuously in a place ⟨physicians in *residence* in a hospital⟩ ⟨*residence* abroad⟩   **2 a** : the place where one lives   **b** : the status of a legal resident   **3 a** : the period during which a person resides in a place   **b** : a period of actual study, research, or teaching at a college or university

res·i·den·cy \'rez-əd-ən-sē, -ə-,den(t)-\ *n, pl* **-cies**   **1** : a usually official place of residence   **2** : a period of advanced resident training especially in a medical specialty

¹res·i·dent \'rez-əd-ənt, -ə-,dent\ *adj*   **1** : living in a place for some length of time   **2** : working on a regular or full-time basis ⟨a *resident* physician⟩   **3** : not migrating to other areas ⟨*resident* birds⟩

²resident *n*   **1** : one who resides in a place   **2** : a person (as a physician) serving a residency

res·i·den·tial \,rez-(ə)-'den-chəl\ *adj*   **1** : used as a residence or by residents ⟨a *residential* hotel⟩   **2** : suitable for or containing residences ⟨a *residential* neighborhood⟩   **3** : of or relating to residence or residences — **res·i·den·tial·ly** \-'dench-(ə-)lē\ *adv*

¹re·sid·u·al \ri-'zij-(ə-)wəl, -'zij-əl\ *adj* : leaving a residue that is effective for some time afterward — **re·sid·u·al·ly** \-ē\ *adv*

²residual *n* : a residual product, substance, or result

res·i·due \'rez-ə-,d(y)ü\ *n* : whatever remains after a part is taken, set apart, or lost

re·sign \ri-'zīn\ *vb*   **1** : to give up by a formal or official act ⟨*resign* an office⟩   **2** : to give up an office or position   **3** : to accept something usually unpleasant ⟨*resign* oneself to disappointment⟩

res·ig·na·tion \,rez-ig-'nā-shən\ *n*   **1 a** : an act of resigning   **b** : a written notice of this act   **2** : the quality or the feeling of a person who is resigned

re·signed \ri-'zīnd\ *adj* : giving in patiently (as to loss, sorrow, or misfortune) — **re·sign·ed·ly** \-'zī-nəd-lē\ *adv* — **re·sign·ed·ness** \-'zī-nəd-nəs\ *n*

re·sil·ience \ri-'zil-yən(t)s\ *n*   **1** : the ability of a body to regain its original size and shape after being compressed, bent, or stretched : ELASTICITY   **2** : the ability to recover from or adjust to misfortune or change

re·sil·ien·cy \ri-'zil-yən-sē\ *n* : RESILIENCE

re·sil·ient \ri-'zil-yənt\ *adj* : marked by resilience [from Latin *resilient-, resiliens,* present participle of *resilire* "to jump back, rebound", from *re-* "back, again" and *salire* "to leap, spring" — related to ASSAULT, INSULT, SOMERSAULT] — **re·sil·ient·ly** *adv*

res·in \'rez-ᵉn\ *n*   **1** : any of various yellowish or brownish substances (as rosin) that are obtained from the gum or sap of some trees (as the pine) and are used in varnishes and plastics and in medicine   **2** : any of various manufactured products that are similar to natural resins in properties and are used chiefly as plastics — **res·in·ous** \'rez-nəs, -ᵉn-əs\ *adj*

re·sist \ri-'zist\ *vb*   **1** : to fight against : OPPOSE   **2** : to withstand the force or effect of — **re·sist·er** *n*

re·sis·tance \ri-'zis-tən(t)s\ *n*   **1 a** : an act or instance of resisting : OPPOSITION   **b** : a method of resisting   **2** : the ability to resist ⟨the body's *resistance* to disease⟩   **3** : an opposing or slowing force   **4** : the opposition offered by a body or substance to the passage through it of a steady electric current   **5** : a source of resistance   **6** *often cap*

: a secret organization in a conquered country fighting against enemy forces

re·sis·tant \ri-'zis-tənt\ *adj* : giving or capable of resistance — often used in combination ⟨wrinkle-*resistant* clothes⟩

re·sist·ibil·i·ty \ri-,zis-tə-'bil-ət-ē\ *n*   **1** : the quality or state of being resistible   **2** : the ability to resist

re·sist·ible \ri-'zis-tə-bəl\ *adj* : capable of being resisted

re·sist·less \ri-'zist-ləs\ *adj*   **1** : IRRESISTIBLE   **2** : giving no resistance — **re·sist·less·ly** *adv*

re·sis·tor \ri-'zis-tər\ *n* : a device offering electrical resistance

res·o·lute \'rez-ə-,lüt\ *adj* : firmly determined — **res·o·lute·ly** *adv* — **res·o·lute·ness** *n*

res·o·lu·tion \,rez-ə-'lü-shən\ *n*   **1 a** : the act or process of changing to simpler form   **b** : the act of answering : SOLVING ⟨the *resolution* of a problem⟩   **c** : the act of determining   **2** : the process or ability by which a lens or system of lenses (as in a microscope) produces an image in which points that are very close to each other can be seen as separate instead of blurred together — compare MAGNIFICATION 2b   **3 a** : something that is resolved ⟨New Year *resolutions*⟩   **b** : DETERMINATION 4   **4** : a formal statement of the feelings, wishes, or decision of a group   **5** : the point in a work of literature at which the main conflict is worked out

¹re·solve \ri-'zälv, -'zólv\ *vb* **re·solved; re·solv·ing**   **1** : to break up or separate into individual parts   **2 a** : to clear up : DISPEL ⟨*resolve* doubts⟩   **b** : to find an answer or solution to   **3** : to reach a decision about : DETERMINE, DECIDE ⟨*resolve* to study harder⟩   **4** : to declare or decide by a formal resolution and vote — **re·solv·able** \-'zäl-və-bəl, -'zól-\ *adj* — **re·solv·er** *n*

²resolve *n*   **1** : something resolved : RESOLUTION   **2** : firmness of purpose

re·solved \ri-'zälvd, -'zólvd\ *adj* : RESOLUTE

res·o·nance \'rez-ᵉn-ən(t)s, -nən(t)s\ *n*   **1** : the quality or state of being resonant   **2** : a reinforcement of sound (as a musical tone) in a vibrating body or system caused by waves from another body vibrating at nearly the same rate   **3** : a vibrating quality of a voice sound

res·o·nant \'rez-ᵉn-ənt, 'rez-nənt\ *adj*   **1** : continuing to sound   **2** : of, relating to, or showing resonance   **3** : strengthened and enriched by resonance — **res·o·nant·ly** *adv*

res·o·nate \'rez-ᵉn-,āt\ *vb* **-nat·ed; -nat·ing**   **1** : to produce or exhibit resonance   **2** : REECHO, RESOUND

res·o·na·tor \'rez-ᵉn-,āt-ər\ *n* : something (as a device for increasing the resonance of a musical instrument) that resounds or resonates

¹re·sort \ri-'zó(ə)rt\ *n*   **1 a** : someone or something that is looked to for help ⟨a last *resort*⟩   **b** : RECOURSE 1 ⟨have *resort* to force⟩   **2 a** : frequent, habitual, or general visiting   **b** : a frequently visited place : HANGOUT   **c** : a place providing recreation and entertainment especially to vacationers ⟨a ski *resort*⟩

²resort *vb*   **1** : to go especially frequently or habitually   **2** : to turn to for aid, relief, or advantage ⟨*resort* to violence⟩ — **re·sort·er** *n*

re·sound \ri-'zaund\ *vb*   **1** : to become filled with sound : REVERBERATE ⟨the hall *resounded* with cheers⟩   **2** : to sound loudly ⟨the organ *resounds* throughout the hall⟩   **3** : to become renowned

re·sound·ing *adj*   **1** : producing or marked by resonant sound   **2** : ¹CLEAR 4, UNMISTAKABLE ⟨a *resounding* success⟩ — **re·sound·ing·ly** \-'zaun-diŋ-lē\ *adv*

re·source \'rē-,só(ə)rs, -,zó(ə)rs, -,só(ə)rs, -,zó(ə)rs; ri-'só(ə)rs, -'zó(ə)rs, -'só(ə)rs, -'zó(ə)rs\ *n*   **1** : a new or a reserve source of supply or support   **2** *pl* : a usable stock or supply (as of money, products, or energy) ⟨mineral *resources*⟩   **3** : the possibility of relief or recovery ⟨left helpless without *resource*⟩   **4** : the ability to meet and deal with difficult situations

re·source·ful \ri-'sōrs-fəl, -'sȯrs-, -'zōrs-, -'zȯrs-\ *adj* : able to deal well with new or difficult situations — **re·source·ful·ly** \-fə-lē\ *adv* — **re·source·ful·ness** *n*

¹**re·spect** \ri-'spekt\ *n* **1** : relation to or concern with something specified : REFERENCE ⟨with *respect* to your last letter⟩ **2 a** : high or special regard : ESTEEM **b** *pl* : expressions of regard or courtesy ⟨pay my *respects* to your family⟩ **3** : ¹DETAIL 1b ⟨perfect in all *respects*⟩

²**respect** *vb* **1** : to consider worthy of high regard : ESTEEM **2** : to pay attention to ⟨*respected* their wishes⟩ — **re·spect·er** *n*

re·spect·able \ri-'spek-tə-bəl\ *adj* **1** : worthy of respect : REPUTABLE **2** : decent or correct in character or behavior : PROPER ⟨*respectable* people⟩ **3** : fair in size, quality, or quantity ⟨a *respectable* amount of money⟩ **4** : fit to be seen : PRESENTABLE ⟨*respectable* clothes⟩ — **re·spect·abil·i·ty** \-,spek-tə-'bil-ət-ē\ *n* — **re·spect·able·ness** \-'spek-tə-bəl-nəs\ *n* — **re·spect·ably** \-blē\ *adv*

re·spect·ful \ri-'spekt-fəl\ *adj* : marked by or showing respect ⟨a *respectful* manner⟩ ⟨*respectful* of the rights of others⟩ — **re·spect·ful·ly** \-fə-lē\ *adv* — **re·spect·ful·ness** *n*

re·spect·ing *prep* : CONCERNING

re·spec·tive \ri-'spek-tiv\ *adj* : not the same or shared : SEPARATE ⟨they hurried to their *respective* homes⟩

re·spec·tive·ly \ri-'spek-tiv-lē\ *adv* : each in the order given ⟨John and Mary were 12 and 13 years old *respectively*⟩

re·spell \(')rē-'spel\ *vb* : to spell again or in another way; *esp* : to spell out according to a phonetic system — **re·spell·ing** *n*

res·pi·ra·tion \,res-pə-'rā-shən\ *n* **1** : the act or process of breathing **2** : the physical and chemical processes (as breathing and oxidation) by which a living thing obtains the oxygen it needs to produce energy and eliminates waste gases (as carbon dioxide) **3** : any of various chemical reactions that release energy from food molecules and occur in living things

res·pi·ra·tor \'res-pə-,rāt-ər\ *n* **1** : a device covering the mouth or nose especially to prevent the breathing in of harmful substances **2** : a device used to maintain artificial respiration

respirator 1

re·spi·ra·to·ry \'res-p(ə-)rə-,tōr-ē, ri-'spī-rə-, -,tȯr-\ *adj* : of or relating to respiration or the organs of respiration ⟨*respiratory* diseases⟩

respiratory system *n* : a system of organs used in breathing that in air-breathing vertebrates consists of the lungs with their nerves and blood vessels and the organs by which the lungs connect with the outside air

re·spire \ri-'spī(ə)r\ *vb* **re·spired; re·spir·ing** : to engage in respiration; *esp* : BREATHE 1

re·spite \'res-pət *also* ri-'spīt\ *n* **1** : a short delay : POSTPONEMENT **2** : a period of rest or relief

re·splen·dent \ri-'splen-dənt\ *adj* : so bright and colorful as to seem to glow ⟨fields *resplendent* with flowers⟩ ⟨*resplendent* in a new red coat⟩ — **re·splen·dence** \-dən(t)s\ *n* — **re·splen·den·cy** \-dən-sē\ *n* — **re·splen·dent·ly** *adv*

re·spond \ri-'spänd\ *vb* **1** : to say something in return : make an answer **2 a** : to react in response ⟨note how the animal's eyes *respond* to light⟩ **b** : to have a favorable reaction ⟨the patient is *responding* to treatment⟩

re·sponse \ri-'spän(t)s\ *n* **1** : an act or instance of replying : ANSWER **2** : words said or sung by the people or choir in a religious service **3** : a reaction of a living thing to a stimulus

re·spon·si·bil·i·ty \ri-,spän(t)-sə-'bil-ət-ē\ *n, pl* **-ties 1** : the quality or state of being responsible **2** : the quality of being dependable **3** : something for which one is responsible

re·spon·si·ble \ri-'spän(t)-sə-bəl\ *adj* **1 a** : being the one who must answer or account for something ⟨the committee *responsible* for the job⟩ **b** : being the cause or explanation ⟨the germ *responsible* for the disease⟩ **2 a** : able to meet one's obligations : TRUSTWORTHY, RELIABLE ⟨a *responsible* citizen⟩ **b** : able to choose for oneself between right and wrong **3** : requiring a person to take charge of or be trusted with important matters ⟨a *responsible* job⟩ — **re·spon·si·ble·ness** *n* — **re·spon·si·bly** \-blē\ *adv*

re·spon·sive \ri-'spän(t)-siv\ *adj* **1** : giving response : being an answer ⟨a *responsive* smile⟩ **2** : quick to respond or react sympathetically : SENSITIVE ⟨*responsive* to the needs of the poor⟩ — **re·spon·sive·ly** *adv* — **re·spon·sive·ness** *n*

¹**rest** \'rest\ *n* **1** : ¹SLEEP 1 **2 a** : freedom from activity **b** : a state marked by lack of motion or activity **3** : a place for resting or lodging **4 a** : a silence in music

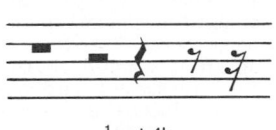

¹rest 4b

equal in time to a note of the same name **b** : a character standing for such a silence **5** : something used for support ⟨a head *rest*⟩

²**rest** *vb* **1 a** : to get rest by lying down : SLEEP **b** : to give rest to **c** : to lie dead **2** : to not take part in work or activity **3** : to place or be placed for or as if for support **4 a** : to be based or founded **b** : to fix or be fixed in hope or confidence ⟨*rested* their hopes on their children⟩ **5** : to stop presenting evidence in a law case ⟨the defense *rests*⟩

³**rest** *n* : something that is left over or behind : REMAINDER ⟨ate the *rest* of the soup⟩

re·state \(')rē-'stāt\ *vb* : to state again or in another way — **re·state·ment** \-mənt\ *n*

res·tau·rant \'res-t(ə-)rənt, -tə-,ränt\ *n* : a public eating place [from French *restaurant* "food that restores, restaurant", from *restaurer* "to restore, renew"]

res·tau·ra·teur \,res-tə-rə-'tər\ *also* **res·tau·ran·teur** \-,rän-\ *n* : a person who owns or runs a restaurant

rest·ful \'rest-fəl\ *adj* : giving or suggesting rest : QUIET ⟨a *restful* scene⟩ — **rest·ful·ly** \-fə-lē\ *adv* — **rest·ful·ness** *n*

rest home *n* : a place that provides housing and general care for the aged or sick

rest house *n* : a building used for shelter by travelers

rest·ing *adj* : not growing or active : DORMANT ⟨a *resting* spore⟩

res·ti·tu·tion \,res-tə-'t(y)ü-shən\ *n* : the giving of something back to its rightful owner or the giving of something of equal value (as for loss or damage)

res·tive \'res-tiv\ *adj* **1** : stubbornly fighting control : BALKY ⟨a *restive* horse⟩ **2** : showing impatience or restlessness : FIDGETY ⟨the crowd grew *restive*⟩ — **res·tive·ly** *adv* — **res·tive·ness** *n*

rest·less \'rest-ləs\ *adj* **1** : being without rest : giving no rest ⟨a *restless* night⟩ **2** : never resting or settled : always moving ⟨the *restless* sea⟩ **3** : showing one to be uneasy ⟨*restless* pacing back and forth⟩ — **rest·less·ly** *adv* — **rest·less·ness** *n*

res·to·ra·tion \,res-tə-'rā-shən\ *n* **1** : an act of restoring

\ə\ abut		\au̇\ out	\i\ tip	\o̅\ saw	\u̇\ foot
\ər\ further		\ch\ chin	\ī\ life	\oi̇\ coin	\y\ yet
\a\ mat		\e\ pet	\j\ job	\th\ thin	\yü\ few
\ā\ take		\ē\ easy	\ŋ\ sing	\th\ this	\yu̇\ cure
\ä\ cot, cart		\g\ go	\ō\ bone	\ü\ food	\zh\ vision

or the condition of being restored **2** : something (as a building) that has been restored

¹re·stor·ative \ri-'stōr-ət-iv, -'stȯr-\ *adj* : of or relating to restoration; *esp* : having power to restore ⟨the *restorative* value of food and rest⟩

²restorative *n* : something that serves to restore to consciousness or health

re·store \ri-'stō(ə)r, -'stȯ(ə)r\ *vb* **re·stored; re·stor·ing** **1** : ¹RETURN 5 ⟨*restored* the purse to its owner⟩ **2** : to put or bring back into existence or use ⟨*restore* harmony after an argument⟩ **3** : to bring back to or put back into an earlier or original state ⟨*restore* an old house⟩ **4** : to put again in possession of something ⟨*restore* the king to the throne⟩ — **re·stor·able** \-'stȯr-ə-bəl, -'stȯr-\ *adj* — **re·stor·er** *n*

re·strain \ri-'strān\ *vb* **1 a** : to prevent from doing something **b** : to keep back : CURB ⟨*restrain* one's anger⟩ **c** : to limit or keep under control ⟨*restrain* trade⟩ **2** : to take away liberty; *esp* : to place under arrest or restraint — **re·strain·able** \-'strā-nə-bəl\ *adj* — **re·strain·er** *n*

re·strained \ri-'strānd\ *adj* : marked by restraint : showing careful control — **re·strain·ed·ly** \-'strā-nəd-lē\ *adv*

re·straint \ri-'strānt\ *n* **1** : the act of restraining : the state of being restrained ⟨held in *restraint*⟩ **2** : a restraining force or influence **3** : control over one's behavior ⟨act with *restraint*⟩

re·strict \ri-'strikt\ *vb* **1** : to keep within bounds **2** : to place under limits as to use

re·strict·ed *adj* : being or placed under limits or restrictions ⟨a *restricted* outlook⟩ ⟨a *restricted* area⟩

re·stric·tion \ri-'strik-shən\ *n* **1** : something (as a law or rule) that restricts **2** : an act of restricting : the condition of being restricted

re·stric·tive \ri-'strik-tiv\ *adj* **1** : serving or likely to restrict **2** : limiting the reference of a modified word or phrase — **restrictive** *n* — **re·stric·tive·ly** *adv* — **re·stric·tive·ness** *n*

rest room *n* : a room or set of rooms that includes sinks and toilets

¹re·sult \ri-'zəlt\ *vb* **1** : to come about as an effect ⟨disease *results* from infection⟩ **2** : to have as an effect ⟨the disease *results* in death⟩

²result *n* **1** : something that comes about as an effect or end **2** : a good or clear effect ⟨this method gets *results*⟩ — **re·sult·ful** \-fəl\ *adj* — **re·sult·less** \-ləs\ *adj*

¹re·sul·tant \ri-'zəlt-ᵊnt\ *adj* : coming from or resulting from something else : being a resultant — **re·sul·tant·ly** *adv*

²resultant *n* : something that results : OUTCOME; *esp* : the single vector that is the sum of a given set of vectors

re·sume \ri-'züm\ *vb* **re·sumed; re·sum·ing** **1** : to take again : occupy again ⟨*resume* your seats⟩ **2** : to begin again or go back to ⟨*resumed* the game the next day⟩

ré·su·mé *or* **re·su·me** *or* **re·su·mé** \'rez-ə-,mā\ *n* : a brief statement : SUMMARY ⟨a *résumé* of the news⟩; *esp* : a short account of one's career and qualifications for a job

re·sump·tion \ri-'zəm(p)-shən\ *n* : the action of resuming

re·sur·gence \ri-'sər-jən(t)s\ *n* : a rising again into life, activity, or notice — **re·sur·gent** \-jənt\ *adj*

res·ur·rect \,rez-ə-'rekt\ *vb* **1** : to raise from the dead : bring back to life **2** : to bring to attention or into use again

res·ur·rec·tion \,rez-ə-'rek-shən\ *n* **1 a** *cap* : the rising of Jesus from the dead **b** *often cap* : the rising again to life of all the human dead before the final judgment **2** : RESURGENCE, REVIVAL — **res·ur·rec·tion·al** \-shnəl, -shən-ᵊl\ *adj*

re·sus·ci·tate \ri-'səs-ə-,tāt\ *vb* **-tat·ed; -tat·ing** **1** : to bring back from apparent death or from unconsciousness **2** : REVIVE 1

re·sus·ci·ta·tion \ri-,səs-ə-'tā-shən\ *n* : an act or proce-

dure that attempts to resuscitate; *also* : the state of being resuscitated — compare CARDIOPULMONARY RESUSCITATION

re·sus·ci·ta·tor \ri-'səs-ə-,tāt-ər\ *n* : one that resuscitates; *esp* : a device used to restore or assist the respiration of a person who is not breathing normally

ret \'ret\ *vb* **ret·ted; ret·ting** : to partially rot a plant (as flax or hemp) to loosen the fiber from the woody tissue

¹re·tail \'rē-,tāl\ *vb* : to sell in small amounts to people for their own use — **re·tail·er** *n*

²retail *n* : the sale of products or goods in small quantities to people for their own use

³retail *adj* : of, relating to, or engaged in selling by retail ⟨*retail* stores⟩

⁴retail *adv* : in small quantities : from a retailer

re·tain \ri-'tān\ *vb* **1 a** : to keep in possession or use ⟨you will *retain* your rights as a citizen⟩ **b** : to keep in pay or in one's service; *esp* : to employ by paying a retainer ⟨*retain* an attorney⟩ **2** : to hold secure or unchanged ⟨land *retains* heat longer than water⟩

¹re·tain·er \ri-'tā-nər\ *n* : a fee paid (as to a lawyer) for advice or services or for a claim upon services in case of need

²retainer *n* **1** : one that retains **2** : a servant or follower in a wealthy household

¹re·take \(')rē-'tāk\ *vb* **-took** \-'tùk\; **-tak·en** \-'tā-kən\; **-tak·ing** : to take again; *esp* : to photograph again

²re·take \'rē-,tāk\ *n* : a second photographing or photograph

re·tal·i·ate \ri-'tal-ē-,āt\ *vb* **-at·ed; -at·ing** : to return (as an injury) in kind : get revenge — **re·tal·i·a·tion** \-,tal-ē-'ā-shən\ *n* — **re·tal·ia·to·ry** \-'tal-yə-,tōr-ē, -,tȯr-\ *adj*

re·tard \ri-'tärd\ *vb* : to slow up especially by preventing or checking progress : HINDER — **re·tard·er** *n*

re·tar·dant \ri-'tärd-ᵊnt\ *adj* : serving or tending to retard ⟨flame-*retardant* fabrics⟩

re·tar·da·tion \,rē-,tär-'dā-shən\ *n* **1** : an act or instance of retarding **2** : the extent to which something is retarded **3** : an unusual slowness especially of mental or physical development

re·tard·ed \ri-'tärd-əd\ *adj* : slow or limited in mental or emotional development

retch \'rech, *British* rēch\ *vb* **1** : ²VOMIT 1 **2** : to try to vomit

re·ten·tion \ri-'ten-chən\ *n* **1** : the act of retaining : the state of being retained **2** : power of retaining **3** : something retained

re·ten·tive \ri-'tent-iv\ *adj* : having ability to retain ⟨a *retentive* memory⟩ — **re·ten·tive·ness** *n*

ret·i·cent \'ret-ə-sənt\ *adj* **1** : tending not to talk or give out information **2** : quiet in tone or appearance **syn** see SILENT — **ret·i·cence** \-sən(t)s\ *n* — **ret·i·cen·cy** \-sən-sē\ *n* — **ret·i·cent·ly** *adv*

re·tic·u·lar \ri-'tik-yə-lər\ *adj* : RETICULATE

re·tic·u·late \ri-'tik-yə-lət\ *adj* : resembling a net

ret·i·cule \'ret-i-,kyü(ə)l\ *n* : a handbag that is closed by pulling a string

ret·i·na \'ret-ᵊn-ə, 'ret-nə\ *n, pl* **retinas** *or* **ret·i·nae** \-ᵊn-,ē, -,ī\ : the light-sensitive nerve membrane lining the back of the eye that receives images formed by the lens and is connected with the brain by the optic nerve — **ret·i·nal** \-ᵊn-əl, -nəl\ *adj*

ret·i·nol \'ret-ᵊn-,ȯl, -,ōl\ *n* : VITAMIN A

ret·i·nue \'ret-ᵊn-,(y)ü\ *n* : a group of helpers, servants, or followers

re·tire \ri-'tī(ə)r\ *vb* **re·tired; re·tir·ing** **1** : to get away from action or danger : RETREAT **2** : to go away especially to be alone **3** : to give up or cause to give up one's job **4** : to go to bed **5** : to put out (a batter or side) in baseball

re·tired *adj* **1** : SECLUDED 1 ⟨a *retired* village⟩ **2** : not working at active duties or business

re·tire·ment \ri-'tī(ə)r-mənt\ *n* : an act of retiring : the state of being retired; *esp* : the leaving of one's job permanently

re·tir·ing \ri-'tī(ə)r-iŋ\ *adj* : RESERVED 1, SHY — **re·tir·ing·ly** \-iŋ-lē\ *adv* — **re·tir·ing·ness** *n*

re·tool \(')rē-'tül\ *vb* : to equip again with new or different tools ⟨*retool* a factory⟩

¹re·tort \ri-'to(ə)rt\ *vb* **1** : to answer back : reply angrily or sharply **2** : to reply to an argument with an opposing argument [from Latin *retortus*, past participle of *retorquēre*, literally "to twist back, hurl back", from *re-* "back, again" and *torquēre* "to twist" — related to DISTORT, EXTORT, TORTURE]

²retort *n* : a quick, witty, or angry reply

³re·tort \ri-'to(ə)rt, 'rē-,to(ə)rt\ *n* : a container in which substances are distilled or broken down by heat [from early French *retorte* "a vessel in which substances are distilled", derived from Latin *retortus*, past participle of *retorquēre* "to twist"; probably so called from its shape]

re·touch \(')rē-'təch\ *vb* : TOUCH UP; *esp* : to change (as a photographic negative) in order to produce a more desirable appearance — **re·touch** \'rē-,təch, (')rē-'təch\ *n* — **re·touch·er** \(')rē-'təch-ər\ *n*

re·trace \(')rē-'trās\ *vb* : to go over again or back

re·tract \ri-'trakt\ *vb* **1** : to draw or pull back or in ⟨a cat can *retract* its claws⟩ **2** : to withdraw (as an offer, a statement, or a claim) ⟨the newspaper *retracted* the story⟩ — **re·tract·able** \-'trak-tə-bəl\ *adj*

re·trac·tile \ri-'trak-tᵊl, -,tīl\ *adj* : capable of being drawn back or in ⟨the *retractile* claws of a cat⟩

re·trac·tion \ri-'trak-shən\ *n* **1** : a statement taking back something previously said **2** : an act of retracting : the state of being retracted **3** : the ability to retract

re·trac·tor \ri-'trak-tər\ *n* : one that retracts; *esp* : a muscle that draws an organ or part in or back

¹re·tread \(')rē-'tred\ *vb* **re·tread·ed; re·tread·ing** : to put a new tread on (a worn tire)

²re·tread \'rē-,tred\ *n* **1** : a new tread on a tire **2** : a retreaded tire

¹re·treat \ri-'trēt\ *n* **1 a** : an act of going away especially from something difficult, dangerous, or disagreeable **b** : a military retreat from the enemy **c** : a signal for retreating **2** : a place of privacy or safety : REFUGE

²retreat *vb* **1** : to make a retreat **2** : to slope backward

re·trench \ri-'trench\ *vb* **1** : LESSEN, REDUCE **2** : to reduce expenses : ECONOMIZE — **re·trench·ment** \-mənt\ *n*

re·tri·al \(')rē-'trī(-ə)l\ *n* : a second trial, experiment, or test

ret·ri·bu·tion \,re-trə-'byü-shən\ *n* : something given in payment for a wrong : PUNISHMENT

re·trib·u·tive \ri-'trib-yət-iv\ *adj* : of, relating to, or marked by retribution ⟨*retributive* justice⟩ — **re·trib·u·tive·ly** *adv*

re·trib·u·to·ry \ri-'trib-yə-,tōr-ē, -,tȯr-\ *adj* : RETRIBUTIVE

re·triev·al \ri-'trē-vəl\ *n* : an act or process of retrieving

re·trieve \ri-'trēv\ *vb* **re·trieved; re·triev·ing** **1** : to find and bring in killed or wounded game ⟨teach a dog how to *retrieve*⟩ **2** : to recover or make good a loss or damage **3** : to get and bring back; *esp* : to recover (as information) from storage — **re·triev·able** \-'trē-və-bəl\ *adj*

re·triev·er \ri-'trē-vər\ *n* : one that retrieves; *esp* : a dog (as a golden retriever) of any of several breeds having a heavy water-resistant coat and used especially for retrieving game

retro- *prefix* : backward : back ⟨*retro*-rocket⟩ [derived from Latin *re-* "back, again" and Latin *-tro* (the final part of *intro* "within")]

³retort

ret·ro·ac·tive \,re-trō-'ak-tiv\ *adj* : intended to apply or take effect at a date in the past ⟨a *retroactive* pay raise⟩ — **ret·ro·ac·tive·ly** *adv*

re·tro·fire \'re-trō-,fī(-ə)r\ *vb* : to ignite a retro-rocket — **re·trofire** *n*

ret·ro·grade \'re-trə-,grād\ *adj* : having a backward direction, motion, or tendency

ret·ro·gress \,re-trə-'gres\ *vb* : to move backward — **ret·ro·gres·sion** \-'gresh-ən\ *n*

ret·ro–rock·et \'re-trō-,räk-ət\ *n* : a rocket (as on a space vehicle) used to slow forward motion

ret·ro·spect \'re-trə-,spekt\ *n* : a looking back on things past : a thinking of past events

ret·ro·spec·tion \,re-trə-'spek-shən\ *n* **1** : the act or power of recalling the past **2** : RETROSPECT

ret·ro·spec·tive \,re-trə-'spek-tiv\ *adj* : of, relating to, or given to retrospection — **ret·ro·spec·tive·ly** *adv*

retro-rocket

retted *past and past participle of* RET

retting *present participle of* RET

¹re·turn \ri-'tərn\ *vb* **1** : to come or go back **2** : ¹REPLY 3, ANSWER **3** : to make an official report of ⟨the jury *returned* a verdict⟩ **4** : to elect to office **5** : to bring, carry, send, or put back ⟨*return* a book to the library⟩ ⟨*return* borrowed money⟩ **6** : to bring in (as profit) : YIELD **7** : to send or say in response or reply ⟨*return* thanks⟩ — **re·turn·er** *n*

²return *n* **1 a** : the act of coming back to or from a place or condition **b** : a regular or frequent occurrence : RECURRENCE ⟨the *return* of spring⟩ **2 a** : a report of the results of voting — usually used in pl. ⟨election *returns*⟩ **b** : a statement of income to be taxed ⟨a tax *return*⟩ **3** : a means for bringing something (as water) back to its starting point **4** : the profit from labor, investment, or business : YIELD **5 a** : the act of returning something to an earlier place, condition, or ownership **b** : something returned **6** : something given in payment or exchange ⟨ask nothing in *return* for a favor⟩ **7** : the action or an instance of returning a ball (as in tennis or football)

³return *adj* **1** : played or given in return ⟨a *return* call⟩ ⟨a *return* game⟩ **2** : used for returning ⟨a *return* ticket⟩

re·turn·able \ri-'tər-nə-bəl\ *adj* : that may or must be returned ⟨*returnable* bottles⟩

re·turn·ee \ri-,tər-'nē\ *n* : one who returns

re·uni·fy \(')rē-'yü-nə-,fī\ *vb* : to restore unity to — **re·uni·fi·ca·tion** \(,)rē-,yü-nə-fə-'kā-shən\ *n*

re·union \(')rē-'yün-yən\ *n* **1** : the act of reuniting : the state of being reunited **2** : a reuniting of persons ⟨a class *reunion*⟩

re·unite \,rē-yù-'nīt\ *vb* : to come or bring together again after a separation

re·use \(')rē-'yüz\ *vb* : to use again — **re·us·able** \-'yü-zə-bəl\ *adj* — **re·use** \-'yüs\ *n*

¹rev \'rev\ *n* : a revolution of a motor

²rev *vb* **revved; rev·ving** : to increase the revolutions per minute of (a motor)

re·val·u·ate \(')rē-'val-yə-,wāt\ *vb* **-at·ed; -at·ing** : REVALUE — **re·val·u·a·tion** \(,)rē-,val-yə-'wā-shən\ *n*

re·val·ue \(')rē-'val-yü\ *vb* : to make a new valuation of : REAPPRAISE

\ə\ **abut**	\au̇\ **out**	\i\ **tip**	\ȯ\ **saw**	\u̇\ **foot**
\ər\ **further**	\ch\ **chin**	\ī\ **life**	\ȯi\ **coin**	\y\ **yet**
\a\ **mat**	\e\ **pet**	\j\ **job**	\th\ **thin**	\yü\ **few**
\ā\ **take**	\ē\ **easy**	\ŋ\ **sing**	\t̲h̲\ **this**	\yu̇\ **cure**
\ä\ **cot, cart**	\g\ **go**	\ō\ **bone**	\ü\ **food**	\zh\ **vision**

re·vamp \(')rē-'vamp\ *vb* **1** : to make like new again : RENOVATE **2** : [1]REVISE

re·veal \ri-'vē(ə)l\ *vb* **1** : to make known : DIVULGE **2** : to show plainly : DISPLAY — **re·veal·er** *n*

> **syn** REVEAL, DISCLOSE, TELL, BETRAY mean to make known what has been or should be concealed. REVEAL may apply to making known ordinary information or to making known truths that are usually beyond the range of human vision or reason ⟨*revealed* his age to the interviewer⟩ ⟨their mission was *revealed* to them in a dream⟩ DISCLOSE most often involves the giving out of information previously kept secret ⟨*disclosed* to the media that the leaders of the two countries had met privately⟩ TELL stresses that the information made known is necessary or useful ⟨why didn't you *tell* her that the concert was canceled?⟩ BETRAY implies either that disclosing the information involves wrongdoing or that the disclosure is against one's will ⟨*betrayed* plans for a new computer to the firm's chief rival⟩ ⟨though I said nothing, my face *betrayed* my concern⟩

rev·eil·le \'rev-ə-lē\ *n* **1** : a signal to get up in the morning **2** : a bugle call at about sunrise signaling the first military formation of the day [from French *réveillez* "wake up!"]

[1]rev·el \'rev-əl\ *vb* **-eled** *or* **-elled; -el·ing** *or* **-el·ling** \'rev-(ə-)liŋ\ **1** : to take part in a revel : be noisy in a festive manner **2** : to take great delight in something — **rev·el·er** *or* **rev·el·ler** \-(ə-)lər\ *n*

[2]revel *n* : a noisy or merry celebration

rev·e·la·tion \,rev-ə-'lā-shən\ *n* **1** : an act of revealing or making known divine truth **2 a** : an act of revealing to view **b** : something that is revealed; *esp* : a surprising or astonishing disclosure

Rev·e·la·tion \,rev-ə-'lā-shən\ *n* — see BIBLE table

re·ve·la·to·ry \'rev-ə-lə-,tōr-ē, -,tȯr-, ri-'vel-ə-\ *adj* : of or relating to revelation

rev·el·ry \'rev-əl-rē\ *n, pl* **-ries** : rough and noisy merrymaking

[1]re·venge \ri-'venj\ *vb* **re·venged; re·veng·ing** **1** : to get even for a wrong done **2** : to give injury in return for — **re·veng·er** *n*

[2]revenge *n* **1** : a desire to pay back injury for injury **2** : an act or instance of revenging **3** : a chance for getting satisfaction — **re·venge·ful** \-fəl\ *adj* — **re·venge·ful·ly** \-fə-lē\ *adv* — **re·venge·ful·ness** *n*

rev·e·nue \'rev-ə-,n(y)ü\ *n* **1** : the income produced by a given source **2** : the income that a government collects for public use

rev·e·nu·er \'rev-ə-,n(y)ü-ər\ *n* : a revenue officer or boat

re·ver·ber·ant \ri-'vər-b(ə-)rənt\ *adj* : tending to reverberate — **re·ver·ber·ant·ly** *adv*

re·ver·ber·ate \ri-'vər-bə-,rāt\ *vb* **-at·ed; -at·ing** : to continue in or as if in a series of echoes — **re·ver·ber·a·tion** \-,vər-bə-'rā-shən\ *n*

re·vere \ri-'vi(ə)r\ *vb* **re·vered; re·ver·ing** : to show devotion and honor to : think of with reverence

[1]rev·er·ence \'rev-(ə-)rən(t)s, 'rev-ərn(t)s\ *n* **1** : honor or respect felt or shown : DEFERENCE **2** : the state of being revered or honored

[2]reverence *vb* **-enced; -enc·ing** : to think of or treat with reverence

[1]rev·er·end \'rev-(ə-)rənd, 'rev-ərnd\ *adj* **1** : worthy of reverence : REVERED ⟨these *reverend* halls⟩ **2** — used as a title for a member of the clergy ⟨the *Reverend* Mr. Doe⟩ ⟨the *Reverend* John Doe⟩ ⟨the *Reverend* Mother Superior⟩

[2]reverend *n* : a member of the clergy

rev·er·ent \'rev-(ə-)rənt, 'rev-ərnt\ *adj* : very respectful : showing reverence — **rev·er·ent·ly** *adv*

rev·er·en·tial \,rev-ə-'ren-chəl\ *adj* **1** : showing or having a quality of reverence **2** : inspiring reverence — **rev·er·en·tial·ly** \-'rench-(ə-)lē\ *adv*

rev·er·ie *also* **rev·ery** \'rev-(ə-)rē\ *n, pl* **-er·ies** **1** : [1]DAYDREAM **2** : the condition of being lost in thought

re·ver·sal \ri-'vər-səl\ *n* : an act or the process of reversing

[1]re·verse \ri-'vərs\ *adj* **1** : opposite or contrary to a previous or normal condition ⟨*reverse* order⟩ **2** : acting or working in a manner opposite to the usual **3** : bringing about backward movement ⟨*reverse* gear⟩ — **re·verse·ly** *adv*

[2]reverse *vb* **re·versed; re·vers·ing** **1** : to turn completely about or upside down or inside out **2 a** : to overthrow or set aside a legal decision by an opposite decision **b** : to change to the contrary ⟨*reverse* a policy⟩ **3 a** : to go or cause to go in the opposite direction **b** : to put (as a car) into reverse [Middle English *reversen* "cause to return, turn around", from early French *reverser* (same meaning), from Latin *reversare* "to turn around", from *revertere* "to turn back", from *re-* "again" and *vertere* "to turn" — related to CONVERSE, VERSATILE, VERTICAL, VICE VERSA] — **re·vers·er** *n*

[3]reverse *n* **1** : something directly opposite to something else **2** : an act or instance of reversing; *esp* : a change for the worse **3** : the back part of something **4** : a gear that reverses something

[1]re·vers·ible \ri-'vər-sə-bəl\ *adj* **1** : capable of being reversed or of reversing ⟨a *reversible* chemical reaction⟩ **2 a** : having two finished usable sides ⟨*reversible* fabrics⟩ **b** : wearable with either side out ⟨a *reversible* coat⟩ — **re·vers·ibil·i·ty** \-,vər-sə-'bil-ət-ē\ *n* — **re·vers·ibly** \-'vər-sə-blē\ *adv*

[2]reversible *n* : a reversible cloth or garment

re·ver·sion \ri-'vər-zhən\ *n* **1** : a right of future possession (as of property or a title) **2 a** : an act or the process of returning (as to an earlier condition) **b** : a product of reversion **3** : an act or instance of turning the opposite way : the state of being so turned

re·vert \ri-'vərt\ *vb* **1** : to come or go back ⟨*reverted* to the customs of their ancestors⟩ **2** : to experience reversion

[1]re·view \ri-'vyü\ *n* **1** : a formal inspection of troops by officers **2** : a general survey **3** : an act of looking something over especially for flaws **4 a** : a discussion by a critic of the quality of something (as a book or play) **b** : a magazine filled mostly with reviews and essays **5 a** : a look at past events **b** : a fresh study of material studied before **6** : REVUE

[2]review *vb* **1** : to look at a thing again : study or examine again ⟨*review* a lesson⟩; *esp* : to reexamine judicially **2** : to make a formal inspection of (as troops) **3** : to discuss the quality of (as a book or play) **4** : to look back on ⟨*review* one's accomplishments⟩ — **re·view·er** *n*

re·vile \ri-'vī(ə)l\ *vb* **re·viled; re·vil·ing** : to speak to or about in an insulting way — **re·vile·ment** \-mənt\ *n* — **re·vil·er** *n*

[1]re·vise \ri-'vīz\ *vb* **re·vised; re·vis·ing** **1** : to look over again in order to correct or improve ⟨*revise* a book report⟩ **2** : to make a new, corrected, improved, or up-to-date version or arrangement of ⟨*revise* a dictionary⟩ — **re·vis·er** *or* **re·vi·sor** \-'vī-zər\ *n*

[2]re·vise \'rē-,vīz, ri-'vīz\ *n* : an act of revising : REVISION

Revised Standard Version *n* : a revision of the American Standard Version of the Bible published in 1946 and 1952

Revised Version *n* : a British revision of the Authorized Version of the Bible published in 1881 and 1885

re·vi·sion \ri-'vizh-ən\ *n* **1** : an act of revising (as an essay) **2** : a revised version — **re·vi·sion·ary** \-'vizh-ə-,ner-ē\ *adj*

re·vi·tal·ize \(')rē-'vīt-ᵊl-,īz\ *vb* **-ized; -iz·ing** : to give new life or vigor to — **re·vi·tal·i·za·tion** \(,)rē-,vīt-ᵊl-ə-'zā-shən\ *n*

re·viv·al \ri-'vī-vəl\ *n* **1** : a reviving of interest (as in art, literature, or religion) **2** : a new presentation of a play or movie **3** : a new growth or increase ⟨a *revival* of business⟩ **4** : a meeting or series of meetings conducted by a preacher to arouse religious emotions or to make converts

re·viv·al·ism \ri-'vī-və-,liz-əm\ *n* : the spirit or methods found at religious revivals

re·viv·al·ist \ri-'vīv-(ə-)ləst\ *n* : one who conducts revivals

re·vive \ri-'vīv\ *vb* **re·vived; re·viv·ing** **1** : to bring back or come back to life, consciousness, or activity : make or become fresh or strong again **2** : to bring back into use ⟨trying to *revive* an old custom⟩ — **re·viv·er** *n*

re·vo·ca·ble \'rev-ə-kə-bəl\ *adj* : capable of being revoked

re·vo·ca·tion \,rev-ə-'kā-shən\ *n* : an act or instance of revoking

re·voke \ri-'vōk\ *vb* **re·voked; re·vok·ing** : to put an end to (as a law, order, or privilege) by taking away or canceling [Middle English *revoken* "to take back, withdraw", from early French *revoquer* (same meaning), from Latin *revocare* "to call back", from *re-* "back, again" and *vocare* "to call" — related to ADVOCATE, PROVOKE, VOCATION] — **re·vok·er** *n*

¹re·volt \ri-'vōlt\ *vb* **1** : to rise up against the authority of a ruler or government **2** : to feel or cause to feel disgust or shock — **re·volt·er** *n*

²revolt *n* **1** : an act or instance of revolting **2** : an open and often violent rising up against authority

re·volt·ing *adj* : very offensive : DISGUSTING — **re·volt·ing·ly** *adv*

rev·o·lu·tion \,rev-ə-'lü-shən\ *n* **1 a** : the action by a heavenly body of going round in an orbit **b** : the time taken to complete one orbit **2** : completion of a course (as of years) : CYCLE **3 a** : the action or motion of revolving : a turning round a center or axis : ROTATION **b** : a single complete turn (as of a wheel or a phonograph record) **4 a** : a sudden, extreme, or complete change **b** : a basic change in government; *esp* : the overthrow of one government and the substitution of another by the governed **syn** see REBELLION

rev·o·lu·tion·ary \,rev-ə-'lü-shə-,ner-ē\ *adj* **1 a** : of, relating to, or involving a revolution ⟨*revolutionary* war⟩ **b** : favoring revolution **c** : ¹RADICAL 2a, EXTREMIST **2** *cap* : of or relating to the American Revolution — **revolutionary** *n*

rev·o·lu·tion·ist \,rev-ə-'lü-sh(ə-)nəst\ *n* **1** : a person who takes part in a revolution **2** : a person who believes in revolution as a means of bringing about change — **revolutionist** *adj*

rev·o·lu·tion·ize \,rev-ə-'lü-shə-,nīz\ *vb* **-ized; -iz·ing** **1** : to overthrow the established government of **2** : to cause a person to become a revolutionist **3** : to change greatly or completely ⟨an invention that *revolutionized* the industry⟩ — **rev·o·lu·tion·iz·er** *n*

re·volve \ri-'välv, -'vȯlv\ *vb* **re·volved; re·volv·ing** **1** : to think over carefully **2 a** : to move in an orbit **b** : to turn on or as if on an axis : ROTATE **3** : RECUR 3 **4** : to have as a main point ⟨the argument *revolved* around wages⟩ [Middle English *revolven* "to turn over in the mind, cause to go around (on an axis)", from Latin *revolvere* "to roll back, cause to return", from *re-* "back, again" and *volvere* "to roll" — related to VOLUME; see *Word History* at VOLUME] — **re·volv·able** \-'väl-və-bəl, -'vȯl-\ *adj*

re·volv·er \ri-'väl-vər, -'vȯl-\ *n* : a handgun having a revolving cylinder holding several bullets all of which may be shot without loading again

re·volv·ing *adj* : likely to revolve or recur

revolving credit *n* : credit which may be used repeatedly up to a certain amount after partial or total repayments have been made

revolver

re·vue \ri-'vyü\ *n* : a theatrical entertainment consisting usually of brief and often funny sketches and songs

re·vul·sion \ri-'vəl-shən\ *n* **1** : a strong pulling or drawing away : WITHDRAWAL **2 a** : a sudden or strong reaction or change **b** : a sense of complete dislike — **re·vul·sive** \-'vəl-siv\ *adj*

revved *past and past participle of* REV

revving *present participle of* REV

re·wake \(')rē-'wāk\ *vb* **-waked** *or* **-woke** \-'wōk\; **-waked** *or* **-wo·ken** \-'wō-kən\ *or* **-woke; -wak·ing** : to waken again

¹re·ward \ri-'wȯrd\ *vb* : to give a reward to or for — **re·ward·er** *n*

²reward *n* **1** : something (as money) given or offered in return for a service (as the return of something lost) **2** : a stimulus that is given to an organism after a correct or desired way of behaving and that makes the behavior more probable in the future

re·ward·ing *adj* : giving satisfaction ⟨a *rewarding* experience⟩

re·word \(')rē-'wərd\ *vb* : to state in different words

re·work \(')rē-'wərk\ *vb* : to work again or anew: as **a** : ¹REVISE 2, REWRITE **b** : to reprocess (as used material) for further use

¹re·write \(')rē-'rīt\ *vb* **-wrote** \-'rōt\; **-writ·ten** \-'rit-ən\; **-writ·ing** \-'rīt-ing\ : to write over again : REVISE — **re·writ·er** \-'rīt-ər\ *n*

²re·write \'rē-,rīt\ *n* : something rewritten

rey·nard \'rān-ərd, 'ren-\ *n, often cap* : ¹FOX 1a [derived from *Renart, Renard,* the name of a fox who was the hero of an early French epic poem *Roman de Renart*]

re·zone \(')rē-'zōn\ *vb* : to alter the zoning of ⟨*rezoned* the neighborhood for business⟩

rhap·so·dize \'rap-sə-,dīz\ *vb* **-dized; -diz·ing** : to speak or write with great praise

rhap·so·dy \'rap-səd-ē\ *n, pl* **-dies** **1** : a written or spoken expression of great praise or delight **2** : a musical composition of irregular form — **rhap·sod·ic** \rap-'säd-ik\ *also* **rhap·sod·i·cal** \-i-kəl\ *adj* — **rhap·sod·i·cal·ly** \-i-k(ə-)lē\ *adv*

rhea \'rē-ə\ *n* : any of several large three-toed South American birds that cannot fly and are smaller than the related African ostrich

rhe·ni·um \'rē-nē-əm\ *n* : a rare heavy metallic element that is chemically similar to manganese and is obtained either as a powder or as a hard silver-white metal — see ELEMENT table

rheo·stat \'rē-ə-,stat\ *n* : a resistor for regulating an electric current by the use of variable resistances — **rheo·stat·ic** \,rē-ə-'stat-ik\ *adj*

rhe·sus monkey \'rē-səs-\ *n* : a pale brown Asian monkey frequently used in medical research

rhea

rhet·o·ric \'ret-ə-rik\ *n* **1** : the art of speaking or writing effectively **2** : the study or use of the principles and rules of composition **3 a** : skill in the effective use of speech **b** : language that is not honest, sincere, or meaningful — **rhet·o·ri·cian** \,ret-ə-'rish-ən\ *n*

rhe·tor·i·cal \ri-'tȯr-i-kəl, -'tär-\ *adj* **1** : of, relating to, or dealing with rhetoric ⟨*rhetorical* studies⟩ **2** : used only for a colorful effect and not expected to be answered ⟨a *rhetorical* question⟩ — **rhe·tor·i·cal·ly** \-k(ə-)lē\ *adv*

rheum \'rüm\ *n* **1** : a watery discharge from the mucous

\ə\ **abut**	\au̇\ **out**	\i\ **tip**	\o̧\ **saw**	\u̇\ **foot**
\ər\ **further**	\ch\ **chin**	\ī\ **life**	\o̧i\ **coin**	\y\ **yet**
\a\ **mat**	\e\ **pet**	\j\ **job**	\th\ **thin**	\yü\ **few**
\ā\ **take**	\ē\ **easy**	\ŋ\ **sing**	\th\ **this**	\yu̇\ **cure**
\ä\ **cot, cart**	\g\ **go**	\ō\ **bone**	\ü\ **food**	\zh\ **vision**

membranes especially of the eyes or nose   **2** : a condition (as a cold) marked by a rheum — **rheumy** \'rü-mē\ *adj*

rheu·mat·ic \rù-'mat-ik\ *adj* : of, relating to, characteristic of, or suffering from rheumatism — **rheu·mat·i·cal·ly** \-'mat-i-k(ə-)lē\ *adv*

rheumatic fever *n* : a disease especially of young people that is characterized by fever, by inflammation and pain in and around the joints, and by inflammation of the membranes surrounding the heart and the heart valves

rheu·ma·tism \'rü-mə-,tiz-əm\ *n* : any of various conditions marked by stiffness, pain, or swelling in muscles or joints

Rh factor \är-'ach-\ *n* : any of several inherited substances present in the red blood cells that help to classify the blood groups [from *rh*esus monkey, the animal in which the Rh factor was found]

rhine·stone \'rīn-,stōn\ *n* : a colorless imitation diamond of high luster made usually of glass or paste [named after the *Rhine* river in Europe, near where were found the rock crystals that were originally used as substitutes for diamonds]

rhi·no \'rī-nō\ *n, pl* **rhino** *or* **rhinos** : RHINOCEROS

rhi·noc·er·os \rī-'näs-(ə-)rəs\ *n, pl* **-er·os·es** *or* **-eros** : any of various large plant-eating mammals of Africa and Asia that have a thick skin, three toes on each foot, and one or two heavy upright horns on the snout

rhinoceros

Word History One of the largest animals found on land today is the thick-skinned rhinoceros. Another of the animal's characteristics, besides large size, is found on its snout. All rhinoceroses have at least one horn, and some have two horns. The English name for this animal with a horn or horns on its snout was borrowed from Latin *rhinoceros*. The Latin name, in turn, came from the Greek word *rhinokerōs*, which literally means "horned nose". This word is made up of the Greek word *rhin-, rhis,* meaning "nose" and the word *keras,* meaning "horn". [Middle English *rinoceros* "rhinoceros", from Latin *rhinocerot-, rhinoceros* (same meaning), from Greek *rhinokerōt-, rhínokerōs,* literally "horned nose", from *rhin-, rhis* "nose" and *keras* "horn"]

rhi·zoid \'rī-,zòid\ *n* : a structure (as a hypha of a fungus) that functions like a root

rhi·zome \'rī-,zōm\ *n* : a fleshy, rootlike, and usually horizontal underground plant stem that produces shoots above and roots below

Rh–negative \,är-,ach-\ *adj* : lacking Rh factors in the red blood cells

rho \'rō\ *n* : the 17th letter of the Greek alphabet — P or ρ

Rhode Is·land Red \rō-,dī-lən(d)-\ *n* : any of an American breed of domestic chickens with rich brownish red feathers

rho·di·um \'rōd-ē-əm\ *n* : a white hard metallic element that is resistant to attack by acids, occurs in platinum ores, and is used in metals with platinum — see ELEMENT table

rho·do·den·dron \,rōd-ə-'den-drən\ *n* : any of a genus of trees and shrubs usually of northern regions that often have leathery evergreen leaves and showy clusters of yellow, white, pink, red, or purple flowers [from scientific Latin *rhododendron* "rhododendron", derived from Greek *rhodon* "rose" and Greek *dendron* "tree"]

rhom·bic \'räm-bik\ *adj* **1** : having the form of a rhombus   **2** : of, relating to, or being a form of crystal having three unequal axes at right angles to each other

rhom·boid \'räm-,bòid\ *n* : a parallelogram in which the angles are not right angles and adjacent sides are unequal

rhom·bus \'räm-bəs\ *n, pl* **rhom·bus·es** *or* **rhom·bi** \-,bī, -,bē\ : a parallelogram having all four sides equal

Rh–pos·i·tive \,är-,ach-'päz-ət-iv, -'päz-tiv\ *adj* : containing Rh factors in the red blood cells

rhu·barb \'rü-,bärb\ *n* **1** : a plant related to buckwheat and having large green leaves and thick juicy pink or red stems that are used for food   **2** : a heated dispute or argument

rhumba *variant of* RUMBA

¹rhyme *or* **rime** \'rīm\ *n* **1 a** : close similarity in the final sounds of two or more words or lines of verse   **b** : one of two or more words having this similarity in sound   **2 a** : rhyming verse·   **b** : a composition in verse that rhymes

²rhyme *or* **rime** *vb* **rhymed** *or* **rimed; rhym·ing** *or* **rim·ing 1 a** : to make rhymes : put into rhyme   **b** : to compose rhyming verse   **2** : to end in syllables that rhyme ⟨find the two lines that *rhyme*⟩   **3** : to cause to rhyme : use as rhyme ⟨*rhymed* "moon" with "June"⟩ — **rhym·er** *or* **rim·er** *n*

rhyme scheme *n* : the arrangement of rhymes in a stanza or a poem

rhy·o·lite \'rī-ə-,līt\ *n* : a very acid volcanic rock that is the lava form of granite — **rhy·o·lit·ic** \,rī-ə-'lit-ik\ *adj*

rhythm \'rith-əm\ *n* **1** : a flow of rising and falling sounds in language that is produced in verse by a regular repeating of stressed and unstressed syllables   **2** : a flow of sound in music having regular accented beats   **3** : a particular or typical pattern of rhythm   **4** : a movement or activity in which some action repeats regularly ⟨the *rhythm* of breathing⟩

rhythm and blues *n* : popular music with elements of blues and Negro folk music

rhyth·mic \'rith-mik\ *or* **rhyth·mi·cal** \-mi-kəl\ *adj* : of, relating to, or having rhythm — **rhyth·mi·cal·ly** \-mi-k(ə-)lē\ *adv*

rhythm method *n* : a method of birth control in which a couple does not have sexual intercourse during the time when ovulation is most likely to occur

ri·a·ta \rē-'at-ə, -'ät-\ *n* : LARIAT

¹rib \'rib\ *n* **1 a** : one of the series of curved bones of the chest of most vertebrates that are joined to the spinal column in pairs and help to support the body wall and protect the organs inside   **b** : a cut of meat including a rib   **2** : something (as a piece of wire supporting the fabric of an umbrella) resembling a rib   **3 a** : a major vein of an insect's wing or of a leaf   **b** : one of the parallel ridges in a knitted or woven fabric

²rib *vb* **ribbed; rib·bing 1** : to furnish or enclose with ribs   **2** : to form ribs in a fabric in knitting or weaving — **rib·ber** *n*

rib 1a

³rib *vb* **ribbed; rib·bing** : to make jokes about : KID — **rib·ber** *n*

rib·ald \'rib-əld\ *adj* : marked by or using coarse or indecent language or humor — **rib·ald·ry** \-əl-drē\ *n*

rib·bon \'rib-ən\ *n* **1 a** : a narrow usually closely woven strip of colorful fabric (as silk) used especially for decoration   **b** : a ribbon worn as a military decoration or as a symbol of a medal   **c** : a ribbon given as an award in a competition   **2 a** : a long narrow strip like a ribbon   **b** : a strip of inked fabric (as in a typewriter)   **3** : TATTER 1, SHRED — usually used in pl. ⟨torn to *ribbons*⟩ — **rib·bon·like** \-,līk\ *adj*

rib cage *n* : the bony enclosing wall of the chest consisting chiefly of the ribs and their connecting parts

ri·bo·fla·vin \,rī-bə-'flā-vən\ *n* : a substance of the vitamin B complex that helps growth and is found both free (as in milk) and combined with other substances (as in liver) — called also VITAMIN B₂

ri·bo·nu·cle·ic acid \,rī-bō-n(y)ù-,klē-ik-, -,klā-\ *n* : RNA

ri·bose \'rī-,bōs\ *n* : a sugar that has five carbon atoms and five oxygen atoms in each molecule and is part of RNA —

compare DEOXYRIBOSE

ri·bo·som·al RNA \,rī-bə-'sō-məl-\ *n* : an RNA that is one of the structural elements of ribosomes — called also *rRNA*

ri·bo·some \'rī-bə-,sōm\ *n* : one of numerous small RNA-containing particles in a cell that are sites of protein synthesis

rice \'rīs\ *n* **1** : an annual grass widely grown in warm wet areas for its seed that is used for food and for its by-products **2** : the seed or grain of rice

rice paper *n* : a thin papery material made from a small Asian tree or shrub of the ginseng family

ric·er \'rī-sər\ *n* : a kitchen utensil in which soft foods (as boiled potatoes) are pressed through a strainer

rich \'rich\ *adj* **1** : having great wealth : WEALTHY **2 a** : having high value ⟨a *rich* harvest⟩ **b** : COSTLY 1, VALUABLE ⟨*rich* robes⟩ **3 a** : having a large supply of some usually desirable quality or thing ⟨a land *rich* in resources⟩ **b** : of pleasingly strong odor ⟨*rich* perfumes⟩ **c** : very productive : FRUITFUL, FERTILE ⟨a *rich* mine⟩ ⟨*rich* soils⟩ **d** : containing much seasoning, fat, or sugar ⟨*rich* food⟩ **e** : high in fuel content ⟨a *rich* mixture⟩ **4 a** : vivid and deep in color ⟨*rich* red⟩ **b** : full and mellow in tone and quality ⟨*rich* voice⟩ **5** : very amusing ⟨a play with many *rich* lines⟩ — **rich·ness** *n*

Rich·ard Roe \,rich-ər-'drō\ *n* : a party to legal proceedings whose true name is unknown

rich·en \'rich-ən\ *vb* **rich·ened; rich·en·ing** \-(ə-)niŋ\ : to make rich or richer

rich·es \'rich-əz\ *n pl* : things that make one rich : WEALTH [Middle English *richesse*, originally not a plural but a singular noun meaning "richness"]

rich·ly \'rich-lē\ *adv* **1** : in a rich manner ⟨*richly* dressed⟩ **2** : in full measure : AMPLY ⟨*richly* deserved⟩

Rich·ter scale \'rik-tər-\ *n* : a scale for expressing the strength of an earthquake

rick \'rik\ *n* : a stack or pile (as of hay or grain) in the open air

rick·ets \'rik-əts\ *n* : a disease of young people and animals in which the bones are soft and deformed due to an inability of the body to use calcium and phosphorus because of a lack of vitamin D

rick·ett·sia \rik-'et-sē-ə\ *n, pl* **-si·as** *or* **-si·ae** \-sē-,ē, -sē-,ī\ : any of various microorganisms that are closely related to bacteria, live in cells, and include several that cause serious diseases (as typhus) — **rick·ett·si·al** \-sē-əl\ *adj*

rick·ety \'rik-ət-ē\ *adj* **1** : feeble in the joints **2** : UNSOUND 3, SHAKY ⟨a *rickety* wagon⟩

rick·ey \'rik-ē\ *n, pl* **rickeys** : a soft drink flavored with lime

rick·rack *or* **ric·rac** \'rik-,rak\ *n* : a flat braid woven to form zigzags and used especially as trimming on clothing

rick·sha *or* **rick·shaw** \'rik-,shò\ *n* : a small hooded carriage with two wheels that is pulled by one person and was used originally in Japan

¹ric·o·chet \'rik-ə-,shā, *British also* -,shet\ *n* **1** : a bouncing off at an angle (as of a bullet off a flat surface) **2** : an object that ricochets

r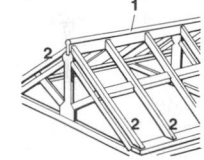icksha

²ricochet *vb* **-cheted** \-,shād\ *or* **-chet·ted** \-,shet-əd\; **-chet·ing** \-,shā-iŋ\ *or* **-chet·ting** \-,shet-iŋ\ : to bounce off at an angle

ri·cot·ta \ri-'kät-ə\ *n* : a white cheese that resembles cottage cheese and originally came from Italy

rid \'rid\ *vb* **rid** *also* **rid·ded; rid·ding** : to make free : RELIEVE ⟨*rid* yourself of worries⟩ ⟨get *rid* of that junk⟩

rid·able *or* **ride·able** \'rīd-ə-bəl\ *adj* : fit for riding on or over ⟨a *ridable* horse⟩ ⟨a *ridable* road⟩

rid·dance \'rid-ᵊn(t)s\ *n* : the act of ridding : the state of being rid of

¹rid·dle \'rid-ᵊl\ *n* **1** : a baffling, misleading, or puzzling question presented as a problem to be solved or guessed : CONUNDRUM **2** : something or someone difficult to understand [Old English *rǣdelse* "opinion, riddle"]

²riddle *vb* **rid·dled; rid·dling** \'rid-liŋ, -ᵊl-iŋ\ **1** : to find the answer for a riddle or mystery **2** : to create a riddle for : MYSTIFY **3** : to speak in riddles — **rid·dler** \-lər, -ᵊl-ər\ *n*

³riddle *n* : a coarse sieve [Old English *hriddel* "a coarse sieve"]

⁴riddle *vb* **rid·dled; rid·dling** \'rid-liŋ, -ᵊl-iŋ\ **1** : to sift or separate with or as if with a riddle **2 a** : to pierce with many holes ⟨*riddled* the car with bullets⟩ **b** : to spread through ⟨a book *riddled* with mistakes⟩

¹ride \'rīd\ *vb* **rode** \'rōd\; **rid·den** \'rid-ᵊn\; **rid·ing** \'rīd-iŋ\ **1 a** : to go or be carried along on an animal's back or on or in a vehicle (as a boat, automobile, or airplane) **b** : to sit on and control so as to be carried along ⟨*ride* a bicycle⟩ **2 a** : to be supported and usually carried along by ⟨a surfboard *rides* the waves⟩ **b** : to float at anchor **c** : to remain afloat through : SURVIVE ⟨*ride* out a storm⟩ **3 a** : ¹CARRY 1 ⟨*rode* the child on my back⟩ **b** : to travel over a surface ⟨the car *rides* well⟩ **4 a** : ¹TEASE 2a **b** : OPPRESS 1 ⟨*ridden* by fears⟩ **5** : to depend on something

²ride *n* **1** : an act of riding; *esp* : a trip on horseback or by vehicle ⟨a *ride* in the country⟩ **2** : a mechanical device (as at an amusement park) for riding on **3** : a means of transportation ⟨needs a *ride* to work⟩

rid·er \'rīd-ər\ *n* **1** : one that rides **2 a** : an addition to a document **b** : an additional clause to a legislative bill **3** : something that lies over or moves along on another piece ⟨the scale had *riders* to measure weight⟩ — **rid·er·less** \-ləs\ *adj*

¹ridge \'rij\ *n* : a raised or elevated part or area: as **a** : a range of hills or mountains **b** : the line made where two sloping surfaces come together ⟨the *ridge* of a roof⟩ — **ridged** \'rijd\ *adj*

²ridge *vb* **ridged; ridg·ing** : to form into or extend in ridges

ridge·pole \'rij-,pōl\ *n* **1** : the horizontal pole at the top of a tent **2** : the highest horizontal timber in a sloping roof to which the upper ends of the rafters are fastened

ridgy \'rij-ē\ *adj* : having or rising in ridges

¹rid·i·cule \'rid-ə-,kyü(ə)l\ *n* : the act of making fun of someone or something : DERISION

ridgepole 2: *1* ridgepole, *2* rafter

²ridicule *vb* **-culed; -cul·ing** : to make fun of : DERIDE — **rid·i·cul·er** *n*

ri·dic·u·lous \rə-'dik-yə-ləs\ *adj* : causing or deserving ridicule : ABSURD, PREPOSTEROUS — **ri·dic·u·lous·ly** *adv* — **ri·dic·u·lous·ness** *n*

rid·ing \'rīd-iŋ\ *adj* **1** : used for or when riding **2** : operated by a rider

rife \'rīf\ *adj* **1** : WIDESPREAD 1, PREVALENT ⟨lands where famine is *rife*⟩ **2** : supplied in large amounts ⟨the town was *rife* with rumors⟩ — **rife·ly** *adv*

¹rif·fle \'rif-əl\ *vb* **rif·fled; rif·fling** \'rif-(ə-)liŋ\ **1** : to form, flow over, or move in riffles **2** : to ruffle slightly : RIPPLE **3 a** : to flip or leaf through in a hurry **b** : to shuffle playing cards by separating the deck into two parts and sliding the thumbs along the edges so that the cards are mixed

²riffle *n* **1 a** : a shallow extending across a stream bed and causing broken water **b** : a stretch of water flowing over a riffle **2** : a small wave or succession of small waves : RIPPLE **3** : the act or process of shuffling (as cards)

riff•raff \'rif-ˌraf\ *n* **1** : RABBLE 2 **2** : RUBBISH — **riffraff** *adj*

¹ri•fle \'rī-fəl\ *vb* **ri•fled; ri•fling** \-f(ə)liŋ\ **1** : to search through fast and roughly especially in order to steal ⟨*rifled* the coat pockets for loose change⟩ **2** : ¹STEAL 2a — **ri•fler** \-f(ə-)lər\ *n*

> **Word History** The basic meaning of the early French verb *rifler* was "to scratch or file", but it also had a second sense, "to rob or carry away, especially in a military action". In those days, soldiers were paid poorly, if at all. They were expected to steal anything of value they could carry away from a conquered people or even a neutral country. To pillage or plunder, as it was called, was a normal part of war everywhere, so the word *rifle* came into English with that meaning. *Rifle* is still used today to mean "to plunder or loot". Hundreds of years later, the French used the same verb *rifler* to describe the process of cutting grooves in a spiral inside the barrels of firearms. When a lead ball having the same diameter as the inside of these grooves was forced by an explosion of gunpowder along the barrel, the ball would squeeze into the grooves and turn. When it came out the muzzle, it would continue to turn and be more stable in flight than a ball from a barrel that was smooth inside. This made the *rifle,* as the firearm came to be called, more accurate. The English also borrowed this sense, "to cut spiral grooves in a barrel", for the verb *rifle.* [Middle English *riflen* "to steal or carry away by force", from early French *rifler* "to scratch or file, plunder"; of Germanic origin]

²rifle *vb* **ri•fled; ri•fling** \-f(ə-)liŋ\ : to cut spiral grooves on the inside of a barrel of ⟨*rifled* arms⟩ [from French *rifler* "to cut spiral grooves in the inside of the barrel of a weapon", from early French *rifler* "to scratch or file, plunder" — related to ¹RIFLE]

³rifle *n* **1 a** : a weapon with a long rifled barrel that is designed to be fired from the shoulder **b** : a rifled artillery piece **2** *pl* : a body of soldiers armed with rifles

⁴rifle *vb* **ri•fled; ri•fling** \-f(ə-)liŋ\ : to hit or throw a ball with great force

ri•fle•man \'rī-fəl-mən\ *n* **1** : a soldier armed with a rifle **2** : a person skilled in shooting with a rifle

ri•fle•ry \'rī-fəl-rē\ *n* **1** : rifle fire **2** : rifle shooting especially at targets

ri•fling \'rī-f(ə-)liŋ\ *n* **1** : the act or process of making spiral grooves **2** : a system of spiral grooves inside the barrel of a gun causing a bullet when fired to spin about its longer axis

¹rift \'rift\ *n* **1 a** : an opening made by splitting or separation : CLEFT **b** : a normal geological fault **2** : a break in friendly relations : BREACH

²rift *vb* : ²CLEAVE, SPLIT

rift valley *n* : a long valley formed by the sinking of the earth's crust between two parallel or nearly parallel faults or groups of faults

¹rig \'rig\ *vb* **rigged; rig•ging** **1** : to fit out (as a ship) with rigging **2** : CLOTHE 1a, DRESS — usually used with *out* **3 a** : to furnish with gear : EQUIP **b** : to set up usually for temporary use : CONSTRUCT ⟨*rig* up a temporary shelter⟩ [Middle English *riggen* "to fit out a ship with rigging"] — **rig•ger** *n*

²rig *n* **1** : the shape, number, and arrangement of sails and masts of a ship that sets it apart from ships of other types ⟨the *rig* of a schooner⟩ **2** : EQUIPAGE 2; *esp* : a carriage with its horse **3** : CLOTHING 1 **4** : tackle, equipment, or machinery fitted for a certain purpose ⟨an oil-drilling *rig*⟩

³rig *vb* **rigged; rig•ging** : to fix in advance so that the outcome will be known ⟨*rig* an election⟩ [from earlier *rig* (noun) "a cheating trick", of unknown origin]

Ri•gel \'rī-jəl, -gəl\ *n* : a bright star in the left foot of the Orion star group

rig•ging \'rig-iŋ, -ən\ *n* **1** : the ropes and chains used aboard a ship especially in working sail and supporting masts and spars **2** : equipment for supporting and working something (as theater scenery)

¹right \'rīt\ *adj* **1** : RIGHTEOUS 1, UPRIGHT **2** : following what is just, good, or proper ⟨*right* conduct⟩ **3** : agreeing with a standard, facts, or truth ⟨*right* answer⟩ **4** : ²APPROPRIATE, SUITABLE ⟨the *right* person for the job⟩ ⟨*right* tool⟩ **5** : STRAIGHT 1 ⟨a *right* line⟩ **6** : GENUINE 1, REAL **7 a** : of, relating to, situated on, or being the side of the body which is away from the heart and on which the hand is stronger and more skilled in most people ⟨*right* leg⟩ **b** : located nearer to the right side of the body ⟨the *right* arm of the chair⟩ **8** : having the line drawn from the top or the middle of the top to the middle of the base perpendicular to the base ⟨*right* cone⟩ **9** : being or meant to be the side on top, in front, or on the outside ⟨landed *right* side up⟩ ⟨*right* side out⟩ **10** : acting or judging in a way that agrees with truth or fact ⟨time proved us *right*⟩ **11** : healthy in mind or body ⟨did not feel *right*⟩ **12** : most worth having or seeking ⟨the *right* neighborhoods⟩ ⟨the *right* people⟩ — **right•ness** *n*

²right *n* **1** : the ideal of what is just and good **2** : something to which one has a just claim — often used in pl. ⟨the *right* to freedom of religion⟩ ⟨the movie *rights* to a story⟩ **3** : something that one may properly claim as due **4** : the cause of truth or justice ⟨fighting for *right*⟩ **5** : the right side or the part on the right side **6** : the quality or state of being factually correct ⟨there's both *right* and wrong in that argument⟩ **7** : the members of a European legislative body sitting to the right of the officer in charge and holding more conservative political views than other members **8** *cap* : political conservatives — **by rights** : with reason or justice : PROPERLY — **to rights** : into proper order ⟨put your room *to rights*⟩

³right *adv* **1** : according to right ⟨live *right*⟩ **2** : in the exact location or position : PRECISELY ⟨*right* where you left it⟩ **3** : in a suitable, proper, or desired manner ⟨hold your pen *right*⟩ **4** : in a direct line or course ⟨go *right* home⟩ **5** : according to fact or truth : TRULY ⟨guess *right*⟩ ⟨heard *right*⟩ **6** : all the way ⟨windows *right* to the floor⟩ **7** : without delay : IMMEDIATELY ⟨*right* at 2 o'clock⟩ **8** : to a great degree : VERY ⟨a *right* pleasant day⟩

⁴right *vb* **1** : to make right (something wrong or unjust) **2 a** : to adjust or restore to the proper state or condition **b** : to bring or restore to an upright position **3** : to become upright — **right•er** *n*

right angle *n* : an angle whose measure is 90° : an angle whose sides are perpendicular to each other — **right–an•gled** \'rīt-'aŋ-gəld\ *or* **right–an•gle** \-gəl\ *adj*

right away *adv* : without delay : IMMEDIATELY

right circular cone *n* : CONE 2a

right circular cylinder *n* : a cylinder with bases that are circles and with the line joining the two centers of the bases perpendicular to the planes of the two bases

right angle

righ•teous \'rī-chəs\ *adj* **1** : acting rightly : UPRIGHT **2 a** : according to what is right ⟨*righteous* actions⟩ **b**

: caused by an insult to one's sense of what is right ⟨*righteous* anger⟩ — **righ·teous·ly** *adv* — **righ·teous·ness** *n*

right field *n* **1** : the part of the baseball outfield to the right looking out from the home plate **2** : the position of the player defending right field — **right fielder** *n*

right·ful \'rīt-fəl\ *adj* **1** : ¹JUST 2a **2** : having a just or legal claim : LEGITIMATE ⟨the *rightful* owner⟩ — **right·ful·ly** \-fə-lē\ *adv* — **right·ful·ness** *n*

right–hand \'rīt-,hand\ *adj* **1** : located on the right **2** : RIGHT-HANDED 1 **3** : relied on most of all ⟨*right-hand* man⟩

right–hand·ed \'rīt-'han-dəd\ *adj* **1** : using the right hand more easily than the left **2** : done or made with or for the right hand **3** : having or moving with a clockwise turn or twist — **right–hand·ed·ly** *or* **right–hand·ed** *adv* — **right–hand·ed·ness** *n* — **right–hand·er** \-'han-dər\ *n*

right·ist \'rīt-əst\ *n, often cap* : a person with conservative political views — **rightist** *adj, often cap*

right·ly \'rīt-lē\ *adv* **1** : in agreement with right conduct **2** : in the right or proper manner **3** : in agreement with truth or fact

right–mind·ed \'rīt-'mīn-dəd\ *adj* : likely to do what is right

right now *adv* **1** : RIGHT AWAY **2** : at the present time

right–of–way \,rīt-ə(v)-'wā\ *n* **1** : a legal right to pass over another person's land **2** : the area over which a right-of-way exists **3** : the right of certain traffic to go ahead of other traffic **4** : PRIORITY 1 ⟨gave the bill the *right-of-way* in the senate⟩

right on *interj* — used to show agreement or to give encouragement

right prism *n* : a prism all of whose lateral faces are rectangles

right triangle *n* : a triangle having a right angle

right·ward \'rīt-wərd\ *also* **right·wards** \-wərdz\ *adv* : toward or on the right — **rightward** *adj*

rig·id \'rij-əd\ *adj* **1** : not flexible : STIFF, HARD **2 a** : very fixed in one's opinion or habits : UNYIELDING **b** : carefully observed : SCRUPULOUS ⟨follows a *rigid* exercise program⟩ **3** : exact and accurate in procedure [from early French *rigide* or Latin *rigidus,* both meaning "rigid", from Latin *rigēre* "to be stiff" — related to RIGOR MORTIS] — **ri·gid·i·ty** \rə-'jid-ət-ē\ *n* — **rig·id·ly** \'rij-əd-lē\ *adv* — **rig·id·ness** *n*

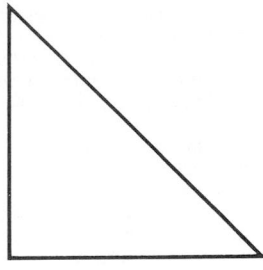

right triangle

rig·ma·role \'rig-(ə-)mə-,rōl\ *n* **1** : confused or meaningless talk : NONSENSE **2** : a complicated and often unnecessary procedure

rig·or \'rig-ər\ *n* **1 a** : the quality of not being flexible or yielding **b** : an act or instance of being strict or harsh **2** : a shuddering caused by a chill **3** : a condition that makes life difficult or uncomfortable; *esp* : extreme cold **4** : strict precision : EXACTNESS ⟨logical *rigor*⟩

rig·or mor·tis \,rig-ər-'mȯrt-əs\ *n* : temporary stiffness of muscles occurring after death [from scientific Latin, literally "stiffness of death", from Latin *rigēre* "to be stiff" — related to RIGID]

rig·or·ous \'rig-(ə-)rəs\ *adj* **1** : very strict **2** : marked by great differences of temperature or climate **3** : very accurate : PRECISE — **rig·or·ous·ly** *adv* — **rig·or·ous·ness** *n*

rile \'rī(ə)l\ *vb* **riled; ril·ing** **1** : to make angry **2** : ROIL 1

rill \'ril\ *n* : a very small brook

¹rim \'rim\ *n* **1 a** : an outer edge especially of something curved **b** : BRINK 1 **2** : the outer part of a wheel joined to the hub usually by spokes — **rim·less** \-ləs\ *adj*

²rim *vb* **rimmed; rim·ming** **1** : to provide with a rim : serve as a rim for : BORDER **2** : to run around the rim of ⟨the putt *rimmed* the cup⟩

¹rime \'rīm\ *n* **1** : ¹FROST 2 **2** : CRUST 3a, INCRUSTATION — **rimy** \'rī-mē\ *adj*

²rime *vb* **rimed; rim·ing** : to cover with or as if with rime

³rime, rimer *variant of* RHYME, RHYMER

rim·rock \'rim-,räk\ *n* **1** : the top layer or layers of rock on a plateau that remains as a vertical surface after the land near it is worn away **2** : the edge or surface of a layer of rimrock

rind \'rīnd\ *n* : the bark of a tree; *also* : a usually hard or tough outer layer (as the skin of a fruit)

¹ring \'riŋ\ *n* **1** : a circular band for holding, connecting, hanging, or pulling or for packing or sealing ⟨a key *ring*⟩ ⟨a towel *ring*⟩ **2** : a circular band usually of precious metal worn on the finger **3** : something circular in shape ⟨smoke *rings*⟩ **4** : an often circular space for shows and contests ⟨a circus *ring*⟩ ⟨a boxing *ring*⟩ **5** : ANNUAL RING **6** : a group of persons involved in selfish or dishonest activities ⟨police broke up a *ring* of car thieves⟩ [Old English *hring* "a circular band"] — **ringed** \'riŋd\ *adj* — **ring·like** \'riŋ-,līk\ *adj*

²ring *vb* **ringed; ring·ing** \'riŋ-iŋ\ **1** : to place or form a ring around : ENCIRCLE **2** : to provide with a ring **3** : to throw a ring over (the mark) in a game where curved objects (as horseshoes) are tossed at a mark **4** : to form or take the shape of a ring

³ring *vb* **rang** \'raŋ\; **rung** \'rəŋ\; **ring·ing** \'riŋ-iŋ\ **1** : to make a clear and vibrating sound when struck ⟨church bells *ringing*⟩ **2** : to cause to sound especially by striking ⟨*rang* the bell⟩ **3** : to announce by or as if by ringing ⟨*ring* an alarm⟩ ⟨*ring* in the new year⟩ **4** : to sound loudly ⟨cheers *rang* out⟩ **5 a** : to be filled with echoing sound : RESOUND ⟨the whole hall *rang* with their cheers⟩ **b** : to have the feeling of being filled with a humming sound ⟨his ears were *ringing*⟩ **6** : to be filled with talk or news ⟨the whole town *rang* with news of the victory⟩ **7** : to seem to have some particular quality ⟨her story *rings* true⟩ **8 a** : to call for especially by bell ⟨*ring* for the servants⟩ **b** *chiefly British* : to call on the telephone [Old English *hringan* "to ring"] — **ring a bell** : to sound familiar ⟨yes, that name *rings a bell*⟩

⁴ring *n* **1** : a set of bells **2** : a clear sound made by or as if by vibrating metal **3** : a tone like that of a bell **4** : a continuous or repeating loud noise **5** : something that suggests a certain quality ⟨a story with the *ring* of truth⟩ **6 a** : the act or an instance of ringing **b** : a telephone call

ring·bolt \'riŋ-,bōlt\ *n* : a bolt with a ring through a loop at one end

¹ring·er \'riŋ-ər\ *n* **1** : one that sounds especially by ringing **2 a** : one that enters a competition with a false identity **b** : one that strongly resembles another — often used with *dead* ⟨a dead *ringer* for the senator⟩

²ringer *n* : a quoit or horseshoe that falls right over a peg

ring finger *n* : the third finger of the left hand counting the index finger as one

ring·lead·er \'riŋ-,lēd-ər\ *n* : a leader especially of a group of persons who cause trouble

ring·let \'riŋ-lət\ *n* **1** *archaic* : a small ring or circle **2** : a long curl (as of hair)

ring·mas·ter \'riŋ-,mas-tər\ *n* : one in charge of performances in a ring (as of a circus)

ring–necked \'riŋ-'nekt\ *adj* : having a ring of color around the neck

ring–necked pheasant *n* : any of various Eurasian pheas-

\ə\ **abut**	\au̇\ **out**	\i\ **tip**	\ȯ\ **saw**	\u̇\ **foot**
\ər\ **further**	\ch\ **chin**	\ī\ **life**	\ȯi\ **coin**	\y\ **yet**
\a\ **mat**	\e\ **pet**	\j\ **job**	\th\ **thin**	\yü\ **few**
\ā\ **take**	\ē\ **easy**	\ŋ\ **sing**	\th\ **this**	\yu̇\ **cure**
\ä\ **cot, cart**	\g\ **go**	\ō\ **bone**	\ü\ **food**	\zh\ **vision**

ants with white neck rings that have been widely introduced in temperate regions as game birds

ring·side \'riŋ-ˌsīd\ *n* : the area just outside a ring (as at a prizefight) — **ringside** *adj*

ring stand *n* : a metal stand consisting of a long upright rod attached to a heavy rectangular base used with rings and clamps for supporting laboratory equipment

ring-necked pheasant

ring–tailed \'riŋ-ˈtā(ə)ld\ *adj* : having a tail marked with rings of different colors

ring up *vb* : to add up and record on a cash register

ring·worm \'riŋ-ˌwərm\ *n* : a contagious skin disease caused by fungi and marked by ring-shaped discolored patches

rink \'riŋk\ *n* **1** : a sheet of ice laid out for curling, ice hockey, or ice-skating **2** : an enclosed place for roller-skating

¹rinse \'rin(t)s\ *vb* **rinsed; rins·ing 1 a** : to wash lightly with water ⟨*rinse* out your mouth⟩ ⟨*rinse* the apple before you eat it⟩ **b** : to clean off with clear water the soap left over from washing ⟨*rinse* the dishes⟩ **2** : to treat (hair) with a rinse — **rins·er** *n*

²rinse *n* **1** : an act of rinsing **2 a** : liquid used for rinsing **b** : a solution that temporarily tints hair

¹ri·ot \'rī-ət\ *n* **1** : public violence, disturbance, or disorder **2** : a varied display of color **3** : something or someone very funny

²riot *vb* : to create or take part in a riot — **ri·ot·er** *n*

riot act *n* : a strong scolding or warning — used in the phrase *read the riot act*

ri·ot·ous \'rī-ət-əs\ *adj* **1 a** : of the nature of a riot **b** : taking part in rioting **2** : ABUNDANT — **ri·ot·ous·ly** *adv*

¹rip \'rip\ *vb* **ripped; rip·ping 1** : to tear, cut apart, or open **2** : to slash or slit with or as if with a sharp blade **3** : to go with a rush [probably from a word in Flemish (a Dutch language used in northern Belgium) *rippen* "to strip off roughly"] — **rip·per** *n*

²rip *n* : a torn place : TEAR

³rip *n* : a body of water made rough by the meeting of opposing currents or by passing over a rough bottom

⁴rip *n* : a person who acts wild or gets into trouble [probably a shortened and altered form of *reprobate* (noun)]

rip cord *n* : a cord or wire pulled by a parachute jumper to release a small parachute which lifts the main parachute out of its container

ripe \'rīp\ *adj* **rip·er; rip·est 1** : fully grown and developed ⟨a *ripe* tomato⟩ **2** : having mature knowledge, understanding, or judgment **3** : ¹READY 1 ⟨*ripe* for action⟩ **4** : brought to just the right state — **ripe·ly** *adv* — **ripe·ness** *n*

rip·en \'rī-pən\ *vb* **rip·ened; rip·en·ing** \'rīp-(ə-)niŋ\ : to make or become ripe

rip–off \'rip-ˌȯf\ *n* : an act or an instance of ripping off

rip off \'rip-'ȯf\ *vb* **1** : ROB 1a; *also* : to cheat someone : DEFRAUD **2** : ¹STEAL 2a

ri·poste \ri-'pōst\ *n* **1** : a fencer's quick return thrust **2** : a quick reply or action in return

rip·ping \'rip-iŋ\ *adj* **1** : very good ⟨had a *ripping* time⟩ **2** : very angry ⟨your mother's going to be *ripping*⟩

¹rip·ple \'rip-əl\ *vb* **rip·pled; rip·pling** \-(ə-)liŋ\ **1 a** : to become or cause to become covered with small waves **b** : to flow in small waves **2** : to make a sound like that of water flowing in small waves **3** : to move with a wavy motion

²ripple *n* **1 a** : the disturbing of the surface of water **b** : a

small wave or a mark like a small wave **2** : a sound like that of rippling water ⋅

rip·ply \'rip-lē\ *adj* : having ripples

rip–roar·ing \'rip-'rȯr-iŋ, -'ror-\ *adj* : noisily excited or exciting

rip·saw \'rip-ˌsȯ\ *n* : a saw for cutting wood in the direction of the grain

¹rise \'rīz\ *vb* **rose** \'rōz\; **ris·en** \'riz-ᵉn\; **ris·ing** \'rī-ziŋ\ **1 a** : to get up from lying, kneeling, or sitting **b** : to get up from sleep or from one's bed **2** : to return from death **3** : to take up arms ⟨the people *rose* in rebellion⟩ **4** : to appear above the horizon ⟨sun *rises* at six⟩ **5 a** : to move upward : ASCEND ⟨smoke *rises*⟩ **b** : to extend upward ⟨hill *rises* to a great height⟩ **6** : to swell in size or volume ⟨the river was *rising*⟩ ⟨bread dough *rises*⟩ **7 a** : to become encouraged ⟨their spirits *rose*⟩ **b** : to grow stronger ⟨felt her anger *rising*⟩ **8 a** : to gain a higher rank or position ⟨*rose* to colonel⟩ **b** : to increase in quantity or number ⟨prices were *rising*⟩ **9 a** : ARISE 2b ⟨an ugly rumor had *risen*⟩ **b** : to come into being : ORIGINATE ⟨river *rises* in the hills⟩ **10** : to show oneself equal to a demand or test ⟨*rise* to the occasion⟩

²rise \'rīz\ *n* **1** : an act of rising : a state of being risen **2** : BEGINNING 1, ORIGIN **3** : the distance of one point above another **4** : an increase in amount, number, or volume **5 a** : an upward slope **b** : a spot higher than surrounding ground **6** : an angry reaction

ris·er \'rī-zər\ *n* **1** : one that rises (as from sleep) ⟨an early *riser*⟩ **2** : the upright board between two stair treads

ris·i·ble \'riz-ə-bəl\ *adj* **1** : able to laugh **2** : arousing laughter : FUNNY

¹risk \'risk\ *n* **1** : possibility of loss or injury **2** : someone or something that presents a risk ⟨a bad *risk*⟩ ⟨a good credit *risk*⟩ **syn** see DANGER

²risk *vb* **1** : to expose to danger ⟨*risked* her life⟩ **2** : to take the risk or danger of ⟨*risked* breaking his neck⟩

risky \'ris-kē\ *adj* **risk·i·er; -est** : having or bringing risk : DANGEROUS

ri·tar·dan·do \ri-ˌtär-'dän-dō, ˌrē-\ *adv or adj* : with a gradual slowing of tempo — used as a direction in music — **ritardando** *n*

rite \'rīt\ *n* **1 a** : a fixed form for a ceremony **b** : LITURGY **2** : a ceremonial act or action

¹rit·u·al \'rich(ə-)wəl, 'rich-əl\ *adj* **1** : of or relating to rites or a ritual ⟨a *ritual* dance⟩ **2** : according to religious law or social custom — **rit·u·al·ly** \-ē\ *adv*

²ritual *n* **1** : an established form for a ceremony **2 a** : a system of rites **b** : a ceremonial act or action **c** : a formal and customarily repeated act or series of acts

rit·u·al·ism \'rich-(ə-)wəl-ˌiz-əm, 'rich-əl-\ *n* : the use of ritual — **rit·u·al·is·tic** \ˌrich-(ə-)wəl-'is-tik, ˌrich-əl-\ *adj*

ritzy \'rit-sē\ *adj* **ritz·i·er; -est 1** : very fashionable **2** : STUCK-UP, SNOBBISH [from *Ritz*, name of a group of elegant hotels]

¹ri·val \'rī-vəl\ *n* **1 a** : one of two or more trying to get what only one can have **b** : COMPETITOR **2** : one that equals another : PEER

Word History The English word *rival* can be traced to the Latin word *rivus*, meaning "a stream". From *rivus* came the Latin *rivalis*, which meant "one who uses the same stream as another". Those who must share a stream may argue about who has the right to use the water. Such disputes are common when two people want the same thing. The Latin word *rivalis* in time came to be used for other people who are also likely to fight with each other. It meant "a man in love with the same woman as another man". This sense of *rivalis* came into English as *rival*. [from early French *rival* "rival", from Latin *rivalis* "one using the same stream as another, a rival in love", from *rivalis* (adjective) "of a stream", from *rivus* "stream"]

²rival *adj* : of, relating to, or being a rival

³**rival** *vb* **ri·valed** *or* **ri·valled; ri·val·ing** *or* **ri·val·ling** \ˈrɪv-(ə-)lɪŋ\ **1** : to be in competition with **2** : to be as good as or almost as good as ⟨manufacture linens that *rival* the world's best⟩

ri·val·ry \ˈrɪ-vəl-rē\ *n, pl* **-ries** : the act of rivaling : the state of being a rival : COMPETITION

rive \ˈrɪv\ *vb* **rived** \ˈrɪvd\; **riv·en** \ˈrɪv-ən\ *also* **rived; riv·ing** \ˈrɪ-vɪŋ\ **1** : to tear apart **2** : to become split or cause to split

riv·er \ˈrɪv-ər\ *n* **1** : a natural stream of water larger than a brook or creek **2** : a large stream or flow ⟨the jet stream is a *river* of air⟩ [Middle English *rivere* "river", from early French *rivere* (same meaning), derived from Latin *riparius* "related to or located on the bank of a river", from *ripa* "shore"]

riv·er·bank \ˈrɪv-ər-ˌbaŋk\ *n* : the bank of a river

riv·er·bed \-ˌbed\ *n* : the channel occupied or once occupied by a river

river blindness *n* : a human disease that is caused by a worm related to those causing malaria, is passed on by several biting flies, occurs in Africa and tropical America, and often causes blindness — called also *onchocerciasis*

riv·er·boat \-ˌbōt\ *n* : a boat used (as for carrying passengers or freight) on a river

riv·er·boat·man \-ˌmən\ *n* : an owner of or worker on a riverboat

riv·er·side \-ˌsīd\ *n* : the side or bank of a river

¹**riv·et** \ˈrɪv-ət\ *n* : a metal bolt with a head at one end used for uniting two or more pieces by passing the shank through a hole in each piece and then beating or pressing down the plain end so as to make a second head

²**rivet** *vb* **1** : to fasten with or as if with rivets **2** : to attract and hold (as one's eyes or attention) completely — **riv·et·er** *n*

riv·u·let \ˈrɪv-(y)ə-lət\ *n* : a small stream

RNA \ˌär-ˌen-ˈā\ *n* : any of several nucleic acids found especially in the cytoplasm of cells that have ribose as the five-carbon sugar and are associated with protein synthesis — called also *ribonucleic acid;* compare MESSENGER RNA, RIBOSOMAL RNA, TRANSFER RNA

¹**roach** \ˈrōch\ *n, pl* **roach** *also* **roach·es** : any of various fishes including some sunfishes and shiners

²**roach** *n* **1** : COCKROACH **2** : the butt of a marijuana cigarette

road \ˈrōd\ *n* **1** : ROADSTEAD — often used in pl. **2 a** : an open way for vehicles, persons, and animals **b** : ROADBED 2 **3** : PATH 2b ⟨the *road* to success⟩ **4** : ¹RAILROAD **5** : a series of visits to several places or the travel necessary to get there ⟨the team plays five games on the *road*⟩ ⟨traveled with the *road* company of the play⟩

road·bed \-ˌbed\ *n* **1** : the foundation of a road or railroad **2** : the part of the surface of a road that vehicles travel on

road·block \-ˌbläk\ *n* : a blocking of a road (as by police officers looking for an escaped prisoner or for drunk drivers)

road·house \-ˌhau̇s\ *n* : a nightclub usually outside city limits

road·run·ner \ˈrō-ˌdrən-ər\ *n* : a long-tailed ground-dwelling bird of the southwestern U.S. that usually travels by running — called also *chaparral bird, chaparral cock*

roadrunner

¹**road·side** \ˈrōd-ˌsīd\ *n* : the strip of land along a road : the side of a road

²**roadside** *adj* : located by the side of a road ⟨*roadside* hamburger stand⟩

road·stead \ˈrōd-ˌsted\ *n* : a place less enclosed than a harbor where ships may ride at anchor

road·ster \ˈrōd-stər\ *n* : an automobile with an open body and a folding fabric top that seats two

road test *n* : a test (as of a vehicle or of a person's ability to drive) made on the road

road·way \ˈrōd-ˌwā\ *n* **1 a** : the strip of land over which a road passes **b** : ROAD 2a **2** : the part of a bridge used by vehicles

roam \ˈrōm\ *vb* : to go or go over from place to place without a plan ⟨*roam* the hills⟩ ⟨cattle *roaming* in search of water⟩ **syn** see WANDER — **roam·er** *n*

¹**roan** \ˈrōn\ *adj* : of a dark color (as black, red, or brown) sprinkled with white ⟨a *roan* horse⟩

²**roan** *n* : an animal (as a horse) with a roan coat

¹**roar** \ˈrō(ə)r, ˈrȯ(ə)r\ *vb* **1** : to utter a long full loud sound **2** : to laugh loudly **3** : to say with a roar — **roar·er** \ˈrȯr-ər, ˈrȯr-\ *n*

²**roar** *n* **1 a** : the deep cry of a wild beast **b** : a loud deep cry or shout **2** : a loud confused sound ⟨the *roar* of the crowd⟩

roar·ing \ˈrōr-iŋ, ˈrȯr-\ *adj* : very active or strong ⟨a *roaring* fire⟩ ⟨does a *roaring* business⟩ ⟨a *roaring* headache⟩ ⟨*roaring* inflation⟩

¹**roast** \ˈrōst\ *vb* **1** : to cook with dry heat (as in an oven) **2** : to be or make very hot **3** : to criticize severely in either a serious or joking way

²**roast** *n* **1** : a piece of meat roasted or suitable for roasting **2** : an outing at which food is roasted **3** : severe criticism or kidding

³**roast** *adj* : cooked by roasting ⟨*roast* beef⟩ ⟨*roast* pork⟩

roast·er \ˈrō-stər\ *n* **1** : a device for roasting meat **2** : something (as a young chicken) suitable for roasting

rob \ˈräb\ *vb* **robbed; rob·bing** **1 a** : to take something away from a person or place in secrecy or by force, threat, or trickery **b** : ¹STEAL 2a **2** : to keep from getting something due, expected, or desired — **rob·ber** *n*

robber fly *n* : any of various flies that eat insects and are covered with coarse bristly hairs

rob·bery \ˈräb-(ə-)rē\ *n, pl* **-ber·ies** : the act, practice, or an instance of robbing

¹**robe** \ˈrōb\ *n* **1** : a long loose or flowing garment **2** : a covering or wrap for the lower body

²**robe** *vb* **robed; rob·ing** **1** : to clothe or cover with or as if with a robe **2** : ¹DRESS 2a

rob·in \ˈräb-ən\ *n* **1** : a small European thrush with a yellowish red throat and breast **2** : a large North American thrush with a grayish back, a streaked throat, and a chiefly dull reddish breast

ro·bot \ˈrō-ˌbät, -bət\ *n* **1 a** : a machine that looks and acts like a human being **b** : a capable but unfeeling person **2** : a device that automatically performs tasks that are complicated and often continuously repeated — **ro·bot·ic** *adj*

Word History In 1923 a play by the Czech author Karel Čapek introduced the word *robot* to English. The title of the play, *R.U.R.,* stood for "Rossum's Universal Robots", a fictional company that manufactured robots. These humanlike machines were supposed to perform all the hard, dull, and dangerous work for people, but they finally became resentful and rebelled, killing all humans. Čapek formed the word *robot* for his machines from the Czech *robota,* meaning "forced labor". The play was very popular and its ideas made a strong impression. As a result, the word *robot* came to have several meanings, including "a human being who has become brutal and insensitive or machinelike because

\ə\ abut	\au̇\ out	\i\ tip	\ȯ\ saw	\u̇\ foot
\ər\ further	\ch\ chin	\ī\ life	\ȯi\ coin	\y\ yet
\a\ mat	\e\ pet	\j\ job	\th\ thin	\yü\ few
\ā\ take	\ē\ easy	\ŋ\ sing	\th\ this	\yu̇\ cure
\ä\ cot, cart	\g\ go	\ō\ bone	\ü\ food	\zh\ vision

of overwork and mistreatment". It is used today for machines that may not look human but do perform the kind of dangerous or dull work that Rossum's Universal Robots were supposed to have done. [from Czech *robot* "a machine that looks like a human being and performs dull or dangerous work", from *robota* "forced labor, work"]

ro·bust \rō-'bəst, 'rō-(₁)bəst\ *adj* : being strong and vigorously healthy — **ro·bust·ly** *adv* — **ro·bust·ness** \-'bəs(t)-nəs, -(₁)bəs(t)-\ *n*

roc \'räk\ *n* : a bird of fable so big it was supposed to be able to carry off an elephant

Ro·chelle salt \rō-₁shel-\ *n* : a salt of potassium and sodium that is a laxative

¹rock \'räk\ *vb* **1** : to move back and forth as in a cradle **2 a** : to sway or cause to sway back and forth **b** : to cause to be upset ⟨*rocked* by the news⟩ [Old English *roccian* "to move back and forth as in a cradle"]

²rock *n* **1** : a rocking movement **2** : popular music usually having a fast tempo, strong beat, and much repetition — **rock** *adj*

³rock *n* **1** : a large mass of stone **2 a** : solid mineral deposits **b** : a lump or piece of rock **3** : something like a rock in firmness : SUPPORT [Middle English *rokke* "stone, rock", from an early French dialect word *roque* (same meaning)] — **rock·like** *adj*

rock–and–roll *n* : ²ROCK 2

rock bass *n* **1** : a sunfish found especially in the upper Mississippi valley and Great Lakes region **2** : any of various sea basses (as a striped bass) native to the coastal waters of America

rock bottom *n* : the lowest point or level

rock·bound \'räk-₁baund\ *adj* : surrounded or covered with rocks

rock candy *n* : boiled sugar crystallized on a string

rock crystal *n* : transparent quartz

rock·er \'räk-ər\ *n* **1 a** : a curving piece of wood or metal on which an object (as a cradle) rocks **b** : a structure or device (as a chair) that rocks on rockers **2** : a device that works with a rocking motion **3** : a rock singer, musician, or song — **off one's rocker** : CRAZY 1

¹rock·et \'räk-ət\ *n* **1** : a firework that is driven through the air by the gases produced by a burning substance **2** : a jet engine that operates like a firework rocket but carries its own oxygen for burning the fuel and is therefore able to run without the oxygen of the air **3** : an object (as a missile) that is driven by a rocket [from Italian *rocchetta*, literally "a small stick or rod on which wool is held for spinning", from *rocca* "distaff"; probably so called because of its shape]

²rocket *vb* **1** : to transport by a rocket ⟨*rocket* a satellite into orbit⟩ **2** : to rise swiftly ⟨a singer who *rocketed* to stardom⟩ **3** : to travel rapidly in or as if in a rocket

rock·et·ry \'räk-ə-trē\ *n* : the study of, experimenting with, or use of rockets

rocket ship *n* : a spaceship driven by rockets

rocket sled *n* : a rocket-propelled vehicle that runs usually on a single rail and that is used especially in aviation research

rock garden *n* : a garden laid out among rocks or decorated with rocks

rock hound *n* : a person who collects rocks and minerals as a hobby

rocking chair *n* : a chair mounted on rockers

rocking horse *n* : a toy horse mounted on rockers

rock lobster *n* : SPINY LOBSTER

rock 'n' roll \₁räk-ən-'rōl\ *n*

rocking horse

: ²ROCK 2

rock salt *n* : common salt in large crystals or masses

rock·weed \'räk-₁wēd\ *n* : FUCUS

rock wool *n* : a material resembling wool made by blowing a jet of steam through melted rock and used chiefly for heat and sound insulation

¹rocky \'räk-ē\ *adj* **rock·i·er; -est** : full of or consisting of rocks — **rock·i·ness** *n*

²rocky *adj* **rock·i·er; -est** : weak and confused and unsteady on one's feet — **rock·i·ly** \'räk-ə-lē\ *adv* — **rock·i·ness** \-ē-nəs\ *n*

Rocky Mountain sheep *n* : BIGHORN

Rocky Mountain spotted fever *n* : a serious disease caused by a rickettsia and passed on by the bite of a tick that is characterized by chills, fever, headache, pains in the muscles and joints, and a red to purple rash

ro·co·co \rə-'kō-kō, rō-kə-'kō\ *adj* : of or relating to a style of artistic expression common in the 18th century marked by fancy curved forms and much ornament — **rococo** *n*

rod \'räd\ *n* **1 a** : a straight slender stick or bar **b** : a stick or bundle of twigs used in whipping a person **c** : a light flexible pole with a line and usually a reel attached for fishing **2 a** : a unit of length — see MEASURE table **b** : a square rod **3** : any of the sensory bodies in the retina that are shaped like rods and respond to dim light **4** *slang* : HANDGUN — **rod·less** \-ləs\ *adj* — **rod·like** \-₁līk\ *adj*

rode *past of* RIDE

ro·dent \'rōd-ᵊnt\ *n* : any of an order of fairly small mammals (as mice, squirrels, or beavers) that have sharp front teeth used for gnawing — compare LAGOMORPH [derived from Latin *rodent-, rodens*, a form of *rodere* "to gnaw" — related to ERODE] — **rodent** *adj*

muskrat, an aquatic rodent

ro·den·ti·cide \rō-'dent-ə-₁sīd\ *n* : a chemical substance used to kill rodents

ro·deo \'rōd-ē-₁ō, rə-'dā-ō\ *n, pl* **-de·os 1** : a roundup of cattle **2** : an exhibition featuring cowboy skills (as riding and roping) [from Spanish *rodeo* "a roundup", from *rodear* "to surround", from *rueda* "a wheel"]

roe \'rō\ *n* : the eggs of a fish especially while still bound together in a membrane

roent·gen \'rent-gən, 'rənt-, -jən\ *n* : the international unit of measurement for X rays and gamma rays equal to the amount of radiation that produces in one kilogram of dry air at 0°C and standard atmospheric pressure charged particles having a total charge of .000258 coulomb

roentgen ray *n, often cap 1st R* : X RAY

Ro·ga·tion Day \rō-'gā-shən-\ *n* : one of the days of prayer especially for the harvest observed on the three days before Ascension Day and by Roman Catholics also on April 25

rog·er \'räj-ər\ *interj* — used especially in radio and signaling to say that a message has been received and understood

rogue \'rōg\ *n* **1** : a dishonest or wicked person **2** : a playfully mischievous individual

rogue elephant *n* : a vicious elephant that separates from the herd and roams alone

rogues' gallery *n* : a collection of pictures of persons arrested as criminals

rogu·ish \'rō-gish\ *adj* **1** : of, relating to, or being a rogue **2** : playfully mischievous — **rogu·ish·ly** *adv* — **rogu·ish·ness** *n*

roil \'rȯ(ə)l, *sense 2 is also* 'rī(ə)l\ *vb* **1** : to make cloudy or muddy by stirring up ⟨*roil* the water of a brook⟩ **2** : to rouse the anger of

rois·ter \ˈrȯi-stər\ *vb* **rois·tered; rois·ter·ing** \-st(ə-)riŋ\ : to have a noisy good time — **rois·ter·er** \-stər-ər\ *n*

role *also* **rôle** \ˈrōl\ *n* **1 a** : a character assigned or taken on **b** : a part played by an actor or singer ⟨a starring *role*⟩ **2** : ¹FUNCTION 2a ⟨the *role* of enzymes in digestion⟩ [from French *rôle* "part played by an actor", literally "scroll"; so called because before the use of books, the actor's parts were written on scrolls]

role model *n* : a person whose behavior in a certain role is imitated by others

role–play \ˈrōl-ˌplā, -ˈplā\ *vb* : to act out ⟨*role-play* an interview⟩

¹roll \ˈrōl\ *n* **1 a** : a written document that may be rolled up : SCROLL **b** : an official list of names **2 a** : something or a quantity of something that is rolled up or rounded as if rolled **b** : a small piece of baked bread dough **c** : paper money folded or rolled

²roll *vb* **1** : to move or cause to move by turning over and over on a surface without sliding **2 a** : to put a wrapping around **b** : to form into a ball or roll **3** : to make smooth, even, or firm with or as if with a roller **4 a** : to move on rollers or wheels **b** : to begin or cause to begin operating or moving ⟨*roll* the cameras⟩ ⟨let's get *rolling*⟩ **5** : to sound with a full echoing tone or with a continuous beating sound ⟨*roll* a drum⟩ ⟨thunder *rolled*⟩ **6** : to have an abundant supply ⟨*rolling* in money⟩ **7 a** : to move onward or around as if on a wheel or scroll ⟨the days *roll* by⟩ ⟨lines *rolling* off the screen of a computer⟩ **b** : to rotate on an axis **8** : to flow in a continuous stream ⟨money was *rolling* in⟩ **9** : to move with a side-to-side sway : ROCK ⟨the ship heaved and *rolled*⟩

³roll *n* **1 a** : a sound produced by rapid strokes on a drum **b** : a heavy echoing sound ⟨the *roll* of thunder⟩ **2** : a rolling movement or an action involving such movement

roll bar *n* : an overhead metal bar in an automobile that is designed to protect riders in case the automobile overturns

roll call *n* : the action of calling off a list of names (as for checking attendance); *also* : a time for a roll call

roll·er \ˈrō-lər\ *n* **1 a** : a turning cylinder over or on which something is moved or which is used to press, shape, spread, or smooth something **b** : a rod on which something (as a map or a shade) is rolled up **c** : a small wheel (as of a roller skate) **2** : a long heavy wave on the sea **3** : one that rolls or rolls over

roller bearing *n* : a bearing in which a rotating part turns on rollers held in a circular frame or cage

roll·er coast·er \ˈrō-lər-ˌkō-stər, ˈrō-lē-ˌkō-\ *n* : an elevated railway (as in an amusement park) with sharp curves and steep slopes on which cars roll

roller rink *n* : RINK 2

roller skate *n* : a skate that goes on wheels instead of a runner — **roller–skate** *vb*

rol·lick \ˈräl-ik\ *vb* : ²FROLIC — **rollick** *n*

rol·lick·ing \ˈräl-ik-iŋ\ *adj* : full of fun and good spirits

rolling pin *n* : a cylinder (as of wood) used to roll out dough

rolling stock *n* : wheeled vehicles owned or used by a railroad or trucking company

roll·top desk \ˌrōl-ˌtäp-\ *n* : a desk with a cover that can be slid up or down

roll up *vb* : to build up by many additions one after the other ⟨the winning candidate *rolled up* a large majority⟩

¹ro·ly–po·ly \ˌrō-lē-ˈpō-lē\ *adj* : being short and fat

²roly–poly *n, pl* **-lies** : a roly-poly person or thing

ROM \ˈräm\ *n* : READ-ONLY MEMORY

ro·maine \rō-ˈmān\ *n* : a lettuce with a tall loose head of long crisp leaves — called also *romaine lettuce*

¹Ro·man \ˈrō-mən\ *n* **1 a** : a person born or living in Rome **b** : a citizen of the Roman Empire **2** *not cap* : roman letters or type

²Roman *adj* **1** : of or relating to Rome or the Romans or the empire of which Rome was the original capital **2 a** : ¹LATIN 2 **b** : of or relating to the Latin language **3** *not*

cap : of or relating to a type style with upright characters (as in "these definitions") **4** : of or relating to the Roman Catholic Church

Roman candle *n* : a firework that is a long tube that shoots out balls or stars of fire one at a time

Roman Catholic *adj* : of or relating to the body of Christians having levels of authority under the pope, a liturgy centered in the Mass, and a body of beliefs laid down by the church as the only interpreter of revealed truth — **Roman Catholic** *n* — **Roman Catholicism** *n*

¹ro·mance \rō-ˈman(t)s, ˈrō-ˌman(t)s\ *n* **1 a** : an old tale of knights and noble ladies **b** : an adventure story **c** : a love story **2** : LOVE AFFAIR **3** : an attraction or appeal to one's feelings ⟨the *romance* of the old West⟩

Word History As the Roman Empire spread throughout Europe, the Latin language developed many dialects. In these dialects, the original Latin was changed by the native languages spoken before the conquest. These dialects were called *romans* in early French and became the bases of what we call Romance languages today. Even after the fall of Rome, serious writing was done in Latin. But in what is now France, popular verse stories about knights, dragons, ghosts, and battles were written in the local dialect. Soon *romans* came to mean one of these stories, and the word was borrowed into Middle English. Since many of the stories were about love affairs, *romance* came to mean "a love story", and then "a love affair". In the late 18th and early 19th centuries, a group of poets, including Shelley, Byron, Keats, and Wordsworth, were labeled *Romantic* because they wrote poetry about the same kinds of things as were found in the old romances — noble love, courage, and ghostly beings. [Middle English *romauns* "a story of adventure or legend", from early French *romans* "French language, something written in French", from Latin *romanice* "in the Roman manner", from *romanicus* "Roman", from *Romanus* "one who lives in Rome"]

²romance *vb* **ro·manced; ro·manc·ing** **1** : to have romantic thoughts or ideas **2** : to carry on a love affair with

Ro·mance \rō-ˈman(t)s, ˈrō-ˌman(t)s\ *adj* : of, relating to, or being the languages (as French, Italian, or Spanish) developed from Latin

Ro·man·esque \ˌrō-mə-ˈnesk\ *adj* : relating to or being an old style of architecture (as for churches) coming before Gothic architecture and having round arches, thick heavy walls, and few small windows

Ro·ma·ni·an \rù-ˈmā-nē-ən, rō-\ *n* **1** : a person born or living in Romania **2** : RUMANIAN 2 — **Romanian** *adj*

Roman numeral *n* : a numeral in a system of figures based on the ancient Roman system — see NUMBER table

Ro·ma·no \rə-ˈmän-ō, rō-\ *n* : a hard sharp cheese used grated

Ro·mans \ˈrō-mənz\ *n* — see BIBLE table

Ro·mansch *or* **Ro·mansh** \rō-ˈmänch\ *n* : a Romance language spoken in parts of Switzerland

¹ro·man·tic \rō-ˈmant-ik\ *n* : a romantic person; *esp* : a romantic writer, composer, or artist

²romantic *adj* **1 a** : of, relating to, or resembling a romance ⟨*romantic* writing⟩ **b** : not founded on fact : IMAGINARY **2** : IMPRACTICAL ⟨a *romantic* scheme⟩ **3 a** : stressing or appealing to the emotions or imagination ⟨a *romantic* spot⟩ **b** *often cap* : of or relating to romanticism **4** : of, relating to, or associated with love — **ro·man·ti·cal·ly** \-i-k(ə-)lē\ *adv*

ro·man·ti·cism \rō-ˈmant-ə-ˌsiz-əm\ *n* **1** *often cap* : a literary and artistic movement marked chiefly by an empha-

\ə\ abut	\au̇\ out	\i\ tip	\o̊\ saw	\u̇\ foot
\ər\ further	\ch\ chin	\ī\ life	\o̊i\ coin	\y\ yet
\a\ mat	\e\ pet	\j\ job	\th\ thin	\yü\ few
\ā\ take	\ē\ easy	\ŋ\ sing	\th\ this	\yu̇\ cure
\ä\ cot, cart	\g\ go	\ō\ bone	\ü\ food	\zh\ vision

sis on the imagination and emotions **2** : the quality or state of being romantic — **ro·man·ti·cist** \-səst\ *n, often cap*

ro·man·ti·cize \rō-'mant-ə-,sīz\ *vb* **-cized; -ciz·ing** **1** : to make romantic : show in a romantic way **2** : to have romantic ideas — **ro·man·ti·ci·za·tion** \-,mant-ə-sə-'zā-shən\ *n*

Rom·a·ny \'räm-ə-nē, 'rō-mə-\ *n, pl* **-nies** **1** : GYPSY 1 **2** : the Indic language of the Gypsies — **Romany** *adj*

¹romp \'rämp\ *n* : rough and noisy play : FROLIC

²romp *vb* : to play in a rough and noisy way

romp·er \'räm-pər\ *n* : a child's one-piece garment with the lower part shaped like bloomers — usually used in pl.

rood \'rüd\ *n* : ¹CROSS 1b, CRUCIFIX

¹roof \'rüf, 'rùf\ *n, pl* **roofs** \'rüfs, 'rùfs, 'rüvz, 'rùvz\ **1 a** : the upper covering part of a building **b** : a place to live : HOME ⟨a *roof* over one's head⟩ **2** : the upper boundary of the mouth **3** : something resembling a roof in form, position, or purpose — **roofed** \'rüft, 'rùft\ *adj* — **roof·less** \'rüf-ləs, 'rùf-\ *adj* — **roof·like** \-,līk\ *adj*

²roof *vb* **1** : to cover with or as if with a roof **2** : to provide with roofing — **roof·er** *n*

roof·ing *n* : material for a roof

roof·top \'rüf-,täp, 'rùf-\ *n* : ¹ROOF 1a; *esp* : the outer surface of a flat roof

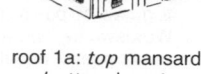

roof 1a: *top* mansard, *bottom* lean-to

roof·tree \-,trē\ *n* : RIDGEPOLE

¹rook \'rùk\ *n* : a common Old World bird about the size and color of the related crows [Old English *hrōc* "crowlike bird"]

²rook *vb* : ¹CHEAT 1, SWINDLE

³rook *n* : a chessman that can move parallel to the sides of the board across any number of unoccupied squares [Middle English *rok* "chess piece", from early French *roc* (same meaning), from Arabic *rukhkh* (same meaning); of Persian origin]

rook·ery \'rùk-ə-rē\ *n, pl* **-er·ies** : the place where a group of birds or social mammals breed, nest, or raise their young

rook·ie \'rùk-ē\ *n* : BEGINNER, RECRUIT; *esp* : a first-year player in a professional sport

¹room \'rüm, 'rùm\ *n* **1** : space used or available for something ⟨houseplants that take up little *room*⟩ ⟨enough *room* to run and play⟩ **2 a** : a part of the inside of a building that is divided off **b** : such a part used as a lodging **3** : the people in a room **4** : a suitable opportunity : CHANCE ⟨*room* for improvement⟩

²room *vb* : to live in or share a room as a lodger

room·er \'rü-mər, 'rùm-ər\ *n* : LODGER

room·ful \'rüm-,fùl, 'rùm-\ *n, pl* **roomfuls** \-,fùlz\ *or* **rooms·ful** \'rümz-,fùl, 'rùmz-\ **1** : as much or as many as a room will hold **2** : the persons or objects in a room

rooming house *n* : a house where rooms are rented to lodgers

room·mate \'rüm-,māt, 'rùm-\ *n* : one of two or more persons sharing a room or dwelling

roomy \'rü-mē, 'rùm-ē\ *adj* **room·i·er; -est** : having plenty of room — **room·i·ness** *n*

¹roost \'rüst\ *n* **1** : a support on which birds rest **2** : a place where birds often roost

²roost *vb* **1** : to settle down for rest or sleep : PERCH **2** : to supply a roost for

roost·er \'rü-stər\ *n* **1** : an adult male domestic chicken **2** : an adult male bird

¹root \'rüt, 'rùt\ *n* **1 a** : the leafless usually underground part of a plant that absorbs and stores water and minerals and holds the plant in place **b** : an underground plant part especially when fleshy and edible **2 a** : the part of a tooth within the socket **b** : the base or end of a bodily part (as a hair or a fingernail) or that by which it is attached to the body **3 a** : an original cause : SOURCE ⟨the *roots* of evil⟩ **b** : the ancestors of a person or a group of persons ⟨people tracing their *roots*⟩ **c** : something that lies under and supports ⟨the *roots* of a mountain chain⟩ **d** : ¹CORE 1, HEART ⟨get to the *root* of the problem⟩ **e** : a special relationship with a social environment ⟨has *roots* deep in Southern life⟩ **4 a** : a number that when taken as a factor an indicated number of times gives a specified number ⟨2 is a 4th *root* of 16⟩ **b** : a solution of a polynomial equation having one unknown **5** : a word or part of a word from which other words are formed ("butler" and "bottle" come from the same Latin *root*) ("hold" is the *root* of "holder") [Old English *rōt* "root of a plant"; of Norse origin] — **root·ed** \-əd\ *adj* — **root·less** \-ləs\ *adj* — **root·like** \-,līk\ *adj*

²root *vb* **1 a** : to form or enable to form roots **b** : to fix or become fixed by or as if by roots : take root **2** : to remove by or as if by pulling out the roots ⟨cut down a tree and *root* out the stump⟩ ⟨*root* out dissenters⟩

³root *vb* : to turn up or dig with the snout

⁴root \'rüt, 'rùt\ *vb* **1** : ²CHEER 2 **2** : to wish for the success of someone or something ⟨*rooting* for the underdog⟩ [perhaps an altered form of *rout*, a rare word meaning "to low or bellow like cattle"] — **root·er** *n*

root beer *n* : a sweet carbonated drink flavored with extracts of roots and herbs

root cap *n* : a layer of dead cells that forms a protective cover over the growing tip of a root

root hair *n* : one of the threadlike outgrowths near the tip of a rootlet that function in absorption of water and minerals

root·let \'rüt-lət, 'rùt-\ *n* : a small root

root pressure *n* : the pressure that is caused by the absorption of soil water and that helps to push water up the plant stem from the roots

root·stock \'rüt-,stäk, 'rùt-\ *n* : an underground part of a plant that resembles a rhizome

¹rope \'rōp\ *n* **1 a** : a large stout cord of strands (as of fiber or wire) twisted or braided together **b** : LARIAT **c** : a noose used for hanging **2** : a row or string (as of beads) made by or as if by braiding, twining, or threading **3** *pl* : the special way things are done (as on a job) ⟨learn the *ropes*⟩

²rope *vb* **roped; rop·ing** **1 a** : to bind, fasten, or tie with a rope **b** : to set off or divide by a rope ⟨*rope* off a street for a neighborhood carnival⟩ **c** : to catch with a lasso **2** : to draw as if with a rope ⟨*roped* her friends into helping with the project⟩ — **rop·er** *n*

rope·walk \-,wòk\ *n* : a place where rope is made

rope·walk·er \-,wò-kər\ *n* : an acrobat who performs on a tightrope

ropy \'rō-pē\ *adj* **rop·i·er; -est** **1** : capable of being drawn into a sticky thread : VISCOUS **2** : resembling rope — **rop·i·ness** *n*

Roque·fort \'rōk-fərt\ *trademark* — used for a blue cheese made in France of sheep's milk

ro·que·laure \,rō-kə-'lō(ə)r\ *n* : a knee-length cape

Ror·schach test \'rò(ə)r-,shäk-\ *n* : a psychological test in which a person is asked to tell what he or she sees in and thinks about ink blots of varying designs and colors and which is used to measure certain traits of personality

ro·sa·ry \'rōz-(ə-)rē\ *n, pl* **-ries** **1** *often cap* : a Roman Catholic devotion consisting of meditation on usually five sacred mysteries during recitation of five decades of Hail Marys of which each is preceded by the Lord's Prayer and followed by the Gloria Patri **2** : a string of beads used in counting prayers and especially those of the Roman Catholic rosary

Word History *Rosary* comes from the Latin word *rosarium*, which at first meant "a rose garden". It was later used to refer to a series of prayers, thought of perhaps as a garden of prayers. This second meaning of *rosa-rium* may also have developed partly because in Christianity the rose is associated with Mary, the mother of Jesus, and the rose garden with paradise. *Rosarium* in time came to be used not only for the prayers themselves but also for the string of beads used in counting them. [from Latin *rosarium* "rosary prayers, rosary beads", from earlier *rosarium* "rose garden", derived from *rosa* "rose"]

¹rose *past of* RISE

²rose \'rōz\ *n* **1 a** : any of a genus of usually prickly often climbing shrubs that have compound leaves and showy often fragrant white, yellow, red, pink, or orange flowers **b** : the flower of a rose **2** : a medium purplish red — **rose-like** \-,līk\ *adj*

³rose *adj* **1** : of, relating to, resembling, or used for the rose or roses **2** : of the color rose

rose–breast·ed grosbeak \,rōz-,bres-təd-\ *n* : a grosbeak of eastern North America of which the male is chiefly black and white with a rose-red breast and the female is a streaky grayish brown with the lining of the wings orange

rose·bud \'rōz-,bəd\ *n* : the bud of a rose

rose·bush \-,bush\ *n* : a shrub that produces roses

rose–col·ored \-,kəl-ərd\ *adj* **1** : having a rose color ⟨a lamp with a *rose-colored* shade⟩ **2** : OPTIMISTIC ⟨a *rose-colored* view of the problem⟩

rose·mary \'rōz-,mer-ē\ *n* : a fragrant mint that is used in cooking and perfumes [an altered form of Middle English *rosmarine* "rosemary", from Latin *rosmarinus,* literally "dew of the sea", from *ros* "dew" and *marinus* "of the sea"]

Ro·set·ta stone \rō-,zet-ə-\ *n* : a black stone with inscriptions in Egyptian hieroglyphics and Greek that gave the first clue to understanding hieroglyphics

ro·sette \rō-'zet\ *n* **1** : a badge or ornament of ribbon gathered in the shape of a rose **2** : a design of leaves or flowers used as a decoration **3** : a circular cluster of leaves developed on a plant (as at the base of a dandelion)

rose·wood \'rōz-,wud\ *n* **1** : any of various tropical trees with hard dark red to purplish wood that is streaked with black and is used especially for making furniture and musical instruments **2** : the wood of a rosewood

rosette 2

Rosh Ha·sha·nah \,rōsh-hə-'shō-nə, ,rōsh-ə-, ,räsh-, -'shän-ə\ *n* : the Jewish New Year observed as a religious holiday in September or October [from Hebrew *rōsh hash-shānāh,* literally "head of the year"]

¹ros·in \'räz-ᵊn, 'rōz-\ *n* : an amber-colored to almost black brittle resin obtained especially from pine trees and used in making varnish and soap and on violin bows

²rosin *vb* : to rub (as the bow of a violin) with rosin

ros·ter \'räs-tər\ *n* : a list usually of people belonging to some group

ros·trum \'räs-trəm\ *n, pl* **rostrums** *or* **ros·tra** \-trə\ **1** : a stage or platform from which to give a speech **2** : a bodily part (as a snout) that resembles a bird's beak

Word History   *R* rostrum 2

Rostrum, a "raised platform for speakers", goes back to the collecting of war souvenirs by the ancient Romans. Warships in those days had pointed beams, called "beaks", sticking out from the bows. They were used to ram and sink enemy ships. To celebrate a great naval victory, the Romans gathered the beaks of the losers' ships. They hung them in back of the speaker's platform in the Forum in Rome. The Latin word for the ship's beak was *rostum.* The plural, *rostra,* soon came to be used for the speaker's platform. In time *rostra* came to be used for any speaker's platform, not just one decorated with the beaks of ships. In the 18th century English began using the Latin singular form *rostrum* to mean "a speaker's platform". [from Latin *Rostra* "the speaker's platform in the Forum", from *rostra,* plural of *rostrum* "ship's beak"]

rosy \'rō-zē\ *adj* **ros·i·er; -est** **1** : of the color rose **2** : PROMISING, HOPEFUL ⟨the outlook was *rosy*⟩ ⟨*rosy* prospects⟩ — **ros·i·ly** \-zə-lē\ *adv* — **ros·i·ness** \-zē-nəs\ *n*

¹rot \'rät\ *vb* **rot·ted; rot·ting** **1 a** : to decay due to the action of fungi or microorganisms **b** : to become unsafe or weak (as from use or chemical action) **2** : to go to ruin **3** : to cause to rot

²rot *n* **1 a** : the process of rotting : the state of being rotten **b** : something rotten or rotting **2 a** : a disease of plants or animals marked by the decay of tissue **b** : an area of decayed tissue ⟨pruned the *rot* from the tree trunk⟩ **3** : NONSENSE 1 ⟨don't talk *rot*⟩

¹ro·ta·ry \'rōt-ə-rē\ *adj* **1 a** : turning on an axis like a wheel ⟨a *rotary* blade⟩ **b** : taking place about an axis ⟨*rotary* motion⟩ **2** : having a rotating part ⟨a *rotary* lawn mower⟩

²rotary *n, pl* **-ries** **1** : a rotary machine **2** : a road junction formed around a central circle about which traffic moves in one direction only

ro·tate \'rō-,tāt\ *vb* **ro·tat·ed; ro·tat·ing** **1** : to turn or cause to turn about an axis or a center ⟨the earth *rotates*⟩ **2 a** : to do or cause to do something in turn **b** : to pass in a series ⟨the seasons *rotate*⟩ **3** : to cause to grow in rotation ⟨*rotate* alfalfa and corn⟩ — **ro·tat·able** \-,tāt-ə-bəl\ *adj* — **ro·ta·tor** \-,tāt-ər\ *n*

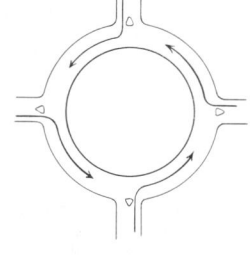

rotary 2

ro·ta·tion \rō-'tā-shən\ *n* **1 a** : the act of rotating especially on an axis **b** : one complete turn **2** : the growing of different crops in the same field usually in a regular order — **ro·ta·tion·al** \-shnəl, -shən-ᵊl\ *adj*

¹rote \'rōt\ *n* **1** : the use of memory usually without thinking about it ⟨learn by *rote*⟩ ⟨repeat something by *rote*⟩ **2** : something done time after time in an automatic way or without thinking

²rote *adj* **1** : done or learned by rote ⟨*rote* learning of multiplication tables⟩ ⟨a *rote* phrase⟩ **2** : done or carried out without engaging the mind or feelings ⟨*rote* duties⟩ ⟨ask a *rote* question⟩

ro·te·none \'rōt-ᵊn-,ōn\ *n* : a substance obtained from tropical plants that is usually harmless to warm-blooded animals but is poisonous especially to insects

ro·ti·fer \'rōt-ə-fər\ *n* : any of a class of usually microscopic aquatic animals with circles of cilia on one end that look

\ə\ abut	\aù\ out	\i\ tip	\ò\ saw	\ù\ foot	
\ər\ further	\ch\ chin	\ī\ life	\òi\ coin	\y\ yet	
\a\ mat	\e\ pet	\j\ job	\th\ thin	\yü\ few	
\ā\ take	\ē\ easy	\ŋ\ sing	\th\ this	\yù\ cure	
\ä\ cot, cart	\g\ go	\ō\ bone	\ü\ food	\zh\ vision	

like moving wheels when moving

ro·tis·ser·ie \rō-'tis-(ə-)rē\ *n* : an appliance fitted with a spit on which food is rotated before or over a source of heat

ro·tor \'rōt-ər\ *n* **1** : a part that rotates in a stationary part (as in an electrical machine) **2** : a complete system of horizontal rotating blades that support a helicopter in flight

rot·ten \'rät-ᵊn\ *adj* **1** : having rotted **2** : morally bad **3** : very unpleasant or worthless ⟨did a *rotten* job⟩ ⟨played a *rotten* game⟩ — **rot·ten·ly** *adv* — **rot·ten·ness** \-ᵊn-(n)əs\ *n*

ro·tund \rō-'tənd, 'rō-,tənd\ *adj* **1** : somewhat round **2** : ⁵PLUMP — **ro·tun·di·ty** \rō-'tən-dət-ē\ *n*

ro·tun·da \rō-'tən-də\ *n* **1** : a round building; *esp* : one covered by a dome **2 a** : a large round room **b** : a large central area (as in a hotel)

rouble *variant of* RUBLE

¹rouge \'rüzh, *especially Southern* 'rüj\ *n* **1** : a cosmetic used to give a red color to the cheeks or lips **2** : a red powder consisting essentially of ferric oxide used for polishing (as glass or metal)

²rouge *vb* **rouged; roug·ing** : to put rouge on

¹rough \'rəf\ *adj* **1 a** : having an uneven surface : not smooth **b** : covered with or made up of coarse and often shaggy hair or bristles ⟨a *rough*-coated terrier⟩ **2 a** : not calm ⟨*rough* seas⟩ **b** : being harsh or violent ⟨*rough* treatment⟩ **c** : difficult to take or deal with ⟨we've had some *rough* times⟩ **3 a** : harsh to the ear **b** : coarse or rugged in nature or look **4** : not complete or exact ⟨a *rough* draft⟩ ⟨*rough* estimate⟩; *also* : ¹APPROXIMATE ⟨this will give you a *rough* idea of the house⟩ — **rough·ish** \'rəf-ish\ *adj* — **rough·ly** *adv* — **rough·ness** *n*

syn ROUGH, HARSH, RUGGED mean not smooth or even. ROUGH implies having points, bristles, ridges, or projections on the surface ⟨*rough* wood⟩ HARSH implies having a surface that is unpleasant to the touch ⟨a *harsh* brush⟩ *rugged* implies an uneven land surface and suggests difficulty of travel ⟨*rugged* mountain roads⟩

²rough *n* **1** : uneven ground covered with high grass, brush, and stones **2** : the rugged or unpleasant part of something ⟨nature in the *rough*⟩ **3** : something in a crude or unfinished state; *also* : such a state ⟨a diamond in the *rough*⟩

³rough *adv* : in a rough way : not smoothly ⟨the engine idled *rough*, but ran smoothly at high speed⟩

⁴rough *vb* **1** : ¹ROUGHEN **2** : to handle roughly : BEAT ⟨*roughed* up by hoodlums⟩ **3** : to shape or make in a rough way ⟨*rough* out a plan⟩ — **rough it** : to live without ordinary comforts

rough·age \'rəf-ij\ *n* : coarse bulky food (as bran) with much indigestible matter that stimulates the intestine to move its contents along — called also *fiber*

rough·en \'rəf-ən\ *vb* **rough·ened; rough·en·ing** \-(ə-)niŋ\ : to make or become rough

rough·hewn \'rəf-'hyün\ *adj* **1** : being rough or unfinished ⟨*roughhewn* beams⟩ **2** : lacking smooth manners or social grace

¹rough·house \'rəf-,haus\ *n* : violence or rough noisy play

²rough·house \-,haus, -,hauz\ *vb* **rough·housed; rough·hous·ing** : to take part in roughhouse

rough·neck \'rəf-,nek\ *n* **1** : a rough person : ROWDY **2** : a worker on a crew drilling oil wells

Rough Rider *n* : a member of the cavalry led by Theodore Roosevelt in the Spanish-American War

rough·shod \'rəf-'shäd\ *adv* : with no consideration for the wishes or feelings of others — usually used in the phrase *ride roughshod over* or *run roughshod over*

rou·lette \rü-'let\ *n* **1** : a gambling game in which players bet on which compartment of a revolving wheel a small ball will come to rest in **2** : a wheel or disk with teeth around the outside [from French *roulette,* literally "small wheel"]

¹round \'raund\ *adj* **1 a** : having every part of the surface or circumference the same distance from the center **b**

: shaped like a cylinder ⟨a *round* peg⟩ **c** : nearly round ⟨a *round* face⟩ **2** : ⁵PLUMP **3 a** : ¹COMPLETE **1** ⟨a *round* dozen⟩ **b** : nearly correct or exact ⟨in *round* numbers⟩ **c** : LARGE ⟨a good *round* sum⟩ **4** : moving in or forming a circle **5** : having lifelike fullness ⟨a *round* character in a story⟩ **6** : having fullness of tone **7** : having curves rather than angles — **round·ish** \'raun-dish\ *adj* — **round·ness** \'raun(d)-nəs\ *n*

²round *adv* : ¹AROUND

³round *n* **1** : something (as a circle, globe, or ring) that is round **2** : a song in which three or four singers sing the same melody and words one after another at intervals **3** : ²RUNG **4** : an indirect or circling path **5 a** : a regularly covered route ⟨a watchman's *rounds*⟩ **b** : a series of calls or stops regularly made ⟨a doctor on her *rounds* in the hospital⟩ **6** : a drink apiece served at one time to each person in a group **7** : a series or cycle of repeated actions or events ⟨opened a new *round* of disarmament talks⟩ **8 a** : one shot fired by a soldier or weapon **b** : ammunition for one shot **9** : a unit of play in a contest or game ⟨a *round* of golf⟩ **10** : a cut of beef especially between the rump and the lower leg — **in the round 1** : in full sculptured form unattached to a background **2** : with a center stage surrounded by an audience on all sides ⟨theater *in the round*⟩

⁴round *vb* **1 a** : to make or become round **b** : to pronounce a sound with rounding of the lips **2** : to go or pass around ⟨*rounded* the curve⟩ **3** : to bring to completion — often used with *off* or *out* **4** : to express as a round number especially by dropping decimal figures to the right of a specified number of places and increasing the final remaining figure by 1 if the first digit dropped is 5 or greater ⟨4.57268 *rounded* off to three decimal places is 4.573⟩ **5** : to follow a winding course

⁵round \(')raund\ *prep* : ²AROUND

round·about \'raun-də-,baut\ *adj* : not direct ⟨went a *roundabout* way⟩

round dance *n* **1** : a folk dance in which participants form a ring and move in a certain direction **2** : a series of movements performed by a bee to indicate that a source of food is nearby

round·ed \'raun-dəd\ *adj* : curving or round in shape

roun·de·lay \'raun-də-,lā\ *n* : a simple song with refrain

round·house \'raund-,haus\ *n* **1 a** : a circular building where locomotives are kept or repaired **2** : a blow with the hand made with a wide swing

round·ly \'raun-(d)lē\ *adv* **1** : in a thorough way : COMPLETELY ⟨was punished *roundly*⟩ ⟨was *roundly* ignored⟩ **2** : in plain or strong language ⟨*roundly* criticized the plan⟩

roundhouse 1

round–robin \'raun-,dräb-ən\ *n* **1** : a letter (as of protest) whose signers put their signatures in a circle so the receiver cannot tell who signed first **2** : a tournament in which every contestant plays once against every other contestant

round–shoul·dered \'raun(d)-'shōl-dərd\ *adj* : having the shoulders stooping or rounded

round steak *n* : a steak cut from the round of beef

round table \'raun(d)-,tā-bəl\ *n* **1** *cap R&T* : the large round table of King Arthur and his knights **2** *usually* **round·ta·ble** : a meeting of several persons for discussion

round·up \'raun-,dəp\ *n* **1** : the gathering together of animals on the range by riding around them and driving them in **2** : a gathering together of scattered persons or things

3 : ²SUMMARY ⟨a *roundup* of the day's news⟩

round up \'raủn-'dəp\ *vb* **1** : to collect (as cattle) by circling and driving **2** : to gather in or bring together

round·worm \'raủn-,dwərm\ *n* : a nematode worm (as a hookworm); *also* : a related round-bodied worm without segments as compared to a flatworm

rouse \'raủz\ *vb* **roused; rous·ing 1** : ¹AWAKE 1, 3 **2** : to make or become active : stir up

rous·ing \'raủ-ziŋ\ *adj* **1** : having the power to rouse one ⟨sang a *rousing* hymn⟩ ⟨a *rousing* speech⟩ **2** : very good : EXCEPTIONAL ⟨a *rousing* business⟩

roust·about \'raủ-stə-,baủt\ *n* : a person (as a deckhand, dock worker, or oil field worker) who does heavy labor

¹**rout** \'raủt\ *vb* **rout·ed; rout·ing 1** : to poke around with the snout : ROOT **2** : to dig or cut a groove in (as wood or metal) **3 a** : to drive by force ⟨*routed* out of their homes⟩ **b** : to cause to come out especially from bed

²**rout** *n* **1** : a state of wild confusion and disorderly retreat **2** : a disastrous defeat

³**rout** *vb* **rout·ed; rout·ing 1** : to put to flight **2** : to defeat completely

¹**route** \'rüt, 'raủt\ *n* **1** : ROAD 2a, HIGHWAY ⟨U.S. *Route* 66⟩ **2** : a course of action toward a goal ⟨the best *route* to peace⟩ **3 a** : an established, selected, or assigned course of travel ⟨explorers looking for a new *route* to the Indies⟩ ⟨air *routes* to Europe⟩ **b** : a territory to be gone over regularly ⟨a newspaper *route*⟩

²**route** *vb* **rout·ed; rout·ing** : to send or transport by a certain route ⟨*route* heavy traffic around the city⟩

rout·er \'raủt-ər\ *n* : a machine for cutting out the surface of wood or metal

¹**rou·tine** \rü-'tēn\ *n* **1** : a standard or regular way of doing something **2** : an often repeated speech or formula **3** : a part (as of an act or a sports performance) that is carefully worked out so it can be repeated often ⟨a comedy *routine*⟩ ⟨a dance *routine*⟩ ⟨a gymnastic *routine*⟩ **4** : a set of computer instructions that will perform a certain job

²**routine** *adj* **1** : ²COMMONPLACE, ORDINARY **2** : done or happening in a usual or standard way — **rou·tine·ly** *adv*

rove \'rōv\ *vb* **roved; rov·ing** : ROAM

¹**ro·ver** \'rō-vər\ *n* : ¹PIRATE

²**rov·er** \'rō-vər\ *n* : a person who roves around : ROAMER

rov·ing \'rō-viŋ\ *n* : a slightly twisted roll or strand of textile fibers

¹**row** \'rō\ *vb* **1** : to move a boat by means of oars **2** : to travel or carry in a rowboat **3** : to pull an oar in a crew [Old English *rōwan* "to propel a boat with oars"] — **row·er** \'rō(-ə)r\ *n*

²**row** *n* : an act or instance of rowing

³**row** *n* **1 a** : a series of persons or things arranged in a usually straight line; *esp* : a horizontal arrangement of items **b** : the line along which such objects are arranged ⟨planted the corn in parallel *rows*⟩ **2** : ¹WAY 1a, STREET [Middle English *rawe* "a number of objects arranged in a line"]

⁴**row** \'raủ\ *n* : a noisy disturbance or quarrel [origin unknown]

⁵**row** \'raủ\ *vb* : to have a row : FIGHT, QUARREL

row·boat \'rō-,bōt\ *n* : a boat made to be rowed

¹**row·dy** \'raủd-ē\ *adj* **row·di·er; -est** : rough or loud in behavior — **row·di·ness** *n*

²**rowdy** *n, pl* **rowdies** : a rowdy person

row·el \'raủ-(ə)l\ *n* : a disk on the end of a spur that has sharp points around its edge

row house \'rō-\ *n* : any of a row of houses connected by common sidewalls

rowboat

row·ing \'rō-iŋ\ *n* : the sport of racing long narrow boats rowed by oars

row·lock \'räl-ək, 'rel-; 'rō-,läk\ *n, chiefly British* : OARLOCK

roy·al \'rȯi-(ə)l\ *adj* **1** : of or relating to a sovereign : REGAL **2** : fit for a king or queen ⟨a *royal* welcome⟩ — **roy·al·ly** \'rȯi-ə-lē\ *adv*

royal blue *n* : a purplish blue

roy·al·ist \'rȯi-ə-ləst\ *n* : a person who supports a sovereign — **royalist** *adj*

royal jelly *n* : a substance rich in vitamins and proteins that is secreted from glands in the head of honeybees and is fed to all very young larvae and to all maturing queen bees

roy·al·ty \'rȯi-(ə)l-tē\ *n, pl* **-ties 1** : royal status or power **2** : royal character or conduct **3** : members of a royal family **4 a** : a share of a product or profit (as of a mine) claimed by the owner for allowing another to use the property **b** : a payment made to the owner of a patent or copyright for the use of it

rRNA \,är-,är-,en-'ā\ *n* : RIBOSOMAL RNA

¹**rub** \'rəb\ *vb* **rubbed; rub·bing 1 a** : to move along the surface of a body with pressure **b** : to wear away or chafe with friction **2** : to scour, polish, erase, spread, or smear by pressure and friction — **rub elbows** *or* **rub shoulders** : to associate in a friendly way : MINGLE — **rub the wrong way** : to cause to be angry : IRRITATE

²**rub** *n* **1 a** : something that gets in the way : DIFFICULTY **b** : something that is annoying **2** : the act of rubbing

¹**rub·ber** \'rəb-ər\ *n* **1** : something used in rubbing, polishing, scraping, or cleaning **2 a** : an elastic substance obtained from the milky juice of various tropical plants **b** : any of various synthetic substances like rubber **3** : something made of or resembling rubber: as **a** : a rubber overshoe **b** : a rectangular slab of white rubber in the middle of a baseball infield on which a pitcher stands while pitching **4** : CONDOM — **rub·ber·like** \-,līk\ *adj* — **rub·bery** \'rəb-(ə-)rē\ *adj*

²**rubber** *n* **1** : a contest that consists of an odd number of games (as card games) and is won by the side that takes a majority (as two out of three) **2** : an extra game played to decide the winner of a tie

³**rubber** *vb* : RUBBERNECK

rubber band *n* : a continuous band made of rubber for holding things together : ELASTIC

rub·ber·ized \'rəb-ə-,rīzd\ *adj* : coated or soaked with rubber

rub·ber·neck \'rəb-ər-,nek\ *vb* : to look around or stare with great curiosity

rubber plant *n* : a plant that produces rubber; *esp* : an Asian tree related to the mulberry that is widely raised as a houseplant

rubber stamp *n* : a stamp with a printing face made of rubber

rubber tree *n* : a tree that produces rubber; *esp* : a South American tree that is often grown on plantations as a commercial source of rubber

rub·bing \'rəb-iŋ\ *n* : an image of a raised or indented surface made by placing paper over it and rubbing the paper with something colored

rubbing alcohol *n* : a cooling and soothing solution for use on the outside of the body that contains an alcohol and water

rub·bish \'rəb-ish\ *n* : useless waste or stuff that has been thrown away : TRASH — **rub·bishy** \-ē\ *adj*

rub·ble \'rəb-əl\ *n* **1** : rough broken stones or bricks used

\ə\ abut		\aủ\ **out**	\i\ **tip**	\ȯ\ **saw**	\ủ\ **foot**
\ər\ **further**	\ch\ **chin**		\ī\ **life**	\ȯi\ **coin**	\y\ **yet**
\a\ **mat**	\e\ **pet**		\j\ **job**	\th\ **thin**	\yü\ **few**
\ā\ **take**	\ē\ **easy**		\ŋ\ **sing**	\th\ **this**	\yủ\ **cure**
\ä\ **cot, cart**	\g\ **go**		\ō\ **bone**	\ü\ **food**	\zh\ **vision**

in building **2** : a confused mass of rough or broken things

rub·down \'rəb-,daůn\ *n* : a brisk rubbing of the body

ru·bel·la \rü-'bel-ə\ *n* : GERMAN MEASLES

ru·bi·cund \'rü-bi-(,)kənd\ *adj* : RUDDY 1

ru·bid·i·um \rü-'bid-ē-əm\ *n* : a soft silvery metallic element that reacts violently with water — see ELEMENT table

rub in *vb* : to keep reminding someone of something unpleasant ⟨you don't have to *rub* it *in*⟩

ru·ble *also* **rou·ble** \'rü-bəl\ *n* **1** : the basic unit of money of the U.S.S.R. **2** : a coin representing one ruble

rub off *vb* : to become transferred ⟨be careful that the ink doesn't *rub off* on your fingers⟩ ⟨a cheerful attitude can *rub off* on others⟩

rub out *vb* : to remove by or as if by erasing

ru·bric \'rü-brik\ *n* : a name or heading under which something is classified : CLASSIFICATION ⟨different problems under the general *rubric* of ecology⟩

¹ru·by \'rü-bē\ *n, pl* **rubies** **1** : a precious stone of a deep red color **2** : the dark red color of the ruby

²ruby *adj* : dark red in color

ru·by–throat·ed hummingbird \,rü-bē-,thrōt-əd-\ *n* : a hummingbird of eastern North America that has a bright shiny green back, a white belly, and in the adult male a shiny red throat

ruck·sack \'rək-,sak, 'růk-\ *n* : KNAPSACK

ruck·us \'rək-əs, 'růk-, 'růk-\ *n* : ⁴ROW

ruc·tion \'rək-shən\ *n* : a noisy disturbance : UPROAR

rud·der \'rəd-ər\ *n* : a flat movable piece (as of wood or metal) attached to the rear of a ship or aircraft for steering

rud·dy \'rəd-ē\ *adj* **rud·di·er; -est** **1** : having a healthy reddish color **2** : ¹RED 1, REDDISH — **rud·di·ly** \'rəd-ᵊl-ē\ *adv* — **rud·di·ness** \'rəd-ē-nəs\ *n*

rude \'rüd\ *adj* **rud·er; rud·est** **1** : being in a rough or unfinished state : roughly made **2** : not refined or cultured : UNCOUTH **3** : IMPOLITE **4** : being sudden and forceful ⟨a *rude* awakening⟩ — **rude·ly** *adv* — **rude·ness** *n*

rudder

ru·di·ment \'rüd-ə-mənt\ *n* **1** : a basic principle or skill — usually used in pl. ⟨the *rudiments* of grammar⟩ **2 a** : something unformed or undeveloped : BEGINNING — usually used in pl. **b** : a body part so underdeveloped in size or structure that it is unable to perform its normal function

ru·di·men·ta·ry \,rüd-ə-'ment-ə-rē, -'men-trē\ *adj* **1** : ELEMENTARY 1, FUNDAMENTAL **2** : very imperfectly developed or represented only by a small part compared to the fully developed form

¹rue \'rü\ *vb* **rued; ru·ing** : to feel sorrow or regret for

²rue *n* : ²REGRET 1, SORROW

rue·ful \'rü-fəl\ *adj* **1** : exciting pity or sympathy **2** : MOURNFUL 1, REGRETFUL — **rue·ful·ly** \-fə-lē\ *adv*

ruff \'rəf\ *n* **1** : a large round collar of pleated muslin or linen worn by men and women in the 16th and 17th centuries **2** : a fringe of long hairs or feathers growing around or on the neck — **ruffed** \'rəft\ *adj*

ruffed grouse *n* : a North American grouse with tufts of shiny black feathers on the sides of the neck

ruf·fi·an \'rəf-ē-ən\ *n* : a brutal person : BULLY — **ruffian** *adj* — **ruf·fi·an·ly** *adj*

¹ruf·fle \'rəf-əl\ *vb* **ruf·fled; ruf·fling** \'rəf-(ə-)liŋ\ **1 a** : to

ruff 1

disturb the smoothness of **b** : ¹TROUBLE 1a, VEX **2** : to erect (as feathers) in or like a ruff **3** : to make into a ruffle

²ruffle *n* **1** : a state or cause of irritation **2 a** : a strip of fabric gathered or pleated on one edge **b** : RUFF 2 — **ruf·fly** \'rəf-(ə-)lē\ *adj*

³ruffle *n* : a low vibrating drumbeat that is less loud than a roll

rug \'rəg\ *n* : a piece of thick heavy fabric usually with a nap or pile used as a floor covering

rug·by \'rəg-bē\ *n, often cap* : a football game for teams of 15 players each in which play is continuous and the team that has the ball may run with it, kick it, or pass it sideways or backward but is not allowed to block or make forward passes [named for *Rugby* School in England where the game was first played]

rug·ged \'rəg-əd\ *ad* **1** : having a rough uneven surface ⟨hiking on *rugged* trails⟩ ⟨the *rugged* surface of the moon⟩ **2** : having wrinkles or uneven features ⟨their *rugged* faces⟩ ⟨*rugged* good looks⟩ **3** : having a rough but strong or sturdy character ⟨*rugged* pioneers⟩ ⟨the *rugged* dignity of an oak⟩ **4** : involving hardship : presenting a severe test of physical, mental, or moral strength ⟨a *rugged* winter⟩ ⟨*rugged* training⟩ ⟨the *rugged* life of a sailor⟩ **5** : being strong and tough ⟨*rugged* enough to stand hard use⟩ **syn** see ROUGH — **rug·ged·ly** *adv* — **rug·ged·ness** *n*

¹ru·in \'rü-ən, -,in\ *n* **1** : complete collapse or destruction **2** : the remains of something destroyed — usually used in pl. ⟨the *ruins* of a city⟩

²ruin *vb* **1** : to reduce to ruins **2 a** : to damage beyond repair **b** : ²BANKRUPT — **ru·in·er** *n*

ru·in·a·tion \,rü-ə-'nā-shən\ *n* : ¹RUIN 1

ru·in·ous \'rü-ə-nəs\ *adj* : causing or tending to cause ruin : DESTRUCTIVE — **ru·in·ous·ly** *adv*

¹rule \'rül\ *n* **1 a** : a guide or principle for conduct or action **b** : an accepted method, custom, or habit **c** : REGULATION 2, BYLAW **2** : a broad statement generally found to be true ⟨as a *rule* we don't have much snow here⟩ **3** : the exercise of authority or control : GOVERNMENT **4** : RULER 2 [Middle English *reule* "a guide for proper actions", from early French *reule* (same meaning), from Latin *regula* "straightedge, ruler", from *regere* "to lead straight, govern, rule" — related to ¹RAIL, REGENT, REGULATE]

²rule *vb* **ruled; rul·ing** **1** : to have power over : CONTROL, DIRECT **2 a** : to exercise authority or power over **b** : to be supreme or outstanding in **3** : to give or state as a considered decision **4** : to mark with lines drawn along or as if along the straight edge of a ruler **syn** see GOVERN

rule of thumb **1** : a method based on experience and common sense **2** : a general principle that is roughly correct

rule out *vb* : to eliminate the possibility of

rul·er \'rü-lər\ *n* **1** : ¹SOVEREIGN 1 **2** : a straight strip of material (as wood or metal) marked off in units and used as a guide in drawing lines or for measuring

rul·ing \'rü-liŋ\ *n* : an official decision (as by a judge)

rum \'rəm\ *n* : an alcoholic liquor made from molasses or sugarcane

Ru·ma·ni·an \rü-'mā-nē-ən\ *n* **1** : ROMANIAN 1 **2** : the Romance language of the Romanians

rum·ba *also* **rhum·ba** \'rəm-bə, 'rům-\ *n* : a dance of Cuban origin

¹rum·ble \'rəm-bəl\ *vb* **rum·bled; rum·bling** \-b(ə-)liŋ\ : to make or move with a low heavy rolling sound ⟨thunder *rumbled* in the distance⟩

²rumble *n* : a low heavy rolling sound

rumble seat *n* : a folding seat in the back of an old-fashioned automobile that is not covered by the top

rumble seat

over the front seat

ru·men \'rü-mən\ *n, pl* **ru·mi·na** \-mə-nə\ *or* **ru·mens** : the large first compartment of the stomach of a cud-chewing mammal (as a cow) in which cellulose is broken down by the action of microorganisms and in which food is stored prior to chewing

¹ru·mi·nant \'rü-mə-nənt\ *n* : a cud-chewing mammal

²ruminant *adj* **1 a** : chewing the cud   **b** : of or relating to a group of hoofed mammals (as sheep, giraffes, deer, and camels) that chew the cud and have a complex 3- or 4-chambered stomach   **2** : given to or engaged in contemplation : MEDITATIVE

ru·mi·nate \'rü-mə-,nāt\ *vb* **-nat·ed; -nat·ing** **1** : to spend time thinking : MEDITATE   **2** : to chew the cud : bring up and chew again what has been chewed slightly and swallowed — **ru·mi·na·tion** \,rü-mə-'nā-shən\ *n*

¹rum·mage \'rəm-ij\ *vb* **rum·maged; rum·mag·ing** : to make an active search especially by moving, turning, or looking through the contents of a place or container ⟨*rummaging* through the attic⟩

²rummage *n* : a confused miscellaneous collection of articles

rummage sale *n* : a sale of miscellaneous articles especially to raise money (as for a church or charity)

rum·my \'rəm-ē\ *n* : a card game in which each player tries to lay down cards in groups of three or more

¹ru·mor \'rü-mər\ *n* **1** : a widely held opinion having no known source : HEARSAY   **2** : a statement or story that is in circulation but has not been proved to be true

²rumor *vb* **ru·mored; ru·mor·ing** \'rüm-(ə-)riŋ\ : to tell by rumor : spread a rumor

rump \'rəmp\ *n* **1** : the back part of an animal's body where the hips and thighs join that generally includes the buttocks   **2** : a cut of beef between the loin and round

rum·ple \'rəm-pəl\ *vb* **rum·pled; rum·pling** \-p(ə-)liŋ\ : ²WRINKLE, MUSS

rum·pus \'rəm-pəs\ *n* : a noisy commotion

¹run \'rən\ *vb* **ran** \'ran\; **run; run·ning** **1 a** : to go at a pace faster than a walk   **b** : to take to flight : FLEE ⟨made the enemy *run*⟩   **2** : to move or allow to move freely about ⟨chickens *running* loose⟩ ⟨*running* around without a coat⟩   **3 a** : to go or cause to go rapidly or hurriedly ⟨*run* and get the doctor⟩   **b** : to go in pursuit of ⟨had *run* the woodchuck into its hole⟩   **4** : to do something by or as if by running ⟨*run* errands⟩   **5 a** : to take part in a race   **b** : to be or cause to be a candidate in an election ⟨*ran* for mayor⟩   **6 a** : to move on or as if on wheels   **b** : to ravel lengthwise ⟨stockings guaranteed not to *run*⟩   **7 a** : to go back and forth ⟨the bus *runs* every hour⟩   **b** : to migrate or move in schools; *esp* : to go up a river to spawn ⟨shad are *running* in the river⟩   **8 a** : OPERATE 1 ⟨I can *run* that machine⟩ ⟨left the engine *running*⟩   **b** : to cause to be treated or operated on : PROCESS ⟨*ran* my program on the computer⟩   **9** : to continue in force or operation ⟨the contract has two years to *run*⟩ ⟨the play *ran* for six months⟩   **10** : to pass into a specified condition ⟨*run* into debt⟩   **11 a** : to move as a liquid : FLOW   **b** : to dissolve and spread out ⟨colors guaranteed not to *run*⟩   **c** : to give off liquid ⟨my nose is *running*⟩   **12** : to tend to develop a specified quality or feature ⟨one of those people who *run* to fat⟩   **13 a** : EXTEND 4 ⟨the boundary line *runs* east⟩   **b** : to be in a certain form or order   **14 a** : to occur again and again ⟨a song *running* through my head⟩ ⟨a condition that *runs* in their family⟩   **b** : to exist or occur in a continuous range of variation   **15** : to be in circulation ⟨there's a story *running* that the prime minister will resign⟩   **16** : ²TRACE 2a ⟨*ran* the rumor to its source⟩   **17** : to slip through or past ⟨*run* a blockade⟩   **18** : to pass over, across, or through   **19 a** : to cause or allow to go ⟨*ran* the rascals out of town⟩ ⟨*ran* the car off the road⟩   **b** : to be in charge of : MANAGE ⟨*run* a factory⟩   **20** : to make oneself liable to : INCUR ⟨*ran* the risk of discovery⟩ — **run across** : to meet or find by chance — **run into** : to meet by chance — **run riot 1**

: to behave wildly   **2** : to occur in great quantity — **run short** *or* **run low** : to be running out ⟨supplies were *running short*⟩ ⟨*run low* on fuel⟩

²run *n* **1 a** : an act or the action of running   **b** : a fast gallop   **c** : an annual migration of fish up a river especially to spawn   **d** : a group of fish migrating especially to spawn   **e** : a running race ⟨the 1500-meter *run*⟩   **f** : a score made in baseball by a base runner reaching home plate   **2 a** *chiefly Midland* : CREEK 2   **b** : something that flows especially during a certain time ⟨the first *run* of maple sap⟩   **3 a** : the horizontal distance from one point to another   **b** : general tendency or direction   **4** : a continuous series especially of similar things ⟨a long *run* of cloudy days⟩   **5** : sudden heavy demands from depositors, creditors, or customers ⟨a *run* on a bank⟩   **6** : the quantity of work turned out in a continuous operation; *also* : a period of continuous operation   **7** : the usual or normal kind ⟨average *run* of students⟩   **8 a** : the distance covered in a period of continuous traveling   **b** : regular course or trip ⟨the bus makes four *runs* daily⟩   **c** : freedom of movement ⟨has the *run* of the house⟩   **9 a** : a way, track, or path often traveled by animals   **b** : an enclosure for animals where they may feed or exercise   **10 a** : an inclined course (as for skiing)   **b** : a track or guide on which something runs   **11** : a ravel in a knitted fabric — **on the run 1** : while running : without stopping   **2** : running away

run·about \'rən-ə-,baùt\ *n* : a small motorboat used especially for pleasure

run·a·gate \'rən-ə-,gāt\ *n* **1** : ²VAGABOND   **2** : ¹RUNAWAY 1

run·around \'rən-ə-,raùnd\ *n* : deceptive or delaying action especially in response to a request

¹run·away \'rən-ə-,wā\ *n* **1** : a person who runs away : FUGITIVE   **2** : the act of running away out of control; *also* : something (as a horse) that is running out of control

²runaway *adj* **1** : running away : FUGITIVE   **2** : being out of control

run away \,rən-ə-'wā\ *vb* **1** : to leave in a hurry especially to escape from danger or confinement   **2** : to leave home

run·back \'rən-,bak\ *n* : ²RETURN 7

run·down \'rən-,daùn\ *n* : an item by item report : SUMMARY

run–down \'rən-'daùn\ *adj* **1** : being in poor condition ⟨a *run-down* farm⟩   **2** : being in or indicating poor health ⟨that *run-down* feeling⟩

run down \'rən-'daùn\ *vb* **1** : to collide with and knock down   **2 a** : to chase until exhausted or captured   **b** : to find by search : trace the source of   **3** : to stop operating because of the exhaustion of an energy source ⟨the battery *ran down*⟩

rune \'rün\ *n* : any of the characters of an alphabet used by the Germanic peoples from about the 3d to the 13th centuries — **ru·nic** \'rü-nik\ *adj*

rune

¹rung *past participle of* ³RING

²rung \'rəŋ\ *n* : a rounded part placed as a crosspiece between the legs of a chair; *also* : one of the crosspieces of a ladder

run–in \'rən-,in\ *n* : an angry dispute : QUARREL

run·ner \'rən-ər\ *n* **1 a** : one that runs   **b** : BASE RUNNER   **2** : MESSENGER   **3** : a thin piece or part on which something slides   **4 a** : a slender creeping branch of a plant; *esp* : STOLON 1   **b** : a plant that forms or spreads by run-

\ə\ abut	\aù\ out	\i\ tip	\o'\ saw	\ù\ foot
\ər\ further	\ch\ chin	\ī\ life	\oi\ coin	\y\ yet
\a\ mat	\e\ pet	\j\ job	\th\ thin	\yü\ few
\ā\ take	\ē\ easy	\ŋ\ sing	\th\ this	\yù\ cure
\ä\ cot, cart	\g\ go	\ō\ bone	\ü\ food	\zh\ vision

ners **5 a** : a long narrow carpet (as for a hall) **b** : a narrow decorative cloth cover for a table or dresser top

run·ner–up \'rən-ə-,rəp\ *n, pl* **runners–up** : the competitor in a contest who finishes next to the winner

¹run·ning \'rən-iŋ\ *n* : the action of running — **in the running** : having a chance to win a contest — **out of the running** : having no chance to win a contest

²running *adj* **1** : going on steadily : CONTINUOUS ⟨a *running* battle⟩ **2** : measured in a straight line **3** : done while running or with a running start ⟨a *running* jump⟩ **4** : made or trained for running ⟨a *running* track⟩ ⟨*running* shoes⟩

³running *adv* : one after another : in a row : CONSECUTIVELY ⟨for three days *running*⟩

running board *n* : a narrow step at the side of an automobile

running knot *n* : a knot (as a slipknot) that slides along the line around which it is tied

running light *n* : any of the lights on a vehicle (as a ship) that show size, position, or direction

running board

running mate *n* : a candidate running for a lesser office (as vice president) who is on the same ticket with the candidate for the top office

running stitch *n* : a small even stitch run in and out in cloth

run·ny \'rən-ē\ *adj* **run·ni·er; -est** **1** : too soft and liquid ⟨the pudding is *runny*⟩ **2** : giving off a liquid ⟨a *runny* nose⟩

run·off \'rən-,of\ *n* **1** : water from rain or snow that flows over the surface of the ground and finally into streams **2** : a final contest or election to decide an earlier one that has not given the victory to one competitor

run off \'rən-'of, ,rən-\ *vb* **1** : to produce rapidly **2** : to decide by a runoff **3** : to drive away **4** : RUN AWAY 1 — **run off with** : to carry off : STEAL

run–of–the–mill \,rən-ə(v)-the-'mil\ *adj* : ²AVERAGE 2, ORDINARY

¹run–on \'rən-,on, -'än\ *adj* : continuing without pause from one line of verse to another

²run–on \'rən-,on, -,än\ *n* **1** : a dictionary entry that is run on **2** : RUN-ON SENTENCE

run on \'rən-'on, ,rən-, -'än\ *vb* **1** : to keep going : CONTINUE **2** : to talk or tell at length **3** : to place or add (as an entry in a dictionary) at the end of an entry

run–on sentence *n* : a sentence formed from two or more sentences improperly joined (as "I didn't see the red light, officer, I was looking the other way")

run out *vb* **1** : to come to an end : EXPIRE ⟨time *ran out* before we could tie the game⟩ **2** : to become exhausted or used up ⟨our supplies were *running out*⟩ — **run out of** : to use up the available supply of ⟨better stop before we *run out* of gas⟩

run over *vb* **1** : ¹OVERFLOW 2, 3 **2** : to go beyond a limit ⟨the show may *run over* a minute or two⟩ **3** : to go over or rehearse quickly ⟨let's *run over* those lines again⟩ **4** : to collide with, knock down, and often drive over

runt \'rənt\ *n* : an unusually small person or animal — **runty** \-ē\ *adj*

run through *vb* **1** : to pierce with or as if with a sword **2** : to spend or use up wastefully ⟨*ran through* the money in no time⟩ **3** : to read or rehearse without pausing

run up *vb* : to cause to pile up : ACCUMULATE ⟨*ran up* a big telephone bill⟩

run·way \'rən-,wā\ *n* **1** : ²RUN 9a **2** : a paved strip of ground (as at an airport) for the landing and takeoff of aircraft **3** : a support (as a track, pipe, or trough) on which something runs

ru·pee \rü-'pē, 'rü-,pē\ *n* **1** : the basic unit of money of

India, Mauritius, Nepal, Pakistan, Seychelles, and Sri Lanka **2** : a coin representing one rupee [from a word in Hindi (the main language of India) *rūpaiyā* "a unit of money", of Sanskrit origin]

¹rup·ture \'rəp-chər\ *n* **1** : a break in peaceful or friendly relations **2** : a breaking or tearing apart (as of body tissue) ⟨a *rupture* in an artery⟩ **3** : HERNIA [Middle English *ruptur* "a breach of the peace", from early French *rupture* "a breach of the peace" or Latin *ruptura* "fracture, break", from Latin *ruptus*, past participle of *rumpere* "to break" — related to CORRUPT, INTERRUPT]

²rupture *vb* **rup·tured; rup·tur·ing** **1** : to part by violence : BREAK **2** : to produce a rupture in **3** : to have a rupture

ru·ral \'rur-əl\ *adj* : of or relating to the country, country people or life, or agriculture

rural free delivery *n* : the free delivery of mail on routes in country districts

rural route *n* : a postal route in a rural free delivery area

ruse \'rüs, 'rüz\ *n* : a clever way to fool someone : TRICK

¹rush \'rəsh\ *n* : any of various marsh plants that are related to the grasses but belong to a different family and that often have hollow stems used to weave chair seats and mats [Old English *risc* "the rush plant"]

²rush *vb* **1** : to move forward or act with haste or eagerness **2** : to perform in a short time or at high speed ⟨*rushed* the job through⟩ **3** : to urge on to greater speed ⟨don't *rush* me⟩ **4** : to run toward or against in attack : CHARGE [Middle English *russhen* "to rush", from early French *ruser* "to cause to flee, drive off", from Latin *recusare* "to refuse"] — **rush·er** *n*

³rush *n* **1** : a violent forward motion ⟨a *rush* of wind⟩ **2** : a burst of activity or speed **3** : an eager migration of people usually to a new place in search of wealth ⟨the gold *rush*⟩

⁴rush *adj* : demanding special speed or hurry ⟨*rush* orders⟩ ⟨the *rush* season⟩

rush hour *n* : a period of the day when traffic is very heavy or business is very brisk

rusk \'rəsk\ *n* : a sweet or plain bread baked, sliced, and baked again until dry and crisp

¹rus·set \'rəs-ət\ *n* **1** : coarse homespun usually reddish brown cloth **2** : a strong brown **3** : any of various late-ripening apples that have rough russet-colored skins and keep well in winter

²russet *adj* : of the color russet

Rus·sian \'rəsh-ən\ *n* **1** : a person born or living in Russia **2** : a Slavic language of the Russian people — **Russian** *adj*

Russian dressing *n* : a salad dressing usually containing mayonnaise and chili sauce

Russian wolfhound *n* : BORZOI

Rus·so- \'rəs-ō, 'rəsh-; ,rəs-ə\ *combining form* **1** : Russian **2** : Russian and ⟨*Russo*-Japanese⟩ [from the English words *Russia, Russian*]

¹rust \'rəst\ *n* **1** : a reddish brittle coating formed on iron especially when chemically attacked by moist air and composed chiefly of ferric oxide **2 a** : any of numerous destructive diseases of plants caused by fungi and characterized by reddish brown spots **b** : any of an order of fungi that cause plant rusts **3** : a reddish brown

²rust *vb* : to form or cause to form rust ⟨iron *rusts*⟩

¹rus·tic \'rəs-tik\ *adj* : of, relating to, or suitable for the country or country people : RURAL — **rus·ti·cal·ly** \-ti-k(ə-)lē\ *adv* — **rus·tic·i·ty** \,rəs-'tis-ət-ē\ *n*

²rustic *n* : a person living or raised in the country

¹rus·tle \'rəs-əl\ *vb* **rus·tled; rus·tling** \'rəs-(ə-)liŋ\ **1** : to make or cause to make a rustle **2** : to act or move with energy **3** : to steal (as cattle) from the range — **rus·tler** \'rəs-(ə-)lər\ *n*

²rustle *n* : a quick series of small sounds ⟨the *rustle* of leaves⟩

rust·proof \'rəst-'prüf\ *adj* : protected against rusting

rusty \'rəs-tē\ *adj* **rust·i·er; -est** **1** : affected by or as if by rust **2** : less skilled and slow through lack of practice or old age **3** : of the color rust — **rust·i·ly** \-tə-lē\ *adv* — **rust·i·ness** \-tē-nəs\ *n*

¹rut \'rət\ *n* : a state of sexual excitement especially in the male deer; *also* : a period in which rut occurs [Middle English *rutte* "state of sexual excitement", from early French *rut* "a roar", derived from Latin *rugitus,* past participle of *rugire* "to roar"]

²rut *vb* **rut·ted; rut·ting** : to be in or enter into a state of rut

³rut *n* **1** : a track worn by a wheel or by frequent passage **2** : a usual or fixed routine ⟨I need a change — I'm getting in a *rut*⟩ [probably derived from early French *route* "route, way"] — **rut·ty** \'rət-ē\ *adj*

⁴rut *vb* **rut·ted; rut·ting** : to make a rut in

ru·ta·ba·ga \,rüt-ə-'bā-gə, ,rüt-, -'beg-ə\ *n* : a turnip with a very large yellowish root — called also *swede*

Ruth \'rüth\ *n* — see BIBLE table

ru·the·ni·um \rü-'thē-nē-əm\ *n* : a hard brittle grayish rare metallic element found in platinum ores — see ELEMENT table

ruth·less \'rüth-ləs\ *adj* : having no pity : MERCILESS, CRUEL — **ruth·less·ly** *adv* — **ruth·less·ness** *n*

-ry \rē\ *n suffix, pl* **-ries** : -ERY ⟨wizard*ry*⟩ ⟨citizen*ry*⟩ [derived from early French *-erie* (a noun suffix)]

rye \'rī\ *n* **1** : a hardy annual cereal grass widely grown for grain and as a cover crop; *also* : its seeds **2** : RYE BREAD **3** : whiskey distilled from rye or from rye and malt

rye bread *n* : bread made entirely or partly from rye flour

rye 1

S

s \'es\ *n, often cap* **1** : the 19th letter of the English alphabet **2** : a grade rating a student's work as satisfactory

¹-s \s *after a voiceless consonant sound, z after a voiced consonant sound or a vowel sound*\ *n pl suffx* — used to form the plural of most nouns that do not end in *s, z, sh,* or *ch* or in *y* following a consonant ⟨head*s*⟩ ⟨book*s*⟩ ⟨boy*s*⟩ ⟨belief*s*⟩, to form the plural of proper nouns that end in *y* following a consonant ⟨Mary*s*⟩, and with or without a preceding apostrophe to form the plural of abbreviations, numbers, letters, and symbols used as nouns ⟨MC*s*⟩ ⟨4*s*⟩ ⟨#*s*⟩ ⟨B'*s*⟩ [derived from Old English *-as,* an ending on plural nouns]

²-s *adv suffix* — used to form adverbs indicating usual or repeated action or state ⟨at home Sunday*s*⟩ ⟨shops morning*s*⟩

³-s *vb suffix* — used to form the third person singular present of most verbs that do not end in *s, z, sh,* or *ch* or in *y* following a consonant ⟨fall*s*⟩ ⟨take*s*⟩ ⟨play*s*⟩

-'s \s *after voiceless consonant sounds other than* s, sh, ch; *z after vowel sounds and voiced consonant sounds other than* z, zh, j; *əz after* s, sh, ch, z, zh, j\ *n suffix or pron suffix* — used to form the possessive of singular nouns ⟨boy'*s*⟩, of plural nouns not ending in *s* ⟨children'*s*⟩, of some pronouns ⟨anyone'*s*⟩, and of word groups functioning as nouns ⟨the man in the corner'*s* hat⟩ or pronouns ⟨someone else'*s*⟩

¹'s *like* -'s\ *vb* **1 a** : IS ⟨she'*s* here⟩ **b** : WAS ⟨when'*s* the last time you ate?⟩ **2** : HAS ⟨he'*s* seen them⟩ **3** : DOES ⟨what'*s* he want?⟩

²'s \s\ *pron* : US — used with *let* ⟨let'*s*⟩

Sab·bath \'sab-əth\ *n* **1** : the 7th day of the week observed from Friday evening to Saturday evening as a day of rest and worship by Jews and some Christians **2** : the day of the week (as among Christians) set aside in a religion for rest and worship [Middle English *sabat* "the seventh day of the week for rest and worship", from early French *sabat* and Old English *sabat* (both, same meaning), both from Latin *sabbatum* "Sabbath", from Greek *sabbaton* (same meaning), from Hebrew *shabbāth,* literally "rest"]

sab·bat·i·cal \sə-'bat-i-kəl\ *or* **sab·bat·ic** \-'bat-ik\ *adj* **1** : of or relating to the Sabbath ⟨*sabbatical* laws⟩ **2** : of or relating to a leave granted usually every seventh year (as to a professor) for rest, travel, or research

sa·ber *or* **sa·bre** \'sā-bər\ *n* : a cavalry sword with a curved blade

sa·ber–toothed tiger \,sā-bər-,tüth(t)-\ *n* : any of various large prehistoric cats with very long curved upper canine teeth

Sa·bine \'sā-,bīn\ *n* : a member of an ancient Italic people conquered by Rome in 290 B.C. — **Sabine** *adj*

sa·ble \'sā-bəl\ *n, pl* **sables** **1** : the color black **2 a** *or pl* **sable** : a meat-eating mammal of northern Europe and Asia related to the martens and valued for its soft rich brown fur **b** : the fur or pelt of a sable — **sable** *adj*

¹sab·o·tage \'sab-ə-,täzh\ *n* **1** : destruction of an employer's property or the action of making it difficult to work by discontented workers **2** : destructive or blocking action carried on by enemy agents or sympathizers to make a nation's war effort more difficult

saber

sable 2a

Word History In French the word *sabot* refers to "a wooden work shoe". Naturally, walking around in such shoes can be noisy, so the verb *saboter* was formed and used to mean "to clatter with sabots". From this verb the French derived the noun *sabotage,* meaning "the making of sabots". In time *sabotage* acquired the added sense of "the botching or bungling of something". Apparently, walking in these clumsy, clattering shoes became associated with working in a careless or slipshod way. Later the word was used for "the deliberate destruction of an employer's property". This kind of

\ə\ abut	\aú\ out	\i\ tip	\ó\ saw	\ú\ foot
\ər\ further	\ch\ chin	\ī\ life	\ói\ coin	\y\ yet
\a\ mat	\e\ pet	\j\ job	\th\ thin	\yü\ few
\ā\ take	\ē\ easy	\ŋ\ sing	\th\ this	\yú\ cure
\ä\ cot, cart	\g\ go	\ō\ bone	\ü\ food	\zh\ vision

sabotage was done by workers in order to force employers to agree to their demands. This sense of *sabotage* was borrowed into English around 1890. The term was especially appropriate during the great French railway strike of 1910 when the strikers destroyed the wooden devices (also called *sabots*) holding the rails in place. Since World War I *sabotage* has been commonly used for "actions taken by enemy agents against a nation's war effort". [from French *sabotage* "destruction of property to hinder a manufacturing or war effort", from *saboter* "to clatter around wearing sabots, botch", from *sabot* "a wooden shoe"]

²sabotage *vb* **-taged; -tag•ing** : to practice sabotage on : WRECK

sab•o•teur \,sab-ə-'tər, -'t(y)ù(ə)r\ *n* : a person who performs sabotage

sac \'sak\ *n* : a pouch in an animal or plant often containing a fluid ⟨a food-storage *sac*⟩ — **sac•like** \-,līk\ *adj*

sac•cha•rin \'sak-(ə-)rən\ *n* : a very sweet white substance that comes from coal tar and is used as a calorie-free sweetener [derived from Latin *saccharum* "sugar", from Greek *sakcharon* "sugar"; of Sanskrit origin]

sac•cha•rine \'sak-(ə-)rən, -ə-,rēn, -ə-,rīn\ *adj* **1 a** : of, relating to, or resembling sugar or its characteristics ⟨*saccharine* taste⟩ **b** : producing or containing sugar ⟨*saccharine* fluids⟩ **2** : overly sweet ⟨a *saccharine* smile⟩

sac•er•do•tal \,sas-ər-'dōt-ᵉl, ,sak-\ *adj* : of or relating to priests or a priesthood : PRIESTLY — **sac•er•do•tal•ly** \-ᵉl-ē\ *adv*

sac fungus *n* : ASCOMYCETE

sa•chem \'sā-chəm\ *n* : a North American Indian chief

sa•chet \sa-'shā\ *n* : a small bag containing a perfumed powder for scenting clothes and linens

¹sack \'sak\ *n* **1** : a flexible container (as of paper) : BAG **2** : SACKFUL **3** : discharge from employment — usually used with *get* or *give* **4** : ¹BUNK 2, BED [Middle English *sak* "bag, sackcloth", from early French *sacc* (same meaning), from Latin *saccus* "bag" and later Latin *saccus* "sackcloth", both from Greek *sakkos* "bag, sackcloth" — related to ⁴SACK] — **sack•like** \-,līk\ *adj*

²sack *vb* **1** : to put in a sack **2** : DISMISS 2, FIRE

³sack *n* : any of several white wines imported to England from Spain and the Canary islands in the 16th and 17th centuries [from early French *sec* "dry to the taste, not sweet", from Latin *siccus* (same meaning)]

⁴sack *vb* **1** : to loot after capture **2** : ²PILLAGE, LOOT [from early French *sachier* "to loot, pillage", from *sac* "the action of looting", from early Italian *sacco*, literally "a bag", from Latin *saccus* "bag" — related to ¹SACK]

⁵sack *n* : the looting of a captured town

sack•cloth \'sak-,(k)lòth\ *n* **1** : rough cloth for sacks **2** : a garment of sackcloth worn as a sign of sorrow

sack coat *n* : a man's jacket with a straight back

sack•ful \'sak-,fùl\ *n, pl* **sackfuls** \-,fùlz\ : the quantity that fills a sack

sack•ing \'sak-iŋ\ *n* : strong rough cloth from which sacks are made

sac•ra•ment \'sak-rə-mənt\ *n* **1** : a religious act that is a sign or symbol of a spiritual existence **2** *cap* : BLESSED SACRAMENT — **sac•ra•men•tal** \,sak-rə-'ment-ᵉl\ *adj* — **sac•ra•men•tal•ly** \-ᵉl-ē\ *adv*

sa•cred \'sā-krəd\ *adj* **1** : set apart in honor of someone (as a god) ⟨a mountain *sacred* to Jupiter⟩ **2** : HOLY 1 ⟨the *sacred* name of Jesus⟩ **3** : ¹RELIGIOUS 2 ⟨*sacred* songs⟩ **4** : deserving respect or honor ⟨a *sacred* right⟩ [Middle English *sacred* "sacred", derived from early French *sacrer* "to make holy, dedicate to God", from Latin *sacrare* (same meaning), from *sacr-, sacer* "sacred, holy" — related to CONSECRATE, SACRIFICE] — **sa•cred•ly** *adv* — **sa•cred•ness** *n*

¹sac•ri•fice \'sak-rə-,fīs, -fəs\ *n* **1** : an act of offering something precious to God or a god; *esp* : the killing of a

victim on an altar **2** : something offered in sacrifice **3** : a giving up of something especially for the sake of someone else; *also* : something so given up **4** : loss of profit ⟨sell goods at a *sacrifice*⟩ [Middle English *sacrifise, sacrifice* "the act of offering something to God or a god", from early French *sacrifise* (same meaning), from Latin *sacrificium* "sacrifice", from *sacr-, sacer* "sacred" and *-ficium*, from *facere* "to do, make" — related to SACRED]

²sac•ri•fice \'sak-rə-,fīs, -,fīz\ *vb* **-ficed; -fic•ing** **1** : to offer or perform as a sacrifice **2** : to give up for the sake of something else **3** : to sell at a loss **4** : to make a sacrifice hit — **sac•ri•fic•er** *n*

sacrifice fly *n* : an outfield fly in baseball caught by a fielder after which a base runner scores

sacrifice hit *n* : a bunt in baseball that allows a runner to advance one base while the batter is put out

sac•ri•fi•cial \,sak-rə-'fish-əl\ *adj* : of or relating to sacrifice — **sac•ri•fi•cial•ly** \-ə-lē\ *adv*

sac•ri•lege \'sak-rə-lij\ *n* : theft or violation of something sacred — **sac•ri•le•gious** \,sak-rə-'lij-əs, -'lē-jəs\ *adj* — **sac•ri•le•gious•ly** *adv* — **sac•ri•le•gious•ness** *n*

sac•ris•tan \'sak-rə-stən\ *n* **1** : a church officer in charge of the sacristy **2** : SEXTON

sac•ris•ty \'sak-rə-stē\ *n, pl* **-ties** : VESTRY

sac•ro•sanct \'sak-rō-,saŋ(k)t\ *adj* : most sacred or holy : INVIOLABLE — **sac•ro•sanc•ti•ty** \,sak-rō-'saŋ(k)-tət-ē\ *n*

sa•crum \'sak-rəm, 'sā-krəm\ *n, pl* **sa•cra** \'sak-rə, 'sā-krə\ : a triangular bone at the base of the spinal column that connects with or forms a part of the pelvis and in human beings consists of five united vertebrae

sad \'sad\ *adj* **sad•der; sad•dest** **1** : filled with or expressing grief or unhappiness ⟨*sad* songs⟩ **2** : causing grief or unhappiness : DEPRESSING ⟨*sad* news⟩ — **sad•ly** *adv*

sad•den \'sad-ᵉn\ *vb* **sad•dened; sad•den•ing** \-niŋ, -ᵉn-iŋ\ : to make or become sad

¹sad•dle \'sad-ᵉl\ *n* **1 a** : a padded and leather-covered seat for a horseback rider **b** : a padded part of a harness **c** : a bicycle or motorcycle seat **2** : something like a saddle in shape, position, or use; *esp* : a support for an object — **in the saddle** : in control or command

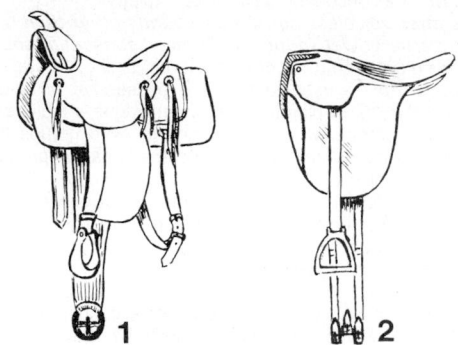

saddle 1a: *1* western, *2* English

²saddle *vb* **sad•dled; sad•dling** \'sad-liŋ, -ᵉl-iŋ\ **1** : to put a saddle on **2** : ENCUMBER 1, BURDEN

sad•dle•bag \'sad-ᵉl-,bag\ *n* : one of a pair of covered pouches laid across the back of a horse behind the saddle or hanging over the rear wheel of a bicycle or motorcycle

sad•dle•bow \-,bō\ *n* : the raised front part of a saddle

saddle horse *n* : a horse suited for or trained for riding

sad•dler \'sad-lər\ *n* : one that makes, repairs, or sells horse equipment (as saddles)

sad•dlery \'sad-lə-rē, 'sad-ᵉl-rē\ *n, pl* **-dler•ies** : the work, articles of trade, or shop of a saddler

saddle shoe n : a shoe having a piece of different color or leather across the instep

saddle sore n **1** : a sore on the back of a horse caused by an ill-fitting or improperly adjusted saddle **2** : an irritation or sore on parts of the rider's body caused by rubbing against the saddle

sad·dle·tree \'sad-ᵊl-,trē\ n : the frame of a saddle

sa·dism \'sā-,diz-əm, 'sad-,iz-\ n **1** : abnormal sexual behavior in which sexual pleasure is obtained by hurting another **2** : very great cruelty — **sa·dis·tic** \sə-'dis-tik also sā-\ adj

sa·dist \'sād-əst, 'sad-\ n : an individual who practices sadism

sad·ness \'sad-nəs\ n : the quality, state, or fact of being sad

sa·fa·ri \sə-'fär-ē, -'far-\ n : a hunting expedition especially in eastern Africa

¹safe \'sāf\ adj **saf·er; saf·est 1** : freed or secure from danger, harm, or loss **2** : successful at getting to a base in baseball without being put out ⟨the runner was *safe*⟩ **3** : providing safety **4** : not threatening danger ⟨*safe* medicine⟩ **5 a** : CAUTIOUS ⟨a *safe* driver⟩ **b** : TRUSTWORTHY [Middle English *sauf* "safe, unhurt", from early French *sauf* (same meaning), from Latin *salvus* "safe, healthy" — related to ³SAGE, SAVE] — **safe·ly** adv — **safe·ness** n

²safe n : a container to keep articles (as valuables) safe

safe–deposit box n : a box (as in the vault of a bank) for the safe storage of valuables

¹safe·guard \'sāf-,gärd\ n : something that protects and gives safety : DEFENSE

²safeguard vb : to make safe or secure : PROTECT

safe·keep·ing \'sāf-'kē-piŋ\ n : PROTECTION 1, CUSTODY

safe·light \'sā-,flīt\ n : a darkroom lamp with a filter to screen out light that is harmful to film or paper

safe sex n : sexual activity and especially sexual intercourse in which various measures (as the use of latex condoms) are taken to avoid disease (as AIDS) transmitted by sexual contact

safe·ty \'sāf-tē\ n, pl **safeties 1** : the state of being safe : SECURITY **2** : a protective device (as on a pistol) to prevent accidental operation **3 a** : a score of two points for the defensive team in football when an offensive ballcarrier is tackled behind the offensive team's goal line **b** : a defensive football player whose position is far back from the line of scrimmage

safety belt n : a belt for fastening a person to an object to prevent falling or injury

safety match n : a match that can be struck only on a specially prepared surface

safety pin n : a pin that is bent back on itself to form a spring and has a guard covering its point

safety razor n : a razor with a guard for the blade to prevent deep cuts

safety valve n **1** : a valve that opens automatically (as when steam pressure becomes too great) **2** : OUTLET 2

saf·flow·er \'saf-,laû(-ə)r\ n : a widely grown Old World herb related to the daisies that has large orange or red flower heads that are the source of a dye and seeds rich in edible oil

safflower oil n : a polyunsaturated edible oil obtained from the seeds of the safflower

saf·fron \'saf-rən\ n **1** : an orange powder that is used especially to color or flavor foods and consists of the dried stigmas of a crocus with purple flowers **2** : an orange to orange yellow color

¹sag \'sag\ vb **sagged; sag·ging 1** : to droop or sink below the normal or right level **2** : to become less firm or strong

²sag n **1** : a sagging part or area ⟨the *sag* in a rope⟩ **2** : an instance or amount of sagging

sa·ga \'säg-ə\ n **1** : a tale of figures and events of Norway and Iceland from history or legend **2** : a story of heroic deeds

sa·ga·cious \sə-'gā-shəs\ adj : quick and wise in understanding and judgment — **sa·ga·cious·ness** n — **sa·gac·i·ty** \-'gas-ət-ē\ n

sag·a·more \'sag-ə-,mō(ə)r, -,mȯ(ə)r\ n **1** : an Algonquian Indian chief **2** : SACHEM

¹sage \'sāj\ adj **sag·er; sag·est** : ²WISE 1, PRUDENT ⟨*sage* advice⟩ [Middle English *sage* "wise", from early French *sage* (same meaning), derived from Latin *sapere* "to be wise, taste, have flavor" — related to INSIPID, SAVANT] — **sage·ly** adv — **sage·ness** n

²sage n : a very wise person

³sage n **1** : a mint with fragrant leaves that is used especially to flavor meat **2** : SAGEBRUSH [Middle English *sage* "sage plant", from early French *sauge* (same meaning), from Latin *salvia* "sage plant used for health", from *salvus* "safe, healthy" — related to SAFE, SAVE]

sage·brush \'sāj-,brəsh\ n : any of several low shrubby North American plants related to the daisies; esp : a common plant with a bitter juice that smells like sage and is widespread on the plains of the western U.S.

Sag·it·tar·i·us \,saj-ə-'ter-ē-əs\ n **1** : a group of stars between Scorpio and Capricorn usually pictured as a creature that is half man half horse with a bow and arrow **2 a** : the ninth sign of the zodiac — see ZODIAC table **b** : a person whose sign of the zodiac is Sagittarius [from Latin *Sagittarius*, literally "archer"]

sa·go \'sā-gō\ n, pl **sagos** : a dry granulated or powdered starch prepared from spongy tissue inside the stem of a sago palm

sago palm n : any of a genus of tall tropical palms that have leaves with numerous leaflets and are a source of sago

sa·gua·ro \sə-'wär-ə, -'wär-ō, -'gwär-ō\ n, pl **-ros** : a cactus of desert regions of the southwestern U.S. and Mexico that has a spiny branched trunk of up to 20 meters and bears white flowers and edible fruit

saguaro

said past and past participle of SAY

¹sail \'sā(ə)l, as last element in compounds often səl\ n **1 a** : a sheet of fabric (as canvas) used to catch wind to move a craft through water or over ice **b** : the sails of a ship ⟨under full *sail*⟩ **c** pl usually **sail** : a ship with sails **2** : something like a sail **3** : a journey by ship

²sail vb **1** : to travel on water in a ship ⟨*sail* the seas⟩ **2** : to travel by a sailing craft **3** : to move or glide along ⟨*sailed* into the room⟩ **4** : to manage the sailing of — **sail into** : to go at something eagerly ⟨*sailed into* their dinner⟩

sail·boat \'sā(ə)l-,bōt\ n : a boat equipped with sails

sail·cloth \-,klȯth\ n : a heavy canvas

sail·fish \-,fish\ n : any of a genus of large sea fishes related to the swordfish that have teeth, scales, and a very large fin like a sail on the back

sail·or \'sā-lər\ n : a person who sails : SEAMAN

sail·plane \'sā(ə)l-,plān\ n : a glider designed to rise in an upward current of air

¹saint \'sānt; when a name follows (,)sānt or sənt\ n **1** : a holy and godly person; esp : one who is declared to be worthy of special honor **2** : a person who is very good

\ə\ abut	\aú\ out	\i\ tip	\ȯ\ saw	\ú\ foot
\ər\ further	\ch\ chin	\ī\ life	\ȯi\ coin	\y\ yet
\a\ mat	\e\ pet	\j\ job	\th\ thin	\yü\ few
\ā\ take	\ē\ easy	\ŋ\ sing	\<u>th</u>\ this	\yú\ cure
\ä\ cot, cart	\g\ go	\ō\ bone	\ü\ food	\zh\ vision

especially about helping others

²saint \'sānt\ *vb* : CANONIZE

Saint Ag·nes's Eve \sānt-,ag-nə-səz-\ *n* : the night of January 20 when girls were traditionally thought to dream of their future husbands

Saint An·drew's cross \-,an-,drüz-\ *n* : a cross shaped like the letter X

Saint Ber·nard \,sānt-bər-'närd\ *n* : any of a breed of large powerful dogs developed in the Swiss Alps and formerly used in aiding lost travelers

Saint Bernard

saint·ed \'sānt-əd\ *adj* : SAINTLY

saint·hood \'sānt-,hůd\ *n* **1** : the quality or state of being a saint **2** : saints as a group

saint·ly \'sānt-lē\ *adj* **saint·li·er; -est** : relating to, resembling, or proper for a saint : HOLY — **saint·li·ness** *n*

Saint Pat·rick's Day \-'pa-triks-\ *n* : March 17 celebrated in honor of St. Patrick

saint·ship \'sānt-,ship\ *n* : SAINTHOOD 1

Saint Val·en·tine's Day \-'val-ən-,tīnz-\ *n* : February 14 observed in honor of St. Valentine and as a time for exchanging valentines

saith \(')seth, 'sā-əth\ *archaic present third sing of* SAY

¹sake \'sāk\ *n* **1** : GOAL 2, PURPOSE ⟨for the *sake* of argument⟩ **2** : the good of something : ADVANTAGE ⟨the *sake* of our country⟩ [Old English *sacu* "guilt, legal action"]

²sa·ke *or* **sa·ki** \'säk-ē\ *n* : a Japanese alcoholic drink made from rice [Japanese]

sa·laam \sə-'läm\ *n* : a greeting performed by bowing very low with the palm on the forehead [from Arabic *salām* "a greeting", literally "peace"] — **salaam** *vb*

sal·able *or* **sale·able** \'sā-lə-bəl\ *adj* : capable of being or good enough to be sold — **sal·abil·i·ty** \,sā-lə-'bil-ət-ē\ *n*

sal·ad \'sal-əd\ *n* **1** : green vegetables (as lettuce) often with tomato, cucumber, or radish served with dressing **2** : a cold dish (as of meat, shellfish, fruit, or vegetables) served with a dressing

salad bar *n* : a self-service counter in a restaurant featuring a selection of salad makings and dressings

salad dressing *n* : a sauce for a salad

salad oil *n* : an oil from plants suitable for use in salad dressings

sal·a·man·der \'sal-ə-,man-dər\ *n* **1** : an imaginary creature not harmed by fire **2** : any of an order of amphibians that are covered with scaleless usually smooth moist skin and look like lizards

sa·la·mi \sə-'läm-ē\ *n* : highly seasoned sausage of pork and beef

sal am·mo·ni·ac \,sal-ə-'mō-nē-,ak\ *n* : AMMONIUM CHLORIDE

sal·a·ried \'sal-(ə-)rēd\ *adj* : receiving or paying a salary ⟨a *salaried* position⟩

sal·a·ry \'sal-(ə-)rē\ *n, pl* **-ries** : money paid at regular times for work or services : STIPEND

> **Word History** Salt was a very valuable substance in ancient times. In addition to being used to flavor food, it was also used to keep foods from spoiling. Because of its importance, soldiers in the Roman army were given a special sum of money with which to buy salt for themselves. The Latin word for "salt" was *sal*, and the "salt money" given to the soldiers was called *salarium*. *Salarium* later came to be used for the regular pension or salary paid to the soldiers. Still later it was used for payments made to officials of the empire. The English word *salary* comes from the Latin *salarium*. [Middle English *salarie* "money paid to a worker", from Latin *salarium* "salt money, pension, salary," derived from *sal* "salt"]

sale \'sā(ə)l\ *n* **1** : the act of selling; *esp* : the exchange of property for a price **2** : ¹AUCTION **3** : a selling of goods at bargain prices **4** *pl* **a** : the business of selling **b** : total amounts of money received — **for sale** : available for purchase — **on sale** **1** : available for purchase **2** : selling at a bargain price

sales·clerk \'sā(ə)lz-,klərk\ *n* : a person employed to sell goods in a store

sales·man \-mən\ *n* : one who sells in a specific territory or in a store — **sales·man·ship** \-,ship\ *n*

sales·peo·ple \-,pē-pəl\ *n pl* : people employed to sell goods or services

sales·per·son \-,pərs-ᵉn\ *n* : a person employed to sell goods or services

sales tax *n* : a tax paid on the purchase of goods and services and collected by the seller

sales·wom·an \'sā(ə)lz-,wům-ən\ *n* : a woman employed to sell goods especially in a store

sal·i·cyl·ic acid \,sal-ə-,sil-ik-\ *n* : a weak acid used especially in the form of salts to relieve pain and fever and in the treatment of rheumatism

sa·lient \'sā-lyənt, 'sā-lē-ənt\ *adj* **1** : sticking outward ⟨a *salient* angle⟩ **2** : OUTSTANDING **3** — **sa·lient·ly** *adv*

sa·line \'sā-,lēn, -,līn\ *adj* **1** : consisting of or containing salt ⟨a *saline* solution⟩ **2** : of, relating to, or resembling salt — **sa·lin·i·ty** \sā-'lin-ət-ē, sə-\ *n*

sa·li·va \sə-'lī-və\ *n* : a fluid containing water, protein, salts, and often a starch-splitting enzyme that is secreted into the mouth by salivary glands

sal·i·vary \'sal-ə-,ver-ē\ *adj* : of or relating to saliva or the salivary glands

salivary gland *n* : any of various glands that secrete saliva into the mouth cavity

sal·i·vate \'sal-ə-,vāt\ *vb* **-vat·ed; -vat·ing** : to produce or secrete saliva especially in large amounts — **sal·i·va·tion** \,sal-ə-'vā-shən\ *n*

Salk vaccine \'só(l)k-\ *n* : a polio vaccine that contains inactivated virus and is given by injection [named for Jonas *Salk* born 1914 an American doctor who developed the vaccine]

sal·low \'sal-ō\ *adj* : of a grayish greenish yellow color ⟨*sallow* complexion⟩

¹sal·ly \'sal-ē\ *n, pl* **sallies** **1** : an action of rushing or bursting out; *esp* : a sudden attack of surrounded troops upon the attackers **2** : a witty remark : QUIP **3** : EXCURSION 1a, JAUNT

²sally *vb* **sal·lied; sal·ly·ing** **1** : to leap or burst out suddenly **2** : SET OUT 2, DEPART ⟨*sallied* out to see the town⟩

salm·on \'sam-ən\ *n, pl* **salmon** *also* **salmons** **1** : any of various large food and game fishes that are related to the trouts, have reddish or pinkish flesh, live in oceans or large lakes, and swim up rivers to lay eggs: as **a** : a large game fish

salmon 1b

of the northern Atlantic that lays eggs in rivers on both sides of the Atlantic — called also *Atlantic salmon* **b** : any of a genus of fishes that breed in rivers emptying into the northern Pacific **2** : SALMON PINK

salm·on·ber·ry \-,ber-ē\ *n* : a showy red-flowered raspberry of the Pacific coast; *also* : its edible salmon-colored fruit

sal·mo·nel·la \,sal-mə-'nel-ə\ *n, pl* **-nellas** *or* **-nella** *also* **-nel·lae** \-'nel-ē, -,ī\ : any of a genus of rod-shaped bacteria that cause various illnesses (as food poisoning) in human beings and warm-blooded animals

salmon pink *n* : a strong yellowish pink

sa·lon \sə-'län, 'sal-,än\ *n* **1** : an apartment or living room of stylish design **2** : a social gathering held in a salon **3 a** : an art gallery **b** : an annual exhibition of art **4** : a stylish business establishment

sa·loon \sə-'lün\ *n* **1** : a public room for socializing especially on a ship **2** : BARROOM

sal·sa \'sȯl-sə, 'säl-\ *n* **1** : a spicy sauce of tomatoes, onions, and hot peppers **2** : popular music of Latin American origin with elements of rhythm and blues, jazz, and rock

¹salt \'sȯlt\ *n* **1 a** : a compound in the form of crystals that consists of sodium chloride and is used especially for seasoning or preserving food and in industry — called also *common salt* **b** : any of numerous compounds formed by replacement of part or all of the hydrogen of an acid by a metal or by a group acting like a metal **2** : an element that gives flavor **3** : SAILOR

²salt *vb* : to treat, prepare for future use, flavor, or supply with salt

³salt *adj* **1 a** : containing salt : SALINE, SALTY ⟨*salt* water⟩ **b** : having or being one of the four basic taste sensations — compare BITTER 1, ¹SOUR 1, ¹SWEET 1b **2** : prepared for use or seasoned with salt ⟨*salt* pork⟩ — **salt·ness** *n*

salt away *vb* : to lay away safely : SAVE

salt·bush \'sȯlt-,bu̇sh\ *n* : any of various shrubby plants of dry regions that are related to the goosefoots

salt·cel·lar \'sȯlt-,sel-ər\ *n* : a small container for holding salt at table

salt flat *n* : an area of land covered with a crust of salt left by evaporation of water

sal·tine \sȯl-'tēn\ *n* : a square crisp cracker usually sprinkled with salt

salt lake *n* : a lake that has become salty through evaporation

salt lick *n* : ²LICK 3

salt marsh *n* : flat land that is overflowed by salt water

salt·shak·er \'sȯlt-,shā-kər\ *n* : a container having a top with holes in it for sprinkling salt

salt·wa·ter \,sȯlt-,wȯt-ər, -,wät-\ *adj* : relating to, living in, or consisting of salt water

salty \'sȯl-tē\ *adj* **salt·i·er; -est** **1** : seasoned with or containing salt : tasting of or like salt **2** : having the flavor of or suggesting the sea or things related to the sea **3** : ¹RACY 2 ⟨a *salty* remark⟩ — **salt·i·ness** *n*

sa·lu·bri·ous \sə-'lü-brē-əs\ *adj* : favorable to health — **sa·lu·bri·ous·ly** *adv* — **sa·lu·bri·ous·ness** *n*

sal·u·tary \'sal-yə-,ter-ē\ *adj* **1** : producing a good result **2** : furthering good health — **sal·u·tari·ness** *n*

sal·u·ta·tion \,sal-yə-'tā-shən\ *n* **1** : an expression of greeting, goodwill, or courtesy **2** : the word or phrase of greeting that begins a letter — **sal·u·ta·tion·al** \-shnəl, -shən-ᵊl\ *adj*

sa·lu·ta·to·ri·an \sə-,lüt-ə-'tȯr-ē-ən, -'tȯr-\ *n* : the graduating student usually second highest in rank

¹sa·lu·ta·to·ry \sə-'lüt-ə-,tȯr-ē, -,tȯr-\ *adj* : expressing salutations or welcome

²salutatory *n, pl* **-ries** : a salutatory address

¹sa·lute \sə-'lüt\ *vb* **sa·lut·ed; sa·lut·ing** **1** : to greet with courteous words or a bow **2 a** : to honor by a standard military ceremony **b** : to show respect to by taking the proper position ⟨*salute* an officer⟩ — **sa·lut·er** *n*

²salute *n* **1** : SALUTATION 1, GREETING **2 a** : a sign or ceremony of goodwill, compliment, or respect **b** : the position taken by a person saluting a military officer

¹sal·vage \'sal-vij\ *n* **1** : money paid for saving a wrecked or endangered ship or its cargo or passengers **2** : the act of saving a ship or possessions in danger of being lost **3** : something saved or recovered (as from a wreck or fire)

²salvage *vb* **sal·vaged; sal·vag·ing** : to rescue or save especially from wreckage or ruin — **sal·vage·able** \-ə-bəl\ *adj* — **sal·vag·er** *n*

sal·va·tion \sal-'vā-shən\ *n* **1** : the saving of a person from sin **2** : something that saves **3** : the saving from danger or evil

¹salve \'sav, 'sàv\ *n* : a healing ointment

²salve *vb* **salved; salv·ing** : to ease or soothe with or as if with a salve

sal·ver \'sal-vər\ *n* : a serving tray

sal·vo \'sal-vō\ *n, pl* **salvos** *or* **salvoes** **1 a** : the firing of two or more guns at the same time at one target or in a salute **b** : the release all at once of a rack of bombs or rockets **2** : the firing of one gun after another in a group of artillery pieces **3** : a sudden burst (as of cheers)

sa·mar·i·um \sə-'mer-ē-əm, -'mar-\ *n* : a pale gray shiny metallic element — see ELEMENT table

¹same \'sām\ *adj* **1** : resembling in every respect ⟨the *same* answer as before⟩ **2** : not another ⟨the *same* school⟩ **3** : very much alike ⟨on the *same* day last year⟩

syn SAME, IDENTICAL, EQUAL mean not different or not differing from one another. SAME suggests that the things being compared are really one thing and not two or more ⟨saw the *same* truck at different times⟩ IDENTICAL usually suggests that two or more things are like each other in every way ⟨these plates are *identical*⟩ EQUAL suggests that the things being compared are like each other in some specific way ⟨two singers of *equal* talent⟩

²same *pron* : the same one or ones

same·ness \'sām-nəs\ *n* **1** : the quality or state of being the same : IDENTITY **2** : MONOTONY 2, UNIFORMITY

Samoa time *n* : the time of the 11th time zone west of Greenwich that includes American Samoa

sam·o·var \'sam-ə-,vär\ *n* : a container with a faucet used especially in Russia for tea

Sam·o·yed \'sam-ə-,yed, 'sam-,ȯi-,ed\ *n* : any of a breed of medium-sized white or cream-colored dogs developed in Siberia

sam·pan \'sam-,pan\ *n* : a flat-bottomed Chinese boat usually moved by oars

sampan

¹sam·ple \'sam-pəl\ *n* **1** : a part or thing that shows the quality of the whole or group **2** : a part (as a set of individuals chosen from a whole population) used for investigating the whole

²sample *vb* **sam·pled; sam·pling** \-p(ə-)liŋ\ : to judge the quality of by a sample

¹sam·pler \'sam-plər\ *n* : a piece of needlework typically having letters or verses on it done in various stitches as an example of skill

²sam·pler \'sam-p(ə-)lər\ *n* **1** : one that collects or examines samples **2** : a collection of samples

sample space *n* : the set of all possible results of an experiment (as tossing a pair of dice) in probability or statistics

Sam·u·el \'sam-yə-(wə)l\ *n* — see BIBLE table

sam·u·rai \'sam-(y)ə-,rī\ *n, pl* **samurai** : a Japanese knight

san·a·to·ri·um \,san-ə-'tȯr-ē-əm, -'tȯr-\ *n, pl* **-ri·ums** *or* **-ria** \-ē-ə\ : an establishment for the care and treatment especially of people recovering from illness or having a disease likely to last a long time — called also *sanitarium*

sanc·ti·fy \'saŋ(k)-tə-,fī\ *vb* **-fied; -fy·ing** **1** : to set apart as sacred **2** : to make free from sin — **sanc·ti·fi·ca·tion** \,saŋ(k)-tə-fə-'kā-shən\ *n*

sanc·ti·mo·ni·ous \,saŋ(k)-tə-'mō-nē-əs\ *adj* : pretending

\ə\ abut	\au̇\ **out**	\i\ **tip**	\ȯ\ **saw**	\u̇\ **foot**
\ər\ **further**	\ch\ **chin**	\ī\ **life**	\ȯi\ **coin**	\y\ **yet**
\a\ **mat**	\e\ **pet**	\j\ **job**	\th\ **thin**	\yü\ **few**
\ā\ **take**	\ē\ **easy**	\ŋ\ **sing**	\th\ **this**	\yu̇\ **cure**
\ä\ **cot, cart**	\g\ **go**	\ō\ **bone**	\ü\ **food**	\zh\ **vision**

to be devoted — **sanc·ti·mo·ni·ous·ly** *adv* — **sanc·ti·mo·ni·ous·ness** *n*

¹sanc·tion \'saŋ(k)-shən\ *n* **1** : an action taken to enforce a law or rule **2** : official permission or approval

²sanction *vb* **sanc·tioned; sanc·tion·ing** \-sh(ə-)niŋ\ : RATIFY, PERMIT

sanc·ti·ty \'saŋ(k)-tət-ē\ *n, pl* **-ties** **1** : HOLINESS 1, SAINTLINESS **2** : the quality or state of being holy or sacred

sanc·tu·ary \'saŋ(k)-chə-ˌwer-ē\ *n, pl* **-ar·ies** **1** : a holy or sacred place **2** : the most sacred part of a place of worship **3** : a building or room for religious worship **4** : a place that provides shelter or protection ⟨wildlife *sanctuary*⟩ **5** : protection provided by a sanctuary

sanc·tum \'saŋ(k)-təm\ *n, pl* **sanctums** *also* **sanc·ta** \-tə\ **1** : a sacred place **2** : a place where one is free from being bothered

¹sand \'sand\ *n* **1** : loose material in grains produced by the natural breaking up of rocks **2** : a soil made up mostly of sand

²sand *vb* **1** : to sprinkle with sand **2** : to smooth by rubbing with sandpaper

san·dal \'san-dᵊl\ *n* : a shoe consisting of a sole strapped to the foot

san·dal·wood \-ˌwu̇d\ *n* : the close-grained fragrant yellowish wood of an Asian tree often used in carving and cabinetwork; *also* : the tree itself

sand·bag \'san(d)-ˌbag\ *n* : a bag filled with sand

sand·bank \-ˌbaŋk\ *n* : a large deposit of sand

sand·bar \-ˌbär\ *n* : a ridge of sand formed in water by tides or currents

sand·blast \-ˌblast\ *vb* : to cut or clean with sand driven at high speed by or as if by compressed air — **sand·blast·er** *n*

sand·box \-ˌbäks\ *n* : a box for holding sand especially for children to play in

sand·bur \'san(d)-ˌbər\ *n* : any of a genus of grasses native to warm sandy areas that produce spine-covered seeds; *also* : one of these seeds

sand dollar *n* : any of numerous round flat sea urchins that usually live in shallow water and on sandy bottoms

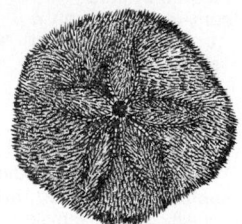

sand·er \'san-dər\ *n* : one that sands: as **a** : a device for spreading sand (as on icy roads); *also* : a truck that carries such a device **b** : a power tool that smooths or polishes using a rough material (as sandpaper)

sand dollar

sand flea *n* **1** : a flea found in sandy places **2** : BEACH FLEA

sand fly *n* : any of various small two-winged flies that bite

sand·glass \'san(d)-ˌglas\ *n* : an instrument (as an hourglass) for measuring time by the running of sand

sand·hill crane \ˌsand-ˌhil-\ *n* : a crane of eastern and central North America that is chiefly bluish gray with a touch of sandy yellow

sand·lot \'san-ˌ(d)lät\ *n* : a vacant lot especially when used by youngsters for unorganized sports — **sandlot** *adj* — **sand·lot·ter** \-ˌ(d)lät-ər\ *n*

sand·man \'san(d)-ˌman\ *n* : the magical being of folklore who is said to make children sleepy by sprinkling sand in their eyes

¹sand·pa·per \-ˌpā-pər\ *n* : paper with rough material (as sand) glued on one side and used for smoothing and polishing

²sandpaper *vb* : to rub with or as if with sandpaper

sand·pip·er \-ˌpī-pər\ *n* : any of numerous small shorebirds with a soft-tipped bill that is longer than the bill of the related plovers

sand·spit \-ˌspit\ *n* : ¹SPIT 2

sand·spur \'san(d)-ˌspər\ *n* : SANDBUR

sand·stone \-ˌstōn\ *n* : a rock made of sand held together by a natural cement

sand·storm \-ˌstȯ(ə)rm\ *n* : a storm of wind (as in a desert) that drives clouds of sand

sand trap *n* : a hazard on a golf course consisting of a hollow containing sand

¹sand·wich \'san-(ˌ)(d)wich\ *n* **1** : one or more slices of bread or a roll with a filling or spread **2** : something resembling a sandwich

Word History John Montagu, 4th Earl of Sandwich, was famous in 18th century England as a powerful political figure. He was also known to be fond of playing cards. The story was told that he once spent an entire night at the card table. Instead of leaving the game to have dinner, he ordered that slices of meat be brought to him between two pieces of bread. In that way he could continue playing while he ate. This convenient type of food soon became popular throughout England. Because of the story about the Earl, it became known as the *sandwich*. [named for John Montagu, 4th Earl of *Sandwich* died 1792 English diplomat]

²sandwich *vb* **1** : to insert between two or more things **2** : to make a place for : CROWD

sandwich man *n* : one who advertises or pickets a place of business by wearing an advertising board in front and behind

sandy \'san-dē\ *adj* **sand·i·er; -est** **1** : consisting of, containing, or sprinkled with sand **2** : of a yellowish gray color

sane \'sān\ *adj* **san·er; san·est** **1** : mentally sound and healthy **2** : proceeding from a sound mind : RATIONAL, SENSIBLE — **sane·ly** *adv* — **sane·ness** \'sān-nəs\ *n*

sang *past of* SING

san·gui·nary \'saŋ-gwə-ˌner-ē\ *adj* **1** : willing or even eager to cause blood to flow : BLOODTHIRSTY, MURDEROUS **2** : BLOODY 2

san·guine \'saŋ-gwən\ *adj* **1** : having the color of blood **2 a** : SANGUINARY 1 **b** : RUDDY 1 **3** : CHEERFUL 1a, HOPEFUL ⟨a *sanguine* disposition⟩ **4** : CONFIDENT, OPTIMISTIC ⟨*sanguine* of success⟩ [Middle English *sanguin* "having the color of blood", from early French *sanguin* (same meaning), from Latin *sanguineus* (same meaning), from *sanguin-, sanguis* "blood" — see *Word History* at HUMOR] — **san·guine·ly** *adv* — **san·guin·i·ty** \saŋ-ˈgwin-ət-ē, san-\ *n*

san·i·tar·i·an \ˌsan-ə-ˈter-ē-ən\ *n* : a person who specializes in public health and matters of sanitation

san·i·tar·i·um \ˌsan-ə-ˈter-ē-əm\ *n, pl* **-i·ums** *or* **-ia** \-ē-ə\ : SANATORIUM

san·i·tary \'san-ə-ˌter-ē\ *adj* **1** : of or relating to health : HYGIENIC ⟨*sanitary* laws⟩ **2** : free from filth, infection, or dangers to health

sanitary landfill *n* : LANDFILL

sanitary napkin *n* : a disposable absorbent pad with a gauze covering that is used to absorb uterine flow (as during menstruation)

san·i·ta·tion \ˌsan-ə-ˈtā-shən\ *n* **1** : the act or process of making sanitary **2** : the promotion of community hygiene and disease prevention especially by keeping up sewage systems, by collecting and disposing of trash and garbage, and by cleaning streets

san·i·tize \'san-ə-ˌtīz\ *vb* **-tized; -tiz·ing** : to make sanitary (as by cleaning or sterilizing)

san·i·ty \'san-ət-ē\ *n* : the quality or state of being sane

San Jo·se scale \ˌsan-ə-ˌzā-\ *n* : a scale insect introduced into North America from Asia that is very destructive to fruit trees

sank *past of* SINK

sans \(ˌ)sanz\ *prep* : ¹WITHOUT 2a

san·se·vie·ria \ˌsan(t)-sə-ˈvir-ē-ə\ *n* : any of a genus of tropical herbs of the Old World that are related to the lilies and have spotted or striped sword-shaped leaves — called also *snake plant*

San·skrit \'san-ˌskrit\ *n* : an ancient Indic language of India and of Hinduism — **Sanskrit** *adj*

San·ta Claus \'sant-ē-ˌklȯz, 'sant-ə-\ *n* : the spirit of Christmas represented by a fat jolly old man in a red suit who gives toys to children [from Dutch *Sinterklaas*, an altered form of Dutch *Sint Nikolaas* "Saint Nicholas"]

San·ta Ger·tru·dis \ˌsant-ə-(ˌ)gər-'trüd-əs\ *n* : any of a breed of red beef cattle that were developed from a cross between Brahmans and shorthorns and that are resistant to hot climates

¹**sap** \'sap\ *n* **1** : the fluid part of a plant; *esp* : a watery solution that circulates through a higher plant and carries food and nutrients **2** : VITALITY 3b **3** : a foolish person who is easily tricked or cheated

²**sap** *vb* **sapped; sap·ping 1** : UNDERMINE 2 **2** : to weaken gradually

sa·pi·ence \'sā-pē-ən(t)s, 'sap-ē-\ *n* : WISDOM 1a, SAGENESS

sa·pi·ent \'sā-pē-ənt, 'sap-ē-\ *adj* : ²WISE 1, DISCERNING — **sa·pi·ent·ly** *adv*

sap·ling \'sap-liŋ\ *n* : a young tree

sap·o·dil·la \ˌsap-ə-'dil-ə\ *n* : a tropical American evergreen tree with hard reddish wood, a rough-skinned brownish fruit that is used for food, and a milky sap that is the source of chicle

sap·phire \'saf-ˌī(ə)r\ *n* **1** : a clear bright blue precious stone **2** : a deep purplish blue — **sapphire** *adj*

> **Word History** In ancient India each planet was believed to have its own god. The god of the planet Saturn was thought of as a dark man with dark clothes. This god was fond of a dark gemstone. In Sanskrit, the ancient language of India, the favorite stone of Saturn's god was called *śanipriya*, meaning "dear to the planet Saturn". It is likely that this gemstone was the dark-blue sapphire. English borrowed *sapphire* from French *safir*, a word that can be traced back through several languages to the ancient Indians' name for the stone. [Middle English *safir* "sapphire", from early French *safir* (same meaning), from Latin *sapphirus* "sapphire", from Greek *sappheiros* (same meaning), derived from Sanskrit *śanipriya*, literally "dear to the planet Saturn"]

sap·py \'sap-ē\ *adj* **sap·pi·er; -est 1** : full of sap **2 a** : foolishly sentimental **b** : FOOLISH, SILLY — **sap·pi·ness** *n*

sap·ro·phyte \'sap-rə-ˌfīt\ *n* : a living thing and especially a plant that lives on the dead or decaying material of plants and animals — **sap·ro·phyt·ic** \ˌsap-rə-'fit-ik\ *adj*

sap·suck·er \'sap-ˌsək-ər\ *n* : any of various small American woodpeckers that drill holes in trees in order to obtain sap and insects for food

sap·wood \-ˌwùd\ *n* : the young sap-containing and usually lighter-colored wood found just beneath the bark of a tree — compare HEARTWOOD

sa·ran \sə-'ran\ *n* : a tough flexible plastic resin

sarape *variant of* SERAPE

sar·casm \'sär-ˌkaz-əm\ *n* **1** : a remark made usually to hurt someone's feelings or show scorn **2** : the use of sarcasms

> **Word History** Anyone who has suffered from the sarcastic remarks of others will not be too surprised to learn that *sarcasm*, "a cutting remark", comes from a Greek verb, *sarkazein*, that literally means "to tear flesh like a dog". Very early, though, this Greek verb came to mean "to bite one's lip in rage", and "to gnash one's teeth", and finally "to sneer". The Greek noun *sarkasmos*, from which the English *sarcasm* comes, meant "a sneering or hurtful remark". But even today sarcasm is often described as sharp, cutting, or wounding, recalling in a faint way the original meaning of the Greek verb. [from French *sarcasme* or Latin *sarcasmos*, both meaning

"sarcasm", from Greek *sarkasmos* "sarcasm", from *sarkazein* "to tear flesh, bite the lips in rage, sneer", from *sark-, sarx* "flesh"]

sar·cas·tic \sär-'kas-tik\ *adj* **1** : containing sarcasm ⟨a *sarcastic* remark⟩ **2** : being in the habit of using sarcasm — **sar·cas·ti·cal·ly** \-ti-k(ə-)lē\ *adv*

sar·coph·a·gus \sär-'käf-ə-gəs\ *n, pl* **-gi** \-ˌgī, -ˌjī, -ˌgē\ *also* **-gus·es** : a stone coffin

sar·dine \sär-'dēn\ *n, pl* **sardines** *also* **sardine** : any of various young or very small fish often preserved in oil for food

sar·don·ic \sär-'dän-ik\ *adj* : SCORNFUL, MOCKING — **sar·don·i·cal·ly** \-'dän-i-k(ə-)lē\ *adv*

sar·gas·so \sär-'gas-ō\ *n, pl* **-sos 1** : SARGASSUM **2** : a mass of floating plants and especially sargassums

sar·gas·sum \sär-'gas-əm\ *n* : any of a genus of brown algae that have a leafy branching body and air bladders and that often grow in free-floating masses in the ocean

sa·ri *also* **sa·ree** \'sär-ē\ *n* : a garment worn by women in southern Asia that consists of a long cloth draped around the body and head or shoulder

sa·rong \sə-'rȯŋ, -'räŋ\ *n* : a loose skirt made of a long strip of cloth wrapped loosely around the body and worn by men and women of the Malay island group and many Pacific islands

sar·sa·pa·ril·la \ˌsas-(ə-)pə-'ril-ə, ˌsärs-\ *n* **1** : the dried roots of any of several tropical American woody plants used especially as a flavoring; *also* : a plant that produces sarsaparilla **2** : a sweetened carbonated beverage flavored with sassafras and an oil from a birch

sar·to·ri·al \sär-'tōr-ē-əl, -'tȯr-\ *adj* : of or relating to a tailor or tailored clothes — **sar·to·ri·al·ly** \-ē-ə-lē\ *adv*

sari

¹**sash** \'sash\ *n* : a broad band (as of silk) worn around the waist or over the shoulder

²**sash** *n, pl* **sash** *also* **sash·es 1** : the frame in which panes of glass are set in a window or door **2** : the movable part of a window

Sas·quatch \'sas-ˌkwach, -ˌkwäch\ *n* : BIGFOOT

sass \'sas\ *vb* : to reply to in a rude impolite way — **sass** *n*

sas·sa·fras \'sas-(ə-)ˌfras\ *n* : a tall eastern North American tree that is related to the laurel and has fragrant yellow flowers and blue-black berries; *also* : its dried root bark used especially in medicine or as a flavoring

sassy \'sas-ē\ *adj* **sass·i·er; -est** : IMPUDENT, SAUCY

sat *past and past participle of* SIT

Sa·tan \'sāt-ᵊn\ *n* : ¹DEVIL 1 [Middle English *Satan* "Satan", from early French *Satan* (same meaning), from Latin *Satan* (same meaning), from Greek *Satan* "Satan", from Hebrew *śātān* "someone who opposes"] — **sa·tan·ic** \sə-'tan-ik, sā-\ *adj* — **sa·tan·i·cal·ly** \-'tan-i-k(ə-)lē\ *adv*

satch·el \'sach-əl\ *n* : a small bag often with a shoulder strap

sate \'sāt\ *vb* **sat·ed; sat·ing 1** : to fill especially with food beyond desire : GLUT **2** : to satisfy fully

sa·teen \sa-'tēn\ *n* : a glossy cotton fabric resembling satin

sat·el·lite \'sat-ᵊl-ˌīt\ *n* **1** : a follower resembling a slave **2 a** : a heavenly body orbiting another of larger size **b** : a man-made vehicle intended to orbit a heavenly body (as the earth or the moon) **3** : a country controlled by a more powerful country — **satellite** *adj*

> **Word History** Although it is now closely connected with

\ə\ abut	\aù\ out	\i\ tip	\ȯ\ saw	\ù\ foot
\ər\ further	\ch\ chin	\ī\ life	\ȯi\ coin	\y\ yet
\a\ mat	\e\ pet	\j\ job	\th\ thin	\yü\ few
\ā\ take	\ē\ easy	\ŋ\ sing	\t͟h\ this	\yù\ cure
\ä\ cot, cart	\g\ go	\ō\ bone	\ü\ food	\zh\ vision

the modern world of space exploration, *satellite* is actually a very old word. Its origin can be traced to the Latin word *satelles,* meaning "one who escorts or follows after an important person". This is also the original meaning of *satellite* in English. Because such heavenly bodies as the moon can be thought of as "escorts" of the planets they orbit, they also became known as *satellites.* The satellites of modern times made by humans got their name because they, like the moon, orbit the earth. [from early French *satellite* "a person who follows or escorts someone of importance", from Latin *satellit-, satelles* "escort, attendant"]

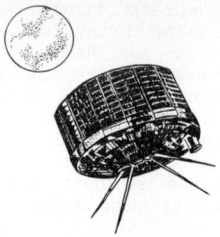

satellite 2b

¹**sa·ti·ate** \'sā-sh(ē-)ət\ *adj* : filled to excess

²**sa·ti·ate** \'sā-shē-,āt\ *vb* **-at·ed; -at·ing** : SATE 2 — **sa·ti·a·tion** \,sā-shē-'ā-shən, -sē-\ *n*

sa·ti·ety \sə-'tī-ət-ē\ *n* : ²GLUT

sat·in \'sat-ᵊn\ *n* : a fabric (as of silk) with smooth shiny face and dull back — **satin** *adj* — **sat·iny** \'sat-nē, 'sat-ᵊn-ē\ *adj*

satin weave *n* : a weave that produces a fabric with a smooth face

sat·ire \'sa-,tī(ə)r\ *n* : something meant to make fun of and show the weaknesses of human nature or a particular person — **sa·tir·ic** \sə-'tir-ik\ *or* **sa·tir·i·cal** \-'tir-i-kəl\ *adj* — **sa·tir·i·cal·ly** \-i-k(ə-)lē\ *adv*

sat·i·rist \'sat-ə-rəst\ *n* : a person who satirizes

sat·i·rize \'sat-ə-,rīz\ *vb* **-rized; -riz·ing** : to make fun of or show the weaknesses of by using satire

sat·is·fac·tion \,sat-əs-'fak-shən\ *n* **1 a** : the quality or state of being satisfied **b** : a cause of satisfaction **2** : something that makes up for a loss or injury **3** : ASSURANCE 2

sat·is·fac·to·ry \,sat-əs-'fak-t(ə-)rē\ *adj* : giving satisfaction — **sat·is·fac·to·ri·ly** \-t(ə-)rə-lē\ *adv* — **sat·is·fac·to·ri·ness** \-t(ə-)rē-nəs\ *n*

sat·is·fy \'sat-əs-,fī\ *vb* **-fied; -fy·ing** **1** : to do what has been agreed upon in (as a contract) **2 a** : to make happy : PLEASE **b** : to meet the needs of : APPEASE ⟨satisfied their hunger⟩ **3** : CONVINCE ⟨satisfied that they are innocent⟩ **4** : FULFILL 2, MEET ⟨satisfy requirements⟩ [Middle English *satisfien* "fulfill an obligation", from early French *satisfier* (same meaning), from Latin *satisfacere* (same meaning), from *satis* "enough" and *facere* "to do, make" — related to FASHION, PERFECT] — **sat·is·fi·able** \-,fī-ə-bəl\ *adj* — **sat·is·fy·ing·ly** \-,fī-iŋ-lē\ *adv*

sa·trap \'sā-,trap, 'sa-\ *n* **1** : the governor of a division of ancient Persia **2** : a ruler who is controlled by a higher authority

sat·u·rate \'sach-ə-,rāt\ *vb* **-rat·ed; -rat·ing** **1** : to soak or fill with something to the point where no more can be absorbed or dissolved ⟨saturate water with salt⟩ **2** : to fill completely with something that penetrates : STEEP **syn** see SOAK

sat·u·rat·ed \'sach-ə-,rāt-əd\ *adj* **1** : full of moisture **2 a** : being a mixture that is unable to absorb or dissolve any more of a substance at a given temperature and pressure **b** : being a carbon compound having no double or triple bonds between carbon atoms ⟨saturated fatty acids⟩

sat·u·ra·tion \,sach-ə-'rā-shən\ *n* **1** : the act or process of saturating **2** : the state of being saturated

Sat·ur·day \'sat-ərd-ē\ *n* : the seventh day of the week

Word History Several of the days of the week, such as Tuesday and Wednesday, get their English names from Germanic gods, but Saturday gets its name from a Roman one. *Saturnus* was the name of an important Roman god of agriculture, known in English as *Saturn.* The Old English word *sæterndæg,* "Saturn's day", came originally from the god's Latin name. The modern English *Saturday* comes from the Old English *sæterndæg.* [Old English *sæterndæg,* literally "Saturn's day", derived from Latin *Saturnus* "Saturn"]

Sat·urn \'sat-ərn\ *n* : the planet sixth in order from the sun — see PLANET table

sat·ur·na·lia \,sat-ər-'nāl-yə\ *n sing or pl* **1** *cap* : the festival of the god Saturn celebrated in ancient Rome with feasting and wild revelry **2** : a celebration involving wicked or lawless behavior : ORGY — **sat·ur·na·lian** \-yən\ *adj*

sat·ur·nine \'sat-ər-,nīn\ *adj* : SULLEN 1a

sa·tyr \'sāt-ər, 'sat-\ *n* **1** *often cap* : a forest god believed by the ancient Greeks to have the ears and tail of a horse or goat and to enjoy rowdy pleasures **2** : a man having strong sexual desire

¹**sauce** \'sȯs, *sense 3 is usually* 'sas\ *n* **1** : an often fluid relish for food : DRESSING **2** : boiled or canned fruit **3** : rude or impolite language or actions

²**sauce** \'sȯs, *sense 2 is usually* 'sas\ *vb* **sauced; sauc·ing** **1** : to add sauce to : SEASON **2** : to be rude or sassy to

sauce·pan \'sȯs-,span\ *n* : a small cooking pan with a handle

sau·cer \'sȯ-sər\ *n* **1** : a small round shallow dish in which a cup is set **2** : something like a saucer especially in shape

saucy \'sas-ē *also* 'sȯs-ē\ *adj* **sauc·i·er; -est** **1** : IMPUDENT **2** : IRREPRESSIBLE, PERT **3** : ²SMART 6a, TRIM ⟨a saucy ship⟩ — **sauc·i·ly** \-ə-lē\ *adv* — **sauc·i·ness** \-ē-nəs\ *n*

sau·er·bra·ten \'saů(-ə)r-,brät-ᵊn\ *n* : beef soaked in vinegar and seasonings before being roasted

sau·er·kraut \'saů(-ə)r-,kraůt\ *n* : finely cut cabbage fermented in brine [German, literally "sour cabbage"]

sau·na \'saů-nə, 'sȯ-nə\ *n* : a Finnish steam bath

saun·ter \'sȯnt-ər, 'sänt-\ *vb* : to walk along in an idle or leisurely manner : STROLL — **saunter** *n* — **saun·ter·er** \-ər-ər\ *n*

sau·ri·an \'sȯr-ē-ən\ *n* : any of a group of reptiles including the lizards and in older classifications the crocodiles and various extinct forms (as the dinosaurs) that look like lizards — **saurian** *adj*

sau·sage \'sȯ-sij\ *n* **1** : highly seasoned ground meat (as pork) usually stuffed in casings **2** : a roll of sausage meat in a casing

sau·té \sȯ-'tā, sō-\ *vb* **sau·téed** *or* **sau·téd; sau·té·ing** : to fry in a small amount of fat

sau·terne \sō-'tərn, sȯ-, -'te(ə)rn\ *n* : a semisweet golden table wine

¹**sav·age** \'sav-ij\ *adj* **1** : not tamed **2** : CRUEL 2, FEROCIOUS **3 a** : ¹WILD 1b **b** : IMPOLITE **c** : UNCIVILIZED 1 — **sav·age·ly** *adv* — **sav·age·ness** *n*

Word History In ancient times woods, forests, and other wild areas were frightening to many people who lived in towns and cities. Dangerous animals, like wolves and bears, lived in the wilds, and many humans who lived there were probably thought to be dangerous, too. The Latin word for "woods, forest" was *silva,* and from this came the adjective *silvaticus,* meaning "of the woods, wild". Later, the Latin word *silvaticus* came to be spelled *salvaticus,* and this spelling appeared in the French of the Middle Ages as *sauvage,* meaning "wild, untamed". Eventually it took on other meanings that city people associated with the forests: "cruel, brutal, fierce". All of these meanings were carried over into English when the word was borrowed as *savage.* [Middle English *sauvage* "untamed, wild", from early French *sauvage* (same meaning), from Latin *salvaticus,* an altered form of earlier *silvaticus* "of the woods, wild", from *silva* "woods, forest"]

²**savage** *n* **1** : a person belonging to a group with a low level of civilization **2** : a brutal person

sav·age·ry \'sav-ij-(ə-)rē\ *n, pl* **-ries** **1** : savage disposition or action : CRUELTY **2** : the state of being savage

sa·van·na *also* **sa·van·nah** \sə-'van-ə\ *n* : a grassland containing scattered trees

sa·vant \sa-'vänt, -'vän; sə-'vant, 'sav-ənt\ *n* : SCHOLAR 2b [from French *savant,* a form of the verb *savoir* "to know", from Latin *sapere* "to be wise, taste, have flavor" — related to INSIPID, ¹SAGE]

¹**save** \'sāv\ *vb* **saved; sav·ing** **1 a** : to deliver from sin **b** : to rescue or deliver from danger or harm **c** : to keep from injury, destruction, waste, or loss ⟨*save* your computer program on a disk⟩ **2** : to put aside for future use ⟨*save* a little for later⟩ **3 a** : to make unnecessary : AVOID ⟨it will *save* your having to go back again⟩ **b** : to keep from being lost to an opponent ⟨*saved* the game⟩ ⟨*saved* the day⟩ **4 a** : to put aside money **b** : ECONOMIZE 2 ⟨*save* on heat⟩ [Middle English *saven* "to deliver from sin", from early French *salver* (same meaning), from Latin *salvare* "to save", from earlier *salvus* "safe, healthy" — related to SAFE, ³SAGE] — **sav·er** *n*

²**save** *n* **1** : a play that prevents an opponent from scoring or winning **2** : a game that has been saved

³**save** \(ˌ)sāv\ *prep* : ²EXCEPT 2 ⟨no hope *save* one⟩

¹**sav·ing** \'sā-viŋ\ *n* **1** : the act of rescuing **2 a** : something saved **b** *pl* : money saved over a period of time

²**saving** *prep* **1** : ²EXCEPT 2, SAVE **2** : without disrespect to

³**saving** *conj* : ³EXCEPT

savings account *n* : an account (as in a bank) on which interest is usually paid and from which withdrawals can be made

savings and loan association *n* : an association organized to hold savings of members and to invest chiefly in mortgage loans

savings bank *n* : a bank that receives and invests savings and pays interest to depositors

savings bond *n* : a registered U.S. bond that comes in values of $50 to $10,000

sav·ior *or* **sav·iour** \'sāv-yər\ *n* : one that saves from danger or destruction; *esp, cap* : Jesus

¹**sa·vor** \'sā-vər\ *n* **1** : the taste and odor of something **2** : something clearly marking one as different from others — **sa·vor·less** \-ləs\ *adj*

²**savor** *vb* **sa·vored; sa·vor·ing** \'sav-(ə-)riŋ\ **1** : to have a specified smell or quality **2** : to give flavor to **3** : to taste or smell with pleasure : RELISH — **sa·vor·er** \'sā-vər-ər\ *n*

¹**sa·vory** \'sāv-(ə-)rē\ *adj* : pleasing to the taste or smell — **sa·vor·i·ness** *n*

²**sa·vo·ry** \'sāv-(ə-)rē\ *n, pl* **-ries** : any of a genus of mints used in cooking as seasonings

¹**sav·vy** \'sav-ē\ *vb* **sav·vied; sav·vy·ing** : COMPREHEND 1, UNDERSTAND

²**savvy** *n* : useful understanding : SHREWDNESS

¹**saw** *past of* SEE

²**saw** \'sȯ\ *n* : a hand or power tool or a machine used to cut hard material and equipped usually with a tooth-edged blade

³**saw** *vb* **sawed** \'sȯd\; **sawed** *or* **sawn** \'sȯn\; **saw·ing** \'sȯ(-)iŋ\ : to cut or shape with a saw

⁴**saw** *n* : a common saying : PROVERB

saw·buck \'sȯ-ˌbək\ *n* **1** : SAWHORSE **2** *slang* : a 10-dollar bill

saw·dust \'sȯd-(ˌ)əst\ *n* : tiny particles (as of wood) made by a saw in cutting

sawed–off \'sȯ-ˌdȯf\ *adj* : having an end sawed off ⟨a *sawed-off* shotgun⟩

saw·fish \'sȯ-ˌfish\ *n* : any of several mostly tropical fish

related to the rays that have a long flat snout with sharp toothlike structures along both edges

sawhorse

saw·fly \-ˌflī\ *n* : any of numerous insects which are related to the wasps and bees and in which the female has a pair of organs used to cut holes in plants where she lays eggs

saw grass *n* : a sedge with leaves that have sharp jagged edges

saw·horse \'sȯ-ˌhȯ(ə)rs\ *n* : a frame on which wood is laid for sawing by hand

saw·mill \-ˌmil\ *n* : a mill or machine for sawing logs

saw–toothed \-'tütht\ *adj* : having an edge or outline like the teeth of a saw

saw·yer \'sȯ-yər, 'sȯi-ər\ *n* : a person who saws timber

sax \'saks\ *n* : SAXOPHONE

Sax·on \'sak-sən\ *n* : a member of a Germanic people conquering England with the Angles and Jutes in the 5th century A.D. and joining with them to form the Anglo-Saxon people

sax·o·phone \'sak-sə-ˌfōn\ *n* : a musical instrument of the woodwind class consisting of a usually curved metal tube with finger keys and a reed mouthpiece [named for Antoine "Adolph" *Sax* 1814–1894 a Belgian maker of musical instruments] — **sax·o·phon·ist** \-ˌfō-nəst\ *n*

saxophone

¹**say** \'sā\ *vb* **said** \'sed\; **say·ing** \'sā-iŋ\; **says** \'sez\ **1 a** : to express in words : STATE **b** : to state as opinion or belief : DECLARE ⟨*said* to be the best you can get⟩ **2 a** : ²UTTER 2, PRONOUNCE **b** : RECITE 1, REPEAT ⟨*said* my prayers⟩ **3** : INDICATE 2, SHOW ⟨the clock *says* five after⟩ — **say·er** \'sā-ər\ *n*

²**say** *n* **1** : an expression of opinion ⟨had my *say*⟩ **2** : the power to decide or help decide ⟨had no *say* in making the plans⟩

³**say** *adv* **1** : about as much or as many as ⟨the property is worth, *say,* four million dollars⟩ **2** : as an example : AS ⟨if we compress any gas, *say* oxygen⟩

say·ing \'sā-iŋ\ *n* : something frequently said : PROVERB

say–so \'sā-ˌsō\ *n* **1 a** : one's unsupported word **b** : a judgment coming from a person of authority **2** : a right of last decision : AUTHORITY

¹**scab** \'skab\ *n* **1** : scabies of domestic animals **2** : a crust of hardened blood that forms over and protects a wound **3** : a worker who takes the place of a striking worker **4** : a plant disease in which crusted spots form on stems or leaves

²**scab** *vb* **scabbed; scab·bing** **1** : to become covered with a scab **2** : to act as a scab

scab·bard \'skab-ərd\ *n* : a protective case for a sword, dagger, or bayonet

scab·by \'skab-ē\ *adj* **scab·bi·er; -est** **1 a** : covered with or full of scabs ⟨*scabby* skin⟩ **b** : diseased with scab ⟨a *scabby* plant⟩ **2** : CONTEMPTIBLE ⟨a *scabby* trick⟩

\ə\ abut	\au̇\ out	\i\ tip	\ȯ\ saw	\u̇\ foot
\ər\ further	\ch\ chin	\ī\ life	\ȯi\ coin	\y\ yet
\a\ mat	\e\ pet	\j\ job	\th\ thin	\yü\ few
\ā\ take	\ē\ easy	\ŋ\ sing	\th\ this	\yu̇\ cure
\ä\ cot, cart	\g\ go	\ō\ bone	\ü\ food	\zh\ vision

sca·bies \'skā-bēz\ *n, pl* **scabies** : an itch or mange caused by mites living as parasites under the skin

scads \'skadz\ *n pl* : a great quantity

scaf·fold \'skaf-əld *also* -,ōld\ *n* **1** : an elevated platform built as a support for workers **2** : a platform on which a criminal is executed

scaf·fold·ing \'skaf-əl-diŋ, -,ōl-\ *n* **1** : a system of scaffolds **2** : materials for scaffolds

¹**sca·lar** \'skā-lər, -,lär\ *adj* **1** : arranged like a ladder : GRADUATED ⟨*scalar* chain of authority⟩ **2** : describable by a number that can be represented by a point on a scale ⟨*scalar* quantity⟩

²**scalar** *n* **1** : a real number rather than a vector **2** : a quantity (as mass or time) having a magnitude that can be described by a real number but having no direction

sca·la·re \skə-'la(ə)r-ē, -'le(ə)r-, -'lär-\ *n* : ANGELFISH 2

scal·a·wag \'skal-i-,wag\ *n* **1** : RASCAL 1 **2** : a white Southerner acting as a Republican in the time of reconstruction after the Civil War

¹**scald** \'skȯld\ *vb* **1** : to burn with or as if with hot liquid or steam **2 a** : to cover with boiling water or steam **b** : to bring to a temperature just below the boiling point ⟨*scald* milk⟩ **3** : ¹SCORCH 1

²**scald** *n* : an injury to the body caused by scalding

scald·ing \'skȯl-diŋ\ *adj* **1** : causing the sensation of scalding or burning **2** : as hot as if boiling ⟨*scalding* water⟩ **3** : very hot **4** : BITING, SCATHING

¹**scale** \'skā(ə)l\ *n* **1 a** : either pan of a balance **b** : ¹BALANCE 1 — usually used in pl. **2** : a device for weighing ⟨a bathroom *scale*⟩ [Middle English *scale* "bowl, pan or tray of a balance", of Norse origin]

²**scale** *vb* **scaled; scal·ing** **1** : to weigh in scales **2** : to have a specified weight

³**scale** *n* **1 a** : any of the small stiff flat plates that form an outer covering on the body of some animals and especially fishes and reptiles **b** : a small thin plate that resembles an animal scale ⟨*scales* of mica⟩ ⟨the *scales* on a moth's wing⟩ **2** : a small thin flake (as of dandruff) shed from the skin **3** : a thin layer or coating formed especially on metal (as iron) ⟨boiler *scale*⟩ **4** : a special leaf that covers a bud of a seed plant **5 a** : SCALE INSECT **b** : a disease of plants caused by a scale insect [Middle English *scale* "a plate on the skin of a fish", from early French *escale* (same meaning); of Germanic origin] — **scale·less** \'skā(ə)l-ləs\ *adj* — **scale·like** \'skā(ə)l-,līk\ *adj*

⁴**scale** *vb* **scaled; scal·ing** **1** : to remove scale or the scales from ⟨*scale* a boiler⟩ ⟨*scale* fish⟩ **2** : to take off in scales or thin layers ⟨*scale* the bark off a tree⟩ **3** : to come off in scales or shed scales : FLAKE **4** : to throw a flat object so as to sail in air or skip on water

⁵**scale** *n* **1** : a series of tones going up or down in pitch with each tone having a fixed relationship to those above and below it **2 a** : a series of spaces marked by lines and used to measure distances or to register something (as the height of the mercury in a thermometer) **b** : a divided line on a map or chart indicating the length (as a centimeter) used to represent a larger unit of measure (as a kilometer) **c** : an instrument consisting of a strip (as of wood, plastic, or metal) with spaces on its surface that are evenly divided and numbered for measuring distances or amounts **3** : a series divided into classes **4** : the size of a picture, plan, or model of a thing compared to the size of the thing itself **5** : size in comparison ⟨do things on a large *scale*⟩ **6** : a rule by which something can be measured or judged [Middle English *scale* "ladder", from Latin *scala* "ladder, staircase", from earlier *scalae* (plural) "stairs, rungs, ladder"]

⁶**scale** *vb* **scaled; scal·ing** **1** : to climb by or as if by a ladder ⟨*scale* a wall⟩ ⟨*scale* a cliff⟩ **2 a** : to arrange in order from the highest assigned one value (as a grade of A) and the lowest another value (as a grade of D) with the rest placed in groups between the two ⟨*scale* a test⟩ **b** : to measure by or as if by a scale **c** : to make, regulate,

or estimate by a rule ⟨*scale* down the budget⟩ — **scal·er** *n*

scaled \'skā(ə)ld\ *adj* : furnished with or adjusted to a scale ⟨a *scaled* line⟩

scale insect *n* : any of numerous small insects related to the plant lice and including many destructive plant pests in which the males have wings, the females are scale-covered and are often permanently attached to a host plant, and the young suck the juices of plants

sca·lene \'skā-,lēn, skā-'lēn\ *adj* : having the sides unequal ⟨a *scalene* triangle⟩

scal·lion \'skal-yən\ *n* : GREEN ONION

¹**scal·lop** \'skäl-əp, 'skal-\ *n* **1 a** : any of a family of marine mollusks with a two-part ribbed shell **b** : a muscle of the scallops that is often used for food **2** : one of the two parts of a scallop shell **3** : one of a continuous series of rounded half-circles forming a border (as on lace)

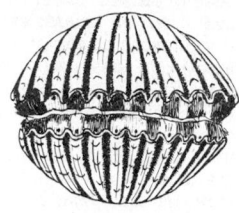
scallop 1a

²**scallop** *or* **es·cal·lop** \is-'käl-əp, -'kal-\ *vb* **1** : to bake in a sauce usually covered with seasoned bread or cracker crumbs ⟨*scalloped* potatoes⟩ **2** : to shape, cut, or make an edge in scallops

¹**scalp** \'skalp\ *n* **1** : the part of the skin and flesh of the head usually covered with hair **2** : a part of the human scalp cut or torn from an enemy especially as a sign of victory

²**scalp** *vb* **1** : to remove the scalp from **2** : to buy and resell at much higher prices ⟨*scalp* theater tickets⟩ — **scalp·er** *n*

scal·pel \'skal-pəl *also* skal-'pel\ *n* : a small straight thin-bladed knife used especially in surgery

scaly \'skā-lē\ *adj* **scal·i·er; -est** **1 a** : covered with, composed of, or resembling scale or scales **b** : FLAKY 2 **2** : infested with scale insects

scamp \'skamp\ *n* : RASCAL 1

scam·per \'skam-pər\ *vb* **scam·pered; scam·per·ing** \-p(ə-)riŋ\ : to run lightly and playfully about — **scamper** *n*

¹**scan** \'skan\ *vb* **scanned; scan·ning** **1** : to read or mark verses so as to show stress and rhythm **2 a** : to examine thoroughly ⟨*scanned* their faces⟩ **b** : to make a wide sweeping search of ⟨*scanning* the field with binoculars⟩ **c** : to look through or over hastily ⟨*scanned* the headlines⟩ **3** : to move across in successive lines to form an image on a cathode-ray tube ⟨the electron beam *scans* the face of the picture tube⟩ **4** : to check (as a magnetic tape) for recorded data by means of a mechanical or electronic device

²**scan** *n* **1** : the act or process of scanning **2** : a picture of the distribution of radioactive material in something; *also* : a picture of part of the body made by combining separate pictures taken from different angles or of different sections

scan·dal \'skan-dᵊl\ *n* **1** : a crime against faith that causes another to sin **2** : loss of or damage to one's reputation : DISGRACE ⟨brought *scandal* on the school⟩ **3** : something that offends accepted moral standards or disgraces those associated with it ⟨the slum is a *scandal*⟩

scan·dal·ize \'skan-də-,līz\ *vb* **-ized; -iz·ing** **1** : to speak of in a false or vicious way **2** : to shock the moral sense of

scan·dal·ous \'skan-d(ə-)ləs\ *adj* **1** : harmful to one's reputation : DEFAMATORY ⟨a *scandalous* story⟩ **2** : SHOCKING ⟨*scandalous* behavior⟩ — **scan·dal·ous·ly** *adv*

scan·di·um \'skan-dē-əm\ *n* : a white metallic element found together with other rare elements — see ELEMENT table

scan·ner \'skan-ər\ *n* : one that scans: as **a** : a device that senses recorded information **b** : a device used for scanning or in making scans

scan·sion \'skan-chən\ *n* : the scanning of verse to show its meter

¹scant \'skant\ *adj* **1 a** : barely or scarcely enough; *esp* : not quite coming up to a certain measure ⟨a *scant* cup of milk⟩ **b** : lacking in size or quantity : MEAGER, SCANTY **2** : having a small or short supply ⟨*scant* of breath⟩ — **scant·ly** *adv*

²scant *vb* : SKIMP 1, STINT

scant·ling \'skant-liŋ, -lən\ *n* : a small piece of lumber; *esp* : one of the upright pieces in the frame of a house

scanty \'skant-ē\ *adj* **scant·i·er; -est** : very small in size or amount ⟨*scanty* nourishment⟩ ⟨*scanty* bikinis⟩ **syn** see MEAGER — **scant·i·ly** \'skant-ᵊl-ē\ *adv* — **scant·i·ness** \'skant-ē-nəs\ *n*

scape·goat \'skāp-ˌgōt\ *n* : a person or thing taking the blame for others

scap·u·la \'skap-yə-lə\ *n, pl* **-lae** \-ˌlē, -ˌlī\ *or* **-las** : SHOULDER BLADE

scap·u·lar \'skap-yə-lər\ *n* **1** : a long wide band of cloth with an opening for the head worn front and back over the shoulders by monks **2** : a pair of small cloth squares joined by shoulder tapes and worn under the clothing on the breast and back especially for religious purposes

¹scar \'skär\ *n* **1** : a mark left (as on the skin) after injured tissue has healed **2** : a mark on a stem or branch where a leaf or fruit has separated **3** : a mark (as on furniture) resembling a scar **4** : a lasting injury from a bad experience

²scar *vb* **scarred; scar·ring** *vb* **1** : to mark with or form a scar **2** : to do lasting injury to **3** : to become scarred

scar·ab \'skar-əb\ *n* **1** : any of a family of large stout beetles (as a dung beetle) **2** : an ornament or a gem made to represent a scarab; *esp* : one used in ancient Egypt as a symbol of eternal life

scarce \'ske(ə)rs, 'ska(ə)rs\ *adj* **scarc·er; scarc·est** : lacking in quantity or number : not plentiful ⟨food is *scarce*⟩ **syn** see RARE — **scarce·ly** *adv* — **scarce·ness** *n*

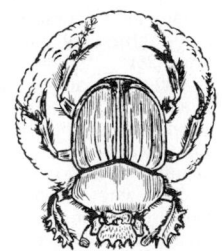

scarab 1

scar·ci·ty \'sker-sət-ē, 'skar-\ *n, pl* **-ties** : the quality or condition of being scarce : a very small supply

¹scare \'ske(ə)r, 'ska(ə)r\ *vb* **scared; scar·ing** **1** : to frighten suddenly : ALARM **2** : to become scared

²scare *n* **1** : a sudden fright **2** : a widespread state of alarm : PANIC

scare·crow \'ske(ə)r-ˌkrō, 'ska(ə)r-\ *n* : an object usually suggesting a human figure that is set up to scare birds away from crops

scare up *vb* : to bring to light or get together with much labor or difficulty

scarf \'skärf\ *n, pl* **scarves** \'skärvz\ *or* **scarfs** **1** : a broad band of cloth worn about the shoulders, around the neck, over the head, or about the waist **2** : RUNNER 5b

scar·i·fy \'skar-ə-ˌfī, 'sker-\ *vb* **-fied; -fy·ing** : to make scratches or small cuts in

scar·let \'skär-lət\ *n* **1** : scarlet cloth or clothes **2** : a bright red — **scarlet** *adj*

scarlet fever *n* : a contagious disease characterized by fever, swelling, and pain in the nose, throat, and mouth, and by a red rash

scarlet runner *n* : a tropical American high-climbing bean with large bright red flowers and red-and-black seeds

scarlet tanager *n* : an American tanager of which the male

is scarlet with black wings and the female is olive

scarp \'skärp\ *n* **1** : a line of cliffs produced by faulting or erosion **2** : a low steep slope along a beach caused by wave erosion — **scarped** *adj*

scar tissue *n* : connective tissue forming a scar

scary \'ske(ə)r-ē, 'ska(ə)r-\ *adj* **scar·i·er; -est** **1** : causing fright : ALARMING ⟨a *scary* movie⟩ **2** : easily scared : TIMID **3** : feeling alarm or fright : SCARED, FRIGHTENED ⟨*scary* feeling⟩

¹scat \'skat\ *vb* **scat·ted; scat·ting** **1** : to go away quickly — often used to drive away an animal (as a cat) **2** : to move fast : SCOOT

²scat *n* : jazz singing with meaningless syllables

³scat *vb* **scat·ted; scat·ting** : to sing by making up meaningless syllables to go with the music

¹scathe \'skāth\ *n* : HARM 1, INJURY — **scathe·less** \-ləs\ *adj*

²scathe *vb* **scathed; scath·ing** **1** : to do harm to : INJURE; *esp* : to injure by fire : SCORCH, SEAR **2** : to attack with very harsh accusations

scath·ing \'skā-thiŋ\ *adj* : painfully harsh ⟨a *scathing* look⟩ — **scath·ing·ly** \-thiŋ-lē\ *adv*

scat·ter \'skat-ər\ *vb* **1** : to cause to separate widely ⟨wind *scattered* the dry leaves⟩ **2** : to place or leave here and there ⟨*scattered* their toys all over the house⟩ **3** : to sow widely and without pattern **4** : to separate and go in different directions ⟨the crowd *scattered*⟩ **5** : to occur or fall without pattern ⟨lakes *scattered* everywhere in the hills⟩

scat·ter·brain \'skat-ər-ˌbrān\ *n* : a silly careless person incapable of concentration — **scat·ter·brained** \-ˌbrānd\ *adj*

¹scat·ter·ing \'skat-ə-riŋ\ *n* **1** : an act or process in which something scatters or is scattered **2** : something scattered; *esp* : a small number or amount placed or found here and there ⟨a *scattering* of visitors⟩

²scattering *adj* **1** : going in various directions **2** : found or placed far apart and in no pattern

scatter rug *n* : a rug of such a size that several can be used (as to fill vacant places) in a room

scav·enge \'skav-ənj, -inj\ *vb* **scav·enged; scav·eng·ing** : to collect usable things from what has been discarded

scav·en·ger \'skav-ən-jər\ *n* **1** : someone or something that scavenges **2** : an organism (as a vulture) that usually feeds on dead or decayed material

Word History In the United States, *scavenger* is not the title of a particular occupation, but it is in Great Britain. There it means "street cleaner", which is a use close to the original meaning. In English towns in the Middle Ages, a tax was placed on goods offered for sale by merchants who came from another town for market day. This tax was called a *skawage,* from an early French dialect word *escauwage,* meaning "a showing or inspection (of goods)". The *skawage* gave the local merchants an advantage and discouraged outsiders from selling in the town. In this way it was like our modern-day *tarrif,* or "tax on imports". The official whose duty it was to collect this tax was called the *skawager.* This word was later spelled *scavager* and then *scavenger.* When the towns came to need someone to keep the streets clean, this duty also became the job of the scavenger. The word *scavenger* is now used in the British Isles for all street cleaners. By the time British colonists started towns in America, the skawage tax was no longer collected, and the word *scavenger* came to be used here in its more general sense of "someone who collects usable things from what has been discarded".

\ə\ **abut**	\au̇\ **out**	\i\ **tip**	\ȯ\ **saw**	\u̇\ **foot**
\ər\ **further**	\ch\ **chin**	\ī\ **life**	\ȯi\ **coin**	\y\ **yet**
\a\ **mat**	\e\ **pet**	\j\ **job**	\th\ **thin**	\yü\ **few**
\ā\ **take**	\ē\ **easy**	\ŋ\ **sing**	\th\ **this**	\yu̇\ **cure**
\ä\ **cot, cart**	\g\ **go**	\ō\ **bone**	\ü\ **food**	\zh\ **vision**

[from earlier *scavager*, an altered form of Middle English *skawager* "one who collects a tax on goods sold by merchants from another town", from an early French dialect word *escauwage* "a showing or inspection (of goods)"]

scavenger hunt *n* : a party contest in which players are sent out usually in pairs to obtain without buying unusual objects within a fixed length of time

sce·nar·io \sə-'nar-ē-,ō, -'ner-, -'när-\ *n, pl* **-i·os**　**1 a** : an outline of a play　**b** : the text of an opera　**2** : SCREENPLAY

sce·nar·ist \sə-'nar-əst, -'ner-, -'när-\ *n* : a writer of scenarios

scene \'sēn\ *n*　**1 a** : a division of an act during which there is no change of scene or break in time　**b** : a single situation or conversation in a play ⟨a famous fight *scene*⟩　**c** : a small part of a motion picture or a television program　**2 a** : a stage setting ⟨change *scenes*⟩　**b** : a view or sight that looks like a picture ⟨a winter *scene*⟩　**3 a** : the place and time of the action in a play or story　**b** : the place of an event or action : LOCALE ⟨*scene* of a riot⟩　**4** : a display of anger or misconduct ⟨made a *scene* when accused of the crime⟩　**5 a** : area of activity ⟨the music *scene*⟩　**b** : SITUATION 3 ⟨the *scene* got serious when the police arrived⟩ — **behind the scenes**　**1** : out of public view ⟨decisions reached *behind the scenes*⟩　**2** : in a position to see or control the hidden workings ⟨the lawyer *behind the scenes*⟩

scen·ery \'sēn-(ə-)rē\ *n*　**1** : the painted scenes or hangings and accessories used on a theater stage　**2** : a view or landscape resembling a beautiful painting ⟨mountain *scenery*⟩

scene–steal·er \'sēn-,stē-lər\ *n* : an actor who draws attention though he or she is not intended to be the center of attraction

sce·nic \'sē-nik\ *adj*　**1** : of or relating to stage scenery　**2** : of or relating to natural scenery ⟨a *scenic* route⟩　**3** : representing an action or event in pictured form ⟨*scenic* wallpaper⟩

¹scent \'sent\ *n*　**1 a** : an odor left by an animal　**b** : a particular and usually agreeable odor ⟨a keen *scent*⟩　**2 a** : sense of smell　**b** : power of detection　**3** : a course of pursuit or discovery ⟨throw them off the *scent*⟩　**4** : ¹HINT 1, INKLING ⟨a *scent* of trouble⟩　**5** : ¹PERFUME 2　**6** : something that attracts animals with its odor

²scent *vb*　**1 a** : to become aware of or follow through the sense of smell ⟨the dog *scented* a rabbit⟩　**b** : to get a hint of ⟨*scent* trouble⟩　**2** : to fill with an odor : PERFUME ⟨*scent* a handkerchief⟩

scent·ed *adj* : having scent; *esp* : filled with perfume

scep·ter \'sep-tər\ *n*　**1** : a baton carried by a ruler as an emblem of authority　**2** : authority of an empire or a ruler : SOVEREIGNTY — **scep·tered** \-tərd\ *adj*

scep·tic *variant of* SKEPTIC

¹sched·ule \'skej-ü(ə)l, -əl, *Canadian also* 'shej-, *British usually* 'shed-yü(ə)l\ *n*　**1 a** : a written or printed list or catalog ⟨a *schedule* of social events⟩　**b** : TIMETABLE ⟨a plane *schedule*⟩ ⟨a *schedule* for completion of the school⟩　**2** : ¹PROGRAM 3, AGENDA ⟨my *schedule* for tomorrow⟩

²schedule *vb* **sched·uled; sched·ul·ing**　**1** : to place in a schedule ⟨*schedule* a meeting⟩　**2** : to make a schedule of ⟨*scheduled* my income and debts⟩

scepter 1

sche·mat·ic \ski-'mat-ik\ *adj* : of, relating to, or forming a scheme, plan, or diagram : DIAGRAMMATIC — **sche·mat·i·cal·ly** \-'mat-i-k(ə-)lē\ *adv*

sche·ma·tize \'skē-mə-,tīz\ *vb* **-tized; -tiz·ing** : to form or form into a scheme or regular arrangement

¹scheme \'skēm\ *n*　**1** : a pictorial sketch or outline　**2** : a brief statement in an outline, table, or list　**3** : a plan or program of action ⟨a new *scheme* for better insurance coverage⟩; *esp* : a sly or secret one ⟨a *scheme* to seize control⟩　**4** : a regular or organized design ⟨color *scheme* of a room⟩ ⟨your whole *scheme* of life⟩　**syn** *see* PLAN

²scheme *vb* **schemed; schem·ing**　**1** : to form a scheme for　**2** : to form plans; *esp* : to engage in a plot — **schem·er** *n*

schem·ing \'skē-miŋ\ *adj* : being in the habit of forming schemes

Schick test \'shik-\ *n* : a test to determine whether a person might catch diphtheria

schil·ling \'shil-iŋ\ *n*　**1** : the basic unit of money of Austria　**2** : a coin representing one schilling

schism \'siz-əm, 'skiz-\ *n*　**1 a** : DIVISION 6, SEPARATION　**b** : lack of harmony : DISCORD　**2** : division in or separation from a church or religious body

¹schis·mat·ic \siz-'mat-ik, skiz-\ *n* : one who creates or takes part in schism

²schismatic *adj* : of, relating to, or guilty of schism

schist \'shist\ *n* : a metamorphic rock that can be split along nearly parallel planes

schizo·phre·nia \,skit-sə-'frē-nē-ə\ *n* : a serious mental illness that is a psychosis and is characterized by a twisted view of the real world, by greatly reduced ability to carry out one's daily tasks, and by abnormal ways of thinking, feeling, and behaving

¹schizo·phren·ic \,skit-sə-'fren-ik\ *adj* : of, relating to, or affected with schizophrenia

²schizophrenic *n* : a person affected with schizophrenia

schle·miel \shlə-'mē(ə)l\ *n* : an unlucky clumsy person : CHUMP

schmaltz *also* **schmalz** \'shmölts\ *n* : sentimental music or art — **schmaltzy** \'shmölt-sē\ *adj*

schnau·zer \'shnaut-sər, 'shnaú-zər, snaú-\ *n* : any of a breed of terriers with a long head, small ears, and wiry coat

schnauzer

schol·ar \'skäl-ər\ *n*　**1** : one who attends a school or studies under a teacher : PUPIL　**2 a** : one who has done advanced study in a special area　**b** : a learned person　**3** : a holder of a scholarship — **schol·ar·ly** *adj*

schol·ar·ship \'skäl-ər-,ship\ *n*　**1** : money given (as by a college) to a student to help pay for further education　**2** : the character, qualities, or achievements of a scholar　**syn** *see* KNOWLEDGE

scho·las·tic \skə-'las-tik\ *adj* : of or relating to schools or scholars — **scho·las·ti·cal·ly** \-ti-k(ə-)lē\ *adv*

¹school \'skül\ *n*　**1 a** : a place or establishment for teaching and learning ⟨public *schools*⟩ ⟨a music *school*⟩　**b** : a faculty or division within an institution for higher education devoted to teaching, study, and research in a particular area of knowledge : COLLEGE ⟨*school* of law⟩ ⟨graduate *school*⟩　**2 a** : a session of school ⟨missed *school* yesterday⟩　**b** : SCHOOLHOUSE　**c** : the students or students and teachers of a school ⟨the whole *school* was at the assembly⟩　**3** : persons having the same opinions and beliefs or accepting the same methods or leaders

Word History The English word *school* comes from the Greek *scholē*. The original meaning of *scholē* was "leisure". To the Greeks it seemed natural that one's leisure should be spent learning and thinking. *Scholē* therefore came to mean not only "leisure" but also "a place for learning". Many Greeks were later employed by the Romans as teachers, and the Romans borrowed the Greek word as *schola*. The Latin word *schola* in time came into Old English as *scōl*. [Old English *scōl* "a place for learning", from Latin *schola* (same meaning), from Greek *scholē* "leisure, discussion, lecture, school"]

²school *vb* : TEACH 2, TRAIN; *esp* : to drill in or make used to something

³school *n* : a large number of water animals of one kind (as fish) swimming together

school·bag \'skül-,bag\ *n* : a bag for carrying schoolbooks and school supplies

school board *n* : a board in charge of local public schools

school·book \'skül-,bük\ *n* : a school textbook

school·boy \-,bȯi\ *n* : a boy attending school

school bus *n* : a vehicle for transporting children to and from school

school·child \'skül-,chīld\ *n* : a child attending school

school·fel·low \-,fel-ō\ *n* : SCHOOLMATE

school·girl \-,gər(-ə)l\ *n* : a girl attending school

school·house \-,haůs\ *n* : a building used as a school

school·ing \'skül-iŋ\ *n* **1** : instruction in school : EDUCATION **2** : the cost of going to school

school·marm \'skül-,mä(r)m\ *or* **school·ma'am** \-,mäm, -,mam\ *n* : a woman schoolteacher especially in a rural or small-town school

school·mas·ter \-,mas-tər\ *n* : a male schoolteacher

school·mate \-,māt\ *n* : a school companion

school·mis·tress \-,mis-trəs\ *n* : a woman schoolteacher

school·room \-,rüm, -,rům\ *n* : CLASSROOM

school·teach·er \-,tē-chər\ *n* : a person who teaches in a school

school·time \-,tīm\ *n* : the time for beginning a session of school or during which school is held

school·work \-,wərk\ *n* : lessons done in classes at school or assigned to be done at home

school·yard \-,yärd\ *n* : the playground of a school

schoo·ner \'skü-nər\ *n* **1** : a ship with a fore-and-aft rig and two or more masts **2** : a large tall glass (as for beer) **3** : PRAIRIE SCHOONER

schot·tische \'shät-ish, shä-'tēsh\ *n* : a slow dance with steps similar to those of a polka; *also* : music for this dance

schooner 1

schuss \'shůs, 'shüs\ *vb* : to ski directly down a slope at high speed — **schuss** *n*

schwa \'shwä\ *n* **1** : a vowel that is not stressed and is the usual sound of the first and last vowels of the English word *America* **2** : the symbol ə commonly used for a schwa and sometimes also for a similarly pronounced stressed vowel (as in *cut*)

sci·at·i·ca \sī-'at-i-kə\ *n* : pain along the course of a sciatic nerve especially in the back of the thigh; *also* : pain in or near the hips

sciatic nerve \sī-,at-ik-\ *n* : a nerve that runs down the back of the thigh and is the largest nerve in the body

sci·ence \'sī-ən(t)s\ *n* **1 a** : an area of knowledge that is an object of study **b** : something (as a sport or technique) that may be studied or learned like a science **c** : any of the natural sciences (as biology, physics, or chemistry) **2** : knowledge covering general truths or the operation of general laws especially as obtained and tested through the scientific method [Middle English *science* "the state of knowing, knowledge", from early French *science* (same meaning), from Latin *scientia* (same meaning), from *scient-, sciens* "knowing", from *scire* "to know" — related to CONSCIOUS, NICE, OMNISCIENT; see *Word History* at NICE]

science fiction *n* : fiction that deals with the influence of real

or imagined science on society or individuals

sci·en·tif·ic \,sī-ən-'tif-ik\ *adj* : of, relating to, or exhibiting the methods or rules of science — **sci·en·tif·i·cal·ly** \-'tif-i-k(ə-)lē\ *adv*

scientific method *n* : the rules and methods for the pursuit of knowledge involving the finding and stating of a problem, the collection of facts through observation and experiment, and the making and testing of ideas that need to be proven right or wrong

scientific notation *n* : the expression of numbers as a decimal greater than or equal to 1 and less than 10 multiplied by a power of 10 ⟨999.9 is expressed in *scientific notation* as 9.999×10^2⟩

sci·en·tist \'sī-ənt-əst\ *n* : a person skilled in science and especially natural science : a scientific investigator

sci–fi \'sī-'fī\ *n* : SCIENCE FICTION — **sci–fi** *adj*

scim·i·tar \'sim-ət-ər, -ə-,tär\ *n* : a sword with a curved blade used chiefly by Arabs and Turks

scin·til·late \'sint-ᵊl-,āt\ *vb* **-lat·ed; -lat·ing** **1** : to give off sparks **2** : to flash or gleam as if throwing off sparks ⟨eyes *scintillating* with anger⟩ — **scin·til·lant** \'ᵊl-ənt\ *adj* — **scin·til·la·tion** \,sint-ᵊl-'ā-shən\ *n*

sci·on *also* **ci·on** \'sī-ən\ *n* **1** : a living stem or branch that is cut from a plant and joined to another plant in grafting **2** : ²DESCENDANT 1, CHILD

¹scis·sor \'siz-ər\ *n* : SCISSORS

²scissor *vb* **scis·sored; scis·sor·ing** \-(ə-)riŋ\ : to cut with scissors or shears

scis·sors \'siz-ərz\ *n sing or pl* : a cutting instrument having two blades so fastened together that the sharp edges slide against each other

scissors kick *n* : a swimming kick in which the legs move like scissors

sclera \'skler-ə\ *n* : the dense fibrous white or bluish white tissue that forms the outer covering of the back five-sixths of the eye and is replaced in front by the transparent cornea with which it is continuous

scle·ro·sis \sklə-'rō-səs\ *n* : an abnormal increase in the hardness of a tissue or body part (as arteries or muscles) that occurs in several serious diseases — called also *hardening*; compare MULTIPLE SCLEROSIS

¹scle·rot·ic \sklə-'rät-ik\ *adj* **1** : being or relating to the sclera **2** : of, relating to, or affected with sclerosis

²sclerotic *n* : SCLERA

sclerotic coat *n* : SCLERA

¹scoff \'skäf, 'skȯf\ *n* : an expression of scorn or mockery

²scoff *vb* : JEER, RIDICULE — **scoff·er** *n*

¹scold \'skōld\ *n* : a person who scolds constantly

²scold *vb* **1** : to find fault noisily **2** : to criticize severely or angrily

sco·li·o·sis \,skō-lē-'ō-səs\ *n, pl* **-o·ses** \-,sēz\ : an abnormal curving of the spine

sconce \'skän(t)s\ *n* : a candlestick or group of candlesticks fastened to a wall

scone \'skōn, 'skän\ *n* : a quick bread baked on a griddle or in an oven

¹scoop \'sküp\ *n* **1 a** : a large shovel (as for shoveling coal) **b** : a tool or utensil shaped like a shovel for digging into a soft substance and lifting out a portion **c** : a round utensil with a handle for dipping out soft food (as ice cream)

sconce

\ə\ **abut**		\aů\ **out**	\i\ **tip**	\ȯ\ **saw**	\ů\ **foot**
\ər\ **further**		\ch\ **chin**	\ī\ **life**	\ȯi\ **coin**	\y\ **yet**
\a\ **mat**		\e\ **pet**	\j\ **job**	\th\ **thin**	\yü\ **few**
\ā\ **take**		\ē\ **easy**	\ŋ\ **sing**	\th\ **this**	\yů\ **cure**
\ä\ **cot, cart**		\g\ **go**	\ō\ **bone**	\ü\ **food**	\zh\ **vision**

d : a small tool for cutting or gouging   **2** : an act or the action of scooping : a motion made with or as if with a scoop   **3 a** : the amount held by a scoop ⟨a *scoop* of ice cream⟩   **b** : a hole made by scooping   **4 a** : information of immediate interest ⟨what's the *scoop*⟩   **b** : the reporting of a news story ahead of competitors — **scoop·ful** \-ˌful\ *n*

²**scoop** *vb*   **1** : to take out or up with or as if with a scoop   **2** : to make hollow   **3** : to report a news story ahead of — **scoop·er** *n*

scoot \ˈsküt\ *vb* : to go suddenly and swiftly : DART — **scoot** *n*

scoot·er \ˈsküt-ər\ *n*   **1** : a child's vehicle consisting of a narrow base between a front and a back wheel and guided by a handle attached to the front wheel   **2** : a low vehicle resembling a child's scooter but having two or three wheels, a motor, and a seat

¹**scope** \ˈskōp\ *n*   **1** : space or opportunity for action or thought ⟨full *scope* for the exercise of your talents⟩   **2** : area or amount included, reached, or viewed : RANGE ⟨a subject broad in *scope*⟩ [from Italian *scopo* "aim, purpose, goal", from Latin *scopus* (same meaning), from Greek *skopos* "watcher, goal, aim" — related to BISHOP, EPISCOPAL, HOROSCOPE; see *Word History* at BISHOP]

²**scope** *n* : any of various instruments for viewing: as   **a** : MICROSCOPE   **b** : ¹TELESCOPE   **c** : OSCILLOSCOPE [by shortening]

-scope *combining form* : means for viewing : instrument for viewing ⟨kaleido*scope*⟩ [derived from Greek *skopos* "watcher, goal, aim"]

sco·pol·amine \skō-ˈpäl-ə-ˌmēn\ *n* : a poisonous substance that is found in some plants related to the potato and that is used as a drug with effects similar to those of atropine but also with sedative and tranquilizing effects

¹**scorch** \ˈskorch\ *vb*   **1** : to burn on the surface   **2** : to burn so as to dry, wilt, or turn brown

²**scorch** *n*   **1** : a result of scorching   **2** : a browning of plant tissues usually caused by disease or heat

scorched earth *n* : land stripped of anything that could be of use to an invading enemy force

scorch·er \ˈskor-chər\ *n* : someone or something that scorches; *esp* : a very hot day

¹**score** \ˈskō(ə)r, ˈsko(ə)r\ *n, pl* **scores**   **1** *or pl* **score**   **a** : TWENTY   **b** : a group of 20 things — often used in combination with a cardinal number ⟨five*score*⟩   **2** : a line made with or as if with a sharp instrument   **3** : a duty or injury kept in mind for later action ⟨had some old *scores* to settle⟩   **4** : ¹REASON 1b, GROUND ⟨you have nothing to worry about on that *score*⟩   **5** : the complete written music showing all of the individual parts of a large piece (as a symphony)   **6 a** : a number expressing accomplishment (as in a game or a test) or worth (as of a product) ⟨had a *score* of 80 out of a possible 100⟩   **b** : a record of points made by competing teams or players ⟨the final *score* was 4–3⟩   **7** : the facts of a situation ⟨we won't know what the *score* is until the laboratory results are in⟩ — **score·less** \-ləs\ *adj*

²**score** *vb* **scored; scor·ing**   **1 a** : to set down in an account : RECORD   **b** : to keep score in a game or contest   **2** : to mark with lines, grooves, scratches, or notches   **3** : BERATE, SCOLD   **4 a** : to make or cause to make a score in or as if in a game : TALLY ⟨*score* a run⟩   **b** : ACHIEVE 2, WIN ⟨*scored* a big success⟩   **5** : ¹GRADE 3, MARK   **6** : to arrange (a musical composition) for performance — **scor·er** *n*

score·board \ˈskō(ə)r-ˌbō(ə)rd, ˈsko(ə)r-ˌbo(ə)rd\ *n* : a large board for displaying the score of a game or match

score·card \-ˌkärd\ *n* : a card for recording the score (as of a game)

score·keep·er \-ˌkē-pər\ *n* : a person appointed to record the score during the progress of a game or contest

sco·ria \ˈskōr-ē-ə, ˈskor-\ *n, pl* **-ri·ae** \-ē-ˌē, -ē-ˌī\ : rough cindery lava

¹**scorn** \ˈsko(ə)rn\ *n*   **1** : a feeling of anger and disgust   **2** : someone or something very much disliked

²**scorn** *vb*   **1** : to show scorn for   **2** : to refuse because of scorn : DISDAIN — **scorn·er** *n*

scorn·ful \ˈskorn-fəl\ *adj* : feeling or showing scorn   **syn** see CONTEMPTUOUS — **scorn·ful·ly** \-fə-lē\ *adv*

Scor·pio \ˈskor-pē-ˌō\ *n*   **1** : a group of stars between Libra and Sagittarius usually pictured as a scorpion   **2 a** : the eighth sign of the zodiac — see ZODIAC table   **b** : a person whose sign of the zodiac is Scorpio

scor·pi·on \ˈskor-pē-ən\ *n* : any of an order of animals that are arthropods related to the spiders and that have a long jointed body and a slender tail with a poisonous stinger at the end

scorpion

Scot \ˈskät\ *n* : a person born or living in Scotland

scotch \ˈskäch\ *vb*   **1** *archaic* : to injure so as to make temporarily harmless   **2** : to stamp out : CRUSH; *esp* : to put an end to by showing the untruth of ⟨*scotch* a rumor⟩

¹**Scotch** \ˈskäch\ *adj* : of, relating to, or characteristic of Scotland or its people

²**Scotch** *n*   **1** **Scotch** *pl* : the people of Scotland   **2** *often not cap* : whiskey made in Scotland especially from barley

Scotch·man \ˈskäch-mən\ *n* : a person born or living in Scotland

Scotch terrier *n* : SCOTTISH TERRIER

Scotch·wom·an \ˈskäch-ˌwum-ən\ *n* : a woman born or living in Scotland

sco·ter \ˈskōt-ər\ *n, pl* **scoters** *or* **scoter** : any of several ducks of northern coasts of Europe and North America

scot–free \ˈskät-ˈfrē\ *adj* : completely free from duty, harm, or penalty ⟨get off *scot-free*⟩ [from earlier *scot* "money owed"]

Scot·land Yard \ˌskät-lən(d)-ˈyärd\ *n* : the detective division of the London area police

¹**Scots** \ˈskäts\ *adj* : ¹SCOTCH

²**Scots** *n* : the English language of Scotland

Scots·man \ˈskät-smən\ *n* : SCOTCHMAN

scot·tie \ˈskät-ē\ *n*   **1** *cap* : SCOTCHMAN   **2** : SCOTTISH TERRIER

¹**Scot·tish** \ˈskät-ish\ *adj* : ¹SCOTCH

²**Scottish** *n* : ²SCOTS

Scottish terrier *n* : any of an old Scottish breed of terrier with short legs, large head, small ears that stand straight up, a broad deep chest, and a thick rough coat

scoun·drel \ˈskaun-drəl\ *n* : a mean or wicked person : VILLAIN — **scoun·drel·ly** \-drə-lē\ *adj*

Scottish terrier

¹**scour** \ˈskau(ə)r\ *vb*   **1** : to move about or through quickly especially in search ⟨*scoured* the woods for the missing child⟩   **2** : to examine thoroughly and rapidly ⟨*scoured* the legal documents⟩ — **scour·er** *n*

²**scour** *vb*   **1 a** : to rub hard with something rough in order to clean   **b** : to remove by rubbing hard and washing ⟨*scour* spots from the stove⟩   **2** : to free from foreign substances or impurities by or as if by washing   **3** : to wear away (as by water) : ERODE ⟨a stream *scouring* its banks⟩

— **scour·er** *n*

³**scour** *n* : an action or result of scouring

¹**scourge** \'skərj\ *n* **1** : ²WHIP 1, LASH **2** : someone or something that is an instrument of punishment or criticism **3** : AFFLICTION 2

²**scourge** *vb* **scourged; scourg·ing** **1** : to whip severely : FLOG **2** : to cause severe suffering to : DEVASTATE

scouring rush *n* : EQUISETUM

¹**scout** \'skaut\ *vb* **1** : to go about and observe in search of information : RECONNOITER **2 a** : to make a search ⟨*scout* about for firewood⟩ **b** : to find by searching ⟨*scouted* up the necessary supplies⟩ [Middle English *scouten* "to explore an area for information", from early French *escouter* "to listen", from Latin *auscultare* "to listen"]

²**scout** *n* **1** : the act or an instance of scouting : RECONNAISSANCE **2 a** : one sent to obtain information and especially to survey in preparation for military action in war **b** : a person who searches for talented newcomers ⟨a baseball *scout*⟩ **3** *often cap* **a** : BOY SCOUT **b** : GIRL SCOUT **4** : ²INDIVIDUAL 2, PERSON ⟨you're a good *scout*⟩

³**scout** *vb* **1** : DERIDE, MOCK **2** : to reject as foolish [of Scandinavian origin]

scout·ing \'skaut-iŋ\ *n* **1** : the action of one that scouts **2** *often cap* : the activities of the various Boy Scout and Girl Scout groups

scout·mas·ter \'skaut-,mas-tər\ *n* : the leader of a band of scouts and especially of a troop of Boy Scouts

scow \'skau\ *n* : a large flat-bottomed boat with broad square ends used chiefly for transporting sand, gravel, or refuse

¹**scowl** \'skau(ə)l\ *vb* **1** : to make a frowning expression of displeasure **2** : to exhibit or express with a scowl — **scowl·er** *n*

²**scowl** *n* : an expression of displeasure on the face : FROWN

¹**scrab·ble** \'skrab-əl\ *vb* **scrab·bled; scrab·bling** \-(ə-)liŋ\ **1** : to scratch or scrape about frantically with hands or paws **2** : ¹SCRAMBLE 2 **3** : to struggle by or as if by scraping or scratching ⟨*scrabble* for a living⟩ — **scrab·bler** \-(ə-)lər\ *n*

²**scrabble** *n* : an act or instance of scrabbling

scrag \'skrag\ *n* : a lean person or animal

scrag·gly \'skrag-(ə-)lē\ *adj* **scrag·gli·er; -est** : of rough or uneven outline : RAGGED, UNKEMPT ⟨a *scraggly* beard⟩

scrag·gy \'skrag-ē\ *adj* **scrag·gi·er; -est** **1** : ¹ROUGH 3b, JAGGED ⟨*scraggy* cliffs⟩ **2** : being lean and long : SCRAWNY

scram \'skram\ *vb* **scrammed; scram·ming** : to go away at once ⟨*scram*, you're not wanted⟩

¹**scram·ble** \'skram-bəl\ *vb* **scram·bled; scram·bling** \-b(ə-)liŋ\ **1** : to move or climb hastily on all fours **2** : to strive or struggle for something ⟨*scramble* for front seats⟩ **3 a** : to toss or mix together : JUMBLE **b** : to cook the mixed whites and yolks of eggs by stirring them while frying — **scram·bler** \-b(ə-)lər\ *n*

²**scramble** *n* **1** : a scrambling movement **2** : a disordered mess

¹**scrap** \'skrap\ *n* **1** *pl* : pieces of discarded or leftover food **2** : a small bit : FRAGMENT **3** : things discarded as worthless [Middle English *scrap* "discarded bits of food"; of Norse origin]

²**scrap** *vb* **scrapped; scrap·ping** **1** : to break up into scrap **2** : to discard as worthless

³**scrap** *n* : ¹QUARREL 2, FIGHT [origin unknown]

⁴**scrap** *vb* **scrapped; scrap·ping**: ²QUARREL 2, FIGHT — **scrap·per** *n*

scrap·book \'skrap-,buk\ *n* : a book of blank pages for miscellaneous items (as clippings and pictures)

¹**scrape** \'skrāp\ *vb* **scraped; scrap·ing** **1 a** : to remove by repeated strokes of an edged tool ⟨*scrape* off rust⟩ **b** : to clean or smooth by rubbing **2 a** : to rub or cause to rub so as to make a harsh noise **b** : to damage or injure by dragging against a rough surface ⟨*scrape* a fender⟩ **3 a** : to gather with difficulty and little by little ⟨*scrape* together a few dollars⟩ **b** : to barely get by ⟨*scraped* through with low marks⟩ — **scrap·er** *n*

²**scrape** *n* **1 a** : the act or process of scraping **b** : a sound, mark, or injury made by scraping **2** : a bow made with a pulling back of the foot **3** : a disagreeable situation

scrap·ing \'skrā-piŋ\ *n* : something scraped off or together — usually used in pl.

scrap·ple \'skrap-əl\ *n* : a seasoned mush of meat scraps and cornmeal set in a mold and served in fried slices

scrap·py \'skrap-ē\ *adj* **scrap·pi·er; -est** **1** : QUARRELSOME **2** : having an aggressive and determined spirit — **scrap·pi·ness** *n*

¹**scratch** \'skrach\ *vb* **1** : to scrape, rub, or injure with or as if with the claws or nails **2** : to make a living by hard work and saving **3** : ERASE, CANCEL ⟨*scratch* a name from a list⟩ ⟨*scratch* a runner from a race⟩ **4** : to write or draw especially hastily or carelessly : SCRAWL **5** : to make a thin harsh sound ⟨this pen *scratches*⟩ — **scratch·er** *n*

²**scratch** *n* **1** : a mark (as a line) or injury made by scratching **2** : the sound of scratching **3 a** : the line from which competitors start in a race **b** : ³NOTHING 1a ⟨start from *scratch*⟩ **4** : satisfactory state or performance ⟨not up to *scratch*⟩

scratch hit *n* : a batted ball that is not hit hard but that results in a base hit

scratch test *n* : a test that is used to determine if a person is allergic to a substance and is made by rubbing some of that substance into small scratches on the skin

scratchy \'skrach-ē\ *adj* **scratch·i·er; -est** **1** : likely to scratch or make sore or raw : PRICKLY ⟨*scratchy* woolens⟩ **2** : making a scratching noise **3** : marked or made with scratches ⟨a *scratchy* surface⟩ ⟨*scratchy* handwriting⟩ **4** : uneven in quality : RAGGED ⟨played a *scratchy* game of golf⟩ — **scratch·i·ness** *n*

scrawl \'skrol\ *vb* : to write or draw awkwardly, hastily, or carelessly : SCRIBBLE — **scrawl** *n* — **scrawly** \'skro-lē\ *adj*

scraw·ny \'skro-nē\ *adj* **scraw·ni·er; -est** : poorly nourished : SKINNY — **scraw·ni·ness** *n*

¹**scream** \'skrēm\ *vb* **1** : to cry out, sound, or utter loudly and shrilly **2** : to produce or give a vivid, startling, or alarming effect or expression — **scream·er** *n*

²**scream** *n* **1** : a loud shrill long cry or noise ⟨*screams* of terror⟩ **2** : one that is very funny ⟨you're a *scream* when you get going⟩

scream·ing \'skrē-miŋ\ *adj* **1** : noticeable as if by screaming ⟨*screaming* headlines⟩ ⟨a *screaming* red⟩ **2** : very funny — **scream·ing·ly** *adv*

¹**screech** \'skrēch\ *n* **1** : a shrill harsh cry usually expressing pain or terror **2** : a sound like a screech ⟨*screech* of brakes⟩

²**screech** *vb* **1** : to cry out usually in terror or pain **2** : to make a sound like a screech ⟨the car *screeched* to a halt⟩ **syn** see SHOUT — **screech·er** *n*

screech owl *n* : any of numerous small American owls that are reddish brown or gray and have two tufts of feathers on the head that look like ears

screech owl

¹**screen** \'skrēn\ *n* **1** : a device used to hide or protect ⟨a window *screen*⟩ **2** : something that serves to

shelter, protect, or conceal ⟨a *screen* of fighter planes⟩ **3** : a network of wire set in a frame and used for separating different-sized parts (as of sand) **4 a** : a flat surface on which a picture or series of pictures is projected **b** : the surface (as of a cathode-ray tube) on which the image appears in an electronic display (as in a television set or computer terminal) **5** : the motion-picture industry ⟨a star of stage and *screen*⟩

²**screen** *vb* **1** : to guard from injury or danger **2 a** : to shelter, protect, or separate with or as if with a screen **b** : to pass through a screen to separate the parts of different sizes ⟨*screen* gravel⟩ **c** : to remove by or as if by a screen ⟨*screens* out much harmful radiation⟩ **d** : to examine in order to separate into groups or to select or eliminate ⟨carefully *screened* everyone applying for the job⟩ **3** : to provide with a screen ⟨*screen* a porch⟩ **4** : to project on a screen ⟨*screen* a movie⟩

screen·ing \ˈskrē-niŋ\ *n* : a net (as of metal or plastic) used especially for screens

screen·play \ˈskrēn-ˌplā\ *n* : the written form of a story prepared for film production

screen·writ·er \-ˌrīt-ər\ *n* : a writer of screenplays

¹**screw** \ˈskrü\ *n* **1 a** : a simple machine consisting of a solid cylinder with a winding groove around it and a correspondingly grooved hollow cylinder into which it fits **b** : a nail-shaped or rod-shaped metal piece with a winding groove used for fastening solid pieces together **2 a** : something having the shape of a screw : SPIRAL **b** : the act of screwing tight : TWIST **c** : a screw-shaped device (as a corkscrew) **3** : PROPELLER — **screw·like** \-ˌlīk\ *adj*

²**screw** *vb* **1 a** : to attach, fasten, or close with a screw **b** : to operate, tighten, or adjust with a screw **c** : to turn or twist on a screwlike thread **2** : to twist out of shape ⟨a face *screwed* up in pain⟩ **3** : to increase in amount ⟨trying to *screw* up enough nerve to ask⟩ — **screw·er** *n*

¹**screw·ball** \ˈskrü-ˌbȯl\ *n* **1** : a baseball pitch that moves away from a straight path in a direction opposite to a curve **2** : a crazy person : NUT

²**screwball** *adj* : ²ZANY, NUTTY

screw·driv·er \ˈskrü-ˌdrī-vər\ *n* : a tool for turning screws

screw eye *n* : a screw having a head in the form of a loop

screw propeller *n* : PROPELLER

screw·worm \ˈskrü-ˌwərm\ *n* : the larva of a fly of the warm parts of America that matures in the wounds or sores of mammals and may cause disease or death

screwy \ˈskrü-ē\ *adj* **screw·i·er; -est** **1** : oddly different and unfamiliar ⟨knew something was *screwy*⟩ **2** : CRAZY 1, INSANE ⟨completely *screwy* people⟩

scrib·ble \ˈskrib-əl\ *vb* **scrib·bled; scrib·bling** \-(ə-)liŋ\ : to write or draw hastily or carelessly [Middle English *scriblen* "to write hurriedly or carelessly", from Latin *scribillare* (same meaning), from earlier *scribere* "to write" — related to SCRIBE] — **scribble** *n* — **scrib·bler** \ˈskrib-(ə-)lər\ *n*

¹**scribe** \ˈskrīb\ *n* **1** : a scholar of the Jewish law in New Testament times **2 a** : a public secretary or clerk **b** : a person who copies manuscripts [Middle English *scribe* "one of a class of scholars and copiers of the Scriptures in ancient Israel", from Latin *scriba* "official writer", from *scribere* "to write" — related to CIRCUMSCRIBE, DESCRIPTION, SCRIBBLE, SCRIPTURE, SHROVE TUESDAY]

²**scribe** *vb* **scribed; scrib·ing** : to mark or make by cutting or scratching with a pointed instrument

¹**scrim·mage** \ˈskrim-ij\ *n* **1** : a minor battle : SKIRMISH **2** : the play between two football teams that begins with the snap of the ball **3** : practice play between a team's squads or a practice game between two teams

²**scrimmage** *vb* **scrim·maged; scrim·mag·ing** : to take part in a scrimmage — **scrim·mag·er** *n*

scrimp \ˈskrimp\ *vb* **1** : to make too small or short : SKIMP **2** : ECONOMIZE 1

scrip \ˈskrip\ *n* **1** : a document showing that the holder has

the right to something (as stock or land) **2** : paper money made by the government for temporary use in an emergency

script \ˈskript\ *n* **1 a** : something written : TEXT **b** : the written text of a stage play, screenplay, or broadcast **2** : letters and figures written by hand : HANDWRITING

scrip·to·ri·um \skrip-ˈtōr-ē-əm, -ˈtȯr-\ *n, pl* **-ria** \-ē-ə\ : a copying room in a monastery for use by scribes in the Middle Ages

scrip·tur·al \ˈskrip-chə-rəl, ˈskrip-shrəl\ *adj* : of, relating to, or agreeing with a sacred writing; *esp* : BIBLICAL — **scrip·tur·al·ly** \-ē\ *adv*

scrip·ture \ˈskrip-chər\ *n* **1 a** *cap* : the books of the Old and New Testaments or of either of them : BIBLE — often used in pl. **b** *often cap* : a portion of writing from the Bible **2** : the sacred writings of a religion [Middle English *scripture, Scripture* "the books of the Bible", from Latin *scriptura* (same meaning), from earlier *scriptura* "the act or product of writing", from *scriptus,* past participle of *scribere* "to write" — related to SCRIBE]

script·writ·er \ˈskrip-ˌtrīt-ər\ *n* : a person who writes scripts (as for television shows)

scriv·en·er \ˈskriv-(ə-)nər\ *n* : a professional copyist or writer : SCRIBE

scrod \ˈskräd\ *n* : a young fish (as a cod or haddock); *esp* : one split and boned for cooking

scroll \ˈskrōl\ *n* **1** : a roll of paper or animal skin that has been prepared as a writing surface; *esp* : one on which something is written or engraved **2** : an ornament resembling a loosely or partly rolled scroll

scroll·work \-ˌwərk\ *n* : ornamental work (as in metal or wood) having a scroll or scrolls

scrooge \ˈskrüj\ *n, often cap* : a miserly person

scroll 1

scro·tum \ˈskrōt-əm\ *n, pl* **scro·ta** \ˈskrōt-ə\ *or* **scro·tums** : the pouch on the outside of the body that in most mammals contains the testes

scrounge \ˈskraunj\ *vb* **scrounged; scroung·ing** **1** : to collect by or as if by rummaging ⟨*scrounge* around for firewood⟩ **2** : to get by coaxing or persuading ⟨*scrounge* a dollar from a friend⟩ — **scroung·er** *n*

¹**scrub** \ˈskrəb\ *n* **1 a** : a thick growth of small or stunted shrubs or trees **b** : an area of land covered with scrub **2** : a domestic animal of mixed or unknown parentage and usually inferior build **3** : a person of small size or low social rank **4** : a player not belonging to the first team — **scrub** *adj*

²**scrub** *vb* **scrubbed; scrub·bing** : to rub hard in cleaning or washing ⟨*scrub* clothes⟩ — **scrub·ber** *n*

³**scrub** *n* : an act or instance of scrubbing

scrub·by \ˈskrəb-ē\ *adj* **scrub·bi·er; -est** **1** : of small size or poor quality : STUNTED ⟨*scrubby* cattle⟩ **2** : covered with or consisting of scrub

scrub·land \ˈskrəb-ˌland\ *n* : land covered with scrub

scruff \ˈskrəf\ *n* : the skin of the back of the neck : NAPE

scruffy \ˈskrəf-ē\ *adj* **scruff·i·er; -est** : dirty or shabby in appearance

scrump·tious \ˈskrəm(p)-shəs\ *adj* : DELIGHTFUL, EXCELLENT

scrunch \ˈskrənch\ *vb* **1 a** : ¹CRUNCH 1, CRUSH, CRUMPLE ⟨*scrunch* a paper cup⟩ **b** : to make or move with a crunching sound ⟨cinders *scrunching* underfoot⟩ **2** : CROUCH, SQUEEZE

¹**scru·ple** \ˈskrü-pəl\ *n* **1** — see MEASURE table **2** : a tiny part or quantity [Middle English *scriple* "a unit of weight",

from Latin *scrupulus* "small sharp stone"]

²scruple *n* **1** : a moral consideration or rule of conduct that makes one uneasy or makes action difficult **2** : a sense of guilt felt when one does wrong ⟨acted without *scruple*⟩ **syn** see QUALM

> **Word History** Having a sharp pebble in your shoe can be painful enough to keep you from walking until you remove it. That fact was well known by the ancient Romans, who regularly wore sandals. *Scruple* comes from the Latin word *scrupulus*, which originally meant "a small sharp stone". The ancient Romans also used *scrupulus* to refer to a feeling or thought that might keep a person from doing something that was not quite right. It seemed to them to affect the conscience in the same way that a tiny stone in the shoe would keep a person from being able to walk. This second meaning of *scrupulus* is the one that still survives in our English word *scruple*. [from early French *scrupule* "scruple", from Latin *scrupulus* "scruple, a small sharp stone"]

³scruple *vb* **scru·pled; scru·pling** \-p(ə-)liŋ\ : to have scruples

scru·pu·lous \'skrü-pyə-ləs\ *adj* : full of or having scruples : STRICT — **scru·pu·lous·ly** *adv* — **scru·pu·lous·ness** *n*

scru·ti·nize \'skrüt-ᵊn-,īz\ *vb* **-nized; -niz·ing** : to examine very closely : INSPECT

scru·ti·ny \'skrüt-ᵊn-ē, 'skrüt-nē\ *n, pl* **-nies** : a close inspection : EXAMINATION

scu·ba \'sk(y)ü-bə\ *n* : equipment used for breathing while swimming under water [*s*elf-*c*ontained *u*nderwater *b*reathing *a*pparatus]

¹scud \'skəd\ *vb* **scud·ded; scud·ding** : to move or run swiftly ⟨clouds *scudding* across the sky⟩

²scud *n* **1** : the act of scudding **2** : light clouds driven by the wind

¹scuff \'skəf\ *vb* **1** : to scrape the feet in walking : SHUFFLE **2** : to become rough or scratched through wear

²scuff *n* : a noise or act of scuffing

scuf·fle \'skəf-əl\ *vb* **scuf·fled; scuf·fling** \-(ə-)liŋ\ **1** : to struggle roughly at close quarters **2 a** : to move with a scuff : SCURRY **b** : to scuff one's feet — **scuffle** *n*

¹scull \'skəl\ *n* **1 a** : an oar used at the stern of a boat to drive it forward **b** : one of a pair of short oars for use by one person **2** : a boat driven by one or more pairs of sculls

²scull *vb* : to move a boat by a scull or sculls — **scull·er** *n*

scul·lery \'skəl-(ə-)rē\ *n, pl* **-ler·ies** : a room for cleaning and storing dishes and utensils, washing vegetables, and similar work

scul·lion \'skəl-yən\ *n* : a kitchen helper

scul·pin \'skəl-pən\ *n, pl* **sculpins** *also* **sculpin** : any of numerous spiny large-headed broad-mouthed usually scaleless fishes that have one or more poisonous spines on the fin on the back; *esp* : one of the southern California coast used for food and sport

sculpt \'skəlpt\ *vb* : ²SCULPTURE, CARVE

sculp·tor \'skəlp-tər\ *n* : a person who sculptures

sculp·tress \'skəlp-trəs\ *n* : a woman who sculptures

¹sculp·ture \'skəlp-chər\ *n* **1** : the act, process, or art of carving or cutting hard substances, modeling plastic substances, or casting melted metals into works of art **2 a** : work produced by sculpture **b** : a piece of such work — **sculp·tur·al** \-chə-rəl, -shrəl\ *adj*

²sculpture *vb* **sculp·tured; sculp·tur·ing** \'skəlp-chə-riŋ, 'skəlp-shriŋ\ **1** : to make sculptures **2** : to shape by or as if by carving or molding

scum \'skəm\ *n* **1 a** : a film or impurities risen to or formed on the surface of a liquid **b** : a slimy coating especially on still water **2** : the lowest class : RABBLE — **scum·my** \'skəm-ē\ *adj*

scup·per \'skəp-ər\ *n* : an opening above the upper deck in the side of a boat through which water drains overboard

scup·per·nong \'skəp-ər-,noŋ, -,näŋ\ *n* : a large yellowish green plum-flavored grape

scur·ri·lous \'skər-ə-ləs, 'skə-rə-\ *adj* **1** : being vulgar and evil ⟨*scurrilous* crooks⟩ **2** : containing indecent words or harsh abuse ⟨*scurrilous* attacks on the senator⟩ — **scur·ri·lous·ly** \'skər-ə-ləs-lē, 'skə-rə-\ *adv*

scur·ry \'skər-ē, 'skə-rē\ *vb* **scur·ried; scur·ry·ing** : to move briskly : SCAMPER — **scurry** *n*

¹scur·vy \'skər-vē\ *n* : a disease caused by lack of vitamin C and characterized by loosening of the teeth, softening of the gums, and bleeding under the skin

²scurvy *adj* **scur·vi·er; -est** : CONTEMPTIBLE, MEAN ⟨a *scurvy* practice⟩

scutch·eon \'skəch-ən\ *n* : ESCUTCHEON

¹scut·tle \'skət-ᵊl\ *n* : a metal pail for carrying coal [Middle English *scutel* "a shallow basket for carrying things", from Latin *scutella* "drinking bowl"]

²scuttle *n* : a small opening (as in the deck of a ship or the roof of a house) with a lid or cover [Middle English *skottell* "a small covered opening in the deck of a ship"]

³scuttle *vb* **scut·tled; scut·tling** \'skət-liŋ, -ᵊl-iŋ\ **1** : to sink by cutting holes through the bottom or sides ⟨*scuttle* a ship⟩ **2** : to put an end to by a deliberate act ⟨*scuttle* a conference⟩

⁴scuttle *vb* **scut·tled; scut·tling** \'skət-liŋ, -ᵊl-iŋ\ : SCURRY [probably a combination of ¹*scud* and ²*shuttle*]

⁵scuttle *n* **1** : a quick scuffing pace **2** : short swift run

scut·tle·butt \'skət-ᵊl-,bət\ *n* : ¹RUMOR 1, GOSSIP

scythe \'sīth̶, sī\ *n* : a tool that has a curved blade on a long curved handle and is used for mowing grass or grain by hand

sea \'sē\ *n* **1 a** : a great body of salty water that covers much of the earth; *also* : the waters of the earth **b** : a body of salt water not as large as an ocean ⟨the Mediterranean *sea*⟩ **c** : OCEAN 1 **d** : an inland body of water either salt or fresh ⟨the *Sea* of Galilee⟩ **2** : rough water ⟨a high *sea* swept the deck⟩ **3** : something suggesting the sea (as in great size or depth) ⟨a golden *sea* of wheat⟩ **4** : a life involving marine travel ⟨hoped to make a career of the *sea*⟩ **5** : ²MARE — **sea** *adj* — **at sea 1** : on the sea; *esp* : on a sea voyage **2** : without landmarks for guidance : LOST, BEWILDERED — **to sea** : to or upon the open sea

scythe

sea anemone *n* : any of several invertebrate sea animals that are coelenterates, look like flowers, and have clusters of brightly colored tentacles around the mouth

sea·bag \'sē-,bag\ *n* : a canvas bag used especially by a sailor for gear (as clothes)

sea bass *n* : any of numerous marine fishes that are usually smaller and more active than the related groupers; *esp* : a food and sport fish of the Atlantic coast of the U.S.

sea·bird \'sē-,bərd\ *n* : a bird (as a gull or albatross) that lives on or near the open ocean

sea·board \'sē-,bō(ə)rd, -,bȯ(ə)rd\ *n* : SEACOAST; *also* : the country bordering a seacoast — **seaboard** *adj*

sea breeze *n* : a cooling daytime breeze blowing inland from the sea

sea·coast \'sē-,kōst\ *n* : the shore of the sea

sea cow *n* : MANATEE, DUGONG

\ə\ **abut**	\au̇\ **out**	\i\ **tip**	\ȯ\ **saw**	\u̇\ **foot**
\ər\ **further**	\ch\ **chin**	\ī\ **life**	\ȯi\ **coin**	\y\ **yet**
\a\ **mat**	\e\ **pet**	\j\ **job**	\th\ **thin**	\yü\ **few**
\ā\ **take**	\ē\ **easy**	\ŋ\ **sing**	\th̶\ **this**	\yu̇\ **cure**
\ä\ **cot, cart**	\g\ **go**	\ō\ **bone**	\ü\ **food**	\zh\ **vision**

sea cucumber *n* : a sea animal related to the starfishes and sea urchins that has a long flexible muscular body shaped like a cucumber

sea devil *n* : DEVILFISH 1

sea dog *n* : an experienced sailor

sea·far·er \'sē-,far-ər, -,fer-\ *n* : a person who travels over the ocean : MARINER

sea·far·ing \'sē-,far-iŋ, -,fer-\ *n* : a traveling over the sea as work or recreation — **seafaring** *adj*

sea·floor \-,flō(ə)r, -,flȯ(ə)r\ *n* : the floor of a sea or ocean

sea·food \-,füd\ *n* : edible marine fish and shellfish

sea·go·ing \-,gō-iŋ\ *adj* : designed or used for sea travel

sea green *n* **1** : a medium green or bluish green **2** : a medium yellow green

sea gull *n* : a gull that lives near the sea

sea horse *n* **1** : a fictitious animal half horse and half fish **2** : a small fish with bony plates covering its body and a head that looks like a horse's head

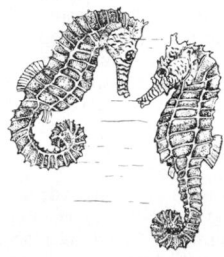

sea horse 2

¹seal \'sē(ə)l\ *n, pl* **seals** *also* **seal 1** : any of numerous marine mammals that live mostly in cold regions, feed especially on fish, mate and give birth to young on land, and use short webbed flippers to swim and dive **2 a** : the soft dense fur of a seal **b** : leather made from the skin of a seal [Old English *seolh* "seal (marine animal)"]

²seal *vb* : to hunt seals

³seal *n* **1 a** : something (as a pledge) that makes safe or secure ⟨under *seal* of secrecy⟩ **b** : a device with a cut or raised design or figure that can be pressed or stamped into paper or wax to form a mark (as for certifying a signature) **c** : a usually ornamental adhesive stamp that may be used to close a letter or package ⟨Christmas *seals*⟩ **2 a** : something that is attached to a closed container and has to be broken in order to open the container **b** : a tight and perfect closing ⟨test the *seal* of the jars⟩ [Middle English *seel* "pledge, guarantee", from early French *seel* (same meaning), from Latin *sigillum* "seal", literally "small sign, small image", from *signum* "mark, sign, image" — related to ¹SIGN]

⁴seal *vb* **1** : to mark with a seal ⟨*seal* a deed⟩ **2** : to close with or as if with a seal ⟨the sheriff *sealed* the area⟩ ⟨ice *sealed* the ships into the harbor⟩ **3** : to decide finally

sea lamprey *n* : a large lamprey that is a pest destroying native fish of the Great Lakes and that is sometimes used for food

sea·lane \'sē-,lān\ *n* : an established sea route

sea lavender *n* : any of a genus of mostly coastal plants that produce clusters of tiny pink to purplish flowers

sea legs *n pl* : bodily adjustment to the motion of a ship at sea indicated especially by ability to walk steadily and by freedom from seasickness

¹seal·er \'sē-lər\ *n* **1** : an official who certifies weights and measures **2** : a substance used on a surface to be painted that prevents the paint from sinking in

²seal·er *n* : a person or a ship engaged in hunting seals

sea lettuce *n* : any of several marine green algae that are thin and edible — called also *ulva*

sea level *n* : the height of the surface of the sea midway

sea lettuce

between the average high and low tides

sea lily *n* : CRINOID; *esp* : a crinoid that has a stalk

sealing wax *n* : a composition that is plastic when warm and is used for sealing (as letters)

sea lion *n* : any of several large Pacific seals that have small ears on the outside of the body

seal·skin \'sē(ə)l-,skin\ *n* **1** : the fur or pelt of a fur seal **2** : a garment (as a coat) of sealskin — **sealskin** *adj*

¹seam \'sēm\ *n* **1** : the fold, line, or groove made by sewing together or joining two edges or two pieces ⟨the *seams* of a dress⟩ ⟨the *seams* of a boat⟩ **2 a** : a raised or sunken line : GROOVE, FURROW, WRINKLE **b** : a layer (as of rock) between clearly different layers ⟨coal *seams*⟩ — **seam·less** \-ləs\ *adj*

²seam *vb* **1** : to join with a seam **2** : to mark with a line, scar, or wrinkle ⟨creeks *seam* the valley⟩ ⟨a face *seamed* with age⟩

sea·man \'sē-mən\ *n* **1** : SAILOR, MARINER **2** : a naval enlisted person with a rank below those of petty officers; *esp* : an enlisted person with a rank just below that of petty officer third class

seaman apprentice *n* : a naval enlisted person with a rank just below that of seaman

seaman recruit *n* : a naval enlisted person of the lowest rank

sea·man·ship \'sē-mən-,ship\ *n* : the art or skill of handling, working, and navigating a ship

sea mile *n* : NAUTICAL MILE

sea·mount \'sē-,maúnt\ *n* : a submarine mountain

seam·stress \'sēm(p)-strəs\ *n* : a woman who sews especially for a living

seamy \'sē-mē\ *adj* **seam·i·er; -est** : not pleasing or presentable : SORDID ⟨the *seamy* side of life⟩ — **seam·i·ness** *n*

sé·ance \'sā-,än(t)s\ *n* **1** : a meeting for discussion : SESSION **2** : a meeting to receive the communications of spirits

sea otter *n* : a large marine otter of northern Pacific coasts that feeds mostly on shellfish and can grow to nearly two meters in length

sea·plane \'sē-,plān\ *n* : an airplane designed to take off from and land on the water

sea otter

sea·port \-,pō(ə)rt, -,pȯ(ə)rt\ *n* : a port, harbor, or town within reach of seagoing ships

sea·quake \'sē-,kwāk\ *n* : a submarine earthquake

¹sear \'si(ə)r\ *vb* **1** : to cause withering or drying : PARCH, SHRIVEL ⟨harsh winds that *sear* and burn⟩ **2** : to burn, scorch, or injure with or as if with sudden heat

²sear *n* : a mark or scar left by searing

¹search \'sərch\ *vb* **1 a** : to go through or look carefully and thoroughly in an effort to find or discover ⟨*search* a room⟩ ⟨*search* for a lost child⟩ **b** : to look in the pockets or the clothing of for something hidden ⟨*search* an arrested person⟩ **2** : to find or come to know by or as if by careful investigation or examination **syn** see SEEK — **search·er** *n* — **search·ing·ly** \'sər-chiŋ-lē\ *adv*

²search *n* : an act of searching : an attempt to get, find, or seek out

search·light \'sərch-,līt\ *n* : a device for casting a beam of light; *also* : a beam of light cast by it

search warrant *n* : a warrant making legal a search of a specified place (as a house) for stolen goods or unlawful possessions (as burglars' tools)

sea·scape \'sē-,skāp\ *n* **1** : a view of the sea **2** : a picture representing a scene at sea

Sea Scout *n* : one enrolled in the Boy Scouts of America program that provides training in seamanship

sea serpent *n* : a large marine animal resembling a snake often reported to have been seen but never proved to be real

sea·shell \'sē-,shel\ *n* : the shell of a marine animal and especially a mollusk

sea·shore \-,shō(ə)r, -,shȯ(ə)r\ *n* : the shore of a sea : SEA-COAST

sea·sick \-,sik\ *adj* : sick or as if sick in the stomach from the pitching or rolling of a ship — **sea·sick·ness** *n*

sea·side \-,sīd\ *n* : the land bordering the sea : SEACOAST

sea slug *n* **1** : SEA CUCUMBER **2** : any of several marine mollusks that have no shell

¹**sea·son** \'sēz-ᵊn\ *n* **1 a** : a suitable or natural time or occasion ⟨a *season* for all things⟩ **b** : a usually brief period of time ⟨willing to wait a *season*⟩ **2 a** : a period of the year associated with something in particular that happens every year ⟨the baseball *season*⟩ **b** : a period in which a place is most often visited ⟨tourists at all *seasons*⟩ **c** : one of the four quarters into which the year is commonly divided — compare AUTUMN 1, SPRING, SUMMER 1, WINTER 1 **d** : the time of a major holiday — **in season 1** : at the right or fitting time **2** : in a state or at the stage of greatest fitness (as for eating) ⟨peaches are *in season*⟩ **3** : at the legally established time for being hunted or caught — **out of season** : not in season ⟨fined for hunting *out of season*⟩

²**season** *vb* **sea·soned; sea·son·ing** \'sēz-niŋ, -ᵊn-iŋ\ **1** : to make pleasant to the taste by adding seasoning ⟨a *seasoned* stew⟩ **2 a** : to make or become suitable for use (as by drying) ⟨*season* lumber⟩ **b** : to make fit by experience — **sea·son·er** \'sēz-nər, -ᵊn-ər\ *n*

sea·son·able \'sēz-nə-bəl, -ᵊn-ə-bəl\ *adj* : suitable to the season or situation : TIMELY ⟨a *seasonable* frost⟩ ⟨*seasonable* advice⟩ — **sea·son·ably** \-blē\ *adv*

sea·son·al \'sēz-nəl, -ᵊn-əl\ *adj* : of, relating to, or restricted to a particular season ⟨*seasonal* industries⟩ — **sea·son·al·ly** \-nə-lē, -ᵊn-ə-lē\ *adv*

sea·son·ing \'sēz-niŋ, -ᵊn-iŋ\ *n* : something (as a spice or herb) that seasons

season ticket *n* : a ticket (as to all of a club's games) good for a specified season

sea star *n* : STARFISH

¹**seat** \'sēt\ *n* **1 a** : something (as a chair) intended to be sat in or on **b** : the part of something on which one rests in sitting ⟨*seat* of the trousers⟩ ⟨a chair *seat*⟩ **c** : the part of the body on which a person sits : BUTTOCK 2 **2 a** : the place on or at which a person sits ⟨had three *seats* for the game⟩ **b** : a right of sitting usually as a member ⟨a *seat* in the senate⟩ **c** : MEMBERSHIP 1 **3** : a place or area where something is located ⟨the *seat* of the pain⟩ ⟨*seats* of learning⟩; *esp* : a place (as a city) from which authority is exercised ⟨the new *seat* of the government⟩ **4** : posture in or way of sitting especially on horseback **5** : a part or surface on which another part or surface rests — **seat·ed** \-əd\ *adj*

²**seat** *vb* **1 a** : to place in or on a seat ⟨*seat* a guest⟩ **b** : to provide seats for ⟨a theater *seating* 1000 persons⟩ **2** : to repair the seat of or provide a new seat for ⟨*seat* a chair⟩ — **seat·er** *n*

seat belt *n* : a strap (as in an automobile or airplane) designed to hold a person in a seat

sea trout *n* **1** : a trout or char that lives mostly in the ocean but goes up rivers to breed and lay eggs **2** : any of various sea fishes (as the weakfish) that look like trout

sea turtle *n* : any of numerous large marine turtles (as the green turtle or the loggerhead) that have paddle-shaped feet to aid in swimming

sea urchin *n* : any of a class of invertebrate animals that are echinoderms related to the starfish, live on or burrow in the sea bottom, and are covered with spines

sea·wall \'sē-,wȯl\ *n* : a wall or bank to prevent sea waves from wearing away the shore

¹**sea·ward** \'sē-wərd\ *n* : the direction or side away from land and toward the open sea

²**seaward** *adj* **1** : going or located toward the sea **2** : coming from the sea ⟨a *seaward* wind⟩

³**seaward** *also* **sea·wards** \-wərdz\ *adv* : toward the sea

sea urchin

sea·wa·ter \'sē-,wȯt-ər, -,wät-\ *n* : water in or from the sea

sea·way \-,wā\ *n* **1 a** : a route for travel on the sea **b** : an ocean traffic lane **2** : a rough sea **3** : a deep inland waterway that admits ocean shipping

sea·weed \-,wēd\ *n* : a plant growing in the sea; *esp* : a marine alga (as a kelp)

sea·wor·thy \-,wər-thē\ *adj* : fit or safe for a sea voyage ⟨a *seaworthy* ship⟩ — **sea·wor·thi·ness** *n*

se·ba·ceous gland \si-'bā-shəs-\ *n* : any of the skin glands that secrete an oily lubricating substance at the base of hairs or onto the skin

se·cant \'sē-,kant, -kənt\ *n* **1** : a straight line cutting a curve at two or more points **2** : the ratio between the hypotenuse in a right triangle and the side next to an acute angle

se·cede \si-'sēd\ *vb* **se·ced·ed; se·ced·ing** : to withdraw from an organization (as a nation, church, or political party)

se·ces·sion \si-'sesh-ən\ *n* : the act of seceding — **se·ces·sion·ism** \-'sesh-ə-,niz-əm\ *n* — **se·ces·sion·ist** \-'sesh-(ə-)nəst\ *n*

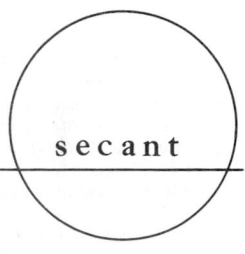

secant 1

se·clude \si-'klüd\ *vb* **se·clud·ed; se·clud·ing** **1** : to keep away from others : SECRETE, HIDE ⟨*secluded* themselves⟩ **2** : to shut away : SCREEN, ISOLATE ⟨a cottage *secluded* by forests⟩

se·clud·ed *adj* **1** : hidden from view ⟨a *secluded* valley⟩ **2** : living in seclusion : SOLITARY ⟨*secluded* monks⟩ — **se·clud·ed·ness** *n*

se·clu·sion \si-'klü-zhən\ *n* **1** : the act of secluding : the state of being secluded **2** : a secluded place

¹**sec·ond** \'sek-ənd *also* -ənt\ *adj* **1** — see NUMBER table **2 a** : next to the first in time, order, importance, or rank ⟨*second* violin⟩ ⟨*second* place⟩ **b** : ¹OTHER 2 ⟨elects a mayor every *second* year⟩ **c** : resembling or suggesting an original : ANOTHER ⟨a *second* Washington⟩ [Middle English *second* "next to the first in position, order, or time", from early French *second* (same meaning), from Latin *secundus* "second, following, favorable", from *sequi* "to follow" — related to SEQUEL] — **second** *adv* — **sec·ond·ly** *adv*

²**second** *n* **1 a** — see NUMBER table **b** : one next after the first in time, order, importance, or rank **2** : one who assists another (as in a duel or prizefight) **3** : the difference in pitch between the first tone and the second tone of a scale **4** : a damaged or imperfect article (as of merchandise) **5** : the act of seconding a motion **6** : SECOND BASE **7** : the second gear or speed in an automobile **8** *pl* : a second helping of food

\ə\ abut	\au̇\ **out**	\i\ tip	\ȯ\ **saw**	\u̇\ **foot**
\ər\ **further**	\ch\ **chin**	\ī\ life	\ȯi\ **coin**	\y\ **yet**
\a\ mat	\e\ **pet**	\j\ **job**	\th\ **thin**	\yü\ **few**
\ā\ take	\ē\ **easy**	\ŋ\ **sing**	\th\ **this**	\yu̇\ **cure**
\ä\ cot, cart	\g\ **go**	\ō\ **bone**	\ü\ **food**	\zh\ **vision**

³second n **1 a** : the 60th part of a minute of angular measure **b** : the 60th part of a minute of time; *esp* : the international unit of time related to the period of the radiation corresponding to a change between the two levels of the ground state of a particular isotope of the cesium atom **2** : ¹INSTANT, MOMENT (I'll be back in a *second*) [Middle English *secunde* "the 60th part of a minute", from Latin *secunda* (same meaning), derived from earlier *secundus* (adjective) "second (in order), following, favorable"; so called from the fact that the minute is the first level of division of a degree or hour and this is the second level]

⁴second vb **1** : to give support or encouragement to : ASSIST **2** : to encourage that something be debated or voted on (*second* a motion) [from Latin *secundare* "to give support to, assist", from *secundus* (adjective) "second, following, favorable"] — **sec·ond·er** n

¹sec·ond·ary \'sek-ən-ˌder-ē\ adj **1 a** : of second rank, importance, or value (*secondary* considerations) **b** : of, relating to, or being the second strongest of the three or four levels of stress (the last syllable of "refrigerate" has *secondary* stress) **2 a** : coming from something original or basic **b** : of, relating to, or being the current created by a change in the primary current or the circuit of the created current in an induction coil or transformer (a *secondary* coil) (*secondary* voltage) **3 a** : of, relating to, or being a second rank or grade in a series **b** : of or relating to a school between elementary or grammar school and college — **sec·ond·ari·ly** \ˌsek-ən-'der-ə-lē\ adv

²secondary n, pl **-ar·ies** **1** : the defensive football players who line up behind the line of scrimmage **2** : any of the quill feathers attached to the ulna of the wing of a bird **3** : the coil through which the secondary current passes in an induction coil or transformer — called also *secondary coil*

secondary color n : a color formed by mixing equal amounts of basic colors

secondary school n : a school for students above elementary or grammar school level and below college level

secondary sex characteristic n : a physical characteristic (as the breasts of a female mammal or the showy feathers of a male bird) that appears in members of one sex at puberty or in seasonal breeders at breeding season and is not directly concerned with reproduction

second base n : the base that must be touched second by a base runner in baseball or the position of the player defending the area around it

second baseman n : the player defending the area to the right of second base

second–class adj **1** : of or relating to a class next below the first or highest class **2 a** : ¹INFERIOR 3, MEDIOCRE **b** : deprived of wealth or social rank

second–degree burn n : a burn characterized by pain, blistering, and destruction of the top layers of the skin that is accompanied by the accumulation of blood and fluid in the tissues beneath the burned area

second fiddle n : a person who fills a secondary role

second growth n : forest trees that come up naturally after removal of the first growth by cutting or by fire

sec·ond–guess \ˌsek-ᵊn-'ges, -ən-\ vb **1** : to think out substitute strategies or explanations for after the event **2 a** : OUTWIT **b** : PREDICT — **sec·ond–guess·er** n

sec·ond·hand \ˌsek-ən-'hand\ adj **1** : not original : taken from someone else (*secondhand* reports) **2 a** : having had a previous owner (a *secondhand* car) **b** : selling used goods (a *secondhand* store) — **secondhand** adv

second lieutenant n : a military commissioned officer of the lowest rank

second person n : a set of words or forms (as pronouns or verb forms) referring to the one to whom the utterance in which they occur is addressed

sec·ond–rate \ˌsek-ən-'(d)rāt\ adj : of second or ordinary quality or value : MEDIOCRE

second wind n : new energy or ability to continue

se·cre·cy \'sē-krə-sē\ n, pl **-cies** **1** : the habit of keeping secrets : SECRETIVENESS **2** : the quality or state of being hidden or concealed

¹se·cret \'sē-krət\ adj **1 a** : hidden or kept from knowledge or view **b** : working in secret as a spy or detective : UNDERCOVER (a *secret* agent) **2** : SECLUDED 1 (a *secret* valley) — **se·cret·ly** adv

²secret n **1 a** : something that cannot be explained : MYSTERY **b** : something kept from the knowledge of others or shared only privately with a few **2** : something taken to be necessary to gain a desired end (the *secret* of a long life) — **in secret** : in a private place or manner

sec·re·tar·i·at \ˌsek-rə-'ter-ē-ət, -ē-ˌat\ n **1** : the secretaries of an organization **2** : the division of administration of a governmental organization (the United Nations *secretariat*)

sec·re·tary \'sek-rə-ˌter-ē\ n, pl **-tar·ies** **1** : a person employed to handle records, letters, and routine work for another person **2** : an officer of a business corporation or society who has charge of the letters and records **3** : a government official in charge of a division (*Secretary* of State) **4** : a desk with a top section for books — **sec·re·tar·i·al** \ˌsek-rə-'ter-ē-əl\ adj

secretary–general n, pl **secretaries–general** : a principal officer of administration (*secretary-general* of the United Nations)

¹se·crete \si-'krēt\ vb **se·cret·ed; se·cret·ing** : to produce and give off a secretion (glands that *secrete* saliva)

²se·crete \si-'krēt, 'sē-krēt\ vb **se·cret·ed; se·cret·ing** : to deposit or conceal in a hiding place

secretary 4

se·cre·tion \si-'krē-shən\ n **1 a** : the act or process of secreting **b** : a substance produced and given off by a gland; *esp* : one (as an enzyme) that performs a specific useful function in the body **2** : a concealing of something

se·cre·tive \'sē-krət-iv, si-'krēt-\ adj : not frank or open — **se·cre·tive·ly** adv — **se·cre·tive·ness** n

secret police n : a police organization operating mostly in secrecy and especially for the political purposes of its government and often using methods of terrorists

sect \'sekt\ n **1 a** : a religious group having beliefs that differ greatly from those of the main body **b** : a religious body consisting of members having similar beliefs **2 a** : a group of people having the same beliefs or following the same leader **b** : PARTY 1 **c** : FACTION

¹sec·tar·i·an \sek-'ter-ē-ən\ adj **1** : of, relating to, or characteristic of a sect or sectarian **2** : not willing to consider other points of view (a *sectarian* mind) — **sec·tar·i·an·ism** \-ē-ə-ˌniz-əm\ n

²sectarian n **1** : a member of a sect **2** : a person who won't consider the ideas or opinions of others

¹sec·tion \'sek-shən\ n **1** : a part cut off or separated (a *section* of an orange) **2** : a part of a written work (sports *section* of the newspaper) **3** : the appearance that a thing has or would have if cut straight through (a drawing of a ship in *section*) **4** : a part of an area, community, or group of people (the business *section* of town) **5** : one of several parts (as of a bookcase) that may be assembled or reassembled **6** : a part of an orchestra composed of one class of instruments (brass *section*) [from Latin *section-, sectio* "section, the act of cutting", from *sectus,* past participle of *secare* "to cut" — related to DISSECT, INSECT] **syn** see PART

²section vb **sec·tioned; sec·tion·ing** \-sh(ə-)niŋ\ **1** : to cut or separate into or become cut or separated into parts or sections **2** : to represent in sections (as by a drawing)

sec·tion·al \'sek-shnəl, -shən-ᵊl\ *adj* **1 a** : of or relating to a section **b** : local or regional in type ⟨*sectional* interests⟩ **2** : consisting of or divided into sections ⟨*sectional* furniture⟩ — **sec·tion·al·ly** \-ē\ *adv*

sec·tion·al·ism \'sek-shnə-,liz-əm, -shən-ᵊl-,iz-\ *n* : too much devotion to the interests of a region

sec·tor \'sek-tər, -,tȯ(ə)r\ *n* **1 a** : the part of a circle included between two radii **b** : an area assigned to a military commander to defend **2** : a part of society ⟨the public *sector*⟩ ⟨the industrial *sector*⟩

sec·u·lar \'sek-yə-lər\ *adj* **1 a** : not spiritual : WORLDLY ⟨*secular* concerns⟩ **b** : not religious ⟨*secular* music⟩ **c** : of, relating to, or regulated by the state rather than the church ⟨*secular* courts⟩ **2** : of or relating to members of the clergy who do not belong to a religious community ⟨a *secular* priest⟩ — **sec·u·lar·ly** *adv*

sec·u·lar·ism \'sek-yə-lə-,riz-əm\ *n* : the belief that religion and religious considerations should be ignored — **sec·u·lar·ist** \-rəst\ *n* — **secularist** *or* **sec·u·lar·is·tic** \,sek-yə-lə-'ris-tik\ *adj*

sec·u·lar·ize \'sek-yə-lə-,rīz\ *vb* **-ized; -iz·ing** **1** : to make secular **2** : to transfer to civil use, possession, or control from that of the church — **sec·u·lar·iza·tion** \,sek-yə-lə-rə-'zā-shən\ *n*

¹se·cure \si-'kyu̇(ə)r\ *adj* **se·cur·er; se·cur·est** **1** : easy in mind : CONFIDENT ⟨*secure* in the knowledge that help was near⟩ **2 a** : providing safety : SAFE ⟨*secure* hideaway⟩ ⟨*secure* against attack⟩ **b** : TRUSTWORTHY, DEPENDABLE ⟨*secure* foundation⟩ **3** : ¹SURE 5a, CERTAIN ⟨victory is *secure*⟩ [from Latin *securus* "safe, secure", literally "without care", from *se* "without" and *cura* "care" — related to CURE, SURE; see *Word History* at CURE] — **se·cure·ly** *adv*

²secure *vb* **se·cured; se·cur·ing** **1 a** : to make safe : GUARD, SHIELD ⟨*secure* a supply line from enemy raids⟩ **b** : to assure payment of **2 a** : to take into custody ⟨*secure* a prisoner⟩ **b** : to fasten tightly ⟨*secure* a door⟩ **3** : to acquire as the result of effort ⟨*secure* employment⟩
syn see GET

se·cure·ment \si-'kyu̇(ə)r-mənt\ *n* : the act or process of making secure

se·cu·ri·ty \si-'kyu̇r-ət-ē\ *n, pl* **-ties** **1** : the state of being secure : SAFETY **2** : something given as a pledge ⟨*security* for a loan⟩ **3** : an evidence of debt or of property (as a stock certificate or bond) ⟨government *securities*⟩ **4** : something that secures : PROTECTION; *esp* : measures taken to guard against spying or destructive actions ⟨a senate committee concerned with national *security*⟩

se·dan \si-'dan\ *n* **1** : a portable often covered chair that is designed to hold one person and to be carried on poles by two people **2** : an enclosed automobile that seats four to seven persons including the driver in a single compartment and has a permanent top

se·date \si-'dāt\ *adj* : quiet in manner or conduct : STAID, SOBER — **se·date·ly** *adv* — **se·date·ness** *n*

¹sed·a·tive \'sed-ət-iv\ *adj* : tending to calm or to ease tension

²sedative *n* : a sedative medicine

sed·en·tary \'sed-ᵊn-,ter-ē\ *adj* **1** : not migratory : SETTLED ⟨*sedentary* birds⟩ **2** : doing or requiring much sitting ⟨a *sedentary* job⟩

sedge \'sej\ *n* : any of a family of plants of marshy areas that are related to the grasses and have solid often three-sided stems

sed·i·ment \'sed-ə-mənt\ *n* **1** : the material from a liquid that settles to the bottom **2** : material (as stones and sand) deposited by water,

sedge

wind, or glaciers — **sed·i·ment·** \-,ment\ *vb*

sed·i·men·ta·ry \,sed-ə-'ment-ə-rē, -'men-trē\ *adj* **1** : of, relating to, or containing sediment **2** : formed by or from sediment ⟨*sedimentary* rock⟩ — compare IGNEOUS, META-MORPHIC

sed·i·men·ta·tion \,sed-ə-mən-'tā-shən, -,men-\ *n* : the action or process of depositing sediment

se·di·tion \si-'dish-ən\ *n* : the stirring up of feelings against lawful authority

se·di·tious \si-'dish-əs\ *adj* : of, relating to, or stirring up sedition ⟨*seditious* statements⟩

se·duce \si-'d(y)üs\ *vb* **se·duced; se·duc·ing** **1** : to persuade to be disobedient or disloyal **2** : to persuade to do wrong ⟨*seduced* into crime⟩ **3** : to persuade to have sexual intercourse especially for the first time — **se·duc·er** *n* — **se·duc·tion** \-'dək-shən\ *n*

se·duc·tive \si-'dək-tiv\ *adj* : tending to seduce : ALLURING, TEMPTING — **se·duc·tive·ly** *adv* — **se·duc·tive·ness** *n*

sed·u·lous \'sej-ə-ləs\ *adj* : steadily industrious : DILIGENT — **sed·u·lous·ly** *adv*

se·dum \'sēd-əm\ *n* : any of a genus of herbs that have fleshy leaves and clusters of yellow, white, or pink flowers

¹see \'sē\ *vb* **saw** \'sȯ\; **seen** \'sēn\; **see·ing** \'sē-iŋ\ **1 a** : to become aware of by means of the eyes or have the power of sight ⟨*see* a bird⟩ ⟨a person who cannot *see*⟩ **b** : to give or pay attention ⟨*see*, the bus is coming⟩ **2 a** : to have experience of : UNDERGO ⟨had *seen* something of life⟩ **b** : to know or find out by investigation ⟨*see* what's wrong with the car⟩ **3** : to understand the meaning or importance of ⟨I *see* what you mean⟩ **4 a** : to provide for ⟨*see* them through⟩ **b** : to make sure ⟨*see* that the job gets done⟩ **5 a** : to call on : VISIT ⟨*see* a sick friend⟩ **b** : to grant an interview to : RECEIVE ⟨the president will *see* you⟩ **6** : ACCOMPANY 1, ESCORT ⟨I'll *see* you home⟩ — **see eye to eye** : to have a common point of view : AGREE — **see to** : to provide for the needs of ⟨*saw* to the children's education⟩

²see *n* **1** : the city in which a bishop's church is located **2** : the area in which a bishop has authority : DIOCESE

see·able \'sē-ə-bəl\ *adj* : capable of being seen

¹seed \'sēd\ *n, pl* **seed** *or* **seeds** **1 a** : the grains of plants used for sowing **b** : a fertilized ripened ovule of a flowering plant that contains an embryo and is capable of producing a new plant; *also* : a plant structure (as a spore or small dry fruit) capable of producing a new plant **c** : MILT, SEMEN **2** : the children of one individual ⟨the *seed* of David⟩ **3** : something from which growth takes place : GERM — **seed** *adj* — **seed·ed** \-əd\ *adj* — **seed·like** \-,līk\ *adj* — **go to seed** *or* **run to seed** : to lose effectiveness : DECAY

²seed *vb* **1** : ²SOW 1a, c, PLANT ⟨*seed* a field⟩ **2** : to produce or shed seeds ⟨weeds that *seed* freely⟩ **3** : to treat (a cloud) with solid particles to convert water droplets into ice crystals in an attempt to produce rain **4** : to remove seeds from **5** : to rank (a player or team) in a tournament on the basis of previous record ⟨was *seeded* second in the state tournament⟩

seed·bed \'sēd-,bed\ *n* : soil or a bed of soil prepared for planting seed

seed·case \-,kās\ *n* : a dry hollow fruit (as a pod) that contains seeds

seed coat *n* : the hard protective outer covering of a seed

seed·eat·er \'sēd-,ēt-ər\ *n* : a bird (as a finch) that eats mostly seeds

seed·er \'sēd-ər\ *n* : a machine for planting or sowing seeds

\ə\ abut		\au̇\ out		\i\ tip		\ȯ\ saw	\u̇\ foot
\ər\ further		\ch\ chin		\ī\ life		\ȯi\ coin	\y\ yet
\a\ mat		\e\ pet		\j\ job		\th\ thin	\yü\ few
\ā\ take		\ē\ easy		\ŋ\ sing		\th\ this	\yu̇\ cure
\ä\ cot, cart		\g\ go		\ō\ bone		\ü\ food	\zh\ vision

seed leaf *n* : COTYLEDON

seed·less \'sēd-ləs\ *adj* : having no seeds ⟨*seedless* grapes⟩

seed·ling \'sēd-liŋ\ *n* **1** : a young plant grown from seed **2** : a tree before it becomes a sapling — **seedling** *adj*

seed plant *n* : a plant that bears seeds : SPERMATOPHYTE

seed·pod \'sēd-,päd\ *n* : ¹POD 1

seedy \'sēd-ē\ *adj* **seed·i·er; -est 1** : containing or full of seeds ⟨a *seedy* fruit⟩ **2** : not being in good shape : SHABBY ⟨*seedy* clothes⟩ — **seed·i·ness** *n*

see·ing \'sē-iŋ\ *conj* : in consideration of the fact that

Seeing Eye *trademark* — used for a dog trained to guide the blind

seek \'sēk\ *vb* **sought** \'sȯt\; **seek·ing 1** : to go to ⟨*seek* the shade on a sunny day⟩ **2 a** : to go in search of : look for ⟨*seek* out the guilty person⟩ **b** : to try to discover ⟨*seek* the truth⟩ **3** : to ask for : REQUEST ⟨*seeks* advice⟩ **4** : to try to acquire or gain : aim at ⟨*seeking* public office⟩ **5** : to make an attempt : TRY ⟨*seek* to find a way⟩ ⟨*sought* to improve my work⟩ — **seek·er** *n*

> **syn** SEEK, SEARCH, HUNT mean to look for something. SEEK may imply looking for either material or mental things ⟨*seeking* new friends⟩ ⟨*seek* the truth⟩ SEARCH suggests looking for something in a careful, thorough way ⟨we *searched* all over the house for the letter⟩ HUNT suggests a long pursuit, as if one were going after game ⟨I *hunted* all day for the right gift⟩

seem \'sēm\ *vb* **1** : to give the impression of being : APPEAR ⟨the request *seems* reasonable⟩ **2 a** : to appear to a person's own mind or opinion ⟨can't *seem* to solve the problem⟩ **b** : to appear to be ⟨there *seems* no reason for worry⟩

seem·ing \'sē-miŋ\ *adj* : appearing to be real or true : APPARENT ⟨suspicious of their *seeming* enthusiasm⟩ — **seem·ing·ly** *adv*

seem·ly \'sēm-lē\ *adj* **seem·li·er; -est 1** : ATTRACTIVE, HANDSOME **2** : being in good taste : PROPER ⟨*seemly* behavior⟩ **3** : suitable for the occasion, purpose, or person : FIT ⟨a *seemly* reply⟩ — **seem·li·ness** *n* — **seemly** *adv*

seen *past participle of* SEE

see out *vb* : to continue with until the end : FINISH

seep \'sēp\ *vb* : to flow or pass slowly through small openings : OOZE

seep·age \'sē-pij\ *n* **1** : the process of seeping **2** : a quantity of fluid that has seeped through something

seer \'si(ə)r, *especially for sense 1 also* 'sē-ər\ *n* **1** : someone or something that sees **2** : a person who foresees or foretells events

seer·suck·er \'si(ə)r-,sək-ər\ *n* : a light fabric usually striped and having parallel wrinkles

¹see·saw \'sē-,sȯ\ *n* **1 a** : an up-and-down or backward-and-forward motion or movement **b** : a contest or struggle in which now one side now the other has the lead **2 a** : a game in which two children or groups of children ride on opposite ends of a plank balanced in the middle so that one end goes up as the other goes down **b** : the plank used in the game of seesaw — **seesaw** *adj*

²seesaw *vb* **see·sawed; see·saw·ing 1** : to move like a seesaw **2** : to play on a seesaw

seesaw 2b

seethe \'sēth\ *vb* **seethed; seeth·ing 1** : to churn or foam as if boiling ⟨the river rapids *seethed*⟩ **2** : to be in a state of great excitement or upset ⟨was *seething* with rage⟩

¹seg·ment \'seg-mənt\ *n* **1** : any of the parts into which a thing is divided or naturally separates : SECTION, DIVISION **2 a** : a part cut off from a figure by a line; *esp* : a region of a circle bounded by a chord and an arc **b** : a part of a straight line included between two points — called also *line segment* — **seg·ment·ed** \'seg-,ment-əd, seg-'ment-\ *adj*

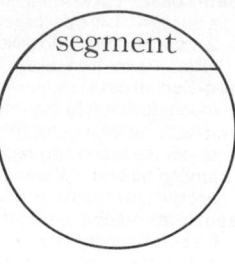

segment 2a

²seg·ment \'seg-,ment\ *vb* : to separate into segments

seg·men·ta·tion \,seg-mən-'tā-shən, -,men-\ *n* : the process of dividing into segments; *esp* : the formation of many cells from a single cell (as in a developing egg)

sego lily \,sē-gō-\ *n* : a western North American herb related to the lilies and having mostly white and in some areas mostly yellow flowers with some streaking or spotting with a darker color

seg·re·gate \'seg-ri-,gāt\ *vb* **-gat·ed; -gat·ing** : to separate from others or from the general mass : ISOLATE; *esp* : to separate by races [from Latin *segregatus* "set apart", from *segregare* "to set apart", from *se-* "apart, without" and *gregare* "gather together into a flock or herd", from *greg-, grex* "flock, herd" — related to AGGREGATE, CONGREGATE]

seg·re·ga·tion \,seg-ri-'gā-shən\ *n* **1** : the act or process of segregating : the state of being segregated **2** : the separation or isolation of a race, class, or group (as by restriction to an area or by separate schools)

seg·re·ga·tion·ist \,seg-ri-'gā-sh(ə-)nəst\ *n* : a person who believes in, practices, or encourages segregation especially of races

sei·gneur \sān-'yər\ *n, often cap* : ¹LORD 1, SEIGNIOR

sei·gnior \sān-'yó(ə)r, 'sān-,yó(ə)r\ *n* : a man of rank or authority

sei·gniory *or* **sei·gnory** \'sān-yə-rē\ *n, pl* **-gnior·ies** *or* **-gnor·ies** : the territory of a lord : DOMAIN

seine \'sān\ *n* : a large fishing net kept hanging in the water by weights and floats

seism- *or* **seismo-** *combining form* : earthquake : vibration ⟨*seismo*graph⟩ [derived from Greek *seismos* "earthquake", from *seiein* "to shake"]

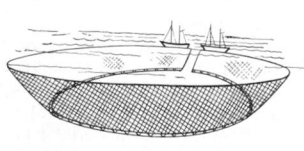

seine

seis·mic \'sīz-mik, 'sīs-\ *adj* : of, subject to, or caused by an earthquake or an earth vibration caused by something else (as an explosion)

seis·mo·gram \'sīz-mə-,gram, 'sīs-\ *n* : the record of an earth tremor as made by a seismograph

seis·mo·graph \'sīz-mə-,graf, 'sīs-\ *n* : a device to measure and record vibrations of the earth — **seis·mo·graph·ic** \,sīz-mə-'graf-ik, ,sīs-\ *adj* — **seis·mog·ra·phy** \sīz-'mäg-rə-fē, sīs-\ *n*

seis·mol·o·gy \sīz-'mäl-ə-jē, sīs-\ *n* : a science that deals with earthquakes and with artificially produced vibrations of the earth — **seis·mo·log·i·cal** \,sīz-mə-'läj-i-kəl, ,sīs-\ *adj* — **seis·mol·o·gist** \sīz-'mäl-ə-jəst, sīs-\ *n*

seis·mom·e·ter \sīz-'mäm-ət-ər, sīs-\ *n* : a seismograph that measures the actual movements of the ground

seize \'sēz\ *vb* **seized; seiz·ing 1** : to take possession of by force ⟨the wind *seized* the hat off my head⟩ **2** : to take prisoner : ARREST **3 a** : to take hold of suddenly or with force : CLUTCH **b** : to understand fully and clearly : COMPREHEND ⟨*seize* an idea quickly⟩ **4** : to attack or overwhelm suddenly (as with fever) — **seiz·er** *n*

sei·zure \'sē-zhər\ *n* **1** : the act of seizing : the state of being seized   **2** : a sudden attack (as of disease) : FIT

se·lag·i·nel·la \sə-ˌlaj-ə-'nel-ə\ *n* : any of a genus of plants that are related to the ferns and club mosses and have branching stems and scalelike leaves

sel·dom \'sel-dəm\ *adv* : not often : RARELY

¹se·lect \sə-'lekt\ *adj*   **1** : chosen from a number or group to include the best or most suitable individuals ⟨invited only a few *select* employees⟩   **2** : of special value or excellence : SUPERIOR, CHOICE ⟨a *select* hotel⟩

²select *vb* : to pick out from a number or group : CHOOSE

se·lec·tion \sə-'lek-shən\ *n*   **1** : the act of selecting : the state of being selected ⟨*selection* of the best poem was difficult⟩ ⟨cheered my *selection* as athlete of the year⟩   **2 a** : one that is selected : CHOICE   **b** : a collection of selected things   **3** : any natural or artificial process that tends to favor the survival and reproduction of some individuals but not of others with the result that only the inherited characteristics of the favored individuals continue to be passed on

se·lec·tive \sə-'lek-tiv\ *adj* : of or relating to selection : selecting or tending to select ⟨*selective* shoppers⟩

se·lect·man \si-'lek(t)-ˌman, -mən; -ˌlek(t)-'man\ *n* : one of a group of town officials elected annually in some of the New England states

se·lec·tor \sə-'lek-tər\ *n* : someone or something that selects

se·le·ni·um \sə-'lē-nē-əm\ *n* : a nonmetallic element that chemically resembles sulfur and tellurium, is obtained chiefly from copper refining, and is used in electronic devices — see ELEMENT table

¹self \'self, *Southern also* 'sef\ *pron* : MYSELF 1, HIMSELF, HERSELF ⟨check that can be paid to *self*⟩ ⟨a room for *self*, son, and daughter⟩

²self \'self\ *n, pl* **selves** \'selvz, *Southern also* 'sevz\   **1** : a person thought of as an individual apart from everyone else   **2** : a particular side of a person's disposition ⟨your better *self*⟩   **3** : personal interest ⟨without thought of *self*⟩

self- *combining form*   **1 a** : oneself or itself ⟨*self*-pitying⟩   **b** : of oneself or itself ⟨*self*-destructive⟩ ⟨*self*-sacrifice⟩   **c** : by oneself or itself ⟨*self*-made⟩ ⟨*self*-propelled⟩   **2 a** : to, with, for, or toward oneself or itself ⟨*self*-addressed⟩   **b** : of or in oneself or itself ⟨*self*-evident⟩   **c** : from or by means of oneself or itself ⟨*self*-fertile⟩ [derived from Old English *self* "myself, himself, herself"]

self–act·ing \'sel-'fak-tiŋ\ *adj* : acting or capable of acting of or by itself : AUTOMATIC

self–ac·tu·al·iza·tion \ˌsel-ˌfak-ch(ə-w)ə-lə-'zā-shən, -ˌfaksh-wə-\ *n* : the full development of one's abilities

self–ad·dressed \ˌsel-fə-'drest, 'sel-'fad-ˌrest\ *adj* : addressed for return to the sender ⟨*self-addressed* envelope⟩

self–ad·mi·ra·tion \ˌsel-ˌfad-mə-'rā-shən\ *n* : SELF-CONCEIT

self–ap·point·ed \ˌsel-fə-'pȯint-əd\ *adj* : appointed by oneself usually without qualifications ⟨a *self-appointed* guardian⟩

self–as·ser·tion \ˌsel-fə-'sər-shən\ *n*   **1** : the act of asserting oneself or one's own rights or claims   **2** : the act of asserting that one is better than others — **self–as·ser·tive** \-'sərt-iv\ *adj*

self–as·sur·ance \ˌsel-fə-'shùr-ən(t)s\ *n* : SELF-CONFIDENCE

self–as·sured \ˌsel-fə-'shú(ə)rd\ *adj* : sure of oneself : having self-confidence

self–aware·ness \ˌsel-fə-'wa(ə)r-nəs, -'we(ə)r-\ *n* : an awareness of one's own personality or individuality

self–cen·tered \'sel-'sent-ərd\ *adj* : interested chiefly in one's own self : SELFISH — **self–cen·tered·ness** *n*

self–con·ceit \ˌself-kən-'sēt\ *n* : an exaggerated opinion of oneself : VANITY — **self–con·ceit·ed** \-əd\ *adj*

self–con·cept \'self-'kän-ˌsept\ *n* : the mental image one has of oneself

self–con·fessed \ˌself-kən-'fest\ *adj* : openly admitted by

oneself ⟨a *self-confessed* forger⟩

self–con·fi·dence \'self-'kän-fəd-ən(t)s, -fə-ˌden(t)s\ *n* : confidence in oneself and in one's powers and abilities — **self–con·fi·dent** \-fəd-ənt, -fə-ˌdent\ *adj* — **self–con·fi·dent·ly** *adv*

self–con·scious \'self-'kän-chəs\ *adj* : uncomfortably conscious of oneself as an object of the observation of others — **self–con·scious·ly** *adv* — **self–con·scious·ness** *n*

self–con·tained \ˌself-kən-'tānd\ *adj*   **1** : enough or complete in itself   **2 a** : showing self-control   **b** : keeping one's thoughts and feelings to oneself — **self–con·tain·ment** \-'tān-mənt\ *n*

self–con·trol \ˌself-kən-'trōl\ *n* : control of oneself — **self–con·trolled** \-'trōld\ *adj*

self–de·cep·tion \ˌself-di-'sep-shən\ *n* : the act of deceiving oneself : the state of being deceived by oneself

self–de·feat·ing \ˌself-di-'fēt-iŋ\ *adj* : acting to defeat its own purpose

self–de·fense \ˌself-di-'fen(t)s\ *n* : the act of defending oneself, one's property, or a close relative

self–de·ni·al \ˌself-di-'nī(-ə)l\ *n* : the refusal to satisfy one's own desires

self–de·struc·tion \ˌself-di-'strək-shən\ *n* : destruction of oneself; *esp* : SUICIDE 1 — **self–de·struc·tive** \-'strək-tiv\ *adj*

self–de·ter·mi·na·tion \ˌself-di-ˌtər-mə-'nā-shən\ *n*   **1** : free choice of one's own acts without outside pressure   **2** : the deciding by the people of a place of the form of government they will have

self–di·rect·ed \ˌself-də-'rek-təd, -dī-\ *adj* : directed by oneself and not by an outside force or agency ⟨a *self-directed* personality⟩

self–dis·ci·pline \'self-'dis-ə-plən\ *n* : correction or regulation of oneself for the sake of improvement

self–doubt \'self-'daůt\ *n* : a lack of faith in oneself — **self–doubt·ing** \-iŋ\ *adj*

self–ed·u·cat·ed \'self-'ej-ə-ˌkāt-əd\ *adj* : educated by one's own efforts without formal instruction

self–em·ployed \ˌsel-fim-'plȯid\ *adj* : earning income from one's own business or profession rather than salary or wages from an employer

self–es·teem \ˌsel-fə-'stēm\ *n*   **1** : a confidence and satisfaction in oneself : SELF-RESPECT   **2** : an exaggerated opinion of one's own abilities : SELF-CONCEIT

self–ev·i·dent \'sel-'fev-əd-ənt, -ə-ˌdent\ *adj* : having no need of proof ⟨*self-evident* truths⟩

self–ex·plan·a·to·ry \'self-ik-'splan-ə-ˌtōr-ē, -ˌtȯr-\ *adj* : understandable without explanation

self–ex·pres·sion \ˌsel-fik-'spresh-ən\ *n* : the expression of one's own personality

self–fer·til·iza·tion \ˌself-ˌfərt-ᵊl-ə-'zā-shən\ *n* : fertilization of a plant or animal by its own pollen or sperm — **self–fer·til·ize** \'self-'fərt-ᵊl-ˌīz\ *vb*

self–gov·ern·ment \'self-'gəv-ər(n)-mənt, -'gəv-ᵊm-ənt\ *n*   **1** : control over one's own actions : SELF-CONTROL   **2** : government by action of the people making up a community; *esp* : democratic government — **self–gov·erned** \-'gəv-ərnd\ *adj* — **self–gov·ern·ing** \-ər-niŋ\ *adj*

self–help \'self-'help\ *n* : the act of providing for or helping oneself without dependence on others

self·hood \'self-ˌhůd\ *n* : INDIVIDUALITY 1

self–iden·ti·ty \ˌsel-ˌfī-'den(t)-ət-ē\ *n* : INDIVIDUALITY 1

self–im·age \'sel-'fim-ij\ *n* : one's ideas about oneself or one's role

self–im·por·tance \ˌsel-fim-'pȯrt-ᵊn(t)s, -ᵊn(t)s\ *n* : an exaggerated opinion of one's own importance — **self–im-**

\ə\ abut	\aů\ out	\i\ tip	\ȯ\ saw	\ů\ foot
\ər\ further	\ch\ chin	\ī\ life	\ȯi\ coin	\y\ yet
\a\ mat	\e\ pet	\j\ job	\th\ thin	\yü\ few
\ā\ take	\ē\ easy	\ŋ\ sing	\ṯẖ\ this	\yů\ cure
\ä\ cot, cart	\g\ go	\ō\ bone	\ü\ food	\zh\ vision

por·tant \-ᵊnt, -ənt\ *adj* — **self·im·por·tant·ly** *adv*

self–im·posed \,sel-fim-'pōzd\ *adj* : imposed on one by oneself : voluntarily assumed

self·im·prove·ment \,sel-,fim-'prüv-mənt\ *n* : improvement of oneself by one's own actions

self·in·crim·i·na·tion \,sel-fin-,krim-ə-'nā-shən\ *n* : incrimination of oneself; *esp* : the giving of evidence or answering of questions which would leave one liable to be tried for a crime

self·in·dul·gence \,sel-fin-'dəl-jən(t)s\ *n* : the quality or state of being self-indulgent

self–in·dul·gent \,sel-fin-'dəl-jənt\ *adj* : pleasing one's own desires too easily

self–in·flict·ed \,sel-fin-'flik-təd\ *adj* : inflicted by oneself ⟨a *self-inflicted* wound⟩

self–in·ter·est \'self-'fin-trəst, -'fint-ə-rəst\ *n* **1** : a concern for one's own advantage ⟨acted out of *self-interest* and fear⟩ **2** : one's own interest or advantage ⟨our *self-interest* demands that we help others⟩

self·ish \'sel-fish\ *adj* : taking care of oneself without thought for others — **self·ish·ly** *adv* — **self·ish·ness** *n*

self·less \'sel-fləs\ *adj* : having no concern for self : UN-SELFISH — **self·less·ly** *adv* — **self·less·ness** *n*

self–made \'self-'mād\ *adj* **1** : made by one's own actions **2** : raised from poverty by one's own efforts ⟨a *self-made* person⟩

self–pity \'self-'pit-ē\ *n* : pity for oneself; *esp* : too much attention to one's misfortunes — **self–pity·ing** \-ē-iŋ\ *adj*

self–pol·li·na·tion \,self-,päl-ə-'nā-shən\ *n* : pollination of a flower by its own pollen or sometimes by pollen from another flower on the same plant — **self–pol·li·nate** \'self-'päl-ə-,nāt\ *vb*

self–por·trait \'self-'pōr-trət, -'pòr-, -,trāt\ *n* : a portrait of oneself made by oneself

self–pos·sessed \,self-pə-'zest\ *adj* : having or showing self-possession : CALM

self–pos·ses·sion \,self-pə-'zesh-ən\ *n* : control of one's emotions or reactions : COMPOSURE

self–pres·er·va·tion \,self-,prez-ər-'vā-shən\ *n* : the keeping of oneself from destruction or harm

self–pro·claimed \,self-prō-'klāmd\ *adj* : SELF-STYLED

self–pro·duced \,self-prə-'d(y)üst\ *adj* : produced by oneself or itself

self–pro·pelled \,self-prə-'peld\ *adj* : having within itself the means for its own movement

self–pro·pel·ling \,self-prə-'pel-iŋ\ *adj* : SELF-PROPELLED

self–pro·tec·tive \,self-prə-'tek-tiv\ *adj* : serving or tending to protect oneself

self–re·gard \,sel-fri-'gärd\ *n* : regard for or consideration of oneself or one's own interests

self–re·li·ance \,sel-fri-'lī-ənts\ *n* : trust in one's own efforts and abilities — **self–re·li·ant** \-ənt\ *adj*

self–re·proach \,sel-fri-'prōch\ *n* : the act of blaming or accusing oneself

self–re·spect \,sel-fri-'spekt\ *n* **1** : a proper respect for oneself as a human being **2** : regard for one's own standing or position — **self–re·spect·ing** \-'spek-tiŋ\ *adj*

self–re·straint \,sel-fri-'strānt\ *n* : proper control over one's actions or emotions

self–righ·teous \'self-'frī-chəs\ *adj* : strongly convinced of the rightness of one's actions or beliefs — **self–righ·teous·ly** *adv* — **self–righ·teous·ness** *n*

self–ris·ing flour \,sel-,frī-ziŋ-\ *n* : a mixture of flour, salt, and a leavening agent

self–rule \'sel-'frül\ *n* : SELF-GOVERNMENT 2

self–sac·ri·fice \'self-'sak-rə-,fīs, -fəs\ *n* : an unselfish giving over of oneself or one's own interest for others — **self–sa·cri·fic·ing** \-,fī-siŋ\ *adj*

self·same \'self-,sām\ *adj* : exactly the same : IDENTICAL

self–sat·is·fac·tion \,self-,sat-əs-'fak-shən\ *n* : a usually overly satisfied feeling about oneself or one's own achievements

self–sat·is·fied \'self-'sat-əs-,fīd\ *adj* : feeling or showing self-satisfaction

self–seal·ing \'self-'sē-liŋ\ *adj* : capable of sealing itself (as after puncture) ⟨a *self-sealing* tire⟩

self–seek·er \'self-'sē-kər\ *n* : one who selfishly advances one's own ends — **self–seek·ing** \-kiŋ\ *n or adj*

self–serve \'self-'sərv\ *adj* : permitting self-service

self–ser·vice \'self-'sər-vəs\ *n* : the serving of oneself (as in a restaurant or service station) with things to be paid for at a cashier's desk or by means of a mechanism that is operated by coins — **self–service** *adj*

self–start·er \'self-'stärt-ər\ *n* : a person who is ambitious

self–styled \'self-'stī(ə)ld\ *adj* : called by oneself ⟨*self-styled* experts⟩

self–suf·fi·cien·cy \,self-sə-'fish-ən-sē\ *n* : the quality or state of being self-sufficient

self–suf·fi·cient \,self-sə-'fish-ənt\ *adj* : able to take care of oneself without outside help : INDEPENDENT

self–sup·port \,self-sə-'pō(ə)rt, -'pò(ə)rt\ *n* : independent support of oneself or itself — **self–sup·port·ing** \-iŋ\ *adj*

self–taught \'self-'tòt\ *adj* **1** : having knowledge or skills acquired by one's own efforts without formal instruction ⟨a *self-taught* musician⟩ **2** : learned by oneself ⟨*self-taught* knowledge⟩

self–will \'self-'wil\ *n* : a stubborn sticking to one's own desires or ideas — **self–willed** \-'wild\ *adj*

self–wind·ing \'self-'wīn-diŋ\ *adj* : not needing to be wound by hand ⟨a *self-winding* watch⟩

sell \'sel\ *vb* **sold** \'sōld\; **sell·ing** **1** : to betray a person or duty — often used with *out* **2** : to exchange in return for money or something else of value ⟨*sell* groceries⟩ **3 a** : to develop a belief in the truth, value, or desirability of ⟨trying to *sell* a program to Congress⟩ **b** : to bring around to a favorable way of thinking ⟨tried to *sell* the children on reading⟩ **4** : to achieve a sale; *also* : to achieve satisfactory sales ⟨hoped that the new car would *sell*⟩ **5** : to be sold or priced ⟨these *sell* for a dollar apiece⟩ — **sell·er** *n* — **sell short** : to put too low a value on the ability, strength, or importance of

sell·out \'sel-,aút\ *n* **1** : the act or an instance of selling out **2** : a show, contest, or exhibition for which all seats are sold

sell out \(')sel-'aút\ *vb* : to dispose of all of one's goods by sale

sel·vage *or* **sel·vedge** \'sel-vij\ *n* : an edge of cloth so woven that it will not ravel

selves *pl of* ²SELF

se·man·tic \si-'mant-ik\ *adj* **1** : of or relating to meaning in language **2** : of or relating to semantics — **se·man·ti·cal·ly** \-'mant-i-k(ə-)lē\ *adv*

se·man·tics \si-'mant-iks\ *n sing or pl* : the study of meanings and changes of meaning — **se·man·ti·cist** \si-'mant-ə-səst\ *n*

sema·phore \'sem-ə-,fō(ə)r, -,fò(ə)r\ *n* **1** : a device for sending signals that can be seen by the receiver **2** : a system of sending signals with two flags held one in each hand

sem·blance \'sem-blən(t)s\ *n* **1** : outward and often misleading appearance or show **2** : one that resembles another : LIKE-NESS, IMAGE

se·men \'sē-mən\ *n* : a sticky whitish fluid of the male reproductive tract that contains the sperm

se·mes·ter \sə-'mes-tər\ *n* : either of two terms of about 18 weeks each that make up a school year

semi- \,sem-i, 'sem-, -,ī\ *prefix* **1** : half in amount or value ⟨*semi-*

semaphore 2

tone⟩ **2** : occurring halfway through a certain time period ⟨*semi*annual⟩ **3** : to some extent : partly : incompletely ⟨*semi*tropical⟩ **4** : partial : incomplete ⟨*semi*darkness⟩ [derived from Latin *semi-* "half"]

semi·an·nu·al \,sem-ē-'an-yə(-wə)l, ,sem-,ī-\ *adj* : occurring every six months or twice a year — **semi·an·nu·al·ly** \-ē\ *adv*

semi·aquat·ic \,sem-ē-ə-'kwät-ik, ,sem-,ī-, -'kwät-\ *adj* : growing well in or very near water; *also* : living near and often entering water but not living in it

semi·ar·id \,sem-ē-'ar-əd, ,sem-,ī-\ *adj* : marked by light rainfall; *esp* : having from about 25 to 55 centimeters of annual precipitation

semi·cir·cle \'sem-i-,sər-kəl\ *n* **1** : half of a circle **2** : an object or arrangement of objects in the form of a half circle — **semi·cir·cu·lar** \,sem-i-'sər-kyə-lər\ *adj*

semicircular canal *n* : any of the loop-shaped tubes in the ear that contain fluid and tiny hairs and help to maintain the body's sense of balance

semi·clas·si·cal \,sem-i-'klas-i-kəl, ,sem-,ī-\ *adj* **1** : having some of the characteristics of the classical **2** : of or relating to a classical musical composition that has become generally popular

semi·co·lon \'sem-i-,kō-lən\ *n* : a punctuation mark that can be used to separate parts of a sentence which need clearer separation than would be shown by a comma, to separate main clauses which have no conjunction between, and to separate phrases and clauses containing commas

semi·con·duc·tor \,sem-i-kən-'dək-tər, ,sem-,ī-\ *n* : any of a class of solids (as germanium) that have an ability to conduct electricity between that of a conductor and that of an insulator — **semi·con·duct·ing** \-tiŋ\ *adj*

semi·con·scious \,sem-i-'kän-chəs, ,sem-,ī-\ *adj* : partially conscious — **semi·con·scious·ness** *n*

semi·dark·ness \,sem-i-'därk-nəs, ,sem-,ī-\ *n* : partial darkness

¹**semi·fi·nal** \,sem-i-'fīn-ºl\ *adj* **1** : coming before the final round in a tournament **2** : of or taking part in a semifinal

²**semi·fi·nal** \'sem-i-,fīn-ºl\ *n* : a semifinal match or game — **semi·fi·nal·ist** \,sem-i-'fīn-ºl-əst\ *n*

semi·for·mal \,sem-i-'for-məl, ,sem-,ī-\ *adj* : being or suitable for an event that is not too formal

¹**semi·month·ly** \,sem-i-'mən(t)th-lē, ,sem-,ī-\ *n* : a semimonthly publication

²**semimonthly** *adj* : occurring twice a month

³**semimonthly** *adv* : twice a month

sem·i·nar \'sem-ə-,när\ *n* **1** : a course of study followed by a group of advanced students **2** : a meeting of a seminar or a room for such meetings **3** : a meeting for giving and discussing information ⟨a sales *seminar*⟩

sem·i·nar·i·an \,sem-ə-'ner-ē-ən\ *n* : a student in a seminary

sem·i·nary \'sem-ə-,ner-ē\ *n, pl* **-nar·ies** **1** : a private school at or above the high school level **2** : a school for the training of priests, ministers, or rabbis

> **Word History** The Latin word for "seed" is *semen*. When the Romans needed a word for a place where seeds were sprouted and young plants raised, they used the basic part of their word for seed and the ending *-arium*, meaning "a place having to do with". They joined them to create *seminarium*, meaning "seedbed, nursery". When academies and schools for young people were set up, the idea of a place where young things were protected, sheltered, and encouraged to grow mentally must have called to mind the seminarium. Thus, the Romans used the same word. Only this last sense of the word survives in English as *seminary*, especially in the sense "a school for training of priests, ministers, or rabbis". [Middle English *seminary* "nursery, school", from Latin *seminarium* "seedbed, nursery, school", from *semen* "seed"]

sem·i·nif·er·ous tubule \,sem-ə-'nif-(ə-)rəs-\ *n* : any of the coiled threadlike tubes that make up most of the testis and are lined with an epithelium from which sperm are produced

Sem·i·nole \'sem-ə-,nōl\ *n* : a member of an American Indian people of Florida

semi·of·fi·cial \,sem-ē-ə-'fish-əl, ,sem-,ī-\ *adj* : having some official authority or standing

semi·per·me·able \,sem-i-'pər-mē-ə-bəl, ,sem-,ī-\ *adj* : partially but not freely or entirely permeable; *esp* : permeable to some usually small molecules but not to other usually larger particles — **semi·per·me·abil·i·ty** \-,pər-mē-ə-'bil-ət-ē\ *n*

semi·pre·cious \,sem-i-'presh-əs, ,sem-,ī-\ *adj* : of less value than a precious stone

semi·pri·vate \,sem-i-'prī-vət, ,sem-,ī-\ *adj* : of or relating to hospital service that gives a patient more services than a patient in a ward but not as many as a patient in a private room ⟨a *semiprivate* room⟩

semi·pro \'sem-i-,prō, 'sem-,ī-\ *adj or n* : SEMIPROFESSIONAL

semi·pro·fes·sion·al \,sem-i-prə-'fesh-nəl, -ən-ºl, ,sem-,ī-\ *adj* **1** : engaging in an activity for pay but not as a full-time occupation **2** : engaged in by semiprofessional players ⟨*semiprofessional* football⟩ — **semiprofessional** *n*

semi·re·li·gious \,sem-i-ri-'lij-əs, ,sem-,ī-\ *adj* : somewhat religious in character

semi·skilled \,sem-i-'skild, ,sem-,ī-\ *adj* : having or requiring less training than skilled labor and more than unskilled labor

semi·soft \,sem-i-'soft, ,sem-,ī-\ *adj* : moderately soft; *esp* : firm but easily cut ⟨*semisoft* cheese⟩

semi·sol·id \,sem-i-'säl-əd, ,sem-,ī-\ *adj* : having the qualities of both a solid and a liquid — **semisolid** *n*

semi·sweet \,sem-i-'swēt, ,sem-,ī-\ *adj* : slightly sweetened ⟨*semisweet* chocolate⟩

Sem·ite \'sem-,īt\ *n* : a member of any of a group of peoples of southwestern Asia chiefly represented by the Jews and Arabs

Se·mit·ic \sə-'mit-ik\ *adj* : of or relating to the Semites; *esp* : of, relating to, or characteristic of the Jews

semi·tone \'sem-i-,tōn, 'sem-,ī-\ *n* : the smallest difference in pitch between any two tones of a scale

semi·trail·er \'sem-i-,trā-lər, 'sem-,ī-\ *n* **1** : a freight trailer that when attached is supported at its forward end by the truck tractor **2** : a trucking rig made up of a tractor and a semitrailer

semi·trop·i·cal \,sem-i-'träp-i-kəl, ,sem-,ī-\ *also* **semi·trop·ic** \-ik\ *adj* : SUBTROPICAL

¹**semi·week·ly** \,sem-i-'wē-klē, ,sem-,ī-\ *adj* : occurring twice a week — **semiweekly** *adv*

²**semiweekly** *n* : a publication that comes out twice a week

sem·o·li·na \,sem-ə-'lē-nə\ *n* : a grainy powder that is milled from hard wheat (as durum wheat) and is often used to make pasta (as spaghetti)

sen·ate \'sen-ət\ *n* : an official law-making group or council: as **a** : the supreme council of the ancient Roman republic and empire **b** : the higher branch of a legislature of a nation, state, or province [Middle English *senat* "lawmaking council of ancient Rome", from early French *senat* (same meaning), from Latin *senatus*, literally "council of elders", from *sen-, senex* "old" — related to SENIOR]

sen·a·tor \'sen-ət-ər\ *n* : a member of a senate — **sen·a·tor·ship** \-,ship\ *n*

sen·a·to·ri·al \,sen-ə-'tōr-ē-əl, -'tȯr-\ *adj* : of or relating to a senator or a senate ⟨*senatorial* office⟩

\ə\ abut		\aù\ out	\i\ tip	\ȯ\ saw	\ù\ foot
\ər\ further		\ch\ chin	\ī\ life	\ȯi\ coin	\y\ yet
\a\ mat		\e\ pet	\j\ job	\th\ thin	\yü\ few
\ā\ take		\ē\ easy	\ŋ\ sing	\th\ this	\yù\ cure
\ä\ cot, cart		\g\ go	\ō\ bone	\ü\ food	\zh\ vision

send \'send\ *vb* **sent** \'sent\; **send·ing** **1** : to cause to go ⟨*sent* the pupil home⟩ ⟨*sent* a message⟩; *esp* : to set in motion by physical force ⟨*sent* the ball into right field⟩ ⟨*send* a rocket to the moon⟩ **2** : to cause to happen ⟨whatever fate may *send*⟩ **3** : to put or bring into a certain condition ⟨*sent* them into a rage⟩ **4 a** : to cause someone to pass a message on or do an errand — often used with *out* ⟨*send* out for lunch⟩ **b** : to dispatch a request or order — often used with *away* ⟨*sent* away for skates⟩ — **send·er** *n* — **send for** : to request by message to come ⟨the principal *sent for* the child⟩ — **send packing** : to send off roughly or in disgrace

send–off \'sen-,dòf\ *n* : a demonstration of goodwill and enthusiasm for the beginning of something new (as a trip)

Sen·e·ca \'sen-i-kə\ *n* : a member of an American Indian people of western New York

sen·e·schal \'sen-ə-shəl\ *n* : an agent or bailiff who managed a lord's estate in feudal times

se·nile \'sēn-,īl *also* 'sen-\ *adj* : of, relating to, or characteristic of old age ⟨*senile* weakness⟩; *esp* : showing a loss of mental ability usually associated with old age [from Latin *senilis* "showing the features of old age", from *sen-, senex* "old" — related to SENIOR]

se·nil·i·ty \si-'nil-ət-ē\ *n* : the quality or state of being senile; *esp* : the physical and mental weakness of old age

¹se·nior \'sē-nyər\ *n* **1** : a person who is older than another ⟨five years my *senior*⟩ **2 a** : a person with higher standing or rank **b** : a student in the final year of high school or college [Middle English *senior* "a person older than another specific person", from Latin *senior* (same meaning), from *senior* (adjective) "older, elder", from *sen-, senex* "old" — related to SENATE, SENILE, SENOR, SIR]

²senior *adj* **1** : being older — used to distinguish a father from a son with the same name ⟨John Doe, *Senior*⟩ **2** : higher ranking ⟨*senior* officers⟩ ⟨the *senior* partner of the law firm⟩ **3** : of or relating to seniors in an educational institution ⟨the *senior* class⟩

senior airman *n* : a temporary rank in the air force just below that of a sergeant

senior chief petty officer *n* : a naval petty officer with a rank just below that of a master chief petty officer

senior citizen *n* : an elderly person; *esp* : one who has retired

se·nior·i·ty \sēn-'yòr-ət-ē, -'yär-\ *n* **1** : the quality or state of being senior **2** : a privileged position arrived at by length of service

senior master sergeant *n* : a noncommissioned officer in the air force with a rank just below that of chief master sergeant

sen·na \'sen-ə\ *n* **1** : CASSIA 2; *esp* : one used as a medicine **2** : the dried leaves or pods of various cassias used as a strong laxative

se·nor *or* **se·ñor** \sān-'yò(ə)r\ *n, pl* **senors** *or* **se·ño·res** \-'yō(ə)r-ās, -'yò(ə)r-\ : a Spanish or Spanish-speaking man — used as a title equivalent to *Mr.* [from Spanish *señor* "man", from Latin *senior* "superior, lord", from earlier *senior* (adjective) "elder, older", from *sen-, senex* "old" — related to SENIOR]

se·no·ra *or* **se·ño·ra** \sān-'yōr-ə, -'yòr-\ *n* : a married Spanish or Spanish-speaking girl or woman — used as a title equivalent to *Mrs.*

se·no·ri·ta *or* **se·ño·ri·ta** \,sān-yə-'rēt-ə\ *n* : an unmarried Spanish or Spanish-speaking girl or woman — used as a title equivalent to *Miss*

sen·sa·tion \sen-'sā-shən, sən-\ *n* **1 a** : a mental process (as seeing, hearing, or smelling) that is due to bodily stimulation **b** : awareness (as of heat or pain) due to stimulation of a sense organ **c** : an indefinite bodily feeling **2 a** : a state of excited interest or feeling **b** : a cause of such excitement

sen·sa·tion·al \sen-'sā-shnəl, -shən-³l, sən-\ *adj* **1** : of or relating to sensation or the senses **2** : arousing a strong

and usually shallow interest or emotional reaction ⟨*sensational* news⟩ **3** : exceedingly or unexpectedly excellent or great ⟨a *sensational* diving catch⟩ — **sen·sa·tion·al·ly** \-ē\ *adv*

¹sense \'sen(t)s\ *n* **1** : a meaning or one of a set of meanings a word, phrase, or story may have **2 a** : the power to become aware of by means of sense organs **b** : a specialized function or mechanism (as sight, hearing, smell, taste, or touch) of the body that involves the action and effect of a stimulus on a sense organ ⟨the pain *sense*⟩ **3 a** : a particular sensation or kind of sensation ⟨a good *sense* of balance⟩ **b** : awareness arrived at through or as if through the senses ⟨a vague *sense* of danger⟩ **c** : an awareness and appreciation of something ⟨a fine *sense* of humor⟩ **4 a** : INTELLIGENCE 1 **b** : good reason or excuse ⟨no *sense* in waiting⟩

²sense *vb* **sensed; sens·ing** **1** : to become aware of through the senses **2** : to be or become conscious of ⟨*sense* danger⟩ **3** : to detect automatically and especially to respond to a physical quantity (as light or movement)

sense·less \'sen(t)-sləs\ *adj* **1** : ¹UNCONSCIOUS 2 ⟨knocked *senseless*⟩ **2** : FOOLISH, STUPID **3** : POINTLESS 2, MEANINGLESS ⟨a *senseless* act⟩ — **sense·less·ly** *adv* — **sense·less·ness** *n*

sense organ *n* : a body part (as an eye or ear) that receives stimuli (as light or sound) which excite nerve cells to send information to the brain

sen·si·bil·i·ty \,sen(t)-sə-'bil-ət-ē\ *n, pl* **-ties** **1** : ability to receive sensations : SENSITIVENESS **2** : the emotion or feeling of which a person is capable

sen·si·ble \'sen(t)-sə-bəl\ *adj* **1** : possible to take in by the senses or by reason or understanding ⟨felt a *sensible* chill⟩ ⟨her distress was *sensible* from the way she acted⟩ **2** : capable of being made aware of or of feeling ⟨*sensible* to pain⟩ **3** : AWARE ⟨*sensible* of the increasing heat⟩ **4** : showing or containing good sense or reason : REASONABLE ⟨a *sensible* arrangement⟩ — **sen·si·ble·ness** *n* — **sen·si·bly** \-blē\ *adv*

sen·si·tive \'sen(t)-sət-iv, 'sen(t)-stiv\ *adj* **1** : capable of responding to stimulation **2 a** : easily or strongly affected or hurt ⟨a *sensitive* child⟩ **b** : capable of showing very small differences : DELICATE ⟨*sensitive* scales⟩ **c** : readily affected or changed by the action of a certain thing ⟨plants *sensitive* to light⟩ — **sen·si·tive·ly** *adv* — **sen·si·tive·ness** *n*

sensitive plant *n* : any of several mimosas with leaves that fold or droop when touched

sen·si·tiv·i·ty \,sen(t)-sə-'tiv-ət-ē\ *n, pl* **-ties** : the quality or state of being sensitive

sen·si·tize \'sen(t)-sə-,tīz\ *vb* **-tized; -tiz·ing** : to make or become sensitive

sen·sor \'sen-,sò(ə)r, 'sen(t)-sər\ *n* : a device that detects a physical quantity (as a movement or a beam of light) and responds by transmitting a signal (as for operating a control)

sen·so·ry \'sen(t)s-(ə-)rē\ *adj* **1** : of or relating to sensation or to the senses **2** : carrying nerve impulses from the sense organs toward or to the brain : AFFERENT ⟨a *sensory* nerve⟩

sen·su·al \'sench-(ə-)wəl, 'sen-shəl\ *adj* **1** : relating to or consisting in the pleasing of the senses **2** : devoted to the pleasures of the senses — **sen·su·al·i·ty** \,sen-chə-'wal-ət-ē\ *n* — **sen·su·al·ly** \'sench-(ə-)wə-lē, 'sen-shə-lē\ *adv*

sen·su·ous \'sench-(ə-)wəs\ *adj* **1 a** : having to do with the senses or with things perceived by the senses **b** : producing an agreeable effect on the senses ⟨mild *sensuous* breezes⟩ **2** : able to be easily influenced through the senses — **sen·su·ous·ly** *adv* — **sen·su·ous·ness** *n*

sent *past and past participle of* SEND

¹sen·tence \'sent-³n(t)s, -³nz\ *n* **1 a** : JUDGMENT 2; *esp*

: one pronounced by a court in a criminal proceeding and specifying the punishment ⟨**b** : the punishment set by a court ⟩ **2 a** : a grammatically self-contained group of words that expresses a statement, a question, a command, a wish, or an exclamation **b** : a mathematical or logical statement (as an equation) in words or symbols — **sen·ten·tial** \sen-'ten-chəl\ *adj*

²**sentence** *vb* **sen·tenced; sen·tenc·ing 1** : to impose a judgment on ⟨*sentenced* them to prison⟩ **2** : to cause to suffer something

sentence fragment *n* : a word, phrase, or clause that lacks the self-contained structure of a sentence but is written and punctuated like a complete sentence

sen·ten·tious \sen-'ten-chəs\ *adj* : containing or using phrases which sound more important than they are

sen·tient \'sen-ch(ē-)ənt\ *adj* **1** : capable of sensing or feeling ⟨*sentient* beings⟩ **2** : AWARE ⟨*sentient* of one's surroundings⟩

sen·ti·ment \'sent-ə-mənt\ *n* **1 a** : a thought or attitude influenced by feeling **b** : a certain notion : OPINION **2** : tender feelings of affection or yearning

sen·ti·men·tal \,sent-ə-'ment-ᵊl\ *adj* **1 a** : marked by feeling or sentiment **b** : resulting from feeling rather than reason or thought **2** : having an excess of sentiment or sensibility — **sen·ti·men·tal·ly** \-ᵊl-ē\ *adv*

sen·ti·men·tal·ism \,sent-ə-'ment-ᵊl-,iz-əm\ *n* **1** : a tendency to be sentimental **2** : an overly sentimental idea or statement — **sen·ti·men·tal·ist** \-ᵊl-əst\ *n*

sen·ti·men·tal·i·ty \,sent-ə-,men-'tal-ət-ē, -mən-\ *n, pl* **-ties 1** : the quality or state of being sentimental and especially overly sentimental **2** : a sentimental idea or its expression

sen·ti·nel \'sent-(ə-)nəl\ *n* : SENTRY

sen·try \'sen-trē\ *n, pl* **sen·tries** : ¹GUARD 3a; *esp* : a soldier standing guard at a point of passage

se·pal \'sēp-əl, 'sep-\ *n* : one of the specialized leaves that form the calyx of a flower

sep·a·ra·ble \'sep-(ə-)rə-bəl\ *adj* : capable of being separated or distinguished — **sep·a·ra·bil·i·ty** \,sep-(ə-)rə-'bil-ət-ē\ *n*

¹**sep·a·rate** \'sep-ə-,rāt\ *vb* **-rat·ed; -rat·ing 1 a** : to set or keep apart ⟨*separate* the pages with a slip of paper⟩ **b** : to make a distinction between : DISTINGUISH ⟨*separate* fact from fiction⟩ **c** : ²SORT 1 ⟨*separate* mail⟩ **d** : to spread widely in space or time : SCATTER ⟨widely *separated* homesteads⟩ **2** : to end a relationship with that is bound by a contract ⟨*separated* from the army⟩ **3** : to isolate or become isolated from a mixture ⟨*separate* cream from milk⟩ **4** : to become divided or detached : come apart **5** : to cease to live together as man and wife **6** : to go in different directions

    syn SEPARATE, PART, DIVIDE mean to break into parts or to keep apart. SEPARATE may suggest that things have been put into different groups, or that a thing has been removed from a group, or that something has been put between like things ⟨*separate* the good eggs from the bad eggs⟩ ⟨a fence *separates* the yards⟩ PART suggests that the things to be separated are closely joined in some way ⟨only death could *part* the two friends⟩ DIVIDE suggests separating by cutting or breaking into pieces or sections ⟨*divide* the pie into six equal servings⟩

²**sep·a·rate** \'sep-(ə-)rət\ *adj* **1** : set or kept apart ⟨the motel contains fifty *separate* units⟩ **2** : not shared with another : INDIVIDUAL ⟨*separate* rooms⟩ **3** : having independent existence ⟨the *separate* pieces of a puzzle⟩ — **sep·a·rate·ly** *adv* — **sep·a·rate·ness** *n*

³**sep·a·rate** \'sep-(ə-)rət\ *n* : an article of dress designed to be worn interchangeably with others to form different outfits — usually used in pl.

sep·a·ra·tion \,sep-ə-'rā-shən\ *n* **1** : the act or process of separating : the state of being separated **2 a** : a point

or line of division **b** : a space that comes between things : GAP **3 a** : a formal separating of husband and wife by agreement but without divorce **b** : the ending of a relationship that is bound by a contract (as employment or military service)

sep·a·rat·ist \'sep-(ə-)rət-əst\ *n* : a person who favors separation (as from a church or party) — **sep·a·rat·ism** \-rə-,tiz-əm\ *n* — **separatist** *adj*

sep·a·ra·tor \'sep-ə-,rāt-ər\ *n* : one that separates; *esp* : a device for separating liquids (as cream from milk) of different densities or liquids from solids

¹**se·pia** \'sē-pē-ə\ *n* **1** : a brown pigment made from the ink of cuttlefishes **2** : a brownish gray

²**sepia** *adj* : of the color sepia

se·poy \'sē-,pȯi\ *n* : a native of India employed as a soldier in the service of a European power

Sep·tem·ber \sep-'tem-bər, səp-\ *n* : the ninth month of the year

    Word History The ancient Romans originally used a calendar which began the year with the month of March. The seventh month of the year was called *September,* from *septem,* a Latin word meaning "seven". The name was spelled *Septembre* when it was borrowed from early French into Middle English, but eventually the English spelling was changed to that of the original Latin. [Middle English *Septembre* "the month of September", from Old English *September* and early French *Septembre* (both, same meaning), both from Latin *September* "the seventh month", from *septem* "seven"]

sep·tet *also* **sep·tette** \sep-'tet\ *n* **1** : a musical composition for seven instruments or voices **2** : a group or set of seven; *esp* : the musicians that perform a septet

sep·tic sore throat \'sep-tik-\ *n* : a sore throat that is marked by inflammation of the throat and pharynx and by fever and weakness and is caused by infection with streptococci

septic tank *n* : a tank in which solid sewage is broken down by bacteria

sep·til·lion \sep-'til-yən\ *n* — see NUMBER table

sep·tu·a·ge·nar·i·an \(,)sep-,t(y)ü-ə-jə-'ner-ē-ən, ,sep-tə-,waj-ə-\ *n* : a person who is 70 or more but less than 80 years old — **septuagenarian** *adj*

Sep·tu·a·ges·i·ma \,sep-tə-wə-'jes-ə-mə, -'jā-zə-\ *n* : the third Sunday before Lent

sep·tum \'sep-təm\ *n, pl* **sep·ta** \-tə\ : a dividing wall or membrane especially between bodily spaces or masses of soft tissue

sep·ul·cher *or* **sep·ul·chre** \'sep-əl-kər\ *n* **1** : a place of burial : TOMB **2** : a container for religious relics especially in an altar

se·pul·chral \sə-'pəl-krəl\ *adj* **1** : of or relating to the burial of the dead **2** : DISMAL, GLOOMY

sep·ul·ture \'sep-əl-chù(ə)r\ *n* **1** : BURIAL **2** : SEPULCHER

se·quel \'sē-kwəl\ *n* **1** : an event that follows or comes afterward : RESULT **2** : a book that continues a story begun in another [Middle English *sequel, sequele* "follower, series", from early French *sequelle* (same meaning), from Latin *sequella, sequela* "follower", from *sequi* "to follow" — related to CONSECUTIVE, PURSUE, ¹SECOND, SEQUENCE]

se·quence \'sē-kwən(t)s, -,kwen(t)s\ *n* **1 a** : a continuous or connected series **b** : a set of several shots or scenes developing a single subject (as in a movie) ⟨a chase *sequence* in a spy movie⟩ **2** : the order in which things are or should be connected, related, or dated ⟨the *sequence* of events⟩ **3 a** : ²RESULT 1, CONSEQUENCE **b** : a development that follows something else [Middle English *se-*

quence "a hymn, a connected series", derived from Latin *sequentia* "state or fact of following, succession", from *sequent-, sequens,* a form of the verb *sequi* "to follow" — related to SEQUEL]

se·quen·tial \si-'kwen-chəl\ *adj* **1** : of, relating to, or arranged in a sequence ⟨*sequential* file systems⟩ **2** : following in sequence — **se·quen·tial·ly** \-'kwench-(ə-)lē\ *adv*

se·ques·ter \si-'kwes-tər\ *vb* **-tered; -ter·ing** \-t(ə-)riŋ\ **1** : to set apart : SEGREGATE ⟨the jury was *sequestered* until a verdict was reached⟩ **2** : to take custody of (as personal property) until a demand is satisfied

se·ques·tra·tion \,sēk-wəs-'trā-shən, ,sek-\ *n* : the act of sequestering : the state of being sequestered

se·quin \'sē-kwən\ *n* : a small piece of shiny metal or plastic used as an ornament especially on clothes

se·quined *or* **se·quinned** \'sē-kwənd\ *adj* : ornamented with or as if with sequins

se·quoia \si-'kwȯi-(y)ə\ *n* : either of two huge cone-bearing California trees that are related to the pines and may grow to a height of over 90 meters: **a** : BIG TREE **b** : REDWOOD

sera *pl of* SERUM

se·ra·glio \sə-'ral-yō\ *n, pl* **-glios** : the rooms assigned to women in a Muslim household

se·ra·pe *or* **sa·ra·pe** \sə-'räp-ē\ *n* : a colorful woolen shawl worn over the shoulders especially by Mexican men

ser·aph \'ser-əf\ *n, pl* **ser·a·phim** \-ə-,fim\ *or* **seraphs** : SERAPHIM — **se·raph·ic** \sə-'raf-ik\ *adj*

ser·a·phim \'ser-ə-,fim\ *n, pl* **seraphim** : one of the six-winged angels standing in the presence of God

Serb \'sərb\ *n* : a person born or living in Serbia

Ser·bi·an \'sər-bē-ən\ *adj* : of, relating to, or characteristic of Serbia or its people

Ser·bo–Cro·atian \,sər-(,)bō-krō-'ā-shən\ *n* : the Slavic language of the Serbs and Croats

sere \'si(ə)r\ *adj* : being dry and withered

¹ser·e·nade \,ser-ə-'nād\ *n* : music as sung or played outdoors at night for a woman

²serenade *vb* **-nad·ed; -nad·ing** : to entertain with or perform a serenade — **ser·e·nad·er** *n*

ser·en·dip·i·ty \,ser-ən-'dip-ət-ē\ *n* : the gift of finding valuable or agreeable things not looked for

se·rene \sə-'rēn\ *adj* **1** : showing complete calm **2 a** : clear and free of storms ⟨*serene* skies⟩ **b** : shining bright and steady **syn** see CALM — **se·rene·ly** *adv* — **se·rene·ness** \-'rēn-nəs\ *n*

se·ren·i·ty \sə-'ren-ət-ē\ *n* : the quality or state of being serene : PEACEFULNESS

serf \'sərf\ *n* : a servant or laborer of olden times who was treated as part of the land worked on and went along with the land if it was sold [from French *serf* "a slave bound to a certain piece of land", from Latin *servus* "slave, servant" — related to SERVANT; see Word History at SLAVE] — **serf·dom** \-dəm\ *n*

serge \'sərj\ *n* : a durable cloth woven with diagonal ridges.

ser·geant \'sär-jənt\ *n* **1** : a military noncommissioned officer with any of the ranks above corporal in the army or the marines or above airman first class in the air force; *esp* : an enlisted person with the rank just below that of staff sergeant **2** : a police officer ranking in the U.S. just below captain or sometimes lieutenant [Middle English *sergeant* "sergeant, attendant, servant", from early French *sergent, serjant* (same meaning), from Latin *servient-, serviens,* a form of the verb *servire* "to serve"]

sergeant at arms : an officer of a court of law or a lawmak-

ing body appointed to keep order

sergeant first class *n* : an enlisted person in the army with a rank just below that of master sergeant

sergeant major *n, pl* **sergeants major** *or* **sergeant majors** **1** : a noncommissioned officer (as in the army) serving as chief enlisted assistant in a headquarters **2** : an enlisted person of the highest rank in the army or marines

sergeant major of the army : a sergeant major who advises the senior commanding officer of the army

sergeant major of the marine corps : a sergeant major who advises the senior commanding officer of the marines

¹se·ri·al \'sir-ē-əl\ *adj* **1** : consisting of or arranged in a series, rank, or row ⟨*serial* order⟩ **2** : appearing in parts or numbers that follow regularly ⟨a *serial* story⟩ **3** : being or relating to a connection in a computer system in which the bits of a byte are transmitted one at a time over a single wire — **se·ri·al·ly** \-ē-ə-lē\ *adv*

²serial *n* **1** : a work appearing (as in a magazine or on television) in parts at regular intervals **2** : one part of a serial work — **se·ri·al·ist** \'sir-ē-ə-ləst\ *n*

se·ri·al·ize \'sir-ē-ə-,līz\ *vb* **-ized; -iz·ing** : to arrange or publish in serial form

serial number *n* : a number showing place in a series and used as a means of identification

seri·cul·ture \'ser-ə-,kəl-chər\ *n* : the production of raw silk by raising silkworms

se·ries \'si(ə)r-ēz\ *n, pl* **series** **1** : a number of things or events arranged in order and connected by being alike in some way ⟨a concert *series*⟩ ⟨a *series* of talks⟩ **2** : a division of rock formations smaller than a system comprising rocks deposited during an epoch **3** : an arrangement of the parts of or elements in an electric circuit whereby the whole current passes through each part or element without branching **4** : a group of sentence elements of the same rank that follow one after another and are joined together ⟨the phrase "a bowl of oranges, apples, and bananas" has a *series* of three nouns⟩ — **in series** : in a serial arrangement

ser·if \'ser-əf\ *n* : any of the short lines crossing the upper and lower ends of the strokes of a printed letter

se·ri·ous \'sir-ē-əs\ *adj* **1** : thoughtful or quiet in appearance or manner **2 a** : requiring much thought or work ⟨*serious* study⟩ **b** : of or relating to a matter of importance ⟨a *serious* novel⟩ **3** : not joking or funny **4** : having important or dangerous possible consequences ⟨a *serious* injury⟩ — **se·ri·ous·ly** *adv* — **se·ri·ous·ness** *n*

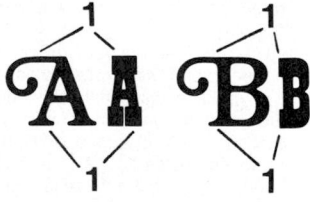

1 serif

syn SERIOUS, SOLEMN, EARNEST mean not funny or not playful. SERIOUS suggests being concerned or seeming to be concerned about really important things ⟨doctors are *serious* about finding a cure⟩ SOLEMN stresses dignity along with full seriousness ⟨the new governor took the oath of office in a *solemn* voice⟩ EARNEST stresses that one is sincere and has serious intentions ⟨an *earnest* student working hard for a prize in math⟩

se·ri·ous–mind·ed \,sir-ē-ə-'smīn-dəd\ *adj* : having a serious disposition or trend of thought

ser·mon \'sər-mən\ *n* **1** : a public speech usually by a priest, minister, or rabbi for the purpose of giving religious instruction **2** : a speech on conduct or duty

se·rous membrane \'sir-əs-\ *n* : a thin membrane (as the peritoneum) with cells that secrete a watery fluid

ser·pent \'sər-pənt\ *n* : a usually large snake

ser·pen·tine \'sər-pən-,tēn, -,tīn\ *adj* **1** : of or resembling a serpent **2** : winding or turning one way and another ⟨a

serape

serpentine path through the woods⟩

ser·rate \'se(ə)r-ˌāt, sə-'rāt\ *adj* : having a saw-toothed edge ⟨a *serrate* leaf⟩

ser·rat·ed \'ser-ˌāt-əd, sə-'rāt-\ *adj* : notched or toothed on the edge ⟨a knife with a *serrated* blade⟩ [derived from Latin *serratus,* past participle of *serrare* "to saw", from *serra* "a saw" — related to SIERRA]

ser·ried \'ser-ēd\ *adj* : crowded or pressed together

se·rum \'sir-əm\ *n, pl* **serums** *or* **se·ra** \'sir-ə\ **1** : the liquid part that can be separated from blood when it clots and that contains antibodies **2** : a preparation of animal serum that contains specific antibodies and is used to prevent or cure disease

ser·vant \'sər-vənt\ *n* : one that serves others; *esp* : a person hired to perform household or personal services [Middle English *servant* "servant", from early French *servant* (same meaning), derived from Latin *servire* "to be a slave, serve", from *servus* "slave, servant" — related to SERF; see *Word History* at SLAVE]

¹serve \'sərv\ *vb* **served; serv·ing 1 a** : to be a servant **b** : to give the service and respect due **c** : to work through or perform a term of service ⟨*served* five years in the marines⟩ **d** : to be in prison for or during ⟨*serving* two years for robbery⟩ ⟨*served* a 10-year sentence⟩ **2 a** : to act officially as a clergyman or priest ⟨*serve* mass⟩ **b** : to assist at mass **3 a** : to be of use : answer a purpose ⟨the tree *serves* as shelter⟩ **b** : to be favorable or convenient ⟨when the time *serves*⟩ **c** : to hold an office : perform a duty ⟨*serve* on a jury⟩ **4** : to be enough for ⟨a pie that will *serve* eight people⟩ **5 a** : to help persons to food ⟨as at a table or counter⟩ **b** : to set out portions of food or drink **6 a** : to furnish or supply with something needed or desired **b** : to wait on customers **7** : to treat or act toward in a certain way ⟨they *served* me ill⟩ **8** : to bring to notice, deliver, or carry out as required by law ⟨*serve* a summons⟩ **9** : to make a serve ⟨as in tennis⟩ — **serve one right** : to be deserved

²serve *n* : the act of putting the ball or shuttlecock in play ⟨as in tennis or badminton⟩

serv·er \'sər-vər\ *n* **1** : a person who serves food or drink **2** : the player who puts a ball in play **3** : something ⟨as a tray⟩ used in serving food or drink

¹ser·vice \'sər-vəs\ *n* **1 a** : the occupation or function of serving ⟨in active *service*⟩ **b** : employment as a servant ⟨entered the queen's *service*⟩ **2 a** : the work or action performed by one that serves ⟨gives good *service*⟩ **b** : ²HELP 1, USE, BENEFIT ⟨be of *service* to them⟩ **c** : availability for use ⟨I'll place a car at your *service*⟩ **3** : a religious ceremony or rite ⟨the burial *service*⟩ **4 a** : the act of serving **b** : a helpful act : good turn ⟨did us a *service*⟩ **c** : useful labor that does not produce goods — usually used in pl. ⟨charge for professional *services*⟩ **d** : ²SERVE **5** : a set of articles for a particular use ⟨a tea *service*⟩ **6 a** : a branch of public employment or the people working in it ⟨the consular *service*⟩ **b** : a nation's armed forces ⟨called into the *service*⟩ **7** : an organization for supplying some public demand or keeping up and repairing something ⟨bus *service*⟩ ⟨television sales and *service*⟩ — **service** *adj*

²service *vb* **ser·viced; ser·vic·ing** : to work at taking care of and repairing ⟨*service* cars⟩

ser·vice·able \'sər-və-sə-bəl\ *adj* **1** : prepared for or capable of service : USEFUL **2** : lasting or wearing well in use — **ser·vice·abil·i·ty** \ˌsər-və-sə-'bil-ət-ē\ *n* — **ser·vice·able·ness** \'sər-və-sə-bəl-nəs\ *n*

ser·vice·ber·ry \'sər-vəs-ˌber-ē *also* 'sär-\ *n* : any of various North American trees or shrubs related to the roses that are sometimes grown for their showy white flowers and edible purplish to red fruit — called also *Juneberry, shadbush*

service charge *n* : a fee charged for a particular service often in addition to a basic fee

service club *n* **1** : a club of business or professional men or women organized for their common benefit and active in community service **2** : a recreation center for enlisted persons provided by one of the armed services

ser·vice·man \'sər-və-ˌsman, -smən\ *n* : a member of the armed forces

service mark *n* : a mark used to identify a service offered to customers

service module *n* : a part of a space vehicle containing oxygen, water, fuel cells, fuel tanks, and the main rocket engine

service station *n* : a place for servicing motor vehicles especially with gasoline and oil

ser·vice·wom·an \'sər-və-ˌswum-ən\ *n* : a female member of the armed forces

ser·vile \'sər-vəl, -ˌvīl\ *adj* **1** : of or appropriate to a slave **2** : lacking spirit or independence : SUBMISSIVE — **ser·vile·ly** \-və(l)-lē, -ˌvīl-lē\ *adv* — **ser·vil·i·ty** \(ˌ)sər-'vil-ət-ē\ *n*

serv·ing \'sər-vin\ *n* : a helping of food or drink ⟨another *serving* of meat⟩

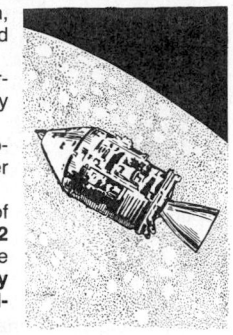

service module

ser·vi·tor \'sər-vət-ər, -və-ˌtȯ(ə)r\ *n* : a male servant

ser·vi·tude \'sər-və-ˌt(y)üd\ *n* : a condition in which one does not have the freedom to determine one's own life

ses·a·me \'ses-ə-mē\ *n* **1** : a hairy herb of warm regions that is grown for food; *also* : its small somewhat flat seeds that are used as a source of oil and to flavor food **2** : something that always brings about a desired result

sesqui- *combining form* : one and a half times ⟨*sesqui*centennial⟩ [from Latin *sesqui-* "one and a half", literally "and a half", derived from *semi-* "half"]

ses·qui·cen·ten·ni·al \ˌses-kwi-sen-'ten-ē-əl\ *n* : a 150th anniversary or its celebration — **sesquicentennial** *adj*

ses·sile \'ses-ˌīl, -əl\ *adj* **1** : attached directly by the base and not raised upon a stalk ⟨a *sessile* leaf⟩ **2** : permanently attached and not free to move about : SEDENTARY ⟨*sessile* polyps⟩

ses·sion \'sesh-ən\ *n* **1** : a meeting or series of meetings of a body ⟨as a court or legislature⟩ for the carrying on of business **2** : the period between the first meeting of a legislative or judicial body and the last meeting **3** : the period during the year or day in which a school has classes

ses·tet \se-'stet\ *n* : a group of six lines of poetry ⟨as the last six lines of a sonnet⟩

¹set \'set\ *vb* **set; set·ting 1** : to cause to sit **2** : to give ⟨a fowl⟩ eggs to hatch or provide ⟨eggs⟩ with suitable conditions for hatching **3** : to put or fix in a place, condition, or position ⟨*set* a dish on the table⟩ ⟨*set* a trap⟩ ⟨*set* a watch⟩ **4** : to direct with fixed attention ⟨had *set* my heart on a new bike⟩ **5** : to cause to be, become, or do ⟨slaves were *set* free⟩ **6** : to start on purpose ⟨*set* a fire⟩ **7** : to fix or decide on as a time, limit, or regulation ⟨*set* a price⟩ ⟨*set* a wedding day⟩ **8 a** : to establish as the best performance ⟨*set* a record⟩ **b** : to furnish as a pattern or model ⟨*set* an example⟩ **9** : to restore to normal position or connection ⟨*set* a broken bone⟩ **10 a** : to put in order for immediate use ⟨*set* the table⟩ **b** : to put in order for printing ⟨*set* type by hand⟩ **c** : to put into type or something like type ⟨as on photographic film⟩ ⟨*set* the first word in

\ə\ **abut**	\au̇\ **out**	\i\ **tip**	\ȯ\ **saw**	\u̇\ **foot**
\ər\ **further**	\ch\ **chin**	\ī\ **life**	\ȯi\ **coin**	\y\ **yet**
\a\ **mat**	\e\ **pet**	\j\ **job**	\th\ **thin**	\yü\ **few**
\ā\ **take**	\ē\ **easy**	\ŋ\ **sing**	\th\ **this**	\yu̇\ **cure**
\ä\ **cot, cart**	\g\ **go**	\ō\ **bone**	\ü\ **food**	\zh\ **vision**

italic⟩ **11** : to wave, curl, or arrange hair by wetting and drying **12** : to fix in a setting or frame ⟨*set* diamonds in a ring⟩ **13** : ²VALUE 1, RATE ⟨*set* the loss at $2000⟩ **14** : to put and fix in a direction ⟨*set* our faces toward home once more⟩ **15** : to fix firmly : give rigid form to ⟨*set* his jaw in determination⟩ **16** : to become or cause to become firm or solid ⟨the gelatin is *setting*⟩ **17** : to form and bring to maturity ⟨the old tree still *sets* a good crop of apples⟩ **18** *chiefly dialect* : SIT 1a, b **19** : to cover and warm eggs to hatch them ⟨the hen has been *setting* for several days⟩ **20** : to pass below the horizon ⟨the sun *sets*⟩ **21** : to apply oneself to some activity ⟨*set* to work⟩ **22** : to have a certain direction in motion : FLOW **23** : to become permanent ⟨if you don't wash that fast the stain will *set*⟩ — **set about** : to begin to do — **set apart** **1** : to reserve for a certain use **2** : to make noticeable — **set aside** **1** : ¹DISCARD 2 **2** : to set apart for some purpose : RESERVE, SAVE **3** : ANNUL 2, OVERRULE ⟨the verdict was *set aside* by the court⟩ — **set eyes on** : to catch sight of : SEE ⟨loved her from the minute he *set eyes on* her⟩ — **set foot in** : ENTER 1 — **set foot on** : to step onto — **set forth** **1** : to make known ⟨*set forth* an idea⟩ **2** : to start out on a journey : SET OUT — **set one's hand to** : to become engaged in : UNDERTAKE — **set one's sights on** : to determine to get or accomplish ⟨*set their sights on* winning the game⟩ — **set store** : to consider valuable or trustworthy — used with *by* or *on* — **set to music** : to provide music for — **set upon** : to attack usually with violence : ASSAULT

²set *n* **1 a** : the act or action of setting **b** : the condition of being set **2** : a number of persons or things of the same kind that belong or are used together ⟨the social *set*⟩ ⟨a *set* of dishes⟩ **3** : direction of flow ⟨the *set* of the wind⟩ **4** : the form or movement of the body or of its parts ⟨the *set* of the shoulders⟩ **5** : an artificial setting for a scene of a play or movie **6** : a group of tennis games that make up a match **7** : a collection of mathematical elements (as numbers or points) **8** : an electronic device ⟨a television *set*⟩

³set *adj* **1** : showing great determination ⟨*set* against going⟩ **2** : fixed by authority ⟨a *set* rule⟩ **3** : not very willing to change ⟨*set* in their ways⟩ **4 a** : FIXED 1a, RIGID ⟨a *set* smile⟩ **b** : BUILT-IN ⟨a *set* tub for washing⟩ **5** : prepared for use or action : READY ⟨are you all *set*⟩

se·ta \'sēt-ə\ *n, pl* **se·tae** \'sē-,tē\ : a slender usually rigid or bristly and springy organ or part of an animal or plant

set·back \'set-,bak\ *n* : a slowing of progress : a temporary defeat

set down *vb* **1** : to cause to sit down : SEAT **2** : to place at rest on a surface or on the ground **3** : to land (an airplane) on the ground or water **4** : ESTABLISH 2 ⟨the government *set down* laws⟩ **5** : to put in writing

set–in \,set-,in\ *adj* : cut separately and stitched in ⟨*set-in* sleeves⟩

set in *vb* **1** : ¹INSERT 2 **2** : to make its appearance : BEGIN ⟨winter *set in* early⟩

set off *vb* **1 a** : to cause to show up clearly ⟨bright flowers *set off* by dark shadows⟩ **b** : to separate from others : make noticeable ⟨a direct quotation *set off* by quotation marks⟩ **2 a** : to cause to go off or explode ⟨*set off* an alarm⟩ ⟨*set off* a firecracker⟩ **b** : to cause to start : BEGIN ⟨*set* an argument *off* by your remarks⟩ **3** : to start out on a course or a trip ⟨*set off* for home⟩ ⟨*set off* in a boat⟩ ⟨*set off* on a journey⟩

set out *vb* **1** : to begin with a definite purpose : UNDERTAKE ⟨deliberately *set out* to win⟩ **2** : to start out on a course, a journey, or a career ⟨*set out* to be a doctor⟩ ⟨*set out* for Spain⟩

set·tee \se-'tē\ *n* **1** : a long seat with a back **2** : a medium-sized sofa with arms and a back

set·ter \'set-ər\ *n* **1** : someone or something that sets **2** : a large long-coated dog used in hunting birds

set theory *n* : a branch of mathematics that deals with sets

and with relations between sets — **set–the·o·ret·ic** \-,thē-ə-'ret-ik\ *adj*

set·ting \'set-iŋ\ *n* **1** : the manner, position, or direction in which something is set ⟨change a thermostat *setting*⟩ **2** : a frame or holder in which something is mounted ⟨a *setting* for a diamond⟩ **3** : the background (as time and place) of the action of a story or play **4** : the articles of tableware required for setting a place at table ⟨two *settings* of silver⟩ **5** : a batch of eggs for hatching

settle

¹set·tle \'set-ªl\ *n* : a long wooden bench with arms and a solid back

²settle *vb* **set·tled; set·tling** \'set-liŋ, -ªl-iŋ\ **1** : to place so as to stay ⟨*settled* into a chair⟩ **2 a** : to establish in a place to live : COLONIZE ⟨*settled* the West⟩ **b** : to make one's home ⟨*settle* in the country⟩ **3** : to make or become quiet : CALM ⟨rocking *settled* the baby⟩ **4** : DECIDE 1 ⟨*settle* the question⟩ **5** : to put in order : make final arrangements ⟨*settle* an estate⟩ ⟨*settle* a bill⟩ **6** : to adjust differences ⟨*settle* a quarrel⟩ **7 a** : to come to rest ⟨birds *settling* on a branch⟩ **b** : to descend usually slowly and stay down ⟨mist *settling* in the valley⟩ **8 a** : to sink gradually or to the bottom ⟨the foundations of the house *settled*⟩ — often used with *out* ⟨dust particles *settling* out⟩ **b** : to sink in a liquid ⟨sediment *settles* to the bottom⟩ **9** : to apply oneself — usually used with *down* ⟨*settle* down to study⟩ **10** : to take up an ordered life — often used with *down* ⟨marry and *settle* down⟩ — **settle for** : to be content with ⟨would not *settle* for a tie score⟩

set·tle·ment \'set-ªl-mənt\ *n* **1** : the act of settling : the condition of being settled **2** : final payment (as of a bill) **3 a** : a place or region newly settled **b** : a small village **4** : SETTLEMENT HOUSE

settlement house *n* : an institution providing various community services to people in a crowded part of a city

set·tler \'set-lər, -ªl-ər\ *n* : a person who settles in a new region : COLONIST

set·up \'set-,əp\ *n* : the way in which something is set up : ORGANIZATION, ARRANGEMENT

set up \(')set-'əp\ *vb* **1** : to place in position ⟨*set up* a target⟩ **2 a** : ²ERECT 1 ⟨*set up* a building⟩ **b** : to assemble the parts of ⟨*set up* a machine⟩ **3** : to cause to happen ⟨the wind *sets up* a humming in the wires⟩ **4** : to put in operation : FOUND, INAUGURATE ⟨*set up* a school⟩ **5** : to put in operation as a way of living ⟨*set up* housekeeping⟩ — **set up shop** : to establish one's business

sev·en \'sev-ən\ *n* **1** — see NUMBER table **2** : the seventh in a set or series ⟨the *seven* of hearts⟩ — **seven** *adj or pron*

sev·en–league \'sev-ən-,lēg\ *adj* : crossing seven leagues at a stride ⟨*seven-league* boots⟩

seven seas *n pl* : all the waters or oceans of the world ⟨had sailed the *seven seas*⟩

sev·en·teen \,sev-ən-'tēn\ *n* — see NUMBER table — **sev·enteen** *adj or pron* — **sev·en·teenth** \-'tēn(t)th\ *adj or n*

seventeen–year locust *n* : a cicada of the U.S. with a life span of seventeen years in the North and of thirteen years in the South that spends only a few weeks as a winged adult and lives most of its life as a wingless underground nymph which feeds on roots

sev·enth \'sev-ən(t)th\ *n* **1** — see NUMBER table **2** : the difference in pitch between the first tone and the seventh tone of a scale — **seventh** *adj or adv*

sev·en·ty \'sev-ən-tē\ *n, pl* **-ties** — see NUMBER table — **sev·en·ti·eth** \-tē-əth\ *adj or n* — **seventy** *adj or pron*

sev·er \'sev-ər\ *vb* **sev·ered; sev·er·ing** \-(ə-)riŋ\ **1** : to put or keep apart : DIVIDE; *esp* : to cut off or through **2** : to come or break apart

¹sev·er·al \'sev-(ə-)rəl\ *adj* **1** : separate or distinct from one another : DIFFERENT 〈federal union of the *several* states〉 **2** : being more than two but not very many 〈*several* persons〉 — **sev·er·al·ly** \-ē\ *adv*

²several *pron* : a small number : more than two but not very many 〈*several* of the guests〉

sev·er·ance \'sev-(ə-)rən(t)s\ *n* : the act or process of severing : the state of being severed

se·vere \sə-'vi(ə)r\ *adj* **se·ver·er; -est** **1 a** : strict in judgment, discipline, or government 〈a *severe* ruler〉 **b** : serious in feeling or manner : GRAVE **2** : not using unnecessary ornament : PLAIN 〈a *severe* style〉 **3** : inflicting pain, distress, or hardship 〈*severe* wounds〉 〈a *severe* winter〉 **4** : requiring great effort 〈a *severe* test〉 — **se·vere·ly** *adv*

se·ver·i·ty \sə-'ver-ət-ē\ *n, pl* **-ties** : the quality or state of being severe

sew \'sō\ *vb* **sewed; sewn** \'sōn\ *or* **sewed; sew·ing** **1** : to join or fasten by stitches 〈*sew* on a button〉 **2** : to work with needle and thread

sew·age \'sü-ij\ *n* : waste materials carried off by sewers

¹sew·er \'sō-(ə)r\ *n* : one that sews

²sew·er \'sü-ər, 'sù(-ə)r\ *n* : a usually covered drain to carry off water and sewage

sew·er·age \'sü-ə-rij, 'sù(-ə)r-ij\ *n* **1** : SEWAGE **2** : the removal and disposal of sewage and surface water by sewers **3** : a system of sewers

sew·ing \'sō-iŋ\ *n* **1** : the act, method, or occupation of one that sews **2** : material that has been or is to be sewed

sewing machine *n* : a machine for sewing

sew up *vb* **1** : to get exclusive use or control of **2** : to make certain of

sex \'seks\ *n* **1** : either of two groups into which many living things are divided according to their roles in reproduction and which consist of males or females **2** : the physical and behavioral characteristics that make males and females different from each other **3** : sexual activity; *esp* : SEXUAL INTERCOURSE [Middle English *sex* "category of living things according to reproductive roles", from Latin *sexus* (same meaning)]

sex- *or* **sexi-** *combining form* : six 〈*sextet*〉 [from Latin *sex* "six"]

sex·a·ge·nar·i·an \,sek-sə-jə-'ner-ē-ən, (,)sek-,saj-ə-\ *n* : a person who is 60 or more but less than 70 years old — **sexagenarian** *adj*

sex cell *n* : an egg cell or a sperm cell

sex chromosome *n* : either of a pair of chromosomes (as the human X chromosome or the human Y chromosome) in a sexually reproducing organism that are concerned with the determination of sex and are represented differently in the two sexes either by being present in one sex and not the other or by being present a different number of times in one sex compared to the other

sex gland *n* : GONAD

sex hormone *n* : a hormone that affects the growth or function of the reproductive organs or the development of secondary sex characteristics

sex·ism \'sek-,siz-əm\ *n* : distinction and especially unjust distinction based on sex and made against one person or group in favor of another; *esp* : distinctions made against women — **sex·ist** \'sek-səst\ *adj or n*

sex–linked \'sek-,sliŋ(k)t\ *adj* **1** : located on a sex chromosome 〈a *sex-linked* gene〉 **2** : controlled by a sex-linked gene 〈a *sex-linked* characteristic〉 — **sex–link·age** \-,sliŋ-kij\ *n*

sex·tant \'sek-stənt\ *n* : a navigational instrument for measuring the angle between the horizon and the sun or a star in order to find out the latitude (as of a ship)

sex·tet \sek-'stet\ *n* **1** : a musical composition for six instruments or voices **2** : a group or set of six

sex·til·lion \sek-'stil-yən\ *n* — see NUMBER table

sex·ton \'sek-stən\ *n* : an official of a church who takes care of church buildings and property

¹sex·tu·ple \sek-'st(y)üp-əl, -'stəp-; 'sek-stəp-\ *adj* **1** : having six units or members **2** : being six times as great or as many — **sextuple** *n*

²sextuple *vb* **sex·tu·pled; sex·tu·pling** \-(ə)liŋ\ : to make or become six times as much or as many

sextant

sex·tu·plet \sek-'stəp-lət, -'st(y)üp-; 'sek-st(y)əp-\ *n* **1** : a combination of six of a kind **2** : one of six offspring born at one birth

sex·u·al \'seksh-(ə-)wəl, 'sek-shəl\ *adj* **1** : of or relating to sex or the sexes 〈*sexual* differences〉 **2** : having or involving sex 〈*sexual* reproduction〉 〈*sexual* spores〉 — **sex·u·al·ly** \'seksh-(ə-)wə-lē, 'seksh-(ə-)lē\ *adv*

sexual intercourse *n* : sexual union especially involving penetration of the vagina by the penis

sex·u·al·i·ty \,sek-shə-'wal-ət-ē\ *n* : the quality or state of being sexual

sexually transmitted disease *n* : STD

sexual relations *n pl* : SEXUAL INTERCOURSE

sexy \'sek-sē\ *adj* **sex·i·er; -est** : sexually exciting : EROTIC — **sex·i·ness** *n*

sfor·zan·do \sfȯrt-'sän-dō, -'san-\ *adj* : played with special stress or accent — used as a direction in music

shab·by \'shab-ē\ *adj* **shab·bi·er; -est** **1** : dressed in worn clothes **2 a** : worn and faded from wear 〈a *shabby* sofa〉 **b** : ill kept : DILAPIDATED 〈a *shabby* neighborhood〉 **3** : not fair or generous 〈*shabby* treatment〉 — **shab·bi·ly** \'shab-ə-lē\ *adv* — **shab·bi·ness** \'shab-ē-nəs\ *n*

Sha·bu·oth \shə-'vü-,ōt(h), -,ōs, -əs\ *n* : a Jewish holiday celebrated in May or June to commemorate the revelation of the Ten Commandments at Mount Sinai

shack \'shak\ *n* **1** : HUT, SHANTY **2** : a room or similar enclosed structure for a particular person or use 〈a radio *shack*〉

¹shack·le \'shak-əl\ *n* **1** : a ring or band that prevents free use of the legs or arms **2** : something that prevents free action — usually used in pl. **3** : a U-shaped metal device for joining or fastening something

²shackle *vb* **shack·led; shack·ling** \'shak-(ə-)liŋ\ **1 a** : to bind with shackles 〈the guard *shackled* the prisoner〉 **b** : to make fast with a shackle **2** : to deprive of freedom of action : HINDER 〈*shackled* by poverty〉 — **shack·ler** \-(ə-)lər\ *n*

shad \'shad\ *n, pl* **shad** : any of several sea fishes that are related to the herrings, swim up rivers to spawn, and are important food fish

shad·bush \'shad-,bùsh\ *n* : SERVICEBERRY

¹shade \'shād\ *n* **1** : partial darkness 〈the trees cast *shade*〉 **2** : space sheltered from light or heat and especially from the sun 〈sit in the *shade* of a tree〉 **3** *pl* : the shadows that gather as darkness falls 〈the *shades* of night〉 **4** : ¹SPIRIT 2b, GHOST **5** : something that blocks off or cuts down light, sun, or heat 〈a lamp *shade*〉 〈a window *shade*〉 **6** : the darkening of some objects in a painting or drawing to suggest that they are in shade **7** : the darkness or lightness of a color 〈four *shades* of brown〉 **8** : a

\ə\ abut	\aú\ out	\i\ tip	\ȯ\ saw	\ú\ foot
\ər\ further	\ch\ chin	\ī\ life	\ȯi\ coin	\y\ yet
\a\ mat	\e\ pet	\j\ job	\th\ thin	\yü\ few
\ā\ take	\ē\ easy	\ŋ\ sing	\th\ this	\yú\ cure
\ä\ cot, cart	\g\ go	\ō\ bone	\ü\ food	\zh\ vision

very small difference or amount ⟨just a *shade* taller⟩ ⟨*shades* of meaning⟩ — **shade·less** \-ləs\ *adj*

²**shade** *vb* **shad·ed; shad·ing** **1** : to shelter from light or heat **2** : to mark with changes of light or color ⟨*shade* a drawing⟩ **3** : to show or begin to have slight differences of color, value, or meaning — **shad·er** *n*

shade tree *n* : a tree grown chiefly to make shade

¹**shad·ow** \'shad-ō\ *n* **1** : shade within certain bounds ⟨the valley was in *shadow*⟩ **2** : a reflected image (as in a mirror) **3** : shelter from danger or view **4 a** : an imperfect and faint representation **b** : an imitation of something **5** : the dark figure cast on a surface by a body that is between the surface and the light ⟨my *shadow* stays with me⟩ **6** : ¹PHANTOM **7** *pl* : darkness caused by the setting of the sun ⟨twilight *shadows*⟩ **8** : a shaded part of a picture **9** : a form from which the substance has departed : REMNANT, VESTIGE **10 a** : an inseparable companion or follower **b** : a person who shadows as a spy or detective **11** : a very little bit : TRACE ⟨not a *shadow* of a doubt⟩ **12** : a source of gloom or unhappiness — **shad·ow·less** \-ləs\ *adj* — **shad·ow·like** \-ˌlīk\ *adj*

²**shadow** *vb* **1** : to cast a shadow on **2** : to follow especially secretly : TRAIL — **shad·ow·er** \'shad-ə-wər\ *n*

shad·ow·box \'shad-ō-ˌbäks\ *vb* : to box with an imaginary opponent as a form of training

shad·owy \'shad-ə-wē\ *adj* **1 a** : not realistic ⟨*shadowy* dreams of glory⟩ **b** : dim as a shadow ⟨the *shadowy* area between good and bad⟩ **2** : full of shade ⟨a *shadowy* lane⟩

shady \'shād-ē\ *adj* **shad·i·er; -est** **1** : casting a shadow : giving shade **2** : sheltered from the sun's rays ⟨a *shady* grove⟩ **3** : not right or honest ⟨a *shady* business deal⟩ — **shad·i·ly** \'shād-ᵊl-ē\ *adv* — **shad·i·ness** \'shād-ē-nəs\ *n*

shaft \'shaft\ *n, pl* **shafts** \'shaf(t)s, *in sense 1c also* 'shavz\ **1 a** : the long handle of a weapon (as a spear) **b** : ¹SPEAR 1, LANCE **c** *or pl* **shaves** \'shavz\ : ¹POLE 1; *esp* : one of two poles between which a horse is hitched to pull a vehicle **d** : an arrow especially for a longbow **2** : a narrow beam of light **3** : something suggestive of the shaft of an arrow or spear ⟨the *shaft* or trunk of a tree⟩ **4** : the handle of a tool or instrument (as a hammer or golf club) **5** : a tall monument (as a column) **6** : an opening or passage straight down through the floors of a building ⟨an air *shaft*⟩ **7** : a commonly cylindrical bar used to support rotating pieces or to transmit power or motion by rotation **8** : a mine opening for finding or mining ore **9** : the midrib of a feather

¹**shag** \'shag\ *n* **1 a** : a shaggy tangled mass or covering **b** : a rug or carpeting with long yarns that do not stand up **2** : a strong coarse tobacco cut into fine shreds

²**shag** *vb* **shagged; shag·ging** **1** : to chase after and return a ball **2** : to catch a ball

shag·bark hickory \'shag-ˌbärk-\ *n* : a hickory of the eastern U.S. and Canada with a gray shaggy outer bark that peels off in long strips — called also *shagbark*

shag·gy \'shag-ē\ *adj* **shag·gi·er; -est** **1** : covered with or made up of long, coarse, or tangled growth **2** : having a rough or hairy surface — **shag·gi·ly** \'shag-ə-lē\ *adv* — **shag·gi·ness** \'shag-ē-nəs\ *n*

shah \'shä, 'shò\ *n* : a ruler of Iran until the 1979 revolution

¹**shake** \'shāk\ *vb* **shook** \'shůk\; **shak·en** \'shā-kən\; **shak·ing** **1** : to move irregularly to and fro : QUIVER, TREMBLE ⟨*shaking* with cold⟩ **2** : to become unsteady : TOTTER **3** : to cause to move in a usually quick jerky manner **4** : to free oneself from ⟨*shake* off a cold⟩ **5** : to cause to become weaker ⟨*shake* one's faith⟩ **6** : to force out of a place by quick jerky movements ⟨*shake* dust from a blanket⟩ **7** : to clasp (hands) in greeting or as a sign of goodwill or agreement — **shak·able** \'shā-kə-bəl\ *adj* — **shake a leg** : to hurry up

²**shake** *n* **1** : an act of shaking **2** *pl* : a condition of trem-

bling (as from chill) **3** : something produced by shaking; *esp* : MILK SHAKE **4** : a very brief period of time ⟨ready in two *shakes*⟩ **5** *pl* : one that stands out especially in importance, ability, or merit — usually used in the phrase *no great shakes* **6** : a long shingle **7** : ³DEAL 2 ⟨a fair *shake*⟩

shake·down \'shāk-ˌdaůn\ *n* : a testing under operating conditions of something new (as a ship) for possible faults or for the operators to become more familiar with it ⟨a *shakedown* cruise⟩

shak·er \'shā-kər\ *n* **1** : a utensil or machine used in shaking **2** *cap* : a member of a religious group originating in England and practicing a communal life

Shake·spear·ean *or* **Shake·spear·ian** \shāk-'spir-ē-ən\ *adj* : of, relating to, or having the characteristics of Shakespeare or his writings

shake–up \'shā-ˌkəp\ *n* : an act or instance of shaking up; *esp* : a reorganization that has extreme effects ⟨lost their jobs in an office *shake-up*⟩

shake up \(')shā-'kəp\ *vb* **1** : to jar by or as if by a physical shock ⟨the accident *shook up* both drivers⟩ ⟨the news *shook* us *up*⟩ **2** : to bring about an extensive reorganization of

sha·ko \'shak-ō, 'shāk-\ *n, pl* **sha·kos** *or* **sha·koes** : a stiff military cap with a high crown and plume

shaky \'shā-kē\ *adj* **shak·i·er; -est** **1 a** : lacking firmness **b** : lacking in authority or reliability : QUESTIONABLE **2** : marked by shaking : TREMBLING **3** : likely to give way or break down — **shak·i·ly** \-kə-lē\ *adv* — **shak·i·ness** \-kē-nəs\ *n*

shale \'shā(ə)l\ *n* : a rock with a fine grain formed from clay, mud, or silt — **shal·ey** \'shā-lē\ *adj*

shall \shəl, (')shal\ *helping verb, past* **should** \shəd, (')shůd\; *present sing & pl* **shall** **1** : am or are going to or expecting to : WILL ⟨I *shall* write today⟩ **2** : is or are compelled to : MUST ⟨they *shall* not pass⟩

shako

shal·lop \'shal-əp\ *n* : a small open boat moved by oars or sails

¹**shal·low** \'shal-ō\ *adj* **1** : having little depth ⟨*shallow* water⟩ **2** : showing little knowledge, thought, or feeling — **shal·low·ly** *adv* — **shal·low·ness** *n*

²**shallow** *n* : a shallow place or area in a body of water — usually used in pl.

shalt \shəlt, (')shalt\ *archaic present 2d sing of* SHALL

¹**sham** \'sham\ *n* **1** : a trick that deceives : HOAX **2** : something resembling an article of personal or household linen and used in place of or over it **3** : an imitation or counterfeit giving the impression of being real

²**sham** *vb* **shammed; sham·ming** : to act in a deceiving way

³**sham** *adj* : not real : FALSE ⟨*sham* pearls⟩

sham·ble \'sham-bəl\ *vb* **sham·bled; sham·bling** \-b(ə-)liŋ\ : to walk awkwardly with dragging feet : SHUFFLE — **shamble** *n*

sham·bles \'sham-bəlz\ *n sing or pl* **1** : a place or state of destruction ⟨the war left the country in a *shambles*⟩ **2** : a scene or state of disorder or confusion : MESS ⟨this room is a *shambles*⟩

¹**shame** \'shām\ *n* **1 a** : a painful emotion caused by having done something wrong or improper **b** : ability to feel shame ⟨have you no *shame*⟩ **2** : ¹DISHONOR 1, DISGRACE **3** : something that brings disgrace or causes shame or strong regret **4** : something to be regretted : PITY ⟨it's a *shame* you'll miss the show⟩

²**shame** *vb* **shamed; sham·ing** **1** : to bring shame to : DISGRACE **2** : to cause to feel shame **3** : to force by

causing to feel guilty ⟨they were *shamed* into confessing⟩

shame·faced \'shām-'fāst\ *adj* **1** : showing modesty : BASHFUL **2** : showing shame : ASHAMED — **shame·faced·ly** \-'fā-səd-lē, -'fāst-lē\ *adv* — **shame·faced·ness** \-'fā-səd-nəs, -'fās(t)-nəs\ *n*

> **Word History** The Old English word *scamfæst* was formed by a combination of the noun *scamu,* meaning "shame", and the adjective *fæst,* meaning "firmly fixed or bound, fast". The meaning of *scamfæst* was "bound by shame" or, more simply, "bashful". Over the course of many years, the Old English *scamfæst* was changed to the modern English *shamefaced.* The change from *-fæst* to *-faced* occurred because many people misunderstood *-fæst.* They substituted a more familiar word for one they did not know. The belief that bashfulness shows in a person's face probably also influenced the change. [an altered form of earlier *shamefast,* from Old English *scamfæst,* "bound by shame, bashful", from *scamu* "shame" and *fæst* "fixed, fast"]

shame·ful \'shām-fəl\ *adj* **1** : bringing shame ⟨*shameful* behavior⟩ **2** : arousing the feeling of shame ⟨a *shameful* sight⟩ — **shame·ful·ly** \-fə-lē\ *adv* — **shame·ful·ness** \-fəl-nəs\ *n*

shame·less \'shām-ləs\ *adj* **1** : having no shame **2** : showing lack of shame — **shame·less·ly** *adv* — **shame·less·ness** *n*

¹sham·poo \sham-'pü\ *vb* : to wash (as the hair) with soap and water or with a special preparation — **sham·poo·er** *n*

²shampoo *n* **1** : an act or instance of shampooing **2** : a cleaner used in shampooing

sham·rock \'sham-,räk\ *n* : a plant of folk legend with leaves composed of three leaflets that is associated with St. Patrick and Ireland; *also* : any of several plants (as a clover or a wood sorrel) or their leaves that resemble, are worn to represent, or are held to be the shamrock of legend [from Irish Gaelic (the ancient language of Ireland) *seamróg,* literally "little clover"]

shang·hai \shaŋ-'hī\ *vb* **shang·haied; shang·hai·ing** **1** : to put aboard a ship by force often with the help of liquor or a drug **2** : to put by threat or force into or as if into a place of detention [from *Shanghai,* a major seaport in China; so called because this method was formerly sometimes used to get sailors for ships sailing to the Orient]

shank \'shaŋk\ *n* **1 a** : the part of the leg between the knee and the ankle in humans or a similar part in various other vertebrates **b** : a cut of meat from usually the upper part of a leg **2 a** : the straight shaft (as of a nail, pin, or fishhook) **b** : the narrow part of the sole of a shoe beneath the instep **3** : a part of a tool that connects the acting part with a part by which it is held or moved ⟨the *shank* of a drill bit⟩ ⟨the *shank* of a key⟩ **4** : a part of something by which it can be attached: as **a** : a part that sticks out on the back of a solid button **b** : a short stem of thread that holds a sewn button away from the cloth — **shanked** \'shaŋ(k)t\ *adj*

shan't \(')shant, (')shȧnt\ : shall not

shan·ty \'shant-ē\ *n, pl* **shanties** : SHACK, HUT

shan·ty·town \-,taún\ *n* : a usually poor town or section of a town made up mostly of shanties

¹shape \'shāp\ *vb* **shaped; shap·ing** **1** : to give a certain form or shape to ⟨*shape* the dough into loaves⟩ **2** : to change in shape so as to fit neatly and closely ⟨a hat *shaped* close to the head⟩ **3** : DEVISE 1, PLAN **4** : to make fit especially for some purpose ⟨*shaping* the minds of future leaders⟩ **5** : to take on or approach a definite form — often used with *up* — **shap·er** *n*

²shape *n* **1** : outward appearance : FORM ⟨the *shape* of a pearl⟩ **2** : the outline of a body : FIGURE ⟨a square *shape*⟩ **3** : definite form and arrangement ⟨a plan now taking *shape*⟩ **4** : something having a certain form **5** : the condition in which something or someone is at a certain time

⟨the car was in poor *shape*⟩ — **shaped** \,shāpt\ *adj*

shape·less \'shā-pləs\ *adj* **1** : having no fixed or regular shape **2 a** : deprived of usual or normal shape **b** : not shapely — **shape·less·ly** *adv* — **shape·less·ness** *n*

shape·ly \'shā-plē\ *adj* **shape·li·er; -est** : having a regular or pleasing shape — **shape·li·ness** *n*

shape up \(')shā-'pəp\ *vb* : to improve to a good condition or standard ⟨*shape up* and start studying⟩

shard \'shärd\ *n* : a piece or fragment of something brittle (as pottery)

¹share \'she(ə)r, 'sha(ə)r\ *n* **1** : a portion belonging to, due to, or contributed by an individual **2** : the part given or belonging to one of a number owning something together ⟨sold my *share* of the business⟩ **3** : any of the equal portions or interests into which the property of a corporation is divided ⟨100 *shares* of stock⟩

²share *vb* **shared; shar·ing** **1** : to divide and distribute in portions ⟨*shared* the lunch⟩ **2** : to use, experience, or enjoy with others **3** : to give or be given a share : take a part ⟨*share* in planning the program⟩ **syn** see PARTAKE — **shar·er** *n*

share·crop \'she(ə)r-,kräp, 'sha(ə)r-\ **share·cropped; share·crop·ping** *vb* : to farm or produce as a sharecropper

share·crop·per \'she(ə)r-,kräp-ər, 'sha(ə)r-\ *n* : a farmer who works land for the owner in return for a share of the value of the crop

share·hold·er \-,hōl-dər\ *n* : one that owns or holds a share in property; *esp* : STOCKHOLDER

¹shark \'shärk\ *n* : any of numerous marine fishes that have rough grayish skin and a skeleton made of cartilage, that usually prey on other animals and are dangerous to people, and that include some caught for the oil in their livers or for their hide from which a leather is made — **shark·like** \'shär-,klīk\ *adj*

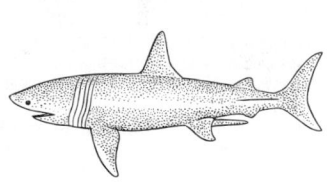

¹shark

²shark *n* **1** : a sly greedy person who takes advantage of others ⟨a loan *shark*⟩ **2** : a person who outdoes others especially in a certain area ⟨a *shark* at arithmetic⟩

shark·skin \'shärk-,skin\ *n* **1** : the hide of a shark or leather made from it **2** : a smooth durable material with small woven designs that looks like the hide of a shark

¹sharp \'shärp\ *adj* **1 a** : having a thin keen edge or fine point ⟨a *sharp* knife⟩ **b** : briskly cold : NIPPING ⟨*sharp* biting wind⟩ **2 a** : alert in understanding : QUICK-WITTED ⟨a *sharp* student⟩ **b** : having very good ability to see or hear ⟨you have *sharp* eyes⟩ **c** : keen in attention to one's own interest sometimes to the point of being dishonest ⟨a *sharp* customer⟩ **3 a** : full of activity or energy : BRISK ⟨keep up a *sharp* pace⟩ **b** : EAGER ⟨a *sharp* appetite⟩ **4 a** : CURT, ANGRY ⟨a *sharp* reply⟩ **b** : very trying to the feelings : causing distress ⟨a *sharp* pain⟩ ⟨*sharp* criticism⟩ **5** : having a strong odor or flavor ⟨*sharp* cheese⟩ **6 a** : ending in a point or edge ⟨*sharp* features⟩ ⟨*sharp* mountain peaks⟩ **b** : involving an abrupt change ⟨a *sharp* turn⟩ ⟨a *sharp* drop in the temperature⟩ **c** : clear in outline or detail : DISTINCT ⟨a *sharp* image⟩ **d** : set forth with clarity and distinctness ⟨*sharp* contrast⟩ **7 a** : higher by a half step than the pitch of the note indicated by the letter name **b**

\ə\ **abut**	\aú\ **out**	\i\ **tip**	\ò\ **saw**	\ú\ **foot**
\ər\ **further**	\ch\ **chin**	\ī\ **life**	\ói\ **coin**	\y\ **yet**
\a\ **mat**	\e\ **pet**	\j\ **job**	\th\ **thin**	\yü\ **few**
\ā\ **take**	\ē\ **easy**	\ŋ\ **sing**	\th\ **this**	\yú\ **cure**
\ä\ **cot, cart**	\g\ **go**	\ō\ **bone**	\ü\ **food**	\zh\ **vision**

: higher than the true pitch   **8** : STYLISH, DRESSY —
sharp·ly *adv* — **sharp·ness** *n*

    syn SHARP, KEEN, ACUTE mean having or showing alertness and clear understanding. SHARP suggests quick understanding, cleverness, and sometimes trickery ⟨*sharp* traders⟩ KEEN suggests quickness, enthusiasm, and a mind of deep understanding ⟨a *keen* student of baseball in the major leagues⟩ ACUTE suggests the power to think clearly and to see small differences ⟨*acute* powers of reasoning⟩

²sharp *adv*   **1** : in a sharp manner : SHARPLY ⟨sang *sharp*⟩   **2** : at an exact time ⟨four o'clock *sharp*⟩

³sharp *n*   **1** : a musical note or tone one half step higher than the note or tone indicated by the letter name; *also* : a character ♯ on a line or space of the staff indicating such a note or tone   **2** : a needle with a small eye for sewing by hand

⁴sharp *vb*   **1** : to raise in pitch especially by a half step   **2** : to sing or play above the true pitch

sharp·en \'shär-pən\ *vb* **sharp·ened; sharp·en·ing** \'shärp-(ə-)niŋ\ : to make or become sharp or sharper — **sharp·en·er** \'shärp-(ə-)nər\ *n*

sharp·er \'shär-pər\ *n* : ²CHEAT 2, SWINDLER

sharp–eyed \'shär-'pīd\ *adj* : having keen sight; *also* : keen in observing or seeing through

sharp·shoot·er \'shärp-,shüt-ər\ *n* : one skilled in shooting : a good marksman — **sharp·shoot·ing** \-,shüt-iŋ\ *n*

sharp·wit·ted \'shärp-'wit-əd\ *adj* : having or showing a quick keen mind

shat·ter \'shat-ər\ *vb*   **1** : to break or fall to pieces   **2** : to damage badly : RUIN, WRECK

shat·ter·proof \,shat-ər-'prüf\ *adj* : made so as not to shatter ⟨*shatterproof* glass⟩

shat·ters \'shat-ərz\ *n pl* : broken pieces ⟨the vase lay in *shatters*⟩

¹shave \'shāv\ *vb* **shaved; shaved** *or* **shav·en** \'shā-vən\; **shav·ing**   **1 a** : to cut off in thin layers or shreds   **b** : to cut off closely   **2 a** : to cut the hair from (as the head) close to the roots   **b** : to cut off hair or beard close to the skin   **3** : to come close to or touch lightly in passing

²shave *n*   **1** : SHAVER 2   **2** : an act or process of shaving especially the beard   **3** : a narrow escape ⟨a close *shave*⟩

shav·er \'shā-vər\ *n*   **1** : a person who shaves   **2** : a tool or machine for shaving; *esp* : an electric-powered razor   **3** : BOY 1, YOUNGSTER

shaves *pl of* SHAFT

shav·ing \'shā-viŋ\ *n*   **1** : the act of one that shaves   **2** : something shaved off ⟨wood *shavings*⟩

¹shawl \'shȯl\ *n* : a square or oblong piece of woven or knitted fabric used especially as a covering for the head or shoulders

²shawl *vb* : to wrap in or as if in a shawl

Shaw·nee \shȯ-'nē, shä-\ *n* : a member of an American Indian people originally of the central Ohio valley

shay \'shā\ *n, chiefly dialect* : a two-wheeled carriage; *esp* : CHAISE

¹she \(')shē\ *pron* : that female one ⟨*she* is my wife⟩

²she \'shē\ *n* : a female person or animal — often used in combination ⟨*she*-cat⟩

sheaf \'shēf\ *n, pl* **sheaves** \'shēvz\   **1** : a bundle of stalks and ears of grain   **2** : a group of things often fastened together and resembling a sheaf of grain ⟨a *sheaf* of arrows⟩ ⟨a *sheaf* of papers⟩ — **sheaf·like** \'shē-,flīk\ *adj*

¹shear \'shi(ə)r\ *vb* **sheared; sheared** *or* **shorn** \'shō(ə)rn, 'shȯ(ə)rn\; **shear·ing**   **1** : to cut the hair or wool from : CLIP ⟨*shearing* sheep⟩   **2** : to deprive of by or as if by cutting off ⟨*shorn* of power⟩   **3** : to become divided under the action of a shear ⟨the bolt may *shear* off⟩ — **shear·er** *n*

²shear *n*   **1 a** : a cutting tool similar or identical to a pair of scissors but typically larger — usually used in pl.   **b** : any of various cutting tools or machines operating by the action

of opposed cutting edges of metal — usually used in pl.   **2** : an action or force that causes or tends to cause two parts of a body to slide on each other in a direction parallel to their plane of contact

shear·wa·ter \'shi(ə)r-,wȯt-ər, -,wät-\ *n* : any of numerous marine birds related to the petrels and albatrosses that often skim close to the water during flight

sheath \'shēth\ *n, pl* **sheaths** \'shēthz, 'shēths\   **1** : a case for a blade (as of a knife)   **2** : a covering especially of a body part that is like a sheath in form or use

sheathe \'shēth\ *vb* **sheathed; sheath·ing**   **1** : to put into a sheath ⟨*sheathe* your sword⟩   **2** : to cover with something that protects ⟨*sheathe* a ship's bottom with copper⟩ — **sheath·er** *n*

sheath·ing \'shē-thiŋ, -thiŋ\ *n* : material used to sheathe something; *esp* : the first covering of boards or of waterproof material on the outside wall of a frame house or on a timber roof

sheath knife *n* : a knife having a fixed blade and designed to be carried in a sheath

¹sheave \'shiv, 'shēv\ *n* : a grooved wheel : PULLEY

²sheave \'shēv\ *vb* **sheaved; sheav·ing** : to gather and bind into a sheaf

she·bang \shi-'baŋ\ *n* : everything involved that is under consideration — usually used in the phrase *the whole shebang*

¹shed \'shed\ *vb* **shed; shed·ding**   **1** : to keep out : REPEL ⟨raincoats *shed* water⟩   **2 a** : to cause (blood) to flow from a cut or wound   **b** : to pour forth in drops ⟨*shed* tears⟩   **c** : to give off or out ⟨the sun *sheds* light and heat⟩   **3 a** : to cast (as a natural covering) aside ⟨a snake *sheds* its skin⟩   **b** : to let fall (as leaves)   **4** : to rid oneself of : DISCARD ⟨*shed* extra pounds⟩ — **shed·der** *n*

²shed *n* : a structure built for shelter or storage

she'd \(,)shēd\ : she had : she would

sheen \'shēn\ *n* : a bright or shining condition ⟨the *sheen* of satin⟩

sheep \'shēp\ *n, pl* **sheep**   **1** : any of a genus of cud-chewing mammals that are stockier than the related goats and lack a beard in the male; *esp* : one that is raised for meat or for its wool or skin   **2** : a weak helpless person who is easily led

sheep·dog \'shēp-,dȯg\ *n* : a dog used to tend, drive, or guard sheep

sheep·fold \'shēp-,fōld\ *n* : a pen or shelter for sheep

sheep·herd·er \'shēp-,hərd-ər\ *n* : a worker in charge of a flock of sheep — **sheep·herd·ing** \-,hərd-iŋ\ *n*

sheep·ish \'shē-pish\ *adj*   **1** : resembling a sheep (as in being meek or shy)   **2** : embarrassed especially over being found out in a fault ⟨a *sheepish* look⟩ — **sheep·ish·ly** *adv* — **sheep·ish·ness** *n*

sheeps·head \'shēps-,hed\ *n* : any of several fishes; *esp* : a food fish of the Atlantic and Gulf coasts of the U.S.

sheep·skin \'shēp-,skin\ *n*   **1** : the skin of a sheep or leather made from it   **2** : DIPLOMA

¹sheer \'shi(ə)r\ *adj*   **1** : very thin or transparent ⟨*sheer* stockings⟩   **2 a** : being such to the fullest degree : UTTER ⟨*sheer* nonsense⟩   **b** : taken or acting apart from everything else ⟨by *sheer* force⟩   **3** : very steep : being almost straight up and down ⟨a *sheer* drop to the sea⟩ [from earlier *sheer* "shining", from Middle English *sheer* "freed from guilt", probably derived from an early Norse word *skærr* "pure"] — **sheer·ly** *adv* — **sheer·ness** *n*

²sheer *adv*   **1** : in a complete manner : ALTOGETHER   **2**

sheep 1: *top* karakul, *bottom* merino

: straight up or down without a break : PERPENDICULARLY

³**sheer** *vb* : to swerve from a course [perhaps an altered form of *shear* "cut, cut off"]

⁴**sheer** *n* : a turn or change in the course of a ship

¹**sheet** \'shēt\ *n* **1** : a broad piece of cloth (as an article of bedding used next to the body) **2 a** : a usually rectangular piece of paper **b** : an unbound page of a book — usually used in pl. **c** : a newspaper, magazine, or occasional publication ⟨a gossip *sheet*⟩ **d** : the unseparated postage stamps printed by one impression of a plate on a single piece of paper; *also* : PANE 2 **3** : a broad surface of something ⟨a *sheet* of ice⟩ **4** : a portion of something that is thin in comparison to its length and width ⟨a *sheet* of iron⟩ [Old English *scȳte* "broad piece of cloth, sheet"] — **sheet·like** *adj*

²**sheet** *vb* : to cover with a sheet : SHROUD

³**sheet** *n* : a rope or chain that regulates the angle at which a sail is set in relation to the wind [Old English *scēata* "lower corner of a sail"]

sheet erosion *n* : erosion that removes surface material more or less evenly from a large area

sheet·ing \'shēt-iŋ\ *n* : material in the form of sheets or suitable for forming into sheets

sheet metal *n* : metal in the form of a sheet

sheet music *n* : music printed on unbound sheets of paper

Sheet·rock \'shēt-,räk\ *trademark* — used for plasterboard

sheikh *or* **sheik** \'shēk, *for sense 1 also* 'shāk\ *n* **1** : an Arab chief **2** *usually* **sheik** : a man supposed to be irresistibly attractive to romantic young women — **sheik·dom** \-dəm\ *n*

shek·el \'shek-əl\ *n* **1** : an ancient unit of weight or value; *esp* : a Hebrew unit equal to about 252 grains troy **2** : a coin weighing one shekel

shelf \'shelf\ *n, pl* **shelves** \'shelvz\ **1** : a flat piece (as of wood or metal) set parallel to and above a floor (as on a wall or in a bookcase) to hold objects **2** : something (as a sandbar or ledge of rock) that suggests a shelf — **shelf·like** \'shel-,flīk\ *adj* — **on the shelf** : in a state of idleness or uselessness

shelf fungus *n* : a fungus that forms shelflike fruiting bodies

shelf life *n* : the period of time something may be stored and still be good enough to use

¹**shell** \'shel\ *n* **1 a** : a hard stiff covering of an animal (as a turtle or beetle) **b** : the outer covering of an egg and especially of a bird's egg **2** : the outer covering of a nut, fruit, or seed especially when hard or tough **3** : shell material or shells especially of mollusks **4** : something like a shell: as **a** : a framework or outside structure **b** : a bottom crust for a pie ⟨a *pastry* shell⟩ **c** : a concrete arched roof (as over an outdoor stage) ⟨a band *shell*⟩ **5** : a way of behaving that hides one's feelings ⟨coming out of one's *shell*⟩ **6** : a shell-bearing mollusk **7** : a narrow light racing boat rowed by one or more persons using long oars **8 a** : an object filled with an explosive to be shot from cannon **b** : a metal or paper case holding the explosive charge and shot or bullet used in small arms — **shell** *adj*

²**shell** *vb* **1 a** : to remove from a natural enclosing cover (as a shell or husk) : SHUCK ⟨*shell* peas⟩ **b** : to remove the grains from (as an ear of Indian corn) **2** : to shoot shells at or upon **3** : to fall out of the pod or husk

she'll \(,)shē(ə)l, shil\ : she shall : she will

¹**shel·lac** \shə-'lak\ *n* **1** : purified lac **2** : a preparation of lac dissolved in alcohol and used as a wood filler or finish

²**shellac** *vb* **shel·lacked; shel·lack·ing** : to coat or treat with shellac

shel·lack·ing \shə-'lak-iŋ\ *n* : a lopsided defeat

shell bean *n* **1** : a bean grown primarily for its edible seeds — compare SNAP BEAN **2** : the edible seed of a bean

shelled \'sheld\ *adj* **1** : having a shell especially of a specified kind ⟨pink-*shelled*⟩ ⟨hard-*shelled*⟩ **2 a** : having the shell removed ⟨*shelled* nuts⟩ ⟨*shelled* oysters⟩ **b** : removed from the cob ⟨*shelled* corn⟩

shell·fish \'shel-,fish\ *n* : an invertebrate animal that lives in water and has a shell; *esp* : an edible mollusk (as an oyster) or crustacean (as a crab) — compare FINFISH

shell shock *n* : any of numerous nervous conditions appearing in soldiers exposed to modern warfare

shell–shocked \'shel-,shäkt\ *adj* **1** : affected with shell shock **2** : mentally confused, upset, or exhausted as the result of being under too much stress

shelly \'shel-ē\ *adj* **shell·i·er; -est** **1** : full of or covered with shells and especially seashells ⟨a *shelly* beach⟩ **2** : consisting of a shell or shells ⟨the hermit crab in its *shelly* home⟩

¹**shel·ter** \'shel-tər\ *n* **1** : something that covers or protects ⟨an air raid *shelter*⟩ ⟨fallout *shelter*⟩ **2** : the state of being protected ⟨take *shelter* from a storm⟩

²**shelter** *vb* **shel·tered; shel·ter·ing** \-t(ə-)riŋ\ **1** : to be a shelter for : provide with shelter **2** : to find and use a shelter

shelve \'shelv\ *vb* **shelved; shelv·ing** **1** : to place on a shelf ⟨*shelve* books⟩ **2** : to put off or aside : DEFER ⟨*shelve* a project⟩ — **shelv·er** *n*

shelv·ing \'shel-viŋ\ *n* : material to make shelves from; *also* : the shelves themselves

she·nan·i·gans \shə-'nan-i-gənz\ *n pl* : funny or mischievous activity

¹**shep·herd** \'shep-ərd\ *n* **1** : a person who takes care of sheep **2** : GERMAN SHEPHERD

²**shepherd** *vb* : to care for as or as if a shepherd

shep·herd·ess \'shep-ərd-əs\ *n* : a woman who takes care of sheep

shepherd's check *n* : a pattern of small black-and-white checks especially in a fabric

sher·bet \'shər-bət\ *n* : a frozen dessert of fruit juice to which milk, egg white, or gelatin is added before freezing

sher·iff \'sher-əf\ *n* : an official of a county who is in charge of enforcing the law [Middle English *shirreve* "sheriff", from Old English *scirgerēfa* "sheriff", from *scir* "shire, county" and *gerēfa* "a government agent"]

sher·pa \'she(ə)r-pə, 'shər-\ *n* : a member of a people living on the high southern slopes of the Himalayas who are skilled in mountain climbing

sher·ry \'sher-ē\ *n, pl* **sherries** : a wine with a nutty flavor

Word History It is common to name wines after the part of a country where they are made. The wine with a nutty taste called *sherry* today was first made in a town originally called, in Spanish, *Xeres*. The closest the English could come to the Spanish pronunciation was \'sher-ēz\. They spelled the word *sherris*. After a time, people thought that *sherris* was a plural and so made a singular form, *sherry,* by cutting off the supposed plural ending. The name of the Spanish town from which the wine came changed in spelling from *Xeres* to *Jerez,* so it no longer sounds very much like *sherris* or *sherry.* [named for *Xeres* (now spelled *Jerez*), a city in Spain where the wine was originally made]

she's \(,)shēz\ : she is : she has

Shet·land pony \,shet-lən(d)-\ *n* : any of a breed of small strong short-legged ponies developed in the Shetland islands

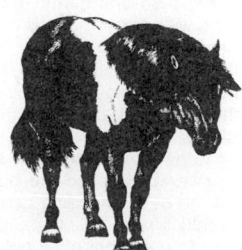

Shetland pony

\ə\ abut	\au̇\ out	\i\ tip	\ȯ\ saw	\u̇\ foot
\ər\ further	\ch\ chin	\ī\ life	\ȯi\ coin	\y\ yet
\a\ mat	\e\ pet	\j\ job	\th\ thin	\yü\ few
\ā\ take	\ē\ easy	\ŋ\ sing	\th\ this	\yu̇\ cure
\ä\ cot, cart	\g\ go	\ō\ bone	\ü\ food	\zh\ vision

Shetland sheepdog n : any of a breed of small dogs that have a long thick coat and look like miniature collies

shib·bo·leth \'shib-ə-ləth also -ˌleth\ n **1 a** : a slogan especially of a party or group **b** : an idea or saying that is commonly believed **2** : some behavior or use of language that identifies a person as belonging to a group

shied past and past participle of SHY

¹shield \'shē(ə)ld\ n **1** : a broad piece of armor carried on the arm to protect oneself in battle **2** : something that serves as a defense or protection **3** : the ancient mass of hard rock that forms the core of a continent

²shield vb : to cover or screen with or as if with a shield

shield volcano n : a broad rounded volcano that is built up from many layers of lava

shier comparative of SHY

shies pl of SHY

shiest superlative of SHY

¹shift \'shift\ vb **1** : to exchange for another of the same kind **2 a** : to change the place, position, or direction of **b** : to make a change in place, position, or direction **c** : to change the gear rotating the transmission shaft of an automobile **3** : to get along without help : FEND ⟨left the others to shift for themselves⟩

²shift n **1** : a means or device for getting something done **2** : the act of shifting **3** : a group of workers who work together during a scheduled period of time; also : the period of time during which they work **4** : GEARSHIFT

shift key n : a key on a keyboard (as of a typewriter) that when pressed allows a different set of characters to be printed

shift·less \'shif(t)-ləs\ adj : lacking in ambition and energy : LAZY — **shift·less·ly** adv — **shift·less·ness** n

shifty \'shif-tē\ adj **shift·i·er; -est** **1** : not worthy of trust : TRICKY **2** : indicating a tricky character ⟨shifty eyes⟩ ⟨a shifty expression⟩ — **shift·i·ly** \-tə-lē\ adv — **shift·i·ness** \-tē-nəs\ n

shil·le·lagh \shə-'lā-lē\ n : a club used as a weapon or to punish someone : CUDGEL [named for Shillelagh, a town in Ireland noted for its oak trees]

shil·ling \'shil-iŋ\ n **1** : a former unit of British money equal to ¹⁄₂₀ pound **2** : a coin equal to ¹⁄₂₀ pound in any of several countries of the Commonwealth **3** : any of several early American coins **4 a** : the basic unit of money of Kenya, Somalia, Tanzania, and Uganda **b** : a coin representing this unit

shilly–shally \'shil-ē-ˌshal-ē\ vb **shilly–shal·lied; shilly–shal·ly·ing** : to be unable to make up one's mind : show hesitation

shim·mer \'shim-ər\ vb **shim·mered; shim·mer·ing** \-(ə-)riŋ\ : to shine with a wavering light : GLIMMER — **shimmer** n

¹shin \'shin\ n : the front part of the leg below the knee

²shin vb **shinned; shin·ning** : to climb (as a pole) by grasping with arms and legs and moving oneself up by repeated jerks

shin·bone \'shin-ˌbōn, -ˌbōn\ n : TIBIA 1

shin·dig \'shin-ˌdig\ n : a big fancy party

shin·dy \'shin-dē\ n, pl **shindies** : ⁴ROW

¹shine \'shīn\ vb **shone** \'shōn\ or **shined; shin·ing** **1** : to give light ⟨the stars shone brightly⟩ **2** : to be glossy : GLEAM ⟨polished the buttons until they shone like gold⟩ **3** : to be outstanding : show talent ⟨on stage where I could really shine⟩ **4** : to cause to give light ⟨shine a flashlight⟩ **5** : to make bright by polishing ⟨shined my shoes⟩

²shine n **1** : brightness from light given off or reflected **2** : fair weather : SUNSHINE ⟨rain or shine⟩ **3** : LIKING, FANCY ⟨took a shine to them⟩ **4** : a polish given to shoes

shin·er \'shī-nər\ n **1** : one that shines **2** : a silvery fish; esp : any of numerous small freshwater American fishes related to the carp **3** : an eye discolored by injury : BLACK EYE

¹shin·gle \'shiŋ-gəl\ n **1** : a small thin piece of building material for laying in overlapping rows as a covering for the roof or sides of a building **2** : a small sign **3** : a woman's short haircut — **shin·gle·like** \-ˌlīk\ adj

²shingle vb **shin·gled; shin·gling** \-g(ə-)liŋ\ **1** : to cover with or as if with shingles **2** : to cut and shape the hair in a shingle

shin·ing \'shī-niŋ\ adj **1** : giving forth or reflecting a steady light : GLOWING **2** : OUTSTANDING 2 ⟨a shining example⟩ **syn** see BRIGHT — **shin·ing·ly** adv

shin·ny \'shin-ē\ vb **shin·nied; shin·ny·ing** : ²SHIN

Shin·to \'shin-tō\ n : a religion native to Japan

shiny \'shī-nē\ adj **shin·i·er; -est** : bright in appearance

¹ship \'ship\ n **1** : a large seagoing boat **2** : a ship's crew **3** : AIRSHIP, AIRPLANE, SPACECRAFT

²ship vb **shipped; ship·ping** **1 a** : to place or receive on board a ship for transportation by water **b** : to cause to be transported **2** : to take into a ship or boat ⟨ship oars⟩ **3** : to sign on as a crew member of a ship **4** : to take in (as water) over the side

-ship \ˌship\ n suffix **1** : state : condition : quality ⟨friendship⟩ ⟨apprenticeship⟩ **2** : position : office : duties ⟨professorship⟩ **3** : art : skill : activity ⟨horsemanship⟩ ⟨penmanship⟩ **4** : one having or entitled to be called by a (specified) title ⟨his Lordship⟩ ⟨her Ladyship⟩ **5** : the whole body of persons included in a class ⟨a large readership⟩ [Old English -scipe "condition, something having a certain quality"]

ship·board \'ship-ˌbō(ə)rd, -ˌbȯ(ə)rd\ n **1** : the side of a ship **2** : ¹SHIP 1 ⟨met on shipboard⟩

ship·build·er \-ˌbil-dər\ n : one who designs or builds ships — **ship·build·ing** \-diŋ\ n

ship·load \-'lōd, -ˌlōd\ n : as much or as many as a ship will hold ⟨a shipload of corn⟩ ⟨shiploads of settlers⟩

ship·mate \-ˌmāt\ n : a fellow sailor

ship·ment \'ship-mənt\ n **1** : the act of shipping **2** : the goods shipped

ship·pa·ble \'ship-ə-bəl\ adj : suitable for shipping

ship·per \'ship-ər\ n : one who ships goods

ship·ping \'ship-iŋ\ n **1** : the body of ships in one place or belonging to one port or country **2** : the act or business a person who ships goods

ship·shape \'ship-'shāp\ adj : being neat and orderly : TIDY

ship·worm \-ˌwərm\ n : any of various marine clams that have long bodies and specialized shells, look like worms, burrow in underwater wood, and often damage wooden ships and wharves — called also teredo

¹ship·wreck \-ˌrek\ n **1** : a wrecked ship **2** : the destruction or loss of a ship

²shipwreck vb **1** : to cause to experience shipwreck **2** : to destroy a ship by driving ashore or sinking

ship·yard \'ship-ˌyärd\ n : a place where ships are built or repaired

shire \'shī(ə)r, in place-name compounds ˌshi(ə)r, shər\ n **1** : a territorial division of England usually identical with a present or old county **2** : any of a British breed of tall draft horses

shirk \'shərk\ vb **1** : to get out of doing what one ought to do **2** : AVOID 2 ⟨had shirked telling them the bad news⟩ — **shirk·er** n

shire 2

shirr \'shər\ vb **1** : to draw cloth together in a shirring **2** : to cook eggs removed from the shell by baking

shirr·ing \'shər-iŋ\ n : a decorative gathering (as of cloth) made by drawing up the material along two or more parallel lines of stitching

shirt \'shərt\ n **1** : a garment for the upper part of the body usually with a collar, sleeves, a front opening, and a tail long enough to be tucked inside pants or a skirt **2** : UN-DERSHIRT

shirt·sleeve \-,slēv\ *n* : the sleeve of a shirt — **in shirt-sleeves** : wearing a shirt but no coat

shirt·tail \-,tāl\ *n* : the part of a shirt that reaches below the waist especially in the back

shirt·waist \-,wāst\ *n* : a woman's tailored garment (as a dress or blouse) with details copied from men's shirts

shirty \'shərt-ē\ *adj, chiefly British* : being annoyed : AN-GRY

shish ke·bab \'shish-kə-,bäb\ *n* : cubes of meat (as lamb) cooked on skewers

¹shiv·er \'shiv-ər\ *n* : one of the small pieces into which a brittle thing is broken by sudden violence [Middle English *shiver* "a small piece of something that is broken"]

²shiver *vb* **shiv·ered; shiv·er·ing** \'shiv-(ə-)riŋ\ : to break into many small pieces : SHATTER

³shiver *vb* **shiv·ered; shiv·er·ing** \'shiv-(ə-)riŋ\ : to be made to shake (as by cold or fear) [Middle English *shiveren,* an altered form of *chiveren* "to tremble, shiver"]

⁴shiver *n* **1** : an instance of shivering **2** : a thrill of emotion and especially of fear — usually used in pl. ⟨a ghost story that would give you the *shivers*⟩ ⟨it sent *shivers* up my spine⟩

shiv·ery \'shiv-(ə-)rē\ *adj* **1** : marked by shivers **2** : causing shivers

¹shoal \'shōl\ *adj* : ¹SHALLOW 1 ⟨*shoal* water⟩ [Old English *sceald* "shallow"]

²shoal *n* **1** : a place where a sea, lake, or river is shallow **2** : a sandbank or sandbar just below the surface of the water

³shoal *n* : ³SCHOOL ⟨a *shoal* of pilot fish⟩ [Old English *scolu* "great number"]

shoat \'shōt\ *n* : a young hog usually less than one year old

¹shock \'shäk\ *n* : a bunch of sheaves of grain or stalks of corn set on end in a field [Middle English *shock* "bunch of stalks"]

²shock *n* **1** : the sudden violent collision of bodies in a fight ⟨the *shock* of battle⟩ **2** : a violent shake or jerk ⟨an earthquake *shock*⟩ **3** : a sudden or violent disturbance of the mind or feelings **4** : a state of bodily collapse that is often marked by a drop in blood pressure and volume and that is usually caused by a severe injury, burn, or hemorrhage **5** : the effect of a strong charge of electricity passing through the body of a person or animal [from early French *choc* "a violent collision, shock", from earlier *choquer* (verb) "to strike against", from earlier *choquier* (same meaning); of Germanic origin]

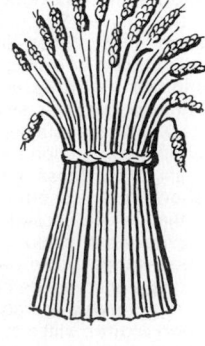
¹shock

³shock *vb* **1** : to strike with surprise, horror, or disgust ⟨were *shocked* by the way the law was broken⟩ **2** : to affect by electrical shock **3** : to drive into or out of by or as if by a shock ⟨*shocked* the public into action⟩ — **shock·er** *n*

⁴shock *n* : a thick bushy mass ⟨a *shock* of hair⟩ [from earlier *shock* (adjective) "bushy", probably derived from *shock* (noun) "a bunch of stalks" because of the similarity of the appearance of bushy hair to a bunch of stalks of grain]

shock absorber *n* : a device for absorbing the energy of sudden shocks in machinery or structures

shock·ing *adj* : causing horror or disgust ⟨a *shocking* crime⟩ ⟨*shocking* behavior⟩ — **shock·ing·ly** \-iŋ-lē\ *adv*

shock wave *n* : a wave formed by the sudden compression (as by an earthquake or supersonic aircraft) of the substance through which the wave travels

shod·dy \'shäd-ē\ *adj* **shod·di·er; -est** : poorly done or made — **shod·di·ly** \'shäd-°l-ē\ *adv* — **shod·di·ness** \'shäd-ē-nəs\ *n*

¹shoe \'shü\ *n* **1 a** : an outer covering for the human foot usually having a thick and somewhat stiff sole and heel and a lighter upper part **b** : HORSESHOE 1 **2** *pl* : another's place or point of view ⟨suppose you were in your friend's *shoes*⟩ **3** : the part of a brake that presses on the wheel of a vehicle

²shoe *vb* **shod** \'shäd\ *also* **shoed** \'shüd\; **shoe·ing** \'shü-iŋ\ : to put a shoe on : furnish with shoes

shoe·box \'shü-,bäks\ *n* : a paperboard box designed to hold a pair of shoes for retail sale

shoe·horn \-,hȯrn\ *n* : a curved piece (as of metal) to help in putting on a shoe

shoe·lace \-,lās\ *n* : a lace or string for fastening a shoe

shoe·mak·er \-,mā-kər\ *n* : a person who makes or repairs shoes

shoe·string \-,striŋ\ *n* **1** : SHOELACE **2** : a small sum of money ⟨start a business on a *shoestring*⟩

shoe tree *n* : a foot-shaped device that can be put into a shoe to preserve its shape

sho·gun \'shō-gən\ *n* : any of a line of military governors ruling Japan until the revolution of 1867–68

shone *past and past participle of* SHINE

shoo \'shü\ *vb* : to scare, drive, or send away by or as if by crying shoo

shoo·fly pie \'shü-,flī-\ *n* : a pie made of molasses or brown sugar with a crumbly topping

shook *past of* SHAKE

¹shoot \'shüt\ *vb* **shot** \'shät\; **shoot·ing** **1 a** : to let fly or cause to be driven forward with force ⟨*shoot* an arrow⟩ **b** : to cause a missile to be driven out of ⟨*shoot* a gun⟩ **c** : to cause a weapon to discharge a missile ⟨*shoot* at a target⟩ **2 a** : to send (a marble) forward by snapping the thumb **b** : to hit or throw (as a ball or puck) toward a goal **c** : to score by shooting ⟨*shoot* a basket⟩ **d** : ²PLAY 5a ⟨*shoot* a round of golf⟩ ⟨*shoot* craps⟩ **3** : to strike with a missile from a bow or gun ⟨*shot* a deer⟩ **4** : to push or slide into or out of a fastening ⟨*shot* the door bolt⟩ **5 a** : to push or thrust forward swiftly ⟨lizards *shooting* out their tongues⟩ **b** : to grow rapidly ⟨the corn is *shooting* up⟩ **6 a** : to go, move, or pass rapidly ⟨they *shot* past on skis⟩ **b** : to pass swiftly along ⟨*shoot* the rapids in a canoe⟩ **c** : to stream out suddenly : SPURT **7** : to take the altitude of ⟨*shoot* the sun with a sextant⟩ **8** : to take a picture or series of pictures or television images of — **shoot·er** *n* — **shoot at** *or* **shoot for** : to try to accomplish : strive for — **shoot the breeze** : ¹TALK 5a, CHAT — **shoot the works** : to put forth all one's efforts

²shoot *n* **1** : a sending out of new growth or the new growth sent out: as **a** : a plant stem with its leaves and branches especially when not yet mature **b** : OFFSHOOT 1 **2 a** : an act of shooting **b** : a hunting trip or party **c** : a shooting match

shooting star *n* : a meteor appearing as a temporary streak of light in the night sky

shoot·out \'shüt-,aut\ *n* : a battle fought with handguns or rifles

¹shop \'shäp\ *n* **1** : a worker's place of business **2** : a building or room where goods are sold retail **3** : a place where workers are doing a particular kind of work especially with machinery : FACTORY **4** : a school laboratory equipped for manual training ⟨metal *shop*⟩ **5** : SHOPTALK

²shop *vb* **shopped; shop·ping** : to visit shops for the purpose of looking over and buying goods; *also* : to look for

\ə\	abut	\au̇\	out	\i\	tip	\ȯ\	saw	\u̇\	foot
\ər\	further	\ch\	chin	\ī\	life	\ȯi\	coin	\y\	yet
\a\	mat	\e\	pet	\j\	job	\th\	thin	\yü\	few
\ā\	take	\ē\	easy	\ŋ\	sing	\th\	this	\yu̇\	cure
\ä\	cot, cart	\g\	go	\ō\	bone	\ü\	food	\zh\	vision

the best buy — **shop·per** *n*

shop·keep·er \'shäp-,kē-pər\ *n* : STOREKEEPER 2

shop·lift \-,lift\ *vb* : to steal merchandise on display in stores

shop·lift·er \-,lif-tər\ *n* : a thief who steals merchandise on display in stores

shoppe \'shäp\ *n* : ¹SHOP 2

shopping center *n* : a group of retail stores located in a suburban area and having a large parking lot

shopping mall *n* : a shopping center in which the stores face an enclosed pedestrian mall

shop·talk \'shäp-,tȯk\ *n* : talk about or related to one's work or special interests

shop·worn \-,wō(ə)rn, -,wȯ(ə)rn\ *adj* : faded or soiled from being too long in a store

¹**shore** \'shō(ə)r, 'shȯ(ə)r\ *n* : the land along the edge of a body of water (as the sea) [Middle English *shore* "the land on the edge of a body of water"]

²**shore** *vb* **shored; shor·ing** : to support with one or more bracing timbers [Middle English *shoren* "to support, brace"]

³**shore** *n* : a prop or support placed under or against something to support it

shore·bird \'shō(ə)r-,bərd, 'shȯ(ə)r-\ *n* : any of a group of birds that frequent the seashore

shore·line \-,līn\ *n* : the line where a body of water touches the shore

shore patrol *n* : a branch of a navy with guard and police functions

shore·ward \'shō(ə)r-wərd, 'shȯ(ə)r-\ *or* **shore·wards** \-wərdz\ *adv* : toward the shore

³shore

shor·ing \'shōr-iŋ, 'shȯr-\ *n* : a group of things that shore something up

shorn *past participle of* SHEAR

¹**short** \'shȯ(ə)rt\ *adj* **1** : having little length or height : not long or tall **2 a** : not long in time : BRIEF ⟨a *short* delay⟩ **b** : not great in distance ⟨a *short* walk⟩ **3** : not remembering for long ⟨a *short* memory⟩ **4** : of, relating to, or being one of the vowel sounds \ə, a, e, i, ů\ and sometimes \ä\ and \ȯ\ **5 a** : not coming up to the regular standard or to what is needed ⟨gave *short* measure⟩ ⟨in *short* supply⟩ **b** : not reaching far enough ⟨the throw was *short*⟩ **c** : not having enough ⟨*short* of cash⟩ ⟨*short* on brains⟩ **6** : easily upset ⟨has a *short* temper⟩ **7** : FLAKY 2, CRUMBLY **8** : cut down to a brief length ⟨a *short* tax form⟩ ⟨"doc" is *short* for "doctor"⟩ — **short·ish** \-ish\ *adj* — **in short order** : with speed and promptness

²**short** *adv* **1** : with suddenness ⟨stopped *short*⟩ **2** : so as not to reach as far as expected ⟨fell *short* of the mark⟩

³**short** *n* **1** : something that is shorter than the usual or regular length **2** *pl* **a** : pants that reach to the knees or above the knees **b** : short underpants **3** : SHORT CIRCUIT — **for short** : as an abbreviation ⟨named Katherine or Kate *for short*⟩ — **in short** : as a brief summary

⁴**short** *vb* : SHORT-CIRCUIT

short·age \'shȯrt-ij\ *n* : a lack in the amount needed : DEFICIT ⟨a *shortage* of cash⟩ ⟨a gasoline *shortage*⟩

short·bread \'shȯrt-,bred\ *n* : a cookie made of flour, sugar, and lots of shortening

short·cake \-,kāk\ *n* : a dessert made of rich biscuit dough baked and served with sweetened fruit ⟨strawberry *shortcake*⟩

short·change \-'chānj\ *vb* **1** : to give less than the correct amount of change to **2** : to give less than expected : CHEAT

short–cir·cuit \-'sər-kət\ *vb* : to make a short circuit in or

have a short circuit

short circuit *n* : an electrical connection made between points in an electric circuit between which current does not normally flow

short·com·ing \'shȯrt-,kəm-iŋ, (')shȯrt-'kəm-\ *n* : ¹FAULT 1a

¹**short·cut** \'shȯrt-,kət, -'kət\ *n* : a shorter, quicker, or easier way

²**shortcut** *vb* **-cut; -cut·ting** : to take or use a shortcut

short division *n* : mathematical division in which the steps are performed one after another without writing out the remainders

short·en \'shȯrt-ⁿn\ *vb* **short·ened; short·en·ing** \'shȯrt-niŋ, -ⁿn-iŋ\ **1** : to make or become short or shorter **2** : to add shortening to (as pastry) — **short·en·er** \-nər, -ⁿn-ər\ *n*

short·en·ing \'shȯrt-niŋ, -ⁿn-iŋ\ *n* **1** : a making or becoming short or shorter **2** : a fat (as butter or lard) used in baking especially to make pastry flaky

short·hand \'shȯrt-,hand\ *n* **1** : a method of rapid writing by using symbols for sounds, words, or phrases **2** : a short or quick way of showing or saying something — **shorthand** *adj*

short·hand·ed \-'han-dəd\ *adj* : having or working with fewer than the usual number of people

short–haul \-,hȯl\ *adj* : traveling or involving a short distance ⟨*short-haul* flights⟩

short·horn \-,hȯ(ə)rn\ *n* : any of a breed of red, roan, or white beef and dairy cattle that have short horns and were originally developed in England

short–horned grasshopper \,shȯrt-,hȯrn(d)-\ *n* : any of a family of grasshoppers with short antennae

short hundredweight *n* : HUNDREDWEIGHT 1

shorthorn

short–lived \'shȯrt-'līvd, -'livd\ *adj* : living or lasting only a short time

short·ly \'shȯrt-lē\ *adv* **1** : in a few words : BRIEFLY **2** : in or within a short time : SOON ⟨will arrive *shortly*⟩ ⟨*shortly* after sunset⟩

short·ness \'shȯrt-nəs\ *n* : the quality or state of being short ⟨*shortness* of breath⟩

short–order \,shȯrt-,ȯrd-ər\ *adj* : preparing or serving food that can be cooked quickly when a customer orders it ⟨a *short-order* cook⟩

short–range \-'rānj\ *adj* : involving or taking into account only a short period of time ⟨*short-range* weather forecasting⟩ ⟨*short-range* goals⟩

short shrift *n* : little or no attention or consideration

short·sight·ed \'shȯrt-'sīt-əd\ *adj* **1** : NEARSIGHTED, MYOPIC **2** : showing a failure to think ahead : lacking foresight — **short·sight·ed·ly** *adv* — **short·sight·ed·ness** *n*

short·stop \'shȯrt-,stäp\ *n* : the baseball infielder whose position is between second and third base

short story *n* : a short work of fiction usually dealing with a few characters and a single event

short–tem·pered \'shȯrt-'tem-pərd\ *adj* : easily angered

short–term \-'tərm\ *adj* : SHORT-RANGE ⟨*short-term* goals⟩

short ton *n* — see MEASURE table

short–wave \'shȯrt-'wāv\ *n* : a radio wave with a wavelength between 10 and 100 meters

Sho·shone \shə-'shōn(-ē), 'shō-,shōn\ *or* **Sho·sho·ni** \shə-'shō-nē\ *n, pl* **Shoshones** *or* **Shoshoni** : a member of a group of American Indian peoples of California, Colorado, Idaho, Nevada, Utah, and Wyoming

¹**shot** \'shät\ *n* **1 a** : an action of shooting **b** : an aimed discharge of a gun or cannon **c** : a stroke or throw in a game; *esp* : an attempt at scoring **d** : an injection of

something (as a medicine or vaccine) into the body ⟨penicillin *shots*⟩ **2 a** *pl* **shot** : something sent by shooting; *esp* : small lead or steel pellets forming a charge for a shotgun **b** : a heavy metal ball thrown for distance in the shot put **3** : the flight of a missile or the distance it travels : RANGE ⟨within rifle *shot*⟩ **4** : a person who shoots ⟨a good *shot*⟩ **5** : ²ATTEMPT 1, TRY ⟨take another *shot* at the puzzle⟩ **6 a** : ¹PHOTOGRAPH **b** : a single portion of a movie or a television program shot by one camera without stopping **7 a** : a small measure or amount of alcoholic liquor **b** : a small amount applied at one time : DOSE

²shot *past and past participle of* SHOOT

³shot *adj* **1** : marked or streaked with a different color ⟨blue *shot* with silver⟩ ⟨hair *shot* with gray⟩ **2** : brought to a state of ruin or uselessness ⟨my nerves were *shot*⟩ ⟨the tires are *shot*⟩

shot·gun \'shät-,gən\ *n* : a firearm used to fire small shot at short range

shot put *n* : a track-and-field event in which a heavy metal ball is heaved for distance — **shotput·ter** \-,pùt-ər\ *n*

should \shəd, (')shùd\ *past of* SHALL **1** : ought to ⟨you *should* study harder⟩ ⟨they *should* be here soon⟩ **2** : happen to ⟨if you *should* see them, say hello for me⟩ **3** — used as a more polite or less assured form of *shall* ⟨*should* I turn out the lights?⟩

¹shoul·der \'shōl-dər\ *n* **1** : the part of the body of a person or animal where the arm or foreleg joins the body **2** : a cut of meat including the upper joint of the foreleg and attached parts **3** : the part of a garment at the wearer's shoulder **4** : a part that resembles a person's shoulder ⟨*shoulder* of a hill⟩ **5** : the edge of a road

shot put

²shoulder *vb* **shoul·dered; shoul·der·ing** \-d(ə-)riŋ\ **1** : to push with one's shoulder **2** : to accept as one's burden or responsibility ⟨*shoulder* the blame⟩

shoulder blade *n* : the flat triangular bone of the back of the shoulder that forms a joint with the bone of the upper arm — called also *scapula*

shoulder strap *n* : a strap worn over the shoulder to hold up an article or a garment

should·est \'shùd-əst\ *archaic past 2d sing of* SHALL

shouldn't \'shùd-ᵊnt\ : should not

shouldst \shədst, (')shùdst\ *archaic past 2d sing of* SHALL

¹shout \'shaùt\ *vb* : to utter a sudden loud cry ⟨*shouted* with delight⟩ — **shout·er** *n*

    syn SHOUT, SHRIEK, SCREECH mean to utter a loud cry. SHOUT suggests any kind of loud cry that is meant to be heard either far away or above other noise ⟨we *shouted* to them across the street⟩ SHRIEK suggests a high-pitched, shrill cry that is a sign of strong feeling ⟨the children *shrieked* with excitement⟩ SCREECH suggests a drawn-out shriek that is usually without words and is very harsh and unpleasant ⟨the cats fought and *screeched*⟩

²shout *n* : a sudden loud cry

¹shove \'shəv\ *vb* **shoved; shov·ing** **1** : to push with steady force **2** : to push along or away carelessly or rudely ⟨*shove* a person out of the way⟩ **3** : ¹LEAVE 7 ⟨time to *shove* off for home⟩ — **shov·er** *n*

²shove *n* : an act or instance of shoving

¹shov·el \'shəv-əl\ *n* **1** : a broad scoop with a long handle used for lifting and throwing loose material (as snow) **2** : SHOVELFUL

²shovel *vb* **-eled** *or* **-elled; -el·ing** *or* **-el·ling** \'shəv-(ə-)liŋ\

1 : to lift and throw with a shovel **2** : to dig or clean out with a shovel **3** : to throw or carry roughly or in a mass as if with a shovel ⟨*shoveling* the food into your mouth⟩

shov·el·er *or* **shov·el·ler** \'shəv-(ə-)lər\ *n* **1** : one that shovels **2** : any of several ducks having a large and very broad bill

shov·el·ful \'shəv-əl-,fùl\ *n, pl* **shovelfuls** \-,fùlz\ *also* **shov·els·ful** \-əlz-,fùl\ : as much as a shovel will hold

¹show \'shō\ *vb* **showed; shown** \'shōn\ *or* **showed; show·ing** **1** : to place in sight : present so as to be seen **2** : REVEAL 2 ⟨*showed* strong feeling⟩ **3** : to give from or as if from a position of authority ⟨we'll *show* them no mercy⟩ **4** : TEACH 1, INSTRUCT ⟨*showed* me a few chords on the guitar⟩ **5** : PROVE 2a ⟨that *shows* we're right⟩ **6** : to point out the way for : USHER, GUIDE ⟨*showed* them to a seat⟩ **7** : to be noticeable ⟨the patch hardly *shows*⟩ ⟨the determination *showed* in her face⟩ **8** : to be third or at least third (as in a horse race)

    syn SHOW, EXHIBIT, DISPLAY, PARADE mean to present something in a way that will draw attention. SHOW suggests letting another see or examine ⟨*show* me a picture of your family⟩ EXHIBIT suggests putting something out in public ⟨the children *exhibited* their drawings at the fair⟩ DISPLAY stresses putting something out in the open where others may see it clearly ⟨*display* sale items in front of the store⟩ PARADE suggests making a great show of something ⟨look at them *parading* their new bikes⟩

²show *n* **1** : a display made for effect ⟨a *show* of strength⟩ **2 a** : a false outward appearance ⟨made a *show* of friendship⟩ **b** : a true indication : SIGN ⟨a *show* of reason⟩ **3** : a ridiculous spectacle **4** : an entertainment or exhibition especially by performers (as on TV or the stage) **5** : third place at the finish (as of a horse race)

show biz \-,biz\ *n* : SHOW BUSINESS

show·boat \'shō-,bōt\ *n* : a river steamboat used as a traveling theater

show business *n* : the arts, occupations, and companies that make up the entertainment industry

show·case \-,kās\ *n* : a protective glass case in which things are displayed

show·down \-,daùn\ *n* : the test of strength that finally settles a dispute

¹show·er \'shaù(-ə)r\ *n* **1 a** : a short fall of rain over a small area **b** : a like fall of sleet, hail, or snow **2** : something resembling a shower ⟨a *shower* of sparks⟩ ⟨a *shower* of tears⟩ **3** : a party where gifts are given especially to a bride or pregnant woman **4** : a bath in which water is sprayed on a person; *also* : a device for providing such a bath

²shower *vb* **1** : to rain or fall in or as if in a shower **2** : to bathe in a shower **3** : to wet with fine spray or drops **4** : to provide in great quantity ⟨*showered* them with attention⟩

show·man \'shō-mən\ *n* **1** : the producer of a theatrical show **2** : a person having a special skill for presenting something in a dramatic way — **show·man·ship** \-,ship\ *n*

show–off \'shō-,óf\ *n* **1** : the act of showing off **2** : a person who shows off

show off \(')shō-'óf\ *vb* **1** : to display proudly **2** : to try to attract attention by conspicuous behavior

show·piece \'shō-,pēs\ *n* : a very fine example used for exhibition

show·place \-,plās\ *n* : a place (as an estate or building) that is regarded as a very fine example

show·room \-,rüm, -,rùm\ *n* : a room where merchandise

\ə\ abut	\aù\ out	\i\ tip	\ó\ saw	\ù\ foot
\ər\ further	\ch\ chin	\ī\ life	\oi\ coin	\y\ yet
\a\ mat	\e\ pet	\j\ job	\th\ thin	\yü\ few
\ā\ take	\ē\ easy	\ŋ\ sing	\th\ this	\yù\ cure
\ä\ cot, cart	\g\ go	\ō\ bone	\ü\ food	\zh\ vision

is displayed for sale

show up *vb* **1** : to reveal the true nature of : EXPOSE ⟨were *shown up* for what they really are⟩ **2** : to be where one is expected to be : ARRIVE ⟨*showed up* an hour late⟩

showy \'shō-ē\ *adj* **show·i·er; -est** **1** : attracting attention : STRIKING ⟨*showy* blossoms⟩ **2** : given to or being too much outward display : GAUDY — **show·i·ly** \'shō-ə-lē\ *adv* — **show·i·ness** \'shō-ē-nəs\ *n*

shrap·nel \'shrap-nᵊl\ *n, pl* **shrapnel** **1** : a shell designed to burst and scatter metal balls with which it is filled along with jagged fragments of the case **2** : metal pieces from an exploded bomb, shell, or mine

¹shred \'shred\ *n* **1 a** : a long narrow piece cut or torn off : SCRAP ⟨*shreds* of cloth⟩ **b** *pl* : a shredded, damaged, or ruined condition ⟨an air attack tore the village to *shreds*⟩ ⟨reputation was in *shreds*⟩ **2** : a small amount : BIT ⟨not a *shred* of evidence⟩

²shred *vb* **shred·ded; shred·ding** : to cut or tear into shreds ⟨*shred* paper⟩ ⟨*shred* cabbage⟩ — **shred·der** *n*

shrew \'shrü\ *n* **1** : any of numerous small mammals related to the moles that have a long pointed snout, very small eyes, and velvety fur **2** : a scolding or bad-tempered woman

shrew 1

shrewd \'shrüd\ *adj* : showing quick practical cleverness : ASTUTE ⟨a *shrewd* observer⟩ — **shrewd·ly** *adv* — **shrewd·ness** *n*

¹shriek \'shrēk\ *vb* **1** : to utter a sharp shrill cry **2** : to cry out in a high-pitched voice **syn** see SHOUT

²shriek *n* : a sharp shrill cry

shrift \'shrift\ *n, archaic* : the confession of sins to a priest or the hearing of a confession by a priest

¹shrill \'shril\ *vb* : to make a high sharp piercing sound : SCREAM

²shrill *adj* : having a sharp high sound ⟨a *shrill* whistle⟩ — **shrill** *adv* — **shrill·ness** *n* — **shril·ly** \'shril-lē\ *adv*

³shrill *n* : a shrill sound

¹shrimp \'shrimp\ *n, pl* **shrimp** *or* **shrimps** **1** : any of numerous small mostly marine shellfish that are crustaceans related to the lobsters and have a long slender body, an abdomen that is very thin from side to side, and long legs **2** : a very small or unimportant person or thing — **shrimp·like** \-ˌlīk\ *adj*

²shrimp *vb* : to fish for or catch shrimp

shrimp·er \'shrimp-ər\ *n* : a boat that goes out fishing for shrimp

shrine \'shrīn\ *n* **1** : a case or box for sacred relics (as the bones of a saint) **2** : the tomb of a holy person (as a saint) **3** : a place that is considered sacred ⟨visited the *shrines* of American independence⟩

shrink \'shrink\ *vb* **shrank** \'shrank\ *also* **shrunk** \'shrəŋk\; **shrunk** *or* **shrunk·en** \'shrən-kən\; **shrink·ing** **1** : to curl up or withdraw in or as if in fear or pain ⟨*shrink* in horror⟩ **2** : to make or become smaller ⟨the sweater *shrank* when it was washed⟩ ⟨meat *shrinks* in cooking⟩ — **shrink·er** *n*

shrink·age \'shrin-kij\ *n* : the amount by which something shrinks or becomes less

shrive \'shrīv\ *vb* **shrived** *or* **shrove** \'shrōv\; **shriv·en** \'shriv-ən\ *or* **shrived; shriv·ing** \'shrī-viŋ\ **1** : to hear the confession of and administer the sacrament of penance to : PARDON **2** *archaic* : to confess one's sins especially to a priest

shriv·el \'shriv-əl\ *vb* **-eled** *or* **-elled; -el·ing** *or* **-el·ling** \-(ə-)liŋ\ : to shrink and become dry and wrinkled

¹shroud \'shraúd\ *n* **1** : the cloth placed over or around a dead body **2** : something that covers or shelters like a shroud ⟨a *shroud* of secrecy⟩ **3** : one of the ropes that go from the masthead of a ship to the sides to provide support to the mast

²shroud *vb* : to cover with or as if with a shroud

Shrove·tide \'shrōv-ˌtīd\ *n* : the three days just before Ash Wednesday

Shrove Tuesday \'shrōv-\ *n* : the Tuesday before Ash Wednesday [Middle English *schroftewesday* "Shrove Tuesday", from *schrof*, from *shriven* "to shrive, give a penance or pardon to", and *tewesday* "Tuesday"; *shriven* from Old English *scrifan* "to shrive, prescribe", from Latin *scribere* "to write" — related to SCRIBE, TUESDAY; see *Word History* at TUESDAY]

1 shroud 3

shrub \'shrəb\ *n* : a woody plant that has several stems and is smaller than most trees

shrub·bery \'shrəb-(ə-)rē\ *n, pl* **-ber·ies** : a group of shrubs or an area where shrubs are grown

shrub·by \'shrəb-ē\ *adj* **shrub·bi·er; -est** **1** : consisting of or covered with shrubs **2** : resembling a shrub

shrug \'shrəg\ *vb* **shrugged; shrug·ging** : to draw or hunch up the shoulders usually to express doubt, uncertainty, or lack of interest — **shrug** *n*

shrug off *vb* **1** : to brush aside as not important **2** : to take off (a garment) by wriggling out

¹shuck \'shək\ *n* **1** : the outer covering of a nut or of Indian corn **2** : the shell of an oyster or clam

²shuck *vb* **1** : to remove the shucks of **2** : to throw aside — often used with *off*

¹shud·der \'shəd-ər\ *vb* **shud·dered; shud·der·ing** \-(ə-)riŋ\ **1** : to tremble with fear or horror or from cold ⟨*shuddered* just thinking about it⟩ **2** : ¹SHAKE 1, QUIVER ⟨the train slowed and *shuddered* to a halt⟩

²shudder *n* : an act of shuddering : SHIVER — **shud·dery** \-(ə-)rē\ *adj*

¹shuf·fle \'shəf-əl\ *vb* **shuf·fled; shuf·fling** \-(ə-)liŋ\ **1** : to mix in a disorderly mass **2** : to push out of sight **3 a** : to mix cards to change their order in the pack **b** : to move from place to place **4** : to move in a clumsy dragging way — **shuf·fler** \-(ə-)lər\ *n*

²shuffle *n* **1 a** : an act of shuffling **b** : a disorderly mass or pile **2** : a clumsy dragging walk

shuf·fle·board \'shəf-əl-ˌbō(ə)rd, -ˌbȯ(ə)rd\ *n* : a game in which players try to push disks into scoring areas of a diagram marked on a smooth surface

shul \'shúl\ *n* : SYNAGOGUE

shun \'shən\ *vb* **shunned; shun·ning** : to avoid purposely or by habit — **shun·ner** *n*

¹shunt \'shənt\ *vb* : to turn off to one side or out of the way : SHIFT; *esp* : to switch (as a train) from one track to another — **shunt·er** *n*

²shunt *n* : a method or device for turning or pushing aside; *esp* : a conductor joining two points in an electrical circuit so as to form a path through which a portion of the current may pass

shush \'shəsh, 'shùsh\ *vb* : to urge to be quiet — **shush** *n*

shut \'shət\ *vb* **shut; shut·ting** **1** : to close or become closed ⟨*shut* the door⟩ **2** : to close so as to forbid entrance or leaving ⟨*shut* the cottage for the winter⟩ **3** : to keep in a place by enclosing or by blocking the way out : IMPRISON ⟨*shut* them in jail⟩ **4** : to close by bringing parts together ⟨*shut* your eyes⟩ **5** : to stop or cause to stop operation ⟨*shut* both stores for a week⟩ ⟨the plant *shut* down⟩

shut·down \'shət-ˌdaún\ *n* : an ending of an activity

shute *variant of* CHUTE

shut–in \'shət-,in\ *n* : a sick person kept indoors

shut·off \'shət-,óf\ *n* **1** : something that shuts off **2** : an instance of shutting off : INTERRUPTION, STOPPAGE

shut off \,shət-'óf\ *vb* **1** : to stop the flow of ⟨*shut off* the water⟩ **2** : to stop the operation of ⟨*shut* the motor *off*⟩ **3** : to keep something away ⟨the mountains *shut off* the western winds⟩

shut·out \'shət-,aút\ *n* : a game in which one side fails to score

shut out \,shət-'aút\ *vb* **1** : to keep something out : EXCLUDE **2** : to keep an opponent from scoring in a game

¹shut·ter \'shət-ər\ **1** : a movable cover for a window that swings on hinges like a door **2** : a device in a camera that opens to expose the film when a picture is taken

²shutter *vb* : to close with or by shutters

shut·ter·bug \'shət-ər-,bəg\ *n* : a photography enthusiast

¹shut·tle \'shət-ᵊl\ *n* **1** : an instrument used in weaving to carry the thread back and forth from side to side through the threads that run lengthwise **2** : a vehicle that goes back and forth over a short route ⟨a *shuttle* bus⟩ ⟨a *shuttle* train⟩

²shuttle *vb* **shut·tled; shut·tling** \'shət-liŋ, -ᵊl-iŋ\ *n* : to move back and forth rapidly or often

shut·tle·cock \'shət-ᵊl-,käk\ *n* : a small and very light cone-shaped object that is used in playing badminton

shut up *vb* **1** : to cause a person to stop talking **2** : to stop writing or speaking

shuttlecock

¹shy \'shī\ *adj* **shi·er** *or* **shy·er** \'shī(-ə)r\; **shi·est** *or* **shy·est** \'shī-əst\ **1 a** : easily frightened : TIMID **b** : not feeling comfortable around people : not wanting or able to call attention to oneself **2** : having less than a full or an expected amount or number ⟨we were *shy* about ten dollars⟩ — **shy·ly** *adv* — **shy·ness** *n*

syn SHY, BASHFUL, DIFFIDENT mean feeling awkward around others. SHY suggests not wanting to meet or talk with people either by habit or for special reasons ⟨at the new school I was *shy* at first⟩ BASHFUL suggests being shy and afraid like a very young child ⟨they were *bashful* and would hide when company came⟩ DIFFIDENT suggests not putting oneself forward because of a lack of self-confidence ⟨in art class he was *diffident* about his work⟩

²shy *vb* **shied; shy·ing** **1** : to draw back in sudden dislike or distaste ⟨*shied* from publicity⟩ **2** : to move quickly to one side in fright ⟨the horse *shied*⟩

³shy *n, pl* **shies** : a sudden move to one side

shy·ster \'shī-stər\ *n* : a crooked lawyer or politician

si \'sē\ *n* : the seventh note of a scale : TI

¹Si·a·mese \,sī-ə-'mēz, -'mēs\ *adj* : of or relating to Thailand, the Thais, or their language

²Siamese *n, pl* **Siamese** **1** : THAI 1 **2** : THAI 2

Siamese cat *n* : a slender blue⸗eyed short-haired domestic cat that has a light-colored body and darker ears, paws, tail, and face

Siamese twin *n* : either of a pair of human or animal twins born joined together

Si·be·ri·an husky \sī-,bir-ē-ən-\ *n* : any of a breed of medium⸗sized dogs developed to pull sleds

¹sib·i·lant \'sib-ə-lənt\ *adj* : having or producing the sound of or

Siberian husky

a sound like the *s* or the *sh* in *sash*

²sibilant *n* : a sibilant speech sound (as English \s\, \z\, \sh\, \zh\, \ch (=tsh)\, or \j (=dzh)\)

sib·ling \'sib-liŋ\ *n* : one of two or more individuals having the same parents or sometimes only one parent in common

sick \'sik\ *adj* **1 a** : affected with disease or ill health **b** : of, relating to, or intended for use in sickness ⟨*sick* pay⟩ ⟨a *sick* ward⟩ **c** : affected with or accompanied by nausea **2 a** : badly upset by strong emotion (as shame or fear) **b** : tired of something from having too much of it ⟨*sick* of flattery⟩ **c** : filled with disgust ⟨such gossip makes me *sick*⟩ **3** : mentally or emotionally unsound or disturbed ⟨*sick* thoughts⟩

sick bay *n* : a place on a ship used as a hospital

sick·bed \'sik-,bed\ *n* : the bed on which a sick person lies

sick·en \'sik-ən\ *vb* **sick·ened; sick·en·ing** \-(ə-)niŋ\ : to make or become sick

sick·en·ing \'sik-(ə-)niŋ\ *adj* : causing sickness or disgust — **sick·en·ing·ly** *adv*

sick·ish \'sik-ish\ *adj* **1** : somewhat nauseated **2** : somewhat sickening ⟨a *sickish* odor⟩

¹sick·le \'sik-əl\ *n* : a tool with a sharp curved metal blade and a short handle used to cut grass

²sickle *vb* **sick·led; sick·ling** \'sik-(ə-)liŋ\ : to change into a sickle cell ⟨the ability of red blood cells to *sickle*⟩

sickle cell *n* : an abnormal red blood cell that is crescent⸗shaped

sickle–cell anemia *n* : a serious inherited disease in which many of the red blood cells become sickled and cannot carry oxygen properly and which occurs especially in blacks

sick·ly \'sik-lē\ *adj* **sick·li·er; -est** **1** : somewhat sick : often ailing ⟨was *sickly* as a child⟩ **2** : caused by or associated with ill health ⟨a *sickly* complexion⟩ **3 a** : appearing as if sick **b** : not growing well : SPINDLING ⟨a *sickly* plant⟩

sick·ness \'sik-nəs\ *n* **1** : ill health : ILLNESS **2** : a specific disease : MALADY **3** : NAUSEA 1

sick·room \'sik-,rüm, -,rum\ *n* : a room in which a sick person stays

¹side \'sīd\ *n* **1 a** : the right or left part of the trunk of the body **b** : the entire right or left half of the animal body ⟨a *side* of beef⟩ **2** : a place, space, or direction away from or beyond a central point or line ⟨set it to one *side*⟩ **3** : a surface or line forming a border or face of an object **4** : an outer part of a thing considered as facing in a certain direction ⟨the upper *side*⟩ **5 a** : a straight-line segment forming part of the boundary of a geometric figure ⟨*side* of a square⟩ **b** : one of the surfaces that form the boundary of a solid **c** : either surface of a thin object ⟨one *side* of a record⟩ **6** : a position or part of something viewed as opposite another ⟨my *side* of the story⟩ **7** : a body of contestants ⟨our *side* won⟩ **8** : a line of ancestors traced back from either parent — **on the side** **1** : in addition to the main portion ⟨an order of cole slaw *on the side*⟩ **2** : in addition to one's main occupation ⟨selling insurance *on the side*⟩

²side *adj* **1** : of, relating to, or located on the side ⟨*side* window⟩ **2** : going toward or coming from the side ⟨*side* wind⟩ **3** : being in addition to something more important : INCIDENTAL ⟨a *side* issue⟩

³side *vb* **sid·ed; sid·ing** **1** : to take the same side ⟨*sided* with our friend in the argument⟩ **2** : to put siding on ⟨*side* a house⟩

side·arm \'sīd-,ärm\ *adj* : done with the arm extending out

\ə\	abut	\aú\	**out**	\i\	tip	\ó\	**saw**	\ú\ **foot**
\ər\	further	\ch\	**chin**	\ī\	life	\ói\	**coin**	\y\ **yet**
\a\	mat	\e\	**pet**	\j\	**job**	\th\	**thin**	\yü\ **few**
\ā\	take	\ē\	**easy**	\ŋ\	**sing**	\t̲h̲\	**this**	\yu̇\ **cure**
\ä\	cot, cart	\g\	**go**	\ō\	**bone**	\ü\	**food**	\zh\ **vision**

to the side ⟨a *sidearm* pitch in baseball⟩ — **sidearm** *adv*

side arm *n* : a weapon (as a sword or revolver) worn at the side or in the belt

side·board \'sīd-,bō(ə)rd, -,bȯ(ə)rd\ *n* : a piece of furniture for holding dishes, silverware, and table linen

side·burns \'sīd-,bərnz\ *n pl* : hair growing on the side of the face in front of the ears

> **Word History** During the American Civil War, the Union general Ambrose Everett Burnside became known for the long bushy whiskers he wore on the sides of his face. Burnside was a popular figure in the city of Washington during the early days of the war. His unusual appearance caught the public eye, and other men soon began growing long whiskers like his. Such whiskers, which became the fashion throughout America, were originally called *burnsides* after the general. The modern word *sideburns* was formed by rearranging the letters of the older word *burnsides*. [an altered form of *burnsides* "long whiskers at the side of the face", named for Ambrose Everett *Burnside* 1824–1881 American general]

side by side *adv* : beside one another

side·car \'sīd-,kär\ *n* : a car attached to the side of a motorcycle for a passenger

sid·ed \'sīd-əd\ *adj* : having sides often of a stated number or kind ⟨glass-*sided*⟩ ⟨four-*sided* figures⟩

side dish *n* : food served separately along with the main course

side effect *n* : an often harmful and unwanted effect (as of a drug) that occurs along with the basic desired effect ⟨the harmful *side effects* on the environment of using DDT to kill insects⟩

side·kick \'sīd-,kik\ *n* : one who is another's pal, partner, or helper

side·light \-,līt\ *n* 1 : light from the side 2 : incidental or extra information

side·line \-,līn\ *n* 1 : a line marking the side of a playing field or court 2 : a business or job done in addition to one's regular occupation

¹side·long \'sīd-,lȯŋ\ *adv* : out of the corner of one's eye ⟨glanced *sidelong* at the food on the table⟩

²sidelong \,sīd-,lȯŋ\ *adj* 1 : made to one side or out of the corner of one's eye ⟨a *sidelong* glance⟩ 2 : INDIRECT 2

side·sad·dle \-,sad-ᵊl\ *n* : a saddle for women in which the rider sits with both legs on the same side of the horse — **sidesaddle** *adv*

side·show \-,shō\ *n* : a small show off to the side offered in addition to a main show (as of a circus)

side·slip \-,slip\ *vb* : to slide sideways — **sideslip** *n*

side·spin \-,spin\ *n* : motion that causes a ball to spin sideways

side–split·ting \-,split-iŋ\ *adj* : very funny

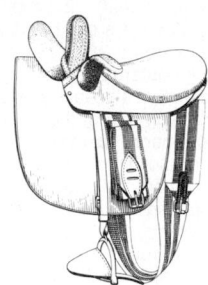

sidesaddle

side·step \-,step\ *vb* 1 : to take a step to the side 2 : to avoid by a step to the side 3 : to avoid answering or dealing with ⟨*sidestep* a question⟩

side·stroke \-,strōk\ *n* : a swimming stroke made while lying on the side by sweeping the arms downward and backward underwater while the legs do a scissors kick

¹side·swipe \-,swīp\ *vb* : to hit along the side with a blow that bounces off at an angle ⟨*sideswiped* a parked car⟩

²sideswipe *n* : an instance of sideswiping : a blow from an angle that bounces off

¹side·track \'sīd-,trak\ *n* : SIDING 1

²sidetrack *vb* 1 : to transfer from a main railroad line to a siding 2 : to turn aside from a main purpose or use

side·walk \'sīd-,wȯk\ *n* : a usually paved walk at the side of a street or road

side·wall \-,wȯl\ *n* 1 : a wall forming the side of something 2 : the side of an automotive tire between the tread shoulder and the rim

side·ward \'sīd-wərd\ *or* **side·wards** \-wərdz\ *adv or adj* : toward the side

side·ways \'sīd-,wāz\ *adv or adj* 1 : from one side 2 : with one side forward 3 : to one side

side·wind·er \-,wīn-dər\ *n* : a small rattlesnake of the southwestern U.S. that moves by thrusting its body diagonally forward in a series of flat S-shaped loops

sidewinder

side·wise \'sīd-,wīz\ *adv or adj* : SIDEWAYS

sid·ing \'sīd-iŋ\ *n* 1 : a short railroad track connected with the main track 2 : material used to cover the outside walls of frame buildings ⟨aluminum *siding*⟩ ⟨*siding* boards⟩

si·dle \'sīd-ᵊl\ *vb* **si·dled; si·dling** \'sīd-liŋ, -ᵊl-iŋ\ : to go or move with one side forward ⟨the waiter *sidled* around the end of the counter⟩

siege \'sēj\ *n* 1 : the placing of an army around a fortified place to capture it 2 : a continued attempt to get something 3 : a lasting attack (as of illness)

si·en·na \sē-'en-ə\ *n* : an artist's pigment that is either brownish yellow or reddish brown

si·er·ra \sē-'er-ə\ *n* : a range of mountains especially with jagged peaks [from Spanish *sierra* "a range of jagged mountains", literally "a saw", from Latin *serra* "a saw" — related to *serrated*]

si·es·ta \sē-'es-tə\ *n* : a nap or rest especially in the afternoon

> **Word History** In the ancient Roman way of keeping track of time, the hours of the day were counted from sunrise to sunset. The hour when the sun was most nearly directly overhead was their sixth hour, or *sexta hora* in Latin. Later on, the Spanish kept *sexta* as their name for noontime but spelled it *siesta*. In some countries, like Spain, it may be too hot to work in the middle of the day. There it is the custom to take a short nap until the heat begins to lessen. This rest period is called *siesta* in Spanish, and this word has come directly into English with the same meaning. [from Spanish *siesta* "an afternoon nap or rest period", from Latin *sexta (hora)* "sixth (hour), noon"; so called because the Romans counted the hours from sunrise]

¹sieve \'siv\ *n* : a device with meshes or holes to separate finer particles from coarser ones or solids from liquids

²sieve *vb* **sieved; siev·ing** : to put through a sieve : SIFT

sieve tube *n* : a tube that is composed of an end-to-end series of thin-walled living cells, transports food substances in plants, and is found in the phloem

sift \'sift\ *vb* 1 a : to put through a sieve ⟨*sift* flour⟩ b : to separate or separate out by or as if by putting through a sieve 2 : to test or examine closely ⟨*sift* evidence⟩ — **sift·er** *n*

sigh \'sī\ *vb* 1 : to take or let out a long loud breath often as an expression of sadness or weariness 2 : to make a sound like sighing ⟨wind *sighing* in the branches⟩ 3 : YEARN 1 ⟨*sighing* for the good old days⟩ — **sigh** *n*

¹sight \'sīt\ *n* 1 : something that is seen : SPECTACLE 2 a : something that is worth seeing ⟨showed us the *sights* of the city⟩ b : something that is peculiar, funny, or messy ⟨you're a *sight*⟩ 3 : the process, power, or function of seeing; *esp* : the animal sense of which the sense organ is the eye and by which the position, shape, and color of objects are perceived   **4** : the act of seeing   **5** : the presence of an object within the visual field ⟨can't stand the *sight* of it⟩   **6** : the distance a person can see ⟨a ship came into *sight*⟩   **7** : a device that aids the eye in aiming or in finding the direction of an object — **out of sight** : very good — **sight for sore eyes** : someone or something one is very glad to see

²**sight** *vb*   **1** : to get sight of   **2** : to look at through or as if through a sight

sight·ed \'sīt-əd\ *adj* : having sight

sight·less \'sīt-ləs\ *adj* : lacking sight : BLIND — **sight·less·ness** *n*

sight·ly \'sīt-lē\ *adj* : pleasant to look at — **sight·li·ness** *n*

sight–read \'sīt-,rēd\ *vb* **-read** \-,red\; **-read·ing** \-,rēd-iŋ\ : to read something written in a foreign language or play music without first practicing or studying it

sight·se·er \-,sē-ər, -,si(ə)r\ *n* : a person who goes about to see places and things of interest

sight–see·ing \-,sē-iŋ\ *adj* : engaged in, devoted to, or used for seeing things and places of interest ⟨a *sight-seeing* bus⟩ — **sight–seeing** *n*

sight unseen *adv* : without inspection or estimate of worth ⟨bought it *sight unseen*⟩

sig·ma \'sig-mə\ *n* : the 18th letter of the Greek alphabet — Σ or σ or ς

¹**sign** \'sīn\ *n*   **1 a** : a motion, action, or movement of the hand by which a thought is expressed or a command made known ⟨made a *sign* for them to be quiet⟩   **b** : ¹SIGNAL 1   **c** : SIGN LANGUAGE   **2** : a mark having a generally understood meaning and used in place of words   **3** : one of the 12 parts of the zodiac   **4 a** : a symbol (as a flat or sharp) used in musical notation   **b** : a symbol (as ÷ or √⎺) indicating a mathematical operation; *also* : one of two symbols + and − characterizing a number as positive or negative   **5** : a public notice that advertises something or gives information   **6 a** : something that indicates what is present or is to come ⟨no *sign* of life⟩ ⟨first *signs* of spring⟩   **b** : something that provides evidence of plant or animal disease — compare SYMPTOM 1 [Middle English *signe* "a gesture that conveys a thought or command", from early French *signe* (same meaning), from Latin *signum* "mark, sign, image" — related to DESIGNATE, ³SEAL, ¹SIGNAL, SIGNIFICANT]

²**sign** *vb*   **1 a** : to make or place a sign on   **b** : to represent or indicate by a sign   **2** : to write one's name on to show that one accepts, agrees with, or is responsible for ⟨*sign* a check⟩ ⟨*sign* a letter⟩ ⟨*sign* a contract⟩   **3** : to hire by getting to sign something (as a contract) ⟨*sign* a new ball player⟩ — **sign·er** *n*

¹**sig·nal** \'sig-nᵊl\ *n*   **1** : an act, event, or word that serves to start some action   **2** : a sound or motion of a part of the body made to give warning or command   **3** : an object placed to give notice or warning ⟨a traffic *signal*⟩   **4 a** : the message, sound, or effect transmitted in electronic communication (as radio or television)   **b** : a radio wave or electric current that transmits a message or effect (as in radio or television) [Middle English *signal* "signal, sign", from early French *signal* (same meaning), derived from Latin *signalis* "of a sign", from earlier *signum* "mark, sign, image" — related to SIGN]

²**signal** *vb* **-naled** *or* **-nalled; -nal·ing** *or* **-nal·ling** \-nə-liŋ\   **1** : to notify by a signal   **2** : to communicate by signals — **sig·nal·er** *n*

³**signal** *adj*   **1** : unusually great ⟨a *signal* honor⟩ ⟨a *signal* achievement⟩   **2** : used in signaling ⟨a *signal* light⟩ — **sig·nal·ly** \-nə-lē\ *adv*

sig·nal·ize \'sig-nə-,līz\ *vb* **-ized; -iz·ing** : to make well-known : point out clearly

sig·nal·man \'sig-nᵊl-mən, -,man\ *n* : a person who sends signals or works with signals

sig·na·ture \'sig-nə-,chú(ə)r, -chər\ *n*   **1** : the name of a

person written by that person   **2** : a notation used in music to indicate the key or the rhythm

sign·board \'sīn-,bō(ə)rd, -,bȯ(ə)rd\ *n* : a board with a notice or sign on it

sig·nif·i·cance \sig-'nif-i-kən(t)s\ *n*   **1** : ¹MEANING 1   **2** : the quality of being of notable worth or influence   **syn** see IMPORTANCE

sig·nif·i·cant \sig-'nif-i-kənt\ *adj*   **1** : having meaning and especially a hidden or special meaning ⟨gave us a *significant* wink⟩   **2** : having much importance   **3** : of, relating to, or being significant digits [from Latin *significant-, significans,* present participle of *significare* "to signify, indicate", from *signum* "mark, sign, image" — related to SIGN] — **sig·nif·i·cant·ly** *adv*

significant digit *n* : any of the figures of a number beginning with the first figure to the left that is not zero and ending with the last figure to the right that is not zero or is a zero that is considered to be exact — called also *significant figure*

sig·ni·fi·ca·tion \,sig-nə-fə-'kā-shən\ *n* : the meaning that a term or symbol has or is meant to have

sig·ni·fy \'sig-nə-,fī\ *vb* **-fied; -fy·ing**   **1** : ²MEAN 2, DENOTE   **2** : to show especially by a sign : make known ⟨*signified* their agreement by nodding⟩   **3** : to have importance

sign in *vb* : to make a record of one's arrival or presence ⟨use a password to *sign in* on the computer⟩

sign language *n* : a system of hand movements used for communication (as by the deaf)

sign off \(')sī-'nȯf\ *vb* : to announce the end (as of a program or broadcast)

sign of the cross : a movement of the hand forming a cross especially on forehead, shoulders, and breast to profess Christian faith or ask divine protection or blessing

sign on \(')sī-'nȯn, -'nän\ *vb*   **1** : to hire oneself by or as if by a signature ⟨*signed on* as a member of the crew⟩   **2** : to announce the beginning of broadcasting

sign·post \'sīn-,pōst\ *n*   **1** : a post with signs on it to direct travelers   **2** : something that points the way

sign up \(')sī-'nəp\ *vb* : to sign one's name in order to get, do, or take something ⟨*signed up* for Spanish⟩ — **sign–up** *n or adj*

Sikh \'sēk\ *n* : a believer in a religion of India that was founded about 1500 by a Hindu under Islamic influence and that believes in one God and rejects idols and caste — **Sikh·ism** \-,iz-əm\ *n*

si·lage \'sī-lij\ *n* : fodder fermented (as in a silo) to produce a rich moist feed for livestock

¹**si·lence** \'sī-lən(t)s\ *n*   **1** : the state of keeping or being silent   **2** : the state of there being no sound or noise : STILLNESS   **3** : a state of not mentioning

²**silence** *vb* **si·lenced; si·lenc·ing**   **1** : to stop the noise or speech of : cause to be silent   **2** : SUPPRESS 1

si·lenc·er \'sī-lən-sər\ *n*   **1** : one that silences   **2** : a device placed on the muzzle of a handgun to reduce the sound of firing

si·lent \'sī-lənt\ *adj*   **1** : not speaking ⟨stood *silent* before the court⟩   **2** : tending not to say much ⟨a very *silent* person⟩   **3** : free from sound or noise : STILL   **4** : done or felt without speaking ⟨*silent* prayer⟩ ⟨*silent* reading⟩   **5 a** : making no mention ⟨history is *silent* about this incident⟩   **b** : not active in running a business ⟨*silent* partner⟩   **6** : not pronounced ⟨*silent* "e" in "came"⟩ ⟨the "b" in "doubt" is *silent*⟩   **7** : made without recorded sound ⟨*silent* movies⟩ — **si·lent·ly** *adv*

syn SILENT, TACITURN, RETICENT, RESERVED mean tend-

\ə\ abut	\aú\ out	\i\ tip	\ȯ\ saw	\ú\ foot
\ər\ further	\ch\ chin	\ī\ life	\ȯi\ coin	\y\ yet
\a\ mat	\e\ pet	\j\ job	\th\ thin	\yü\ few
\ā\ take	\ē\ easy	\ŋ\ sing	\th\ this	\yú\ cure
\ä\ cot, cart	\g\ go	\ō\ bone	\ü\ food	\zh\ vision

ing not to talk. SILENT suggests a habit of never saying more than one must ⟨a *silent* person who leads by example rather than words⟩ TACITURN suggests that by nature one dislikes talking and may also prefer being alone ⟨a *taciturn* farmer who did not welcome visitors⟩ RETICENT suggests a dislike of talking about one's own business ⟨the new neighbor was *reticent* about her job⟩ RESERVED suggests that one is rigid and quiet during conversation ⟨the *reserved* couple did not join in the lively talk at dinner⟩

¹sil·hou·ette \,sil-ə-'wet\ *n* **1 a** : a picture (as a drawing or cutout) of the outline of an object filled in with a solid usually black color **b** : a profile portrait done in silhouette **2** : the outline of an object seen or as if seen against the light

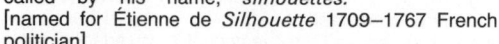

Word History Étienne de Silhouette served as the French controller general of finances in 1759. He became noted for being extremely stingy with the government's money. He would not allow any unnecessary expenses and reduced government pensions. People began making fun of his overly strict regulations for saving money. It was said that he was so cheap that he decorated his walls with cutout outline drawings instead of paintings. Such outline or profile drawings came to be called by his name, *silhouettes.* [named for Étienne de *Silhouette* 1709–1767 French politician]

silhouette 1b

²silhouette *vb* **-ett·ed; -ett·ing** : to represent by a silhouette; *also* : to show against a light background ⟨ducks *silhouetted* against the evening sky⟩

sil·i·ca \'sil-i-kə\ *n* : a compound that consists of silicon dioxide and occurs in various forms (as in quartz, opal, and sand)

sil·i·cate \'sil-i-ˌkāt, 'sil-ə-kət\ *n* : a chemical salt that consists of a metal combined with silicon and oxygen and is used especially in building materials (as bricks)

sil·i·con \'sil-i-kən, 'sil-ə-ˌkän\ *n* : a nonmetallic element that occurs combined as the most abundant element after oxygen in the earth's crust and is used especially in electronic devices — see ELEMENT table

silicon dioxide *n* : SILICA

sil·i·cone \'sil-ə-ˌkōn\ *n* : any of various silicon compounds that contain carbon and hydrogen, are obtained as oily or greasy substances or plastics, and are used especially for water-resistant and heat-resistant lubricants and varnishes

sil·i·co·sis \,sil-ə-'kō-səs\ *n* : a serious lung disease that is characterized by scar tissue in the lungs and shortness of breath and is caused by inhaling silica dusts for a long time

silk \'silk\ *n* **1** : a fine continuous protein fiber produced by various insect larvae usually to form their cocoons; *esp* : a strong glossy elastic fiber produced by silkworms and used to weave cloth **2** : thread, yarn, or fabric made from silk **3** : something resembling silk: as **a** : the thread produced by a spider **b** : the cluster of thin threadlike parts at the end of an ear of Indian corn that are styles of the ovaries

silk·en \'sil-kən\ *adj* **1** : made of or with silk **2** : resembling silk especially in soft smooth feel

silk moth *n* : the silkworm moth

silk screen *n* : a method of printing in which a design is produced by forcing colored ink through a piece of fabric that has been treated so that the ink cannot pass through some parts

silk·worm \'sil-ˌkwərm\ *n* : any of various moth larvae that spin a large amount of silk to make a cocoon; *esp* : the wrinkled hairless yellowish caterpillar that is the larva of an Asian moth, is raised in captivity on mulberry leaves, and

produces a strong silk that is the silk most often used for thread or cloth

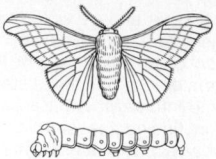

silkworm: *top* moth, *bottom* larva

silky \'sil-kē\ *adj* **silk·i·er; -est** **1** : soft and smooth as silk **2** : having or covered with fine soft hairs, plumes, or scales — **silk·i·ly** \-kə-lē\ *adv*

sill \'sil\ *n* **1** : a horizontal piece (as a timber) that forms the lowest part of a supporting structure: as **a** : the horizontal piece at the base of a window **b** : the timber or stone at the foot of a door : THRESHOLD **2** : a flat mass of igneous rock injected while melted between other rocks

sil·ly \'sil-ē\ *adj* **sil·li·er; -est** **1** : weak in mind **2** : not agreeing with reason : ABSURD **3** : lacking in seriousness or importance **4** : being stunned or dazed ⟨scared *silly*⟩ — **sil·li·ness** \'sil-ē-nəs\ *n*

si·lo \'sī-lō\ *n, pl* **silos** **1** : a trench, pit, or especially a tall cylinder (as of wood or concrete) used for making and storing silage **2** : an underground structure for housing a missile

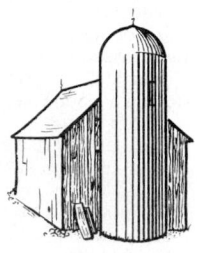

silo 1

¹silt \'silt\ *n* **1** : very small particles left as sediment from water; *also* : a soil made up mostly of silt with little clay **2** : a deposit of sediment (as by a river) — **silty** \'sil-tē\ *adj*

²silt *vb* : to make or become choked, blocked, filled, or covered with silt

Si·lu·ri·an \sī-'lür-ē-ən, sə-\ *adj* : of, relating to, or being a period of the Paleozoic era of geological history marked by the first appearance of land plants; *also* : relating to the corresponding system of rocks — see GEOLOGIC TIME table — **Silurian** *n*

silvan *variant of* SYLVAN

¹sil·ver \'sil-vər\ *n* **1** : a soft white metallic element that takes a high polish and is a better conductor of heat and electricity than any other substance — see ELEMENT table **2 a** : coin made of silver **b** : articles (as tableware) made of or plated with silver **c** : tableware made of other metals (as stainless steel) **3** : a medium gray

²silver *adj* **1** : relating to, made of, or yielding silver ⟨*silver* jewelry⟩ ⟨*silver* ore⟩ **2** : SILVERY 1

³silver *vb* **sil·vered; sil·ver·ing** \'silv-(ə-)riŋ\ : to coat with or as if with silver — **sil·ver·er** \'sil-vər-ər\ *n*

silver bromide *n* : a compound that is easily affected by light and is much used in photography

sil·ver·fish \'sil-vər-ˌfish\ *n* : any of various small wingless insects; *esp* : one that is found in houses and feeds on paper products, clothing, and other starchy materials

silver fox *n* : a color form of the common red fox in which the pelt is black tipped with white

silver iodide *n* : a compound that darkens when exposed to light and is used in photography, rainmaking, and medicine

silver nitrate *n* : a compound used especially in photography and in medicine

silver plate *n* **1** : a plating of silver **2** : tableware plated with silver

sil·ver·smith \'sil-vər-ˌsmith\ *n* : a person who makes articles of silver

sil·ver·ware \-ˌwa(ə)r, -ˌwe(ə)r\ *n* **1** : tableware made of or plated with silver **2** : ¹SILVER 2c

sil·very \'silv-(ə-)rē\ *adj* **1** : having a shine like silver **2** : containing or consisting of silver

Sim·chas To·rah \,sim-kə-'stör-ə, -'stör-\ *n* : a Jewish holiday observed in October or November in celebration of the completion of the annual reading of the Torah [from

Hebrew *śimḥath tōrāh* "rejoicing of the Torah"]

¹sim·i·an \'sim-ē-ən\ *adj* : of, relating to, or resembling monkeys or apes

²simian *n* : ¹MONKEY 1, APE

sim·i·lar \'sim-(ə-)lər\ *adj* **1** : having qualities in common **2** : not differing in shape but only in size or position ⟨*similar* triangles⟩ — **sim·i·lar·ly** *adv*

sim·i·lar·i·ty \,sim-ə-'lar-ət-ē\ *n, pl* **-ties 1** : the quality or state of being similar : RESEMBLANCE **2** : a point in which things are similar : CORRESPONDENCE

sim·i·le \'sim-ə-(,)lē\ *n* : a figure of speech in which things different in kind or quality are compared by the use of the word *like* or *as* (as in *eyes like stars*) — compare METAPHOR

si·mil·i·tude \sə-'mil-ə-,t(y)üd\ *n* **1** : a visible likeness **2** : a comparison based on an imagined likeness **3** : SIMILARITY 2

sim·mer \'sim-ər\ *vb* **sim·mered; sim·mer·ing** \-(ə-)riŋ\ : to stew gently below or just at the boiling point — **simmer** *n*

sim·per \'sim-pər\ *vb* **sim·pered; sim·per·ing** \-p(ə-)riŋ\ : to smile in a foolish insincere manner — **simper** *n* — **sim·per·er** \-pər-ər\ *n*

sim·ple \'sim-pəl\ *adj* **sim·pler** \-p(ə-)lər\; **sim·plest** \-p(ə-)ləst\ **1** : free from dishonesty or vanity : INNOCENT **2** : not wealthy ⟨*simple* folks⟩ **3** : lacking in education, experience, or intelligence **4 a** : free from complications ⟨a *simple* melody⟩ ⟨neat *simple* clothing⟩ **b** : consisting of only one main clause and no subordinate clauses ⟨*simple* sentence⟩ **c** : consisting of only the verb ⟨*simple* predicate⟩ **5** : not compound ⟨a *simple* eye⟩ **6 a** : not divided into branches or leaflets ⟨*simple* leaf⟩ **b** : developing from a single ovary ⟨*simple* fruits⟩ **7** : ¹UTTER, ABSOLUTE ⟨the *simple* truth⟩ **8** : ¹EASY 1 ⟨a *simple* explanation⟩ — **sim·ple·ness** \-pəl-nəs\ *n*

simple fracture *n* : a breaking of a bone in such a way that the skin is not broken and bone fragments do not stick out

simple interest *n* : interest paid or figured on the original amount only of a loan or on the amount of an account

simple machine *n* : any of various elementary devices formerly considered as the elements of which all machines are composed and including the lever, the wheel and axle, the pulley, the inclined plane, the wedge, and the screw

sim·ple·mind·ed \,sim-pəl-'mīn-dəd\ *adj* **1** : UNSOPHISTICATED 1 **2** : FOOLISH

simplest form *n* : LOWEST TERMS

simple sugar *n* : MONOSACCHARIDE

sim·ple·ton \'sim-pəl-tən\ *n* : a person lacking in common sense

sim·plic·i·ty \sim-'plis-ət-ē\ *n, pl* **-ties 1** : the quality or state of being simple **2** : HONESTY, STRAIGHTFORWARDNESS **3 a** : clearness of expression **b** : the quality or state of being plain **4** : FOLLY 1, SILLINESS

sim·pli·fy \'sim-plə-,fī\ *vb* **-fied; -fy·ing** : to make simple or simpler — **sim·pli·fi·ca·tion** \,sim-plə-fə-'kā-shən\ *n* — **sim·pli·fi·er** \'sim-plə-,fī(-ə)r\ *n*

sim·ply \'sim-plē\ *adv* **1 a** : in a clear manner ⟨stated the directions *simply*⟩ **b** : in a plain manner ⟨*simply* dressed⟩ **c** : in a direct manner : CANDIDLY ⟨told the story as *simply* as a child would⟩ **2 a** : for nothing more than ⟨eats *simply* to keep alive⟩ **b** : without any question : TRULY ⟨*simply* marvelous⟩

sim·u·late \'sim-yə-,lāt\ *vb* **-lat·ed; -lat·ing** : to give the appearance or effect of : IMITATE — **sim·u·la·tor** \-,lāt-ər\ *n*

sim·u·la·tion \,sim-yə-'lā-shən\ *n* **1** : the act or process of simulating **2** : an object that is not genuine **3** : the imitation by one system or process of the way in which another system or process works ⟨a computer *simulation* of spaceflight⟩

si·mul·ta·neous \,sī-məl-'tā-nē-əs, -nyəs\ *adj* **1** : existing or occurring at the same time **2** : satisfied by the same

values of the variables ⟨*simultaneous* equations⟩ [probably from a Latin word *simultaneus* "simultaneous", from earlier *simul* "at the same time, together" — related to ASSEMBLE, ENSEMBLE] — **si·mul·ta·neous·ly** *adv*

¹sin \'sin\ *n* **1** : a breaking of a moral law **2** : an action that is or is felt to be bad **syn** see OFFENSE

²sin *vb* **sinned; sin·ning** : to commit a sin

¹since \(')sin(t)s\ *adv* **1** : from a definite past time until now ⟨has stayed there ever *since*⟩ **2** : before the present time : AGO ⟨long *since* dead⟩ **3** : after a time in the past ⟨has *since* become rich⟩

²since *prep* : from or after a specified time in the past

³since *conj* **1** : at a time or times in the past after or later than **2** : from the time in the past when **3** : for the reason that : BECAUSE

sin·cere \sin-'si(ə)r\ *adj* **sin·cer·er; sin·cer·est 1** : TRUSTWORTHY, STRAIGHTFORWARD ⟨a *sincere* friend⟩ **2** : GENUINE 1, REAL ⟨*sincere* interest in painting⟩ — **sin·cere·ly** *adv* — **sin·cer·i·ty** \-'ser-ət-ē, -'sir-\ *n*

sine \'sīn\ *n* : a function that for an acute angle in a right triangle is the ratio of the side opposite the angle to the hypotenuse

sin·ew \'sin-yü *also* 'sin-ü\ *n* **1** : TENDON; *esp* : one prepared for use as a cord or thread **2** : solid strength : POWER

sin·ewy \'sin-yə-wē *also* 'sin-ə-\ *adj* **1** : full of sinews : STRINGY **2** : STRONG 1 ⟨*sinewy* arms⟩

sin·ful \'sin-fəl\ *adj* : marked by or full of sin : WICKED — **sin·ful·ly** \-fə-lē\ *adv* — **sin·ful·ness** *n*

¹sing \'siŋ\ *vb* **sang** \'saŋ\ *or* **sung** \'səŋ\; **sung; sing·ing** \'siŋ-iŋ\ **1 a** : to produce musical sounds by means of the voice ⟨*sing* for joy⟩ **b** : to utter with musical sounds ⟨*sing* a song⟩ **c** : ¹CHANT 2, INTONE ⟨parts of the mass were *sung*⟩ **2** : to make pleasing musical sounds ⟨birds *singing* at dawn⟩ **3** : to make a slight shrill sound ⟨a kettle *singing* on the stove⟩ **4** : to express enthusiastically ⟨*sing* the praises of life in the city⟩ **5** : ¹BUZZ 1, RING ⟨ears *singing* from the sudden descent⟩ **6** : to act on or affect by singing ⟨*sing* a baby to sleep⟩ ⟨*sing* the blues away⟩ **7** : to call aloud : cry out ⟨*sing* out when you find them⟩ — **sing·able** \'siŋ-ə-bəl\ *adj*

²sing *n* : a singing especially in company ⟨a community *sing*⟩

¹singe \'sinj\ *vb* **singed** \'sinjd\; **singe·ing** \'sin-jiŋ\ : to burn slightly; *esp* : to remove hair, down, or fuzz from usually by passing briefly over a flame

²singe *n* : a slight burn : SCORCH

¹sing·er \'siŋ-ər\ *n* : one that sings

²sing·er \'sin-jər\ *n* : one that singes

¹sin·gle \'siŋ-gəl\ *adj* **1** : not married; *esp* : never having been married **2** : being alone : being the only one **3** : consisting of one ⟨a *single* standard⟩ **4** : having only one row of petals or ray flowers around the center of a blossom ⟨a *single* rose⟩ **5 a** : consisting of a separate whole : INDIVIDUAL ⟨each *single* citizen⟩ **b** : of, relating to, or involving only one person **6** : being a whole ⟨a *single* world⟩ **7** : engaged in between one person and another ⟨fight in *single* combat⟩ **8** : designed for the use of one person or family only ⟨a *single* house⟩ — **sin·gle·ness** *n*

²single *n* **1 a** : a separate individual person or thing **b** : an unmarried adult **c** : a phonograph record with one song on each side **2** : a hit in baseball that enables a batter to reach first base safely **3** *pl* : a game (as of tennis) between two players

³single *vb* **sin·gled; sin·gling** \'siŋ-g(ə-)liŋ\ **1** : to select (a person or thing) from a number or group **2** : to make a single in baseball

\ə\ abut	\au̇\ out	\i\ tip	\o̅\ saw	\u̇\ foot
\ər\ further	\ch\ chin	\ī\ life	\oi\ coin	\y\ yet
\a\ mat	\e\ pet	\j\ job	\th\ thin	\yü\ few
\ā\ take	\ē\ easy	\ŋ\ sing	\th\ this	\yu̇\ cure
\ä\ cot, cart	\g\ go	\ō\ bone	\ü\ food	\zh\ vision

single bond *n* : a chemical bond in which one pair of electrons is shared by two atoms in a molecule especially when the atoms can share more than one pair of electrons — compare DOUBLE BOND, TRIPLE BOND

sin·gle–breast·ed \,siŋ-gəl-'bres-təd\ *adj* : having a center closing with one row of buttons and no overlapping lapel ⟨*single-breasted* coat⟩

single file *n* : a line of persons or things arranged one behind another — **single file** *adv*

sin·gle–hand·ed \,siŋ-gəl-'han-dəd\ *adj* **1** : managed or done by one person **2** : working alone : lacking help — **sin·gle–hand·ed·ly** *adv*

sin·gle–mind·ed \-'mīn-dəd\ *adj* **1** : TRUSTWORTHY, SINCERE **2** : having only one purpose ⟨a *single-minded* devotion to stopping crime⟩ — **sin·gle–mind·ed·ly** *adv*

sin·glet \'siŋ-glət\ *n, chiefly British* : UNDERSHIRT

sin·gle·tree \'siŋ-gəl-,trē\ *n* : WHIFFLETREE

sin·gly \'siŋ-g(ə-)lē\ *adv* **1** : by or with oneself : INDIVIDUALLY **2** : in a single-handed manner

¹sing·song \'siŋ-,soŋ\ *n* : a monotonous rhythm or a monotonous rise and fall of pitch

²singsong *adj* : having a monotonous rhythm

¹sin·gu·lar \'siŋ-gyə-lər\ *adj* **1 a** : of or relating to a separate person or thing : INDIVIDUAL **b** : of, relating to, or constituting a word form denoting one person, thing, or instance **c** : of or relating to a single instance or to something considered by itself **2 a** : EXCEPTIONAL 1 **b** : UNIQUE 2 **3** : PECULIAR 1 — **sin·gu·lar·ly** *adv*

²singular *n* : something that is singular; *esp* : the singular number, the inflectional form denoting it, or a word in that form

sin·gu·lar·i·ty \,siŋ-gyə-'lar-ət-ē\ *n, pl* **-ties** **1** : the quality or state of being singular **2** : something that is singular : PECULIARITY

sin·is·ter \'sin-əs-tər\ *adj* **1** : especially evil or leading to evil : BAD **2** : threatening evil, harm, or danger : OMINOUS [Middle English *sinistre* "unlucky, unfavorable", from Latin *sinistr-, sinister* "left, on the left side, awkward, unfavorable"; so called because the ancient Romans believed that omens seen on the left side told of bad things to come] — **sin·is·ter·ly** *adv*

¹sink \'siŋk\ *vb* **sank** \'saŋk\ *or* **sunk** \'səŋk\; **sunk; sink·ing** **1 a** : to move or cause to move downward usually so as to be below the surface or swallowed up ⟨feet *sinking* into deep mud⟩ ⟨*sink* a ship⟩ **b** : to descend gradually lower and lower ⟨the sun *sank* behind the hills⟩ **2** : to lessen in amount or strength **3** : to fall to or into a lower status (as of quality, worth, or number) : DECLINE ⟨*sink* into decay⟩ **4 a** : to penetrate or cause to penetrate ⟨*sank* my ax into the tree⟩ **b** : to become absorbed ⟨the water *sank* into the dry ground⟩ **5** : to form by digging or boring ⟨*sink* a well⟩ **6** : ²INVEST 1 ⟨*sank* a million dollars in the new company⟩ — **sink·able** \'siŋ-kə-bəl\ *adj*

²sink *n* **1 a** : CESSPOOL **b** : ²SEWER **2** : a stationary basin for washing (as in a kitchen) connected with a drain and usually a water supply

sink·er \'siŋ-kər\ *n* **1** : one that sinks; *esp* : a weight for sinking a line or net **2** : DOUGHNUT 1

sink·hole \'siŋk-,hōl\ *n* : a hollow place in which drainage collects

sinking fund *n* : a fund set up for paying off the original amount of a debt when it falls due

sinned *past and past participle of* SIN

sin·ner \'sin-ər\ *n* : one that sins

sinning *present participle of* SIN

Si·no- \,sī-nō, 'sī-\ : Chinese : Chinese and ⟨*Sino*-American⟩ [derived from Greek *Sinai* "Chinese"; of Arabic origin]

sin·u·os·i·ty \,sin-yə-'wäs-ət-ē\ *n, pl* **-ties** **1** : the quality or state of being sinuous **2** : something that is sinuous : winding turn

sin·u·ous \'sin-yə-wəs\ *adj* : of a snakelike or wavy form : WINDING — **sin·u·ous·ly** *adv*

si·nus \'sī-nəs\ *n* : a hollow place : CAVITY; *esp* : any of several cavities in the skull that usually connect with the nostrils

si·nus·itis \,sī-n(y)ə-'sīt-əs\ *n* : inflammation of a sinus

Siou·an \'sü-ən\ *n* **1** : a language stock of central and eastern North America **2** : a member of any of the American Indian peoples speaking Siouan languages

Sioux \'sü\ *n, pl* **Sioux** \'sü(z)\ **1** : DAKOTA **2** : SIOUAN

¹sip \'sip\ *vb* **sipped; sip·ping** **1** : to drink in small quantities or little by little **2** : to take sips from : TASTE — **sip·per** *n*

²sip *n* **1** : the act of sipping **2** : a small amount taken by sipping

¹si·phon *also* **sy·phon** \'sī-fən\ *n* **1** : a bent tube through which a liquid can be drawn by means of air pressure up and over the edge of one container and into another container at a lower level **2** : any of various tube-shaped organs in animals and especially mollusks that are used to draw in or pass off fluids

siphon 1

²siphon *also* **syphon** *vb* **si·phoned** *also* **sy·phoned; si·phon·ing** *also* **sy·phon·ing** \'sīf-(ə-)niŋ\ : to draw off or pass off by or as if by a siphon

sir \(')sər\ *n* **1** : a man having the right to be addressed as *sir* — used as a title before the given name of a knight or baronet **2** : a title of respect used in addressing a man without using his name [Middle English *sir* "a man of rank or position", from *sire* "a father", from early French *sire* (same meaning), from Latin *senior* (adjective) "older, elder" — related to SENIOR]

¹sire \'sī(ə)r\ *n* **1** : ¹FATHER 1a **2** *archaic* : a male ancestor : FOREFATHER **3** : the male parent of an animal and especially of a domestic animal

²sire *vb* **sired; sir·ing** : BEGET 1, PROCREATE — used especially of domestic animals

si·ren \'sī-rən *for sense 3 also* sī-'rēn\ *n* **1** *often cap* : one of a group of womanlike creatures in Greek mythology that lured mariners to destruction by their singing **2** : a tempting woman **3** : a device often electrically operated for producing a loud shrill warning sound ⟨ambulance *siren*⟩

Word History In the Greek epic poem *The Odyssey*, Homer tells of the adventures of Odysseus on his voyage home after the Trojan War. One of these adventures involves a couple of sea nymphs, called Sirens, who are half woman and half bird. They attract sailors by the beauty of their singing, which causes the ships to crash on the rocks. To avoid such a fate, Odysseus has his sailors' ears filled with wax so that they cannot hear the Sirens' song. He has himself tied to a mast so that he cannot steer the ship toward the rocks. It works. The ship succeeds in getting past the Sirens, who are then so upset that they drown themselves. The word *siren* lives on, however. It was taken into Latin, French, and English. It has been used for "a tempting woman", but its chief use is for "a loud-sounding warning device". Its sound is far from beautiful, but it does signal danger. [Middle English *siren* "a partly female creature in Greek legend whose beautiful singing lured sailors to their deaths", from early French *siren* and Latin *siren* (both, same meaning), from Greek *seirēn* (same meaning)]

Sir·i·us \'sir-ē-əs\ *n* : the brightest star in the night sky — called also *Dog Star* [Middle English *Sirius* "the brightest star", from Latin *Sirius* (same meaning), from Greek *Seirios* "the brightest star", literally "burning, scorching" —

see *Word History* at DOG DAYS]

sir·loin \'sər-ˌlȯin\ *n* : a cut of meat and especially of beef from the part just in front of the rump

sirup *variant of* SYRUP

si·sal \'sī-səl, -zəl\ *n* **1** : a strong durable white fiber used to make ropes and twine **2** : a widely grown tropical American agave with leaves that produce sisal

sis·sy \'sis-ē\ *n, pl* **sissies** **1** : a man or boy who appears feminine or behaves in a feminine manner **2** : a fearful or cowardly person — **sissy** *adj*

¹sis·ter \'sis-tər\ *n* **1** : a female who has one or both parents in common with another individual **2** : a female relative **3** : a fellow female member of a group **4** : one related to another by common ties or interests **5** *often cap* : a member of a religious community of women : NUN **6** *chiefly British* : ¹NURSE 2 — **sis·ter·ly** *adj or adv*

²sister *adj* : having or suggesting the relationship of a sister ⟨*sister* ships⟩

sis·ter·hood \'sis-tər-ˌhu̇d\ *n* **1** : the state of being a sister **2** : a community or society of sisters

sis·ter–in–law \'sis-t(ə-)rən-ˌlȯ, -tərn-ˌlȯ\ *n, pl* **sis·ters–in–law** \-tər-zən-\ **1** : the sister of one's spouse **2** : the wife of one's brother

sit \'sit\ *vb* **sat** \'sat\; **sit·ting** **1 a** : to rest on the buttocks or haunches ⟨*sit* in a chair⟩ **b** : to cause to be seated ⟨*sit* yourself down⟩ **c** : ²PERCH 2, ROOST **2** : to provide seats or seating room for ⟨the car *sits* five people⟩ **3** : to occupy a place as a member of an official body ⟨*sit* in Congress⟩ **4** : to hold a session ⟨the court is now *sitting*⟩ **5** : to cover eggs for hatching : BROOD **6** : to pose for a portrait or photograph : serve as a model **7** : to lie or rest in a condition or location ⟨the vase *sits* on the table⟩ **8** : to remain inactive ⟨the car *sits* in the garage⟩ **9** : BABY-SIT — **sit on one's hands** : to fail to take action — **sit pretty** : to be in a highly favorable situation — **sit tight** : to keep one's position without change

sit·com \'sit-ˌkäm\ *n* : SITUATION COMEDY

sit–down \'sit-ˌdau̇n\ *n* : a strike in which the workers stop work and refuse to leave their places of employment — called also *sit-down strike*

site \'sīt\ *n* **1** : local position (as of a building, town, or monument) **2** : the place or scene of something

sit–in \'sit-ˌin\ *n* : an act of occupying seats (as in a restaurant or office) as a means of organized protest

Sit·ka spruce \ˌsit-kə-\ *n* : a tall spruce of the northern Pacific coast with thin reddish brown bark and flat needles; *also* : its wood

sit·ter \'sit-ər\ *n* : one that sits; *esp* : a person who baby-sits

¹sit·ting \'sit-iŋ\ *n* **1** : an act of one that sits; *esp* : a single occasion of continuous sitting ⟨finished the portrait in one *sitting*⟩ **2 a** : a brooding over eggs for hatching **b** : SETTING 5 **3** : SESSION 1, 2 ⟨*sitting* of the legislature⟩

²sitting *adj* : used in or for sitting ⟨a *sitting* position⟩

sitting duck *n* : an easy or defenseless target

sitting room *n* : LIVING ROOM

sit·u·ate \'sich-ə-ˌwāt\ *vb* **-at·ed; -at·ing** : to place in a site or situation : LOCATE

sit·u·at·ed \'sich-ə-ˌwāt-əd\ *adj* **1** : placed in a site or situation **2** : placed in certain circumstances ⟨not rich but comfortably *situated*⟩

sit·u·a·tion \ˌsich-ə-'wā-shən\ *n* **1 a** : the way in which something is placed in relation to its surroundings **b** : SITE 1 **2 a** : a position or place of employment : POST, JOB **b** : position in life : STATUS **3** : position with respect to conditions and circumstances ⟨the military *situation*⟩

situation comedy *n* : a radio or television comedy series that involves a continuing cast of characters in different stories not related to each other

sit–up \'sit-ˌəp\ *n* : an exercise done by lying on the back and rising up to a sitting position by bending forward at the waist

six \'siks\ *n* **1** — see NUMBER table **2** : the sixth in a set or series — **six** *adj or pron* — **at sixes and sevens** : in disorder : CONFUSED

six–gun \'siks-ˌgən\ *n* : a revolver with six chambers

six·pence \'sik-spən(t)s, *US also* -ˌspen(t)s\ *n* : the sum of six pence; *also* : a coin representing six pence

six–shoot·er \'sik(s)-ˈshüt-ər\ *n* : SIX-GUN

six·teen \(')sik-'stēn\ *n* — see NUMBER table — **six·teen** *adj or pron* — **six·teenth** \-'tēn(t)th\ *adj or n*

sixteenth note *n* : a musical note with a time value one sixteenth that of a whole note

sixth \'siks(t)th, 'siks(t)\ *n* **1** — see NUMBER table **2** : the difference in pitch between the first tone and the sixth tone of a scale — **sixth** *adj or adv* — **sixth·ly** \'siksth-lē, 'sikst-\ *adv*

sixth sense *n* : a special ability to sense something that does not involve the five senses

six·ty \'sik-stē\ *n, pl* **sixties** — see NUMBER table — **six·ti·eth** \-stē-əth\ *adj or n* — **sixty** *adj or pron*

six–year molar \ˌsik-ˌsyi(ə)r-\ *n* : one of the first permanent molar teeth of which there are four including one on each side of the upper and lower jaws and which erupt at about six years of age — called also *sixth-year molar*

siz·able *or* **size·able** \'sī-zə-bəl\ *adj* : fairly large : CONSIDERABLE — **siz·ably** \-blē\ *adv*

¹size \'sīz\ *n* **1** : physical extent or bulk **2 a** : the measurements of a thing **b** : relative amount or number **3** : one of a series of measures especially of manufactured articles (as of clothing) [Middle English *sise* "a law, a law controlling weights and measures used in the marketplace, a fixed portion of food and drink", from early French *sise* (same meaning), from earlier *assise* "a lawmaking session, settlement, judgment", from *asseoir* "to seat", derived from Latin *assidere* "to sit beside, assist (a judge)", from *ad-* "toward, near" and *sedere* "to sit"]

²size *vb* **sized; siz·ing** **1** : to make a particular size **2** : to arrange, grade, or classify according to size **3** : to form a judgment of — usually used with *up* ⟨*sizing* up the candidates⟩

³size \'sīz, ˌsīz\ *adj* : SIZED 1 ⟨medium-*size*⟩

⁴size \'sīz\ *n* : a gluey material (as a preparation of glue, flour, or varnish) used for filling the pores in a surface (as of plaster), as a stiffener (as of fabric), or as an adhesive [Middle English *sise* "something gluey used as a filler, stiffener, or adhesive"]

⁵size *vb* **sized; siz·ing** : to apply size to

sized \'sīzd, ˌsīzd\ *adj* **1** : having a specified size ⟨small-*sized*⟩ **2** : arranged or adjusted according to size

siz·ing \'sī-ziŋ\ *n* : ⁴SIZE

siz·zle \'siz-əl\ *vb* **siz·zled; siz·zling** \-(ə-)liŋ\ : to make a hissing sound in or as if in burning or frying — **sizzle** *n* — **siz·zler** \-(ə-)lər\ *n*

¹skate \'skāt\ *n* : any of numerous rays that have broad winglike fins

²skate *n* **1** : a metallic runner fitting the sole of a shoe or a shoe with a permanently attached runner used for gliding on ice **2** : ROLLER SKATE

³skate *vb* **skat·ed; skat·ing** **1** : to glide along on skates **2** : to slide or move as if on skates — **skat·er** *n*

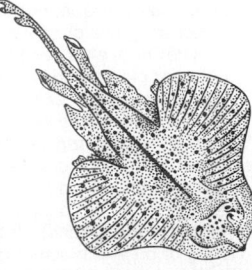

¹skate

\ə\ abut	\au̇\ out	\i\ tip	\ȯ\ saw	\u̇\ foot
\ər\ further	\ch\ chin	\ī\ life	\ȯi\ coin	\y\ yet
\a\ mat	\e\ pet	\j\ job	\th\ thin	\yü\ few
\ā\ take	\ē\ easy	\ŋ\ sing	\th\ this	\yu̇\ cure
\ä\ cot, cart	\g\ go	\ō\ bone	\ü\ food	\zh\ vision

skate·board \'skāt-ˌbō(ə)rd, -ˌbȯ(ə)rd\ *n* : a short board mounted on small wheels that is used for coasting and often for performing athletic stunts — **skate·board·er** \-ˌbȯrd-ər, -ˌbȯrd-\ *n* — **skate·board·ing** \-iŋ\ *n*

skat·ing \'skāt-iŋ\ *n* : the act, art, or sport of gliding on skates

skeet \'skēt\ *n* : trapshooting in which clay targets are thrown in such a way as to simulate the angle of flight of a flushed game bird

skein \'skān\ *n* : a looped length of yarn or thread put up in a loose twist after it is taken from the reel

skel·e·tal \'skel-ət-ᵊl\ *adj* : of, relating or attached to, forming, or resembling a skeleton ⟨*skeletal* muscles⟩ ⟨the *skeletal* system⟩

¹**skel·e·ton** \'skel-ət-ᵊn\ *n* **1** : a firm supporting or protecting structure or framework of a living thing; *esp* : a framework made of bone or sometimes cartilage that supports the soft tissues and protects the internal organs of a vertebrate (as a fish or human being) — compare ENDOSKELETON, EXOSKELETON **2** : a very thin person or animal **3** : something forming a structural framework

²**skeleton** *adj* **1** : of, consisting of, or resembling a skeleton ⟨a *skeleton* hand⟩ **2** : consisting of the smallest possible number of persons who can get a job done ⟨a *skeleton* crew⟩

skeleton key *n* : a key made to open many locks

skep·tic \'skep-tik\ *n* : a person slow to believe or ready to question : DOUBTER

skep·ti·cal \'skep-ti-kəl\ *adj* : relating to or marked by doubt — **skep·ti·cal·ly** \-k(ə-)lē\ *adv*

skep·ti·cism \'skep-tə-ˌsiz-əm\ *n* : an attitude of doubt

¹**sketch** \'skech\ *n* **1 a** : a rough drawing representing the chief features of an object or scene **b** : a rough draft (as of a story) **2** : a brief description or outline **3** : a short comedy piece

²**sketch** *vb* **1** : to make a sketch, rough draft, or outline of **2** : to draw or paint sketches — **sketch·er** *n*

sketch·book \'skech-ˌbůk\ *n* : a book of or for sketches

sketchy \'skech-ē\ *adj* **sketch·i·er; -est** **1** : of the nature of a sketch : roughly outlined **2** : lacking completeness, clearness, or substance : SLIGHT, VAGUE

¹**skew** \'skyü\ *vb* **1** : to take a slanting course : move or turn aside : TWIST, SWERVE **2** : to distort from a true value or symmetrical form ⟨*skewed* the facts to fit their theory⟩

²**skew** *adj* : being straight lines in space that are neither parallel nor intersecting and do not lie in the same plane

¹**skew·er** \'skyü-ər, 'skyü-(-ə)r\ *n* **1** : a long pin for keeping meat in form while roasting or for holding small pieces of meat and vegetables for broiling **2** : something shaped or used like a meat skewer

²**skewer** *vb* : to fasten or pierce with or as if with a skewer

skew·ness \'skyü-nəs\ *n* : lack of straightness or of agreement in size, shape, or position of parts on opposite sides of a dividing line or center

¹**ski** \'skē\ *n, pl* **skis** : one of a pair of narrow strips of wood, metal, or plastic curving upward in front that are used for gliding over snow or water [from Norwegian *ski* "a ski", from an early Norse word *skīth* "a stick of wood"]

²**ski** *vb* **skied; ski·ing** : to glide on skis — **ski·er** *n*

ski boot *n* : a boot or shoe used for skiing; *esp* : a heavy rigid boot that extends above the ankle

¹**skid** \'skid\ *n* **1** : a log or plank for supporting something (as above the ground) **2** : one of the logs, planks, or rails along or on which something heavy is rolled or slid **3** : a device placed under a carriage wheel to prevent its turning **4** : a runner used as part of the landing gear of an airplane or helicopter **5** : the act of skidding : SLIDE

²**skid** *vb* **skid·ded; skid·ding** **1** : to haul along, slide, hoist, or store on skids **2** : to slide without rotating ⟨the wheels *skidded*⟩ **3** : to fail to grip the roadway; *esp* : to slip sideways on the road ⟨the car *skidded* on an icy road⟩

skid row \-'rō\ *n* : a district of cheap saloons and cheap rooming houses in which migrant workers, tramps, and alcoholics live

skies *pl of* SKY

skiff \'skif\ *n* **1** : a light rowboat **2** : a sailboat light enough to be rowed

ski·ing \'skē-iŋ\ *n* : the art or sport of gliding and jumping on skis

ski jump *n* **1** : a jump made by a person wearing skis **2** : a specially prepared course or track from which a skier makes a jump — **ski jump** *vb* — **ski jump·er** *n*

ski lift *n* : a machine that consists usually of a series of bars or seats hanging from a moving cable and that is used to carry skiers or sightseers up a long slope

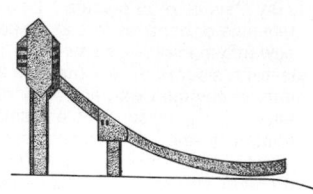

ski jump 2

skill \'skil\ *n* **1** : ability that comes from training or practice **2 a** : a particular art or science **b** : a developed or acquired ability : ACCOMPLISHMENT ⟨reading *skills*⟩

skilled \'skild\ *adj* **1** : having skill : EXPERT ⟨*skilled* workers⟩ **2** : requiring skill and training ⟨a *skilled* trade⟩

skil·let \'skil-ət\ *n* : FRYING PAN

skill·ful *or* **skil·ful** \'skil-fəl\ *adj* **1** : having or showing skill **2** : accomplished with skill ⟨a *skillful* defense⟩ — **skill·ful·ly** \-fə-lē\ *adv* — **skill·ful·ness** *n*

syn SKILLFUL, PROFICIENT, ADEPT, EXPERT mean having the knowledge and experience needed to succeed at what one does. SKILLFUL suggests being very able at doing a particular job ⟨a *skillful* truck driver⟩ PROFICIENT suggests a sure ability that comes from training and practice ⟨a *proficient* waiter who can handle several tables at once⟩ ADEPT suggests having a native ability as well as a learned skill at something (she is *adept* at getting people to work together⟩ EXPERT suggests having a thorough knowledge of a subject as well as being very skillful at working in it ⟨*expert* guides led us through the cave⟩

¹**skim** \'skim\ *vb* **skimmed; skim·ming** **1 a** : to clear a liquid of scum or floating substance : remove (as film or scum) from the surface of a liquid **b** : to remove cream from by skimming **2** : to glance through (as a book) for the chief ideas or the plot **3** : to throw so as to bounce along the surface of water **4** : to pass swiftly or lightly over : glide or skip along, above, or near a surface

²**skim** *n* **1** : a thin layer, coating, or film **2** : the act of skimming **3** : something skimmed; *esp* : SKIM MILK

³**skim** *adj* : having been skimmed

skim·mer \'skim-ər\ *n* : one that skims; *esp* : a flat scoop or spoon with holes that is used for skimming

skim milk *n* : milk from which the cream has been taken — called also *skimmed milk*

skimp \'skimp\ *vb* **1** : to give not enough or barely enough attention or effort to or funds for **2** : to save by or as if by skimping : SCRIMP

skimpy \'skim-pē\ *adj* **skimp·i·er; -est** : barely enough : SCANTY — **skimp·i·ly** \-pə-lē\ *adv* — **skimp·i·ness** \-pē-nəs\ *n*

¹**skin** \'skin\ *n* **1 a** : ²HIDE, PELT **b** : a sheet of parchment or fine-grained leather made from a hide **c** : ¹BOTTLE 1b **2 a** : the usually tough flexible outer layer of an animal body that in vertebrates is made up of two layers including an inner dermis and an outer epidermis **b** : an outer or surface layer ⟨a sausage *skin*⟩ ⟨apple *skins*⟩ **3** : the life or physical well-being of a person ⟨made sure to save his *skin*⟩ — **skin·less** \-ləs\ *adj* — **skinned** \'skind\ *adj*

²**skin** *vb* **skinned; skin·ning** **1** : to cover or become covered with or as if with skin **2** : to strip, scrape, or rub off

the skin of ⟨*skin* a rabbit⟩ ⟨*skinned* my knee⟩ **3** : ¹CHEAT 1, FLEECE **4 a** : ²SHIN ⟨*skin* up and down a rope⟩ **b** : to pass or get by with little room to spare

skin–deep \'skin-'dēp\ *adj* **1** : as deep as the skin **2** : not thorough or lasting in impression : SUPERFICIAL

skin–dive \'skin-,dīv\ *vb* : to swim underwater with a face mask and flippers and sometimes with a portable breathing device — **skin diver** *n*

skin·flint \'skin-,flint\ *n* : a person who is very stingy in money matters : MISER

skin graft *n* : skin transferred from a donor area to grow new skin at a place where the skin has been destroyed or stripped away (as by burning)

skink \'skiŋk\ *n* : any of a family of mostly small lizards with small scales

skin·ner \'skin-ər\ *n* **1** : one that removes and processes or deals in skins, pelts, or hides **2** : a driver of draft animals; *esp* : MULE SKINNER

skin·ny \'skin-ē\ *adj* **skin·ni·er; -est** **1** : resembling skin : MEMBRANOUS ⟨a *skinny* layer⟩ **2** : very thin **syn** see LEAN — **skin·ni·ness** *n*

skin·ny–dip \'skin-ē-,dip\ *vb* : to swim in the nude — **skin·ny–dip·per** *n*

skin·tight \'skin-'tīt\ *adj* : closely fitted to the figure

¹**skip** \'skip\ *vb* **skipped; skip·ping** **1 a** : to move or proceed with leaps and bounds **b** : to bounce or cause to bounce off one point after another ⟨*skipping* stones⟩ **c** : to leap over lightly **2** : to leave hurriedly or secretly ⟨*skip* town⟩ **3 a** : to pass over or leave out (as a section, item, or step) ⟨*skipped* the dull parts of the book⟩ **b** : to promote or cause to be promoted to a grade higher than the next grade in school **c** : to fail to attend ⟨*skipped* the meeting⟩

²**skip** *n* **1 a** : a light bouncing step **b** : a manner of moving by alternating hops and steps **2** : a failure to do something; *also* : something not done

ski pole *n* : a pole that has an encircling disk set a little above the point and a strap for the hand at the top and is used as an aid in skiing

¹**skip·per** \'skip-ər\ *n* **1** : one that skips **2** : any of a group of stout-bodied insects that are related to the butterflies and fly with quick darting movements [*skip* (verb) and *-er* (noun suffix)]

²**skipper** *n* : the master of a ship; *esp* : the master of a fishing, small trading, or pleasure boat [Middle English *skipper* "the master of a ship", from early Dutch *schipper* (same meaning), from *schip* "ship"]

¹**skir·mish** \'skər-mish\ *n* **1** : a minor fight between small bodies of troops **2** : a minor dispute or contest

²**skirmish** *vb* **1** : to engage in a skirmish **2** : to search about (as for supplies) — **skir·mish·er** *n*

¹**skirt** \'skərt\ *n* **1 a** : a free hanging part of a garment extending from the waist down **b** : a separate free hanging garment for women and girls covering the body from the waist down **c** : either of two flaps on a saddle covering the bars on which the stirrups are hung **2** *pl* : OUTSKIRTS **3** : a part or attachment serving as a rim, border, or edging

²**skirt** *vb* **1 a** : to go or pass around or about; *esp* : to go around or keep away from in order to avoid danger or discovery **b** : to escape or miss by a narrow margin **2** : to be, lie, or move along an edge, border, or margin

skit \'skit\ *n* : a humorous story or sketch; *esp* : a sketch included in a dramatic performance

ski tow *n* **1** : a machine that consists usually of a moving rope which a skier grasps to be pulled to the top of a slope **2** : SKI LIFT

skit·ter \'skit-ər\ *vb* : to glide or skip lightly or quickly : skim along a surface

skit·tish \'skit-ish\ *adj* **1** : lively or frisky in action **2** : easily frightened : RESTIVE ⟨a *skittish* horse⟩ **3** : BASHFUL — **skit·tish·ly** *adv* — **skit·tish·ness** *n*

skiv·vy \'skiv-ē\ *n*, *pl* **skivvies** : underwear consisting of shorts and a T-shirt — usually used in pl.

skoal \'skōl\ *n* : ²TOAST 3, HEALTH — often used as an interjection

skul·dug·gery *or* **skull·dug·gery** \,skəl-'dəg-(ə-)rē\ *n*, *pl* **-ger·ies** : sneaky or dishonest behavior : TRICKERY

skulk \'skəlk\ *vb* **1** : to move in a sly or secret manner : SNEAK **2** : to hide or conceal oneself from cowardice or fear or with treacherous intention **syn** see LURK — **skulk·er** *n*

skull \'skəl\ *n* **1** : the case of bone or cartilage that forms the skeleton of the head and face, encloses the brain, and supports the jaws of vertebrates **2** : the location of understanding or intelligence : MIND — **skulled** \'skəld\ *adj*

skull and cross·bones \-'kròs-,bōnz\ *n*, *pl* **skulls and crossbones** : a representation of a human skull over crossbones formerly pictured on pirates' flags and now used as a warning of danger to life

skull·cap \'skəl-,kap\ *n* : a close-fitting cap; *esp* : a light cap without brim for indoor wear

¹**skunk** \'skəŋk\ *n*, *pl* **skunks** *also* **skunk** **1** : any of various black-and-white North American mammals related to the weasels that give off a fluid with a sharp and unpleasant smell when startled **2** : a mean hateful person [from a word in an American Indian language]

²**skunk** *vb* : to defeat completely; *esp* : to shut out in a game

skunk cabbage *n* : an eastern North American herb of marshy areas that has a spotted brownish purple hood-shaped covering around the flowering stalk containing many tiny flowers; *also* : a related herb of the Pacific coast region having a yellow hood-shaped covering around the flowering stalk

skunk 1

sky \'skī\ *n*, *pl* **skies** **1** : the upper atmosphere : the vast arch or dome that seems to spread over the earth **2** : HEAVEN 2 **3** : ¹WEATHER, CLIMATE ⟨the forecast is for sunny *skies* tomorrow⟩

sky blue *n* : a pale to light blue

sky·cap \'skī-,kap\ *n* : one employed to carry hand luggage at an airport

sky·div·ing \-,dī-viŋ\ *n* : the sport of jumping from an airplane and carrying out various body maneuvers before opening a parachute — **sky diver** *n*

sky–high \-'hī\ *adv or adj* **1 a** : high into the air **b** : to a high level or degree **2** : in an enthusiastic manner **3** : to bits : APART

sky·jack·er \-,jak-ər\ *n* : a person who takes control of a flying airplane by threat of violence

¹**sky·lark** \'skī-,lärk\ *n* : a common Old World lark that sings as it rises in almost perpendicular flight

²**skylark** *vb* : to play wild pranks : FROLIC — **sky·lark·er** *n*

sky·light \'skī-,līt\ *n* : a window or group of windows in a roof or ceiling

sky·line \-,līn\ *n* **1** : the line where earth and sky or water and sky seem to meet : HORIZON **2** : an outline against the sky

¹**sky·rock·et** \'skī-,räk-ət\ *n* : ¹ROCKET 1

²**skyrocket** *vb* **1** : to shoot up suddenly ⟨costs have *skyrocketed*⟩ **2** : to cause to rise or increase rapidly

\ə\ abut	\aú\ out	\i\ tip	\ò\ saw	\ú\ foot
\ər\ further	\ch\ chin	\ī\ life	\òi\ coin	\yet
\a\ mat	\e\ pet	\j\ job	\th\ thin	\yü\ few
\ā\ take	\ē\ easy	\ŋ\ sing	\th\ this	\yù\ cure
\ä\ cot, cart	\g\ go	\ō\ bone	\ü\ food	\zh\ vision

sky·scrap·er \'skī-ˌskrā-pər\ n : a very tall building

sky·ward \'skī-wərd\ adv or adj **1** : toward the sky ⟨gaze *skyward*⟩ **2** : to a higher level

sky·writ·ing \'skī-ˌrīt-iŋ\ n : writing formed in the sky by means of smoke or vapor released from an airplane — **sky·writ·er** \-ˌrīt-ər\ n

slab \'slab\ n : a thick flat piece or slice (as of stone, wood, or bread)

¹slack \'slak\ adj **1** : CARELESS 2 **2** : not energetic ⟨a *slack* pace⟩ **3 a** : not tight : not tense or taut ⟨*slack* rope⟩ **b** : lacking in firmness : WEAK, SOFT ⟨*slack* control⟩ **4** : not busy ⟨*slack* season⟩ — **slack·ly** adv — **slack·ness** n

²slack vb **1 a** : to be or become slack or careless in performing or doing **b** : LESSEN **2** : to avoid work or duty **3** : LOOSEN 2 **4 a** : to cause to lessen **b** : SLAKE 4

³slack n **1** : a stopping of movement or flow **2** : a part of something that hangs loose without strain ⟨take up the *slack* of a rope⟩ **3** pl : trousers especially for casual wear **4** : a dull season or period : LULL

slack·en \'slak-ən\ vb **slack·ened; slack·en·ing** \-(ə-)niŋ\ **1** : to make or become slower or less energetic ⟨*slacken* speed⟩ **2** : to make less taut : LOOSEN ⟨*slacken* sail⟩ **3** : to become careless

slack·er \'slak-ər\ n : one who avoids work or a duty

slag \'slag\ n : waste left after the melting of ores and the separation of the metal from them

slain *past participle of* SLAY

slake \'slāk, *senses 3 & 4 are also* 'slak\ vb **slaked; slak·ing** **1** *archaic* : ABATE, MODERATE **2** : to relieve or satisfy with water or liquid : QUENCH ⟨*slaked* our thirst⟩ **3** : to become slaked **4** : to cause (lime) to heat and crumble by treatment with water

sla·lom \'släl-əm\ n **1** : skiing in a zigzag or wavy course between upright poles **2** : a skiing race against time over such a course

¹slam vb **slammed; slam·ming** **1** : to strike or beat hard **2** : to shut with force and noise : BANG ⟨*slammed* the door⟩ **3** : to set or slap down violently or noisily ⟨*slammed* the books down on the table⟩ **4** : to make a banging noise **5** : to criticize harshly

²slam n **1** : a heavy blow **2 a** : a noisy violent closing **b** : a banging noise especially from the slamming of a door **3** : a cutting or violent criticism

slam–bang \'slam-'baŋ\ adv or adj **1** : with noisy violence **2** : ¹HEADLONG 2, RECKLESSLY

slam dunk n : DUNK SHOT — **slam–dunk** \'slam-'dəŋk\ vb

¹slan·der \'slan-dər\ n **1** : the making of false statements that damage another's reputation **2** : a false and harmful oral statement about a person — **slan·der·ous** \-d(ə-)rəs\ adj — **slan·der·ous·ly** adv

²slander vb **slan·dered; slan·der·ing** \-d(ə-)riŋ\ : to utter slander against : DEFAME — **slan·der·er** \-dər-ər\ n

slang \'slaŋ\ n **1** : special language used by a particular group **2** : an informal nonstandard vocabulary composed of invented words, changed words, and exaggerated or humorous figures of speech — **slang** adj

slangy \'slaŋ-ē\ adj **slang·i·er; -est** **1** : of, relating to, or being slang : containing slang **2** : being in the habit of using slang — **slang·i·ness** n

¹slant \'slant\ vb **1** : to turn or incline from a straight line or a level : SLOPE **2** : to interpret or present according to a special viewpoint

²slant n **1** : a slanting direction, line, or plane : SLOPE **2** : something that slants **3** : a way of looking at something ⟨get a new *slant* on the problem⟩ — **slant** adj

slant height n **1** : the length of a line segment lying in the lateral surface of a right circular cone **2** : the altitude of one of the triangular faces on the side of a regular pyramid

slant·ways \'slant-ˌwāz\ adv : SLANTWISE

slant·wise \'slant-ˌwīz\ adv or adj : so as to slant : in a slanting direction or position

¹slap \'slap\ n **1** : a quick sharp blow especially with the open hand **2** : a noise like that of a slap

²slap vb **slapped; slap·ping** **1 a** : to strike with or as if with the open hand **b** : to make a sound like that of slapping **2** : to put, place, or throw with careless haste or force ⟨*slapped* the book down on the desk⟩

³slap adv **1** : ¹DIRECTLY 2, SMACK

slap·dash \'slap-ˌdash, -'dash\ adj : HAPHAZARD, SLIPSHOD

slap·jack \'slap-ˌjak\ n **1** : PANCAKE **2** : a card game in which each player tries to be the first to slap his or her hand on any jack that appears faceup

slap shot n : a hard shot in ice hockey that is made with a swinging stroke

slap·stick \'slap-ˌstik\ n : comedy stressing horseplay — **slapstick** adj

¹slash \'slash\ vb **1** : to cut by sweeping and pointless blows **2** : to whip or strike with or as if with a cane **3** : to criticize without mercy **4** : to cut slits in (as a skirt) to reveal a different color or material **5** : to reduce sharply : CUT ⟨*slash* prices⟩ — **slash·er** n

²slash n **1** : the act of slashing; *also* : a long cut or stroke made by slashing **2** : an ornamental slit in a garment **3** : a mark / used to mean "or" (as in *and/or*), "and or" (as in *bottles/cans*), or "per" (as in *kilometers/hour*) or as a division sign (as in ¾)

slash pine n : an American pine that is an important source of turpentine and lumber in the southeastern U.S.

slat \'slat\ n : a thin narrow flat strip of wood, plastic, or metal ⟨the *slats* of a venetian blind⟩ — **slat·ted** \'slat-əd\ adj

¹slate \'slāt\ n **1** : a piece of construction material (as layered rock) prepared as a shingle for roofing and siding **2** : a dense fine-grained rock formed by compression of shales or other rocks that splits readily into thin layers or plates **3** : a tablet of material (as slate) used for writing on **4 a** : a written or unwritten record (as of deeds) **b** : a list of candidates for nomination or election **5 a** : a dark purplish gray **b** : a gray similar in color to common roofing slate — **slate** adj — **slate·like** \-ˌlīk\ adj

²slate vb **slat·ed; slat·ing** **1** : to cover with slate or a slatelike substance ⟨*slate* a roof⟩ **2** : to register or schedule on or as if on a slate ⟨*slate* a meeting⟩ — **slat·er** n

slat·tern \'slat-ərn\ n : an untidy sloppy woman — **slat·tern·ly** \-lē\ adj or adv

slaty \'slāt-ē\ adj **1** : of, containing, or characteristic of slate **2** : of a purplish gray color

¹slaugh·ter \'slȯt-ər\ n **1** : the act of killing; *esp* : the butchering of livestock for market **2** : destruction of human lives in large numbers (as in war or a massacre)

²slaughter vb **1** : to kill an animal for food : BUTCHER **2** : to kill without mercy or in large numbers : MASSACRE — **slaugh·ter·er** \'slȯt-ər-ər\ n

slaugh·ter·house \'slȯt-ər-ˌhau̇s\ n : an establishment where animals are butchered

Slav \'släv, 'slav\ n : a native speaker of a Slavic language

¹slave \'slāv\ n **1** : a person who is owned by another person and can be sold at the owner's will **2** : a person who has lost self-control and is controlled by something or someone else ⟨a *slave* to bad habits⟩ **3** : ²DRUDGE — **slave** adj

Word History In the Middle Ages, Germanic people fought and raided other peoples, especially the Slavic peoples to the east. They took a great many captives there and sold them as slaves throughout Europe. The Slavic people were so common as slaves that writers of the time used the Latin word for "Slav", *Sclavus,* to mean "a personal slave". The Latin word became *sclave* in Middle English and then *slave* in Modern English. Of course slavery and slaves had existed long before the Middle Ages. The ancient Romans used the Latin word *servus* for "slave". This Latin word is the ancestor of our word *servant.* In French, *servus* became *serf* and was used for a slave who belonged to a piece of land rather than to an individual. *Serf* has continued to mean this in both French and English, although serfs themselves no longer exist. [Middle English *sclave* "slave", from early French *esclave* (same meaning), derived from Latin *Sclavus* "Slav"]

²**slave** *vb* **slaved; slav·ing** : to work like a slave : DRUDGE

slave driver *n* **1** : a supervisor of slaves at work **2** : a harsh boss

slave·hold·er \'slāv-ˌhōl-dər\ *n* : an owner of slaves — **slave·hold·ing** \-diŋ\ *adj or n*

¹**sla·ver** \'slav-ər, 'slāv-\ *vb* **sla·vered; sla·ver·ing** \-(ə-)riŋ\ : DROOL 2, SLOBBER

²**slav·er** \'slā-vər\ *n* : a person or ship engaged in the slave trade

slav·ery \'slāv-(ə-)rē\ *n* **1** : DRUDGERY, TOIL **2 a** : the state of being a slave **b** : the practice of slaveholding

¹**Slav·ic** \'slav-ik, 'släv-\ *adj* : of, relating to, or characteristic of the Slavs or their languages

²**Slavic** *n* : a branch of the Indo-European language family including Bulgarian, Czech, Polish, Serbo-Croatian, Slovene, Russian, and Ukrainian

slav·ish \'slā-vish\ *adj* **1** : of or characteristic of a slave **2** : lacking in independence or originality especially of thought ⟨*slavish* imitators⟩ — **slav·ish·ly** *adv* — **slav·ish·ness** *n*

¹**Sla·von·ic** \slə-'vän-ik\ *adj* : ¹SLAVIC

²**Slavonic** *n* : ²SLAVIC

slaw \'slȯ\ *n* : COLESLAW

slay \'slā\ *vb* **slew** \'slü\; **slain** \'slān\; **slay·ing** : to put to death violently — **slay·er** *n*

slea·zy \'slē-zē *also* 'slā-\ *adj* **slea·zi·er; -est** **1** : not firmly or closely woven : FLIMSY **2** : made carelessly of poor material : SHODDY — **slea·zi·ly** \-zə-lē\ *adv* — **slea·zi·ness** \-zē-nəs\ *n*

¹**sled** \'sled\ *n* **1** : a vehicle on runners for transportation especially over snow or ice **2** : a small sled used by children for coasting on snow-covered slopes

²**sled** *vb* **sled·ded; sled·ding** : to ride or carry on a sled or sleigh — **sled·der** *n*

sled dog *n* : a dog trained to draw a sled especially in the Arctic regions

¹**sledge** \'slej\ *n* : SLEDGEHAMMER

²**sledge** *n* : a strong heavy sled

³**sledge** *vb* **sledged; sledg·ing** : to travel with or transport on a sledge

sledge·ham·mer \'slej-ˌham-ər\ *n* : a large heavy hammer usually used with both hands — **sledgehammer** *adj or vb*

¹**sleek** \'slēk\ *vb* : to make or become sleek

²**sleek** *adj* **1 a** : smooth and glossy as if polished ⟨*sleek* dark hair⟩ **b** : having a smooth healthy well-groomed look ⟨*sleek* cattle grazing⟩ **2** : having a prosperous look or manner — **sleek·ly** *adv* — **sleek·ness** *n*

¹**sleep** \'slēp\ *n* **1** : the natural periodic loss of consciousness during which the powers of the body are restored **2** : a state resembling sleep: as **a** : a state of inactivity like sleep **b** : DEATH 4 ⟨put my pet cat to *sleep*⟩; *also* : ¹COMA, TRANCE — **sleep·like** \'slē-ˌplīk\ *adj*

²**sleep** *vb* **slept** \'slept\; **sleep·ing** **1** : to rest or be in a state of sleep **2** : to have sexual intercourse **3** : to get rid of or spend in or by sleep **4** : to provide sleeping space for

sleep·er \'slē-pər\ *n* **1** : one that sleeps **2** : a horizontal beam to support something on or near ground level **3** : SLEEPING CAR **4** : something considered unlikely to succeed that suddenly becomes successful

sleeping bag *n* : a bag that is warmly lined for sleeping outdoors or in a camp or tent

sleeping car *n* : a railroad passenger car having berths for sleeping

sleeping pill *n* : a drug that is taken as a tablet or capsule to bring on sleep

sleeping sickness *n* **1** : a serious disease found in tropical Africa that is characterized by fever, sleepiness, and loss of weight and is passed on by tsetse flies **2** : any of various virus diseases in which sleepiness is a major symptom

sleep·less \'slē-pləs\ *adj* **1** : not able to sleep **2** : marked by the absence of sleep ⟨a *sleepless* night⟩ **3** : unceasingly alert or active — **sleep·less·ly** *adv* — **sleep·less·ness** *n*

sleep·walk·er \'slēp-ˌwȯ-kər\ *n* : a person who walks while asleep — **sleep·walk·ing** \-kiŋ\ *n*

sleepy \'slē-pē\ *adj* **sleep·i·er; -est** **1** : ready to fall asleep **2** : quietly inactive ⟨a *sleepy* village⟩ — **sleep·i·ly** \-pə-lē\ *adv* — **sleep·i·ness** \-pē-nəs\ *n*

syn SLEEPY, SOMNOLENT, DROWSY mean having the urge or tendency to sleep. SLEEPY may suggest that one is merely aware of a desire to go to sleep ⟨felt *sleepy* after a long day⟩ SOMNOLENT is more likely to suggest the slowness or laziness of one who is sleepy by nature ⟨a *somnolent* child who did not take part in games⟩ DROWSY suggests strong feelings of numbness and sleepiness that can be hard to get rid of ⟨felt *drowsy* after a big meal⟩

sleepy·head \-ˌhed\ *n* : a sleepy person

¹**sleet** \'slēt\ *n* : frozen or partly frozen rain — **sleety** \'slēt-ē\ *adj*

²**sleet** *vb* : to shower sleet

sleeve \'slēv\ *n* **1** : the part of a garment covering the arm **2** : a part that fits over or around something like a sleeve — **sleeved** \'slēvd\ *adj* — **sleeve·less** \'slēv-ləs\ *adj*

¹**sleigh** \'slā\ *n* : an open usually horse-drawn vehicle with runners for use on snow or ice

²**sleigh** *vb* : to drive or travel in a sleigh

sleight \'slīt\ *n* **1 a** : sly trickery **b** : ¹TRICK 1d, STRATAGEM **2** : DEXTERITY, SKILL

sleigh

sleight of hand **1** : skill especially in juggling or magical tricks **2** : a magical or juggling trick requiring sleight of hand

slen·der \'slen-dər\ *adj* **1** : ¹THIN 1, SLIM **2** : limited or not enough in amount : MEAGER ⟨a *slender* income⟩ — **slen·der·ly** *adv* — **slen·der·ness** *n*

¹**sleuth** \'slüth\ *n* : ²DETECTIVE

Word History In Middle English the word *sleuth* meant "the track or trail left by an animal or person". After the 15th century *sleuth* was seldom used except in such words as *sleuth-dog* and *sleuthhound*. These were terms for a dog trained to follow a track or trail. The sleuthhound became well known for its eager and thorough pursuit of an object. Later the word *sleuthhound* came to be used for a "detective". The modern word *sleuth* first came into use as a shortened form of *sleuthhound*. [a shortened form of *sleuthhound* "a dog that follows a track or trail by scent", from Middle English *sleuth* "a track or trail"; of Norse origin]

²**sleuth** *vb* : to act as a detective

¹**slew** \'slü\ *past of* SLAY

²**slew** *also* **slue** *vb* : to turn, twist, or swing about especially out of a course : VEER

³**slew** *n* : a large number

\ə\ abut	\au̇\ **out**	\i\ **tip**	\ȯ\ **saw**	\u̇\ **foot**
\ər\ **further**	\ch\ **chin**	\ī\ **life**	\ȯi\ **coin**	\y\ **yet**
\a\ **mat**	\e\ **pet**	\j\ **job**	\th\ **thin**	\yü\ **few**
\ā\ **take**	\ē\ **easy**	\ŋ\ **sing**	\th\ **this**	\yu̇\ **cure**
\ä\ **cot, cart**	\g\ **go**	\ō\ **bone**	\ü\ **food**	\zh\ **vision**

¹slice \'slīs\ *n* **1** : a thin flat piece cut from something ⟨a *slice* of bread⟩ **2** : the flight of a ball curving to the right when hit by a right-hander or to the left when hit by a left-hander

²slice *vb* **sliced; slic·ing** **1 a** : to cut with or as if with a knife **b** : to cut into slices **2** : to hit a ball so that a slice results — **slic·er** *n*

¹slick \'slik\ *vb* : to make sleek or smooth

²slick *adj* **1 a** : having a smooth surface : SLIPPERY ⟨a *slick* road⟩ **b** : having or showing skill and style but no depth ⟨*slick* writing⟩ **2 a** : CLEVER 3; *esp* : TRICKY 1 **b** : quick and neat in action : SKILLFUL — **slick·ly** *adv* — **slick·ness** *n*

³slick *n* : something that is smooth or slippery; *esp* : a smooth patch of water covered with a film of oil

slick·er \'slik-ər\ *n* **1** : a long loose raincoat often of rubberized cloth or plastic **2** : a sly clever tricky person

¹slide \'slīd\ *vb* **slid** \'slid\; **slid·ing** \'slīd-iŋ\ **1 a** : to move or cause to move smoothly over a surface **b** : to coast on snow or ice **2** : to slip and fall by a loss of footing, balance, or support **3 a** : to move or pass smoothly and easily **b** : to move, pass, or put so as not to be noticed

²slide *n* **1** : the act or motion of sliding **2** : a loosened mass that slides ⟨a rock *slide*⟩ **3 a** : a sloping surface down which a person or thing slides **b** : something (as a cover for an opening) that operates or adjusts by sliding **4 a** : a small transparent picture or image that can be projected on a screen **b** : a small usually rectangular glass plate used to hold an object to be examined under a microscope

slid·er \'slīd-ər\ *n* : one that slides or operates a slide

slide rule *n* : an instrument used for rapid calculation that in its simple form consists of a ruler with a movable middle piece

slide rule

slide·way \'slīd-,wā\ *n* : a way along which something slides

slier *comparative of* SLY

sliest *superlative of* SLY

¹slight \'slīt\ *adj* **1 a** : having a slim or delicate build : not stout **b** : lacking in strength or substance : FLIMSY, FRAIL **c** : lacking weight, solidity, or importance : TRIVIAL **2** : small of its kind or in amount — **slight·ly** *adv* — **slightness** *n*

²slight *vb* **1** : to treat with disrespect **2** : to perform or attend to carelessly and without proper attention to detail

³slight *n* **1** : an act or an instance of slighting **2** : a humiliating discourtesy

slight·ing \'slīt-iŋ\ *adj* : characterized by disregard or disrespect — **slight·ing·ly** *adv*

¹slim \'slim\ *adj* **slim·mer; slim·mest** **1** : of small diameter or thickness in comparison with the height or length **2 a** : low in quality or quantity : SLIGHT **b** : SCANTY, SMALL ⟨has a *slim* chance of winning⟩ — **slim·ly** *adv* — **slimness** *n*

²slim *vb* **slimmed; slim·ming** : to make or become slender

slime \'slīm\ *n* **1** : soft moist earth or clay; *esp* : sticky slippery mud **2** : a soft slippery substance; *esp* : a thick slippery fluid that various animals (as slugs or catfishes) secrete onto their skin

slime mold *n* : any of a group of organisms that reproduce by spores and can live either as single cells resembling amebas or in groups as a mass of protoplasm resembling fungi — called also *myxomycete*

slimy \'slī-mē\ *adj* **slim·i·er; -est** **1 a** : of, relating to, or resembling slime : VISCOUS **b** : covered with or producing slime **2** : VILE 1a, OFFENSIVE — **slim·i·ness** *n*

¹sling \'sliŋ\ *vb* **slung** \'sləŋ\; **sling·ing** \'sliŋ-iŋ\ **1** : to throw with a sudden sweeping motion ⟨*slung* the sweater over her shoulder⟩ **2** : to throw with a sling — **sling·er** \'sliŋ-ər\ *n*

²sling *n* **1 a** : a short strap with strings fastened to its ends that is whirled round to throw something (as a stone) **b** : SLINGSHOT **2** : something (as a rope or chain) used to hoist, lower, support, or carry something; *esp* : a bandage hanging from the neck to support an arm or hand **3** : a slinging or hurling of or as if of a missile

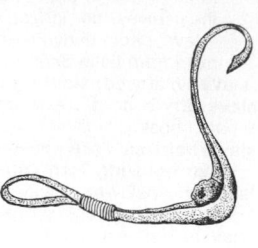

sling 1a

³sling *vb* **slung** \'sləŋ\; **sling·ing** \'sliŋ-iŋ\ **1** : to put in or move or support with a sling **2** : to hang from two points ⟨*sling* a hammock⟩

sling·shot \'sliŋ-,shät\ *n* : a forked stick with an elastic band attached for shooting small stones

slink \'sliŋk\ *vb* **slunk** \'sləŋk\; **slink·ing** : to move or go sneakily : creep along (as in fear or shame)

slinky \'sliŋ-kē\ *adj* **slink·i·er; -est** **1** : sneakily quiet ⟨*slinky* movements⟩ **2** : following the lines of the figure in a gracefully flowing manner ⟨*slinky* dresses⟩

¹slip \'slip\ *vb* **slipped; slip·ping** **1 a** : to move easily and smoothly : SLIDE ⟨*slip* the knife into its sheath⟩ **b** : to move or place quietly or sneakily ⟨*slipped* from the room⟩ **c** : to pass without being noticed or used ⟨let the opportunity *slip*⟩ **2 a** : to get away from ⟨*slipped* his pursuers⟩ **b** : to free from : SHED ⟨the dog *slipped* its collar⟩ **c** : to escape the attention of ⟨it *slipped* my mind⟩ **d** : to express or become expressed unintentionally ⟨the secret *slipped* out⟩ **e** : to cause to slide open : RELEASE, DISENGAGE ⟨*slip* a bolt⟩ **f** : to let a knitting stitch pass from one needle to another without working a new stitch **3 a** : to slide out of place, away from a support, or from one's grasp **b** : to slide so as to fall or lose balance ⟨*slip* on a grease spot⟩ **c** : to cause to slide especially in putting, passing, or inserting easily or quickly ⟨*slip* into a coat⟩ **d** : to fail to progress or hold normally from or as if from sliding ⟨the loose belt continued to *slip*⟩ **4** : to fall from some level or standard usually gradually or by degrees [Middle English *slippen* "to move by sliding, to move quietly or unnoticed"; of Germanic origin] — **slip something over** : to get the better of another by trickery

²slip *n* **1 a** : a sloping ramp that extends out into the water and serves for landing or repairing ships **b** : a place for a ship between two piers **2** : the act or an instance of departing secretly or hurriedly **3** : a mistake in judgment, selected course of action, or way of doing things : BLUNDER, MISSTEP **4** : the act or an instance of slipping down or out of place ⟨a *slip* on the ice⟩; *also* : a sudden mishap **5 a** : an undergarment made in dress length with shoulder straps **b** : PILLOWCASE

³slip *n* **1** : a small shoot or twig cut for planting or grafting : CUTTING **2 a** : a long narrow strip of material **b** : a piece of paper used for a record ⟨sales *slip*⟩ [Middle English *slippe* "a small shoot or twig for planting or grafting"; probably of Germanic origin]

⁴slip *n* : thin wet clay used in pottery for casting, for decoration, or as a cement [Old English *slypa* "slime, paste"]

slip·cov·er \'slip-,kəv-ər\ *n* : a removable protective covering for a piece of furniture

slip·knot \-,nät\ *n* : a knot that slips along a line around which it is made

slip·page \'slip-ij\ *n* **1** : an act, instance, or process of slipping **2** : a loss in transmission of power

slipped disk *n* : an injury in which one of the disks of cartilage between the vertebrae slips out of place, puts pressure on spinal nerves, and causes back pain

slip·per \'slip-ər\ *n* : a light low shoe without laces that is easily slipped on or off — **slip·pered** \-ərd\ *adj*

slip·pery \'slip-(ə-)rē\ *adj* **slip·peri·er; -est** **1** : having a surface smooth enough to cause one to slide or lose one's hold **2** : not worthy of trust : TRICKY, CRAFTY — **slip·peri·ness** *n*

slip·shod \'slip-'shäd\ *adj* : very careless : SLOVENLY

slip·up \'slip-,əp\ *n* **1** : ²MISTAKE 2 **2** : MISCHANCE 2

slip up \slip-'əp\ *vb* : to make a mistake : BLUNDER

¹slit \'slit\ *vb* **slit; slit·ting 1 a** : to make a slit in : SLASH **b** : to cut off or away : SEVER **2** : to cut into long narrow strips — **slit·ter** *n*

²slit *n* : a long narrow cut or opening — **slit** *adj* — **slit·like** \-,līk\ *adj*

slith·er \'slith-ər\ *vb* **1** : to slide or cause to slide on or as if on a loose gravelly surface **2** : to slip or slide like a snake

slith·ery \'slith-ə-rē\ *adj* : having a slippery surface, texture, or quality

¹sliv·er \'sliv-ər\ *n* : a long slender piece cut or torn off : SPLINTER

²sliver *vb* **sliv·ered; sliv·er·ing** \'sliv-(ə-)riŋ\ : to cut or form into slivers : SPLINTER

slob \'släb\ *n* : a dirty, nasty, or rude person

¹slob·ber \'släb-ər\ *vb* **slob·bered; slob·ber·ing** \-(ə-)riŋ\ **1** : to let saliva or liquid dribble from the mouth : DROOL **2** : to show feeling in an exaggerated way : GUSH

²slobber *n* **1** : dripping saliva **2** : silly exaggerated show of feeling

sloe \'slō\ *n* : the tart bluish black globe-shaped fruit of the blackthorn; *also* : BLACKTHORN 1

sloe—eyed \'slō-'īd\ *adj* **1** : having soft dark bluish or purplish black eyes **2** : having slanted eyes

sloe gin *n* : a sweet reddish liqueur flavored chiefly with sloes

slog \'släg\ *vb* **slogged; slog·ging 1** : to hit hard : BEAT **2** : to work in a steady determined manner — **slog·ger** *n*

slo·gan \'slō-gən\ *n* **1** : a word or phrase that calls to battle **2** : a word or phrase used by a party, a group, or a business to attract attention

> **Word History** The clans of Scotland were groups of related families that joined together, especially to defend against outsiders. In the old days these outsiders might be other clans, but usually they were the English to the south. When it was time to gather members of the clan for a battle, the Scots would shout the *sluagh-ghairm,* which meant "army cry". It is made up of the Scottish Gaelic word *sluagh,* meaning "army", and *ghairm,* meaning "call, cry". This came into English as *slogorn* and later became *slogan.* At first *slogan* meant a "battle cry" or "rallying cry". Later it came to be used for "a motto or phrase used by a group to attract attention". [from earlier *slogorn* "war cry, rallying cry", from Scottish Gaelic, the ancient language of Scotland, *sluagh-ghairm* "army cry", from *sluagh* "army" and *ghairm* "call, cry"]

sloop \'slüp\ *n* : a sailboat with one mast and a fore= and-aft mainsail and jib

¹slop \'släp\ *n* **1** : soft mud : SLUSH **2** : thin tasteless drink or liquid food — usually used in pl. **3** : liquid spilled or splashed **4 a** : food waste (as garbage) fed to animals : SWILL **b** : waste given off by the body — usually used in pl.

²slop *vb* **slopped; slop·ping 1** : to spill on or over **2** : to feed slop to ⟨*slop* the pigs⟩ **3** : to behave or

sloop

deal with in a sloppy manner

¹slope \'slōp\ *adj* : that slants : SLOPING

²slope *vb* **sloped; slop·ing** : to take a slanting direction : give a slant to : INCLINE — **slop·er** *n*

³slope *n* **1** : ground that forms a natural or artificial incline **2** : upward or downward slant or degree of slant **3** : the ratio of the change in a vertical direction to the change in a horizontal direction between any two points on the graph of a straight line

slop·py \'släp-ē\ *adj* **slop·pi·er; -est 1 a** : wet so as to spatter easily : SLUSHY **b** : wet with or as if with something slopped over **2** : SLOVENLY, CARELESS **3** : overly sentimental — **slop·pi·ly** \'släp-ə-lē\ *adv* — **slop·pi·ness** \'släp-ē-nəs\ *n*

¹slosh \'släsh\ *n* **1** : SLUSH 1 **2** : the slap or splash of liquid

²slosh *vb* **1** : to struggle through or splash about in or with water, mud, or slush **2** : to move with a splashing motion

¹slot \'slät\ *n* : a long narrow opening, groove, or passage : SLIT, NOTCH

²slot *vb* **slot·ted; slot·ting** : to cut a slot in

slot car *n* : a toy racing car that fits into a groove and is guided electrically by remote control

sloth \'slòth, 'slōth\ *n* **1** : the quality or state of being lazy **2** : any of several slow-moving mammals of the tropical forests of Central and South America that are related to the armadillos, live in trees, and feed on leaves, shoots, and fruits

sloth·ful \'slòth-fəl, 'slōth-\ *adj* : LAZY 1, SLUGGISH, INDOLENT — **sloth·ful·ly** \-fə-lē\ *adv*

slot machine *n* **1** : a machine whose operation is begun when a coin is dropped into a slot **2** : a coin-operated gambling machine that pays off for the matching of symbols on wheels spun by a handle

sloth 2

¹slouch \'slaùch\ *n* **1** : an awkward, lazy, or unqualified person **2** : a manner of walking, sitting, or standing characterized by an awkward stooping of head and shoulders

²slouch *vb* : to walk, sit, or stand with a slouch — **sloucher** *n*

slouchy \'slaù-chē\ *adj* **slouch·i·er; -est** : slouching or untidy especially in appearance

¹slough \'slü, 'slaù; in the U.S. (except New England) 'slü is usual for sense 1; 'slaù is more frequent for sense 2\ *n* **1** *also* **slue** : a wet and marshy or muddy place (as a swamp or backwater) **2** : a discouraged, degraded, or hopeless state [Old English *slōh* "swamp"]

²slough \'sləf\ *also* **sluff** *n* **1** : the cast-off skin of a snake **2** : a mass of dead tissue separating from living tissue **3** : something that may be shed or cast off [Middle English *slughe* "the cast-off skin of a snake"]

³slough \'sləf\ *also* **sluff** *vb* **1 a** : to cast off or become cast off **b** : to cast off one's skin **c** : to separate dead tissue from living tissue **d** : to get rid of or discard as bothersome, objectionable, or not to one's advantage **2** : to crumble slowly and fall away

Slo·vak \'slō-,väk, -,vak\ *n* **1** : a member of a Slavic people of eastern Czechoslovakia **2** : the Slavic language of the Slovak people — **Slovak** *adj* — **Slo·va·ki·an** \slō-'väk-ē-ən, -'vak-\ *adj or n*

slov·en \'sləv-ən\ *n* : a slovenly person : SLOB

\ə\ abut	\aù\ out	\i\ tip	\ò\ saw	\ù\ foot	
\ər\ further	\ch\ chin	\ī\ life	\òi\ coin	\y\ yet	
\a\ mat	\e\ pet	\j\ job	\th\ thin	\yü\ few	
\ā\ take	\ē\ easy	\ŋ\ sing	\th\ this	\yù\ cure	
\ä\ cot, cart	\g\ go	\ō\ bone	\ü\ food	\zh\ vision	

Slo·vene \'slō-,vēn\ *n* **1 a** : a member of a southern Slavic people living in Yugoslavia **b** : a person born or living in Slovenia **2** : the language of the Slovenes — **Slovene** *adj* — **Slo·ve·ni·an** \slō-'vē-nē-ən\ *adj or n*

slov·en·ly \'sləv-ən-lē\ *adj* **1 a** : untidy especially in dress or person **b** : lazily careless **2** : characteristic of a sloven — **slov·en·li·ness** *n* — **slovenly** *adv*

¹slow \'slō\ *adj* **1 a** : mentally dull : STUPID **b** : naturally slow-moving **2 a** : unwilling to take prompt action **b** : not easily aroused or excited **3 a** : moving, flowing, or proceeding without speed or at less than usual speed **b** : not vigorous or active ⟨a *slow* fire⟩ **c** : taking place at a low rate or over a considerable period of time **4** : having qualities that hinder or stop rapid progress or action ⟨a *slow* racetrack⟩ **5 a** : registering behind or below what is correct ⟨the clock is *slow*⟩ **b** : that is behind the time at a specified time or place **6** : lacking in activity or liveliness ⟨a *slow* market⟩ — **slow·ish** \'slō-ish\ *adj* — **slow·ly** *adv* — **slow·ness** *n*

²slow *adv* : in a slow manner

³slow *vb* : to make or go slow or slower — often used with *down* or *up*

slow cooker *n* : a covered electric cooking pot that cooks food slowly at low temperatures

slow·down \'slō-,daun\ *n* : a slowing down

slow motion *n* : action in a film or television picture apparently taking place more slowly than it actually occurred

slow·poke \'slō-,pōk\ *n* : a very slow person

sludge \'sləj\ *n* **1** : MUD, MIRE **2** : a muddy or slushy mass; *esp* : solid matter produced by water and sewage treatment processes — **sludgy** \'sləj-ē\ *adj*

¹slue \'slü\ *variant of* ¹SLOUGH

²slue *variant of* ²SLEW

¹slug \'sləg\ *n* **1** : SLUGGARD **2** : any of numerous long wormlike land mollusks that are related to the snails but have only an underdeveloped shell or none at all [Middle English *slugge* "a lazy person"; of Scandinavian origin]

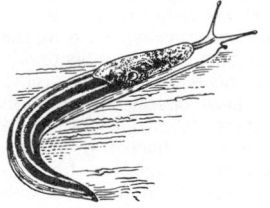

¹slug 2

²slug *n* **1 a** : a small piece of shaped metal (as a bullet) **b** : a metal disk used in place of a coin in a coin-operated machine **2** : a single drink of liquor : SHOT

³slug *n* : a heavy blow especially with the fist [probably from *slug* (noun) "a bullet" or earlier *slug* (verb) "to load (a weapon) with slugs"]

⁴slug *vb* **slugged; slug·ging** : to strike heavily with or as if with the fist or a bat — **slug·ger** *n*

slug·gard \'sləg-ərd\ *n* : a lazy person — **sluggard** *adj*

slug·gish \'sləg-ish\ *adj* : slow in movement or reaction by habit or condition — **slug·gish·ly** *adv* — **slug·gish·ness** *n*

¹sluice \'slüs\ *n* **1** : an artificial passage for water with a gate for controlling its flow or changing its direction **2** : a body of water held back by a gate or a stream flowing through a gate **3** : a device (as a floodgate) for controlling the flow of water **4** : a channel that carries off surplus water **5** : a long sloping trough (as for floating logs to a sawmill)

²sluice *vb* **sluiced; sluic·ing** **1** : to draw off by or through a sluice **2 a** : to wash with or in water running through or from a sluice **b** : DRENCH, FLUSH

¹slum \'sləm\ *n* : a thickly populated section especially of a city marked by crowding, dirty run-down housing, and generally poor living conditions

²slum *vb* **slummed; slum·ming** : to visit slums especially out of curiosity — **slum·mer** *n*

¹slum·ber \'sləm-bər\ *vb* **slum·bered; slum·ber·ing** \-b(ə-)rin̥\ **1** : to sleep usually lightly **2** : to exist without being active ⟨a *slumbering* volcano⟩

²slumber *n* : ¹SLEEP — **slum·ber·er** \-bər-ər\ *n*

slum·ber·ous *or* **slum·brous** \'sləm-b(ə-)rəs\ *adj* **1** : very sleepy **2** : causing or tending to cause sleep : SOPORIFIC

slum·lord \'sləm-,lo(ə)rd\ *n* : a landlord who receives high profits from renting substandard housing

¹slump \'sləmp\ *vb* **1** : to drop or slide down suddenly : COLLAPSE **2** : ²SLOUCH **3** : to fall off sharply

²slump *n* : a marked or continued reduction especially in economic activity or prices

slung *past and past participle of* SLING

slunk *past and past participle of* SLINK

¹slur \'slər\ *vb* **slurred; slur·ring** **1 a** : to slide or slip over without proper mention, consideration, or emphasis **b** : to perform hurriedly : SKIMP **2** : to sing or play successive musical notes of different pitch in a smooth or connected manner **3** : to speak unclearly usually as a result of carelessness or haste

²slur *n* **1 a** : a curved line ⌢ or ⌣ connecting notes to be sung or played without a break **b** : the combination of two or more slurred tones **2** : a slurring manner of speech

³slur *vb* **slurred; slur·ring** **1** : to make an insulting remark about : DISPARAGE **2** : to make unclear : OBSCURE

⁴slur *n* **1 a** : damaging criticism **b** : ¹DISHONOR 1, SHAME **2** : a blurred spot in printed matter : SMUDGE

slurp \'slərp\ *vb* : to eat or drink noisily or with a sucking sound — **slurp** *n*

slush \'sləsh\ *n* **1** : partly melted or watery snow **2** : soft mud : MIRE **3** : RUBBISH, DRIVEL

slushy \'sləsh-ē\ *adj* **slush·i·er; -est** : full of or resembling slush ⟨a *slushy* road⟩

slut \'slət\ *n* **1** : a dirty or sloppy woman **2** : an indecent woman; *esp* : ²PROSTITUTE — **slut·tish** \'slət-ish\ *adj*

sly \'slī\ *adj* **sli·er** *also* **sly·er** \'slī-(ə)r\; **sli·est** *also* **sly·est** \'slī-əst\ **1 a** : skillful or clever at tricks **b** : tending to secrecy or concealment **2** : lightly mischievous **syn** see CUNNING — **sly·ly** *adv* — **sly·ness** *n* — **on the sly** : in a secret manner

¹smack \'smak\ *n* **1** : characteristic or slight taste or flavor **2** : a small quantity [Old English *smæc* "a characteristic taste or flavor"]

²smack *vb* : to have a flavor, trace, or suggestion

³smack *vb* **1** : to close and open the lips noisily especially in eating **2** : to kiss usually loudly **3** : to make or give a sharp slap or blow

⁴smack *n* **1** : a quick sharp noise made by rapidly opening and closing the lips **2** : a loud kiss **3** : a sharp slap or blow

⁵smack *adv* : in a square and sharp manner : DIRECTLY ⟨*smack* in the face⟩

⁶smack *n, slang* : HEROIN [perhaps from Yiddish *shmek* "sniff, pinch of snuff"]

smack–dab \'smak-'dab\ *adv* : EXACTLY 1b

¹small \'smol\ *adj* **1** : little in size **2** : few in numbers or members ⟨a *small* crowd⟩ **3** : little in amount ⟨a *small* supply⟩ **4** : not very much ⟨*small* success⟩ **5** : not important ⟨a *small* matter⟩ **6** : operating on a limited scale ⟨*small* dealers⟩ **7** : ¹SOFT 1c ⟨a *small* voice⟩ **8** : not generous : MEAN ⟨a *small* nature⟩ **9** : made up of small units **10** : ¹HUMBLE 1, MODEST ⟨a *small* beginning⟩ **11** : having been humiliated or humbled ⟨felt very *small* to be caught cheating⟩ — **small·ish** \'smo-lish\ *adj* — **small·ness** \'smol-nəs\ *n*

²small *adv* **1** : in or into small pieces ⟨cut the meat *small*⟩ **2** : in a small manner ⟨most businesses begin *small*⟩

³small *n* : a part smaller and especially narrower than the rest ⟨the *small* of the back⟩

small arm *n* : a firearm fired while held in the hands

small calorie *n* : CALORIE 1a

small claims court *n* : a court intended to simplify the settling of disputes over small debts

small–fry \'smȯl-ˌfrī\ *adj* **1** : ¹MINOR 1, UNIMPORTANT **2** : of or relating to children : CHILDISH

small intestine *n* : the long narrow part of the intestine between the stomach and the colon in which food is mostly digested, from which digested food is absorbed into the body, and which consists of the duodenum, jejunum, and ileum

small–mind·ed \'smȯl-'mīn-dəd\ *adj* **1** : having narrow interests, sympathies, or outlook **2** : typical of a small-minded person : PETTY — **small–mind·ed·ness** *n*

small·mouth bass \ˌsmȯl-ˌmaùth-\ *n* : a black bass that lives in clear rivers and lakes and is bronze green above and lighter below — called also *smallmouth black bass*

smallmouth bass

small·pox \'smȯl-ˌpäks\ *n* : a deadly disease that is caused by a virus and characterized by fever and a rash

small talk *n* : light or informal conversation

¹**smart** \'smärt\ *vb* **1** : to cause or feel a sharp stinging pain **2** : to feel mental distress (as regret, resentment, or embarrassment)

²**smart** *adj* **1** : causing smarting : STINGING **2** : marked by forceful activity or vigorous strength **3** : BRISK 1, SPIRITED **4 a** : mentally alert : BRIGHT ⟨a *smart* teacher⟩ **b** : sharp in scheming : SHREWD **5 a** : WITTY, CLEVER **b** : IMPUDENT, FLIPPANT **6 a** : stylish or elegant in dress or appearance **b** : WORLDLY-WISE, KNOWING **c** : FASHIONABLE — **smart·ly** *adv* — **smart·ness** *n*

³**smart** *adv* : in a smart manner

⁴**smart** *n* : a smarting pain; *esp* : a stinging pain in one small part of the body

smart al·eck \'smärt-ˌal-ik, -ˌel-\ *n* : a person who likes to show off in a clever or witty but annoying way — **smart–al·ecky** \-ˌal-ə-kē, -ˌel-\ *or* **smart–aleck** *adj*

smart·en \'smärt-ᵊn\ *vb* **smart·ened; smart·en·ing** \'smärt-niŋ, -ᵊn-iŋ\ **1** : to make smart or smarter; *esp* : SPRUCE, FRESHEN ⟨*smartened* themselves for the party⟩ **2** : to make or become more alert ⟨*smarten* up, before it's too late⟩

smarty *or* **smart·ie** \'smärt-ē\ *n, pl* **smart·ies** : SMART ALECK

¹**smash** \'smash\ *vb* **1** : to break into pieces by violence : SHATTER **2** : to drive, throw, or move violently especially with a destructive effect **3** : to destroy completely : WRECK **4** : to go to pieces suddenly : COLLAPSE — **smash·er** *n*

²**smash** *n* **1 a** : a heavy blow or attack **b** : a hard overhand stroke (as in tennis) **2** : the condition of being smashed **3 a** : the action or sound of smashing; *esp* : a wreck due to collision : CRASH **b** : complete collapse : RUIN; *esp* : BANKRUPTCY **4** : a striking success : HIT ⟨the new play is a *smash*⟩

smash·up \'smash-ˌəp\ *n* **1** : a complete collapse **2** : a destructive collision of motor vehicles

smat·ter·ing \'smat-ə-riŋ\ *n* **1** : a small amount of knowledge ⟨a *smattering* of French⟩ **2** : a small scattered number

¹**smear** \'smi(ə)r\ *n* **1** : a spot made by or as if by an oily or sticky substance : SMUDGE **2** : material smeared on a surface; *esp* : material prepared for microscopic examination by smearing on a slide — compare PAP SMEAR **3** : a usually unproven charge or accusation

²**smear** *vb* **1 a** : to spread with something oily or sticky **b** : to spread over a surface **2 a** : to stain, smudge, or dirty by or as if by smearing **b** : to blacken the reputation of **3** : to blot out or blur by or as if by smearing — **smear·er** *n*

smear·case *also* **smier·case** \'smi(ə)r-ˌkās\ *n, chiefly Midland* : COTTAGE CHEESE

smeary \'smi(ə)r-ē\ *adj* **1** : marked by smears **2** : likely to cause smears

¹**smell** \'smel\ *vb* **smelled** \'smeld\ *or* **smelt** \'smelt\; **smell·ing** **1** : to become aware of an odor by means of the sense organs located in the nose **2** : to detect or become aware of as if by the sense of smell ⟨*smell* trouble⟩ **3** : to use the sense of smell **4 a** : to have or give off an odor **b** : to give a hint or trace of something and especially of something harmful or evil ⟨the plan *smells* of trickery⟩ — **smell·er** *n* — **smell a rat** : to have a suspicion of something wrong

²**smell** *n* **1 a** : the process or power of smelling **b** : the special sense concerned with detecting odor **2** : the quality of a thing that affects the organs of smell : ODOR, SCENT **3** : a special quality associated with a given source : AURA ⟨the *smell* of adventure⟩ **4** : an act of smelling

smelling salts *n pl* : a strong-smelling preparation of ammonia in water used to reawaken someone who has fainted

smelly \'smel-ē\ *adj* **smell·i·er; -est** : having a smell and especially a bad smell

¹**smelt** \'smelt\ *n, pl* **smelts** *or* **smelt** : any of several very small food fishes that look like the related trouts, live in coastal sea waters, and usually swim up rivers to spawn

²**smelt** *vb* **1** : to melt (as ore) usually in order to separate the metal **2** : REFINE 1, REDUCE

smelt·er \'smel-tər\ *n* **1** : a person whose work or business is smelting **2** : an establishment for smelting

smid·gen *also* **smid·geon** *or* **smid·gin** \'smij-ən\ *n* : a small amount : BIT

¹**smile** \'smī(ə)l\ *vb* **smiled; smil·ing** **1** : to have, produce, or exhibit a smile **2 a** : to look with amusement or ridicule **b** : to be fortunate or agreeable ⟨the weather *smiled* on our plans⟩ **3** : to express by a smile ⟨both parents *smiled* their approval⟩ — **smil·er** *n* — **smil·ing·ly** \'smī-liŋ-lē\ *adv*

²**smile** *n* : a change of facial expression in which the eyes brighten and the lips curve slightly upward especially in expression of amusement, pleasure, approval, or sometimes scorn

smirch \'smərch\ *vb* **1** : to make dirty, stained, or discolored especially by smearing with something that soils **2** : to bring discredit or disgrace on — **smirch** *n*

smirk \'smərk\ *vb* : to smile in an insincere manner : SIMPER — **smirk** *n*

smirky \'smər-kē\ *adj* : suggesting or being a smirk

smite \'smīt\ *vb* **smote** \'smōt\; **smit·ten** \'smit-ᵊn\ *or* **smote; smit·ing** \'smīt-iŋ\ **1** : to strike sharply or heavily especially with the hand or a hand weapon **2 a** : to kill or injure by smiting **b** : to attack or afflict suddenly and harmfully ⟨*smitten* by disease⟩ **3** : to affect like a sudden hard blow ⟨*smitten* with terror⟩ — **smit·er** \'smīt-ər\ *n*

smith \'smith\ *n* **1** : a worker in metals : BLACKSMITH **2** : one who constructs, builds, or produces something : MAKER — often used in combination ⟨gun*smith*⟩

smith·er·eens \ˌsmith-ə-'rēnz\ *n pl* : small broken pieces : BITS

smithy \'smith-ē *also* 'smith-\ *n, pl* **smith·ies** **1** : the workshop of a smith **2** : BLACKSMITH

\ə\ abut	\aù\ out	\i\ tip	\o\̇ saw	\ù\ foot
\ər\ further	\ch\ chin	\ī\ lite	\oi\̇ coin	\y\ yet
\a\ mat	\e\ pet	\j\ job	\th\ thin	\yü\ few
\ā\ take	\ē\ easy	\ŋ\ sing	\t͟h\ this	\yu̇\ cure
\ä\ cot, cart	\g\ go	\ō\ bone	\ü\ food	\zh\ vision

¹smock \'smäk\ *n* **1** *archaic* : a woman's undergarment; *esp* : CHEMISE 1 **2** : a light loose garment worn usually over regular clothing for protection from dirt

²smock *vb* : to embroider or shirr with smocking

smock·ing \'smäk-iŋ\ *n* : a decorative embroidery or shirring made by gathering cloth in regularly spaced round tucks

smog \'smäg *also* 'smȯg\ *n* : a thick haze caused by the action of sunlight on air polluted by smoke and automobile exhaust fumes [from *smoke* and *fog*]

smog·gy \'smäg-ē *also* 'smȯg-ē\ *adj* **smog·gi·er; -est** : having a lot of smog

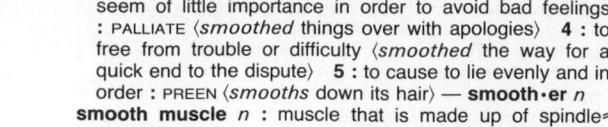

smock 2

¹smoke \'smōk\ *n* **1** : the gas of burning materials (as coal, wood, or tobacco) made visible by small particles of carbon floating in it **2** : a mass or column of smoke **3** : something that has little substance or value or that doesn't last very long **4** : something that hides **5 a** : something to smoke (as a cigarette) **b** : an act of smoking tobacco — **smoke·like** \'smō-ˌklīk\ *adj*

²smoke *vb* **smoked; smok·ing** **1 a** : to give off or exhale smoke **b** : to give off too much smoke **2 a** : to inhale and exhale the fumes of a burning substance (as tobacco) **b** : to use in smoking ⟨*smoke* a pipe⟩ **3 a** : to drive away by smoke **b** : to blacken or discolor with smoke **c** : to use smoke to give (as meat or cheese) flavor and keep from spoiling — **smok·er** *n*

smoke·house \'smōk-ˌhaús\ *n* : a building where meat or fish is given flavor and kept from spoiling by the use of smoke

smoke jumper *n* : a forest-fire fighter who parachutes to locations otherwise difficult to reach

smoke·less \'smō-kləs\ *adj* : producing or containing little or no smoke ⟨*smokeless* powder⟩

smoke screen *n* : a screen of or as if of smoke to make observation or detection difficult

smoke·stack \'smōk-ˌstak\ *n* : a large chimney or pipe for carrying away smoke (as on a factory or ship)

smoke tree *n* : either of two shrubs or small trees that are related to the sumacs and produce large clusters of tiny flowers that look like clouds of smoke

smoky *also* **smok·ey** \'smō-kē\ *adj* **smok·i·er; -est** : giving off smoke especially in large quantities ⟨*smoky* stoves⟩ **2** : like that of smoke ⟨a *smoky* flavor⟩ **3** : filled with or darkened by smoke ⟨a *smoky* room⟩ — **smok·i·ly** \-kə-lē\ *adv* — **smok·i·ness** \-kē-nəs\ *n*

¹smol·der *or* **smoul·der** \'smōl-dər\ *n* : a slow smoky fire

²smolder *or* **smoulder** *vb* **smol·dered** *or* **smoul·dered; smol·der·ing** *or* **smoul·der·ing** \-d(ə-)riŋ\ **1** : to burn slowly with smoke and usually without flame ⟨fire was *smoldering* in the pit⟩ **2** : to exist or continue in a hidden or controlled state ⟨discontent *smoldered* for years before the revolt⟩ **3** : to burn inwardly ⟨anger *smoldered* in my heart⟩

smooch \'smüch\ *vb* : ¹KISS 1, PET — **smooch** *n*

¹smooth \'smüth\ *adj* **1 a** : having a continuous even surface : not rough ⟨a *smooth* skin⟩ **b** : not hairy **2** : free from obstacles or difficulties ⟨a *smooth* path⟩ **3** : even and uninterrupted in flow or flight **4** : flattering but not truthfully so ⟨a *smooth* talker⟩ **5 a** : SERENE 1, EQUABLE ⟨a *smooth* disposition⟩ **b** : AMIABLE, COURTEOUS **6** : not having a strong or sour odor or flavor : BLAND ⟨a *smooth* sherry⟩ — **smooth·ly** *adv* — **smooth·ness** *n*

²smooth *vb* **1 a** : to free from what is harsh or disagreeable : POLISH ⟨*smoothed* out my style⟩ **b** : to make calm : SOOTHE **2** : to make smooth **3** : to make (as a fault)

seem of little importance in order to avoid bad feelings : PALLIATE ⟨*smoothed* things over with apologies⟩ **4** : to free from trouble or difficulty ⟨*smoothed* the way for a quick end to the dispute⟩ **5** : to cause to lie evenly and in order : PREEN ⟨*smooths* down its hair⟩ — **smooth·er** *n*

smooth muscle *n* : muscle that is made up of spindle-shaped cells with a single nucleus and no cross stripes, that is found in many internal organs (as the stomach and the bladder), and that is not under voluntary control — called also *involuntary muscle*; compare STRIATED MUSCLE

smooth–tongued \'smüth-'təŋd\ *adj* : flattering but not truthfully so

smoothy *or* **smooth·ie** \'smü-thē\ *n, pl* **smooth·ies** **1** : a smooth-tongued person **2** : a person with well-bred manners

smor·gas·bord \'smȯr-gəs-ˌbō(ə)rd, -ˌbȯ(ə)rd\ *n* : a self-service luncheon or supper offering a large variety of foods and dishes [from Swedish *smörgåsbord* "a buffet meal", from *smörgås* "open sandwich" and *bord* "table"]

smote *past of* SMITE

smoth·er \'sməth-ər\ *vb* **smoth·ered; smoth·er·ing** \-(ə-)riŋ\ **1** : to be overcome or killed through lack of air **2** : to overcome or kill by depriving of air or exposing to smoke or fumes **3 a** : to prevent the development or actions of ⟨*smother* a child with too much care⟩ **b** : to cover up : SUPPRESS ⟨*smother* a yawn⟩ **c** : to cover thickly ⟨steak *smothered* with mushrooms⟩

¹smudge \'sməj\ *vb* **smudged; smudg·ing** **1 a** : to make a smudge on **b** : to soil as if by smudging **2** : to make a smudge **3** : to become smudged

²smudge *n* **1 a** : a blurry spot or streak : SMEAR **b** : ²STAIN 2 **2** : a fire made to smoke (as for protecting fruit from frost) — **smudgy** \'sməj-ē\ *adj*

smug \'sməg\ *adj* **smug·ger; smug·gest** : highly satisfied with oneself : COMPLACENT — **smug·ly** *adv* — **smug·ness** *n*

smug·gle \'sməg-əl\ *vb* **smug·gled; smug·gling** \-(ə-)liŋ\ **1** : to export or import secretly and unlawfully especially to avoid paying taxes ⟨*smuggle* jewels⟩ **2** : to take, bring, or introduce secretly — **smug·gler** \'sməg-lər\ *n*

¹smut \'smət\ *vb* **smut·ted; smut·ting** **1** : to stain, soil, or affect (a crop or plant) with smut **2** : to become affected by smut

²smut *n* **1** : matter that soils or blackens; *esp* : a particle of soot **2** : any of various destructive diseases of plants caused by fungi that transform plant organs (as seeds) into dark masses of spores; *also* : a fungus that causes a smut **3** : indecent language, pictures, or writing

smut·ty \'smət-ē\ *adj* **smut·ti·er; -est** **1** : soiled or tainted with smut ⟨a *smutty* face⟩ **2** : affected with smut fungus **3** : OBSCENE, INDECENT ⟨*smutty* jokes⟩ — **smut·ti·ly** \'smət-ᵊl-ē\ *adv* — **smut·ti·ness** \'smət-ē-nəs\ *n*

snack \'snak\ *n* : a light meal : LUNCH

snack bar *n* : a public eating place where snacks are served usually at a counter

¹snag \'snag\ *n* **1** : a stump or stub of a tree branch especially when stuck under water and not visible from the surface **2** : an uneven or broken part sticking out from a smooth surface ⟨caught my sweater on a *snag*⟩ **3** : a concealed or unexpected difficulty ⟨our plans hit a *snag*⟩

²snag *vb* **snagged; snag·ging** : to catch on or as if on a snag

snag·gle·tooth \'snag-əl-ˌtüth\ *n* : a tooth that sticks out, is uneven, or is broken — **snag·gle·toothed** \ˌsnag-əl-'tütht\ *adj*

snail \'snā(ə)l\ *n* **1** : any of numerous

snail 1

small mollusks that are gastropods usually with a spiral shell and that include some living on land and others living in water **2** : a slow-moving person or thing

¹snake \'snāk\ *n* **1** : any of numerous limbless reptiles that have a long body and eat large insects or small mammals and birds **2** : a mean or treacherous person — **snake-like** \'snā-ˌklīk\ *adj*

²snake *vb* **snaked; snak·ing** : to crawl, wind, or move like a snake

snake·bird \'snāk-ˌbərd\ *n* : any of a genus of large fish-eating birds that are related to the cormorants but have a longer thinner neck and a sharp-pointed bill

snake·bite \-ˌbīt\ *n* : the bite of a snake and especially a poisonous snake

snake in the grass : a secretly unfaithful friend

snake plant *n* : SANSEVIERIA

snake·root \'snā-ˌkrüt, -ˌkrut\ *n* : any of numerous plants sometimes believed to be a cure for snakebites or illness; *also* : the roots of a snakeroot

snake·skin \'snāk-ˌskin\ *n* : the skin of a snake or leather made from it

snaky *also* **snak·ey** \'snā-kē\ *adj* **1** : of or resembling a snake **2** : full of snakes — **snak·i·ly** \-kə-lē\ *adv*

¹snap \'snap\ *vb* **snapped; snap·ping** **1 a** : to make a sudden closing of the jaws : seize something sharply with the mouth ⟨fish *snapping* at the bait⟩ **b** : to grasp at something eagerly ⟨*snapped* at the chance to travel⟩ **c** : to take possession of at once — usually used with *up* ⟨*snap* up a bargain⟩ **2** : to speak sharply or irritably ⟨*snap* at a questioner⟩ **3 a** : to break or break apart suddenly especially with a sharp sound ⟨the twig *snapped*⟩ ⟨*snapped* the bone in two⟩ **b** : to give way or cause to give way suddenly under stress ⟨the rope *snapped*⟩ **c** : to bring to a sudden end ⟨*snapped* the opposing team's winning streak⟩ **4** : to make or cause to make a sharp or crackling sound ⟨*snap* a whip⟩ **5 a** : to close or fit in place with a quick movement ⟨the lid *snapped* shut⟩ **b** : to put into or remove from a position by a sudden movement or with a snapping sound ⟨*snap* off a switch⟩ **c** : to close by snaps or fasteners ⟨*snapped* up the snowsuit⟩ **6 a** : to move briskly or sharply ⟨*snapped* to attention⟩ **b** : to put (a football) in play especially by passing or handing backward between the legs **c** : to take a snapshot of

²snap *n* **1** : a quick closing (as of the mouth in biting or of scissors in cutting); *esp* : a biting or snatching with the teeth or jaws **2** : something that is easy and presents no problems : CINCH **3** : a small amount : BIT ⟨don't care a *snap*⟩ **4 a** : a sudden snatching at something **b** : a quick short movement **c** : a sudden sharp breaking **5** : a sound made by snapping something ⟨shut the book with a *snap*⟩ **6** : a sudden spell of harsh weather ⟨a cold *snap*⟩ **7** : a catch or fastening that closes or locks with a click ⟨*snap* of a bracelet⟩ **8** : a thin brittle cookie **9** : SNAP-SHOT **10** : smartness of movement or speech : ENERGY **11** : an act or instance of snapping a football

³snap *adj* **1** : made suddenly or without careful thought ⟨a *snap* judgment⟩ **2** : shutting or fastening with a click or by means of a device that snaps ⟨a *snap* lock⟩ **3** : unusually easy ⟨a *snap* course⟩

snap·back \'snap-ˌbak\ *n* : a sudden rebound or recovery

snap back \(ˈ)snap-ˈbak\ *vb* : to make a quick recovery ⟨*snap back* after an illness⟩

snap bean *n* : a bean grown primarily for its pods that are usually broken into pieces and cooked as a vegetable while they are still young and tender and before their seeds have become enlarged — compare SHELL BEAN

snap·drag·on \'snap-ˌdrag-ən\ *n* : any of several garden plants having showy white, crimson, or yellow two-lipped flowers

snap·per \'snap-ər\ *n, pl* **snappers** **1 a** : something that snaps **b** : SNAPPING TURTLE **2** *pl also* **snapper** **a** : any of a large family of active flesh-eating fishes of warm seas

that are important as food and sport fishes **b** : any of several immature fishes (as the young of the bluefish) that resemble a snapper

snapping turtle *n* : any of several large American freshwater turtles that have powerful jaws and are sometimes used for food

snapping turtle

snap·pish \'snap-ish\ *adj* **1** : marked by snapping irritable speech : IRASCIBLE ⟨a *snappish* disposition⟩ **2** : apt to bite ⟨a *snappish* dog⟩ — **snap·pish·ly** *adv*

snap·py \'snap-ē\ *adj* **snap·pi·er; -est** **1** : SNAPPISH 1 **2 a** : quickly made or done **b** : full of life : LIVELY **c** : briskly cold **d** : STYLISH, SMART ⟨a *snappy* dresser⟩ — **snap·pi·ly** \'snap-ə-lē\ *adv*

snap·shot \'snap-ˌshät\ *n* : a photograph taken usually with an inexpensive hand-held camera

¹snare \'sna(ə)r, 'sne(ə)r\ *n* **1 a** : a trap often consisting of a noose for catching small animals or birds **b** : something by which one is entangled, trapped, or deceived **2** : one of the catgut strings or metal spirals stretched across the bottom of a snare drum

²snare *vb* **snared; snar·ing** **1** : to capture or entangle by or as if by use of a snare **2** : to win by skillful or deceptive measures **syn** see CATCH — **snar·er** *n*

snare drum *n* : a small two-headed drum that can be worn at the side while marching and that has a band of snares stretched across the lower head to rattle when the head vibrates to give the drum its special sound

¹snarl \'snär(-ə)l\ *n* **1** : a tangle especially of hairs or thread : KNOT **2** : a tangled situation ⟨a traffic *snarl*⟩ [Middle English *snarle* "a tangle or knot of hairs or thread", probably derived from *snare* "noose, trap"]

²snarl *vb* : to get into a tangle

³snarl *vb* **1** : to growl with a snapping of teeth **2** : to speak in an angry way **3** : to utter with a snarl [from obsolete *snar* "to growl"] — **snarl·er** *n*

⁴snarl *n* : an angry growl

¹snatch \'snach\ *vb* **1** : to seize or try to seize something quickly or suddenly **2** : to grasp or take suddenly or hastily : GRAB — **snatch·er** *n*

²snatch *n* **1 a** : a brief period ⟨slept in *snatches*⟩ **b** : something brief, hurried, or in small bits **2** : a snatching at or of something

snaz·zy \'snaz-ē\ *adj* **snaz·zi·er; -est** : attractive in a flashy way ⟨a *snazzy* tie⟩

¹sneak \'snēk\ *vb* **sneaked** \'snēkt\ *or* **snuck** \'snək\; **sneak·ing** **1** : to go about in a sly or secret manner **2** : to put, bring, or take in a sly manner **syn** see LURK

²sneak *n* **1** : a person who acts in a secret or sly manner **2** : the act or an instance of sneaking

³sneak *adj* **1** : carried on secretly : CLANDESTINE **2** : occurring without warning ⟨a *sneak* attack⟩

sneak·er \'snē-kər\ *n* **1** : one that sneaks **2** : a sports shoe (as of canvas) with a rubber sole

sneak·ing \'snē-kiŋ\ *adj* **1** : FURTIVE, UNDERHAND **2 a** : not openly expressed ⟨a *sneaking* admiration for an opponent⟩ **b** : being a thought, feeling, or suspicion that makes one uneasy ⟨a *sneaking* feeling that we're going to have a test today⟩

sneaky \'snē-kē\ *adj* **sneak·i·er; -est** **1** : behaving in a sly or secret manner **2** : marked by secrecy or slyness ⟨a

\ə\ abut	\au̇\ out	\i\ tip	\ȯ\ saw	\u̇\ foot
\ər\ further	\ch\ chin	\ī\ life	\ȯi\ coin	\y\ yet
\a\ mat	\e\ pet	\j\ job	\th\ thin	\yü\ few
\ā\ take	\ē\ easy	\ŋ\ sing	\th\ this	\yu̇\ cure
\ä\ cot, cart	\g\ go	\ō\ bone	\ü\ food	\zh\ vision

sneaky trick⟩ — **sneak·i·ly** \-kə-lē\ *adv* — **sneak·i·ness** \-kē-nəs\ *n*

¹**sneer** \'sni(ə)r\ *vb* **1** : to smile or laugh with expressions of scorn **2** : to speak or write in a scorning manner — **sneer·er** *n*

²**sneer** *n* : a sneering expression or remark

sneeze \'snēz\ *vb* **sneezed; sneez·ing** : to force a breath out mostly through the nose in a sudden violent noisy action — **sneeze** *n* — **sneez·er** *n* — **sneeze at** : to treat lightly : DISDAIN

¹**snick** \'snik\ *vb* : to make or cause to make a snick

²**snick** *n* : a slight often metallic sound : CLICK

¹**snick·er** \'snik-ər\ *vb* **snick·ered; snick·er·ing** \-(ə-)riŋ\ : to give a small and often mean or sly laugh

²**snicker** *n* : an act or sound of snickering

snide \'snīd\ *adj* **1** : ²LOW 9b, MEAN ⟨a *snide* trick⟩ **2** : slyly uncomplimentary or insulting ⟨*snide* remarks⟩

¹**sniff** \'snif\ *vb* **1** : to draw air into the nose in short breaths loud enough to be heard **2** : to show or express scorn ⟨*sniffed* at simple jobs⟩ **3** : to smell or inhale by taking short breaths ⟨*sniff* perfume⟩ **4** : to detect by or as if by smelling ⟨*sniff* out trouble⟩ — **sniff·er** *n*

²**sniff** *n* **1** : the act or sound of sniffing **2** : an odor or amount sniffed

sniff·ish \'snif-ish\ *adj* : SCORNFUL, DISDAINFUL ⟨a *sniffish* boss⟩ — **sniff·ish·ly** *adv*

snif·fle \'snif-əl\ *vb* **snif·fled; snif·fling** \-(ə-)liŋ\ **1** : to sniff repeatedly **2** : to speak with or as if with sniffling

snif·fles \'snif-əls\ *n pl* : a common cold in which the main symptom is a runny nose

snig·ger \'snig-ər\ *vb* **snig·gered; snig·ger·ing** \-(ə-)riŋ\ : ¹SNICKER — **snigger** *n*

¹**snip** \'snip\ *n* **1** : a small piece that is snipped off : FRAGMENT **2** : an act or sound of snipping **3** : a rude person

²**snip** *vb* **snipped; snip·ping** : to cut or cut off with or as if with shears or scissors; *esp* : to clip suddenly or by bits

¹**snipe** \'snīp\ *n, pl* **snipes** *or* **snipe** : any of various birds that have a long slender bill; *esp* : any of several game birds that live in marshy areas and resemble the related woodcocks

²**snipe** *vb* **sniped; snip·ing** **1** : to shoot at exposed individuals of an enemy's forces from a usually concealed point **2** : to attack with sly or cutting remarks — **snip·er** *n*

snipe

snip·pet \'snip-ət\ *n* : a small part, piece, or thing

snip·py \'snip-ē\ *adj* **snip·pi·er; -est** **1** : SHORT-TEMPERED, SNAPPISH **2** : rudely brief : CURT

snips \'snips\ *n pl* : hand shears used especially for cutting sheet metal ⟨tin *snips*⟩

snitch \'snich\ *vb* **1** : INFORM 2, TATTLE ⟨always *snitching* on someone⟩ **2** : to take by sly or secret action; *esp* : PILFER ⟨*snitched* a dime from the kid next door⟩ — **snitch·er** *n*

sniv·el \'sniv-əl\ *vb* **-eled** *or* **-elled; -el·ing** *or* **-el·ling** \-(ə-)liŋ\ **1** : SNUFFLE 2 **2** : to cry or whine with sniffling **3** : to speak or act in a whining manner — **sniv·el·er** \-(ə-)lər\ *n*

snob \'snäb\ *n* **1** : one who imitates, admires, or seeks association with those of higher social position **2** : one who looks down upon those felt to be less important

Word History *Snob* is an old word in English for "a cobbler, a person who makes or repairs shoes". Cobblers came to be thought of as representative of all of the working-class or lower-class people. In time the name *snob* came to be applied to the lower classes as distin-guished from the nobility, the landowners, and the rich merchants. From its being used for any member of the lower class, *snob* soon came to mean "a person who pretends to be a member of a higher class, one who imitates the clothing, speech, and manners of the nobility". Nowadays the word means "anyone who acts as if he or she were better than others". [from obsolete *snob* "a member of the lower classes", from a dialect word *snob* "cobbler, shoemaker"]

snob appeal *n* : the appeal (as from high price) that a product has for a snobbish person

snob·bery \'snäb-(ə-)rē\ *n* : snobbish conduct

snob·bish \'snäb-ish\ *adj* : of, relating to, or being a snob — **snob·bish·ly** *adv* — **snob·bish·ness** *n* — **snob·bism** \'snäb-,iz-əm\ *n*

snob·by \'snäb-ē\ *adj* **snob·bi·er; -est** : SNOBBISH

snood \'snüd\ *n* : a net or fabric bag for holding hair pinned or tied on at the back of the head

¹**snoop** \'snüp\ *vb* : to look or search especially in a sneaking or meddlesome manner — **snoop·er** *n*

²**snoop** *n* : one that snoops : SNOOPER

snoop·er·scope \'snü-pər-,skōp\ *n* : a device that makes it easier for a person to see an object (as in darkness)

snoopy \'snü-pē\ *adj* : being in the habit of snooping especially for personal information about others

snoot \'snüt\ *n* **1** : SNOUT 1 **2** : ¹NOSE 1a

snooty \'snüt-ē\ *adj* **snoot·i·er; -est** : SNOBBISH — **snoot·i·ly** \'snüt-ᵊl-ē\ *adv* — **snoot·i·ness** \'snüt-ē-nəs\ *n*

snooze \'snüz\ *vb* **snoozed; snooz·ing** : to take a nap : DOZE — **snooze** *n*

snore \'snō(ə)r, 'snȯ(ə)r\ *vb* : to breathe with a rough hoarse noise while sleeping — **snore** *n* — **snor·er** *n*

¹**snor·kel** \'snȯr-kəl\ *n* **1** : a tube or tubes that can be extended above the surface of the water to supply air to and remove exhaust from a submerged submarine **2** : a tube used by swimmers for breathing with the head under water

²**snorkel** *vb* **snor·keled; snor·kel·ing** \-k(ə-)liŋ\ : to swim underwater using a snorkel

¹**snort** \'snȯ(ə)rt\ *vb* **1** : to force air violently through the nose with a rough harsh sound **2** : to express scorn, anger, or surprise by a snort **3** : to take in (a drug) by inhaling through the nose — **snort·er** *n*

snorkel 2

²**snort** *n* **1** : an act or sound of snorting **2** : a drink of liquor usually taken by itself in one swallow

snout \'snaút\ *n* **1 a** : a long nose or muzzle (as of a pig) that sticks out **b** : a front part of the head of an animal that sticks out like the snout of a pig **c** : the human nose especially when large or ugly **2** : something resembling a snout — **snout·ed** \-əd\ *adj*

snout beetle *n* : WEEVIL

¹**snow** \'snō\ *n* **1 a** : small white ice crystals formed directly from the water vapor of the air **b** : a fall of snow crystals : a mass of snow crystals that have fallen to earth **2** : something resembling snow: as **a** : a dessert made of stiffly beaten egg whites, sugar, and fruit ⟨pineapple *snow*⟩ **b** *slang* : COCAINE

²**snow** *vb* **1** : to fall or cause to fall in or as snow **2** : to cover, shut in, or imprison with or as if with snow **3** : to deceive, persuade, or charm with insincere or flattering talk

¹**snow·ball** \'snō-,bȯl\ *n* **1** : a round mass of snow pressed or rolled together **2** : a viburnum widely grown for its ball-shaped clusters of white sterile flowers — called also *snowball bush*

²**snowball** *vb* **1** : to throw snowballs at **2** : to increase or expand at a rapidly accelerating rate ⟨problems *snowball*

when early trouble signs are ignored⟩

snow·bank \'snō-ˌbaŋk\ *n* : a mound or slope of snow

snow·bird \-ˌbərd\ *n* : any of several small birds (as a junco) seen chiefly in winter

snow–blind \-ˌblīnd\ *or* **snow–blind·ed** \-ˈblīn-dəd\ *adj* : affected with snow blindness

snow blindness *n* : inflammation and inability to stand light caused by glare reflected from snow or ice

snow·blow·er \'snō-ˌblō-(ə)r\ *n* : a machine in which a rotating device picks up and throws snow aside

snow·bound \-'baund\ *adj* : shut in or blockaded by snow

snow·cap \-ˌkap\ *n* : a covering cap of snow (as on a mountain peak) — **snow·capped** \-ˌkapt\ *adj*

snow·drift \-ˌdrift\ *n* : a bank of drifted snow

snow·drop \-ˌdräp\ *n* : a European plant that is related to the amaryllis and produces nodding white flowers that often appear while snow is still on the ground

snow·fall \-ˌfȯl\ *n* **1** : a fall of snow **2** : the amount of snow that falls in a single storm or in a certain period

snow fence *n* : a fence placed across the usual path of the wind to protect something (as a road) from snowdrifts

snow·flake \'snō-ˌflāk\ *n* : a flake or crystal of snow

snowflake

snow leopard *n* : a large cat of central Asia with a long heavy pelt blotched with brownish black in summer and almost pure white in winter

snow line *n* : the lower edge of an area of permanent snow (as a mountain peak)

snow·man \'snō-ˌman, -ˈman\ *n* : snow shaped to resemble a person

snow·mo·bile \'snō-mō-ˌbēl\ *n* : any of various motor vehicles for travel on snow — **snow·mo·bil·er** \-ˌbē-lər\ *n* — **snow·mo·bil·ing** \-ˌbē-liŋ\ *n*

snow·pea \-ˌpē\ *n* : any of a variety of the cultivated pea that has edible pods — called also *sugar pea*

snow·plow \-ˌplau̇\ *n* : any of various devices used for clearing away snow

¹snow·shoe \-ˌshü\ *n* : a light wooden frame strung with a net that is attached to the foot to prevent sinking in soft snow

²snowshoe *vb* **snow·shoed; snow·shoe·ing** : to travel on snowshoes

snowshoe rabbit *n* : a rather large hare of northern North America with heavily furred hind feet and a coat that is brown in summer but usually white in winter — called also *snowshoe hare*

snow·slide \'snō-ˌslīd\ *n* : an avalanche of snow

snow·storm \-ˌstȯrm\ *n* : a storm of falling snow

snow·suit \-ˌsüt\ *n* : a one-piece or two-piece lined garment worn by children

snow tire *n* : an automobile tire with a tread designed to give added traction on snow

snow under *vb* **1** : to overwhelm especially beyond the ability to absorb or deal with something **2** : to defeat by a large amount

snow–white \'snō-ˈhwīt, -ˈwīt\ *adj* : white as snow

snowy \'snō-ē\ *adj* **snow·i·er; -est** **1** : marked by or covered with snow ⟨a *snowy* day⟩ ⟨*snowy* mountaintops⟩ **2 a** : whitened by or as if by snow ⟨an orchard *snowy* with apple blossoms⟩ **b** : SNOW-WHITE

snowy owl *n* : a large chiefly arctic owl that is white or white spotted with brown

¹snub \'snəb\ *vb* **snubbed; snub·bing** **1** : to check or stop with a reply that hurts : REBUKE **2 a** : to check (as a line) suddenly while running out especially by turning around a fixed object (as a post) **b** : to check the motion of by snubbing a line **3** : to deliberately ignore or treat rudely **4**

: to put out by crushing — **snub·ber** *n*

²snub *n* : an act or an instance of snubbing; *esp* : ²REBUFF

³snub *or* **snubbed** \'snəbd\ *adj* : STUBBY, BLUNT

snub–nosed \'snəb-ˈnōzd\ *adj* : having a stubby and usually slightly turned-up nose

snowy owl

¹snuff \'snəf\ *vb* **1** : to cut or pinch off the burned end of the wick of a candle so as to brighten the light **2** : to put an end to : EXTINGUISH ⟨*snuff* out a candle⟩ ⟨*snuff* out a life⟩ [Middle English *snoffe* "the burned end of a candle wick"]

²snuff *vb* **1** : to draw forcibly through or into the nostrils **2** : to sniff so as to smell [perhaps derived from Dutch *snuffen* "to sniff"]

³snuff *n* : powdered tobacco especially for snuffing up the nose [from Dutch *snuf*, a shortened form of *snuftabak* "powdered tobacco", from *snuffen* "to snuff, sniff" and *tabak* "tobacco"] — **up to snuff** : in good shape

snuff·box \'snəf-ˌbäks\ *n* : a small box for snuff

¹snuf·fle \'snəf-əl\ *vb* **snuf·fled; snuf·fling** \-(ə-)liŋ\ **1** : to snuff or sniff usually loudly and over and over again **2** : to breathe through a partly blocked nose with a sniffing sound **3** : ¹WHINE 1

²snuffle *n* : the sound made in snuffling

¹snug \'snəg\ *vb* **snugged; snug·ging** **1** : to settle or lie down : SNUGGLE **2** : to make snug

²snug *adj* **snug·ger; snug·gest** **1 a** : SEAWORTHY **b** : ²TRIM, NEAT **c** : fitting closely and comfortably ⟨a *snug* coat⟩ **2** : enjoying or providing warm secure shelter and comfort : COZY ⟨a *snug* little cottage⟩ **3** : fairly large : AMPLE ⟨a *snug* fortune⟩ **4** : offering safe concealment ⟨a *snug* harbor⟩ — **snug** *adv* — **snug·ly** *adv* — **snug·ness** *n*

snug·gery \'snəg-(ə-)rē\ *n, pl* **-ger·ies** *chiefly British* : a snug place; *esp* : DEN 4

snug·gle \'snəg-əl\ *vb* **snug·gled; snug·gling** \-(ə-)liŋ\ **1** : to curl up comfortably or cozily : CUDDLE **2** : to pull in close especially for comfort or in affection : NESTLE

¹so \(ˈ)sō, *especially before adj or adv followed by* "that" sə\ *adv* **1 a** : in a manner or way that is indicated or suggested ⟨said I'd attend and did *so*⟩ ⟨it *so* happened that all were wrong⟩ **b** : in the same manner or way : ALSO ⟨worked hard and *so* did we⟩ **c** : ¹THEN 2 ⟨and *so* home and to bed⟩ **2 a** : to an indicated or suggested amount or way ⟨had never been *so* happy⟩ **b** : very much ⟨I loved them *so*⟩ **c** : to a definite but not specified amount ⟨can only do *so* much in a day⟩ **d** : most certainly : INDEED ⟨you did *so* do it⟩ **3** : for a reason that has just been stated : THEREFORE ⟨is honest and *so* returned the wallet⟩

²so \(ˈ)sō\ *conj* **1 a** : with the result that ⟨the way you speak is good, *so* every word is clear⟩ **b** : in order that ⟨be quiet *so* I can sleep⟩ — often followed by *that* **2** *archaic* : provided that — often used with *just* **3** : for that reason ⟨don't want to, *so* I won't⟩

³so \'sō\ *adj* **1** : agreeing with actual facts : TRUE ⟨said things that were not *so*⟩ **2** : marked by a definite order ⟨my books are always just *so*⟩

⁴so \ˌsō, 'sō\ *pron* **1** : such as has been specified : the same ⟨became our supervisor and remained *so*⟩ **2** : approximately that ⟨20 years or *so*⟩

⁵so \'sō\ *n* : ¹SOL

\ə\ abut	\au̇\ out	\i\ tip	\ȯ\ saw	\u̇\ foot
\ər\ further	\ch\ chin	\ī\ life	\ȯi\ coin	\y\ yet
\a\ mat	\e\ pet	\j\ job	\th\ thin	\yü\ few
\ā\ take	\ē\ easy	\ŋ\ sing	\th\ this	\yu̇\ cure
\ä\ cot, cart	\g\ go	\ō\ bone	\ü\ food	\zh\ vision

¹soak \'sōk\ *vb* **1 a :** to lie covered with a liquid **b :** to place in a liquid to wet or as if to wet thoroughly **2 a :** to enter or pass through something by or as if by pores **: PERMEATE b :** to penetrate or affect the mind or feelings **3 :** to draw out by or as if by steeping ⟨*soak* the dirt out⟩ **4 :** to draw in by or as if by suction or absorption ⟨*soaked* up the sunshine⟩ **5 :** to cause to pay too much — **soak·er** *n*

syn SOAK, SATURATE, STEEP, DRENCH mean to pass or to be passed through a liquid. SOAK suggests dunking something in a liquid for a long time in order to soften or clean it ⟨let the dirty clothes *soak* for several hours⟩ SATURATE stresses soaking something to the point where no more liquid can be absorbed ⟨the cloth is *saturated* with the dye⟩ STEEP applies to the soaking of something so that some part of the thing passes into the liquid ⟨allow the tea to *steep* for five minutes⟩ DRENCH suggests a thorough wetting from something that pours down ⟨the rain *drenched* our clothes⟩

²soak *n* **1 :** the act or process of soaking **:** the state of being soaked **2 :** DRUNKARD

so–and–so \'sō-ən-ˌsō\ *n, pl* **so–and–sos** *or* **so–and–so's** \-ən-ˌsōz\ **:** an unnamed or unspecified person or thing

¹soap \'sōp\ *n* **1 :** a substance that is usually made by the action of alkali on fat, dissolves in water, and is used for washing **2 :** a salt of a fatty acid **3 :** SOAP OPERA — **soap·mak·ing** \-ˌmā-kiŋ\ *n*

²soap *vb* **:** to rub soap over or into

soap·ber·ry \'sōp-ˌber-ē\ *n* **:** any of a genus of mostly tropical woody plants having leaves composed of a number of leaflets; *also* **:** the fruit of a soapberry that is sometimes used as a substitute for soap

soap·box \-ˌbäks\ *n* **:** something used as a platform (as on a street) by someone giving a speech to passersby — **soapbox** *adj*

soap opera *n* **:** a radio or television drama presented in a series of continuing stories and characters and intended to appeal to the emotions [so called from the fact that the advertisers on these programs were usually soap manufacturers; see *Word History* at HORSE OPERA]

soap·stone \'sōp-ˌstōn\ *n* **:** a soft stone having a soapy feel and composed essentially of talc, chlorite, and often some magnetite

soap·suds \-ˌsədz\ *n pl* **:** SUDS 1

soapy \'sō-pē\ *adj* **soap·i·er; -est 1 :** smeared with or full of soap ⟨a *soapy* face⟩ **2 :** containing or combined with soap **3 :** resembling or having the qualities of soap — **soap·i·ness** \-pē-nəs\ *n*

¹soar \'sō(ə)r, 'so(ə)r\ *vb* **1 a :** to fly aloft or about **b :** to sail in the air often at a great height **:** GLIDE **2 :** to rise or increase very noticeably (as in position, value, or price)

²soar *n* **:** the act of soaring **:** upward flight

¹sob \'säb\ *vb* **sobbed; sob·bing 1 :** to weep with heavings of the chest or with short gasping sounds in the throat **2 :** to bring to a specified state by sobbing ⟨*sobbed* myself to sleep⟩ **3 a :** to make a sound like that of sobbing ⟨the wind *sobbed* through the trees⟩ **b :** to utter with sobs ⟨*sobbed* out their story⟩

²sob *n* **1 :** an act of sobbing **2 :** a sound of or like that of sobbing

¹so·ber \'sō-bər\ *adj* **so·ber·er** \-bər-ər\; **so·ber·est** \-b(ə-)rəst\ **1 a :** sparing especially in the use of food and drink **b :** not drunk **2 :** having a serious attitude **:** SOLEMN **3 :** having a quiet tone or color **4 :** well reasoned and balanced ⟨a *sober* decision⟩ — **so·ber·ly** \-bər-lē\ *adv* — **so·ber·ness** *n*

²sober *vb* **so·bered; so·ber·ing** \-b(ə-)riŋ\ **:** to make or become sober

so·bri·ety \sə-'brī-ət-ē\ *n* **:** the quality or state of being sober

so·bri·quet *or* **sou·bri·quet** \'sō-bri-ˌkā, -ˌket; ˌsō-bri-'kā,

-'ket\ *n* **:** a descriptive name or phrase **:** NICKNAME

so–called \'sō-'kȯld\ *adj* **:** commonly or popularly but often inaccurately so named ⟨your *so-called* friend⟩

soc·cer \'säk-ər\ *n* **:** a football game with 11 players on a side in which a round ball is advanced by kicking it or by hitting it with any part of the body except the hands and arms

Word History Soccer is the world's most popular sport. In most countries, however, its name is not *soccer* but *football*. In England where the modern game started, it is usually called either *football* or *association football*. The latter name comes from the fact that the rules of the game were standardized when the *Football Association* was founded in England in 1863. The word *soccer* comes from the last three letters of the abbreviation *assoc.*, which stands for "association". Although the word *soccer* was first used in England, the only countries where it is now the usual name for the sport are the United States and Canada. [by shortening and alteration of *association football*]

so·cia·bil·i·ty \ˌsō-shə-'bil-ət-ē\ *n, pl* **-ties 1 :** the quality or state of being sociable **:** AFFABILITY **2 :** the act or an instance of being sociable

¹so·cia·ble \'sō-shə-bəl\ *adj* **1 :** likely to seek or enjoy companionship **:** AFFABLE, FRIENDLY ⟨*sociable* people⟩ **2 :** leading to friendliness or pleasant social relations [from early French *sociable* "social, sociable", from Latin *sociabilis* (same meaning), from *sociare* "to join, associate", from *socius* "ally, companion" — related to ASSOCIATE] — **so·cia·bly** \-blē\ *adv*

²sociable *n* **:** a friendly gathering usually for a special reason ⟨a club *sociable*⟩

¹so·cial \'sō-shəl\ *adj* **1 a :** devoted to or engaged in for sociability ⟨*social* events⟩ ⟨my *social* life⟩ **b :** ¹SOCIABLE 1 **2 :** of or relating to human society ⟨*social* institutions⟩ **3 a :** tending to form cooperative relationships with others ⟨we are *social* beings⟩ **b :** living or growing by nature in groups or communities ⟨bees are *social* insects⟩ **4 a :** of, relating to, or based on rank in a particular society ⟨not accepted as their *social* equal⟩ **b :** of or relating to fashionable society ⟨a *social* leader⟩

²social *n* **:** ²SOCIABLE

social climber *n* **:** one who attempts to gain a higher social position or be accepted in fashionable society

so·cial·ism \'sō-shə-ˌliz-əm\ *n* **:** any of various social systems based on shared or governmental ownership and administration of the means of production and distribution of goods — **so·cial·ist** \'sōsh-(ə-)ləst\ *n* — **socialist** *or* **so·cial·is·tic** \ˌsō-shə-'lis-tik\ *adj* — **so·cial·is·ti·cal·ly** \-ti-k(ə-)lē\ *adv*

so·cial·ite \'sō-shə-ˌlīt\ *n* **:** a person well-known in fashionable society

so·cial·ize \'sō-shə-ˌlīz\ *vb* **-ized; -iz·ing 1 :** to make social; *esp* **:** to train for group living **2 :** to use for social purposes **3 :** to take part in the social life around one — **so·cial·iza·tion** \ˌsōsh-(ə-)lə-'zā-shən\ *n* — **so·cial·iz·er** \'sō-shə-ˌlī-zər\ *n*

so·cial·ly \'sōsh-(ə-)lē\ *adv* **1 :** in a social manner ⟨*socially* popular⟩ **2 :** with respect to society ⟨*socially* improper⟩

social science *n* **1 :** a science that deals with human society or its elements (as family, state, or race) and with institutions and relationships in an organized community **2 :** a science (as economics) dealing with a particular side of human society

social scientist *n* **:** a person who specializes in social science

social security *n* **1 :** the idea or system by which the public provides for the security of individuals and their families **2** *often cap both Ss* **:** a U.S. government program established in 1935 to include old-age and survivors insurance, contributions to state unemployment insurance, and old-age assistance

social studies *n pl* : the studies dealing with human relationships and the way society works (as history, civics, economics, and geography)

social work *n* : the art, system, or profession of extending the benefits of organized society especially by assistance to the underprivileged — **social worker** *n*

¹so·ci·ety \sə-'sī-ət-ē\ *n, pl* **-et·ies** **1** : companionship with one's fellows : COMPANY **2** : the community life thought of as a system within which the individual lives ⟨rural *society*⟩ **3** : people for the most part ⟨the benefit of *society*⟩ **4** : an association of persons for some purpose ⟨the school French *society*⟩ **5** : a part of a community thought of as a unit set apart by common interests or values; *esp* : the group or set of fashionable persons **6** : a system or group of living things that depend on each other and usually form a social unit (as a hive of bees) — **so·ci·etal** \-ət-ºl\ *adj*

²society *adj* : of, relating to, or characteristic of fashionable society

so·cio·log·i·cal \ˌsō-sē-ə-'läj-i-kəl, ˌsō-sh(ē-)ə-\ *also* **so·cio·log·ic** \-ik\ *adj* **1** : of or relating to sociology or its methods **2** : concerned with or relating to social needs and problems — **so·cio·log·i·cal·ly** \-i-k(ə-)lē\ *adv*

so·ci·ol·o·gist \ˌsō-sē-'äl-ə-jəst, ˌsō-shē-\ *n* : a person who specializes in sociology

so·ci·ol·o·gy \ˌsō-sē-'äl-ə-jē, ˌsō-shē-\ *n* : the science of society, social institutions, and social relationships

¹sock \'säk\ *n, pl* **socks** *or* **sox** \'säks\ : a knitted or woven covering for the foot usually extending above the ankle and sometimes to the knee [Old English *socc* "a low shoe or slipper", from Latin *soccus* (same meaning)]

²sock *vb* : to hit, strike, or apply forcefully : deliver a blow [probably of Scandinavian origin]

³sock *n* : a violent blow : PUNCH

sock·et \'säk-ət\ *n* : an opening or hollow that forms a holder for something ⟨the eye *socket*⟩ ⟨light-bulb *socket*⟩

¹sod \'säd\ *n* **1 a** : TURF 1 **b** : the grass-covered and herb-covered surface of the ground **2** : one's native land

²sod *vb* **sod·ded; sod·ding** : to cover with sod or turfs

so·da \'sōd-ə\ *n* **1 a** : SODIUM CARBONATE **b** : SODIUM BICARBONATE **2 a** : SODA WATER **b** : SODA POP **c** : a sweet drink consisting of soda water, flavoring, and often ice cream

soda cracker *n* : a cracker leavened with bicarbonate of soda and cream of tartar

soda fountain *n* **1** : a device for drawing soda water **2** : the equipment and counter for the preparation and serving of carbonated drinks, sodas, sundaes, and ice cream

soda jerk *n* : one who prepares and serves soft drinks and ice cream at a soda fountain

so·dal·i·ty \sō-'dal-ət-ē\ *n, pl* **-ties** : an organized society or fellowship; *esp* : a Roman Catholic association for the purposes of devotion or charity

soda pop *n* : a soft drink consisting of soda water with added flavoring and a sweet syrup

soda water *n* : a beverage consisting of carbonated water

sod·den \'säd-ºn\ *adj* **1 a** : dull or lacking in expression **b** : SLUGGISH, UNIMAGINATIVE ⟨*sodden* minds⟩ **2** : heavy with moisture : SOAKED, SATURATED — **sod·den·ly** *adv*

so·di·um \'sōd-ē-əm\ *n* : a soft waxy silver-white metallic element that is chemically very active and is common in nature in combined form — see ELEMENT table

sodium bicarbonate *n* : a white weakly alkaline salt used especially in baking powders, fire extinguishers, and medicine

sodium carbonate *n* : a sodium salt used especially in making soaps and chemicals, In water softening, in cleaning and bleaching, and in photography

sodium chloride *n* : a chemical compound that consists of crystals having equal numbers of sodium and chlorine atoms : SALT 1a

sodium citrate *n* : a salt used especially to prevent stored blood from clotting

sodium fluoride *n* : a salt that is used in tiny amounts to prevent tooth decay by fluoridation of drinking water or by being applied directly to teeth, is poisonous to human tissue in more than very small amounts, and is sometimes used as an insecticide

sodium hydroxide *n* : a white brittle solid that is strongly alkaline and is used especially in making soap, rayon, and paper

sodium nitrate *n* : a salt used as a fertilizer and to preserve meat

sodium sulfate *n* : a bitter salt used especially in detergents, in the manufacture of rayon, and in dyeing and finishing textiles

sodium thio·sul·fate \-ˌthī-ə-'səl-ˌfāt\ *n* : a chemical compound used especially in photography to make images permanent and in bleaching — called also *hypo*

so·fa \'sō-fə\ *n* : a long upholstered seat usually with arms and a back and often convertible into a bed

sofa bed *n* : a sofa that can be made to serve as a bed

¹soft \'sȯft\ *adj* **1 a** : having a pleasing, comfortable, or soothing effect : GENTLE, MILD ⟨*soft* breezes⟩ **b** : not bright or glaring ⟨*soft* lighting⟩ **c** : pleasing to the ear : quiet in pitch or volume ⟨*soft* voices⟩ **d** : smooth or delicate in appearance or feel ⟨a *soft* silk⟩ **2** : demanding little effort : EASY ⟨a *soft* job⟩ **3** : sounding as in *ace* and *gem* — used of *c* and *g* **4** : gently or gradually curved or rounded : not harsh or jagged ⟨*soft* hills⟩ **5 a** : having a mild gentle disposition : DOCILE **b** : showing sympathetic understanding ⟨took a *soft* stand toward the rebels⟩ **6** : lacking in strength : FEEBLE ⟨*soft* from easy living⟩ **7** : mentally weak **8 a** : yielding to physical pressure ⟨a *soft* mattress⟩ ⟨*soft* metals such as lead⟩ **b** : not as hard as others of its kind **9** : free from substances (as calcium and magnesium salts) that prevent lathering of soap ⟨*soft* water⟩ **10** : occurring at such a speed and in such a way that a destructive crash is avoided ⟨a *soft* landing on the moon⟩ **11** *of a drug*: considered less harmful than an addictive drug — **soft·ly** *adv* — **soft·ness** \'sȯf(t)-nəs\ *n*

²soft *adv* : in a soft manner

soft·ball \'sȯf(t)-ˌbȯl\ *n* : baseball played on a small diamond with a ball that is larger than a baseball and that is pitched underhand; *also* : the ball used in this game

soft–boiled \-'bȯi(ə)ld\ *adj* : lightly boiled so that the contents are soft ⟨*soft-boiled* eggs⟩

soft coal *n* : BITUMINOUS COAL

soft drink *n* : a sweet flavored beverage containing no alcohol

soft·en \'sȯ-fən\ *vb* **soft·ened; soft·en·ing** \'sȯf-(ə-)niŋ\ **1** : to make or become soft or softer **2** : to lessen the strength of — **soft·en·er** \'sȯf-(ə-)nər\ *n*

soft·heart·ed \'sȯft-'härt-əd\ *adj* : MERCIFUL, SYMPATHETIC — **soft·heart·ed·ly** *adv* — **soft·heart·ed·ness** *n*

soft–shell \'sȯf(t)-ˌshel\ *or* **soft–shelled** \-'sheld\ *adj* : having a soft or fragile shell especially as a result of recent shedding ⟨*soft-shell* crab⟩

soft–shoe \'sȯf(t)-'shü\ *n* : a form of stage dancing developed from tap dancing but done with soft-soled shoes and at a slower tempo and more relaxed rhythm

soft soap *n* **1** : a partly liquid soap **2** : FLATTERY 2

soft–soap \'sȯf(t)-'sōp\ *vb* : to soothe or coax with flattery — **soft–soap·er** *n*

soft·ware \'sȯf-ˌtwa(ə)r, -ˌtwe(ə)r\ *n* : the programs and related information used by a computer

\ə\ abut	\au̇\ out	\i\ tip	\ȯ\ saw	\u̇\ foot
\ər\ further	\ch\ chin	\ī\ life	\ȯi\ coin	\y\ yet
\a\ mat	\e\ pet	\j\ job	\th\ thin	\yü\ few
\ā\ take	\ē\ easy	\ŋ\ sing	\th\ this	\yu̇\ cure
\ä\ cot, cart	\g\ go	\ō\ bone	\ü\ food	\zh\ vision

soft wheat *n* : a wheat with soft starchy kernels high in starch but usually low in protein

soft·wood \'sȯf-ˌtwu̇d\ *n* **1** : the wood of a tree (as a pine or fir) that produces cones as compared to that of a tree producing enclosed seeds **2** : a tree that produces softwood

softy *or* **soft·ie** \'sȯf-tē\ *n, pl* **soft·ies** **1** : WEAKLING **2** : a silly or sentimental person

sog·gy \'säg-ē, 'sȯg-\ *adj* **sog·gi·er; -est** : heavy with water or moisture : SOAKED, SODDEN — **sog·gi·ly** \'säg-ə-lē, 'sȯg-\ *adv* — **sog·gi·ness** \'säg-ē-nəs, 'sȯg-\ *n*

¹soil \'sȯi(ə)l\ *vb* : to make or become dirty [Middle English *soilen* "to corrupt, make dirty", from early French *soiller* "to wallow", from *soil* "pigsty"]

²soil *n* **1 a** : SOILAGE, STAIN **b** : moral soilage : CORRUPTION **2** : something that soils or pollutes

³soil *n* **1** : firm land : EARTH **2** : the loose surface material of the earth in which plants grow **3** : ¹COUNTRY 2b, LAND **4** : an environment in which something may take root and grow ⟨slums are fertile *soil* for crime⟩ [Middle English *soil* "earth", derived from Latin *solium* "a seat"]

soil·age \'sȯi-lij\ *n* : the act of soiling : the state of being soiled

soil conservation *n* : management of soil designed to obtain the largest possible crops while improving and protecting the soil

soil·less \'sȯi(ə)l-ləs\ *adj* : carried on without soil ⟨*soilless* agriculture⟩

soil profile *n* : PROFILE 3

soil science *n* : the science of soils

soil scientist *n* : a person who specializes in soil science

soi·ree *or* **soi·rée** \swä-'rā\ *n* : an evening party or social gathering

¹so·journ \'sō-ˌjərn, sō-'jərn\ *n* : a temporary stay

²sojourn *vb* : to stay as a temporary resident : STOP ⟨*sojourned* for a month at a resort⟩ — **so·journ·er** *n*

¹sol \'sōl\ *n* : the fifth note of the musical scale [from Latin *sol* "the fifth note of the scale"]

²sol \'säl, 'sȯl\ *n* : a colloid in which tiny solid particles are scattered throughout a liquid [derived from *sol*ution]

¹so·lace \'säl-əs *also* 'sōl-\ *n* **1** : comfort in times of grief or worry : CONSOLATION **2** : something that gives comfort

²solace *vb* **so·laced; so·lac·ing** **1** : to give solace to : CONSOLE **2** : to make cheerful

so·lar \'sō-lər, -ˌlär\ *adj* **1** : of, derived from, or relating to the sun **2** : measured by the earth's course in relation to the sun ⟨*solar* time⟩ ⟨*solar* year⟩ **3 a** : produced or operated by the action of the sun's light or heat ⟨*solar* energy⟩ **b** : using the sun's rays especially to produce heat or electricity ⟨a *solar* house⟩ [Middle English *solar* "derived from or related to the sun", from Latin *solaris* (same meaning), from *sol* "sun" — related to SUNDAY; see *Word History* at SUNDAY]

solar cell *n* : a photoelectric cell that converts sunlight into electrical energy and is used as a power source

solar collector *n* : any of various devices for the absorption of solar radiation for the heating of water or buildings or the production of electricity

solar flare *n* : a sudden temporary outburst of energy from a small area of the sun's surface

solar collector

so·lar·i·um \sō-'lar-ē-əm, sə-, -'ler-\ *n, pl* **-ia** \-ē-ə\ *also* **-i·ums** : a room exposed to the sun (as for treatment of illness)

solar panel *n* : a group of solar cells forming a flat surface (as on a spacecraft)

so·lar plexus \'sō-lər-\ *n* **1** : a nerve plexus in the abdomen behind the stomach that contains ganglia sending nerve fibers to the internal organs of the abdomen **2** : the general area of the stomach below the sternum

solar system *n* : a star with the group of heavenly bodies that revolve around it; *esp* : the sun with the planets, asteroids, comets, and meteors that orbit it

solar wind *n* : the continuous radiation of charged particles from the sun's surface

sold *past and past participle of* SELL

¹sol·der \'säd-ər, 'sȯd-\ *n* : a metal or a mixture of metals (as of lead and tin) used when melted to join metallic surfaces

²solder *vb* **sol·dered; sol·der·ing** \-(ə-)riŋ\ **1** : to unite or repair with solder ⟨*solder* wires together⟩ ⟨*solder* a leak⟩ **2** : to become joined or renewed by or as if by the use of solder — **sol·der·er** \-ər-ər\ *n*

soldering iron *n* : a usually electrical device used for soldering

¹sol·dier \'sōl-jər\ *n* **1** : a person in military service usually as an enlisted man or woman **2** : a worker in something strongly believed in **3** : a member of a caste of wingless individuals with large heads and jaws among termites and some ants — **sol·dier·ly** *adj*

²soldier *vb* **sol·diered; sol·dier·ing** \ˌsōlj-(ə-)riŋ\ : to serve as or act like a soldier

soldier of fortune *n* : one who follows a military career wherever there is promise of profit, adventure, or pleasure

sol·diery \'sōlj-(ə-)rē\ *n* : a body of soldiers

¹sole \'sōl\ *n* **1** : the underside of a foot **2** : the part of footwear on which the sole of the foot rests [Middle English *sole* "the underside of the foot or shoe", from early French *sole* (same meaning), from Latin *solea* "sandal, a flatfish"] — **soled** \'sōld\ *adj*

²sole *vb* **soled; sol·ing** : to furnish with a sole ⟨*sole* shoes⟩

³sole *n* : any of various flatfishes that have a small mouth, small fins, and small closely set eyes and that include some fishes used for food [Middle English *sole* "a type of flatfish", from early French *sole* (same meaning), from Latin *solea* "sandal, a flatfish"]

⁴sole *adj* **1** *archaic* : having no companion : ALONE **2 a** : having no sharer ⟨*sole* owner⟩ **b** : being the only one **3** : acting independently and without assistance or interference ⟨the *sole* judge⟩ **4** : belonging only to the one person, unit, or group named ⟨given *sole* authority⟩ [Middle English *sole* "alone", from early French *seul* (same meaning), from Latin *solus* "alone" — related to DESOLATE, SOLITUDE, SOLO] — **sole·ness** *n*

so·le·cism \'säl-ə-ˌsiz-əm, 'sō-lə-\ *n* **1** : a combination of words in a sentence that does not show proper grammar **2** : a social blunder

sole·ly \'sō(l)-lē\ *adv* **1** : without another : SINGLY, ALONE **2** : ²ONLY 1a ⟨done *solely* for money⟩

sol·emn \'säl-əm\ *adj* : being serious and dignified in appearance or behavior **syn** see SERIOUS — **so·lem·ni·ty** \sə-'lem-nət-ē\ *n* — **sol·emn·ly** \'säl-əm-lē\ *adv*

sol·em·nize \'säl-əm-ˌnīz\ *vb* **-nized; -niz·ing** **1** : to observe or honor with solemnity **2** : to perform with ceremony; *esp* : to unite in marriage with religious ceremony **3** : to make solemn : DIGNIFY — **sol·em·ni·za·tion** \ˌsäl-əm-nə-'zā-shən\ *n*

so·le·noid \'sō-lə-ˌnȯid, 'säl-ə-\ *n* : a coil of wire commonly in the form of a long cylinder that when carrying a current acts as a magnet so that a movable core is drawn into the coil when a current flows

soli *pl of* SOLO

so·lic·it \sə-'lis-ət\ *vb* **1** : ENTREAT, BEG; *esp* : to approach with a request or appeal **2** : to appeal for ⟨*solicited* the help of neighbors⟩ **3 a** : to lead especially into evil **b** : to approach for sinful purposes — **so·lic·i·ta·tion** \-ˌlis-ə-'tā-shən\ *n*

so·lic·i·tor \sə-'lis-ət-ər\ *n* **1** : one that solicits **2** : a British lawyer   **3** : the chief law officer of a city, town, county, or government division

so·lic·i·tous \sə-'lis-ət-əs\ *adj*   **1** : full of concern or fears : APPREHENSIVE   **2** : very careful   **3** : anxiously willing : EAGER — **so·lic·i·tous·ly** *adv*

so·lic·i·tude \sə-'lis-ə-,t(y)üd\ *n*   **1** : the state of being solicitous : ANXIETY   **2** : too much care or attention

¹sol·id \'säl-əd\ *adj*   **1 a** : not hollow   **b** : written as one word ⟨a *solid* compound⟩   **2** : having, involving, or dealing with solids : CUBIC 3a   **3 a** : not loose or spongy : COMPACT ⟨a *solid* mass of rock⟩   **b** : neither gaseous nor liquid   **4** : of good sturdy quality or kind ⟨*solid* comfort⟩ ⟨*solid* reasons⟩   **5 a** : not interrupted ⟨for three *solid* hours⟩   **b** : being in complete agreement : UNANIMOUS, UNITED ⟨*solid* for pay increases⟩   **6 a** : thoroughly dependable : RELIABLE ⟨a *solid* citizen⟩   **b** : earnest or important in purpose ⟨*solid* reading⟩   **7** : of one material, kind, or color ⟨*solid* gold⟩   **syn** see HARD — **solid** *adv* — **sol·id·ly** *adv* — **sol·id·ness** *n*

²solid *n*   **1** : an enclosed region (as a cube or a sphere) of three-dimensional space   **2** : a solid substance : a substance that keeps its size and shape

sol·i·dar·i·ty \,säl-ə-'dar-ət-ē\ *n* : unity (as of a group) that produces or is based on shared interests and goals

so·lid·i·fy \sə-'lid-ə-,fī\ *vb* **-fied; -fy·ing** : to make or become solid, compact, or hard

so·lid·i·ty \sə-'lid-ət-ē\ *n, pl* **-ties**   **1** : the quality or state of being solid   **2** : something solid

solid–state *adj*   **1** : relating to the characteristics and structure of solid material   **2** : not using vacuum tubes ⟨a *solid-state* radio⟩

so·lil·o·quize \sə-'lil-ə-,kwīz\ *vb* **-quized; -quiz·ing** : to give a soliloquy : talk to oneself

so·lil·o·quy \sə-'lil-ə-kwē\ *n, pl* **-quies**   **1** : the act of talking to oneself   **2** : a dramatic speech that seems like a series of unspoken thoughts

sol·i·taire \'säl-ə-,ta(ə)r, -,te(ə)r\ *n*   **1** : a single gem (as a diamond) set alone   **2** : a card game played by one person alone

¹sol·i·tary \'säl-ə-,ter-ē\ *adj*   **1** : all alone ⟨a *solitary* traveler⟩   **2** : seldom visited : LONELY   **3** : being the only one : SOLE ⟨*solitary* example⟩   **4** : growing or living alone : not forming part of a group or cluster ⟨flowers at the end of the stalk and *solitary*⟩ ⟨the *solitary* wasps⟩ — **sol·i·tari·ly** \,säl-ə-'ter-ə-lē\ *adv* — **sol·i·tari·ness** \'säl-ə-,ter-ē-nəs\ *n*

²solitary *n, pl* **-tar·ies** : one who lives or seeks to live a solitary life : RECLUSE, HERMIT

sol·i·tude \'säl-ə-,t(y)üd\ *n*   **1** : the quality or state of being alone or far-off from society : SECLUSION, LONELINESS   **2** : a lonely place (as a desert) [Middle English *solitude* "the state of being alone", from early French *solitude* (same meaning), from Latin *solitudin-, solitudo* (same meaning), from *solus* "alone" — related to DESOLATE, ⁴SOLE, SOLO]

¹so·lo \'sō-lō\ *n, pl* **solos**   **1** *or pl* **so·li** \'sō-lē\ : a piece of music written to be performed by one voice or one instrument   **2** : an action in which there is only one performer [from Italian *solo* "a part in music performed without accompaniment", from *solo* (adjective) "alone", from Latin *solus* "alone" — related to DESOLATE, ⁴SOLE, SOLITUDE]

²solo *adv or adj* : without a companion : ALONE

³solo *vb* **so·loed; so·lo·ing** \-(,)lō-iŋ, -lə-wiŋ\ : to perform by oneself; *esp* : to fly an airplane without one's instructor

so·lo·ist \'sō-lə-wəst, -(,)lō-əst\ *n* : one who performs a solo

so·lon \'sō-lən, -,län\ *n*   **1** : a wise and skillful giver of a collection of laws   **2** : a member of a legislative body

so long \sō-'lòn\ *interj* — used to express good-bye or farewell

so long as *conj*   **1** : during and up to the end of the time that : WHILE   **2** : provided that

sol·stice \'säl-stəs, 'sōl-, 'sòl-\ *n*   **1** : the point in the apparent path of the sun at which the sun is farthest north or south of the equator   **2** : the time of the sun's passing a solstice which occurs on June 22d and on December 22d

sol·u·bil·i·ty \,säl-yə-'bil-ət-ē\ *n*   **1** : the quality or state of being soluble   **2** : the amount of a substance that will dissolve in a given amount of another substance

sol·u·ble \'säl-yə-bəl\ *adj*   **1** : capable of being dissolved in a liquid ⟨sugar is *soluble* in water⟩   **2** : capable of being solved or explained : SOLVABLE ⟨a *soluble* problem⟩

so·lu·tion \sə-'lü-shən\ *n*   **1 a** : an act or process of solving   **b** : an answer to a problem : EXPLANATION   **c** : SOLUTION SET   **2 a** : an act or the process by which a solid, liquid, or gaseous substance is dissolved in a liquid   **b** : a liquid in which something has been dissolved   **c** : the condition of being dissolved

solution set *n* : a set of values that are solutions for an equation; *also* : TRUTH SET

solv·able \'säl-və-bəl, 'sòl-\ *adj* : capable of being solved

Sol·vay process \'säl-,vā-\ *n* : a process for making sodium carbonate from common salt using carbon dioxide and ammonia

solve \'sälv, 'sòlv\ *vb* **solved; solv·ing** : to find a solution for

sol·ven·cy \'säl-vən-sē, 'sòl-\ *n* : the quality or state of being solvent

¹sol·vent \'säl-vənt, 'sòl-\ *adj* : able to pay all legal debts

²solvent *n* : a usually liquid substance capable of dissolving one or more other substances

so·mat·ic \sō-'mat-ik, sə-\ *adj* : of, relating to, or affecting the body especially as compared to the mind or the tissue producing the germ cells

somatic cell *n* : any cell of an animal or plant other than a germ cell

som·ber *or* **som·bre** \'säm-bər\ *adj*   **1** : so shaded as to be dark and gloomy   **2** : ²MELANCHOLY 1, GRAVE ⟨a *somber* mood⟩   **3** : dull or dark colored — **som·ber·ly** *adv* — **som·ber·ness** *n*

som·bre·ro \səm-'bre(ə)r-ō, säm-\ *n, pl* **-ros** : a tall hat with a very wide brim worn especially in the Southwest and Mexico [from Spanish *sombrero* "a wide-brimmed hat", from *sombra* "shade"]

¹some \'səm, *for sense 2b* səm *without stress*\ *adj*   **1** : being one unknown, unnamed, or unspecified unit or thing ⟨*some* person knocked⟩   **2 a** : being one, a part, or an unspecified number of something (as a class or group) named ⟨*some* birds can't fly⟩   **b** : being of an unspecified amount or number ⟨give me *some* water⟩ ⟨have *some* apples⟩   **3** : worthy of notice or consideration ⟨that was *some* party⟩

²some \'səm\ *pron* : a part or quantity of something ⟨*some* of the milk⟩ ⟨*some* of the apples⟩

³some \'səm, ,səm\ *adv* : reasonably close to : ABOUT ⟨*some* eighty houses⟩

-some \səm\ *adj suffix*   **1** : having the quality or nature of the thing specified ⟨burden*some*⟩   **2** : causing a (specified) feeling or condition ⟨fear*some*⟩ [Old English *-sum* "having a particular quality, action, or effect"]

¹some·body \'səm-,bäd-ē, -bəd-\ *pron* : one or some person of no certain or known identity ⟨did *somebody* knock?⟩

²somebody *n* : a person of position or importance ⟨wanted to be *somebody*⟩

some·day \'səm-,dā\ *adv* : at some future time

some·how \-,haù\ *adv* : in one way or another

some·one \-(,)wən\ *pron* : ¹SOMEBODY

some·place \-,plās\ *adv* : ¹SOMEWHERE 1

\ə\ abut	\aù\ out	\i\ tip	\ò\ saw	\ù\ foot	
\ər\ further	\ch\ chin	\ī\ life	\òi\ coin	\y\ yet	
\a\ mat	\e\ pet	\j\ job	\th\ thin	\yü\ few	
\ā\ take	\ē\ easy	\ŋ\ sing	\th\ this	\yù\ cure	
\ä\ cot, cart	\g\ go	\ō\ bone	\ü\ food	\zh\ vision	

¹som·er·sault \'səm-ər-ˌsȯlt\ *n* : a leap or roll in which a person turns heels over head [from early French *sombresaut* "somersault", derived from Latin *super* "over" and *saltus* "leap", from *saltus*, past participle of *salire* "to leap, spring" — related to RESILIENT]

²somersault *vb* : to perform a somersault

¹som·er·set \'səm-ər-ˌset\ *n* : ¹SOMERSAULT

²somerset *vb* : ²SOMERSAULT

¹some·thing \'səm(p)-thiŋ, *especially in rapid speech or for sense 2* 'səmp-ᵊm\ *pron* **1** : some unnamed or unspecified thing **2** : an important person or thing ⟨decided to make *something* of myself⟩ — **something else** : something or someone special or extraordinary

²something *adv* **1** : ²SOMEWHAT **2** : ²VERY 1 ⟨snores *something* awful⟩

¹some·time \'səm-ˌtīm\ *adv* **1** : at some time in the future ⟨I'll do it *sometime*⟩ **2** : at some unspecified or uncertain point of time ⟨*sometime* last night⟩

²sometime *adj* : having been at an earlier time : FORMER, LATE ⟨*sometime* mayor⟩

some·times \'səm-ˌtīmz, (ˌ)səm-'tīmz\ *adv* : at times : now and then — used OCCASIONALLY

some·way \'səm-ˌwā\ *also* **some·ways** \-ˌwāz\ *adv* : in some way : SOMEHOW

¹some·what \'səm-ˌ(h)wät, -ˌ(h)wət; (ˌ)səm-'(h)wät, -'(h)wət\ *pron* : some unspecified part or amount : SOMETHING

²somewhat *adv* : in some measure : SLIGHTLY ⟨*somewhat* comfortable⟩

¹some·where \'səm-ˌ(h)we(ə)r, -ˌ(h)wa(ə)r, -(ˌ)(h)wər\ *adv* **1** : in, at, or to a place unknown or unspecified **2** : reasonably close to ⟨*somewhere* around nine o'clock⟩

²somewhere *n* : an unnamed place

some·wheres \'səm-ˌ(h)we(ə)rz, -ˌ(h)wa(ə)rz, -(ˌ)(h)wərz\ *adv* : ¹SOMEWHERE

som·no·lence \'säm-nə-lən(t)s\ *n* : the state of being sleepy or ready to fall asleep : DROWSINESS

som·no·lent \'säm-nə-lənt\ *adj* : showing signs of not being fully awake **syn** see SLEEPY

so much as *adv* : ³EVEN 5 ⟨nobody would *so much as* look at you⟩

son \'sən\ *n* **1 a** : a male offspring especially of human parents **b** : a male descendant **2** *cap* : the second person of the Trinity **3** : a man or boy closely associated with or thought of as a child of something (as a country, race, or religion)

so·nar \'sō-ˌnär\ *n* : a device for detecting the presence and location of submerged objects (as submarines) by sound waves

so·na·ta \sə-'nät-ə\ *n* : a piece of music written for instruments and usually having three or four main parts in different styles and different keys

song \'sȯŋ\ *n* **1** : the act or art of singing **2** : poetical composition : POETRY **3** : a short piece of music with words intended to be sung **4 a** : a melody for a lyric poem or ballad **b** : a poem easily set to music **5** : a small amount ⟨can be bought for a *song*⟩

song·bird \-ˌbərd\ *n* : a bird that sings

song·fest \'sȯŋ-ˌfest\ *n* : an informal session of group singing of popular or folk songs

Song of Sol·o·mon \-'säl-ə-mən\ — see BIBLE table

Song of Songs — see BIBLE table

song sparrow *n* : a common sparrow of eastern North America that is brownish above and white below and is noted for its sweet cheerful song

song·ster \'sȯŋ(k)-stər\ *n* **1** : a person that sings **2** : a book of songs

song·stress \'sȯŋ(k)-strəs\ *n* : a woman who is a singer

song·writ·er \'sȯŋ-ˌrīt-ər\ *n* : a person who composes words or music or both especially for popular songs

son·ic \'sän-ik\ *adj* : using, produced by, or relating to sound waves

sonic boom *n* : a sound like that of an explosion produced when a shock wave formed at the nose of an aircraft traveling at supersonic speed reaches the ground

son–in–law \'sən-ən-ˌlȯ\ *n, pl* **sons–in–law** \'sən-zən-\ : the husband of one's daughter

son·net \'sän-ət\ *n* : a poem of 14 lines usually rhyming by a fixed scheme

son·ne·teer \ˌsän-ə-'ti(ə)r\ *n* : a writer of sonnets

son·ny \'sən-ē\ *n* : a young boy — used chiefly as a term of address

so·nom·e·ter \sə-'näm-ət-ər\ *n* : an instrument for showing how musical tones are related mathematically that consists of a single string stretched over a movable arch on a board

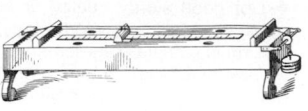

sonometer

so·nor·i·ty \sə-'nȯr-ət-ē, -'när-\ *n, pl* **-ties** : the quality or state of being sonorous : RESONANCE

so·no·rous \sə-'nȯr-əs, -'nȯr-; 'sän-ə-rəs\ *adj* **1** : producing sound (as when struck) **2** : full or loud in sound : RESONANT — **so·no·rous·ly** *adv*

soon \'sün, *especially New England* 'su̇n\ *adv* **1** : before long : without delay ⟨*soon* after sunrise⟩ **2** : in a speedy way ⟨as *soon* as possible⟩ **3** : before the usual time **4** : by choice ⟨would as *soon* do it now⟩

soot \'su̇t, 'sət, 'süt\ *n* : a black powder formed when something is burned; *esp* : the fine powder consisting chiefly of carbon that colors smoke

sooth \'süth\ *n, archaic* : the quality or state of being true : TRUTH, REALITY

soothe \'süth\ *vb* **soothed; sooth·ing** **1** : to please by or as if by attention or concern : PLACATE **2** : ALLEVIATE, RELIEVE **3** : to bring comfort : calm down

sooth·ing \'sü-thiŋ\ *adj* : tending to soothe

sooth·say·er \'süth-ˌsā-ər\ *n* : a person who claims to foretell events — **sooth·say·ing** \-ˌsā-iŋ\ *n*

sooty \'su̇t-ē, 'sət-, 'süt-\ *adj* **soot·i·er; -est** **1 a** : of, relating to, or producing soot **b** : soiled with soot **2** : of the color of soot — **soot·i·ness** \-ē-nəs\ *n*

¹sop \'säp\ *n* **1** *chiefly dialect* : a piece of food dipped or soaked in a liquid (as bread dipped in milk or gravy) **2** : a bribe or gift for soothing or winning approval

²sop *vb* **sopped; sop·ping** **1 a** : to soak or dip in or as if in liquid **b** : to wet thoroughly **2** : to mop or soak up ⟨*sopping* up gravy with bread⟩

soph·ism \'säf-ˌiz-əm\ *n* : a misleading argument that seems reasonable

soph·ist \'säf-əst\ *n* : one who argues by the use of sophisms

¹so·phis·ti·cate \sə-'fis-tə-ˌkāt\ *vb* **-cat·ed; -cat·ing** : to cause to become sophisticated — **so·phis·ti·ca·tion** \-ˌfis-tə-'kā-shən\ *n*

²so·phis·ti·cate \sə-'fis-ti-kət, -tə-ˌkāt\ *n* : a sophisticated person

so·phis·ti·cat·ed \sə-'fis-tə-ˌkāt-əd\ *adj* **1 a** : deprived of native or original plainness **b** : very complicated : COMPLEX ⟨*sophisticated* instruments⟩ **c** : WORLDLY-WISE, KNOWING ⟨a *sophisticated* young graduate⟩ **2 a** : finely experienced and aware ⟨a *sophisticated* observer⟩ **b** : appealing to one's intelligence ⟨a *sophisticated* novel⟩ — **so·phis·ti·cat·ed·ly** *adv*

soph·ist·ry \'säf-ə-strē\ *n* : reasoning or arguments typical of a sophist

soph·o·more \'säf-ˌmō(ə)r, -ˌmȯ(ə)r; 'säf-ᵊm-ˌō(ə)r, -ˌȯ(ə)r\ *n* : a student in his or her second year at a high school or college

soph·o·mor·ic \ˌsäf-ə-'mōr-ik, -'mȯr-, -'mär-\ *adj* **1** : very sure of one's knowledge but poorly informed and immature **2** : of, relating to, or characteristic of a sophomore

So·pho·ni·as \,säf-ə-'nī-əs, ,sō-fə-\ *n* — see BIBLE table

sop·ping \'säp-iŋ\ *adj* : thoroughly wet

sop·py \'säp-ē\ *adj* **sop·pi·er; -est** **1** : soaked through **2** : very wet

¹so·pra·no \sə-'pran-ō, -'prän-\ *adj* **1** : relating to the soprano voice or part **2** : having a high range ⟨*soprano* sax⟩ [from Italian *soprano* "relating to a soprano or soprano part", from *sopra* "above", from Latin *supra* "above"]

²soprano *n, pl* **-nos** **1** : the highest voice part in harmony for four parts with men's and women's voices — compare ALTO 1b, ²BASS 1a, TENOR 2a **2** : the highest female singing voice or a person with this voice

sor·cer·er \'sòrs-(ə-)rər\ *n* : a person who practices sorcery : WIZARD

sor·cer·ess \'sòrs-(ə-)rəs\ *n* : a woman who practices sorcery : WITCH

sor·cery \'sòrs-(ə-)rē\ *n* : the use of powers gotten with the help of or by the control of evil spirits : WITCHCRAFT

sor·did \'sòrd-əd\ *adj* **1** : very dirty : FILTHY ⟨*sordid* surroundings⟩ **2** : VILE 1a ⟨a *sordid* life⟩ **3** : MISERLY, NIGGARDLY, COVETOUS — **sor·did·ly** *adv* — **sor·did·ness** *n*

¹sore \'sō(ə)r, 'sò(ə)r\ *adj* **sor·er; sor·est** **1 a** : causing pain or distress **b** : full of pain : TENDER ⟨*sore* muscles⟩ **c** : hurt or red and swollen so as to be or seem painful ⟨*sore* runny eyes⟩ **2** : accompanied by difficulties, hardship, or exertion ⟨a *sore* subject⟩ **3** : made angry ⟨my neighbor is *sore* at me⟩ — **sore·ness** *n*

²sore *n* **1** : a sore spot on the body; *esp* : one (as an ulcer) with the tissues broken and usually infected **2** : a cause of pain : AFFLICTION

³sore *adv* : SORELY

sore·head \'sō(ə)r-,hed, 'sò(ə)r-\ *n* : a person easily angered or discontented — **sorehead** *or* **sore·head·ed** \-'hed-əd\ *adj*

sore·ly \'sō(ə)r-lē, 'sò(ə)r-\ *adv* : in a sore manner

sore throat *n* : a throat that is painful because of inflammation

sor·ghum \'sòr-gəm\ *n* **1** : any of a genus of Old World tropical grasses that look like Indian corn; *esp* : one cultivated for grain, forage, or syrup **2** : syrup made from a sorghum

so·ror·i·ty \sə-'ròr-ət-ē, -'rär-\ *n, pl* **-ties** : a club of girls or women especially at a college [from Latin *sororitas* "sisterhood", from earlier *soror* "sister"]

¹sor·rel \'sòr-əl, 'sär-\ *n* **1** : a sorrel-colored animal; *esp* : a light reddish brown horse often with cream mane and tail **2** : a brownish orange to light brown

²sorrel *n* : any of various plants (as wood sorrel) with sour juice

¹sor·row \'sär-ō, 'sòr-\ *n* **1 a** : sadness felt after a loss (as of something loved) **b** : a cause of grief or sadness **2** : CONTRITION, REPENTANCE

 syn SORROW, GRIEF, WOE mean distress of mind. SORROW suggests a feeling that something has been lost and often feelings of guilt and regret ⟨expressed *sorrow* for having caused the accident⟩ GRIEF stresses feeling great sorrow usually for a special reason ⟨their *grief* when their pet died⟩ WOE suggests feeling hopeless and miserable ⟨all my troubles left me in a state of *woe*⟩

²sorrow *vb* : to feel or express sorrow : GRIEVE

sor·row·ful \'sär-ō-fəl, 'sòr-, -ə-fəl\ *adj* **1** : full of or showing sorrow **2** : expressive of or causing sorrow — **sor·row·ful·ly** \-f(ə-)lē\ *adv*

sorghum 1

sor·ry \'sär-ē, 'sòr-\ *adj* **sor·ri·er; -est** **1** : feeling sorrow or regret **2** : MOURNFUL 2, SAD **3** : causing sorrow, pity, or scorn : WRETCHED — **sor·ri·ness** \-ē-nəs\ *n*

¹sort \'sò(ə)rt\ *n* **1 a** : a group of persons or things that have something in common : CLASS **b** : PERSON 1, INDIVIDUAL ⟨not a bad *sort*⟩ **2 a** : method or manner of acting : WAY, MANNER **b** : general disposition : NATURE — **of sorts** *or* **of a sort** : of an unimportant or just average kind ⟨a poet of sorts⟩ — **out of sorts** **1** : somewhat ill **2** : easily angered : IRRITABLE

²sort *vb* **1** : to separate and arrange by kind or class : CLASSIFY ⟨*sort* mail⟩ ⟨*sort* out socks by color⟩ **2** : AGREE 6, SUIT — **sort·er** *n*

sor·tie \'sòrt-ē, sòr-'tē\ *n* : a sudden rushing out of troops from a position of defense against the enemy : SALLY — **sortie** *vb*

sort of \,sòrt-ə(v), -ər\ *adv* : ²SOMEWHAT, RATHER

so·rus \'sòr-əs, 'sòr-\ *n, pl* **so·ri** \'sō(ə)r-,ī, 'sò(ə)r-, -,ē\ : any of the dots on the underside of a fertile fern frond consisting of a cluster of spores

SOS \,es-(,)ō-'es, ,es-ə-'wes\ *n* **1** : an international radio code distress signal used by ships and aircraft calling for help **2** : a call for help

¹so-so \'sō-'sō\ *adv* : fairly well : TOLERABLY, PASSABLY

²so-so *adj* : neither very good nor very bad : MIDDLING

sot \'sät\ *n* : DRUNKARD

sot·to vo·ce \,sät-ō-'vō-chē\ *adv or adj* **1** : in a whisper; *also* : in private **2** : very softly ⟨play the last part *sotto voce*⟩ [from Italian *sottovoce*, literally "under the voice"]

sou \'sü\ *n* : a French bronze coin of the period before 1914 worth 5 centimes

soubriquet *variant of* SOBRIQUET

¹souf·flé \sü-'flā, 'sü-,flā\ *n* : a delicate spongy hot dish lightened in baking by stiffly beaten egg whites ⟨cheese *soufflé*⟩ [derived from French *soufflé*, past participle of *souffler* "to blow up, inflate"]

²soufflé *or* **souf·fléed** \-'flād, -,flād\ *adj* : puffed by or in cooking ⟨*soufflé* omelet⟩

sough \'saù, 'səf\ *vb* : to make a moaning or sighing sound — **sough** *n*

sought *past and past participle of* SEEK

¹soul \'sōl\ *n* **1** : the spiritual part of a person believed to give life to the body and in many religions thought to live forever **2 a** : the necessary part of something **b** : a person who leads or stirs others to action : LEADER ⟨the *soul* of the campaign⟩ **3 a** : the part of one's personality having to do with feelings and the sense of what is right and wrong ⟨felt my *soul* rebel against injustice⟩ **b** : spiritual force : FERVOR **4** : a human being : PERSON ⟨a kind *soul*⟩ **5** : practices or traditions of black Americans — **souled** \'sōld\ *adj*

²soul *adj* **1** : of or relating to black Americans or their culture ⟨*soul* food⟩ ⟨*soul* music⟩ **2** : designed for or controlled by blacks ⟨*soul* radio stations⟩

soul·ful \'sōl-fəl\ *adj* : full of or expressing feeling — **soul·ful·ly** \-fə-lē\ *adv* — **soul·ful·ness** *n*

soul·less \'sōl-ləs\ *adj* : having no soul or no greatness or nobleness of mind or feeling — **soul·less·ly** *adv*

soul–search·ing \'sōl-,sər-chin\ *n* : examination of one's conscience and especially one's reasons and values

¹sound \'saùnd\ *adj* **1 a** : not diseased or weak : HEALTHY ⟨a *sound* mind in a *sound* body⟩ **b** : free from imperfection or rot **2** : ¹SOLID 4, FIRM ⟨a building of *sound* construction⟩ **3** : not faulty : VALID, RIGHT ⟨a *sound* argument⟩ **4 a** : THOROUGH 1 **b** : not disturbed ⟨a *sound* sleep⟩ **c** : SEVERE 3 ⟨a *sound* beating⟩ [Old English *gesund* "free

\ə\	abut	\aù\	out	\i\	tip	\ò\ saw	\ù\ foot
\ər\	further	\ch\	chin	\ī\	life	\òi\ coin	\y\ yet
\a\	mat	\e\	pet	\j\	job	\th\ thin	\yü\ few
\ā\	take	\ē\	easy	\ŋ\	sing	\th\ this	\yù\ cure
\ä\	cot, cart	\g\	go	\ō\	bone	\ü\ food	\zh\ vision

from injury or disease"] — **sound·ly** \'saún-(d)lē\ *adv* — **sound·ness** \'saún(d)-nəs\ *n*

²**sound** *adv* : in a sound manner : SOUNDLY ⟨*sound* asleep⟩

³**sound** *n* **1 a** : the sensation of hearing **b** : a particular impression obtained by hearing : NOISE, TONE **c** : the energy of vibration that causes the sensation of hearing **2 a** : one of the noises that together make up human speech ⟨the *sound* of "th" in "this"⟩ **b** : a series of spoken noises **3 a** : meaningless noise **b** : the suggestion carried or given by something heard or said ⟨the excuse has a suspicious *sound*⟩ **4** : hearing distance : EARSHOT ⟨within *sound* of my voice⟩ [Middle English *soun* "a sound, something that can be heard", from early French *son* (same meaning), from Latin *sonus* "a sound" — related to UNISON]

⁴**sound** *vb* **1 a** : to make or cause to make a sound **b** : RESOUND 1, 2 **c** : to give a signal by sound **2** : PRONOUNCE 3a ⟨*sound* each word clearly⟩ **3** : to put into words : VOICE **4 a** : to make known : PROCLAIM **b** : to order, signal, or indicate by a sound **5** : to make or give an impression : SEEM ⟨*sounds* incredible⟩

⁵**sound** *n* : a long passage of water that is wider than a strait and often connects two larger bodies of water or forms a channel between the mainland and an island [Old English *sund* "a sea, swimming"]

⁶**sound** *vb* **1 a** : to measure the depth of (as with a sounding line) : FATHOM **b** : to look into or investigate the possibility **2** : to try to find out the views or intentions of : PROBE ⟨*sounded* me out on the idea⟩ **3** : to dive down suddenly ⟨a *sounding* whale⟩ [Middle English *sounden* "to measure the depth of", from early French *sonder* (same meaning), from *sonde* "a line used for measuring depths"; probably of Germanic origin]

sound barrier *n* : the sudden large increase in resistance that the air offers to an aircraft nearing the speed of sound

sound·board \'saún(d)-,bō(ə)rd, -,bò(ə)rd\ *n* **1** : a thin board under the strings of a musical instrument (as a piano) that vibrates slightly from the sound made by the strings and serves to strengthen the sound given off by the instrument **2** : SOUNDING BOARD 1

S soundboard 1

sound effects *n pl* : effects that imitate sounds called for in the script of a play, radio or television program, or motion picture

sound·er \'saún-dər\ *n* : one that sounds; *esp* : a device for making soundings

sound·ing \'saún-diŋ\ *n* **1 a** : measurement of depth especially with a sounding line **b** : the depth found by sounding **2** : an investigation, test, or sampling of opinion or intention

sounding board *n* **1** : a structure behind or over a speaker's platform to make sound uttered from it clear **2** : a means for helping to spread opinions **3** : a person or group on whom new ideas or opinions are tested

sounding line *n* : a line, wire, or cord weighted at one end for sounding

sound·less \'saún-(d)ləs\ *adj* : making no sound : SILENT — **sound·less·ly** *adv*

sound off *vb* **1** : to count while marching **2** : to voice one's opinions freely with force

sound pollution *n* : NOISE POLLUTION

sound·proof \'saún(d)-'prüf\ *adj* : designed to prevent sound from entering or leaving — **soundproof** *vb*

sound track *n* : the area on a motion-picture film that carries the sound record

sound truck *n* : a truck equipped with a loudspeaker

sound wave *n* : a wave formed by compression of the material (as air) through which it travels regardless of whether it can be heard

¹**soup** \'süp\ *n* **1** : a liquid food with a meat, fish, or vegetable stock as a base and often containing pieces of solid food **2** : something like or suggesting soup (as a heavy fog) [from French *soupe* "soup"; of Germanic origin]

²**soup** *vb* : to increase the power or better the performance of ⟨*soup* up an engine⟩ [from an earlier slang word *soup* "a dope injected into a racehorse before a race to make him run faster"] — **souped–up** \'süpt-'əp\ *adj*

soupy \'sü-pē\ *adj* **soup·i·er; -est 1** : resembling soup **2** : thickly foggy or cloudy

¹**sour** \'saú(ə)r\ *adj* **1** : having or being an acid or tart taste that is one of the four taste sensations — compare BITTER 1, ³SALT 1b, ¹SWEET 1b **2 a** : having become acid through spoiling ⟨*sour* milk⟩ **b** : indicating decay : PUTRID ⟨a *sour* odor⟩ **3** : UNPLEASANT, DISAGREEABLE ⟨a *sour* look⟩ ⟨played a *sour* note⟩ **4** : acid in reaction ⟨*sour* soil⟩ — **sour·ly** *adv* — **sour·ness** *n*

²**sour** *n* **1 a** : something sour **b** : the basic taste sensation produced by acid stimuli **2** : a cocktail made with liquor, lemon or lime juice, sugar, and sometimes soda water

³**sour** *vb* : to become or make sour

sour ball *n* : a round piece of hard candy having a sour flavor

source \'sō(ə)rs, 'sò(ə)rs\ *n* **1 a** : a force that gives rise to something : CAUSE ⟨a *source* of strength⟩ **b** : a point where something begins **c** : a person or a publication that supplies information **2** : the beginning of a stream of water ⟨the *source* of the Nile⟩ **3** : a firsthand document or main reference work

sour cherry *n* : a small Old World cherry tree widely grown for its soft tart bright red to nearly black fruits; *also* : its fruit

sour cream *n* : a thick cream soured by the addition of a special kind of bacterium and used in cooking

sour·dough \'saú(ə)r-,dō\ *n* **1** : a dough in which fermentation is active and which is used to start fermentation in other dough (as in making bread) **2** : an old-time prospector in Alaska or northwestern Canada

sour grapes *n pl* : the act of making something seem unimportant after it becomes impossible to gain

sou·sa·phone \'sü-zə-,fōn\ *n* : a large circular tuba that goes over the player's shoulder and has a wide bell that faces forward [named for John Philip *Sousa* 1854–1932 American band leader and composer]

¹**souse** \'saús\ *vb* **soused; sous·ing 1** : ²PICKLE **2 a** : to plunge in liquid : IMMERSE **b** : to wet thoroughly : DRENCH **3** : to make or become drunk

²**souse** *n* **1** : something pickled; *esp* : seasoned and chopped meat trimmed from pork, fish, or shellfish **2** : an act of sousing : WETTING **3** : DRUNKARD

sousaphone

¹**south** \'saúth\ *adv* : to or toward the south

²**south** *adj* **1** : situated toward or at the south ⟨the *south* entrance⟩ **2** : coming from the south ⟨a *south* wind⟩

³**south** *n* **1 a** : the direction to the right of one facing east **b** : the compass point opposite to north **2** *cap* : regions or countries south of a point that is mentioned or understood; *esp* : the southeastern part of the U.S.

south·bound \'saúth-,baúnd\ *adj* : headed south

¹**south·east** \saú-'thēst, *nautical* saú-'ēst\ *adv* : to or toward the southeast

²**southeast** *n* **1** : the direction between south and east **2**

cap : regions or countries southeast of a point that is mentioned or understood

³southeast *adj* **1** : situated toward or at the southeast ⟨the *southeast* corner⟩ **2** : coming from the southeast ⟨a *southeast* wind⟩

south·east·er \saủ-'thē-stər, saủ-'ē-\ *n* : a storm, strong wind, or gale coming from the southeast

south·east·er·ly \saủ-'thē-stər-lē, saủ-'ē-\ *adv or adj* **1** : from the southeast **2** : toward the southeast

south·east·ern \saủ-'thē-stərn, saủ-'ē-\ *adj* **1** *often cap* : of, relating to, or characteristic of the Southeast **2** : lying toward or coming from the southeast

South·east·ern·er \saủ-'thē-stə(r)-nər, saủ-'ē-\ *n* : a person born or living in a southeastern region (as of the U.S.)

south·east·ward \saủ-'thēs-twərd, saủ-'ēs-\ *adv or adj* : toward the southeast — **south·east·wards** \-twərdz\ *adv*

south·er·ly \'səth-ər-lē\ *adv or adj* **1** : toward the south **2** : coming from the south

south·ern \'səth-ərn\ *adj* **1** *cap* : of, relating to, or characteristic of the South **2** : lying toward or coming from the south — **south·ern·most** \-,mōst\ *adj*

Southern Cross *n* : four bright stars in the southern hemisphere that are placed as if at the ends of a cross; *also* : the group of stars of which these four are the brightest

South·ern·er \'səth-ə(r)-nər\ *n* : a person born or living in the South (as of the U.S.)

southern hemisphere *n, often cap S & H* : the half of the earth that lies south of the equator

southern lights *n pl* : AURORA AUSTRALIS

south·land \'saủth-,land, -lənd\ *n, often cap* : land in the south : the south of a country or region

south·paw \'saủth-,pỏ\ *n* : a left-handed person; *esp* : a left-handed baseball pitcher — **southpaw** *adj*

south pole *n* **1** *often cap S & P* : the southernmost point of the earth : the southern end of the earth's axis **2** : the pole of a magnet that points toward the south

south–seeking pole *n* : SOUTH POLE 2

south·ward \'saủth-wərd\ *adv or adj* : toward the south — **south·wards** \-wərdz\ *adv*

¹south·west \saủth-'west, *nautical* saủ-'west\ *adv* : to or toward the southwest

²southwest *n* **1** : the direction between south and west **2** *cap* : regions or countries southwest of a point that is mentioned or understood

³southwest *adj* **1** : coming from the southwest **2** : situated toward or at the southwest

south·west·er \saủ(th)-'wes-tər\ *n* : a storm or wind from the southwest

south·west·er·ly \saủ(th)-'wes-tər-lē\ *adv or adj* **1** : from the southwest **2** : toward the southwest

south·west·ern \saủ(th)-'wes-tərn\ *adj* **1** : lying toward or coming from the southwest **2** *often cap* : of, relating to, or characteristic of the Southwest

South·west·ern·er \saủ(th)-'wes-tə(r)-nər\ *n* : a person born or living in a southwestern region (as of the U.S.)

south·west·ward \saủ(th)-'wes-twərd\ *adv or adj* : toward the southwest — **south·west·wards** \-twərdz\ *adv*

sou·ve·nir \'sü-və-,ni(ə)r, ,sü-və-'ni(ə)r\ *n* : something that serves as a reminder : MEMENTO

sou'·west·er \saủ-'wes-tər\ *n* **1** : a long waterproof coat worn especially at sea during stormy weather **2** : a waterproof hat with a wide slanting brim longer in back than in front

sou'wester 2

¹sov·er·eign \'säv-(ə-)rən, 'säv-ərn,

'səv-\ *n* **1** : a person, body of persons, or a state possessing sovereignty; *esp* : a monarch exercising supreme authority in a state **2** : an old British gold coin

²sovereign *adj* **1** : ²CHIEF 2, HIGHEST ⟨a citizen's *sovereign* duty⟩ **2** : supreme in power or authority ⟨a *sovereign* prince⟩ **3** : having independent authority ⟨a *sovereign* state⟩

sov·er·eign·ty \'säv-(ə-)rən-tē, 'säv-ərn-, 'səv-\ *n, pl* **-ties** **1 a** : supreme power especially over a politically organized unit : DOMINION **b** : freedom from outside control : AUTONOMY **c** : the condition of being sovereign or a sovereign **2** : one (as a country) that is sovereign

so·vi·et \'sōv-ē-,et, 'säv-, -ē-ət\ *n* **1 a** : one of the representative councils of workers, peasants, or soldiers formed during the Russian revolution **b** : one of the ranks of governing councils in the U.S.S.R. **2** *pl, cap* : the people and especially the political and military leaders of the U.S.S.R. [from Russian *sovet* "council"] — **soviet** *adj, often cap*

so·vi·et·ize \'sōv-ē-ə-,tīz, 'säv-, -ē-ət-\ *vb* **-ized; -iz·ing** *often cap* **1** : to bring under Soviet control **2** : to force to be like the Soviets — **so·vi·et·iza·tion** \,sōv-ē-,et-ə-'zā-shən, ,säv-ē-, -ət-\ *n, often cap*

¹sow \'saủ\ *n* : an adult female hog

²sow \'sō\ *vb* **sowed; sown** \'sōn\ *or* **sowed; sow·ing** **1 a** : to plant seed for growth especially by scattering **b** : ¹PLANT 1a **c** : to scatter with or as if with seed **d** : to put into a selected environment : IMPLANT **2** : to set in motion : FOMENT ⟨*sowing* the seeds of suspicion⟩ **3** : to spread over a wide area : DISPERSE, DISSEMINATE — **sow·er** \'sō(-ə)r\ *n*

sow·bel·ly \'saủ-,bel-ē\ *n* : fat salt pork or bacon

sow bug \'saủ-\ *n* : WOOD LOUSE

sox *pl of* SOCK

soy \'sỏi\ *n* **1** : SOY SAUCE **2** : SOYBEAN

soya \'sỏi-(y)ə\ *n* : SOYBEAN

soy·bean \'sỏi-,bēn, -,bēn\ *n* : a hairy annual Asian plant of the legume family widely grown for its edible seeds rich in oil and proteins, as food for livestock, and for soil improvement; *also* : its seed

soy sauce *n* : Chinese and Japanese sauce consisting of a brown liquid made from soybeans

spa \'spä, 'spỏ\ *n* **1 a** : a mineral spring **b** : a resort area with mineral springs **2** : a commercial establishment offering programs and equipment for healthful exercise [named for *Spa*, a place in Belgium that has a natural mineral spring and health resort]

soybean

¹space \'spās\ *n* **1** : a period of time **2 a** : a limited extent in one, two, or three dimensions : DISTANCE, AREA, VOLUME **b** : an area set apart or available ⟨parking *space*⟩ ⟨floor *space*⟩ **3** : the limitless three-dimensional extent in which all things exist and move **4** : the region beyond the earth's atmosphere **5** : a blank area separating words or lines **6** : an available seat on a public vehicle

²space *vb* **spaced; spac·ing** : to place with space between

space–age \'spā-,sāj\ *adj* : of or relating to the age of space exploration; *esp* : ¹MODERN 1

space·craft \'spā-,skraft\ *n, pl* **spacecraft** : a vehicle for travel beyond the earth's atmosphere

\ə\ abut	\aủ\ **out**	\i\ tip	\ỏ\ **saw**	\ủ\ **foot**
\ər\ **further**	\ch\ **chin**	\ī\ **life**	\ỏi\ **coin**	\y\ **yet**
\a\ **mat**	\e\ **pet**	\j\ **job**	\th\ **thin**	\yü\ **few**
\ā\ **take**	\ē\ **easy**	\ŋ\ **sing**	\th\ **this**	\yủ\ **cure**
\ä\ **cot, cart**	\g\ **go**	\ō\ **bone**	\ü\ **food**	\zh\ **vision**

space·flight \'spās-ˌflīt\ *n* : flight beyond the earth's atmosphere

space heater *n* : a device for heating an enclosed space; *esp* : an often portable device that heats the space in which it is located and has no outside pipes

space heating *n* : heating of spaces especially for human comfort by any method

space·man \'spā-ˌsman, -smən\ *n* : one who travels outside the earth's atmosphere

space medicine *n* : a branch of medicine concerned with the effects on the human body of flight beyond the earth's atmosphere

space opera *n* : science fiction that deals with fantastic situations involving space travelers and beings from other worlds [from *space* and *opera,* following the pattern of *soap opera, horse opera;* see *Word History* at HORSE OPERA]

space·port \'spā-ˌspō(ə)rt, -ˌspȯ(ə)rt\ *n* : a place for testing and launching spacecraft

space·ship \'spās-ˌship, 'spāsh-\ *n* : SPACECRAFT

space shuttle *n* : a spacecraft designed to transport people and cargo between earth and space that can be used repeatedly

space station *n* : an artificial satellite designed to stay in orbit permanently and to be occupied by humans for long periods

space suit *n* : a suit equipped to make life in space possible for its wearer

space walk *n* : a period of movement in space outside a spacecraft by an astronaut

spac·ing \'spā-siŋ\ *n* 1 : an arrangement in space 2 : the distance between any two objects in an arranged series

spa·cious \'spā-shəs\ *adj* : large or vast in size or capacity — **spa·cious·ly** *adv* — **spa·cious·ness** *n*
syn SPACIOUS, COMMODIOUS, CAPACIOUS mean larger than average in size or capacity. SPACIOUS suggests great length and width ⟨a house with a *spacious* front lawn⟩ COMMODIOUS stresses that something is roomy and comfortable ⟨a *commodious* and airy workroom⟩ CAPACIOUS stresses the ability to hold, contain, or keep more than average ⟨a *capacious* closet⟩

space suit

¹spade \'spād\ *n* 1 : a digging tool like a shovel made so that it can be pushed into the ground with the foot 2 : a spade-shaped instrument [Old English *spadu* "a digging tool"] — **spade·ful** \-ˌfúl\ *n*

²spade *vb* **spad·ed; spad·ing** : to dig with or use a spade

³spade *n* 1 : a black figure resembling an inverted heart with a short stem at the bottom used to indicate a suit of playing cards 2 : a card of the suit of spades [from Italian *spada* or Spanish *espada,* both meaning "broad sword" and both from Latin *spatha* "spatula, broad sword"]

spade·work \'spād-ˌwərk\ *n* 1 : work done with the spade 2 : the hard plain work that must be done at the beginning of a project

spa·ghet·ti \spə-'get-ē\ *n* : a food made chiefly of a mixture of flour and water dried in the form of thin solid strings
Word History The Italian word *spago* means "cord, string". The suffix *-etto* in Italian, like the suffix *-ette* in English, means "little one". Added together, *spago* and *-etto* become *spaghetto,* which means "little string". "Little string" describes very well the shape of a strand of spaghetti. The word *spaghetti* is actually the plural form of *spaghetto.* [from Italian *spaghetti* "pasta made in long strings", from *spaghetti,* pl. of *spaghetto* "little string", from *spago* "string"]

spake \'spāk\ *archaic past of* SPEAK

¹span \'span\ *n* 1 : the distance from the end of the thumb to the end of the little finger of a spread hand; *also* : an English unit of length equal to 9 inches (about 23 centimeters) 2 **a** : a limited portion of time ⟨*span* of life⟩ **b** : the spread (as of an arch) from one support to another **c** : the portion supported to form a span [Old English *spann* "distance measured by the outstretched hand"]

²span *vb* **spanned; span·ning** 1 **a** : to measure by or as if by the hand with fingers and thumb extended **b** : ²MEASURE 2 2 **a** : to reach or extend across ⟨a bridge *spans* the river⟩ **b** : to place or construct a span over

³span *n* : a pair of animals (as mules) driven together [from Dutch *span* "a pair of animals driven together", derived from earlier *spannen* "to hitch up"]

span·dex \'span-ˌdeks\ *n* : any of various synthetic elastic textile fibers

¹span·gle \'spaŋ-gəl\ *n* 1 : a small piece of shining metal or plastic used for ornamentation on clothing 2 : a small glittering object

²spangle *vb* **span·gled; span·gling** \'spaŋ-g(ə-)liŋ\ : to set or sprinkle with or as if with spangles

Span·glish \'spaŋ-glish, -lish\ *n* : Spanish marked by many borrowings from English; *also* : any of various combinations of Spanish and English

Span·iard \'span-yərd\ *n* : a person born or living in Spain

span·iel \'span-yəl\ *n* : any of numerous small or medium-sized mostly short-legged dogs that usually have long wavy hair and large drooping ears
Word History There are several kinds of spaniels, and each comes from a different area of Europe. The Brittany spaniel comes from France and the cocker spaniel comes from England. Other spaniels come from Ireland and Wales. But the ancestors of all of these spaniels came from Spain, and that is why they are called *spaniels.* The Latin word for Spain was *Hispania.* From this was derived the early French word *espaignol,* meaning "one that lives in or comes from Spain". This word was used for the little dogs that were bred in Spain. Later in English the word became first *spaniell* and finally *spaniel.* It was used for any of several kinds of silky-haired, long-eared dogs like those that originally came from Spain. [Middle English *spaniell* "spaniel", from early French *espaignol* "spaniel", literally "Spaniard", derived from Latin *Hispania* "Spain"]

Span·ish \'span-ish\ *n* 1 : the Romance language of Spain and of the countries colonized by Spaniards 2 **Spanish** *pl* : the people of Spain — **Spanish** *adj*

Spanish American *n* 1 : a person living in the U.S. whose native language is Spanish and whose culture is of Spanish origin 2 : a person born or living in one of the countries of America in which Spanish is the national language — **Spanish–American** *adj*

Spanish moss *n* : a plant related to the pineapple that forms hanging tufts of grayish green threadlike strands on trees in the southern U.S. and the West Indies

Spanish rice *n* : rice cooked with onions, green peppers, and tomatoes

spank \'spaŋk\ *vb* : to strike on the buttocks with the open hand — **spank** *n*

spank·ing \'spaŋ-kiŋ\ *adj* : BRISK 1, LIVELY ⟨a *spanking* breeze⟩

span·ner \'span-ər\ *n, chiefly British* : ²WRENCH 2

¹spar \'spär\ *n* 1 : a stout pole 2 : a long rounded wood or metal piece (as a mast, boom, or yard) to which a sail is fastened [Middle English *sparre* "a stout pole, a pole used to support a sail on a ship"]

1 spar 2

²spar *vb* **sparred; spar·ring** **1** : to box or make boxing movements with the fists for practice or in fun **2** : ²SKIRMISH 1 [probably an altered form of *spur* "to urge (a horse) on with spurs"]

¹spare \'spa(ə)r, 'spe(ə)r\ *vb* **spared; spar·ing** **1** : to keep from being punished or harmed : show mercy ⟨*spared* the prisoners⟩ **2** : to free of the need to do something ⟨*spare* yourself the trouble⟩ **3** : to hold off from doing or spending ⟨*spare* no cost⟩ **4** : to use or give out in small amounts ⟨more pancakes, please, and don't *spare* the syrup⟩ **5 a** : to give up as not really needed ⟨can you *spare* me a few minutes⟩ ⟨couldn't *spare* a dime⟩ **b** : to have left over ⟨got there with time to *spare*⟩ [Old English *sparian* "to refrain from harming"]

²spare *adj* **spar·er; spar·est** **1** : held in reserve ⟨a spare tire⟩ **2** : being over what is needed ⟨spare time⟩ **3** : not generous or wasteful : SPARING **4** : somewhat thin **5** : SCANTY [Middle English *spare* "being extra or more than is needed"] — **spare·ly** *adv* — **spare·ness** *n*

³spare *n* **1** : a spare or duplicate piece or part **2** : the knocking down of all 10 bowling pins with the first two balls

spare·ribs \'spa(ə)r-,(r)ibz, 'spe(ə)r-\ *n pl* : a cut of pork ribs separated from the bacon strips [derived from a German dialect word *ribbesper* "pickled pork ribs roasted on a spit", derived from *ribbe* "rib" and *sper* "spear, spit"; probably spelled *spareribs* in English because of the misunderstanding of the meaning of the German word *sper*]

spar·ing \'spa(ə)r-iŋ, 'spe(ə)r-\ *adj* : careful in the use of money or supplies — **spar·ing·ly** \-iŋ-lē\ *adv*

¹spark \'spärk\ *n* **1 a** : a small bit of a burning material **b** : a hot glowing bit struck from a mass **2** : a short bright flash of electricity between two points **3** : ²SPARKLE 1 **4** : ¹TRACE 2 [Old English *spearca* "spark"]

²spark *vb* **1** : to give off or cause to give off sparks **2** : to cause to get going ⟨the question *sparked* quite an argument⟩ ⟨*sparked* the team to victory⟩

³spark *vb* : WOO 1, COURT [from earlier *spark* (noun) "a foolish young man, boyfriend"; perhaps of Scandinavian origin]

¹spar·kle \'spär-kəl\ *vb* **spar·kled; spar·kling** \-k(ə-)liŋ\ **1 a** : to throw out sparks **b** : to give off small flashes of light ⟨the diamond *sparkled*⟩ **2** : to do or play very well ⟨*sparkled* at shortstop⟩ **3** : EFFERVESCE 1 ⟨*sparkling* wine⟩ **4** : to become lively or active ⟨the conversation *sparkled*⟩

²sparkle *n* **1** : a little flash of light **2** : the quality of sparkling **3** : the quality or state of being effervescent

spar·kler \'spär-klər\ *n* **1** : DIAMOND 1b **2** : a firework that throws off very bright sparks as it burns

spark plug *n* **1** : a device used in an engine to produce a spark that ignites a fuel mixture **2** : one that begins something or drives something forward

sparky \'spär-kē\ *adj* **spark·i·er; -est** : being lively and active

sparred *past and past participle of* SPAR

sparring *present participle of* SPAR

sparring partner *n* : a person with whom a boxer spars for practice during training

spar·row \'spar-ō\ *n* **1** : any of several small songbirds that have usually brownish or grayish feathers and are related to the finches; *esp* : HOUSE SPARROW **2** : any of various finches (as the song sparrow) that resemble the true sparrows

sparrow hawk *n* : any of various small hawks or falcons

sparse \'spärs\ *adj* **spars-**

sparrow hawk

er; **spars·est** : of few and scattered elements; *esp* : not thickly grown or settled **syn** see MEAGER — **sparse·ly** *adv* — **sparse·ness** *n* — **spar·si·ty** \'spär-sət-ē\ *n*

¹Spar·tan \'spärt-ᵊn\ *n* : a person born or living in ancient Sparta

²Spartan *adj* **1** : of or relating to Sparta in ancient Greece **2** : marked by absence of comfort and luxury

spasm \'spaz-əm\ *n* **1** : a sudden uncontrolled contracting of muscles ⟨back *spasms*⟩ **2** : a sudden violent and temporary effort, emotion, or outburst

spas·mod·ic \spaz-'mäd-ik\ *adj* **1 a** : relating to or affected or characterized by spasm ⟨*spasmodic* movements⟩ **b** : resembling a spasm especially in sudden violence **2** : acting or going now and then : INTERMITTENT — **spas·mod·i·cal·ly** \-'mäd-ik(ə-)lē\ *adv*

¹spas·tic \'spas-tik\ *adj* **1** : of, relating to, or characterized by spasms ⟨*spastic* colon⟩ **2** : affected with spasms ⟨a *spastic* child⟩

²spastic *n* : a spastic person

¹spat \'spat\ *past and past participle of* SPIT

²spat *n, pl* **spat** *or* **spats** : a young oyster [origin unknown]

³spat *n* : a cloth or leather covering for the instep and ankle [a shortened form of *spatterdash* "a protective covering for the ankle or leg"]

⁴spat *n* **1** : a brief unimportant quarrel : DISPUTE **2** : a sound like that of rain falling in large drops

⁵spat *vb* **spat·ted; spat·ting** **1** : to have a spat : QUARREL **2** : to strike with a sound like that of rain falling in large drops

spate \'spāt\ *n* : a sudden flood or rush

spa·tial \'spā-shəl\ *adj* : of or relating to space — **spa·tial·ly** \'spāsh-(ə-)lē\ *adv*

¹spat·ter \'spat-ər\ *vb* **1** : to splash with drops or small bits of something wet **2** : to scatter by splashing ⟨*spatter* mud⟩

²spatter *n* **1** : the act or sound of spattering **2** : a drop or splash spattered on something : a spot or stain due to spattering

spat·u·la \'spach-ə-lə\ *n* : an instrument with a thin flexible blade used especially for spreading or mixing soft substances or lifting

spav·in \'spav-ən\ *n* : a disease of horses characterized by swelling of the hock and associated with strain

spav·ined \'spav-ənd\ *adj* : lame and crippled by or as by spavin

¹spawn \'spón, 'spän\ *vb* **1** : to produce or deposit eggs or spawn **2** : to produce young especially in large numbers **3** : GENERATE, BRING FORTH — **spawn·er** *n*

²spawn *n* **1** : the eggs of aquatic animals (as fishes or oysters) that lay many small eggs **2** : PRODUCT 2, OFFSPRING; *also* : offspring produced in large quantities

spay \'spā\ *vb* : to remove the ovaries of (a female animal)

speak \'spēk\ *vb* **spoke** \'spōk\; **spo·ken** \'spō-kən\; **speak·ing** **1** : to utter words : TALK **2** : to utter in words ⟨*speak* the truth⟩ **3** : to mention in speech or writing ⟨*spoke* of being ill⟩ **4** : to be spokesman ⟨*spoke* for the group⟩ **5** : to express feelings in ways other than by words ⟨actions *speak* louder than words⟩ **6** : to use or be able to use in talking ⟨*speaks* Spanish⟩ — **speak·able** \'spē-kə-bəl\ *adj* — **to speak of** : worth mentioning or noticing ⟨there was nothing else *to speak of*⟩

speak·easy \'spē-,kē-zē\ *n, pl* **-eas·ies** : a place where alcoholic drinks are illegally sold

speak·er \'spē-kər\ *n* **1** : a person who speaks **2** : a person who conducts a meeting (as of a legislature) **3** : LOUDSPEAKER

\ə\ abut	\au̇\ out	\i\ tip	\ȯ\ saw	\u̇\ foot
\ər\ further	\ch\ chin	\ī\ llfe	\ȯi\ coin	\y\ yet
\a\ mat	\e\ pet	\j\ job	\th\ thin	\yü\ few
\ā\ take	\ē\ easy	\ŋ\ sing	\th\ this	\yu̇\ cure
\ä\ cot, cart	\g\ go	\ō\ bone	\ü\ food	\zh\ vision

speak·er·ship \'spē-kər-,ship\ *n* : the position of speaker of a legislature

speak out *vb* **1** : to speak loudly and clearly **2** : to speak freely and without fear

speak up *vb* : SPEAK OUT

¹spear \'spi(ə)r\ *n* **1** : a weapon with a long straight handle and sharp head or blade used for throwing or jabbing **2** : an instrument with a sharp point and curved hooks used in spearing fish — **spear·like** \-,līk\ *adj*

²spear *vb* : to pierce or strike with or as if with a spear — **spear·er** *n*

³spear *n* : a usually young blade, shoot, or sprout (as of grass)

spear·fish \'spi(ə)r-,fish\ *vb* : to fish with a spear

spear·gun \-,gən\ *n* : a gun that shoots a spear and is used for spearfishing

¹spear·head \-,hed\ *n* **1** : the head or point of a spear **2** : a person, thing, or group that is the leading force (as in a development or attack)

²spearhead *vb* : to serve as leader of (*spearhead* a campaign for better schools)

spearhead 1

spear·man \'spi(ə)r-mən\ *n* : a soldier armed with a spear

spear·mint \-,mint, -mənt\ *n* : a common mint grown for flavoring and especially for its fragrant oil

spear·point \-,pȯint\ *n* : the point of a spear

¹spe·cial \'spesh-əl\ *adj* **1 a** : being unusual and especially better in some way (a *special* occasion) **b** : being very dear or liked very well (a *special* friend) **2** : different from others of the same kind : UNIQUE (a *special* case) **3** : being or having more than the usual : ADDITIONAL, EXTRA (a *special* edition) **4** : designed for a certain purpose or occasion (a *special* diet) — **spe·cial·ly** \'spesh-(ə-)lē\ *adv*

²special *n* : something (as a television program) that is not part of a regular series

special delivery *n* : delivery of mail by messenger for an extra fee

special education *n* : classes for students (as the handicapped) with special educational needs

spearmint

spe·cial·ist \'spesh-(ə-)ləst\ *n* **1** : a person who studies or works at a special occupation or branch of learning (an eye *specialist*) **2** : an enlisted person in the army with any of four ranks similar to those of corporal to sergeant first class — **specialist** *or* **spe·cial·is·tic** \,spesh-ə-'lis-tik\ *adj*

spe·ci·al·i·ty \,spesh-ē-'al-ət-ē\ *n, pl* **-ties** : SPECIALTY

spe·cial·iza·tion \,spesh-(ə-)lə-'zā-shən\ *n* **1** : a making or becoming specialized **2 a** : a change in the structure of a body part so that it becomes suited for performing a particular function or of a whole plant or animal so that it is suited for life in a particular environment **b** : a body part or an organism changed by specialization

spe·cial·ize \'spesh-ə-,līz\ *vb* **-ized; -iz·ing** **1** : to limit one's attention or energy to one business, subject, or study **2** : to undergo specialization

specialized *adj* **1** : designed or fitted for one particular purpose or occupation **2** : characterized by or exhibiting biological specialization

spe·cial·ty \'spesh-əl-tē\ *n, pl* **-ties** **1** : a product of a special kind or of special excellence (eggs were the cook's

specialty) **2** : something a person specializes in or has special knowledge of

spe·cie \'spē-shē, -sē\ *n* : money in coin

spe·cies \'spē-shēz, -sēz\ *n, pl* **species** **1** : a class of things of the same kind and with the same name : KIND, SORT **2** : a category of living things that ranks below a genus, is made up of related individuals able to produce fertile offspring, and is identified by a two-part scientific name

¹spe·cif·ic \spi-'sif-ik\ *adj* **1** : relating to or being an example of a certain kind of thing (a *specific* case) (was the question *specific* or general?) **2 a** : having one particular effect or influence (as on a body part or a disease) (quinine is *specific* for malaria) **b** : capable of reacting only in usually one way or with one particular thing in a chemical or an immune reaction (*specific* antibodies) (a *specific* enzyme) **3** : clearly and exactly presented or stated (gave them *specific* directions) **4** : of, relating to, or being a species — **spe·cif·i·cal·ly** \-'sif-i-k(ə-)lē\ *adv*

²specific *n* **1** : something specially adapted to a purpose or use; *esp* : a drug or remedy specific for a particular disease **2** *pl* : things that are specific : DETAILS, PARTICULARS (get down to *specifics*)

spec·i·fi·ca·tion \,spes-(ə-)fə-'kā-shən\ *n* **1** : the act or process of specifying **2 a** : a description of work to be done or materials to be used — usually used in pl. (the architect's *specifications* for a new building) **b** : a single specified item

specific gravity *n* : the ratio of the density of a substance to the density of some substance (as water) taken as a standard when both densities are obtained by weighing in air

specific heat *n* : the heat in calories required to raise the temperature of one gram of a substance one degree Celsius

spec·i·fic·i·ty \,spes-ə-'fis-ət-ē\ *n* : the quality or condition of being specific; *esp* : the condition of taking part in or acting as a catalyst in only one or a few chemical reactions (the *specificity* of an enzyme)

spec·i·fy \'spes-ə-,fī\ *vb* **-fied; -fy·ing** **1** : to name or mention exactly and clearly (*specify* the cause) **2** : to include in a specification (*specify* oak flooring)

spec·i·men \'spes-(ə-)mən\ *n* **1** : a part or a single thing that shows what the whole thing or group is like : SAMPLE **2** : PERSON 1, SORT, INDIVIDUAL (a tough *specimen*)

spe·cious \'spē-shəs\ *adj* : having a false look of being fair, just, or right (a *specious* argument) — **spe·cious·ly** *adv* — **spe·cious·ness** *n*

¹speck \'spek\ *n* **1** : a small spot or blemish **2** : a very small amount : BIT (just a *speck* more milk)

²speck *vb* : to make specks on or in

¹speck·le \'spek-əl\ *n* : a small mark (as of color)

²speckle *vb* **speck·led; speck·ling** \'spek-(ə-)liŋ\ : to mark with speckles

specs \'speks\ *n pl* **1** : ¹GLASS 2b **2** : SPECIFICATION 2a

spec·ta·cle \'spek-ti-kəl\ *n* **1 a** : an unusual or impressive public display **b** : an object of curious or annoyed attention (made a *spectacle* of yourself at the party) **2** *pl* : ¹GLASS 2b [Middle English *spectacle* "spectacle", from early French *spectacle* (same meaning), derived from Latin *spectare* "to watch", derived from *specere* "to look, look at" — related to AUSPICE, EXPECT]

spec·ta·cled \'spek-ti-kəld\ *adj* : having markings that look like a pair of spectacles (a *spectacled* snake)

spec·tac·u·lar \spek-'tak-yə-lər, spək-\ *adj* : of, relating to, or being a spectacle : exciting to see : SENSATIONAL (a *spectacular* sunset) (a *spectacular* play in a football game) — **spec·tac·u·lar·ly** *adv*

spec·ta·tor \'spek-,tāt-ər, spek-'tāt-\ *n* : a person who looks on (as at a sports event) — **spectator** *adj*

spec·ter *or* **spec·tre** \'spek-tər\ *n* **1** : GHOST **2** : something that bothers the mind

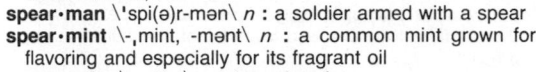

spec·tral \'spek-trəl\ *adj* **1** : of, relating to, or suggesting a specter : GHOSTLY **2** : of, relating to, or made by a spectrum

spec·tro·graph \'spek-t(r)ə-ˌgraf\ *n* : an instrument for spreading radiation (as of light or sound) into a spectrum and photographing or mapping the spectrum

spec·tro·pho·tom·e·ter \ˌspek-trō-fə-'täm-ət-ər\ *n* : an instrument for measuring the strengths of the light in different parts of a spectrum

spec·tro·scope \'spek-trə-ˌskōp\ *n* : an instrument that produces spectra from or by the use of electromagnetic waves (as of light)

spec·trum \'spek-trəm\ *n, pl* **spec·tra** \-trə\ *or* **spectrums** **1 a** : the group of different colors including red, orange, yellow, green, blue, indigo, and violet arranged in the order of their wavelengths and seen when white light passes through a prism and falls on a surface or when sunlight is scattered by water droplets to form a rainbow **b** : ELECTROMAGNETIC SPECTRUM **2** : a continuous range or series ⟨a wide *spectrum* of interests⟩

spec·u·late \'spek-yə-ˌlāt\ *vb* **-lat·ed; -lat·ing** **1** : to think or wonder about a subject : MEDITATE ⟨*speculating* about the future⟩ **2** : to engage in a business deal in which much profit may be made although at a big risk ⟨*speculating* on the stock market⟩ — **spec·u·la·tor** \-ˌlāt-ər\ *n*

spec·u·la·tion \ˌspek-yə-'lā-shən\ *n* **1** : thoughts or guesses about something ⟨much *speculation* about who the new teacher would be⟩ **2** : the taking of a big risk in business in hopes of making a big profit

spec·u·la·tive \'spek-yə-lət-iv, -ˌlāt-\ *adj* **1 a** : of or relating to mental speculation **b** : CURIOUS 1 **2** : of or relating to financial speculation — **spec·u·la·tive·ly** *adv*

spec·u·lum \'spek-yə-ləm\ *n, pl* **-la** \-lə\ *also* **-lums** : a metal instrument that is inserted into a bodily passage in order to help in inspection or the giving of medicine

speech \'spēch\ *n* **1** : the communication or expression of thoughts in spoken words **2 a** : something that is spoken **b** : a public talk **3** : a form of communication (as a language or dialect) used by a particular group **4** : the power of expressing or communicating thoughts by speaking

speech·less \'spēch-ləs\ *adj* **1** : unable to speak **2** : not speaking for a time : SILENT ⟨*speechless* with surprise⟩ — **speech·less·ly** *adv* — **speech·less·ness** *n*

¹speed \'spēd\ *n* **1 a** : the act or state of moving swiftly : SWIFTNESS **b** : rate of motion : VELOCITY **2** : quickness in movement or action **3** : a transmission gear in motor vehicles or bicycles ⟨a 10-*speed* bicycle⟩ **4** : a drug that is related to amphetamine, is used as a stimulant of the central nervous system, and is sometimes involved in drug abuse; *also* : a related drug

²speed *vb* **sped** \'sped\ *or* **speed·ed; speed·ing** **1 a** : to move or cause to move fast **b** : to go or drive at too high a speed **3** : to increase the speed of : ACCELERATE — often used with *up*

³speed *adj* : of, relating to, or regulating speed

speed·boat \'spēd-ˌbōt\ *n* : a fast motorboat

speed bump *n* : a low raised ridge across a roadway (as in a parking lot) to limit vehicle speed

speed·er \'spēd-ər\ *n* : a person who drives faster than the legal speed limit

speed limit *n* : the highest or lowest speed allowed by law in a certain area

speed·om·e·ter \spi-'däm-ət-ər\ *n* **1** : an instrument that measures speed **2** : an instrument that both measures speed and records distance traveled

speed–read·ing \'spēd-ˌrēd-iŋ\ *n* : a method of reading rapidly by skimming

speed·ster \'spēd-stər\ *n* : one that goes or can go very fast

speed·way \'spēd-ˌwā\ *n* : a racetrack for racing cars or motorcycles

speedy \'spēd-ē\ *adj* **speed·i·er; -est** : moving or taking

place fast — **speed·i·ly** \'spēd-ᵊl-ē\ *adv* **speed·i·ness** \'spēd-ē-nəs\ *n*

spe·le·ol·o·gy \ˌspē-lē-'äl-ə-jē, ˌspel-ē-\ *n* : the scientific study or exploration of caves — **spe·le·o·log·i·cal** \-ə-'läj-i-kəl\ *adj*

¹spell \'spel\ *n* **1 a** : a spoken word or form of words believed to have magic power **b** : a state of enchantment **2** : a very strong influence [Old English *spell* "a tale, story told"]

²spell *vb* : to put under a spell : BEWITCH

³spell *vb* **spelled** \'speld\; **spell·ing** : to take the place of for a time : RELIEVE ⟨if we *spell* each other we won't get tired⟩ [Old English *spelian* "to take the place of, relieve"]

⁴spell *vb* **spelled** \'speld, 'spelt\; **spell·ing** **1 a** : to name, write, or print the letters of in order **b** : to be the letters of ⟨"c-a-t" *spells* "cat"⟩ **3** : to amount to : MEAN ⟨what you do could *spell* the difference between life and death⟩ ⟨that usually *spells* trouble⟩ [Middle English *spellen* "to read slowly and with difficulty", from early French *espeller* (same meaning); of Germanic origin]

⁵spell *n* **1** : one's turn at work or duty **2** : a period spent in a job or occupation **3 a** : a short period of time **b** : a stretch of a specified type of weather ⟨a hot *spell*⟩ **4** : a period of bodily or mental distress or disorder : ATTACK, FIT ⟨a *spell* of coughing⟩ ⟨fainting *spell*⟩ [probably an altered form of Old English *spale* "a substitute"; the spelling probably influenced in Middle English by the similar word *spelen* "to substitute for, relieve"]

spell·bind \'spel-ˌbīnd\ *vb* **-bound** \-ˌbaúnd\; **-bind·ing** : to hold by or as if by a spell : FASCINATE

spell·bind·er \'spel-ˌbīn-dər\ *n* : a very powerful speaker

spell·bound \'spel-'baúnd\ *adj* : held by or as if by a spell

spell·er \'spel-ər\ *n* **1** : a person who spells words **2** : a book with exercises for teaching spelling

spell·ing \'spel-iŋ\ *n* : the forming of words from letters; *also* : the letters composing a word

spelling bee *n* : a spelling contest in which each contestant who spells a word wrong is eliminated

spell out *vb* : to make very plain ⟨each one's duties were *spelled out* in detail⟩

spelt \'spelt\ *chiefly British past and past participle of* SPELL

spe·lunk·er \spi-'ləŋ-kər, 'spē-ˌləŋ-\ *n* : a person who makes a hobby of exploring or studying caves

spend \'spend\ *vb* **spent** \'spent\; **spend·ing** **1** : to pay out : USE UP, EXPEND **2 a** : ¹EXHAUST 1, WEAR OUT **b** : to use wastefully : SQUANDER **3** : to cause or allow (as time) to pass ⟨*spent* the summer at the beach⟩ — **spend·er** *n*

spend·able \'spen-də-bəl\ *adj* : available for spending

spending money *n* : money for small personal expenses

spend·thrift \'spen(d)-ˌthrift\ *n* : one who spends wastefully — **spendthrift** *adj*

spent \'spent\ *adj* **1** : used up **2** : drained of energy

sperm \'spərm\ *n, pl* **sperm** *or* **sperms** **1** : SEMEN **2** : a mobile male gamete that has a long and thin or rounded head and a long thin tail that acts as a flagellum — called also *spermatozoon, sperm cell*

sper·ma·ce·ti \ˌspər-mə-'sēt-ē, -'set-\ *n* : a waxy solid that is obtained from the oil of some sea-dwelling mammals (as the sperm whale) and is used in ointments, cosmetics, and candles

sper·ma·tid \'spər-mət-əd\ *n* : any of the cells produced in meiosis that form sperms

sper·mato·gen·e·sis \(ˌ)spər-ˌmat-ə-'jen-ə-səs\ *n, pl* **-e·ses** \-ə-ˌsēz\ : the process of male gamete formation including meiosis and formation of sperms

\ə\	abut	\aú\	out	\i\	tip	\ó\	saw	\ú\	foot
\ər\	further	\ch\	chin	\ī\	life	\ói\	coin	\y\	yet
\a\	mat	\e\	pet	\j\	job	\th\	thin	\yü\	few
\ā\	take	\ē\	easy	\ŋ\	sing	\th\	this	\yú\	cure
\ä\	cot, cart	\g\	go	\ō\	bone	\ü\	food	\zh\	vision

sper·mato·phyte \(,)spər-'mat-ə-,fīt\ *n* : any of a group of plants that produce seeds and include the gymnosperms and angiosperms

sper·ma·to·zo·on \(,)spər-,mat-ə-'zō-ən, ,spər-mət-\ *n, pl* **-zoa** \-'zō-ə\ : SPERM 2

sperm cell *n* : SPERM 2

sper·mi·cide \'spər-mə-,sīd\ *n* : a preparation or substance (as in a contraceptive) used to kill sperm

sperm whale *n* : a large toothed whale with a large chamber in the skull that contains a fluid mixture of spermaceti and oil

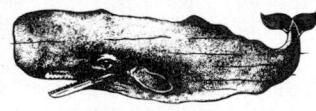

sperm whale

¹**spew** \'spyü\ *vb* : to send or come out in a flood or gush

²**spew** *n* : matter that is spewed out

sphag·num \'sfag-nəm\ *n* **1** : any of a large genus of mosses that usually grow in marshes and bogs **2** : a mass of sphagnum plants

sphere \'sfi(ə)r\ *n* **1 a** : a globe-shaped body : BALL, GLOBE **b** : a solid that has a boundary consisting of all points at a given distance from a point that is the center **c** : the surface that forms the boundary of a sphere **2** : a field of influence or activity ⟨countries within the Soviet *sphere*⟩ — **sphe·ric·i·ty** \sfir-'is-ət-ē\ *n*

spher·i·cal \'sfir-i-kəl, 'sfer-\ *adj* : relating to or having the form of a sphere or part of a sphere — **spher·i·cal·ly** \-k(ə-)lē\ *adv*

spher·oid \'sfi(ə)r-,óid, 'sfe(ə)r-\ *n* : a figure resembling a flattened sphere

sphinc·ter \'sfiŋ(k)-tər\ *n* : a ringlike muscle surrounding a body opening that is able to make the opening smaller or close it

sphinx \'sfiŋ(k)s\ *n, pl* **sphinx·es** *or* **sphin·ges** \'sfin-,jēz\ **1** : an ancient Egyptian image having the body of a lion and the head of a man, ram, or hawk **2** : HAWK-MOTH — called also *sphinx moth*

sphinx 1

sphyg·mo·ma·nom·e·ter \,sfig-mō-mə-'näm-ət-ər\ *n* : an instrument for measuring blood pressure

¹**spice** \'spīs\ *n* **1** : a plant product (as pepper or nutmeg) that has a strong pleasant smell and is used to season or flavor food **2** : something that adds interest ⟨variety is the *spice* of life⟩ **3** : a fragrant odor : PERFUME

²**spice** *vb* **spiced; spic·ing** : to season with or as if with spices

spice·bush \'spīs-,bush\ *n* : a fragrant shrub of the eastern U.S. and Canada that is related to the laurel and has small yellow flowers which come out early in the spring

spick–and–span *or* **spic–and–span** \,spik-ən-'span\ *adj* **1** : quite new and unused **2** : very clean and neat ⟨kept the cabin *spick-and-span*⟩

spic·ule \'spik-yü(ə)l\ *n* : a small hard needlelike structure; *esp* : one of the tiny calcium- or silica-containing bodies that support the tissues of various invertebrates and especially sponges

spicy \'spī-sē\ *adj* **spic·i·er; -est** **1** : flavored with or containing spice **2** : somewhat shocking or indecent ⟨a *spicy* story⟩ — **spic·i·ly** \-sə-lē\ *adv* — **spic·i·ness** \-sē-nəs\ *n*

spi·der \'spīd-ər\ *n* **1** : any of numerous arachnids that have a two-part body, eight legs, and two or more pairs of abdominal organs for spinning threads of silk used in making cocoons for their eggs, nests for themselves, or webs for catching their prey **2** : a cast-iron frying pan

spider crab *n* : any of numerous crabs with very long legs and nearly triangular bodies

spider plant *n* : any of several plants of the lily family that have long narrow leaves and wiry stems often producing small plants at the end and that are often grown as houseplants

spi·der·web \'spīd-ər-,web\ *n* : the silken web spun by most spiders and used as a resting place and a trap for small prey

spi·dery \'spīd-ə-rē\ *adj* **1** : resembling a spider; *also* : long and thin like the legs of a spider **2** : resembling a spiderweb **3** : full of spiders

spied *past and past participle of* ¹SPY

¹**spiel** \'spē(ə)l\ *vb* : to talk in a fast, smooth, and usually colorful manner — **spiel·er** \'spē-lər\ *n*

²**spiel** *n* : fast smooth usually colorful talk often intended to sell something

spies *pl of* ²SPY

spiffy \'spif-ē\ *adj* **spiff·i·er; -est** : fine looking : SMART

spig·ot \'spig-ət, 'spik-ət\ *n* **1** : a plug used to stop the vent in a barrel **2** : FAUCET

¹**spike** \'spīk\ *n* **1** : a very large nail **2** : one of the metal objects set in the sole and heel of a shoe (as a baseball shoe) to prevent slipping **3** : an unbranched antler of a young deer **4** : a pointed element (as in a graph) [Middle English *spike* "a large nail"; probably of Dutch origin]

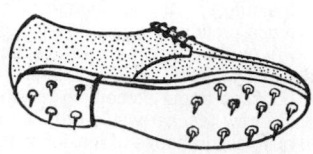

¹spike 2

²**spike** *vb* **spiked; spik·ing** **1** : to fasten or furnish with spikes **2** : to pierce or cut with or on a spike **3** : to add alcoholic liquor to a drink **4** : to drive (as a volleyball) sharply downward

³**spike** *n* **1** : an ear of grain **2** : a long usually rather narrow cluster of flowers in which the blossoms grow close to the central stem [Middle English *spik* "a head of a stalk of grain, ear", from Latin *spica* (same meaning)]

spiked \'spīkt\ *adj* : SPIKY 2

spike·let \'spī-klət\ *n* : one of the small few-flowered spikes that occur in grasses and sedges

spike·nard \'spīk-,närd\ *n* : an American herb with a fragrant root and clusters of small white flowers

spiky \'spī-kē\ *adj* **spik·i·er; -est** **1** : resembling a spike **2** : having spikes

spile \'spī(ə)l\ *n* : a spout inserted in a tree to draw off sap

¹**spill** \'spil\ *vb* **spilled** \'spild, 'spilt\ *also* **spilt** \'spilt\; **spill·ing** **1** : to cause (blood) to flow by wounding or killing **2 a** : to cause or allow to fall, flow, or run out by accident ⟨*spilled* some flour on the floor⟩ **b** : to fall or run out so as to be lost or wasted ⟨the milk *spilled*⟩ **c** : to spread beyond limits **3** : to throw off or out ⟨a horse *spilled* its rider⟩ **4** : to let out : GIVE AWAY ⟨*spilled* the secret⟩ — **spill·able** \'spil-ə-bəl\ *adj* — **spill the beans** : to give a secret away by talking without thinking

²**spill** *n* **1 a** : an act or instance of spilling **b** : a fall from a horse or vehicle **2** : something spilled ⟨cleaning up an oil *spill*⟩

spill·age \'spil-ij\ *n* **1** : the act or process of spilling **2** : the quantity that spills

spill·way \'spil-,wā\ *n* : a passage for extra water to run over or around a dam

¹**spin** \'spin\ *vb* **spun** \'spən\; **spin·ning** **1** : to draw out and twist into yarn or thread ⟨*spun* the fleece into thread⟩ **2 a** : to produce by drawing out and twisting fibers ⟨*spin* thread⟩ **b** : to form threads or a web or cocoon by giving off a sticky fluid that quickly hardens into silk **3** : to turn or cause to turn round and round rapidly **4** : to feel as if in a whirl ⟨my head was *spinning*⟩ **5** : to tell using the

imagination ⟨*spin* a yarn⟩ **6 :** to move swiftly on wheels or in a vehicle **7 :** to make, shape, or produce by or as if by spinning ⟨*spun* sugar⟩

²**spin** *n* **1 a :** the act of spinning something **b :** a rapid whirling motion **2 :** a short trip in a vehicle ⟨go for a *spin*⟩ **3 a :** a plunging descent or downward spiral **b :** a state of mental confusion **4 :** a special point of view, emphasis, or interpretation

spin·ach \'spin-ich\ *n* : a dark green leafy plant that is grown for use as food

spi·nal \'spīn-ᵊl\ *adj* **1 :** of, relating to, or located near the backbone **2 :** of, relating to, or affecting the spinal cord

spinal column *n* : BACKBONE 1

spinal cord *n* : the cord of nervous tissue that extends from the brain along the back in the cavity of the backbone, branches to form the spinal nerves, carries nerve impulses to and from the brain, and helps to control reflex actions

spinal nerve *n* : any of the paired nerves which arise from the spinal cord and pass to various parts of the body and of which there are normally 31 pairs in human beings

¹**spin·dle** \'spin-dᵊl\ *n* **1 a :** a slender round rod or stick with tapered ends by which thread or yarn is twisted in spinning by hand and on which it is wound **b :** a device consisting of a long spike fixed so that papers can be stuck on it for filing **2 :** something shaped like a spindle: as **a** : a figure along which the chromosomes are distributed during cell division **b :** MUSCLE SPINDLE **3 :** something (as an axle or shaft) shaped or turned like a spindle or on which something turns

²**spindle** *vb* **spin·dled; spin·dling** \'spin-(d)liŋ, -dᵊl-iŋ\ : to stick (as a piece of paper) on a spindle ⟨do not fold, *spindle,* or mutilate⟩

spin·dle–shanked \,spin-dᵊl-'shaŋ(k)t\ *adj* : having long thin legs

spin·dling \'spin-(d)liŋ, -dᵊl-iŋ\ *adj* : being long or tall and thin and usually feeble or weak ⟨*spindling* stems⟩

spin·dly \'spin-(d)lē, -dᵊl-ē\ *adj* **spin·dli·er; -est** : SPIN-DLING

spin·drift \'spin-,drift\ *n* : spray blown from waves

spine \'spīn\ *n* **1 a :** BACKBONE 1 **b :** something resembling a backbone **c :** the backbone of a book **2 :** a stiff pointed process; *esp* : one on a plant that is formed from a leaf or leaf part ⟨cactus *spines*⟩ **3 :** a sharp stiff process on an animal: as **a :** SPICULE **b :** a stiff fin ray of a fish **c :** a sharp bump that sticks out from a bone [Middle English *spine* "thorn, spinal column", from Latin *spina* "thorn, spinal column" — related to PORCUPINE]

spine·less \'spīn-ləs\ *adj* **1 :** having no spines, thorns, or prickles **2 a :** having no backbone : INVERTEBRATE **b :** lacking spirit, courage, or determination — **spine·less·ly** *adv* — **spine·less·ness** *n*

spin·et \'spin-ət\ *n* : a low piano built with the strings running up and down

spin·na·ker \'spin-i-kər\ *n* : a large triangular sail set on a long light pole and used when sailing with the wind pushing from behind or nearly so

spin·ner \'spin-ər\ *n* **1 :** one that spins **2 :** a fishing lure that spins when drawn through the water

spin·ner·et \,spin-ə-'ret\ *n* : an organ especially of a spider or caterpillar that has a small hole through which the sticky fluid produced by the silk glands is forced and hardens to form a silk thread

spinning *present participle of* SPIN

spinning jen·ny \'spin-iŋ-,jen-ē\ *n* : an early machine for spinning wool or cotton by means of many spindles

spinning reel *n* : a fishing reel that has a moving arm which

1 spinnaker

winds the line around the spool and which locks out of the way during casting so the line can wind off freely

spinning wheel *n* : a small machine driven by the hand or foot for spinning yarn or thread

spin–off \'spin-,of\ *n* : something that results from work done to produce a different product : BY-PRODUCT ⟨household products that are *spin-offs* of space research⟩

spin·ster \'spin(t)-stər\ *n* : an unmarried woman past the usual age for marrying — **spin·ster·hood** \-,hud\ *n* — **spin·ster·ish** \-st(ə-)rish\ *adj*

spiny \'spī-nē\ *adj* **spin·i·er; -est** **1 :** having or covered with spines, thorns, or prickles **2 :** full of difficulties, obstacles, or problems : THORNY — **spin·i·ness** *n*

spiny anteater *n* : ECHIDNA

spiny lobster *n* : an edible crustacean that differs from the related true lobster in having a simple unenlarged first pair of legs and a spiny carapace

spi·ra·cle \'spir-i-kəl, 'spī-ri-\ *n* : any of the openings in the body of an arthropod and especially of an insect through which air enters a trachea

¹**spi·ral** \'spī-rəl\ *adj* **1 :** winding or circling around a center and gradually getting closer to or farther away from it ⟨*spiral* curve of a watch spring⟩ **2 :** winding around an axis like the thread of a screw ⟨a *spiral* staircase⟩ — **spi·ral·ly** \-rə-lē\ *adv*

²**spiral** *n* **1 a :** a curve in a plane that winds around a point while getting closer to or farther away from it **b :** a curve (as a helix) in space that winds around an axis **2 :** a single turn or coil in a spiral object **3 :** something having a spiral form

³**spiral** *vb* **-raled** *or* **-ralled; -ral·ing** *or* **-ral·ling** : to move in a spiral path

spire \'spī(ə)r\ *n* **1 :** a blade or stalk (as of grass) that gradually becomes thinner and narrower near the top **2** : a sharp pointed tip (as of a tree or antler) **3 a :** a pointed roof especially of a tower **b :** STEEPLE — **spired** \'spī(ə)rd\ *adj*

spi·rea *or* **spi·raea** \spī-'rē-ə\ *n* : any of a genus of shrubs related to the roses and having small white or pink flowers in dense clusters

spi·ril·lum \spī-'ril-əm\ *n, pl* **-ril·la** \-'ril-ə\ : any of a genus of long curved bacteria with a bunch of flagella at one or at both ends; *also* : any spiral thread-shaped bacterium (as a spirochete)

¹**spir·it** \'spir-ət\ *n* **1 :** a force within a human being thought to give the body life, energy, and power : SOUL **2 a** *cap* : the active presence of God in human life : the third person of the Trinity **b :** a being (as a ghost) whose existence cannot be explained by the known laws of nature **3 :** ¹MOOD ⟨in good *spirits*⟩ **4 :** a lively or brisk quality ⟨answered with *spirit*⟩ **5 :** real meaning or intention ⟨the *spirit* of the law⟩ **6 :** an attitude governing one's actions ⟨said in a *spirit* of fun⟩ **7 a :** a distilled alcoholic liquor — usually used in pl. **b :** a solution in alcohol — often used in pl. ⟨*spirits* of camphor⟩ [Middle English *spirit* "a life-giving force", derived from Latin *spiritus,* literally "breath"]

²**spirit** *vb* : to carry off secretly or mysteriously

spir·it·ed \'spir-ət-əd\ *adj* : full of courage or energy — **spir·it·ed·ly** *adv*

spir·it·less \'spir-ət-ləs\ *adj* : lacking courage or energy — **spir·it·less·ly** *adv* — **spir·it·less·ness** *n*

¹**spir·i·tu·al** \'spir-ich-(ə-)wəl, -ich-əl\ *adj* **1 :** of, relating to, or consisting of spirit : not bodily or material **2 :** of or relating to sacred or religious matters **3 :** related or joined in spirit ⟨our *spiritual* home⟩ — **spir·i·tu·al·i·ty** \,spir-ich-ə-'wal-ət-ē\ *n* — **spir·i·tu·al·ly** \'spir-ich-(ə-)wəl-ē,

\ə\ abut	\aù\ out	\i\ tip	\o\ saw	\ù\ foot
\ər\ further	\ch\ chin	\ī\ life	\oi\ coin	\y\ yet
\a\ mat	\e\ pet	\j\ job	\th\ thin	\yü\ few
\ā\ take	\ē\ easy	\ŋ\ sing	\th\ this	\yu\ cure
\ä\ cot, cart	\g\ go	\ō\ bone	\ü\ food	\zh\ vision

-ich-əl-ē\ *adv*

²**spir·i·tu·al** *n* : a religious folk song developed especially among blacks in the southern U.S.

spir·i·tu·al·ism \'spir-ich-(ə-)wə-‚liz-əm, -ich-ə-‚liz-\ *n* : a belief that the spirits of the dead communicate with the living

spi·ro·chete *also* **spi·ro·chaete** \'spī-rə-‚kēt\ *n* : any of a group of slender coiled bacteria including one that causes syphilis

spi·ro·gy·ra \‚spī-rə-'jī-rə\ *n* : any of a genus of freshwater green algae with bands of chlorophyll arranged in spirals

¹**spit** \'spit\ *n* **1** : a thin pointed rod for holding meat over a fire **2** : a small point of land that runs out into a body of water [Old English *spitu* "a long rod for holding meat over a fire to cook"]

²**spit** *vb* **spit** *or* **spat** \'spat\; **spit·ting** **1 a** : to cause (as saliva) to spurt from the mouth : EXPECTORATE **b** : to express by or as if by spitting : make a spitting sound **2 a** : to give off briskly : EMIT **b** : to rain lightly or snow in flurries [Old English *spittan* "to spit (saliva) from the mouth"] — **spit·ter** *n*

³**spit** *n* **1 a** : SALIVA **b** : the act of spitting **2** : a foamy secretion produced by spittlebugs **3** : perfect likeness ⟨the *spit* and image of her father⟩

¹**spite** \'spīt\ *n* : dislike or hatred for another person with a wish to torment, anger, or defeat — **in spite of** : without being prevented by ⟨failed *in spite of* all our work⟩ ⟨went ahead *in spite of* the difficulties⟩

²**spite** *vb* **spit·ed; spit·ing** : ANNOY, OFFEND ⟨did it to *spite* me⟩

spite·ful \'spīt-fəl\ *adj* : filled with or showing spite : MALICIOUS — **spite·ful·ly** \-fə-lē\ *adv* — **spite·ful·ness** *n*

spit·tle \'spit-ᵊl\ *n* **1** : SALIVA **2** : ³SPIT 2

spit·tle·bug \-‚bəg\ *n* : any of numerous leaping bugs that produce and cover themselves with foam in the young stages

spittle insect *n* : SPITTLEBUG

spit·toon \spi-'tün\ *n* : a container to spit into

spit up *vb* **1** : REGURGITATE **2** : ²VOMIT 1

spitz \'spits\ *n* : any of several heavy-coated dogs with ears standing straight up and a tail carried over the back

¹**splash** \'splash\ *vb* **1 a** : to hit (something liquid or sloppy) and cause to move and scatter roughly ⟨*splash* water⟩ **b** : to wet or soil by spattering with water or mud ⟨*splashed* by a passing car⟩ **2** : to move or strike with a splashing sound ⟨*splash* through a puddle⟩ ⟨a brook *splashing* over rocks⟩ **3** : to spread or scatter like a splashed liquid ⟨sunset *splashed* the sky with red⟩ — **splash·er** *n*

spitz

²**splash** *n* **1 a** : splashed material **b** : a spot or smear from or as if from splashed liquid **2** : the sound or action of splashing

splash·down \'splash-‚daun\ *n* : the landing of a spacecraft in the ocean

splashy \'splash-ē\ *adj* **splash·i·er; -est** **1** : attracting attention or meant to attract attention ⟨would have preferred a less *splashy* debut⟩ **2** : being bright, bold, and colorful ⟨a *splashy* shirt⟩ ⟨*splashy* posters⟩

splat·ter \'splat-ər\ *vb* : ¹SPLASH, SPATTER — **splatter** *n*

splay \'splā\ *vb* : to spread out or apart ⟨a colt with legs *splayed* out⟩

spleen \'splēn\ *n* **1** : an organ containing many blood vessels that is located near the stomach or intestine of most vertebrates, destroys worn-out red blood cells, filters the blood, and produces some white blood cells **2** : ANGER, MALICE, SPITE

splen·did \'splen-dəd\ *adj* **1** : having or showing splendor : BRILLIANT **2** : impressive in beauty, grandeur, or excellence ⟨a *splendid* job⟩ ⟨a *splendid* palace⟩ **3** : ¹GRAND 6 ⟨had a *splendid* time at the beach⟩ [from Latin *splendidus* "splendid, brilliant", from *splendēre* "to shine"] — **splen·did·ly** *adv*

syn SPLENDID, GORGEOUS, GLORIOUS, SUBLIME mean very impressive. SPLENDID suggests that something is far above the ordinary in excellence, beauty, or grandeur ⟨a *splendid* jewel⟩ GORGEOUS suggests a rich splendor especially in a display of color ⟨a *gorgeous* purple robe trimmed with fur⟩ GLORIOUS suggests that something is radiant with light or beauty ⟨a *glorious* sunset⟩ SUBLIME suggests a noble grandeur almost beyond human understanding ⟨the Grand Canyon is a *sublime* sight⟩

splen·dif·er·ous \splen-'dif-(ə-)rəs\ *adj* : SPLENDID 1

splen·dor \'splen-dər\ *n* **1** : great brightness : BRILLIANCE ⟨the *splendor* of the sun⟩ **2** : gorgeous show : POMP, GLORY ⟨the *splendor* of ancient Rome⟩ **3** : something splendid

sple·net·ic \spli-'net-ik\ *adj* : marked by bad temper : TESTY, GRUMPY

¹**splice** \'splīs\ *vb* **spliced; splic·ing** **1** : to unite (as two ropes) by weaving the strands together **2** : to unite (as rails or pieces of film) by connecting the ends together — **splic·er** *n*

²**splice** *n* : a joining or joint made by splicing

¹**splint** \'splint\ *n* **1** : a thin flexible strip of wood woven together with others in making a chair seat or basket **2** : ¹SPLINTER 1 **3** : material or a device used to protect a body part (as a broken arm) and keep it in place

²**splint** *vb* : to support and hold in place with or as if with a splint or splints

splint bone *n* : one of the small slender bones in the leg of a horse

¹**splin·ter** \'splint-ər\ *n* : a thin piece split or torn off lengthwise : SLIVER — **splinter** *adj*

²**splinter** *vb* **splin·tered; splin·ter·ing** \'splint-ə-riŋ, 'splin-triŋ\ : to divide or break into splinters

splice

¹**split** \'split\ *vb* **split; split·ting** **1 a** : to divide lengthwise or by layers ⟨*split* a log⟩ **b** : to divide or separate as if by forcing apart ⟨a river *split* the town⟩ ⟨families were often *split* up when some members decided to move westward⟩ **2 a** : to burst or break apart or in pieces **b** : to affect as if by breaking up or tearing apart **3 a** : to divide into shares ⟨we *split* the profit⟩ **b** : to divide into groups or parts ⟨we'll *split* up; you take the left fork⟩ **c** : to mark a ballot or cast a vote for candidates of different parties **4** *British* : INFORM 2, TELL — usually used with *on* — **split·ter** *n* — **split hairs** : to make small and unimportant distinctions

²**split** *n* **1** : a narrow break made by or as if by splitting : CRACK **2** : the act or process of splitting : DIVISION **3** : the feat of lowering oneself to the floor or leaping into the air with the legs extended in a straight line and in opposite directions

³**split** *adj* : divided by or as if by splitting

split infinitive *n* : an infinitive with *to* having a modifier between the *to* and the verbal (as in "to really mean what you say")

split–lev·el \'split-‚lev-əl\ *n* : a house divided so that the floor in one part is about halfway between two floors in the other

split pea *n* : a dried pea that has had the outer skin removed

split personality *n* : SCHIZOPHRENIA; *also* : a mental and emotional disorder which is a neurosis and in which the personality becomes separated into two or more parts each of which controls behavior part of the time

split second *n* : a small fraction of a second : FLASH

split·ting \'split-iŋ\ *adj* : seeming likely to cause something to split ⟨a *splitting* headache⟩

splotch \'spläch\ *n* : BLOTCH 2, SPOT — **splotch** *vb* — **splotchy** \'spläch-ē\ *adj*

¹**splurge** \'splərj\ *n* : an instance of spending more than usual

²**splurge** *vb* **splurged; splurg·ing** : to spend more than usual especially on oneself

¹**splut·ter** \'splət-ər\ *n* **1** : a confused noise (as of trying to talk too fast) **2** : a splashing or sputtering sound

²**splutter** *vb* **1** : to make a noise as if spitting **2** : to speak or say in haste or confusion

¹**spoil** \'spȯi(ə)l\ *n* : stolen goods : PLUNDER

²**spoil** *vb* **spoiled** \'spȯi(ə)ld, 'spȯi(ə)lt\ *or* **spoilt** \'spȯi(ə)lt\; **spoil·ing 1** : PLUNDER, ROB **2 a** : to damage badly : RUIN ⟨*spoiled* my new sweater⟩ **b** : to damage the quality or effect of ⟨a quarrel *spoiled* the party⟩ **c** : to decay or lose freshness, value, or usefulness by being kept too long ⟨the milk *spoiled*⟩ **3** : to damage the disposition of by letting get away with too much ⟨*spoil* a child⟩ **4** : to have an eager desire ⟨*spoiling* for a fight⟩ — **spoil·er** *n*

spoil·age \'spȯi-lij\ *n* : the action of spoiling or the condition of being spoiled

spoil·sport \'spȯi(ə)l-,spō(ə)rt, -,spȯ(ə)rt\ *n* : a person who spoils other persons' fun

¹**spoke** \'spōk\ *past and archaic past participle of* SPEAK

²**spoke** *n* **1** : one of the small bars extending from the hub of a wheel to support the rim **2** : something resembling the spoke of a wheel

spo·ken \'spō-kən\ *adj* **1** : given by or using speech ⟨a *spoken* message⟩ ⟨the *spoken* language⟩ **2** : speaking in a specified manner ⟨soft-*spoken*⟩ ⟨plain*spoken*⟩

spokes·man \'spōk-smən\ *n* : a person who speaks for another or for a group

spokes·per·son \'spōk-,spərs-ᵉn\ *n* : SPOKESMAN

spokes·wom·an \'spōk-,swum-ən\ *n* : a woman who speaks for another or for a group

spon·dee \'spän-,dē\ *n* : a metrical foot consisting of two accented syllables (as in *tom-tom*) — **spon·da·ic** \spän-'dā-ik\ *adj*

¹**sponge** \'spənj\ *n* **1 a** : a springy mass of fibers and calcium- or silica-containing spicules that forms the skeleton of aquatic animals of a phylum and is able to absorb water freely; *also* : a piece of this material or of a natural or synthetic product with similar properties used especially for cleaning **b** : any of the phylum of primitive aquatic animals

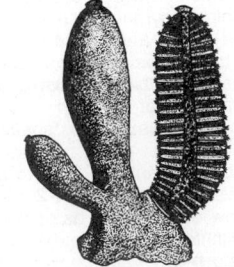

sponge 1b

that are the source of natural sponges, usually form double-walled cell colonies, and live permanently attached to a solid surface as adults **2** : a pad (as of folded gauze) used in surgery and medicine (as to soak up fluids or apply medicine) **3** : one who lives on others : SPONGER **4 a** : raised dough (as for yeast bread) **b** : a whipped dessert usually containing egg whites

²**sponge** *vb* **sponged; spong·ing 1** : to clean or wipe with or as if with a sponge **2** : to absorb with or like a sponge **3** : to get something or live at the expense of another — **spong·er** *n*

sponge cake *n* : a light cake made without shortening

spon·gin \'spən-jən\ *n* : a protein that is the main element making up the flexible fibers in sponge skeletons

spongy \'spən-jē\ *adj* **spong·i·er; -est** : resembling a sponge in appearance or in ability to absorb : soft and full of holes or moisture — **spong·i·ness** *n*

spongy cell *n* : one of the chlorophyll-containing cells of the spongy layer of a plant leaf

spongy layer *n* : a layer of loosely packed and irregularly shaped chlorophyll-shaped cells that fills the part of a leaf between the palisade layer and the lower epidermis — called also *spongy parenchyma, spongy tissue*

¹**spon·sor** \'spän(t)-sər\ *n* **1** : a person who takes the responsibility for some other person or thing ⟨agreed to be our *sponsor* at the club⟩ **2** : GODPARENT **3 a** : a person or an organization that pays for or plans and carries out a project or activity **b** : a person or an organization that pays the cost of a radio or television program — **spon·sor·ship** \-,ship\ *n*

²**sponsor** *vb* **spon·sored; spon·sor·ing** \'spän(t)s-(ə-)riŋ\ : to act as sponsor for

spon·ta·ne·ity \,spänt-ən-'ē-ət-ē, ,spänt-ᵉn-, -'ā-ət-\ *n* : the quality or state of being spontaneous

spon·ta·ne·ous \spän-'tā-nē-əs\ *adj* **1** : done, said, or produced freely and naturally ⟨*spontaneous* laughter⟩ **2** : acting or taking place without any outside force or cause — **spon·ta·ne·ous·ly** *adv* — **spon·ta·ne·ous·ness** *n*

spontaneous combustion *n* : a bursting of material into flame from the heat produced within itself by chemical action (as oxidation)

spontaneous generation *n* : the coming into existence of living things directly from lifeless matter instead of from other living things

spoof \'spüf\ *vb* : to make good-natured fun of — **spoof** *n*

¹**spook** \'spük\ *n* **1** : GHOST, SPECTER **2** : ²SPY 2

²**spook** *vb* : to make or become frightened : SCARE

spooky \'spü-kē\ *adj* **spook·i·er; -est 1** : relating to, resembling, or suggesting ghosts ⟨a *spooky* movie⟩ ⟨*spooky* houses⟩ **2** : SKITTISH 2 ⟨a *spooky* horse⟩ — **spook·i·ness** *n*

spool \'spül\ *n* **1** : a cylinder which has a rim at each end and on which something (as thread, wire, or tape) is wound **2** : material wound on a spool

¹**spoon** \'spün\ *n* **1** : a utensil with a small shallow bowl and a handle that is used especially in eating and cooking **2** : something (as a fishing lure) that resembles a spoon in shape [Old English *spōn* "a chip of wood"]

²**spoon** *vb* : to take up in or as if in a spoon

spoon·bill \'spün-,bil\ *n* : any of several wading birds related to the ibises that have a bill with a broad flat tip

spoon bread *n* : soft bread made of cornmeal mixed with milk, eggs, and shortening and served with a spoon

spoo·ner·ism \'spü-nə-,riz-əm\ *n* : a mixing up of usually the initial sounds of two or more words (as in "tons of soil" for "sons of toil")

spoonbill

spoon–feed \'spün-,fēd\ *vb* **–fed** \-,fed\; **–feed·ing** : to feed by means of a spoon

\ə\ **abut**	\aů\ **out**	\i\ **tip**	\ȯ\ **saw**	\ů\ **foot**
\ər\ **further**	\ch\ **chin**	\ī\ **life**	\ȯi\ **coin**	\y\ **yet**
\a\ **mat**	\e\ **pet**	\j\ **job**	\th\ **thin**	\yü\ **few**
\ā\ **take**	\ē\ **easy**	\ŋ\ **sing**	\th\ **this**	\yů\ **cure**
\ä\ **cot, cart**	\g\ **go**	\ō\ **bone**	\ü\ **food**	\zh\ **vision**

spoon·ful \'spün-ˌfùl\ *n, pl* **spoonfuls** \-ˌfùlz\ *or* **spoons-ful** \'spünz-ˌfùl\ : as much as a spoon can hold

spoor \'spù(ə)r, 'spō(ə)r, 'spó(ə)r\ *n* : a track, a trail, a scent, or droppings especially of a wild animal

spo·rad·ic \spə-'rad-ik\ *adj* : occurring or done now and then — **spo·rad·i·cal·ly** \-'rad-i-k(ə-)lē\ *adv*

spo·ran·gi·um \spə-'ran-jē-əm\ *n, pl* **-gia** \-jē-ə\ : a sac or case within which spores are produced and stored

¹spore \'spō(ə)r, 'spó(ə)r\ *n* : a reproductive body produced by various plants, numerous microbes (as some bacteria), and some lower animals that usually consists of a single cell and is able to produce a new individual either by developing by itself or after fusion with another spore — **spored** \'spō(ə)rd, 'spó(ə)rd\ *adj*

²spore *vb* **spored; spor·ing** : to produce or reproduce by spores

spore case *n* : SPORANGIUM

spo·ro·phyte \'spōr-ə-ˌfīt, 'spór-\ *n* : the individual or generation of a plant having alternating sexual and asexual generations that produces asexual spores — compare GAMETOPHYTE

spo·ro·zo·an \ˌspōr-ə-'zō-ən, ˌspór-\ *n* : any of a large group of parasitic one-celled animals (as the parasites that cause malaria) that have a complicated life cycle usually involving both asexual and sexual generations often in different hosts — **sporozoan** *adj*

spor·ran \'spór-ən, 'spär-\ *n* : a pouch of skin with the fur on that is worn in front of the kilt by Highlanders in full dress

¹sport \'spō(ə)rt, 'spó(ə)rt\ *vb* **1** : to amuse oneself : FROLIC **2** : to speak or act in fun **3** : SHOW OFF 1

²sport *n* **1 a** : PASTIME, RECREATION **b** : physical activity (as hunting, running, or an athletic game) engaged in for pleasure **2 a** : JEST 2 **b** : ¹FUN 3 ⟨make *sport* of someone⟩ **3** : a person who shows good sportsmanship **4** : an individual that shows a sudden major change from the normal type usually as a result of a mutation ⟨a yellow *sport* among the red apples⟩

1 sporran

³sport *or* **sports** *adj* : of, relating to, or suitable for sports ⟨*sports* equipment⟩; *also* : made in a style suitable for casual or informal wear ⟨a *sport* coat⟩

sport·ing \'spōrt-iŋ, 'spórt-\ *adj* **1** : of, relating to, or suitable for sport ⟨*sporting* events⟩ ⟨*sporting* dogs⟩ **2** : involving about as much risk as a sports competitor would expect to take ⟨a *sporting* chance⟩

sport·ive \'spōrt-iv, 'spórt-\ *adj* : FROLICSOME, PLAYFUL, MERRY — **sport·ive·ly** *adv* — **sport·ive·ness** *n*

sports car *n* : a low small usually two-passenger automobile designed for high-speed driving

sports·cast \'spō(ə)rt-ˌskast, 'spó(ə)rt-\ *n* : a broadcast of a sports event — **sports·cast·er** *n*

sports·man \'spō(ə)rt-smən, 'spó(ə)rt-\ *n* : a person who engages in or is interested in sports and especially outdoor sports **2** : ²SPORT 3 — **sports·man·like** \-ˌlīk\ *adj* — **sports·man·ly** \-lē\ *adj*

sports·man·ship \'spō(ə)rt-smən-ˌship, 'spó(ə)rt-\ *n* : fair play, respect for opponents, and gracious behavior in winning or losing

sports·wear \'spō(ə)rt-ˌswa(ə)r, 'spó(ə)rt-, -ˌswe(ə)r\ *n* : clothes suitable for sports or for casual or informal wear

sports·wom·an \-ˌswùm-ən\ *n* : a woman who engages in or is interested in sports and especially outdoor sports

sports·writ·er \'spō(ə)rts-ˌrīt-ər, 'spó(ə)rts-\ *n* : a person who writes about sports (as for a newspaper)

sporty \'spōrt-ē, 'spórt-\ *adj* **sport·i·er; -est** : of or relating

to sports; *also* : being or having the look of being suitable for sports ⟨*sporty* clothes⟩ — **sport·i·ly** \'spōrt-ᵊl-ē, 'spórt-\ *adv* — **sport·i·ness** \'spōrt-ē-nəs, 'spórt-\ *n*

spor·u·la·tion \ˌspōr-(y)ə-'lā-shən, ˌspór-\ *n* : formation of or division into spores

¹spot \'spät\ *n* **1** : something bad that others know about one : FAULT **2 a** : a small area that is different (as in color) from the main part **b** : an area marred or marked (as by dirt) **c** : a small diseased or decayed area on the body surface of a plant or animal ⟨*spots* of rot on a leaf⟩ ⟨*spots* of chicken pox⟩ **3 a** : a small quantity or amount **b** : a particular place ⟨a good *spot* for a picnic⟩ ⟨a sore *spot*⟩ **4** : a particular position (as in an organization or on a program) **5** : ¹SPOTLIGHT 2 **6** : a position usually of difficulty or embarrassment ⟨put someone in a *spot*⟩ **7** : a short broadcast announcement or advertisement — **on the spot 1** : at once : IMMEDIATELY **2** : at the place of action **3** : in difficulty or danger

²spot *vb* **spot·ted; spot·ting 1** : to mark or become marked with or as if with spots **2** : to single out : IDENTIFY ⟨*spot* a friend in a crowd⟩

³spot *adj* **1 a** : done or paid on the spot ⟨*spot* cash⟩ **b** : involving cash payment ⟨the *spot* market for oil⟩ **c** : broadcast between scheduled programs ⟨*spot* announcements⟩ **3** : made from time to time or in a few places or instances ⟨a *spot* check⟩

spot–check \'spät-ˌchek\ *vb* : to make a spot check

spot·less \'spät-ləs\ *adj* : free from spots or blemishes : perfectly clean or pure — **spot·less·ly** *adv* — **spot·less·ness** *n*

¹spot·light \'spät-ˌlīt\ *n* **1 a** : a spot of light used to show up a particular area, person, or thing (as on a stage) **b** : public notice **2** : a light designed to direct a narrow strong beam of light on a small area

²spotlight *vb* **-light·ed** *or* **-lit; -light·ing 1** : to light up with a spotlight **2** : to bring to public attention

spot·ted \'spät-əd\ *adj* : marked with spots ⟨a *spotted* cat⟩

spotted fever *n* : any of various diseases that are characterized by spots on the skin

spotted owl *n* : a rare dark brown owl with white spots above and dark stripes below that is found from British Columbia to Southern California and Central Mexico

spotted turtle *n* : a small American freshwater turtle that has a blackish shell covered with round yellow spots

spot·ter \'spät-ər\ *n* **1** : a person who removes spots **2** : a person who keeps watch : OBSERVER **3** : a person who helps a gymnast in practice

spot·ty \'spät-ē\ *adj* **spot·ti·er; -est 1** : having spots **2** : not always the same especially in quality ⟨your work has been *spotty*⟩ — **spot·ti·ly** \'spät-ᵊl-ē\ *adv* — **spot·ti·ness** \'spät-ē-nəs\ *n*

spouse \'spaùs *also* 'spaùz\ *n* : a married person : HUSBAND, WIFE

¹spout \'spaùt\ *vb* **1** : to shoot (as liquid) out with force ⟨wells *spouting* oil⟩ **2** : to speak with a long and quick flow of words so as to sound important **3** : to flow out with force : SPURT ⟨blood *spouted* from the wound⟩ — **spout·er** *n*

²spout *n* **1** : a tube, pipe, or hole through which something (as rainwater) spouts **2** : a sudden strong stream of fluid

¹sprain \'sprān\ *n* **1** : a sudden or severe twisting of a joint with stretching or tearing of ligaments **2** : a sprained condition

²sprain *vb* : to injure by a sudden or severe twist

sprawl \'spról\ *vb* **1** : to lie or sit with arms and legs spread out **2** : to spread out in an uneven or awkward way ⟨a *sprawling* city⟩ — **sprawl** *n*

¹spray \'sprā\ *n* : a usually flowering branch or shoot

²spray *n* **1** : liquid flying in fine drops like water blown from a wave **2 a** : a burst of fine mist (as from an atomizer) **b** : a device (as an atomizer) for scattering a spray

³spray *vb* **1** : to scatter or let fall in a spray **2** : to scatter spray on or into — **spray·er** *n*

spray gun *n* : a device for spraying liquids (as paints and insecticides)

¹**spread** \'spred\ *vb* **spread; spread·ing** **1 a** : to open over a larger area ⟨*spread* out a map⟩ **b** : to stretch out : EXTEND ⟨*spread* her arms wide⟩ **2 a** : to scatter over an area ⟨*spread* fertilizer⟩ **b** : to give out over a period or among a group ⟨*spread* the work over several weeks⟩ **c** : to put a layer of on a surface ⟨*spread* butter on bread⟩ **d** : to cover something with ⟨*spread* the cloth on the table⟩ **e** : to prepare for a meal : SET ⟨*spread* a table⟩ **3 a** : to become or cause to become widely known ⟨*spread* the news⟩ ⟨the panic *spread* rapidly⟩ **b** : to extend the range or occurrence of ⟨*spread* a disease⟩ **4** : to stretch or move apart ⟨*spread* one's fingers⟩

²**spread** *n* **1 a** : the act or process of spreading ⟨the *spread* of education⟩ **b** : the extent of spreading ⟨the *spread* of a bird's wings⟩ **2** : a very noticeable display in a newspaper or magazine ⟨a two-page *spread*⟩ **3 a** : a food to be spread on bread or crackers ⟨sandwich *spread*⟩ **b** : a very fine meal : FEAST **c** : a cloth cover for a table or bed **4** : distance between two points

spread–ea·gle \'spred-,ē-ggl\ *vb* **spread–ea·gled; spread–ea·gling** \-,ē-g(g)liŋ\ : to stand or move with arms and legs spread wide

spread·er \'spred-gr\ *n* : one that spreads: as **a** : an implement for scattering material **b** : a small knife for spreading butter

spread·sheet \'spred-,shēt\ *n* : an accounting program for a computer; *also* : the ledger layout simulated by such a program

spree \'sprē\ *n* : an outburst of activity ⟨a buying *spree*⟩

sprier *comparative of* SPRY

spriest *superlative of* SPRY

sprig \'sprig\ *n* : a small shoot or twig especially with leaves or flowers

spright·ly \'sprīt-lē\ *adj* **spright·li·er; -est** : full of spirit : LIVELY — **spright·li·ness** *n* — **sprightly** *adv*

¹**spring** \'spriŋ\ *vb* **sprang** \'spraŋ\ *or* **sprung** \'sprəŋ\; **sprung; spring·ing** \'spriŋ-iŋ\ **1 a** : to appear or grow quickly ⟨the weeds *sprang* up overnight⟩ **b** : to come from by birth or descent ⟨*sprang* from an immigrant family⟩ **c** : to come into being : ARISE ⟨hope *springs* eternal⟩ **2** : to move suddenly forward or upward : LEAP ⟨a lion crouched and waiting to *spring*⟩ ⟨*sprang* up the path⟩ ⟨*sprang* to my feet⟩ **3** : to have (a leak) appear **4 a** : to move by elastic force ⟨the lid *sprang* shut⟩ ⟨the muscular wall of the artery stretches and *springs* back⟩ **b** : to become warped or bent ⟨the door has *sprung*⟩ **5 a** : to cause to operate suddenly ⟨*spring* a trap⟩ **b** : to produce suddenly ⟨*sprung* a surprise on us⟩ **6** : ¹PAY 1 — usually used with *for* ⟨*spring* for a new pair of shoes⟩ **7** : to release or cause to be released from confinement (as jail)

²**spring** *n* **1** : a source of supply; *esp* : a source of water coming up from the ground **2 a** : the season between winter and summer including in the northern hemisphere usually the months of March, April, and May **b** : a time or season of growth or development **3** : an elastic body or device that recovers its original shape when released after being squeezed or stretched **4 a** : the act or an instance of leaping up or forward **b** : elastic power or force ⟨the *spring* in your step⟩

spring beauty *n* : a spring herb that sends up a two-leaved stem and has delicate pink flowers

spring·board \'spriŋ-,bō(ə)rd, -,bȯ(ə)rd\ *n* **1** : a flexible board usually fastened at one end and used for jumping high in gymnastics or diving **2** : a point of departure ⟨a *springboard* to success in business⟩

spring·er spaniel \,spriŋ-ər-\ *n* : a medium-sized sporting dog of either of two breeds used chiefly for finding small game and driving it from cover: **a** : ENGLISH SPRINGER SPANIEL **b** : WELSH SPRINGER SPANIEL

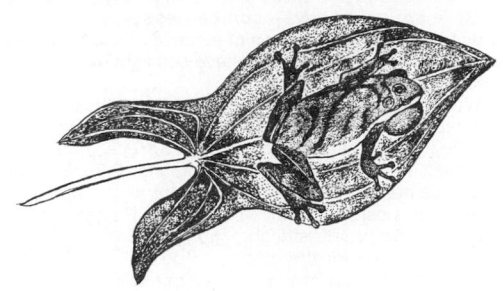

spring peeper

spring fever *n* : a lazy or restless feeling often associated with the coming of spring

spring peeper *n* : a small brown tree toad of the eastern U.S. and Canada with a shrill piping call

spring tide *n* : a greater than usual tide that occurs at each new moon and full moon

spring·time \'spriŋ-,tīm\ *n* : the season of spring

spring·wood \-,wůd\ *n* : the soft light-colored part of an annual ring of wood that develops early in the growing season — compare SUMMERWOOD

springy \'spriŋ-ē\ *adj* **spring·i·er; -est** **1** : having an elastic quality **2** : having or showing a lively and energetic movement ⟨walks with a *springy* step⟩ — **spring·i·ly** \'spriŋ-ə-lē\ *adv* — **spring·i·ness** \'spriŋ-ē-nəs\ *n*

¹**sprin·kle** \'spriŋ-kəl\ *vb* **sprin·kled; sprin·kling** \-k(ə-)liŋ\ **1** : to scatter in drops or particles ⟨*sprinkle* water⟩ ⟨*sprinkle* grass seed over the soil⟩ **2 a** : to scatter over or in or among ⟨*sprinkle* the spaghetti with grated cheese⟩ **b** : to wet lightly ⟨*sprinkle* clothes before ironing⟩ **3** : to rain lightly in scattered drops — **sprin·kler** \-k(ə-)lər\ *n*

²**sprinkle** *n* **1** : the act or an instance of sprinkling; *esp* : a light rain **2** : SPRINKLING

sprin·kling \'spriŋ-kliŋ\ *n* : a very small number or amount

¹**sprint** \'sprint\ *vb* : to run at top speed especially for a short distance — **sprint·er** *n*

²**sprint** *n* **1** : a short run at top speed **2** : a race over a short distance

sprite \'sprīt\ *n* : ELF, FAIRY

sprock·et \'spräk-ət\ *n* **1** : one of many points that stick up on the rim of a wheel shaped so as to fit into the links of a chain **2** : a wheel having sprockets

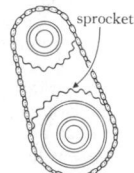

sprocket 1 and 2

¹**sprout** \'spraůt\ *vb* **1** : to grow or spring up as or as if a sprout **2** : to send out new growth ⟨potatoes kept too warm will *sprout* in the bag⟩ **3** : to send forth or up : cause to develop : GROW

²**sprout** *n* **1 a** : ²SHOOT 1 a; *esp* : a young shoot (as from a seed or root) **b** *pl* : edible shoots of a plant of the mustard family **2** *pl* : a plant (as brussels sprouts) that produces sprouts

¹**spruce** \'sprüs\ *vb* **spruced; spruc·ing** : to make or make oneself spruce ⟨*spruce* up a room⟩ ⟨*spruce* up a bit before

\ə\ **abut**	\aů\ **out**	\i\ **tip**	\ȯ\ **saw**	\ů\ **foot**
\ər\ **further**	\ch\ **chin**	\ī\ **life**	\ȯi\ **coin**	\y\ **yet**
\a\ **mat**	\e\ **pet**	\j\ **job**	\th\ **thin**	\yü\ **few**
\ā\ **take**	\ē\ **easy**	\ŋ\ **sing**	\th\ **this**	\yů\ **cure**
\ä\ **cot, cart**	\g\ **go**	\ō\ **bone**	\ü\ **food**	\zh\ **vision**

going out to dinner⟩

²spruce *adj* **spruc·er; spruc·est** : neat or stylish in appearance — **spruce·ly** *adv* — **spruce·ness** *n*

³spruce *n* **1** : any of a genus of pyramid-shaped evergreen trees related to the pines that have soft light wood **2** : the wood of a spruce

Word History Before the 19th century, Prussia was an independent German kingdom. In Middle English it was called *Pruce* or more commonly *Spruce.* Prussia exported many fine products to England. All Spruce leather, Spruce iron, and Spruce canvas were all well thought of. But the most important import from Prussia was the spruce tree, a tall, straight, strong, and light evergreen that was used for the masts of England's sailing ships. Long after the country was no longer called *Spruce,* the name of the tree remained, and it is still called *spruce.* Spruce leather, which was used to make jackets that were fashionable in England in the 16th century, apparently was also the source of the verb *spruce,* meaning "to make oneself stylish in appearance". From the verb we get the adjective *spruce.* [Middle English *Spruce, Pruce* "Prussia (a former German kingdom)"]

sprung *past and past participle of* SPRING

spry \'sprī\ *adj* **spri·er** *or* **spry·er** \'sprī(-ə)r\; **spri·est** *or* **spry·est** \'sprī-əst\ : light and easy in motion : NIMBLE, SPRIGHTLY ⟨64 and still *spry* as a sparrow⟩ — **spry·ly** *adv* — **spry·ness** *n*

spud \'spəd\ *n* : POTATO 2b

spume \'spyüm\ *n* : ¹FOAM 1

spu·mo·ni *or* **spu·mo·ne** \spù-'mō-nē\ *n* : ice cream in layers of different colors and flavors often with candied fruits and nuts [from Italian *spumone,* a form of *spuma* "foam"]

spun *past and past participle of* SPIN

spun glass *n* : FIBERGLASS

spunk \'spəŋk\ *n* : COURAGE, SPIRIT, PLUCK

Word History *Spunk* now means "spirit, readiness to fight against odds, courage". It is somewhat surprising to learn that it comes from a Latin word for something that seems quite the opposite: "sponge". The Latin word for "sponge", *spongia,* came into Scottish Gaelic, the original language of Scotland, as *spong* and meant "sponge". But it also came to mean "tinder", the light, dry material used to start a fire. Tinder was often dry, spongy wood that would ignite easily and looked like sponge. A person who fought courageously and without complaining, especially against strong opponents, was thought of as catching fire. This flaring up of the human spirit was compared to the bursting into flame of tinder. Thus, a person who had this quality was said to have spunk. [from earlier *spunk* "tinder", from Scottish Gaelic (the original language of Scotland) *spong* "sponge, tinder", from Latin *spongia* "sponge"]

spunky \'spəŋ-kē\ *adj* **spunk·i·er; -est** : full of spunk : SPIRITED — **spunk·i·ly** \-kə-lē\ *adv* — **spunk·i·ness** \-kē-nəs\ *n*

spun sugar *n* : sugar that has been boiled and spun into fine threads usually for cotton candy

¹spur \'spər\ *n* **1 a** : a pointed device fastened to the back of a rider's boot and used to urge a horse on **b** *pl* : recognition for achievement **2** : something that makes one want to do something : INCENTIVE **3 a** : a stiff sharp pointed part (as a horny spine on the leg of a rooster) **b** : a hollow flower part that sticks out especially on a petal (as of a columbine) or on a sepal (as of a larkspur) **4** : a mass of jagged rock coming out from the side of a mountain **5** : a short section of railway track coming away from the main line — **on the spur of the moment** : by a sudden decision : without thinking about it long

²spur *vb* **spurred; spur·ring** **1** : to urge a horse on with spurs **2** : to move to action : INCITE, STIMULATE

spu·ri·ous \'spyùr-ē-əs\ *adj* : not genuine or authentic

: FALSE — **spu·ri·ous·ly** *adv* — **spu·ri·ous·ness** *n*

spurn \'spərn\ *vb* : to reject or thrust aside with scorn — **spurn·er** *n*

spur–of–the–moment *adj* : made or done by the sudden making up of one's mind

spurred \'spərd\ *adj* **1** : wearing spurs **2** : having one or more spurs ⟨a *spurred* violet⟩

¹spurt \'spərt\ *vb* **1** : to pour out suddenly : SPOUT **2** : ¹SQUIRT 1

²spurt *n* : a sudden pouring out : JET

³spurt *n* **1** : a short period of time : MOMENT **2** : a brief burst of increased effort or activity

⁴spurt *vb* : to make a spurt

sput·nik \'spùt-nik, 'spət-\ *n* : SATELLITE 2b

¹sput·ter \'spət-ər\ *vb* **1** : to spit or squirt pieces of food or saliva noisily from the mouth **2** : to speak or utter hastily or explosively in confusion or excitement ⟨*sputtered* out protests⟩ **3** : to make explosive popping sounds ⟨the motor *sputtered* and died⟩ — **sput·ter·er** \-ər-ər\ *n*

²sputter *n* : the act or sound of sputtering

spu·tum \'sp(y)üt-əm\ *n, pl* **spu·ta** \-ə\ : material that is spit or coughed up and is made up of saliva and mucus from the respiratory passages

¹spy \'spī\ *vb* **spied; spy·ing** **1** : to watch, inspect, or examine secretly : act as a spy **2** : to catch sight of : SEE ⟨*spied* a friend in the crowd⟩

²spy *n, pl* **spies** **1** : one that watches the movement or actions of others especially in secret **2** : a person who tries secretly to obtain information for one country in the territory of another usually unfriendly country

spy·glass \'spī-,glas\ *n* : a small telescope

squab \'skwäb\ *n, pl* **squabs** *or* **squab** : a young bird; *esp* : a young pigeon about four weeks old and ready for use as food

spyglass

¹squab·ble \'skwäb-əl\ *n* : a noisy quarrel usually over unimportant things

²squabble *vb* **squab·bled; squab·bling** \'skwäb-(ə-)liŋ\ : to quarrel noisily for little or no reason : WRANGLE — **squab·bler** \-(ə-)lər\ *n*

squad \'skwäd\ *n* **1** : a small organized group of soldiers; *esp* : a small unit that can be easily directed in the field **2** : a small group engaged in a common effort or occupation ⟨a football *squad*⟩ ⟨a rescue *squad*⟩

squad car *n* : a police car connected by radio with headquarters

squad·ron \'skwäd-rən\ *n* : any of several units of military organization

squal·id \'skwäl-əd\ *adj* **1** : filthy or degraded as a result of neglect or the lack of money **2** : VILE 1a **syn** see DIRTY — **squal·id·ly** *adv* — **squal·id·ness** *n*

¹squall \'skwòl\ *vb* : to cry out with a harsh sound : SCREAM — **squall·er** *n*

²squall *n* : a harsh cry or scream

³squall *n* **1** : a sudden violent wind often with rain or snow **2** : a short-lived commotion

⁴squall *vb* : to blow as a squall

squally \'skwò-lē\ *adj* **squall·i·er; -est** : marked by squalls : GUSTY, STORMY

squa·lor \'skwäl-ər\ *n* : the quality or state of being squalid

squa·mous \'skwā-məs, 'skwä-\ *adj* : of, relating to, or being an epithelium that consists at least in its outer layers of small scalelike cells

squan·der \'skwän-dər\ *vb* **squan·dered; squan·der·ing** \-d(ə-)riŋ\ : to spend foolishly or wastefully — **squan·der·er** \-dər-ər\ *n*

¹square \'skwa(ə)r, 'skwe(ə)r\ *n* **1** : an instrument having at least one right angle and two straight edges used to lay out or test right angles   **2** : a rectangle with all four sides equal   **3** : any of the four-sided spaces marked out on a board for playing games   **4** : the product of a number multiplied by itself   **5 a** : an open place or area formed at the meeting of two or more streets   **b** : ¹BLOCK 7a — **on the square**   **1** : at right angles   **2** : in a fair open manner : HONESTLY — **out of square** : not at an exact right angle

²**square** *adj* **squar·er; squar·est**   **1 a** : having four sides of equal measure and four right angles   **b** : forming a right angle ⟨a *square* corner⟩   **c** : having a square base ⟨a *square* pyramid⟩   **2** : raised to the second power   **3 a** : of a shape suggesting strength and toughness ⟨a *square* jaw⟩ ⟨*square* shoulders⟩   **b** : rectangular and equal-sided in section ⟨a *square* tower⟩   **c** : having an outline like a rectangle rather than a curve   **4 a** : being a unit of area equal in measure to a square each side of which measures one unit of a specified unit of length ⟨a *square* foot⟩   **b** : being of a specified length in each of two equal dimensions ⟨10 feet *square*⟩   **5 a** : exactly adjusted : well made   **b** : ¹JUST 2a, FAIR   **c** : leaving no balance : SETTLED   **d** : being tied in score ⟨the golfers were all *square* after five holes⟩   **e** : large enough to satisfy ⟨three *square* meals a day⟩   **6** : not knowing or following the latest styles — **square·ly** *adv* — **square·ness** *n* — **squar·ish** \'skwa(ə)r-ish, 'skwe(ə)r-\ *adj*

³**square** *vb* **squared; squar·ing**   **1** : to form with right angles, straight edges, and flat surfaces : make square or rectangular ⟨*square* a timber⟩   **2** : to bring to a right angle ⟨*squared* his shoulders⟩   **3 a** : to multiply (a number) by itself   **b** : to find a square equal in area to ⟨*square* a circle⟩   **4** : to agree or make agree ⟨his story does not *square* with the facts⟩   **5** : ²BALANCE 1, SETTLE ⟨*square* an account⟩   **6** : to mark off into squares   **7** : ²BRIBE, FIX   **8** : to take a fighting stance ⟨the two *squared* off⟩

⁴**square** *adv* : in a direct, firm, or honest manner

square away *vb* : to put in order or readiness

square bracket *n* : ¹BRACKET 3a

square dance *n* : a lively dance for sets of four couples who form a hollow square — **square dancer** *n* — **square dancing** *n*

square knot *n* : a knot made of two reverse half-knots and typically used to join the ends of two cords

square measure *n* : a unit or system of units for measuring area — see MEASURE table, METRIC SYSTEM table

square number *n* : a number (as 1, 4, or 9) that is the square of an integer

square–rigged \'skwa(ə)r-'rigd, 'skwe(ə)r-\ *adj* : having the principal sails extended on yards fastened in a horizontal position to the masts at their center

square–rig·ger \-'rig-ər\ *n* : a square-rigged ship

square-rigger

square root *n* : either of the two numbers whose squares are equal to a given number ⟨either +3 or −3 is the *square root* of 9⟩

square shooter *n* : a just or honest person

¹**squash** \'skwäsh, 'skwȯsh\ *vb*   **1** : to press or beat into a pulp or a flat mass : CRUSH ⟨*squash* a beetle⟩   **2** : to put an end to by force : SUPPRESS, SQUELCH   **3** : ¹SQUEEZE 1c, PRESS ⟨*squashed* into the seat⟩ [from early French *esquasser* "to press or beat into pulp, crush flat", derived from Latin *ex-* "out" and Latin *quassare* "to shake"]

²**squash** *n*   **1** : the sudden fall of a heavy soft body or the sound of such a fall   **2** : a crushing sound   **3** : a crushed mass   **4** : a game played in a four-walled court with a racket and a rubber ball

³**squash** *n, pl* **squash·es** *or* **squash** : a fruit of any of several plants related to the gourds that is cooked as a vegetable or used for animal feed; *also* : a plant and especially a vine that produces squashes [a shortened and altered form of earlier *quoutersquash* "the squash plant or fruit"; of American Indian origin]

squash bug *n* : a large black American bug that is destructive to squash vines

squash racquets *n* : ²SQUASH 4

squashy \'skwäsh-ē, 'skwȯsh-\ *adj* **squash·i·er; -est** : easily squashed : SOFT

¹**squat** \'skwät\ *vb* **squat·ted; squat·ting**   **1** : to sit or cause (oneself) to sit on one's heels   **2** : to occupy land as a squatter   **3** : to crouch close to the ground ⟨*squatting* hare⟩

²**squat** *n*   **1** : the act of squatting   **2** : a squatting posture

³**squat** *adj* **squat·ter; squat·test**   **1** : being in a squatting posture   **2** : low to the ground   **3** : being short and thick — **squat·ly** *adv* — **squat·ness** *n*

squat·ter \'skwät-ər\ *n*   **1** : one that squats   **2 a** : one that settles on land without right or title or payment of rent   **b** : one that settles on public land under government regulation with the purpose of acquiring title

squat·ty \'skwät-ē\ *adj* **squat·ti·er; -est** : ³SQUAT 3, THICKSET

squaw \'skwȯ\ *n* : an American Indian woman

¹**squawk** \'skwȯk\ *vb*   **1** : to utter a harsh short scream   **2** : to complain or protest loudly or forcefully — **squawk·er** *n*

²**squawk** *n*   **1** : a harsh short scream   **2** : a noisy complaint

¹**squeak** \'skwēk\ *vb*   **1** : to make a short shrill cry or noise   **2** : to pass, succeed, or win by a narrow margin ⟨barely *squeaked* by⟩   **3** : to utter in a shrill tone

²**squeak** *n*   **1** : a sharp shrill cry or sound   **2** : ²ESCAPE 1 ⟨a close *squeak*⟩

squeaky \'skwē-kē\ *adj* **squeak·i·er; -est** : making or likely to make a shrill sound ⟨a *squeaky* door⟩

¹**squeal** \'skwē(ə)l\ *vb*   **1** : to make a long shrill cry or noise   **2 a** : INFORM 2   **b** : COMPLAIN 1, PROTEST   **3** : to utter with or as if with a squeal — **squeal·er** *n*

²**squeal** *n* : a long shrill cry or noise

squea·mish \'skwē-mish\ *adj*   **1 a** : easily made sick : QUEASY   **b** : affected with nausea : NAUSEATED   **2** : easily shocked or disgusted — **squea·mish·ly** *adv* — **squea·mish·ness** *n*

squee·gee \'skwē-,jē\ *n* : a blade of leather or rubber set on a handle and used for spreading or wiping liquid material on, across, or off a surface (as a window) — **squeegee** *vb*

¹**squeeze** \'skwēz\ *vb* **squeezed; squeez·ing**   **1 a** : to press together from the opposite sides of : COMPRESS   **b** : to get by squeezing ⟨*squeeze* juice from a lemon⟩   **c** : to force or thrust by compression : CROWD ⟨*squeezed* into the car⟩   **2 a** : to force (as by threats) money, goods, or services from ⟨*squeezed* their tenants mercilessly⟩   **b** : to reduce the amount of ⟨rising costs *squeezed* profits⟩   **3** : to gain or win by a narrow margin — **squeez·er** *n*

²**squeeze** *n*   **1** : an act or instance of squeezing   **2** : financial pressure ⟨put the *squeeze* on someone⟩

¹**squelch** \'skwelch\ *n*   **1** : a sound of or as if of a squishy substance under suction ⟨the *squelch* of mud⟩   **2** : a remark that silences an opponent

²**squelch** *vb*   **1 a** : to fall or stamp on so as to crush   **b** : to put an end to by force : QUELL, SILENCE   **2** : to make or cause to make a sucking sound   **3** : to splash through water, slush, or mire — **squelch·er** *n*

\ə\ abut	\au̇\ **out**	\i\ **tip**	\ȯ\ **saw**	\u̇\ **foot**
\ər\ **further**	\ch\ **chin**	\ī\ **life**	\ȯi\ **coin**	\y\ **yet**
\a\ **mat**	\e\ **pet**	\j\ **job**	\th\ **thin**	\yü\ **few**
\ā\ **take**	\ē\ **easy**	\ŋ\ **sing**	\th̲\ **this**	\yu̇\ **cure**
\ä\ **cot, cart**	\g\ **go**	\ō\ **bone**	\ü\ **food**	\zh\ **vision**

squib \'skwib\ *n* : a short humorous or witty writing or speech

squid \'skwid\ *n, pl* **squid** *or* **squids** : any of numerous 10-armed sea mollusks that are cephalopods and have a long thin body with a fin on each side and a slender internal shell

squig·gle \'skwig-əl\ *n* : a short wavy twist or line : CURLICUE

squinch \'skwinch\ *vb* **1** : to screw up (the face or eyes) : SQUINT ⟨*squinched* in the bright light⟩ **2** : to make more compact **3** : to crouch down or draw together

¹squint \'skwint\ *vb* **1 a** : to look in a squint-eyed manner **b** : to be cross-eyed **2** : to look or peer with eyes partly closed — **squint·er** *n*

²squint *n* : inability to direct both eyes to the same object due to a fault of the muscles of the eyeball; *also* : the act or an instance of squinting — **squinty** \'skwint-ē\ *adj*

squint–eyed \'skwint-'īd\ *adj* **1** : having eyes that are partly closed **2** : looking with a side glance (as in envy or ill will)

¹squire \'skwī(ə)r\ *n* **1** : one who carries the shield or armor of a knight **2 a** : a male servant **b** : a lady's escort **3 a** : an owner of a country estate **b** : JUSTICE OF THE PEACE

²squire *vb* **squired; squir·ing** : to attend as a squire or escort

squirm \'skwərm\ *vb* **1** : to twist about like an eel or a worm **2** : to feel very embarrassed — **squirmy** \'skwər-mē\ *adj*

¹squir·rel \'skwər(-ə)l, 'skwə-rəl\ *n, pl* **squirrels** *also* **squir·rel** **1** : any of various small or medium-sized rodents; *esp* : one with a long bushy tail and strong hind legs **2** : the fur of a squirrel

> **Word History** Squirrels come in different sizes and colors, but they all have one thing in common — a long, bushy tail. When a squirrel sits up to eat or to look around, it often raises its tail up against its back and over its head as if to shade itself. The ancient Greeks noticed this habit, and they called the animal *skiouros.* This word was made up of *skia,* meaning "shadow", and *oura,* "tail". The Romans turned this into the Latin word *sciurus,* which made its way into early French as *esquireul.* English *squirrel* was borrowed from the French. [Middle English *squirel* "squirrel" from early French *esquireul* (same meaning), derived from Latin *sciurus* (same meaning), from Greek *skiouros* "squirrel", from *skia* "shadow" and *oura* "tail"]

²squirrel *vb* **-reled** *or* **-relled; -rel·ing** *or* **-rel·ling** : to store up for future use — often used with *away*

¹squirt \'skwərt\ *vb* **1** : to come forth or shoot out in a sudden rapid stream : SPURT **2** : to wet with a sudden rapid stream

²squirt *n* **1 a** : a small quick stream : JET **b** : the action of squirting **2** : a disrespectful youngster

squishy \'skwish-ē\ *adj* **squish·i·er; -est** : being soft, yielding, and damp

S–shaped \'es-,shāpt, 'esh-\ *adj* : having the shape of a capital S

SST \,es-(,)es-'tē\ *n* : an airplane used to transport people and goods at supersonic speeds

-st — see ²-EST

¹stab \'stab\ *n* **1** : a wound produced by a pointed weapon **2** : a thrust of a pointed weapon **3** : EFFORT 2, TRY

²stab *vb* **stabbed; stab·bing** **1** : to wound or pierce by or as if by the thrust of a pointed weapon **2** : ¹THRUST 1, DRIVE — **stab·ber** *n*

sta·bil·i·ty \stə-'bil-ət-ē\ *n, pl* **-ties** : the condition of being stable

sta·bi·lize \'stā-bə-,līz\ *vb* **-lized; -liz·ing** **1** : to make or become stable, fixed, or firm **2** : to hold steady (as by means of a stabilizer) — **sta·bi·li·za·tion** \,stā-bə-lə-'zā-shən\ *n*

sta·bi·liz·er \'stā-bə-,lī-zər\ *n* : one (as a chemical or a device) that stabilizes something; *esp* : a fixed surface for stabilizing the motion of an airplane

¹sta·ble \'stā-bəl\ *n* **1** : a building in which domestic animals are sheltered and fed; *esp* : such a building having stalls or compartments ⟨horse *stable*⟩ **2 a** : the race-horses of one owner **b** : a group of athletes (as boxers) under one management [Middle English *stable* "a place where animals are sheltered", from early French *estable* (same meaning), from Latin *stabulum* (same meaning), from *stare* "to stand"]

²stable *vb* **sta·bled; sta·bling** \-b(ə-)liŋ\ : to put, keep, or live in or as if in a stable

³stable *adj* **sta·bler** \-b(ə-)lər\; **sta·blest** \-b(ə-)ləst\ **1 a** : firmly established : FIXED, STEADFAST ⟨a *stable* community⟩ **b** : not easily changed or affected ⟨a *stable* government⟩ **c** : not likely to change suddenly or greatly ⟨a *stable* income⟩ **2 a** : steady in purpose : CONSTANT **b** : not subject to insecurity or emotional illness : SANE, RATIONAL ⟨*stable* personalities⟩ **3** : not readily changing in chemical composition or physical state ⟨a *stable* compound⟩ [Middle English *stable* "fixed, not moving or changing", from early French *estable* (same meaning), from Latin *stabilis* (same meaning), from *stare* "to stand"] — **sta·bly** \-b(ə-)lē\ *adv*

sta·bler \'stā-b(ə-)lər\ *n* : one that keeps a stable

stac·ca·to \stə-'kät-ō\ *adj* **1** : cut short so as not to sound connected ⟨*staccato* notes⟩ **2** : made up of rapid disconnected elements or sounds ⟨*staccato* blasts of a horn⟩ — **staccato** *adv* — **staccato** *n*

¹stack \'stak\ *n* **1** : a large pile (as of hay, straw, or grain) usually shaped like a cone **2 a** : an orderly pile of objects usually one on top of the other ⟨a *stack* of dishes⟩ **b** : a large number or amount **3** : CHIMNEY 1, SMOKESTACK **4** : a structure with shelves for storing books — usually used in pl.

²stack *vb* : to arrange in or form a stack : PILE ⟨*stacked* the dishes on the table⟩ — **stack·er** *n*

stack·able \'stak-ə-bəl\ *adj* : easily stacked

stack up *vb* : MEASURE UP 2, COMPARE ⟨see how you *stack up* against the champion⟩

sta·di·um \'stād-ē-əm\ *n, pl* **-dia** \-ē-ə\ *or* **-di·ums** **1** : a course for footraces in ancient Greece with rows of seats for spectators **2** *pl usually* **stadiums** : a large usually roofless building with rows of seats for spectators at modern sports events

> **Word History** A *stadion* in ancient Greece was a unit of measurement equal to about 180 meters. One of the most important events in the ancient Olympic Games was a footrace exactly one stadion long. The course on which the race was run, including the raised seats from which spectators watched, was also known as a *stadion.* This word was later borrowed into Latin as *stadium.* In time, it also came to be used to refer to larger structures in which different kinds of athletic contests were held. That is how the English word *stadium* is usually used. [Middle Enlglish *stadium* "a course for races in ancient Greece, a large structure for sports events", from Latin *stadium* (same meaning), from Greek *stadion* "a course for foot races, a unit of measurement"]

¹staff \'staf\ *n, pl* **staffs** \'stafs, 'stavz\ *or* **staves** \'stavz, 'stāvz\ **1 a** : a pole, stick, rod, or bar used as a support or as a sign of authority ⟨a flag hanging limp on its *staff*⟩ **b** : the long handle of a weapon (as a lance or pike) **c** : ¹CLUB 1a, CUDGEL **2** : something that is a source of strength ⟨bread is the *staff* of life⟩ **3** : the five horizontal lines and the spaces between them on which music is written **4** *pl* **staffs** **a** : a group of persons serving as assistants to or employees under a chief ⟨a hospital *staff*⟩ **b** : military officers who

staff 3

assist a commanding officer in planning and management but who do not take part in actual combat — **staff** *adj*

²staff *vb* : to supply with a staff or with workers

staff·er \'staf-ər\ *n* : a member of a staff and especially a newspaper staff

staff sergeant *n* : a military enlisted person with a rank just below that of platoon sergeant in the army, below that of gunnery sergeant in the marines, and below that of technical sergeant in the air force

¹stag \'stag\ *n, pl* **stag** *or* **stags** **1** : an adult male deer especially of one of the larger kinds **2 a** : a social gathering of men only **b** : a man who attends a dance or party unaccompanied by a woman

²stag *adj* **1** : intended for men only ⟨a *stag* party⟩ **2** : unaccompanied by someone of the opposite sex

¹stage \'stāj\ *n* **1 a** : one of the levels into which a structure can be divided **b** : a floor of a building **c** : a shelf or layer especially as one of a series **2 a** : a raised platform **b** : a part of a theater including the acting area **c** : the small platform of a microscope on which an object is placed for examination **3 a** : a center of attention : scene of action **b** : the theatrical profession or art **4 a** : a stopping place especially for a stagecoach providing fresh horses and refreshments **b** : the distance between stopping places in a journey **c** : a period or step in a process, activity, or development ⟨an early *stage* of a disease⟩ **d** : one of the periods of the growth and development of a plant or animal ⟨the larval *stage* of a beetle⟩; *also* : an individual in such a stage **e** : one complete process or step in a series or cycle **5** : STAGECOACH **6** : one of two or more sections of a rocket each having its own fuel and engine ⟨a three-*stage* missile⟩ — **on the stage** : in or into the acting profession

²stage *vb* **staged; stag·ing** : to produce or show publicly on or as if on the stage ⟨*stages* two plays each year⟩ ⟨*stage* a track meet⟩

stage·coach \'stāj-,kōch\ *n* : a coach pulled by horses that carries passengers and mail and runs on a schedule between established stops

stage direction *n* : a playwright's instruction to a director and actors

stage fright *n* : nervousness felt at appearing before an audience

stage·hand \'stāj-,hand\ *n* : a stage worker who handles scenery, properties, or lights

stage manager *n* : a person who is in charge of the stage and the related details of a theatrical production

stage·struck \'stāj-,strək\ *adj* : fascinated by the stage; *esp* : having an eager desire to become an actor

stage whisper *n* : a loud whisper by an actor intended to be heard by the spectators but supposed not to be heard by persons on the stage

¹stag·ger \'stag-ər\ *vb* **stag·gered; stag·ger·ing** \-(ə-)riŋ\ **1** : to move or cause to move unsteadily from side to side as if about to fall **2 a** : to begin to doubt and waver **b** : become less confident **b** : to cause to doubt, waver, or hesitate : OVERWHELM ⟨were *staggered* by the problems they had to face⟩ **3** : to place or arrange in a zigzag or alternate but regular way — **stag·ger·er** \-ər-ər\ *n*

²stagger *n* **1** *pl* : an abnormal condition of domestic mammals and birds associated with damage to the central nervous system and marked by unsteady movements and falling **2** : a reeling or unsteady gait or stance

stag·ger·ing *adj* : so great as to cause one to stagger : ASTONISHING, OVERWHELMING ⟨*staggering* medical bills⟩ — **stag·ger·ing·ly** \'stag-(ə-)riŋ-lē\ *adv*

stag·hound \'stag-,haúnd\ *n* : a large heavy hound once used in hunting deer and other large animals

stag·ing \'stā-jiŋ\ *n* **1** : SCAFFOLDING 1 **2** : the putting of a play on the stage

stag·nant \'stag-nənt\ *adj* **1** : not flowing in a current or stream : MOTIONLESS **2** : not active or brisk ⟨*stagnant* business⟩

stag·nate \'stag-,nāt\ *vb* **stag·nat·ed; stag·nat·ing** : to be or become stagnant — **stag·na·tion** \stag-nā-shən\ *n*

¹staid \'stād\ *adj* **1** : not easily changed : SETTLED, FIXED ⟨a *staid* opinion⟩ **2 a** : calm and serious in manner, attitude, or style **b** : not bold, bright, or showy ⟨*staid* colors⟩ — **staid·ly** *adv* — **staid·ness** *n*

²staid *past and past participle of* STAY

¹stain \'stān\ *vb* **1** : to soil or discolor especially in spots **2** : to give color to (as by dyeing) : TINGE **3 a** : ¹CORRUPT 1 **b** : ¹DISGRACE — **stain·er** *n*

²stain *n* **1** : a soiled or discolored spot **2** : a mark of guilt or disgrace **3 a** : something (as a dye) used in staining **b** : a dye or mixture of dyes used in microscopy to make very small and transparent structures visible, to color tissue elements so that they can be told apart, and to produce specific chemical reactions — **stain·less** \'stā-ləs\ *adj*

stained glass *n* : glass colored or stained for use in windows

stainless steel *n* : an alloy of steel and chromium that is highly resistant to stain, rust, and corrosion

stair \'sta(ə)r, 'ste(ə)r\ *n* **1** : a series of steps or flights of steps for passing from one level to another — often used in pl. ⟨ran down the *stairs*⟩ **2** : one step of a stairway

stair·case \-,kās\ *n* : a flight of stairs with the supporting structures

stair·way \-,wā\ *n* : one or more flights of stairs usually with landings to pass from one level to another

stair·well \-,wel\ *n* : a vertical shaft around which stairs are located

¹stake \'stāk\ *n* **1** : a pointed piece (as of wood or metal) driven or to be driven into the ground especially as a marker or support **2** : a post to which a person is bound for execution by burning **3 a** : something that is staked for gain or loss **b** : the prize in a contest **c** : an interest or share in a business **4** : GRUBSTAKE — **at stake** : in a position to be lost or won

²stake *vb* **staked; stak·ing** **1 a** : to mark the limits of by stakes ⟨*stake* out a mining claim⟩ **b** : to tie to a stake **c** : to fasten up or support (as plants) with stakes **2 a** : ²BET 1 **b** : to back financially

sta·lac·tite \stə-'lak-,tīt\ *n* : a deposit of calcium carbonate resembling an icicle hanging from the roof or sides of a cavern [from scientific Latin *stalactites* "stalactite", from Greek *stalaktos*

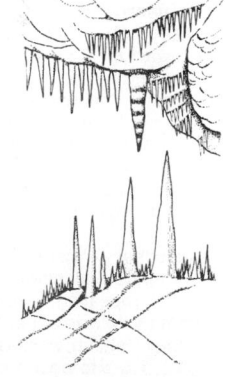

stalactite and stalagmite

\ə\ **abut**	\aú\ **out**	\i\ **tip**	\ó\ **saw**	\ú\ **foot**
\ər\ **further**	\ch\ **chin**	\ī\ **life**	\ói\ **coin**	\y\ **yet**
\a\ **mat**	\e\ **pet**	\j\ **job**	\th\ **thin**	\yü\ **few**
\ā\ **take**	\ē\ **easy**	\ŋ\ **sing**	\th\ **this**	\yú\ **cure**
\ä\ **cot, cart**	\g\ **go**	\ō\ **bone**	\ü\ **food**	\zh\ **vision**

(adjective) "dripping"]

sta·lag·mite \stə-'lag-,mīt\ *n* : a deposit like an inverted stalactite formed on the floor of a cave by the drip of water containing calcium carbonate [from scientific Latin *stalagmites* "stalagmite", from Greek *stalagma* "a drop" or Greek *stalagmos* "the act or result of dripping"]

¹stale \'stā(ə)l\ *adj* **stal·er; stal·est** **1** : having lost a good taste or quality from age ⟨*stale* food⟩ **2** : used or heard so often as to be dull ⟨*stale* news⟩ **3** : not so strong, effective, or energetic as before ⟨felt *stale* from lack of exercise⟩ — **stale·ly** \'stā(ə)l-lē\ *adv* — **stale·ness** *n*

²stale *vb* **staled; stal·ing** : to make or become stale

¹stale·mate \'stā(ə)l-,māt\ *n* **1** : a position in chess that results in a draw when the only piece to be moved is the king which cannot be moved without being exposed to attack by the other player's piece **2** : a drawn or undecided contest : DEADLOCK

²stalemate *vb* **stale·mat·ed; stale·mat·ing** : to bring into a stalemate

¹stalk \'stȯk\ *n* **1** : a plant stem especially of a plant that is not woody ⟨*stalks* of asparagus⟩ **2** : a slender upright object or supporting or connecting structure ⟨the *stalk* of a goblet⟩ — **stalked** \'stȯkt\ *adj* — **stalk·line** \-,līk\ *adj* — **stalky** \'stȯ-kē\ *adj*

²stalk *vb* **1 a** : to hunt slowly and quietly ⟨*stalk* deer⟩ **b** : to cover an area in stalking prey **2** : to walk in a stiff or proud manner ⟨*stalked* out of the room⟩ — **stalk·er** *n*

³stalk *n* **1** : the act of stalking **2** : a stalking manner of walking

¹stall \'stȯl\ *n* **1** : a compartment for a domestic animal in a stable or barn **2 a** : a seat in the choir of a church with back and sides wholly or partly enclosed **b** *British* : a front orchestra seat in a theater **3** : a booth, stand, or counter at which articles are displayed for sale **4** : a small compartment ⟨a shower *stall*⟩ [Old English *steall* "stall for an animal"]

²stall *vb* **1** : to put into or keep in a stall **2** : to stop or cause to stop usually by accident ⟨*stall* an engine⟩

³stall *n* : the condition of an aircraft or a wing of an aircraft in which lift is lost and the aircraft or wing tends to drop

⁴stall *n* : a trick to deceive or delay [an altered form of earlier *stale* "lure"]

⁵stall *vb* : to distract attention or make excuses to gain time ⟨try to *stall* them until I get the place cleaned up⟩

stal·lion \'stal-yən\ *n* : a male horse; *esp* : one kept especially for breeding

¹stal·wart \'stȯl-wərt\ *adj* **1** : STURDY 1 **2** : ¹BRAVE 1, RESOLUTE — **stal·wart·ly** *adv*

²stalwart *n* **1** : a stalwart person **2** : a loyal supporter (as in politics)

sta·men \'stā-mən\ *n, pl* **stamens** *also* **sta·mi·na** \'stā-mə-nə, 'stam-ə-\ : an organ of a flower that consists of an anther and a filament and produces the pollen

stam·i·na \'stam-ə-nə\ *n* : VIGOR 1, ENDURANCE

sta·mi·nate \'stā-mə-nət, 'stam-ə-, -,nāt\ *adj* : having stamens; *esp* : having stamens but no pistils ⟨*staminate* flowers⟩

¹stam·mer \'stam-ər\ *vb* **stam·mered; stam·mer·ing** \-(ə-)riŋ\ : to speak or utter with involuntary stops and much repeating — **stam·mer·er** \-ər-ər\ *n*

²stammer *n* : an act or instance of stammering

¹stamp \'stamp; *senses 1b & 2 are also* 'stamp *or* 'stȯmp\ *vb* **1 a** : to pound or crush with a heavy instrument **b** : to strike or beat forcibly with the bottom of the foot **c** : to put an end to or destroy by or as if by stamping with the foot **2** : to walk heavily or noisily **3 a** : ¹IMPRESS 1, IMPRINT ⟨*stamp* the bill "paid"⟩ **b** : to attach a stamp to ⟨*stamp* a letter⟩ **4** : to form with a stamp or die **5** : CHARACTERIZE 1 — **stamp·er** *n*

²stamp *n* **1** : a device or instrument for stamping **2** : the mark made by stamping **3** : a sign of a special quality ⟨*stamp* of genius⟩ **4** : the act of stamping **5 a** : a

stamped or printed paper attached to something to show that a tax or fee has been paid **b** : POSTAGE STAMP

¹stam·pede \stam-'pēd\ *n* **1** : a wild rush or flight of frightened animals **2** : a sudden movement of a crowd of people [from a word in the Spanish of Mexico and the American Southwest, *estampida* "stampede", from Spanish *estampida* "a crash, loud noise", from *estamper* "to pound, stamp"]

²stampede *vb* **stam·ped·ed; stam·ped·ing** **1** : to run away or cause (as cattle) to run away in panic **2** : to act together or cause to act together suddenly and without thought

stance \'stan(t)s\ *n* : way of standing or being placed : POSTURE

¹stanch *also* **staunch** \'stȯnch, 'stänch\ *vb* : to stop the flow of ⟨*stanch* tears⟩; *also* : to stop the flow of blood from (a wound)

²stanch *variant of* ²STAUNCH

stan·chion \'stan-chən\ *n* **1** : an upright bar, post, or support **2** : a device that fits loosely around an animal's neck and limits forward and backward motion (as in a stall)

stanchion 2

¹stand \'stand\ *vb* **stood** \'stu̇d\; **stand·ing** **1 a** : to support oneself on the feet in an erect position **b** : to rise to one's feet **2** : to take up and keep a usually specified position or attitude ⟨*stand* aside⟩ ⟨where do we *stand* on this question⟩ **3** : to be in a particular state or situation ⟨*stands* accused⟩ **4** *chiefly British* : to be a candidate : RUN **5 a** : to rest remain, or set upright on a base or lower end ⟨the spade *stood* in the sod⟩ **b** : to occupy a place or location ⟨a house *standing* on a hill⟩ **6 a** : to remain without moving ⟨rainwater *standing* in stagnant pools⟩ **b** : to remain in effect ⟨the order *stands*⟩ **7** : to exist in a certain form ⟨you must take or leave our offer as it *stands*⟩ **8 a** : to put up with or resist successfully : BEAR ⟨*stand* pain⟩ ⟨the building *stood* the pressure of the storm⟩ **b** : to go through the experience of ⟨*stand* trial⟩ **9** : to pay for ⟨I'll *stand* dinner⟩ — **stand·er** *n* — **stand by** **1** : to be loyal to ⟨*stood* by their friends⟩ — **stand for** **1** : to be a symbol for : REPRESENT **2** : to put up with : PERMIT ⟨would not *stand for* bad manners⟩ — **stand pat** : to oppose or resist change

²stand *n* **1** : an act or instance of stopping or staying in one place **2 a** : a halt for defense or resistance **b** : a stop made to give a theatrical performance **3 a** : a place or post where one stands **b** : a position especially with respect to an issue **4 a** : the place occupied by a witness testifying in court **b** : a row of seats for spectators of an outdoor sport or spectacle **c** : a raised platform (as for a speaker) **5** : a small often open-air structure for a small retail business ⟨a hot-dog *stand*⟩ **6** : a support (as a rack or table) on or in which something may be placed ⟨umbrella *stands*⟩ ⟨a bicycle *stand*⟩ **7** : a group of plants growing in a continuous area ⟨a good *stand* of wheat⟩

¹stan·dard \'stan-dərd\ *n* **1 a** : a figure used as an emblem by an organized body of people ⟨the eagle was the Roman legion's *standard*⟩ **b** : the personal flag of the ruler of a state **2 a** : something set up by authority or general consent as a rule for measuring or as a model ⟨a *standard* of weight⟩ ⟨*standards* of good manners⟩ **b** : the basis of value in a monetary system ⟨gold *standard*⟩ **3** : a structure that serves as a support ⟨a lamp *standard*⟩

²standard *adj* **1** : used as or meeting a standard established by law or custom ⟨*standard* weight⟩ **2** : regularly and widely used ⟨*standard* practice in the trade⟩ **3** : having recognized and permanent value ⟨*standard* reference works⟩ **4** : well established by usage in the speech or writing of the educated and widely recognized as acceptable ⟨*standard* spelling⟩

stan·dard–bear·er \'stan-dərd-,bar-ər, -,ber-\ *n* **1** : one that bears a standard or banner **2** : the leader of an organization or movement

stan·dard·bred \-,bred\ *n* : any of an American breed of trotting and pacing horses noted for speed and strength

standard deviation *n* : the square root of the arithmetic mean of the squares of differences between the arithmetic mean of a frequency distribution and the values of the variable

stan·dard·ize \'stan-dərd-,īz\ *vb* **-ized; -iz·ing** : to compare with or make agree with a standard — **stan·dard·iza·tion** \,stan-dərd-ə-'zā-shən\ *n*

standard of living : the necessities, comforts, and luxuries that a person or group is accustomed to

standard time *n* : the time established by law or by general usage over a region or country

stand·by \'stan(d)-,bī\ *n, pl* **stand·bys** \-,bīz\ : one available or to be relied on especially in emergencies

stand by \(')stan(d)-'bī\ *vb* **1** : to be present **2** : to be or to get ready to act

stand·ee \stan-'dē\ *n* : one who occupies standing room

stand·in \'stan-,din\ *n* **1** : someone employed to occupy an actor's place while lights and camera are readied **2** : [1]SUBSTITUTE

stand in \(')stan-'din\ *vb* : to act as a stand-in

[1]stand·ing \'stan-din\ *adj* **1** : upright on the feet or base : ERECT ⟨*standing* grain⟩ **2 a** : not flowing : STAGNANT ⟨*standing* water⟩ **b** : remaining at the same level, degree, or amount until canceled ⟨*standing* offer⟩ **c** : continuing in existence or use for an unlimited length of time : PERMANENT ⟨a *standing* army⟩ ⟨*standing* committees⟩ **3** : done from a standing position ⟨*standing* jump⟩ ⟨a *standing* ovation⟩

[2]standing *n* **1** : the action or position of one that stands **2** : length of existence or service : DURATION ⟨a quarrel of long *standing*⟩ **3 a** : position or rank as compared with others ⟨had the highest *standing* in the class⟩ **b** : good reputation ⟨people of *standing* in the community⟩

standing room *n* : space available for spectators or passengers to stand in after all seats are filled

standing wave *n* : a vibration of a body or physical system in which the amplitude varies from place to place, is constantly zero at fixed points, and does not appear to move

stand·off \'stan-,dȯf\ *n* : a contest or game in which there is no winner : DRAW

stand·off·ish \stan-'dȯ-fish\ *adj* : not friendly : ALOOF

stand·out \'stan-,daůt\ *n* : one that is well-known or outstanding especially because of excellence

stand out \(')stan-'daůt\ *vb* **1** : to stick out from a surface : PROJECT **2** : to be easily seen or recognized

stand·point \'stan(d)-,pȯint\ *n* : a position from which things are viewed and according to which they are compared and judged

stand·still \-,stil\ *n* : a state marked by absence of motion or activity : STOP ⟨business was at a *standstill*⟩

stand up *vb* **1** : to remain in good condition **2** : to fail to keep an appointment with — **stand up for** : to defend against attack or criticism — **stand up to** **1** : to meet fairly and fully **2** : to face boldly

stank *past of* STINK

stan·za \'stan-zə\ *n* : a division of a poem consisting of a series of lines arranged together in a usually repeating pattern of rhythm and rhyme — **stan·za·ic** \stan-'zā-ik\ *adj*

sta·pes \'stā-pēz\ *n, pl* **stapes** *or* **sta·pe·des** \'stā-pə-,dēz\ : STIRRUP 2

staph \'staf\ *n* : STAPHYLOCOCCUS; *also* : an infection with staphylococci

staph·y·lo·coc·cus \,staf-(ə-)lō-'käk-əs\ *n, pl* **-coc·ci** \-'käk-,(s)ī, -(,)(s)ē\ : any of various round bacteria that occur especially in irregular clusters and include many disease-causing parasites of the skin and mucous membranes — **staph·y·lo·coc·cal** \-'käk-əl\ *also* **staph·y·lo·coc·cic** \-'käk-(s)ik\ *adj*

[1]sta·ple \'stā-pəl\ *n* **1** : a U-shaped piece of metal with sharp points to be driven into a surface to hold something (as a hook, rope, or wire) **2** : a U-shaped piece of thin wire that is driven through papers and bent over at the ends to fasten them together or driven through thin material to fasten it to something else [Old English *stapol* "post"]

[2]staple *vb* **sta·pled; sta·pling** \-p(ə-)lin\ : to fasten with staples

[3]staple *n* **1** : a chief product of business or farming of a place **2 a** : something in widespread and constant use or demand **b** : the chief part of something ⟨potatoes are the *staple* of their diet⟩ **3** : RAW MATERIAL **4** : textile fiber (as wool or rayon) suitable for spinning into yarn [Middle English *staple* "a major market town, place for exporting"; of Dutch origin]

[4]staple *adj* **1** : used, needed, or enjoyed constantly usually by many individuals **2** : produced regularly or in large quantities **3** : [1]PRINCIPAL, CHIEF ⟨*staple* crop⟩

sta·pler \'stā-p(ə-)lər\ *n* : a device that staples

[1]star \'stär\ *n* **1 a** : a natural body visible in the sky especially at night that gives off light or shines by reflection **b** : a ball-shaped gaseous celestial body (as the sun) of great mass that shines by its own light **2** : a planet or an arrangement of the planets that is believed in astrology to influence one's life — usually used in pl. **3** : a figure or thing (as an asterisk or badge) with five or more points that represents or resembles a star **4 a** : the principal member of a theater or opera company **b** : a very talented or popular performer ⟨football *stars*⟩ ⟨TV *stars*⟩ — **star·like** \-,līk\ *adj*

[2]star *vb* **starred; star·ring** **1** : to sprinkle or adorn with stars **2 a** : to mark with a star as being superior **b** : to mark with an asterisk **3** : to present in the role of a star **4** : to play the most important role ⟨will produce and *star* in a new play⟩ **5** : to perform outstandingly ⟨*starred* at shortstop in the series⟩

[3]star *adj* **1** : of, relating to, or being a star **2** : being of outstanding excellence : PREEMINENT ⟨*star* athlete⟩ ⟨our *star* trumpeter⟩

[1]star·board \'stär-bərd\ *n* : the right side of a ship or aircraft looking forward

> **Word History** The word *starboard* has nothing whatever to do with stars. The *star-* part of the word used to be spelled *stēor-* in Old English and referred to the steering oar or rudder of a ship. In those days the rudder was located on the side of the ship to the right of a person facing toward the bow. Nowadays, of course, the rudder is at the stern. The *-board* part of the word refers not to a plank but to a whole side of a ship. This meaning survives today in the verb to *board* a ship or airplane. The side opposite the starboard is usually called the *port*. The name probably comes from the fact that this side faced the port or dock when the ship was steered into a harbor. The port side is sometimes also called the *larboard*. The *lar-* part of this word was spelled *lade-* in Old English. It probably came from the verb *laden*, meaning "to load". So the *larboard* was the side from which the cargo was loaded and unloaded. [Old English *stēorbord* "starboard, side of a ship from which it is steered", from *stēor* "steering oar" and *bord* "the side of a ship"]

\ə\ abut	\aů\ out	\i\ tip	\ȯ\ saw	\ů\ foot
\ər\ further	\ch\ chin	\ī\ life	\ȯi\ coin	\y\ yet
\a\ mat	\e\ pet	\j\ job	\th\ thin	\yü\ few
\ā\ take	\ē\ easy	\ŋ\ sing	\th\ this	\yů\ cure
\ä\ cot, cart	\g\ go	\ō\ bone	\ü\ food	\zh\ vision

²**starboard** *adj* : of, relating to, or situated to starboard

¹**starch** \'stärch\ *vb* : to stiffen with or as if with starch

²**starch** *n* 1 : a white odorless tasteless carbohydrate that is the chief form in which carbohydrate is stored in plants, is an important food, and is used also in adhesives, in laundering, and in pharmacy and medicine 2 : a stiff formal manner : FORMALITY 2, VITALITY 2, SPUNK

starchy \'stär-chē\ *adj* **starch·i·er; -est** 1 : containing, consisting of, or resembling starch 2 : consisting of or marked by formality or stiffness — **starch·i·ness** *n*

star–crossed \'stär-ˌkròst\ *adj* : UNLUCKY 1, UNFORTUNATE [so called from the idea that stars control the lives and actions of people]

star·dom \'stärd-əm\ *n* : the status or position of a star

¹**stare** \'sta(ə)r, 'ste(ə)r\ *vb* **stared; star·ing** : to look hard and long often with wide-open eyes ⟨*stare* at a stranger⟩
syn see GAZE — **star·er** *n*

²**stare** *n* : the act or an instance of staring

star·fish \'stär-ˌfish\ *n*
: any of a class of echinoderms usually having five arms arranged evenly around a central disk and feeding largely on mollusks (as oysters)

star·gaze \-ˌgāz\ *vb* **star·gazed; star·gaz·ing** 1 : to gaze at stars 2 : to stare absentmindedly : DAYDREAM — **star·gaz·er** *n*

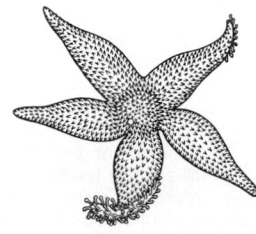
starfish

¹**stark** \'stärk\ *adj* 1 : STRONG 1, ROBUST 2 a : STIFF 1, MOTIONLESS ⟨*stark* in death⟩ b : INFLEXIBLE 3, STRICT ⟨*stark* discipline⟩ 3 : ¹SHEER 2a, UTTER ⟨*stark* nonsense⟩ 4 a : ¹BARREN 2a, DESOLATE ⟨a *stark* landscape⟩ b : having few or no ornaments : BARE 5 : UNADORNED, HARSH ⟨*stark* realism⟩ — **stark·ly** *adv*

²**stark** *adv* : WHOLLY, ABSOLUTELY ⟨*stark* mad⟩

star·let \'stär-lət\ *n* : a young movie actress

star·light \'stär-ˌlīt\ *n* : the light given by the stars

star·ling \'stär-liŋ\ *n* : any of a family of usually dark-colored social birds; *esp* : a dark brown or in summer glossy greenish black European bird that has been brought to the U.S. and is often a pest

star·lit \'stär-ˌlit\ *adj* : lighted by the stars

Star of Da·vid \-'dā-vəd\ : a six-pointed star used as a symbol of Judaism

star·ry \'stär-ē\ *adj* **star·ri·er; -est** 1 : full of stars ⟨*starry* heavens⟩ 2 : of, relating to, or consisting of stars : STELLAR ⟨*starry* light⟩ 3 : shining like stars : SPARKLING ⟨*starry* eyes⟩

Stars and Bars *n sing or pl* : the first flag of the Confederate States of America

Stars and Stripes *n sing or pl* : the flag of the United States

star·shine \'stär-ˌshīn\ *n* : STARLIGHT

star·ship \'stär-ˌship\ *n* : a vehicle designed for travel beyond the earth's atmosphere

star–span·gled \'stär-ˌspaŋ-gəld\ *adj* : adorned with stars

¹**start** \'stärt\ *vb* 1 : to move suddenly and sharply : give a sudden twitch or jerk (as in surprise) 2 : to come or bring into being, activity, or operation ⟨who *started* the rumor⟩ ⟨*started* a camp for youngsters⟩ ⟨fire *started* in the cellar⟩ ⟨the game *started* late⟩ 3 : to stick out or seem to stick out : PROTRUDE ⟨eyes that *started* from their sockets⟩ 4 : SET OUT 2, BEGIN ⟨*start* to school⟩ 5 : to take part or cause to take part in a game or contest 6 : to cause to move, act, or operate ⟨*start* the motor⟩

²**start** *n* 1 a : a quick unwilled bodily reaction b : a brief and sudden action or movement 2 : a beginning of movement, activity, or development ⟨get an early *start*⟩ 3 : a lead or advantage at the beginning of a race or competition

: HEAD START 4 : a place of beginning

start·er \'stärt-ər\ *n* : someone or something that starts something or causes something else to start ⟨the *starter* of a motor⟩

star·tle \'stärt-ᵊl\ *vb* **star·tled; star·tling** \'stärt-liŋ, -ᵊl-iŋ\ 1 : to move or jump suddenly (as in surprise or fright) 2 : to frighten suddenly and usually not seriously — **startle** *n*

star·tling *adj* : causing a sudden fright, surprise, or astonishment — **star·tling·ly** \'stärt-liŋ-lē, -ᵊl-iŋ-\ *adv*

star·va·tion \stär-'vā-shən\ *n* : the act or an instance of starving : the state of being starved

starve \'stärv\ *vb* **starved; starv·ing** 1 : to suffer or die or cause to suffer or die from lack of food 2 : to suffer or die or cause to suffer or die from a lack of something other than food ⟨a child *starving* for affection⟩ [Old English *steorfan* "to die (from any cause)"]

starve·ling \'stärv-liŋ\ *n* : one thin and weakened by or as if by lack of food

¹**stash** \'stash\ *vb* : to store in a usually secret place for future use

²**stash** *n* 1 : a hiding place 2 : something stored or hidden away

¹**state** \'stāt\ *n* 1 a : manner or condition of being ⟨a *state* of readiness⟩ b : condition of mind or disposition ⟨in a highly nervous *state*⟩ 2 a : a condition or stage of the physical makeup of something ⟨water in the gaseous *state*⟩ b : a stage in the growth or development of a plant or animal ⟨the larval *state*⟩ 3 a : a politically organized body of people usually occupying a definite territory b : the political organization of such a body of people 4 : one of the units of a nation having a federal government ⟨the United *States* of America⟩ 5 : the territory of a state — **state·less** \-ləs\ *adj*

²**state** *adj* 1 : suitable or used for ceremonies or official occasions ⟨*state* robes⟩ 2 : of or relating to a national state or to one state of a federal government ⟨a *state* church⟩ ⟨a *state* legislature⟩ 3 : of or relating to the government : GOVERNMENTAL ⟨*state* secrets⟩

³**state** *vb* **stated; stat·ing** 1 : to set by regulation or authority ⟨*stated* times⟩ 2 : to express in words ⟨*state* an opinion⟩

state bird *n* : a bird selected (as by the legislature) as an emblem of a state of the U.S.

state·craft \'stāt-ˌkraft\ *n* : the art of conducting state affairs : STATESMANSHIP

stat·ed \'stāt-əd\ *adj* 1 : being set or fixed (as by rule or custom) 2 : set down clearly ⟨*stated* goals⟩

state flower *n* : a flowering plant selected (as by the legislature) as an emblem of a state of the U.S.

state·hood \'stāt-ˌhud\ *n* : the condition of being a state; *esp* : the condition or status of one of the states of the U.S.

state·house \'stāt-ˌhaus\ *n* : the building in which a state legislature meets

state·ly \'stāt-lē\ *adj* **state·li·er; -est** : impressively grand in appearance, manner, or size — **state·li·ness** *n*

state·ment \'stāt-mənt\ *n* 1 : the act or process of stating 2 a : something stated : REPORT, ASSERTION b : PROPOSITION 2 3 : a brief summarized record of a financial account ⟨a monthly bank *statement*⟩ 4 : an instruction in a computer program

state·room \'stāt-ˌrüm, -ˌrum\ *n* : a private room on a ship or on a railroad car

state·side \'stāt-ˌsīd\ *adj* : of or relating to the United States as considered from outside its continental limits

states·man \'stāt-smən\ *n* : a person engaged in fixing the policies and conducting the affairs of a government; *esp* : one having unusual wisdom and skill in such matters — **states·man·like** \-ˌlīk\ *adj* — **states·man·ly** \-lē\ *adj* — **states·man·ship** \-ˌship\ *n*

states' rights *n pl* : all rights not given to the federal government by the U.S. Constitution nor forbidden by it to the separate states

state·wide \'stāt-'wīd\ *adj* : including all parts of a state

¹**stat·ic** \'stat-ik\ *adj* **1** : of or relating to bodies at rest or forces that are balanced ⟨*static* friction⟩ **2** : marked by a lack of movement, liveliness, or progress **3** : of, relating to, or producing stationary charges of electricity (as those produced by friction)

²**static** *n* : noise produced in a radio or television receiver by atmospheric or electrical disturbances

static line *n* : a cord attached to a parachute pack and to an airplane to open the parachute after a jumper clears the plane

¹**sta·tion** \'stā-shən\ *n* **1** : the place or position in which something or someone stands or is assigned to stand or remain **2** : a regular stopping place : DEPOT ⟨drove him to the bus *station*⟩ **3 a** : a post or area of duty or occupation **b** : a stock farm or ranch of Australia or New Zealand **4** : social or official position : RANK ⟨a person of high *station*⟩ **5** : a place for specialized scientific observation and study especially in or near the field or in natural surroundings ⟨a biological *station*⟩ ⟨a weather *station*⟩ **6** : a place established to provide a public service ⟨police *station*⟩ ⟨fire *station*⟩ ⟨power *station*⟩ **7 a** : a complete collection of radio or television equipment for transmitting or receiving **b** : the place in which such a station is located

²**station** *vb* **sta·tioned; sta·tion·ing** \'stā-sh(ə-)niŋ\ : to assign to or set in a station or position : POST

sta·tion·ary \'stā-shə-,ner-ē\ *adj* **1** : fixed in a station, course, or position : IMMOBILE ⟨a *stationary* loudspeaker⟩ **2** : unchanging in condition ⟨a *stationary* population⟩

station break *n* : a pause in a radio or television broadcast for announcement of the identity of the network or station

sta·tio·ner \'stā-sh(ə-)nər\ *n* : one that sells stationery

sta·tio·nery \'stā-shə-,ner-ē\ *n* **1** : materials (as paper, pens, and ink) for writing or typing **2** : letter paper usually accompanied with matching envelopes

sta·tion·mas·ter \'stā-shən-,mas-tər\ *n* : an official in charge of the operation of a railroad station

station wagon *n* : an automobile that has an interior longer than a sedan's, has one or more folding or removable rear seats to make carrying luggage or cargo easier, and usually has a door at the rear end

sta·tis·tic \stə-'tis-tik\ *n* : a single item of information in a collection of statistics

stat·is·ti·cian \,stat-ə-'stish-ən\ *n* : a person who specializes in statistics

sta·tis·tics \stə-'tis-tiks\ *n sing or pl* : a branch of mathematics dealing with the collection and study of masses of facts in numerical form; *also* : a collection of such numerical facts — **sta·tis·ti·cal** \-'tis-ti-kəl\ *adj* — **sta·tis·ti·cal·ly** \-ti-k(ə-)lē\ *adv*

stat·u·ary \'stach-ə-,wer-ē\ *n, pl* **-ar·ies** **1** : ¹SCULPTURE 1 **2** : a collection of statues — **statuary** *adj*

stat·ue \'stach-ü\ *n* : a likeness (as of a person) sculptured, modeled, or cast in a solid substance (as marble)

stat·u·esque \,stach-ə-'wesk\ *adj* : resembling a statue especially in size, gracefulness, or beauty

stat·u·ette \,stach-ə-'wet\ *n* : a small statue

stat·ure \'stach-ər\ *n* **1** : natural height (as of a person) in an upright position **2** : quality or status gained by growth, development, or achievement ⟨artists of *stature*⟩

sta·tus \'stāt-əs, 'stat-\ *n* **1** : position or rank in relation to others : STANDING **2** : state of affairs : SITUATION

sta·tus quo \,stāt-ə-'skwō, ,stat-\ *n* : the existing state of affairs

stat·ute \'stach-üt, -ət\ *n* : a law put into effect by the legislative branch of a government

statute mile *n* : MILE 1

stat·u·to·ry \'stach-ə-,tōr-ē, -,tor-\ *adj* **1** : of or relating to statutes **2** : regulated by statute **3** : punishable by statute

¹**staunch** *variant of* ¹STANCH

²**staunch** *or* **stanch** \'stȯnch, 'stänch\ *adj* **1 a** : WATERTIGHT 1, SOUND ⟨a *staunch* ship⟩ **b** : strongly built : SUBSTANTIAL ⟨*staunch* foundations⟩ **2** : steadfast in loyalty or principle ⟨a *staunch* friend⟩ **syn** see FAITHFUL — **staunch·ly** *adv*

¹**stave** \'stāv\ *n* **1** : a wooden stick **2** : one of the narrow strips of wood or iron plates placed edge to edge to form the sides, covering, or lining of a vessel (as a barrel or cask) or structure **3** : STANZA **4** : ¹STAFF 3

²**stave** *vb* **staved** *or* **stove** \'stōv\; **stav·ing** **1** : to break in the staves of (a cask) **2** : to smash a hole in ⟨*stave* in a boat⟩

stave off *vb* : to force or keep away : fend off ⟨*stave off* trouble⟩

staves *pl of* STAFF

stave

stave 2

¹**stay** \'stā\ *n* : a strong rope or wire used to steady or brace something (as a mast) [Old English *stæg* "a strong rope used to steady or support something"]

²**stay** *vb* : to fasten (as a smokestack) with stays

³**stay** *vb* **1** : to stop going forward : PAUSE **2** : to continue in a place or condition : REMAIN ⟨*stayed* at home⟩ **3** : to stand firm **4** : to take up residence : LODGE ⟨*stayed* in a hotel⟩ **5** : ¹WAIT 1a **6** : to last out (as a race) **7** : ²CHECK 2, HALT ⟨*stay* an execution⟩ [Middle English *stayen* "to stop going forward", from early French *ester* "to stand, stay", from Latin *stare* "to stand"]

⁴**stay** *n* **1** : the action of halting : the state of being stopped **2** : a residence or visit in a place

⁵**stay** *n* **1** : something that serves as a prop : SUPPORT **2** : a thin firm strip (as of plastic) used for stiffening a garment (as a corset) or part (as a shirt collar) [from early French *estaie* "a support, prop"; of Germanic origin]

⁶**stay** *vb* : to provide support for

staying power *n* : ability or strength enough to keep going through a difficult task

STD \,es-,tē-'dē\ *n* : any of various diseases transmitted by direct sexual contact that include the classic venereal diseases (as syphilis and gonorrhea) and other diseases (as hepatitis and AIDS) that are often or sometimes contracted by other than sexual means

stead \'sted\ *n* **1** : ADVANTAGE 3, SERVICE ⟨their knowledge of French stood them in good *stead*⟩ **2** : the place usually taken or duty carried out by the one mentioned ⟨acted in the mayor's *stead*⟩

stead·fast \'sted-,fast\ *adj* **1 a** : firmly fixed in place **b** : not subject to change ⟨a *steadfast* purpose⟩ **2** : firm in belief, determination, or allegiance ⟨*steadfast* friends⟩ **syn** see FAITHFUL — **stead·fast·ly** *adv* — **stead·fast·ness** \-,fas(t)-nəs\ *n*

¹**steady** \'sted-ē\ *adj* **stead·i·er; -est** **1 a** : firm in position : FIXED **b** : direct or sure in movement ⟨took *steady* aim⟩ **2 a** : ¹REGULAR 3, UNIFORM ⟨a *steady* pace⟩ **b** : not changing much : STABLE ⟨*steady* prices⟩ **3 a** : not easily moved or upset : RESOLUTE **b** : constant in feeling, principle, purpose, or attachment : DEPENDABLE — **steadi·ly** \'sted-ᵊl-ē\ *adv* — **steadi·ness** \'sted-ē-nəs\ *n*

²**steady** *vb* **stead·ied; steady·ing** : to make, keep, or become steady

³**steady** *adv* : in a steady manner : STEADILY

⁴**steady** *n, pl* **stead·ies** : one that is steady; *esp* : a boy-

\ə\ **abut**	\au̇\ **out**	\i\ **tip**	\ȯ\ **saw**	\u̇\ **foot**
\ər\ **further**	\ch\ **chin**	\ī\ **life**	\ȯi\ **coin**	\y\ **yet**
\a\ **mat**	\e\ **pet**	\j\ **job**	\th\ **thin**	\yü\ **few**
\ā\ **take**	\ē\ **easy**	\ŋ\ **sing**	\th\ **this**	\yu̇\ **cure**
\ä\ **cot, cart**	\g\ **go**	\ō\ **bone**	\ü\ **food**	\zh\ **vision**

friend or girlfriend with whom one goes steady

steady state *n* : a state or condition of a system or process that does not change in time; *also* : a condition that changes only slightly over a specified time ⟨on the average a living cell maintains a *steady state*⟩

steady state theory *n* : a theory in astronomy that states that the universe has always existed and has always been expanding

steak \'stāk\ *n* **1** : a slice of meat and especially beef **2** : a slice of a large fish (as swordfish)

¹steal \'stē(ə)l\ *vb* **stole** \'stōl\; **sto·len** \'stō-lən\; **steal·ing** **1** : to come or go secretly or quietly ⟨*stole* out of the room⟩ **2 a** : to take and carry away without right and with the intention of keeping the property of another : ROB **b** : to take entirely to oneself or beyond one's proper share ⟨*steal* the show⟩ **3 a** : SMUGGLE 2 **b** : to accomplish or get in a concealed or unobserved manner ⟨*steal* a nap⟩ **4 a** : to seize, gain, or win by trickery, skill, or daring ⟨the basketball player *stole* the ball⟩ **b** : to gain a base in baseball by running without the aid of a hit or an error — **steal·er** *n*

²steal *n* **1** : the act or an instance of stealing **2** : something offered or purchased at a low price : BARGAIN

stealth \'stelth\ *n* : sly or secret action

stealthy \'stel-thē\ *adj* **stealth·i·er; -est** **1** : slow, deliberate, and secret in action or character **2** : intended to escape observation : FURTIVE — **stealth·i·ly** \-thə-lē\ *adv*

¹steam \'stēm\ *n* **1 a** : the invisible vapor into which water is changed when heated to the boiling point **b** : the mist formed when water vapor cools **2** : water vapor kept under pressure so as to supply energy for heating, cooking, or mechanical work; *also* : the power so generated **3 a** : driving force : POWER ⟨arrived under their own *steam*⟩ **b** : built-up tension ⟨let off a little *steam*⟩

²steam *vb* **1** : to rise or pass off as vapor **2** : to give off steam or vapor **3** : to move or travel by or as if by the power of steam ⟨*steamed* up the river⟩ **4** : to be angry : BOIL ⟨was *steaming* over the insult⟩ **5** : to expose to the action of steam (as for softening or cooking) ⟨*steamed* clams⟩

steam·boat \'stēm-,bōt\ *n* : a boat driven by steam

steam engine *n* : an engine driven by steam

steam·er \'stē-mər\ *n* **1** : a container in which something is steamed **2 a** : a ship driven by steam **b** : an engine, machine, or vehicle run by steam

steam iron *n* : a pressing iron with a compartment holding water that is converted to steam by the iron's heat and given off through holes in the bottom onto the fabric being pressed

steam·roll·er \'stēm-'rō-lər\ *n* : a machine formerly driven by steam that has wide heavy rollers for pressing down and smoothing roads

steam·ship \'stēm-,ship\ *n* : STEAMER 2a

steam shovel *n* : a power machine for digging that was formerly operated by steam

steam turbine *n* : a turbine that is driven by the pressure of steam discharged at high speed against the turbine blades

steamy \'stē-mē\ *adj* **steam·i·er; -est** : consisting of, characterized by, or full of steam — **steam·i·ly** \-mə-lē\ *adv*

ste·ap·sin \stē-'ap-sən\ *n* : a fat-digesting enzyme in pancreatic juice

stea·ric acid \stē-,ar-ik-, ,sti(ə)r-ik-\ *n* : acid obtained by the hydrolysis of a hard fat (as tallow) with alkali

stea·rin \'stē-ə-rən, 'sti(ə)r-ən\ *n* : a chemical compound that is the chief substance in beef fat

steed \'stēd\ *n* : ¹HORSE 1a; *esp* : a lively horse

¹steel \'stē(ə)l\ *n* **1** : commercial iron that contains carbon in any amount up to 1.7 percent as a necessary part **2** : an article (as a sword) made of steel **3** : a hard cold quality ⟨answered with *steel* in her voice⟩

²steel *vb* : to fill with courage or determination

³steel *adj* **1** : made of or like steel **2** : of or relating to the

production of steel

steel·head \'stē(ə)l-,hed\ *n* : a large silvery western North American trout that usually migrates to the sea to mature and returns to rivers to breed and that is usually considered to be a race of the rainbow trout

steel wool *n* : a rough material composed of long fine steel shavings and used especially for cleaning and polishing

steely \'stē-lē\ *adj* **steel·i·er; -est** **1** : made of steel **2** : resembling steel (as in hardness or color) ⟨a *steely* gaze⟩ — **steel·i·ness** *n*

steel·yard \'stē(ə)l-,yärd\ *n* : a balance on which something to be weighed is hung from the shorter arm of a lever and is balanced by a weight that slides along the longer arm which is marked with a scale

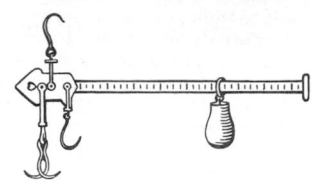

steelyard

¹steep \'stēp\ *adj* **1** : having a very sharp slope : almost straight up-and-down **2** : being or characterized by a very rapid decline or increase **3** : too great or high ⟨*steep* prices⟩ — **steep·ly** *adv*

²steep *n* : a sharply sloping place

³steep *vb* **1 a** : to soak in liquid (as for drawing out a flavor) at a temperature under the boiling point ⟨*steep* tea⟩ **b** : to undergo the process of soaking in a liquid **2** : to fill with or involve deeply ⟨*steeped* in learning⟩ **syn** see SOAK

steep·en \'stē-pən\ *vb* **steep·ened; steep·en·ing** \'stēp-(ə-)niŋ\ : to make or become steeper

stee·ple \'stē-pəl\ *n* **1** : a tall structure usually having a small spire at the top and built on top of a church tower **2** : a church tower — **stee·pled** \-pəld\ *adj*

stee·ple·chase \'stē-pəl-,chās\ *n* **1 a** : a race over the countryside on horses **b** : a horse race on a special course with obstacles (as hedges and walls) **2** : a footrace of usually 3,000 meters over hurdles and a water jump [so called from the fact that originally the races were across the countryside in a direct line toward a distant church steeple sighted rising above the other buildings] — **stee·ple·chas·er** \-,chā-sər\ *n*

¹steer \'sti(ə)r\ *n* **1** : a male bovine animal castrated before sexual maturity and especially one raised for beef **2** : an ox less than four years old

²steer *vb* **1** : to direct the course or the course of : GUIDE ⟨*steer* by the stars⟩ ⟨*steer* a boat⟩ ⟨*steer* a conversation⟩ **2** : to follow a course of action **3** : to be guided ⟨an automobile that *steers* well⟩ — **steer·able** \'stir-ə-bəl\ *adj* — **steer·er** \'stir-ər\ *n* — **steer clear** : to keep entirely away ⟨*steer clear* of arguments⟩

steer·age \'sti(ə)r-ij\ *n* **1** : the act or practice of steering; *also* : DIRECTION 1 **2** : a section in a passenger ship for passengers paying the lowest fares

steering wheel *n* : a wheel for steering something by hand

stego·sau·rus \,steg-ə-'sȯr-əs\ *n* : any of a genus of large armored dinosaurs whose fossil remains are found in the Upper Jurassic rocks of Colorado and Wyoming

stein \'stīn\ *n* : a pottery mug for beer

stel·lar \'stel-ər\ *adj* **1** : of or relating to the stars ⟨*stellar* light⟩ **2 a** : ¹PRINCIPAL, LEADING ⟨a *stellar* role⟩ **b** : OUTSTANDING 3 ⟨a *stellar* performance⟩

¹stem \'stem\ *n* **1 a** : the main stalk of a plant that develops buds and shoots and usually grows above the ground **b** : a plant part (as the stalk of a leaf or flower) that supports some other part **2** : the bow of a ship **3** : the basic part of a word to which prefixes or suffixes may be added **4** : something held to resemble a plant stem: as **a** : the short upright line from the head of a musical note **b** : the part of a tobacco pipe from the bowl outward [Old English *stefn, stemn* "stem of a plant, stem of a ship"] — **stem-**

less \-ləs\ *adj* — **from stem to stern** : [1]THROUGHOUT 1, THOROUGHLY

[2]**stem** *vb* **stemmed; stem·ming** **1** : to have or trace a beginning or growth : DERIVE **2** : to remove the stem from

[3]**stem** *vb* **stemmed; stem·ming** : to make progress against

[4]**stem** *vb* **stemmed; stem·ming** **1** : to stop or check by or as if by damming **2** : to become checked or stopped [Middle English *stemmen* "to dam up"; of Norse origin]

stemmed \'stemd\ *adj* : having a stem

stench \'stench\ *n* : a very disagreeable smell : STINK

[1]**sten·cil** \'sten(t)-səl\ *n* **1** : a piece of material (as a sheet of paper) with lettering or a design that is cut out and through which ink or paint is forced onto a surface to be printed **2** : a design or print produced with a stencil

stencil 1

[2]**stencil** *vb* **-ciled** *or* **-cilled; -cil·ing** *or* **-cil·ling** \-s(ə-)liŋ\ **1** : to paint with a stencil **2** : to produce by a stencil

steno \'sten-ō\ *n, pl* **sten·os** : STENOGRAPHER

ste·nog·ra·pher \stə-'näg-rə-fər\ *n* **1** : a writer of shorthand **2** : one employed chiefly to take and make a copy of dictation

ste·nog·ra·phy \stə-'näg-rə-fē\ *n* : the art or process of writing in shorthand — **steno·graph·ic** \,sten-ə-'graf-ik\ *adj* — **steno·graph·i·cal·ly** \-'graf-i-k(ə-)lē\ *adv*

sten·tor \'sten-,tȯ(ə)r, 'stent-ər\ *n* : any of a genus of trumpet-shaped one-celled animals that are protozoans living in fresh water and moving by means of cilia

sten·to·ri·an \sten-'tȯr-ē-ən, -'tȯr-\ *adj* : very loud ⟨a *stentorian* voice⟩ [so called from *Stentōr*, a Greek messenger at the time of the Trojan War noted for having a very loud voice]

[1]**step** \'step\ *n* **1** : a rest for the foot in going up or down : STAIR, RUNG **2 a** : a movement made by raising the foot and bringing it down elsewhere **b** : a combination of foot or foot and body movements in a repeated pattern **c** : manner of walking : STRIDE ⟨knows me by my *step*⟩ **d** : FOOTPRINT **e** : the sound of a footstep **3 a** : the space passed over in one step **b** : a short distance ⟨only a *step* away⟩ **c** : the height of one stair **4** *pl* : [1]COURSE 2, WAY ⟨guided their *steps* down the path⟩ **5 a** : a level or rank in a scale ⟨one *step* nearer graduation⟩ **b** : a stage in a process **6** : an action, proceeding, or measure often occurring as one in a series ⟨took *steps* to correct the situation⟩ **7** : a musical scale degree — **step·like** \-,līk\ *adj* — **stepped** \'stept\ *adj*

[2]**step** *vb* **stepped; step·ping** **1 a** : to move or take by raising the foot and bringing it down elsewhere or by moving each foot in order ⟨*step* three paces⟩ ⟨*stepped* ashore⟩ **b** : [1]DANCE 1 **2 a** : to go on foot : WALK ⟨*step* outside⟩ **b** : to move briskly ⟨really *stepped* along⟩ **3** : to press down with the foot ⟨*step* on a nail⟩ **4** : to come as if at a single step ⟨*step* into a good job⟩ **5** : to measure by steps — **step·per** *n*

step·broth·er \'step-,brəth-ər\ *n* : a son of one's stepparent by a past marriage

step–by–step \,step-bə-'step\ *adj* : GRADUAL

step·child \'step-,chīld\ *n* : a child of one's wife or husband by a past marriage

step·daugh·ter \-,dȯt-ər\ *n* : a daughter of one's wife or husband by a past marriage

step down \(')step-'daún\ *vb* **1** : to lower the voltage of (a current) using a transformer **2** : RESIGN 2, RETIRE — **step–down** \-,daún\ *adj*

step·fa·ther \'step-,fäth-ər\ *n* : the husband of one's mother by a later marriage

step–in \-,in\ *n* : an article of clothing (as a dress or shoes) that can be put on by being stepped into

step·lad·der \-,lad-ər\ *n* : a short ladder that has broad flat steps and two pairs of legs connected by a hinge at the top and that opens at the bottom to become freestanding

step·moth·er \-,məth-ər\ *n* : the wife of one's father by a later marriage

step out *vb* : to go away from a place usually for a short distance and for a short time

step·par·ent \'step-,par-ənt, -,per-\ *n* : the husband or wife of one's mother or father by a later marriage

steppe \'step\ *n* : land in regions of wide temperature range (as in southeastern Europe and parts of Asia) that is dry, usually rather level, and covered with grass

step·ping–stone \'step-iŋ-,stōn\ *n* **1** : a stone on which to step (as in crossing a stream) **2** : something aiding in progress or advancement

step·sis·ter \'step-,sis-tər\ *n* : a daughter of one's stepparent by a past marriage

step·son \-,sən\ *n* : a son of one's husband or wife by a past marriage

step stool *n* : a stool with one or two steps beneath the seat

step up *vb* **1** : to increase the voltage of (a current) using a transformer **2** : to increase or advance ⟨*step up* production⟩ — **step–up** \'step-,əp\ *adj*

-ster \stər\ *n combining form* **1** : one that does or handles or operates ⟨team*ster*⟩ **2** : one that makes or uses ⟨song*ster*⟩ ⟨prank*ster*⟩ **3** : one that is associated with or participates in ⟨gang*ster*⟩ **4** : one that is ⟨young*ster*⟩ [Old English *-estre* "female agent"]

[1]**ste·reo** \'ster-ē-,ō, 'stir-\ *n* **1** : stereophonic reproduction **2** : a stereophonic sound system

[2]**stereo** *adj* **1** : of or relating to the seeing of objects in three dimensions **2** : STEREOPHONIC

ste·reo·phon·ic \,ster-ē-ə-'fän-ik, ,stir-\ *adj* : of or relating to sound reproduction designed to create the effect of listening to the original

ste·re·op·ti·con \,ster-ē-'äp-ti-kən, ,stir-\ *n* : a projector for transparent slides

ste·reo·scope \'ster-ē-ə-,skōp, 'stir-\ *n* : an optical instrument that blends two slightly different pictures of the same subject to give the effect of depth — **ster·e·o·scop·ic** \,ster-ē-ə-'skäp-ik\ *adj*

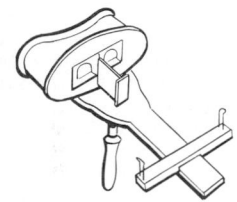
stereoscope

[1]**ste·reo·type** \'ster-ē-ə-,tīp, 'stir-\ *n* **1** : a printing plate made by casting melted metal in a mold **2** : something agreeing with a pattern; *esp* : an idea that many people have about a thing or a group and that may often be untrue or only partly true

[2]**stereotype** *vb* **1** : to make a stereotype from **2** : to develop a mental stereotype about

ste·reo·typed \'ster-ē-ə-,tīpt, 'stir-\ *adj* : following a pattern : lacking originality

ster·ile \'ster-əl\ *adj* **1** : not able to produce fruit, crops, or offspring : not fertile ⟨*sterile* soil⟩ **2** : free from living things and especially microbes ⟨a *sterile* dressing for a wound⟩ — **ste·ril·i·ty** \stə-'ril-ət-ē\ *n*

ster·il·ize \'ster-ə-,līz\ *vb* **-ized; -iz·ing** : to make sterile: as **a** : to deprive of the power of reproduction ⟨had their cat *sterilized*⟩ **b** : to free of living things and especially microbes (as bacteria) ⟨*sterilize* the dental instruments⟩ — **ster·il·iza·tion** \,ster-ə-lə-'zā-shən\ *n*

\ə\ abut	\aú\ out	\i\ tip	\ȯ\ saw	\ú\ foot
\ər\ further	\ch\ chin	\ī\ life	\ȯi\ coin	\y\ yet
\a\ mat	\e\ pet	\j\ job	\th\ thin	\yü\ few
\ā\ take	\ē\ easy	\ŋ\ sing	\th\ this	\yu̇\ cure
\ä\ cot, cart	\g\ go	\ō\ bone	\ü\ food	\zh\ vision

ster·il·iz·er \'ster-ə-,lī-zər\ *n* : one that sterilizes something; *esp* : a device used for sterilizing by steam, boiling water, or dry heat

¹ster·ling \'stər-liŋ\ *n* **1** : British money **2** : sterling silver or articles of it [so called from the phrase "a pound sterling", meaning the British pound as a monetary unit, but originally "a pound (by weight) of sterlings", from Middle English *sterling* "silver penny"]

²sterling *adj* **1** : of or relating to British sterling **2** : being or made of an alloy of 925 parts of silver with 75 parts of copper ⟨*sterling* silver⟩ **3** : EXCELLENT

¹stern \'stərn\ *adj* **1 a** : hard and severe in nature or manner ⟨a *stern* judge⟩ **b** : expressing severe displeasure : HARSH ⟨a *stern* look⟩ **2** : not inviting or attractive : FORBIDDING, GRIM **3** : firm and not changeable : STOUT, RESOLUTE ⟨*stern* determination⟩ — **stern·ly** *adv* — **stern·ness** \'stərn-nəs\ *n*

²stern *n* **1** : the rear end of a boat **2** : a rear part

ster·num \'stər-nəm\ *n, pl* **sternums** *or* **ster·na** \-nə\ : a flat narrow piece of bone or cartilage in the chest that connects the ribs in most vertebrates above the fishes — called also *breastbone*

stern–wheel·er \'stərn-'hwē-lər\ *n* : a paddle-wheel steamer having a stern wheel instead of side wheels

stetho·scope \'steth-ə-,skōp *also* 'steth-\ *n* : an instrument used for listening to sounds produced in the body and especially in the chest

Stet·son \'stet-sən\ *trademark* — used for a felt hat with a wide brim and high crown

ste·ve·dore \'stēv(-ə)-,dō(ə)r, -,dȯ(ə)r\ *n* : a person who loads and unloads boats in port [from Spanish *estibador* "stevedore", from *estibar* "to pack"]

stethoscope

¹stew \'st(y)ü\ *n* **1** : food (as meat with vegetables) prepared by slow boiling **2** : a state of excitement, worry, or confusion ⟨in a *stew* over nothing⟩

²stew *vb* **1** : to boil slowly : SIMMER **2** : to become excited or worried : FRET

stew·ard \'st(y)ü-ərd, 'st(y)ú(-ə)rd\ *n* **1** : a manager of a large home, estate, or organization **2 a** : a person employed to manage the supply and distribution of food (as on a ship) **b** : a worker who serves and attends the needs of passengers (as on a train, airplane, or ship) [Old English *stīweard*, literally "keeper of the hall, keeper of the sty", from *stī* "hall, sty" and *weard* "ward, guard, keeper"]

stew·ard·ess \'st(y)ü-ərd-əs, 'st(y)ú(-ə)rd-\ *n* : a woman who does the job of a steward; *esp* : one who attends the needs of passengers (as on an airplane)

stew·ard·ship \'st(y)ü-ərd-,ship, 'st(y)ú(-ə)rd-\ *n* : the office and duties of a steward

¹stick \'stik\ *n* **1** : a cut or broken branch of twig especially when dry and dead **2 a** : a long slender piece of wood : CLUB, STAFF **b** : WALKING STICK 1 **3** : something used for striking or moving an object in a game **4** : something like a stick in shape or use ⟨a *stick* of dynamite⟩ **5** : something prepared in a long and slender form ⟨carrot *sticks*⟩ ⟨a *stick* of butter⟩ **6** : a person who is dull or lifeless **7** *pl* : rural districts ⟨way out in the *sticks*⟩

²stick *vb* **stuck** \'stək\; **stick·ing** **1 a** : to stab with something pointed : PIERCE **b** : to kill by piercing **2** : to cause to penetrate ⟨*stuck* a needle in my finger⟩ **3 a** : to fasten by pushing in : ATTACH ⟨*stuck* a flower in my buttonhole⟩ **b** : to push out, up, or under ⟨*stuck* out my hand⟩ **4** : to put or set in a specified place or position ⟨*stuck* the cap on my head⟩ **5** : to cling to a surface ⟨snowflakes *stuck* on the windowpane⟩ **6 a** : to halt the movement or action of

b : ¹BAFFLE 1, STUMP ⟨were all *stuck* by the question⟩ **7 a** : ¹CHEAT 1, DEFRAUD **b** : to burden with something disagreeable ⟨*stuck* with the job of cleaning up⟩ **8** : to hold to something firmly by or as if by clinging ⟨car *stuck* in mud⟩ **9 a** : to remain in a place, situation, or environment **b** : to hold to something tightly : CLING **10** : to become blocked or jammed **11** : to be unable to proceed through fear or conscience

stick around *vb* : to stay or wait about : LINGER

stick·ball \'stik-,bȯl\ *n* : baseball played on the street or in a small area with a broomstick and a lightweight ball

stick·er \'stik-ər\ *n* **1** : something that pierces with a point **2 a** : something that clings or causes clinging **b** : a slip of paper with gummed back that clings to a surface — **stick·er·like** \-,līk\ *adj*

stick insect *n* : WALKINGSTICK 2

stick–in–the–mud \'stik-ən-the̱-,məd\ *n* : one who is slow, old-fashioned, or unprogressive

stick·le \'stik-əl\ *vb* **stick·led; stick·ling** \-(ə-)liŋ\ : to fight for something especially stubbornly

stick·le·back \'stik-əl-,bak\ *n* : any of numerous small scaleless fishes that have two or more sharp spines on the back

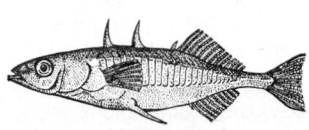

stickleback

stick·ler \'stik-(ə)lər\ *n* **1** : one who insists on exactness or completeness in the observance of something ⟨a *stickler* for the rules⟩ **2** : something that baffles or puzzles

stick out *vb* **1 a** : to extend out : PROJECT **b** : to be noticeable **2** : to put up with : ENDURE ⟨*stuck* it *out* to the bitter end⟩

stick·pin \'stik-,pin\ *n* : an ornamental pin worn in a necktie

stick·tight \-,tīt\ *n* : BUR MARIGOLD

stick up \'stik-'əp\ *vb* : to rob at the point of a gun — **stick·up** \-,əp\ *n*

sticky \'stik-ē\ *adj* **stick·i·er; -est** **1 a** : ¹ADHESIVE, GLUEY **b** : coated with a sticky substance **2** : MUGGY, HUMID **3** : tending to stick ⟨*sticky* windows⟩ — **stick·i·ly** \'stik-ə-lē\ *adv* — **stick·i·ness** \'stik-ē-nəs\ *n*

stiff \'stif\ *adj* **1 a** : not easily bent : RIGID **b** : not easily moved ⟨*stiff* muscles⟩ ⟨*stiff* valves⟩ **2 a** : ¹FIRM 3, RESOLUTE **b** : not easy or graceful in manner **3** : hard fought ⟨a *stiff* fight⟩ **4 a** : STRONG 1, VIGOROUS ⟨*stiff* wind⟩ **b** : POTENT 2b ⟨a *stiff* dose⟩ **5** : not flowing easily : THICK, HEAVY ⟨beat egg whites until *stiff*⟩ **6 a** : HARSH 3, SEVERE ⟨a *stiff* penalty⟩ **b** : difficult to do ⟨a *stiff* task⟩ **7** : EXPENSIVE 2, STEEP ⟨a *stiff* price⟩ — **stiff·ly** *adv* — **stiff·ness** *n*

stiff·en \'stif-ən\ *vb* **stiff·ened; stiff·en·ing** \-(ə-)niŋ\ : to make or become stiff or stiffer — **stiff·en·er** \-(ə-)nər\ *n*

sti·fle \'stī-fəl\ *vb* **sti·fled; sti·fling** \-f(ə-)liŋ\ : to kill by depriving of or die from lack of oxygen or air **1** : SMOTHER **2** : to keep in check by deliberate effort : REPRESS ⟨trying to *stifle* a sneeze⟩ — **sti·fling·ly** \-f(ə-)liŋ-lē\ *adv*

stig·ma \'stig-mə\ *n, pl* **stig·ma·ta** \stig-'mät-ə, 'stig-mət-ə\ *or* **stigmas** **1** : a mark of shame : STAIN **b** : an identifying mark or characteristic; *esp* : a specific sign that indicates the presence of a disease **2** *pl* : bodily marks or pains resembling the wounds of Christ when nailed on the cross **3 a** : a small spot, scar, or opening on a plant or animal **b** : the upper part of the pistil of a flower which receives the pollen grains and on which they start to grow — **stig·mat·ic** \stig-'mat-ik\ *adj*

stig·ma·tize \'stig-mə-,tīz\ *vb* **-tized; -tiz·ing** : to mark with a stigma; *esp* : to describe or identify as disgraceful

stile \'stī(ə)l\ *n* **1** : a step or set of steps for passing over a fence or wall **2** : TURNSTILE

sti·let·to \stə-'let-ō\ *n, pl* **-tos** *or* **-toes** : a slender dagger

¹still \'stil\ *adj* **1 a** : having no motion **b** : of, relating to, or being an ordinary photograph rather than a motion picture   **2** : uttering no sound : QUIET   **3 a** : TRANQUIL, CALM   **b** : free from noise or commotion : PEACEFUL [Old English *stille* "not moving"] — **still·ness** *n*

²**still** *vb*   **1 a** : ALLAY 2, CALM   **b** : to put to an end : SETTLE   **2** : to make or become still : QUIET

³**still** *adv*   **1** : without motion ⟨sit *still*⟩   **2** : up to this or that time ⟨*still* lives there⟩ ⟨while it's *still* hot⟩   **3** : in spite of that : NEVERTHELESS ⟨those who take care can *still* make mistakes⟩   **4 a** : ³EVEN 4 ⟨a *still* more difficult problem⟩   **b** : beyond this : IN ADDITION, YET ⟨won *still* another tournament⟩

⁴**still** *n*   **1** : ¹QUIET, SILENCE   **2** : a still photograph

⁵**still** *n*   **1** : DISTILLERY   **2** : a device used in distillation [from earlier *still* (verb) "to distill", from Middle English *stillen*, a shortened form of *distillen* "to distill"]

still·birth \'stil-,bərth, -'bərth\ *n* : the birth of a dead baby

still·born \-'bó(ə)rn\ *adj* : dead at birth

still life *n*, *pl* **still lifes** \-'līfs, -'līvz\ : a picture of an arrangement of objects

stil·ly \'stil-ē\ *adj* : showing stillness : CALM, QUIET

stilt \'stilt\ *n*   **1** : one of two poles each with a rest or strap for the foot used to elevate the wearer above the ground in walking   **2** : a stake or post used to support a structure above ground or water level

stilt·ed \'stil-təd\ *adj* : not easy and natural ⟨a *stilted* speech⟩

stim·u·lant \'stim-yə-lənt\ *n*   **1** : something (as a drug) that temporarily increases the activity or efficiency of the body or one of its parts ⟨a heart *stimulant*⟩   **2** : STIMULUS 1 — **stimulant** *adj*

stim·u·late \'stim-yə-,lāt\ *vb* **-lat·ed; -lat·ing**   **1** : to make active or more active : ANIMATE, AROUSE ⟨*stimulate* industry⟩   **2** : to act toward as a bodily stimulus or stimulant   **syn** see PROVOKE

stim·u·la·tion \,stim-yə-'lā-shən\ *n* : the act or result of stimulating

stim·u·lus \'stim-yə-ləs\ *n*, *pl* **-li** \-,lī, -,lē\   **1** : something that rouses or stirs to action : INCENTIVE   **2** : something (as an environmental change) that acts to partly change bodily activity (as by exciting a sensory organ) ⟨heat, light, and sound are common physical *stimuli*⟩

¹**sting** \'stiŋ\ *vb* **stung** \'stəŋ\; **sting·ing** \'stiŋ-iŋ\   **1 a** : to prick painfully especially with a sharp or poisonous stinger ⟨*stung* by a bee⟩   **b** : to affect with or feel quick piercing pain or smart ⟨hail *stung* their faces⟩   **2** : to cause to suffer mentally ⟨*stung* with regret⟩   **3** : OVERCHARGE 1, CHEAT ⟨got *stung* on the deal⟩   **4** : to use a stinger

²**sting** *n*   **1 a** : the act of stinging   **b** : a wound or pain caused by or as if by stinging   **2** : STINGER 2 — **sting·less** \'stiŋ-ləs\ *adj*

sting·er \'stiŋ-ər\ *n*   **1** : one that stings; *esp* : a piercing blow or remark   **2** : a sharp organ of some animals (as bees or scorpions) that is used to wound, paralyze, or kill prey or an enemy by piercing and injecting a poisonous fluid

sting·ray \'stiŋ-,rā\ *n* : any of numerous rays that have one or more large sharp stinging spines near the base of the whip-like tail

stin·gy \'stin-jē\ *adj* **stin·gi·er; -est**   **1** : not generous : giving or spending as little as possible   **2** : SCANTY, MEAGER ⟨*stingy* portion⟩ — **stin·gi·ly** \-jə-lē\ *adv* — **stin·gi·ness** \-jē-nəs\ *n*

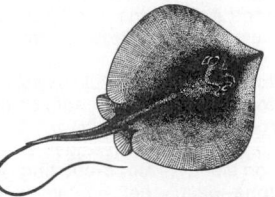
stingray

¹**stink** \'stiŋk\ *vb* **stank** \'staŋk\ *or* **stunk** \'stəŋk\; **stunk; stink·ing**   **1** : to give or cause to have an unpleasant smell   **2** : to be of very bad quality — **stink·er** *n*

²**stink** *n*   **1** : a strong unpleasant odor : STENCH   **2** : a public outcry against something thought to be bad — **stinky** \'stiŋ-kē\ *adj*

stink·bug \'stiŋk-,bəg\ *n* : any of various true bugs that give off a bad smell

¹**stint** \'stint\ *vb*   **1** : to be sparing or stingy   **2** : to limit in share or allowance — **stint·er** *n*

²**stint** *n*   **1** : RESTRICTION 1, LIMITATION ⟨gave without *stint*⟩   **2** : a quantity of work assigned

stipe \'stīp\ *n* : a short stalk supporting the cap of a mushroom

sti·pend \'stī-,pend, -pənd\ *n* : a sum of money paid at regular times for services or expenses

stip·ple \'stip-əl\ *vb* **stip·pled; stip·pling** \-(ə-)liŋ\ : to apply (as paint or ink) by repeated small touches — **stipple** *n* — **stip·pler** \-(ə-)lər\ *n*

stip·u·late \'stip-yə-,lāt\ *vb* **-lat·ed; -lat·ing** : to demand or insist on as part of an agreement

stip·u·la·tion \,stip-yə-'lā-shən\ *n* : something required as part of an agreement

stip·ule \'stip-yü(ə)l\ *n* : either of a pair of small leaflike parts at the base of the leaf in many plants — see LEAF illustration

¹**stir** \'stər\ *vb* **stirred; stir·ring**   **1 a** : to make or cause to make an especially small movement or change of position   **b** : to disturb the quiet of : AGITATE   **2** : to mix, dissolve, or make especially by a continued circular movement   **3** : to rouse to action : INCITE, QUICKEN ⟨*stir* up trouble⟩   **4** : to be active or busy ⟨not a creature was *stirring*⟩ — **stir·rer** *n*

²**stir** *n*   **1 a** : a state of disturbance, upset, or action   **b** : widespread notice and discussion : IMPRESSION   **2** : a small movement   **3** : a stirring movement

stir–fry \'stər-'frī\ *vb* : to fry quickly over high heat while stirring continuously

stir·ring \'stər-iŋ\ *adj* : LIVELY 3, MOVING

stir·rup \'stər-əp *also* 'stir-əp *or* 'stə-rəp\ *n*   **1** : either of a pair of small light frames often of metal hung by straps from a saddle and used as a support for the foot of a horseback rider   **2** : the innermost bone of the chain of three small bones in the ears of a mammal — called also *stapes*

¹**stitch** \'stich\ *n*   **1** : a sudden sharp pain especially in the side   **2 a** : one in-and-out movement of a threaded needle in sewing or embroidering   **b** : a portion of thread left in the material after one stitch   **3** : a single loop of thread or yarn around a tool (as a knitting needle)   **4** : a series of stitches — **in stitches** : in a state of uncontrollable laughter

²**stitch** *vb*   **1 a** : to join with or as if with stitches   **b** : to make, mend, or decorate with or as if with stitches   **2** : to do needlework : SEW — **stitch·er** *n*

stoat \'stōt\ *n* : the European ermine especially in its brown summer coat

¹**stock** \'stäk\ *n*   **1 a** : ¹STUMP 2   **b** *archaic* : a log or block of wood   **c** : something without life or consciousness   **d** : a dull, stupid, or lifeless person   **2 a** *pl* : a timber frame with holes to contain the feet or feet and hands of a wrong-doer as public punishment   **b** : the part of a crossbow or

\ə\ **abut**	\au̇\ **out**	\i\ **tip**	\ȯ\ **saw**	\u̇\ **foot**
\ər\ **further**	\ch\ **chin**	\ī\ **life**	\ȯi\ **coin**	\y\ **yet**
\a\ **mat**	\e\ **pet**	\j\ **job**	\th\ **thin**	\yü\ **few**
\ā\ **take**	\ē\ **easy**	\ŋ\ **sing**	\th\ **this**	\yu̇\ **cure**
\ä\ **cot, cart**	\g\ **go**	\ō\ **bone**	\ü\ **food**	\zh\ **vision**

long gun that is held against the shoulder or in the hand when in use **3 a :** the main stem of a plant : TRUNK **b :** a plant or plant part that will produce mostly underground parts in a graft **4 a :** the original (as a human being, race, or language) from which others descend : SOURCE **b :** ANCESTRY 2, LINEAGE **5 a :** the equipment or goods of an establishment **b :** farm animals : LIVESTOCK **6 a :** the ownership element of a corporation divided to give the owners an interest and usually voting power **b :** a portion of such stock **7 :** a wide band or scarf worn about the neck **8 a :** liquid in which meat, fish, or vegetables have been simmered and which is used to make soup, stew, or gravy **b :** RAW MATERIAL **9 :** confidence placed in one **10 :** the production and presentation of plays by a stock company — **in stock** : in the store and ready for delivery

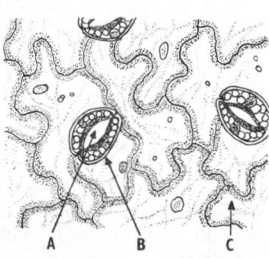

S stock 3b

²**stock** *vb* **1 :** to fit to or with a stock **2 :** to provide with or acquire stock or a stock ⟨*stock* up on food⟩ **3 :** to get or keep a stock of ⟨a store that *stocks* only the finest goods⟩

³**stock** *adj* **1 :** kept regularly in stock ⟨a *stock* model⟩ **2** : commonly used or brought forward : STANDARD ⟨the *stock* answer⟩

¹**stock·ade** \stä-'kād\ *n* **1 :** a line of stout posts set firmly to form a defense **2 a :** an enclosure or pen made with posts and stakes **b :** an enclosure in which prisoners are kept

²**stockade** *vb* **stock·ad·ed; stock·ad·ing :** to protect or surround with a stockade

stock·bro·ker \'stäk-ˌbrō-kər\ *n* **:** one that handles orders to buy and sell stocks

stock car *n* **:** a racing car that is similar to regular cars

stock company *n* **1 :** a corporation whose resources are represented by stock **2 :** a theatrical company without outstanding stars

stock exchange *n* **1 :** a place where the buying and selling of stocks is conducted **2 :** an association of stockbrokers

stock·fish \'stäk-ˌfish\ *n* **:** fish (as cod, haddock, or hake) dried hard in the open air without salt

stock·hold·er \'stäk-ˌhōl-dər\ *n* **:** an owner of stocks

stock·ing \'stäk-iŋ\ *n* **:** a close-fitting usually knit covering for the foot and leg

stocking cap *n* **:** a long knitted cone-shaped cap usually with an ornament at the pointed end

stock market *n* **:** STOCK EXCHANGE 1

stock·pile \'stäk-ˌpīl\ *n* **:** an extra supply especially of something necessary accumulated within a country for use during a shortage — **stockpile** *vb*

stock·room \-ˌrüm, -ˌru̇m\ *n* **:** a storage place for supplies or goods used in a business

stock–still \-'stil\ *adj* **:** very still : MOTIONLESS

stocky \'stäk-ē\ *adj* **stock·i·er; -est :** compact, sturdy, and quite thick in build : THICKSET — **stock·i·ly** \'stäk-ə-lē\ *adv*

stock·yard \'stäk-ˌyärd\ *n* **:** a yard in which livestock are kept temporarily for slaughter, market, or shipping

stodgy \'stäj-ē\ *adj* **stodg·i·er; -est 1 :** moving in a slow struggling way especially as a result of physical bulkiness **2 :** having no excitement or interest : DULL, BORING **3** : very old-fashioned in attitude or point of view — **stodg·i·ly** \'stäj-ə-lē\ *adv*

¹**sto·ic** \'stō-ik\ *n* **:** one not easily excited or upset

²**stoic** *or* **sto·i·cal** \'stō-i-kəl\ *adj* **:** unconcerned about pleasure or pain — **sto·ical·ly** \-i-k(ə-)lē\ *adv*

stoke \'stōk\ *vb* **stoked; stok·ing 1 :** to stir up or tend (as a fire) **2 :** to supply (as a furnace) with fuel **3 :** to feed plentifully — **stok·er** *n*

¹**stole** \'stōl\ *past of* STEAL

²**stole** *n* **1 :** a long narrow band worn around the neck by bishops and priests in ceremonies **2 :** a long wide scarf or similar covering worn by women usually across the shoulders

stolen *past participle of* STEAL

stol·id \'stäl-əd\ *adj* **:** having or expressing little or no feeling : not easily stirred or excited — **stol·id·ly** *adv*

sto·lon \'stō-lən, -ˌlän\ *n* **1 :** a horizontal branch from the base of a plant that produces new plants from buds at its tip or nodes (as in the strawberry) **2 :** an extension of the body wall of some lower animals (as hydrozoans) producing buds that form new individuals

sto·ma \'stō-mə\ *n, pl* **sto·ma·ta** \-mət-ə\ **:** a small opening which is surrounded by two guard cells and through which moisture and gases pass in and out of the epidermis of a leaf

¹**stom·ach** \'stəm-ək, -ik\ *n* **1 a :** a pouch of the vertebrate digestive system into which food goes for further mixing and digestion after it leaves the mouth and passes down the throat

A stoma; *B* guard cell; *C* leaf epidermis cell

b : a cavity with a similar function in an invertebrate animal **c :** the part of the body that contains the stomach : BELLY, ABDOMEN **2 a :** desire for food caused by hunger : APPETITE **b :** ²DESIRE 1, INCLINATION ⟨had no *stomach* for a quarrel⟩

²**stomach** *vb* **:** TOLERATE 1 ⟨could not *stomach* the smell⟩

stom·ach·ache \'stəm-ək-ˌāk, -ik-\ *n* **:** pain in or near the stomach

stom·ach·er \'stəm-i-kər\ *n* **:** the center front section of an upper part of a woman's dress appearing between the laces of an outer garment (as in 16th century costume)

sto·mate \'stō-ˌmāt\ *n* **:** STOMA

stomp \'stämp, 'stȯmp\ *vb* **:** ¹STAMP 2 ⟨*stomped* angrily out of the room⟩ — **stomp** *n* — **stomp·er** *n*

¹**stone** \'stōn\ *n* **1 a :** earth or mineral matter hardened in a mass **b :** a piece of rock not as fine as gravel ⟨throw *stones*⟩ **c :** a piece of rock used for some special purpose (as for a monument or in construction) **d :** GEM 1b **2 a :** CALCULUS 1 **b :** a stony seed or one (as of a plum) enclosed in a stony cover **3** *pl usually* **stone :** any of various units of weight; *esp* **:** a British unit equal to 14 pounds (6.3 kilograms)

²**stone** *adj* **:** of, relating to, or made of stone

³**stone** *vb* **stoned; ston·ing 1 :** to throw stones at; *esp* : to kill by hitting with stones **2 :** to remove the stones of (a fruit) — **ston·er** *n*

Stone Age *n* **:** the oldest period in which human beings are known to have existed : the age during which stone tools were used

stone–blind \'stōn-'blīnd\ *adj* **:** totally blind

stone–broke \-'brōk\ *adj* **:** completely broke

stone·cut·ter \-ˌkət-ər\ *n* **1 :** a person who cuts, carves, or puts a finish on stone **2 :** a machine for putting a finish on stone — **stone·cut·ting** \-ˌkət-iŋ\ *n*

stone–deaf \-'def\ *adj* **:** totally deaf

stone fly *n* **:** any of an order of 4-winged insects of which the immature stages have gills and live in water and the adults are useful to fishermen for bait

stone–ground \'stōn-'grau̇nd\ *adj* **:** ground by the use of millstones ⟨*stone-ground* flour⟩

stone·ma·son \'stōn-ˌmās-ᵊn\ *n* **:** a mason who builds with stone

stone·ware \-ˌwa(ə)r, -ˌwe(ə)r\ *n* **:** a clay pottery used for storage utensils, tile, and ornamental wares

stone·work \-,wərk\ *n* **1** : a structure or part built of stone : MASONRY **2** : the shaping, preparation, or setting of stone — **stone·work·er** *n*

stony *also* **ston·ey** \'stō-nē\ *adj* **ston·i·er; -est** **1 a** : full of stones ⟨*stony* soil⟩ **b** : hard as stone ⟨a *stony* seed⟩ **2** : PITILESS, UNFEELING ⟨a *stony* stare⟩ — **ston·i·ly** \'stōn-°l-ē\ *adv*

stood *past and past participle of* STAND

stooge \'stüj\ *n* **1** : one who follows or serves another without thinking **2** : an actor who usually by asking questions prepares the way for a principal comedian's jokes — **stooge** *vb*

stool \'stül\ *n* **1 a** : a seat without back or arms supported by three or four legs or by a central post **b** : FOOTSTOOL **2 a** : a seat used while urinating or having a bowel movement **b** : a mass of bodily waste discharged from the intestine in a bowel movement

stool pigeon *n* : a person acting as a spy or informer for the police [from earlier *stool pigeon* "a pigeon tied to a stool and used as a decoy to draw other birds into a net"]

¹stoop \'stüp\ *vb* **1 a** : to bend down or over **b** : to carry the head and shoulders or the upper part of the body bent forward **2** : to degrade oneself ⟨*stoop* to lying⟩ [Old English *stūpian* "to stoop, bend over"]

²stoop *n* **1** : an act of bending the body forward **2** : a forward bend of the back and shoulders that is temporary or by habit

³stoop *n* : a porch, platform, or entrance stairway at a house door [from Dutch *stoep* "porch, stoop"]

¹stop \'stäp\ *vb* **stopped; stop·ping** **1** : to close an opening by filling or blocking it : PLUG ⟨nose *stopped* up by a cold⟩ **2** : RESTRAIN 1a ⟨*stopped* me from going⟩ **3** : to interrupt or prevent from continuing or occurring : CHECK **4** : to instruct one's bank not to pay ⟨*stop* payment on a check⟩ **5** : to halt the movement or progress of ⟨*stop* the car⟩ **6** : to change the pitch of (as a violin string) by pressing with the finger **7 a** : to bring action or operation to an end **b** : to come to an end **8** : to make a visit ⟨*stopping* with friends for a week⟩

²stop *n* **1** : CESSATION, END **2 a** : a series of similar organ pipes that vary by pitch but have the same tone quality **b** : STOP KNOB **3** : something that delays, blocks, or brings to a halt : IMPEDIMENT, OBSTACLE **4** : a device for halting or limiting motion ⟨door was held open by a *stop*⟩ **5** : the act of stopping : the state of being stopped **6** : a halt in a journey : STAY **7** : a stopping place ⟨a bus *stop*⟩ **8** *chiefly British* : any of several punctuation marks **9** : a consonant in the uttering of which there is a step (as in the "p" of "apt" or the "g" of "tiger") when the breath passage is completely closed

³stop *adj* : serving to stop : designed to stop ⟨*stop* line⟩ ⟨*stop* signal⟩

stop bath *n* : an acid bath used to stop the development of a photographic negative or print

stop·cock \'stäp-,käk\ *n* : a faucet for stopping or regulating flow (as through a pipe)

stop·gap \'stäp-,gap\ *n* : something that fills a gap : a temporary substitute

stop knob *n* : one of the handles by which an organist draws or shuts off a particular stop

stop·light \'stäp-,līt\ *n* : TRAFFIC SIGNAL

stop·over \-,ō-vər\ *n* **1** : a stop in the course of one's journey **2** : a stopping place on a journey

stop·page \'stäp-ij\ *n* : the act of stopping : the state of being stopped

¹stop·per \'stäp-ər\ *n* **1** : one that brings to a halt : CHECK

stopcock

2 : one that closes, shuts, or fills up; *esp* : something used to plug an opening

²stopper *vb* : to close or fasten with or as if with a stopper

stop·watch \'stäp-,wäch\ *n* : a watch having a hand that can be started and stopped for exact timing (as of a race)

stor·age \'stōr-ij, 'stȯr-\ *n* **1 a** : space or a place for storing **b** : an amount stored **c** : MEMORY 5 **2 a** : the act of storing : the state of being stored **b** : the price charged for storing something

storage battery *n* : a cell or connected group of cells that converts chemical energy into electrical energy by reversible chemical reactions and that may be recharged by passing a current through it in the direction opposite to that of its discharge — called also *storage cell*

¹store \'stō(ə)r, 'stȯ(ə)r\ *vb* **stored; stor·ing** **1** : to provide with what is needed : FURNISH, SUPPLY ⟨*store* a ship with provisions⟩ **2** : LAY AWAY, ACCUMULATE ⟨*store* vegetables for winter use⟩ **3 a** : to deposit in a place (as a warehouse) for safekeeping or disposal ⟨*stored* my furniture until I found a new apartment⟩ **b** : to record information in a device (as a computer) — **stor·able** \'stōr-ə-bəl, 'stȯr-\ *adj*

²store *n* **1 a** : something stored ⟨a *store* of good jokes⟩ **b** : accumulated supplies (as of food) : STOCK ⟨a ship's *stores*⟩ **2** : ¹VALUE 3, IMPORTANCE ⟨a family that set great *store* by tradition⟩ **3** : a place where goods are sold : SHOP — **in store** : ready for use or action

³store *adj* : purchased from a store : READY-MADE ⟨*store* clothes⟩ ⟨*store* bread⟩

store·house \'stō(ə)r-,haus, 'stȯ(ə)r-\ *n* **1** : a building for storing goods **2** : a large supply : REPOSITORY

store·keep·er \-,kē-pər\ *n* **1** : one who is in charge of stores **2** : one who manages a store or shop

store·room \-,rüm, -,rüm\ *n* : a room for the storing of goods or supplies

store·wide \-'wīd\ *adj* : including all or most merchandise in a store ⟨a *storewide* sale⟩

¹sto·ried \'stōr-ēd, 'stȯr-\ *adj* **1** : decorated with designs representing scenes from story or history **2** : having an interesting history ⟨a *storied* castle⟩

²storied *or* **sto·reyed** \'stōr-ēd, 'stȯr-\ *adj* : having stories ⟨a two-*storied* house⟩

stork \'stȯ(ə)rk\ *n* : any of various large mostly Old World wading birds that have long stout bills, are related to the herons and ibises, and include one that often nests on roofs and chimneys

stork

¹storm \'stȯ(ə)rm\ *n* **1 a** : a disturbance of the atmosphere accompanied by wind and usually by rain, snow, hail, sleet, or thunder and lightning **b** : a heavy fall of rain, snow, or hail **c** : a serious disturbance of any element of nature **2** : a disturbed state : a sudden or violent commotion **3** : a heavy discharge of objects or actions ⟨fired a *storm* of arrows at the castle⟩ **4** : a violent outburst ⟨a *storm* of protest⟩ **5** : a violent attack on a defended position ⟨taken by *storm*⟩

²storm *vb* **1 a** : to blow with violence **b** : to rain, hail, snow, or sleet heavily **2** : to attack by storm ⟨*stormed* ashore⟩ ⟨*storm* the fort⟩ **3** : to show violent feeling : RAGE ⟨*storming* at the unusual delay⟩ **4** : to rush about vio-

\ə\ abut	\au̇\ out	\i\ tip	\o̅\ saw	\u̇\ foot
\ər\ further	\ch\ chin	\ī\ life	\oi\ coin	\y\ yet
\a\ mat	\e\ pet	\j\ job	\th\ thin	\yü\ few
\ā\ take	\ē\ easy	\ŋ\ sing	\th\ this	\yu̇\ cure
\ä\ cot, cart	\g\ go	\ō\ bone	\ü\ food	\zh\ vision

lently ⟨the mob *stormed* through the streets⟩

storm window *n* : a glass window that is placed outside an ordinary window as a protection against severe weather

stormy \'stȯr-mē\ *adj* **storm·i·er; -est** **1** : relating to, marked by, or being a sign of a storm ⟨a *stormy* day⟩ ⟨*stormy* skies⟩ **2** : displaying anger and excitement ⟨a *stormy* conference⟩ — **storm·i·ly** \-mə-lē\ *adv* — **storm·i·ness** \-mē-nəs\ *n*

stormy petrel *n* : a person who is fond of conflict or disagreement

¹sto·ry \'stōr-ē, 'stȯr-\ *n, pl* **stories** **1 a** : an account of incidents or events **b** : ANECDOTE **2 a** : a fictional tale shorter than a novel; *esp* : SHORT STORY **b** : the main tale of a written work **3** : a widely told rumor **4** : FIB, LIE, FALSEHOOD **5** : a news article or broadcast

²story *also* **sto·rey** \'stōr-ē, 'stȯr-\ *n, pl* **stories** *also* **storeys** : a set of rooms or an area making up one floor level of a building

sto·ry·tell·er \'stōr-ē-ˌtel-ər, 'stȯr-\ *n* : a teller of stories

stoup \'stüp\ *n* **1** : a container (as a large glass) for beverages **2** : a basin for holy water at the entrance of a church

¹stout \'staủt\ *adj* **1** : strong of character : BRAVE, BOLD **2** : physically or materially strong : STURDY, VIGOROUS **3** : FORCEFUL **4** : bulky in body : THICKSET — **stout·ly** *adv* — **stout·ness** *n*

²stout *n* : a dark heavy beer

stout·heart·ed \'staủt-'härt-əd\ *adj* : COURAGEOUS, BOLD — **stout·heart·ed·ly** *adv*

¹stove \'stōv\ *n* **1** : an appliance that burns fuel or uses electricity to provide heat (as for cooking or heating) **2** : KILN

²stove *past and past participle of* ²STAVE

stove·pipe \'stōv-ˌpīp\ *n* **1** : a metal pipe for carrying off smoke from a stove **2** : a tall silk hat

stow \'stō\ *vb* **1** : to put away : STORE **2 a** : ARRANGE 1, PACK **b** : ²LOAD 1a **3** : to cram in ⟨*stow* away a meal⟩

stow·age \'stō-ij\ *n* **1 a** : an act or process of stowing **b** : goods stowed or to be stowed **2 a** : ability to store **b** : a place for storage

stow·away \'stō-ə-ˌwā\ *n* : one who stows away : an unregistered passenger

stow away \ˌstō-ə-'wā\ *vb* : to hide aboard a vehicle to obtain transportation

¹strad·dle \'strad-ᵊl\ *vb* **strad·dled; strad·dling** \'strad-liŋ, -ᵊl-iŋ\ **1** : to stand, sit, or walk with the legs wide apart **2** : to approve or seem to approve two apparently opposite sides ⟨*straddle* a question⟩ — **strad·dler** \-lər, -ᵊl-ər\ *n*

²straddle *n* : the act or position of one that straddles

strafe \'strāf\ *vb* **strafed; straf·ing** : to fire on at close range and especially with machine guns from low-flying airplanes ⟨*strafed* the village⟩ — **straf·er** *n*

strag·gle \'strag-əl\ *vb* **strag·gled; strag·gling** \-(ə-)liŋ\ **1** : to wander from a course or way : ROVE, STRAY **2** : to trail off from others of its kind — **strag·gler** \-(ə-)lər\ *n*

¹straight \'strāt\ *adj* **1** : free from curves, bends, angles, or unevenness ⟨*straight* hair⟩ ⟨*straight* timber⟩ **2 a** : holding to a proper course or method ⟨*straight* thinker⟩ **b** : FRANK, CANDID ⟨a *straight* answer⟩ **3 a** : exhibiting truth, fairness, and honesty : JUST, VIRTUOUS **b** : correctly ordered or arranged ⟨set the kitchen *straight*⟩ **c** : having nothing added ⟨*straight* humor without a serious purpose⟩ **d** : making no exceptions in one's voting for a political party **e** : not varying ⟨*straight* pay⟩ **f** : CONVENTIONAL **g** : not using or under the influence of drugs **h** : ¹HETEROSEXUAL **4** : being the only form of payment ⟨on *straight* commission⟩ — **straight·ness** *n*

²straight *adv* : in a straight manner, course, or line

¹straight·away \'strāt-ə-ˌwā\ *adj* **1** : proceeding in a straight line : continuous in direction : STRAIGHTFORWARD **2** : IMMEDIATE 4 ⟨made a *straightaway* reply⟩

²straightaway *n* : the straight part of a racetrack : STRETCH

³straight·away \ˌstrāt-ə-'wā\ *adv* : without delay : IMMEDIATELY

straight·edge \'strāt-ˌej\ *n* : a bar or piece of wood, metal, or plastic with a straight edge for testing straight lines and surfaces or drawing straight lines

straight·en \'strāt-ᵊn\ *vb* **straight·ened; straight·en·ing** \'strāt-niŋ, -ᵊn-iŋ\ : to make or become straight — usually used with *up* or *out* ⟨*straighten* up a room⟩ ⟨*straightened* out the problem⟩ — **straight·en·er** \'strāt-nər, -ᵊn-ər\ *n*

straight face *n* : a face giving no evidence of feeling and especially of amusement — **straight–faced** \'strāt-'fāst\ *adj*

¹straight·for·ward \(')strāt-'fȯr-wərd\ *adj* **1** : OUTSPOKEN, CANDID ⟨a *straightforward* reply⟩ **2** : proceeding in a straight course or manner : DIRECT — **straight·for·ward·ly** *adv* — **straight·for·ward·ness** *n*

²straightforward *also* **straight·for·wards** \-wərdz\ *adv* : in a straightforward manner

straight line *n* : the path of a point moving always in the same direction

straight·way \'strāt-'wā, -ˌwā\ *adv* : IMMEDIATELY 2, FORTHWITH

¹strain \'strān\ *n* **1 a** : LINEAGE, ANCESTRY **b** : a group of plants or animals that look alike but have characteristics (as the ability to resist disease) that make them slightly different : VARIETY 3b ⟨a strong *strain* of winter wheat⟩ **2 a** : a quality or disposition that is natural or runs through a family ⟨a *strain* of madness in the family⟩ **b** : a small amount : TRACE, STREAK ⟨a *strain* of sadness⟩ **3** : MELODY 2, TUNE, AIR **4** : the manner or style of something said or of a course of action or conduct

²strain *vb* **1 a** : to draw tight : cause to clasp firmly **b** : to stretch to maximum extension and tightness **2 a** : to try one's hardest : STRIVE **b** : to injure or be injured by overuse, misuse, or pressure ⟨*strained* the heart by overwork⟩ ⟨*strain* one's back by lifting⟩ **3 a** : to pass or cause to pass through or as if through a strainer : FILTER **b** : to remove by straining ⟨*strain* lumps out of the gravy⟩ **4** : to stretch beyond a proper limit ⟨*strain* the truth⟩

³strain *n* **1** : an act of straining or the state of being strained **2** : bodily injury caused by too much tension, effort, or use ⟨heart *strain*⟩; *esp* : one resulting from a wrench or twist and involving severe stretching of muscles or ligaments ⟨back *strain*⟩

strained \'strānd\ *adj* **1** : not easy or natural : FORCED ⟨a *strained* smile⟩ **2** : brought close to war ⟨*strained* relations between countries⟩

strain·er \'strā-nər\ *n* : one that strains; *esp* : a device (as a screen or filter) to hold solid pieces while a liquid passes through

strait \'strāt\ *n* **1 a** : a narrow channel connecting two large bodies of water — often used in pl. **b** : ISTHMUS **2 a** : a situation of confusion or distress — often used in pl. ⟨in difficult *straits*⟩

strait·en \'strāt-ᵊn\ *vb* **strait·ened; strait·en·ing** \'strāt-niŋ, -ᵊn-iŋ\ : to limit or restrict especially in resources ⟨*straitened* by misfortune⟩

strait·jack·et *also* **straight·jack·et** \'strāt-ˌjak-ət\ *n* : a cover or outer garment of strong material (as canvas) used to restrict the movement of the arms as a means of controlling a violent prisoner or patient

strait·laced *or* **straight·laced** \'strāt-'lāst\ *adj* : very strict or proper in actions, beliefs, or point of view

¹strand \'strand\ *n* : the land bordering a body of water : SHORE, BEACH [Old English *strand* "shore"]

²strand *vb* **1** : to run aground : BEACH **2** : to leave in a strange or an unfavorable place especially without a way of departing ⟨*stranded* in a strange city⟩

³strand *n* **1** : one of the fibers, threads, strings, or wires twisted or braided to make a cord, rope, or cable **2** : something resembling a strand ⟨a *strand* of pearls⟩ ⟨a *strand* of DNA⟩ **3** : one of the elements of a complicated whole ⟨the *strands* of a legal argument⟩ [Middle English *strond* "strand, fiber"]

strange \'strānj\ *adj* **strang·er; strang·est** **1** : of or relating to some other person or place ⟨the cuckoo lays eggs in a *strange* nest⟩ **2 a** : not well known ⟨*strange* surroundings⟩ **b** : exciting surprise or wonder because not usual : noticeably unusual ⟨*strange* clothes⟩ **3** : UNEASY 1 ⟨feels *strange* on the first day of school⟩ [Middle English *strange* "foreign", from early French *estrange* (same meaning), from Latin *extraneus,* literally "external, coming from the outside", from *extra* "outside" — related to EXTRA-] — **strange·ly** *adv* — **strange·ness** *n*

strang·er \'strān-jər\ *n* **1** : one who is strange **2 a** : FOREIGNER **b** : GUEST 1, VISITOR **c** : a person with whom one is unacquainted

stran·gle \'straŋ-gəl\ *vb* **stran·gled; stran·gling** \-g(ə-)liŋ\ **1** : to choke to death by squeezing the throat **2** : to cause (someone or something) to choke or suffocate **3** : to suppress or hinder the rise, growth, or expression of **4** : to become strangled **5** : to die by or as if by interference with breathing — **stran·gler** \-g(ə-)lər\ *n*

stran·gle·hold \'straŋ-gəl-ˌhōld\ *n* **1** : a wrestling hold by which one's opponent is choked **2** : a force or influence that chokes or blocks freedom of development or expression

stran·gu·la·tion \ˌstraŋ-gyə-'lā-shən\ *n* **1** : an act or process of strangling **2** : the state of being strangled

¹strap \'strap\ *n* **1** : a band, plate, or loop of metal for tying objects together or for clamping an object in position **2 a** : a narrow usually flat strip of a flexible material and especially leather used variously (as for fastening, holding together, or wrapping) **b** : something made of a strap forming a loop ⟨boot *strap*⟩ **c** : a strip of leather used for whipping **d** : ¹STROP

²strap *vb* **strapped; strap·ping** **1** : to fasten with or attach by a strap **2** : to beat or punish with a strap **3** : ²STROP

strap·less \'strap-ləs\ *adj* : having no strap; *esp* : made or worn without shoulder straps ⟨*strapless* evening gown⟩

strap·ping \'strap-iŋ\ *adj* : ROBUST

strat·a·gem \'strat-ə-jəm\ *n* **1** : a trick in war for deceiving and outwitting the enemy **2** : a clever trick or scheme

stra·te·gic \strə-'tē-jik\ *adj* **1** : of, relating to, or showing strategy ⟨*strategic* value of the position⟩ ⟨a *strategic* retreat⟩ **2 a** : important in strategy : required for the conduct of war ⟨*strategic* supplies⟩ **b** : of great importance within a whole or for a planned purpose ⟨mentioned *strategic* points⟩ **3** : designed or trained to strike at what makes an enemy powerful ⟨*strategic* bomber⟩ — **stra·te·gi·cal** \-ji-kəl\ *adj* — **stra·te·gi·cal·ly** \-ji-k(ə-)lē\ *adv*

strat·e·gist \'strat-ə-jəst\ *n* : one skilled in strategy

strat·e·gy \'strat-ə-jē\ *n, pl* **-gies** **1** : the science and art of employing the forces of a country in peace or war; *esp* : the science and art of military command exercised to meet the enemy in combat **2 a** : a careful plan or method **b** : the art of making or employing plans or tricks to achieve a goal

strat·i·fi·ca·tion \ˌstrat-ə-fə-'kā-shən\ *n* **1** : the act or process of arranging or becoming arranged in layers or strata **2** : the state of being arranged in layers or strata

strat·i·fied \'strat-ə-ˌfīd\ *adj* : arranged in layers ⟨*stratified* rock⟩ ⟨*stratified* epithelial tissue⟩

stra·tig·ra·phy \strə-'tig-rə-fē\ *n* : geology that deals with the beginnings, composition, distribution, and succession of the layers of rock in the earth's crust

stra·to·cu·mu·lus \ˌstrat-ō-'kyü-myə-ləs, ˌstrat-\ *n* : layered cumulus consisting of large balls or rolls of dark cloud which often cover the whole sky especially in winter

strato·sphere \'strat-ə-ˌsfi(ə)r\ *n* : an upper portion of the atmosphere more than 11 kilometers above the earth where temperature changes little and clouds rarely form

stra·tum \'strāt-əm, 'strat-\ *n, pl* **stra·ta** \-ə\ **1** : a layer of a substance; *esp* : one of a series of layers ⟨a rock *stratum*⟩ ⟨a *stratum* of earth⟩ ⟨deep *stratum* of the skin⟩ **2** : a level of society consisting of persons of the same or similar rank or position

stra·tus \'strāt-əs, 'strat-\ *n, pl* **stra·ti** \'strāt-ˌī, 'strat-\ : a cloud form extending over a large area at an altitude of from 600 to 2100 meters

¹straw \'strȯ\ *n* **1 a** : stalks of grain after threshing; *also* : any dry stalky plant part used like grain straw (as for bedding or in packing) ⟨pine *straw*⟩ **b** : a natural or artificial fiber used for weaving or braiding **2** : a dry coarse stem especially of a cereal grass **3 a** : something of small worth or importance **b** : something too weak to provide help in a desperate situation ⟨clutch at any *straw* in a crisis⟩ **4** : a prepared tube for sucking up a beverage — **straw·like** \-ˌlīk\ *adj* — **strawy** \'strȯ(-)i\ *adj*

²straw *adj* **1** : made of straw ⟨a *straw* rug⟩ **2** : of the pale yellow color of straw

straw·ber·ry \'strȯ-ˌber-ē, -b(ə-)rē\ *n* : an edible juicy usually red pulpy fruit of a low herb with white flowers and long slender runners; *also* : this plant

straw boss *n* : a person in charge of a small gang of workers

straw vote *n* : an unofficial vote

¹stray \'strā\ *n* **1** : a domestic animal that is wandering loose or is lost **2** : a person or thing that strays

strawberry

²stray *vb* **1** : to wander from a group or from the proper place : ROAM **2** : DEVIATE — **stray·er** *n*

³stray *adj* **1** : having strayed or been lost ⟨a *stray* cow⟩ **2** : occurring in one place and another or at random ⟨a few *stray* hairs⟩

¹streak \'strēk\ *n* **1** : a line or mark of a different color or composition from its background : STRIPE **2** : the color of the fine powder of a mineral obtained by scratching or rubbing against a hard white surface **3 a** : a narrow band of light **b** : a lightning bolt **4 a** : a small amount : TRACE, STRAIN ⟨*streak* of stubbornness⟩ **b** : a brief period or series ⟨a *streak* of luck⟩ ⟨winning *streak*⟩ **5** : a narrow layer ⟨a *streak* of fat in bacon⟩

²streak *vb* **1** : to make or have streaks on or in **2** : to move swiftly : RUSH ⟨*streaked* through the streets⟩

streaked \'strēkt, 'strē-kəd\ *adj* : marked with streaks or lines of color

streaky \'strē-kē\ *adj* **streak·i·er; -est** **1** : having or showing streaks **2** : ¹VARIABLE 1a — **streak·i·ness** *n*

¹stream \'strēm\ *n* **1** : a body of running water (as a river or brook) flowing on the earth; *also* : any body of flowing fluid (as water or gas) **2** : a steady flow ⟨a *stream* of words⟩ **3** : a ray of light

²stream *vb* **1** : to flow or cause to flow in or as if in a stream **2 a** : to give off a bodily fluid in large amounts ⟨face *streaming* with sweat⟩ **b** : to become wet with a discharge of bodily fluid (as sweat) **3** : to trail out at full length ⟨hair *streaming* in the wind⟩ **4** : to pour in large numbers ⟨the people *streamed* into the hall⟩

stream·er \'strē-mər\ *n* **1 a** : a flag that streams in the wind; *esp* : PENNANT 1 **b** : a long narrow wavy strip suggesting a banner floating in the wind **2** *pl* : AURORA BOREALIS

stream·let \'strēm-lət\ *n* : a small stream

\ə\ abut	\au̇\ out	\i\ tip	\ȯ\ saw	\u̇\ foot
\ər\ further	\ch\ chin	\ī\ life	\ȯi\ coin	\y\ yet
\a\ mat	\e\ pet	\j\ job	\th\ thin	\yü\ few
\ā\ take	\ē\ easy	\ŋ\ sing	\th\ this	\yu̇\ cure
\ä\ cot, cart	\g\ go	\ō\ bone	\ü\ food	\zh\ vision

stream·line \'strēm-,līn, -'līn\ *vb* **1** : to design or construct with an outline which makes motion through water or air easier **2** : to bring up to date : MODERNIZE **3** : to make simpler, more effective, or more productive

stream·lined \-,līnd, -'līnd\ *adj* **1 a** : designed or constructed to make or as if to make motion through water or air easier **b** : stripped of everything unnecessary : SIMPLIFIED **2** : made more modern

¹**street** \'strēt\ *n* **1 a** : a public way especially in a city, town, or village usually including sidewalks and being wider than an alley or lane **b** : the part of a street reserved for vehicles **c** : a public way with the property along it ⟨lived on Maple *Street*⟩ **2** : the people occupying property on a street ⟨the whole *street* was excited⟩ [Old English *strǣt* "street", from Latin *strata* "paved road", derived from earlier *stratus*, past participle of *sternere* "to spread out"]

²**street** *adj* **1** : of or relating to the street or streets ⟨a *street* door⟩ ⟨a *street* map⟩ ⟨*street* clothes⟩ **2** : of or relating to the environment of the street ⟨*street* people⟩

street·car \-,kär\ *n* : a passenger vehicle that runs on rails and typically operates on city streets

street·light \-,līt\ *n* : a light usually on a pole that is one of a series spaced along a public road

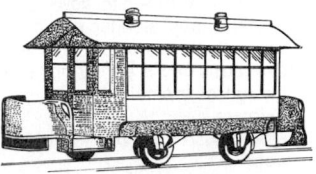

streetcar

street–smart \'strēt-,smärt\ *adj* : STREETWISE

street smarts *n pl* : the quality of being streetwise

street·wise \'strēt-,wīz\ *adj* : possessing the skills and attitudes necessary to survive in an often violent urban environment

strength \'stren(k)th\ *n* **1** : the quality or state of being strong **2** : power to resist force **3** : power to resist attack **4 a** : the power to have an effect **b** : degree of concentration ⟨the *strength* of a liquid cleaner⟩ **c** : intensity of light, color, sound, or odor **5** : force as measured in numbers ⟨army at full *strength*⟩ **6** : ²SUPPORT 1 **syn** see POWER

strength·en \'stren(k)-thən\ *vb* **strength·ened; strength·en·ing** \'stren(k)th-(ə-)niŋ\ : to make or become stronger — **strength·en·er** \-(ə-)nər\ *n*

stren·u·ous \'stren-yə-wəs\ *adj* **1 a** : very active : ENERGETIC **b** : FERVENT, ZEALOUS ⟨*strenuous* protest⟩ **2** : showing or requiring great energy ⟨*strenuous* tasks⟩ **syn** see VIGOROUS — **stren·u·ous·ly** *adv*

strep \'strep\ *adj* : of, relating to, or caused by streptococci

strep·to·coc·cus \,strep-tə-'käk-əs\ *n, pl* **-coc·ci** \-'käk-,(s)ī, -(,)(s)ē\ : any of various mostly parasitic round bacteria that divide only in one direction, occur in pairs or chains, and include some that cause diseases in human beings and animals

strep·to·my·ces \,strep-tə-'mī-,sēz\ *n, pl* **streptomyces** : any of a genus of mostly soil bacteria including some that form antibiotics as by-products of their normal bodily processes

strep·to·my·cin \,strep-tə-'mīs-ᵊn\ *n* : an antibiotic produced by a soil streptomyces and used especially in the treatment of some infections (as tuberculosis)

¹**stress** \'stres\ *n* **1 a** : a force that acts when one body or part of a body presses on, pulls on, pushes against, or tends to squeeze or twist another body or part of a body **b** : the change in shape caused in a body by such a force **c** : a physical, chemical, or emotional factor that causes bodily or mental tension and may be involved in causing some diseases **d** : a state of tension resulting from a stress **2** : special importance given to something : EMPHASIS, WEIGHT ⟨lay *stress* on a point⟩ **3** : relative prominence of sound **4** : ¹ACCENT 4 — **stress·less** \-ləs\ *adj*

²**stress** *vb* **1** : to subject to physical or emotional stress **2** : to pronounce with stress **3** : EMPHASIZE

stressed–out \'strest-'aut\ *adj* : suffering from high levels of physical or especially psychological stress

stress·ful \'stres-fəl\ *adj* : full of stress — **stress·ful·ly** \-fə-lē\ *adv*

stress mark *n* : a mark used with (as before, after, or over) a written syllable in the respelling of a word to show that this syllable is to be stressed when spoken : ACCENT MARK

¹**stretch** \'strech\ *vb* **1** : to extend (as one's body) in a flat position ⟨*stretched* out on the bed⟩ **2** : to reach out ⟨*stretched* my arm⟩ **3 a** : to extend in length or width or both : SPREAD **b** : to extend over a continuous period **4** : to draw up (one's body) from a cramped, stooping, or relaxed position **5** : to pull tight **6 a** : to enlarge or expand especially by force **b** : ²STRAIN 2b **7** : to cause to reach or continue ⟨*stretch* a wire between two posts⟩ **8** : EXAGGERATE ⟨*stretch* the truth⟩ **9** : to become extended without breaking — **stretch·abil·i·ty** \,strech-ə-'bil-ət-ē\ *n* — **stretch·able** \'strech-ə-bəl\ *adj*

²**stretch** *n* **1** : an exercise of something beyond ordinary or normal limits ⟨*stretch* of the imagination⟩ **2** : the extent to which something may be stretched **3** : the act of stretching : the state of being stretched **4 a** : an extent in length or area ⟨a *stretch* of woods⟩ **b** : a continuous period of time ⟨silent for a *stretch*⟩ **5** : an act or instance of stretching the body or one of its parts **6** : a term of imprisonment **7** : either of the straight sides of a racecourse; *esp* : HOMESTRETCH 1 **8** : the ability to be stretched

³**stretch** *adj* : easily stretched : ELASTIC ⟨*stretch* socks⟩

stretch·er \'strech-ər\ *n* **1** : one that stretches; *esp* : a device or machine for stretching or expanding something ⟨placed curtains on the *stretcher*⟩ **2** : a device (as of canvas) that resembles a cot and is used for carrying an injured or dead person

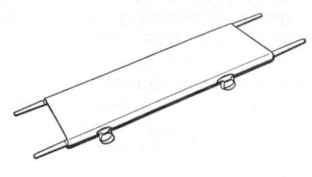

stretcher 2

stretch·er–bear·er \-,bar-ər, -,ber-\ *n* : one who carries one end of a stretcher

stretch receptor *n* : MUSCLE SPINDLE

strew \'strü\ *vb* **strewed; strewed** *or* **strewn** \'strün\; **strew·ing** **1** : to spread (as seeds) by scattering **2** : to cover by or as if by scattering something over or on **3** : to spread around or as if sowing seeds : DISSEMINATE

stri·at·ed \'strī-,āt-əd\ *adj* : having or showing lines, bands, or grooves — **stri·a·tion** \strī-'ā-shən\ *n*

striated muscle *n* : muscle tissue that is made up of long thin cells with many nuclei and with alternate light and dark stripes, that usually connects to and moves the vertebrate skeleton, and that is mostly under voluntary control — compare SMOOTH MUSCLE

strick·en \'strik-ən\ *adj* **1** : hit or wounded by or as if by an object that was thrown **2** : troubled with disease, misfortune, or sorrow

strict \'strikt\ *adj* **1** : permitting no avoidance or escape ⟨under *strict* orders⟩ **2 a** : kept with great care : ABSOLUTE ⟨*strict* secrecy⟩ **b** : carefully obeying rules or a code of conduct ⟨a *strict* Catholic⟩ **3** : completely correct : EXACT, PRECISE — **strict·ly** \'strik-(t)lē\ *adv* — **strict·ness** \'strik(t)-nəs\ *n*

stric·ture \'strik-chər\ *n* : a negative criticism : CENSURE

¹**stride** \'strīd\ *vb* **strode** \'strōd\; **strid·den** \'strid-ᵊn\; **strid·ing** \'strīd-iŋ\ **1** : to move over, through, or along with or as if with long even steps **2** : to take a very long step — **strid·er** \'strīd-ər\ *n*

²**stride** *n* **1** : a step or the distance covered by a step **2** : a way of striding **3** : a step forward : ADVANCE ⟨the

strides made in the control of tuberculosis⟩

stri·dent \'strīd-ᵊnt\ *adj* : harsh sounding : GRATING, SHRILL — **stri·dent·ly** *adv*

strife \'strīf\ *n* **1** : bitter sometimes violent disagreement ⟨political *strife*⟩ **2** : ²STRUGGLE 2, FIGHT

¹strike \'strīk\ *vb* **struck** \'strək\; **struck** *also* **strick·en** \'strik-ən\; **strik·ing** \'strī-kiŋ\ **1** : to take a course : GO ⟨*strike* across the field⟩ **2 a** : to deliver a stroke or blow : HIT **b** : to attack or seize especially with fangs or claws ⟨*struck* by a snake⟩ **3** : to come into contact or collision with : COLLIDE **4** : to remove or cancel with or as if with a stroke of the pen ⟨*struck* out a word in the text⟩ **5** : to lower, take down, or take apart ⟨*strike* a flag⟩ ⟨*strike* camp⟩ **6 a** : to indicate or become indicated by a clock, bell, or chime **b** : to indicate by sounding **7** : to pierce or penetrate or to cause to pierce or penetrate **8** : to make a military attack : FIGHT ⟨*strike* for freedom⟩ **9** : to seize the bait ⟨a fish *struck*⟩ **10** : to take root or cause to take root : GERMINATE ⟨some plant cuttings *strike* quickly⟩ **11** : to stop work for the purpose of forcing an employer to meet demands **12** : to make a beginning : LAUNCH ⟨the orchestra *struck* into another waltz⟩ **13** : to cause to suffer pain or distress suddenly ⟨*struck* down at the height of her career⟩ **14 a** : to bring into forceful contact **b** : to fall on ⟨sunlight *strikes* your face⟩ **15** : to affect with a strong feeling ⟨*struck* by its beauty⟩ **16 a** : to produce by stamping with a die or punch ⟨*strike* a medal⟩ **b** : to cause to ignite by friction ⟨*strike* a match⟩ **17** : to produce on a musical instrument by hitting or plucking strings ⟨*strike* a chord on the piano⟩ **18 a** : to come to mind **b** : to appear remarkable or make a strong impression on : IMPRESS **19** : to come to ⟨*strike* the main road⟩ **20** : to take on : ASSUME ⟨*strike* a pose⟩

²strike *n* **1** : an act or instance of striking **2 a** : a stopping of work by a body of workers to force an employer to meet demands **b** : a temporary stopping of normal activities in protest against an act or condition ⟨a hunger *strike*⟩ **3** : a pull on a line by a fish in striking **4** : a stroke of good luck; *esp* : a discovery of a valuable mineral deposit **5** : a baseball pitch that passes through the strike zone or that is swung at without being hit fair **6** : ¹DISADVANTAGE 2a, HANDICAP ⟨started the job with two *strikes* against them⟩ **7** : the knocking down of all the pins with the first ball in bowling **8** : a military attack

strike·bound \'strīk-,baund\ *adj* : experiencing a strike ⟨a *strikebound* factory⟩

strike·break·er \-,brā-kər\ *n* : a person hired to help break up a strike of workers

strike·break·ing \-,brā-kiŋ\ *n* : action designed to break up a strike

strike off *vb* : to produce in an effortless manner ⟨*strike off* a poem for the occasion⟩

strike·out \'strī-,kaut\ *n* : an out in baseball resulting from a batter's being charged with three strikes

strike out \(')strī-'kaut\ *vb* **1** : to enter upon a course of action ⟨*struck out* on my own after graduation⟩ **2** : to make an out or cause to make an out in baseball by a strikeout ⟨the shortstop *struck out*⟩ ⟨the pitcher *struck* him *out* with a curve⟩

strike·over \'strī-,kō-vər\ *n* : an act or instance of striking a typewriter letter, number, or symbol on a spot already occupied by another

strik·er \'strī-kər\ *n* : a worker on strike

strike up *vb* **1** : to begin or cause to begin to sing or play ⟨*strike up* the band⟩ **2** : to cause to begin ⟨*strike up* a conversation⟩

strike zone *n* : the area (as from the armpits to the tops of the knees of a batter) over home plate through which a baseball pitch must pass to be called a strike

strik·ing \'strī-kiŋ\ *adj* : attracting attention : REMARKABLE, IMPRESSIVE ⟨a *striking* costume⟩ ⟨a *striking* resemblance⟩ — **strik·ing·ly** *adv*

¹string \'striŋ\ *n* **1** : a small cord used to fasten or tie **2** : a thin tough plant structure (as the fiber connecting the halves of a bean pod) **3 a** : the gut, wire, or plastic cord that is plucked, bowed, or struck to produce a sound **b** *pl* : the stringed instruments of an orchestra **4 a** : a group of objects threaded on a string ⟨a *string* of pearls⟩ **b** : a series of things arranged in or as if in a line ⟨a *string* of automobiles⟩ **c** : a series of like items (as units of information, marks, or words) **d** : the animals and especially horses belonging to or used by one individual **5** : any of several squads of players on a team that are grouped together according to skill ⟨the second *string* of a football team⟩ **6** : a series in time : SUCCESSION, SEQUENCE **7** *pl* : requirements or obligations connected with something ⟨an agreement with no *strings* attached⟩

²string *vb* **strung** \'strəŋ\; **string·ing** \'striŋ-iŋ\ **1** : to equip with strings **2 a** : to thread on or as if on a string ⟨*string* beads⟩ **b** : to tie, hang, or fasten with string **3** : to hang by the neck ⟨*strung* up from a high tree⟩ **4** : to remove the strings of ⟨*string* beans⟩ **5 a** : to extend or stretch like a string ⟨*string* wires from tree to tree⟩ **b** : to set out in a line or series

string along *vb* **1** : to go along : AGREE ⟨*string along* with the majority⟩ **2** : DECEIVE 1, FOOL ⟨would *string* us *along* with false promises⟩

string bass *n* : DOUBLE BASS

string bean *n* **1** : a bean of one of the older varieties of kidney bean that have stringy fibers on the lines of separation of the pods; *also* : SNAP BEAN **2** : a very tall thin person

stringed instrument \'striŋd-\ *n* : any of a group of musical instruments (as the violin, harp, or piano) that is played by plucking or striking or by drawing a bow across tense strings — compare BRASS INSTRUMENT, PERCUSSION INSTRUMENT, WOODWIND 1

string bean 1

strin·gent \'strin-jənt\ *adj* **1** : tying, drawing, or pressing tight **2** : strict in setting standards and following rules ⟨*stringent* training⟩ — **strin·gent·ly** *adv*

string·er \'striŋ-ər\ *n* **1** : one that strings **2** : a long piece of wood or metal used for support or strengthening in a building (as under a floor)

string·ing \'striŋ-iŋ\ *n* : the material with which a racket is strung

stringy \'striŋ-ē\ *adj* **string·i·er; -est** : containing, consisting of, or resembling string ⟨*stringy* roots⟩ ⟨*stringy* hair⟩ — **string·i·ness** *n*

¹strip \'strip\ *vb* **stripped** \'stript\ *also* **stript; strip·ping** **1 a** : to remove clothing, covering, or surface substance from **b** : to remove (as clothing) from a person : UNDRESS **c** : PLUNDER, SPOIL ⟨troops *stripped* the town after capturing it⟩ **d** : to take away all duties, honors, or special rights **2 a** : to remove a layer that covers : SKIN, PEEL ⟨*strip* bark from a tree⟩ **b** : to remove unimportant material from **c** : to remove furniture, equipment, or accessories from **3** : to make bare or clear (as by cutting or grazing) **4** : to tear or damage the screw thread of (as a bolt or nut) — **strip·per** *n*

²strip *n* **1** : a long narrow piece or area ⟨*strips* of bacon⟩

\ə\ abut		\au\ out		\i\ tip		\ȯ\ saw		\u̇\ foot
\ər\ further		\ch\ chin		\ī\ life		\ȯi\ coin		\y\ yet
\a\ mat		\e\ pet		\j\ job		\th\ thin		\yü\ few
\ā\ take		\ē\ easy		\ŋ\ sing		\th\ this		\yu̇\ cure
\ä\ cot, cart		\g\ go		\ō\ bone		\ü\ food		\zh\ vision

⟨a *strip* of land⟩ **2** : AIRSTRIP

strip—crop·ping \'strip-ˌkräp-iŋ\ *n* : the growing of a food crop (as corn) in alternate strips with a crop (as hay) that forms sod and helps keep the soil from being worn away — **strip—crop** \-ˌkräp\ *vb*

¹stripe \'strīp\ *n* : a stroke or blow with a rod or part of a whip

²stripe *vb* **striped** \'strīpt\; **strip·ing** : to make stripes on

³stripe *n* **1** : a line or long narrow section differing in color or appearance from the background **2** : a piece of braid (as on the sleeve) to indicate military rank or length of service — **stripe·less** \'strī-pləs\ *adj*

striped \'strīpt, 'strī-pəd\ *adj* : having stripes or streaks

striped bass *n* : a large marine food and sport fish that occurs along the Atlantic coast of the U.S. and has been introduced along the Pacific coast

strip·ling \'strip-liŋ\ *n* : a youth just passing from boyhood to manhood

strip mine *n* : a mine that is worked from the earth's surface by the stripping away of covering material — **strip—mine** *vb*

strive \'strīv\ *vb* **strove** \'strōv\ *also* **strived** \'strīvd\; **striv·en** \'striv-ən\ *or* **strived; striv·ing** \'strī-viŋ\ **1** : to struggle against : CONTEND **2** : to try hard : ENDEAVOR ⟨*strive* to win⟩ — **striv·er** \'strī-vər\ *n*

strobe \'strōb\ *n* : a device that produces a very brief strong flash of light (as for photography) and that can be used repeatedly

strode *past of* STRIDE

¹stroke \'strōk\ *vb* **stroked; strok·ing** **1** : to rub gently in one direction **2** : to pass the hand over gently in kindness or tenderness [Old English *strācian* "stroke, caress"] — **strok·er** *n*

²stroke *n* **1** : the act of striking; *esp* : a blow with a weapon or instrument **2** : a single unbroken movement; *esp* : one of a series of repeated or to-and-fro movements **3** : a striking of the ball in a game; *esp* : a striking or attempt to strike the ball that counts as the scoring unit in golf **4 a** : a sudden action or process that results in something being struck ⟨*stroke* of lightning⟩ **b** : an unexpected result ⟨*stroke* of luck⟩ **5** : sudden weakening or loss of consciousness or the power to feel or move caused by the breaking of a blood vessel in the brain or the cutting off of the supply of blood to the brain by a clot in a blood vessel — called also *apoplexy* **6** : one of a series of movements that pushes against something ⟨*stroke* of an oar⟩ **7** : the movement or the distance of the movement in either direction of a mechanical part (as a piston) having a forward and backward motion **8** : the sound of a bell being struck **9 a** : a mark made by a single movement of a tool ⟨*stroke* of the pen⟩ **b** : one of the lines of a letter of the alphabet [Middle English *stroke* "act of striking"]

³stroke *vb* **stroked; strok·ing** **1** : to show or cancel with a line **2** : ¹HIT 1a ⟨gently *stroked* the ball toward the hole⟩

stroll \'strōl\ *vb* : to walk in a leisurely or idle manner : RAMBLE — **stroll** *n*

stroll·er \'strō-lər\ *n* **1** : one that strolls **2** : a small carriage in which a baby sits and can be pushed around

strong \'stroŋ\ *adj* **strong·er** \'stroŋ-gər\; **strong·est** \'stroŋ-gəst\ **1** : marked by great physical power : ROBUST **2** : having moral or mental power **3** : having great resources (as of wealth) **4** : of a specified number ⟨an army ten thousand *strong*⟩ **5** : FORCEFUL, COGENT ⟨*strong* arguments⟩ **6** : not mild or weak : having much of some quality ⟨*strong* coffee⟩ ⟨*strong* acid⟩ ⟨*strong* glasses⟩ **7** : moving with rapidity or force ⟨*strong* wind⟩ **8** : ENTHUSIASTIC, ZEALOUS ⟨a *strong* believer in peace⟩ **9** : not easily captured or overcome ⟨a *strong* fort⟩ **10** : well established : FIRM ⟨*strong* traditions⟩ **11** : having a disgusting or powerful odor or flavor : RANK **12** : of, relating to, or being a verb that forms the past tense by a change in the root vowel and the past participle usually by the addition of *-en* with or without change of the root vowel (as *strive, strove, striven* or *drink, drank, drunk*) — **strong** *adv* — **strong·ly** \'stroŋ-lē\ *adv*

syn STRONG, STURDY, TOUGH mean showing the power to hold out against opposing force. STRONG suggests great power of body or material ⟨a *strong* person is needed to lift that⟩ ⟨a *strong* rope for pulling heavy loads⟩ STURDY suggests the ability to endure pressure or hard use ⟨a *sturdy* table⟩ TOUGH suggests that something is very firm and elastic ⟨this meat is *tough*⟩ ⟨a *tough* fabric that will last many years⟩

strong·box \'stroŋ-ˌbäks\ *n* : a strongly made container for money or valuables

strong force *n* : the force between the particles of an atomic nucleus that acts to hold the nucleus together and is the strongest known force

strong·hold \'stroŋ-ˌhōld\ *n* : FORTRESS

stron·tium \'strän-ch(ē-)əm, 'stränt-ē-əm\ *n* : a soft metallic element that can be hammered and shaped, occurs only in combination, and is used in color TV tubes and red fireworks — see ELEMENT table

strontium 90 *n* : a heavy radioactive form of strontium having the mass number 90 that is present in the fallout from nuclear explosions

¹strop \'sträp\ *n* : a usually leather band for sharpening a razor

²strop *vb* **stropped; strop·ping** : to sharpen on a strop ⟨*strop* a razor⟩

stro·phe \'strō-fē\ *n* : a division of a poem : STANZA — **stro·phic** \'strō-fik, 'sträf-ik\ *adj*

strove *past and chiefly dialect past participle of* STRIVE

struck *past and past participle of* STRIKE

struc·tur·al \'strək-chə-rəl, 'strək-shrəl\ *adj* **1** : of, relating to, or affecting structure ⟨*structural* weaknesses⟩ **2** : used or formed for use in construction ⟨*structural* steel⟩ — **struc·tur·al·ly** \-ē\ *adv*

structural formula *n* : an expanded molecular formula showing the arrangement within the molecule of atoms and of bonds

¹struc·ture \'strək-chər\ *n* **1** : the action of building : CONSTRUCTION **2** : something constructed or arranged in a definite pattern of organization **3** : manner of construction : the arrangement or relationship of elements (as particles, parts, or organs) in a substance, body, or system ⟨soil *structure*⟩ ⟨the *structure* of a plant⟩ ⟨molecular *structure*⟩ ⟨social *structure*⟩ ⟨the *structure* of a language⟩ — **struc·ture·less** \-ləs\ *adj*

²structure *vb* **struc·tured; struc·tur·ing** \'strək-chə-riŋ, 'strək-shriŋ\ : to form into a structure : ORGANIZE

stru·del \'strüd-ᵊl, 'shtrüd-\ *n* : a pastry made of thin dough rolled up with filling and baked

¹strug·gle \'strəg-əl\ *vb* **strug·gled; strug·gling** \-(ə-)liŋ\ **1** : to make a great effort to overcome someone or something : STRIVE **2** : to proceed with difficulty or with great effort ⟨*struggled* through the snow⟩ — **strug·gler** \-(ə-)lər\ *n*

²struggle *n* **1** : ²FIGHT 1a, CONTEST **2** : a violent effort or exertion

struggle for existence : competition (as for food, space, or light) of members of a natural population that tends to eliminate weaker or less efficient individuals and thereby to increase the chance of the stronger or more efficient individuals to pass on their traits

strum \'strəm\ *vb* **strummed; strum·ming** : to play a stringed instrument by brushing the strings with the fingers — **strum·mer** *n*

strung *past and past participle of* STRING

¹strut \'strət\ *vb* **strut·ted; strut·ting** **1** : to walk in a stiff proud way **2** : to parade (as clothes) with a show of pride

strop

— **strut·ter** n

²**strut** n **1** : a bar or brace to resist pressure in the direction of its length **2** : a strutting step or walk

strych·nine \'strik-,nīn, -nən, -,nēn\ n : a bitter poison that is obtained from certain plants and is used in rat poison and in medicine as a stimulant to the central nervous system

¹**stub** \'stəb\ n **1** : ¹STUMP 2 **2** : a pen with a short blunt point **3** : a short part left after a larger part has been broken off or used up ⟨pencil stub⟩ **4 a** : a small part of a check kept as a record of the contents of the check **b** : the part of a ticket returned to the user

²**stub** vb **stubbed**; **stub·bing** **1** : to put out (as a cigarette) by crushing **2** : to strike (as one's toe) against an object

stub·ble \'stəb-əl\ n **1** : the stem ends of herbs and especially cereal grasses left in the ground after harvest **2** : a rough surface or growth resembling stubble — **stub·bly** \-(ə-)lē\ adj

stub·born \'stəb-ərn\ adj **1 a** : hard to convince, persuade, or move ⟨stubborn as a mule⟩ **b** : having a firm idea or purpose : DETERMINED **2** : done or continued in a firm and determined manner ⟨stubborn refusal⟩ **3** : difficult to handle, manage, or treat ⟨stubborn hair⟩ **syn** see OBSTINATE — **stub·born·ly** adv — **stub·born·ness** \-ərn-(n)əs\ n

stub·by \'stəb-ē\ adj : resembling a stub especially in shortness and broadness ⟨stubby fingers⟩

¹**stuc·co** \'stək-ō\ n, pl **stuccos** or **stuccoes** : a plaster used to cover exterior walls or decorate interior walls

²**stucco** vb : to coat or decorate with stucco

stuck past and past participle of STICK

stuck–up \'stək-'əp\ adj : having too high an opinion of one's own worth or ability : CONCEITED

¹**stud** \'stəd\ n **1** : a group of animals and especially horses kept primarily for breeding **2** : a male animal (as a stallion) kept for breeding

²**stud** n **1** : one of the smaller uprights in the framing of the walls of a building to which the wall materials are fastened **2 a** : a knob, pin, bolt, or nail with a large head used for ornament or protection **b** : a solid button used on a garment as a fastener or ornament **3** : one of the metal cleats used on a snow tire to provide a better grip

³**stud** vb **stud·ded**; **stud·ding** **1** : to furnish with studs **2** : to decorate, cover, or protect with studs **3** : to set or be set thickly together ⟨water studded with islands⟩

stu·dent \'st(y)üd-ᵊnt, chiefly Southern -ənt\ n **1** : SCHOLAR 1; esp : one who attends a school or college **2** : one who studies ⟨a student of life⟩

student council n : a group elected from a body of students to serve as representatives in student government

student government n : the organization and management of student life, recreation, or discipline by various student organizations in a school or college

stud·ied \'stəd-ēd\ adj **1** : carefully thought out or prepared : THOUGHTFUL ⟨your judgments are always studied and fair⟩ **2** : INTENTIONAL, DELIBERATE ⟨a studied insult⟩ — **stud·ied·ly** adv

stu·dio \'st(y)üd-ē-,ō\ n, pl **-dios** **1 a** : the working place of an artist **b** : a place for the study of an art **2** : a place where motion pictures are made **3** : a place for the transmission of radio or television programs

studio couch n : an upholstered usually backless couch that can be made to serve as a double bed by sliding from underneath it the frame of a single cot

stu·di·ous \'st(y)üd-ē-əs\ adj **1** : devoted to, fond of, or concerned with study ⟨a studious child⟩ ⟨studious habits⟩ **2** : ²EARNEST 1 ⟨made a studious effort to obey the rules⟩ — **stu·di·ous·ly** adv — **stu·di·ous·ness** n

¹**study** \'stəd-ē\ n, pl **stud·ies** **1** : a state of thinking about something steadily : REVERIE **2 a** : use of the mind to acquire knowledge **b** : a careful examination or investigation of something **c** : a report or publication based on a study **3** : a building or room devoted to study, reading, or writing **4 a** : a division or area of learning : SUBJECT **b** : the actions or work of a student

²**study** vb **stud·ied**; **study·ing** **1** : to engage in study or the study of ⟨studied hard⟩ ⟨liked to study geography⟩ **2** : to give close attention to ⟨study a part in a play⟩ ⟨studied the request carefully⟩

study hall n **1** : a room in a school where students can study **2** : a period in a student's day set aside for study and homework

¹**stuff** \'stəf\ n **1** : supplies or equipment that people need or use **2** : writing, conversation, or ideas often of little or temporary worth **3** : something mentioned or understood but not named ⟨sold tons of the stuff⟩ **4 a** : basic part of something : SUBSTANCE ⟨stuff of greatness⟩ **b** : body of knowledge ⟨teachers who know their stuff⟩ **5 a** : actions or talk of a particular kind ⟨how do they get away with such stuff⟩ **b** : special knowledge or ability ⟨a person who has the right stuff will do well here⟩

²**stuff** vb **1 a** : to fill by or as if by packing things in **b** : to eat too much **c** : to fill with a stuffing **2** : to fill with ideas or information **3** : to stop up : PLUG **4** : to put or push into something especially carelessly or with little concern ⟨stuffed the clothes into the drawer⟩ **syn** see PACK — **stuff·er** n

stuff·ing \'stəf-iŋ\ n : material used to stuff something; esp : a seasoned mixture used to stuff meat or poultry

stuffy \'stəf-ē\ adj **stuff·i·er**; **-est** **1** : SULLEN 1, ILL-HUMORED **2 a** : lacking fresh air ⟨a stuffy room⟩ **b** : stuffed or choked up ⟨had a stuffy feeling in my head⟩ **3** : lacking in pep or interest : DULL, STODGY **4** : SELF-RIGHTEOUS — **stuff·i·ly** \'stəf-ə-lē\ adv — **stuff·i·ness** \'stəf-ē-nəs\ n

stul·ti·fy \'stəl-tə-,fī\ vb **-fied**; **-fy·ing** **1** : to cause to appear or be stupid, foolish, or very unreasonable **2** : to make worthless or useless

stum·ble \'stəm-bəl\ vb **stum·bled**; **stum·bling** \-b(ə-)liŋ\ **1** : to trip in walking or running **2 a** : to walk unsteadily **b** : to speak or act in a blundering or clumsy manner **3** : to come or happen unexpectedly or by chance ⟨stumbled onto the ruins of an old fort⟩ — **stumble** n — **stum·bler** \-b(ə-)lər\ n — **stum·bling·ly** \-b(ə-)liŋ-lē\ adv

stum·bling block \'stəm-bliŋ-\ n **1** : an obstacle to belief or understanding **2** : an obstacle to progress

¹**stump** \'stəmp\ n **1** : the base of a bodily part (as an arm or leg) remaining after the rest is removed **2** : the part of a plant and especially a tree remaining attached to the root after the top is cut off **3** : a part remaining after the rest is worn away or lost : STUB **4** : a place or occasion for political public speaking

²**stump** vb **1 a** : ¹CHALLENGE 3 **b** : PERPLEX 1, CONFOUND **2 a** : to walk or walk over heavily or clumsily **b** : ²STUB 2 **3** : to go about making political speeches ⟨stump the state for a candidate⟩ [probably an altered form of earlier stump (noun) "a challenge"] — **stumper** n

stumpy \'stəm-pē\ adj **1** : being short and thick : SQUAT **2** : full of stumps

stun \'stən\ vb **stunned**; **stun·ning** **1** : to make senseless or dizzy by or as if by a blow **2** : BEWILDER, STUPEFY ⟨stunned by the news⟩ — **stun** n

stung past and past participle of STING

stunk past and past participle of STINK

stun·ner \'stən-ər\ n : one that stuns; esp : an unusually attractive person

stun·ning \'stən-iŋ\ adj : unusually lovely or pleasing ⟨a stunning dress⟩ — **stun·ning·ly** adv

¹**stunt** \'stənt\ vb : to hold back the normal growth or prog-

\ə\ abut	\aů\ out	\i\ tip	\ȯ\ saw	\ů\ foot
\ər\ further	\ch\ chin	\ī\ life	\ȯi\ coin	\y\ yet
\a\ mat	\e\ pet	\j\ job	\th\ thin	\yü\ few
\ā\ take	\ē\ easy	\ŋ\ sing	\t̲h̲\ this	\yů\ cure
\ä\ cot, cart	\g\ go	\ō\ bone	\ü\ food	\zh\ vision

ress of [from a dialect word *stunt* "stubborn, abrupt, stunted"; probably of Scandinavian origin]

²**stunt** *n* : an unusual or difficult feat performed or attempted usually to gain attention or publicity

³**stunt** *vb* : to perform stunts

stu·pe·fy \'st(y)ü-pə-ˌfī\ *vb* **-fied; -fy·ing** **1** : ASTONISH, BEWILDER **2** : to make stupid, groggy, or numb especially by or as if by drugs

stu·pen·dous \st(y)ù-'pen-dəs\ *adj* : amazing especially because of great size or height ⟨*stupendous* gorges⟩ **syn** see MONSTROUS — **stu·pen·dous·ly** *adv* — **stu·pen·dous·ness** *n*

stu·pid \'st(y)ü-pəd\ *adj* **1 a** : dull of mind : DENSE **b** : UNTHINKING 1, FOOLISH **2** : dulled in feeling or sensation : TORPID **3** : showing or resulting from dullness : SENSELESS ⟨a *stupid* mistake⟩ **4** : not interesting or worthwhile : DREARY, BORING ⟨a *stupid* movie⟩ — **stu·pid·ly** *adv* — **stu·pid·ness** *n*

stu·pid·i·ty \st(y)ù-'pid-ət-ē\ *n, pl* **-ties** **1** : the quality or state of being stupid **2** : something (as an idea or act) that is stupid

stu·por \'st(y)ü-pər\ *n* **1** : a condition of greatly dulled or completely suspended sense or feeling ⟨drifted into a pleasant, dreamy *stupor*⟩ **2** : a state of dullness or lack of interest resulting often from stress or shock

stur·dy \'stərd-ē\ *adj* **stur·di·er; -est** **1 a** : firmly built or made ⟨a *sturdy* ship⟩ **b** : strong and healthy in body : HARDY, ROBUST **2** : ¹FIRM 3, RESOLUTE ⟨*sturdy* self-reliance⟩ ⟨*sturdy* peasants⟩ — **stur·di·ly** \'stərd-ᵊl-ē\ *adv* — **stur·di·ness** \'stərd-ē-nəs\ *n*

stur·geon \'stər-jən\ *n* : any of various usually large long-bodied fishes having a thick skin covered with rows of bony plates that are prized especially for their eggs which are made into caviar

sturgeon

¹**stut·ter** \'stət-ər\ *vb* : to speak or say in an uneven way with involuntary repeating or interruption of sounds — **stut·ter·er** \-ər-ər\ *n*

²**stutter** *n* **1** : an act or instance of stuttering **2** : a speech disorder involving stuttering

¹**sty** \'stī\ *n, pl* **sties** *also* **styes** : a pen for swine [Old English *stig* "a pen for swine"]

²**sty** *or* **stye** \'stī\ *n, pl* **sties** *or* **styes** : a painful red swelling of a skin gland on the edge of an eyelid [a shortened form of obsolete *styan* "a painful swelling of a gland on the edge of the eyelid", probably derived from Old English *stīgan* "to rise up"]

¹**style** \'stī(ə)l\ *n* **1 a** : a way of expressing oneself (as in speaking or writing) **b** : a particular way by which something is done, created, or performed ⟨a unique *style* of horseback riding⟩ ⟨the classical *style* of dance⟩ **2 a** : STYLUS 1 **b** : the shadow-producing pin of a sundial **c** : the narrow middle part of the pistil of a flower **3 a** : fashionable elegance **b** : beauty, grace, or ease of doing something **4** : the custom or plan followed in spelling, capitalization, punctuation, and arrangement and display of type — **style·less** \-ləs\ *adj*

²**style** *vb* **styled; styl·ing** **1** : to call by an identifying term : CALL **2 a** : to give a particular style to ⟨cuts and *styles* hair⟩ **b:** to design and make in agreement with an accepted way of doing something — **styl·er** *n*

styl·ish \'stī-lish\ *adj* : having style; *esp* : FASHIONABLE — **styl·ish·ly** *adv* — **styl·ish·ness** *n*

styl·ist \'stī-ləst\ *n* **1** : a person known for an outstanding style ⟨a song *stylist*⟩ ⟨a prose *stylist*⟩ **2** : one who develops, designs, or advises on styles ⟨a hair *stylist*⟩ — **sty·lis·tic** \stī-'lis-tik\ *adj* — **sty·lis·ti·cal·ly** \-ti-k(ə-)lē\ *adv*

styl·ize \'stī(ə)l-ˌīz\ *vb* **styl·ized; styl·iz·ing** : to represent or design according to a style or pattern rather than according to nature

sty·lus \'stī-ləs\ *n, pl* **sty·li** \'stī(ə)l-ˌī\ *also* **sty·lus·es** \'stī-lə-səz\ **1** : an instrument used by the ancients for writing on wax tablets **2** : ¹NEEDLE 4

Sty·ro·foam \'stī-rə-ˌfōm\ *trademark* — used for an expanded stiff plastic

Styx \'stiks\ *n* : the principal river of Hades in Greek mythology

sua·sion \'swā-zhən\ *n* : the act of influencing or persuading ⟨moral *suasion*⟩

suave \'swäv\ *adj* : persuasively pleasing : smoothly polite and aggreeable — **suave·ly** *adv* — **suave·ness** *n* — **sua·vi·ty** \'swäv-ət-ē\ *n*

¹**sub** \'səb\ *n* : ¹SUBSTITUTE

²**sub** *vb* **subbed; sub·bing** : to act as a substitute

³**sub** *n* : ²SUBMARINE

sub- *prefix* **1** : under : beneath : below ⟨*sub*soil⟩ ⟨*sub*freezing⟩ **2 a** : being at a lower rank or secondary level ⟨*sub*station⟩ **b** : division or lesser part of ⟨*sub*committee⟩ ⟨*sub*topic⟩ **3** : involving a secondary stage or process ⟨*sub*let⟩ ⟨*sub*contract⟩ **4 a** : less than completely, perfectly, or typically : somewhat ⟨*sub*dominant⟩ **b** : bordering upon ⟨*sub*arctic⟩ [derived from Latin *sub-* "under, below"]

sub·ant·arc·tic \ˌsəb-ant-'ärk-tik, -'ärt-ik\ *adj* : of, relating to, or being a region just outside the antarctic circle

sub·arc·tic \ˌsəb-'ärk-tik, 'səb-'ärt-ik\ *adj* : of, relating to, or being regions immediately outside of the arctic circle or regions similar to these in climate or conditions of life

sub·com·mit·tee \'səb-kə-ˌmit-ē, ˌsəb-kə-'mit-ē\ *n* : a part of a committee usually organized for a certain purpose

sub·com·pact \'səb-'käm-ˌpakt\ *n* : an automobile smaller than a compact

¹**sub·con·scious** \ˌsəb-'kän-chəs, 'səb-\ *adj* : existing in the mind but not immediately available to consciousness — **sub·con·scious·ly** *adv*

²**subconscious** *n* : the mental activities just below the limit of consciousness

sub·con·ti·nent \'səb-'känt-ᵊn-ənt, -'känt-nənt, -ˌkänt-\ *n* : a large area of land smaller than a continent; *esp* : a major subdivision of a continent ⟨the Indian *subcontinent*⟩ — **sub·con·ti·nen·tal** \ˌsəb-ˌkänt-ᵊn-'ent-ᵊl\ *adj*

sub·con·tract \'səb-'kän-ˌtrakt, -ˌkän-\ *n* : a contract between a party to an original contract and a third party who usually agrees to supply work or materials required in the original contract — **sub·con·tract** \ˌsəb-'kän-ˌtrakt, 'səb-; ˌsəb-kən-'trakt\ *vb* — **sub·con·trac·tor** \ˌsəb-'kän-ˌtrak-tər, 'səb-; ˌsəb-kən-'trak-tər\ *n*

sub·cu·ta·ne·ous \ˌsəb-kyü-'tā-nē-əs\ *adj* : being, living, used, or made under the skin

sub·di·vide \ˌsəb-də-'vīd\ *vb* **1** : to divide the parts of something into more parts **2** : to divide into several parts; *esp* : to divide a piece of land into building lots

sub·di·vi·sion \ˌsəb-də-'vizh-ən\ *n* **1** : the act or process of subdividing **2** : one of the parts into which something is subdivided

sub·dom·i·nant \ˌsəb-'däm(-ə)-nənt, 'səb-\ *n* **1** : something dominant to a lesser or partial degree **2** : the fourth tone of the major or minor scale (as F in the scale of C) — **subdominant** *adj*

sub·due \səb-'d(y)ü\ *vb* **sub·dued; sub·du·ing** **1** : to overcome in battle ⟨*subdued* the enemy⟩ **2** : to bring under control ⟨how the tiger had been caught and *subdued*⟩ **3** : to reduce the brightness or strength of : SOFTEN ⟨*subdued* light⟩ — **sub·du·er** *n*

sub·en·try \'səb-ˌen-trē\ *n* : an entry (as in a catalog) made under a more general entry

sub·freez·ing \'səb-'frē-ziŋ\ *adj* : being or marked by temperature below the freezing point (as of water) ⟨*subfreezing* weather⟩

sub·group \'səb-ˌgrüp\ *n* : a group whose members usually share some common quality that makes them different from the other members of a major group to which they belong

sub·head \'səb-ˌhed\ *n* **1** : a heading under which one of the divisions of a subject is listed **2** : a title or headline coming after the main title or headline

sub·head·ing \'səb-ˌhed-iŋ\ *n* : SUBHEAD

¹sub·ject \'səb-jikt\ *n* **1 a** : a person under the authority or control of another **b** : a person who owes loyalty to a monarch or state **2 a** : a department of knowledge or learning **b** : an individual that is studied or experimented on **c** : the person or thing discussed : TOPIC ⟨the *subject* of an essay⟩

²subject *adj* **1** : owing obedience or loyalty to another **2 a** : likely to be affected by ⟨*subject* to temptation⟩ **b** : having a tendency ⟨*subject* to catching colds⟩ **3** : depending on ⟨*subject* to your approval⟩

³sub·ject \səb-'jekt\ *vb* **1 a** : to bring under control or rule **b** : to make responsive to the discipline and control of a superior **2** : to make liable **3** : to cause or force to put up with ⟨unwilling to *subject* us to embarrassment⟩ — **sub·jec·tion** \səb-'jek-shən\ *n*

sub·jec·tive \(ˌ)səb-'jek-tiv\ *adj* **1** : of, relating to, or being a subject **2** : of, relating to, or arising within one's self or mind : PERSONAL — **sub·jec·tive·ly** *adv* — **sub·jec·tiv·i·ty** \(ˌ)səb-ˌjek-'tiv-ət-ē\ *n*

sub·ju·gate \'səb-ji-ˌgāt\ *vb* **-gat·ed; -gat·ing 1** : to bring under control and rule as a subject : CONQUER **2** : to make willing to submit to others : SUBDUE — **sub·ju·ga·tion** \ˌsəb-ji-'gā-shən\ *n* — **sub·ju·ga·tor** \'səb-ji-ˌgāt-ər\ *n*

¹sub·junc·tive \səb-'jəŋ(k)-tiv\ *adj* : of, relating to, or being the grammatical mood that represents an act or state not as fact but as conditional or possible or viewed emotionally (as with doubt or desire) ⟨the *subjunctive* mood⟩

²subjunctive *n* : the subjunctive mood of a verb or a verb in this mood

sub·lease \'səb-ˌlēs, -ˌlēs\ *n* : a lease by a tenant of part or all of leased property to another person — **sublease** *vb*

sub·let \'səb-'let\ *vb* **sub·let; sub·let·ting 1** : to lease or rent all or part of a leased or rented property **2** : to hire a third party to perform under a subcontract the work included in an original contract : SUBCONTRACT

sub·li·mate \'səb-lə-ˌmāt\ *vb* **-mat·ed; -mat·ing** : to direct the expression of (a desire or emotion) from a crude or simple form to a form that is considered proper by one's culture or society — **sub·li·ma·tion** \ˌsəb-lə-'mā-shən\ *n*

sub·lime \sə-'blīm\ *adj* **1** : grand or noble in thought, expression, or manner ⟨*sublime* truths⟩ **2** : having an impressive beauty that excites wonder **syn** see SPLENDID — **sub·lime·ly** *adv* — **sub·lime·ness** *n*

sub·lim·i·nal \(ˌ)səb-'lim-ən-ᵊl, 'səb-\ *adj* **1** : not strong enough to produce a sensation or a mental awareness ⟨*subliminal* stimuli⟩ **2** : existing or functioning below the level of conscious awareness ⟨the *subliminal* mind⟩ ⟨*subliminal* advertising⟩ — **sub·lim·i·nal·ly** \-ē\ *adv*

sub·ma·chine gun \ˌsəb-mə-'shēn-ˌgən\ *n* : a lightweight automatic portable firearm

sub·mar·gin·al \ˌsəb-'märj-nəl, 'səb-, -ən-ᵊl\ *adj* **1** : located near or beneath a margin or a marginal structure **2** : falling below a necessary minimum ⟨farming *submarginal* land⟩ — **sub·mar·gin·al·ly** \-ē\ *adv*

¹sub·ma·rine \'səb-mə-ˌrēn, ˌsəb-mə-'rēn\ *adj* : UNDERWATER; *esp* : UNDERSEA

²submarine *n* **1** : a naval vessel designed to operate un-

submarine 1

derwater **2** : a large sandwich on a long split roll

sub·ma·ri·ner \'səb-mə-ˌrē-nər, ˌsəb-mə-'rē-nər *also* ˌsəb-'mar-ə-\ *n* : a member of a submarine crew

sub·me·di·ant \ˌsəb-'mēd-ē-ənt, 'səb-\ *n* : the sixth tone above the tonic

sub·merge \səb-'mərj\ *vb* **sub·merged; sub·merg·ing 1** : to put or go underwater ⟨the whale *submerged*⟩ **2** : to cover or become covered with or as if with water ⟨floods *submerged* the town⟩

sub·merse \səb-'mərs\ *vb* **sub·mersed; sub·mers·ing** : SUBMERGE — **sub·mer·sion** \-'mər-zhən, -shən\ *n*

¹sub·mers·ible \səb-'mər-sə-bəl\ *adj* : capable of being submerged

²submersible *n* : something that is submersible; *esp* : ²SUBMARINE 1

sub·min·ia·ture \ˌsəb-'min-ē-ə-ˌchü(ə)r, 'səb-, -'min-i-ˌchü(ə)r, -'min-yə-, -chər\ *adj* : very small

sub·mis·sion \səb-'mish-ən\ *n* **1** : an act of submitting something (as for consideration or comment) **2** : the condition of being humble or obedient **3** : an act of submitting to the authority or control of another

sub·mis·sive \səb-'mis-iv\ *adj* : inclined or willing to submit to others [from Latin *submissus,* past participle of *submittere* "to let down", from *sub-* "under, below" and *mittere* "to send, throw" — related to MESSAGE] — **sub·mis·sive·ly** *adv* — **sub·mis·sive·ness** *n*

sub·mit \səb-'mit\ *vb* **sub·mit·ted; sub·mit·ting 1** : to subject to a process or treatment ⟨the metal was *submitted* to analysis⟩ **2** : to present to another for review or decision ⟨*submit* a question to the court⟩ **3** : to put forward an opinion, reason, or idea ⟨we *submit* that the facts have not been established⟩ **4** : to give in to the authority, control, or choice of another **syn** see YIELD

sub·nor·mal \ˌsəb-'nòr-məl, 'səb-\ *adj* **1** : lower or smaller than normal **2** : having less of something and especially of intelligence than is normal — **sub·nor·mal·i·ty** \ˌsəb-nòr-'mal-ət-ē\ *n* — **sub·nor·mal·ly** \ˌsəb-'nòr-mə-lē, 'səb-\ *adv*

¹sub·or·di·nate \sə-'bórd-ᵊn-ət, -'bórd-nət\ *adj* **1** : placed in or occupying a lower class or rank **2** : yielding to or controlled by authority **3 a** : of, relating to, or being a clause that functions as a noun, adjective, or adverb **b** : SUBORDINATING — **sub·or·di·nate·ly** *adv* — **sub·or·di·nate·ness** *n*

²subordinate *n* : one that is subordinate

³sub·or·di·nate \sə-'bórd-ᵊn-ˌāt\ *vb* **-nat·ed; -nat·ing** : to make subordinate — **sub·or·di·na·tion** \-ˌbórd-ᵊn-'ā-shən\ *n* — **sub·or·di·na·tive** \-'bórd-ᵊn-ˌāt-iv\ *adj*

sub·or·di·nat·ing \sə-'bórd-ᵊn-ˌāt-iŋ\ *adj* : introducing and linking a subordinate clause to a main clause ⟨*subordinating* conjunction⟩

sub·phy·lum \'səb-ˌfī-ləm\ *n* : a primary division of a phylum

sub·plot \'səb-ˌplät\ *n* : a subordinate plot in fiction or drama

¹sub·poe·na \sə-'pē-nə\ *n* : an order in writing commanding a person named in it to appear in court under a penalty for failure to appear [from the Latin phrase *sub poena* "under penalty"; used as the beginning words of the order]

²subpoena *vb* **-naed; -na·ing** : to serve or summon with a subpoena

sub·po·lar \ˌsəb-'pō-lər, 'səb-\ *adj* : SUBARCTIC, SUBANTARCTIC

sub·rou·tine \ˌsəb-(ˌ)rü-'tēn\ *n* : a sequence of computer instructions for performing a specified task that can be used repeatedly

\ə\ abut	\au̇\ out	\i\ tip	\ò\ saw	\u̇\ foot
\ər\ further	\ch\ chin	\ī\ life	\òi\ coin	\y\ yet
\a\ mat	\e\ pet	\j\ job	\th\ thin	\yü\ few
\ā\ take	\ē\ easy	\ŋ\ sing	\th\ this	\yu̇\ cure
\ä\ cot, cart	\g\ go	\ō\ bone	\ü\ food	\zh\ vision

sub–Sa·ha·ran \ˌsəb-sə-'har-ən, 'səb-, -'her-, -'här-\ *adj* : of, relating to, or being the part of Africa south of the Sahara

sub·scribe \səb-'skrīb\ *vb* **sub·scribed; sub·scrib·ing** **1** : to make known one's approval by or as if by signing 〈we *subscribe* to your plan〉 **2** : to agree to give or contribute by signing one's name with the amount promised 〈*subscribe* fifty dollars to the fund〉 **3 a** : to enter one's name for a publication or service **b** : to receive a periodical or service regularly on order — **sub·scrib·er** *n*

sub·script \'səb-ˌskript\ *n* : a distinguishing symbol (as a letter or number) immediately below or below and to the right or left of another written character — **subscript** *adj*

sub·scrip·tion \səb-'skrip-shən\ *n* **1** : an act or instance of subscribing **2** : something that is subscribed **3** : a purchase of a certain number of future issues (as of a magazine)

sub·sense \'səb-ˌsen(t)s\ *n* : a subordinate division of a sense (as in a dictionary)

sub·se·quent \'səb-si-kwənt, -sə-ˌkwent\ *adj* : following in time, order, or place 〈*subsequent* events〉 — **subsequent** *n* — **sub·se·quent·ly** \-ˌkwent-lē, -kwənt-\ *adv*

sub·ser·vi·ence \səb-'sər-vē-ən(t)s\ *n* **1** : a subordinate place or function **2** : behavior that shows lack of self‑respect

sub·ser·vi·en·cy \səb-'sər-vē-ən-sē\ *n* : SUBSERVIENCE

sub·ser·vi·ent \səb-'sər-vē-ənt\ *adj* **1** : useful in an inferior capacity : SUBORDINATE **2** : inclined or willing to submit to others : SUBMISSIVE — **sub·ser·vi·ent·ly** *adv*

sub·set \'səb-ˌset\ *n* : a mathematical set each of whose elements is also an element of a set that includes the given set

sub·side \səb-'sīd\ *vb* **sub·sid·ed; sub·sid·ing** **1** : to sink or fall to the bottom : SETTLE **2** : to become quiet or less : ABATE 〈as the fever *subsides*〉 〈my anger *subsided*〉 — **sub·si·dence** \səb-'sīd-ᵊn(t)s, 'səb-səd-ən(t)s\ *n*

¹sub·sid·iary \səb-'sid-ē-ˌer-ē, -'sid-ə-rē\ *adj* : of secondary importance 〈*subsidiary* streams〉

²subsidiary *n, pl* **-iar·ies** : one that is subsidiary; *esp* : a company wholly controlled by another

sub·si·dize \'səb-sə-ˌdīz, -zə-\ *vb* **-dized; -diz·ing** : to aid or furnish with a subsidy — **sub·si·di·za·tion** \ˌsəb-səd-ə-'zā-shən, ˌsəb-zəd-\ *n* — **sub·si·diz·er** *n*

sub·si·dy \'səb-səd-ē, -zəd-\ *n, pl* **-dies** : a grant or gift especially of money; *esp* : a grant by a government to a private person or company or to another government to assist an undertaking thought helpful to the public

sub·sist \səb-'sist\ *vb* **1** : to have or continue to have existence : BE, PERSIST **2** : to have or get the necessities of life (as food and clothing); *esp* : to nourish oneself 〈*subsisting* on roots and berries〉

sub·sis·tence \səb-'sis-tən(t)s\ *n* **1 a** : real being : EXISTENCE **b** : CONTINUATION 1, PERSISTENCE **2 a** : means of subsisting **b** : the minimum (as of food and shelter) necessary to support life — **sub·sis·tent** \-tənt\ *adj*

sub·soil \'səb-ˌsȯil\ *n* : a layer of weathered material that lies just under the surface soil

sub·son·ic \ˌsəb-'sän-ik, 'səb-\ *adj* **1** : of, relating to, or being a speed less than that of sound in air **2** : moving, capable of moving, or using air currents moving at a subsonic speed

sub·spe·cies \'səb-ˌspē-shēz, -sēz\ *n* : a subdivision of a species: as **a** : a category in biological classification that ranks just below a species and includes a physically recognizable and geographically separate group of individuals whose members can breed successfully with members of other subspecies of the same species where their ranges overlap **b** : a named subdivision (as a race) of a biological species — **sub·spe·cif·ic** \ˌsəb-spi-'sif-ik\ *adj*

sub·stance \'səb-stən(t)s\ *n* **1 a** : essential nature : ESSENCE 〈divine *substance*〉 **b** : the fundamental or essential part, quality, or meaning 〈the *substance* of the speech〉

2 a : physical material from which something is made **b** : material of particular or definite chemical constitution 〈an oily *substance*〉 **c** : something (as drugs or alcoholic beverages) considered harmful and usually subject to legal restriction 〈has a *substance* problem〉 **3** : material possessions : PROPERTY 〈a person of *substance*〉

substance abuse *n* : excessive use of a drug (as alcohol or narcotics) : use of a drug without medical justification — **substance abuser** *n*

sub·stan·dard \ˌsəb-'stan-dərd, 'səb-\ *adj* **1** : varying from or falling short of a standard or norm **2** : following a pattern of linguistic usage that is not considered standard especially for writing

sub·stan·tial \səb-'stan-chəl\ *adj* **1 a** : consisting of or relating to substance : MATERIAL **b** : not imaginary : REAL 〈the *substantial* world〉 **c** : IMPORTANT 1, ESSENTIAL 〈*substantial* differences〉 **2** : enough to satisfy and nourish 〈a *substantial* meal〉 **3 a** : PROSPEROUS 1 〈a *substantial* farmer〉 **b** : considerable in quantity : significantly large **4** : firmly constructed — **sub·stan·ti·al·i·ty** \-ˌstan-chē-'al-ət-ē\ *n* — **sub·stan·tial·ly** \-'stanch-(ə-)lē\ *adv*

sub·stan·ti·ate \səb-'stan-chē-ˌāt\ *vb* **-at·ed; -at·ing** **1** : to give substance or form to : EMBODY **2** : to establish by proof or evidence 〈*substantiate* a claim〉 — **sub·stan·ti·a·tion** \-ˌstan-chē-'ā-shən\ *n*

¹sub·stan·tive \'səb-stən-tiv\ *n* : a word or word group that functions in a sentence as a noun — **sub·stan·ti·val** \ˌsəb-stən-'tī-vəl\ *adj*

²substantive *adj* **1** : of, relating to, or being something real or independent **2** : having the function of a grammatical substantive 〈a *substantive* clause〉 **3** : considerable in amount or numbers **4** : creating and defining rights and duties 〈*substantive* law〉 — **sub·stan·tive·ly** *adv*

sub·sta·tion \'səb-ˌstā-shən\ *n* **1** : a branch post office **2** : a subsidiary station in which electric current is transformed

¹sub·sti·tute \'səb-stə-ˌt(y)üt\ *n* : a person or thing that takes the place of another — **substitute** *adj*

²substitute *vb* **-tut·ed; -tut·ing** **1** : to put in the place of another : REPLACE **2** : to serve as a substitute — **sub·sti·tu·tion** \ˌsəb-stə-'t(y)ü-shən\ *n*

sub·struc·ture \'səb-ˌstrək-chər\ *n* : an underlying or supporting part of a structure

sub·teen \'səb-ˌtēn\ *n* : a child not yet in the teens

sub·ter·fuge \'səb-tər-ˌfyüj\ *n* **1** : the action of deceiving usually by slyness in order to avoid some unpleasant circumstance (as to escape blame) **2** : a plan or trick that employs sly deception

sub·ter·ra·nean \ˌsəb-tə-'rā-nē-ən, -nyən\ *adj* **1** : being, lying, or operating under the surface of the earth **2** : existing or working in secret : HIDDEN

sub·ti·tle \'səb-ˌtīt-ᵊl\ *n* **1** : a secondary or explanatory title **2** : a printed statement or bit of dialogue appearing on the screen between the scenes of a silent motion picture or appearing as a translation at the bottom of the screen during the scenes — **subtitle** *vb*

sub·tle \'sət-ᵊl\ *adj* **sub·tler** \'sət-lər, -ᵊl-ər\; **sub·tlest** \'sət-ləst, -ᵊl-əst\ **1 a** : DELICATE 1, ELUSIVE 〈a *subtle* fragrance〉 **b** : difficult to understand or distinguish 〈*subtle* differences in vowel sounds〉 **2** : marked by a keen ability to understand 〈a *subtle* mind〉 **3** : SLY 1a, CRAFTY 〈*subtle* flattery〉 **4** : INSIDIOUS 2 〈a *subtle* poison〉 [Middle English *sutil, sotil* "delicate", from early French *soutil* (same meaning), from Latin *subtilis* "delicate", literally "finely woven", from *sub* "under, close to" and *tela* "fabric woven on a loom"] — **sub·tle·ness** \'sət-ᵊl-nəs\ *n* — **sub·tly** \'sət-lē, 'sət-ᵊl-(l)ē\ *adv*

sub·tle·ty \'sət-ᵊl-tē\ *n, pl* **-ties** **1** : the quality or state of being subtle **2** : something subtle

sub·ton·ic \ˌsəb-'tän-ik, 'səb-\ *n* : LEADING TONE

sub·top·ic \'səb-ˌtäp-ik\ *n* : a topic (as in a composition) that is a division of a main topic

sub·to·tal \'səb-ˌtōt-ᵊl\ *n* : the sum of part of a series of figures

sub·tract \səb-'trakt\ *vb* **1** : to take away (as one part or number) from another : DEDUCT ⟨*subtract* 5 from 9⟩ **2** : to perform a subtraction

sub·trac·tion \səb-'trak-shən\ *n* **1** : an act or instance of subtracting **2** : the operation of deducting one number from another

sub·trac·tive \səb-'trak-tiv\ *adj* : being or involving subtraction

sub·tra·hend \'səb-trə-ˌhend\ *n* : a number that is to be subtracted from another number

sub·trop·i·cal \ˌsəb-'träp-i-kəl, 'səb-\ *also* **sub·trop·ic** \-'träp-ik\ *adj* : of, relating to, or being the regions bordering on the tropical zone

sub·trop·ics \ˌsəb-'träp-iks, 'səb-\ *n pl* : subtropical regions

sub·urb \'səb-ˌərb\ *n* **1 a** : a part of a city or town near its outer edge **b** : a smaller community close to a city **2** *pl* : the area of homes close to or surrounding a city [Middle English *suburb* "part around the outer edge of a city", from Latin *suburbium* (same meaning), from *sub* "under, close to" and *urbs* "city"] — **sub·ur·ban** \sə-'bər-bən\ *adj or n*

sub·ur·ban·ite \sə-'bər-bə-ˌnīt\ *n* : a person who lives in the suburbs

sub·ur·bia \sə-'bər-bē-ə\ *n* : the suburbs of a city

sub·ver·sion \səb-'vər-zhən\ *n* : the act of overthrowing : the state of being overthrown; *esp* : an attempt to overthrow or undermine a government or political system by persons working secretly within the country involved — **sub·ver·sive** \-'vər-siv, -ziv\ *adj or n* — **sub·ver·sive·ly** *adv*

sub·vert \səb-'vərt\ *vb* **1** : to overturn or overthrow from the foundation **2** : to undermine the morals, allegiance, or faith of : CORRUPT — **sub·vert·er** *n*

sub·vo·cal·ize \ˌsəb-'vō-kə-ˌlīz, 'səb-\ *vb* **-ized; -iz·ing** : to move one's lips while reading silently

sub·way \'səb-ˌwā\ *n* **1** : an underground passage **2** : a usually electric underground railway

sub·ze·ro \ˌsəb-'zē-rō\ *adj* : being or marked by temperature below zero

suc·ceed \sək-'sēd\ *vb* **1 a** : to come next after another in office or position or in possession of an estate; *esp* : to inherit sovereignty **b** : to follow after another in order **2 a** : to turn out well **b** : to be successful [Middle English *succeden* "to come after", from Latin *succedere* "to go up, follow after", from *sub-* "under, near" and *cedere* "to go, yield" — related to CONCEDE, NECESSARY] — **suc·ceed·er** *n*

suc·cess \sək-'ses\ *n* **1 a** : degree or measure of succeeding **b** : satisfactory completion of something **c** : the gaining of wealth, respect, or fame **d** : a desired or favorable event or happening especially in an experiment in probability or statistics **2** : a person or thing that succeeds

suc·cess·ful \sək-'ses-fəl\ *adj* **1** : resulting or ending in success **2** : gaining or having gained success — **suc·cess·ful·ly** \-fə-lē\ *adv* — **suc·cess·ful·ness** *n*

suc·ces·sion \sək-'sesh-ən\ *n* **1** : the order, action, or right of succeeding to a throne, title, or property **2 a** : a repeated following of one person or thing after another **b** : a series of one-way changes in the composition of a biological community in which one group of plants or animals is replaced by a different group — **suc·ces·sion·al** \-'sesh-nəl, -ən-ᵊl\ *adj*

suc·ces·sive \sək-'ses-iv\ *adj* : following in order : following each other without interruption — **suc·ces·sive·ly** *adv* — **suc·ces·sive·ness** *n*

suc·ces·sor \sək-'ses-ər\ *n* : one that follows; *esp* : a person who succeeds to a throne, title, estate, or office

suc·cinct \ˌsək-'siŋ(k)t, sə-'siŋ(k)t\ *adj* : marked by short concise expression without wasted words — **suc·cinct·ly**

adv — **suc·cinct·ness** *n*

¹**suc·cor** \'sək-ər\ *n* : RELIEF 1a

²**succor** *vb* **suc·cored; suc·cor·ing** \'sək-(ə-)riŋ\ : to go to the aid of : RELIEVE — **suc·cor·er** \'sək-ər-ər\ *n*

suc·co·tash \'sək-ə-ˌtash\ *n* : lima or shell beans and green corn cooked together

suc·cu·lence \'sək-yə-lən(t)s\ *n* : the state of being succulent

¹**suc·cu·lent** \'sək-yə-lənt\ *adj* **1 a** : full of juice : JUICY **b** : having fleshy tissues that conserve moisture ⟨*succulent* plants⟩ **2** : rich in interest — **suc·cu·lent·ly** *adv*

²**succulent** *n* : a succulent plant (as a cactus)

suc·cumb \sə-'kəm\ *vb* **1** : to yield to force or pressure ⟨*succumb* to temptation⟩ **2** : ¹DIE 1

¹**such** \(')səch,(ˌ)sich\ *adj* **1** : of a kind or character to be indicated or suggested ⟨a bag *such* as a doctor carries⟩ **2** : having a quality already specified ⟨deeply moved by *such* acts of kindness⟩ **3** : so great : so remarkable ⟨*such* a storm⟩ ⟨*such* courage⟩ **4** : of the same class, type, or sort : SIMILAR ⟨opened three *such* stores⟩

²**such** *pron* **1** : such a person or thing ⟨has a plan if it may be called *such*⟩ **2** : someone or something stated, implied, or exemplified ⟨*such* was the result⟩ ⟨*such* were the Romans⟩ **3** : someone or something of the same kind ⟨ships and planes and *such*⟩

³**such** *adv* **1** : to such a degree : SO ⟨*such* tall buildings⟩ ⟨*such* a fine person⟩ **2** : ²VERY 1 ⟨hasn't been in *such* good spirits lately⟩

¹**such·like** \'səch-ˌlīk\ *adj* : of like kind : SIMILAR

²**suchlike** *pron* : someone or something of the same sort : a similar person or thing

¹**suck** \'sək\ *vb* **1 a** : to draw in liquid and especially mother's milk with the mouth **b** : to draw liquid from by action of the mouth ⟨*suck* an orange⟩ **c** : to allow to dissolve gradually in the mouth ⟨*suck* a cough drop⟩ **d** : to apply the mouth to in order to or as if to suck out a liquid ⟨*sucked* my burned finger⟩ **2** : to take something in or up or remove something from by or as if by suction ⟨plants *sucking* moisture from the soil⟩

²**suck** *n* **1** : a sucking movement or force **2** : the act of sucking

suck·er \'sək-ər\ *n* **1 a** : one that sucks **b** : a part of an animal's body used for sucking or for clinging by suction **2** : a shoot from the roots or lower part of the stem of a plant **3** : any of numerous freshwater fishes related to the carps that usually have thick soft lips for sucking in food **4** : LOLLIPOP **5** : a person easily fooled or cheated

suck·ing louse *n* : any of an order of wingless insects that include the true lice and have mouthparts used for sucking body fluids

suck·le \'sək-əl\ *vb* **suck·led; suck·ling** \-(ə-)liŋ\ : to feed from the breast or udder

suck·ling \'sək-liŋ\ *n* : a young mammal still sucking milk from its mother

su·crase \'sü-ˌkrās\ *n* : an enzyme that splits sucrose into glucose and fructose

su·crose \'sü-ˌkrōs\ *n* : a sweet sugar obtained especially from sugarcane or sugar beets

suc·tion \'sək-shən\ *n* **1** : the act or process of sucking **2 a** : the action or process of drawing something (as liquid or dust) into a space (as a vacuum cleaner or a pump) by removing air from the space **b** : the force caused by suction

suction cup *n* : a cup of glass or of a flexible material (as rubber) in which a partial vacuum is produced when applied to a surface

\ə\ abut	\au̇\ out	\i\ tip	\ȯ\ saw	\u̇\ foot
\ər\ further	\ch\ chin	\ī\ life	\ȯi\ coin	\y\ yet
\a\ mat	\e\ pet	\j\ job	\th\ thin	\yü\ few
\ā\ take	\ē\ easy	\ŋ\ sing	\th\ this	\yu̇\ cure
\ä\ cot, cart	\g\ go	\ō\ bone	\ü\ food	\zh\ vision

sud·den \'səd-ᵊn\ adj **1 a** : happening or coming unexpectedly ⟨a *sudden* shower⟩ **b** : changing angle or character all at once ⟨a *sudden* turn in the road⟩ ⟨a *sudden* descent to the sea⟩ **2** : marked by or showing haste ⟨a *sudden* decision⟩ **3** : made or brought about in a short time ⟨a *sudden* cure⟩ — **sud·den·ly** adv — **sud·den·ness** \'səd-ᵊn-(n)əs\ n — **all of a sudden** : sooner than was expected : SUDDENLY

sudden death n : extra play to break a tie in a sports contest in which the first to go ahead wins

¹suds \'sədz\ n pl **1** : soapy water especially when frothy **2** : the froth on soapy water

²suds vb : to form suds

sudsy \'səd-zē\ adj **suds·i·er; -est** : full of suds : FROTHY, FOAMY

sue \'sü\ vb **sued; su·ing 1** : to seek justice from a person by bringing a legal action **2** : to make a request or application : PLEAD — usually used with *for* or *to* ⟨the weaker nation *sued* for peace⟩ — **su·er** n

suede *or* **suède** \'swād\ n **1** : leather rubbed on one side to produce a velvety surface **2** : a cloth fabric that looks and feels like suede [from *suede gloves,* a partial translation of French *gants de Suède* "Swedish gloves" ("gloves of Sweden"), from *Suède* "Sweden"]

su·et \'sü-ət\ n : the hard fat around the kidneys in beef and mutton from which tallow is made

suf·fer \'səf-ər\ vb **suf·fered; suf·fer·ing** \-(ə-)riŋ\ **1** : to feel or endure pain **2** : to experience something unpleasant ⟨*suffer* a defeat⟩ **3** : to bear loss or damage ⟨the business *suffered* during the storm⟩ **4** : ¹PERMIT 1, ALLOW — **suf·fer·able** \'səf-(ə)rə-bəl\ adj — **suf·fer·able·ness** n — **suf·fer·ably** \-blē\ adv — **suf·fer·er** \'səf-ər-ər\ n

suf·fer·ance \'səf-(ə)rən(t)s\ n **1** : consent or approval implied by a lack of interference or failure to enforce a prohibition **2** : power or ability to put up with

suf·fer·ing n **1** : the state or experience of one that suffers **2** : a pain or injury endured

suf·fice \sə-'fīs\ vb **suf·ficed; suf·fic·ing 1** : to meet or satisfy a need : be sufficient ⟨a brief note will *suffice*⟩ **2** : to be competent or capable **3** : to be enough for

suf·fi·cien·cy \sə-'fish-ən-sē\ n, pl **-cies 1** : sufficient means to meet one's needs **2** : the quality or state of being sufficient : ADEQUACY

suf·fi·cient \sə-'fish-ənt\ adj : enough to achieve a goal or fill a need — **suf·fi·cient·ly** adv

¹suf·fix \'səf-ˌiks\ n : a letter or group of letters that comes at the end of a word and has a meaning of its own — **suf·fix·al** \-ˌik-səl\ adj — **suf·fix·less** \-ˌiks-ləs\ adj

²suf·fix \'səf-ˌiks, (ˌ)sə-'fiks\ vb : to attach as a suffix — **suf·fix·ation** \ˌsəf-ˌik-'sā-shən\ n

suf·fo·cate \'səf-ə-ˌkāt\ vb **-cat·ed; -cat·ing 1 a** : to stop the breathing of (as by strangling) **b** : to deprive of oxygen **c** : to make uncomfortable by want of cool fresh air **2** : to become suffocated; *esp* : to die or suffer from being unable to breathe — **suf·fo·ca·tion** \ˌsəf-ə-'kā-shən\ n

suf·frage \'səf-rij\ n : the right of voting; *also* : the exercise of such right

suf·frag·ette \ˌsəf-ri-'jet\ n : a woman who supports voting rights for her sex

suf·frag·ist \'səf-ri-jəst\ n : a person who supports extending voting rights especially to women

suf·fuse \sə-'fyüz\ vb **suf·fused; suf·fus·ing** : to spread over or through in the manner of fluid or light — **suf·fu·sion** \-'fyü-zhən\ n — **suf·fu·sive** \-'fyü-siv, -ziv\ adj

¹sug·ar \'shùg-ər\ n **1** : a sweet substance that is made up wholly or mostly of sucrose, is colorless or white when pure, is obtained from plants (as sugarcane or sugar beets), is a source of dietary carbohydrate, and is used as a sweetener and preservative of other foods **2** : any of various water-soluble compounds that vary widely in sweetness and make up the simpler carbohydrates

²sugar vb **sug·ared; sug·ar·ing** \'shùg-(ə-)riŋ\ **1** : to make something less hard to take or put up with ⟨*sugar* advice with praise⟩ **2** : to sprinkle or mix with sugar **3** : to change to crystals of sugar ⟨candy *sugars* when cooked too long⟩ **4** : to make maple syrup or maple sugar

sugar beet n : a white-rooted beet grown for the sugar in its roots

sugar bush n : woods in which sugar maples are more numerous than other kinds of trees

sug·ar·cane \'shùg-ər-ˌkān\ n : a stout tall tropical grass that has broad leaves and a jointed stem and is widely grown in warm regions as a source of sugar

sugarcane

sug·ar·coat \ˌshùg-ər-'kōt\ vb : to coat with or as if with sugar

sug·ar·house \'shùg-ər-ˌhaùs\ n : a building where maple sap is boiled to make maple syrup and maple sugar

sug·ar·less \'shùg-ər-ləs\ adj : containing no sugar ⟨*sugarless* gum⟩

sug·ar·loaf \-ˌlōf\ n **1** : refined sugar molded into a cone **2** : a hill or mountain shaped like a sugarloaf — **sugarloaf** adj

sugar maple n : a maple tree that has sweet sap; *esp* : a maple of eastern North America with hard wood that is much used for cabinetwork and sap that is the chief source of maple syrup and maple sugar

sugar pea n : SNOWPEA

sug·ar·plum \'shùg-ər-ˌpləm\ n : a round piece of candy

sug·ary \'shùg-(ə-)rē\ adj **1** : too sweetly sentimental **2** : containing, resembling, or tasting of sugar

sug·gest \sə(g)-'jest\ vb **1 a** : to put (as a thought) into a person's mind **b** : to propose as an idea or possibility ⟨*suggest* going for a walk⟩ **2** : to call to mind through close connection or association ⟨the fire *suggests* arson⟩ — **sug·gest·er** n

sug·gest·ible \sə(g)-'jes-tə-bəl\ adj : easily influenced by suggestion — **sug·gest·ibil·i·ty** \-ˌjes-tə-'bil-ət-ē\ n

sug·ges·tion \sə(g)-'jes-chən, -'jesh-\ n **1 a** : the act or process of suggesting **b** : something (as a thought or plan) that is suggested **2 a** : the process by which one thought leads to another especially through association of ideas **b** : a way of influencing attitudes and behavior hypnotically **3** : a slight indication ⟨a *suggestion* of a smile⟩

sug·ges·tive \sə(g)-'jes-tiv\ adj **1 a** : giving a suggestion : INDICATIVE ⟨*suggestive* of a past era⟩ **b** : full of suggestions : stimulating thought **c** : stirring mental associations **2** : suggesting something improper or indecent — **sug·ges·tive·ly** adv — **sug·ges·tive·ness** n

sui·cide \'sü-ə-ˌsīd\ n **1 a** : the act of killing oneself purposely **b** : ruin of one's own interests ⟨risking political *suicide*⟩ **2** : a person who commits or attempts suicide — **sui·cid·al** \ˌsü-ə-'sīd-ᵊl\ adj

suing *present participle of* SUE

¹suit \'süt\ n **1** : an action or process in a court for enforcing a right or claim **2** : an act or instance of requesting earnestly; *esp* : COURTSHIP **3** : a number of things used together : SET **4 a** : an outer costume of two or more pieces **b** : a costume to be worn for a special purpose or under particular conditions ⟨gym *suit*⟩ **5 a** : all the cards of one kind (as spades or hearts) in a pack of playing cards **b** : all the dominoes bearing the same number

²suit vb **1** : to outfit with clothes : DRESS **2** : to make suitable : ADAPT ⟨*suit* the action to the word⟩ **3 a** : to be proper for **b** : to be becoming to **4** : to meet the needs or desires of : PLEASE ⟨*suits* me fine⟩ **5** : to be in accordance : AGREE **6** : to be appropriate or satisfactory ⟨if their flavor and quality do not *suit*⟩

suit·able \'süt-ə-bəl\ adj **1** : adapted to a use or purpose

⟨food *suitable* for human consumption⟩ **2** : being fit or right for a use or group ⟨clothes *suitable* to the occasion⟩ ⟨a movie *suitable* for children⟩ **3** : QUALIFIED 1, CAPABLE ⟨looking for a *suitable* replacement⟩ **syn** see FIT — **suit·abil·i·ty** \ˌsüt-ə-'bil-ət-ē\ *n* — **suit·able·ness** \'süt-ə-bəl-nəs\ *n* — **suit·ably** \-blē\ *adv*

suit·case \'süt-ˌkās\ *n* : a flat rectangular traveling bag

suite \'swēt, *sense 2c is also* 'süt\ *n* **1** : the personal staff accompanying a ruler, diplomat, or dignitary on official business **2** : a group of things forming a unit or making up a collection: as **a** : a group of rooms occupied as a unit **b** : a piece of music for an orchestra usually consisting of several independent pieces written in the form of special dances or taken as selections from a larger work (as a ballet) **c** : a set of matched furniture for a room ⟨a bedroom *suite*⟩

suit·or \'süt-ər\ *n* **1** : one that petitions or pleads **2** : a party to a suit at law **3** : a man who courts a woman or seeks to marry her

Suk·koth \'súk-əs, -ˌōt, -ˌōth, -ˌōs\ *n* : a Jewish harvest festival celebrated in September or October to commemorate the temporary shelters used by the Jews during their wanderings in the wilderness

sul·fa \'səl-fə\ *adj* : of, relating to, or containing sulfanilamide or the sulfa drugs

sul·fa·di·a·zine \ˌsəl-fə-'dī-ə-ˌzēn\ *n* : a sulfa drug that is used especially in the treatment of meningitis, pneumonia, and intestinal infections

sulfa drug *n* : any of various synthetic drugs that stop or slow the growth of bacteria and are closely related chemically to sulfanilamide

sul·fa·nil·amide \ˌsəl-fə-'nil-ə-ˌmīd, -məd\ *n* : a compound in the form of crystals that is the parent compound of most of the sulfa drugs

sul·fate \'səl-ˌfāt\ *n* : a compound and especially a salt formed by the reaction of sulfuric acid with another substance

sul·fide \'səl-ˌfīd\ *n* : a compound of sulfur with one or more other elements : a salt of hydrogen sulfide

sul·fur *or* **sul·phur** \'səl-fər\ *n* : a nonmetallic element that occurs either free or combined especially in sulfides and sulfates, is found in proteins, exists in several forms including yellow crystals, and is used especially in the chemical and paper industries, in strengthening rubber, and in medicine for treating skin diseases — see ELEMENT table

sulfur dioxide *n* : a heavy strong-smelling gas that is used especially in making sulfuric acid, in bleaching, in preserving things, and as a refrigerant and that is a major substance in air pollution especially in industrial areas

sul·fu·ric \ˌsəl-'fyú(ə)r-ik\ *adj* : of, relating to, or containing sulfur

sulfuric acid *n* : a heavy oily strong acid that is colorless when pure and eats away at many solid substances

sul·fu·rous \'səl-f(y)ə-rəs *also for sense 1* ˌsəl-'fyúr-əs\ *adj* **1** : of, relating to, or containing sulfur **2** *or* **sulphu·rous a** : of, relating to, or dealing with the fire of hell : INFERNAL **b** : FIERY 3a, INFLAMED ⟨*sulfurous* sermon⟩ **c** : PROFANE 2, BLASPHEMOUS ⟨*sulfurous* language⟩

sulfurous acid *n* : a weak acid known especially in mixtures of sulfur dioxide with water and through its salts and used in bleaching

sulfur oxide *n* : any of several oxides of sulfur: as **a** : SULFUR DIOXIDE **b** : SULFUR TRIOXIDE

sulfur tri·ox·ide \-(')trī-'äk-ˌsīd\ *n* : a compound that consists of molecules having three oxygen atoms bonded to one sulfur atom, that is formed when sulfur dioxide and oxygen combine, that is a heavy strongly acid liquid when first produced at ordinary temperatures, and that gives off toxic fumes in air and combines violently with water producing much heat and forming sulfuric acid

¹sulk \'səlk\ *vb* : to be sullenly silent or irritable

²sulk *n* **1** : the state of one sulking — often used in pl. ⟨had

a case of the *sulks*⟩ **2** : a sulky mood or spell ⟨was in a sulk⟩

¹sulky \'səl-kē\ *adj* : sulking or given to spells of sulking — **sulk·i·ly** \-kə-lē\ *adv* — **sulk·i·ness** \-kē-nəs\ *n*

²sulky *n, pl* **sulk·ies** : a light two-wheeled vehicle that is pulled by a horse and has a seat for the driver only and usually no body

sulky

sul·len \'səl-ən\ *adj* **1 a** : gloomily or resentfully silent : not sociable **b** : suggesting a sullen state ⟨*sullen* refusal⟩ **2** : dull in sound or color **3** : DISMAL, GLOOMY ⟨a *sullen* sky⟩ — **sul·len·ly** *adv* — **sul·len·ness** \'səl-ən-(n)əs\ *n*

sul·ly \'səl-ē\ *vb* **sul·lied; sul·ly·ing** : to make soiled or tarnished

sul·tan \'səlt-ᵊn\ *n* : a king or ruler especially of a Muslim state

sul·ta·na \(ˌ)səl-'tan-ə\ *n* **1** : a female member of a sultan's family; *esp* : a sultan's wife **2 a** : a pale yellow seedless grape grown for raisins and wine **b** : a raisin prepared by drying a sultana

sul·tan·ate \'səlt-ᵊn-ˌāt\ *n* **1** : a state or country governed by a sultan **2** : the power or position of a sultan

sul·try \'səl-trē\ *adj* **sul·tri·er; -est 1** : very hot and humid ⟨a *sultry* day⟩ **2** : burning hot ⟨*sultry* sun⟩ **3** : exciting or capable of exciting sexual desire ⟨*sultry* glances⟩ — **sul·tri·ly** \-trə-lē\ *adv* — **sul·tri·ness** \-trē-nəs\ *n*

¹sum \'səm\ *n* **1** : an indefinite or specified amount of money **2** : the whole amount ⟨the *sum* of your experience⟩ **3 a** : a summary of the chief points or thoughts **b** : the main point ⟨the *sum* and substance of an argument⟩ **4 a** : the result of adding numbers ⟨the *sum* of 5 and 7 is 12⟩ **b** : a problem in arithmetic

²sum *vb* **summed; sum·ming 1** : to calculate the sum of : COUNT **2** : to reach a sum : AMOUNT

su·mac *also* **su·mach** \'sü-ˌmak, 'shü-\ *n* **1** : a material used in tanning and dyeing made of the leaves and other parts of sumac **2** : any of a genus of trees, shrubs, and woody vines with feathery compound leaves turning to brilliant colors in autumn, spikes or loose clusters of red or whitish berries, and in some cases leaves or berries that are poisonous to the touch — compare POISON IVY, POISON OAK

Su·me·ri·an \sü-'mer-ē-ən, -'mir-\ *n* **1** : a native of Sumer **2** : the language of the Sumerians that has no known relationships to other languages — **Sumerian** *adj*

sum·ma cum lau·de \ˌsúm-ə-ˌkúm-'laúd-ə, -'laúd-ē; ˌsəm-ə-ˌkəm-'lôd-ē\ *adv or adj* : with highest distinction ⟨graduated *summa cum laude*⟩

sum·ma·ri·za·tion \ˌsəm-(ə-)rə-'zā-shən\ *n* **1** : the act of summarizing **2** : ²SUMMARY

sum·ma·rize \'səm-ə-ˌrīz\ *vb* **-rized; -riz·ing 1** : to tell in or reduce to a summary **2** : to make a summary — **sum·ma·riz·er** *n*

¹sum·ma·ry \'səm-ə-rē\ *adj* **1** : expressing or covering the main points briefly : CONCISE ⟨a *summary* account⟩ **2** : done without delay or formality : quickly carried out ⟨a *summary* dismissal⟩ — **sum·mari·ly** \(ˌ)sə-'mer-ə-lē\ *adv*

²summary *n, pl* **-ries** : a short statement of the main points

\ə\ **abut**	\aú\ **out**	\i\ **tip**	\ó\ **saw**	\ú\ **foot**	
\ər\ **further**	\ch\ **chin**	\ī\ **life**	\ói\ **coin**	\y\ **yet**	
\a\ **mat**	\e\ **pet**	\j\ **job**	\th\ **thin**	\yü\ **few**	
\ā\ **take**	\ē\ **easy**	\ŋ\ **sing**	\th\ **this**	\yú\ **cure**	
\ä\ **cot, cart**	\g\ **go**	\ō\ **bone**	\ü\ **food**	\zh\ **vision**	

(as in a book or report)

sum·ma·tion \(,)sə-'mā-shən\ *n* **1** : the act or process of forming a sum : ADDITION **2** : ¹SUM 2, TOTAL **3** : a final part of an argument reviewing points made and expressing conclusions

¹**sum·mer** \'səm-ər\ *n* **1** : the season between spring and autumn that usually includes the months of June, July, and August in the northern hemisphere **2** : the warmer half of the year **3** : one of the years of one's life ⟨a child of eight *summers*⟩ **4** : a time of fulfillment

²**summer** *adj* : of or for the summer ⟨*summer* flowers⟩ ⟨a *summer* job⟩

³**summer** *vb* **sum·mered; sum·mer·ing** \'səm-(ə-)riŋ\ **1** : to pass the summer **2** : to keep or carry through the summer; *esp* : to provide (as cattle or sheep) with pasture during the summer

sum·mer·house \'səm-ər-,haùs\ *n* : a covered structure in a garden or park designed to provide a shady resting place in summer

summer school *n* : a school or school session conducted in summer especially to help students make faster progress toward a degree, to make up credits lost through absence or failure, or to round out professional education

summer squash *n* : any of various garden squashes closely related to the pumpkins and used as a vegetable before they are fully ripe

sum·mer·time \'səm-ər-,tīm\ *n* : the summer season or a period like summer

sum·mer·wood \-,wùd\ *n* : the harder and heavier outer portion of an annual ring of wood that is made up of small thick-walled cells and develops late in the growing season — compare SPRINGWOOD

sum·mery \'səm-(ə-)rē\ *adj* : of, resembling, or fit for summer

sum·mit \'səm-ət\ *n* **1** : ¹TOP 1a, APEX; *esp* : the highest point (as of a mountain) **2** : the topmost level that can be reached **3** : the highest level of officials; *esp* : the diplomatic level of heads of government ⟨a *summit* conference⟩

sum·mon \'səm-ən\ *vb* **sum·moned; sum·mon·ing** \-(ə-)niŋ\ **1** : to call or send for in order to meet : CONVENE **2** : to order to appear before a court of law **3** : to send for ⟨*summon* a physician⟩ **4** : to call into being ⟨*summon* up courage⟩ — **sum·mon·er** \-(ə-)nər\ *n*

¹**sum·mons** \'səm-ənz\ *n, pl* **sum·mons·es** **1** : the act of summoning; *esp* : a call by authority to appear at a place named or to attend to some duty **2** : a warning or notice to appear in court **3** : a call, signal, or knock that summons

²**summons** *vb* : SUMMON 2

su·mo \'sü-mō\ *n* : a Japanese form of wrestling in which a contestant loses if forced out of the ring or if any part of the body except the soles of the feet touches the ground [Japanese]

sump \'səmp\ *n* : a pit or reservoir serving as a container or as a drain for liquids

sump·tu·ous \'səm(p)-ch(ə-w)əs\ *adj* : involving large expense : LAVISH, LUXURIOUS ⟨a *sumptuous* feast⟩ — **sump·tu·ous·ly** *adv* — **sump·tu·ous·ness** *n*

sum total *n* : total result : TOTALITY

sum up 1 : to state concisely ⟨a sentence that *sums up* the important ideas⟩ **2** : to present a summary

¹**sun** \'sən\ *n* **1 a** : the star around which the planets revolve, from which they receive heat and light, and which has an average distance from the earth of 150,000,000 kilometers, a diameter of 1,390,000 kilometers, and a mass 332,000 times greater than earth **b** : a star like the sun **2** : the heat or light given off by the sun : SUNSHINE **3** : one resembling the sun usually in brilliance **4** : the rising or setting of the sun ⟨from *sun* to *sun*⟩ — **in the sun** : in the public eye — **under the sun** : in the world : on earth

²**sun** *vb* **sunned; sun·ning 1** : to expose to or as if to the rays of the sun **2** : to sun oneself

sun·baked \'sən-,bākt\ *adj* **1** : heated, parched, or compressed especially by too much sunlight **2** : baked by exposing to sunshine ⟨*sunbaked* bricks⟩

sun·bath \'sən-,bath, -,bàth\ *n* : the action of sunbathing

sun·bathe \-,bāth\ *vb* : to expose oneself to sunlight or a sunlamp especially to get a tan — **sun·bath·er** \-,bā-thər\ *n*

sun·beam \-,bēm\ *n* : a ray of sunlight

Sun·belt \-,belt\ *n* : the southern and southwestern states of the U.S.

sun·block \-,bläk\ *n* : a preparation designed to block out more of the sun's rays than a sunscreen

sun·bon·net \-,bän-ət\ *n* : a woman's bonnet with a wide brim framing the face and usually having a ruffle at the back to protect the neck from the sun

¹**sun·burn** \-,bərn\ *vb* **-burned** \-,bərnd\ *or* **-burnt** \-,bərnt\; **-burn·ing 1** : to burn or discolor by the sun **2** : to become sunburned

²**sunburn** *n* : a sore red state of the skin caused by too much sunlight

sunbonnet

sun·burst \'sən-,bərst\ *n* **1** : a flash of sunlight especially through a break in the clouds **2** : a jeweled pin representing a sun surrounded by rays

sun·dae \'sən-dē\ *n* : a serving of ice cream topped with fruit, syrup, or nuts

¹**Sun·day** \'sən-dē\ *n* : the first day of the week : the Christian Sabbath

> **Word History** It was believed in ancient times that there were seven "planets", including the sun and the moon. The days of the week were named in Latin for these "planets". One of the days was named *dies solis*, meaning "day of the sun." The Latin name was later translated into other languages. *Dies solis* became *sunnandæg* in Old English. The modern English *Sunday* comes from the Old English *sunnandæg*. [Old English *sunnandæg* "Sunday", derived from Latin *dies solis* "day of the sun", from *dies* "day" and *sol* "sun" — related to DIARY, SOLAR]

²**Sunday** *adj* **1** : of, relating to, or associated with Sunday **2** : ¹BEST 1 ⟨*Sunday* suit⟩

Sunday school *n* : a school held on Sunday for religious education

sun·der \'sən-dər\ *vb* **sun·dered; sun·der·ing** \-d(ə-)riŋ\ : to break or force apart or in two

sun·dew \'sən-d(y)ü\ *n* : any of a genus of wetland herbs that trap and digest insects with the sticky hairlike glands on their leaves

sun·di·al \-,dī(-ə)l\ *n* : a device to show the time of day by the position of the shadow cast on a marked plate or disk usually by an object with a straight edge

sun·down \-,daún\ *n* : SUNSET 2

sun·down·er \-,daù-nər\ *n, Australian* : ²TRAMP 1, HOBO

sun·dries \'sən-drēz\ *n pl* : miscellaneous small articles (as pins or needles)

sundial

sun·dry \'sən-drē\ *adj* : MISCELLANEOUS, SEVERAL, VARIOUS ⟨for *sundry* reasons⟩

sun·fish \'sən-,fish\ *n* **1** : a sea fish that is flattened from side to side with the head much larger than the shortened body and that has high fins and a small mouth **2** : any of a family of American freshwater fishes that are related to the perches, are often brightly colored, and usually have a body that is flattened from side to side

sun·flow·er \-,flaů(-ə)r\ *n* : any of a genus of tall herbs that are often grown for their showy flower heads with yellow ray flowers and for their oil-rich seeds

sung *past and past participle of* SING

sun·glass·es \'sən-,glas-əz\ *n pl* : glasses to protect the eyes from the sun

sun god *n* : a god that represents the sun in various religions

sunk *past and past participle of* SINK

sunk·en \'sən-kən\ *adj* **1** : being submerged; *esp* : lying at the bottom of a body of water ⟨*sunken* ships⟩ **2** : fallen in : HOLLOW ⟨*sunken* cheeks⟩ **3 a** : lying in a depression ⟨a *sunken* garden⟩ **b** : constructed below the normal floor level ⟨a *sunken* living room⟩

sun·lamp \'sən-,lamp\ *n* : an electric lamp that is made to give off radiation of wavelengths from ultraviolet to infrared

sun·less \'sən-ləs\ *adj* : lacking sunshine : DARK

sun·light \'sən-,līt\ *n* : the light of the sun : SUNSHINE

sun·lit \-,lit\ *adj* : lighted by or as if by the sun

Sun·ni \'sůn-(n)ē\ *n* : the Muslims of the branch of Islam that follows the orthodox tradition

sun·ny \'sən-ē\ *adj* **sun·ni·er; -est** **1** : bright with sunshine **2** : MERRY 1 ⟨a *sunny* smile⟩ — **sun·ni·ly** \'sən-ᵊl-ē\ *adv* — **sun·ni·ness** \'sən-ē-nəs\ *n*

sun·rise \'sən-,rīz\ *n* **1** : the apparent rising of the sun above the horizon; *also* : the accompanying atmospheric effects (as color) **2** : the time at which the sun rises

sun·screen \-,skrēn\ *n* : a substance used in suntan preparations to protect the skin from excessive ultraviolet radiation

sun·set \-,set\ *n* **1** : the apparent sinking of the sun below the horizon; *also* : the accompanying atmospheric effects **2** : the time at which the sun sets

sun·shade \-,shād\ *n* : something (as a parasol) used to protect from the sun's rays

sun·shine \-,shīn\ *n* **1 a** : the sun's light or direct rays **b** : the warmth and light given by the sun's rays **2** : one (as a person or a condition) that spreads warmth, cheer, or happiness — **sun·shiny** \-,shī-nē\ *adj*

sun·spot \-,spät\ *n* : one of the dark spots that appear from time to time on the sun's surface and are usually visible only through a telescope

sun·stroke \-,strōk\ *n* : a bodily condition caused by staying in the sun for too long and often marked by a high fever and collapse — compare HEATSTROKE

sun·tan \-,tan\ *n* : a browning of the skin from being exposed to the rays of the sun — **sun·tanned** \-,tand\ *adj*

sun·up \-,əp\ *n* : SUNRISE 2

¹sun·ward \'sən-wərd\ *adv* : toward the sun

²sunward *adj* : facing the sun

¹sup \'səp\ *vb* **supped; sup·ping** : to take or drink in swallows or gulps [Old English *sūpan, suppan* "to eat or drink in gulps"]

²sup *n* : a mouthful especially of liquid : SIP

³sup *vb* **supped; sup·ping** **1** : to eat the evening meal **2** : to make one's supper — used with *on* or *off* ⟨*supped* on roast beef⟩ [Middle English *suppen, soupen* "to eat the evening meal", from early French *souper* (same meaning), from *soupe* "soup, sop"]

¹su·per \'sü-pər\ *adj* **1** — used as an overall term of approval ⟨a *super* cook⟩ **2** : very large or powerful ⟨a *super* atom bomb⟩ **3** : showing the characteristics of its type to an extreme degree ⟨*super* secrecy⟩

²super *n* **1** : an actor not listed with the regular cast **2** : SUPERINTENDENT, SUPERVISOR

³super *adv* **1** : ²VERY 1, EXTREMELY ⟨a *super* fast car⟩ **2** : to a degree exceeding the usual or normal ⟨*super* critical⟩

super- *prefix* **1 a** : over and above : higher in quantity, quality, or degree than : more than ⟨*super*fine⟩ ⟨*super*human⟩ **b** : exceeding or so as to exceed what is usual or

normal ⟨*super*cool⟩ **c** : bigger, better, or more important than others of the same kind ⟨*super*highway⟩ ⟨*super*star⟩ **2 a** : situated or placed above, on, or at the top of ⟨*super*impose⟩ **b** : next above or higher ⟨*super*tonic⟩ [derived from Latin *super* "over, above"]

su·per·abun·dant \,sü-pə-rə-'bən-dənt\ *adj* : more than ample : EXCESSIVE — **su·per·abun·dance** \-dən(t)s\ *n* — **su·per·abun·dant·ly** *adv*

su·per·an·nu·ate \,sü-pə-'ran-yə-,wāt\ *vb* **-at·ed; -at·ing** **1** : to retire and pension because of age or infirmity **2** : to become retired **3** : to become outdated — **su·per·an·nu·a·tion** \-,ran-yə-'wā-shən\ *n*

su·per·an·nu·at·ed *adj* : too old for work or use

su·perb \su-'pərb\ *adj* : outstandingly excellent, impressive, or beautiful — **su·perb·ly** *adv* — **su·perb·ness** *n*

su·per·cil·ious \,sü-pər-'sil-ē-əs, -'sil-yəs\ *adj* : coolly and disdainfully proud : SNOBBISH — **su·per·cil·ious·ly** *adv* — **su·per·cil·ious·ness** *n*

su·per·com·put·er \'sü-pər-kəm-,pyüt-ər\ *n* : a large very fast mainframe used especially for scientific computations

su·per·con·ti·nent \'sü-pər-,känt-ᵊn-ənt, -,känt-nənt\ *n* : a former large continent which is assumed to have existed and from which other continents broke off and drifted away

su·per·cool \,sü-pər-'kül\ *vb* : to cool below the freezing point while remaining liquid

su·per·fi·cial \,sü-pər-'fish-əl\ *adj* **1 a** : of or relating to a surface **b** : lying on, not going below, or affecting only the surface ⟨*superficial* wounds⟩ **2** : not thorough : SHALLOW ⟨a *superficial* inspection⟩ — **su·per·fi·ci·al·i·ty** \-,fish-ē-'al-ət-ē\ *n* — **su·per·fi·cial·ly** \-'fish-(ə-)lē\ *adv*

su·per·fine \,sü-pər-'fīn\ *adj* **1** : overly refined or nice **2** : extremely fine ⟨*superfine* toothbrush bristles⟩ **3** : of high quality or grade — used especially of merchandise

su·per·flu·ity \,sü-pər-'flü-ət-ē\ *n, pl* **-ties** **1** : an amount in excess **2** : something unnecessary or superfluous

su·per·flu·ous \su-'pər-flə-wəs\ *adj* : going beyond what is enough or necessary : EXTRA [Middle English *superfluous* "more than is needed", from Latin *superfluus*, literally "running over", from *superfluere* "to overflow", from *super-* "over, in addition", and *fluere* "to flow" — related to FLUID] — **su·per·flu·ous·ly** \su-'pər-flə-wəs-lē\ *adv*

su·per·glue \'sü-pər-,glü\ *n* : a very strong glue

su·per·heat \,sü-pər-'hēt\ *vb* **1 a** : to heat (steam) to a higher temperature than the normal boiling point of water **b** : to heat a liquid above the boiling point without converting into vapor **2** : to heat very much or excessively

su·per·he·ro \'sü-per-,hē-rō, -,hi(ə)r-ō\ *n* : a fictional hero having extraordinary or superhuman powers; *also* : a very successful person

su·per·high·way \,sü-pər-'hī-,wā\ *n* : a highway designed for high-speed traffic

su·per·hu·man \,sü-pər-'hyü-mən, -'yü-\ *adj* **1** : being above the human ⟨*superhuman* beings⟩ **2** : going beyond normal human power, size, or capability ⟨a *superhuman* effort⟩ — **su·per·hu·man·ly** *adv*

su·per·im·pose \,sü-pə-rim-'pōz\ *vb* : to place or lay over or above something — **su·per·im·po·si·tion** \-,rim-pə-'zish-ən\ *n*

su·per·in·tend \,sü-p(ə-)rin-'tend, ,sü-pərn-\ *vb* : to be in charge of : DIRECT

su·per·in·ten·dence \,sü-p(ə-)rin-'ten-dən(t)s, ,sü-pərn-\ *n* : the act or function of superintending or directing

su·per·in·ten·den·cy \,sü-p(ə-)rin-'ten-dən-sē\ *n, pl* **-cies** : the office or post of a superintendent

su·per·in·ten·dent \,sü-p(ə-)rin-'ten-dənt, ,sü-pərn-\ *n* : a person who directs or manages something

\ə\ abut	\aů\ out	\i\ tip	\ȯ\ saw	\ů\ foot
\ər\ further	\ch\ chin	\ī\ life	\ȯi\ coin	\yů\ yet
\a\ mat	\e\ pet	\j\ job	\th\ thin	\yü\ few
\ā\ take	\ē\ easy	\ŋ\ sing	\th\ this	\yů\ cure
\ä\ cot, cart	\g\ go	\ō\ bone	\ü\ food	\zh\ vision

¹su·pe·ri·or \su̇-'pir-ē-ər\ *adj* **1** : situated higher up : UPPER **2** : of higher rank, quality, or importance **3** : courageously or calmly indifferent (as to something painful) **4 a** : greater in quantity or numbers ⟨escaped by *superior* speed⟩ **b** : excellent of its kind : BETTER ⟨a *superior* memory⟩ **5** : covering or including more things ⟨a genus is *superior* to a species⟩ **6** : feeling that one is better or more important than others — **su·pe·ri·or·ly** *adv*

²superior *n* **1** : one who is above another in rank, station, or office; *esp* : the head of a religious house or order **2** : one that goes beyond another in quality or merit

su·pe·ri·or·i·ty \su̇-,pir-ē-'ȯr-ət-ē, -'är-\ *n, pl* **-ties** : the state or fact of being superior

superior vena cava *n* : a large vein that returns blood to the heart from the upper or front part of the body including the head and front limbs

¹su·per·la·tive \su̇-'pər-lət-iv\ *adj* **1** : of, relating to, or being the form of an adjective or adverb that shows the highest or lowest degree of comparison **2** : better than all others : SUPREME — **su·per·la·tive·ly** *adv*

²superlative *n* **1** : the superlative degree or a superlative form in a language **2** : the superlative or utmost degree of something **3** : a superlative person or thing

su·per·man \'sü-pər-,man\ *n* : a person with extraordinary or superhuman power

su·per·mar·ket \'sü-pər-,mär-kət\ *n* : a self-service market selling foods and household merchandise

su·per·mi·cro \-,mī-krō\ *n* : a very fast and powerful microcomputer

su·per·mini \-,min-ē\ *n* : SUPER-MINICOMPUTER

su·per·mini·com·put·er \-'min-ē-kəm-,pyüt-ər\ *n* : a very fast and powerful minicomputer

su·per·nal \su̇-'pərn-ᵊl\ *adj* **1 a** : being or coming from on high **b** : HEAVENLY **3** ⟨*supernal* lamb chops⟩ **2** : located in or belonging to the sky — **su·per·nal·ly** \-ᵊl-ē\ *adv*

su·per·nat·u·ral \,sü-pər-'nach-(ə-)rəl\ *adj* **1** : of or relating to an order of existence beyond the visible observable universe; *esp* : of or relating to God or a god, demigod, spirit, or devil **2 a** : departing from what is usual or normal especially so as to appear to go beyond the laws of nature **b** : attributed to an invisible agent (as a ghost or spirit) — **supernatural** *n* — **su·per·nat·u·ral·ly** \-'nach-(ə-)rə-lē, -'nach-ər-lē\ *adv*

su·per·no·va \,sü-pər-'nō-və\ *n* : the explosion of a very large star in which the star temporarily gives off up to one billion times more energy than the sun

¹su·per·nu·mer·ary \,sü-pər-'n(y)ü-mə-,rer-ē\ *adj* : exceeding the usual or needed number : EXTRA

²supernumerary *n, pl* **-ar·ies** **1** : a supernumerary person or thing **2** : an actor employed to play a small usually nonspeaking part

su·per·phos·phate \,sü-pər-'fäs-,fāt\ *n* : a soluble mixture of phosphates used as fertilizer

su·per·pose \,sü-pər-'pōz\ *vb* **-posed; -pos·ing** : to place or lay over or above another especially so as to make all like parts coincide ⟨congruent triangles can be *superposed*⟩ — **su·per·po·si·tion** \-pə-'zish-ən\ *n*

su·per·pow·er \'sü-pər-,pau̇(-ə)r\ *n* : an extremely powerful nation (as the United States)

su·per·sat·u·rat·ed \,sü-pər-'sach-ə-,rāt-əd\ *adj* : containing an amount of something greater than the amount required for saturation by having been cooled from a higher temperature to a temperature below that at which saturation occurs ⟨a *supersaturated* solution⟩ ⟨air *supersaturated* with water vapor⟩

su·per·scribe \'sü-pər-,skrīb\ *vb* **-scribed; -scrib·ing** **1** : to write (as a name or address) on the outside or cover of **2** : to write or engrave on the top or outside

su·per·script \'sü-pər-,skript\ *n* : a distinguishing symbol (as a numeral or letter) written immediately above or above and to the side of another character — **superscript** *adj*

su·per·scrip·tion \,sü-pər-'skrip-shən\ *n* **1** : something

superscribed **2** : the act of superscribing

su·per·sede \,sü-pər-'sēd\ *vb* **-sed·ed; -sed·ing** **1** : to force out of use as inferior **2** : to take the place, room, or position of : REPLACE **3** : to remove in favor of another [Middle English *superceden* "to supercede", from early French *superseder* "to refrain from", from Latin *supersedēre* "to be superior to, refrain from", literally "to sit above", from *super* "over, above", and *sedēre* "to sit"] — **su·per·se·dure** \-'sē-jər\ *n*

su·per·sen·si·tive \,sü-pər-'sen(t)-sət-iv, -'sen(t)-stiv\ *adj* : HYPERSENSITIVE

su·per·ses·sion \,sü-pər-'sesh-ən\ *n* : the act of superseding : the state of being superseded

su·per·son·ic \,sü-pər-'sän-ik\ *adj* **1** : ULTRASONIC **2** : of, being, or relating to speeds from one to five times the speed of sound in air **3** : moving, capable of moving, or using air currents moving at supersonic speed ⟨a *supersonic* airplane⟩ — **su·per·son·i·cal·ly** \-i-k(ə-)lē\ *adv*

su·per·star \'sü-pər-,stär\ *n* : a star (as in sports or the movies) who is considered extremely talented, has great public appeal, and can usually command a high salary

su·per·sti·tion \,sü-pər-'stish-ən\ *n* **1** : a belief or practice resulting from ignorance, fear of the unknown, or trust in magic **2** : an unreasoning fear of nature, the unknown, or God resulting from superstition

su·per·sti·tious \,sü-pər-'stish-əs\ *adj* : of, relating to, or influenced by superstition — **su·per·sti·tious·ly** *adv*

su·per·tank·er \'sü-pər-,taŋ-kər\ *n* : a very large cargo ship fitted with tanks for carrying large amounts of liquid

su·per·ton·ic \,sü-pər-'tän-ik\ *n* : the second tone of the musical scale

su·per·vene \,sü-pər-'vēn\ *vb* **-vened; -ven·ing** : to take place as an additional or unlooked-for development — **su·per·ven·tion** \-'ven-chən\ *n*

su·per·ve·nient \,sü-pər-'vē-nyənt\ *adj* : coming or occurring as something additional or unexpected

su·per·vise \'sü-pər-,vīz\ *vb* **-vised; -vis·ing** : SUPERINTEND, OVERSEE [from Latin *supervisus*, past participle of *supervidēre* "to oversee", from *super-* "over, above" and *vidēre* "to see" — related to VISION]

su·per·vi·sion \,sü-pər-'vizh-ən\ *n* : the act of supervising; *esp* : a critical watching and directing (as of activities)

su·per·vi·sor \'sü-pər-,vī-zər\ *n* : a person who supervises; *esp* : an officer in charge of a unit or an operation of a business, government, or school — **su·per·vi·so·ry** \,sü-pər-'vīz-(ə-)rē\ *adj*

su·pine \su̇-'pīn\ *adj* **1** : lying on the back or with the face upward **2** : showing mental or moral indifference : LAZY — **su·pine·ly** *adv* — **su·pine·ness** \-'pīn-nəs\ *n*

supped *past and past participle of* SUP

sup·per \'səp-ər\ *n* **1 a** : the evening meal especially when dinner is eaten at midday **b** : a social affair having a supper **2** : a light meal served late in the evening

supping *present participle of* SUP

sup·plant \sə-'plant\ *vb* **1** : to take the place of (another) especially by force or treachery **2 a** : to root out and supply a substitute for **b** : to gain the place of and serve as a substitute for especially by reason of superior excellence or power — **sup·plan·ta·tion** \(,)sə-,plan-'tā-shən\ *n* — **sup·plant·er** \sə-'plant-ər\ *n*

¹sup·ple \'səp-əl\ *adj* **sup·pler** \'səp-(ə-)lər\; **sup·plest** \'səp-(ə-)ləst\ **1** : readily adaptable to new situations ⟨a *supple* mind⟩ **2 a** : capable of being bent without creases or breaks : PLIANT **b** : able to bend or twist with ease and grace : LIMBER — **sup·ple·ness** \-əl-nəs\ *n*

²supple *vb* **sup·pled; sup·pling** \'səp-(ə-)liŋ\ : to make soft and easy to bend

¹sup·ple·ment \'səp-lə-mənt\ *n* **1** : something that supplies what is needed or makes an addition ⟨diet *supplements*⟩ **2** : an arc or angle that when added to a given arc or angle equals 180 degrees — **sup·ple·men·tal** \,səp-lə-'ment-ᵊl\ *adj*

²sup·ple·ment \'səp-lə-ˌment\ *vb* : to add to ⟨*supplement* their incomes by doing odd jobs⟩ — **sup·ple·men·ta·tion** \ˌsəp-lə-ˌmen-'tā-shən, -mən-\ *n*

sup·ple·men·ta·ry \ˌsəp-lə-'ment-ə-rē, -'men-trē\ *adj* **1** : added as a supplement : ADDITIONAL **2** : being or related to a supplement or a supplementary angle

supplementary angle *n* : either of two angles whose sum is 180 degrees — usually used in pl.

¹sup·pli·ant \'səp-lē-ənt\ *n* : one who asks earnestly

²suppliant *adj* : humbly asking — **sup·pli·ant·ly** *adv*

sup·pli·cant \'səp-li-kənt\ *n* : one who asks earnestly — **suppliant** *adj* — **sup·pli·cant·ly** *adv*

sup·pli·cate \'səp-lə-ˌkāt\ *vb* **-cat·ed; -cat·ing** **1** : to make a humble appeal; *esp* : to pray to God **2** : to ask earnestly and humbly — **sup·pli·ca·tion** \ˌsəp-lə-'kā-shən\ *n*

¹sup·ply \sə-'plī\ *vb* **sup·plied; sup·ply·ing** **1** : to add as a supplement **2 a** : to provide for : SATISFY ⟨enough to *supply* the demand⟩ **b** : to make available for use ⟨*supplied* the necessary money⟩ **c** : to satisfy the needs or wishes of — **sup·pli·er** \-'plī(-ə)r\ *n*

²supply *n, pl* **supplies** **1 a** : the quantity or amount of something that is needed or available ⟨the nation's oil *supply*⟩ **b** : ²STORE 1b — usually used in pl. **2** : the act or process of filling a want or need **3** : the quantities of goods or services offered for sale at a particular time or at one price

¹sup·port \sə-'pō(ə)rt, -'pȯ(ə)rt\ *vb* **1** : to endure bravely or quietly : BEAR **2 a** : to promote the interests or cause of **b** : to uphold or defend as true or right : ADVOCATE **c** : to argue or vote for ⟨*support* a candidate⟩ **d** : ¹ASSIST, HELP **e** : to provide evidence for : VERIFY ⟨they cannot *support* the claim⟩ **3** : to pay the costs of : MAINTAIN ⟨*supports* a large family⟩ **4 a** : to hold up or in position or serve as a foundation or prop for ⟨posts *support* the porch roof⟩ **b** : to keep up the price of (as milk or wheat) by buying large amounts to store at a certain price **5** : to keep something going : SUSTAIN ⟨not enough air to *support* life⟩ — **sup·port·able** \-ə-bəl\ *adj* — **sup·port·ive** \-'pōrt-iv, -'pȯrt-\ *adj*

²support *n* **1** : the act or process of supporting : the condition of being supported **2** : someone or something that supports

sup·port·er \sə-'pōrt-ər, -'pȯrt-\ *n* : one that supports; *esp* : one who argues or votes for someone or something

support hose *n* : elastic stockings

sup·pose \sə-'pōz\ *vb* **sup·posed; sup·pos·ing** **1** : to take as true or as a fact for the sake of argument ⟨*suppose* a fire should break out⟩ **2** : to hold as an opinion : BELIEVE ⟨they *supposed* they were on the right bus⟩ **3** : to come to a conclusion arrived at by guessing ⟨who do you *suppose* will win⟩

sup·posed \sə-'pōzd; *sense 1 usually* -'pō-zəd, *senses 2 & 3 often* -'pōst\ *adj* **1** : believed to be true or real ⟨a *supposed* cure⟩ **2** : considered probable or certain : EXPECTED ⟨they are *supposed* to be here tomorrow⟩ **3** : required by or as if by authority ⟨you are *supposed* to listen to your parents⟩ — **sup·pos·ed·ly** \-'pō-zəd-lē *also* -'pōz-dlē\ *adv*

sup·po·si·tion \ˌsəp-ə-'zish-ən\ *n* **1** : something that is supposed **2** : the act of supposing — **sup·po·si·tion·al** \-'zish-nəl, -ən-ᵊl\ *adj*

sup·press \sə-'pres\ *vb* **1** : to put down by authority or force ⟨*suppress* a rebellion⟩ **2 a** : to keep from being known ⟨tried to *suppress* the news⟩ **b** : to stop the publication or distribution of ⟨ordered the magazine *suppressed*⟩ **3** : to hold back : REPRESS ⟨*suppress* feelings of jealousy⟩ ⟨*suppressed* a cough⟩ **4** : to slow or stop the growth or development of : STUNT — **sup·press·ible** \-ə-bəl\ *adj* — **sup·pres·sion** \-'presh-ən\ *n* — **sup·pres·sive** \-'pres-iv\ *adj* — **sup·pres·sor** \-'pres-ər\ *n*

sup·pu·rate \'səp-yə-ˌrāt\ *vb* **-rat·ed; -rat·ing** : to form or

give off pus — **sup·pu·ra·tion** \ˌsəp-yə-'rā-shən\ *n*

supra- *prefix* **1** : SUPER- 2a ⟨*supra*renal⟩ **2** : going beyond ⟨*supra*national⟩ [derived from Latin *supra* "above, beyond"]

su·pra·na·tion·al \ˌsü-prə-'nash-nəl, -ən-ᵊl\ *adj* : going beyond national boundaries or authority

¹su·pra·re·nal \ˌsü-prə-'rēn-ᵊl\ *adj* : situated above or in front of the kidneys; *esp* : ¹ADRENAL

²suprarenal *n* : a suprarenal part; *esp* : ADRENAL GLAND

su·prem·a·cist \sə-'prem-ə-səst\ *n* : a person who believes that one group (as the white race) should control all others

su·prem·a·cy \sə-'prem-ə-sē\ *n, pl* **-cies** **1** : the quality or state of being supreme **2** : supreme authority or power

su·preme \sə-'prēm, sü-\ *adj* **1** : highest in rank or authority **2** : highest in degree or quality **3** : greatest in degree ⟨giving one's life is the *supreme* sacrifice⟩ [from Latin *supremus,* a form of *superus* "upper", from *super* "over, above"] — **su·preme·ly** *adv* — **su·preme·ness** *n*

Supreme Being *n* : GOD 1

supreme court *n* : the highest court in a political unit (as the U.S. or one of its states)

sur- *prefix* : over ⟨*sur*print⟩ ⟨*sur*tax⟩ [derived from Latin *super* "over, above"]

sur·cease \'sər-ˌsēs, (ˌ)sər-'sēs\ *n* : a stopping of action; *esp* : a temporary halt

¹sur·charge \'sər-ˌchärj\ *vb* **1 a** : OVERCHARGE 1 **b** : to charge an extra fee **2** : ¹OVERLOAD **3** : to mark a new value or a surcharge on a stamp

²surcharge *n* **1** : an additional tax or charge **2** : a burden that is too great **3 a** : a mark on top of a stamp that changes the value **b** : a stamp bearing such a mark

sur·cin·gle \'sər-ˌsiŋ-gəl\ *n* : a belt or band passing around the body of a horse to bind a saddle or pack fast to the horse's back

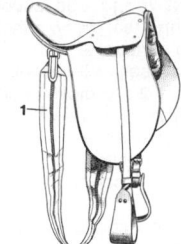

1 surcingle

sur·coat \'sər-ˌkōt\ *n* : an outer coat or cloak; *esp* : one worn over armor

¹sure \'shu̇(ə)r, *especially Southern* 'shō(ə)r\ *adj* **1** : firmly established : STEADFAST **2** : RELIABLE, TRUSTWORTHY **3** : having no doubt : CONFIDENT **4** : not to be doubted : CERTAIN **5 a** : bound to happen : INEVITABLE ⟨*sure* disaster⟩ **b** : bound as if by fate ⟨we are *sure* to win⟩ [Middle English *sure* "established, steadfast", from early French *sur* (same meaning), from *securus* "secure" — related to SECURE] — **sure·ness** *n* — **for sure** : without doubt : with certainty — **to be sure** : it must be admitted

²sure *adv* : SURELY 1b, 2

sure·fire \ˌshu̇r-'fī(ə)r\ *adj* : certain to get results

sure·foot·ed \'shu̇(ə)r-'fu̇t-əd\ *adj* : not likely to stumble or fall — **sure·foot·ed·ly** *adv* — **sure·foot·ed·ness** *n*

sure·ly \'shu̇(ə)r-lē\ *adv* **1 a** : with confidence ⟨answered quickly and *surely*⟩ **b** : without doubt : CERTAINLY ⟨they will *surely* be heard from again⟩ **2** : beyond question : TRULY ⟨I *surely* am tired this afternoon⟩

sure·ty \'shu̇r-ət-ē, 'shu̇(ə)rt-ē\ *n, pl* **-ties** **1** : sure knowledge : CERTAINTY **2** : a formal agreement to do something : GUARANTEE **3** : one who takes legal responsibility for another's debt or failure in duty

\ə\ abut	\au̇\ out	\i\ tip	\ȯ\ saw	\u̇\ foot
\ər\ further	\ch\ chin	\ī\ life	\ȯi\ coin	\y\ yet
\a\ mat	\e\ pet	\j\ job	\th\ thin	\yü\ few
\ā\ take	\ē\ easy	\ŋ\ sing	\th\ this	\yu̇\ cure
\ä\ cot, cart	\g\ go	\ō\ bone	\ü\ food	\zh\ vision

¹surf \'sərf\ *n* **1** : waves that break upon the shore **2** : the foam, splash, and sound of breaking waves

²surf *vb* : to ride the surf (as on a surfboard)

¹sur·face \'sər-fəs\ *n* **1** : the outside of an object or body **2** : any plane or curved region in space which is two-dimensional but has no thickness at any point and often for which any two points contained in it can be connected by a straight or curving line lying completely in the region ⟨*surface* of a sphere⟩ **3** : the outside appearance ⟨on the *surface* the plan seems good⟩ — **surface** *adj*

²surface *vb* **sur·faced; sur·fac·ing** **1** : to give a surface to ⟨*surface* a road⟩ **2** : to come to the surface

surface tension *n* : the attractive force felt by surface molecules of a liquid from the molecules beneath that tends to draw the surface molecules into the mass of the liquid and makes the liquid take the shape having the least surface area

sur·fac·ing *n* : material forming or used to form a surface

surf·board \'sərf-,bō(ə)rd, -,bo(ə)rd\ *n* : a lightweight board used in the sport of surfing — **surfboard** *vb* — **surf·board·er** *n*

surfboard

¹sur·feit \'sər-fət\ *n* **1** : a supply that is more than enough : EXCESS **2** : an enjoyment of something (as food or drink) beyond what is good or necessary **3** : disgust caused by excess

²surfeit *vb* : to feed, supply, or enjoy to the point of excess

surf·ing \'sər-fiŋ\ *n* : the sport of riding the surf especially on a surfboard

¹surge \'sərj\ *vb* **surged; surg·ing** **1** : to rise and fall actively **2** : to move in or as if in waves

²surge *n* **1** : a swelling, rolling, or sweeping forward like that of a wave : an onward rush ⟨a *surge* of support for the candidate⟩ **2** : a large wave or billow : SWELL

sur·geon \'sər-jən\ *n* : a physician who specializes in surgery

sur·gery \'sərj-(ə-)rē\ *n, pl* **-ger·ies** **1** : medical science concerned with the correction of physical defects, the repair and healing of injuries, and the treatment of diseased conditions especially by operations **2** : the work done by a surgeon **3** : a room or area where surgery is performed [Middle English *surgerie* "surgery", from early French *cirurgie, surgerie* (same meaning), from Latin *chirurgia* (same meaning), derived from Greek *cheirourgos* "surgeon", from *cheirourgos* "working with the hand", from *cheir* "hand" and *ergon* "work"]

sur·gi·cal \'sər-ji-kəl\ *adj* : of, relating to, or associated with surgeons or surgery ⟨*surgical* skills⟩ ⟨*surgical* equipment⟩ ⟨a *surgical* fever⟩ — **sur·gi·cal·ly** \-k(ə-)lē\ *adv*

sur·ly \'sər-lē\ *adj* **sur·li·er; -est** : having a rude unfriendly disposition — **sur·li·ness** *n*

> **Word History** The word *surly,* which describes someone with a very bad temper, was originally spelled *sirly.* It comes from the familiar word *sir,* which has been used for centuries as a title of respect for a gentleman or nobleman. *Sirly* was originally used to describe a person who behaves in a very proud way — the kind of person who might insist on being called "sir". It was similar in meaning to the word *lordly.* Many years of use brought about the changes in spelling and in meaning that have given us the modern word *surly.* [Middle English *sirly* "lordly, imperious", from *sir* "a man of rank"]

¹sur·mise \sər-'mīz\ *vb* **sur·mised; sur·mis·ing** : to form an idea on very little evidence : GUESS

²sur·mise \sər-'mīz, 'sər-,mīz\ *n* : a thought or idea based on little evidence : CONJECTURE

sur·mount \sər-'maunt\ *vb* **1** : OVERCOME 1 ⟨*surmount* an obstacle⟩ **2** : to get to the top of : CLIMB **3** : to stand or lie at the top of : CROWN ⟨a weather vane *surmounts* the roof⟩ — **sur·mount·able** \-ə-bəl\ *adj*

sur·name \'sər-,nām\ *n* **1** : an added name : NICKNAME **2** : the name held in common by members of a family — **surname** *vb*

sur·pass \sər-'pas\ *vb* **1** : to be greater, better, or stronger than **2** : to go beyond the reach, powers, or capacity of — **sur·pass·able** \-ə-bəl\ *adj* **syn** see EXCEED

sur·plice \'sər-pləs\ *n* : a loose white outer garment worn at church services

sur·plus \'sər-(,)pləs\ *n* **1** : the amount more than what is required or necessary : EXCESS **2** : an excess of income over spending — **surplus** *adj*

¹sur·prise \sə(r)-'prīz\ *n* **1 a** : an attack made without warning **b** : an act or an instance of coming upon someone suddenly **2** : something that surprises **3** : the state of being surprised : ASTONISHMENT

²surprise *also* **sur·prize** *vb* **sur·prised** *also* **sur·prized; sur·pris·ing** *also* **sur·priz·ing** **1 a** : to attack without warning **b** : to capture by an unexpected attack **2** : to come upon unexpectedly **3** : to fill with wonder or amazement because unexpected

sur·pris·ing \sə(r)-'prī-ziŋ\ *adj* : causing surprise : AMAZING — **sur·pris·ing·ly** *adv*

¹sur·ren·der \sə-'ren-dər\ *vb* **-dered; -der·ing** \-d(ə-)riŋ\ **1** : to give over to the power, control, or possession of another especially by force **2** : to give oneself over to something **syn** see YIELD

²surrender *n* : the giving of oneself or something into the power of another person or thing

sur·rep·ti·tious \,sər-əp-'tish-əs, ,sə-rəp-\ *adj* : done, made, or acquired in secret — **sur·rep·ti·tious·ly** *adv* — **sur·rep·ti·tious·ness** *n*

sur·rey \'sər-ē, 'sə-rē\ *n, pl* **surreys** : a horse-drawn carriage that has two wide seats and four wheels [from earlier *Surrey cart,* named for *Surrey,* a county in England where it was first made]

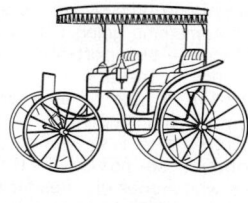

surrey

sur·ro·gate \'sər-ə-,gāt, 'sə-rə-, -gət\ *n* **1** : one appointed to act in place of another : DEPUTY **2** : a court officer in some states who handles the settling of wills

¹sur·round \sə-'raund\ *vb* : to enclose on all sides : ENCIRCLE

²surround *n* : something (as a border) that surrounds

sur·round·ings \sə-'raun-diŋz\ *n pl* : the circumstances, conditions, or objects by which one is surrounded

sur·tax \'sər-,taks\ *n* : an additional tax over and above a general tax

sur·veil·lance \sər-'vā-lən(t)s *also* -'vāl-yən(t)s *or* -'vā-ən(t)s\ *n* : close watch ⟨under *surveillance*⟩

¹sur·vey \sər-'vā, 'sər-,vā\ *vb* **sur·veyed; sur·vey·ing** **1** : to look over and examine closely **2** : to find out the size, shape, and position of (as an area of land) **3** : to gather information from or about : make a survey of

²sur·vey \'sər-,vā, sər-'vā\ *n, pl* **surveys** : the act or an instance of surveying or of applying the principles and methods of surveying; *also* : something that is surveyed

sur·vey·ing \sər-'vā-iŋ\ *n* : a branch of mathematics concerned with finding for any part of the earth's surface the area, the lengths and directions of the boundary lines, and the contour lines of the surface and with accurately showing the results on paper

sur·vey·or \sər-'vā-ər\ *n* : one that surveys; *esp* : one

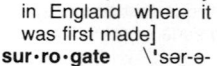

whose occupation is surveying land

sur·viv·al \sər-'vī-vəl\ *n* **1** : a living or continuing longer than another person or thing ⟨*survival* of half the population after an epidemic⟩ **2** : a continuation of life despite difficult conditions ⟨skills for *survival* in the desert⟩ **3** : one that survives

survival of the fittest : NATURAL SELECTION

sur·vive \sər-'vīv\ *vb* **sur·vived; sur·viv·ing 1** : to remain alive : continue to exist **2** : to remain alive after the death of ⟨*survived* by three children⟩ **3** : to continue to exist or live after ⟨*survived* the flood⟩ — **sur·vi·vor** \-'vī-vər\ *n*

sus·cep·ti·bil·i·ty \sə-,sep-tə-'bil-ət-ē\ *n, pl* **-ties 1** : the quality or state of being susceptible; *esp* : lack of ability to resist some outside agent (as a disease-causing germ or drug) **2 a** : a susceptible disposition or nature **b** *pl* : one's emotional state : FEELINGS

sus·cep·ti·ble \sə-'sep-tə-bəl\ *adj* **1** : being of such a nature as to permit some action or operation ⟨a theory *susceptible* to proof⟩ **2** : having little resistance ⟨persons *susceptible* to colds⟩ **3** : easily affected or impressed ⟨*susceptible* to flattery⟩ — **sus·cep·ti·bly** \-blē\ *adv*

su·shi \'sü-shē, 'sush-ē\ *n* : cold rice shaped in small cakes and topped or wrapped with pieces of raw fish

¹sus·pect \'səs-,pekt, sə-'spekt\ *adj* : regarded with suspicion

²sus·pect \'səs-,pekt\ *n* : one who is suspected

³sus·pect \sə-'spekt\ *vb* **1** : to have doubts about **2** : to believe to be guilty without proof ⟨*suspect* someone of theft⟩ **3** : to suppose to be true or likely ⟨I *suspect* that it will rain⟩

sus·pend \sə-'spend\ *vb* **1** : to force to give up some right or position for a time ⟨*suspend* a student from school⟩ **2 a** : to stop or do away with for a time ⟨*suspend* bus service⟩ **b** : to put off on certain conditions ⟨*suspend* a lawbreaker's sentence⟩ **3 a** : to hang so as to be free on all sides except at the point of support **b** : to keep from falling or sinking by some invisible support ⟨dust *suspended* in the air⟩

sus·pend·er \sə-'spen-dər\ *n* **1** : one that suspends **2** : one of two bands worn across the shoulders to hold up one's pants or skirt — usually used in pl. ⟨a pair of *suspenders*⟩

sus·pense \sə-'spen(t)s\ *n* **1** : the state of being suspended : SUSPENSION **2 a** : mental uncertainty : ANXIETY **b** : pleasant excitement caused by wondering what will happen ⟨a novel of *suspense*⟩ **3** : the state of being undecided — **sus·pense·ful** \-fəl\ *adj*

sus·pen·sion \sə-'spen-chən\ *n* **1 a** : the act or an instance of suspending **b** : the state of being suspended **c** : the period during which someone or something is suspended **2** : the act of hanging : the state of being hung **3** : the state of a substance when its particles are mixed with but not dissolved in a fluid or solid; *also* : a substance in this state **4** : something suspended **5** : the system of devices (as springs) supporting the upper part of a vehicle on the axles

suspension bridge *n* : a bridge that has its roadway suspended from two or more cables usually passing over towers and strongly anchored at the ends

¹sus·pi·cion \sə-'spish-ən\ *n* **1** : the act or an instance of suspecting or being suspected **2** : a feeling that something is wrong without definite evidence **3** : a small amount **syn** see DOUBT

²suspicion *vb* **sus·pi·cioned; sus·pi·cion·ing** \-'spish-(ə-)niŋ\ *chiefly substandard* : ³SUSPECT

sus·pi·cious \sə-'spish-əs\ *adj* **1** : likely to arouse suspicion : QUESTIONABLE ⟨*suspicious* behavior⟩ **2** : likely to suspect or distrust ⟨*suspicious* of strangers⟩ **3** : showing suspicion ⟨a *suspicious* glance⟩ — **sus·pi·cious·ly** *adv* — **sus·pi·cious·ness** *n*

sus·tain \sə-'stān\ *vb* **1** : to give support or relief to **2** : to supply with nourishment ⟨food *sustains* our bodies⟩ **3** : to keep up : PROLONG ⟨a book that will *sustain* your interest⟩ **4** : to support the weight of : CARRY **5** : to keep up the spirits of ⟨hope *sustained* the people⟩ **6 a** : to bear up under : ENDURE **b** : ²EXPERIENCE, UNDERGO ⟨*sustained* a serious wound⟩ **7 a** : to support as true, legal, or just **b** : to allow or admit as right ⟨the court *sustained* the motion⟩ **8** : PROVE 2a, CONFIRM — **sus·tain·able** \-'stā-nə-bəl\ *adj* — **sus·tain·er** *n*

sus·te·nance \'səs-tə-nən(t)s\ *n* **1 a** : means of support, maintenance, or existence **b** : NOURISHMENT 1 **2** : the act of sustaining : the state of being sustained; *esp* : a supplying with the necessities of life **3** : something that gives support, help, or strength

¹su·ture \'sü-chər\ *n* **1 a** : a stitch made with a suture **b** : a strand or fiber used to sew parts of the living body **c** : the act or process of sewing with sutures **2** : the line of connection in an immovable joint (as between the bones of the skull); *also* : such a joint

²suture *vb* **su·tured; su·tur·ing** \'süch-(ə-)riŋ\ : to unite, close, or secure with sutures ⟨*suture* a wound⟩

svelte \'sfelt\ *adj* : slender and graceful in form [from French *svelte* "slender, sleek", from Italian *svelto* (same meaning), derived from *svellere* "to pull or stretch out", derived from Latin *evellere* "to pull out"]

¹swab \'swäb\ *n* **1 a** : ¹MOP 1 **b** : a wad of absorbent material usually wound around one end of a small stick and used for applying medicine or for removing material (as from a wound); *also* : a sample taken with a swab **2** : SAILOR

²swab *vb* **swabbed; swab·bing** : to use a swab on

swad·dle \'swäd-ᵊl\ *vb* **swad·dled; swad·dling** \'swäd-liŋ, -ᵊl-iŋ\ : to wrap an infant with swaddling clothes

swaddling clothes *n pl* : narrow strips of cloth wrapped around an infant to restrict movement

swag \'swag\ *n* : goods acquired by unlawful means

¹swag·ger \'swag-ər\ *vb* **swag·gered; swag·ger·ing** \-(ə-)riŋ\ **1** : to behave in a very proud manner; *esp* : to walk with a proud strut **2** : ²BOAST 1 — **swag·ger·er** \-ər-ər\ *n* — **swag·ger·ing·ly** \-(ə-)riŋ-lē\ *adv*

²swagger *n* : an act or instance of swaggering

swag·man \'swag-mən\ *n, chiefly Australian* : ²TRAMP 1, HOBO

Swa·hi·li \swä-'hē-lē\ *n, pl* **Swahili** *or* **Swahilis 1** : a member of a Bantu-speaking people of Zanzibar and the adjacent coast of Africa **2** : a Bantu language that is a trade and governmental language over much of East Africa and in the Congo region

swain \'swān\ *n* **1** : ²RUSTIC; *esp* : ¹SHEPHERD 1 **2** : a male admirer or lover

¹swal·low \'swäl-ō\ *n* **1** : any of a family of small long-winged birds that migrate, are noted for their graceful flight, and have usually a deeply forked tail **2** : any of several swifts that look like true swallows [Old English *swealwe* "the swallow"]

¹swallow 1

²swallow *vb* **1 a** : to take into the stomach through the mouth and throat **b** : to perform the actions used in swallowing something ⟨clear your throat and *swallow* before answering⟩ **2** : to take in as if by swallowing : ENGULF **3** : to accept or believe without question, protest, or anger ⟨a hard story to *swallow*⟩ **4** : to keep from expressing or showing : REPRESS ⟨*swallowed* my anger⟩ [Old English *swelgan* "to swallow"] — **swal·low·er** \'swäl-ə-wər\ *n*

³swallow *n* **1** : an act of swallowing **2** : an amount that can be swallowed at one time

swal·low·tail \'swäl-ō-,tāl\ *n* **1** : a deeply forked and tapering tail (as of a swallow) **2** : any of various large butterflies in which the hind wing is drawn out into a process that resembles a tail — **swal·low–tailed** \,swäl-ō-'tāld\ *adj*

swam *past of* SWIM

swa·mi \'swäm-ē\ *n* **1** : a Hindu priest or religious teacher — used as a title **2** : SEER 2

¹swamp \'swämp, 'swomp\ *n* : wet spongy land often partly covered with water

²swamp *vb* **1** : to fill or become filled with or as if with water **2** : OVERWHELM 2 ⟨was *swamped* with work⟩

swamp·land \'swäm-,pland, 'swom-\ *n* : ¹SWAMP

swampy \'swäm-pē, 'swom-\ *adj* **swamp·i·er; -est** : consisting of, relating to, or resembling swamp — **swamp·i·ness** *n*

swan \'swän\ *n, pl* **swans** *also* **swan** : any of various heavy-bodied long-necked usually pure white water birds that are related to but larger than the geese

¹swank \'swaŋk\ *vb* : SHOW OFF 2, SWAGGER

²swank *n* **1** : showy display or pride in dress or manners **2** : ELEGANCE 2

³swank *or* **swanky** \'swaŋ-kē\ *adj* **swank·er** *or* **swank·i·er; -est** **1** : marked by showy display : OSTENTATIOUS **2** : fashionably elegant ⟨a *swank* restaurant⟩ — **swank·i·ly** \'swaŋ-kə-lē\ *adv* — **swank·i·ness** \-kē-nəs\ *n*

swan song *n* : a farewell appearance or final act or public statement [from the legend that a dying swan sings a beautiful song]

swap *also* **swop** \'swäp\ *vb* **swapped** *also* **swopped; swap·ping** *also* **swop·ping** : to give in exchange : make an exchange : TRADE — **swap** *n*

sward \'sword\ *n* : the grassy surface of land : TURF

¹swarm \'sworm\ *n* **1** : a great number of honeybees leaving together from a hive with a queen to start a new colony elsewhere; *also* : a colony of honeybees settled in a hive **2** : a large number grouped together and usually in motion ⟨*swarms* of sightseers⟩ ⟨a *swarm* of meteors⟩

²swarm *vb* **1** : to form and leave a hive in a swarm **2** : to move or gather in a swarm : THRONG ⟨spectators *swarmed* into the stadium⟩ **3** : to contain or fill with a swarm

swar·thy \'swor-thē, -thē\ *adj* **swar·thi·er; -est** : having a dark complexion — **swar·thi·ness** *n*

¹swash \'swäsh, 'swosh\ *vb* **1** : ¹BLUSTER 2 **2** : to make violent noisy movements **3** : to move with a splashing sound

²swash *n* **1** : ²SWAGGER **2** : a dashing of water against or upon something

swash·buck·ler \'swäsh-,bək-lər, 'swosh-\ *n* : a swaggering or daring soldier or adventurer; *also* : a story or movie about such a man

swash·buck·ling \'swäsh-,bək-(ə-)liŋ, 'swosh-\ *adj* : being, resembling, or resembling that of a swashbuckler ⟨*swashbuckling* adventure⟩ ⟨a *swashbuckling* tale⟩

swas·ti·ka \'swäs-ti-kə *also* swä-'stē-kə\ *n* : a symbol in the form of a cross with the ends of the arms bent at right angles all in the same direction [from a word in Sanskrit (the ancient language of India) *svastika* "a symbol in the form of a cross with bent arms", from *svasti* "well-being"]

swat \'swät\ *vb* **swat·ted; swat·ting** : to hit with a quick hard blow — **swat** *n* — **swat·ter** *n*

swatch \'swäch\ *n* **1** : a sample piece (as of fabric) or a collection of samples **2** : ¹PATCH 3 ⟨*swatches* of hair⟩

swath \'swäth, 'swoth\ *or* **swathe** \'swäth, 'swoth, 'swoth, 'swäth\ *n* **1 a** : the sweep of a scythe or machine in mowing or the path cut in one course **b** : a row of cut grain or grass **2** : a long broad strip or belt **3** : a path of destruction made as if by a mowing machine

¹swathe \'swäth, 'swoth, 'swäth\ *vb* **swathed; swath·ing** **1** : to bind, wrap, or swaddle with or as if with a bandage **2** : ENVELOP

²swathe \'swäth, 'swoth, 'swäth\ *or* **swath** \'swäth, 'swäth, 'swoth, 'swoth\ *n* : a band used in swathing

¹sway \'swā\ *n* **1** : the action or an instance of swaying or of being swayed **2** : a bending or twisting caused by or as if by swaying **3** : controlling force or influence : RULE

²sway *vb* **1 a** : to swing or cause to swing slowly back and forth **b** : to move gently from an upright to a leaning position **2** : to change often between one point, position, or opinion and another **3** : to have a strong influence upon — **sway·er** *n*

sway·backed \'swā-'bakt\ *also* **sway·back** \-'bak, -,bak\ *adj* : having an unusually hollow or sagging back ⟨a *sway-backed* mare⟩ — **sway·back** *n*

swear \'swa(ə)r, 'swe(ə)r\ *vb* **swore** \'swō(ə)r, 'swo(ə)r\; **sworn** \'swō(ə)rn, 'swo(ə)rn\; **swear·ing** **1** : to make a statement or promise under oath **2 a** : to state as true under oath ⟨a *sworn* statement⟩ **b** : to state or promise strongly or sincerely ⟨I *swear* that I was there⟩ **3 a** : to give an oath to ⟨the witness was *sworn*⟩ **b** : to bind by an oath ⟨*swore* us to secrecy⟩ **4** : to take an oath **5** : to use bad or vulgar language — **swear·er** *n* — **swear by** : to place great confidence in — **swear off** : to promise to give up ⟨*swear off* desserts⟩

swear in *vb* : to place into office by the giving of an oath

swear·word \'swa(ə)r-,wərd, 'swe(ə)r-\ *n* : a bad or vulgar word

¹sweat \'swet\ *vb* **sweat** *or* **sweat·ed; sweat·ing** **1** : to give off salty moisture through the pores of the skin : PERSPIRE **2** : to give off or cause to give off moisture **3** : to collect drops of moisture on the surface ⟨a pitcher of ice water *sweats* on a hot day⟩ **4 a** : to work very hard : TOIL ⟨*sweat* to succeed⟩ **b** : to worry greatly ⟨*sweat* off weight⟩ **5** : to get rid of or lose by perspiring ⟨*sweat* off weight⟩

²sweat *n* **1** : hard work **2** : moisture coming from the sweat glands of the skin : PERSPIRATION **3** : moisture gathering in drops on a surface

sweat·er \'swet-ər\ *n* **1** : one that sweats or causes sweating **2** : a knitted or crocheted jacket or pullover

sweat gland *n* : a gland of the skin that gives off perspiration and opens by a tiny pore in the skin

sweat lodge *n* : a hut, lodge, or cavern heated by steam from water poured on hot stones and used especially by American Indians for ritual or therapeutic sweating

sweat out *vb* : to suffer or wait through the course of ⟨*sweated out* the afternoon waiting for the results⟩

sweat·pants \'swet-,pan(t)s\ *n pl* : pants of soft absorbent material worn especially by athletes

sweat·shirt \-,shərt\ *n* : a loose collarless usually long-sleeved pullover of soft absorbent material

sweat·shop \-,shäp\ *n* : a shop or factory in which workers work long hours at low wages under unhealthy conditions

sweaty \'swet-ē\ *adj* **sweat·i·er; -est** **1** : causing sweat ⟨*sweaty* work⟩ **2** : wet or stained with or smelling of sweat — **sweat·i·ly** \'swet-ᵊl-ē\ *adv* — **sweat·i·ness** \'swet-ē-nəs\ *n*

swede \'swēd\ *n* **1** *cap* **a** : a person born or living in Sweden **b** : a person of Swedish ancestry **2** : RUTABAGA

Swed·ish \'swēd-ish\ *n* **1** : the Germanic language spoken in Sweden **2 Swedish** *pl* : the people of Sweden — **Swedish** *adj*

¹sweep \'swēp\ *vb* **swept** \'swept\; **sweep·ing** **1 a** : to remove from a surface with or as if with a broom or brush ⟨*sweep* the dirt off the rug⟩ **b** : to remove or take with a single continuous forceful action ⟨*swept* the books off the desk⟩ **c** : to drive or carry along with great force **2 a** : to clean with or as if with a broom or brush ⟨*sweep* the floor⟩ **b** : to move across or along swiftly, violently, or overwhelmingly ⟨a storm *swept* across the plains⟩ **c** : to win all of ⟨*swept* the western states⟩ **3** : to move with stately or sweeping movements ⟨*swept* into the room⟩ **4** : to move or extend in a wide curve or range — **sweep·er** *n*

²sweep *n* **1** : a long movable pole on a post that is used to raise and lower a bucket (as in a well) **2 a** : an act or instance of sweeping **b** : a complete victory ⟨a *sweep* of all the state elections⟩ **3 a** : a movement of great range and force

sweep 1

b : a curving or circular course or line   **c** : ¹RANGE 6, SCOPE ⟨outside the *sweep* of our vision⟩ **4** : CHIMNEY SWEEP **5** : SWEEPSTAKES

¹sweep·ing *n* **1** : the act or action of one that sweeps **2** *pl* : things collected by sweeping

²sweeping *adj* **1 a** : moving or extending in a wide curve or over a wide area   **b** : having a curving line or form **2** : BROAD 5 ⟨*sweeping* reforms⟩ ⟨*sweeping* generalizations⟩ — **sweep·ing·ly** \'swē-piŋ-lē\ *adv*

sweep–second \'swēp-,sek-ənd, -ənt\ *n* : a hand marking seconds on a timepiece that is read from the same dial as the minute hand

sweep·stakes \'swēp-,stāks\ *also* **sweep·stake** \-,stāk\ *n*, *pl* **sweepstakes** **1 a** : a race or contest in which the entire prize may be awarded to the winner   **b** : ²CONTEST, COMPETITION   **2** : any of various lotteries

¹sweet \'swēt\ *adj* **1 a** : pleasing to the taste   **b** : being or causing the one of the four basic taste sensations that is caused especially by table sugar and is identified especially by the taste buds at the front of the tongue — compare BITTER 1, ³SALT 1b, ¹SOUR 1   **c** : having a relatively large sugar content ⟨*sweet* wine⟩ **2 a** : pleasing to the mind or feelings : AGREEABLE ⟨victory is *sweet*⟩   **b** : marked by gentle good humor or kindliness ⟨a *sweet* elderly couple⟩   **c** : FRAGRANT   **d** : delicately pleasing to the ear or eye   **3** : much loved : DEAR   **4 a** : not sour, stale, or spoiled : WHOLESOME ⟨*sweet* milk⟩   **b** : not salt or salted : FRESH ⟨*sweet* butter⟩   **c** : not having too much acid ⟨*sweet* soil⟩   **d** : free from foul gases and odors — **sweet·ish** \-ish\ *adj* — **sweet·ly** *adv* — **sweet·ness** *n* — **sweet on** : in love with

²sweet *adv* : in a sweet way

³sweet *n* **1 a** : a food (as a candy) having a high sugar content   **b** *British* : DESSERT   **2** : a sweet taste sensation **3** : a pleasant or agreeable experience, possession, or state   **4** : ¹DARLING 1

sweet basil *n* : a mint that has clusters of white flowers tinged with purple and leaves often used as a seasoning in cooking

sweet·bread \'swēt-,bred\ *n* : the thymus or pancreas of a young animal (as a calf) used as food

sweet·bri·er *also* **sweet·bri·ar** \-,brī(-ə)r\ *n* : a rose with stout curved prickles and white to deep rosy pink single flowers — called also *eglantine*

sweet clover *n* : any of a genus of tall upright plants of the legume family widely grown for soil improvement or hay

sweet corn *n* : an Indian corn with kernels containing much sugar that is cooked as a vegetable while immature — compare FIELD CORN

sweet·en \'swēt-ᵊn\ *vb* **sweet·ened; sweet·en·ing** \'swēt-niŋ, -ᵊn-iŋ\ : to make or become sweet — **sweet·en·er** \'swēt-nər, -ᵊn-ər\ *n*

sweet·en·ing *n* **1** : the act or process of making sweet **2** : something that sweetens

sweet gum *n* : a North American tree that has lobed leaves, hard wood, and a long-stemmed woody globe-shaped fruit;

also : its wood

sweet·heart \'swēt-,härt\ *n* : a person whom one loves

sweet·meat \-,mēt\ *n* : a food (as a candied fruit or piece of candy) rich in sugar

sweet pea *n* **1** : a garden plant with slender climbing stems and large fragrant flowers   **2** : the flower of a sweet pea

sweet pepper *n* : a large mild-flavored thick-walled pepper; *also* : a plant related to the potato that produces sweet peppers

sweet potato *n* **1** : a tropical vine related to the morning glory that has variously shaped leaves and purplish flowers; *also* : its large sweet starchy root that is cooked and eaten as a vegetable   **2** : OCARINA

sweet tooth *n* : a craving or fondness for sweets

sweet wil·liam \,swēt-'wil-yəm\ *n*, *often cap W* : a widely grown Eurasian pink with small white to deep red or purple flowers that are often spotted or banded and grow in flat clusters on upright stems

sweet william

¹swell \'swel\ *vb* **swelled; swelled** *or* **swol·len** \'swō-lən\; **swell·ing** **1 a** : to expand (as in size, volume, or numbers) gradually beyond a normal or original limit ⟨the population *swelled*⟩   **b** : to become abnormally enlarged or puffed up ⟨the sprained ankle *swelled* badly⟩   **c** : to form a bulge or lump   **2** : to fill or become filled with pride   **3** : to fill or become filled with emotion   **syn** see EXPAND

²swell *n* **1 a** : a rounded lump   **b** : the condition of bulging **2** : a long rolling wave or series of waves in the open sea **3 a** : a gradual increase and decrease of the loudness of a musical sound   **b** : a sign marking a swell   **4 a** : a fashionably dressed person

³swell *adj* : very good : EXCELLENT

swell·ing \'swel-iŋ\ *n* **1** : something that is swollen; *esp* : a swollen part of the body   **2** : the condition of being swollen

¹swel·ter \'swel-tər\ *vb* **swel·tered; swel·ter·ing** \-t(ə-)riŋ\ **1** : to suffer, sweat, or be faint from heat   **2** : to overcome with heat

²swelter *n* : a state of great heat

swel·ter·ing *adj* : very hot — **swel·ter·ing·ly** *adv*

swept *past and past participle of* SWEEP

swept–back \'swep(t)-'bak\ *adj* : slanting toward the tail of an airplane to form an acute angle with the body ⟨*swept-back* wings⟩

swerve \'swərv\ *vb* **swerved; swerv·ing** : to turn aside suddenly from a straight line or course — **swerve** *n*

¹swift \'swift\ *adj* **1** : moving or capable of moving with great speed   **2** : occurring suddenly or within a very short time   **syn** see FAST — **swift·ly** *adv* — **swift·ness** \'swif(t)-nəs\ *n*

²swift *adv* : in a swift manner

³swift *n* : any of numerous small plainly colored birds that are related to the hummingbirds but look like the swallows

¹swig \'swig\ *n* : a quantity drunk at one time

²swig *vb* **swigged; swig·ging** : to drink in long gulps

¹swill \'swil\ *vb* **1** : DRENCH   **2** : to drink or eat greedily **3** : to feed (as a pig) with swill — **swill·er** *n*

²swill *n* **1** : food for animals (as pigs) made from scraps of food mixed with water or skimmed or sour milk   **2** : GAR-

---

\ə\ abut	\au̇\ out	\i\ tip	\ȯ\ saw	\u̇\ foot
\ər\ further	\ch\ chin	\ī\ life	\ȯi\ coin	\y\ yet
\a\ mat	\e\ pet	\j\ job	\th\ thin	\yü\ few
\ā\ take	\ē\ easy	\ŋ\ sing	\th\ this	\yu̇\ cure
\ä\ cot, cart	\g\ go	\ō\ bone	\ü\ food	\zh\ vision

BAGE, REFUSE **3** : ¹SWIG

¹swim \'swim\ *vb* **swam** \'swam\; **swum** \'swəm\; **swim-ming** **1** : to move through water by moving arms, legs, fins, or tail **2** : to float on or in or be covered with or as if with a liquid **3** : to feel dizzy ⟨my head *swam* in the stuffy room⟩ **4** : to cross by swimming ⟨*swim* a stream⟩ — **swim-mer** *n*

²swim *n* **1** : an act or period of swimming **2** : the main current of activity ⟨be in the *swim* of things⟩

swim-ming \'swim-iŋ\ *adj* : marked by, capable of, or used in or for swimming

swim-ming-ly \'swim-iŋ-lē\ *adv* : very well : SPLENDIDLY

swimming pool *n* : an indoor or outdoor tank built for swimming

swim-suit \'swim-,süt\ *n* : a suit for swimming or bathing

swim-wear \-,wa(ə)r, -,we(ə)r\ *n* : clothing suitable for swimming

¹swin-dle \'swin-dᵊl\ *vb* **swin-dled**; **swin-dling** \-(d)liŋ, -dᵊl-iŋ\ : to get money or property from by dishonest means : CHEAT — **swin-dler** \-(d)lər, -dᵊl-ər\ *n*

²swindle *n* : an act or instance of swindling : FRAUD

swine \'swīn\ *n, pl* **swine** **1** : any of a family of stout-bodied short-legged hoofed mammals with a thick bristly skin and a long snout; *esp* : a domestic animal developed from the European wild boar and raised for meat : PIG **2** : a nasty person

swine-herd \'swīn-,hərd\ *n* : a person who tends swine

¹swing \'swiŋ\ *vb* **swung** \'swəŋ\; **swing-ing** \'swiŋ-iŋ\ **1 a** : to move quickly in a sweeping curve ⟨*swing* an ax⟩ **b** : to sway or cause to sway to and fro or turn on an axis or hinge ⟨*swung* the door open⟩ **c** : to face or move in another direction ⟨go forward, then *swing* to the right⟩ **2 a** : to hang or be hung so as to permit swaying or turning **b** : to die by hanging **c** : to hang freely from support **d** : to change quickly between extremes ⟨sales *swung* up sharply⟩ **3** : to handle successfully : MANAGE ⟨can you *swing* the purchase of a car⟩ **4 a** : to move along with free swaying movements **b** : to start up in a smooth vigorous manner ⟨ready to *swing* into action⟩ **c** : to hit at something with a sweeping movement **5** : to be lively and up-to-date ⟨a town that really *swings*⟩ — **swing-er** \'swiŋ-ər\ *n*

²swing *n* **1** : an act of swinging **2** : a swinging movement, blow, or rhythm **3** : the distance through which something swings ⟨a pendulum with a 30-centimeter *swing*⟩ **4** : a swinging seat usually hung by ropes or chains **5** : a curving course or outline or one beginning and ending at the same point ⟨took a *swing* through the hills⟩ — **swing** *adj*

swin-ish \'swī-nish\ *adj* : of, suggesting, or characteristic of swine : BEASTLY — **swin-ish-ly** *adv* — **swin-ish-ness** *n*

¹swipe \'swīp\ *vb* **swiped**; **swip-ing** **1** : to strike or wipe with a sweeping motion **2** : PILFER

²swipe *n* : a strong sweeping blow

¹swirl \'swər(-ə)l\ *n* **1** : a whirling mass or motion : EDDY **2** : whirling confusion ⟨lost in the *swirl* of events⟩ **3** : a twisting shape, mark, or pattern

²swirl *vb* **1** : to move with or pass in a swirl **2** : to be marked with or arranged in swirls **3** : to cause to swirl — **swirl-ing-ly** \'swər-liŋ-lē\ *adv*

¹swish \'swish\ *vb* : to make, move, or strike with a soft rubbing, hissing, or splashing sound

²swish *n* **1** : a hissing sound (as of a whip cutting the air) or a sound of soft surfaces rubbing against each other **2** : a swishing movement — **swishy** \-ē\ *adj*

Swiss \'swis\ *n* **1** *pl* **Swiss a** : a person born or living in Switzerland **b** : a person of Swiss ancestry **2** : a pale yellow firm cheese with many large holes — **Swiss** *adj*

Swiss chard *n* : CHARD

Swiss steak *n* : a steak pounded with flour and cooked usually with vegetables and seasonings

¹switch \'swich\ *n* **1** : a slender flexible whip, rod, or twig **2** : an act or an instance of switching **3** : a bunch of long

hairs at the end of the tail of an animal (as a cow) **4 a** : a device made usually of two movable rails and necessary connections and designed to turn a train or streetcar from one track to another **b** : SIDING 1 **5** : a device for making, breaking, or changing the connections in an electrical circuit

²switch *vb* **1** : to strike or whip with or as if with a switch **2** : to lash from side to side **3** : to turn, shift, or change by or as if by operating a switch ⟨*switch* off the light⟩ ⟨*switched* to a different channel⟩ — **switch-er** *n*

switch-back \'swich-,bak\ *n* : a zigzag road, trail, or section of railroad tracks for climbing a steep hill

switch-blade \-,blād\ *n* : a pocketknife with a spring-operated blade

switch-board \-,bō(ə)rd, -,bȯ(ə)rd\ *n* : a device (as in a telephone exchange) consisting of a panel on which are mounted electric switches so arranged that a number of circuits may be connected, combined, and controlled

switch-man \-mən\ *n* : one who attends a railroad switch

switch-yard \-,yärd\ *n* : a place where railroad cars are switched from one track to another and trains are made up

¹swiv-el \'swiv-əl\ *n* : a device joining two parts so that one or both can turn freely

²swivel *vb* **-eled** *or* **-elled**; **-el-ing** *or* **-el-ling** \'swiv-(ə-)liŋ\ : to turn on or as if on a swivel

swivel chair *n* : a chair that swivels on its base

swollen *past participle of* SWELL

¹swoon \'swün\ *vb* **1** : ²FAINT **2** : to drift or fade gradually — **swoon-er** *n* — **swoon-ing-ly** \'swü-niŋ-lē\ *adv*

²swoon *n* **1** : a partial or total loss of consciousness **2** : a dreamlike state

¹swoop \'swüp\ *vb* : to dive or pounce suddenly like a hawk on its prey

²swoop *n* : an act or instance of swooping

swoosh \'swüsh, 'swu̇sh\ *vb* : to make or move with a rushing sound — **swoosh** *n*

swop *variant of* SWAP

swivel

sword \'sō(ə)rd, 'sȯ(ə)rd\ *n* **1** : a weapon having a long blade usually with a sharp point and edge **2** : the use of force — **sword-like** \-,līk\ *adj*

sword-fish \-,fish\ *n* : a very large ocean food fish having a long swordlike beak formed by the bones of the upper jaw

sword-play \-,plā\ *n* : the art or skill of using a sword especially in fencing

swordfish

swords-man \'sō(ə)rdz-mən, 'sȯ(ə)rdz-\ *n* **1** : one who fights with a sword **2** : one skilled in the use of the sword

swords-man-ship \'sō(ə)rdz-mən-,ship, 'sȯ(ə)rdz-\ *n* : SWORDPLAY

sword-tail \'sō(ə)rd-,tāl, 'sȯ(ə)rd-\ *n* : a small brightly marked Central American fish often kept in tropical aquariums and bred in many colors

swore *past of* SWEAR

sworn *past participle of* SWEAR

swum *past participle of* SWIM

swung *past and past participle of* SWING

syc-a-more \'sik-ə-,mō(ə)r, -,mȯ(ə)r\ *n* **1** : a Eurasian maple with yellowish green flowers that is widely planted as a shade tree **2** : a large spreading tree of eastern and central North America that has light-brown flaky bark and small round fruits hanging on long stalks

sy-co-phant \'sik-ə-fənt *also* -,fant\ *n* : a person who flatters another in order to get ahead — **sy-co-phan-tic**

\,sik-ə-'fant-ik\ *adj* — **sy·co·phan·ti·cal·ly** \-'fant-i-k(ə-)lē\ *adv*

sy·e·nite \'sī-ə-ˌnīt\ *n* : an igneous rock composed chiefly of feldspar

syl·la·bary \'sil-ə-ˌber-ē\ *n, pl* **-bar·ies** : a set of written characters each of which stands for a syllable

syl·lab·ic \sə-'lab-ik\ *adj* : of, relating to, or being syllables — **syl·lab·i·cal·ly** \-i-k(ə-)lē\ *adv*

syl·lab·i·ca·tion \sə-ˌlab-ə-'kā-shən\ *n* : the forming of syllables : the division of words into syllables — **syl·lab·i·cate** \-'lab-ə-ˌkāt\ *vb*

syl·lab·i·fi·ca·tion \sə-ˌlab-ə-fə-'kā-shən\ *n* : SYLLABICATION

syl·lab·i·fy \sə-'lab-ə-ˌfī\ *vb* **-fied; -fy·ing** : to form or divide into syllables

syl·la·ble \'sil-ə-bəl\ *n* **1** : a unit of spoken language that consists of one or more vowel sounds alone or with one or more consonant sounds preceding or following **2** : one or more letters (as *syl, la,* and *ble)* in a word (as *syl·la·ble)* usually set off from the rest of the word by a centered dot or a hyphen and treated as guides to division at the end of a line

syl·la·bus \'sil-ə-bəs\ *n, pl* **-bi** \-ˌbī, -ˌbē\ *or* **-bus·es** : a brief outline (as of a course of study)

syl·lo·gism \'sil-ə-ˌjiz-əm\ *n* : a brief form for stating an argument that consists of two statements and a conclusion that must be true if these two statements are true — **syl·lo·gis·tic** \ˌsil-ə-'jis-tik\ *adj*

sylph \'silf\ *n* : a slender graceful woman or girl — **sylph·like** \'sil-ˌflīk\ *adj*

syl·van *also* **sil·van** \'sil-vən\ *adj* **1 a** : living or located in the woods or forest **b** : of, relating to, or characteristic of the woods or forest **2** : having lots of woods or trees : WOODED

sym·bi·ont \'sim-ˌbī-ˌänt, -bē-\ *n* : an individual living in symbiosis; *esp* : the smaller member of a symbiotic pair

sym·bi·o·sis \ˌsim-ˌbī-'ō-səs, -bē-\ *n, pl* **-o·ses** \-'ō-ˌsēz\ **1** : the living together in close association of two different kinds of organisms (as a fungus and an alga making up a lichen) especially when such a relationship is of benefit to both **2** : a cooperative relationship (as between two persons or groups) — **sym·bi·ot·ic** \-'ät-ik\ *adj* — **sym·bi·ot·i·cal·ly** \-i-k(ə-)lē\ *adv*

sym·bol \'sim-bəl\ *n* **1** : something that stands for something else; *esp* : something real that stands for or suggests another thing that cannot in itself be pictured or shown (the lion is a *symbol* of courage) **2** : a letter, character, or sign used instead of a word or group of words (the sign + is the *symbol* for addition) **syn** see EMBLEM

sym·bol·ic \sim-'bäl-ik\ *also* **sym·bol·i·cal** \-i-kəl\ *adj* **1** : of, relating to, or using symbols or symbolism (a *symbolic* meaning) (*symbolic* art) **2** : having the function or meaning of a symbol — **sym·bol·i·cal·ly** \-i-k(ə-)lē\ *adv*

sym·bol·ism \'sim-bə-ˌliz-əm\ *n* **1** : the art or practice of using symbols **2** : a system of symbols or representations

sym·bol·ist \'sim-bə-ləst\ *n* **1** : a user of symbols or symbolism (as in poetry) **2** : an expert in the explaining of symbols — **symbolist** *or* **sym·bol·is·tic** \ˌsim-bə-'lis-tik\ *adj*

sym·bol·ize \'sim-bə-ˌlīz\ *vb* **-ized; -iz·ing** : to serve as a symbol of — **sym·bol·iza·tion** \ˌsim-bə-lə-'zā-shən\ *n*

sym·met·ri·cal \sə-'me-tri-kəl\ *or* **sym·met·ric** \-trik\ *adj* : having, involving, or showing symmetry — **sym·met·ri·cal·ly** \-tri-k(ə-)lē\ *adv*

sym·me·try \'sim-ə-trē\ *n, pl* **-tries** **1** : balanced proportions **2** : close agreement in size, shape, and relative position of parts arranged on opposite sides of a dividing line or plane or around a central point

sym·pa·thet·ic \ˌsim-pə-'thet-ik\ *adj* **1** : fitting one's mood or disposition (a *sympathetic* atmosphere for quiet study) **2 a** : feeling favorable (*sympathetic* with their aims) **b** : marked by kindly or pleased appreciation (a

sympathetic study of modern music) **3** : given to or arising from sympathy and sensitivity to others (a *sympathetic* personality) **4 a** : of or relating to the sympathetic nervous system **b** : controlled by or acting on the sympathetic nerves — **sym·pa·thet·i·cal·ly** \-i-k(ə-)lē\ *adv*

sympathetic nervous system *n* : the part of the autonomic nervous system that is concerned especially with preparing the body to react to situations of stress or emergency, that controls expansion of the pupil of the eye, increases the activity of the heart and the blood pressure, and narrows systemic blood vessels and especially those vessels supplying the abdominal organs, and that acts on organs mostly by releasing norepinephrine at the ends of the nerve fibers supplying them — compare PARASYMPATHETIC NERVOUS SYSTEM

sympathetic vibration *n* : a vibration produced in one body by vibrations of exactly the same period in a neighboring body

sym·pa·thize \'sim-pə-ˌthīz\ *vb* **-thized; -thiz·ing** **1** : to share in suffering or grief : to feel or show sympathy **2** : to be in favor of something — **sym·pa·thiz·er** *n*

sym·pa·thy \'sim-pə-thē\ *n, pl* **-thies** **1** : a relationship between persons or things in which whatever affects one also affects the other **2 a** : the readiness to think or feel alike that makes for a common bond **b** : readiness to favor or support **3** : the act of or capacity for entering into or sharing the feelings or interests of another **4** : a showing of sorrow for another's loss, grief, or misfortune

sym·phon·ic \sim-'fän-ik\ *adj* **1** : HARMONIOUS 1 **2** : of, relating to, or having the form of a symphony or symphony orchestra — **sym·phon·i·cal·ly** \-i-k(ə-)lē\ *adv*

sym·pho·ny \'sim(p)-fə-nē\ *n, pl* **-nies** **1** : harmonious arrangement (as of sound or color) (a *symphony* of sounds in the forest) **2** : a usually long musical composition for a full orchestra **3** : SYMPHONY ORCHESTRA [Middle English *symphonie* "pleasing arrangement of sounds", from early French *symphonie* (same meaning), derived from Greek *syn-* "together" and *phōnē* "voice, sound" — related to EUPHONY, PHONETIC]

symphony orchestra *n* : a large orchestra of wind, string, and percussion instruments that plays symphonic works

sym·po·sium \sim-'pō-zē-əm *also* -zh(ē-)əm\ *n, pl* **-sia** \-zē-ə, -zh(ē-)ə\ *or* **-siums** **1** : a group meeting at which there are several speeches and often a group discussion **2** : a collection of opinions on a subject [from earlier *symposium* "a social gathering at which there is a free exchange of ideas", from Latin *symposium* "a party with much drinking and conversation", derived from Greek *sympinein* "to drink together", from *syn-* "together with" and *pinein* "to drink" — related to SYNONYMOUS]

symp·tom \'sim(p)-təm\ *n* **1** : a change in a living thing that indicates the presence of a disease or other physical disorder; *esp* : one (as a headache) that can be felt or sensed only by the individual affected — compare ¹SIGN 6b **2** : something that shows that something else exists : INDICATION — **symp·tom·less** \-ləs\ *adj*

symp·tom·at·ic \ˌsim(p)-tə-'mat-ik\ *adj* **1 a** : being a symptom (as of disease) **b** : concerned with or affecting symptoms **2** : showing a quality or identity : CHARACTERISTIC — **symp·tom·at·i·cal·ly** \-i-k(ə-)lē\ *adv*

syn·a·gogue *or* **syn·a·gog** \'sin-ə-ˌgäg\ *n* **1** : a Jewish congregation **2** : the house of worship of a Jewish congregation [Middle English *synagoge* "a Jewish congregation", from early French *synagoge* (same meaning), from Latin *synagoga* (same meaning), from Greek *synagōgē* "synagogue, assembly", from *synagein* "to bring to-

\ə\ abut	\au̇\ out	\i\ tip	\ȯ\ saw	\u̇\ foot	
\ər\ further	\ch\ chin	\ī\ life	\ȯi\ coin	\y\ yet	
\a\ mat	\e\ pet	\j\ job	\th\ thin	\yü\ few	
\ā\ take	\ē\ easy	\ŋ\ sing	\th\ this	\yu̇\ cure	
\ä\ cot, cart	\g\ go	\ō\ bone	\ü\ food	\zh\ vision	

gether", from *syn-* "together with" and *agein* "to lead" — related to SYNONYMOUS]

syn·apse \'sin-,aps, sə-'naps\ *n* : the point at which a nerve impulse passes from one neuron to another

syn·chro·nize \'siŋ-krə-,nīz, 'sin-\ *vb* **-nized; -niz·ing** : to cause to agree in time ⟨*synchronize* your watches⟩

syn·chro·nous \'siŋ-krə-nəs, 'sin-\ *adj* : happening or existing at the same time : SIMULTANEOUS [from Latin *synchronos* "synchronous", from Greek *synchronos* (same meaning), from *syn-* "together, along with" and *chronos* "time" — related to CHRONICLE, SYNONYMOUS]

syn·cline \'sin-,klīn\ *n* : a place in the earth's crust where the rock layers curve downward — compare ANTICLINE

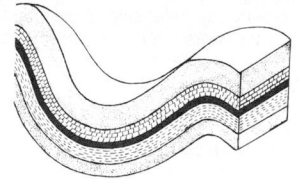

syncline

syn·co·pate \'siŋ-kə-,pāt, 'sin-\ *vb* **-pat·ed; -pat·ing** **1** : to cut short : CLIP, ABBREVIATE **2** : to change or affect (musical rhythm) by syncopation — **syn·co·pa·tor** \-,pāt-ər\ *n*

syn·co·pa·tion \,siŋ-kə-'pā-shən, ,sin-\ *n* **1** : a temporary accenting of a normally weak beat in music to vary the rhythm **2** : a syncopated rhythm, passage, or dance step

syn·co·pe \'siŋ-kə-(,)pē, 'sin-\ *n* : the loss of one or more sounds or letters in the middle of a word

¹syn·di·cate \'sin-di-kət\ *n* **1** : an association of persons involved in some official duty or business **2** : an association of people involved in organized crime **3** : a business concern that sells materials for publication at the same time in a number of newspapers or magazines

²syn·di·cate \'sin-də-,kāt\ *vb* **-cat·ed; -cat·ing** **1** : to operate as a syndicate **2** : to sell (as a cartoon) for publication in several newspapers or magazines at once **3** : to join to form a syndicate — **syn·di·ca·tion** \,sin-də-'kā-shən\ *n* — **syn·di·ca·tor** \'sin-də-,kāt-ər\ *n*

syn·drome \'sin-,drōm\ *n* : a group of signs and symptoms that occur together and characterize a particular abnormality

syn·er·gism \'sin-ər-,jiz-əm\ *n* : action between individual parts or forces that produces a total result that is greater than the sum of the individual results — **syn·er·gist** \-jəst\ *n*

syn·er·gis·tic \,sin-ər-'jis-tik\ *adj* : of, relating to, or able to function in synergism ⟨*synergistic* drugs⟩

syn·od \'sin-əd\ *n* **1** : a meeting of church leaders **2** : the governing or advisory council of a church — **syn·od·al** \'sin-əd-ᵊl\ *adj* — **syn·od·i·cal** \sə-'näd-i-kəl\ *adj*

syn·onym \'sin-ə-,nim\ *n* : a word having the same or almost the same meaning as another word in the same language — **syn·onym·i·ty** \,sin-ə-'nim-ət-ē\ *n*

syn·on·y·mize \sə-'nän-ə-,mīz\ *vb* **-mized; -miz·ing** : to list or discuss the synonyms of a word

syn·on·y·mous \sə-'nän-ə-məs\ *adj* **1** : alike in meaning **2** : suggesting the same thing ⟨a brand name that is *synonymous* with quality⟩ [from Latin *synonymus* "synonymous", from Greek *synōnymos*, literally "having the same name", from *syn-* "together, along with" and *onyma, onoma* "name" — related to ANONYMOUS, SYMPOSIUM, SYNAGOGUE, SYNCHRONOUS] — **syn·on·y·mous·ly** *adv*

syn·on·y·my \sə-'nän-ə-mē\ *n, pl* **-mies** **1 a** : the study or discussion of synonyms **b** : a list or collection of synonyms often defined and discussed **2** : the quality or state of being synonymous

syn·op·sis \sə-'näp-səs\ *n, pl* **-op·ses** \-'näp-,sēz\ : a brief statement or outline (as of a story)

syn·tac·tic \sin-'tak-tik\ *or* **syn·tac·ti·cal** \-ti-kəl\ *adj* : of, relating to, or according to the rules of syntax — **syn·tac-**

ti·cal·ly \-ti-k(ə-)lē\ *adv*

syn·tax \'sin-,taks\ *n* : the way in which words are put together to form phrases, clauses, or sentences

syn·the·sis \'sin(t)-thə-səs\ *n, pl* **-the·ses** \-thə-,sēz\ **1** : the combination of parts or elements so as to form a whole; *esp* : the production of a substance by union of chemically simpler substances **2 a** : the combining of often very different ideas into an ordered whole **b** : the product so formed

syn·the·size \'sin(t)-thə-,sīz\ *vb* **-sized; -siz·ing** : to combine or produce by synthesis — **syn·the·siz·er** *n*

¹syn·thet·ic \sin-'thet-ik\ *adj* **1** : relating to or involving synthesis **2** : of, relating to, or produced by chemical synthesis; *esp* : produced artificially ⟨*synthetic* drugs⟩ ⟨*synthetic* fibers⟩ — **syn·thet·i·cal·ly** \-'thet-i-k(ə-)lē\ *adv*

²synthetic *n* : a product of chemical synthesis

syph·i·lis \'sif-(ə-)ləs\ *n* : a venereal disease that is caused by a spirochete, is usually passed on by sexual intercourse, and if left untreated is marked by a series of three stages extending over many years — **syph·i·lit·ic** \,sif-ə-'lit-ik\, *adj or n*

sy·phon *variant of* SIPHON

Syr·i·ac \'sir-ē-,ak\ *n* **1** : a literary language based on an eastern Aramaic dialect and used as the literary and liturgical language by several eastern Christian churches **2** : Aramaic spoken by Christian communities — **Syriac** *adj*

sy·rin·ga \sə-'riŋ-gə\ *n* : any of a genus of shrubs grown for their showy white flowers — called also *mock orange*

¹sy·ringe \sə-'rinj *also* 'sir-inj\ *n* : a device used to inject fluids into or withdraw them from the body or its cavities

²syringe *vb* **sy·ringed; sy·ring·ing** : to flush or cleanse with or as if with a syringe

syr·up *or* **sir·up** \'sər-əp, 'sir-əp, 'sə-rəp\ *n* **1** : a thick solution of sugar and water often containing a flavoring or a medicine **2** : the juice of a fruit or plant with some of the water removed — **syr·upy** \-ē\ *adj*

sys·op \'sis-,äp\ *n* : the administrator of a computer bulletin board [*system operator*]

sys·tem \'sis-təm\ *n* **1 a** : a group of objects or units combined to form a whole and to move or work together ⟨railroad *system*⟩ ⟨a park *system*⟩ **b** : a body that functions as a whole ⟨a *system* weakened by disease⟩ **c** : a group of bodily organs that together carry on one or more vital functions ⟨the nervous *system*⟩ — compare ORGAN 2 **d** : an orderly plan or method of governing or arranging ⟨a democratic *system* of government⟩ **e** : a major division of rocks usually larger than a series and including all formed during a period or era **2** : a set of ideas or statements that explains the order or functioning of a whole — **sys·tem·less** \-ləs\ *adj*

sys·tem·at·ic \,sis-tə-'mat-ik\ *also* **sys·tem·at·i·cal** \-i-kəl\ *adj* **1** : relating to or forming a system ⟨*systematic* thought⟩ **2** : presented or worked out as a system **3** : carried out or acting with thoroughness or regularity ⟨*systematic* efforts⟩ — **sys·tem·at·i·cal·ly** \-i-k(ə-)lē\ *adv* — **sys·tem·at·ic·ness** \-ik-nəs\ *n*

sys·tem·a·tize \'sis-tə-mə-,tīz\ *vb* **-atized; -atiz·ing** : to make into or arrange according to a system

sys·tem·ic \sis-'tem-ik\ *adj* : of, relating to, or common to a system: as **a** : of or relating to the body as a whole ⟨a *systemic* disease⟩ **b** : concerned with the circulation that supplies blood to the bodily tissues through the aorta rather than the circulation involved in carrying blood through the pulmonary artery

systems analyst *n* : a person who studies a procedure or business to find out its goals and purposes and to discover the best ways to accomplish them

sys·to·le \'sis-tə-lē\ *n* : the contraction of the heart by which the blood is forced onward and the circulation kept up

sys·tol·ic \sis-'täl-ik\ *adj* : of, relating to, or caused by systole ⟨*systolic* movement⟩ ⟨*systolic* blood pressure⟩

T

t \tē\ *n, pl* **t's** *or* **ts** \'tēz\ *often cap* : the 20th letter of the English alphabet — **to a T** : in a perfect manner : EXACTLY

't \t\ *pron* : ¹IT \'twill do\

¹tab \'tab\ *n* **1 a** : a short flap or tag used as an aid in filing, pulling, or hanging **b** : something inserted **2 a** : a close watch ⟨keep *tab* on the situation⟩ **b** : ³BILL 2, CHECK

²tab *vb* **tabbed; tab·bing 1** : to furnish or ornament with tabs **2** : to select or name for a special purpose : DESIGNATE ⟨*tabbed* as the team's next captain⟩

tab·ard \'tab-ərd\ *n* **1** : a cloak worn by a knight over his armor and ornamented with his arms **2** : a herald's cape or coat ornamented with the lord's arms

tab·by \'tab-ē\ *n, pl* **tab·bies 1** : a domestic cat with a gray or brown coat striped and spotted with black **2** : a female cat

tabby 1

Word History A silk cloth with a striped or wavy pattern was once made in a section of the ancient city of Baghdad in what is now Iraq. The Arabic name for the cloth was *'attābī,* from *Al-'Attābīya,* the name of the part of the city where it was made. Through Latin, the French borrowed this word for the cloth, calling it *tabis.* This word in turn became *tabby* in English. People saw a resemblance between the striped or wavy pattern of the silk and cats that had striped or spotted markings on their fur. Thus these cats came to be called *tabby* cats after the cloth. [from French *tabis* "a silk fabric with a lustrous wavy finish", from Latin *attabi* (same meaning), from Arabic *'attābī* (same meaning), from *Al-'Attābīya,* name of a part of Baghdad where the cloth was made]

tab·er·na·cle \'tab-ər-,nak-əl\ *n* **1 a** *often cap* : a tent used as a place of worship by the Israelites during their wanderings in the wilderness with Moses **b** : a dwelling place **2** : a locked box usually fixed to the altar and used to hold Communion breads **3** : a house of worship

¹ta·ble \'tā-bəl\ *n* **1** : TABLET 1a **2 a** : a piece of furniture with a smooth flat top fixed on legs **b** : food served at a meal **c** : a group of people assembled at a table **3 a** : an orderly arrangement of facts or figures in rows or columns for quick reference ⟨*table* of weights⟩ ⟨multiplication *table*⟩ **b** : a short list ⟨*table* of contents⟩ **4** : PLATEAU 1

²table *vb* **ta·bled; ta·bling** \-b(ə-)liŋ\ **1** : TABULATE **2** : to remove a parliamentary motion from consideration for an unspecified period of time **3** : to put on a table

tab·leau \'tab-,lō, ta-'blō\ *n, pl* **tableaus** *or* **tab·leaux** \-,lōz, -blōz\ : a scene or event shown by a group of persons in costume who remain silent and motionless

ta·ble·cloth \'tā-bəl-,klȯth\ *n* : a covering spread over a dining table before the places are set

ta·ble·land \'tā-bəl-,(l)and\ *n* : PLATEAU 1

table salt *n* : salt for use on food and in cooking

ta·ble·spoon \'tā-bəl-,spün\ *n* **1** : a large spoon used for serving rather than eating food **2** : TABLESPOONFUL

ta·ble·spoon·ful \,tā-bəl-'spün-,fúl, 'tā-bəl-,spün-\ *n, pl* **-spoonfuls** \-,fúlz\ *or* **-spoons·ful** \-'spünz-,fúl, -,spünz-\ **1** : as much as a tablespoon can hold **2** : a unit of measure used in cooking equal to one half fluidounce (about 15 milliliters) or three teaspoonfuls

table sugar *n* : ¹SUGAR 1; *esp* : white sugar crystals

tab·let \'tab-lət\ *n* **1 a** : a flat slab suited for an inscription **b** : ²PAD 4 **2 a** : a compressed or molded block of a solid

material **b** : a small usually round mass of material containing medicine ⟨aspirin *tablet*⟩

table talk *n* : informal conversation at or as if at a dining table

table tennis *n* : a game resembling tennis that is played on a table with wooden paddles and a small hollow plastic ball

ta·ble·top \'tā-bəl-,täp\ *n* : the top of a table

ta·ble·ware \'tā-bəl-,wa(ə)r, -,we(ə)r\ *n* : utensils (as of china, glass, or silver) for table use

table wine *n* : a wine suitable for serving with food

tab·loid \'tab-,lȯid\ *n* : a newspaper about half the page size of an ordinary newspaper containing short often sensational news stories and many photographs

¹ta·boo *also* **ta·bu** \tə-'bü, ta-\ *adj* : prohibited by a taboo [from *tabu,* a word in a language of the people of a South Sea island, meaning "taboo"]

²taboo *also* **tabu** *n, pl* **taboos** *also* **tabus 1** : a prohibition against touching, saying, or doing something for fear of immediate harm by a superhuman force **2** : a prohibition established by social custom

ta·bor \'tā-bər\ *n* : a small drum with one head used to accompany a pipe played by the same person

tab·u·lar \'tab-yə-lər\ *adj* **1** : having a flat surface **2 a** : arranged or entered in a table **b** : computed by means of a table

tab·u·late \'tab-yə-,lāt\ *vb* **-lat·ed; -lat·ing** : to count and record in an orderly way ⟨*tabulate* votes⟩ — **tab·u·la·tion** \,tab-yə-'lā-shən\ *n*

tab·u·la·tor \'tab-yə-,lāt-ər\ *n* : one that tabulates: as **a** : a business machine that sorts and selects information from marked or punched cards **b** : a device on a typewriter for arranging data in columns

tabor

ta·chom·e·ter \ta-'käm-ət-ər, tə-\ *n* : a device for indicating speed of rotation [from Greek *tachos* "speed" and English *meter* "an instrument for measuring"]

tac·it \'tas-ət\ *adj* **1** : expressed without words or speech **2** : understood or made known though not actually expressed ⟨*tacit* approval⟩ — **tac·it·ly** *adv* — **tac·it·ness** *n*

tac·i·turn \'tas-ə-,tərn\ *adj* : silent by habit **syn** see SILENT — **tac·i·tur·ni·ty** \,tas-ə-'tər-nət-ē\ *n* — **tac·i·turn·ly** \'tas-ə-,tərn-lē\ *adv*

¹tack \'tak\ *vb* **1** : to fasten or attach especially with tacks **2** : to join in a slight or hasty manner **3** : to add on in order to complete **4 a** : to change the direction of a sailing ship by shifting the sails **b** : to change from one tack to another **5** : to follow a zigzag course — **tack·er** *n*

²tack *n* **1** : a small short sharp-pointed nail usually with a broad flat head ⟨carpet *tack*⟩ **2 a** : the direction a ship is sailing as shown by the position the sails are set in ⟨on the port *tack*⟩ **b** : a change of course from one tack to another **3** : a zigzag movement on land **4** : a course or method of action ⟨try a new *tack*⟩ **5** : a slight or temporary sewing or fastening

\ə\ abut	\aú\ out	\i\ tip	\ȯ\ saw	\ú\ foot
\ər\ further	\ch\ chin	\ī\ life	\ȯi\ coin	\y\ yet
\a\ mat	\e\ pet	\j\ job	\th\ thin	\yü\ few
\ā\ take	\ē\ easy	\ŋ\ sing	\th\ this	\yú\ cure
\ä\ cot, cart	\g\ go	\ō\ bone	\ü\ food	\zh\ vision

³tack *n* : stable gear; *esp* : articles of harness (as a saddle and bridle) for use on a saddle horse

tacki·ness \'tak-ē-nəs\ *n* : the quality or state of being tacky

¹tack·le \'tak-əl, *nautical often* 'tāk-\ *n* **1** : a set of special equipment : GEAR ⟨fishing *tackle*⟩ **2** : an arrangement of ropes and wheels for hoisting or pulling something heavy **3 a** : the act or an instance of tackling **b** : a football player who is positioned on the line of scrimmage

²tackle *vb* **tack·led; tack·ling** \'tak-(ə-)liŋ\ **1** : to seize or take hold of especially in order to stop or throw down **2** : to set about dealing with ⟨*tackle* a problem⟩ — **tack·ler** \-(ə-)lər\ *n*

¹tacky \'tak-ē\ *adj* **tack·i·er; -est** : barely sticky to the touch ⟨*tacky* varnish⟩

²tacky *adj* **tack·i·er; -est 1** : SHABBY 2b, SEEDY **2** : marked by lack of style or good taste

tackle 2

ta·co \'täk-ō\ *n, pl* **tacos** \-ōz, -ōs\ : a tortilla usually fried and rolled or folded and filled [from the Spanish spoken in Mexico *taco* "taco"]

tac·o·nite \'tak-ə-,nīt\ *n* : a flinty rock high enough in iron content to be used as a low-grade iron ore

tact \'takt\ *n* : the ability to deal with others without offending them — **tact·less** \'tak-tləs\ *adj* — **tact·less·ly** *adv* — **tact·less·ness** *n*

tact·ful \'takt-fəl\ *adj* : having or showing tact — **tact·ful·ly** \-fə-lē\ *adv* — **tact·ful·ness** *n*

tac·tic \'tak-tik\ *n* **1** : a method of arranging and moving forces in combat **2** : a planned action for a particular purpose

tac·ti·cal \'tak-ti-kəl\ *adj* : of or relating to tactics — **tac·ti·cal·ly** \-k(ə-)lē\ *adv*

tac·ti·cian \tak-'tish-ən\ *n* : one skilled in tactics

tac·tics \'tak-tiks\ *n sing or pl* **1 a** : the science and art of arranging and moving forces in combat **b** : the art or skill of using available means to accomplish an end **2** : a system or method of proceeding

tac·tile \'tak-t⁰l, -,tīl\ *adj* : of, relating to, or used in the sense of touch [from French *tactile* or Latin *tactilis*, both meaning "capable of being touched or felt", from Latin *tactus* "was touched", from *tangere* "to touch" — related to TANGENT, TANGIBLE]

tad \'tad\ *n* : BOY 1

tad·pole \'tad-,pōl\ *n* : the larva of a frog or toad that has a rounded body and a long tail, breathes with gills, and lives in water — called also *pollywog*

Word History A young tadpole looks like a large head with a tail. In time it will develop back legs and then front legs. Finally it will lose its tail and become a toad or a frog. Our word for this immature form of a toad or frog comes from Middle English *taddepol.* This word was a combination of two others, *tode,* meaning "toad", and *polle,* meaning "head". [Middle English *taddepol* "tadpole", from *tode* "toad" and *polle* "head"]

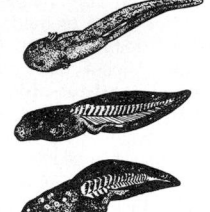

tadpole: from top to bottom, different stages of development

taf·fe·ta \'taf-ət-ə\ *n* : a crisp shiny fabric used especially for women's clothing

taff·rail \'taf-,rāl, -rəl\ *n* : the rail around the stern of a ship

taf·fy \'taf-ē\ *n, pl* **taffies** : a candy usually of molasses or brown sugar boiled and pulled until soft and chewy

¹tag \'tag\ *n* **1** : a loose hanging piece of cloth : TATTER **2** : a metal or plastic binding on an end of a shoelace **3** : TAG LINE **4** : something (as a marker) used for identification [Middle English *tagge* "a hanging piece of loose cloth"; of Germanic origin]

²tag *vb* **tagged; tag·ging 1** : to provide or mark with or as if with a tag **2** : to follow closely and continuously **3** : ²LABEL 3

³tag *n* **1** : a game in which one player who is it chases the others and tries to touch one of them to make that person it **2** : an act or instance of tagging a runner in baseball [origin unknown]

⁴tag *vb* **tagged; tag·ging 1** : to touch in a game of tag **2** : to put out (a runner) in baseball by touching with the ball or with the gloved hand holding the ball

Ta·ga·log \tə-'gäl-əg, -,òg\ *n, pl* **Tagalog** *or* **Tagalogs 1** : a member of the native people of the Philippine island of Luzon **2** : the language of the Tagalog people

tag·along \'tag-ə-,lòŋ\ *n* : one that tags along

tag along \,tag-ə-'lòŋ\ *vb* : to follow another's lead especially in going from one place to another

tag end *n* : TAIL END

tag line *n* : a final line (as in a joke)

tag up *vb* : to touch a base in baseball before running after a fly ball is caught

tai·ga \'tī-gə\ *n* : a moist northern forest that consists mostly of cone-producing trees (as pines, spruces, and firs) and ends where the tundra begins

¹tail \'tā(ə)l\ *n* **1** : the rear end or a lengthened growth from the rear end of the body of an animal **2** : something resembling an animal's tail ⟨*tail* of a kite⟩ ⟨*tail* of a comet⟩ **3** *pl* : full evening dress for men **4** : the back, last, lower, or rear part of something ⟨the *tail* of an airplane⟩ **5** : the reverse of a coin **6** : one (as a detective) who follows or keeps watch on someone **7** : a location not far behind ⟨a posse on the outlaw's *tail*⟩ — **tailed** \'tā(ə)ld\ *adj* — **tail·less** \'tā(ə)l-ləs\ *adj* — **tail·like** \-,līk\ *adj*

²tail *adj* : being at or coming from the rear

³tail *vb* **1** : to make or furnish with a tail **2 a** : to follow or be drawn behind like a tail **b** : to follow closely to observe : SHADOW

tail·board \'tā(ə)l-,bō(ə)rd, -,bò(ə)rd\ *n* : ¹TAILGATE

tail end *n* : the last part ⟨the *tail end* of summer⟩

¹tail·gate \'tā(ə)l-,gāt\ *n* : a panel at the back end of a vehicle (as a station wagon) that can be let down for loading and unloading

²tailgate *vb* **tail·gat·ed; tail·gat·ing** : to drive dangerously close behind another vehicle

tail·light \'tā(ə)l-,līt\ *n* : a red warning light mounted at the rear of a vehicle

¹tai·lor \'tā-lər\ *n* : a person whose occupation is making or making adjustments in outer garments

²tailor *vb* **1** : to make or fashion as the work of a tailor **2** : to make or make suitable for a special need or purpose — **tai·lored** \'tā-lərd\ *adj* — **tail·or·ing** \'tā-lə-riŋ\ *n*

tai·lor·bird \'tā-lər-,bərd\ *n* : any of a genus of warblers native to Asia and Africa that stitch leaves together to support and hide their nests

tai·lor–made \,tā-lər-'mād\ *adj* **1** : made by or as if by a tailor; *esp* : marked by exact fit and simple style **2** : made or seeming to have been made to take care of a particular need

tailor's ham \'tā-lərz-\ *n* : a cushion used especially by tailors for pressing curved areas of garments

tailor's tack *n* : a long loose stitch with a double thread to fasten seams before thorough sewing

tail·piece \'tā(ə)l-,pēs\ *n* **1** : a piece added at the end **2** : a device to which the strings of a stringed instrument are fastened

tail pipe *n* : an outlet by which the exhaust gases are removed from an engine (as of an automobile or jet aircraft)

tail·spin \'tā(ə)l-,spin\ *n* : ²SPIN 3

tail wind *n* : a wind having the same general direction as the course of a moving object (as an aircraft)

¹taint \'tānt\ *vb* **1** : to touch or affect slightly with something bad **2** : ²SPOIL 2c, DECAY

²taint *n* **1** : a trace of decay : STAIN **2** : a spoiling influence — **taint·less** \-ləs\ *adj*

¹take \'tāk\ *vb* **took** \'tuk\; **tak·en** \'tā-kən\; **tak·ing** **1** : to lay hold of : GRASP ⟨*take* my hand⟩ **2** : ²CAPTURE 1 ⟨*take* a fort⟩ **3** : ¹WIN 3a ⟨*take* first prize⟩ **4** : to get possession of (as by buying, capturing, or killing) ⟨*took* several trout with hook and line⟩ **5** : to seize and affect suddenly ⟨*taken* with a fever⟩ **6** : CAPTIVATE, DELIGHT ⟨was much *taken* with the new neighbors⟩ **7** : ¹EXTRACT 4 ⟨*take* material from an encyclopedia⟩ **8** : SUBTRACT 1 ⟨*take* 78 from 112⟩ **9** : to put an end to (as life) **10** : to find out by testing or examining ⟨*take* a patient's temperature⟩ **11** : ²SELECT, CHOOSE ⟨I *took* the red one⟩ **12** : ASSUME 1 ⟨*take* office⟩ ⟨*take* charge⟩ **13 a** : to let in and hold : ADMIT, ACCOMMODATE ⟨the boat was *taking* water fast⟩ ⟨the suitcase won't *take* another thing⟩ **b** : to be affected harmfully by (as a disease) : CONTRACT ⟨*take* a cold⟩ ⟨*take* a fit⟩ **c** : to become soaked with or make part of itself : ABSORB ⟨this cloth *takes* dye very well⟩ ⟨plants *take* up water⟩ **14** : to be guided by : FOLLOW ⟨*take* my advice⟩ **15** : to introduce into the body ⟨*take* medicine⟩ **16 a** : to submit to ⟨*took* the punishment without complaining⟩ **b** : WITHSTAND ⟨can *take* a lot of punishment⟩ **17 a** : to subscribe to ⟨*takes* two newspapers⟩ **b** : to enroll in for study ⟨*take* a course in history⟩ ⟨*take* piano lessons⟩ **c** : to keep from swinging at (a baseball pitch) ⟨*take* a strike⟩ **18 a** : UNDERSTAND 3, INTERPRET ⟨I *took* it to mean something different⟩ **b** : CONSIDER 3 ⟨wanted to be *taken* for a genius⟩ **19** : to react in a certain way ⟨*take* pride in one's work⟩ ⟨*take* offense⟩ **20** : to be formed or used with ⟨this verb *takes* an object⟩ **21** : CONVEY 1, CONDUCT, CARRY ⟨*take* a package home⟩ ⟨*take* me to your leader⟩ **22 a** : to make use of ⟨*take* a vacation⟩ **b** : to proceed to occupy ⟨*take* a chair⟩ **23** : ²NEED 2, REQUIRE ⟨this job *takes* a lot of time⟩ ⟨I *take* a larger size⟩ **24** : to obtain an image or copy of ⟨*take* a photograph⟩ ⟨*take* fingerprints⟩ **25** : to set out to make, do, or perform ⟨*take* a walk⟩ ⟨*took* a new job⟩ **26** : to have effect ⟨the vaccination *took*⟩ — **tak·er** *n* — **take advantage of** **1** : to use to advantage : profit by **2** : to treat (someone) unfairly : EXPLOIT — **take after** **1** : to take as an example : FOLLOW **2** : to look like : RESEMBLE ⟨*take* after their parents⟩ — **take care** : to be careful — **take care of** : to attend to or provide for the needs, operation, or treatment of — **take effect** **1** : to go into effect **2** : to have an expected or intended effect : be effective — **take for** : to suppose to be; *esp* : to suppose mistakenly to be — **take for granted** : to assume as true, real, or expected — **take hold** : to become attached or established — **take into account** : to make allowance for : CONSIDER — **take in vain** : to use a name without proper respect — **take part** : PARTICIPATE, SHARE — **take place** : to come about or occur : HAPPEN — **take stock** : to make a study or survey : ASSESS — **take the floor** : to rise (as in a meeting) to speak — **take to** : to be drawn or attracted to — **take to task** : to scold for a fault

²take *n* **1** : an act or the action of taking **2** : something taken : PROCEEDS, CATCH **3 a** : a scene filmed or televised at one time without stopping the camera **b** : a sound recording made during a single recording period **4** : a bodily reaction that indicates a successful vaccination against smallpox **5** : mental response or reaction

take back *vb* : RETRACT 2, WITHDRAW ⟨*take back* an insulting remark⟩

take·down \'tāk-,daun\ *n* : the action or an act of taking down — **take·down** \,tāk-,daun\ *adj*

take down \(')tāk-'daun\ *vb* **1 a** : to pull to pieces **b** : DISASSEMBLE **2** : to lower the spirit or pride of : HUMBLE

3 : to write down or record by mechanical means

take–home pay \,tāk-,hōm-\ *n* : the part of one's salary or wages remaining after deductions (as of income tax payments or union dues)

take in *vb* **1 a** : to reduce the length of ⟨*take in* a slack line⟩ **b** : to make smaller by enlarging seams or tucks ⟨*take in* a coat⟩ **2 a** : to receive as a guest or resident **b** : to give shelter to **3** : to receive and do at home for pay ⟨*take in* washing⟩ **4** : to include within fixed limits ⟨the camp *took in* several acres⟩ **5** : ATTEND 4 ⟨*take in* a movie⟩ **6** : to observe and think about so as to understand ⟨paused to *take* the situation *in*⟩ **7** : to deceive so as to take advantage of ⟨*taken in* by a hard luck story⟩

taken *past participle of* TAKE

take–off \'tā-,kòf\ *n* **1** : ¹IMITATION 2; *esp* : PARODY 1 **2 a** : a rise or leap from a surface in making a jump or flight in an aircraft or spacecraft **b** : an action of starting out **3** : a spot at which one takes off

take off \(')tā-'kòf\ *vb* **1 a** : ¹REMOVE 2 ⟨*take* your hat *off*⟩ **b** : to take away : DEDUCT ⟨*take off* 10 percent⟩ **2** : ¹RELEASE 1 ⟨*take* the brake *off*⟩ **3** : to spend (some time) away from an activity or occupation ⟨*took* two weeks *off* in August⟩ **4** : ³MIMIC 2 **5 a** : to start off or away ⟨*took off* without saying goodbye⟩ **b** : to begin flight ⟨planes *taking off*⟩

take on *vb* **1** : to struggle with as an opponent **2** : ¹EMPLOY 2 ⟨*took on* more workers⟩ **3** : to acquire (as an appearance or quality) as one's own ⟨*take on* weight⟩ ⟨*take on* dignity with age⟩ **4** : to make an unusual show of one's feelings especially of grief or anger ⟨don't *take on* so⟩

take out \(')tā-'kaut\ *vb* **1** : to find release for : VENT ⟨*took out* their anger on me⟩ **2** : to conduct or escort into the open or to a public entertainment **3** : to take as payment in another form ⟨*took* the debt *out* in goods⟩ **4** : to obtain from the proper authority ⟨*take out* a charter⟩ **5** : to start on a course : SET OUT — **take·out** \'tā-,kaut\ *n*

take over \(')tā-'kō-vər\ *vb* : to get control or possession of or responsibility for something — **take·over** \'tā-,kō-vər\ *n*

take–up \'tā-,kəp\ *n* **1** : a device in a sewing machine for drawing up the slack thread as the needle rises in completing a stitch **2** : a device for winding photographic film on a reel, core, or spool

take up \(')tā-'kəp\ *vb* **1** : to begin to occupy ⟨*took up* their positions⟩ **2** : to begin to engage in : UNDERTAKE ⟨*took up* swimming⟩ **3** : to pull up or in so as to tighten or to shorten ⟨*take up* the slack⟩ — **take up for** : to take the part or side of — **take up with** : to begin to associate with

tak·ing \'tā-kin\ *adj* : ATTRACTIVE, PLEASING

tak·ings \'tā-kinz\ *n pl* : receipts especially of money

talc \'talk\ *n* : a soft mineral that consists of a silicate of magnesium, has a soapy feel, and is used in making talcum powder and for coloring

tal·cum powder \'tal-kəm-\ *n* : a usually mildly antiseptic powder composed of perfumed talc for sprinkling or rubbing over the skin

tale \'tā(ə)l\ *n* **1** : something told ⟨a *tale* of woe⟩ **2** : a story about an imaginary event ⟨a fairy *tale*⟩ **3** : a false story : LIE **4** : a piece of harmful gossip ⟨spread *tales* about us⟩

tale·bear·er \-,bar-ər, -,ber-\ *n* : a person who spreads gossip, scandal, and rumors — **tale·bear·ing** \-in\ *adj or n*

tal·ent \'tal-ənt\ *n* **1** : an ancient unit of weight and money **2** : the natural abilities of a person **3** : a special often creative or artistic ability **4** : persons of talent in a field or

\ə\ abut		\au\ out	\i\ tip	\o\ saw	\u\ foot
\ər\ further	\ch\ chin		\ī\ life	\oi\ coin	\y\ yet
\a\ mat		\e\ pet	\j\ job	\th\ thin	\yü\ few
\ā\ take		\ē\ easy	\ŋ\ sing	\th\ this	\yu\ cure
\ä\ cot, cart	\g\ go		\ō\ bone	\ü\ food	\zh\ vision

activity [Middle English *talent, talente* "an ancient unit of weight and money"; in sense 1 from Old English *talente* (same meaning), from Latin *talenta*, plural of *talentum* "unit of weight or money", from Greek *talanton* (same meaning); in senses 2–4 so called from the parable of the talents told by Jesus (Matthew 25:14–30)] **syn** see ABIL-ITY — **tal·ent·ed** \-ən-təd\ *adj*

talent scout *n* : a person engaged in discovering and recruiting people with special talents

talent show *n* : a show consisting of a series of performances by amateurs who may be selected for special recognition as performers

tal·is·man \'tal-ə-smən, -əz-mən\ *n, pl* **talismans** : a ring or stone carved with symbols and believed to have magical powers : CHARM

¹talk \'tȯk\ *vb* **1** : to express in speech 〈*talk* sense〉 **2** : to speak about : DISCUSS 〈*talk* business〉 **3** : to influence, affect, or cause by talking 〈*talked* us into agreeing〉 **4** : to use for communicating 〈*talk* sign language〉 **5 a** : to express or exchange ideas by means of spoken words **b** : to communicate in any way 〈*talk* to a computer〉 **6 a** : to spread gossip **b** : to reveal secret information 〈tried to make the suspect *talk*〉 — **talk·er** *n* — **talk back** : to answer disrespectfully

²talk *n* **1** : the act or an instance of talking **2** : a way of speaking **3** : pointless or useless discussion **4** : a formal discussion or exchange of views : CONFERENCE **5** : ¹RUMOR 1, GOSSIP **6** : the topic of comment or gossip 〈it's the *talk* of the town〉

talk·a·tive \'tȯ-kət-iv\ *adj* : fond of talking — **talk·a·tive·ness** *n*

   syn TALKATIVE, LOQUACIOUS, GARRULOUS, VOLUBLE mean fond of talking. TALKATIVE suggests a regular willingness to talk or join in a conversation 〈a good group discussion needs a few *talkative* people〉 LOQUACIOUS suggests the ability of a person who speaks easily and smoothly 〈the *loquacious* host of a television show〉 GARRULOUS suggests a wish to talk that often continues to the point of being foolish and boring 〈a *garrulous* person running on about the good old days〉 VOLUBLE suggests a ready, rapid, and seemingly endless flow of speech 〈a *voluble* salesclerk who told customers more than they cared to know〉

talk down *vb* : to speak in an overly simple manner as if to a person who does not know much

talking book *n* : a recording of a reading of a book or magazine for the use of the blind

talk·ing–to \'tȯ-kiŋ-,tü\ *n* : an often wordy scolding

talk over *vb* : DISCUSS 1

talk show *n* : a radio or television program in which persons engage in discussions or are interviewed

talky \'tȯ-kē\ *adj* : TALKATIVE

tall \'tȯl\ *adj* **1 a** : having unusually great height **b** : of a specified height 〈five feet *tall*〉 **2 a** : large in amount, extent, or degree 〈*tall* order to fill〉 **b** : greatly exaggerated : IMPROBABLE 〈a *tall* tale〉 **syn** see HIGH — **tall** *adv* — **tall·ness** *n*

tal·lith \'täl-əs, -ət, -əth\ *n* : a shawl with fringed corners traditionally worn over the head or shoulders by Jewish men during morning prayers

tal·low \'tal-ō\ *n* : the solid fat of cattle and sheep used chiefly in soap, margarine, candles, and lubricants

¹tal·ly \'tal-ē\ *n, pl* **tallies** **1** : a device for keeping a count **2 a** : a recorded account **b** : a total

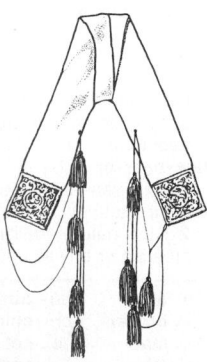

tallith

recorded **3** : a score or point made (as in a game)

²tally *vb* **tal·lied; tal·ly·ing** **1** : to keep a count of **2** : to make a tally : SCORE **3** : CORRESPOND 1, AGREE

tal·ly·ho \,tal-ē-'hō\ *n, pl* **tallyhos** : a call of a huntsman at sight of the fox

tally mark *n* : one of a group of lines or marks drawn for the purpose of counting

Tal·mud \'täl-,mu̇d, 'tal-məd\ *n* : the writings that declare Jewish law and tradition

tal·on \'tal-ən\ *n* : the claw of an animal and especially of a bird of prey

ta·lus \'tā-ləs\ *n* : a pile of rocks broken off from and found at the base of a cliff or steep slope

ta·ma·le \tə-'mäl-ē\ *n* : ground meat seasoned usually with chili, rolled in cornmeal dough, wrapped in corn husks, and steamed

tam·a·rack \'tam-(ə-),rak\ *n* **1** : any of several American larches; *esp* : a larch of the northern U.S. and Canada **2** : the wood of a tamarack

tam·a·rind \'tam-ə-rənd, -rind\ *n* : a tropical tree of the legume family that has hard yellowish wood, feathery leaves, and red-striped yellow flowers; *also* : its fruit which has an acid pulp used for preserves or in drinks

tam·a·risk \'tam-ə-,risk\ *n* : any of a genus of chiefly desert shrubs that have small narrow leaves and clusters of tiny flowers

tam·bou·rine \,tam-bə-'rēn\ *n* : a shallow drum with one head and loose metal disks at the sides that is played by shaking or striking with the hand

¹tame \'tām\ *adj* **tam·er; tam·est** **1** : changed from the wild state so as to become useful and obedient to human beings : DOMESTICATED **2** : made gentle and obedient **3** : lacking spirit or interest : DULL — **tame·ly** *adv* — **tame·ness** *n*

²tame *vb* **tamed; tam·ing** **1 a** : to make or become tame **b** : CULTIVATE 1 **2** : to bring under control : SUBDUE 〈*tame* your temper〉 — **tam·er** *n*

tam-o'-shan·ter \'tam-ə-,shant-ər\ *n* : a Scottish cap with a tight headband, wide flat circular crown, and usually a pompon [named for *Tam o' Shanter*, hero of a poem by Robert Burns 1759–1796 Scottish poet]

tamp \'tamp\ *vb* : to drive in or down by a series of blows — **tamp·er** *n*

tam-o'-shanter

tam·per \'tam-pər\ *vb* **tam·pered; tam·per·ing** \-p(ə-)riŋ\ **1** : to interfere in a secret or wrongful way **2 a** : to interfere so as to cause a weakening or change for the worse **b** : to try foolish or dangerous experiments **syn** see MEDDLE

¹tan \'tan\ *vb* **tanned; tan·ning** **1** : to change hide into leather especially by soaking in a tannin solution **2** : to make or become tan or brown especially by exposing to the sun **3** : THRASH 2a, WHIP

²tan *adj* **tan·ner; tan·nest** : of the color tan

³tan *n* **1** : a brown color given to the skin by the sun or weather **2** : a light yellowish brown

tan·a·ger \'tan-i-jər\ *n* : any of numerous small American birds that are related to the finches but have larger thicker bills, are mostly tropical but include several found in the U.S., and are brightly colored especially in the males — compare SCARLET TANAGER

¹tan·dem \'tan-dəm\ *n* **1 a** : a two-seated carriage drawn by horses hitched one behind the other **b** : TANDEM BICYCLE **2** : a group of two or more arranged one behind the other

   Word History *Tandem* is used to describe many things that involve the connecting of one object to another similar object behind it. A tandem tractor-trailer truck has one trailer hitched behind another, which is attached to the truck body, or tractor. A bicycle built for two is called a tandem bicycle because it has one seat and set of pedals behind another. The first use of the word *tandem* in English was for a carriage pulled by one horse hitched behind, rather than beside, another. Whoever first used the term in English apparently was making a play on words. The Latin word *tandem* meant "at length" referring to time, but in English *tandem* came to mean "at length" or "lengthwise", referring to position. [from Latin *tandem* "at length, at last"]

²**tandem** *adv or adj* : one behind another

tandem bicycle *n* : a bicycle for two or more persons sitting tandem

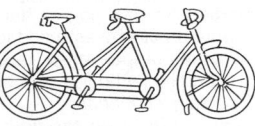

tandem bicycle

tang \'taŋ\ *n* **1** : a sharp often lingering flavor **2** : a sharp odor

tan·ge·lo \'tan-jə-ˌlō\ *n, pl* **-los** : a citrus tree that is a hybrid between a tangerine and a grapefruit; *also* : its fruit

¹**tan·gent** \'tan-jənt\ *adj* **1** : lying in the plane of a circle and touching it at only one point ⟨a straight line *tangent* to a circle⟩ ⟨a circle inside another and *tangent* to it⟩ **2** : touching a sphere at only one point ⟨a plane *tangent* to a sphere⟩ [from Latin *tangent-, tangens* "touching", from *tangere* "to touch" — related to CONTACT, TACTILE, TANGIBLE]

²**tangent** *n* **1** : the mathematical function that for an acute angle in a right triangle is the ratio of the side opposite to the side adjacent **2** : a tangent line, circle, or sphere **3** : a sudden change of course ⟨the speaker went off on a *tangent*⟩ — **tan·gen·tial** \tan-'jen-chəl\ *adj* — **tan·gen·tial·ly** \-'jench-(ə-)lē\ *adv*

tan·ger·ine \'tan-jə-ˌrēn, ˌtan-jə-'rēn\ *n* **1** : a citrus tree that belongs to any of several varieties of mandarin orange and is grown for its deep orange loose-skinned fruit **2** : the fruit of the tangerine

¹**tan·gi·ble** \'tan-jə-bəl\ *adj* **1** : capable of being touched **2** : capable of being understood and appreciated [from Latin *tangibilis* "tangible", from *tangere* "to touch" — related to CONTACT, TACTILE, TANGENT] — **tan·gi·bil·i·ty** \ˌtan-jə-'bil-ət-ē\ *n* — **tan·gi·bly** \'tan-jə-blē\ *adv*

²**tangible** *n* : something tangible

¹**tan·gle** \'taŋ-gəl\ *vb* **tan·gled; tan·gling** \-g(ə-)liŋ\ **1** : to make or become involved so as to complicate or confuse : be or become entangled **2** : to twist or become twisted together into a mass hard to straighten out again

²**tangle** *n* **1** : a tangled twisted mass (as of vines) confusedly woven together : SNARL **2** : a complicated or confused state or condition

tan·go \'taŋ-gō\ *n, pl* **tangos** **1** : a ballroom dance of Latin American origin to music in ²/₄ time and marked by pauses between steps and a variety of body postures; *also* : the music for a tango — **tango** *vb*

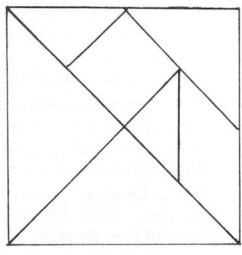

tangram

tan·gram \'taŋ-grəm, 'tan-\ *n* : a Chinese puzzle made by cutting a square of thin material into a number of pieces which can be recombined into many different figures

tangy \'taŋ-ē\ **tang·i·er; -est** *adj* : having or suggestive of a tang

¹**tank** \'taŋk\ *n* **1** : a usually large container for holding, transporting, or storing liquids **2** : an enclosed heavily armed and armored combat vehicle that moves on beltlike tracks

²**tank** *vb* : to place, store, or treat in a tank

tan·kard \'taŋ-kərd\ *n* : a tall one-handled drinking vessel; *esp* : a silver or pewter mug with a lid

tank·er \'taŋ-kər\ *n* : a vehicle (as a ship, truck, or aircraft) designed for the transportation of liquids

tank top *n* : a sleeveless pullover knitted shirt with a low neckline

tanned *past and past participle of* TAN

tan·ner \'tan-ər\ *n* : a person who tans hides

tan·nery \'tan-(ə-)rē\ *n, pl* **tan·ner·ies** : a place where hides are tanned

tannest *superlative of* TAN

tan·nic acid \ˌtan-ik-\ *n* : TANNIN

tan·nin \'tan-ən\ *n* : any of various substances from plants (as the oak or sumac) used in tanning, dyeing, the making of ink, and in medicine

tan·ning \'tan-iŋ\ *n* **1** : the art or process by which a skin is tanned **2** : a browning of the skin by the sun **3** : a usually severe whipping

tan·ta·lite \'tant-ᵊl-ˌīt\ *n* : a mineral consisting of a heavy dark shiny oxide of iron, manganese, tantalum, and niobium

tan·ta·lize \'tant-ᵊl-ˌīz\ *vb* **-lized; -liz·ing** : to tease or torment by or as if by presenting something desirable to the view but continually keeping it out of reach — **tan·ta·liz·ing·ly** \-ˌī-ziŋ-lē\ *adv*

Word History In Greek mythology, King Tantalus offended the gods, so they punished him in a truly terrible way. He was forced to stand in a lake whose water came up to his neck. But every time Tantalus became thirsty and bent over to drink, the water level dropped so that he could never reach it. Above his head were branches loaded with delicious fruits. Yet every time Tantalus reached up to take a fruit, the branches moved up out of reach, leaving him hungry. Thus, Tantalus was always in torment, and from his name comes the English word for tormenting or teasing someone in a similar way. [from Greek *Tantalus,* name of a king in mythology]

tan·ta·lum \'tant-ᵊl-əm\ *n* : a hard gray-white metallic element that is resistant to attack by acid and is found combined in rare minerals — see ELEMENT table

tan·ta·mount \'tant-ə-ˌmaunt\ *adj* : equal in value, meaning, or effect

tan·trum \'tan-trəm\ *n* : a fit of bad temper

¹**tap** \'tap\ *n* **1** : FAUCET, SPIGOT **2** : the procedure of removing fluid from a container or cavity by tapping [Old English *tæppa* "a plug for a hole (as in a wine cask)"] — **on tap** **1** : ready to be drawn ⟨root beer *on tap*⟩ **2** : on hand : AVAILABLE

²**tap** *vb* **tapped; tap·ping** **1** : to release or cause to flow by making a hole or by drawing a plug from a container or cavity ⟨*tap* wine from a cask⟩ **2 a** : to make a hole in so as to let out or draw off a fluid ⟨*tap* maple trees⟩ **b** : to draw from or upon ⟨*tap* the nation's resources⟩ — **tap·per** *n*

³**tap** *vb* **tapped; tap·ping** : to strike or cause to strike lightly especially with a slight sound ⟨*tapping* the desk with a pencil⟩ ⟨*tap* on a window⟩ ⟨*tap* one's foot⟩ [Middle English *tappen* "to strike lightly, tap", from early French *taper* (same meaning); of Germanic origin] — **tap·per** *n*

⁴**tap** *n* **1** : a light blow or its sound **2** : a small metal plate for the sole or heel of a shoe (as for tap dancing)

tap dance *n* : a dance tapped out loudly by means of shoes to which taps have been added — **tap–dance** *vb* — **tap**

\ə\ abut	\au\ out	\i\ tip	\o\ saw	\u\ foot
\ər\ further	\ch\ chin	\ī\ life	\oi\ coin	\y\ yet
\a\ mat	\e\ pet	\j\ job	\th\ thin	\yü\ few
\ā\ take	\ē\ easy	\ŋ\ sing	\th\ this	\yu̇\ cure
\ä\ cot, cart	\g\ go	\ō\ bone	\ü\ food	\zh\ vision

dancer *n* — **tap dancing** *n*

¹tape \'tāp\ *n* **1** : a narrow band of woven fabric **2** : a string stretched breast-high above the finishing line of a race **3** : a narrow flexible strip or band; *esp* : MAGNETIC TAPE **4** : a recording made on magnetic tape

²tape *vb* **taped; tap·ing 1** : to fasten, tie, bind, cover, or support with tape **2** : to measure with a tape measure **3** : TAPE-RECORD

tape deck *n* : a device used to play back and often to record on magnetic tapes that usually has to be connected to an audio system

tape measure *n* : a tape marked off in units (as inches or centimeters) and used for measuring

¹ta·per \'tā-pər\ *n* **1 a** : a long waxed wick used especially for lighting lamps, pipes, or fires **b** : a slender candle **2 a** : a tapering form or figure **b** : gradual lessening of thickness, diameter, or width in a long object **c** : a gradual decrease

²taper *vb* **ta·pered; ta·per·ing** \'tā-p(ə-)riŋ\ **1** : to make or become gradually smaller toward one end **2** : to become gradually less and less

tape–re·cord \,tā-pri-'kȯ(ə)rd\ *vb* : to make a recording of on magnetic tape ⟨*tape-record* a concert⟩

tape recorder *n* : a device for recording on and playing back magnetic tapes

taper off *vb* : to stop or lessen gradually

tap·es·try \'tap-ə-strē\ *n, pl* **-tries** : a heavy cloth that has designs or pictures woven into it and is used especially as a wall hanging — **tap·es·tried** \-strēd\ *adj*

tape·worm \'tāp-,wərm\ *n* : a flatworm with a segmented body that is a parasite of the intestines of vertebrate animals including human beings

tap·i·o·ca \,tap-ē-'ō-kə\ *n* : grains or flakes of starch from the cassava root that are used especially in puddings and as a thickening in liquid foods; *also* : a dish (as pudding) that contains tapioca

ta·pir \'tā-pər\ *n, pl* **tapir** or **tapirs** : any of several large hoofed mammals of tropical America, Malaya, and Sumatra that are related to the horses and rhinoceroses and have a long flexible snout, a very short tail, and stout legs

tapir

tap·root \'tap-,rüt, -,rủt\ *n* : a large main root that grows straight down and gives off many smaller side roots — compare FIBROUS ROOT

taps \'taps\ *n sing or pl* : the last bugle call at night blown as a signal to put out the lights **2** : a similar call blown at military funerals and memorial services

¹tar \'tär\ *n* **1 a** : a dark usually thick sticky liquid obtained by distilling wood, coal, or peat **b** : a substance that resembles tar; *esp* : a waste substance present in tobacco smoke that contains the by-products of burning **2** : SAILOR

²tar *vb* **tarred; tar·ring** : to smear with or as if with tar

ta·ran·tu·la \tə-'ranch-(ə-)lə, -'rant-ᵊl-ə\ *n* : any of a family of large hairy American spiders that usually move slowly and have a sharp bite but are not very poisonous to human beings

tar·dy \'tärd-ē\ *adj* **tar·di·er; -est 1** : moving slowly : SLUGGISH **2** : not on time : LATE — **tar·di·ly** \'tärd-ə-lē\ *adv* — **tar·di·ness** \'tärd-ē-nəs\ *n*

tare \'ta(ə)r, 'te(ə)r\ *n* : a weed of grainfields especially of biblical times

tar·get \'tär-gət\ *n* **1** : a mark to shoot at **2** : a person or thing that is talked about, criticized, or laughed at **3** : a goal to be achieved : OBJECTIVE

tar·iff \'tar-əf\ *n* **1 a** : a list of taxes placed by a govern-

ment on imported or in some countries exported goods **b** : a tax or rate of tax set up in a tariff list **2** : a list of rates or charges of a business or public service company

tar·mac \'tär-,mak\ *n* : a road, apron, or runway paved with layers of crushed stone covered with tar

¹tar·nish \'tär-nish\ *vb* **1** : to make or become dull, dim, or discolored ⟨silver *tarnishes*⟩ **2** : to bring disgrace or cast doubt on ⟨*tarnished* the family's good name⟩

²tarnish *n* : something that tarnishes; *esp* : a film of chemically changed material on the surface of a metal (as silver)

ta·ro \'tär-ō, 'tar-, 'ter-\ *n, pl* **taros** : a plant grown throughout the tropics for its edible starchy and fleshy rootstocks; *also* : this rootstock

tar paper *n* : a heavy paper coated with or soaked in tar for use especially in building

tar·pau·lin \tär-'pȯ-lən, 'tär-pə-\ *n* : a piece of material (as waterproof canvas) used for protecting exposed objects

tar·pon \'tär-pən\ *n, pl* **tarpon** or **tarpons** : a large silvery sport fish found in warm coastal waters of the Atlantic especially off Florida

¹tar·ry \'tar-ē\ *vb* **tar·ried; tar·ry·ing 1** : to be slow in coming or going **2** : to stay in or at a place

²tar·ry \'tär-ē\ *adj* : of, resembling, or covered with tar

¹tar·sal \'tär-səl\ *adj* : of or relating to the tarsus

²tarsal *n* : a tarsal part (as a bone or cartilage)

tar sand *n* : sand or sandstone that is naturally soaked with heavy sticky portions of petroleum

tar·si·er \'tär-sē-ər, -sē-,ā\ *n* : any of several small tree-dwelling primate mammals of the East Indies related to the lemurs that are active at night

tar·sus \'tär-səs\ *n, pl* **tar·si** \-,sī, -,sē\ **1** : the part of the foot of a vertebrate between the metatarsus and the leg : ANKLE; *also* : the small bones that support this part of the foot **2** : the shank of a bird's leg **3** : the part of the limb of an arthropod (as an insect) most distant from the body

¹tart \'tärt\ *adj* **1** : pleasantly sharp or sour to the taste **2** : having a sharp or biting quality ⟨a *tart* voice⟩ — **tart·ly** *adv* — **tart·ness** *n*

²tart *n* : a small pie or pastry shell containing jelly, custard, or fruit

tar·tan \'tärt-ᵊn\ *n* **1** : a plaid textile design of Scottish origin **2** : a fabric or garment with tartan design

¹tar·tar \'tärt-ər\ *n* **1** : a substance consisting mostly of cream of tartar that is found in the juice of grapes and is deposited in wine casks as a reddish crust or sediment **2** : a hard crust of saliva, bits of food, and various calcium salts that forms on the teeth

²tartar *n* **1** *cap* : a member of any of the chiefly Mongolian peoples who invaded parts of Asia and eastern Europe during the Middle Ages **2** : a bad-tempered or unexpectedly violent person

tar·tar sauce or **tar·tare sauce** \,tärt-ər-\ *n* : a sauce made chiefly of mayonnaise and chopped pickles

task \'task\ *n* : a piece of assigned work

syn TASK, DUTY, JOB, CHORE mean a piece of work assigned or to be done. TASK suggests work given by a person in a position of authority ⟨the boss used to give me every hard *task*⟩ DUTY stresses that one is responsible for doing the work ⟨the *duty* of the police is to protect the people⟩ JOB may suggest that the work is necessary, hard, or important ⟨we all have to do our *job*⟩ CHORE suggests a small routine piece of work that is necessary for keeping a house or farm ⟨taking out the garbage is a daily *chore*⟩

task·mas·ter \-,mas-tər\ *n* : one that assigns a task or burdens another with labor

Tas·ma·ni·an devil

Tasmanian devil

\(,)taz-,mā-nē-ən-\ *n* : a powerful stocky burrowing marsupial of Tasmania that eats other animals, is about the size of a large cat or badger, and has a black coat marked with white on the chest

¹**tas·sel** \'tas-əl *also especially of corn* 'täs-, 'tòs-\ *n* **1** : a hanging ornament made of a bunch of cords fastened at one end **2** : something resembling a tassel; *esp* : the male flower cluster on the top of some plants and especially Indian corn

²**tassel** *vb* **-seled** *or* **-selled; -sel·ing** *or* **-sel·ling** \-(ə-)liŋ\ : to adorn with or put forth tassels

¹**taste** \'tāst\ *vb* **tast·ed; tast·ing** **1** : ²EXPERIENCE, UNDERGO ⟨*taste* the joy of flying⟩ **2** : to test the flavor of something by taking a little into the mouth **3** : to eat or drink especially in small quantities **4** : to recognize by or as if by the sense of taste ⟨can *taste* the onion in it⟩ **5** : to have a specific flavor ⟨this milk *tastes* sour⟩

²**taste** *n* **1 a** : a small amount tasted **b** : a small sample of experience ⟨first *taste* of success⟩ **2** : the sense that recognizes and tells apart the sweet, sour, bitter, or salty quality of a dissolved substance and is controlled by receptors in the taste buds of the tongue **3 a** : the quality of a dissolved substance that can be identified by the sense of taste **b** : a sensation obtained from a substance in the mouth that is usually produced by the sense of taste in combination with those of touch and smell : FLAVOR **4** : a personal liking ⟨had expensive *tastes*⟩ **5 a** : the ability to choose and enjoy what is good and beautiful ⟨a person of *taste*⟩ **b** : aesthetic quality : STYLE ⟨in bad *taste*⟩

taste bud *n* : any of the sense organs by means of which taste is recognized and which are usually on the surface of the tongue

taste·ful \'tāst-fəl\ *adj* : having or showing good taste — **taste·ful·ly** \-fə-lē\ *adv* — **taste·ful·ness** *n*

taste·less \'tāst-ləs\ *adj* **1** : lacking flavor : FLAT **2** : not having or showing good taste — **taste·less·ly** *adv* — **taste·less·ness** *n*

tast·er \'tā-stər\ *n* : one that tastes: as **a** : a person who has the duty of tasting food or drink prepared for another person especially to test for poison **b** : a person who is able to taste the chemical phenylthiocarbamide

tasty \'tā-stē\ *adj* **tast·i·er; -est** **1** : pleasing to the taste : SAVORY **2** : very attractive or interesting — **tast·i·ly** \-stə-lē\ *adv* — **tast·i·ness** \-stē-nəs\ *n*

tat \'tat\ *vb* **tat·ted; tat·ting** : to work at or make by tatting

tat·ter \'tat-ər\ *n* **1** : a part torn and left hanging : SHRED **2** *pl* : tattered clothing : RAGS — **tatter** *vb*

tat·tered \'tat-ərd\ *adj* **1** : wearing ragged clothes ⟨a *tattered* barefoot child⟩ **2** : torn in shreds : RAGGED ⟨a *tattered* flag⟩

tat·ting \'tat-iŋ\ *n* **1** : a delicate handmade lace formed usually by looping and knotting with a single thread and a small shuttle **2** : the act or process of making tatting

¹**tat·tle** \'tat-ᵊl\ *vb* **tat·tled; tat·tling** \'tat-liŋ, -ᵊl-iŋ\ : to tell secrets : BLAB

²**tattle** *n* **1** : idle talk : CHATTER **2** : GOSSIP 2a

tat·tler \'tat-lər, -ᵊl-ər\ *n* : TATTLETALE

tat·tle·tale \'tat-ᵊl-,tāl\ *n* : a person who tattles

¹**tat·too** \ta-'tü\ *n* **1** : a call sounded shortly before taps as notice to go to quarters **2** : a rapid rhythmic rapping [from earlier *taptoo* "a call to go to quarters for the night", from Dutch *taptoe* (same meaning), from the phrase *tap toe!* "taps shut!", used as a signal that the taps, or faucets, on the wine casks in a barroom were closed for the night]

²**tattoo** *vb* : to mark or color the skin with a tattoo [from a word in the native language of Tahiti *tatan* (noun) "the act of marking or coloring the skin"]

³**tattoo** *n* : a mark or figure fixed upon the body by using a needle to put color under the skin

tau \'tau̇, 'tò\ *n* : the 19th letter of the Greek alphabet — T or τ

taught *past and past participle of* TEACH

taunt \'tònt, 'tänt\ *vb* : to provoke or challenge in a mocking or insulting manner : jeer at — **taunt** *n* — **taunt·er** *n* — **taunt·ing·ly** \-iŋ-lē\ *adv*

taupe \'tōp\ *n* : a brownish gray

Tau·rus \'tòr-əs\ *n* **1** : a group of stars between Aries and Gemini usually pictured as a bull **2 a** : the second sign of the zodiac — see ZODIAC table **b** : a person whose sign of the zodiac is Taurus

taut \'tòt\ *adj* **1 a** : drawn to the limit : not slack ⟨*taut* rope⟩ **b** : HIGH-STRUNG, TENSE ⟨*taut* nerves⟩ **2** : kept in proper order or condition ⟨a *taut* ship⟩ **syn** see TIGHT — **taut·ly** *adv* — **taut·ness** *n*

tau·tol·o·gy \tò-'täl-ə-jē\ *n, pl* **-gies** : needless repetition of an idea, statement, or word; *also* : an instance of such repetition ⟨"a beginner who has just started" is a *tautology*⟩ — **tau·to·log·i·cal** \,tòt-ᵊl-'äj-i-kəl\ *adj*

tav·ern \'tav-ərn\ *n* **1** : an establishment where alcoholic liquors are sold to be drunk on the premises **2** : INN

taw \'tò\ *n* **1** : a marble used as a shooter **2** : the line from which players shoot at marbles

taw·dry \'tòd-rē, 'täd-\ *adj* **taw·dri·er; -est** : cheap and showy — **taw·dri·ly** \-rə-lē\ *adv* — **taw·dri·ness** \-rē-nəs\ *n*

¹**taw·ny** \'tò-nē, 'tän-ē\ *adj* **taw·ni·er; -est** : of the color tawny — **taw·ni·ness** *n*

²**tawny** *n, pl* **tawnies** : a brownish orange to light brown color

¹**tax** \'taks\ *vb* **1** : to require to pay a tax **2** : to accuse of something ⟨*taxed* them with carelessness⟩ **3** : to make heavy demands on : STRAIN ⟨*taxed* our strength⟩ — **tax·er** *n*

²**tax** *n* **1** : a charge usually of money set by authority on persons or property for public purposes **2** : something (as an effort or duty) that makes heavy demands : STRAIN

tax·able \'tak-sə-bəl\ *adj* : subject to tax ⟨*taxable* property⟩

tax·a·tion \tak-'sā-shən\ *n* : the action of taxing; *esp* : the establishing of taxes

¹**taxi** \'tak-sē\ *n, pl* **tax·is** \-sēz\ *also* **tax·ies** : TAXICAB; *also* : a similarly operated boat or airplane

²**taxi** *vb* **tax·ied; taxi·ing** *or* **taxy·ing; tax·is** *or* **tax·ies** **1** : to operate an airplane slowly on the ground under its own power **2** : to ride in or transport by taxi

taxi·cab \'tak-sē-,kab\ *n* : an automobile that carries passengers for a fare usually based on the distance traveled

Word History In the days of horse-drawn vehicles, one type of carriage was called a *cabriolet*, from a French word meaning "leap". This name was fitting since the carriage was so light it bounced or "leaped" about on the rough roads of the time. In time the name *cabriolet* was shortened to *cab*. These cabs were popular as vehicles carrying passengers for a fee. They were equipped with a taximeter, a device that automatically recorded the distance traveled and showed what fee or "tax" the passenger owed. In time this carriage or "cab" with its taximeter came to be called a *taximeter cab*. When the automobile took over from carriages the job of carrying passengers for a fee, it took over the name *taximeter cab* as well. This name was soon shortened to *taxicab*, and that was later shortened to *taxi* and sometimes just *cab*. [from earlier *taximeter cab*, from French *taximètre*, literally "tax meter", and English *cab*, a shortened form of *cabriolet* "a one-horse carriage"]

\ə\ abut	\au̇\ out	\i\ tip	\ò\ saw	\u̇\ foot
\ər\ further	\ch\ chin	\ī\ life	\ȯi\ coin	\y\ yet
\a\ mat	\e\ pet	\j\ job	\th\ thin	\yü\ few
\ā\ take	\ē\ easy	\ŋ\ sing	\th\ this	\yu̇\ cure
\ä\ cot, cart	\g\ go	\ō\ bone	\ü\ food	\zh\ vision

taxi·der·mist \'tak-sə-,dər-məst\ *n* : a person who practices taxidermy

taxi·der·my \'tak-sə-,dər-mē\ *n* : the skill or occupation of preparing, stuffing, and mounting skins of animals [derived from Greek *taxis* "arrangement" and Greek *derma* "skin" and English *-y,* noun suffix] — **taxi·der·mic** \,tak-sə-'dər-mik\ *adj*

tax·is \'tak-səs\ *n, pl* **tax·es** \'tak-,sēz\ : a reflex movement by a freely moving organism in relation to a stimulus (as a light or a change in temperature); *also* : a reflex reaction involving such movement — compare TROPISM

tax·on·o·mist \tak-'sän-ə-məst\ *n* : a person who specializes in taxonomy and especially the taxonomy of plants and animals

tax·on·o·my \tak-'sän-ə-mē\ *n* **1** : the study of scientific classification 2 : CLASSIFICATION 2a; *esp* : orderly classification of plants and animals according to their presumed natural relationships — **tax·o·nom·ic** \,tak-sə-'näm-ik\ *adj*

tax·pay·er \'tak-,spā-ər\ *n* : one that pays or is responsible for paying a tax

Tay–Sachs disease \'tā-'saks-\ *n* : a fatal hereditary disease that is caused by the absence of an enzyme needed to break down fatty material and is characterized by a buildup of lipids in the nervous tissue — called also *Tay⸗ Sachs*

TB \(')tē-'bē\ *n* : TUBERCULOSIS

T cell *n* : any of the lymphocytes (as a helper T cell) that usually mature in the thymus and take an active part in immune responses

tea \'tē\ *n* **1 a** : a shrub related to the camellias that has fragrant white flowers and is grown mainly in China, Japan, India, and Sri Lanka **b** : the leaves and leaf buds of the tea prepared for use in beverages **c** : a beverage prepared from tea by soaking the prepared leaves and buds in boiling water **2** : a drink or medicine made by soaking plant parts (as dried roots) ⟨ginger *tea*⟩

tea 1a

3 a : a late afternoon serving of tea and a light meal **b** : a party at which tea is served

tea bag *n* : a filter-paper bag holding enough tea for an individual serving

teach \'tēch\ *vb* **taught** \'tȯt\; **teach·ing** **1** : to assist in learning how to do something : show how ⟨*teach* a child to read⟩ **2** : to guide the studies of : INSTRUCT ⟨*teach* a class⟩ **3** : to give lessons in : instruct pupils in ⟨*teach* music⟩ **4** : to be a teacher **5** : to cause to learn : cause to know the effects of an action

teach·able \'tē-chə-bəl\ *adj* : capable of being taught; *esp* : able and willing to learn — **teach·abil·i·ty** \,tē-chə-'bil-ət-ē\ *n*

teach·er \'tē-chər\ *n* : one that teaches; *esp* : a person whose occupation is to instruct

teach·ing *n* **1** : the act, practice, or profession of a teacher **2** : something taught; *esp* : DOCTRINE

tea·cup \'tē-,kəp\ *n* : a cup used with a saucer for hot beverages

teak \'tēk\ *n* **1** : a tall timber tree of southeastern Asia **2** : the hard durable yellowish brown wood of a teak — called also *teak wood* \'tē-,kwu̇d\

tea·ket·tle \'tē-,ket-ᵊl\ *n* : a covered kettle that is used for boiling water and has a handle and a spout

teal \'tē(ə)l\ *n, pl* **teal** *or* **teals** : any of several small short⸗ necked ducks of Europe and America

¹team \'tēm\ *n* **1** : two or more animals used to pull the same vehicle or piece of machinery; *also* : these animals with their harness and attached vehicle **2** : a number of persons associated together in work or activity

²team *vb* **1** : to join in a team **2** : to haul with or drive a team **3** : to form a team

team·mate \'tēm-,māt\ *n* : a fellow member of a team

team·ster \'tēm(p)-stər\ *n* : a person who drives a team or truck

team·work \'tēm-,wərk\ *n* : the work or activity of a number of persons acting together as a team

tea·pot \'tē-,pät\ *n* : a pot that is used for brewing and serving tea and that has a spout

¹tear \'ti(ə)r\ *n* **1** : a drop of the salty liquid that keeps the eye and the inner eyelids moist **2** *pl* : an act of crying or grieving ⟨burst into *tears*⟩ [Old English *tēar* "a drop of liquid from the eye"] — **teary** \'ti(ə)r-ē\ *adj*

²tear *vb* : to fill with tears : shed tears ⟨eyes *tearing* in the wind⟩

³tear \'ta(ə)r, 'te(ə)r\ *vb* **tore** \'tō(ə)r, 'tȯ(ə)r\; **torn** \'tō(ə)rn, 'tȯ(ə)rn\; **tear·ing** **1 a** : to separate or pull apart by force ⟨*tore* a page from the pad⟩ **b** : to injure by slashing or tearing ⟨*tear* the skin⟩ **2** : to divide or throw into disorder by the pull of contrary forces ⟨a mind *torn* by doubts⟩ **3** : to remove by force ⟨children *torn* from their parents⟩ **4** : to cause by force or violent means ⟨*tore* a hole in the wall⟩ **5** : to move or act with violence, haste, or force ⟨*tearing* down the street⟩ [Old English *teran* "to pull apart"] — **tear·er** *n*

⁴tear \'ta(ə)r, 'te(ə)r\ *n* **1** : the act of tearing **2** : damage from being torn; *esp* : a torn place ⟨mending a *tear* in my sleeve⟩

tear down *vb* : to knock down and break into pieces ⟨*tear down* an old building⟩

tear·drop \'ti(ə)r-,dräp\ *n* **1** : ¹TEAR 1 **2** : something (as a pendent gem) shaped like a dropping tear

tear·ful \'ti(ə)r-fəl\ *adj* : flowing with, accompanied by, or causing tears — **tear·ful·ly** \-fə-lē\ *adv*

tear·gas \'ti(ə)r-,gas\ *vb* : to use tear gas on

tear gas *n* : any of various substances that cause eye irritation and blind the eyes with tears when released into the air and that are used mostly to scatter mobs

tea·room \'tē-,rüm, -,ru̇m\ *n* : a restaurant serving light meals

¹tease \'tēz\ *vb* **teased; teas·ing** **1** : to untangle and lay parallel by combing or carding ⟨*tease* wool⟩ **2 a** : to annoy continually : PESTER, TORMENT **b** : TANTALIZE — **teas·er** *n* — **teas·ing·ly** \'tē-ziŋ-lē\ *adv*

²tease *n* **1 a** : the act of teasing **b** : the state of being teased **2** : one that teases

tea·sel \'tē-zəl\ *n* : an Old World prickly herb with flower heads covered with stiff hooked bracts

tea·spoon \'tē-,spün, -'spün\ *n* **1** : a small spoon used especially for eating soft foods and stirring beverages **2** : TEASPOONFUL

tea·spoon·ful \'tē-,spün-,fu̇l, -'spün-\ *n, pl* **-spoonfuls** \-,fu̇lz\ *or* **-spoons·ful** \-,spünz-,fu̇l, -'spünz-\ **1** : as much as a teaspoon can hold **2** : a unit of measure used especially in cooking equal to 1⅓ fluidrams (about 5 milliliters) or one third of a tablespoonful

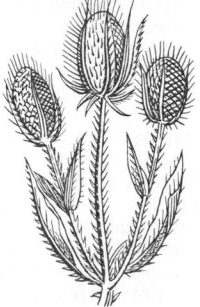

teasel

teat \'tit, 'tēt\ *n* : the part of a breast or udder through which milk is drawn : NIPPLE

tech·ne·tium \tek-'nē-sh(ē-)əm\ *n* : a metallic element obtained by bombarding molybdenum (as with neutrons) and in the fission of uranium — see ELEMENT table

tech·ni·cal \'tek-ni-kəl\ *adj* **1 a** : having special knowledge especially of a mechanical or scientific subject ⟨*tech-*

nical experts⟩ **b** : used in special fields of knowledge ⟨*technical* language⟩ **2** : of or relating to a particular subject; *esp* : of or relating to a practical subject organized on scientific principles ⟨*technical* training⟩ **3** : existing by laws or rules ⟨a *technical* knockout⟩ **4** : of or relating to technique ⟨*technical* skill⟩ — **tech·ni·cal·ly** \-k(ə-)lē\ *adv*

tech·ni·cal·i·ty \ˌtek-nə-'kal-ət-ē\ *n, pl* **-ties** **1** : something technical; *esp* : a detail that means something only to a specialist ⟨a legal *technicality*⟩ **2** : the quality or state of being technical

technical sergeant *n* : an enlisted person in the air force with a rank just below a master sergeant

tech·ni·cian \tek-'nish-ən\ *n* **1** : a specialist in the technical details of a subject or occupation ⟨a medical *technician*⟩ **2** : a person skilled in the techniques especially of an art

tech·nique \tek-'nēk\ *n* **1 a** : the manner in which details are treated (as by a writer) or basic physical movements are used (as by a dancer) **b** : ability in such treatment or use ⟨perfect piano *technique*⟩ **2 a** : technical methods especially in scientific research ⟨laboratory *technique*⟩ **b** : a method of accomplishing a desired aim ⟨a *technique* for handling complaints⟩

tech·nol·o·gist \tek-'näl-ə-jəst\ *n* : a person who specializes in technology

tech·nol·o·gy \tek-'näl-ə-jē\ *n, pl* **-gies** **1** : the use of science in solving problems (as in industry or engineering) **2** : a technical method of doing something — **tech·no·log·i·cal** \ˌtek-nə-'läj-i-kəl\ *adj*

tec·ton·ic \tek-'tän-ik\ *adj* : of or relating to changes in the shape of the crust of a moon or planet (as earth), the forces involved in or producing such changes, and the resulting forms

tec·ton·ics \tek-'tän-iks\ *n* **1** : a branch of geology concerned with the structure of the earth's crust and especially with the formation of folds and faults in it **2** : the process of change in the earth's crust that produces continents, ocean basins, plateaus, mountains, folds, and faults

ted·dy bear \'ted-ē-\ *n* : a stuffed toy bear

te·dious \'tēd-ē-əs, 'tē-jəs\ *adj* : tiring because of length or dullness : BORING — **te·dious·ly** *adv* — **te·dious·ness** *n*

te·di·um \'tēd-ē-əm\ *n* : the quality or state of being tedious : BOREDOM

¹tee \'tē\ *n* **1** : a small peg on which a golf ball is set to be struck **2** : the area from which a golf ball is struck in starting play on a hole

²tee *vb* **teed; tee·ing** : to place on a tee ⟨*teed* up the ball⟩

teem \'tēm\ *vb* : to become filled : ABOUND ⟨a stream *teeming* with fish⟩

teen \'tēn\ *adj* : TEENAGE

teen·age \'tē-ˌnāj\ *or* **teen·aged** \-ˌnājd\ *adj* : of, being, or relating to people in their teens

teen·ag·er \'tē-ˌnā-jər\ *n* : a person in his or her teens

teens \'tēnz\ *n pl* **1** : the numbers 13 through 19; *esp* : the years 13 through 19 in a lifetime or century **2** : teenage persons : TEENAGERS

tee·ny \'tē-nē\ *adj* **tee·ni·er; -est** : TINY

teeny·bop·per \'tē-nē-ˌbäp-ər\ *n* : a person in his or her early teens

tee·ny–wee·ny \ˌtē-nē-'wē-nē\ *adj* : TINY

tee off *vb* : to hit a golf ball from a tee in starting play on a hole

teepee *variant of* TEPEE

tee shirt *variant of* T-SHIRT

tee·ter \'tēt-ər\ *vb* **1 a** : to move unsteadily ⟨*teetered* on the edge and fell over the side⟩ **b** : WAVER 1 **2** : ²SEESAW 2 — **teeter** *n*

tee·ter–board \-ˌbȯ(ə)rd, -ˌbȯ(ə)rd\ *n* **1** : ¹SEESAW 2b **2** : a board placed on a raised support so that a person standing on one end of the board is thrown into the air if another person jumps on the opposite end

tee·ter–tot·ter \'tēt-ər-ˌtät-ər\ *n* : ¹SEESAW 2b

teeth *pl of* TOOTH

teethe \'tēth\ *vb* **teethed; teeth·ing** : to cut one's teeth : grow teeth

Tef·lon \'tef-ˌlän\ *trademark* — used for synthetic fluorine-containing resins used especially for molded articles and for nonstick coatings (as for frying pans)

tele- *combining form* **1** : at a distance ⟨*tele*gram⟩ ⟨*tele*vision⟩ **2** : television ⟨*tele*cast⟩ [derived from Greek *tēle* "far off"]

tele·cast \'tel-i-ˌkast\ *vb* **telecast** *also* **tele·cast·ed; tele·cast·ing** : to broadcast by television — **telecast** *n* — **tele·cast·er** *n*

tele·gram \'tel-ə-ˌgram, *Southern also* -grəm\ *n* : a message sent by telegraph

¹tele·graph \'tel-ə-ˌgraf\ *n* : an electric device or system for sending messages by a code over wires — **tele·graph·ic** \ˌtel-ə-'graf-ik\ *adj* — **tele·graph·i·cal·ly** \-'graf-i-k(ə-)lē\ *adv*

²telegraph *vb* **1** : to send by or as if by telegraph ⟨*telegraphed* a message⟩ **2** : to send a telegram to ⟨*telegraphed* home for money⟩ — **te·leg·ra·pher** \tə-'leg-rə-fər\ *n*

te·leg·ra·phy \tə-'leg-rə-fē\ *n* : the use or operation of a telegraph system or equipment

tele·me·ter \'tel-ə-ˌmēt-ər\ *vb* : to transmit measurements taken by automatic instruments especially by radio to be recorded or indicated at a distant station

te·lem·e·try \tə-'lem-ə-trē\ *n* : the process of telemetering measurements

te·lep·a·thy \tə-'lep-ə-thē\ *n* : apparent communication from one mind to another without speech or signs — **tele·path·ic** \ˌtel-ə-'path-ik\ *adj* — **tele·path·i·cal·ly** \-'path-i-k(ə-)lē\ *adv*

¹tele·phone \'tel-ə-ˌfōn\ *n* : an instrument for transmitting and receiving sounds over long distances by electricity

²telephone *vb* **-phoned; -phon·ing** **1** : to communicate by telephone **2** : to send by telephone **3** : to speak to by telephone

telephone booth *n* : an enclosure within which one may stand or sit while making a telephone call

tele·pho·to \ˌtel-ə-'fōt-ō\ *adj* : being a camera lens designed to give a large image of a distant object

tele·print·er \'tel-ə-ˌprint-ər\ *n* : a device that produces hard copy from signals received over a communications circuit; *esp* : TELETYPEWRITER

¹tele·scope \'tel-ə-ˌskōp\ *n* : a cylindrical instrument that has lenses or mirrors for viewing distant objects and especially for observing objects in outer space

²telescope *vb* **-scoped; -scop·ing** **1** : to slide or cause to slide one within another like the cylindrical sections of a hand telescope **2** : to run together like the sections of a telescope

tele·scop·ic \ˌtel-ə-'skäp-ik\ *adj* **1** : of, relating to, or performed with a telescope **2** : seen or discoverable only by a telescope ⟨*telescopic* stars⟩ **3** : able to discern objects at a distance **4** : having parts that telescope — **tele·scop·i·cal·ly** \-i-k(ə-)lē\ *adv*

tele·thon \'tel-ə-ˌthän\ *n* : a long television program usually to raise funds for a charity

Tele·type \'tel-ə-ˌtīp\ *trademark* — used for a teletypewriter

tele·type·writ·er \ˌtel-ə-'tīp-ˌrīt-ər\ *n* : a printing device resembling a typewriter that is used to send and receive signals over telephone lines

\ə\ **abut**	\au̇\ **out**	\i\ **tip**	\ȯ\ **saw**	\u̇\ **foot**
\ər\ **further**	\ch\ **chin**	\ī\ **life**	\ȯi\ **coin**	\y\ **yet**
\a\ **mat**	\e\ **pet**	\j\ **job**	\th\ **thin**	\yü\ **few**
\ā\ **take**	\ē\ **easy**	\ŋ\ **sing**	\th\ **this**	\yu̇\ **cure**
\ä\ **cot, cart**	\g\ **go**	\ō\ **bone**	\ü\ **food**	\zh\ **vision**

tele·vise \'tel-ə-ˌvīz\ *vb* **-vised; -vis·ing** : to pick up and usually to broadcast by television ⟨*televised* the ball game⟩

tele·vi·sion \'tel-ə-ˌvizh-ən\ *n* 1 : an electronic system of transmitting images with sound over a wire or through space by devices that change light and sound into electrical waves and then change these back into light and sound 2 : a television receiving set 3 : the television broadcasting industry

tel·ex \'tel-ˌeks\ *n* : a communication service involving teletypewriters connected by wire through automatic exchanges

tell \'tel\ *vb* **told** \'tōld\; **tell·ing** 1 : ¹COUNT 1a, ENUMERATE 2 a : to describe item by item : NARRATE ⟨*tell* a story⟩ b : ¹SAY 1a, UTTER ⟨*tell* a lie⟩ 3 a : to make known : REVEAL ⟨*tell* a secret⟩ b : to express in words ⟨can't *tell* you how pleased we are⟩ 4 : to report to : INFORM ⟨*tell* me as soon as the package gets here⟩ 5 : ¹ORDER 2a, DIRECT ⟨*told* us to wait⟩ 6 : to find out by observing ⟨can *tell* the child is honest⟩ 7 : to act as a tattletale ⟨*tell* on a cheater⟩ 8 : to have a noticeable effect ⟨the pressure began to *tell* on them⟩ 9 : to be evidence of : INDICATE ⟨smiles *telling* of success⟩ **syn** see REVEAL

tell·er \'tel-ər\ *n* 1 : one that tells ⟨a *teller* of tales⟩ 2 : a person who counts votes (as in a legislative body) 3 : a bank employee who receives and pays out money

tell·ing \'tel-iŋ\ *adj* : producing a noticeable effect : EFFECTIVE ⟨the most *telling* evidence⟩ — **tell·ing·ly** \-iŋ-lē\ *adv*

¹tell·tale \'tel-ˌtāl\ *n* 1 : TALEBEARER, INFORMER 2 : an outward sign : INDICATION

²telltale *adj* : indicating or giving evidence of something ⟨*telltale* fingerprints⟩

tel·lu·ri·um \tə-'lur-ē-əm, te-\ *n* : an element related to selenium and sulfur that may occur as a silvery white brittle form having a metallic shine or in combination with metals — see ELEMENT table

telo·phase \'tel-ə-ˌfāz, 'tēl-\ *n* 1 : the final stage of mitosis in which separate nuclei form 2 : the final stage of the first or second division of meiosis

te·mer·i·ty \tə-'mer-ət-ē\ *n* : the quality or state of being recklessly or foolishly bold

¹tem·per \'tem-pər\ *vb* **tem·pered; tem·per·ing** \-p(ə-)riŋ\ 1 : ²MODERATE 1, SOFTEN ⟨*temper* justice with mercy⟩ 2 a : to bring (as steel) to the desired hardness by heating and cooling b : to toughen (glass) by heating and cooling 3 : to be or become tempered

²temper *n* 1 : characteristic manner of feeling ⟨the *temper* of the times⟩ 2 : the hardness or toughness of a substance ⟨*temper* of a knife blade⟩ 3 a : a characteristic state of mind or state of feeling : DISPOSITION b : calmness of mind : COMPOSURE ⟨lost my *temper*⟩ c : state of feeling or state of mind at a particular time d : a state of anger ⟨left in a *temper*⟩ e : the quality of being easily angered ⟨has a hot *temper*⟩

tem·pera \'tem-pə-rə\ *n* : a process of painting in which the colors are mixed with substances (as egg, glue, or gum) other than oil

tem·per·a·ment \'tem-p(ə-)rə-mənt\ *n* 1 : a person's attitude as it affects what he or she says or does ⟨nervous *temperament*⟩ 2 : the quality of being very excitable or irritable

tem·per·a·men·tal \ˌtem-p(ə-)rə-'ment-ᵊl\ *adj* 1 : of or relating to temperament ⟨*temperamental* peculiarities⟩ 2 a : likely to be easily upset ⟨a *temperamental* movie star⟩ b : unpredictable in performance ⟨a *temperamental* motor⟩ — **tem·per·a·men·tal·ly** \-ᵊl-ē\ *adv*

tem·per·ance \'tem-p(ə-)rən(t)s, -pərn(t)s\ *n* 1 : control over one's acts, thoughts, or feelings : MODERATION, RESTRAINT 2 : the use of little or no alcoholic drink

tem·per·ate \'tem-p(ə-)rət\ *adj* 1 : being or kept within limits 2 : not going too far in satisfying one's needs or desires 3 : not drinking much liquor 4 : marked by self-control : RESTRAINED ⟨*temperate* speech⟩ 5 : having or

associated with a climate that is usually mild — **tem·per·ate·ly** *adv* — **tem·per·ate·ness** *n*

temperate rain forest *n* : woodland that has a temperate climate with heavy rainfall and that usually includes numerous kinds of trees but differs from a tropical rain forest in having one or two very common major trees

temperate zone *n, often cap T & Z* : either of two regions of the earth that lie between the torrid zones and the frigid zones and are characterized by a usually mild climate with four separate seasons — compare FRIGID ZONE, TORRID ZONE

tem·per·a·ture \'tem-pə(r)-ˌchu̇r, 'tem-p(ə-)rə-ˌchu̇r, -chər\ *n* 1 : the degree of hotness or coldness of something (as air, water, or the body) as shown by a thermometer 2 : FEVER 1a ⟨have a *temperature*⟩

temperature inversion *n* : INVERSION 3

tem·pered \'tem-pərd\ *adj* 1 : having a particular kind of temper ⟨a bad-*tempered* dog⟩ 2 : brought to the desired state (as of hardness, toughness, or flexibility) ⟨*tempered* steel⟩ ⟨*tempered* glass⟩

tem·pest \'tem-pəst\ *n* 1 : a violent wind; *esp* : one accompanied by rain, hail, or snow 2 : a violent commotion : UPROAR

tem·pes·tu·ous \tem-'pes-chə-wəs, -'pesh-\ *adj* : VIOLENT 1, STORMY ⟨a *tempestuous* sea⟩ ⟨a *tempestuous* romance⟩ — **tem·pes·tu·ous·ly** *adv* — **tem·pes·tu·ous·ness** *n*

tem·plate \'tem-plət\ *n* : a gauge, pattern, or mold (as a thin plate or board) used as a guide to the form of a piece being made

¹tem·ple \'tem-pəl\ *n* : a building for worship

²temple *n* : the flattened space on each side of the forehead of some mammals including human beings

tem·po \'tem-pō\ *n, pl* **tem·pi** \-pē\ *or* **tempos** 1 : the rate of speed at which a musical piece or passage is to be played or sung 2 : rate of motion or activity

tem·po·ral \'tem-p(ə-)rəl\ *adj* 1 : of or relating to time as opposed to eternity 2 a : of or relating to earthly life b : of or relating to material as opposed to spiritual concerns — **tem·po·ral·ly** \-ē\ *adv*

temporal bone *n* : a compound bone that is located on the side of the skull of some mammals including human beings and is composed of four major parts

tem·po·rary \'tem-pə-ˌrer-ē\ *adj* : not permanent : lasting for a time only [from Latin *temporarius* "lasting for only a short time", from *tempus* "time" — related to ¹TENSE] — **tem·po·rari·ly** \ˌtem-pə-'rer-ə-lē\ *adv*

tem·po·rize \'tem-pə-ˌrīz\ *vb* **-rized; -riz·ing** 1 : to act to suit the time or occasion : COMPROMISE 2 : to draw out discussions so as to gain time : DELAY — **tem·po·riz·er** \'tem-pə-ˌrī-zər\ *n*

tempt \'tem(p)t\ *vb* 1 : to persuade or try to persuade to do wrong by promise of pleasure or gain 2 : to risk the dangers of 3 a : to get to do something b : to cause to have a certain feeling ⟨was *tempted* to quit⟩ — **tempt·able** \'tem(p)-tə-bəl\ *adj* — **tempt·er** *n*

temp·ta·tion \tem(p)-'tā-shən\ *n* 1 : the act of tempting : the state of being tempted especially to evil 2 : something tempting

tempt·ing \'tem(p)-tiŋ\ *adj* : having a strong attraction ⟨the food all looked *tempting*⟩ — **tempt·ing·ly** *adv*

tempt·ress \'tem(p)-trəs\ *n* : a woman who tempts

ten \'ten\ *n* 1 — see NUMBER table 2 : the tenth in a set or series ⟨the *ten* of hearts⟩ 3 : something having ten units or members — **ten** *adj or pron*

ten·a·ble \'ten-ə-bəl\ *adj* : capable of being held, maintained, or defended

te·na·cious \tə-'nā-shəs\ *adj* 1 a : not easily pulled apart b : tending to stick 2 a : holding fast or tending to hold fast : PERSISTENT ⟨people *tenacious* of their opinions⟩ ⟨old ideas are *tenacious*⟩ b : RETENTIVE ⟨a *tenacious* memory⟩ — **te·na·cious·ly** *adv* — **te·na·cious·ness** *n*

te·nac·i·ty \tə-'nas-ət-ē\ *n* : the quality or state of being tenacious

ten·an·cy \'ten-ən-sē\ *n, pl* **-cies** **1 a** : the temporary possession or use of another's property **b** : the period of such use or possession **2** : the ownership of property

¹ten·ant \'ten-ənt\ *n* **1** : one who occupies property of another especially for rent **2** : OCCUPANT

²tenant *vb* : to hold or occupy as a tenant : INHABIT

Ten Commandments *n pl* : the commandments of God given to Moses on Mount Sinai

¹tend \'tend\ *vb* **1** : to pay attention ⟨*tend* to business⟩ **2** : to take care of : CULTIVATE **3** : to have responsibility for as caretaker **4** : to manage the operation of

²tend *vb* **1** : to move or turn in a certain direction ⟨the road *tends* to the right⟩ **2** : to be likely ⟨a person who *tends* to slouch⟩

ten·den·cy \'ten-dən-sē\ *n, pl* **-cies** **1** : a direction or approach toward a place, object, result, or limit **2** : a leaning toward a particular kind of thought or action : INCLINATION

¹ten·der \'ten-dər\ *adj* **1** : having a soft or yielding quality ⟨*tender* steak⟩ **2 a** : physically weak : DELICATE ⟨a *tender* plant⟩ **b** : IMMATURE, YOUNG ⟨children of *tender* years⟩ **3** : LOVING, AFFECTIONATE ⟨a *tender* look⟩ **4** : showing care : CONSIDERATE **5** : not harsh or stern : GENTLE, MILD **6** : sensitive to touch : very easily hurt ⟨a *tender* scar⟩ **7** : demanding careful and sensitive handling ⟨a *tender* subject⟩ [Middle English *tender* "tender, fragile", from early French *tendre* (same meaning), from Latin *tener* "having a soft yielding texture, tender, young"] — **ten·der·ly** *adv* — **ten·der·ness** *n*

²tender *n* **1** : an offer of money in payment of a debt **2** : an offer made for acceptance; *esp* : a bid for a contract **3** : something that may by law be offered in payment; *esp* : MONEY [from early French *tendre* "to stretch out, offer", from Latin *tendere* "to stretch" — related to ²TENSE]

³tender *vb* **ten·dered; ten·der·ing** \-d(ə-)riŋ\ **1** : to offer in payment **2** : to present for acceptance ⟨*tendered* my resignation⟩

⁴tend·er \'ten-dər\ *n* : one that tends or takes care: as **a** : a ship used to attend other ships (as to supply food) **b** : a boat that carries passengers or freight between shore and a larger ship **c** : a car attached to a locomotive for carrying fuel and water [from *tend* "to look after" and *-er,* noun suffix]

ten·der·foot \'ten-dər-,fut\ *n, pl* **-feet** \-,fēt\ *also* **-foots** \-,futs\ **1** : a person who is not hardened to a rough outdoor life **2** : BEGINNER

ten·der·heart·ed \,ten-dər-'härt-əd\ *adj* : easily moved to love, pity, or sorrow : COMPASSIONATE

ten·der·ize \'ten-də-,rīz\ *vb* **-ized; -iz·ing** : to make (meat or meat products) tender by using a process or substance that breaks down connective tissue — **ten·der·iza·tion** \,ten-d(ə-)rə-'zā-shən\ *n* — **ten·der·iz·er** \'ten-də-,rī-zər\ *n*

ten·der·loin \'ten-dər-,loin\ *n* : a strip of tender meat on each side of the backbone of beef or pork

ten·don \'ten-dən\ *n* : a tough cord or band of dense white connective tissue that links a muscle to some other part (as a bone)

ten·dril \'ten-drəl\ *n* **1** : a slender leafless winding stem by which some climbing plants fasten themselves to a support **2** : something that curls like a tendril ⟨*tendrils* of hair⟩

ten·e·ment \'ten-ə-mənt\ *n* **1 a** : a house used as a dwelling **b** : APARTMENT 1, FLAT **c** : TENEMENT HOUSE **2** : DWELLING

T tendril 1

tenement house *n* : APARTMENT HOUSE; *esp* : one housing poorer families in a city

te·net \'ten-ət\ *n* : a widely held belief; *esp* : one held in common by members of a group or profession

ten·fold \'ten-,fōld, -'fōld\ *adj* **1** : having 10 units or members **2** : 10 times as much or as many — **ten·fold** *adv*

ten·nis \'ten-əs\ *n* : a game played with rackets and a light elastic ball by two players or two pairs of players on a level court divided by a low net

tennis shoe *n* : a lightweight sneaker suitable for wear when playing tennis

ten·on \'ten-ən\ *n* : a projecting part in a piece of material (as wood) for insertion into a mortise to make a joint

ten·or \'ten-ər\ *n* **1** : the general meaning of something spoken or written ⟨the *tenor* of the book⟩ **2 a** : the next to lowest musical part in harmony for four parts — compare ALTO 1b, ²BASS 1a, ²SOPRANO 1 **b** : the highest natural adult male voice or a person who has such a voice **c** : a person or instrument performing a part next above a bass part **3** : a continuing in a course, movement, or activity ⟨the *tenor* of my life⟩ — **tenor** *adj*

ten·pen·ny nail \,ten-,pen-ē-\ *n* : a nail three inches (about 7.6 centimeters) long

ten·pin \'ten-,pin\ *n* **1** : a large bottle-shaped bowling pin **2** *pl* : a bowling game using 10 tenpins and a large ball

tens digit \'tenz-\ *n* : the numeral (as 5 in 456) in the tens place in a number expressed in the Arabic system of writing numbers

¹tense \'ten(t)s\ *n* : a form of a verb used to show the time of the action or state [Middle English *tens* "time, tense", from early French *tens* (same meaning), from Latin *tempus* "time" — related to TEMPORARY]

²tense *adj* **tens·er; tens·est** **1** : stretched tight : made taut : RIGID ⟨*tense* muscles⟩ **2** : feeling or showing nervous tension **3** : marked by strain or uncertainty ⟨a *tense* moment⟩ [from Latin *tensus* "stretched tight", from *tendere* "to stretch" — related to ²TENDER] **syn** see TIGHT — **tense·ly** *adv* — **tense·ness** *n*

³tense *vb* **tensed; tens·ing** : to make or become tense

ten·sion \'ten-chən\ *n* **1 a** : the act or action of stretching or the condition or degree of being stretched to stiffness ⟨*tension* of a muscle⟩ **b** : ¹STRESS 1c **2 a** : a state of mental unrest that is often accompanied by physical signs (as perspiring) of emotion **b** : a state of unfriendliness between individuals or groups

ten·sor \'ten(t)-sər, 'ten-,sò(ə)r\ *n* : a muscle that stretches a part

ten–speed \'ten-,spēd\ *n* : a bicycle with a derailleur that has ten possible combinations of gears

tens place *n* : the place two to the left of the decimal point in a number expressed in the Arabic system of writing numbers

¹tent \'tent\ *n* **1** : a portable shelter (as of nylon) stretched and supported by poles **2 a** : something that resembles a tent or that serves as a shelter; *esp* : an enclosure placed over the head and shoulders to hold in oxygen or vapors given for medical reasons ⟨an oxygen *tent*⟩ **b** : the web of a tent caterpillar

²tent *vb* **1** : to live in a tent **2** : to cover with or as if with a tent

ten·ta·cle \'tent-i-kəl\ *n* **1** : one of the long flexible structures that stick out usually around the head or mouth of an animal (as a worm or fish) and are used especially for feeling or grasping **2** : something that resembles a tentacle; *esp* : a sensitive hair on a plant — **ten·ta·cled** \-kəld\ *adj*

ten·ta·tive \'tent-ət-iv\ *adj* **1** : not fully worked out or de-

\ə\ abut	\au̇\ **out**	\i\ **tip**	\ȯ\ **saw**	\u̇\ **foot**
\ər\ **further**	\ch\ **chin**	\ī\ **life**	\ȯi\ **coin**	\y\ **yet**
\a\ **mat**	\e\ **pet**	\j\ **job**	\th\ **thin**	\yü\ **few**
\ā\ **take**	\ē\ **easy**	\ŋ\ **sing**	\th\ **this**	\yu̇\ **cure**
\ä\ **cot, cart**	\g\ **go**	\ō\ **bone**	\ü\ **food**	\zh\ **vision**

veloped ⟨*tentative* plans⟩ **2** : HESITANT, UNCERTAIN ⟨a *tentative* smile⟩ — **ten·ta·tive·ly** *adv*

tent caterpillar *n* : any of several destructive caterpillars that live in groups and construct large silken webs on trees

tenth \'ten(t)th\ *n, pl* **tenths** \'ten(t)s, 'ten(t)ths\ **1** — see NUMBER table **2** : one of 10 equal parts of something **3** : the one numbered 10 in a countable series — **tenth** *adj or adv*

tenths digit *n* : the numeral (as 5 in 4.56) in the tenths place in a number expressed in the Arabic system of writing numbers

tenths place *n* : the first place to the right of the decimal point in a number expressed in the Arabic system of writing numbers

ten·u·ous \'ten-yə-wəs\ *adj* : having little substance or strength : FLIMSY, WEAK — **ten·u·ous·ly** *adv*

ten·ure \'ten-yər\ *n* : the act, right, manner, or term of holding something (as property, a position, or an office) — **ten·ur·i·al** \te-'nyúr-ē-əl\ *adj*

te·pee *or* **ti·pi** *also* **tee·pee** \'tē-pē\ *n* : a cone-shaped tent usually of skins used as a home by some American Indians [from *tipi,* a word in the language of the Dakota Indians meaning "a dwelling tent", from *ti* "to dwell" and *pi* "to use for"]

tep·id \'tep-əd\ *adj* : LUKEWARM

te·qui·la \tə-'kē-lə, tä-\ *n* : a usually colorless Mexican liquor made from the fermented juice of a plant

ter·bi·um \'tər-bē-əm\ *n* : a metallic element that reacts readily to form compounds — see ELEMENT table

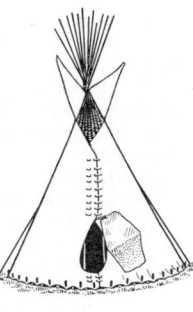

tepee

ter·cet \'tər-sət\ *n* : a unit or group of three lines of verse

te·re·do \tə-'rēd-ō, -'räd-\ *n, pl* **-re·dos** *or* **-red·i·nes** \-'red-ə-,nēz\ : SHIPWORM

¹term \'tərm\ *n* **1** : ¹END 1b **2** : a period of time fixed especially by law or custom ⟨served two *terms*⟩ ⟨the new school *term*⟩ **3** *pl* : conditions that limit the nature and scope of something (as an agreement) ⟨could not accept their *terms*⟩ **4 a** : a word or expression that has an exact meaning in some uses or is limited to a particular field ⟨legal *terms*⟩ **b** *pl* : words of a particular kind ⟨spoke in glowing *terms*⟩ **5 a** : a mathematical expression connected with another by a plus or minus sign **b** : an element (as a numerator) of a fraction or proportion **6** *pl* : personal relationship ⟨on good *terms* with the neighbors⟩ — **in terms of** : with respect to

²term *vb* : to apply a term to : CALL, NAME

¹ter·ma·gant \'tər-mə-gənt\ *n* : a nagging woman

²termagant *adj* : noisily nagging

¹ter·mi·nal \'tərm-nəl, -ən-ᵊl\ *adj* **1 a** : of, relating to, or forming an end ⟨a *terminal* pillar of a temple⟩ **b** : growing at the end of a branch or stem ⟨a *terminal* bud⟩ **2 a** : of, relating to, or occurring in a term or each term ⟨make *terminal* payments on a car⟩ **b** : leading finally to death ⟨*terminal* cancer⟩ **3** : occurring at or being the end of a period or series : CONCLUDING — **ter·mi·nal·ly** \-ē\ *adv*

²terminal *n* **1** : a part that forms the end **2** : a device attached to the end of a wire or cable or to electrical equipment for making connections **3 a** : either end of a transportation line (as a railroad or shipping line) with its offices and freight and passenger stations **b** : a freight or passenger station that serves a large area or acts as a junction between lines ⟨a bus *terminal*⟩ **c** : a town at the end of a transportation line **4** : a device that is connected to a communication network and is used to enter, receive, and display information

ter·mi·nate \'tər-mə-,nāt\ *vb* **-nat·ed; -nat·ing** **1 a** : to bring or come to an end : CLOSE **b** : to form the conclusion of ⟨review questions *terminate* each chapter⟩ **2** : to serve as a limit to : BOUND **3** : to reach an end point or line ⟨the race course *terminates* at the park entrance⟩ — **ter·mi·na·ble** \'tərm-(ə-)nə-bəl\ *adj* — **ter·mi·na·tion** \,tər-mə-'nā-shən\ *n* — **ter·mi·na·tor** \'tər-mə-,nāt-ər\ *n*

ter·mi·nat·ing decimal *n* : a decimal which can be expressed in a finite number of figures or for which all figures to the right of some place are zero — compare REPEATING DECIMAL

ter·mi·nol·o·gy \,tər-mə-'näl-ə-jē\ *n, pl* **-gies** : the special terms or expressions used in a field ⟨the *terminology* of law⟩

term insurance *n* : insurance that covers a limited period of time and pays only for losses that occur during that period

ter·mi·nus \'tər-mə-nəs\ *n, pl* **-ni** \-,nī, -,nē\ *or* **-nus·es** **1** : final goal : finishing point **2** : a post or stone marking a boundary **3 a** : either end of a transportation line or travel route **b** : the station or town at such a place

ter·mite \'tər-,mīt\ *n* : any of a group of pale-colored soft-bodied social insects that feed on wood, that have winged sexual forms, wingless sterile workers, and often soldiers, and that include some very destructive to wooden structures and trees — called also *white ant*

tern \'tərn\ *n* : any of numerous sea birds that usually have a forked tail, black cap, and white body and that in comparison to the related gulls have a smaller and slenderer body and bill and narrower wings

tern

¹ter·race \'ter-əs\ *n* **1 a** : a flat roof or open platform **b** : a level area next to a building **2** : a raised piece of land with the top leveled off or with a series of level banks or ridges **3** : a row of houses on raised ground or a sloping site

²terrace *vb* **ter·raced; ter·rac·ing** : to make into a terrace or supply with terraces

ter·ra·cot·ta \,ter-ə-'kät-ə\ *n, pl* **terra–cottas** **1** : a glazed or unglazed baked clay used for pottery, statues, and building materials **2** : a brownish orange [from Italian *terra cotta,* literally "baked earth", derived from Latin *terra* "earth" and Latin *coquere* "to cook"]

ter·rain \tə-'rān *also* te-\ *n* : the surface features of an area of land ⟨rough *terrain*⟩

Ter·ra·my·cin \,ter-ə-'mīs-ᵊn\ *trademark* — used for an antibiotic

ter·ra·pin \'ter-ə-pən, 'tar-\ *n* : any of various edible North American turtles living in fresh or somewhat salt water

ter·rar·i·um \tə-'rar-ē-əm, -'rer-\ *n, pl* **-ia** \-ē-ə\ *or* **-i·ums** : an enclosure usually of glass used for keeping and observing small animals and plants indoors

terrapin

ter·res·tri·al \tə-'res-trē-əl, -'res-chəl, -'resh-chəl\ *adj* **1** : of or relating to the earth or its living things **2 a** : of or relating to land as distinct from air or water **b** : living on or in or growing from land ⟨*terrestrial* plants⟩ ⟨*terrestrial* birds⟩

ter·ri·ble \'ter-ə-bəl\ *adj* **1** : causing terror or awe : FEARFUL, DREADFUL ⟨a *terrible* disaster⟩ **2 a** : very great in degree ⟨made a *terrible* mess of things⟩ ⟨a *terrible* cold⟩ **b** : very bad in quality ⟨*terrible* music⟩ — **ter·ri·bly** \-blē\ *adv*

ter·ri·er \'ter-ē-ər\ *n* : any of various usually small dogs

originally used by hunt-
ers to drive game ani-
mals from their holes

Word History Today
most terriers are kept
as pets. However,
there was a time when
the dogs were widely
used for hunting. Ter-
riers are usually small
dogs with short legs,
and they were used to
dig game animals
such as foxes, bad-

terrier

gers, and weasels out of their holes. The dogs were also
trained to go into a hole after a game animal and drive
it out. The French name for these dogs was *chien terrier*, meaning "earth dog". English borrowed only the
word *terrier*, which can be traced back to Latin *terra*,
meaning "earth". [Middle English *terrier* "a small dog
used for hunting burrowing animals", from early French
(chien) terrier, literally "earth dog", from *terrier* (adjective) "of the earth", derived from Latin *terra* "earth"]

ter·rif·ic \tə-'rif-ik\ *adj* **1** : causing terror : TERRIBLE ⟨*terrific*
destruction⟩ **2** : very great in degree : EXTRAORDINARY ⟨a
car going at *terrific* speed⟩ **3** : unusually good ⟨makes
terrific chili⟩ — **ter·rif·i·cal·ly** \-i-k(ə-)lē\ *adv*

ter·ri·fy \'ter-ə-,fī\ *vb* **-fied; -fy·ing** : to fill with terror —
ter·ri·fy·ing·ly \-,fī-iŋ-lē\ *adv*

ter·ri·to·ri·al \,ter-ə-'tōr-ē-əl, -'tór-\ *adj* **1** : of or relating
to a territory ⟨*territorial* claims⟩ **2** : organized chiefly for
territorial defense ⟨a *territorial* army⟩ **3** : of, relating to,
or showing territoriality ⟨*territorial* birds⟩ — **territorial** *n* —
ter·ri·to·ri·al·ly \-ē-ə-lē\ *adv*

ter·ri·to·ri·al·i·ty \,ter-ə-,tōr-ē-'al-ət-ē, -,tór-\ *n* : the pattern of behavior associated with the defense of an animal's
territory

ter·ri·to·ry \'ter-ə-,tōr-ē, -,tór-\ *n, pl* **-ries** **1 a** : a geographical area belonging to or under the control of a government **b** : a part of the U.S. not included within any
state but having a separate governing body **2 a** : an assigned area ⟨a sales representative's *territory*⟩ **b** : an
area that is occupied and defended by an animal or group
of animals

ter·ror \'ter-ər\ *n* **1** : a state of great fear **2** : a cause of
great fear **3** : violence (as bombing) committed by a
group as a means of achieving its goals

ter·ror·ism \'ter-ər-,iz-əm\ *n* : the use of terror as a means
of achieving a goal — **ter·ror·ist** \-ər-əst\ *adj or n*

ter·ror·ize \'ter-ər-,īz\ *vb* **-ized; -iz·ing** **1** : to fill with terror **2** : to force by threat or violence — **ter·ror·iza·tion**
\,ter-ər-ə-'zā-shən\ *n*

ter·ry \'ter-ē\ *n, pl* **terries** : an absorbent fabric with an
even surface of uncut loops — called also *terry cloth*

terse \'tərs\ *adj* **ters·er; ters·est** : being brief and to the
point : CONCISE — **terse·ly** *adv* — **terse·ness** *n*

ter·ti·ary \'tər-shē-,er-ē\ *adj* **1** : of third rank, importance,
or value **2** *cap* : of, relating to, or being the earliest period
of the Cenozoic era of geological history marked by the
formation of high mountains (as the Alps and Himalayas)
and the rise in importance of mammals on land; *also* : relating to the corresponding system of rocks — see GEO-
LOGIC TIME table

Tertiary *n* : the Tertiary period or system of rocks

¹test \'test\ *n* **1** : a means of finding out the nature, quality,
or value of something ⟨put the new car to the *test*⟩ **2** : a
procedure or method for identifying something ⟨a *test* for
starch⟩ ⟨allergy *tests*⟩ **3** : a set of questions or problems
designed to find out a person's knowledge, skills, or intelligence

²test *vb* **1** : to put to test or proof : TRY ⟨*test* your strength⟩
2 a : to take part in a test ⟨actors *testing* for roles in the

play⟩ **b** : to achieve a rating on the basis of tests ⟨the
class *tested* high in math⟩ **3** : to use tests as a way to
analyze or identify ⟨*test* for copper⟩ — **test·able** \'tes-tə-
bəl\ *adj*

tes·ta \'tes-tə\ *n, pl* **tes·tae** \-,tē, -,tī\ : the hard outer coat
of a seed

tes·ta·ment \'tes-tə-mənt\ *n* **1** *cap* : either of the two chief
parts of the Bible **2 a** : actual proof : EVIDENCE **b** : an
expression of belief : CREDO **3** : the legal instructions for
the distribution of a person's belongings after death : WILL
— **tes·ta·men·ta·ry** \,tes-tə-'ment-ə-rē, -'men-trē\ *adj*

tes·ta·tor \'tes-,tāt-ər, tes-'tāt-\ *n* : a person who leaves a
will in force at the time of death

test·ed \'tes-təd\ *adj* : examined or qualified through testing
⟨time-*tested* principles⟩

¹tes·ter \'tēs-tər, 'tes-\ *n* : a canopy or a frame for a canopy
over a bed, pulpit, or altar

²test·er \'tes-tər\ *n* : one that
tests

tes·ti·cle \'tes-ti-kəl\ *n* : TESTIS

tes·ti·fy \'tes-tə-,fī\ *vb* **-fied;
-fy·ing** **1** : to make a formal
statement of what one swears
is true **2** : to give outward
proof : serve as a sign of —
tes·ti·fi·er \-,fī-(ə)r\ *n*

¹tester

¹tes·ti·mo·ni·al \,tes-tə-'mō-
nē-əl\ *adj* : being a testimonial

²testimonial *n* **1 a** : a recommendation of a product or service ⟨an athlete's *testimonial* for a tennis racket⟩ **b** : a
letter of recommendation **2** : something given or said to
show affection or respect : TRIBUTE

tes·ti·mo·ny \'tes-tə-,mō-nē\ *n, pl* **-nies** **1** : firsthand evidence ⟨according to the *testimony* of eyewitnesses⟩ **2**
: a statement made by a witness under oath especially in
a court **3** : a public declaration of religious experience

tes·tis \'tes-təs\ *n, pl* **tes·tes** \'tes-,tēz\ : an oval-shaped
male reproductive organ which is usually located in the
scrotum, which in vertebrates produces and secretes various male hormones and especially testosterone, and in
which sperm are produced

tes·tos·ter·one \te-'stäs-tə-,rōn\ *n* : a male hormone produced by the testes that causes the development of the
male reproductive system and secondary sex characteristics

test pilot *n* : a pilot who puts new aircraft through tests

test tube *n* : a tube of thin glass closed at one end and used
especially in chemistry and biology

tes·ty \'tes-tē\ *adj* **tes·ti·er; -est** : easily annoyed : IRRIT-
ABLE — **tes·ti·ly** \-tə-lē\ *adv* — **tes·ti·ness** \-tē-nəs\ *n*

tet·a·nus \'tet-ə-nəs\ *n* **1** : a dangerous infectious disease
marked by stiffness and spasms of the muscles with locking of the jaws and caused by a poison made by a bacterium that usually enters the body through a wound **2**
: contraction of a muscle for a much longer time than normal that results from rapidly repeated motor nerve impulses

¹tête-à-tête \,tāt-ə-'tāt\ *adv* : face to face : PRIVATELY
[French, literally "head-to-head"]

²tête-à-tête \'tāt-ə-,tāt\ *n* : a private conversation between
two persons

³tête-à-tête \,tāt-ə-,tāt\ *adj* : being face to face : PRIVATE

¹teth·er \'teth-ər\ *n* : a line by which something (as an animal or a balloon) is fastened

²tether *vb* **teth·ered; teth·er·ing** \'teth-(ə-)riŋ\ : to fasten

\ə\ abut	\au̇\ out	\i\ tip	\o̊\ saw	\u̇\ foot
\ər\ further	\ch\ chin	\ī\ life	\o̊i\ coin	\y\ yet
\a\ mat	\e\ pet	\j\ job	\th\ thin	\yü\ few
\ā\ take	\ē\ easy	\ŋ\ sing	\t̲h̲\ this	\yu̇\ cure
\ä\ cot, cart	\g\ go	\ō\ bone	\ü\ food	\zh\ vision

or hold with or as if with a tether

tet·ra \'te-trə\ *n* : any of various small brightly colored South American fishes often bred in tropical aquariums

tetra- *combining form* : four : having four : having four parts [derived from Greek *tetra-* "four"]

tet·ra·chord \'te-trə-,kȯ(ə)rd\ *n* : a series of four tones : half an octave

tet·ra·eth·yl lead \,te-trə-,eth-əl-'led\ *n* : a heavy oily poisonous liquid added to gasoline to prevent engines from knocking

tet·ra·he·dron \,te-trə-'hē-drən\ *n, pl* **-drons** *or* **-dra** \-drə\ : a polyhedron that has four faces — **tet·ra·he·dral** \-drəl\ *adj*

te·tram·e·ter \te-'tram-ət-ər\ *n* : a line of verse consisting of four metrical feet

Teu·ton \'t(y)üt-ᵊn\ *n* **1** : a member of an ancient probably Germanic or Celtic people **2** : a member of a people speaking a Germanic language; *esp* : GERMAN 1 — **Teu·ton·ic** \t(y)ü-'tän-ik\ *adj*

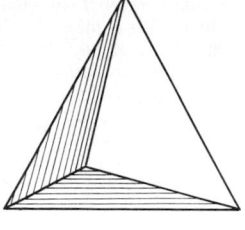

tetrahedron

Teutonic *n* : the Germanic languages

Tex–Mex \'tek-'smeks\ *adj* : of, relating to, or being the Mexican-American culture or food found especially in southern Texas [from *Tex*as and *Mex*ico]

text \'tekst\ *n* **1** : the original words of a work of literature **2 a** : the main body of printed or written matter on a page **b** : the main part of a book **3 a** : a passage from the Bible chosen for the subject of a sermon **b** : a subject on which one writes or speaks **4** : matter handled with a computer that is chiefly in the form of words **5** : TEXTBOOK

text·book \'teks(t)-,bu̇k\ *n* : a book used in the study of a subject

tex·tile \'tek-,stīl, 'teks-tᵊl\ *n* : CLOTH 1; *esp* : a woven or knit cloth

tex·tu·al \'teks-chə-(-wə)l\ *adj* : of, relating to, or based on a text — **tex·tu·al·ly** \-ē\ *adv*

¹tex·ture \'teks-chər\ *n* **1** : the structure, feel, and appearance of something (as a fabric) (the smooth *texture* of silk) (wood with a rough *texture*) **2** : a quality that identifies something

²texture *vb* **tex·tured; tex·tur·ing** : to give a particular texture to (*textured* fabrics)

textured vegetable protein *n* : protein that is obtained from some vegetables and especially soybeans and is used as a substitute for or added to meat

tex·tur·ize \'teks-chə-,rīz\ *vb* **-ized; -iz·ing** : ²TEXTURE

¹-th — see ¹-ETH

²-th *or* **-eth** *adj suffix* — used to form ordinal numbers (hundredth) (forti*eth*) [Old English *-tha, -ta* (a suffix used in forming ordinal numbers)]

Thai \'tī\ *n* **1** : a person born or living in Thailand **2** : the official language of Thailand

thal·a·mus \'thal-ə-məs\ *n, pl* **-mi** \-,mī, -,mē\ : a subdivision of the forebrain that receives nerve impulses and sends them on to the appropriate parts of the brain cortex

tha·lid·o·mide \thə-'lid-ə-,mīd, -məd\ *n* : a drug that was formerly used in tranquilizers and sleeping pills in some countries outside the U.S. and that has caused serious birth defects in some babies born to mothers who used it during pregnancy

thal·li·um \'thal-ē-əm\ *n* : a poisonous metallic element that has characteristics similar to lead — see ELEMENT table

thal·lo·phyte \'thal-ə-,fīt\ *n* : any of a large group of plants having single-celled sex organs or sex organs of which all cells form egg cells or sperm cells and including the algae, fungi, and lichens

¹than \thən, (')than\ *conj* **1** : when compared to the way, extent, or degree in or to which (10 is less *than* 20) (older *than* I am) (easier said *than* done) **2** : different from in kind, manner, or identity (adults other *than* parents)

²than *prep* : in comparison with (taller *than* me)

thane \'thān\ *n* **1** : a man in England during the Middle Ages who received lands from the king in return for military service **2** : a lord in Scotland during the Middle Ages

thank \'thaŋk\ *vb* **1** : to express gratitude to (*thanked* her for the present) **2** : to hold responsible (had only myself to *thank* for my loss)

thank·ful \'thaŋk-fəl\ *adj* : feeling or showing thanks — **thank·ful·ly** \-fə-lē\ *adv* — **thank·ful·ness** *n*

thank·less \'thaŋ-kləs\ *adj* **1** : not showing or feeling gratitude **2** : not appreciated by others (a *thankless* job) — **thank·less·ly** *adv* — **thank·less·ness** *n*

thanks \'thaŋ(k)s\ *n pl* **1** : kindly or grateful thoughts : GRATITUDE (express my *thanks* for their kindness) **2** : an expression of gratitude (give *thanks* before the meal) (many *thanks*)

thanks·giv·ing \thaŋ(k)s-'giv-iŋ\ *n* **1** : the act of giving thanks **2** : a prayer expressing gratitude **3** *cap* : THANKSGIVING DAY

Thanksgiving Day *n* : the fourth Thursday in November observed as a legal holiday in the U.S. for public thanksgiving to God

thank–you \'thaŋ-,kyü\ *n* : a polite expression of one's gratitude

¹that \(')that\ *pron, pl* **those** \(')thōz\ **1 a** : the person, thing, or idea shown, mentioned, or understood from the situation (*that* is my father) **b** : the one : the thing : the kind (the richest ore is *that* found higher up) **2** : the one farther away (*those* are elms and these are maples)

²that *adj, pl* **those** **1** : being the one named or understood (*that* boy did it) **2** : being the one farther away (this chair or *that* one)

³that \thət, (,)that\ *conj* **1 a** — used to introduce a noun clause serving especially as the subject or object of a verb (*that* she has succeeded is certain) (said *that* I was afraid) (the reason for his absence is *that* he is ill) **b** — used to introduce a clause that modifies a noun or adjective (certain *that* this is true) (the fact *that* you are here) **2** — used alone or after *so* or *in order* to introduce a clause expressing purpose (saved money so *that* I could buy a bicycle) **3** — used to introduce a clause giving a reason (delighted *that* you could visit) **4** — used especially after an expression including the word *so* or *such* to introduce a clause naming a result (worked so hard *that* they became exhausted)

⁴that \thət, (,)that\ *pron* **1** : WHO, WHOM, ²WHICH (the girl *that* smiled) (the person *that* you spoke to) (the house *that* Jack built) **2** : at, in, or on which : by, to, or with which (each year *that* the awards are given)

⁵that \'that\ *adv* : to such an extent (need a nail about *that* long)

¹thatch \'thach\ *vb* : to cover with or as if with thatch

²thatch *n* : a plant material (as straw) used to cover the roof of a building

¹thaw \'thȯ\ *vb* **1** : to melt or cause to melt (ice on the pond is *thawing*) **2** : to become free of the effects of cold temperatures by being exposed to warmth (frozen foods *thawed* before cooking)

²thaw *n* **1** : the action, fact, or process of thawing **2** : a period of weather warm enough to thaw ice and snow

¹the \thə (*especially before consonant sounds and sometimes vowel sounds in Southern speech*), thē (*before vowel sounds*); 1e *is often* 'thē\ *definite article* **1 a** : that or those mentioned, seen, or clearly understood (put *the* cat out) **b** : that one existing as only one at a time (*the* Lord) (*the* sky) (*the* sun) **c** : that or those near in space, time, or thought (news of *the* day) **d** : that or those best known to the speaker or writer or to the hearer or reader ⟨*the* President⟩ ⟨*the* courts will decide⟩ **e** : that or those considered best, most typical, or most worth selecting ⟨*the* poet of her day⟩ ⟨it's *the* car to own⟩ **f** : any one typical of or standing for an entire class so named ⟨good advice for *the* beginner⟩ ⟨good for *the* soul⟩ **2** — used before names of some parts of the body or of clothing in place of a possessive adjective ⟨grabbed me by *the* collar⟩ ⟨*the* ankle is better today⟩ **3** : ¹EACH, EVERY ⟨80 crackers to *the* box⟩ **4 a** : that which is ⟨an essay on *the* beautiful⟩ **b** : those that are ⟨*the* Greeks⟩ ⟨*the* wise⟩

²**the** *adv* **1** : than before : than otherwise ⟨none *the* wiser for attending⟩ **2 a** : to what extent ⟨*the* sooner the better⟩ **b** : to that extent ⟨the sooner *the* better⟩

the·ater *or* **the·atre** \'thē-ət-ər, 'thi-ət-\ *n* **1** : a building or area for dramatic performances or for showing motion pictures **2** : a place like a theater; *esp* : a room often with rising rows of seats (as for a lecture) **3** : a place of significant events or action ⟨a *theater* of war⟩ **4** : plays or the performance of plays ⟨a course in American *theater*⟩ [Middle English *theatre* "outdoor structure for watching public performances (in ancient Greece and Rome)", from early French *theatre* (same meaning), from Latin *theatrum* (same meaning), from Greek *theatron,* literally "a place for viewing", from *theasthai* "to view", from *thea* "action of seeing, sight, view" — related to THEORY]

the·ater·go·er \-,gō(-ə)r\ *n* : a person who frequently goes to the theater

the·at·ri·cal \thē-'a-tri-kəl\ *adj* **1** : of or relating to the theater ⟨*theatrical* costume⟩ **2** : marked by pretended or excessive emotion ⟨a *theatrical* speech⟩ — **the·at·ri·cal·ly** \-k(ə-)lē\ *adv*

the·at·ri·cals \thē-'a-tri-kəlz\ *n pl* : the performance of plays

thee \(')thē\ *pron, objective case of* THOU

theft \'theft\ *n* : the act of stealing

their \thər, (,)the(ə)r, (,)tha(ə)r\ *adj* : of or relating to them or themselves ⟨*their* clothes⟩ ⟨they all have *their* theories⟩ ⟨*their* being seen⟩

theirs \'the(ə)rz, 'tha(ə)rz\ *pron* : their one : their ones ⟨the house is *theirs*⟩ ⟨these books are *theirs*⟩ ⟨*theirs* are on the table⟩

the·ism \'thē-,iz-əm\ *n* : belief in the existence of God as creator and ruler of the universe — **the·ist** \'thē-əst\ *n* — **the·is·tic** \thē-'is-tik\ *adj*

them \th̲əm, (')them, *after* p, b, v, f, *also* əm\ *pron, objective case of* THEY

theme \'thēm\ *n* **1** : a subject for a work of literature, art, or music **2** : a written exercise : COMPOSITION — **the·mat·ic** \thi-'mat-ik\ *adj*

them·selves \th̲əm-'selvz, them-\ *pron* : their own selves ⟨nations that govern *themselves*⟩ ⟨they *themselves* were present⟩

¹**then** \(')then\ *adv* **1** : at that time ⟨it was *then* believed the world was flat⟩ **2** : soon after that ⟨walked to the door, *then* turned⟩ **3 a** : following next after in order **b** : in addition : BESIDES **4 a** : in that case **b** : according to that ⟨your mind is made up, *then*⟩ **c** : as it appears ⟨the case, *then,* is closed⟩ **d** : as a necessary result ⟨if you were there, *then* you saw me⟩

²**then** \'then\ *n* : that time ⟨wait until *then*⟩

³**then** \'then\ *adj* : existing or acting at or belonging to the time mentioned ⟨the *then* governor⟩

thence \'then(t)s *also* 'then(t)s\ *adv* **1** : from that place **2** : from that fact or circumstance

thence·forth \'then(t)s-,fō(ə)rth, -,fò(ə)rth *also* 'then(t)s-\ *adv* : from that time forward : THEREAFTER

thence·for·ward \then(t)s-'fòr-wərd *also* then(t)s-\ *also* **thence·for·wards** \-wərdz\ *adv* : onward from that place or time

the·oc·ra·cy \thē-'äk-rə-sē\ *n, pl* **-cies** **1** : government of a country by officials believed to have divine guidance **2** : a country governed by a theocracy

the·od·o·lite \thē-'äd-ᵊl-,īt\ *n* : a very precise surveyor's transit

the·ol·o·gy \thē-'äl-ə-jē\ *n, pl* **-gies** **1** : the study of religion **2** : a set of religious beliefs — **theo·lo·gian** \,thē-ə-'lō-jən\ *n* — **theo·log·i·cal** \-'läj-i-kəl\ *adj*

the·o·rem \'thē-ə-rəm, 'thi(-ə)r-əm\ *n* **1** : a formula or proposition especially in geometry that has been or is to be proved from other formulas or propositions **2** : an idea accepted and proposed as a demonstrable truth

the·o·ret·i·cal \,thē-ə-'ret-i-kəl, ,thi(-ə)r-'et-\ *also* **the·o·ret·ic** \-ik\ *adj* **1 a** : relating to or having the character of theory : ABSTRACT **b** : limited to theory or speculation : SPECULATIVE ⟨*theoretical* mechanics⟩ **2** : existing only in theory : HYPOTHETICAL ⟨a *theoretical* situation⟩ — **the·o·ret·i·cal·ly** \-i-k(ə-)lē\ *adv*

theodolite

the·o·rist \'thē-ə-rəst, 'thi(-ə)r-əst\ *n* : a person who theorizes

the·o·rize \'thē-ə-,rīz\ *vb* **-rized; -riz·ing** : to form a theory : SPECULATE — **the·o·riz·er** *n*

the·o·ry \'thē-ə-rē, 'thi(-ə)r-ē\ *n, pl* **-ries** **1** : the general ideas or principles of an art or science ⟨music *theory*⟩ **2** : a general principle or set of principles that explains facts or events of the natural world ⟨wave *theory* of light⟩ **3** : an idea that is the starting point for argument or investigation [from Latin *theoria* "a looking at or considering of facts, theory", from Greek *theōria* "theory, action of viewing, consideration", from *theōrein* "to look at, consider", from *theōros* "spectator", from *thea* "action of seeing, sight, view" — related to THEATER]

ther·a·peu·tic \,ther-ə-'pyüt-ik\ *adj* : of or relating to the treatment of diseases or disorders by using healing agents or methods

ther·a·peu·tics \,ther-ə-'pyüt-iks\ *n* : a branch of medical and dental science dealing with the use of remedies

ther·a·pist \'ther-ə-pəst\ *n* : a person who specializes in therapy; *esp* : a person trained in methods of treatment other than the use of drugs or surgery ⟨a speech *therapist*⟩

ther·a·py \'ther-ə-pē\ *n, pl* **-pies** : treatment of an abnormal state of the mind or body

¹**there** \'tha(ə)r, 'the(ə)r\ *adv* **1** : in or at that place ⟨stand over *there*⟩ **2** : to or into that place ⟨went *there* every year⟩ **3** : at that point or stage ⟨*there* it begins to get interesting⟩ **4** : in that matter, respect, or relation ⟨*there* you have a choice⟩ **5** — used as an interjection to show satisfaction, approval, soothing, or defiance ⟨*there,* it's finished at last⟩ ⟨so *there*⟩

²**there** \(,)tha(ə)r, (,)the(ə)r *also* thər\ *pron* — used to introduce a sentence or clause in which the subject comes after the verb ⟨*there* will come a time⟩

³**there** \ike ¹\ *n* : that place : that point ⟨get away from *there*⟩ ⟨you take it from *there*⟩

there·abouts *or* **there·about** \,thar-ə-'baut(s), ,ther-; 'thar-ə-,baut(s), 'ther-\ *adv* **1** : near that place or time **2** : near that number, degree, or quantity ⟨fifty people or *thereabouts*⟩

there·af·ter \tha-'raf-tər, the-\ *adv* : after that

there·at \tha-'rat, the-\ *adv* **1** : at that place **2** : at that occurrence : on that account

there·by \tha(ə)r-'bī, the(ə)r-; 'tha(ə)r-,bī, 'the(ə)r-\ *adv* **1**

\ə\ abut	\au̇\ **out**	\i\ **tip**	\ȯ\ **saw**	\u̇\ **foot**	
\ər\ **further**	\ch\ **chin**	\ī\ **life**	\ȯi\ **coin**	\y\ **yet**	
\a\ **mat**	\e\ **pet**	\j\ **job**	\th\ **thin**	\yü\ **few**	
\ā\ **take**	\ē\ **easy**	\ŋ\ **sing**	\th̲\ **this**	\yu̇\ **cure**	
\ä\ **cot, cart**	\g\ **go**	\ō\ **bone**	\ü\ **food**	\zh\ **vision**	

: by that : by that means ⟨make a friend *thereby*⟩ **2** : connected with or with reference to that ⟨*thereby* hangs a tale⟩

there·for \tha(ə)r-'fò(ə)r, the(ə)r-\ *adv* : for or in return for that

there·fore \'tha(ə)r-,fō(ə)r, 'the(ə)r-, -,fò(ə)r\ *adv* : for that reason : CONSEQUENTLY

there·from \tha(ə)r-'frəm, the(ə)r-, -'främ\ *adv* : from that or it ⟨learned much *therefrom*⟩

there·in \tha-'rin, the-\ *adv* **1** : in or into that place, time, or thing ⟨the world and all *therein*⟩ **2** : in that particular or respect ⟨*therein* they disagreed⟩

there·of \tha-'rəv, -'räv, the-\ *adv* **1** : of that or it **2** : from that cause or particular

there·on \tha-'ròn, -'rän, the-\ *adv* : on that

there·to \tha(ə)r-'tü, the(ə)r-\ *adv* : to that

there·to·fore \'thart-ə-,fō(ə)r, 'thert-, -,fò(ə)r\ *adv* : up to that time

there·un·to \tha-'rən-tü, the-; ,thar-ən-'tü, ,ther-\ *adv, archaic* : THERETO

there·upon \'thar-ə-,pòn, 'ther-, -,pän\ *adv* **1** : on that matter ⟨they disagreed *thereupon*⟩ **2** : THEREFORE **3** : immediately after that

there·with \tha(ə)r-'with, the(ə)r-, -'with\ *adv* : with that

there·with·al \'tha(ə)r-with-'òl, 'the(ə)r-, -with-\ *adv* : THEREWITH

¹ther·mal \'thər-məl\ *adj* : of, relating to, caused by, or saving heat ⟨*thermal* energy⟩ ⟨*thermal* underwear⟩ — **ther·mal·ly** \-mə-lē\ *adv*

²thermal *n* : a rising body of warm air

thermal pollution *n* : the release of heated liquid (as water used by a factory) into a natural body of water at a temperature harmful to the environment

thermal spring *n* : HOT SPRING

ther·mo·cou·ple \'thər-mə-,kəp-əl\ *n* : a device for measuring temperature in which a pair of wires of different metals (as copper and iron) are joined and the free ends of the wires are connected to an instrument (as a voltmeter) that measures the difference in potential created at the junction of the two metals

ther·mo·gram \'thər-mə-,gram\ *n* : a photograph that shows differences in temperature between different parts of an object (as the body or a building)

ther·mo·graph \'thər-mə-,graf\ *n* : a recording thermometer

ther·mom·e·ter \thə(r)-'mäm-ət-ər\ *n* : an instrument for measuring temperature consisting typically of a glass bulb attached to a fine glass tube with a numbered scale and containing a liquid (as mercury or colored alcohol) that is sealed in and rises and falls with changes of temperature — **ther·mo·met·ric** \,thər-mə-'me-trik\ *adj*

ther·mo·nu·cle·ar \,thər-mō-'n(y)ü-klē-ər\ *adj* : of or relating to the transformations in the nucleus of atoms of low atomic weight (as hydrogen) that require a very high temperature (as in the hydrogen bomb or in the sun) ⟨*thermonuclear* reaction⟩ ⟨*thermonuclear* weapon⟩

ther·mo·plas·tic \,thər-mə-'plas-tik\ *adj* : capable of softening or melting when heated and of hardening again when cooled ⟨*thermoplastic* synthetic fibers⟩

ther·mos \'thər-məs\ *n* : VACUUM BOTTLE

ther·mo·stat \'thər-mə-,stat\ *n* : a device that automatically controls temperature — **ther·mo·stat·ic** \,thər-mə-'stat-ik\ *adj* — **ther·mo·stat·i·cal·ly** \-i-k(ə-)lē\ *adv*

ther·mo·tax·is \,thər-mə-'tak-səs\ *n* : a taxis in which a change in temperature is the stimulus directing the movement of an organism

the·sau·rus \thi-'sòr-əs\ *n, pl* **-sau·ri** \-'sò(ə)r-,ī, -,ē\ *or* **-sau·rus·es** \-'sòr-ə-səz\ : a book of words and their synonyms [from scientific Latin *thesaurus* "treasury, storehouse, book of words", from Latin *thesaurus* "treasury, wealth", from Greek *thēsauros* (same meaning) — related to TREASURE]

these *pl of* THIS

the·sis \'thē-səs\ *n, pl* **the·ses** \'thē-,sēz\ **1** : a statement put forth for discussion or proof : HYPOTHESIS **2** : a long essay presenting the results of original research

Thes·sa·lo·nians \,thes-ə-'lō-nyənz, -nē-ənz\ *n* — see BIBLE table

the·ta \'thāt-ə, 'thēt-\ *n* : the eighth letter of the Greek alphabet — Θ *or* θ

they \(')thā\ *pron* **1** : those ones ⟨*they* won the game⟩ **2** : some people ⟨*they* say it will be a hard winter⟩

they'd \(,)thād\ : they had : they would

they'll \(,)thā(ə)l, thel\ : they shall : they will

they're \thər, (,)the(ə)r\ : they are

they've \(,)thāv\ : they have

thi·a·mine \'thī-ə-,mən, -,mēn\ *also* **thi·a·min** \-mən\ *n* : a vitamin of the B complex that is necessary for normal metabolism and nerve function and is found in many plants and animals — called also *vitamin B_1*

¹thick \'thik\ *adj* **1** : having or being of great depth or extent from one surface to its opposite ⟨a *thick* plank⟩ **2** : heavily built : THICKSET **3 a** : having units closely packed together : DENSE ⟨a *thick* forest⟩ **b** : NUMEROUS ⟨flies were *thick* in the barn⟩ **c** : VISCOUS 2 ⟨*thick* syrup⟩ **4** : marked by haze, fog, or mist ⟨*thick* weather⟩ **5** : measuring in thickness ⟨two meters *thick*⟩ **6** : not clearly spoken ⟨*thick* speech⟩ **7** : STUPID 1a **8** : ²INTIMATE 3a ⟨those two are really *thick*⟩ **9** : going beyond what is proper or enough ⟨the flattery was a bit *thick*⟩ — **thick·ish** \-ish\ *adj* — **thick·ly** *adv*

²thick *n* **1** : the most crowded or active part ⟨in the *thick* of things⟩ **2** : the part of greatest thickness

³thick *adv* : in a thick manner : so as to be thick : THICKLY

thick and thin *n* : every difficulty and problem ⟨through *thick and thin*⟩

thick·en \'thik-ən\ *vb* **thick·ened; thick·en·ing** \-(ə-)niŋ\ **1** : to make or become thick, dense, or viscous **2** : to become complicated ⟨the plot *thickens*⟩ — **thick·en·er** \-(ə-)nər\ *n*

thick·en·ing *n* **1** : the act of making or becoming thick **2** : a thickened part or place **3** : something used to thicken

thick·et \'thik-ət\ *n* : a thick usually small patch of shrubbery, small trees, or underbrush

thick·head·ed \'thik-'hed-əd\ *adj* : STUPID 1a

thick·ness \'thik-nəs\ *n* **1** : the quality or state of being thick **2** : the smallest of three dimensions ⟨length, width, and *thickness*⟩ **3** : the thick part of something **4** : ¹LAYER 2 ⟨a single *thickness* of canvas⟩

thick·set \'thik-'set\ *adj* **1** : closely placed or planted **2** : of short stout build : STOCKY

thick–skinned \-'skind\ *adj* **1** : having a thick skin **2** : not easily bothered by criticism or insult

thief \'thēf\ *n, pl* **thieves** \'thēvz\ : one that steals

thieve \'thēv\ *vb* **thieved; thiev·ing** \: ¹STEAL 2a, ROB

thiev·ery \'thēv-(ə-)rē\ *n, pl* **-er·ies** : the action of stealing : THEFT

thiev·ish \'thē-vish\ *adj* **1** : of, relating to, or characteristic of a thief **2** : given to stealing — **thiev·ish·ly** *adv* — **thiev·ish·ness** *n*

thigh \'thī\ *n* : the part of the leg that extends from the hip to the knee and is supported by a single large bone

thigh·bone \-'bōn, -,bōn\ *n* : FEMUR 1

thig·mo·tax·is \,thig-mə-'tak-səs\ *n* : a taxis in which contact especially with a solid object is the stimulus directing the movement of an organism

thig·mot·ro·pism \thig-'mä-trə-,piz-əm\ *n* : a tropism in which contact (as with a rigid surface) is the stimulus directing the movement of an organism

thim·ble \'thim-bəl\ *n* : a cap or cover used in sewing to protect the finger that pushes the needle

¹thin \'thin\ *adj* **thin·ner; thin·nest** **1** : having little extent from one surface to its opposite ⟨*thin* paper⟩ **2** : having widely scattered units ⟨*thin* hair⟩ **3** : having too little flesh

4 : less dense than normal ⟨*thin* air⟩ **5 :** lacking substance or strength ⟨*thin* broth⟩ ⟨*thin* excuses⟩ **6 :** somewhat weak or shrill ⟨*thin* voice⟩ **syn** see LEAN — **thin·ly** *adv* — **thin·ness** \'thin-nəs\ *n*

²**thin** *vb* **thinned; thin·ning 1 :** to make or become thin **2 :** to reduce in number especially to prevent crowding ⟨*thin* young carrots in the garden⟩

thine \'thīn\ *pron, archaic* : thy one : thy ones

thing \'thiŋ\ *n* **1 a :** a matter of concern : AFFAIR ⟨many *things* to do⟩ **b** *pl* : state of affairs ⟨*things* are improving⟩ **c** : SITUATION 3 ⟨look at this *thing* another way⟩ **d** : EVENT 1a, CIRCUMSTANCE ⟨the flood was a terrible thing⟩ **e** : something one does well or likes to do ⟨do your *thing*⟩ **2 a :** ¹DEED 1, ACT ⟨do great *things*⟩ **b** : a product of work or activity ⟨likes to build *things*⟩ **c** : the aim of effort or activity ⟨the *thing* is to get well⟩ **3 :** a particular object; *esp* : a lifeless object ⟨how do you work this *thing*?⟩ **4 a** *pl* : BELONGINGS ⟨pack your *things*⟩ **b** : an article of clothing ⟨not a *thing* to wear⟩ **5 a :** ¹DETAIL 1b ⟨checks every little *thing*⟩ **b** : a material or substance of a particular kind ⟨avoid starchy *things*⟩ **6 :** IDEA 2, NOTION ⟨says the first *thing* that comes to mind⟩ **7 :** ²INDIVIDUAL ⟨poor little *thing*⟩

think \'thiŋk\ *vb* **thought** \'thot\; **think·ing 1 :** to form or have in the mind ⟨afraid to *think* what might happen⟩ **2 :** to have as an opinion : BELIEVE ⟨*think* it's so⟩ **3 :** to hold in the mind for some time : PONDER ⟨*think* the matter over⟩ ⟨*think* about it⟩ **4 :** to call to mind : REMEMBER ⟨never *thought* to ask⟩ **5 :** to use the power of reason ⟨*think* before you write your answer⟩ **6 :** to have an opinion ⟨they *think* highly of you⟩ **7 :** to have concern ⟨I must *think* of my family first⟩ **8 :** to invent by thinking — usually used with *up* ⟨always *thinking* up new schemes⟩ — **think·able** \'thiŋ-kə-bəl\ *adj* — **think·er** *n* — **think·ing** *adj*

think tank *n* : an organization formed to think up new solutions especially for social and scientific problems

thin·ner \'thin-ər\ *n* : one that thins; *esp* : a liquid (as turpentine) used to thin paint

thin–skinned \'thin-'skind\ *adj* **1 :** having a thin skin **2 :** easily bothered by criticism or insult

¹**third** \'thərd\ *adj* **1 a** — see NUMBER table **b** : next after the second in time, order, or importance **2 :** being one of three equal parts of something — **third** *adv* — **third·ly** *adv*

²**third** *n* **1 :** — see NUMBER table **2 :** one of three equal parts of something **3 :** the difference in pitch between the first tone and the third tone of a scale **4 :** the third forward gear or speed of a motor vehicle **5 :** one next after a second in time, order, or importance

third base *n* : the base that must be touched third by a base runner in baseball or the position of the player defending the area around it

third baseman *n* : the player defending the area around third base

third class *n* : the class next below second class in a classification — **third–class** *adj*

third degree *n* : brutal treatment of a prisoner by the police in order to get a confession

third–degree burn *n* : a burn in which the whole thickness of the skin and sometimes deeper tissues are destroyed with loss of fluid and often shock

third person *n* : a set of words or forms (as verb forms or pronouns) referring to someone or something that is neither the speaker or writer of the utterance in which they occur nor the one to whom that utterance is addressed; *also* : a word or form belonging to such a set

third world *n, often cap T & W* **1 :** nations especially in Africa and Asia that are not part of either the Communist or the non-Communist groups **2 :** the underdeveloped nations of the world

¹**thirst** \'thərst\ *n* **1 a :** a feeling of dryness in the mouth and throat that accompanies a desire for liquids; *also* : the bodily condition (as of dehydration) that causes thirst **b** : a strong desire to drink **2 :** a strong desire : CRAVING ⟨a *thirst* for fame⟩

²**thirst** *vb* **1 :** to feel thirsty **2 :** to have a strong desire : CRAVE

thirsty \'thər-stē\ *adj* **thirst·i·er; -est 1 a :** feeling thirst **b** : needing moisture ⟨*thirsty* land⟩ **2 :** having a strong desire ⟨*thirsty* for knowledge⟩ — **thirst·i·ly** \-stə-lē\ *adv*

thir·teen \,thər(t)-'tēn, 'thər(t)-\ *n* — see NUMBER table — **thirteen** *adj or pron* — **thir·teenth** \-'tēn(t)th\ *adj or n*

thir·ty \'thərt-ē\ *n, pl* **thirties 1 :** — see NUMBER table **2** *pl* : the numbers 30 to 39; *esp* : the years 30 to 39 in a lifetime or century — **thir·ti·eth** \-ē-əth\ *n or adj* — **thirty** *adj or pron*

¹**this** \('¹)this, thəs\ *pron, pl* **these** \('¹)thēz\ **1 :** the person, thing, or idea present or near in place, time, or thought, or just mentioned ⟨*these* are my friends⟩ **2 :** the one nearer ⟨*this* is iron and that is tin⟩

²**this** *adj, pl* **these 1 :** being the one present or near in place, time, or thought, or just mentioned ⟨*this* book is mine⟩ ⟨early *this* morning⟩ ⟨friends all *these* years⟩ **2 :** the nearer at hand ⟨*this* car or that one⟩ ⟨I like *these* colors better than those⟩

³**this** \'this\ *adv* : to the degree suggested by something in the present situation ⟨didn't expect to wait *this* long⟩

this·tle \'this-əl\ *n* : any of various prickly plants related to the daisies that have often showy heads of mostly tubular flowers — **this·tly** \'this-(ə-)lē\ *adj* — **this·tle·like** \-,līk\ *adj*

thistle

this·tle·down \'this-əl-,daùn\ *n* : the mass of seed-carrying fluffy bristles from the ripe flower head of a thistle

thistle tube *n* : a usually glass funnel tube with a mouth that spreads out and a bulging top

¹**thith·er** \'thith-ər *also* 'thith-\ *adv* : to that place : THERE

²**thither** *adj* : being on the other and farther side

tho *variant of* THOUGH

thole \'thōl\ *also* **thole·pin** \-,pin\ *n* : a peg or pin on the rim of a boat that holds an oar in place

thong \'thoŋ\ *n* **1 :** a strip of leather used especially for fastening something **2 :** a sandal held on the foot by a thong fitting between the toes

tho·rac·ic \thə-'ras-ik\ *adj* : of, relating to, located in, or involving the thorax

tho·rax \'thō(ə)r-,aks, 'thò(ə)r-\ *n, pl* **tho·rax·es** *or* **tho·ra·ces** \'thòr-ə-,sēz, 'thòr-\ **1 :** the part of the body of a mammal between the neck and the abdomen; *also* : its cavity in which the heart and lungs lie **2 :** the middle of the three main divisions of the body of an insect

tho·ri·um \'thōr-ē-əm, 'thòr-\ *n* : a radioactive metallic element that occurs combined in minerals — see ELEMENT table

thorn \'thò(ə)rn\ *n* **1 :** a woody plant bearing sharp processes (as briers, prickles, or spines); *esp* : HAWTHORN **2 :** a sharp stiff process on a plant; *esp* : a short, stiff, sharp-pointed, and leafless branch **3 :** something or someone that causes distress or irritation — **thorned** \'thò(ə)rnd\ *adj* — **thorn·less** \'thò(ə)rn-ləs\ *adj*

\ə\ abut	\aù\ out	\i\ tip	\o\ saw	\ù\ foot
\ər\ further	\ch\ chin	\ī\ life	\oi\ coin	\y\ yet
\a\ mat	\e\ pet	\j\ job	\th\ thin	\yü\ few
\ā\ take	\ē\ easy	\ŋ\ sing	\th\ this	\yù\ cure
\ä\ cot, cart	\g\ go	\ō\ bone	\ü\ food	\zh\ vision

thorny \'thȯr-nē\ adj **thorn·i·er; -est** **1** : full of or covered with thorns **2** : full of difficulties ⟨a *thorny* problem⟩ — **thorn·i·ness** n

thor·ough \'thər-ō, 'thə-rō\ adj **1** : marked by or carried out to completion : EXHAUSTIVE ⟨a *thorough* search⟩ **2** : careful about detail ⟨a *thorough* worker⟩ [Middle English *thorow* "thorough", from Old English *thuruh, thurh* "through" — related to THRILL, THROUGH; see *Word History* at THRILL] — **thor·ough·ly** adv — **thor·ough·ness** n

¹thor·ough·bred \'thər-ə-ˌbred, 'thə-rə-\ adj **1** : bred from the best stock through a long line : PUREBRED ⟨*thoroughbred* dogs⟩ **2** cap : of, relating to, or being a member of the Thoroughbred breed of horses

²thoroughbred n **1** cap : any of an English breed of light speedy horses kept chiefly for racing **2** : a purebred or pedigreed animal

thor·ough·fare \'thər-ə-ˌfa(ə)r, 'thə-rə-, -ˌfe(ə)r\ n **1** : a street or road open at both ends **2** : a main road

thor·ough·go·ing \ˌthər-ə-'gō-iŋ, ˌthə-rə-\ adj : THOROUGH 1

Thoroughbred

those pl of THAT

¹thou \(')thau̇\ pron, archaic : the person addressed

²thou \'thau̇\ n, pl **thou** : a thousand of something (as dollars)

¹though also **tho** \'thō\ adv : ²HOWEVER 2, NEVERTHELESS ⟨not for long, *though*⟩

²though also **tho** \(ˌ)thō\ conj : in spite of the fact or possibility that ⟨*though* it was raining, we went hiking⟩

¹thought past and past participle of THINK

²thought \'thȯt\ n **1** : the act or process of thinking **2** : serious consideration : careful attention **3** : power of thinking and especially of reasoning and judging **4** : power of imagining **5** : a product of thinking (as an idea, fancy, or invention) ⟨share your *thoughts* with us⟩

thought·ful \'thȯt-fəl\ adj **1 a** : lost in thought **b** : marked by careful thinking **2** : considerate of the needs of others — **thought·ful·ly** \-fə-lē\ adv — **thought·ful·ness** n

thought·less \'thȯt-ləs\ adj **1 a** : not careful and alert **b** : done without thinking beforehand **2** : lacking concern for others : INCONSIDERATE — **thought·less·ly** adv

thou·sand \'thau̇z-ᵊn(d)\ n, pl **thousands** or **thousand** **1** — see NUMBER table **2** : a very large number — **thousand** adj

thou·sand–leg·ger \ˌthau̇z-ᵊn-'(d)leg-ər, -'(d)lāg-\ n : MILLIPEDE

thousands digit \'thau̇z-ᵊn(d)z-\ n : the numeral (as 1 in 1456) in the thousands place

thousands place n : the place four to the left of the decimal point in a number expressed in the Arabic system of writing numbers

thou·sandth \'thau̇z-ᵊn(t)th\ n **1** : one of 1000 equal parts of something **2** : the one numbered 1000 in a countable series — see NUMBER table — **thousandth** adj

thrall \'thrȯl\ n **1** : ¹SLAVE 1 **2 a** : a state of slavery **b** : a state of complete attention ⟨the play held me in *thrall*⟩ — **thrall·dom** or **thral·dom** \'thrȯl-dəm\ n

thrash \'thrash\ vb **1** : THRESH 1 **2 a** : to strike forcefully especially with a long instrument (as a whip) : FLOG **b** : ¹DEFEAT 2 **3** : to move or stir about violently ⟨something was *thrashing* wildly in the water⟩ **4** : to go over again and again ⟨*thrash* the matter over⟩ ⟨*thrash* out a plan⟩

¹thrash·er \'thrash-ər\ n : one that thrashes or threshes

²thrasher n : any of numerous long-tailed American songbirds that resemble thrushes

¹thread \'thred\ n **1** : a thin fine cord formed by spinning and twisting short fibers into a continuous strand **2** : something that resembles a thread **3** : the ridge or groove that winds around a screw **4** : a train of thought — **thread·like** \-ˌlīk\ adj

²thread vb **1** : to put a thread in working position in ⟨*thread* a needle⟩ **2** : to pass through in the manner of a thread ⟨*thread* film through a camera⟩ **3** : to make a way through or between ⟨a river *threading* narrow valleys⟩; *also* : to make (one's way) carefully ⟨had to *thread* their way between the mountains⟩ **4** : to put together on a thread : STRING ⟨*thread* beads⟩ **5** : to weave together with or as if with threads : INTERSPERSE ⟨dark hair *threaded* with gray⟩ — **thread·er** n

thread·bare \'thred-ˌba(ə)r, -ˌbe(ə)r\ adj **1** : worn so much that the thread shows : SHABBY **2** : TRITE

thready \'thred-ē\ adj **1** : consisting of or bearing fine threads or fibers ⟨a *thready* bark⟩ **2** : lacking in fullness or vigor : THIN ⟨a *thready* voice⟩

threat \'thret\ n **1** : an expression of an intent to do harm **2** : something that threatens ⟨a *threat* of rain⟩

threat·en \'thret-ᵊn\ vb **threat·ened; threat·en·ing** \'thret-niŋ, -ᵊn-iŋ\ **1** : to utter threats : make threats against **2** : to give warning of by a threat or sign ⟨clouds *threatening* rain⟩ **3** : to give signs of trouble to come — **threat·en·ing·ly** \'thret-niŋ-lē, -ᵊn-iŋ-\ adv

three \'thrē\ n **1** — see NUMBER table **2** : the third in a set or series **3** : something having three units or members — **three** adj or pron

3–D \'thrē-'dē\ n : the three-dimensional form or a picture produced in it

three–deck·er \'thrē-'dek-ər\ n : something made with three floors or layers

three–dimensional adj **1** : of, relating to, or having three dimensions (as length, width, and height) **2** : giving the appearance of depth or varying distances

three·fold \'thrē-ˌfōld, -'fōld\ adj **1** : having three units or members **2** : being three times as great or as many — **threefold** adv

three·pence \'threp-ən(t)s, 'thrip-, 'thrəp-, US also 'thrē-ˌpen(t)s\ n, pl **threepence** or **three·penc·es** **1** : a coin worth three pennies **2** : the sum of three British pennies

three·pen·ny \'threp-(ə-)nē, 'thrip-, 'thrəp-, US also 'thrē-ˌpen-ē\ adj : costing or worth threepence

three R's n pl : the basic subjects (as reading, writing, arithmetic) taught in elementary school

three·score \'thrē-'skō(ə)r, -'skȯ(ə)r\ adj : SIXTY

three·some \'thrē-səm\ n : a group of three

three–toed sloth \ˌthrē-ˌtōd-\ n : any of a genus of sloths having three claws on each foot — compare TWO-TOED SLOTH

thren·o·dy \'thren-əd-ē\ n, pl **-dies** : a song of mourning or sorrow

thresh \'thrash, 'thresh\ vb **1** : to separate seed from a harvested plant especially by using a machine or tool ⟨*thresh* wheat⟩ **2** : THRASH 4 **3** : THRASH 3

thresh·er \'thrash-ər, 'thresh-\ n **1 a** : a person who threshes **b** : a machine used for separating grain or seeds from straw **2** : THRESHER SHARK

thresher shark n : a large shark that has a long curved upper lobe on its tail which it is reported to use in rounding up and killing fish to feed on

thresher shark

threshing machine n : THRESHER 1b

thresh·old \'thresh-ˌ(h)ōld\ n **1** : the section of wood or stone that lies under a door **2 a** : ¹ENTRANCE 2a **b** : the place or point of beginning ⟨at the *threshold* of an adventure⟩ **3** : the point or level at which a physical or mental effect begins to be produced ⟨the *threshold* of hearing⟩

threw past of THROW

thrice \ˈthrīs\ adv **1** : three times **2** : to a high degree

thrift \ˈthrift\ n : careful management especially of money

thrift·less \ˈthrift-ləs\ adj : careless in the handling of money or resources

thrift shop n : a shop that sells secondhand articles and is often run by a charity

thrifty \ˈthrif-tē\ adj **thrift·i·er; -est** **1** : doing well because of hard work and thrift : PROSPEROUS **2** : growing strongly ⟨*thrifty* cattle⟩ **3** : tending to save money **syn** see FRUGAL — **thrift·i·ly** \-tə-lē\ adv

¹thrill \ˈthril\ vb **1** : to experience or cause to experience a sudden sharp feeling of excitement **2** : VIBRATE 2, TREMBLE

> **Word History** Today when we speak of being thrilled, we are referring to a very pleasing experience. But it was not always so. The Old English word *thyrlian*, which gave us *thrill*, meant "to pierce" as with an arrow or spear. The Old English word came from an earlier word *thyrel*, meaning "hole". *Thyrel* has also given us two other Modern English words, *through* and *thorough*. It has also given us the last half of the word *nostril*, which literally means "nose hole". During the Middle English period the verb *thyrlian* became *thirlen* and continued to mean "to pierce". It also was the basis of the new verb *thrillen*, meaning "to penetrate". Then a connection was made between the physical sensation of being pierced and the emotional feeling of being suddenly and sharply excited. A new sense was born, which became the chief meaning of our *thrill*. [Middle English *thrillen* "to penetrate", an altered form of *thirlen* "to pierce", from Old English *thyrlian* "to pierce", from *thyrel* (noun) "a hole", from *thurh* "through" — related to NOSTRIL, THOROUGH, THROUGH]

²thrill n **1** : a tingling sensation that accompanies a sudden sharp emotion ⟨felt a *thrill* of excitement⟩ **2** : VIBRATION 1b

thril·ler \ˈthril-ər\ n : one that thrills; esp : a work of fiction or drama with a great deal of action, mystery, adventure, or suspense

thrive \ˈthrīv\ vb **throve** \ˈthrōv\ or **thrived; thriv·en** \ˈthriv-ən\ also **thrived; thriv·ing** \ˈthrī-viŋ\ **1** : to grow vigorously : do well : FLOURISH **2** : to gain in wealth or possessions : PROSPER

throat \ˈthrōt\ n **1** : the part of the neck in front of the spinal column; also : the passages that run through the neck to the stomach and lungs **2** : something (as an end part) that resembles the throat — **throat·ed** \-əd\ adj

throaty \ˈthrōt-ē\ adj **throat·i·er; -est** : uttered or produced in deep, low tones from or as if from low in the throat — **throat·i·ly** \ˈthrōt-ᵊl-ē\ adv

throb \ˈthräb\ vb **throbbed; throb·bing** **1** : to beat hard or fast **2** : to beat or vibrate with a steady rhythm — **throb** n

throe \ˈthrō\ n **1** : PANG ⟨death *throes*⟩ ⟨*throes* of childbirth⟩ **2** pl : a hard or painful struggle ⟨a state in the *throes* of revolution⟩

throm·bo·sis \thräm-ˈbō-səs\ n, pl **-bo·ses** \-ˈbō-ˌsēz\ : the formation or presence of a blood clot within a blood vessel during life

throm·bus \ˈthräm-bəs\ n, pl **throm·bi** \-ˌbī, -ˌbē\ : a clot of blood formed within a blood vessel and remaining attached to its place of origin — compare EMBOLUS

¹throne \ˈthrōn\ n **1** : the chair of state of a monarch or bishop **2** : royal power and dignity

²throne vb **throned; thron·ing** : to seat on a throne : ENTHRONE

¹throng \ˈthrȯŋ\ n : a large number of people gathered together **syn** see MULTITUDE

²throng vb **thronged; throng·ing** \ˈthrȯŋ-iŋ\ **1** : to crowd upon or into ⟨shoppers *thronged* the mall⟩ **2** : to crowd together in great numbers

¹throt·tle \ˈthrät-ᵊl\ vb **throt·tled; throt·tling** \ˈthrät-liŋ, -ᵊl-iŋ\ **1** : to slow or stop the breathing of : CHOKE, STRANGLE **2** : to reduce the speed of (an engine) by closing the throttle — **throt·tler** \-lər, -ᵊl-ər\ n

²throttle n **1** : a valve controlling the flow of steam or fuel to an engine **2** : a lever controlling a throttle

¹through also **thru** \ˈthrü\ prep **1 a** : in at one side and out at the opposite side of ⟨drove *through* the town⟩ **b** : by way of ⟨left *through* the window⟩ **c** : in the midst of : AMONG ⟨a path *through* the trees⟩ **2 a** : by means of ⟨succeeded *through* hard work⟩ **b** : because of ⟨failed *through* lack of planning⟩ **3** : over the whole of ⟨all *through* the country⟩ **4 a** : from the beginning to the end of : DURING ⟨worked *through* the summer⟩ **b** : to and including ⟨Monday *through* Friday⟩ [Old English *thurh* "through" — related to THOROUGH, THRILL; see *Word History* at THRILL]

²through also **thru** \ˈthrü\ adv **1 a** : from one end or side to the other ⟨let these people go *through*, please⟩ **b** : over the whole distance ⟨shipped *through* to Des Moines⟩ **2 a** : from beginning to end ⟨read the book *through* at one sitting⟩ **b** : to completion, conclusion, or accomplishment ⟨see the job *through*⟩ **3** : in or to every part : COMPLETELY ⟨wet *through*⟩ **4** : into the open : OUT

³through also **thru** \ˈthrü\ adj **1** : allowing free or continuous passage ⟨a *through* road⟩ **2** : going from point of origin to destination without changes or transfers ⟨a *through* train⟩ **3** : coming from and going to points outside a local area ⟨a lane for *through* traffic only⟩ **4** : having reached the end ⟨is *through* with the job⟩

¹through·out \thrü-ˈaut\ adv **1** : in or to every part : EVERYWHERE **2** : during the whole time or action : from beginning to end

²throughout prep **1** : in or to every part of ⟨*throughout* the house⟩ **2** : during the whole time of ⟨*throughout* the evening⟩

throughway variant of THRUWAY

throve past of THRIVE

¹throw \ˈthrō\ vb **threw** \ˈthrü\; **thrown** \ˈthrōn\; **throw·ing** **1** : to send through the air especially with a quick forward motion of the arm ⟨*threw* the ball over the fence⟩ **2 a** : to cause to fall ⟨a horse jumped and *threw* its rider⟩ **b** : to get the better of : OVERCOME ⟨the problem didn't *throw* her⟩ **3** : to put suddenly in a certain condition or position ⟨*thrown* out of work⟩ **4** : to put on or take off quickly ⟨*throw* on a coat⟩ **5** : to form or shape on a potter's wheel **6** : to move to an open or closed position ⟨*throw* a switch⟩ **7** : to lose (a game or contest) on purpose **8** : to give for entertainment ⟨*throw* a party⟩ — **throw·er** \ˈthrō(-ə)r\ n

syn THROW, TOSS, FLING, HURL mean to drive something swiftly through space often by a movement of the arm. THROW is the broadest word and can be used of almost any motion and driving force ⟨*throw* a ball⟩ ⟨the sudden stop *threw* the groceries to the floor of the car⟩ TOSS suggests a light or careless throwing ⟨*toss* a coin to see which side comes up⟩ ⟨*tossed* the paper away⟩ FLING suggests a quick tossing often at no particular target ⟨*flung* the coat on the chair and ran out of the room⟩ HURL suggests a throwing with strong force ⟨*hurled* rocks at the old cans they were using as targets⟩

²throw n **1** : an act of throwing **2** : a method of throwing an opponent in wrestling or judo **3** : the distance something is or may be thrown ⟨a stone's *throw*⟩ **4** : a loose covering (as for a sofa) **5** : a woman's light wrap

¹throw·away \ˈthrō-ə-ˌwā\ n : something that is or designed to be thrown away especially after one use

\ə\ **abut**	\au\ **out**	\i\ **tip**	\o\ **saw**	\u\ **foot**	
\ər\ **further**	\ch\ **chin**	\ī\ **life**	\oi\ **coin**	\y\ **yet**	
\a\ **mat**	\e\ **pet**	\j\ **job**	\th\ **thin**	\yü\ **few**	
\ā\ **take**	\ē\ **easy**	\ŋ\ **sing**	\th\ **this**	\yu\ **cure**	
\ä\ **cot, cart**	\g\ **go**	\ō\ **bone**	\ü\ **food**	\zh\ **vision**	

²throw·away \ˌthrō-ə-ˌwā\ *adj* : designed to be thrown away : DISPOSABLE ⟨*throwaway* cans and bottles⟩

throw away \ˌthrō-ə-ˈwā\ *vb* **1** : to get rid of : DISCARD ⟨*threw* the old ones *away*⟩ **2** : SQUANDER, WASTE ⟨careful not to *throw* money *away*⟩

throw·back \ˈthrō-ˌbak\ *n* : something that has changed back to an earlier type or phase

throw off *vb* : to send out : EMIT ⟨a sparkler *throws off* sparks⟩

throw out *vb* **1** : THROW AWAY 1, DISCARD **2** : to remove from a place, position, or participation

throw up *vb* **1** : to build or raise hurriedly or quickly ⟨*threw up* the window⟩ **2** : ¹STOP 7a, QUIT ⟨just wanted to *throw* the whole thing *up*⟩ **3** : ²VOMIT 1

thru *variant of* THROUGH

thrum \ˈthrəm\ *vb* **thrummed; thrum·ming** : to sound or speak with a steady or boring rhythm — **thrum** *n*

thrush \ˈthrəsh\ *n* : any of a large family of small or medium-sized songbirds that are mostly of a plain color often with spotted underparts

thrush

¹thrust \ˈthrəst\ *vb* **thrust; thrust·ing** **1** : to push or drive with force : SHOVE **2** : to cause to enter or pierce something by pushing **3** : to press or force the acceptance of upon someone

²thrust *n* **1 a** : a push or lunge with a pointed weapon **b** : a military attack **2** : the force produced by a propeller or jet or rocket engine that drives an aircraft or rocket forward **3 a** : a forward or upward push **b** : a movement (as by a group of people) in a particular direction

thrust·er \ˈthrəs-tər\ *n* : one that thrusts; *esp* : an engine that produces thrust by discharging a jet of fluid or a stream of particles

thru·way *or* **through·way** \ˈthrü-ˌwā\ *n* : EXPRESSWAY

¹thud \ˈthəd\ *vb* **thud·ded; thud·ding** : to move or strike so as to make a dull sound

²thud *n* **1** : ⁴BLOW 1 **2** : a dull sound : THUMP 1

thug \ˈthəg\ *n* : RUFFIAN

Word History *Thug* was the name given by the British in India in the 19th century to a member of a band of thieves and murderers. A thug would pretend to be friendly with a traveler and offer to share a journey. Then as soon as it was safe to do so, the thug would strangle and rob his companion. The word *thug* comes from *thag,* a word in the Indian language Hindi meaning one of these robbers. The Hindi word in turn came from *sthagati,* a word in the ancient Indian language Sanskrit meaning "he covers up, he hides". Since thugs made travel dangerous, the British government rounded up most of them, and in a few years they were no longer a threat. The word *thug,* however, has lasted till today and even taken on the broader meaning of "ruffian". [from Hindi *thag,* literally "thief", derived from Sanskrit *sthagati* "he covers up, he hides"]

thu·li·um \ˈth(y)ü-lē-əm\ *n* : a rare metallic element — see ELEMENT table

¹thumb \ˈthəm\ *n* **1 a** : the short thick first finger of the human hand next to the forefinger **b** : the similar structure in lower animals **2** : the part of a glove or mitten that covers the thumb

²thumb *vb* **1** : to turn pages with the thumb ⟨*thumb* through a book⟩ **2** : to seek or get a ride in a passing automobile by sticking out one's thumb

¹thumb·nail \ˈthəm-ˌnāl, -ˈnā(ə)l\ *n* : the nail of the thumb

²thumb·nail \ˌthəm-ˌnāl\ *adj* : ¹BRIEF ⟨wrote a *thumbnail* sketch of the poet⟩

thumb·print \ˈthəm-ˌprint\ *n* : an impression made by the thumb

thumb·tack \ˈthəm-ˌtak\ *n* : a tack with a broad flat head for pressing into a board or wall with the thumb

thump \ˈthəmp\ *vb* **1** : to strike or beat with something thick or heavy so as to cause a dull sound **2** : ²POUND 2a — **thump** *n*

¹thun·der \ˈthən-dər\ *n* **1** : the loud sound that follows a flash of lightning **2** : a noise like thunder

²thunder *vb* **thun·dered; thun·der·ing** \-d(ə-)riŋ\ **1 a** : to produce thunder **b** : to produce a sound like thunder ⟨horses *thundered* down the road⟩ **2** : to utter loudly ⟨the people *thundered* their approval⟩ — **thun·der·er** \-dər-ər\ *n*

thun·der·bolt \ˈthən-dər-ˌbōlt\ *n* : a flash of lightning and the thunder that follows it

thun·der·clap \-ˌklap\ *n* **1** : a clap of thunder **2** : something sharp, loud, or sudden like a clap of thunder

thun·der·cloud \-ˌklaüd\ *n* : a dark storm cloud that produces lightning and thunder

thun·der·head \-ˌhed\ *n* : a large cumulus cloud often appearing before a thunderstorm

thunder lizard *n* : BRONTOSAURUS

thun·der·ous \ˈthən-d(ə-)rəs\ *adj* : producing thunder; *also* : making a noise like thunder ⟨*thunderous* applause⟩ — **thun·der·ous·ly** *adv*

thun·der·show·er \ˈthən-dər-ˌshaü(-ə)r\ *n* : a shower accompanied by lightning and thunder

thun·der·storm \-ˌstȯ(ə)rm\ *n* : a storm accompanied by lightning and thunder

thun·der·struck \-ˌstrək\ *adj* : stunned as if struck by a thunderbolt : ASTONISHED

Thurs·day \ˈthərz-dē\ *n* : the fifth day of the week

Word History Among the many gods worshiped by the Germanic people who lived in northern Europe in ancient times was one whose name was *Thor.* Thor was the god of thunder, weather, and crops. In the early Norse language, the fifth day of the week was known as *thōrsdagr,* literally "day of Thor", in his honor. The Norse name came into Old English as *thursdæg,* which in time became the Modern English *Thursday.* [Old English *thursdæg,* from early Norse *thōrsdagr,* literally "day of Thor"]

thus \ˈthəs\ *adv* **1** : in this or that manner or way **2** : to this degree or extent : so ⟨a mild winter *thus* far⟩ **3** : because of this or that : HENCE **4** : as an example

thwack \ˈthwak\ *vb* : to strike with or as if with something flat or heavy : WHACK — **thwack** *n*

¹thwart \ˈthwȯ(ə)rt\ *vb* **1** : to stand in the way of : hinder by opposing **2** : to oppose successfully [Middle English *thwerten* (verb) "oppose, hinder", from *thwert* (adverb) "across"] **syn** see FRUSTRATE — **thwart·er** *n*

²thwart \ˈthwȯ(ə)rt, *nautical often* ˈthȯ(ə)rt\ *adv* : ¹ACROSS 1 [Middle English *thwert* "across"; of Norse origin]

³thwart *adj* : situated or placed across something else

⁴thwart *n* : a rower's seat extending across a boat

thy \(ˌ)thī\ *adj, archaic* : of, relating to, or done by or to thee or thyself

thyme \ˈtīm *also* ˈthīm\ *n* : any of a genus of mints with small fragrant leaves; *esp* : one grown for use as a seasoning for food

thy·mine \ˈthī-ˌmēn\ *n* : a pyrimidine base that is one of the bases coding hereditary information in DNA — compare ADENINE, CYTOSINE, GUANINE, URACIL

thy·mus \ˈthī-məs\ *n, pl* **thy·mus·es** *or* **thy·mi** \-ˌmī\ : a gland that is found in most young vertebrates usually at the base of the neck, that before and for a time after birth has very important effects on the production, development, and activity of the white blood cells which attack and destroy or make inactive cells and substances foreign to the body, and that becomes less active and gradually shrinks or disappears with age

¹thy·roid \'thī-,ròid\ *adj* : of, relating to, or being a thyroid gland

²thyroid *n* **1** : a large endocrine gland at the base of the neck of most vertebrates that produces several iodine-containing hormones that affect growth, development, and metabolism — called also *thyroid gland* **2** : a preparation of the thyroid gland of animals that is used as a medicine to treat thyroid disorders

thyroid–stimulating hormone *n* : THYROTROPIN

thy·ro·tro·pin \,thī-rə-'trō-pən\ *n* : a hormone secreted by the pituitary gland that controls the formation and release of the thyroid hormones

thy·rox·in *also* **thy·rox·ine** \thī-'räk-sən, -,sēn\ *n* : an iodine-containing hormone that is produced by the thyroid gland and is used to treat thyroid disorders

thy·self \thī-'self\ *pron, archaic* : YOURSELF

ti \'tē\ *n* : the seventh note of the musical scale

ti·ara \tē-'ar-ə, -'er-, -'är-\ *n* **1** : a crown worn by the pope **2** : a decorative headband worn by women on special occasions

tiara 2

Ti·bet·an \tə-'bet-ᵊn\ *n* **1** : a member of the native race of Tibet **2** : the language of the Tibetan people — **Tibetan** *adj*

tib·ia \'tib-ē-ə\ *n, pl* **-i·ae** \-ē-,ē, -ē-,ī\ *also* **-i·as** **1** : the inner and usually larger of the two bones of the vertebrate hind leg between the knee and the ankle — called also *shinbone* **2** : the fourth joint of the leg of an insect between the femur and the tarsus — **tib·i·al** \-ē-əl\ *adj*

tib·io·fib·u·la \,tib-ē-ō-'fib-yə-lə\ *n* : a single bone that replaces the tibia and fibula in a frog or toad

tic \'tik\ *n* **1** : a regularly repeated twitching movement of a particular muscle and especially one of the face muscles **2** : a particular form of behavior that is often repeated

¹tick \'tik\ *n* : any of numerous bloodsucking animals that are arachnids larger than the related mites, attach themselves to warm-blooded animals to feed, and include important carriers of infectious diseases [Middle English *tyke, teke* "tick"]

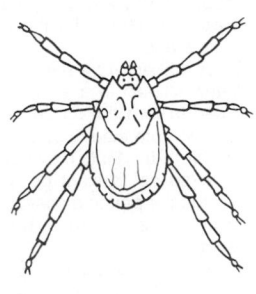

¹tick

²tick *n* **1** : the fabric case of a mattress, pillow, or cushion **2** : TICKING [Middle English *tike* "a fabric case for a mattress"; probably of Dutch origin]

³tick *n* **1** : a light rhythmic tap or beat ⟨the *tick* of a clock⟩ **2** : a small mark used to direct attention to something or to check an item on a list [Middle English *tek* "a rhythmic tap or beat"]

⁴tick *vb* **1 a** : to make the sound of a tick or a series of ticks **b** : to mark, count, or announce by or as if by ticking beats **2** : to work at a regular or proper pace : RUN **3** : to mark with a written tick : CHECK

⁵tick *n* : ¹CREDIT 3a, TRUST ⟨bought on *tick*⟩ [a shortened form of *ticket* "a slip recording a business deal"]

tick·er \'tik-ər\ *n* **1** : ²WATCH 4 **2** : a telegraphic machine that receives stock prices and news and prints them out on a paper ribbon **3** *slang* : HEART 1a

ticker tape *n* : the paper ribbon on which a telegraphic ticker prints

¹tick·et \'tik-ət\ *n* **1** : ¹TAG 4, LABEL ⟨price *ticket*⟩ **2** : a summons or warning issued to a traffic offender ⟨got a *ticket* for speeding⟩ **3** : a paper or token showing that a fare or admission fee has been paid **4** : a list of candidates **5** : a slip or card recording a business deal [from obsolete French *etiquet* "a notice attached to something", derived from early French *estiquier* "to attach"; of Dutch origin — related to ETIQUETTE]

²ticket *vb* **1** : to attach a ticket to : LABEL **2** : to give a traffic ticket to

tick·ing \'tik-iŋ\ *n* : a strong fabric used especially as a covering for mattresses and pillows

tick·le \'tik-əl\ *vb* **tick·led; tick·ling** \-(ə-)liŋ\ **1** : to have a tingling or prickling sensation **2 a** : to excite or stir up agreeably : PLEASE ⟨food that *tickles* your taste buds⟩ **b** : to stir to laughter or merriment ⟨were *tickled* by the clown's antics⟩ **3** : to touch a body part lightly so as to cause uneasiness, laughter, or jerky movements — **tickle** *n* — **tick·ler** \'tik-(ə-)lər\ *n*

tick·lish \'tik-(ə-)lish\ *adj* **1** : TOUCHY 1 ⟨*ticklish* about his baldness⟩ **2** : requiring delicate handling ⟨a *ticklish* subject⟩ **3** : sensitive to tickling — **tick·lish·ly** *adv* — **tick·lish·ness** *n*

tick·tack·toe *also* **tic–tac–toe** \,tik-,tak-'tō\ *n* : a game in which two players by turns put crosses and zeros in compartments of a figure formed by two vertical lines crossing two horizontal lines and each tries to get a row of three crosses or three zeros before the opponent does

tid·al \'tīd-ᵊl\ *adj* : of or relating to tides : rising and falling or flowing and ebbing at regular times

tidal wave *n* **1** : an unusually high sea wave that sometimes follows an earthquake **2** : an unusual rise of water alongshore due to strong winds

tid·bit \'tid-,bit\ *or* **tit·bit** \'tit-,bit\ *n* **1** : a small tasty piece of food **2** : a pleasing bit (as of news)

tid·dle·dy·winks *or* **tid·dly·winks** \'tid-ᵊl-(d)ē-,win(k)s, 'tid-lē-,win(k)s\ *n* : a game in which players snap small disks from a flat surface into a small container

¹tide \'tīd\ *n* **1** : the alternate rising and falling of the surface of the ocean that occurs twice a day and is caused by the gravitational attraction of the sun and moon occurring unequally on different parts of the earth **2** : the flow of the incoming or outgoing tide **3** : something that rises and falls like the tides of the sea

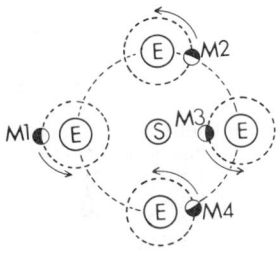

tide 1: M1 and M3, position of moon at spring tides; M2 and M4, moon at neap tides

²tide *vb* **tid·ed; tid·ing** : to enable to overcome or put up with a difficulty ⟨money to *tide* us over⟩

tide·land \'tīd-,land, -lənd\ *n* : land overflowed during high tide

tide·wa·ter \-,wòt-ər, -,wät-\ *n* **1** : water overflowing land at high tide **2** : low-lying coastal land

tid·ings \'tīd-iŋz\ *n pl* : NEWS 3 ⟨good *tidings*⟩

¹ti·dy \'tīd-ē\ *adj* **ti·di·er; -est** **1** : well ordered and cared for **2** : LARGE, SUBSTANTIAL ⟨a *tidy* price⟩ **syn** see NEAT

²tidy *vb* **ti·died; ti·dy·ing** **1** : to put in order **2** : to make things tidy

³tidy *n, pl* **tidies** : a fancy covering used to protect the back, arms, or headrest of a chair or sofa from wear or soiling

¹tie \'tī\ *n* **1** : a line, ribbon, or cord used for fastening,

\ə\ abut	\aù\ out	\i\ tip	\ò\ saw	\ù\ foot	
\ər\ further	\ch\ chin	\ī\ life	\òi\ coin	\y\ yet	
\a\ mat	\e\ pet	\j\ job	\th\ thin	\yü\ few	
\ā\ take	\ē\ easy	\ŋ\ sing	\th\ this	\yù\ cure	
\ä\ cot, cart	\g\ go	\ō\ bone	\ü\ food	\zh\ vision	

uniting, or drawing something closed   **2 a** : a structural part (as a beam) holding two pieces together   **b** : one of the cross supports to which railroad rails are fastened   **3** : a bond of kinship or affection 〈family *ties*〉   **4 a** : an equality in number : DEADLOCK 〈the game ended in a *tie*〉   **b** : a contest that ends with an equal score   **5** : NECKTIE

²tie *vb* **tied; ty·ing** \'tī-iŋ\ *or* **tie·ing**   **1 a** : to fasten, attach, or close by means of a tie   **b** : to form a knot or bow in   **2** : to limit the freedom or actions of 〈responsibilities *tied* us down〉   **3 a** : to make or have an equal score with in a contest 〈the two teams *tied*〉   **b** : to come up with something equal to 〈*tied* the score〉

tie–dye·ing \'tī-,dī-iŋ\ *n* : a hand method of ornamenting textiles by tying portions of the fabric so that they will not absorb the dye — **tie–dye** \-,dī\ *vb* — **tie–dyed** *adj*

tie in \(')tī-'in\ *vb* : to become connected — **tie–in** \'tī-,in\ *n*

¹tier \'ti(ə)r\ *n* : a row, rank, or layer usually arranged in a series one above the other — **tiered** \'ti(ə)rd\ *adj*

²tier *vb*   **1** : to place or arrange in tiers   **2** : to rise in tiers

³ti·er \'tī(-ə)r\ *n* : a person or thing that ties

tie–up \'tī-,əp\ *n*   **1** : a slowing or stopping especially of traffic or business   **2** : CONNECTION 2, ASSOCIATION

tie up \(')tī-'əp\ *vb*   **1** : to fasten securely   **2 a** : to use in such a manner as not to be available for other purposes 〈money *tied up* in stocks〉   **b** : to keep from working or going 〈traffic was *tied up* for hours〉   **3** : to have a relationship with something else 〈this *ties up* with what you said before〉

tiff \'tif\ *n* : a minor quarrel

ti·ger \'tī-gər\ *n, pl* **ti·gers** *also* **tiger**   **1** : a large Asian flesh= eating mammal of the cat family with a coat that is light brown to orange with black stripes   **2** : any of several large wildcats (as the jaguar or cougar); *esp* : one with a striped or spotted coat   **3** : a domestic cat with a striped coat

tiger 1

tiger beetle *n* : any of numerous active beetles with strong jaws that eat other insects, have larvae which build tunnels in the soil, and include some capable of giving a painful bite

tiger cat *n*   **1** : any of various medium-sized wildcats (as the ocelot) with a striped or spotted coat   **2** : a striped or spotted tabby cat

ti·ger·ish \'tī-g(ə-)rish\ *adj* : of or resembling a tiger

tiger lily *n* : an Asian garden lily that has nodding orange= colored flowers densely spotted with black; *also* : any of various lilies with similar flowers

tiger moth *n* : any of a family of stout-bodied moths usually with broad striped or spotted wings

tiger shark *n* : a large brown or gray shark of warm seas that sometimes attacks human beings

tiger swallowtail *n* : any of several large swallowtails of North America that are mostly yellow with black borders and black stripes on the wings

¹tight \'tīt\ *adj*   **1** : so close in structure as not to allow something (as liquid, gas, or light) to pass through 〈a *tight* roof〉   **2 a** : fixed very firmly in place 〈loosen a *tight* jar cover〉   **b** : firmly stretched or drawn   **c** : fitting too closely 〈*tight* shoes〉   **3** : difficult to get through or out of 〈in a *tight* spot〉 〈on a *tight* schedule〉   **4 a** : firm in control 〈kept a *tight* hand on affairs〉   **b** : STINGY 1   **5** : very closely packed or compressed   **6** : low in supply : SCARCE 〈*tight* money〉 — **tight·ly** *adv* — **tight·ness** *n*

syn TIGHT, TAUT, TENSE mean drawn or stretched to the limit. TIGHT may suggest that one thing is drawn around

another as closely as possible 〈the collar fit snugly around the dog's neck but was not too *tight*〉 TAUT suggests pulling (as of a rope) until there is no give or slack 〈a *taut* line between two poles〉 TENSE suggests that something is so strained that it cannot function correctly 〈if your muscles are too *tense,* you won't be able to run well〉

²tight *adv*   **1 a** : in a tight manner 〈hold on *tight*〉   **b** : so as to be tight 〈shut the door *tight*〉 〈wound the spring *tight*〉   **2** : in a deep and uninterrupted manner : SOUNDLY 〈sleep *tight*〉

tight·en \'tīt-ᵊn\ *vb* **tight·ened; tight·en·ing** \'tīt-niŋ, -ᵊn-iŋ\ : to make or become tight or tighter — **tight·en·er** \-nər, -ᵊn-ər\ *n*

tight·fist·ed \'tīt-'fis-təd\ *adj* : STINGY 1

tight–lipped \-'lipt\ *adj*   **1** : having the lips closed tight (as in determination)   **2** : not liking to speak : TACITURN

tight·rope \-,rōp\ *n* : a rope or wire stretched tight for acrobats to perform on

tights \'tīts\ *n pl* : a garment closely fitted to the body and covering it from the neck down or from the waist down

tight·wad \'tīt-,wäd\ *n* : a stingy person

ti·gress \'tī-grəs\ *n* : a female tiger

tike *variant of* TYKE

til·de \'til-də\ *n* : a mark ˜ placed especially over the letter *n* (as in Spanish *señor*) to indicate a sound that is approximately \ny\

¹tile \'tī(ə)l\ *n*   **1** *pl* **tiles** *or* **tile**   **a** : a flat or curved piece (as of fired clay, stone, or concrete) used especially for roofs or floors   **b** : a pipe of earthenware used for a drain   **2** : thin piece of material (as linoleum or rubber) for covering floors or walls

²tile *vb* **tiled; til·ing** : to cover with tiles

¹till \tᵊl, təl, (,)til\ *prep or conj* : UNTIL 〈won't finish *till* next week〉 [Old English *til* "until"]

²till \'til\ *vb* : to work by plowing, sowing, and raising crops on [Old English *tilian* "to work (land) by plowing and raising crops"] — **till·able** \-ə-bəl\ *adj*

³till \'til\ *n* : a drawer for money

⁴till \'til\ *n* : a mixture of clay, sand, gravel, and boulders deposited by a glacier [origin unknown]

till·age \'til-ij\ *n*   **1** : the process of tilling land   **2** : cultivated land

¹till·er \'til-ər\ *n* : a person who tills or a tool used for tilling

²til·ler \'til-ər\ *n* : a lever used to turn the rudder of a boat from side to side

¹tilt \'tilt\ *vb*   **1** : to move or shift so as to slant or tip   **2** : to take part in a contest with lances : JOUST — **tilt·er** *n*

²tilt *n*   **1** : a contest on horseback in which two opponents charging with lances try to unhorse each other : JOUST   **2** : a contest with words between opponents   **3** : ¹SPEED 1b 〈at full *tilt*〉   **4** : the act of tilting : the state or position of being tilted

tile 1a

tilth \'tilth\ *n*   **1** : TILLAGE 2   **2** : the state of a soil with respect to the suitability of its particle size and structure for growing crops

tilt·me·ter \'tilt-,mēt-ər\ *n* : an instrument that measures the tilt of the earth's surface

tim·ber \'tim-bər\ *n*   **1** : wood for use in making something   **2** : a usually large piece of wood squared or finished for use   **3** : wooded land or growing trees forming a source of timber — **timber** *adj*

tim·ber·land \-,land\ *n* : wooded land

tim·ber·line \-,līn\ *n* : the upper limit beyond which trees do not grow (as on mountains)

timber wolf *n* : a large powerful gray to brownish white wolf of northern regions — called also *gray wolf*

tim·bre \'tam-bər, 'tim-\ *n* : the quality of a sound or musical tone determined by its overtones and different for each voice or instrument

tim·brel \'tim-brəl\ *n* : a small hand drum or tambourine

¹time \'tīm\ *n* **1 a** : the period during which an action, process, or condition exists or continues : DURATION **b** : part of the day when one is free to do as one pleases ⟨find *time* for reading⟩ **2** : a point or period when something occurs : OCCASION ⟨remember the *time* you entered the pie-eating contest⟩ **3** : a set or usual moment or hour for something to happen, begin, or end ⟨arrived ahead of *time*⟩ **4 a** : an historical period : AGE ⟨in your grandparents' *time*⟩ **b** : conditions of a specified period ⟨*times* are hard⟩ ⟨move with the *times*⟩ **5** : a prison sentence ⟨doing *time* for robbery⟩ **6** : the rhythmic grouping of beats in music shown in the time signature as a fraction (as ¾, ⁴⁄₄, or ⁶⁄₈) with the top number showing the number of beats in a measure and the bottom number showing the kind of note (as quarter note or eighth note) for each beat **7 a** : a moment, hour, day, or year as indicated by a clock or calendar ⟨what *time* is it⟩ **b** : a system of determining time **8 a** : one of a series of repeated instances or actions ⟨told you many *times*⟩ **b** *pl* : added or accumulated quantities or examples ⟨five *times* greater⟩ **c** *pl* : equal parts of which an indicated number make up a greater quantity ⟨five *times* smaller⟩ **d** : ²TURN 5b ⟨three *times* at bat⟩ **9** : a person's experience during a certain period ⟨had the *time* of their lives⟩ ⟨had quite a *time* staying in the saddle⟩ **10** : TIME-OUT ⟨called *time*⟩ — **at times** : now and then — **from time to time** : once in a while : OCCASIONALLY — **in no time** : in the shortest possible time — **in time 1** : early enough **2** : in the course of time : EVENTUALLY **3** : at the correct speed in music — **on time 1** : at the time set **2** : on an installment payment plan — **time after time** : over and over again — **time and again** : over and over again

²time *vb* **timed; tim·ing 1** : to arrange or set the time or rate at which something happens **2** : to measure or record the time, duration, or rate of ⟨*timed* the race⟩

time and a half *n* : payment of a worker (as for working overtime) at one and one half times the regular wage rate

time card *n* : a card used with a time clock to record an employee's starting and quitting times each day

time clock *n* : a clock that stamps an employee's starting and quitting times on his or her time card

time deposit *n* : a deposit in a bank that is to be paid after a specified time has gone by

time exposure *n* : a photograph taken by the exposure of film for a definite time usually of more than one half second

time–hon·ored \'tī-,män-ərd\ *adj* : being in use for a long time ⟨*time-honored* traditions⟩

time·keep·er \'tīm-,kē-pər\ *n* **1** : a clerk who keeps records of the time worked by employees **2** : an official who keeps track of the playing time in a sports contest

time lag *n* : the period of time between two related happenings (as a cause and its effect)

time·less \'tīm-ləs\ *adj* : not restricted to a certain time or date — **time·less·ly** *adv* — **time·less·ness** *n*

time·ly \'tīm-lē\ *adj* **time·li·er; -est 1** : coming early or at the right time **2** : especially suitable for the time ⟨a *timely* book⟩ — **time·li·ness** *n*

time machine *n* : a fictional machine that allows one to travel backward or forward in time

time–out \'tī-'maut\ *n* : a stopping of play (as in a game) usually for a short time

time·piece \'tīm-,pēs\ *n* : a device (as a clock or watch) to measure time

tim·er \'tī-mər\ *n* **1 a** : TIMEPIECE **b** : TIMEKEEPER 2 **2** : a clocklike device that turns something on or off at a set time or gives a signal at the end of a period of time

times \,tīmz\ *prep* : multiplied by ⟨two *times* seven is fourteen⟩

time·sav·ing \'tīm-,sā-viŋ\ *adj* : designed to get something done quicker — **time–sav·er** \-,sā-vər\ *n*

time–shar·ing \'tīm-,she(ə)r-iŋ, -,sha(ə)r-\ *n* : use of a computer system by many users at the same time

times sign \'tīm(z-)\ *n* : the symbol × used to indicate multiplication

time·ta·ble \'tīm-,tā-bəl\ *n* **1** : a table telling when a plane, bus, or train leaves or arrives **2** : a list showing the order in which something is planned to be done

time–test·ed \-,tes-təd\ *adj* : proven effective over a long period of time ⟨*time-tested* methods⟩

time zone *n* : a geographical region within which the same standard time is used

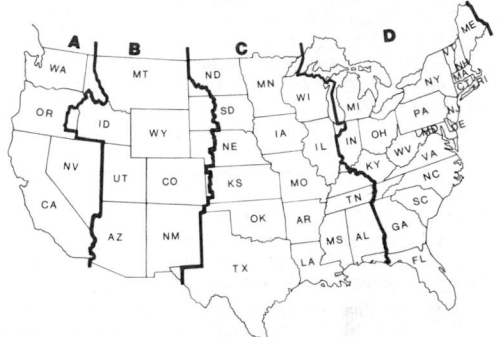

time zone: *A* Pacific time, *B* mountain time, *C* central time, *D* eastern time

tim·id \'tim-əd\ *adj* : feeling or showing a lack of courage or self-confidence : SHY — **ti·mid·i·ty** \tə-'mid-ət-ē\ *n* — **tim·id·ly** \'tim-əd-lē\ *adv* — **tim·id·ness** *n*

tim·ing \'tī-miŋ\ *n* **1** : selection for best effect of the exact moment for beginning or doing something **2** : observation and recording (as by a stopwatch) of the time taken by something

tim·o·rous \'tim-(ə-)rəs\ *adj* : easily frightened : FEARFUL — **tim·o·rous·ly** *adv* — **tim·o·rous·ness** *n*

tim·o·thy \'tim-ə-thē\ *n* : a grass that has long cylinder-shaped spikes and is widely grown in the U.S. for hay

Tim·o·thy \'tim-ə-thē\ *n* — see BIBLE table

tim·pa·ni *or* **tym·pa·ni** \'tim-pə-nē\ *n pl* : a set of two or three kettledrums played by one performer — **tim·pa·nist** \-nəst\ *n*

¹tin \'tin\ *n* **1** : a soft shiny bluish white metallic element that is used in combination with other metals, as a protective coating, and in tinfoil — see ELEMENT table **2 a** : a container made of metal (as tinplate) ⟨a pie *tin*⟩ **b** : a sealed can holding food — **tin** *adj*

²tin *vb* **tinned; tin·ning 1** : to cover or plate with tin or a mixture of tin with another metal **2** : to put up or pack in tins : CAN

tin can *n* : a container for food made of metal (as tinplate or aluminum)

tinc·ture \'tiŋ(k)-chər\ *n* **1** : a substance that colors, dyes, or stains **2** : a solution that contains a medical substance (as a drug) mixed with alcohol ⟨*tincture* of iodine⟩

tin·der \'tin-dər\ *n* : a material that burns easily and can be used as kindling

tin·der·box \-,bäks\ *n* **1** : a metal box for holding tinder and usually a flint and steel for striking a spark **2** : something that can easily catch fire

tine \'tīn\ *n* : a slender pointed part : PRONG ⟨the *tines* of a fork⟩

tin·foil \'tin-,fȯil\ *n* : a thin metal sheeting usually of aluminum or an alloy of tin and lead

¹tinge \'tinj\ *vb* **tinged; tinge·ing** *or* **ting·ing** \'tin-jin\ : to color or flavor slightly

²tinge *n* : a slight coloring, flavor, or quality ⟨a reddish *tinge*⟩ ⟨a tinge of mystery⟩

tin·gle \'tin-gəl\ *vb* **tin·gled; tin·gling** \'tin-g(ə-)lin\ : to feel or cause a prickling or thrilling sensation — **tingle** *n* — **tin·gly** \-g(ə-)lē\ *adj*

¹tin·ker \'tin-kər\ *n* : a person who travels around and earns a living by repairing household utensils (as pots and pans)

²tinker *vb* **tin·kered; tin·ker·ing** \'tin-k(ə-)rin\ : to repair or adjust something in an unskilled or experimental manner — **tin·ker·er** \-kər-ər\ *n*

tin·kle \'tin-kəl\ *vb* **tin·kled; tin·kling** \-k(ə-)lin\ : to make or cause to make a series of short high ringing or clinking sounds — **tinkle** *n*

tin liz·zie \-'liz-ē\ *n, often cap T & L* : a small cheap usually old automobile

tin·ny \'tin-ē\ *adj* **tin·ni·er; -est** : resembling or suggesting tin

tin·plate \'tin-'plāt\ *n* : thin sheet iron or steel coated with tin — **tin–plate** *vb*

tin·sel \'tin(t)-səl\ *n* **1** : a thread, strip, or sheet of metal, paper, or plastic used to produce a glittering effect **2** : something that seems attractive but is of little worth

tin·smith \'tin-,smith\ *n* : a worker in tin or sometimes other metals

¹tint \'tint\ *n* **1 a** : a slight or pale coloring **b** : any of various shades of a color **2** : a variation of a color made by adding white to it

²tint *vb* : to give or apply a tint or color to ⟨*tinted* glasses⟩

tin·tin·nab·u·la·tion \,tin-tə-,nab-yə-'lā-shən\ *n* : the ringing of bells or a similar sound

tin·type \-,tīp\ *n* : an early photograph consisting of a positive image taken directly on a thin iron plate having a darkened surface

tin·ware \'tin-,wa(ə)r, -,we(ə)r\ *n* : objects made of tinplate

ti·ny \'tī-nē\ *adj* **ti·ni·er; -est** : very small : MINUTE — **ti·ni·ness** *n*

¹tip \'tip\ *vb* **tipped; tip·ping** **1** : TURN OVER 1a ⟨*tipped* over a glass⟩ **2** : to bend from a straight position : SLANT ⟨the bench *tips* on the uneven floor⟩ **3** : to raise and tilt forward ⟨*tipped* his hat⟩ [Middle English *tipen* "to upset, overturn"]

²tip *n* : the act or an instance of tipping ⟨a *tip* of the hat⟩

³tip *n* **1** : the pointed or rounded end of something **2** : a small piece or part serving as an end, cap, or point [Middle English *tip* "a pointed end"] — **tipped** \'tipt\ *adj*

⁴tip *vb* **tipped; tip·ping** **1** : to attach a tip to **2** : to cover or decorate the tip of

⁵tip *n* : a light touch or blow : TAP [Middle English *tippe* "a light touch or blow"]

⁶tip *vb* **tipped; tip·ping** : to hit a baseball so that it glances off the bat

⁷tip *n* : a piece of useful or secret information given ⟨got a *tip* on how to prepare for the test⟩ [origin unknown]

⁸tip *vb* **tipped; tip·ping** : to give useful or secret information to ⟨someone must have *tipped* them off⟩

⁹tip *vb* **tipped; tip·ping** : to give a tip to ⟨*tip* the waiter⟩ [probably derived from earlier *tip* (verb) "to strike lightly"]

¹⁰tip *n* : a small sum of money given for a service

tipi *variant of* TEPEE

tip–off \'tip-,ȯf\ *n* : a warning that something is going to happen

tip·per \'tip-ər\ *n* : one that tips

tip·pet \'tip-ət\ *n* **1** : a long hanging part of a garment (as on a sleeve or cape) **2** : a shoulder cape usually with

hanging ends

tip·ple \'tip-əl\ *vb* **tip·pled; tip·pling** \-(ə-)lin\ : to drink liquor especially by habit — **tip·pler** \-(ə-)lər\ *n*

tip·sy \'tip-sē\ *adj* **tip·si·er; -est** : unsteady or foolish from drinking

¹tip·toe \'tip-,tō, -'tō\ *n* **1** : the tip of a toe **2** : the ends of the toes

²tiptoe *adv or adj* : on or as if on tiptoe

³tiptoe *vb* **tip·toed; tip·toe·ing** : to walk on tiptoe

¹tip–top \'tip-'täp, -,täp\ *n* : the highest point

²tip–top *adj* : very good : EXCELLENT ⟨in *tip-top* shape⟩ — **tip–top** *adv*

ti·rade \tī-'rād, 'tī-,rād\ *n* : a long violent angry speech : HARANGUE

¹tire \'tī(ə)r\ *vb* **tired; tir·ing** **1** : to become weary **2** : to decrease greatly or completely the physical strength of **3** : to wear out the patience or attention of : BORE

syn TIRE, WEARY, FATIGUE, EXHAUST mean to make someone unwilling or unable to continue doing something. TIRE suggests a loss of strength or patience ⟨all that lifting really *tired* me⟩ WEARY suggests that one has reached a point where one cannot put up with something any more ⟨I'm *wearied* by these endless complaints⟩ FATIGUE suggests very great tiredness brought about by much effort or strain ⟨the long climb up the mountain greatly *fatigued* her⟩ EXHAUST suggests that one's energy of mind or body has been all used up ⟨the race had *exhausted* him and he fell asleep at once⟩

²tire *n* **1** : a metal hoop that forms the tread of a wheel **2** : a rubber cushion that usually contains compressed air and fits around a wheel ⟨automobile *tires*⟩

¹tired \'tī(ə)rd\ *adj* **1** : ¹WEARY 1 **2** : used over and over again ⟨the same *tired* old excuse⟩ — **tired·ly** *adv* — **tired·ness** *n*

²tired *adj* : having tires

tire·less \'tī(ə)r-ləs\ *adj* : seeming never to get tired — **tire·less·ly** *adv*

tire·some \'tī(ə)r-səm\ *adj* : likely to tire one because of length or dullness : BORING — **tire·some·ly** *adv*

'tis \'tiz, (,)tiz\ : it is

tis·sue \'tish-ü\ *n* **1** : a fine lightweight fabric **2** : a piece of soft absorbent paper **3** : a mass or layer of cells usually of one kind together with the uniting or enclosing substance around and between that form the basic structural materials of a plant or an animal — compare ORGAN 2, CONNECTIVE TISSUE, PARENCHYMA

tissue paper *n* : a thin paper used especially to wrap delicate articles

¹tit \'tit\ *n* : TEAT

²tit *n* **1** : TITMOUSE **2** : any of various small plump often long-tailed birds

ti·tan \'tīt-ⁿn\ *n* **1** *cap* : one of a family of giants overthrown by the gods of ancient Greece **2** : one of gigantic size, power, or achievement

ti·tan·ic \tī-'tan-ik\ *adj* : enormous in size, force, or power : GIGANTIC

ti·ta·ni·um \tī-'tān-ē-əm, tə-\ *n* : a silvery gray light strong metallic element found combined in various minerals and used in combination with other metals (as in steel) — see ELEMENT table

titbit *variant of* TIDBIT

¹tithe \'tīth\ *vb* **tithed; thith·ing** : to pay or give a tithe [Old English *teogothian* "to give a tenth part", from *teogotha* "tenth"] — **tith·er** *n*

²tithe *n* : a tenth part (as of one's income) given especially as a contribution to a church

tit·il·late \'tit-ⁿl-,āt\ *vb* **-lat·ed; -lat·ing** **1** : TICKLE 3 **2** : to excite pleasurably — **tit·il·la·tion** \,tit-ⁿl-'ā-shən\ *n*

¹ti·tle \'tīt-ⁿl\ *n* **1 a** : a legal right to the ownership of property **b** : the document that is evidence of a right **2** : the name given to something (as a book, song, or job) to identify or describe it **3** : a word or group of words attached

to a person's name to show honor, rank, or office **4**
: CHAMPIONSHIP 2 ⟨won the batting *title*⟩
²**title** *vb* **ti·tled; ti·tling** \'tīt-liŋ, -ᵊl-iŋ\ : to call by a title
ti·tled \'tīt-ᵊld\ *adj* : having a title especially of nobility
title page *n* : a page of a book bearing the title
tit·mouse \'tit-ˌmaüs\ *n, pl* **tit·mice** \-ˌmīs\ : any of numerous small birds that eat insects, are found in trees, and are related to the nuthatches but have longer tails
ti·tra·tion \tī-'trā-shən\ *n* : the process of finding out the strength of a liquid mixture (as of an acid in water) by dripping another mixture (as of a base) of known strength into a known amount of the first mixture with usually another substance that will change color and measuring the amount of the second mixture required to make the first mixture change color
tit·ter \'tit-ər\ *vb* : to laugh in a nervous manner or while trying to hold the laugh back — **titter** *n*
tit·tle \'tit-ᵊl\ *n* **1** : a point or small sign (as the dot over an *i*) in writing or printing **2** : a very small part
tit·u·lar \'tich-(ə-)lər\ *adj* : being something in title only : NOMINAL ⟨the *titular* head of a nation⟩ — **tit·u·lar·ly** *adv*
Ti·tus \'tīt-əs\ *n* — see BIBLE table
tiz·zy \'tiz-ē\ *n, pl* **tizzies** : a very excited and mixed-up state of mind
TNT \ˌtē-ˌen-'tē\ *n* : a flammable poisonous compound used as a high explosive
¹**to** \tə, tü, (')tü\ *prep* **1 a** — used to indicate movement or something suggesting movement toward a place, person, or thing reached ⟨walked *to* school⟩ ⟨send data *to* disk storage⟩ ⟨went back *to* my first idea⟩ **b** — used to indicate direction ⟨a mile *to* the south⟩ ⟨your back *to* the window⟩ **c** — used to indicate contact ⟨apply polish *to* the table⟩ **d** — used to indicate a limit ⟨stripped *to* the waist⟩ **2** — used to indicate purpose, result, or end ⟨came *to* our aid⟩ ⟨broke *to* pieces⟩ ⟨sentenced *to* death⟩ **3 a** : ²BEFORE 3 ⟨at quarter *to* five⟩ **b** : ¹UNTIL ⟨from nine *to* five⟩ **4** — used to indicate belonging, accompanying, or responding ⟨the key *to* the lock⟩ ⟨dance *to* live music⟩ ⟨not much you could say *to* that⟩ **5 a** — used to indicate a relation of likeness or unlikeness ⟨similar *to* mine⟩ **b** — used to indicate agreement ⟨salt *to* taste⟩ **c** — used to indicate a proportion in terms of number or amount ⟨packed 10 *to* the box⟩ **6 a** — used to indicate the relation of adjective to noun ⟨agreeable *to* all of us⟩ or verb to complement ⟨sticks *to* business⟩ **b** — used to indicate one that receives an action ⟨spoke *to* the teacher⟩ ⟨give it *to* me⟩ **7** : for no one but ⟨had the house *to* ourselves⟩ **8** — used to mark an infinitive ⟨likes *to* swim⟩ and often used by itself in place of an infinitive ⟨I didn't mean *to*⟩
²**to** \'tü\ *adv* **1** : in the direction toward ⟨run *to* and fro⟩ **2** : into contact especially with a frame ⟨snapped her purse *to*⟩ ⟨wind blew the door *to*⟩ **3** : to a state of consciousness or awareness ⟨brings him *to* with smelling salts⟩

toad \'tōd\ *n* : any of numerous tailless leaping amphibians that as compared with the related frogs live mostly on land though they lay their eggs in water, are shorter and thicker in build, have weaker hind limbs, and have rough, dry, and warty skin rather than skin that is smooth and moist

toad

toad·stool \-ˌstül\ *n* : a fungus that has an umbrella-shaped cap : MUSHROOM; *esp* : one that is poisonous or unfit for food
¹**toady** \'tōd-ē\ *n, pl* **toad·ies** : a person who flatters another in the hope of receiving favors
²**toady** *vb* **toad·ied; toady·ing** : to behave like a toady — **toady·ism** \-ē-ˌiz-əm\ *n*

to–and–fro \ˌtü-ən-'frō\ *adj* : forward and backward
¹**toast** \'tōst\ *vb* **1** : to make crisp, hot, and brown by heat ⟨*toast* bread⟩ **2** : to warm completely
²**toast** *n* **1** : sliced toasted bread **2 a** : a person in whose honor other people drink **b** : a highly admired person ⟨the *toast* of the town⟩ **3** : an act of drinking in honor of a person
³**toast** *vb* : to suggest or drink to as a toast
toast·er \'tō-stər\ *n* : an electrical appliance for toasting
toaster oven *n* : an electrical kitchen appliance that bakes, broils, and toasts and that fits on a countertop
toasty \'tō-stē\ *adj* **toast·i·er; -est** : comfortably warm
to·bac·co \tə-'bak-ō\ *n, pl* **-cos** **1** : any of a genus of chiefly American plants of the nightshade family that have sticky leaves and tube-shaped flowers; *esp* : a tall upright South American herb with pink or white flowers that is grown for its leaves **2** : the leaves of cultivated tobacco prepared for use in smoking or chewing or as snuff

tobacco 1

tobacco mosaic *n* : any of a group of virus diseases of tobacco and related plants
To·bi·as \tə-'bī-əs\ *n* — see BIBLE table
To·bit \'tō-bət\ *n* — see BIBLE table
¹**to·bog·gan** \tə-'bäg-ən\ *n* : a long light sled made without runners and curved up at the front
²**toboggan** *vb* : to slide on a toboggan
to·coph·er·ol \tō-'käf-ə-ˌról, -ˌrōl\ *n* : VITAMIN E
toc·sin \'täk-sən\ *n* **1** : an alarm bell or the ringing of it **2** : a warning signal
¹**to·day** \tə-'dā\ *adv* **1** : on or for this day **2** : at the present time : NOWADAYS
²**today** *n* : the present day, time, or age
tod·dle \'täd-ᵊl\ *vb* **tod·dled; tod·dling** \'täd-liŋ, -ᵊl-iŋ\ : to walk with short unsteady steps like a young child — **toddle** *n*
tod·dler \'täd-lər, -ᵊl-ər\ *n* : a young child — **tod·dler·hood** \-ˌhúd\ *n*
to–do \tə-'dü\ *n, pl* **to–dos** \-'düz\ : ¹FUSS, STIR, COMMOTION
¹**toe** \'tō\ *n* **1 a** : one of the jointed parts of the front end of a vertebrate foot **b** : the front end or part of a foot or hoof **c** : the front end or part of something worn on the foot **2** : something that resembles a toe
²**toe** *vb* **toed; toe·ing** : to touch, reach, or kick with the toes
toed \'tōd\ *adj* : having a toe or toes especially of a specified kind or number ⟨five-*toed*⟩ ⟨round-*toed* shoes⟩
toe·hold \'tō-ˌhōld\ *n* : a hold or support for the toes (as in climbing)
toe·nail \-ˌnāl, -'nā(ə)l\ *n* : a nail of a toe
tof·fee *or* **tof·fy** \'tó-fē, 'täf-ē\ *n, pl* **tof·fees** *or* **toffies** : candy made by boiling sugar and butter together
to·ga \'tō-gə\ *n* : the loose outer garment worn in public by citizens of ancient Rome

toga

\ə\ abut	\aú\ out	\i\ tip	\ó\ saw	\ú\ foot
\ər\ further	\ch\ chin	\ī\ life	\ói\ coin	\y\ yet
\a\ mat	\e\ pet	\j\ job	\th\ thin	\yü\ few
\ā\ take	\ē\ easy	\ŋ\ sing	\th\ this	\yú\ cure
\ä\ cot, cart	\g\ go	\ō\ bone	\ü\ food	\zh\ vision

to·geth·er \tə-'geth-ər\ adv **1** : in or into one group, body, or place ⟨gathered *together*⟩ **2** : in touch or in partnership with each other ⟨in business *together*⟩ ⟨the doors banged *together*⟩ **3 a** : at one time ⟨they all cheered *together*⟩ **b** : one after the other : in order ⟨work for hours *together*⟩ **4 a** : in or by combined effort ⟨worked *together* to clear the road⟩ **b** : in or into agreement ⟨get *together* on a plan⟩ **c** : in or into an organized or orderly arrangement ⟨pull yourself *together*⟩ **5 a** : to each other ⟨add the numbers *together*⟩ **b** : considered as a whole ⟨all *together* there were 15 of us⟩ — **to·geth·er·ness** n

tog·gle \'täg-əl\ n : a crosspiece attached to the end of or to a loop in a rope, chain, or belt to prevent slipping or to serve as a fastening or as a grip for tightening ⟨used a stick as a *toggle* in tightening a rope⟩

toggle bolt n : a bolt that has a nut with wings that close for passage through a small hole and spring open after passing through the hole to keep the bolt from slipping back through

toggle switch n : an electric switch operated by pushing a lever through a small angle

togs \'tägz, 'tȯgz\ n pl : CLOTHING 1; *esp* : a set of clothes and accessories for a specified use ⟨riding *togs*⟩ ⟨skiing *togs*⟩

¹**toil** \'tȯi(ə)l\ n : long hard labor

Word History Even though we have machines to do much of our hard work today, much long, hard toil must still be done by hand. Our Modern English word *toil*, however, comes from a Latin word for a laborsaving machine. The ancient Romans built a machine for crushing olives to produce olive oil. This machine was called a *tudicula*. This Latin word was formed from the word *tudes*, meaning "hammer", because the machine had little hammers to crush the olives. From this came the Latin verb *tudiculare*, meaning "to crush or grind". Early French used this Latin verb as the basis for its verb, spelled *tooiller* or *toeillier*, which meant "to crush, stir, disturb, dispute". From this came the noun *tooil* or *toeil*, meaning "battle, disturbance, confusion". This early French noun in time was taken into Middle English as *toile*, meaning "argument, battle". The earliest sense of our Modern English *toil* was "a long, hard struggle in battle". It is natural enough that in time this came to be used to refer to any long hard effort. [Middle English *toile* "battle, argument", derived from early French *tooil*, *toeil* "battle, disturbance, confusion", from *tooiller*, *toeillier* (verb) "crush, disturb, stir", from Latin *tudiculare* "crush, grind", from *tudicula* "machine with hammers for beating olives", from *tudes* "hammer"]

²**toil** vb **1** : to work hard and long **2** : to go on with effort ⟨*toiling* up a steep hill⟩ **syn** see WORK — **toil·er** n

toi·let \'tȯi-lət\ n **1** : the act or process of dressing and making oneself neat **2 a** : BATHROOM **b** : a fixture for removing body wastes that consists essentially of a bowl that is flushed with water

toilet paper n : a thin soft sanitary absorbent paper for bathroom use

toi·let·ry \'tȯi-lə-trē\ n, pl **-ries** : something (as a soap, lotion, cosmetic, or cologne) used in grooming oneself

toilet water n : a scented liquid (as cologne) for use especially after bathing

toil·some \'tȯi(ə)l-səm\ adj : requiring much effort

to·ken \'tō-kən\ n **1** : an outward sign **2** : something (as an act, gesture, or object) that serves as a sign or symbol **3 a** : SOUVENIR **b** : INDICATION 2 **4** : a piece resembling a coin that has a special use ⟨a bus *token*⟩ **syn** see EMBLEM — **by the same token** : for the same reason

told past and past participle of TELL

tol·er·able \'täl-(ə-)rə-bəl, 'täl-ər-bəl\ adj **1** : capable of being put up with **2** : fairly good — **tol·er·ably** \-blē\ adv

tol·er·ance \'täl-(ə-)rən(t)s\ n **1 a** : ability to put up with something harmful or unpleasant **b** : the ability to adjust to a food or drug so that its effects are experienced less strongly **2** : sympathy for or acceptance of feelings, habits, or beliefs that are different from one's own

tol·er·ant \'täl-(ə-)rənt\ adj : showing tolerance — **tol·er·ant·ly** adv

tol·er·ate \'täl-ə-,rāt\ vb **-at·ed; -at·ing** **1** : to allow something to be or be done without making a move to stop it : put up with **2** : to withstand the action of ⟨plants that *tolerate* drought⟩ ⟨*tolerate* a drug⟩ — **tol·er·a·tion** \,täl-ə-'rā-shən\ n

¹**toll** \'tōl\ n **1** : a tax paid for a privilege (as the use of a highway or bridge) **2** : a charge paid for a service **3** : the cost in life or health [Middle English *toll* "a tax or fee paid to be allowed to do something", from early French *toll* (same meaning), derived from Latin *telonium* "a house where duties on imports are paid and ships' cargoes are checked", derived from Greek *telos* "tax, toll"]

²**toll** vb **1** : to announce or call by the sounding of a bell **2** : to sound with slow strokes [Middle English *tollen* "to announce or call by sounding a bell", probably from earlier *tollen* "to attract, arouse desire in"]

³**toll** n : the sound of a tolling bell

toll·booth \'tōl-,büth\ n : a booth where tolls are paid

toll bridge n : a bridge at which a toll is charged for crossing

toll call n : a long-distance telephone call

toll·gate \'tōl-,gāt\ n : a point where vehicles stop to pay a toll

toll·house \-,haús\ n : a house or booth where tolls are collected

tom \'täm\ n : the male of various animals; *esp* : TOMCAT

tom·a·hawk \'täm-i-,hȯk\ n : a light ax used as a weapon by North American Indians — **tomahawk** vb

to·ma·to \tə-'māt-ō *also* -'mät-\ n, pl **-toes** **1** : the usually large rounded and red or yellow pulpy berry of a tomato **2** : any of a genus of South American herbs of the nightshade family; *esp* : one widely grown for its edible fruit [derived from Spanish *tomate* "tomato", from the name for this plant in the ancient language of the Aztecs]

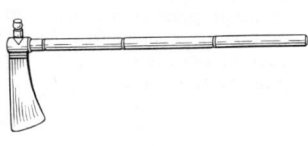

tomahawk

tomb \'tüm\ n **1** : ²GRAVE 1 **2** : a house or burial chamber for dead people

tom·boy \'täm-,bȯi\ n : a girl who enjoys things some people think are more suited to boys — **tom·boy·ish** \-ish\ adj — **tom·boy·ish·ness** n

tomb·stone \'tüm-,stōn\ n : GRAVESTONE

tom·cat \'täm-,kat\ n : a male cat

tome \'tōm\ n : a big thick book

tom·fool·ery \täm-'fül-(ə-)rē\ n : playful or foolish behavior : NONSENSE, MONKEYSHINES

tom·my gun \'täm-ē-,gən\ n : SUBMACHINE GUN

to·mo·gram \'tō-mə-,gram\ n : an X-ray photograph of a section of the body in which the shadows of structures in front of and behind the section under study do not show

¹**to·mor·row** \tə-'mär-ō, -'mȯr-\ adv : on or for the day after today

²**tomorrow** n : the day after today

tom–tom \'täm-,täm, 'təm-,təm\ n : a usually long and narrow drum beaten with the hands

ton \'tən\ n, pl **tons** *also* **ton** **1** — see MEASURE table **2** : METRIC TON

ton·al \'tōn-°l\ adj : of or relating to a musical tone — **ton·al·ly** \-°l-ē\ adv

to·nai·i·ty \tō-'nal-ət-ē\ n, pl **-ties** : the quality of a piece of music of being based on a particular keynote

¹tone \'tōn\ *n* **1 a** : a musical sound having a definite pitch : the sound of a note **b** : WHOLE STEP **2** : accent or pitch of the voice especially when used to express an emotion or a change in meaning ⟨spoke in a sharp *tone*⟩ **3** : style or manner of expression ⟨reply in a friendly *tone*⟩ ⟨the author's *tone* shows his or her attitude toward the subject⟩ **4 a** : a shade of color ⟨decorated in soft *tones*⟩ **b** : a color that changes another ⟨gray with a blue *tone*⟩ **5 a** : a healthy state of the body or any of its parts **b** : normal tension or ability to respond to stimuli; *esp* : the state of normal tension of a muscle in which it is partly contracted **6** : common character or quality [Middle English *tone* "a musical sound, a sound from the voice", from Latin *tonus* "tension, tone, pitch", from Greek *tonos* "act of stretching, tension, tone, pitch"; so called because the pitch of the tone of a stringed musical instrument is related to how tightly the strings are stretched]

²tone *vb* **toned; ton·ing** **1** : to give tone to : STRENGTHEN ⟨vitamins to *tone* up the system⟩ **2** : to soften in color, appearance, or sound — often used with *down*

tone–deaf \'tōn-,def\ *adj* : not noticing small differences in musical pitch

tone language *n* : a language (as Chinese) in which changes in tone of words that otherwise sound alike indicate different meanings

tongs \'täŋz, 'tȯŋz\ *n pl* : a device for taking hold of something that consists usually of two movable pieces joined at one end

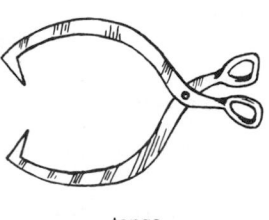

tongs

¹tongue \'təŋ\ *n* **1** : a fleshy movable process of the floor of the mouth of most vertebrates that has sensory organs (as taste buds) and small glands and functions especially in taking and swallowing food and in human beings as a speech organ **2** : the flesh of a tongue (as of beef) used as food **3** : the power of communication : SPEECH **4** : LANGUAGE 1a **5** : something resembling a tongue (as in being long and fastened at one end) — **tongue·less** \-ləs\ *adj* — **tongue·like** \-,līk\ *adj*

²tongue *vb* **tongued; tongu·ing** \'təŋ-iŋ\ **1** : to touch or lick with or as if with the tongue **2** : to separate individual notes when playing a musical instrument by using the tongue

tongue–in–cheek *adj* : not meant to be taken seriously

tongue in cheek *adv* : in a tongue-in-cheek manner

tongue–lash·ing \'təŋ-,lash-iŋ\ *n* : a severe scolding

tongue roller *n* : a person who can roll the tongue into the shape of a U due to the presence of a dominant gene

tongue–tied \-,tīd\ *adj* : unable to speak clearly or freely (as from shyness)

tongue twister *n* : a word, phrase, or sentence that is hard to say because of a series of similar consonant sounds (as in "twin-screw steel cruiser" or "rubber baby-buggy bumpers")

¹ton·ic \'tän-ik\ *adj* **1** : making (as the mind or body) stronger or healthier **2** : relating to or based on the first tone of a scale ⟨*tonic* chord⟩ ⟨*tonic* harmony⟩

²tonic *n* **1 a** : a tonic medicine **b** : a liquid to be used on the hair or scalp **c** *chiefly New England* : SODA POP **d** : TONIC WATER **2** : the first tone of a scale

tonic water *n* : a carbonated beverage flavored with a small amount of quinine, lemon, and lime

¹to·night \tə-'nīt\ *adv* : on this present night or the night following this present day

²tonight *n* : the present or the coming night

ton·nage \'tən-ij\ *n* **1** : a tax on ships based on tons carried **2** : ships in terms of the total number of tons that are or can be carried **3** : total weight in tons shipped, carried, or mined

ton·sil \'tän(t)-səl\ *n* : either of a pair of oval-shaped masses of spongy tissue that lie one on each side of the throat at the back of the mouth

ton·sil·lec·to·my \,tän(t)-sə-'lek-tə-mē\ *n, pl* **-mies** : the surgical removal of the tonsils

ton·sil·li·tis \,tän(t)-sə-'līt-əs\ *n* : inflammation of the tonsils

ton·sure \'tän-chər\ *n* : a haircut with the top of the head shaved worn especially by monks [Middle English *tonsure* "the act of shaving a part of the top of the head", derived from Latin *tonsura* "the act of shearing", from *tonsus*, past participle of *tondēre* "to shear"] — **ton·sured** \-chərd\ *adj*

too \(')tü\ *adv* **1** : in addition : ALSO ⟨sell the house and the furniture *too*⟩ **2** : to a degree greater than wanted or needed ⟨the soup is *too* hot⟩ ⟨this has gone on *too* long⟩ **3** : ²VERY 1 ⟨the climb was not *too* hard⟩

took *past of* TAKE

¹tool \'tül\ *n* **1** : a device (as a hammer, saw, knife, or wrench) used or worked by hand or by a machine **2 a** : something used in doing one's job as if it were a tool **b** : something that helps to gain an end **3** : a person used by another : DUPE **syn** see IMPLEMENT

²tool *vb* **1** : to shape, form, or finish with a tool **2** : to equip a plant or industry with machines and tools for production

tool·box \'tül-,bäks\ *n* : a chest to store tools in

tool·mak·er \-,mā-kər\ *n* : one (as an animal or a human being) that makes tools — **tool·mak·ing** \-kiŋ\ *n*

tool·shed \-,shed\ *n* : a small building to store tools in

¹toot \'tüt\ *vb* **1** : to sound a short blast ⟨a horn *tooted*⟩ **2** : to blow or sound an instrument (as a horn) especially in short blasts ⟨*toot* a whistle⟩ — **toot·er** *n*

²toot *n* : a short blast (as on a horn)

tooth \'tüth\ *n, pl* **teeth** \'tēth\ **1 a** : one of the hard bony structures that are usually located on the jaws of vertebrates and are used for seizing and chewing food and as weapons **b** : any of various usually hard and sharp structures especially around the mouth of an invertebrate **2 a** : something like or suggesting the tooth of an animal in shape, arrangement, or action ⟨the *tooth* of a saw⟩ **b** : one of the projections on the rim of a cogwheel that fit between the projections on another part especially to transmit force : COG — **tooth·less** \'tüth-ləs\ *adj* — **tooth·like** \-,līk\ *adj*

tooth·ache \'tü-,thāk\ *n* : pain in or near a tooth

tooth and nail *adv* : as hard as one can ⟨fighting *tooth and nail*⟩

tooth·brush \'tüth-,brəsh\ *n* : a brush for cleaning the teeth

toothed \'tütht\ *adj* **1** : having teeth especially of a specified kind or number **2** : JAGGED, NOTCHED

toothed whale *n* : any of a group of whales, dolphins, and porpoises with numerous sharp cone-shaped teeth — compare WHALEBONE WHALE

tooth·paste \'tüth-,pāst\ *n* : a paste for cleaning the teeth

tooth·pick \-,pik\ *n* : a pointed instrument for removing substances caught between the teeth

tooth powder *n* : a powder for cleaning the teeth

tooth·some \'tüth-səm\ *adj* : pleasing to the taste : DELICIOUS ⟨*toothsome* pies⟩

toothy \'tü-thē\ *adj* **tooth·i·er; -est** : having or showing many usually large teeth ⟨a *toothy* grin⟩ — **tooth·i·ly** \-thə-lē\ *adv*

\ə\ abut	\au̇\ out	\i\ tip	\ȯ\ saw	\u̇\ foot
\ər\ further	\ch\ chin	\ī\ life	\ȯi\ coin	\y\ yet
\a\ mat	\e\ pet	\j\ job	\th\ thin	\yü\ few
\ā\ take	\ē\ easy	\ŋ\ sing	\t͟h\ this	\yu̇\ cure
\ä\ cot, cart	\g\ go	\ō\ bone	\ü\ food	\zh\ vision

¹**top** \'täp\ *n* **1 a** : the highest point, level, or part of something ⟨the *top* of the hill⟩ ⟨sang at the *top* of her voice⟩ **b** : the upper end, edge, or surface ⟨the *top* of the page⟩ ⟨filled the glass to the *top*⟩ **c** : the stalk and leaves of a plant and especially one with edible roots ⟨beet *tops*⟩ **2** : an upper piece, lid, or covering ⟨blouses, shirts, and *tops*⟩ ⟨put the *top* on the jar⟩ **3** : the highest position ⟨reached the *top* of the profession⟩ [Old English *top* "highest point"] — **topped** \'täpt\ *adj* — **on top of** : in addition to

²**top** *vb* **topped; top·ping** **1** : to remove or cut the top of ⟨*top* a tree⟩ **2** : to cover with a top or on the top ⟨*topped* the sundae with nuts⟩ **3** : to be better than **4** : to go over the top of **5** : to hit the top part of ⟨*top* a golf ball⟩

³**top** *adj* : of, relating to, or being at the top

⁴**top** *n* : a child's toy that has a point on which it can be made to spin [Old English *top* "a spinning toy"]

to·paz \'tō-,paz\ *n* : a mineral in the form of usually yellow to brownish yellow crystals that is valued as a gem

top·coat \'täp-,kōt\ *n* : a lightweight overcoat

top–dress \-,dres\ *vb* : to apply material to (as land or a road) without working it in; *esp* : to scatter fertilizer over ⟨land⟩

top·dress·ing \-,dres-iŋ\ *n* : a material used to top-dress soil

top·gal·lant \(')täp-'gal-ənt, tə-'gal-\ *n* **1** : a mast or sail next above the topmast or topsail **2** : the topmost point

top hat *n* : a man's hat with a tall crown

top–heavy \'täp-,hev-ē\ *adj* : having the top part too heavy for the lower part

top·ic \'täp-ik\ *n* **1** : a heading in an outline of a subject or explanation **2** : the subject or a section of a subject (as of a speech or a report)

top·i·cal \'täp-i-kəl\ *adj* **1** : designed to be applied to or to work on a specific place or part (as of the body) ⟨a *topical* medicine⟩ **2 a** : of or relating to topics ⟨*topical* outline⟩ **b** : referring to the topics of the day or place ⟨*topical* jokes⟩ — **top·i·cal·ly** \-k(ə-)lē\ *adv*

top hat

topic sentence *n* : a sentence that states the main thought of a paragraph

top·knot \'täp-,nät\ *n* : a tuft of feathers or hair on the top of the head

top·mast \-,mast, -məst\ *n* : the mast next above the lower mast

top·min·now \-,min-ō\ *n* : any of several small surface-feeding fishes

top·most \-,mōst\ *adj* : highest of all

top–notch \-'näch\ *adj* : of the highest quality : FIRST-RATE ⟨a *top-notch* performance⟩

to·po·graph·ic \,täp-ə-'graf-ik, ,tōp-ə-\ *or* **to·po·graph·i·cal** \-'graf-i-kəl\ *adj* : of, relating to, or showing topography ⟨a *topographic* map⟩ — **to·po·graph·i·cal·ly** \-k(ə-)lē\ *adv*

to·pog·ra·phy \tə-'päg-rə-fē\ *n* **1** : the art or practice of showing on maps or charts the heights and depths of the features of a place **2** : the shape and height and depth of the features of a place

to·pol·o·gy \tə-'päl-ə-jē, tō-\ *n* : a branch of mathematics concerned with the properties of geometric figures that do not change when the figure is twisted or stretched in a continuous way without breaking — **to·po·log·i·cal** \,täp-ə-'läj-i-kəl, ,tōp-\ *adj*

top·per \'täp-ər\ *n* **1** : one that tops **2** : TOP HAT

top·ping \'täp-iŋ\ *n* : a food served on top of another to make it look or taste better

top·ple \'täp-əl\ *vb* **top·pled; top·pling** \-(ə-)liŋ\ **1** : to fall over from being too heavy at the top **2** : to push over

top·sail \'täp-,sāl, -səl\ *also* **top·s'l** \-səl\ *n* **1** : the sail next above the lowermost sail on a mast in a square-rigged ship **2** : the sail set above and sometimes on the gaff in a fore-and-aft rigged ship

top–secret *adj* : containing information that is very important to the safety and defense of a nation

top·side \'täp-'sīd\ *adv* : on or onto the deck of a ship

T topsail 2

top·soil \-,sȯil\ *n* : surface soil usually including the rich upper layer in which plants have most of their roots and which the farmer turns over in plowing

top·spin \-,spin\ *n* : a forward spinning motion of a ball

top·stitch \-,stich\ *vb* : to make a line of stitches on the outside of a garment near a seam

top·sy–tur·vy \,täp-sē-'tər-vē\ *adv* : UPSIDE DOWN — **topsy–turvy** *adj*

toque \'tōk\ *n* : a woman's small hat usually without a brim

tor \'tȯ(ə)r\ *n* : a high rocky hill

To·rah \'tōr-ə, 'tȯr-; 'tȯi-rə\ *n* **1** : the wisdom and law contained in Jewish Scripture and other sacred writings and in oral tradition **2** : a scroll containing the first five books of the Old Testament used in a synagogue for religious services

toque

torch \'tȯ(ə)rch\ *n* **1** : a flaming light made of something that burns brightly and usually is carried in the hand **2** : something that guides or gives light or heat like a torch **3** : any of various portable devices for producing a hot flame — compare BLOWTORCH **4** *chiefly British* : FLASHLIGHT

torch·light \-,līt\ *n* : the light given by torches

tore *past of* ³TEAR

to·re·ador \'tȯr-ē-ə-,dȯ(ə)r, 'tōr-, 'tär-\ *n* : a person who fights bulls : a performer in a bullfight

to·re·ro \tə-'re(ə)r-ō\ *n, pl* **-ros** : TOREADOR

¹**tor·ment** \'tȯr-,ment\ *n* **1** : extreme pain or distress of body or mind **2** : a cause of suffering in mind or body

²**tor·ment** \tȯr-'ment, 'tȯr-,ment\ *vb* **1** : to cause severe suffering of body or mind to **2** : to cause worry, distress, or trouble to : HARASS — **tor·men·tor** \tȯr-'ment-ər, 'tȯr-,ment-\ *n*

torn *past participle of* ³TEAR

tor·na·do \tȯr-'nād-ō\ *n, pl* **-does** *or* **-dos** : a violent destructive whirling wind accompanied by a funnel-shaped cloud that moves in a narrow path over the land

¹**tor·pe·do** \tȯr-'pēd-ō\ *n, pl* **-does** **1** : a thin cylindrical self-propelled submarine weapon **2** : a small firework that explodes when thrown against a hard object

Word History The Latin verb *torpēre*, meaning "to be numb", gave rise to the noun *torpedo*, "numbness". This noun was borrowed into English in the 16th century to refer to a long round fish that gave a numbing electric shock to anyone who touched it. This fish was also called an electric ray, a crampfish, or a numbfish. In the early 19th century, the American inventor Robert Fulton developed a floating device that exploded when it touched a ship. He called this device a *torpedo* because it reminded him of the electric ray. Since then the torpedo has been modernized and is fired at its target. Although it still looks somewhat like the fish, its effects can certainly be more than numbing. [from Latin *torpedo*, literally "numbness", from *torpēre* "to be numb" — related to TORPID]

²torpedo *vb* **-doed; do·ing** \tȯr-ˈpēd-ə-wiŋ\ : to hit or sink with or as if with a torpedo

torpedo boat *n* : a small very fast boat for firing torpedoes

tor·pid \ˈtȯr-pəd\ *adj* **1** : having lost motion or the power of exertion or feeling ⟨a bear *torpid* in winter sleep⟩ **2** : having too little energy or strength [from Latin *torpidus* "having lost motion or power of moving or feeling, numb", from *torpēre* "to be numb" — related to TORPEDO; see *Word History* at TORPEDO]

tor·por \ˈtȯr-pər\ *n* **1** : the quality or state of being torpid **2** : a state marked by little or no mental or physical activity and by a total or partial loss of feeling ⟨the *torpor* of bears in winter⟩

tor·rent \ˈtȯr-ənt, ˈtär-\ *n* **1** : a rushing stream of a liquid ⟨a *torrent* of rain⟩ **2** : a mountain stream or its channel **3** : a sudden rush like a stream of liquid [from French *torrent* "a violent stream of liquid", from Latin *torrent-, torrens* (same meaning), from *torrens* (adjective) "burning, flowing with great force", derived from *torrēre* "to heat so as to dry up or burn" — related to TORRID; see *Word History* at TORRID]

tor·ren·tial \tȯ-ˈren-chəl, tə-\ *adj* : relating to or resembling a torrent ⟨*torrential* rains⟩ — **tor·ren·tial·ly** \-ˈrench-(ə-)lē\ *adv*

tor·rid \ˈtȯr-əd, ˈtär-\ *adj* : very hot and usually dry — **tor·rid·ly** *adv*

Word History The Latin verb *torrēre*, meaning "to heat so as to dry up or burn", gave rise to two quite different English words. They are *torrid* and *torrent*. The Latin adjective *torridus*, meaning "dried or burnt by heat", was formed from *torrēre*. It became our *torrid*. Another Latin adjective, *torrens*, meaning "scorching, burning", was also formed from *torrēre*. It, however, gained a second sense of "flowing with great force and speed, rushing". This second sense led to the use of *torrens* as a noun for "a rushing or violent stream". This noun was borrowed into English as *torrent*. It came to refer not only to rushing water, but also to any kind of outpouring, such as of words, information, sounds, or feelings. [from Latin *torridus* "dried or burnt by heat, torrid", derived from *torrēre* "to heat so as to dry up or burn" — related to TORRENT]

torrid zone *n* : the region of the earth between the tropic of Cancer and the tropic of Capricorn in which the sun is often almost directly overhead and which is usually hot all year long — compare FRIGID ZONE, TEMPERATE ZONE

tor·sion \ˈtȯr-shən\ *n* **1** : the act or process of turning or twisting **2** : the state of being twisted

torsion bar *n* : a long metal piece in an automobile suspension that has one end firmly attached to the frame and the other twisted and connected to the axle and that acts as a spring

tor·so \ˈtȯr-sō\ *n, pl* **torsos** *or* **tor·si** \-ˌsē\ : the human body except for the head, arms, and legs

torte \ˈtȯrt-ə, ˈtȯ(ə)rt\ *n, pl* **tortes** *or* **tor·ten** \ˈtȯrt-ᵊn\ : a rich cake

tor·ti·lla \tȯr-ˈtē-(y)ə\ *n* : a round thin cake of unleavened cornmeal or wheat flour bread [American Spanish, literally "little cake", from Spanish *torta* "cake"]

tor·toise \ˈtȯrt-əs\ *n* : ²TURTLE; *esp* : a land turtle

¹tor·toise·shell \ˈtȯrt-əs-ˌshel, -əsh-ˌshel\ *n* **1** : a spotted hornlike substance that covers the shell of some turtles and is used to make ornamental objects **2** : any of several showy butterflies

²tortoiseshell *adj* **1** : made of or resembling tortoiseshell especially in spotted brown and yellow coloring **2** : of,

relating to, or being a color pattern of the domestic cat that consists of patches of black, orange, and light yellow

tor·tu·ous \ˈtȯrch-(ə-)wəs\ *adj* : having many twists and turns — **tor·tu·ous·ly** *adv*

¹tor·ture \ˈtȯr-chər\ *n* **1** : distress of body or mind **2** : the causing of great pain especially to punish or to obtain a confession [from French *torture* "causing of intense pain or agony", from Latin *tortura* "act of twisting", from earlier *tortus,* past participle of *torquēre* "to twist" — related to DISTORT, EXTORT, RETORT]

²torture *vb* **tor·tured; tor·tur·ing** \ˈtȯrch-(ə-)riŋ\ **1** : to cause great suffering to **2** : to punish or force someone to do or say something by causing great pain — **tor·tur·er** \ˈtȯr-chər-ər\ *n*

tor·tur·ous \ˈtȯrch-(ə-)rəs\ *adj* : causing great pain — **tor·tur·ous·ly** *adv*

To·ry \ˈtȯr-ē, ˈtȯr-\ *n, pl* **Tories** **1** : ²CONSERVATIVE **2** : an American on the side of the British during the American Revolution — **Tory** *adj*

Word History In the 17th century, many of the Irish had their property taken from them by the English. Some of them lived by plundering English settlements and robbing English soldiers. Such an outlaw was called a *tōraidhe* in Gaelic, an early language of Ireland. This word literally meant "one who is pursued" and "robber". Later, this term was also applied to an armed Irish supporter of the Roman Catholic faith. In English the word was shortened to *Tory* and was used for a member of the conservative political party in England. Tories strongly supported the authority of the monarch. During the American Revolution, the term *Tory* was used for an American who supported British authority rather than independence. [from *tōraidhe,* a word in Irish Gaelic, the original language of Ireland, meaning "robber, pursued man"]

toss \ˈtȯs, ˈtäs\ *vb* **1** : to throw or swing to and fro or up and down ⟨waves *tossed* the ship about⟩ **2** : to throw with a quick light motion ⟨*toss* a ball into the air⟩ **3** : to lift with a sudden motion ⟨*toss* the head⟩ **4** : to be thrown about rapidly ⟨the river surged and *tossed*⟩ **5** : to move about restlessly **6** : to stir or mix lightly ⟨*toss* a salad⟩ **7** : to drink quickly **syn** see THROW — **toss** *n*

toss–up \-ˌəp\ *n* : something that offers no clear choice ⟨it's a *toss-up* who will win⟩

tos·ta·da \tō-ˈstäd-ə\ *n* : a fried tortilla [Mexican Spanish *tostada,* a feminine form of *tostado* "fried", from Spanish *tostado* "toasted"]

tot \ˈtät\ *n* : a small child

¹to·tal \ˈtōt-ᵊl\ *adj* **1** : of or relating to the whole of something ⟨a *total* eclipse of the sun⟩ **2** : making up the whole ⟨the *total* amount⟩ **3** : being such to the fullest degree ⟨*total* ruin⟩ **4** : making use of every means to do something ⟨*total* war⟩

²total *n* **1** : a product of addition : SUM **2** : an entire amount

³total *vb* **to·taled** *or* **to·talled; to·tal·ing** *or* **to·tal·ling** **1** : ADD **2** : to amount to ⟨donations *totaled* $120⟩ **3** : to make a total wreck of ⟨*totaled* the car⟩

to·tal·i·tar·i·an \(ˌ)tō-ˌtal-ə-ˈter-ē-ən\ *adj* : of or relating to a political system in which the government has complete control over the people — **to·tal·i·tar·i·an·ism** \-ē-ə-ˌniz-əm\ *n*

to·tal·i·ty \tō-ˈtal-ət-ē\ *n, pl* **-ties** **1** : a combined amount : SUM, WHOLE **2** : the quality or state of being total : ENTIRETY ⟨rejected the scheme in its *totality*⟩

to·tal·ly \ˈtōt-ᵊl-ē\ *adv* **1** : in a total manner : WHOLLY **2**

\ə\ abut	\au̇\ out	\i\ tip	\ȯ\ saw	\u̇\ foot
\ər\ further	\ch\ chin	\ī\ life	\ȯi\ coin	\y\ yet
\a\ mat	\e\ pet	\j\ job	\th\ thin	\yü\ few
\ā\ take	\ē\ easy	\ŋ\ sing	\th\ this	\yu̇\ cure
\ä\ cot, cart	\g\ go	\ō\ bone	\ü\ food	\zh\ vision

: as a whole

tote \\'tōt\\ *vb* **tot·ed; tot·ing** : to carry by hand — **tot·er** *n*

tote bag *n* : a large handbag

tote·board \\'tōt-ˌbō(ə)rd, -ˌbȯ(ə)rd\\ *n* : a scoreboard for a horse race

to·tem \\'tōt-əm\\ *n* **1** : an object (as an animal or plant) serving as the emblem of a family or clan **2** : something usually carved or painted to represent a totem — **to·tem·ic** \\tō-'tem-ik\\ *adj*

totem pole *n* : a pole carved and painted with symbols of totems that is set up before the houses of Indian tribes of the northwest coast of North America

tot·ter \\'tät-ər\\ *vb* **1 a** : to sway or rock as if about to fall **2** : to move unsteadily : STAGGER — **tot·tery** \\-ə-rē\\ *adj*

tou·can \\'tü-ˌkan, tü-'kan\\ *n* : any of a family of fruit-eating birds of tropical America with brilliant coloring and a very large beak

¹touch \\'təch\\ *vb* **1** : to feel or handle (as with fingers) especially so as to be aware of by the sense of touch **2 a** : to be or cause to be in contact with something **b** : to be or come next to **3** : to hit lightly **4 a** : to do harm to **b** : to make use of ⟨never *touches* meat⟩ **5** : to refer to in passing : MENTION **6** : to affect the interest of ⟨a matter that *touches* every parent⟩ **7** : to move emotionally ⟨*touched* by their friend's kindness⟩ — **touch·able** \\-ə-bəl\\ *adj* — **touch·er** *n*

²touch *n* **1** : a light stroke or tap **2** : the act or fact of touching or being touched **3 a** : the special sense by which one is aware of light pressure especially on the skin ⟨soft to the *touch*⟩ **b** : an impression gotten through the sense of touch ⟨the soft *touch* of silk⟩ **4** : a state of contact or communication ⟨keeping in *touch* with friends⟩ **5** : a small amount : TRACE ⟨a *touch* of garlic in the salad⟩

touch and go *adj* : not certain of having a good result

touch·back \\'təch-ˌbak\\ *n* : the act of downing a football behind the goal line after receiving a kick or intercepting a pass

touch·down \\'təch-ˌdaůn\\ *n* **1** : the act of touching a football to the ground behind an opponent's goal **2** : the act of scoring six points in American football by carrying the ball over the opponent's goal line

touch down \\(')təch-'daůn\\ *vb* : to reach the ground : LAND

touch·ing \\'təch-iŋ\\ *adj* : causing a feeling of tenderness or pity — **touch·ing·ly** *adv*

touch·line \\'təch-ˌlīn\\ *n* : either of the lines that mark the sides of the field of play in rugby and soccer

touch–me–not \\'təch-mē-ˌnät\\ *n* : IMPATIENS

touch off *vb* : to start by or as if by touching with fire ⟨the announcement *touched off* riots⟩

touch pad *n* : a keypad for an electronic device (as a microwave oven) that consists of a flat surface divided into several differently marked areas which are touched to choose options

touch·stone \\'təch-ˌstōn\\ *n* **1** : a black stone formerly used to test the purity of gold and silver by the streak left on the stone when rubbed by the metal **2** : a test for judging something

Touch–Tone \\-ˌtōn\\ *trademark* — used for a telephone having push buttons that produce tones corresponding to

totem pole

toucan

numbers

touch–up \\'təch-ˌəp\\ *n* : an act or instance of touching up

touch up \\(')təch-'əp\\ *vb* : to improve by or as if by small changes : fix the little imperfections of

touchy \\'təch-ē\\ *adj* **touch·i·er; -est 1** : easily hurt or insulted **2** : calling for tact or careful handling ⟨a *touchy* subject⟩

¹tough \\'təf\\ *adj* **1 a** : able to take great force : flexible and not brittle ⟨*tough* fibers⟩ **b** : not easily chewed ⟨*tough* meat⟩ **2** : marked by firmness or determination ⟨a *tough* policy⟩ **3** : able to stand hard work and hardship ⟨a *tough* body⟩ **4** : hard to influence : STUBBORN ⟨a *tough* bargainer⟩ **5** : very difficult ⟨a *tough* problem⟩ **6** : having much crime or bad behavior ⟨a *tough* neighborhood⟩ **syn** see STRONG — **tough·ly** *adv* — **tough·ness** *n*

²tough *n* : a tough person : ROWDY

tough·en \\'təf-ən\\ *vb* **tough·ened; tough·en·ing** \\'təf-(ə-)niŋ\\ : to make or become tough

tough·ie \\'təf-ē\\ *n* **1** : ²TOUGH **2** : a hard problem or question

tou·pee \\tü-'pā\\ *n* : a small wig worn to cover a bald spot

¹tour \\'tů(ə)r, *sense 1 is also* 'taů(ə)r\\ *n* **1 a** : one's turn in a schedule **b** : a period of time during which one is on duty or in a certain place **2** : a trip usually ending at the point of beginning ⟨a *tour* of the city⟩ **3** : a series of related sports events held regularly at varied locations ⟨the golf *tour*⟩ **syn** see JOURNEY

²tour *vb* : to make a tour of : travel as a tourist

tour·ism \\'tů(ə)r-ˌiz-əm\\ *n* : the practice of traveling for pleasure or the business of encouraging and serving such traveling

tour·ist \\'tůr-əst\\ *n* : a person who travels for pleasure — **tourist** *adj*

tourist class *n* : economy accommodations (as on a ship)

tour·ma·line \\'tůr-mə-lən, -ˌlēn\\ *n* : a mineral of variable color that makes a striking gem when transparent and cut

tour·na·ment \\'tůr-nə-mənt *also* 'tər- *or* 'tȯr-\\ *n* **1** : a contest of skill and courage between knights wearing armor and fighting with blunted lances or swords **2** : a contest or series of contests played for a championship

tour·ney \\'tů(ə)r-nē *also* 'tər- *or* 'tȯr-\\ *n, pl* **tourneys** : TOURNAMENT

tour·ni·quet \\'tůr-ni-kət, 'tər-\\ *n* : a device (as a tight bandage) used to stop or slow bleeding or blood flow

tou·sle \\'taů-zəl, -səl\\ *vb* **tou·sled; tou·sling** \\'taůz-(ə-)liŋ, 'taůs-\\ : to put into disorder by rough handling

tout \\'taůt, 'tüt\\ *vb* : to give much praise or publicity to

¹tow \\'tō\\ *vb* : to draw or pull along behind [Old English *togian* "to tow"]

²tow *n* **1** : a line or rope for towing **2** : an act or instance of towing or the fact or condition of being towed **3** : something (as a barge) that tows or is towed — **in tow** : under guidance or protection ⟨taken *in tow* by a friendly guide⟩

³tow *n* **1** : short broken fiber from flax, hemp, or jute used for yarn, twine, or stuffing **2** : yarn or cloth made of tow [Old English *tow-* "spinning"]

to·ward *or* **to·wards** \\(')tō(-ə)rd(z), (')tȯ(-ə)rd(z), tə-'wȯrd(z), (')twȯrd(z), (')twȯrd(z)\\ *prep* **1** : in the direction of ⟨heading *toward* town⟩ **2 a** : along a course leading to ⟨efforts *toward* peace⟩ **b** : in regard to ⟨attitude *toward* life⟩ **3** : so as to face ⟨turn the chair *toward* the window⟩ **4** : not long before : NEAR ⟨*toward* noon⟩ **5** : as part of the payment for ⟨$100 *toward* a new sofa⟩

tow·boat \\'tō-ˌbōt\\ *n* **1** : TUGBOAT **2** : a compact shallow-draft boat for pushing barges on inland waterways

¹tow·el \\'taů(-ə)l\\ *n* : a cloth or piece of absorbent paper for wiping or drying

²towel *vb* **-eled** *or* **-elled; -el·ing** *or* **-el·ling** : to rub or dry with a towel : use a towel to dry off

tow·el·ing *or* **tow·el·ling** \\'taů-(ə-)liŋ\\ *n* : material for towels

¹tow·er \\'taů(-ə)r\\ *n* **1** : a building or structure that is higher than it is long or wide, is high with respect to its surroundings, and may stand by itself or be attached to a larger structure   **2** : CITADEL 1 — **tow·ered** \'taù(-ə)rd\ *adj*

²tower *vb* : to reach or rise to a great height

tow·er·ing *adj*   **1** : rising high : TALL ⟨*towering* mountain peaks⟩ ⟨*towering* skyscrapers⟩   **2** : reaching a high point of strength or force ⟨a *towering* rage⟩   **3** : going beyond proper bounds ⟨*towering* ambitions⟩

tow·head \'tō-,hed\ *n* : a person having soft whitish blond hair

to·whee \'tō-,hē, 'tō-ē, tō-'hē\ *n* : any of several North American birds; *esp* : one of eastern North America in which the male has a black back, a white belly, and reddish sides

tow·line \'tō-,līn\ *n* : a line used in towing

towhee

town \'taùn\ *n*   **1 a** : a compactly settled area that is usually larger than a village but smaller than a city   **b** : CITY 1   **2** : the people of a town — **town** *adj*

town clerk *n* : an official who keeps the town records

town crier *n* : an official who makes public announcements

town hall *n* : a public building used for offices and meetings of town government

town house *n* : a house connected to the next house by a common sidewall

town·ie \'taù-nē\ *n* : a permanent resident of a town

town meeting *n* : a meeting of townspeople to pass laws for the town

towns·folk \'taùnz-,fōk\ *n pl* : TOWNSPEOPLE

town·ship \'taùn-,ship\ *n*   **1** : a unit of local government in some northeastern and north central states   **2** : a division of territory in surveys of U.S. public land containing 36 square miles (about 93 square kilometers)

towns·peo·ple \'taùnz-,pē-pəl\ *n pl* : the people who live in a town or city

tow·path \'tō-,path, -,pàth\ *n* : a path traveled by people or animals towing boats

tow·rope \-,rōp\ *n* : a line used in towing

tow truck *n* : WRECKER 1b

tox·emia \tàk-'sē-mē-ə\ *n* : a disorder caused by toxic substances in the blood

tox·ic \'tàk-sik\ *adj*   **1** : of, relating to, or caused by a poison or toxin   **2** : POISONOUS [from Latin *toxicus* "relating to or caused by a poison", from earlier *toxicum* "poison", from Greek *toxikon* "a poison put on the tips of arrows", from *toxikos* "of a bow and arrows", from *toxon* "bow, arrow" — related to INTOXICATE, TOXIN; see *Word History* at INTOXICATE] — **tox·ic·i·ty** \tàk-'sis-ət-ē\ *n*

tox·in \'tàk-sən\ *n* : a complicated substance produced by a living organism (as a bacterium) that is very poisonous when it enters directly into the tissues (as through a wound) but is usually destroyed in digestion when taken by mouth and that usually causes antibody formation — compare ANTITOXIN, TOXOID [derived from Latin *tox-* "poisonous" and English *-in* "chemical compound"; *tox-* from *toxicum* "poison", from Greek *toxikon* "arrow poison", from *toxon* "bow, arrow" — related to INTOXICATE, TOXIC; see *Word History* at INTOXICATE]

tox·in–an·ti·tox·in \'tàk-sə-'nant-i-,tàk-sən\ *n* : a mixture of a toxin and its antitoxin used especially formerly as a vaccine against some diseases (as diphtheria)

tox·oid \'tàk-,soid\ *n* : a toxin of a disease-causing organism treated so as to destroy its poisonous effects while leaving it still capable of causing antibodies to form when it is injected into the body

¹toy \'toi\ *n*   **1** : something of little or no value or importance   **2** : something for a child to play with   **3** : something small

for its kind; *esp* : an animal of a breed or variety marked by exceptionally small size — **toy** *adj* — **toy·like** \-,līk\ *adj*

²toy *vb* : to amuse oneself as if with a toy

¹trace \'trās\ *n*   **1** : ROAD 2a   **2** : a mark left by something that has passed or is past   **3** : a very small amount [Middle English *trace* "a course, a mark left by something that passes", from early French *trace* (same meaning), from *tracier* (verb) "to move over, mark a route or course on something, make a record of by marks or a picture", derived from Latin *tractus,* past participle of *trahere* "to pull, drag" — related to ABSTRACT, ATTRACT, ³TRACE, TRAIT]

²trace *vb* **traced; trac·ing**   **1 a** : ²SKETCH 1   **b** : to form (as letters) carefully   **c** : to copy (as a drawing or pattern) by following the lines or letters as seen through a transparent sheet placed over the thing copied   **d** : to make a graphic record of by a recording instrument ⟨*trace* the heart action⟩   **2 a** : to follow the footprints, track, or trail of   **b** : to study, follow, or show the development and progress of in detail — **trace·able** \'trā-sə-bəl\ *adj*

³trace *n* : either of two straps, chains, or lines of a harness for attaching a horse to something (as a wagon or plow) to be pulled [Middle English *trais* (plural) "two straps used for connecting a horse to a vehicle to be pulled", from early French *trais,* plural of *trait* "a strap used in pairs for connecting a horse to a vehicle to be pulled", literally "act of pulling", from Latin *tractus,* past participle of *trahere* "to pull, drag" — related to ABSTRACT, ATTRACT, ¹TRACE, TRAIT]

trace element *n* : a chemical element present in tiny amounts; *esp* : one that is used by a living thing and is considered essential to the functions necessary for life

trac·er \'trā-sər\ *n*   **1 a** : a person who traces missing persons or property   **b** : an inquiry sent out in tracing a shipment lost in transit   **2 a** : ammunition containing a chemical composition to mark the flight of projectiles by a trail of smoke or fire   **b** : a substance and especially a labeled element or atom used to trace the course of a chemical or biological process

trac·ery \'trās-(ə-)rē\ *n, pl* **-er·ies** : ornamental work with many branching lines

tra·chea \'trā-kē-ə\ *n, pl* **-che·ae** \-kē-,ē, -kē-,ī\ *also* **-che·as**   **1** : the main part of the system of tubes by which air passes to and from the lungs in vertebrates — called also *windpipe*   **2** : one of the tiny air-carrying tubes that form the respiratory system of most insects and many other arthropods (as spiders) — **tra·che·al** \-kē-əl\ *adj*

tracery

tra·cheid \'trā-kē-əd, -,kēd\ *n* : a long tube-shaped cell that is found in the xylem of plants, grows narrower near the ends, has strong thickened walls, and functions in support and in the transport of water and solutions

tra·cho·ma \trə-'kō-mə\ *n* : a serious contagious eye disease that is marked by swelling of the conjunctiva, is caused by a microbe closely related to the rickettsias, and often results in blindness if left untreated

trac·ing \'trā-siŋ\ *n*   **1** : the act of one that traces   **2** : something that is traced

tracing paper *n* : a thin paper through which something (as a picture) may be traced; *also* : a thin paper for transfer-

\ə\ **abut**	\aù\ **out**	\i\ **tip**	\ò\ **saw**	\ù\ **foot**
\ər\ **further**	\ch\ **chin**	\ī\ **life**	\òi\ **coin**	\y\ **yet**
\a\ **mat**	\e\ **pet**	\j\ **job**	\th\ **thin**	\yü\ **few**
\ā\ **take**	\ē\ **easy**	\ŋ\ **sing**	\th\ **this**	\yù\ **cure**
\ä\ **cot, cart**	\g\ **go**	\ō\ **bone**	\ü\ **food**	\zh\ **vision**

ring a clothing pattern to cloth

tracing wheel *n* : a small plain or toothed wheel attached to a handle and used to transfer clothing patterns to cloth

¹track \'trak\ *n* **1 a** : a mark left by something that has gone by **b** : PATH 1, TRAIL **2 a** : a course laid out for racing **b** : the parallel rails of a railroad **3** : the course along which something moves **4** : awareness of things or the order in which things happen or ideas come ⟨lose *track* of the time⟩ ⟨keep *track* of expenses⟩ **5** : either of two continuous metal belts on which a vehicle (as a tank or bulldozer) travels **6** : track-and-field sports; *esp* : those performed on a running track — **track·less** \'trak-ləs\ *adj* — **in one's tracks** : where one is at the moment : on the spot

²track *vb* **1 a** : to follow the tracks or traces of : TRAIL ⟨*track* a deer⟩ **b** : to search for until found ⟨*tracking* down the causes of cancer⟩ **2** : to observe the moving path of ⟨*track* a missile with radar⟩ **3** : to make tracks upon or with ⟨*track* up the floor⟩ ⟨*track* mud all over the floor⟩ — **track·er** *n*

track–and–field \,trak-ən-'fē(ə)ld\ *adj* : of, relating to, or being sports events (as racing, throwing, and jumping contests) held on a running track and on an enclosed field

¹tract \'trakt\ *n* **1 a** : an indefinite stretch of land ⟨a large *tract* of forest⟩ **b** : a defined area of land ⟨garden *tract*⟩ **2** : a system of body parts or organs that serves some special purpose ⟨the digestive *tract*⟩

²tract *n* : a pamphlet of political or religious ideas and beliefs

trac·ta·ble \'trak-tə-bəl\ *adj* : easily led, taught, or controlled

tract house *n* : a house that is one of a number of very similar houses built on a tract of land

trac·tion \'trak-shən\ *n* **1** : the act of drawing : the state of being drawn **2** : the adhesive friction of a body on a surface on which it moves (as of a wheel on a rail) **3** : a pulling force applied to a skeletal structure (as a broken bone) by using a special device ⟨a *traction* splint⟩; *also* : a state of tension created by such a pulling force ⟨a leg in *traction*⟩

trac·tor \'trak-tər\ *n* **1** : a vehicle that has large rear wheels or moves on tracks and is used especially for pulling farm implements **2** : a short truck with no body used in combination with a trailer for hauling freight

¹trade \'trād\ *n* **1** : the business or work in which a person takes part regularly : OCCUPATION **2** : an occupation requiring manual or mechanical skill **3** : the persons working in an occupation, business, or industry **4** : the business of buying and selling items : COMMERCE **5 a** : an act or instance of trading : TRANSACTION **b** : an exchange of property without use of money : SWAP **6** : a firm's customers **7** : TRADE WIND

²trade *vb* **trad·ed; trad·ing** **1 a** : to give in exchange for something else **b** : to make an exchange of **2 a** : to take part in the exchange, purchase, or sale of goods **b** : to deal regularly as a customer

³trade *adj* : of, relating to, or used in trade

trade–in \'trād-,in\ *n* : something given in trade usually as part payment for a purchase

trade in \(')trād-'in\ *vb* : to turn in as a payment or part payment for a purchase

trade·mark \'trād-,märk\ *n* **1** : a device (as a word) that points clearly to the origin or ownership of merchandise to which it is applied and that is legally reserved for use only by the owner **2** : something that identifies a person or thing — **trademark** *vb*

trade–off \'trād-,óf\ *n* **1** : a balancing of things all of which cannot be had at the same time **2** : a giving up of one thing in return for another

trad·er \'trād-ər\ *n* **1** : a person who trades **2** : a ship engaged in trade

trade school *n* : a secondary school teaching the skilled trades

trades·man \'trādz-mən\ *n* **1** : a worker in a skilled trade : CRAFTSMAN **2** : one who runs a retail store : SHOPKEEPER

trades·peo·ple \-,pē-pəl\ *n pl* : people engaged in trade

trade union *n* : LABOR UNION — **trade unionist** *n*

trade wind *n* : a wind blowing almost constantly toward the equator from an easterly direction

trading post *n* : a station or store of a trader or trading company established in a thinly settled region where local products (as furs) are exchanged for manufactured goods

tra·di·tion \trə-'dish-ən\ *n* **1** : the handing down of information, beliefs, or customs from one generation to another **2** : a belief or custom handed down by tradition [Middle English *tradicion, tradicioun* "tradition", from early French *tradition* (same meaning) and Latin *tradition-, traditio* "the action of handing over, tradition, betrayal" — related to TREASON; see *Word History* at TREASON]

tra·di·tion·al \trə-'dish-nəl, -ən-ᵊl\ *adj* **1** : handed down from age to age without writing **2** : based on custom ⟨our *traditional* Thanksgiving dinner⟩ — **tra·di·tion·al·ly** \-ē\ *adv*

tra·duce \trə-'d(y)üs\ *vb* **tra·duced; tra·duc·ing** : ²SLANDER — **tra·duc·er** *n*

¹traf·fic \'traf-ik\ *n* **1** : the business of carrying passengers or goods ⟨the tourist *traffic*⟩ **2** : the business of buying and selling : COMMERCE **3** : communication or dealings between persons or groups ⟨had no *traffic* with the enemy⟩ **4 a** : the passengers or goods carried by train, boat, or airplane or passing along a road, river, or air route **b** : the pedestrians or vehicles passing along a route **c** : the movement (as of pedestrians or vehicles) through an area or along a route ⟨heavy *traffic* in the kitchen before dinner⟩ ⟨rush-hour *traffic*⟩

²traffic *vb* **traf·ficked; traf·fick·ing** : to carry on traffic : TRADE, DEAL — **traf·fick·er** *n*

traffic circle *n* : ²ROTARY 2

traffic light *n* : an electrically operated visual signal (as a system of green, yellow, and red lights) for controlling traffic

traffic signal *n* : a signal (as a traffic light) for controlling traffic

tra·ge·di·an \trə-'jēd-ē-ən\ *n* **1** : a writer of tragedies **2** : an actor of tragic roles

trag·e·dy \'traj-əd-ē\ *n, pl* **-dies** **1** : a serious drama with a sorrowful or disastrous conclusion **2** : a disastrous event

Word History Tragedy as a form of drama began in ancient Greece. It developed from the public performances of songs and dances at religious festivals. These festivals were held in honor of Dionysus, the god of wine and fertility. The Greeks called these performances *tragōidia*, which meant literally "goat song". The word came from *tragos*, meaning "goat" and *aeidein*, meaning "to sing". These performances were at first given by a chorus. Later, however, it became popular to have one member of the chorus stand apart from the others and give a spoken introduction to or interpretation of the story. This speaker soon took over a larger and larger role in the performances. In time, this person was joined by more speakers until the dramas came to be like our modern plays with many parts acted out. It is not certain why these performances were named with a word for "goat". One explanation is that a goat was given as a prize to the person presenting the best drama. Another is that the goat was sacred to the god Dionysus and was sacrificed to him at these festivals. The early tragedies were stories of the misfortunes of heroes of legend or history, and that idea of misfortune carries on today in the common meaning of our word *tragedy*. [Middle English *tragedie* "tragedy as a drama, misfortune", from early French *tragedie* (same meaning), from Latin *tragoedia* (same meaning), from Greek *tragōidia* "a drama about the misfortunes of heroes", literally "goat song", from *tragos* "goat" and *aeidein* "to sing"]

trag·ic \'traj-ik\ *adj* **1** : of, marked by, or expressive of tragedy **2** : dealing with or appearing in tragedy **3** : very unfortunate : DEPLORABLE — **trag·i·cal·ly** \-i-k(ə-)lē\ *adv*

tragic flaw *n* : a defect in the character of a good person (as the hero of a tragedy) that causes his or her destruction

tragi·com·edy \,traj-i-'käm-əd-ē\ *n* : a play or situation which blends tragic and comic elements — **tragi·com·ic** \-'käm-ik\ *adj*

¹trail \'trā(ə)l\ *vb* **1** : to drag or draw along behind **2** : to lag behind **3** : to follow in the tracks of : PURSUE ⟨dogs *trailing* a fox⟩ **4** : to hang down or rest on or creep over the ground ⟨*trailing* vines⟩ ⟨a *trailing* skirt⟩ **5** : to form a trail ⟨smoke *trailed* from the chimney⟩ **6** : to become less and less : DWINDLE ⟨the voice *trailed* off⟩ **syn** see CHASE

²trail *n* **1** : something that trails or is trailed **2** : a trace or mark left by something that has passed or been drawn along **3 a** : a track made by passage : a beaten path **b** : a path marked to show a route through a wilderness region **c** : an established course or routine ⟨hit the campaign *trail*⟩

trail·blaz·er \'trā(ə)l-,blā-zər\ *n* : someone who prepares the way for others who follow: as **a** : PATHFINDER **b** : ¹PIONEER 1

trail·er \'trā-lər\ *n* **1** : one that trails **2 a** : a vehicle designed to be hauled (as by a tractor) **b** : a vehicle designed to serve wherever parked as a dwelling or as a place of business **3** : ²PREVIEW 2

trailing arbutus *n* : a trailing plant of eastern North America that belongs to the heath family and produces fragrant pinkish flowers in early spring — called also *arbutus*

trailing arbutus

¹train \'trān\ *n* **1** : a part of a gown that trails behind the wearer **2** : a number of followers or attendants : RETINUE **3** : a moving file of persons, vehicles, or animals ⟨wagon *train*⟩ **4 a** : an orderly connected series of events, actions, or ideas ⟨*train* of thought⟩ **b** : ²RESULT 1, AFTERMATH **5** : a series of moving machine parts (as gears) for transmitting and modifying motion **6** : a connected line of railroad cars

²train *vb* **1** : to direct the growth of (a plant) usually by bending, pruning, and tying **2 a** : to teach in an art, profession, or trade **b** : to teach (an animal) to obey **3** : to make ready for a test of skill or strength **4** : to aim at an object or target ⟨*trained* their eyes on the horizon⟩ — **train·abil·i·ty** \,trā-nə-'bil-ət-ē\ *n* — **train·able** \'trā-nə-bəl\ *adj* — **train·er** *n*

train·ee \trā-'nē\ *n* : a person who is being trained for a job

train·ing *n* **1** : the course followed by one who trains or is being trained **2** : the knowledge, experience, or condition acquired by one who trains **syn** see EDUCATION

traipse \'trāps\ *vb* **traipsed; traips·ing** : to walk or wander about

trait \'trāt\ *n* **1** : a quality that sets one person or thing off from another : PECULIARITY **2** : an inherited characteristic ⟨dominant and recessive *traits*⟩ [from early French *trait* "the act of pulling", from Latin *tractus,* past participle of *trahere* "to pull, drag" — related to ¹TRACE, ³TRACE] **syn** see CHARACTERISTIC

trai·tor \'trāt-ər\ *n* **1** : one who betrays another's trust or is false to an obligation or duty **2** : one who commits treason [Middle English *traitre* "traitor", from early French *traitre* (same meaning), from Latin *traditor* (same meaning), derived from *tradere* "to hand over, betray" — related to TREASON; see *Word History* at TREASON]

trai·tor·ous \'trāt-ə-rəs, 'trā-trəs\ *adj* **1** : guilty or capable of treason **2** : amounting to treason ⟨*traitorous* acts⟩

tra·jec·to·ry \trə-'jek-t(ə-)rē\ *n, pl* **-ries** : the curve that a body (as a planet in its orbit or a rocket) travels along in space

tram \'tram\ *n* **1** : a cart or wagon running on rails (as in a mine) **2** *chiefly British* : STREETCAR **3** : an overhead cable car

¹tram·mel \'tram-əl\ *n* : something preventing free movement or activity — usually used in pl.

²trammel *vb* **-meled** *or* **-melled; -mel·ing** *or* **-mel·ling** \-(ə-)liŋ\ : to prevent or restrict the free movement of

tram 1

¹tramp \'tramp, *senses 1 & 2 are also* 'trämp, 'trómp\ *vb* **1** : to walk heavily **2** : to tread on forcibly and repeatedly **3** : to travel or wander through on foot ⟨*tramp* the streets⟩ — **tramp·er** *n*

²tramp \'tramp, *sense 3 is also* 'trämp, 'trómp\ *n* **1** : a homeless wanderer who may beg or steal for a living **2** : a walking trip : HIKE **3** : the sound made by many marching feet **4** : a ship not making regular trips but taking cargo to any port — called also *tramp steamer*

tram·ple \'tram-pəl\ *vb* **tram·pled; tram·pling** \-p(ə-)liŋ\ **1** : to tramp or tread heavily so as to bruise, crush, or injure **2** : to crush underfoot **3** : to injure or harm by ruthless or heartless treatment — **tram·pler** \-p(ə-)lər\ *n*

tram·po·line \,tram-pə-'lēn, 'tram-pə-,lēn\ *n* : a canvas sheet supported by springs in a metal frame used for springing and landing in acrobatic tumbling

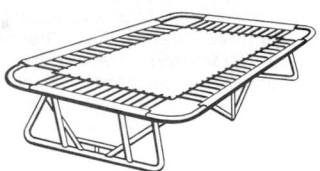

trampoline

trance \'tran(t)s\ *n* **1** : a living state in which the important bodily and mental activities slow down greatly or almost stop **2** : a sleeplike state (as of deep hypnosis) **3** : a state of being so deeply absorbed in something as to be unaware of one's surroundings

tran·quil \'traŋ-kwəl, 'tran-\ *adj* : free from disturbance or turmoil : QUIET **syn** see CALM — **tran·quil·ly** \-kwə-lē\ *adv*

tran·quil·ize *also* **tran·quil·lize** \'traŋ-kwə-,līz, 'tran-\ *vb* **-ized** *also* **-lized; -iz·ing** *also* **-liz·ing** : to make or become tranquil or relaxed; *esp* : to ease the nervous tension and anxiety of usually by means of drugs

tran·quil·iz·er *also* **tran·quil·liz·er** \'traŋ-kwə-,lī-zər, 'tran-\ *n* : one that tranquilizes; *esp* : a drug used to reduce anxiety and nervous tension

tran·quil·li·ty *or* **tran·quil·i·ty** \tran-'kwil-ət-ē, traŋ-\ *n* : the quality or state of being tranquil

trans- *prefix* **1** : on or to the other side of : across : beyond ⟨*trans*atlantic⟩ **2** : so or such as to change in form or position or transfer [derived from Latin *trans-* "across, beyond, so as to change"]

trans·act \tran(t)s-'akt, tranz-\ *vb* **1** : to carry through ⟨*transact* a sale of property⟩ **2** : ²CONDUCT 2, CARRY ON ⟨*transact* business⟩ — **trans·ac·tor** \-'ak-tər\ *n*

\ə\ abut	\au̇\ out	\i\ tip	\ȯ\ saw	\u̇\ foot
\ər\ further	\ch\ chin	\ī\ life	\ȯi\ coin	\y\ yet
\a\ mat	\e\ pet	\j\ job	\th\ thin	\yü\ few
\ā\ take	\ē\ easy	\ŋ\ sing	\th\ this	\yu̇\ cure
\ä\ cot, cart	\g\ go	\ō\ bone	\ü\ food	\zh\ vision

trans·ac·tion \tran(t)s-'ak-shən, tranz-\ *n* **1 a** : something transacted; *esp* : a business deal **b** *pl* : the record of the meeting of an organization **2 a** : an act, process, or instance of transacting **b** : an act of communication between two people who influence or change each other

trans·at·lan·tic \,tran(t)s-ət-'lant-ik, ,tranz-\ *adj* **1** : crossing or extending across the Atlantic ocean ⟨a *transatlantic* cable⟩ **2** : located or coming from beyond the Atlantic ocean ⟨our *transatlantic* friends⟩

tran·scend \tran(t)s-'end\ *vb* **1** : to rise above or go beyond the limits of : EXCEED **2** : to be greatly superior to : SURPASS

tran·scen·dence \tran(t)s-'en-dən(t)s\ *n* : the quality or state of being transcendent

tran·scen·dent \tran(t)s-'en-dənt\ *adj* **1** : superior to or going beyond the usual : EXTRAORDINARY **2** : going beyond the limits of ordinary experience

tran·scen·den·tal \,tran(t)s-,en-'dent-ᵊl, -ən-\ *adj* : TRANSCENDENT 2 — **tran·scen·den·tal·ly** \-ᵊl-ē\ *adv*

tran·con·ti·nen·tal \,tran(t)s-,känt-ᵊn-'ent-ᵊl\ *adj* : extending or going across a continent

tran·scribe \tran(t)s-'krīb\ *vb* **tran·scribed; tran·scrib·ing** **1 a** : to make a written copy of **b** : to make a copy of (dictated or recorded matter) by hand or on a typewriter **2** : to represent speech sounds with phonetic symbols — **tran·scrib·er** *n*

tran·script \'tran(t)s-,kript\ *n* **1** : a written, printed, or typed copy **2** : an official copy (as of a student's educational record)

tran·scrip·tion \tran(t)s-'krip-shən\ *n* **1** : an act, process, or instance of transcribing **2** : ¹COPY 1, TRANSCRIPT

tran·sept \'tran(t)s-,ept\ *n* : the section of a church with a cross-shaped floor plan that lies at right angles to the nave

¹trans·fer \tran(t)s-'fər, 'tran(t)s-,fər\ *vb* **trans·ferred; trans·fer·ring** **1 a** : to pass from one person, place, or situation to another **b** : to cause to pass from one to another **2** : to give over the possession or ownership of **3** : to move to a different place, region, or situation; *esp* : to withdraw from one school to enroll at another **4** : to change from one vehicle or transportation line to another [Middle English *transferren* "to transfer", from Latin *transferre* (same meaning), from *trans-* "across, through" and *ferre* "to bear, carry" — related to ¹DEFER, FERTILE] — **trans·fer·able** \tran(t)s-'fər-ə-bəl\ *adj* — **trans·fer·al** \-'fər-əl\ *n*

²trans·fer \'tran(t)s-,fər\ *n* **1** : a giving over of right, title, or interest in property by one person to another **2** : an act, process, or example of transferring **3** : one that transfers or is transferred **4** : a graphic image transferred by contact from one surface to another **5** : a place where a transfer is made (as from trains to ferries) **6** : a ticket permitting a passenger on a bus or train to continue the journey by another route

trans·fer·ence \tran(t)s-'fər-ən(t)s\ *n* : an act, process, or example of transferring

transfer RNA \'tran(t)s-,fər-\ *n* : a relatively small RNA molecule that functions in the transfer of a particular amino acid to the site of protein synthesis — compare MESSENGER RNA

trans·fig·u·ra·tion \(,)tran(t)s-,fig-(y)ə-'rā-shən\ *n* **1** : a great change of form or appearance; *esp* : a change that beautifies, glorifies, or makes more spiritual **2** *cap* : a Christian festival on August 6 celebrating Christ's transfiguration on the mountain as witnessed by his disciples

trans·fig·ure \tran(t)s-'fig-yər, *especially British* -'fig-ər\ *vb* **-ured; -ur·ing** **1** : to change the form or appearance of : TRANSFORM **2** : to make or become more glorious or ideally beautiful : EXALT, GLORIFY

trans·fix \tran(t)s-'fiks\ *vb* **1** : to pierce through with or as if with a pointed weapon **2** : to hold motionless by or as if by piercing

trans·form \tran(t)s-'fó(ə)rm\ *vb* **1 a** : to change completely in composition, structure, or character **b** : to change in outward appearance **2** : to substitute for or change (a mathematical expression) into another using a mathematical rule — **trans·for·ma·tive** \-'fór-mət-iv\ *adj*

trans·for·ma·tion \,tran(t)s-fər-'mā-shən, -fór-\ *n* : an act, process, or example of transforming or being transformed — **trans·for·ma·tion·al** \-shnəl, -shən-ᵊl\ *adj*

trans·form·er \tran(t)s-'fór-mər\ *n* : a device for changing an electric current into one of different voltage

trans·fuse \tran(t)s-'fyüz\ *vb* **trans·fused; trans·fus·ing** **1 a** : to cause to pass from one to another **b** : to spread through or be filled with ⟨a room *transfused* with light⟩ **2** : to transfer (as blood) into a blood vessel of a person or animal

trans·fu·sion \tran(t)s-'fyü-zhən\ *n* **1** : an act, process, or example of transfusing; *esp* : the process of transfusing a fluid and especially blood into a blood vessel **2** : something transfused

trans·gress \tran(t)s-'gres, tranz-\ *vb* **1** : to go beyond limits set by : VIOLATE ⟨*transgress* the divine law⟩ **2** : to pass beyond or go over a limit or boundary **3** : to violate a command or law [from French *transgresser* "to transgress", from Latin *transgressus*, past participle of *transgredi* "to step across or beyond", from *trans-* "across, beyond" and *gradi* "to step"] — **trans·gres·sor** \-'gres-ər\ *n*

trans·gres·sion \tran(t)s-'gresh-ən, tranz-\ *n* : an act, process, or example of transgressing

¹tran·sient \'tranch-ənt\ *adj* : not lasting or staying long — **tran·sient·ly** *adv*

syn TRANSIENT, TRANSITORY, MOMENTARY, FLEETING mean lasting or staying only a short time. TRANSIENT applies to what is actually short in its duration or stay ⟨a hotel for *transient* guests⟩ TRANSITORY applies to what is by its nature likely to change, pass, or come to an end ⟨fame in the movies is *transitory*⟩ MOMENTARY suggests a quick coming and going as a brief interruption of a more lasting state ⟨my feeling of joy was only *momentary*⟩ FLEETING applies to something that passes very quickly and cannot be brought back ⟨a happy life with only *fleeting* moments of sorrow⟩

²transient *n* **1** : a temporary guest **2** : a person traveling about usually in search of work

tran·sis·tor \tranz-'is-tər, tran(t)s-\ *n* **1** : a small solid electronic device that consists of a small block of a semiconductor (as germanium) with at least three electrodes and is used to control the flow of electricity in electronic equipment (as a radio or television) **2** : a radio having transistors — called also *transistor radio*

¹tran·sit \'tran(t)s-ət, 'tranz-\ *n* **1** : an act, process, or example of passing through or over : PASSAGE **2** : the transporting of persons or things from one place to another ⟨goods lost in *transit*⟩ **3** : local transportation of people in public vehicles; *also* : the vehicles or system used in such transportation **4** : a surveyor's instrument for measuring angles [from Latin *transitus* "passage, journey", from *transire* "to go across, pass", from *trans-* "across, beyond" and *ire* "to go" — related to ISSUE, ITINERARY]

transit 4

²transit *vb* : to pass or cause to pass over, through, or across

tran·si·tion \tran(t)s-'ish-ən, tranz-\ *n* **1** : a changing from one state, stage, place, or subject to another **2** : a musical passage leading from one section of a piece to another

— **tran·si·tion·al** \-'ish-nəl, -'izh-, -ən-ᵊl\ *adj* — **tran·si·tion·al·ly** \-ē\ *adv*

transition element *n* : any of various metallic elements (as chromium, iron, and nickel) that can form bonds using electrons from two energy levels instead of only one

tran·si·tive \'tran(t)s-ət-iv, 'tranz-; 'tran(t)s-tiv\ *adj* **1** : having or containing a direct object ⟨a *transitive* verb⟩ **2** : of, relating to, or characterized by transition — **tran·si·tive·ly** *adv*

tran·si·to·ry \'tran(t)s-ə-,tōr-ē, 'tranz-, -,tȯr-\ *adj* : lasting only a short time : SHORT-LIVED, TEMPORARY **syn** see TRANSIENT — **tran·si·to·ri·ly** \,tran(t)s-ə-'tōr-ə-lē, ,tranz-, -'tȯr-\ *adv*

trans·late \tran(t)s-'lāt, tranz-\ *vb* **trans·lat·ed; trans·lat·ing** **1** : to change from one place, state, or form to another : TRANSFORM **2** : to transport miraculously to heaven without death **3 a** : to change from one language or set of symbols into another ⟨*translate* Japanese into English⟩ **b** : to express in different words : PARAPHRASE **c** : to explain in a clearer way : INTERPRET **4** : to be translated — **trans·lat·able** \-'lāt-ə-bəl\ *adj* — **trans·la·tor** \-'lāt-ər\ *n*

trans·la·tion \tran(t)s-'lā-shən, tranz-\ *n* : an act, process, or product of translating

trans·lit·er·ate \tran(t)s-'lit-ə-,rāt, tranz-\ *vb* **-at·ed; -at·ing** : to represent or spell in the characters of another alphabet — **trans·lit·er·a·tion** \(,)tran(t)s-,lit-ə-'rā-shən, (,)tranz-\ *n*

trans·lu·cen·cy \tran(t)s-'lü-sən-sē\ *n* : the quality or state of being translucent

trans·lu·cent \tran(t)s-'lüs-ᵊnt, tranz-\ *adj* **1** : clear and pure as if shining from within **2** : not transparent but clear enough to allow light to pass through ⟨frosted glass is *translucent*⟩

trans·mi·gra·tion \,tran(t)s-, mī-'grā-shən, ,tranz-\ *n* : the passing of a soul into another body after death

trans·mis·si·ble \tran(t)s-'mis-ə-bəl, tranz-\ *adj* : capable of being transmitted

trans·mis·sion \tran(t)s-'mish-ən, tranz-\ *n* **1** : an act, process, or example of transmitting **2** : the passage of radio waves in the space between transmitting and receiving stations **3** : the gears by which the power is transmitted from the engine to the axle that gives motion to a motor vehicle **4** : something transmitted

trans·mit \tran(t)s-'mit, tranz-\ *vb* **trans·mit·ted; trans·mit·ting** **1 a** : to transfer from one person or place to another **b** : to pass on by or as if by inheritance **c** : to cause or allow to spread abroad or to another ⟨*transmit* a disease⟩ **2 a** : to pass or cause to pass through space or a material : allow the passage of **b** : to send a signal by radio waves or over a wire [Middle English *transmitten* "to send to another person or place", from Latin *transmittere* (same meaning), from *trans-* "across, to the other side" and *mittere* "to send, throw" — related to EMIT] — **trans·mit·ta·ble** \-'mit-ə-bəl\ *adj* — **trans·mit·tal** \-'mit-ᵊl\ *n*

trans·mit·ter \tran(t)s-'mit-ər, tranz-\ *n* **1** : one that transmits **2** : the instrument in a telegraph system that sends out messages **3** : the part of a telephone that includes the mouthpiece and a device that picks up sound waves and sends them over the wire **4** : a device that sends out radio or television signals or the building which contains it

trans·mu·ta·tion \,tran(t)s-myü-'tā-shən, ,tranz-\ *n* : an act or example of transmuting or being transmuted; *esp* : the changing of one element into another (as of base metals into gold or silver)

trans·mute \tran(t)s-'myüt, tranz-\ *vb* **trans·mut·ed; trans·mut·ing** **1** : to change in kind, appearance, or value : CONVERT **2** : to change into another substance or element : to undergo transmutation

trans·oce·an·ic \tran(t)s-,ō-shē-'an-ik, tranz-\ *adj* **1** : lying or dwelling beyond the ocean **2** : crossing or extending across the ocean

tran·som \'tran(t)-səm\ *n* **1** : a horizontal crossbar in a window, over a door, or between a door and a window or fanlight above it **2** : a window above a door or other window built on and commonly hinged to a transom

trans·pa·cif·ic \,tran(t)s-pə-'sif-ik\ *adj* **1** : crossing or extending across the Pacific ocean **2** : located or occurring beyond the Pacific ocean

trans·par·en·cy \tran(t)s-'par-ən-sē, -'per-\ *n, pl* **-cies** **1** : the quality or state of being transparent **2** : a picture or design on glass, thin cloth, paper, or film viewed by shining light through it or by projection

T transom 1

trans·par·ent \tran(t)s-'par-ənt, -'per-\ *adj* **1 a** : transmitting light so that objects lying beyond are entirely visible **b** : fine or sheer enough to be seen through ⟨*transparent* gauze⟩ **2** : easily detected or understood : OBVIOUS ⟨*transparent* falsehood⟩ — **trans·par·ent·ly** *adv*

tran·spi·ra·tion \tran(t)s-pə-'rā-shən\ *n* : the process by which green plants give off water vapor through the stomata in their leaves

tran·spire \tran(t)s-'pī(ə)r\ *vb* **tran·spired; tran·spir·ing** **1** : to pass or give off in the form of water vapor through stomata in leaves **2** : to become known or apparent : become revealed **3** : to come to pass : HAPPEN

¹trans·plant \tran(t)s-'plant\ *vb* **1** : to dig up and plant in another soil or situation ⟨*transplant* seedlings⟩ **2** : to remove from one place and settle or introduce elsewhere **3** : to transfer (an organ or tissue) from one part or individual to another — **trans·plan·ta·tion** \,tran(t)s-,plan-'tā-shən\ *n* — **trans·plant·er** \tran(t)s-'plant-ər\ *n*

²trans·plant \'tran(t)s-,plant\ *n* **1** : something transplanted **2** : the act or process of transplanting

¹trans·port \tran(t)s-'pō(ə)rt, -'pȯ(ə)rt\ *vb* **1** : to carry from one place to another **2** : to fill with delight **3** : to send to a penal colony overseas [Middle English *transporten* "to transport", from early French *transporter* or Latin *transportare* (both, same meaning), from Latin *trans-* "across, through, so as to change" and *portare* "to carry" — related to PORTABLE] — **trans·port·able** \-ə-bəl\ *adj* — **trans·port·er** *n*

²trans·port \'tran(t)s-,pō(ə)rt, -,pȯ(ə)rt\ *n* **1** : an act or process of transporting : TRANSPORTATION **2** : strong or extremely pleasurable emotion ⟨*transports* of joy⟩ **2 a** : a ship for carrying soldiers or military equipment **b** : a vehicle used to transport persons or goods

trans·por·ta·tion \,tran(t)s-pər-'tā-shən\ *n* **1** : an act, process, or instance of transporting or being transported **2** : exile to a penal colony **3 a** : a means or method of transport ⟨was left without *transportation* when the car died⟩ **b** : the transporting of passengers or goods usually for a price

trans·pose \tran(t)s-'pōz\ *vb* **trans·posed; trans·pos·ing** **1** : to change the position, order, or sequence of **2** : to write or perform (a musical composition) in a different key **3** : to bring (a term) from one side of an algebraic equation to the other with change of sign — **trans·po·si·tion** \,tran(t)s-pə-'zish-ən\ *n*

tran·sub·stan·ti·a·tion \,tran(t)s-əb-,stan-chē-'ā-shən\ *n* : the miraculous transformation by which according to Roman Catholic and Eastern Orthodox belief the consecrated

\ə\ abut	\au̇\ out	\i\ tip	\ȯ\ saw	\u̇\ foot
\ər\ further	\ch\ chin	\ī\ life	\ȯi\ coin	\y\ yet
\a\ mat	\e\ pet	\j\ job	\th\ thin	\yü\ few
\ā\ take	\ē\ easy	\ŋ\ sing	\th\ this	\yu̇\ cure
\ä\ cot, cart	\g\ go	\ō\ bone	\ü\ food	\zh\ vision

bread and wine at Mass are changed in substance but not in appearance to the body and blood of Christ

trans·ver·sal \tran(t)s-'vər-səl, tranz-\ *n* : a line that intersects a system of lines

trans·verse \tran(t)s-'vərs, tranz-; 'tran(t)s-ˌvərs, 'tranz-\ *adj* : lying or being across : set crosswise — **transverse·ly** *adv*

transverse wave *n* : a wave in which the vibrating element moves in a direction perpendicular to the direction of advance of the wave

¹**trap** \'trap\ *n* **1** : a device for catching animals; *esp* : one that catches by springing shut suddenly **2** : something by which one is caught unawares **3 a** : a device for hurling clay pigeons into the air **b** : a hazard on a golf course consisting of a depression containing sand **4** : a light usually one-horse carriage with springs **5 a** : any of various devices for preventing passage of one thing often while allowing something else to proceed **b** : a device for drains or sewers consisting of a bend or chamber in which the liquid forms a seal to prevent the passage of sewer gas **6** *pl* : a group of percussion instruments (as in a dance band)

²**trap** *vb* **trapped; trap·ping 1 a** : to catch in or as if in a trap **b** : to place in a restricted position : CONFINE **2** : to provide with a trap **3** : to engage in trapping animals (as for fur) **syn** see CATCH — **trap·per** *n*

trap·door \'trap-'dō(ə)r, -'dȯ(ə)r\ *n* : a lifting or sliding door covering or hiding an opening in a roof, ceiling, or floor

trap–door spider *n* : any of various spiders that build silk-lined underground nests topped with a hinged lid

tra·peze \tra-'pēz\ *n* : a gymnastic or acrobatic device consisting of a short horizontal bar hung from two parallel ropes

trap·e·zoid \'trap-ə-ˌzȯid\ *n* : a four-sided plane figure having two and only two sides parallel — **trap·e·zoi·dal** \ˌtrap-ə-'zȯid-ᵊl\ *adj*

trap·line \'trap-ˌlīn\ *n* : a line or series of traps especially for fur-bearing animals; *also* : the route along which such traps are set

trapezoid

trap·pings \'trap-iŋz\ *n pl* **1** : an ornamental covering especially for a horse **2** : outward decoration or dress

trap·shoot·ing \'trap-ˌshüt-iŋ\ *n* : shooting at clay pigeons sprung into the air from a trap — **trap·shoot·er** \-ˌshüt-ər\ *n*

tra·pun·to \tra-'pün-tō, -'pùn-\ *n, pl* **-tos** : a type of quilting in which a design outlined with a single row of stitches is padded from behind to produce a decorative raised effect

trash \'trash\ *n* **1** : something of little or no value: as **a** : JUNK 2, RUBBISH **b** : silly or worthless ideas or works (as books) **2** : a low or worthless person; *also* : RABBLE 2 — **trashy** \'trash-ē\ *adj*

tra·vail \trə-'vā(ə)l, 'trav-ˌāl\ *n* **1** : work especially of a painful or difficult nature : TOIL **2** : AGONY 1, TORMENT [Middle English *travail* "hard labor", from early French *travail* (same meaning), from *travaillier* (verb) "to labor hard, torture" — related to TRAVEL; see *Word History* at TRAVEL] — **travail** *vb*

¹**trav·el** \'trav-əl\ *vb* **-eled** *or* **-elled; -el·ing** *or* **-el·ling** \-(ə-)liŋ\ **1** : to journey from place to place or to a distant place **2** : to move or advance from one place to another
Word History With our modern cars, ships, and airplanes and our many restaurants and hotels, travel today is not difficult. But in the Middle Ages roads were poor and places to eat and sleep were far apart. Travel was hard, uncomfortable work — even torture. In fact, our word *travel* comes from an ancient Latin word that

meant "torture". Many devices were used in the Middle Ages for torture in an effort to force confessions from persons accused of crimes. One of these devices, called in Latin a *tripalium,* gave us our word *travel.* The word *tripalium,* literally "three stakes", was derived from Latin *tri-,* meaning "three" and *palus,* meaning "stake, pale". This word is thought to have been the source of the Latin verb *tripaliare,* meaning "to torture". In early French the word became *travaillier,* with both the meaning "to torture" and the meaning "to work hard". This early French word was taken into Middle English as *travailen,* with the meaning "to work hard" and "to travel". In time these two meanings became separated into different words, *travail,* which means "hard work", and *travel,* which means "to go on a trip". [Middle English *travailen* "to travel, to work hard", from early French *travailler* "to work hard, to torture", probably from an unrecorded Latin verb *tripaliare* "to torture", from Latin *tripalium* "an instrument of torture", literally "three stakes", derived from *tri-* "three" and *palus* "stake, pale" — related to ³PALE, TRAVAIL]

²**travel** *n* **1 a** : the act or means of traveling ⟨air *travel* is fast⟩ **b** : ¹JOURNEY, TRIP — often used in pl. **2** *pl* : an account of one's travels

travel agency *n* : a business that plans and arranges for tours, transportation, and lodgings for travelers — **travel agent** *n*

trav·eled *or* **trav·elled** \'trav-əld\ *adj* **1** : having traveled widely : experienced in travel **2** : used by travelers ⟨a heavily-*traveled* road⟩

trav·el·er *or* **trav·el·ler** \'trav-(ə-)lər\ *n* : one that travels

traveler's check *n* : a check that is paid for in advance like a money order, that is difficult to forge, and that will be replaced if lost or stolen

trav·el·ing *or* **trav·el·ling** \'trav-(ə-)liŋ\ *adj* **1** : that travels ⟨a troupe of *traveling* actors⟩ **2** : used by or accompanying a traveler ⟨a *traveling* alarm clock⟩ ⟨a *traveling* companion⟩

traveling bag *n* : a bag carried by hand and designed to hold a traveler's clothing and personal articles

traveling salesman *n* : a traveling representative of a business concern who solicits orders

trav·el·ogue *also* **trav·el·og** \'trav-ə-ˌlȯg, -ˌläg\ *n* : an illustrated lecture or film about travel

tra·vers·al \trə-'vər-səl\ *n* : the act or an instance of traversing

¹**trav·erse** \'trav-ərs\ *n* **1** : something that crosses or lies across **2** : a curved or zigzag path along the face of a steep slope **3** : an act of traversing

²**tra·verse** \trə-'vərs\ *vb* **tra·versed; tra·vers·ing 1** : to pass through, across, or over **2** : to move back and forth or from side to side

³**trav·erse** \'trav-(ˌ)ərs, trə-'vərs\ *adj* : lying across : TRANSVERSE

trav·er·tine \'trav-ər-ˌtēn, -tən\ *n* : a mineral consisting of a massive usually layered calcium carbonate formed as deposits from spring waters or especially from hot springs

trav·es·ty \'trav-ə-stē\ *n, pl* **-ties 1** : an imitation that makes crude fun of something **2** : an inferior imitation or likeness ⟨a *travesty* of justice⟩ — **travesty** *vb*

tra·vois \trə-'vȯi, 'trav-ˌȯi\ *n, pl* **tra·vois** \-'vȯiz, -ˌȯiz\ *also* **tra·voises** \-'vȯiz, -ˌȯiz\ : an animal-drawn vehicle made of two crossed trailing poles used by Plains Indians to transport a load

¹**trawl** \'trȯl\ *vb* : to fish or catch with a trawl

²**trawl** *n* **1** : a large cone-shaped net dragged along

travois

the sea bottom in fishing **2** : a long heavy line to which a row of hooks are attached

trawl·er \'trȯ-lər\ *n* : a boat used for trawling

tray \'trā\ *n* : an open container with flat bottom and low rim for holding, carrying, or exhibiting articles — **tray·ful** \-,fu̇l\ *n*

treach·er·ous \'trech-(ə-)rəs\ *adj* **1 a** : guilty of treachery **b** : likely to betray : UNRELIABLE ⟨a *treacherous* memory⟩ **2** : giving a false appearance of safety or solidity ⟨a *treacherous* stretch of bog⟩ — **treach·er·ous·ly** *adv*

treach·ery \'trech-(ə-)rē\ *n, pl* **-er·ies** **1** : violation of allegiance or of faith and confidence : TREASON **2** : an act of treason

trea·cle \'trē-kəl\ *n, chiefly British* : MOLASSES

¹tread \'tred\ *vb* **trod** \'träd\; **trod·den** \'träd-ᵊn\ *or* **trod**; **tread·ing** **1 a** : to step or walk on or over **b** : to walk along : FOLLOW **2** : to beat or press with the feet : TRAMPLE **3 a** : to form by treading : BEAT ⟨*tread* a path⟩ **b** : to perform by stepping or dancing ⟨*tread* a measure⟩ — **tread·er** *n* — **tread water** : to keep the body nearly upright in the water and the head above water by a treading motion of the feet usually aided by the hands

²tread *n* **1** : a mark made by or as if by treading **2** : the action, manner, or sound of treading or stepping **3 a** : the part of a sole that touches the ground **b** : the part of a wheel or tire that makes contact with a road or rail; *esp* : the ridges or grooves on the surface of a tire **4** : the horizontal part of a step

¹trea·dle \'tred-ᵊl\ *n* : a lever or other device pressed by the foot to operate a machine

²treadle *vb* **trea·dled; trea·dling** \'tred-liŋ, -ᵊl-iŋ\ : to operate a treadle on a machine

tread·mill \'tred-,mil\ *n* **1** : a device moved by persons treading on steps set around the rim of a wide wheel or by animals walking on an endless belt **2** : a tiring or monotonous routine

trea·son \'trēz-ᵊn\ *n* **1** : the betrayal of a trust : TREACHERY **2** : the crime of attempting to overthrow the government of one's country or of assisting its enemies during war

    Word History The words *treason* and *tradition* both come from the same Latin source. The Latin word *traditio* meant "teaching" or "tradition". These senses developed from its basic meaning, which was "the act of handing something over". Tradition is maintained by passing information from one generation to another. One kind of treason is committed when someone who has been entrusted with secret information passes it on to someone else. The word *tradition* was borrowed directly from the Latin *traditio*. *Treason*, on the other hand, came to us through early French, where *traditio* had changed into the word *traison*. [Middle English *tresoun* "treason", from early French *traison* (same meaning), derived from Latin *tradition-, traditio* "the action of handing over, tradition, betrayal", from *traditus,* past participle of *tradere* "to hand over, betray", from *tra-, trans-* "across" and *dare* "to give" — related to TRADITION, TRAITOR]

trea·son·able \'trēz-nə-bəl, -ᵊn-ə-bəl\ *adj* : relating to, consisting of, or involving treason — **trea·son·ably** \-blē\ *adv*

¹trea·sure \'trezh-ər, 'trāzh-\ *n* **1** : wealth (as money, jewels, or precious metals) stored up or held in reserve **2** : someone or something that is valued highly [Middle English *tresor* "treasure", from early French *tresor* (same meaning), from Latin *thesaurus* "treasure, collection" — related to THESAURUS]

²treasure *vb* **trea·sured; trea·sur·ing** \-(ə-)riŋ\ : to value highly : CHERISH

trea·sur·er \'trezh-rər, 'trezh-ər-ər, 'trāzh-\ *n* : an officer of a club, business, or government who has charge of money taken in and paid out

treasure trove \-,trōv\ *n* **1** : treasure of unknown owner-

ship found buried or hidden **2** : a valuable discovery

trea·sury \'trezh-(ə-)rē, 'trāzh-\ *n, pl* **trea·sur·ies** **1 a** : a place in which stores of wealth are kept **b** : the place where collected funds are stored and paid out **2** *cap* : a government department in charge of finances

¹treat \'trēt\ *vb* **1** : to discuss terms of agreement with : NEGOTIATE ⟨*treat* with the enemy⟩ **2 a** : to have as a subject especially in writing **b** : to deal with : HANDLE **3 a** : to pay for another's food or entertainment **b** : to provide with free food, entertainment, or enjoyment **4** : to handle, use, or act toward in a usually stated way ⟨*treat* a horse cruelly⟩ ⟨*treat* this as top-secret⟩ **5** : to give medical or surgical care to ⟨*treat* a patient⟩ ⟨*treat* a cold⟩ **6** : to subject to some action or process to bring about a desired result

²treat *n* **1** : an entertainment given without expense to those invited **2** : a usually unexpected or unusual source of pleasure or amusement

trea·tise \'trēt-əs\ *n* : a book or article examining a subject carefully and completely

treat·ment \'trēt-mənt\ *n* **1** : the act or manner or an instance of treating someone or something **2** : a substance or method used in treating ⟨a beauty *treatment*⟩ ⟨waste *treatment* plant⟩

trea·ty \'trēt-ē\ *n, pl* **treaties** : an agreement or arrangement made by negotiation; *esp* : one between two or more states or rulers

¹tre·ble \'treb-əl\ *n* **1 a** : the highest of the four voice parts in vocal music : SOPRANO **b** : a singer or instrument taking this part **2** : a high-pitched or shrill voice, tone, or sound **3** : the upper half of the musical pitch range — compare ²BASS

²treble *adj* **1 a** : having three parts **b** : triple in number or amount. **2 a** : relating to or having the range of a musical treble ⟨*treble* voice⟩ **b** : high-pitched : SHRILL — **tre·bly** \'treb-(ə-)lē\ *adv*

³treble *vb* **tre·bled; tre·bling** \'treb-(ə-)liŋ\ : to make or become three times the size, amount, or number

treble clef *n* **1** : a clef that places G above middle C on the second line of the staff **2** : TREBLE STAFF

treble staff *n* : the musical staff carrying the treble clef

¹tree \'trē\ *n* **1 a** : a woody plant that lives for years and has a usually single tall main stem with few or no branches on its lower part — compare HERB 1, SHRUB **b** : a shrub or herb that has a form like a tree ⟨rose *trees*⟩ ⟨a banana *tree*⟩ **2** : a piece of wood (as a post or pole) put to a particular use of forming part of a structure or device **3** : something shaped like or arranged in a form like a tree; *esp* : a diagram or graph in branching form — compare FACTOR TREE, FAMILY TREE 2 — **tree·less** \-ləs\ *adj* — **tree·like** \-,līk\ *adj*

²tree *vb* **treed; tree·ing** **1** : to drive up or as if up a tree **2** : to furnish or fit with a tree ⟨*tree* an axle⟩

tree farm *n* : an area of forest land managed to ensure continuous commercial production — **tree farmer** *n* — **tree farming** *n*

tree fern *n* : a tropical fern with a woody stalk and a top of large often feathery fronds

tree frog *n* : any of a family of tailless tree-dwelling amphibians (as the spring peeper)

tree hopper *n* : any of several small leaping insects that are related to the leafhoppers and live on sap from branches and twigs

tree house *n* : a structure (as a playhouse) built among the branches of a tree

tree line *n* : TIMBERLINE

\ə\ **abut**	\au̇\ **out**	\i\ **tip**	\ȯ\ **saw**	\u̇\ **foot**
\ər\ **further**	\ch\ **chin**	\ī\ **life**	\ȯi\ **coin**	\y\ **yet**
\a\ **mat**	\e\ **pet**	\j\ **job**	\th\ **thin**	\yü\ **few**
\ā\ **take**	\ē\ **easy**	\ŋ\ **sing**	\th\ **this**	\yu̇\ **cure**
\ä\ **cot, cart**	\g\ **go**	\ō\ **bone**	\ü\ **food**	\zh\ **vision**

tree of heaven : an Asian ailanthus that has leaves resembling those of the sumacs and that is widely grown as a shade and ornamental tree

tree ring *n* : ANNUAL RING

tree toad *n* : TREE FROG

tree-top \'trē-,täp\ *n* **1** : the highest part of a tree **2** *pl* : the height or line marked by the tops of a group of trees

tre-foil \'trē-,fȯil, 'tref-,ȯil\ *n* **1** : any of several herbs (as a clover) of the legume family that have leaves with three leaflets **2** : an ornament or symbol shaped like a leaf with three parts

trefoil 2

¹trek \'trek\ *vb* **trekked; trek-king** **1** *chiefly southern Africa* : to travel or migrate by ox wagon or in a train of such wagons **2** : to make one's way slowly and painfully [from *trek,* a word in Afrikaans (an official language in South Africa that is based on Dutch) meaning "to travel by ox wagon", from Dutch *trecken* "to haul, pull"]

²trek *n* **1** *chiefly southern Africa* : an organized journey or migration of a group of settlers traveling by ox wagon **2** : a slow or difficult journey

trel-lis \'trel-əs\ *n* : a frame of lattice used especially as a screen or a support for climbing plants — **trel-lised** \'trel-əst\ *adj*

trem-a-tode \'trem-ə-,tōd\ *n* : any of a class of parasitic flatworms including the flukes — **trematode** *adj*

¹trem-ble \'trem-bəl\ *vb* **trem-bled; trem-bling** \-b(ə-)liŋ\ **1** : to shake uncontrollably (as with fear or cold) : SHIVER **2** : to move, sound, or happen as if shaken ⟨the building *trembled* from the blast⟩ ⟨my voice *trembled*⟩ **3** : to have strong fear or doubt ⟨I *tremble* to think what might happen⟩ — **trem-bler** \-b(ə-)lər\ *n*

²tremble *n* **1** : a fit or spell of uncontrollable shaking or quivering **2** : a tremor or series of tremors

tre-men-dous \tri-'men-dəs\ *adj* **1** : causing dread, awe, or terror : DREADFUL **2** : astonishing because of great size or power **syn** see MONSTROUS — **tre-men-dous-ly** *adv*

trem-o-lo \'trem-ə-,lō\ *n, pl* **-los** **1** : the rapid repetition of a musical tone or of alternating tones to produce a rapid wavering sound **2** : a mechanical device in an organ for causing a rapid wavering sound

trem-or \'trem-ər\ *n* **1** : a trembling or shaking usually caused by weakness or disease **2** : a quivering or vibrating motion; *esp* : a small movement of the earth before or after an earthquake

trem-u-lous \'trem-yə-ləs\ *adj* **1** : marked by or affected with trembling or tremors ⟨*tremulous* hands⟩ **2** : FEARFUL 2, TIMID ⟨a shy *tremulous* person⟩ **3** : caused by or displaying a tremulous state or condition ⟨a *tremulous* smile⟩

trench \'trench\ *n* **1 a** : a long narrow cut in the ground : DITCH **b** : a ditch protected by a bank of earth used to shelter soldiers **2** : a long narrow steep-sided depression in the ocean floor

tren-chant \'tren-chənt\ *adj* **1** : having a sharp edge or point : CUTTING **2** : sharply clear and to the point : PENETRATING ⟨a *trenchant* analysis⟩ **3** : forceful and effective in expressing ideas — **tren-chant-ly** *adv*

trench coat *n* : a loose double-breasted raincoat with deep pockets, belt, and straps on the shoulders

tren-cher \'tren-chər\ *n* : a wooden platter for serving food

tren-cher-man \'tren-chər-mən\ *n* : a hearty eater

trench mouth *n* : a destructive infectious inflammation of the mouth caused by bacteria

¹trend \'trend\ *vb* **1** : to extend in a general direction **2** : to show a tendency : INCLINE

²trend *n* **1** : general direction taken **2 a** : a general tendency or movement **b** : a current style or liking

trep-i-da-tion \,trep-ə-'dā-shən\ *n* : a state of alarm

¹tres-pass \'tres-pəs, -,pas\ *n* **1** : ¹SIN, OFFENSE **2** : an unlawful act committed on the person, property, or rights of another; *esp* : unlawful entry on someone else's land

²trespass *vb* **1** : ERR 1, SIN **2** : to commit a trespass; *esp* : to enter unlawfully upon the land of another — **tres-pass-er** *n*

tress \'tres\ *n* : a long lock of hair

tres-tle \'tres-əl\ *n* **1** : a braced frame consisting usually of a horizontal piece with spreading legs at each end that supports something (as the top of a table) **2** : a structure of timbers or steel for carrying a road or railroad over a valley

trey \'trā\ *n, pl* **treys** : a card or dice with three spots

tri- *prefix* **1** : three **2** : having three elements or parts **2** : into three ⟨*tri*sect⟩ **3 a** : three times ⟨*tri*weekly⟩ **b** : every third ⟨*tri*weekly⟩ [derived from Latin *tri-, tres* and Greek *tri-, treis* "three"]

tri-ac-e-tate \(')trī-'as-ə-,tāt\ *n* : a textile fiber or fabric made by the chemical addition of acetate groups to cellulose

tri-ad \'trī-,ad *also* -əd\ *n* **1** : a union or group of three usually closely related persons or things **2** : a chord made up usually of the first, third, and fifth notes of a scale — **tri-ad-ic** \trī-'ad-ik\ *adj*

¹tri-al \'trī(-ə)l\ *n* **1** : the action or process of testing or trying **2** : the hearing and judgment of a case in court **3** : a test of faith, patience, or strength **4** : an experiment to test quality, value, or usefulness **5** : ²ATTEMPT 1, EFFORT

²trial *adj* **1** : of, relating to, or used in a trial **2** : made or done as a test or experiment ⟨a *trial* run⟩

trial and error *n* : the trying of this and that until something succeeds

tri-an-gle \'trī-,aŋ-gəl\ *n* **1** : a figure that has three sides and three angles : a polygon having three sides **2** : a percussion instrument made of a steel rod bent into a triangle open at one corner which is played by striking with a metal rod **3** : a drafting instrument consisting of a thin flat right-angled triangle

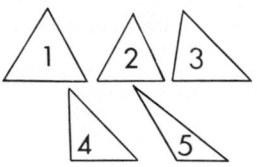

triangle 1: *1* equilateral, *2* isosceles, *3* scalene, *4* right, *5* obtuse

tri-an-gu-lar \trī-'aŋ-gyə-lər\ *adj* **1** : of, relating to, or having the form of a triangle **2** : having one or more triangular bases or principal surfaces ⟨a *triangular* pyramid⟩

triangular numbers *n pl* : numbers (as 1, 3, 6, 10, 15) that are of the general form $\frac{n(n + 1)}{2}$ where $n = 1, 2, 3, \ldots$ and represent the number of dots in the figures formed starting with one dot and adding rows one after another to form triangles each row of which has one more dot than the one before

tri-an-gu-la-tion \(,)trī-,aŋ-gyə-'lā-shən\ *n* : the method in surveying of making measurements and using trigonometry to find where places are located on the earth's surface using points whose exact location is known and especially by constructing a network of triangles

Tri-as-sic \trī-'as-ik\ *adj* : of, relating to, or being the earliest period of the Mesozoic era of geological history marked by the first appearance of dinosaurs; *also* : relating to the corresponding system of rocks — see GEOLOGIC TIME table — **Triassic** *n*

tri-atom-ic \,trī-ə-'täm-ik\ *adj* : having three atoms in the molecule ⟨ozone is *triatomic* oxygen⟩

trib-al \'trī-bəl\ *adj* : of, relating to, or characteristic of a tribe — **trib-al-ly** \-bə-lē\ *adv*

tribe \'trīb\ *n* **1** : a social group made up of many families, clans, or generations that share the same language, customs, and beliefs **2** : a group of persons with a common character, occupation, or interest **3** : a group of related plants or animals

tribes·man \'trībz-mən\ *n* : a member of a tribe

trib·u·la·tion \,trib-yə-'lā-shən\ *n* **1** : distress or suffering resulting from cruel or unjust treatment or misfortune **2** : a trying experience

tri·bu·nal \trī-'byün-ᵊl, trib-'yün-\ *n* **1** : the seat of a judge **2** : a court of justice **3** : something that decides or determines ⟨the *tribunal* of public opinion⟩

tri·bune \'trib-,yün, trib-'yün\ *n* **1** : a Roman official who protected plebeian citizens from unjust action by patrician magistrates **2** : a defender of the people especially against injustice — **tri·bune·ship** \-,ship\ *n*

¹trib·u·tary \'trib-yə-,ter-ē\ *adj* **1** : paying tribute to another : SUBJECT **2** : paid or owed as tribute **3** : contributing or adding to something larger or more important; *esp* : flowing into a larger stream or lake

²tributary *n, pl* **-tar·ies** **1** : a ruler or state that pays tribute **2** : a stream flowing into a larger stream or a lake

trib·ute \'trib-,yüt, -yət\ *n* **1 a** : a payment made by one ruler or nation to another to show obedience or to obtain peace or protection **b** : a tax to raise money for a tribute **c** : the obligation to pay tribute ⟨nations under *tribute*⟩ **2** : something (as a gift or speech of praise) that is given or performed to show appreciation, respect, or affection ⟨floral *tribute*⟩

trice \'trīs\ *n* : a brief space of time : INSTANT — used chiefly in the phrase *in a trice*

tri·ceps \'trī-,seps\ *n, pl* **tri·ceps·es** *also* **triceps** : a large muscle along the back of the upper arm that is attached at its upper end by three main parts and that acts to extend the arm at the elbow joint

tri·cer·a·tops \(')trī-'ser-ə-,täps\ *n* : any of a genus of large plant-eating Cretaceous dinosaurs with three horns, a bony hood or crest on the neck, and hoofed toes

tri·chi·na \trik-'ī-nə\ *n, pl* **-nae** \-nē\ *also* **-nas** **1** : a small slender nematode worm which enters the body of flesh-eating mammals (as the hog and human beings) when infected meat is eaten and whose larvae form cysts in voluntary muscles causing trichinosis **2** : TRICHINOSIS

trich·i·no·sis \,trik-ə-'nō-səs\ *n, pl* **-no·ses** \-'nō-,sēz\ : a dangerous and painful disease caused by trichinae

tricho·mo·ni·a·sis \,trik-ə-mə-'nī-ə-səs\ *n, pl* **-a·ses** \-,sēz\ : an infection of the vagina by a protozoan parasite that is marked by itching and a frothy discharge having a bad odor and that also occurs in the male urethra

¹trick \'trik\ *n* **1 a** : an action meant to deceive or cheat **b** : a mischievous act : PRANK **c** : an unwise or childish action **d** : a skillful or clever feat designed to puzzle or amuse ⟨a juggler's *tricks*⟩ **2** : an habitual peculiarity of behavior or manner **3 a** : a quick or artful way of getting a result : KNACK **b** : a technical device (as of an art or craft) **4** : the cards played in one round of a card game

²trick *vb* **1** : to deceive with tricks : CHEAT **2** : to dress or decorate especially oddly or ornately ⟨*tricked* out in a gaudy uniform⟩

³trick *adj* : of or relating to or involving tricks or trickery ⟨*trick* photography⟩

trick·ery \'trik-(ə-)rē\ *n, pl* **-er·ies** : the use of tricks to deceive or cheat

trick·le \'trik-əl\ *vb* **trick·led; trick·ling** \-(ə-)liŋ\ **1** : to flow or fall in drops **2** : to flow in a thin slow stream — **trickle** *n*

trick or treat *n* : a children's Halloween practice of going around usually in costume asking for treats — **trick–or–treat** *vb*

trick·ster \'trik-stər\ *n* : one who tricks: as **a** : a dishonest person who cheats others by trickery **b** : MAGICIAN 2

tricky \'trik-ē\ *adj* **trick·i·er; -est** **1** : likely to use or characterized by tricks or trickery **2** : requiring skill or caution : DIFFICULT ⟨a *tricky* situation⟩

¹tri·col·or \'trī-,kəl-ər\ *n* : a flag of three colors

²tricolor *or* **tri·col·ored** \'trī-kəl-ərd\ *adj* : having or using three colors

tri·corn \'trī-,kó(ə)rn\ *adj* : having three horns or corners

tri·cot \'trē-kō, 'trī-kət\ *n* : a knitted fabric (as for underwear) that is resistant to runs

tri·cus·pid valve \(,)trī-'kəs-pəd-\ *n* : a valve on the right side of the heart between the atrium and the ventricle that has three flaps and prevents the backward flow of blood from the ventricle to the atrium

tri·cy·cle \'trī-,sik-əl\ *n* : a three-wheeled vehicle usually moved by pedals

tri·dent \'trīd-ᵊnt\ *n* : a spear with three prongs [from Latin *trident-, tridens* "trident", from *tridens* (adjective) "having three teeth", from *tri-* "three" and *dens* "tooth" — related to DENTAL] — **trident** *adj*

¹tried \'trīd\ *past and past participle of* TRY

²tried *adj* : found good, faithful, or trustworthy through experience or testing ⟨a *tried* recipe⟩

tried–and–true *adj* : known to be reliable ⟨a *tried-and-true* friend⟩ ⟨a *tried-and-true* remedy⟩

tri·en·ni·al \(')trī-'en-ē-əl\ *adj* **1** : consisting of or lasting for three years **2** : occurring or being done every three years — **triennial** *n* — **tri·en·ni·al·ly** \-ē-ə-lē\ *adv*

¹tri·fle \'trī-fəl\ *n* **1** : something of little value or importance; *esp* : a small amount of money **2** : a dessert of sponge cake spread with jam or jelly covered with a custard and whipped cream — **a trifle** : to a small degree : SLIGHTLY ⟨only *a trifle* overweight⟩

²trifle *vb* **tri·fled; tri·fling** \-f(ə-)liŋ\ **1 a** : to talk in a joking manner **b** : to act in a silly or careless manner : PLAY **2** : to waste time in trifling or on trifles **3** : to handle something idly : TOY — **tri·fler** \-f(ə-)lər\ *n*

tri·fling \'trī-fliŋ\ *adj* **1** : having little meaning or seriousness : FRIVOLOUS ⟨*trifling* talk⟩ **2** : of little value ⟨a *trifling* sum⟩

trig \'trig\ *n* : TRIGONOMETRY

¹trig·ger \'trig-ər\ *n* : a movable lever that activates a device when it is squeezed; *esp* : the part of the lock of a firearm that releases the hammer and so fires the gun — **trigger** *adj* — **trig·gered** \-ərd\ *adj*

²trigger *vb* **trig·gered; trig·ger·ing** \-(ə-)riŋ\ **1** : to fire by pulling a trigger **2** : to begin, stir up, or set in motion as if by pulling a trigger

trig·o·no·met·ric \,trig-ə-nə-'me-trik\ *also* **trig·o·no·met·ri·cal** \-tri-kəl\ *adj* : of, relating to, or involving trigonometry — **trig·o·no·met·ri·cal·ly** \-tri-k(ə-)lē\ *adv*

trigonometric function *n* : any of a group of functions (as the sine, cosine, and tangent) that for an acute angle are most easily expressed as ratios between the sides of a right triangle containing the angle

trig·o·nom·e·try \,trig-ə-'näm-ə-trē\ *n* : a branch of mathematics concerned with the study of the properties of triangles and trigonometric functions and of their practical uses [from scientific Latin *trigonometria*, literally "triangle measurement", derived from Greek *tri-* "three" and Greek *gonia* "angle" and Greek *-metria* "art or science of measuring"]

tri·hy·brid \(')trī-'hī-brəd\ *adj* : of, involving, or being an individual or stock that is hybrid with respect to three different pairs of genes

tri·lat·er·al \(')trī-'lat-ə-rəl, -'la-trəl\ *adj* : having three sides

¹trill \'tril\ *n* **1 a** : the alternation of two musical tones a whole step apart **b** : VIBRATO **2** : ¹WARBLE 1 **3 a** : the

\ə\ abut	\au̇\ out	\i\ tip	\ȯ\ saw	\u̇\ foot
\ər\ further	\ch\ chin	\ī\ life	\ȯi\ coin	\y\ yet
\a\ mat	\e\ pet	\j\ job	\th\ thin	\yü\ few
\ā\ take	\ē\ easy	\ŋ\ sing	\t̲h̲\ this	\yu̇\ cure
\ä\ cot, cart	\g\ go	\ō\ bone	\ü\ food	\zh\ vision

rapid vibration of one speech organ against another (as of the tip of the tongue against the teeth) **b** : a speech sound produced by a trill

²trill *vb* **1** : to utter as or with a trill **2** : to play or sing with a trill : QUAVER

tril·lion \'tril-yən\ *n* — see NUMBER table — **trillion** *adj* — **tril·lionth** \-yən(t)th\ *adj* — **trillionth** *n*

tril·li·um \'tril-ē-əm\ *n* : any of a genus of herbs related to the lilies that have three large leaves arranged around the upright stem at the same level and a single flower with three petals at the end of the stem — called also *wake-robin*

trillium

tri·lo·bite \'trī-lə-ˌbīt\ *n* : any of a group of extinct invertebrate animals that lived in Paleozoic seas, have a body composed of segments and divided lengthwise along the back into three parts, and are classified as arthropods

tril·o·gy \'tril-ə-jē\ *n, pl* **-gies** : a series of three literary or musical works that are closely related and develop a single theme

¹trim \'trim\ *vb* **trimmed; trim·ming** **1 a** : to decorate with ribbons, lace, or ornaments : ADORN ⟨*trim* a Christmas tree⟩ **b** : to arrange a display of goods in ⟨*trim* a shop window⟩ **2** : to defeat in a game or contest **3 a** : to make trim and neat especially by cutting or clipping **b** : to free of excess or unnecessary matter by or as if by cutting ⟨*trim* a steak⟩ ⟨*trim* a budget⟩ **4** : to cause (as a ship) to take the right position in the water by balancing the load carried **5** : to adjust (as an airplane or submarine) for horizontal movement or for motion upward or downward **6** : to adjust (as a sail) to a desired position — **trim·mer** *n*

²trim *adj* **trim·mer; trim·mest** : neat, orderly, and compact in line or structure ⟨a *trim* figure⟩ **syn** see NEAT — **trim·ly** *adv* — **trim·ness** *n*

³trim *adv* : in a trim manner : TRIMLY

⁴trim *n* **1** : good or healthy condition : FITNESS **2 a** : material used for ornament or trimming **b** : the woodwork in the finish of a building especially around doors and windows **3 a** : the position of a ship or boat especially with reference to the horizontal **b** : the relation between the plane of a sail and the direction of the ship **c** : the position of an airplane at which it will continue in level flight with no adjustments to the controls **4** : something that is trimmed off or cut out

trim·e·ter \'trim-ət-ər\ *n* : a line of verse consisting of three metrical feet

trim·ming \'trim-iŋ\ *n* **1** : the action of one that trims **2** : ²DEFEAT 2, BEATING **3** : something that trims, ornaments, or completes **4** *pl* : parts removed by trimming

tri·month·ly \(')trī-'mən(t)th-lē\ *adj* : occurring every three months

trin·i·ty \'trin-ət-ē\ *n, pl* **-ties** **1** *cap* : the unity of Father, Son, and Holy Spirit existing as three persons in one Godhead according to some Christian doctrines **2** : TRIAD 1

Trinity Sunday *n* : the eighth Sunday after Easter

trin·ket \'triŋ-kət\ *n* **1** : a small ornament (as a jewel or ring) **2** : a thing of little value

¹tri·no·mi·al \trī-'nō-mē-əl\ *n* : a polynomial of three terms

²trinomial *adj* : consisting of three terms

trio \'trē-ō\ *n, pl* **tri·os** **1 a** : a musical composition for three voices or instruments **b** : the performers of a musical trio **2** : a group or set of three

tri·ode \'trī-ˌōd\ *n* : a vacuum tube with three electrodes

¹trip \'trip\ *n* **1** : an act of causing another to stumble or fall **2 a** : a traveling from one place to another **b** : a brief errand or journey with a purpose that often takes

place on a regular basis ⟨a *trip* to the dentist⟩ **3** : ERROR 4, MISSTEP **4** : a quick light step **5 a** : the action of releasing something mechanically **b** : a device (as a catch) for releasing a mechanism **syn** see JOURNEY

²trip *vb* **tripped; trip·ping** **1** : to move (as in dancing or walking) with light quick steps **2** : to catch one's foot while walking or running : cause to stumble **3 a** : to make or cause to make a mistake **b** : to catch making a false statement, error, or blunder **4** : to release or start a device by moving a catch

tri·par·tite \(')trī-'pär-,tīt\ *adj* **1** : divided into or made of three parts **2** : made between or involving three parties ⟨a *tripartite* treaty⟩

tripe \'trīp\ *n* **1** : stomach tissue of a cud-chewing animal (as the ox) used as food **2** : something poor, worthless, or ridiculous

¹tri·ple \'trip-əl\ *vb* **tri·pled; tri·pling** \'trip-(ə-)liŋ\ **1** : to make or become three times as great or as many : multiply by three **2** : to make a triple in baseball

²triple *n* **1 a** : a triple sum, quantity, or number **b** : a combination, group, or series of three **2** : a hit that permits a batter to reach third base safely

³triple *adj* **1** : being three times as great or as many **2** : having three units or parts **3** : three times repeated

triple bond *n* : a chemical bond in which three pairs of electrons are shared by two atoms in a molecule — compare SINGLE BOND, DOUBLE BOND

triple jump *n* : a track-and-field event in which competitors make three jumps in a row after a running start

triple play *n* : a play in baseball by which three base runners are put out

triple point *n* : the condition of temperature and pressure under which the gaseous, liquid, and solid forms of a substance change into each other at equal rates so that the amount of each always remains the same

trip·let \'trip-lət\ *n* **1** : a unit of three lines of verse **2** : a combination, set, or group of three **3** : one of three offspring born at one birth **4** : a group of three notes played in the time of two of the same value

¹tri·plex \'trip-,leks, 'trī-,pleks\ *adj* : ³TRIPLE 2

²triplex *n* : something that has three parts (as an apartment with three floors)

¹trip·li·cate \'trip-li-kət\ *adj* : made in three identical copies

²trip·li·cate \'trip-lə-,kāt\ *vb* **-cat·ed; -cat·ing** : to make triple or provide in triplicate

³trip·li·cate \'trip-li-kət\ *n* : three copies all alike — used with *in* ⟨typed in *triplicate*⟩

tri·ply \'trip-(ə-)lē\ *adv* : in a triple degree, amount, or manner

tri·pod \'trī-,päd\ *n* **1** : something (as a container or stool) resting on three legs **2** : a three-legged stand (as for a camera)

trip·per \'trip-ər\ *n* **1** *chiefly British* : one that takes a trip : TOURIST **2** : a tripping device (as for operating a railroad signal)

trip·ping·ly \'trip-iŋ-lē\ *adv* : in a quick and lively manner

tri·sect \'trī-,sekt, trī-'sekt\ *vb* : to divide into three usually equal parts — **tri·sec·tion** \'trī-,sek-shən, trī-'sek-\ *n* — **tri·sec·tor** \'trī-,sek-tər, trī-'sek-\ *n*

tri·syl·lab·ic \,trī-sə-'lab-ik\ *adj* : having three syllables — **tri·syl·la·ble** \'trī-,sil-ə-bəl, (')trī-'sil-\ *n*

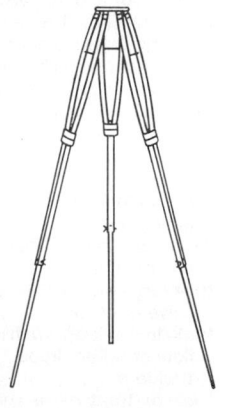

tripod 2

trite \'trīt\ *adj* **trit·er; trit·est** : so common that the newness or cleverness has worn off — **trite·ly** *adv* — **trite·ness** *n*

tri·ti·um \'trit-ē-əm, 'trish-ē-\ *n* : a rare radioactive form of hydrogen having atoms with three times the mass of ordinary light hydrogen atoms

tri·ton \'trīt-ᵊn\ *n* : any of various large sea snails with a heavy cone-shaped shell; *also* : the shell of a triton

¹tri·umph \'trī-əm(p)f\ *n*   **1** : an ancient Roman ceremony honoring a victorious general   **2** : the joy of victory or success   **3 a** : a military victory or conquest   **b** : any great success

²triumph *vb*   **1** : to celebrate victory or success with much rejoicing   **2** : to gain victory : WIN

tri·um·phal \trī-'əm(p)-fəl\ *adj* : of, relating to, or honoring a triumph ⟨a *triumphal* procession⟩

tri·um·phant \trī-'əm(p)-fənt\ *adj*   **1** : VICTORIOUS, CONQUERING   **2** : rejoicing for or celebrating victory or success — **tri·um·phant·ly** *adv*

tri·um·vir \trī-'əm-vər\ *n* : one of a council or ruling body of three especially in ancient Rome

tri·um·vi·rate \trī-'əm-və-rət\ *n*   **1** : government by three persons who share authority and responsibility   **2** : the office or term of office of a triumvir   **3** : a group of three persons or things having something in common

triv·et \'triv-ət\ *n*   **1** : a three-legged stand : TRIPOD   **2** : an ornamental metal or ceramic plate used under a hot dish to protect the table

triv·ia \'triv-ē-ə\ *n sing or pl*   **1** : unimportant matters or details   **2** : interesting little-known facts

triv·i·al \'triv-ē-əl\ *adj*   **1** : ²ORDINARY 2, COMMONPLACE   **2** : of little worth or importance : INSIGNIFICANT ⟨a *trivial* mistake⟩ — **triv·i·al·ly** \-ē-ə-lē\ *adv*

   Word History The words *trivial* and *trivia* can be traced back to the Latin noun *trivium,* meaning "a place where three roads meet". The Latin word was made from *tri-*, meaning "three", and *via* "way, road". The adjective form of *trivium* was *trivialis.* It was used to mean "common, ordinary". This sense probably developed from the use of these three-road junctions as meeting places for the common people to exchange ordinary bits of news. In the 16th century, the adjective *trivial* came to be used in English with the same meaning. In time, this adjective also took on the sense of "of little worth or importance". This is its main meaning today. It wasn't until the 1920s that the word *trivia* began being used for "unimportant matters". This word is the plural form of the Latin word *trivium.* [from Latin *trivialis* "found everywhere, commonplace, trivial", from *trivium* "a place where three roads meet", from *tri-* "three" and *via* "way"]

triv·i·al·i·ty \,triv-ē-'al-ət-ē\ *n, pl* **-ties**   **1** : the quality or state of being trivial   **2** : something trivial : TRIFLE

¹tri·week·ly \(')trī-'wē-klē\ *adj*   **1** : occurring or appearing three times a week   **2** : occurring or appearing every three weeks — **triweekly** *adv*

²triweekly *n* : a triweekly publication

tro·chee \'trō-kē\ *n* : a metrical foot consisting of one accented syllable followed by one unaccented syllable (as in *hungry*) — **tro·cha·ic** \trō-'kā-ik\ *adj*

trod *past and past participle of* TREAD

trodden *past participle of* TREAD

Tro·jan \'trō-jən\ *n* : a person born or living in ancient Troy — **Trojan** *adj*

Trojan War *n* : a 10-year war between the ancient Greeks and Trojans

¹troll \'trōl\ *vb*   **1 a** : to sing the parts of (as a round)   **b** : to sing or recite loudly or merrily   **2** : to fish for with a hook and line drawn through the water [Middle English *trollen* "to cause to move round and round"] — **troll·er** *n*

²troll *n*   **1** : a lure or a line with its bait and hook used in trolling   **2** : a song in which different people sing the same part one after another

³troll *n* : a dwarf or giant of folklore living in caves or hills [from Norwegian *troll* and Danish *trold,* both meaning "a giant or dwarf of folklore"]

trol·ley *or* **trol·ly** \'träl-ē\ *n, pl* **trolleys** *or* **trollies**   **1 a** : a

device for carrying current from a wire to an electrically driven vehicle   **b** : a streetcar that runs on tracks and gets its electric power through a trolley — called also *trolley car*   **2** : a wheeled carriage running on an overhead rail or track

trom·bone \träm-'bōn, (,)trəm-\ *n* : a brass wind instrument with a section that can slide in and out to make different tones [from Italian *trombone,* literally "large trumpet", from *tromba* "trumpet"] — **trom·bon·ist** \-'bō-nəst\ *n*

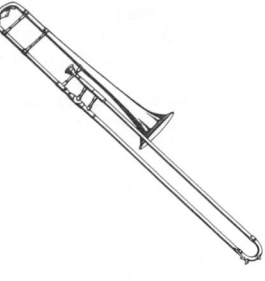

trombone

tromp \'trämp, 'tròmp\ *vb* : ¹TRAMP 1, TRAMPLE

¹troop \'trüp\ *n*   **1 a** : a group of soldiers   **b** *pl* : ARMED FORCES, MILITARY   **2** : a collection of beings or things : COMPANY   **3** : a unit of Boy Scouts or Girl Scouts under an adult leader

²troop *vb* : to move or gather in crowds

troop·er \'trü-pər\ *n*   **1** : a cavalry soldier   **2 a** : a mounted police officer   **b** : a state police officer

tro·phic \'trō-fik\ *adj* : of or relating to the process of getting and eating food : NUTRITIONAL

tro·phy \'trō-fē\ *n, pl* **trophies**   **1** : something taken from the enemy during battle or conquest and kept as proof of one's bravery or victory ⟨warriors took scalps as *trophies*⟩   **2** : something given in recognition of a victory or as an award for achievement ⟨a golf *trophy*⟩ — **tro·phied** \-fēd\ *adj*

¹trop·ic \'träp-ik\ *n*   **1** : either of the two parallels of the earth's latitude that are approximately 23½ degrees north of the equator and approximately 23½ degrees south of the equator   **2** *pl, often cap* : the region lying between the two tropics [Middle English *tropik* (noun) "tropic", from Latin *tropicus* (adjective) "of the solstice", from Greek *tropikos* (same meaning), from *tropē* "turn"; so called because it marks the turning point in the sun's apparent progression up the sky]

²tropic *adj* : TROPICAL

³tro·pic \'trō-pik\ *adj* : of, relating to, or being a tropism ⟨a *tropic* movement of a plant⟩

trop·i·cal \'träp-i-kəl\ *adj* : of, relating to, occurring in, or used in the tropics — **trop·i·cal·ly** \-k(ə-)lē\ *adv*

tropical aquarium *n* : an aquarium kept at a warm and constant temperature and used especially for tropical fish

tropical fish *n* : any of various small usually brightly colored fishes that occur wild especially in the tropics and are often kept in tropical aquariums

tropical rain forest *n* : RAIN FOREST 1

tropic of Cancer : the parallel of latitude that is 23½ degrees north of the equator and is the northernmost latitude reached by the overhead sun

tropic of Capricorn : the parallel of latitude that is 23½ degrees south of the equator and is the southernmost latitude reached by the overhead sun

tro·pism \'trō-,piz-əm\ *n* : an automatic movement by an organism unable to move about from place to place and especially by a plant that involves a turning or growing toward or away from a stimulus (as light or moisture); *also* : a reflex reaction involving such a movement — compare TAXIS — **tro·pis·tic** \trō-'pis-tik\ *adj*

tro·po·pause \'trōp-ə-,póz, 'träp-\ *n* : the region at the top

\ə\ **abut**	\au̇\ **out**	\i\ **tip**	\ȯ\ **saw**	\u̇\ **foot**
\ər\ **further**	\ch\ **chin**	\ī\ **life**	\ȯi\ **coin**	\y\ **yet**
\a\ **mat**	\e\ **pet**	\j\ **job**	\th\ **thin**	\yü\ **few**
\ā\ **take**	\ē\ **easy**	\ŋ\ **sing**	\t͟h\ **this**	\yu̇\ **cure**
\ä\ **cot, cart**	\g\ **go**	\ō\ **bone**	\ü\ **food**	\zh\ **vision**

of the troposphere

tro·po·sphere \'trōp-ə-ˌsfi(ə)r, 'trāp-\ *n* : the portion of the atmosphere which extends from the earth's surface to about 11 to 16 kilometers and in which temperature generally decreases rapidly with altitude and clouds form — **tro·po·spher·ic** \ˌtrōp-ə-'sfi(ə)r-ik, ˌtrāp-, -'sfer-\ *adj*

¹trot \'trät\ *n* **1** : a moderately fast gait of a four-footed animal (as a horse) in which a front foot and the opposite hind foot move at the same time **2** : a human jogging pace between a walk and a run

²trot *vb* **trot·ted; trot·ting** **1** : to ride, drive, go, or cause to go at a trot **2** : to go along quickly : HURRY

¹troth \'träth, 'trȯth, 'trōth, *or with* th\ *n* **1** : loyal or pledged faithfulness : FIDELITY **2** : one's pledged word; *also* : BETROTHAL

²troth *vb* : BETROTH, PLEDGE

trot·ter \'trät-ər\ *n* : one that trots; *esp* : a standardbred horse trained for harness racing

trou·ba·dour \'trü-bə-ˌdō(ə)r, -ˌdȯ(ə)r, -ˌdu̇(ə)r\ *n* : a poet= musician of the Middle Ages in France and Italy

¹trou·ble \'trəb-əl\ *vb* **trou·bled; trou·bling** \'trəb-(ə-)liŋ\ **1 a** : to disturb or become disturbed mentally or spiritually : WORRY **b** : to produce physical disorder in : AFFLICT **c** : to put to exertion or inconvenience **2** : to put into confused motion **3** : to make an effort

²trouble *n* **1 a** : the quality or state of being troubled : MISFORTUNE ⟨help people in *trouble*⟩ **b** : an instance of distress or annoyance ⟨made light of their *troubles*⟩ **2** : disorder or public unrest ⟨labor *trouble*⟩ **3** : a state or condition of distress, annoyance, or difficulty ⟨in big financial *trouble*⟩: as **a** : physical distress or ill health : AILMENT ⟨heart *trouble*⟩ **b** : failure to work properly ⟨engine *trouble*⟩ **c** : a condition of doing something badly or with great difficulty ⟨had *trouble* reading⟩ **4** : an effort made : PAINS ⟨took the *trouble* to write⟩ **5 a** : a cause of distress, annoyance, or inconvenience **b** : a negative feature or characteristic ⟨laziness is your biggest *trouble*⟩ **c** : an unpleasant fact ⟨the *trouble* is I'm broke⟩

trou·ble·mak·er \'trəb-əl-ˌmā-kər\ *n* : a person who causes problems or disagreements

trou·ble·some \'trəb-əl-səm\ *adj* **1** : DIFFICULT 2a, BURDENSOME **2** : giving trouble or anxiety ⟨a *troublesome* infection⟩ — **trou·ble·some·ly** *adv*

trou·blous \'trəb-(ə-)ləs\ *adj* **1** : full of trouble : STORMY ⟨these *troublous* times⟩ **2** : causing trouble : TROUBLESOME

trough \'trȯf\ *n, pl* **troughs** \'trȯfs, 'trȯvz\ **1** : a long shallow container for the drinking water or feed of domestic animals **2** : a pipe, drain, or channel for water; *esp* : ¹GUTTER 1a **3** : a long and narrow or shallow hollow (as between waves or hills)

trounce \'traun(t)s\ *vb* **trounced; trounc·ing** **1** : to thrash or punish severely : FLOG **2** : to defeat thoroughly

¹troupe \'trüp\ *n* : a company or troop especially of stage performers

²troupe *vb* **trouped; troup·ing** **1** : to travel in a troupe **2** : to perform as a member of a theatrical troupe — **troup·er** *n*

trou·ser \'trau̇-zər\ *adj* : of or relating to trousers

trou·sers \'trau̇-zərz\ *n pl* : PANTS 1

trous·seau \'trü-ˌsō\ *n, pl* **trous·seaux** \-ˌsōz\ *or* **trous·seaus** : the clothes and personal possessions (as household linens) of a bride

trout \'trau̇t\ *n, pl* **trout** *also* **trouts** **1** : any of various edible fishes mostly smaller than the related salmons, restricted to cool clear fresh waters, and often speckled with dark colors **2** : any of various fishes that resemble the

trout 1

true trouts

¹trow·el \'trau̇(-ə)l\ *n* **1** : a small hand tool consisting of a flat blade with a handle used for spreading and smoothing mortar or plaster **2** : a small hand tool with a curved blade used by gardeners

²trowel *vb* **-eled** *or* **-elled; -el·ing** *or* **-el·ling** : to smooth, mix, or apply with a trowel

troy \'trȯi\ *adj* : expressed in troy weight

troy weight *n* : a series of units of weight based on a pound of 12 ounces and the ounce of 20 pennyweights or 480 grains — see MEASURE table

tru·an·cy \'trü-ən-sē\ *n, pl* **-cies** : an act or an instance of being a truant

tru·ant \'trü-ənt\ *n* **1** : a person who neglects duty **2** : a student who stays out of school without permission — **truant** *adj*

truant officer *n* : a school officer whose duty is to check on truants

truce \'trüs\ *n* **1** : a temporary stopping of fighting (as in a war) **2** : a short rest especially from something unpleasant

¹truck \'trək\ *n* **1** : ²BARTER **2** : goods for barter or for small trade **3** : close association ⟨have no *truck* with such people⟩ **4** : vegetables grown for market **5 a** : small articles of little value **b** : RUBBISH [from earlier *truck* (verb) "to exchange goods, swap", from Middle English *trukken* (same meaning), from early French *troquer* (same meaning)]

²truck *n* : a wheeled vehicle for moving heavy articles [from *truck* "a small wheel", probably from Latin *trochus* "iron hoop"]

³truck *vb* : to transport on or by truck

truck·er \'trək-ər\ *n* **1** : a person whose business is transporting goods by truck **2** : a truck driver

truck farm *n* : a farm growing vegetables for market — **truck farmer** *n*

truck garden *n* : a garden where vegetables are raised for market

truck·load \'trək-ˌlōd, -ˌlȯd\ *n* : a load that fills a truck

truc·u·lence \'trək-yə-lən(t)s *also* 'trük-\ *n* : the quality or state of being truculent

tru·cu·lent \'trək-yə-lənt *also* 'trük-\ *adj* : ready and willing to fight or quarrel — **tru·cu·lent·ly** *adv*

¹trudge \'trəj\ *vb* **trudged; trudg·ing** : to walk or march steadily and usually with much effort — **trudg·er** *n*

²trudge *n* : a long tiring walk : TRAMP

¹true \'trü\ *adj* **tru·er; tru·est** **1** : completely loyal : FAITHFUL **2** : that can be relied on : CERTAIN **3** : agreeing with the facts : ACCURATE **4** : ¹HONEST 1, SINCERE ⟨*true* friendship⟩ **5** : properly so called : GENUINE ⟨lichens have no *true* stems⟩ **6** : placed or formed accurately : EXACT ⟨*true* pitch⟩ **7** : being or holding by right : LEGITIMATE ⟨the *true* owner⟩ **syn** see REAL

²true *n* : the quality or state of being accurate (as in adjustment) — used in the phrases *in true* and *out of true*

³true *vb* **trued; true·ing** *also* **tru·ing** : to bring to exactly correct condition as to place, position, or shape

⁴true *adv* **1** : in agreement with fact : TRUTHFULLY **2** : in an accurate manner : ACCURATELY ⟨the bullet flew straight and *true*⟩ **3** : without variation from type ⟨breed *true*⟩

true–blue \'trü-'blü\ *adj* : very faithful

true bug *n* : ¹BUG 1b

true–false test \'trü-'fȯls-\ *n* : a test made up of items that are to be marked as true or false

true seal *n* : HAIR SEAL

truf·fle \'trəf-əl, 'trüf-\ *n* : the usually dark and wrinkled fruiting body of a European fungus that grows in the ground; *also* : this fungus

tru·ism \'trü-ˌiz-əm\ *n* : an obvious truth

tru·ly \'trü-lē\ *adv* : in a true manner

¹trump \'trəmp\ *n* : a card of a suit any of whose cards will win over a card that is of a different suit; *also* : the suit whose cards are trumps for a particular hand — often used in pl.

²trump *vb* **1** : to take with a trump ⟨*trump* another player's card⟩ **2** : to play a trump

trumped–up \'trəm(p)-'təp\ *adj* : MADE-UP 1, FALSE ⟨arrested on *trumped-up* charges⟩

trum·pery \'trəm-p(ə-)rē\ *n, pl* **-per·ies** : things of no value — **trumpery** *adj*

¹trum·pet \'trəm-pət\ *n* **1**
: a wind instrument consisting of a long cylindrical metal tube commonly once or twice curved and ending in a bell **2** : something shaped like a trumpet **3** : a sound like that of a trumpet

²trumpet *vb* **1** : to blow a trumpet **2** : to make a sound like that of a trumpet

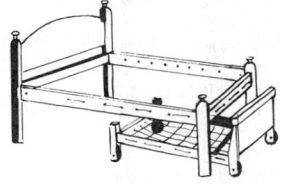
trumpet 1

trumpet creeper *n* : a North American woody vine with feathery leaves and large red trumpet-shaped flowers — called also *trumpet vine*

trum·pet·er \'trəm-pət-ər\ *n* : a trumpet player

trumpeter swan *n* : a rare pure white wild swan of western North America with a loud call that sounds like a trumpet

¹trun·cate \'trən-,kāt, 'trən-\ *adj* : having the end square or blunt ⟨a *truncate* leaf⟩

²truncate *vb* **trun·cat·ed; trun·cat·ing** : to shorten by or as if by cutting off — **trun·ca·tion** \trən-'kā-shən, trən-\ *n*

trun·cheon \'trən-chən\ *n* : a police officer's club

¹trun·dle \'trən-dᵊl\ *n* **1** : a small wheel or roller **2** : a cart or truck with low wheels

²trundle *vb* **trun·dled; trun·dling** \'trən-dliŋ, -dᵊl-iŋ\ : to roll along : WHEEL

trundle bed *n* : a low bed usually on small wheels that can be rolled under a higher bed

¹trunk \'trəŋk\ *n* **1 a** : the main stem of a tree apart from branches or roots **b** : the body of a person or animal apart

trundle bed

from the head, arms, and legs **c** : the main or central part of something ⟨*trunk* of an artery⟩ **2 a** : a box or chest for holding clothes or other articles especially for traveling **b** : the enclosed space usually in the rear of an automobile for carrying articles **3** : the long flexible muscular nose of an elephant or a related mammal **4** *pl* : men's shorts worn chiefly for sports ⟨swimming *trunks*⟩

²trunk *adj* : being or relating to a main line of a system

¹truss \'trəs\ *vb* **1 a** : to tie up tightly : BIND **b** : to tie the wings or legs of for cooking ⟨*truss* a turkey⟩ **2** : to support, strengthen, or stiffen by a truss

²truss *n* **1** : a rigid framework of beams, bars, or rods ⟨a *truss* for a roof⟩ **2** : a device worn to hold a hernia in place

¹trust \'trəst\ *n* **1 a** : firm belief in the character, ability, strength, or truth of someone or something **b** : a person or thing in which confidence is placed **2 a** : confident hope **b** : financial credit **3 a** : property held or managed by one person or organization (as a bank) for the benefit of another **b** : a combination of firms or corporations formed by a legal agreement and often held to reduce competition **4 a** : something (as a public office) held or managed by someone for the benefit of another **b** : responsibility for safety and well-being

²trust *vb* **1 a** : to place confidence : DEPEND ⟨*trust* in God⟩ ⟨*trust* to luck⟩ **b** : to be confident : HOPE **2** : to place in one's care or keeping : ENTRUST **3** : to rely on the truth of : BELIEVE **4** : to give financial credit to — **trust·er** *n*

trust company *n* : a corporation (as a bank) organized to act as a trustee

trust·ee \,trəs-'tē\ *n* : a person who has been given responsibility for someone else's property

trust·ee·ship \,trəs-'tē-,ship\ *n* : the office or job of a trustee

trust·ful \'trəst-fəl\ *adj* : full of trust — **trust·ful·ly** \-fə-lē\ *adv*

trust·ing \'trəs-tiŋ\ *adj* : having trust, faith, or confidence — **trust·ing·ly** *adv*

trust·wor·thy \'trəst-,wər-thē\ *adj* : deserving confidence : DEPENDABLE — **trust·wor·thi·ness** \-thē-nəs\ *n*

¹trusty \'trəs-tē\ *adj* **trust·i·er; -est** : TRUSTWORTHY, RELIABLE

²trusty \'trəs-tē *also* ,trəs-'tē\ *n, pl* **trust·ies** : a convict considered trustworthy and allowed special privileges

truth \'trüth\ *n, pl* **truths** \'trüthz, 'trüths\ **1** : the quality or state of being true **2** : a true or accepted statement **3** : the body of real events or facts **4** : agreement with fact or reality — **in truth** : in fact : ACTUALLY, REALLY

truth·ful \'trüth-fəl\ *adj* : telling or being in the habit of telling the truth — **truth·ful·ly** \-fə-lē\ *adv* — **truth·ful·ness** *n*

truth set *n* : a set of the elements that can be substituted in an open sentence to make it true

¹try \'trī\ *vb* **tried; try·ing** **1 a** : to examine or investigate in a court of law **b** : to conduct the trial of **2 a** : to put to a test ⟨*try* out something new⟩ ⟨*try* your luck⟩ **b** : to test to the limit ⟨you're *trying* my patience⟩ **3** : to melt down (as tallow) and obtain in a pure state : RENDER ⟨*try* out whale oil from blubber⟩ **4** : to make an effort to do ⟨I'll *try*⟩

²try *n, pl* **tries** : an effort to do something : ATTEMPT

try·ing \'trī-iŋ\ *adj* : hard to bear or put up with ⟨these are *trying* times⟩

try on *vb* : to put on (as a garment) in order to test the fit

try·out \'trī-,aut\ *n* : a test of the ability (as of an actor or athlete) to fill a part or meet standards

try out \(')trī-'aut\ *vb* : to take part in a tryout for a position on an athletic team or a part in a play

tryp·sin \'trip-sən\ *n* : an enzyme from pancreatic juice that helps to digest proteins

tryp·sin·o·gen \trip-'sin-ə-jən\ *n* : the inactive form of trypsin present in the pancreas

tryp·to·phan \'trip-tə-,fan\ *n* : an amino acid that is found in many proteins and is necessary for life but cannot be manufactured by the human body and must be obtained in food

¹tryst \'trist, *especially British* 'trīst\ *n* : a meeting arranged especially by lovers

²tryst *vb* : to keep a tryst

try·works \'trī-,wərks\ *n* : a brick furnace (as on a whaling ship) for melting down blubber to produce whale oil

tsar *variant of* CZAR

tset·se fly \'(t)set-sē-, 'tet-, '(t)sēt-, 'tēt-\ *n* : any of a genus of two-winged flies found mostly in Africa south of the Sahara desert and including some forms that pass on a one-celled animal causing a fatal sickness in cattle and sleeping sickness in human beings — called also *tsetse*

T–shirt *also* **tee shirt** \'tē-,shərt\ *n* **1** : a cotton undershirt with short sleeves and no collar **2** : a jersey outer shirt designed like a T-shirt

\ə\ abut	\au̇\ out	\i\ tip	\o̊\ saw	\u̇\ foot
\ər\ further	\ch\ chin	\ī\ life	\oi\ coin	\y\ yet
\a\ mat	\e\ pet	\j\ job	\th\ thin	\yü\ few
\ā\ take	\ē\ easy	\ŋ\ sing	\th\ this	\yu̇\ cure
\ä\ cot, cart	\g\ go	\ō\ bone	\ü\ food	\zh\ vision

T square *n* : a ruler with a piece fixed at right angles at one end used to draw parallel lines

tsu·na·mi \(t)sù-'näm-ē\ *n* : a great sea wave produced by an earthquake or volcano eruption under the sea : TIDAL WAVE [Japanese]

Tua·reg \'twä-,reg\ *n* : a member of a nomadic people of Africa

tu·a·ta·ra \,tü-ə-'tär-ə\ *n* : a large spiny reptile of the islands off the coast of New Zealand that looks like a lizard

¹tub \'təb\ *n* **1** : a wide low container **2** : an old or slow boat **3 a** : BATHTUB **b** : BATH 1 **4** : the amount that a tub will hold

²tub *vb* **tubbed; tub·bing** : to wash or bathe in a tub

tu·ba \'t(y)ü-bə\ *n* : a brass musical instrument of lowest pitch with an oval shape and valves for producing different tones

tuba

tub·by \'təb-ē\ *adj* **tub·bi·er; -est** : ⁵PLUMP, FLESHY

tube \'t(y)üb\ *n* **1 a** : a slender channel within a plant or animal body : DUCT **b** : a long hollow cylinder; *esp* : one to carry fluids **c** : the part of a wind instrument that connects the mouthpiece with the open end **2** : a soft container shaped something like a tube whose contents (as toothpaste or glue) can be removed by squeezing **3** : an airtight tube of rubber inside a tire to hold air under pressure **4** : ELECTRON TUBE **5** : TELEVISION 2 **6** : an article of clothing shaped like a tube ⟨*tube* socks⟩ — **tubed** \'t(y)übd\ *adj* — **tube·like** \'t(y)ü-,blīk\ *adj*

tube foot *n* : one of the tiny tubes of most echinoderms (as starfish or sea urchins) that are part of the water-vascular system and are used especially in movement and grasping

tube·less \'t(y)ü-bləs\ *adj* : lacking a tube; *esp* : being a tire that does not depend on an inner tube to keep it airtight

tube nucleus *n* : a nucleus of a pollen grain that is believed to control the growth of the pollen tube

tu·ber \'t(y)ü-bər\ *n* **1** : a short fleshy usually underground stem (as of a potato plant) having tiny scalelike leaves each with a bud at its base that can produce a new plant — compare BULB 1a, CORM **2** : a fleshy root or rhizome that resembles a tuber

tu·ber·cle \'t(y)ü-bər-kəl\ *n* **1** : a small knobby lump or outgrowth especially on a plant or animal **2** : a small diseased growth in an organ or on the skin; *esp* : one caused by tuberculosis

tu·ber·cu·lar \t(y)ù-'bər-kyə-lər\ *adj* : of, relating to, or affected with tuberculosis : TUBERCULOUS ⟨*tubercular* meningitis⟩

tu·ber·cu·lin \t(y)ù-'bər-kyə-lən\ *n* : a sterile liquid containing substances taken from the bacteria that cause tuberculosis and used in the diagnosis of the disease especially in children and cattle

tuberculin test *n* : a test for sensitivity to tuberculin as a sign of a past or present infection with the bacterium causing tuberculosis

tu·ber·cu·lo·sis \t(y)ù-,bər-kyə-'lō-səs\ *n* : a disease of human beings and some other vertebrates caused by a bacterium and usually marked by wasting, fever, and formation of cheesy tubercles that in human beings occur mostly in the lungs — **tu·ber·cu·lous** \t(y)ù-'bər-kyə-ləs\ *adj*

tube·rose \'t(y)ü-,brōz; 't(y)ü-bə-,rōz, -bə-,rōs\ *n* : an herb related to the amaryllises that is grown for its spike of fragrant white flowers

tu·ber·os·i·ty \,t(y)ü-bə-'räs-ət-ē\ *n, pl* **-ties** : a rounded lump; *esp* : one on a bone usually serving for the attachment of muscles or ligaments

tu·ber·ous \'t(y)ü-b(ə-)rəs\ *adj* **1** : consisting of, resembling, or producing a tuber **2** : of, relating to, or being a plant tuber

tub·ing \'t(y)ü-biŋ\ *n* **1** : material in the form of a tube **2** : a series or system of tubes

tu·bu·lar \'t(y)ü-byə-lər\ *adj* **1** : having the form of or consisting of a tube **2** : made or provided with tubes

tu·bule \'t(y)ü-(,)byü(ə)l\ *n* : a small tube; *esp* : a long slender channel in the body of a living thing — compare SEMINIFEROUS TUBULE

¹tuck \'tək\ *vb* **1 a** : to pull up into a fold **b** : to make a stitched fold in **2** : to put or fit into a snug or safe place ⟨*tucked* their money away in the bank⟩ ⟨our lunch *tucked* in a basket⟩ **3 a** : to push in the loose end of so as to hold tightly ⟨*tuck* in your shirt⟩ **b** : to cover by tucking in bedclothes ⟨a child *tucked* in for the night⟩

²tuck *n* **1** : a stitched fold (as in a garment) **2** : an act or instance of tucking

tuck·er \'tək-ər\ *vb* **tuck·ered; tuck·er·ing** \'tək-(ə-)riŋ\ : to cause to tire ⟨*tuckered* out by the hard work⟩

Tues·day \'t(y)üz-dē\ *n* : the third day of the week

> **Word History** The Germanic people who lived in northern Europe in ancient times worshiped many gods. One of the most important of these was a war god whose name in Old English was *Tiw*. The third day of the week was known as *tīwesdæg*, "day of Tiw", in honor of this god. Modern English *Tuesday* comes from Old English *tīwesdæg*. [Old English *tīwesdæg*, literally, "day of Tiw (god of war)"]

tuf·fet \'təf-ət\ *n* : a low seat

¹tuft \'təft\ *n* **1** : a small cluster of long flexible outgrowths that are attached or close together at the base and free at the opposite end; *esp* : a growing bunch of grass or of plants set close together **2** : a bunch of soft fluffy threads cut off short and used as ornament — **tuft·ed** \'təf-təd\ *adj*

²tuft *vb* **1** : to provide or decorate with a tuft **2** : to make (as upholstery) firm by stitching through the stuffing here and there

¹tug \'təg\ *vb* **tugged; tug·ging** **1 a** : to pull hard **b** : to move by pulling hard : DRAG **2** : to tow with a tugboat — **tug·ger** *n*

²tug *n* **1 a** : an act or instance of tugging : PULL **b** : a strong pulling force **3** : a struggle between two people or forces **4** : TUGBOAT

tug·boat \'təg-,bōt\ *n* : a strongly built powerful boat used for towing and pushing ships

tugboat

tug–of–war \,təg-ə(v)-'wô(ə)r\ *n, pl* **tugs–of–war** **1** : a struggle to win **2** : a contest in which two teams pull against each other at opposite ends of a rope

tu·ition \t(y)ù-'ish-ən\ *n* : money paid for instruction (as at a college)

tu·la·re·mia \,t(y)ü-lə-'rē-mē-ə\ *n* : an infectious disease especially of wild rabbits, rodents, human beings, and some domestic animals that is caused by a bacterium and passed on by the bites of insects

tu·lip \'t(y)ü-ləp\ *n* : any of a genus of Eurasian herbs related to the lilies that grow from bulbs, have large lance-shaped leaves, and are widely grown for their showy cup-shaped flowers; *also* : the flower or bulb of a tulip

> **Word History** We often think of the tulip as a Dutch flower. The Dutch certainly do grow many tulips, but they first got the plant from Turkey. The Turkish word for the

tulip was *tülbent,* meaning literally "turban". Perhaps it was the flower's shape that reminded the Turks of a turban. Or perhaps it was the bright colors and velvety petals. In any case, scientists picking a universal word for the flower chose the scientific Latin *tulipa,* taken from the Turkish word. The word came into English from the scientific Latin and was spelled *tulip.* [from scientific Latin *tulipa* "the tulip", from Turkish *tülbent* "tulip", literally "turban"]

tulip tree *n* : a tall North American timber tree with large greenish yellow tulip-shaped flowers and soft white wood used especially for cabinetwork

tulle \'tül\ *n* : a fine netlike fabric used chiefly for veils, evening dresses, or ballet costumes

¹**tum·ble** \'təm-bəl\ *vb* **tum·bled; tum·bling** \-b(ə-)liŋ\ **1 a** : to perform gymnastic feats of rolling and turning **b** : to turn end over end in falling or in flight ⟨the satellite was *tumbling* out of control⟩ **2 a** : to fall suddenly and helplessly **b** : to suffer a sudden downward turn or defeat **3** : to move or go in a hurried or confused way ⟨everyone came *tumbling* out at closing time⟩ **4** : to come to understand ⟨I thought you'd *tumble* to what I meant⟩ **5** : to toss about or together into a confused mass ⟨*tumble* the ingredients lightly⟩

²**tumble** *n* **1** : a messy state or collection **2** : an act or instance of tumbling

tum·ble·bug \'təm-bəl-,bəg\ *n* : a large stout-bodied beetle that rolls dung into small balls, buries them in the ground, and lays its eggs in them

tum·ble·down \,təm-bəl-,daùn\ *adj* : DILAPIDATED ⟨a *tumbledown* shack⟩

tumble dry *vb* **tumble dried; tumble drying** : to dry (as clothes) in a dryer

tum·bler \'təm-blər\ *n* **1** : a person (as an acrobat) who tumbles **2** : a pigeon that often somersaults backward in flight **3** : a drinking glass ⟨a water *tumbler*⟩ **4** : a movable part in a lock that must be adjusted (as by a key) before the lock will open

tum·ble·weed \'təm-bəl-,wēd\ *n* : a plant that breaks away from its roots in autumn and is blown about by the wind

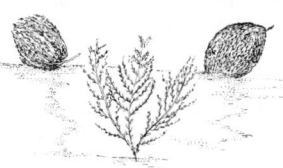

tumbleweed

tu·mid \'t(y)ü-məd\ *adj* : marked by swelling

tum·my \'təm-ē\ *n, pl* **tummies** : ¹STOMACH 1c

tu·mor \'t(y)ü-mər\ *n* : an abnormal mass of tissue that arises from normal tissue cells and serves no useful purpose in the body — **tu·mor·ous** \'t(y)üm-(ə-)rəs\ *adj*

tump·line \'təm-,plīn\ *n* : a strap placed over the forehead or chest and used to support or help support a pack on the back or to haul a load

tu·mult \'t(y)ü-,məlt\ *n* **1** : UPROAR ⟨a great *tumult* arose in the stands⟩ **2** : great confusion of mind

tu·mul·tu·ous \t(y)ü-'məlch-(ə-)wəs, -'məl-chəs\ *adj* : being or suggesting a tumult ⟨a *tumultuous* welcome for the astronauts⟩ — **tu·mul·tu·ous·ly** *adv*

tu·mu·lus \'t(y)ü-myə-ləs, 'təm-yə-\ *n, pl* **-li** \-,lī, -,lē\ : a mound usually over an ancient grave

tu·na \'t(y)ü-nə\ *n, pl* **tuna** *or* **tunas** **1** : any of several mostly large sea fishes (as an albacore or bonito) related to the mackerels and caught for food and sport **2** : the flesh of a tuna especially when canned for use as food — called also *tuna fish*

tun·dra \'tən-drə *also* 'tùn-\ *n* : a treeless plain especially of arctic regions

¹**tune** \'t(y)ün\ *n* **1** : a succession of pleasing musical tones : MELODY **2** : correct musical pitch or consonance ⟨the piano was not in *tune*⟩ **3** : AGREEMENT 1b, HARMONY ⟨in

tune with the times⟩ **4** : general attitude ⟨changed their *tune* after reading the report⟩

²**tune** *vb* **tuned; tun·ing** **1** : to adjust in musical pitch ⟨*tuned* my guitar⟩ ⟨the orchestra was *tuning* up⟩ **2** : to come or bring into harmony **3** : to adjust a radio or television set so that it receives clearly — often used with *in* **4** : to put (as an engine) in good working order — often used with *up*

tune·ful \'t(y)ün-fəl\ *adj* : MELODIOUS, MUSICAL — **tune·ful·ly** \-fə-lē\ *adv*

tune out *vb* : to stop paying attention to ⟨thinking about the work and *tuning* everything else *out*⟩

tun·er \'t(y)ü-nər\ *n* **1** : one that tunes ⟨a piano *tuner*⟩ **2** : something used for tuning; *esp* : the part of a receiving set that converts radio signals into sound or pictures

tune–up \'t(y)ü-,nəp\ *n* : a general adjustment to get everything in good working order ⟨an engine *tune-up*⟩

tung oil \'təŋ\ *n* : an oil that is obtained from the seeds of any of several trees and especially from a Chinese tree widely grown in warm regions and that is used chiefly in quick-drying varnishes and paints and for waterproofing

tung·sten \'təŋ-stən\ *n* : a gray-white heavy hard metallic element that has many characteristics similar to chromium and molybdenum and is used especially for electrical purposes and to harden other metals and blends of metals (as steel) — called also *wolfram;* see ELEMENT table [from Swedish *tungsten,* literally "heavy stone", from *tung* "heavy" and *sten* "stone"]

tu·nic \'t(y)ü-nik\ *n* **1** : a usually belted knee-length garment worn by ancient Greeks and Romans **2** : a shirt or jacket reaching to or just below the hips

tu·ni·cate \'t(y)ü-ni-kət, -nə-,kāt\ *n* : any of a major group of marine chordates that secrete a thick covering layer and that have a reduced nervous system and a heart able to reverse the direction of blood flow by changing its contractions

tuning fork *n* : a metal instrument that gives a fixed tone when struck and is useful in tuning musical instruments

¹**tun·nel** \'tən-ᵊl\ *n* : a passage under the ground — **tun·nel·like** \-ᵊl-,(l)īk\ *adj*

²**tunnel** *vb* **-neled** *or* **-nelled; -nel·ing** *or* **-nel·ling** \'tən-liŋ, -ᵊl-iŋ\ : to make a tunnel

tun·ny \'tən-ē\ *n, pl* **tunnies** *also* **tunny** : TUNA

tuppence *variant of* TWOPENCE

tur·ban \'tər-bən\ *n* **1** : a head covering worn especially by Muslims and made of a long cloth wrapped around the head or around a cap **2** : a woman's small soft hat with no brim — **tur·baned** *or* **tur·banned** \-bənd\ *adj*

turban 1

tur·bid \'tər-bəd\ *adj* : clouded or discolored by sediment ⟨a *turbid* stream⟩ — **tur·bid·i·ty** \,tər-'bid-ət-ē\ *n*

tur·bine \'tər-bən, -,bīn\ *n* : an engine whose central driving shaft is fitted with a series of blades spun around by the pressure of a fluid (as water, steam, or air) [from French *turbine* "turbine", from Latin *turbin-, turbo* "top (for spinning), whirlwind"]

tur·bo·jet \'tər-bō-,jet\ *n* : an airplane powered by turbojet engines

turbojet engine *n* : a jet engine in which a turbine drives a compressor that supplies air to a burner and hot gases from the burner drive the turbine before being discharged

\ə\ **abut**	\aù\ **out**	\i\ **tip**	\ò\ **saw**	\ù\ **foot**
\ər\ **further**	\ch\ **chin**	\ī\ **life**	\òi\ **coin**	\y\ **yet**
\a\ **mat**	\e\ **pet**	\j\ **job**	\th\ **thin**	\yü\ **few**
\ā\ **take**	\ē\ **easy**	\ŋ\ **sing**	\th\ **this**	\yù\ **cure**
\ä\ **cot, cart**	\g\ **go**	\ō\ **bone**	\ü\ **food**	\zh\ **vision**

to the rear

tur·bo·prop \'tər-bō-,präp\ *n* : an airplane powered by turboprop engines

turboprop engine *n* : a jet engine that produces power principally through a propeller driven by a turbine but also usually by the rearward discharge of hot exhaust gases

tur·bu·lence \'tər-byə-lən(t)s\ *n* : the quality or state of being turbulent; *esp* : irregular atmospheric motion with up and down currents

tur·bu·lent \'tər-byə-lənt\ *adj* : causing or being in a state of unrest, violence, or disturbance — **tur·bu·lent·ly** *adv*

tu·reen \tə-'rēn, tyu̇-\ *n* : a deep bowl from which food (as soup) is served

turf \'tərf\ *n* **1 a** : the upper layer of soil bound by grass and plant roots into a thick mat; *also* : a piece of this **b** : an artificial substitute for turf (as on a playing field) **2** : the sport or business of horse racing **3** : an area or a place that is or is felt to be under one's control ⟨on my own *turf*⟩

tur·gid \'tər-jəd\ *adj* : being in a swollen state; *esp* : exhibiting turgor ⟨a *turgid* plant cell⟩

tur·gor \'tər-gər, -,gȯ(ə)r\ *n* : the normal state of firmness and tension of living cells

Turk \'tərk\ *n* : a person born or living in Turkey

tur·key \'tər-kē\ *n* **1** : a large American bird that is related to the domestic chicken, has a wide range in North America, and is domesticated in most parts of the world **2** : something that is a failure ⟨the new play was a *turkey*⟩ **3** : a stupid or foolish person

> **Word History** The bird we now call the guinea fowl was once called the *turkey*. *Turkey* was the shortened version of *turkey-cock* and *turkey-hen.* The guinea fowl's original home was in Africa. However, Europeans discovered that it was good to eat and did well in captivity, so they brought it back to Europe. Some people mistakenly thought that the birds came from Turkey, and the name stuck. Later, when English settlers first arrived in America, they found a large bird living here that was also good to eat. They called this new bird *turkey* because it reminded them of the turkey they were familiar with back in Europe. [from *turkey-cock,* an old word for "guinea fowl", from *Turkey,* a country in Asia Minor; so called because at one time people thought guinea fowl came from Turkey]

tur·key–cock \'tər-kē-,käk\ *n* : GOBBLER

turkey vulture *n* : an American vulture common in South and Central America and in the U.S. — called also *turkey buzzard*

¹Turk·ish \'tər-kish\ *adj* : of or relating to Turkey, the Turks, or Turkish

²Turkish *n* : the language of the Turks

Turkish towel *n* : a towel made of cotton terry cloth

tur·moil \'tər-,mȯil\ *n* : a very confused or disturbed state or condition

¹turn \'tərn\ *vb* **1 a** : to move or cause to move around an axis or center : ROTATE, REVOLVE ⟨wheels *turning* slowly⟩ ⟨*turn* a crank⟩ **b** : to twist so as to bring about a desired end ⟨*turned* the knob and swung the door open⟩ **c** : to do by revolving ⟨*turn* handsprings⟩ **d** : to twist out of line or shape : WRENCH ⟨*turn* an ankle⟩ **2 a** : to change in position usually by moving through an arc of a circle ⟨they *turned* and walked away⟩ ⟨*turn* the page⟩ ⟨*turn* a pancake⟩ **b** : to examine as if by turning over : think about ⟨*turned* the problem over in her mind⟩ **3** : to make over (as a garment) by reversing the material and sewing back together ⟨*turn* a collar⟩ **4 a** : to upset the order of ⟨everything was *turned* topsy-turvy⟩ **b** : to set in another and

turkey 1

especially opposite direction **5 a** : to change course or direction ⟨the road *turns* to the left⟩ ⟨*turning* to a different subject⟩ **b** : to go around ⟨*turn* a corner⟩ **6** : to direct toward or away from something ⟨we *turned* toward home⟩ **7** : to seek out as a source of something ⟨*turn* to a friend for help⟩ **8 a** : to change or cause to change ⟨water *turned* to ice⟩ ⟨the witch *turned* the prince into a frog⟩ **b** : to cause to spoil : SOUR ⟨the milk had *turned*⟩ **c** : to change in color ⟨leaves *turning* in the fall⟩ **d** : to pass from one state to another : BECOME ⟨hair *turned* gray⟩ ⟨had just *turned* fourteen⟩ **9** : TRANSLATE 3a **10** : to give a rounded form to (as on a lathe) — **turn a hair** : to be or become upset or frightened — **turn loose** : to set free : let go — **turn one's hand** *or* **turn a hand** : to set to work : apply oneself — **turn tail** : to turn away so as to flee — **turn the tables** : to bring about a switch in the positions or fortunes of two opposing people or sides — **turn the trick** : to bring about the desired result — **turn turtle** : OVERTURN 1

²turn *n* **1** : the action or an act of turning about a center **2 a** : a change or changing of direction, course, or position ⟨a left *turn*⟩ ⟨*turn* of the tide⟩ **b** : a place where something turns ⟨at the *turn* of the road⟩ **c** : a change or changing of general state or condition ⟨took a *turn* for the better⟩ ⟨a *turn* in the weather⟩ **3** : a short walk or ride ⟨took a *turn* through the park⟩ **4** : an act affecting another ⟨I may be able to do you a *turn* some day⟩ **5 a** : a period of action or activity : SPELL ⟨a *turn* as guard⟩ **b** : proper place in a waiting line or time in a schedule ⟨wait your *turn*⟩ ⟨take *turns*⟩ **6** : a special purpose ⟨that will serve the *turn*⟩ **7 a** : a special quality ⟨a neat *turn* of phrase⟩ **b** : the shape or form in which something is molded : CAST ⟨an odd *turn* of mind⟩ **8** : a single circle or loop (as of rope passed around an object) **9** : natural or special skill ⟨a *turn* for languages⟩ — **at every turn** : on every occasion : all the time : CONSTANTLY — **by turns** : one after another — **in turn** : one after the other in order — **to a turn** : precisely right : PERFECTLY

turn·about \'tər-nə-,baut\ *n* : a change from one direction or one way of thinking or acting to the opposite

turn·around \'tər-nə-,raund\ *n* **1** : TURNABOUT **2** : the time needed for one complete cycle or round trip from start to destination and back

turn away *vb* : to refuse to let in : send away ⟨all the seats were sold and a large crowd had to be *turned away*⟩

turn back *vb* **1** : to go in the reverse direction : RETURN ⟨*turned back* for home⟩ **2** : to stop the advance of : CHECK ⟨*turned back* the enemy⟩

turn·coat \'tərn-,kōt\ *n* : a person on one side who goes over to the other

turn down *vb* **1** : to fold back or down **2** : to lower by turning a control ⟨*turn down* the heat⟩ **3** : ¹REJECT 1 ⟨*turned down* the job⟩

turn·er \'tər-nər\ *n* : one that turns; *esp* : a kitchen tool for lifting and turning foods

turn in *vb* **1** : to give up or hand back ⟨*turned in* my tools when I was finished⟩ **2** : to hand over to authorities ⟨the escaped prisoner *turned* himself *in*⟩ **3** : ¹DO 1a ⟨*turned in* a fine job⟩ **4** : to go to bed

turning point *n* : a point (as in an action or situation) where an important change occurs

tur·nip \'tər-nəp\ *n* : either of two herbs related to cabbage with thick roots that are eaten as a vegetable or fed to stock: **a** : one with hairy leaves and usually white and flattened roots **b** : RUTABAGA

turn·off \'tər-,nȯf\ *n* : a place where one turns off or turns something off

turn off \,tər-'nȯf, 'tər-\ *vb* **1** : to turn aside ⟨*turned off* onto a side road⟩ **2** : to stop by or as if by turning a control ⟨*turn off* the light⟩ ⟨*turn* the alarm *off*⟩ **3** : to cause dislike or loss of interest ⟨that sort of thing *turns* me *off*⟩

turn on \(')tər-'nȯn, -'nän\ *vb* **1** : to cause to work by or as if by turning a control 〈*turn* the water *on*〉 〈*turn on* the computer〉 **2** : to cause interest or enjoyment 〈the kind of music that *turns* me *on*〉 — **turn–on** *n*

turn·out \'tər-ˌnaut\ *n* : the number of people who attend or who do something (as vote) 〈a good *turnout* at the meeting〉 〈expected a light voter *turnout*〉

turn out \ˌtər-'naut, 'tər-\ *vb* **1** : to put or empty out of a container **2** : to make by or as if by machine 〈factories *turn out* pottery〉 〈*turns out* a new story every month〉 **3** : TURN OFF 2 〈who *turned out* the light?〉 **4** : to come or go out from home 〈thousands *turned out* to see them〉 **5** : to prove to be 〈it *turned out* to be only the cat〉 〈of course, I *turned out* to be right〉

turn·over \'tər-ˌnō-vər\ *n* **1** : an act or the action of turning over **2** : a filled pastry with one half of the crust turned over the other **3 a** : movement (as of people) into, through, and out of a place **b** : the purchase, sale, and replacement of a stock of goods (as in a store) **c** : the number of persons hired to replace those leaving

turn over \ˌtər-'nō-vər, 'tər-\ *vb* **1 a** : to shift in position **b** : to rotate the crankshaft (of an engine) especially by a device (as a starter or crank) outside the engine to attempt to get the cylinders to fire **2** : to give to another to take care of : HAND OVER **3** *of one's stomach* : to feel sick

turn·pike \'tərn-ˌpīk\ *n* **1** : a road one must pay to use **2** : a main road

Word History In the Middle Ages, a spiked barrier would sometimes be placed on a road or bridge to protect against sudden attack. The barrier would have to be turned to allow passage. The Middle English word for such a barrier was *turnepike*. This word was formed from the verb *turnen*, meaning "to turn", and the noun *pike*, meaning "a sharp-tipped weapon". With a slight change in spelling, *turnpike* later came to be used as the word for a simple gate placed across a road. In order to pass through the turnpike, travelers would have to pay a fee or toll. A road on which these tollgates were found was called a *turnpike road*. Such a road in time became known simply as a *turnpike*. [Middle English *turnepike* "a turning frame bearing spikes that is used as a barrier", from ·*turnen* "to turn" and *pike* "a pointed weapon"]

turn·stile \-ˌstīl\ *n* : a post having arms which turn around that is set in an entrance or exit so that persons can pass through only on foot one by one

turn·ta·ble \-ˌtā-bəl\ *n* **1** : a platform that can be turned around **2** : a round flat plate that turns a phonograph record

turnstile

turn up *vb* **1** : to be found or happen usually unexpectedly 〈the papers will *turn up*〉 **2** : to raise by or as if by using a control 〈*turn up* the heat〉 **3** : ARRIVE 1 〈*turned up* late〉 — **turn up one's nose** : to show scorn

tur·pen·tine \'tər-pən-ˌtīn\ *n* **1** : a mixture of oil and resin obtained from pines and some related trees **2** : an oil made from turpentine and used especially as a solvent and paint thinner

tur·quoise \'tər-ˌk(w)oiz\ *n* **1** : a blue, bluish green, or greenish gray mineral that contains copper and aluminum, takes a high polish, and is used in jewelry **2** : a light greenish blue [Middle English *turkeis, turcas* "turquoise", from early French *turquoyse* (same meaning), derived from *turquoys*, literally "Turkish (stone)"; so called because it was first brought to Europe from a part of Turkey]

tur·ret \'tər-ət, 'tə-rət, tur-ət\ *n* **1** : a little tower often at a corner of a building **2** : a low usually rotating structure (as in a tank, warship, or airplane) in which guns are mounted

¹tur·tle \'tərt-ᵊl\ *n, archaic* : TURTLEDOVE [Old English *turtla* "turtledove", from Latin *turtur* (same meaning)]

²turtle *n, pl* **turtles** *also* **turtle** : any of an order of land, freshwater, and marine reptiles with a toothless horny beak and a bony shell which encloses the body and into which the head, legs, and tail usually may be withdrawn [probably derived from French *tortue* "tortoise, turtle" and influenced by the earlier English *turtle* "turtledove"]

tur·tle·dove \'tərt-ᵊl-ˌdəv\ *n* : any of several small wild pigeons especially of an Old World genus noted for cooing

tur·tle·neck \-ˌnek\ *n* **1** : a high turned-over collar (as of a sweater) **2** : a sweater or jersey with a turtleneck

turves *pl of* TURF

¹tusk \'təsk\ *n* **1** : a very long large tooth (as of an elephant, walrus, or boar) that sticks out when the mouth is closed and is used for digging food or as a weapon **2** : a tooth-shaped part — **tusked** \'təskt\ *adj*

²tusk *vb* : to dig up or gash with a tusk

tusk·er \'təs-kər\ *n* : an animal with tusks; *esp* : a male elephant with two normally developed tusks

¹tus·sle \'təs-əl\ *vb* **tus·sled; tus·sling** \'təs-(ə-)liŋ\ : SCUFFLE 1

²tussle *n* **1** : a physical contest or struggle **2** : a rough argument or a struggle against difficult odds

tus·sock \'təs-ək\ *n* : a compact bunch especially of grass or sedge — **tus·socky** \-ə-kē\ *adj*

tussock moth *n* : any of numerous dull-colored moths that usually have wingless females and larvae with long tufts of hair

tu·te·lage \'t(y)üt-ə-lij\ *n* **1** : an act of guarding or protecting : GUARDIANSHIP **2** : INSTRUCTION

¹tu·tor \'t(y)üt-ər\ *n* : a person who has the responsibility of instructing and guiding another

²tutor *vb* : to teach usually individually

¹tu·to·ri·al \t(y)ü-'tōr-ē-əl, -'tȯr-\ *adj* : of or relating to a tutor

²tutorial *n* : something written to give practical information about a subject

tux \'təks\ *n* : TUXEDO

tux·e·do \ˌtək-'sēd-ō\ *n, pl* **-dos** *or* **-does** : a suit for men to be worn on special occasions

Word History *Tuxedo* can be traced back to an American Indian word for "wolf", but this doesn't mean that Indians invented the garment. An Indian tribe living in eastern North America was divided into three groups. Each group used a different animal as its emblem. One group used the wolf as its emblem. They took the name *P'tuksit* from their name for the animal. In the 18th century, European Americans gave the name of the P'tuksit Indians to a village in southeastern New York. The Indian name was spelled *Tuxedo* in English. In the 1880s, an area called Tuxedo Park, near the village of Tuxedo, became a popular vacation community. It was here, around the turn of the century, that young men began wearing a new kind of dress jacket. The new style was soon called *tuxedo*. [named for *Tuxedo Park*, a resort in New York State, from *P'tuksit*, a word in an American Indian language meaning "wolf"; so called because the jacket was first popular in Tuxedo Park]

TV \(')tē-'vē\ *n* : TELEVISION

TV dinner \ˌtē-ˌvē-\ *n* : a quick-frozen packaged dinner that requires only heating before it is served

twad·dle \'twäd-ᵊl\ *n* : silly idle talk

twain \'twān\ *n* **1** : TWO 1 **2** : two persons or things

\ə\ **abut**		\au\ **out**	\i\ **tip**	\o\ **saw**	\u\ **foot**
\ər\ **further**		\ch\ **chin**	\ī\ **life**	\oi\ **coin**	\y\ **yet**
\a\ **mat**		\e\ **pet**	\j\ **job**	\th\ **thin**	\yü\ **few**
\ā\ **take**		\ē\ **easy**	\ŋ\ **sing**	\th\ **this**	\yu\ **cure**
\ä\ **cot, cart**		\g\ **go**	\ō\ **bone**	\ü\ **food**	\zh\ **vision**

: COUPLE, PAIR

¹twang \'twaŋ\ *n* **1** : a harsh quick ringing sound **2** : nasal speech

²twang *vb* **twanged; twang·ing** \'twaŋ-iŋ\ **1** : to sound or cause to sound with a twang **2** : to speak with a nasal twang

tweak \'twēk\ *vb* : to pinch and pull with a sudden jerk and twist — **tweak** *n*

tweed \'twēd\ *n* **1** : a rough woolen cloth **2** *pl* : tweed clothing (as a suit)

tweedy \'twēd-ē\ *adj* : of or resembling tweed

tween \('twēn\ *prep* : ¹BETWEEN

¹tweet \'twēt\ *n* : a chirping sound

²tweet *vb* : CHIRP

tweet·er \'twēt-ər\ *n* : a small loudspeaker that responds only to high sound frequencies and produces sounds of high pitch — compare WOOFER

twee·zers \'twē-zərz\ *n pl* : a small instrument that is used like pincers in grasping or pulling something

twelfth \'twelf(t)th\ *n* — see NUMBER table — **twelfth** *adj or adv*

Twelfth Day *n* : EPIPHANY

Twelfth Night *n* **1** : the eve preceding Epiphany **2** : the evening of Epiphany

twelve \'twelv\ *n* **1** — see NUMBER table **2** *cap* : the twelve original disciples of Jesus **3** : the 12th in a set or series — **twelve** *adj or pron*

twelve·month \-,mən(t)th\ *n* : YEAR

twen·ti·eth \'twent-ē-əth\ *n* — see NUMBER table — **twentieth** *adj*

twen·ty \'twent-ē\ *n, pl* **twenties** — see NUMBER table — **twenty** *adj or pron*

twen·ty–twen·ty \,twent-ē-'twent-ē\ *adj* : having normal visual sharpness — often written 20/20

twenty–two \,twent-ē-'tü\ *n* **1** : a firearm cartridge of .22 caliber **2** : a firearm of .22 caliber

twerp \'twərp\ *n* : a silly or unimportant person

twice \'twīs\ *adv* : two times ⟨use it *twice*⟩ ⟨*twice* as large⟩

twid·dle \'twid-ᵊl\ *vb* **twid·dled; twid·dling** \'twid-liŋ, -ᵊl-iŋ\ : to rotate lightly or idly ⟨*twiddle* one's thumbs⟩

twig \'twig\ *n* : a small shoot or branch — **twig·gy** \'twig-ē\ *adj*

twi·light \'twī-,līt\ *n* : the period or the light from the sky between full night and sunrise or between sunset and full night

¹twill \'twil\ *n* : a way of weaving cloth that produces a pattern of diagonal lines

²twill *vb* : to make (cloth) with a twill weave

¹twin \'twin\ *adj* **1** : born with one other or as a pair at one birth ⟨*twin* brother⟩ ⟨*twin* girls⟩ **2 a** : made up of two similar, related, or connected members or parts **b** : being one of a pair ⟨*twin* city⟩

²twin *vb* **twinned; twin·ning** : to produce or give birth to twins

³twin *n* **1** : either of two offspring produced at a birth — compare FRATERNAL TWIN, IDENTICAL TWIN

twin bed *n* : one of a pair of single beds that match

¹twine \'twīn\ *n* : a string made of two or more strands twisted together

²twine *vb* **twined; twin·ing** **1 a** : to twist together **b** : INTERLACE **2** : to coil or cause to coil around a support

¹twinge \'twinj\ *vb* **twinged; twing·ing** \'twin-jiŋ\ *or* **twinge·ing** : to affect with or feel a sudden sharp pain

²twinge *n* : a sudden sharp stab (as of pain)

¹twin·kle \'twiŋ-kəl\ *vb* **twin·kled; twin·kling** \-k(ə-)liŋ\ **1** : to shine or cause to shine with a flickering or sparkling light **2** : to appear bright with amusement **3** : to move or flutter rapidly — **twin·kler** \-k(ə-)lər\ *n*

²twinkle *n* **1** : a very short time **2** : ²SPARKLE 1, FLICKER — **twin·kly** \-k(ə-)lē\ *adj*

twin·kling \'twiŋ-kliŋ\ *n* **1** : a winking of the eye **2** : ²TWINKLE 1

¹twirl \'twər(-ə)l\ *vb* : to turn or cause to turn rapidly ⟨*twirl* a baton⟩ — **twirl·er** *n*

²twirl *n* : an act of twirling

¹twist \'twist\ *vb* **1** : to unite by winding one thread, strand, or wire around another **2** : ²TWINE 2 **3 a** : to turn so as to sprain or hurt ⟨*twisted* my ankle⟩ **b** : to change the meaning of ⟨*twisted* the facts⟩ **c** : to pull off, rotate, or break by a turning force ⟨*twisted* a small branch off the tree⟩ **4** : to follow a winding course

²twist *n* **1** : a thread, yarn, or cord made by twisting two or more strands together **2** : an act of twisting : the state of being twisted **3** : a spiral turn or curve **4** : a strong personal tendency : BENT **5** : a changing of meaning **6** : something (as a plan of action) that is both surprising and strange **7** : a lively dance in which the hips are twisted

twist·er \'twis-tər\ *n* **1** : one that twists **2 a** : TORNADO **b** : WATERSPOUT 2

¹twitch \'twich\ *vb* **1** : to move or pull with a sudden motion : JERK **2** : ²QUIVER

²twitch *n* **1** : an act of twitching **2 a** : a short sharp contraction of muscle fibers **b** : a slight jerk of a body part

¹twit·ter \'twit-ər\ *vb* **1** : to make a series of chirping sounds **2** : to talk in a chattering fashion **3** : to make or become very nervous and upset

²twitter *n* **1** : a nervous upset state **2** : the chirping of birds **3** : a light chattering

two \'tü\ *n, pl* **twos** **1** — see NUMBER table **2** : the second in a set or series — **two** *adj or pron*

two–bit \,tü-,bit\ *adj* : of the value of two bits

two bits *n sing or pl* **1** : the value of a quarter of a dollar **2** : something of little worth or importance

two–by–four \,tü-bə-'fō(ə)r, -'fȯ(ə)r\ *n* : a piece of lumber approximately 2 by 4 inches (5 by 10 centimeters) as sawed and usually 1⅝ by 3⅝ inches (4 by 9 centimeters) if dressed

two–dimensional *adj* : having two dimensions (as length and width)

two–faced \'tü-'fāst\ *adj* : pretending to feel or act one way while acting another

two·fold \-,fōld, -'fōld\ *adj* : twice as great or as many — **twofold** *adv*

2, 4–D \,tü-,fȯr-'dē, -,fȯr-\ *n* : a white compound used as a weed killer

two–hand·ed \'tü-'han-dəd\ *adj* **1** : used with both hands ⟨a *two-handed* sword⟩ **2** : requiring two persons ⟨a *two-handed* saw⟩

two·pence *also* **tup·pence** \'təp-ən(t)s, *US also* 'tü-,pen(t)s\ *n* : the sum of two pence

two·some \'tü-səm\ *n* : a group of two persons or things

two–toed sloth \,tü-,tōd-\ *n* : either of two species of sloth that have two claws on each front foot and three on each back foot — compare *three-toed sloth*

two–way *adj* **1** : moving or acting or allowing movement or action in either direction ⟨*two-way* traffic⟩ ⟨a *two-way* street⟩ **2 a** : involving two persons or groups ⟨communication is a *two-way* process⟩ **b** : made to send and receive messages ⟨a *two-way* radio⟩

two–winged fly \,tü-,wiŋ(d)-\ *n* : any of a large order of insects (as the housefly, mosquitoes, and gnats) that produce often headless, eyeless, and legless larvae and that usually use the front wings for flying and have the back wings reduced to balancers

ty·coon \tī-'kün\ *n* : a very wealthy and powerful business person

    Word History Commodore Matthew Perry of the U.S. Navy led an expedition to Japan in 1853. He wanted to force Japan to give up its isolation from the West. He wanted the Japanese to open their ports and allow trade with America. At that time, the hereditary emperor was the official ruler. Power, though, was in the hands of the commander of the army, called *shogun,* meaning "general". For the benefit of Western visitors the shogun was given the more impressive title of *taikun,* from the Chinese *ta chun,* meaning "great ruler". When Perry was introduced to the *taikun,* he mistakenly thought he was dealing with the emperor. Perry's trip so captured public attention in America that *taikun* was borrowed into English as *tycoon.* At first it was applied, often with humor, to anyone who was considered great, powerful, or outstanding. By the end of the 19th century, *tycoon* was being used chiefly of the founders of the great American businesses, industries, and banking empires. Its meaning today still has this specific relation to business. [Japanese *taikun* "shogun", from Chinese (Pekingese dialect), *ta chun* (same meaning), literally "great ruler", from *ta* "great" + *chun* "ruler"]

ty·ing *present participle of* TIE
tyke *also* **tike** \'tīk\ *n* : a small child
tympani *variant of* TIMPANI
tym·pan·ic membrane \tim-'pan-ik-\ *n* : EARDRUM
tym·pa·num \'tim-pə-nəm\ *n, pl* **-na** \-nə\ *also* **-nums** 1 : EARDRUM 2 : a thin tense membrane covering an organ of hearing or of sound-production of an insect

¹**type** \'tīp\ *n* 1 a : a rectangular block usually of metal with a raised letter or number from which an inked print is made b : a set of letters or figures that are used for printing or the letters or figures printed by them 2 a : the special things by which members of a group are set apart from other groups (horses of the draft *type*) b : a particular kind, class, or group (a seedless *type* of orange) (I don't like people of that *type*)

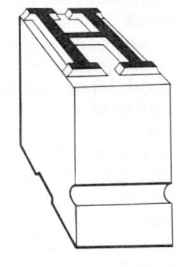

type 1a

²**type** *vb* **typed; typ·ing** 1 : to write with a keyboard : TYPEWRITE 2 : to identify as belonging to a type
type·write \'tī-,prīt\ *vb* **-wrote; -writ·ten; -writ·ing** : to write with a typewriter
type·writ·er \'tī-,prīt-ər\ *n* : a machine that prints letters or figures when a person pushes its keys down
type·writ·ing \'tī-,prīt-iŋ\ *n* 1 : the use of a typewriter 2 : printing done with a typewriter

¹**ty·phoid** \'tī-,fóid, (')tī-'fóid\ *adj* : of, relating to, or being typhoid fever
²**typhoid** *n* : TYPHOID FEVER
typhoid fever *n* : a disease that is caused by a bacteria, is characterized especially by fever, diarrhea, weakness, headache, and an inflamed intestine, and is passed from one person to another in dirty food or water
ty·phoon \tī-'fün\ *n* : a tropical cyclone occurring in the region of the Philippines or the China sea
ty·phus \'tī-fəs\ *n* : a severe infectious disease that is marked by high fever, stupor and delirium, intense headache, and a dark red rash, that is caused by a rickettsia, and that is passed on especially by body lice — called also *typhus fever*
typ·i·cal \'tip-i-kəl\ *adj* : combining or showing the special characteristics of a group or kind (a *typical* school lunch) — **typ·i·cal·ly** \-k(ə-)lē\ *adv*
typ·i·fy \'tip-ə-,fī\ *vb* **-fied; -fy·ing** 1 : REPRESENT 2 2 : to have or include the special or main characteristics of
typ·ist \'tī-pəst\ *n* : a person who uses a typewriter or a keyboard (as of a computer)
ty·ran·ni·cal \tə-'ran-i-kəl, tī-\ *also* **ty·ran·nic** \-'ran-ik\ *adj* : of, relating to, or characteristic of a tyrant or tyranny — **ty·ran·ni·cal·ly** \-'ran-i-k(ə-)lē\ *adv*
tyr·an·nize \'tir-ə-,nīz\ *vb* **-nized; -niz·ing** : to act like a tyrant
ty·ran·no·saur \tə-'ran-ə-,só(ə)r, tī-\ *n* : TYRANNOSAURUS
ty·ran·no·sau·rus \tə-,ran-ə-'sór-əs, (,)tī-\ *n* : a very large American flesh-eating dinosaur of the Cretaceous that had small forelegs and walked on its hind legs
tyr·an·nous \'tir-ə-nəs\ *adj* : TYRANNICAL — **tyr·an·nous·ly** *adv*
tyr·an·ny \'tir-ə-nē\ *n, pl* **-nies** 1 : a government in which all power is in the hands of a single ruler 2 : harsh, cruel, and severe government or conduct 3 : a tyrannical act
ty·rant \'tī-rənt\ *n* 1 : a ruler who has no legal limits on his or her power by law or constitution 2 a : a ruler who exercises total power harshly or cruelly b : a person who uses authority or power harshly
tyre *chiefly British variant of* TIRE
ty·ro \'tī-rō\ *n, pl* **tyros** : a beginner in learning
tzar *variant of* CZAR

U

u \'yü\ *n, often cap* : the 21st letter of the English alphabet
ubiq·ui·tous \yü-'bik-wət-əs\ *adj* : being everywhere at the same time : OMNIPRESENT — **ubiq·ui·tous·ly** *adv* — **ubiq·ui·tous·ness** *n* — **ubiq·ui·ty** \-wət-ē\ *n*
U–boat \'yü-,bōt\ *n* : a German submarine
ud·der \'əd-ər\ *n* 1 : a large bag-shaped organ (as of a cow) consisting of two or more mammary glands enclosed in a common pouch but with each having a separate nipple 2 : MAMMARY GLAND
UFO \,yü-(,)ef-'ō\ *n, pl* **UFO's** *or* **UFOs** \-'ōz\ : an unidentified flying object; *esp* : FLYING SAUCER
ugh *often read as* 'əg *or* 'ək *or* 'ə\ *interj* — used for various sounds that express disgust or horror
ug·li·fy \'əg-li-,fī\ *vb* **-fied; -fy·ing** : to make ugly
ug·ly \'əg-lē\ *adj* **ug·li·er; -est** 1 : horrid or unpleasant especially to the sight : UNSIGHTLY, HIDEOUS 2 : ¹OFFENSIVE 2, REPULSIVE (*ugly* habits) 3 a : likely to cause bother or discomfort : TROUBLESOME (an *ugly* situation) b : QUARRELSOME (an *ugly* disposition) — **ug·li·ness** *n*
ugly duckling *n* : a child or thing capable of developing into

a person or thing worthy of attention or respect to people's surprise
ukase \yü-'kās, -'kāz; 'yü-,kāz, ü-'käz\ *n* : a ruling especially of a Russian emperor or government
uke \'yük\ *n* : UKULELE
Ukrai·ni·an \yü-'krā-nē-ən\ *n* 1 : a person born or living in the Ukrainian Soviet Socialist Republic 2 : the language of the Ukrainian people — **Ukrainian** *adj*
uku·le·le \,yü-kə-'lā-lē, ,ü-\ *n* : a usually four-stringed

ukulele

\ə\ **abut**	\au̇\ **out**	\i\ tip	\ȯ\ **saw**	\u̇\ **foot**
\ər\ **further**	\ch\ **chin**	\ī\ **life**	\ȯi\ **coin**	\y\ **yet**
\a\ **mat**	\e\ **pet**	\j\ **job**	\th\ **thin**	\yü\ **few**
\ā\ **take**	\ē\ **easy**	\ŋ\ **sing**	\th\ **this**	\yu̇\ **cure**
\ä\ **cot, cart**	\g\ **go**	\ō\ **bone**	\ü\ **food**	\zh\ **vision**

small guitar popularized in Hawaii

Word History In the 19th century, a former British army officer named Edward Purvis lived in Hawaii as an official at the royal court. Purvis is said to have been given the Hawaiian nickname of *'ukulele,* which means "jumping flea", because he was small and lively. In 1879 Portuguese immigrants arrived in the Hawaiian islands. They brought several of their native instruments, among them a small four-stringed guitar. Purvis liked this new instrument. He quickly learned to play it. In time the small guitar became a general favorite, and it took the nickname of the man who had made it popular. [from Hawaiian *'ukulele* "ukulele", literally "jumping flea", from *'uku* "flea" + *lele* "jumping"]

ul·cer \'əl-sər\ *n* **1** : a slow-healing open sore in which tissue breaks down **2** : something that rots and gets worse like an open sore

ul·cer·ate \'əl-sə-ˌrāt\ *vb* **-at·ed; -at·ing** : to cause or become affected with an ulcer ⟨an *ulcerated* wound⟩

ul·cer·ation \ˌəl-sə-'rā-shən\ *n* **1** : the process of forming or state of having an ulcer **2** : ULCER 1

ul·na \'əl-nə\ *n* : the bone on the little-finger side of the human forearm; *also* : a corresponding part of the forelimb of vertebrates above the fishes — **ul·nar** \-nər\ *adj*

ul·ster \'əl-stər\ *n* : a long loose heavy overcoat

ul·te·ri·or \ˌəl-'tir-ē-ər\ *adj* : going beyond what is openly said or shown and especially what is proper ⟨*ulterior* motives⟩

ul·ti·ma \'əl-tə-mə\ *n* : the last syllable of a word

ul·ti·mate \'əl-tə-mət\ *adj* **1 a** : ¹FARTHEST ⟨*ultimate* reaches of the universe⟩ **b** : last in a progression : FINAL **c** : ¹EXTREME 1 **2** : arrived at as the last result ⟨the *ultimate* question⟩ ⟨the *ultimate* damage of the hurricane⟩ **3 a** : ¹BASIC 1 ⟨*ultimate* control⟩ **b** : incapable of further division or separation : ELEMENTAL ⟨*ultimate* particles⟩ **4** : being the greatest : MAXIMUM ⟨*ultimate* speed of an airplane⟩ — **ultimate** *n* — **ul·ti·mate·ly** *adv*

ul·ti·ma·tum \ˌəl-tə-'māt-əm, -'mät-\ *n pl* **-tums** *or* **-ta** \-ə\ : a demand that if rejected will bring about an end of peaceful talks and could lead to forceful action

ul·tra \'əl-trə\ *adj* : going beyond others : EXTREME

ultra- *prefix* **1** : beyond : exceeding the range or limits of ⟨*ultra*violet⟩ **2** : more than is usual ⟨*ultra*modern⟩ [derived from Latin *ultra* "beyond"]

ul·tra·high frequency \ˌəl-trə-'hī-\ *n* : any radio frequency in the range between 300 and 3000 megahertz — abbr. *UHF*

ul·tra·ma·rine \ˌəl-trə-mə-'rēn\ *n* : a vivid blue

ul·tra·mod·ern \ˌəl-trə-'mäd-ərn\ *adj* : very modern in idea, style, or direction — **ul·tra·mod·ern·ist** \-ər-nəst\ *n*

ul·tra·son·ic \ˌəl-trə-'sän-ik\ *adj* : relating to or being vibrations that are of the same kind as sound waves but have too high a frequency to be heard by the human ear — **ul·tra·son·i·cal·ly** \-'sän-i-k(ə-)lē\ *adv*

ul·tra·sound \'əl-trə-ˌsaund\ *n* **1** : ultrasonic vibrations **2** : the use of ultrasound for medical diagnosis or treatment and especially a technique involving the formation of a two-dimensional image used for examining internal body structures and detecting abnormalities in the body

ul·tra·vi·o·let \ˌəl-trə-'vī-ə-lət\ *adj* **1** : located beyond the visible spectrum at its violet end and having a wavelength shorter than those of visible light but longer than those of X rays **2** : relating to, producing, or using ultraviolet radiation — **ultraviolet** *n*

ul·va \'əl-və\ *n* : SEA LETTUCE

um·bel \'əm-bəl\ *n* : a flat-topped or ball-shaped flower cluster (as in the carrot) in which the stalks of the individual flowers all grow from one point on the main stem like the ribs of an umbrella

um·ber \'əm-bər\ *n* **1** : an artist's pigment that is either greenish brown or reddish brown **2** : a medium to dark brown or yellowish brown — **umber** *adj*

um·bil·i·cal cord \ˌəm-'bil-i-kəl-\ *n* : a cord that contains blood vessels and connects the navel of a fetus with the placenta of the mother

um·bil·i·cus \ˌəm-'bil-i-kəs\ *n, pl* **-bil·i·ci** \-'bil-ə-ˌkī, -ˌkē, -ˌsī\ *or* **-bil·i·cus·es** *n* : a cavity in the wall of the abdomen at the place where the umbilical cord is attached

um·bra \'əm-brə\ *n, pl* **umbras** *or* **um·brae** \-brē, -ˌbrī\ **1** : a shaded area **2** : the cone-shaped part of the shadow of a celestial body from which the light of the sun is completely blocked

um·brage \'əm-brij\ *n* : RESENTMENT, OFFENSE ⟨take *umbrage* at a remark⟩

um·brel·la \ˌəm-'brel-ə\ *n* **1** : a collapsible covering for protection against weather consisting of fabric stretched over a hinged frame coming out from a center pole; *esp* : a small one for carrying in the hand **2** : something resembling an umbrella in shape or purpose [from Italian *ombrella* "umbrella", from Latin *umbella,* literally "little shade", from *umbra* "shade, shadow"]

Um·bri·an \'əm-brē-ən\ *n* : a member of a people of ancient Italy occupying Umbria — **Umbrian** *adj*

umi·ak \'ü-mē-ˌak\ *n* : an open Eskimo boat made of an open frame covered with hide

umiak

um·laut \'um-ˌlaut, 'üm-\ *n* **1** : the change of a vowel brought about by a following sound **2** : a diacritical ¨ mark placed especially over a German vowel to indicate umlaut

um·pire \'əm-ˌpī(ə)r\ *n* **1** : one having authority to decide an argument or a question **2** : an official in a sport (as baseball) who rules on plays — **umpire** *vb*

Word History The meaning of the Latin word *par* was "equal". From *par* came the early French word *per,* which also meant "equal". *Per* was combined with the prefix *non-, nom-,* meaning "not", to form the early French word *nomper,* which meant "not equal". *Nomper* came into Middle English as a noun, *noumpere.* The meaning of *noumpere* was "a person who is not equal, a person who has authority over others". Many people who heard the words *a noumpere* thought they were actually hearing *an oumpere.* Because of that misunderstanding, the letter *n* in time came to be dropped from *noumpere.* Other changes over the course of many years have given us the modern word *umpire.* [Middle English *oumpere,* an altered form of *noumpere* "one having authority to decide an issue or dispute", from early French *nomper* (adjective) "not equal", from *non-, nom-* "not" and *per* "equal", from Latin *par* "equal" — related to COMPARE, PAIR, PAR, PEER]

ump·teen \'əm(p)-'tēn, ˌəm(p)-\ *adj* : numerous but not fixed in amount ⟨*umpteen* million things to do⟩

¹un- \ˌən, 'ən\ *prefix* **1** : not ⟨*un*skilled⟩ ⟨*un*kindness⟩ **2** : opposite of : contrary to ⟨*un*constitutional⟩ ⟨*un*godly⟩ [Old English *un-* "not"]

unabsorbed	unadapted	unaired
unabsorbent	unadjusted	unalike
unacademic	unadmirable	unallied
unaccented	unadventurous	unaltered
unaccentuated	unadvertised	unambiguous
unacceptable	unadvisable	unambitious
unacceptably	unaesthetic	unanchored
unaccepted	unaffiliated	unanimated
unacclimated	unafraid	unannounced
unaccredited	unaggressive	unanswered
unachievable	unaided	unanticipated
unacquainted	unaimed	unapologetic

unapparent
unappeased
unappetizing
unappreciated
unappreciative
unapproved
unarmored
unarticulated
unartistic
unashamed
unaspiring
unassailed
unassigned
unassisted
unassociated
unathletic
unattainable
unattempted
unattended
unattractive
unauthentic
unauthenticated
unauthorized
unavailable
unavenged
unawakened
unawed
unbaked
unbaptized
unbeautiful
unbeloved
unblamed
unbleached
unblemished
unblinking
unborrowed
unbought
unbranded
unbreakable
unbridgeable
unbridged
unbrotherly
unbruised
unbrushed
unbudging
unburied
unburned
unburnished
unburnt
uncalibrated
uncalled
uncanceled
uncapitalized
uncared–for
uncaring
uncarpeted
uncashed
uncataloged
uncaught
uncelebrated
uncensored
uncensured
unchallenged
unchambered
unchanged
unchanging
unchaperoned
unchecked
unchristened
unclaimed
uncleaned
unclear

uncleared
unclimbed
unclog
unclouded
uncluttered
uncoated
uncoiled
uncollectable
uncollected
uncolored
uncombed
uncombined
uncomic
uncommercial
uncompensated
uncompetitive
uncomplaining
uncomplainingly
uncompleted
uncomplicated
unconcealable
unconcealed
unconfined
unconfirmed
unconfused
uncongenial
unconnected
unconquered
unconsecrated
unconsolidated
uncontaminated
uncontested
uncontradicted
uncontrolled
unconverted
unconvinced
unconvincing
uncooked
uncooperative
uncoordinated
uncordial
uncorrected
uncorrupted
uncorruptible
uncountable
uncourteous
uncreative
uncredited
uncrippled
uncritical
uncritically
uncrowded
uncultivated
uncultured
uncurbed
uncured
uncurious
uncurtained
uncustomary
undamaged
undamped
undated
undazzled
undecked
undeclared
undecorated
undefeated
undefended
undefiled
undefinable
undefined
undelayed

undemanding
undemocratic
undenominational
undependable
undeserved
undeserving
undesired
undetected
undetermined
undeterred
undeveloped
undigested
undignified
undiluted
undiminished
undimmed
undiplomatic
undiscerning
undisciplined
undisclosed
undiscovered
undiscriminating
undisguised
undismayed
undisputed
undissolved
undistinguished
undisturbed
undivided
undomesticated
undramatic
undreamed
undreamt
undrinkable
undyed
uneager
uneaten
uneconomic
unedifying
uneducated
unembarrassed
unemotional
unemphatic
unenclosed
unendorsed
unendurable
unenforceable
unenforced
unengaged
unenjoyable
unenlarged
unenterprising
unentertaining
unenthusiastic
unequipped
unessential
unethical
unexaggerated
unexamined
unexceptional
unexcited
unexciting
unexpanded
unexpended
unexperienced
unexpired
unexplainable
unexplained
unexploded
unexplored
unexposed
unexpressed

unexpurgated
unextinguished
unfaded
unfaltering
unfashionable
unfathomable
unfed
unfeminine
unfenced
unfermented
unfertilized
unfilled
unfiltered
unflagging
unflattering
unflavored
unfocused
unforced
unforeseen
unforested
unforgivable
unforgiving
unframed
unfree
unfrozen
unfulfilled
unfunny
unfurnished
unfussy
ungentle
ungentlemanly
ungoverned
ungraded
ungrammatical
unguided
unhampered
unhandsome
unhanged
unhardened
unharmed
unharmonious
unharvested
unhatched
unhealed
unheated
unheeded
unheeding
unhelpful
unheroic
unhesitating
unhindered
unhired
unhomogenized
unhonored
unhoused
unhurt
unidentified
unidiomatic
unilluminated
unillustrated
unimaginable
unimaginably
unimaginative
unimpaired
unimpeded
unimportant

unimposing
unimpressed
unimpressionable
unimpressive
uninclined
unincorporated
unindexed
uninfected
uninflammable
uninflected
uninfluenced
uninformed
uninhabitable
uninhabited
uninitiated
uninjured
uninoculated
uninspected
uninspired
uninspiring
uninstructed
uninstructive
uninsulated
uninsured
unintegrated
unintended
uninteresting
uninvested
uninvited
unjointed
unjustifiable
unjustified
unlabeled
unladylike
unlamented
unleavened
unlicensed
unlighted
unlikable
unlined
unlit
unliterary
unlivable
unlobed
unlovable
unloved
unloving
unmagnetized
unmalicious
unmanageable
unmanufactured
unmapped
unmarked
unmarketable
unmarried
unmasculine
unmatched
unmatching
unmated
unmeasured
unmelodious
unmentioned
unmindful
unmixed
unmodified
unmotivated

unmounted
unmovable
unmusical
unnamed
unneighborly
unnewsworthy
unnoted
unnoticeable
unnoticed
unobjectionable
unobliging
unobservant
unobserved
unobserving
unobstructed
unobtainable
unopened
unopposed
unordered
unoriginal
unowned
unpaid
unpainted
unpalatable
unpardonable
unpardoned
unpasteurized
unpatriotic
unpatterned
unpaved
unperceived
unperceiving
unperceptive
unperformed
unperturbed
unpitied
unpitying
unplanned
unplanted
unplayable
unpleasing
unpledged
unplowed
unpoetic
unpolarized
unpolished
unpolled
unpolluted
unposed
unpowered
unpracticed
unprejudiced
unpremeditated
unprepared
unpreparedness
unprepossessing
unprescribed
unpressed
unpretending
unpretty
unprinted
unprivileged
unprocessed
unproductive
unproductively
unprogrammed

\ə\ abut	\aú\ out	\i\ tip	\ȯ\ saw	\ù\ foot
\ər\ further	\ch\ chin	\ī\ life	\ȯi\ coin	\y\ yet
\a\ mat	\e\ pet	\j\ job	\th\ thin	\yü\ few
\ā\ take	\ē\ easy	\ŋ\ sing	\th\ this	\yù\ cure
\ä\ cot, cart	\g\ go	\ō\ bone	\ü\ food	\zh\ vision

unprogressive
unprompted
unprotected
unprotesting
unproved
unproven
unprovided
unprovoked
unpruned
unpunished
unpure
unquenchable
unquenched
unquestioned
unraised
unranked
unransomed
unrated
unratified
unrationed
unreachable
unready
unreal
unrealistic
unrealized
unreasonable
unreasonableness
unreasoned
unreasoning
unrecognizable
unrecognized
unreconciled
unrecorded
unrecoverable
unredeemable
unredeemed
unrefined
unreflecting
unreflective
unreformed
unregimented
unregistered
unregulated
unrehearsed
unrelated
unreliable
unrelieved
unreligious
unreluctant
unremarkable
unremembered
unremovable
unrepaired
unrepealed
unrepentant
unrepentantly
unreported
unrepresented
unrequited
unresistant
unresisted
unresisting
unresolved
unresourceful
unresponsive
unrestful
unrestricted
unreturnable
unreturned
unrevealed
unrevenged
unreviewed

unrevised
unrewarded
unrewarding
unrhymed
unrhythmic
unrinsed
unripened
unromantic
unromantically
unruled
unrushed
unsafe
unsaid
unsaintly
unsalable
unsalaried
unsalted
unsanctified
unsanctioned
unsanitary
unsaponified
unsatisfactorily
unsatisfactoriness
unsatisfactory
unsatisfiable
unsatisfied
unsatisfying
unscarred
unscented
unscreened
unsealed
unseasoned
unseaworthy
unsecured
unseeable
unseeded
unseeing
unsegmented
unselected
unsensational
unsent
unsentimental
unseparated
unserved
unsexual
unshaded
unshadowed
unshakable
unshaken
unshapely
unshared
unshaved
unshaven
unshed
unsheltered
unshielded
unshorn
unshrinkable
unshrinking
unshut
unsifted
unsigned
unsingable
unsinkable
unsized
unskillful
unslaked
unsmiling
unsociable
unsoiled
unsold
unsoldierly

unsolicited
unsolicitous
unsolvable
unsolved
unsorted
unsounded
unsown
unspecialized
unspecified
unspectacular
unspent
unspiritual
unsplit
unspoiled
unspoken
unsponsored
unsportsmanlike
unsquared
unstained
unsterile
unsterilized
unstinted
unstinting
unstrained
unstratified
unstriated
unstriped
unstructured
unstylish
unstylishly
unsubdued
unsubstantiated
unsubtle
unsuited
unsullied
unsupervised
unsupportable
unsupported
unsuppressed
unsure
unsureness
unsurpassable
unsurpassed
unsuspected
unsuspecting
unsuspenseful
unsuspicious
unsustained
unsweetened
unsympathetic
unsystematic
untainted
untalented
untamed
untanned
untapped
untarnished
untaxed
unteachable
untenable
untended
untested
unthanked
unthankful
unthawed
untheatrical
unthoughtful
unthreatened
unthrifty
untilled
untired
untiring

untouched
untracked
untrained
untranslated
untrapped
untraveled
untraversed
untreated
untrimmed
untrod
untrodden
untroubled
untrustworthy
untwisted
unusable
unuttered
unvaried

unvarying
unveiled
unventilated
unverified
unvulcanized
unwanted
unwarranted
unwashed
unwatched
unwatered
unwavering
unweaned
unwearable
unwearying
unweathered
unwed
unweeded

unweighted
unwelcome
unwelded
unwilled
unwished
unwitnessed
unwomanly
unwon
unwooded
unworkable
unworked
unworn
unworried
unwounded
unwoven
unwrinkled

²un- *prefix* **1** : do the opposite of : reverse ⟨*undress*⟩ **2** : remove a specified thing from ⟨*unburden*⟩ [Old English *un-, on-,* an altered form of *and-* "against"]

un·abashed \,ən-ə-'basht\ *adj* : not abashed : not embarrassed or ashamed — **un·abash·ed·ly** \-'bash-əd-lē\ *adv*

un·abat·ed \,ən-ə-'bāt-əd\ *adj* : not abated : at full strength or force — **un·abat·ed·ly** *adv*

un·able \,ən-'ā-bəl, 'ən-\ *adj* : not able : INCAPABLE

un·abridged \,ən-ə-'brijd\ *adj* **1** : not abridged : COMPLETE ⟨an *unabridged* reprint of a novel⟩ **2** : complete of its class : not based on one larger ⟨an *unabridged* dictionary⟩

un·ac·com·mo·dat·ed \,ən-ə-'käm-ə-,dāt-əd\ *adj* : not accommodated : UNPROVIDED

un·ac·com·pa·nied \,ən-ə-'kəmp-(ə-)nēd\ *adj* : not accompanied; *esp* : being without instrumental accompaniment

un·ac·count·able \,ən-ə-'kaůnt-ə-bəl\ *adj* **1** : INEXPLICABLE, STRANGE **2** : not to be called to account : not responsible — **un·ac·count·ably** \-blē\ *adv*

un·ac·count·ed \,ən-ə-'kaůnt-əd\ *adj* : not accounted : UNEXPLAINED — often used with *for* ⟨their absence was *unaccounted* for⟩

un·ac·cus·tomed \,ən-ə-'kəs-təmd\ *adj* **1** : UNUSUAL, UNFAMILIAR ⟨*unaccustomed* scenes⟩ **2** : not used to something : not accustomed ⟨*unaccustomed* to travel⟩

un·adorned \,ən-ə-'dò(ə)rnd\ *adj* : not adorned : lacking decoration : SIMPLE

un·adul·ter·at·ed \,ən-ə-'dəl-tə-,rāt-əd\ *adj* : PURE 1, 3, UNMIXED ⟨*unadulterated* foods⟩ ⟨*unadulterated* beauty⟩ ⟨*unadulterated* happiness⟩

un·ad·vised \,ən-əd-'vīzd\ *adj* : done without proper consideration

un·af·fect·ed \,ən-ə-'fek-təd\ *adj* **1** : not influenced or changed mentally, physically, or chemically **2** : free from false behavior intended to impress others : GENUINE — **un·af·fect·ed·ly** *adv*

un·alien·able \,ən-'āl-yə-nə-bəl, -'ā-lē-ə-nə-\ *adj* : INALIENABLE

un·aligned \,ən-ᵊl-'īnd\ *adj* : not associated with any one of competing groups of nations

un·al·loyed \,ən-ᵊl-'òid\ *adj* : not alloyed : UNMIXED, PURE ⟨*unalloyed* metals⟩ ⟨*unalloyed* happiness⟩

un·al·ter·able \,ən-'òl-t(ə-)rə-bəl, 'ən-\ *adj* : not capable of being altered or changed ⟨*unalterable* opposition⟩ — **un·al·ter·ably** \-blē\ *adv*

un–Amer·i·can \,ən-ə-'mer-ə-kən\ *adj* : not American — **un–Amer·i·can·ism** \-kə-,niz-əm\ *n*

unan·i·mous \yů-'nan-ə-məs\ *adj* **1** : being of one mind : agreeing completely ⟨the councilors were *unanimous* in their approval of the report⟩ **2** : agreed to by all ⟨a *unanimous* vote⟩ — **una·nim·i·ty** \,yü-nə-'nim-ət-ē\ *n* — **unan·i·mous·ly** \yů-'nan-ə-məs-lē\ *adv*

un·an·swer·able \,ən-'an(t)s-(ə-)rə-bəl, 'ən-\ *adj* : not answerable; *esp* : IRREFUTABLE ⟨the arguments were *unanswerable*⟩

un·ap·peal·ing \,ən-ə-'pē-liŋ\ *adj* : not appealing : UNATTRACTIVE

un·ap·peas·able \,ən-ə-'pē-zə-bəl\ *adj* : not to be appeased : IMPLACABLE

un·apt \,ən-'apt, 'ən-\ *adj* **1** : UNSUITABLE, INAPPROPRIATE ⟨an *unapt* quotation⟩ **2** : not accustomed and not likely ⟨*unapt* to run from danger⟩ **3** : not qualified or skilled ⟨*unapt* students⟩ — **un·apt·ly** \-'ap-(t)lē\ *adv*

un·arm \,ən-'ärm, 'ən-\ *vb* : DISARM 1

un·armed \,ən-'ärmd, 'ən-\ *adj* : not armed or armored

un·asked \,ən-'as(k)t, 'ən-\ *adj* **1** : not asked ⟨*unasked* questions⟩ **2** : not asked for ⟨*unasked* advice⟩

un·as·sail·able \,ən-ə-'sā-lə-bəl\ *adj* : not assailable : not open to doubt, attack, or question — **un·as·sail·ably** \-blē\ *adv*

un·as·ser·tive \,ən-ə-'sərt-iv\ *adj* : not assertive : MODEST, SHY

un·as·sum·ing \,ən-ə-'sü-miŋ\ *adj* : MODEST 1, RETIRING — **un·as·sum·ing·ly** *adv*

un·at·tached \,ən-ə-'tacht\ *adj* **1** : not attached **2** : not married or engaged

un·avail·ing \,ən-ə-'vā-liŋ\ *adj* : of no use : not successful : FUTILE — **un·avail·ing·ly** *adv*

un·avoid·able \,ən-ə-'vóid-ə-bəl\ *adj* : not avoidable : INEVITABLE — **un·avoid·ably** \-blē\ *adv*

¹un·aware \,ən-ə-'wa(ə)r, -'we(ə)r\ *adv* : UNAWARES

²unaware *adj* : not aware : IGNORANT — **un·aware·ness** *n*

un·awares \,ən-ə-'wa(ə)rz, -'we(ə)rz\ *adv* **1** : without knowing : UNINTENTIONALLY **2** : without warning : by surprise ⟨taken *unawares*⟩

un·backed \,ən-'bakt, 'ən-\ *adj* : not backed or encouraged

un·bal·ance \,ən-'bal-ən(t)s\ *vb* : to put out of balance

un·bal·anced \,ən-'bal-ən(t)st\ *adj* **1** : not in a state of balance **2** : not completely sane **3** : not adjusted so as to make credits equal to debits ⟨an *unbalanced* account⟩

un·bar \,ən-'bär, 'ən-\ *vb* **-barred; -bar·ring** : to remove a bar from : UNBOLT

un·bear·able \,ən-'bar-ə-bəl, 'ən-, -'ber-\ *adj* : greater than can be borne ⟨*unbearable* pain⟩ — **un·bear·ably** \-blē\ *adv*

un·beat·able \,ən-'bēt-ə-bəl\ *adj* : not capable of being defeated

un·beat·en \,ən-'bēt-°n\ *adj* **1** : not pounded, beaten, or whipped **2** : not defeated

un·be·com·ing \,ən-bi-'kəm-iŋ\ *adj* : not becoming ⟨an *unbecoming* dress⟩; *esp* : UNSUITABLE, IMPROPER ⟨conduct *unbecoming* an officer⟩ — **un·be·com·ing·ly** *adv*

un·be·knownst \,ən-bi-'nōn(t)st\ *also* **un·be·known** \-'nōn\ *adj* : happening without one's knowledge : UNKNOWN ⟨events *unbeknownst* to me⟩

un·be·lief \,ən-bə-'lēf\ *n* : the withholding or absence of belief : DOUBT

un·be·liev·able \,ən-bə-'lē-və-bəl\ *adj* : too unlikely for belief — **un·be·liev·ably** \-blē\ *adv*

un·be·liev·er \,ən-bə-'lē-vər\ *n* **1** : one who does not believe : DOUBTER **2** : one who does not believe in a particular religious faith : INFIDEL — **un·be·liev·ing** \-'lē-viŋ\ *adj* — **un·be·liev·ing·ly** *adv*

un·bend \,ən-'bend\ *vb* **-bent** \-'bent\; **-bend·ing** **1** : to free from being bent : make or become straight **2** : RELAX 3

un·bend·ing \,ən-'ben-diŋ\ *adj* **1** : INFLEXIBLE 2, RESOLUTE **2** : not relaxed and easy in manner : ALOOF

un·bi·ased \,ən-'bī-əst, 'ən-\ *adj* : free from bias ⟨*unbiased* estimate⟩; *esp* : IMPARTIAL, UNPREJUDICED

un·bid·den \,ən-'bid-°n\ *also* **un·bid** \-'bid\ *adj* : not bidden : UNASKED, UNINVITED

un·bind \,ən-'bīnd\ *vb* **-bound** \-'baùnd\; **-bind·ing** **1** : UNFASTEN, UNTIE, LOOSE **2** : to set free : RELEASE

un·blush·ing \,ən-'bləsh-iŋ\ *adj* **1** : not blushing **2** : UN-

ABASHED, SHAMELESS — **un·blush·ing·ly** *adv*

un·bolt \,ən-'bōlt, 'ən-\ *vb* : to open or unfasten by withdrawing a bolt

un·born \,ən-'bò(ə)rn\ *adj* : not born; *esp* : still to appear : FUTURE ⟨*unborn* generations⟩

un·bo·som \,ən-'bùz-əm\ *vb* **1** : to give expression to : DISCLOSE, REVEAL **2** : to reveal one's thoughts or feelings

un·bound \,ən-'baùnd\ *adj* **1 a** : not fastened or tied up ⟨*unbound* hair⟩ **b** : not kept within bounds ⟨*unbound* spirit⟩ **2** : not having a binding ⟨an *unbound* book⟩

un·bound·ed \,ən-'baùn-dəd\ *adj* : having no bounds or limits ⟨*unbounded* space⟩ ⟨*unbounded* enthusiasm⟩

un·bowed \,ən-'baùd, 'ən-\ *adj* **1** : not bowed down ⟨*unbowed* heads⟩ **2** : not conquered ⟨*unbowed* by failure⟩

un·braid \,ən-'brād\ *vb* : UNRAVEL 1

un·branched \,ən-'brancht\ *adj* : free from or not divided into branches ⟨a palm tree with a straight *unbranched* trunk⟩

un·bri·dled \,ən-'brīd-°ld\ *adj* : UNRESTRAINED, UNGOVERNED ⟨*unbridled* enthusiasm⟩

un·bro·ken \,ən-'brō-kən\ *adj* **1** : not broken : WHOLE **2** : not tamed; *esp* : not trained for use ⟨*unbroken* colts⟩ **3** : not interrupted : CONTINUOUS ⟨an *unbroken* row of trees⟩ ⟨*unbroken* sleep⟩

un·buck·le \,ən-'bək-əl\ *vb* : to unfasten the buckle of (as a belt)

un·built \,ən-'bilt\ *adj* **1** : not yet built ⟨an *unbuilt* house⟩ **2** : not built on ⟨an *unbuilt* plot⟩

un·bur·den \,ən-'bərd-°n\ *vb* **1** : to free or bring relief from a burden **2** : to free oneself from (as cares)

un·but·ton \,ən-'bət-°n\ *vb* : to unfasten the buttons of (as a garment)

un·but·toned \,ən-'bət-°nd\ *adj* **1 a** : not buttoned **b** : not provided with buttons **2** : free and unrestricted in action or expression

un·cage \,ən-'kāj, 'ən-\ *vb* : to release from or as if from a cage

un·called–for \,ən-'kòl(d)-,fò(ə)r\ *adj* **1** : not called for : UNNECESSARY **2 a** : not justified ⟨your jealousy is *uncalled-for*⟩ **b** : IMPOLITE, RUDE ⟨*uncalled-for* comments⟩

un·can·ny \,ən-'kan-ē\ *adj* **1** : MYSTERIOUS **2** : being beyond what is normal ⟨an *uncanny* sense of direction⟩ — **un·can·ni·ly** \-'kan-°l-ē\ *adv*

un·cap \,ən-'kap\ *vb* : to remove a cap or covering from

un·ceas·ing \,ən-'sē-siŋ\ *adj* : never ceasing : CONTINUOUS, INCESSANT — **un·ceas·ing·ly** *adv*

un·cer·e·mo·ni·ous \,ən-,ser-ə-'mō-nē-əs\ *adj* : acting without or lacking ordinary courtesy — **un·cer·e·mo·ni·ous·ly** *adv*

un·cer·tain \,ən-'sərt-°n, 'ən-\ *adj* **1** : not definite or fixed ⟨an *uncertain* quantity⟩ **2 a** : not sure ⟨*uncertain* of the truth⟩ **b** : not known for sure **3** : likely to change : not dependable ⟨*uncertain* weather⟩ — **un·cer·tain·ly** *adv*

un·cer·tain·ty \,ən-'sərt-°n-tē\ *n* **1** : lack of certainty **2** : something that is uncertain **syn** see DOUBT

un·chain \,ən-'chān, 'ən-\ *vb* : to free by or as if by removing a chain : set loose

un·change·able \,ən-'chān-jə-bəl\ *adj* : not changing or to be changed : IMMUTABLE — **un·change·able·ness** *n* — **un·change·ably** \-blē\ *adv*

un·charged \,ən-'chärjd\ *adj* : having no electric charge

un·char·i·ta·ble \,ən-'char-ət-ə-bəl\ *adj* : not charitable; *esp* : severe in judging others — **un·char·i·ta·ble·ness** *n* — **un·char·i·ta·bly** \-blē\ *adv*

un·chart·ed \,ən-'chärt-əd\ *adj* : not recorded or located

\ə\ abut	\aù\ out	\i\ tip	\ò\ saw	\ù\ foot
\ər\ further	\ch\ chin	\ī\ life	\òi\ coin	\y\ yet
\a\ mat	\e\ pet	\j\ job	\th\ thin	\yü\ few
\ā\ take	\ē\ easy	\ŋ\ sing	\th\ this	\yù\ cure
\ä\ cot, cart	\g\ go	\ō\ bone	\ü\ food	\zh\ vision

on a map, chart, or plan : UNKNOWN ⟨vast *uncharted* wilderness⟩

un·chaste \,ən-'chāst\ *adj* : not chaste : lacking in chastity — **un·chas·ti·ty** \-'chas-tət-ē\ *n*

un·chris·tian \,ən-'kris-chən\ *adj* **1** : not of the Christian faith **2 a** : not suitable to or like a Christian **b** : UNCIVILIZED 1, BARBAROUS

un·civ·il \,ən-'siv-əl\ *adj* **1** : not civilized : BARBAROUS **2** : lacking in courtesy : ILL-MANNERED

un·civ·i·lized \,ən-'siv-ə-,līzd\ *adj* **1** : not civilized : BARBAROUS **2** : far from civilization : WILD

un·clad \,ən-'klad\ *adj* : not clothed : UNDRESSED, NAKED

un·clasp \,ən-'klasp\ *vb* : to release from a clasp

un·clas·si·fied \,ən-'klas-ə-,fīd\ *adj* : not classified; *esp* : not requiring special treatment for purposes of security ⟨*unclassified* documents⟩

un·cle \'əŋ-kəl\ *n* **1** : the brother of one's father or mother **2** : the husband of one's aunt

un·clean \,ən-'klēn\ *adj* **1** : not pure and innocent : WICKED **2** : prohibited by religious law for use or contact **3** : ¹DIRTY 1, FILTHY — **un·clean·ness** \-'klēn-nəs\ *n*

un·clean·ly \,ən-'klen-lē\ *adj* : UNCLEAN 1, DIRTY — **un·clean·li·ness** *n*

un·clench \,ən-'klench\ *vb* : to open from a clenched position : RELAX ⟨*unclenched* my hands⟩

Un·cle Sam \,əŋ-kəl-'sam\ *n* **1** : the U.S. government thought of or represented as a person **2** : the American nation or people

Uncle Tom \-'täm\ *n* : a black eager to win the approval of whites and willing to cooperate with them [from *Uncle Tom*, name of a slave in the novel *Uncle Tom's Cabin* by Harriet Beecher Stowe]

un·clinch \,ən-'klinch\ *vb* : UNCLENCH

un·cloak \,ən-'klōk\ *vb* **1** : to remove a cloak or cover from **2** : REVEAL 1, UNMASK

un·close \,ən-'klōz\ *vb* : ²OPEN 1a

un·clothe \,ən-'klōth\ *vb* : to strip of clothes or a covering

un·coil \,ən-'kȯi(ə)l, 'ən-\ *vb* : to release or become released from a coiled state : UNWIND

un·com·fort·able \,ən-'kəm(p)(f)-tə(r)-bəl, -'kəm(p)-fə(r)t-ə-bəl, 'ən-\ *adj* **1** : causing discomfort ⟨an *uncomfortable* chair⟩ **2** : feeling discomfort : UNEASY — **un·com·fort·ably** \-blē\ *adv*

un·com·mit·ted \,ən-kə-'mit-əd\ *adj* : not committed; *esp* : not pledged to a particular belief, allegiance, or program

un·com·mon \,ən-'käm-ən, 'ən-\ *adj* **1** : not ordinarily found or experienced : UNUSUAL ⟨not *uncommon* to catch a cold⟩ **2** : EXTRAORDINARY, REMARKABLE, EXCEPTIONAL ⟨has *uncommon* ability⟩ — **un·com·mon·ly** *adv* — **un·com·mon·ness** \-ən-nəs\ *n*

un·com·mu·ni·ca·tive \,ən-kə-'myü-nə-,kāt-iv, -ni-kət-\ *adj* : not tending to talk or give out information : RESERVED

un·com·pli·men·ta·ry \'ən-,käm-plə-'ment-ə-rē, -'men-trē\ *adj* : not complimentary ⟨an *uncomplimentary* remark⟩

un·com·pro·mis·ing \,ən-'käm-prə-,mī-ziŋ\ *adj* : not making or accepting a compromise : UNYIELDING — **un·com·pro·mis·ing·ly** *adv*

un·con·cern \,ən-kən-'sərn\ *n* : lack of care or interest : INDIFFERENCE ⟨*unconcern* for world problems⟩

un·con·cerned \,ən-kən-'sərnd\ *adj* **1** : not involved : not having a party or interest **2** : the anxious or upset : free of worry — **un·con·cern·ed·ly** \-'sər-nəd-lē\ *adv*

un·con·di·tion·al \,ən-kən-'dish-nəl, -'dish-ən-əl\ *adj* : not limited : ABSOLUTE, UNQUALIFIED ⟨*unconditional* surrender⟩ — **un·con·di·tion·al·ly** \-ē\ *adv*

un·con·quer·able \,ən-'käŋ-k(ə-)rə-bəl, 'ən-\ *adj* : incapable of being conquered or overcome — **un·con·quer·ably** \-blē\ *adv*

un·con·scio·na·ble \,ən-'känch-(ə-)nə-bəl\ *adj* **1** : not guided or controlled by conscience **2** : not being in agreement with what is right or just : UNREASONABLE, EXCESSIVE — **un·con·scio·na·bly** \-blē\ *adv*

¹**un·con·scious** \,ən-'kän-chəs, 'ən\ *adj* **1** : not aware ⟨*unconscious* of having made a mistake⟩ **2** : having lost consciousness ⟨knocked *unconscious* by a fall⟩ **3** : not realized : not consciously done ⟨an *unconscious* mistake⟩ ⟨*unconscious* humor⟩ — **un·con·scious·ly** *adv* — **un·con·scious·ness** *n*

²**unconscious** *n* : the part of one's mental life of which one is not aware but which is often a powerful force in controlling behavior

un·con·sid·ered \,ən-kən-'sid-ərd\ *adj* **1** : not considered or worth consideration **2** : not resulting from consideration or study ⟨*unconsidered* opinions⟩

un·con·sti·tu·tion·al \'ən-,kän(t)-stə-'t(y)üsh-nəl, -ən-əl\ *adj* : not according to or agreeing with the constitution of a state or society — **un·con·sti·tu·tion·al·i·ty** \-,t(y)ü-shə-'nal-ət-ē\ *n* — **un·con·sti·tu·tion·al·ly** \-'t(y)üsh-nə-lē, -ən-əl-ē\ *adv*

un·con·trol·la·ble \,ən-kən-'trō-lə-bəl\ *adj* : incapable of being controlled : UNGOVERNABLE — **un·con·trol·la·bly** \-blē\ *adv*

un·con·ven·tion·al \,ən-kən-'vench-nəl, -ən-əl\ *adj* : not conventional : not bound by or in agreement with convention ⟨*unconventional* behavior⟩ — **un·con·ven·tion·al·i·ty** \-,vench-ə-'nal-ət-ē\ *n* — **un·con·ven·tion·al·ly** \-'vench-nə-lē, -ən-əl-ē\ *adv*

un·cork \,ən-'kȯ(ə)rk, 'ən-\ *vb* **1** : to draw a cork from **2 a** : to release from a sealed or shut up state ⟨*uncork* a surprise⟩ **b** : to let go : RELEASE ⟨*uncork* a wild pitch⟩

un·count·ed \,ən-'kaȯnt-əd\ *adj* **1** : not counted ⟨a stack of *uncounted* bills⟩ **2** : too many to be counted : INNUMERABLE ⟨*uncounted* millions of people⟩

un·cou·ple \,ən-'kəp-əl\ *vb* **-cou·pled; -cou·pling** \-'kəp-(ə-)liŋ\ : DISCONNECT ⟨*uncouple* railroad cars⟩

un·couth \,ən-'küth\ *adj* **1** : strange, awkward, and clumsy in shape or appearance **2** : vulgar in conduct or speech : RUDE

un·cov·er \,ən-'kəv-ər\ *vb* **1** : to make known : DISCLOSE, REVEAL ⟨*uncover* a plot⟩ **2** : to expose to view by removing some covering ⟨*uncover* the ruins of an ancient city⟩ **3 a** : to take the cover from ⟨*uncover* the box⟩ **b** : to remove the hat from **c** : to take off one's hat as a sign of respect

un·cov·ered \,ən-'kəv-ərd\ *adj* : not covered or supplied with a covering

un·cre·at·ed \,ən-krē-'āt-əd\ *adj* **1** : not occurring by creation : ETERNAL **2** : not yet created

un·cross \,ən-'krȯs\ *vb* : to change from a crossed position ⟨*uncrossed* my legs⟩

un·crown \,ən-'kraȯn\ *vb* : to take the crown from : DEPOSE, DETHRONE

unc·tion \'əŋ(k)-shən\ *n* **1** : the act of anointing as a ceremony of healing **2** : exaggerated earnestness of language or manner

unc·tu·ous \'əŋ(k)-chə-(wə)s, 'əŋ(k)sh-wəs\ *adj* **1** : smooth and greasy like an ointment : OILY **2** : too smooth, polite, and agreeable in speech or manner — **unc·tu·ous·ly** *adv* — **unc·tu·ous·ness** *n*

un·curl \,ən-'kər(-ə)l, 'ən-\ *vb* : to make or become straightened out from a curled or coiled position

un·cut \,ən-'kət, 'ən-\ *adj* **1** : not cut down or cut into **2** : not shaped by cutting ⟨an *uncut* diamond⟩ **3** : not having the folds of the leaves slit ⟨*uncut* books⟩ **4** : not shortened ⟨an *uncut* text⟩

un·daunt·ed \,ən-'dȯnt-əd, -'dänt-\ *adj* : not discouraged or frightened : FEARLESS — **un·daunt·ed·ly** *adv*

un·de·ceive \,ən-di-'sēv\ *vb* : to free from deception or error

un·de·cid·ed \,ən-di-'sīd-əd\ *adj* **1** : not yet decided : not settled ⟨the question is still *undecided*⟩ **2** : not having decided : uncertain what to do ⟨still *undecided* about it⟩ — **un·de·cid·ed·ly** *adv*

un·de·mon·stra·tive \ˌən-di-ˈmän(t)-strət-iv\ *adj* : not demonstrative : RESERVED

un·de·ni·able \ˌən-di-ˈnī-ə-bəl\ *adj* **1** : plainly true : INCONTESTABLE **2** : positively excellent or genuine — **un·de·ni·ably** \-blē\ *adv*

¹un·der \ˈən-dər\ *adv* **1** : in or into a position below or beneath something ⟨the duck surfaced, then went *under* again⟩ **2** : below some quantity, level, or average ⟨ten dollars or *under*⟩ — often used in combination ⟨*under*played the part⟩ **3** : in or into a losing, lower, or unconscious state or condition ⟨kept my disappointment *under*⟩ ⟨the ether put you *under*⟩ **4** : so as to be covered or hidden ⟨turned *under* by the plow⟩

²un·der \ˈən-dər, ˈən-\ *prep* **1** : below or beneath and topped or sheltered by ⟨*under* sunny skies⟩ ⟨*under* a tree⟩ ⟨swimming *under* water⟩ ⟨wearing a sweater *under* my jacket⟩ **2 a** : bound by the authority or guidance of ⟨served *under* the general⟩ **b** : affected or influenced by the action or result of ⟨the disease is *under* treatment⟩ **3** : within the group or division of ⟨*under* this heading⟩ **4 a** : less or lower than (as in size, amount, or rank) ⟨all masses *under* 90 kilograms⟩ ⟨nobody *under* a colonel⟩ **b** : below the required level of ⟨*under* legal age⟩

³un·der \ˈən-dər\ *adj* **1 a** : lying or placed below — often used in combination ⟨the sea's *under*currents⟩ ⟨the *under*side of an animal⟩ **b** : facing or bulging downward — often used in combination ⟨*under*surface of a leaf⟩ **2** : lower in position or authority : SUBORDINATE ⟨*under* bookkeepers⟩ **3** : lower than usual, proper, or desired in amount or quality ⟨*under* dose of medicine⟩

un·der·achiev·er \ˌən-də-rə-ˈchē-vər\ *n* : a student who fails to do as well as he or she can

un·der·ac·tive \ˌən-də-ˈrak-tiv\ *adj* : having an abnormally low level of activity ⟨an *underactive* gland⟩

un·der·age \ˌən-də-ˈrāj\ *adj* : of less than mature or legal age

¹un·der·arm \ˌən-də-ˈrärm\ *adj* **1** : ²UNDERHAND 2 ⟨an *underarm* toss⟩ **2** : placed under or on the underside of the arm ⟨*underarm* seams⟩ — **un·der·arm** \ˈən-də-ˌrärm\ *n*

²un·der·arm \ˌən-də-ˈrärm\ *adv* : with an underarm motion

un·der·bel·ly \ˈən-dər-ˌbel-ē\ *n* : the under part of a body or mass ⟨*underbelly* of a bomber⟩; *also* : an area open to attack or damage ⟨the *underbelly* of the enemy's defenses⟩

un·der·bid \ˌən-dər-ˈbid\ *vb* **-bid; -bid·ding** **1** : to bid less than a competing bidder **2** : to bid too low (as in cards) — **un·der·bid·der** *n*

un·der·body \ˈən-dər-ˌbäd-ē\ *n* : the lower part or underside of something (as an animal or car)

un·der·brush \ˈən-dər-ˌbrəsh\ *n* : shrubs and small trees growing among large trees : UNDERGROWTH

un·der·car·riage \ˈən-dər-ˌkar-ij\ *n* **1** : a supporting structure (as of an automobile) **2** : the landing gear of an airplane

U undercarriage 2

un·der·charge \ˌən-dər-ˈchärj\ *vb* : to charge too little ⟨was *undercharged* by the salesclerk⟩ — **un·der·charge** \ˈən-dər-ˌchärj\ *n*

un·der·class·man \ˌən-dər-ˈklas-mən\ *n* : a student in the first or second year of a four-year high school or college

un·der·clothes \ˈən-dər-ˌklō(th)z\ *n pl* : UNDERWEAR

un·der·cloth·ing \-ˌklō-thiŋ\ *n* : UNDERWEAR

un·der·coat \-ˌkōt\ *n* **1** : a coat or jacket worn under another **2** : a growth of short hair or fur partly concealed by a longer growth **3** : a coat of paint under another — **un·dercoat** *vb*

un·der·cov·er \-ˌkəv-ər\ *adj* : acting or performed in secret ⟨*undercover* scheme⟩; *esp* : employed or engaged in spying or secret investigation ⟨*undercover* agent⟩

un·der·cur·rent \-ˌkər-ənt, -ˌkə-rənt\ *n* **1** : a current below the upper currents or surface ⟨*undercurrents* of water⟩ **2** : a hidden current of opinion or feeling often different from the one openly shown

¹un·der·cut \ˌən-dər-ˈkət\ *vb* **-cut; -cut·ting** **1** : to cut away the under part of or beneath something **2** : to offer to sell at lower prices than or to work for lower wages than ⟨*undercut* a competitor⟩ **3** : to strike so as to give a backspin or height to the shot ⟨a tennis player *undercutting* the ball⟩

²un·der·cut \ˈən-dər-ˌkət\ *n* : the action or result of undercutting

un·der·de·vel·oped \ˌən-dər-di-ˈvel-əpt\ *adj* **1** : not developed normally or enough ⟨*underdeveloped* muscles⟩ **2** : having a low level of industrial production and standard of living ⟨the *underdeveloped* nations⟩

un·der·dog \ˈən-dər-ˌdȯg\ *n* : the loser or predicted loser in a struggle

un·der·done \ˌən-dər-ˈdən\ *adj* : not thoroughly cooked : RARE

un·der·draw·ers \-ˌdrȯ(-ə)rz\ *n pl* : UNDERPANTS

un·der·es·ti·mate \ˌən-də-ˈres-tə-ˌmāt\ *vb* **1** : to estimate as being less than the actual size, quantity, or number ⟨*underestimate* the cost of a new building⟩ **2** : to place too low a value on : UNDERRATE ⟨*underestimate* an opponent⟩ — **un·der·es·ti·mate** \-mət\ *n* — **un·der·es·ti·ma·tion** \-ˌres-tə-ˈmā-shən\ *n*

un·der·ex·pose \ˌən-də-rik-ˈspōz\ *vb* : to expose for less time than is needed ⟨the film was *underexposed*⟩ — **un·der·ex·po·sure** \-ˈspō-zhər\ *n*

un·der·fed \ˌən-dər-ˈfed\ *adj* : fed with too little food : UNDERNOURISHED

un·der·foot \-ˈfu̇t\ *adv* **1** : under the feet ⟨flowers trampled *underfoot*⟩ **2** : close about one's feet : in the way ⟨a puppy always *underfoot*⟩

un·der·fur \ˈən-dər-ˌfər\ *n* : the thick soft undercoat of fur lying beneath the longer and coarser hair of a mammal

un·der·gar·ment \ˈən-dər-ˌgär-mənt\ *n* : a garment to be worn under another

un·der·gird \ˌən-dər-ˈgərd\ *vb* : to make secure : brace up : STRENGTHEN ⟨a life *undergirded* by religion⟩

un·der·go \ˌən-dər-ˈgō\ *vb* **-went** \-ˈwent\; **-gone** \-ˈgȯn *also* -ˈgän\, **-go·ing** \-ˈgō-iŋ\ **1** : ENDURE **2** ⟨*undergo* an operation⟩ **2** : to pass through : EXPERIENCE ⟨*undergoing* a change⟩

un·der·grad·u·ate \ˌən-dər-ˈgraj-(ə-)wət, -ə-ˌwät\ *n* : a student at a college or university who has not been granted a degree

¹un·der·ground \ˌən-dər-ˈgraund\ *adv* **1** : below the surface of the earth **2** : in or into hiding or secret operation ⟨the political party went *underground*⟩

²un·der·ground \ˈən-dər-ˌgraund\ *n* **1** : a space under the surface of the ground; *esp* : SUBWAY 2 **2** : a secret political group; *esp* : an organized body working in secret to overthrow a government or an occupying power

³un·der·ground \ˈən-dər-ˌgraund\ *adj* **1** : being, growing, operating, or located below the surface of the ground ⟨an *underground* stream⟩ **2** : conducted secretly

Underground Railroad *n* : a system of cooperation in the United States before 1863 by which slaves were secretly helped to reach the North or Canada

un·der·growth \ˈən-dər-ˌgrōth\ *n* : low growth on the floor of a forest including seedlings and saplings, shrubs, and herbs

¹un·der·hand \ˈən-dər-ˌhand\ *adv* **1** : in an underhand or secret manner **2** : with an underhand motion ⟨throw *underhand*⟩

²under·hand *adj* **1** : done in secret or so as to deceive : SLY ⟨*underhand* methods⟩ **2** : performed with the hand kept below the level of the shoulder ⟨an *underhand* pitch⟩

un·der·hand·ed \,ən-dər-'han-dəd\ *adj or adv* : ¹UNDERHAND, ²UNDERHAND 1 — **un·der·hand·ed·ly** *adv* — **un·der·hand·ed·ness** *n*

un·der·lay \,ən-dər-'lā\ *vb* **-laid** \-'lād\; **-lay·ing** **1** : to cover, line, or cross the bottom of ⟨shingles *underlaid* with tar paper⟩ **2** : to raise or hold up by something laid under — **un·der·lay** \'ən-dər-,lā\ *n*

un·der·lie \,ən-dər-'lī\ *vb* **-lay** \-'lā\; **-lain** \-'lān\; **-ly·ing** \-'lī-iŋ\ **1** : to lie or be located under **2** : to form the foundation of : SUPPORT ⟨ideas *underlying* the revolution⟩

un·der·line \'ən-dər-,līn, ,ən-dər-'līn\ *vb* **1** : to draw a line under : UNDERSCORE **2** : EMPHASIZE — **un·der·line** \'ən-dər-,līn\ *n*

un·der·ling \'ən-dər-liŋ\ *n* : one who is under the orders of another : SUBORDINATE

un·der·ly·ing \,ən-dər-,lī-iŋ\ *adj* **1** : lying under or below ⟨the *underlying* rock⟩ **2** : ¹FUNDAMENTAL 1

un·der·mine \,ən-dər-'mīn\ *vb* **1** : to dig out or wear away the earth beneath ⟨*undermine* a wall⟩ **2** : to weaken or ruin secretly or gradually ⟨*undermine* a government⟩

un·der·most \'ən-dər-,mōst\ *adj* : lowest in position compared to others — **undermost** *adv*

¹un·der·neath \,ən-dər-'nēth\ *prep* **1** : right under ⟨wore their bathing suits *underneath* their clothes⟩ **2** : under the control of

²underneath *adv* **1** : under or below an object or an outside part ⟨soaked through the jacket to the shirt *underneath*⟩ **2** : on the lower side ⟨a pot blackened *underneath*⟩

un·der·nour·ished \,ən-dər-'nər-isht, -'nə-risht\ *adj* : supplied with too little nourishment for health and growth — **un·der·nour·ish·ment** \-'nər-ish-ment, -'nə-rish-\ *n*

un·der·pants \'ən-dər-,pan(t)s\ *n pl* : short or long pants worn under an outer garment

un·der·part \-,pärt\ *n* : a part lying on the lower side especially of a bird or mammal

un·der·pass \-,pas\ *n* : a passage underneath something (as for a road passing under another road)

un·der·pay \,ən-dər-'pā\ *vb* **-paid** \-'pād\; **-pay·ing** : to pay too little

un·der·pin \-'pin\ *vb* **1** : to form part of, strengthen, or replace the foundation of ⟨*underpin* a structure⟩ **2** : to give support to

underpass

un·der·pin·ning \'ən-dər-,pin-iŋ\ *n* **1** : the foundation used for support of a structure **2** : ¹PROP, SUPPORT **3** : a person's legs — usually used in pl.

un·der·play \,ən-dər-'plā\ *vb* : to handle carefully; *esp* : to play a role without much force

un·der·priv·i·leged \-'priv-(ə)lijd\ *adj* : having fewer privileges than others : POOR

un·der·pro·duc·tion \-prə-'dək-shən\ *n* : the production of less than enough to satisfy the demand or of less than the usual supply

un·der·rate \,ən-də(r)-'rāt\ *vb* : to rate too low : UNDERVALUE

un·der·score \'ən-dər-,skō(ə)r, -,skȯ(ə)r\ *vb* **1** : to draw a line under : UNDERLINE **2** : EMPHASIZE — **underscore** *n*

un·der·sea \,ən-dər-,sē\ *adj* **1** : being or carried on under the sea or under the surface of the sea ⟨*undersea* oil de-

posits⟩ ⟨*undersea* warfare⟩ **2** : designed for use under the surface of the sea ⟨*undersea* fleet⟩

under secretary *n* : a secretary right under a principal secretary ⟨*under secretary* of state⟩

un·der·sell \,ən-dər-'sel\ *vb* **-sold** \-'sōld\; **-sell·ing** : to sell articles cheaper than ⟨*undersell* a competitor⟩

un·der·shirt \'ən-dər-,shərt\ *n* : a collarless undergarment for the upper body

un·der·side \'ən-dər-,sīd, ,ən-dər-'sīd\ *n* : the side or part lying underneath

un·der·signed \'ən-dər-,sīnd\ *n, pl* **undersigned** : one who signs his or her name at the end of a document ⟨the *undersigned* testifies⟩ ⟨the *undersigned* all agree⟩

un·der·sized \,ən-dər-'sīzd\ *adj* : smaller than is usual or standard ⟨*undersized* fruit⟩

un·der·skirt \'ən-dər-,skərt\ *n* : a skirt worn under an outer skirt; *esp* : ¹PETTICOAT

un·der·stand \,ən-dər-'stand\ *vb* **-stood** \-'stúd\; **-stand·ing** **1 a** : to get the meaning of : COMPREHEND **b** : to have thorough acquaintance with ⟨*understand* the arts⟩ **2** : to have reason to believe : GATHER, INFER ⟨I *understand* that they will arrive today⟩ **3** : to take as meaning something not openly made known : INTERPRET, EXPLAIN ⟨*understand* the letter to be a refusal⟩ **4** : to have a sympathetic attitude ⟨my cousin doesn't *understand* about these things⟩ **5** : to supply in thought as if expressed ⟨"to be married" is commonly *understood* after the word *engaged*⟩ — **un·der·stand·able** \-'stan-də-bəl\ *adj* — **un·der·stand·ably** \-blē\ *adv*

¹un·der·stand·ing \,ən-dər-'stan-diŋ\ *n* **1** : knowledge and ability to judge : INTELLIGENCE ⟨a person of *understanding*⟩ **2 a** : agreement of opinion or feeling ⟨had never been much *understanding* between them⟩ **b** : something agreed to by both sides and entered into silently or without ceremony ⟨an *understanding* between two nations over trade⟩

²understanding *adj* : having or showing understanding : TOLERANT, SYMPATHETIC ⟨you seem very *understanding*⟩ — **un·der·stand·ing·ly** \-diŋ-lē\ *adv*

un·der·state \,ən-dər-'stāt\ *vb* **1** : to represent as less than is the case ⟨*understate* taxable income⟩ **2** : to state mildly especially on purpose — **un·der·state·ment** \-mənt\ *n*

un·der·stat·ed \,ən-dər-'stāt-əd\ *adj* : expressed or done in a quiet or simple fashion

un·der·stood \,ən-dər-'stúd\ *adj* **1** : fully known **2** : agreed upon **3** : IMPLICIT 1

un·der·study \'ən-dər-,stəd-ē, ,ən-dər-'stəd-ē\ *vb* : to study another actor's part in order to be his or her substitute in an emergency — **understudy** *n*

un·der·sur·face \'ən-dər-,sər-fəs\ *n* : UNDERSIDE

un·der·take \,ən-dər-'tāk\ *vb* **-took** \-'túk\; **-tak·en** \-'tā-kən\; **-tak·ing** **1** : to take upon oneself as a task : enter upon ⟨*undertake* a journey⟩ **2** : to take on as a duty : AGREE, CONTRACT ⟨*undertake* to deliver a package⟩

un·der·tak·er \'ən-dər-,tā-kər\ *n* : a person whose business is to prepare the dead for burial or cremation and to take charge of funerals

un·der·tak·ing \'ən-dər-,tā-kiŋ, ,ən-dər-'tā-kiŋ; sense 1b is 'ən-dər-,tā-kiŋ *only*\ **1 a** : the act of a person who undertakes something **b** : the business of an undertaker **2** : something undertaken

un·der·tone \'ən-dər-,tōn\ *n* **1** : a low or quiet tone **2** : a faint color as seen through and changing another color

un·der·tow \'ən-dər-,tō\ *n* : a current beneath the surface of the water that moves away from or along the shore while the surface water above it moves toward the shore

un·der·val·ue \,ən-dər-'val-yü\ *vb* **1** : to value below the real worth **2** : to set little value on — **un·der·val·u·a·tion** \-,val-yə-'wā-shən\ *n*

un·der·wa·ter \,ən-dər-,wȯt-ər, -,wät-\ *adj* : lying, growing, worn, or operating below the surface of the water — **un-**

der·wa·ter \-'wȯt-, -'wät-\ *adv*

under way *adv or adj* **1** : in or into motion ⟨a ship getting *under way*⟩ **2** : in progress : AFOOT ⟨preparations are *under way*⟩

un·der·wear \'ən-dər-ˌwa(ə)r, -ˌwe(ə)r\ *n* : clothing or an article of clothing worn next to the skin and under other clothing

un·der·weight \ˌən-dər-'wāt\ *adj* : weighing less than what is normal, average, or necessary

underwent *past of* UNDERGO

un·der·wood \'ən-dər-ˌwu̇d\ *n* : UNDERBRUSH

un·der·world \'ən-dər-ˌwərld\ *n* **1** : the place of the dead : HADES **2** : the side of the earth opposite to one **3** : the world of organized crime

un·der·write \'ən-də(r)-ˌrīt, ˌən-də(r)-'rīt\ *vb* **-wrote** \-ˌrōt, -'rōt\; **-writ·ten** \-ˌrit-ᵊn, -'rit-ᵊn\; **-writ·ing** \-ˌrīt-iŋ, -'rīt-\ **1** : to write under or at the end of something else **2** : to set one's name to (an insurance policy) and thereby agree to insure against specified loss or damage **3** : to agree to **4 a** : to attempt the sale of and agree to purchase on a fixed date any remaining unsold **b** : to guarantee financial support of ⟨*underwrite* an expedition⟩ — **un·der·writ·er** \'ən-də(r)-ˌrīt-ər\ *n*

un·de·sir·able \ˌən-di-'zī-rə-bəl\ *adj* : not desirable : UNWANTED — **un·de·sir·abil·i·ty** \-ˌzī-rə-'bil-ət-ē\ *n* — **undesirable** *n* — **un·de·sir·able·ness** \-'zī-rə-bəl-nəs\ *n* — **un·de·sir·ably** \-blē\ *adv*

un·de·vi·at·ing \ˌən-'dē-vē-ˌāt-iŋ, 'ən-\ *adj* : keeping a true course : UNSWERVING

un·dies \'ən-dēz\ *n pl* : UNDERWEAR; *esp* : women's underwear

un·di·rect·ed \ˌən-də-'rek-təd, -dī-\ *adj* : not directed ⟨*undirected* efforts⟩

un·do \ˌən-'dü, 'ən-\ *vb* **-did** \-'did\; **-done** \-'dən\; **-do·ing** \-'dü-iŋ\ **1** : to make or become unfastened or loosened : OPEN, UNTIE ⟨*undo* a knot⟩ **2** : to destroy the effect of : NULLIFY, REVERSE **3 a** : to cause the ruin of ⟨your stubbornness *undid* you⟩ ⟨*undone* by greed⟩ **b** : to disturb the calmness of : UPSET — **un·do·er** *n*

un·do·ing \ˌən-'dü-iŋ\ *n* **1** : an act or instance of unfastening **2 a** : ¹RUIN 1 ⟨parental neglect helped lead to their *undoing*⟩ **b** : a cause of ruin ⟨my quick temper was my *undoing*⟩ **3** : REVERSAL, ANNULMENT

un·done \ˌən-'dən\ *adj* : not done ⟨an *undone* task⟩

un·doubt·ed \ˌən-'dauṫ-əd\ *adj* : not doubted or open to doubt : CERTAIN ⟨*undoubted* proof of guilt⟩ — **un·doubt·ed·ly** *adv*

un·drape \ˌən-'drāp, 'ən-\ *vb* : to strip of drapery : UNCOVER, UNVEIL

¹un·dress \ˌən-'dres\ *vb* : to remove the clothes or covering of : STRIP, DISROBE

²undress *n* **1** : ordinary dress **2** : a state of nudity

un·dressed \ˌən-'drest, 'ən-\ *adj* **1** : partially dressed or wearing clothing that is ordinary or unsuitable **2** : not fully processed or finished ⟨*undressed* hides⟩ **3** : not cared for or tended ⟨an *undressed* wound⟩ ⟨*undressed* fields⟩

un·due \ˌən-'d(y)ü\ *adj* **1** : not due **2** : EXCESSIVE ⟨*undue* profit⟩

un·du·lant \'ən-jə-lənt, 'ən-d(y)ə-\ *adj* : rising and falling in waves

undulant fever *n* : a human disease that is caused by a bacterium and is marked by a fever that comes and goes, by pain and swelling in the joints, and by great weakness

un·du·late \'ən-jə-ˌlāt, 'ən-d(y)ə-\ *vb* **-lat·ed; -lat·ing** **1** : to form or move in waves : FLUCTUATE **2** : to rise and fall in volume, pitch, or rhythm **3** : to present a wavy appearance [from Latin *undula* "small wave", derived from earlier *unda* "wave"]

un·du·la·tion \ˌən-jə-'lā-shən, ˌən-d(y)ə-\ *n* **1** : the action of undulating **2** : a wavy appearance or form : WAVINESS

un·du·ly \ˌən-'d(y)ü-lē, 'ən-\ *adv* : in an undue manner;

esp : EXCESSIVELY ⟨*unduly* upset⟩

un·dy·ing \ˌən-'dī-iŋ\ *adj* : not dying : IMMORTAL, PERPETUAL ⟨*undying* gratitude⟩

un·earned \ˌən-'ərnd, 'ən-\ *adj* : not gained by labor, service, or skill ⟨*unearned* income⟩

un·earth \ˌən-'ərth, 'ən-\ *vb* **1** : to drive or draw from the earth : dig up ⟨*unearth* buried treasure⟩ **2** : to bring to light : DISCOVER ⟨*unearth* a secret⟩

un·earth·ly \ˌən-'ərth-lē, 'ən-\ *adj* **1** : not of or belonging to the earth ⟨*unearthly* terrain⟩ **2** : SUPERNATURAL 2, WEIRD, TERRIFYING ⟨an *unearthly* scream⟩ — **un·earth·li·ness** *n*

un·easy \ˌən-'ē-zē\ *adj* **1** : not easy in manner : AWKWARD ⟨*uneasy* among strangers⟩ **2** : disturbed by pain or worry : RESTLESS ⟨rain made the crew *uneasy*⟩ — **un·eas·i·ly** \-'ēz-ə-lē\ *adv* — **un·eas·i·ness** \-'ē-zē-nəs\ *n*

un·ed·u·cat·ed \ˌən-'ej-ə-ˌkāt-əd\ *adj* : seriously lacking in education and especially in formal schooling **syn** *see* IGNORANT

un·em·ploy·able \ˌən-im-'plȯi-ə-bəl\ *adj* : not capable of being employed; *esp* : not capable of holding a job — **unemployable** *n*

un·em·ployed \ˌən-im-'plȯid\ *adj* **1** : not being used ⟨*unemployed* tools⟩ **2** : not employed : having no job ⟨*unemployed* workers⟩ — **unemployed** *n*

un·em·ploy·ment \ˌən-im-'plȯi-mənt\ *n* : the state of being out of work

un·end·ing \ˌən-'en-diŋ, 'ən-\ *adj* : having no ending : ENDLESS — **un·end·ing·ly** *adv*

un·equal \ˌən-'ē-kwəl, 'ən-\ *adj* **1 a** : not of the same measurement, quantity, or number as another **b** : not like or not the same as another in value or worth **2** : ¹VARIABLE 3, UNEVEN **3** : badly balanced or matched ⟨an *unequal* fight⟩ **4** : INADEQUATE, INSUFFICIENT — **un·equal·ly** \-kwə-lē\ *adv*

un·equaled \ˌən-'ē-kwəld, 'ən-\ *adj* : not equaled : UNPARALLELED

un·equiv·o·cal \ˌən-i-'kwiv-ə-kəl\ *adj* : leaving no doubt : CLEAR, UNAMBIGUOUS ⟨an *unequivocal* refusal⟩ — **un·equiv·o·cal·ly** \-k(ə-)lē\ *adv*

un·err·ing \ˌən-'e(ə)r-iŋ, -'ər-, 'ən-\ *adj* : making no errors : CERTAIN, UNFAILING — **un·err·ing·ly** *adv*

un·even \ˌən-'ē-vən, 'ən-\ *adj* **1** : not level or smooth : RUGGED, RAGGED ⟨large *uneven* teeth⟩ ⟨*uneven* handwriting⟩ **2** : varying from the straight or parallel **3** : not constant : IRREGULAR ⟨*uneven* earnings⟩ **4** : varying in quality ⟨an *uneven* performance⟩ — **un·even·ly** *adv* — **un·even·ness** *n*

un·event·ful \ˌən-i-'vent-fəl\ *adj* : not eventful : lacking happenings that are interesting or worth noting ⟨an *uneventful* vacation⟩ — **un·event·ful·ly** \-fə-lē\ *adv*

un·ex·am·pled \ˌən-ig-'zam-pəld\ *adj* : having no example or match : UNPRECEDENTED ⟨an *unexampled* record of achievement⟩

un·ex·cep·tion·able \ˌən-ik-'sep-sh(ə-)nə-bəl\ *adj* : UNIMPEACHABLE

un·ex·pect·ed \ˌən-ik-'spek-təd\ *adj* : not expected : UNFORSEEN ⟨an *unexpected* happening⟩ — **un·ex·pect·ed·ly** *adv*

un·fail·ing \ˌən-'fā-liŋ, 'ən-\ *adj* **1** : not likely to fail : CONSTANT, UNFLAGGING ⟨*unfailing* support⟩ **2** : not likely to run out or be used up : EVERLASTING, INEXHAUSTIBLE ⟨an *unfailing* supply⟩ **3** : INFALLIBLE 2 ⟨the *unfailing* mark of an amateur⟩ — **un·fail·ing·ly** *adv*

un·fair \ˌən-'fa(ə)r, 'ən-, -'fe(ə)r\ *adj* **1** : not fair, honest, or just : UNJUST, DISHONEST ⟨an *unfair* trial⟩ **2** : not fair in

\ə\ **abut**		\au̇\ **out**		\i\ **tip**		\ȯ\ **saw**		\u̇\ **foot**
\ər\ **further**		\ch\ **chin**		\ī\ **life**		\ȯi\ **coin**		\y\ **yet**
\a\ **mat**		\e\ **pet**		\j\ **job**		\th\ **thin**		\yü\ **few**
\ā\ **take**		\ē\ **easy**		\ŋ\ **sing**		\th\ **this**		\yu̇\ **cure**
\ä\ **cot, cart**		\g\ **go**		\ō\ **bone**		\ü\ **food**		\zh\ **vision**

doing business ⟨*unfair* to labor⟩ — **un·fair·ly** *adv* — **un·fair·ness** *n*

un·faith·ful \,ən-'fāth-fəl, 'ən-\ *adj* **1** : not observing vows, allegiance, or duty : DISLOYAL **2** : not faithful to marriage vows **3** : INACCURATE, UNTRUSTWORTHY — **un·faith·ful·ly** \-fə-lē\ *adv* — **un·faith·ful·ness** *n*

un·fa·mil·iar \,ən-fə-'mil-yər\ *adj* **1** : not well-known : STRANGE ⟨an *unfamiliar* place⟩ **2** : not well acquainted ⟨*unfamiliar* with the subject⟩ — **un·fa·mil·iar·i·ty** \-,mil-'yar-ət-ē, -,mil-ē-'(y)ar-\ *n*

un·fas·ten \,ən-'fas-ᵊn\ *vb* : to make or become loose : UNDO, DETACH, UNTIE ⟨*unfasten* a belt⟩

un·fa·vor·able \,ən-'fāv-(ə-)rə-bəl\ *adj* **1** : expressing disapproval ⟨*unfavorable* comments⟩ **2** : likely to make difficult or unpleasant ⟨*unfavorable* weather for a camping trip⟩ — **un·fa·vor·ably** \-blē\ *adv*

un·feel·ing \,ən-'fē-liŋ\ *adj* **1** : lacking feeling : INSENSATE **2** : lacking kindness or sympathy : HARDHEARTED, CRUEL — **un·feel·ing·ly** *adv*

un·feigned \,ən-'fānd\ *adj* : not false or pretended : GENUINE ⟨an *unfeigned* interest in people⟩ — **un·feigned·ly** \-'fā-nəd-lē, -'fān-dlē\ *adv*

un·fet·ter \,ən-'fet-ər\ *vb* : to free from fetters ⟨*unfetter* the prisoner⟩

un·fil·ial \,ən-'fil-ē-əl, -ən-, -'fil-yəl\ *adj* : not observing the duties of a child to a parent

un·fin·ished \,ən-'fin-isht\ *adj* : not finished; *esp* : not brought to the desired state ⟨*unfinished* furniture⟩

¹un·fit \,ən-'fit\ *adj* **1** : UNSUITABLE ⟨*unfit* to eat⟩ **2** : INCAPABLE, INCOMPETENT ⟨removed *unfit* candidates by testing⟩ **3** : physically or mentally unhealthy ⟨*unfit* for army service⟩

²unfit *vb* : to make unfit : DISABLE, DISQUALIFY

un·flap·pa·ble \,ən-'flap-ə-bəl\ *adj* : not easily upset or panicked : unusually calm

un·fledged \,ən-'flejd, 'ən-\ *adj* **1** : not feathered or ready for flight **2** : IMMATURE, CALLOW

un·flinch·ing \,ən-'flin-chiŋ\ *adj* : not flinching or shrinking : STEADFAST — **un·flinch·ing·ly** *adv*

un·fold \,ən-'fōld\ *vb* **1 a** : to spread or cause to spread or straighten out from a folded position or arrangement **b** : UNWRAP **2** : ²BLOOM 1 **3** : DEVELOP 1a **4** : to open out or cause to open out gradually to the view or understanding

un·for·get·ta·ble \,ən-fər-'get-ə-bəl\ *adj* : not to be forgotten : lasting in memory — **un·for·get·ta·bly** \-blē\ *adv*

un·formed \,ən-'fȯ(ə)rmd\ *adj* **1** : not arranged in regular shape, order, or relations; *esp* : SHAPELESS **2** : IMMATURE, UNDEVELOPED ⟨an *unformed* thought⟩

¹un·for·tu·nate \,ən-'fȯrch-(ə-)nət\ *adj* **1 a** : not fortunate : UNLUCKY **b** : showing, accompanied by, or resulting in misfortune ⟨an *unfortunate* experience⟩ ⟨*unfortunate* investments⟩ **2 a** : UNSUITABLE, INFELICITOUS ⟨an *unfortunate* choice of words⟩ **b** : DEPLORABLE 1 — **un·for·tu·nate·ly** *adv*

²unfortunate *n* : an unfortunate person

un·found·ed \,ən-'faún-dəd, 'ən-\ *adj* : lacking a sound base : GROUNDLESS ⟨*unfounded* suspicions⟩

un·fre·quent·ed \,ən-frē-'kwent-əd; ,ən-'frē-kwənt-, 'ən-\ *adj* : not often visited or traveled over

un·friend·ly \,ən-'fren-(d)lē\ *adj* **1** : not friendly or kind : HOSTILE ⟨an *unfriendly* greeting⟩ **2** : not agreeable ⟨an *unfriendly* environment⟩ — **un·friend·li·ness** *n*

un·fruit·ful \,ən-'früt-fəl\ *adj* **1** : not bearing fruit or offspring **2** : not producing a desired result ⟨*unfruitful* efforts⟩

un·furl \,ən-'fər(-ə)l\ *vb* : to loose from a furled state : open or spread : UNFOLD ⟨*unfurl* sails⟩ ⟨*unfurl* a flag⟩

un·gain·ly \,ən-'gān-lē\ *adj* : CLUMSY 1a, AWKWARD — **un·gain·li·ness** *n*

un·glazed \,ən-'glāzd\ *adj* : not having a glaze

un·god·ly \,ən-'gäd-lē *also* -'gȯd-\ *adj* **1 a** : denying God : IMPIOUS, IRRELIGIOUS **b** : SINFUL, WICKED **2** : OUTRAGEOUS ⟨gets up at an *ungodly* hour⟩ — **un·god·li·ness** *n*

un·gov·ern·able \,ən-'gəv-ər-nə-bəl\ *adj* : not capable of being governed, guided, or controlled ⟨an *ungovernable* temper⟩ **syn** see UNRULY — **un·gov·ern·ably** \-blē\ *adv*

un·grace·ful \,ən-'grās-fəl\ *adj* : not graceful : AWKWARD — **un·grace·ful·ly** \-fə-lē\ *adv*

un·gra·cious \,ən-'grā-shəs\ *adj* **1** : not courteous : RUDE **2** : not pleasing : DISAGREEABLE — **un·gra·cious·ly** *adv* — **un·gra·cious·ness** *n*

un·grate·ful \,ən-'grāt-fəl, 'ən-\ *adj* **1** : not thankful for favors **2** : not pleasing : DISAGREEABLE ⟨an *ungrateful* task⟩ — **un·grate·ful·ly** \-fə-lē\ *adv* — **un·grate·ful·ness** *n*

un·ground·ed \,ən-'graún-dəd, 'ən-\ *adj* **1** : UNFOUNDED, BASELESS **2** : not instructed or informed

un·guard·ed \,ən-'gärd-əd\ *adj* **1** : open to attack : UNPROTECTED **2** : not cautious : UNWARY — **un·guard·ed·ly** *adv*

un·guent \'əŋ-gwənt, 'ən-; 'ən-jənt\ *n* : a soothing or healing salve : OINTMENT

¹un·gu·late \'əŋ-gyə-lət, 'ən-, -,lāt\ *adj* **1** : having hoofs **2** : of or relating to the ungulates

²ungulate *n* : any of a group of animals consisting of the hoofed mammals and including the ruminants, swine, horses, tapirs, rhinoceroses, elephants, and hyraxes

un·hal·lowed \,ən-'hal-ōd, 'ən-\ *adj* : UNHOLY, UNCONSECRATED

un·hand \,ən-'hand, 'ən-\ *vb* : to remove the hand from : let go

un·handy \,ən-'han-dē\ *adj* **1** : hard to handle : INCONVENIENT **2** : lacking in skill : AWKWARD

un·hap·py \,ən-'hap-ē\ *adj* **1** : not fortunate : UNLUCKY ⟨the result of an *unhappy* mistake⟩ **2** : not cheerful : SAD, MISERABLE **3** : INAPPROPRIATE ⟨an *unhappy* color combination⟩ — **un·hap·pi·ly** \-'hap-ə-lē\ *adv* — **un·hap·pi·ness** \-'hap-i-nəs\ *n*

un·health·ful \,ən-'helth-fəl\ *adj* : not healthful

un·healthy \-,ən-'hel-thē\ *adj* **1** : UNHEALTHFUL ⟨an *unhealthy* climate⟩ **2** : not in good health : SICKLY, DISEASED **3 a** : RISKY, UNSOUND **b** : INJURIOUS, BAD — **un·health·i·ly** \-thə-lē\ *adv* — **un·health·i·ness** \-thē-nəs\ *n*

un·heard \,ən-'hərd\ *adj* **1** : not heard by the ear **2** : not given a hearing

un·heard-of \-,əv, -,äv\ *adj* : previously unknown : UNPRECEDENTED

un·hinge \,ən-'hinj\ *vb* **1** : to remove (as a door) from the hinges **2** : UNSETTLE 2, DISRUPT ⟨a mind *unhinged* by grief⟩

un·hitch \,ən-'hich\ *vb* : to free from being hitched

un·ho·ly \,ən-'hō-lē, 'ən-\ *adj* : not holy : PROFANE, WICKED — **un·ho·li·ness** *n*

un·hook \,ən-'húk\ *vb* **1** : to remove from a hook **2** : to unfasten the hooks of

un·horse \,ən-'hȯ(ə)rs\ *vb* : to cause to fall from a horse : OVERTHROW, UNSEAT

un·hur·ried \,ən-'hər-ēd, -'hə-rēd\ *adj* : not hurried : LEISURELY

uni·cam·er·al \,yü-ni-'kam-(ə-)rəl\ *adj* : having or consisting of a single legislative body

uni·cel·lu·lar \,yü-ni-'sel-yə-lər\ *adj* : having or consisting of a single cell

uni·corn \'yü-nə-,kȯ(ə)rn\ *n* : an imaginary animal generally represented with the body and head of a horse and a single horn in the middle of the forehead [Middle English *unicorne* "unicorn", from early French *unicorne* (same meaning), derived from Latin *unicornis* "having one horn", from *uni-* "one" and *cornu* "horn" — related to ³CORN, UNIVERSE]

uni·cy·cle \'yü-ni-,sī-kəl\ *n* : a vehicle having a single wheel and usually moved forward by pedals

¹uni·form \'yü-nə-ˌform\ *adj* **1** : not varying ⟨*uniform* temperature⟩ **2** : of the same form with others ⟨*uniform* procedures in the courts⟩ — **uni·form·ly** *adv*

²uniform *vb* : to dress with a uniform

³uniform *n* : uniform dress worn by members of a particular group (as an army or a police force)

uni·for·mi·tar·i·an·ism \ˌyü-nə-ˌfor-mə-'ter-ē-ə-ˌniz-əm\ *n* : a principle in geology that states that knowledge of processes going on in nature at the present time can help to explain geological changes in the past

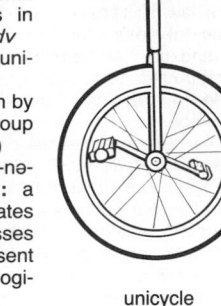

unicycle

uni·for·mi·ty \ˌyü-nə-'for-mət-ē\ *n, pl* **-ties** : the quality or state or an instance of being uniform

uni·fy \'yü-nə-ˌfī\ *vb* **-fied; -fy·ing** : UNITE 1a — **uni·fi·ca·tion** \ˌyü-nə-fə-'kā-shən\ *n*

uni·lat·er·al \ˌyü-ni-'lat-ə-rəl, -'la-trəl\ *adj* : done or carried out by only one of two or more parties ⟨*unilateral* disarmament⟩ — **uni·lat·er·al·ly** \-ē\ *adv*

un·im·peach·able \ˌən-im-'pē-chə-bəl\ *adj* : not impeachable : not to be doubted or questioned : IRREPROACHABLE ⟨an *unimpeachable* reputation⟩ ⟨information from an *unimpeachable* source⟩ — **un·im·peach·ably** \-blē\ *adv*

un·in·hib·it·ed \ˌən-in-'hib-ət-əd\ *adj* : not inhibited; *esp* : marked by an open showing of feelings and informal behavior ⟨an *uninhibited* party⟩ — **un·in·hib·it·ed·ly** *adv*

un·in·tel·li·gent \ˌən-in-'tel-ə-jənt\ *adj* : lacking intelligence : UNWISE, STUPID ⟨an *unintelligent* use of your money⟩ — **un·in·tel·li·gent·ly** *adv*

un·in·tel·li·gi·ble \ˌən-in-'tel-ə-jə-bəl\ *adj* : impossible to understand — **un·in·tel·li·gi·bly** \-blē\ *adv*

un·in·ten·tion·al \ˌən-in-'tench-nəl, -'ten-chən-ᵊl\ *adj* : not intentional — **un·in·ten·tion·al·ly** \-ē\ *adv*

un·in·ter·est·ed \ˌən-'int-ə-ˌres-təd, 'ən-; -'in-trəs-, -ˌtres-; -'int-ərs-, -'int-ə-rəs-\ *adj* : not interested : not paying attention

un·in·ter·rupt·ed \ˌən-ˌint-ə-'rəp-təd\ *adj* : not interrupted : CONTINUOUS — **un·in·ter·rupt·ed·ly** *adv*

union \'yün-yən\ *n* **1 a** : an act or instance of uniting two or more things into one ⟨the *union* of Scotland and England⟩ ⟨*union* of a man and a woman in marriage⟩ **b** : COMBINATION 1 ⟨the *union* of science and technology to solve modern problems⟩ **2 a** : something (as a nation) formed by a combining of parts or members **b** : LABOR UNION **c** : the set of all elements that belong to one or more of a collection of two or more sets **3** : a device for connecting parts (as of a machine)

Union *adj* : of, relating to, or being the side favoring the federal union in the U.S. Civil War ⟨the *Union* army⟩

union·ism \'yün-yə-ˌniz-əm\ *n* **1** : the principle or policy of forming or keeping a union **2** *cap* : support of a strong federal union before or during the U.S. Civil War **3** : a theory or policy that supports trade unions — **union·ist** \-yə-nəst\ *n, often cap*

union·ize \'yün-yə-ˌnīz\ *vb* **-ized; -iz·ing** : to form into a labor union — **union·iza·tion** \ˌyün-yə-nə-'zā-shən\ *n*

union jack *n* **1** : a flag consisting of the part of a national flag that signifies union; *esp* : a U.S. flag consisting of a blue field

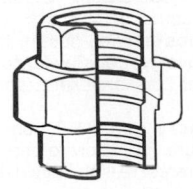

union 3

with one white star for each state **2** *cap U & J* : the national flag of the United Kingdom

union suit *n* : an undergarment with shirt and pants in one piece

unique \yu̇-'nēk\ *adj* **1 a** : being the only one of its kind **b** : PECULIAR 1 **2** : very unusual : NOTABLE **3** : being the one and only possible result of one or more mathematical operations ⟨a *unique* solution⟩; *also* : having only one possible result ⟨addition of integers is *unique*⟩ — **unique·ly** *adv* — **unique·ness** *n*

uni·sex \'yü-nə-ˌseks\ *adj* : suitable or designed for both males and females ⟨*unisex* clothing⟩

uni·sex·u·al \ˌyü-nə-'seksh-(ə-)wəl, -'sek-shəl\ *adj* **1** : having only male or only female sex organs **2** : UNISEX

uni·son \'yü-nə-sən, -zən\ *n* **1** : sameness of musical pitch **2** : the condition of being tuned or sounded at the same pitch or at an octave ⟨sing in *unison* rather than in harmony⟩ **3** : exact agreement : ACCORD ⟨all are in *unison* on the next move⟩ [from early French *unison* "having the same musical pitch", from Latin *unisonus* "having the same sound", from *uni-* "one" (from *unus* "one") and *sonus* "a sound" — related to ³SOUND, UNITE]

¹unit \'yü-nət\ *n* **1 a** : the first and smallest natural number : ONE **b** : a single quantity regarded as a whole in calculation **2** : a definite quantity (as of length, time, or value) used as a standard of measurement ⟨the dollar is the *unit* of American money⟩ **3 a** : a single thing or person or group that is a part of a whole **b** : a part or arrangement of parts performing one function ⟨a train drawn by two diesel *units*⟩ **c** : a part of a school course with a central theme

²unit *adj* : being, relating to, or measuring one unit of ⟨*unit* length⟩ ⟨*unit* angle⟩

uni·tar·i·an \ˌyü-nə-'ter-ē-ən\ *n, often cap* : one who believes that God exists only in one person — **unitarian** *adj, often cap* — **uni·tar·i·an·ism** \-ē-ə-ˌniz-əm\ *n, often cap*

uni·tary \'yü-nə-ˌter-ē\ *adj* **1 a** : of or relating to a unit **b** : based on or marked by unity or units **2** : having the character of a unit : WHOLE

unite \yu̇-'nīt\ *vb* **unit·ed; unit·ing** **1 a** : to put or come together to form a single unit **b** : to cause to cling together ⟨*unite* two pieces of wood⟩ **c** : to link by a legal or moral bond **2** : to become one or as if one ⟨two elements *unite* to form a compound⟩ **3** : to join in action : act as if one ⟨*unite* in song⟩ [Middle English *uniten* "to unite", from Latin *unitus*, past participle of *unire* "to unite, make into one", from earlier *unus* "one" — related to INCH, OUNCE, UNISON] **syn** see JOIN — **unit·er** *n*

unit·ed \yu̇-'nīt-əd\ *adj* **1** : made one : COMBINED **2** : relating to or produced by joint action ⟨a *united* drive against drug abuse⟩ **3** : being in agreement : HARMONIOUS ⟨a *united* family⟩ — **unit·ed·ly** *adv*

unit·ize \'yü-nət-ˌīz\ *vb* **-ized; -iz·ing** : to form into a unit

unit price *n* : the price of a product per unit of a standard weight or measure (as a pound or a pint)

unit pricing *n* : the pricing of products (as packaged foods) whereby the unit price is shown along with the total price

units digit *n* : the numeral (as 6 in 456) occupying the units place — called also *ones digit*

units place *n* : the place immediately to the left of the decimal point in a number expressed in the Arabic system of writing numbers — called also *ones place*

uni·ty \'yü-nət-ē\ *n, pl* **-ties** **1** : the quality or state of being one **2** : the state of those that are in full agreement : HARMONY **3** : a mathematical quantity or combination of

\ə\ abut	\au̇\ out	\i\ tip	\o̊\ saw	\u̇\ foot
\ər\ further	\ch\ chin	\ī\ life	\o̊i\ coin	\y\ yet
\a\ mat	\e\ pet	\j\ job	\th\ thin	\yu̇\ few
\ā\ take	\ē\ easy	\ŋ\ sing	\th\ this	\yu̇\ cure
\ä\ cot, cart	\g\ go	\ō\ bone	\ü\ food	\zh\ vision

quantities taken as one or for which 1 is made to stand in a calculation   **4** : the combination or arrangement of parts in a work of art or literature that produces a total effect

¹uni·valve \'yü-ni-ˌvalv\ *adj* : having a shell made up of only one piece

²univalve *n* : a univalve mollusk shell or a mollusk having such a shell

uni·ver·sal \ˌyü-nə-'vər-səl\ *adj* **1** : including or covering all or a whole without limit or exception ⟨*universal* human characteristics⟩ **2** : present or existing everywhere or under all conditions ⟨the family is a *universal* social unit⟩ **3 a** : including or involving a major part or the greatest portion **b** : very broad in range ⟨a *universal* genius⟩ **4** : adapted or adjustable to meet varied requirements (as of use, shape, or size) ⟨a *universal* wrench⟩ — **uni·ver·sal·ly** \-s(ə-)lē\ *adv*

universal donor *n* : a person with type O blood

uni·ver·sal·i·ty \ˌyü-nə-(ˌ)vər-'sal-ət-ē\ *n* : the quality or state of being universal (as in range, occurrence, or appeal)

uni·ver·sal·ize \ˌyü-nə-'vər-sə-ˌlīz\ *vb* **-ized; -iz·ing** : to make universal : GENERALIZE — **uni·ver·sal·iza·tion** \-ˌvər-sə-lə-'zā-shən\ *n*

universal joint *n* : a shaft coupling capable of transmitting rotation from one shaft to another not in a straight line with it

universal joint

Universal Product Code *n* : a bar code that identifies a product's type and price for entry into a computer or cash register (as at a supermarket checkout)

universal recipient *n* : a person with type AB blood

universal set *n* : UNIVERSE 2

uni·verse \'yü-nə-ˌvərs\ *n* **1** : the whole body of things observed or assumed : COSMOS **2** : a set that contains all elements relating to a particular discussion or problem — called also *universal set* [from Latin *universum* "whole body of things that exist", from *universus* "whole, entire", literally "turned into one", from *uni-* "one" and *versus* "turned", from *vertere* "to turn" — related to ANNIVERSARY, CONVERSE, UNICORN, VERSATILE]

uni·ver·si·ty \ˌyü-nə-'vər-sət-ē, -'vər-stē\ *n, pl* **-ties** : an institution of higher learning that grants degrees in special fields (as law or medicine) as well as in the arts and sciences

un·just \ˌən-'jəst, 'ən-\ *adj* : not just : UNFAIR ⟨an *unjust* way of picking the winner⟩ — **un·just·ly** *adv* — **un·just·ness** \-'jəs(t)-nəs\ *n*

un·kempt \ˌən-'kem(p)t\ *adj* **1** : lacking in order or neatness : UNTIDY **2** : not combed

un·kind \ˌən-'kīnd\ *adj* : not kind or sympathetic ⟨an *unkind* remark⟩ — **un·kind·ly** *adv* — **un·kind·ness** \-'kīn(d)-nəs\ *n*

un·kind·ly \ˌən-'kīn-(d)lē\ *adj* : UNKIND — **un·kind·li·ness** *n*

un·know·able \ˌən-'nō-ə-bəl, 'ən-\ *adj* : not knowable ⟨some facts in the case may remain *unknowable*⟩

un·know·ing \ˌən-'nō-iŋ\ *adj* : not knowing — **un·know·ing·ly** *adv*

¹un·known \ˌən-'nōn\ *adj* : not known; *also* : having an unknown value ⟨*unknown* quantity⟩

²unknown *n* : something that is unknown and usually to be discovered; *esp* : an unknown quantity usually symbolized in mathematics by one of the last letters of the alphabet

un·lace \ˌən-'lās, 'ən-\ *vb* : to loose by undoing a lacing

un·lade \ˌən-'lād\ *vb* **-lad·ed; -laded** *or* **-lad·en** \-'lād-ᵊn\; **-lad·ing** **1** : to take the load or cargo from **2** : UNLOAD 1a

un·lash \ˌən-'lash\ *vb* : to untie the lashing of : LOOSE, UNDO

un·latch \ˌən-'lach\ *vb* **1** : to open or loose by lifting the latch **2** : to become loosed or opened

un·law·ful \ˌən-'lò-fəl, 'ən-\ *adj* : not lawful : being against the law : ILLEGAL — **un·law·ful·ly** \-f(ə-)lē\ *adv* — **un·law·ful·ness** \-fəl-nəs\ *n*

un·lead·ed \ˌən-'led-əd\ *adj* : not mixed with lead or lead compounds ⟨*unleaded* gasoline⟩

un·learn \ˌən-'lərn\ *vb* : to put out of one's knowledge or memory

un·learned *adj* \ˌən-'lər-nəd *for sense 1,* ˌən-'lərnd *for senses 2 & 3*\ **1** : not learned : UNEDUCATED, ILLITERATE ⟨a good but *unlearned* man⟩ **2** : not learned by study : not known ⟨lessons *unlearned* by many⟩ **3** : not learned by previous experience ⟨breathing is *unlearned* behavior⟩

un·leash \ˌən-'lēsh\ *vb* : to free from or as if from a leash ⟨*unleash* a dog⟩ ⟨the storm *unleashed* its fury⟩

un·less \ən-ˌles, ˌən-, *in some contexts* ᵊn-, ᵊm-, *or* ᵊŋ-\ *conj* : except on the condition that : if not ⟨will fail *unless* she works harder⟩

un·let·tered \ˌən-'let-ərd, 'ən-\ *adj* **1** : not having knowledge especially of the kind gained from books **2** : ILLITERATE 1 **syn** see IGNORANT

¹un·like \ˌən-'līk, 'ən-\ *adj* **1** : marked by differences ⟨people are all *unlike*⟩ **2** : UNEQUAL 1a ⟨contributed *unlike* amounts⟩ — **un·like·ness** *n*

²unlike *prep* **1** : different from ⟨feeling completely *unlike* a hero⟩ **2** : not typical of ⟨it was *unlike* her to be late⟩ **3** : in a different manner from ⟨behaving *unlike* all the other children⟩

un·like·li·hood \ˌən-'lī-klē-ˌhůd, 'ən-\ *n* : the quality or state of being unlikely

un·like·ly \ˌən-'lī-klē, 'ən-\ *adj* **1** : not likely : IMPROBABLE ⟨an *unlikely* story⟩ **2** : likely to fail : UNPROMISING ⟨an *unlikely* place for fishing⟩ — **un·like·li·ness** *n*

un·lim·ber \ˌən-'lim-bər, 'ən-\ *vb* : to prepare for action or performance

un·lim·it·ed \ˌən-'lim-ət-əd, 'ən-\ *adj* **1** : lacking any controls ⟨*unlimited* freedom⟩ **2** : ¹INFINITE 1 ⟨there is an *unlimited* number of natural numbers⟩ **3** : not bounded by exceptions : UNDEFINED ⟨an *unlimited* and unconditional surrender⟩

un·link \ˌən-'liŋk, 'ən-\ *vb* : to unfasten the links of : SEPARATE, DISCONNECT

un·list·ed \ˌən-'lis-təd, 'ən-\ *adj* : not appearing on a list ⟨an *unlisted* telephone number⟩

un·load \ˌən-'lōd, 'ən-\ *vb* **1 a** : to take away or off : REMOVE ⟨*unload* cargo from a hold⟩ **b** : to take a load from ⟨*unload* a ship⟩; *also* : to rid or set free : UNBURDEN ⟨*unload* your mind of worries⟩ **2** : to get rid of or be freed of a load or burden ⟨the ship is *unloading* now⟩ **3** : to sell in large quantities : DUMP ⟨*unload* surplus goods⟩

un·lock \ˌən-'läk, 'ən-\ *vb* **1** : to open or unfasten through release of a lock ⟨*unlock* the door⟩ ⟨the chest won't *unlock*⟩ **2** : to set free : RELEASE ⟨*unlock* a flood of emotions⟩ **3** : to make known ⟨scientists *unlocking* the secrets of nature⟩

un·looked-for \ˌən-'lůk-ˌtfó(ə)r, 'ən-\ *adj* : UNEXPECTED ⟨an *unlooked-for* bonus⟩

un·loose \ˌən-'lüs, 'ən-\ *vb* **1** : to make looser : RELAX ⟨*unloose* a grip⟩ **2** : to set free ⟨the new rules *unloosed* a flood of complaints⟩

un·loos·en \ˌən-'lüs-ᵊn, 'ən-\ *vb* : UNLOOSE

un·love·ly \ˌən-'ləv-lē, 'ən-\ *adj* : having no charm or appeal : DISAGREEABLE ⟨an *unlovely* story about selfish people⟩

un·lucky \ˌən-'lək-ē, 'ən-\ *adj* **1** : marked by bad luck or failure **2** : likely to bring misfortune **3** : causing distress or regret — **un·luck·i·ly** \-'lək-ə-lē\ *adv* — **un·luck·i·ness** \-'lək-ē-nəs\ *n*

un·make \ˌən-'māk, 'ən-\ *vb* **-made** \-'mād\; **-mak·ing** **1**

: to cause to disappear : DESTROY ⟨a reputation can be quickly *unmade*⟩ **2** : to remove from rank or office : DEPOSE

un·man \‚ən-'man, 'ən-\ *vb* : to deprive of vigor or courage

un·man·ly \‚ən-'man-lē, 'ən-\ *adj* : not manly: as **a** : being of weak character : COWARDLY **b** : EFFEMINATE

un·manned \‚ən-'mand, 'ən-\ *adj* : having no crew aboard ⟨*unmanned* spacecraft⟩

un·man·ner·ly \‚ən-'man-ər-lē, 'ən-\ *adj* : IMPOLITE — **unmannerly** *adv*

un·mask \‚ən-'mask, 'ən-\ *vb* : to strip of a mask or a disguise : EXPOSE ⟨*unmask* a traitor⟩

un·men·tion·able \‚ən-'mench-(ə-)nə-bəl, 'ən-\ *adj* : not fit or proper to be talked about

un·mer·ci·ful \‚ən-'mər-si-fəl, 'ən-\ *adj* : not merciful : MERCILESS, CRUEL — **un·mer·ci·ful·ly** \-f(ə-)lē\ *adv*

un·mis·tak·able \‚ən-mə-'stā-kə-bəl, 'ən-\ *adj* : not capable of being mistaken or misunderstood : CLEAR, OBVIOUS — **un·mis·tak·ably** \-blē\ *adv*

un·mit·i·gat·ed \‚ən-'mit-ə-‚gāt-əd, 'ən-\ *adj* **1** : not lessened or made less severe ⟨*unmitigated* poverty⟩ **2** : ABSOLUTE 3, DOWNRIGHT ⟨an *unmitigated* liar⟩

un·mor·al \‚ən-'mȯr-əl, -'mär-, 'ən-\ *adj* : having no moral quality or relation : being neither moral nor immoral — **un·mor·al·ly** \-ə-lē\ *adv*

un·moved \‚ən-'müvd, 'ən-\ *adj* **1** : not moved : remaining in the same place **2** : holding to the same position ⟨*unmoved* by their arguments⟩ **3** : not disturbed emotionally ⟨*unmoved* by the sad news⟩

un·muf·fle \‚ən-'məf-əl, 'ən-\ *vb* : to free from something that muffles

un·muz·zle \‚ən-'məz-əl, 'ən-\ *vb* : to remove a muzzle from

un·nat·u·ral \‚ən-'nach-(ə-)rəl, 'ən-\ *adj* **1** : not following nature or a normal course of events **2 a** : not being in agreement with normal feelings or behavior **b** : lacking ease and naturalness — **un·nat·u·ral·ly** \-'nach-(ə-)rə-lē, -'nach-ər-lē\ *adv* — **un·nat·u·ral·ness** \-'nach-(ə-)rəl-nəs\ *n*

un·nec·es·sar·i·ly \‚ən-‚nes-ə-'ser-ə-lē\ *adv* **1** : not by necessity ⟨spent money *unnecessarily*⟩ **2** : to an unnecessary degree ⟨an *unnecessarily* harsh punishment⟩

un·nec·es·sary \‚ən-'nes-ə-‚ser-ē, 'ən-\ *adj* : not necessary

un·nerve \‚ən-'nərv, 'ən-\ *vb* **-nerved; -nerv·ing** : to deprive of nerve, courage, or self-control ⟨the accident *unnerved* me⟩

un·nil·hex·i·um \‚yün-ᵊl-'hek-sē-əm\ *n* : the chemical element of atomic number 106 — see ELEMENT table

un·nil·pen·ti·um \‚yün-ᵊl-'pent-ē-əm\ *n* : the chemical element of atomic number 105 — see ELEMENT table

un·nil·qua·di·um \‚yün-ᵊl-'kwäd-ē-əm\ *n* : the chemical element of atomic number 104 — see ELEMENT table

un·num·bered \‚ən-'nəm-bərd, 'ən-\ *adj* **1** : COUNTLESS **2** : not having an identifying number ⟨*unnumbered* pages⟩

un·ob·tru·sive \‚ən-əb-'trü-siv, -ziv\ *adj* : not obtrusive or bold : INCONSPICUOUS — **un·ob·tru·sive·ly** *adv*

un·oc·cu·pied \‚ən-'äk-yə-‚pīd, 'ən-\ *adj* **1** : not busy : UNEMPLOYED **2** : not occupied : EMPTY

un·of·fi·cial \‚ən-ə-'fish-əl\ *adj* : not official — **un·of·fi·cial·ly** \-'fish-(ə-)lē\ *adv*

un·or·ga·nized \‚ən-'ȯr-gə-‚nīzd, 'ən-\ *adj* : not organized: as **a** : not formed or brought into an ordered whole **b** : not organized into unions ⟨*unorganized* labor⟩

un·or·tho·dox \‚ən-'ȯr-thə-‚däks, 'ən-\ *adj* : not orthodox : not usual ⟨a tennis player with an *unorthodox* serve⟩

un·owned \‚ən-'ōnd, 'ən-\ *adj* : not owned : not belonging to anybody

un·pack \‚ən-'pak, 'ən-\ *vb* **1** : to separate and remove things packed **2** : to open and remove the contents of ⟨*unpack* a trunk⟩

un·paired \‚ən-'pa(ə)rd, -'pe(ə)rd, 'ən-\ *adj* : not paired;

esp : not matched or mated ⟨an *unpaired* shoe⟩

un·par·al·leled \‚ən-'par-ə-‚leld, -‚leld, 'ən-\ *adj* : having no parallel; *esp* : having no equal or match : UNSURPASSED ⟨a scene of *unparalleled* beauty⟩

un·par·lia·men·ta·ry \‚ən-‚pär-lə-'ment-ə-rē, -‚pärl-yə-, -'men-trē\ *adj* : not being in agreement with parliamentary practice

un·pile \‚ən-'pī(ə)l, 'ən-\ *vb* : to take or pull out from a pile

un·pin \‚ən-'pin, 'ən-\ *vb* : to remove a pin from : UNFASTEN

un·pleas·ant \‚ən-'plez-ᵊnt, 'ən-\ *adj* : not pleasant : not friendly or agreeable : DISPLEASING — **un·pleas·ant·ly** *adv* — **un·pleas·ant·ness** *n*

un·plug \‚ən-'pləg, 'ən-\ *vb* **1** : to remove (as an electric plug) from a socket or opening **2** : to disconnect from an electric circuit by removing a plug ⟨*unplug* the television⟩

un·plumbed \‚ən-'pləmd, 'ən-\ *adj* **1** : not tested or measured with a plumb line **2** : not explored completely ⟨many *unplumbed* areas in science⟩

un·po·lit·i·cal \‚ən-pə-'lit-i-kəl\ *adj* : not interested or active in politics

un·pop·u·lar \‚ən-'päp-yə-lər, 'ən-\ *adj* : not popular : disliked by many people — **un·pop·u·lar·i·ty** \‚ən-‚päp-yə-'lar-ət-ē\ *n*

un·prec·e·dent·ed \‚ən-'pres-ə-‚dent-əd, 'ən-\ *adj* : having no precedent : not done or experienced before ⟨an *unprecedented* achievement⟩

un·pre·dict·able \‚ən-pri-'dik-tə-bəl\ *adj* : not predictable — **un·pre·dict·abil·i·ty** \-‚dik-tə-'bil-ət-ē\ *n* — **un·pre·dict·ably** \-'dik-tə-blē\ *adv*

un·pre·ten·tious \‚ən-pri-'ten-chəs\ *adj* : not pretentious : not showy : SIMPLE, MODEST ⟨pleasant but *unpretentious* homes⟩ — **un·pre·ten·tious·ly** *adv*

un·prin·ci·pled \‚ən-'prin(t)-s(ə-)pəld, -sə-bəld, 'ən-\ *adj* : lacking moral principles : UNSCRUPULOUS

un·print·able \‚ən-'print-ə-bəl, 'ən-\ *adj* : unfit to be printed

un·pro·fes·sion·al \‚ən-prə-'fesh-nəl, -ən-ᵊl\ *adj* : not professional; *esp* : not up to the standards of one's profession — **un·pro·fes·sion·al·ly** \-ē\ *adv*

un·prof·it·able \‚ən-'präf-ət-ə-bəl, -'präf-tə-bəl, 'ən-\ *adj* : not profitable — **un·prof·it·ably** \-blē\ *adv*

un·prom·is·ing \‚ən-'präm-ə-siŋ, 'ən-\ *adj* : appearing unlikely to prove worthwhile or successful — **un·prom·is·ing·ly** *adv*

un·qual·i·fied \‚ən-'kwäl-ə-‚fīd, 'ən-\ *adj* **1** : not fit : not having required qualifications ⟨*unqualified* for the job⟩ **2** : not having any exceptions : ABSOLUTE ⟨an *unqualified* denial⟩ — **un·qual·i·fied·ly** \-‚fī(-ə)d-lē\ *adv*

un·ques·tion·able \‚ən-'kwəs-chə-nə-bəl, -'kwesh-, *in rapid speech* -'kwesh-nə-; 'ən-\ *adj* : not questionable : INDISPUTABLE ⟨*unquestionable* evidence⟩ — **un·ques·tion·ably** \-blē\ *adv*

un·ques·tion·ing \‚ən-'kwəs-chə-niŋ, -'kwesh-, 'ən-\ *adj* : not questioning : accepting without thinking or doubting ⟨*unquestioning* obedience⟩ — **un·ques·tion·ing·ly** *adv*

un·qui·et \‚ən-'kwī-ət, 'ən-\ *adj* **1** : not quiet : AGITATED, TURBULENT **2** : UNEASY 2 — **un·qui·et·ly** *adv*

un·quote \'ən-‚kwōt\ *n* — used orally to mark the end of a direct quotation

un·rav·el \‚ən-'rav-əl, 'ən-\ *vb* **1** : to separate the threads of : DISENTANGLE ⟨*unravel* a snarl⟩ **2** : SOLVE ⟨*unravel* a mystery⟩ **3** : to become unraveled

un·read \‚ən-'red, 'ən-\ *adj* **1** : not read ⟨an *unread* book⟩ **2** : not well informed through reading : UNEDUCATED

un·read·able \‚ən-'rēd-ə-bəl, 'ən-\ *adj* **1** : too dull or unattractive to read ⟨a long, *unreadable* essay⟩ **2** : ILLEGIBLE ⟨*unreadable* handwriting⟩

\ə\	**abut**	\au̇\	**out**	\i\	**tip**	\ȯ\	**saw**	\u̇\	**foot**
\ər\	**further**	\ch\	**chin**	\ī\	**life**	\ȯi\	**coin**	\y\	**yet**
\a\	**mat**	\e\	**pet**	\j\	**job**	\th\	**thin**	\yü\	**few**
\ā\	**take**	\ē\	**easy**	\ŋ\	**sing**	\t͟h\	**this**	\yu̇\	**cure**
\ä\	**cot, cart**	\g\	**go**	\ō\	**bone**	\ü\	**food**	\zh\	**vision**

un·re·al \ˌən-'rē(-ə)l, -'ri(-ə)l, 'ən-\ *adj* **1** : not real, actual, or genuine : ILLUSORY **2** : FANTASTIC 2

un·re·al·i·ty \ˌən-rē-'al-ət-ē\ *n* **1 a** : the quality or state of being unreal : NONEXISTENCE ⟨an air of *unreality* about the place⟩ **b** : something unreal or imaginary : FIGMENT **2** : inability to deal with reality

un·rea·son·ing \ˌən-'rēz-niŋ, -°n-iŋ, 'ən-\ *adj* : not reasoning; *esp* : not using or showing the use of reason as a guide or control ⟨*unreasoning* fear⟩

un·reel \ˌən-'rē(ə)l, 'ən-\ *vb* : to unwind from or as if from a reel

un·re·gen·er·ate \ˌən-ri-'jen-(ə-)rət\ *adj* : not feeling or showing sorrow or the willingness to reform ⟨an *unregenerate* criminal⟩

un·re·lent·ing \ˌən-ri-'lent-iŋ\ *adj* **1** : not softening or giving in easily : HARD, STERN **2** : not letting up or weakening in energy or pace ⟨our *unrelenting* struggle for freedom⟩ — **un·re·lent·ing·ly** *adv*

un·re·mit·ting \ˌən-ri-'mit-iŋ\ *adj* : not stopping : UNCEASING

un·re·served \ˌən-ri-'zərvd\ *adj* **1** : not held in reserve : not kept back ⟨*unreserved* enthusiasm⟩ **2** : having or showing no reserve in manner or speech — **un·re·serv·ed·ly** \-'zər-vəd-lē\ *adv*

un·rest \ˌən-'rest, 'ən-\ *n* : lack of rest : a disturbed or uneasy state : TURMOIL

un·re·strained \ˌən-ri-'strānd\ *adj* **1** : not restrained : not held back ⟨*unrestrained* praise for the political candidate⟩ **2** : free of outside forces or limits

un·re·straint \ˌən-ri-'strānt\ *n* : lack of restraint

un·righ·teous \ˌən-'rī-chəs, 'ən-\ *adj* **1** : not righteous : SINFUL, WICKED **2** : UNJUST — **un·righ·teous·ly** *adv* — **un·righ·teous·ness** *n*

un·ripe \ˌən-'rīp, 'ən-\ *adj* : not ripe : IMMATURE ⟨*unripe* fruit⟩

un·ri·valed *or* **un·ri·valled** \ˌən-'rī-vəld, 'ən-\ *adj* : having no rival : INCOMPARABLE, UNEQUALED ⟨a palace of *unrivaled* magnificence⟩

un·roll \ˌən-'rōl, 'ən-\ *vb* **1** : to unwind a roll of : open out ⟨*unroll* a carpet⟩ **2** : DISCLOSE ⟨the government *unrolled* a new welfare program⟩ **3** : to become unrolled or spread out : UNFOLD ⟨a great view of snowcapped mountains *unrolled* before their eyes⟩

un·round \ˌən-'raúnd, 'ən-\ *vb* : to pronounce a sound without, or with decreased, rounding of the lips — **un·round·ed** *adj*

un·ruf·fled \ˌən-'rəf-əld, 'ən-\ *adj* **1** : not upset or disturbed ⟨a speaker *unruffled* by noisy children⟩ **2** : not ruffled : SMOOTH ⟨*unruffled* water⟩

un·ruly \ˌən-'rü-lē, 'ən-\ *adj* : not yielding easily to rule or restriction : UNCONTROLLABLE ⟨an *unruly* temper⟩ ⟨an *unruly* horse⟩

syn UNRULY, UNGOVERNABLE, WILLFUL, HEADSTRONG mean not yielding to discipline or control. UNRULY suggests a lack of self-control or control by others and also often suggests bad behavior ⟨*unruly* children broke the lamp⟩ UNGOVERNABLE suggests either a loss of control or an inability to be controlled by oneself or by others ⟨sometimes an *ungovernable* rage comes over them⟩ WILLFUL suggests a strong determination to have one's own way ⟨a *willful* disregard for the rights of others⟩ HEADSTRONG suggests stubbornness and lack of patience with suggestions, advice, or control by others ⟨a *headstrong* refusal to listen to skilled workers⟩

un·sad·dle \ˌən-'sad-°l, 'ən-\ *vb* : to remove the saddle from a horse

un·sat·u·rat·ed \ˌən-'sach-ə-ˌrāt-əd, 'ən-\ *adj* : not saturated: as **a** : capable of absorbing or dissolving more of something ⟨an *unsaturated* solution⟩ **b** : able to form products by combining chemically with other substances; *esp* : containing double or triple bonds between carbon atoms ⟨an *unsaturated* fat⟩

un·saved \ˌən-'sāvd, 'ən-\ *adj* : not saved; *esp* : not rescued from eternal punishment

un·sa·vory \ˌən-'sāv(-ə)-rē, 'ən-\ *adj* **1** : having little or no taste **2** : having a bad taste or smell **3** : morally bad

un·say \ˌən-'sā, 'ən-\ *vb* **-said** \-'sed\; **-say·ing** \-'sā-iŋ\ : to take back something said : RETRACT

un·scathed \ˌən-'skāthd, 'ən-\ *adj* : completely unharmed : not injured

un·schooled \ˌən-'sküld, 'ən-\ *adj* : not schooled : UNTAUGHT, UNTRAINED

un·sci·en·tif·ic \ˌən-ˌsī-ən-'tif-ik\ *adj* **1** : not being in agreement with the principles and methods of science **2** : not showing scientific knowledge or familiarity with scientific methods — **un·sci·en·tif·i·cal·ly** \-'tif-i-k(ə-)lē\ *adv*

un·scram·ble \ˌən-'skram-bəl, 'ən-\ *vb* : to make orderly or clear again ⟨trying to *unscramble* a mix-up with the test scores⟩ ⟨*unscramble* a radio message⟩

un·screw \ˌən-'skrü, 'ən-\ *vb* **1** : to remove the screws from **2** : to loosen or withdraw by turning ⟨*unscrew* a light bulb⟩

un·scru·pu·lous \ˌən-'skrü-pyə-ləs, 'ən-\ *adj* : not scrupulous : UNPRINCIPLED — **un·scru·pu·lous·ly** *adv* — **un·scru·pu·lous·ness** *n*

un·seal \ˌən-'sē(ə)l, 'ən-\ *vb* : to break or remove the seal of

un·sea·son·able \ˌən-'sēz-nə-bəl, -'sēz-°n-ə-\ *adj* : not seasonable : happening or coming at the wrong time : UNTIMELY — **un·sea·son·ably** \-blē\ *adv*

un·seat \ˌən-'sēt, 'ən-\ *vb* **1** : to throw from one's seat especially on horseback **2** : to remove from a place or position; *esp* : to remove from political office

un·seem·ly \ˌən-'sēm-lē, 'ən-\ *adj* : not seemly : not polite or proper ⟨*unseemly* arguing in public⟩

un·seen \ˌən-'sēn, 'ən-\ *adj* : not seen : INVISIBLE

un·seg·re·gat·ed \ˌən-'seg-ri-ˌgāt-əd, 'ən-\ *adj* : not segregated; *esp* : free from racial segregation

un·self·ish \ˌən-'sel-fish, 'ən-\ *adj* : not selfish : GENEROUS — **un·self·ish·ly** *adv* — **un·self·ish·ness** *n*

un·set·tle \ˌən-'set-°l, 'ən-\ *vb* **1** : to move or loosen from a settled state **2** : to make uneasy ⟨rapid changes *unsettle* some people⟩

un·set·tled \ˌən-'set-°ld, 'ən-\ *adj* **1** : not settled : not fixed (as in position or nature) ⟨*unsettled* weather⟩ **2** : not calm : DISTURBED ⟨*unsettled* waters⟩ **3** : not decided in mind : UNDETERMINED ⟨*unsettled* about what to do⟩ **4** : not paid ⟨an *unsettled* account⟩ **5** : not lived in by settlers ⟨an *unsettled* region⟩

un·shaped \ˌən-'shāpt, 'ən-\ *adj* : not shaped; *esp* : not finished to final form ⟨an *unshaped* timber⟩ ⟨*unshaped* ideas⟩

un·shap·en \ˌən-'shā-pən, 'ən-\ *adj* : UNSHAPED

un·sheathe \ˌən-'shēth, 'ən-\ *vb* : to draw from or as if from a sheath ⟨*unsheathe* a sword⟩

un·ship \ˌən-'ship, 'ən-\ *vb* **1** : to remove from a ship **2** : to remove or become removed from position ⟨*unship* an oar⟩

un·shod \ˌən-'shäd, 'ən-\ *adj* **1** : BAREFOOT **2** : not shod ⟨an *unshod* horse⟩

un·sight·ly \ˌən-'sīt-lē, 'ən-\ *adj* : unpleasant to the sight : UGLY ⟨an *unsightly* scar⟩ — **un·sight·li·ness** *n*

un·skilled \ˌən-'skild, 'ən-\ *adj* **1** : not skilled; *esp* : not skilled in a branch of work : lacking mechanical training **2** : not requiring skill ⟨*unskilled* jobs⟩ **3** : marked by lack of skill ⟨an *unskilled* painting⟩

un·sling \ˌən-'sliŋ, 'ən-\ *vb* **-slung** \-'sləŋ\; **-sling·ing** \-'sliŋ-iŋ\ : to remove from being slung

un·snap \ˌən-'snap, 'ən-\ *vb* : to loosen or free by or as if by undoing a snap

un·snarl \ˌən-'snär(-ə)l, 'ən-\ *vb* : to remove a snarl in

un·so·cial \ˌən-'sō-shəl, 'ən-\ *adj* : having or showing a lack of desire for the company of others

un·so·phis·ti·cat·ed \,ən(t)-sə-'fis-tə-,kāt-əd\ *adj* **1** : not sophisticated ⟨was still innocent and *unsophisticated*⟩ **2** : not complex : PLAIN, SIMPLE ⟨*unsophisticated* designs⟩ — **un·so·phis·ti·ca·tion** \-,fis-tə-'kā-shən\ *n*

un·sought \,ən-'sot, 'ən-\ *adj* **1** : not searched for or asked for ⟨*unsought* advice⟩

un·sound \,ən-'saůnd, 'ən-\ *adj* **1** : not healthy or whole **2** : not mentally normal : not wholly sane **3** : not firmly made, placed, or fixed **4** : not based on truth or logic ⟨*unsound* arguments⟩ — **un·sound·ly** \-'saůn-(d)lē\ *adv* — **un·sound·ness** \-'saůn(d)-nəs\ *n*

un·spar·ing \,ən-'spa(ə)r-iŋ, -'spe(ə)r-, 'ən-\ *adj* **1** : not merciful or forgiving : HARD, RUTHLESS ⟨*unsparing* attacks⟩ **2** : not stingy : LIBERAL ⟨*unsparing* in their gifts to charity⟩ — **un·spar·ing·ly** *adv*

un·speak·able \,ən-'spē-kə-bəl, 'ən-\ *adj* **1** : impossible to express in words ⟨*unspeakable* beauty of the sunset⟩ **2** : extremely bad ⟨*unspeakable* conduct⟩ — **un·speak·ably** \-blē\ *adv*

un·spot·ted \,ən-'spät-əd, 'ən-\ *adj* : not spotted : free from spot or stain; *esp* : free from moral stain ⟨an *unspotted* record in public office⟩

un·sta·ble \,ən-'stā-bəl, 'ən-\ *adj* **1** : not stable : not firm or fixed : FLUCTUATING ⟨*unstable* prices⟩ **2** : readily changing in chemical composition or physical state or properties (as by breaking down into parts) ⟨an *unstable* atomic nucleus⟩

un·steady \,ən-'sted-ē, 'ən-\ *adj* : not steady : UNSTABLE — **un·steadi·ly** \-'sted-ə̇l-ē\ *adv* — **un·steadi·ness** \-'sted-ē-nəs\ *n*

un·stick \,ən-'stik, 'ən-\ *vb* **-stuck** \-'stək\; **-stick·ing** : to free from being stuck or bound

un·stint·ing \,ən-'stint-iŋ, 'ən-\ *adj* : giving or being given freely or generously ⟨*unstinting* praise⟩ — **un·stint·ing·ly** *adv*

un·stop \,ən-'stäp, 'ən-\ *vb* **1** : to free from blockage : OPEN **2** : to remove a stopper from

un·strap \,ən-'strap, 'ən-\ *vb* : to remove or loosen a strap from

un·stressed \,ən-'strest, 'ən-\ *adj* : not stressed; *esp* : not bearing a stress or accent

un·string \,ən-'striŋ, 'ən-\ *vb* **-strung** \-'strəŋ\; **-string·ing** \-'striŋ-iŋ\ **1** : to loosen or remove the strings of **2** : to remove from a string ⟨*unstrung* the beads⟩ **3** : to damage mentally or emotionally ⟨*unstrung* by bad news⟩

un·stud·ied \,ən-'stəd-ēd, 'ən-\ *adj* : not studied or planned with a certain effect in mind : NATURAL, UNFORCED ⟨moved with an *unstudied* grace⟩

un·sub·stan·tial \,ən(t)-səb-'stan-chəl\ *adj* : lacking substance, firmness, or strength

un·suc·cess·ful \,ən(t)-sək-'ses-fəl\ *adj* : not successful : not having or producing success — **un·suc·cess·ful·ly** \-fə-lē\ *adv*

un·suit·able \,ən-'süt-ə-bəl, 'ən-\ *adj* : not suitable or fitting : UNBECOMING, INAPPROPRIATE — **un·suit·ably** \-blē\ *adv*

un·sung \,ən-'səŋ, 'ən-\ *adj* **1** : not sung **2** : not celebrated in song or verse ⟨*unsung* heroes⟩

un·swerv·ing \,ən-'swər-viŋ, 'ən-\ *adj* **1** : not swerving or turning aside **2** : ¹STEADY 3a ⟨*unswerving* loyalty⟩

un·sym·met·ri·cal \,ən(t)-sə-'me-tri-kəl\ *adj* : not symmetrical : ASYMMETRIC

un·tan·gle \,ən-'taŋ-gəl, 'ən-\ *vb* **1** : to remove a tangle from : DISENTANGLE **2** : to straighten out : RESOLVE ⟨*untangle* financial problems⟩

un·taught \,ən-'tot, 'ən-\ *adj* **1** : not instructed or trained : IGNORANT **2** : ¹NATURAL 1 ⟨*untaught* animal behavior⟩

un·teth·er \,ən-'teth-ər, 'ən-\ *vb* : to free from a tether

un·think·able \,ən-'thiŋ-kə-bəl, 'ən-\ *adj* : not to be thought of or considered as possible ⟨*unthinkable* cruelty⟩

un·think·ing \,ən-'thiŋ-kiŋ, 'ən-\ *adj* **1** : not thinking : IN-ATTENTIVE, THOUGHTLESS ⟨*unthinking* people who litter the

streets⟩ **2** : not having the power of thought — **un·think·ing·ly** *adv*

un·thought–of \,ən-'thot-,əv, -,äv, 'ən-\ *adj* : not thought of : not considered : not imagined

un·thread \,ən-'thred, 'ən-\ *vb* **1** : to draw or take out a thread from **2** : to loosen the threads or connections of **3** : to make one's way through ⟨*unthread* a maze⟩

un·throne \,ən-'thrōn, 'ən-\ *vb* **-throned; -thron·ing** : to remove from or as if from a throne

un·ti·dy \,ən-'tīd-ē, 'ən-\ *adj* **1** : not neat : CARELESS **2 a** : not neatly organized or carried out **b** : marked by a lack of neatness — **un·ti·di·ly** \-'tīd-ə̇l-ē\ *adv* — **un·ti·di·ness** \-'tīd-ē-nəs\ *n*

un·tie \,ən-'tī, 'ən-\ *vb* **-tied; -ty·ing** *or* **-tie·ing** **1** : to free from something that ties or fastens : UNBIND ⟨*untie* a horse⟩ **2 a** : to undo the knotted parts of ⟨*untied* her scarf⟩ **b** : to straighten out : RESOLVE ⟨*untie* a traffic jam⟩ **3** : to become loosened or unbound ⟨the strings *untied* easily⟩

¹un·til \ən-,til, -t°l, -,tel, ,ən-, *in some contexts* ᵊn-, ᵊm-, *or* ᵊŋ-\ *prep* : up to the time of ⟨stayed *until* morning⟩

²until *conj* **1** : up to the time that ⟨played *until* it got dark⟩ **2** : to the point or degree that ⟨ran *until* I was breathless⟩

un·time·ly \,ən-'tīm-lē, 'ən-\ *adj* **1** : occurring or done before the expected, natural, or proper time : PREMATURE ⟨*untimely* death⟩ **2** : coming at the wrong time ⟨an *untimely* joke⟩

un·ti·tled \,ən-'tīt-ᵊld, 'ən-\ *adj* : not named ⟨an *untitled* poem⟩

un·to \,ən-tə, 'ən-tü\ *prep* : ¹TO

un·told \,ən-'tōld, 'ən-\ *adj* **1** : not told : not revealed ⟨*untold* secrets⟩ ⟨a story yet *untold*⟩ **2** : not counted : VAST, NUMBERLESS ⟨*untold* wealth⟩

¹un·touch·able \,ən-'təch-ə-bəl, 'ən-\ *adj* **1 a** : not to be touched or handled **b** : not to be criticized or controlled **2** : lying beyond the reach

²untouchable *n* : one that is untouchable; *esp* : a member of the lowest social class in India

un·to·ward \,ən-'tō-(ə)rd, 'ən-, -'to(-ə)rd; ,ən-tə-'wo̊(ə)rd\ *adj* **1** : hard to manage : STUBBORN, WILLFUL ⟨an *untoward* child⟩ **2** : causing trouble : UNLUCKY ⟨an *untoward* accident⟩

un·tried \,ən-'trīd, 'ən-\ *adj* **1** : not tested or proved by experience or trial ⟨*untried* soldiers⟩ **2** : not yet tried in court ⟨a long list of *untried* cases⟩

un·true \,ən-'trü, 'ən-\ *adj* **1** : not faithful : DISLOYAL **2** : not meeting a standard of correctness : not level or exact **3** : not agreeing with the facts : FALSE — **un·tru·ly** \-'trü-lē\ *adv*

un·truth \,ən-'trüth, 'ən-\ *n* **1** : lack of truthfulness : FAL-SITY **2** : something that is untrue : FALSEHOOD, LIE

un·truth·ful \,ən-'trüth-fəl, 'ən-\ *adj* : not containing or telling the truth : FALSE, INACCURATE ⟨*untruthful* reports⟩ — **un·truth·ful·ly** \-fə-lē\ *adv* — **un·truth·ful·ness** *n*

un·tuck \,ən-'tək, 'ən-\ *vb* : to free from a tuck or from being tucked up

un·tu·tored \,ən-'t(y)üt-ərd, 'ən-\ *adj* : having no formal learning or training

un·twine \,ən-'twīn, 'ən-\ *vb* **1** : to unwind the twisted or tangled parts of : DISENTANGLE **2** : to remove by unwinding **3** : to become untangled or unwound

un·twist \,ən-'twist, 'ən-\ *vb* **1** : to separate the twisted parts of : UNTWINE **2** : to become untwined

un·used \,ən-'yüzd, 'ən-, *in the phrase "unused to"* usually -'yüs(t)\ *adj* **1** : not accustomed **2 a** : not having been used before ⟨an *unused* paintbrush⟩ **b** : not being

\ə\ abut	\aů\ out	\i\ tip	\o̊\ saw	\ů\ foot
\ər\ further	\ch\ chin	\ī\ life	\oi\ coin	\y\ yet
\a\ mat	\e\ pet	\j\ job	\th\ thin	\yü\ few
\ā\ take	\ē\ easy	\ŋ\ sing	\th\ this	\yů\ cure
\ä\ cot, cart	\g\ go	\ō\ bone	\ü\ food	\zh\ vision

in use : IDLE   **c** : available for future use ⟨*unused* vacation time⟩

un·usu·al \ˌən-'yüzh-(ə-)wəl, -'yü-zhəl\ *adj* : not usual : UNCOMMON, RARE — **un·usu·al·ly** \-ē\ *adv* — **un·usu·al·ness** *n*

un·ut·ter·able \ˌən-'ət-ə-rə-bəl, 'ən-\ *adj* **1** : not capable of being pronounced **2** : not capable of being put into words : INEXPRESSIBLE ⟨*unutterable* sorrow⟩ — **un·ut·ter·ably** \-blē\ *adv*

un·val·ued \ˌən-'val-yüd, -yəd, 'ən-\ *adj* **1** : not important or prized : DISREGARDED **2** : not having an estimated value ⟨a box of *unvalued* goods⟩

un·var·nished \ˌən-'vär-nisht, 'ən-\ *adj* **1** : not adorned or exaggerated : PLAIN ⟨the *unvarnished* truth⟩ **2** : not varnished

un·veil \ˌən-'vā(ə)l, 'ən-\ *vb* **1 a** : to remove a veil or covering from ⟨*unveil* a statue⟩ **b** : DISCLOSE, REVEAL ⟨*unveiled* plans for a new housing complex⟩ **2** : to remove a veil; *esp* : to reveal oneself

un·voiced \ˌən-'vóist, 'ən-\ *adj* **1** : not actually said : UNSPOKEN ⟨an *unvoiced* agreement⟩ **2** : VOICELESS 2

un·war·rant·able \ˌən-'wór-ənt-ə-bəl, -'wär-, 'ən-\ *adj* : not justifiable : INEXCUSABLE

un·wary \ˌən-'wa(ə)r-ē, -'we(ə)r-, 'ən-\ *adj* : not alert : easily fooled or surprised : HEEDLESS, GULLIBLE ⟨the *unwary* buyer⟩ — **un·wari·ly** \-'war-ə-lē, -'wer-\ *adv* — **un·wari·ness** \-'war-ē-nəs, -'wer-\ *n*

un·wea·ried \ˌən-'wi(ə)r-ēd, 'ən-\ *adj* : not tired or bored : FRESH

un·well \ˌən-'wel, 'ən-\ *adj* : being in poor health : AILING, SICK

un·wept \ˌən-'wept, 'ən-\ *adj* : not mourned : UNLAMENTED ⟨died *unwept* and unsung⟩

un·whole·some \ˌən-'hōl-səm, 'ən-\ *adj* : bad for the well-being of the body, mind, or soul : UNHEALTHY

un·wieldy \ˌən-'wē(ə)l-dē, 'ən-\ *adj* : not easily handled or managed because of size or weight : AWKWARD, CUMBERSOME ⟨an *unwieldy* tool⟩

un·will·ing \ˌən-'wil-iŋ, 'ən-\ *adj* : not willing — **un·will·ing·ly** *adv* — **un·will·ing·ness** *n*

un·wind \ˌən-'wīnd, 'ən-\ *vb* **-wound** \-'waúnd\; **-wind·ing** **1 a** : to cause to uncoil : wind off   **b** : to become uncoiled or untangled **2** : to make or become free of tension : RELAX ⟨wanted to *unwind* after a hard day⟩

un·wise \ˌən-'wīz, 'ən-\ *adj* : not wise : FOOLISH — **un·wise·ly** *adv*

un·wit·ting \ˌən-'wit-iŋ, 'ən-\ *adj* **1** : not intended : INADVERTENT ⟨an *unwitting* mistake⟩ **2** : not knowing : UNAWARE — **un·wit·ting·ly** *adv*

un·wont·ed \ˌən-'wónt-əd, -'wōnt-, 'ən-\ *adj* : being out of the ordinary : RARE, UNUSUAL

un·world·ly \ˌən-'wər(-ə)l-dlē, -'wərl-lē, 'ən-\ *adj* **1** : not of this world; *esp* : ¹SPIRITUAL 1 **2** : not wise in the ways of the world : UNSOPHISTICATED — **un·world·li·ness** \-'wərl-(d)lē-nəs\ *n*

un·worn \ˌən-'wō(ə)rn, -'wó(ə)rn, 'ən-\ *adj* : not worn : NEW

un·wor·thy \ˌən-'wər-thē, 'ən-\ *adj* : lacking in excellence or worth : UNDESERVING — **un·wor·thi·ly** \-thə-lē\ *adv* — **un·wor·thi·ness** \-thē-nəs\ *n*

un·wrap \ˌən-'rap, 'ən-\ *vb* : to remove the wrapping from

un·writ·ten \ˌən-'rit-ᵊn, 'ən-\ *adj* **1** : not put in writing : ORAL, TRADITIONAL ⟨an *unwritten* law⟩ **2** : containing no writing : BLANK ⟨*unwritten* pages⟩

un·yield·ing \ˌən-'yē(ə)l-diŋ, 'ən-\ *adj* **1** : not soft or flexible : HARD **2** : marked by firmness or stubbornness

un·yoke \ˌən-'yōk, 'ən-\ *vb* **1** : to free from a yoke ⟨*un-yoke* oxen⟩ **2** : to take apart : DISCONNECT

un·zip \ˌən-'zip, 'ən-\ *vb* **-zipped; -zip·ping** : to open by means of a zipper

¹up \'əp\ *adv* **1 a** : in or to a higher position or level : away from the center of the earth ⟨held *up* my hand⟩ **b** : from beneath a surface (as ground or water) ⟨pulling *up* weeds⟩

c : from below the horizon ⟨watched the moon come *up*⟩ **d** : in or into an upright position ⟨stand *up*⟩ **e** : out of bed ⟨stayed *up* late⟩ **2** : with greater force ⟨speak *up*⟩ **3 a** : in or into a better or more advanced state ⟨worked our way *up* in the world⟩ **b** : in or into a state of greater activity ⟨stir *up* a fire⟩ **4 a** : into existence, evidence, or knowledge ⟨the missing ring turned *up*⟩ **b** : into consideration ⟨brought the matter *up*⟩ **5** : into possession or control ⟨gave himself *up*⟩ **6** : WHOLLY, ENTIRELY, COMPLETELY ⟨eat it *up*⟩ ⟨the house burned *up*⟩ **7** : in or into storage : ASIDE, BY ⟨lay *up* supplies⟩ ⟨put our boat *up* for the winter⟩ **8** : into a closed state ⟨button *up* your coat⟩ ⟨seal *up* a package⟩ **9 a** : so as to arrive or approach ⟨came *up* the drive⟩ **b** : so as to be even with, overtake, or arrive at ⟨catch *up*⟩ ⟨keep *up* with the times⟩ **10** : in or into parts ⟨tear *up* paper⟩ ⟨blow *up* a bridge⟩ **11** : to a stop ⟨pull *up*⟩ ⟨drew *up* at the curb⟩ **12 a** : in advance ⟨went one *up* on her opponent⟩ **b** : for each side ⟨score was 15 *up*⟩

²up *adj* **1 a** : risen above the horizon or ground ⟨the sun was *up*⟩ **b** : being out of bed   **c** : higher than usual ⟨the river is *up*⟩ **d** : raised so as to be open : LIFTED ⟨windows are *up*⟩ **e** : put together : BUILT ⟨the house is *up* but not finished⟩ **f** : grown above a surface ⟨the corn is *up*⟩ **g** : moving or going upward ⟨the *up* escalator⟩ **2 a** : being on one's feet and busy ⟨was eager to be *up* and doing⟩ **b** : well prepared ⟨the team was *up* for the game⟩ **c** : going on : taking place ⟨find out what is *up*⟩ **3** : come to an end : EXPIRED, ENDED ⟨your time is *up*⟩ **4** : well informed ⟨always *up* on the news⟩ **5** : being ahead of an opponent ⟨was three games *up* in the series⟩ **6 a** : presented for or under consideration ⟨*up* for reelection⟩ **b** : charged before a court ⟨was *up* for robbery⟩ — **up to 1** : capable of performing or dealing with ⟨feels *up to* the role⟩ **2** : engaged in ⟨what are they *up to*⟩ **3** : being the responsibility of ⟨it's *up to* me⟩

³up \(ˌ)əp, 'əp\ *prep* **1** : to, toward, or at a higher point of ⟨*up* the hill⟩ **2 a** : toward the beginning of ⟨going *up* the river⟩ **b** : toward the northern part of ⟨sailed *up* the coast⟩ **c** : to, toward, or in the inner part of ⟨stuck *up* a dead end street⟩ **3** : ¹ALONG 1 ⟨walking *up* the street⟩

⁴up \'əp\ *n* **1** : an upward course or slope **2** : a period or state of success ⟨had had my *ups* and downs⟩

⁵up *vb* **upped** *or in sense 1* **up; upped; up·ping; ups** *or in sense 1* **up 1** : to act suddenly or surprisingly ⟨*up* and left town⟩ **2** : to rise from a lying or sitting position **3** : to move or cause to move upward : ASCEND, RAISE ⟨*upped* the prices⟩

up–and–down *adj* **1** : marked by alternate upward and downward movement, action, or surface **2** : ¹PERPENDICULAR 1

¹up·beat \'əp-ˌbēt\ *n* : an unaccented beat in a musical measure; *esp* : the last beat of the measure

²upbeat *adj* : OPTIMISTIC, CHEERFUL ⟨a story with an *upbeat* ending⟩

up·braid \ˌəp-'brād\ *vb* : to criticize or scold severely

up·bring·ing \'əp-ˌbriŋ-iŋ\ *n* : the process of bringing up and training

up·com·ing \ˌəp-ˌkəm-iŋ\ *adj* : coming soon

¹up–coun·try \'əp-ˌkən-trē\ *adj* : of or relating to the interior of a country or a region — **up–country** \'əp-\ *n*

²up–coun·try \'əp-'kən-trē\ *adv* : to or in the interior of a country or a region

up·date \ˌəp-'dāt\ *vb* : to bring up to date

up·draft \'əp-ˌdraft, -ˌdrȧft\ *n* : an upward movement of gas (as air)

up·end \ˌə-'pend\ *vb* : to set, stand, or rise on end

¹up·grade \'əp-ˌgrād\ *n* **1** : an upward grade or slope **2** : ²RISE 4 ⟨crime has been on the *upgrade*⟩

²up·grade \'əp-ˌgrād, ˌəp-'grād\ *vb* : to raise to a higher grade or position

up·heav·al \ˌəp-'hē-vəl, (ˌ)ə-'pē-\ *n* **1** : the action or an instance of heaving or lifting up from beneath especially of part of the earth's crust   **2** : an instance of violent disorder or change 〈student *upheavals*〉

¹up·hill \'əp-'hil\ *adv*   **1** : in an upward direction   **2** : against difficulties

²up·hill \,əp-,hil\ *adj*   **1** : being on high ground   **2** : going up : ASCENDING   **3** : DIFFICULT 1 〈an *uphill* struggle〉

up·hold \(,)əp-'hōld\ *vb* **-held** \-'held\; **-hold·ing**   **1** : to give support to 〈promise to *uphold* the law〉   **2 a** : to keep elevated   **b** : to lift up — **up·hold·er** *n*

up·hol·ster \(,)əp-'hōl-stər, (,)ə-'pōl-\ *vb* **-stered; -ster·ing** \-st(ə-)riŋ\ : to provide with or as if with upholstery — **up·hol·ster·er** \-stər-ər\ *n*

up·hol·stery \(,)əp-'hōl-st(ə-)rē, (,)ə-'pōl-\ *n, pl* **-ster·ies** : materials (as fabric, padding, and springs) used to make a soft covering especially for a seat

up·keep \'əp-,kēp\ *n* : the act or cost of maintaining in good condition : MAINTENANCE

up·land \'əp-lənd, -,land\ *n* : high land especially at some distance from the sea — **upland** *adj*

¹up·lift \(,)əp-'lift\ *vb*   **1** : to lift up : ELEVATE   **2** : to improve the spiritual, mental, or social condition of

²up·lift \'əp-,lift\ *n*   **1** : an act, process, or result of uplifting; *esp* : the uplifting of a part of the earth's surface   **2** : moral or social improvement or a movement to make such improvement

up·load \,əp-'lōd, 'əp-,\ *vb* : to transfer (information) from a microcomputer to a remote computer usually with a modem

up·most \'əp-,mōst\ *adj* : being in the highest or most important position

up·on \ə-'pȯn, -'pän, -(,)pən\ *prep* : ¹ON

upped *past and past participle of* UP

¹up·per \'əp-ər\ *adj*   **1** : higher in physical position, rank, or order   **2** : being the smaller and more restricted branch of a two-house legislature   **3** *cap* : of, relating to, or being a later geologic period or formation   **4** : being toward the interior : further inland 〈the *upper* Amazon〉   **5** : NORTHERN 〈*upper* New York state〉

²upper *n*   **1** : the parts of a shoe or boot above the sole   **2** : an upper tooth or set of teeth   **3** : an upper berth   **4** : a stimulant drug; *esp* : AMPHETAMINE

up·per·case \,əp-ər-'kās\ *adj* : ¹CAPITAL 2 — **uppercase** *n*

upper class *n* : the highest class in society — **upper–class** *adj*

up·per·class·man \,əp-ər-'klas-mən\ *n* : a student in the third or fourth year of a four-year college or a high school

upper crust *n* : the highest social class or group

up·per·cut \'əp-ər-,kət\ *n* : a swinging blow (as in boxing) directed upward with a bent arm — **uppercut** *vb*

upper hand *n* : the position of being ahead or in control

up·per·most \'əp-ər-,mōst\ *adv* : in or into the highest or most prominent position — **uppermost** *adj*

upping *present participle of* UP

up·pish \'əp-ish\ *adj* : UPPITY

up·pi·ty \'əp-ət-ē\ *adj* : acting as if better or more important than others : ARROGANT

up·raise \,əp-'rāz\ *vb* : to raise or lift up : ELEVATE

¹up·right \'əp-,rīt\ *adj*   **1 a** : ¹VERTICAL 2 〈an *upright* posture〉   **b** : having the main axis or a main part perpendicular   **2** : living by high moral standards : HONORABLE — **up·right·ness** *n*

    syn UPRIGHT, HONEST, JUST mean having or showing a great concern for what is right. UPRIGHT suggests having high moral standards in all areas of life 〈an *upright* person whose life was an example to the whole town〉 HONEST suggests dealing with others in a fair and truthful way 〈an *honest* merchant who would not cheat anyone〉 JUST stresses that one's fairness comes from conscious choice and is practiced steadily 〈a *just* principal who knows she must treat all students equally〉

²upright *n*   **1** : an upright or vertical position   **2** : something upright

upright piano *n* : a piano whose strings run vertically

---

up·rise \,ə-'prīz\ *vb* **-rose** \-'prōz\; **-ris·en** \-'priz-ᵊn\; **-ris·ing** \-'prī-ziŋ\   **1** : to rise to a higher position   **2** : to get up (as from sleep or a sitting position)

up·ris·ing \'əp-,rī-ziŋ\ *n* : an act or instance of rising up   **syn** see REBELLION

up·riv·er \'əp-'riv-ər\ *adv or adj* : toward or at a point nearer the start of a river

upright piano

up·roar \'əp-,rō(ə)r, -,rȯ(ə)r\ *n* : a state of commotion, excitement, or violent disturbance

    Word History The *-roar* part of the word *uproar* has no connection with the sounds made by some animals and crowds. The first use of *uproar* was as the translation of the Dutch word *oproer,* meaning "uprising, rebellion, revolt". Thus, the first meaning of *uproar* was the same as the Dutch meaning of *oproer.* Nowadays, this sense of *uproar* is no longer used. Because people thought that the *roar* of *uproar* referred to loud cries and sounds, they began to use the word to mean "a noisy disturbance or commotion". This is the sense of *uproar* that has survived. [from Dutch *oproer* "revolt, uprising", from *op* "up" and *roer* "motion"; the English spelling and meaning influenced by the similarity of the English *roar* to Dutch *roer*]

up·roar·i·ous \,ə-'prōr-ē-əs, -'prȯr-\ *adj*   **1** : marked by uproar   **2** : extremely funny — **up·roar·i·ous·ly** *adv*

up·root \(,)ə-'prüt, -'prut\ *vb* : to remove by or as if by pulling up by the roots 〈*uproot* a vine〉 〈families *uprooted* by war〉

¹up·set \(,)əp-'set\ *vb* **-set; -set·ting**   **1** : to force or be forced out of the usual position : OVERTURN   **2 a** : to worry or cause unhappiness to   **b** : to make somewhat ill   **3 a** : to throw into disorder   **b** : to defeat unexpectedly

²up·set \'əp-,set\ *n*   **1** : an act or result of upsetting : a state of being upset   **2 a** : a minor illness 〈a stomach *upset*〉   **b** : a period of worry or unhappiness

up·shot \'əp-,shät\ *n* : final result : OUTCOME

up·side down \,əp-,sīd-'daun\ *adv*   **1** : with the upper part underneath and the lower part on top   **2** : in or into great disorder — **upside–down** *adj*

upside–down cake *n* : a cake baked with a layer of fruit (as pineapple) on the bottom and served fruit side up

up·si·lon \'yüp-sə-,län, 'əp-, -lən\ *n* : the 20th letter of the Greek alphabet — Υ or υ

¹up·stage \'əp-,stāj\ *adv or adj* : toward or at the part of the stage or set farthest from the audience or the motion picture or television camera

²up·stage \,əp-'stāj\ *vb* : to steal the show from 〈children *upstaging* adult performers〉

¹up·stairs \'əp-'sta(ə)rz, -'ste(ə)rz\ *adv*   **1** : up the stairs : to or on a higher floor   **2** : to or at a higher position or level

²up·stairs \,əp-,sta(ə)rz, -,ste(ə)rz\ *adj* : of or relating to the upper floors

³up·stairs \'əp-'sta(ə)rz, -'ste(ə)rz; 'əp-,sta(ə)rz, -,ste(ə)rz\ *n* : the part of a building above the ground floor

up·stand·ing \,əp-'stan-diŋ, 'əp-,stan-\ *adj*   **1** : ¹VERTICAL 2   **2** : ¹HONEST 3

up·start \'əp-,stärt\ *n* : a person who has risen suddenly (as from a low position to wealth or power); *esp* : one who

---

\ə\ **abut**	\au̇\ **out**	\i\ **tip**	\ȯ\ **saw**	\u̇\ **foot**
\ər\ **further**	\ch\ **chin**	\ī\ **life**	\ȯi\ **coin**	\y\ **yet**
\a\ **mat**	\e\ **pet**	\j\ **job**	\th\ **thin**	\yü\ **few**
\ā\ **take**	\ē\ **easy**	\ŋ\ **sing**	\th\ **this**	\yu̇\ **cure**
\ä\ **cot, cart**	\g\ **go**	\ō\ **bone**	\ü\ **food**	\zh\ **vision**

makes a great show of success

up·state \'əp-ˌstāt\ *adj* : of, relating to, or typical of a part of a state away from a large city and especially to the north — **upstate** *n*

up·stream \'əp-'strēm\ *adv or adj* : at or toward the beginning of a stream : against the current ⟨salmon swimming *upstream*⟩

up·stroke \'əp-ˌstrōk\ *n* : an upward stroke (as of a pen)

up·surge \'əp-ˌsərj\ *n* : a rapid or sudden rise ⟨an *upsurge* of popularity⟩

up·sweep \'əp-ˌswēp\ *vb* **-swept** \-ˌswept\; **-sweep·ing** : to sweep upward : curve or slope upward — **upsweep** *n*

up·swept \'əp-ˌswept\ *adj* : swept upward ⟨an *upswept* hairdo⟩

up·swing \'əp-ˌswiŋ\ *n* : an upward swing; *esp* : a marked increase or rise (as in activity) ⟨business is on the *upswing*⟩

up·take \'əp-ˌtāk\ *n* **1** : ¹UNDERSTANDING 1, COMPREHENSION ⟨quick on the *uptake*⟩ **2** : a process especially in a living organism of absorbing and combining with something

up·tight \'əp-'tīt, (ˌ)əp-'tīt, ˌəp-ˌtīt\ *adj* : being tense, nervous, or uneasy

up·tilt \ˌəp-'tilt\ *vb* : to tilt upward

up to *prep* **1** : as far as a named part or place ⟨sank *up to* my hips⟩ **2** : in accordance with ⟨the game was not *up to* our standards⟩ **3 a** : to the limit of ⟨come in sizes *up to* 10⟩ **b** : as many or as much as ⟨carry *up to* 10 tons⟩ **4** : ¹UNTIL, TILL ⟨from dawn *up to* dusk⟩

up–to–date *adj* **1** : coming up to the present time ⟨*up-to-date* maps⟩ **2** : knowing, being, or making use of what is new or recent ⟨*up-to-date* information⟩ — **up–to–date·ness** *n*

up·town \'əp-'taùn\ *adv* : toward, to, or in the upper part of a town — **uptown** *adj*

up·trend \'əp-ˌtrend\ *n* : a rise especially in business or activity

¹up·turn \'əp-ˌtərn, ˌəp-'tərn\ *vb* **1** : to turn up or over ⟨an *upturned* boat⟩ **2** : to turn or direct upward ⟨*upturned* faces⟩

²up·turn \'əp-ˌtərn\ *n* : an upward turning (as toward better conditions or higher prices)

¹up·ward \'əp-wərd\ *or* **up·wards** \-wərdz\ *adv* **1** : in a direction from lower to higher ⟨the land rises *upward*⟩ **2** : toward a higher or better condition ⟨worked my way *upward* in the business⟩ **3** : toward a greater amount or higher number, degree, or rate ⟨prices shot *upward*⟩

²upward *adj* : directed toward or located in a higher place or level : ASCENDING — **up·ward·ly** *adv*

upwards of *also* **upward of** *adv* : more than ⟨*upwards of* half a million people⟩

up·well·ing \ˌəp-'wel-iŋ\ *n* : the process or an example of rising or appearing to rise to the surface and flowing outward; *esp* : the process of movement of deeper cooler layers of ocean water that are often rich in nourishing substances to the surface

up·wind \'əp-'wind\ *adv or adj* : in the direction from which the wind is blowing

ura·cil \'yùr-ə-ˌsil, -səl\ *n* : a pyrimidine base that is one of the four bases coding hereditary information in RNA — compare ADENINE, CYTOSINE, GUANINE, THYMINE

ura·ni·nite \yù-'rā-nə-ˌnīt\ *n* : a mineral that is a black oxide of uranium, contains also various metals (as thorium and lead), and is the chief ore of uranium

ura·ni·um \yò-'rā-nē-əm\ *n* : a silvery heavy radioactive metallic element that exists naturally as a mixture of three forms having atomic mass numbers 234, 235, and 238 — see ELEMENT table

Word History The ancient Greek word *ouranos* meant "sky, heaven". It was fitting, then, for the Greeks to name their god of heaven *Ouranos* and their muse of astronomy *Ourania*. In Latin these names became *Ura-*

nus and *Urania.* Uranus was the father of the god Saturn and the grandfather of Jupiter. In 1781 the English astronomer Sir William Herschel discovered by telescope the seventh planet of our solar system. It was the custom to name planets after Roman gods. Following this custom, the German astronomer Johann Bode suggested the name *Uranus* for this planet. It seemed a good idea since the fifth planet was called Jupiter and the sixth was Saturn. Eight years after the discovery of Uranus, the German chemist Martin Klaproth discovered a new element. He called it *uranium* after the new planet Uranus. [scientific Latin; named for the planet Uranus, from Latin *Uranus,* name of the god of heaven]

uranium hexa·flu·o·ride \-ˌhek-sə-'flù(-ə)r-ˌīd\ *n* : a compound of uranium and fluorine that is used in one major process for the separation of uranium 235 from ordinary uranium

uranium 238 *n* : the most common form of uranium that has an atomic mass number of 238, breaks down in a series of nuclear changes into a form of lead, and can absorb neutrons and then go through a series of nuclear transformations to change into a form of plutonium

uranium 235 *n* : a light form of uranium of mass number 235 that when bombarded with neutrons splits rapidly into smaller atoms with the release of neutrons and atomic energy

Ura·nus \'yùr-ə-nəs, yù-'rā-\ *n* : the planet seventh in order from the sun — see PLANET table

ur·ban \'ər-bən\ *adj* : of, relating to, typical of, or being a city ⟨*urban* life⟩ ⟨an *urban* area⟩

ur·bane \ˌər-'bān\ *adj* : very polite and smooth in manner — **ur·ban·i·ty** \-'ban-ət-ē\ *n*

ur·ban·ite \'ər-bə-ˌnīt\ *n* : one living in a city

ur·ban·ize \'ər-bə-ˌnīz\ *vb* **-ized; -iz·ing** **1** : to cause to have an urban appearance ⟨*urbanized* areas⟩ **2** : to cause to take on an urban way of life ⟨*urbanized* the peasant population⟩ — **ur·ban·iza·tion** \ˌər-bə-nə-'zā-shən\ *n*

urban renewal *n* : a construction program for replacing or restoring old or run-down buildings in an urban area

urban sprawl *n* : the spreading of urban structures into areas surrounding a city

ur·chin \'ər-chən\ *n* : a mischievous child

-ure *n suffix* **1** : act : process : being ⟨expo*sure*⟩ **2** : office : function; *also* : body performing (such) a function ⟨legislat*ure*⟩ [derived from Latin *-ura* (noun suffix) "-ure"]

urea \yù-'rē-ə\ *n* : a soluble nitrogen-containing compound that is the chief solid substance in the urine of mammals

ure·ter \'yùr-ət-ər\ *n* : a tube that carries urine from a kidney to the bladder or cloaca

ure·thra \yù-'rē-thrə\ *n, pl* **-thras** *or* **-thrae** \-thrē\ : a canal that in most mammals carries off urine from the bladder and in the male serves as a passage for the release of semen from the body — **ure·thral** \-thrəl\ *adj*

¹urge \'ərj\ *vb* **urged; urg·ing** **1** : to ask for or support earnestly ⟨continually *urging* reform⟩ **2** : to try to persuade ⟨*urge* a guest to stay longer⟩ **3** : to force or drive to some course or activity (as greater speed) ⟨riders *urging* their horses on⟩

²urge *n* **1** : the act or process of urging **2** : a strong desire especially to achieve a goal ⟨the *urge* to win⟩

ur·gen·cy \'ər-jən-sē\ *n* : the quality or state of being urgent

ur·gent \'ər-jənt\ *adj* **1 a** : calling for immediate attention : PRESSING ⟨an *urgent* need for food⟩ **b** : indicating an urgent desire or need ⟨an *urgent* manner⟩ **2** : urging very earnestly — **ur·gent·ly** *adv*

uric \'yù(ə)r-ik\ *adj* : of, relating to, or found in urine

uric acid *n* : a white odorless nitrogen-containing acid that is present only in small quantities in the urine of mammals but is the chief form in which nitrogen is eliminated from the body in birds and many lower animals

uri·nal \'yùr-ən-ᵊl\ *n* : a container for receiving urine; *also*

: a place for urinating

uri·nal·y·sis \ˌyūr-ə-ˈnal-ə-səs\ *n, pl* **-nal·y·ses** \-ə-ˌsēz\ : the analysis of urine

uri·nary \ˈyūr-ə-ˌner-ē\ *adj* **1** : relating to, occurring in, or making up the organs concerned with producing and giving off urine **2** : of, relating to, or used for urine

uri·nate \ˈyūr-ə-ˌnāt\ *vb* **-nat·ed; -nat·ing** : to release or give off urine — **uri·na·tion** \ˌyūr-ə-ˈnā-shən\ *n*

urine \ˈyūr-ən\ *n* : waste material that is secreted by the kidneys, is rich in the end products of protein metabolism, and is usually a yellowish liquid in mammals but semisolid in birds and reptiles

urn \ˈərn\ *n* **1** : a container that has the form of a vase on a base and often is used for keeping the ashes of the dead **2** : a closed vessel usually with a faucet for serving a hot beverage ⟨coffee *urn*⟩

Ur·sa Ma·jor \ˌər-sə-ˈmā-jər\ *n* : the northern group of stars that is the easiest to pick out, is located near the north pole of the heavens, and contains the stars forming the Big Dipper two of which are in a line pointing in the direction of the North Star — called also *Great Bear*

Ursa Mi·nor \-ˈmī-nər\ *n* : the group of stars that includes the north pole of the heavens and the stars which form the Little Dipper with the North Star at the tip of the handle — called also *Little Bear*

urn 2

us \(ˈ)əs\ *pron, objective case of* WE

us·able \ˈyü-zə-bəl\ *adj* : suitable or fit for use ⟨*usable* waste⟩

us·age \ˈyü-sij, -zij\ *n* **1 a** : usual practice or procedure **b** : the way in which words and phrases are actually used **2 a** : the action of using : USE ⟨increasing *usage* of the nation's highways⟩ **b** : manner of treating ⟨restaurant dishes receive rough *usage*⟩ **syn** see HABIT

¹use \ˈyüs\ *n* **1 a** : the act or practice of using something : APPLICATION ⟨put knowledge to *use*⟩ **b** : the fact or state of being used ⟨a dish in daily *use*⟩ **c** : way of using ⟨the proper *use* of tools⟩ **2 a** : the privilege or benefit of using something ⟨gave me the *use* of their car⟩ **b** : the ability or power to use something (as a limb) ⟨after the operation you'll again have the *use* of your leg⟩ **3 a** : a particular service or end ⟨no *use* in crying all the time⟩ **b** : the quality of being useful ⟨old clothes that are still of some *use*⟩ **c** : a reason or need to use ⟨took only what he had *use* for⟩ **4** : LIKING ⟨had no *use* for modern art⟩

²use \ˈyüz\ *vb* **used** \ˈyüzd, *in the phrase "used to" usually* ˈyüs(t)\; **us·ing** \ˈyü-ziŋ\ **1** : to put into action or service : EMPLOY ⟨pronunciations *used* by different people⟩ **2** : to take into the body ⟨never *uses* tobacco⟩ **3** : to carry out an action by means of : UTILIZE ⟨*use* caution⟩ **4** : to make use of ⟨likes to *use* herbs in cooking⟩ **5** : to behave toward : TREAT ⟨*used* the prisoners cruelly⟩ **6** — used in the past with *to* to show a former practice, fact, or state ⟨claims winters *used* to be harder⟩ — **us·er** \ˈyü-zər\ *n*

used \ˈyüzd, *in the phrase "used to" usually* ˈyüs(t)\ *adj* **1** : employed in accomplishing something ⟨a much *used* excuse⟩ **2** : that has been used; *esp* : SECONDHAND 2a ⟨*used* cars⟩ **3** : having the habit of doing or experiencing ⟨is *used* to flying⟩

use·ful \ˈyüs-fəl\ *adj* **1** : capable of being put to use : USABLE ⟨*useful* scraps of material⟩ **2** : having practical value ⟨a *useful* invention⟩ — **use·ful·ly** \-fə-lē\ *adv* — **use·ful·ness** *n*

use·less \ˈyüs-ləs\ *adj* : having or being of no use — **use·less·ly** *adv* — **use·less·ness** *n*

use up *vb* : to make complete use of : EXHAUST

¹ush·er \ˈəsh-ər\ *n* : a person who leads other persons to seats (as in a theater or at a wedding)

²usher *vb* **ush·ered; ush·er·ing** \ˈəsh-(ə-)riŋ\ **1** : to lead to a place **2** : to come before as if to lead in or announce ⟨*usher* in a new era⟩

usu·al \ˈyüzh-(ə-)wəl, ˈyüzh-əl\ *adj* : done, found, or used in the ordinary course of events : NORMAL, REGULAR ⟨less than the *usual* fee⟩ ⟨the *usual* route to work⟩ — **usu·al·ly** \ˈyüzh-(ə-)wə-lē, ˈyüzh-(ə-)lē, *in rapid speech* ˈyüz-lē\ *adv*

usu·rer \ˈyü-zhər-ər, ˈyüzh-rər\ *n* : one who lends money especially at a very high rate of interest

usu·ri·ous \yū-ˈzhūr-ē-əs, -ˈzūr-\ *adj* : practicing, involving, or being usury ⟨*usurious* interest⟩

usurp \yū-ˈsərp *also* -ˈzərp\ *vb* : to seize and hold by force or without right ⟨*usurp* power from the king⟩

usu·ry \ˈyüzh-(ə-)rē\ *n, pl* **usu·ries** **1** : the lending of money with an interest charge for its use **2** : a rate of interest that is very high or higher than the usual rate

uten·sil \yū-ˈten(t)-səl\ *n* **1** : a device or container used in a household and especially a kitchen **2** : an article serving a useful purpose ⟨writing *utensils*⟩ **syn** see IMPLEMENT

uter·ine \ˈyüt-ə-ˌrīn, -rən\ *adj* : of, relating to, or affecting the uterus ⟨the *uterine* lining⟩ ⟨*uterine* cancer⟩

uter·us \ˈyüt-ə-rəs\ *n, pl* **uteri** \-ˌrī\ *also* **uter·us·es** : the muscular organ of a female mammal in which the young develop before birth — called also *womb*

util·i·tar·i·an \(ˌ)yü-ˌtil-ə-ˈter-ē-ən\ *adj* **1** : of or relating to utility **2** : aiming at usefulness rather than beauty ⟨*utilitarian* furniture⟩

¹util·i·ty \yü-ˈtil-ət-ē\ *n, pl* **-ties** **1** : the quality or state of being useful : USEFULNESS **2** : something useful or designed for use **3 a** : PUBLIC UTILITY **b** : a public service (as power or water) provided by a public utility

²utility *adj* **1** : capable of serving as a substitute in various roles or positions ⟨*utility* infielder⟩ **2** : being of a usable but poor quality ⟨*utility* beef⟩ **3** : serving chiefly for usefulness rather than beauty : UTILITARIAN **4** : designed for general use ⟨*utility* bag⟩

uti·lize \ˈyüt-ᵊl-ˌīz\ *vb* **-lized; -liz·ing** : to make use of especially for a certain job — **uti·li·za·tion** \ˌyüt-ᵊl-ə-ˈzā-shən\ *n*

ut·most \ˈət-ˌmōst, *especially Southern* -məst\ *adj* **1** : located at the farthest or most distant point **2** : of the greatest or highest degree, quantity, number, or amount ⟨a matter of the *utmost* urgency⟩ [Old English *ūtmest* "outermost", from *ūt* "out" and *-mest* (a superlative adjective suffix similar to *-est*)] — **utmost** *n*

uto·pia \yū-ˈtō-pē-ə\ *n* **1** *often cap* : a place of ideal perfection especially in laws, government, and social conditions **2** : an impractical scheme for social improvement — **uto·pi·an** \-pē-ən\ *adj or n*

Word History In 1516 the English statesman Sir Thomas More published a book that compared the condition of his England to that of a perfect and imaginary country, *Utopia*. Everything that was wrong in England was perfect in Utopia. More was trying to show how people could live together in peace and happiness if they only did what he thought was right. But the name he gave his imaginary country showed that he did not really believe perfection could ever be reached. *Utopia* means, literally, "no place", since it was formed from the Greek *ou,* meaning "no, not", and *topos,* "place". Since More's time, *utopia* has come to mean "a place of ideal perfection". Over the years many books similar to *Uto-*

\ə\	abut	\au̇\	out	\i\	tip	\ȯ\	saw	\u̇\	foot
\ər\	further	\ch\	chin	\ī\	life	\ȯi\	coin	\y\	yet
\a\	mat	\e\	pet	\j\	job	\th\	thin	\yü\	few
\ā\	take	\ē\	easy	\ŋ\	sing	\th\	this	\yu̇\	cure
\ä\	cot, cart	\g\	go	\ō\	bone	\ü\	food	\zh\	vision

pia have been written, and many plans for perfect societies proposed, most of them impractical. *Utopia* has also come to mean any such scheme or plan. [from *Utopia*, name of an imaginary ideal country in a book *Utopia* written by Sir Thomas More 1478–1535 English statesman and author; from Greek *ou* "not, no" and Greek *topos* "place"]

¹ut·ter \'ət-ər\ *adj* : complete in extent or degree ⟨an *utter* impossibility⟩ ⟨*utter* strangers⟩ — **ut·ter·ly** *adv*

²utter *vb* **1** : to send forth usually as a sound ⟨*uttered* a laugh⟩ **2** : to express in words ⟨forced to *utter* the truth⟩

ut·ter·ance \'ət-ə-rən(t)s\ *n* **1** : something uttered; *esp* : an oral or written statement **2** : the action of uttering with the voice : SPEECH **3** : power, style, or manner of speaking

ut·ter·most \'ət-ər-ˌmōst\ *adj* : UTMOST 2 — **uttermost** *n*

uvu·la \'yü-vyə-lə\ *n, pl* **-las** *or* **-lae** \-ˌlē, -ˌlī\ : the small fleshy fingerlike part hanging down from the back part of the roof of the mouth

V

v \'vē\ *n, often cap* **1** : the 22d letter of the English alphabet **2** : five in Roman numerals

va·can·cy \'vā-kən-sē\ *n, pl* **-cies** **1** : something (as an office or hotel room) that is vacant **2** : empty space **3** : the state of being vacant

va·cant \'vā-kənt\ *adj* **1** : not filled, used, or lived in ⟨a *vacant* house⟩ **2** : free from duties or care ⟨a few *vacant* hours⟩ **3** : showing lack of thought : FOOLISH ⟨a *vacant* stare⟩ — **va·cant·ly** *adv*

va·cate \'vā-ˌkāt, vā-'kāt\ *vb* **va·cat·ed; va·cat·ing** : to leave vacant

¹va·ca·tion \vā-'kā-shən, və-\ *n* **1** : a period during which activity (as of a school) is stopped for a time **2** : a period spent away from home or business in travel or amusement

²vacation *vb* **-tioned; -tion·ing** \-sh(ə-)niŋ\ : to take or spend a vacation — **va·ca·tion·er** \-sh(ə-)nər\ *n*

va·ca·tion·ist \vā-'kā-sh(ə-)nəst\ *n* : a person taking a vacation

va·ca·tion·land \vā-'kā-shən-ˌland\ *n* : a place where many people go on vacation

vac·ci·nate \'vak-sə-ˌnāt\ *vb* **-nat·ed; -nat·ing** : to inoculate (a person) with cowpox virus in order to produce immunity to smallpox; *also* : to give a vaccine to usually by injection — **vac·ci·na·tor** \-ˌnāt-ər\ *n*

vac·ci·na·tion \ˌvak-sə-'nā-shən\ *n* **1** : the act of vaccinating **2** : the scar left by vaccinating

vac·cine \vak-'sēn, 'vak-ˌsēn\ *n* **1** : a preparation containing the virus causing cowpox that is used for vaccination **2** : a preparation of killed, weakened, or fully infectious microbes that is given (as by injection) to produce or increase immunity to a particular disease

Word History Toward the end of the 18th century, Edward Jenner, an English physician, made an important discovery. He observed that dairymaids who had the disease cowpox did not get smallpox, a much more serious disease. Working from this observation, he injected a person with material taken from another person's cowpox sores. He found out that this injection protected that person against the dreaded smallpox. He reported these findings in an article in which he used the Latin translation of *cowpox*, *variolae vaccinae*. The Latin word *vaccinae* was formed from the adjective *vaccinus* meaning "of or relating to cows". This word, in turn, was based on the noun *vacca*, meaning "cow". The cowpox material used for injections was then called *vaccine*. The injection itself was called *vaccination*. From this noun we created the verb *vaccinate* and the noun *vaccinator*. [from Latin *vaccinus* (adjective) "of or from cows", from *vacca* "cow" — related to BUCKAROO, VAQUERO]

vac·il·late \'vas-ə-ˌlāt\ *vb* **-lat·ed; -lat·ing** : to hesitate between courses or opinions : be unable to choose — **vac·il·la·tion** \ˌvas-ə-'lā-shən\ *n* — **vac·il·la·tor** \'vas-ə-ˌlāt-ər\ *n*

va·cu·ity \va-'kyü-ət-ē, və-\ *n, pl* **-ities** **1** : an empty space **2** : the quality or state of being vacuous

vac·u·ole \'vak-yə-ˌwōl\ *n* : a cavity in bodily tissues or in the protoplasm of a single cell that is usually filled with fluid — **vac·u·o·lar** \ˌvak-yə-'wō-lər, -ˌlär\ *adj*

vac·u·ous \'vak-yə-wəs\ *adj* : lacking ideas or intelligence — **vac·u·ous·ly** *adv*

¹vac·u·um \'vak-yüm, -yü-əm, -yəm\ *n, pl* **vac·u·ums** *or* **vac·ua** \-yə-wə\ **1 a** : a space completely empty of matter **b** : a space from which most of the air has been removed (as by a pump) **2** : VACUUM CLEANER [from Latin *vacuum* "emptiness", from *vacuus* "empty"]

²vacuum *adj* : of, containing, producing, or using a partial vacuum ⟨the *vacuum* method of making coffee⟩

³vacuum *vb* : to use a vacuum cleaner on

vacuum bottle *n* : a cylindrical container with a vacuum between an inner and an outer wall used to keep liquids hot or cold — called also *thermos*

vacuum cleaner *n* : an electrical appliance for cleaning (as floors or rugs) by suction

vac·u·um–packed \ˌvak-yüm-'pakt, -yü-əm-, -yəm-\ *adj* : having much of the air removed before being sealed

vacuum pump *n* : a pump for removing gas from an enclosed space

vacuum tube *n* : an electron tube from which most of the air has been removed

¹vag·a·bond \'vag-ə-ˌbänd\ *adj* : moving from place to place without a fixed home [Middle English *vagabond* "moving about with no fixed home", from early French *vagabond* (same meaning), from Latin *vagabundus* (same meaning), from *vagari* "to wander about" — related to EXTRAVAGANT]

²vagabond *n* : a person who leads a vagabond life

va·ga·ry \'vā-gə-rē; və-'ge(ə)r-ē, -'ga(ə)r-\ *n, pl* **-ries** : an odd or unpredictable idea or happening

va·gi·na \və-'jī-nə\ *n, pl* **-nae** \-nē\ *or* **-nas** : a canal that leads from the uterus to the outside opening of the female sex organs — **vag·i·nal** \'vaj-ən-ᵊl\ *adj*

va·gran·cy \'vā-grən(t)-sē\ *n, pl* **-cies** : the state or action of being vagrant

¹va·grant \'vā-grənt\ *n* : a person who has no steady job and wanders from place to place

²vagrant *adj* **1** : wandering about from place to place **2** : having no fixed course ⟨*vagrant* breezes⟩

vague \'vāg\ *adj* **vagu·er; vagu·est** **1** : not clearly expressed ⟨a *vague* answer⟩ **2** : not clearly understood or sensed ⟨only a *vague* idea of where we were⟩ **3** : not clearly outlined : INDISTINCT, SHADOWY ⟨*vague* figures in the mist⟩ — **vague·ly** *adv* — **vague·ness** *n*

vain \'vān\ *adj* **1** : having no success : FUTILE ⟨a *vain* attempt to escape⟩ **2** : proud of one's looks or abilities — **vain·ly** *adv* — **vain·ness** *n* — **in vain** **1** : without success **2** : in an unholy way

vain·glo·ri·ous \(')vān-'glōr-ē-əs, -'glȯr-\ *adj* : being vain and boastful : showing vainglory — **vain·glo·ri·ous·ly**

adv — **vain·glo·ri·ous·ness** *n*

vain·glo·ry \'vān-ˌglōr-ē, -ˌglȯr-\ *n* : too much pride especially in what one has done

va·lance \'val-ən(t)s, 'val-\ *n* : a short drapery or wood or metal frame (as across the top of a window)

vale \'vā(ə)l\ *n* : VALLEY

vale·dic·to·ri·an \ˌval-ə-ˌdik-'tōr-ē-ən, -'tȯr-\ *n* : the student usually of the highest rank in a graduating class who gives the farewell speech at graduation ceremonies

vale·dic·to·ry \ˌval-ə-'dik-t(ə-)rē\ *adj* : of or relating to a leaving

va·lence \'vā-lən(t)s\ *n* : the combining power of an atom as shown by the number of electrons in its outermost energy level that are lost, gained, or shared in the formation of chemical bonds

valance

val·en·tine \'val-ən-ˌtīn\ *n* **1** : a sweetheart given something as a sign of affection on St. Valentine's Day **2** : a gift or greeting sent or given on St. Valentine's Day

Valentine Day *or* **Valentine's Day** *n* : SAINT VALENTINE'S DAY

va·let \'val-ā, va-'lā, 'val-ət\ *n* **1** : a male servant who takes care of a man's clothes and does personal services **2** : a hotel employee who does personal services for guests

Val·hal·la \val-'hal-ə\ *n* : the hall of Odin in Norse mythology to which the Valkyries take heroes killed in battle [derived from an early Norse word *Valhǫll*, literally "hall of the slain", from *valr* "those slain (in battle)" and *hǫll* "hall"]

¹**val·iant** \'val-yənt\ *adj* **1** : boldly brave **2** : done with courage : HEROIC — **val·iant·ly** *adv*

²**valiant** *n* : a valiant person

val·id \'val-əd\ *adj* **1** : legally binding **2** : founded on truth or fact — **val·id·ly** *adv*

val·i·date \'val-ə-ˌdāt\ *vb* **-dat·ed; -dat·ing** : to make valid — **val·i·da·tion** \ˌval-ə-'dā-shən\ *n*

va·lid·i·ty \və-'lid-ət-ē, va-\ *n* : the quality or state of being valid

va·lise \və-'lēs\ *n* : TRAVELING BAG

Val·kyr·ie \val-'kir-ē\ *n* : any of the maidens in Norse mythology who take slain heroes to Valhalla

val·ley \'val-ē\ *n, pl* **valleys** : an area of lowland between ranges of hills or mountains

val·or \'val-ər\ *n* : personal bravery in combat **syn** see COURAGE

val·or·ous \'val-ə-rəs\ *adj* : having or showing valor : BRAVE

¹**val·u·able** \'val-yə-(wə-)bəl\ *adj* **1** : worth a large amount of money **2** : of great use or service — **val·u·able·ness** *n* — **val·u·ably** \-blē\ *adv*

²**valuable** *n* : a possession (as a jewel) of great value — usually used in pl.

val·u·a·tion \ˌval-yə-'wā-shən\ *n* : the value placed on something

¹**val·ue** \'val-yü\ *n* **1** : a fair return in goods, services, or money for something exchanged **2** : the amount of money something is worth **3** : worth, utility, or importance in comparison with something else **4** : a numerical quantity that is assigned or is found by calculation or measurement **5** : the length of time a musical note is to be held **6** : the lightness or darkness of a color **7** : something (as a belief) that is valuable or desirable — **val·ue·less** \-yü-ləs, -yə-\ *adj*

²**value** *vb* **val·ued; valu·ing 1** : to estimate the worth of ⟨was *valued* at $200⟩ **2** : to think highly of ⟨*values* your advice⟩ — **valu·er** \-yə-wər\ *n*

value judgment *n* : a judgment assigning a value (as good or bad) to something

valve \'valv\ *n* **1** : a structure in a tube of the body (as a vein) that closes temporarily to prevent passage of material or that allows movement of a fluid in one direction only **2 a** : a mechanical device by which the flow of liquid, gas, or loose material in bulk may be controlled by a movable part; *also* : the movable part of such a device **b** : a device in a brass musical instrument for quickly changing the tube length in order to make the tone higher or lower **3** : one of the separate pieces that make up the shell of some animals (as clams) and are often hinged **4** : one of the pieces into which a ripe seed capsule or pod separates — **valved** \'valvd\ *adj*

val·vu·lar \'val-vyə-lər\ *adj* : of, relating to, or affecting a valve especially of the heart ⟨*valvular* heart disease⟩

vam·pire \'vam-ˌpī(ə)r\ *n* **1** : the body of a dead person believed to come from the grave at night and suck the blood of sleeping persons **2** : any of various bats of Mexico and Central and South America that feed on blood and are dangerous to human beings and domestic animals because they carry and pass on diseases (as rabies); *also* : any of several other bats that do not feed on blood but are sometimes said to do so

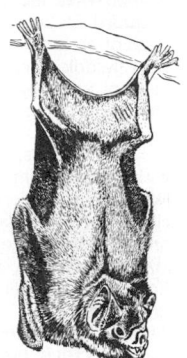

vampire 2

¹**van** \'van\ *n* : VANGUARD [a shortened form of *vanguard*]

²**van** *n* **1** : a usually closed wagon or truck for transporting goods or animals **2** : an enclosed motor vehicle shaped like a box that is used for a variety of purposes and has rear or side doors and side panels often with windows [a shortened form of *caravan* "vehicle"]

va·na·di·um \və-'nād-ē-əm\ *n* : a grayish metallic element found combined in minerals and used especially to form alloys (as of steel) — see ELEMENT table

Van Al·len belt \va-ˌnal-ən-, və-\ *n* : a belt of high-energy charged particles that surrounds the earth in the outer atmosphere [named for James A. *Van Allen* born 1914 American physicist]

van·dal \'van-dᵊl\ *n* **1** *cap* : a member of a Germanic people overrunning Gaul, Spain, and northern Africa in the fourth and fifth centuries A.D. **2** : a person who destroys or damages property on purpose

Word History The Vandals were a Germanic people who originally lived in northern Europe. In the fourth and fifth centuries, however, other barbarian peoples, especially the Huns, forced the Vandals to migrate westward and southward through what are now the lands of France and Spain. They finally settled in northern Africa. But as they migrated, the Vandals did not just pass through an area. They destroyed many cities and towns. They probably were no worse than other barbarians, but they became widely known for destruction. This probably happened because they invaded and looted the city of Rome in 455. They destroyed or ruined much of what they could not take with them. The Vandals were later defeated by the Roman army but their bad reputation caused their name to be used for "a deliberately destructive person". [from Latin *Vandalii* (plural) "The

\ə\ abut	\au̇\ out	\i\ tip	\ȯ\ saw	\u̇\ foot
\ər\ further	\ch\ chin	\ī\ life	\ȯi\ coin	\y\ yet
\a\ mat	\e\ pet	\j\ job	\th\ thin	\yü\ few
\ā\ take	\ē\ easy	\ŋ\ sing	\th\ this	\yu̇\ cure
\ä\ cot, cart	\g\ go	\ō\ bone	\ü\ food	\zh\ vision

Vandals"; of Germanic origin]

van·dal·ism \\'van-d^əl-ˌiz-əm\\ *n* : intentional destruction or damage to property

van·dal·ize \\'van-d^əl-ˌīz\\ *vb* **-ized; -iz·ing** : to destroy or damage property on purpose

Van de Graaff generator \\ˌvan-də-ˌgraf-\\ *n* : a generator of high voltages in which electric charges on a moving belt are transferred to a hollow sphere [named for Robert J. *Van de Graaff* 1901–1967 American physicist]

Van·dyke \\van-'dīk\\ *n* : a trim pointed beard

vane \\'vān\\ *n* **1** : a movable device attached to something high to show which way the wind is blowing **2** : a thin flat or curved object that is rotated about an axis by a flow of fluid (as air or water) or that rotates to cause a fluid to flow or that changes the direction of a flow of fluid ⟨the *vanes* of a windmill⟩ **3** : the web or flat expanded part of a feather — **vaned** \\'vānd\\ *adj*

van·guard \\'van-ˌgärd\\ *n* **1** : the troops moving at the head of an army **2** : FOREFRONT; *also* : those at the forefront [Middle English *vantgard* "the troops moving at the head of an army", from early French *avant-garde* (same meaning), derived from *avant-* "fore-, in front" and *garde* "guard"]

va·nil·la \\və-'nil-ə, -'nel-\\ *n* : a flavoring made from the long beanlike pods of a tropical American climbing orchid; *also* : this orchid or one of the same genus

van·ish \\'van-ish\\ *vb* : to pass from sight or existence — **van·ish·er** *n*

vanishing cream *n* : a cosmetic like cold cream but less greasy

vanishing point *n* : a point at which parallel lines seem to meet (as in a drawing)

van·i·ty \\'van-ət-ē\\ *n, pl* **-ties 1** : something that is vain **2** : the quality or fact of being vain **3 a** : ³COMPACT 1 **b** : DRESSING TABLE

vanilla: orchid and pods

van·quish \\'van-kwish, 'van-\\ *vb* : to defeat and gain control of completely **syn** *see* CONQUER — **van·quish·er** *n*

van·tage \\'vant-ij\\ *n* : a position giving advantage or a wide view

vantage point *n* : POINT OF VIEW

vap·id \\'vap-əd\\ *adj* : being dull or uninteresting — **vap·id·ly** *adv*

va·por \\'vā-pər\\ *n* **1** : fine particles of matter (as fog or smoke) floating in the air and clouding it **2** : a substance in the gaseous state

va·por·ize \\'vā-pə-ˌrīz\\ *vb* **-ized; -iz·ing** : to turn from a liquid or solid into vapor — **va·por·iza·tion** \\ˌvā-pə-rə-'zā-shən\\ *n*

va·por·iz·er \\'vā-pə-ˌrī-zər\\ *n* : a device that vaporizes something (as a liquid containing medicine)

vapour *chiefly British variant of* VAPOR

va·que·ro \\vä-'ke(ə)r-ō\\ *n, pl* **-ros** : a cowboy especially of Central or South America [from Spanish *vaquero* "cowboy", from *vaca* "cow", from Latin *vacca* "cow" — related to BUCKAROO, VACCINE; see *Word History* at VACCINE]

vari·abil·i·ty \\ˌver-ē-ə-'bil-ət-ē, ˌvar-\\ *n* : the quality or fact of being variable

¹**vari·able** \\'ver-ē-ə-bəl, 'var-\\ *adj* **1** : able to change : likely to be changed : CHANGEABLE ⟨winds light and *variable*⟩ **2** : having the characteristics of a variable **3** : not true to the usual or normal type : ABERRANT ⟨a *variable* species of wheat⟩ — **vari·able·ness** \\'ver-ē-ə-bəl-nəs, 'var-\\ *n* — **vari·ably** \\-blē\\ *adv*

²**variable** *n* **1 a** : a quantity that may take on any one of a

set of values **b** : a mathematical symbol representing a variable **2** : something that is variable

variable star *n* : a star whose brightness changes usually in more or less regular periods

vari·ance \\'ver-ē-ən(t)s, 'var-\\ *n* **1** : the quality or state of being variable or variant **2** : DISSENSION, DISPUTE **3** : the square of the standard deviation — **at variance** : not in harmony or agreement

¹**vari·ant** \\'ver-ē-ənt, 'var-\\ *adj* : differing from others of its kind or class

²**variant** *n* **1** : an individual that shows variation from a type **2** : one of two or more different spellings or pronunciations of the same word

vari·a·tion \\ˌver-ē-'ā-shən, ˌvar-\\ *n* **1 a** : a change in form, position, or condition **b** : amount of change or difference **2** : the repeating of a musical passage with a change in rhythm, tune, harmony, or key ⟨*variations* on a theme by Haydn⟩ **3 a** : change in the characteristics that are usual for a species or group **b** : an individual or group showing variation — **vari·a·tion·al** \\-shnəl, -shən-^əl\\ *adj*

vari·col·ored \\'ver-i-ˌkəl-ərd, 'var-\\ *adj* : having various colors ⟨*varicolored* marble⟩

var·i·cose \\'var-ə-ˌkōs\\ *adj* : abnormally swollen or made larger or wider ⟨*varicose* veins⟩

var·ied \\'ve(ə)r-ēd, 'va(ə)r-\\ *adj* **1** : having many forms or types : DIVERSE **2** : VARIEGATED 2 — **var·ied·ly** *adv*

var·ie·gat·ed \\'ver-ē-ə-ˌgāt-əd, 'ver-i-ˌgāt-, 'var-\\ *adj* **1** : having patches, stripes, or marks of different colors ⟨*variegated* flowers⟩ **2** : full of variety ⟨a *variegated* career⟩

va·ri·ety \\və-'rī-ət-ē\\ *n, pl* **-et·ies 1** : the quality or state of having different forms or types **2** : a number or collection of different things : ASSORTMENT **3 a** : something differing from others of the class to which it belongs **b** : any of various groups of plants or animals within a species that are separated from other groups by characteristics not constant enough or too unimportant to separate species

variety meat *n* : an edible part of a slaughter animal other than skeletal muscle

variety show *n* : entertainment made up of performances (as dances and songs) that follow one another and are not related

variety store *n* : a retail store that stocks a variety of goods

var·i·ous \\'ver-ē-əs, 'var-\\ *adj* **1** : of different kinds **2** : different one from another : UNLIKE ⟨animals as *various* as cat and mouse⟩ **3** : having many different characteristics ⟨spring is a *various* season⟩ **4** : made up of an indefinite number greater than one ⟨stopped at *various* places along the way⟩ — **var·i·ous·ly** *adv* — **var·i·ous·ness** *n*

var·let \\'vär-lət\\ *n* : RASCAL 1

var·mint \\'vär-mənt\\ *n* : an animal or bird that is considered a pest and is not protected by game laws

¹**var·nish** \\'vär-nish\\ *n* **1** : a liquid that when spread and allowed to dry on a surface forms a hard shiny typically transparent coating **b** : the covering or shiny coating given by varnish

²**varnish** *vb* : to cover with or as if with varnish

var·si·ty \\'vär-sət-ē, -stē\\ *n, pl* **-ties** : the main team representing a college, school, or club in contests [an altered form of *versity*, itself an old, shortened form of *university*]

varve \\'värv\\ *n* : a pair of layers of alternately finer and coarser silt or clay believed to be deposited annually in a body of still water

vary \\'ve(ə)r-ē, 'va(ə)r-\\ *vb* **var·ied; vary·ing 1** : to make a minor or partial change in **2** : to give variety to **3** : to show or undergo change **4 a** : to be different **b** : to change in bodily structure or function away from what is usual for members of a group — **vary·ing·ly** \\-iŋ-lē\\ *adv*

varying hare *n* : any of several hares (as a snowshoe rabbit) having white fur in winter

vas·cu·lar \'vas-kyə-lər\ *adj* : of or relating to a tube or channel for carrying a body fluid (as blood of an animal or sap of a plant) or to a system of such channels or tubes; *also* : supplied with or made up of such channels or tubes ⟨a *vascular* system⟩ ⟨*vascular* tissue⟩

vascular bundle *n* : a unit of the vascular system of a higher plant consisting usually of vessels and sieve tubes together with parenchyma cells and fibers — called also *fibrovascular bundle*

vascular plant *n* : a plant having a specialized system for carrying fluids that includes xylem and phloem

varying hare: *top* winter, *bottom* summer

vascular ray *n* : a band of tissue in a root or stem of a vascular plant that looks in cross section like a spoke of a wheel and that carries fluids along a radius away from the center of the root or stem

vas·cu·lum \'vas-kyə-ləm\ *n* : an often cylinder-shaped box usually of metal that is used for the temporary storage of plants collected in the field

vas def·er·ens \'vas-'def-ə-rənz, -,renz\ *n, pl* **va·sa def·er·en·tia** \,vä-zə-,def-ə-'ren-ch(ē-)ə\ : a bodily tube especially in a higher vertebrate that serves to carry sperm

vase \'vās, 'vāz\ *n* : an often round container of greater depth than width used chiefly for ornament or for flowers

Vas·e·line \'vas-ə-,lēn, ,vas-ə-'lēn\ *trademark* — used for petroleum jelly

vas·sal \'vas-əl\ *n* : a person in the Middle Ages who received protection and land from a lord in return for loyalty and service

vast \'vast\ *adj* : very great in extent, size, amount, degree, or intensity **syn** see ENORMOUS — **vast·ly** *adv* — **vast·ness** \'vas(t)-nəs\ *n*

vasty \'vas-tē\ *adj* **vast·i·er; -est** : VAST, IMMENSE

vat \'vat\ *n* : a large container (as a tub) especially for holding liquids in manufacturing processes

vaude·ville \'vȯd-(ə)-vəl, 'väd-, 'vōd-, -,vil\ *n* : theatrical entertainment made up of a variety of songs, dances, and comic acts

Word History In the 15th century, a number of humorous songs became popular in France. The songs were said to have been written by a man who lived in the valley of the river Vire, which is located in northwest France. The songs became known as *chansons de vau de Vire,* meaning "songs of the valley of Vire". Other people were soon writing and performing similar songs. Before long, people no longer connected such songs with the valley of Vire. The name *chansons de vau de Vire* was shortened to one word, *vaudevire.* Further changes in spelling and pronunciation have given us the modern word *vaudeville,* which refers not only to humorous songs, but also to other forms of popular entertainment. [from French *vaudeville* "a humorous song or skit", derived from early French *vaudevire* "a song that makes fun of something", from *chansons de vau de Vire* "songs of the valley of Vire"]

¹vault \'vȯlt\ *n* **1 a** : an arched structure of stone or concrete forming a ceiling or roof **b** : an arch or dome suggesting a vault ⟨the *vault* of the sky⟩ **2** : a room or compartment for storage or safekeeping ⟨a bank *vault*⟩ **3** : a burial chamber

²vault *vb* : to leap or leap over with the aid of the hands or a pole — **vault·er** *n*

³vault *n* : an act of vaulting : LEAP

vaunt·ed \'vȯnt-əd, 'vänt-\ *adj* : much praised or boasted of

VCR \,vē-(,)sē-'är\ *n* : a device for recording (as television programs) on videocassettes and playing them back [*videocassette recorder*]

¹vault 1a

've \v, əv\ *vb* : HAVE ⟨we've been there⟩

veal \'vē(ə)l\ *n* : a young calf or its flesh for use as meat

vec·tor \'vek-tər\ *n* **1** : a quantity that has magnitude and direction and that is usually represented by a line segment with the given direction and with a length representing the magnitude **2** : an organism (as an insect) that carries and passes on a disease-causing microbe

vee·jay \'vē-,jā\ *n* : an announcer of a program (as on television) that features music videos

veer \'vi(ə)r\ *vb* : to change direction or course — **veer** *n*

veg·an \'vej-ən, -,an; 'vē-gən\ *n* : a strict vegetarian; *esp* : one who does not use animals or dairy products for food

¹veg·e·ta·ble \'vej-tə-bəl, 'vej-ət-ə-bəl\ *adj* **1** : of, relating to, consisting of, or growing like plants ⟨*vegetable* growth⟩ **2** : made of or obtained from plants ⟨*vegetable* oils⟩

²vegetable *n* **1** : ²PLANT 1 **2** : a leafy plant (as a cabbage, bean, or potato) usually without woody tissue grown for an edible part that is usually eaten as part of a meal; *also* : such an edible part

¹veg·e·tar·i·an \,vej-ə-'ter-ē-ən\ *n* **1** : a person who lives on a diet made up of vegetables, fruits, grains, nuts, and sometimes animal products (as milk and cheese) **2** : HERBIVORE

²vegetarian *adj* **1** : of or relating to vegetarians **2** : consisting wholly of vegetables ⟨a *vegetarian* diet⟩

veg·e·tar·i·an·ism \,vej-ə-'ter-ē-ə-,niz-əm\ *n* : the theory and practice of living on a vegetarian diet

veg·e·tate \'vej-ə-,tāt\ *vb* **-tat·ed; -tat·ing** **1** : to live or grow in the manner of a plant **2** : to lead a lazy life by doing little but eating and growing

veg·e·ta·tion \,vej-ə-'tā-shən\ *n* **1** : the act or process of vegetating **2** : an inactive way of life **3** : plant life or cover (as of an area)

veg·e·ta·tive \'vej-ə-,tāt-iv\ *adj* **1** : of, relating to, or functioning in nutrition and growth rather than reproduction **2** : of, relating to, or involving reproduction by other than sexual means — **veg·e·ta·tive·ly** *adv*

veg·gie \'vej-ē\ *n* : VEGETABLE

ve·he·mence \'vē-ə-mən(t)s\ *n* : the quality or state of being vehement

ve·he·ment \'vē-ə-mənt\ *adj* **1** : showing great force or energy **2** : highly emotional — **ve·he·ment·ly** *adv*

ve·hi·cle \'vē-,(h)ik-əl, 'vē-ə-kəl\ *n* **1** : a means by which something is passed along, expressed, achieved, or shown **2** : something used to transport persons or goods ⟨space *vehicle*⟩

ve·hic·u·lar \vē-'hik-yə-lər\ *adj* : of, relating to, or designed for vehicles

¹veil \'vā(ə)l\ *n* **1** : a piece of cloth or net worn usually by women over the head and shoulders and sometimes over the face **2** : something that covers or hides like a veil

²veil *vb* : to cover with or as if with a veil

vein \'vān\ *n* **1** : a long narrow opening in rock filled with mineral matter ⟨a *vein* of gold⟩ **2 a** : one of the blood vessels that carry blood from the capillaries back to the

\ə\ **abut**		\au̇\ **out**		\i\ tip		\ȯ\ **saw**	\u̇\ **foot**
\ər\ **further**		\ch\ **chin**		\ī\ life		\ȯi\ **coin**	\y\ **yet**
\a\ **mat**		\e\ **pet**		\j\ **job**		\th\ **thin**	\yü\ **few**
\ā\ **take**		\ē\ **easy**		\ŋ\ **sing**		\t̲h̲\ **this**	\yu̇\ **cure**
\ä\ **cot, cart**		\g\ **go**		\ō\ **bone**		\ü\ **food**	\zh\ **vision**

heart   **b** : one of the vascular bundles forming the frame-work of a leaf   **c** : one of the thickened ribs that stiffen the wings of an insect   **3** : a wavy band or streak (as of a different color or texture) ⟨a marble with greenish *veins*⟩   **4** : a style of expression

veined \'vānd\ *adj* : marked with or as if with veins : having venation

vein·ing \'vā-niŋ\ *n* : a pattern of veins : VENATION

Vel·cro \'vel-krō\ *trademark* — used for a nylon fabric that can be fastened to itself

veld *or* **veldt** \'felt, 'velt\ *n* : an area of grassy land with few trees or shrubs especially in southern Africa

vel·lum \'vel-əm\ *n*   **1** : a fine-grained lambskin, kidskin, or calfskin prepared especially for writing on or for binding books   **2** : a strong cream-colored paper resembling vellum — **vellum** *adj*

ve·loc·i·pede \və-'läs-ə-,pēd\ *n* : ¹BICYCLE — used especially of early forms

ve·loc·i·ty \və-'läs-ət-ē, -'läs-tē\ *n, pl* **-ties**   **1** : quickness of motion : SPEED   **2** : the rate of change of position along a straight line with respect to time   **3** : rate of occurrence or action

ve·lour \və-'lù(ə)r\ *n* : a fabric resembling velvet

vel·vet \'vel-vət\ *n*   **1** : a fabric with short soft raised fibers   **2** : the soft skin covering the developing antler of a deer — **velvet** *adj*

vel·ve·teen \,vel-və-'tēn\ *n* : a fabric resembling velvet

vel·vety \'vel-vət-ē\ *adj* : soft and smooth like velvet

ve·na ca·va \,vē-nə-'kā-və\ *n, pl* **ve·nae ca·vae** \,vē-ni-'kā-vē\ : one of the large veins by which the blood is re-turned to the right atrium of the heart in an air-breathing vertebrate

ve·nal \'vēn-ᵊl\ *adj* : ready to take or influenced by bribes : CORRUPT — **ve·nal·i·ty** \vi-'nal-ət-ē\ *n* — **ve·nal·ly** \'vēn-ᵊl-ē\ *adv*

ve·na·tion \ve-'nā-shən, vē-\ *n* : an arrangement or system of veins ⟨the *venation* of the hand⟩ ⟨the *venation* of a leaf⟩

vend \'vend\ *vb* : to offer for sale (as in a vending machine) : SELL — **vend·er** *n*

ven·det·ta \ven-'det-ə\ *n* : a feud in which the relatives of a murdered person try to kill the murderer or the murderer's relatives

venation

vending machine *n* : a machine from which one may get merchandise after putting in coins

ven·dor \'ven-dər\ *n* : one that sells : SELLER

¹ve·neer \və-'ni(ə)r\ *n*   **1** : a thin layer of wood bonded to other wood usually to provide a finer surface or a stronger structure   **2** : a protective or ornamental facing (as of brick)

²veneer *vb* : to cover with a veneer

ven·er·a·ble \'ven-ər-(ə-)bəl, 'ven-rə-bəl\ *adj*   **1** : deserving to be venerated — often used as a religious title   **2** : deserving honor or respect   **3** : very old

ven·er·ate \'ven-ə-,rāt\ *vb* **-at·ed; -at·ing** : to show deep respect for

ven·er·a·tion \,ven-ə-'rā-shən\ *n*   **1** : the act of venerating : the state of being venerated   **2** : a feeling of deep respect

ve·ne·re·al \və-'nir-ē-əl\ *adj* : of or relating to sexual intercourse or to diseases that are passed from person to person by it ⟨a *venereal* infection⟩

venereal disease *n* : a contagious disease (as gonorrhea or syphilis) that is usually acquired by having sexual intercourse with someone who already has it

Ve·ne·tian \və-'nē-shən\ *adj* : of, relating to, or characteristic of Venice or its people — **Venetian** *n*

ve·ne·tian blind \və-,nē-shən-\ *n* : a blind having thin horizontal slats that can be adjusted to keep out light or to let light come in between them

ven·geance \'ven-jən(t)s\ *n* : punishment given in return for an injury or offense

venge·ful \'venj-fəl\ *adj* : wanting revenge — **venge·ful·ly** \-fə-lē\ *adv* — **venge·ful·ness** *n*

ve·nial \'vē-nē-əl, -nyəl\ *adj* : not being a serious offense : FORGIVABLE ⟨a *venial* sin⟩

ven·i·son \'ven-ə-sən *also* -ə-zən\ *n* : the flesh of a deer used as food [Middle English *venison* "the flesh of a game animal hunted for food", from early French *veneison* "hunting, animals hunted", from Latin *venation-, venatio*, past participle of *venari* "to hunt"]

Venn diagram \'ven-\ *n* : a diagram using circles or ellipses to represent relations between and operations on sets

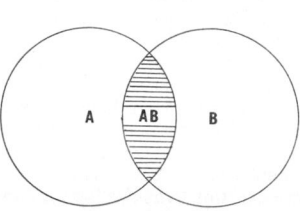

Venn diagram: *AB* represents the intersection of sets *A* and *B*

ven·om \'ven-əm\ *n*   **1** : poison produced by an animal (as a snake, scorpion, or bee) and passed to a victim usually by biting or stinging   **2** : ¹SPITE, MALICE

ven·om·ous \'ven-ə-məs\ *adj* : having or producing venom ⟨*venomous* snakes⟩ — **ven·om·ous·ly** *adv*

ve·nous \'vē-nəs\ *adj*   **1** : of, relating to, or full of veins ⟨a *venous* rock⟩   **2** : being blood which has passed through the capillaries, given up oxygen to the tissues, and become loaded with carbon dioxide

¹vent \'vent\ *vb*   **1 a** : to provide with an outlet   **b** : to serve as an outlet for ⟨chimneys *vent* smoke⟩   **2** : to give expression to

²vent *n*   **1** : OUTLET 1, 2   **2** : an opening (as a flue) for the escape of a gas or liquid or for the relief of pressure

³vent *n* : an opening in the lower part of a seam (as of a jacket or skirt)

ven·ti·late \'vent-ᵊl-,āt\ *vb* **-lat·ed; -lat·ing**   **1** : to discuss freely and openly   **2 a** : to expose to air and especially to a current of fresh air   **b** : to provide with ventilation

ven·ti·la·tion \,vent-ᵊl-'ā-shən\ *n*   **1** : the act or process of ventilating   **2** : a system or means of providing fresh air

ven·ti·la·tor \'vent-ᵊl-,āt-ər\ *n* : a device for letting in fresh air or driving out bad or stale air

ven·tral \'ven-trəl\ *adj*   **1** : of or relating to the belly : ABDOMINAL   **2** : of or relating to or located on or near the surface of the body that in human beings is the front but in most other animals is the lower surface ⟨a fish's *ventral* fins⟩ — **ven·tral·ly** \-trə-lē\ *adv*

ven·tri·cle \'ven-tri-kəl\ *n*   **1** : a chamber of the heart which receives blood from an atrium and from which blood is forced into the arteries   **2** : one of the cavities in the brain that are continuous with the central canal of the spinal cord

ven·tril·o·quist \ven-'tril-ə-kwəst\ *n* : a person skilled in speaking in such a way that the voice seems to come from a source other than the speaker [from Latin *ventriloquus* "ventriloquist", from *ventr-, venter* "stomach, belly" and *loqui* "to speak"; so called from the early belief that the voice is produced in the ventroloquist's stomach] — **ven·tril·o·quism** \-,kwiz-əm\ *n*

¹ven·ture \'ven-chər\ *vb* **ven·tured; ven·tur·ing** \'vench-(ə-)riŋ\   **1** : to expose to risk   **2** : to face the risks and dangers of   **3** : to offer at the risk of being criticized ⟨*venture* an opinion⟩ ⟨*venture* to disagree⟩   **4** : to go ahead in spite of danger — **ven·tur·er** \'vench-(ə-)rər\ *n*

²**venture** *n* : an undertaking involving chance, risk, or danger; *esp* : a speculative business enterprise

ven·ture·some \'ven-chər-səm\ *adj* **1** : tending to take risks **2** : involving risk : RISKY, DANGEROUS **syn** see ADVENTUROUS — **ven·ture·some·ness** *n*

ven·tur·ous \'vench-(ə-)rəs\ *adj* : VENTURESOME

ven·ue \'ven-,yü\ *n* : the place in which a trial is held

ve·nule \'ven-yü(ə)l, 'vēn-\ *n* : a small vein; *esp* : one of the minute veins connecting blood capillaries with larger veins

Ve·nus \'vē-nəs\ *n* : the planet second in order from the sun — see PLANET table

Ve·nus's–flower–basket \,vē-nəs(-əz)-\ *or* **Venus flower basket** *n* : a tube-shaped sponge with a delicate glassy silica-containing skeleton

Ve·nus's–fly·trap \,vē-nəs(-əz)-'flī-,trap\ *or* **Venus flytrap** *n* : an insect-eating plant that grows along the Carolina coast and has the tip of each leaf formed into an insect trap

Venus's-flytrap

ve·ra·cious \və-'rā-shəs\ *adj* **1** : telling the truth : TRUTHFUL, HONEST **2** : being truthful or accurate — **ve·ra·cious·ly** *adv*

ve·rac·i·ty \və-'ras-ət-ē\ *n, pl* **-ties** **1** : devotion to the truth : TRUTHFULNESS **2** : agreement with truth or fact

ve·ran·da *or* **ve·ran·dah** \və-'ran-də\ *n* : a long open porch usually with a roof

verb \'vərb\ *n* : a word that is usually the grammatical center of a predicate and expresses an act, occurrence, or state of being and that in various languages is inflected (as for agreement with the subject or for tense)

¹**ver·bal** \'vər-bəl\ *adj* **1** : of, relating to, or consisting of words **2** : of, relating to, or formed from a verb ⟨a *verbal* adjective⟩ **3** : spoken rather than written ⟨a *verbal* agreement⟩ **syn** see ORAL — **ver·bal·ly** \-bə-lē\ *adv*

²**verbal** *n* : a word that combines characteristics of a verb with those of a noun or adjective

ver·bal·ize \'vər-bə-,līz\ *vb* **-ized; -iz·ing** : to express in words

verbal noun *n* : a noun derived directly from a verb or verb stem

ver·ba·tim \(,)vər-'bāt-əm\ *adv or adj* : in the same words : word for word

ver·be·na \(,)vər-'bē-nə\ *n* : any of a genus of numerous plants including some that are often grown in gardens for their showy spikes of white, pink, red, or blue flowers

ver·bi·age \'vər-bē-ij\ *n* : many words and especially many hard words used to say very little

ver·bose \(,)vər-'bōs\ *adj* : using more words than are needed — **ver·bose·ly** *adv* — **ver·bose·ness** *n* — **ver·bos·i·ty** \-'bäs-ət-ē\ *n*

verb phrase *n* : a verb consisting of a past or present participle preceded by one or more helping verbs

ver·dant \'vərd-ᵊnt\ *adj* : green with growing plants ⟨*verdant* fields⟩ — **ver·dant·ly** *adv*

ver·dict \'vər-(,)dikt\ *n* **1** : the decision reached by a jury **2** : JUDGMENT 3b, OPINION [an altered form of Middle English *verdit* "a decision by a jury", derived from early French *ver* "true" and *dit* "saying, formal pronouncement"; *ver* from Latin *verus* "true" and *dit* from Latin *dictum* "formal pronouncement", derived from *dicere* "to say" — related to DICTATE, VERIFY, VERY]

ver·dure \'vər-jər\ *n* : green vegetation

¹**verge** \'vərj\ *n* : something that borders, limits, or bounds : EDGE ⟨walking on the grassy *verge* at the side of a country road⟩ **2** : BRINK 2, THRESHOLD ⟨the company was on the *verge* of bankruptcy⟩

²**verge** *vb* **verged; verg·ing** : to come near to being ⟨misconduct *verging* on treason⟩

verg·er \'vər-jər\ *n* : a minor church official

verier *comparative of* VERY

veriest *superlative of* VERY

ver·i·fi·able \'ver-ə-,fī-ə-bəl\ *adj* : able to be verified — **ver·i·fi·ably** \-blē\ *adv*

ver·i·fi·ca·tion \,ver-ə-fə-'kā-shən\ *n* : the act or process of verifying : the state of being verified

ver·i·fy \'ver-ə-,fī\ *vb* **-fied; -fy·ing** **1** : to prove to be true or correct : CONFIRM **2** : to check or test the accuracy of [Middle English *verifien* "to establish the truth of", from early French *verifier* (same meaning), from Latin *verificare* (same meaning), from earlier *verus* "true" — related to VERDICT, VERY] — **ver·i·fi·er** \-,fī(-ə)r\ *n*

ver·i·ly \'ver-ə-lē\ *adv* : in fact : CERTAINLY

veri·si·mil·i·tude \,ver-ə-sə-'mil-ə-,t(y)üd\ *n* : the appearance of being true or real

ver·i·ta·ble \'ver-ət-ə-bəl\ *adj* : ACTUAL, TRUE — **ver·i·ta·bly** \-blē\ *adv*

ver·i·ty \'ver-ət-ē\ *n, pl* **-ties** **1** : the quality or state of being true or real **2** : a statement or thing that is true : FACT **3** : VERACITY 1, HONESTY

ver·mi·cel·li \,vər-mə-'chel-ē, -'sel-\ *n* : a pasta that is thinner than spaghetti [from Italian *vermicelli* "pasta similar to but thinner than spaghetti", literally "little worms", from *verme* "worm", from Latin *vermis* "worm" — related to VERMIN; see *Word History* at VERMIN]

ver·mic·u·lite \(,)vər-'mik-yə-,līt\ *n* : any of various minerals that result usually from the expansion of small grains of mica at high temperatures to give a lightweight highly water-absorbent material

ver·mi·form appendix \'vər-mə-,fôrm-\ *n* : the appendix of the intestine

ver·mil·ion *or* **ver·mil·lion** \vər-'mil-yən\ *n* : a bright reddish orange

ver·min \'vər-mən\ *n, pl* **vermin** : small common harmful or objectionable animals (as fleas or mice) that are difficult to get rid of

> **Word History** The word *vermin* is used for any small harmful or annoying insect or animal that is difficult to get rid of or control. Fleas, lice, mice, rats, and even rabbits when they destroy gardens have been called vermin. However, the word *vermin* comes from a Latin word for a creature that is not usually thought of as troublesome. The word is *vermis*, meaning "worm". The word *vermicelli*, which English borrowed from Italian, can also be traced back to Latin *vermis*. The Italians used this word for "thin spaghetti" because the strands look like "little worms", which is what *vermicelli* means literally. [Middle English *vermin* "small animal pests", from early French *vermin* (same meaning), derived from Latin *vermis* "worm" — related to VERMICELLI]

ver·mouth \vər-'müth\ *n* : a wine flavored with herbs

¹**ver·nac·u·lar** \və(r)-'nak-yə-lər\ *adj* : of, relating to, or using ordinary especially spoken language

²**vernacular** *n* **1** : ordinary spoken language rather than literary language **2** : a common name of a plant or animal in contrast to its taxonomic name

ver·nal \'vərn-ᵊl\ *adj* : of, relating to, or occurring in the spring ⟨the *vernal* equinox⟩

ver·ni·er \'vər-nē-ər\ *n* : a short scale made to slide along the divisions of an instrument marked for measuring or indicating parts of divisions

vernier caliper *n* : a measuring device that consists of a

\ə\ abut	\aů\ out	\i\ tip	\ȯ\ saw	\ů\ foot
\ər\ further	\ch\ chin	\ī\ life	\ȯi\ coin	\y\ yet
\a\ mat	\e\ pet	\j\ job	\th\ thin	\yü\ few
\ā\ take	\ē\ easy	\ŋ\ sing	\th\ this	\yů\ cure
\ä\ cot, cart	\g\ go	\ō\ bone	\ü\ food	\zh\ vision

main scale with a fixed jaw and a sliding jaw with an attached vernier

ver·sa·tile \'vər-sət-ºl\ *adj* : able to do many different kinds of things [from French *versatile* or Latin *versatilis,* both meaning "versatile, able to change", derived from Latin *versari* "to turn, change, reside (in a place)", from *vertere* "to turn" — related to CONVERSE, REVERSE, UNIVERSE, VERTICAL, VICE VERSA] — **ver·sa·til·i·ty** \,vər-sə-'til-ət-ē\ *n*

verse \'vərs\ *n* **1** : a line of writing in which words are arranged in a rhythmic pattern **2** : writing in which words are arranged in a rhythmic pattern **3** : STANZA **4** : one of the short parts of a chapter of the Bible

versed \'vərst\ *adj* : having knowledge or skill as a result of experience, study, or skill

ver·si·fi·ca·tion \,vər-sə-fə-'kā-shən\ *n* : the making of verses

ver·si·fy \'vər-sə-,fī\ *vb* **-fied; -fy·ing** : to write or turn into verse — **ver·si·fi·er** \-,fī(-ə)r\ *n*

ver·sion \'vər-zhən\ *n* **1** : a translation especially of the Bible ⟨the Douay *version*⟩ ⟨the King James *version*⟩ **2** : an account or description from one point of view ⟨your *version* of what happened⟩

ver·sus \'vər-səs, -səz\ *prep* : AGAINST 2a

ver·te·bra \'vərt-ə-brə\ *n, pl* **-brae** \-,brā, -brē, -brə\ *or* **-bras** : one of the sections of bone or cartilage that make up the spinal column

ver·te·bral \(,)vər-'tē-brəl, 'vərt-ə-\ *adj* : of, relating to, or made up of vertebrae : SPINAL

vertebral column *n* : BACKBONE 1

¹ver·te·brate \'vərt-ə-brət, -,brāt\ *adj* **1** : having a spinal column **2** : of or relating to the vertebrates

²vertebrate *n* : any of a group of chordate animals with a spinal column (as in mammals, birds, reptiles, amphibians, and fishes) divided into sections or a notochord (as in the lamprey) remaining in the adult and with a tubular nervous system arranged along the back and divided into a brain and spinal cord

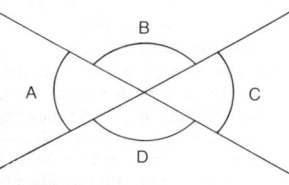

vertebra

ver·tex \'vər-,teks\ *n, pl* **ver·ti·ces** \'vərt-ə-,sēz\ *also* **ver·tex·es** \-əz\ **1** : the point of a figure that is opposite to and farthest from its base **2** : the common endpoint of the sides of an angle or of three or more edges of a polyhedron (as a cube)

¹ver·ti·cal \'vərt-i-kəl\ *adj* **1** : directly overhead **2** : going straight up or down from a level surface **3** : of or relating to persons of higher or lower standing ⟨a *vertical* social order⟩ [from early French *vertical* or Latin *verticalis,* both meaning "relating to a vertex, at the highest point overhead", from earlier Latin *vertic-, vertex* "top, highest point, pole (turning point), whirl", from *vertere* "to turn" — related to CONVERSE, REVERSE, UNIVERSE, VERSATILE] — **ver·ti·cal·ly** \-k(ə-)lē\ *adv*

²vertical *n* **1** : something (as a line or plane) that is vertical **2** : a vertical direction

vertical angle *n* : either of a pair of angles that have the same vertex and are on opposite sides of two intersecting straight lines — called also *opposite angle*

vertical file *n* : a collection especially of pamphlets maintained (as in a library) for reference

vertical angle: *A, C* and *B, D* are vertical angles

ver·ti·go \'vərt-i-,gō\ *n, pl* **-goes** *or* **-gos** : a dizzy state

verve \'vərv\ *n* : lively enthusiasm

¹very \'ver-ē\ *adj* **ver·i·er; -est** **1** : being actual or real **2 a** : ²EXACT 1, PRECISE ⟨*very* heart of the city⟩ **b** : exactly suitable or necessary ⟨the *very* thing for the purpose⟩ **3** : ²MERE, BARE ⟨the *very* thought terrified them⟩ **4** : exactly the same ⟨the *very* one I saw yesterday⟩ [Middle English *verray, verry* "true, real", from early French *verai* (same meaning), derived from Latin *verus* "true" — related to VERDICT, VERIFY]

²very *adv* **1** : to a great degree : EXTREMELY ⟨a *very* hot day⟩ **2** : in actual fact : TRULY ⟨told the *very* same story⟩

very high frequency *n* : a radio frequency in the range between 30 and 300 megahertz — abbr. VHF

ves·i·cle \'ves-i-kəl\ *n* : a small cavity, cyst, or blister usually filled with fluid

ves·per \'ves-pər\ *n, archaic* : EVENING 1

ves·pers \'ves-pərz\ *n pl, often cap* : a late afternoon or evening church service

ves·sel \'ves-əl\ *n* **1** : a hollow utensil (as a cup or bowl) for holding something **2** : a craft bigger than a rowboat for navigation of the water; *esp* : ¹SHIP 1 **3** : a tube or canal (as a vein or artery) in which a body fluid is contained and carried or circulated

¹vest \'vest\ *vb* **1** : to place or give into the possession or control of some person or authority **2** : to clothe in vestments [Middle English *vesten* "to give into the possession or control of someone", from early French *vestir* "to dress with clothes, to give power or authority to", from Latin *vestire* "to clothe", from *vestis* "clothing, garment"]

²vest *n* **1** : a sleeveless garment usually worn under a suit coat **2** : a protective garment (as a life preserver) that reaches to the waist **3** : a knitted undershirt for women [from French *veste* "robe, garment", from Italian *veste* (same meaning), from Latin *vestis* "clothing, garment"]

ves·ti·bule \'ves-tə-,byü(ə)l\ *n* : a hall or room between the outer door and the inside part of a building

ves·tige \'ves-tij\ *n* **1** : a tiny amount or visible sign of something lost or vanished : TRACE **2** : a small and imperfectly developed bodily part or organ that is the remains of one that was more fully developed in an earlier stage of the individual, in a past generation, or in a closely related form [from French *vestige* "sign of something vanished or lost", from Latin *vestigium* "footprint" — related to INVESTIGATE] — **ves·ti·gial** \ve-'stij-(ē-)əl\ *adj*

vest·ment \'ves(t)-mənt\ *n* : an outer garment especially for wear during ceremonies or by an official

ves·try \'ves-trē\ *n, pl* **vestries** : a room in a church building for sacred furnishings (as vestments)

¹vet \'vet\ *n* : VETERINARIAN, VETERINARY

²vet *n* : VETERAN

vetch \'vech\ *n* : any of a genus of twining herbs that are legumes related to the peas and include plants used to feed domestic animals and to build soil

vet·er·an \'vet-ə-rən, 've-trən\ *n* **1** : a person who has had long experience (as in politics) **2** : a former member of the armed forces especially during wartime — **veteran** *adj*

Veterans Day *n* : November 11 observed as a legal holiday in the U.S. in honor of the veterans of U.S. wars

vet·er·i·nar·i·an \,vet-ə-rən-'er-ē-ən, ,ve-trən-, ,vet-ºn-\ *n* : a person who is qualified and has been given the authority to treat diseases and injuries of animals

¹vet·er·i·nary \'vet-ə-rən-,er-ē, 've-trən-, 'vet-ºn-\ *adj* : of, relating to, or being the medical care of animals ⟨*veterinary* medicine⟩

²veterinary *n, pl* **-naries** : VETERINARIAN

¹ve·to \'vēt-ō\ *n, pl* **vetoes** **1** : a forbidding of something by a person in authority **2 a** : the power of the head of a government to prevent a bill passed by a legislature from becoming law **b** : the use of such authority [from Latin *veto* "I forbid", from *vetare* "to forbid"]

²veto *vb* : PROHIBIT 1; *esp* : to use one's power of veto — **ve·to·er** \-ˌō(-ə)r\ *n*

vex \'veks\ *vb* **vexed** *also* **vext; vex·ing** 1 : to bring trouble, distress, or worry to 2 : to annoy continually with little irritations

vex·a·tion \vek-'sā-shən\ *n* 1 : the quality or state of being vexed : IRRITATION 2 : the act of vexing : ANNOYANCE 3 : a cause of trouble or worry

vex·a·tious \vek-'sā-shəs\ *adj* : causing vexation : ANNOYING, DISTRESSING — **vex·a·tious·ly** *adv* — **vex·a·tiousness** *n*

via \ˌvī-ə, ˌvē-ə\ *prep* : by way of

vi·a·ble \'vī-ə-bəl\ *adj* 1 : capable of living; *esp* : capable of surviving outside the mother's womb ⟨a *viable* human fetus⟩ 2 : capable of growing or developing ⟨*viable* seeds⟩ ⟨*viable* eggs⟩ 3 a : capable of being put into practice : WORKABLE ⟨a *viable* solution to the problem⟩ b : capable of succeeding ⟨a *viable* candidate⟩ — **vi·a·bil·i·ty** \ˌvī-ə-'bil-ət-ē\ *n*

via·duct \'vī-ə-ˌdəkt\ *n* : a bridge for carrying a road or railroad over something (as a gorge or a highway)

vi·al \'vī-(ə)l\ *n* : a small container (as for medicines) made usually of glass or plastic

viaduct

vi·and \'vī-ənd\ *n* 1 : an article of food 2 *pl* : food supplies

vi·at·i·cum \vī-'at-i-kəm, vē-\ *n, pl* **-cums** *or* **-ca** \-kə\ 1 : Communion given to a person in danger of death 2 : money or supplies for a journey

vibes \'vībz\ *n pl* 1 : VIBRAPHONE 2 *slang* : VIBRATION 3

vi·bran·cy \'vī-brən-sē\ *n* : the quality or state of being vibrant

vi·brant \'vī-brənt\ *adj* 1 a : vibrating rapidly b : having or giving a sense of life, vigor, or activity ⟨a *vibrant* personality⟩ 2 : sounding as a result of vibration : RESONANT — **vi·brant·ly** *adv*

vi·bra·phone \'vī-brə-ˌfōn\ *n* : a musical instrument resembling the xylophone but having metal bars and devices for increasing the vibrations — **vi·bra·phon·ist** \-ˌfō-nəst\ *n*

vi·brate \'vī-ˌbrāt\ *vb* **vi·brat·ed; vi·brat·ing** : to move or cause to move back and forth or from side to side

vi·bra·tion \vī-'brā-shən\ *n* 1 a : a rapid motion of the particles of an elastic body or substance back and forth (as when a stretched cord produces a musical tone or molecules in the air transmit sounds to the ear) b : the action of vibrating : the state of being vibrated 2 : a trembling motion ⟨*vibration* of a house caused by a passing truck⟩ 3 *pl* : a feeling or impression that someone or something gives off ⟨good *vibrations*⟩ — **vi·bra·tion·al** \-shnəl, -shən-ᵊl\ *adj*

vibraphone

vi·bra·to \vi-'brät-ō, vī-\ *n, pl* **-tos** : a slightly trembling effect given to vocal or instrumental tone by slight and rapid variations in pitch

vi·bra·tor \'vī-ˌbrāt-ər\ *n* : one that vibrates or causes vibration

vi·bra·to·ry \'vī-brə-ˌtōr-ē, -ˌtȯr-\ *adj* : consisting of, capable of, or causing vibration

vi·bur·num \vī-'bər-nəm\ *n* : any of a genus of widely distributed shrubs or trees that are related to the honey-suckles and have simple leaves and white or rarely pink flowers in broad clusters

vic·ar \'vik-ər\ *n* 1 : a minister in charge of a church who serves under the authority of another minister 2 : a church official who takes the place of or represents a higher official

vic·ar·age \'vik-(ə)rij\ *n* : a vicar's home

vi·car·i·ous \vī-'ker-ē-əs, və-, -'kar-\ *adj* 1 : serving or acting for another 2 : done or suffered for the benefit of someone else ⟨*vicarious* sacrifice⟩ 3 : sharing in someone else's experience through the use of the imagination or sympathetic feelings — **vi·car·i·ous·ly** *adv* — **vi·car·i·ous·ness** *n*

vice \'vīs\ *n* 1 a : evil conduct or habits : WICKEDNESS b : a moral fault or weakness ⟨thought gambling was a *vice*⟩ 2 : an unimportant fault ⟨eating too much is my *vice*⟩ 3 : behavior that is unwanted in a domestic animal (as pulling out feathers by a bird) **syn** see OFFENSE

vice- \(')vīs, ˌvīs\ *prefix* : one that takes the place of [derived from Latin *vice,* a form of *vicis* "a change, another's place or role or job"]

vice admiral *n* : a naval commissioned officer with a rank just below that of admiral

vice presidency *n* : the office of vice president

vice president *n* : an official whose rank is next below that of the president and who takes the place of the president when necessary

vice·re·gal \(')vīs-'rē-gəl\ *adj* : of or relating to a viceroy or viceroyalty — **vice·re·gal·ly** \-gə-lē\ *adv*

vice·roy \'vīs-ˌrȯi\ *n* 1 : the governor of a country or province who represents the sovereign 2 : a showy American butterfly resembling but smaller than the monarch

vi·ce ver·sa \ˌvī-si-'vər-sə, (')vīs-'vər-\ *adv* : with the order turned around [from Latin *vice versa* "with the order turned around", from *vice* "in place of, instead" and *versa,* form of *versus* "turned", from *vertere* "to turn" — related to CONVERSE, REVERSE, VERSATILE]

vi·cin·i·ty \və-'sin-ət-ē\ *n, pl* **-ties** : a surrounding area or district

vi·cious \'vish-əs\ *adj* 1 a : likely to do evil : WICKED b : of the nature of evil : IMMORAL 2 : very dangerous ⟨a *vicious* dog⟩ 3 : having or showing hateful feelings ⟨*vicious* gossip⟩ — **vi·cious·ly** *adv* — **vi·cious·ness** *n*

vicious circle *n* : a situation or condition that endlessly repeats itself

vi·cis·si·tude \və-'sis-ə-ˌt(y)üd, vī-\ *n* : a surprising or irregular change

vic·tim \'vik-təm\ *n* 1 : a living being offered as a sacrifice in a religious rite 2 : an individual injured or killed 3 : a person cheated, fooled, or harmed by another

vic·tim·ize \'vik-tə-ˌmīz\ *vb* **-ized; -iz·ing** : to make a victim of especially by cheating

vic·tor \'vik-tər\ *n* : one that defeats an enemy or opponent : WINNER

vic·to·ria \vik-'tōr-ē-ə, -'tȯr-\ *n* : a low four-wheeled carriage with a folding top and a raised seat in front for the driver [named in honor of *Victoria* 1819–1901 queen of England]

victoria

Vic·to·ri·an \vik-'tōr-ē-ən, -'tȯr-\ *adj* : of, relating to, or typical of the reign of Queen Victoria of En-

\ə\ abut	\au̇\ out	\i\ tip	\ȯ\ saw	\u̇\ foot
\ər\ further	\ch\ chin	\ī\ life	\ȯi\ coin	\y\ yet
\a\ mat	\e\ pet	\j\ job	\th\ thin	\yü\ few
\ā\ take	\ē\ easy	\ŋ\ sing	\th\ this	\yu̇\ cure
\ä\ cot, cart	\g\ go	\ō\ bone	\ü\ food	\zh\ vision

gland or of the literature, art, and tastes of her time

vic·to·ri·ous \vik-'tōr-ē-əs, -'tȯr-\ *adj* : having won a victory — **vic·to·ri·ous·ly** *adv*

vic·to·ry \'vik-t(ə-)rē\ *n, pl* **-ries** **1** : the overcoming of an enemy or opponent **2** : success in a struggle

[1]**vict·ual** \'vit-ᵊl\ *n* **1** : food fit for humans **2** *pl* : supplies of food : PROVISIONS

[2]**victual** *vb* **-ualed** *or* **-ualled; -ual·ing** *or* **-ual·ling** **1** : to supply with food **2** : to store provisions

vict·ual·ler *or* **vict·ual·er** \'vit-ᵊl-ər\ *n* : one that supplies provisions (as to an army or a ship)

vi·cu·ña *or* **vi·cu·na** \vi-'kün-yə, vī-; vī-'k(y)ü-nə, və-\ *n* **1** : a wild cud-chewing animal of the Andes that is related to the domesticated llama and alpaca **2** : the wool of the vicuña

[1]**vid·eo** \'vid-ē-,ō\ *n* : TELEVISION 1

[2]**video** *adj* **1** : relating to or used in the sending or receiving of television images — compare [1]AUDIO 2b **2** : being, relating to, or involving images on a television screen or computer display ⟨a *video* terminal⟩

vicuña 1

vid·eo·cas·sette \,vid-ē-ō-kə-'set\ *n* **1** : a case containing videotape for use with a VCR **2** : a recording (as of a movie) on a videocassette

videocassette recorder *n* : VCR

video game *n* : a game played with images on a video screen

vid·eo·phone \'vid-ē-ə-,fōn\ *n* : a telephone equipped for transmission of a picture as well as sound so that users can see each other

[1]**vid·eo·tape** \'vid-ē-ō-,tāp\ *n* : a recording of visual images and sound (as of a television production) made on magnetic tape; *also* : the magnetic tape used for such a recording

[2]**videotape** *vb* : to make a videotape of ⟨*videotape* a show⟩

video tape recorder *n* : a device for recording on videotape — called also *video recorder*

vie \'vī\ *vb* **vied; vy·ing** \'vī-iŋ\ : to strive to win over another : CONTEND — **vi·er** \'vī(-ə)r\ *n*

Viet·cong \vē-'et-'käŋ, -'kȯŋ\ *n, pl* **Vietcong** : a guerrilla soldier in the Vietnamese communist movement [from the Vietnamese phrase *Viêt Nam công-san* "Vietnam communist"]

Viet·nam·ese \vē-,et-nə-'mēz, ,vyet-, ,vē-ət-, ,vēt-, -nä, -'mēs\ *n, pl* **Vietnamese** **1** : a person born or living in Vietnam **2** : the official language of Vietnam — **Vietnamese** *adj*

[1]**view** \'vyü\ *n* **1 a** : the act of seeing or examining **b** : a brief study or description **2** : OPINION 2 ⟨state your *views*⟩ **3** : all that can be seen from a certain point ⟨a house with a *view* of the lake⟩ **4** : range of vision ⟨out of *view*⟩ **5** : GOAL 2 ⟨with a *view* to winning honors⟩ **6** : a picture of a place — **in view of** : in regard to

[2]**view** *vb* **1** : [1]SEE 1a **2** : to look at carefully : STUDY ⟨*view* an exhibit on birds⟩

view·er \'vyü-ər\ *n* : one that views; *esp* : an optical device used in viewing ⟨a *viewer* for slides⟩

view·find·er \'vyü-,fīn-dər\ *n* : FINDER b

view·point \-,pȯint\ *n* : POINT OF VIEW

vig·il \'vij-əl\ *n* **1 a** : the day before a religious feast **b** : prayers or religious services held in the evening or at night — usually used in pl. **2** : a staying awake to keep watch when one normally would be sleeping

vig·i·lance \'vij-ə-lən(t)s\ *n* : the quality or state of being vigilant

vig·i·lant \'vij-ə-lənt\ *adj* : alert to signs of danger — **vig·i·lant·ly** *adv*

vig·i·lan·te \,vij-ə-'lant-ē\ *n* : a member of a group of volunteers who decide on their own to stop crime and to pun-

ish criminals

vi·gnette \vin-'yet, vēn-\ *n* : a brief word picture : SKETCH

vig·or \'vig-ər\ *n* **1** : active strength or energy of body or mind **2** : active strength or force

vig·or·ous \'vig-(ə)rəs\ *adj* **1** : having vigor : ROBUST ⟨*vigorous* youth⟩ ⟨a *vigorous* plant⟩ **2** : done with force and energy ⟨a *vigorous* protest⟩ — **vig·or·ous·ly** *adv* — **vig·or·ous·ness** *n*

> **syn** VIGOROUS, ENERGETIC, STRENUOUS mean having or demanding great life and force. VIGOROUS suggests active strength and unfailing freshness and health ⟨people who are still *vigorous* in old age⟩ ENERGETIC suggests an ability to take lots of activity ⟨*energetic* travelers always going places⟩ STRENUOUS suggests the making or meeting of hard and challenging demands ⟨tough athletes doing *strenuous* exercise⟩ ⟨a *strenuous* opponent of the loss of freedom⟩

Vi·king \'vī-kiŋ\ *n* : one of the Scandinavians who raided or invaded the coasts of Europe in the 8th to 10th centuries

vile \'vī(ə)l\ *adj* **vil·er** \'vī-lər\; **vil·est** \-ləst\ **1 a** : morally bad ⟨*vile* deeds⟩ **b** : physically ugly ⟨a *vile* slum⟩ **2** : of little worth **3** : very or completely bad ⟨a *vile* temper⟩ — **vile·ly** \'vī(ə)l-lē\ *adv* — **vile·ness** *n*

vil·i·fy \'vil-ə-,fī\ *vb* **-fied; -fy·ing** : to speak of as wicked — **vil·i·fi·ca·tion** \,vil-ə-fə-'kā-shən\ *n* — **vil·i·fi·er** \'vil-ə-,fī(-ə)r\ *n*

vil·la \'vil-ə\ *n* **1** : a country estate **2** : a large expensive house usually located in the country

vil·lage \'vil-ij\ *n* **1** : a place somewhat smaller than a town **2** : the people living in a village

vil·lag·er \'vil-ij-ər\ *n* : a person living in a village

vil·lain \'vil-ən\ *n* **1** : VILLEIN **2** : an evil person : SCOUNDREL

vil·lain·ous \'vil-ə-nəs\ *adj* **1** : typical of a villain : WICKED **2** : very objectionable — **vil·lain·ous·ly** *adv*

vil·lainy \'vil-ə-nē\ *n, pl* **-lain·ies** : conduct or actions of or typical of a villain

vil·lein \'vil-ən, 'vil-,ān, vil-'ān\ *n* **1** : a free peasant **2** : an unfree peasant having the status of a slave to a lord

vil·lus \'vil-əs\ *n, pl* **vil·li** \'vil-,ī, -ē\ : one of the tiny finger-shaped processes of the mucous membrane of the small intestine through which digested food is absorbed

vim \'vim\ *n* : robust energy and enthusiasm

vi·nal \'vī-,nal\ *n* : a synthetic textile fiber

vin·cu·lum \'viŋ-kyə-ləm\ *n, pl* **-lums** *or* **-la** \-lə\ : a straight horizontal mark placed over two or more members of a compound mathematical expression as a symbol of grouping (as in a − $\overline{b − c}$ = a − [b − c])

vin·di·cate \'vin-də-,kāt\ *vb* **-cat·ed; -cat·ing** **1** : to free from blame or guilt ⟨evidence that will *vindicate* me⟩ **2** : CONFIRM 4 ⟨later discoveries *vindicated* the claim⟩ — **vin·di·ca·tion** \,vin-də-'kā-shən\ *n* — **vin·di·ca·tor** \'vin-də-,kāt-ər\ *n*

vin·dic·tive \vin-'dik-tiv\ *adj* : likely to seek revenge — **vin·dic·tive·ly** *adv* — **vin·dic·tive·ness** *n*

vine \'vīn\ *n* **1** : GRAPE 2 **2 a** : a plant whose stem requires support and which climbs by tendrils or twining or creeps along the ground **b** : the stem of a vine [Middle English *vine* "grape, a climbing plant", from early French *vine, vigne* (same meaning), from Latin *vinea* "vine, vineyard", derived from *vinum* "wine, grape" — related to VINEGAR, VINTAGE]

vin·e·gar \'vin-i-gər\ *n* : a sour liquid obtained from cider, wine, or malt and used to flavor or preserve foods [Middle English *vinegre* "vinegar", from early French *vinaigre* (same meaning), literally "sour wine", from *vin* "wine" and *aigre* "sharp, sour, eager"; *vin* from Latin *vinum* "wine, grape", and *aigre* from Latin *acer* "sharp, sour, spirited" — related to EAGER, VINE, VINTAGE]

vinegar eel *n* : a tiny nematode roundworm often found in vinegar or other fermenting vegetable substances

vinegar fly *n* : DROSOPHILA

vin·e·gary \'vin-i-g(ə-)rē\ *adj* : resembling vinegar : SOUR

vine·yard \'vin-yərd\ *n* : a field of grapevines

vin·tage \'vint-ij\ *n* **1 a** : the grapes or wine produced during one season **b** : [1]WINE 1 **2** : a period in which something was made or was begun [Middle English *vintage,* an altered form of *vindage* "the grapes picked during a season", from early French *vendenge* (same meaning), from Latin *vindemia* (same meaning), from *vinum* "wine, grape" and *demere* "to take off" — related to VINE, VINEGAR] — **vintage** *adj*

vint·ner \'vint-nər\ *n* : a wine merchant

viny \'vī-nē\ *adj* **vin·i·er; -est** : of, relating to, or resembling vines ⟨*viny* plants⟩

vi·nyl \'vīn-ᵊl\ *n* **1** : a chemical obtained from ethylene by the removal of one hydrogen atom **2** : a polymer of a vinyl compound or a product (as a textile fiber) made from such a polymer

vi·ol \'vī-(-ə)l\ *n* : an old bowed stringed instrument like the violin

1vi·o·la \vī-'ō-lə, vē-\ *n* : VIOLET 1a; *esp* : any of various hybrid garden plants that have white, yellow, purple, or variously colored flowers and that resemble but are smaller than the related pansies

2vi·o·la \vē-'ō-lə\ *n* : a stringed musical instrument like a violin but slightly larger and lower in pitch

vi·o·late \'vī-ə-,lāt\ *vb* **-lat·ed; -lat·ing** **1** : to fail to keep : BREAK ⟨*violate* the law⟩ **2** : to do harm or damage to **3** : to treat with great disrespect ⟨*violate* a house of worship⟩ **4** : DISTURB 1a ⟨don't *violate* their privacy⟩ — **vi·o·la·tor** \-,lāt-ər\ *n*

vi·o·la·tion \,vī-ə-'lā-shən\ *n* : an act or an instance of violating : the state of being violated

vi·o·lence \'vī-ə-lən(t)s\ *n* **1** : the use of force in a way that harms a person or property **2** : great force or energy especially of a destructive kind ⟨the *violence* of the storm caused great fear⟩

vi·o·lent \'vī-ə-lənt\ *adj* **1** : marked by great force or sudden activity ⟨a *violent* attack⟩ **2 a** : especially furious ⟨a *violent* denial of guilt⟩ **b** : INTENSE 1 ⟨*violent* pain⟩ **3** : caused by force ⟨a *violent* death⟩ — **vi·o·lent·ly** *adv*

vi·o·let \'vī-ə-lət\ *n* **1 a** : any of a genus of herbs or woody-stemmed plants that produce both often fragrant white, blue, purple, or yellow flowers above ground and small closed self-pollinated flowers underground **b** : any of several plants of other genera — compare DOGTOOTH VIOLET **2** : a reddish blue

violet 1a

vi·o·lin \,vī-ə-'lin\ *n* **1** : a stringed musical instrument with four strings that is usually held against the shoulder under the chin and played with a bow **2** : VIOLINIST

vi·o·lin·ist \,vī-ə-'lin-əst\ *n* : a violin player

vi·o·lon·cel·lo \,vī-ə-lən-'chel-ō, ,vē-\ *n* : CELLO

VIP \,vē-,ī-'pē\ *n, pl* **VIPs** \-'pēz\ : a person of great importance or fame [from *v*ery *i*mportant *p*erson]

vi·per *n* \'vī-pər\ *n* **1** : any of various sluggish Old World poisonous snakes that have heavy bodies, broad heads, and hollow tube-shaped fangs **2** : PIT VIPER **3** : any snake that is poisonous or that is believed to be poisonous

vi·per·ine \'vī-pə-,rīn\ *adj* : of, relating to, or resembling a viper : VENOMOUS

vi·ra·go \və-'räg-ō, -'rāg-; 'vir-ə-,gō\ *n, pl* **-goes** *or* **-gos** : a scolding quarrelsome woman

vi·ral \'vī-rəl\ *adj* : of, relating to, or caused by a virus

vir·eo \'vir-ē-,ō\ *n, pl* **-e·os** : any of various small insect-eating songbirds that are chiefly olive-green or grayish in color

1vir·gin \'vər-jən\ *n* : a person who has not had sexual intercourse — **vir·gin·al** \'vər-jən-ᵊl, 'vərj-nəl\ *adj* — **vir·gin·al·ly** \-ē\ *adv*

2virgin *adj* **1** : being a virgin **2** : not soiled ⟨*virgin* snow⟩; *esp* : not altered by human activity ⟨*virgin* soil⟩ **3** : being used or worked for the first time ⟨*virgin* wool⟩

vir·gin·al \'vər-jən-ᵊl, 'vərj-nəl\ *n* : a musical instrument resembling a small piano with no legs

Vir·gin·ia creeper \vər-,jin-yə-, -,jin-ē-ə-\ *n* : a common North American climbing vine related to the grapes and having leaves with five leaflets and bluish black berries — called also *woodbine*

Virginia reel *n* : an American dance in which two lines of couples face each other and in which all couples in turn do a series of movements

vir·gin·i·ty \(,)vər-'jin-ət-ē\ *n, pl* **-ties** : the quality or state of being virgin

Virgo \'vər-gō, 'vi(ə)r-\ *n* **1** : a group of stars between Leo and Libra usually pictured as a young woman **2 a** : the sixth sign of the zodiac — see ZODIAC table **b** : a person whose sign of the zodiac is Virgo

vir·ile \'vir-əl, 'vi(ə)r-, -,īl\ *adj* **1** : having the nature, powers, or qualities of an adult male **2 a** : VIGOROUS 1 **b** : marked by unusual vigor : FORCEFUL [from early French *viril* "having the qualities of a man", from Latin *virilis* (same meaning), from *vir* "man, male" — related to VIRTUE]

vi·ril·i·ty \və-'ril-ət-ē\ *n* : the quality or state of being virile

vi·rol·o·gist \vī-'räl-ə-jəst\ *n* : a person who specializes in virology

vi·rol·o·gy \vī-'räl-ə-jē\ *n* : a branch of science concerned with viruses

vir·tu·al \'vərch-(ə-)wəl, 'vər-chəl\ *adj* : being in effect but not in fact or name — **vir·tu·al·ly** \-ē\ *adv*

vir·tue \'vər-chü\ *n* **1** : conduct that agrees with what is morally right **2** : a particular moral quality **3** : a desirable quality [Middle English *virtu* "behavior that fits with a standard of what is right or moral", from early French *virtu* (same meaning), from Latin *virtus* "strength, virtue, manly quality", from *vir* "man, male" — related to VIRILE] — **by virtue of** *or* **in virtue of** : through the force of : by authority of

vir·tu·os·i·ty \,vər-chə-'wäs-ət-ē\ *n, pl* **-ties** : great performing ability in the fine arts

vir·tu·o·so \,vər-chə-'wō-sō, -zō\ *n, pl* **-sos** *or* **-si** \-sē, -zē\ : a person who excels in the performance of an art; *esp* : a skilled musician — **virtuoso** *adj*

vir·tu·ous \'vərch-(ə-)wəs\ *adj* : having or showing moral virtue — **vir·tu·ous·ly** *adv* — **vir·tu·ous·ness** *n*

vir·u·lence \'vir-(y)ə-lən(t)s\ *n* : the quality or state of being virulent

vir·u·lent \'vir-(y)ə-lənt\ *adj* **1 a** : marked by a rapid, severe, and often deadly course ⟨a *virulent* infection⟩ **b** : able to overcome or break down the defenses of the body ⟨a *virulent* germ⟩ **2** : extremely poisonous : NOXIOUS **3** : full of hate : SPITEFUL — **vir·u·lent·ly** *adv*

vi·rus \'vī-rəs\ *n* **1** : any of a large group of very tiny infectious agents that are too small to be seen with the ordinary light microscope but can often be seen with the electron microscope, that are considered either very simple microorganisms or very complicated molecules, that have an outside coat of protein around a core of RNA or DNA, that can grow and multiply only in living cells, and that cause important diseases in human beings, lower animals, and

\ə\ abut	\aú\ out	\i\ tip	\ó\ saw	\ú\ foot
\ər\ further	\ch\ chin	\ī\ life	\ói\ coin	\y\ yet
\a\ mat	\e\ pet	\j\ job	\th\ thin	\yü\ few
\ā\ take	\ē\ easy	\ŋ\ sing	\th\ this	\yú\ cure
\ä\ cot, cart	\g\ go	\ō\ bone	\ü\ food	\zh\ vision

plants — compare FILTERABLE VIRUS **2** : a disease caused by a virus [from Latin *virus* "slime, poison, terrible smell"]

¹vi·sa \'vē-zə *also* -sə\ *n* : a mark on a passport that is a sign of approval and permission for a traveler to go ahead

²visa *vb* **vi·saed** \-zəd, -səd\; **vi·sa·ing** \-zə-iŋ, -sə-\ : to give a visa to

vis·age \'viz-ij\ *n* : ¹FACE 1, 3a, 4a

viscera *pl of* VISCUS

vis·cer·al \'vis-ə-rəl\ *adj* **1** : felt in or as if in the viscera **2** : of, relating to, or being the viscera — **vis·cer·al·ly** \-rə-lē\ *adv*

vis·cid \'vis-əd\ *adj* : VISCOUS

vis·cos·i·ty \vis-'käs-ət-ē\ *n, pl* **-ties** : the quality or state of being viscous; *esp* : the characteristic of a fluid that resists flow

vis·count \'vī-,kaůnt\ *n* : a British nobleman ranking below an earl and above a baron

vis·count·ess \'vī-,kaůnt-əs\ *n* **1** : the wife or widow of a viscount **2** : a woman holding the rank of viscount

vis·cous \'vis-kəs\ *adj* **1** : having the characteristic of stickiness **2** : having or marked by viscosity

vis·cus \'vis-kəs\ *n, pl* **vis·cera** \'vis-ə-rə\ : an organ located inside of the body; *esp* : one (as the heart, liver, or intestine) located in the large cavity of the main part of the body

vise \'vīs\ *n* : any of various tools with two jaws for holding work that close usually by a screw or lever — **vise·like** *adj*

vis·i·bil·i·ty \,viz-ə-'bil-ət-ē\ *n* **1** : the quality or state of being visible **2** : the degree of clearness of the atmosphere

vis·i·ble \'viz-ə-bəl\ *adj* **1** : capable of being seen ⟨stars *visible* to the naked eye⟩ **2** : easily seen or understood : OBVIOUS ⟨no *visible* means of support⟩ — **vis·i·bly** \-blē\ *adv*

¹vi·sion \'vizh-ən\ *n* **1 a** : something seen in the mind (as during a dream) **b** : a vivid picture created by the imagination **c** : GHOST **2 a** : the act or power of imagination **b** : unusual ability to think or plan ahead ⟨people with *vision* building for the future⟩ **3 a** : the act or power of seeing : SIGHT **b** : the sense by which the qualities of an object (as color, shape, and size) are perceived **4** : something seen; *esp* : a lovely or charming sight [Middle English *vision* "something seen in a dream or trance", from early French *vision* (same meaning), from Latin *vision-, visio* (same meaning), derived from *vidēre* "to see" — related to CLAIRVOYANCE, EVIDENT, PROVIDE, SUPERVISE, VISIT]

²vision *vb* : IMAGINE 1

¹vi·sion·ary \'vizh-ə-,ner-ē\ *adj* **1** : resembling a vision especially in being impractical ⟨*visionary* plans for underwater cities⟩ **2** : likely to dream or imagine

²visionary *n, pl* **-ar·ies** **1** : a person whose ideas or plans are impractical : DREAMER **2** : a person who sees visions : SEER

¹vis·it \'viz-ət\ *vb* **vis·it·ed** \'viz-ət-əd, 'viz-təd\; **vis·it·ing** \'viz-ət-iŋ, 'viz-tiŋ\ **1** : to go to see in order to comfort or help **2 a** : to pay a call upon as an act of friendship or courtesy **b** : to go or come to see on business **c** : to live with for a time as a guest **3** : to go to for pleasure ⟨*visit* the zoo⟩ **4** : to make a visit or frequent or regular visits **5** : ¹CHAT [Middle English *visiten* "to go to a person especially to give comfort", from early French *visiter* (same meaning), derived from Latin *visere* "to go to see", from *vidēre* "to see" — related to VISION] — **vis·i·tor**

\'viz-ət-ər, 'viz-tər\ *n*

²visit *n* **1** : a brief stay : CALL **2** : a stay as a guest **3** : a business call

vis·i·tant \'viz-ət-ənt, 'viz-tənt\ *n* : one that visits; *esp* : a visitor from another world

vis·i·ta·tion \,viz-ə-'tā-shən\ *n* : an instance of visiting; *esp* : a visit by an important person for a reason (as an inspection)

vi·sor *also* **vi·zor** \'vī-zər\ *n* **1** : a movable front upper piece on a helmet **2** : a projecting part (as on a cap) to protect or shade the eyes — **vi·sored** \-zərd\ *adj*

vis·ta \'vis-tə\ *n* **1** : a distant view through an opening or along an avenue : PROSPECT **2** : a mental view over a long period of time

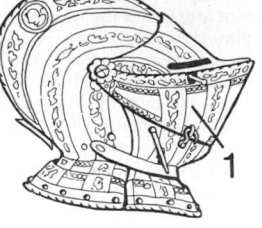

1 visor 1

¹vi·su·al \'vizh-(ə-)wəl, 'vizh-əl\ *adj* **1** : of, relating to, or used in vision **2** : received by sight **3** : VISIBLE 1 **4** : of, relating to, or using visual aids — **vi·su·al·ly** \-ē\ *adv*

²visual *n* : something (as a picture, chart, or film) that appeals to the sight and is used to illustrate, demonstrate, or advertise — usually used in pl.

visual aid *n* : an instructional device (as a chart, map, or model) that appeals chiefly to vision; *esp* : an educational motion picture or filmstrip

visual field *n* : the entire space visible at a given instant without moving the eyes — called also *field of vision*

vi·su·al·iza·tion \,vizh-(ə-)wə-lə-'zā-shən, ,vizh-ə-lə-\ *n* **1** : the formation of visual mental images **2** : the act or process of putting into visual form

vi·su·al·ize \'vizh-(ə-)wə-,līz, 'vizh-ə-,līz\ *vb* **-ized; -iz·ing** : to make visible; *esp* : to form a mental image of

visual purple *n* : a red or purple pigment in the retina of various vertebrates including human beings that is sensitive to dim light and functions in night vision

vi·tal \'vīt-ᵊl\ *adj* **1** : concerned with or necessary to the continuation of life ⟨*vital* organs⟩ **2** : full of vitality : ANIMATED **3** : characteristic of life or of living things ⟨*vital* activities⟩ **4** : destructive of life : FATAL **5** : of first importance ⟨matters *vital* to national defense⟩ [Middle English *vital* "alive, full of life, relating to life", from early French *vital* (same meaning), from Latin *vitalis* "of life", from *vita* "life"] — **vi·tal·ly** \-ᵊl-ē\ *adv*

vital capacity *n* : the breathing capacity of the lungs expressed as the number of cubic inches or cubic centimeters of air that can be forcibly exhaled after one full act of breathing in

vi·tal·i·ty \vī-'tal-ət-ē\ *n, pl* **-ties** **1 a** : the property by which the living can be separated from the nonliving : LIFE **b** : capacity to live and develop **2** : energy of mind or body **3 a** : the ability to last **b** : lively and animated spirit

vi·tal·ize \'vīt-ᵊl-,īz\ *vb* **-ized; -iz·ing** : to give vitality to

vi·tals \'vīt-ᵊlz\ *n pl* **1** : vital organs **2** : essential parts

vital statistics *n pl* : statistics about births, marriages, health, and disease

vi·ta·min \'vīt-ə-mən\ *n* : any of various organic substances that are needed in very small amounts by most animals and some plants, that are important to the control of growth and development but do not produce energy or serve as building units, and that are present in natural foods or in some cases are produced within the body

vitamin A *n* : any of several vitamins or a mixture of them that are found especially in animal products (as egg yolk, milk, or fish-liver oils) and are needed especially for good vision

vitamin B *n* **1** : VITAMIN B COMPLEX **2** : THIAMINE
vitamin B complex *n* : a group of vitamins that are found widely in foods and are essential for normal function of certain enzymes and for growth — called also *B complex*
vitamin B₁ \-'bē-'wən\ *n* : THIAMINE
vitamin B₆ \-'bē-'siks\ *n* : PYRIDOXINE; *also* : a closely related compound
vitamin B₁₂ \-'bē-'twelv\ *n* : a member of the vitamin B complex that contains cobalt, occurs especially in liver, and is needed for normal blood formation, nerve function, and growth; *also* : any of several other compounds with similar activity
vitamin B₂ \-'bē-'tü\ *n* : RIBOFLAVIN
vitamin C *n* : a vitamin that is present especially in fruits and vegetables and is needed by the body to prevent scurvy — called also *ascorbic acid*
vitamin D *n* : any or all of several vitamins that are needed for normal bone and tooth structure, and are found especially in fish-liver oils, egg yolk, and milk or are produced in response to ultraviolet light
vitamin E *n* : any of various oily liquid compounds that can be dissolved in fats, are found especially in plants, and are necessary in the body to prevent such ailments as infertility, the breakdown of muscles, and vascular problems
vitamin K *n* : any of several vitamins that are needed in order for blood to clot properly
vi·tel·line membrane \vī-'tel-ən-, -,ēn-, -,īn-\ *n* : a membrane enclosing the egg and corresponding to the cell membrane of an ordinary cell
vi·ti·ate \'vish-ē-,āt\ *vb* **-at·ed; -at·ing** **1** : to harm the quality of : SPOIL **2** : to destroy the effect or force of — **vi·ti·a·tion** \,vish-ē-'ā-shən\ *n*
vit·re·ous humor \'vi-trē-əs-\ *n* : the clear colorless transparent jelly that fills the eyeball behind the lens
vit·ri·ol \'vi-trē-əl\ *n* : something (as written or spoken words) thought to be as harsh and burning as acid
vit·tles \'vit-ᵊlz\ *n pl* : VICTUALS
vi·tu·per·ate \vī-'t(y)ü-pə-,rāt, və-\ *vb* **-at·ed; -at·ing** : to criticize harshly : SCOLD
vi·tu·per·a·tion \(,)vī-,t(y)ü-pə-'rā-shən\ *n* : lengthy harsh bitter criticism or abuse
vi·va·ce \vē-'väch-ā, -ē\ *adv or adj* : in a brisk spirited manner — used as a direction in music
vi·va·cious \və-'vā-shəs *also* vī-\ *adj* : full of life and good spirits **syn** see LIVELY — **vi·va·cious·ly** *adv* — **vi·va·cious·ness** *n*
vi·vac·i·ty \və-'vas-ət-ē *also* vī-\ *n* : the quality or state of being vivacious
vi·var·i·um \vī-'var-ē-əm, -'ver-\ *n, pl* **-ia** \-ē-ə\ *or* **-i·ums** : an enclosure for keeping or studying animals or plants indoors; *esp* : one for animals that live on land
viv·id \'viv-əd\ *adj* **1** : having the appearance of vigorous life ⟨a *vivid* sketch of the children⟩ **2** : very strong or bright ⟨a *vivid* red⟩ **3** : producing a strong or clear impression : SHARP; *esp* : producing distinct mental pictures ⟨a *vivid* description⟩ **4** : acting clearly and powerfully ⟨a *vivid* imagination⟩ **syn** see GRAPHIC — **viv·id·ly** *adv* — **viv·id·ness** *n*
viv·i·fy \'viv-ə-,fī\ *vb* **-fied; -fy·ing** **1** : to put life into : ANIMATE **2** : to make vivid — **viv·i·fi·ca·tion** \,viv-ə-fə-'kā-shən\ *n* — **viv·i·fi·er** \'viv-ə-,fī(-ə)r\ *n*
vi·vip·a·rous \vī-'vip-(ə-)rəs, və-\ *adj* : giving birth to living young from within the body rather than laying eggs
vivi·sec·tion \,viv-ə-'sek-shən\ *n* : the operating or experimenting on a living animal for scientific or medical study
vix·en \'vik-sən\ *n* : a female fox
viz·ard \'viz-ərd, -,ärd\ *n* : a mask for disguise or protection
vi·zier \və-'zi(ə)r\ *n* : a high official in a Muslim country
vizor *variant of* VISOR
vo·cab·u·lary \vō-'kab-yə-,ler-ē\ *n, pl* **-lar·ies** **1** : a list or collection of words defined or explained **2** : a stock of words used in a language, by a group or individual, or in

relation to a subject
¹vo·cal \'vō-kəl\ *adj* **1** : uttered by the voice : ORAL **2** : composed or arranged for or sung by the human voice ⟨*vocal* music⟩ **3** : speaking freely or loudly : OUTSPOKEN ⟨a *vocal* opponent of the new law⟩ **4** : of, relating to, or resembling the voice — **vo·cal·ly** \-kə-lē\ *adv*
²vocal *n* **1** : a vocal sound **2** : a piece of vocal music
vocal cords *n pl* : either of two pairs of elastic folds of mucous membrane in the larynx that function in the production of vocal sounds
vo·cal·ic \vō-'kal-ik\ *adj* **1** : marked by or consisting of vowels **2** : of, relating to, or functioning as a vowel
vo·cal·ist \'vō-kə-ləst\ *n* : ¹SINGER
vo·cal·ize \'vō-kə-,līz\ *vb* **-ized; -iz·ing** : to give voice to; *esp* : ¹SING 1a — **vo·cal·iza·tion** \,vō-kə-lə-'zā-shən\ *n* — **vo·cal·iz·er** \'vō-kə-,lī-zər\ *n*
vo·ca·tion \vō-'kā-shən\ *n* **1** : a strong desire or leaning for a certain career or course of action; *esp* : a divine call to the religious life **2 a** : the work a person regularly does : OCCUPATION **b** : the persons in a particular occupation [Middle English *vocacioun* "a strong inclination to a particular course of action or way of life", from Latin *vocation-*, *vocatio* "summons", derived from *vocare* "to call" — related to ADVOCATE, PROVOKE, REVOKE]
vo·ca·tion·al \vō-'kā-shnəl, -shən-ᵊl\ *adj* **1** : of, relating to, or concerned with a vocation **2** : concerned with choice of or training in a skill or trade to be followed as a career ⟨*vocational* school⟩ — **vo·ca·tion·al·ly** \-ē\ *adv*
vo·cif·er·ate \vō-'sif-ə-,rāt\ *vb* **-at·ed; -at·ing** : to cry out loudly : SHOUT
vo·cif·er·ous \vō-'sif-(ə-)rəs\ *adj* : making a loud outcry : NOISY, CLAMOROUS — **vo·cif·er·ous·ly** *adv*
vod·ka \'väd-kə\ *n* : a colorless alcoholic liquor [Russian, literally "little water", from *voda* "water"]
vogue \'vōg\ *n* **1** : the quality or state of being popular **2** : a period in which something is popular or in fashion **3** : something in fashion at a particular time — **vogue** *adj*
¹voice \'vois\ *n* **1 a** : sound produced by vertebrates by means of vocal organs; *esp* : sound so produced by human beings **b** : the power of speaking ⟨lost my *voice*⟩ **2 a** : musical sound produced by the vocal cords **b** : the ability to sing ⟨a singer with a great *voice*⟩ **c** : ¹SINGER ⟨one of the finest *voices* of our time⟩ **d** : one of the melodic parts in a vocal or instrumental composition **e** : condition of the vocal organs for singing ⟨in good *voice*⟩ **3** : a sound like a vocal sound ⟨the *voice* of the cricket⟩ **4** : a medium of expression ⟨the *voice* of the people⟩ **5 a** : wish, choice, or opinion openly or formally expressed **b** : the right to express a wish, choice, or opinion ⟨students want a *voice* in school affairs⟩ **6** : a grammatical form showing the relation between the subject of a verb and the action which the verb expresses — **with one voice** : in total agreement
²voice *vb* **voiced; voic·ing** **1** : to express in words ⟨*voice* a complaint⟩ **2** : to vibrate the vocal cords in pronouncing ⟨*voice* a consonant⟩
voice box *n* : LARYNX
voiced \'voist\ *adj* : uttered with the vocal cords vibrating ⟨a *voiced* consonant like \v\⟩
voice·less \'voi-sləs\ *adj* **1** : having no voice : MUTE **2** : not voiced ⟨a *voiceless* consonant like \f\⟩ — **voice·less·ness** *n*
voice–over \'voi-,sō-vər\ *n* : the voice in a film or television program of a person who is heard but not seen or not seen actually talking
¹void \'void\ *adj* **1** : containing nothing : EMPTY **2** : DE-

\ə\ abut	\au̇\ out	\i\ tip	\ȯ\ saw	\u̇\ foot
\ər\ further	\ch\ chin	\ī\ life	\ȯi\ coin	\y\ yet
\a\ mat	\e\ pet	\j\ job	\th\ thin	\yü\ few
\ā\ take	\ē\ easy	\ŋ\ sing	\th\ this	\yu̇\ cure
\ä\ cot, cart	\g\ go	\ō\ bone	\ü\ food	\zh\ vision

VOID **3** : of no legal force or effect

²void *n* **1** : empty space **2** : a feeling of want or hollowness

³void *vb* : to make void ⟨*void* a contract⟩

voile \'vȯi(ə)l\ *n* : a soft sheer fabric used for summer dresses and for curtains

vol·a·tile \'väl-ət-ᵊl\ *adj* **1** : easily becoming a vapor at a fairly low temperature ⟨a *volatile* solvent⟩ **2** : likely to change suddenly or quickly ⟨a *volatile* temper⟩ ⟨the stock market is *volatile*⟩ — **vol·a·til·i·ty** \,väl-ə-'til-ət-ē\ *n*

vol·ca·nic \väl-'kan-ik, vȯl-\ *adj* **1 a** : of, relating to, or produced by a volcano ⟨a *volcanic* eruption⟩ **b** : made of materials from volcanoes ⟨*volcanic* dust⟩ **2** : explosively violent ⟨a *volcanic* rage⟩

vol·ca·no \väl-'kā-nō, vȯl-\ *n, pl* **-noes** *or* **-nos** : a vent in the earth's crust from which melted or hot rock and steam come out; *also* : a hill or mountain composed entirely or in part of the material thrown out

> **Word History** The ancient Greeks and Romans had many gods and goddesses. Each of these deities was in charge of a special kind of work or an aspect of nature. Many of the happenings in nature were explained in myth as the actions of one or more of these gods or goddesses. The Roman god of fire was known as *Vulcanus* in Latin (*Vulcan* in English). He was thought to live inside Mount Etna, a volcano on the island of Sicily. Vulcan was a giant who worked as a blacksmith, forging the thunderbolts for Jupiter, king of the gods. The smoke and occasional fiery rocks and lava that came from Mount Etna were thought to be from Vulcan's forge. That is how his name came to be applied to a mountain that sometimes spews forth fire and smoke. [from Italian *vulcano* "volcano", from Latin *Volcanus, Vulcanus* "Vulcan (Roman god of fire)"]

vole \'vōl\ *n* : any of various small rodents that are closely related to the lemmings and muskrats but in general look like fat mice or rats and that are sometimes harmful to crops

vole

vo·li·tion \vō-'lish-ən, və-\ *n* : the act or power of making one's choices or decisions : WILL — **vo·li·tion·al** \-'lish-nəl, -ən-ᵊl\ *adj*

¹vol·ley \'väl-ē\ *n, pl* **volleys** **1** : a group of missiles (as arrows or bullets) passing through the air **2** : a firing of a number of weapons (as rifles) at the same time **3** : a bursting forth of many things at once **4** : the act of volleying

²volley *vb* **vol·leyed; vol·ley·ing** **1** : to shoot in a volley **2** : to hit an object (as a ball) while it is in the air before it touches the ground

vol·ley·ball \'väl-ē-,bȯl\ *n* : a game played by volleying a large air-filled ball over a net; *also* : the ball used to play this game

volt \'vōlt\ *n* : a unit of electrical potential difference and electromotive force equal to the difference in potential between two points in a conducting wire carrying a constant current of one ampere when the power used between these two points is equal to one watt

volt·age \'vōl-tij\ *n* : potential difference measured in volts

vol·ta·ic \väl-'tā-ik, vōl-, vȯl-\ *adj* : of, relating to, or producing direct electric current by chemical action (as in a battery) : GALVANIC ⟨*voltaic* cell⟩

volt·me·ter \'vōlt-,mēt-ər\ *n* : an instrument for measuring in volts the difference in potential between different points of an electrical circuit

vol·u·ble \'väl-yə-bəl\ *adj* : having a smooth and fast flow of words in speaking **syn** see TALKATIVE — **vol·u·bil·i-**

ty \,väl-yə-'bil-ət-ē\ *n* — **vol·u·bly** \'väl-yə-blē\ *adv*

vol·ume \'väl-yəm, -yüm\ *n* **1** : ¹BOOK 2a **2** : one of a series of books forming a complete work or collection ⟨the fifth *volume* of an encyclopedia⟩ **3** : space included within limits as measured in cubic units ⟨the *volume* of a cylinder⟩ **4** : a large amount : MASS **5** : the degree of loudness of a sound

> **Word History** The earliest books were written on long rolls made from a plant called papyrus. The Roman name for such a roll was *volumen*, a word which came from the verb *volvere*, meaning "to roll". Later, books were made of a material called parchment, which, unlike papyrus, could be folded and bound together. This advance made it unnecessary to use rolls any more. The French word *volume*, which came from the Latin *volumen*, was originally used to refer to papyrus rolls but later was used for bound books as well. The French word was borrowed into English in the 14th century. By the 16th century, *volume* had also come to mean "the size (of a book)". This meaning led to a more general sense, "the quantity or amount (of anything)". In the 19th century, *volume* acquired still another meaning, "the strength or loudness of a sound". [Middle English *volume* "a book", from early French *volume* "a book of bound sheets, a scroll of papyrus", from Latin *volumen* "roll, scroll", from *volvere* "to roll" — related to REVOLVE]

vo·lu·mi·nous \və-'lü-mə-nəs\ *adj* : having or marked by great volume or bulk : LARGE — **vo·lu·mi·nous·ly** *adv* — **vo·lu·mi·nous·ness** *n*

vol·un·tari·ly \,väl-ən-'ter-ə-lē\ *adv* : of one's own free will

¹vol·un·tary \'väl-ən-,ter-ē\ *adj* **1** : done, given, or made with one's own free will ⟨*voluntary* assistance⟩ **2** : not accidental : INTENTIONAL ⟨*voluntary* manslaughter⟩ **3** : of, relating to, or controlled by the will ⟨*voluntary* behavior⟩

> **syn** VOLUNTARY, INTENTIONAL, DELIBERATE mean done or brought about of one's own will. VOLUNTARY suggests free choice ⟨joining the club is *voluntary*⟩ or control by the will ⟨*voluntary* blinking of the eyes⟩ INTENTIONAL suggests that something is done for a reason and only after some thought ⟨took an *intentional* fall to get a laugh⟩ DELIBERATE suggests that one is fully aware of what one is doing and of the likely results of the action ⟨a *deliberate* insult⟩

²voluntary *n, pl* **-tar·ies** : a musical piece played usually on the organ at a religious service

voluntary muscle *n* : muscle (as most striated muscle) that is under voluntary control; *also* : a muscle especially of the skeleton that is composed of voluntary muscle

¹vol·un·teer \,väl-ən-'ti(ə)r\ *n* : a person who volunteers for a service

²volunteer *adj* : of, relating to, or consisting of volunteers : VOLUNTARY

³volunteer *vb* **1** : to offer voluntarily ⟨*volunteered* my services⟩ **2** : to offer oneself as a volunteer ⟨*volunteered* to do the job⟩

vo·lup·tuous \və-'ləp-chə(-wə)s\ *adj* : giving pleasure to the senses — **vo·lup·tuous·ly** *adv* — **vo·lup·tuous·ness** *n*

vol·vox \'väl-,väks\ *n* : any of a genus of green flagellates that form ball-shaped colonies

¹vom·it \'väm-ət\ *n* : an act of throwing up the contents of the stomach through the mouth; *also* : the matter thrown up

²vomit *vb* : to throw up the contents of the stomach through the mouth — **vom·it·er** *n*

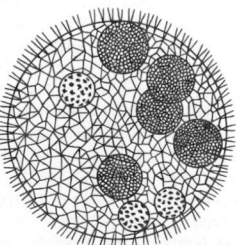

volvox

voo·doo \'vüd-ü\ *n, pl* **voo·doos** **1** : VOODOOISM **2** : one who deals in spells and magic [from Louisiana French *voudou* "voodoo"; of African origin] — **voodoo** *adj*

voo·doo·ism \'vüd-(,)ü-,iz-əm\ *n* **1** : a religion based on African ancestor worship and practiced chiefly in Haiti **2** : WITCHCRAFT — **voo·doo·ist** \'vüd-ü-əst\ *n*

vo·ra·cious \vò-'rā-shəs, və-\ *adj* **1** : having a huge appetite : RAVENOUS **2** : very eager ⟨a *voracious* reader⟩ — **vo·ra·cious·ly** *adv* — **vo·rac·i·ty** \-'ras-ət-ē\ *n*

vor·tex \'vòr-,teks\ *n, pl* **vor·ti·ces** \'vòrt-ə-,sēz\ *also* **vor·tex·es** : a mass of whirling fluid forming a cavity in the center toward which things are drawn : WHIRLPOOL

vor·ti·cel·la \,vòrt-ə-'sel-ə\ *n, pl* **-cel·lae** \-'sel-ē\ *or* **-cel·las** : any of a genus of ciliates that look like a bell on the end of a stalk

vo·ta·ry \'vōt-ə-rē\ *n, pl* **-ries** : a devoted follower; *esp* : a devout or eager worshiper

¹vote \'vōt\ *n* **1 a** : a formal expression of opinion or will (as by ballot in an election) **b** : the result reached by voting **c** : ¹BALLOT 1 **2** : the general opinion expressed by voters ⟨the *vote* is to lower taxes⟩ **3** : the right to cast a vote : SUFFRAGE ⟨gave women the *vote*⟩ **4 a** : the act or process of voting ⟨bring the issue to a *vote*⟩ **b** : a method of voting ⟨a voice *vote*⟩ **5 a** : VOTER **b** : a group of voters with a common interest or quality ⟨the farm *vote*⟩ — **vote·less** \-ləs\ *adj*

²vote *vb* **vot·ed; vot·ing** **1** : to express one's wish or choice by a vote : cast a vote **2** : to elect, decide, pass, defeat, grant, or make legal by a vote **3** : to declare by general agreement **4** : to put forth as a suggestion ⟨I *vote* we all go home⟩

vot·er \'vōt-ər\ *n* : one that votes or has the legal right to vote

voting machine *n* : a mechanical device for recording and counting votes cast in an election

vo·tive \'vōt-iv\ *adj* : consisting of or expressing a vow, wish, or desire ⟨a *votive* prayer⟩

vouch \'vaùch\ *vb* **1** : to give a guarantee ⟨*vouch* for the truth of a story⟩ **2** : to supply supporting evidence or testimony

vouch·er \'vaù-chər\ *n* **1** : one who vouches for another **2** : a paper that records a business dealing (as payment of a bill or credit for a future purchase)

vouch·safe \vaùch-'sāf, 'vaùch-,sāf\ *vb* **vouch·safed; vouch·saf·ing** : to grant as a special favor

¹vow \'vaù\ *n* : a solemn promise or statement

²vow *vb* **1** : to make a vow or as a vow **2** : to bind or make holy by a vow

vow·el \'vaù(-ə)l\ *n* **1** : a speech sound produced without obstruction or audible friction in the mouth **2** : a letter (as *a, e, i, o, u,* and sometimes *y*) representing a vowel

¹voy·age \'vòi-ij, 'vò(-)ij\ *n* : a journey especially by water from one place or country to another

²voyage *vb* **voy·aged; voy·ag·ing** : to take a trip : TRAVEL — **voy·ag·er** *n*

vul·ca·nize \'vəl-kə-,nīz\ *vb* **-nized; -niz·ing** : to treat rubber or similar plastic material chemically in order to give it useful properties (as elasticity or strength)

vul·gar \'vəl-gər\ *adj* **1** : generally used, applied, or accepted **2** : of or relating to common speech : ¹VERNACULAR **3** : of or relating to the common people **4 a** : lacking in good manners or taste : COARSE **b** : morally crude **c** : tastelessly showy : PRETENTIOUS **5** : offensive in language : OBSCENE — **vul·gar·ly** *adv*

vul·gar·ism \'vəl-gə-,riz-əm\ *n* : a vulgar expression

vul·gar·i·ty \,vəl-'gar-ət-ē\ *n, pl* **-ties** **1** : the quality or state of being vulgar **2** : something vulgar

vul·gar·ize \'vəl-gə-,rīz\ *vb* **-ized; -iz·ing** : to make vulgar

Vul·gate \'vəl-,gāt\ *n* : a Latin version of the Bible authorized and used by the Roman Catholic Church

vul·ner·a·ble \'vəln-(ə-)rə-bəl, 'vəl-nər-bəl\ *adj* **1** : capable of being wounded **2** : open to attack or damage ⟨a *vulnerable* position⟩ — **vul·ner·a·bil·i·ty** \,vəln-(ə-)rə-'bil-ət-ē\ *n*

vul·ture \'vəl-chər\ *n* **1** : any of various large birds that feed mostly on animals found dead and that are related to the hawks and eagles but have weaker claws and the head usually naked **2** : a greedy or predatory person

vul·va \'vəl-və\ *n, pl* **vul·vae** \-,vē, -,vī\ : the parts of the female genital organs that are on the outside of the body

vying *present participle of* VIE

W

w \'dəb-əl-(,)yü, -yə, 'dəb-(ə)-yə\ *n, often cap* : the 23d letter of the English alphabet

Wac \'wak\ *n* : a member of the Women's Army Corps

wacky \'wak-ē\ *adj* **wack·i·er; -est** : ODD 5, CRAZY — **wack·i·ly** \'wak-ə-lē\ *adv* — **wack·i·ness** \'wak-ē-nəs\ *n*

¹wad \'wäd\ *n* **1** : a small mass, bundle, or tuft ⟨a *wad* of cotton⟩ **2** : a soft pad or plug used to hold a powder charge in a gun or cartridge **3 a** : a roll of paper money **b** : a large amount (as of money) ⟨spent a *wad* on clothes⟩

²wad *vb* **wad·ded; wad·ding** **1** : to form into a wad or wadding ⟨*wad* up a handkerchief⟩ **2** : to stuff or line with soft material

wad·ding \'wäd-iŋ\ *n* **1** : wads or material for making wads **2** : a soft mass or sheet of fibers used for stuffing or padding

¹wad·dle \'wäd-°l\ *vb* **wad·dled; wad·dling** \'wäd-liŋ, -°l-iŋ\ **1** : to walk with short steps swaying from side to side like a duck **2** : to move slowly and awkwardly — **wad·dler** \-lər, -°l-ər\ *n*

²waddle *n* : a waddling walk

wade \'wād\ *vb* **wad·ed; wad·ing** **1** : to step in or through a substance (as water, mud, or sand) that is thicker than air **2 a** : to move or proceed slowly or with difficulty ⟨*wade* through a dull book⟩ **b** : to attack or work energetically ⟨*waded* into their chores⟩ **3** : to pass or cross by wading

wad·er \'wād-ər\ *n* **1** : one that wades **2** *pl* : high waterproof boots or trousers for wading

wa·di \'wäd-ē\ *n* : the bed or valley of a stream in regions of southwestern Asia and northern Africa that is usually dry except during the rainy season

wading bird *n* : any of many long-legged birds including the shorebirds (as sandpipers) and the inland waterbirds (as cranes and herons) that wade in water in search of food

Waf \'waf\ *n* : a member of the women's branch of the U.S. Air Force

wa·fer \'wā-fər\ *n* **1 a** : a thin crisp cake or cracker **b** : a round thin piece of bread used in the sacrament of Communion **2** : something (as a piece of candy or a computer chip) resembling a wafer especially in thin round form

\ə\ abut	\aù\ out	\i\ tip	\ò\ saw	\ù\ foot
\ər\ further	\ch\ chin	\ī\ life	\òi\ coin	\y\ yet
\a\ mat	\e\ pet	\j\ job	\th\ thin	\yü\ few
\ā\ take	\ē\ easy	\ŋ\ sing	\th\ this	\yù\ cure
\ä\ cot, cart	\g\ go	\ō\ bone	\ü\ food	\zh\ vision

waf·fle \'wäf-əl, 'wȯf-\ *n* : a crisp cake with an indented crust made by cooking batter in a waffle iron

waffle iron *n* : a cooking utensil with two hinged metal parts that shut upon each other to make a grid-shaped pattern on a waffle being cooked

¹waft \'wäft, 'waft\ *vb* : to move or be moved lightly by or as if by the action of wind or waves

²waft *n* : a slight breeze : PUFF

¹wag \'wag\ *vb* **wagged; wag·ging** : to move or swing to and fro or up and down especially with quick jerky movements ⟨the dog *wagged* its tail⟩ ⟨*wagged* his finger as he scolded⟩ [Middle English *waggen* "to be in motion, move about"] — **wag·ger** *n*

²wag *n* : a wagging movement

³wag *n* : JOKER 1, WIT [probably a shortened form of obsolete *waghalter* "a person who should be hanged"]

¹wage \'wāj\ *vb* **waged; wag·ing** **1** : to engage in or carry on ⟨*wage* war⟩ ⟨*wage* a campaign⟩ **2** : to be in the process of occurring ⟨the battle *waged* for several hours⟩

²wage *n* **1** : a payment for work or services usually calculated on an hourly, daily, or piecework basis — often used in pl. **2** *sing or pl* : something given or received because of one's actions : REWARD

¹wa·ger \'wā-jər\ *n* **1 a** : something risked on an uncertain event : BET **b** : something on which a bet is made **2** : an act of betting : GAMBLE

²wager *vb* **wa·gered; wa·ger·ing** \'wāj-(ə-)riŋ\ : to bet on the outcome of a contest or question — **wa·ger·er** \'wā-jər-ər\ *n*

wage scale *n* : a list of wage rates for related tasks; *also* : the general level of wages for an area or region

wag·ery \'wag-ə-rē\ *n, pl* **-ger·ies** **1** : mischievous fun **2** : JEST 1; *esp* : PRACTICAL JOKE

wag·gish \'wag-ish\ *adj* : displaying or done in a spirit of good-humored mischief ⟨*waggish* pranks⟩

wag·gle \'wag-əl\ *vb* **wag·gled; wag·gling** \-(ə-)liŋ\ : ¹WAG — **waggle** *n*

wag·on \'wag-ən\ *n* **1 a** : a usually four-wheeled vehicle for transporting goods or passengers; *esp* : one drawn by animals **b** : PATROL WAGON **2** : a low four-wheeled vehicle with an open rectangular body for the play or use of a child **3** : STATION WAGON — **wag·on·er** \'wag-ə-nər\ *n* — **on the wagon** : choosing not to drink alcoholic beverages

wagon 1a

waif \'wāf\ *n* : a stray person or animal; *esp* : a homeless child

¹wail \'wā(ə)l\ *vb* **1** : to express sorrow by mournful cries : LAMENT **2** : to make a sound like a mournful cry **3** : to express dissatisfaction : COMPLAIN — **wail·er** \'wā-lər\ *n*

²wail *n* **1** : a long cry or sound of grief or pain **2** : a sound like a wail ⟨the *wail* of a siren⟩

wain \'wān\ *n* : a heavy wagon or two-wheeled cart for farm use

wain·scot \'wān-skət, -ˌskōt, -ˌskät\ *n* **1** : a usually paneled wooden lining of the wall of a room **2** : the lower three or four feet of an interior wall when finished differently from the rest

wain·scot·ing *or* **wain·scot·ting** \'wān-ˌskōt-iŋ, -ˌskät-, -skət-\ *n* **1** : WAINSCOT **2** : material used to line a surface with wainscot

waist \'wāst\ *n* **1 a** : the part of the body between the chest and hips **b** : the narrow front part of the abdomen of some insects (as a wasp) **2** : the central portion of something that is usually thinner or narrower than the ends ⟨the *waist* of a ship⟩ ⟨the *waist* of a violin⟩ **3** : a garment or the part of a garment that covers the body from the neck

to the waist — **waist·ed** \'wā-stəd\ *adj*

waist·band \'wās(t)-ˌband\ *n* : a band (as of trousers or a skirt) fitting around the waist

waist·coat \'wes-kət, 'wās(t)-ˌkōt\ *n, chiefly British* : ²VEST 1

waist·line \'wāst-ˌlīn\ *n* **1 a** : WAIST 1a **b** : body circumference at the waist **2** : the part of a garment surrounding the waist; *also* : the line at which the waist and skirt of a dress meet

¹wait \'wāt\ *vb* **1 a** : to remain in place in readiness or expectation of something : AWAIT ⟨*wait* your turn⟩ ⟨*wait* for orders⟩ **b** : to pause to let someone catch up ⟨hey, *wait* for me⟩ **2** : POSTPONE, DELAY ⟨*wait* dinner for a guest⟩ **3** : to serve as a waiter or waitress ⟨*wait* tables⟩ ⟨*wait* at a luncheon⟩ — **wait on** *or* **wait upon** **1 a** : to work for as a servant **b** : to supply the wants of : SERVE ⟨*wait on* a customer⟩ **2** : to make a formal call on **3** : to wait for — **wait up** : to delay going to bed ⟨I'll be late; don't *wait up*⟩

²wait *n* **1 a** : a hidden position : AMBUSH — used chiefly in the expression *lie in wait* **b** : a state of watchful expectation **2** : an act or period of waiting ⟨a long *wait* in line⟩

wait·er \'wāt-ər\ *n* : one that waits; *esp* : a boy or man who waits on table (as in a restaurant)

waiting list *n* : a list containing names of people who are waiting for something

waiting room *n* : a room or area (as at a doctor's office) for the use of persons waiting

wait·ress \'wā-trəs\ *n* : a girl or woman who waits on table (as in a restaurant)

waive \'wāv\ *vb* **waived; waiv·ing** : to give up claim to ⟨*waive* her right to answer⟩

waiv·er \'wā-vər\ *n* **1** : the act of intentionally giving up a right, claim, or privilege **2** : a document containing a declaration of a waiver

¹wake \'wāk\ *vb* **woke** \'wōk\ *also* **waked** \'wākt\; **wo·ken** \'wō-kən\ *also* **waked** *or* **woke; wak·ing** **1** : to be or remain awake **2** : to stand watch over (as a dead body) **3** : to arouse from or as if from sleep : AWAKE — often used with *up* [from Old English *wacan* "to awake" and Old English *waccian* "to be awake"] — **wak·er** *n*

²wake *n* : a watch held over the body of a dead person before burial

³wake *n* **1** : a track or path left by a moving body (as a ship) in the water **2** : AFTERMATH 2 [of Scandinavian origin] — **in the wake of** **1** : close behind and following the same course **2** : as a result of

wake·ful \'wāk-fəl\ *adj* : not sleeping or able to sleep — **wake·ful·ly** \-fə-lē\ *adv* — **wake·ful·ness** *n*

wak·en \'wā-kən\ *vb* **wak·ened; wak·en·ing** \'wāk-(ə-)niŋ\ : AROUSE 1

wake–rob·in \'wā-ˌkräb-ən\ *n* : TRILLIUM

Wal·dorf salad \ˌwȯl-ˌdȯrf-\ *n* : a salad usually containing apples, celery, nuts, and mayonnaise [named for the *Waldorf*-Astoria Hotel in New York City]

wale \'wā(ə)l\ *n* : a narrow raised surface or ridge; *esp* : one of a series of even ribs on a fabric (as corduroy)

¹walk \'wȯk\ *vb* **1** : to move or cause to move along on foot at a natural slow gait ⟨*walk* to town⟩ ⟨*walk* a horse up a hill⟩ **2** : to pass over, through, or along by walking ⟨*walk* the streets⟩ **3** : to perform or affect by walking **4** : to take or cause to take first base with a base on balls — **walk off with** **1** : ¹STEAL 2 **2** : to win or gain especially without difficulty ⟨*walked off with* the state championship⟩ — **walk over** : to disregard the wishes or feelings of

²walk *n* **1** : a going on foot ⟨go for a *walk*⟩ **2** : a place, path, or course for walking **3** : distance to be walked ⟨it's a long *walk*⟩ **4 a** : manner of living : CONDUCT, BEHAVIOR **b** : social or economic status ⟨various *walks* of life⟩ **5 a** : manner of walking **b** : a way of moving by a four-footed animal in which there are always at least two feet on the ground; *esp* : a slow way of moving by a horse in which the feet strike the ground in the sequence of left hind foot, left front foot, right hind foot, right front foot   **6** : BASE ON BALLS

walk·er \'wȯ-kər\ *n*   **1** : one that walks   **2** : something used in walking; *esp* : a framework that supports a baby learning to walk or a crippled or handicapped person

walk·ie–talk·ie \,wȯ-kē-'tȯ-kē\ *n* : a small portable radio set for receiving and sending messages

walk–in \,wȯ-,kin\ *adj* : large enough to be walked into ⟨a *walk-in* closet⟩

walking leaf *n* : any of a family of tropical insects that are related to the walkingsticks and have wings and legs resembling leaves

walking stick *n*   **1** : a stick used in walking   **2** *usually* **walk·ing·stick** : any of various usually wingless insects that have a long body resembling a stick — called also *stick insect*

Walk·man \'wȯk-mən, -,man\ *trademark* — used for a small portable radio or cassette player listened to by means of headphones or earphones

walk·out \'wȯ-,kau̇t\ *n*   **1** : ²STRIKE 2a   **2** : the action of leaving a meeting or organization as an expression of disapproval

walk out \(')wȯ-'kau̇t\ *vb*   **1** : to go on strike   **2** : to leave suddenly often as an expression of disapproval — **walk out on** : ¹ABANDON 3, DESERT

walk–up \'wȯ-,kəp\ *n* : a building or apartment house without an elevator — **walk–up** *adj*

walk–way \'wȯ-,kwā\ *n* : a path or passageway for pedestrians ⟨a *walkway* over the busy street⟩

¹wall \'wȯl\ *n*   **1** : a structure (as of brick or stone) meant to enclose or shut off a space; *esp* : a side of a room or building   **2** : something resembling a wall; *esp* : something that acts as a barrier or defense ⟨a tariff *wall*⟩   **3** : a layer of material that encloses space ⟨the heart *wall*⟩ ⟨the *walls* of a container⟩ — **walled** \'wȯld\ *adj*

²wall *vb*   **1** : to provide, separate, or surround with or as if with a wall ⟨*wall* in the garden⟩   **2** : to close off an opening with or as if with a wall ⟨*wall* up a door⟩

wal·la·by \'wäl-ə-bē\ *n, pl* **-bies** *also* **-by** : any of various small or medium-sized kangaroos

wall·board \'wȯl-,bō(ə)rd, -,bȯ(ə)rd\ *n* : a building material (as of wood pulp, gypsum, or plastic) made in large stiff sheets and used especially for inside walls and ceilings

wal·let \'wäl-ət\ *n*   **1** : a bag or sack for carrying things on a journey   **2** : a small flat folding pocketbook with compartments (as for coins, paper money, and cards); *also* : BILLFOLD

wallaby

wall·eye \'wȯ-,lī\ *n* : a large vigorous American freshwater food and sport fish that is related to the perches but resembles the true pike — called also *walleyed pike*

wall·flow·er \'wȯl-,flau̇(-ə)r\ *n* : a person who from shyness or unpopularity remains alone (as at a dance)

¹wal·lop \'wäl-əp\ *n*   **1** : a powerful blow or impact   **2** : the ability to hit hard

²wallop *vb*   **1** : to beat thoroughly : TROUNCE   **2** : to hit with force : SOCK — **wal·lop·er** *n*

¹wal·low \'wäl-ō\ *vb*   **1** : to roll about in or as if in deep mud ⟨elephants *wallowing* in the river⟩   **2** : to devote oneself to something pleasurable   **3** : to become or remain helpless ⟨allowed them to *wallow* in their ignorance⟩ — **wal·low·er** \'wäl-ə-wər\ *n*

²wallow *n*   **1** : an act of wallowing   **2** : a muddy or dust-filled hollow where animals wallow

wall·pa·per \'wȯl-,pā-pər\ *n* : decorative paper for covering the walls of a room — **wallpaper** *vb*

Wall Street \'wȯl-\ *n* : the powerful financial interests that control or influence the U.S. economy [from *Wall Street* in New York City, site of a major stock trading exchange]

wall–to–wall *adj*   **1** : covering the entire floor ⟨*wall-to-wall* carpeting⟩   **2** : filling an entire space ⟨a beach that was *wall-to-wall* sunbathers⟩

wal·nut \'wȯl-(,)nət\ *n*   **1 a** : an edible nut of any of a genus of trees related to the hickories; *esp* : the large edible nut of a Eurasian tree   **b** : a tree that produces walnuts — compare BLACK WALNUT   **c** : the usually reddish to dark brown wood of a walnut that is widely used for cabinetwork and veneers   **2** : a medium reddish brown

   Word History Long before walnut trees were introduced into England, they were cultivated for their tasty nuts in southern Europe. The nut tree native to the more northern areas of Europe was the hazel. In order to tell apart the native hazelnut and the less familiar walnut, Old English called the walnut *wealhhnutu,* which means "foreign nut". This word is a compound of *wealh,* "foreigner" and *hnutu* "nut". The Old English word *wealh* has supplied us with another word as well. While *wealh* meant "foreigner" in a general sense, it was applied specifically by the Anglo-Saxon invaders of Britain to the native people they found living on the island. *Wealh* gave rise to the modern forms *Welsh, Welshman,* and *Welshwoman.* [Old English *wealhhnutu,* literally "foreign nut", from *Wealh* "Welshman, foreigner" + *hnutu* "nut" — related to WELSH]

Wal·pur·gis Night \väl-'pu̇r-gəs-\ *n* : the evening before May 1, when witches were believed to gather to worship the devil [named for Saint *Walburga* (German *Walpurgis*) died 779 an English saint whose feast day falls on May Day]

wal·rus \'wȯl-rəs, 'wäl-\ *n, pl* **walrus** *or* **wal·rus·es** : either of two large mammals of northern seas that are related to the seals and are hunted especially for their hides, the ivory tusks of the males, and oil obtained from their blubber

walrus

¹waltz \'wȯl(t)s\ *n* : a ballroom dance in ¾ time with strong accent on the first beat

²waltz *vb*   **1 a** : to dance a waltz   **b** : to dance a waltz with   **2** : to approach or proceed with bold self-confidence : BREEZE

wam·pum \'wäm-pəm\ *n*   **1** : beads of polished shells formerly used by North American Indians as money and ornaments   **2** *slang* : MONEY 1 [from *wamponpeag,* a word in an American Indian language literally meaning "white strings"]

wan \'wän\ *adj* **wan·ner; wan·nest**   **1 a** : ¹PALE 1b, SICKLY   **b** : lacking vitality : FEEBLE   **2** : ¹DIM 1, FAINT   **3** : showing little effort : LANGUID ⟨a *wan* smile⟩ — **wan·ly** *adv* — **wan·ness** \'wän-nəs\ *n*

wand \'wänd\ *n*   **1** : a slender rod used in performing magic   **2** : a light rod or tube

wan·der \'wän-dər\ *vb* **wan·dered; wan·der·ing** \-d(ə-)riŋ\   **1** : to move about without a purpose   **2** : to follow a winding course : MEANDER   **3 a** : to get off the right course : STRAY   **b** : to lose one's normal mental state —

\ə\ abut	\au̇\ **out**	\i\ tip	\ȯ\ **saw**	\u̇\ foot
\ər\ **further**	\ch\ **chin**	\ī\ life	\ȯi\ **coin**	\y\ **yet**
\a\ mat	\e\ **pet**	\j\ job	\th\ **thin**	\yü\ few
\ā\ take	\ē\ **easy**	\ŋ\ **sing**	\th\ **this**	\yu̇\ cure
\ä\ cot, cart	\g\ **go**	\ō\ bone	\ü\ **food**	\zh\ vision

wander *n* — **wan·der·er** \-dər-ər\ *n*
syn WANDER, ROAM, RAMBLE, MEANDER mean to move about from place to place without a reason or plan. WANDER suggests that one does not follow a fixed course while moving about ⟨the nomads *wandered* in the desert for hundreds of years⟩ ROAM suggests a carefree wandering over a wide area often for pleasure ⟨I *roamed* over the hills and through the meadows⟩ RAMBLE suggests that one wanders in a careless way and without concern for where one goes ⟨tourists *rambling* through the park⟩ MEANDER suggests following a winding course and may also suggest moving lazily ⟨the youngsters *meandered* on the way home⟩

wandering Jew *n* : any of several creeping or trailing plants

wan·der·lust \'wän-dər-ˌləst\ *n* : strong longing to travel

¹wane \'wān\ *vb* **waned; wan·ing** **1** : to grow gradually smaller or less ⟨the moon *wanes*⟩ **2** : to lose power, prosperity, or influence ⟨the nation *waned* as its commerce declined⟩ **3** : to draw toward an end ⟨summer is *waning*⟩

²wane *n* **1** : the act or process of waning **2** : a period or time of waning; *esp* : the period from the full phase of the moon to the new moon

wan·gle \'waŋ-gəl\ *vb* **wan·gled; wan·gling** \-g(ə-)liŋ\ : to achieve or obtain by sly, tricky, or indirect methods ⟨*wangled* a free ticket to the show⟩

¹want \'wȯnt *also* 'wänt, 'wənt\ *vb* **1** : to be without : LACK ⟨this coat is *wanting* a button⟩ **2** : to fall short by **3** : to feel or have the need of : REQUIRE ⟨our house *wants* painting⟩ **4** : to desire, wish, or long for something **5** : to seek in order to arrest ⟨was *wanted* for murder⟩

²want *n* **1 a** : a lack of a required or usual amount **b** : a state of great poverty **2** : something wanted : NEED, DESIRE

want ad *n* : a newspaper advertisement stating that something (as an employee, job, or item) is wanted

¹want·ing *adj* **1** : not present or noticeable : ABSENT, LACKING **2 a** : falling below standards or expectations **b** : lacking in ability : DEFICIENT

²wanting *prep* **1** : ¹WITHOUT 2a ⟨a book *wanting* a cover⟩ **2** : ¹MINUS 1 ⟨a month *wanting* two days⟩

wan·ton \'wȯnt-ⁿn, 'wänt-\ *adj* **1** : FRISKY, PLAYFUL ⟨a *wanton* kitten⟩ **2** : INDECENT, LEWD **3 a** : MERCILESS, INHUMANE ⟨*wanton* cruelty⟩ **b** : being without just cause : MALICIOUS ⟨a *wanton* attack⟩ **4** : UNRESTRAINED 1, EXTRAVAGANT ⟨a life of *wanton* luxury⟩ — **wan·ton·ly** *adv* — **wan·ton·ness** \-ⁿn-nəs\ *n*

wa·pi·ti \'wäp-ət-ē\ *n, pl* **wapiti** *or* **wapitis** : ELK 2

¹war \'wȯ(ə)r\ *n* **1 a** : a state or period of armed hostile conflict between states, nations, or groups **b** : the science of warfare **2 a** : a state of hostility, antagonism, or conflict **b** : a struggle between opposing forces or for a particular goal ⟨a *war* on disease⟩

²war *vb* **warred; war·ring** **1** : to engage in warfare ⟨*warring* nations⟩ **2** : to be in conflict

¹war·ble \'wȯr-bəl\ *n* **1** : low pleasing sounds forming a melody **2** : the action of warbling : TRILL

²warble *vb* **war·bled; war·bling** \-b(ə-)liŋ\ **1** : to sing with trills **2** : to express by warbling

war·bler \'wȯr-blər\ *n* **1** : one that warbles **2 a** : any of numerous small Old World singing birds many of which are noted songsters and which are closely related to the thrushes **b** : any of numerous small brightly colored American songbirds with a usually weak and unmusical song

war·bon·net \'wȯr-ˌbän-ət\ *n* : a long feathered ceremonial American Indian headdress

war cry *n* : a cry or yell used by

warbonnet

fighters in battle

¹ward \'wȯ(ə)rd\ *n* **1** : the action or process of guarding or of being under guard; *esp* : CUSTODY 1 **2 a** : a division in a hospital **b** : a division (as a cell or block) of a prison **3** : an electoral or administrative division of a city **4** : a person (as a child or lunatic) under the protection of a court or guardian

²ward *vb* **1** : to keep watch over : GUARD **2** : to turn aside : DEFLECT — usually used with *off* ⟨*ward* off a cold⟩

¹-ward \wərd\ *also* **-wards** \wərdz\ *adj suffix* **1** : that moves, tends, faces, or is directed toward ⟨wind*ward*⟩ **2** : that occurs or is located in the direction of ⟨rear*ward*⟩ [Old English *-weard* (adjective suffix) "being or moving in the direction of"]

²-ward *or* **-wards** *adv suffix* **1** : in a (specified) direction ⟨rear*wards*⟩ ⟨after*ward*⟩ **2** : toward a (specified) point, position, or area ⟨sky*ward*⟩

war·den \'wȯrd-ⁿn\ *n* **1** : one who has charge or care of something : GUARDIAN, KEEPER **2** : the governor of a town, district, or fortress **3** : an official charged with special duties or with the enforcement of specified laws or regulations ⟨game *warden*⟩ ⟨air-raid *warden*⟩ **4** : an official in charge of a prison **5 a** : a lay officer of an Episcopal parish **b** : any of various British college officials

ward·er \'wȯrd-ər\ *n* : WATCHMAN, WARDEN

ward·robe \'wȯr-ˌdrōb\ *n* **1** : a room, closet, or chest where clothes are kept **2** : a collection of clothes (as of one person or for one activity)

ward·room \'wȯr-ˌdrüm, -ˌdru̇m\ *n* : the space in a warship assigned to the officers except the captain as living quarters or a dining room

ware \'wa(ə)r, 'we(ə)r\ *n* **1 a** : manufactured articles or products of art or craft : GOODS — often used in combination ⟨tin*ware*⟩ **b** : an article of merchandise ⟨peddlers hawking their *wares*⟩ **2** : items (as dishes) made from fired clay : POTTERY

ware·house \'wa(ə)r-ˌhau̇s, 'we(ə)r-\ *n* : a building for the storage of goods — **ware·house·man** \-ˌhau̇-smən\ *n*

war·fare \'wȯr-ˌfa(ə)r, -ˌfe(ə)r\ *n* **1 a** : military fighting between enemies : WAR **b** : activity undertaken by one country or group to weaken or destroy another ⟨economic *warfare*⟩ **2** : a struggle between competitors : CONFLICT ⟨industrial *warfare*⟩

war·head \'wȯr-ˌhed\ *n* : the section of a missile containing the charge

war–horse \'wȯ(ə)r-ˌhȯ(ə)rs\ *n* **1** : a horse used in war : CHARGER **2** : a veteran soldier or politician

warier *comparative of* WARY

wariest *superlative of* WARY

war·like \'wȯ(ə)r-ˌlīk\ *adj* **1** : fond of war ⟨*warlike* people⟩ **2** : of, relating to, or used in war

war·lock \'wȯ(ə)r-ˌläk\ *n* : a man who practices witchcraft : SORCERER, WIZARD

war·lord \'wȯ(ə)r-ˌlȯ(ə)rd\ *n* **1** : an important military leader **2** : a military leader who governs an area by force

¹warm \'wȯ(ə)rm\ *adj* **1 a** : having or giving off heat to a moderate or adequate degree ⟨*warm* food⟩ ⟨a *warm* stove⟩ **b** : serving to keep in heat (as of the body) ⟨*warm* clothes⟩ **c** : feeling or causing sensations of heat ⟨*warm* from exertion⟩ ⟨a long *warm* walk⟩ **2 a** : showing or marked by strong feeling : ARDENT ⟨a *warm* hug⟩ **b** : marked by tense excitement or anger ⟨a *warm* political campaign⟩ **3** : marked by or tending toward injury, distress, or pain ⟨gave the enemy a *warm* reception⟩ **4 a** : newly made : FRESH ⟨a *warm* scent⟩ **b** : near to a goal, answer, or object sought ⟨keep going; you're getting *warm*⟩ **5** : of a color in the range yellow to orange to red — **warm·ly** *adv* — **warm·ness** *n*

²warm *vb* **1** : to make or become warm ⟨*warm* yourself in front of the fire⟩ **2 a** : to give a feeling of warmth or pleasure to ⟨it *warms* my heart to see you⟩ **b** : to experience feelings of affection or pleasure ⟨*warmed* to her young guests⟩ **3** : to reheat for eating ⟨*warm* over some potatoes⟩ **4 a** : to make or become ready for action or performing by doing special exercises or actions beforehand ⟨swimmers *warm* up before a race⟩ **b** : to become increasingly interested or enthusiastic ⟨a speaker *warming* to his topic⟩

warm–blood·ed \'worm-'bləd-əd\ *adj* **1** : able to keep up a body temperature that is mostly independent of that of the surrounding environment **2** : warm in feeling — **warm–blood·ed·ness**

warm·er \'wor-mər\ *n* : one that warms; *esp* : a device for keeping something warm ⟨a foot *warmer*⟩

warm front *n* : an advancing edge of a warm air mass

warm·heart·ed \'wo(ə)rm-'härt-əd\ *adj* : marked by warmth of feeling — **warm·heart·ed·ness** *n*

warming pan *n* : a long-handled covered pan filled with hot coals and used to warm beds in earlier times

war·mon·ger \'wo(ə)r-,məŋ-gər, -,mäŋ-\ *n* : one who urges or attempts to stir up war — **war·mon·ger·ing** \-g(ə-)riŋ\ *n*

warmth \'wo(ə)rm(p)th\ *n* **1** : the quality or state of being warm in temperature **2 a** : the quality or state of being warm in feeling ⟨enjoyed the *warmth* of their praise⟩ **b** : a glowing effect produced by the use of warm colors

warm–up \'wor-,məp\ *n* **1** : the act or an instance of warming up **2** : a practice or set of exercises done before a game, contest, or workout

warn \'wo(ə)rn\ *vb* **1 a** : to give notice to beforehand especially of danger or evil **b** : to give advice to : COUNSEL **2** : to order to go or stay away ⟨*warned* us off their land⟩ — **warn·er** *n*

warn·ing \'wor-niŋ\ *n* **1** : the act of warning : the state of being warned ⟨he had *warning* of his illness⟩ **2** : something that warns ⟨storm *warnings*⟩ — **warning** *adj* — **warn·ing·ly** *adv*

¹warp \'wo(ə)rp\ *n* **1** : a series of yarns going lengthwise in a loom and crossed by the woof **2** : a twist or curve in something once flat or straight ⟨a *warp* in a door⟩

²warp *vb* **1 a** : to turn or twist out of shape **b** : to cause to judge, choose, or act wrongly : PERVERT **2** : to arrange so as to form a warp ⟨*warp* yarns⟩ — **warp·er** *n*

warp 1: *dark* warp, *light* woof

war·path \'wo(ə)r-,path, -,pȧth\ *n* : the route taken by a group of American Indians on their way to fight the enemy — **on the warpath** : ready to fight or argue

warp knit *n* : a knit fabric produced by a machine in which the knitting is done with the yarns running in a lengthwise direction — compare WEFT KNIT — **warp knitting** *n*

¹war·rant \'wor-ənt, 'wär-\ *n* **1** : evidence or a reason for thinking, deciding, or doing something : JUSTIFICATION **2** : evidence of permission; *esp* : a legal paper giving an officer the power to carry out the law **3** : a certificate of appointment issued to an officer of lower rank than a commissioned officer

²warrant *vb* **1** : to declare or insist with certainty ⟨I'll *warrant* they know the answer⟩ **2** : to guarantee something to be as it appears or is represented to be **3** : to give legal or official approval to : AUTHORIZE **4** : to call for : REQUIRE ⟨this report *warrants* careful study⟩ — **war·rant·able** \-ə-bəl\ *adj* — **war·ran·tor** \,wor-ən-'to(ə)r, ,wär-, -ənt-ər\ *n*

warrant officer *n* : a military or naval officer with any of the ranks between those of commissioned officers and those of noncommissioned officers; *esp* : a warrant officer of

lowest rank

war·ran·ty \'wor-ənt-ē, 'wär-\ *n, pl* **-ties** : a written statement guaranteeing the good condition of a product and stating the maker's responsibility for the repair or replacement of faulty parts

warred *past and past participle of* WAR

war·ren \'wor-ən, 'wär-\ *n* : a place where small game (as rabbits) are kept or raised

warring *present participle of* WAR

war·rior \'wor-yər; 'wor-ē-ər, 'wär-ē-\ *n* : a person who is or has been in warfare

war·ship \'wo(ə)r-,ship\ *n* : a ship armed for combat

wart \'wo(ə)rt\ *n* **1** : a small hard growth on the skin often caused by a virus **2** : something that sticks out (as on a plant) and resembles a wart — **warty** \'wort-ē\ *adj*

wart·hog \'wo(ə)rt-,hog, -,häg\ *n* : an African wild hog with two pairs of rough warty growths on the face and large tusks

war·time \'wo(ə)r-,tīm\ *n* : a period when a war is going on

wary \'wa(ə)r-ē, 'we(ə)r-\ *adj* **wari·er; -est** : very cautious; *esp* : being on guard against danger or trickery **syn** see CAREFUL — **wari·ly** \'war-ə-lē, 'wer-\ *adv* — **wari·ness** \'war-ē-nəs, 'wer-\ *n*

warthog

was *past 1st & 3d sing of* BE

¹wash \'wosh, 'wäsh\ *vb* **1** : to clean with water and usually a cleaning substance (as soap or detergent) ⟨*wash* clothes⟩ **2 a** : to wet thoroughly with liquid **b** : to pass water over or through especially so as to carry off material from the surface or interior **3** : to flow along or splash or overflow against ⟨waves *wash* the shore⟩ **4** : to pour or flow in a stream or current ⟨the river *washes* against its banks⟩ **5** : to move or carry by the action of water ⟨a child *washed* overboard⟩ **6** : to cover or smear lightly with a liquid (as whitewash or varnish) **7** : to run water over in order to separate out valuable matter ⟨*wash* sand for gold⟩ **8** : to hold up under washing ⟨this dress *washes* well⟩ **9** : to stand a test for truthfulness ⟨that story won't *wash*⟩ **10** : to be worn away by washing ⟨the heavy rain caused the bridge to *wash* out⟩

²wash *n* **1** : the act or process or an instance of washing **2** : articles to be or being washed **3 a** : a piece of ground washed by the sea or river **b** *Western* : the dry bed of a stream **4** : worthless especially liquid waste : REFUSE **5 a** : a thin coat of paint (as watercolor) **b** : a liquid used for coating a surface (as a wall) or for washing **6** : material carried along or deposited by running water **7 a** : BACKWASH **b** : a disturbance in the air produced by the passage of a wing or propeller

³wash *adj* : WASHABLE

wash·able \'wosh-ə-bəl, 'wäsh-\ *adj* : capable of being washed without damage ⟨a *washable* silk⟩ — **wash·abil·i·ty** \,wosh-ə-'bil-ət-ē, ,wäsh-\ *n*

wash–and–wear *adj* : of, relating to, or being a fabric or garment needing little or no ironing after washing

wash·ba·sin \'wosh-,bās-ᵊn, 'wäsh-\ *n* : WASHBOWL

wash·board \'wosh-,bō(ə)rd, 'wäsh-, -,bo(ə)rd\ *n* : a grooved board to scrub clothes on

wash·bowl \-,bōl\ *n* : a large bowl for water that is used to wash one's hands and face

\ə\ **abut**		\au̇\ **out**	\i\ **tip**	\o̅\ **saw**	\u̇\ **foot**
\ər\ **further**		\ch\ **chin**	\ī\ **life**	\oi\ **coin**	\y\ **yet**
\a\ **mat**		\e\ **pet**	\j\ **job**	\th\ **thin**	\yü\ **few**
\ā\ **take**		\ē\ **easy**	\ŋ\ **sing**	\th\ **this**	\yu̇\ **cure**
\ä\ **cot, cart**		\g\ **go**	\ō\ **bone**	\ü\ **food**	\zh\ **vision**

wash·cloth \-,klȯth\ *n* : a cloth for washing one's face and body

washed–out \'wȯsh-'taut, 'wäsh-\ *adj* **1** : faded in color **2** : empty of life or energy : EXHAUSTED

washed–up \'wȯsh-'təp, 'wäsh-\ *adj* : no longer successful, popular, or needed

wash·er \'wȯsh-ər, 'wäsh-\ *n* **1** : a ring (as of metal) used to make something fit tightly or to prevent rubbing **2** : one that washes; *esp* : WASHING MACHINE

wash·er·wom·an \'wȯsh-ər-,wum-ən, 'wäsh-\ *n* : a woman who takes in washing

wash·ing \'wȯsh-iŋ, 'wäsh-\ *n* : articles washed or to be washed

washing machine *n* : a machine used especially for washing clothes and household linen

washing soda *n* : SODIUM CARBONATE

Washington's Birthday *n* **1** : February 22 formerly observed as a legal holiday in most states of the U.S. **2** : the third Monday in February observed as a legal holiday in most states of the U.S. — called also *Presidents' Day*

wash·out \'wȯsh-,aut, 'wäsh-\ *n* **1 a** : the washing away of earth (as from a road) **b** : a place where earth is washed away **2** : a complete failure

wash out \(')wȯsh-'aut, (')wäsh-\ *vb* **1** : to fade or cause to fade by or as if by laundering **2** : to exhaust the strength or energy **3** : to fail to measure up to a standard **4** : to destroy by the force or action of water

wash·room \'wȯsh-,rüm, 'wäsh-, -,rum\ *n* : a room with washbowls and toilets

wash·stand \-,(s)tand\ *n* **1** : a stand holding articles for washing one's face and hands **2** : WASHBOWL

wash·tub \-,təb\ *n* : a tub for washing or soaking clothes

wash up *vb* : to bring to an end the force or value of ⟨a scandal would *wash* you *up* as a sports hero⟩

wasn't \'wəz-ᵊnt, 'wäz-\ : was not

wasp \'wäsp, 'wȯsp\ *n* : any of numerous winged insects related to the bees and ants that have a slender body with the abdomen attached by a narrow stalk and that in females and workers are usually capable of giving a very painful sting

WASP *or* **Wasp** *n* : an American of northern European and Protestant background

wasp

wasp·ish \'wäs-pish, 'wȯs-\ *adj* **1** : easily annoyed : SNAPPISH **2** : like a wasp in form; *esp* : very thin — **wasp·ish·ly** *adv* — **wasp·ish·ness** *n*

wasp waist *n* : a very slender waist

¹was·sail \'wäs-əl *also* wä-'sā(ə)l\ *n* **1** : an early English toast to someone's health **2** : wild drinking : REVELRY [Middle English *wæs hæil* "a toast to someone's health", from early Norse *ves heill* "be of good health", from *heill* "healthy" — related to ³HAIL, ¹HALE]

²wassail *vb* : to go on a wild drinking spree — **was·sail·er** *n*

wast \wəst, (')wäst\ *archaic past 2d sing of* BE

wast·age \'wā-stij\ *n* : loss, decrease, or destruction of something (as by use, decay, erosion, or leakage); *esp* : wasteful or avoidable loss of something valuable

¹waste \'wāst\ *n* **1 a** : a region that has few people or is empty of most signs of life : DESERT **b** : uncultivated land **2 a** : the act or an instance of wasting **b** : the state of being wasted **3 a** : material left over, rejected, or thrown away **b** : an unwanted product obtained in the course of a manufacturing or chemical process **c** : material (as carbon dioxide in the lungs or urine in the kidneys) produced in and of no further use to the living body

²waste *vb* **wast·ed; wast·ing** **1** : to destroy completely **2** : to wear away or grow smaller gradually **3** : to spend carelessly or uselessly : SQUANDER **4** : to lose or cause to lose weight, strength, or energy ⟨illness caused her to *waste* away⟩

³waste *adj* **1** : being wild and without people or crops : DESOLATE, BARREN **2** : being in a ruined condition **3** : thrown away as worthless after being used **4** : of no further use to a person, animal, or plant ⟨means by which the body gives off *waste* materials⟩

waste·bas·ket \'wās(t)-,bas-kət\ *n* : an open container for wastepaper

waste·ful \'wāst-fəl\ *adj* : given to or marked by waste : PRODIGAL ⟨a *wasteful* use of our natural resources⟩ — **waste·ful·ly** \-fə-lē\ *adv* — **waste·ful·ness** *n*

waste·land \'wāst-,land\ *n* : land that is barren or not fit for crops

waste·pa·per \'wās(t)-'pā-pər\ *n* : paper thrown away as used, not needed, or not fit for use

wast·er \'wā-stər\ *n* : one that uses or uses up carelessly or needlessly

wast·rel \'wā-strəl\ *n* : SPENDTHRIFT

¹watch \'wäch, 'wȯch\ *vb* **1** : to stay awake especially during the night (as at the bedside of a sick person) **2** : to be on the alert or on the lookout **3** : to keep guard ⟨*watch* outside the door⟩ **4** : to keep one's eyes on : keep in view ⟨*watch* a game⟩ **5** : to keep in view so as to prevent harm or warn of danger ⟨*watch* a brush fire carefully⟩ **6** : to keep oneself informed about ⟨*watch* his career⟩ **7** : to be on the alert for the chance to make use of ⟨*watched* her opportunity and took it⟩ — **watch·er** *n*

²watch *n* **1 a** : the act of keeping awake to guard, protect, or attend **b** : a state of alert and continuous attention ⟨a tornado *watch*⟩ **c** : close observation ⟨kept a *watch* over the prisoner⟩ **2 a** : WATCHMAN **b** : a body of watchmen **3 a** : a period during which a part of a ship's company is on duty **b** : the part of a ship's company on duty during a watch **4** : a portable timepiece designed to be worn (as on the wrist) or carried in the pocket

watch·dog \'wäch-,dȯg, 'wȯch-\ *n* **1** : a dog kept to guard property **2** : one that guards against loss, waste, theft, or dishonesty

watch·ful \'wäch-fəl, 'wȯch-\ *adj* : continually on the lookout especially for danger — **watch·ful·ly** \-fə-lē\ *adv* — **watch·ful·ness** *n*

watch·mak·er \'wäch-,mā-kər, 'wȯch-\ *n* : one that makes or repairs watches or clocks — **watch·mak·ing** \-kiŋ\ *n*

watch·man \-mən\ *n* : a person assigned to watch : GUARD

watch out *vb* : to be on the lookout ⟨*watch out* for cars⟩

watch·tow·er \'wäch-,tau(-ə)r, 'wȯch-\ *n* : a tower for a lookout

watch·word \-,wərd\ *n* **1** : a secret word used as a signal or password **2** : a motto used as a slogan or cry for common support

¹wa·ter \'wȯt-ər, 'wät-\ *n* **1** : the liquid that descends from the clouds as rain, forms streams, lakes, and seas, and is a major part of all living material and that is an odorless and tasteless compound having two atoms of hydrogen and one atom of oxygen per molecule **2** *pl* : an area of seawater bordering on and under the control of a country ⟨sailing Canadian *waters*⟩ **3** : travel or transportation on water ⟨came by *water*⟩ **4** : the level of water at a particular state of the tide : TIDE **5** : a liquid containing or resembling water; *esp* : a watery fluid (as tears, urine, or sap) formed or circulating in a living body — **wa·ter·less** \-ləs\ *adj*

²water *vb* **1** : to wet or supply with water ⟨*water* horses⟩ ⟨*water* the lawn⟩ **2** : to weaken by or as if by the addition of water ⟨someone *watered* down the punch⟩ **3** : to form or give off water or watery matter (as tears or saliva) ⟨smog makes my eyes *water*⟩ — **wa·ter·er** \-ər-ər\ *n*

water bed *n* : a bed whose mattress is a plastic bag filled with water

water beetle *n* : any of numerous oval flattened beetles that are found in water and swim by means of their fringed hind legs which act together as oars

wa·ter·bird \'wȯt-ər-,bərd\ *n* : a swimming or wading bird — compare WATERFOWL

wa·ter·buck \'wȯt-ər-,bək, 'wät-\ *n, pl* **waterbuck** *or* **waterbucks** : any of several African antelopes that are found within range of streams or wet lands

water buffalo *n* : an Asian buffalo that is often domesticated and somewhat resembles a large ox

water buffalo

water bug *n* : any of various insects (as a true bug or a cockroach) that live in or near water or in moist places

water chestnut *n* : any of several water-dwelling plants (as a Chinese sedge) with edible underground parts or fruits; *also* : the edible part

water clock *n* : a device or machine for measuring time by the fall or flow of water

water closet *n*   **1** : a compartment or room with a toilet bowl   **2** : a toilet bowl with its fixtures

wa·ter·col·or \'wȯt-ər-,kəl-ər, 'wät-\ *n*   **1** : a paint whose liquid part is water   **2** : a picture painted with watercolor   **3** : the art of painting with watercolor — **wa·ter·col·or·ist** \-,kəl-ə-rəst\ *n*

wa·ter·course \-,kō(ə)rs, -,kȯ(ə)rs\ *n*   **1** : a channel in which water flows   **2** : a stream of water (as a river or brook)

wa·ter·craft \-,kraft\ *n* : craft for water transportation

wa·ter·cress \-,kres\ *n* : a plant that is related to the mustards and the cabbage, grows especially in clear running water, and has crisp peppery-tasting leaves used especially in salads

water cycle *n* : HYDROLOGIC CYCLE

wa·ter·fall \'wȯt-ər-,fȯl, 'wät-\ *n* : a fall of water usually from a great height

water flea *n* : any of various small active dark or brightly colored freshwater crustaceans (as a daphnia)

wa·ter·fowl \'wȯt-ər-,faul, 'wät-\ *n*   **1** : a bird that is found in or near water   **2 waterfowl** *pl* : birds with webbed feet of the family including ducks, geese, and swans; *esp* : wild ducks and geese hunted as game

wa·ter·front \-,frənt\ *n* : land or a section of a town bordering on a body of water

water gas *n* : a poisonous flammable gaseous mixture that consists chiefly of carbon monoxide and hydrogen, that is usually made by blowing air and then steam over red-hot coke or coal, and that is used as a fuel

water glass *n* : a glass container (as a drinking glass) for holding water

water hole *n* : a natural hole or hollow containing water especially for drinking

water hyacinth *n* : a floating water plant often clogging waterways in the southern U.S.

water ice *n* : a frozen dessert of water, sugar, and flavoring

water jump *n* : an obstacle (as in a steeplechase) consisting of a pool, stream, or ditch of water

water lily *n* : any of a family of water plants with

water lily

rounded floating leaves and usually showy flowers

wa·ter·line \'wȯt-ər-,līn, 'wät-\ *n* : any of several lines that are marked on the outside of a ship and that match the surface of the water when the ship floats evenly

wa·ter·logged \'wȯt-ər-,lȯgd, 'wät-, -,lägd\ *adj* : so filled or soaked with water as to be heavy or hard to manage (a *waterlogged* boat)

¹wa·ter·mark \'wȯt-ər-,märk, 'wät-\ *n*   **1** : a mark that shows a line to which water has risen   **2** : a mark (as the maker's name or trademark) made in paper during manufacture and visible when the paper is held up to the light

²watermark *vb* : to mark with a watermark

wa·ter·mel·on \'wȯt-ər-,mel-ən, 'wät-\ *n*   **1** : a large oblong or rounded fruit with a hard outer shell, a sweet red juicy pulp, and many seeds   **2** : a widely grown African vine that is related to the squashes and produces watermelons

water moccasin *n* : a poisonous pit viper of the southern U.S. that is closely related to the copperhead — called also *cottonmouth, cottonmouth moccasin*

water ouzel *n* : DIPPER 1

water pistol *n* : a toy pistol designed to squirt a stream of water

water polo *n* : a ball game played in water by teams of swimmers

wa·ter·pow·er \'wȯt-ər-,pau̇(-ə)r, 'wät-\ *n* : the power of moving water used to run machinery (as for generating electricity)

¹wa·ter·proof \-,prüf\ *adj* : not letting water through; *esp* : covered or treated with a material to prevent penetration by water

²waterproof *n, chiefly British* : RAINCOAT

³waterproof *vb* : to make waterproof

water rat *n* : a rodent that is found in or near water

wa·ter·re·pel·lent \,wȯt-ə(r)-ri-'pel-ənt, ,wät-\ *adj* : treated with a finish that resists but does not completely prevent penetration by water

wa·ter·re·sis·tant \-ri-'zis-tənt\ *adj* : WATER-REPELLENT

wa·ter·shed \'wȯt-ər-,shed, 'wät-\ *n*   **1** : a dividing ridge (as a mountain range) separating one drainage area from others   **2** : the area that drains into a river or lake

water–ski \-,skē\ *vb* : to ski on water while being towed by a speedboat — **wa·ter–ski·er** *n*

water ski *n* : a ski used in water-skiing

water snake *n* : any of numerous snakes found in or near fresh waters and feeding largely on water-dwelling animals

water spaniel *n* : a rather large spaniel of either of two breeds with heavy curly coats

wa·ter·spout \'wȯt-ər-,spaut, 'wät-\ *n*   **1** : a pipe for carrying off water from a roof   **2** : a slender cloud that is shaped like a funnel and extends down to a cloud of spray torn up from the surface of a body of water by a whirlwind

water strider *n* : any of various long-legged bugs that move about swiftly on the surface of the water

water table *n* : the upper limit of the portion of the ground completely soaked with water

wa·ter·tight \,wȯt-ər-'tīt, ,wät-\ *adj*   **1** : made to keep water out (a *watertight* compartment)   **2** : allowing no possibility for doubt or uncertainty (a *watertight* case against the accused)

water vapor *n* : water in a gaseous form especially when below boiling temperature and spread through the atmosphere

water–vascular system *n* : a system of vessels in echinoderms containing a circulating watery fluid that is used especially for the movement of tentacles and tube feet

\ə\ abut	\au̇\ out	\i\ tip	\ȯ\ saw	\u̇\ foot
\ər\ further	\ch\ chin	\ī\ life	\ȯi\ coin	\y\ yet
\a\ mat	\e\ pet	\j\ job	\th\ thin	\yü\ few
\ā\ take	\ē\ easy	\ŋ\ sing	\th\ this	\yu̇\ cure
\ä\ cot, cart	\g\ go	\ō\ bone	\ü\ food	\zh\ vision

wa·ter·way \'wȯt-ər-,wā, 'wät-\ *n* **1** : a channel for water **2** : a body of water through which ships can travel

wa·ter·weed \-,wēd\ *n* : a weedy water plant usually with small flowers

wa·ter·wheel \-,hwēl, -,wēl\ *n* : a wheel made to turn by a flow of water against it

water wings *n pl* : an air-filled device to give support to the body of a swimmer

wa·ter·works \'wȯt-ər-,wərks, 'wät-\ *n pl* : a system of reservoirs, pumps, and pipes for supplying water (as to a city)

waterwheel

wa·tery \'wȯt-ə-rē, 'wät-\ *adj* **1 a** : consisting of or filled with water **b** : containing or giving out water or a thin liquid ⟨a *watery* mixture⟩ ⟨*watery* eyes⟩ **2** : being like water especially in thinness, sogginess, paleness, or lack of taste ⟨*watery* lemonade⟩ ⟨*watery* blood⟩

watt \'wät\ *n* : the metric unit of power equal to the work done at the rate of one joule per second [named for James Watt 1736–1819 Scottish engineer]

watt·age \'wät-ij\ *n* : amount of power expressed in watts

¹wat·tle \'wät-ᵊl\ *n* **1 a** : a framework of poles interwoven with slender branches or reeds and used in building **b** : material for such a framework **2** : a fleshy flap of skin hanging usually from the neck (as of a bird) — **wat·tled** \-ᵊld\ *adj*

²wattle *vb* **wat·tled; wat·tling** \'wät-liŋ, -ᵊl-iŋ\ **1** : to form or build of or with wattle **2 a** : to weave (as branches) together to form wattle **b** : to unite or make solid by weaving together light flexible material

¹wave \'wāv\ *vb* **waved; wav·ing** **1** : to float or shake in an air current : FLUTTER ⟨flags *waving* in the breeze⟩ **2** : to signal or salute with the hand or with something held in it **3** : BRANDISH ⟨*waved* a pistol and made threats⟩ **4** : to move before the wind with a wavelike motion ⟨a field of *waving* grain⟩ **5** : to follow or cause to follow a curving line or take a wavy form ⟨*waved* her hair⟩

²wave *n* **1** : a moving ridge on the surface of water **2** : a wavelike formation or shape ⟨a *wave* in the hair⟩ **3** : the action or process of making wavy or curly **4** : a waving motion ⟨a *wave* of my hand⟩ **5** : a steady flowing movement ⟨a *wave* of color swept the speaker's face⟩ **6** : a sudden or rapid increase ⟨a *wave* of buying⟩ **7** : a disturbance similar to a wave in water that transfers energy progressively from point to point ⟨a light *wave*⟩ **8** : a period of hot or cold weather — **wave·like** \-,līk\ *adj*

Wave \'wāv\ *n* : a woman serving in the U.S. Navy

wave·length \'wāv-,leŋ(k)th\ *n* **1** : the distance (as from crest to crest) in the line of advance of a wave from any one point to the next corresponding point **2** : a certain line of thought or behavior that reveals a common understanding ⟨a project is easier when everyone is on the same *wavelength*⟩

wave·let \'wāv-lət\ *n* : a little wave : RIPPLE

wa·ver \'wā-vər\ *vb* **wa·vered; wa·ver·ing** \'wāv-(ə-)riŋ\ **1** : to go back and forth between choices **2** : to weave or sway to and fro **3** : to move unsteadily — **wa·ver·er** \'wā-vər-ər\ *n*

wavy \'wā-vē\ *adj* **wav·i·er; wav·i·est** : having or moving in waves ⟨*wavy* hair⟩ — **wav·i·ness** \-vē-nəs\ *n*

¹wax \'waks\ *n* **1** : a yellowish plastic substance produced and given off by bees and used by them for making the honeycomb — called also *beeswax* **2** : any of various substances like beeswax [Old English *weax* "wax produced by bees"] — **wax·like** \'wak-,slīk\ *adj*

²wax *vb* : to treat or rub with wax

³wax *vb* **1** : to grow larger, stronger, fuller, or more numerous **2** : BECOME 1 ⟨*waxed* angry as I heard the story⟩ [Old English *weaxan* "to increase"]

wax bean *n* : a kidney bean with pods that are yellow when ripe for use as snap beans

waxed paper *or* **wax paper** *n* : paper treated with wax to make it resistant to water and grease and used especially as a wrapping

wax·en \'wak-sən\ *adj* : of or like wax

wax myrtle *n* : any of several trees or shrubs with fragrant leaves; *esp* : an American evergreen shrub that produces small hard berries with a thick coating of white wax used for candles — compare BAYBERRY 2a

wax·wing \'wak-,swiŋ\ *n* : any of a genus of American and Eurasian birds that are mostly brown with a showy crest and velvety feathers

waxwing

waxy \'wak-sē\ *adj* **wax·i·er; -est** **1** : full of or covered with wax ⟨a *waxy* surface⟩ ⟨*waxy* berries⟩ **2** : WAXEN — **wax·i·ness** *n*

¹way \'wā\ *n* **1 a** : a track for travel : PATH **b** : an opening for passage (as through a crowd or a gate) ⟨tried to find my *way* in the mob⟩ **2 a** : a course traveled : ROUTE **b** : DIRECTION 3 ⟨come this *way*⟩ ⟨the wrong *way*⟩ **3 a** : a course of action ⟨chose the easy *way*⟩ **b** : opportunity or power of doing as one pleases ⟨have your own *way*⟩ **c** : POSSIBILITY 1 ⟨there are no two *ways* about it⟩ **4 a** : the manner in which something is done or happens ⟨this *way* of thinking⟩ ⟨a new *way* of painting⟩ **b** : a noticeable part or detail ⟨a good worker in many *ways*⟩ **c** : ¹STATE 1a ⟨the *way* things are⟩ **5** : a particular or typical manner of behavior ⟨it's just his *way*⟩ ⟨a nice *way* with his pets⟩ **6 a** : ¹DISTANCE 1b ⟨a short *way* down the road⟩ **b** : progress along a course ⟨earning her *way* through school⟩ ⟨made her *way* with difficulty⟩ **7** : LOCALITY ⟨out our *way*⟩ **8** : room or chance to pass or advance ⟨make *way* for the queen⟩ **9** : CATEGORY 1 ⟨get what you need in the *way* of supplies⟩ — **by way of** **1** : for the purpose of ⟨mentioned her *by way of* example⟩ **2** : by the route through : VIA — **in one's way** *also* **in the way** **1** : in or along one's course **2** : in a position to hinder or obstruct — **out of the way** **1** : IMPROPER ⟨said nothing *out of the way* during dinner⟩ **2** : in or to a place away from public view ⟨found a cottage that was *out of the way*⟩ — **under way** **1** : in motion through the water **2** : in progress ⟨the show was *under way* when we came in⟩

²way *adv* : ¹FAR 1

way·far·er \'wā-,far-ər, -,fer-\ *n* : a traveler especially on foot — **way·far·ing** \-,far-iŋ, -,fer-\ *adj*

way·lay \'wā-,lā\ *vb* **-laid** \-,lād\; **-lay·ing** : to attack from a hiding place

way–out \'wā-'aut\ *adj* : very unusual or odd ⟨*way-out* ideas⟩

-ways \,wāz\ *adv suffix* : in such a way, course, direction, or manner ⟨side*ways*⟩ [derived from Middle English *way* "course, route"]

way·side \'wā-,sīd\ *n* : the side or border of a road or path — **wayside** *adj*

way station *n* : a station or stopping place along a line of travel (as a railroad line)

way·ward \'wā-wərd\ *adj* **1** : tending to do as one pleases : DISOBEDIENT ⟨*wayward* children⟩ **2** : not following a rule or regular course of action — **way·ward·ly** *adv* — **way·ward·ness** *n*

we \(')wē\ *pron* **1** : I and one or more others **2** : I — used

by a monarch or an editor or writer

weak \'wēk\ *adj* **1** : lacking physical strength **2** : not able to stand much weight, pressure, or strain ⟨a *weak* rope⟩ **3 a** : lacking strength of mind or character **b** : resulting from or showing a lack of mental or moral firmness ⟨a *weak* policy⟩ **4** : not rich in some usual or important element ⟨*weak* tea⟩ **5** : not able to stand the test of logic ⟨a *weak* argument⟩ **6** : lacking skill or ability **7** : lacking in force of expression ⟨a *weak* writing style⟩ **8** : not having or using authority ⟨*weak* government⟩ **9** : of, relating to, or being a verb or verb conjugation that forms the past tense and past participle by adding the suffix *-ed* or *-d* or *-t* **10** : of, relating to, or being the lightest of three levels of stress in pronunciation ⟨a *weak* syllable⟩ **11** : ionizing only slightly in solution ⟨*weak* acids⟩ — **weak·ly** *adv*

　syn WEAK, FEEBLE, FRAIL mean not strong enough to stand pressure or hard effort. WEAK can be used of either a temporary or permanent loss of strength or power ⟨felt *weak* after the illness⟩ ⟨I have *weak* lungs⟩ FEEBLE stresses very great and pitiful weakness ⟨*feeble* with hunger, the dog was found wandering in the streets⟩ FRAIL can be used of a person who since birth has had a delicate body ⟨a *frail* child always getting sick⟩ or of any kind of flimsy construction ⟨the *frail* boat was wrecked in the first storm⟩

weak·en \'wē-kən\ *vb* **weak·ened; weak·en·ing** \'wēk-(ə-)niŋ\ : to make or become weak or weaker ⟨disease *weakens* the body⟩

weak·fish \'wēk-ˌfish\ *n* : a common fish of the eastern coast of the U.S. that is related to the perches and is caught for sport or for sale in markets; *also* : any of several related fishes used for food

weak force *n* : a fundamental force experienced by elementary particles that causes some forms of radioactivity and also causes some types of particles to break down into other particles

weak·ling \'wē-kliŋ\ *n* : one that is weak in body, character, or mind — **weakling** *adj*

weak·ly \'wē-klē\ *adj* **weak·li·er; -est** : not strong or healthy

weak–mind·ed \'wēk-'mīn-dəd\ *adj* **1** : lacking in judgment or good sense **2** : FEEBLE-MINDED

weak·ness \'wēk-nəs\ *n* **1** : the quality or state of being weak **2** : a weak point : FAULT, DEFECT ⟨a person with few *weaknesses*⟩ **3** : an object of special desire or fondness ⟨movies are my *weakness*⟩

¹weal \'wē(ə)l\ *n* : a sound or prosperous state : WELL-BEING [Old English *wela* "healthy state"]

²weal *n* : WELT [an altered form of *wale* "a streak or ridge made on the skin from a blow"]

wealth \'welth\ *n* **1** : a great amount of money or possessions : AFFLUENCE **2** : a large amount or number : PROFUSION ⟨a *wealth* of detail⟩

wealthy \'wel-thē\ *adj* **wealth·i·er; -est** **1** : having wealth : RICH **2** : marked by plenty : ABUNDANT — **wealth·i·ness** \-thē-nəs\ *n*

wean \'wēn\ *vb* **1** : to get a child or young animal used to food other than its mother's milk **2** : to turn (one) away from something long desired or followed ⟨*wean* a child from a bad habit⟩

weap·on \'wep-ən\ *n* **1** : something (as a gun, knife, or club) used to injure, defeat, or destroy **2** : something with which one fights or struggles against another

weap·on·ry \'wep-ən-rē\ *n* : weapons as a whole

¹wear \'wa(ə)r, 'we(ə)r\ *vb* **wore** \'wō(ə)r, 'wȯ(ə)r\; **worn** \'wō(ə)rn, 'wȯ(ə)rn\; **wear·ing** **1 a** : to use as an article of clothing ⟨*wears* blue jeans all the time⟩ **b** : to carry on the person ⟨*wear* a watch⟩ **2** : to have or show an appearance of ⟨*wore* a happy smile⟩ **3 a** : to damage, destroy, or make less by use or by scraping or rubbing ⟨*wore* the shoes to pieces⟩ **b** : to produce gradually by wearing ⟨*wear* a hole in the rug⟩ **c** : to tire or weaken : FATIGUE

⟨soldiers *worn* by the strain of war⟩ **4** : to stand up under use ⟨a silk that *wears* well⟩ **5 a** : to lessen or end with the passage of time ⟨the effect of the medicine *wore* off⟩ ⟨the day *wore* on⟩ **b** : to reach a certain condition gradually — **wear·er** *n*

²wear *n* **1 a** : the act of wearing : USE **b** : the state of being worn **2** : clothing or an article of clothing usually of a particular kind or for a special occasion or use ⟨children's *wear*⟩ **3** : wearing quality : durability under use **4** : the result of wearing or use ⟨a carpet showing signs of *wear*⟩

wear·able \'war-ə-bəl, 'wer-\ *adj* : capable of being worn : suitable to be worn — **wear·abil·i·ty** \ˌwar-ə-'bil-ət-ē, ˌwer-\ *n*

wear and tear *n* : the loss or damage that occurs to something in the course of normal use

wea·ri·some \'wir-ē-səm\ *adj* : causing weariness : TIRESOME — **wea·ri·some·ly** *adv* — **wea·ri·some·ness** *n*

wear out *vb* **1** : to tire gradually ⟨*worn out* from exercising⟩ **2** : to make or become useless by wear

¹wea·ry \'wi(ə)r-ē\ *adj* **wea·ri·er; -est** **1** : worn out in strength, energy, or freshness **2** : showing or marked by weariness **3** : having one's patience, interest, or pleasure exhausted ⟨*weary* of their attacks⟩ **4** : WEARISOME — **wea·ri·ly** \'wir-ə-lē\ *adv* — **wea·ri·ness** \'wir-ē-nəs\ *n*

²weary *vb* **wea·ried; wea·ry·ing** : to become or make weary **syn** see TIRE

wea·sel \'wē-zəl\ *n, pl* **weasel** *or* **weasels** : any of various small slender active mammals that are related to the minks and eat small birds and mammals

weasel

weasel word *n* : a word used in order to mislead a person or to avoid a straight answer

¹weath·er \'weth-ər\ *n* **1** : the state of the atmosphere in regard to heat or cold, wetness or dryness, calm or storm, clearness or cloudiness **2** : disagreeable atmospheric conditions ⟨stormy *weather*⟩ — **under the weather** : somewhat ill or drunk

²weather *vb* **weath·ered; weath·er·ing** \'weth-(ə-)riŋ\ **1 a** : to expose to the weather **b** : to change (as in color or structure) by exposure **2** : to bear up against and come safely through ⟨*weather* a storm⟩

³weather *adj* : ¹WINDWARD

weath·er–beat·en \'weth-ər-ˌbēt-ᵊn\ *adj* : worn or changed by exposure to weather ⟨a *weather-beaten* old barn⟩

weath·er·cock \-ˌkäk\ *n* : a weather vane shaped like a rooster

weath·er·ing \'weth-(ə-)riŋ\ *n* : the action of the forces of nature that changes the color, texture, composition, or form of exposed objects; *esp* : the physical and chemical breakdown of earth materials at or near the earth's surface

weath·er·man \'weth-ər-ˌman\ *n* : a person who reports and forecasts the weather : METEOROLOGIST

weath·er·proof \ˌweth-ər-'prüf\ *adj* : able to stand up under exposure to weather — **weatherproof** *vb*

weather station *n* : a station for taking, recording, and reporting observations of the weather

weather stripping *n* : material used to seal a door or window around the edges

weather vane *n* : VANE 1

¹weave \'wēv\ *vb* **wove** \'wōv\ *or* **weaved; wo·ven** \'wō-

\ə\ abut	\au̇\ out	\i\ tip	\o̅\ saw	\u̇\ foot
\ər\ further	\ch\ chin	\ī\ life	\o̅i\ coin	\y\ yet
\a\ mat	\e\ pet	\j\ job	\th\ thin	\yü\ few
\ā\ take	\ē\ easy	\ŋ\ sing	\th\ this	\yu̇\ cure
\ä\ cot, cart	\g\ go	\ō\ bone	\ü\ food	\zh\ vision

vən\ or **weaved; weav·ing 1 a** : to form by lacing together strands of material; *esp* : to make on a loom by lacing together threads going lengthwise with threads going crosswise ⟨*weave* cloth⟩ **b** : to form into a fabric ⟨*weave* wool into tweeds⟩ **2** : ¹SPIN 2b **3 a** : to make by or as if by lacing together parts ⟨*wove* an exciting adventure tale⟩ **b** : to insert as a part : work in ⟨*weave* a moral into a tale⟩ **4** : to move back and forth or from side to side ⟨*weaving* his way through a crowd of holiday shoppers⟩ — **weav·er** *n*

²**weave** *n* : a pattern or method of weaving

weav·er·bird \'wē-vər-ˌbərd\ *n* : any of numerous Old World birds that resemble finches and usually build a complicated nest by weaving together plant materials

¹**web** \'web\ *n* **1** : a fabric on a loom in the process of being removed from a loom **2 a** : a thread or network of threads spun by a spider or insect larva : SPIDERWEB **b** : something that catches and holds one ⟨spies caught in a *web* of plots⟩ **3** : a membrane of an animal or plant; *esp* : one uniting toes (as of many birds) **4** : NETWORK 2

²**web** *vb* **webbed; web·bing 1** : to cover or provide with webs or a web **2** : to make or form a web

webbed \'webd\ *adj* : having or being toes or fingers joined by webs ⟨the *webbed* feet of ducks⟩

web·bing \'web-iŋ\ *n* : a strong closely woven tape used especially for straps, harness, or upholstery

web–foot·ed \'web-'fut-əd\ *adj* : having webbed feet

wed \'wed\ *vb* **wed·ded** *also* **wed; wed·ding 1** : to take, give, or join in marriage : MARRY **2** : to unite firmly as if by marriage

we'd \(ˌ)wēd\ : we had : we should : we would

wed·ding \'wed-iŋ\ *n* : a marriage ceremony usually with accompanying festivities : NUPTIALS

¹**wedge** \'wej\ *n* **1** : a piece of wood or metal with a pointed edge used especially to split wood or rocks and to lift heavy weights **2** : something (as a piece of pie or land) shaped like a triangle **3** : something that serves to open the way for an action or development

²**wedge** *vb* **wedged; wedg·ing 1** : to fasten or tighten by or as if by driving in a wedge **2** : to press or force into a narrow space ⟨*wedged* a stick into the crack⟩

wed·lock \'wed-ˌläk\ *n* : the state of being married : MARRIAGE

Wednes·day \'wenz-dē\ *n* : the fourth day of the week

wedge 1

Word History Many gods were worshiped by the Germanic people who lived in northern Europe in ancient times. The chief of all the Germanic gods was one who is now usually called *Odin.* His name in Old English was *Woden,* and the fourth day of the week was called *wōdnesdæg,* "day of Woden", or "Woden's day" in his honor. The Old English *wōdnesdæg* eventually became the Modern English *Wednesday.* [Old English *wōdnesdæg,* literally, "Woden's day"]

wee \'wē\ *adj* **1** : very small : TINY **2** : very early ⟨the *wee* hours of the morning⟩

¹**weed** \'wēd\ *n* : a plant that tends to grow thickly where it is not wanted and to choke out more desirable plants

²**weed** *vb* **1** : to remove weeds from ⟨*weed* a garden⟩ **2** : to get rid of (something unwanted) ⟨*weed* out the loafers from the crew⟩ — **weed·er** *n*

weeds \'wēdz\ *n pl* : mourning clothes

weedy \'wēd-ē\ *adj* **1** : full or consisting of weeds ⟨a *weedy* field⟩ **2** : like a weed especially in having strong

rapid growth **3** : very skinny

week \'wēk\ *n* **1 a** : seven days in a row ⟨was sick for a *week*⟩ **b** : a period of seven days beginning with Sunday and ending with Saturday ⟨the last *week* of the month⟩ **2** : the working or school days of the calendar week

week·day \'wēk-ˌdā\ *n* : a day of the week except Sunday or except Saturday and Sunday

¹**week·end** \'wē-ˌkend\ *n* : the end of the week; *esp* : the period between the close of one working or school week and the beginning of the next

²**weekend** *vb* : to spend the weekend ⟨families *weekending* at the seashore⟩

¹**week·ly** \'wē-klē\ *adj* **1** : occurring, done, produced, or published every week **2** : figured by the week ⟨a *weekly* wage⟩ — **weekly** *adv*

²**weekly** *n, pl* **weeklies** : a weekly publication

ween \'wēn\ *vb, archaic* : SUPPOSE 2, IMAGINE

weep \'wēp\ *vb* **wept** \'wept\; **weep·ing 1** : to show emotion and especially sorrow by shedding tears : CRY **2** : to give off liquid slowly or in drops : OOZE — **weep·er** *n*

weep·ing \'wē-piŋ\ *adj* **1** : TEARFUL **2** : having slender drooping branches

weeping willow *n* : an Asian willow with weeping branches

wee·vil \'wē-vəl\ *n* : any of a large group of mostly small beetles that have the head long and usually curved downward to form a snout bearing the jaws at the tip and that include many very harmful to plants or plant products — called also *snout beetle* — **wee·vily** or **wee·vil·ly** \'wēv-(ə-)lē\ *adj*

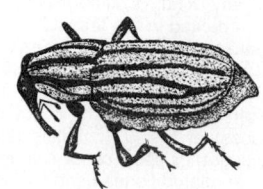

weevil

weft \'weft\ *n* **1 a** : ¹WOOF 1 **b** : yarn used for the woof **2 a** : woven fabric **b** : an article of woven fabric

weft knit *n* : a knit fabric in which the knitting is done with the yarns running in a crosswise or circular direction (as in ordinary hand knitting) — compare WARP KNIT — **weft knit·ting** *n*

weigh \'wā\ *vb* **1 a** : to find the heaviness of **b** : to have weight or a certain weight **2 a** : to consider carefully : PONDER ⟨*weigh* your chances of winning⟩ **b** : to be important : COUNT ⟨the evidence will *weigh* heavily against him⟩ **3** : to raise before sailing ⟨*weigh* anchor⟩ **4** : to measure on or as if on a scale ⟨*weigh* out several kilograms of rice⟩ **5** : to press down with or as if with a weight ⟨her worries *weigh* heavily on her⟩ — **weigh·er** *n*

¹**weight** \'wāt\ *n* **1 a** : the amount that something weighs **b** : the standard amount that something should weigh ⟨fined for selling meat under *weight*⟩ **2** : a quantity or portion weighing usually a certain amount ⟨equal *weights* of flour and butter⟩ **3** : a unit (as a pound or kilogram) of weight or mass — see METRIC SYSTEM table **4 a** : an object (as a piece of metal) of known weight for balancing a scale in weighing other objects **b** : a heavy object used to hold, press down, or balance something else ⟨clock *weights*⟩ **c** : a heavy object (as a metal ball) used in athletic exercises and contests **5 a** : something heavy : LOAD **b** : a mental or emotional burden ⟨had a *weight* on my conscience⟩ **6** : the force with which a body is attracted toward the earth or a heavenly body by gravitation **7 a** : the importance given to something ⟨opinions that carry *weight*⟩ **b** : the greater or more impressive part ⟨the *weight* of the evidence is for a verdict of guilty⟩

²**weight** *vb* **1** : to load or make heavy with a weight **2** : to trouble with a burden ⟨*weighted* down with cares⟩

weight·less \'wāt-ləs\ *adj* : having little weight : lacking apparent gravitational pull — **weight·less·ness** *n*

weight lifter *n* : one who lifts barbells in competition or as

an exercise — **weight lifting** *n*

weighty \'wāt-ē\ *adj* **weight·i·er; -est**   **1** : having much weight : HEAVY   **2 a** : of much importance : SERIOUS ⟨*weighty* problems⟩   **b** : showing seriousness : SOLEMN ⟨a *weighty* expression on her face⟩   **3** : having the power to influence or persuade ⟨*weighty* arguments⟩ — **weight·i·ly** \'wāt-ᵊl-ē\ *adv* — **weight·i·ness** *n*

wei·ma·ra·ner \,vī-mə-'rän-ər, 'wī-mə-,rän-ər\ *n* : any of a German breed of large gray short-haired sporting dogs [German, from *Weimar*, a city in Germany]

weimaraner

weir \'wa(ə)r, 'we(ə)r, 'wi(ə)r\ *n*   **1** : a fence set in a stream to catch fish   **2** : a dam in a stream to raise the water level or change the direction and course of its flow

weird \'wi(ə)rd\ *adj*   **1** : of, relating to, or caused by witchcraft or magic   **2** : very unusual or strange : FANTASTIC — **weird·ly** *adv* — **weird·ness** *n*

> **Word History** The belief in some form of fate, a force that cannot be explained, predicted, or controlled, has been a part of many cultures. When people understood very little of the laws of nature, such a belief may have helped to make it easier to live with life's misfortunes even if it did not make life any more comfortable. The Old English word for "fate" was *wyrd.* When the English began translating Latin works, they used this word for the Roman Fates, goddesses who were believed to control the events in human lives. When the Fates were described as "weird sisters", the first use of *weird* as an adjective occurred. People practicing witchcraft were thought to be controlling the *wyrd,* and in time the Modern English word *weird* came to refer to things that seemed to happen by magic or that were strange, unusual, or mysterious. [Old English *wyrd* (noun) "fate"]

weirdo \'wi(ə)rd-ō\ *n, pl* **weird·os** : a strange person

¹wel·come \'wel-kəm\ *interj* — used to greet a guest or newcomer upon arrival

²welcome *vb* **wel·comed; wel·com·ing**   **1** : to greet in a warm and friendly manner   **2** : to receive or accept with pleasure ⟨*welcomes* a challenge⟩ — **wel·com·er** *n*

³welcome *adj*   **1** : received gladly ⟨a *welcome* visitor⟩   **2** : giving pleasure : PLEASING ⟨*welcome* news⟩   **3** : willingly permitted to do, have, or enjoy something ⟨anyone is *welcome* to use the pool⟩   **4** — used in the phrase "You're welcome" as a reply to an expression of thanks

⁴welcome *n* : a friendly greeting or reception

¹weld \'weld\ *vb*   **1** : to join pieces of metal or plastic by heating and allowing the edges to flow together or by hammering or pressing together   **2** : to join as if by welding ⟨*welded* together in friendship⟩   **3** : to become or be capable of being welded ⟨certain metals *weld* easily⟩ — **weld·er** *n*

²weld *n*   **1** : a welded joint   **2** : union by welding

wel·fare \'wel-,fa(ə)r, -,fe(ə)r\ *n*   **1** : the state of doing well especially in relation to happiness, well-being, or success   **2** : WELFARE WORK   **3** : aid in the form of money or necessities for people who are poor, aged, or disabled — **welfare** *adj*

welfare state *n* : a social system in which the government takes on much of the responsibility for the individual and group welfare of its people

welfare work *n* : work done by a community or organization for the benefit of some group in society — **welfare worker** *n*

¹well \'wel\ *n*   **1** : a source of supply ⟨was a *well* of information⟩   **2** : a hole made in the earth to reach a natural deposit (as of water, oil, or gas)   **3** : an open space extending up through floors of a structure (as for a staircase)   **4** : something suggesting a well

²well *vb* : to rise to the surface and flow out

³well *adv* **bet·ter** \'bet-ər\; **best** \'best\   **1** : so as to be right : in a satisfactory way ⟨did *well* on the test⟩   **2** : in a friendly or generous way ⟨they always speak *well* of you⟩   **3** : in a skillful or expert manner ⟨plays the trumpet *well*⟩   **4** : by as much as possible : COMPLETELY ⟨we are *well* aware of the problem⟩   **5** : with reason or courtesy ⟨cannot *well* refuse⟩   **6** : in such a way as to be pleasing : as one would wish ⟨everything has gone *well* this week⟩   **7** : without trouble ⟨we could *well* afford it⟩   **8** : in a thorough manner ⟨shake *well* before using⟩   **9** : in a familiar manner ⟨knew them *well*⟩   **10** : by quite a lot ⟨was *well* ahead⟩ ⟨*well* over a million⟩ — **as well**   **1** : in addition : ALSO ⟨other features *as well*⟩   **2** : with the same result ⟨might *as well* tell them now⟩

⁴well *interj*   **1** — used to begin a conversation or continue one that was interrupted   **2** — used to express surprise or doubt

⁵well *adj*   **1** : being in a satisfactory or good state ⟨all is *well*⟩   **2** : free or recovered from ill health : HEALTHY   **3** : FORTUNATE 1 ⟨it was *well* that we left⟩

we'll \(,)wē(ə)l\ : we shall : we will

well–be·ing \'wel-'bē-iŋ\ *n* : WELFARE 1

well·born \-'bȯrn\ *adj* : coming from a good family : of gentle or noble birth

well–bred \-'bred\ *adj* : having or showing good manners : POLITE

well–dis·posed \-dis-'pōzd\ *adj* : having a good disposition

well–done \-'dən\ *adj*   **1** : done right   **2** : cooked thoroughly

well–found·ed \-'faùn-dəd\ *adj* : based on good reasons

well·head \'wel-,hed\ *n* : the top of or a structure built over a well

well–heeled \'wel-'hē(ə)ld\ *adj* : having plenty of money

well–known \'wel-'nōn\ *adj* : known by many people

well–mean·ing \-'mē-niŋ\ *adj* : having or based on good intentions

well–ness \-nəs\ *n* : the quality or state of being in good health especially as an actively sought goal ⟨lifestyles that promote *wellness*⟩

well–nigh \-'nī\ *adv* : ALMOST, NEARLY

well–off \-'ȯf\ *adj*   **1** : being in good condition or in a good situation   **2** : WELL-TO-DO

well–read \-'red\ *adj* : well informed by much reading

well–round·ed \-'raùn-dəd\ *adj* : including many details or much variety ⟨a *well-rounded* education⟩

well–spo·ken \-'spō-kən\ *adj*   **1** : having a good command of language : speaking well and especially courteously   **2** : spoken in a fitting and proper manner ⟨*well-spoken* words⟩

well·spring \'wel-,spriŋ\ *n*   **1** : a source of continual supply   **2** : FOUNTAINHEAD

well–to–do \,wel-tə-'dü\ *adj* : having plenty of money and possessions : PROSPEROUS

well–wish·er \'wel-,wish-ər, -'wish-\ *n* : a person who wishes good fortune to another

Welsh \'welsh *also* 'welch\ *n*   **1** Welsh *pl* : people born or living in Wales   **2** : the Celtic language of the Welsh people [Old English *Wealh* "Welshman, foreigner"; of Celtic origin — related to WALNUT; see *Word History* at WALNUT] — **Welsh** *adj*

Welsh cor·gi \-'kȯr-gē\ *n* : a Welsh dog with a foxy head and a long low body that occurs in two breeds: **a** : CARDIGAN WELSH CORGI   **b** : PEMBROKE WELSH CORGI

\ə\ abut	\aú\ out	\i\ tip	\ȯ\ saw	\ú\ foot
\ər\ further	\ch\ chin	\ī\ life	\ȯi\ coin	\y\ yet
\a\ mat	\e\ pet	\j\ job	\th\ thin	\yü\ few
\ā\ take	\ē\ easy	\ŋ\ sing	\th\ this	\yú\ cure
\ä\ cot, cart	\g\ go	\ō\ bone	\ü\ food	\zh\ vision

Welsh·man \'welsh-mən\ *n* : a person born or living in Wales

Welsh rabbit *n* : melted cheese served over toast or crackers

Welsh rare·bit \-'ra(ə)r-bət, -'re(ə)r-\ *n* : WELSH RABBIT

Welsh springer spaniel *n* : any of a breed of red and white or orange and white springer spaniels

welt \'welt\ *n* : a ridge or lump raised on the skin by a blow

¹**wel·ter** \'wel-tər\ *vb* **wel·tered; wel·ter·ing** \-t(ə-)riŋ\ **1** : to twist or roll one's body about **2** : to rise and fall or toss about in or with waves **3** : to become deeply sunk or bogged down

²**welter** *n* **1** : a state of wild confusion **2** : a confused jumble

wel·ter·weight \'wel-tər-,wāt\ *n* : a boxer in a weight division having the approximate range of 60 to 67 kilograms

wen \'wen\ *n* : a cyst formed by blocking a skin gland and filled with fatty material

wench \'wench\ *n* **1** : a young woman : GIRL **2** : a female servant

wend \'wend\ *vb* : to go one's way : PROCEED ⟨*wending* their way home⟩

went *past of* GO

wept *past and past participle of* WEEP

were *past 2d sing, past pl, or past subjunctive of* BE

we're \(,)wi(ə)r, (,)wər\ : we are

weren't \(')wərnt, 'wər-ənt\ : were not

were·wolf \'wi(ə)r-,wůlf, 'we(ə)r-, 'wər-\ *n, pl* **were·wolves** \-,wůlvz\ : a person changed or able to change into a wolf

Word History Many countries have legends about people who changed into savage wolflike creatures. Often these people were thought to keep their human shape during the day. At night, however, they were transformed into hungry monsters that killed and then ate their human victims. A full moon was sometimes seen as the force that turned people into werewolves. People who changed into these monsters were thought to have inherited the condition or to have been bitten by another werewolf. No one is sure how these stories got started or why so many different groups of people believed in them. We are sure, though, that Modern English *werewolf* comes from Old English *werwulf,* a compound of *wer,* meaning "man", and *wulf,* "wolf". [Old English *werwulf* "werewolf", from *wer* "man" and *wulf* "wolf"]

wert \(')wərt\ *archaic past 2d sing of* BE

¹**west** \'west\ *adv* : to or toward the west

²**west** *adj* **1** : situated toward or at the west **2** : coming from the west

³**west** *n* **1** : the direction of sunset : the compass point opposite to east **2** *cap* : regions or countries west of a point that is mentioned or understood

west·bound \'wes(t)-,bau̇nd\ *adj* : going west

west·er \'wes-tər\ *vb* **west·ered; west·er·ing** \-t(ə-)riŋ\ : to turn or move westward

¹**west·er·ly** \'wes-tər-lē\ *adv or adj* **1** : toward the west **2** : from the west ⟨a *westerly* wind⟩

²**westerly** *n, pl* **-lies** : a wind blowing from the west

¹**west·ern** \'wes-tərn\ *adj* **1** *often cap* : of, relating to, or resembling that of the West **2** : lying toward or coming from the west

²**western** *n* : a story, film, or radio or television show about life in the western U.S. in the last part of the 19th century

West·ern·er \'wes-tə(r)-nər\ *n* : a person born or living in the West (as of the U.S.)

western hemisphere *n, often cap W&H* : the half of the earth including North America, South America, and surrounding waters

western hemlock *n* : a hemlock of commercial importance as a timber tree that ranges from Alaska to California and has leaves without pale lines on the underside; *also* : its wood

western omelet *n* : an omelet made with chopped ham, green pepper, and onion

western saddle *n* : a large saddle having a deep broad seat and a high front and back

West Highland white terrier *n* : a small white dog of a breed developed in Scotland

¹**west·ward** \'wes-twərd\ *adv or adj* : toward the west — **west·wards** \-twərdz\ *adv*

²**westward** *n* : westward direction or part

West Highland white terrier

¹**wet** \'wet\ *adj* **wet·ter; wet·test** **1** : containing, covered with, or soaked with liquid (as water) **2** : RAINY ⟨*wet* weather⟩ **3** : not yet dry ⟨*wet* paint⟩ — **wet·ly** *adv* — **wet·ness** *n* — **all wet** : completely wrong : MISTAKEN

²**wet** *n* **1** : ¹WATER 1 **2** : MOISTURE **3** : rainy weather : RAIN

³**wet** *vb* **wet** *or* **wet·ted; wet·ting** **1** : to make or become wet **2** : URINATE

wet·land \'wet-,land\ *n* : land or areas having much soil moisture — usually used in pl.

wet suit *n* : a rubber suit for swimmers that traps a layer of water against the body to save body heat (as while swimming in cold water)

we've \(,)wēv\ : we have

¹**whack** \'hwak, 'wak\ *vb* : to hit or cut with a hard noisy blow — **whack·er** *n*

²**whack** *n* **1** : a hard noisy blow; *also* : its sound **2** : ²TRY, ATTEMPT ⟨take a *whack* at it⟩ — **out of whack** : not in good working order or shape

¹**whack·ing** \'hwak-iŋ, 'wak-\ *adj* : very big ⟨a *whacking* sum of money⟩

²**whacking** *adv* : ²VERY 1 ⟨a *whacking* good story⟩ ⟨a *whacking* big bill⟩

¹**whale** \'hwā(ə)l, 'wā(ə)l\ *n, pl* **whale** *or* **whales** **1** : any of an order of water-dwelling mammals that do not have hind limbs and have the front limbs represented by flippers, that have the tail flattened and extended to the sides as flukes, and that usually breathe through an opening on top of the head; *esp* : one of the larger members of the order **2** : something large enough to catch attention ⟨it made a *whale* of a difference⟩ [Old English *hwæl* "whale"]

²**whale** *vb* **whaled; whal·ing** : to hunt whales

³**whale** *vb* **whaled; whal·ing** **1** : THRASH 3 **2** : to hit hard [origin unknown]

whale·boat \'hwā(ə)l-,bōt, 'wā(ə)l-\ *n* : a long narrow rowboat originally used by whalers

whale·bone \-,bōn\ *n* : a horny substance found in two rows of long plates attached along the upper jaw of whalebone whales

whalebone whale *n* : any of various usually large whales having whalebone instead of teeth — called also *baleen whale;* compare TOOTHED WHALE

whale oil *n* : an oil obtained from the blubber of whales and formerly used especially in lamps

whal·er \'hwā-lər, 'wā-\ *n* : a person or ship that hunts for whales

whale shark *n* : a very large harmless shark of tropical seas

wharf \'hwȯrf, 'wȯrf\ *n, pl* **wharves** \'hwȯrvz, 'wȯrvz\ *also* **wharfs** : a structure built on the shore at which ships can load and unload

¹**what** \(')hwät, (')hwət, (')wät, (')wət\ *pron* **1 a** : which thing or things ⟨*what* happened?⟩ **b** : which sort of thing or person ⟨*what* is this?⟩ ⟨*what* are they — doctors?⟩ **2** : that which ⟨do *what* you're told⟩ — **what for** : ¹WHY — **what have you** : ¹WHATNOT — **what if** **1** : what would happen if ⟨*what if* they find out?⟩ **2** : what does it matter

if ⟨so *what if* they do? I don't care⟩

²**what** *adv* **1** : in what way : HOW ⟨*what* does it matter⟩ — used before one or more phrases that tell a cause ⟨*what* with the cold and the hunger, they nearly died⟩

³**what** *adj* **1 a** — used to ask about the identity of a person, object, or matter ⟨*what* books do you read⟩ **b** : how remarkable or surprising ⟨*what* an idea⟩ **2** : ²WHATEVER 1

¹**what·ev·er** \hwät-'ev-ər, (ˌ)hwət-, wät-, (ˌ)wət-\ *pron* **1** : anything that ⟨take *whatever* you need⟩ **2** : no matter what ⟨*whatever* you do, don't cheat⟩ **3** : what in the world ⟨*whatever* made you think that⟩

²**whatever** *adj* **1** : any and all : any . . . that ⟨take *whatever* action is needed⟩ **2** : of any kind at all ⟨no food *whatever*⟩

¹**what·not** \'hwät-ˌnät, 'hwət-, 'wät-, 'wət-\ *pron* : any of various other things that might also be mentioned ⟨hummingbirds and hawks and owls and *whatnot*⟩

²**whatnot** *n* : a light open set of shelves

what·so·ev·er \ˌhwät-sə-'wev-ər, ˌhwət-, ˌwät-, ˌwət-\ *pron or adj* : WHATEVER

wheat \'hwēt, 'wēt\ *n* **1** : a cereal grain that can be made into a fine white flour, is the chief source of bread in temperate regions, and is used in animal feeds **2** : any of a genus of grasses grown in most temperate areas for the wheat they produce; *esp* : a grass with long dense flower spikes and white to dark red grains that is the chief source of wheat and is known only in cultivation

wheat·en \'hwēt-ᵊn, 'wēt-\ *adj* : containing or made from wheat ⟨*wheaten* bread⟩

wheat germ *n* : the embryo of the wheat kernel separated in milling and used especially as a source of vitamins

wheat rust *n* : a harmful disease of wheat caused by rust fungi; *also* : a fungus causing a wheat rust

whee·dle \'hwēd-ᵊl, 'wēd-\ *vb* **whee·dled; whee·dling** \'hwēd-liŋ, -ᵊl-iŋ, 'wēd-\ **1** : to get (someone) to think or act a certain way by flattering or coaxing **2** : to gain or get by coaxing or flattering

¹**wheel** \'hwē(ə)l, 'wē(ə)l\ *n* **1** : a disk or circular frame turning on a central point **2** : a device whose main part is a wheel **3** : something resembling a wheel (as in being round or turning) **4** : a curving or circular movement **5** : moving power : necessary parts ⟨the *wheels* of government⟩ — **wheeled** \'hwē(ə)ld, 'wē(ə)ld\ *adj*

²**wheel** *vb* **1** : to turn on or as if on a central point : REVOLVE **2** : to change direction as if turning on a central point **3** : to move in a circle or curve **4** : to carry or move on wheels or in a vehicle

wheel and axle *n* : a simple machine consisting of a grooved wheel turned by a cord or chain with a firmly attached axle (as for winding up a weight) together with supports

wheel·bar·row \'hwē(ə)l-ˌbar-ō, 'wē(ə)l-\ *n* : a small cart that has two handles and usually one wheel, is used for carrying small loads, and is usually pushed

wheel·base \-ˌbās\ *n* : the distance between the front and rear axles of a motor vehicle

wheel·chair \-ˌche(ə)r, -ˌcha(ə)r\ *n* : a chair with wheels used especially by sick or injured people to get about

wheel·er \'hwē-lər, 'wē-\ *n* : one of a team of animals (as horses) that pulls from the position nearest the front wheels of a wagon

wheel·house \-ˌhaús\ *n* : PILOTHOUSE

¹**wheeze** \'hwēz, 'wēz\ *vb* **wheezed; wheez·ing** **1** : to breathe with difficulty especially with a whistling sound **2** : to make a sound like wheezing

²**wheeze** *n* : a wheezing sound — **wheezy** \'hwē-zē, 'wē-\ *adj*

whelk \'hwelk, 'welk, 'wilk\ *n* : any of nu-

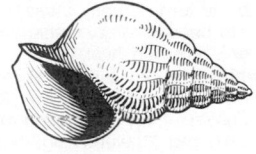

whelk

merous large marine snails; *esp* : one used for food in Europe

whelm \'hwelm, 'welm\ *vb* : OVERWHELM 2

¹**whelp** \'hwelp, 'welp\ *n* **1** : one of the young of a flesh-eating animal and especially a dog **2** : a rude or disrespectful young person

²**whelp** *vb* : to give birth to whelps

¹**when** \(')hwen, hwən, (')wen, wən\ *adv* **1** : at what time ⟨*when* will you return⟩ **2** : at or during which time ⟨a time *when* things were upset⟩

²**when** *conj* **1 a** : at or during the time that : WHILE ⟨went fishing *when* we were on vacation⟩ **b** : just after the time that ⟨left *when* the bell rang⟩ **c** : every time that ⟨my mouth waters *when* I see food⟩ **2** : in the event that : IF ⟨*when* you have no family, you are really on your own⟩ **3** : ²THOUGH

³**when** \ˌhwen, ˌwen\ *pron* : what or which time ⟨since *when* have you known that⟩

whence \(')hwen(t)s, (')wen(t)s\ *adv* **1** : from what place, source, or cause ⟨*whence* come all these doubts⟩ **2** : from or out of which ⟨the land *whence* they came⟩

¹**when·ev·er** \hwe-'nev-ər, hwə-, we-, wə-\ *conj* : at any or every time that ⟨stop *whenever* you wish⟩

²**whenever** *adv* : at whatever time ⟨come tomorrow or *whenever*⟩

when·so·ev·er \'hwen(t)-sə-ˌwev-ər, 'wen(t)-\ *conj* : WHENEVER

¹**where** \(')hwe(ə)r, (')hwa(ə)r, (ˌ)hwər, (')we(ə)r, (')wa(ə)r, (ˌ)wər\ *adv* **1** : at, in, or to what place ⟨*where* are we going⟩ **2** : at, in, or to what situation, position, direction, or circumstances ⟨*where* will this course of action lead⟩

²**where** *conj* **1 a** : at, in, or to what place ⟨knows *where* the house is⟩ **b** : at, in, or to what situation, position, direction, or circumstances ⟨see *where* that behavior leads⟩ **2** : at, in, or to which place ⟨the town *where* we live⟩ **3 a** : at, in, or to the place at, in, or to which ⟨stay *where* you are⟩ **b** : in a situation or circumstances in which ⟨no good *where* careful work is needed⟩

³**where** \'hwe(ə)r, 'hwa(ə)r, 'we(ə)r, 'wa(ə)r\ *pron* : what place, source, or cause ⟨*where* are you from⟩

¹**where·abouts** \-ə-ˌbaúts\ *also* **where·about** \-ˌbaút\ *adv* : about where ⟨*whereabouts* is the house⟩

²**whereabouts** *n sing or pl* : the place where a person or thing is ⟨do you know their *whereabouts*⟩

where·as \hwer-'az, hwar-, wer-, war-, (ˌ)hwər-, (ˌ)wər\ *conj* **1** : in view of the fact that : SINCE **2** : while just the opposite ⟨water puts out fire, *whereas* gasoline feeds it⟩

where·at \-'at\ *conj* **1** : at or toward which **2** : as a result of which

where·by \hwe(ə)r-'bī, hwa(ə)r-, we(ə)r-, wa(ə)r-, (ˌ)hwər-, (ˌ)wər-\ *conj* : by, through, or in agreement with which

¹**where·fore** \'hwe(ə)r-ˌfō(ə)r, 'hwa(ə)r-, 'we(ə)r-, 'wa(ə)r-, -ˌfó(ə)r\ *adv* **1** : for what reason or purpose : WHY **2** : THEREFORE

²**wherefore** *n* : ¹REASON 1a ⟨the whys and *wherefores*⟩

where·from \-ˌfrəm, -ˌfräm\ *conj* : from which

¹**where·in** \hwer-'in, hwar-, wer-, war-, (ˌ)hwər-, (ˌ)wər-\ *adv* : in what : in what way ⟨*wherein* was I guilty⟩

²**wherein** *conj* : in which ⟨the city *wherein* we live⟩

where·of \-'əv, -'äv\ *conj* **1** : of what ⟨knows *whereof* she speaks⟩ **2** : of which or whom ⟨wrote many books *whereof* the best are lost⟩

where·on \-'òn, -'än\ *adv* : on which ⟨the base *whereon* the vase rests⟩

where·so·ev·er \'hwer-sə-ˌwev-ər, 'hwar-, 'wer-, 'war-\ *conj* : WHEREVER

\ə\ abut	\aú\ out	\i\ tip	\ò\ saw	\ú\ foot
\ər\ further	\ch\ chin	\ī\ life	\òi\ coin	\y\ yet
\a\ mat	\e\ pet	\j\ job	\th\ thin	\yü\ few
\ā\ take	\ē\ easy	\ŋ\ sing	\th\ this	\yú\ cure
\ä\ cot, cart	\g\ go	\ō\ bone	\ü\ food	\zh\ vision

where·up·on \'hwer-ə-,pȯn, 'hwar-, 'wer-, 'war-, -,pän\ *conj* **1** : on which   **2** : and then : at which time

¹wher·ev·er \hwer-'ev-ər, hwar-, wer-, war-, (,)hwər-, (,)wər-\ *adv* : where in the world 〈*wherever* did you get that hat〉

²wherever *conj* **1** : at, in, or to whatever place 〈succeeds *wherever* he goes〉   **2** : in any situation in which 〈*wherever* it is possible, I try to help〉

where·with \'hwe(ə)r-,with, 'hwa(ə)r-, 'we(ə)r-, 'wa(ə)r-, -,with\ *adv* : with or by means of which

where·with·al \'hwe(ə)r-with-,ȯl, 'hwa(ə)r-, 'we(ə)r-, 'wa(ə)r-, -with-\ *n* : WEALTH 1, RESOURCES; *esp* : MONEY 1b 〈the *wherewithal* to buy a house〉

whet \'hwet, 'wet\ *vb* **whet·ted; whet·ting** **1** : to sharpen by rubbing on or with something (as a stone) 〈*whet* a knife〉   **2** : to make keen : STIMULATE 〈*whet* the appetite〉

wheth·er \'hweth-ər, 'weth-, (,)hweth-ər, (,)weth-\ *conj* **1 a** : if it is or was true that 〈ask *whether* they are going〉   **b** : if it is or was better 〈uncertain *whether* to go or stay〉   **2** — used to introduce two or more situations of which only one can occur 〈*whether* we succeed or fail, we must try〉 〈seated him next to her *whether* by accident or on purpose〉

whet·stone \'hwet-,stōn, 'wet-\ *n* : a stone for sharpening blades

whew *often read as* 'hwü, 'wü, 'hyü; *the interjection is a whistle ending with a voiceless* ü\ *n* : a sound somewhat like a whistle used chiefly to express amazement, discomfort, or relief

whey \'hwā, 'wā\ *n* : the watery part of milk that separates after the milk has soured and thickened

¹which \(')hwich, (')wich\ *adj* **1** : being what one or ones 〈*which* tie should I wear〉 〈knew *which* people had paid〉   **2** : WHICHEVER 〈it will not fit, turn it *which* way you like〉

²which *pron* **1** : what one or ones out of a group 〈*which* of those houses do you live in〉 〈they are swimming or canoeing, I don't know *which*〉   **2** : WHICHEVER 〈take *which* you like〉   **3** — used to introduce a clause referring to something other than human beings 〈the records *which* we bought〉

¹which·ev·er \hwich-'ev-ər, wich-\ *pron* : whatever one or ones out of a group

²whichever *adj* : being whatever one or ones out of a group : no matter which 〈*whichever* way you go〉

¹whiff \'hwif, 'wif\ *n* **1** : a quick puff or slight gust 〈a *whiff* of air〉   **2** : a small quantity of odor, gas, or smoke that is breathed in

²whiff *vb* **1** : to blow out or away in small amounts   **2** : to breathe in an odor

whif·fle·tree \'hwif-əl-(,)trē, 'wif-\ *n* : the swinging bar that connects an animal harness to a vehicle (as a cart) or a plow — called also *whippletree*

whiffletree

Whig \'hwig, 'wig\ *n* **1** : a member or supporter of a British political group of the 18th and early 19th centuries trying to lessen the power of the monarch and to increase the power of the parliament   **2** : an American supporting independence from Great Britain during the American Revolution   **3** : a member or supporter of a 19th century American political party formed to oppose the Democrats

¹while \'hwī(ə)l, 'wī(ə)l\ *n* **1** : a period of time 〈stay here for a *while*〉   **2** : time and effort used 〈worth your *while*〉

²while *conj* **1 a** : during the time that 〈take a nap *while* I'm out〉   **b** : as long as 〈enjoy life *while* we can〉   **2** : THOUGH 〈*while* respected, the mayor is not liked〉

³while *vb* **whiled; whil·ing** : to cause to pass pleasantly or without boredom 〈*while* away the time〉

¹whi·lom \'hwī-ləm, 'wī-\ *adv, archaic* : FORMERLY

²whilom *adj* : FORMER 〈your *whilom* friends〉

whilst \'hwī(ə)lst, 'wī(ə)lst\ *conj, chiefly British* : ²WHILE

whim \'hwim, 'wim\ *n* : an odd or sudden wish, desire, or change of mind

¹whim·per \'hwim-pər, 'wim-\ *vb* **whim·pered; whim·per·ing** \-p(ə-)riŋ\ : to utter weak interrupted cries

²whimper *n* : a whimpering cry

whim·si·cal \'hwim-zi-kəl, 'wim-\ *adj* **1** : full of whims : CAPRICIOUS 〈a *whimsical* person always going off somewhere〉   **2** : resulting from or marked by whim : ERRATIC 〈*whimsical* behavior〉 — **whim·si·cal·i·ty** \,hwim-zə-'kal-ət-ē, ,wim-\ *n* — **whim·si·cal·ly** \'hwim-zi-k(ə-)lē, 'wim-\ *adv*

whim·sy *or* **whim·sey** \'hwim-zē, 'wim-\ *n, pl* **whimsies** *or* **whimseys** **1** : WHIM, CAPRICE   **2** : an imaginative or fantastic object or creation especially in a piece of writing or art

¹whine \'hwīn, 'wīn\ *vb* **whined; whin·ing** **1** : to make a shrill troubled cry or a similar sound 〈a child *whining*〉 〈the electric saw *whined* as it cut the wood〉   **2** : to complain with or as if with a whine — **whin·er** *n* — **whin·ing·ly** \'hwī-niŋ-lē, 'wī-\ *adv*

²whine *n* : a whining cry or sound

¹whin·ny \'hwin-ē, 'win-\ *vb* **whin·nied; whin·ny·ing** : to neigh especially in a low gentle manner

²whinny *n, pl* **whinnies** : a low gentle neigh

¹whip \'hwip, 'wip\ *vb* **whipped; whip·ping** **1** : to move, snatch, or jerk quickly and forcefully 〈*whip* out a gun〉   **2** : to strike with something long and thin or flexible   **3** : to overcome thoroughly : DEFEAT   **4** : to stir up : INCITE 〈*whip* up enthusiasm〉   **5** : to beat into a thick fluffy mass 〈*whip* cream〉   **6** : to flap about in a lively manner 〈sails *whipped* in the strong wind〉 — **whip·per** *n*

²whip *n* **1** : a flexible tool for whipping   **2** : a dessert made by whipping some part of the mixture   **3** : a whipping motion — **whip·like** \'hwip-,līk, 'wip-\ *adj*

whip·cord \'hwip-,kȯ(ə)rd, 'wip-\ *n* **1** : a thin tough braided cord   **2** : a strong cloth with fine diagonal ridges

whip·lash \-,lash\ *n* : the lash of a whip

whip·per·snap·per \'hwip-ər-,snap-ər, 'wip-\ *n* : a small, unimportant, or overly confident person

whip·pet \'hwip-ət, 'wip-\ *n* : any of a breed of small swift slender dogs that are widely used for racing

whip·ping boy *n* : SCAPEGOAT

whip·ple·tree \'hwip-əl-(,)trē, 'wip-\ *n* : WHIFFLETREE

whip·poor·will \'hwip-ər-,wil, ,hwip-ər-'wil, 'wip-, ,wip-\ *n* : an insect-eating bird of the eastern U.S. and Canada that is active at night and is often heard at nightfall and just before dawn

whippoorwill

¹whir *also* **whirr** \'hwər, 'wər\ *vb* **whirred; whir·ring** : to fly, turn, or move rapidly with a buzzing sound

²whir *also* **whirr** *n* : a whirring sound

¹whirl \'hwər(-ə)l, 'wər(-ə)l\ *vb* **1** : to move or drive in a circle or curve especially with force or speed 〈cars *whirling* around the track〉   **2 a** : to turn rapidly in circles : SPIN   **b** : to turn abruptly : WHEEL   **3** : to move or go quickly   **4** : to become dizzy : REEL 〈my head is *whirling*〉 — **whirl·er** \'hwər-lər, 'wər-\ *n*

²whirl *n* **1 a** : a rapid whirling movement   **b** : something whirling 〈a *whirl* of dust〉   **2 a** : a state of busy movement : BUSTLE   **b** : a confused mental state

whirl·i·gig \'hwər-li-,gig, 'wər-\ *n* **1** : a toy that has a whirling motion   **2** : something that continuously whirls or changes

whirligig beetle *n* : any of a family of beetles that swim with a whirling motion and have two pairs of compound eyes by which they can see both above and under the surface of the water at the same time

whirl·pool \'hwər(-ə)l-,pül, 'wər(-ə)l-\ *n* : water moving rapidly in a circle with a hollow in the center into which floating objects are drawn : EDDY

¹whirl·wind \-,wind\ *n* : a small windstorm or rapidly rotating air

²whirlwind *adj* : resembling a whirlwind especially in speed or force ⟨a *whirlwind* campaign⟩ ⟨a *whirlwind* romance⟩

whish \'hwish, 'wish\ *vb* : to move with a whizzing or swishing sound — **whish** *n*

¹whisk \'hwisk, 'wisk\ *n* **1** : a quick brush or sweep ⟨a *whisk* of the hand⟩ **2** : a small kitchen utensil used for beating food **3** : WHISK BROOM

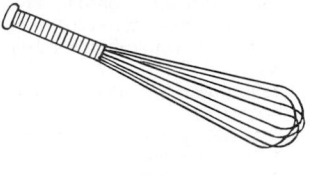

whisk 2

²whisk *vb* **1** : to move easily and quickly ⟨squirrels *whisked* up the trees⟩ **2** : to move or carry briskly ⟨*whisked* the children off to bed⟩ **3** : to mix or fluff up by or as if by beating with a whisk ⟨*whisk* eggs⟩ **4** : to brush or wipe off lightly ⟨*whisk* the lint off your skirt⟩

whisk broom *n* : a small broom with a short handle used especially as a clothes brush

whis·ker \'hwis-kər, 'wis-\ *n* **1 a** : a hair of the beard **b** *pl* : the part of the beard growing on the sides of the face or on the chin **2** : one of the long hairs or bristles growing near the mouth of an animal (as a cat or mouse) — **whis·kered** \-kərd\ *adj*

whis·key *or* **whis·ky** \'hwis-kē, 'wis-\ *n, pl* **whiskeys** *or* **whiskies** : alcoholic liquor made from grain (as rye, corn, or barley) [from *uisce beathadh,* a phrase in Irish Gaelic (the ancient language of Ireland) and *usige beatha,* a phrase in Scottish Gaelic (the ancient language of Scotland), both meaning literally "water of life"]

¹whis·per \'hwis-pər, 'wis-\ *vb* **whis·pered; whis·per·ing** \-p(ə-)riŋ\ **1** : to speak very softly or under the breath **2** : to tell or utter by whispering ⟨*whisper* a secret⟩ **3** : to make a series of little noises ⟨*whispering* leaves⟩ — **whis·per·er** \-pər-ər\ *n*

²whisper *n* **1** : something said by or as if by whispering; *esp* : ¹RUMOR ⟨*whispers* of scandal⟩ **2** : an act or instance of whispering **3** : ¹TRACE 3

whis·pery \'hwis-p(ə-)rē, 'wis-\ *adj* : resembling a whisper ⟨a *whispery* voice⟩

whist \'hwist, 'wist\ *n* : a card game for four players in two partnerships

¹whis·tle \'hwis-əl, 'wis-\ *n* **1** : a device making a shrill sound ⟨tin *whistle*⟩ ⟨steam *whistle*⟩ **2 a** : a shrill clear sound made by forcing air through puckered lips **b** : a sound or signal produced by a whistle or as if by whistling

²whistle *vb* **whis·tled; whis·tling** \'hwis-(ə-)liŋ, 'wis-\ **1** : to make a whistle through puckered lips **2** : to move, pass, or go with a shrill sound ⟨an arrow *whistled* by me⟩ **3** : to blow or sound a whistle ⟨the teakettle *whistled*⟩ **4** : to utter by whistling ⟨*whistle* a tune⟩ — **whis·tler** \'hwis-(ə-)lər, 'wis-\ *n*

whit \'hwit, 'wit\ *n* : the smallest part or particle : BIT ⟨cared not a *whit* about money⟩

¹white \'hwīt, 'wīt\ *adj* **whit·er; whit·est** **1 a** : having no color **b** : of the color of new snow or milk **c** : light or pale in color ⟨*white* wine⟩ ⟨lips *white* with fear⟩ **d** : pale gray : SILVERY **2** : of, relating to, or being a member of a group or race having light skin **3** : unmarked by writing or printing : BLANK **4** : not intended to cause harm ⟨a *white* lie⟩ ⟨*white* magic⟩ **5** : marked by the presence of snow ⟨a *white* Christmas⟩ — **white·ness** *n*

²white *n* **1** : the color of fresh snow **2** : a white or light-colored thing or part (as the material around the yolk of an egg or the white part of the ball of the eye) **3** : a person belonging to a light-skinned race

white ant *n* : TERMITE

white blood cell *n* : a blood cell that does not contain hemoglobin : LEUKOCYTE — called also *white cell, white blood corpuscle, white corpuscle*

white·cap \'hwīt-,kap, 'wīt-\ *n* : the top of a wave breaking into foam

white cedar *n* **1** : any of several North American timber trees: as **a** : an evergreen swamp tree of the eastern coast of the U.S. **b** : a common arborvitae especially of Canada and the northern U.S. **2** : the wood of a white cedar

white clover *n* : a Eurasian clover with heads of white flowers that is widely used in grass-seed mixtures and is an important source of nectar for bees

white–collar \'hwīt-'käl-ər, 'wīt-\ *adj* : of, relating to, or being a member of the class of workers (as clerks and salespersons) whose jobs often require certain mental skills and not much heavy physical labor

white crappie *n* : an edible silvery North American sunfish that is often stocked in small ponds

white dwarf *n* : a small whitish star of low brightness that has a mass approximately equal to that of the sun but that is many times more dense

white elephant *n* : something requiring much care and expense and giving little profit or enjoyment [so called from the fact that in India and neighboring countries, light-colored elephants are treated as sacred and kept without being put to work]

white·fish \'hwīt-,fish, 'wīt-\ *n* : any of various freshwater food fishes related to the salmons and trouts and mostly greenish above and silvery white below

white flag *n* : a flag of plain white used as a flag of truce or as a sign of surrender

white gold *n* : a pale mixture of gold especially with nickel or palladium that resembles platinum in appearance

white goods *n pl* **1** : articles of cloth used in the bedroom, bathroom, or kitchen **2** : major household appliances (as stoves) that typically are white-colored

white·head \'hwīt-,hed, 'wīt-\ *n* : a small whitish lump in the skin caused by the fluid given off by an oil gland when the canal leading from the gland is blocked

white lead *n* : a heavy white poisonous carbonate of lead used chiefly as a coloring matter in exterior paints

white matter *n* : whitish nerve tissue that consists largely of nerve fibers enclosed in a fatty material and that lies under the gray matter of the brain and spinal cord or is collected into nerves

whit·en \'hwīt-ᵊn, 'wīt-\ *vb* **whit·ened; whit·en·ing** \-ᵊn-iŋ, -niŋ\ : to make or become white or whiter — **whit·en·er** \-nər, -ᵊn-ər\ *n*

white oak *n* : any of various oaks with acorns that mature in one year and with leaf veins that never extend beyond the margin of the leaf; *also* : the hard, strong wood of a white oak that lasts well and is not easily rotted by water

white pepper *n* : a seasoning with a sharp flavor that is prepared by grinding the fruit of the East Indian pepper after the black outer husk is removed

white pine *n* : a tall-growing pine of eastern North America with leaves in clusters of five; *also* : its wood

white–pine blister rust *n* : a harmful disease of white pine caused by a rust fungus that passes part of its life on currant or gooseberry bushes; *also* : this fungus

\ə\ **abut**	\au̇\ **out**	\i\ **tip**	\ȯ\ **saw**	\u̇\ **foot**
\ər\ **further**	\ch\ **chin**	\ī\ **life**	\ȯi\ **coin**	\y\ **yet**
\a\ **mat**	\e\ **pet**	\j\ **job**	\th\ **thin**	\yü\ **few**
\ā\ **take**	\ē\ **easy**	\ŋ\ **sing**	\th\ **this**	\yu̇\ **cure**
\ä\ **cot, cart**	\g\ **go**	\ō\ **bone**	\ü\ **food**	\zh\ **vision**

white potato *n* : POTATO 2b

white sauce *n* : a sauce made from seasoned milk, cream, or broth and thickened with flour

white shark *n* : a large and dangerous shark of warm seas that is quick to attack human beings and is bluish when young but becomes whitish with age — called also *great white shark*

white·tail \'hwīt-ˌtāl, 'wīt-\ *n* : WHITE-TAILED DEER

white–tailed deer \ˌhwīt-ˌtāl-'di(ə)r, ˌwīt-\ *n* : a North American deer that has a long tail which is white on the underside and antlers which arch forward

white-tailed deer

white·throat \'hwīt-ˌthrōt, 'wīt-\ *n* : WHITE-THROATED SPARROW

white–throated sparrow \ˌhwīt-ˌthrōt-əd-, ˌwīt-\ *n* : a common brown sparrow of eastern North America with stripes on the top of its head and with a white patch on its throat

¹white·wash \'hwīt-ˌwȯsh, -ˌwäsh, 'wīt-\ *vb* **1** : to whiten with whitewash **2** : to clear of a charge of wrongdoing by offering excuses, hiding facts, or conducting a careless investigation ⟨accused the city council of *whitewashing* the mayor⟩ **3** : to prevent an opponent in a game or contest from scoring — **white·wash·er** *n*

²whitewash *n* **1** : a mixture (as of lime and water) for whitening a surface **2** : a clearing of wrongdoing by whitewashing

white water *n* : rough foamy water (as in rapids or waterfalls)

whith·er \'hwith-ər, 'with-\ *adv* **1** : to what place or situation ⟨*whither* will they go⟩ **2** : to which place

whit·ish \'hwīt-ish, 'wīt-\ *adj* : somewhat white

whit·low \'hwit-ˌlō, 'wit-\ *n* : a deep inflammation of a finger or toe usually with pus and located especially near the end or around the nail

Whit·sun·day \hwit-'sən-dē, -sən-ˌdā, 'wit-\ *n* : PENTECOST 2 [Old English *hwīta sunnandæg*, literally "white Sunday"; probably so called from the fact that at this season there were many people who were newly baptized and who wore white robes]

Whit·sun·tide \'hwit-sən-ˌtīd, 'wit-\ *n* : the week beginning with Whitsunday; *esp* : the first three days of this week

whit·tle \'hwit-ᵊl, 'wit-\ *vb* **whit·tled; whit·tling** \-liŋ, -ᵊl-iŋ\ **1 a** : to shave or cut off chips from the surface of wood with a knife **b** : to shape or form by so shaving or cutting **2** : to reduce gradually : PARE ⟨*whittle* down expenses⟩ — **whit·tler** \-lər, -ᵊl-ər\ *n*

¹whiz *or* **whizz** \'hwiz, 'wiz\ *vb* **whizzed; whiz·zing** **1** : to hum, buzz, or hiss like a speeding object (as an arrow) passing through air **2** : to fly, pass, or move swiftly with a buzzing sound [probably coined in imitation of the sound of a speeding object going by] — **whiz·zer** *n*

²whiz *or* **whizz** *n, pl* **whiz·zes** : a humming, buzzing, or hissing sound

³whiz *n, pl* **whiz·zes** : WIZARD 2 [probably a shortened and altered form of *wizard*]

who *pron* \(')hü, ü\ **1** : what or which person or persons ⟨*who* was elected president⟩ ⟨find out *who* did it⟩ **2** — used to introduce a clause that talks about a person or persons ⟨my father, *who* was a lawyer⟩

whoa \'wō, 'hō, 'hwō\ *imperative verb* — used as a command to an animal to stop pulling or moving

who·dun·it \hü-'dən-ət\ *n* : a detective or mystery story presented as a novel, play, or motion picture

who·ev·er \hü-'ev-ər\ *pron* : whatever person ⟨*whoever* wants to come along must be ready⟩

¹whole \'hōl\ *adj* **1** : being in healthy or sound condition : free from sickness or injury : WELL **2 a** : having all its proper parts or elements ⟨*whole* grain⟩ ⟨*whole* milk⟩ **b** : not cut up or in pieces **3** : made up of all its parts ⟨the *whole* family⟩ **4** : not divided or scattered ⟨your *whole* attention⟩ **5** : being the total or full amount or extent of something ⟨owns the *whole* island⟩ **6** : each or all of the ⟨the *whole* 10 days⟩ [Old English *hāl* "healthy" — related to ¹HALE]

²whole *n* **1** : a complete amount or sum **2** : something whole or entire ⟨the *whole* of an apple⟩ — **in whole** : to the full or entire extent : WHOLLY — **on the whole** **1** : in view of all the facts : all things considered ⟨*on the whole* you did a good job⟩ **2** : in general : in most cases

whole·heart·ed \'hōl-'härt-əd\ *adj* : not lacking in enthusiasm, determination, or devotion : HEARTY ⟨*wholehearted* effort⟩ — **whole·heart·ed·ly** *adv* — **whole·heart·ed·ness** *n*

whole note *n* : a musical note equal to one measure of four beats

whole number *n* **1** : any of the set of natural numbers together with zero **2** : INTEGER

¹whole·sale \'hōl-ˌsāl\ *n* : the sale of goods in large quantity to dealers

²wholesale *adj* **1** : of, relating to, or working in wholesaling ⟨a *wholesale* grocer⟩ ⟨*wholesale* prices⟩ **2** : done on a large scale : GENERAL — **wholesale** *adv*

³wholesale *vb* **whole·saled; whole·sal·ing** : to sell to dealers usually in large amounts — **whole·sal·er** *n*

whole·some \'hōl-səm\ *adj* **1** : helping to keep or improve the good condition of the mind, body, or spirit **2** : sound in body, mind, or morals : HEALTHY **syn** SEE HEALTHFUL — **whole·some·ly** *adv* — **whole·some·ness** *n*

whole step *n* : the basic unit of measurement of the difference in pitch between two tones equal to that between a C and the D just above it

whole wheat *adj* : made from wheat kernels that were ground in their entirety

whol·ly \'hōl-(l)ē\ *adv* : to the full or entire extent : COMPLETELY

whom \(')hüm, üm\ *pron, objective case of* WHO

whom·ev·er \hü-'mev-ər\ *pron, objective case of* WHOEVER

whom·so·ev·er \ˌhüm-sə-'wev-ər\ *pron, objective case of* WHOSOEVER

¹whoop \'hüp, 'hùp, *least frequently for sense 2* 'hwüp *or* 'hwùp\ *vb* **1** : to shout or call loudly and energetically especially in enthusiasm or enjoyment ⟨the children *whooped* with joy⟩ **2** : to make the sound that follows an attack of coughing in whooping cough — **whoop it up** **1** : to celebrate loudly : CAROUSE **2** : to stir up enthusiasm

²whoop *n* **1** : a whooping sound **2** : the cry of an owl : HOOT

whooping cough *n* : a disease especially of children that is caused by a bacterium and is marked by severe attacks of coughing often followed by a shrill gasping intake of breath — called also *pertussis*

whooping crane *n* : a large white nearly extinct North American crane that has a loud whooping call

¹whoosh \'hwüsh, 'wüsh, 'hwùsh, 'wùsh\ *n* : the sound made by swiftly moving or expanding air

²whoosh *vb* : to pass or move along with a whoosh

whop·per \'hwäp-ər, 'wäp-\ *n* **1** : something unusually large **2** : a monstrous lie

whooping crane

whop·ping \'hwäp-iŋ, 'wäp-\ *adj* : extremely large

whore \'hō(ə)r, 'hò(ə)r, 'hù(ə)r\ *n* : ²PROSTITUTE

whorl \'hwȯr(-ə)l, 'wȯr(-ə)l, 'hwər(-ə)l, 'wər(-ə)l\ n 1 : a row of parts (as leaves or petals) forming a circle around a point and especially a stem 2 : something that whirls or winds around a center ⟨a *whorl* of smoke⟩ 3 : one of the turns of a shell (as of a snail) having just one valve 4 : a fingerprint in which the central ridges on the skin turn through at least one complete circle

whorled \'hwȯr(-ə)ld, 'wȯr(-ə)ld, 'hwər(-ə)ld, 'wər(-ə)ld\ adj : having or arranged in whorls ⟨*whorled* leaves⟩

whorl 1

¹**whose** \(')hüz, üz\ adj : of or relating to whom or which ⟨*whose* bag is it⟩ ⟨the book *whose* cover is torn⟩

²**whose** pron : whose one : whose ones

who·so \'hü-,sō\ pron : WHOEVER

who·so·ev·er \,hü-sə-'wev-ər\ pron : WHOEVER

¹**why** \('))hwī, (')wī\ adv : for what cause or reason ⟨*why* did you do it⟩

²**why** conj 1 : the cause or reason for which ⟨know *why* you did it⟩ 2 : for which : on account of which ⟨the reason *why* she did it⟩

³**why** \'hwī, 'wī\ n, pl **whys** : ¹REASON 1a ⟨explained the *whys* and wherefores of the sudden price increase⟩

⁴**why** \(,)wī, (,)hwī\ interj — used to express surprise, indecision, approval, disapproval, or impatience ⟨*why,* I didn't know that⟩

wick \'wik\ n : a cord, strip, or ring of loosely woven material through which a liquid (as wax or oil) is drawn to the top in a candle, lamp, or oil stove for burning

wick·ed \'wik-əd\ adj 1 : morally bad : EVIL 2 : given to mischief : ROGUISH 3 : very bad or unpleasant ⟨a *wicked* storm⟩ — **wick·ed·ly** adv — **wick·ed·ness** n

wick·er \'wik-ər\ n 1 : a flexible twig (as of willow) 2 : WICKERWORK — **wicker** adj

wick·er·work \-,wərk\ n : something (as a basket or chair) made of wicker

wick·et \'wik-ət\ n 1 : a small gate or door; esp : one in or near a larger one 2 : a small window (as at a ticket office) through which one does business 3 : either of the two sets of three rods topped by two crosspieces at which the ball is bowled in cricket 4 : a hoop (as of wire) through which a ball is hit in croquet

wick·i·up \'wik-ē-,əp\ n : a cone-shaped Indian hut consisting of a rough frame covered with reed mats, grass, or branches

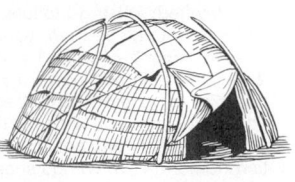
wickiup

¹**wide** \'wīd\ adj **wider**; **wid·est** 1 : covering a large area ⟨the *wide* world⟩ 2 : measured across or at right angles to length ⟨cloth 100 centimeters *wide*⟩ 3 : having a great measure across : BROAD ⟨a *wide* river⟩ 4 : opened as far as possible ⟨eyes *wide* with wonder⟩ 5 : not limited : EXTENSIVE ⟨a job calling for *wide* experience⟩ 6 : far from the thing in question ⟨a charge *wide* of the truth⟩ — **wide·ly** adv — **wide·ness** n

²**wide** adv 1 : over a great distance or extent : WIDELY ⟨searched far and *wide*⟩ 2 a : so as to leave much space between ⟨*wide* apart⟩ b : so as to clear by a wide distance ⟨ran *wide* around left end⟩ 3 : to the limit : COMPLETELY ⟨opened his eyes *wide*⟩

wide–awake \,wīd-ə-'wāk\ adj 1 : fully awake 2 : ¹ALERT 1b

wide–eyed \'wīd-'īd\ adj 1 : having the eyes wide open 2 : struck with wonder or astonishment 3 : NAIVE 2 ⟨a *wide-eyed* belief in the goodness of everybody⟩

wide·mouthed \-'mau̇thd, -'mau̇tht\ adj 1 : having a wide mouth ⟨*widemouthed* jars⟩ 2 : having one's mouth opened wide (as in awe)

wid·en \'wīd-°n\ vb **wid·ened**; **wid·en·ing** \'wīd-niŋ, -°n-iŋ\ : to make or become wide or wider : BROADEN

wide·spread \'wīd-'spred\ adj 1 : scattered or found over a wide area ⟨*widespread* interest in the election⟩ 2 : spread out over a wide area

¹**wid·ow** \'wid-ō\ n : a woman who has lost her husband by death — **wid·ow·hood** \-,hu̇d\ n

²**widow** vb : to cause to become a widow ⟨*widowed* by war⟩

wid·ow·er \'wid-ə-wər\ n : a man who has lost his wife by death

width \'width, 'witth\ n 1 : the measurement of the short or shorter side of something : BREADTH 2 : largeness of area or range 3 : a measured piece of material ⟨a *width* of cloth⟩ ⟨a *width* of lumber⟩

wield \'wē(ə)ld\ vb 1 : to put (as a tool) to good use ⟨*wield* a broom⟩ 2 : to use one's authority by means of ⟨*wield* influence⟩ **syn** see HANDLE — **wield·er** n

wie·ner \'wē-nər, 'wē-nē\ n : FRANKFURTER [from German *wienerwurst* "Vienna sausage", from *Vienna,* capital of Austria]

wife \'wīf\ n, pl **wives** \'wīvz\ 1 dialect : WOMAN 1 2 : a married woman

wife·ly \'wī-flē\ adj : of, relating to, or suitable for a wife

wig \'wig\ n : a manufactured covering of natural or artificial hair for the head

wi·geon or **wid·geon** \'wij-ən\ n, pl **wigeon** or **wigeons** or **widgeon** or **widgeons** : any of several freshwater ducks with a large white patch on the upper side of the front part of each wing

wig·gle \'wig-əl\ vb **wig·gled**; **wig·gling** \-(ə-)liŋ\ 1 : to move to and fro with quick jerky or shaking motions : JIGGLE ⟨*wiggled* my toes⟩ 2 : to move along with twisting and turning movements — **wiggle** n

wig·gler \'wig-(ə-)lər\ n 1 : a larva or pupa of a mosquito — called also *wriggler* 2 : one that wiggles

wig·gly \'wig-(ə-)lē\ adj **wig·gli·er**; **-est** 1 : tending to wiggle ⟨a *wiggly* worm⟩ 2 : WAVY ⟨*wiggly* lines⟩

wight \'wīt\ n : a living being : CREATURE

¹**wig·wag** \'wig-,wag\ vb **wig·wagged**; **wig·wag·ging** : to signal especially by a flag or light waved according to a code

²**wigwag** n 1 : the art or practice of wigwagging 2 : a wigwagged message

wig·wam \'wig-,wäm\ n : a hut of the Indians of the Great Lakes region and eastward that usually has an arched frame of poles covered with bark, rush mats, or hides [from a word *wikwām* of American Indian origin meaning literally "their dwelling"]

wigwam

¹**wild** \'wī(ə)ld\ adj 1 a : living in a state of nature and not under human control and care ⟨*wild* animals⟩ b : growing or produced without human aid and care ⟨*wild* honey⟩ c

\ə\ **abut**	\au̇\ **out**	\i\ **tip**	\ȯ\ **saw**	\u̇\ **foot**
\ər\ **further**	\ch\ **chin**	\ī\ **life**	\ȯi\ **coin**	\y\ **yet**
\a\ **mat**	\e\ **pet**	\j\ **job**	\th\ **thin**	\yü\ **few**
\ā\ **take**	\ē\ **easy**	\ŋ\ **sing**	\th\ **this**	\yu̇\ **cure**
\ä\ **cot, cart**	\g\ **go**	\ō\ **bone**	\ü\ **food**	\zh\ **vision**

: of or relating to wild organisms ⟨the *wild* state⟩ **2** : not inhabited or cultivated ⟨*wild* land⟩ **3 a** : not being under control ⟨*wild* rage⟩ **b** : marked by disturbance and confusion ⟨a *wild* night⟩ **c** : going beyond what is usual : FANTASTIC ⟨*wild* colors⟩ ⟨*wild* ideas⟩ **4** : not civilized : SAVAGE **5** : being far off the intended course ⟨a *wild* pitch⟩ — **wild·ly** \'wī(ə)l-(d)lē\ *adv* — **wild·ness** \'wī(ə)l(d)-nəs\ *n*

²wild *n* : WILDERNESS

³wild *adv* **1** : in a wild manner : WILDLY **2** : without rules or control ⟨running *wild*⟩

wild boar *n* : an Old World wild hog from which most domestic swine have been developed

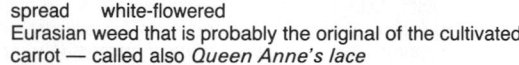
wild boar

wild carrot *n* : a widespread white-flowered Eurasian weed that is probably the original of the cultivated carrot — called also *Queen Anne's lace*

wild·cat \'wī(ə)l(d)-ˌkat\ *n, pl* **wildcats** *or* **wildcat** **1** : any of various small or medium-sized cats (as the lynx or ocelot) **2** : a savage quick-tempered person

wildcat 1

wil·de·beeste \'wil-də-ˌbēst\ *n, pl* **wildebeestes** *also* **wildebeeste** : GNU

wil·der·ness \'wil-dər-nəs\ *n* : an area in which few people live that is not used for farming and is more or less in its natural state

wild·fire \'wī(ə)l(d)-ˌfī(ə)r\ *n* : an uncontrollable fire that destroys a wide area

wild·flower \-ˌflaů(-ə)r\ *n* : the flower of a wild plant or the plant bearing it

wild·fowl \-ˌfaůl\ *n* : a bird and especially a waterfowl (as a wild duck) hunted as game

wild geranium *n* : a geranium of the eastern U.S. with rosy purple flowers

wild·life \'wī(ə)l-ˌ(d)līf\ *n* : nonhuman living things and especially wild animals living in their natural environment

wild rice *n* : a tall North American grass that grows in water and produces an edible grain

wild·wood \'wī(ə)l-ˌ(d)wůd\ *n* : woodland untouched by human activity

¹wile \'wī(ə)l\ *n* **1** : a trick intended to deceive or trap **2** : GUILE

²wile *vb* **wiled; wil·ing** : to lure by or as if by a magic spell

¹will \wəl, (ə)l, ⁰l, (')wil\ *vb, past* **would** \wəd, (ə)d, (')wůd\; *present sing & pl* **will** **1** : ¹WISH 1 ⟨call it what you *will*⟩ **2** — used as a helping verb to express (1) desire, willingness, or in negative sentences refusal ⟨*will* you have another⟩ ⟨no one *would* do it⟩ ⟨they *won't* stop⟩, (2) regular or usual action ⟨*will* get angry over nothing⟩, (3) future action ⟨tomorrow we *will* go shopping⟩, (4) capacity or ability ⟨the back seat *will* hold three people⟩, (5) determination or willfulness ⟨I *will* go despite the weather⟩, or (6) a command ⟨you *will* do as I say⟩

²will \'wil\ *n* **1** : firm desire or determination ⟨the *will* to win⟩ **2** : the desire or choice especially of someone in power or authority ⟨the king's *will*⟩ **3** : the process or power of wishing, choosing, desiring, or intending **4** : the power of control over one's own actions or emotions ⟨has an iron *will*⟩ **5** : a legal document that instructs how a person's property is to be divided after death

³will \'wil\ *vb* **1** : to leave by or as if by a will : BEQUEATH **2** : to bring about by the power of the will **3** : ¹ORDER 2a

⟨it will happen if God *wills* it⟩ **4** : to decide on by choice ⟨went wherever they *willed*⟩

willed \'wild\ *adj* : having a will especially of a certain kind ⟨strong-*willed*⟩

will·ful *or* **wil·ful** \'wil-fəl\ *adj* **1** : stubbornly determined to have one's own way **2** : done deliberately : INTENTIONAL ⟨*willful* murder⟩ **syn** see UNRULY — **will·ful·ly** \-fə-lē\ *adv* — **will·ful·ness** *n*

wil·lies \'wil-ēz\ *n pl* : a fit of nervousness : JITTERS

will·ing \'wil-iŋ\ *adj* **1** : feeling no objection : READY ⟨*willing* to go⟩ **2** : prompt to act or respond ⟨*willing* workers⟩ **3** : done, made, or given by choice : VOLUNTARY ⟨*willing* obedience⟩ — **will·ing·ly** *adv* — **will·ing·ness** *n*

wil·li·waw \'wil-i-ˌwò\ *n* : a sudden violent gust of cold land air common along mountainous coasts of high latitudes

will-o'-the-wisp \ˌwil-ə-t͟hə-'wisp\ *n* **1** : a light that sometimes appears in the night over marshy ground **2** : a false or unreachable goal

wil·low \'wil-ō\ *n* **1** : any of a genus of trees and shrubs that often have narrow leaves, produce catkins for flowers, and include some used for their wood, for making baskets, or as ornamentals **2** : an object made of willow wood — **wil·low·like** \-ˌlīk\ *adj*

wil·lowy \'wil-ə-wē\ *adj* **1** : having many willows **2 a** : bending easily without breaking : PLIANT **b** : gracefully tall and slender ⟨a *willowy* young dancer⟩

will·pow·er \'wil-ˌpaů(-ə)r\ *n* : strong determination

wil·ly-nil·ly \ˌwil-ē-'nil-ē\ *adv or adj* : by force : without choice ⟨rushed us along *willy-nilly*⟩ [an altered form of the phrase *will I nill I* or *will ye nill ye; nill*, an ancient negative form of *will*, from Old English *nyllan*, a combination of *ne* "not" and *wyllan* "to wish, will"]

¹wilt \wəlt, (')wilt\ *archaic present 2d sing of* WILL

²wilt \'wilt\ *vb* **1** : to lose or cause to lose freshness and become limp : DROOP ⟨*wilting* roses⟩ **2** : to grow weak or faint

³wilt \'wilt\ *n* : a plant disease (as one caused by a fungus) marked by wilting and drooping of the soft parts of the plant

wily \'wī-lē\ *adj* **wil·i·er; -est** : full of deceit : TRICKY **syn** see CUNNING — **wil·i·ness** *n*

wim·ple \'wim-pəl\ *n* : a cloth covering worn over the head and around the neck and chin by women in earlier times and by some nuns today

¹win \'win\ *vb* **won** \'wən\; **win·ning** **1** : to achieve victory in a contest **2** : to get especially by effort ⟨*won* praise for my hard work⟩ **3 a** : to gain in or as if in battle or contest **b** : to be the victor in ⟨*won* the war⟩ **4** : to make friendly or favorable to oneself or one's cause ⟨*won* the voters with her warm sense of humor⟩

²win *n* : VICTORY; *esp* : first place in a horse race

wince \'win(t)s\ *vb* **winced; winc·ing** : to shrink back (as from pain) : FLINCH — **wince** *n*

winch \'winch\ *n* : a machine that has a roller on which rope is wound for pulling or lifting

¹wind \'wind\ *n* **1** : a movement of air **2** : something that has force or influence ⟨the changing *winds* of political opinion⟩ **3** : BREATH 2a ⟨the fall knocked the *wind* out of me⟩ **4** : gas produced in the stomach or the intestines **5** : something unimportant; *esp* : idle words **6 a** : air carrying a scent (as of a hunter or game) **b** : slight information especially about something secret ⟨got *wind* of our plans⟩ **7** *pl* : the wind instruments of a band or orchestra **8** : the direction from which the wind is blowing [Old English *wind* "the natural movement of air"] — **in the wind** : about to happen : ASTIR, AFOOT

²wind *vb* **1** : to get a scent of ⟨the dogs *winded* game⟩ **2** : to cause to be out of breath ⟨the long climb *winded* us⟩ **3** : to allow to rest so as to recover breath ⟨*wind* a horse⟩

³wind \'wīnd, 'wind\ *vb* **wound** \'waůnd\; **wind·ing** : to sound by blowing ⟨*wind* a horn⟩

⁴wind \'wīnd\ *vb* **wound** \'waůnd\ *also* **wind·ed; wind-**

ing   **1** : to move in a series of twists and turns ⟨a river winding through the valley⟩ **2** : ENTANGLE **2** **3 a** : to encircle or cover with something flexible **b** : to coil completely or repeatedly about an object : TWINE ⟨*wind* thread on a spool⟩ **4** : to lift, pull, move, or operate by means of a rope or chain and a winch ⟨*wind* up a pail⟩ **5** : to tighten the spring of ⟨*wind* a clock⟩ ⟨*wind* up a toy train⟩ [Old English *windan* "to twist, move with force"] — **wind·er** *n*

⁵**wind** \ˈwīnd\ *n* : something curved or twisted : BEND

wind·age \ˈwin-dij\ *n* **1** : the influence of the wind in turning the course of a bullet or shell **2** : the amount of turning aside caused by the wind

wind·blown \ˈwin(d)-ˌblōn\ *adj* : blown by the wind ⟨*windblown* pollen⟩; *also* : having the appearance of being blown by the wind ⟨*windblown* hair⟩

wind·break \-ˌbrāk\ *n* : something (as a growth of trees) that serves as a shelter from the wind

wind·break·er \-ˌbrā-kər\ *n* : a light jacket made of material that can resist the wind

wind·burn \-ˌbərn\ *n* : skin irritation caused by wind — **wind·burned** \-ˌbərnd\ *adj*

wind·fall \-ˌföl\ *n* **1** : something (as a tree or fruit) blown down by the wind **2** : an unexpected gift, gain, or help

wind·flow·er \-ˌflau̇(-ə)r\ *n* : ANEMONE 1

¹**wind·ing** \ˈwīn-diŋ\ *n* **1** : material (as wire) wound or coiled about an object **2** : a single turn of wound material

²**winding** *adj* : marked by winding: as **a** : having a noticeable curve **b** : having a course that winds

wind·ing–sheet \-ˌshēt\ *n* : a sheet used to wrap a corpse for burial : SHROUD

wind instrument *n* : a musical instrument (as a flute or horn) sounded by the vibration of a stream of air and especially by the player's breath

wind·jam·mer \ˈwin(d)-ˌjam-ər\ *n* : a sailing ship

wind·lass \ˈwin-dləs\ *n* : a winch used especially on ships for pulling and lifting

wind·mill \ˈwin(d)-ˌmil\ *n* : a mill or a machine (as for pumping water) worked by the wind turning sails or vanes at the top of a tower

win·dow \ˈwin-dō\ *n* **1** : an opening in a wall for letting in light or air **2** : WINDOWPANE **3** : any of the areas into which a computer display may be divided and on which distinctly different types of information are displayed

> **Word History** The English word *window* comes from an early Norse word *vindauga*. *Vindauga* was formed by a combination of *vindr*, meaning "wind", and *auga*, meaning "eye". *Vindauga* could be translated as "wind's eye". A window can be thought of as an eye, or hole, through which the wind can enter. [from early Norse *vindauga*, literally "wind's eye", from *vindr* "wind" and *auga* "eye"]

window box *n* : a box for growing plants in or by a window

win·dow·pane \ˈwin-dō-ˌpān\ *n* : a pane in a window

window shade *n* : a shade or curtain for a window

win·dow–shop \ˈwin-dō-ˌshäp, -də-\ *vb* : to look at the displays in store windows without going inside to buy — **win·dow–shop·per** *n*

win·dow·sill \-ˌsil\ *n* : the horizontal piece at the bottom of a window

wind·pipe \ˈwin(d)-ˌpīp\ *n* : TRACHEA 1

wind·row \ˈwin-ˌ(d)rō\ *n* **1** : hay raked up into a row to dry **2** : a row of something (as sand or dry leaves) heaped up by or as if by the wind

wind·shield \ˈwin(d)-ˌshēld\ *n* : a clear screen (as of glass) in front of the riders of a vehicle

wind·storm \-ˌstö(ə)rm\ *n* : a storm with strong wind and little or no rain

wind·swept \-ˌswept\ *adj* : swept by or as if by wind ⟨a *windswept* beach⟩

wind tunnel *n* : a passage like a tunnel through which air is blown at a known speed to test the effect of wind pressure on an object (as an airplane part or model) placed in the passage

¹**wind·up** \ˈwīn-ˌdəp\ *n* **1 a** : the act of bringing to an end **b** : a last act or part : FINISH **2** : a swing of a baseball pitcher's arm before the pitch is thrown

²**windup** *adj* : having a spring wound by hand ⟨*windup* toys⟩

wind up \(ˈ)wīn-ˈdəp\ *vb* **1** : to bring or come to a conclusion : END ⟨let's *wind up* the meeting quickly⟩ **2** : to put in order : SETTLE **3** : to arrive in a place, situation, or state ⟨*wound up* as millionaires⟩ **4** : to swing the arm before pitching a baseball

¹**wind·ward** \ˈwin-(d)wərd\ *adj* : moving or placed toward the direction from which the wind is blowing

²**windward** *n* : the side or direction from which the wind is blowing ⟨sail to *windward*⟩

windy \ˈwin-dē\ *adj* **wind·i·er; -est** **1** : having strong winds ⟨a *windy* prairie⟩ **2** : marked by or given to too much talk ⟨a *windy* speaker⟩ — **wind·i·ness** *n*

¹**wine** \ˈwīn\ *n* **1** : fermented grape juice containing a percentage of alcohol **2** : the usually fermented juice of a plant product (as a fruit) used as a beverage **3** : a dark red color

²**wine** *vb* **wined; win·ing** **1** : to drink wine **2** : to serve wine to ⟨*wined* and dined my friends⟩

¹**wing** \ˈwiŋ\ *n* **1** : one of the movable feathered or membranous paired appendages by means of which a bird, bat, or insect flies **2** : an extension or part resembling a wing in shape, appearance, or position **3** : an extension from the side of

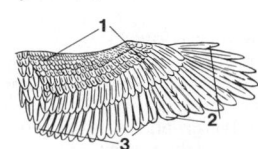

wing 1: *1* covering feathers, *2* primary feathers, *3* secondary feathers

an armchair **4** : a part that extends from the side of an airplane **5** : the act or manner of flying : FLIGHT **6** : a part sticking out from a main part ⟨the rear *wing* of the house⟩ **7** *pl* : the area at the side of the stage out of sight of the audience **8** : one of the positions or players on each side of a center position or line **9** : a particular group within an organization : FACTION **10** : a unit of a military force and especially an air force — **winged** \ˈwiŋd, ˈwiŋ-əd\ *adj* — **wing·like** \-ˌlīk\ *adj* — **on the wing** : in flight : FLYING — **under one's wing** : under one's protection : in one's care

²**wing** *vb* **1** : to pass through in flight : FLY **2** : to wound in the wing; *also* : to wound without killing

wing case *n* : ELYTRON

wing chair *n* : an upholstered armchair with a high back and side sections

wing·less \ˈwiŋ-ləs\ *adj* : having no wings or very undeveloped wings

wing·span \ˈwiŋ-ˌspan\ *n* : the distance between the tips of a pair of wings and especially between the tips of an airplane's wings

wing·spread \-ˌspred\ *n* : WINGSPAN; *esp* : the distance between the tips of the fully extended wings of a bird, bat, or insect

¹**wink** \ˈwiŋk\ *vb* **1** : to close and open one eye quickly as a signal or hint **2** : to close and open the eyes quickly : BLINK **3** : to avoid seeing or noting ⟨*wink* at a parking violation⟩ **4** : to gleam or shine on and off : TWINKLE

²**wink** *n* **1** : a brief period of sleep : NAP **2 a** : a hint or sign given by winking **b** : an act of winking **3** : the time of a wink : INSTANT ⟨quick as a *wink* she did the job⟩

\ə\ **abut**	\au̇\ **out**	\i\ **tip**	\ȯ\ **saw**	\u̇\ **foot**
\ər\ **further**	\ch\ **chin**	\ī\ **life**	\ȯi\ **coin**	\y\ **yet**
\a\ **mat**	\e\ **pet**	\j\ **job**	\th\ **thin**	\yü\ **few**
\ā\ **take**	\ē\ **easy**	\ŋ\ **sing**	\th\ **this**	\yu̇\ **cure**
\ä\ **cot, cart**	\g\ **go**	\ō\ **bone**	\ü\ **food**	\zh\ **vision**

win·ner \'win-ər\ *n* : one that wins

¹win·ning \'win-iŋ\ *n* **1** : the act of one that wins : VICTORY **2** : something won; *esp* : money won in a game or contest — usually used in pl.

²winning *adj* **1 a** : of, relating to, or used for or in the act of winning 〈the *winning* ticket〉 **b** : successful especially in competition 〈a *winning* team〉 **2** : tending to please or delight 〈a *winning* smile〉 — **win·ning·ly** *adv*

win·now \'win-ō\ *vb* **1 a** : to remove by a current of air the parts separated from grain in threshing **b** : to expose grain to a current of air to remove waste **2** : to sort or separate as if by winnowing 〈*winnow* out the bad cherries from the basket〉 — **win·now·er** \'win-ə-wər\ *n*

win·some \'win(t)-səm\ *adj* **1** : having a charming or pleasing quality **2** : CHEERFUL 1a — **win·some·ly** *adv* — **win·some·ness** *n*

¹win·ter \'wint-ər\ *n* **1** : the season between autumn and spring usually including in the northern half of the globe the months of December, January, and February **2** : YEAR 2 〈happened many *winters* ago〉 **3** : a time or season of idleness or decay

²winter *vb* **win·tered; win·ter·ing** \'wint-ə-riŋ, 'win-triŋ\ **1** : to pass or live through the winter 〈the cattle *wintered* on the range〉 **2** : to keep, feed, or manage during the winter 〈*winter* livestock〉

³winter *adj* **1** : of, relating to, or suitable for winter 〈*winter* clothes〉 **2** : sown in autumn and harvested in the following spring or summer 〈*winter* wheat〉

win·ter·green \'wint-ər-,grēn\ *n* **1 a** : a low evergreen plant of the heath family with white bell-shaped flowers and spicy red berries — called also *checkerberry* **b** : any of several plants related to the wintergreen **2** : an oil from the common wintergreen or its flavor; *also* : something flavored with wintergreen

win·ter·ize \'wint-ə-,rīz\ *vb* **-ized; -iz·ing** : to make ready for winter 〈*winterize* the car〉

win·ter–kill \'wint-ər-,kil\ *vb* : to cause the death of (as a plant) through the effects of winter and especially cold; *also* : to die as a result of the effects of winter conditions and especially cold

winter squash *n* : any of various squashes or pumpkins that keep well in storage

win·ter·time \'wint-ər-,tīm\ *n* : the winter season

win·try \'win-trē\ *adj* **win·tri·er; -est** **1** : of, relating to, or typical of winter **2** : not warm and friendly : CHEERLESS 〈a *wintry* welcome〉 — **win·tri·ness** *n*

¹wipe \'wīp\ *vb* **wiped; wip·ing** **1** : to clean or dry by rubbing 〈*wipe* dishes〉 **2** : to remove by or as if by rubbing 〈*wipe* away tears〉 **3** : to pass or draw over a surface 〈*wiped* my hand across my forehead〉 — **wip·er** *n*

²wipe *n* : an act or instance of wiping

wipe out *vb* : to destroy completely 〈the company of soldiers was *wiped out*〉

¹wire \'wī(ə)r\ *n* **1 a** : metal in the form of a usually flexible thread or slender rod **b** : a thread or rod of metal **2 a** : a line of wire for conducting electrical current **b** : a telephone or telegraph wire or system **c** : TELEGRAM, CABLEGRAM — **wire·like** \-,līk\ *adj* — **under the wire** **1** : at the finish line **2** : at the last moment

²wire *vb* **wired; wir·ing** **1** : to provide or equip with wire or electricity 〈*wire* a house〉 **2** : to bind, string, or mount with wire **3** : to send or send word to by telegraph 〈*wire* me some money right away〉

wire grass *n* : any of various grasses or rushes having wiry stems or leaves

wire·haired \'wī(ə)r-'ha(ə)rd, -'he(ə)rd\ *adj* : having a stiff wiry outer coat of hair

¹wire·less \'wī(ə)r-ləs\ *adj* **1** : having no wire or wires **2** *chiefly British* : of or relating to radiotelegraphy, radiotelephony, or radio

²wireless *n* **1** : wireless telegraphy **2** *chiefly British* : ¹RADIO

wire service *n* : a news organization that sends out news stories by wire to subscribers (as newspapers)

¹wire·tap \'wī(ə)r-,tap\ *n* : the act or an instance of wiretapping

²wiretap *vb* : to tap a telephone or telegraph wire to get information — **wire·tap·per** *n*

wire·worm \'wī(ə)r-,wərm\ *n* : the slender hard-coated larva of various beetles that is especially destructive to plant roots

wiry \'wī(ə)r-ē\ *adj* **wir·i·er** \'wī-rē-ər\; **wir·i·est** **1** : of, relating to, or resembling wire **2** : being slender yet strong and muscular

wis·dom \'wiz-dəm\ *n* **1 a** : learning acquired over a period of time : KNOWLEDGE **b** : ability to see beneath the surface of things : INSIGHT **c** : good sense : JUDGMENT **2** : a wise attitude or course of action

Wisdom *n* — see BIBLE table

Wisdom of Sol·o·mon \-'säl-ə-mən\ — see BIBLE table

wisdom tooth *n* : the last tooth of the full set of teeth on each half of each jaw in a human being

¹wise \'wīz\ *n* : MANNER 2b — used in such phrases as *in any wise, in no wise, in this wise* [Old English *wīse* "way, manner"]

²wise *adj* **wis·er; wis·est** **1** : having or showing wisdom : SENSIBLE **2** : having special or secret information : INFORMED 〈I was *wise* to their plans〉 [Old English *wīs* "showing good judgment or intelligence"] — **wise·ly** *adv*

³wise *vb* **wised; wis·ing** : to make or become informed or smart — used with *up* 〈*wise up* if you want to get ahead〉

-wise \,wīz\ *adv combining form* **1 a** : in the manner of 〈crab*wise*〉 〈fan*wise*〉 **b** : in the position or direction of 〈slant*wise*〉 〈clock*wise*〉 **2** : with regard to : in respect of 〈dollar*wise*〉 [derived from Old English *wīse* "manner"]

wise·acre \'wī-,zā-kər\ *n* : SMART ALECK [a modified form of early Dutch *wijssegger* "one who is thought to be able to foretell events"]

wise·crack \'wīz-,krak\ *n* : a clever, smart, or joking remark — **wisecrack** *vb* — **wise·crack·er** *n*

wise guy \'wīz-,gī\ *n* : WISEACRE

¹wish \'wish\ *vb* **1** : to have a desire : long for : WANT 〈*wish* you were here〉 〈*wish* for a puppy〉 **2** : to form or express a desire concerning 〈*wished* them a happy New Year〉 **3** : ²REQUEST 1 〈I *wish* you to go now〉 — **wish·er** *n*

²wish *n* **1 a** : an act or instance of wishing or desire **b** : an object of desire : GOAL 〈I got my *wish* — a good score on the test〉 **2** : a wishing of good fortune 〈sends her best *wishes*〉

wish·bone \'wish-,bōn\ *n* : a bone in front of a bird's breastbone that is shaped like a V

wish·ful \'wish-fəl\ *adj* **1** : having a wish : DESIROUS **2** : based on wishes rather than fact 〈*wishful* thinking〉 — **wish·ful·ly** \-fə-lē\ *adv* — **wish·ful·ness** *n*

wishy–washy \'wish-ē-,wȯsh-ē, -,wäsh-\ *adj* : lacking spirit, courage, or determination : WEAK

wisp \'wisp\ *n* **1** : a small bunch of hay or straw **2 a** : a thin piece or strand **b** : a faint streak 〈a *wisp* of smoke〉 **c** : something weak, slight, or delicate 〈a *wisp* of a smile〉 — **wispy** \'wis-pē\ *adj*

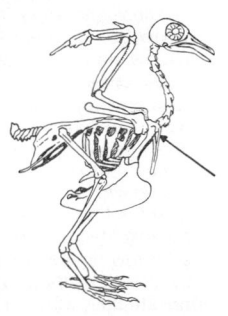

wishbone

wis·te·ria \wis-'tir-ē-ə\ *or* **wis·tar·ia** \-'tir-ē-ə *also* -'ter-\ *n* : any of a genus of chiefly Asian mostly woody vines of the legume family that have leaves with numerous leaflets and showy blue, white, purple, or rose flowers in long hanging clusters [named for Caspar *Wistar* 1761–1818 American physician]

wist·ful \'wist-fəl\ *adj* : feeling or showing a timid desire ⟨a *wistful* look on his face⟩ — **wist·ful·ly** \-fə-lē\ *adv* — **wist·ful·ness** *n*

¹wit \'wit\ *vb* **wist** \'wist\; **wit·ting;** *present 1st & 3d sing* **wot** \'wät\ *archaic* : KNOW, LEARN [Old English *witan* "to know"]

²wit *n* **1** : ability to think or reason : INTELLIGENCE **2 a** : normal mental state — usually used in pl. ⟨scared out of my *wits*⟩ **b** : practical good judgment ⟨had the *wit* to leave quickly⟩ **3 a** : a talent for making clever and usually amusing remarks **b** : clever remarks **c** : one noted for making witty remarks [Old English *wit* "mind"] — **at one's wit's end** *or* **at one's wits' end** : at a loss for a means of solving a problem

witch \'wich\ *n* **1** : a woman believed to have magic powers **2** : a mean or ugly old woman

witch·craft \-ˌkraft\ *n* : the power or doings of a witch : SORCERY

witch doctor *n* : a person in a primitive society who uses magic to treat sickness and to fight off evil spirits

witch·ery \'wich-(ə-)rē\ *n, pl* **-er·ies 1** : WITCHCRAFT **2** : a power to charm or fascinate

witch ha·zel \'wich-ˌhā-zəl\ *n* **1** : any of a genus of shrubs that produce yellow flowers with very thin petals in late fall or early spring; *esp* : one of eastern North America that blooms in the fall **2** : a soothing alcoholic lotion made from the bark of the witch hazel [from *witch*, an old name for any of several trees with branches that bend easily, from Old English *wice* (same meaning)]

witch–hunt \-ˌhənt\ *n* : a searching out and persecution of persons accused of witchcraft

witch·ing \'wich-in\ *adj* : of, relating to, or suitable for witchcraft ⟨the *witching* hour⟩

with \(')with, (')with\ *prep* **1 a** : in opposition to : AGAINST ⟨fought *with* his sister⟩ **b** : FROM 2 ⟨parting *with* friends⟩ **2** : in shared relation to ⟨talking *with* a friend⟩ ⟨trade *with* other countries⟩ **3** : in regard to : TOWARD ⟨angry *with* her⟩ ⟨on friendly terms *with* all nations⟩ **4 a** : compared to ⟨on equal terms *with* the others⟩ **b** : on the side of ⟨voted *with* the majority⟩ **c** : in a way that can be compared to ⟨I can scream *with* the best of them⟩ **5 a** : in the judgment or opinion of ⟨it's all right *with* me⟩ **b** : in the experience or practice of ⟨*with* them a promise is a real duty⟩ **6 a** : by means of ⟨write *with* a pen⟩ **b** : because of ⟨danced *with* joy⟩ **7** : having or showing as a manner of action or an accompanying fact ⟨spoke *with* vigor⟩ ⟨stood there *with* my hat on⟩ **8 a** : in possession of : HAVING ⟨animals *with* horns⟩ **b** : marked by ⟨a person *with* a hot temper⟩ **9 a** : in the company of ⟨went to the movies *with* us⟩ **b** : having or including as a part ⟨costs $5 *with* the tax⟩ ⟨tea *with* lemon⟩ **10 a** : at the same time as ⟨rose *with* the sun⟩ **b** : in proportion to ⟨the pressure varies *with* the depth⟩ **11** : in spite of ⟨*with* all her cleverness, she failed⟩ **12** : in the direction of ⟨cut *with* the grain of the fabric⟩

with·al \with-'ol, with-\ *adv* **1** : together with this : BESIDES **2** : on the other hand : NEVERTHELESS

with·draw \with-'dro, with-\ *vb* **-drew** \-'drü\; **-drawn** \-'dron\; **-draw·ing** \-'dro(-)in\ **1** : to take back or away : draw away : REMOVE ⟨*withdraw* money from the bank⟩ **2 a** : to call back : RECALL ⟨*withdrew* the charge of theft⟩ **b** : to take back (one's words) : RETRACT **3** : to go away : RETREAT ⟨*withdrew* to the country⟩

with·draw·al \with-'dro(-ə)l, with-\ *n* **1** : an act or instance of withdrawing; *esp* : a removal of money from a bank account **2** : the stopping of the use or giving of a drug and especially a habit-forming drug; *also* : the bodily process that takes place when use of such a drug is stopped

with·drawn \with-'dron, with-\ *adj* **1** : removed from close or easy contact : ISOLATED **2** : not socially active or interested : INTROVERTED

withe \'with, 'with, 'with\ *n* : a slender flexible branch or twig

with·er \'with-ər\ *vb* **with·ered; with·er·ing** \-(ə-)rin\ **1** : to shrivel from or as if from loss of bodily moisture and especially sap **2** : to lose liveliness, force, or freshness

with·ers \'with-ərz\ *n pl* : the ridge between the shoulder bones of a horse

with·hold \with-'hōld, with-\ *vb* **-held** \-'held\; **-holding 1** : to hold back : RETAIN **2** : to refuse to grant, give, or allow ⟨*withhold* permission⟩ **3** : to deduct (withholding tax) from income — **with·hold·er** *n*

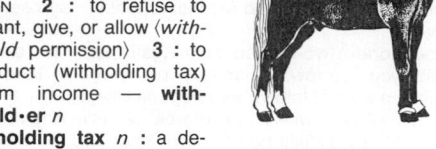

W withers

withholding tax *n* : a deduction (as from one's wages) taken at a source of income (as one's employer) as an advance payment of income tax

¹with·in \with-'in, with-\ *adv* **1** : in or into the interior : INSIDE **2** : inside oneself : INWARDLY

²within *prep* **1** : in or into the inner part of ⟨*within* the house⟩ **2** : not beyond the bounds or limits of ⟨*within* sight⟩

³within *n* : an inner place or area

with–it \'with-ət\ *adj* : very aware of what is up-to-date and in fashion

¹with·out \with-'aut, with-\ *prep* **1** : ⁴OUTSIDE 1, 2 **2 a** : not having : LACKING ⟨*without* food⟩ **b** : not accompanied by or showing ⟨spoke *without* thinking⟩

²without *adv* **1** : on the outside **2** : with something lacking or absent ⟨learn to do *without*⟩

³without *n* : an outer place or area

with·stand \with-'stand, with-\ *vb* **-stood** \-'stud\; **-standing** : to stand against : RESIST; *esp* : to oppose successfully

wit·less \'wit-ləs\ *adj* : lacking wit : FOOLISH — **wit·less·ly** *adv* — **wit·less·ness** *n*

¹wit·ness \'wit-nəs\ *n* **1** : TESTIMONY 1 ⟨bear false *witness*⟩ **2** : one who gives evidence especially before a court of law **3 a** : one present at an action (as a wedding) who can testify to its having taken place **b** : one who has personal knowledge or experience of something **4** : something serving as evidence or proof : SIGN

²witness *vb* **1** : to give testimony to : TESTIFY **2** : to act as legal witness of ⟨*witness* a document⟩ **3** : to be or give proof of ⟨their actions *witness* their guilt⟩ **4** : to have personal knowledge of : see for oneself ⟨had *witnessed* the accident⟩

wit·ted \'wit-əd\ *adj* : having wit or understanding — used in combination ⟨dull-*witted*⟩

wit·ti·cism \'wit-ə-ˌsiz-əm\ *n* : a witty saying

witting *present participle of* WIT

wit·ting·ly \'wit-in-lē\ *adv* : with knowledge or awareness of what one is doing : CONSCIOUSLY ⟨you *wittingly* insulted them⟩

wit·ty \'wit-ē\ *adj* **wit·ti·er; -est** : marked by or full of wit : AMUSING ⟨a *witty* writer⟩ ⟨a *witty* remark⟩ — **wit·ti·ly** \'wit-ᵊl-ē\ *adv* — **wit·ti·ness** \'wit-ē-nəs\ *n*

wives *pl of* WIFE

wiz·ard \'wiz-ərd\ *n* **1** : a person skilled in magic : SORCERER, MAGICIAN **2** : a very clever or skillful person [Middle English *wysard* "wise man, a person skilled in magic", from *wis, wys* "wise", from Old English *wis* "wise"]

wiz·ard·ry \'wiz-ə(r)-drē\ *n, pl* **-ries** **1** : the art or practices of a wizard : SORCERY **2** : a seemingly magical power or influence ⟨the *wizardry* of modern computers⟩

wiz·en \'wiz-ᵊn\ *vb* : to become shrunken or wrinkled often as a result of aging

wob·ble \'wäb-əl\ *vb* **wob·bled; wob·bling** \-(ə-)liŋ\ **1 a** : to move or cause to move with a jerky rocking or side-to-side motion **b** : ¹TREMBLE 1 **2** : WAVER 1 — **wobble** *n* — **wob·bler** \'wäb-(ə-)lər\ *n* — **wob·bly** \-(ə-)lē\ *adj*

woe \'wō\ *n* **1** : great suffering from loss, misfortune, or trouble **2** : ²TROUBLE 1b ⟨economic *woes*⟩ **syn** see SORROW

woe·be·gone \'wō-bi-ˌgȯn *also* -ˌgän\ *adj* **1** : showing great woe, sorrow, or misery ⟨*woebegone* faces⟩ **2** : being in a sad state ⟨a *woebegone* village⟩

woe·ful \'wō-fəl\ *adj* **1** : full of woe **2** : involving or bringing woe **3** : pitifully bad ⟨*woeful* ignorance⟩ — **woe·ful·ly** \-f(ə-)lē\ *adv* — **woe·ful·ness** \-fəl-nəs\ *n*

wok \'wäk\ *n* : a bowl-shaped cooking utensil used especially in making Chinese food [Chinese]

woke *past and past participle of* WAKE

woken *past participle of* WAKE

wold \'wōld\ *n* : a high plain or hilly area usually without woods

¹wolf \'wu̇lf\ *n, pl* **wolves** \'wu̇lvz\ *also* **wolf** **1** : any of several large bushy-tailed mammals with ears standing straight up that resemble the related dogs, that prey on other animals, and that often hunt in packs — compare COYOTE, JACKAL **2** : a person who resembles a wolf — **wolf·ish** \'wu̇l-fish\ *adj* — **wolf·like** \'wu̇l-ˌflīk\ *adj*

²wolf *vb* : to eat greedily : DEVOUR ⟨*wolfed* down the sandwiches⟩

wolf dog *n* **1** : any of various large dogs formerly kept for hunting wolves **2** : a hybrid offspring of a wolf and a domestic dog

wolf·hound \'wu̇lf-ˌhau̇nd\ *n* : any of several large dogs used in hunting large animals (as wolves)

wol·fram \'wu̇l-frəm\ *n* : TUNGSTEN

wol·fram·ite \'wu̇l-frə-ˌmīt\ *n* : a brownish or grayish black mineral that contains tungsten in combination with iron, manganese, and oxygen, that occurs as crystals and grainy masses, and that is used as a source of tungsten

wolf spider *n* : any of various active wandering spiders of which most do not build a web but chase and catch their prey

wol·ver·ine \ˌwu̇l-və-'rēn\ *n* : a blackish mammal with shaggy fur that is related to the weasels, martens, and sables, eats flesh, and is found chiefly in the northern parts of North America

wom·an \'wu̇m-ən\ *n, pl* **wom·en** \'wim-ən\ **1** : an adult female person **2** : WOMANKIND **3** : a female servant or attendant [Old English *wīfman* "a female person", from *wīf* "woman, wife" and *man* "person"]

wolverine

wom·an·hood \'wu̇m-ən-ˌhu̇d\ *n* **1** : the state of being a woman **2** : womanly qualities **3** : women considered as a group

wom·an·ish \'wu̇m-ə-nish\ *adj* **1** : typical of a woman **2** : suitable to a woman rather than to a man

wom·an·kind \'wu̇m-ən-ˌkīnd\ *n* : female human beings : WOMEN

wom·an·like \'wu̇m-ən-ˌlīk\ *adj* : resembling or typical of a woman : WOMANLY

wom·an·ly \'wu̇m-ən-lē\ *adj* : marked by qualities typical of a woman

womb \'wüm\ *n* **1** : UTERUS **2** : a place where something is begun or developed

wom·bat \'wäm-ˌbat\ *n* : any of several stocky burrowing Australian marsupials that resemble small bears

wom·en·folk \'wim-ən-ˌfōk\ *or* **wom·en·folks** \-ˌfōks\ *n pl* : women especially of one family or group

women's rights *n pl* : legal, political, and social rights for women equal to those of men

won *past and past participle of* WIN

¹won·der \'wən-dər\ *n* **1** : something extraordinary or surprising : MARVEL **2 a** : a feeling (as awe or astonishment) caused by something extraordinary **b** : the quality of exciting wonder

²wonder *vb* **won·dered; won·der·ing** \-d(ə-)riŋ\ **1** : to feel surprise or amazement **2** : to have curiosity or doubt ⟨I always *wondered* about that⟩ — **won·der·er** \-dər-ər\ *n*

wonder drug *n* : MIRACLE DRUG

won·der·ful \'wən-dər-fəl\ *adj* **1** : exciting wonder : MARVELOUS **2** : unusually good ⟨having a *wonderful* time⟩ — **won·der·ful·ly** \-f(ə-)lē\ *adv*

won·der·land \'wən-dər-ˌland, -lənd\ *n* : a place filled with wonders or surprises

won·der·ment \'wən-dər-mənt\ *n* **1** : AMAZEMENT **2** : curiosity about something

won·drous \'wən-drəs\ *adj* : WONDERFUL — **wondrous** *adv, archaic* — **won·drous·ly** *adv* — **won·drous·ness** *n*

¹wont \'wȯnt, 'wōnt\ *adj* : being in the habit of doing

²wont *n* : usual custom

won't \(')wōnt, 'wənt\ : will not

wont·ed \'wȯnt-əd, 'wōnt-\ *adj* : CUSTOMARY 2 ⟨acted with their *wonted* politeness⟩

woo \'wü\ *vb* **1** : to try to gain the love of : COURT **2** : to seek to gain or bring about ⟨political candidates *wooing* public support⟩

¹wood \'wu̇d\ *n* **1** : a dense growth of trees usually smaller than a forest — often used in pl. ⟨a thick *woods* runs along the ridge⟩ **2** : a hard fibrous substance that is basically xylem and makes up the greater part of the stems and branches of trees or shrubs beneath the bark; *also* : this material prepared for some use (as burning or building) **3** : something made of wood; *esp* : a golf club having a wooden head — **out of the woods** : escaped from danger or difficulty

²wood *adj* **1** : WOODEN 1 **2** : suitable for cutting or working wood ⟨*wood* chisels⟩ **3** *or* **woods** \'wu̇dz\ : living or growing in woods

wood alcohol *n* : METHANOL

wood·bine \'wu̇d-ˌbīn\ *n* : any of several climbing vines (as a honeysuckle or the Virginia creeper) of Europe and America

wood·block \'wu̇d-ˌbläk\ *n* : WOODCUT

wood–carv·er \-ˌkär-vər\ *n* : a person who carves objects of wood — **wood carv·ing** \-viŋ\ *n*

wood·chop·per \-ˌchäp-ər\ *n* : WOODCUTTER

wood·chuck \-ˌchək\ *n* **1** : a stocky marmot of the northeastern U.S. and Canada — called also *groundhog* **2** : any of several marmots of mountainous western North America [from either of two American Indian words *otchig* or *otcheck* "an animal related to the weasel"; the spelling influenced by the similarity of sound to the more familiar English words *wood* and *chuck*]

woodchuck 1

wood·cock \-ˌkäk\ *n, pl* **wood·cocks** *or* **woodcock** : a brown game bird with a short neck and long bill that is related to the snipe; *also* : a related and similar bird that is widespread in the Old World

wood·craft \-ˌkraft\ *n* : knowledge about the woods and how to take care of oneself in them

wood·cut \-ˌkət\ *n* **1** : a printing surface having a raised design carved from a block of wood **2** : a print from a woodcut

wood·cut·ter \-ˌkət-ər\ *n* : one that cuts wood especially as an occupation

wood duck *n* : a showy American duck which nests in trees and the male of which has a large crest on the head and feathers colored with green, black, purple, white, and brown

wood·ed \ˈwu̇d-əd\ *adj* : covered with trees

wood·en \ˈwu̇d-ᵊn\ *adj* **1** : made of wood **2** : lacking in spirit, ease, or charm ⟨written in a *wooden* style⟩ — **wood·en·ly** *adv* — **wood·en·ness** \-ᵊn-(n)əs\ *n*

woodcock

wood engraving *n* **1** : a printing surface consisting of a design cut into a block of wood **2** : a print from a wood engraving

¹wood·land \ˈwu̇d-lənd, -ˌland\ *n* : land covered with trees and shrubs : FOREST

²woodland *adj* **1** : growing or living in woodland **2** : of, relating to, or being woodland

wood·lot \ˈwu̇d-ˌlät\ *n* : a small area of trees kept usually to meet fuel and timber needs

wood louse *n* : a small flat grayish crustacean that is an isopod and lives especially under stones and bark — called also *pill bug, sow bug*

wood·man \ˈwu̇d-mən\ *n* : WOODSMAN

wood·peck·er \-ˌpek-ər\ *n* : any of numerous brightly marked birds with stiff tail feathers used for support in climbing or resting on tree trunks, a long flexible tongue, and a very hard bill used to drill into trees to get insects for food and to dig out holes for nesting

wood·pile \-ˌpīl\ *n* : a pile of wood and especially firewood

wood rat *n* : any of numerous native small rodents of the southern and western U.S. that have soft pale fur, furry tails, and large ears

wood·shed \-ˌshed\ *n* : a shed for storing wood and especially firewood

woods·man \ˈwu̇dz-mən\ *n* : a person who visits or works in the woods; *esp* : one skilled in woodcraft

wood sorrel *n* : any of a genus of herbs with acid sap, leaves having leaflets, and flowers with five petals; *esp* : a stemless herb having leaves with three leaflets that is sometimes considered to be the original shamrock

woodsy \ˈwu̇d-zē\ *adj* : of, relating to, or suggestive of woods ⟨a *woodsy* smell⟩

wood·wind \ˈwu̇d-ˌwind\ *n* **1** : one of a group of musical instruments including flutes, clarinets, oboes, bassoons, and sometimes saxophones — compare BRASS INSTRUMENT, PERCUSSION INSTRUMENT, STRINGED INSTRUMENT **2** : the woodwind section of a band or orchestra — **woodwind** *adj*

wood·work \-ˌwərk\ *n* : work made of wood; *esp* : interior fittings (as window frames or stairways) of wood

wood·work·ing \-ˌwər-kiŋ\ *n* : the act, process, or occupation of working with wood — **wood·work·er** \-kər\ *n*

woody \ˈwu̇d-ē\ *adj* **wood·i·er; -est** **1** : having or covered with trees ⟨a *woody* piece of land⟩ **2** : of or containing wood or wood fibers **3** : characteristic of or similar to wood ⟨a *woody* texture⟩

woo·er \ˈwü-ər\ *n* : one that woos : SUITOR

¹woof \ˈwu̇f, ˈwüf\ *n* **1** : the threads that cross the warp in a woven fabric **2** : a woven fabric or its texture [Old English *ōwef*, literally "to weave onto"]

²woof \ˈwu̇f\ *vb* : to make the sound of a woof

³woof *n* : a low gruff sound made by a dog [a word created in imitation of the sound]

woof·er \ˈwu̇f-ər\ *n* : a loudspeaker larger than a tweeter that responds only to low sound frequencies and produces sounds of low pitch — compare TWEETER

¹woof 1: *light* woof, *dark* warp

wool \ˈwu̇l\ *n* **1** : the heavy soft wavy or curly hair of various mammals and especially the sheep **2** : a fabric or garment made of wool **3** : material that resembles a mass of wool — **wooled** \ˈwu̇ld\ *adj*

¹wool·en *or* **wool·len** \ˈwu̇l-ən\ *adj* **1** : made of wool **2** : of or relating to the manufacture or sale of woolen products

²woolen *or* **woollen** *n* **1** : a fabric made of wool **2** : garments of woolen fabric — usually used in pl.

wool·gath·er·ing \ˈwu̇l-ˌgath-(ə-)riŋ\ *n* : the act of daydreaming

¹wool·ly *also* **wooly** \ˈwu̇l-ē\ *adj* **wool·li·er; -est** **1 a** : of, relating to, or bearing wool ⟨*woolly* animals⟩ **b** : resembling wool **2** : marked by mental confusion ⟨*woolly* thinking⟩ **3** : marked by much noise and roughness ⟨the wild and *woolly* West⟩ — **wool·li·ness** *n*

²wool·ly *also* **wool·lie** *or* **wooly** \ˈwu̇l-ē\ *n, pl* **wool·lies** : a woolen garment; *esp* : underclothing of knitted wool — usually used in pl.

woolly bear *n* : any of various rather large very hairy moth caterpillars; *esp* : one that is the larva of a tiger moth

woolly mammoth *n* : an extinct mammal with a heavy coat that is known from fossils, from the drawings of prehistoric human beings, and from entire dead frozen bodies dug up in Siberia

woo·zy \ˈwü-zē\ *adj* **woo·zi·er; -est** : slightly dizzy, sick, or weak

¹word \ˈwərd\ *n* **1** : a sound or combination of sounds that has meaning and is spoken by a human being **2** : a written or printed letter or letters standing for a spoken word **3** : a brief remark or conversation ⟨could I have a *word* with you⟩ **4** : ¹ORDER 5b ⟨give the *word* to begin⟩ **5** : NEWS 1 ⟨any *word* on how they are⟩ **6** : ¹PROMISE 1 ⟨I give you my *word*⟩ **7** : a remark or conversation uttered in anger — usually used in pl. ⟨*words* were exchanged and a fight broke out⟩ — **good word** : a favorable statement ⟨put in a *good word* for me⟩ — **word for word** : in the exact words : VERBATIM — **word·less** \ˈwərd-ləs\ *adj*

²word *vb* : to express in words : PHRASE ⟨*worded* their request with great care⟩

word·age \ˈwərd-ij\ *n* : a quantity or number of words

word·book \ˈwərd-ˌbu̇k\ *n* : VOCABULARY 1, DICTIONARY

word·ing \ˈwərd-iŋ\ *n* : the way in which something is put into words

word order *n* : the order or arrangement of words in a phrase, clause, or sentence

word·play \ˈwərd-ˌplā\ *n* : wit that is based on the clever use of words

word processing *n* : the production of typewritten docu-

\ə\ abut	\au̇\ out	\i\ tip	\ȯ\ saw	\u̇\ foot
\ər\ further	\ch\ chin	\ī\ life	\ȯi\ coin	\y\ yet
\a\ mat	\e\ pet	\j\ job	\th\ thin	\yü\ few
\ā\ take	\ē\ easy	\ŋ\ sing	\th\ this	\yu̇\ cure
\ä\ cot, cart	\g\ go	\ō\ bone	\ü\ food	\zh\ vision

ments (as business letters) with automated and usually computerized equipment for preparing text

word processor *n* : a keyboard-operated terminal usually with a video display and a magnetic storage device for use in word processing; *also* : software (as for a computer system) to perform word processing

wordy \'wərd-ē\ *adj* **word·i·er; -est** : using or containing too many words — **word·i·ly** \'wərd-°l-ē\ *adv* — **word·i·ness** \'wərd-ē-nəs\ *n*

wore *past of* WEAR

¹**work** \'wərk\ *n* **1 a** : the use of one's strength or ability to get something done or to achieve a result : LABOR, TOIL **b** : the work done as one's regular job **c** : something to be done : TASK ⟨have *work* to do⟩ **2** : the energy used when a force is applied over a given distance **3 a** : something that results from a particular manner or method of working, operating, or devising ⟨careful police *work*⟩ **b** : something that results from the use or shaping of a particular material **4** : a fortified structure **5** *pl* : a place where industrial labor is done : PLANT, FACTORY ⟨a cement *works*⟩ **6** *pl* : the working or moving parts of a mechanical device ⟨the *works* of a watch⟩ **7** : something produced by hard work or skill ⟨a writer's first *work*⟩ **8** : manner of working : WORKMANSHIP ⟨careless *work*⟩ **9** *pl* **a** : everything available, possessed, or belonging ⟨a hamburger with the *works*⟩ **b** : the harshest treatment possible ⟨gave him the *works*⟩ [Old English *werc, weorc* "work, activity directed toward accomplishing something"] — **at work** **1** : doing work : BUSY; *esp* : taking part in one's regular occupation **2** : having effect : OPERATING ⟨medicine *at work* in the body⟩ — **out of work** : without a regular job

²**work** *adj* **1** : used for work ⟨a *work* elephant⟩ **2** : suitable for wear while working ⟨*work* clothes⟩

³**work** *vb* **worked** \'wərkt\ *or* **wrought** \'rȯt\; **work·ing** **1** : to bring about : EFFECT ⟨*work* a cure⟩ **2 a** : to prepare by stirring or shaping ⟨*work* dough⟩ **b** : to bring into a desired form by a manufacturing process ⟨*work* cold steel⟩ **3** : to set or keep in motion or operation ⟨a pump *worked* by hand⟩ **4** : to solve by reasoning or figuring ⟨*work* an arithmetic problem⟩ **5 a** : to cause to labor ⟨*worked* the crew hard⟩ **b** : to make use of : EXPLOIT ⟨*work* a mine⟩ **6** : to pay for with labor ⟨*work* off a debt⟩ **7 a** : to get into or out of a state or position by stages ⟨*worked* the boat loose⟩ **b** : CONTRIVE 3 ⟨*work* it so that you can leave soon⟩ **8 a** : to make an effort especially for a long period **b** : to perform a task requiring extended effort or repeated operations **c** : to perform work regularly for wages ⟨*works* on the railroad⟩ **9** : to function or operate properly ⟨hinges *work* better with oil⟩ **10** : to produce a desired effect : SUCCEED ⟨my plan *worked*⟩ **11** : to move gradually into a certain position or state ⟨the knot *worked* loose⟩ [Old English *wyrcan* "to create, cause to happen, shape"]

syn WORK, LABOR, TOIL mean to exert oneself at a physical or mental task. WORK applies to any effort, pleasant or not, that achieves a goal ⟨*worked* to discover a cure⟩ LABOR applies especially to physical work that is often hard and unpleasant ⟨*labored* for weeks to harvest all the crops⟩ TOIL applies to work that is long, hard, and very tiring ⟨*toiled* all day in the hot sun⟩

— **work on** : to try to influence or persuade ⟨*working on* them to change their votes⟩

work·able \'wər-kə-bəl\ *adj* **1** : capable of being worked **2** : FEASIBLE ⟨a *workable* solution to the problem⟩

work·a·day \'wər-kə-,dā\ *adj* : EVERYDAY ⟨writing that makes *workaday* events interesting⟩

work·bench \'wərk-,bench\ *n* : a bench on which work is done

work·book \-,bůk\ *n* : a book made up of a series of problems or practice examples for a student to use as part of a course of study

work·day \-,dā\ *n* **1** : a day on which work is performed **2** : the period of time in a day during which work is per-

formed — **workday** *adj*

worked up *adj* : emotionally excited

work·er \'wər-kər\ *n* **1 a** : one that works **b** : a member of the working class **2** : one of the members of a colony of social ants, bees, wasps, or termites that are only partially developed sexually and that perform most of the labor and protective duties of the colony

work·horse \'wərk-,hȯ(ə)rs\ *n* **1** : a horse used for hard work (as on a farm) **2 a** : a person who does most of the work of a group task **b** : a strong useful machine or vehicle

work·house \'wərk-,haůs\ *n* **1** *British* : POORHOUSE **2** : a place where persons who have committed minor wrongdoings are kept

work·ing \'wər-kiŋ\ *adj* **1 a** : doing work especially for a living ⟨hours that suit most *working* people⟩ **b** : being in an operating state ⟨a *working* model of the car⟩ **2** : relating to work **3** : good enough to allow work to be done ⟨a *working* majority⟩ ⟨a *working* arrangement⟩

working class *n* : the class of people who work for wages usually in manual labor — **working–class** *adj*

work·ing·man \'wər-kiŋ-,man\ *n* : one who works for wages usually at manual labor or in industry

work·man \'wərk-mən\ *n* **1** : WORKINGMAN **2** : a skilled worker (as an electrician or carpenter)

work·man·like \'wərk-mən-,līk\ *adj* : worthy of a good worker ⟨did a *workmanlike* job on the boat⟩

work·man·ship \'wərk-mən-,ship\ *n* **1** : the art or skill of a workman : CRAFTSMANSHIP **2** : the quality of a piece of work

work·out \'wər-,kaůt\ *n* : a practice or exercise to test or improve one's fitness especially in athletics

work out \,wər-'kaůt, 'wər-\ *vb* **1** : to bring about by effort or by clearing up difficulties **2 a** : SOLVE ⟨*work out* a math problem⟩ **b** : DEVELOP 2 ⟨*work out* a plan⟩ **3** : to be successful ⟨our plans for reorganization *worked out*⟩ **4** : to perform athletic exercises ⟨*working out* in the gym⟩

work·room \'wər-,krüm, -,krům\ *n* : a room used especially for manual work

work·shop \'wərk-,shäp\ *n* : a shop where manufacturing or handicrafts are carried on

world \'wər(-ə)ld\ *n* **1** : the earth and all the people and things upon it **2** : people in general : HUMANITY **3** : the system of created things : UNIVERSE **4** : human affairs ⟨leave the *world* and enter a convent⟩ **5** : a part or section of the earth and the people who live in it ⟨the musical *world*⟩ **7** : the scene of one's life and action **8** : a great number or amount ⟨a *world* of troubles⟩ **9** : a heavenly body especially if lived upon — **in the world** : EVER ⟨what *in the world* is it⟩ — **out of this world** : very good : SUPERB

world·ling \'wər(-ə)l-dliŋ, 'wərl-liŋ\ *n* : a person busy with the affairs of this world

world·ly \'wər(-ə)l-dlē, 'wərl-lē\ *adj* **1** : of, relating to, or concerned with the affairs of this world rather than with spiritual affairs **2** : WORLDLY-WISE — **world·li·ness** *n*

world·ly–wise \'wərl-dlē-,wīz, -lē-\ *adj* : wise as to things and ways of this world

world war *n* : a war involving all or most of the chief nations of the world; *esp, cap both Ws* : either of two such wars of the 20th century

world·wide \'wər(-ə)l-'dwīd\ *adj* : going all over the world — **worldwide** *adv*

¹**worm** \'wərm\ *n* **1 a** : EARTHWORM **b** : any of various long creeping or crawling animals (as an insect larva or a planarian) that usually have soft bodies **2** : a person who is hated or pitied : WRETCH **3** *pl* : infection with or disease caused by parasitic worms **4** : something in the form of a coil — **worm·like** \-,līk\ *adj*

²**worm** *vb* **1** : to free from worms ⟨*worm* a puppy⟩ **2** : to obtain by cleverness or trickery ⟨*wormed* the truth out of him⟩ **3** : to move, go, or work slowly in the manner of a

worm ⟨*wormed* out of the trap⟩ ⟨*wormed* my way into a job⟩ — **worm·er** *n*

worm gear *n* : a mechanical linkage consisting of a short rotating screw whose threads fit together with the teeth of a gear wheel

worm·hole \'wərm-,hōl\ *n* : a hole or passage made by a worm

worm·wood \'wərm-,wu̇d\ *n* : something bitter or painful

worm gear

wormy \'wər-mē\ *adj* **worm·i·er; -est** **1** : containing, swarming with, or damaged by worms **2** : resembling or suggestive of a worm

worn *past participle of* WEAR

worn–out \'wō(ə)r-'nȧu̇t, 'wȯ(ə)r-\ *adj* **1** : useless from long or hard wear **2** : very weary

wor·ried \'wər-ēd, 'wə-rēd\ *adj* : having worries : marked by or showing worry ⟨very *worried* about the test⟩ ⟨a *worried* look⟩ — **wor·ried·ly** *adv*

wor·ri·some \'wər-ē-səm, 'wə-rē-\ *adj* **1** : causing worry **2** : given to worrying

¹**wor·ry** \'wər-ē, 'wə-rē\ *vb* **wor·ried; wor·ry·ing** **1** : to shake and tear or mangle with the teeth ⟨a puppy *worrying* an old shoe⟩ **2** : to make anxious or upset : FRET **3** : to feel or express great concern — **wor·ri·er** *n*

²**worry** *n, pl* **worries** **1** : ANXIETY 1 **2** : a cause of anxiety : TROUBLE

¹**worse** \'wərs\ *adj, comparative of* BAD *or of* ILL **1** : of poorer quality, value, or condition **2** : being in poorer health ⟨the child was *worse* the next day⟩ **3** : bad or evil in greater degree

²**worse** *n* **1** : something worse **2** : a greater degree of ill or badness ⟨a turn for the *worse*⟩

³**worse** *adv, comparative of* ILL *or of* BAD *or* BADLY : in a worse manner : to a worse extent or degree

wors·en \'wərs-ᵊn\ *vb* **wors·ened; wors·en·ing** \'wərs-niŋ, -ᵊn-iŋ\ : to make or become worse

¹**wor·ship** \'wər-shəp\ *n* **1** *chiefly British* : an important person — used as a title for some officials **2 a** : great respect toward God, a god, or a sacred object **b** : the outward showing of such respect **3** : too great admiration or devotion [Old English *weorthscipe* "worship, respect, worthiness", literally "worthyship", from *weorth* "worth, worthy" and *-scipe* "-ship (quality, condition)"]

²**worship** *vb* **-shiped** *or* **-shipped; -ship·ing** *or* **-ship·ping** **1** : to honor or respect as a divine being or supernatural power **2** : to treat with too great respect, honor, or devotion : IDOLIZE ⟨*worshipped* popular singers⟩ **3** : to perform or take part in worship — **wor·ship·er** *or* **wor·ship·per** *n*

wor·ship·ful \'wər-shəp-fəl\ *adj* : giving worship

¹**worst** \'wərst\ *adj, superlative of* BAD *or of* ILL : most bad, evil, or ill

²**worst** *adv, superlative of* ILL *or of* BAD *or* BADLY : to the greatest degree of badness

³**worst** *n* **1** : one that is worst **2** : the greatest degree of ill or badness

⁴**worst** *vb* : to get the better of : DEFEAT

wor·sted \'wu̇s-təd, 'wər-stəd\ *n* **1** : a fabric made from worsted yarns **2** : a smooth compact yarn from long wool fibers [named for *Worsted* (now *Worstead*) a village in England famous for the fabrics made there] — **worsted** *adj*

wort \'wərt, 'wȯ(ə)rt\ *n* : a dilute solution of sugars obtained by steeping malt and fermented to make beer

¹**worth** \'wərth\ *prep* **1 a** : equal in value to **b** : having possessions or income equal to ⟨an actress *worth* millions⟩ **2** : deserving of ⟨well *worth* the effort⟩ **3** : capable of ⟨ran for all I was *worth*⟩

²**worth** *n* **1 a** : value in terms of money ⟨furniture of little

worth⟩ **b** : the equivalent of a certain amount or figure ⟨five dollars *worth* of gas⟩ **2** : the value of something measured by its qualities **3** : EXCELLENCE 1

worth·less \'wərth-ləs\ *adj* **1 a** : lacking worth : VALUELESS **b** : USELESS **2** : deserving of hatred or pity ⟨a *worthless* coward⟩ — **worth·less·ly** *adv* — **worth·less·ness** *n*

worth·while \'wərth-'hwī(ə)l, -'wī(ə)l\ *adj* : being worth the time or effort spent

¹**wor·thy** \'wər-thē\ *adj* **wor·thi·er; -est** **1 a** : having worth or value **b** : HONORABLE 1 **2** : having enough value or excellence ⟨a student *worthy* of the prize⟩ — **wor·thi·ly** \-thə-lē\ *adv* — **wor·thi·ness** \-thē-nəs\ *n*

²**worthy** *n, pl* **worthies** : a worthy person

wot *present 1st & 3d sing of* WIT

would \wəd, əd, d, (')wu̇d\ *past of* WILL **1** : strongly desire : WISH ⟨I *would* I were young again⟩ **2** — used as a helping verb to express (1) preference or willingness ⟨I *would* sooner die than face them⟩, (2) wish or intent ⟨those who *would* forbid free access to books⟩, (3) custom or usual behavior ⟨we *would* meet often for lunch⟩, (4) possibility ⟨if they were coming, they *would* be here now⟩, (5) completion of a statement of desire, request, or advice ⟨I wish that you *would* go⟩, or (6) probability or likelihood in past or present time ⟨*would* have won if she had not tripped⟩ **3** : COULD ⟨the pitcher *would* hold two liters⟩ **4** — used as a helping verb to word a polite request or to show doubt or uncertainty ⟨*would* you please help us⟩ ⟨the explanation *would* seem satisfactory⟩ **5** : SHOULD ⟨knew I *would* enjoy the trip⟩ ⟨*would* be glad to know the answer⟩

would–be \,wu̇d-'bē\ *adj* : desiring or pretending to be ⟨a *would-be* poet⟩

wouldn't \'wu̇d-ᵊnt\ : would not

wouldst \wədst, (')wu̇dst, wətst\ *archaic past 2d sing of* WILL

¹**wound** \'wu̇nd\ *n* **1** : an injury involving cutting or breaking of bodily tissue (as by violence, accident, or surgery) **2** : an injury to a person's feelings

²**wound** *vb* **1** : to hurt by cutting or breaking bodily tissue **2** : to hurt the feelings or pride of

³**wound** \'wau̇nd\ *past and past participle of* WIND

wound·ed \'wu̇n-dəd\ *n pl* : persons that have been wounded

wove *past of* WEAVE

woven *past participle of* WEAVE

wrack \'rak\ *n* : violent or total destruction : RUIN

wraith \'rāth\ *n* **1** : GHOST **2** : a bodiless appearance : SHADOW

¹**wran·gle** \'raŋ-gəl\ *vb* **wran·gled; wran·gling** \-g(ə-)liŋ\ **1** : to have an angry quarrel **2** : to take part in an argument **3** : to herd and care for livestock and especially horses on the range

²**wrangle** *n* : an angry, noisy, or lengthy dispute or quarrel

wran·gler \'raŋ-g(ə-)lər\ *n* **1** : a person who quarrels **2** : a ranch hand who takes care of the saddle horses

¹**wrap** \'rap\ *vb* **wrapped; wrap·ping** **1 a** : to cover especially by winding or folding ⟨*wrap* a baby in a blanket⟩ **b** : to enclose and prepare for transportation or storage **c** : ¹EMBRACE 1 ⟨*wrapped* my arms around her⟩ **d** : to coil, fold, or draw about something ⟨*wrap* a rubber band around the sticks⟩ **2 a** : ENVELOP **b** : to involve completely : ENGROSS

²**wrap** *n* **1 a** : WRAPPER 1, 3 **b** : material for wrapping ⟨plastic *wrap*⟩ **2** : a warm loose outer garment (as a coat or shawl)

wrap·per \'rap-ər\ *n* **1** : a covering or enclosure for something **2** : one that wraps **3** : a garment worn wrapped

\ə\ abut	\au̇\ out	\i\ tip	\ȯ\ saw	\u̇\ foot
\ər\ further	\ch\ chin	\ī\ life	\ȯi\ coin	\y\ yet
\a\ mat	\e\ pet	\j\ job	\th\ thin	\yü\ few
\ā\ take	\ē\ easy	\ŋ\ sing	\th\ this	\yu̇\ cure
\ä\ cot, cart	\g\ go	\ō\ bone	\ü\ food	\zh\ vision

around the body

wrap·ping \'rap-iŋ\ n : WRAPPER 1

wrap–up \'rap-,əp\ n : a summarizing news report

wrap up \(')rap-'əp\ vb 1 : SUMMARIZE 2 : to bring to a conclusion ⟨quickly *wrapped up* the meeting⟩

wrath \'rath\ n 1 : violent anger 2 : punishment for sin or crime **syn** see ANGER

wrath·ful \'rath-fəl\ adj 1 : filled with wrath : very angry 2 : showing wrath ⟨a *wrathful* expression⟩ — **wrath·ful·ly** \-fə-lē\ adv — **wrath·ful·ness** n

wreak \'rēk\ vb : to bring down in or as if in punishment ⟨*wreak* revenge on the enemy⟩ ⟨the storm *wreaked* destruction⟩

wreath \'rēth\ n, pl **wreaths** \'rēthz, 'rēths\ : something twisted or woven into a circular shape ⟨a *wreath* of flowers⟩

wreathe \'rēth\ vb **wreathed**; **wreath·ing** 1 : to form into a wreath 2 : to crown, decorate, or cover with or as if with a wreath ⟨faces *wreathed* in smiles⟩

¹wreck \'rek\ n 1 : goods cast upon the land by the sea after a shipwreck 2 : ¹SHIPWRECK 2 3 : the action of wrecking 4 : the broken remains of something wrecked or ruined 5 : a person in poor health or spirits

²wreck vb 1 : ²SHIPWRECK 2 2 : to damage or ruin by breaking up

wreck·age \'rek-ij\ n 1 a : the act of wrecking b : the state of being wrecked 2 : the remains of a wreck

wreck·er \'rek-ər\ n 1 a : one that searches for or works on the wrecks of ships b : a truck equipped to remove wrecked or broken-down cars c : one that salvages junked automobile parts and material 2 : one that wrecks

wren \'ren\ n 1 : any of a large family of small mostly brown singing birds with short rounded wings and a short tail that points upward 2 : any of various small singing birds resembling the true wrens in size and habits

¹wrench \'rench\ vb 1 : to move with a violent twist 2 : to pull, strain, or tighten with violent twisting or force 3 : to injure by a violent twisting or straining ⟨*wrenched* my knee while playing football⟩ 4 : to snatch forcibly : WREST

²wrench n 1 a : a violent twisting or pull b : a sharp twist or sudden jerk that strains muscles or ligaments; also : the injury caused by this 2 : a tool for holding, twisting, or turning (as nuts and bolts)

wren 1

wrest \'rest\ vb 1 : to pull, force, or move by violent wringing or twisting movements 2 : to gain by or as if by force or violence

¹wres·tle \'res-əl\ vb **wres·tled**; **wres·tling** \-(ə-)liŋ\ 1 : to struggle with and try to throw down an opponent 2 : to compete against in wrestling 3 : to struggle for control (as of something difficult) — **wres·tler** \'res-lər\ n

²wrestle n : the action or an instance of wrestling

wres·tling \'res-liŋ\ n : the sport in which two contestants wrestle each other

wretch \'rech\ n 1 : a miserable unhappy person 2 : a mean or evil person

wretch·ed \'rech-əd\ adj 1 : very miserable or unhappy 2 : causing misery or distress ⟨that *wretched* accident⟩ 3 : deserving of hatred or disgust ⟨a *wretched* trick⟩ 4 : very poor in quality or ability ⟨*wretched* work⟩ — **wretch·ed·ly** adv — **wretch·ed·ness** n

wrig·gle \'rig-əl\ vb **wrig·gled**; **wrig·gling** \-(ə-)liŋ\ 1 : to twist or move to and fro like a worm : SQUIRM ⟨*wriggle* in one's chair⟩ ⟨*wriggle* one's toes⟩ 2 : to move along by twisting and turning ⟨a snake *wriggled* along the path⟩ — **wriggle** n — **wrig·gly** \-(ə-)lē\ adj

wrig·gler \'rig-(ə-)lər\ n : one that wriggles; esp : WIGGLER 1

wright \'rīt\ n : a worker especially in wood — usually used in combination

wring \'riŋ\ vb **wrung** \'rəŋ\; **wring·ing** \'riŋ-iŋ\ 1 : to squeeze or twist especially so as to make dry or to rid of moisture or liquid ⟨*wring* wet clothes⟩ 2 : to get by or as if by twisting or pressing ⟨*wring* the truth out of them⟩ 3 : to twist so as to strain, sprain, or strangle ⟨*wring* a chicken's neck⟩ : CONTORT 4 : to cause pain to as if by wringing : TORMENT ⟨their troubles *wrung* our hearts⟩

wring·er \'riŋ-ər\ n : one that wrings; esp : a device for squeezing out liquid or moisture ⟨clothes *wringer*⟩

¹wrin·kle \'riŋ-kəl\ n 1 : a crease or small fold on a surface (as in the skin or in cloth) 2 : a clever or new method, trick, or idea — **wrin·kly** \-k(ə-)lē\ adj

²wrinkle vb **wrin·kled**; **wrin·kling** \-k(ə-)liŋ\ : to develop or cause to develop wrinkles

wrist \'rist\ n : the joint or the region of the joint between the human hand and the arm; also : a corresponding part of a lower animal

wrist·band \'ris(t)-,band\ n : a band or a part of a sleeve encircling the wrist

wrist·let \'ris(t)-lət\ n : WRISTBAND; esp : a close-fitting knitted band at the end of a glove or sleeve

wrist·watch \'ris-,twäch\ n : a small watch attached to a bracelet or strap to fasten about the wrist

writ \'rit\ n 1 : something written : WRITING ⟨Holy *Writ*⟩ 2 : a written legal order signed by a court officer

write \'rīt\ vb **wrote** \'rōt\; **writ·ten** \'rit-ᵊn\ also **writ** \'rit\; **writ·ing** \'rīt-iŋ\ 1 : to form letters or words on a surface with an instrument (as a pen or pencil) ⟨learn to read and *write*⟩ 2 : to form the letters or the words of (as on paper) ⟨*write* your name⟩ ⟨*write* a check⟩ 3 : to spell in writing 4 : to put down on paper : express in writing ⟨*write* what you felt about the circus⟩ 5 a : to make up and set down for others to read ⟨*write* a book⟩ b : to compose music 6 : to write a letter to ⟨*write* your senator⟩ 7 : to communicate by letter : CORRESPOND 8 : to transfer information in a computer to a storage area or output device

write off vb 1 : to reduce the estimated value of : DEPRECIATE 2 : to take off the books : CANCEL ⟨*write off* a bad debt⟩ 3 : to consider to be lost ⟨the candidate has already *written off* the southern states⟩; also : DISMISS 3 ⟨*wrote off* my losing as bad luck⟩

writ·er \'rīt-ər\ n : one that writes especially as a business or occupation

writer's cramp n : a painful cramp of the muscles of the hand or fingers brought on by too much use in writing

write–up \'rīt-,əp\ n : a written account (as in a newspaper); esp : a flattering article

write up \(')rīt-'əp\ vb : to write an account of : DESCRIBE

writhe \'rīth\ vb **writhed**; **writh·ing** : to twist and turn this way and that ⟨*writhe* in pain⟩

writ·ing \'rīt-iŋ\ n 1 a : the act or process of one that writes : the formation of letters to express words and ideas b : HANDWRITING 2 2 : something that is written or printed 3 : a style or form of composition 4 : the occupation of a writer

writing paper n : paper that has a smooth surface so that it can be written on with ink

¹wrong \'róŋ\ n 1 : a harmful, unfair, or unjust act 2 : something that is wrong : wrong principles, practices, or conduct ⟨know right from *wrong*⟩ 3 : the state, position, or fact of being or doing wrong ⟨in the *wrong*⟩

²wrong adj 1 : not according to the moral standard : SINFUL, IMMORAL 2 : not agreeing with proper behavior ⟨it was *wrong* not to thank the hostess⟩ 3 : not suitable ⟨wore the *wrong* clothes for a wedding⟩ 4 : not true or correct : FALSE ⟨a *wrong* answer on the test⟩ 5 : not satisfactory ⟨there's something *wrong* about the story's ending⟩ 6 : made so as to be placed down or under and not

to be seen ⟨the *wrong* side of a fabric⟩ — **wrong** *adv* —
wrong·ly *adv* — **wrong·ness** *n*
³**wrong** *vb* **wronged; wrong·ing** \'ròŋ-iŋ\   **1** : to do wrong
to : INJURE, HARM   **2** : to make unjust remarks about
wrong·do·er \'ròŋ-'dü-ər\ *n* : a person who does wrong
and especially moral wrong — **wrong·do·ing** \-'dü-iŋ\ *n*
wrong·ful \'ròŋ-fəl\ *adj*   **1** : ²WRONG 1   **2** : UNLAWFUL —
wrong·ful·ly \-fə-lē\ *adv* — **wrong·ful·ness** *n*
wrong·head·ed \'ròŋ-'hed-əd\ *adj* : stubborn in clinging to
wrong opinion or principles — **wrong·head·ed·ly** *adv* —
wrong·head·ed·ness *n*
wrote *past of* WRITE
wroth \'ròth *also* 'rōth\ *adj* : filled with wrath : ANGRY
¹**wrought** \'ròt\ *past and past participle of* WORK

²**wrought** *adj*   **1** : worked into shape by skill or effort   **2**
: decorated with fancy designs   **3** : beaten into shape by
tools : HAMMERED ⟨*wrought* metals⟩   **4** : very excited ⟨gets
wrought up over nothing⟩
wrought iron *n* : a commercial form of iron that is tough but
soft and that can be hammered and shaped
wrung *past and past participle of* WRING
wry \'rī\ *adj* **wry·er** \'rī(-ə)r\; **wry·est** \'rī-əst\   **1** : having
a bent or twisted shape or condition ⟨a *wry* smile⟩; *esp*
: turned abnormally to one side ⟨a *wry* neck⟩   **2** : cleverly
humorous — **wry·ly** *adv* — **wry·ness** *n*
wy·an·dotte \'wī-ən-,dät\ *n* : any of an American breed of
medium-sized domestic chickens raised especially for
meat and eggs

X

¹**x** \'eks\ *n, often cap*   **1** : the 24th letter of the English
alphabet   **2** : ten in Roman numerals   **3** : an unknown
quantity
²**x** *vb* **x—ed** *also* **x'd** *or* **xed** \'ekst\; **x—ing** *or* **x'ing** \'ek-siŋ\
1 : to mark with an *x*   **2** : to cancel with a series of *x*'s
X \'eks\ *adj, of a motion picture* : of such a nature that
admission is denied to persons under a certain age (as 17)
— compare G, PG, R
x—ax·is \'ek-,sak-səs\ *n* : the axis of a graph or a system
of coordinates in a plane parallel to which the abscissas
are measured
X chromosome *n* : a sex chromosome that usually occurs
paired in each female cell and single in each male cell in
organisms (as human beings) in which the male normally
has two unlike sex chromosomes — compare Y CHROMO-
SOME
xe·bec \'zē-,bek, zi-
'bek\ *n* : a usually
three-masted Mediter-
ranean   sailing   ship
with long overhanging
bow and stern
xe·non \'zē-,nän, 'zen-
,än\ *n* : a heavy color-
less   gaseous   element
that occurs in air in
minute quantities and
is used in specialized
electric lamps — see ELEMENT table

xebec

xe·no·pho·bia \,zen-ə-'fō-bē-ə, ,zēn-\ *n* : fear of foreigners or foreign things [from Latin *xeno-* "strange, foreign,
foreigner" (from Greek *xenos* "foreigner") and English
phobia'an exaggerated fear"]
xe·rog·ra·phy \zə-'räg-rə-fē, zir-'äg-\ *n* : a process for
copying printed material by the action of light on an electrically charged surface in which the image is developed
with a powder — **xe·ro·graph·ic** \,zir-ə-'graf-ik\ *adj*
xe·ro·phyte \'zir-ə-,fīt\ *n* : a plant (as an agave, cactus,
sagebrush, or yucca) suited for growth in dry or desert
conditions — **xe·ro·phyt·ic** \,zir-ə-'fit-ik\ *adj*
xi \'zī, 'ksī\ *n* : the 14th letter of the Greek alphabet — Ξ or
ξ
x—in·ter·cept \'ek-'sint-ər-,sept\ *n* : the abscissa of a point
where a line or curve intersects the x-axis — compare Y–
INTERCEPT
Xmas \'kris-məs *also* 'ek-sməs\ *n* : CHRISTMAS [from *X*, an
ancient symbol for Jesus Christ, and *-mas*, from *Christmas*; the *X* is from the Greek letter *X* "chi", the first letter
in the Greek word *Christos* "Christ"]
x—ray \'eks-,rā\ *vb, often cap X* : to examine, treat, or pho-

tograph with X rays
X ray \'eks-,rā\ *n*   **1** : an electromagnetic radiation of the
same nature as visible light but of an extremely short
wavelength that is produced by bombarding a metallic target with fast electrons in vacuum and that is able to penetrate various thicknesses of solids and to act on photographic film as light does   **2** : a photograph taken by the
use of X rays — **X–ray** *adj*
   Word History In 1895, a German scientist, Wilhelm
   Conrad Röntgen, was experimenting with an electric current passing through a vacuum in a glass tube. He found
   that a piece of material that glows only when electricity
   passes through it began to glow even though it was not
   inside the tube. Röntgen tried to shield the material from
   the tube. However, he found that the material glowed
   even when it was shielded by paper or wood. Only a
   shield of metal stopped the glowing. He guessed that an
   unknown invisible ray created inside the glass tube was
   causing this to happen. Since he knew nothing about
   this mysterious ray, Röntgen called it *x-strahl* in German, which translates as *X ray* in English. He was using
   the letter *x*, which had long been used in mathematics
   for an unknown value. [from German *x-strahl* "X ray",
   from the use of *x* to represent an unknown value]
xy·lem \'zī-ləm, -,lem\ *n* : a tissue of higher plants that carries water and dissolved materials upward, functions also
in support and storage, lies deeper inside the plant than
the phloem, and usually makes up the woody parts (as of
a plant stem) — compare PHLOEM
xy·lo·phone \'zī-lə-
,fōn\ *n* : a musical in-
strument   consisting
of a series of wooden
bars varying in length
and sounded by strik-
ing with two wooden
hammers [from Latin
xylo- "wood, of
wood" (derived from
Greek *xylon* "wood")
and English *-phone*
"sound, a sound-producing device"] — **xy·lo·phon·ist**
\-,fō-nəst\ *n*

xylophone

\ə\ **abut**	\aù\ **out**	\i\ **tip**	\ò\ **saw**	\ù\ **foot**	
\ər\ **further**	\ch\ **chin**	\ī\ **life**	\òi\ **coin**	\y\ **yet**	
\a\ **mat**	\e\ **pet**	\j\ **job**	\th\ **thin**	\yü\ **few**	
\ā\ **take**	\ē\ **easy**	\ŋ\ **sing**	\th\ **this**	\yù\ **cure**	
\ä\ **cot, cart**	\g\ **go**	\ō\ **bone**	\ü\ **food**	\zh\ **vision**	

Y

y \'wī\ *n, often cap* : the 25th letter of the English alphabet

¹-y *also* **-ey** \ē\ *adj suffix* **-i·er; -i·est** **1 a** : marked by : full of ⟨blossom*y*⟩ ⟨dirt*y*⟩ ⟨mudd*y*⟩ ⟨clay*ey*⟩ **b** : composed of ⟨ic*y*⟩ ⟨wax*y*⟩ **c** : like : like that of ⟨home*y*⟩ ⟨wintr*y*⟩ ⟨stag*y*⟩ **d** : devoted to : enthusiastic over ⟨hors*ey*⟩ **2 a** : tending to ⟨sleep*y*⟩ ⟨chatt*y*⟩ **b** : causing or performing (a certain) action ⟨tear*y*⟩ **3 a** : somewhat : rather : -ISH ⟨chill*y*⟩ **b** : having (certain) characteristics that are put on for show ⟨French*y*⟩ [Old English *-ig* (adjective suffix) "having the character of"]

²-y \ē\ *n suffix, pl* **-ies** **1** : state : condition : quality ⟨jealous*y*⟩ **2** : activity, place of business, or goods dealt with ⟨grocer*y*⟩ ⟨laundr*y*⟩ **3** : whole body or group ⟨soldier*y*⟩ [derived from Greek *-ia* (noun suffix) "state, condition, quality"]

³-y *n suffix, pl* **-ies** : instance of a (certain) action ⟨entreat*y*⟩ ⟨inquir*y*⟩ [derived from Latin *-ium* (noun suffix) "an instance of a certain action"]

⁴-y — see -IE

¹yacht \'yät\ *n* : a fairly small ship used for pleasure cruising or racing

> **Word History** In the 16th century, the Dutch were being attacked by pirates and smugglers who managed to escape after their raids because their ships were much faster than the heavy warships used by the Dutch. To solve the problem, the Dutch began building smaller, sleeker, faster craft. This new kind of craft was called a *jaght* (later spelled *jacht*) in Dutch. The word was derived from the early German word *jachtschiff,* literally meaning "chase ship". The German word derived from *jagen* "to hunt, chase" and *schiff* "ship". In 1660, the Dutch East India Company presented one of these boats to England's King Charles II. He used it for a pleasure boat rather than for chasing pirates. Soon, other wealthy Englishmen wanted boats just like the king's. The style was then copied and improved over the years. The name for this craft also went through a number of changes over the years, from the original *jaght,* taken from the Dutch, to the *yacht* spelling we have today. [from obsolete Dutch *jaght* (now *jacht*) "chase boat", from early German *jaghtschiff,* literally "chase ship", derived from *jagen* "to hunt, chase" and *schiff* "ship"]

²yacht *vb* : to race or cruise in a yacht

yacht·ing *n* : the sport of racing or cruising in a yacht

yachts·man \'yät-smən\ *n* : a person who owns or sails a yacht

yak \'yak\ *n, pl* **yaks** *also* **yak** : a large long-haired wild or domesticated ox of Tibet and nearby elevated parts of central Asia

yam \'yam\ *n* **1** : an edible starchy root that is an important food in tropical areas; *also* : a plant distantly related to the lilies that produces them **2** : a sweet potato with usually orange flesh

yak

yam·mer \'yam-ər\ *vb* **yam·mered; yam·mer·ing** \-(ə-)riŋ\ : to utter repeated cries of sorrow, distress, or complaint

¹yank \'yaŋk\ *n* : a strong sudden pull : JERK

²yank *vb* : to pull suddenly or forcefully

Yank \'yaŋk\ *n* : YANKEE

Yan·kee \'yaŋ-kē\ *n* **1** : a person born or living in New England **2** : a person born or living in the northern U.S. **3** : a person born or living in the U.S.

¹yap \'yap\ *vb* **yapped; yap·ping** **1** : to bark in yaps **2** : to talk sharply or continuously

²yap *n* : a quick shrill bark

¹yard \'yärd\ *n* **1 a** : a small often enclosed area open to the sky and next to a building **b** : the grounds of a building **2 a** : an enclosure for livestock **b** : an area with its buildings and equipment set aside for a particular activity ⟨a navy *yard*⟩ **c** : a system of railroad tracks for keeping and repairing cars [Old English *geard* "an enclosed space, yard"]

²yard *n* **1** : any of various units of measure; *esp* : a unit of length equal in the U.S. to 0.9144 meter — see MEASURE table **2** : a long pole tapered toward the ends that supports and spreads the top of a sail [Old English *gierd* "twig, measure"]

yard·age \'yärd-ij\ *n* **1** : a total number of yards **2** : the length or size of something measured in yards

yard·arm \'yärd-,ärm\ *n* : either end of the yard of a square-rigged ship

yard·mas·ter \-,mas-tər\ *n* : the person in charge of a railroad yard

yard sale *n* : GARAGE SALE

yard·stick \-,stik\ *n* **1** : a measuring stick a yard long **2** : a rule or standard by which something is measured

¹yarn \'yärn\ *n* **1 a** : a natural or manufactured fiber (as cotton, wool, or rayon) formed as a continuous thread for use in knitting or weaving **b** : a similar thread of metal, glass, asbestos, paper, or plastic **2** : an interesting or exciting story

²yarn *vb* : to tell a yarn

yaw \'yȯ\ *vb* : to turn suddenly from a straight course : SWERVE, VEER — **yaw** *n*

yawl \'yȯl\ *n* : a sailboat having two masts with the shorter one behind the rudder

¹yawn \'yȯn, 'yän\ *vb* **1** : to open wide : GAPE **2** : to open the mouth wide usually as a reaction to being tired or bored — **yawn·er** *n*

²yawn *n* : a deep drawing in of breath through the wide-open mouth

¹yawp *or* **yaup** \'yȯp\ *vb* : to make a loud harsh noise

yawl

²yawp *also* **yaup** *n* : a loud harsh noise

yaws \'yȯz\ *n sing or pl* : a tropical contagious skin disease caused by a spirochete

y–ax·is \'wī-,ak-səs\ *n* : the axis of a graph or a system of coordinates in a plane parallel to which the ordinates are measured

Y chromosome *n* : a sex chromosome that is characteristic of male cells in organisms (as human beings) in which the male normally has two unlike sex chromosomes — compare X CHROMOSOME

yclept \i-'klept\ *or* **ycleped** \-'klept, -'klept\ *adj, archaic* : being named : CALLED [Old English *geclipod,* past participle of *clipian* "to call, cry out"]

¹ye \(')yē\ *pron, archaic* : YOU **1** [Old English *gē* "you"]

²ye \yē, yə, *or like* THE\ *definite article, archaic* : THE ⟨*Ye* Olde Gifte Shoppe⟩ [an altered form of Old English *þē* "the"; because the handwritten forms of þ and *y* in old manuscripts looked much alike, early printers used *y* when the obsolete þ was not available]

¹yea \'yā\ *adv* **1** : ¹YES **1** — used in oral voting **2** — used to give special force to a phrase that follows ⟨most people, *yea* everyone, would agree with that⟩

²yea *n* **1** : a vote in favor of something **2** : a person casting a yea vote

yeah \'ye-ə, 'yeù, 'ya-ə\ *adv* : ¹YES

year \'yi(ə)r\ *n* **1** : the period of about 365¼ days required for the earth to make one complete trip around the sun **2** : a period of 365 days or in leap year 366 days beginning January 1 **3** : a period of time usually shorter than a calendar year ⟨a school *year* of nine months⟩

year·book \-,bùk\ *n* **1** : a book published yearly **2** : a school publication recording the history and activities of a graduating class

year·ling \'yi(ə)r-liŋ\ *n* **1** : one that is a year old or in the second year after birth **2** : a racehorse between January 1st of the year after the year in which it was born and the next January 1st — **yearling** *adj*

year·ly \'yi(ə)r-lē\ *adj* **1** : occurring, made, done, or produced every year : ANNUAL **2** : calculated in terms of one year — **yearly** *adv*

yearn \'yərn\ *vb* **1** : to desire eagerly **2** : to feel tenderness or sympathy — **yearn·er** *n*

　　syn YEARN, LONG, PINE mean to desire something very much. YEARN suggests an eager desire along with restless, painful feelings ⟨*yearning* for the day when they would be on their own⟩ LONG suggests wanting something with one's whole heart and often striving to get it as well ⟨*longing* to succeed as a writer⟩ PINE suggests that one grows weak while continuing to want something that one will never have ⟨*pining* away for an absent friend⟩

yearn·ing *n* : a tender or eager longing

year–round \'yi(ə)r-'raùnd, 'yiə-'raùnd\ *adj* : being in operation for the whole year ⟨a *year-round* resort⟩

yeast \'yēst, 'ēst\ *n* **1 a** : material that may be found on the surface or at the bottom of sweet liquids, is made up mostly of the cells of a tiny fungus, and causes a reaction in which alcohol is produced **b** : a commercial product containing living yeast plants and used especially to make bread dough rise **c** : any of the group of tiny fungi that form alcohol or cause bread to rise **2** : something that causes motion or activity — **yeasty** \'yē-stē, 'ē-stē\ *adj*

¹yell \'yel\ *vb* **1** : to utter a loud cry, scream, or shout **2** : to give a cheer usually as part of a crowd — **yell·er** *n*

²yell *n* **1** : ²SCREAM 1, SHOUT **2** : a cheer used especially in schools or colleges to encourage athletic teams

¹yel·low \'yel-ō\ *adj* **1 a** : of the color yellow **b** : yellowish from age, disease, or discoloring **c** : having a yellow or light brown complexion or skin **2** : COWARDLY 1 — **yellow** *vb* — **yel·low·ness** *n*

²yellow *n* **1** : a color like that of ripe lemons **2** : something yellow or yellowish

yellow fever *n* : a destructive infectious disease of warm regions marked by yellowness of the skin, intestinal bleeding, and vomiting and caused by a virus transmitted by a mosquito — called also *yellow jack*

yellow–green alga *n* : any of a division of algae (as diatoms) with the chlorophyll masked by brown or yellow coloring substances

yel·low·ham·mer \'yel-ō-,ham-ər, 'yel-ə-\ *n* : YELLOW⸗SHAFTED FLICKER

yel·low·ish \'yel-ə-wish\ *adj* : somewhat yellow

yellow jack *n* : YELLOW FEVER

yellow jacket *n* : any of various small social wasps with yellow markings that commonly nest in the ground

yellow pages *n pl* : the section of a telephone directory that lists businesses and professional firms by category and includes advertising

yellow perch *n* : ³PERCH 1

yel·low–shaft·ed flicker \,yel-ō-,shaf-təd-, ,yel-ə-\ *n* : a flicker of the form found in the more eastern parts of North America that is golden yellow on the underside of the tail and wings, has a red mark on the back of the neck, and in the male has a black streak on each side of the base of the bill — called also *yellowhammer*

yelp \'yelp\ *vb* : to utter a sharp quick shrill cry or bark — **yelp** *n* — **yelp·er** *n*

¹yen \'yen\ *n, pl* **yen** **1** : the basic unit of money of Japan **2** : a coin or bill worth one yen

²yen *n* : an intense desire : LONGING

yeo·man \'yō-mən\ *n* **1 a** : a servant in a royal or noble household **b** : a naval petty officer who works as a clerk **2** : a small landowning farmer

yellow-shafted flicker

yeo·man·ly \'yō-mən-lē\ *adj* : becoming to a yeoman : STURDY, LOYAL

yeo·man·ry \'yō-mən-rē\ *n* : a body of yeomen

-yer — see ²-ER

yer·ba ma·té \,yer-bə-'mä-,tā, ,yər-\ *n* : MATÉ

¹yes \'yes, 'yeù, 'e-(y)ə *are three of many variants*\ *adv* **1** — used to express agreement ⟨are you ready? *Yes,* I am⟩ **2** — used to correct or contradict what another has said ⟨don't say that! *Yes,* I will⟩ **3** — used to introduce a phrase with greater force or clearness ⟨we are glad, *yes,* very glad to see you⟩ **4** — used to show interest or attention ⟨*yes,* what is it you want⟩

²yes \'yes\ *n* : a positive reply

ye·shi·va *or* **ye·shi·vah** \yə-'shē-və\ *n, pl* **yeshivas** *or* **ye·shi·voth** \-,shē-'vōt(h)\ : a Jewish school especially for religious instruction

yes–man \'yes-,man\ *n* : a person who agrees with every opinion or suggestion of a boss

¹yes·ter·day \'yes-tərd-ē\ *adv* **1** : on the day before today **2** : at a time not long past

²yesterday *n* **1** : the day next before the present **2** : recent time : time not long past

yes·ter·year \'yes-tər-,yi(ə)r\ *n* **1** : last year **2** : the recent past

¹yet \(')yet\ *adv* **1 a** : in addition : BESIDES ⟨gives *yet* another reason⟩ **b** : ³EVEN 4 ⟨a *yet* higher speed⟩ **2 a** : up to now : so far ⟨hasn't done much *yet*⟩ **b** : at this time : so soon as now ⟨not time to go *yet*⟩ **c** : ³STILL 2 ⟨is *yet* a new country⟩ **d** : at a later time ⟨may *yet* see the light⟩ **3** : NEVERTHELESS ⟨strong, *yet* not strong enough⟩

²yet *conj* : despite that fact : BUT

ye·ti \'yet-ē, 'yät-\ *n* : ABOMINABLE SNOWMAN

yew \'yü\ *n* **1** : any of a genus of evergreen trees and shrubs with stiff poisonous needles and fleshy fruits **2** : the wood of a yew; *esp* : the heavy fine-grained wood of an Old World yew that is used for bows and small articles

Yid·dish \'yid-ish\ *n* : a language that began among the Jews of eastern Europe and is based on German [from Yiddish *yidish,* a shortened form of *yidish daytsh,* literally "Jewish German (language)", derived from early German *jüdisch* "Jewish" and *diutsch* "the German language"] — **Yiddish** *adj*

¹yield \'yē(ə)ld\ *vb* **1** : to give up possession of on claim or demand : SURRENDER **2** : to give oneself up to a liking, temptation, or habit **3 a** : to bear as a natural product ⟨trees that *yield* much fruit⟩ **b** : to produce as a result **c**

\ə\ abut	\aù\ **out**	\i\ **tip**	\ò\ **saw**	\ù\ **foot**
\ər\ **further**	\ch\ **chin**	\ī\ **life**	\òi\ **coin**	\y\ **yet**
\a\ **mat**	\e\ **pet**	\j\ **job**	\th\ **thin**	\yü\ **few**
\ā\ **take**	\ē\ **easy**	\ŋ\ **sing**	\th\ **this**	\yù\ **cure**
\ä\ **cot, cart**	\g\ **go**	\ō\ **bone**	\ü\ **food**	\zh\ **vision**

: to return as profit or interest   **4** : to bring good results **5** : to give up and stop fighting   **6** : to give way to urging, persuasion, or pleading   **7** : to give way under physical force so as to bend, stretch, or break   **8** : to admit that someone else is better — **yield·er** \'yēl-dər\ n

syn YIELD, SUBMIT, SURRENDER mean to give way to someone or something that one can no longer oppose. YIELD applies to any kind of giving way or giving in (as to physical force, argument, or persuasion) ⟨the roof *yielded* to the heavy load of snow⟩ ⟨she refused to *yield* to the pressure to change her vote⟩ SUBMIT stresses giving in to the will of another and going against one's own wishes ⟨*submitted* to the plan but under protest⟩ SURRENDER applies to a total giving in and the placing of oneself at the mercy of another ⟨finally the lord of the castle *surrendered* it to the enemy⟩

²yield n : something yielded : PRODUCT; *esp* : the amount or quantity produced or returned

yield·ing \'yēl-diŋ\ adj   **1** : not rigid or stiff : FLEXIBLE   **2** : tending to give in to the wishes of another

y–in·ter·cept \'wī-'int-ər-,sept\ n : the ordinate of a point where a line or curve intersects the y-axis — compare X–INTERCEPT

yip \'yip\ vb **yipped**; **yip·ping** : YELP — used chiefly of a dog — **yip** n

yip·pee \'yip-ē\ interj — used to express delight or triumph

YMCA \,wī-,em-(,)sē-'ā\ n : an international organization originally for young men [Young Men's Christian Association]

YMHA \,wī-,em-,ā-'chä\ n : an international organization of Jewish young men [Young Men's Hebrew Association]

yo·del \'yōd-ᵊl\ vb **-deled** or **-delled**; **-del·ing** or **-del·ling** \'yōd-liŋ, -ᵊl-iŋ\ : to sing while frequently going back and forth between the range of one's natural voice and a higher range; *also* : to shout or call in this manner — **yodel** n — **yo·del·er** \'yōd-lər, -ᵊl-ər\ n

yo·ga \'yō-gə\ n   **1** cap : a Hindu philosophy teaching that by holding back the activity of one's body, mind, and will one can know one's true self and be free   **2** : a system of exercises for gaining bodily or mental control and well–being

yo·gi \'yō-gē\ also **yo·gin** \-gən, -,gin\ n   **1** : a person who practices yoga   **2** cap : a follower of Yoga

yo·gurt also **yo·ghurt** \'yō-gərt\ n : a slightly acid semisolid food that is often flavored and is made of cow's milk or milk solids that have been soured by the addition of bacteria

¹yoke \'yōk\ n, pl **yokes**   **1 a** : a wooden bar or frame by which two work animals (as oxen) are harnessed at their heads or necks for drawing a plow or load   **b** : a frame fitted to a person's shoulders to carry a load in two equal portions   **c** : a clamp or brace that holds or unites two parts   **2** pl usu **yoke** : two animals yoked together   **3 a** : something that brings about a state of hardship, pain, or slavery   **b** : SLAVERY 2a   **4** : a fitted or shaped piece at the top of a skirt or at the shoulder of a garment

²yoke vb **yoked**; **yok·ing**   **1** : to put a yoke on   **2** : to attach (a work animal) to ⟨*yoke* a plow⟩   **3** : to join as if by a yoke   **4** : to put to work

yoke·fel·low \'yōk-,fel-ō\ n : a close companion

yo·kel \'yō-kəl\ n : a country person with little education or experience

yolk \'yōk, 'yelk also 'yōlk\ n   **1** : the yellow inner mass of the egg of a bird or reptile   **2** : the material stored in an ovum that supplies food material to the developing embryo

Yom Kip·pur \,yōm-ki-'pur, ,yòm-, ,yäm-, -'kip-ər\ n : a Jewish holiday observed in September or October with fasting and prayer as ways of making up for sins

¹yon \'yän\ adj : ²YONDER

²yon adv   **1** : ¹YONDER   **2** : ¹THITHER ⟨hither and *yon*⟩

yond \'yänd\ adv, archaic : ¹YONDER

¹yon·der \'yän-dər\ adv : at or to that place : over there

²yonder adj   **1** : more distant   **2** : being at a distance within view

yore \'yō(ə)r, 'yo(ə)r\ n : time long past — usually used in the phrase *of yore*

York·shire pudding \'yò(ə)rk-,shi(ə)r-, -shər-\ n : batter made from eggs, flour, and milk and baked in meat drippings

Yorkshire terrier n : any of a breed of small toy terriers with long straight silky hair mostly bluish gray but tan on the head and chest

you \(')yü, yə, yē\ pron   **1** : the one or ones spoken to ⟨can I pour *you* a cup of tea⟩ ⟨*you* are my friends⟩   **2** : ²ONE 2 ⟨*you* never know what will happen⟩

you–all \(')yü-'òl, 'yü-,òl, 'yòl\ pron : YOU — usually used in addressing two or more persons or sometimes one person as representing also another or others

you'd \(,)yüd, (,)yud, yəd\ : you had : you would

you'll \(,)yü(ə)l, (,)yul, yəl\ : you shall : you will

¹young \'yəŋ\ adj **youn·ger** \'yəŋ-gər\; **youn·gest** \'yəŋ-gəst\   **1 a** : being in the early stage of life, growth, or development   **b** : ¹JUNIOR 1a   **2** : lacking in experience   **3** : recently come into being : NEW ⟨*young* rock strata⟩   **4** : of, relating to, or having the characteristics of youth or a young person ⟨*young* at heart⟩ — **young·ness** \'yəŋ-nəs\ n

²young n pl   **1** : young persons : YOUTH ⟨music that appeals to the *young*⟩   **2** : immature or recently born offspring ⟨a bear and her *young*⟩ — **with young** : PREGNANT 1 — used of animals

youn·gest \'yəŋ-gəst\ n : the least old member especially of a family

young·ish \'yəŋ-ish\ adj : somewhat young

young·ster \'yəŋ(k)-stər\ n   **1** : a young person : YOUTH   **2** : CHILD 2a

your \yər, (')yu(ə)r, (')yō(ə)r, (')yò(ə)r\ adj   **1** : of or relating to you or yourself or yourselves ⟨*your* house⟩ ⟨*your* contributions⟩ ⟨*your* friends⟩   **2** : of or relating to one ⟨when you face the north, east is at *your* right⟩   **3** — used before a title of honor in address ⟨*your* Honor⟩

you're \yər, (,)yu(ə)r, (,)yō(ə)r, (,)yò(ə)r\ : you are

yours \'yu(ə)rz, 'yō(ə)rz, 'yò(ə)rz\ pron : your one : your ones — often used with an adverb and as part of the closing of a letter ⟨*yours* truly⟩

your·self \yər-'self\ pron   **1 a** : that one that is you ⟨don't hurt *yourself*⟩ ⟨carry them *yourself*⟩   **b** : your normal or healthy self ⟨you're not *yourself* today⟩   **2** : ONESELF

your·selves \yər-'selvz\ pron pl   **1** : those identical ones that are you   **2** : your normal or healthy selves

youth \'yüth\ n, pl **youths** \'yüthz, 'yüths\   **1** : the time of life when one is young; *esp* : the period between childhood and adulthood   **2 a** : a young man   **b** : young people ⟨the *youth* of today⟩ — usually used with a pl. verb   **3** : the quality or state of being young

youth·ful \'yüth-fəl\ adj   **1** : of, relating to, or suitable for youth   **2** : being young and not yet mature   **3** : having the freshness and energy of youth — **youth·ful·ly** \-fə-lē\ adv — **youth·ful·ness** n

youth hostel n : HOSTEL 2

you've \(,)yüv, yəv\ : you have

yowl \'yau̇(ə)l\ vb : to utter a loud long often mournful cry or howl — **yowl** n

yo-yo \'yō-,yō\ n, pl **yo–yos** also **yo–yoes**   **1** : a thick divided disk that is made to fall and rise to the hand by unwinding and rewinding on a string   **2** : ¹FOOL 1

yt·ter·bi·um \i-'tər-bē-əm\ n : a metallic element that resembles yttrium and occurs with it and related elements in several minerals — see ELEMENT table

yt·tri·um \'i-trē-əm\ n : a metallic element that occurs in minerals along with other similar uncommon elements — see ELEMENT table

yu·an \'yü-ən, yü-'än\ n, pl **yuan**   **1** : the basic unit of money in China   **2** : a coin or bill worth one yuan

yuc·ca \ˈyək-ə\ *n* : any of a genus of plants that are related to the lilies, grow in dry regions, and have stiff pointed leaves at the base of a tall stiff stalk with whitish flowers

yule \ˈyü(ə)l\ *n, often cap* : CHRISTMAS

yule log *n, often cap Y* : a large log formerly put on the hearth on Christmas Eve as the foundation of the fire

yule·tide \ˈyü(ə)l-ˌtīd\ *n, often cap* : the Christmas season

yum·my \ˈyəm-ē\ *adj* : very pleasing especially to the taste

yurt \ˈyù(ə)rt\ *n* : a light round tent of skins or felt used by nomads in Siberia [from Russian *yurta* "a domed tent, yurt"; of Turkish origin]

YWCA \ˌwī-ˌdəb-əl-yù-(ˌ)sē-ˈā\ *n* : an international organization originally for young women [*Young Women's Christian Association*]

YWHA \ˌwī-ˌdəb-əl-yù-ˌā-ˈchä\ *n* : an international organization of Jewish young women [*Young Women's Hebrew Association*]

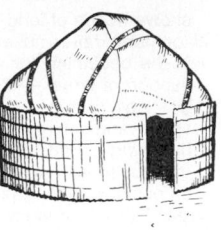

yurt

Z

z \ˈzē, *British & Canadian* ˈzed\ *n, often cap* : the 26th letter of the English alphabet

Zach·a·ri·as \ˌzak-ə-ˈrī-əs\ *n* — see BIBLE table

¹za·ny \ˈzā-nē\ *n, pl* **zanies** **1** : ¹CLOWN 2 **2** : a silly or foolish person

²zany *adj* **za·ni·er; -est** : being, typical of, or resembling a zany — **za·ni·ly** \ˈzā-nə-lē, ˈzān-ᵊl-ē\ *adv* — **za·ni·ness** \ˈzā-nē-nəs\ *n*

zap \ˈzap\ *vb* **zapped; zap·ping** **1** : to destroy or kill by or as if by shooting **2** : to hit suddenly and forcefully

zeal \ˈzē(ə)l\ *n* : eager desire in going for a goal

zeal·ot \ˈzel-ət\ *n* : a zealous person; *esp* : an overly zealous supporter

zeal·ous \ˈzel-əs\ *adj* : filled with or showing zeal — **zeal·ous·ly** *adv* — **zeal·ous·ness** *n*

ze·bra \ˈzēb-rə\ *n, pl* **zebras** *also* **zebra** **1** : any of several fleet African mammals that are related to the horse and have a hide striped in black and white or black and buff **2** : a small Indian fish with blue and silver stripes that is often kept in tropical aquariums

ze·bu \ˈzē-b(y)ü\ *n* : an Asian domesticated ox that differs from European cattle with which it crosses freely by a large fleshy hump over the shoulders and a loose skin with hanging folds

Zech·a·ri·ah \ˌzek-ə-ˈrī-ə\ *n* — see BIBLE table

zed \ˈzed\ *n, chiefly British* : the letter z

ze·nith \ˈzē-nəth\ *n* **1** : the point in the heavens directly overhead **2** : the highest point

Zeph·a·ni·ah \ˌzef-ə-ˈnī-ə\ *n* — see BIBLE table

zeph·yr \ˈzef-ər\ *n* **1** : a breeze from the west **2** : a gentle breeze

zep·pe·lin \ˈzep-(ə-)lən\ *n* : a long cylindrical passenger balloon that has a metal frame and is driven through the air by engines carried on its underside

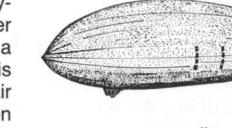

zeppelin

¹ze·ro \ˈzē-rō, ˈzi(ə)r-ō\ *n, pl* **zeros** *also* **zeroes** **1** : the numerical symbol 0 or the number represented by it — see NUMBER table **2 a** : a point (as on a scale) from which measurements are made **b** : a value or reading of zero; *esp* : the temperature shown by the zero mark on a thermometer **3** : something or someone of no importance **4** : the lowest point

²zero *adj* **1** : of, relating to, or being a zero **2** : showing no change in the word form ("sheep" is a noun with a *zero* plural)

³zero *vb* **1** : to find out or adjust the zero of (as a balance) **2** : to aim or concentrate on a target or goal 〈*zero* in on my problems with algebra〉

zero hour *n* **1** : the hour at which a military action is scheduled to start **2** : a moment of crisis

zest \ˈzest\ *n* **1** : a quality that increases enjoyment **2** : keen enjoyment : RELISH — **zest·ful** \-fəl\ *adj* — **zest·ful·ly** \-fə-lē\ *adv* — **zest·ful·ness** *n* — **zesty** \ˈzes-tē\ *adj*

> **Word History** *Zest* was borrowed into English in the 17th century from the French *zest* (now spelled *zeste*), meaning "an orange or lemon peel". Where the French got the word we do not know. The peels of oranges and lemons are sometimes used to add flavor to food and drinks. The earliest uses of *zest* in English refer to the peel of such fruit used in this way. By the early 18th century, however, *zest* had developed another meaning. It was used to refer to a quality that adds enjoyment to something, in the same way that the *zest* of an orange or lemon adds flavor to food. [from obsolete French *zest* (now *zeste*) "orange or lemon peel used for flavoring"]

ze·ta \ˈzāt-ə\ *n* : the sixth letter of the Greek alphabet — Z or ζ

¹zig·zag \ˈzig-ˌzag\ *n* **1** : one of a series of short sharp turns, angles, or changes in a course; *also* : something having the form or appearance of such a series

²zigzag *adv* : in or by a zigzag path or course

³zigzag *adj* : having short sharp turns or angles 〈a *zigzag* road〉

⁴zigzag *vb* **zig·zagged; zig·zag·ging** : to form, move along, or consist of a zigzag course

zilch \ˈzilch\ *n* : ³NOTHING, ZERO

zil·lion \ˈzil-yən\ *n* : a large number 〈*zillions* of ants〉

zinc \ˈziŋk\ *n* : a bluish white metallic element of low to medium hardness that in the commercial form is brittle at ordinary temperatures, is commonly found in minerals, and is used especially as a protective coating for iron and steel — see ELEMENT table

zinc oxide *n* : a white substance that is used as a white pigment, is added to rubber, and is used in medical preparations (as calamine)

zinc sulfide *n* : a white to yellowish compound used especially as a white coloring matter

zinc white *n* : a white coloring matter that consists of a compound made up of zinc and oxygen

zing \ˈziŋ\ *n* **1** : a shrill humming sound **2** : a lively or energetic quality 〈a musical show with lots of *zing*〉

zin·nia \ˈzin-ē-ə, ˈzin-yə, ˈzēn-\ *n* : any of a small genus of tropical American herbs related to the daisies and having

\ə\ abut	\aù\ out	\i\ tip	\ȯ\ saw	\ù\ foot
\ər\ further	\ch\ chin	\ī\ life	\ȯi\ coin	\y\ yet
\a\ mat	\e\ pet	\j\ job	\th\ thin	\yü\ few
\ā\ take	\ē\ easy	\ŋ\ sing	\th\ this	\yù\ cure
\ä\ cot, cart	\g\ go	\ō\ bone	\ü\ food	\zh\ vision

showy heads of long-lasting flowers

Zi·on·ism \'zī-ə-ˌniz-əm\ *n* : an international effort working in the beginning for a Jewish homeland and later for the support of Israel — **Zi·on·ist** \-nəst\ *n*

¹zip \'zip\ *vb* **zipped; zip·ping 1** : to move or act with speed and energy **2** : to travel with a sharp hissing or humming sound **3** : to add energy, interest, or life to — often used with *up* [a word created to imitate the sound of an object speeding past]

²zip *n* **1** : a sudden sharp hissing sound **2** : VIM

³zip *vb* **zipped; zip·ping** : to close or open with a zipper [from *zipper*]

⁴zip *n* : ¹ZERO 1 — often used in giving scores ⟨won the game 7–*zip*⟩ [origin unknown]

⁵zip *n, often cap Z & I & P* : ZIP CODE

zip code *n* : a number that identifies each postal delivery area in the U.S.

zip gun *n* : a crude homemade pistol

zip·per \'zip-ər\ *n* : a fastener consisting of two rows of metal or plastic teeth on strips of tape and a sliding piece that closes an opening by drawing the teeth together — **zip·pered** \-ərd\ *adj*

zip·py \'zip-ē\ *adj* **zip·pi·er; -est** : full of zip : BRISK, SNAPPY

zir·con \'zər-ˌkän, -kən\ *n* : a mineral that consists of a silicate of zirconium and occurs usually as brown or grayish crystals or sometimes as transparent forms which are used as gems

zir·co·ni·um \ˌzər-'kō-nē-əm\ *n* : a steel-gray strong metallic element with a high melting point that occurs widely in combined form (as in zircon) and is used especially in combination with other metals — see ELEMENT table

zith·er \'zith-ər, 'zith-\ *n* : a stringed instrument with thirty to forty tuned strings that are plucked with the fingers or with a pick

zlo·ty \'zlȯt-ē, zə-'lȯt-ē\ *n, pl* **zlotys** \-ēz\ *or* **zloty 1** : the basic unit of money in Poland **2** : a coin worth one zloty

zo·di·ac \'zōd-ē-ˌak\ *n* **1** : an imaginary belt in the heavens that includes the apparent paths of most of the planets and is divided into 12 star groups or signs **2** : a figure showing the signs of the zodiac [Middle English *zodiac* "zodiac", from early French *zodiaque* (same meaning), from Latin *zodiacus* (same meaning), derived from Greek *zōidion* "carved or painted figure, sign of the zodiac", from *zōion* "living being, animal, figure"] — **zo·di·a·cal** \zō-'dī-ə-kəl\ *adj*

THE SIGNS OF THE ZODIAC

NUMBER	NAME	SYMBOL	SUN ENTERS
1	Aries the Ram	♈	March 21
2	Taurus the Bull	♉	April 20
3	Gemini the Twins	♊	May 21
4	Cancer the Crab	♋	June 22
5	Leo the Lion	♌	July 23
6	Virgo the Virgin	♍	August 23
7	Libra the Balance	♎	September 23
8	Scorpio the Scorpion	♏	October 24
9	Sagittarius the Archer	♐	November 22
10	Capricorn the Goat	♑	December 22
11	Aquarius the Water Bearer	♒	January 20
12	Pisces the Fishes	♓	February 19

zom·bie *also* **zom·bi** \'zäm-bē\ *n* : a person who is believed to have died and been brought back to life without speech or free will

Word History In western Africa at one time the *zombie* was a god in the shape of a python, a very large snake. Worshipers believed that this snake-god had the power to enter the bodies of the dead. A dead person possessed by this power was capable of movement, but not speech or thought. The power, like the god, was called *zombie,* and the possessed body was called a *zombie* as well. When Africans arrived in the West Indies and the southern United States, they brought their languages and their beliefs with them. Their word for the living dead was borrowed into English. [of African origin]

zon·al \'zōn-ᵊl\ *adj* : of, relating to, or having the form of a zone

¹zone \'zōn\ *n* **1** : any of five great divisions of the earth's surface with respect to latitude and temperature **2** : a region or area set off from surrounding or neighboring parts ⟨a *zone* of trees⟩ **3** : one of the sections of an area or territory created for a particular purpose ⟨a business *zone*⟩ **4** : an area on a playing field

²zone *vb* **zoned; zon·ing** : to divide into zones; *esp* : to divide (as a city) into sections for different purposes (as manufacturing)

zoo \'zü\ *n, pl* **zoos** : a collection of living animals kept for showing to the public : ZOOLOGICAL GARDEN

zoo·keep·er \-ˌkē-pər\ *n* : a person who keeps or cares for animals in a zoo

zoo·log·i·cal garden \ˌzō-ə-'läj-i-kəl-\ *n* : a garden or park where wild animals are kept for showing to the public

zo·ol·o·gist \zō-'äl-ə-jəst, zə-'wäl-\ *n* : a person who specializes in zoology

zo·ol·o·gy \zō-'äl-ə-jē, zə-'wäl-\ *n* : a branch of biology concerned with the animal kingdom and animal life — **zoo·log·i·cal** *adj*

¹zoom \'züm\ *vb* **1** : to speed along with a loud low hum or buzz ⟨cars *zooming* down the highway⟩ **2** : to gain altitude quickly ⟨the rocket *zoomed* into the sky⟩

²zoom *n* **1** : an act or process of zooming **2** : a zooming sound

zoom lens *n* : a lens on a camera or projector in which the size of the image can be continuously changed while the image remains in focus

zoo·plank·ton \ˌzō-ə-'plaŋ(k)-tən, -ˌtän\ *n* : animal life that is part of plankton

Zo·ro·as·tri·an \ˌzōr-ə-'was-trē-ən\ *adj* : of or relating to the Persian prophet Zoroaster or the religion founded by him and marked by belief in a great war between good and evil in the universe — **Zoroastrian** *n* — **Zo·ro·as·tri·an·ism** \-trē-ə-ˌniz-əm\ *n*

zounds \'z(w)aun(d)z, 'z(w)ün(d)z\ *interj* — used as a mild oath

zuc·chi·ni \zu̇-'kē-nē\ *n, pl* **-ni** *or* **-nis** : a summer squash of bushy growth with smooth slender cylinder-shaped dark green fruits; *also* : its fruit

Zu·lu \'zü-lü\ *n* : a member of a Bantu-speaking people of South Africa

Zu·ni \'zü-nē\ *or* **Zu·ñi** \'zün-yē\ *n, pl* **Zuni** *or* **Zunis** *or* **Zuñi** *or* **Zuñis** : an American Indian people of western New Mexico

zwie·back \'swē-ˌbak, 'swī-, 'zwē-, 'zwī-, -ˌbäk\ *n* : a usually sweet bread made with eggs that is baked and then sliced and toasted until dry and crisp

zy·gote \'zī-ˌgōt\ *n* : a cell formed by the union of two sex cells; *also* : the developing individual produced from such a cell — **zy·got·ic** \zī-'gät-ik\ *adj*

ABBREVIATIONS AND SYMBOLS FOR CHEMICAL ELEMENTS

Most of these abbreviations have been entered according to one standard form. There is, however, variation in the use of periods and of capital letters (as *mph, m.p.h., Mph,* and *MPH*). Therefore, stylings other than those given in this dictionary are often acceptable.

a absent, acre, alto, answer, are, atto-

A ace, ampere, area, argon, assist

Å angstrom unit

AA associate in arts

AAA American Automobile Association

A and M agricultural and mechanical

AB able-bodied seaman, at bat, bachelor of arts [modern Latin *artium baccalaureus*]

abbr abbreviation

ABC American Broadcasting Company

abl ablative

abp archbishop

abs absolute, abstract

abstr abstract

ac account

Ac actinium

AC alternating current, before Christ [Latin *ante Christum*], area code

acad academic, academy

acc, accus accusative

accel accelerando

acct account, accountant

act active, actor, actual

ACT Australian Capital Territory

AD after date, anno Domini

ADC aide-de-camp, Aid to Dependent Children

addn addition

adj adjective, adjutant

ad loc to or at the place [Latin *ad locum*]

ADM admiral

admin administration

adv adverb

advt advertisement

AF air force, audio frequency

AFDC Aid to Families with Dependent Children

AFL–CIO American Federation of Labor and Congress of Industrial Organizations

Afr Africa, African

Ag silver [Latin *argentum*]

agcy agency

agric agricultural, agriculture

agt agent

AK Alaska

aka also known as

Al aluminum

AL Alabama, American League

Ala Alabama

Alb Albania, Albanian

alc alcohol

ald alderman

alg algebra

alk alkaline

alt alternate, altitude

Alta Alberta

a.m., A.M. ante meridiem

Am America, American, americium

AM master of arts [modern Latin *artium magister*]

amb ambassador

amdt amendment

Amer America, American

Amerind Amerindian

amp ampere

amt amount

AMU atomic mass unit

anat anatomical, anatomy

anc ancient

ann annual

anon anonymous

ans answer

ant antonym

Ant Antarctica

anthrop anthropology

AP Associated Press

APB all points bulletin

APO army post office

approx approximate, approximately

appt appointment

Apr April

apt apartment, aptitude

aq aqua, aqueous

ar arrive, arrive

Ar argon, Arkansas

AR Arkansas

Arab Arabian, Arabic

arch architect, architecture

arith arithmetic

Ariz Arizona

Ark Arkansas

arr arranged, arrival, arrive

art article, artificial

ARV American Revised Version

As arsenic

AS Anglo-Saxon

assn association

assoc associate, association

asst assistant

ASV American Standard Version

AT astatine

Atl Atlantic

atm atmosphere, atmospheric

at. no. atomic number

att attached, attention, attorney

attn attention

attrib attributive, attributively

atty attorney

at. wt. atomic weight

Au gold [Latin *aurum*]

Aug August

Austral Australia

auth author

aux, auxil auxiliary

av avenue, average, avoirdupois

AV audiovisual, Authorized Version

avdp avoirdupois

ave avenue

avg average

AZ Arizona

b back, base, bishop, book, born

B bachelor, Bible, boron

Ba barium

BA bachelor of arts

bal balance

Bart baronet

BBC British Broadcasting Corporation

bbl barrel, barrels

BC before Christ, British Columbia

bd board, bound

bd ft board foot

bdl, bdle bundle

Be beryllium

Belg Belgian, Belgium

bet between

bf boldface

bg background, bag

Bi bismuth

bib Bible, biblical

biog biographer, biographical, biography

biol biologic, biological, biologist, biology

bk bank, book, break

Bk berkelium

bkt basket, bracket

bl bale, barrel

BL bats left

bldg building

blk black, block

BLT bacon, lettuce, tomato

blvd boulevard

BM basal metabolism, bowel movement

BMR basal metabolic rate

BO body odor, box office

bor borough

bp baptized, birthplace, bishop

BP blood pressure, blueprint, boiling point

bpl birthplace

BPW Board of Public Works

br branch

BR Britain, British, bromine

Braz Brazil, Brazilian

brig brigade, brigadier

Brit Britain, British

bro brother, brothers

bros brothers

BS, BSc bachelor of science

BSA Boy Scouts of America

bskt basket

Bt baronet

Btu British thermal unit

bu bureau, bushel

bull bulletin

bur bureau

bus business

BV Blessed Virgin

BWI British West Indies

bx box

BX base exchange

c carat, cent, centi-, centimeter, century, chapter, circa, circumference, copyright, cubic, cup

C capacitance, carbon, Celsius, centigrade

Ca calcium

CA California

CAD computer-aided design

cal calendar, caliber, small calorie

Cal California, large calorie

Calif California

Can, Canad Canada, Canadian

canc canceled

C & W country and western

cap capital

caps capitals, capsule

Capt captain

CARE Cooperative for American Remittances to Everywhere
cat catalog
CATV community antenna television
Cb columbium
CBC Canadian Broadcasting Corporation
CBS Columbia Broadcasting System
cc cubic centimeter
cd candela, candle, cord
Cd cadmium
CD civil defense
CDR commander
CDT Central daylight time
cent centigrade, central, century
CEO chief executive officer
cert certificate, certification, certified, certify
Cf californium
cg, cgm centigram
CG coast guard
cgs centimeter-gram-second
ch chapter, church
chap chapter
chem chemical, chemist, chemistry
chg change, charge
Chin Chinese
chm, chmn chairman
CIA Central Intelligence Agency
C in C commander in chief
cir circle
civ civil, civilian
ck cask, check
cl centiliter, class
Cl chlorine
clk clerk
cm centimeter
Cm curium
CNS central nervous system
co company, county
Co cobalt
CO Colorado, commanding officer
c/o care of
COD cash on delivery, collect on delivery
col colonial, colony, color, colored, column, counsel
Col colonel, Colorado
Colo Colorado
com commander, committee
comm commission, commonwealth
comp comparative, compensation, compiled, compiler, composition, compound
conc concentrated
cond condition, conductivity
conf conference, confidential
confed confederate
cong congress

conj conjunction
Conn Connecticut
cons consonant
const constant, constitution, constitutional
constr construction
cont containing, contents, continent, continental, continued, control
contr contract, contraction
CORE Congress of Racial Equality
corp corporal, corporation
corr corrected, correction
cos cosine
CP candlepower, chemically pure, communist party
CPA certified public accountant
cpd compound
Cpl corporal
CPR cardiopulmonary resuscitation
cps cycles per second
CPU central processing unit
cr credit, creditor
Cr chromium
cresc crescendo
crit critical, criticism
CRT cathode ray tube
cryst crystalline, crystallized
Cs cesium
c/s cycles per second
CSA Confederate States of America
csc cosecant
CST Central standard time
ct carat, cent, count, court
CT Central time, certified teacher, Connecticut
ctn carton, cotangent
ctr center, counter
cu cubic
Cu copper [Latin *cuprum*]
cur currency, current
CV cardiovascular
cwt hundredweight
cyl cylinder
CZ Canal Zone

d date, daughter, day, density, died, penny, pence [Latin *denarius, denarii*]
D Democrat, Democratic, deuterium, diameter, doctor
DA district attorney
dag dekagram
dal dekaliter
dam dekameter
Dan Danish
DAR Daughters of the American Revolution
dB decibel
dbl double
DC da capo, direct current, District of Columbia
DDD direct distance dialing
DDS doctor of dental science, doctor of dental

surgery
DE Delaware
dec deceased, decrease
Dec December
def definite, definition
deg degree
del delegate, delegation
Del Delaware
Dem Democrat, Democratic
Den Denmark
dent dental, dentist, dentistry
dep deposit
dept department
der, deriv derivation, derivative
dg decigram
DH designated hitter
dia, diam diameter
diag diagonal, diagram
dial dialect, dialectal
dict dictionary
dif, diff difference
dil dilute
dir director
disc discount
dist distance, district
distn distillation
div divided, dividend, division, divorced
DJ disc jockey
dk dark, deck, dock
dkg dekagram
dkl dekaliter
dkm dekameter
dl deciliter
dm decimeter
DMD doctor of dental medicine
dn down
do direct object, ditto
DO doctor of osteopathy
DOA dead on arrival
doc document
dol dollar
dom domestic
DOS disk operating system
doz dozen
DP data processing, double play
dpt department
dr dram, drive, drum
Dr doctor
DS dal segno
DST daylight saving time
DTP diphtheria, tetanus, pertussis
Du Dutch
dup duplex, duplicate
DV Douay Version
DVM doctor of veterinary medicine
dwt pennyweight
dz dozen

e edge
E east, eastern, energy, English, error, excellent
ea each
EB eastbound
eccl ecclesiastic, ecclesiastical

ecol ecological, ecology
econ economics, economist, economy
Ecua Ecuador
ed edited, edition, editor, education
EDT Eastern daylight time
educ education, educational
e.g. for example [Latin *exempli gratia*]
Eg Egypt, Egyptian
EHF extremely high frequency
el, elev elevation
elec electric, electrical, electricity
elem elementary
emf electromotive force
EMT emergency medical training
ency, encyc encyclopedia
ENE east-northeast
eng engine, engineer, engineering
Eng England, English
ENS ensign
env envelope
eq equal, equation
Er erbium
ER earned run
ERA earned run average, equal rights amendment
Es einsteinium
ESE east-southeast
Esk Eskimo
esp especially
ESP extrasensory perception
Esq, Esqr esquire
est established, estimate, estimated
EST Eastern standard time
ET eastern time
ETA estimated time of arrival
et al. and others [Latin *et alii*]
etc et cetera
ETD estimated time of departure
Eu europium
Eur Europe, European
evap evaporate
ex example, executive, extra
exc excellent, except
exp expense, export, express
expt experiment
exptl experimental
ext extension, extra

f and the following one, false, female, feminine, focal length, folio, forte, frequency
F Fahrenheit, fluorine, French
Fah, Fahr Fahrenheit
fath fathom
FBI Federal Bureau of In-

vestigation
FD fire department
FDA Food and Drug Administration
Fe iron [Latin *ferrum*]
Feb February
fem female, feminine
ff and the following ones, fortissimo
FFA Future Farmers of America
FHA Future Homemakers of America
FICA Federal Insurance Contributions Act
fig figure
fin finish
Finn Finnish
fl fluid
FL, Fla Florida
Flem Flemish
fl oz fluidounce
Fm fermium
FOB free on board
for foreign, forestry
fp freezing point
FPC fish protein concentrate
fpm feet per minute
FPO fleet post office
fps feet per second, foot-pound-second
fr father, friar, from
Fr francium, French
freq frequency, frequent, frequently
Fri Friday
frt freight
frwy freeway
FSH follicle-stimulating hormone
ft feet, foot, fort
ft lb foot-pound
fwd foreword, forward
FYI for your information

g acceleration of gravity, gram, gravity
G German, goal, good
Ga gallium, Georgia
GA Georgia
gal gallon
gar garage
GB Great Britain
GCD greatest common divisor
GCF greatest common factor
Gd gadolinium
Ge germanium
gen general, genitive
geog geographic, geographical, geography
geol geologic, geological, geology
geom geometric, geometrical, geometry
ger gerund
Ger German, Germany
gi gill
GI gastrointestinal, general issue, government issue

Gib Gibraltar
Gk Greek
gm gram
GM general manager
GMT Greenwich mean time
GNP gross national product
GOP Grand Old Party (Republican)
gov government, governor
govt government
gp group
GP games played, general practitioner
GPO general post office
GQ general quarters
gr grade, grain, gram, gravity, gross
Gr Greece, Greek
grad graduate, graduated
gro gross
GSA Girl Scouts of America
gt great
Gt Brit Great Britain
GU Guam

h hard, hardness, height, heroin, hour, husband
H hit, hydrogen
ha hectare
hd head
HD heavy-duty
hdbk handbook
hdkf handkerchief
He helium
Heb Hebrew
hf half
Hf hafnium
HF high frequency
hg hectogram
Hg mercury [Latin *hydrargyrum*]
hgt height
hgwy highway
HI Hawaii
hist historian, historical, history
hl hectoliter
hm hectometer
HM Her Majesty, Her Majesty's, His Majesty, His Majesty's
HMS Her Majesty's ship, His Majesty's ship
Ho holmium
hon honor, honorable, honorary
hor horizontal
hort horticultural, horticulture
hosp hospital
hp horse power
HP high pressure
HQ headquarters
hr here, hour
HR home run, House of Representatives
HRH Her Royal Highness, His Royal Highness
HS high school
ht height
HT Hawaii time, high-tension

Hung Hungarian, Hungary
hwy highway
Hz hertz

I electric current, intransitive, iodine, island, isle
Ia, IA Iowa
ICSH interstitial cell-stimulating hormone
ID Idaho, identification
i.e. that is [Latin *id est*]
IL, Ill Illinois
ill, illus, illust illustrated, illustration
imp imperative, imperfect
in inch
In Indium
IN Indiana
inc incomplete, incorporated, increase
ind independent, index, industrial, industry
Ind Indian, Indiana
indef indefinite
indic indicative
inf infantry, infinitive
INP International News Photo
INRI Jesus of Nazareth, King of the Jews [Latin *Iesus Nazarenus Rex Iudaeorum*]
inst instant, institute, institution, institutional
instr instructor
int interest, intermediate, international, intransitive
interj interjection
interrog interrogative
intrans intransitive
io indirect object
I/O input/output
Ir iridium, Irish
Ire Ireland
irreg irregular
IRS Internal Revenue Service
is island
ISBN International Standard Book Number
Isr Israel, Israeli
It Italian, Italy
ital italic, italicized
Ital Italian
IU international unit
IV intravenous, intravenously
IW Isle of Wight
IWW Industrial Workers of the World

J joule
Jam Jamaica
Jan January
JCC Junior Chamber of Commerce
jct junction
JD juvenile delinquent
Je June
JP justice of the peace
Jpn Japan, Japanese
jr, jun junior

JRC Junior Red Cross
jt, jnt joint
junc junction
juv juvenile
JV junior varsity

k karat, knit
K kelvin, potassium [Latin *kalium*], strikeout
Kans Kansas
kc kilocycle
KC Kansas City
kcal kilocalorie
kc/s kilocycles per second
kg kilogram
KIA killed in action
KKK Ku Klux Klan
kl kiloliter
km kilometer
Kr krypton
KS Kansas
kv kilovolt
kw kilowatt
kwhr, kwh kilowatt-hour
Ky, KY Kentucky

l left, length, line, liter, long
L large, Latin
La lanthanum, Louisiana
LA law agent, Los Angeles, Louisiana
Lab Labrador
lang language
lat latitude
Lat Latin
lb pound [Latin *libra*]
LCD least common denominator, lowest common denominator
LCM least common multiple, lowest common multiple
LD lethal dose
lect lecture, lecturer
leg legal, legato, legislative, legislature
LEM lunar excursion module
LF low frequency
lg large, long
LH left hand, luteinizing hormone
Li lithium
LI Long Island
lib liberal, librarian, library
lieut lieutenant
liq liquid
ll lines
LLD doctor of laws
LM lunar module
ln lane
LNG liquefied natural gas
Lond London
long longitude
loq he speaks, she speaks [Latin *loquitur*]
LPG liquefied petroleum gas
Lr lawrencium
LS left side
LSI large-scale integration
Lt lieutenant

ltd limited
ltr letter
Lu lutetium
lub lubricant, lubricating
lv leave

m male, married, masculine, mass, meter, mile, milli-, minute, noon [Latin *meridies*]
M medium, mega-, monsieur, thousand [Latin *mille*]
ma milliampere
MA Massachusetts, master of arts
mach machine, machinery, machinist
mag magazine, magnetism
Maj major
man manual
Man Manitoba
manuf manufacture, manufacturing
Mar March
masc masculine
Mass Massachusetts
MAT master of arts in teaching
math mathematical, mathematician
max maximum
mb millibar
mc megacycle
MC member of Congress
Md Maryland, mendelevium
MD doctor of medicine, Maryland, muscular dystrophy
mdse merchandise
Me Maine
ME Maine
meas measure
mech mechanical, mechanics
med medical, medicine, medieval, medium
mem member
MeV million electron volts
Mex Mexican, Mexico
MF medium frequency, mezzo forte, microfiche
mfd manufactured
mfg manufacturing
mfr manufacturer
mg milligram
Mg magnesium
mgr manager, monseigneur, monsignor
MHz megahertz
MI, Mich Michigan
MIA missing in action
mid middle
mil military
min minimum, minute
Minn Minnesota
misc miscellaneous
Miss Mississippi
mixt mixture
mk mark
ml milliliter
Mlle mademoiselle

mm millimeter
Mme madame
Mn manganese
MN Minnesota
mo month
Mo Missouri, molybdenum
MO Missouri
mol molecular, molecule
mol wt molecular weight
Mon Monday
Mont Montana
mos months
MP melting point, member of parliament, military police
mpg miles per gallon
mph miles per hour
mRNA messenger RNA
MS manuscript, master of science, Mississippi, multiple sclerosis
msec millisecond
MSG monosodium glutamate
msgr monseigneur, monsignor
MSS manuscripts
MST Mountain standard time
mt mount, mountain
MT metric ton, Montana, Mountain time
mus museum, music
mv millivolt
Mv mendelevium
MVP most valuable player

n neuter, note, noun
N newton, nitrogen, north, northern
Na sodium [Latin *natrium*]
NA North America, not applicable, not available
NAACP National Association for the Advancement of Colored People
NASA National Aeronautics and Space Administration
natl national
NATO North Atlantic Treaty Organization
nav naval, navigation
Nb niobium
NB New Brunswick, northbound
NBC National Broadcasting Company
NBS National Bureau of Standards
NC no charge, North Carolina
NCO noncommissioned officer
Nd neodymium
ND, N Dak North Dakota
Ne neon
NE Nebraska, New England, northeast, northeastern
Neb, Nebr Nebraska
neg negative
Neth Netherlands

neut neuter
Nev Nevada
Nfld Newfoundland
NG national guard, no good
NH New Hampshire
Ni nickel
NJ New Jersey
NL National League
NM, N Mex New Mexico
NNE north-northeast
NNW north-northwest
no north, number
No nobelium
nom nominative
Nor Norway, Norwegian
Nov November
NOW National Organization for Women
Np neptunium
NP noun phrase
NS Nova Scotia
NT New Testament
NTP normal temperature and pressure
nt wt, n wt net weight
num number, numeral
NV Nevada
NW northwest, northwestern
NWT Northwest Territories
NY New York
NYC New York City
NZ New Zealand

o ocean, ohm
O Ohio, oxygen
OAS Organization of American States
obj object, objective
obs obsolete
occas occasionally
Oct October
OD officer of the day
OF outfield
off office, officer, official
OH Ohio
OK, Okla Oklahoma
Ont Ontario
op opus
OPEC Organization of Petroleum Exporting Countries
opp opposite
opt optical, optician, optional
OR operating room, Oregon
orch orchestra
ord order
Oreg, Ore Oregon
org organization
orig original, originally
Os osmium
OT Old Testament
oz ounce, ounces [obsolete Italian *onza*]

p page, participle, past, pint
P phosphorus, pressure
Pa pascal, Pennsylvania
PA Pennsylvania, public address
Pac Pacific

pam pamphlet
Pan Panama
par paragraph, parallel
part participle, particular
pass passenger, passive
pat patent
path, pathol pathological, pathology
payt payment
Pb lead [Latin *plumbum*]
PBS Public Broadcasting System
PC Peace Corps, percent, postcard
pct percent, percentage
pd paid
Pd palladium
PD police department
PE physical education
PEI Prince Edward Island
pen peninsula
Penn, Penna Pennsylvania
per period, person
perf perfect
perh perhaps
perm permanent
perp perpendicular
pers person, personal
Pers Persia, Persian
PFC private first class
pg page
pharm pharmaceutical, pharmacist, pharmacy
PhD doctor of philosophy [Latin *philosophiae doctor*]
photog photographic, photography
phr phrase
phys physical, physician, physics
physiol physiologist, physiology
PI Philippine Islands
pizz pizzicato
pk park, peak, peck
pkg package
PKU phenylketonuria
pkwy parkway
pl place, plural
p.m., P.M. post meridiem
Pm promethium
pmt payment
Po polonium
PO post office
Pol Poland, Polish
pop popular, poulation
Port Portugal, Portuguese
pos positive
poss possessive
POW prisoner of war
pp pages, pianissimo
PP past participle
ppd postpaid, prepaid
PPS an additional postscript [Latin *post postscriptum*]
PQ Province of Quebec
pr pair, price, printed
Pr praseodymium
PR public relations, Puerto Rico

pred predicate
pref preface, prefix
prep preparatory, preposition
pres present, president
prev previous, previously
prf proof
prim primary
prin principal, principle
prob probably, problem
prod production
prof professional, professor
pron pronoun, pronunciation
prop property, proprietor
Prot Protestant
prov province
PS postscript [Latin *postscriptum*], public school
pseud pseudonym
PST Pacific standard time
psych psychology
psychol psychologist, psychology
pt part, pint, point
Pt platinum
PT Pacific time, physical therapy, physical training
PTA Parent-Teacher Association
PTO Parent-Teacher Organization
PTV public television
Pu plutonium
pub public
pwt pennyweight
PX post exchange

q quart, question
Q queen
QED which was to be demonstrated [Latin *quod erat demonstrandum*]
qr quarter
qt quart
Que Quebec
quot quotation

r radius, rate, right, river
R rabbi, regular, Republican, resistance
Ra radium
rad radio, radius
R&B rhythm and blues
Rb rubidium
RBC red blood cells
RBI run batted in
RC Red Cross, Roman Catholic
rd road, rod
RD rural delivery
RDA recommended daily allowance, recommended dietary allowance
Re rhenium
rec receipt, record, recording, recreation
recd received
rect rectangle, rectangular
ref reference
reg region, regular
rel relating, relative, reli-

gion, religious
rep representative, republic
Rep Republican
repl replace, replacement
rept report
req require
res residence
resp respective, respectively
rev review, revolution
Rev reverend
RF radio frequency
RFD rural free delivery
Rh rhodium
RH right hand
RI Rhode Island
rit ritardando
riv river
rm ream, room
Rn radon
RN registered nurse
Rom Roman, Romania, Romanian
ROTC Reserve Officers' Training Corps
RP relief pitcher
rpm revolutions per minute
rps revolutions per second
RR railroad, rural route
RS right side
RSFSR Russian Soviet Federated Socialist Republic
RSV Revised Standard Version
RSVP please reply [French *répondez s'il vous plaît*]
rt right
rte route
Ru ruthenium
Rum Rumania, Rumanian
Russ Russia, Russian
RV recreational vehicle
rwy, ry railway

s second
S small, south, southern, sulfur
SA Salvation Army, South Africa, South America
Sask Saskatchewan
sat saturate, saturated, saturation
Sat Saturday
sb substantive
Sb antimony [Latin *stibium*]
SB bachelor of science [scientific Latin *scientiae baccalaureus*], southbound, stolen base
sc science
Sc scandium, Scots
SC South Carolina
Scand Scandinavia, Scandinavian
sch school
sci science, scientific
Scot Scotland, Scottish
SD, S Dak South Dakota
Se selenium
SE southeast, southeastern

SEATO Southeast Asia Treaty Organization
sec secant, second, secretary, section
secy secretary
sel select, selected, selection
sem seminary
sen senate, senator, senior
Sept, Sep September
ser series
serg, sergt sergeant
serv service
sf, sfz sforzando
SF sacrifice fly, science fiction
Sgt sergeant
sh share
Si silicon
SI International System of Units [French *Système International d'Unités*]
sin sine
sing singular
sm small
Sm samarium
SM master of science [scientific Latin *scientiae magister*]
Sn tin [Latin *stannum*]
so south, southern
SO strikeout
soc social, society
sociol sociologist, sociology
soph sophomore
sp special, species, specimen, spelling
Sp Spain, Spanish
Span Spanish
SPCA Society for the Prevention of Cruelty to Animals
SPCC Society for the Prevention of Cruelty to Children
spec special, specifically
specif specific, specifically
sp gr specific gravity
spp species
sq square
sr senior
Sr senior, senor, sister, strontium
Sra senora
Sres señores
SRO standing room only
Srta senorita
SS steamship, Sunday school
SSE south-southeast
ssp subspecies
SSR Soviet Socialist Republic
SSS Selective Service System
SSW south-southwest
st state, street
St saint
sta station
Ste saint (female) [French *sainte*]

stud student
subj subject, subjunctive
suff sufficient, suffix
Sun Sunday
sup supplement, supply
supt superintendent
surg surgeon, surgery, surgical
Sw, Swed Sweden, Swedish
SW southwest, southwestern
SWA South-West Africa
Switz Switzerland
syl, syll syllable
sym symbol, symmetrical
syn synonym, synonymous, synonymy
syst system

t metric ton, teaspoon, temperature, tense, ton, transitive, true
T tablespoon, tritium
Ta tantalum
tan tangent
taxon taxonomic, taxonomy
tb tablespoon, tablespoonful
Tb terbium
TAB to be announced
tbs, tbsp tablespoon, tablespoonful
Tc technetium
TD touchdown
Te tellurium
tech technical, technically, technician, technological, technology
tel telegram, telegraph, telephone
temp temperature, temporary
Tenn Tennessee
ter terrace
terr territory
Tex Texas
TGIF thank God it's Friday
Th thorium, Thursday
therm thermometer
Thurs, Thu Thursday
Ti titanium
Tl thallium
TLC tender loving care
Tm thulium
TM trademark
tn ton, town
TN Tennessee
tnpk turnpike
tot total
tp township
tpk, tpke turnpike
trans transitive, transportation
trib tributary
TSH thyroid-stimulating hormone
tsp teaspoon, teaspoonful
TT Trust Territories
Tues, Tue Tuesday
Turk Turkey, Turkish
TVA Tennessee Valley Au-

thority
TX Texas

u unit
U university, uranium
UHF ultrahigh frequency
UK United Kingdom
ult ultimate, ultimo
UN United Nations
UNESCO United Nations Educational, Scientific, and Cultural Organization
Unh unnilhexium
UNICEF United Nations Children's Fund
univ universal, university
Unp unnilpentium
Unq unnilquadium
UPC Universal Product Code
UPI United Press International
US United States
USA United States Army, United States of America
USAF United States Air Force
USCG United States Coast Guard
USDA United States Department of Agriculture
USM United Sates Mail
USMC United States Marine Corps

USN United States Navy
USO United Service Organizations
USPS United States Postal Service
USS United States ship
USSR Union of Soviet Socialist Republics
usu usual, usually
UT Utah
UV ultraviolet

v speed, velocity, verb, verse
V vanadium, victory, volt, voltage, volume
Va Virginia
VA Veterans Administration, Virginia
var variant
vb verb, verbal
VD venereal disease
veg vegetable
Ven venerable
vert vertical
VFD volunteer fire department
VFW Veterans of Foreign Wars
VHF very high frequency
vi verb intransitive
VI Virgin Islands
vil village
vis visual

VISTA Volunteers in Service to America
viz namely [Latin *videlicet*]
vocab vocabulary
vol volume, volunteer
VP verb phrase, vice president
vs versus
vt verb transitive
Vt, VT Vermont
VTOL vertical takeoff and landing
Vulg Vulgate
vv verses

w water, watt, week, weight, wide, width, wife, with
W tungsten [German *wolfram*], west, western, wins
WA Washington
WAC Women's Army Corps
WAF Women in the Air Force
Wash Washington
WAVES Women Accepted for Volunteer Emergency Service
WB westbound
WBC white blood cells
WC water closet
Wed Wednesday
wh watt-hour, which, white
WHO World Health Organi-

zation
whr watt-hour
WI West Indies, Wisconsin
Wis, Wisc Wisconsin
wk week, work
WNW west-northwest
w/o without
wpm words per minute
WSW west-southwest
wt weight
WV, W Va West Virginia
WW world war
WY, Wyo Wyoming

Xe xenon
XL extra large, extra long

y yard, year
Y yttrium
Yb ytterbium
yd yard
yr year, your
YT Yukon Territory
Yug Yugoslavia

z zero
Zn zinc
zool zoological, zoology
ZPG zero population growth
Zr zirconium

BIOGRAPHICAL, BIBLICAL, AND MYTHOLOGICAL NAMES

This section is a listing of the names of important figures from recorded history, biblical tradition, classical mythology, popular legend, and current events. Figures from the Bible, myth, or legend are clearly identified as such. In cases where figures have alternate names, they are entered under the name by which they are best known. The part of the name shown in boldface type is either the family name or the common shorter name for that figure. The dates following the name or pronunciation are the birth and death dates. Other dates in the entry refer to the dates of a particular office, honor, or achievement. Italicized names within an entry refer to a person's nickname, original name, title, or other name.

Aar·on \\'ar-ən, 'er-\\ brother of Moses and first high priest of the Hebrews in the Bible

Abel \\'ā-bəl\\ son of Adam and Eve and brother of Cain in the Bible

Abra·ham \\'ā-brə-,ham\\ patriarch and founder of the Hebrew people in the Bible

Achil·les \\ə-'kil-ēz\\ Greek hero in the Trojan War in mythology

Ad·am \\'ad-əm\\ the first man in the Bible

Ad·ams \\'ad-əmz\\ Abigail 1744–1818 American writer; wife of John Adams

Adams John 1735–1826 2d president of the U.S. (1797–1801)

Adams John Quin·cy \\'kwin-zē, 'kwin(t)-sē\\ 1767–1848 6th president of the U.S. (1825–29); son of John and Abigail Adams

Adams Samuel 1722–1803 patriot in the American Revolutionary War

Ad·dams \\'ad-əmz\\ Jane 1860–1935 American social worker; Nobel Prize winner (1931)

Ado·nis \\ə-'dän-əs, -'dō-nəs\\ beautiful youth in Greek mythology who is loved by Aphrodite

Ae·ne·as \\i-'nē-əs\\ Trojan hero in Greek and Roman mythology

Ae·o·lus \\'ē-ə-ləs\\ god of the winds in Greek mythology

Aes·chy·lus \\'es-kə-ləs, 'ēs-\\ 525–456 B.C. Greek dramatist

Aes·cu·la·pi·us \\,es-kyə-'lā-pē-əs\\ god of medicine in Roman mythology — compare ASCLEPIUS

Ae·sop \\'ē-,säp, -səp\\ legendary Greek writer of fables

Ag·a·mem·non \\,ag-ə-'mem-,nän, -nən\\ leader of the Greeks during the Trojan War in Greek mythology

Ag·nes \\'ag-nəs\\ Saint died 304 A.D. Christian martyr

Ahab \\'ā-,hab\\ king of Israel in the 9th century B.C. and husband of Jezebel

Ajax \\'ā-,jaks\\ hero in Greek mythology who kills himself because the armor of Achilles is awarded to Odysseus during the Trojan War

Alad·din \\ə-'lad-ᵊn\\ youth in the *Arabian Nights' Entertainments* who comes into possession of a magic lamp and ring

Al·cott \\'ȯl-kət, 'al-, -,kät\\ Louisa May 1832–1888 American author

Al·ex·an·der \\,al-ig-'zan-der, ,el-\\ name of eight popes: especially **VI** (Rodrigo Lanzol y Borja) 1431–1503 (pope 1492–1503)

Alexander III of Macedon 356–323 B.C. *the Great* king (336–323)

Al·fred \\'al-frəd, -fərd\\ 849–899 *the Great* king of the West Saxons (871–899)

Ali Ba·ba \\,al-ē-'bäb-ə\\ a woodcutter in the *Arabian Nights' Entertainments* who enters the cave of the Forty Thieves by using the password *Sesame*

Al·len \\'al-ən\\ Ethan 1738–1789 American Revolutionary soldier

Amerigo Vespucci — see VESPUCCI

Am·herst \\'am-(,)ərst\\ Jeffrey 1717–1797 *Baron Amherst* British general in America

Amund·sen \\'äm-ən-sən\\ Roald 1872–1928 Norwegian explorer and discoverer of the South Pole (1911)

An·a·ni·as \\,an-ə-'nī-əs\\ early Christian struck dead for lying

An·der·sen \\'an-dər-sən\\ Hans Christian 1805–1875 Danish writer of fairy tales

An·der·son \\'an-dər-sən\\ Marian 1897–1993 American contralto

Anne \\'an\\ 1665–1714 queen of Great Britain (1702–14)

An·tho·ny \\'an(t)-thə-nē\\ Susan Brownell 1820–1906 American suffragist

An·tig·o·ne \\an-'tig-ə-nē\\ daughter of Oedipus and Jocasta in Greek mythology

An·to·ni·us \\an-'tō-nē-əs\\ Marcus *about* 82–30 B.C. *Mark* or *Marc An·to·ny* or *An·tho·ny* \\'an(t)-thə-nē, *chiefly British* 'an-tə-nē\\ Roman general

Aph·ro·di·te \\,af-rə-'dīt-ē\\ goddess of love and beauty in Greek mythology — compare VENUS

Apol·lo \\ə-'päl-ō\\ god of sunlight, prophecy, music, and poetry in Greek and Roman mythology

Aqui·nas \\ə-'kwī-nəs\\ Saint Thomas 1224 (or 1225)–1274 Italian theologian

Ar·chi·me·des \\,är-kə-'mēd-ēz\\ *about* 287–212 B.C. Greek mathematician

Ares \\'a(ə)r-ēz, 'e(ə)r-\\ god of war in Greek mythology — compare MARS

Ar·is·toph·a·nes \\,ar-ə-'stäf-ə-,nēz\\ *about* 450– *about* 388 B.C. Greek dramatist

Ar·is·tot·le \\'ar-ə-,stät-ᵊl\\ 384–322 B.C. Greek philosopher

Arm·strong \\'ärm-,strȯŋ\\ Louis 1901–1971 *Satch·mo* \\'sach-,mō\\ American jazz musician

Armstrong Neil Alden 1930– American astronaut and first man on the moon (1969)

Ar·nold \\'ärn-ᵊld\\ Benedict 1741–1801 American Revolutionary general and traitor

Ar·te·mis \\'ärt-ə-məs\\ goddess of the moon, wild animals, and hunting in Greek mythology — compare DIANA

Ar·thur \\'är-thər\\ legendary king of the Britons whose story is based on traditions of a 6th century military leader — **Ar·thu·ri·an** \\är-'th(y)ùr-ē-ən\\ *adj*

Arthur Chester Alan 1829–1886 21st president of the U.S. (1881–85)

As·cle·pi·us \\ə-'sklē-pē-əs\\ god of medicine in Greek my-

\\ə\\ abut	\\au̇\\ out	\\i\\ tip	\\ȯ\\ saw	\\u̇\\ foot
\\ər\\ further	\\ch\\ chin	\\ī\\ life	\\ȯi\\ coin	\\y\\ yet
\\a\\ mat	\\e\\ pet	\\j\\ job	\\th\\ thin	\\yü\\ few
\\ā\\ take	\\ē\\ easy	\\ŋ\\ sing	\\th\\ this	\\yu̇\\ cure
\\ä\\ cot, cart	\\g\\ go	\\ō\\ bone	\\ü\\ food	\\zh\\ vision

thology — compare AESCULAPIUS

As·tor \'as-tər\ John Jacob 1763–1848 American (German-born) fur trader and capitalist

Athe·na \ə-'thē-nə\ *or* **Athe·ne** \-nē\ goddess of wisdom in Greek mythology — compare MINERVA

At·las \'at-ləs\ Titan in Greek mythology forced to bear the heavens on his shoulders

At·ti·la \ə-'til-ə, 'at-ºl-ə\ 406?–453 A.D. *the Scourge of God* king of the Huns

At·tucks \'at-əks\ Crispus 1723?–1770 American patriot; one of five men killed in Boston Massacre

Au·du·bon \'òd-ə-,bän, -bən\ John James 1785–1851 American (Haitian-born) artist and naturalist

Au·gus·tine \'ò-gə-,stēn; ò-'gəs-tən, ə-\ Saint 354–430 A.D. church father; bishop of Hippo (396–430)

Au·gus·tus \ò-'gəs-təs, ə-\ *or* **Augustus Caesar** *or* **Oc·ta·vi·an** \äk-'tā-vē-ən\ 63 B.C.–14 A.D. 1st Roman emperor (27 B.C.–14 A.D.)

Aus·ten \'òs-tən, 'äs-\ Jane 1775–1817 English author

Bac·chus \'bak-əs\ — see DIONYSUS

Bach \'bäk̠, 'bäk\ Johann Sebastian 1685–1750 German composer and organist

Ba·con \'bā-kən\ Francis 1561–1626 English philosopher and author

Ba·den-Pow·ell \,bād-ºn-'pō-əl\ Robert Stephenson Smyth 1857–1941 English founder of Boy Scout movement

Baf·fin \'baf-ən\ William *about* 1584–1622 English navigator

Bal·boa, de \bal-'bō-ə\ Vasco Núñez 1475–1519 Spanish explorer and discoverer of Pacific Ocean (1513)

Bal·ti·more \'bòl-tə-,mō(ə)r, -,mò(ə)r\ Lord — see George CALVERT

Bal·zac, de \'bòl-,zak, 'bal-\ Honoré 1799–1850 French author

Ba·rab·bas \bə-'rab-əs\ prisoner released in preference to Jesus at the demand of the multitude

Bar·num \'bär-nəm\ Phineas Taylor 1810–1891 American show-business manager

Bar·rie \'bar-ē\ Sir James Matthew 1860–1937 Scottish author

Bar·thol·di \bär-'täl-dē, -'tòl-, -'thäl-, -'thòl-\ Frédéric² Auguste 1834–1904 French sculptor who designed the Statue of Liberty

Bar·ton \'bärt-ºn\ Clara 1821–1912 founder of American Red Cross Society

Beau·re·gard \'bōr-ə-,gärd, 'bòr-\ Pierre Gustave Toutant 1818–1893 American Confederate general

Beck·et, à \ə-'bek-ət, ä-\ Saint Thomas *about* 1118–1170 archbishop of Canterbury (1162–1170)

Bee·tho·ven \'bā-,tō-vən\ Ludwig van 1770–1827 German composer

Bell \'bel\ Alexander Graham 1847–1922 American (Scottish-born) inventor of the telephone

Ben·e·dict \'ben-ə-,dikt\ name of 15 popes: especially **XIV** (*Prospero Lambertini*) 1675–1758 (pope 1740–58); **XV** (*Giacomo della Chiesa*) 1854–1922 (pope 1914–22)

Be·nét \bə-'nā\ Stephen Vincent 1898–1943 American author

Ben·ja·min \'benj-(ə-)mən\ youngest son of Jacob and ancestor of one of the 12 tribes of Israel in the Bible

Ben·ton \'bent-ºn\ Thomas Hart 1889–1975 American painter

Be·o·wulf \'bā-ə-,wùlf\ legendary warrior and hero of the Old English poem *Beowulf*

Be·ring \'bi(ə)r-iŋ, 'be(ə)r-\ Vitus 1681–1741 Danish navigator; discovered Bering strait and Bering sea

Ber·lin \(,)bər-'lin\ Irving 1888–1989 American (Russianborn) composer

Ber·ni·ni \bər-'nē-nē\ Gian Lorenzo 1598–1680 Italian sculptor, architect, and painter

Bes·se·mer \'bes-ə-mər\ Sir Henry 1813–1898 English engineer and inventor

Be·thune \bə-'th(y)ün\ Mary 1875–1955 *née McLeod* American educator

Bi·zet \bē-'zā\ Alexandre-César-Léopold 1838–1875 called *Georges* French composer

Black Hawk \'blak-,hòk\ 1767–1838 American Indian chief

Black·well \'blak-,wel, -wəl\ Elizabeth 1821–1910 American (English-born) physician

Blake \'blāk\ William 1757–1827 English poet and artist

Bloom·er \'blü-mər\ Amelia Jenks 1818–1894 American social reformer

Boc·cac·cio \bō-'käch-(ē-,)ō\ Giovanni 1313–1375 Italian author

Bohr \'bō(ə)r, 'bò(ə)r\ Niels 1885–1962 Danish physicist

Bo·leyn \bù-'lin, 'bùl-ən\ Anne 1507?–1536 2d wife of Henry VIII and mother of Elizabeth I of England

Bo·lí·var Si·món \sē-,mōn-bə-'lē-,vär, ,sī-mən-'bäl-ə-vər\ 1783–1830 South American liberator

Bon·i·face \'bän-ə-fəs, -,fās\ name of nine popes: especially **VIII** (*Benedetto Caetani*) about 1235 (or 1240)–1303 (pope 1294–1303)

Boone \'bün\ Daniel 1734–1820 American pioneer

Booth \'büth\ John Wilkes 1838–1865 assassin of Abraham Lincoln

Bo·re·as \'bōr-ē-əs, 'bòr-\ god of the north wind in Greek mythology

Bot·ti·cel·li \,bät-ə-'chel-ē\ Sandro 1445–1510 Italian painter

Bow·ie \'bü-ē, 'bō-\ James 1796–1836 hero of Texas revolution

Boyle \'bòi(ə)l\ Robert 1627–1691 English physicist and chemist

Brad·bury \'brad-,ber-ē, -b(ə-)rē\ Ray Douglas 1920– American author

Brad·dock \'brad-ək\ Edward 1695–1755 British general in America

Brad·ford \'brad-fərd\ William 1590–1657 Pilgrim leader

Brad·street \'brad-,strēt\ Anne *about* 1612–1672 American poet

Bra·dy \'brād-ē\ Mathew B. 1823?–1896 American photographer

Brah·ma \'bräm-ə\ creator god of the Hindu sacred triad — compare SIVA, VISHNU

Brahms \'brämz\ Johannes 1833–1897 German composer

Braille \'brā(ə)l, 'brī\ Louis 1809–1852 French blind teacher of the blind

Braun \'braùn\ Wernher von 1912–1977 American (German-born) engineer

Brezh·nev \'brezh-,nef\ Leonid Ilyich 1906–1982 Russian politician; 1st secretary of Communist party (1964–82); president of the U.S.S.R. (1960–64; 1977–82)

Brid·ger \'brij-ər\ James 1804–1881 American pioneer and scout

Bron·të \'bränt-ē, 'brän-,tā\ family of English writers: Charlotte 1816–1855 and her sisters Emily 1818–1848 and Anne 1820–1849

Brooks \'brùks\ Gwendolyn Elizabeth 1917– American poet

Brown \'braùn\ John *Old Brown of Osa·wat·o·mie* \,ō-sə-'wät-ə-mē\ 1800–1859 American abolitionist

Brow·ning \'braù-niŋ\ Elizabeth Barrett 1806–1861 English poet; wife of Robert

Browning Robert 1812–1889 English poet; husband of Elizabeth

Bru·tus \'brüt-əs\ Marcus Junius 85–42 B.C. Roman politician; one of Julius Caesar's assassins

Bry·an \'brī-ən\ William Jennings 1860–1925 American lawyer and politician

Bu·chan·an \byü-'kan-ən, bə-\ James 1791–1868 15th president of the U.S. (1857–61)

Buck \'bək\ Pearl 1892–1973 American author; Nobel Prize winner (1938)

Buddha — see GAUTAMA BUDDHA

Buffalo Bill — see William Frederick CODY

Bun·yan \'bən-yən\ John 1628–1688 English preacher and author

Bur·bank \'bər-,baŋk\ Luther 1849–1926 American horticulturist

Bur·goyne \(,)bər-'gȯin, 'bər-,gȯin\ John 1722–1792 British general in America

Burns \'bərnz\ Robert 1759–1796 Scottish poet

Burn·side \'bərn-,sīd\ Ambrose Everett 1824–1881 American general

Burr \'bər\ Aaron 1756–1836 vice president of the U.S. (1801–05)

Bush \'bush\ George Herbert Walker 1924–   41st president of the U.S. (1989–93)

By·ron \'bī-rən\ Lord 1788–1824 *George Gordon Byron* English poet

Cab·ot \'kab-ət\ John *about* 1450–*about* 1499 Italian navigator; explored coast of North America for England

Cabot Sebastian 1476?–1557 English navigator; son of John Cabot

Ca·bri·ni \kə-'brē-nē\ Saint Frances Xavier 1850–1917 *Mother Cabrini* first American (Italian-born) saint (1946)

Cae·sar \'sē-zər\ Gaius Julius 100–44 B.C. Roman general, political leader, and writer

Cain \'kān\ brother of Abel in the Bible

Cal·houn \kal-'hün\ John Caldwell 1782–1850 vice president of the U.S. (1825–32)

Ca·lig·u·la \kə-'lig-yə-lə\ 12–41 A.D. *Gaius Caesar* Roman emperor (37–41)

Cal·li·ope \kə-'lī-ə-,pē\ muse of heroic poetry in Greek mythology

Cal·vert \'kal-vərt\ George 1580?–1632 1st Baron *Baltimore* English colonist in America

Cal·vin \'kal-vən\ John 1509–1564 French theologian and reformer

Ca·nute \kə-'n(y)üt\ *died* 1035 *the Great* king of England (1016–35); of Denmark (1018–35); of Norway (1028–35)

Car·ne·gie \'kär-nə-gē, kär-'neg-ē\ Andrew 1835–1919 American (Scottish-born) industrialist and philanthropist

Carroll Lewis — see Charles Lutwidge DODGSON

Car·son \'kärs-ᵊn\ Christopher 1809–1868 *Kit* American soldier and guide

Carson Rachel Louise 1907–1964 American scientist

Car·ter \'kärt-ər\ James Earl, Jr. 1924–   *Jimmy* 39th president of the U.S. (1977–81)

Car·tier \kär-'tyā, 'kärt-ē-,ā\ Jacques 1491–1557 French navigator; discovered Saint Lawrence river

Ca·ru·so \kə-'rü-sō, -zō\ En·ri·co \en-'rē-kō\ 1873–1921 Italian tenor

Car·ver \'kär-vər\ George Washington *about* 1864–1943 American botanist

Ca·sa·no·va \,kaz-ə-'nō-və, ,kas-\ Giovanni Giacomo 1725–1798 Italian adventurer

Cas·san·dra \kə-'san-drə\ daughter of Priam in Greek mythology who is endowed with the gift of prophecy but fated never to be believed

Cas·satt \kə-'sat\ Mary 1845–1926 American painter

Cas·tro \'kas-trō, 'käs-\ **(Ruz)** \'rüs\ Fi·del \fē-'del\ 1926–   Cuban premier (1959–   )

Cath·er \'kath-ər\ Willa Sibert 1873–1947 American author

Cath·er·ine \'kath-(ə-)rən\ name of 1st, 5th, and 6th wives of Henry VIII of England: Catherine of Aragon 1485–1536; Catherine Howard 1520?–1542; Catherine Parr 1512–1548

Catherine I 1684–1727 wife of Peter the Great; empress of Russia (1725–27)

Catherine II 1729–1796 *the Great* empress of Russia (1762–96)

Cav·en·dish \'kav-ən-(,)dish\ Henry 1731–1810 English scientist

Ce·ci·lia \sə-'sēl-yə, -'sil-\ Saint 2d or 3d century A.D. Roman martyr; patron saint of music

Ce·res \'si(ə)r-,ēz\ the goddess of agriculture in Roman mythology — compare DEMETER

Cer·van·tes \sər-'van-,tēz\ Miguel de 1547–1616 Spanish author

Cé·zanne \sā-'zan\ Paul 1839–1906 French painter

Cha·gall \shə-'gäl, -'gal\ Marc 1887–1985 Russian painter

Cham·plain \(')sham-'plān\ Samuel de *about* 1567–1635 French explorer in America; founder of Quebec

Chap·lin \'chap-lən\ Sir Charles Spencer 1889–1977 British actor and producer

Chap·man \'chap-mən\ John 1774–1845 *Johnny Ap·ple·seed* \'ap-əl-,sēd\ American pioneer

Char·le·magne \'shär-lə-,mān\ 742–814 A.D. *Charles the Great* or *Charles I* Frankish king (768–814); emperor of the West (800–814)

Charles \'chär(-ə)lz\ name of 10 kings of France: especially **I** 823–877 A.D. (reigned 840–77) *the Bald*; Holy Roman emperor as *Charles II* (875–77); **IV** 1294–1328 (reigned 1322–28) *the Fair*; **V** 1337–1380 (reigned 1364–80) *the Wise*; **VI** 1368–1422 (reigned 1380–1422) *the Mad* or *the Beloved*; **VII** 1403–1461 (reigned 1422–61) *the Victorious*; **IX** 1550–1574 (reigned 1560–74); **X** 1757–1836 (reigned 1824–30)

Charles name of two kings of Great Britain: **I** 1600–1649 (reigned 1625–49) *Charles Stuart;* **II** 1630–1685 (reigned 1660–85) son of Charles I

Charles V 1500–1558 Holy Roman emperor (1519–56); king of Spain as *Charles I* (1516–56)

Charles Edward Stuart 1720–1788 *the Young Pretender; (Bonnie) Prince Charlie* English prince

Charles Mar·tel \mär-'tel\ *about* 688–741 A.D. Frankish ruler (719–41); grandfather of Charlemagne

Cha·ryb·dis \kə-'rib-dəs, shə-, chə-\ a whirlpool off the coast of Sicily personified in Greek mythology as a female monster

Chau·cer \'chȯ-sər\ Geoffrey *about* 1342–1400 English poet

Che·khov \'chek-,ȯf, -,ȯv\ Anton Pavlovich 1860–1904 Russian author

Cheops — see KHUFU

Ches·ter·ton \'ches-tərt-ᵊn\ Gilbert Keith 1874–1936 English author

Cho·pin \'shō-,pan\ Frédéric François 1810–1849 Polish pianist and composer

Chou En-lai \'jō-'en-'lī\ 1898–1976 Chinese Communist politician; premier (1949–76)

Christ Jesus — see JESUS

Chris·tie \'kris-tē\ Agatha 1890–1976 English author

Chur·chill \'chər-,chil, 'chərch-,hil\ Sir Winston Leonard Spencer 1874–1965 British prime minister (1940–45; 1951–55)

Clark \'klärk\ George Rogers 1752–1818 American soldier and pioneer

Clark William 1770–1838 American explorer

Clay \'klā\ Henry 1777–1852 American politician and orator

Clem·ens \'klem-ənz\ Samuel Langhorne 1835–1910 pseudonym *Mark Twain* \'twān\ American author

Cle·o·pa·tra \,klē-ə-'pa-trə, -'pā-, -'pä-\ 69–30 B.C. queen of Egypt (51–30)

Cleve·land \'klēv-lənd\ (Stephen) Grover 1837–1908 22d and 24th president of the U.S. (1885–89; 1893–97)

Clin·ton \'klin-tᵊn\ William Jefferson 1946–   42d president of the U.S. (1993–   )

Cly·tem·nes·tra \,klīt-əm-'nes-trə\ wife of Agamemnon in Greek mythology

\ə\ **abut**	\aủ\ **out**	\i\ **tip**	\ȯ\ **saw**	\ủ\ **foot**
\ər\ **further**	\ch\ **chin**	\ī\ **life**	\ȯi\ **coin**	\y\ **yet**
\a\ **mat**	\e\ **pet**	\j\ **job**	\th\ **thin**	\yü\ **few**
\ā\ **take**	\ē\ **easy**	\ŋ\ **sing**	\th\ **this**	\yủ\ **cure**
\ä\ **cot, cart**	\g\ **go**	\ō\ **bone**	\ü\ **food**	\zh\ **vision**

Cobb \\'käb\\ Tyrus Raymond 1886–1961 *Ty* American baseball player

Co·chise \\kō-'chēs\\ 1812?–1874 Apache Indian chief

Co·dy \\'kōd-ē\\ William Frederick 1846–1917 *Buffalo Bill* American hunter, guide, and entertainer

Co·han \\'kō-,han\\ George Michael 1878–1942 American actor and composer

Cole·ridge \\'kōl-rij, 'kō-lə-rij\\ Samuel Taylor 1772–1834 English poet

Co·lette \\kò-'let\\ Sidonie-Gabrielle 1873–1954 French author

Co·lum·bus \\kə-'ləm-bəs\\ Christopher 1451–1506 Italian navigator; discovered America for Spain (1492)

Con·fu·cius \\kən-'fyü-shəs\\ 551–479 B.C. Chinese philosopher

Con·rad \\'kän-,rad\\ Joseph 1857–1924 British (Ukrainian-born of Polish parents) author

Con·sta·ble \\'kən(t)-stə-bəl, 'kän(t)-\\ John 1776–1837 English painter

Con·stan·tine \\'kän(t)-stən-,tēn, -,tīn\\ *died* 337 A.D. *the Great* Roman emperor (306–37)

Cook \\'kủk\\ Captain James 1728–1779 English navigator

Coo·lidge \\'kü-lij\\ (John) Calvin 1872–1933 30th president of the U.S. (1923–29)

Coo·per \\'kü-pər, 'kủp-ər\\ James Fen·i·more \\'fen-ə-,mō(ə)r, -,mò(ə)r\\ 1789–1851 American author

Co·per·ni·cus \\kō-'pər-ni-kəs\\ Nicolaus 1473–1543 Polish astronomer

Cop·land \\'kō-plənd\\ Aaron 1900–1990 American composer

Cop·ley \\'käp-lē\\ John Sin·gle·ton \\'siŋ-gəl-tən\\ 1738–1815 American portrait painter

Corn·wal·lis \\kòrn-'wäl-əs\\ 1st Marquis 1738–1805 *Charles Cornwallis* British general in America

Co·ro·na·do \\,kòr-ə-'näd-ō, ,kär-\\ Francisco Vásquez de *about* 1510–1554 Spanish explorer of southwestern U.S.

Cor·tés \\kòr-'tez, 'kòr-,tez\\ Hernán *or* Hernando 1485–1547 Spanish conqueror of Mexico

Cous·teau \\kü-'stō\\ Jacques-Yves 1910– French marine explorer

Crane \\'krān\\ Stephen 1871–1900 American author

Crazy Horse \\'krā-zē-,hòrs\\ 1842–1877 Sioux Indian chief

Crock·ett \\'kräk-ət\\ David 1786–1836 *Davy* American pioneer

Crom·well \\'kräm-,wel, 'krəm-, -wəl\\ Oliver 1599–1658 English general and political leader; lord protector of England (1653–58)

Cro·nus \\'krō-nəs, 'krän-əs\\ a Titan in Greek mythology overthrown by his son Zeus

Cum·mings \\'kəm-inz\\ Edward Estlin 1894–1962 known as *e. e. cummings* American poet

Cu·pid \\'kyü-pəd\\ god of love in Roman mythology — compare EROS

Cu·rie \\kyủ-'rē, 'kyủ(ə)r-ē\\ Marie 1867–1934 French (Polish-born) chemist; Nobel Prize winner (1903, 1911)

Curie Pierre 1859–1906 French chemist; Nobel Prize winner (1903)

Cus·ter \\'kəs-tər\\ George Armstrong 1839–1876 American general

Cy·ra·no de Ber·ge·rac \\,sir-ə-,nō-də-'ber-zhə-,rak\\ Savinien de 1619–1655 French poet and soldier

Dae·da·lus \\'ded-ᵊl-əs, 'dēd-\\ builder in Greek mythology of the Cretan labyrinth and inventor of wings by which he and his son Icarus escape from it

Dal·ton \\'dòlt-ᵊn\\ John 1766–1844 English chemist and physicist

Da·na \\'dā-nə\\ Richard Henry 1815–1882 American author

Dan·iel \\'dan-yəl\\ a prophet in the Bible who is held captive in Babylon and delivered by God from a den of lions

Dan·te \\'dän-tā, 'dan-, -tē\\ 1265–1321 Italian poet

Dare \\'da(ə)r, 'de(ə)r\\ Virginia 1587–? first child born in America of English parents

Da·ri·us I \\də-'rī-əs\\ 550–486 B.C. *the Great* king of Persia (522–486)

Dar·row \\'dar-ō\\ Clarence Seward 1857–1938 American lawyer

Dar·win \\'där-wən\\ Charles Robert 1809–1882 English naturalist

Da·vid \\'dā-vəd\\ a youth in the Bible who slays Goliath and succeeds Saul as king of Israel

Da·vis \\'dā-vəs\\ Jefferson 1808–1889 president of the Confederate States of America (1861–65)

Dawes \\'dòz\\ William 1745–1799 American patriot

Debs \\'debz\\ Eugene Victor 1855–1926 American socialist

De·bus·sy \\,deb-yủ-'sē, ,däb-; də-'byü-sē\\ (Achille-) Claude 1862–1918 French composer

De·ca·tur \\di-'kāt-ər\\ Stephen 1779–1820 American naval officer

De·foe \\di-'fō\\ Daniel 1660–1731 English author

De·gas \\də-'gä\\ (Hilaire-Germain-) Edgar 1834–1917 French painter

de Gaulle \\di-'gōl, -'gòl\\ Charles-André-Joseph-Marie 1890–1970 French general; president of Fifth Republic (1958–69)

De·li·lah \\di-'lī-lə\\ mistress and betrayer of Samson in the Bible

De·me·ter \\di-'mēt-ər\\ goddess of agriculture in Greek mythology — compare CERES

de Mille \\də-'mil\\ Agnes George 1909?– American dancer and choreographer

Des·cartes \\dā-'kärt\\ René 1596–1650 French mathematician and philosopher

de So·to \\di-'sōt-ō\\ Hernando 1496 (or 1499 or 1500)–1542 Spanish explorer in America

Dew·ey \\'d(y)ü-ē\\ George 1837–1917 American admiral

Dewey John 1859–1952 American philosopher and educator

Dewey Melvil 1851–1931 American librarian

Di·ana \\dī-'an-ə\\ goddess of the forest and of childbirth in ancient Italian mythology who was identified with Artemis by the Romans

Dick·ens \\'dik-ənz\\ Charles John Huffam 1812–1870 pseudonym *Boz* \\'bäz, 'bōz\\ English author

Dick·in·son \\'dik-ən-sən\\ Emily Elizabeth 1830–1886 American poet

Di·do \\'dīd-ō\\ legendary queen of Carthage who falls in love with Aeneas and kills herself when he leaves her

Di·o·ny·sus \\,dī-ə-'nī-səs, -'nē-\\ god of wine and ecstasy in Greek mythology — **Di·o·ny·sian** \\dī-ə-'nizh-ē-ən\\ *adj*

Dis·ney \\'diz-nē\\ Walter Elias 1901–1966 American film producer

Dis·rae·li \\diz-'rā-lē\\ Benjamin 1804–1881 1st Earl of *Bea·cons·field* \\'bē-kənz-,fēld\\ British prime minister (1868; 1874–80)

Dix \\'diks\\ Dorothea Lynde 1802–1887 American social reformer

Dodg·son \\'däj-sən, 'däd-\\ Charles Lut·widge \\'lət-wij\\ 1832–1898 pseudonym *Lewis Car·roll* \\'kar-əl\\ English author and mathematician

Donne \\'dən\\ John 1572–1631 English poet and minister

Don Qui·xote \\,dän-kē-'(h)ōt-ē, ,däŋ-; dän-'kwik-sət\\ the idealistic and impractical hero of Cervantes' *Don Quixote*

Dos·to·yev·ski \\,däs-tə-'yef-skē, -'yev-\\ Fyodor Mikhaylovich 1821–1881 Russian novelist

Doug·las \\'dəg-ləs\\ Stephen Arnold 1813–1861 American politician

Doug·lass \\'dəg-ləs\\ Frederick 1817–1895 American abolitionist

Doyle \\'dòi(ə)l\\ Sir Arthur Co·nan \\'kō-nən\\ 1859–1930 British physician, novelist, and detective-story writer

Drake \\'drāk\\ Sir Francis 1540 (or 1543)–1596 English navigator and admiral

Drei·ser \\'drī-sər, -zər\\ Theodore 1871–1945 American author

Du Bois \\d(y)ü-'bòis\\ William Edward Burghardt 1868–1963 American educator and writer

Du·mas \d(y)ü-ˈmä, ˈd(y)ü-ˌmä\ Alexandre 1802–1870 *Dumas père* \ˈpe(ə)r\ French author

Dumas Alexandre 1824–1895 *Dumas fils* \ˈfēs\ French author

Dun·can \ˈdəŋ-kən\ Isadora 1877–1927 American dancer

Dü·rer \ˈd(y)ùr-ər\ Albrecht 1471–1528 German painter and engraver

Ea·kins \ˈā-kənz\ Thomas 1843–1916 American artist

Ear·hart \ˈe(ə)r-ˌhärt, ˈi(ə)r-\ Amelia 1897–1937 American aviator

Ed·dy \ˈed-ē\ Mary Baker 1821–1910 American founder of the Christian Science Church

Ed·i·son \ˈed-ə-sən\ Thomas Alva 1847–1931 American inventor

Ed·ward \ˈed-wərd\ name of eight post-Norman kings of England: **I** 1239–1307 (reigned 1272–1307) *Longshanks;* **II** 1284–1327 (reigned 1307–27); **III** 1312–1377 (reigned 1327–77); **IV** 1442–1483 (reigned 1461–70; 1471–83); **V** 1470–1483 (reigned 1483); **VI** 1537–1553 (reigned 1547–53) son of Henry VIII and Jane Seymour; **VII** 1841–1910 (reigned 1901–10) *Albert Edward* son of Queen Victoria; **VIII** 1894–1972 (reigned 1936; abdicated) *Duke of Windsor* son of George V

Ein·stein \ˈīn-ˌstīn\ Albert 1879–1955 American (German-born) physicist; Nobel Prize winner (1921)

Ei·sen·how·er \ˈīz-ᵊn-ˌhaù(-ə)r\ Dwight David 1890–1969 American general; 34th president of the U.S. (1953–61)

Elec·tra \i-ˈlek-trə\ sister of Orestes in Greek mythology who with her brother avenges their father's murder

Eli·jah \i-ˈlī-jə\ Hebrew prophet of the 9th century B.C.

El·i·ot \ˈel-ē-ət, ˈel-yət\ George 1819–1880 pseudonym of *Mary Ann Evans* English author

Eliot Thomas Stearns 1888–1965 British (American-born) poet and critic

Eliz·a·beth I \i-ˈliz-ə-bəth\ 1533–1603 daughter of Henry VIII and Anne Boleyn; queen of England (1558–1603)

Elizabeth II 1926– queen of the United Kingdom (1952–)

Em·er·son \ˈem-ər-sən\ Ralph Waldo 1803–1882 American essayist and poet

En·dym·i·on \en-ˈdim-ē-ən\ beautiful youth in Greek mythology loved by the goddess of the moon

Ep·i·cu·rus \ˌep-i-ˈkyùr-əs\ 341–270 B.C. Greek philosopher

Er·ik \ˈer-ik\ *the Red* 10th century Norwegian navigator; explored Greenland coast

Eriksson Leif — see LEIF ERIKSSON

Eros \ˈe(ə)r-ˌäs, ˈi(ə)r-\ god of love in Greek mythology — compare CUPID

Esau \ˈē-(ˌ)sò\ son of Isaac and Rebekah and elder twin brother of Jacob in the Bible

Es·ther \ˈes-tər\ Hebrew woman in the Bible who as the queen of Persia delivers her people from destruction

Eu·clid \ˈyü-kləd\ *flourished about* 300 B.C. Greek mathematician

Eu·rip·i·des \yù-ˈrip-ə-ˌdēz\ *about* 484–406 B.C. Greek dramatist

Eu·ro·pa \yù-ˈrō-pə\ a princess in Greek mythology who was carried off by Zeus disguised as a white bull

Eu·ryd·i·ce \yù-ˈrid-ə-sē\ the wife of Orpheus whom he attempts to bring back from Hades

Eve \ˈēv\ the first woman in the Bible

Eze·kiel \i-ˈzē-kyəl, -kē-əl\ Hebrew prophet of the 6th century B.C.

Fahr·en·heit \ˈfar-ən-ˌhīt, ˈfär-\ Daniel Gabriel 1686–1736 German physicist

Far·a·day \ˈfar-ə-ˌdā, -əd-ē\ Michael 1791–1867 English chemist and physicist

Far·ra·gut \ˈfar-ə-gət\ David Glasgow 1801–1870 American admiral

Faulk·ner \ˈfòk-nər\ William 1897–1962 American author; Nobel Prize winner (1949)

Faust \ˈfaùst\ *or* **Fau·stus** \ˈfaù-stəs, ˈfò-\ a legendary German magician who sells his soul to the devil

Fawkes \ˈfòks\ Guy 1570–1606 English conspirator

Fer·di·nand \ˈfərd-ᵊn-ˌand\ **II** of Aragon *or* **V** of Castile 1452–1516 *the Catholic* king of Castile (1474–1504); of Aragon (1479–1516); of Naples (1504–16); founder of the Spanish monarchy

Fer·mi \ˈfe(ə)r-mē\ Enrico 1901–1954 American (Italian-born) physicist; Nobel Prize winner (1938)

Fiel·ding \ˈfē(ə)l-diŋ\ Henry 1707–1754 English author

Fill·more \ˈfil-ˌmō(ə)r, -ˌmò(ə)r\ Millard 1800–1874 13th president of the U.S. (1850–53)

Fitz·ger·ald \fits-ˈjer-əld\ Francis Scott Key 1896–1940 American author

Flem·ing \ˈflem-iŋ\ Sir Alexander 1881–1955 British bacteriologist; Nobel Prize winner (1945)

Flo·ra \ˈflōr-ə, ˈflòr-\ goddess of flowers in Roman mythology

Flying Dutchman legendary Dutch mariner condemned to sail the seas until Judgment Day

Ford \ˈfō(ə)rd, ˈfò(ə)rd\ Gerald Rudolph 1913– 38th president of the U.S. (1974–77)

Ford Henry 1863–1947 American automobile manufacturer

Fos·ter \ˈfòs-tər, ˈfäs-\ Stephen Collins 1826–1864 American songwriter

Francis \ˈfran(t)-səs\ **of As·si·si** \ə-ˈsis-ē, -ˈsē-zē, -ˈsē-sē, -ˈsiz-ē\ Saint 1181 (or 1182)–1226 Italian friar; founder of Franciscan order

Frank·lin \ˈfraŋ-klən\ Benjamin 1706–1790 American patriot, author, and inventor

Fred·er·ick I \ˈfred-(ə-)rik\ *about* 1123–1190 *Frederick Bar·ba·ros·sa* \ˌbär-bə-ˈräs-ə, -ˈròs-\ Holy Roman emperor (1152–90)

Frederick II 1712–1786 *the Great* king of Prussia (1740–86)

Fré·mont \ˈfrē-ˌmänt\ John Charles 1813–1890 American general and explorer

French \ˈfrench\ Daniel Chester 1850–1931 American sculptor

Freud \ˈfròid\ Sigmund 1856–1939 Austrian neurologist; founder of psychoanalysis

Frig·ga \ˈfrig-ə\ wife of Odin and goddess of married love and the hearth in Norse mythology

Frost \ˈfròst\ Robert Lee 1874–1963 American poet

Ful·ler \ˈfùl-ər\ (Richard) Buckminster 1895–1983 American engineer

Fuller (Sarah) Margaret 1810–1850 American author and reformer

Ful·ton \ˈfùlt-ᵊn\ Robert 1765–1815 American inventor

Ga·bri·el \ˈgā-brē-əl\ one of the four archangels named in Hebrew tradition — compare MICHAEL, RAPHAEL, URIEL

Ga·ga·rin \gə-ˈgär-ən\ Yu·ry \ˈyù(ə)r-ē\ Alekseyevich 1934–1968 Russian astronaut; first man in space

Gage \ˈgāj\ Thomas 1721–1787 British general in America

Gal·a·had \ˈgal-ə-ˌhad\ knight of the Round Table who finds the Holy Grail

Gal·a·tea \ˌgal-ə-ˈtē-ə\ a female figure sculpted by Pygmalion in Greek mythology and given life by Aphrodite in answer to the sculptor's prayer

Ga·len \ˈgā-lən\ 129–*about* 199 A.D. Greek physician and writer

Ga·li·lei \ˌgal-ə-ˈlā-ˌē\ Ga·li·leo \ˌgal-ə-ˈlē-ō, -ˈlā-\ 1564–1642 usually called *Galileo* Italian astronomer and physicist — **Gal·i·le·an** \ˌgal-ə-ˈlē-ən\ *adj*

Gall \ˈgòl\ 1840?–1894 Sioux Indian leader

Ga·ma, da \ˈgam-ə, ˈgäm-\ Vasco *about* 1460–1524 Portuguese navigator

\ə\ **abut**	\aù\ **out**	\i\ **tip**	\ò\ **saw**	\ù\ **foot**
\ər\ **further**	\ch\ **chin**	\ī\ **life**	\òi\ **coin**	\y\ **yet**
\a\ **mat**	\e\ **pet**	\j\ **job**	\th\ **thin**	\yü\ **few**
\ā\ **take**	\ē\ **easy**	\ŋ\ **sing**	\th\ **this**	\yù\ **cure**
\ä\ **cot, cart**	\g\ **go**	\ō\ **bone**	\ü\ **food**	\zh\ **vision**

Gan·dhi \'gän-dē, 'gan-\ Mohandas Karamchand 1869–1948 *Ma·hat·ma* \mə-'hät-mə, -'hat-\ Indian leader

Gar·field \'gär-ˌfēld\ James Abram 1831–1881 20th president of the U.S. (1881)

Gar·i·bal·di \ˌgar-ə-'bȯl-dē\ Giuseppe 1807–1882 Italian patriot

Gar·ri·son \'gar-ə-sən\ William Lloyd 1805–1879 American abolitionist

Gau·guin \gō-'gan\ (Eugène-Henri-) Paul 1848–1903 French painter

Gau·ta·ma Bud·dha \ˌgauṫ-ə-mə-'büd-ə, -'bu̇d-\ *about* 563–*about* 483 B.C. *The Buddha* Indian philosopher; founder of Buddhism

Gen·ghis Khan \ˌjeŋ-gə-'skän, ˌgeŋ-\ *about* 1162–1227 Mongol conqueror

George \'jȯ(ə)rj\ name of six kings of Great Britain: **I** 1660–1727 (reigned 1714–27); **II** 1683–1760 (reigned 1727–60); **III** 1738–1820 (reigned 1760–1820); **IV** 1762–1830 (reigned 1820–30); **V** 1865–1936 (reigned 1910–36); **VI** 1895–1952 (reigned 1936–52)

Ge·ron·i·mo \jə-'rän-ə-ˌmō\ 1829–1909 Apache Indian leader

Gersh·win \'gərsh-wən\ George 1898–1937 American composer

Gid·e·on \'gid-ē-ən\ Hebrew hero in the Bible

Gil·bert \'gil-bərt\ Sir William Schwenck 1836–1911 English librettist and poet; collaborator with Sir Arthur Sullivan

Glad·stone \'glad-ˌstōn, *chiefly British* -stən\ William Ewart 1809–1898 British prime minister (1868–74; 1880–85; 1886; 1892–94)

Glenn \'glen\ John Herschel 1921– American astronaut and politician; first American to orbit the earth (1962)

Go·di·va \gə-'dī-və\ an English gentlewoman who in legend rode naked through Coventry to save its citizens from a tax

Goe·thals \'gō-thəlz\ George Washington 1858–1928 American general and engineer

Goe·the \'gə(r)-tə\ Johann Wolfgang von 1749–1832 German author

Gogh, van \van-'gō, -'gäk̲, -'k̲ȯk̲\ Vincent Willem 1853–1890 Dutch painter

Go·li·ath \gə-'lī-əth\ Philistine giant who is killed by David in the Bible

Gom·pers \'gäm-pərz\ Samuel 1850–1924 American (British-born) labor leader

Good·year \'gu̇d-ˌyi(ə)r, 'gu̇j-ˌi(ə)r\ Charles 1800–1860 American inventor

Gor·gas \'gȯr-gəs\ William Crawford 1854–1920 American army surgeon

Gra·ham \'grā-əm, 'gra(-ə)m\ Martha 1893–1991 American dancer and choreographer

Grant \'grant\ Ulysses 1822–1885 originally *Hiram Ulysses Grant* American general; 18th president of the U.S. (1869–77)

Gre·co, El \el-'grek-ō\ 1541–1614 *Doménikos Theotokópoulos* Spanish (Cretan-born) painter

Gree·ley \'grē-lē\ Horace 1811–1872 American journalist and politician

Greene \'grēn\ Graham 1904–1991 British novelist

Greene Nathanael 1742–1786 American Revolutionary general

Greg·o·ry \'greg-(ə-)rē\ name of 16 popes: especially **I** Saint *about* 540–604 *the Great* (pope 590–604); **VII** Saint *about* 1020–1085 (pope 1073–85); **XIII** 1502–1585 (pope 1572–85)

Grey \'grā\ Lady Jane 1537–1554 English noblewoman beheaded as a possible rival for the throne of Mary I

Grey Zane 1875–1939 American novelist

Grimm \'grim\ Jacob 1785–1863 and his brother Wilhelm 1786–1859 German philologists and folklorists

Guin·e·vere \'gwin-ə-ˌvi(ə)r\ wife of King Arthur and lover of Lancelot

Gu·ten·berg \'güt-ᵊn-ˌbərg\ Johannes *about* 1390–1468 German inventor of printing from movable type

Ha·des \'hād-ˌēz\ — see PLUTO

Ha·dri·an \'hā-drē-ən\ 76–138 A.D. Roman emperor (117–138)

Ha·gar \'hā-ˌgär, -gər\ mistress of Abraham and mother of Ishmael in the Bible

Hai·le Se·las·sie \ˌhī-lē-sə-'las-ē, -'läs-\ 1892–1975 emperor of Ethiopia (1930–36; 1941–74)

Hale \'hā(ə)l\ Edward Everett 1822–1909 American minister and author

Hale Nathan 1755–1776 American Revolutionary hero

Hal·ley \'hal-ē, 'hā-lē\ Edmond *or* Edmund 1656–1742 English astronomer

Hal·sey \'hȯl-sē, -zē\ William Frederick 1882–1959 American admiral

Ham·il·ton \'ham-əl-tən\ Alexander 1755–1804 American political leader

Ham·mu·ra·bi \ˌham-ə-'räb-ē\ *or* **Ham·mu·ra·pi** \-'räp-ē\ *died* 1750 B.C. king of Babylon (1792–50)

Han·cock \'han-ˌkäk\ John 1737–1793 American Revolutionary patriot

Han·del \'han-dᵊl\ George Frideric 1685–1759 British (German-born) composer

Han·dy \'han-dē\ William Christopher 1873–1958 American blues musician

Han·ni·bal \'han-ə-bəl\ 247–183 B.C. Carthaginian general

Har·ding \'härd-iŋ\ Warren Gamaliel 1865–1923 29th president of the U.S. (1921–23)

Har·dy \'härd-ē\ Thomas 1840–1928 English author

Har·ri·son \'har-ə-sən\ Benjamin 1833–1901 23d president of the U.S. (1889–93); grandson of William Henry Harrison

Harte \'härt\ Francis Brett 1836–1902 known as *Bret* American author

Har·vey \'här-vē\ William 1578–1657 English physician and anatomist

Haw·thorne \'hȯ-ˌthȯ(ə)rn\ Nathaniel 1804–1864 American author

Hayes \'hāz\ Rutherford Birchard 1822–1893 19th president of the U.S. (1877–81)

Hearst \'hərst\ William Randolph 1863–1951 American newspaper publisher

Hec·tor \'hek-tər\ son of Priam and Trojan hero slain by Achilles in Greek mythology

Hec·u·ba \'hek-yə-bə\ wife of Priam in Greek mythology

Hel·en of Troy \ˌhel-ə-nəv-'trȯi\ wife of Menelaus whose abduction by Paris in Greek mythology caused the Trojan War

He·li·os \'hē-lē-əs, -ōs\ god of the sun in Greek mythology

Hem·ing·way \'hem-iŋ-ˌwā\ Ernest Miller 1899–1961 American author; Nobel Prize winner (1954)

Hen·ry \'hen-rē\ name of eight kings of England: **I** 1068–1135 (reigned 1100–35); **II** 1133–1189 (reigned 1154–89); **III** 1207–1272 (reigned 1216–72); **IV** 1367–1413 (reigned 1399–1413); **V** 1387–1422 (reigned 1413–22); **VI** 1421–1471 (reigned 1422–61; 1470–71); **VII** 1457–1509 (reigned 1485–1509); **VIII** 1491–1547 (reigned 1509–47)

Henry name of 4 kings of France: **I** 1008–1060 (reigned 1031–60); **II** 1519–1559 (reigned 1547–59); **III** 1551–1589 (reigned 1574–89); **IV** 1553–1610 *Henry of Navarre* (reigned 1589–1610)

Henry O. — see William Sydney PORTER

Henry Patrick 1736–1799 American patriot and orator

He·phaes·tus \hi-'fes-təs, -'fēs-\ god of fire and of metalworking in Greek mythology — compare VULCAN

He·ra \'hir-ə, 'hē-rə\ sister and wife of Zeus and goddess of women and marriage in Greek mythology — compare JUNO

Her·cu·les \'hər-kyə-ˌlēz\ *or* **Her·a·cles** \'her-ə-ˌklēz\ hero in Greek mythology noted for his strength and for performing 12 labors imposed on him by Hera

Her·maph·ro·di·tus \(,)hər-,maf-rə-'dīt-əs\ son of Hermes and Aphrodite who in Greek mythology is joined with a nymph into one body

Her·mes \'hər-mēz\ god of commerce, eloquence, invention, travel, and theft who serves as herald and messenger of the other gods in Greek mythology

Her·od \'her-əd\ 73–4 B.C. *the Great* Roman king of Judea (37–4)

Herod An·ti·pas \'ant-ə-,pas, -pəs\ 21 B.C.–39 A.D. Roman governor of Galilee (4 B.C.–39 A.D.); son of Herod the Great

Hey·er·dahl \'hā-ər-,däl, 'hī-\ Thor 1914–   Norwegian explorer and author

Hi·a·wa·tha \,hī-ə-'wò-thə, ,hē-ə-, -'wäth-ə\ legendary Indian chief

Hick·ok \'hik-,äk\ James Butler 1837–1876 *Wild Bill* American scout and United States marshal

Hil·ton \'hilt-ºn\ James 1900–1954 English novelist

Hip·poc·ra·tes \hip-'äk-rə-,tēz\ *about* 460–*about* 377 B.C. *founder of medicine* Greek physician

Hi·ro·hi·to \,hir-ō-'hē-tō\ 1901–1989 emperor of Japan (1926–1989)

Hit·ler \'hit-lər\ Adolf 1889–1945 German (Austrian-born) chancellor (1933–45)

Holmes \'hōmz, 'hōlmz\ Oliver Wendell 1809–1894 American physician and author

Holmes Oliver Wendell 1841–1935 American jurist; son of the preceding

Ho·mer \'hō-mər\ 9th–8th? century B.C. Greek epic poet — **Ho·mer·ic** \hō-'mer-ik\ *adj*

Homer Winslow 1836–1910 American painter

Hooke \'hùk\ Robert 1635–1703 English scientist

Hook·er \'hùk-ər\ Thomas 1586?–1647 English colonist; a founder of Connecticut

Hoo·ver \'hü-vər\ Herbert Clark 1874–1964 31st president of the U.S. (1929–33)

Hoover John Edgar 1895–1972 American criminologist; director of the Federal Bureau of Investigation (1924–72)

Hou·di·ni \hü-'dē-nē\ Harry 1874–1926 originally *Ehrich Weiss* American magician

Hous·ton \'(h)yü-stən\ Samuel 1793–1863 *Sam* American general; president of the Republic of Texas (1836–38; 1841–44)

Howe \'haù\ Elias 1819–1867 American inventor

Howe Julia 1819–1910 née *Ward* American suffragist and reformer

Hud·son \'həd-sən\ Henry *died* 1611 English navigator and explorer

Hughes \'hyüz *also* 'yüz\ (James) Langston 1902–1967 American author

Hus·sein I \hü-'sān\ 1935–   king of Jordan (1952–   )

Hutch·in·son \'həch-ə(n)-sən\ Anne 1591–1643 religious leader in America

Hutchinson Thomas 1711–1780 American colonial administrator

Hux·ley \'hək-slē\ Aldous Leonard 1894–1963 English author

Hy·men \'hī-mən\ god of marriage in Greek mythology

Ib·sen \'ib-sən, 'ip-\ Henrik 1828–1906 Norwegian dramatist and poet

Ic·a·rus \'ik-ə-rəs\ son of Daedalus who in Greek mythology falls into the sea when the wax of his artificial wings melts as he flies too near the sun

Ig·na·tius \ig-'nā-sh(ē-)əs\ *Saint Ignatius of Loy·o·la* \lòi-'ō-lə\ 1491–1556 Spanish soldier and priest; founded the Society of Jesus

In·no·cent \'in-ə-sənt\ name of 13 popes: especially **II** *died* 1143 (pope 1130–43); **III** 1160 (or 1161)–1216 (pope 1198–1216); **IV** *died* 1254 (pope 1243–54); **XI** 1611–1689 (pope 1676–89)

Ir·ving \'ər-viŋ\ Washington 1783–1859 American author

Isaac \'ī-zik, -zək\ son of Abraham and father of Jacob in the Bible

Is·a·bel·la I \,iz-ə-'bel-ə\ 1451–1504 queen of Castile (1474–1504) and of Aragon (1479–1504); wife of Ferdinand V of Castile

Isa·iah \ī-'zā-ə\ Hebrew prophet of the 8th century B.C.

Ish·ma·el \'ish-(,)mā-əl, -mē-\ outcast son of Abraham and Hagar in the Bible

Ives \'īvz\ Charles Edward 1874–1954 American composer

Jack·son \'jak-sən\ Andrew 1767–1845 American general; 7th president of the U.S. (1829–37)

Jackson Thomas Jonathan 1824–1863 *Stonewall* American Confederate general

Ja·cob \'jā-kəb\ son of Isaac and Rebekah and younger twin brother of Esau in the Bible

James \'jāmz\ one of the 12 apostles in the Bible

James *the Less* one of the 12 apostles in the Bible

James name of two kings of Great Britain: **I** 1566–1625 (reigned 1603–25); king of Scotland as *James VI* (reigned 1567–1603); **II** 1633–1701 (reigned 1685–88)

James Henry 1843–1916 British (American-born) author

Ja·nus \'jā-nəs\ god of gates and doors and of beginnings and endings in Roman mythology who is usually pictured as having two opposite faces

Ja·son \'jās-ºn\ hero in Greek mythology noted for his successful quest of the Golden Fleece

Jay \'jā\ John 1745–1829 American jurist and political leader; 1st chief justice of the U.S. Supreme Court (1789–95)

Jef·fer·son \'jef-ər-sən\ Thomas 1743–1826 3d president of the U.S. (1801–09) — **Jef·fer·so·nian** \,jef-ər-'sō-nē-ən, -nyən\ *adj*

Jer·e·mi·ah \,jer-ə-'mī-ə\ Hebrew prophet of the 6th and 7th centuries B.C.

Je·sus \'jē-zəs, -zəz\ *or* **Jesus Christ** \'krīst\ *or* **Christ Je·sus** *about* 6 B.C.–*about* 30 A.D. source of the Christian religion and Savior in the Christian faith

Jez·e·bel \'jez-ə-,bel\ queen of Israel and wife of Ahab who was noted for her wickedness

Joan of Arc \,jō-nə-'värk\ *Saint about* 1412–1431 *the Maid of Orleans* French national heroine

Job \'jōb\ man in the Bible who has many sufferings but keeps his faith

Jo·cas·ta \jō-'kas-tə\ queen of Thebes in Greek mythology who unknowingly marries her son Oedipus

John \'jän\ *the Baptist* prophet and baptizer of Jesus in the Bible

John one of the 12 apostles believed to be the author of the fourth Gospel, three Epistles, and the Book of Revelation

John name of 21 popes: especially **XXIII** 1881–1963 (pope 1958–63)

John 1167–1216 *John Lack·land* \'lak-,land\ king of England (1199–1216)

John·son \'jän(t)-sən\ Andrew 1808–1875 17th president of the U.S. (1865–69)

Johnson Lyndon Baines 1908–1973 36th president of the U.S. (1963–69)

Johnson Samuel 1709–1784 *Dr. Johnson* English lexicographer and author

Jol·iet *or* **Jo·liet** \zhòl-'yā, ,jō-lē-'et\ Louis 1645–1700 French explorer in America

Jo·nah \'jō-nə\ Hebrew prophet who in the Bible spends three days in the belly of a great fish

Jones \'jōnz\ John Paul 1747–1792 American (Scottish=born) naval officer

Jop·lin \'jäp-lən\ Scott 1868–1917 American pianist and composer

\ə\ abut	\aù\ out	\i\ tip	\ò\ saw	\ù\ foot
\ər\ further	\ch\ chin	\ī\ life	\òi\ coin	\y\ yet
\a\ mat	\e\ pet	\j\ job	\th\ thin	\yü\ few
\ā\ take	\ē\ easy	\ŋ\ sing	\th\ this	\yù\ cure
\ä\ cot, cart	\g\ go	\ō\ bone	\ü\ food	\zh\ vision

Jo·seph \\'jō-zəf *also* -səf\\ a son of Jacob in the Bible who rose to high office in Egypt after being sold into slavery by his brothers

Joseph *about* 1840–1904 Nez Percé Indian chief

Joseph *Saint* husband of Mary, the mother of Jesus, in the Bible

Josh·ua \\'jäsh-(ə-)wə\\ Hebrew leader in the Bible who succeeds Moses during the settlement of the Israelites in Canaan

Ju·dah \\'jüd-ə\\ son of Jacob and ancestor of one of the 12 tribes of Israel in the Bible

Ju·das \\'jüd-əs\\ or **Judas Is·car·i·ot** \\-is-'kar-ē-ət\\ one of the 12 apostles and the betrayer of Jesus in the Bible

Ju·no \\'jü-nō\\ the queen of heaven in Roman mythology, wife of Jupiter, and goddess of light, birth, women, and marriage — compare HERA

Ju·pi·ter \\'jü-pət-ər\\ the chief god in Roman mythology, husband of Juno, and the god of light, of the sky and weather, and of the state

Kalb \\'kälp, 'kalb\\ Johann 1721–1780 Baron *de Kalb* \\di-'kalb\\ German general in American Revolutionary army

Keats \\'kēts\\ John 1795–1821 English poet

Kel·ler \\'kel-ər\\ Helen Adams 1880–1968 American deaf and blind lecturer

Kel·vin \\'kel-vən\\ 1st Baron 1824–1907 *William Thomson* British mathematician and physicist

Ken·ne·dy \\'ken-əd-ē\\ John Fitzgerald 1917–1963 35th president of the U.S. (1961–63)

Kennedy Robert Francis 1925–1968 American politician; attorney general of the U.S. (1961–64); brother of John F. Kennedy

Ke·o·kuk \\'kē-ə-, kək\\ 1788?–?1848 American Indian chief

Key \\'kē\\ Francis Scott 1779–1843 American lawyer; author of "The Star-Spangled Banner"

Khayyám Omar — see OMAR KHAYYÁM

Khru·shchev \\krüsh-'(ch)óf, -'(ch)óv, -'(ch)ef\\ Ni·ki·ta \\nə-'kēt-ə\\ Sergeyevich 1894–1971 premier of U.S.S.R. (1958–64)

Khu·fu \\'kü-fü\\ or Greek **Che·ops** \\'kē-, äps\\ 26th century B.C. king of Egypt and pyramid builder

Kidd \\'kid\\ William *about* 1645–1701 *Captain Kidd* Scottish pirate

King \\'kiŋ\\ Martin Luther, Jr. 1929–1968 American minister and civil rights leader; Nobel Prize winner (1964)

Kip·ling \\'kip-liŋ\\ Rud·yard \\'rəd-yərd, 'rəj-ərd\\ 1865–1936 English author

Kis·sin·ger \\'kis-ᵊn-jər\\ Henry Alfred 1923–   American (German-born) scholar and government official; U.S. secretary of state (1973–77); Nobel Prize winner (1973)

Knox \\'näks\\ John *about* 1514–1572 Scottish religious reformer

Koch \\'kók, 'kók\\ Robert 1843–1910 German bacteriologist; Nobel Prize winner (1905)

Koś·ciusz·ko \\, käs-ē-'əs-, kō, kósh-'chùsh-kō\\ Tadeusz 1746–1817 Polish patriot and general in American Revolutionary army

Krish·na \\'krish-nə\\ god worshipped in later Hinduism

Kriss Kringle — see SANTA CLAUS

Ku·blai Khan \\, kü-blə-'kän, -, blī-\\ 1215–1294 founder of Mongol dynasty in China

La·fa·yette \\, läf-ē-'et, , laf-\\ Marquis de 1757–1834 French general in American Revolutionary army

La·ius \\'lā-(y)əs, 'lī-əs\\ king of Thebes who in Greek mythology is killed by his son Oedipus

Lan·ce·lot \\'lan(t)-sə-, lät\\ legendary knight of the Round Table and lover of Queen Guinevere

La Salle \\lə-'sal\\ Sieur de 1643–1687 French explorer in America

La·voi·sier \\lǝv-'wäz-ē-, ā\\ Antoine-Laurent 1743–1794 French chemist

Law·rence \\'lòr-ən(t)s, 'lär-\\ Thomas Edward 1888–1935 *Lawrence of Arabia* later surnamed *Shaw* British archaeologist, soldier, and author

Laz·a·rus \\'laz-(ə-)rəs\\ brother of Mary and Martha who in the Bible is raised by Jesus from the dead

Lazarus beggar in the biblical parable of the rich man and the beggar

Le·da \\'lēd-ə\\ a queen of Sparta in Greek mythology who is courted by Zeus in the form of a swan

Lee \\'lē\\ Ann 1736–1784 English mystic; founder of Shaker society in the U.S.

Lee Henry 1756–1818 *Light-Horse Harry* American general

Lee Robert Edward 1807–1870 American Confederate general

Leeu·wen·hoek \\'lā-vən-, hùk\\ Antonie van 1632–1723 Dutch naturalist

Leif Er·iks·son \\, lā-'ver-ik-sən, , lē-'fer-\\ or **Er·ics·son** *flourished* 1000 Norwegian explorer; son of Erik the Red

Le·nin \\'len-ən\\ 1870–1924 originally *Vladimir Ilyich Ul·ya·nov* \\ùl-'yän-əf, -, óf, -, óv\\ Russian Communist leader

Leo \\'lē-ō\\ name of 13 popes: especially **I** Saint *died* 461 (pope 440–61); **III** Saint *died* 816 (pope 795–816); **XIII** 1810–1903 (pope 1878–1903)

Le·o·nar·do da Vin·ci \\, lē-ə-'närd-, ōd-ə-'vin-chē, , lā-, -'vēn-\\ 1452–1519 Italian painter, sculptor, architect, and engineer

Lew·is \\'lü-əs\\ John Llewellyn 1880–1969 American labor leader

Lewis Meriwether 1774–1809 American explorer (with William Clark)

Lewis (Harry) Sinclair 1885–1951 American author; Nobel Prize winner (1930)

Lin·coln \\'liŋ-kən\\ Abraham 1809–1865 16th president of the U.S. (1861–65)

Lind·bergh \\'lin(d)-, bərg\\ Charles Augustus 1902–1974 American aviator

Lin·nae·us \\lə-'nē-əs, -'nā-\\ Carolus 1707–1778 Swedish *Carl von Lin·né* \\lə-'nā\\ Swedish botanist

Lis·ter \\'lis-tər\\ Joseph 1827–1912 English surgeon

Liszt \\'list\\ Franz 1811–1886 Hungarian pianist and composer

Liv·ing·stone \\'liv-iŋ-stən\\ David 1813–1873 Scottish explorer in Africa

Long·fel·low \\'lòŋ-, fel-ō\\ Henry Wads·worth \\'wädz-(,)wərth\\ 1807–1882 American poet

Lou·is \\'lü-ē, 'lü-əs\\ name of 18 kings of France: especially **IX** Saint 1214–1270 (reigned 1226–70); **XI** 1423–1483 (reigned 1461–83); **XII** 1462–1515 (reigned 1498–1515); **XIII** 1601–1643 (reigned 1610–43); **XIV** 1638–1715 (reigned 1643–1715); **XV** 1710–1774 (reigned 1715–74); **XVI** 1754–1793 (reigned 1774–92; guillotined); **XVII** 1785–1795 (reigned in name 1793–95); **XVIII** 1755–1824 (reigned 1814–15; 1815–24)

Low \\'lō\\ Juliette Gordon 1860–1927 American founder of the Girl Scouts

Low·ell \\'lō-əl\\ Amy 1874–1925 American poet

Lowell James Russell 1819–1891 American author

Luke \\'lük\\ physician and companion of the apostle Paul believed to be the author of the third Gospel and the Book of Acts

Lu·ther \\'lü-thər\\ Martin 1483–1546 German Reformation leader

Ly·on \\'lī-ən\\ Mary 1797–1849 American educator

Mac·Ar·thur \\mə-'kär-thər\\ Douglas 1880–1964 American general

Mc·Car·thy \\mə-'kär-thē\\ Joseph Raymond 1908–1957 American politician

Mc·Clel·lan \\mə-'klel-ən\\ George Brinton 1826–1885 American general

Mc·Cor·mick \\mə-'kòr-mik\\ Cyrus Hall 1809–1884 American inventor

Mc·Kin·ley \\mə-'kin-lē\\ William 1843–1901 25th president of the U.S. (1897–1901)

Ma·cy \\'mā-sē\\ Anne Sullivan 1866–1936 American educator; teacher of Helen Keller

Mad·i·son \'mad-ə-sən\ James 1751–1836 4th president of the U.S. (1809–17)

Ma·gel·lan \mə-'jel-ən\ Ferdinand *about* 1480–1521 Portuguese navigator

Mal·colm X \,mal-kə-'meks\ 1925–1965 American civil rights leader

Ma·net \ma-'nā, mä-\ Édouard 1832–1883 French painter

Mann \'man\ Horace 1796–1859 American educator

Mao Tse-tung \,maù(d)-zə-'dùŋ, ,maùt-sə-\ 1893–1976 Chinese Communist; leader of People's Republic of China (1949–76)

Mar·co·ni \mär-'kō-nē\ Guglielmo 1874–1937 Italian physicist and inventor; Nobel Prize winner (1909)

Ma·rie An·toi·nette \mə-'rē-,an-t(w)ə-'net\ 1755–1793 wife of Louis XVI

Mar·i·on \'mer-ē-ən, 'mar-ē-\ Francis 1732?–1795 *the Swamp Fox* American commander in Revolution

Mark \'märk\ evangelist believed to be the author of the second Gospel

Mar·quette \mär-'ket\ Jacques 1637–1675 French-born Jesuit missionary and explorer in America

Mars \'märz\ the god of war in Roman mythology

Mar·shall \'mär-shəl\ George Catlett 1880–1959 American general and diplomat

Marshall John 1755–1835 American jurist; chief justice of the U.S. Supreme Court (1801–35)

Mar·tha \'mär-thə\ sister of Lazarus and Mary and friend of Jesus in the Bible

Mar·tin \'märt-ᵊn\ Saint *about* 316–397 *Martin of Tours* \-'tü(ə)r\ patron saint of France

Marx \'märks\ Karl 1818–1883 German political philosopher and socialist

Mary \'me(ə)r-ē, 'ma(ə)r-ē, 'mā-rē\ mother of Jesus

Mary sister of Lazarus and Martha in the Bible

Mary I 1516–1558 *Mary Tudor; Bloody Mary* queen of England (1553–58)

Mary II 1662–1694 joint British sovereign with William III (1689–94)

Mary Mag·da·lene \-'mag-də-,lən, -,lēn\ woman in the Bible who was healed of evil spirits by Jesus and who later saw the risen Christ

Mary Stuart 1542–1587 *Mary, Queen of Scots* queen of Scotland (1542–87)

Mas·sa·soit \,mas-ə-'sòit\ *died* 1661 Indian chief in eastern Massachusetts

Math·er \'math-ər, 'math-\ Cotton 1663–1728 American religious leader and author

Mather Increase 1639–1723 American minister and author; father of Cotton Mather

Mat·thew \'math-yü\ apostle believed to be the author of the first Gospel

Mau·pas·sant \,mō-pə-'sänt\ (Henri-René-Albert-) Guy de 1850–1893 French short-story writer

Mead \'mēd\ Margaret 1901–1978 American anthropologist

Meade \'mēd\ George Gordon 1815–1872 American general

Mea·ny \'mē-nē\ George 1894–1980 American labor leader

Me·dea \mə-'dē-ə\ woman with magic powers in Greek mythology who helps Jason to win the Golden Fleece and who kills her children when he leaves her

Me·di·ci, de' \'med-ə-chē\ Catherine 1519–1589 French *Catherine de Médicis* \,mād-ə-'sē(s)\ queen of Henry II of France

Me·ir \me-'i(ə)r\ Golda 1898–1978 prime minister of Israel (1969–74)

Mel·ville \'mel-,vil\ Herman 1819–1891 American author

Men·del \'men-dᵊl\ Gregor Johann 1822–1884 Austrian botanist

Men·e·la·us \,men-ᵊl-'ā-əs\ king of Sparta, brother of Agamemnon, and husband of Helen of Troy in Greek mythology

Meph·is·toph·e·les \,mef-ə-'stäf-ə-,lēz\ chief devil in the Faust legend

Mer·ca·tor \(,)mər-'kāt-ər\ Gerardus 1512–1594 Flemish mapmaker

Mer·cu·ry \'mər-kyə-rē, -k(ə-)rē\ god of commerce, eloquence, travel, and theft who serves as herald and messenger of the other gods in Roman mythology

Mer·lin \'mər-lən\ prophet and magician in the legend of King Arthur

Mi·chael \'mī-kəl\ one of the four archangels named in Hebrew tradition — compare GABRIEL, RAPHAEL, URIEL

Mi·chel·an·ge·lo \,mī-kə-'lan-jə-,lō, ,mik-ə-'lan-, ,mē-kə-'län-\ 1475–1564 Italian sculptor, painter, architect, and poet

Mi·das \'mīd-əs\ legendary king who was given the power to turn everything he touched into gold

Mil·lay \mil-'ā\ Edna St. Vincent 1892–1950 American poet

Mil·ler \'mil-ər\ Arthur 1915– American author

Mil·ton \'milt-ᵊn\ John 1608–1674 English poet

Mi·ner·va \mə-'nər-və\ goddess of wisdom in Roman mythology — compare ATHENA

Mi·no·taur \'min-ə-,tò(ə)r, 'mī-nə-\ monster in Greek mythology shaped half like a man and half like a bull

Min·u·it \'min-yə-wət\ Peter 1580–1638 Dutch colonial administrator in America

Mitch·ell \'mich-əl\ Maria 1818–1889 American astronomer

Mo·lière \mōl-'ye(ə)r, 'mōl-,ye(ə)r\ 1622–1673 originally *Jean-Baptiste Poquelin* French actor and dramatist

Mo·net \mō-'nā\ Claude 1840–1926 French painter

Mon·roe \mən-'rō\ James 1758–1831 5th president of the U.S. (1817–25)

Mont·calm de Saint-Vé·ran \mänt-'käm-də-,san-vā-'rän, -'kälm-\ Marquis de 1712–1759 French field marshal in Canada

Mon·tes·so·ri \,mänt-ə-'sòr-ē, -'sòr-\ Maria 1870–1952 Italian physician and educator

Mon·te·zu·ma II \,mänt-ə-'zü-mə\ 1466–1520 last Aztec emperor of Mexico (1502–20)

Moore \'mō(ə)r, 'mò(ə)r, 'mù(ə)r\ Marianne Craig 1887–1972 American poet

More \'mō(ə)r, 'mò(ə)r\ Sir Thomas 1478–1535 *Saint* English public official and author

Mor·gan \'mòr-gən\ John Pierpont 1837–1913 American financier

Morse \'mò(ə)rs\ Samuel Finley Breese 1791–1872 American artist and inventor

Mo·ses \'mō-zez *also* -zəs\ Hebrew prophet and lawgiver who in the Bible freed the Israelites from slavery in Egypt

Mott \'mät\ Lucretia 1793–1880 American reformer

Mo·zart \'mōt-,särt\ Wolfgang Amadeus 1756–1791 Austrian composer

Mu·ham·mad \mō-'ham-əd, -'häm- *also* mü-\ *about* 570–632 Arab prophet and founder of Islam

Mus·so·li·ni \,mü-sə-'lē-nē, ,mùs-ə-\ Be·ni·to \bə-'nēt-ō\ 1883–1945 *Il Du·ce* \ēl-'dü-chā\ Italian fascist premier (1922–43)

Na·po·leon I \nə-'pōl-yən, -'pō-lē-ən\ *or* Napoleon Bo·na·parte \'bō-nə-,pärt\ 1769–1821 emperor of the French (1804–15) — **Na·po·le·on·ic** \nə-,pō-lē-'än-ik\ *adj*

Nar·cis·sus \när-'sis-əs\ a beautiful youth in Greek mythology who pines away for love of his own reflection and is then turned into the narcissus flower

Nash \'nash\ Ogden 1902–1971 American poet

Na·tion \'nā-shən\ Car·ry \'kar-ē\ Amelia 1846–1911 American social reformer

\ə\ abut	\aù\ out	\i\ tip	\ò\ saw	\ù\ foot
\ər\ further	\ch\ chin	\ī\ life	\òi\ coin	\y\ yet
\a\ mat	\e\ pet	\j\ job	\th\ thin	\yü\ few
\ā\ take	\ē\ easy	\ŋ\ sing	\th\ this	\yù\ cure
\ä\ cot, cart	\g\ go	\ō\ bone	\ü\ food	\zh\ vision

Neb·u·cha·drez·zar II \‚neb-(y)ə-kə-'drez-ər\ *also* **Neb·u·chad·nez·zar** \-kəd-'nez-\ *about* 630–562 B.C. Chaldean king of Babylon (605–562)

Neh·ru \'ne(ə)r-‚ü, 'nā-rü\ Ja·wa·har·lal \jə-'wä-hər-‚läl\ 1889–1964 Indian nationalist; 1st prime minister (1947–64)

Nel·son \'nel-sən\ Horatio 1758–1805 Viscount *Nelson* British admiral

Nem·e·sis \'nem-ə-səs\ the goddess of reward and punishment in Greek mythology

Nep·tune \'nep-‚t(y)ün\ the god of the sea in Roman mythology

Ne·ro \'nē-‚rō, 'ni(ə)r-ō\ 37–68 A.D. Roman emperor (54–68)

New·ton \'n(y)üt-ᵊn\ Sir Isaac 1642–1727 English mathematician and physicist

Nich·o·las \'nik-(ə-)ləs\ Saint 4th century Christian bishop

Nicholas I 1796–1855 czar of Russia (1825–55)

Nicholas II 1868–1918 czar of Russia (1894–1917)

Night·in·gale \'nīt-ᵊn-‚gäl, -iŋ-\ Florence 1820–1910 English nurse and philanthropist

Ni·ke \'nī-kē\ the goddess of victory in Greek mythology

Ni·o·be \'nī-ə-bē\ a daughter of Tantalus in Greek mythology who while weeping for her slain children is turned into a stone from which her tears continue to flow

Nix·on \'nik-sən\ Richard Mil·hous \'mil-‚haús\ 1913– 37th president of the U.S. (1969–74)

No·ah \'nō-ə\ Old Testament builder of the ark in which he, his family, and living creatures of every kind survived the Flood

No·bel \nō-'bel\ Alfred Bernhard 1833–1896 Swedish manufacturer, inventor, and philanthropist

Oce·anus \ō-'sē-ə-nəs\ a Titan who rules over a great river encircling the earth in Greek mythology

Odin \'ōd-ᵊn\ *or* **Wo·den** \'wōd-ᵊn\ god of war and patron of heroes in Norse mythology

Odys·seus \ō-'dis-ē-əs, -'dis-yəs, -'dish-əs, -'dish-‚üs\ *or* **Ulys·ses** \yú-'lis-ēz\ king of Ithaca and hero in Greek mythology who after the Trojan war wanders for 10 years before reaching home

Oe·di·pus \'ed-ə-pəs, 'ēd-\ son of Laius and Jocasta who in Greek mythology kills his father and marries his mother not knowing their identity

Ogle·thorpe \'ō-gəl-‚thòrp\ James Edward 1696–1785 English general and philanthropist; founder of Georgia

O'·Keeffe \ō-'kēf\ Georgia 1887–1986 American painter

Omar Khay·yám \‚ō-‚mär-‚kī-'(y)äm, ‚ō-mər-, -'(y)am\ 1048?–1122 Persian poet and astronomer

O'·Neill \ō-'nē(ə)l\ Eugene Gladstone 1888–1953 American dramatist; Nobel Prize winner (1936)

Or·pheus \'òr-‚fyüs, -fē-əs\ poet and musician in Greek mythology who almost rescues his wife Eurydice from Hades by charming Pluto and Persephone with his lyre

Or·well \'òr-‚wel, -wəl\ George 1903–1950 pseudonym of *Eric Blair* English author — **Or·well·ian** \òr-'wel-ē-ən\ *adj*

Osce·o·la \‚äs-ē-'ō-lə, ‚ō-sē-\ *about* 1800–1838 Seminole Indian chief

Otis \'ōt-əs\ James 1725–1783 American Revolutionary patriot

Ov·id \'äv-əd\ 43 B.C.–17A.D.? Roman poet

Ow·en \'ō-ən\ Robert 1771–1858 Welsh social reformer

Ow·ens \'ō-ənz\ Jesse 1913–1980 originally *James Cleveland* American athlete

Paine \'pān\ Thomas 1737–1809 American (English-born) political philosopher and author

Pan \'pan\ god of forests, pastures, flocks, and shepherds in Greek mythology who is represented as having the legs, ears, and horns of a goat

Pan·do·ra \pan-'dōr-ə, -'dòr-\ woman in Greek mythology who out of curiosity opened a box and let loose all of the evils that trouble humans

Par·is \'par-əs\ son of Priam whose abduction of Helen of Troy in Greek mythology led to the Trojan War

Park·man \'pärk-mən\ Francis 1823–1893 American historian

Pas·cal \pas-'kal\ Blaise 1623–1662 French mathematician and philosopher

Pas·ter·nak \'pas-tər-‚nak\ Boris Leonidovich 1890–1960 Russian author; Nobel Prize winner (1958)

Pas·teur \pas-'tər\ Louis 1822–1895 French chemist and microbiologist

Pat·rick \'pa-trik\ Saint 5th century apostle and patron saint of Ireland

Pat·ton \'pat-ᵊn\ George Smith 1885–1945 American general

Paul \'pòl\ Saint *died between* 62 *and* 68 A.D. author of several New Testament epistles — **Pau·line** \'pò-‚līn\ *adj*

Paul name of six popes: especially **III** 1468–1549 (pope 1534–49); **V** 1552–1621 (pope 1605–21); **VI** 1897–1978 (pope 1963–78)

Paul Bun·yan \'pòl-'bən-yən\ giant lumberjack in American folklore

Pau·ling \'pò-liŋ\ Linus Carl 1901–   American chemist; Nobel Prize winner (1954, 1962)

Pav·lov \'päv-‚lòf, 'pav-, -‚lòv\ Ivan Petrovich 1849–1936 Russian physiologist; Nobel Prize winner (1904)

Pa·vlo·va \'pav-lə-və, pav-'lō-və\ Anna 1882–1931 Russian ballerina

Pea·ry \'pi(ə)r-ē\ Robert Edwin 1856–1920 American arctic explorer

Pe·cos Bill \‚pā-kəs-'bil\ a cowboy in American folklore known for his extraordinary feats

Peg·a·sus \'peg-ə-səs\ winged horse in Greek mythology

Penn \'pen\ William 1644–1718 English Quaker; founder of Pennsylvania

Per·i·cles \'per-ə-‚klēz\ *about* 495–429 B.C. Athenian political leader

Per·ry \'per-ē\ Matthew Calbraith 1794–1858 American commodore

Perry Oliver Hazard 1785–1819 American naval officer

Per·seph·o·ne \pər-'sef-ə-nē\ daughter of Zeus and Demeter who in Greek mythology is abducted by Pluto to rule with him over the underworld

Per·shing \'pər-shiŋ, -zhiŋ\ John Joseph 1860–1948 American general

Pe·ter \'pēt-ər\ Saint *died about* 64 A.D. *Si·mon Peter* \'sī-mən-\ one of the 12 apostles in the Bible

Peter I 1672–1725 *the Great* czar of Russia (1682–1725)

Phil·ip \'fil-əp\ one of the 12 apostles in the Bible

Philip 1639?–1676 American Indian chief

Philip name of six kings of France: especially **II** *or* **Philip Augustus** 1165–1223 (reigned 1179–1223); **IV** 1268–1314 (reigned 1285–1314) *the Fair;* **VI** 1293–1350 (reigned 1328–50)

Philip name of five kings of Spain: especially **II** 1527–1598 (reigned 1556–98); **V** 1683–1746 (reigned 1700–46)

Philip II 382–336 B.C. king of Macedon (359–336); father of Alexander the Great

Pi·cas·so \pi-'käs-ō, -'kas-\ Pablo 1881–1973 Spanish painter and sculptor in France

Pick·ett \'pik-ət\ George Edward 1825–1875 American Confederate general

Pierce \'pi(ə)rs\ Franklin 1804–1869 14th president of the U.S. (1853–57)

Pi·late \'pī-lət\ Pon·tius \'pän-chəs, 'pən-chəs\ *died* after 36 A.D. Roman governor of Judea

Pitt \'pit\ William 1759–1806 English prime minister (1783–1801; 1804–6)

Pi·us \'pī-əs\ name of 12 popes: especially **VII** 1742–1823 (pope 1800–23); **IX** 1792–1878 (pope 1846–78); **X** 1835–1914 (pope 1903–14); **XI** 1857–1939 (pope 1922–39); **XII** 1876–1958 (pope 1939–58)

Pi·zar·ro \pə-'zär-ō\ Francisco *about* 1475–1541 Spanish conqueror of Peru

Pla·to \'plāt-ō\ *about* 428–348 (*or* 347) B.C. Greek philosopher

Plu·to \'plüt-ō\ god of the dead and the underworld in Greek mythology

Po·ca·hon·tas \ˌpō-kə-'hänt-əs\ *about* 1595–1617 American Indian princess

Poe \'pō\ Edgar Allan 1809–1849 American author

Polk \'pōk\ James Knox 1795–1849 11th president of the U.S. (1845–49)

Po·lo \'pō-lō\ Mar·co \'mär-kō\ 1254–1324 Venetian traveler

Poly·phe·mus \ˌpäl-ə-'fē-məs\ a Cyclops in Greek mythology who is blinded by Odysseus

Ponce de Le·ón \ˌpän(t)-sə-ˌdā-lē-'ōn, ˌpän(t)s-də-'lē-ən\ Juan 1460–1521 Spanish explorer and discoverer of Florida (1513)

Pon·ti·ac \'pänt-ē-ˌak\ *about* 1720–1769 American Indian chief

Por·ter \'pōrt-ər, 'pȯrt-\ Cole Albert 1891–1964 American composer and songwriter

Porter David Dixon 1813–1891 American admiral

Porter Katherine Anne 1890–1980 American author

Porter William Sydney 1862–1910 pseudonym *O. Henry* \(')ō-'hen-rē\ American author

Po·sei·don \pə-'sīd-ᵊn\ god of the sea in Greek mythology — compare NEPTUNE

Pot·ter \'pät-ər\ Beatrix 1866–1943 British author and illustrator

Pow·ha·tan \ˌpaù-ə-'tan, paù-'hat-ᵊn\ 1550?–1618 American Indian chief

Pri·am \'prī-əm, -ˌam\ king of Troy during the Trojan War in Greek mythology

Pro·me·theus \prə-'mē-th(y)üs, -thē-əs\ a Titan in Greek mythology who is punished by Zeus for stealing fire from heaven and giving it to human beings

Pro·teus \'prō-ˌt(y)üs, 'prōt-ē-əs\ sea god in Greek mythology who is capable of assuming different forms

Puc·ci·ni \pü-'chē-nē\ Giacomo 1858–1924 Italian composer

Pu·las·ki \pə-'las-kē, pyü-\ Kazimierz 1747–1779 Polish soldier in American Revolutionary army

Pu·lit·zer \'pùl-ət-sər, 'pyü-lət-sər\ Joseph 1847–1911 American (Hungarian-born) journalist

Pyg·ma·lion \pig-'māl-yən, -'mā-lē-ən\ a sculptor in Greek mythology who falls in love with a statue which is then brought to life

Py·thag·o·ras \pə-'thag-ə-rəs, pī-\ *about* 580–*about* 500 B.C. Greek philosopher and mathematician

Ra \'rä, 'rȯ\ god of the sun and chief deity of ancient Egypt

Ra·leigh *or* **Ra·legh** \'rȯl-ē, 'räl- *also* 'ral-\ Sir Walter 1554–1618 English navigator and historian

Ram·ses \'ram-ˌsēz\ *or* **Ram·e·ses** \'ram-ə-ˌsēz\ name of 12 kings of Egypt: especially **II** (reigned 1304–1237 B.C.); **III** (reigned 1198–66 B.C.)

Ran·dolph \'ran-ˌdälf\ Asa Philip 1889–1979 American labor leader

Ra·pha·el \'raf-ē-əl, 'rā-fē-\ one of the four archangels named in Hebrew tradition — compare GABRIEL, MICHAEL, URIEL

Ra·pha·el \'raf-ē-əl, 'rā-fē-, 'räf-ē-\ 1483–1520 Italian painter

Ras·pu·tin \ra-'sp(y)üt-ᵊn, -'spùt-\ Grigory Yefimovich 1872–1916 Russian mystic

Rea·gan \'rā-gən *also* 'rē-\ Ronald Wilson 1911–   40th president of the U.S. (1981–89)

Re·bek·ah *or* **Re·bec·ca** \ri-'bek-ə\ wife of Isaac in the Bible

Red Cloud \'red-ˌklaùd\ 1822–1909 American Indian chief

Reed \'rēd\ Walter 1851–1902 American army surgeon

Rem·brandt \'rem-ˌbrant *also* -ˌbränt\ 1606–1669 Dutch painter

Re·mus \'rē-məs\ son of Mars who in Roman mythology is killed by his twin brother Romulus

Re·noir \'ren-ˌwär, rən-'wär\ Pierre-Auguste 1841–1919 French painter

Re·vere \ri-'vi(ə)r\ Paul 1735–1818 American patriot and silversmith

Rich·ard \'rich-ərd\ name of three kings of England: **I** 1157–1199 (reigned 1189–99) *the Lion-Hearted;* **II** 1367–1400 (reigned 1377–99); **III** 1452–1485 (reigned 1483–85)

Rob·in Good·fel·low \ˌräb-ən-'gùd-ˌfel-ō\ mischievous elf in English folklore

Rob·in·son \'räb-ən-sən\ Edwin Arlington 1869–1935 American poet

Rob·in·son Cru·soe \ˌräb-ə(n)-sən-'krü-sō\ a shipwrecked sailor in Daniel Defoe's *Robinson Crusoe* who lives for many years on a desert island

Ro·cham·beau \ˌrō-ˌsham-'bō\ Comte de 1725–1807 French general in American Revolution

Rocke·fel·ler \'räk-i-ˌfel-ər, 'räk-ˌfel-\ John Davison father 1839–1937 and son 1874–1960 American oil magnates and philanthropists

Ro·ma·nov *or* **Ro·ma·noff** \rō-'män-əf, 'rō-mə-ˌnäf\ Michael 1596–1645 1st czar (1613–45) of Russian Romanov dynasty (1613–1917)

Rom·u·lus \'räm-yə-ləs\ son of Mars in Roman mythology who was the twin brother of Remus and the founder of Rome

Rönt·gen *or* **Roent·gen** \'rent-gən, 'rənt-, -jən\ Wilhelm Conrad 1845–1923 German physicist; Nobel Prize winner (1901)

Roo·se·velt \'rō-zə-vəlt *(Roosevelts' usual pronunciation)*, -ˌvelt *also* 'rü-\ (Anna) Eleanor 1884–1962 American lecturer and writer; wife of Franklin Delano Roosevelt

Roosevelt Franklin Del·a·no \'del-ə-ˌnō\ 1882–1945 32d president of the U.S. (1933–45)

Roosevelt Theodore 1858–1919 26th president of the U.S. (1901–09); Nobel Prize winner (1906)

Ross \'rȯs\ Betsy 1752–1836 reputed maker of first American flag

Ros·si·ni \rȯ-'sē-nē, rə-\ Gioacchino Antonio 1792–1868 Italian composer

Ru·bens \'rü-bənz\ Peter Paul 1577–1640 Flemish painter

Rus·sell \'rəs-əl\ Bertrand Arthur William 1872–1970 English mathematician and philosopher; Nobel Prize winner (1950)

Ruth \'rüth\ woman in the Bible who was one of the ancestors of King David

Ruth George Herman 1895–1948 *Babe* American baseball player

Ruth·er·ford \'rəth-ə(r)-fərd, 'rəth-\ Ernest 1871–1937 1st Baron *Rutherford of Nelson* British physicist

Sa·bin \'sā-bin\ Albert Bruce 1906–1993 American physician

Sac·a·ga·wea \ˌsak-ə-jə-'wē-ə, -'wä-ə\ 1786?–1812 American Indian guide to Lewis and Clark

Sa·dat \sə-'dat, -'dät\ Anwar as- 1918–1981 president of Egypt (1970–81)

Saint Nicholas — see NICHOLAS, SANTA CLAUS

Sal·in·ger \'sal-ən-jər\ Jerome David 1919–   American author

Salk \'sȯk, 'sȯlk\ Jonas Edward 1914–   American physician

Sa·lo·me \sə-'lō-mē\ niece of Herod Antipas who in the Bible is given the head of John the Baptist as a reward for her dancing

\ə\ **abut**		\aù\ **out**	\i\ **tip**	\ȯ\ **saw**		\ù\ **foot**
\ər\ **further**		\ch\ **chin**	\ī\ **life**	\ȯi\ **coin**		\y\ **yet**
\a\ **mat**		\e\ **pet**	\j\ **job**	\th\ **thin**		\yü\ **few**
\ā\ **take**		\ē\ **easy**	\ŋ\ **sing**	\th\ **this**		\yù\ **cure**
\ä\ **cot, cart**		\g\ **go**	\ō\ **bone**	\ü\ **food**		\zh\ **vision**

Sa·mo·set \'sam-ə-ˌset, sə-'mäs-ət\ *died about* 1653 American Indian leader

Sam·son \'sam(p)-sən\ powerful Hebrew hero in the Bible who fought against the Philistines

Sam·u·el \'sam-yə(-wə)l\ Hebrew judge in the Bible who appointed Saul and then David king

Sand·burg \'san(d)-ˌbərg\ Carl 1878–1967 American author

San·ta Claus \'sant-ē-ˌklȯz, 'sant-ə-\ *or* **Saint Nich·o·las** \sȧnt-'nik-(ə-)ləs, sənt-\ *or* **Kriss Krin·gle** \'kris-'kriŋ-gəl\ a fat jolly old man in modern folklore who delivers presents to good children at Christmastime

Sap·pho \'saf-ō\ *flourished about* 610–*about* 580 B.C. Greek poet

Sa·rah \'ser-ə, 'sar-ə, 'sā-rə\ wife of Abraham and mother of Isaac in the Bible

Sar·gent \'sär-jənt\ John Singer 1856–1925 American painter

Sat·urn \'sat-ərn\ a god of agriculture in Roman mythology

Saul \'sȯl\ first king of Israel in the Bible

Saul *or* **Saul of Tar·sus** \-'tär-səs\ the apostle Paul

Sche·her·a·zade \shə-ˌher-ə-'zäd(-ə), -'zäd(-ē)\ fictional oriental queen and narrator of the tales in the *Arabian Nights' Entertainments*

Schu·bert \'shü-bərt, -ˌbərt\ Franz Peter 1797–1828 Austrian composer

Schweit·zer \'shwīt-sər, 'swīt-, 'shvīt-\ Albert 1875–1965 French Protestant minister, philosopher, physician, and music scholar; Nobel Prize winner (1952)

Scott \'skät\ Dred \'dred\ 1795?–1858 American slave

Scott Sir Walter 1771–1832 Scottish author

Scott Winfield 1786–1866 American general

Scyl·la \'sil-ə\ a nymph in Greek mythology who is changed into a monster and inhabits a cave opposite the whirlpool Charybdis off the coast of Sicily

Se·quoya \si-'kwȯi-ə\ *about* 1760–1843 Cherokee Indian leader

Ser·ra \'ser-ə\ Junípero 1713–1784 Spanish missionary in Mexico and California

Se·ton \'sēt-ᵊn\ Saint Elizabeth Ann Bayley 1774–1821 *Mother Seton* American religious leader

Sew·ard \'sü-ərd, 'sü(-ə)rd\ William Henry 1801–1872 American politician; secretary of state (1861–69)

Shake·speare \'shāk-ˌspi(ə)r\ William 1564–1616 English dramatist and poet

Shaw \'shȯ\ George Bernard 1856–1950 British author

Shel·ley \'shel-ē\ Mary Woll·stone·craft \'wul-stən-ˌkraft\ 1797–1851 English novelist; wife of Percy Bysshe Shelley

Shelley Percy Bysshe \'bish\ 1792–1822 English poet

Shep·ard \'shep-ərd\ Alan Bartlett 1923– American astronaut; first American in space (1961)

Sher·i·dan \'sher-əd-ᵊn\ Philip Henry 1831–1888 American general

Sher·lock Holmes \'shər-ˌläk-'hōmz, -'hōlmz\ detective in stories by Sir Arthur Conan Doyle

Sher·man \'shər-mən\ John 1823–1900 American politician

Sherman William Tecumseh 1820–1891 American general

Sieg·fried \'sig-ˌfrēd, 'sēg-\ hero in Germanic legend who kills a dragon guarding a gold hoard

Si·mon \'sī-mən\ *or* **Simon the Zealot** one of the 12 apostles

Sind·bad the Sailor \'sin-ˌbad-\ citizen of Baghdad whose adventures are narrated in the *Arabian Nights' Entertainments*

Sis·y·phus \'sis-ə-fəs\ king of Corinth who in Greek mythology is condemned to roll a heavy stone up a hill in Hades only to have it roll down again as it nears the top

Sit·ting Bull \ˌsit-iŋ-'bul\ *about* 1831–90 Sioux Indian leader

Si·va \'shiv-ə, 'siv-; 'shē-və, 'sē-\ god of destruction in the Hindu sacred triad — compare BRAHMA, VISHNU

Smith \'smith\ Bessie 1894 (or 1898)–1937 American blues singer

Smith John *about* 1580–1631 English colonist in America

Smith Joseph 1805–1844 American founder of the Mormon Church

Soc·ra·tes \'säk-rə-ˌtēz\ *about* 470–399 B.C. Greek philosopher

Sol·o·mon \'säl-ə-mən\ son of David and 10th-century B.C. king of Israel noted for his wisdom

Soph·o·cles \'säf-ə-ˌklēz\ *about* 496–406 B.C. Greek dramatist

Sou·sa \'sü-zə, 'sü-sə\ John Philip 1854–1932 American bandmaster and composer

Spar·ta·cus \'spärt-ə-kəs\ *died* 71 B.C. Roman slave and gladiator; leader of a slave rebellion

Sphinx \'sfiŋ(k)s\ monster in Greek mythology having a lion's body, wings, and the head and bust of a woman

Squan·to \'skwän-tō\ *died* 1622 Indian friend of the Pilgrims

Sta·lin \'stäl-ən, 'stal-, -ˌēn\ Joseph 1879–1953 Soviet leader

Stan·dish \'stan-dish\ Myles *or* Miles 1584?–1656 American colonist

Stan·ley \'stan-lē\ Sir Henry Morton 1841–1904 British explorer in Africa

Stan·ton \'stant-ᵊn\ Elizabeth Cady 1815–1902 American suffragist

Stein \'stīn\ Gertrude 1874–1946 American author

Stein·beck \'stīn-ˌbek\ John Ernst 1902–1968 American author; Nobel Prize winner (1962)

Steu·ben, von \'st(y)ü-bən, 'shtȯi-\ Baron Friedrich Wilhelm Ludolf Gerhard Augustin 1730–1794 Prussian-born general in American Revolution

Ste·ven·son \'stē-vən-sən\ Adlai Ewing 1900–1965 American politician

Stevenson Robert Louis Balfour 1850–1894 Scottish author

Stowe \'stō\ Harriet Elizabeth Beecher 1811–1896 American author

Stra·di·va·ri \ˌstrad-ə-'vär-ē, -'var-, -'ver-\ Antonio 1644–1737 Latin *Antonius Strad·i·var·i·us* \ˌstrad-ə-'var-ē-əs, -'ver-\ Italian violin maker

Strauss \'straus, 'shtraus\ Johann father 1804–1849 and his sons Johann 1825–1899 and Josef 1827–1870 Austrian composers

Stu·art \'st(y)ü-ərt, 'st(y)ü(-ə)rt\ — see CHARLES I, MARY STUART

Stuart Charles — CHARLES EDWARD STUART

Stuart Gilbert Charles 1755–1828 American painter

Stuart James Ewell Brown 1833–1864 *Jeb* American Confederate general

Stuy·ve·sant \'stī-və-sənt\ Peter *about* 1610–1672 Dutch colonial administrator in America

Sul·li·van \'səl-ə-vən\ Sir Arthur Seymour 1842–1900 English composer; collaborator with Sir William Gilbert

Sullivan Louis Henri 1856–1924 American architect

Sum·ner \'səm-nər\ Charles 1811–1874 American politician

Swift \'swift\ Jonathan 1667–1745 English author

Taft \'taft\ William Howard 1857–1930 27th president of the U.S. (1909–13); chief justice of the U.S. Supreme Court (1921–30)

Ta·ney \'tȯ-nē\ Roger Brooke 1777–1864 American jurist; chief justice of the U.S. Supreme Court (1836–64)

Tan·ta·lus \'tant-ᵊl-əs\ king in Greek mythology who is condemned to stand up to his chin in a pool of water in Hades and beneath fruit-laden boughs only to have the water or fruit go out of reach at each attempt to drink or eat

Tay·lor \'tā-lər\ Zachary 1784–1850 12th president of the U.S. (1849–50)

Tchai·kov·sky \chī-'kȯf-skē, chə-, -'kȯv-\ Pyotr Ilich 1840–1893 Russian composer

Te·cum·seh \tə-'kəm(p)-sə, -sē\ 1768–1813 Shawnee Indian chief

Ten·ny·son \'ten-ə-sən\ Alfred 1809–1892 known as *Alfred, Lord Tennyson* English poet

Te·re·sa \tə-'rā-zə, -'rē-sə\ **of Ávi·la** \'äv-i-lə\ Saint 1515–1582 Spanish nun and mystic

The·seus \'thē-,süs, -sē-əs\ hero in Greek mythology who kills the Minotaur and conquers the Amazons

Thom·as \'täm-əs\ apostle in the Bible who demanded proof of Christ's resurrection

Thomas à Becket — see BECKET, À

Thor \'thȯ(ə)r\ god of thunder, weather, and crops in Norse mythology

Tho·reau \thə-'rō, thȯ-; 'thȯr-ō\ Henry David 1817–1862 American author

Thur·ber \'thər-bər\ James Grover 1894–1961 American author

Ti·be·ri·us \tī-'bir-ē-əs\ 42 B.C.–37 A.D. Roman emperor (14–37)

Tocque·ville \'tōk-,vil, 'tȯk-, 'täk-, -,vēl, -vəl\ Alexis⸗ Charles-Henri Clérel de 1805–1859 French politician and author

Tol·kien \'tȯl-,kēn, 'tōl-, 'täl-\ John Ronald Reuel 1892–1973 English author

Tol·stoy \'tȯl-,stȯi, tōl-'stȯi, täl-'stȯi, 'tȯl-,stȯi, 'tōl-,stȯi, 'täl-,stȯi\ Count Lev Nikolayevich 1828–1910 Russian author

Tri·ton \'trīt-ᵊn\ sea god in Greek mythology who is half man and half fish

Trots·ky \'trät-skē, 'trȯt-\ Leon 1879–1940 originally *Lev Davidovich Bronstein* Russian Communist

Tru·man \'trü-mən\ Harry S 1884–1972 33d president of the U.S. (1945–53)

Truth \'trüth\ Sojourner 1797?–1883 American abolitionist

Tub·man \'təb-mən\ Harriet *about* 1820–1913 American abolitionist

Tut·ankh·a·men \,tü-,taŋ-'käm-ən, -,täŋ-\ *or* **Tut·ankh·a·ten** \-'kät-ᵊn\ *about* 1370–1352 B.C. king of Egypt (1361–1352 B.C.)

Twain Mark — see CLEMENS

Tweed \'twēd\ William Marcy 1823–1878 *Boss Tweed* American politician

Ty·ler \'tī-lər\ John 1790–1862 10th president of the U.S. (1841–45)

Ulysses — see ODYSSEUS

Ura·nus \'yur-ə-nəs, yu-'rā-\ the sky personified as a god and father of the Titans in Greek mythology

Ur·ban \'ər-bən\ name of eight popes: especially **II** *about* 1035–1099 (pope 1088–99)

Uri·el \'yur-ē-əl\ one of the four archangels named in Hebrew tradition — compare GABRIEL, MICHAEL, RAPHAEL

Val·en·tine \'val-ən-,tīn\ Saint 3d century Christian martyr

Van Bu·ren \van-'byur-ən, vən-\ Martin 1782–1862 8th president of the U.S. (1837–41)

Van Dyck *or* **Van·dyke** \van-'dīk, vən-\ Sir Anthony 1599–1641 Flemish painter

Ve·láz·quez \və-'las-kəs\ Diego Rodríguez de Silva 1599–1660 Spanish painter

Ve·nus \'vē-nəs\ the goddess of love and beauty in Roman mythology — compare APHRODITE

Ver·di \'ve(ə)rd-ē\ Giuseppe Fortunio Francesco 1813–1901 Italian composer

Ver·meer \vər-'me(ə)r, -'mi(ə)r\ Jan 1632–1675 also called *Jan van der Meer van Delft* Dutch painter

Verne Jules \'jülz-'vərn\ 1828–1905 French author

Ves·puc·ci \ve-'spü-chē\ Ame·ri·go \,äm-ə-'rē-gō\ 1454–1512 Latin *Amer·i·cus Ves·pu·cius* \ə-'mer-ə-kəs-,ves-'pyü-sh(ē-)əs\ Italian navigator for whom America was named

Vic·to·ria \vik-'tōr-ē-ə, -'tȯr-\ 1819–1901 *Alexandrina Victoria* queen of Great Britain (1837–1901)

Vinci, da Leonardo — see LEONARDO DA VINCI

Vir·gil *also* **Ver·gil** \'vər-jəl\ 70–19 B.C. Roman poet

Vish·nu \'vish-nü\ god of preservation in the Hindu sacred triad — compare BRAHMA, SIVA

Vol·ta \'vōl-tə, 'väl-, 'vȯl-\ Count Alessandro Giuseppe Antonio Anastasio 1745–1827 Italian physicist

Vol·taire \vōl-'ta(ə)r, vȯl-, väl-, -'te(ə)r\ 1694–1778 originally *François-Marie Arouet* French author

Vul·can \'vəl-kən\ the god of fire and metalworking in Roman mythology — compare HEPHAESTUS

Wag·ner \'väg-nər\ (Wilhelm) Ri·chard \'rik-,ärt, 'rik-\ 1813–1883 German composer

War·ren \'wȯr-ən, 'wär-\ Earl 1891–1974 American jurist; chief justice of the U.S. Supreme Court (1953–69)

Wash·ing·ton \'wȯsh-iŋ-tən, 'wäsh-\ Book·er \'buk-ər\ Tal·ia·ferro \'täl-ə-vər\ 1856–1915 American educator

Washington George 1732–1799 American general; 1st president of the U.S. (1789–97)

Watt \'wät\ James 1736–1819 Scottish inventor

Wayne \'wān\ Anthony 1745–1796 *Mad Anthony* American general

Web·ster \'web-stər\ Daniel 1782–1852 American politician

Webster Noah 1758–1843 American lexicographer

Wel·ling·ton \'wel-iŋ-tən\ 1st Duke of 1769–1852 *Arthur Wellesley; the Iron Duke* British general and politician

Wells \'welz\ Herbert George 1866–1946 English author and historian

Wes·ley \'wes-lē, 'wez-\ John 1703–1791 English founder of Methodism

Wes·ting·house \'wes-tiŋ-,haus\ George 1846–1914 American inventor

Whar·ton \'hwȯrt-ᵊn, 'wȯrt-\ Edith Newbold 1862–1937 American author

Whis·tler \'hwis-lər, 'wis-\ James Abbott McNeill 1834–1903 American artist

Whit·man \'hwit-mən, 'wit-\ Walt 1819–1892 American poet

Whit·ney \'hwit-nē, 'wit-\ Eli 1765–1825 American inventor

Whit·ti·er \'hwit-ē-ər, 'wit-\ John Greenleaf 1807–1892 American poet

Wilde \'wī(ə)ld\ Oscar Fingal O'Flahertie Wills 1854–1900 Irish author

Wil·der \'wīl-dər\ Thornton Niven 1897–1975 American author

Wil·liam \'wil-yəm\ name of four kings of England: **I** *(the Conqueror) about* 1028–1087 (reigned 1066–87); **II** *(Rufus* \'rü-fəs\) *about* 1056–1100 (reigned 1087–1100); **III** 1650–1702 (reigned 1689–1702); **IV** 1765–1837 (reigned 1830–37)

Wil·liam Tell \,wil-yəm-'tel\ legendary Swiss patriot commanded to shoot an apple from his son's head

Wil·liams \'wil-yəmz\ Roger 1603?–1683 English colonist; founder of Rhode Island

Williams Tennessee 1911–1983 originally *Thomas Lanier Williams* American dramatist

Wil·son \'wil-sən\ (Thomas) Wood·row \'wud-,rō\ 1856–1924 28th president of the U.S. (1913–21); Nobel Prize winner (1919)

Win·throp \'win(t)-thrəp\ John 1588–1649 1st governor of Massachusetts Bay Colony

Woden — see ODIN

Woolf \'wulf\ Virginia 1882–1941 English author

Words·worth \'wərdz-(,)wərth\ William 1770–1850 English poet

Wren \'ren\ Sir Christopher 1632–1723 English architect

Wright \'rīt\ Frank Lloyd 1867–1959 American architect

Wright Or·ville \'ȯr-vəl\ 1871–1948 and his brother Wilbur 1867–1912 American pioneers in aviation

Wright Richard 1908–1960 American author

Wy·eth \'wī-əth\ Andrew Newell 1917–   American painter

Yeats \'yāts\ William Butler 1865–1939 Irish author

Young \'yəŋ\ Brig·ham \'brig-əm\ 1801–1877 American

\ə\ **abut**	\au̇\ **out**	\i\ **tip**	\ȯ\ **saw**	\u̇\ **foot**
\ər\ **further**	\ch\ **chin**	\ī\ **life**	\ȯi\ **coin**	\y\ **yet**
\a\ **mat**	\e\ **pet**	\j\ **job**	\th\ **thin**	\yü\ **few**
\ā\ **take**	\ē\ **easy**	\ŋ\ **sing**	\th̲\ **this**	\yu̇\ **cure**
\ä\ **cot, cart**	\g\ **go**	\ō\ **bone**	\ü\ **food**	\zh\ **vision**

Mormon leader

Zech·a·ri·ah \ˌzek-ə-ˈrī-ə\ Hebrew prophet of the 6th century B.C.

Zeng·er \ˈzeŋ-(g)ər\ John Peter 1697–1746 American (German-born) journalist and printer

Zeph·y·rus \ˈzef-ə-rəs\ god of the west wind in Greek mythology

Zeus \ˈzüs\ chief god, ruler of the sky and weather (as lightning and rain), and husband of Hera in Greek mythology

GEOGRAPHICAL NAMES

This section contains definitions of current and historical place names likely to be of interest to the student. It adds to the general vocabulary by entering many adjectives and nouns formed from geographical names, such as **Florentine** at **Florence** and **Libyan** at **Libya.**

In the entries the letters Ⓝ, Ⓔ, Ⓢ, and Ⓦ singly or in combination indicate direction and are not part of a place name. They may represent either the name of the direction (as *north*) or the adjective derived from it (as *northern*); thus, west-northwest of Santiago appears as Ⓦ Ⓝ Ⓦ of Santiago and southern California appears as Ⓢ California. The only other special abbreviations used in this section are U.S. for United States, and U.S.S.R. for Union of Soviet Socialist Republics. All heights and distances are given in metric units.

Ab·er·deen \,ab-ər-'dēn\ city Ⓝ Ⓔ Scotland in Grampian region — **Ab·er·do·ni·an** \-'dō-nē-ən\ *adj or n*

Ab·i·djan \,ab-i-'jän\ city, capital of Ivory Coast

Abu Dha·bi \,äb-ü-'däb-ē\ city, capital of United Arab Emirates

Abu·ja \ä-'bü-jä\ city, official capital of Nigeria

Ab·ys·sin·ia \,ab-ə-'sin-ē-ə, -'sin-yə\ — see ETHIOPIA — **Ab·ys·sin·i·an** \-ē-ən, -yən\ *adj or n*

Aca·dia \ə-'kād-ē-ə\ *or French* **Aca·die** \à-kà-dē\ NOVA SCOTIA — an early name — **Aca·di·an** \-ē-ən\ *adj or n*

Aca·pul·co \,äk-ə-'pül-kō, ,ak-\ city Ⓢ Mexico on the Pacific

Ac·cra \ə-'krä\ city, capital of Ghana

Acon·ca·gua \,ak-ən-'käg-wə, ,äk-, -əŋ-\ mountain 6960 meters Ⓦ Argentina; highest in the Andes & in North America & South America

Ad·dis Aba·ba \,ad-ə-'sab-ə-bə\ city, capital of Ethiopia

Ad·e·laide \'ad-ᵊl-,ād\ city, capital of South Australia

Aden \'äd-ᵊn, 'äd-, 'ad-\ city Ⓢ Yemen; formerly capital of People's Democratic Republic of Yemen

Aden, Gulf of arm of Indian ocean between Yemen (Arabia) & Somalia (Africa)

Ad·i·ron·dack \,ad-ə-'rän-,dak\ mountains Ⓝ Ⓔ New York; highest Mount Marcy 1629 meters

Ad·mi·ral·ty \'ad-m(ə-)rəl-tē\ **1** island Ⓢ Ⓔ Alaska in Ⓝ Alexander island group **2** islands Ⓦ Pacific Ⓝ of New Guinea; belong to Papua New Guinea

Adri·at·ic \,ā-drē-'at-ik, ,ad-rē-\ sea arm of Mediterranean between Italy & Balkan peninsula

Ae·ge·an \i-'jē-ən\ sea arm of Mediterranean between Asia Minor & Greece

Af·ghan·i·stan \af-'gan-ə-,stan\ country Ⓦ Asia Ⓔ of Iran; capital, Kabul

Af·ri·ca \'af-ri-kə\ continent Ⓢ of Mediterranean

Aga·na \ə-'gän-yə\ town, capital of Guam

Ag·as·siz Lake \'ag-ə-sē-\ prehistoric lake 1130 kilometers long in region consisting of present Ⓢ Manitoba, Ⓔ Saskatchewan, Ⓝ Ⓦ Minnesota, & Ⓔ North Dakota

Agra \'äg-rə\ city Ⓝ India

Aguas·ca·lien·tes \,äg-wə-,skäl-'yen-,tās\ city central Mexico, Ⓝ Ⓔ of Guadalajara

Agul·has, Cape \-ə-'gəl-əs\ cape Republic of South Africa in Ⓢ Cape Province; most southerly point of Africa, at 34° 50′ Ⓢ latitude

Ahag·gar \ə-'häg-ər, ,ä-hə-'gär\ mountains Ⓢ Algeria in Ⓦ central Sahara

Ah·mad·abad *or* **Ah·med·abad** \'äm-əd-ə-,bäd\ city Ⓦ India

Ak·ron \'ak-rən\ city Ⓝ Ⓔ Ohio

Al·a·bama \,al-ə-'bam-ə\ state Ⓢ Ⓔ U.S.; capital, Montgomery — **Al·a·bam·i·an** \-'bam-ē-ən\ *or* **Al·a·bam·an** \-'bam-ən\ *adj or n*

Alas·ka \ə-'las-kə\ **1** peninsula Ⓢ Ⓦ Alaska Ⓢ Ⓦ of Cook inlet **2** state of U.S. in Ⓝ Ⓦ North America; capital, Juneau **3** mountain range Ⓢ Alaska extending from Alaska peninsula to Yukon boundary — **Alas·kan** \-kən\ *adj or n*

Alaska, Gulf of inlet of Pacific off Ⓢ Alaska between Alaska peninsula on Ⓦ & Alexander island group on Ⓔ

Al·ba·nia \al-'bā-nē-ə, -nyə\ country Ⓢ Europe in Balkan peninsula on Adriatic; capital, Tirane

Al·ba·ny \'ȯl-bə-nē\ city, capital of New York

Al·be·marle \'al-bə-,märl\ inlet of Atlantic in Ⓝ Ⓔ North Carolina

Al·bert, Lake \-'al-bərt\ lake Ⓔ Africa between Uganda & Zaire in course of Nile

Al·ber·ta \al-'bərt-ə\ province Ⓦ Canada; capital, Edmonton — **Al·ber·tan** \-'bərt-ᵊn\ *adj or n*

Al·bu·quer·que \'al-b(y)ə-,kər-kē\ city central New Mexico

Al·ca·traz \'al-kə-,traz\ island California in San Francisco Bay

Al·da·bra \'al-də-brə\ island Ⓝ Ⓦ Indian ocean Ⓝ of Madagascar; belongs to Seychelles

Al·der·ney \'ȯl-dər-nē\ island in English channel — see CHANNEL

Alep·po \ə-'lep-ō\ city Ⓝ Syria

Aleu·tian \ə-'lü-shən\ islands Ⓢ Ⓦ Alaska extending 1930 kilometers Ⓦ from Alaska peninsula

Al·ex·an·der \,al-ig-'zan-dər, ,el-\ island group Ⓢ Ⓔ Alaska

Al·ex·an·dria \,al-ig-'zan-drē-ə, ,el-\ **1** city Ⓝ Virginia **2** city Ⓝ Egypt on Mediterranean — **Al·ex·an·dri·an** \-drē-ən\ *adj or n*

Al·ge·ria \al-'jir-ē-ə\ country Ⓝ Ⓦ Africa on Mediterranean; capital, Algiers — **Al·ge·ri·an** \-ē-ən\ *adj or n*

Al·giers \al-'ji(ə)rz\ city, capital of Algeria — **Al·ge·rine** \,al-jə-'rēn\ *adj or n*

Al·lah·abad \'al-ə-hə-,bad, -,bäd\ city Ⓝ India

Al·le·ghe·ny \,al-ə-'gā-nē\ **1** river 523 kilometers long Ⓦ Pennsylvania & Ⓢ Ⓦ New York **2** mountains of Appalachian system Ⓔ U.S. in Pennsylvania, Maryland, Virginia, & West Virginia

Al·len·town \'al-ən-,taûn\ city Ⓔ Pennsylvania

Al·ma–Ata \,al-mə-ə-'tä\ city, capital of Kazakhstan

Alps \'alps\ mountain system central Europe — see MONT BLANC

Al·tai \'al-,tī\ mountain system central Asia between Mongolia & Ⓦ China & between Kazakhstan & Russia; highest peak Tabun Bogdo 4653 meters

Ama·ga·sa·ki \,am-ə-gə-'säk-ē\ city Japan in Ⓦ central Honshu

---

\ə\ abut	\aû\ out	\i\ tip	\ȯ\ saw	\ù\ foot
\ər\ further	\ch\ chin	\ī\ life	\ȯi\ coin	\y\ yet
\a\ mat	\e\ pet	\j\ job	\th\ thin	\yü\ few
\ā\ take	\ē\ easy	\ŋ\ sing	\t͟h\ this	\yù\ cure
\ä\ cot, cart	\g\ go	\ō\ bone	\ü\ food	\zh\ vision

Am·a·ril·lo \‚am-ə-'ril-ō, -'ril-ə\ city ⃞NW Texas

Am·a·zon \'am-ə-‚zän, -zən\ river about 6275 kilometers long ⃞N South America flowing from Peruvian Andes into Atlantic in ⃞N Brazil

Amer·i·ca \ə-'mer-ə-kə\ **1** either continent (North America or South America) of western hemisphere **2** *or* **the Amer·i·cas** \-kəz\ lands of western hemisphere including North, Central, & South America & West Indies **3** UNITED STATES OF AMERICA

American Falls — see NIAGARA FALLS

American Samoa *or* **Eastern Samoa** islands ⃞SW central Pacific; capital, Pago Pago (on Tutuila island)

Am·man \ä-'män, -'man\ city, capital of Jordan

Am·ster·dam \'am(p)-stər-‚dam\ city, official capital of the Netherlands

Amur \ä-'mü(ə)r\ river 2865 kilometers long ⃞E Asia flowing into the Pacific & forming part of boundary between China & Russia

An·a·heim \'an-ə-‚hīm\ city ⃞SW California ⃞E of Long Beach

An·a·to·lia \‚an-ə-'tō-lē-ə, -'tōl-yə\ — see ASIA MINOR — **An·a·to·li·an** \-'tō-lē-ən, -'tōl-yən\ *adj or n*

An·chor·age \'aŋ-k(ə)rij\ city ⃞S central Alaska

An·da·man \'an-də-mən, -‚man\ **1** islands India in Bay of Bengal ⃞S of Myanmar & ⃞N of Nicobar islands **2** sea arm of Bay of Bengal ⃞S of Myanmar — **An·da·man·ese** \‚an-də-mə-'nēz, -'nēs\ *adj or n*

An·des \'an-dēz\ mountain system ⃞W South America extending from Panama to Tierra del Fuego — see ACONCAGUA — **An·de·an** \'an-(‚)dē-ən, an-'dē-\ *adj* — **An·dine** \'an-‚dēn, -‚dīn\ *adj*

An·dor·ra \an-'dôr-ə, -'där-ə\ country ⃞SW Europe in ⃞E Pyrenees between France & Spain; capital, Andorra la Vella — **An·dor·ran** \-ən\ *adj or n*

An·dros \'an-drəs\ island, largest of Bahamas

An·gel Falls \‚än-jəl-\ waterfall 979 meters ⃞SE Venezuela; world's highest waterfall

Ang·kor \'aŋ-‚kô(ə)r\ ruins of ancient city ⃞NW Cambodia

An·gle·sey \'aŋ-gəl-sē\ island ⃞NW Wales

An·go·la \aŋ-'gō-lə, an-\ country ⃞SW Africa ⃞S of mouth of Congo river; until 1975 a dependency of Portugal; capital, Luanda — **An·go·lan** \-lən\ *adj or n*

An·i·ak·chak Crater \‚an-ē-'ak-‚chak-\ volcano 1347 meters ⃞SW Alaska on Alaska peninsula; crater 10 kilometers in diameter

An·ka·ra \'an-kə-rə, 'än-\ city, capital of Turkey in ⃞N central Anatolia

An·nap·o·lis \ə-'nap-(ə)ləs\ city, capital of Maryland

Ann Ar·bor \a-'när-bər\ city ⃞SE Michigan

An·shan \'än-'shän\ city ⃞NE China

An·ta·na·na·ri·vo \‚an-tə-‚nan-ə-'rē-vō\ city, capital of Madagascar

Ant·arc·ti·ca \(')ant-'ärk-ti-kə, -'ärt-i-\ *or* **Ant·arc·tic con·tinent** \-'ärk-tik-, -'ärt-ik-\ body of land around the South Pole; plateau covered by great ice cap

An·ti·gua \an-'tē-gə\ island West Indies in the Leewards ⃞E of Nevis; capital, Saint Johns; part of independent Antigua and Barbuda

Antigua and Barbuda country West Indies in the Leewards; capital, St. Johns

An·til·les \an-'til-ēz\ the West Indies except for the Bahamas — see GREATER ANTILLES, LESSER ANTILLES — **An·til·le·an** \-'til-ē-ən\ *adj*

An·trim \'an-trəm\ **1** district ⃞E Northern Ireland **2** town in Antrim district

Aorangi — see COOK, MOUNT

Ap·en·nines \'ap-ə-‚nīnz\ mountain chain Italy extending length of the peninsula; highest point Monte Corno (⃞NE of Rome) 2914 meters — **Ap·en·nine** \-‚nīn\ *adj*

Apia \ə-'pē-ə\ town, capital of Western Samoa

Apo, Mount \-'äp-ō\ volcano Philippines in ⃞SE Mindanao 2594 meters; highest peak in the Philippines

Ap·pa·la·chia \‚ap-ə-'lā-chə, -'lach-ə, -'lā-shə\ region ⃞E U.S. including Appalachian mountains from ⃞S central New York to central Alabama

Ap·pa·la·chian \‚ap-ə-'lā-ch(ē-)ən, -'lach(-ē)-ən, -'lā-sh(ē-)ən\ mountain system ⃞E North America extending from ⃞S Quebec to central Alabama — see MITCHELL, MOUNT

'Aqa·ba, Gulf of \-'äk-ə-bə, -'ak-\ arm of Red sea ⃞E of Sinai peninsula

Aquid·neck Island \ə-'kwid-‚nek-\ *or* **Rhode Island** island ⃞SE Rhode Island in Narragansett Bay

Ara·bia \ə-'rā-bē-ə\ peninsula of ⃞SW Asia including Saudi Arabia, Yemen, Oman, & Persian Gulf States

Ara·bi·an \ə-'rā-bē-ən\ sea ⃞NW section of Indian ocean between Arabia & India

Ar·a·fu·ra \‚ar-ə-'fúr-ə\ sea between ⃞N Australia & ⃞W New Guinea

Ar·al sea \'ar-əl-\ *or formerly* **Lake Aral** lake ⃞W Asia between Kazakhstan & Uzbekistan

Ar·a·rat \'ar-ə-‚rat\ mountain 5165 meters ⃞E Turkey near border of Iran

Arc·tic \'ärk-tik, 'ärt-ik\ **1** ocean ⃞N of Arctic circle **2** Arctic regions **3** island group ⃞N Canada in ⃞N & ⃞E Northwest Territories

Ar·da·bil *or* **Ar·de·bil** \‚är-də-'bē(ə)l\ city ⃞NW Iran

Ards \'ärdz\ district ⃞E Northern Ireland

Ar·gen·ti·na \‚är-jən-'tē-nə\ country ⃞S South America between the Andes & the Atlantic; capital, Buenos Aires — **Argentine** \'är-jən-‚tēn, -‚tīn\ *adj or n* — **Ar·gen·tin·ean** *or* **Ar·gen·tin·i·an** \‚är-jən-'tin-ē-ən\ *adj or n*

Ar·gos \'är-‚gäs, -gəs\ ancient Greek city & state ⃞S Greece

Ar·i·zo·na \‚ar-ə-'zō-nə\ state ⃞SW U.S.; capital, Phoenix — **Ar·i·zo·nan** \-nən\ *or* **Ar·i·zo·nian** \-nē-ən, -nyən\ *adj or n*

Ar·kan·sas \'är-kən-‚sò; *1 is also* är-'kan-zəs\ **1** river 2335 kilometers long ⃞SW central U.S. flowing ⃞SE into the Mississippi **2** state ⃞S central U.S.; capital, Little Rock — **Ar·kan·san** \är-'kan-zən\ *adj or n*

Ar·ling·ton \'är-liŋ-tən\ city ⃞N Texas

Ar·magh \är-'mä, 'är-‚mä\ **1** district ⃞S Northern Ireland **2** town in Armagh district

Ar·me·nia \är-'mē-nē-ə, -nyə\ **1** region ⃞W Asia in mountainous area ⃞SE of Black sea & ⃞SW of Caspian sea divided between Iran, Turkey, & Armenia (country) **2** country ⃞E Europe; capital, Yerevan; a republic of U.S.S.R. 1936–91 — **Ar·me·ni·an** \-nē-ən, -nyən\ *adj or n*

Arn·hem Land \'är-nəm-\ region ⃞N Australia on ⃞N coast of Northern Territory

Ar·no \'är-nō\ river 225 kilometers long central Italy flowing through Florence

Aru·ba \ə-'rü-bə\ island Netherlands Antilles off coast of ⃞NW Venezuela

Ashkh·a·bad \'ash-kə-‚bad, -‚bäd\ city, capital of Turkmenistan

Asia \'ā-zhə, -shə\ continent of eastern hemisphere ⃞N of equator — see EURASIA

Asia Mi·nor \-'mī-nər\ *or* **Anatolia** peninsula in modern Turkey between Black sea on ⃞N & the Mediterranean on ⃞S

As·syr·ia \ə-'sir-ē-ə\ ancient empire ⃞W Asia extending along the middle Tigris & over foothills to the ⃞E — **As·syr·i·an** \-ən\ *adj or n*

Asun·ción \ə-‚sün(t)-sē-'ōn, (‚)ä-\ city, capital of Paraguay

As·wân \a-'swän, ä-\ city ⃞S Egypt on the Nile near site of **Aswân High Dam**

Ata·ca·ma \‚at-ə-'käm-ə\ desert ⃞N Chile

Atchaf·a·laya \(ə-)‚chaf-ə-'lī-ə\ river 362 kilometers long ⃞S Louisiana flowing ⃞S into Gulf of Mexico

Ath·a·bas·ca *or* **Ath·a·bas·ka** \‚ath-ə-'bas-kə\ river 1231 kilometers long ⃞NE Alberta flowing into Lake Athabasca

Athabasca, Lake lake W central Canada on Alberta-Saskatchewan border

Ath·ens \'ath-ənz\ city, capital of Greece — **Athe·nian** \ə-'thē-nē-ən, -nyən\ adj or n

At·lan·ta \ət-'lant-ə, at-\ city, capital of Georgia

At·lan·tic \ət-'lant-ik, at-\ ocean separating North America & South America from Europe & Africa — **Atlantic** adj

At·las \'at-ləs\ mountains NW Africa extending from SW Morocco to N Tunisia

At·ti·ca \'at-i-kə\ ancient division & state E Greece; chief city Athens — **At·tic** \'at-ik\ adj

Auck·land \'ȯ-klənd\ city N New Zealand on NW North island

Au·gus·ta \ȯ-'gəst-ə, ə-\ city, capital of Maine

Au·ro·ra \ə-'rȯr-ə, ȯ-, -'rȯr-\ city NE central Colorado

Aus·tin \'ȯs-tən, 'äs-\ city, capital of Texas

Aus·tral·asia \,ȯs-trə-'lā-zhə, ,äs-, -'lā-shə\ Australia, Tasmania, New Zealand, & Melanesia — **Aus·tral·asian** \-zhən, -shən\ adj or n

Aus·tra·lia \ȯ-'strāl-yə, ä-, ə-\ **1** continent of eastern hemisphere SE of Asia **2** independent country in the Commonwealth including continent of Australia & island of Tasmania; capital, Canberra — **Aus·tra·lian** \-yən\ adj or n

Australian Alps mountain range SE Australia in E Victoria & SE New South Wales; part of Great Dividing range

Australian Capital Territory district SE Australia including two areas, one containing Canberra (capital of Australia) & the other on Jervis Bay; surrounded by New South Wales

Aus·tria \'ȯs-trē-ə, 'äs-\ country central Europe; capital, Vienna — **Aus·tri·an** \-ən\ adj or n

Aus·tria–Hun·ga·ry \-'həŋ-gə-rē\ country 1867–1918 central Europe including Bohemia, Moravia, Bukovina, Transylvania, Galicia, and what are now Austria, Hungary, Slovenia, Croatia, & part of NE Italy — **Aus·tro–Hun·gar·i·an** \'ȯs-(,)trō-,həŋ-'gar-ē-ən, 'äs-, -'ger-\ adj or n

Aus·tro·ne·sia \,ȯs-trə-'nē-zhə, ,äs-, -'nē-shə\ **1** islands of the S Pacific **2** area extending from Madagascar through Malay peninsula & island group to Hawaii & Easter island — **Aus·tro·ne·sian** \-zhən, -shən\ adj or n

Avon \'ā-vən, 'av-ən, in the U.S. also 'ā-,vän\ **1** river 155 kilometers long central England flowing WSW into the Severn **2** county SW England

Ayles·bury \'ā(ə)lz-b(ə-)rē, in the U.S. also -,ber-ē\ borough SE central England in Buckinghamshire

Ayr \'a(ə)r, 'e(ə)r\ or **Ayr·shire** \-,shi(ə)r, -shər\ former county SW Scotland

Az·ca·po·tzal·co \,äs-kə-pət-'säl-(,)kō, ,äz-gə-\ city central NW Mexico City

Azer·bai·jan \,az-ər-,bī-'jän, ,äz-\ country SE Europe bordering on Caspian sea; capital, Baku; a republic of U.S.S.R. 1936–91

Azores \'ā-,zō(ə)rz, -,zȯ(ə)rz; ə-'zō(ə)rz, -'zȯ(ə)rz\ islands N Atlantic belonging to Portugal & lying 1290 kilometers W of Portuguese coast — **Azor·e·an** or **Azor·i·an** \ā-'zōr-ē-ən, ə-, -'zȯr-\ adj or n

Bab·y·lon \'bab-ə-lən, -,län\ ancient city, capital of Babylonia; site about 80 kilometers S of Baghdad near the Euphrates — **Bab·y·lo·nian** \,bab-ə-'lō-nyən, -nē-ən\ adj or n

Bab·y·lo·nia \,bab-ə-'lō-nyə, -nē-ə\ ancient country W Asia in valley of lower Euphrates and Tigris rivers; capital, Babylon — **Bab·y·lo·nian** \-nyən, -nē-ən\ adj or n

Bac·tria \'bak-trē-ə\ ancient country W Asia in present NE Afghanistan — **Bac·tri·an** \-ən\ adj or n

Bad Lands barren region SW South Dakota & NW Nebraska

Baf·fin \'baf-ən\ island NE Canada in Arctic island group N of Hudson strait

Baffin Bay inlet of the Atlantic between W Greenland & E Baffin island

Bagh·dad \'bag-,dad\ city, capital of Iraq on the Tigris

Ba·guio \,bäg-ē-'ō\ city, summer capital of the Philippines in NW central Luzon

Ba·ha·ma \bə-'häm-ə, by outsiders also -'hä-mə\ islands in N Atlantic SE of Florida; an independent member of the Commonwealth; capital, Nassau — **Ba·ha·mi·an** \-'hä-mē-ən, -'häm-ē-ən\ or **Ba·ha·man** \-'hä-mən, -'häm-ən\ adj or n

Bahia — see SALVADOR

Bah·rain \bä-'rān\ islands in Persian gulf off coast of Arabia; an independent country; capital, Manama

Bai·kal, Lake \-bī-'kȯl, -'käl\ lake Russia, in mountains N of Mongolia

Ba·ja California \,bä-(,)hä-\ peninsula NW Mexico W of Gulf of California

Ba·kers·field \'bā-kərz-,fēld\ city S California

Ba·ku \bä-'kü\ city, capital of Azerbaijan on W coast of Caspian sea

Bal·a·ton \'bal-ə-,tän, 'bȯl-ə-,tōn\ lake W Hungary

Bal·boa Heights \(,)bal-,bō-ə-\ town Panama; formerly the center of administration for Canal Zone

Ba·li \'bäl-ē\ island Indonesia off E end of Java — **Ba·li·nese** \,bäl-i-nēz, ,bal-, -'nēs\ adj or n

Bal·kan \'bȯl-kən\ **1** mountains N Bulgaria extending from Yugoslavia border to Black sea; highest about 2380 meters **2** peninsula SE Europe between Adriatic & Ionian seas on the W & Aegean & Black seas on the E

Bal·kans \'bȯl-kənz\ or **Balkan States** countries occupying the Balkan peninsula: Solvenia, Croatia, Bosnia and Herzegovina, Macedonia, Yugoslavia, Romania, Bulgaria, Albania, Greece, Turkey (in Europe)

Bal·ly·cas·tle \,bal-ē-'kas-əl\ town N Northern Ireland in Moyle district

Bal·ly·me·na \,bal-ē-'mē-nə\ district NE central Northern Ireland

Bal·ly·mon·ey \,bal-ē-'mən-ē\ district N central Northern Ireland

Bal·tic \'bȯl-tik\ sea arm of the Atlantic N Europe E of Scandinavian peninsula

Bal·ti·more \'bȯl-tə-,mō(ə)r, -,mȯ(ə)r; 'bȯl-(tə-)mər\ city N central Maryland

Ba·ma·ko \,bäm-ə-'kō\ city, capital of Mali on the Niger

Ba·na·ras or **Be·na·res** \bə-'när-əs, -ēz\ or **Va·ra·na·si** \və-'rän-ə-(,)sē\ city N India

Ban·bridge \ban-'brij\ district SE central Northern Ireland

Ban·dar Se·ri Be·ga·wan \,bən-dər-,ser-ē-bə-'gä-wən\ town, capital of Brunei

Ban·dung \'bän-,dùŋ\ city Indonesia in W Java SE of Djakarta

Ban·ga·lore \'baŋ-gə-,lō(ə)r, -,lȯ(ə)r\ city S India W of Madras

Bang·kok \'baŋ-,käk, baŋ-'käk\ city, capital of Thailand

Ban·gla·desh \,bäŋ-gle-'desh, ,baŋ-, -'däsh\ country S Asia E of India; formerly part of Pakistan; an independent state since 1971; capital, Dacca — see EAST PAKISTAN

Ban·gor \'baŋ-,gȯ(ə)r, 'ban-,gȯ(ə)r, 'baŋ-gər\ city area E Northern Ireland in North Down district

Ban·gui \bäŋ-'gē\ city, capital of Central African Republic

Ban·jul \'bän-,jül\ or formerly **Bath·urst** \'bath-(,)ərst\ city, capital of Gambia

Baotou or **Pao-t'ou** \'baù-'tō\ city N China

Bar·ba·dos \bär-'bād-əs, -ōz, -äs, -ōs\ island West Indies in Lesser Antilles E of Windward Islands; an independent country in the Commonwealth since 1966; capital, Bridgetown — **Bar·ba·di·an** \-'bād-ē-ən\ adj or n

\ə\ **abut**	\aù\ **out**	\i\ **tip**	\ȯ\ **saw**	\ù\ **foot**
\ər\ **further**	\ch\ **chin**	\ī\ **life**	\ȯi\ **coin**	\y\ **yet**
\a\ **mat**	\e\ **pet**	\j\ **job**	\th\ **thin**	\yü\ **few**
\ā\ **take**	\ē\ **easy**	\ŋ\ **sing**	\th\ **this**	\yù\ **cure**
\ä\ **cot, cart**	\g\ **go**	\ō\ **bone**	\ü\ **food**	\zh\ **vision**

Bar·bu·da \bär-'büd-ə\ island West Indies; part of independent Antigua and Barbuda

Bar·ce·lo·na \,bär-sə-'lō-nə\ city [NE] Spain on the Mediterranean; chief city of Catalonia

Bar·king \'bär-kiŋ\ city area of [E] Greater London county, England

Bar·na·ul \,bär-nə-'ül\ city [S] Russia

Bar·net \'bär-nət\ city area of [N] Greater London county, England

Bar·ran·qui·lla \,bar-ən-'kē-(y)ə\ city [N] Colombia

Barren Grounds treeless plains [N] Canada [W] of Hudson bay

Bar·row, Point \-'bar-ō\ most northerly point of Alaska & of United States at about 71°25'N latitude

Ba·si·lan \bä-'sē-,län\ island [S] Philippines

Bas·il·don \'baz-əl-dən\ town [SE] England in Essex county

Bass \'bas\ strait separating Tasmania & continent of Australia

Basse·terre \bas-'te(ə)r, bäs-\ seaport St. Christopher, capital of Saint Christopher-Nevis

Basutoland — see LESOTHO

Batavia — see DJAKARTA

Bathurst — see BANJUL

Bat·on Rouge \,bat-ᵊn-'rüzh\ city, capital of Louisiana

Ba·var·ia \bə-'ver-ē-ə, -'var-\ *or German* **Bay·ern** \'bī-ərn\ state [SE] Germany bordering on Czech Republic & Austria — **Ba·var·i·an** \bə-'ver-ē-ən, -'var-\ *adj or n*

Ba·ya·mon \,bī-ə-'mōn\ city [NE] central Puerto Rico

Beau·fort \'bō-fərt\ sea consisting of part of Arctic ocean [NE] of Alaska & [NW] of Canada

Beau·mont \'bō-,mänt, bō-'mänt\ city [SE] Texas

Bech·u·a·na·land \,bech-(ə-)'wän-ə-,land\ **1** region [S] Africa [N] of Orange river **2** — see BOTSWANA — **Bech·u·a·na** \,bech-(ə-)'wän-ə\ *adj or n*

Bed·ford·shire \'bed-fərd-,shi(ə)r, -shər\ *or* **Bedford** county [SE] England

Bedloe's *or* **Bedloe** — see LIBERTY

Bei·jing \'bā-'jiŋ\ *or* **Pe·king** \'pē-'kiŋ, 'pā-\ city, capital of China

Bei·rut \bā-'rüt\ city, capital of Lebanon

Be·la·rus \,bē-lə-'rüs, ,byel-ə-\ *or* **Bye·la·rus** \bē-,el-ə-, ,byel-ə-\ country central Europe; capital, Minsk

Be·lau \bə-'laú\ *or formerly* **Pa·lau** \pə-'laú\ island group [W] Pacific in the [W] Carolines

Be·lém \bə-'lem\ city [N] Brazil

Bel·fast \'bel-,fast, bel-'fast\ **1** district [E] Northern Ireland **2** city, capital of Northern Ireland in Antrim district

Belgian Congo — see ZAIRE

Bel·gium \'bel-jəm\ *or French* **Bel·gique** \bel-zhēk\ *or Flemish* **Bel·gië** \'bel-gē-ə\ county [W] Europe; capital, Brussels — **Bel·gian** \'bel-jən\ *adj or n*

Bel·grade \'bel-,gräd, -,gråd, -,grad\ *or* **Beo·grad** \'beú-,gräd\ city, capital of Yugoslavia on the Danube

Be·lize \bə-'lēz\ *or formerly* **British Honduras** country Central America on the Caribbean; capital, Belmopan

Bel·mo·pan \,bel-mō-'pan\ city, capital of Belize

Be·lo Ho·ri·zon·te \'bā-lō-,hòr-ə-'zänt-ē, 'bel-ō-, -,här-\ city [E] Brazil [N] of Rio de Janeiro

Be·lo·rus·sia \,bel-ō-'rəsh-ə, ,byel-\ *or* **Bye·lo·rus·sia** \bē-,el-ō-, ,byel-ō-\ former republic of U.S.S.R.; became independent Belarus in 1991 — **Belorussian** *adj or n*

Benares — see BANARAS

Ben·gal \ben-'gòl, beŋ-\ region [S] Asia including delta of Ganges & Brahmaputra rivers; divided between Bangladesh & India — **Ben·gal·ese** \,beŋ-gə-'lēz, ,ben-, -'lēs\ *adj or n*

Bengal, Bay of arm of Indian ocean between India & Myanmar

Be·nin \bə-'nin, -'nēn; 'ben-ən\ *or formerly* **Da·ho·mey** \də-'hō-mē\ country [W] Africa on Gulf of Guinea; capital,

Porto-Novo — **Ben·i·nese** \bə-,nin-'ēz, -,nēn-; ,ben-i-'nēz, -'nēs\ *adj or n*

Ben Nev·is \ben-'nev-əs\ mountain 1343 meters [W] Scotland in the Grampians; highest in Great Britain

Ber·gen \'bər-gən, 'be(ə)r-\ city [SW] Norway

Be·ring \'bi(ə)r-iŋ, 'be(ə)r-\ **1** sea arm of the [N] Pacific between Alaska & [NE] Siberia **2** strait about 90 kilometers wide between North America (Alaska) and Asia (Russia)

Berke·ley \'bər-klē\ city [W] California on San Francisco Bay [N] of Oakland

Berk·shire \'bərk-,shi(ə)r, -shər, *for 2 British usually* 'bärk-\ **1** hills [W] Massachusetts; highest point Mount Greylock 1064 meters **2** county [S] England [W] of London

Ber·lin \(,)bər-'lin\ city, official capital of Germany; divided 1945–90 into **East Berlin** (capital of East Germany) & **West Berlin** (city of West Germany lying within East Germany) — **Ber·lin·er** \-'lin-ər\ *n*

Ber·mu·da \(,)bər-'myüd-ə\ islands [W] Atlantic [ESE] of Cape Hatteras; a British colony; capital, Hamilton — **Ber·mu·dan** \-'myüd-ᵊn\ *or* **Ber·mu·di·an** \-'myüd-ē-ən\ *adj or n*

Bern *or* **Berne** \'bərn, 'be(ə)rn\ city, capital of Switzerland — **Ber·nese** \(,)bər-'nēz, -'nēs\ *adj or n*

Bes·sa·ra·bia \,bes-ə-'rā-bē-ə\ region [SE] Europe now chiefly in Moldova — **Bes·sa·ra·bi·an** \-bē-ən\ *adj or n*

Beth·le·hem \'beth-li-,hem, -lē-həm, -lē-əm\ town of ancient Palestine in Judea [SW] of Jerusalem in area occupied by Israel since 1967

Bev·er·ly Hills \,bev-ər-lē-'hilz\ city [SW] California within city of Los Angeles

Bex·ley \'bek-slē\ city area of [E] Greater London county, England

Bho·pal \bō-'päl\ city [N] central India

Bhu·tan \bü-'tan, -'tän\ country [S] Asia in the Himalayas on [NE] border of India; capital, Thimbu — **Bhu·ta·nese** \,büt-ᵊn-'ēz, -'ēs\ *adj or n*

Bi·ki·ni \bə-'kē-nē\ island [W] Pacific in Marshall islands

Bil·lings \'bil-iŋz\ city [S] central Montana; largest in state

Bi·lox·i \bə-'lək-sē, -'läk-\ city [SE] Mississippi on Gulf of Mexico

Bi·o·ko \bē-'ō-kō\ *or formerly* **Fer·nan·do Po** \fər-,nan-(,)dō-'pō\ *or 1973–79* **Ma·cí·as Ngue·ma Bi·yo·go** \'mä-thē-ə-səŋ-'(g)wä-mə-bi-'yō-(,)gō\ island portion of Equatorial Guinea in Gulf of Guinea

Bir·ken·head \'bər-kən-,hed, ,bər-kən-'hed\ city area [NW] England in Merseyside county

Bir·ming·ham \'bər-miŋ-,ham, *British usually* -miŋ-əm\ **1** city [N] central Alabama **2** city [W] central England in West Midlands county

Bisayas — see VISAYAN

Bis·cay, Bay of \-'bis-,kā, -kē\ inlet of the Atlantic between [W] coast of France & [N] coast of Spain

Bish·kek \bish-'kek\ *or 1926–91* **Frunze** \'frün-zə\ city, capital of Kyrgyzstan

Bis·marck \'biz-,märk\ **1** city, capital of North Dakota **2** island group [W] Pacific [N] of [E] end of New Guinea

Bis·sau \bis-'aú\ city, capital of Guinea-Bissau

Bi·thyn·ia \bə-'thin-ē-ə\ ancient country [NW] Asia Minor bordering on Sea of Marmara and Black sea — **Bi·thyn·i·an** \-ē-ən\ *adj or n*

Bit·ter·root Range \'bit-ə(r)-,rüt-, -,rút-\ range of the Rockies along Idaho-Montana boundary

Black·burn \'blak-(,)bərn\ city area [NW] England in Lancashire

Black Forest forested mountain region [SW] Germany along [E] bank of the upper Rhine

Black hills mountains [W] South Dakota & [NE] Wyoming; highest Harney Peak 2207 meters

Black·pool \'blak-,pül\ city area [NW] England in Lancashire

Black sea *or ancient* **Pon·tus Eux·i·nus** \'pänt-əs-,yük-'sī-nəs\ *or* **Pon·tus** sea between Europe & Asia connected with Aegean sea through the Bosporus, Sea of Marmara, & Dardanelles

Blanc, Mont — see MONT BLANC

Bloem·fon·tein \'blüm-fən-,tān, -,fän\ city Republic of South Africa, capital of Orange Free State & judicial capital of the country

Blue Ridge E range of the Applachians E U.S. extending from S Pennsylvania to N Georgia

Boe·o·tia \bē-'ō-sh(ē-)ə\ ancient state E central Greece NW of Attica; chief ancient city, Thebes — **Boe·o·tian** \bē-'ō-shən\ *adj or n*

Bo·go·tá \,bō-gə-'tȯ, -'tä\ city, capital of Colombia

Bo Hai *or* **Po Hai** \'bō-'hī\ *or* **Gulf of Chih·li** \'chē-lē, 'jir-\ arm of Yellow Sea NE China

Bo·he·mia \bō-'hē-mē-ə\ region W Czech Republic; once a kingdom; chief city, Prague

Bo·hol \bō-'hȯl\ island S central Philippines

Boi·se \'bȯi-sē, -zē\ city, capital of Idaho

Bo·liv·ia \bə-'liv-ē-ə\ country W central South America; administrative capital, La Paz; constitutional capital, Sucre — **Bo·liv·i·an** \-ē-ən\ *adj or n*

Bol·ton \'bōlt-ᵊn\ *or in full* **Bolton—le—Moors** \-lə-,mu̇(ə)rz\ city area NW England in Greater Manchester county

Bom·bay \bäm-'bā\ city W India

Bonn \'bän, 'bȯn\ city W Germany on the Rhine SSE of Cologne; formerly capital of West Germany

Boo·thia \'bü-thē-ə\ peninsula N Canada W of Baffin island; its N tip is most northerly point in North America except for islands

Bor·ders \'bȯrd-ərz\ region SE Scotland; established 1975

Bor·neo \'bȯr-nē-,ō\ island Malay group SW of the Philippines; divided between Brunei, Indonesia, and Malaysia

Bos·nia \'bäz-nē-ə\ region S Europe; with Herzegovina forms independent **Bosnia and Her·ze·go·vi·na** \,hert-sə-gō-'vē-nə, ,hərt-, -'gō-və-nə\; capital, Sarajevo — **Bos·ni·an** \-nē-ən\ *adj or n*

Bos·po·rus \'bäs-p(ə-)rəs\ *or ancient* **Bosporus Thra·ci·us** \-'thrā-sh(ē-)əs\ strait about 29 kilometers long between Turkey in Europe & Turkey in Asia connecting Sea of Marmara & Black sea

Bos·ton \'bȯ-stən\ city, capital of Massachusetts — **Bos·to·nian** \bȯ-'stō-nē-ən, -nyən\ *adj or n*

Bot·a·ny Bay \bät-ᵊn-ē-, 'bät-nē-\ inlet S Pacific SE Australia in New South Wales S of Sydney

Both·nia, Gulf of \-'bäth-nē-ə\ arm of Baltic sea between Sweden & Finland

Bo·tswa·na \bät-'swän-ə\ country S Africa; formerly (as Bechuanaland) dependent on Britain; now an independent state; capital, Gaborone

Boul·der \'bōl-dər\ city N central Colorado

Boulder Dam — see HOOVER DAM

Bourne·mouth \'bō(ə)rn-məth, 'bȯ(ə)rn-, 'bu̇(ə)rn-\ town S England in Dorset county on English channel

Brad·ford \'brad-fərd\ city N England in West Yorkshire

Brah·ma·pu·tra \,bräm-ə-'p(y)ü-trə\ river 2705 kilometers long S Asia flowing from the Himalayas in Tibet to Ganges delta

Bra·síl·ia \brə-'zil-yə\ city, capital of Brazil

Bra·ti·sla·va \,brat-ə-'släv-ə, ,brät-\ city on the Danube; capital of Slovakia

Bra·zil \brə-'zil\ country E & central South America; capital, Brasília — **Bra·zil·ian** \brə-'zil-yən\ *adj or n*

Braz·za·ville \'braz-ə-,vil, 'bräz-ə-,vēl\ city, capital of Congo on W bank of lower Congo river

Bre·men \'brem-ən, 'brā-mən\ city NW Germany

Bren·ner \'bren-ər\ pass 1397 meters in the Alps between Austria & Italy

Brent \'brent\ city area of W Greater London county, England

Bret·on, Cape \kāp-'bret-ᵊn, kə-'bret-, -'brit-\ cape Canada; most easterly point of Cape Breton Island & of Nova Scotia

Bridge·port \'brij-,pō(ə)rt, -,pȯ(ə)rt\ city SW Connecticut

Bridge·town \'brij-,tau̇n\ city, capital of Barbados

Brigh·ton \'brīt-ᵊn\ city area S England in East Sussex county on English channel

Bris·bane \'briz-bən, -,bān\ city E Australia, capital of Queensland

Bris·tol \'bris-tᵊl\ **1** city SW England in Avon **2** channel between S Wales & SW England

Brit·ain \'brit-ᵊn\ **1** the island of Great Britain **2** UNITED KINGDOM

British Columbia province W Canada on Pacific coast; capital, Victoria

British Commonwealth of Nations — see COMMONWEALTH, THE

British Guiana — see GUYANA

British Honduras — see BELIZE

British India the part of India formerly under direct British administration

British Indian Ocean Territory British colony in Indian ocean consisting of Chagos island group

British Isles island group W Europe consisting of Great Britain, Ireland, & nearby islands

British Virgin Islands E islands of Virgin islands group; a British possession

British West Indies islands of the West Indies belonging to the Commonwealth & including Jamaica, Trinidad and Tobago, & the Bahama & Cayman islands, Windward Islands, Leeward Islands, & British Virgin Islands

Brit·ta·ny \'brit-ᵊn-ē\ region NW France SW of Normandy

Brom·ley \'bräm-lē\ city area of SE Greater London county, England

Bronx \'brän(k)s\ *or* **The Bronx** section of New York City NE of Manhattan island

Brook·lyn \'bru̇k-lən\ section of New York City at SW end of Long Island

Brooks Range \'bru̇ks-\ mountains N Alaska

Browns·ville \'brau̇nz-,vil, -vəl\ city S Texas on the Rio Grande

Bru·nei \bru̇-'nī, 'brü-,nī\ country NE Borneo; formerly under British authority; capital, Bandar Seri Begawan

Brus·sels \'brəs-əlz\ city, capital of Belgium

Bu·cha·rest \'b(y)ü-kə-,rest\ city, capital of Romania

Buck·ing·ham·shire \'bək-iŋ-əm-,shi(ə)r, -shər, *in the* U.S. *also* -iŋ-,ham-\ *or* **Buckingham** county SE central England

Bu·da·pest \'büd-ə-,pest *also* 'byüd-, 'bu̇d-, -,pesht\ city, capital of Hungary

Bue·nos Ai·res \,bwä-nə-'sa(ə)r-ēz, ,bō-nə-, -'se(ə)r-, -'sī(ə)r-\ city, capital of Argentina

Buf·fa·lo \'bəf-ə-,lō\ city W New York on Lake Erie

Bu·jum·bu·ra \,bü-jəm-'bu̇r-ə\ city, capital of Burundi

Bu·ko·vi·na \,bü-kə-'vē-nə\ region E central Europe in foothills of E Carpathians

Bul·gar·ia \,bəl-'gar-ē-ə, bu̇l-, -'ger-\ country SE Europe on Black sea; capital, Sofia

Bull Run \'bu̇l-'rən\ stream NE Virginia

Bun·ker Hill \,bəŋ-kər-\ height in Boston, Massachusetts

Bur·gun·dy \'bər-gən-dē\ region E France — **Bur·gun·di·an** \(,)bər-'gən-dē-ən\ *adj or n*

Bur·ki·na Fa·so \bu̇r-'kē-nə-'fä-sō\ *or formerly* **Upper Volta** \-'vōl-tə, -'vȯl-\ country W Africa N of Ivory Coast, Ghana, & Togo; capital, Ouagadougou

Bur·ling·ton \'bər-liŋ-tən\ city NW Vermont; largest in state

\ə\ **abut**	\au̇\ **out**	\i\ **tip**	\ȯ\ **saw**	\u̇\ **foot**
\ər\ **further**	\ch\ **chin**	\ī\ **life**	\ȯi\ **coin**	\y\ **yet**
\a\ **mat**	\e\ **pet**	\j\ **job**	\th\ **thin**	\yü\ **few**
\ā\ **take**	\ē\ **easy**	\ŋ\ **sing**	\th\ **this**	\yu̇\ **cure**
\ä\ **cot, cart**	\g\ **go**	\ō\ **bone**	\ü\ **food**	\zh\ **vision**

Burma — see MYANMAR

Bu·run·di \bú-'rün-dē\ country [E] central Africa; capital, Bujumbura — see RUANDA-URUNDI

Bute \'byüt\ island [SW] Scotland in Firth of Clyde

Butte \'byüt\ city [SW] Montana

Byelarus — see BELARUS

Byelorussia — see BELORUSSIA

By·zan·tine Empire \'biz-ᵊn-,tēn, 'bīz-, -,tīn; bə-'zan-,tēn, -tīn, bī-\ empire of [SE] and [S] Europe and [W] Asia from 4th to 15th century

By·zan·ti·um \bə-'zan-sh(ē-)əm, -'zant-ē-əm\ ancient city on site of modern Istanbul

Caer·nar·von \kär-'när-vən, kə(r)-\ city area [NW] Wales in Gwynedd county

Cai·ro \'kī-rō\ city, capital of Egypt — **Cai·rene** \kī-'rēn\ adj or n

Ca·la·bria \kə-'lā-brē-ə, -'läb-rē-\ district of ancient Italy consisting of area forming heel of Italian peninsula — **Ca·la·bri·an** \kə-'lā-brē-ən, -'läb-rē-\ adj or n

Cal·cut·ta \kal-'kət-ə\ city [E] India on Hooghly river — **Cal·cut·tan** \-'kət-ᵊn\ adj or n

Cal·e·do·nia \,kal-ə-'dō-nyə, -nē-ə\ — see SCOTLAND — **Cal·e·do·nian** \-nyən, -nē-ən\ adj or n

Cal·ga·ry \'kal-gə-rē\ city [SW] Alberta, Canada

Ca·li \'käl-ē\ city [W] Colombia

Cal·i·for·nia \,kal-ə-'fór-nyə\ state [SW] U.S.; capital, Sacramento — **Cal·i·for·nian** \-nyən\ adj or n

California, Gulf of arm of the Pacific [NW] Mexico

Cal·va·ry \'kalv-(ə-)rē\ place outside ancient Jerusalem where Christ was crucified

Cam·bay, Gulf of \-kam-'bā\ inlet of Arabian sea India [N] of Bombay

Cam·bo·dia \kam-'bōd-ē-ə\ or **Kam·pu·chea** \,kam-pə-'chē-ə\ or 1970–75 **Khmer Republic** \kə-'me(ə)r-\ country [SE] Asia in [S] Indochina; capital, Phnom Penh

Cam·bria \'kam-brē-ə\ WALES — an old name

Cam·bridge \'kām-brij\ city [E] England in Cambridgeshire

Cam·bridge·shire \'kām-brij-,shi(ə)r, -shər\ or **Cambridge** county [E] England

Cam·den \'kam-dən\ city area of [N] Greater London county, England

Cam·er·oon or French **Cam·er·oun** \,kam-ə-'rün\ country [W] Africa; capital, Yaoundé — **Cam·er·oo·nian** \-'rü-nē-ən, -rü-nyən\ adj or n

Ca·mi·guin \,kam-ə-'gēn\ island Philippines, off [N] coast of Mindanao

Ca·naan \'kā-nən\ ancient region [SW] Asia; approximately the area later called Palestine — **Ca·naan·ite** \'kā-nə-,nīt\ adj or n

Can·a·da \'kan-ə-də\ country [N] North America; independent state in the Commonwealth; capital, Ottawa — **Ca·na·di·an** \kə-'nād-ē-ən\ adj or n

Canadian Falls — see NIAGARA FALLS

Canadian Shield — see LAURENTIAN HIGHLANDS

Canal Zone or **Panama Canal Zone** former strip of territory Panama leased to U.S. for Panama canal

Ca·nary \kə-'ne(ə)r-ē\ islands in the Atlantic off [NW] coast of Africa belonging to Spain

Ca·nav·er·al, Cape \-kə-'nav-(ə-)rəl\ or 1963–1973 **Cape Ken·ne·dy** \-'ken-ə-dē\ cape [E] Florida in the Atlantic on Canaveral peninsula [E] of Indian river

Can·ber·ra \'kan-b(ə-)rə, -,ber-ə\ city, capital of Australia in Australian Capital Territory

Can·on City \,kan-yən-\ city [S] central Colorado on Arkansas river

Can·ter·bury \'kant-ə(r)-,ber-ē, -b(ə-)rē\ **1** city [SE] Australia in [E] New South Wales **2** city [SE] England in Kent county

Canton — see GUANGZHOU

Cape Bret·on Island \kāp-'bret-ᵊn-, kə-'bret-, -'brit-\ island [NE] Nova Scotia

Cape Horn — see HORN, CAPE

Cape of Good Hope 1 — see GOOD HOPE, CAPE OF **2** — see CAPE PROVINCE

Cape Province or **Cape of Good Hope** or formerly **Cape Colony** province [S] Republic of South Africa; capital, Cape Town

Cape Town \'kāp-,taún\ city Republic of South Africa, capital of Cape Province & legislative capital of the country

Cape Verde \-'vərd\ islands in the [N] Atlantic off [W] Africa; an independent country; capital, Praia; until 1975 belonged to Portugal

Cape York peninsula \-'yó(ə)rk-\ peninsula [NE] Australia in [N] Queensland

Ca·pri \kə-'prē, kə-; 'kāp-rē, 'kap-\ island Italy [S] of Bay of Naples

Ca·ra·cas \kə-'rak-əs, -'räk-\ city, capital of Venezuela

Car·diff \'kärd-əf\ city, capital of Wales in South Glamorgan county

Ca·rib·be·an \,kar-ə-'bē-ən, kə-'rib-ē-\ sea arm of the Atlantic; on [N] & [E] are the West Indies, on [S] is South America, & on [W] is Central America — **Caribbean** adj

Car·lisle \kär-'lī(ə)l, kər-, 'kär-,lī(ə)l\ city [NW] England in Cumbria county

Carls·bad Caverns \'kär(-ə)lz-,bad-\ series of caves [SE] New Mexico

Car·mar·then \kär-'mär-thən, kə(r)-\ port [S] Wales in Dyfed county

Car·o·li·na \,kar-ə-'lī-nə\ English colony on [E] coast of North America founded 1663 & divided 1729 into North Carolina & South Carolina (the **Carolinas**) — **Car·o·lin·i·an** \-'lin-e-ən\ adj or n

Ca·ro·li·na \,kär-ə-'lē-nə\ city [NE] Puerto Rico

Car·o·line \'kar-ə-,līn, -lən\ islands [W] Pacific [E] of [S] Philippines; formerly part of Trust Territory of the Pacific Islands

Car·pa·thi·an \kär-'pā-thē-ən\ mountains [E] central Europe along boundary between Slovakia & Poland & in [N] & central Romania; highest Gerlachovka 2663 meters

Car·pen·tar·ia, Gulf of \-,kär-pən-'ter-ē-ə, -tar-\ inlet of Arafura sea [N] of Australia

Car·rick·fer·gus \,kar-ik-'fər-gəs\ district [E] Northern Ireland

Car·son City \'kärs-ᵊn-\ city, capital of Nevada

Car·thage \'kär-thij\ ancient city [N] Africa [NE] of modern Tunis; capital of an empire that once included much of [NW] Africa, [E] Spain, & Sicily — **Car·tha·gin·ian** \,kär-thə-'jin-yən, -'jin-ē-ən\ adj or n

Ca·sa·blan·ca \,kas-ə-'blaŋ-kə, ,kaz-\ city [W] Morocco on the Atlantic

Cas·cade Range \(')kas-'kād-\ mountains [NW] U.S. in Washington, Oregon, & [N] California — see RAINIER, MOUNT

Cas·per \'kas-pər\ city [E] central Wyoming; largest in state

Cas·pi·an sea \'kas-pē-ən-\ salt lake between Europe and Asia about 27 meters below sea level

Cas·tile \kas-'tē(ə)l\ or Spanish **Cas·ti·lla** \kä-'stē-yä\ region & ancient kingdom central & [N] Spain

Cast·le·reagh \'kas-əl-rā\ district [E] Northern Ireland

Cas·tries \'kas-,trēz, -,trēs\ seaport, capital of Saint Lucia

Cat·a·lo·nia \,kat-ᵊl-'ō-nyə, -nē-ə\ region [NE] Spain bordering on France & the Mediterranean; chief city, Barcelona — **Cat·a·lo·nian** \-'ō-nyən, -nē-ən\ adj or n

Ca·tan·dua·nes \,kät-ən-'dwän-əs\ island [E] Philippines

Ca·thay \kath-'ā\ an old name for China

Cats·kill \'kat-,skil\ mountains in Appalachian system [SE] New York [W] of the Hudson

Cau·ca·sus \'kó-kə-səs\ mountain system [SE] Europe between Black and Caspian seas in Russia, Georgia, Azerbaijan, & Armenia

Cay·enne \kī-'en, kā-\ city, capital of French Guiana

Cay·man \(')kā-'man, 'kā-mən\ islands West Indies [NW] of Jamaica; a British colony

Ce·bu \sā-'bü\ island [E] central Philippines

Ce·dar Rapids \'sēd-ər-\ city [E] Iowa

Celebes — see SULAWESI

Cel·tic \'kel-tik, 'sel-\ sea inlet of the Atlantic in British Isles ⬚SE of Ireland, ⬚SW of Wales, & ⬚W of Cornwall and Isles of Scilly county, England

Central region central Scotland; established 1975

Central African Republic country ⬚N central Africa; capital, Bangui

Central America narrow portion of North America from ⬚S border of Mexico to South America — **Central American** *adj or n*

Central Valley valley of Sacramento & San Joaquin rivers in California between Sierra Nevada & Coast ranges

Cey·lon \si-'län, sā-\ **1** island in Indian ocean off ⬚S India **2** — see SRI LANKA — **Cey·lon·ese** \,sā-lə-'nēz, ,sē-lə-, ,sel-ə-, -'nēs\ *adj or n*

Chad \'chad\ country ⬚N central Africa; capital, N'Djamena — **Chad·ian** \'chad-ē-ən\ *adj or n*

Chad, Lake shallow lake ⬚N central Africa at junction of boundaries of Chad, Niger, & Nigeria

Cha·gos \'chä-gəs\ island group central Indian ocean; forms British Indian Ocean Territory — see DIEGO GARCIA

Chal·dea \kal-'dē-ə\ ancient region ⬚SW Asia on Euphrates river & Persian gulf — **Chal·de·an** \-'dē-ən\ *adj or n* — **Chal·dee** \'kal-,dē\ *n*

Cham·pagne \sham-'pān\ region ⬚NE France

Champlain, Lake \sham-'plān\ lake between New York & Vermont extending ⬚N into Quebec

Chan·di·garh \'chən-dē-gər\ city ⬚N India ⬚N of Delhi

Chang \'chäŋ\ *or* **Yang·tze** \'yaŋ-'sē, 'yaŋ(k)t-'sē\ river 4990 kilometers long central China flowing into East China sea

Chang·chun \'chäŋ-'chùn\ city ⬚NE China

Chang·sha \'chäŋ-'shä\ city ⬚SE central China

Channel **1** — see SANTA BARBARA **2** islands in English channel including Jersey, Guernsey, & Alderney & belonging to United Kingdom

Charles \'chär(ə)lz\ river 76 kilometers long ⬚E Massachusetts flowing into Boston harbor

Charles, Cape cape ⬚E Virginia ⬚N of entrance to Chesapeake Bay

Charles·ton \'chärl-stən\ **1** seaport ⬚SE South Carolina **2** city, capital of West Virginia

Char·lotte \'shär-lət\ city ⬚S North Carolina

Charlotte Ama·lie \-'am-ə-lē\ city, capital of Virgin Islands of the U.S.; on Saint Thomas island

Char·lottes·ville \'shär-ləts-,vil, -vəl\ city central Virginia

Char·lotte·town \'shär-lət-,taùn\ city, capital of Prince Edward Island, Canada

Chat·ta·noo·ga \,chat-ə-'nü-gə, ,chat-ºn-'ü-\ city ⬚SE Tennessee

Chelms·ford \'chelm-sfərd, 'chem-\ city area ⬚SE England in Essex county

Che·lya·binsk \chel-'yä-bən(t)sk\ city ⬚W Russia, ⬚S of Sverdlovsk

Cheng–chou — see ZHENGZHOU

Cheng·du *or* **Ch'eng–tu** \'chəŋ-'dü\ city ⬚SW central China

Ches·a·peake \'ches-(ə-),pēk\ city ⬚SE Virginia

Chesapeake Bay inlet of the Atlantic in Virginia & Maryland

Chesh·ire \'chesh-ər, 'chesh-,i(ə)r\ *or* **Ches·ter** \'ches-tər\ county ⬚W England bordering on Wales

Ches·ter \'ches-tər\ city ⬚NW England in Cheshire

Chev·i·ot \'chev-ē-ət, 'chē-vē-ət\ hills along English-Scottish border

Chey·enne \shī-'an, -'en\ city, capital of Wyoming

Chi·ba \'chē-bə\ city ⬚E Japan in Honshu on Tokyo Bay ⬚E of Tokyo

Chi·ca·go \shə-'käg-ō, -'kog-\ city ⬚NE Illinois — **Chi·ca·go·an** \-'käg-ə-wən, -'kog-\ *n*

Chi·chén It·zá \chə-,chən-ət-'sä\ ruined Mayan city ⬚OE Mexico in Yucatán

Chich·es·ter \'chich-ə-stər\ city ⬚S England in West Sussex county

Ch'i–ch'i–ha–erh — see QIQIHAR

Chihli, Gulf of — see BO HAI

Chi·le \'chil-ē\ country ⬚SW South America; capital, Santiago — **Chil·ean** \'chil-ē-ən, chə-'lā-ən\ *adj or n*

Chim·bo·ra·zo \,chim-bə-'räz-ō, ,shim-\ mountain 6267 meters ⬚W central Ecuador

Chi·na \'chī-nə\ **1** country ⬚E Asia; capital, Beijing — see TAIWAN **2** sea section of the ⬚W Pacific; divided at Taiwan strait into East China & South China seas

Chin–chou *or* **Chinchow** — see JINZHOU

Chit·ta·gong \'chit-ə-,gäŋ, -,goŋ\ city ⬚SE Bangladesh on Bay of Bengal

Chong·qing *or* **Ch'ung–ch'ing** \'chùŋ-'chiŋ\ *or* **Chungking** \'chùŋ-'kiŋ\ city ⬚SW central China

Christ·church \'krīs(t)-,chərch\ city New Zealand on ⬚E coast of South island

Christ·mas \'kris-məs\ island ⬚E Indian ocean ⬚SW of Java; governed by Australia

Cin·cin·na·ti \,sin(t)-sə-'nat-ē, -'nat-ə\ city ⬚SW Ohio

Ciudad Trujillo — see SANTO DOMINGO

Cleve·land \'klēv-lənd\ **1** city ⬚NE Ohio **2** county ⬚N England ⬚N of North Yorkshire

Clwyd \'klüid\ county ⬚NE Wales; established 1974

Clyde \'klīd\ river 171 kilometers long ⬚SW Scotland flowing into **Firth of Clyde** (estuary)

Coast mountains mountain range ⬚W British Columbia, Canada; the ⬚N continuation of Cascade range

Coast ranges chain of mountain ranges ⬚W North America extending along Pacific coast ⬚W of Sierra Nevada & Cascade range & through Vancouver island into ⬚S Alaska to Kenai peninsula & Kodiak island

Cod, Cape \-'käd\ peninsula ⬚SE Massachusetts

Coim·ba·tore \,kòim-bə-'tō(ə)r, -'tò(ə)r\ city ⬚S India

Cole·raine \kōl-'rān, 'kōl-,ran\ **1** county ⬚N Northern Ireland **2** port in Coleraine county

Co·logne \kə-'lōn\ city ⬚W Germany on the Rhine

Co·lom·bia \kə-'ləm-bē-ə\ country ⬚NW South America; capital, Bogotá — **Co·lom·bi·an** \-bē-ən\ *adj or n*

Co·lom·bo \kə-'ləm-bō\ city, capital of Sri Lanka

Col·o·ra·do \,käl-ə-'rad-ō, -'räd-\ **1** river 2335 kilometers long ⬚SW U.S. & ⬚NW Mexico flowing from ⬚N Colorado into Gulf of California **2** desert ⬚SE California **3** plateau region ⬚SW U.S. ⬚W of Rocky mountains **4** state ⬚W U.S.; capital, Denver – **Col·o·rad·an** \-'rad-ºn, -'räd-\ *or* **Co·lo·ra·do·an** \-'rad-ə-wən, -'räd-\ *adj or n*

Colorado Springs city central Colorado

Co·lum·bia \kə-'ləm-bē-ə\ **1** river 2045 kilometers long ⬚SW Canada & ⬚NW U.S. flowing ⬚S & ⬚W from ⬚SE British Columbia into the Pacific **2** plateau in Columbia river basin in ⬚E Washington, ⬚E Oregon, & ⬚SW Idaho **3** city, capital of South Carolina **4** — see UNITED STATES OF AMERICA

Co·lum·bus \kə-'ləm-bəs\ **1** city ⬚W Georgia **2** city, capital of Ohio

Com·mon·wealth, the \'käm-ən-,wel(t)th\ *or* **Commonwealth of Nations** *or formerly* **British Commonwealth of Nations** the United Kingdom & most of the countries formerly dependent on it

Com·o·ro \'käm-ə-,rō\ islands off ⬚SE Africa ⬚NW of Madagascar; formerly a French possession; an independent country (except for Mayotte Island remaining French) since 1975; capital, Moroni

Con·a·kry \'kän-ə-krē\ city, capital of Guinea

Con·cord \'kän-kərd\ **1** city ⬚W California **2** city, capital of New Hampshire **3** town ⬚E Massachusetts ⬚NW of Boston

\ə\ **abut**	\aù\ **out**	\i\ **tip**	\ò\ **saw**	\ù\ **foot**
\ºr\ **further**	\ch\ **chin**	\ī\ **life**	\òi\ **coin**	\y\ **yet**
\a\ **mat**	\e\ **pet**	\j\ **job**	\th\ **thin**	\yü\ **few**
\ā\ **take**	\ē\ **easy**	\ŋ\ **sing**	\th\ **this**	\yù\ **cure**
\ä\ **cot, cart**	\g\ **go**	\ō\ **bone**	\ü\ **food**	\zh\ **vision**

Con·go \'käŋ-gō\ **1** *or* **Zaire** \'zī(ə)r, zä-'i(ə)r\ river 4830 kilometers long W Africa flowing into the Atlantic **2** — see ZAIRE **3** country W central Africa W of lower Congo river; capital, Brazzaville — **Con·go·lese** \,käŋ-gə-'lēz, -'lēs\ *adj or n*

Con·nacht \'kän-,ȯt\ province W Ireland

Con·nect·i·cut \kə-'net-i-kət\ **1** river 655 kilometers long NE U.S. flowing S from N New Hampshire into Long Island Sound **2** state NE U.S.; capital, Hartford

Constantinople — see ISTANBUL

Con·ti·nen·tal Di·vide \,känt-ᵊn-,ent-ᵊl-di-'vīd\ line of highest points of land separating the waters flowing W from those flowing N or E and extending SSE from NW Canada across W U.S. through Mexico & Central America to South America where it joins the Andes mountains

Cook \'kúk\ **1** inlet of the Pacific S Alaska W of Kenai peninsula **2** islands S Pacific SW of Society islands belonging to New Zealand **3** strait New Zealand between North island & South island

Cook, Mount *or formerly* **Ao·rangi** \aủ-'räŋ-ē\ mountain 3764 meters New Zealand in W central South island in Southern Alps; highest in New Zealand

Cooks·town \'kúk-,staủn\ district central Northern Ireland

Co·pen·ha·gen \,kō-pən-'hā-gən, -'häg-ən\ city, capital of Denmark

Cor·al \'kȯr-əl, 'kär-\ sea arm of the W Pacific NE of Australia

Cór·do·ba \'kȯrd-ə-bə, -ə-və\ city N central Argentina

Cor·inth \'kȯr-ən(t)th, 'kär-\ **1** region of ancient Greece **2** ancient city, its capital; site SW of present city of Corinth — **Co·rin·thi·an** \kə-'rin(t)-thē-ən\ *adj or n*

Corinth, Gulf of inlet of Ionian sea central Greece N of the Peloponnisos

Cork \'kȯ(ə)rk\ city S Ireland in Munster

Corn·wall \'kȯrn-,wȯl, -wəl\ area and once a county SW England

Cornwall and Isles of Scilly county SW England

Cor·pus Chris·ti \,kȯr-pə-'skris-tē\ city S Texas

Cor·reg·i·dor \kə-'reg-ə-,dȯ(ə)r\ island Philippines at entrance to Manila Bay

Cor·si·ca \'kȯr-si-kə\ island France in the Mediterranean N of Sardinia — **Cor·si·can** \'kȯr-si-kən\ *adj or n*

Cos·ta Ri·ca \,käs-tə-'rē-kə, ,kȯs-, ,kōs-\ country Central America between Nicaragua & Panama; capital, San José — **Cos·ta Ri·can** \-'rē-kən\ *adj or n*

Cots·wold \'kät-,swōld\ hills SW central England

Cov·en·try \'kəv-ən-trē, 'kəv-\ city central England in West Midlands county

Cow·pens \'kaủ-,penz\ town NW South Carolina

Craig·av·on \krā-'gav-ən\ district central Northern Ireland

Cra·ter \'krāt-ər\ lake 589 meters deep SW Oregon in Cascade range — see MAZAMA, MOUNT

Crete \'krēt\ island Greece in E Mediterranean — **Cre·tan** \'krēt-ᵊn\ *adj or n*

Cri·mea \krī-'mē-ə, krə-\ peninsula SE Europe, extending into Black sea — **Cri·me·an** \krī-'mē-ən, krə-\ *adj*

Cro·atia \krō-'ā-sh(ē-)ə\ country SE Europe; capital, Zagreb; a republic of Yugoslavia 1946–91

Croy·don \'krȯid-ᵊn\ city area of S Greater London county, England

Cu·ba \'kyü-bə\ island in the West Indies; an independent country; capital, Havana — **Cu·ban** \-bən\ *adj or n*

Cum·ber·land \'kəm-bər-lənd\ river 1106 kilometers long S Kentucky & N Tennessee

Cumberland Gap pass through Cumberland plateau NE Tennessee

Cumberland plateau *or* **Cumberland mountains** mountain region E U.S.; part of S Appalachian mountains extending from S West Virginia to NE Alabama

Cum·bria \'kəm-brē-ə\ county NW England — **Cum·bri·an** \-ən\ *adj or n*

Cumbrian mountains NW England chiefly in Cumbria county

Cu·par \'kü-pər\ town E Scotland in Fife region

Cu·ri·ti·ba \,kúr-ə-'tē-bə\ city S Brazil SW of São Paulo

Cush \'kəsh, 'kúsh\ ancient country NE Africa in upper Nile valley S of Egypt — **Cush·ite** \-,īt\ *n* — **Cush·it·ic** \,kəsh-'it-ik, kúsh-\ *adj*

Cuz·co \'kü-skō\ city S central Peru

Cymru — see WALES

Cy·prus \'sī-prəs\ island E Mediterranean S of Turkey; an independent country in the Commonwealth; capital, Nicosia — **Cyp·ri·ot** \'sip-rē-ət, -rē-,ät\ *or* **Cyp·ri·ote** \-,ōt, -ət\ *adj or n*

Cy·re·na·ica \,sir-ə-'nā-ə-kə, ,sī-rə-\ ancient region N Africa on coast E of Egypt; capital, Cyrene — **Cy·re·na·i·can** \-kən\ *adj or n*

Czecho·slo·va·kia \,chek-ə-slō-'väk-ē-ə, -'vak-\ former country central Europe; capital, Prague; since January 1, 1993 divided into the independent states of the **Czech Republic** (capital, Prague) & **Slovakia** (capital, Bratislava) — **Czecho·slo·vak** \-'slō-,väk, -,vak\ *adj or n* — **Czecho·slo·va·ki·an** \-slō-'väk-ē-ən, -'vak-\ *adj or n*

Dac·ca *or* **Dha·ka** \'dak-ə, 'däk-ə\ city, capital of Bangladesh

Dahomey — see BENIN

Dairen — see LÜDA

Da·kar \'dak-,är, də-'kär\ city, capital of Senegal

Da·ko·ta Territory \də-'kōt-ə-\ territory 1861–89 NW U.S. divided 1889 into states of North Dakota & South Dakota (the **Da·ko·tas** \-əz\)

Dal·las \'dal-əs, -is\ city NE Texas

Dal·ma·tia \dal-'mā-sh(ē-)ə\ region W Balkan peninsula on the Adriatic — **Dal·ma·tian** \-shən\ *adj or n*

Da·mas·cus \də-'mas-kəs\ city, capital of Syria

Dan·ube \'dan-yüb\ river 2776 kilometers long S Europe flowing from SW Germany into Black sea — **Da·nu·bi·an** \da-'nyü-bē-ən\ *adj*

Dar·da·nelles \,därd-ᵊn-'elz\ *or* **Hel·les·pont** \'hel-ə-,spänt\ strait NW Turkey connecting Sea of Marmara & the Aegean

Dar es Sa·laam \,där-,es-sə-'läm\ city, capital of Tanzania

Dar·ling \'där-liŋ\ river 1865 kilometers long SE Australia in Queensland & New South Wales flowing SW into the Murray

Dar·win \'där-wən\ city Australia, capital of Northern Territory

Da·vao \'däv-,aủ, dä-'vaủ\ city S Philippines in E Mindanao on Davao Gulf

Dav·en·port \'dav-ən-,pō(ə)rt, -,pȯ(ə)rt\ city E Iowa

Da·vis \'dā-vəs\ strait between SW Greenland & E Baffin island connecting Baffin Bay & the Atlantic

Day·ton \'dāt-ᵊn\ city SW Ohio

Dead sea \'ded-\ salt lake between Israel & Jordan; 397 meters below sea level

Death Valley \'deth-\ dry valley E California & S Nevada containing lowest point in U.S. (86 meters below sea level)

Dec·can \'dek-ən, -,an\ plateau region S India

Del·a·ware \'del-ə-,wa(ə)r, -,we(ə)r, -wər\ **1** river 476 kilometers long E U.S. flowing S from S New York into Delaware Bay **2** state E U.S.; capital, Dover — **Del·a·war·ean** *or* **Del·a·war·ian** \,del-ə-'war-ē-ən, -'wer-\ *adj or n*

Delaware Bay inlet of the Atlantic between SW New Jersey & E Delaware

Del·hi \'del-ē\ city N India — see NEW DELHI

De·los \'dē-,läs\ island Greece — **De·lian** \'dē-lē-ən, 'dēl-yən\ *adj or n*

Del·phi \'del-,fī\ ancient town central Greece on S slope of Parnassus

Democratic Republic of the Congo — see ZAIRE

Denali — see MCKINLEY, MOUNT

Den·mark \'den-,märk\ country N Europe occupying most of Jutland & neighboring islands; capital, Copenhagen

Den·ver \'den-vər\ city, capital of Colorado

Der·by \'där-bē, *chiefly in the U.S.* 'dər-bē\ city area N central England in Derbyshire

Der·by·shire \'där-bē-,shi(ə)r, -shər, *U.S. also* 'dər-\ *or* **Derby** county N central England

Der·ry \'der-ē\ *or* **Lon·don·der·ry** \,lən-dən-'der-ē; 'lən-dən-,der-ē, -d(ə-)rē\ **1** district NW Northern Ireland **2** seaport in Londonderry district

Des Moines \di-'mȯin\ city, capital of Iowa

De·troit \di-'trȯit\ **1** river 50 kilometers long between SE Michigan & Ontario connecting Lake Saint Clair & Lake Erie **2** city SE Michigan

Dev·on \'dev-ən\ *or* **De·von·shire** \-,shi(ə)r, -shər\ county SW England

Dhaka — see DACCA

Die·go Gar·cia \dē-,ā-gō-,gär-'sē-ə\ island in Indian ocean; chief island of Chagos island group

Di·nar·ic Alps \də-,nar-ik-\ range of the E Alps in W Slovenia, W Croatia, Bosnia and Herzegovina, & Montenegro

District of Co·lum·bia \-kə-'ləm-bē-ə\ federal district E U.S. coextensive with city of Washington

Dja·kar·ta *or* **Ja·kar·ta** \jə-'kärt-ə\ *or formerly* **Ba·ta·via** \bə-'tā-vē-ə\ city, capital of Indonesia in NW Java

Dji·bou·ti \jə-'büt-ē\ **1** country E Africa on Gulf of Aden **2** city, its capital

Dne·pro·pe·trovsk \'nep-(,)rō-pə-'trȯfsk\ city E central Ukraine

Dodge City \'däj-\ city S Kansas on Arkansas river

Do·ha \'dō-hä\ city & port, capital of Qatar on Persian gulf

Dom·i·ni·ca \,däm-ə-'nē-kə, də-'min-ə-kə\ island West Indies in the Leeward Islands; an independent country; capital, Roseau

Do·min·i·can Republic \də-,min-i-kən\ country West Indies in E Hispaniola; capital, Santo Domingo — **Do·min·i·can** \də-'min-i-kən\ *adj or n*

Don \'dän\ river 1930 kilometers long SW Russia

Do·netsk \də-'netsk\ city E Ukraine

Dor·ches·ter \'dȯr-chə-stər, -,ches-tər\ city area S England in Dorset county

Dor·set \'dȯr-sət\ *or* **Dor·set·shire** \-,shi(ə)r, -shər\ county S England on English channel

Dort·mund \'dȯrt-,mu̇nt, -mənd\ city W Germany in the Ruhr

Dou·ro \'dōr-ü, 'dȯr-\ *or Spanish* **Due·ro** \'dwe(ə)r-ō\ *or ancient* **Du·ri·us** \'d(y)u̇r-ē-əs\ river 780 kilometers long N Spain & N Portugal flowing into the Atlantic

Do·ver \'dō-vər\ city, capital of Delaware

Dover, Strait of channel between SE England & N France; the most easterly section of English channel

Down \'dau̇n\ district SE Northern Ireland

Down·pat·rick \dau̇n-'pa-trik\ city district E Northern Ireland in Down district

Dra·kens·berg \'dräk-ənz-,bərg\ mountain range E Republic of South Africa & Lesotho; highest peak Thabana Ntlenyana 3482 meters

Dres·den \'drez-dən\ city E Germany

Dub·lin \'dəb-lən\ *or ancient* **Eb·la·na** \'eb-lə-nə\ city, capital of Ireland in Leinster

Dud·ley \'dəd-lē\ city area W central England in West Midlands county

Duis·burg \'dü-əs-,bərg; 'd(y)üz-,bərg\ city W Germany at junction of Rhine & Ruhr rivers

Du·luth \də-'lüth\ city NE Minnesota

Dum·fries \,dəm-'frēs\ town S Scotland in Dumfries and Galloway region

Dumfries and Gal·lo·way \-'gal-ə-,wā\ region S Scotland; established 1975

Dun·dee \,dən-'dē\ city E Scotland in Tayside region

Dun·gan·non \dən-'gan-ən\ district W Northern Ireland

Dur·ban \'dər-bən\ city E Republic of South Africa in E Natal

Dur·ham \'dər-əm, 'də-rəm, 'du̇r-əm\ **1** city N central North Carolina **2** county N England on North sea **3** city area in Durham county

Du·shan·be \d(y)ü-'sham-bə, -'shäm-\ city, capital of Tajikistan

Düs·sel·dorf \'d(y)üs-əl-,dȯrf\ city W Germany on the Rhine

Dutch East Indies — see NETHERLANDS EAST INDIES

Dy·fed \'dəv-ed, -əd\ county SW Wales; established 1974

Ea·ling \'ē-liŋ\ city area of W Greater London county, England

East An·glia \-aŋ-glē-ə\ region E England including Norfolk & Suffolk counties

East China sea — see CHINA

Eas·ter \'ē-stər\ island SE Pacific 3220 kilometers W of Chilean coast; belongs to Chile

Eastern Ghats \-'gȯts\ chain of low mountains SE India along coast

Eastern Roman Empire the Byzantine Empire from 395 to 474

Eastern Samoa — see AMERICAN SAMOA

East Germany the German Democratic Republic — see GERMANY

East Indies the Malay island group — **East Indian** *adj or n*

East London city S Republic of South Africa in SE Cape Province

East Pakistan the former E division of Pakistan consisting of E portion of Bengal; now the independent country of Bangladesh

East river strait SE New York connecting upper New York Bay & Long Island Sound & separating Manhattan island and Long Island

East Sus·sex \-'səs-iks, *U.S. also* -,eks\ county SE England

Eblana — see DUBLIN

Ebro \'ā-brō\ river 775 kilometers long NE Spain flowing into the Mediterranean

Ec·ua·dor \'ek-wə-,dȯ(ə)r\ country W South America; capital, Quito — **Ec·ua·dor·an** \,ek-wə-'dȯr-ən, -'dȯr-\ *or* **Ec·ua·dor·ean** *or* **Ec·ua·dor·ian** \-ē-ən\ *adj or n*

Ed·in·burgh \'ed-ən-,bər-ə, -,bə-rə, -b(ə-)rə\ city, capital of Scotland, in Lothian region

Ed·mon·ton \'ed-mən-tən\ city, capital of Alberta, Canada

Edom \'ēd-əm\ ancient country SW Asia S of Judea & Dead sea — **Edom·ite** \'ēd-ə-,mīt\ *n*

Egypt \'ē-jəpt\ country NE Africa & Sinai peninsula of SW Asia bordering on Mediterranean & Red seas; capital, Cairo

Eire — see IRELAND

Elam \'ē-ləm\ ancient country SW Asia at head of Persian gulf E of Babylonia — **Elam·ite** \'ē-lə-,mīt\ *n*

Elbe \'el-bə, 'elb\ river 1160 kilometers long N Czech Republic & NE Germany flowing NW into North sea

El·bert, Mount \-'el-bərt\ mountain 4399 meters W central Colorado; highest in Colorado & the Rocky mountains

El·burz \el-'bu̇(ə)rz\ mountains N Iran

Eliz·a·beth \i-'liz-ə-bəth\ city NE New Jersey

Elles·mere \'elz-,mi(ə)r\ island N Canada in Northwest Territories

Ellice — see TUVALU

El Paso \el-'pas-ō\ city W Texas on Rio Grande

El Sal·va·dor \el-'sal-və-,dȯ(ə)r, -,sal-və-'dȯ(ə)r\ country

\ə\ abut	\au̇\ **out**	\i\ **tip**	\ȯ\ **saw**	\u̇\ **foot**	
\ər\ further	\ch\ **chin**	\ī\ **life**	\ȯi\ **coin**	\y\ **yet**	
\a\ **mat**	\e\ **pet**	\j\ **job**	\th\ **thin**	\yü\ **few**	
\ā\ **take**	\ē\ **easy**	\ŋ\ **sing**	\th\ **this**	\yu̇\ **cure**	
\ä\ **cot, cart**	\g\ **go**	\ō\ **bone**	\ü\ **food**	\zh\ **vision**	

Central America bordering on the Pacific; capital, San Salvador

Ely, Isle of \-'ē-lē\ district [E] England in Cambridgeshire

En·field \'en-ˌfēld\ city area of [N] Greater London county, England

En·gland \'iŋ-glənd *also* 'iŋ-lənd\ country [S] Great Britain; a division of United Kingdom; capital, London

English channel arm of the Atlantic between [S] England & [N] France

En·nis·kil·len \ˌen-ə-'skil-ən\ city district [SW] Northern Ireland in Fermanagh district

Ephra·im \'ē-frē-əm\ **1** hilly region [N] Jordan [E] of Jordan river **2** — see ISRAEL — **Ephra·im·ite** \'ē-frē-ə-ˌmīt\ n

Equatorial Guinea *or formerly* **Spanish Guinea** country [W] Africa including Río Muni & Bioko; capital, Malabo

Erie \'i(ə)r-ē\ **1** city [NW] Pennsylvania **2** canal New York between Hudson river at Albany & Lake Erie at Buffalo; built 1817–25; now superseded by New York State Barge Canal

Erie, Lake lake [E] central North America in U.S. & Canada; one of the Great Lakes

Er·in \'er-ən\ poetic name of Ireland

Española — see HISPANIOLA

Es·sen \'es-ᵊn\ city [W] Germany in the Ruhr

Es·sex \'es-iks\ county [SE] England on North sea

Es·to·nia \e-'stō-nē-ə, -nyə\ country [E] Europe on Baltic sea; capital, Tallinn; a republic of U.S.S.R. 1940–91

Ethi·o·pia \ˌē-thē-'ō-pē-ə\ *or* **Ab·ys·sin·ia** \ˌab-ə-'sin-yə, -'sin-ē-ə\ country [E] Africa; capital, Addis Ababa — **Ethi·o·pi·an** \-pē-ən\ *adj or n*

Et·na \'et-nə\ volcano 3323 meters Italy in [NE] Sicily

Eto·bi·coke \e-'tō-bi-ˌkō\ city Canada in [SE] Ontario

Etru·ria \i-'trür-ē-ə\ ancient country central Italy

Eu·gene \yü-'jēn\ city [W] Oregon

Eu·phra·tes \yü-'frāt-ēz\ river 2735 kilometers long [SW] Asia flowing from [E] Turkey & uniting with the Tigris to form the Shatt-al-Arab

Eur·asia \yü-'rā-zhə, -shə\ landmass consisting of Europe & Asia — **Eur·asian** \-zhən, -shən\ *adj or n*

Eu·rope \'yür-əp\ continent of the eastern hemisphere between Asia & the Atlantic

Ev·ans·ville \'ev-ənz-ˌvil\ city [SW] Indiana

Ev·er·est, Mount \-'ev-(ə-)rəst\ mountain 8848 meters [S] Asia in the Himalayas on border between Nepal & Tibet; highest in the world

Ev·er·glades \'ev-ər-ˌglādz\ swamp region [S] Florida now partly drained

Ex·e·ter \'ek-sət-ər\ **1** town [SE] New Hampshire **2** city [SW] England in Devon county

Faer·oe *or* **Far·oe** \'fa(ə)r-ō, 'fe(ə)r-\ islands [NE] Atlantic [NW] of the Shetlands belonging to Denmark — **Faero·ese** \ˌfar-ə-'wēz, -fer-, -'wēs\ *adj or n*

Fair·field \'fa(ə)r-ˌfēld, 'fe(ə)r-\ city [SE] Australia in [E] New South Wales

Fai·sa·la·bad \ˌfī-ˌsäl-ə-'bäd, -ˌsal-ə-'bad\ *or formerly* **Ly·all·pur** \lē-ˌäl-'pü(ə)r\ city [NE] Pakistan in [E] Lahore

Falk·land \'fö(l)-klənd\ *or Spanish* **Is·las Mal·vi·nas** \ˌēz-läz-mäl-'vē-näs\ islands [SW] Atlantic [E] of [S] end of Argentina; a British colony; capital, Stanley

Far East the countries of [E] Asia & the Malay island group — usually thought to consist of the Asian countries bordering on the Pacific but sometimes including also India, Sri Lanka, Bangladesh, Tibet, & Myanmar — **Far Eastern** *adj*

Far·go \'fär-gō\ city [E] North Dakota; largest in state

Fear, Cape \-'fi(ə)r\ cape [SE] North Carolina at mouth of Cape Fear river

Fer·man·agh \fər-'man-ə\ district [SW] Northern Ireland

Fernando Po — see BIOKO

Fez \'fez\ city [N] central Morocco

Fife \'fīf\ *or* **Fife·shire** \-ˌshi(ə)r, -shər\ region [E] Scotland

Fi·ji \'fē-jē\ islands [SW] Pacific; an independent country in the Commonwealth; capital, Suva — **Fi·ji·an** \-jē-ən\ *adj or n*

Fin·land \'fin-lənd\ country [NE] Europe; capital, Helsinki — **Fin·land·er** *n*

Flan·ders \'flan-dərz\ region [W] Belgium & [N] France on North sea

Flat·tery, Cape \-'flat-ə-rē\ cape [NW] Washington at entrance to Strait of Juan de Fuca

Flint \'flint\ city [SE] Michigan

Flor·ence \'flór-ən(t)s, 'flär-\ *or Italian* **Fi·ren·ze** \fē-'rent-sä\ *or ancient* **Flo·ren·tia** \flə-'ren-chə, -chē-ə\ city central Italy — **Flor·en·tine** \'flór-ən-ˌtēn, 'flär-, -, -ˌtīn\ *adj or n*

Flor·i·da \'flór-əd-ə, 'flär-\ state [SE] U.S.; capital, Tallahassee — **Flo·rid·i·an** \flə-'rid-ē-ən\ *or* **Flor·i·dan** \'flór-əd-ᵊn, 'flär-\ *adj or n*

Florida, Straits of channel between Florida Keys on [NW] & Cuba & Bahamas on [S] & [E] connecting Gulf of Mexico & the Atlantic

Florida Keys chain of islands off [S] tip of Florida

Foochow — see FUZHOU

For·a·ker, Mount \-'fór-i-kər, -'fär-\ mountain 5304 meters [S] central Alaska in Alaska range

For·mo·sa \fór-'mō-sə, fər-, -zə\ — see TAIWAN — **For·mo·san** \-'mōs-ᵊn, -'mōz-\ *adj or n*

For·ta·le·za \ˌfórt-ᵊl-'ā-zə\ city [NE] Brazil

Fort–de–France \ˌfórd-ə-'fräns\ city West Indies, capital of Martinique on [W] coast

Forth \'fō(ə)rth, 'fó(ə)rth\ river 183 kilometers long [S] central Scotland flowing [E] into North sea through **Firth of Forth**

Fort Knox \-'näks\ military reservation [N] central Kentucky [SSW] of Louisville; location of U.S. Gold Bullion Depository

Fort Lau·der·dale \-'lòd-ər-ˌdāl\ city [SE] Florida

Fort Wayne \-'wān\ city [NE] Indiana

Fort Worth \-'wərth\ city [NE] Texas

Fox \'fäks\ islands [SW] Alaska in the [E] Aleutians

Foxe Basin \'fäks-\ inlet of the Atlantic [N] Canada in [E] Northwest Territories [W] of Baffin island

France \'fran(t)s\ country [W] Europe between the English channel & the Mediterranean; capital, Paris

Frank·fort \'fraŋ-fərt\ city, capital of Kentucky

Frank·furt \'fraŋk-fərt, 'frän-ˌfú(ə)rt\ *or in full* **Frankfurt am Main** \-(ˌ)äm-'mīn\ *or* **Frankfort on the Main** city [W] Germany on Main river

Frank·lin \'fraŋ-klən\ former district [N] Canada in Northwest Territories including Arctic islands & Boothia & Melville peninsulas

Fra·ser \'frā-zər, -zhər\ river 1370 kilometers long Canada in [S] central British Columbia flowing into the Pacific

Fred·er·ic·ton \'fred-(ə-)rik-tən\ city, capital of New Brunswick, Canada

Free·town \'frē-ˌtaún\ city, capital of Sierra Leone

Fre·mont \'frē-mänt\ city [W] California

French Guiana country [N] South America on the Atlantic; an overseas division of France; capital, Cayenne

French Indochina — see INDOCHINA

Fres·no \'frez-nō\ city [S] central California

Frunze — see BISHKEK

Fu·ji \'f(y)ü-jē\ *or* **Fu·ji·ya·ma** \ˌf(y)ü-jē-'(y)äm-ə\ mountain 3776 meters Japan in [S] central Honshu; highest in Japan

Fu·ku·o·ka \ˌfü-kə-'wō-kə\ city Japan in [N] Kyushu

Ful·ler·ton \'fúl-ərt-ᵊn\ city [SW] California

Fu·na·fu·ti \ˌf(y)ü-nə-'f(y)üt-ē\ city, capital of Tuvalu

Fun·dy, Bay of \-'fən-dē\ inlet of the Atlantic [SE] Canada between New Brunswick & Nova Scotia

Fu·shun \'fü-'shùn\ city [NE] China [S] of Shenyang

Fu·zhou \'fü-'jō\ *or* **Foo·chow** \'fü-'jō, -'chaú\ city [SE] China

Ga·bon \ga-'bōn\ country [W] Africa on the equator; capital, Libreville — **Gab·o·nese** \ˌgab-ə-'nēz, -'nēs\ *adj or n*

Ga·bo·rone \ˌgäb-ə-ˈrōn\ city, capital of Botswana

Gads·den Purchase \ˈgadz-dən-\ area of land ⑤ of Gila river in present Arizona & New Mexico purchased 1853 by the U.S. from Mexico

Ga·la·pa·gos islands \gə-ˈläp-ə-gəs-, -ˈlap-\ island group Ecuador in the Pacific 965 kilometers Ⓦ of South America

Ga·la·tia \gə-ˈlā-sh(ē-)ə\ ancient country central Asia Minor in region around modern Ankara, Turkey — **Ga·la·tian** \-shən\ adj or n

Ga·li·cia \gə-ˈlish-(ē-)ə\ **1** region Ⓔ central Europe now divided between Poland & Ukraine **2** region ⓃⓌ Spain on the Atlantic — **Ga·li·cian** \-ˈlish-ən\ adj or n

Gal·i·lee \ˈgal-ə-,lē\ hilly region Ⓝ Israel — **Gal·i·le·an** \ˌgal-ə-ˈlē-ən\ adj or n

Galilee, Sea of or **Lake of Gen·nes·a·ret** \-gə-ˈnes-ə-,ret, -rət\ lake Ⓝ Israel on Syrian border; crossed by Jordan river

Gal·lo·way \ˈgal-ə-,wā\ district ⓈⓌ Scotland — see DUM-FRIES AND GALLOWAY

Gam·bia \ˈgam-bē-ə\ country Ⓦ Africa; capital, Banjul — **Gam·bi·an** \-bē-ən\ adj or n

Gan·ges \ˈgan-,jēz\ river 2495 kilometers long Ⓝ India flowing from the Himalayas ⓈⒺ & Ⓔ to unite with the Brahmaputra & empty into Bay of Bengal through a vast delta — **Gan·get·ic** \gan-ˈjet-ik\ adj

Garden Grove city ⓈⓌ California

Gar·land \ˈgär-lənd\ city Ⓝ Texas

Ga·ronne \gə-ˈrän, -ˈrōn\ river 571 kilometers long Ⓢ Ⓔ France flowing ⓃⓌ

Gary \ˈga(ə)r-ē, ˈge(ə)r-ē\ city ⓃⓌ Indiana on Lake Michigan

Gas·co·ny \ˈgas-kə-nē\ region ⓈⓌ France — **Gas·con** \ˈgas-kən\ adj or n

Gas·pé \gas-ˈpā, ˈgas-,pā\ peninsula ⓈⒺ Quebec Ⓔ of mouth of the Saint Lawrence — **Gas·pe·sian** \ga-ˈspē-zhən\ adj or n

Gaul \ˈgȯl\ or Latin **Gal·lia** \ˈgal-ē-ə\ ancient country Ⓦ Europe chiefly consisting of region occupied by modern France & Belgium but at one time including also Po valley in Ⓝ Italy

Ga·za Strip \ˈgäz-ə-\ district ⓃⒺ Sinai peninsula on the Mediterranean

Gee·long \jə-ˈlȯŋ\ city ⓈⒺ Australia in Ⓢ Victoria

Ge·ne·va \jə-ˈnē-və\ city ⓈⓌ Switzerland on Lake of Geneva — **Ge·ne·van** \-vən\ adj or n — **Gen·e·vese** \ˌjen-ə-ˈvēz, -ˈvēs\ adj or n

Geneva, Lake of lake on border between ⓈⓌ Switzerland & Ⓔ France; crossed by the Rhone

Gen·oa \ˈjen-ə-wə\ or Italian **Ge·no·va** \ˈje-nō-vä\ city ⓃⓌ Italy — **Gen·o·ese** \ˌjen-ə-ˈwēz, -ˈwēs\ or **Gen·o·vese** \-ə-ˈvēz, -ˈvēs\ adj or n

George·town \ˈjȯ(ə)rj-,taùn\ **1** a Ⓦ section of Washington, District of Columbia **2** city, capital of Guyana

Geor·gia \ˈjȯr-jə\ **1** state ⓈⒺ U.S.; capital, Atlanta **2** or **Republic of Georgia** country ⓈⒺ Europe on Black sea Ⓢ of Caucasus mountains; capital, Tiflis; a republic of U.S.S.R. 1936–91 — **Georgian** adj or n

Georgia, Strait of channel Canada & U.S. between Vancouver Island & main part of British Columbia ⓃⓌ of Puget Sound

Georgian Bay inlet of Lake Huron in Ⓢ Ontario

Ger·man·town \ˈjər-mən-,taùn\ a ⓃⓌ section of Philadelphia, Pennsylvania

Ger·ma·ny \ˈjərm-(ə-)nē\ country central Europe bordering on North & Baltic seas; official capital, Berlin; divided 1946–90 into two independent states: the Federal Republic of Germany (capital, Bonn) & the German Democratic Republic (capital, East Berlin)

Get·tys·burg \ˈget-ēz-,bȯrg\ town Ⓢ Pennsylvania

Gha·na \ˈgän-ə, ˈgan-ə\ or formerly **Gold Coast** country Ⓦ Africa on Gulf of Guinea; an independent state in the Commonwealth; capital, Accra — **Gha·na·ian** \gä-ˈnā-ən,

ga-, -yən; -ˈnī-ən\ or **Gha·ni·an** \ˈgän-ē-ən, ˈgän-yən, ˈgan-\ adj or n

Ghats \ˈgȯts\ two mountain chains Ⓢ India — see EASTERN GHATS, WESTERN GHATS

Ghent \ˈgent\ city ⓃⓌ central Belgium

Gi·bral·tar \jə-ˈbrȯl-tər\ British colony on Ⓢ coast of Spain including Rock of Gibraltar

Gibraltar, Rock of cape on Ⓢ coast of Spain in Gibraltar colony at Ⓔ end of Strait of Gibraltar; highest point 426 meters

Gibraltar, Strait of passage between Spain & Africa connecting the Atlantic & the Mediterranean

Gi·la \ˈhē-lə\ river 1015 kilometers long ⓈⓌ New Mexico and Ⓢ Arizona flowing Ⓦ into the Colorado

Gil·bert and El·ice Islands \ˈgil-bərt-ən(d)-ˈel-əs-\ island group Ⓦ Pacific; until 1976 a British colony; now divided into the independent states of Kiribati and Tuvalu

Gil·e·ad \ˈgil-ē-əd\ mountain region ⓃⒺ Palestine Ⓔ of Jordan river; now in ⓃⓌ Jordan — **Gil·e·ad·ite** \-ē-ə-,dīt\ n

Gi·za \ˈgē-zə\ city Ⓝ Egypt on the Nile ⓈⓌ of Cairo

Gla·cier Bay \ˌglā-shər-\ inlet ⓈⒺ Alaska at Ⓢ end of Saint Elias range

Glas·gow \ˈglas-kō, ˈglas-gō, ˈglaz-gō\ city Ⓢ central Scotland in Strathclyde region on the Clyde — **Glas·we·gian** \glas-ˈwē-jən\ adj or n

Glen·dale \ˈglen-,dāl\ city Ⓢ California ⓃⒺ of Los Angeles

Glouces·ter \ˈgläs-tər, ˈglȯs-\ city area ⓈⓌ central England in Gloucestershire

Glouces·ter·shire \ˈgläs-tər-,shi(ə)r, ˈglȯs-, -shər\ or **Gloucester** county ⓈⓌ central England

Goa \ˈgō-ə\ district Ⓦ India on Malabar coast belonging to Portugal before 1962

Goat Island island Ⓦ New York in Niagara river — see NIAGARA FALLS

Go·bi \ˈgō-bē\ desert Ⓔ central Asia in Mongolia & Ⓝ China

Godt·haab \ˈgȯt-,hȯb, ˈgät-\ town, capital of Greenland on ⓈⓌ coast

Godwin Austen — see K2

Go·lan Heights \ˌgō-,län-, -lən-\ hilly region ⓃⒺ of Sea of Galilee

Gol·con·da \gäl-ˈkän-də\ ruined city central India Ⓦ of Hyderabad

Gold Coast **1** — see GHANA **2** coast region Ⓦ Africa on Ⓝ shore of Gulf of Guinea Ⓔ of Ivory Coast

Golden Gate strait Ⓦ California

Good Hope, Cape of \-,gùd-ˈhōp\ cape Ⓢ Republic of South Africa in ⓈⓌ Cape Province

Gor'kiy or **Gorky** — see NIZHNI NOVGOROD

Gram·pi·an \ˈgram-pē-ən\ **1** hills Ⓝ central Scotland **2** region ⓃⒺ central Scotland; established 1975

Grand Banks shallow area in the Ⓦ Atlantic ⓈⒺ of Newfoundland

Grand Canyon gorge of Colorado river ⓃⓌ Arizona

Grand Canyon of the Snake — see HELLS CANYON

Grande, Rio — see RIO GRANDE

Grand Rapids city ⓈⓌ Michigan

Great Australian Bight wide bay on Ⓢ coast of Australia

Great Barrier Reef coral reef Australia off ⓃⒺ coast of Queensland

Great Basin region Ⓦ U.S. between Sierra Nevada & Wasatch mountains including most of Nevada & parts of California, Idaho, Utah, Wyoming, and Oregon; has no drainage to ocean

Great Bear lake Canada in Ⓦ Northwest Territories drain-

\ə\ abut	\aù\ out	\i\ tip	\ȯ\ saw	\ù\ foot	
\ər\ further	\ch\ chin	\ī\ life	\ȯi\ coin	\y\ yet	
\a\ mat	\e\ pet	\j\ job	\th\ thin	\yü\ few	
\ā\ take	\ē\ easy	\ŋ\ sing	\th\ this	\yù\ cure	
\ä\ cot, cart	\g\ go	\ō\ bone	\ü\ food	\zh\ vision	

through Great Bear river into Mackenzie river

Great Brit·ain \-'brit-°n\ **1** island W Europe NW of France consisting of England, Scotland, & Wales **2** UNITED KINGDOM

Great Dividing range mountain system E Australia & Tasmania extending S from Cape York peninsula — see KOSCIUSKO, MOUNT

Greater An·til·les \-an-'til-ēz\ group of islands of the West Indies including Cuba, Hispaniola, Jamaica, & Puerto Rico — see LESSER ANTILLES

Greater London county SE England consisting of City of London & 32 surrounding city areas

Greater Manchester county NW England including city of Manchester

Great Lakes chain of five lakes (Superior, Michigan, Huron, Erie, & Ontario) central North America in U.S. & Canada

Great Plains elevated plains region W central U.S. & W Canada E of the Rockies; extending from W Texas to NE British Columbia & NW Alberta

Great Rift valley \-'rift-\ basin SW Asia & E Africa extending with several breaks from valley of the Jordan S to central Mozambique

Great Salt lake N Utah having salty waters & no outlet

Great Slave lake NW Canada in S Northwest Territories drained by Mackenzie river

Great Smoky mountains between W North Carolina & E Tennessee; highest Clingmans Dome 2024 meters

Greece \'grēs\ country S Europe at S end of Balkan peninsula; capital, Athens

Green \'grēn\ **1** mountains E North America in the Appalachians extending from S Quebec S through Vermont into W Massachusetts **2** river 1175 kilometers long W U.S. flowing from S Wyoming S into the Colorado in SE Utah

Green Bay inlet of NW Lake Michigan 193 kilometers long in NW Michigan & NE Wisconsin

Green·land \'grēn-lənd, -,land\ island in the N Atlantic off NE North America belonging to Denmark; capital, Godthaab

Greens·boro \'grēnz-,bər-ə, -,bə-rə\ city N central North Carolina

Green·wich \'grin-ij, 'gren-, -ich\ city area of SE Greater London county, England

Green·wich Village \,gren-ich-, ,grin-, -ij-\ section of New York City in Manhattan on lower W side

Gre·na·da \grə-'nād-ə\ island West Indies in S Windward Islands; an independent country; capital, Saint George's

Gua·da·la·ja·ra \,gwäd-ə-lə-'här-ə\ city W central Mexico

Gua·dal·ca·nal \,gwäd-°l-kə-'nal, ,gwäd-ə-kə-\ island W Pacific in the SE Solomons

Gua·dal·qui·vir \,gwäd-°l-'kwiv-ər, -ki-'vi(ə)r\ river 602 kilometers long S Spain flowing into the Atlantic

Gua·de·loupe \'gwäd-°l-,üp\ two islands separated by a narrow channel in West Indies in central Leeward Islands; an overseas division of France

Gua·lla·ti·ri \,gwä-yə-'tir-ē, ,gwī-ə-\ volcano 6060 meters N Chile; highest volcano in world

Guam \'gwäm\ island W Pacific in S Marianas belonging to U.S.; capital, Agana — **Gua·ma·ni·an** \gwä-'mä-nē-ən\ adj or n

Gua·na·ba·ra Bay \,gwän-ə-'bar-ə, -'bär-\ inlet of the Atlantic SE Brazil on which city of Rio de Janeiro is located

Guang·zhou \'gwäŋ-'jō\ or **Can·ton** \'kan-,tän, kan-'\ city SE China

Guan·tá·na·mo Bay \gwän-'tän-ə-,mō\ inlet of the Caribbean in SE Cuba; site of U.S. naval station

Gua·te·ma·la \,gwät-ə-'mäl-ə\ **1** country Central America **2** or **Guatemala City** city, its capital — **Gua·te·ma·lan** \-'mäl-ən\ adj or n

Gua·ya·quil \,gwī-ə-'kē(ə)l, -'kil\ city W Ecuador

Guern·sey \'gərn-zē\ island in English channel — see CHANNEL

Gui·a·na \gē-'an-ə, -'än-ə; gī-'an-ə\ region N South America on the Atlantic; includes Guyana, French Guiana, Suriname, & nearby parts of Brazil & Venezuela — **Gui·a·nan** \-ən\ adj or n

Guin·ea \'gin-ē\ **1** region W Africa on the Atlantic extending along coast from Gambia to Angola **2** country W Africa N of Sierra Leone & Liberia; capital, Conakry — **Guin·ean** \'gin-ē-ən\ adj or n

Guinea, Gulf of arm of the Atlantic W central Africa

Guin·ea–Bis·sau \,gin-ē-bis-'aù\ country W Africa; an independent state since 1974; capital, Bissau

Gui·yang \'gwē-'yäŋ\ or **Kuei–yang** \'gwā-'yäŋ\ city S China

Gulf States states of U.S. bordering on Gulf of Mexico: Florida, Alabama, Mississippi, Louisiana, and Texas

Gulf Stream warm current of the Atlantic ocean flowing from Gulf of Mexico NE along coast of U.S. to Nantucket island and from there eastward

Guy·ana \gī-'an-ə\ or formerly **British Guiana** country N South America on the Atlantic; an independent state in the Commonwealth since 1970; capital, Georgetown

Gwent \'gwent\ county SE Wales; established 1974

Gwyn·edd \'gwin-eth\ county NW Wales; established 1974

Hack·ney \'hak-nē\ city area of N Greater London county, England

Hague, The \the-'hāg\ city SW Netherlands; a capital of the Netherlands

Haidarabad — see HYDERABAD

Hai·kou \'hī-'kō\ city SE China

Hai·ti \'hāt-ē\ **1** — see HISPANIOLA **2** country West Indies in W Hispaniola; capital, Port-au-Prince — **Hai·tian** \'hā-shən\ adj or n

Ha·le·a·ka·la Crater \,häl-ē-,äk-ə-'lä\ crater 829 meters deep & 32 kilometers in circumference Hawaii in E Maui Island

Hal·i·fax \'hal-ə-,faks\ city, capital of Nova Scotia, Canada

Ham·burg \'ham-,bərg, 'häm-,bù(ə)rg\ city N Germany on the Elbe — **Ham·burg·er** \-,bər-gər, -,bür-\ n

Ham·il·ton \'ham-əl-tən, -əlt-°n\ **1** city S Ontario, Canada **2** town, capital of Bermuda

Ham·mer·smith \'ham-ər-,smith\ city area of SW Greater London county, England

Hamp·shire \'ham(p)-,shi(ə)r, -shər\ county S England on English channel

Hamp·ton \'ham(p)-tən\ city SE Virginia

Hampton Roads channel SE Virginia through which James river flows into Chesapeake Bay

Hang·zhou \'häŋ-'jō\ or **Hang·chow** \'haŋ-'chaù, 'häŋ-'jō\ or **Hang–chou** \'häŋ-'jō\ city E China

Han·ni·bal \'han-ə-bəl\ city NE Missouri on the Mississippi river

Han·no·ver or **Han·o·ver** \'han-,ō-vər, 'han-ə-vər; German hä-'nō-vər\ city N central Germany

Ha·noi \ha-'nòi, hə-, hä-\ city, capital of Vietnam

Ha·ra·re \hə-'rä-rā\ or formerly **Salis·bury** \'sòlz-,ber-ē, -b(ə-)rē\ city, capital of Zimbabwe

Har·bin \'här-bən, här-'bin\ or **Ha–erh–pin** \'hä-'er-'bin\ city NE China

Har·in·gey \'har-iŋ-,gā\ city area of N Greater London county, England

Har·lem \'här-ləm\ section of New York City in N Manhattan

Har·ris·burg \'har-əs-,bərg\ city, capital of Pennsylvania

Har·row \'har-ō\ city area of NW Greater London county, England

Hart·ford \'härt-fərd\ city, capital of Connecticut

Hat·ter·as, Cape \'hat-ə-rəs, -'ha-trəs\ cape, North Carolina on Cape Hatteras Island

Ha·vana \hə-'van-ə\ city, capital of Cuba

Hav·ant and Wa·ter·loo \'hav-ənt-°n-,wòt-ər-'lü, -,wät-\ town S England in Hampshire

Ha·ver·ing \'hāv-(ə-)riŋ\ city area of NE Greater London county, England

Ha·waii \hə-'wä-(y)ē, -'wī-, -'wȯ-\ **1** or **Ha·wai·ian Is·lands** or formerly **Sand·wich islands** \,san-(d)wich-\ group of islands central Pacific belonging to U.S. **2** island, largest of the group **3** state of U.S. consisting of Hawaiian Islands except Midway; capital, Honolulu

Heb·ri·des \'heb-rə-,dēz\ islands Ⓦ Scotland in the Atlantic consisting of **Outer Hebrides** (to Ⓦ) and **Inner Hebrides** (to Ⓔ) — see WESTERN ISLES — **Heb·ri·de·an** \,heb-rə-'dē-ən\ adj or n

Hel·e·na \'hel-ə-nə\ city, capital of Montana

Hellespont — see DARDANELLES

Hells Canyon \'helz-\ or **Grand Canyon of the Snake** canyon of Snake river on Idaho-Oregon boundary

Hel·sin·ki \'hel-,siŋ-kē, hel-'siŋ-\ city, capital of Finland

Henry, Cape \-'hen-rē\ cape Ⓔ Virginia Ⓢ of entrance to Chesapeake Bay

Her·e·ford and Wor·ces·ter \'her-ə-fərd-°n-'wús-tər, in the U.S. also 'hər-fərd-\ county Ⓦ England bordering on Wales

Hert·ford·shire \'härt-fərd-,shi(ə)r, -shər, also 'härt-, in the U.S. also 'hərt-\ or **Hertford** county Ⓢ England

Hi·a·le·ah \,hī-ə-'lē-ə\ city Ⓢ Florida

Hi·ber·nia \hī-'bər-nē-ə\ — see IRELAND — **Hi·ber·ni·an** \-ən\ adj or n

Hi·ga·shi·ōsa·ka \hē-,gä-shē-ō-'säk-ə\ city Japan in Ⓢ Honshu Ⓔ of Osaka

High·land \'hī-lənd\ region Ⓝ Scotland

High·lands \'hī-lən(d)z\ the mountainous Ⓝ part of Scotland lying Ⓝ & Ⓦ of the Lowlands

High Plains the Great Plains especially from Nebraska southward

Hil·ling·don \'hil-iŋ-dən\ city area of Ⓦ Greater London county, England

Hi·ma·la·ya \,him-ə-'lā-ə, hə-'mäl-(ə-)yə\ mountain system Ⓢ Asia on border between India & Tibet & in Kashmir, Nepal, & Bhutan — see EVEREST, MOUNT — **Hi·ma·la·yan** \,him-ə-'lā-ən, hə-'mäl-(ə-)yən\ adj

Hin·du Kush \,hin-(,)dü-'kúsh, -'kəsh\ mountain range central Asia ⓈⓌ of the Pamirs on border of Kashmir & in Afghanistan

Hin·du·stan \,hin-(,)dü-'stan, -də-, -'stän\ **1** region Ⓝ India **2** the subcontinent of India **3** the country of India

Hi·ro·shi·ma \,hir-ə-'shē-mə, hə-'rō-shə-mə\ city Japan in Ⓢ Ⓦ Honshu on Inland sea

His·pan·io·la \,his-pən-'yō-lə\ or Spanish **Es·pa·ño·la** \,es-,pañ-'yō-lə\ or formerly **Hai·ti** \'hāt-ē\ island West Indies in Greater Antilles divided between Haiti on Ⓦ & Dominican Republic on Ⓔ

Ho·bart \'hō-,bärt\ city Australia, capital of Tasmania

Ho Chi Minh City \,hō-,chē-,min-, -,shē-\ or formerly **Saigon** \'sī-'gän, 'sī-,gän\ city Ⓢ Vietnam

Hoh·hot \'hō-'hōt\ or **Hu·he·hot** \'hü-,hä-'hōt\ city Ⓝ China, capital of Inner Mongolia

Hok·kai·do \hä-'kīd-ō\ island Ⓝ Japan Ⓝ of Honshu

Hol·land \'häl-ənd\ **1** county of Holy Roman Empire bordering on North sea & consisting of area now forming part of Ⓦ Netherlands **2** — see NETHERLANDS — **Hol·land·er** \-ən-dər\ n

Hol·ly·wood \'häl-ē-,wúd\ **1** section of Los Angeles, California, Ⓝ Ⓦ of downtown district **2** city Ⓢ Ⓔ Florida

Holy Land PALESTINE

Holy Roman Empire empire consisting mainly of German and Italian territories and existing from the 9th or 10th century to 1806

Hon·du·ras \hän-'d(y)úr-əs\ country Central America; capital, Tegucigalpa — **Hon·du·ran** \-ən\ or **Hon·du·ra·ne·an** or **Hon·du·ra·ni·an** \,hän-d(y)ù-'rā-nē-ən\ adj or n

Hong Kong \'häŋ-,käŋ, -'käŋ; 'hòŋ-,kòŋ, -'kòŋ\ British colony on coast of Ⓢ Ⓔ China including Hong Kong Island & Kowloon peninsula; capital, Victoria

Ho·ni·a·ra \,hō-nē-'är-ə\ town, capital of Solomon Islands

Ho·no·lu·lu \,hän-°l-'ü-lü, ,hōn-°l-\ city, capital of Hawaii on Oahu Island

Hon·shu \'hän-shü\ or **Hon·do** \'hän-dō\ island Japan; largest of the four chief islands

Hood, Mount \-'húd\ mountain 3424 meters Ⓝ Ⓦ Oregon in Cascade Range

Hoo·ghly or **Hu·gli** \'hü-glē\ river 193 kilometers long Ⓔ India flowing Ⓢ into Bay of Bengal; most westerly channel of the Ganges in its delta

Hoo·ver Dam \,hü-vər-\ or **Boul·der Dam** \,bōl-dər-\ dam 221 meters high in Colorado river between Arizona & Nevada — see MEAD, LAKE

Horn, Cape \-'hȯ(ə)rn\ cape Ⓢ Chile on an island in Tierra del Fuego; the most southerly point of South America at 55°59' Ⓢ latitude

Horseshoe Falls — see NIAGARA FALLS

Houns·low \'haúnz-,lō\ city area of Ⓢ Ⓦ Greater London county, England

Hous·ton \'(h)yü-stən\ city Ⓢ Ⓔ Texas

How·rah \'haú-rə\ city Ⓔ India on Hooghly river opposite Calcutta

Huang or **Hwang** \'hwäŋ\ or **Yellow** river 4830 kilometers long Ⓝ China flowing into Bo Hai

Hud·ders·field \'həd-ərz-,fēld\ city area Ⓝ England in West Yorkshire Ⓝ Ⓔ of Manchester

Hud·son \'həd-sən\ **1** river 492 kilometers long Ⓔ New York flowing Ⓢ **2** bay inlet of the Atlantic in Ⓝ Canada **3** strait Ⓝ Ⓔ Canada connecting Hudson bay & the Atlantic

Huhehot — see HOHHOT

Hull \'həl\ or **Kings·ton upon Hull** \'kiŋ(k)-stən-\ city Ⓝ England in Humberside county

Hum·ber·side \'həm-bər-,sīd\ county Ⓔ England

Hun·ga·ry \'həŋ-g(ə-)rē\ country central Europe; capital, Budapest

Hunt·ing·ton Beach \'hənt-iŋ-tən-\ city Ⓢ Ⓦ California

Hunts·ville \'hən(t)s-,vil, -vəl\ city Ⓝ Alabama

Hu·ron, Lake \-'(h)yúr-ən, -'(h)yú(ə)r-,än\ lake Ⓔ central North America in U.S. & Canada; one of the Great Lakes

Hy·der·abad \'hīd-(ə-)rə-,bad, -,bäd\ **1** or **Hai·dar·abad** city Ⓢ central India **2** city Ⓢ Ⓔ Pakistan on the Indus

Iba·dan \i-'bäd-°n, -'bad-\ city Ⓢ Ⓦ Nigeria

Ibe·ri·an \ī-'bir-ē-ən\ peninsula Ⓢ Ⓦ Europe occupied by Spain & Portugal

Ice·land \'ī-slənd, -,sland\ island Ⓢ Ⓔ of Greenland between Arctic & Atlantic oceans; capital, Reykjavik — **Ice·land·er** \-,slan-dər, -slən-dər\ n

Ida·ho \'īd-ə-,hō\ state Ⓝ Ⓦ U.S.; capital, Boise — **Ida·ho·an** \,īd-ə-'hō-ən\ adj or n

Igua·çu or Spanish **Igua·zú** \,ē-gwə-'sü\ river 612 kilometers long Ⓢ Brazil flowing Ⓦ

IJs·sel or **Ijs·sel** \'ī-səl\ river 113 kilometers long Ⓔ Netherlands flowing out of Rhine Ⓝ into IJsselmeer

IJs·sel·meer \,ī-səl-'me(ə)r\ or **Lake Ijs·sel** freshwater lake Ⓝ Netherlands separated from North sea by a dike; part of former Zuider Zee (inlet of North sea)

Ilium or **Ilion** — see TROY

Il·li·nois \,il-ə-'nȯi also -'nȯiz\ state Ⓝ central U.S.; capital, Springfield — **Il·li·nois·an** \-'nȯi-ən, -'nȯiz-°n\ adj or n

Il·lyr·ia \il-'ir-ē-ə\ ancient country Ⓢ Europe and Balkan peninsula on the Adriatic — **Il·lyr·i·an** \-ē-ən\ adj or n

Im·pe·ri·al Valley \im-'pir-ē-əl-\ valley Ⓢ Ⓔ corner of California & partly in Baja California, Mexico

In·chon \'in-,chän\ city South Korea on Yellow sea

In·de·pen·dence \,in-də-'pen-dən(t)s\ city Ⓦ Missouri Ⓔ of Kansas City

\ə\ abut		\aú\ out	\i\ tip	\ȯ\ saw	\ú\ foot
\ər\ further		\ch\ chin	\ī\ life	\ȯi\ coin	\y\ yet
\a\ mat		\e\ pet	\j\ job	\th\ thin	\yü\ few
\ā\ take		\ē\ easy	\ŋ\ sing	\th\ this	\yú\ cure
\ä\ cot, cart		\g\ go	\ō\ bone	\ü\ food	\zh\ vision

In·dia \'in-dē-ə\ **1** subcontinent ⑤ Asia ⑤ of the Himalayas between Bay of Bengal & Arabian sea **2** *or* **Bharat** \'bər-ət, 'bə-rət\ country consisting of major portion of the subcontinent; an independent state in the Commonwealth; capital, New Delhi **3** *or* **Indian Empire** before 1947 those parts of the Indian subcontinent under British rule or protection

In·di·an \'in-dē-ən\ ocean ⑤ of Africa, ⑤ of Asia, ⑥ of Australia, & ⑥ of Antarctica

In·di·ana \,in-dē-'an-ə\ state ⑥ central U.S.; capital, Indianapolis — **In·di·an·an** \-'an-ən\ *or* **In·di·an·i·an** \-'an-ē-ən\ *adj or n*

In·di·a·nap·o·lis \,in-dē-ə-'nap-(ə-)ləs\ city, capital of Indiana

Indian river lagoon 266 kilometers long ⑥ Florida between main part of the state & coastal islands

Indian Territory former territory ⑤ U.S. in present state of Oklahoma

In·dies \'in-dēz\ **1** EAST INDIES **2** WEST INDIES

In·do·chi·na \'in-(,)dō-'chī-nə\ **1** peninsula ⑤ Asia including Myanmar, Malay peninsula, Thailand, Cambodia, Laos, & Vietnam **2** *or* **French Indochina** former country ⑤ Asia consisting of area now forming Cambodia, Laos, & Vietnam — **In·do–Chi·nese** \-chī-'nēz, -'nēs\ *adj or n*

In·do·ne·sia \,in-də-'nē-zhə, -shə\ country ⑤ Asia in Malay island group consisting of Sumatra, Java, ⑤ & ⑥ Borneo, Sulawesi, ⑥ New Guinea, & many smaller islands; capital, Djakarta — *see* NETHERLANDS EAST INDIES — **In·do·ne·sian** \-zhən, -shən\ *adj or n*

In·dore \in-'dō(ə)r, -'dȯ(ə)r\ city ⑥ central India

In·dus \'in-dəs\ river 2900 kilometers long ⑤ Asia flowing from Tibet ⑥ & ⑤ through Pakistan into Arabian sea

In·gle·wood \'iŋ-gəl-,wùd\ city ⑤ California

In·land \'in-,land, -lənd\ sea inlet of the Pacific in ⑤ Japan between Honshu on ⑥ and Shikoku and Kyushu on ⑤

Inner Hebrides — *see* HEBRIDES

Inner Mon·go·lia \-män-'gōl-yə, mäŋ-, -'gō-lē-ə\ region ⑥ China

Inside Passage *or* **Inland Passage** protected shipping route between Puget Sound, Washington, & Skagway, Alaska

In·ver·ness \,in-vər-'nes\ town ⑥ Scotland in Highland region

Io·ni·an \ī-'ō-nē-ən\ **1** sea arm of the Mediterranean between ⑤ Italy & ⑥ Greece **2** islands ⑥ Greece in Ionian sea

Io·wa \'ī-ə-wə\ state ⑥ central U.S.; capital, Des Moines — **Io·wan** \-wən\ *adj or n*

Ips·wich \'ip-(,)swich\ city area ⑤ England in Suffolk county

Iran \i-'rän, -'ran; ī-'ran\ *or formerly* **Per·sia** \'pər-zhə\ country ⑤ Asia; capital, Tehran — **Irani** \i-'rän-ē, -'ran-\ *adj or n* — **Ira·nian** \ir-'ā-nē-ən, -'an-ē-, -'än-ē-\ *adj or n*

Iraq \i-'räk, -'rak\ country ⑤ Asia in Mesopotamia; capital, Baghdad — **Iraqi** \-'räk-ē, -'rak-\ *adj or n*

Ire·land \'ī(ə)r-lənd\ **1** *or Latin* **Hi·ber·nia** \hī-'bər-nē-ə\ island ⑥ Europe in the Atlantic; one of the British Isles **2** *or* **Irish Republic** *or* **Ei·re** \'ar-ə, 'ar-ē, 'er-, 'är-, 'īr-\ country occupying major portion of the island; capital, Dublin

Irish sea \'īr-ish-\ arm of the Atlantic between Great Britain & Ireland

Ir·kutsk \i(ə)r-'kütsk, ,ər-\ city ⑤ Russia near Lake Baikal

Ir·ra·wad·dy \,ir-ə-'wäd-ē\ river 2175 kilometers long Myanmar flowing ⑤ into Bay of Bengal

Ir·tysh \i(ə)r-'tish, ,ər-\ river 3540 kilometers long central Asia flowing ⑥ & ⑥ from Altai mountains in China, through Kazakhstan, and into ⑥ central Russia

Ir·ving \'ər-viŋ\ city ⑥ Texas ⑥ of Dallas

Is·fa·han \,is-fə-'hän, -'han\ *or formerly* **Is·pa·han** \,is-pə-\ city ⑥ central Iran

Is·lam·abad \is-'läm-ə-,bäd, iz-'lam-ə-,bad\ city, capital of Pakistan

Isle of Man — *see* MAN, ISLE OF

Isle of Wight \-'wīt\ island and county ⑤ England in English channel

Isle Roy·ale \(')ī(ə)l-'rȯi(-ə)l\ island Michigan in Lake Superior

Isles of Scilly — *see* CORNWALL AND ISLES OF SCILLY; SCILLY

Is·ling·ton \'iz-liŋ-tən\ city area of ⑥ Greater London county, England

Is·ra·el \'iz-rē-əl, -rā-əl, -rəl\ **1** ancient kingdom Palestine consisting of lands occupied by the Hebrew people **2** *or* **Ephra·im** \'ē-frē-əm\ the ⑥ part of the Hebrew kingdom after about 933 B.C. **3** country ⑤ Asia in Palestine; established 1948; capital, Jerusalem — **Is·rae·li** \iz-'rā-lē\ *adj or n*

Is·tan·bul \,is-təm-'bül, -,täm-, -,tam-, -,tän-\ *or formerly* **Con·stan·ti·no·ple** \,kän-,stant-°n-'ō-pəl\ city ⑥ Turkey on the Bosporus & Sea of Marmara; former capital of Turkey

Is·tria \'is-trē-ə\ peninsula in Croatia & Slovenia extending into the ⑥ Adriatic — **Is·tri·an** \-trē-ən\ *adj or n*

It·a·ly \'it-ºl-ē\ **1** peninsula 1225 kilometers long ⑤ Europe extending into the Mediterranean between Adriatic & Tyrrhenian seas **2** country including the peninsula of Italy, Sicily, & Sardinia; capital, Rome

Itas·ca, Lake \-ī-'tas-kə\ lake ⑥ central Minnesota; source of the Mississippi

Ivory Coast country ⑥ Africa on Gulf of Guinea; capital, Abidjan

Iwo Ji·ma \,ē-(,)wō-'jē-mə\ island Japan in ⑥ Pacific about 1130 kilometers ⑤ of Tokyo

Ix·ta·pa·la·pa \,ē-stə-pə-'läp-ə\ city ⑤ central Mexico ⑤ of Mexico City

Izhevsk \'ē-,zhefsk\ *or 1985–87* **Usti·nov** \'üs-ti-,nóf, -,nȯv\ city ⑥ Russia

Iz·mir \iz-'mi(ə)r\ *or formerly* **Smyr·na** \'smər-nə\ city ⑥ Turkey

Jack·son \'jak-sən\ city, capital of Mississippi

Jack·son·ville \'jak-sən-,vil\ city ⑥ Florida

Jai·pur \'jī-,pù(ə r\ city ⑥ India

Jakarta — *see* DJAKARTA

Ja·mai·ca \jə-'mā-kə\ island West Indies in Greater Antilles; an independent country in the Commonwealth; capital, Kingston — **Ja·mai·can** \-kən\ *adj or n*

James \'jāmz\ **1** river 1145 kilometers long North Dakota and South Dakota flowing ⑤ into the Missouri **2** river 550 kilometers long Virginia flowing ⑥ into Chesapeake Bay

James Bay the ⑤ extension of Hudson bay between ⑥ Ontario & ⑥ Quebec

James·town \'jām-,staùn\ ruined village ⑥ Virginia on James river; first permanent English settlement in America (1607)

Jam·shed·pur \'jäm-,shed-,pù(ə)r\ city ⑥ India

Ja·pan \jə-'pan, ji-, ja-\ *or Japanese* **Nip·pon** \nip-'än\ country ⑥ Asia consisting of Honshu, Hokkaido, Kyushu, Shikoku, & other islands in the ⑥ Pacific; capital, Tokyo

Japan, Sea of arm of the Pacific between Japan & main part of Asia

Ja·va \'jäv-ə, 'jav-ə\ island Indonesia ⑤ of Borneo; chief city, Djakarta — **Ja·van** \-ən\ *adj or n*

Jef·fer·son City \'jef-ər-sən-\ city, capital of Missouri

Jer·sey \'jər-zē\ island in English channel — *see* CHANNEL — **Jer·sey·ite** \-zē-,īt\ *n*

Jersey City city ⑥ New Jersey on Hudson river

Je·ru·sa·lem \jə-'rü-s(ə-)ləm, -'rüz-(ə-)ləm\ city ⑥ of Dead sea divided 1948–67 between Israel & Jordan; capital of Israel since 1950 & formerly of ancient kingdom of Israel

Jid·da \'jid-ə\ city ⑥ Saudi Arabia on Red sea

Ji·lin \'jē-'lin\ *or* **Ki·rin** \'kē-'rin\ city [NE] China
Ji·nan *or* **Tsi·nan** \'jē-'nän\ city [E] China
Jinzhou *or* **Chin–chou** *or* **Chinchow** \'jin-'jō\ city [NE] China
Jo·han·nes·burg \jō-'han-əs-,bərg, -'hän-\ city [NE] Republic of South Africa in [S] Transvaal province
Jor·dan \'jòrd-ᵊn\ **1** river 320 kilometers long Israel & Jordan flowing [S] from Syria into Dead sea **2** country [SW] Asia in [NW] Arabia; capital, Amman — **Jor·da·ni·an** \jòr-'dā-nē-ən\ *adj or n*
Juan de Fu·ca, Strait of \-,(h)wän-də-'fyü-kə\ strait 160 kilometers long between Vancouver Island, British Columbia, & Olympic peninsula, Washington
Ju·dea *or* **Ju·daea** \jü-'dē-ə, -'dā-\ ancient region Palestine forming the [S] division (Judah) of the country under Persian, Greek, & Roman rule — **Ju·dean** \-ən\ *adj or n*
Ju·go·sla·via \,yü-gō-'släv-ē-ə\ — see YUGOSLAVIA — **Ju·go·slav** \,yü-gō-'släv, -'slav\ *or* **Ju·go·sla·vi·an** \-'släv-ē-ən\ *adj or n*
Ju·neau \'jü-nō, jü-'nō\ city, capital of Alaska
Ju·ra \'jùr-ə\ mountain range extending along boundary between France & Switzerland [W] of Lake of Geneva
Jut·land \'jət-lənd\ **1** peninsula [N] Europe extending into North sea & consisting of main part of Denmark & [N] portion of Germany **2** the main part of Denmark
Ka·bul \'käb-əl, kä-'bül\ city, capital of Afghanistan
Ka Lae \kä-'lä-ä\ *or* **South Cape** *or* **South Point** most southerly point of Hawaii & of U.S.
Kal·a·ha·ri \,kal-ə-'här-ē\ desert region [S] Africa [N] of Orange river in [S] Botswana & [NW] Republic of South Africa
Kalgan — see ZHANGJIAKOU
Ka·li·man·tan \,kal-ə-'man-,tan, ,käl-ə-'män-,tän\ **1** BORNEO — its Indonesian name **2** the [S] & [E] portion of Borneo belonging to Indonesia; formerly part of Netherlands East Indies
Kam·chat·ka \kam-'chat-kə\ peninsula 1205 kilometers long [E] Russia
Kam·pa·la \käm-'päl-ə\ city, capital of Uganda
Kampuchea — see CAMBODIA
Ka·no \'kän-ō\ city [N] central Nigeria
Kan·pur \'kän-,pù(ə)r\ city [N] India on the Ganges
Kan·sas \'kan-zəs\ state [W] central U.S.; capital, Topeka — **Kan·san** \-zən\ *adj or n*
Kansas City **1** city [NE] Kansas bordering on Kansas City, Missouri **2** city [W] Missouri
Kao·hsiung \'kaù-shē-'ùŋ, 'gaù-\ city China in [SW] Taiwan
Ka·ra·chi \kə-'räch-ē\ city [S] Pakistan on Arabian sea
Ka·ra·gan·da \,kar-ə-gən-'dä\ city central Kazakhstan
Ka·re·lia \kə-'rē-lē-ə, -'rēl-yə\ region [NE] Europe in Finland & Russia — **Ka·re·lian** \-'rē-lē-ən, -'rēl-yən\ *adj or n*
Kar·roo \kə-'rü\ plateau region [W] Republic of South Africa [W] of Drakensberg mountains
Kash·mir \'kash-,mi(ə)r, 'kazh-, kash-'mi(ə)r, kazh-'mi(ə)r\ region and former state [N] Indian subcontinent — **Kash·miri** \kash-'mi(ə)r-ē, kazh-\ *adj or n*
Ka·thi·a·war \,kät-ē-ə-'wär\ peninsula [W] India [N] of Gulf of Cambay
Kath·man·du *or* **Kat·man·du** \,kat-,man-'dü\ city, capital of Nepal
Kat·mai, Mount \-'kat-,mī\ volcano 2047 meters [S] Alaska on Alaska peninsula
Kat·te·gat \'kat-i-,gat\ arm of North sea between Sweden & [E] coast of Jutland peninsula of Denmark
Kau·ai \'kaù-,ī\ island Hawaii [NW] of Oahu
Ka·wa·sa·ki \,kä-wə-'säk-ē\ city Japan in [E] Honshu [S] of Tokyo
Ka·zakh·stan \kə-,zak-'stan; kə-,zäk-'stän, ,kä-\ country [NW] central Asia; capital, Alma-Ata; a republic (**Ka·zakh Soviet Socialist Republic** \kə-,zak-, -,zäk-\) of U.S.S.R. 1936-91
Ka·zan \kə-'zan, -'zän(-yə)\ city [W] Russia

Kee·wa·tin \kē-'wāt-ᵊn\ former district [N] Canada in [E] Northwest Territories [NW] of Hudson bay
Ke·me·ro·vo \'kem-ə-rə-və, -,rō-və, -rə-,vō\ city [S] central Russia
Ke·nai \'kē-,nī\ peninsula [S] Alaska [E] of Cook inlet
Kennedy, Cape — see CANAVERAL, CAPE
Ken·sing·ton and Chel·sea \'ken-ziŋ-tən-ən-'chel-sē, 'ken(t)-siŋ-\ city area of [W] Greater London county, England
Kent \'kent\ county [SE] England — **Kent·ish** \'kent-ish\ *adj*
Ken·tucky \kən-'tək-ē\ state [E] central U.S.; capital, Frankfort — **Ken·tuck·i·an** \-ē-ən\ *adj or n*
Ken·ya \'ken-yə, 'kēn-\ **1** mountain 5194 meters central Kenya **2** country [E] Africa [S] of Ethiopia; capital, Nairobi — **Ken·yan** \-yən\ *adj or n*
Key West \'kē-'west\ city [SW] Florida on Key West island
Kha·ba·rovsk \kə-'bär-əfsk\ city [SE] Russia
Khar·kov \'kär-,kòf, -,kòv, -kəf\ city [NE] Ukraine
Khar·toum \kär-'tüm\ city, capital of Sudan
Khmer Republic — see CAMBODIA
Khy·ber \'kī-bər\ pass 53 kilometers long on border between Afghanistan & Pakistan
Ki·bo \'kē-bō\ mountain peak 5888 meters [NE] Tanzania; highest peak of Kilimanjaro & highest point in Africa
Kiel \'kē(ə)l\ canal 98 kilometers long [N] Germany across base of Jutland peninsula connecting Baltic sea & North sea
Ki·ev *or Russian* **Ki·yev** \'kē-,(y)ef, -(y)ev, -(y)əf\ city, capital of Ukraine
Ki·ga·li \ki-'gäl-ē\ city, capital of Rwanda
Ki·lau·ea \,kē-,laù-'ā-ə\ volcanic crater Hawaii on Hawaii island on [E] slope of Mauna Loa
Kil·i·man·ja·ro \,kil-ə-mən-'jär-ō, -'jar-\ mountain [NE] Tanzania; highest in Africa — see KIBO
Kil·lar·ney, Lakes of \-kil-'är-nē\ three lakes [SW] Ireland
Kings·ton \'kiŋ-stən\ city, capital of Jamaica
Kingston upon Hull — see HULL
Kingston upon Thames \-'temz\ city area of [SW] Greater London county, England
Kings·town \'kiŋ-,staùn\ seaport, capital of Saint Vincent and the Grenadines
Kin·sha·sa \kin-'shäs-ə\ city, capital of Zaire
Kirgiz Republic *or* **Kirghiz Republic** *or* **Kirghizia** — see KYRGYZSTAN
Ki·ri·bati \'kir-ə-,bas\ island group [W] Pacific; an independent country; capital, Tarawa
Kirin — see JILIN
Kirk·wall \'kər-,kwòl\ town and port [N] Scotland in Orkney region
Ki·shi·nev \'kish-ə-,nef, -nev\ city central Moldova; its capital
Ki·ta·kyu·shu \kē-'tä-kē-'ü-shü\ city Japan in [N] Kyushu
Kitch·e·ner \'kich-(ə-)nər\ city [SE] Ontario, Canada
Kit·ty Hawk \'kit-ē-,hòk\ village [E] North Carolina
Klon·dike \'klän-,dīk\ region [NW] Canada in central Yukon Territory in valley of Klondike river
Knox·ville \'näks-,vil, -vəl\ city [E] Tennessee
Ko·be \'kō-bē, -,bā\ city Japan in [S] Honshu
Ko·di·ak \'kōd-ē-,ak\ island [S] Alaska [E] of Alaska peninsula
Ko·la \'kō-lə\ peninsula [NW] Russia
Ko·rea \kə-'rē-ə, *especially South* kō-\ country [E] Asia between Yellow sea & Sea of Japan; capital, Seoul; divided after World War II at 38th parallel of latitude into independent countries of **North Korea** (capital, Pyongyang) & **South Korea** (capital, Seoul)

\ə\ abut	\aù\ out	\i\ tip	\ò\ saw	\ù\ foot
\ər\ further	\ch\ chin	\ī\ life	\òi\ coin	\y\ yet
\a\ mat	\e\ pet	\j\ job	\th\ thin	\yü\ few
\ā\ take	\ē\ easy	\ŋ\ sing	\th\ this	\yù\ cure
\ä\ cot, cart	\g\ go	\ō\ bone	\ü\ food	\zh\ vision

Kos·ci·us·ko, Mount \-,käz-ē-'əs-kō\ mountain 2230 meters SE Australia in SE New South Wales; highest in Greater Dividing range & in Australia

Kow·loon \'kaù-'lün\ **1** penninsula SE China in Hong Kong colony opposite Hong Kong Island **2** city on Kowloon peninsula

Krak·a·toa \,krak-ə-'tō-ə\ or **Krak·a·tau** \-'taù\ island & volcano Indonesia between Sumatra & Java

Kra·kow \'kräk-,aù, 'krak-, 'kräk-, -ō, Polish 'kräk-,üf\ city S Poland

Kras·no·dar \'kras-nə-,där\ city SW Russia

Kras·no·yarsk \,kras-nə-'yärsk\ city S central Russia

Kri·voy Rog \,kriv-,ȯi-'rōg, -'rȯk\ city SE central Ukraine

K2 \'kā-'tü\ or **God·win Aus·ten** \,gäd-wə-'nȯs-tən, -'näs-tən\ mountain 8611 meters N Kashmir in Karakoram range; second highest in the world

Kua·la Lum·pur \,kwäl-ə-'lùm-,pù(ə)r, -'ləm-\ city, capital of Malaysia

Kuei–yang — see GUIYANG

Kun·lun \'kün-lün\ mountain system W China extending E from the Pamirs; highest peak Ulugh Muztagh 7724 meters

Kun·ming \'kùn-'miŋ\ city S China

Kur·di·stan \,kùr-də-'stan, ,kər-, -'stän; 'kər-də-,\ region SW Asia chiefly in E Turkey, NW Iran, & N Iraq

Ku·ril or **Ku·rile** \'kyùr-,ēl, 'kùr-; kyù-'rē(ə)l, kù-\ islands Russia in W Pacific between Kamchatka peninsula & Hokkaido island

Ku·wait \kə-'wāt\ **1** country SW Asia in Arabia at head of Persian gulf **2** city, its capital — **Ku·waiti** \-'wāt-ē\ adj or n

Kuybyshev — see SAMARA

Kuz·netsk basin \kùz-'netsk-\ or **Kuz·bass** or **Kuz·bas** \'kùz-,bas\ basin S central Russia

Kwa·ja·lein \'kwäj-ə-lən, -,lān\ island W Pacific in Marshall islands

Kwang·ju \'gwäŋ-jü, 'kwäŋ-\ city SW South Korea

Kyo·to \kē-'ōt-ō\ city Japan in W central Honshu; formerly capital of Japan

Kyr·gyz·stan \,kir-gi-'stan, -'stän; 'kir-gi-,\ country W central Asia; capital, Bishkek; a republic (**Kir·giz Republic** or **Kir·ghiz Republic** \(,)kir-'gēz-\ or **Kir·ghi·zia** \kir-'gē-zh(ē-)ə, -zē-ə\) of U.S.S.R. 1936–91

Kyu·shu \kē-'ü-shü\ island Japan S of W end of Honshu

Lab·ra·dor \'lab-rə-,dò(ə)r\ **1** peninsula E Canada between Hudson bay & the Atlantic divided between Quebec & Newfoundland **2** the part of the peninsula belonging to Newfoundland — **Lab·ra·dor·ean** or **Lab·ra·dor·ian** \,lab-rə-'dòr-ē-ən, -'dōr-\ adj or n

Lac·ca·dive \'lak-ə-,dēv, -,dīv\ islands India in Arabian sea N of Maldive islands

Lac·e·dae·mon \,las-ə-'dē-mən\ — see SPARTA — **Lac·e·dae·mo·nian** \,las-əd-i-'mō-nē-ən, -nyən\ adj or n

La·co·nia \lə-'kō-nē-ə, -nyə\ ancient country S Greece in SE Peloponnisos; capital, Sparta — **La·co·nian** \-nē-ən, -nyən\ adj or n

La·gos \'lä-,gäs\ city, former capital of Nigeria

La·hore \lə-'hō(ə)r, -'hò(ə)r\ city E Pakistan

Lake District region NW England in Cumbria county & NW Lancashire containing many lakes & mountains

Lake·hurst \'lāk-(,)hərst\ town E New Jersey

Lake·wood \'lā-,kwùd\ city central Colorado

Lam·beth \'lam-bəth, -,beth\ city area of S Greater London county, England

La·nai \lə-'nī\ island Hawaii W of Maui

Lan·ca·shire \'laŋ-kə-,shi(ə)r, -shər\ or **Lan·cas·ter** \'laŋ-kə-stər\ county NW England — **Lan·cas·tri·an** \laŋ-'kas-trē-ən, lan-\ adj or n

Lan·cas·ter \'laŋ-,kas-tər; 'lan,kas-tər, 'laŋ-\ city area, capital of Lancashire, England

Land's End \'lan(d)-'zend\ cape SW England; most westerly point of England, at 5° 41′ W longitude

Lan·sing \'lan(t)-siŋ\ city, capital of Michigan

Lan·zhou or **Lan–chou** \'län-'jō\ city W central China

Laos \'laùs, 'lä-,äs, 'lä-ōs\ country SE Asia in Indochina NE of Thailand; capital, Vientiane

La Paz \lə-'paz, -'päz, -'päs\ city, administrative capital of Bolivia

Lap·land \'lap-,land, -lənd\ region N Europe above the arctic circle in N Norway, N Sweden, N Finland, & Kola peninsula of Russia — **Lap·land·er** \-,lan-dər, -lən-\ n

La·re·do \lə-'rā-(,)dō\ city S Texas on the Rio Grande

Larne \'lärn\ district NE Northern Ireland

Las·sen Peak \'las-ᵊn-\ volcano 3187 meters N California at S end of Cascade Range

Las Ve·gas \läs-'vā-gəs\ city SE Nevada

Latin America **1** Spanish America and Brazil **2** all of the Americas S of the U.S. — **Latin–American** adj — **Latin American** n

Latin Quarter section of Paris, France S of the Seine

Lat·via \'lat-vē-ə\ country E Europe on Baltic sea; capital, Riga; a republic of U.S.S.R. 1940–91

Lau·ren·tian \lȯ-'ren-chən\ hills E Canada in S Quebec N of the Saint Lawrence on S edge of Laurentian Highlands

Laurentian Highlands or **Canadian Shield** plateau region E Canada & NE U.S. extending from Mackenzie basin E to Davis strait & S to S Quebec, S central Ontario, NE Minnesota, N Wisconsin, NW Michigan, and NE New York including the Adirondacks

La·val \lə-'val\ city S Quebec NW of Montreal

Law·rence \'lȯr-ən(t)s, 'lär-\ city NE corner of Massachusetts

Leb·a·non \'leb-ə-nən, -,nän\ **1** mountains Lebanon running parallel to coast; highest Dahr el Qadib 3088 meters **2** country SW Asia on the Mediterranean; capital, Beirut — **Leb·a·nese** \,leb-ə-'nēz, -'nēs\ adj or n

Leeds \'lēdz\ city N England in West Yorkshire

Lee·ward Islands \'lē-wərd-\ **1** islands Hawaii extending WNW from main islands of the group **2** islands S Pacific in W Society islands **3** islands West Indies in N Lesser Antilles extending from Virgin islands (on N) to Dominica (on S)

Le Ha·vre \lə-'hävrᵊ\ city N France on English channel

Leh·man Caves \'lē-mən-\ limestone caverns E Nevada

Leices·ter \'les-tər\ city central England in Leicestershire ENE of Birmingham

Leices·ter·shire \'les-tər-,shi(ə)r, -shər\ or **Leicester** county central England

Lein·ster \'len(t)-stər\ province E Ireland

Leip·zig \'līp-sig, -sik\ city E Germany

Le·na \'lē-nə, 'lā-\ river 4830 kilometers long E Russia, flowing NE & N from mountains W of Lake Baikal into Arctic ocean

Leningrad — see SAINT PETERSBURG

Le·ón \lā-'ōn\ city central Mexico

Ler·wick \'lər-(')wik, 'le(ə)r-\ town and port N Scotland in Shetland region

Le·so·tho \lə-'sō-tō, -'sü-(,)tü\ country S Africa surrounded by Republic of South Africa; formerly British territory of **Ba·su·to·land** \bə-süt-ə-,land\, now an independent country in the Commonwealth; capital, Maseru

Lesser An·til·les \-an-'til-ēz\ islands in the West Indies including Virgin Islands, Leeward Islands, & Windward Islands, Barbados, Trinidad, Tobago, & islands in the S Caribbean N of Venezuela — see GREATER ANTILLES

Le·vant \lə-'vant\ the countries bordering on the E Mediterranean — **Lev·an·tine** \'lev-ən-,tīn, -,tēn, lə-'van-\ adj or n

Lew·es \'lü-əs\ city area S England in East Sussex county

Lew·i·sham \'lü-ə-shəm\ city area of SE Greater London county, England

Lew·is with Har·ris \,lü-ə-swẹth-'har-əs, -swẹth-\ island

[NW] Scotland in Outer Hebrides

Lex·ing·ton \'lek-siŋ-tən\ town [NE] Massachusetts

Lexington–Fayette \'lek-siŋ-tən-fā-'et\ city [N] central Kentucky

Ley·te \'lāt-ē\ island Philippines [S] of Samar

Lha·sa \'läs-ə, 'las-\ city [SW] China, capital of Tibet

Li·be·ria \lī-'bir-ē-ə\ country [W] Africa on the Atlantic; capital, Monrovia — **Li·be·ri·an** \-ē-ən\ adj or n

Lib·er·ty \'lib-ərt-ē\ or formerly **Bed·loe's** \'bed-,lōz\ or **Bed·loe** \-lō\ island [SE] New York; the Statue of Liberty is on it

Li·bre·ville \'lē-brə-,vil, -,vē(ə)l\ city, capital of Gabon

Lib·ya \'lib-ē-ə\ **1** the part of Africa [N] of the Sahara and just [W] of Egypt — an ancient name **2** northern Africa [W] of Egypt — an ancient name **3** country [N] Africa on the Mediterranean [W] of Egypt; capital, Tripoli — **Lib·y·an** \'lib-ē-ən\ adj or n

Libyan desert [N] Africa [W] of the Nile in Libya, Egypt, & Sudan

Liech·ten·stein \'lik-tən-,stīn, -,shtīn\ country [W] Europe between Austria & Switzerland; capital, Vaduz — **Liech·ten·stein·er** \-,stī-nər, -,shtī-\ n

Lif·fey \'lif-ē\ river 80 kilometers long [E] Ireland

Li·gu·ria \lə-'gyůr-ē-ə\ ancient region [SW] Europe — **Li·gu·ri·an** \-ē-ən\ adj or n

Ligurian sea arm of the Mediterranean [N] of Corsica

Li·lon·gwe \li-'lòŋ-wā\ city, capital of Malawi

Li·ma \'lē-mə\ city, capital of Peru

Lim·a·vady \,lim-ə-'vad-ē\ district [NW] Northern Ireland

Lim·po·po \lim-'pō-pō\ river 1610 kilometers long Africa flowing from Transvaal into Indian ocean in Mozambique

Lin·coln \'liŋ-kən\ **1** city, capital of Nebraska **2** city [E] England in Lincolnshire

Lin·coln·shire \'liŋ-kən-,shi(ə)r, -shər\ or **Lincoln** county [E] England

Line \'līn\ islands Kiribati [S] of Hawaii; formerly divided between U.S. & United Kingdom

Lis·bon \'liz-bən\ or Portuguese **Lis·boa** \lēzh-'vō-ə\ city, capital of Portugal

Lis·burn \'liz-(,)bərn\ district [E] Northern Ireland

Lith·u·a·nia \,lith-(y)ə-'wā-nē-ə, -nyə\ country [E] Europe; capital, Vilnius; a republic of U.S.S.R. 1940–91

Lit·tle Rock \'lit-ºl-,räk\ city, capital of Arkansas

Liv·er·pool \'liv-ər-,pül\ city [NW] England in Merseyside county

Li·vo·nia \lə-'vō-nē-ə, -nyə\ city [SE] Michigan

Lju·blja·na \lē-,ü-blē-'än-ə\ city, capital of Slovenia

Llan·drin·dod Wells \hlan-'drin-,dòd-, lan-\ town [E] Wales in Powys county

Lla·no Es·ta·ca·do \'lan-(,)ō-,es-ta-'käd-ō, 'län-\ or **Staked Plain** \'stāk(t)-\ plateau region [SE] New Mexico & [NW] Texas

Lodz \'lüj, 'lädz\ city central Poland [WSW] of Warsaw

Lo·fo·ten \'lō-,fōt-ºn\ islands Norway

Lo·gan, Mount \-'lō-gən\ mountain 6050 meters [NW] Canada in Saint Elias range; highest in Canada & second highest in North America

Loire \lə-'wär\ river 1005 kilometers long central France flowing [NW] & [W] into Bay of Biscay

Lo·mé \lō-'mā\ city, capital of Togo

Lo·mond, Loch \-'lō-mənd\ lake [S] central Scotland

Lon·don \'lən-dən\ **1** city [S] Ontario, Canada **2** city, capital of England & of United Kingdom on the Thames; consists of **City of London** & Greater London county — **Lon·don·er** \-də-nər\ n

Londonderry — see DERRY

Long Beach city [SW] California [S] of Los Angeles

Long Island island 190 kilometers long [SE] New York [S] of Connecticut

Long Island Sound inlet of the Atlantic between Connecticut & Long Island, New York

Lon·gueuil \lòŋ-'gā(ə)l\ city Canada in [S] Quebec [E] of Montreal

Lor·raine \lə-'rān, lò-\ region [NE] France

Los An·ge·les \lò-'san-jə-ləs also -'saŋ-g(ə-)ləs\ city [SW] California

Lo·thi·an \'lō-thē-ən\ region [SE] Scotland [S] of Firth of Forth; established 1975; includes Edinburgh

Lou·ise, Lake \-lú-'ēz\ lake [SW] Alberta, Canada

Lou·i·si·ana \lú-,ē-zē-'an-ə, ,lü-ə-zē-, ,lü-zē-\ state [S] U.S.; capital, Baton Rouge — **Lou·i·si·an·ian** \-'an-ē-ən, -'an-yən\ or **Lou·i·si·an·an** \-'an-ən\ adj or n

Louisiana Purchase area [W] central U.S. between Rocky mountains & the Mississippi purchased 1803 from France

Lou·is·ville \'lü-i-,vil, -vəl\ city [N] Kentucky on the Ohio river

Low Countries region [W] Europe consisting of modern Belgium, Luxembourg, & the Netherlands

Lower 48 the continental states of the U.S. excluding Alaska

Low·lands \'lō-lən(d)z, -,lan(d)z\ the central & [E] part of Scotland

Lu·an·da \lü-'an-də\ city, capital of Angola

Lub·bock \'ləb-ək\ city [NW] Texas

Luck·now \'lək-,naů\ city [N] India

Lü·da or **Lü–ta** \'lü;'dä\ or **Dai·ren** \'dī-'ren\ city [NE] China

Lu·ray Caverns \'lü-,rā-, lü-'rā-\ series of caves [N] Virginia

Lu·sa·ka \lü-'säk-ə\ city, capital of Zambia

Lü·shun \'lü-'shùn\ or **Port Ar·thur** \-'är-thər\ city [NE] China

Lu·ton \'lüt-ºn\ city area [SE] central England in Bedfordshire

Lux·em·bourg or **Lux·em·burg** \'lək-səm-,bərg, 'lůk-səm-,bů(ə)rg\ **1** country [W] Europe bordered by Belgium, France, & Germany **2** city, its capital — **Lux·em·bourg·er** \-,bər-gər, -,bůr-\ n — **Lux·em·bourg·ian** \,lək-səm-'bər-gē-ən, ,lůk-səm-'bůr-\ adj

Lu·zon \lü-'zän\ island [N] Philippines

Lvov \lə-'vòf, -'vòv\ or Polish **Lwów** \lə-'vüf, -'vüv\ or Ukrainian **Lwiw** \lə-'věf\ city [W] Ukraine

Lyallpur — see FAISALABAD

Lyd·ia \'lid-ē-ə\ ancient country [W] Asia Minor on the Aegean — **Lyd·i·an** \-ē-ən\ adj or n

Lynn \'lin\ city [NE] corner of Massachusetts

Ma·cao or Portuguese **Ma·cau** \mə-'kaů\ **1** Portuguese territory on coast of [SE] China [W] of Hong Kong **2** city, its capital — **Mac·a·nese** \,mak-ə-'nēz, -'nēs\ n

Mac·e·do·nia \,mas-ə-'dō-nyə, -nē-ə\ **1** region [S] Europe in Balkan peninsula in [NE] Greece, the country of Macedonia, and [SW] Bulgaria including territory of ancient kingdom of Macedonia (**Mac·e·don** \'mas-əd-ən, -ə-,dän\) **2** country [S] central Balkan peninsula; capital, Skopje; a former republic of Yugoslavia — **Mac·e·do·nian** \,mas-ə-'dō-nyən, -nē-ən\ adj or n

Mac·gil·li·cud·dy's Reeks \mə-,gil-ə-,kəd-ēz-'rēks\ mountains [SW] Ireland; highest Carrantuohill 1041 meters

Ma·chu Pic·chu \,mäch-ü-'pēk-chü\ site [SE] Peru of ancient Inca city

Macías Nguema Biyogo — see BIOKO

Mac·ken·zie \mə-'ken-zē\ **1** river 1800 kilometers long [NW] Canada flowing from Great Slave lake [NW] into Beaufort sea **2** former district [W] Canada in [W] Northwest Territories in basin of Mackenzie river

Mack·i·nac, Straits of \-'mak-ə-,nak, -,nò\ channel [N] Michigan connecting Lake Huron & Lake Michigan

Mc·Kin·ley, Mount \-mə-'kin-lē\ or **De·na·li** \də-'näl-ē\ mountain 6194 meters [S] central Alaska in Alaska range; highest in U.S. & North America

\ə\ **abut**	\aů\ **out**	\i\ **tip**	\ò\ **saw**	\ů\ **foot**	
\ər\ **further**	\ch\ **chin**	\ī\ **life**	\òi\ **coin**	\y\ **yet**	
\a\ **mat**	\e\ **pet**	\j\ **job**	\th\ **thin**	\yü\ **few**	
\ā\ **take**	\ē\ **easy**	\ŋ\ **sing**	\th\ **this**	\yů\ **cure**	
\ä\ **cot, cart**	\g\ **go**	\ō\ **bone**	\ü\ **food**	\zh\ **vision**	

Ma·con \'mā-kən\ city central Georgia

Mad·a·gas·car \,mad-ə-'gas-kər\ *or formerly* **Mal·a·gasy Re·public** \,mal-ə-,gas-ē-\ island W Indian ocean off SE Africa; an independent country; capital, Antananarivo — **Mad·a·gas·can** \,mad-ə-'gas-kən\ *adj or n*

Ma·dei·ra \mə-'dir-ə, -'der-\ 1 river 3380 kilometers long W Brazil flowing NE into the Amazon 2 islands in the N Atlantic W of the Canary islands belonging to Portugal 3 island; chief of the Madeira group — **Ma·dei·ran** \-ən\ *adj or n*

Ma·di·nat ash Sha'b \mə-'dē-,nət-ash-'shab\ town S Yemen

Mad·i·son \'mad-ə-sən\ city, capital of Wisconsin

Ma·dras \mə-'dras, -'dräs\ city SE India

Ma·drid \mə-'drid\ city, capital of Spain

Ma·du·rai \,mäd-ə-'rī\ city S India

Magh·er·a·felt \'mär-ə-,felt, 'mak-ə-rə-,felt\ district central Northern Ireland

Maid·stone \'mād-stən, -,stōn\ city district SE England in Kent county

Main \'mīn, 'män\ river 490 kilometers long S central Germany flowing W into the Rhine

Maine \'mān\ state NE U.S.; capital, Augusta

Ma·jor·ca \mə-'jór-kə, -'yór-\ *or Spanish* **Ma·llor·ca** \mə-'yór-kə\ island Spain in W Mediterranean — **Ma·jor·can** \-'jór-kən, -'yór-\ *adj or n*

Mal·a·bar \'mal-ə-,bär\ coast region SW India on Arabian sea

Ma·la·bo \mä-'lä-bō\ city, capital of Equatorial Guinea

Ma·lac·ca, Strait of \-mə-'lak-ə, -'läk-\ channel between S Malay peninsula & island of Sumatra

Ma·la·wi \mə-'lä-wē, -'laú-ē\ *or formerly* **Ny·asa·land** \nī-'as-ə-,land, nē-\ country SE Africa on Lake Nyasa; an independent state since 1964; capital, Lilongwe

Ma·lay \mə-'lā, 'mā-lā\ 1 island group SE Asia including Sumatra, Java, Borneo, Sulawesi, Moluccas, & Timor; usually thought to include the Philippines & sometimes New Guinea 2 peninsula about 1100 kilometers long SE Asia divided between Thailand and Malaysia (country)

Ma·laya \mə-'lā-ə, mä-\ 1 the Malay peninsula 2 former country SE Asia on Malay peninsula; since 1963 part of Malaysia — see MALAYSIA

Ma·lay·sia \mə-'lā-zh(ē-)ə, -sh(ē-)ə\ 1 the Malay island group 2 the Malay peninsula & Malay island group 3 country SE Asia, a union of Malaya, Sabah, Sarawak, & (until 1965) Singapore; capital, Kuala Lumpur — **Ma·lay·sian** \mə-'lā-zhən, -shən\ *adj or n*

Mal·dive \'mól-,dēv, -,dīv\ islands in Indian ocean S of the Laccadives; formerly under British protection; since 1965 an independent country; capital, Male — **Mal·div·i·an** \mól-'div-ē-ən\ *adj or n*

Ma·li \'mäl-ē, 'mal-ē\ country W Africa; capital, Bamako — **Ma·li·an** \-ē-ən\ *adj or n*

Mal·ta \'mól-tə\ islands in the Mediterranean S of Sicily; a former British colony; an independent country since 1964; capital, Valletta

Malvinas, Islas — see FALKLAND

Mam·moth Cave \,mam-əth-\ limestone caverns SW central Kentucky

Man, Isle of \-'man\ island British Isles in Irish sea; has own legislature & laws

Ma·na·gua \mə-'näg-wə\ city, capital of Nicaragua

Ma·na·ma \mə-'nam-ə\ city, capital of Bahrain

Man·ches·ter \'man-,ches-tər, -chə-stər\ 1 city S central New Hampshire; largest in state 2 city NW England in Greater Manchester county

Man·chu·ria \man-'chúr-ē-ə\ region NE China S of the Amur — **Man·chu·ri·an** \man-'chúr-ē-ən\ *adj or n*

Man·hat·tan \man-'hat-°n, mən-\ 1 island SE New York in New York City 2 section of New York City consisting chiefly of Manhattan island

Ma·nila \mə-'nil-ə\ city, capital of Philippines in W Luzon

Man·i·to·ba \,man-ə-'tō-bə\ province central Canada; capital, Winnipeg — **Man·i·to·ban** \-'tō-bən\ *adj or n*

Man·i·tou·lin \,man-ə-'tü-lən\ island 130 kilometers long S Ontario in Lake Huron

Ma·pu·to \mä-'pü-tō\ city, capital of Mozambique

Mar·a·cai·bo \,mar-ə-'kī-bō\ city NW Venezuela

Maracaibo, Lake extension of a gulf NW Venezuela

Mar·a·thon \'mar-ə-,thän, -thən\ plain E Greece NE of Athens

Mar·i·ana \,mar-ē-'an-ə, ,mer-\ islands W Pacific N of Caroline islands; comprise Commonwealth of Northern Mariana Islands & Guam

Mariana Trench ocean trench W Pacific extending from SE of Guam to NW of Mariana islands; deepest in world

Ma·rin·du·que \,mar-ən-'dü-kā, ,mär-\ island central Philippines

Maritime Provinces the Canadian provinces of New Brunswick, Nova Scotia, & Prince Edward Island & sometimes thought to include Newfoundland

Ma·ri·u·pol \,mar-ē-'ü-,pól\ *or 1949–89* **Zhda·nov** \zhə-'dän-əf\ city E Ukraine

Mar·ma·ra, Sea of \-'mär-mə-rə\ sea NW Turkey connected with Black sea by the Bosporus & with Aegean sea by the Dardanelles

Marne \'märn\ river 523 kilometers long NE France flowing W into the Seine

Mar·que·sas \mär-'kā-zəz, -zəs, -səz, -səs\ islands S Pacific — **Mar·que·san** \-zən, -sən\ *adj or n*

Mar·seilles \mär-'sā, -'sā(ə)lz\ *or* **Mar·seille** \mär-'sā\ *or ancient* **Mas·sil·ia** \mə-'sil-ē-ə\ city SE France

Mar·shall \'mär-shəl\ islands W Pacific E of the Carolines; formerly part of Trust Territory of the Pacific Islands

Mar·tha's Vineyard \,mär-thəz-\ island SE Massachusetts off SW coast of Cape Cod WNW of Nantucket

Mar·ti·nique \,märt-°n-'ēk\ island West Indies in the Windward Islands; an overseas division of France; capital, Fort=de-France

Mary·land \'mer-ə-lənd\ state E U.S.; capital, Annapolis — **Mary·land·er** \-lən-dər, -,lan-\ *n*

Mas·ba·te \mäz-'bät-ē\ island central Philippines

Mas·e·ru \'maz-ə-,rü\ city, capital of Lesotho

Mash·had \mə-'shad\ city NE Iran

Ma·son–Dix·on line \,mäs-°n-'dik-sən-\ boundary between Maryland & Pennsylvania; was in part boundary between free & slave states

Mas·sa·chu·setts \,mas(-ə)-'chü-səts, -zəts\ state NE U.S.; capital, Boston

Mat·a·be·le·land \,mat-ə-'bē-lē-,land\ region SW Zimbabwe

Mat·lock \'mat-,läk\ town N England in Derbyshire

Mat·ter·horn \'mat-ər-,hó(ə)rn, 'mät-\ mountain 4478 meters on border between Switzerland & Italy

Maui \'maú-ē\ island Hawaii NW of Hawaii island

Mau·na Kea \,maú-nə-'kā-ə\ extinct volcano 4205 meters Hawaii in N central Hawaii island

Mau·na Loa \,maú-nə-'lō-ə\ volcano 4170 meters Hawaii in S central Hawaii island

Mau·re·ta·nia *or* **Mau·ri·ta·nia** \,mór-ə-'tā-nē-ə, ,mär-, -nyə\ ancient country NW Africa in modern Morocco & W Algeria — **Mau·re·ta·ni·an** \-nē-ən, -nyən\ *adj or n*

Mauritania country NW Africa on the Atlantic N of Senegal river; capital, Nouakchott — **Mauritanian** *adj or n*

Mau·ri·tius \mó-'rish-(ē-)əs\ island in Indian ocean E of Madagascar; an independent country in the Commonwealth; capital, Port Louis — **Mau·ri·tian** \-'rish-ən\ *adj or n*

May, Cape \-'mā\ cape S New Jersey at entrance to Delaware Bay

Ma·yon, Mount \-mä-'yón\ volcano 2525 meters Philippines in SE Luzon

Ma·yotte Island \mä-'yät-\ island Comoro group — see COMORO

Ma·za·ma, Mount \-mə-'zäm-ə\ prehistoric mountain SW Oregon the collapse of whose top formed Crater lake

Mba·bane \,em-bə-'bän\ city, capital of Swaziland

Mbi·ni \em-'bē-nē\ *or formerly* **Río Mu·ni** \,rē-ō-'mü-nē\ mainland portion of Equatorial Guinea

Mead, Lake \-'mēd\ reservoir NW Arizona & SE Nevada formed by Hoover Dam in Colorado river

Mec·ca \'mek-ə\ city W Saudi Arabia containing the Great Mosque of Islam

Me·dan \mä-'dän\ city Indonesia, in N Sumatra

Me·de·llín \,med-ªl-'ēn, ,mä-<u>th</u>ə-'yēn\ city N Colombia

Med·i·ter·ra·nean \,med-ə-tə-'rā-nē-ən, -nyən\ sea 3750 kilometers long between Europe & Africa connecting with the Atlantic through Strait of Gibraltar

Me·kong \'mā-'kòŋ, -'käŋ\ river 4185 kilometers long SE Asia flowing from E Tibet S & SE into South China sea in S Vietnam

Mel·a·ne·sia \,mel-ə-'nē-zhə, -shə\ islands of the Pacific NE of Australia & S of Micronesia including Bismarck, the Solomons, Vanuatu, New Caledonia, & the Fijis

Mel·bourne \'mel-bərn\ city SE Australia, capital of Victoria

Me·los \'mē-,läs\ island Greece — **Me·li·an** \'mē-lē-ən\ *adj or n*

Mel·ville \'mel-,vil\ **1** island N Canada in N Northwest Territories **2** peninsula E Northwest Territories, Canada

Mem·phis \'mem(p)-fəs\ **1** city SW Tennessee **2** ancient city N Egypt S of modern Cairo

Men·do·ci·no, Cape \-,men-də-'sē-nō\ cape NW California

Mer·cia \'mər-sh(ē-)ə\ ancient Anglo-Saxon kingdom central England — **Mer·cian** \'mər-shən\ *adj or n*

Mer·sey \'mər-zē\ river 110 kilometers long NW England flowing NW & W into Irish sea

Mer·sey·side \'mər-zē-,sīd\ county NW England; includes Liverpool

Mer·ton \'mərt-ªn\ city area of SW Greater London county, England

Me·sa \'mā-sə\ city S central Arizona

Me·sa·bi range \mə-'säb-ē\ region NE Minnesota that contains iron ore

Mes·o·po·ta·mia \,mes-(ə-)pə-'tä-mē-ə, -myə\ **1** region SW Asia between Euphrates & Tigris rivers **2** the entire Tigris-Euphrates valley — **Mes·o·po·ta·mian** \-mē-ən, -myən\ *adj or n*

Meuse \'myüz, 'mə(r)z\ river 925 kilometers long W Europe flowing from NE France into North sea in the Netherlands

Mex·i·co \'mek-si-,kō\ **1** country S North America **2** *or* **Mexico City** city, its capital

Mexico, Gulf of inlet of the Atlantic SE North America

Mi·ami \mī-'am-ē, -'am-ə\ city SE Florida

Miami Beach city SE Florida

Mich·i·gan \'mish-i-gən\ state N central U.S.; capital, Lansing — **Mich·i·gan·der** \,mish-i-'gan-dər\ *n* — **Mich·i·gan·ite** \'mish-i-gə-,nīt\ *n*

Michigan, Lake lake N central U.S.; one of the Great Lakes

Mi·cro·ne·sia \,mī-krə-'nē-zhə, -shə\ islands of the W Pacific E of the Philippines & N of Melanesia including Caroline, Kiribati, Mariana, & Marshall groups — **Mi·cro·ne·sian** \-zhən, -shən\ *adj or n*

Middle East the countries of SW Asia & N Africa — usually thought to include the countries extending from Libya on the W to Afghanistan on the E — **Middle Eastern** *or* **Mid·east·ern** \'mid-'ē-stərn\ *adj*

Mid·dles·brough \'mid-ªlz-brə\ town N England in Cleveland county

Mid Gla·mor·gan \'mid-glə-'mòr-gən\ county SE Wales; established 1974

Mid·i·an \'mid-ē-ən\ ancient region NW Arabia E of Gulf of 'Aqaba — **Mid·i·an·ite** \-ē-ə-,nīt\ *n*

Mid·lands \'mid-lən(d)z\ the central counties of England usually thought to consist of Bedfordshire, Buckinghamshire, Cambridgeshire, Derbyshire, Leicestershire, Lincolnshire, Northamptonshire, Nottinghamshire, Oxfordshire, Staffordshire, Warwickshire, West Midlands, & part of Hereford and Worcester

Mid·way \'mid-,wā\ islands central Pacific in Hawaiian group 2090 kilometers WNW of Honolulu belonging to U.S.; not included in state of Hawaii

Mid·west \,mid-'west\ *or* **Middle West** region N central U.S. including area around Great Lakes & in upper Mississippi valley from Ohio on the E to North Dakota, South Dakota, Nebraska, & Kansas on the W — **Mid·wes·tern** \,mid-'wes-tərn\ *or* **Middle Western** *adj* — **Mid·west·ern·er** \,mid-'wes-tə(r)-nər\ *or* **Middle Westerner** *n*

Mi·lan \mə-'lan, -'län\ *or Italian* **Mi·la·no** \mi-'län-ō\ city NW Italy — **Mi·la·nese** \,mil-ə-'nēz, -'nēs\ *adj or n*

Mil·wau·kee \mil-'wò-kē\ city SE Wisconsin

Mi·nas Basin \,mī-nəs-\ bay central Nova Scotia; NE extension of Bay of Fundy

Min·da·nao \,min-də-'nä-ō, -'naù\ island S Philippines

Min·do·ro \min-'dòr-ō, -'dòr-\ island central Philippines

Min·ne·ap·o·lis \,min-ē-'ap-(ə-)ləs\ city SE Minnesota

Min·ne·so·ta \,min-ə-'sōt-ə\ state N central U.S.; capital, Saint Paul — **Min·ne·so·tan** \-'sōt-ªn\ *adj or n*

Mi·nor·ca \mə-'nòr-kə\ island Spain in W Mediterranean — **Mi·nor·can** \mə-'nòr-kən\ *adj or n*

Minsk \'min(t)sk\ city, capital of Belarus

Mis·sis·sip·pi \,mis-(ə-)'sip-ē\ **1** river 3975 kilometers long central U.S. flowing into Gulf of Mexico — see ITASCA, LAKE **2** state S U.S.; capital, Jackson

Mis·sou·ri \mə-'zù(ə)r-ē, -'zùr-ə\ **1** river 4345 kilometers long N U.S. flowing from SW Montana to the Mississippi in E Missouri **2** state central U.S.; capital, Jefferson City — **Mis·sou·ri·an** \-'zùr-ē-ən\ *adj or n*

Mitch·ell, Mount \-'mich-əl\ mountain 2037 meters W North Carolina in the Appalachians; highest in U.S. E of the Mississippi

Mo·bile \mō-'bē(ə)l, 'mō-,bēl\ city SW Alabama on Mobile Bay

Mo·des·to \mə-'dəs-tō\ city central California

Mog·a·di·shu \,mäg-ə-'dish-ü, -'dēsh-\ *or* **Mog·a·di·scio** \-ō\ city, capital of Somalia

Mo·hawk \'mō-,hók\ river E central New York flowing into the Hudson

Mo·ja·ve *or* **Mo·ha·ve** \mə-'häv-ē\ desert S California SE of S end of Sierra Nevada

Mold \'mōld\ town NE Wales in Clwyd county

Mol·da·via \mäl-'dā-vē-ə, -vyə\ **1** region E Europe in NE Romania & Moldova **2** former republic of U.S.S.R. bordered by Ukraine, Black sea, & Romania; became independent (as Moldova) 1991 — **Mol·da·vian** \-vē-ən, -vyən\ *adj or n*

Mol·do·va \mäl-'dō-və, mòl-\ country E Europe in E Moldavia region; capital, Kishinev

Mol·o·kai \,mäl-ə-'kī, ,mō-lə-\ island Hawaii ESE of Oahu

Mo·luc·cas \mə-'lək-əz\ islands Indonesia E of Sulawesi — **Mo·luc·ca** \mə-'lək-ə\ *adj* — **Mo·luc·can** \-ən\ *adj or n*

Mo·na·co \'män-ə-,kō *also* mə-'näk-ō\ country W Europe on Mediterranean coast of France; capital, Monaco — **Mo·na·can** \'män-ə-kən, mə-'näk-ən\ *adj or n* — **Mon·e·gasque** \,män-i-'gask\ *n*

Mon·go·lia \män-'gōl-yə, mäŋ-, -'gō-lē-ə\ **1** region E Asia E of Altai mountains; includes Gobi desert **2** coun-

\ə\ **abut**	\aù\ **out**	\i\ **tip**	\ò\ **saw**	\ù\ **foot**
\ər\ **further**	\ch\ **chin**	\ī\ **life**	\òi\ **coin**	\y\ **yet**
\a\ **mat**	\e\ **pet**	\j\ **job**	\th\ **thin**	\yü\ **few**
\ā\ **take**	\ē\ **easy**	\ŋ\ **sing**	\<u>th</u>\ **this**	\yù\ **cure**
\ä\ **cot, cart**	\g\ **go**	\ō\ **bone**	\ü\ **food**	\zh\ **vision**

try [E] Asia consisting of major portion of Mongolia region; capital Ulan Bator

Mo·non·ga·he·la \mə-ˌnän-gə-ˈhē-lə, -ˌnäŋ-gə-, -ˈhā-lə\ river [N] West Virginia & [SW] Pennsylvania

Mon·ro·via \(ˌ)mən-ˈrō-vē-ə\ city, capital of Liberia

Mon·tana \män-ˈtan-ə\ state [NW] U.S.; capital, Helena — **Mon·tan·an** \-ən\ adj or n

Mont Blanc \ˈmōn-ˈblän(k)\ mountain 4807 meters [SE] France on Italian border; highest in the Alps

Mon·te·ne·gro \ˌmän-tə-ˈnē-(ˌ)grō, -ˈnä-\ region [SW] Yugoslavia on the Adriatic sea

Mon·ter·rey \ˌmänt-ə-ˈrā\ city [NE] Mexico

Mon·te·vi·deo \ˌmänt-ə-və-ˈdā-ō, -ˈvid-ē-ˌō\ city, capital of Uruguay

Mont·gom·ery \(ˌ)mən(t)-ˈgəm-(ə-)rē, män(t)-, -ˈgäm-\ city, capital of Alabama

Mont·pe·lier \mänt-ˈpēl-yər, -ˈpil-\ city, capital of Vermont

Mon·tre·al \ˌmän-trē-ˈȯl, ˌmən-\ city [S] Quebec, Canada on Montreal Island in the Saint Lawrence

Mont·ser·rat \ˌmän(t)-sə-ˈrat\ island West Indies in the Leeward Islands

Mo·ra·via \mə-ˈrā-vē-ə\ region [E] Czech Republic — **Mo·ra·vi·an** \mə-ˈrā-vē-ən\ adj or n

Mo·rea \mə-ˈrē-ə\ PELOPONNISOS — an old name — **Mo·re·an** \-ˈrē-ən\ adj or n

Mo·roc·co \mə-ˈräk-ō\ country [NW] Africa; a kingdom; capital, Rabat — **Mo·roc·can** \-ˈräk-ən\ adj or n

Mo·ro·ni \mȯ-ˈrō-nē\ city, capital of Comoro

Mos·cow \ˈmäs-ˌkaù, -kō\ or Russian **Mos·kva** \mäsk-ˈvä\ city, capital of Russia and formerly of U.S.S.R. and of Russian Soviet Federated Socialist Republic

Mourne \ˈmō(ə)rn, ˈmȯ(ə)rn\ district [S] Northern Ireland

Moyle \ˈmȯi(ə)l\ district [N] Northern Ireland

Mo·zam·bique \ˌmō-zəm-ˈbēk\ 1 channel [SE] Africa between Mozambique & Madagascar 2 country [SE] Africa; capital, Maputo

Mukden — see SHENYANG

Mul·tan \mùl-ˈtän\ city [NE] Pakistan [SW] of Lahore

Mu·nich \ˈmyü-nik\ or German **Mün·chen** \ˈm(y)ün-kən\ city [S] Germany in Bavaria

Mun·ster \ˈmən(t)-stər\ province [S] Ireland

Mur·cia \ˈmər-sh(ē-)ə\ region & ancient kingdom [SE] Spain — **Mur·cian** \-shən\ adj or n

Mur·ray \ˈmər-ē, ˈmə-rē\ river 1930 kilometers long [SE] Australia flowing [W] from [E] Victoria into Indian ocean in South Australia — see DARLING

Mur·rum·bidg·ee \ˌmər-əm-ˈbij-ē, ˌmə-rəm-\ river 1610 kilometers long [SE] Australia in New South Wales flowing [W] into the Murray

Mus·cat \ˈməs-ˌkat, -kət\ town [E] Arabia, capital of Oman

Myan·mar \ˈmyän-ˌmär\ or **Myan·ma** \-ˌmä\ or formerly **Bur·ma** \ˈbər-mə\ country [SE] Asia; capital, Yangon

My·ce·nae \mī-ˈsē-nē\ ancient city [S] Greece in [NE] Peloponnisos

My·sore \mī-ˈsō(ə)r, -ˈsȯ(ə)r\ city [S] India

Nab·a·taea or **Nab·a·tea** \ˌnab-ə-ˈtē-ə\ ancient Arab kingdom [SE] of Palestine — **Nab·a·tae·an** or **Nab·a·te·an** \-ˈtē-ən\ adj or n

Na·goya \nə-ˈgȯi-ə, ˈnäg-ə-ˌyä\ city Japan in [S] central Honshu

Nag·pur \ˈnäg-ˌpù(ə)r\ city [E] central India

Nai·ro·bi \nī-ˈrō-bē\ city, capital of Kenya

Na·mib·ia \nə-ˈmib-ē-ə\ or formerly **South–West Africa** country [SW] Africa on the Atlantic; capital, Windhoek

Nan·chang \ˈnän-ˈjäŋ\ city [SE] China

Nan·jing \ˈnän-ˈjiŋ\ or **Nan·king** \ˈnan-ˈkiŋ, ˈnän-\ city [E] China

Nan·tuck·et \nan-ˈtək-ət\ island [SE] Massachusetts [S] of Cape Cod

Na·ples \ˈnā-pəlz\ or Italian **Na·po·li** \ˈnäp-ə-lē\ or ancient **Ne·ap·o·lis** \nē-ˈap-ə-ləs\ city [S] Italy on Bay of Naples — **Ne·a·pol·i·tan** \ˌnē-ə-ˈpäl-ət-°n\ adj or n

Nar·ra·gan·sett Bay \ˌnar-ə-ˈgan(t)-sət\ inlet of the Atlantic [SE] Rhode Island

Nash·ville \ˈnash-ˌvil, -vəl\ city, capital of Tennessee

Nas·sau \ˈnas-ˌȯ\ city, capital of Bahamas on New Providence island

Na·tal \nə-ˈtal, -ˈtäl\ province [E] Republic of South Africa; capital, Pietermaritzburg

Na·u·ru \nä-ˈü-rü\ island [W] Pacific 42 kilometers [S] of the equator; formerly a shared British, New Zealand, & Australian trust territory; an independent country in the Commonwealth since 1968

Naz·a·reth \ˈnaz-(ə-)rəth\ town of ancient Palestine in central Galilee; now a city of [N] Israel

N'Dja·me·na \en-ˈjäm-ə-nə\ city, capital of Chad

Neagh, Lough \läk-ˈnā\ lake Northern Ireland; largest in British Isles

Near East the countries of [NE] Africa & [SW] Asia — **Near Eastern** adj

Ne·bras·ka \nə-ˈbras-kə\ state central U.S.; capital, Lincoln — **Ne·bras·kan** \-kən\ adj or n

Neg·ev \ˈneg-ˌev\ desert region [S] Israel

Ne·gros \ˈnā-(ˌ)grōs\ island central Philippines

Ne·pal \nə-ˈpȯl, -ˈpäl, -ˈpal\ country Asia on [NE] border of India in the Himalayas; a kingdom; capital, Kathmandu — **Nep·a·lese** \ˌnep-ə-ˈlēz, -ˈlēs\ adj or n — **Ne·pali** \nə-ˈpȯl-ē, -ˈpäl-, -ˈpal-\ adj or n

Ness, Loch \-ˈnes\ lake [NW] Scotland

Neth·er·lands \ˈneth-ər-lən(d)z\ 1 or Dutch **Ne·der·land** \ˈnād-ər-ˌlänt\ also Holland country [NW] Europe on North sea; a kingdom; capitals, Amsterdam and The Hague 2 LOW COUNTRIES — an historical usage — **Neth·er·land** \ˈneth-ər-lənd\ adj — **Neth·er·land·er** \-ˌlan-dər, -lən-\ n — **Neth·er·land·ish** \-dish\ adj

Netherlands An·til·les \-an-ˈtil-ēz\ islands of the West Indies belonging to the Netherlands

Netherlands East Indies or **Netherlands India** or **Dutch East Indies** former Dutch possessions in the East Indies including Indonesia

Ne·va \ˈnē-və, ˈnā-\ river 65 kilometers long [W] Russia; flows through Saint Petersburg

Ne·vada \nə-ˈvad-ə, -ˈväd-ə\ state [W] U.S.; capital, Carson City — **Ne·vad·an** \-ˈvad-°n, -ˈväd-°n\ or **Ne·vad·i·an** \-ˈvad-ē-ən, -ˈväd-\ adj or n

Ne·vis \ˈnē-vəs\ island West Indies in the Leeward Islands — see SAINT CHRISTOPHER

New Am·ster·dam \-ˈam(p)-stər-ˌdam\ town founded 1625 on Manhattan island by the Dutch; renamed New York 1664 by the British

New·ark \ˈn(y)ü-ərk, ˈn(y)ù-(ə)rk\ city [NE] New Jersey

New Brit·ain \-ˈbrit-°n\ island [W] Pacific

New Bruns·wick \-ˈbrənz-(ˌ)wik\ province [SE] Canada; capital, Fredericton

New Cal·e·do·nia \-ˌkal-ə-ˈdō-nyə, -nē-ə\ island [SW] Pacific [SW] of Vanuatu; an overseas department of France; capital, Nouméa

New·cas·tle \ˈn(y)ü-ˌkas-əl\ city [SE] Australia in [E] New South Wales

Newcastle or **New·cas·tle up·on Tyne** \n(y)ü-ˈkas-əl-ə-ˌpȯn-ˈtīn\ city [N] England in Tyne and Wear county

New Del·hi \-ˈdel-ē\ city, capital of India [S] of Delhi

New England section of U.S. consisting of states of Maine, New Hampshire, Vermont, Massachusetts, Rhode Island, & Connecticut — **New En·gland·er** \-ˈiŋ-glən-dər also -ˈiŋ-lən-\ n

New·found·land \ˈn(y)ü-fən-(d)lənd, -ˌ(d)land; ˌn(y)ü-fən-ˈ(d)land\ 1 island Canada in the Atlantic 2 province [E] Canada consisting of Newfoundland island & Labrador; capital, Saint John's — **New·found·land·er** \-(d)lən-dər, -ˈ(d)lan-dər\ n

New France the possessions of France in North America before 1763

New Guin·ea \-ˈgin-ē\ 1 island [W] Pacific [N] of [E] Australia divided between West Irian & Papua New Guinea **2** the NE portion of the island of New Guinea together with some nearby islands; now part of Papua New Guinea — **New Guin·e·an** \-'gin-ē-ən\ *adj or n*

New·ham \'n(y)ü-əm\ city area of E Greater London county, England

New Hamp·shire \-'ham(p)-shər, -,shi(ə)r\ state NE U.S.; capital, Concord — **New Hamp·shire·man** \-mən\ *n* — **New Hamp·shir·ite** \-,īt\ *n*

New Ha·ven \-'hā-vən\ city S Connecticut

New Hebrides — see VANUATU

New Jer·sey \-'jər-zē\ state E U.S.; capital, Trenton — **New Jer·sey·ite** \-,īt\ *n*

New Mex·i·co \-'mek-si-,kō\ state SW U.S.; capital, Santa Fe — **New Mex·i·can** \-si-kən\ *adj or n*

New Neth·er·land \-'neth-ər-lənd\ former Dutch colony (1613–64) North America along Hudson & lower Delaware rivers; capital, New Amsterdam

New Or·leans \-'ór-lē-ənz, -'órl-(y)ənz, -(,)ór-'lēnz\ city SE Louisiana

New·port \'n(y)ü-,pō(ə)rt, -,pò(ə)rt\ **1** city area S England in Isle of Wight **2** city SE Wales in Gwent county

Newport News \,n(y)ü-,pōrt-'n(y)üz, -,pòrt-, -pərt-\ city SE Virginia

New Prov·i·dence \-'präv-əd-ən(t)s, -ə-,den(t)s\ island NW central Bahamas; chief town, Nassau

New·ry \'n(y)ù(ə)r-ē\ city district S Northern Ireland in Mourne district

New South Wales state SE Australia; capital, Sydney

New Spain former Spanish possessions in North America, Central America, West Indies, & the Philippines; capital, Mexico City

New Sweden former Swedish colony (1638–55) North America on W bank of Delaware river

New·town·ab·bey \,n(y)üt-ᵊn-'ab-ē\ district E Northern Ireland

New·town·ards \,n(y)üt-ᵊn-'ärdz\ city area E Northern Ireland in Ards district

Newtown Saint Bos·wells \-sənt-'bäz-wəlz, -sänt-\ village S Scotland in Borders region

New World the western hemisphere including North America and South America

New York \-'yò(ə)rk\ **1** state NE U.S.; capital, Albany **2** *or* **New York City** city SE New York — **New York·er** \-'yòr-kər\ *n*

New York State Barge Canal — see ERIE

New Zea·land \-'zē-lənd\ country SW Pacific ESE of Australia; an independent country in the Commonwealth; capital, Wellington — **New Zea·land·er** \-lən-dər\ *n*

Ni·ag·a·ra Falls \(,)nī-'ag-(ə-)rə-\ falls New York & Ontario in **Niagara river** (58 kilometers long flowing N from Lake Erie into Lake Ontario); divided by Goat Island into Horseshoe Falls, or Canadian Falls (48 meters high, 917 meters wide) & American Falls (51 meters high, 323 meters wide)

Nia·mey \nē-'äm-ā, nyä-'mā\ city, capital of Niger

Ni·caea \nī-'sē-ə\ *or* **Nice** \'nīs\ ancient city W Bithynia; site at modern village in NW Turkey — **Ni·cae·an** \nī-'sē-ən\ *adj or n* — **Ni·cene** \'nī-,sēn, nī-'sēn\ *adj*

Ni·ca·ra·gua \,nik-ə-'räg-wə\ **1** lake 160 kilometers long S Nicaragua **2** country Central America; capital, Managua — **Ni·ca·ra·guan** \-wən\ *adj or n*

Nic·o·bar \'nik-ə-,bär\ islands India in Bay of Bengal S of the Andamans — see ANDAMAN

Nic·o·sia \,nik-ə-'sē-ə\ city, capital of Cyprus

Ni·ger \'nī-jər\ **1** river 4185 kilometers long W Africa flowing into Gulf of Guinea **2** country W Africa N of Nigeria; capital, Niamey

Ni·ge·ria \nī-'jir-ē-ə\ country W Africa on Gulf of Guinea; an independent state in the Commonwealth; official capital, Abuja — **Ni·ge·ri·an** \-ē-ən\ *adj or n*

Nii·hau \'nē-,haú\ island Hawaii WSW of Kauai

Nile \'nī(ə)l\ river 6497 kilometers long E Africa flowing

from Lake Victoria in Uganda N into the Mediterranean in Egypt

Nil·gi·ri \'nil-gə-rē\ hills S India

Nin·e·veh \'nin-ə-və\ ancient city, capital of Assyria; ruins in Iraq on the Tigris

Nip·i·gon, Lake \-'nip-ə-,gän\ lake Canada in W Ontario N of Lake Superior

Nip·pon \nip-'än\ — see JAPAN — **Nip·pon·ese** \,nip-ə-'nēz, -'nēs\ *adj or n*

Nizh·ni Nov·go·rod \,nizh-nē-'näv-gə-,räd, -'nòv-gə-rət\ *or 1932–89* **Gor'·kiy** *or* **Gor·ki** \'gor-kē\ city W Russia

Nor·folk \'nòr-fək, *in the U.S. also* -,fók\ **1** city SE Virginia **2** county E England on North sea

Nor·man·dy \'nòr-mən-dē\ region NW France NE of Brittany

North **1** river estuary of the Hudson between NE New Jersey & SE New York **2** sea arm of the Atlantic E of Great Britain **3** island N New Zealand

North·al·ler·ton \nòr-'thal-ərt-ᵊn\ town N England in North Yorkshire

North America continent of western hemisphere NW of South America & N of the equator — **North American** *adj or n*

North·amp·ton \nòrth-'(h)am(p)-tən\ city area central England in Northamptonshire

North·amp·ton·shire \nòrth-'(h)am(p)-tən-,shi(ə)r, -shər\ *or* **Northampton** county central England

North Cape cape New Zealand at N end of North island

North Car·o·li·na \-,kar-ə-'lī-nə\ state E U.S.; capital, Raleigh — **North Car·o·lin·ian** \-'lin-ē-ən, -'lin-yən\ *adj or n*

North Da·ko·ta \-də-'kōt-ə\ state N U.S.; capital, Bismarck — **North Da·ko·tan** \-'kōt-ᵊn\ *adj or n*

North Down district E Northern Ireland

Northern Cook \-'kúk\ islands S central Pacific N of Cook islands

Northern Ireland region N Ireland comprising 26 districts of Ulster; a division of United Kingdom; capital, Belfast

Northern Mar·i·ana Islands \-,mar-ē-'an-ə-, -,mer-\ islands W Pacific; a U.S. commonwealth since 1986

Northern Rhodesia — see ZAMBIA

Northern Territory territory N & central Australia; capital, Darwin

North Korea — see KOREA

North Slope region N Alaska between Brooks Range & Arctic ocean

North·um·ber·land \nòr-'thəm-bər-lənd\ county N England — **North·um·bri·an** \-'thəm-brē-ən\ *adj or n*

North·um·bria \nòr-'thəm-brē-ə\ ancient country Great Britain in what is now N England and S Scotland — **North·um·bri·an** \-brē-ən\ *adj or n*

North Vietnam — see VIETNAM

Northwest Territories territory N Canada consisting of the arctic islands, the mainland N of 60° between Yukon Territory & Hudson bay, & the islands in Hudson bay

North Yorkshire county N England

Nor·way \'nò(ə)r-,wā\ country N Europe in Scandinavia; a kingdom; capital, Oslo

Nor·wich \'nò(ə)r-(,)wich; 'nòr-ich, 'när-\ city E England in Norfolk county

Not·ting·ham \'nät-iŋ-əm, *in the U.S. also* -,ham\ city N central England in Nottinghamshire

Not·ting·ham·shire \'nät-iŋ-əm-shi(ə)r, -shər, *in the U.S. also* -,ham-\ *or* **Nottingham** county N central England

Nouak·chott \nú-'äk-,shät\ city, capital of Mauritania

Nou·méa \nü-'mā-ə\ city, capital of New Caledonia

No·va Sco·tia \,nō-və-'skō-shə\ province SE Canada;

\ə\ abut	\au̇\ out	\i\ tip	\ò\ saw	\u̇\ foot
\ər\ further	\ch\ chin	\ī\ life	\ò͝i\ coin	\y\ yet
\a\ mat	\e\ pet	\j\ job	\th\ thin	\yü\ few
\ā\ take	\ē\ easy	\ŋ\ sing	\th\ this	\yu̇\ cure
\ä\ cot, cart	\g\ go	\ō\ bone	\ü\ food	\zh\ vision

capital, Halifax — **No·va Sco·tian** \-'skō-shən\ *adj or n*

No·vo·kuz·netsk \,nō-(,)vō-kúz-'netsk\ city ⓢ Russia

No·vo·si·birsk \,nō-(,)vō-sə-'bi(ə)rsk\ city ⓢ Russia

Nu·bia \'n(y)ü-bē-ə\ region ⓃⒺ Africa in Nile valley in ⓢ Egypt & Ⓝ Sudan — **Nu·bi·an** \-bē-ən\ *adj or n*

Nu·ku·a·lo·fa \,nü-kə-wə-'lō-fə\ seaport, capital of Tonga

Nu·mid·ia \n(y)ü-'mid-ē-ə\ ancient country Ⓝ Africa Ⓔ of Mauretania in modern Algeria — **Nu·mid·i·an** \-ē-ən\ *adj or n*

Ny·asa, Lake \-nī-'as-ə, -nē-\ lake ⓈⒺ Africa in Malawi, Mozambique, & Tanzania

Nyasaland — see MALAWI

Oa·hu \ə-'wä-hü\ island Hawaii; site of Honolulu

Oak·land \'ō-klənd\ city Ⓦ California on San Francisco Bay Ⓔ of San Francisco

Oce·a·nia \,ō-shē-'an-ē-ə, -'ä-nē-ə\ lands of the central & ⓢ Pacific: Micronesia, Melanesia, Polynesia including New Zealand, & sometimes Australia & Malay island group — **Oce·a·ni·an** \-'an-ē-ən, -'ä-nē-\ *adj or n*

Oder \'ōd-ər\ *or* **Odra** \'ò-drə\ river 906 kilometers long central Europe flowing from Silesia ⓃⓌ into Baltic sea; forms part of boundary between Poland & Germany

Odes·sa \ō-'des-ə\ city & port ⓢ Ukraine on Black sea

Ohio \ō-'hī-ō\ **1** river 1579 kilometers long Ⓔ U.S. flowing from Ⓦ Pennsylvania into the Mississippi **2** state Ⓔ central U.S.; capital, Columbus — **Ohio·an** \ō-'hī-ə-wən\ *adj or n*

Oka·ya·ma \,ō-kə-'yäm-ə\ city Japan in Ⓦ Honshu on Inland sea

Okee·cho·bee, Lake \,ō-kə-'chō-bē\ lake ⓢ central Florida

Oke·fe·no·kee \,ō-kə-fə-'nō-kē\ swamp ⓈⒺ Georgia & ⓃⒺ Florida

Oki·na·wa \,ō-kə-'nä-wə, -'naú-ə\ **1** islands Japan in central Ryukyus **2** island, chief of group — **Oki·na·wan** \-'nä-wən, -'naú-ən\ *adj or n*

Okla·ho·ma \,ō-klə-'hō-mə\ state ⓢ U.S.; capital, Oklahoma City — **Okla·ho·man** \-mən\ *adj or n*

Oklahoma City city, capital of Oklahoma

Old·ham \'ōl-dəm\ city ⓃⓌ England in Greater Manchester county

Old Point Comfort cape ⓈⒺ Virginia Ⓝ of entrance to Hampton Roads

Ol·du·vai Gorge \'ōl-də-,vī-\ canyon Ⓝ Tanzania ⓈⒺ of Serengeti Plain; site of fossil beds

Old World the half of the earth to the east of the Atlantic ocean including Europe, Asia, and Africa; *esp* : the continent of Europe

Olym·pia \ə-'lim-pē-ə, ō-\ **1** city, capital of Washington **2** plain ⓢ Greece in ⓃⓌ Peloponnisos

Olym·pic \ə-'lim-pik, ō-\ mountains ⓃⓌ Washington on Olympic peninsula; highest Mt. Olympus 2428 meters

Olym·pus \ə-'lim-pəs, ō-\ mountains ⓃⒺ Greece

Omagh \'ō-mə\ **1** district Ⓦ Northern Ireland **2** town in Omagh county

Oma·ha \'ō-mə-,hò, -,hä\ city Ⓔ Nebraska

Oman \ō-'män, -'man\ country ⓈⓌ Asia in ⓈⒺ Arabia; a sultanate; capital, Masqat — see UNITED ARAB EMIRATES

Oman, Gulf of arm of Arabian sea between Oman & ⓈⒺ Iran

Omsk \'òm(p)sk, 'äm(p)sk\ city ⓢ Russia

On·tar·io \än-'ter-ē-,ō, -'tar-\ province Ⓔ Canada; capital, Toronto — **On·tar·i·an** \-ē-ən\ *adj or n*

Ontario, Lake lake Ⓔ central North America in U.S. & Canada; one of the Great Lakes

Or·ange \'òr-inj, 'är-, -ənj\ river 2090 kilometers long ⓢ Africa flowing Ⓦ from Drakensberg mountains into the Atlantic

Orange Free State province Ⓔ central Republic of South Africa; capital, Bloemfontein

Or·e·gon \'òr-i-gən, 'är-, -,gän\ state ⓃⓌ U.S.; capital,

Salem — **Or·e·go·nian** \,òr-i-'gō-nē-ən, ,är-, -nyən\ *adj or n*

Oregon Trail pioneer route to the Pacific Northwest about 3220 kilometers long from Missouri to Washington

Ori·no·co \,ōr-ə-'nō-kō, ,òr-\ river 2575 kilometers long Venezuela flowing into the Atlantic

Ork·ney \'òrk-nē\ islands Ⓝ Scotland forming a region

Or·lan·do \òr-'lan-dō\ city central Florida

Osa·ka \ō-'säk-ə\ city Japan in ⓢ Honshu

Osh·a·wa \'äsh-ə-,wä\ city ⓈⒺ Ontario, Canada on Lake Ontario ⒺⓃⒺ of Toronto

Os·lo \'äz-lō, 'äs-\ city, capital of Norway

Ot·ta·wa \'ät-ə-,wä, -wə, -,wò\ city, capital of Canada in ⓈⒺ Ontario on Ottawa river

Ottoman Empire \,ät-ə-mən-\ former Turkish sultanate in ⓈⒺ Europe, Ⓦ Asia, & Ⓝ Africa

Oua·ga·dou·gou \,wäg-ə-'dü-,gü\ city, capital of Burkina Faso

Outer Hebrides — see HEBRIDES

Ox·ford \'äks-fərd\ city central England in Oxfordshire

Ox·ford·shire \'äks-fərd-,shi(ə)r, -shər\ *or* **Oxford** county central England

Ox·nard \'äk-,snärd\ city ⓈⓌ California

Ozark plateau \'ō-,zärk-\ *or* **Ozark mountains** eroded plateau Ⓝ Arkansas, ⓢ Missouri, & ⓃⒺ Oklahoma with Ⓔ extensions into ⓢ Illinois

Pa·cif·ic \pə-'sif-ik\ ocean extending from arctic circle to the equator (North Pacific) and from the equator to the antarctic regions (South Pacific) & from Ⓦ North America & Ⓦ South America to Ⓔ Asia & Australia — **Pacific** *adj*

Pacific Islands, Trust Territory of the grouping of islands in Ⓦ Pacific formerly under U.S. administration: the Carolines & the Marshalls

Pa·dang \'pä-,däŋ\ city Indonesia in Ⓦ Sumatra

Pa·dre \'päd-rē, 'pad-\ island about 160 kilometers long ⓢ Texas in Gulf of Mexico

Pa·go Pa·go \,päŋ-(g)ō-'päŋ-(g)ō, ,päg-ō-'päg-ō\ town, capital of American Samoa on Tutuila island

Painted Desert region Ⓝ central Arizona

Pak·i·stan \'pak-i-,stan, ,päk-i-'stän\ country ⓃⓌ of India; until 1971 included also an eastern division Ⓔ of India; capital, Islamabad — see EAST PAKISTAN — **Pak·i·stani** \-'stan-ē, -'stän-ē\ *adj or n*

Palau — see BELAU

Pa·la·wan \pə-'lä-wən, -,wän\ island Ⓦ Philippines between South China & Sulu seas

Pa·lem·bang \,päl-əm-'bäŋ\ city Indonesia in ⓈⒺ Sumatra

Pa·ler·mo \pə-'lər-mō, -'le(ə)r-\ city Italy, capital of Sicily

Pal·es·tine \'pal-ə-,stīn, -,stēn\ region ⓈⓌ Asia between Syrian Desert & the Mediterranean now divided between Israel & Jordan — **Pal·es·tin·ian** \,pal-ə-'stin-ē-ən, -'stin-yən\ *adj or n*

Pal·i·sades \,pal-ə-'sädz\ line of high cliffs 24 kilometers long on Ⓦ bank of the Hudson in ⓈⒺ New York & ⓃⒺ New Jersey

Pa·mirs \pə-'mi(ə)rz\ *or* **Pa·mir** \pə-'mi(ə)r\ elevated mountainous region central Asia in Ⓔ Tajikistan & on borders of China, India, Pakistan, & Afghanistan; many peaks over 6000 meters

Pam·li·co \'pam-li-,kō\ inlet of the Atlantic Ⓔ North Carolina between main part of the state & offshore islands

Pam·pa \'pam-pə\ city ⓃⓌ Texas

Pan·a·ma \'pan-ə-,mä, -,mò, ,pan-ə-'mä, -'mò\ **1** country ⓢ Central America **2** *or* **Panama City** city, its capital on the Pacific **3** canal 82 kilometers long Panama connecting Atlantic & Pacific oceans — **Pan·a·ma·ni·an** \,pan-ə-'mä-nē-ən\ *adj or n*

Panama, Isthmus of *or formerly* **Isthmus of Dar·i·en** \-,dar-ē-'en\ strip of land central Panama connecting North America & South America

Panama Canal Zone — see CANAL ZONE

Pa·nay \pə-'nī\ island central Philippines

Pao–t'ou — see BAOTOU

Pap·ua, Territory of \-'pap-yə-wə, -'päp-ə-wə\ former British territory consisting of SE New Guinea & offshore islands; now part of Papua New Guinea

Papua New Guinea country combining former territories of Papua & New Guinea; formerly a United Nations trust territory governed by Australia; independent since 1975; capital, Port Moresby

Par·a·guay \'par-ə-ˌgwī, -ˌgwä\ **1** river 2415 kilometers long central South America flowing from Brazil into the Paraná in Paraguay **2** country central South America; capital, Asunción — **Par·a·guay·an** \ˌpar-ə-'gwī-ən, -'gwä-\ adj or n

Par·a·mar·i·bo \ˌpar-ə-'mar-ə-ˌbō\ city, capital of Suriname

Pa·ra·ná \ˌpar-ə-'nä\ river 3285 kilometers long central South America flowing S from Brazil into Argentina

Pa·ri·cu·tin \pə-'rē-kə-ˌtēn\ **1** former village Mexico **2** volcano on site of former village of Paricutin

Par·is \'par-əs\ city, capital of France — **Pa·ri·sian** \pə-'rizh-ən, -'rēzh-\ adj or n

Par·nas·sus \pär-'nas-əs\ mountain central Greece

Par·os \'par-ˌäs, 'per-\ island Greece — **Par·i·an** \'par-ē-ən, 'per-\ adj

Par·ra·mat·ta \ˌpar-ə-'mat-ə\ city SE Australia in New South Wales NW of Sydney

Par·thia \'pär-thē-ə\ ancient country SW Asia in NE modern Iran — **Par·thi·an** \-thē-ən\ adj or n

Pas·a·de·na \ˌpas-ə-'dē-nə\ **1** city SW California E of Glendale **2** city SE Texas

Pat·a·go·nia \ˌpat-ə-'gō-nyə, -nē-ə\ region South America S of about 40° S latitude in S Argentina & S tip of Chile; sometimes thought to include Tierra del Fuego — **Pat·a·go·nian** \-nyən, -nē-ən\ adj or n

Pat·er·son \'pat-ər-sən\ city NE New Jersey

Pat·mos \'pat-məs\ island Greece SSW of Samos

Pat·na \'pət-nə\ city NE India on the Ganges

Pearl Harbor inlet Hawaii on S coast of Oahu W of Honolulu

Peking — see BEIJING

Pe·li·on \'pē-lē-ən\ mountain 1618 meters NE Greece

Pel·o·pon·ni·sos \ˌpel-ə-pə-'nē-səs\ peninsula forming S part of mainland of Greece

Pen·nine Chain \'pen-ˌīn-\ mountains N England; highest Cross Fell 893 meters

Penn·syl·va·nia \ˌpen(t)-səl-'vā-nyə, -nē-ə\ state E U.S.; capital, Harrisburg

People's Democratic Republic of Yemen — see YEMEN

Pe·o·ria \pē-'ȯr-ē-ə, -'ōr-\ city N central Illinois

Per·ga·mum \'pər-gə-məm\ or **Per·ga·mus** \-məs\ ancient Greek kingdom including most of Asia Minor; at its height 263–133 B.C.; capital, Pergamum (in what is now W Turkey)

Perm \'pərm, 'pe(ə)rm\ city W Russia

Pernambuco — see RECIFE

Persia — see IRAN

Per·sian \'pər-zhən\ gulf arm of Arabian sea between Iran & Arabia

Perth \'pərth\ city, capital of Western Australia

Pe·ru \pə-'rü\ country W South America; capital, Lima — **Pe·ru·vi·an** \pə-'rü-vē-ən\ adj or n

Pe·ter·bor·ough \'pēt-ər-ˌbər-ə, -ˌbə-rə, -b(ə-)rə\ city area central England in Cambridgeshire

Pe·tra \'pē-trə, 'pe-trə\ ancient city NW Arabia; site in SW Jordan

Petrograd — see SAINT PETERSBURG

Phil·a·del·phia \ˌfil-ə-'del-fyə, -fē-ə\ city SE Pennsylvania — **Phil·a·del·phian** \-fyən, -fē-ən\ adj or n

Phil·ip·pines \ˌfil-ə-'pēnz, 'fil-ə-ˌpēnz\ island group approximately 800 kilometers off SE coast of Asia; an independent country; capital, Manila — **Phil·ip·pine** \-'pēn, -ˌpēn\ adj

Phnom Penh \(pə-)'nȯm-'pen, (pə-)'näm-\ city, capital of Cambodia

Phoe·ni·cia \fi-'nish-(ē-)ə, -'nēsh-\ ancient country SW Asia on the Mediterranean in modern Syria & Lebanon

Phoe·nix \'fē-niks\ city, capital of Arizona

Phry·gia \'frij-(ē-)ə\ ancient country W central Asia Minor

Pied·mont \'pēd-ˌmänt\ plateau region E U.S. E of the Appalachians between SE New York & NE Alabama — **Pied·mon·tese** \ˌpēd-mən-'tēz, -(ˌ)män-, -'tēs\ adj or n

Pierre \'pi(ə)r\ city, capital of South Dakota

Pie·ter·mar·itz·burg \ˌpēt-ər-'mar-əts-ˌbərg\ city E Republic of South Africa, capital of Natal

Pikes Peak \'pīks-\ mountain 4301 meters E central Colorado in a range of the Rockies

Pin·dus \'pin-dəs\ mountains W Greece; highest point 2480 meters

Pi·sa \'pē-zə\ city W central Italy W of Florence

Pit·cairn \'pit-ˌka(ə)rn, -ˌke(ə)rn\ island S Pacific; a British colony

Pitts·burgh \'pits-ˌbərg\ city SW Pennsylvania

Plac·id, Lake \-'plas-əd\ lake NE New York

Plym·outh \'plim-əth\ **1** town SE Massachusetts **2** city SW England in Devon county

Po \'pō\ river 673 kilometers N Italy flowing into the Adriatic

Po Hai — see BO HAI

Po·land \'pō-lənd\ country central Europe on Baltic sea; capital, Warsaw

Pol·y·ne·sia \ˌpäl-ə-'nē-zhə, -shə\ islands of the central & S Pacific including Hawaii, the Line, Tonga, Cook, & Samoa islands, & often New Zealand among others

Pom·er·a·nia \ˌpäm-ə-'rā-nē-ə, -nyə\ region N Europe on Baltic sea; formerly in Germany, now mostly in Poland

Pom·peii \päm-'pā, -'pā-ˌē\ ancient city S Italy SE of Naples destroyed 79 A.D. by eruption of Vesuvius — **Pom·pe·ian** \-'pā-ən\ adj or n

Po·na·pe \'pō-nə-ˌpā\ island W Pacific in the E Carolines

Pon·ce \'pȯn(t)-sā\ city S Puerto Rico

Pon·do·land \'pän-(ˌ)dō-ˌland\ territory Republic of South Africa in Transkei

Pon·ta Del·ga·da \ˌpän-tə-del-'gäd-ə, -'gad-\ city & port Portugal, largest in the Azores

Pont·char·train, Lake \-'pän-chər-ˌtrān, -ˌpän-chər-'trān\ lake SE Louisiana E of the Mississippi & N of New Orleans

Pon·tus \'pänt-əs\ **1** ancient country NE Asia Minor **2** or **Pontus Euxinus** — see BLACK SEA — **Pon·tic** \'pänt-ik\ adj or n

Poole \'pül\ city area S England in Dorset county on English Channel

Poo·na \'pü-nə\ city W India, ESE of Bombay

Po·po·ca·te·petl \ˌpō-pə-ˌkat-ə-'pet-ᵊl\ volcano 5452 meters SE central Mexico

Port Arthur — see LÜSHUN

Port–au–Prince \ˌpȯrt-ō-'prin(t)s, ˌpōrt-\ city, capital of Haiti

Port Jack·son \-'jak-sən\ inlet of S Pacific SE Australia in New South Wales; harbor of Sydney

Port·land \'pȯrt-lənd, 'pōrt-\ **1** city SW Maine; largest in state **2** city NW Oregon

Port Lou·is \-'lü-əs, -'lü-ē, -lü-'ē\ city, capital of Mauritius

Port Mores·by \-'mō(ə)rz-bē, -'mȯ(ə)rz-\ city, capital of Papua New Guinea

Pôr·to Ale·gre \ˌpōrt-ō-ə-'leg-rə, ˌpȯrt-\ city S Brazil

Port of Spain city NW Trinidad, capital of Trinidad and Tobago

\ə\ abut		\aů\ out	\i\ tip	\ȯ\ saw	\ů\ foot
\ər\ further		\ch\ chin	\ī\ life	\ȯi\ coin	\y\ yet
\a\ mat		\e\ pet	\j\ job	\th\ thin	\yü\ few
\ā\ take		\ē\ easy	\ŋ\ sing	\th\ this	\yů\ cure
\ä\ cot, cart		\g\ go	\ō\ bone	\ü\ food	\zh\ vision

Por·to–No·vo \,pȯrt-ə-'nō-vō, ,pȯrt-\ city, capital of Benin

Port Phil·lip Bay \-'fil-əp-\ inlet of ⬚S Pacific ⬚SE Australia in Victoria; harbor of Melbourne

Ports·mouth \'pȯrt-sməth, 'pȯrt-\ **1** city ⬚SE Virginia **2** city ⬚S England in Hampshire

Por·tu·gal \'pȯr-chi-gəl, 'pȯr-\ country ⬚SW Europe; capital, Lisbon

Portuguese India former Portuguese possession on ⬚W coast of India; became part of India 1962

Po·to·mac \pə-'tō-mək, -mik\ river 462 kilometers long flowing from West Virginia into Chesapeake Bay & forming boundary between Maryland & Virginia

Pough·keep·sie \pə-'kip-sē, pō-\ city and river port ⬚SE New York on the Hudson

Po·wys \'pō-əs\ county ⬚E central Wales; established 1974

Prague \'präg\ or Czech **Pra·ha** \'prä-hä\ city, capital of Czech Republic & formerly of Czechoslovakia

Praia \'prī-ə\ town, capital of Cape Verde

Prairie Provinces the Canadian provinces of Alberta, Manitoba, & Saskatchewan

Pres·ton \'pres-tən\ city area ⬚NW England in Lancashire

Pre·to·ria \pri-'tōr-ē-ə, -'tȯr-\ city Republic of South Africa, capital of Transvaal & administrative capital of the country

Prib·i·lof \'prib-ə-,lȯf\ islands Alaska in Bering sea

Prince Ed·ward Island \-,ed-wərd-\ island ⬚SE Canada in Gulf of Saint Lawrence; a province; capital, Charlottetown

Prince Ru·pert's Land \-'rü-pərts-\ historical region ⬚N & ⬚W Canada consisting of drainage basin of Hudson bay granted 1670 by King Charles II to Hudson's Bay Company

Prince·ton \'prin(t)-stən\ town ⬚W central New Jersey

Prin·ci·pe \'prin(t)-sə-pe\ island ⬚W Africa in Gulf of Guinea — see SAO TOME AND PRINCIPE

Prom·on·to·ry \'präm-ən-,tōr-ē, -,tȯr-\ locality ⬚NW Utah

Pro·vence \prə-'vän(t)s\ region ⬚SE France on the Mediterranean

Prov·i·dence \'präv-əd-ən(t)s, -ə-,den(t)s\ city, capital of Rhode Island

Prus·sia \'prəsh-ə\ former kingdom &, later, state Germany; capital, Berlin — **Prus·sian** \-ən\ adj or n

Pueb·lo \pü-'eb-lō, 'pweb-, pyü-'eb-\ city ⬚SE central Colorado ⬚SSE of Colorado Springs

Puer·to Ri·co \,pȯrt-ə-'rē-kō, ,pȯrt-, pwert-\ island West Indies ⬚E of Hispaniola; a self-governing commonwealth associated with U.S.; capital, San Juan — **Puer·to Ri·can** \-'rē-kən\ adj or n

Pu·get Sound \,pyü-jət-\ arm of the Pacific ⬚W Washington

Pun·jab \,pən-'jäb, -'jab, 'pen-,jäb, -,jab\ region in Pakistan & ⬚NW India in valley of the Indus

Pu·san \'pü-,sän\ city ⬚SE South Korea

Pyong·yang \pē-'ȯŋ-,yäŋ, pē-'əŋ-, -,yaŋ\ city, capital of North Korea

Pyr·e·nees \'pir-ə-,nēz\ mountains on French-Spanish border extending from Bay of Biscay to the Mediterranean; highest Pico de Aneto 3404 meters

Qa·tar \'kät-ər, 'gät-, 'gət-\ independent country ⬚E Arabia on peninsula extending into Persian gulf; capital, Doha

Qing·dao \'chiŋ-'dau̇\ or **Tsing·tao** \'chiŋ-'dau̇, '(t)siŋ-\ city & port ⬚E China

Qi·qi·har \'chē-'chē-'här\ or **Ch'i·ch'i·ha·erh** \'chē-chē-'hä-'ər\ city ⬚NE China

Que·bec \kwi-'bek, ki-\ or French **Qué·bec** \kā-bek\ **1** province ⬚E Canada **2** city, its capital, on the Saint Lawrence

Queens \'kwēnz\ section of New York City on Long Island ⬚E of Brooklyn

Queens·land \'kwēnz-,land, -lənd\ state ⬚NE Australia; capital, Brisbane — **Queens·land·er** \-ər\ n

Que·zon City \'kā-,sȯn-\ city Philippines in Luzon; formerly capital of the country

Qui·to \'kē-tō\ city, capital of Ecuador

Ra·bat \rə-'bät\ city, capital of Morocco

Rai·nier, Mount \-rə-'ni(ə)r, -rā-\ mountain 4392 meters ⬚W central Washington; highest in Cascade Range

Rajasthan — see RAJPUTANA

Raj·pu·ta·na \,räj-pə-'tän-ə\ or **Ra·ja·sthan** \'räj-ə-,stän\ region ⬚NW India ⬚S of Punjab

Ra·leigh \'rȯ-lē, 'räl-ē\ city, capital of North Carolina

Rand — see WITWATERSRAND

Rand·wick \'ran-(,)dwik\ city ⬚SE Australia in ⬚E New South Wales

Rangoon — see YANGON

Ra·wal·pin·di \,rä-wəl-'pin-dē, rau̇l-'pin-, rȯl-'pin-\ city ⬚NE Pakistan ⬚NNW of Lahore

Read·ing \'red-iŋ\ city area ⬚S England in Berkshire

Re·ci·fe \rə-'sē-fə\ or formerly **Per·nam·bu·co** \,pər-nəm-'b(y)ü-kō, ,per-nəm-'bü-\ city ⬚NE Brazil

Red \'red\ **1** river 1638 kilometers long flowing ⬚E on Oklahoma-Texas boundary & into the Atchafalaya & the Mississippi in Louisiana **2** sea between Arabia & ⬚NE Africa

Red·bridge \'red-(,)brij\ city area of ⬚NE Greater London county, England

Re·gi·na \ri-'jī-nə\ city, capital of Saskatchewan, Canada

Re·no \'rē-nō\ city ⬚NW Nevada

Ré·union \rē-'yün-yən\ island ⬚W Indian ocean; an overseas division of France; capital Saint-Denis

Reyk·ja·vik \'rāk-(y)ə-,vik, -,vēk\ city, capital of Iceland

Rhine \'rīn\ river 1320 kilometers long ⬚W Europe flowing from ⬚SE Switzerland to North sea in the Netherlands — **Rhen·ish** \'ren-ish, 'rē-nish\ adj or n

Rhine·land \'rīn-,land, -lənd\ or German **Rhein·land** \'rīn-,länt\ the part of Germany ⬚W of the Rhine — **Rhine·land·er** \'rīn-,lan-dər, -lən-\ n

Rhode Is·land \rō-'dī-lənd\ **1** or officially **Rhode Island and Providence Plantations** state ⬚NE U.S.; capital, Providence **2** — see AQUIDNECK ISLAND — **Rhode Is·land·er** \-lən-dər\ n

Rho·de·sia \rō-'dē-zh(ē-)ə\ — see ZIMBABWE — **Rho·de·sian** \-zh(ē-)ən\ adj or n

Rhone or French **Rhône** \'rōn\ or ancient **Rhod·a·nus** \'räd-ᵊn-əs\ river 800 kilometers long Switzerland & ⬚SE France

Rich·mond \'rich-mənd\ **1** — see STATEN ISLAND **2** city, capital of Virginia

Richmond upon Thames \-'temz\ city area of ⬚SW Greater London county, England

Ri·ga \'rē-gə\ city, capital of Latvia

Rio \'rē-ō\ RIO DE JANEIRO

Rio de Ja·nei·ro \'rē-ō-,dā-zhə-'ne(ə)r-ō, -,dē-, -də-, -jə-'ne(ə)r-\ city ⬚SE Brazil on Guanabara Bay

Rio Grande \,rē-(,)ō-'grand(-ē)\ or Mexican **Rio Bra·vo** \-'bräv-ō\ river 3035 kilometers long ⬚SW U.S. forming part of U.S.-Mexico boundary & flowing into Gulf of Mexico

Río Muni — see MBINI

Riv·er·side \'riv-ər-,sīd\ city ⬚S California

Riv·i·era \,riv-ē-'er-ə\ coast region ⬚SE France & ⬚NW Italy

Ri·yadh \rē-'(y)äd\ city, capital of Saudi Arabia

Ro·a·noke \'rō-(ə-),nōk\ city ⬚W Virginia

Roanoke Island island North Carolina ⬚S of entrance to Albemarle sound

Rob·son, Mount \-'räb-sən\ mountain 3954 meters ⬚W Canada in ⬚E British Columbia; highest in the Canadian Rockies

Roch·es·ter \'räch-ə-stər, 'räch-,es-tər\ city ⬚W New York

Rock·ford \'räk-fərd\ city ⬚N Illinois

Rocky \'räk-ē\ mountains ⬚W North America extending ⬚SE from ⬚N Alaska to central New Mexico — see ELBERT, MOUNT; ROBSON, MOUNT

Roman Empire the empire of ancient Rome

Ro·ma·nia \rō-'mā-nē-ə, -nyə\ or **Ru·ma·nia** \ru̇-\ country ⬚SE Europe on Black sea; capital, Bucharest

Rom·blon \räm-'blōn\ island group central Philippines

Rome \'rōm\ **1** or Italian **Ro·ma** \'rō-mä\ city, capital of Italy **2** the Roman Empire

Ro·sa·rio \rō-'zär-ē-,ō, -'sär-\ city E central Argentina

Ro·seau \rō-'zō\ seaport, capital of Dominica

Ros·tov \rə-'stóf, -'stóv\ city SW Russia, on the Don

Ros·well \'räz-,wel, -wəl\ city SE New Mexico

Ro·ta \'rōt-ə\ island W Pacific in Marianas

Rot·ter·dam \'rät-ər-,dam\ city SW Netherlands

Ru·an·da-Urun·di \rü-'än-də-ü-'rün-dē\ former territory E central Africa bordering on Lake Tanganyika & administered by Belgium; divided into Burundi & Rwanda 1962

Ru·dolf, Lake \-'rü-,dälf\ lake N Kenya in Great Rift valley

Ruhr \'rü(ə)r\ industrial district W Germany E of the Rhine in valley of Ruhr river

Rupert's Land PRINCE RUPERT'S LAND

Rush·more, Mount \-'rəsh-,mō(ə)r, -,mó(ə)r\ mountain 1890 meters W South Dakota in Black hills

Rus·sia \'rəsh-ə\ **1** former empire largely having the same boundaries as U.S.S.R.; capital, Petrograd (Saint Petersburg) **2** UNION OF SOVIET SOCIALIST REPUBLICS **3** country E Europe & N Asia; capital, Moscow; a republic (**Russian Soviet Federated Socialist Republic** or **Soviet Russia**) of U.S.S.R. 1922–91

Ru·the·nia \rü-'thē-nyə, -nē-ə\ region W Ukraine W of the N Carpathians — **Ru·the·nian** \rü-'thē-nyən, -nē-ən\ adj or n

Ru·wen·zo·ri \,rü-(w)ən-'zōr-ē, -'zór-\ mountain group E central Africa between Uganda & Zaire; highest Mount Margherita 5019 meters

Rwan·da or formerly **Ru·an·da** \rü-'än-də\ country E central Africa, until 1962 part of Ruanda-Urundi trust territory; capital, Kigali — **Rwan·dan** \-dən\ adj or n

Ryu·kyu \rē-'(y)ü-k(y)ü\ islands W Pacific extending in an arc from Kyushu, Japan, to Taiwan, China; belong to Japan — **Ryu·kyu·an** \-,(y)ü-'k(y)ü-ən\ adj or n

Saar \'sär, 'zär\ **1** river 135 kilometers long Europe flowing from E France to W Germany **2** or **Saar·land** \'sär-,land, 'zär-\ district W Europe in valley of Saar river between France and Germany

Sa·bah \'säb-ə\ part of Malaysia in NE Borneo

Sac·ra·men·to \,sak-rə-'ment-ō\ **1** river 615 kilometers long N California flowing S into Suisun Bay **2** city, capital of California

Sag·ue·nay \'sag-ə-,nā, ,sag-ə-'nā\ river 200 kilometers long Canada in S Quebec flowing E into the Saint Lawrence

Sa·ha·ra \sə-'har-ə, -'her-, -'här-\ desert region N Africa N of Sudan region extending from Atlantic coast to Red sea or, as sometimes thought, to the Nile — **Sa·ha·ran** \-ən\ adj

Sa·hel \'sa-hil, sə-'hil\ the S fringe of the Sahara

Saigon — see HO CHI MINH CITY

Saint Al·bans \-'ól-bənz\ city area SE England in Hertfordshire

Saint Cath·a·rines \-'kath-(ə-)rənz\ city Canada in SE Ontario

Saint Chris·to·pher \-'kris-tə-fər\ or **Saint Kitts** \-'kits\ island West Indies in the Leeward Islands; with Nevis forms independent **Saint Christopher–Nevis;** capital, Basseterre (on Saint Christopher)

Saint Clair, Lake \-'kla(ə)r, -'kle(ə)r\ lake SE Michigan & SE Ontario connected by **Saint Clair river** (64 kilometers long) with Lake Huron & draining by Detroit river into Lake Erie

Saint Croix \sänt-'krói, sənt-\ **1** river 120 kilometers long Canada & U.S. on border between New Brunswick & Maine **2** island West Indies; largest of Virgin Islands of the U.S.

Saint Eli·as, Mount \-,sänt-°l-'ī-əs\ mountain 5489 meters on Alaska-Canada boundary in **Saint Elias range**

Saint George's \-'jór-jəz\ town, capital of Grenada

Saint George's Channel channel British Isles between SW Wales & Ireland

Saint Gott·hard \sänt-'gät-ərd, -'gäth-, sənt-\ **1** pass S

central Switzerland in Saint Gotthard range of the Alps **2** tunnel 15 kilometers long near the pass

Saint He·le·na \,sänt-°l-'ē-nə, ,sänt-hə-'lē-\ island S Atlantic; a British colony

Saint Hel·ens \sänt-'hel-ənz, sənt-\ city area NW England in Merseyside county ENE of Liverpool

Saint Helens, Mount volcano S Washington

Saint John \sänt-'jän, sənt-\ city Canada in New Brunswick

Saint Johns \sänt-'jänz, sənt-\ city, capital of Antigua and Barbuda

Saint John's \sänt-'jänz, sənt-\ city, capital of Newfoundland, Canada

Saint Law·rence \sänt-'lór-ən(t)s, sənt-, -'lär-\ **1** river 1225 kilometers long E Canada in Ontario & Quebec bordering on U.S. in New York & flowing from Lake Ontario NE into the **Gulf of Saint Lawrence** (inlet of the Atlantic) **2** seaway Canada & U.S. in & along the Saint Lawrence between Lake Ontario & Montreal

Saint Lou·is \sänt-'lü-əs, sənt-\ city E Missouri on the Mississippi

Saint Lu·cia \sänt-'lü-shə, sənt-\ island West Indies in the Windwards S of Martinique; an independent country; capital, Castries

Saint Paul \-'pól\ city, capital of Minnesota

Saint Pe·ters·burg \-'pēt-ərz-,bərg\ **1** city W Florida **2** or 1914–24 **Pet·ro·grad** \'pe-trə-,grad, -,gräd\ or 1924–91 **Le·nin·grad** \'len-ən-,grad, -,gräd\ city W Russia

Saint Thom·as \-'täm-əs\ island West Indies, one of Virgin Islands of the U.S.; chief town, Charlotte Amalie

Saint Vin·cent \sänt-'vin(t)-sənt, sənt-\ island West Indies in the central Windward Islands; with N Grenadines forms independent **Saint Vincent and the Grenadines;** capital, Kingstown (on Saint Vincent)

Sai·pan \sī-'pan, -'pän; 'sī-,pan, -,pän\ island W Pacific in S central Marianas

Sa·kai \(')sä-'kī\ city Japan in S Honshu

Sa·kha·lin \'sak-ə-,lēn, -lən; ,sak-ə-'lēn\ island SE Russia in W Pacific N of Hokkaido, Japan; until 1945 divided between Japan & U.S.S.R.

Sal·a·mis \'sal-ə-məs\ **1** ancient city Cyprus on E coast **2** island Greece off Attica

Sa·lem \'sā-ləm\ city, capital of Oregon

Sal·ford \'sól-fərd\ city area NW England in Greater Manchester county

Salisbury — see HARARE

Sa·lo·ni·ka \sə-'län-i-kə, ,sal-ə-'nē-kə\ or **Thes·sa·lo·ni·ca** \,thes-ə-lə-'nī-kə, -'län-i-kə\ city N Greece in Macedonia

Sal·op \'sal-əp\ or **Shrop·shire** \'shräp-,shi(ə)r, -shər\ county W England bordering on Wales

Salt Lake City city, capital of Utah

Sal·va·dor \'sal-və-,dó(ə)r, ,sal-və-'dó(ə)r\ or **Ba·hia** \bä-'ē-ə\ city NE Brazil on the Atlantic — **Sal·va·dor·an** \,sal-və-'dór-ən, -'dór-\ or **Sal·va·dor·ean** or **Sal·va·dor·ian** \-ē-ən\ adj or n

Sal·ween \'sal-,wēn\ river 2815 kilometers long SE Asia flowing S

Sa·mar \'säm-,är\ island central Philippines

Sa·ma·ra \sə-'mär-ə\ or 1935–91 **Kuy·by·shev** \'kwē-bə-,shef, -,shev\ city W Russia, on the Volga

Sam·ni·um \'sam-nē-əm\ ancient country S central Italy — **Sam·nite** \'sam-,nīt\ adj or n

Sa·moa \sə-'mō-ə\ islands SW central Pacific N of Tonga islands; divided at longitude 171° W into American Samoa or Eastern Samoa & Western Samoa — **Sa·mo·an** \-ən\ adj or n

\ə\ abut	\au̇\ out	\i\ tip	\ó\ saw	\u̇\ foot
\ər\ further	\ch\ chin	\ī\ life	\ói\ coin	\y\ yet
\a\ mat	\e\ pet	\j\ job	\th\ thin	\yü\ few
\ā\ take	\ē\ easy	\ŋ\ sing	\th\ this	\yu̇\ cure
\ä\ cot, cart	\g\ go	\ō\ bone	\ü\ food	\zh\ vision

Sa·mos \'sā-ˌmäs\ island Greece in the Aegean off coast of Turkey — **Sa·mi·an** \-mē-ən\ adj or n

San·'a \'san-ˌä, san-'ä\ city [SW] Arabia, capital of Yemen & formerly of Yemen Arab Republic

San An·to·nio \ˌsan-ən-'tō-nē-ˌō\ city [S] Texas

San Ber·nar·di·no \ˌsan-ˌbər-nə(r)-'dē-nō\ city [S] California

San Di·ego \ˌsan-dē-'ā-gō\ city [SW] California

Sand·wich \'san-(ˌ)(d)wich\ town [SE] England

Sandwich islands — see HAWAII

San Fran·cis·co \ˌsan-frən-'sis-kō\ city [W] California on San Francisco Bay & Pacific ocean

San Joa·quin \ˌsan-wä-'kēn, -wȯ\ river 563 kilometers long central California flowing [NW] into the Sacramento

San Jo·se \ˌsan-ə-'zā\ city [W] California [SE] of San Francisco

San Jo·sé \ˌsan-ə-'zā, -ō-'zā, -hō-'zā\ city, capital of Costa Rica

San Juan \san-'hwän, -'wän\ city, capital of Puerto Rico

San Ma·ri·no \ˌsan-mə-'rē-nō\ 1 country [S] Europe on Italian peninsula [ENE] of Florence near Adriatic sea 2 town, its capital

San Sal·va·dor \san-'sal-və-ˌdȯ(ə)r\ 1 island central Bahama islands 2 city, capital of El Salvador

San·ta Ana \ˌsant-ə-'an-ə\ city [SW] California [ESE] of Long Beach

San·ta Bar·ba·ra \-'bär-b(ə-)rə\ or **Channel** islands California in the Pacific off [SW] coast

San·ta Fe \ˌsant-ə-'fā\ city, capital of New Mexico

Santa Fe Trail pioneer route to the Southwest 1290 kilometers long used especially 1821–80 from vicinity of Kansas City, Missouri, to Santa Fe, New Mexico

San·ti·a·go \ˌsant-ē-'äg-ō, ˌsänt-\ city, capital of Chile

San·to Do·min·go \ˌsant-əd-ə-'miŋ-gō\ or formerly **Ci·u·dad Tru·ji·llo** \ˌsē-ü-ˌthä-trü-'hē-(y)ō, ˌsē-ü-ˌdad-\ city, capital of Dominican Republic

São Pau·lo \ˌsä-ō-'paủ-lō\ city [SE] Brazil

São To·mé \ˌsä-ō-tō-'mā\ town, capital of Sao Tome and Principe

Sao Tome and Principe country [W] Africa; formerly a Portuguese colony; became independent 1975; capital São Tomé

Sap·po·ro \'säp-ə-ˌrō; sə-'pōr-ō, -'pȯr\ city Japan on [W] Hokkaido

Sa·ra·tov \sə-'rät-əf\ city [W] Russia, on the Volga

Sa·ra·wak \sə-'rä-(ˌ)wä(k), -ˌwak\ part of Malaysia in [N] Borneo

Sar·din·ia \sär-'din-ē-ə, -'din-yə\ island Italy in the Mediterranean [S] of Corsica — **Sar·din·ian** \-'din-ē-ən, -'din-yən\ adj or n

Sar·gas·so sea \sär-ˌgas-ō-\ area of nearly still water in the [N] Atlantic lying chiefly between 25° & 35° [N] latitude & 40° & 70° [W] longitude

Sas·katch·e·wan \sə-'skach-ə-wən, sa-, -ˌwän\ province [W] Canada; capital, Regina

Sas·ka·toon \ˌsas-kə-'tün\ city central Saskatchewan, Canada

Sau·di Ara·bia \ˌsaủd-ē-ə-'rā-bē-ə, ˌsȯd-ē-, sä-ˌüd-ē-\ country [SW] Asia occupying largest part of Arabian peninsula; a kingdom; capital, Riyadh — **Saudi** adj or n — **Saudi Arabian** adj or n

Sault Sainte Ma·rie canals \ˌsü-(ˌ)sänt-mə-'rē-\ or **Soo canals** \ˌsü-\ three ship canals, two in U.S. (Michigan) & one in Canada (Ontario), at rapids in river connecting Lake Superior & Lake Huron

Sa·vaii \sə-'vī-ˌē\ island, largest in Western Samoa

Sa·van·nah \sə-'van-ə\ city [E] Georgia

Sa·voy \sə-'vȯi\ or French **Sa·voie** \sà-vwà\ region [SE] France [SW] of Switzerland bordering on Italy — **Sa·voy·ard** \sə-'vȯi-ˌärd, sav-ˌȯi-'ärd; ˌsav-wä-'yär(d)\ adj or n

Sca·fell Pike \'skȯ-'fel-\ mountain 978 meters [NW] England in Cumbria county; highest in Cumbrian mountains

& in England

Scan·di·na·via \ˌskan-də-'nā-vē-ə, -vyə\ 1 peninsula [N] Europe occupied by Norway & Sweden 2 Denmark, Norway, Sweden, & sometimes also Iceland & Finland — **Scan·di·na·vian** \-vē-ən, -vyən\ adj or n

Scar·bor·ough \'skär-ˌbər-ə, -b(ə-)rə\ city Canada in [SE] Ontario near Toronto

Scheldt \'skelt\ or **Schel·de** \'skel-də\ or ancient **Scal·dis** \'skal-dəs\ river 435 kilometers long [W] Europe flowing from [N] France through Belgium into North sea in Netherlands

Scil·ly \'sil-ē\ islands [SW] England off Land's End in Cornwall and Isles of Scilly county

Sco·tia \'skō-shə\ SCOTLAND — the Medieval Latin name

Scot·land \'skät-lənd\ or Latin **Cal·e·do·nia** \ˌkal-ə-'dō-nyə, -nē-ə\ country [N] Great Britain; a division of United Kingdom of Great Britain and Northern Ireland; capital, Edinburgh

Scyth·ia \'sith-ē-ə, 'sith-\ ancient area of Europe & Asia [N] & [NE] of Black sea & [E] of Aral sea — **Scyth·i·an** \-ē-ən\ adj or n

Se·at·tle \sē-'at-ᵊl\ city [W] Washington

Seine \'sān, 'sen\ river 773 kilometers long [N] France flowing [NW] into English channel

Sel·kirk \'sel-ˌkərk\ range of the Rocky mountains [SE] British Columbia, Canada; highest peak, Mount Sir Donald 3390 meters

Se·ma·rang \sə-'mär-ˌäŋ\ city Indonesia in central Java

Sen·dai \(')sen-'dī\ city Japan in [NE] Honshu

Sen·e·ca Falls \'sen-i-kə-\ village [W] central New York

Sen·e·gal \ˌsen-i-'gȯl\ 1 river 1690 kilometers long [W] Africa flowing [W] into the Atlantic 2 country [W] Africa; capital, Dakar — **Sen·e·ga·lese** \ˌsen-i-gə-'lēz, -'lēs\ adj or n

Seoul \'sōl\ city, capital of South Korea

Ser·bia \'sər-bē-ə\ region in the Balkans comprising the largest part of Yugoslavia

Ser·en·ge·ti Plain \ˌser-ən-'get-ē\ area [N] Tanzania

Seven Hills the seven hills upon and about which was built the city of Rome

Sev·ern \'sev-ərn\ river 338 kilometers long Wales & England flowing from [E] central Wales into Bristol channel

Se·ville \sə-'vil\ or Spanish **Se·vi·lla** \sā-'vē-(y)ä\ city [SW] Spain

Sey·chelles \sā-'shel(z)\ islands [W] Indian ocean [NE] of Madagascar; formerly a British colony; became independent 1976; capital, Victoria

Shang·hai \shaŋ-'hī\ city [E] China

Shan·non \'shan-ən\ river 386 kilometers long [W] Ireland flowing [S] & [W] into the Atlantic

Shas·ta, Mount \-'shas-tə\ mountain 4317 meters [N] California in Cascade Range

Shatt–al–Ar·ab \ˌshat-ˌal-'ar-əb\ river 193 kilometers long [SE] Iraq formed by flowing together of Euphrates & Tigris rivers & flowing [SE] into Persian gulf

Shef·field \'shef-ˌēld\ city [N] England in South Yorkshire

Shen·an·do·ah Valley \ˌshen-ən-'dō-ə, ˌshan-ə-'dō-ə-\ valley Virginia between the Allegheny & Blue Ridge mountains

Shen·yang \'shən-'yäŋ\ or **Muk·den** \'mủk-dən, 'mək-; mủk-'den\ city [NE] China; chief city of Manchuria

Sher·brooke \'shər-ˌbrủk\ city Quebec, Canada [E] of Montreal

Sher·wood Forest \ˌshər-ˌwủd-\ ancient royal forest central England chiefly in Nottinghamshire

Shet·land \'shet-lənd\ 1 islands [N] Scotland [NE] of the Orkneys 2 or **Zet·land** \'zet-\ region consisting of the Shetland islands

Shi·jia·zhuang or **Shih·kia·chwang** \'shi(ə)r-jē-'äj-'wän, 'shē-jē-\ city [NE] China

Shi·ko·ku \shi-'kō-kü\ island [S] Japan [E] of Kyushu

Shreve·port \'shrēv-ˌpō(ə)rt, -ˌpȯ(ə)rt\ city [NW] Louisiana

Shrews·bury \'sh(r)üz-,ber-ē, 'shrōz-\ city area ⓦ England in Salop county

Shropshire — see SALOP

Siam — see THAILAND

Siam, Gulf of or **Gulf of Thailand** arm of South China sea between Indochina and Malay peninsula

Sian — see XI'AN

Si·be·ria \sī-'bir-ē-ə\ region Ⓝ Asia in Russia between the Urals & the Pacific — **Si·be·ri·an** \-ē-ən\ adj or n

Sic·i·ly \'sis-(ə-)lē\ or Italian **Si·ci·lia** \sē-'chēl-yä\ island Ⓢ Italy ⓈⓌ of toe of Italian peninsula; capital, Palermo — **Si·cil·ian** \sə-'sil-yən\ adj or n

Si·er·ra Le·one \sē-,er-ə-lē-'ōn, ,sir-ə-\ country ⓦ Africa on the Atlantic; capital, Freetown — **Si·er·ra Le·on·ean** \-'ō-nē-ən\ adj or n

Si·er·ra Ma·dre \sē-,er-ə-'mäd-rē\ mountain system Mexico including **Sierra Madre Oc·ci·den·tal** \-,äk-sə-,den-'täl\ range ⓦ of the central plateau, **Sierra Madre Ori·en·tal** \-,ōr-ē-,en-'täl, -,ór-\ range Ⓔ of the plateau, & **Sierra del Sur** \sē-,er-ə-,del-'sù(ə)r\ range to the Ⓢ

Sierra Ne·va·da \-nə-'vad-ə, -'väd-\ **1** mountain range Ⓔ California & ⓦ Nevada — see WHITNEY, MOUNT **2** mountain range Ⓢ Spain; highest peak Mulhacén 3477 meters, highest in Spain

Sik·kim \'sik-əm, -,im\ former country ⓈⒺ Asia on Ⓢ slope of the Himalayas between Nepal & Bhutan; part of India (country) since 1975; capital, Gangtok

Si·le·sia \sī-'lē-zh(ē-)ə, -sh(ē-)ə, sə-\ region Ⓔ central Europe in valley of the upper Oder; formerly chiefly in Germany now chiefly in Ⓔ Czech Republic & ⓈⓌ Poland — **Si·le·sian** \-zh(ē-)ən, -sh(ē-)ən\ adj or n

Sim·coe, Lake \-'sim-kō\ lake Canada in ⓈⒺ Ontario

Si·nai \'sī-,nī\ **1** mountain on Sinai peninsula where according to the Bible the Law was given to Moses **2** peninsula extension of continent of Asia ⓃⒺ Egypt between Red sea & the Mediterranean

Sin·ga·pore \'siŋ-(g)ə-,pō(ə)r, -,pò(ə)r\ **1** island off Ⓢ end of Malay peninsula; an independent country in the Commonwealth **2** city, its capital — **Sin·ga·por·ean** \,siŋ-(g)ə-'pōr-ē-ən, -'pór-\ adj or n

Sinkiang Uighur — see XINJIANG UYGUR

Sioux Falls \'sü-\ city ⓈⒺ South Dakota; largest in state

Skag·ge·rak \'skag-ə-,rak\ arm of North sea between Ⓢ Norway & Ⓝ Denmark

Skag·way \'skag-wā\ city ⓈⒺ Alaska

Sla·vo·nia \slə-'vō-nē-ə, -nyə\ region Ⓔ Croatia — **Sla·vo·ni·an** \-nē-ən, -nyən\ adj or n

Slo·va·kia \slō-'väk-ē-ə, -'vak-\ country central Europe; capital, Bratislava; formerly part of Czechoslovakia

Slo·ve·nia \slō-'vē-nē-ə, -nyə\ country Ⓢ Europe; capital, Ljubljana; a republic of Yugoslavia 1946–91

Smyrna — see IZMIR

Snake \'snāk\ river ⓃⓌ U.S. flowing from ⓃⓌ Wyoming into the Columbia in ⓈⒺ Washington

Snow·don \'snōd-ᵊn\ massif 1085 meters ⓃⓌ Wales; highest point in Wales

Snow·do·nia \snō-'dō-nē-ə, -nyə\ mountainous district ⓃⓌ Wales in area around Snowdon

So·ci·e·ty \sə-'sī-ət-ē\ islands Ⓢ Pacific; belong to France; chief island, Tahiti

So·fia \'sō-fē-ə, 'sò-, sō-'fē-\ city, capital of Bulgaria

So·ho \'sō-,hō\ district of central London, England, in Westminster

So·li·hull \,sō-li-'həl\ city area central England in West Midlands county

Sol·o·mon \'säl-ə-mən\ **1** islands ⓦ Pacific Ⓔ of New Guinea divided between Papua New Guinea & independent Solomon Islands (capital, Honiara) **2** sea arm of Coral sea ⓦ of the Solomons

So·ma·lia \sō-'mäl-ē-ə, sə-, -'mäl-yə\ country Ⓔ Africa on Gulf of Aden & Indian ocean; capital, Mogadishu — **So·ma·li·an** \-'mäl-ē-ən, -'mäl-yən\ adj or n

So·ma·li·land \sō-'mäl-ē-,land, sə-\ region Ⓔ Africa consisting of Somalia, Djibouti, & part of Ⓔ Ethiopia — **So·ma·li** \sō-'mäl-ē\ n

Som·er·set \'səm-ər-,set, -sət\ or **Som·er·set·shire** \-,shi(ə)r, -shər\ county ⓈⓌ England

So·nor·an \sə-'nōr-ən, -'nòr-\ or **Sonora** desert ⓈⓌ U.S. & Ⓝ Ⓦ Mexico

Soo canals — see SAULT SAINTE MARIE CANALS

South island Ⓢ New Zealand

South Africa, Republic of country Ⓢ Africa; formerly (as **Union of South Africa**) a British dominion; became independent 1961; administrative capital, Pretoria; legislative capital, Cape Town; judicial capital, Bloemfontein — **South African** adj or n

South America continent of western hemisphere ⓈⒺ of North America & chiefly Ⓢ of the equator — **South American** adj or n

South·amp·ton \saúth-'(h)am(p)-tən\ city Ⓢ England in Hampshire

South Australia state Ⓢ Australia; capital, Adelaide — **South Australian** adj or n

South Bend \-'bend\ city Ⓝ Indiana

South Cape or **South Point** — see KA LAE

South Car·o·li·na \-,kar-ə-'lī-nə\ state ⓈⒺ U.S.; capital, Columbia — **South Car·o·lin·i·an** \-'lin-ē-ən, -'lin-yən\ adj or n

South China sea — see CHINA

South Da·ko·ta \-də-'kōt-ə\ state ⓃⓌ central U.S.; capital, Pierre — **South Da·ko·tan** \-'kōt-ᵊn\ adj or n

South·end on Sea \,saú-,thend-\ city area ⓈⒺ England in Essex county Ⓔ of London

Southern Alps mountain range New Zealand in ⓦ South island extending almost the length of the island

Southern Rhodesia — see ZIMBABWE

South Gla·mor·gan \-glə-'mòr-gən\ county ⓈⒺ Wales; established 1974; includes Cardiff

South Korea — see KOREA

South seas the areas of the Atlantic, Indian, & Pacific oceans in the southern hemisphere

South Shields \-'shē(ə)l(d)z\ city Ⓝ England in Tyne and Wear county

South Vietnam — see VIETNAM

South·wark \'səth-ərk, 'saúth-wərk\ city area of Ⓢ Greater London county, England

South–West Africa territory ⓈⓌ Africa; under administration of Union (later Republic) of South Africa 1919–90 — see NAMIBIA

South Yorkshire county Ⓝ England; includes Barnsley

Soviet Central Asia portion of central & ⓈⓌ Asia formerly belonging to U.S.S.R. & including Kirghiz Soviet Socialist Republic, Tadzhik Soviet Socialist Republic, Turkmen Soviet Socialist Republic, Uzbek Soviet Socialist Republic & sometimes Kazakhstan

Soviet Russia **1** — see RUSSIA **2** — see UNION OF SOVIET SOCIALIST REPUBLICS

Soviet Union — see UNION OF SOVIET SOCIALIST REPUBLICS

Spain \'spān\ country ⓈⓌ Europe in Iberian peninsula; a kingdom; capital, Madrid

Spanish America **1** the Spanish-speaking countries of America **2** the parts of America settled & formerly governed by the Spanish

Spanish Guinea — see EQUATORIAL GUINEA

Spanish Sahara — see WESTERN SAHARA

Spar·ta \'spärt-ə\ or **Lac·e·dae·mon** \,las-ə-'dē-mən\ ancient city Ⓢ Greece in Peloponnisos; capital of Laconia

Spo·kane \spō-'kan\ city Ⓔ Washington

\ə\ abut	\aú\ out	\i\ tip	\ó\ saw	\ù\ foot
\ər\ further	\ch\ chin	\ī\ life	\ói\ coin	\y\ yet
\a\ mat	\e\ pet	\j\ job	\th\ thin	\yü\ few
\ā\ take	\ē\ easy	\ŋ\ sing	\th\ this	\yù\ cure
\ä\ cot, cart	\g\ go	\ō\ bone	\ü\ food	\zh\ vision

Spring·field \'sprin̄-ˌfēld\ **1** city, capital of Illinois **2** city SW Massachusetts **3** city SW Missouri

Sri Lan·ka \(')srē-'län̄-kə, (')shrē-\ *or formerly* **Cey·lon** \si-'län, sā-\ country having the same boundaries as island of Ceylon; an independent state in the Commonwealth; capital, Colombo

Sri·na·gar \sri-'nəg-ər\ city N India

Staked Plain — see LLANO ESTACADO

Staf·ford \'staf-ərd\ city area W central England in Staffordshire

Staf·ford·shire \'staf-ərd-ˌshi(ə)r, -shər\ *or* **Stafford** county W central England

Stam·ford \'stam(p)-fərd\ city SW Connecticut

Stan·ley \'stan-lē\ town, capital of Falkland islands

Stat·en Island \'stat-ᵊn-\ **1** island SE New York SW of mouth of the Hudson **2** *or formerly* **Rich·mond** \'rich-mənd\ section of New York City including Staten Island

Sterling Heights city SE Michigan

Stir·ling \'stər-lin̄\ town central Scotland in Central region

Stock·holm \'stäk-ˌhō(l)m\ city, capital of Sweden

Stock·port \'stäk-ˌpō(ə)rt, -ˌpò(ə)rt\ city area NW England in Greater Manchester county

Stock·ton \'stäk-tən\ city central California

Stoke on Trent \ˌstō-ˌkòn-'trent, -ˌkän-\ city central England in Staffordshire

Stone Mountain mountain 514 meters NW Georgia E of Atlanta

Stor·no·way \'stòr-nə-ˌwā\ town NW Scotland in Western Isles region

Stra·bane \strə-'ban\ district W Northern Ireland

Strath·clyde \strath-'klīd\ region SW Scotland; established 1975; includes Glasgow

Strom·bo·li \'sträm-bə-lē\ volcano 927 meters Italy on Stromboli Island

Stutt·gart \'shtút-ˌgärt, 'stút-, 'stət-\ city SW Germany

Styx \'stiks\ chief river of the underworld in Greek mythology

Süchow — see XUZHOU

Su·cre \'sü-krā\ city, constitutional capital of Bolivia

Su·dan \sü-'dan, -'dän\ **1** region N Africa S of the Sahara between the Atlantic & the upper Nile **2** country NE Africa S of Egypt; capital, Khartoum — **Su·da·nese** \ˌsüd-ᵊn-'ēz, -'ēs\ *adj or n*

Sud·bury \'səd-ˌber-ē, -b(ə-)rē\ city SE Ontario, Canada

Su·ez \sü-'ez, 'sü-ˌez\ canal 148 kilometers long NE Egypt across Isthmus of Suez

Suez, Gulf of arm of Red sea

Suez, Isthmus of isthmus NE Egypt between Mediterranean & Red seas connecting Africa & Asia

Suf·folk \'səf-ək\ county E England on North sea

Sui·sun Bay \sə-'sün-\ inlet of San Francisco Bay, W central California

Su·la·we·si \ˌsü-lə-'wä-sē\ *or* **Ce·le·bes** \'sel-ə-ˌbēz, sə-'lē-bēz\ island Indonesia E of Borneo

Su·lu \'sü-lü\ **1** island group SW Philippines SW of Mindanao **2** sea W Philippines

Su·ma·tra \sù-'mä-trə\ island W Indonesia S of Malay peninsula — **Su·ma·tran** \-trən\ *adj or n*

Su·mer \'sü-mər\ the S division of ancient Babylonia — **Su·me·ri·an** \sü-'mer-ē-ən, -'mir-\ *adj or n*

Sun·da \'sün-də\ strait between Java & Sumatra

Sun·der·land \'sən-dər-lənd\ city area N England in Tyne and Wear county

Sun·ny·vale \'sən-ē-ˌvāl\ city W California

Sun Valley resort center central Idaho

Su·pe·ri·or, Lake \-sù-'pir-ē-ər\ lake E central North America in U.S. & Canada; largest of the Great Lakes

Su·ra·ba·ja \ˌsùr-ə-'bī-ə\ city Indonesia in NE Java

Su·ri·na·me \ˌsùr-ə-'näm-ə\ *or* **Su·ri·nam** \'sùr-ə-ˌnam, ˌsùr-ə-'näm\ country N South America between Guyana & French Guiana; formerly a territory of the Netherlands; became independent 1975; capital, Paramaribo

Sur·rey \'sər-ē, 'sə-rē\ **1** county SE England SW of London **2** city Canada in SW British Columbia

Sut·ton \'sət-ᵊn\ city area of S Greater London county, England

Su·va \'sü-və\ city, capital of Fiji on Viti Levu island

Sverdlovsk — see YEKATERINBURG

Swan·sea \'swän-zē\ city SE Wales in West Glamorgan county

Swa·zi·land \'swäz-ē-ˌland\ country SE Africa between Transvaal & Mozambique; an independent kingdom; capital, Mbabane — **Swa·zi** \'swäz-ē\ *adj or n*

Swe·den \'swēd-ᵊn\ country N Europe on Scandinavian peninsula bordering on Baltic sea; a kingdom; capital, Stockholm

Swit·zer·land \'swit-sər-lənd\ country W Europe in the Alps; capital, Bern

Syd·ney \'sid-nē\ city SE Australia, capital of New South Wales

Syr·a·cuse \'sir-ə-ˌkyüs, -kyüz\ city central New York

Syr·ia \'sir-ē-ə\ **1** ancient region SW Asia bordering on the Mediterranean **2** former area under administration of France (1920–44) including present Syria & Lebanon **3** country S of Turkey; capital, Damascus — **Syr·i·an** \'sir-ē-ən\ *adj or n*

Syrian Desert desert region between Mediterranean coast & the Euphrates in N Saudi Arabia, SE Syria, W Iraq, & NE Jordan

Ta·ble Bay harbor of Cape Town, Republic of South Africa

Ta·briz \tə-'brēz\ city NW Iran

Ta·co·ma \tə-'kō-mə\ city W Washington

Tae·gu \ta-'gü, tī-\ city South Korea NNW of Pusan

Tae·jon \ta-'jòn, tī-\ city South Korea NW of Taegu

Ta·gus \'tā-gəs\ *or Spanish* **Ta·jo** \'tä-hō\ *or Portuguese* **Te·jo** \'tā-zhü\ river 911 kilometers long Spain & Portugal flowing W into the Atlantic

Ta·hi·ti \tə-'hēt-ē\ island S Pacific in Society islands — **Ta·hi·tian** \-'hē-shən\ *adj or n*

Tai·chung \'tī-'chùn̄\ city China in W Taiwan

Tai·nan \'tī-'nän\ city China in SW Taiwan

Tai·pei \'tī-'pā, -'bā\ *or formerly* **Tai·ho·ku** \'tī-'hō-ˌkü\ city, capital of (Nationalist) China in N Taiwan

Tai·wan \'tī-'wän\ *or* **For·mo·sa** \fòr-'mō-sə, fər-, -zə\ **1** island China off SE coast; since 1949 seat of government of (Nationalist) Republic of China; capital, Taipei **2** strait between Taiwan & main part of China connecting East China & South China seas — **Tai·wan·ese** \ˌtī-wə-'nēz, -'nēs\ *adj or n*

Tai·yuan \'tī-yù-'än\ city N China

Ta·jik·i·stan \tä-ˌjik-i-'stan, -'stän, -ˌjik-i-ˌ, -'jēk-\ country W central Asia bordering on China & Afghanistan; capital, Dushanbe; a republic (**Ta·dzhik Soviet Socialist Republic** \tä-'jik-, -'jēk-\ *or* **Ta·dzhik·i·stan** *same as* TAJIKISTAN\) of U.S.S.R. 1929–91

Ta·kli·ma·kan *or* **Ta·kla Ma·kan** \ˌtäk-lə-mə-'kän\ desert W China

Tal·la·has·see \ˌtal-ə-'has-ē\ city, capital of Florida

Tal·linn \'tal-ən, 'täl-\ city, capital of Estonia

Tam·pa \'tam-pə\ city W Florida on Tampa Bay

Tan·gan·yi·ka \ˌtan-gən-'yē-kə, ˌtan̄-gən-, -gə-'nē-\ former country E Africa S of Kenya; became part of Tanzania 1964

Tanganyika, Lake lake E Africa between Tanzania & Zaire

Tang·shan \'dän̄-'shän, 'tän̄-\ city NE China

Tan·za·nia \ˌtan-zə-'nē-ə, ˌtan̄-\ country E Africa on Indian ocean; formed 1964 by union of Tanganyika & Zanzibar; capital, Dar es Salaam — **Tan·za·ni·an** \-'nē-ən\ *adj or n*

Ta·ra·wa \tə-'rä-wə, 'tar-ə-ˌwä\ island central Pacific, capital of Kiribati

Tar·lac \'tär-ˌläk\ city Philippines in central Luzon

Tar·ry·town \'tar-ē-ˌtaún\ village SE New York

Tar·sus \'tär-səs\ ancient city of S Asia Minor; now a city in ⑤ Turkey

Tash·kent \tash-'kent\ city, capital of Uzbekistan

Tas·man \'taz-mən\ sea consisting of the part of the ⑤ Pacific between ⑤Ⓔ Australia & New Zealand

Tas·ma·nia \taz-'mā-nē-ə, -nyə\ *or earlier* **Van Die·men's Land** \van-'dē-mənz-\ island ⑤Ⓔ Australia ⑤ of Victoria; a state; capital, Hobart — **Tas·ma·nian** \-nē-ən, -nyən\ *adj or n*

Ta·try \'tä-trē\ *or* **Ta·tra** \'tä-trə\ mountains Ⓝ Slovakia & ⑤ Poland in central Carpathian mountains

Taun·ton \'tȯnt-ᵊn, 'tänt-, 'tant-\ city area ⑤Ⓦ England in Somerset county

Tay·side \'tā-,sīd\ region Ⓔ central Scotland; established 1975

Tbi·li·si \tə-'bil-ə-sē\ *or* **Tif·lis** \'tif-ləs, tə-'flēs\ city, capital of Republic of Georgia

Te·gu·ci·gal·pa \tə-,gü-sə-'gal-pə\ city, capital of Honduras

Teh·ran \,tā-'ran, -'rän\ city, capital of Iran; at foot of ⑤ slope of Elburz mountains

Tel Aviv \,tel-ə-'vēv\ city Ⓦ Israel

Tem·pe \tem-'pē\ city ⑤ central Arizona

Ten·nes·see \,ten-ə-'sē, 'ten-ə-,sē\ **1** river 1049 kilometers long in Tennessee, Ⓝ Alabama, & Ⓦ Kentucky **2** state Ⓔ central U.S.; capital, Nashville

Te·noch·ti·tlan \tä-,nȯch-tē-'tlän\ ancient name of Mexico City

Tex·as \'tek-səs, -siz\ state ⑤ U.S.; capital, Austin — **Tex·an** \-sən\ *adj or n*

Thai·land \'tī-,land, -lənd\ *or formerly* **Si·am** \sī-'am\ country ⑤Ⓔ Asia on Gulf of Siam; capital, Bangkok — **Thai·land·er** \'tī-,lan-dər, -lən-dər\ *n*

Thames \'temz\ river 338 kilometers long ⑤ England flowing Ⓔ from the Cotswolds in Gloucestershire into the North sea

Thar \'tär\ desert Ⓔ Pakistan & ⓃⓌ India (country) Ⓔ of Indus river

Thebes \'thēbz\ **1** *or ancient* **The·bae** \'thē-bē\ ancient city ⑤ Egypt on the Nile **2** ancient city Ⓔ Greece ⓃⓃⓌ of Athens on site of modern village of Thivai — **The·ban** \'thē-bən\ *adj or n*

Thes·sa·lo·ni·ca \,thes-ə-lə-'nī-kə, -'län-i-kə\ — see SALONIKA — **Thes·sa·lo·nian** \-'lō-nē-ən, -'lō-nyən\ *adj or n*

Thim·bu \'thim-bü\ city, capital of Bhutan

Thousand islands Canada & U.S. in the Saint Lawrence in Ontario & New York

Thrace \'thrās\ *or ancient* **Thra·cia** \'thrā-sh(ē-)ə\ region ⑤Ⓔ Europe in Balkan peninsula Ⓝ of the Aegean now divided between Greece & Turkey; in ancient times extended Ⓝ to the Danube — **Thra·cian** \'thrā-shən\ *adj or n*

Three Rivers *or* **Trois-Ri·vieres** \,t(r)wä-riv-'ye(ə)r\ city ⑤ Quebec, Canada

Thunder Bay city ⑤Ⓦ Ontario, Canada

Thur·rock \'thər-ək, 'thə-rək\ district ⑤Ⓔ England in Essex county

Tian·jin \tē-'än-'jin\ *or* **Tien·tsin** \tē-'en(t)-'sin\ city Ⓝ Ⓔ China ⑤Ⓔ of Beijing

Tian Shan *or* **Tien Shen** \tē-'en-'shän, tē-'än-\ mountain system central Asia extending Ⓝⓔ from Pamirs

Ti·ber \'tī-bər\ *or Italian* **Te·ve·re** \'tā-vā-rā\ *or ancient* **Ti·ber·is** \'tī-bə-rəs\ river 360 kilometers long central Italy flowing through Rome into Tyrrhenian sea

Ti·bes·ti \tə-'bes-tē\ mountains Ⓝ central Africa in central Sahara in ⓃⓌ Chad; highest 3415 meters

Ti·bet \tə-'bet\ region ⑤Ⓦ China on high plateau (average altitude 4875 meters) Ⓝ of the Himalayas; capital, Lhasa

Tier·ra del Fue·go \tē-'er-ə-,del-f(y)ü-'ā-gō\ **1** island group off ⑤ South America **2** chief island of the group; divided between Argentina & Chile

Tiflis — see TBILISI

Ti·gris \'tī-grəs\ river 1850 kilometers long Turkey & Iraq flowing ⑤⑤Ⓔ & uniting with the Euphrates to form the Shatt-al-Arab

Ti·mor \'tē-,mȯ(ə)r, tē-'mȯ(ə)r\ island Indonesia ⑤Ⓔ of Sulawesi; Ⓦ half formerly belonged to Netherlands, Ⓔ half to Portugal

Ti·ra·ne *or* **Ti·ra·na** \ti-'rän-ə\ city, capital of Albania

Ti·rol *or* **Ty·rol** \tə-'rōl; 'tī-,rōl, tī-'rōl; 'tir-əl\ *or Italian* **Ti·ro·lo** \tē-'rȯ-lō\ region in Ⓔ Alps in Ⓦ Austria & Ⓝ Ⓔ Italy — **Ti·ro·le·an** \tə-'rō-lē-ən, tī-; ,tir-ə-'lē-, ,tī-rə-'lē-\ *or* **Tir·o·lese** \,tir-ə-'lēz, ,tī-rə-, -'lēs\ *adj or n*

Ti·ti·ca·ca, Lake \-,tit-i-'käk-ə\ lake on Bolivia-Peru boundary at altitude of 3810 meters

To·ba·go \tə-'bā-gō\ island West Indies Ⓝⓔ of Trinidad; part of independent Trinidad and Tobago

To·go \'tō-gō\ country Ⓦ Africa on Gulf of Guinea; capital, Lomé — **To·go·lese** \,tō-gə-'lēz, -'lēs\ *adj or n*

To·kyo \'tō-kē-,ō\ city, capital of Japan in ⑤Ⓔ Honshu on Tokyo Bay — **To·kyo·ite** \'tō-kē-,(,)ō-,īt\ *n*

To·le·do \tə-'lēd-ō, -'lēd-ə\ city ⓃⓌ Ohio

Tol'·yat·ti \tȯl-'yät-ē\ city Ⓦ Russia; ⓃⓌ of Samara

Ton·ga \'täŋ-(g)ə\ islands ⑤Ⓦ Pacific Ⓔ of Fiji islands; a kingdom in the Commonwealth; capital, Nukualofa — **Ton·gan** \-(g)ən\ *adj or n*

To·pe·ka \tə-'pē-kə\ city, capital of Kansas

Tor·bay \(')tȯr-'bā\ town ⑤Ⓦ England in Devon county

To·ron·to \tə-'ränt-ō, -'ränt-ə\ city, capital of Ontario, Canada

Tor·rance \'tȯr-ən(t)s, 'tär-\ city ⑤Ⓦ California

Tor·res \'tȯr-əs\ strait between New Guinea & Cape York peninsula, Australia

Tower Hamlets city area of Ⓔ Greater London county, England

To·yo·na·ka \,tȯi-ə-'näk-ə\ city Japan on Honshu; a suburb of Osaka

Trans·vaal \tran(t)s-'väl, tranz-\ province Ⓝⓔ Republic of South Africa; capital, Pretoria

Tran·syl·va·nia \,tran(t)s-əl-'vā-nyə, -nē-ə\ region Ⓦ Romania — **Tran·syl·va·nian** \-nyən, -nē-ən\ *adj or n*

Transylvanian Alps a ⑤ extension of Carpathian mountains in central Romania

Tren·ton \'trent-ᵊn\ city, capital of New Jersey

Trin·i·dad \'trin-ə-,dad\ island West Indies off Ⓝⓔ coast of Venezuela; with Tobago forms (since 1962) the independent country of **Trinidad and Tobago;** capital, Port of Spain — **Trin·i·da·di·an** \,trin-ə-'däd-ē-ən, -'dad-\ *adj or n*

Trip·o·li \'trip-ə-lē\ city, capital of Libya

Tris·tan da Cu·nha \,tris-tən-də-'kü-nə, -nyə\ island ⑤ Atlantic, chief of the Tristan da Cunha islands belonging to British colony of Saint Helena

Tri·van·drum \triv-'an-drəm\ city ⑤ India

Tro·bri·and \'trō-brē-,änd\ islands ⑤Ⓦ Pacific in Solomon sea belonging to Papua New Guinea

Trois-Rivieres — see THREE RIVERS

Trow·bridge \'trō-(,)brij\ town ⑤ England in Wiltshire

Troy \'trȯi\ *or* **Il·i·um** \'il-ē-əm\ *or* **Il·i·on** \'il-ē-,än, -ē-ən\ *or ancient* **Troia** \'trȯi-ə, 'trō-yə\ *or* **Tro·ja** \'trō-jə, -yə\ ancient city ⓃⓌ Asia Minor ⑤Ⓦ of the Dardanelles

Truk \'trək, 'trůk\ islands Ⓦ Pacific in central Carolines

Tru·ro \'trů(ə)r-ō\ city ⑤Ⓦ England in Cornwall and Isles of Scilly county

Trust Territory of the Pacific Islands — see PACIFIC ISLANDS, TRUST TERRITORY OF THE

Tsinan — see JINAN

Tsingtao — see QINGDAO

\ə\ **abut**	\aů\ **out**	\i\ **tip**	\ȯ\ **saw**	\ů\ **foot**
\ər\ **further**	\ch\ **chin**	\ī\ **life**	\ȯi\ **coin**	\y\ **yet**
\a\ **mat**	\e\ **pet**	\j\ **job**	\th\ **thin**	\yü\ **few**
\ā\ **take**	\ē\ **easy**	\ŋ\ **sing**	\th\ **this**	\yů\ **cure**
\ä\ **cot, cart**	\g\ **go**	\ō\ **bone**	\ü\ **food**	\zh\ **vision**

Tuc·son \tü-'sän, 'tü-ˌsän\ city [SE] Arizona

Tu·la \'tü-lə\ city [W] Russia [S] of Moscow

Tul·sa \'təl-sə\ city [NE] Oklahoma

Tu·nis \'t(y)ü-nəs\ city, capital of Tunisia

Tu·ni·sia \t(y)ü-'nē-zh(ē-)ə, -'nizh-(ē-)ə\ country [N] Africa on the Mediterranean [E] of Algeria; capital, Tunis — **Tu·ni·sian** \-'nē-zh(ē-)ən, -'nizh-(ē-)ən\ *adj or n*

Tu·rin \'t(y)ür-ən, t(y)ü-'rin\ city [NW] Italy on the Po

Tur·key \'tər-kē\ country [W] Asia & [SE] Europe between Mediterranean & Black seas; capital, Ankara

Turk·men·i·stan \(ˌ)tərk-ˌmen-ə-'stan, -'stän; -'men-ə-ˌ\ country central Asia; capital, Ashkhabad; a republic (**Turkmen Soviet Socialist Republic** \'tərk-mən-\) of U.S.S.R. 1925–91 — **Turk·me·ni·an** \ˌtərk-'mē-nē-ən\ *adj*

Turks and Cai·cos \ˌtərk-sən-'kā-kəs\ two groups of islands West Indies at [SE] end of the Bahamas; a British colony

Tu·tu·ila \ˌtüt-ə-'wē-lə\ island [S] Pacific, chief of American Samoa group

Tu·va·lu \tü-'väl-ü, -'vär-\ *or formerly* **El·lice** \'el-əs\ islands [W] Pacific [N] of Fiji; an independent country in the Commonwealth; capital, Funafuti — see GILBERT AND ELLICE ISLANDS

Tyne and Wear \'tī-nən-'(d)wi(ə)r\ county [N] England; includes Newcastle

Tyre \'tī(ə)r\ ancient city, capital of Phoenicia; now a town of [S] Lebanon — **Tyr·i·an** \'tir-ē-ən\ *adj or n*

Tyrol — see TIROL — **Tyrolean** *adj or n* — **Tyrolese** *adj or n*

Tyr·rhe·ni·an \tə-'rē-nē-ən\ sea, part of the Mediterranean [SW] of Italy, [N] of Sicily, & [E] of Sardinia & Corsica

Ufa \ü-'fä\ city [W] Russia [NE] of Samara

Ugan·da \yü-'gan-də, -'gän-, -'gän-\ country [E] Africa [N] of Lake Victoria; an independent state in the Commonwealth; capital, Kampala — **Ugan·dan** \-dən\ *adj or n*

Ukraine \yü-'krān, 'yü-ˌkrān\ *or* **the Ukraine** country [E] Europe on [N] coast of Black sea; capital, Kiez; a republic of U.S.S.R. 1923–91

Ulan Ba·tor \ˌü-ˌlän-'bä-ˌtò(ə)r\ city, capital of Mongolia

Ul·ster \'əl-stər\ **1** region [N] Ireland (island) consisting of Northern Ireland & [N] Ireland (country) **2** province [N] Ireland (country) **3** NORTHERN IRELAND

Um·bria \'əm-brē-ə\ region central Italy in the Apennines

Un·ga·va \ˌən-'gav-ə\ **1** bay inlet of Hudson strait [NE] Canada **2** peninsula region [NE] Canada in [S] Quebec

Union of South Africa — see SOUTH AFRICA, REPUBLIC OF

Union of Soviet Socialist Republics *or* **Soviet Union** *or* **Soviet Russia** country 1922–91 [E] Europe & [N] Asia; a union of 15 now independent republics; capital, Moscow

United Arab Emir·ates \-i-'mi(ə)r-əts, -ˌāts\ country [E] Arabia on Persian Gulf; composed of seven emirates; capital, Abu Dhabi

United Kingdom *or in full* **United Kingdom of Great Britain and Northern Ireland** country [W] Europe in British Isles consisting of England, Scotland, Wales, Northern Ireland, Channel islands, & Isle of Man; capital, London

United Nations international territory; a small area in New York City in [E] central Manhattan; seat of permanent headquarters of the United Nations

United States of America *or* **United States** country North America bordering on Atlantic, Pacific, & Arctic oceans & including Hawaii; capital, Washington

Upper Volta — see BURKINA FASO — **Upper Vol·tan** \-'vält-ᵊn, -'vòlt-, -'vòlt-\ *adj or n*

Ural \'yùr-əl\ **1** mountains Russia & Kazakhstan extending about 2575 kilometers; usually thought of as dividing line between Europe & Asia; highest about 1830 meters **2** river 2255 kilometers long Russia & Kazakhstan flowing from [S] end of Ural mountains into Caspian sea

Uru·guay \'(y)ùr-ə-ˌgwī, 'yùr-ə-ˌgwä\ **1** river 1577 kilometers long [SE] South America **2** country [SE] South America; capital, Montevideo — **Uru·guay·an** \ˌ(y)ùr-ə-

'gwī-ən, ˌyùr-ə-'gwä-\ *adj or n*

Ürüm·qi \'üē-'rüem-'chē\ *or* **Urum·chi** \ù-'rùm-chē, ˌùr-əm-'chē\ city [NW] China

Us·pa·lla·ta \ˌü-spə-'yät-ə, -'zhät-\ mountain pass 3840 meters [S] South America in the Andes between Argentina & Chile

Ustinov — see IZHEVSK

Utah \'yü-ˌtò, -ˌtä\ state [W] U.S.; capital, Salt Lake City — **Utah·an** \-ˌtò(-ə)n, -ˌtä(-ə)n\ *adj or n* — **Utahn** \-ˌtò(-ə)n, -ˌtä(-ə)n\ *n*

Uz·bek·i·stan \(ˌ)úz-ˌbek-i-'stan, -'stän; -'bek-i-ˌ\ country [W] central Asia between Aral sea & Afghanistan; capital, Tashkent; a republic (**Uz·bek Soviet Socialist Republic**) \'úz-ˌbek, 'əz-; úz-'\ of U.S.S.R 1924–91

Va·duz \vä-'düts\ town, capital of Liechtenstein

Val·dez \val-'dēz\ town and port [S] Alaska

Va·len·cia \və-'len-ch(ē-)ə, -'len(t)-sē-ə\ **1** region & ancient kingdom [E] Spain **2** city, its capital, on the Mediterranean

Valley Forge locality [SE] Pennsylvania

Val·let·ta \və-'let-ə\ city, capital of Malta

Van·cou·ver \van-'kü-vər\ **1** island [W] Canada in [SW] British Columbia **2** city [SW] British Columbia, Canada

Van Diemen's Land — see TASMANIA

Van·u·atu \ˌvan-ˌwä-'tü, ˌvän-, -'wä-ˌtü\ *or formerly* **New Heb·ri·des** \-'heb-rə-ˌdēz\ islands [SW] Pacific [W] of Fiji; formerly under shared British and French administration; became independent 1980; capital, Vila

Varanasi — see BANARAS

Vat·i·can City \ˌvat-i-kən-\ independent state within Rome, Italy; created 1929 as headquarters for the Pope

Ven·e·zu·e·la \ˌven-əz(-ə)-'wä-lə, -'wē-\ country [N] South America; capital, Caracas — **Ven·e·zu·e·lan** \-lən\ *adj or n*

Ven·ice \'ven-əs\ *or Italian* **Ve·ne·zia** \və-'net-sē-ə\ city [N] Italy on islands in Lagoon of Venice

Ve·ra·cruz \ˌver-ə-'krüz, -'krüs\ city [E] Mexico

Ver·mont \vər-'mänt\ state [NE] U.S.; capital, Montpelier — **Ver·mont·er** \-ər\ *n*

Ve·ro·na \və-'rō-nə\ city [N] Italy [W] of Venice

Ve·su·vi·us \və-'sü-vē-əs\ volcano about 1220 meters [S] Italy near Bay of Naples

Vicks·burg \'viks-ˌbərg\ city [W] Mississippi

Vic·to·ria \vik-'tōr-ē-ə, -'tòr-\ **1** city, capital of British Columbia, Canada on Vancouver island **2** island [N] Canada in Arctic island group **3** state [SE] Australia; capital, Melbourne **4** city, capital of Hong Kong **5** seaport, capital of Seychelles — **Vic·to·ri·an** \-ē-ən\ *adj or n*

Victoria, Lake lake [E] Africa in Tanzania, Kenya, & Uganda

Vi·en·na \vē-'en-ə\ *or ancient* **Vin·dob·o·na** \vin-'däb-ə-nə\ *or* **Vin·do·na** \-'däb-nə\ city, capital of Austria on the Danube — **Vi·en·nese** \ˌvē-ə-'nēz, -'nēs\ *adj or n*

Vien·tiane \(')vyen-'tyän\ city, capital of Laos

Viet·nam \vē-'et-'näm, vyet-, ˌvē-ət-, -'nam\ country [SE] Asia in Indochina; capital, Hanoi; established 1945–46 & divided 1954–75 at 17th parallel into the independent states of **North Vietnam** (capital, Hanoi) & **South Vietnam** (capital, Saigon)

Vi·la \'vē-lə\ city, capital of Vanuatu

Vil·ni·us \'vil-nē-əs\ *or Russian* **Vil·na** \'vil-nə\ *or* **Vil·no** \-nō\ city, capital of Lithuania

Vin·land \'vin-lənd\ a portion of the coast of North America visited and so called by Norse voyagers about 1000 A.D.; perhaps Newfoundland

Vir·gin·ia \vər-'jin-yə, -'jin-ē-ə\ state [E] U.S.; capital, Richmond — **Vir·gin·ian** \-yən, -ē-ən\ *adj or n*

Virginia Beach city [SE] Virginia

Virginia City village [W] Nevada

Vir·gin Islands \ˌvər-jən-\ island group West Indies [E] of Puerto Rico — see BRITISH VIRGIN ISLANDS; VIRGIN ISLANDS OF THE UNITED STATES

Virgin Islands of the United States the [W] islands of the

Virgin Islands group; capital, Charlotte Amalie (on Saint Thomas)

Vi·sa·yan \və-'sī-ən\ *or* **Bi·sa·yas** \bə-'sī-əz\ islands central Philippines

Vish·a·kha·pat·nam \vi-,shäk-ə-'pət-nəm\ *or* **Vis·a·kha·pat·nam** \-,sä-\ city E India

Vis·tu·la \'vis(h)-chə-lə, 'vis-tə-lə\ river 1015 kilometers long Poland flowing N from the Carpathians

Vi·ti Le·vu \,vēt-ē-'lev-ü\ island SW Pacific; largest of the Fiji group

Vlad·i·vos·tok \,vlad-ə-və-'stäk, -'väs-,täk\ city & port SE Russia on Sea of Japan

Vol·ga \'väl-gə, 'vȯl-, 'vōl-\ river 3742 kilometers long W Russia; longest river in Europe

Vol·go·grad \'väl-gə-,grad, 'vȯl-, 'vōl-\ city SW Russia, on the Volga

Vol·ta \'väl-tə, 'vȯl-\ river 160 kilometers long Ghana flowing from Lake Volta (reservoir) into Gulf of Guinea

Vo·ro·nezh \və-'rȯ-nish\ city SW Russia

Vosges \'vōzh\ mountains NE France on W side of Rhine valley; highest 1423 meters

Wa·co \'wā-kō\ city central Texas

Wake \'wāk\ island N Pacific N of Marshall islands; belongs to U.S.

Wake·field \'wāk-,fēld\ city N England in West Yorkshire

Wa·la·chia *or* **Wal·la·chia** \wä-'lä-kē-ə\ region S Romania between Transylvanian Alps & the Danube

Wales \'wā(ə)lz\ *or* **Welsh Cym·ru** \'kəm-,rē\ principality SW Great Britain; a division of United Kingdom; capital, Cardiff

Wal·sall \'wȯl-,sȯl, -səl\ city area W central England in West Midlands county

Wal·tham Forest \,wȯl-thəm-\ city area of NE Greater London county, England

Wands·worth \'wän(d)z-(,)wərth\ city area of SW Greater London county, England

War·ley \'wȯr-lē\ city area W central England in West Midlands county

War·ren \'wȯr-ən, 'wär-\ city SE Michigan

War·saw \'wȯr-,sȯ\ *or* **Polish War·sza·wa** \vär-'shäv-ə\ city, capital of Poland

War·wick \'wär-ik\ city area central England in Warwickshire

War·wick·shire \'wär-ik-,shi(ə)r, -shər\ *or* **Warwick** county central England

Wa·satch \'wȯ-,sach\ range of the Rockies SE Idaho & N central Utah; highest Mount Timpanogos 3660 meters (in Utah)

Wash·ing·ton \'wȯsh-iŋ-tən, 'wäsh-\ **1** state NW U.S.; capital, Olympia **2** city, capital of U.S.; having the same boundaries as District of Columbia — **Wash·ing·to·nian** \,wȯsh-iŋ-'tō-nē-ən, ,wäsh-, -nyən\ *adj or n*

Washington, Mount mountain 1917 meters N New Hampshire; highest in White mountains

Wa·ter·bury \'wȯt-ə(r)-,ber-ē, 'wät-\ city W central Connecticut

Wa·ver·ley \'wā-vər-lē\ city SE Australia in E New South Wales

Wei·mar Republic \'vī-,mär-\ the German republic 1919–33

Wel·land \'wel-ənd\ canal 45 kilometers long SE Ontario connecting Lake Erie & Lake Ontario

Wel·ling·ton \'wel-iŋ-tən\ city, capital of New Zealand

Wes·sex \'wes-iks\ ancient kingdom S England; capital, Winchester

West Bank area Palestine W of Jordon river; occupied by Israel since 1967

West Brom·wich \-'brəm-ij, -'bräm-, -ich\ city area W central England in West Midlands county

Western Australia state W Australia; capital, Perth — **Western Australian** *adj or n*

Western Ghats \-'gȯts\ chain of low mountains SW India

Western Isles region W Scotland consisting of the Outer Hebrides; established 1975

Western Sahara *or* **Spanish Sahara** region NW Africa; occupied by Morocco

Western Samoa islands Samoa W of 171° W; an independent country in the Commonwealth since 1962; capital, Apia

West Germany the Federal Republic of Germany — see GERMANY

West Gla·mor·gan \-glə-'mȯr-gən\ county S Wales; established 1974

West Indies islands lying between SE North America & N South America & consisting of the Greater Antilles, Lesser Antilles, & Bahamas — **West Indian** *adj or n*

West Iri·an \-,ir-ē-'än\ *or* **West New Guinea** territory of Indonesia consisting of W half of New Guinea

West Midlands county W central England; includes Birmingham

West·min·ster \'wes(t)-,min(t)-stər\ *or* **City of Westminster** city area of W central Greater London county, England

West Pakistan the former W division of Pakistan now having the same boundaries as Pakistan

West·pha·lia \wes(t)-'fāl-yə, -'fā-lē-ə\ region W Germany E of the Rhine — **West·pha·lian** \-'fāl-yən, -'fā-lē-ən\ *adj or n*

West Point U.S. military post SE New York

West Quod·dy Head \-,kwäd-ē-\ cape; most easterly point of Maine & of the Lower 48 states

West Sus·sex \-'səs-iks\ county SE England

West Virginia state E U.S.; capital, Charleston — **West Virginian** *adj or n*

West York·shire \-'yȯrk-,shi(ə)r, -shər\ county NW England; includes Wakefield

White mountains N New Hampshire in the Appalachians — see WASHINGTON, MOUNT

White·horse \'hwīt-,hȯ(ə)rs, 'wīt-\ city, capital of Yukon Territory, Canada

White sea sea inlet NW Russia

Whit·ney, Mount \-'hwit-nē, -'wit-\ mountain 4418 meters SE central California in Sierra Nevada; highest in U.S. outside of Alaska

Wich·i·ta \'wich-ə-,tȯ\ city S Kansas

Wight, Isle of \-'wīt\ — see ISLE OF WIGHT

Wil·lem·stad \'vil-əm-,stät\ city, capital of Netherlands Antilles

Wil·liams·burg \'wil-yəmz-,bərg\ city SE Virginia

Wil·ming·ton \'wil-miŋ-tən\ city N Delaware; largest in state

Wilt·shire \'wilt-,shi(ə)r, 'wil-chər, 'wilt-shər\ county S England

Win·ches·ter \'win-,ches-tər, -chə-stər\ city area S England in Hampshire

Win·der·mere \'win-də(r)-,mi(ə)r\ lake NW England in Lake District

Wind·hoek \'vint-,hůk\ city, capital of South-West Africa

Wind·sor \'win-zər\ city S Ontario, Canada on Detroit river

Wind·ward Islands \'win-dwərd-\ islands West Indies in the S Lesser Antilles extending S from Martinique but not including Barbados, Tobago, or Trinidad

Win·ni·peg \'win-ə-,peg\ city, capital of Manitoba, Canada

Winnipeg, Lake lake S central Manitoba, Canada

Win·ni·pe·sau·kee, Lake \-,win-ə-pə-'sȯ-kē\ lake central New Hampshire

Win·ston–Sa·lem \,win(t)-stən-'sā-ləm\ city N central North Carolina

\ə\ **abut**		\aů\ **out**	\i\ **tip**	\ȯ\ **saw**	\ů\ **foot**
\ər\ **further**		\ch\ **chin**	\ī\ **life**	\ȯi\ **coin**	\y\ **yet**
\a\ **mat**		\e\ **pet**	\j\ **job**	\th\ **thin**	\yü\ **few**
\ā\ **take**		\ē\ **easy**	\ŋ\ **sing**	\th\ **this**	\yů\ **cure**
\ä\ **cot, cart**		\g\ **go**	\ō\ **bone**	\ü\ **food**	\zh\ **vision**

Wis·con·sin \wis-'kän(t)-sən\ state [N] central U.S.; capital, Madison — **Wis·con·sin·ite** \-sə-,nīt\ n

Wit·wa·ters·rand \'wit-,wȯt-ərz-,rand, -,wät-, -,ränd, -,ränt\ or **Rand** \'rand, 'ränd, 'ränt\ ridge of gold-bearing rock [NE] Republic of South Africa in [S] Transvaal

Wol·lon·gong \'wül-ən-,gäŋ, -,gȯŋ\ city [SE] Australia in [E] New South Wales [S] of Sydney

Wol·ver·hamp·ton \'wül-vər-,ham(p)-tən\ city area [W] central England in West Midlands county [NW] of Birmingham

Worces·ter \'wüs-tər\ **1** city [E] central Massachusetts **2** city [W] central England in Hereford and Worcester county

Wran·gell, Mount \'raŋ-gəl\ volcano 4317 meters [S] Alaska in Wrangell range

Wro·claw \'vrȯt-,släf, -,släv\ city [SW] Poland in Silesia

Wu·han \'wü-'hän\ city [S] China

Wu·sih or **Wu–hsi** \'wü-'shē\ city [E] China

Wy·o·ming \wī-'ō-miŋ\ state [NW] U.S.; capital, Cheyenne — **Wy·o·ming·ite** \-miŋ-,īt\ n

xi·'an or **Si·an** \'shē-'än\ city [E] central China

Xin·jiang Uy·gur or **Sin·kiang Ui·ghur** \'shin-jē-'äŋ-'wē-gər\ region [W] China

Xu·zhou \'shü-'jō\ or **Sü·chow** \'shü-'jō, 'sü-; 'sü-'chaü\ city [E] China

Yak·i·ma \'yak-ə-,mȯ\ city [S] central Washington

Ya·lu \'yäl-ü\ river 480 kilometers long [SE] Manchuria & North Korea

Yan·gon \,yän-'gōn\ or formerly **Ran·goon** \ran-'gün, raŋ-\ city, capital of Myanmar

Yangtze — see CHANG

Yaoun·dé \yaün-'dā\ city, capital of Cameroon

Yap \'yap, 'yäp\ island [W] Pacific in the [W] Carolines

Ya·ro·slavl \,yär-ə-'släv-əl\ city [W] Russia, [NE] of Moscow

Yaz·oo \ya-'zü, 'yaz-ü\ river [W] central Mississippi

Ye·ka·te·rin·burg \yi-'kat-ə-rən-,bərg, -'kät-, -,bərk\ or 1924–91 **Sverd·lovsk** \sverd-'lȯfsk\ city [W] Russia, in central Ural mountains

Yellow **1** — see HUANG **2** sea section of East China sea between [N] China, North Korea, & South Korea

Yel·low·knife \'yel-ə-,nīf\ town, capital of Northwest Territories, Canada

Ye·men \'yem-ən\ country [S] Arabia bordering on Red sea & Gulf of Aden; capital, San'a; before 1990 divided into the independent states of **Yemen Arab Republic** (capital, San'a) & **People's Democratic Republic of Yemen** (capital, Aden) — **Ye·me·ni** \'yem-ə-nē\ adj or n — **Ye·men·ite** \-ə-,nīt\ n

Yen·i·sey \,yen-ə-'sā\ river 4505 kilometers long central Russia, flowing [N] into Arctic ocean

Ye·re·van \,yer-ə-'vän\ city, capital of Armenia

Yo·ko·ha·ma \,yō-kə-'häm-ə\ city Japan in [SE] Honshu on Tokyo Bay [S] of Tokyo

Yon·kers \'yäŋ-kərz\ city [SE] New York [N] of New York City

York \'yȯ(ə)rk\ city [N] England in North Yorkshire

York, Cape cape [NE] Australia in Queensland at [N] tip of Cape York peninsula

York·shire \'yȯrk-,shi(ə)r, -shər\ former county [N] England

Yo·sem·i·te Falls \yō-,sem-ət-ē-\ waterfall [E] California in Yosemite valley; includes two falls, the upper 436 meters & the lower 98 meters

Youngs·town \'yəŋ-,staün\ city [NE] Ohio

Yu·ca·tán \,yü-kə-'tan, -'tän\ peninsula [SE] Mexico & [N] Central America including Belize & [N] Guatemala

Yu·go·sla·via or **Ju·go·sla·via** \,yü-gō-'släv-ē-ə\ country [S] Europe including Serbia & Montenegro and formerly also Slovenia, Croatia, Bosnia and Herzegovina, & Macedonia; capital, Belgrade — **Yu·go·slav** \,yü-gō-'släv, -'slav\ or **Yu·go·sla·vi·an** \-'släv-ē-ən\ adj or n

Yu·kon \'yü-,kän\ **1** river 3185 kilometers long [NW] Canada & Alaska flowing into Bering sea **2** or **Yukon Territory** territory [NW] Canada; capital, Whitehorse

Yu·ma \'yü-mə\ city [SW] corner of Arizona on the Colorado

Za·greb \'zäg-,reb\ city, capital of Croatia

Zaire \zä-'i(ə)r also 'zī(ə)r\ **1** river in Africa — see CONGO **2** or formerly **Democratic Republic of the Congo** or earlier **Belgian Congo** country central Africa consisting of most of Congo river basin [E] of lower Congo river; capital, Kinshasa

Zam·be·zi or **Zam·be·si** \zam-'bē-zē\ river 2655 kilometers long [SE] Africa flowing from [NW] Zambia into Mozambique channel

Zam·bia \'zam-bē-ə\ country [S] Africa [N] of the Zambezi; formerly (as **Northern Rhodesia**) dependent on Britain; became independent 1964; capital, Lusaka

Zan·zi·bar \'zan-zə-,bär\ island Tanzania off [NE] Tanganyika coast; formerly a sultanate; became independent 1963; united 1964 with Tanganyika forming Tanzania

Za·po·ro·zhye \,zäp-ə-'rȯ-zhə\ city [SE] Ukraine

Zetland — see SHETLAND

Zhang·jia·kou \'jäŋ-jē-'ä-'kō\ or **Kal·gan** \'kal-'gan\ city [NE] China [NW] of Beijing

Zhdanov — see MARIUPOL

Zheng·zhou or **Cheng–chou** \'jəŋ-'jō\ city [NE] central China

Zim·ba·bwe \zim-'bäb-wē, -wā\ or formerly **Rhodesia** country [S] Africa [S] of Zambezi river; an independent state in the Commonwealth; capital, Harare

Zui·der Zee \,zīd-ər-'zā, -'zē\ former inlet of North sea [N] Netherlands — see IJSSELMEER

Zu·lu·land \'zü-(,)lü-,land\ territory [E] Republic of South Africa in [NE] Natal on Indian ocean

Zu·rich \'zü(ə)r-ik\ city [N] Switzerland

Signs and Symbols

◆ ASTRONOMY

☉	the sun; Sunday
◗, ☾, *or* ☽	the moon; Monday
●	new moon
☽, ◗, ◗, ☽	first quarter
○ *or* ☺	full moon
☾, ◑, ◐, ☾	last quarter
☿	Mercury; Wednesday
♀	Venus; Friday
⊕, ⊖, *or* ♁	the earth
♂	Mars; Tuesday
♃	Jupiter; Thursday
♄	Saturn; Saturday
♅, ⛢, *or* ♅	Uranus
♆, ♆, *or* ♆	Neptune
♇	Pluto
☄	comet
∗ *or* ✶	fixed star

◆ BIOLOGY

○	an individual, specifically, a female — used chiefly in inheritance charts
□	an individual, specifically, a male — used chiefly in inheritance charts
♀	female
♂ *or* ♁	male
×	crossed with; hybrid

◆ BUSINESS

@	at; each ⟨4 apples @ 5¢ = 20¢⟩
℅	care of
#	number if it precedes a numeral ⟨track #3⟩; pounds if it follows ⟨a 5# sack of sugar⟩
lb	pound; pounds
%	percent
‰	per thousand
$	dollars
¢	cents
£	pounds
/	shillings
©	copyrighted
®	registered trademark

◆ CHEMISTRY

(For element symbols see ELEMENT table)

+   signifies "plus," "and," "together with," and is used between the symbols of substances brought together for, or produced by, a reaction; if placed to the right of a symbol above the line, it signifies a unit charge of positive electricity: Ca^{++} denotes the ion of calcium, which carries two positive charges

−   signifies a single "bond," or unit of attractive force or affinity, and is used between the symbols of elements or groups that unite to form a compound; H—Cl for HCl, H—O—H for H_2O; if placed to the right of a symbol above the line, Cl^- denotes a chlorine ion having a negative charge

·   is often used (1) to indicate a single bond (as H·Cl for H—Cl) or (2) to denote the presence of a single unpaired electron (as H·) or (3) to separate parts of a compound regarded as loosely joined (as $CuSO_4 \cdot 5H_2O$)

=   indicates a double bond

:   indicates a double bond (as $H_2C{:}CH_2$) or an unshared pair of electrons (as :NH_3)

≡   indicates a triple bond

( )   mark groups within a compound [as in $C_6H_4(CH_3)_2$, which contains two methyl groups (CH_3)]

→   gives, leads to, or is converted to

⇌   forms and is formed from; is in equilibrium with

↓   indicates precipitation of the substance

↑   indicates that the substance is given off as a gas

pH   hydrogen-ion concentration

MATHEMATICS

+   plus; positive $\langle a + b = c \rangle$

−   minus; negative

±   plus or minus (the square root of $4a^2$ is ± $2a$); more or less than (an error of ±2)

×   multiplied by; times (6 x 4 = 24) — also indicated by placing a dot between the numbers $\langle 6 \cdot 4 = 24 \rangle$

÷ *or* :   divided by (24 ÷ 6 = 4) — also indicated by writing the divisor under the dividend with a line between $\langle \frac{24}{6} = 4 \rangle$ or by writing the divisor after the dividend with a slash between $\langle 3/8 \rangle$

=   equals (6 + 2 = 8)

≠ *or* ≠   is not equal to

>   is greater than (6 > 5)

<   is less than (3 < 4)

≧ *or* ≥   is greater than or equal to

≦ *or* ≤   is less than or equal to

≯   is not greater than

≮   is not less than

≈   is approximately equal to

≡   is identical to

~   equivalent; similar

≅   is congruent to

:   is to; the ratio of

∴   therefore

∞   infinity

∠   angle; the angle $\langle \angle ABC \rangle$

∟   right angle $\langle \llcorner ABC \rangle$

⊥   the perpendicular; is perpendicular to $\langle AB \perp CD \rangle$

∥   parallel; is parallel to $\langle AB \parallel CD \rangle$

⊙ *or* ○   circle

⌒   arc of a circle

△   triangle

□   square

▭   rectangle

( )   parentheses

[ ]   brackets   } indicate that the qualities enclosed by them are to be taken together

{ }   braces

π   pi; the number 3.14159265+; the ratio of the circumference of a circle to its diameter

°   degree $\langle 60° \rangle$

′   minute; foot $\langle 30' \rangle$

″   second; inch $\langle 30'' \rangle$

!   factorial — used to indicate the product of all the whole numbers up to and including a given preceding number

√ *or* √   root — used without a figure to indicate a square root (as in $\sqrt{4} = 2$) or with an index above the sign to indicate another degree (as in $\sqrt[3]{3}, \sqrt[5]{7}$)

2, 3, etc.   — used as exponents placed above and at the right of an expression to indicate that it is raised to a power indicated by the figure (a^2, the square of a)

∩   union of two sets

∪   intersection of two sets

⊂   is included in; is a subset of

⊃   contains as a subset

∈ *or* ∈   is an element of

∉   is not an element of

Λ *or* 0 *or*   null set; empty set
∅ *or* { }

MISCELLANEOUS

&   and

&c   et cetera; and so forth

/   slash; used to mean "or" (as in *and/or*), "per" (as in *meters/second*); indicates end of a line of verse; separates the figures of a date (9/26/86)

†   died — used especially in genealogies

☧   monogram from Greek XP, signifying Jesus

✡   Star of David

✶   — used in Roman Catholic and Anglican service books to divide each verse of a psalm, indicating where the response begins

✠ *or* +   — used in some service books to indicate where the sign of the cross is to be made; also used by certain Roman Catholic and Anglican prelates as a sign of the cross preceding their signatures

f/ or *f:*   relative aperture of a photographic lens

☠   poison

℞   take — used on prescriptions

🜨   civil defense

☢   radioactive

MUSIC

 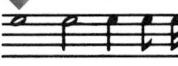   staff with notes — whole note, half note, quarter, eighth, sixteenth; a dot after a note adds to it half the length of the note without the dot

   treble clef; G clef — used to indicate that the second line from the bottom represents the first G above middle C

   bass clef; F clef — used to indicate that the second line from the top represents the first F below middle C

♯   sharp

♭   flat

♮ natural — used to cancel the effect of a previous sharp or flat; the sharps or flats placed at the beginning of a composition or section are called collectively the *key signature*

✕ or ※ double sharp — used to raise a note two half steps

𝄫 double flat — used to lower a note two half steps

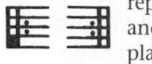 repeat — used to indicate the beginning and end respectively of a passage to be played or sung twice

＜ crescendo

＞ decrescendo; diminuendo

＜＞ swell

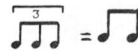 rests — whole, half, quarter, eighth, and sixteenth

 triplet — three notes grouped together under a curved line or a bracket. The three notes have a total duration that two of those notes would ordinarily receive

2/4 two beats per measure; a quarter note gets one beat

3/4 three beats per measure; a quarter note gets one beat

4/4 four beats per measure; a quarter note gets one beat

5/4 five beats per measure; a quarter note gets one beat

6/8 six beats per measure; an eighth note gets one beat

𝄴 common time: same as 4/4

𝄵 cut time: a half note gets one beat

𝄋 dal segno (D.S.) — repeat from the sign

𝄐 fermata — pause, hold

ˆ𝆏 strong accent

·𝆏 staccato — shorten value of note, leaving a small silence between it and the next note

‾𝆏 tenuto — hold note for full value

> accent

REFERENCE MARKS

The first three marks below are placed in text to direct attention to a footnote:

* asterisk *or* star

† dagger

‡ double dagger

§ section *or* numbered clause

‖ parallels

¶ or ℙ paragraph

STAMPS AND STAMP COLLECTING

★ unused

⊙ *or* ○ used

⊞ block of four or more

⊠ entire cover or card

△ on a piece of cover

WEATHER

barometer, changes of:

╱ rising, then falling

╱ rising, then steady; or rising, then rising more slowly

╱ rising steadily, or unsteadily

╱ falling or steady, then rising; or rising, then rising more quickly

— steady, same as 3 hours ago

╲ falling, then rising, same or lower than 3 hours ago

╲ falling, then steady; or falling, then falling more slowly

╲ falling steadily, or unsteadily

╲ steady or rising, then falling; or falling, then falling more quickly

◎ calm

○ clear

◖ cloudy (partly)

● cloudy (completely overcast)

+ drifting or blowing snow

, drizzle

≡ fog

∿ freezing rain

⸺ cold front

⸺ warm front

⸺ occluded front

⸺ stationary front

)(funnel clouds

∞ haze

⚲ hurricane

⚱ tropical storm

● rain

⁂ rain and snow

⩔ frost

S sandstorm or dust storm

∇ shower(s)

∇̇ shower of rain

∮ shower of hail

△ sleet

✳ snow

ℝ thunderstorm

⌇ visibility reduced by smoke

The following list consists of words that are commonly misspelled. Review it regularly to learn the spelling of words that give you trouble. The list will also come in handy for quickly looking up words you are unsure of, while you are writing or proofreading. For information about any of the words on this list, as well as for words not found here, consult the entries in the main section of this dictionary.

Commonly

A

abandon
absence
absolutely
absorption
abundance
acceptance
accidentally
accommodate
accompaniment
accompany
accomplish
accumulate
accurate
accustomed
ache
achieve
acquaintance
acquire
across
actuality
actually
adequately
adjective
administration
adolescent
advertisement
affectionate
again
against
aggressive
agriculture
aisle
almost
always
amateur
ambassador
among
amount
analysis
announce
annual

answer
anticipate
anxiety
anxious
any
apologize
apology
apparatus
apparent
appearance
application
appreciation
approach
appropriate
approval
approximately
arctic
argument
arithmetic
arrangement
article
assignment
assistance
associate
assure
assurance
athlete
attacked
attendance
attitude
attorney
audience
authority
autobiography
available
average
awful

B

background
bacteria
ballad

banana
basically
basis
beginning
belief
believe
beneficial
benefit
bicycle
bough
boundary
bouquet
breathe
brief
brilliant
Britain
build
bulletin
bureau
business
busy

C

calendar
campaign
cancel
candidate
cannot
capacity
captain
career
careless
carrier
carrying
category
cease
ceiling
century
certificate
challenge
changeable
characteristic

chemistry
chief
choice
choir
choose
chorus
chose
circuit
circumstance
civilization
cocoon
college
colonel
column
commencement
commercial
commissioner
commit
commitment
committed
committee
communicate
comparison
competent
competition
completely
conceive
condemn
confidential
confirmation
congratulations
conscience
conscientious
conscious
consequently
conservation
considerable
consistency
constitution
continuous
control
controlled
controversial
convenience
cooperate

cordially
corporation
corps
correspondence
cough
could
country
courteous
criticism
criticize
curiosity
curriculum
cylinder

D

daily
dealt
debtor
decimal
decision
definite
delegate
delicate
denied
deny
describe
description
desirable
despair
despise
develop
diameter
diamond
difference
difficulty
dinosaur
disappearance
disappoint
disaster
disastrous
disciple
discipline
discussion
disguise
dissatisfied

distinction
distinguish
distribution
divide
dividend
divine
doctor
doctrine
doesn't
dominant
don't
done
dormitory
duplicate

E

eager
early
earnest
easily
easy
ecology
economic
efficiency
eighth
elaborate
eligible
eliminate
embarrass
embroidery
emergency
encourage
enemy
engineering
enormous
enough
enthusiasm
environment
equipment
equipped
especially
essential
estimate
etiquette
eventually

Misspelled Words

every
evident
exact
exaggerate
examination
exceed
excellent
exceptional
excessive
excitable
execute
executive
exercise
exhaustion
exhibition
existence
expense
experience
experiment
explanation
extension
extraordinary
extreme

F

fallacy
familiar
fascinate
fatal
faucet
favorably
favorite
February
fictitious
field
fierce
fiery
finally
finance
financial
flourish
flu
foliage
foreign
forfeit

fortunately
forty
fragile
fraternity
frequent
friend
friendliness
fundamental
further

G

gasoline
gene
generally
genius
genuine
glimpse
glorious
government
governor
grabbed
gracious
graduate
grammar
grammatically
grateful
gratitude
gross
guarantee
guardian
guess
guidance
gymnasium

H

handkerchief
happiness
hasten
hatred
having
heard
heavily
heavy
height

heir
heroic
heroine
hesitate
hoarse
hour
humorous
hungrily
hungry
hygiene
hypocrisy
hypocrite

I

icicle
icy
ignorance
illustrate
imaginary
imagination
imitation
immediately
immense
inability
incidentally
independent
indicate
indispensable
individual
inevitable
inferior
influential
initial
innocence
inspiration
instead
institute
insurance
intellect
intelligence
interest
interfere
interference
interpret
interpretation

interrupt
interruption
interval
investigation
involve
irrelevant
irresistible
island

J

jealousy
journal

K

knowledge

L

laboratory
legislature
leisure
lengthen
liability
lieutenant
likelihood
likely
liquor
liveliness
lively
local
loneliness
lonely
luxury

M

magazine
maintenance
majority
mansion
manufacture
marriage
martyr
mathematics
maturity

meant
mechanical
medical
medicine
merchandise
merit
message
metaphor
military
miniature
minimum
minute
mischief
mischievous
missile
misspell
monotony
mortgage
mourn
multiplication
multitude
municipal
muscle
muscular
museum
musician
mutual
mystery
myth

N

narrative
natural
necessary
nervous
niece
ninety
ninth
none
nonsense
noticeable
nuclear
nuisance
numerous

O

obligation
obstacle
obvious
occasion
occasionally
occupy
occur
occurrence
official
often
omit
omitted
once
operation
opinion
opponent
opportunity
oppose
opposite
opposition
optimism
orchestra
ordinary
organization
original
ornament
ounce

P

pageant
paid
pamphlet
parachute
paradise
parallel
parliament
particular
passage
pastime
patience
peaceable
peasant
peculiar

perceive
percentage
performance
peril
permanent
persistent
personal
personality
perspiration
persuade
pertain
petition
phase
philosopher
physical
picnic
picnicked
piece
pigeon
planned
playwright
pleasant
poison
poisonous
policy
politician
popularity
population
positive
possess
possible
possibility
practically
precise
predominant
prefer
preferred
prejudice
preliminary
preparation
preposition
pressure
primitive
priority
prisoner
privilege
probable
probably
procedure
procession
professor
prominent
proportion

prosperous
psychology
publicity
purpose
pursue
pursuit
pyramid

Q

qualify
quality
quantity
questionnaire

R

readily
ready
realize
really
reasonable
receipt
receive
recipe
recognize
recommendation
refer
reference
referred
regard
register
regret
regretted
regular
rehearsal
reign
relief
relieve
religion
religious
remainder
remembrance
removal
renewal
repetition
representative
requirement
rescue
research
residence
resistance
resolution
resource

response
responsibility
restaurant
review
rhythm
ridiculous

S

sacrifice
safety
said
satire
satisfactory
satisfied
saucer
says
scarce
scene
schedule
scheme
scholarship
scissors
security
seize
senate
senator
sense
sensibility
sentiment
separate
several
shepherd
sheriff
shining
shiny
shoe
significance
similar
simile
since
situated
skis
society
solar
solemn
solution
sophomore
source
souvenir
speak
special
species
specific

specimen
speech
spiritual
sponsor
straight
straighten
strength
strenuous
stretch
study
subscription
substantial
substitute
subtle
succeed
success
successful
sufficient
sugar
suggest
summarize
summary
superintendent
superior
suppress
surely
surface
surgeon
surprise
surround
survey
suspense
suspicion
syllable
symbol
sympathy
symphony
synonym

T

tailor
teammate
technique
television
temperament
temperature
temporary
tendency
theme
theory
therefore
thorough
though

tired
tobacco
together
tomorrow
tongue
tonight
tonsils
tough
tournament
tradition
traffic
tragedy
transfer
transferred
treasure
treasury
tremendous
tries
trouble
truly
Tuesday
twelfth
twelve
tying
tyranny

U

unanimous
uncomfortable
undoubtedly
unforgettable
unfortunate
university
unnecessary
unpleasant
unsatisfactory
until
unusual
upon
urgent
useful
using

V

vacancy
vacuum
vague
valuable
varies
variety
various
vegetable

veil
vein
vengeance
vicinity
view
villain
violence

W

warrant
warrior
weapon
Wednesday
weird
welcome
whether
whole
wholly
whose
women
won't
would
wrestle
writing

Y

yield